Langenscheidts New College German Dictionary

German-English
English-German

LANGENSCHEIDT
NEW YORK · BERLIN · MUNICH · VIENNA · ZURICH

First Part

German-English

Completely Revised Edition 1995

By
Sonia Brough

Completely Revised Edition 1995
Langenscheidt's New College German Dictionary, German-English

Printed in Germany

Preface

Revised and enlarged edition

This revised edition of "Langenscheidt's New College German Dictionary German-English" is a classic in a new guise. While retaining the tried and tested features of its predecessor, it has undergone a complete overhaul in the Langenscheidt "workshop" to emerge as a reliable and up-to-date version that is fully-equipped for the 1990's. Its major improvements and innovations are described in the following.

Vocabulary

Updating the dictionary has naturally meant taking up a wealth of new words and phrases from many areas, such as politics (e. g. ***Gipfeldiplomatie, Trendmeldung, Staatsverdrossenheit***), ecology (e. g. ***FCKW-frei, Altlasten, Umweltterrorismus***), transport (e. g. ***Radarpistole, Magermotor, Verkehrsinfarkt***), or tourism (e. g. ***Vielflieger, Landeschleifen ziehen***) etc.

The items of vocabulary have been selected and translated in a way which reflects the full range of language usage, encompassing both colloquial and slang expressions and the elevated registers of written use and literary style. The main emphasis, though, remained on the living language of everyday speech, as entries such as ***Grufti, Dreitagebart, Wohnklo, Rentnerstreß, Organhandel*** or ***Milliardenloch im Haushalt*** show.

One of the aims of this dictionary is to cater also to the demands of those who use foreign languages in the workplace. Thus a wide range of specialist vocabulary from various fields of knowledge has been taken up. Medical vocabulary, for example, covers such entries as ***Östrogenspiegel, Mukoviszidose*** and ***Erythrozytenzählung***, while the selection of economic terms includes ***Kosten-Nutzen-Verhältnis, Zinsschwankungen*** and ***Steuerflüchtling.*** Hi-fi enthusiasts will not search in vain for translations of ***Hochtöner*** or ***Gleichlaufschwankungen***, while for the armchair theatre fans we offer entries such as ***hochauflösendes Fernsehbild*** and ***Schrägspuraufzeichnung.***

Phraseology

Words are rarely used in a vacuum, but appear in specific contexts. To help the user to find the right translation for the right context, this dictionary also contains a host of authentic examples of modern usage. They comprise so-called collocations (e. g. ***nahtlose Bräune, nächtliche Ausgangssperre, runder Geburtstag, schnelle Eingreiftruppe***) and idiomatic expressions (e. g. ***angezwitschert kommen, einen Mordsspektakel machen, ich bin auch nur ein Mensch***).

Translations

We have endeavoured to provide English translations of the German words and phrases that are as accurate, modern and idiomatic as possible, and – where relevant – to offer as many variants as space allowed. Thus the expression ***Otto Normalverbraucher*** is rendered by several equivalents within the same register: *Mr Average, Joe Blow, Joe Bloggs, the man on the Clapham omnibus, your high-street punter*.

Pragmatics has been an important priority in this dictionary. Thus the stylistic register of both the English and the German expressions has been indicated as precisely as possible wherever it deviates from the neutral register, as in the following example (here F stands for "familiar" or "colloquial", and *sl.* for "slang"):

> **Mumm** [mʊm] F *m* (*-s; no pl.*) **1.** gumption, F guts *pl.*, *sl.* bottle; **2.** drive, verve, F get-up-and-go, oomph.

User-friendliness

Easy-to-read, clearly laid out typography makes for good readability and enables words and expressions and their translations to be found more quickly. This is a particular boon in the case of very long entries.

The user will also appreciate the fact that many adjectives derived from verbs are listed as separate entries (e. g. ***gestreßt, geschlaucht, eingeklemmt, ausgeliefert***).

The internal organization of each dictionary entry is also clearly structured and user-friendly. Differences of meaning are distinguished as precisely as possible, the order in which they are given is determined by frequency of use. Thus the entry ***Eintagsfliege***, for example, gives the metaphorical meaning first and the literal zoological meaning second.

Appendices

The appendices offer a useful selection of additional information to complement the main part of the dictionary. Among the names of the states of the Federal Republic of Germany you will find, for example, ***Mecklenburg-Vorpommern*** (*Mecklenburg-Western Pomerania*), while the list of geographical names includes entries of interest to the tourist, such as ***der Wenzelsplatz*** (*Wenceslas Square*) in Prague or ***der Felsendom*** (*the Dome of the Rock*) and ***die Grabeskirche*** (*the Church of the Holy Sepulchre*) in Jerusalem. Music-lovers, finally, may be in for a few surprises when they browse through the list of musical titles. Or did you know that Joseph Haydn's *Surprise Symphony* is known in German-speaking countries as ***Symphonie mit dem Paukenschlag***?

LANGENSCHEIDT

Contents

Guide to the Dictionary

1. Arrangement of entries

a) The entries appear in strict alphabetical order as a rule. Words beginning with the umlauts ä, ö, ü are treated as if they began with a, o, u. Participles are listed on the one hand under the verb entry (e. g. ***schützend*** under **schützen**), but they may also appear as separate entries, in which case the verb entry contains a cross-reference to the participle: e. g. **nerven** → ***genervt.***

The preterite and past participle forms of all irregular verbs are listed as separate entries in alphabetical order.

b) As a guide to hyphenation, syllabification breaks are shown by centred dots in the headwords: **Mä·an·der.**

The vertical bar also indicates a possible end-of-line hyphenation: **Man·del|baum.**

The same applies to a syllable in parentheses: **Schä·del(ba·sis)bruch.**

Difficult syllabic breaks are given in parentheses after the headword: **drücken** ... (*sep.* -k·k-), **Nulleiter** (*sep.* -ll·l-), **Bettuch** (*sep.* -tt·t-).

This information is not, however, given for compound words: **Ma·gen·drücken.**

2. Internal structure of entries

Roman numerals distinguish different parts of speech or grammatical categories within an entry:

> **schwat·zen** ... **I.** *v/i.* a) chat, F natter ...; **II.** *v/t.*: ***dummes Zeug*** ~ ...

As a rule, commas are used to link related translations, while semi-colons separate distinct variants:

> **brül·len** ['brʏlən] (h) **I.** *v/i.* roar (*a. fig. gun, engine etc.*); *cattle*: bellow; low; *person*: shout, scream, ...

Arabic numerals are also used to distinguish between different meanings:

> **'Senk·recht·star·ter** *m* **1.** ✈ vertical takeoff plane, F jump jet; **2.** F *fig.* F whiz(z) kid, high flier

Small letters are used to further structure an entry, occasionally in order to distinguish differences of meaning between the examples of usage:

> **trocken** ... ***auf dem ~en sitzen*** a) be completely on the rocks, b) be staring into an empty glass, c) not to know (*or* have no idea) what's going on ...

> **'An·la·ge** ... **6.** ✝ a) investment, b) invested capital ...

If a reflexive verb pattern is followed by Arabic numerals, it applies to all subsequent sections marked with Arabic numerals, even though further examples of usage may have appeared:

> **küm·mern** ... **I.** *v/refl.*: ***sich ~ um*** *acc.* **1.** look after ...; ***ich muß mich um alles ~*** ... **2.** worry about; ... **3.** pay attention to ...

3. The swung dash or "tilde"

is used for economy of space. The boldface tilde (**~**) replaces the preceding entry word or the part of an entry word preceding the vertical bar (|):

> **Gei·sel** ...; **~be·frei·ung** ...; **~dra·ma** ...; **~gang·ster** ...
> **stink|'faul** ...; **~'fein** ...

The boldface tilde (**~**) in examples of usage replaces the immediately preceding entry word which, in turn, may have been formed using the boldface tilde:

> **klot·zen** ...; ~, ***nicht kleckern!*** ...
> **Mil·li'ar·den|be·trag** ...; **~loch** *n*: ***das ~ im Haushalt*** ...

Where the initial letter of entry words changes from a capital letter to a small letter or vice versa, a circle appears above the tilde:

> **'Knall|kopf** ...; **~kör·per** ...; **~̊'rot** ...; **~tü·te** ...

4. The cross-reference sign (→)

a) serves to indicate a direct cross-reference, e. g. **Ascheimer** *m* → ***Mülleimer*** means that the translations for "Mülleimer" also apply for "Ascheimer";

b) draws attention to further information relating to the entry which can be found elsewhere in the dictionary, e. g. **Bein** ... → ***ausreißen*** I, ***Bauch, Grab, Klotz*** ...

c) cross-refers to another section within an entry:

ba·den ... **III.** *v/refl.*: ***sich ~*** → 1; ...

or, for example, from a derivative noun to its corresponding verb:

Ver·grö·ße·rung ... **1.** enlargement; growth; ...; → ***vergrößern***; ...

5. Differences in meaning

Where necessary, differences in meaning are marked by

a) pictorial signs and abbreviations (listed on pp. 13–14) indicating the field of usage:

Röh·re ... tube; ⚙ pipe; *anat.* duct, canal; ⚗ test tube; ⚡ valve, tube ...

b) brackets indicating synonyms, hypernyms and restrictions on usage:

Tor¹ ... **1.** a) gate (*a. fig.*); archway; (*garage etc.*) door, b) gateway (*a. fig.*) ...

c) clause complements, e. g. the objects of verbs:

wickeln ... **I.** *v/t.* ... tie *bandage etc.*; wrap *blanket etc.*, b) curl *hair*, ...

or the subjects of describing clauses:

kräf·tig ... **I.** *adj.* strong (*a. meteor.*); powerful *engine etc.*, b) heavy, powerful *blow etc.*, c) ... bouncing *baby* ...

d) italics indicating extra contextual information in the absence of a complete translation:

Bauch ... F ***aus dem hohlen ~*** *talk etc.* F off the top of one's head; ...
'nichts·sa·gend ... nondescript *face, person etc.*

If *the* appears in italics, it means that the definite article accompanies the noun.

Volk ..., b) *the* masses *pl.*, ...

e) exponent numerals to distinguish homographs with vastly different meanings:

Schloß¹ ... lock ...
Schloß² ... castle ...

6. Combinations of translations and examples of usage

a) By means of brackets:

Pa·ra·dies ... ***ich fühle mich wie im ~*** (I feel as if) I'm walking on air

(i. e. "I feel as if" can be omitted)

Po'lar·meer *n*: ***nördliches* (*südliches*) *~*** Arctic (Antarctic) Ocean ...

b) Where two examples occur in sequence, the second extending the first, they are arranged as follows:

fin·den ... ***ich kann nichts dabei ~*** I don't see any harm in it, ***daß er ...:*** I can't see any harm in him (*or* his) *ger.* ...

The comma in front of ***daß er*** and the colon after it indicate that the preceding expression must be used at the head of the following example: in this particular case ***ich kann nichts dabei ~, daß er ...***

7. Grammar governing usage

Af·fe ... (-n; -n): des Affen, die Affen
Af·fä·re ... (-; -n): der Affäre, die Affären

The sign ⸚ indicates that an umlaut appears in the inflected form in question:

'Aus·druck¹ *m* (-[e]s; ⸚e): des Ausdruck(e)s, die Ausdrücke

Verbs

a) The past participle is generally formed by prefixing ge- and adding -(e)t to the stem of the verb: **bändigen** – gebändigt, **heiraten** – geheiratet.

Verbs ending with -ieren or -eien do not use the prefix ge-: **reagieren** – reagiert, **prophezeien** – prophezeit.

Verbs with the inseparable prefixes be-, em-, ent-, er-, ge-, ver- and zer- simply add -(e)t to the stem: **begrüßen** – begrüßt, **entbehren** – entbehrt etc.

In all the above cases the entries indicate only whether the perfect tense is formed with "haben" or "sein": **bändigen** ... *v/t.* (h) ..., **klettern** ... *v/i.* (sn) ...

b) The preterite and past participle of an irregular verb are given under the headword: **gehen ...** (ging, gegangen, sn) **I.** *v/i.* **1. ...**: the perfect tense of this verb is formed by means of the auxiliary verb "sein": er ging, er ist gegangen.

c) Separable verbs form the past participle by placing -ge- between the prefix and the stem: **hinausgehen** *v/i.* (*irr.*, *sep.*, -ge-, sn, → ***gehen***): the reference *irr.* indicates that the compound verb "hinausgehen" is conjugated like the root verb "gehen", the → refers the user to the entry "gehen" for the preterite and past participle, *sep.* indicates that the verb is separated: er geht/ging hinaus, er ist hinausgegangen.

d) Homographic verbs like "über'treten", "'übertreten" are differentiated as follows:

'über·tre·ten¹ ... (*irr.*, *sep.*, sn, → ***treten***): er trat über, er ist übergetreten
über'tre·ten² ... (*irr.*, *insep.*, *no* -ge-, h, → ***treten***): er übertrat, er hat übertreten

The case governing the German preposition is always indicated.

Where there are differences between German and English with regard to the grammatical relationship between verbs and their object complements, or between adjectives and the nouns which they describe, the differences are indicated as follows:

a) by giving the relevant grammatical case or preposition after the translation (this information has sometimes been left out to avoid repetition):

her'aus·zie·hen *v/t.* ... pull out (***aus*** *dat.* of); extract (from) ...
'zu·stim·men *v/i.* ... agree (*dat.* to *s.th. or* with *s.o.*)

b) by adding English objects in the relevant case after the translation:

ent'ge·gen·tre·ten ... **3.** ... face *danger etc.*; counter *threats etc.* ...

c) by providing a direct object complement in the English equivalent where it corresponds to an indirect object complement or prepositional object in German:

ent'ge·gen·han·deln ... act against (*dat. s.th.*)
her·um·gei·stern ... flit around (***in*** *dat. a place*) ...

8. Stress marks

are indicated

a) in all entries without phonetic transcription:

Ma·rio'net·ten|re,gie·rung ...
'Mar·ken|al·bum ...; **~ar,ti·kel** ...

b) where different accentuation changes the meaning of the entry word:

'um·rei·ßen¹ ... pull down ...
um'rei·ßen² ... outline ...

c) where a strong stress on an otherwise unstressed word is essential to the meaning of a phrase:

weit ... ***es ~ bringen*** (***im Leben***) ... 'go places ...

9. Word division (hyphenation)

Where hyphens stand at the end of one line and at the beginning of the next, it means that the divided word normally has a hyphen at the point of division:

'haut·far·ben ... *cosmetics*: skin-
-colo(u)red (= skin-colo[u]red)

A single hyphen at the end of the line means that the word does not require a hyphen when not divided:

'Schiff·bau *m* (-[e]s; *no pl.*) shipbuilding (industry); **'Schiff·bau·er** *m* (-s; -) shipbuilder (= shipbuilder)

A hyphen at the beginning of a line inside brackets serves to indicate that the part of the word inside the brackets can be joined to the preceding word, which will then be written together as one word.

10. Stylistic register

In a series of translations used in the same stylistic register, usually only the first expression's stylistic features are indicated:

'Nepp|lo,kal F *n* F clip joint, rip-off place

In this entry, the first F (= familiar, colloquial) refers to the German entry word and the second to both English translations.

The same procedure is used in the case of several figurative uses of an entry word, for these are usually easily recognizable as figurative expressions:

Bein ... *fig.* ***auf schwachen ~en stehen*** be shaky ... ***auf eigenen ~en stehen*** stand on one's own two feet; ***mit beiden ~en im Leben stehen*** have both feet firmly on the ground ...

11. Differences between British and American spelling

have been taken into consideration as far as possible and presented as follows:

grey, *Am.* gray; defen|ce (*Am.* -se)
colo(u)r; travel(l)er; catalog(ue) etc.

12. Pronunciation

As a general rule either full or partial pronunciation is given for every simple entry word. The symbols used are those laid down by the International Phonetic Association. All the phonetic symbols used in the dictionary are explained in the Key to Pronunciation below.

Every headword that does not consist of words listed and phonetically transcribed elsewhere in the dictionary is followed by its pronunciation in square brackets: **Blüte** ['bly:tə] ...

A number of the more common initial and final elements occurring in derivatives and compounds have not been transcribed phonetically after every derivative entry. They have been collected, together with their phonetic transcription, in a comprehensive list on page 12.

13. Key to Pronunciation

The phonetic alphabet used in this German-English dictionary is that of the Association Phonétique Internationale (A.P.I. or I.P.A. = International Phonetic Association). A long vowel is indicated by [:] following the vowel symbol. Main stress is indicated by ['] and secondary stress by [,] preceding the stressed syllable. A glottal stop [ʔ] is the forced stop between one word or syllable and the following one beginning with a stressed vowel, as in "beobachten" [bə'ʔo:baxtən].

Symbol	Examples	Nearest English Equivalents	Remarks
		A. Vowels	
a	Mann [man]		short a as in French "c**a**rte" or in British English "c**a**st" said quickly
aː	Wagen ['vaːgən]	f**a**ther	long a
ɐ	Ober ['oːbɐ]		There is no *-er* sound at the end. It is one pure short vowel-sound.
e	egal [e'gaːl]	b**e**d	
eː	Weg [veːk]		unlike any English sound, though it has a resemblance to the sound in "d**ay**"
ə	Bitte ['bɪtə]	**a**go	a short sound, that of unaccented e
ɛ	Männer ['mɛnɐ] Geld [gɛlt]	f**ai**r	
ɛː	prägen ['prɛːgən]		same sound, but long
ɪ	Wind [vɪnt]	**i**t	
iː	hier [hiːɐ]	m**ee**t	
ɔ	Ort [ɔrt]	l**o**ng	
o	Modell [mo'dɛl]	m**o**lest	
oː	Boot [boːt]		[oː] resembles the English sound in g**o** [gəʊ] but without the [ʊ]
øː	schön [ʃøːn]		as in French "f**eu**". The sound may be acquired by saying [e] through closely rounded lips.
ø	Ödem [ø'deːm]		same sound, but short
œ	öffnen ['œfnən]		as in French "n**euf**". The sound has a resemblance to the English vowel in "h**e**r". Lips, however, must be well rounded as for ɔ.
ʊ	Mutter ['mʊtɐ]	b**oo**k	
uː	Uhr [uːɐ]	b**oo**t	
ʏ	Glück [glʏk]		almost like the French u as in s**u**r. It may be acquired by saying [i] through fairly closely rounded lips.
yː	führen ['fyːrən]		same sound, but long
		B. Diphthongs	
aɪ	Mai [maɪ]	l**i**ke	
aʊ	Maus [maʊs]	m**ou**se	
ɔʏ	Beute ['bɔʏtə] Läufer ['lɔʏfɐ]	b**oy**	
		C. Consonants	
b	besser ['bɛsɐ]	**b**etter	
d	du [duː]	**d**ance	
f	finden ['fɪndən] Vater ['faːtɐ] Photo ['foːto]	**f**ind	
g	Gold [gɔlt] Geld [gɛlt]	**g**old	
ʒ	Genie [ʒe'niː]	mea**s**ure	
h	Haus [haʊs]	**h**ouse	
ç	Licht [lɪçt] manch [manç] traurig ['traʊrɪç]		An approximation to this sound may be produced by assuming the mouth configuration for [i] and emitting a strong current of breath.

Symbol	Examples	Nearest English Equivalents	Remarks
x	Loch [lɔx]	Scotch: lo**ch**	Whereas [ç] is pronounced at the front of the mouth, x is pronounced in the throat.
j	ja [ja:]	**y**ear	
k	keck [kɛk] Tag [ta:k] Chronist [kro'nɪst] Café [ka'fe:]	**k**ick	
l	lassen ['lasən]	**l**ump	pronounced like English initial "clear l"
m	Maus [maʊs]	**m**ouse	
n	nein [naɪn]	**n**ot	
ŋ	klingen ['klɪŋən] sinken ['zɪŋkən]	si**ng** dri**nk**	
p	Paß [pas] Weib [vaɪp] obgleich [ɔp'glaɪç]	**p**ass	
r	rot [ro:t]	**r**ot	There are two pronunciations: the frontal or lingual r and the uvular r (the latter unknown in England).
s	Glas [gla:s] Masse ['masə] Mast [mast] naß [nas]	mi**ss**	unvoiced when final, doubled, or next to a voiceless consonant
z	Sohn [zo:n] Rose ['ro:zə]	**z**ero	voiced when at the beginning of a word or a syllable
ʃ	Schiff [ʃɪf] Charme [ʃarm] Spiel [ʃpi:l] Stein [ʃtaɪn]	**sh**op	
t	Tee [te:] Thron [tro:n] Stadt [ʃtat] Bad [ba:t] Findling ['fɪntlɪŋ] Wind [vɪnt]	**t**ea	
v	Vase ['va:zə] Winter ['vɪntɐ]	**v**ast	

ã, ɛ̃, õ are nasalized vowels. Exmples: Engagement [ãgaʒə'mã:], Terrain [tɛ'rɛ̃:], Feuilleton [fœjə'tõ:].

14. List of Initial and Final Elements normally given without Phonetic Transcription

Initial elements

be- [bə]
er- [ɛr]
ent- [ɛnt]
ge- [gə]
miß- [mɪs]
un- [ʊn]
ver- [fɛr]
zer- [tsɛr]

Final elements

-bar [ba:ɐ]
-chen [çən]
-d [t]
-e [ə]
-ei [aɪ]
-el [əl]
-en [ən]
-end [ənt]
-fach [fax]
-haft [haft]
-halber [halbɐ]
-haltig [haltɪç]
-heit [haɪt]
-ig [ɪç]
-in [ɪn]
-isch [ɪʃ]
-keit [kaɪt]
-kunft [kʊnft]
-lein [laɪn]
-lich [lɪç]
-los [lo:s]
-n [n]
-nis [nɪs]
-s [s]
-sal [za:l]
-sam [za:m]
-schaft [ʃaft]
-st [st]
-ste [stə]
-stel [stəl]
-t [t]
-te [tə]
-tät [tɛ:t]
-tum [tu:m]
-ung [ʊŋ]
-wärts [vɛrts]

Key to Symbols and Abbreviations

1. Symbols

~ }	*See page 8*: The swung dash
F	*familiar; colloquial*
V	*vulgar*
📖	*scientific/technical term*
✿	*botany*
⚙	*technology, engineering*
⚒	*mining*
⚔	*military term*
⚓	*nautical term*
☤	*commercial term*
🚂	*railway*
✈	*aviation; Air Force*
📯	*postal affairs*
♪	*musical term*
△	*architecture*
⚡	*electrical engineering*
⚖	*legal term*
A	*mathematics*
⛏	*agriculture*
⚗	*chemistry*
⚕	*medicine*
→	*See page 8*: The cross-reference sign

2. Abbreviations

a.	*also*
abbr.	*abbreviation*
acc.	*accusative (case)*
adj.	*adjective*
adv.	*adverb*
Am.	*Americanism*
anat.	*anatomy*
art.	*article*
ast.	*astronomy*
attr.	*attributive(ly)*
bibl.	*biblical*
biol.	*biology*
Brit.	*in British usage only*
b.s.	*bad sense*
cj.	*conjunction*
coll.	*collectively*
comp.	*comparative*
contp.	*contemptuously*
cpds.	*compound words*
dat.	*dative (case)*
d-e	deine, *your*
dem.	*demonstrative*
dial.	*dialectal, regional*
dim.	*diminutive*
d-m	deinem, (*to*) *your*
d-n	deinen, *your*
d-r	deiner, *of your, to your*
d-s	deines, *of your*
EC	*European Community*
eccl.	*ecclesiastical*
e-e	eine, *a (an)*
electron.	*electronics*
e-m	einem, *to a (an)*
e-n	einen, *a (an)*
e-r	einer, *of a (an), to a (an)*
e-s	eines, *of a (an)*
esp.	*(e)specially*
et.	etwas, *something*
euphem.	*euphemistically*
f	*feminine*
fig.	*figuratively*
gastr.	*gastronomy*
GB	*Great Britain*
gen.	*genitive (case)*
geogr.	*geography*
geol.	*geology*
ger.	*gerund*
her.	*heraldry*
hist.	*historical*
hum.	*humorously*
impers.	*impersonal*
indef.	*indefinite*
inf.	*infinitive (mood)*
int.	*interjection*
interr.	*interrogative*
iro.	*ironically*
ital.	*Italian*
j-d	jemand, *someone*
j-m	jemandem, (*to*) *someone*
j-n	jemanden, *someone*
j-s	jemandes, *someone's*
ling.	*linguistics*
lit.	*literary, elevated*
m	*masculine*

m-e	meine, *my*
metall.	*metallurgy*
meteor.	*meteorology*
min.	*mineralogy*
m-m	meinem, (*to*) *my*
m-n	meinen, *my*
mot.	*motoring*
m-r	meiner, *of my, to my*
m-s	meines, *of my*
myth.	*mythology*
n	*neuter*
nom.	*nominative* (*case*)
n.s.	*in the narrower sense*
obs.	*obsolescent, obsolete*
opt.	*optics*
o.s.	*oneself*
parl.	*parliamentary term*
ped.	*pedagogics, education*
pers.	*personal*
pharm.	*pharmacy*
phls.	*philosophy*
phot.	*photography*
phys.	*physics*
physiol.	*physiology*
pl.	*plural*
poet.	*poetic*(*ally*)
pol.	*politics*
poss.	*possessive*
p.p.	*past participle*
pred.	*predicative*(*ly*)
pres.p.	*present participle*
pret.	*preterit*(*e*)
pron.	*pronoun*
prp.	*preposition*
psych.	*psychology*
R.C.	*Roman Catholic*
refl.	*reflexive*
rel.	*relative*
rhet.	*rhetoric*
s-e	seine, *his, its, one's*
sep.	*separated*
sg.	*singular*
sl.	*slang*
s-m	seinem, (*to*) *his,* (*to*) *its,* (*to*) *one's*
s-n	seinen, *his, its, one's*
s.o.	*someone*
s-r	seiner, *of his, of its, of oneself*
s-s	seines, *of his, of its, of one's*
s.th.	*something*
su.	*substantive*(*ly*)
sup.	*superlative*
surv.	*surveying*
tel.	*telegraphy*
teleph.	*telephone system*
textil.	*textiles*
thea.	*theatre*
TM	*trademark*
TV	*television*
typ.	*typography, printing*
univ.	*university*
USA	*United States of America*
usu.	*usually*
v/aux.	*auxiliary verb*
vet.	*veterinary medicine*
v/i.	*intransitive verb*
v/impers.	*impersonal verb*
v/refl.	*reflexive verb*
v/t.	*transitive verb*
w.s.	*in the wider sense*
zo.	*zoology*

Alphabetical List of the German Irregular Verbs

Infinitive – Preterite – Past Participle

backen – backte (buk) – gebacken
befehlen – befahl – befohlen
beginnen – begann – begonnen
beißen – biß – gebissen
bergen – barg – geborgen
bersten – barst – geborsten
bewegen – bewog – bewogen
biegen – bog – gebogen
bieten – bot – geboten
binden – band – gebunden
bitten – bat – gebeten
blasen – blies – geblasen
bleiben – blieb – geblieben
bleichen – blich – geblichen
braten – briet – gebraten
brauchen – brauchte – gebraucht (*v/aux.* brauchen)
brechen – brach – gebrochen
brennen – brannte – gebrannt
bringen – brachte – gebracht
denken – dachte – gedacht
dreschen – drosch – gedroschen
dringen – drang – gedrungen
dürfen – durfte – gedurft (*v/aux.* dürfen)
empfehlen – empfahl – empfohlen
erkiesen – erkor – erkoren
erlöschen – erlosch – erloschen
erschrecken – erschrak – erschrocken
essen – aß – gegessen
fahren – fuhr – gefahren
fallen – fiel – gefallen
fangen – fing – gefangen
fechten – focht – gefochten
finden – fand – gefunden
flechten – flocht – geflochten
fliegen – flog – geflogen
fliehen – floh – geflohen
fließen – floß – geflossen
fressen – fraß – gefressen
frieren – fror – gefroren
gären – gor (*esp. fig.* gärte) – gegoren (*esp. fig.* gegärt)
gebären – gebar – geboren
geben – gab – gegeben
gedeihen – gedieh – gediehen
gehen – ging – gegangen
gelingen – gelang – gelungen
gelten – galt – gegolten
genesen – genas – genesen
genießen – genoß – genossen
geschehen – geschah – geschehen
gewinnen – gewann – gewonnen
gießen – goß – gegossen
gleichen – glich – geglichen
gleiten – glitt – geglitten
glimmen – glomm – geglommen
graben – grub – gegraben
greifen – griff – gegriffen
haben – hatte – gehabt
halten – hielt – gehalten
hängen – hing – gehangen
hauen – haute (hieb) – gehauen
heben – hob – gehoben
heißen – hieß – geheißen
helfen – half – geholfen
kennen – kannte – gekannt
klimmen – klomm – geklommen
klingen – klang – geklungen
kneifen – kniff – gekniffen
kommen – kam – gekommen
können – konnte – gekonnt (*v/aux.* können)
kriechen – kroch – gekrochen
laden – lud – geladen
lassen – ließ – gelassen (*v/aux.* lassen)
laufen – lief – gelaufen
leiden – litt – gelitten
leihen – lieh – geliehen
lesen – las – gelesen
liegen – lag – gelegen
lügen – log – gelogen
mahlen – mahlte – gemahlen
meiden – mied – gemieden
melken – melkte (molk) – gemolken (gemelkt)
messen – maß – gemessen
mißlingen – mißlang – mißlungen
mögen – mochte – gemocht (*v/aux.* mögen)
müssen – mußte – gemußt (*v/aux.* müssen)
nehmen – nahm – genommen
nennen – nannte – genannt
pfeifen – pfiff – gepfiffen
preisen – pries – gepriesen
quellen – quoll – gequollen
raten – riet – geraten
reiben – rieb – gerieben
reißen – riß – gerissen
reiten – ritt – geritten
rennen – rannte –gerannt
riechen – roch – gerochen
ringen – rang – gerungen
rinnen – rann – geronnen

rufen – rief – gerufen
salzen – salzte – gesalzen (gesalzt)
saufen – soff – gesoffen
saugen – sog – gesogen
schaffen – schuf – geschaffen
schallen – schallte (scholl) – geschallt (*for* erschallen *a.* erschollen)
scheiden – schied – geschieden
scheinen – schien – geschienen
scheißen – schiß – geschissen
schelten – schalt – gescholten
scheren – schor – geschoren
schieben – schob – geschoben
schießen – schoß – geschossen
schinden – schindete (schund) – geschunden
schlafen – schlief – geschlafen
schlagen – schlug – geschlagen
schleichen – schlich – geschlichen
schleifen – schliff – geschliffen
schließen – schloß – geschlossen
schlingen – schlang – geschlungen
schmeißen – schmiß – geschmissen
schmelzen – schmolz – geschmolzen
schnauben – schnob – geschnoben
schneiden – schnitt – geschnitten
schrecken – schrak – *obs.* geschrocken
schreiben – schrieb – geschrieben
schreien – schrie – geschrie(e)n
schreiten – schritt – geschritten
schweigen – schwieg – geschwiegen
schwellen – schwoll – geschwollen
schwimmen – schwamm – geschwommen
schwinden – schwand – geschwunden
schwingen – schwang – geschwungen
schwören – schwor – geschworen
sehen – sah – gesehen
sein – war – gewesen
senden – sandte – gesandt
sieden – sott – gesotten
singen – sang – gesungen
sinken – sank – gesunken
sinnen – sann – gesonnen
sitzen – saß – gesessen
sollen – sollte – gesollt (*v/aux.* sollen)
spalten – spaltete – gespalten (gespaltet)
speien – spie – gespie(e)n
spinnen – spann – gesponnen
sprechen – sprach – gesprochen
sprießen – sproß – gesprossen
springen – sprang – gesprungen
stechen – stach – gestochen
stecken – steckte (stak) – gesteckt
stehen – stand – gestanden
stehlen – stahl – gestohlen
steigen – stieg – gestiegen
sterben – starb – gestorben
stieben – stob – gestoben
stinken – stank – gestunken
stoßen – stieß – gestoßen
streichen – strich – gestrichen
streiten – stritt – gestritten
tragen – trug – getragen
treffen – traf – getroffen
treiben – trieb – getrieben
treten – trat – getreten
triefen – triefte (troff) – getrieft
trinken – trank – getrunken
trügen – trog – getrogen
tun – tat – getan
verderben – verdarb – verdorben
verdrießen – verdroß – verdrossen
vergessen – vergaß – vergessen
verlieren – verlor – verloren
verschleißen – verschliß – verschlissen
verzeihen – verzieh – verziehen
wachsen – wuchs – gewachsen
wägen – wog (wägte) – gewogen (gewägt)
waschen – wusch – gewaschen
weben – wob – gewoben
weichen – wich – gewichen
weisen – wies – gewiesen
wenden – wandte – gewandt
werben – warb – geworben
werden – wurde – geworden (worden*)
werfen – warf – geworfen
wiegen – wog – gewogen
winden – wand – gewunden
wissen – wußte – gewußt
wollen – wollte – gewollt (*v/aux.* wollen)
wringen – wrang – gewrungen
zeihen – zieh – geziehen
ziehen – zog – gezogen
zwingen – zwang – gezwungen

* only in connection with the past participles of other verbs, *e.g.* ***er ist gesehen worden*** he has been seen.

A

A, a [aː] *n* (-; -) A, a; ♪ A; ***das A und O*** the most important thing, the basics; ***das ist das A und O der Geschichte*** that's what it's all about; ***wer A sagt, muß auch B sagen*** in for a penny, in for a pound; ***von A bis Z*** right down the line; ***von A bis Z durchlesen*** read *book* from cover to cover, read through from beginning to end; ***sie kennt das Thema von A bis Z*** she knows the subject from A to Z (*or* back to front); ***er kennt die Leute von A bis Z*** he knows every single one of them; ***wir haben alles, von A bis Z*** F you name it, we've got it; ***es war ein Erfolg von A bis Z*** it was a success from start to finish; ***er hat es uns von A bis Z erzählt*** he told us everything, right down to the last detail; ***das ist von A bis Z erfunden*** he's *etc.* made the whole thing up; ***das ist von A bis Z erlogen*** there's not a word of truth in it, F it's a pack of lies

à [a] *prp.* at ... each (*or* a piece); ***20 Adreßbücher ~ DM 9,80*** 20 address books at 9.80 DM each

Aal [aːl] *m* (-[e]s; -e) eel; → ***winden*** II

aa·len ['aːlən] F *v/refl.* (h): ***sich ~*** laze around; ***sich in der Sonne ~*** bask in the sun

'Aal|fang *m* eel fishing; **≈glatt** *fig. adj.* (as) slippery as an eel; **~er Typ** F smoothie; **~sup·pe** *f* eel soup

Aas [aːs] *n* (-es) **1.** *pl.* **Aase** carcass; **2.** *pl.* **Äser** F *fig. sl.* swine; F ***kein ~*** *sl.* not a sod; → ***faul*** 2

aa·sen ['aːzən] F *v/i.* (h): ***~ mit*** squander, splash about, throw around, waste; ***er aast mit s-r Gesundheit*** he's ruining his health

'Aas|flie·ge *f* carrion fly; **~fres·ser** *m* scavenger; **~gei·er** *m* vulture (*a. fig.*)

ab [ap] **I.** *prp.* **1.** from; ***~ Brüssel*** from Brussels; ✝ ***~ Berlin*** (***Werk, Lager*** *etc.*) ex Berlin (works, warehouse *etc.*); **2.** from ... (on[wards]), *adm.* as of, with effect from; ***~ heute*** starting today, from today; ***~ 18*** *film etc.*: no admittance to persons under 18; **3.** *order etc.*: from ... (on[wards]); *amount*: from ... (up[wards]); ***~ 30 Leute(n)*** *a.* 30 people and up, for groups of 30 and more; **II.** *adv.* **4.** ***~ mit dir!, ~ (geht) die Post!, ~ nach Kassel!*** off you go now; 🚂 ***Hamburg ~ 20.15*** dep. (= departure) Hamburg 20.15; **5.** from; ***von heute ~*** starting today, from today; ***von jetzt ~*** from now on, in future; ***~ und zu*** now and then, from time to time, occasionally; **6.** *order etc.*: from ... (on[wards]); *amount*: from ... (up[wards]); ***von 4000 Mark ~*** *a.* 4000 marks and up(wards); **7.** *thea.* exit, *pl.* exeunt; ***Romeo ~*** exit Romeo; ***alle ~*** exeunt omnes; **8.** *film*: ***~!*** go ahead; ***Kamera ~!*** roll it!, camera!; ***Ton ~!*** sound!

'ab·ackern (*sep.* -k·k-) F *v/refl.* (*sep*, h): ***sich ~*** slave away, work one's fingers to the bone, *esp. sport*: run o.s. into the ground

'ab·än·der·bar *adj.* open to change *etc.*; → ***Abänderung; es ist noch ~*** it can still be changed *etc.*; → **'ab·än·dern** *v/t.* (*sep*, h) change, alter; revise, modify; *parl.* amend; ⚖ commute; **'Ab·än·de·rung** *f* (-; -en) alteration, change; modification, revision; *parl.* amendment; ⚖ commutation

'Ab·än·de·rungs·an·trag *m parl.* motion for amendment

Aban·don [abãˈdõː] *m* (-s; -s) ✝ abandonment; **aban·do·nie·ren** [abãdoˈniːrən] *v/t.* (h) abandon

'ab·ar·bei·ten (*sep.*, h) **I.** *v/t.* work off; ***s-e Überfahrt ~*** work one's passage; **II.** *v/refl.*: ***sich ~*** slave (away), F work one's fingers to the bone; → ***abgearbeitet***

'ab·är·gern F *v/refl.* (*sep.*, h): ***sich ~*** vex o.s.

'Ab·art *f* (-; -en) ♀, *zo.* variety, species; *fig.* variation (*gen.* of, on); **'ab·ar·tig** *adj.* abnormal; perverse; **'Ab·ar·tig·keit** *f* (-; -en) abnormality; perverseness, perversity

'ab·ät·zen *v/t.* (*sep*, h) ⚕ cauterize

'Ab·bau *m* (-[e]s; *no pl.*) **1.** dismantling; demolition; **2.** reduction (*gen.* in); **3.** decline; **4.** ⚗ decomposition, disintegration; *physiol. a.* breakdown; **5.** ⚒ mining *of coal etc.*; working (of a mine); **'ab·bau·bar** *adj.*: ***biologisch ~*** biodegradable; **'ab·bau·en** (*sep.*, h) **I.** *v/t.* **1.** dismantle; take down *scaffolding etc.*; pull down *house etc.*; **2.** ⚗ break down; **3.** ⚒ mine *coal etc.*; work *a mine*; **4.** reduce; run down *supplies etc.*; remedy *abuses*; get rid of *prejudices etc.*; ***Arbeitskräfte ~*** cut down on manpower (*or* the workforce); **II.** *v/i.* go downhill (*a. mentally*); flag; feel faint; ***er baut in letzter Zeit stark ab*** he's going downhill fast

'Ab·bau|ge·rech·tig·keit *f* mining (*or* mineral) rights *pl.*; **~pro,dukt** *n* degradation product; **~rech·te** *pl.* mining (*or* mineral) rights; **~strecke** (*sep.* -k·k-) *f* gate; **≈wür·dig** *adj.* workable

'ab·bei·ßen *v/t.* (*irr.*, *sep.*, h, → ***beißen***) bite off

'ab·bei·zen *v/t.* (*sep.*, h) strip

'Ab·beiz·mit·tel *n* (paint) stripper, paint remover

'ab·be·kom·men *v/t.* (*irr.*, *sep.*, h, → ***bekommen***) **1.** get off; **2.** F get; ***etwas ~*** a) get one's share, b) *person*: be hit, get hurt, *thing*: be damaged; ***das meiste ~*** bear (*or* take) the brunt

'ab·be·ru·fen *v/t.* (*irr.*, *sep.*, h, → ***berufen***) recall *ambassador etc.*; relieve *s.o.* from office; *fig.* ***~ werden*** pass away

'ab·be·stel·len *v/t.* (*sep.*, h) cancel (the order for); ***j-n ~*** ask s.o. not to come; **'Ab·be·stel·lung** *f* (-; -en) cancellation

'ab·bet·teln *v/t.* (*sep.*, h): ***j-m et. ~*** wheedle s.th. out of s.o.; ***er hat mir den Wagen abgebettelt*** he went on and on at me until I let him have the car

'ab·be·zah·len *v/t.* (*sep.*, h) pay off

'ab·bie·gen (*irr.*, *sep.*, → ***biegen***) **I.** *v/t.* (h) bend; *fig.* head off, stave off; **II.** *v/i.* (sn) *car, road etc.*: turn (off); *road*: branch off; ***nach rechts (links) ~*** turn right (left); **'Ab·bie·ger** *m* (-s; -) car *etc.* turning off; **'Ab·bie·ge·spur** *f* filter lane; **'Ab·bie·gung** *f* (-; -en) turning; bend

'Ab·bild *n* (-[e]s; -er) **1.** image, reflection; **2.** *fig.* image, portrayal; **'ab·bil·den** *v/t.* (*sep.*, h) portray, depict; ***wie oben abgebildet*** as shown above; **'Ab·bil·dung** *f* (-; -en) picture, illustration

'ab·bin·den (*irr.*, *sep.*, h, → ***binden***) **I.** *v/t.* **1.** untie, undo; take off *tie etc.*; **2.** ⚕ ligature; **3.** *gastr.* bind; **II.** *v/i.* *cement etc.*: set

'Ab·bit·te *f* (-; *no pl.*) apology; ***~ tun*** (*or* ***leisten***) apologize (***bei j-m wegen et.*** to s.o. for s.th.); **'ab·bit·ten** *v/t.* (*irr.*, *sep.*, h, → ***bitten***) ***j-m et. ~*** ask s.o.'s pardon for s.th

'ab·bla·sen *v/t.* (*irr.*, *sep.*, h, → ***blasen***) **1.** blow off (*a. steam*); ⚙ (sand)blast *castings*; **2.** F *fig.* call off

'ab·blät·tern *v/i.* (*sep.*, sn) **1.** peel off, *paint*: *a.* flake off; **2.** ♀ shed its leaves

'ab·blei·ben F *v/i.* (*irr.*, *sep.*, sn, → ***bleiben***): ***wo ist es abgeblieben?*** where has it got to?

'ab·blend·bar *adj.* anti-dazzle; **'Ab·blen·de** *f* (-; *no pl.*) *film*: fade-out; **'ab·blen·den** (*sep.*, h) **I.** *v/t.* dim *light etc.*; *mot.* dip (*Am.* dim) *one's headlights*; **II.** *v/i.* *mot.* dip (*Am.* dim) one's headlights; *phot.* stop down; **'Ab·blen·der** *m* (-s; -) dimmer

'Ab·blend|licht *n* anti-dazzle light, *Am.* low beam; **~schal·ter** *m* dipswitch, *Am.* dimmer switch

'ab·blit·zen F *v/i.* (*sep.*, sn) F be told where to go; ***j-n ~ lassen*** F tell s.o. where to go; ***er ist bei ihr abgeblitzt*** F he was given the brush-off

'ab·blocken (*sep.* -k·k-) *v/t.* (*sep.*, h) **1.** *sport*: block; **2.** *fig.* block, *esp. pol. a.* stonewall; ***alle Kompromißvorschläge ~*** stonewall all attempts at compromise

'ab·brau·sen (*sep.*) **I.** *v/t.* (h) shower down; **II.** *v/refl.* (h): ***sich ~*** have (*or* take) a shower; **III.** F *v/i.* (sn) roar (*or* zoom) off

'ab·bre·chen (*irr.*, *sep.*, → ***brechen***) **I.**

v/t. (h) break off; pull down, demolish *house etc.*; take down *scaffolding*; break *camp*; *fig.* break off *negotiations, relations etc.*; *a.* cut short *discussion etc.*; abort *space flight, computer program*; *fig.* **die Zelte ~** pack one's bags and leave; **das Studium ~** drop out of university; F **sich einen ~** nearly kill o.s.; **II.** *v/i.* (sn) break off; *fig. a.* stop; *fig.* **die Gebirgswand bricht dort steil ab** there's a sheer drop at that point

'ab·brem·sen (*sep.*, h) **I.** *v/t.* brake, slow down; deboost *spaceship*; cushion *fall etc.*; **II.** *v/i.* brake, slow down, apply the brakes

'ab·bren·nen (*irr., sep.,* → **brennen**) **I.** *v/t.* (h) burn down; burn off; refine *metal*, temper *steel*; let off *fireworks*; **II.** *v/i.* (sn) burn down (*a. candle etc.*); be destroyed by fire; → **abgebrannt**

'ab·brin·gen *v/t.* (*irr., sep.,* h, → **bringen**) get off; *fig.* **j-n von et. ~** put s.o. off doing s.th., *a.* talk s.o. out of (*or* dissuade s.o. from) doing s.th.; **ich habe versucht, sie davon abzubringen** I tried to talk her out of it; **j-n von e-r Gewohnheit ~** break s.o. of a habit; **j-n von e-m Thema ~** get s.o. off a subject; **j-n vom (rechten) Wege ~** lead s.o. astray; **davon lasse ich mich nicht ~** I'm not going to be talked out of it

'ab·bröckeln (*sep.* -k·k-) *v/i.* crumble away (*or* off); *fig. exchange rates etc.*: drop off, fall

'Ab·bruch *m* (-[e]s; ⸚e) **1.** demolition; **2.** *no pl. fig.* breaking off; **Sieg durch ~** *boxing*: win on a technical knockout; **mit ~ des Spiels drohen** *soccer etc.*: threaten to abandon the match; **3.** *no pl.* damage; **e-r Sache ~ tun** impair (*or* detract) from s.th., be detrimental to s.th.; F **das tut der Liebe keinen ~** that's not going to hurt anyone; **4.** *computer*: abort; **~ar·bei·ten** *pl.* demolition work *sg.*; **~ar·bei·ter** *m* demolition worker; **~haus** *n* condemned building; **≈reif** *adj.* derelict, dilapidated; due for demolition, condemned; ⚙ due to be scrapped; **~sie·ger** *m boxing*: winner on a technical knockout; **~un·ter,neh·men** *n* demolition contractors *pl., Am.* wrecking company

'ab·brü·hen *v/t.* (*sep.*, h) scald; *fig.* → **abgebrüht**

'ab·brum·men F *v/t.* (*sep.*, h): **e-e Strafe ~** F do time; **e-e sechsmonatige Strafe ~** F do six months inside

'ab·bu·chen *v/t.* (*sep.*, h) ✝ debit *a sum to an account*; **'Ab·bu·chung** *f* (-; -en) charge, debit (entry)

'Ab·bu·chungs|auf·trag *m* (direct) debit order, standing order; **~ver·fah·ren** *n* direct debiting service

'ab·bum·meln F *v/t.* → **abfeiern**

'ab·bür·sten *v/t.* (*sep.*, h) **1.** brush (down) *clothes*; **2.** brush off *dust*

'ab·bü·ßen *v/t.* (*sep.*, h) expiate, atone for; **e-e Strafe ~** serve a sentence

Abc [aːbeː'tseː] *n* (-; *no pl.*) ABC, alphabet; *fig. the* basics *pl.*; **nach dem ~** alphabetically, in alphabetical order

'ab·checken (*sep.* -k·k-) *v/t.* (*sep.*, h) **1.** check; **2.** tick (*Am.* check) off

AB'C-Krieg·füh·rung *f* NBC warfare

Ab'c-Schüt·ze *m* school beginner, *formal*: reception child (*or* pupil)

AB'C-Waf·fen *pl.* NBC weapons

'ab·däm·men *v/t.* (*sep.*, h) dam (up)

'Ab·dampf *m* (-[e]s; ⸚e) exhaust steam; **'ab·damp·fen** (*sep.*) **I.** *v/i.* (sn) **1.** evaporate; **2.** F *fig.* F clear off; **II.** *v/t.* (h) (*a.* **~ lassen**) evaporate, vaporize

'Ab·dampf|hei·zung *f* waste-steam heating; **~scha·le** *f* evaporating dish; **~tur,bi·ne** *f* waste-steam turbine

'ab·dan·ken *v/i.* (*sep.*, h) resign; abdicate; **'Ab·dan·kung** *f* (-; -en) resignation; abdication

'Ab·deck|blech *n* metal cover; **~creme** *f* cover-up stick

'ab·decken (*sep.* -k·k-) *v/t.* (*sep.*, h) **1.** uncover; unroof *house*; strip *bed etc.*; clear *the table*; **2.** take off *roof*; **3.** *a.* ⚙ cover (up); **4.** repay *debt*; **5.** *sport*: mark, cover; **6.** ✝ cover

'Ab·decker (*sep.* -k·k-) *m* (-s; -) knacker; **Ab·decke·rei** [apdɛkə'raɪ] (*sep.* -k·k-) *f* (-; -en) knacker's yard

'Ab·deck|hau·be *f* cover; **~pla·ne** *f* tarpaulin; **~stift** *m* cover-up stick

'ab·dich·ten *v/t.* (*sep.*, h) seal; **gegen Luft (Wasser) ~** make airtight (watertight); **gegen Lärm (Zugluft) ~** (make) soundproof (draughtproof, *Am.* draftproof); **'Ab·dich·tung** *f* (-; -en) **1.** *no pl.* sealing *etc.*; **2.** → **Dichtung²**

'ab·die·nen *v/t.* (*sep.*, h): **s-e Zeit ~** serve one's time

ab·ding·bar ['apdɪŋbaːr] *adj.* ⚖ modifiable; **sie sind ~** *a.* they can be modified (*or* altered)

'ab·don·nern F *v/i.* (*sep.*, sn) roar (F zoom) off

'ab·drän·gen *v/t.* (*sep.*, h) push (*or* force) aside; *mot.* force off the road

'ab·dre·hen (*sep.*, h) **I.** *v/t.* **1.** twist off; **2.** turn off *gas, water etc.*; ⚡ *a.* switch off; **3.** turn away (*a.* **sich ~**); **4.** *film*: finish (shooting); **II.** *v/i.* ⚓, ✈ change course; veer off

'Ab·drift *f* (-; *no pl.*) drift; **'ab·drif·ten** *v/i.* (*sep.*, sn) drift (off course)

'ab·dros·seln *v/t.* (*sep.*, h) *mot.* throttle (*a. fig.*)

'Ab·druck¹ *m* (-[e]s; ⸚e) impression, imprint; cast; **~ in Wachs** wax impression; → **Fußabdruck, Fingerabdruck**

'Ab·druck² *m* (-[e]s; -e) **1.** copy; reprint; **2.** *no pl.* (re)printing; **'ab·drucken** (*sep.* -k·k-) *v/t.* (*sep.*, h) print; **wieder ~** reprint

'ab·drücken (*sep.* -k·k-) (*sep.*, h) **I.** *v/t.* **1.** squeeze off; **j-m die Luft ~** choke s.o.; **2.** make an impression (*or* a mo[u]ld) of; **3.** fire, pull the trigger of; **4.** hug, squeeze; **II.** *v/i.* fire, pull the trigger; **III.** *v/refl.*: **sich ~** leave an impression (*or* a mark)

'ab·ducken (*sep.* -k·k-) *v/i.* (*sep.*, h) *boxing*: duck

Ab·duk·tor [ap'dʊktoːɐ] *m* (-s; -en [-'toːrən]) *anat.* abductor

'ab·dun·keln *v/t.* (*sep.*, h) darken, dim, black out *room*; darken *colo(u)r*

'ab·du·schen (*sep.*, h) **I.** *v/t.* spray down; **II.** *v/refl.*: **sich ~** have (*or* take) a shower

'ab·eb·ben *v/i.* (*sep.*, sn) ebb away; *fig.* ebb, die down (*or* away)

Abend ['aːbənt] *m* (-s; -e ['aːbəndə]) evening; **am ~** in the evening; **heute ≈** this evening, tonight; **morgen (gestern) ≈** tomorrow (last) night; **Sonntag ≈** Sunday evening; **guten ~!** good evening!; **zu ~ essen** have supper (*or* dinner); **es wird ~** it's getting dark; *fig.* **man soll den Tag nicht vor dem ~ loben** don't count your chickens before they're hatched; → **bunt, heilig**; **~an·dacht** *f* evening prayer(s *pl.*), evensong; **~an·zug** *m* evening dress; **~aus·ga·be** *f* evening edition; **~blatt** *n* evening paper; **~brot** *n* supper, tea; **~däm·me·rung** *f* twilight, dusk; **in der ~** at dusk

aben·de·lang ['aːbəndəlaŋ] **I.** *adj.*: **~e Gespräche** *etc.* discussions *etc.* that go (*or* went) on for evenings on end; **II.** *adv.* for evenings on end, night after night

'Abend|es·sen *n* dinner, supper; **≈fül·lend** *adj.* full-length *film etc.*; **~kas·se** *f thea.* box office; **Karten an der ~ bekommen** get tickets on the night; **~kleid** *n* evening dress (*Am.* gown); **~kurs** *m* evening classes *pl*

'Abend·land *n* (-[e]s; *no pl.*): **das ~** (*a.* **das christliche ~**) the Occident, the West; Western civilization; **'abend·län·disch** [-lɛndɪʃ] *adj.* western, *formal*: occidental

'abend·lich I. *adj.* evening ...; **II.** *adv.* in the evening(s)

'Abend|mahl *n* (-[e]s; *no pl.*) *eccl.* (Holy) Communion, *the* Lord's Supper; **das ~ empfangen (reichen)** receive (administer) Holy Communion; **~mahls·kelch** *m* Communion chalice; **~nach·rich·ten** *pl.* evening news *sg.*; **~pro,gramm** *n*: **das heutige ~** tonight's (*or* this evening's) program(me)s; **das ~ ist meistens ganz gut** the evening program(me)s are usually quite good; **~rot** *n*, **~rö·te** *f* sunset

abends ['aːbənts] *adv.* in the evening(s); **um 7 Uhr ~** at 7 o'clock in the evening, at 7 p.m.

'Abend|schu·le *f* evening classes *pl.*, night school; **~son·ne** *f* evening (*or* late afternoon) sun; **~spa,zier·gang** *m* evening walk; **~stern** *m* evening star; **~stun·de** *f*: **in den ~n** in the evening(s); **zu später ~** late at night, at a late hour; **~toi,let·te** *f* evening dress; **~vor·stel·lung** *f* evening performance; **~zeit** *f* evening (hours *pl.*); **~zei·tung** *f* evening paper

Aben·teu·er ['aːbəntɔʏɐ] *n* (-s; -) adventure; **er stürzt sich gern in ~** a) he likes getting involved in dangerous and exciting things, b) he's not afraid of taking risks; **~film** *m* adventure film; **~geist** *m* adventurous spirit; **~ge·schich·te** *f* adventure story

'aben·teu·er·lich *adj.* adventurous; *fig.* risky; odd, curious; wild, fantastic

'Aben·teu·er·lust *f* love of (*or* thirst for) adventure

aben·teu·ern ['aːbəntɔʏɐn] *v/i.* (sn): **durch die Welt ~** roam (through) the world

'Aben·teu·er|ro,man *m* adventure story (*or* novel); **~spiel·platz** *m* adventure playground; **~ur·laub** *m* adventure holiday

Aben·teu·rer ['aːbəntɔʏrɐ] *m* (-s; -) adventurer; **~na,tur** *f* **1.** adventurous spirit; **2.** adventurer

aber ['aːbɐ] **I.** *cj.* but; **~ dennoch** yet, (but) still, nevertheless; **oder ~** or alternatively; **II.** *int.*: **~, ~!** now, now!, come, come!; **~ ja!, ~ sicher!** (but) of course; **~ nein!** oh no, of course not; **das ist ~ nett von dir** that's really nice of you; **III.** *adv.*: **Tausende und ~ Tausende** thousands upon (*or* and) thousands; **IV. ≈** *n* (-s; -) but; **die Sache hat ein ~** there's just one snag (*or* catch to it); → **wenn**

'Aber·glau·be *m* (-ns; *no pl.*) superstition; **aber·gläu·bisch** ['a:bɐglɔʏbɪʃ] *adj.* superstitious

'ab·er·ken·nen *v/t.* (*irr., sep.,* h, → ***erkennen***) **1.** ***Höflichkeit*** *etc.* ***kann man ihm nicht*** ~ you can't say he isn't polite *etc.*; **2.** *a.* ⚖ ***j-m et.*** ~ deny s.o. s.th., deprive s.o. of s.th.; **'Ab·er·ken·nung** *f* (-; -en) denial; ⚖ deprivation, dispossession

aber·ma·lig ['a:bɐma:lɪç] *adj.* further, renewed; **aber·mals** ['a:bɐma:ls] *adv.* (once) again, once more

'ab·ern·ten *v/t.* (*sep.,* h) harvest; pick *fruit*; ***das Getreide*** ~ *a.* bring in the crops (*or* corn *etc.*)

Ab·er·ra·ti·on [apʔɛra'tsi̯o:n] *f* (-; -en) aberration

'aber·tau·send *adj.* thousands and thousands of

'Aber·witz *m* (-es; *no pl.*) madness, lunacy; **'aber·wit·zig** *adj.* insane

'ab·er·zie·hen *v/t.* (*irr., sep.,* h, → ***erziehen***) ***j-m et.*** ~ get s.o. out of the habit of *ger.*; ***das müssen wir ihm*** ~ we'll have to get him out of that habit

'ab·es·sen *v/t.* (*irr., sep.,* h, → ***essen***) ***den Teller*** ~ eat the plate clean

'ab·fackeln (*sep.* -k·k-) *v/t.* (*sep.,* h) burn off

'ab·fah·ren (*irr., sep.,* → ***fahren***) **I.** *v/i.* (sn) **1.** leave, set out *or* off (**nach** for); ski downhill; *film etc.*: start, run; **2.** F ~ ***auf*** (*acc.*) F be wild about; ***da fahr' ich echt drauf ab*** F that really does things to me; **3.** F *fig.* → ***abblitzen***; **II.** *v/t.* (h) **4.** cart off, remove; **5.** cover, F do *a distance*; patrol *an area etc.*; **6.** wear down *tires etc.*; **7.** ***ihm wurde ein Bein abgefahren*** he was run over and lost a leg

'Ab·fahrt *f* (-; -en) departure; *skiing*: downhill run; **2be·reit** *adj.* ready to leave (*or* start)

'Ab·fahrts|lauf *m skiing*: downhill (race); **~läu·fer** *m* downhill racer, downhiller; **~ren·nen** *n* → ***Abfahrtslauf***; **~zeit** *f* departure time

'Ab·fall *m* (-[e]s; ⸚e) **1.** *a. pl.* rubbish, *esp. Am.* garbage, trash; *formal*: refuse; ***Abfälle*** *in the street*: litter; **2.** *a. radioactive*: waste; **3.** drop, (steep) slope; **4.** *no pl. fig.* decrease; drop (*a.* ⚡); **5.** *no pl.* defection (**von** from *a party etc.*); *eccl. a.* falling away; **2arm** *adj.* low-waste, low-residue; **~auf·be·rei·tung** *f* waste treatment; **~be·sei·ti·gung** *f* waste disposal; **~ei·mer** *m* rubbish bin, *Am.* trashcan, garbage can

'ab·fal·len *v/i.* (*irr., sep.,* sn, → ***fallen***) **1.** fall (*or* drop) off; **2.** *terrain*: fall away, drop (***steil*** steeply); **3.** fall off, drop; *esp. sport*: fall behind; ***gegen den Koreaner fiel er stark ab*** he was no match for the Korean; ***neben s-n früheren Werken fällt der Roman ab*** compared with his earlier works the novel is disappointing; **4.** break away, defect (***von*** from *a party etc.*); *eccl.* fall away; **5.** F ***es wird dabei für ihn etwas*** ~ there'll be something in it for him too; **'ab·fal·lend** *adj.* sloping; ***steil*** ~ steep, precipitous

'Ab·fall|ent·sor·gung *f* waste disposal; **~hau·fen** *m* rubbish (*Am.* trash) heap

ab·fäl·lig ['apfɛlɪç] **I.** *adj.* disparaging, deprecating, F snide *remark etc.*; adverse *criticism etc.*, unfavo(u)rable *opinion etc.*; **II.** *adv.* disparagingly *etc.*; ~ ***sprechen über j-n*** *a.* run s.o. down

'Ab·fall|korb *m* waste-paper basket; **~kü·bel** *m* → ***Abfalleimer***; **~pro,dukt** *n* **1.** waste product; **2.** by-product, spin-off; **~stof·fe** *pl.* waste products; **~ver·mei·dung** *f* waste avoidance; **~ver·wer·tung** *f* waste recovery

'ab·fäl·schen *v/t.* (*sep.,* h) deflect *ball*

'ab·fan·gen *v/t.* (*irr., sep.,* h, → ***fangen***) intercept *ball, letter, aircraft etc., a.* catch *s.o.*; check *tendency*; parry *blow etc.*; catch up with *s.o.*; bring *car etc.* under control; *a.* pull *plane* out (of a dive); waylay *s.o.*

'Ab·fang|jä·ger *m* ⚔ interceptor; **~sa·tel,lit** *m* hunter-killer satellite

'ab·fär·ben *v/i.* (*sep.,* h) **1.** ***dieses Hemd färbt ab*** the dye comes off this shirt, this shirt runs; ***die Wand färbt ab*** the paint comes off the wall; **2.** *fig.* ~ ***auf*** *acc.* rub off on

'ab·fas·sen *v/t.* (*sep.,* h) write (up); draft, *esp. adm.* draw up; word, formulate; **'Ab·fas·sung** *f* (-; -en) writing; drafting; report, letter, draft *etc*

'ab·fau·len *v/i.* (*sep.,* sn) rot off (*or* away)

'ab·fe·dern (*sep.,* h) **I.** *v/t.* ⚙ spring(-load); suspend; cushion; **II.** *v/i.* ⚙ absorb the shock(s); *sport*: push off; ***gut*** (***schlecht***) ~ land smoothly (stiffly)

'ab·fe·gen *v/t.* (*sep.,* h) sweep off

'ab·fei·ern F *v/t.* (*sep.,* h): ***Überstunden*** ~ use up one's overtime

'ab·fei·len *v/t.* (*sep.,* h) file off

'ab·fer·ti·gen *v/t.* (*sep.,* h) **1.** get *s.th.* ready for dispatch; clear *through customs*; deal with *customers etc.*; check in *passengers*; ***wir wurden an der Grenze sehr schnell abgefertigt*** we got through customs very quickly; **2.** ***j-n kurz*** ~ give s.o. short shrift; **'Ab·fer·ti·gung** *f* (-; -en) **1.** dispatch; (*customs*) clearance; service; **2.** *fig.* rebuff; **3.** → ***Abfertigungsschalter***

'Ab·fer·ti·gungs|ge·bäu·de *n*, **~hal·le** *f* ✈ terminal; **~schal·ter** *m* dispatch counter; ✈ check-in desk

'ab·feu·ern (*sep.,* h) **I.** *v/t.* **1.** fire; **2.** ***e-n Schuß aufs Tor*** ~ fire a shot at goal; **II.** *v/i.* **3.** fire; **4.** *soccer*: shoot

'ab·fin·den (*irr., sep.,* h, → ***finden***) **I.** *v/t.* pay off; indemnify, compensate; **II.** *v/refl.*: ***sich mit j-m*** (***et.***) ~ come to terms with s.o. (s.th.); ***sich mit et.*** ~ *a.* resign o.s. to s.th., ***müssen***: have to face up to s.th.; ***sich mit den Tatsachen*** ~ *a.* face the facts; **'Ab·fin·dung** *f* (-; -en) settlement, arrangement; compensation; severance (*or* redundancy) pay, lump sum settlement, F golden handshake; **'Ab·fin·dungs·sum·me** *f* compensation; severance (*or* redundancy) pay, F golden handshake

ab·fla·chen ['apflaxən] (*sep.,* h) **I.** *v/t.* flatten (*or* level) out; **II.** *v/i. fig.* go flat; level off (*or* out); **III.** *v/refl.*: ***sich*** ~ flatten out, *a. fig.* level out

ab·flau·en ['apflaʊən] *v/i.* (*sep.,* sn) *wind*: die down, drop; *fig.* ebb, subside; *interest etc.*: flag; *prices*: sag; *exchange rates*: ease off; *business*: slacken (off)

'ab·flie·gen (*irr., sep.,* → ***fliegen***) **I.** *v/i.* (sn) *zo.* fly off; *person*: fly; ✈ take off; **II.** *v/t.* (h) patrol

'ab·flie·ßen *v/i.* (*irr., sep.,* sn, → ***fließen***) **1.** run off; drain (off); drain (***in*** *acc.* into); **2.** *fig. capital*: flow off, drain (***nach*** *dat.* into)

'Ab·flug *m* (-[e]s; ⸚e) takeoff; departure; **2be·reit** *adj.* ready for takeoff; **~ha·fen** *m* departure airport; **~hal·le** *f* departure lounge; **~zeit** *f* departure (time)

'Ab·fluß *m* (-sses; ⸚sse) **1.** *no pl.* flowing off, draining off; **2.** outlet, drain; **3.** *no pl.* outflow *of capital*; **~gra·ben** *m* drain(age ditch); **~hahn** *m* drain cock; **~rohr** *n* waste pipe; drainpipe

'Ab·fol·ge *f* (-; -n) succession; sequence; ***in rascher*** ~ in quick succession; ***die*** ~ ***der Ereignisse*** the sequence of events

'ab·for·dern *v/t.* (*sep.,* h): ***j-m et.*** ~ *a. fig.* demand s.th. of (*or* from) s.o.; ***j-m ein Versprechen*** ~ make s.o promise s.th., force a promise out of s.o.; *fig.* ***j-m viel*** ~ make high demands on s.o.; ***j-m alles*** ~ push s.o. to the limit

'ab·for·men *v/t.* (*sep.,* h) mo(u)ld, model

'ab·fo·to·gra,fie·ren *v/t.* (*sep.,* h) take a photo of

'Ab·fra·ge *f* (-; -n) *computer*: query, polling; **'ab·fra·gen** *v/t.* (*sep.,* h) **1.** ***j-n et.*** ~ quiz (*or* test) s.o. on s.th.; → ***abhören*** 5; **2.** *computer*: query, poll; **'Ab·fra·ge·spra·che** *f computer*: query language

'ab·fres·sen *v/t.* (*irr., sep.,* h, → ***fressen***) graze (down), crop; eat bare

'ab·frie·ren (*irr., sep.,* → ***frieren***) **I.** *v/i.* (sn) be frostbitten; ***ihm sind drei Zehen abgefroren*** he lost three toes through frostbite; **II.** F *v/t.* (h): ***sich einen*** ~ F freeze to death; ***ich hab' mir die Füße abgefroren*** my feet were (absolutely) frozen

'ab·frot,tie·ren *v/t.* (*sep.,* h) rub down; ***sich*** ~ rub o.s. down

'Ab·fuhr *f* (-; -en) removal; *sport and fig.*: defeat, beating; rebuff, brush-off; *fig.* ***j-m e-e*** ~ ***erteilen*** give s.o. the brush-off, *sport*: trounce s.o., F beat s.o. hollow; ***sich e-e*** ~ ***holen*** be snubbed, *sport*: get a trouncing

'ab·füh·ren (*sep.,* h) **I.** *v/t.* lead off (*or* away); take *s.o.* into custody; drain off *liquid*; carry off *heat*; draw off *gas*; pay *money, taxes* over (**an** *acc.* to); *fig.* ***j-n vom*** (***rechten***) ***Wege*** ~ lead s.o. astray; ***j-n vom Thema*** ~ lead s.o. away from the subject; **II.** *v/i.* ⚕ act as a laxative, have a purgative effect; **'ab·füh·rend** *adj.* ⚕ laxative

'Ab·führ|mit·tel *n* laxative; **~ta,blet·te** *f* laxative tablet

'Ab·füll|an·la·ge *f* bottling plant; **~da·tum** *n* bottling date

'ab·fül·len *v/t.* (*sep.,* h) fill; rack *wine*; bottle; bag

'Ab·füll·ma,schi·ne *f* bottling machine

'ab·füt·tern *v/t.* (*sep.,* h) **1.** feed *animals*, *a.* F *people*; **2.** line *coat etc.*

'Ab·ga·be *f* (-; -n) **1.** *no pl.* delivery; handing over; handing in; **2.** *soccer*: pass; firing *of a shot*; **3.** *no pl.* emission *of heat, steam etc.*; release *of energy*; **4.** *no pl.* sale; **5.** tribute; duty; tax; → ***Kommunalabgaben, Sozialabgaben***

'ab·ga·ben·frei *adj.* duty-free; tax-exempt

'ab·ga·ben·pflich·tig *adj.* taxable; dutiable

'Ab·ga·be·ter,min *m* deadline; closing date

'Ab·gang *m* (-[e]s; ⸚e) **1.** *no pl.* departure (*a. fig.*), *a. thea.* exit; retirement; leaving *school etc.*; 🚂 *etc.* departure; ⚓ sailing; ***nach s-m*** ~ ***von der Schule*** *etc.* when (*or* after) he left school *etc.*; *fig.* ***sich e-n guten*** ~ ***verschaffen*** make a graceful exit; **2.** *gym.* dismount; **3.** a) *no pl.* ✝ dispatch; b) *banking*: items *pl.* disposed of; → ***Absatz*** 3; **4.** ⚕ a) *no pl.* discharge; passing *of stones etc.*; b) miscarriage; **5.** decease, demise

'Ab·gangs|al·ter *n* school-leaving age; **~prü·fung** *f* leaving (*Am.* final) examination; **~zeug·nis** *n* school-leaving certificate, *Am.* diploma

'Ab·gas *n* (-es; -e) waste gas; *mot.* exhaust fumes *pl.*; **2arm** *adj. mot.* low-emission, F clean; **~ent·gif·tung** *f* waste gas cleaning; **2frei** *adj.* emission-free; **~ka·ta·ly,sa·tor** *m mot.* catalytic converter, catalyst; **~son·der·un·ter,su·chung** *f* (*abbr.* ***ASU***), **~test** *m* exhaust emission test; **~tur,bi·ne** *f* exhaust(-gas) turbine; **~ver·wer·tung** *f* waste gas utilization; **~wer·te** *pl.* exhaust pollution standards

'ab·gau·nern F *v/t.* (*sep.*, h): ***j-m et.*** ~ swindle s.o. out of s.th.

'ab·ge·ar·bei·tet I. *p.p. of* ***abarbeiten***; **II.** *adj.* exhausted, worn-out ..., *pred.* worn out; run-down

'ab·ge·ben (*irr.*, *sep.*, h, → ***geben***) **I.** *v/t.* **1.** hand in; deliver; surrender, F hand over *ticket*; hand in, ✈ check in *baggage*; ~ ***bei*** deliver *s.th.* to; leave *one's baggage* with; **2.** give away; sell (***an*** *acc.* to); ***er gab ihr e-n Keks ab*** he gave her one of his biscuits; **3.** *fig.* hand over; **4.** give up, pass on (***an*** *acc.* to); **5.** radiate, emit *heat etc.*; release *energy*; **6.** fire *shot*; **7.** *sport*: pass *ball*; concede *a point etc.*, lose *game, set etc.*; ***ohne e-n Satz abzugeben*** *a.* without dropping a set; **8.** ***e-e Erklärung*** *etc.* ~ make a statement *etc.*; ***s-e Stimme*** ~ cast one's vote; → ***abgegeben*** II; **9.** ***e-n guten Polizisten*** *etc.* ~ make a good policeman *etc.*; **II.** *v/refl.* **10.** ***sich mit et. (j-m)*** ~ concern o.s. with s.th. (s.o.); ***er gibt sich zu wenig mit s-m Sohn ab*** he doesn't spend enough time with his boy; ***sie gibt sich gern mit Tieren ab*** she loves (to look after) animals; ***mit ihm gebe ich mich nicht ab*** I don't associate (*or* have anything to do) with him; **III.** *v/i.* **11.** share things; ***er mag nicht*** ~ he doesn't like to share (things); **12.** *sport*: pass the ball

'ab·ge·brannt I. *p.p. of* ***abbrennen***; **II.** *adj.* **1.** *house etc., a. candle*: burnt down; **2.** F *fig.* F broke, *Brit. a.* F skint

'ab·ge·brüht I. *p.p. of* ***abbrühen***; **II.** *fig. adj.* hard-boiled; hardened, callous

'ab·ge·dreht I. *p.p. of* ***abdrehen***; **II.** *adj. film*: wrapped up

'ab·ge·dro·schen *adj.* hackneyed, trite; ***~e Redewendung*** *a.* cliché

ab·ge·feimt ['apgəfaımt] *adj.* crafty, wily

'ab·ge·ge·ben I. *p.p. of* ***abgeben***; **II.** *adj.*: ***~e Stimmen*** votes cast

ab·ge·grast ['apgəgra:st] *fig. adj.*: ***das Thema*** *etc.* ***ist*** ~ the subject *etc.* has been flogged (*or* done) to death

'ab·ge·grif·fen I. *p.p. of* ***abgreifen***; **II.** *adj.* (well-)worn; well-thumbed *book*; *fig.* → ***abgedroschen***

'ab·ge·hackt I. *p.p. of* ***abhacken***; **II.** *fig. adj.* disjointed *sentences*, choppy *speech*

'ab·ge·half·tert F *adj.* F sacked

'ab·ge·han·gen I. *p.p. of* ***abhängen***[1]; **II.** *adj.* well-hung *meat*

'ab·ge·hängt I. *p.p. of* ***abhängen***[2]; **II.** *adj.*: ***~e Decke*** suspended ceiling

'ab·ge·härmt I. *p.p. of* ***abhärmen***; **II.** *adj.* drawn, care-worn *face*

'ab·ge·här·tet I. *p.p. of* ***abhärten***; **II.** *adj. physically*: tough, hardy; *emotionally*: hardened (***gegen*** *acc.* against), inured (to)

'ab·ge·hen (*irr.*, *sep.*, sn, → ***gehen***) **I.** *v/i.* **1.** 🚂, ✈ leave; ⚓ *a.* sail; *mail*: go; **2.** *thea.* make one's exit (*a. fig.*); ***... geht*** (***gehen***) ***ab*** exit (exeunt) ...; **3.** ***von der Schule*** ~ leave school; **4.** *button etc.*: come off; **5.** *fig.* be deducted, be taken off; **6.** ✝ sell; **7.** *shot*: go off, be fired; **8.** *road etc.*: branch off; *a.* fork; **9.** ***von e-m Thema*** ~ digress; **10.** ***von e-m Vorhaben*** ~ give up a plan; ***von e-r Meinung*** ~ change one's mind (*or* views); ***nicht*** ~ ***von et.*** persist in s.th., insist on s.th.; ***davon gehe ich nicht ab*** nothing's going to change my mind about that; ***er geht nicht davon ab*** *a.* he won't give up; **11.** ***vom rechten Weg*** ~ go astray, *fig. a.* stray from the straight and narrow; **12.** ***er geht mir sehr ab*** I miss him badly; → *a.* ***fehlen*** 3; **13.** go; ***es ging alles gut ab*** everything went (*or* passed off) well *or* smoothly; **II.** *v/t.* **14.** pace out; **15.** patrol

'ab·ge·hetzt I. *p.p. of* ***abhetzen***; **II.** *adj.* exhausted, F shattered; rushed off one's feet; breathless, out of breath

'ab·ge·kämpft *adj.* worn-out ..., *pred.* worn out

'ab·ge·kap·selt I. *p.p. of* ***abkapseln***; **II.** *adj. person*: cut off; *state*: cocooned; ~ ***leben*** keep o.s. to o.s

'ab·ge·kar·tet I. *p.p. of* ***abkarten***; **II.** *adj.*: ***~es Spiel*** put-up job

'ab·ge·klärt I. *p.p. of* ***abklären***; **II.** *fig. adj.* mellow

'ab·ge·la·gert I. *p.p. of* ***ablagern***; **II.** *adj.* matured, aged *wine*; seasoned *wood*; well-seasoned *tobacco*

'ab·ge·le·gen *adj.* off the beaten track; remote, faraway ..., *pred.* far away; secluded; out-of-the-way ..., *pred.* out of the way

'ab·ge·legt I. *p.p. of* ***ablegen***; **II.** *adj.*: ***~e Kleider*** cast-offs

'ab·gel·ten *v/t.* (*irr.*, *sep.*, h, → ***gelten***) pay off, settle *claim*; compensate for *loss*; **'Ab·gel·tung** *f* (-; -en) payment, compensation

'ab·ge·macht I. *p.p. of* ***abmachen***; **II.** *adj.*: ~! done, (okay,) it's a deal; ~ ***ist*** ~ a deal's a deal

'ab·ge·ma·gert I. *p.p. of* ***abmagern***; **II.** *adj.* emaciated; ***er sieht furchtbar*** ~ ***aus*** *a.* he's just skin and bones

'ab·ge·mes·sen I. *p.p. of* ***abmessen***; **II.** *adj.* precise, exact; *fig.* measured; stiff; formal

'ab·ge·neigt *adj.*: ~ ***sein, et. zu tun*** be disinclined (*or* loath, reluctant, unwilling) to do s.th.; ***e-r Sache*** ~ ***sein*** be averse to s.th., dislike s.th.; ***ich wäre nicht*** ~, ***etwas zu trinken*** I wouldn't mind a drink

'ab·ge·nutzt *adj.* worn; F a bit frayed around the edges

Ab·ge·ord·ne·te ['apgəˀɔrdnətə] *m*, *f* (-n; -n) delegate, representative; member of parliament; *in GB*: Member of Parliament (*abbr.* MP); *in the USA*: Congressman (Congresswoman); ***der Herr*** (***die Frau***) ~ the Hono(u)rable Member; **'Ab·ge·ord·ne·ten·haus** *n* parliament; *in GB*: House of Commons; *in the USA*: House of Representatives

'ab·ge·packt I. *p.p. of* ***abpacken***; **II.** *adj.* prepacked, packaged

'ab·ge·ris·sen I. *p.p. of* ***abreißen***; **II.** *adj.* **1.** ragged, tattered; *person*: down-at-heel; **2.** *fig.* disjointed, incoherent

'ab·ge·run·det I. *p.p. of* ***abrunden***; **II.** *adj.* round *number*; *fig.* well-rounded; ***e-e ~e Leistung*** a finished performance

'Ab·ge·sand·te *m*, *f* (-n; -n) envoy, emissary; → ***Gesandte***

'Ab·ge·sang *m* (-[e]s; ᵘe) **1.** ♪ abgesang; **2.** swan song; ***den*** ~ ***e-r Epoche darstellen*** mark the end of an era

'ab·ge·schie·den I. *p.p. of* ***abscheiden***; **II.** *adj.* **1.** solitary, secluded; **2.** deceased; **'Ab·ge·schie·den·heit** *f* (-; *no pl.*) seclusion

'ab·ge·schlafft F **I.** *p.p. of* ***abschlaffen***; **II.** *adj.* drained, F shattered, whacked; ***ein ~er Typ*** F a real drip

'ab·ge·schla·gen I. *p.p of* ***abschlagen***; **II.** *adj. sport*: far behind

'ab·ge·schlos·sen I. *p.p. of* ***abschließen***; **II.** *adj.* **1.** self-contained *flat*; **2.** completed; ***~es Studium*** degree; ***e-e ~e Ausbildung haben*** be fully qualified (for a job), ***als Sekretärin*** *etc.*: be a (fully) qualified secretary *etc.*; **3.** ~ ***leben*** lead a secluded life, have cut o.s. off; **'Ab·ge·schlos·sen·heit** *f* (-; *no pl.*) seclusion, isolation

ab·ge·schmackt ['apgəʃmakt] *fig. adj.* in bad taste, tasteless; tactless; fatuous

'ab·ge·schnit·ten I. *p.p. of* ***abschneiden***; **II.** *adj.*: ***von der Außenwelt*** ~ cut off from the outside world

'ab·ge·se·hen I. *p.p. of* ***absehen***; **II.** *adv.*: ~ ***von*** apart (*esp. Am.* aside) from, excepting; ~ ***davon, daß er krank ist*** apart from his being ill, apart from the fact that he's ill

'ab·ge·son·dert I. *p.p. of* ***absondern***; **II.** *adj.* separate; isolated

'ab·ge·spannt I. *p.p. of* ***abspannen***; **II.** *fig. adj.* exhausted, worn-out ..., *pred.* worn out; drawn *look*; **'Ab·ge·spannt·heit** *f* (-; *no pl.*) exhaustion, fatigue

'ab·ge·spielt I. *p.p. of* ***abspielen***; **II.** *adj. record*: scratchy, worn-out ..., *pred.* worn out; *film*: worn, in bad condition, rainy; old, used *playing cards*

'ab·ge·stan·den I. *p.p. of* ***abstehen***; **II.** *adj.* stale (*a. fig.*); flat *beer etc*

'ab·ge·stor·ben I. *p.p. of* ***absterben***; **II.** *adj.* numb *leg etc.*; dead *nerve, tree etc.*

'ab·ge·stumpft I. *p.p. of* ***abstumpfen***; **II.** *adj.* blunted, dulled *emotions*; insensitive *person*; **'Ab·ge·stumpft·heit** *f* (-; *no pl.*) apathy, indifference (***gegen*** towards)

'ab·ge·ta·kelt I. *p.p. of* ***abtakeln***; **II.** *fig. adj.* down-at-heel

'ab·ge·tan I. *p.p. of* ***abtun***; **II.** *adj.* finished

'ab·ge·tra·gen I. *p.p. of* ***abtragen***; **II.** *adj.* worn, shabby *clothes*; worn-down *shoes*, *pred.* worn down

'ab·ge·tre·ten I. *p.p. of* ***abtreten***; **II.** *adj.* **1.** *shoes*: → ***abgetragen***; **2.** ***~e Gebiete*** ceded territory

'ab·ge·win·nen *v/t.* (*irr.*, *sep.*, h, → ***gewinnen***): ***j-m et.*** ~ win s.th. from s.o., *fig.* get *a smile etc.* out of s.o.; ***dem Meer Land*** ~ reclaim land from the sea; ***e-r Sache Geschmack*** ~ acquire a taste for s.th.; ***ich kann dem Buch nichts*** ~ I can't get anything out of the book; ***ich kann dieser Art von Musik nichts*** ~ I don't get anything out of this kind of music, this kind of music doesn't do anything for me

'ab·ge·wirt·schaf·tet I. *p.p. of* ***abwirt-***

***schaften*; II.** *adj.* run-down *business etc.*
'**ab·ge·wöh·nen** *v/t.* (*sep.*, h) **1.** ***j-m et.*** ~ break (*or* cure) s.o. of s.th.; ***sich das Rauchen*** *etc.* ~ give up smoking *etc.*; ***das muß er sich langsam*** ~ it's time he gave that up; **2.** F ***zum*** ♀ ***sein*** *film, game etc.*: F be enough to make you weep; *food, drink*: F be diabolical; *person*: F be a (real) creep; ***komm, noch einen zum*** ♀ come on, one for the road
'**ab·ge·wrackt I.** *p.p. of* ***abwracken*; II.** F *fig. adj.* shattered; ***ich bin total*** ~ *a.* I feel like a wreck
'**ab·ge·zehrt I.** *p.p. of* ***abzehren*; II.** *adj.* emaciated
'**ab·gie·ßen** *v/t.* (*irr.*, *sep.*, h, → ***gießen***) pour away *liquid*; strain *potatoes etc.*; cast *metal*
'**Ab·glanz** *m* (-es; *no pl.*) reflection; *fig.* ***ein schwacher*** ~ a pale reflection
'**Ab·gleich** *m* (-[e]s; -e) ⚙, ⚡ adjustment, balance, alignment; '**ab·glei·chen** *v/t.* (*irr.*, *sep.*, h, → ***gleichen***) adjust, balance, align
'**ab·glei·ten** *v/i.* (*irr.*, *sep.*, sn, → ***gleiten***) slip (off); ✝ *exchange rates*: fall; *fig.* lapse (***in*** *acc.* into); ***d-e Leistungen gleiten ab*** your standards are slipping; ***Kritik*** *etc.* ***gleitet von ihm ab*** he's deaf to criticism *etc.*; ***es gleitet alles von ihm ab*** it's like water off a duck's back
'**Ab·gott** *m* (-[e]s; ⸗er) idol; ***j-n zu s-m*** ~ ***machen*** idolize s.o., make an idol of s.o.; **Ab·göt·te·rei** [apgœtə'raɪ] *f* (-; *no pl.*) idolatry; ~ ***treiben*** worship idols, ***mit j-m*:** idolize s.o.; **ab·göt·tisch** ['apgœtɪʃ] **I.** *adj.* idolatrous; **II.** *fig. adv.*: ~ ***lieben*** idolize, adore; dote on
'**ab·gra·ben** *v/t.* (*irr.*, *sep.*, h, → ***graben***) dig away; level; drain (*or* draw) off; *fig.* ***j-m das Wasser*** ~ pull the rug from under s.o.'s feet
'**ab·gra·sen** *v/t.* (*sep.*, h) graze; *fig.* scour, comb; → ***abgegrast*** II
'**ab·grei·fen** *v/t.* (*irr.*, *sep.*, h, → ***greifen***) feel; measure out (with one's hands); *fig.* stake out; → ***abgegriffen*** II
'**ab·gren·zen** *v/t.* (*sep.*, h) **1.** divide; mark off; demarcate *territory etc.*; **2.** *fig.* differentiate; define; ***voneinander*** ~ draw a clear dividing line between; ***sich*** ~ ***von*** distance (*or* dissociate) o.s. from; '**Ab·gren·zung** *f* (-; -en) demarcation; *fig.* definition; '**Ab·gren·zungs·po·li,tik** *f* policy of separation (*or* polarization)
'**Ab·grund** *m* (-[e]s; ⸗e) **1.** abyss, chasm; precipice; **2.** *fig.* gulf, chasm, great divide; ***die Abgründe der menschlichen Seele*** the unplumbed depths of the human soul; ***am Rande des*** ~***s*** (***stehen*** be) on the brink of ruin (*or* disaster), ***stehen*:** *a.* be staring disaster in the face; ♀'**häß·lich** *adj.* unbelievably ugly, F ugly as hell
ab·grün·dig ['apgrʏndɪç] *adj.* mysterious; unfathomable; cryptic
'**ab·grund'tief I.** *adj.* unfathomable; all-consuming *hatred etc.*; **II.** *adv.*: ~ ***hassen*** hate with every fib|re (*Am.* -er) of one's being
'**ab·gucken** (*sep.* -k·k-) *v/t.* (*sep.*, h): ***j-m et.*** ~ learn (*or* copy) s.th. from s.o
'**Ab·guß** *m* (-sses; ⸗sse) **1.** cast, mo(u)ld; **2.** *no pl.* casting
'**ab·ha·ben** F *v/t.* (*irr.*, *sep.*, h, → ***haben***) **1.** ***willst du etwas*** ~? do you want some (of it)?; **2.** have *one's hat etc.* off
'**ab·hacken** (*sep.* -k·k-) *v/t.* (*sep.*, h) chop off; *fig.* clip; → ***abgehackt*** II
'**ab·ha·ken** *v/t.* (*sep.*, h) **1.** unhook; **2.** tick (*Am.* check) off; *fig.* cross off one's list; F knock off *a. contp. sights etc.*
'**ab·hal·ten** *v/t.* (*irr.*, *sep.*, h, → ***halten***) **1.** keep away (*or* off); ward off; ***j-n davon*** ~ ***zu*** *inf.* keep (*or* prevent, stop) s.o. from *ger.*, deter s.o. from *ger.*; ***lassen Sie sich nicht*** ~! don't let me disturb you; **2.** hold *meeting*, *examination etc.*; give *lecture etc.*; ***abgehalten werden*** be held, take place; **3.** hold *a child* out (*or* over the pot)
'**ab·han·deln** *v/t.* (*sep.*, h) **1.** ***j-m et.*** ~ get s.o. to sell one s.th. cheaply; ***etwas vom Preis*** ~ beat down the price; **2.** deal with, treat, discuss
ab·han·den [ap'handən] *adv.*: ~ ***kommen*** go astray, get lost, be mislaid; ***mir sind m-e Schlüssel*** ~ ***gekommen*** I've lost my keys
'**Ab·hand·lung** *f* (-; -en) treatise, paper (***über*** *acc.* on); essay; article
'**Ab·hang** *m* (-[e]s; ⸗e) slope
'**ab·hän·gen**[1] *v/i.* (*irr.*, *sep.*, h, → ***hängen***[1]) *fig.* ~ ***von*** depend on, *a. financially etc.*: be dependent on, rely on; ***letztlich*** ~ ***von*** hinge (up)on; ***es hängt davon ab, ob*** it depends (on) whether; ***es hängt ganz davon ab*** it all depends
'**ab·hän·gen**[2] (*sep.*, h) **I.** *v/t.* **1.** take down; *mot.* uncouple, unhitch; **2.** F *fig.* shake off *competitor*, F leave *s.o.* trailing; shake off *pursuer*, give *s.o.* the slip
ab·hän·gig ['aphɛŋɪç] *adj.* dependent (***von*** on); ~ ***sein von*** → ***abhängen***[1]; ***voneinander*** ~ interdependent; *ling.* ~***er Satz*** subordinate (*or* dependent) clause; → ***drogenabhängig*; Ab·hän·gi·ge** ['aphɛŋɪgə] *m, f* (-n; -n) dependent; '**Ab·hän·gig·keit** *f* (-; -en) **1.** dependence (***von*** *dat.* on); *a.* addiction (***von*** *dat.* to *drugs etc.*); ~ ***von*** *dat. a.* reliance on; ***gegenseitige*** ~ interdependence; **2.** *ling.* subordination
'**Ab·hän·gig·keits|ge·fühl** *n* feeling of dependency; ~**ver·hält·nis** *n* dependent relationship (***zu*** to); interdependence
'**ab·här·men** *v/refl.* (*sep.*, h): ***sich*** ~ fret (***über*** *acc.* over); → ***abgehärmt*** II
'**ab·här·ten** (*sep.*, h) **I.** *v/t.* harden, toughen; **II.** *v/refl.*: ***sich*** ~ become hardened (***gegen*** against); *esp. physically*: build up one's resistance (to), F toughen o.s. up; → ***abgehärtet*** II; '**Ab·här·tung** *f* (-; *no pl.*) hardening
'**ab·hau·en** (*sep.*) **I.** F *v/i.* (sn) F clear off, push off; F do a bunk; ***hau ab!*** F push off!, get lost!, beat it!; ***von zu Hause*** ~ run away from home; **II.** *v/t.* (h) chop (*or* cut) off *or* down
'**ab·häu·ten** *v/t.* (*sep.*, h) skin
'**ab·he·ben** (*irr.*, *sep.*, h, → ***heben***) **I.** *v/t.* **1.** lift off, take off; cut *the cards*; → ***Hörer*** 2; **2.** slip *stitches*; **3.** draw *money* (***von*** from); **4.** set apart (***von*** from); **II.** *v/i.* **5.** ✈ take off; F *fig.* ***du brauchst nicht gleich abzuheben*** don't let it go to your head; **6.** answer the phone; ***kannst du mal*** ~? *a.* can you get it?; **7.** *card game*: cut the cards; **III.** *v/refl.*: ***sich*** ~ ***von*** contrast with, stand out from; ***sich gegen et.*** ~ stand out (*or* be set off) against s.th.
'**Ab·he·bung** *f* (-; -en) withdrawal
'**ab·hef·ten** *v/t.* (*sep.*, h) file (away)
'**ab·hei·len** *v/i.* (*sep.*, sn) heal (up)
'**ab·hel·fen** *v/i.* (*irr.*, *sep.*, h, → ***helfen***) remedy; redress *abuses etc.*; supply, meet *a need etc.*; ***dem ist leicht abzuhelfen*** that's no problem (at all)
'**ab·het·zen** *v/refl.* (*sep.*, h): ***sich*** ~ wear (*or* tire) o.s. out
'**Ab·hil·fe** *f* (-; -n) remedy; ~ ***schaffen*** put things right
'**ab·ho·beln** *v/t.* (*sep.*, h) plane (off *or* down)
'**Ab·hol·dienst** *m* pickup service
'**ab·ho·len** *v/t.* (*sep.*, h) fetch; *a.* call for, come for, pick up, collect *s.o., a letter etc.*; ***j-n vom Bahnhof*** ~ meet s.o. at the station; ~ ***lassen*** send for
'**Ab·hol|markt** *m* cash-and-carry (store); ~**preis** *m* → ***Mitnahmepreis***
'**ab·hol·zen** *v/t.* (*sep.*, h) cut down *trees*; clear *area* (of trees); '**Ab·hol·zung** *f* (-; -en) deforestation; clearing, chopping down *of a forest*
'**Ab·hör|af,fä·re** *f* bugging affair (*or* scandal); ~**ak·ti,on** *f* bugging campaign; ~**an·la·ge** *f* bugging system
'**ab·hor·chen** *v/t.* (*sep.*, h) ⚒ sound, 🕮 auscultate; ***j-m die Brust*** ~ listen to s.o.'s chest
'**Ab·hör·dienst** *m* monitoring service
'**ab·hö·ren** *v/t.* (*sep.*, h) **1.** ⚒ → ***abhorchen*; 2.** intercept *radio messages*; bug, listen in on (*telephone*) *conversations*; **3.** listen to *tape recordings*; **4.** monitor; **5.** ***j-m ein Gedicht*** *etc.* ~ listen to s.o. recite a poem *etc.*; → ***abfragen*** 1
'**Ab·hör|ge·rät** *n* bugging device; monitor; ~**ka,bi·ne** *f* listening booth; ♀**si·cher** *adj.* bug-proof; ~**skan,dal** *m* bugging scandal
'**ab·hun·gern** (*sep.*, h) **I.** *v/refl.*: ***sich*** ~ starve (o.s.); **II.** *v/t.*: ***sich et.*** ~ scrimp and save to be able to afford s.th.; ***sich zehn Pfund*** ~ starve off ten pounds
'**ab·hu·sten** (*sep.*, h) **I.** *v/t.* cough up, bring up; **II.** *v/i.* clear one's lungs
Abi ['abi] F *n* → ***Abitur***
'**ab·ir·ren** *v/i.* (*sep.*, sn) stray; ***vom Weg*** ~ lose one's way; *fig.* ***vom Thema*** ~ go off the subject, go off at a tangent
'**ab·iso,lie·ren** *v/t.* (*sep.*, h) strip
'**Ab·iso,lier·zan·ge** *f*: (***e-e*** ~ a pair of) wire strippers *pl.*
Abi·tur [abi'tuːr] *n* (-s; -e) school-leaving exam; school-leaving certificate, *Am.* high-school diploma; ***das*** ~ ***machen*** a) take one's school-leaving exam, b) get one's school-leaving certificate (*Am.* high-school diploma); **Abi·tu·ri·ent** [abitu'rĭɛnt] *m* (-en; -en), **Abi·tu·ri'en·tin** *f* (-; -nen) a) candidate for the school-leaving exam (*Am.* high-school diploma), *Brit.* sixth-former, b) school-leaver with the ***Abitur***, *Am.* high-school graduate
Abi'tur|prü·fung *f* school-leaving exam; ~**zeug·nis** *n* school-leaving certificate, *Am.* high-school diploma
'**ab·ja·gen** *v/t.* (*sep.*, h): ***j-m et.*** ~ get s.th. off s.o.; ***j-m die Kunden*** ~ steal s.o.'s customers
'**ab·käm·men** *v/t.* (*sep.*, h) **1.** comb *wool*; **2.** *fig.* comb (***nach*** *dat.* for)
'**ab·kan·zeln** *v/t.* (*sep.*, h): ***j-n*** ~ give s.o. a dressing-down (F wigging)
'**ab·kap·seln** *v/refl.* (*sep.*, h): ***sich*** ~ cut o.s. off
ab·kar·ten ['apkartən] *v/t.* (*sep.*, h) fix, rig; → ***abgekartet*** II
'**ab·kas,sie·ren** (*sep.*, h) **I.** *v/i.* **1.** ***bei j-m*** ~ be paid by s.o.; ***ich hab' an dem Tisch***

schon abkassiert that table's paid; **2.** *fig.* cash in (***bei*** on); **II.** *v/t.*: ***j-n ~*** take s.o.'s fare

'**ab·kau·en** *v/t.* (*sep.*, h) chew off; ***sich die Fingernägel ~*** bite one's nails

'**ab·kau·fen** *v/t.* (*sep.*, h) **1.** ***j-m et. ~*** buy s.th. from s.o.; **2.** F *fig.* ***das kauf' ich dir nicht ab!*** tell me another; you don't expect me to believe that, do you?

Ab·kehr ['apke:r] *f* (-; *no pl.*) turning away; *fig. a.* break (***von*** with); renunciation (of); '**ab·keh·ren** (*sep.*, h) **I.** *v/t.* **1.** → ***abfegen***; **2.** turn away, avert *one's eyes*; ***den Blick ~*** look away; **II.** *v/refl*: ***sich ~ von*** turn away from; *fig.* turn one's back on; *fig.* ***sich ~ von*** abandon, give up *a policy etc.*

'**ab·ket·ten** *v/t.* (*sep.*, h) unchain

'**ab·klap·pern** F *v/t.* (*sep.*, h) comb, scour; F do, knock off *the sights etc.*; ***ich hab' alle Häuser*** (***Läden***) ***abgeklappert*** I've been round all the houses (I've been in and out of all the shops); ***ich hab' das ganze Einkaufszentrum nach ihm abgeklappert*** I've been all over the shopping cent|re (*Am.* -er) looking for him

'**ab·klä·ren** *v/t.* (*sep.*, h) clarify, clear; → ***abgeklärt*** II

'**Ab·klatsch** *m* (-[e]s; -e): (***schwacher ~*** poor) imitation

'**ab·klem·men** *v/t.* (*sep.*, h) clamp; *a.* ↯ disconnect

'**Ab·kling·becken** (*sep.* -k·k-) *n reactor*: cooling chamber

'**ab·klin·gen** *v/i.* (*irr.*, *sep.*, sn, → ***klingen***) die (*or* fade) away; *pain*: ease; *effect*: wear off; ✝ *boom etc.*: taper off

'**ab·klop·fen** *v/t.* (*sep.*, h) **1.** knock off; dust off; beat *carpet*; brush down *clothes*; ⚕ tap, ▢ percuss; **2.** F *fig.* sound out; ***et. auf s-e Relevanz etc. hin ~*** check to see whether s.th. is relevant *etc.*; ***die Argumente auf ihre Stichhaltigkeit hin ~*** see whether the arguments hold water

'**ab·knab·bern** *v/t.* (*sep.*, h) nibble (*or* gnaw) off; pick *bone* clean

'**ab·knal·len** F *v/t.* (*sep.*, h): ***j-n ~*** F put a bullet through s.o.'s head, bump s.o. off

'**ab·knap·sen** F *v/t.* (*sep.*, h): ***sich*** (***j-m***) ***et. ~*** stint o.s. (s.o.) of s.th.

'**ab·knei·fen** *v/t.* (*irr.*, *sep.*, h, → ***kneifen***) nip off

'**ab·knicken** (*sep.* -k·k-) *v/t.* (*sep.*, h) *and v/i.* (*sep.*, sn) snap off

'**ab·knip·sen** *v/t.* (*sep.*, h) clip off; nip off

'**ab·knöp·fen** *v/t.* (*sep.*, h) unbutton; F *fig.* ***j-m et. ~*** F wangle s.th. out of s.o.

'**ab·knut·schen** F *v/t.* (*sep.*, h) *sl.* have a good old snog with *s.o.*; ***du hast dich einfach von ihm ~ lassen?*** you let him kiss you just like that?

'**ab·ko·chen** (*sep.*, h) **I.** *v/t.* **1.** boil; ⚕ sterilize; **2.** *fig.* ***j-n ~*** a) give s.o. a good going-over, b) fleece s.o.; **3.** ***einige Pfunde ~*** *boxing etc.*: sweat off a few pounds (to make the weight); **II.** *v/i.* **4.** cook out in the open; **5.** *boxing etc.*: sweat off a few pounds

'**ab·kom·man,die·ren** *v/t.* (*sep.*, h) ⚔ detach, detail, assign

'**ab·kom·men** *v/i.* (*irr.*, *sep.*, sn, → ***kommen***) **1.** ***vom Weg ~*** lose one's way; ***vom Kurs ~*** drift off course; ***von der Fahrbahn ~*** get (*or* skid) off the road; *fig.* ***vom Thema ~*** stray from the point; **2.** ***von et. ~*** give up; ***von e-r Ansicht ~*** change one's views; ***von diesem Brauch ist man abgekommen*** that custom has died out

'**Ab·kom·men** *n* (-s; -) *a. pol.* agreement, settlement; ***ein ~ treffen*** conclude an agreement

ab·kömm·lich ['apkœmlıç] *adj.* dispensable; available; ***er ist zur Zeit nicht ~*** he can't get away (*or* he's very much in demand) at the moment

Ab·kömm·ling ['apkœmlıŋ] *m* (-s; -e) **1.** descendant; **2.** ⚗ derivative

'**ab·kön·nen** *dial. v/t.* (*irr.*, *sep.*, h, → ***können***) be able to take; ***er kann nur wenig ab*** he can't take much

'**ab·kop·peln** *v/t.* (*sep.*, h) uncouple; undock *spaceship etc.*

'**ab·krat·zen** (*sep.*) **I.** *v/t.* (h) scrape off; **II.** V *v/i.* (sn) F kick the bucket, snuff it

'**ab·krie·gen** F *v/t.* → ***abbekommen***

'**ab·küh·len** (*sep.*) **I.** *v/t.* (h) cool (off *or* down) (*a. fig.*); **II.** *v/refl.* (h): ***sich ~*** cool off (*or* down) (*a. fig.*); **III.** *v/i.* (sn) cool (off *or* down); '**Ab·küh·lung** *f* (-; *no pl.*) cooling

Ab·kunft ['apkʊnft] *f* (-; *no pl.*) descent, origin; birth; ***von spanischer ~*** of Spanish descent (*or* extraction); ***von hoher ~*** of noble descent; ***von niedriger ~*** of humble (*or* low) birth

ab·kup·fern ['apkʊpfərn] F *v/t.* (*sep.*, h) copy, F crib, lift

'**ab·kup·peln** *v/t.* (*sep.*, h) uncouple

'**ab·kür·zen** *v/t.* (*sep.*, h) **1.** shorten; **2.** cut short *one's stay etc.*; **3.** condense *book etc.*; **4.** curtail *speech*; **5.** abbreviate, shorten *word etc.*; **6.** ***e-n Weg ~*** take a short cut; '**Ab·kür·zung** *f* (-; -en) **1.** abbreviation; **2.** short cut (*a. fig.*); '**Ab·kür·zungs·ver·zeich·nis** *n* list of abbreviations

'**ab·küs·sen** *v/t.* (*sep.*, h) smother with kisses

'**ab·la·den** *v/t.* (*irr.*, *sep.*, h, → ***laden***) unload; dump *waste etc.*; ***Müll ~ verboten*** no tipping; *fig.* ***s-e Sorgen bei j-m ~*** cry on s.o.'s shoulder, unburden o.s. to s.o.; ***s-e Wut bei j-m ~*** take one's anger out on s.o

'**Ab·la·de·platz** *m* unloading point; dump

'**Ab·la·ge** *f* (-; -n) **1.** place to put s.th.; file; filing cabinet; **2.** *no pl.* filing; **3.** files *pl.*, records *pl.*; **~sy,stem** *n* filing system

'**ab·la·gern** (*sep.*, h) **I.** *v/t.* **1.** store *goods*; deposit *waste*; **2.** *geol.*, ⚕, ⚗ deposit; **3.** store, mature *wine*; season *wood*, *tobacco*; **II.** *v/i.* (*a.* sn) *wine*: mature; *wood*, *tobacco*: season; **III.** *v/refl.*: ***sich ~*** *geol.*, ⚕, ⚗ settle, form a deposit; '**Ab·la·ge·rung** *f* (-; -en) **1.** *no pl.* storage, maturing; *geol.*, ⚕, ⚗ deposition; **2.** deposit, sediment

Ab·laß ['aplas] *m* (Ablasses; Ablässe ['aplɛsə]) **1.** drain; **2.** *eccl.* indulgence; **~brief** *m eccl.* letter of indulgence

'**ab·las·sen** (*irr.*, *sep.*, h, → ***lassen***) **I.** *v/t.* **1.** drain off *liquid*; drain *pond etc.*; broach *cask*; let out *air*; let off *steam*; ***Luft aus den Reifen ~*** let the tyres (*Am.* tires) down; → ***Dampf***; **2.** ***et. vom Preis ~*** F knock s.th. off the price; **II.** *v/i.*: ***von et. ~*** stop doing s.th., give s.th. up; ***von j-m ~*** leave s.o. alone

'**Ab·laß·ven,til** *n* drain valve

Ab·la·tiv ['ablati:f] *m* (-s; -e) *ling.* ablative (case)

'**Ab·lauf** *m* (-[e]s; ⸚e) **1.** *no pl.* flowing, outflow; **2.** outlet, drain; waste pipe; **3.** *no pl.* expiry; ***nach ~ von zwei Wochen*** at the end of two weeks, after two weeks; **4.** order of events; ***der ~ von Ereignissen*** the course (*or* sequence) of events; ***für e-n glatten ~ sorgen*** make sure things run smoothly; **~dia,gramm** *n computer*: chart

'**ab·lau·fen** (*irr.*, *sep.*, → ***laufen***) **I.** *v/i.* (sn) **1.** run (*or* flow) off, *a. bathwater*: drain off; *flood*: subside; ***im Bad läuft das Wasser schlecht ab*** the bath isn't draining properly; *fig.* ***das läuft an ihm alles ab*** it's like water off a duck's back; **2.** *deadline*, *passport etc.*: run out, expire; *term of office etc.*: wind down; **3.** go; turn out; **4.** *clock*: run down; *fig.* ***d-e Uhr ist abgelaufen*** your hour is come; **5.** ***~ lassen*** run, show *film*; play *tape*; run off, drain off *water etc.*; **II.** *v/t.* (h) **6.** wear out *shoes*; wear down *heels*; F *fig.* ***sich die Hacken ~*** F walk one's legs off (***nach*** trying to find); **7.** cover *distance*, scour *territory*, *sport*: check out *the route*; ***alle Geschäfte ~*** run round all the shops; → ***Rang*** 1

'**ab·lauf|fä·hig** *adj. computer program*: active; **2frist** *f* time limit; **2plan** *m* sequence, order of events *etc.*; *TV etc.* running order

'**Ab·laut** *m* (-[e]s; -e) *ling.* vowel gradation, ablaut

'**ab·le·ben I.** *v/i.* (*sep.*, sn) die, pass away; **II. 2** *n* (-s; *no pl.*) death, demise, *a.* ⚖ decease

'**ab·lecken** (*sep.* -k·k-) (*sep.*, h) **I.** *v/t.* **1.** ***den Teller ~*** lick the plate clean; ***sich die Lippen*** (***Finger***) ***~*** lick one's lips (fingers); ***j-n ~*** *dog*: lick s.o. all over; ***j-m das Gesicht ~*** lick s.o.'s face; **2.** lick off; **II.** *v/refl.*: ***sich ~*** *cat*: wash itself

'**ab·le·dern** *v/t.* (*sep.*, h) polish with a chamois (leather)

'**ab·le·gen** (*sep.*, h) **I.** *v/t.* **1.** file *records etc.*; **2.** take off *one's coat etc.*; get rid of *old clothes*; → ***abgelegt*** II; **3.** *fig.* give up, drop *a habit*; **4.** throw out *cards*; **5.** ***e-e Prüfung ~*** take (*or* pass) an exam(ination); → ***Eid, Gelübde, Geständnis, Probe, Rechenschaft, Zeugnis***; **II.** *v/i.* **6.** take one's coat off; **7.** *card game*: throw a card out; **8.** ⚓ (set) sail

'**Ab·le·ger** *m* (-s; -) **1.** ♣ shoot; **2.** ✝ subsidiary

'**ab·leh·nen** (*sep.*, h) **I.** *v/t.* refuse, turn down, decline *invitation etc.*; *a.* reject *offer*, *argument*, *proposal*, *bill etc.*; dislike; disapprove of; turn down *applicant etc.*; **II.** *v/i.* refuse, decline; **III.** *v/impers.*: ***es*** (***strikt***) ***~ zu*** *inf.* (flatly) refuse to *inf.*; '**ab·leh·nend I.** *adj.* negative; **II.** *adv.*: ***~ gegenüberstehen*** *dat.* disapprove of; '**Ab·leh·nung** *f* (-; -en) refusal; rejection; dislike; disapproval; → ***ablehnen***

'**ab·lei·ern** *v/t.* (*sep.*, h) reel off, rattle off

'**ab·lei·sten** *v/t.* (*sep.*, h) fulfil(l), perform; ***s-n Militärdienst ~*** do one's military service

'**ab·lei·ten** (*sep.*, h) **I.** *v/t.* **1.** draw off, drain off *water etc.*; deflect *lightning*; abduct *heat*; **2.** derive *claim etc.* (***aus, von*** from); **3.** deduce; *ling.*, ⚕, *phls.* derive; **4.** ***s-e Herkunft ~ von*** trace one's descent from; **II.** *v/refl.*: ***sich ~*** derive, be derived (***von*** from); '**Ab·lei·tung** *f* (-; -en) **1.** drainage; **2.** *ling.*, *phls.*, ⚕ derivation, derivative; deduction, inference

'**ab·len·ken** (*sep.*, h) **I.** *v/t.* **1.** divert; **2.**

avert, ward off; ***den Verdacht von sich*** ~ avert suspicion, divert suspicion from o.s.; **3.** *sport*: parry *blow*; deflect *the ball, in the goalmouth*: turn *the ball* away; **4.** *phys.* deflect *rays*; diffract *light*; **5.** distract; divert; sidetrack; ***j-n von s-n Sorgen*** *etc.* ~ take s.o.'s mind off his (*or* her) worries *etc.*; **II.** *v/i.* change the subject, sidetrack; **'Ab·len·kung** *f* (-; -en) **1.** diversion, deflection *etc.*; → ***ablenken*; 2.** diversion, distraction; **'Ab·len·kungs·kam͵pa·gne** *f* diversion campaign; **'Ab·len·kungs·ma͵nö·ver** *n* diversionary maneuver (*Brit.* manoeuvre); ***das ist ein*** ~ they're *etc.* just trying to take people's attention away (from the issue *etc.*)

'Ab·le·se·feh·ler *m* reading error

'ab·le·sen *v/t.* (*irr.*, *sep.*, h, → ***lesen***) **1.** read *speech etc.* (from notes); **2.** read *instrument etc.*; ***Gas*** (***Strom***) ~ read the gas (electricity) meter; **3.** ***man konnte ihm s-e Enttäuschung*** *etc.* ***vom Gesicht*** ~ his disappointment *etc.* showed in his face; ***man kann ihm alles vom Gesicht*** ~ you can read him like a book; ***ich konnte es ihr von den Augen*** ~ I could see it in her eyes; ***j-m jeden Wunsch von den Augen*** ~ anticipate s.o.'s every wish; **'Ab·le·sung** *f* (-; -en) ⚙ reading

'ab·leuch·ten *v/t.* (*sep.*, h) search *s.th.* with a lamp (*or* torch); *floodlight*: sweep

'ab·leug·nen *v/t.* (*sep.*, h) deny; repudiate

'ab·lich·ten *v/t.*, **'Ab·lich·tung** *f* → ***fotokopieren, Fotokopie***

'ab·lie·fern *v/t.* (*sep.*, h) deliver; hand in (*dat.* to); F ***ich habe die Kinder zu Hause abgeliefert*** I took the kids home; **'Ab·lie·fe·rung** *f* (-; -en) delivery; ✝ ***bei*** (*or* ***nach***) ~ on delivery; **'Ab·lie·fe·rungs·frist** *f* delivery date

'ab·lie·gen *v/i.* (*irr.*, *sep.*, h, → ***liegen***) be quite a way off; ***weit*** ~ be a long way away; *fig.* ***weit vom Thema*** ~ be off the subject, have nothing to do with the subject (at hand)

'ab·li·sten *v/t.* (*sep.*, h): ***j-m et.*** ~ trick s.o. out of s.th.

'ab·locken (*sep.* -k·k-) *v/t.* (*sep.*, h): ***j-m et.*** ~ wheedle (*or* coax) s.th. out of s.o.; ***j-m ein Lächeln*** ~ draw a smile from s.o., get s.o. to smile

'ab·lö·schen *v/t.* (*sep.*, h) **1.** put out, extinguish; **2.** wipe off *blackboard*; clean *slate*; blot *ink etc.*; **3.** *gastr.* add water (*or* wine *etc.*) to

Ab·lö·se ['aplø:zə] *f* (-; -n) **1.** *sport*: transfer fee; **2.** key money *for a flat*; *in advertisements*: furnishings (and fittings) *pl.*

'ab·lö·sen (*sep.*, h) **I.** *v/t.* remove, take off; ⚔ relieve *guard etc.*; take over from *a colleague*; replace *s.o. in office*; ✝ pay off *debts*, redeem *mortgage*; ***sich*** (*or* ***einander***) ~ take turns (***bei*** at), ***bei der Arbeit***: *a.* work in shifts; ***sich mit j-m*** ~ take it in turns with s.o., rotate with s.o.; **II.** *v/refl.*: ***sich*** ~ *paint, skin etc.*: come off

'Ab·lö·se·sum·me *f sport*: transfer fee

'Ab·lö·sung *f* (-; -en) detachment, removal; ⚔ *etc.* relief; replacement; ✝ discharge *of debts*; redemption *of mortgage etc.*; withdrawal *of capital*

'Ab·lö·sungs·mann·schaft *f* relief team

'ab·luch·sen F *v/t.* (*sep.*, h): ***j-m et.*** ~ F wangle s.th. out of s.o.

'Ab·luft *f* (-; *no pl.*) ⚙ waste air

'ab·ma·chen *v/t.* (*sep.*, h) **1.** take off, remove; *a.* undo *rope etc.*; **2.** *fig.* arrange, agree (on); settle, decide; → ***abgemacht*** II; **3.** *fig.* settle, sort out; ***das mußt du mit dir selbst*** ~ that's for you to sort out (for yourself); **4.** F *fig.* F do *time*; **'Ab·ma·chung** *f* (-; -en) agreement, arrangement; settlement; ***e-e*** ~ ***treffen*** come to an agreement (***über*** *acc.* on)

'ab·ma·gern *v/i.* (*sep.*, sn) go (very) thin; ***er ist sehr abgemagert*** *a.* he's lost an awful lot of weight; → ***abgemagert*** II; **'Ab·ma·ge·rung** *f* (-; -en) emaciation; **'Ab·ma·ge·rungs·kur** *f* (slimming) diet; ***e-e*** ~ ***machen*** be on a (strict) diet, be slimming

'ab·mä·hen *v/t.* (*sep.*, h) mow

'ab·mah·nen *v/t.* (*sep.*, h) ⚖ give *s.o.* a (written) warning; **'Ab·mah·nung** *f* (-; -en) (written) warning

'ab·ma·len *v/t.* (*sep.*, h) paint; copy

'Ab·marsch *m* (-[e]s; ⁼e) marching off; *fig.* start; ~ ***um 8 Uhr*** moving off at 8 a.m., *fig.* we leave at 8 o'clock; **⌐be·reit** *adj.* ready to march (*fig.* set off)

'ab·mar͵schie·ren *v/i.* (*sep.*, sn) march off

'ab·mar·tern *v/refl.* (*sep.*, h): ***sich*** ~ torture o.s., torment o.s. (***mit*** with *reproaches, doubts etc.*; F nearly kill o.s. (*trying to inf.*)

'ab·mel·den (*sep.*, h) **I.** *v/t.* cancel; ***sein Auto*** ~ take one's car off the road; ***j-n*** ~ take s.o.'s name off the list, cancel s.o.'s membership; ***sein Telefon*** ~ have one's (tele)phone disconnected; ***j-n*** ~ *sport*: mark s.o. out of the game; F ***bei mir ist er abgemeldet*** F I'm through with him; **II.** *v/refl.*: ***sich*** ~ sign out; *hotel*: check out; give notification *to the authorities* that one is moving; have one's name taken off the list; cancel one's membership; ***sich bei j-m*** ~ report to s.o. that one is leaving; **'Ab·mel·dung** *f* (-; -en) notice of departure; cancellation *etc.*; → ***abmelden***

'ab·mes·sen *v/t.* (*irr.*, *sep.*, h, → ***messen***) measure; *fig.* assess; *fig.* ***s-e Worte*** ~ weigh one's words; **'Ab·mes·sung** *f* (-; -en) measurement; dimension

'ab·mil·dern *v/t.* (*sep.*, h) moderate

'ab·mon͵tie·ren *v/t.* (*sep.*, h) dismantle; take off, remove

'ab·mü·hen *v/refl.* (*sep.*, h): ***sich*** ~ slave away; ***sich*** ~, ***et. zu tun*** take great pains to do s.th.; ***sich*** ~ ***mit*** struggle (*or* wrestle) with

'ab·murk·sen F *v/t.* (*sep.*, h) F do in, bump off

'ab·mu·stern ⚓ (*sep.*, h) **I.** *v/t.* pay off; **II.** *v/i.* sign off

ab·na·beln ['apna:bəln] (*sep.*, h) **I.** *v/t.*: ***ein Kind*** ~ cut the umbilical cord; **II.** F *fig.* *v/refl.*: ***sich*** ~ cut the cord

'ab·na·gen *v/t.* (*sep.*, h) gnaw off; gnaw *bone*

'ab·nä·hen *v/t.* (*sep.*, h) take in; **'Ab·nä·her** *m* (-s; -) dart

Ab·nah·me ['apna:mə] *f* (-; *no pl.*) **1.** taking down (*or* off); removal; ⚕ amputation; **2.** administering *of an oath*; **3.** acceptance *of goods etc.*; purchase; ***bei*** ~ ***von*** on orders of; **4.** ⚙ a) (final) inspection, b) acceptance; **5.** decrease, decline; *a.* drop (*all gen.* in); shortening *of the days*; waning *of the moon*; loss *of weight*; ~ ***der Kräfte*** weakening; **~prü·fung** *f* specification test; inspection test; **~test** *m computer*: acceptance test; **~ver·wei·ge·rung** *f* rejection; **~vor·schrif·ten** *pl.* quality specifications

ab·nehm·bar ['apne:mba:r] *adj.* removable, detachable; **'ab·neh·men** (*irr.*, *sep.*, h, → ***nehmen***) **I.** *v/t.* **1.** take off (*or* down); remove (*all a.* ⚙); ⚕ amputate, take off; shave off *beard*; decrease *stitches*; ***den Hörer*** ~ pick up the receiver, answer the phone; ***j-m et.*** ~ take s.th. away from s.o.; relieve s.o. of s.th.; F charge s.o. s.th.; ***j-m zuviel*** ~ overcharge s.o.; ***j-m Blut*** ~ take a blood sample (from s.o.); *fig.* ***das nimmt ihm keiner ab*** nobody will buy that; **2.** ✝ buy (*dat.* from); take delivery of; **3. *10 Pfund*** *etc.* ~ lose 10 pounds *etc.*; **4.** ⚙ accept; inspect, test; hold *examination*; → ***Beichte, Eid, Versprechen***; **II.** *v/i.* **5.** decrease, decline, diminish; *strength*: diminish, dwindle; lose weight, be slimming; slacken (off), slow down; *moon*: (be on the) wane; *storm*: abate, subside; *days*: grow shorter; *fig. power etc.*: decline, wane; **6.** *teleph.* answer the phone; ***nimmst du mal ab?*** can you get it?

'Ab·neh·mer *m* (-s; -) ✝ buyer, purchaser, taker; customer; consumer; ***keine*** ~ ***finden*** find no market; **~kreis** *m* market, customers *pl.*; **~land** *n* importing country

'Ab·nei·gung *f* (-; -en) dislike (***gegen*** of, for), aversion (to); ***e-e*** ~ ***gegen j-n fassen*** take a dislike to s.o.; ***ich habe e-e ausgesprochene*** ~ ***dagegen*** I can't stand it; ⚖ ***unüberwindliche*** ~ irreconcilable differences

ab·norm [ap'nɔrm] *adj.* abnormal; exceptional, unusual; **Ab·nor·mi·tät** [apnɔrmi'tɛ:t] *f* (-; -en) abnormality

'ab·nö·ti·gen *v/t.* (*sep.*, h): ***j-m et.*** ~ wring s.th. from s.o.; ***j-m Respekt*** ~ command s.o.'s respect; ***er nötigt mir Bewunderung ab*** I can't help admiring him

'ab·nut·zen, 'ab·nüt·zen (*sep.*, h) **I.** *v/t.* wear out; **II.** *v/refl.*: ***sich*** ~ wear (out), get worn out

'Ab·nut·zung *f* (-; *no pl.*) wear (and tear); **'Ab·nut·zungs·er·schei·nung** *f a.* ⚕ sign of wear (and tear)

Abo ['abo] F *n* → ***Abonnement***

'A-Bombe *f* A bomb

Abon·ne·ment [abɔnə'mã:] *n* (-s; -s) subscription; *thea. a.* season ticket (***bei*** *dat.* for)

Abon·ne'ment(s)|fern·se·hen *n* pay TV; **~kon͵zert** *n* subscription concert; **~vor·stel·lung** *f* subscription performance

Abon·nent [abɔ'nɛnt] *m* (-en; -en) (*thea.* ticket) subscriber

abon·nie·ren [abɔ'ni:rən] *v/t.* (h) subscribe to; have a season ticket for; ***wir haben zwei Tageszeitungen abonniert*** *a.* we get (*or* we have a subscription for) two daily newspapers; *fig.* ***er scheint das Glück*** (***Pech***) ***abonniert zu haben*** he seems to have a monopoly on (bad) luck; **abon'niert I.** *p.p. of* ***abonnieren*; II.** *fig. adj.*: ***sie scheint auf den dritten Platz*** *etc.* ~ ***zu sein*** they seem to have reserved third place *etc.* just for her; ***er scheint auf Autounfälle*** *etc.* ~ ***zu sein*** he seems to have a standing order for car accidents *etc.*

'ab·ord·nen *v/t.* (*sep.*, h) delegate, *Am. a.* deputize; **'Ab·ord·nung** *f* (-; -en) delegation

Ab·ort[1] [a'bɔrt; 'apˀɔrt] *m* (-[e]s; -e) toilet,

lavatory, *Am. a.* bathroom; ***auf den ~ gehen*** go to the toilet *etc.*
Ab·ort² [a'bɔrt] *m* (-s; -e) ⚕ miscarriage; **ab·or·tie·ren** [abɔr'tiːrən] *v/i.* (h) have a miscarriage
'ab·packen (*sep.* -k·k-) *v/t.* (*sep.*, h) pack; → ***abgepackt*** II
'ab·pas·sen *v/t.* (*sep.*, h) wait for; *a.* be on the lookout for *s.o.*, waylay *s.o.*; ***e-n günstigen Moment ~*** wait for the right moment; ***et. gut*** (***schlecht***) **~** time s.th. well (badly)
'ab·pa·trouil,lie·ren *v/t.* (*sep.*, h) patrol
'ab·pau·sen *v/t.* (*sep.*, h) trace
'ab·per·len *v/i.* (*sep.*, sn) (*a.* **~ *an*** *dat.*) trickle down
'ab·pfei·fen *v/i.* (*irr.*, *sep.*, h, → ***pfeifen***) (*a. v/t.* ***das Spiel ~***) stop the game; blow the final whistle
'Ab·pfiff *m* (-[e]s; -e) final whistle
'ab·pflücken (*sep.* -k·k-) *v/t.* (*sep.*, h) pick
'ab·pla·gen *v/refl.* (*sep.*, h): ***sich ~*** struggle (away), slave away, ***mit***: struggle (*or* grapple) with
ab·plat·ten ['applatən] *v/t.* (*sep.*, h) smooth (off)
'ab·plat·zen *v/i.* (*sep.*, sn) **1.** *button etc.*: pop off; **2.** *paint etc.*: flake off
'ab·prä·gen *v/refl.* (*sep.*, h): ***sich ~*** leave an impression (***auf*** *dat.* on); *fig.* leave its mark (***auf*** *dat.*, ***in*** *dat.* on)
'Ab·prall *m* (-[e]s; *no pl.*) rebound; ricochet; **'ab·pral·len** *v/i.* (*sep.*, sn) rebound, bounce off; ricochet; *fig.* ***an j-m ~*** make no impression on s.o.; ***die Vorwürfe*** *etc.* ***prallen an ihm ab*** *a.* it's like water off a duck's back; **'Ab·pral·ler** *m* (-s; -) ricochet; *sport*: rebound
'ab·pres·sen *v/t.* (*sep.*, h): ***j-m et. ~*** force s.th. out of s.o.; ***sich ein Lächeln ~*** force o.s. to smile; ***es preßte ihm die Luft ab*** his heart almost stopped
'ab·pum·pen *v/t.* (*sep.*, h) pump off
'ab·put·zen *v/t.* (*sep.*, h) clean (up); wipe off (*or* up)
'ab·quä·len (*sep.*, h) **I.** *v/refl.*: ***sich ~*** worry (o.s.), fret; → ***abrackern; sich mit j-m*** (*or* ***et.***) **~** have a hard time with s.o. (*or* s.th.); **II.** *v/t.*: ***sich e-e Antwort*** *etc.* **~** force o.s. to answer *etc.*; ***sich ein Lächeln ~*** *a.* force a smile
'ab·qua·li·fi,zie·ren *v/t.* (*sep.*, h) write off (completely)
'ab·quet·schen *v/t.* (*sep.*, h): ***sich den Finger*** *etc.* **~** get one's finger *etc.* crushed
'ab·rackern (*sep.* -k·k-) *v/refl.* (*sep.*, h): ***sich ~*** sweat away; ***ich habe mich mit dem Aufsatz abgerackert*** F I nearly killed myself getting that essay done
'ab·rah·men *v/t.* (*sep.*, h) skim *milk*
Abra·ka·da·bra [aːbraka'daːbra] *n* (-s; *no pl.*) **1.** *without art.*: abracadabra; **2.** drivel
'ab·ra,sie·ren *v/t.* (*sep.*, h) shave off; *fig.* raze (to the ground); ***sich den Bart ~*** shave off one's beard
'ab·ra·ten *v/i.* (*irr.*, *sep.*, h, → ***raten***): ***j-m von et. ~*** advise (*or* warn) s.o. against (doing) s.th.; ***ich rate Ihnen davon ab*** I advise you not to (*or* against it)
'Ab·raum *m* (-[e]s; *no pl.*) ⚒ overburden
'ab·räu·men (*sep.*, h) **I.** *v/t.* clear up (*or* away); ***den Tisch ~*** clear the table; **II.** *v/i.* clear the table; F *fig.* cream off the profits, *esp. sport*: sweep the board
'ab·rau·schen F *v/i.* (*sep.*, sn) F zoom off, *mot. a.* roar off; *fig.* stalk off (in a temper)

'ab·rea,gie·ren (*sep.*, h) **I.** *v/t.* work off *one's anger* (***an*** *dat.* on); *psych.* abreact; **II.** *v/refl.*: ***sich ~*** get rid of one's aggressions, F let off steam; ***sich ~ an*** *dat.* let one's aggressions (*or* anger *etc.*) out on
'ab·rech·nen (*sep*, h) **I.** *v/t.* deduct, subtract; account for; **II.** *v/i.* do the accounts; settle accounts (***mit j-m*** with s.o.); *fig. a.* get even (with s.o.); **'Ab·rech·nung** *f* (-; -en) deduction; settlement of accounts; account; *fig.* requital; ***laut ~*** as per account rendered; *fig.* ***Tag der ~*** day of reckoning; **'Ab·rech·nungs·zeit·raum** *m* accounting period
'Ab·re·de *f* (-; -n) **1.** agreement; ***e-e ~ treffen*** come to an agreement; **2.** ***in ~ stellen*** deny, contest
'ab·re·gen F *v/refl.* (*sep.*, h): ***reg dich ab!*** F cool it!, take it easy!
'ab·rei·ben (*irr.*, *sep.*, h, → ***reiben***) **I.** *v/t.* rub off; rub down; polish; *gastr.* grate; **II.** *v/refl.*: ***sich ~*** rub o.s. down; *velvet etc.*: wear down, wear off; ⚙ abrade; **'Ab·rei·bung** *f* (-; -en) **1.** rubbing-down, sponge-down; **2.** F thrashing; ***j-m e-e ~ verpassen*** give s.o. a thrashing
'Ab·rei·se *f* (-; -n) departure (***nach*** *dat.* for); ***bei m-r ~*** on my departure; **'ab·rei·sen** *v/i.* (*sep.*, sn) leave (***nach*** *dat.* for)
'Ab·reiß·block *m* tear-off pad
'ab·rei·ßen (*irr.*, *sep.*, → ***reißen***) **I.** *v/t.* (h) **1.** tear off (*or* down); pull (*or* rip) off; pull down *house etc.*; **2.** F *fig.* F do *time*; **II.** *v/i.* (sn) **3.** come off, tear off; break, snap; **4.** *fig.* break off; ***das reißt nicht ab*** there's no end to it, it just goes on and on; ***die Arbeit reißt nicht ab*** the work never lets up
'Ab·reiß·ka,len·der *m* sheet (*Am.* pad) calendar
'ab·rei·ten *v/t.* (*irr.*, *sep.*, h, → ***reiten***) ride along; ride, have a trial run of
'ab·ren·nen F *v/t. and v/refl.* (*irr.*, *sep.*, h, → ***rennen***): ***sich*** (***die Beine***) **~** run one's legs off; ***alle Geschäfte ~*** run round all the shops
'ab·rich·ten *v/t.* (*sep.*, h) train, *w.s. a.* teach *an animal* tricks; break in *horse*; **'Ab·rich·tung** *f* (-; *no pl.*) training; breaking-in
Ab·rieb ['apriːp] *m* (-[e]s ['apriːbəs]; -e) ⚙ **1.** *no pl.* abrasion, wear; **2.** grindings *pl.*, dust; **≈fest** *adj.* non-abrasive
'ab·rie·geln *v/t.* (*sep.*, h) bolt *door etc.*; block *road etc.*; *police*: cordon off, *a.* ⚔ seal off
'ab·rin·gen *v/t.* (*irr.*, *sep.*, h, → ***ringen***): ***et. ~*** *dat.* wring s.th. from, *lit.* wrest s.th. from
'ab·rin·nen *v/i.* (*irr.*, *sep.*, sn, → ***rinnen***) run off (*or* down)
'Ab·riß *m* (-sses; -sse) **1.** *no pl.* demolition; **2.** sketch, brief outline (*or* summary); survey; **~bir·ne** *f* demolition (*or* wrecking) ball
'ab·rol·len (*sep.*) **I.** *v/i.* (sn) unroll; *fig.* pass; **II.** *v/t.* (h) unroll; *a. phot.* unwind; pay out *cable etc.*; roll off; **'Ab·rol·ler** *m* (-s; -) dispenser
'ab·rub·beln (*sep.*, h) **I.** *v/t.* rub off; rub down; **II.** *v/refl.*: ***sich ~*** rub o.s. down
'ab·rücken (*sep.* -k·k-) (*sep.*) **I.** *v/t.* (h) move away; **II.** *v/i.* (sn) move off, ⚔ march off; *fig.* **~ *von*** dissociate (*or* distance) o.s. from
'Ab·ruf *m* (-[e]s; *no pl.*) **1.** ⚕ call (***von*** for); ***auf ~*** on call; **2.** recall; ***auf ~*** subject to recall; **≈be·reit** *adj.* on call

'ab·ru·fen *v/t.* (*irr.*, *sep.*, h, → ***rufen***) call *s.o.* away, recall *s.o.*; ⚕ call; *computer*: (re)call *data*
'Ab·ruf·ta·ste *f computer*: attention key
'ab·run·den *v/t.* (*sep.*, h) round off; ***nach oben*** (***unten***) **~** round up (down); → ***abgerundet*** II
'ab·rup·fen *v/t.* (*sep.*, h) pluck (off)
ab·rupt [ap'rʊpt] *adj.* abrupt, sudden
'ab·rü·sten (*sep.*, h) **I.** *v/t.* take the scaffolding down from; **II.** *v/i.* ⚔ disarm; **'Ab·rü·stung** *f* (-; *no pl.*) disarmament; **'Ab·rü·stungs·ver·hand·lun·gen** *pl.* arms (limitation *or* reduction *or* control) talks
'ab·rut·schen *v/i.* (*sep.*, sn) slip off (*or* down); *knife etc.*: slip; *mot.* skid; *ski*, ✈ sideslip; *fig. standards etc.*: slip; *person*: go downhill
ABS [aːbeː'ɛs] → ***Antiblockiersystem***
'ab·sä·beln F *v/t.* (*sep.*, h) hack off, chop off
'ab·sacken (*sep.* -k·k-) *v/i.* (*sep.*, sn) △ sag, *a.* ⚓ sink; ✈ pitch down, pancake; *fig. standards etc.*: slip; *person*: go to seed
'Ab·sa·ge *f* (-; -n) **1.** cancellation; **2.** refusal, negative reply; **3.** **~ *an*** *acc.* renunciation of; **4.** *TV*, *radio*: signing-off; **'ab·sa·gen** (*sep.*, h) **I.** *v/t.* **1.** cancel, call off; turn down *invitation etc.*; **II.** *v/i.* **2.** cry off; ***j-m ~*** a) tell s.o. s.th. is off, tell s.o. not to come, b) tell s.o. one can't come; ***ich muß leider ~*** I'm afraid I can't come (after all); **3.** ***e-r Sache ~*** renounce s.th., break with s.th.; **4.** *TV*, *radio*: sign off
'ab·sä·gen *v/t.* (*sep.*, h) **1.** saw off; **2.** F *fig.* (give *s.o.* the) axe, *Am.* ax
ab·sah·nen ['apzaːnən] (*sep.*, h) **I.** *v/t.* skim, cream; F *fig.* cream off; **II.** F *fig.* *v/i.* cream off the profits
'ab·sat·teln *v/t.* (*sep.*, h) unsaddle
'Ab·satz *m* (-es; ⸚e) **1.** paragraph (*a.* ⚖); *typ.* break; **2.** heel; **3.** ⚕ sales *pl.*, turnover; **~ *finden*** be sal(e)able, find a ready market; ***reißenden ~ finden*** F sell like hot cakes; **4.** *geol.* terrace; landing; **~be·le·bung** *f* increase in sales; **~chan·cen** *pl.* sales prospects; **≈fä·hig** *adj.* sal(e)able; marketable; **~för·de·rung** *f* sales promotion; **~for·schung** *f* marketing research; **~ga·ran,tie** *f* guaranteed sales *pl.*; **~ge·biet** *n* market(ing area); **~kri·se** *f* slump in sales; **~markt** *m* market, outlet; **~mög·lich·kei·ten** *pl.* sales potential *sg.*; **~rück·gang** *m* decline in sales; **~schwie·rig·kei·ten** *pl.* marketing problems; **~stei·ge·rung** *f* increase in sales; **~vo,lu·men** *n* sales volume
'ab·satz·wei·se *adv.* by (*or* in) paragraphs
'Ab·satz·zei·chen *n typ.* break mark
'ab·sau·fen F *v/i.* (*irr.*, *sep.*, sn, → ***saufen***) ⚓ sink, go down; *person*: drown; *engine*: be flooded
'ab·sau·gen *v/t.* (*sep.*, h) suck off; vacuum *carpet etc.*; ⚕ aspirate
'Ab'saug·pum·pe *f* exhaust pump
'ab·scha·ben *v/t.* (*sep.*, h) scrape (off)
'ab·schaf·fen *v/t.* (*sep.*, h) abolish, do away (with); repeal *law*; get rid of *s.th.*; *a.* give up *car etc.*; **'Ab·schaf·fung** *f* (-; *no pl.*) abolition; ⚖ repeal
'ab·schä·len *v/t.* → ***schälen***
'Ab·schalt·au·to,ma·tik *f* automatic shutoff
'ab·schal·ten (*sep.*, h) **I.** *v/t.* switch (*or* turn) off *radio, light etc.*; *light a.* cut out; ⚡ cut off, disconnect; **II.** F *fig.* *v/i.* F

switch off; relax, forget about everything (for a while)
'**ab·schat|tie·ren** *v/t.* (*sep.*, h) shade
'**ab·schätz·bar** *adj.* foreseeable *consequences etc.*; '**ab·schät·zen** *v/t.* (*sep.*, h) estimate, assess; anticipate, foresee *consequences etc.*; *fig.* size *s.o.* up; '**ab·schät·zend** *adj.* **1.** speculative; **2.** → **ab·schät·zig** ['apʃɛtsɪç] *adj.* disparaging, derogatory
'**Ab·schaum** *m* (-[e]s; *no pl.*) scum; *fig.* (*a.* ~ ***der Menschheit***) scum of the earth
'**ab·schäu·men** *v/t.* (*sep.*, h) *gastr.* skim off
'**ab·schei·den** *v/t.* (*irr.*, *sep.*, h, → ***schei-den***) ⚗ eliminate; *physiol.* secrete, deposit; *metall.* refine; '**Ab·schei·der** *m* (-s; -) ⚙ separator; '**Ab·schei·dung** *f* (-; -en) ⚗ elimination; *physiol.* secretion; *metall.* refining
'**ab·sche·ren** *v/t.* (*irr.*, *sep.*, h, → ***sche-ren***) shear off; ***sich den Bart*** *etc.* ~ shave off one's beard *etc.*
'**Ab·scheu** *m* (-s; *no pl.*) horror (***vor*** *dat.* of), disgust (for, at), loathing (for); ~ ***haben vor*** *dat.* detest, loathe
'**ab·scheu·ern** *v/t.* (*sep.*, h) scrub (off), scour (off); (*a.* ***sich*** ~) wear thin; scrape, rub off; ***sich die Haut*** ~ scrape one's skin off
'**ab·scheu·er·re·gend** *adj.* repulsive
ab·scheu·lich [ap'ʃɔylɪç] *adj.* despicable; dreadful; heinous, atrocious
'**ab·schicken** (*sep.* -k·k-) *v/t.* (*sep.*, h) send off, dispatch; post, *esp. Am.* mail
'**Ab·schie·be·haft** *f* custody prior to deportation
'**ab·schie·ben** (*irr.*, *sep.*, → ***schieben***) **I.** *v/t.* (h) push away; deport; F *fig.* get rid of, F shunt off; ***die Schuld auf j-n*** ~ put the blame on s.o., push the blame onto s.o.; **II.** F *v/i.* (sn) F push off; '**Ab·schie·bung** *f* (-; -en) deportation
'**Ab·schie·bungs·haft** *f* → ***Abschiebehaft***
Ab·schied ['apʃiːt] *m* (-[e]s; -e ['apʃiːdə]) leave-taking, farewell, goodbye(s *pl.*); dismissal, ⚔ discharge; resignation; ~ ***nehmen*** say goodbye (***von*** to); ***s-n*** ~ ***nehmen*** hand in one's resignation; ***der*** ~ ***war schwer*** it was hard saying goodbye
'**Ab·schieds|brief** *m* farewell letter; **~fei·er** *f*, **~fest** *n* farewell (*or* going-away) party; **~ge·such** *n* letter of resignation; ***sein*** ~ ***einreichen*** tender one's resignation; **~kon|zert** *n* farewell concert; **~kuß** *m* goodbye kiss; ***j-m e-n*** ~ ***geben*** kiss s.o. goodbye; **~re·de** *f* farewell speech; **~schmerz** *m* pain of parting, wrench; **~spiel** *n sport*: testimonial (match); **~stun·de** *f* hour of parting; **~wor·te** *pl.* words of farewell
'**ab·schie·ßen** *v/t.* (*irr.*, *sep.*, h, → ***schie-ßen***) **1.** fire *gun etc.*; shoot *arrow etc.*; launch *rocket etc.*; **2.** shoot down; bring down *bird*; *fig.* → ***Vogel***; shoot off *leg etc.*; ⚔ shoot (*or* bring) down *plane*; knock out *tank*; F *fig.* ***j-n*** ~ F put the skids under s.o.
'**ab·schin·den** *v/refl.* (*irr.*, *sep.*, h, → ***schinden***): ***sich*** ~ work one's fingers to the bone
'**Ab·schirm·dienst** *m*: ***Militärischer*** ~ Military Intelligence Service
'**ab·schir·men** *v/t.* (*sep.*, h) guard (***gegen*** against), *a.* ⚡ shield (from); '**Ab·schir·mung** *f* (-; -en) screening, shielding
'**ab·schlach·ten** *v/t.* (*sep.*, h) slaughter, butcher (*both a. fig.*)
'**ab·schlaf·fen** F (*sep.*) **I.** *v/i.* (sn) flag, collapse, F flake out; → ***abgeschlafft*** II; **II.** *v/t.* (h) wear *s.o.* out, F take it out of *s.o.*
'**Ab·schlag** *m* (-[e]s; ⸚e) **1.** ✝ drop in prices; reduction, discount; → ***Abschlags-zahlung; auf*** ~ on account; ***auf*** ~ ***kaufen*** buy in instal(l)ments; **2.** *soccer*: kick-out; *golf*: tee, tee-off; '**ab·schla·gen** (*irr.*, *sep.*, h, → ***schlagen***) **I.** *v/t.* **1.** knock off; cut off *head*; cut down *tree*; **2.** *soccer*: kick *the ball* out, *golf*: tee off; **3.** beat off, repulse *attack etc.*; **4.** turn down; ***j-m e-n Wunsch*** ~ deny s.o. a wish; **II.** *v/i.* *soccer*: kick the ball out; *golf*: tee off
ab·schlä·gig ['apʃlɛːgɪç] *adj.* (*and adv.*) negative(ly); ~***e Antwort*** negative reply; ***e-e*** ~***e Antwort erhalten*** be turned down
'**Ab·schlags|di·vi|den·de** *f* ✝ interim dividend; **~sum·me** *f* instal(l)ment; **~zah·lung** *f* payment on account; part payment
'**ab·schlecken** (*sep.* -k·k-) *v/t.* (h) → ***ab-lecken***
'**ab·schlei·fen** (*irr.*, *sep.*, h, → ***schleifen***) **I.** *v/t.* ⚙ grind off (*or* down); polish; *fig.* polish, refine; **II.** *fig.* *v/refl.*: ***sich*** ~ *habit etc.*: wear off
'**Ab·schlepp·dienst** *m* breakdown (*Am.* towing) service; breakdown men *pl.*, *Am.* wreckers *pl.*
'**ab·schlep·pen** (*sep.*, h) **I.** *v/t.* *mot.*, ⚓ (take in) tow, tow off; F drag *s.o.* off, F pick *s.o.* up; **II.** *v/refl.*: ***sich*** ~ ***mit*** struggle with; ***sie schleppt sich mit dem Koffer ab*** *a.* she's having a hard time with that case
'**Ab·schlepp|ko·sten** *pl.* towing charges; **~kran** *m mot.* salvage (*Am* wrecking) crane; **~seil** *n* towrope; **~stan·ge** *f* tow bar; **~wa·gen** *m* breakdown lorry, *Am.* tow truck, wrecker
'**ab·schließ·bar** *adj.* lockable; ***ist es*** ~**?** *a.* has it got a lock?; '**ab·schlie·ßen** (*irr.*, *sep.*, h, → ***schließen***) **I.** *v/t.* **1.** lock (up); lock up (*or* away); **2.** end, (bring to a) close, wind up; settle; complete; ✝ close, balance *books*; settle *accounts etc.*; **3.** strike *a bargain*, close *a deal*; effect *a sale*; take out *a policy*; conclude, make, sign *contract etc.*; → ***Wette***; **II.** *v/i.* **4.** end, close, conclude; (***mit folgenden Worten***) ~ end (*or* wind up) (by saying); ***mit dem Leben*** ~ prepare to die, come to terms with the fact that one has to die; ***er hat mit dem Leben abgeschlossen*** he's ready to die, *lit.* he's prepared to meet his Maker; ***ich hatte schon mit dem Leben abgeschlossen*** I thought to myself, 'This is the end'; **5.** ✝ close the deal; sign (the contract); ***mit j-m*** ~ *a.* come to terms with s.o.; **6.** ***gut*** (***schlecht***) ~ do well (badly); '**ab·schlie·ßend I.** *adj.* concluding, closing, final; final, definitive; **II.** *adv.* in conclusion; finally; ~ ***sagte er*** he wound up by saying
'**Ab·schluß** *m* (-sses; ⸚sse) **1.** conclusion, end(ing), close; settlement; ***vor dem*** ~ ***stehen*** be drawing to a close; ***zum*** ~ in conclusion, finally; ***zum*** ~ ***bringen*** bring to a close; **2.** ✝ conclusion, signing *of contract etc.*; closing, settlement *of accounts etc.*; balance; → ***Jahres-abschluß***; **3.** → ***Schulabschluß, Universitätsabschluß***; **4.** ⚙ seal; **~ball** *m* end-of-course dance; school leavers' (*Am.* graduation) ball; *univ.* finalist's (*esp. Am.* graduation) ball; **~bi|lanz** *f* final balance (sheet); **~klas·se** *f* final-year class; **~kom·mu·ni|qué** *n pol.* final communiqué; **~prü·fung** *f* final (*Brit.* school-leaving) examination (*or* exam); **~sit·zung** *f* closing session; **~zeug·nis** *n* (school-)leaving certificate, *Am.* (high-school *or* graduation) diploma
'**ab·schmecken** (*sep.* k-·k-) *v/t.* (*sep.*, h) taste; season (to taste)
'**ab·schmei·cheln** *v/t.* (*sep.*, h): ***j-m et.*** ~ wheedle s.th. out of s.o.
'**ab·schmel·zen** (*irr.*, *sep.*, → ***schmelzen***) **I.** *v/t.* (*h*) melt off; fuse *metal*; smelt *ore*; **II.** *v/i.* (sn) melt (off); ⚙ fuse
'**ab·schmet·tern** F *v/t.* (*sep.*, h) reject *s.th.* out of hand, F shoot down *arguments etc.*; F give *s.o.* the brush-off; refuse to listen to *a complaint etc.*
'**ab·schmie·ren** (*sep.*) **I.** *v/t.* (h) **1.** ⚙ lubricate, grease; **2.** scribble down; copy; **II.** F *v/i.* (sn) ✈ (do a) nose-dive
'**Ab·schmier|fett** *n* lubricating grease; **~pres·se** *f* grease gun
'**ab·schmin·ken** (*sep.*, h) **I.** *v/t.* take off *s.o.'s* makeup; F ***das kannst du dir*** ~**!** you can forget about that; **II.** *v/refl.*: ***sich*** ~ take one's makeup off
'**ab·schmir·geln** *v/t.* (*sep.*, h) sand down, sandpaper
'**ab·schmücken** (*sep.* -k·k-) *v/t.* (*sep.*, h): ***den Weihnachtsbaum*** ~ take the decorations down from the Christmas tree
'**ab·schnal·len** (*sep.*, h) **I.** *v/t.* unbuckle, unstrap; take off *skis etc.*; **II.** *v/refl.*: ***sich*** ~ take one's seatbelt off; ✈ *a.* unfasten one's seatbelt; **III.** *v/i.*: F ***da schnallst du ab*** F it's absolutely incredible, F it's mind-boggling
'**ab·schnei·den** (*irr.*, *sep.*, h, → ***schneiden***) **I.** *v/t.* **1.** cut off; slice; cut *nails, hair*; ✂ prune, trim; ***sich die Nägel*** *etc.* ~ cut one's nails *etc.*; → ***Scheibe***; **2.** cut off; ***j-m den Weg*** ~ block s.o.'s path; **3.** cut off, isolate; **4.** ***j-m das Wort*** ~ cut s.o. short; **5.** ***den Weg*** ~ take a short cut; **II.** *v/i.* **6.** take a short cut; **7.** F ***gut*** (***schlecht***) ~ do (*or* come off, fare) well (badly); ***am besten*** ~ come out on top
'**ab·schnel·len** (*sep.*) **I.** *v/t.* (*h*) jerk off, flip off; let fly, shoot *arrow etc.*; **II.** *v/i.* (sn) shoot off, fly off; **III.** *v/refl.* (h): ***sich*** ~ propel o.s. off, bounce off
'**ab·schnip·peln** F *v/t.* (*sep.*, h) snip off
'**Ab·schnitt** *m* (-[e]s; -e) **1.** section, ⅋ segment; ⚔ sector; section *of a road*; section, passage *of a book etc.* (*both a.* ♪), paragraph; stage, leg *of a journey*; phase; period; **2.** stub, counterfoil
'**ab·schnitt(s)·wei·se** *adv.* in sections *etc.*; F bit by bit
'**ab·schnü·ren** *v/t.* (*sep.*, h) **1.** ⚕ strangulate; apply a tourniquet to; **2.** ***j-m die Luft*** ~ choke s.o., *fig.* have a stranglehold on s.o., ruin s.o.
'**ab·schöp·fen** *v/t.* (*sep.*, h) skim off; *fig.* ✝ *a.* siphon off *profits etc.*; cream off
ab·schot·ten ['apʃɔtən] *v/refl.* (*sep.*, h): ***sich*** ~ cut o.s. off
'**ab·schrä·gen** *v/t.* (*sep.*, h) slope, slant; ⚙ bevel, chamfer
'**ab·schrau·ben** *v/t.* (*sep.*, h) unscrew
'**ab·schrecken** (*sep.* -k·k-) *v/t.* (*sep.*, h) **1.** scare off; *w.s.* put off; ***sich*** ~ ***lassen*** be

put off; ***laß dich nicht ~*** don't let it (*or* them *etc.*) put you off; **2.** ⚙ chill, quench; **3.** *gastr.* a) run *an egg* under cold water, b) rinse *noodles etc.*; **'ab·schreckend** (*sep.* -k·k-) **I.** *adj.* off-putting; forbidding; deterrent; ***~es Beispiel*** warning, deterrent; ***~e Strafe*** exemplary punishment; **II.** *adv.*: ***~ wirken*** act as a deterrent (***auf*** *acc.* to); **'Ab·schreckung** (*sep.* -k·k-) *f* (-; -en) **1.** deterrence; **2.** → ***Abschreckungsmittel***

'Ab·schreckungs|mit·tel (*sep.* -k·k-) *n* deterrent; **~po·li͵tik** *f* policy of deterrence; **~waf·fe** *f* deterrent weapon

'ab·schrei·ben (*irr.*, *sep.*, h, → ***schreiben***) **I.** *v/t.* **1.** copy; transcribe; *ped. etc.* copy, F crib; **2.** † write off (*a. fig.*), *partially*: write down; depreciate; deduct; → ***absetzen*** 6; **II.** *v/i.* **3.** copy, F crib; **4.** ***j-m*** ~ write (to s.o.) to say one can't come (*or* that the party *etc.* is off); **'Ab·schrei·bung** *f* (-; -en) † writing off; depreciation

'Ab·schrei·bungs|be·trag *m* depreciation (allowance); **~fonds** *m* depreciation fund

'ab·schrei·ten *v/t.* (*irr.*, *sep.*, h, → ***schreiten***) pace; pace off; ***die Front ~*** inspect the troops

'Ab·schrift *f* (-; -en) copy, duplicate

'ab·schröp·fen *v/t.* (*sep.*, h): ***j-m et.*** ~ F wangle s.th. out of s.o.

'ab·schrub·ben F *v/t.* (*sep.*, h) scrub, scour

'ab·schuf·ten *v/refl.* (*sep.*, h): ***sich*** ~ slave away

'ab·schup·pen (*sep.*, h) **I.** *v/t.* scale; **II.** *v/refl.*: ***sich*** ~ peel (off)

'ab·schür·fen *v/t.* (*sep.*, h): ***sich die Haut*** ~ graze o.s.; ***sich*** (***die Haut***) ***am Knie*** *etc.* ~ scrape (*or* graze) one's knee *etc.*; **'Ab·schür·fung** *f* (-; -en) graze

'Ab·schuß *m* (-sses; ⸚sse) **1.** firing *of gun etc.*; launching *of rocket etc.*; shooting *of deer etc.*; ✈ downing; knocking out *of tanks*; **2.** hit, strike; ***drei Abschüsse wurden gemeldet*** three planes were reported shot down; **~ba·sis** *f* launching site

ab·schüs·sig ['apʃʏsɪç] *adj.* sloping, steep

'Ab·schuß|li·ste *f*: F ***auf der ~ stehen*** F be on the hit list, be (in) for the chop; **~prä·mie** *f* bounty; **~ram·pe** *f* launching pad; **~si·lo** *m*, *n* underground launching pad

'ab·schüt·teln *v/t.* (*sep.*, h) shake off (*a. fig.*)

'ab·schüt·ten *v/t.* (*sep.*, h) pour off (*or* out)

'ab·schwä·chen (*sep.*, h) **I.** *v/t.* weaken, reduce; mitigate; extenuate; tone down; *phot.* reduce; **II.** *v/refl.*: ***sich*** ~ weaken; diminish; **'Ab·schwä·chung** *f* (-; -en) weakening; reduction; mitigation; extenuation; toning down; → ***abschwächen***

'ab·schwat·zen F *v/t.* (*sep.*, h): ***j-m et.*** ~ wheedle s.th. out of s.o.

'ab·schwei·fen *v/i.* (*sep.*, sn) **1.** digress; ***nicht ~!*** keep to the point!; **2.** ***sein Blick schweifte wiederholt ab*** his eyes kept wandering, ***von ...***: his eyes kept straying from ...; **3.** deviate, stray; **'Ab·schwei·fung** *f* (-; -en) deviation; digression

'ab·schwel·len *v/i.* (*irr.*, *sep.*, sn, → ***schwellen***) ⚕ go down; *noise etc.*: die away

'ab·schwem·men *v/t.* (*sep.* h) wash away; *geol. a.* erode

'ab·schwen·ken *v/i.* (*sep.*, sn) swerve, veer (off); ⚔ wheel (off); *fig.* ***~ von*** switch (*or* veer) from

'ab·schwin·deln *v/t.* (*sep.*, h): ***j-m et.*** ~ swindle s.o. out of s.th.

'ab·schwir·ren F *v/i.* (*sep.*, sn) F buzz off

'ab·schwit·zen *v/t.* (*sep.*, h) sweat off; F ***sich einen*** ~ F sweat like a pig

'ab·schwö·ren *v/i.* (*irr.*, *sep.*, h, → ***schwören***) renounce *one's faith*; forswear, F swear off *drink*(*ing*) *etc*

'Ab·schwung *m* (-[e]s; ⸚e) *gym.* dismount; † downswing, downturn

'ab·se·geln *v/i.* (*sep.*, sn) set sail (***nach*** *dat.* for)

'ab·seg·nen F *v/t.* (*sep.*, h) F give one's blessing to; ***es muß noch vom Chef abgesegnet werden*** it still has to have the boss's blessing, it still has to be okayed by the boss

ab·seh·bar ['apze:ba:ɐ] *adj.* foreseeable; ***in ~er Zeit*** in the foreseeable future; ***nicht*** ~ unforeseeable; ***der Schaden ist nicht*** ~ the extent of the damage is not yet known

'ab·se·hen (*irr.*, *sep.*, h, → ***sehen***) **I.** *v/t.* **1.** (fore)see; ***es ist kein Ende abzusehen*** there's no end in sight; ***die Folgen sind nicht abzusehen*** there's no telling how things will turn out; **2.** see (***an*** *dat.* from, by); **3.** ***j-m et.*** ~ learn s.th. by watching s.o.; **4.** F ***es abgesehen haben auf*** *acc.* F be out for (*or* to *inf.*), F have it in for *s.o.*; **II.** *v/i.* **5.** ***~ von*** refrain from; ***von e-m Plan*** *etc.* ~ abandon (*or* drop) a plan *etc.*; → ***Beileidsbezeugung***; **6.** disregard; → ***abgesehen*** II

'ab·sei·fen *v/t.* (*sep.*, h) soap down

'ab·sei·hen *v/t.* (*sep.*, h) strain

ab·sei·len ['apzaɪlən] (*sep.*, h) **I.** *v/t.* **1.** lower (on a rope); **II.** *v/refl.*: ***sich*** ~ **2.** abseil; **3.** F *fig.* F make a getaway

'ab·sein F *v/i.* (*irr.*, *sep.*, sn, → ***sein***) have come off

abseits ['apzaɪts] **I.** *adv.*: ***~ stehen*** stand apart, *sport*: be offside; ***etwas ~ liegen*** be a bit out of the way; ***~ von*** → II; *fig.* ***sich ~ halten*** keep one's distance; **II.** *prp.* (*a.* ***~ von***) off *the road*; **III.** ♀ *n* (-; -) *sport*: offside; ***im ~ stehen*** be offside; ***nicht im ~ stehen*** be onside; *w.s.* ***ins ~ gedrängt werden*** be pushed onto the sidelines, be edged out, be marginalized

'Ab·seits|fal·le *f* offside trap; **~stel·lung** *f*: ***in ~*** in an offside position; **~tor** *n* offside goal

'ab·sen·den *v/t.* (*irr.*, *sep.*, h, → ***senden***) send (off), † *a.* forward, dispatch; send, post, *esp. Am.* mail; **'Ab·sen·der** *m* (-s; -) sender, † *a.* consignor; return address; → ***zurück*** I

'ab·sen·gen *v/t.* (*sep.*, h) singe

'ab·sen·ken *v/t.* (*sep.*, h) ♣ layer; ⚒ sink; lower *water table*; **'Ab·sen·kung** *f* (-; -en) layering; sinking; lowering

'ab·ser͵vie·ren (*sep.*, h) **I.** *v/i.* clear the table; **II.** F *v/t.*: ***j-n*** ~ F give s.o. the boot, F bump s.o. off; ***den Gegner*** ~ F thrash one's opponent(s); → ***abspeisen***

ab·setz·bar ['apzɛtsba:ɐ] *adj.*: (***steuerlich*** ~ tax-)deductible; † marketable; ***leicht*** (***schwer***) ~ easy (hard) to sell

'ab·set·zen (*sep.*, h) **I.** *v/t.* **1.** set (*or* put) down; take off *one's hat*, *glasses etc.*; put down *glass*, *bag*, *rifle etc.*; **2.** drop *s.o.* (off) (***an*** *dat.*, ***bei*** at); **3.** throw *rider*; **4.** *typ.* set (in type); ***die Zeile*** ~ begin a new line; **5.** drop; ***von der Tagesordnung*** *etc.* ~ take off the agenda *etc.*; (***vom Spielplan***) ~ drop (from the program[me]); **6.** † write off (against tax); deduct; **7.** dismiss *official etc.*; depose *ruler*; **8.** † sell; ***sich leicht*** (***schwer***) ***~ lassen*** (not to) sell well; **9.** ⚕ stop taking *pills*, go off *a drug*; break off *treatment*; **10.** ***~ von*** (*or* ***gegen***) set off against, contrast with; **11.** trim; **12.** ⚗ deposit; **II.** *v/refl.*: ***sich ~*** **13.** ⚗ *etc.* settle; **14.** leave, F make off (***nach*** for); ***sich ins Ausland ~*** leave the country; **15.** contrast, form a contrast (***von*** *dat.* with); **16.** ⚔ withdraw, retreat; **17.** F *sport*: F make off, leave the others behind; **III.** *v/i.* stop, break off; ***ohne abzusetzen*** without a break, *a. drink etc.* in one go; *write* straight off; **'Ab·set·zung** *f* (-; -en) dismissal; deposition *etc.*; → ***absetzen***

'ab·si·chern (*sep.*, h) **I.** *v/t.* **1.** make *s.th.* safe; cordon off *site of an accident etc.*; **2.** † hedge *investments*; **II.** *v/refl.*: ***sich ~*** cover o.s.

Ab·sicht ['apzɪçt] *f* (-; -en) intention; aim, object; ***in der ~ zu*** *inf.* with the intention of *ger.*, with a view to *ger.*; ***in der besten ~*** with the best of intentions; ***mit ~*** on purpose, deliberately; ***mit e-r bestimmten ~*** for a purpose; ***mit der festen ~ zu*** *inf.* determined to *inf.*; ***ohne ~*** unintentionally; ***ich habe die ~ zu*** *inf.* I intend to *inf.*, I'm planning to *inf.*; ***es war nicht m-e ~ zu*** *inf.* I didn't mean to *inf.*; ***die ~ war zu*** *inf.* the idea was to *inf.*; F ***~en auf j-n haben*** have designs on s.o.

'ab·sicht·lich **I.** *adj.* intentional, deliberate; ⚖ wil(l)ful; **II.** *adv.* intentionally *etc.*; on purpose

'Ab·sichts·er·klä·rung *f pol.* declaration of intent

'ab·sichts·los *adj.* unintentional

'ab·sin·gen *v/t.* (*irr.*, *sep.*, h, → ***singen***) sing (*a song* through); sing at sight

'ab·sin·ken *v/i.* (*irr.*, *sep.*, sn, → ***sinken***) sink; *water level*: drop; *ground etc.*: subside; *blood pressure*, *fever*: go down; *standards etc.*: drop; *interest*: flag; degenerate (***in*** *acc.* into); ***s-e Leistungen sinken ab*** he's not doing as well as he used to; ***sie ist ganz schön tief abgesunken*** she's hit rock bottom

Ab·sinth [ap'zɪnt] *m* (-[e]s; -e) absinth(e)

'ab·sit·zen (*irr.*, *sep.*, → ***sitzen***) **I.** *v/i.* (sn) (*a.* ***vom Pferd ~***) dismount, get off one's horse; (*a.* ***vom Motorrad*** *or* ***Fahrrad ~***) get off (one's motorbike *or* bicycle); **II.** *v/t.* (h) sit out; ***e-e Strafe*** ~ serve a sentence; ***s-e Strafe*** ~ F do time (***wegen*** for), do a spell inside (for)

ab·so·lut [apzo'lu:t] **I.** *adj.* absolute (*a. monarch*, *majority*, *nonsense etc.*, *a. phys.*, *phls.*, ⚗, ♣, ♪); ***~es Gehör*** perfect pitch; ***es ist sein ~es Recht zu*** *inf.* he has every right to *inf.*; **II.** *adv.* absolutely; ***ich sehe ~ keinen Sinn darin*** I just don't see the point of it; ***er hat ~ keine Skrupel*** he has no scruples whatsoever; ***wenn du ~ gehen willst*** if you simply must go; ***~ nicht!*** not at all

Ab·so·lu·ti·on [apzolu'tsĭo:n] *f* (-; -en) absolution; ***j-m*** (***die***) ***~ erteilen*** give (*or* grant) s.o. absolution

Ab·so·lu·tis·mus [apzolu'tɪsmʊs] *m* (-; *no pl.*) absolutism; **ab·so·lu·ti·stisch** [apzolu'tɪstɪʃ] *adj.* absolutist

Ab·sol·vent [apzɔl'vɛnt] *m* (-en; -en), **Ab·sol'ven·tin** *f* (-; -nen) school-leaver,

Am. (high-school) graduate; *univ.* graduate; **ab·sol·vie·ren** [apzɔl'viːrən] *v/t.* (h) finish *one's degree*; *univ.* finish, *Am.* graduate from; pass *examination*; do, get through; ***hast du dein heutiges Pensum schon absolviert?*** have you done your quota for the day yet?

ab'son·der·lich *adj.* peculiar, strange, odd

'ab·son·dern (*sep.*, h) **I.** *v/t.* **1.** separate, segregate; isolate; ⚕, *physiol.* secrete; ⚗ separate, isolate; **II.** *v/refl.*: ***sich*** ~ **2.** be secreted *etc.*; **3.** *fig.* isolate o.s., cut o.s. off (***von*** from); **'Ab·son·de·rung** *f* (-; -en) separation; isolation; *physiol.* secretion; → ***absondern***

Ab·sor·bens [ap'zɔrbɛns] *n* (-; -benzien [apzɔr'bɛntsĭən]) ⚗ absorbent

Ab·sor·ber [ap'zɔrbɐ] *m* (-s; -) absorber

ab·sor·bie·ren [apzɔr'biːrən] *v/t.* (h) absorb (*a. fig.*); **ab·sor'bie·rend** *adj.* absorbent

Ab·sorp·ti·on [apzɔrp'tsĭoːn] *f* (-; *no pl.*) absorption

ab·sorp·ti'ons|fä·hig *adj.* absorptive; **2ver·mö·gen** *n* powers *pl.* of absorption, absorbing capacity

'ab·spal·ten (*sep.*, h) **I.** *v/t.* split off (***von*** from); **II.** *v/refl.*: ***sich*** ~ splinter off (***von*** from *a party etc.*), form a splinter group

Ab·spann ['apʃpan] *m* (-[e]s; -e) *film*: credits *pl.*

'ab·span·nen (*sep.*, h) **I.** *v/t.* unhitch *horse*; ⚙ rig; → ***abgespannt*** II; **II.** *v/i.* relax; **'Ab·span·nung** *f* (-; *no pl.*) **1.** ⚙ anchoring; **2.** *fig.* exhaustion, fatigue

'ab·spa·ren *v/t.* (*sep.*, h): ***sich et.*** (***vom Munde***) ~ scrimp and save for s.th.

ab·specken ['apʃpɛkən] (*sep.* -k·k-) F *v/i.* (*sep.*, h) slim; ***sie müßte mal ein bißchen*** ~ she could do with losing a few pounds

'ab·spei·sen *v/t.* (*sep.*, h) feed; *fig.* ***j-n*** ~ fob s.o. off (***mit*** *dat.* with)

ab·spen·stig ['apʃpɛnstɪç] *adj.*: ***j-m j-n*** (***die Freundin***) ~ ***machen*** turn s.o. against s.o. (take s.o.'s girlfriend away [from him])

'ab·sper·ren *v/t.* (*sep.*, h) **1.** → ***abschließen*** 1; **2.** block, barricade, *police etc.*: cordon off *road etc.*; **3.** cut off *gas, water etc.*

'Ab·sperr|git·ter *n* crowd barrier; **~hahn** *m* stopcock; **~ket·te** *f* cordon

'Ab·sper·rung *f* (-; -en) **1.** roadblock, *police*: cordon; **2.** cutting off *of gas, water etc.*

'Ab·sperr·ven,til *n* stop valve

'ab·spicken (*sep.* -k·k-) *v/t. and v/i.* (*sep.*, h) copy, crib

'Ab·spiel *n* (-[e]s; *no pl.*) *sport*: pass(ing)

'ab·spie·len (*sep.*, h) **I.** *v/t.* **1.** play; play back *tape etc.*; ♪ play at sight; **2.** *sport*: pass (*a. v/i.* ***den Ball*** ~); **II.** *v/refl.*: ***sich*** ~ happen, take place; be going on; F ***da spielt sich nichts ab*** F nothing doing

'ab·split·tern (*sep.*) **I.** *v/i.* (sn) chip off, splinter; *paint etc.*: flake (*or* peel) off; **II.** *v/t.* (h) splinter, chip off *a. paint etc.*; **III.** *v/refl.*: ***sich*** ~ → ***abspalten*** II

'Ab·spra·che *f* (-; -n) arrangement; ***laut*** ~ according to the agreement; **2ge·mäß** *adv.* as agreed

'ab·spre·chen (*irr.*, *sep.*, h, → ***sprechen***) **I.** *v/t.* **1.** arrange; ***hast du es mit ihm schon abgesprochen?*** have you spoken to him about it?; **2.** deny, dispute; ***sie hat ihm jede Fähigkeit abgesprochen*** she denied that he was capable of anything; ***Talent kann man ihm nicht*** ~ there's no denying his talent, he's certainly got talent; **3.** ⚖ dispossess *s.o.* of *s.th.*, deprive *s.o.* of *s.th.*; **II.** *v/refl.*: ***sich mit j-m*** ~, ***daß*** arrange with s.o. that

'ab·sprei·zen *v/t.* (*sep.*, h) stretch out

'ab·spren·gen *v/t.* (*sep.*, h) blast off

'ab·sprin·gen *v/i.* (*irr.*, *sep.*, sn, → ***springen***) **1.** jump off (*or* down); *sport*: take (*or* jump) off; ✈ jump, bale out; ***vom Pferd*** ~ jump off one's horse; **2.** (*a.* ~ ***von***) bounce off; **3.** (*a.* ~ ***von***) *paint etc.*: come off, *a.* chip off; **4.** *fig.* drop out (***von*** of); back out (of); ***von e-r Partei*** *etc.* ~ leave a party *etc.*; **5.** F *fig.* ***und was springt für mich ab?*** what's in it for me?

'ab·sprit·zen *v/t.* (*sep.*, h) hose (*or* wash) down; spray

'Ab·sprung *m* (-[e]s; ⸚e) jump; *fig.* ***den*** ~ ***wagen*** take the plunge; ***den*** ~ ***schaffen*** make it; **~bal·ken** *m* *sport*: takeoff board; **~hö·he** *f* drop altitude; **~stel·le** *f* jumping-off point

'ab·spu·len *v/t.* (*sep.*, h) unwind; run *a film* through; F *fig.* reel off

'ab·spü·len *v/t.* → ***spülen***

'ab·stam·men *v/i.* (*sep.*, *no p.p.*): ~ ***von*** a) be descended from, b) *ling.* derive from; **'Ab·stam·mung** *f* (-; *no pl.*) **1.** descent, origin; birth; ***von italienischer*** ~ of Italian descent (*or* extraction); **2.** *ling.* derivation

'Ab·stam·mungs·leh·re *f* theory of evolution

'Ab·stand *m* (-[e]s; ⸚e) **1.** distance; space, spacing; interval; ***in regelmäßigen Abständen*** at regular intervals; *fig.* ~ ***halten*** keep one's distance; ~ ***von et. gewinnen*** get s.th. in perspective, get over s.th.; ***mit*** ~ ***besser*** far (F miles) better; ***mit*** ~ ***der Beste*** by far (*or* far and away) the best, F the best by miles; ***mit*** ~ ***gewinnen*** win by a wide margin (F by a long chalk); ~ ***von et. nehmen*** refrain (*or* desist) from *ger.*; **2.** → **'Ab·stands·sum·me** *f* compensation, indemnification; severance pay

ab·stat·ten ['apʃtatən] *v/t.* (*sep.*, h): ***j-m e-n Besuch*** ~ pay s.o. a visit; ***j-m s-n Dank*** ~ thank s.o.

'ab·stau·ben (*sep.*, h) **I.** *v/t.* **1.** dust; **2.** F swipe, snitch; **II.** F *v/i.* *sport*: tap the ball in

'Ab·stau·ber·tor *n* tap-in

'ab·ste·chen (*irr.*, *sep.*, h, → ***stechen***) **I.** *v/t.* cut off; cut *peat*; draw off *wine etc.*; stick *pig*; **II.** *v/i.*: ~ ***von*** *dat.* stand out against

'Ab·ste·cher *m* (-s; -) detour; *fig.* digression; ***e-n kurzen*** ~ ***nach X machen*** take in X along the way, make a quick trip to X; *fig.* ***e-n*** ~ ***machen in*** *acc.* digress briefly on

'ab·stecken (*sep.* -k·k-) *v/t.* (*sep.*, h) **1.** fit; **2.** mark out, stake out, peg out; trace (*or* lay) out; demarcate; *fig.* outline; make clear; *fig.* ***die Fronten*** ~ lay down the battle-lines

'ab·ste·hen *v/i.* (*irr.*, *sep.*, h, → ***stehen***) **1.** stand away (***von*** *dat.* from); stick out (of); **2.** grow stale, go flat; **3.** ~ ***von*** renounce; **'ab·ste·hend** *adj.*: **~*e Ohren*** bat ears; ***er hat*** **~*e Ohren*** *a.* his ears stick out

Ab·stei·ge ['apʃtaɪɡə] F *f* (-; -n) F dosshouse, *Am.* flop-house; F short-time hotel

'ab·stei·gen *v/i.* (*irr.*, *sep.*, sn, → ***steigen***) **1.** descend, climb down; get off (one's horse), dismount; get off (one's bicycle); **2.** *fig. sports club*: be relegated, go down; → ***Ast***; **3.** ***wo seid ihr abgestiegen?*** where did you spend the night?, which hotel *etc.* did you stay at?

'Ab·stei·ge·quar,tier *n* → ***Absteige***

'Ab·stei·ger *m* (-s; -) *sport*: relegated team; F ~ ***des Jahres*** flop of the year

'Ab·stell·bahn·hof *m* railway (*Am.* railroad) yard

'ab·stel·len *v/t.* (*sep.*, h) **1.** put down; park *car*; **2.** turn off *engine, gas, water etc.*; switch off *engine, light, radio etc.*; **3.** *fig.* remedy; **4.** *fig.* ~ ***auf*** *acc.* gear to

'Ab·stell|flä·che *f* storage surface; parking space; **~gleis** *n* siding; *fig.* ***aufs*** ~ ***schieben*** put on the shelf, sideline, F throw *s.o.* on the scrapheap, put *s.o.* out to pasture; ***auf dem*** ~ ***stehen*** have come to the end of the road; **~hahn** *m* stopcock; **~raum** *m* boxroom, lumber room; **~tisch** *m* dumb waiter

'ab·stem·peln *v/t.* (*sep.*, h) stamp; ✉ postmark; *fig.* label (***als, zu et.*** [as] s.th.), dub ([as] s.th.); write *s.o.* off (as)

'ab·step·pen *v/t.* (*sep.*, h) stitch; quilt

'ab·ster·ben *v/i.* (*irr.*, *sep.*, sn, → ***sterben***) die (off); ⚕ necrotize; go numb; *engine*: stall; → ***abgestorben*** II

Ab·stieg ['apʃtiːk] *m* (-[e]s; -['apʃtiːɡə]) **1.** descent, way down; **2.** *fig.* decline; **3.** *sport*: relegation

'ab·stiegs·ge·fähr·det *adj.* threatened by (*or* in danger of) relegation

'ab·stil·len *v/t.* (*sep.*, h) wean

'Ab·stimm·be·reich *m* *radio*: tuning range

'ab·stim·men (*sep.*, h) **I.** *v/t.* ♪ *and radio*: tune (***auf*** *acc.* to); ⚙ *and fig.* coordinate; adjust (to); time; match *colo(u)rs*; **II.** *v/i.* *parl. etc.* vote (***über*** *acc.* on); ~ ***lassen über*** take a vote on; **III.** *v/refl.*: ***sich*** ~ a) come to an agreement (*or* arrangement), b) agree to stick to the same version; ***sich mit j-m*** ~ arrange things with s.o.

'Ab·stimm|knopf *m* tuning knob; **~kreis** *m* tuning circuit; **~schär·fe** *f* selectivity

'Ab·stim·mung *f* (-; -en) **1.** voting, vote; referendum; ~ ***durch Handzeichen*** vote by show of hands; ~ ***durch Zuruf*** vote by acclamation; ***geheime*** ~ (voting by) ballot; ***offene*** ~ vote by open ballot; → ***namentlich***; ***zur*** ~ ***bringen*** (***kommen***) put (be put) to the vote; **2.** coordination (***auf*** *acc.*, ***mit*** with); timing; *radio*: tuning

'Ab·stim·mungs·er·geb·nis *n* results *pl.* of the poll

ab·sti·nent [apsti'nɛnt] *adj.* abstemious, abstinent; **Ab·sti·nenz** [apsti'nɛnts] *f* (-; *no pl.*) (total) abstinence; **Ab·sti·nenz·ler** [apsti'nɛntslɐ] *m* (-s; -) teetotal(l)er

'ab·stop·pen (*sep.*, h) **I.** *v/t.* **1.** stop; **2.** clock, time, take the time of; **II.** *v/i.* stop; reduce speed

'Ab·stoß *m* (-es; ⸚e) *soccer*: goal kick; **'ab·sto·ßen** (*irr.*, *sep.*, h, → ***stoßen***) **I.** *v/t.* **1.** push off; **2.** shed *skin, antlers*; → ***Horn*** 1; **3.** ⚕ reject *tissue etc.*; **4.** chip *crockery etc.*; break off; knock off; scuff *shoes*; knock *furniture*; **5.** *fig.* repel, disgust, revolt; **6.** get rid of; ✝ sell off, unload; **II.** *v/refl.*: ***sich*** ~ (***von***) push o.s. off; **III.** *v/i.* *soccer*: take a goal kick; **'ab·sto·ßend** *adj.* repulsive, disgusting, revolting; **'Ab·sto·ßung** *f* (-; -en) ⚕ rejection

'ab·stot·tern F *v/t.* (*sep.*, h) pay for instal(l)ments; ***er stottert monatlich 100 Mark ab*** he pays 100 marks a month (*or* a monthly instal[l]ment of 100 marks)
ab·stra·hie·ren [apstra'hi:rən] (h) **I.** *v/t.* derive, deduce; abstract, distil(l); conceptualize; **II.** *v/i.* consider s.th. abstractly (*or* in abstraction); *art*: be abstract; ~ ***von*** abstain from, renounce
'ab·strah·len *v/t.* (*sep.*, h) emit, radiate
ab·strakt [ap'strakt] **I.** *adj.* abstract (*a. art*); **II.** *adv.* in the abstract, abstractly
Ab·strak·ti·on [apstrak'tsĭo:n] *f* (-; -en) abstraction; **Ab·strak·ti'ons·ver·mö·gen** *n* capacity for abstract thinking, ability to think in abstract terms
'ab·stram·peln F *v/refl.* (*sep.*, h): ***sich*** ~ F slog away
'ab·strei·chen *v/t.* (*irr.*, *sep.*, h, → ***streichen***) **1.** wipe off; scrape off; take off *froth*; wipe *shoes*, *knife etc.*; **2.** deduct; cut; **3.** scour *area etc.*
'ab·strei·fen (*sep.*, h) **I.** *v/t.* **1.** slip off; wipe *shoes etc.*; **2.** patrol, scour *area etc.*; **II.** *v/i.* stray (*a. fig.*)
'ab·strei·ten *v/t.* (*irr.*, *sep.*, h, → ***streiten***) dispute; deny
'Ab·strich *m* (-[e]s; -e) **1.** deduction; curtailment, cut; *fig.* ~***e machen*** lower one's sights, ***an*** *dat.*: cut back on; *fig.* ***irgendwo muß man ~e machen*** you can't have everything; **2.** ⚕ smear; swab; smear test; ***e-n ~ machen*** take a smear (*or* swab)
ab·strus [ap'stru:s] *adj.* abstruse
'ab·stu·fen *v/t.* (*sep.*, h) terrace; *fig.* grade; *a.* graduate; **'Ab·stu·fung** *f* (-; -en) gradation; shade, *a. fig.* nuance
ab·stump·fen ['apʃtʊmpfən] (*sep.*, h) **I.** *v/t.* **1.** blunt; **2.** dull; harden *s.o.*; **II.** *v/i. and v/refl.* (***sich*** ~) **3.** become blunt; **4.** become dulled; *person*: become hardened (*or* insensible); → ***abgestumpft*** II
'Ab·sturz *m* (-es; ⸗e) **1.** fall; ✈ crash; **2.** *computer*: system crash; **3.** precipice
'ab·stür·zen *v/i.* (*sep.*, sn) **1.** fall; ✈ crash; **2.** *computer*: crash; **3.** drop steeply
'Ab·sturz|ge·fahr *f* danger of falling; ~**stel·le** *f* site (*or* scene) of the *or* a crash; ~**ur·sa·che** *f* cause of the *or* a crash
'ab·stüt·zen *v/t.* (*sep.*, h) support, prop up
'ab·su·chen *v/t.* (*sep.*, h) search (***nach*** *dat.* for); *a.* scour, comb *area etc.* (for); *searchlight*, *radar*: sweep (in search of)
ab·surd [ap'zʊrt] *adj.* absurd; *a.* ridiculous; ~***es Theater*** theat|re (*Am.* -er) of the absurd; **Ab·sur·di·tät** [apzʊrdi'tɛ:t] *f* (-; -en) absurdity
Ab·szeß [aps'tsɛs] *m* (-sses; -sse) abscess
Ab·szis·se [aps'tsɪsə] *f* (-; -n) abscissa
Abt [apt] *m* (-[e]s; Äbte ['ɛptə]) abbot
'ab·ta·keln *v/t.* (*sep.*, h) **1.** ⚓ unrig; lay up; **2.** F *fig.* ***j-n*** ~ F give s.o. the sack
'ab·ta·sten *v/t.* (*sep.*, h) feel (***nach*** *dat.* for); frisk (for); ⚕ palpate; *TV*, *radar etc.*: scan, *computer*: *a.* sample
'Ab·ta·ster *m* (-s; -) scanner
'Ab·tast·feh·ler *m* reading error
'Ab·tau·au·to,ma·tik *f* automatic defroster
'ab·tau·chen *v/i.* (*sep.*, sn) **1.** *submarine*: submerge, go down; **2.** F *fig.* go underground
'ab·tau·en (*sep.*) **I.** *v/i.* (sn) thaw; *window etc.*: clear; **II.** *v/t.* (h) thaw; defrost *refrigerator*
Ab·tei [ap'taɪ] *f* (-; -en) abbey
Ab·teil [ap'taɪl] *n* (-[e]s; -e) **1.** 🚂 compartment; **2.** section
'ab·tei·len *v/t.* (*sep.*, h) divide, split up; partition (off)
'Ab·tei·lung[1] *f* (-; -en) division
Ab'tei·lung[2] *f* (-; -en) department; *adm.* division; ⚕ *etc.* ward; ⚔ detachment, unit, battalion
Ab'tei·lungs·lei·ter *m* head of (a *or* the) department; ⚜ departmental manager; *department store*: floor manager
'ab·te·le·fo,nie·ren *v/i.*, **'ab·te·le·gra·,fie·ren** *v/i.* → ***absagen*** 2
'ab·tip·pen F *v/t.* (*sep.*, h) type up, get *s.th.* typed
Äb·tis·sin [ɛp'tɪsɪn] *f* (-; -nen) abbess
'ab·tö·nen *v/t.* (*sep.*, h) tone down (*a. phot.*); **'Ab·tö·nung** *f* (-; -en) shade
'ab·tö·ten *v/t.* (*sep.*, h) kill *a. nerve*; destroy *a. germs*; *fig.* deaden *feeling etc.*
Ab·trag ['aptra:k] *m*: ***j-m*** (***e-r Sache***) ~ ***tun*** do s.o. (s.th.) harm
'ab·tra·gen *v/t.* (*irr.*, *sep.*, h, → ***tragen***) **1.** take away; remove; clear away; pull *wall etc.* down (bit by bit); level; **2.** pay off *loan etc.*, *a.* amortize *mortgage*; **3.** wear out (*a.* ***sich*** ~)
ab·träg·lich ['aptrɛ:klɪç] *adj.* inimical (*dat.* to), detrimental (to)
'ab·trai,nie·ren *v/t.* (*sep.*, h) work off
'Ab·trans,port *m* (-[e]s; -e) removal; **'ab·trans·por,tie·ren** *v/t.* (*sep.*, h) take away, *a.* take *s.o.* to hospital
'ab·trei·ben (*irr.*, *sep.*, → ***treiben***) **I.** *v/t.* (h) **1.** *current etc.*: carry *or* sweep off (*or* away); **2.** ⚕ abort, F get rid of; ***ein Kind ~ lassen*** have an abortion; **II.** *v/i.* **3.** (sn) ⚓, ✈ drift off (course); **4.** (h) ⚕ have an abortion; ***sie hat schon zweimal abgetrieben*** she's had two abortions already
'Ab·trei·bung *f* (-; -en) ⚕ abortion
'Ab·trei·bungs|ge·setz *n* abortion law(s *pl.*); ~**kli·nik** *f* abortion clinic; ~**pa·ra·,graph** *m* abortion law(s *pl.*)
'ab·trenn·bar *adj.* detachable; **'ab·tren·nen** *v/t.* (*sep.*, h) separate (*a.* ***sich*** ~); tear off; take off *sleeves etc.*, take out *lining etc.*; sever, ⚕ amputate *arm*, *leg etc.*; **'Ab·tren·nung** *f* (-; -en) separation; severing, ⚕ amputation, removal
'ab·tre·ten (*irr.*, *sep.*, → ***treten***) **I.** *v/t.* (h) **1.** wear down *steps*, *shoes etc.*; **2.** ***sich die Schuhe*** ~ wipe one's feet; **3.** ***j-m et.*** ~ hand s.th. over to s.o., ⚖ (*a.* ***et. an j-n*** ~) cede s.th. to s.o., make s.th. over to s.o.; **II.** *v/i.* (sn) withdraw, *a.* retire *from office*; *thea.* go off; ⚔ break ranks; *fig.* make one's exit
'Ab·tre·ter *m* (-s; -) doormat; scraper
'Ab·tre·tung *f* (-; -en) cession, transfer, assignment (***an*** *acc.* to)
'Ab·tre·tungs·ur·kun·de *f* transfer deed; (deed of) conveyance; (deed of) assignment
'Ab·tritt *m* (-[e]s; -e) *thea.* exit; *fig.* retirement
'Ab·trocken·tuch (*sep.* -k·k-) F *n* drying-up cloth, tea towel, *Am.* dishtowel
'ab·trock·nen (*sep.*) **I.** *v/t.* (h) dry; ***sich die Hände*** ~ dry one's hands (***an*** *dat.* on); ***das Geschirr*** ~ dry up, dry the dishes, do the drying-up; **II.** *v/i.* a) (sn) dry; b) (h) dry up, dry the dishes, do the drying-up
ab·trop·fen *v/i.* (*sep.*, sn) drip; ~ ***lassen*** drain, let *the glasses etc.* drain
'ab·trot·zen *v/t.* (*sep.*, h): ***sie hat es ihm abgetrotzt*** she just persisted until he let her have it (*or* until she got what she wanted)
ab·trün·nig ['aptrʏnɪç] *adj.* unfaithful, disloyal; breakaway *group*; *eccl.* lapsed *Catholic etc.*, *formal*: apostate; ~ ***werden von*** *dat.* leave, *a.* fall away from; **Ab·trün·ni·ge** ['aptrʏnɪgə] *m*, *f* (-n; -n) defector, renegade; *eccl.* defector, backslider, lapsed Catholic *etc.*, *formal*: apostate
'ab·tun *v/t.* (*irr.*, *sep.*, *h*, → ***tun***) **1.** F take off; shake off; **2.** brush aside, dismiss *a. s.o.*; ***et. mit e-m Achselzucken*** (***Lachen***) ~ shrug (laugh) s.th. off; **3.** pass off (***als*** as)
'ab·tup·fen *v/t.* (*sep.*, h) dab; dab off; swab
'ab·ur·tei·len *v/t.* (*sep.*, h) pass sentence on; *fig.* condemn (out of hand); **'Ab·ur·tei·lung** *f* (-; -en) trial
'ab·ver·lan·gen *v/t.* (*sep.*, h) demand (*dat.* of)
'ab·wä·gen *v/t.* (*irr.*, *sep.*, h, → ***wägen***) weigh, consider (carefully); ***gegeneinander*** ~ weigh up; **'Ab·wä·gung** *f* (-; -en) consideration; ***bei ~ aller Dinge*** on balance
'ab·wäh·len *v/t.* (*sep.*, h) **1.** vote *s.o.* out of office; **2.** *ped.* drop *a subject*
'ab·wäl·zen *v/t.* (*sep.*, h) shift (***auf*** *acc.* on to); ***die Verantwortung auf e-n anderen*** ~ pass the buck (to someone else)
'ab·wan·deln *v/t.* (*sep.*, h) modify
'ab·wan·dern *v/i.* (*sep.*, sn) migrate, move; *spectators etc.*: drift off; *sport*: leave the club; ⚜ *capital*: flow (out); *meteor.* move (***nach Osten*** *etc.* east *etc.*); **'Ab·wan·de·rung** *f* (-; -en) migration; exodus (***aus*** from); *sport*: move, transfer; ⚜ outflow *of capital*; ~ ***von Wissenschaftlern*** (academic) brain drain
'Ab·wand·lung *f* (-; -en) variation, modification
'Ab·wär·me *f* (-; *no pl.*) waste heat; ~**ver·wer·tung** *f* waste heat recovery
'ab·war·ten (*sep.*, h) **I.** *v/t.* wait for; ***j-n*** (***das Gewitter***) ~ wait till s.o. comes (the storm is over); ***das bleibt abzuwarten*** that remains to be seen; → ***abpassen***; **II.** *v/i.* wait (and see); **'ab·war·tend** *adj.* cautious; ***e-e ~e Haltung einnehmen*** decide to wait and see, *pol.* adopt a wait-and-see policy
ab·wärts ['apvɛrts] *adv.* down(wards); ***den Fluß*** ~ down the river, downstream; **2be·we·gung** *f* ⚜ downward trend, downturn; ~**ge·hen** *v/impers.*: (*irr.*, *sep.*, sn, → ***gehen***): ***es geht mit ihm*** (***mit den Geschäften*** *etc.*) ***abwärts*** he's (business *etc.* is) going downhill; ***mit der Moral geht es abwärts*** their *etc.* morale is steadily slipping
Ab·wasch ['apvaʃ] *m* (-[e]s; *no pl.*) **1.** dirty dishes *pl.*; **2.** washing-up; ***den ~ machen*** → ***abwaschen*** II; *fig.* ***das geht in einem*** ~ that can be done in one go
'ab·wasch·bar *adj.* washable
'Ab·wasch·becken (*sep.* -k·k-) *n* sink
'ab·wa·schen (*irr.*, *sep.*, h, → ***waschen***) **I.** *v/t.* wash off (*a.* ~ ***von***); wash down; wash up *the dishes*; **II.** *v/i.* do the dishes (*or* washing-up)
'Ab·wasch|lap·pen *m* washing-up cloth, dishcloth; ~**mit·tel** *n* washing-up liquid; ~**was·ser** *n* dishwater
'Ab·was·ser *n* (-s; ⸗) *a. pl.* waste water, sewage; (industrial) effluent; ~**auf·be-**

rei·tung *f* sewage treatment; **~be·sei·ti·gung** *f* sewage disposal; **~ka,nal** *m* sewer; **~klär·an·la·ge** *f* sewage (disposal) plant, clarification plant; **~lei·tung** *f* sewage pipe, sewer; **~rei·ni·gung** *f* sewage treatment

'ab·wech·seln (*sep.*, h) **I.** *v/i.* (*and v/t.* ***sich** or **einander** ~*) alternate, take turns (***bei*** *dat.* with, in *doing s.th.*); ***sich am Steuer*** ~ take turns driving (*or* at the wheel); ***Regen und Sonnenschein wechselten (sich) ab*** one minute it was raining, the next the sun was shining; **II.** *v/refl.*: ***sich** ~ **mit*** take turns with; ***sich mit j-m beim Fahren*** *etc.* ~ take turns driving *etc.* with s.o.; **'ab·wech·selnd I.** *adj.* alternate, alternating; **II.** *adv.* alternately; by turns; ~ ***rot und blaß werden*** change colo(u)r several times

'Ab·wechs·lung *f* (-; -en) change; variety; ~ ***brauchen*** need a change; ~ ***bringen in*** *acc.* liven up; ***zur*** ~ for a change

'ab·wechs·lungs·reich *adj.* varied; eventful

'ab·we·deln *phot.* (*sep.*, h) **I.** *v/t.* shade; **II.** *v/i.* dodge, shade

'Ab·weg *m* (-[e]s; -e): *fig.* ***auf ~e geraten*** go astray

ab·we·gig ['apve:gıç] *adj.* bizarre, F off-beat; inept, out of place; weird

Ab·wehr ['apve:ɐ] *f* (-; *no pl.*) **1.** *a. sport*: defen|ce (*Am.* -se); ⚔ repulse; resistance; warding off (*a. fig.*); *fencing etc.*: parrying; **2.** → **~dienst** *m* ⚔ counter-intelligence (service)

'ab·weh·ren *v/t.* (*sep.*, h) beat back, repulse; *fencing*: parry; *boxing*, *soccer*: block, clear; reject; ward off

'Ab·wehr|feh·ler *m sport*: defensive error; **~hal·tung** *f psych.* defensiveness; ***sich in** ~ **befinden*** be on the defensive; **~kampf** *m* ⚔ defensive battle; **~kräf·te** *pl.* resistance *sg.*; **~me·cha,nis·mus** *m biol.*, *psych.* defen|ce (*Am.* -se) mechanism; **~mit·tel** *n* means of defen|ce (*Am.* -se); ⚕ prophylactic; **~re·ak·ti,on** *f* defensive reaction; **~spiel** *n sport*: defensive play; **~spie·ler** *m* defender; *pl. a.* defen|ce (*Am.* -se) *sg.*; **⁓stark** *adj. sport*: strong in defen|ce (*Am.* -se); ***das ist e-e ~e Mannschaft*** they're a good defensive team; **~stoff** *m biol.* antibody; **~waf·fe** *f* ⚔ defensive weapon

'ab·wei·chen¹ *v/i.* (*irr.*, *sep.*, sn, → ***weichen***) deviate; *phys.* vary; (***stark***) ***voneinander*** ~ differ (widely); ***vom Thema*** ~ get off the subject, go off on a tangent; ***von den Regeln*** ~ break the rules; ***er ist nie von dem Vorhaben abgewichen*** he never swerved from that ambition

'ab·wei·chen² *v/t.* (*sep.*, h) soak off

'ab·wei·chend *adj.* divergent; varying, differing

Ab·weich·ler ['apvaıçlɐ] *m* (-s; -) *pol.* deviationist; **'ab·weich·le·risch** *adj.* deviationist; **'Ab·weich·ler·tum** *n* (-s; *no pl.*) deviationism

'Ab·wei·chung *f* (-; -en) divergence, deviation; digression; departure (***von*** *dat.* from *a rule etc.*)

'ab·wei·sen *v/t.* (*irr.*, *sep.*, h, → ***weisen***) reject, turn down; ⚖ dismiss; ⚔ repulse; send (*or* turn) *s.o.* away; refuse to see *s.o.*; ***j-n schroff*** ~ snub s.o.; ***er läßt sich nicht*** ~ he won't take no for an answer; **'ab·wei·send** *adj.* unfriendly, cool, off-putting; dismissive; **'Ab·wei·sung** *f* (-; -en) rejection; ⚖ dismissal; ⚔ repulse; snub, rebuff

'ab·wen·den (*irr.*, *sep.*, h, → ***wenden***) **I.** *v/t.* turn away; ward off *blow*; head off, avert *danger, crisis etc.*; ***den Blick*** ~ look away, *formal*: avert one's gaze; **II.** *v/refl.*: ***sich** ~ → **abkehren*** II; **'Ab·wen·dung** *f* (-; *no pl.*) averting; abandonment (***von*** of)

'ab·wer·ben *v/t.* (*irr.*, *sep.*, h, → ***werben***) poach, F steal *customers etc.*, *a.* head-hunt, *a.* woo away *voters*; **'Ab·wer·ber** *m* (-s; -) headhunter; **'Ab·wer·bung** *f* (-; -en) poaching, F stealing, headhunting, wooing away

'ab·wer·fen *v/t.* (*irr.*, *sep.*, h, → ***werfen***) throw down; throw off *coat, blanket etc.*; ✈ drop; throw *rider*; cast *antlers*, shed *skin*; *fig.* shake off *yoke etc.*; throw away *playing card*; *sport*: knock down; *ball games*: get *s.o.* out; ⚚ yield *profit*; bear *interest*; spin off

'ab·wer·ten *v/t.* (*sep.*, h) ⚚ devalue; *fig.* depreciate, derogate; ~ ***als*** dismiss as; **'ab·wer·tend** *fig. adj.* depreciatory, disparaging; **'Ab·wer·tung** *f* (-; -en) devaluation; *fig.* depreciation

ab·we·send ['apve:zənt] **I.** *adj.* **1.** absent, away; not here; *pred.* out, not in; **2.** *fig.* lost in thought; faraway *look*; **II.** *adv.* absently; **'Ab·we·sen·de** *m, f* (-n; -n) absentee; ***die ~n*** those absent

'Ab·we·sen·heit *f* (-; *no pl.*) absence; *fig.* abstraction; daydreaming; ***in** ~ **von*** in the absence of; *iro.* ***durch** ~ **glänzen*** be conspicuous by one's absence; ⚖ ***in** ~ **verurteilt werden*** *criminal law*: be sentenced in absence, *civil law*: be sentenced by default

'Ab·we·sen·heits|quo·te *f*, **~ra·te** *f* rate of absenteeism, absentee figures *pl.*

'ab·wet·zen (*sep*). **I.** *v/t.* (h) wear *s.th.* smooth; **II.** F *v/i.* (sn) F zoom off

'ab·wich·sen V *v/t.* (*sep.*, h): ***sich einen*** ~ V wank off, jerk off, have a wank

'ab·wickeln (*sep.* -k·k-) (*sep.*, h) **I.** *v/t.* **1.** (*a.* ***sich*** ~) unwind; take off *bandage*; **2.** handle; settle; regulate; ⚚ wind up; **II.** *fig. v/refl.*: ***sich*** ~ go; **'Ab·wick·lung** *f* (-; -n) handling, processing; settlement; ⚚ winding up

ab·wie·geln ['apvi:gəln] (*sep.*, h) **I.** *v/t.* **1.** calm down, appease; **2.** turn away, dismiss; **II.** *v/i.* smooth over the difficulties (*or* ill feelings *etc.*); play down the issue

'ab·wie·gen *v/t.* (*irr.*, *sep.*, h, → ***wiegen***) weigh out

Ab·wieg·ler ['apvi:glɐ] *m* (-s; -) conciliator

'ab·wim·meln F *v/t.* (*sep.*, h) shake off; get out of (doing) *s.th.*

'Ab·wind *m* (-[e]s; -e) ✈ downward current

'ab·win·keln *v/t.* (*sep.*, h) bend

'ab·win·ken (*sep.*, h) **I.** *v/t.* **1.** *motor racing*: flag down *car, driver*; stop *race*; **II.** *v/i.* **2.** give a dismissive gesture; make a gesture of refusal; ***als ich mit m-m Vorschlag kam, hat er gleich abgewinkt*** (*hum.* ***abgewunken***) he wouldn't listen to my suggestion; **3.** stop the orchestra

'ab·wirt·schaf·ten (*sep.*, h) **I.** *v/i. firm etc.*: go to ruin, run itself into the ground; *party etc.*: a) be on the road to ruin (*or* collapse), b) collapse; ***er hat abgewirtschaftet*** he's come to the end of the road; **II.** *v/t.* run *s.th.* down, run *s.th.* into the ground; bring *party etc.* to ruin (*or* to the point of collapse)

'ab·wi·schen *v/t.* (*sep.*, h) wipe off; wipe; ***sich den Mund*** (***die Stirn, die Tränen***) ~ wipe one's mouth (mop one's brow, wipe away one's tears)

ab·wracken ['apvrakən] (*sep.* -k·k-) *v/t.* (*sep.*, h) break up, scrap; *fig.* → ***abgewrackt***

'Ab·wurf *m* (-[e]s; ⸚e) ✈ dropping; *sport*: throw-out; *riding*: knock-down

'ab·wür·gen *v/t.* (*sep.*, h) strangle; *mot.* stall; *fig.* crush; quash; stifle *discussion etc.*

'ab·zah·len *v/t.* (*sep.*, h) pay *s.th.* off, settle; pay for *s.th.* by instal(l)ments

'ab·zäh·len *v/t.* (*sep.*, h) count; count (out) *money*; *fig.* ***das kannst du dir an den Fingern*** ~ it's as clear as day(light)

'Ab·zähl|reim *m*, **~vers** *m* counting-out rhyme

'Ab·zah·lung *f* (-; -en) payment; instal(l)ment; ***auf** ~ **kaufen*** buy on hire purchase, *Am.* buy on the instal(l)ment plan; **'Ab·zah·lungs·ge·schäft** *n* hire purchase (sale)

'ab·zap·fen *v/t.* (*sep.*, h) tap, draw off; ⚕ draw *blood*; *fig.* ***j-m Geld*** *etc.* ~ scrounge money *etc.* off s.o.

ab·zäu·nen ['aptsɔynən] *v/t.* (*sep.*, h) fence off (*or* in)

'ab·zeh·ren *v/t.* (*sep.*, h) emaciate

'Ab·zei·chen *n* (-s; -) badge; ⚔ insignia, stripe; decoration

'ab·zeich·nen (*sep.*, h) **I.** *v/t.* **1.** copy, draw (***von*** *dat.* from); **2.** initial; **II.** *v/refl.*: ***sich*** ~ stand out; be reflected; *fig.* loom on the horizon; be emerging, be evolving; ***e-e neue Entwicklung*** *etc.* ***zeichnete sich ab*** a new development *etc.* could be seen to emerge; ***sich ~d*** emerging, emergent, evolving

'Ab·zieh·bild *n* transfer

'ab·zie·hen (*irr.*, *sep.*, → ***ziehen***) **I.** *v/t.* (h) **1.** take off; skin; strip *bed*; take out *key*; string *beans*; withdraw (*a.* ⚔ *and fig.*); **2.** make a copy (*or* copies) of; *typ.* pull off *a proof*; *phot.* make a print (*or* prints) of; **3.** ⚙ smooth, grind, sharpen; surface *parquet*; **4.** subtract; deduct; ***etwas vom Preis*** ~ deduct something from (F knock something off) the price; **5.** bottle; **6.** F have, throw *a party etc.*; → ***Schau***; **7.** *sport*: thrash; **II.** *v/i.* (sn) **8.** *smoke*: escape, *fog*: clear, disperse; *clouds*: move off; *storm*: pass; **9.** ⚔ withdraw; **10.** *birds of passage*: head south, migrate; **11.** *spectators*: leave, *crowd*: *a.* disperse; **12.** F push off; **13.** *sport*: let fly

'Ab·zieh|pres·se *f* proof press; **~rie·men** *m* strop; **~stein** *m* whetstone

'ab·zie·len *v/i.* (*sep.*, h): ~ ***auf*** *acc.* aim at; *measure, remark etc.*: be designed to *inf.*; ***worauf zielte er ab?*** what was he driving at?

'ab·zir·keln *v/t.* (*sep.*, h) measure out with compasses; *fig.* ***s-e Worte genau*** ~ weigh one's words carefully

'ab·zi·schen F *v/i.* (*sep.*, sn) F zoom off

'Ab·zug *m* (-[e]s; ⸚e) **1.** *no pl.* ⚔ withdrawal, retreat; **2.** ⚚ deduction; discount; ***in** ~ **bringen*** deduct; ***nach** ~ **der Kosten*** charges deducted; ***nach** ~ **der Steuer(n)*** after taxation; **3.** ⚙ outlet, escape; drain; **4.** trigger; **5.** *typ.* proof, copy; *phot.* print

ab·züg·lich ['aptsy:klıç] *adv.* less, minus; ~ ***der Kosten*** charges deducted

'ab·zugs·fä·hig *adj.* deductible

'Ab·zugs|hau·be *f* cooker hood; **~he·bel** *m* trigger arm; **~ka͵nal** *m* sewer, culvert; **~rohr** *n* waste pipe; escape (*or* outlet) pipe; **~schach** *n* discovered check; **~schacht** *m* escape shaft
'Ab·zweig·do·se *f* junction box
'ab·zwei·gen (*sep.*) **I.** *v/i.* (sn) branch off; **II.** *v/t.* (h) earmark, set aside (***für*** *Akk.* for); **'Ab·zwei·gung** *f* (-; -en) 🚂 junction; turning, turnoff, fork
'ab·zwicken (*sep.* -k·k-) *v/t.* (*sep.*, h) nip off
'ab·zwit·schern F *v/i.* (*sep.*, sn) F buzz off
Ac·ces·soires [aksɛ'sŏaːɐs] *pl.* accessories
Ace·tat [atse'taːt] *n* (-s; -e) ⚗ acetate; **~sei·de** *f* acetate rayon
Ace·ton [atse'toːn] *n* (-s; *no pl.*) ⚗ acetone
Ace·ty·len [atsety'leːn] *n* (-s; *no pl.*) ⚗ acetylene
ach [ax] *int.* oh; **~(*, wie schade, wie ärgerlich*** *etc.*)**!** oh no!; **~ *nein?*** you don't say; **~ *so!*** oh, I see; **~ *was!*, ~ *wo!*** oh no, of course not
Ach *n*: ***ℒ und weh schreien*** wail; ***mit ~ und Krach*** by the skin of one's teeth, ***e-e Prüfung bestehen*:** scrape through an exam
Achat [a'xaːt] *m* (-[e]s; -e) agate
Achil·les|fer·se [a'xɪlɛs-] *fig. f* Achilles' heel, weak spot; **~seh·ne** *f anat.* Achilles' tendon
achro·ma·tisch [akro'maːtɪʃ] *adj.* achromatic
Achs... ['aks-] → *a.* ***Achsen...*; ~ab·stand** *m* **1.** 𝒜 cent|er (*Brit.* -re) distance; **2.** *mot.* wheel base; **~an·trieb** *m* final drive
Ach·se ['aksə] *f* (-; -n) **1.** 𝒜, △, *anat.*, *bot.* *etc.* axis, *pl.* axes; → ***drehen*** 12; **2.** ⚙ axle; F *fig.* (***dauernd***) ***auf ~ sein*** be on the move *or* road (all the time)
Ach·sel ['aksəl] *f* (-; -n) shoulder; ***die ~*** (*or* ***mit den ~n***) ***zucken*** shrug one's shoulders; *fig.* ***j-n über die ~ ansehen*** look down on s.o.; **~drü·se** *f* axillary gland; **~höh·le** *f* armpit
'Ach·sel·zucken (*sep.* -k·k-) *n* shrug (of the shoulders); ***mit e-m ~ abtun*** shrug *s.th.* off; **'ach·sel·zuckend** (*sep.* -k·k-) *adv.* shrugging one's shoulders, with a shrug; **~ *über et. hinweggehen*** shrug s.th. off
'Ach·sen|bruch *m* **1.** breaking of an axle; **2.** broken axle; **~dre·hung** *f* (axial) rotation; **~sym·me͵trie** *f* axial symmetry
'Achs|la·ger *n* axle bearing; **~last** *f* axle load; **~schen·kel** *m* ⚙ (axle) journal; *mot.* stub axle, *Am.* steering knuckle; **~stand** *m mot.* wheel base; **~wel·le** *f* axle shaft
acht [axt] **I.** *adj.* **1.** eight; ***in ~ Tagen*** in a week('s time); ***vor ~ Tagen*** a week ago; ***alle ~ Tage*** every week, once a week; **2.** eighth; ***~es Kapitel*** chapter eight; ***am ~en April*** on the eighth of April, on April the eighth; ***8. April*** 8th April, April 8(th); **II.** *adv.* ***wir waren zu ~*** there were eight of us; ***wir gingen zu ~ hin*** eight of us went (there); **III.** → ***Acht¹***
Acht¹ *f* (-; -en) (number) eight (*a.* F *bus line etc.*)
Acht² *f* (-; *no pl.*) outlawry; ***in ~ und Bann tun*** outlaw, *fig.* ostracize
Acht³ *f*: ***außer ℒ lassen*** disregard, ignore, pay no attention to; ***in ℒ nehmen*** watch, look after; ***sich in ℒ nehmen*** watch out (***vor*** *dat.* for)
'acht·bän·dig *adj.* eight-volume ..., in eight volumes
acht·bar ['axtbaːɐ] *adj.* respectable; reputable; **'Acht·bar·keit** *f* (-; *no pl.*) respectability
'Ach·te *m*, *f* (-n; -n) (the) eighth; ***er war ~r*** he was (*or* came) eighth; ***Heinrich VIII.*** Henry VIII (= Henry the Eighth); ***heute ist der ~*** it's the eighth today
'Acht·eck *n* (-s; -e) octagon; **'acht·eckig** (*sep.* -k·k-) *adj.* octagonal
Ach·tel ['axtəl] *n* (-s; -) eighth; **~no·te** *f* quaver, *Am.* eighth note; **~pau·se** *f* quaver (*Am.* eighth note) rest
ach·ten ['axtən] (h) **I.** *v/t.* respect, have a high opinion of *s.o.*; observe, abide by *the law etc.*; respect *feelings etc.*; ***nicht ~*** not to value very highly, ignore *the danger etc.*; → ***beachten, erachten*; II.** *v/i.*: **~ *auf*** *acc.* pay attention to, mind; watch, keep an eye on; watch out for; ***darauf ~, daß*** see to it that
äch·ten ['ɛçtən] *v/t.* (h) outlaw *s.o.*; ban *s.th.*; *fig.* ostracize
ach·tens ['axtəns] *adv.* eighth(ly), eight, in eighth place
'ach·tens·wert *adj.* commendable; highly respectable
Ach·ter ['axtɐ] *m* (-s; -) **1.** *rowing*: eight; **2.** *ice-skating*: figure (of) eight; **3.** F buckled tyre (*Am.* tire); **4.** → ***Achte*; ~bahn** *f* roller coaster; **~deck** *n* quarterdeck
'acht·fach *adj.* eightfold; ***die ~e Menge*** eight times the amount; ***~er Sieger*** eight-time winner (*or* champion)
'acht·ge·ben *v/i.* (*irr.*, *sep.*, h, → ***geben***) be careful; **~ *auf*** *acc.* watch; ***gib acht!*** look out!, (be) careful!
Acht'gro·schen·jun·ge F *m* **1.** male prostitute; **2.** F nark
'acht'hun·dert *adj.* eight hundred
'acht·jäh·rig *adj.* **1.** eight-year-old ...; **2.** eight-year ...; ***ein ~es ...*** *a.* eight years of ...; **'Acht·jäh·ri·ge** *m*, *f* (-n; -n) eight-year-old
'acht·kan·tig *adj.*: F ***j-n ~ hinauswerfen*** F turn s.o. out on his (*or* her) ear, boot s.o. out
'acht·los *adj.* careless; **'Acht·lo·sig·keit** *f* carelessness
'acht·mal *adv.* eight times
Acht'mo·nats·kind *n* ⚕ eight-month baby
'Acht·pfün·der [-pfʏndɐ] *m* eight-pound baby *etc.*; eight-pounder
'acht·sam *adj.* careful
'acht·spu·rig *adj.* eight-lane ...
'acht·stel·lig *adj.* eight-digit ...
'acht·stöckig (*sep.* -k·k-) *adj.* eight-stor(e)y ...
Acht'stun·den·tag *m* eight-hour day
'acht·stün·dig *adj.* eight-hour(-long) ...
'acht·tä·gig *adj.* **1.** eight-day(-long) ..., week-long ...; **2.** eight-day-old ...
Acht'tau·sen·der *m* 8000 met|re (*Am.* -er) peak
'acht·tei·lig *adj.* eight-part ..., in eight parts
'Ach·tung *f* (-; *no pl.*) **1.** **~!** look out!; ⚔ attention!; *sign*: danger!, caution!; **~ *Stufe!*** mind the step; **~*! Fertig! Los!*** on your marks, get set, go!; **2.** respect, esteem, regard (***vor*** *dat.* for); ***alle ~!*** hats off!; **~ *erweisen*** *dat.* pay respect to; **~ *gebieten*** command respect; **~ *genießen*** be highly respected; ***in j-s ~ steigen*** rise in s.o.'s esteem
'Äch·tung *f* (-; -en) outlawing; *fig.* ostracism
'ach·tung·ge·bie·tend *adj.* impressive
'ach·tungs·voll *adj.* respectful
'acht·wö·chig *adj.* **1.** eight-week ...; **2.** eight-week-old ...
'acht·zehn *adj.* eighteen; **'acht·zehnt** *adj.* eighteenth; **'Acht·zehn·tel** *n* (-s; -) eighteenth (part)
acht·zig ['axtsɪç] *adj.* eighty; ***in den ~er Jahren*** in the eighties; ***er ist in den ℒern*** he's in his eighties; F ***j-n auf ~ bringen*** F make s.o. wild (with anger), really get s.o. going; ***auf ~ sein*** F be having a fit, *sl.* be freaking out
Acht·zi·ger ['axtsɪgɐ] *m* (-s; -), **Acht·zi·ge·rin** ['axtsɪgərɪn] *f* (-; -nen) octogenarian, man (*f* woman) in his (her) eighties; F eightysomething
'acht·zig·jäh·rig *adj.* eighty-year-old ...; eighty-year(-long) ...
'acht·zigst *adj.* eightieth; ***sie hat heute ihren ℒen*** she's eighty today, it's her eightieth birthday today
'Acht·zy͵lin·der *m* eight-cylinder (car); eight-cylinder engine
äch·zen ['ɛçtsən] *v/i.* (h) groan (***vor*** *dat.* with; *fig.* ***unter*** *dat.* under)
Acker ['akɐ] (*sep.* -k·k-) *m* (-s; Äcker ['ɛkɐ]) field(s *pl.*); farmland; soil; **~bau** *m* (-[e]s; *no pl.*) agriculture, farming; *n.s.* tillage; **~ *treiben*** till the soil; **~be·stel·lung** *f* cultivation of the soil; **~bo·den** *m* arable land; **~gaul** *m* farmhorse; **~land** *n* (-[e]s; *no pl.*) arable land
ackern ['akɐn] (*sep.* -k·k-) *v/t. and v/i.* (h) plough, *Am.* plow; F *fig.* F slog (away)
'Acker·win·de (*sep.* -k·k-) *f* ❦ bindweed
Acryl [a'kryːl] *n* (-s; *no pl.*) ⚗ acryl; **~fa·ser** *f* acrylic fib|re (*Am.* -er)
Ac·tion·film ['ækʃən-] *m* action-packed film
ad ab·sur·dum [at ap'zʊrdʊm] *adv.*: ***et. ~ führen*** show how absurd (*or* ridiculous) s.th. is, reduce s.th. to absurdity
ad ac·ta [at 'akta] *adv.*: **~ *legen*** forget about *s.th.*, consider *the matter* closed
Adam ['aːdam] *m*: *fig.* ***der alte ~*** the old Adam (*or* man); ***nach ~ Riese*** according to Cocker
'Adams|ap·fel *m*: *anat.* (***der ~*** one's) Adam's apple; **~ko͵stüm** F *n*: ***im ~*** F in the raw
Ad·ap·ta·ti·on [adapta'tsĭoːn] *f* (-; -en) adaptation; **ad·ap·tie·ren** [adap'tiːrən] (h) **I.** *v/t.* adapt; **II.** *v/refl.*: ***sich ~*** adapt (***an*** *acc.* to), adjust (o.s.) (to)
Ad·ap·ter [a'daptɐ] *m* (-s; -) adapter
ad·äquat [adɛ'kvaːt] *adj.* adequate; suitable; effectual
ad·die·ren [a'diːrən] *v/t.* (h) add (up)
Ad'dier·ma͵schi·ne *f* adding machine
Ad·di·ti·on [adi'tsĭoːn] *f* (-; -en) addition; sum
Ad·di·tiv [adi'tiːf] *n* (-s; -e) additive
Adel ['aːdəl] *m* (-s; *no pl.*) **1.** nobility, aristocracy; title; **2.** *fig.* nobility (of mind); **~ *verpflichtet*** noblesse oblige
ade·lig ['aːdəlɪç] *adj.* noble (*a. fig.*), titled; **Ade·li·ge** ['aːdəlɪgə] *m*, *f* (-n; -n) nobleman (*f* noblewoman); aristocrat; ***die ~n*** the nobility, the aristocracy
adeln ['aːdəln] *v/t.* (h) make *s.o.* a peer, raise *s.o.* to the peerage; *fig.* ennoble
Adels|brief *m* patent of nobility; **~herr·schaft** *f* aristocratic rule; **~stand** *m* nobility; *in GB*: peerage; → ***erheben*** 2; **~ti·tel** *m* title (of nobility)

Ad·ept [a'dɛpt] *m* (-en; -en) disciple
Ader ['a:dɐ] *f* (-; -n) *anat.* vein, artery; ♣, *geol., min.* vein; *in wood:* grain; *fig.* vein, bent; streak; *fig.* ***e-e praktische ~ haben*** have a practical bent (of mind); ***j-n zur ~ lassen*** bleed s.o. (white); **Ader·laß** ['a:dɐlas] *m* (-lasses; -lässe [-lɛsə]) bloodletting (*a. fig.*)
Ad·hä·si·on [athɛ'zĭo:n] *f* (-; -en) adhesion; **Ad·hä·si'ons·ver·schluß** *m* adhesion flap
ad hoc [at 'hɔk] *adv.* ad hoc; ***et. ~ entscheiden*** make an ad hoc decision on s.th.
Ad-'hoc|-Bil·dung *f* ad hoc formulation; nonce word; **~-Ko·mi͵tee** *n* ad hoc committee
adieu [a'dĭø:] *int.* goodbye, *lit.* farewell
Ad·jek·tiv ['atjɛkti:f] *n* (-s; -e) *ling.* adjective; **ad·jek·ti·visch** ['atjɛkti:vɪʃ] *adj.* adjectival
Ad·ju·tant [atju'tant] *m* (-en; -en) aide-de-camp
Ad·ler ['a:dlɐ] *m* (-s; -) eagle; **~au·ge** *fig. n* eagle eye; ***mit ~n*** eagle-eyed; ***~n haben*** *a.* have eyes like a hawk; **~horst** *m* eyrie; **~na·se** *f* aquiline nose
'ad·lig *adj.*, **'Ad·li·ge** *m, f* → ***adelig, Adelige***
Ad·mi·ni·stra·ti·on [atminɪstra'tsĭo:n] *f* (-; -en) administration; **ad·mi·ni·stra·tiv** [atminɪstra'ti:f] *adj.* administrative
Ad·mi·ral [atmi'ra:l] *m* (-s; -e) (*zo.* red) admiral; **Ad·mi·ra·li·tät** [atmirali'tɛ:t] *f* (-; -en) admiralty; **Ad·mi'rals·schiff** *n* flagship; **Ad·mi'ral·stab** *m* naval staff
Ado·nis [a'do:nɪs] *fig. m* (-; -se) F good-looker; ***er ist nicht gerade ein ~*** he's not exactly the most handsome (young) man I've seen
ad·op·tie·ren [adɔp'ti:rən] *v/t.* (h) adopt; **Ad·op·ti·on** [adɔp'tsĭo:n] *f* (-; -en) adoption
Ad·op'tiv|el·tern *pl.* adoptive parents; **~kind** *n* adopted (*or* adoptive) child
Ad·re·na·lin [adrena'li:n] *n* (-s; *no pl.*) adrenalin; **~stoß** *m* surge of adrenalin
Adres·sat [adrɛ'sa:t] *m* (-en; -en) addressee
Adreß·buch [a'drɛs-] *n* directory
Adres·se [a'drɛsə] *f* (-; -n) address (*a. computer*); (formal) address; ✝ house, firm; ***per ~*** care of (*abbr.* c/o); *fig.* ***an die falsche ~ geraten*** come to the wrong place; ***an der falschen ~ sein*** have come to the wrong place; ***diese Bemerkung war an d-e ~ gerichtet*** this remark was directed at (*or* meant for) you
adres·sie·ren [adrɛ'si:rən] *v/t.* (h) address (***an*** *acc.* to); ✝ consign; **Adres'sier·ma͵schi·ne** *f* addressing machine
adrett [a'drɛt] *adj.* smart, neat, trim
ad·sor·bie·ren [atzɔr'bi:rən] *v/t.* (h) adsorb; **Ad·sorp·ti·on** [atzɔrp'tsĭo:n] *f* (-; -en) adsorption
Ad·strin·gens [at'strɪŋgɛns] *n* (-; -genzien [-'gɛntsĭən]) astringent
Ad·vent [at'vɛnt] *m* (-s; *no pl.*) Advent
Ad'vents|ka͵len·der *m* Advent calendar; **~kranz** *m* Advent wreath; **~sonn·tag** *m* Sunday in Advent; ***der erste ~*** the first Sunday of (*or* in) Advent; **~zeit** *f* Advent season
Ad·verb [at'vɛrp] *n* (-s; -bien [-bĭən]) *ling.* adverb; **ad·ver·bi·al** [atvɛr'bĭa:l] *adj.* adverbial; **Ad·ver·bi'al·satz** *m* adverbial clause
Ad·vo·kat [atvo'ka:t] *m* (-en; -en) lawyer; → ***Anwalt;*** *fig.* advocate, champion
ae·rob [ae'ro:p] *adj. biol.* aerobic
Ae·ro·bic [ɛ'ro:bɪk] *n* (-s; *no pl.*) aerobics *pl.*
Ae·ro·dy·na·mik [aerody'na:mɪk] *f* aerodynamics *pl.*; **ae·ro·dy·na·misch** [aerody'na:mɪʃ] *adj.* aerodynamic(ally *adv.*); streamlined
Ae·ro·nau·tik [aero'naʊtɪk] *f* aeronautics *pl.*
Ae·ro·sol [aero'zo:l] *n* (-s; -e) aerosol
Ae·ro·sta·tik [aero'sta:tɪk] *f* aerostatics *pl.*
Af·fä·re [a'fɛ:rə] *f* (-; -n) affair; incident; ***sich (geschickt) aus der ~ ziehen*** F get out of it (nicely)
Af·fe ['afə] *m* (-n; -n) monkey; ape; F *fig.* dandy; F twit; F ***eingebildeter ~*** F conceited ass; F ***e-n ~n haben*** F be plastered; F ***e-n ~n an j-m gefressen haben*** F be mad (*or* crazy) about s.o.; F ***ich dachte, mich laust der ~*** I thought I was seeing (*or* hearing) things; F ***s-m ~n Zucker geben*** a) be onto one's favo(u)rite topic again, b) indulge one's vice(s); F ***vom wilden ~n gebissen sein*** F be stark raving mad
Af·fekt [a'fɛkt] *m* (-[e]s; -e) emotion; ***im ~*** in the heat of the moment; **2ge·la·den** *adj.* very emotional; very excited; ***es war e-e ~ Atmosphäre*** *a.* feelings were running high; **~hand·lung** *f psych.* impulsive act; ⚖ crime of passion
af·fek·tiert [afɛk'ti:rt] *adj.* affected, artificial; **Af·fek'tiert·heit** *f* (-; *no pl.*) affectation
af·fek·tiv [afɛk'ti:f] *adj. psych.* affective
Af'fekt|stau *m psych.* emotional block, pent-up emotions *pl.*; **~stö·rung** *f* emotional disturbance
'af·fen·ar·tig *adj.* apelike, *formal:* simian; F ***mit ~er Geschwindigkeit*** F like greased lightning
'Af·fen|arsch V *m* V bastard; **~brot·baum** *m* baobab (tree); **~hit·ze** F *f* scorching (*or* sizzling) heat; ***hier drinnen ist ja e-e ~!*** it's like an oven in here; **~lie·be** *f* doting affection; **~mensch** *m* apeman; **~schan·de** F *f* absolute scandal; **~stall** F *m:* (***wie im ~*** like a) madhouse; **~tem·po** F *n:* ***in e-m ~*** F like the clappers, ***fahren:*** *a.* F belt (along); **~the͵a·ter** F *n* farce; ***das ist ja ein ~*** *a.* F it's crazy; **~zahn** F *m:* ***e-n ~ draufhaben*** F be going at some lick
af·fig ['afɪç] F *adj.* foppish; silly
Äf·fin ['ɛfɪn] *f* (-; -nen) she-ape; she-monkey; female ape (*or* monkey)
af·fi·nie·ren [afi'ni:rən] *v/t.* (h) ⚗ refine
Af·fi·ni·tät [afini'tɛ:t] *f* (-; -en) affinity
Af·fir·ma·ti·on [afɪrma'tsĭo:n] *f* (-; -en) affirmation; **af·fir·ma·tiv** [afɪrma'ti:f] *adj.* affirmative
Af·fix [a'fɪks] *n* (-es; -e) affix
Af·front [a'frõ:] *m* (-s; -s) affront (***gegen*** *acc.* to), insult (to)
Af·gha·ne [af'ga:nə] *m* (-n; -n) **1.** Afghan; **2.** Afghan hound; **Af'gha·nin** *f* (-; -nen) Afghan; **af·gha·nisch** [af'ga:nɪʃ] *adj.* Afghan
Afri·ka·ner [afri'ka:nɐ] *m* (-s; -), **Afri·ka·ne·rin** [afri'ka:nərɪn] *f* (-; -nen), **afri·ka·nisch** [afri'ka:nɪʃ] *adj.* African
Afri·ka·ni·stik [afrika'nɪstɪk] *f* (-; *no pl.*) African studies *pl.*
Afro-Ame·ri'ka·ner(in *f*) *m* ['afro-], **'afro-ame·ri'ka·nisch** *adj.* Afro-American
Afro-Look ['afrolʊk] *m:* (***im ~*** with an) Afro hairstyle
Af·ter ['aftɐ] *m* (-s; -) *anat.* anus; ⚕ *euphem.* back passage
ägä·isch [ɛ'gɛ:ɪʃ] *adj.:* ***das 2e Meer*** the Aegean (Sea)
Aga·ve [a'ga:və] *f* (-; -n) ♣ agave
Agens ['a:gɛns] *n* (-; Agenzien [a'gɛntsĭən]) ⚗ agent; *fig.* driving force
Agent [a'gɛnt] *m* (-en; -en) agent
Agen·ten|aus·tausch *m* spy swap; **~netz** *n* spy ring; **~-Thril·ler** *m* spy thriller
Agen·tur [agɛn'tu:r] *f* (-; -en) agency
Ag·glo·me·rat [aglome'ra:t] *n* (-[e]s; -e) agglomerate
Ag·glu·ti·na·ti·on [aglutina'tsĭo:n] *f* (-; -en) ⚕ *and ling.* agglutination; **ag·glu·ti·nie·ren** [agluti'ni:rən] *v/i.* (h) agglutinate
Ag·gre·gat [agre'ga:t] *n* (-[e]s; -e) ⚙ unit; *phys., biol.,* ♏ aggregate; **~zu·stand** *m* physical state
Ag·gres·si·on [agrɛ'sĭo:n] *f* (-; -en) aggression
Ag·gres·si'ons|po·li͵tik *f* policy of aggression; **~trieb** *m* aggressive instinct
ag·gres·siv [agrɛ'si:f] *adj.* aggressive; *a.* abrasive; *fig. a.* hard-hitting; **Ag·gres·si·vi·tät** [agrɛsivi'tɛ:t] *f* (-; *no pl.*) aggressiveness
Ag·gres·sor [a'grɛsɔɐ] *m* (-s; -en [agrɛ'so:rən]) aggressor
Ägi·de [ɛ'gi:də] *f:* ***unter der ~ von*** under the aegis (*or* auspices) of
agie·ren [a'gi:rən] *v/i.* (h) act (*a. thea.*); gesticulate
agil [a'gi:l] *adj.* agile; ***geistig ~*** mentally alert; **Agi·li·tät** [agili'tɛ:t] *f* (-; *no pl.*) agility
Agio ['a:ʒĭo] *n* (-s; Agien ['a:ʒĭən]) ✝ premium; **~pa͵pier** *n* premium bond
Agi·ta·ti·on [agita'tsĭo:n] *f* (-; -en) *pol.* political agitation
Agi·ta·tor [agi'ta:tɔr] *m* (-s; -en [-ta'to:rən]) political agitator, rabble-rouser; **agi·ta·to·risch** [agita'to:rɪʃ] *adj.* rabble-rousing ...
agi·tie·ren [agi'ti:rən] *v/i.* (h) canvass, campaign (***für*** *acc.* for); ***~ gegen*** *acc.* campaign against
Agit·prop [agɪt'prɔp] *f* (-; *no pl.*) agitprop; **~the͵a·ter** *n* agitprop theat|re (*Am.* -er)
Agno·sti·ker [a'gnɔstikɐ] *m* (-s; -), **agno·stisch** [a'gnɔstɪʃ] *adj.* agnostic
Ago·nie [ago'ni:] *f* (-; -n) death throes *pl.*
Agrar... [a'gra:ɐ-] *in cpds.* agrarian *policy, reform, state etc.*, farm *imports, prices etc.*, agricultural; **~be·völ·ke·rung** *f* rural population; **~ex͵por·te** *pl.* agricultural (*or* farm) exports; **~im͵por·te** *pl.* agricultural (*or* farm) imports; **~kri·se** *f* agricultural (*or* farm[ing]) crisis; **~land** *n* agrarian country; **~markt** *m* agricultural commodities market; **~po·li͵tik** *f* agricultural policy; **~prei·se** *pl.* farm prices; **~pro͵dukt** *n* agricultural (*or* farm) product; **~sub·ven·ti͵o·nen** *pl.* farm subsidies; **~͵über·schuß** *m* farm (*or* agricultural) surplus; **~wirt·schaft** *f* farming; **~wis·sen·schaft** *f* agronomy; **~wis·sen·schaft·ler** *m* agronomist
Agré·ment [agre'mã:] *n* (-s; -s) agrément
Agro·nom [agro'no:m] *m* (-en; -en) agronomist; **Agro·no·mie** [agrono'mi:] *f* (-; *no pl.*) agronomy
Ägyp·ter [ɛ'gʏptɐ] *m* (-s; -), **Ägyp·te·rin** [ɛ'gʏptərɪn] *f* (-; -nen), **ägyp·tisch** [ɛ'gʏptɪʃ] *adj.* Egyptian

aha [a'ha(:)] *int.* I see; there you are; **A'ha-Er·leb·nis** *n psych.* aha experience; ***das war ein*** ~ suddenly everything just fell into place, F it was 'the great revelation
'ahi,sto·risch *adj.* ahistorical
Ah·le ['a:lə] *f* (-; -n) awl; *typ.* point, bodkin; ⚙ reamer, broach
Ahn [a:n] *m* (-[e]s; -en) ancestor, forefather
ahn·den ['a:ndən] *v/t.* (h) punish; **'Ahn·dung** *f* (-; -en) revenge; punishment
äh·neln ['ɛ:nəln] *v/i.* (h) look (*or* be) like, resemble; *fig. a.* be similar (*dat.* to); take after *one's mother, father*; ***sich*** (*or* ***einander***) ~ be (*or* look) alike; *fig. a.* be similar
ah·nen ['a:nən] (h) **I.** *v/t.* foresee; suspect; have a presentiment (*or* foreboding) of; ***ich hab's geahnt*** I had a funny feeling, I knew it; ***wie konnte ich*** ~ how was I to know; F ***du ahnst es nicht!*** F blow me!; **II.** *v/i.*: ***mir ahnt Böses*** I fear the worst
Ah·nen|for·schung *f* genealogy, ancestor research; **~ga·le,rie** *f* ancestral halls *pl.*; *w.s. the* family portraits *pl.*; **~kult** *m* ancestral worship; **~rei·he** *f* line of ancestors; **~ta·fel** *f* genealogical table, family tree; **~ver·eh·rung** *f* ancestor worship
'Ahn|frau *f* (female) ancestor, *formal*: ancestress; progenitor, *formal*: progenitrix; **~herr** *m* ancestor; progenitor
ähn·lich ['ɛ:nlɪç] *adj.* similar (*dat.* to), like; ***so etwas*** **≗*es wie*** something like; ***j-m*** ~ ***sehen*** look (*or* be) like s.o.; *iro.* ***das sieht ihm*** (***dir***) ~ that's him (you) all over, he (you) would; ***und*** **~*e*(*s*)** and the like; **'Ähn·lich·keit** *f* (-; -en) resemblance (***mit*** *dat.* to), likeness; *fig.* similarity (with); ***viel*** ~ ***haben mit*** look very much like, *fig.* be very similar to
'Ah·nung *f* (-; -en) presentiment; *a.* foreboding; suspicion, F hunch; ***ich hatte keine blasse*** (***nicht die leiseste***) ~ ***davon*** I hadn't the faintest idea (F a clue); F ***er hatte von Tuten und Blasen keine*** ~ he didn't know the first thing about it; ***keine*** ~! no idea; ***hast du e-e*** ~! that's what you think
'ah·nungs·los *adj.* unsuspecting; ignorant
'ah·nungs·voll *adj.* full of foreboding
ahoi [a'hɔi] *int.* ⚓ ahoy!
Ahorn ['a:hɔrn] *m* (-s; -e) ♣ maple (tree); **~blatt** *n* maple leaf; **~holz** *n* maple (wood); **~si·rup** *m* maple syrup
Äh·re ['ɛ:rə] *f* (-; -n) ♣ ear (of corn *etc.*); **'Äh·ren·le·se** *f* gleaning
Aids [eɪdz] *n* (-; *no pl.*) ✱ AIDS, Aids; **~be·ra·tung** *f* **1.** advice on AIDS; **2.** AIDS advice cent|re (*Am.* -er); **~ge·fahr** *f* AIDS risk, danger of (catching) AIDS; **~in·fek·ti,on** *f* AIDS infection; **≗krank** *adj.*: ~ ***sein*** have AIDS; **~kran·ke** *m, f* (-n; -n) AIDS sufferer (*or* patient, victim); **~-,po·si·tiv** *adj.* HIV-positive; **~test** *m* AIDS test; ***e-n*** ~ ***machen lassen*** have (*or* go for) an AIDS test
Air|bag ['ɛəbæg] *m* (-s; -s) *mot.* air bag; **~bus** *m* ✈ airbus; **~con,di·tion** *f* air conditioning; **~ho,stess** *f* air hostess
Ais ['a:ɪs] *n* (-; -) ♪ A sharp
Aka·de·mie [akade'mi:] *f* (-; -n) academy; (learned) society; college
Aka·de·mi·ker [aka'de:mikɐ] *m* (-s; -), **Aka·de·mi·ke·rin** [aka'de:mikərɪn] *f* (-; -nen) (university) graduate; university man (woman)
Aka'de·mi·ker·ar·beits·lo·sig·keit *f* graduate unemployment
aka·de·misch [aka'de:mɪʃ] *adj.* academic(ally *adv.*); **~*e Bildung*** university education
Aka·zie [a'ka:tsĭə] *f* (-; -n), **A'ka·zi·en·holz** *n* acacia
Ak·kla·ma·ti·on [aklama'tsĭo:n] *f* (-; -en) acclamation; acclaim; ***durch*** (*or* ***per***) ~ ***wählen*** elect by acclamation
ak·kli·ma·ti·sie·ren [aklimati'zi:rən] (h) **I.** *v/t.* acclimatize (*a. fig.*); **II.** *v/refl.*: ***sich*** ~ become acclimatized (*a. fig.*); **Ak·kli·ma·ti'sie·rung** *f* (-; -en) acclimatization
Ak·kord [a'kɔrt] *m* (-[e]s; -e) **1.** ♪ chord; **2.** ⚖ → ***Vergleich*** 3, ***Vereinbarung***; **3.** ✝ piecework; ***im*** ~ ***arbeiten*** do piecework; **~ar·beit** *f* piecework; **~ar·bei·ter** *m* pieceworker
Ak·kor·de·on [a'kɔrdeɔn] *n* (-s; -s) accordion; **~spie·ler** *m* accordionist, accordion player
Ak'kord|lohn *m* piecework wage; **~satz** *m* piece rate
ak·kre·di·tie·ren [akredi'ti:rən] *v/t.* (h) **1.** *pol.* accredit (***bei*** *dat.* to); **2.** ✝ open a credit in favo(u)r of *s.o.*
Ak·kre·di·tiv [akredi'ti:f] *n* (-s; -e [-'ti:və]) **1.** ✝ letter of credit (*abbr.* L/C); ***j-m ein*** ~ ***eröffnen*** open a credit in favo(u)r of s.o.; **2.** *pol.* credentials *pl.*
Ak·ku ['aku] *m* → ***Akkumulator***
Ak·ku·mu·la·ti·on [akumula'tsĭo:n] *f* (-; -en) accumulation
Ak·ku·mu·la·tor [akumu'la:tɔɐ] *m* (-; -en [-la'to:rən]) ⚙ accumulator, storage battery; **Ak·ku·mu·la'to·ren·bat·te,rie** *f* storage battery
ak·ku·mu·lie·ren [akumu'li:rən] *v/t. and v/refl.* (***sich*** ~) (h) accumulate
ak·ku·rat [aku'ra:t] *adj.* meticulous; precise; neat; **Ak·ku·ra·tes·se** [akura'tɛsə] *f* (-; *no pl.*) meticulousness; precision
Ak·ku·sa·tiv ['akuzati:f] *m* (-s; -e [-ti:və]) *ling.* accusative (case); **~ob,jekt** *n* direct object
Ak·ne ['aknə] *f* (-; -n) ✱ acne
Akon·to·zah·lung [a'kɔnto-] *f* ✝ payment on account
Ak·qui·si·teur [akvizi'tø:ɐ] *m* (-s; -e) ✝ agent, canvasser
Akri·bie [akri'bi:] *f* (-; *no pl.*) meticulousness; **akri·bisch** [a'kri:bɪʃ] *adj.* meticulous, painstaking
'akri·tisch *adj.* acritical
Akro·bat [akro'ba:t] *m* (-en; -en) acrobat; **Akro·ba·tik** [akro'ba:tɪk] *f* (-; *no pl.*) acrobatics *pl.*; **akro·ba·tisch** [akro'ba:tɪʃ] *adj.* acrobatic
Akro·nym [akro'ny:m] *n* (-s; -e) acronym
Akt [akt] *m* (-[e]s; -e) act (*a. thea.*), action; sexual act, coitus; *phot., art*: nude; **~auf·nah·me** *f*, **~bild** *n* nude (photograph)
Ak·te ['aktə] *f* (-; -n) file, record; ***e-e*** ~ ***anlegen über*** *acc.* open a file on; ***die*** **~(*n*) *schließen über*** *acc.* close the file(s) on; ***zu den*** **~*n legen*** file away, *fig.* shelve
'Ak·ten|deckel (*sep.* -k·k-) *m* folder; **~ein·sicht** *f* inspection of records; ~ ***erhalten*** be given access to (the) records (*or* files); **~kof·fer** *m* attaché case; **≗kun·dig** *adj.* on record, on file; *person*: known to the police; **~map·pe** *f* **1.** folder; **2.** → ***Aktentasche***; **~no,tiz** *f* memo(randum); **~ord·ner** *m* file; **~schrank** *m* filing cabinet; **~stoß** *m* pile of documents; **~ta·sche** *f* briefcase; **~wolf** *m* shredder; **~zei·chen** *n* file number; *on letter*: reference
Ak·teur [ak'tø:ɐ] *m* (-s; -e) **1.** protagonist; **2.** *film etc.*: actor; **3.** *sport*: player, competitor, *formal*: protagonist
'Akt|fo·to *n* nude (photograph); **~fo·to·gra,fie** *f* **1.** nude photography; **2.** nude photograph
Ak·tie ['aktsĭə] *f* (-; -n) ✝ share, *Am.* stock; F *fig.* ***wie stehen die*** **~*n?*** how are things?, F how's tricks?; ***s-e*** **~*n steigen*** (***stehen schlecht***) things are looking up (things don't look too good) for him
'Ak·ti·en|bör·se *f* stock exchange; **~ge·sell·schaft** *f* limited company, *Am.* (stock) corporation; **~ka·pi,tal** *n* share capital, *Am.* capital stock; **~kurs** *m* stock (*or* share) price; **~markt** *m* stock market; **~mehr·heit** *f* majority holding; ***die*** ~ ***besitzen*** hold the controlling interest; **~pa,ket** *n* block (*or* parcel) of shares (*Am.* stocks)
Ak·ti·on [ak'tsĭo:n] *f* (-; -en) action (*a. pol.*); measures *pl.*; operation; drive, campaign; *art*: happening; **~en** activities; ***in*** ~ in action; ***sie sind voll in*** ~ F it's all stations go (with them); ***in*** ~ ***treten*** take action, act; ***es wird Zeit, daß wir in*** ~ ***treten*** it's time we did something (about it), it's time for action
Ak·tio·när [aktsĭo'nɛ:ɐ] *m* (-s; -e) shareholder, *Am.* stockholder; **Ak·tio'närs·ver·samm·lung** *f* shareholders' (*Am.* stockholders') meeting
Ak·tio·nis·mus [aktsĭo'nɪsmʊs] *contp. m* (-; *no pl.*) (*a.* ***blinder*** ~) doing things for the sake of doing things
Ak·ti'ons|art *f ling.* aspect; **~be·reich** *m* sphere of action; **~frei·heit** *f* freedom of action; **~ge·mein·schaft** *f pol.* action group; **~ma·ler** *m* action painter; **~ma·le,rei** *f* action painting; **~pro,gramm** *n* program(me) of action; **~ra·di·us** *m* radius (of action); *fig.* sphere of action
ak·tiv [ak'ti:f] *adj. a. phys. etc. and fig.* active; ⚗ *a.* activated *carbon etc.*; ✝ favo(u)rable *balance*; ⚔ regular; **~*er Dienst*** active duty; → ***Wahlrecht***
Ak·tiv ['akti:f] *n* (-s; -e [-ti:və]) *ling.* active (voice)
Ak·ti·va [ak'ti:va] *pl.* ✝ assets; ~ ***und Passiva*** assets and liabilities
Ak'tiv·be·stand *m* **1.** ✝ assets *pl.*; **2.** ⚔ present strength
Ak'ti·ve *m, f* (-n;-n) *sport*: active player (*or* runner *etc.*)
Ak'tiv·ge·schäft *n* credit transaction(s *pl.*)
ak·ti·vie·ren [akti'vi:rən] *v/t.* (h) **1.** activate, get *s.th. or s.o.* going; **2.** *phys. etc.* activate; **3.** ✝ carry as an asset; **Ak·ti'vie·rung** *f* (-; -en) *a. fig.* activation
Ak·ti·vis·mus [akti'vɪsmʊs] *m* (-; *no pl.*) activism; **Ak·ti·vist** [akti'vɪst] *m* (-en; -en) activist (*a. hist. DDR*)
Ak·ti·vi·tät [aktivi'tɛ:t] *f* (-; -en) activity; ***hektische*** ~ ***auslösen*** have (*or* get) everyone rushing around like mad; ***schöpferische*** ~ ***entfalten*** become very creative
Ak'tiv|koh·le *f* activated carbon; **~po·sten** *m* credit item, asset; **~sal·do** *m* credit balance; **~sei·te** *f* asset side; **~ur·laub** *m* activity (*or* active) holiday
'Akt|ma·le,rei *f* nude painting; **~mo,dell** *n* nude model; **~stu·die** *f* nude study; **~zeich·nung** *f* nude drawing

ak·tua·li·sie·ren [aktŭali'zi:rən] *v/t.* (h) update, bring *s.th.* up to date
Ak·tua·li·tät [aktŭali'tɛ:t] *f* (-; *no pl.*) topicality, relevance to the present
ak·tu·ell [ak'tŭɛl] *adj.* topical, of current interest; *report* on current affairs; current-events *lecture*; present-day *problems etc.*; up-to-date ..., *pred.* up to date; *computer*: current; ***das ist nicht mehr*** ~ we've crossed that off the agenda; ***wieder*** ~ ***werden*** come back into fashion, become a burning issue again; *pol.* ~***e Stunde*** special session
Ak·tu'el·le *n*: ~***s aus der Politik*** (***Literatur, Filmbranche*** *etc.*) the latest developments in politics (the latest from the literary world, the movie world *etc.*); ***und jetzt*** ~***s*** and now for a look at what's going on in the world of politics (*or* literature *etc.*)
Aku·pres·sur [akuprɛ'su:ɐ] *f* (-; -en) acupressure
Aku·punk·teur [akupʊŋk'tø:ɐ] *m* (-s; -e) acupuncturist; **aku·punk·tie·ren** [akupʊŋk'ti:rən] *v/t.* (h) give *s.o.* acupuncture treatment; **Aku·punk·tur** [akupʊŋk'tu:ɐ] *f* (-; -en) acupuncture
Aku·stik [a'kʊstɪk] *f* (-; *no pl.*) acoustics *pl.*; ~**kopp·ler** *m computer*: acoustic coupler
aku·stisch [a'kʊstɪʃ] **I.** *adj.* acoustic(al); **II.** *adv.* acoustically; ***ich habe Sie*** ~ ***nicht verstanden*** I didn't quite catch what you said
akut [a'ku:t] *adj.* ⚕ acute, *pain*: *a.* severe (*both a. fig.*); pressing *problem, matter etc.*; 2**kran·ken·haus** *n* emergency hospital
Ak·zent [ak'tsɛnt] *m* (-[e]s; -e) accent; *a.* stress (*a. fig.*); *fig.* ***neue*** ~***e setzen*** point the way to the future; 2**frei** *adj. and adv.* without an (*or* any) accent
ak·zen·tu·ie·ren [aktsɛntu'i:rən] *v/t.* (h) *a. fig.* accentuate
Ak'zent·ver·schie·bung *f* shift of stress (*fig.* emphasis)
Ak·zept [ak'tsɛpt] *n* (-[e]s; -e) ✝ acceptance
ak·zep·ta·bel [aktsɛp'ta:bəl] *adj.* acceptable (***für*** *acc.* to)
Ak·zep·tant [aktsɛp'tant] *m* (-en; -en) ✝ acceptor
Ak·zep·tanz [aktsɛp'tants] *f* (-; *no pl.*) acceptance; ✝ market acceptance
ak·zep·tie·ren [aktsɛp'ti:rən] *v/t.* (h) accept
Ak·zi·denz·druck [aktsi'dɛnts-] *m* job printing; **Ak·zi·denz·drucker** (*sep.* -k·k-) *m* job printer
Ala·ba·ster [ala'bastɐ] *m* (-s; -) alabaster
à la carte [ala'kart] *adv.*: ~ ***bestellen*** (***essen***) order (eat) à la carte
Alarm [a'larm] *m* (-[e]s; -e) alarm, alert; air-raid warning; ***blinder*** ~ false alarm; ~ ***schlagen*** sound the alarm; ~**an·la·ge** *f* alarm system; 2**be·reit** *adj.* on alert, ⚔ *a.* on standby; ~**be·reit·schaft** *f*: ***in*** ~ on alert, ⚔ *a.* on standby; ***in höchster*** ~ in a high state of alert; ***in*** ~ ***versetzen*** put on alert (⚔ *a.* standby); ~**glocke** (*sep.* -k·k-) *f* alarm bell, tocsin
alar·mie·ren [alar'mi:rən] *v/t.* (h) alarm (*a. fig.*), alert; **alar'mie·rend** *fig. adj.* alarming
A'larm|si₍gnal *n* alarm signal; ~**stu·fe** *f* alert phase; ~ ***eins*** high alert; ***höchste*** ~ high state of alert; ~**zei·chen** *n* danger signal (*a. fig.*); ~**zu·stand** *m* state of alert; ***im*** ~ on alert
Alaun [a'laʊn] *m* (-s; -e) alum; ~**stift** *m* styptic
Al·ba·ner [al'ba:nɐ] *m* (-s; -), **Al·ba·ne·rin** [al'ba:nərɪn] *f* (-; -nen), **al·ba·nisch** [al'ba:nɪʃ] *adj.*, **Al'ba·nisch** *n* (-en; *no pl.*) *ling.* Albanian
Al·ba·tros ['albatrɔs] *m* (-; -se) albatross
al·bern ['albɐn] **I.** *adj.* silly; ~***es Zeug*** rubbish, nonsense; ***red doch nicht so ein*** ~***es Zeug!*** stop talking such nonsense; **II.** F *v/i.* (h) fool around; **'Al·bern·heit** *f* (-; -en) silly behavio(u)r
Al·bi·no [al'bi:no] *m* (-s; -s) albino
Al·bum ['albʊm] *n* (-s; Alben ['albən]) album
Al·bu·men [al'bu:mən] *n* (-s; *no pl.*) albumen
Al·bu·min [albu'mi:n] *n* (-s; -e) albumin
Al·chi·mie [alçi'mi:] *f* (-; *no pl.*) alchemy; **Al·chi·mist** [alçi'mɪst] *m* (-en; -en) alchemist
Al·de·hyd [alde'hy:t] *n* (-s; -e) aldehyde
Ale·man·ne [alə'manə] *m* (-n; -n), **Ale'man·nin** *f* (-; -nen) *a. hist.* Alemannian; *hist.* ***die Alemannen*** the Alemanni; **ale·man·nisch** [alə'manɪʃ] *adj.*, **Ale'man·nisch** *n* (-en; *no pl.*) *ling.* Alemannic
Alex·an·dri·ner [alɛksan'dri:nɐ] *m* (-s; -) Alexandrine (verse)
Al·ge ['algə] *f* (-; -n) alga; *pl.* algae, seaweed *sg.*
Al·ge·bra ['algebra] *f* (-; -bren) algebra
'Al·gen|pest *f* algal bloom, proliferation of algae; ~**tep·pich** *m* layer (*or* tide) of algae
Al·ge·ri·er [al'ge:rĭɐ] *m* (-s; -), **Al·ge·rie·rin** [al'ge:rĭərɪn] *f* (-; -nen), **al·ge·risch** [al'ge:rɪʃ] *adj.* Algerian
Al·go·rith·mus [algo'rɪtmʊs] *m* (-; -men) algorithm
ali·as ['a:lĭas] *adv.* alias, also known as, F aka
Ali·bi ['a:libi] *n* (-s; -s) ⚖ alibi (*a. fig.*); ~**frau** *f* token woman; ~**funk·ti₍on** *f*: ***das*** (***er*** *or* ***sie***) ***hat nur e-e*** ~ it's just a cover-up (he's *or* she's just a token); ~**schwar·ze** *m, f* (-n; -n) token black
Ali·men·te [ali'mɛntə] *pl.* maintenance *sg.*, child support *sg.*; alimony; **Ali'men·ten·kla·ge** *f* maintenance (*or* alimony) suit
ali·pha·tisch [ali'fa:tɪʃ] *adj.* ⚗ aliphatic
Al·ka·li [al'ka:li] *n* (-s; -en [-lĭən]) ⚗ alkali; **al·ka·lisch** [al'ka:lɪʃ] *adj.* alkaline
Al·ka·lo·id [alkalo'i:t] *n* (-[e]s; -e [-'i:də]) alkaloid
Al·ko·hol ['alkoho:l] *m* (-s; -e) alcohol; ***s-e Sorgen im*** ~ ***ertränken*** drown one's sorrows in drink (*or* alcohol); ***er steht unter*** ~ he's been drinking; ***ich habe keinen Tropfen*** ~ ***getrunken*** I haven't had (*or* touched) a single drop; 2**ab·hän·gig** *adj.*: ~ ***sein*** be an alcoholic; 2**arm** *adj.* low in alcohol, low-alcohol ...; ~**ein·fluß** *m*: ***er stand unter*** ~ he had been drinking; 2**frei** *adj.* non-alcoholic, alcohol-free; ~***e Getränke*** soft drinks (and beverages); ~**ge·halt** *m* alcoholic content; ~**ge·nuß** *m* consumption of alcohol, drinking; ***übermäßiger*** ~ excessive drinking, too much alcohol; 2**hal·tig** *adj.* alcoholic
Al·ko·ho·li·ka [alko'ho:lika] *pl.* alcohol *sg.*, alcoholic drinks
Al·ko·ho·li·ker [alko'ho:likɐ] *m* (-s; -), **Al·ko·ho·li·ke·rin** [alko'ho:likərɪn] *f* (-; -nen) alcoholic
al·ko·ho·lisch [alko'ho:lɪʃ] *adj.* alcoholic
al·ko·ho·li·sie·ren [alkoholi'zi:rən] *v/t.* (h) **1.** ⚗ alcoholize; **2.** ***j-n*** ~ get s.o. drunk; **al·ko·ho·li'siert** *adj.* drunk; ***in*** ~***em Zustand*** (while) under the influence of alcohol
Al·ko·ho·lis·mus [alkoho'lɪsmʊs] *m* (-; *no pl.*) alcoholism
'Al·ko·hol|kon₍sum *m* consumption of alcohol; ~**₍miß·brauch** *m* alcohol abuse; 2**reich** *adj.* high in alcohol, high-alcohol ...; ~**spie·gel** *m* blood--alcohol level; ~**sucht** *f* alcoholism, dependence on alcohol; 2**süch·tig** *adj.* → ***alkoholabhängig***; ~**sün·der** *m* drunk(en) driver; ~**test** *m* breathalyzer test; ~**ver·bot** *n* ban on alcohol; F ***in diesem Haus herrscht*** ~ no alcohol allowed in this house; ~**ver·brauch** *m* alcohol consumption; ~**ver·gif·tung** *f* alcohol poisoning
Al·ko·ven [al'ko:vən] *m* (-s; -) **1.** alcove, recess; **2.** windowless room
all [al] **I.** *indef. pron.* all; ~***e beide*** both of them; ~***e drei*** all three (of them); ***sie*** (***wir***) ~***e*** all of them (us); ~***e anderen*** all the others, all the rest; ***sind*** ~***e da?*** is everyone (*or* everybody) here?; ~***e, die ein Visum benötigen*** anyone (*or* those) requiring a visa; **II.** *adj.* all (of); every; any; ~***e*** (***zwei***) ***Tage*** every (other) day; ~***e acht Tage*** once a week; ~***e Menschen*** everyone, everybody; ~***e Welt*** the whole world; ~***es Gute*** all the best; → ***alle, alles***
All [al] *n* (-s; *no pl.*) universe; (outer) space; ***ins*** ~ ***schicken*** send into space
all'abend·lich **I.** *adj.* regular evening *visit etc.*; **II.** *adv.* every evening
'all·be·kannt *adj.* well-known; *b.s.* notorious
al·le ['alə] F *pred. adj. and adv.* **1.** finished, all gone; ***mein Geld ist*** ~ I've run out of money, F I'm broke; ***der Zucker ist*** ~ we've *etc.* run out of sugar, there's no sugar left; ~ ***machen*** finish; ***allmählich*** ~ ***werden*** run out; **2.** F whacked, bushed
'al·le·dem: ***trotz*** ~ in spite of all that, in spite of it all
Al·lee [a'le:] *f* (-; -n) avenue, boulevard
Al·le·go·rie [alego'ri:] *f* (-; -n) allegory; **al·le·go·risch** [ale'go:rɪʃ] *adj.* allegorical
al·lein [a'laɪn] **I.** *pred. adj. and adv.* alone, on one's own, by oneself; only; lonely; ***ganz*** ~ all alone *etc.*; ***er war*** ~ ***da*** he was the only one there; ***kann ich dich*** ~ ***lassen?*** will you be all right (*Am.* alright) on your own?; ***kann ich mal mit dir*** ~ ***sprechen?*** could I have a word with you in private?; ***von*** ~ by itself, of one's own accord; ***mit der linken Hand*** ~ just with one's left hand, with one's left hand only; ***er*** ~ ***kann das entscheiden*** he's the only one who can decide that; ~ ***schon ihre Stimme regt mich auf*** just the sound of her voice is enough to get me going; ***schon*** ~ ***der Gedanke*** the mere thought (of it); **II.** *cj.* but, however
Al'lein|be·sitz *m* sole ownership; ~**er·be** *m*, ~**er·bin** *f* sole heir(ess *f*); ~**er·zie·hen·de** *m, f* (-n; -n) single (*or* lone) parent; ~**flug** *m* solo flight; ***im*** ~ ***den Atlantik überqueren*** fly solo across the Atlantic; ~**gang** *m* single-handed effort; ***im*** ~ single-handedly, solo; ~**herr·schaft** *f*

autocracy; **~herr·scher** *m* autocrat, absolute ruler
al'lei·nig *adj.* only, sole, exclusive
Al'lein|in·ha·ber *m* sole owner; **~recht** *n* exclusive right; **2rei·send** *adj.*: ***~e Kinder*** unaccompanied minors; **~rei·sen·de** *m, f* (-n; -n) unaccompanied passenger (*or* travel[l]er); **~schuld** *f* sole responsibility; **~sein** *n* loneliness, solitude; ***Angst vor dem ~ haben*** be afraid of being alone; **2'se·lig·ma·chend** *adj.*: *iro.* ***et. für ~ halten*** think s.th. is the be-all and end-all; **2ste·hend** *adj.* **1.** single, unmarried, unattached; **2.** ***~ sein*** live alone; ***~er Witwer*** widower without dependants; **3.** detached *house*; **~un·ter,hal·ter** *m thea.* solo entertainer, F one-man show (man); **~ver·die·ner** *m* sole (wage) earner; **~ver·kauf** *m* exclusive selling rights *pl.*
Al'lein·ver·tre·ter *m* sole agent; **Al'lein·ver·tre·tungs·recht** *n* right of exclusive representation
Al'lein·ver·trieb *m* → ***Alleinverkauf***
al·le'mal *adv.*: ***ein für ~*** once and for all; F ***~!*** F you bet!; F ***wir schaffen das noch ~*** F we'll manage it no problem
al·len·falls ['alən'fals] *adv.* at most, at best; perhaps
al·ler|'äu·ßerst ['alɐ-] *adj.* outermost; *fig.* utmost; rock-bottom *price*; **~'best I.** *adj.* very best; **II.** *adv.*: ***am ~en*** best of all
al·ler·dings ['alɐ'dɪŋs] *adv.* **1.** *war es ein gutes Konzert?* - ***~!*** it certainly was, indeed it was; **2.** though, but, however; ***sie sagte ~ ...*** she did say, however (*or* though), ...; ***das ist ~ wahr, aber*** that may be true, but
'al·ler|'erst I. *adj.* very first; **II.** *adv.*: ***zu ~*** first of all, F first off; **~'frü·he·stens** *adv.*: ***~ um zwei*** (at) two at the very earliest
Al·ler·gen [alɛr'ge:n] *n* (-s; -e) allergen
Al·ler·gie [alɛr'gi:] *f* (-; -n) allergy; ***e-e ~ gegen et. haben*** be allergic to s.th.; **2ge·prüft** *adj.* allergy-tested; **~paß** *m* allergy ID; **~schock** *m* anaphylactic shock
Al·ler·gi·ker [a'lɛrgikɐ] *m* (-s; -) allergy sufferer; ***er ist ~*** he suffers from an allergy (*or* allergies)
al·ler·gisch [a'lɛrgɪʃ] **I.** *adj. a. fig.* allergic (***gegen*** to); **II.** *adv.*: ***~ reagieren auf*** have an allergic reaction to, *a. fig.*: be allergic to
Al·ler·go·lo·ge [alɛrgo'lo:gə] *m* (-n; -n) allergist
'al·ler'hand F *adj.* **1.** → ***allerlei***; **2.** quite a lot; ***das ist ~!*** a) not bad; b) F that's a bit thick
'Al·ler'hei·li·gen *n* All Saints' Day
'Al·ler'hei·lig·ste *n* (-n; *no pl.*) **1.** holy of holies, *a. fig.* inner sanctum; *R.C.* sanctuary; **2.** Blessed Sacrament
'al·ler|'höchst I. *adj.* highest ... of all; very highest; ***es wird ~e Zeit*** it's high time; **II.** *adv.*: ***am ~en*** highest of all; **~'höch·stens** *adv.* at the very most
al·ler·lei ['alɐ'laɪ] **I.** *adj.* all kinds (*or* sorts) of; **II.** *pron.* all sorts of things; ***wir hatten uns ~ zu erzählen*** we had a lot to tell each other; **III. 2** *n* (-s; -s) medley, potpourri; *contp.* jumble; *gastr.* hotchpotch; ***Leipziger ~*** mixed vegetables
'al·ler|'letzt *adj.* very last; F incredible, dreadful; ***er kam als ~er an*** he was the last to arrive; F ***das ist das 2e!*** that really is the limit!; **~'liebst I.** *adj.* lovely, sweet; favo(u)rite ... of all; **II.** *adv.*: ***am ~en*** best of all; **~'meist I.** *adj.* (very) most; ***die ~en Leute*** most people; **II.** *adv.*: ***am ~en*** most of all; **~mo'dernst** *adj. the* very latest; ⊚ *a.* state-of-the-art ...; **~'nächst** *adj.* very next; (very) nearest; ***in ~er Zeit*** very soon; ***aus ~er Nähe*** at close quarters; **~'neu·est** *adj.* very latest; ⊚ *a.* state-of-the-art; ***die ~e Mode*** the latest fashion (F thing); **~'nö·tigst** *adj.* most necessary; ***nur das 2e*** only what is (*or* was) absolutely necessary; **~'schlimmst I.** *adj.* worst ... of all; **II.** *adv.*: ***am ~en*** worst of all
'Al·ler'see·len *n* All Souls' Day
'al·ler'seits *adv.* on all sides; ***gute Nacht ~!*** good night everybody
'al·ler'spä·te·stens *adv.*: ***~ um 10 Uhr*** (at) 10 o'clock at the very latest
'Al·ler'welts... *in cpds.* (very) common; run-of-the-mill; **~ge'sicht** *n* nondescript face; **~kerl** *m* jack of all trades; **~wort** *n* everyday word; *contp.* meaningless (*or* all-purpose) word
'al·ler'we·nigst I. *adj.*: least ... of all; ***die ~en Leute*** very few people; **II.** *adv.*: ***am ~en*** least of all
'Al·ler'wer·te·ste F *m* (-n; -n) F posterior
al·les ['aləs] *indef. pron.* everything; ***~ in allem*** all in all, overall, on balance, when all is said and done; ***das ~*** all that; ***er kann ~*** he can do anything; ***~ oder nichts!*** it's all or nothing; ***~ zu s-r Zeit*** all in good time; ***auf ~ gefaßt sein*** be prepared for the worst; → ***Mädchen***
'al·le'samt *adv.* all of them (*or* us); ***sie kamen ~*** they all came
'Al·les|fres·ser *m* omnivore; **~kle·ber** *m* all-purpose glue; **~kön·ner** *m* man (*or* woman) of many talents; ***er ist ein ~*** *a.* there's nothing (*or* very little) he can't do; **~schnei·der** *m* food-slicer; **~schrei·ber** *contp. m* hack writer; **~wis·ser** [-vɪsɐ] *contp. m* (-s; -) F know-(it-)all
'all'ge·gen·wär·tig *adj.* (all-)pervasive, *formal*: omnipresent
'all·ge'mein I. *adj.* general; public; ***im ~en*** → **II.** *adv.* generally, in general; on the whole; ***~ gesprochen*** generally speaking; ***~ verbreitet*** widespread; ***es ist ~ üblich, daß man ...*** it's common practi|ce (*Am.* -se) to ...; ***es ist ~ bekannt, daß*** it's a well-known fact that; → ***Wunsch, Zustimmung***
'All·ge'mein|arzt *m* general practitioner; **~be·fin·den** *n* general state of health; **~bil·dung** *f* general education; ***e-e gute ~*** a good, all-round education; **2gül·tig** *adj.* universally applicable (*or* valid), general *rule*; **~gut** *n*: *fig.* ***~ sein, zum ~ gehören*** be part of everyday life, be part of our *etc.* common heritage
'All·ge'mein·heit *f* (-; *no pl.*) general public
'All·ge'mein|kran·ken·haus *n* general hospital; **~me·di,zin** *f* general medicine; ***Arzt für ~*** general practitioner; **~platz** *m* commonplace, platitude; **2ver·bind·lich** *adj.* generally binding; **2ver·ständ·lich** *adj.* comprehensible, simple; **~wis·sen** *n* general knowledge; **~wohl** *n* public welfare (*or* weal); **~zu·stand** *m* (-[e]s; *no pl.*) general condition; general situation
'All·ge·walt *f* omnipotence; **'all·ge·wal·tig** *adj.* omnipotent, *a. fig.* all-powerful
All'heil·mit·tel *n* panacea, cure-all (*both a. fig.*)
Al·li·anz [a'lĭants] *f* (-; -en) alliance
Al·li·ga·tor [ali'ga:tɔr] *m* (-s; -en [-ga-'to:rən]) alligator
al·li·ie·ren [ali'i:rən] *v/refl.* (h): ***sich ~*** form an alliance; **al·li'iert** *adj.*: ***~e Streitkräfte*** allied forces; **Al·li'ier·te** *m, f* (-n; -n) ally
Al·li·te·ra·ti·on [alɪtera'tsĭo:n] *f* (-; -en) alliteration
'all'jähr·lich I. *adj.* yearly, annual; **II.** *adv.* annually, every year
'All·macht *f* (-; *no pl.*) omnipotence; **'all'mäch·tig** *adj.* omnipotent; ***der 2e*** God Almighty; ***2er!*** good lord!
all·mäh·lich [al'mɛ:lɪç] **I.** *adj.* gradual; **II.** *adv.* gradually, bit by bit; ***~ müßtest du das können*** it's time you knew how to do that, you should be able to do that by now; ***er müßte ~ kommen*** he should be here any minute; F ***~ reicht's mir*** I'm beginning to get fed up with it
'all'mo·nat·lich I. *adj.* monthly; **II.** *adv.* every month
Al·lo·path [alo'pa:t] *m* (-en; -en) allopath; **Al·lo·pa·thie** [alopa'ti:] *f* (-; *no pl.*) allopathy; **al·lo·pa·thisch** [alo'pa:tɪʃ] *adj.* allopathic(ally *adv.*)
Al·lo·tria [a'lo:tria] *n* (-s; *no pl.*) larking about, fooling around; ***~ treiben*** lark about, fool around
'All·par'tei·en... *in cpds.* all-party
'All·rad·an·trieb *m mot.* all-wheel drive; ***Wagen mit ~*** all-wheel drive vehicle
All·roun·der ['ɔ:l'raʊndə] *m* (-s; -) all-rounder; **'All'round·sport·ler** *m* all-rounder
all·sei·tig ['alzaɪtɪç] *adj.* general, all-round ...
all·seits ['alzaɪts] *adv.* on all sides; ***~ bekannt*** generally known; ***~ geachtet*** universally respected; ***er war ~ beliebt*** he was very popular, everybody loved him
'All·tag *m* **1.** (ordinary) weekday; **2.** daily routine (*contp.* grind); → ***grau***
'all·täg·lich *adj.* daily; *fig.* everyday ...; ordinary; humdrum; **'All·täg·lich·keit** *f* (-; -en) **1.** everyday occurrence; **2.** *no pl.* ordinariness
'All·tags... *in cpds. usu.* everyday; **~le·ben** *n* day-to-day life; **~trott** *m* daily grind
'all·um'fas·send *adj.* all-embracing
Al·lü·ren [a'ly:rən] *pl.* airs and graces
All'wet·ter... *in cpds.* all-weather; **~platz** *m tennis*: all-weather court
'all'wis·send *adj.* omniscient; **'All'wis·sen·heit** *f* (-; *no pl.*) omniscience
'all'wö·chent·lich I. *adj.* weekly; **II.** *adv.* every week, weekly
'all·zu *adv.* far (*or* much) too; over...; ***nicht ~*** not too; ***er ist nicht ~ freundlich*** *etc.* he's not the friendliest *etc.* person I know; **~'gern** *adv.*: ***ich wäre ~ gekommen*** I would love to have come, I would have loved to come; **~'gut** *adv.* only too well; **~'sehr** *adv.* too much, excessively; **~'viel** *adv.* too much; ***~ ist ungesund*** enough is as good as a feast
'All·zweck... *in cpds.* all-purpose, general-purpose, universal
Alm [alm] *f* (-; -en) alpine pasture
Al·ma ma·ter ['alma 'ma:tɐ] (-; -) *f* alma mater
Al·ma·nach ['almanax] *m* (-[e]s; -e) almanac
'Alm·hüt·te *f* alpine hut
Al·mo·sen [al'mo:zən] *n* (-s; -) alms *pl.*;

contp. pittance, handout; **~emp·fän·ger** *m* receiver of alms
Aloe ['a:loe] *f* (-; -n) ⚘ aloe
Al·pa·ka [al'paka] *n* (-s; *no pl.*), **~wol·le** *f* alpaca
al pa·ri [al 'pa:ri] *adv.* ⚜ at par
Alp|druck ['alp-] *m* (-[e]s; ⁻e) nightmare; **~drücken** (*sep.* -k·k-) *n* (-s; *no pl.*) nightmare(s *pl.*)
Al·pen ['alpən] *pl.* Alps; **~glü·hen** *n* alpenglow
'Al·pen·län·der *pl.* Alpine countries; **'al·pen·län·disch** [-lɛndɪʃ] *adj.* Alpine, alpine
'Al·pen|re·pu,blik *f* Alpine republic; **~ro·se** *f* alpine rose; **~veil·chen** *n* cyclamen; **~ver·ein** *m* Alpine Club
Al·pha·bet [alfa'be:t] *n* (-[e]s; -e) alphabet; **al·pha'be·tisch** **I.** *adj.* alphabetical; **II.** *adv.* → **einordnen** 1, **ordnen**
al·pha·be·ti·sie·ren [alfabeti'zi:rən] *v/t.* (h) **1.** alphabetize, put into alphabetical order; **2.** teach *s.o.* to read and write; **Al·pha·be·ti'sie·rungs·kam,pa·gne** *f* literacy campaign
al·pha·me·risch [alfa'me:rɪʃ], **al·pha·nu·me·risch** [alfanu'me:rɪʃ] *adj.* alphanumeric(ally *adv.*)
'Al·pha|strah·len *pl.* alpha rays; **~teil·chen** *n* alpha particle
'Alp·horn *n* alpenhorn, alphorn
al·pin [al'pi:n] *adj.* alpine; → **Kombination**; **Al·pi·nis·mus** [alpi'nɪsmʊs] *m* (-; *no pl.*) alpinism; **Al·pi·nist** [alpi'nɪst] *m* (-en; -en) alpinist, mountaineer
'Alp·traum *m a. fig.* nightmare
Al·raun [al'raʊn] *m* (-[e]s; -e), **Al'rau·ne** *f* (-; -n) ⚘ mandrake
als [als] *cj.* **1.** *after comp. and rather, other*: than; **er ist älter ~ du** he's older than you; **2.** but, except; **alles andere ~ hübsch** anything but pretty; **3.** as; **~ Entschuldigung** by way of an excuse; **~ Geschenk** as a present; **er starb ~ Held** he died (as) a hero; **4.** as, in one's capacity as *officer, critic etc.*; being (*or* as) *an Englishman etc.*; **er kam ~ letzter rein** he was the last to come in; **5.** when, as, while; **6. ~ ob** as if, as though; **er ist zu anständig, ~ daß er das tun könnte** he's too decent to do a thing like that
al·so ['alzo] **I.** *cj.* so; **~ blieb er zu Hause** so he stayed at home; **lassen wir's ~** let's leave it then; **du kommst ~ nicht?** you're not coming then?; **es ist ~ wahr?** it's true then(, is it)?; **du gehst ~ doch?** so you're going after all?; **~, los!** let's get going then; **~, wie gesagt** so, as I was saying (*or* I say); **~, wenn du mich fragst** (well,) if you ask me; **~ gut!** all right (then), *Am.* alright (then), F okay (then); **na ~!** what did I say?, *a.* there you go; **na ~(, da haben wir's ja)!** there we are(, see?); **er mag modernere Komponisten, ~ Berio, Cage ...** he likes more modern composers - Berio, Cage ...; **II.** *obs. adv.* thus, so
alt [alt] *adj.* a) old; ancient; b) used, second-hand; c) old, stale; d) old, experienced; **~ werden** → **altern**; **~e Sprachen** *the* classics; **~e Geschichte** ancient history; **die ~en Germanen** the ancient Germans; **der ~e Herr Huber** old Herr Huber; **der ~e Goethe** Goethe in his old age; F **ein ~er Säufer** a confirmed drunkard; **ein sechs Jahre ~er Junge** a six-year-old boy; **wie ~ bist du?** how old are you?; **er ist (doppelt) so ~ wie ich** he's (twice) my age; **er sieht gar nicht so ~ aus** he doesn't look it, he looks much younger; **sie ist ganz schön ~ geworden** she really has aged; **es macht dich ~** it makes you look old, it ages you; **alles bleibt beim ~en** nothing's changed; **du bist immer noch der ~e** you haven't changed(, have you?); **Peter ist nicht mehr der ~e** he's not the Peter I used to know; **er ist wieder ganz der ~e** he's back to his usual self; F **hier werde ich nicht ~!** F I won't be sticking around here for very long; → **älter, Eisen, Hase**
Alt *m* (-s; -e) ♪ alto
'alt·an·ge·se·hen *adj.* old-established
Al·tar [al'ta:ɐ] *m* (-s; -e) altar; **~auf·satz** *m* reredos; **~bild** *n* altarpiece; **~raum** *m* chancel
'alt·backen (*sep.* -k·k-) *adj.* stale; F *fig.* old-fashioned; *a.* antiquated, stale *ideas etc.*
'Alt·bau *m* (-[e]s; -ten) old building; **~sa,nie·rung** *f* refurbishment of old buildings; **~woh·nung** *f* old flat (*Am.* apartment)
'alt|be·kannt *adj.* old familiar ...; **~be·währt** *adj.* well-tried; longstanding *friendship etc.*; **in ~er Manier** the tried and tested way
'Alt·block·flö·te *f* treble recorder
'Alt|bun·des·kanz·ler *m* ex-chancellor; ex-German (*or* ex-Austrian) chancellor; **~bun·des·prä·si,dent** *m* ex-president; ex-German (*or* ex-Austrian) president
'alt·deutsch *adj.*: **~e Möbel** old-style German furniture
Al·te¹ ['altə] *f* (-n; -n) old woman; F **m-e ~** F the old woman; *a.* F the missus; F **die ~** the boss
'Al·te² *m* (-n; -n) **1.** old man; F **mein ~r** F the old man; F **der ~** F the boss, *sl.* the guv
'alt|'ehr·wür·dig *adj.* time-hono(u)red; **~'ein·ge·ses·sen** *adj.* old-established
'Alt·ei·sen *n* scrap iron
'alt·eng·lisch *adj.*, **'Alt·eng·lisch** *n* (-en; *no pl.*) *ling.* Old English
'Al·ten|heim *n* old people's home; **~pfle·ge** *f* geriatric care, care of the elderly; **~pfle·ger** *m* geriatric (*or* old people's) nurse; **~ta·ges·stät·te** *f* geriatric day-care cent|re (*Am.* -er); **~teil** *n*: **sich aufs ~ zurückziehen** withdraw from active life; **~wohn·heim** *n* retirement home
Al·ter ['altɐ] *n* (-s; -) a) age; b) (old) age; c) seniority; **er ist in m-m ~** he's (about) my age; **im ~ von 20 Jahren** at the age of twenty; **darf ich Sie nach Ihrem ~ fragen?** may I ask how old you are?; **mittleren ~s, von mittlerem ~** middle-aged; **im besten ~** in the prime of life; **im hohen ~** at a ripe old age; **man sieht ihm sein ~ nicht an** he doesn't look his age; **aus dem ~ müßtest du heraus sein** you should have grown out of that by now; **~ schützt vor Torheit nicht** there's no fool like an old fool
äl·ter ['ɛltɐ] *adj.* older; **der ~e Bruder** her *etc.* elder brother; **ein ~er Herr** an elderly gentleman; **Breughel der 2e (d.Ä.)** Breughel the Elder
Al·ter ego ['altɐ 'e:go] *n* (-; -) alter ego (*a. fig.*)
'al·ter'fah·ren *adj.* seasoned
al·tern ['altɐn] **I.** *v/i.* (sn) grow old, age, *lit.* advance in years; **II.** *v/t.* (h) ⚙ age
al·ter·na·tiv [altɛrna'ti:f] **I.** *adj.* **1.** alternative; **2.** fringe *group etc.*; **II.** *adv.*: **~ leben** have opted out of society; **2be·we·gung** *f* alternative (*or* fringe) movement
Al·ter·na·ti·ve [altɛrna'ti:və] *f* (-; -n) alternative
Al·ter·na'tiv|kost *f* **1.** biological foods *pl.*; **2.** alternative diet; **~kul,tur** *f* counter-culture, alternative culture; **~sze·ne** *f*: **die ~** alternative society, the fringe
al·ter·nie·ren [altɛr'ni:rən] *v/i.* (h) alternate
al·ters *adv.*: **von ~ her, seit ~** from (*or* since) time immemorial
'al·ters·be·dingt *adj.* senile ...; **es ist ~** it's old age
'Al·ters|be·schwer·den *pl.* aches and pains of old age; **~blöd·sinn** *m* ⚕ senile dementia; **~er·schei·nung** *f* sign of old age; **~fleck** *m* age spot; **~for·scher** *m* gerontologist; **~for·schung** *f* gerontology; **~für·sor·ge** *f* welfare for the elderly; **~ge·nos·se** *m*, **~ge·nos·sin** *f* person of the same age, contemporary; **~gren·ze** *f* **1.** *sport etc.*: age limit; **2.** retirement age; **~grün·de** *pl.*: **aus ~n** on grounds of age; **~grup·pe** *f* age group (*or* bracket); **~heil·kun·de** *f* geriatrics *pl.*; **~heim** *n* old people's home; **2los** *adj.* ageless; **~prä·si,dent** *m* chairman by seniority; **~py·ra,mi·de** *f* population pyramid; **~ren·te** *f* old-age pension; **2schwach** *adj.* **1.** infirm, (old and) frail; **2.** dilapidated *building etc.*; rickety *chair etc.*; shaky *car etc.*; **~schwä·che** *f* debility (of old age); **an ~ sterben** die of old age; **~si·che·rung** *f* provision for one's old age; **man muß anfangen, an die ~ zu denken** you've got to start planning ahead for your old age (*or* retirement); **~sitz** *m*: **wir wollen unseren ~ am Bodensee nehmen** we want to retire to Lake Constance; **er sucht e-n ~** he's looking for a place to retire to; **2spe,zi·fisch** *adj.* age-specific; **~struk,tur** *f* age distribution; **~,un·ter·schied** *m* age difference; **~ver·si·che·rung** *f* old-age insurance; **~ver·sor·gung** *f* old-age pension (scheme); **~werk** *n art*: late work; **~zu·schlag** *m* age bonus
'Al·ter·tum *n* (-s; *no pl.*) antiquity; **al·ter·tü·melnd** ['altɐty:məlnt] *adj.* archaic; **Al·ter·tü·mer** ['altɐty:mɐ] *pl.* antiquities; **al·ter·tüm·lich** ['altɐty:mlɪç] *adj.* ancient; antiquated
'Al·ter·tums|for·scher *m* **1.** arch(a)eologist; **2.** classical scholar; **~for·schung** *f* **1.** arch(a)eology; **2.** study of classical antiquity; **~wert** *m*: **~ haben** have antique value
äl·test ['ɛltəst] *adj.* oldest; eldest; **'Äl·te·ste** *m, f* (-n; -n): **unser ~r (unsere ~)** our eldest son (daughter)
'Äl·te·sten|rat *m* council of elders; **~recht** *n* (right of) primogeniture
'Alt·flö·te *f* alto flute
'alt·ge·wohnt *adj.* (long-)familiar
'Alt·glas *n* used glass, *a.* empty bottles *pl.*; ⚙ cullet; **~con,tai·ner** *m* bottle bank; **~ver·wer·tung** *f* recycling of used glass
'alt·grie·chisch *adj.*, **'Alt·grie·chisch** *n* (-en; *no pl.*) *ling.* Ancient Greek
'alt'her·ge·bracht *adj.* traditional, old
'Alt'her·ren·mann·schaft *f* team of players over thirty(-two), *soccer*: *a.* veterans eleven, F old crocks *pl.*
'alt·hoch·deutsch *adj.*, **'Alt·hoch-**

deutsch *n* (-en; *no pl.*) *ling.* Old High German

Al·tist [al'tɪst] *m* (-en; -en) ♪ male alto; **Al'ti·stin** *f* (-; -nen) contralto

'alt·jüng·fer·lich *adj.* old-maidish

'Alt·klei·der·samm·lung *f* old clothes collection

'alt·klug *adj.* precocious

'Alt·la·sten *pl.* **1.** residual pollution *sg.*; contaminated soil *sg.*; abandoned (*or* disused) waste dump *sg.* (*or* dumps); **2.** *fig.* burden *sg.* (*or* burdens, F sins) of the past; F past sins that come back to haunt one

ält·lich ['ɛltlɪç] *adj.* oldish

'Alt|ma·te·ri̦al *n* scrap (material); **~mei·ster** *m* (past) master; *sport*: ex-champion; **~me̦tall** *n* scrap metal

'alt·mo·disch *adj.* old-fashioned

'Alt·öl *n* used oil

'Alt·pa̦pier *n* waste paper; ***aus ~*** made of recycled paper; **~con̦tai·ner** *m* paper bank; **~samm·lung** *f* (news)paper collection; **~ver·wer·tung** *f* waste-paper recycling

'Alt·phi·lo̦lo·ge *m* classicist; **'Alt·phi·lo·lo̦gie** *f* (the) classics *pl.*

'Alt|rei·fen *m* used tyre (*Am.* tire); **≈ro·sa** *adj.*, **~ro·sa** *n* dusky pink; **~schlüs·sel** *m* ♪ alto clef; **~schnee** *m* old snow

'alt·sprach·lich *adj.* classical

'Alt·stadt *f* old part of town; *n.s.* medi(a)eval cent|re (*Am.* -er); **~er·neue·rung** *f*, **~sa̦nie·rung** *f* urban renewal

'Alt·stim·me *f* ♪ alto (voice)

'alt|te·sta·men̦ta·risch *adj.* Old Testament ...; **~vä·ter·lich** *adj.* patriarchal

'Alt·wa·ren·händ·ler *m* junk dealer

Alt'wei·ber|ge·schwätz *n* silly gossip, F twaddle; **~mär·chen** *n* fairytale; **~som·mer** *m* **1.** Indian summer; **2.** gossamer

Alu|-Fel·gen ['a:lu-] *pl.* alloy wheels; **~fo·lie** *f* tin foil; **~kof·fer** *m* alumin(i)um case

Alu·mi·ni·um [alu'mi:nĭʊm] *n* (-s; *no pl.*) alumin(i)um

Alz·hei·mer-Krank·heit ['altshaımɐ-] *f*: ***die ~*** Alzheimer's disease

am (***an dem***) → ***an***

Amal·gam [amal'ga:m] *n* (-s; -e) ⚗ *and fig.* amalgam; **~fül·lung** *f* amalgam filling

amal·ga·mie·ren [amalga'mi:rən] *v/t.* (h) amalgamate

Ama·ryl·lis [ama'rʏlɪs] *f* (-; -ryllen [-'rʏlən]) ⚘ amaryllis

Ama·teur [ama'tø:ɐ] *m* (-s; -e), **~...** *in cpds.* amateur; **~be·stim·mun·gen** *pl.* amateur rules; **~funk** *m* amateur radio; **~fun·ker** *m* radio ham

ama'teur·haft *adj.* amateurish

Ama·zo·ne [ama'tso:nə] *f* (-; -n) Amazon; *fig.* amazon

Am·bi·en·te [am'bĭentə] *n* (-; *no pl.*) ambience; atmosphere

Am·bi·ti·on [ambi'tsĭo:n] *f* (-; -en) ambition; ***~en haben auf*** *acc.* have set one's sights on s.th.; **am·bi·tio·niert** [ambitsĭo'ni:ɐt] *adj.* ambitious

am·bi·va·lent [ambiva'lɛnt] *adj.* ambivalent; **Am·bi·va·lenz** [ambiva'lɛnts] *f* (-; -en) ambivalence

Am·boß ['ambɔs] *m* (-sses; -sse) anvil; *anat. a.* incus

am·bu·lant [ambu'lant] **I.** *adj.* outpatient ...; **II.** *adv.*: ***~ behandelt werden*** get outpatient treatment; ***~ behandelter Patient*** outpatient; **Am·bu·lanz** [ambu'lants] *f* (-; -en) outpatients' department; casualty ward; ambulance

Amei·se ['a:maızə] *f* (-; -n) ant

'Amei·sen|bär *m* anteater; **~hau·fen** *m* anthill; **~säu·re** *f* formic acid; **~staat** *m* ant colony; **~stra·ße** *f* ant's trail

Amen ['a:mən] **I.** *n* (-s; -) amen; ***so sicher wie das ~ in der Kirche*** F as sure as hell; **II.** ≈ *int.* amen; ***zu allem ja und ~ sagen*** say yes to everything

Ame·ri·ka·ner [ameri'ka:nɐ] *m* (-s; -), **Ame·ri·ka·ne·rin** [ameri'ka:nərın] *f* (-; -nen), **ame·ri·ka·nisch** [ameri'ka:nıʃ] *adj.* American; **Ame·ri'ka·nisch** *n* (-en) *ling.* American (English); **Ame·ri·ka·nis·mus** [amerika'nısmʊs] *m* (-; -men) *ling.* Americanism; **Ame·ri·ka·ni·stik** [amerika'nıstık] (-; *no pl.*) *f* (North) American studies *pl.*

Ame·thyst [ame'tʏst] *m* (-[e]s; -e) *min.* amethyst

Ami ['ami] F *m* (-[s]; -[s]) F Yank

Ami·no·säu·re [a'mi:no-] *f* ⚗ amino acid

Ami·sche ['a:mıʃə] *pl.* *the* Amish

Am·me ['amə] *f* (-; -n) (*n.s.* wet) nurse; *zo.* nurse; **'Am·men·mär·chen** *n* fairytale

Am·mer ['amɐ] *f* (-; -n) *zo.* bunting

Am·mo·ni·ak [amo'nĭak] *n* (-s; *no pl.*) ⚗ ammonia; **≈hal·tig** *adj.* ammoniac; **~lö·sung** *f* ammonia solution; **~was·ser** *n* ammonia water

Am·mo·nit [amo'ni:t] *m* (-en; -en) *zo.* ammonite

Am·mo·ni·um [a'mo:nĭʊm] *n* (-s; *no pl.*) ⚗ ammonium

Am·ne·sie [amne'zi:] *f* (-; -n) ⚕ amnesia

Am·ne·stie [amnɛs'ti:] *f* (-; -n) amnesty; ***e-e ~ erlassen*** declare an amnesty; **am·ne·stie·ren** [amnɛs'ti:rən] *v/t.* (h) grant an amnesty to

Amö·be [a'mø:bə] *f* (-; -n) am(o)eba; **Amö·ben·ruhr** [a'mø:bən-] *f* ⚕ am(o)ebic dysentery

Amok ['a:mɔk] *m*: ***~ laufen*** run amok; **~fah·rer** *m* maniac driver; motorway maniac; ***ein ~ raste in e-e Menschenmenge hinein*** a car driver went berserk and ploughed (*Am.* plowed) into a crowd of people; **~läu·fer** *m* runner amok; **~schüt·ze** *m* mad (*or* crazed) gunman; ***der ~ schoß in e-e Menschenmenge hinein*** the gunman fired wildly (*or* indiscriminately) into a crowd of people

Amor ['a:mɔɐ] *m* (-s; *no pl.*) *myth.* Cupid

'amo̦ra·lisch *adj.* amoral

amorph [a'mɔrf] *adj.* amorphous

Amor·ti·sa·ti·on [amɔrtiza'tsĭo:n] *f* (-; -en) amortization, repayment; redemption *of loan*; **amor·ti·sie·ren** [amɔrti'zi:rən] (h) **I.** *v/t.* amortize, pay off; redeem *loan*; **II.** *v/refl.*: ***sich ~*** amortize, pay itself off

amou·rös [amu'rø:s] *adj.* amorous; *iro.* ***ein ~es Abenteuer*** a little affair

Am·pel ['ampəl] *f* (-; -n) **1.** traffic lights *pl.*, *Am. a.* traffic light, stoplight; ***fahren Sie bei der ersten ~ rechts*** turn right at the first set of traffic lights (*Am.* at the first traffic light *or* stoplight); **2.** hanging lamp; **~an·la·ge** *f* (set of) traffic lights *pl.*, *Am.* traffic light, stoplight

Am·pere [am'pe:ɐ] *n* (-[s]; -) ⚡ ampere, amp; **~me·ter** *n* (-s; -) ammeter; **~stun·de** *f* ampere-hour

Amp·fer ['ampfɐ] *m* (-s; -) ⚘ sorrel

Am·phet·amin [amfeta'mi:n] *n* (-s; -e) amphetamine

Am·phi·bie [am'fi:bĭə] *f* (-; -n) *zo.* amphibian; **Am'phi·bien...** *in cpds.* ⚙ amphibian *plane, tank etc.*; **am·phi·bisch** [am'fi:bıʃ] *adj. zo.* amphibious, *a.* ⚙ amphibian

Am·phi·the̦a·ter [am'fi:-] *n* amphitheat|re (*Am. a.* -er); arena

Am·pho·re [am'fo:rə] *f* (-; -n) amphora

Am·pli·tu·de [ampli'tu:də] *f* (-; -n) amplitude; **Am·pli'tu·den·mo·du·la·ti̦on** *f* amplitude modulation

Am·pul·le [am'pʊlə] *f* (-; -n) ampulla (*a. anat.*); *pharm.* ampoule

Am·pu·ta·ti·on [amputa'tsĭo:n] *f* (-; -en) ⚕ amputation; **am·pu·tie·ren** [ampu'ti:rən] *v/t.* (h) amputate; **Am·pu'tier·te** *m, f* (-n; -n) amputee

Am·sel ['amzəl] *f* (-; -n) blackbird

Amt [amt] *n* (-[e]s; Ämter ['ɛmtɐ]) office, department; post; (official) duty, function; *teleph.* exchange; *eccl.* service, *R.C.* mass; ***von ~s wegen*** officially; ***kraft m-s ~es*** by virtue of my office; ***s-s ~es walten*** carry out one's duties; F ***walte d-s ~es!*** do your duty; ***das ist nicht mein ~*** that's not my responsibility; → ***antreten*** 4, ***bekleiden*** 2, ***entheben***

am·tie·ren [am'ti:rən] *v/i.* (h) hold office; *eccl. and fig.* officiate; ***als Vizepräsident*** *etc.* ~ be acting vice-president *etc.*; **am'tie·rend** *adj.* incumbent; acting; F ***~er Meister*** reigning champion(s)

'amt·lich *adj.* official (*a.* F *fig.*)

'Amt·mann *m* (-[e]s; -männer, -leute) **1.** senior clerk (*in the middle grade of the German civil service*); **2.** *hist.* bailiff

'Amts|an·ma·ßung *f* (unlawful) assumption of authority; **~an·tritt** *m* assumption of office; **~an·walt** *m* public prosecutor; **~arzt** *m* public health officer; **~be·fug·nis** *f* (official) authority; **~be·reich** *m* jurisdiction, competence; **~blatt** *n* official gazette; **~dau·er** *f* term of office; **~de̦likt** *n* malpractice (in office); **~deutsch** *n* officialese; **~eid** *m* oath of office; ***den ~ ablegen*** be sworn in; **~ein·füh·rung** *f* inauguration (into office); **~ent·he·bung** *f* removal from office, dismissal; **~füh·rung** *f* administration (of office); **~ge·heim·nis** *n* **1.** official secret; **2.** official secrecy; **~ge·richt** *n* district court; **~ge·schäf·te** *pl.* official business *sg.*; **~ge·walt** *f* authority; **~hand·lung** *f* official act; ***e-e ~ ausführen*** perform an official function (*or* duty); **~hil·fe** *f* support (*or* cooperation) through official channels; ***um ~ bitten*** request official support (*or* cooperation); **~in·ha·ber** *m* holder of an (*or* the) office, incumbent; **~ket·te** *f* chain of office; **~kir·che** *f* church hierarchy; **~kol̦le·ge** *m* **1.** colleague; **2.** *pol.* opposite number, counterpart; **~̦miß·brauch** *m* abuse of office (*or* authority)

'amts·mü·de *adj.* weary of office

'Amts|nie·der·le·gung *f* resignation; **~pe·ri̦o·de** *f* term of office; **~rich·ter** *m* district court judge; **~schim·mel** *m* red tape; ***der ~ wiehert*** it's red tape all the way; **~sitz** *m* **1.** official residence; **2.** office(s *pl.*); **~spra·che** *f* official language; *contp.* officialese; **~stun·den** *pl.* office hours; **~tracht** *f* official dress (*or* robes *pl.*); **~trä·ger** *m* office-bearer; **~un·ter̦schla·gung** *f* peculation; **~ver·ge·hen** *n* misconduct; malfeasance (in office); **~ver·schwie·gen·heit** *f* professional discretion; **~vor·gän·ger** *m* pre-

decessor (in office); **~vor·mund** *m* official guardian; **~vor·stand** *m*, **~vor·steher** *m* head of an office; **~weg** *m*: ***den ~ gehen*** go through the official channels; **~zei·chen** *n teleph.* dialling (*Am.* dial) tone; **~zeit** *f* term of office; term in office; ***nach dreijähriger ~*** after three years in office
Amu·lett [amu'lɛt] *n* (-[e]s; -e) amulet, charm
amü·sant [amy'zant] *adj.* entertaining; amusing
amü·sie·ren [amy'zi:rən] (h) **I.** *v/t.* entertain; amuse; ***die Bemerkung amüsierte ihn*** he was amused by the remark; **II.** *v/refl.*: ***sich ~*** a) amuse o.s., b) enjoy o.s., have fun, have a good time; ***sich ~ über*** *acc.* a) be amused at, b) make fun of
Amü'sier·vier·tel *n* nightclub district; red-light district
'amu·sisch *adj.*: ***~ sein*** have no appreciation for the arts (*or* no artistic sensitivity)
an [an] **I.** *prp.* **1.** on; ***am 1. März*** on March 1st; ***am Abend (Morgen)*** in the evening (morning); ***am Tage*** during the day; ***am Tage*** *gen.* on the day of; **2.** at; on; ***am (ans) Fenster*** at (to) the window; ***~ der Grenze*** at the border; *fig.* → ***Grenze; am Himmel*** in the sky; ***~ e-m Ort*** in a place; ***~ e-r Schule (e-m Theater)*** at a school (theat|re [*Am. a.* -er]); ***~ der Themse*** on the Thames; ***~ der Wand*** against (*or* on) the wall; **3.** by, next to; near; ***am Kamin (Tisch) sitzen*** sit by the fire (at the table); ***am Wald*** by the woods; **4.** ***ein Brief ~ mich*** a letter for me; ***Schaden am Dach*** damage to the roof; ***arbeiten ~*** *dat.* work on; ***denken ~*** *acc.* think of; ***sterben ~*** *dat.* die of; ***~ sich*** as such, per se; *a solution etc.* in itself; ***~ und für sich*** properly speaking; ***arm (reich) ~*** *dat.* poor (rich) in; ***er war am schnellsten*** *etc.* he was the fastest *etc.*; ***was gefällt dir ~ ihm nicht?*** what don't you like about him?; ***er ist am Lesen*** he's reading; → ***glauben*** II, ***Leben, leiden*** I, ***Reihe***; **II.** *adv.* **5.** ***von ... ~*** from ... (on[wards]); ***von nun ~*** from now on; **6.** ***London ~ 19.05*** arr. (= arrival) London 19.05; **7.** ***das Gas ist ~*** the gas is on; ***~ - aus*** on - off; **8.** ***~ die 50 Leute*** about (*or* roughly) 50 people
Ana·bo·li·ka [ana'bo:lika] *pl.* anabolic steroids
Ana·chro·nis·mus [anakro'nɪsmʊs] *m* (-; -men) anachronism; **ana·chro·ni·stisch** [anakro'nɪstɪʃ] *adj.* anachronistic
an·ae·rob [anˀae'ro:p] *adj. biol.* anaerobic
Ana·gramm [ana'gram] *n* (-s; -e) anagram
Ana·kon·da [ana'kɔnda] *f* (-; -s) anaconda
anal [a'na:l] *adj.*, **Anal...** *in cpds.* anal
ana·lep·tisch [ana'lɛptɪʃ] *adj.* analeptic
An·al·ge·ti·kum [anˀal'ge:tikʊm] *n* (-s; -ka [-ka]) *pharm.* analgesic
ana·log [ana'lo:k] **I.** *adj.* analogous (*dat.* to); **II.** *adv.* by analogy (**zu** with); **Ana'log·auf·zeich·nung** *f a. computer*: analog(ue) recording; **Ana·lo·gie** [analo'gi:] *f* (-; -n) analogy; **Ana'log·rech·ner** *m* analog(ue) computer
An·al·pha·bet [anˀalfa'be:t] *m* (-en; -en) illiterate (person); **An·al·pha'be·ten·tum** *n* (-s; *no pl.*), **An·al·pha·be·tis·mus** [anˀalfabe'tɪsmʊs] *m* (-; *no pl.*) illiteracy
Anal|pha·se [a'na:l-] *f psych.* anal stage; **~ver·kehr** *m* anal intercourse, *formal*: buggery, sodomy
Ana·ly·sa·tor [analy'za:toɐ] *m* (-s; -en [-za'to:rən]) *phys., computer*: analy|zer (*Brit.* -ser); **Ana·ly·se** [ana'ly:zə] *f* (-; -n) analysis; **ana·ly·sie·ren** [analy'zi:rən] *v/t.* (h) analy|se (*Brit.* -ze); **Ana·ly·sis** [a'na:lyzɪs] *f* (-; *no pl.*) ⅍ analysis; **Ana·ly·tiker** [ana'ly:tikɐ] *m* (-s; -) analyst; **ana·ly·tisch** [ana'ly:tɪʃ] **I.** *adj.* analytical; **II.** *adv.* analytically; ***~ gesehen*** analytically speaking; ***sie denkt sehr ~*** she's got a very analytical mind
An·ämie [anɛ'mi:] *f* (-; -n) ⚕ an(a)emia; **an·ämisch** [a'nɛ:mɪʃ] *adj.* an(a)emic
Ana·mne·se [anam'ne:zə] *f* (-; -n) ⚕ case (*or* medical) history
Ana·nas ['ananas] *f* (-; -[se]) pineapple; **~schei·be** *f* pineapple slice; **~stück** *n* pineapple chunk
Ana·pher [a'nafɐ] *f* (-; -n) anaphora
An·ar·chie [anar'çi:] *f* (-; -n) anarchy; **An·ar·chis·mus** [anar'çɪsmʊs] *m* (-; *no pl.*) anarchism; **An·ar·chist** [anar'çɪst] *m* (-en; -en), **an·ar·chi·stisch** [anar'çɪstɪʃ] *adj.* anarchist; **An·ar·cho-Sze·ne** [a'narço-] *f* young radicals *pl.*
An·äs·the·sie [anˀɛste'zi:] *f* (-; -n) an(a)esthesia; **an·äs·the·sie·ren** [anˀɛste'zi:rən] *v/t.* (h) an(a)esthetize; **An·äs·the·sist** [anˀɛste'zɪst] *m* (-en; -en) anaesthetist, *Am.* anesthesiologist
Ana·tom [ana'to:m] *m* (-en; -en) anatomist; **Ana·to·mie** [anato'mi:] *f* (-; -n) **1.** *no pl.* anatomy; **2.** institute of anatomy; **Ana·to'mie·saal** *m* dissecting room; **ana·to·misch** [ana'to:mɪʃ] *adj.* anatomical
'an·bah·nen (*sep.*, h) **I.** *v/t.* pave the way for, prepare the ground for; initiate *talks*; **II.** *v/refl.*: ***sich ~*** be in the offing, be coming, be on the way; ***zwischen ihnen scheint sich e-e Freundschaft anzubahnen*** it looks like the beginning of a friendship
an·bän·deln ['anbɛndəln] F *v/i.* (*sep.*, h): ***mit j-m ~*** try to get friendly with s.o.
'An·bau *m* (-[e]s; -ten) **1.** *no pl.* ⚘ cultivation; **2.** ⚠ annex(e), extension; **'an·bau·en** (*sep.*, h) **I.** *v/t.* **1.** ⚘ grow; **2.** ⚠ add (**an** *acc.* to); ⚙ attach; **II.** *v/i.* build an extension; ***wir haben angebaut*** *a.* we've extended the house *etc.*
'an·bau·fä·hig *adj.* **1.** ⚘ arable; **2.** ⚠ suitable for extension
'An·bau|flä·che *f* **1.** (arable) acreage; **2.** area under cultivation; **~kü·che** *f* fitted kitchen; **~mö·bel** *pl.* sectional (*or* unit, modular) furniture *sg.*; **~schrank** *m* cupboard unit; **~wand** *f* wall unit
'An·be·ginn *m*: ***von ~*** from the very start
'an·be·hal·ten *v/t.* (*irr.*, *sep.*, h, → ***behalten***) keep on
an'bei *adv.*: ☤ ***~ (senden wir Ihnen)*** enclosed please find
'an·bei·ßen (*irr.*, *sep.*, h, → ***beißen***) **I.** *v/t.* bite into; **II.** *v/i.* bite; *a. fig.* take the bait; F ***du siehst ja zum ♀ aus*** I could eat you up
'an·be·lan·gen *v/t.* (h): ***was das anbelangt*** as far as that is concerned
'an·bel·len *v/t.* (*sep.*, h) bark at (*a. fig.*)
an·be·rau·men ['anbəraʊmən] *v/t.* (*sep.*, h) fix; call *meeting*; ***e-n Termin ~ für*** fix a date for
'an·be·ten *v/t.* (*sep.*, h) worship; *fig. a.* adore, idolize; → ***angebetet, Angebetete***; **'An·be·ter** *m* (-s; -) worship(p)er; *fig.* admirer
'An·be·tracht *m*: ***in ~*** *gen.* considering, taking ... into consideration
'an·be·tref·fen *v/t.* (*irr.*, *sep.*, h, → ***betreffen***): ***was ... anbetrifft*** in terms of ..., as far as ... is (*or* are) concerned
'an·bet·teln *v/t.* (*sep.*, h): ***j-n ~*** beg from s.o.; ***j-n um et. ~*** beg for s.th. from s.o.; ***da wird man ständig von Kindern angebettelt*** you have children coming up to you all the time begging for things (*or* money *etc.*)
'An·be·tung *f* (-; *no pl.*) worship; *fig.* devotion; **'an·be·tungs·wür·dig** *fig. adj.* adorable
an·bie·dern ['anbi:dɐn] *v/refl.* (*sep.*, h): ***sich (bei) j-m ~*** F toady to s.o
'an·bie·ten (*irr.*, *sep.*, h, → ***bieten***) **I.** *v/t.* offer; ***angeboten werden*** *a.* be on offer; ***j-m et. ~*** offer s.o. s.th.; ***s-n Rücktritt ~*** offer to resign, tender one's resignation; **II.** *v/refl.*: ***sich ~*** offer one's services; *opportunity etc.*: present itself; *solution etc.*: suggest itself; ***sich ~ für*** lend itself to; ***es bietet sich doch an zu*** *inf.* the obvious thing (to do) would be to *inf.*; ***es bietet sich als Beispiel an*** it's an obvious example; ***der Raum bietet sich direkt an*** it's the ideal room
'an·bin·den *v/t.* (*irr.*, *sep.*, h, → ***binden***) tie up, fasten (**an** *dat. or acc.* to); moor; put *dog* on a (*or* the) leash; → ***angebunden*** II
'an·bla·sen *v/t.* (*irr.*, *sep.*, h, → ***blasen***) **1.** blow at; **2.** F yell at, blow *s.o.* up
'an·blen·den *v/t.* (*sep.*, h): ***j-n mit der Taschenlampe ~*** shine one's torch on s.o. (*or* into s.o.'s face)
'An·blick *m* (-[e]s; -e) sight; ***beim ersten ~*** at first sight; ***beim ~ der Wunde*** *wurde mir schlecht*: when I saw the wound; ***ein trauriger ~*** a sorry sight; **'an·blicken** (*sep.* -k·k-) *v/t.* (*sep.*, h) look at; glance at
'an·blin·ken *v/t.* (*sep.*, h) *mot.* flash one's lights at
'an·blin·zeln *v/t.* (*sep.*, h) blink at; wink at
'an·boh·ren *v/t.* (*sep.*, h) ⚙ bore, spot-drill; (drill) open; F *fig.* ***j-n ~*** sound s.o. out (**ob** as to whether)
'an·bran·den *v/i.* (*sep.*, sn) surge (***gegen*** against)
'an·bra·ten *v/t.* (*irr.*, *sep.*, h, → ***braten***) sear, brown
'an·bräu·nen *v/t.* (*sep.*, h) **1.** *gastr.* brown; **2.** → ***angebräunt*** II
'an·brau·sen F *v/i.* (*sep.*, sn) (*a.* ***angebraust kommen***) F come roaring up
'an·bre·chen (*irr.*, *sep.*, → ***brechen***) **I.** *v/t.* (h) **1.** break into *supplies etc.*; start on, open; → ***angebrochen*** II; **2.** fracture; **II.** *v/i.* (sn) begin; *day, a. fig. epoch etc.*: dawn; *night*: fall
'an·bren·nen (*irr.*, *sep.*, → ***brennen***) **I.** *v/i.* (sn) catch fire, (start to) burn; *gastr.* (*a.* ***~ lassen***) burn, scorch *milk etc.*; F *fig.* ***nichts ~ lassen*** not to miss a thing; → ***angebrannt*** II; **II.** *v/t.* (h) kindle, burn; light *cigar etc.*
'an·brin·gen *v/t.* (*irr.*, *sep.*, h, → ***bringen***) **1.** bring; **2.** fix, fasten, ⚙ attach (**an** *dat.* to); instal(l); put up *sign etc.*; **3.** ☤ sell; **4.** present, mention; get in *a word, remark etc.*; display, show off *one's knowledge etc.*; make *a request etc.*, carry out; ***e-e Beschwerde ~*** lodge a complaint

'An·bruch *m* (-[e]s; *no pl.*) **1.** (**bei**) **~ des Tages** (at) daybreak; (**bei**) **~ der Nacht** (at) nightfall; **2.** *fig.* dawning *of a new age*
'an·brül·len *v/t.* (*sep.*, h) scream at, yell at
An·cho·vis [an'ço:vɪs] *f* (-; -) anchovy
An·dacht ['andaxt] *f* (-; -en) **1.** devotion; **2.** *eccl.* devotions *pl.*; (short) service; **mit ~** *a. iro.* reverently; **an·däch·tig** ['andɛçtɪç] *adj.* devout, pious; *fig.* absorbed, rapt
An·dan·te [an'dantə] *n* (-[s]; -s), **an'dan·te** *adv.* ♪ andante
'an·dau·ern *v/i.* (*sep.*, h) continue, go on; last; persist; **der Regen dauert an** it's still raining, *meteor.* it will continue to rain; **das schlechte Wetter dauert an** there's no end of the bad weather in sight; **'an·dau·ernd** *adj.* continual; continuing; continuous, incessant; persistent
'An·den·ken *n* (-s; -) **1.** *no pl.* memory (**an** *acc.* of); **zum ~ an** in memory (*or* remembrance) of; **2.** keepsake, souvenir (**an** *acc.* of); **~la·den** *m* souvenir shop
an·der ['andɐ] **I.** *adj.* other; different; next; opposite; **am ~en Tag** the next day; **die ~en Bücher** the rest of the books; **ich hab' ganz ~e Probleme** I haven't got time to worry about things like that; → **Ansicht** 4, **Geschlecht; II.** *indef. pron.*: **ein ~er, eine ~e** someone else; **die ~en** the others; **kein ~er als** nobody but, no less than; **der eine oder ~e** someone or other, one or the other; **noch viele ~e** many (*or* plenty) more; **~es, andres** other things; **alles ~e** everything else; **alles ~e als** anything but, far from; **unter ~em** among other things; **eins nach dem ~en!** one thing after another; **es kommt eins zum ~en** it's just one thing after another; **es kam eins zum ~en** one thing led to another; **ein Tag wie jeder ~e** a perfectly ordinary day; **der eine sagt dies, der ~e sagt das** you get a different version every time; **von denen ist einer wie der ~e** they're all much of a muchness, *contp.* they're as bad as each other; **das ist was ganz ~es** that's a completely different matter; → **anders, Wort**
an·de·rer·seits ['andərɐ'zaɪts] *adv.* on the other hand
'an·der·mal *adv.*: **ein ~** some other time
än·dern ['ɛndɐn] (h) **I.** *v/t.* change, alter *a. dress etc.*; vary; **ich kann es nicht ~** I can't help it; **das ist nicht zu ~** that can't be helped; **es ändert nichts an der Tatsache, daß** it doesn't alter the fact that; **II.** *v/refl.*: **sich ~** change; vary; *wind*: shift; **sich zum Vorteil** (**Nachteil**) **~** change for the better (worse)
'an·dern'falls *adv.* otherwise
an·ders ['andɐs] **I.** *pred. adj. and adv.* different(ly *adv.*); **~ werden** change; **sie ist ~ als ihre Schwester** she's not like her sister; **~ als s-e Freunde** *treibt er keinen Sport*: unlike his friends; **er denkt ~ als wir** he doesn't see it the same way as us; **~ ausgedrückt** to put it another way; **ich kann nicht ~** a) I can't help it, b) I've got no choice; **es kam ganz ~** things turned out very differently; **ich hab's mir ~ überlegt** I've changed my mind, I've decided not to; **~ Herr X** not so Mr X; **das klingt schon ~!** that's more like it; **Urlaub mal ~** a holiday (*or* holidays) with a difference; → **überlegen¹; II.** *adv.* else; **jemand ~** somebody (*or* anybody) else; **niemand ~** nobody else; **niemand ~ als er** nobody but him; **wer ~** (**als er**)**?** who else (but him)?; **irgendwo ~** somewhere else, F some other place; **nirgendwo ~** nowhere else; **nirgendwo ~ als** nowhere but, no place other than; **wo ~** (**als dort**)**?** where else (but there)?; **~ar·tig** *adj.* different; **~den·kend** *adj.* of a different way of thinking; *pol.* dissenting; **≈den·ken·de** *m, f* (-n; -n) *pol.* dissenter; **~far·big** *adj.* of a different colo(u)r; **~ge·ar·tet** *adj.* different; of a different nature; **~ge·sinnt** *adj.* → **andersdenkend; ~her'um I.** *adv.* the other way round; **II.** F *adj.*: **er ist ~** he's gay, F he's one of them; **~lau·tend** *adj.* different, differing; **~e Berichte** reports to the contrary; **~spra·chig** [-ʃpra:xɪç] *adj.* foreign-language *texts etc.*; **~wo** *adv.* somewhere else, elsewhere; **~wo'her** *adv.* from somewhere else; **~wo'hin** *adv.* somewhere else
an·dert·halb ['andɐt'halp] *adj.* one and a half; **~ Pfund** a pound and a half (of); **~fach** *adj.* one and a half times; **~mal** *adv.* one and a half times; **~ soviel** half as much again
Än·de·rung ['ɛndərʊŋ] *f* (-; -en) change; alteration; modification; **e-e ~ vornehmen** (**erfahren**) make (undergo) a change; **~en vorbehalten** subject to alteration
'Än·de·rungs|an·trag *m parl.* amendment; **~ge·setz** *n* amending law; **~vor·schlag** *m*: **e-n ~ machen** suggest a change; **s-e Änderungsvorschläge wurden akzeptiert** the changes he suggested (*or* proposed) were accepted
an·der·wei·tig ['andɐvaɪtɪç] **I.** *adj.* other, further; **wegen ~er Verpflichtungen** due to prior engagements (*or* commitments); **II.** *adv.* a) otherwise; b) elsewhere; **die Stelle wurde ~ vergeben** the job went (*or* was given) to someone else
'an·deu·ten (*sep.*, h) **I.** *v/t.* hint, intimate, give to understand; *b.s.* insinuate (*all* **daß** that); indicate; *art*: suggest; → **angedeutet** II; **II.** *v/refl.*: **sich ~** be on the way; **es deuten sich Änderungen an** there are changes in the air, changes seem to be on the way; **'An·deu·tung** *f* (-; -en) suggestion, hint (**auf** *acc.* of) (*both a. fig.*); *b.s.* insinuation; indication; *art*: suggestion; **e-e ~ machen** drop a hint; **in ~en reden** beat about (*or* around) the bush; **'an·deu·tungs·wei·se** *adv.* allusively; **et. ~ mitteilen** hint at s.th.; **man sieht ~ ein Haus dahinter** you can just (about) make out a house behind it
'an·dich·ten *v/t.* (*sep*, h): **j-m et. ~** impute s.th. to s.o.
'an·dicken (*sep.* -k·k-) *v/t.* (*sep.*, h) *gastr.* thicken
'an·dis·ku'tie·ren *v/t.* (*sep.*, h) broach *a subject*
'an·docken (*sep.* -k·k-) *v/t. and v/i.* (*sep.*, h) *space travel*: dock
'an·don·nern F *fig. v/t.* (*sep.*, h) roar at
An·dor·ra·ner [andɔ'ra:nɐ] *m* (-s; -), **An·dor·ra·ne·rin** [andɔ'ra:nərɪn] *f* (-; -nen), **an·dor·ra·nisch** [andɔ'ra:nɪʃ] *adj.* Andorran
An·drang ['andraŋ] *m* (-[e]s; *no pl.*) crush; rush (*a.* ⚕ *of blood*); † run (**auf** *acc.* on)
An·dre·as·kreuz [an'dre:as-] *n*: (*a.* **das ~**) St Andrew's Cross
'an·dre·hen *v/t.* (*sep.*, h) turn on *gas etc.*; ⚡ *a.* switch on; tighten *screw etc.*; F **j-m et. ~** palm (*or* fob) s.th. off on s.o., land s.o. with s.th., pass s.th. on to s.o.; **wer hat dir denn diese Stiefel angedreht?** who talked you into (buying) those boots?
An·dro·gen [andro'ge:n] *n* (-s; -e) androgen
an·dro·gyn [andro'gy:n] *adj.* androgynous
'an·dro·hen *v/t.* (*sep.*, h): **j-m et. ~** threaten s.o. with s.th.; **'An·dro·hung** *f* (-; -en) threat; ⚖ **unter ~ von** (*or gen.*) under penalty of
'An·druck *m* (-[e]s; -e) *typ.* proof; **'an·drucken** (*sep.* -k·k-) *v/i.* (*sep.*, h) **1.** (pull a) proof; **2.** start printing
'an·drücken (*sep.* -k·k-) (*sep.*, h) **I.** *v/t.* press (on); **II.** *v/refl.*: **sich** (**fest**) **~ an** *acc.* press (hard) against, cling (*or* hold on) (tightly) to *s.o.*
'an·du·deln F *v/t.* (*sep.*, h): **sich einen ~** F get merry (*or* tiddly); **er hat sich einen angedudelt** F he's had one too many
'an·dün·sten *v/t.* (*sep.*, h) *gastr.* steam
'an·ecken ['anʔɛkən] (*sep.* -k·k-) F *v/i.* (*sep.*, sn): **bei j-m** (**überall**) **~** F rub s.o. (everyone) up the wrong way; **wegen s-r Offenheit** (**Kleidung**) **ist er bei den Kollegen angeeckt** his colleagues didn't take to his openness (to the way he dressed)
'an·eig·nen *v/t.* (*sep.*, h): **sich ~** a) acquire, appropriate; b) learn, acquire *knowledge etc.*, develop *style etc.*, *a.* pick up *habit etc.*; c) misappropriate; **er hat sich die dänische Sprache angeeignet** he learnt (how to speak) Danish; **'An·eig·nung** *f* (-; -en) acquisition; (mis)appropriation; development; learning (**e-r Sprache** a language)
an·ein'an·der *adv.* (to, of *etc.*) each other; *fig.* **~ hängen** be very attached to each other; → **vorbeireden; ~bin·den** *v/t.* (*irr.*, *sep.*, h, → **binden**) tie together; **~fü·gen** *v/t.* (*sep.*, h) join (together); **~ge·ra·ten** *v/i.* (*irr.*, *sep.*, sn, → **geraten**) clash; come to blows; **~gren·zen** *v/i.* (*sep.*, h) border on each other; **~klam·mern** *v/refl.* (*sep.*, h): **sich ~** cling to each other; **~pral·len** *v/i.* (*sep.*, sn) collide (with each other); **~rei·hen** *v/t.* (*sep.*, h) line up; *fig.* string together; **~rücken** (*sep.* -k·k-) *v/t.* (*sep.*, h) *and v/i.* (*sep.*, sn) move closer together; **~schmie·gen** *v/refl.* (*sep.*, h): **sich ~** huddle together; **~sto·ßen** *v/i.* (*irr.*, *sep.*, sn, → **stoßen**) collide; → **aneinandergrenzen**
An·ek·do·te [anɛk'do:tə] *f* (-; -n) anecdote; **an·ek'do·ten·haft** *adj.* anecdotal
'an·ekeln *v/t.* (*sep.*, h): **j-n ~** *food, smell etc.*: make s.o. feel sick, nauseate s.o., *fig. behavio(u)r etc.*: make s.o. sick, revolt s.o., F turn s.o. off
Ane·mo·ne [ane'mo:nə] *f* (-; -n) anemone
'An·er·bie·ten *n* (-s; -) offer, tender
'an·er·kannt *adj.* recognized; accepted; **~e Tatsache** established fact; **ein international ~er Schriftsteller** *etc.* an internationally recognized writer *etc.*, a writer *etc.* of international repute (*or* standing); → **staatlich** II; **'an·er·kann·ter'ma·ßen** *adv.*: **er ist ~ ...** he is acknowledged to be ...
'an·er·ken·nen *v/t.* (*irr.*, *sep.*, h, → **erkennen**) acknowledge, *a. pol.* recognize

(**als** as); accept; approve; allow *claim etc.*; admit *guilt etc.*; ✝ hono(u)r, accept *bill of exchange*; **nicht ~** refuse to recognize, **als** (*or* **für**) **das Seinige:** disown (*a. a child*); (**nicht**) **~** (dis)allow *goal*; → **anerkannt** II; **'an·er·ken·nend I.** *adj.* appreciative; **~e Worte** words of appreciation (*or* praise); **II.** *adv.*: **sich ~ äußern über** *acc.* praise; **er hat sich darüber überhaupt nicht ~ geäußert** he didn't have a positive word to say about it; **'an·er·ken·nens·wert** *adj.* laudable, commendable; **'An·er·ken·nung** *f* (-; -en) acknowledg(e)ment, *a. pol.* recognition; ⚖ legitimation; legalization; ✝ acceptance; **~ finden** win recognition; **~ verdienen** deserve credit; **in ~** *gen.* in recognition of, in tribute to; **in ~ s-r Verdienste** in recognition of his services; **'An·er·ken·nungs·ur·kun·de** *f* citation

'an·er·zie·hen *v/t.* (*irr., sep.,* h, → **erziehen**): **j-m et. ~** instil(l) s.th. into s.o.; **e-m Kind Höflichkeit** *etc.* **~** bring a child up to be polite *etc.*; **'an·er·zo·gen** *adj.* acquired; **das ist ~** I *etc.* was brought up that way

'an·es·sen *v/t.* (*irr., sep.,* h, → **essen**): **du hast dir ein ganz schönes Bäuchlein angegessen** you're developing a nice little paunch

an·fa·chen ['anfaxən] *v/t.* (*sep.,* h) fan; *fig.* rouse, stir up; stoke up *controversy etc.*

'an·fah·ren (*irr., sep.,* → **fahren**) **I.** *v/t.* (h) **1.** deliver; **2.** run into, hit, knock down; *fig.* snap at *s.o.*; **3.** ⚓ call at; **4.** ⚙ start; **II.** *v/i.* (sn) start; *reactor*: start up; **angefahren kommen** drive up; **'Anfahrt** *f* (-; -en) **1.** journey, ride; **2.** approach; drive

'An·fall *m* (-[e]s; ⸚e) **1.** ⚕ attack; *epileptic* fit; bout (*or* touch) *of flu*; → **Schwindel-, Tobsuchtsanfall**; *fig.* **ein ~ von Eifersucht** *etc.* a fit of jealousy *etc.*; F **e-n ~ bekommen** F have (*or* throw) a fit *or* wobbly; **2.** yield; amount *produced etc.*; **'an·fal·len** (*irr., sep.,* → **fallen**) **I.** *v/t.* (h) attack; **II.** *v/i.* (sn) *work*: come up; *interest, profit*: accumulate; *costs*: arise; **im Herbst fällt immer viel Arbeit an** the work always piles up in (the) autumn (*Am.* fall); **alle ~den Reparaturen muß ich übernehmen** I'm responsible for any repairs that crop up

'an·fäl·lig *adj.* **1.** susceptible (**für** *acc.* to); ⚕ *a.* prone (to), liable (to); **2.** delicate *health*

'An·fang *m* (-[e]s; ⸚e) beginning, start; *formal*: commencement; origin; **am ~** at (*or* in) the beginning, at the start (*or* outset); **von ~ an** (right) from the start, F from the word go; **~ Januar** early in January; **~ 1990** early in 1990; **am ~** *gen.* at the beginning of; (**am**) **~ der dreißiger Jahre** in the early thirties; **er ist ~ der Dreißiger** he's in his early thirties; **den ~ machen** start, *a. sport*: lead off; **e-n neuen ~ machen** make a fresh start, start all over again, turn over a new leaf; **das ist der ~ vom Ende** it's the beginning of the end; **aller ~ ist schwer** nothing's easy to start off with, you'll *etc.* get into it; **in den Anfängen stecken** be in its (*or* their) infancy; **zu den Anfängen zurückkehren** get back to the grassroots; **zu ~** → **anfangs**; **'an·fangen** *v/t. and v/i.* (*irr., sep.,* h, → **fangen**) start (**mit** *dat.* with), begin, *formal*: commence (with); **~ zu** *inf.* start *ger.*, begin *ger.*; **immer wieder von et. ~** keep harping on about s.th.; **immer wieder vom gleichen Thema ~** keep harping on the same string, keep harping on about the same (old) thing; **wo ~?** where to start?, where do you start?; **ich weiß nichts damit anzufangen** a) I don't know what to do with it, b) I can't make head or tail of it; **ich kann mit ihm nichts ~** a) I don't know what to do with him, b) we have absolutely nothing in common; **damit** (**mit ihm**) **ist nichts anzufangen** it's useless (he's hopeless); **mit dir ist ja heute nichts anzufangen** F you're a dead loss today; **was wirst du morgen ~?** what are you going to do (with yourself) tomorrow?; **fängst du schon wieder an?** are you at it again?; *iro.* **das fängt ja gut an!** that's a great start

'An·fän·ger *m* (-s; -) beginner (**in** *dat.* at); → **blutig**; **~kurs** *m* beginners' course

an·fäng·lich ['anfɛŋlıç] **I.** *adj.* initial; early; **II.** *adv.* → **anfangs** I

an·fangs ['anfaŋs] **I.** *adv.* at first; **II.** F *prp.* (*gen.*) at the beginning of, early on in

'An·fangs|buch·sta·be *m* first (*or* initial) letter; *pl.* initials; **großer** (**kleiner**) **~** capital (small) letter; **~er·folg** *m* initial success; **~ge·halt** *n* starting salary; **~ka·pi͵tal** *n* starting capital; **~schwie·rig·kei·ten** *pl.* initial difficulties; **~sta·di·um** *n* initial stage; **~͵un·ter·richt** *m* first years *pl.* of teaching; **~zeit** *f* time of commencement; broadcasting time, *a.* scheduled start

'an·fas·sen (*sep.,* h) **I.** *v/t.* **1.** touch; take hold of; **zum ⚲** *politician etc.* for the people; hands-on *art etc.*, tactile *exhibition*; **2.** *fig.* deal with; *a.* approach, tackle *task etc.*; **j-n hart** (**sanft**) **~** be firm (gentle) with s.o.; **II.** *v/i.* (*a.* **mit ~**) lend (*or* give *s.o.*) a hand, help out; **III.** *v/refl.*: **sich weich** *etc.* **~** feel soft *etc.*

'an·fau·chen *v/t.* (*sep.,* h) spit at; *fig.* snap at

'an·fau·len *v/i.* (*sep.,* sn) start to rot (*or* mo[u]lder); → **angefault** II

an·fecht·bar ['anfɛçtbaːɐ] *adj.* contestable; disputable; **'an·fech·ten** *v/t.* (*irr., sep.,* h, → **fechten**) **1.** contest; ⚖ appeal against *sentence*; challenge *witness etc.*; **2.** worry, bother; **'An·fech·tung** *f* (-; -en) **1.** ⚖ challenge; appeal (*gen.* against); **2.** temptation

an·fein·den ['anfaındən] *v/t.* (*sep.,* h) be hostile to(wards); **angefeindet werden** become (*or* make o.s.) unpopular (**wegen** because of), make a lot of enemies; **'An·fein·dung** *f* (-; -en) hostility (*gen.* towards)

'an·fer·ti·gen *v/t.* (*sep.,* h) make, ✝ *a.* manufacture; draw up; do, produce *translation, drawing etc.*; **'An·fer·ti·gung** *f* (-; -en) making; ✝ manufacture; drawing up; producing *of a translation etc.*

an·feuch·ten ['anfɔyçtən] *v/t.* (*sep.,* h) moisten; lick; → **angefeuchtet**

'an·feu·ern *v/t.* (*sep.,* h) fire; *fig.* encourage; cheer (on), *Am.* F root for

'an·fle·hen *v/t.* (*sep.,* h) implore, beseech

'an·flie·gen (*irr., sep.,* → **fliegen**) **I.** *v/t.* (h) approach; land at; fly to; *die Luftgesellschaft* **fliegt Funchal** (**direkt**) **an** has a service (a direct flight) to Funchal, **fliegt Funchal nicht an:** has no service (*or* flight[s]) to Funchal; **II.** *v/i.* (sn) approach; **angeflogen kommen** *a.* F *fig.* come flying (along)

'An·flug *m* (-[e]s; ⸚e) **1.** approach; **im ~ auf München sein** be approaching Munich Airport; **beim ~ auf** *acc.* while approaching, during the approach to; **2.** touch, trace, hint; **~schnei·se** *f*, **~weg** *m* approach corridor

'an·flun·kern F *v/t.* → **anschwindeln**

'an·for·dern *v/t.* (*sep.,* h) request, ask for; demand; **'An·for·de·rung** *f* (-; -en) demand (*gen.* for); *pl.* standard *sg.*, demands; **hohe ~en stellen** make high demands (**an** *acc.* on); **'An·for·de·rungs·pro͵fil** *n* job profile

'An·fra·ge *f* (-; -n) inquiry, enquiry; question (*a. parl.*); **'an·fra·gen** *v/i.* (*sep.,* h) inquire, ask; (**bei j-m**) **nach et. ~** ask (s.o.) about s.th.

'an·fres·sen *v/t.* (*irr., sep.,* h, → **fressen**) **1.** *mouse etc.*: nibble at; *caterpillar* eat; *moth*: eat holes into; *bird*: peck at; **die Motten haben den Mantel angefressen** the moths have been at this coat; → **angefressen** II; **2.** ⚗ corrode, eat into; **3.** F → **anessen**

an·freun·den ['anfrɔyndən] *v/refl.* (*sep.,* h): **sich ~** become friends; make friends (**mit** with *s.o.*); *fig.* **sich mit dem Gedanken** *etc.* **~** get used to the idea *etc.*

'an·frie·ren *v/i.* (*irr., sep.,* sn, → **frieren**) **1. ~ an** *dat.* freeze (on)to; **2.** → **angefroren** II

'an·fü·gen *v/t.* (*sep.,* h) add; ⚙ join, attach

'an·füh·len (*sep.,* h) **I.** *v/t.* feel; touch; **II.** *v/refl.*: **sich weich** *etc.* **~** feel soft *etc.*

An·fuhr ['anfuːɐ] *f* (-; -en) delivery

'an·füh·ren *v/t.* (*sep.,* h) **1.** lead; ⚔ *a.* command; *fig.* head, spearhead *campaign, movement etc.*; *sport*: be at the head of *the table*; **2.** a) state, say; b) put forward, state *reasons etc.*; c) quote, cite *a law etc.*; produce *witness etc.*; state (in *s.o.'s* defen|se [*Brit.* -ce]), plead (as an excuse); **'An·füh·rer** *m* (-s; -) leader; ⚔ commander; *b.s.* ringleader

'An·füh·rungs|stri·che *pl.*, **~zei·chen** *n* quotation mark(s), inverted comma(s)

'an·fül·len *v/t. and v/refl.* (**sich ~**) (*sep.,* h) fill (up)

'An·ga·be *f* (-; -n) **1.** statement; information; description; *pl.* information *sg.*, data, ✝ specifications; **falsche ~** misrepresentation; **genauere** (*or* **nähere**) **~n** particulars, details; **~n zur Person** personal data; **~ des Inhalts** declaration of contents; **2.** *table tennis*: service; **3.** *no pl.* F → **Angeberei**

'an·gaf·fen F *v/t.* (sep., h) F gawk at

'an·ge·ben (*irr., sep.,* h, → **geben**) **I.** *v/t.* **1.** give *name, reason etc.*; declare (*a. at the customs*); quote *prices etc.*; show, indicate, point out; **zu hoch** (**niedrig**) **~** overstate (understate); **falsch ~** misstate; **2.** set, determine; → **Tempo** 2, **Ton**[1]; **3.** claim; pretend; **II.** *v/i.* **4.** *card game*: deal first; *table tennis*: serve; **5.** F brag (**mit** *dat.* with), show off ([with] *s.th. or s.o.*); **'An·ge·ber** F *m* (-s; -) show-off; braggart, F big mouth; **An·ge·be·rei** [angeːbəˈraı] F *f* (-; -en) showing-off; **an·ge·be·risch** ['angeːbərıʃ] F *adj.* bragging; showy

'an·ge·be·tet I. *p.p. of* **anbeten**; **II.** *fig. adj.* adored, idolized; **'An·ge·be·te·te** *m, f* (-n; -n) beloved; idol

an·geb·lich ['angeːplıç] **I.** *adj.* alleged

supposed; ostensible; *contp.* would-be *artist etc.*; **II.** *adv.*: ~ ***ist er ...*** he's supposed to be ..., they say he's ...

'an·ge·bo·ren *adj.* inborn, innate (*dat.* in); ⚕ *a.* congenital, hereditary

'An·ge·bot *n* (-[e]s; -e) offer; *auction*: bid; ✝ quotation; tender; *a. stock exchange*: supply; ~ ***und Nachfrage*** supply and demand

'an·ge·bracht I *p.p. of* ***anbringen***; **II.** *adj.* appropriate; advisable; ***nicht*** ~ inappropriate, *remark*: out of place, uncalled-for; ***er hielt es für*** ~ ***zu*** *inf.* he thought it would be appropriate to *inf.*

'an·ge·brannt I. *p.p. of* ***anbrennen***; **II.** *adj. gastr.* (slightly) burnt; *milk etc.*: scorched; ~ ***schmecken*** taste burnt, have a burnt taste

'an·ge·bräunt I. *p.p. of* ***anbräunen***; **II.** *adj.*: ~ ***sein*** have a bit of a tan

'an·ge·bro·chen I. *p.p. of* ***anbrechen***; **II.** *adj.*: ~***e Flasche*** opened bottle; ~***e Tafel Schokolade*** *etc.* started bar of chocolate *etc.*; *fig.* F ***was machen wir mit dem*** ~***en Abend?*** what are we going to do with the rest of the evening?

'an·ge·bun·den I. *p.p. of* ***anbinden***; **II.** *adj.* **1.** ⚓ moored; *dog* on a (*or* the) leash; **2.** *fig.* tied down; **3.** ***kurz*** ~ curt, abrupt; ***mit j-m kurz*** ~ ***sein*** be (very) short with s.o.

'an·ge·dei·hen *v/i.*: ***j-m et.*** ~ ***lassen*** grant (*or* give) s.o. s.th.

'an·ge·deu·tet I. *p.p. of* ***andeuten***; **II.** *adj.* intimated; ***die*** ~***en Änderungen*** *a.* the changes you *etc.* hinted at

'an·ge·fault I. *p.p. of* anfaulen; **II.** *adj.* rotting, mo(u)ldering

'an·ge·feuch·tet I. *p.p. of* ***anfeuchten***; **II.** *adj.* moist, moistened

'an·ge·fres·sen I. *p.p. of* ***anfressen***; **II.** *adj.* moth-eaten; rusty

'an·ge·fro·ren I. *p.p. of* ***anfrieren***; **II.** *adj.*: ~ ***an*** *dat.* frozen to; ~ ***sein*** have got a touch of frost

'an·ge·gos·sen I. *p.p. of* ***angießen***; **II.** *adj.*: ***wie*** ~ ***sitzen*** fit like a glove, be a perfect fit

an·ge·graut ['angəgraʊt] *adj.* greying, *Am.* graying

'an·ge·grif·fen I. *p.p. of* ***angreifen***; **II.** *adj.* exhausted, worn-out ..., *pred.* worn out; bad *health*; affected *heart etc.*; ~ ***aussehen*** look unwell

'an·ge·gur·tet I. *p.p. of* ***angurten***; **II.** *adj.*: ~ ***sein*** have one's seatbelt on, have fastened one's seatbelt, F be belted up

'an·ge·haucht I. *p.p. of* ***anhauchen***; **II.** *fig. adj.*: ***links*** (***rechts, kommunistisch***) ~ ***sein*** have left-wing (right-wing, communist) leanings; ***künstlerisch*** ~ ***sein*** have an artistic bent

'an·ge·häuft I. *p.p. of* ***anhäufen***; **II.** *adj.* accumulated, amassed; ~***e Waffen*** stockpiles of weapons; ~***e Reserven*** reserve stockpiles

'an·ge·hei·ra·tet *adj.* (related) by marriage; ~***e Verwandte*** in-laws

an·ge·hei·tert ['angəhaɪtɐt] *adj.* F (slightly) merry *or* tiddly

'an·ge·hen (*irr., sep.,* → ***gehen***) **I.** *v/i.* (sn) **1.** F start; **2.** F ***die Schuhe gehen schwer an*** I can hardly get into these shoes; **3.** F work; start; *light*: go on; *fire*: start burning; **4. *das kann nicht*** ~ it can't be true; **5.** ~ ***gegen*** resist, fight (against); **6. *es geht nicht an, daß ...*** there's no excuse for *ger.*; ***das mag*** (***noch***) ~ one can (just about) overlook (*or* excuse) that; **II.** *v/t.* **7.** (h) *a. sport*: attack; **8.** a) (h, sn) tackle *problem etc.*; b) (h) *horse*: approach *fence etc.*; **9.** (h, sn) ***j-n*** ~ approach s.o. (with a request), ***um et.***: ask s.o. for s.th.; **10.** (sn) concern; ***was ihn angeht*** as far as he's concerned, as for him; ***was geht das mich an?*** what's that got to do with me?; ***das geht dich nichts an*** that's none of your business; ***das geht niemanden etwas an*** that's my business; **'an·ge·hend** *adj.* beginning; future, ... in the making; budding *artist, beauty etc.*; trainee ...; ~***er Vater*** (***Arzt*** *etc.*) father-to-be (doctor-to-be *etc.*)

'an·ge·hö·ren *v/i.* (*sep.,* h) belong (*dat.* to) (*a. fig.*); *a.* be a member (of); ***der Vergangenheit*** ~ be a thing of the past;

An·ge·hö·ri·ge ['angəhøːrɪgə] *m, f* (-n; -n) member; national (*gen.* of); relative; ***nächste***(***r***) ~(***r***) next of kin; ***meine*** ~***n*** my family

'an·ge·ket·tet I. *p.p. of* ***anketten***; **II.** *adj.* chained (***an*** *acc.* to); on a (*or* the) chain, chained up

an·ge·keucht ['angəkɔʏçt] *p.p.*: ~ ***kommen*** come panting along

An·ge·klag·te ['angəklaːktə] *m, f* (-n; -n) defendant, (the *or* an) accused

'an·ge·knackst I. *p.p. of* ***anknacksen***; **II.** F *adj.* slightly damaged; chipped *bone etc.*; cracked *rib etc.*; *fig.* shaky *health etc.*; dented *pride etc.*; ***leicht*** ~ F slightly cracked (*or* screwy); ***sein Selbstbewußtsein ist*** ~ his self-confidence has been dented (*or* has taken a beating)

'an·ge·kün·digt I. *p.p. of* ***ankündigen***; **II.** *adj.* planned, scheduled *visit, meeting etc.*; expected *visitor etc.*; ***der*** ~***e Wechsel*** *etc.* the change *etc.* that was announced, the announced (*or* promised) change *etc.*

An·gel[1] ['aŋəl] *f* (-; -n) fishing rod

'An·gel[2] *f* (-; -n) hinge; ***aus den*** ~***n heben*** lift *a door* out of its hinges, *a. fig.* unhinge; → ***Tür***

'an·ge·le·gen *adj.*: ***sich et. sehr*** ~ ***sein lassen*** make s.th. one's concern; ***es sich*** ~ ***sein lassen zu*** *inf.* make a point of *ger.*; **'An·ge·le·gen·heit** *f* (-; -en) matter, concern, affair; ***das ist s-e*** ~ that's his problem; ***kümmere dich um d-e*** ~***en*** mind your own business

'an·ge·legt I. *p.p.of* ***anlegen***; **II.** *adj.* invested; ***fest*** ~***es Geld*** permanent investment(s)

'an·ge·lehnt I. *p.p. of* ***anlehnen***; **II.** *adj.* ajar; ***laß die Tür*** ~ *a.* leave the door open a crack (*or* an inch)

'an·ge·leint I. *p.p. of* ***anleinen***; **II.** *adj.* on a lead (*or* leash)

'an·ge·lernt I. *p.p. of* ***anlernen***; **II.** *adj.* acquired; *knowledge etc.* just for show; put-on *politeness etc.*; ~***er Arbeiter*** semi-skilled worker

'an·ge·le·sen I. *p.p. of* ***anlesen***; **II.** *adj.* **1.** started *book*; ***lauter*** ~***e Bücher*** books started and never finished; **2.** ~***es Wissen*** knowledge out of books

'An·gel|ge·rät *n* fishing tackle; fishing rod; ~**ha·ken** *m* fishhook

an·geln ['aŋəln] *v/t. and v/i.* (h) fish (***nach*** *dat.* for) (*a. fig.*); F *fig.* ***sich j-n*** (***et.***) ~ F hook (*or* land) o.s. s.o. (s.th.)

'An·gel|platz *m* fishing ground; ~**punkt** *m* pivot; *fig.* pivotal point; central issue; hub; linchpin; ~**ru·te** *f* fishing rod

'An·gel·sach·se *m*, **'An·gel·säch·sin** *f*, **'an·gel·säch·sisch** *adj.* Anglo-Saxon

'An·gel|schein *m* fishing *or* angler's licen|ce (*Am.* -se); ~**schnur** *f* fishing line; ~**sport** *m* fishing, angling

'an·ge·macht I. *p.p. of* ***anmachen***; **II.** *adj.*: ~***er Salat*** dressed salad, salad with dressing

'an·ge·mes·sen I. *p.p. of* ***anmessen***; **II.** *adj.* appropriate (*dat.* to); reasonable *price etc.*; adequate; proper, fitting

'an·ge·na·gelt I *p.p. of* ***annageln***; **II.** *adj.*: ***wie*** ~ ***dastehen*** stand rooted to the spot

'an·ge·nehm I. *adj.* pleasant; agreeable; welcome; ~ ***riechen*** smell good; ***das*** ~***e mit dem Nützlichen verbinden*** combine business with pleasure; **II.** *adv.*: ~ ***überrascht*** pleasantly surprised

'an·ge·nom·men I. *p.p. of* ***annehmen***; **II.** *cj.* (let's) suppose, supposing, F let's say

'an·ge·paßt I. *p.p. of* ***anpassen***; **II.** *adj.* conformist; *psych.* (well-)adjusted

'an·ge·peilt I. *p.p.of* ***anpeilen***; **II.** *adj.* targeted, aimed-for

An·ger ['aŋɐ] *m* (-s; -) (village) green

'an·ge·regt I. *p.p. of* ***anregen***; **II.** *adj.* lively, animated; **III.** *adv.*: ***sich*** ~ ***unterhalten*** have a lively conversation

'an·ge·rei·chert I *p.p. of* ***anreichern***; **II.** *adj.* enriched (***mit*** with); ***mit Uran*** ~ uranium-enriched

'an·ge·sagt I. *p.p. of* ***ansagen***; **II.** *pred. adj.*: ~ ***sein*** a) be on the agenda, b) be in; ***wieder*** ~ ***sein*** be back in (fashion); ***Fitneß ist*** ~***!*** fitness is the order of the day; ***es ist besseres Wetter*** ~ the weather's supposed to get better

'an·ge·sam·melt I. *p.p. of* ***ansammeln***; **II.** *adj.* amassed *riches etc.*; *fig.* pent-up *anger etc.*

an·ge·säu·selt ['angəzɔʏzəlt] F *adj.* F (slightly) merry *or* tiddly

'an·ge·schim·melt I. *p.p. of* ***anschimmeln***; **II.** *adj.* slightly mo(u)ldy; ~ ***sein*** *a.* have a touch of mo(u)ld

'an·ge·schla·gen I. *p.p. of* ***anschlagen***; **II.** *adj.* **1.** chipped; **2.** *fig.* groggy; *mentally*: shaken; shaky *health*; ***schwer*** ~ ***sein*** have taken a real beating

'an·ge·schlos·sen I. *p.p. of* ***anschließen***; **II.** *adj.* connected (***an*** *acc.* to, with); *radio station etc.*: linked up (with)

an·ge·schmutzt ['angəʃmʊtst] *adj.* slightly dirty, soiled; ✝ shopsoiled

an·ge·schneit ['angəʃnaɪt] F *fig.*: ~ ***kommen*** F come blowing in

'an·ge·schnit·ten I. *p.p. of* ***anschneiden***; **II.** *adj.* **1. *ein*** ~***es Brot*** a started loaf; **2.** ~***er Ärmel*** dolman sleeve; **3.** ~***er Ball*** ball with a spin on it

'an·ge·schos·sen *adj.* slightly wounded (by bullet-fire)

'an·ge·schrie·ben I. *p.p. of* ***anschreiben***; **II.** *adj.*: ***er ist bei ihr gut*** (***schlecht***) ~ she thinks a lot of him (he doesn't rate very highly with her)

An·ge·schul·dig·te ['angəʃʊldɪçtə] *m, f* (-n; -n) ⚖ accused

'an·ge·schwemmt I. *p.p. of* ***anschwemmen***; **II.** *adj.*: ~***es Land*** alluvium

'an·ge·schwol·len I. *p.p. of* ***anschwellen***; **II.** *adj.* swollen

'an·ge·se·hen I. *p.p. of* ***ansehen***; **II.** *adj.* respected; reputable; distinguished

'An·ge·sicht *n* (-[e]s; -er) face, countenance; ***von*** ~ ***zu*** ~ face to face; ***im*** ~ *gen.* in the face of; → ***Schweiß***

'an·ge·sichts *prp.* (*gen.*) at the sight of; *fig.* given, in view of, considering; ~ ***des Todes*** *etc.* in the face of death *etc.*

'an·ge·spannt I. *p.p. of* ***anspannen*; II.** *adj.* a) strained, tense; b) tense(d up); ***~e Aufmerksamkeit*** rapt attention; **II.** *adv.* intensely; ***~ lauschen*** listen intently (*or* with rapt attention)

an·ge·stammt ['angəʃtamt] *adj.* hereditary; F *fig.* accustomed, usual

an·ge·staubt ['angəʃtaʊpt] *adj.* dusty; *fig.* stale

'an·ge·staut I. *p.p. of* ***anstauen*; II.** *adj.* pent-up *anger etc.*

'an·ge·stellt I. *p.p. of* ***anstellen*; II.** *adj.*: ***~ sein bei*** work for, be employed by (*or* with); ***wo sind Sie ~?*** where do you work?

'An·ge·stell·te *m, f* (-n; -n) (salaried) employee, F white-collar worker; office-worker

'An·ge·stell·ten... *in cpds.* (salaried) employees' *insurance etc.*; **~ge·werk·schaft** *f* white-collar union; **~ver·hält·nis** *n*: ***im ~ stehen*** be employed, be in salaried employment (***bei*** *dat.* with); **~ver·si·che·rung** *f* (salaried) employees' insurance

'an·ge·stie·gen I. *p.p. of* ***ansteigen*; II.** *adj.*: (***stark***) ***~e Preise*** (sharp) price rises

'an·ge·sto·chen I. *p.p. of* ***anstechen*; II.** *adj.* bad, rotten *fruit*; F ***herumrennen wie ein ~er Eber*** run (a)round like a lunatic

'an·ge·strahlt I. *p.p. of* ***anstrahlen*; II.** *adj.* floodlit, illuminated

an·ge·strengt ['angəʃtrɛŋt] **I.** *p.p. of* ***anstrengen*; II.** *adj.* concentrated; ***~e Miene*** look of concentration; ***~ aussehen*** look strained; **III.** *adv.*: ***~ arbeiten*** (***nachdenken***) work (think) hard; ***~ zuhören*** listen intently

'an·ge·tan I. *p.p. of* ***antun*; II.** *pred. adj.* **1.** ***~ sein von*** be taken with; ***er war von dem Gedanken wenig ~*** the idea didn't appeal to him (F grab him); **2.** ***dazu*** (*or* ***danach***) ***~ zu*** *inf.* likely (*or* apt) to *inf.*

'an·ge·taut I. *p.p. of* ***antauen*; II.** *adj.*: ***~ sein*** have started to thaw

'an·ge·trun·ken I. *p.p. of* ***antrinken*; II.** *adj.* slightly drunk; ***er war in ~em Zustand*** he had been drinking

'an·ge·wandt I. *p.p. of* ***anwenden*; II.** *adj.* applied *arts etc.*

'an·ge·wie·sen I. *p.p. of* ***anweisen*; II.** *pred. adj.*: ***~ sein auf*** *acc.* be dependent on, depend on; ***auf sich allein ~ sein*** have to look after o.s.; ***plötzlich war ich auf mich selbst ~*** suddenly I was on my own (*or* was left to paddle my own canoe)

'an·ge·wöh·nen *v/t.* (*sep.*, h): ***j-m et. ~*** get s.o. used to s.th., teach s.o. s.th.; ***sich et. ~*** get into the habit of, take to *smoking etc.*; ***du mußt dir e-e deutlichere Handschrift ~*** you must start writing more legibly

'An·ge·wohn·heit *f* (-; -en): (***aus ~*** from) habit; ***ich mache es aus ~*** *a.* it's a habit (with me)

'an·ge·wur·zelt I. *p.p. of* ***anwurzeln*; II.** *adj.*: ***wie ~ dastehen*** stand rooted to the spot

'an·ge·zeigt I. *p.p. of* ***anzeigen*; II.** *adj.* advisable; ***~ sein*** *a.* be the order of the day; ***es für ~ halten zu*** *inf.* consider it appropriate (*or* advisable) to *inf.*

an·gif·ten ['angɪftən] F *v/t.* (*sep.*, h) get nasty with

An·gi·na [aŋ'giːna] *f* (-; -nen) tonsil(l)itis; **~ pec·to·ris** [aŋ'giːna 'pɛktorɪs] *f* angina (pectoris)

'an·glei·chen *v/t. and v/refl.* (***sich ~***) (*irr.*, *sep.*, h, → ***gleichen***) adapt, adjust (*dat. or* ***an*** *acc.* to); **'An·glei·chung** *f* (-; -en) adaptation, adjustment

An·gler ['aŋlɐ] *m* (-s; -) *a. zo.* angler

'an·glie·dern *v/t.* (*sep.*, h) join, attach (*dat. or* ***an*** *acc.* to); affiliate (with), incorporate (into); *pol.* annex (to); integrate (into); **'An·glie·de·rung** *f* (-; -en) affiliation, incorporation; annexation; integration

An·gli·ka·ner [aŋgli'kaːnɐ] *m* (-s; -), **An·gli·ka·ne·rin** [aŋgli'kaːnərɪn] *f* (-; -nen) Anglican; ***~(in) sein*** *a.* be Church of England; **an·gli·ka·nisch** [aŋgli'kaːnɪʃ] *adj.* Anglican; ***die Anglikanische Kirche*** the Church of England, the Anglican Church

an·gli·sie·ren [aŋgli'ziːrən] *v/t.* (h) Anglicize, anglicize

An·glist [aŋ'glɪst] *m* (-en; -en) English student (*or* lecturer); **An·gli·stik** [aŋ'glɪstɪk] *f* (-; *no pl.*) English language and literature, English studies *pl.*

An·gli·zis·mus [aŋgli'tsɪsmʊs] *m* (-; -men) Anglicism

An·glo... ['aŋglo-] *in cpds.* Anglo-...

an·glo·phil [aŋglo'fiːl] *adj.*, **An·glo·'phi·le** *m, f* (-n; -n) Anglophile

an·glo·phon [aŋglo'foːn] *adj.*, **An·glo·'pho·ne** *m, f* (-n; -n) Anglophone

'an·glot·zen F *v/t.* (*sep.*, h) stare (F gawk) at

An·go·la·ner [aŋgo'laːnɐ] *m* (-s; -), **An·go·la·ne·rin** [aŋgo'laːnərɪn] *f* (-; -nen), **an·go·la·nisch** [aŋgo'laːnɪʃ] *adj.* Angolan

An·go·ra|kat·ze [aŋ'goːra-] *f* Angora cat; **~wol·le** *f* angora (wool)

'an·greif·bar *adj.* open to attack; *a. fig.* vulnerable; **'an·grei·fen** *v/t.* (*irr.*, *sep.*, h, → ***greifen***) **1.** attack (*a. sport and fig.*); ⚖ assault; ***angegriffen werden*** *a. fig.* be attacked, come under attack; **2.** tackle *a task etc.*; **3.** break into *supplies etc.*; **4.** weaken; strain *the eyes etc.*; affect *one's health etc.*; → ***angegriffen*** II; **5.** ⚗ corrode; **'An·grei·fer** *m* (-s; -) attacker, assailant; *pol.* aggressor

'an·gren·zen *v/i.* (*sep.*, h): ***~ an*** *acc.* border on; abut on; **'an·gren·zend** *adj.* adjacent (***an*** *acc.* to), adjoining; neighbo(u)ring; *fig.* related; *fig.* ***~e*** (***Fach-***) ***Gebiete*** related disciplines

'An·griff *m* (-[e]s; -e) attack (*a. sport and fig.*), ⚖ assault; offensive; *fig.* ***~ auf die Persönlichkeitssphäre*** assault on privacy; ***in ~ nehmen*** tackle, get started (F cracking) on, get down to; ***zum ~ übergehen*** take the offensive

'An·griffs|flä·che *fig. f* point of attack; ***e-e ~*** (***keine ~n***) ***bieten*** (not to) lay o.s. open to attack (*dat.* from); **~fuß·ball** *m* attacking football; **~krieg** *m* ⚔ offensive warfare; *pol.* war of aggression

'An·griffs·lust *f* (-; *no pl.*) aggressiveness, belligerence; **'an·griffs·lu·stig** *adj.* aggressive

'An·griffs|punkt *fig. m* weak point; ***e-n ~*** (***keine ~e***) ***bieten*** (not to) lay o.s. open to attack (*dat.* from); **~rei·he** *f sport*: forwards *pl.*; **~spiel** *n* attacking play; **~spie·ler** *m* **1.** striker; **2.** *table tennis*: attacking player; **~spit·ze** *f* spearhead; **~waf·fe** *f* offensive weapon

'an·grin·sen *v/t.* (*sep.*, h) grin at

Angst [aŋst] **I.** *f* (-; Ängste ['ɛŋstə]) fear (***vor*** *dat.* of); *a. psych.* anxiety; dread, terror; ***aus ~*** out of fear; for fear *of being punished etc.*; ***aus ~ lügen*** *etc. a.* be too scared to tell the truth *etc.*; ***~ haben*** be afraid (*or* scared, frightened) (***vor*** *dat.* of); *j-n* ***in ~ versetzen*** frighten, scare; ***keine ~!*** no need to be frightened, don't worry; ***schreckliche Ängste ausstehen*** be frightened out of one's mind; F ***es mit der ~ zu tun kriegen*** F get the wind up; **II.** ♀ *pred. adj.*: ***mir ist ~ und bange*** I'm worried to death, F I'm scared stiff; **♀er·füllt** *adj.* terrified; **♀frei I.** *adj.* free from fear; **II.** *adv.* without fear; **~ge·fühl** *n* frightened feeling; sense of fear (*or* anxiety); **~geg·ner** *m sport*: dreaded opponent; bogey team; **~ha·se** F *m* F scaredy-cat

äng·sti·gen ['ɛŋstɪgən] (h) **I.** *v/t.* alarm, frighten; get *s.o.* worried; **II.** *v/refl.*: ***sich ~*** be afraid (***vor*** *dat.* of), be alarmed (by); be worried (***um*** *acc.* about)

'Angst·käu·fe *pl.* panic buying *sg*

ängst·lich ['ɛŋstlɪç] **I.** *adj.* nervous; timid; anxious; **II.** *adv.*: ***~ bedacht*** (*or* ***bemüht***) ***zu*** *inf.* anxious to *inf.*; ***~ gehütetes Geheimnis*** jealously guarded secret; **'Ängst·lich·keit** *f* (-; *no pl.*) nervousness; timidness

'Angst|ma·cher *m* (-s; -) alarmist; **~neu·ro·se** *f* anxiety psychosis; **~par'tie** *f* F nerve-racking affair; **~schrei** *m* frightened scream; scream of terror; **~schweiß** *m* cold sweat; ***ihr brach der ~ aus*** she broke out in a cold sweat; **~traum** *m* nightmare; *psych.* anxiety dream; **♀ver·zerrt** *adj. face* contorted with fear; *voice* trembling with fear (*or* fright); **~zu·stand** *m* state of anxiety; ***Angstzustände bekommen*** get into a panic

'an·gucken (*sep.* -k·k-) F *v/t.* (*sep.*, h) look at

'an·gur·ten *v/refl.* (*sep.*, h): ***sich ~*** fasten one's seatbelt; → ***angegurtet*** II

'an·ha·ben *v/t.* (*irr.*, *sep.*, h, → ***haben***) **1.** F have on *clothes*, *a. light etc.*; wear; **2.** ***j-m nichts ~ können*** be unable to get at s.o.; ***das kann mir*** (***dem Auto***) ***nichts ~*** that doesn't worry me (that won't do the car any harm)

'an·haf·ten *v/i.* (*sep.*, h) *a. fig.* cling, stick (*dat. or* ***an*** *dat.* to); *fig.* be inherent in; ***ihm haftete etwas Eigentümliches an*** there was something peculiar about him; ***ihr haftete noch der alte Haß an*** she couldn't shake off the old hatred

'an·ha·ken *v/t.* (*sep.*, h) **1.** hook on(to ***an*** *acc.*); **2.** tick off, *Am.* check off

'An·halt *m* → ***Anhaltspunkt*; 'an·hal·ten** (*irr.*, *sep.*, h, → ***halten***) **I.** *v/t.* **1.** stop, bring to a halt; pull up *horse*; → ***Atem*; 2.** ***j-n zu et. ~*** urge s.o. to do s.th.; **II.** *v/i.* **3.** stop, come to a stop (*or* standstill); *car*: *a.* pull up; **4.** last, continue; *weather*: hold; persist; **5.** ***~ um*** apply for (***bei*** *j-m* to); ***er hielt um die Hand s-r Tochter an*** he asked him for the hand of his daughter; **'an·hal·tend** *adj.* continuous, lasting; sustained; persistent; ***~er Regen*** continuous (*or* persistent) rainfall; ***~e Bemühungen*** prolonged efforts; ***~e Nachfrage*** persistent demand

'An·hal·ter F *m* (-s; -) hitchhiker; ***per ~ fahren*** hitchhike, F hitch (a lift)
'An·halts·punkt *m* lead, clue; *a. pl.* something to go by; indication (***für*** *acc.* of); basis
'An·hang *m* (-[e]s; ⸚e) **1.** appendix; supplement; addendum; ⚖ codicil; **2.** followers *pl.*, following; F *iro.* F fan club; dependents *pl.*, family; ***ohne ~*** no dependents
'an·hän·gen[1] (*sep.*, h) **I.** *v/t.* **1.** hang up (***an*** *dat.* on); **2.** connect (***an*** *acc.* to), hook up (to); **3.** add (***an*** *acc.* to), F tag on(to); **4.** *fig.* ***j-m et. ~*** a) pin s.th. on s.o., b) fob s.th. off on s.o.; ***j-m e-n Prozeß ~*** take s.o. to court; **II.** *v/refl.*: ***sich ~ an*** *acc.* latch onto *s.o.*; *sport*: tuck o.s. in behind *s.o.*
'an·hän·gen[2] *fig. v/i.* (*irr.*, *sep.*, h, → ***hängen***[1]) **1.** follow *a fashion, party etc.*; believe in; **2.** ***der Ruf*** (***das Erlebnis***) ***hängt ihm immer noch an*** he just can't shake off that reputation (get over the experience)
'An·hän·ger *m* (-s; -) **1.** follower; disciple; *pol.*, *sport*: supporter; *film etc.*: fan; **2.** pendant; **3.** label, tag; **4.** *mot.* trailer; **'An·hän·ger·schaft** *f* (-; *no pl.*) following, supporters *pl.*; F *iro.* F fan club
'An·hän·ge·schild *n* address tag
an·hän·gig ['anhɛŋɪç] *adj.* ⚖ pending; ***e-n Prozeß gegen j-n ~ machen*** bring an action against s.o., take legal proceedings against s.o.
an·häng·lich ['anhɛŋlɪç] *adj.* devoted; affectionate; *contp.* clinging, too dependent; **'An·häng·lich·keit** *f* (-; *no pl.*) devotion, affection; *contp.* dependence
An·häng·sel ['anhɛŋzəl] *fig. n* (-s; -) appendage (*a.* F *person*)
'an·hau·chen *v/t.* (*sep.*, h) breathe on; blow on; ***hauch mich mal an!*** let me smell your breath; → ***angehaucht*** II
'an·hau·en F *v/t.* (*sep.*, h): ***j-n ~*** F tap s.o., ***um et.***: *a.* F touch s.o. for s.th
'an·häu·fen (*sep.*, h) **I.** *v/t.* pile up, accumulate; amass; hoard; stockpile; **II.** *v/refl.*: ***sich ~*** pile up; accumulate; → ***angehäuft*** II; **'An·häu·fung** *f* (-; -en) accumulation
'an·he·ben (*irr.*, *sep.*, h, → ***heben***) **I.** *v/t.* lift, *a.* ✈ raise, F hike *prices etc.*; **II.** *v/i.* begin; **'An·he·bung** *f* (-; -en) increase (*gen.* in)
'an·hef·ten *v/t.* (*sep.*, h) fasten (***an*** *dat. or acc.* to); pin (to); tack, baste
an·hei·melnd ['anhaɪməlnt] *adj.* homely, *Am.* homey; cosy, *Am.* cozy; familiar
an·heim|fal·len [an'haɪm-] *fig. v/i.* (*irr.*, *sep.*, sn, → ***fallen***) fall prey to; ***der Vergessenheit ~*** sink into oblivion; **~stel·len** *v/t.* (*sep.*, h): ***j-m et. ~*** leave s.th. up to s.o.; ***das stelle ich Ihnen anheim*** that's (*or* I'll leave that) up to you
an·hei·schig ['anhaɪʃɪç] *adj.*: ***sich ~ machen, et. zu tun*** offer (*or* volunteer) to do s.th.
'an·hei·zen *v/t.* (*sep.*, h) fire; *fig.* kindle; fuel, get *the argument etc.* going; liven up; ***die Stimmung ~*** liven things up (a bit)
'An·hei·zer *m* (-s; -) *pol.* agitator
'an·herr·schen *v/t.* (*sep.*, h) bark at
'an·heu·ern *v/t.* (*sep.*, h) (*a.* ***sich ~ lassen***) sign on
'An·hieb *m*: ***auf ~*** straightaway, F right off, *a. recite etc. s.th.* off the cuff; ***auf ~*** (***nicht***) ***mögen*** take an instant liking (dislike) to
an·him·meln ['anhɪməln] *v/t.* (*sep.*, h) idolize; ***er himmelte sie den ganzen Abend an*** he just couldn't take his eyes off her all evening
'An·hö·he *f* (-; -n) rise, elevation; (little) hill
'an·hö·ren (*sep.*, h) **I.** *v/t.* (*a.* ***sich*** *dat.* **~**) listen to, hear; ***et. mit ~*** listen in on s.th.; ***hör dir das mal an!*** just listen to this!, *w.s.* just listen to him *etc.* talking; ***ich kann mir das nicht mehr ~*** I can't stand it (*or* stand listening to that) any longer; ***man hört ihm an, daß er nicht von hier ist*** (***daß er erkältet ist***) you can tell by his accent that he doesn't come from around here (you can tell [by his voice] that he's got a cold); **II.** *v/refl.*: ***sich gut*** (***schlecht***) **~** sound good (bad)
An·hö·rung ['anhø:rʊŋ] *f* (-; -en) *parl.*, ⚖ hearing; **'An·hö·rungs·ver·fah·ren** *n* hearing procedure
'an·hu·sten *v/t.* (*sep.*, h): ***j-n ~*** cough at s.o., cough in(to) s.o.'s face
Ani·lin [ani'li:n] *n* (-s; *no pl.*) anilin(e); **~far·be** *f* anilin(e) dye
ani·ma·lisch [ani'ma:lɪʃ] *adj. a. fig.* animal ...; *fig. a.* brutish
Ani·ma·teur [anima'tø:ɐ] *m* (-s; -e) guest host, entertainments officer
Ani·ma·ti·on [anima'tsǐo:n] *f* (-; -en) **1.** animation; **2.** (animated) cartoons *pl.*;
Ani·ma·tor [ani'ma:to:ɐ] *m* (-s; -en [-ma'to:rən]) animator
Ani·mier·da·me [ani'mi:ɐ-] *f* hostess, *Am.* F B-girl; **ani·mie·ren** [ani'mi:rn] *v/t.* (h) encourage, urge; stimulate; ***animierte Stimmung*** high spirits
Ani·mo·si·tät [animozi'tɛ:t] *f* (-; -en) animosity
Anis [a'ni:s] *m* (-[es]; -e) ⚘ anise; *gastr.* aniseed; **~li͵kör** *m* anisette; **~schnaps** *m* aniseed brandy
'an·kämp·fen *v/i.* (*sep.*, h): **~ *gegen*** fight, battle with, struggle against; ***gegen den Schlaf ~*** fight (*or* struggle) to keep awake
'An·kauf *m* (-[e]s; ⸚e) buying, purchase; acquisition; **'an·kau·fen** *v/t.* (*sep.*, h) buy, purchase
'an·kei·fen *v/t.* (*sep.*, h) scream at
An·ker ['aŋkɐ] *m* (-s; -) **1.** ⚓ anchor; ***vor ~ gehen*** drop anchor; *fig.* ***bei j-m vor ~ gehen*** stop by at s.o.'s house *etc.*, drop in on s.o.; ***den ~ lichten*** weigh anchor; **2.** ⚡ armature; **~bo·je** *f* anchor buoy; **~ket·te** *f* cable
an·kern ['aŋkɐn] *v/i.* (h) (cast) anchor
'An·ker|platz *m* anchoring ground; **~spill** *n* capstan; **~win·de** *f* windlass
'an·ket·ten *v/t.* (*sep.*, h) chain (***an*** *acc.* to); put *a dog etc.* on a (*or* the) chain; → ***angekettet*** II
'an·keu·chen *v/i.* → ***angekeucht***
'an·kip·pen *v/t.* (*sep.*, h) tilt
'an·kläf·fen *v/t.* (*sep.*, h) bark at; yelp at
'An·kla·ge *f* (-; -n) accusation, charge (***gegen*** against); *esp. Am.* impeachment (of); **~ *erheben*** bring a charge (***gegen*** against); → ***anklagen; unter ~ stehen*** be on (*or* stand) trial (***wegen*** for); **~bank** *f* (-; ⸚e): (***auf der ~*** in the) dock; **~er·he·bung** *f* preferment of a charge (*or* charges)
'an·kla·gen *v/t.* (*sep.*, h) accuse (*gen. or* ***wegen*** of), charge (with); **'an·kla·gend** *adj.* (*and adv.*) accusing(ly)
'An·kla·ge·punkt *m* charge
'An·klä·ger *m* (-s; -) accuser; ⚖ prosecutor; ***öffentlicher ~*** public prosecutor
'An·kla·ge|schrift *f* (bill of) indictment; **~ver·tre·ter** *m* counsel for the prosecution
'an·klam·mern (*sep.*, h) **I.** *v/t.* fasten (***an*** *dat. or acc.* to); clip on(to); **II.** *v/refl.*: ***sich ~*** cling (***an*** *dat. or acc.* to)
'An·klang *m* (-[e]s; ⸚e) **1.** reminiscence, echo, suggestion (***an*** *acc.* of); **2.** **~ *finden*** strike a chord (***bei*** *dat.* with), *w.s.* go down well (with), meet with approval (from), find favo(u)r (with), catch on (among)
'an·klat·schen F *v/t.* (*sep.*, h) **1.** slap on *paint etc.*; **2.** sleek (*or* plaster) down *one's hair*
'an·kle·ben (*sep.*, h) **I.** *v/t.* stick on(to ***an*** *dat. or acc.*); **II.** *v/i.* stick, cling (***an*** *dat.* to)
'An·klei·de·ka͵bi·ne *f* cubicle; fitting room
'an·klei·den *v/t. and v/refl.* (***sich ~***) (*sep.*, h) dress
'An·klei·de|pup·pe *f* **1.** dummy; **2.** dress-up doll; **~raum** *m* dressing room
'an·klicken (*sep.* -k·k-) *v/t.* (*sep.*, h) *computer*: click
'an·klin·gen *v/i.* (*irr.*, *sep.*, h, → ***klingen***) be heard; *fig.* **~ *an*** *acc.* be reminiscent of; **~ *lassen*** evoke, suggest; ***in s-n Worten klang ein wenig Resignation an*** there was a hint of resignation in what he said
'an·klop·fen *v/i.* (*sep.*, h) knock (***an*** *dat. or acc.* at, on); *fig.* ***bei j-m ~*** approach s.o. (***wegen*** about), F touch s.o. *for money etc.*
'an·knab·bern *v/t.* (*sep.*, h) nibble at; F *fig.* ***sie sieht zum ~ aus*** F I could eat her up
'an·knack·sen F *v/t.* (*sep.*, h) chip; ***sich den Fuß ~*** chip a bone in one's foot; sprain one's ankle; → ***angeknackst*** II
'an·knip·sen *v/t.* (*sep.*, h) switch on
'an·knüp·fen (*sep.*, h) **I.** *v/t.* tie, fasten (***an*** *dat. or acc.* to); *fig.* start; ***ein Gespräch ~*** *a.* strike up a conversation (***mit*** with); ***Verhandlungen ~*** start (*or* enter into) negotiations (***mit*** with); ***Beziehungen ~*** establish contacts; **II.** *v/i.*: **~ *an*** *acc.* go on from, pick up the thread of, go back to, continue *tradition etc.*; ***an die Romantik*** *etc.* **~** carry on where the Romantics *etc.* left off; **'An·knüp·fungs·punkt** *m* **1.** point of contact; **2.** starting point
'an·koh·len *v/t.* (*sep.*, h): F ***j-n ~*** F pull s.o.'s leg
'an·kom·men (*irr.*, *sep.*, sn, → ***kommen***) **I.** *v/i.* **1.** arrive (***in*** *dat.* at, in); **~ *in*** *a.* reach; ***gut ~*** *person*: arrive safely, *letter etc.*: get there all right (*Am.* alright); F ***dauernd kommt er mit s-n Fragen an*** he keeps coming with all these questions; F ***damit kommt er bei mir nicht an*** F that cuts no ice with me; **2.** F get a job (***bei*** *dat.* with); **3.** F go down well (***bei*** *dat.* with); ***nicht ~*** *a.* F be a flop; ***groß ~ bei*** F go down a bomb with; → ***Publikum*** 2; **4.** **~ *gegen*** be able to cope with, get the better of *s.o.*; ***gegen sie kommt er nicht an*** he's no match for her, he can't compete with her, he hasn't got a chance with her; ***gegen die Opposition*** *etc.* ***kommen wir nicht an*** the opposition *etc.* is too strong for us; **II.** *v/impers.* **5.** **~ *auf*** *acc.* depend on; ***es kommt*** (***ganz***) ***darauf an*** it (all) depends (***ob***

whether); ***worauf es ankommt, ist*** the important thing is; ***es kommt (bei ihm) nicht auf den Preis an*** it doesn't matter how much it costs (money is no object for him); ***wenn es darauf ankommt,*** *ist er immer da*: when it comes to the crunch; **6.** ***es auf et. ~ lassen*** risk s.th.; ***ich lasse es darauf ~*** I'll wait and see what happens; **7.** ***es kommt mich hart (leicht) an*** I find it hard (easy); **III.** *lit. v/t.* befall, come over *s.o.*; ***es kam ihn die Lust an zu*** *inf.* he suddenly had the urge to *inf.*

An·kömm·ling ['ankœmlıŋ] *m* (-s; -e) newcomer; F new arrival

'an·kop·peln (*sep.*, h) **I.** *v/t.* connect (**an** *acc.* to); hitch up (to), couple up (to); *space travel*: dock (with); **II.** *v/i. space travel*: dock (**an** *dat.* with); **'An·kopp·lung** *f* (-; -en) connection (**an** *dat. or acc.* to), linking up (to, with); *space travel*: docking (with)

'an·kot·zen V *fig. v/t.* (*sep.*, h) make *s.o.* sick, *sl.* make *s.o.* (want to) puke

'an·kral·len *v/refl.* (*sep.*, h): ***sich ~ an*** *dat. or acc.* clutch at, cling to; *animal*: dig its claws into

an·krei·den ['ankraıdən] *v/t.* (*sep.*, h): ***j-m et. ~*** a) fault s.o. with s.th., b) hold s.th. against s.o.; ***j-m angekreidet werden*** count against s.o.

'an·kreu·zen *v/t.* (*sep.*, h) put a cross next to, mark with a cross; put a tick in, tick off

'an·kün·di·gen (*sep.*, h) **I.** *v/t.* announce (*dat.* to); *formal*: give *s.o.* notice of; *fig.* ***et. ~*** be a sign that s.th. is on its way, *lit.* herald (*or* presage) s.th.; → ***angekündigt*** II; **II.** *v/refl.*: ***sich ~*** tell s.o. that one is coming, *esp. iro.* announce one's arrival; *fig.* be on its way; ***bei mir kündigt sich e-e Grippe an*** I think I'm due (*or* in) for a bout of flu; **'An·kün·di·gung** *f* (-; -en) announcement

An·kunft ['ankʊnft] *f* (-; *no pl.*) arrival; *fig. a.* advent; ***bei ~, nach ~*** on arrival

'An·kunfts|flug·ha·fen *m* arrival airport; **~hal·le** *f* arrival lounge; **~zeit** *f* arrival time

'an·kup·peln *v/t.* (*sep.*, h) connect (**an** *acc.* to)

'an·kur·beln *v/t.* (*sep.*, h) *mot.* start, crank; *fig.* stimulate; *a.* boost; step up, boost *production*

'an·ku·scheln *v/refl.* (*sep.*, h): ***sich an j-n ~*** snuggle up to s.o.

'an·lä·cheln *v/t.* (*sep.*, h) smile at, give *s.o.* a smile; give *s.o.* the come hither look

'an·la·chen *v/t.* (*sep.*, h) laugh at; *fig.* ***das Stück Kuchen da lacht mich an*** that piece of cake looks very tempting; F ***sich j-n ~*** F pick s.o. up

'An·la·ge *f* (-; -n) **1.** *no pl.* arrangement; construction; **2.** arrangement, layout; **3.** design; structure; **4.** installation; plant; system; F hi-fi (system); gardens *pl.*, grounds *pl.*, park; ***öffentliche ~*** public gardens; **5.** talent, aptitude, gift (**zu** *dat.* for); (natural) tendency (to *inf.*), bent (for), (pre)disposition (to[wards]) (*a.* ⚕); ***die ~ zu e-m Musiker*** *etc.* ***haben*** *a.* have the makings of a musician *etc.*; **6.** ✝ a) investment, b) invested capital; **~n** *balance*: assets; **7.** enclosure; ***in der (or als) ~ senden wir Ihnen*** enclosed please find, enclosed you will find, we enclose

'An·la·ge... ✝ *in cpds.* investment *company, credit, etc.*; **2be·dingt** *adj.* constitutional; congenital; ***die Allergien sind bei ihm ~*** he has a natural tendency towards allergies; **~be·ra·ter** *m* investment consultant; **~be·ra·tung** *f* investment consultancy; **~ka·pi,tal** *n* invested capital; capital assets *pl.*; **~pa,pier** *n* investment security; → ***festverzinslich***; **~ver·mö·gen** *n* **1.** fixed assets *pl.*; **2.** invested capital

'an·lan·den (*sep.*, h) **I.** *v/t.* land; disembark; **II.** *v/i.* (*a.* sn) *geol.* accrete

'an·lan·gen (*sep.*) **I.** *v/i.* (sn) **1.** arrive (**an** *dat.*, **bei, in** *dat.* at, in); **~ in** (*or* **bei**) *a.* reach; **II.** *v/t.* (h) **2.** concern; ***was ... anlangt*** as for, as far as ... is (*or* are) concerned; **3.** → ***anfassen***

An·laß ['anlas] *m* (Anlasses; Anlässe ['anlɛsə]) occasion; *a.* motive, reason (**zu** for); grounds *pl.* (**für** *dat.* for; ***zu tun*** for doing); ***aus ~*** *gen.* on the occasion of; ***aus diesem ~*** for this reason, *w.s.* to mark the occasion; ***~ geben zu*** give rise to; ***j-m ~ geben zu*** give s.o. cause for (*ger.*); ***allen ~ haben zu*** have every reason to *inf.*; ***et. zum ~ nehmen zu*** *inf.* use s.th. as an opportunity (*contp.* excuse) to *inf.*; ***ich möchte diese Zusammenkunft*** *etc.* ***zum ~ nehmen zu*** *inf.* I'd like to take this occasion to *inf.*; ***ohne jeden ~*** for no reason at all; ***beim geringsten ~ feiern*** *etc.* use any excuse to celebrate *etc.*; ***er beschwert sich beim geringsten ~*** he complains about every little thing; ***dem ~ entsprechend*** to suit the occasion

'an·las·sen (*irr.*, *sep.*, h, → ***lassen***) **I.** *v/t.* **1.** keep on *coat etc.*; leave on *light, radio etc.*; **2.** *mot.* start (up); **II.** *v/refl.*: ***sich ~*** start; ***die Sache läßt sich gut an*** it's a good start, things look promising; ***das Wetter läßt sich gut an*** it looks as if it's going to be a nice day; ***die Woche läßt sich gut an*** it's a good start to the week; ***wie läßt er sich an?*** how's he making out?; ***er läßt sich gut an*** he's doing quite nicely

An·las·ser ['anlasɐ] *m* (-s; -) *mot.* starter

an·läß·lich ['anlɛslıç] *prp.* (*gen.*) on the occasion of; ***~ ihres 50. Geburtstags*** *a.* to celebrate her 50th birthday

'an·la·sten *v/t* (*sep.*, h).: ***j-m et. ~*** blame s.o. for s.th., put the blame on s.o. for s.th.

'An·lauf *m* (-[e]s; ⸚e) **1.** *sport*: run-up, *ski jumping*: approach; ***e-n ~ nehmen*** take a run; **2.** *fig.* attempt; ***beim ersten ~*** on the first go; ***beim zweiten ~*** the second time round; ***e-n ~ nehmen zu*** *inf.* get ready to *inf.*; ***e-n neuen ~ machen*** try again, have another go; **3.** ⚙ start; **~adres·se** *f* → ***Anlaufstelle***

'an·lau·fen (*irr.*, *sep.*, → ***laufen***) **I.** *v/i.* (sn) **1.** *sport*: run up (for the jump); ***angelaufen kommen*** come running along; ***~ gegen*** → ***anrennen***; **2.** *mot.* start (up) (*a.* ***~ lassen***); **3.** *fig.* start, get under way, get going; ***der Film läuft nächste Woche an*** the film will be (showing) in the cinemas next week; **4.** ✝ *interests, costs*: accumulate; **5.** steam up; ***rot ~*** go red; ***blau ~*** go blue in the face; **II.** *v/t.* (h) ⚓ call at

'An·lauf|ha·fen *m* port of call; **~ko·sten** *pl.* ✝ initial (*or* startup) cost *sg.*; **~pha·se** *f* initial phase; **~stel·le** *f* place to go; drop-in cent|er (*Brit.* -re); *b.s.* contact address; F ***ich kenne s-e ~n*** F I know where he hangs out; **~zeit** *f* ⚙ starting-up time; *fig.* warm-up period; *a.* period of adjustment; ***e-e ~ von 6 Wochen brauchen*** need 6 weeks to get started (*or* to take off), need 6 weeks to get going (*or* to get into it)

'An·laut *m* (-[e]s; -e) *ling.* initial sound, anlaut; ***im ~*** initial ..., in initial position; **'an·lau·ten** *v/i.* (*sep.*, h) begin (**mit** *dat.* with)

'an·läu·ten (*sep.*, h) **I.** *v/i.*: ***bei j-m ~*** ring s.o. up; **II.** *v/t.* *sport*: ring in

'an·lau·tend *adj.* initial

'An·le·ge·brücke (*sep.* -k·k-) *f* landing stage, jetty

'an·le·gen (*sep.*, h) **I.** *v/t.* **1.** ***et. ~ an*** *acc.* put against, lean against; → ***Hand***; **2.** apply (*dat.*, **an** *acc.* to), put on; ***j-m e-n Verband ~*** put a bandage on s.o., bandage s.o. up; ***j-m Fesseln ~*** put s.o. in chains; **3.** put on *dress, jewelry etc.*; **4.** ***das Gewehr ~*** (take) aim (**auf** *acc.* at); **5.** ***e-n Säugling ~*** give a baby the breast; **6.** design; lay out *park etc.*; instal(l); **7.** start *file, collection etc.*; set up *card index*; open *account*; get in *supplies*; **8.** ✝ invest (**in** *acc.* in), F sink *money* into; F ***wieviel willst du ~?*** how much do you want to spend?; → ***angelegt*** II; **9.** ***es ~ auf*** *acc.* be out for (*or* to *inf.*); **10.** → ***Maßstab***; **II.** *v/i.* **11.** ⚓ land, put in; ***~ in*** *dat.* call (*or* dock) at; **III.** *v/refl.*: ***sich mit j-m ~*** start a fight (*or* an argument) with s.o.

An·le·ger ['anle:gɐ] *m* (-s; -) ✝ investor

'An·le·ge·stel·le *f* landing place, moorings *pl.*; → ***Anlegebrücke***

'an·leh·nen (*sep.*, h) **I.** *v/t.* **1.** lean *the door* to; leave *the door* open a crack; → ***angelehnt*** II; **2.** ***~ an*** *acc.* lean against; **II.** *v/refl.*: **3.** ***sich ~ an*** *acc.* lean on; rest one's head on; **4.** *fig.* ***sich (stark) ~ an*** *acc.* follow (closely), *author etc.*: *a.* lean (heavily) on; **'An·leh·nung** *f* (-; -en) *pol.* dependence (**an** *acc.* on); ***in ~ an*** following, *art etc.*: in the style of; **'an·leh·nungs·be·dürf·tig** *adj.*: ***~ sein*** need to feel protected, need a lot of support and affection

'an·lei·ern F *v/t.* (*sep.*, h) F get *s.o. or s.th.* going

An·lei·he ['anlaıə] *f* (-; -n) **1.** loan; ***e-e ~ bei j-m machen*** borrow money from s.o.; **2.** bond issue; **~ka·pi,tal** *n* loan capital; **~pa,pier** *n* stock, bond; **~schuld** *f* bonded debt

'an·lei·men *v/t.* (*sep.*, h) glue on; ***~ an*** *dat. or acc.* glue (on)to

an·lei·nen ['anlaınən] *v/t.* (*sep.*, h) put *dog* on a lead (*or* leash); → ***angeleint*** II

'an·lei·ten *v/t.* (*sep.*, h) guide; *fig.* ***j-n bei e-r Arbeit*** *etc.* ***~*** show s.o. how to do a job *etc.*; **'An·lei·tung** *f* (-; -en) direction, guidance; ⚙ instructions *pl.*; → ***Bedienungsanleitung***

'An·lern·be·ruf *m* semi-skilled job; **'an·ler·nen** *v/t.* (*sep.*, h) train, show *s.o.* the ropes; → ***angelernt***; **An·lern·ling** ['anlɛrnlıŋ] *m* (-s; -e) trainee

'an·le·sen *v/t.* (*irr.*, *sep.*, h, → ***lesen***) **1.** dip into *a book*; **2.** ***sich et. ~*** get s.th. out of a book (*or* magazine *etc.*), read up on s.th.; → ***angelesen*** II

'an·lie·fern *v/t.* (*sep.*, h) deliver; **'An·lie·fe·rung** *f* (-; -en) delivery

'an·lie·gen (*irr.*, *sep.*, h, → ***liegen***) **I.** *v/i.* **1.** *dress etc.*: fit; ***eng ~*** fit tightly, ***an*** *dat.*: cling to; **2.** ⚓ head *north etc.*; **3.** F ***was liegt heute an?*** what's on the agenda today?, what's got to be done today?; **II.**

♀ *n* (-s; -) request; *w.s.* concern; matter; ***ein nationales* ~** a matter of national concern; ***ich habe ein ~ an Sie*** I want to ask you a favo(u)r; **'an·lie·gend** *adj.* **1.** close-fitting, snug; **2.** → ***angrenzend;*** **3.** *a. adv.* enclosed, attached

An·lie·ger ['anli:gɐ] *m* (-s; -) resident; ~ ***frei*** (access to) residents only; **~staat** *m* neighbo(u)ring (*or* bordering) state, riparian state

'an·locken (*sep.* -k·k-) *v/t.* (*sep.*, h) lure, *fig. a.* attract

'an·lö·ten *v/t.* (*sep.*, h) solder on(to ***an*** *dat. or acc.*)

'an·lü·gen *v/t.* (*irr.*, *sep.*, h, → ***lügen***) ***j-n*** ~ lie to s.o.('s face)

'an·ma·chen *v/t.* (*sep.*, h) **1.** attach, fasten (***an*** *dat.* to); **2.** *gastr.* prepare; dress, toss *salad*; → ***angemacht*** II; **3.** make, light *fire*; switch on *light, radio etc.*; **4.** F *fig.* ***j-n*** ~ a) F chat s.o. up, *sl.* (try to) get off with s.o., b) F turn s.o. on

'An·mach·tour F *f*: ***das gehört zu s-r*** ~ F that's all part of his act; ***ich mag diese ~ nicht*** I don't like the way he sets to work on women

'an·mah·nen *v/t.* (*sep.*, h): ⚖ ***et.*** **(*bei j-m*)** ~ ask (s.o.) for payment (*or* delivery *etc.*) of s.th.

'an·ma·len (*sep.*, h) **I.** *v/t.* paint; **II.** F *v/refl.*: ***sich*** ~ F put one's face (*or* war paint) on

'An·marsch *m* (-[e]s; *no pl.*) approach, advance; F march; ***im ~ sein*** a) be advancing (***auf*** *acc.* towards), b) F be on the way; **'an·mar͵schie·ren** *v/i.* (*sep.*, sn) march up; **'An·marsch·weg** *m* approach (route); F way *to work etc.*

an·ma·ßen ['anma:sən] *v/t.* (*sep.*, -ge-, h): ***sich et.*** ~ claim s.th.; ***sich ~, et. zu tun*** take it upon o.s. to do s.th.; ***ich maße mir kein Urteil darüber an*** who am I to judge?, *formal*: far be it from me to pass judg(e)ment on it; **'an·ma·ßend** *adj.* arrogant, presumptuous; overbearing; **'An·ma·ßung** *f* (-; -en) arrogance; presumption; usurpation; ***diese ~!*** what a cheek!

'An·mel·de|for·mu͵lar *n* registration form; application form; **~frist** *f* registration period; ***die ~ läuft morgen ab*** the deadline for registrations is tomorrow; **~ge·bühr** *f* registration fee

'an·mel·den (*sep.*, h) **I.** *v/t.* register (with the police); announce *visitor etc.*; *ped., univ.* enrol(l); *fig.* raise *objections, doubts etc.*; make *a request*; ***würden Sie mich bei ihm ~?*** would you tell him I'm here, please; ***den Fernseher*** **(*das Radio*)** ~ get a television (radio) licen|ce (*Am.* -se); → ***Konkurs, Patent*** I; **II.** *v/refl.*: ***sich*** ~ register (with the police); let *s.o.* know one has arrived; make an appointment (***bei*** *dat.* with); enrol(l) (***zu*** for); *sport*: enter one's name (for); book in *at a hotel*; *fig.* announce itself

'An·mel·de·pflicht *f* compulsory registration; **'an·mel·de·pflich·tig** *adj.* subject to registration; ⚕ notifiable

'An·mel·dung *f* (-; -en) **1.** registration; announcement; booking; enrol(l)ment; entry; *customs*: declaration; ***nach vorheriger*** ~ by appointment (only); **2.** reception (desk)

'an·mer·ken *v/t.* (*sep.*, h) **1.** mark; make a note of; **2. *j-m s-n Ärger*** *etc.* ~ be able to tell that s.o. is annoyed *etc.* (***an*** *dat.* by); ***sich nichts ~ lassen*** not to show one's feelings; ***man merkt ihm sofort an, daß*** you just have to look at him to see that; ***laß dir nichts ~!*** don't let on!; **3.** remark; **'An·mer·kung** *f* (-; -en) remark (***über*** *acc.* on); comment (on); note; annotation; ~ ***der Redaktion*** (*abbr.* ***Anm. d. Red.***) editor's comment (*abbr.* ed.)

'an·mo·sern F *v/t.* → ***anmotzen***

'an·mot·zen F *v/t.* (*sep.*, h) F have a (real) go at

'an·mu·stern *v/t.* (*sep.*, h) sign on

An·mut ['anmu:t] *f* (-; *no pl.*) grace(fulness); charm

an·mu·ten ['anmu:tən] *v/t.* (*sep.*, h): ***j-n seltsam*** *etc.* ~ strike s.o. as strange *etc.*

'an·mu·tig *adj.* charming

'an·na·geln *v/t.* (*sep.*, h) nail on(to ***an*** *dat. or acc.*); → ***angenagelt*** II

'an·na·gen *v/t.* (*sep.*, h) gnaw at

'an·nä·hen *v/t.* (*sep.*, h) sew on(to ***an*** *dat. or acc.*)

'an·nä·hern (*sep.*, h) **I.** *v/t.* approximate (***an*** *acc.* to); *fig.* reconcile; **II.** *v/refl.*: ***sich*** ~ approach (*dat. s.th.*) (*a. fig.*); *fig.* ***sich j-m*** ~ make contact with s.o., get friendly with s.o.; **'an·nä·hernd I.** *adj.* approximate, rough; **II.** *adv.* roughly; ***nicht*** ~ not nearly; ~ ***richtig*** just about right, more or less right; **'An·nä·he·rung** *f* (-; -en) approach; *fig.* reconciliation; *pol.* rapprochement

'An·nä·he·rungs|po·li͵tik *f* policy of rapprochement; **~ver·such** *m* **1.** advances *pl.*, pass; **2.** *pol.* attempt at rapprochement, overtures *pl.*

'an·nä·he·rungs·wei·se *adv.* approximately

'An·nä·he·rungs·wert *m* approximate value

An·nah·me ['ana:mə] *f* (-; -n) **1.** acceptance (*a. fig.*); adoption *of a child, motion etc.*; passing (*Am. a.* passage) *of a bill*; ⚖ ***die ~ e-r Sache verweigern*** refuse to accept s.th.; ✉ ~ ***verweigert!*** refused; **2.** assumption; 📖 hypothesis; ***in der ~, daß*** on the assumption that, assuming that; ***ich war der ~, daß*** I was under the impression that, I had assumed that; ***wir haben Grund zu der ~, daß*** we have reason to assume that; **~be·stä·ti·gung** *f* acknowledg(e)ment of receipt; **~er·klä·rung** *f* ⚖ notice of acceptance; **~frist** *f* ⚖ period of acceptance; **~stel·le** *f* counter; agency; ⚔ recruiting office; **~ver·wei·ge·rung** *f* non-acceptance

An·na·len [a'na:lən] *pl.* annals; F ***in die ~ eingehen*** go down in history

an·nehm·bar ['ane:mba:ɐ] *adj.* acceptable (***für*** *acc.* to), reasonable *price, conditions etc.*; **'an·neh·men** (*irr.*, *sep.*, h, → ***nehmen***) **I.** *v/t.* **1.** accept (*a. fig.*; *a. v/i.*); *parl.* carry *a motion*; pass *a bill*; take *s.o.'s advice*; take on *employee, student etc.*; take on (*fabric*: take) *dye etc.*; take on, assume *shape, look etc.*; take up (*b.s.* fall into) *a habit etc.*; adopt *child, name etc.*; assume *name, title*; *sport*: take *a ball*; ⚖ ***e-n Wechsel*** **(*nicht*)** ~ (dis-) hono(u)r a bill of exchange; → ***Vernunft;*** **2.** assume; ***nehmen wir an, angenommen*** (let's) suppose, supposing, F (let's) say; **II.** *v/refl.*: ***sich e-r Sache*** ~ take care of s.th.; ***sich j-s Sache*** ~ take up s.o.'s cause; ***sich j-s*** ~ take care of s.o., take s.o. under one's wing

An·nehm·lich·kei·ten ['ane:mlɪçkaɪtən] *pl.* comforts, amenities

an·nek·tie·ren [anɛk'ti:rən] *v/t.* (h) annex

An·ne·xi·on [anɛ'ksǐo:n] *f* (-; -en) *pol.* annexation

An·no ['ano] *adv.* in the year (of); ~ ***Domini*** in the year of our Lord; F ~ ***dazumal*** in the olden days; ***in ~ Tobak*** F donkey's years ago

An·non·ce [a'nõ:sə] *f* (-; -n) advertisement, *Brit. a.* advert; F ad; → ***Anzeige;*** **an·non·cie·ren** [anõ'si:rən] (h) **I.** *v/t.* advertise; **II.** *v/i.* place an ad (*or* advertisement) in a newspaper

an·nul·lie·ren [anʊ'li:rən] *v/t.* (h) annul, ⚖ *a.* declare null and void; cancel *order etc.*; *sport*: disallow *goal*; **An·nul'lie·rung** *f* (-; -en) annulment; cancellation

An·ode [a'no:də] *f* (-; -n) ⚡ anode

an·öden ['anʔø:dən] F *v/t.* (*sep.*, h) **1.** F bore to tears; ***sich gegenseitig*** ~ F be sick of the sight of each other; **2.** molest

an·odisch [a'no:dɪʃ] *adj.* anodal, anodic

ano·mal ['anoma:l] *adj.* abnormal; **Ano·ma·lie** [anoma'li:] *f* (-; -n) anomaly, ⚕ *a.* abnormality

ano·nym [ano'ny:m] *adj.* anonymous; ♀***e Alkoholiker*** (*abbr.* ***AA***) Alcoholics Anonymous; **Ano·ny·mi·tät** [anonymi'tɛ:t] *f* (-; *no pl.*) anonymity

Ano·rak ['anorak] *m* (-s; -s) anorak, *esp. Am.* parka

'an·ord·nen *v/t.* (*sep.*, h) **1.** arrange; **2.** order; **'An·ord·nung** *f* (-; -en) **1.** arrangement; grouping; **2.** order, instruction; **~en *treffen*** give orders (*or* instructions); make arrangements; ***auf ~ von*** (*or gen.*) by order of; **(*auf*) ~ *des Arztes!*** doctor's orders

An·ore·xie [anʔorɛ'ksi:] *f* (-; *no pl.*) ⚕ anorexia (nervosa)

'an·or͵ga·nisch *adj.* inorganic

'anor͵mal *adj.* abnormal; ***das ist ~ a.*** that's not normal

'an·packen (*sep.* -k·k-) (*sep.*, h) **I.** *v/t.* grab; *fig.* treat, handle *s.o.*; tackle *work, problem etc.*; F → ***anfassen;*** F ***packen wir's an!*** let's get down to business, then; *fig.* ***e-e Sache anders ~*** approach s.th. differently; **II.** *v/i.*: ***mit*** ~ lend a hand

'an·pas·sen (*sep.*, h) **I.** *v/t.* fit; *fig.* adapt, adjust (*a.* ⚖, ⚙ *etc.*) (*dat.* to); match (with); **II.** *v/refl.*: ***sich*** ~ adapt (o.s.), adjust (o.s.); *eyes*: accommodate; ***sich e-r Sache ~ a.*** conform to s.th.; ***sich ~ an*** *acc. pol. etc.* align o.s. to; ***er kann sich einfach nicht ~*** he just won't fit in; → ***angepaßt*** II; **'An·pas·sung** *f* (-; -en) adaptation, adjustment; acculturation

'an·pas·sungs·fä·hig *adj.* adaptable; flexible; **'An·pas·sungs·fä·hig·keit** *f* (-; *no pl.*) adaptability, flexibility

'An·pas·sungs|schwie·rig·kei·ten *pl.* difficulties in adapting; *psych.* maladjustment; *psych.* ~ ***haben*** suffer from maladjustment; **~ver·mö·gen** *n* → ***Anpassungsfähigkeit***

'an·pei·len *v/t.* (*sep.*, h) take a bearing on; head for; F make for *s.o.*; aim at; have one's sights set on; → ***angepeilt*** II

'an·peit·schen *fig. v/t.* (*sep.*, h) spur on

'an·pfei·fen *v/t.* (*irr.*, *sep.*, h, → ***pfeifen***) **1.** *sport*: ***das Spiel*** ~ start the game; **2.** F ***j-n*** ~ F give s.o. a roasting, *Am.* F chew s.o. out

'An·pfiff *m* (-[e]s; -e) **1.** *sport*: ***der ~ war um 3 Uhr*** the game started at 3 o'clock, *soccer*: kick-off was at 3 o'clock; **2.** F *fig.* ***e-n ~ bekommen*** be hauled over the coals, F get a roasting, *Am.* F get chewed out

'an·pflan·zen *v/t.* (*sep.*, h) plant; cultivate

an·pflau·men ['anpflaʊmən] F *v/t.* (*sep.*, h) **1.** *j-n* ~ F pull s.o.'s leg; **2.** insult; *ich laß' mich von dir nicht* ~ F don't give me any of your lip

'an·piep·sen F *v/t.* (*sep.*, h) F bleep

'an·pin·seln F *v/t.* (*sep.*, h) paint

'an·pir·schen *v/refl.* (*sep.*, h): *sich ~ an acc.* creep up to, stalk

'an·pö·beln *v/t.* (*sep.*, h) (verbally) accost; shout abuse at, F foul-mouth

An·prall ['anpral] *m* (-[e]s; *no pl.*) impact; **'an·pral·len** *v/i.* (*sep.*, sn) crash (*gegen acc.* into)

an·pran·gern ['anpraŋɐn] *v/t.* (*sep.*, h) pillory; denounce (*als* as)

'an·prei·sen *v/t.* (*irr.*, *sep.*, h, → *preisen*) recommend, F push; plug; praise, extol

'An·pro·be *f* (-; -n) fitting; *zur ~ gehen* go for a fitting; **'an·pro,bie·ren** *v/t.* (*sep.*, h) try on

'an·pum·pen F *v/t.* (*sep.*, h) F tap; *j-n ~ um a.* F touch s.o. for

'an·quat·schen F *v/t.* (*sep.*, h) accost

An·rai·ner·staat ['anraɪnɐ-] *m* littoral state; (Pacific) rim nation

an·ran·zen ['anrantsən] F *v/t.* (*sep.*, h) snarl at

'an·ra·ten (*irr.*, *sep.*, h, → *raten*) **I.** *v/t.*: *j-m ~, et. zu tun* advise s.o. to do s.th.; *j-m et. ~* recommend s.th. to s.o.; **II.** ∿ *n*: *auf ~ des Arztes* on the doctor's advice

'an·rau·schen F *v/i.* (*sep.*, sn): *angerauscht kommen car*: come roaring along, *person*: make one's entry

'an·rech·nen *v/t.* (*sep.*, h) credit; take into account, allow for; count; *sie haben mir die alte Kamera angerechnet* they knocked something off for my old camera; *j-m et. ~* charge s.o. with s.th., charge s.th. to s.o.'s account; *j-m zuviel ~* overcharge s.o.; *fig. j-m et. als Verdienst ~* give s.o. credit for s.th.; *j-s Hilfe etc. hoch ~* greatly appreciate s.o.'s help *etc.*; **'An·rech·nung** *f* (-; *no pl.*) charge; *j-m et. in ~ bringen* charge s.o. for s.th.

'An·recht *n* (-[e]s; -e) right, claim; *(ein) ~ haben auf acc.* have a right to, be entitled to

'An·re·de *f* (-; -n) address; opening; **'an·re·den** *v/t.* (*sep.*, h) **1.** address (*als* as; *mit* with); *j-n mit du (Sie) ~* call s.o. du (Sie), use the familiar (polite) form of address with s.o.; *du mußt ihn nicht mit s-m Doktortitel ~* you don't have to call him by his (*or* use his) doctor's title, you don't have to call him Doctor (X); **2.** approach (*auf et. hin* about *or* on s.th.); **3.** *gegen den Lärm etc. ~* compete against the noise *etc.*; **4.** *gegen j-n ~* argue against s.o.

'an·re·gen *v/t.* (*sep.*, h) **1.** suggest; **2.** encourage; *a. physiol. etc.*: stimulate (*a. v/i.*), *a.* whet *one's appetite*; elicit, prompt; start *a discussion etc.*; *j-n zum Nachdenken ~* set s.o. thinking; → *angeregt* II; **3.** ⚡ excite; **'an·re·gend I.** *adj.* stimulating; **II.** *adv.*: *~ wirken* have a stimulating effect; **'An·re·gung** *f* (-; -en) **1.** stimulation; *fig. a.* encouragement; impulse, *a.* ⚕ stimulus; *zur ~ des Kreislaufs* to get one's circulation going; **2.** suggestion; *auf ~ von* (*or gen.*) at the suggestion of; **3.** ⚡ excitation; **'An·re·gungs·mit·tel** *n* ⚕ stimulant

an·rei·chern ['anraɪçɐn] (*sep.*, h) **I.** *v/t.* enrich; → *angereichert* II; **II.** *v/refl.*: *sich ~* accumulate; **'An·rei·che·rung** *f* (-; -en) enrichment; accumulation

'An·rei·che·rungs|an·la·ge *f* enrichment plant; *~ver·fah·ren n* enrichment method

'an·rei·hen (*sep.*, h) **I.** *v/t.* add; string *beads etc.*; *aneinander ~* join (*esp. contp.* string) together; **II.** *v/refl.*: *sich ~* line up (*an acc.* next to); follow on

'An·rei·se *f* (-; -n) journey; **'an·rei·sen** *v/i.* (*sep.*, sn) travel; arrive, come

'an·rei·ßen *v/t.* (*irr.*, *sep.*, h, → *reißen*) **1.** tear (slightly); F *fig.* start on, open, break into; **2.** trace, mark out; **3.** *fig.* raise *question etc.*, broach *subject*; **4.** start up *engine*; **'An·rei·ßer** F *m* (-s; -) tout; **'an·rei·ße·risch** *adj.* loud

'An·reiz *m* (-es; -e) incentive (*a.* ✱); **'an·rei·zen** *v/t.* (*sep.*, h) stimulate; *fig. a.* encourage; tempt; *~ zu inf. a.* spur to *inf.*

'an·rem·peln *v/t.* (*sep.*, h) jostle (against), bump (*or* barge) into; *fig. j-n wegen e-r Sache ~* F get a dig in at s.o. about s.th., keep on at s.o. about s.th.

'an·ren·nen *v/i.* (*irr.*, *sep.*, sn, → *rennen*): *~ gegen* run against (*or* into); ⚔ charge; *sport*: throw everything at; *fig.* struggle against; *wir rennen gegen die Zeit an* it's a battle against the clock; *angerannt kommen* come running (along)

An·rich·te ['anrɪçtə] *f* (-; -n) sideboard; **'an·rich·ten** *v/t.* (*sep.*, h) **1.** *gastr.* prepare; arrange; *es ist angerichtet!* dinner *etc.* is served!; **2.** *fig.* cause; do *damage*, wreak *havoc*; *da hast du was Schönes angerichtet* now you've done it; → *Blutbad*

'An·riß *m* (-sses; -sse) **1.** (hairline) crack, fissure; **2.** tracing

'an·rol·len *v/i.* (*sep.*, sn) **1.** roll up; *w.s.* be under way; *angerollt kommen a.* F *fig.* roll up; **2.** start moving; ✈ taxi

'an·ro·sten *v/i.* (*sep.*, sn) start to rust

'an·rö·sten *v/t.* (*sep.*, h) *gastr.* brown

an·rü·chig ['anrʏçɪç] *adj.* **1.** disreputable, of ill repute, F shady; **2.** indecent

'an·rücken (*sep.* -k·k-) *v/i.* (*sep.*, sn) approach; ⚔ advance; F *iro.* F show up

'An·ruf *m* (-[e]s; -e) (phone) call; *~be·ant·wor·ter m* (-s; -) (telephone) answering machine, answerphone

'an·ru·fen (*irr.*, *sep.*, h, → *rufen*) **I.** *v/t.* **1.** call (up), ring (up), phone (up); **2.** implore, invoke; **3.** ⚖ appeal to; **II.** *v/i.* ring (up), call (up); make a phone call; *rufen Sie einfach an a.* just give us *etc.* a call; *ich muß mal eben ~* I've just got to make a phone call (*or* ring s.o. up); **'An·ru·fer** *m* (-s; -) caller

'an·rüh·ren *v/t.* (*sep.*, h) **1.** touch; *fig.* touch (on) *a subject etc.*; *Alkohol (Geld etc.) nicht ~* not to touch alcohol (money *etc.*); **2.** mix; **3.** *fig.* touch, move *s.o.*

ans (= *an das*) → *an*

An·sa·ge ['anza:gə] *f* (-; -n) announcement; *card game*: bid(ding); **'an·sa·gen** (*sep.*, h) **I.** *v/t.* announce; *card game*: bid; *Trumpf ~* declare trumps; → *angesagt* II, *Kampf*; **II.** *v/refl.*: *sich ~* say that one is coming, *esp. iro.* announce one's arrival; **An·sa·ger** ['anza:gɐ] *m* (-s; -), **An·sa·ge·rin** ['anza:gərɪn] *f* (-; -nen) announcer

'an·sam·meln (*sep.*, h) **I.** *v/t.* collect; amass, pile up; **II.** *v/refl.*: *sich ~* accumulate; *fig.* build up; → *angesammelt* II; **'An·samm·lung** *f* (-; -en) collection; accumulation; pile; array; crowd

an·säs·sig ['anzɛsɪç] *adj.* resident; *nicht ~* non-resident; *~ werden* take up residence, settle (*in dat.* in); *~ sein in* have settled in; *er ist seit 30 Jahren hier ~* he's lived here for 30 years

'An·satz *m* (-es; ⸚e) **1.** *anat.* base; → *Haaransatz*; **2.** ⚙ → *Ansatzstück*; **3.** ⛏, *geol.* deposit, sediment; **4.** ♪ lip(ping); intonation; **5.** *fig.* first sign(s *pl.*), beginning(s *pl.*); *er zeigt den ~ zum Bauch* he's starting to get a paunch; *gute (gewisse) Ansätze zeigen* show (some) promise; *er zeigt Ansätze zur Besserung* a) he's slowly beginning to get better, b) it looks as if he's turning over a new leaf; *das ist im ~ richtig, aber ...* you've got the right idea, but ...; **6.** *fig.* attempt; approach; **7.** ℞ formulation; **8.** ✱ estimate; *die Kosten mit 10 Millionen Mark in ~ bringen* estimate the costs at 10 million marks; *~punkt fig. m* start, point of departure; *das ist immerhin ein ~* it's a start; *~stück n* ⚙ **1.** attachment; **2.** extension (piece); ∿*wei·se adv.*: *~ zeigen (enthalten etc.)* show (have *etc.*) the beginnings of

'an·säu·ern *v/t.* (*sep.*, h) acidify

'an·sau·gen *v/t.* (*sep.*, h) suck in (*or* up), *a.* draw in *air*

'An·saug|rohr *n* induction pipe; *~takt m* suction (*or* intake) stroke

'an·schaf·fen (*sep.*, h) **I** *v/t.* buy; *sich et. ~ a.* get (o.s.) s.th., F invest in s.th.; *sich Kinder ~* have children; **II.** *v/i.*: F *~ gehen sl.* go hooking, *Am.* go hustling; **'An·schaf·fung** *f* (-; -en) purchase, purchasing (*gen.* of), investment (in); acquisition, object; *die ~ e-s Autos* buying a car; *das war e-e große ~* it was a big investment

'An·schaf·fungs|ko·sten *pl.* (purchase) cost *sg.*; *die ~ e-s Autos* the cost of buying a car; *~preis m* cost price; *~wert m* cost (*or* acquisition) value

'an·schal·ten *v/t.* (*sep.*, h) switch on, turn on

'an·schau·en *v/t.* → *ansehen*

an·schau·lich ['anʃaʊlɪç] **I.** *adj.* graphic; clear; *~ machen* illustrate, explain *s.th.* clearly; *ich will Ihnen ein ~es Beispiel geben* let me give you an example to illustrate what I mean (*or* that will make things clear); **II.** *adv.* graphically; clearly; *~ schildern* give a graphic description of; *~ vermittelt werden* come across vividly; **'An·schau·lich·keit** *f* (-; *no pl.*) clarity; graphic nature (*gen.* of)

'An·schau·ung *f* (-; -en) **1.** view, opinion; idea, notion; conception; *zu der ~ gelangen, daß* come to the conclusion that; **2.** contemplation; *in ~ versunken* lost in contemplation; **3.** visual perception; *s-e Unterrichtsmethode ist auf ~ gegründet* the visual element is crucial to his teaching method

'An·schau·ungs|ma·te·ri,al *n* illustrative material; audiovisual aids *pl.*; *~,un·ter·richt m* visual instruction; *fig.* object lesson; *~ver·mö·gen n* intuitive faculty; *~wei·se f* approach, point of view

'An·schein *m* (-[e]s; *no pl.*) appearance; semblance; *den ~ gen. erwecken* give the impression of (being); *es hat den ~, als ob* it looks (very much) as if; *sich den ~ geben zu inf.* pretend to *inf.*, *et. zu sein*: make o.s. out to be s.th.; *allem ~ nach* to all appearances, *war er es*: *a.*

it looks very much as if it was him; '**an·schei·nend I.** *adv.* apparently; ***er ist ~ krank*** *a.* he seems to be ill; **II.** *adj.* apparent, seeming; '**An·scheins·be·weis** *m* prima facie evidence

'**an·schei·ßen** V *v/t.* (*irr., sep.,* h, → ***scheißen***) **1.** *sl.* give *s.o.* a bollocking; **2.** F do

'**an·schicken** (*sep.* -k·k-) *v/refl.* (*sep.,* h): ***sich zu*** *et.* ~ get ready for; set about (*ger.*); ***sich ~ zu*** *inf.* get ready to *inf.*; be about to *inf.*, be on the point of *ger.*

'**an·schie·ben** *v/t.* (*irr., sep.,* h, → ***schieben***) push (***an*** *acc.* against); give *s.th.* a push, *a.* give *a car* a bump-start

'**an·schie·len** *v/t.* (*sep.,* h) look at *s.o. or s.th.* from the corner of one's eye; squint at

'**an·schie·ßen** *v/t.* (*irr., sep.,* h, → ***schießen***) shoot at (and wound), hit; *sport*: hit *s.o.* with the ball; F *fig.* F get at *s.o.*; ***angeschossen werden*** *a.* be hit by a bullet (*or* several bullets); F *fig.* ***angeschossen kommen*** F come shooting along; → ***angeschossen*** II

'**an·schim·meln** *v/i.* (*sep.,* sn) start to go mo(u)ldy; → ***angeschimmelt*** II

an·schir·ren ['anʃɪrən] *v/t.* (*sep.,* h) harness

'**An·schiß** V *m* (-sses; -sse) *sl.* bollocking; ***e-n ~ bekommen*** be given (*or* get) a bollocking

'**An·schlag** *m* (-[e]s; ⸚e) **1.** poster; notice; ***e-n ~ machen*** put a notice up; **2.** attack; ***ein ~ auf j-n*** (***j-s Leben***) an attempt on s.o.'s life; ***es ist ein ~ auf X verübt worden*** there has been an attempt on X's life, X has been the victim of an (*or* a terrorist) attack; **3.** *typewriter*: stroke; space; ***60 Anschläge pro Zeile*** 60 characters per line; ***220 Anschläge pro Minute*** 220 strokes a minute; ***die Tastatur hat e-n sehr leichten ~*** the keyboard has a very light touch; **4.** ♪ *etc.* touch; **5.** *swimming*: touch; **6.** *gun*: firing position; **7.** ⚙ stop; ***bis zum ~ aufdrehen*** turn *s.th.* as far as it will go, open *s.th.* up completely; **8.** ☤ estimate; **~brett** *n* notice (*or* bulletin) board; ***auf dem ~*** *a.* (up) on the board; **~drucker** (*sep.* -k·k-) *m computer*: impact printer

'**an·schla·gen** (*irr., sep.,* h, → ***schlagen***) **I.** *v/t.* **1.** hit, knock (***an*** *acc.* against); ***sich den Ellbogen*** *etc.* ***~ an*** *dat.* knock one's elbow *etc.* on (*or* against) s.th.; → ***angeschlagen*** II; **2.** fasten, fix; stick up, put up; **3.** ♪ hit, strike; sound, ring *bell*; strike *the hour*; ***den Ton ~*** give the note, *fig.* set the tone; *fig.* ***den richtigen Ton ~*** strike the right note; ***e-n frechen*** (***sarkastischen***) ***Ton ~*** start to get cheeky (sarcastic); **4.** ~ ***auf*** *acc.* aim *gun etc.* at; **5.** ☤ estimate; **II.** *v/i.* **6.** (sn) ~ ***an*** *dat. or acc.* hit (*waves*: break) against; ***mit dem Kopf an die Wand ~*** hit one's head against the wall; **7.** bark; **8.** *swimming*: touch; **9.** *drug etc.*: take effect; **10.** tell; ***bei mir schlägt jedes Stück Kuchen an*** every little piece of cake tells with me

'**An·schlag|säu·le** *f* advertising pillar; **~ta·fel** *f* → ***Anschlagbrett***

'**an·schlei·chen** (*irr., sep.,* → ***schleichen***) **I.** *v/i.* (sn) *and v/refl.* (h): (***sich***) ~ ***an*** *acc.* creep up on, *a.* stalk; ***angeschlichen kommen*** a) come sneaking up, b) F turn up on the doorstep; **II.** *v/t.* (h) creep up on, *a.* stalk

'**an·schlep·pen** *v/t.* (*sep.,* h) **1.** (*a.* ***angeschleppt bringen***) drag along, *a.* F have *s.o.* in tow; **2.** *mot.* give *a car* a tow

'**an·schlie·ßen** (*irr., sep.,* h, → ***schließen***) **I.** *v/t.* **1.** padlock (***an*** *dat. or acc.* to); chain (to); **2.** ⚙ connect (***an*** *dat. or acc.* to), ⚡ *a.* hook up (to); plug in(to); ***angeschlossen werden an*** *acc.* be connected to, get plugged into, get hooked up to; **3.** add (***an*** *acc.* to); **II.** *v/refl.*: ***sich ~*** **4.** follow; ***an den Vortrag schloß sich e-e Diskussion an*** the lecture was followed by a discussion; **5.** (*dat.*) join *s.o.*; take *s.o.'s* side; support, endorse *view etc.*; follow *example etc.*; follow suit; ***der Meinung schließe ich mich an*** I'd like to support that view; **6.** border (***an*** *acc.* on); '**an·schlie·ßend I.** *adv.* afterwards, *formal*: subsequently; **II.** *adj.* subsequent, ... that followed

'**An·schluß** *m* (-sses; ⸚sse) 🚂, ⚡, *teleph.* connection; *teleph.* line; ⚙ supply; affiliation (***an*** *acc.* with *a party etc.*); *pol.* union; ~ ***bekommen*** *teleph.* get through; ~ ***finden*** a) make contact *or* friends (***bei*** *dat.* with), b) *sport*: catch up (***an*** *acc.* with), *soccer etc.*: get back into the game, narrow the gap *in the league table*; ***kein ~ unter dieser Nummer*** number no longer in use; 🚂 ***~ haben*** have a connection; ***den ~ verpassen*** miss one's connection, F *fig.* miss the boat; ~ ***suchen*** look for company; ***im ~ an*** *acc.* after, following, *formal*: subsequent to, ***unser Schreiben***: further to our letter; → ***daran***; **~do·se** *f* ⚡ socket; **~flug** *m* connecting flight, connection; **~gleis** *n* 🚂 siding; **~ka·bel** *n* ⚡ connecting lead; *teleph.* subscriber's cable; **~leitung** *f* connecting pipe; **~rei·se** *f* add-on trip; **~stel·le** *f* (motorway) junction; **~strecke** (*sep.* -k·k-) *f* 🚂 feeder line; **~tor** *n*, **~tref·fer** *m sport*: *goal that gets a team back into the match*; **~zug** *m* connecting train, connection

'**an·schmach·ten** *v/t.* (*sep.,* h) drool over

'**an·schmei·ßen** F *v/t.* (*irr., sep.,* h, → ***schmeißen***) ⚙ F get *s.th.* going

'**an·schmie·gen** *v/refl.* (*sep.,* h): ***sich ~*** fit snugly; ***sich ~ an*** *acc.* snuggle up to; '**an·schmieg·sam** *adj.* affectionate

'**an·schmie·ren** (*sep.,* h) **I.** *v/t.* **1.** smear; **2.** F ***j-n ~*** F take s.o. for a ride; **3.** F ***j-m et. ~*** fob s.th. off on s.o.; **II.** *v/refl.* **4. *sich ~*** a) dirty o.s.; b) F put one's face (*or* war paint) on; **5.** F ***sich bei j-m ~*** F suck up to s.o.

'**an·schmo·ren** *v/t.* (*sep.,* h) *gastr.* braise

'**an·schnal·len** (*sep.,* h) **I.** *v/t.* strap on; put on *skis, skates*; **II.** *v/refl.*: ***sich ~*** ✈ *etc.* fasten one's seatbelt; *mot. a.* belt up, buckle up, wear a seatbelt

'**An·schnall|gurt** *m* ✈, *mot.* seatbelt; **~pflicht** *f* compulsory wearing of seatbelts; ***es besteht ~*** it's compulsory to wear seatbelts; ***die ~ besteht seit ...*** the seatbelt law was introduced in ...

'**an·schnau·zen** F *v/t.* (*sep.,* h) snarl at; '**An·schnau·zer** F *m*: ***e-n ~ bekommen*** F get bawled (*Am.* chewed) out

'**an·schnei·den** *v/t.* (*irr., sep.,* h, → ***schneiden***) cut into, start *bread etc.*; put a spin on *a ball*; *fig.* broach, touch on *a subject etc.*; → ***angeschnitten*** II

'**an·schnei·en** *v/i.* → ***angeschneit***

'**An·schnitt** *m* (-[e]s; -e) first slice, F end bit

'**an·schnor·ren** F *v/t.* (*sep.,* h): ***j-n*** (***um et.***) ~ F scrounge (s.th.) off s.o.

An·scho·vis [an'ʃoːvɪs] *f* (-; *no pl.*) anchovy

'**an·schrau·ben** *v/t.* (*sep.,* h) screw on(to ***an*** *dat. or acc.*)

'**an·schrei·ben** (*irr., sep.,* h, → ***schreiben***) **I.** *v/t.* **1.** write; ***et. an die Tafel ~*** write s.th. up on the (black)board (*Am. a.* chalkboard); **2.** write to *s.o.*; **3. *j-m et. ~*** charge s.th. to s.o.'s account; ***et. ~ lassen*** take s.th. on credit; *fig.* → ***angeschrieben*** II; **II.** 2 *n* (-s; -) ☤ cover note

'**an·schrei·en** *v/t.* (*irr., sep.,* h, → ***schreien***) shout at, scream at

'**An·schrift** *f* (-; -en) address; '**An·schriften·än·de·rung** *f* change of address

an·schul·di·gen ['anʃʊldɪgən] *v/t.* (*sep.,* h) accuse (*gen.* of); '**An·schul·di·gung** *f* (-; -en) accusation, charge

'**an·schwär·men** (*sep.,* h) **I.** *v/t.* idolize, F be crazy about; **II.** *v/i.* (*a.* ***angeschwärmt kommen***) come swarming along

'**an·schwär·zen** *v/t.* (*sep.,* h) **1.** blacken; **2.** *fig.* ***j-n ~*** run s.o. down, blacken s.o.'s name

'**an·schwei·gen** *v/t.* (*irr., sep.,* h, → ***schweigen***) not to say a word to *s.o.*; ***sie haben sich*** (***gegenseitig***) ***angeschwiegen*** they just sat there and didn't say a word to each other, they just sat there in silence

'**an·schwei·ßen** *v/t.* (*sep.,* h) weld on(to ***an*** *dat. or acc.*)

'**an·schwel·len** *v/i.* (*irr., sep.,* sn, → ***schwellen***) ⚕, ♪ swell; *river*: *a.* rise; *fig. noise etc.*: grow louder; *work*: mount; → ***angeschwollen***; '**An·schwel·lung** *f* (-; -en) swelling

'**an·schwem·men** *v/t.* (*sep.,* h) wash ashore (*or* up); *geol.* deposit; → ***angeschwemmt*** II; '**An·schwem·mung** *f* (-; -en) *geol.* alluvial deposits *pl.*, alluvium

'**an·schwim·men** *v/i.* (*irr., sep.,* sn, → ***schwimmen***) → ***Strom*** 1

'**an·schwin·deln** *v/t.* (*sep.,* h): ***j-n ~*** lie to s.o., tell s.o. a lie (*or* fib)

'**an·schwir·ren** *v/i.* (*sep.,* sn) (*a.* ***angeschwirrt kommen***) come flying along; F *fig.* F come breezing along

'**an·schwit·zen** *v/t.* (*sep.,* h) *gastr.* brown lightly

'**an·se·geln** (*sep.*) **I.** *v/i.* (sn) (*a.* ***angesegelt kommen***) come sailing along (*a.* F *fig.*); **II.** *v/t.* (h) make for

'**an·se·hen** (*irr., sep.,* h, → ***sehen***) **I.** *v/t.* look at; ***sich et.*** (***genau***) ~ take (*or* have) a (close *or* good) look at s.th.; ***sich e-n Film ~*** go and see a film; ***et. mit ~*** see (*or* stand by and watch) s.th.; *fig.* ***ich kann es nicht länger mit ~*** I can't take it any longer; ***man sieht's ihm doch an*** you can tell just by looking at him; ***man sieht ihm sein Alter nicht an*** he doesn't look his age; *fig.* ~ ***für*** (*or* ***als***) regard as, consider (to be); ***wie ich die Sache ansehe*** as I see it; F ***sieh mal einer an!*** F well, what do you know!; → ***angesehen, Auge*** 1, ***finster, schief*** II; **II.** 2 *n* (-s; *no pl.*) **1.** respect; ***in hohem ~ stehen*** be held in great esteem; ***in j-s ~ steigen*** rise in s.o.'s estimation; ***ohne ~ der Person*** without respect of persons; **2. *j-n*** (***nur***) ***vom ~ kennen*** know s.o. by sight; ***dem ~ nach*** on the face of it

an·sehn·lich ['anzeːnlɪç] *adj.* **1.** considerable; ***e-e ~e Summe*** a tidy little sum; **2.** handsome, good-looking

an·sei·len ['anzaɪlən] *v/t. and v/refl.* (***sich*** **~**) (*sep.*, h) rope (up)

'an·sen·gen *v/t.* (*sep.*, h) singe

'an·set·zen (*sep.*, h) **I.** *v/t.* **1.** (put into) position; put on; add (***an*** *dat. or acc.* to); sew on(to); put *glass, flute etc.* to one's lips; ***die Feder*** **~** put pen to paper; **2.** *gastr.* make, prepare, mix; **3.** fix, set *a date*; **4.** ***j-n auf j-n*** (***et.***) **~** put s.o. onto s.o. (s.th.); **5.** fix *price*; assess *costs etc.*; ***zu hoch*** (***niedrig***) **~** overestimate (underestimate); **6.** ✎ develop; **7.** ***Fett*** **~** put on weight; ***Rost*** **~** start to rust; ***Schimmel*** **~** start to mo(u)ld (*or* go mo[u]ldy); **II.** *v/i.* **8.** (make a) start; ***zum Sprechen*** *etc.* **~** be about to speak *etc.*; ✈ ***zur Landung*** **~** come in to land; ***zum Sprung*** **~** get ready to jump (*or* for a jump); **9.** *criticism etc.*: set in; **10.** put on weight; **11.** *gastr.* burn, stick to the bottom of the pan; **12.** ✎ ***gut angesetzt haben*** be coming up nicely; **III.** *v/refl.*: ***sich*** **~** accumulate, ⚗ *a.* be deposited; ***am Wagen hat sich Rost angesetzt*** the car's starting to rust

'An·sicht *f* (-; -en) **1.** view; ***~en von London*** views of London; ***mit e-r ~ des Doms*** *postcard etc.* with a view of (*or* showing) the cathedral; **2.** view; **~** ***von vorne*** (***hinten***) front (rear) view; **3.** ✝ ***zur ~ schicken*** send on approval; **4.** opinion, view; ***nach ~ von*** (*or gen.*) in the opinion of, according to; ***ich bin*** (***da***) ***anderer ~*** I don't see it that way; ***die ~en sind geteilt*** opinion is divided; ***der ~ sein*** (*or* ***die ~ vertreten***)***, daß*** take the view that; ***zu der ~ kommen, daß*** come to the conclusion that, decide that

'An·sichts|ex·em,plar *n* specimen (*or* inspection) copy; **~kar·te** *f* picture postcard; **~sa·che** *f*: ***das ist ~*** that's a matter of opinion; **~sen·dung** *f* sample on approval

'an·sie·deln (*sep.*, h) **I.** *v/refl.*: ***sich ~*** settle; **II.** *v/t.* settle; *fig.* place; *das Manuskript* ***ist im 9. Jahrhundert anzusiedeln*** goes back to (*or* belongs to) the 9th century; **'An·sied·ler** *m* (-s; -) settler, colonist; **'An·sied·lung** *f* (-; -en) **1.** settlement, colonization; **2.** settlement, colony

'An·sin·nen *n* (-s; -) (strange) request; ***an j-n das ~ stellen zu*** *inf.* expect s.o. to *inf.*; ***ein freches ~!*** what a nerve (to expect anyone to do that)

an·son·sten [an'zɔnstən] *adv.* **1.** otherwise, apart from that; **2.** otherwise

'an·span·nen (*sep.*, h) **I.** *v/t.* **1.** harness (***an*** *acc.* to); **2.** pull *a rope* taut; **3.** *fig.* exert; strain; flex, tense *muscles*; ***alle Kräfte ~*** strain every nerve; → ***angespannt*** II; **II.** *v/refl.*: ***sich ~*** tense up; **'An·span·nung** *f* (-; -en) strain, exertion; tension (*a. fig.*)

'an·spa·ren *v/t.* (*sep.*, h) save

'an·spei·en *v/t.* (*irr.*, *sep.*, h, → ***speien***) spit at

'An·spiel *n* (-[e]s; -e) *sport*: start of play, *soccer*: kick-off; pass; *card game*: lead; **'an·spie·len** (*sep.*, h) **I.** *v/i.* **1.** *sport*: lead off; *soccer*: kick off; *tennis*: serve; *card game*: (have the) lead; **2.** *fig.* **~** ***auf*** *acc.* allude to, hint at; **II.** *v/t. Sport*: ***j-n ~*** pass (the ball) to s.o.; **'An·spie·lung** *f* (-; -en) allusion (***auf*** *acc.* to), hint (at); ***versteckte ~*** innuendo

'an·spin·nen *fig.* (*irr.*, *sep.*, h, → ***spinnen***) **I.** *v/t.* enter into; **II.** *v/refl.*: ***sich ~*** start up

'an·spit·zen *v/t.* (*sep.*, h) sharpen; F *fig.* ***j-n ~*** F have a go at s.o. (*to do s.th.*); **'An·spit·zer** *m* (-s; -) sharpener

'An·sporn *m* (-[e]s; *no pl.*) incentive (*dat. or* ***für*** to); **'an·spor·nen** *v/t.* (*sep.*, h) spur; *fig.* spur on

'An·spra·che *f* (-; -n) **1.** address, speech (***an*** *acc.* to); ***e-e ~ halten*** give an address, make a speech; **2.** F ***keine ~ haben*** have no-one to talk to

an·sprech·bar ['anʃprɛçbaːɐ] *adj.* responsive; ***er ist nicht ~*** a) he's too busy to see anyone, b) he's dead to the world, c) he's not talking to anyone (today), d) he's unable to communicate; **'an·spre·chen** (*irr.*, *sep.*, h, → ***sprechen***) **I.** *v/t.* **1.** speak to *s.o.* (***auf*** *acc.* about); approach *s.o.* (about, on); accost, solicit; **~** ***als*** address as; ***ich habe ihn einfach angesprochen*** I just started talking to him; ***ich fühle mich nicht angesprochen*** it's got nothing to do with me; ***keiner fühlt sich angesprochen*** nobody wants anything to do with it (*or* wants to know); **2.** appeal to; reach; **3.** touch (up)on *question etc.*; **4.** appeal to; ***e-n breiten Kreis ~*** have wide appeal, be very popular; **II.** *v/i.* **5.** *patient etc.*: respond (***auf*** *acc.* to), *drug etc.*: have the desired effect, work; ***die Medizin spricht bei ihm nicht an*** he's not responding (*or* reacting) to the medicine, the medicine's having no effect on him; **6.** go down well (***bei*** *dat.* with); **'an·spre·chend** *adj.* pleasing, pleasant, attractive; engaging; considerable *achievement etc.*; pleasant, savo(u)ry *wine*

'An·sprech|part·ner *m* **1.** contact; ***wer ist dort mein ~?*** who should I get in touch with?; **2.** somebody to talk to; **~zeit** *f computer*: response time

'an·sprin·gen (*irr.*, *sep.*, → ***springen***) **I.** *v/t.* (h) jump at; **II.** *v/i.* (sn) *engine*: start (up); F *fig.* **~** ***auf*** *acc.* F jump at *an offer etc.*

'an·sprit·zen *v/t.* (*sep.*, h) spray; spatter

'An·spruch *m* (-[e]s; ⸚e) *a.* ⚖ claim (***auf*** *acc.* to), demand (for); ⚖ right; ***große*** (***bescheidene***) ***Ansprüche stellen*** (not to) be very demanding; ***hohe Ansprüche an j-n stellen*** make great demands on s.o., expect a great deal of s.o.; **~** ***erheben auf*** *acc.*, ***für sich in ~ nehmen*** claim, lay claim to; **~** ***haben auf*** *acc.* be entitled to, ⚖ have a legitimate claim to; **~** ***auf Schadenersatz erheben*** (make a) claim for damages; ***das Buch erhebt keinen ~ auf historische Genauigkeit*** the book doesn't claim to be historically accurate; ***in ~ nehmen*** call on *s.o.*, take up, make use of *s.o.'s offer*, take up *room, time*; ***ich will Ihre Zeit nicht zu sehr in ~ nehmen*** I don't want to take up too much of your time; ***ihre Arbeit nimmt sie stark in ~*** her work keeps her very busy (*or* takes up most of her time [and energy])

'an·spruchs·los *adj.* modest, easily satisfied; plain, simple; lowbrow; ***das Stück war ziemlich ~*** there wasn't much to the play; **'An·spruchs·lo·sig·keit** *f* (-; *no pl.*) modesty; simplicity; lack of sophistication

'an·spruchs·voll *adj.* demanding, *a.* highbrow; particular; critical; ✝ upmarket

'an·spucken (*sep.* -k·k-) *v/t.* (*sep.*, h) spit at

'an·spü·len *v/t.* → ***anschwemmen***

'an·sta·cheln *v/t.* (*sep.*, h) spur on; goad (***zu*** into [*doing*] *s.th.*)

An·stalt ['anʃtalt] *f* (-; -en) **1.** establishment; (***öffentliche ~*** public) institution; ⚕ sanatorium, *Am.* sanitarium, F asylum; institute, school; home; **2.** ***~en machen zu*** *inf.* get ready to *inf.*; ***keine ~en machen zu*** *inf.* make no move to *inf.*; ***er machte keine ~en zu gehen*** he wouldn't budge; ***~en zu et. treffen*** make arrangements for s.th.

'An·stalts|arzt *m* resident physician; **~klei·dung** *f* institute clothing (*or* dress); **~lei·ter** *m* director of the (*or* an) institution

An·stand *m* (-[e]s; *no pl.*) (sense of) decency; manners *pl.*; ***j-m ein bißchen ~ beibringen*** teach s.o. how to behave; ***mit ~ verlieren können*** be a good loser; ***den ~ wahren*** preserve a sense of decency (*or* decorum); → ***verletzen***

an·stän·dig ['anʃtɛndɪç] **I.** *adj.* decent (*a.* F *fig.*); proper; reasonable; F ***e-e ~e Tracht Prügel*** a good hiding; **II** *adv.* decently; properly (*a.* F *fig.*); ***sich ~ benehmen*** behave (o.s.) (well); ***er kann sich nicht ~ benehmen*** he doesn't know how to behave (himself); ***j-n ~ behandeln*** treat s.o. like a human being; F ***j-m ~ die Meinung sagen*** F give s.o. a piece of one's mind

'An·stands|be·such *m* courtesy (*or* duty) call; **~da·me** *f* chaperon(e); **~ge·fühl** *n* sense of decency; tact

'an·stands·hal·ber *adv.* for decency's sake

'An·stands·hap·pen F *m* morsel left for manners, F last bit that nobody wants to touch

'an·stands·los *adv.* without further ado, F no bother; freely

'An·stands|re·gel *f* rule of etiquette; *pl. a.* social conventions; **~wau·wau** F *m* chaperon(e)

'an·star·ren *v/t.* (*sep.*, h) stare at

an'statt I. *prp.* (*gen.*) instead of; **II.** *cj.*: **~** ***daß er kam, ~ zu kommen*** instead of coming

'an·stau·en (*sep.*, h) **I.** *v/t. and v/refl.* (***sich ~***) → ***stauen***; **II.** *fig. v/refl.*: ***sich ~*** build up; → ***angestaut*** II

'an·stau·nen *v/t.* (*sep.*, h) gaze at *s.o.*, *s.th.* in amazement; gape at

'an·ste·chen *v/t.* (*irr.*, *sep.*, h, → ***stechen***) prick; puncture, slit *tires etc.*; tap *barrel*; → ***angestochen*** II

'an·stecken (*sep.* -k·k-) (*sep.*, h) **I.** *v/t.* **1.** pin on; put (*or* slip) *ring* on; **2.** set *s.th.* on fire; set *s.th.* alight; light *candle, cigar etc.*; **3.** ⚕ infect (***mit*** with); ***angesteckt werden*** catch a cold *or* the measles *etc.* (from s.o.); ***er hat mich mit s-r Erkältung angesteckt*** he's given me his cold, he's passed his cold on to me; *fig.* ***sie hat uns alle mit ihrem Gelächter angesteckt*** she had us all laughing too, her laughter was contagious; **II.** *v/refl.*: ***sich ~*** catch a cold *or* the measles *etc.* (***bei*** *dat.* from); ***ich habe mich bei X angesteckt*** I caught (*or* got) it from X, X gave it (*or* passed it on) to me; ***steck dich bloß nicht an!*** don't you go and catch it!; **III.** *v/i.* ⚕ *and fig.* be catching (*or* infectious, contagious); **'an·steckend** (*sep.* -k·k-) *adj.* infectious; contagious; F catching (*all a. fig.*)

'An·steck·na·del *f* pin; badge

'**An·steckung** (*sep.* -k·k-) *f* (-; -en) ⚕ infection

'**An·steckungs|ge·fahr** *f* danger of infection; **~herd** *m* focus (of infection)

'**an·ste·hen** (*irr., sep.*, h, → **stehen**) **I.** *v/i.* **1.** stand in a queue (*Am.* line); queue up, *a. Am.* line up, stand in line; (**nach** *dat.* for; **vor** *dat.* at, in front of); **2.** be waiting (**zur Diskussion** for discussion); *work*: be waiting to be done; *date*: be fixed (**auf** *acc.* for); **es steht dringend an** it's top priority, it can't wait; **was steht an?** what's next on the agenda?; **3. ~ lassen** put off, put off paying; **4.** *formal*: **j-m** (**schlecht**) **~** (ill) befit s.o.; **es steht ihm nicht an zu** *inf.* it's not for him to *inf.*

'**an·stei·gen** *v/i.* (*irr., sep.*, sn, → **steigen**) rise; *fig. a.* go up, increase; **jäh ~** rise steeply (*fig. a.* sharply), *fig. a.* escalate; → **angestiegen** II

an'stel·le *prp.*: **~ von** (*or gen.*) instead of, in place of

'**an·stel·len** (*sep.*, h) **I.** *v/t.* **1.** put, lean (**an** *dat.or acc.* against); add; **2.** employ, take on, *esp. Am.* hire; F **j-n zu et. ~** rope s.o. in to do s.th.; → **angestellt**; **3.** start; turn on *light, water etc.*; switch on *light, radio etc.*; **4.** do; **Überlegungen ~ über** *acc.* think about; → **Vergleich** 1; **5.** F be up to; **etwas ~** get (*or* be) up to mischief; **6.** manage, do; F **was soll ich damit ~?** F what am I supposed to do with it?; **was soll ich mit dir ~?** F you're a hopeless (*sl.* right) case, you are; **II.** *v/refl.*: **7. sich ~** queue up, *a. Am.* line up, get in line; **8. sich ~, als ob ...** act as if ...; pretend to *inf.*; **er hat sich sehr (un)geschickt angestellt** he tackled it very well, he made a good (bad) job of it (he made a hash of it); **stell dich nicht so an!** stop making such a fuss, *w.s.* F stop acting stupid

'**An·stel·lung** *f* (-; -en) employment; post, job

'**An·stel·lungs|be·din·gun·gen** *pl.* terms of employment; **~ver·trag** *m* employment contract

'**an·stem·men** *v/refl.* (*sep.*, h): **sich** (**mit der Schulter** *etc.*) **~ gegen** press o.s. (one's shoulder *etc.*) against

'**an·steu·ern** *v/t.* (*sep.*, h) **1.** ⚓, ✈ steer (*or* head, make) for; **2.** *fig.* head for; have one's sights set on

'**An·stich** *m* (-[e]s; *no pl.*) tap; **frischer ~** fresh tap

An·stieg ['anʃti:k] *m* (-[e]s; -e ['anʃti:gə]) ascent; gradient, *Am.* grade; *fig.* rise, increase (*gen.* in); **steiler ~** steep incline, *fig.* steep rise (*gen.* in)

'**an·stie·ren** *v/t.* (*sep.*, h) stare at

'**an·stif·ten** *v/t.* (*sep.*, h) cause; incite, instigate; hatch *a plot*; **j-n zu et. ~** put s.o. up to s.th.; '**An·stif·ter** *m* (-s; -) instigator; ringleader; '**An·stif·tung** *f* (-; -en) instigation; incitement

'**an·stim·men** *v/t.* (*sep.*, h) start singing, F launch into *a song*; start playing, strike up *a tune*; start *screaming*

'**an·stin·ken** F (*irr., sep.*, h, → **stinken**) **I.** *v/t.*: **das stinkt mich allmählich an** F it's beginning to get my goat; **II.** *v/i.*: **gegen die kannst du doch nicht ~** *sl.* you haven't got a chance in hell against them

'**An·stoß** *m* (-es; ⸚e) **1.** *soccer*: kick-off; **der ~ ist um drei** kick-off is at three; **2.** *fig.* impulse, impetus; **den** (**ersten**) **~ geben zu** start off; **er hat den ~ gegeben** *a.* it was his initiative (*or* idea); **3.** offen|ce (*Am.* -se); **~ erregen** cause offen|ce (*Am.* -se) (**bei** *dat.* to); **wir wollen keinen ~ erregen** we don't want to cause any offen|ce (*Am.* -se), we don't want to offend anyone; **~ nehmen an** *dat.* take offen|ce (*Am.* -se) at, take exception to; → **Stein**

'**an·sto·ßen** (*irr., sep.*, h, → **stoßen**) **I.** *v/t.* **1.** give *s.th.* a push; knock, bump (**sich den Kopf** one's head; **an** *dat.* against); kick *ball*; **II.** *v/i.* **2.** (sn) **~ an** *dat.* (*or* **gegen**) bump (*or* knock) against; **mit dem Kopf ~ an** *dat.* (*or* **gegen** *acc.*) knock (*or* bang) one's head on (*or* against) s.th.; **3.** clink glasses; **auf et.** (**j-s Wohl**) **~** drink to s.th. (s.o.'s health); **4. bei j-m ~** offend s.o. (**mit** *dat.* with); **5. mit der Zunge ~** lisp; **6.** *soccer*: kick off; '**an·sto·ßend** *adj.* adjacent, adjoining

an·stö·ßig ['anʃtø:sɪç] *adj.* objectionable, offensive; indecent, improper; '**An·stö·ßig·keit** *f* (-; -en) offensiveness, offensive nature; indecency

'**an·strah·len** *v/t.* (*sep.*, h) shine a light *etc.* on; *thea. etc.* spotlight, turn the spotlight on; illuminate, light up *building etc.*; *fig.* beam at *s.o.*; → **angestrahlt**

'**an·stre·ben** *v/t.* (*sep.*, h) aim at, *formal*: strive for

'**an·strei·chen** *v/t.* (*irr., sep.*, h, → **streichen**) **1.** paint; whitewash; **2.** mark; underline; mark *s.th.* wrong; '**An·strei·cher** *m* (-s; -) painter

an·stren·gen ['anʃtrɛŋən] (*sep.*, h) **I.** *v/t.* **1.** exert, strain, be a strain on; tire (out); exhaust; **übermäßig ~** overtax; **2.** ⚖ → **Prozeß** 2; **II.** *v/refl.*: **sich ~** make an effort, try (hard), exert o.s.; F **streng dich mal an!** you could try a bit harder, *iro.* don't strain yourself; → **angestrengt** II; **III.** *v/i.*: **das strengt an** it's hard work; '**an·stren·gend** *adj.* hard (**für die Augen** *etc.* on the eyes *etc.*), strenuous; '**An·stren·gung** *f* (-; -en) strain; effort, *w.s. a.* endeavo(u)r; **mit äußerster ~** by a supreme effort; **ohne ~** effortlessly; **~en machen** → **anstrengen** II

'**An·strich** *m* (-[e]s; -e) **1.** *no pl.* painting; **2.** coat(ing); paint; **3.** *fig.* air, look; tinge, *pol. etc.* complexion; **sich den ~ geben** *gen.* (*or* **von**) give o.s. the air of (*being*)

'**an·strö·men** *v/i.* (*sep.*, sn) **1.** (*a.* **angeströmt kommen**) come streaming along; **2. ~de Kaltluft** a stream of cold air

'**an·stücke(l)n** (*sep.* -k·k-) *v/t.* (*sep.*, h) **1.** piece on, add; **~ an** *acc.* piece (*or* add) onto; **2.** add to (*a. fig.*)

'**An·sturm** *m* (-[e]s; *no pl.*) assault (**auf** *acc.* on); onslaught (on) (*a. fig.*); *sport*: attack; *fig.* rush; *fig.* **~ auf** *acc.* rush for, run on; '**an·stür·men** *v/i.* (*sep.*, sn) charge (*a.* **~ gegen**); *wind*: storm (**gegen** *acc.* against); **angestürmt kommen** come charging along

'**an·stür·zen** *v/i.* (*only p.p.*): **angestürzt kommen** F come pelting along

'**an·su·chen** (*sep.*, h) **I.** *v/i.*: **bei j-m um et. ~** request s.th. of s.o.; apply to s.o. for s.th.; **II.** 𝔖 *n* (-s; -) request; application

An·ta·go·nis·mus [antago'nɪsmʊs] *m* (-; -men) antagonism; **An·ta·go·nist** [antago'nɪst] *m* (-en; -en) antagonist; **an·ta·go·ni·stisch** [antago'nɪstɪʃ] *adj.* antagonistic(ally *adv.*)

'**an·tan·zen** F *v/i.* (*sep.*, sn) (*a.* **angetanzt kommen**) F turn up; F waltz in

ant·ark·tisch [ant'ʔarktɪʃ] *adj.* Antarctic

'**an·ta·sten** *v/t.* (*sep.*, h) touch (*a. fig.*); *fig.* break into *supplies*; infringe on, encroach on *s.o.'s rights etc.*; broach, touch on *a subject etc.*

'**an·tau·en** *v/i.* (*sep.*, sn) start to thaw; **~ lassen** leave *s.th.* to defrost for a while; → **angetaut** II

'**an·täu·schen** *v/t.* (*sep.*, h) *sport*: fake *a shot*

Ant·azi·dum [ant'ʔa:tsidʊm] *n* (-s; -da) *pharm.* antacid

'**An·teil** *m* (-[e]s; -e) **1.** share (**an** *dat.* of); ⚖ portion; ✝ interest; **e-n ~ an e-r Sache haben** have a part in s.th.; **2.** *fig.* interest; sympathy; **~ nehmen an** take an interest in, sympathize with; **an·tei·lig** ['antaɪlɪç], '**an·teil·mä·ßig** *adj.* (*and adv.*) proportionate(ly)

'**An·teil·nah·me** *f* (-; *no pl.*) **1.** interest; **et. mit reger ~ verfolgen** follow s.th. closely (*or* with great interest); **2.** sympathy; **j-m s-e ~ aussprechen** express one's condolences to s.o.

'**An·teil·schein** *m* share certificate *Am.* share of stock

'**an·te·le·fo,nie·ren** *v/t.* (*sep.*, h) (tele)phone, ring up, call up

An·ten·ne [an'tɛnə] *f* (-; -n) **1.** aerial, antenna; **2.** *zo.* antenna, feeler; **3.** *fig.* feeling

An'ten·nen|ka·bel *n* aerial (*or* antenna) cable; **~mast** *m* radio mast; **~steck·do·se** *f* aerial (*or* antenna) socket; **~stecker** (*sep.* -k·k-) *m* aerial (*or* antenna) plug; **~ver·stär·ker** *m* (aerial *or* antenna) booster; **~wald** *m* sea of aerials (*or* antennae)

An·tho·lo·gie [antolo'gi:] *f* (-; -n) anthology

An·thra·zit [antra'tsi:t] *m* (-s; -e) anthracite; 𝔖**far·ben** *adj.* charcoal grey (*Am.* gray)

An·thro·po·lo·ge [antropo'lo:gə] *m* (-n; -n) anthropologist; **An·thro·po·lo·gie** [antropolo'gi:] *f* (-; *no pl.*) anthropology; **an·thro·po·lo·gisch** [antropo'lo:gɪʃ] *adj.* anthropological

An·thro·po·soph [antropo'zo:f] *m* (-en; -en) anthroposophist; **An·thro·po·so·phie** [antropozo'fi:] *f* (-; *no pl.*) anthroposophy; **an·thro·po·so·phisch** [antro-po'zo:fɪʃ] *adj.* anthroposophical

Anti..., anti... [anti-] *in cpds.* anti(-)..

An·ti·al·ko'ho·li·ker *m* teetotal(l)er

an·ti·au·to·ri'tär *adj.* anti-authoritarian

An·ti'ba·by·pil·le F *f* birth control pill, F *the* pill

an·ti·bak·te·ri'ell *adj.* bactericidal

An·ti·be'schlag·tuch *n mot.* anti-mist cloth

An·ti·bio·ti·kum [anti'bĭo:tikʊm] *n* (-s; -ka) ⚕ antibiotic

An·ti·blockier·sy,stem (*sep.* -k·k-) *n mot.* anti-lock (*or* anti-skid) braking system

An·ti·de·pres·si·vum [antidepre'si:vʊm] *n* (-s; -va) antidepressant

An·ti·fa'schis·mus *m* anti-Fascism; **An·ti·fa'schist** *m*, **an·ti·fa'schi·stisch** *adj.* anti-Fascist

An·ti·gen [anti'ge:n] *n* (-s; -e) antigen

An·ti'haft·be·schich·tung *f*: **mit ~** non-stick

'**An·ti·held** *m* antihero

An·ti·hi·sta·min [antihɪsta'mi:n] *n* (-s; -e) antihistamine

an·tik [an'ti:k] *adj.* **1.** ancient, classical; ***die ~e Philosophie*** ancient (*or* classical) philosophy; ***die ~en Völker*** the peoples of the Ancient World; ***das ~e Rom*** Ancient Rome; **2.** a) antique, period *furniture*; b) reproduction *furniture*; ***auf ~ gemacht*** done up to look old

An·ti·ke [an'ti:kə] *f* (-; -n) **1.** *no pl.* (classical) antiquity; *the* Classical (*or* Ancient) World; ***das Griechenland der ~*** Ancient Greece; ***die Welt der ~*** the Ancient World; **2.** antiquity, antique (*or* ancient) work of art

an·ti·ki·sie·rend [antiki'zi:rənt] *adj.* *poetry etc.*: in classical style; in a classical vein

An·ti'klopf·mit·tel *n mot.* anti-knock agent

An·ti·koa·gu·lans [antiko'ʔa:gulans] *n* (-; -tia [-koʔagu'lantsĭa]) ⚕ anticoagulant

An·ti·kom·mu'nist *m*, **an·ti·kom·mu'nistisch** *adj.* anti-Communist

'An·ti·kör·per *m* antibody

An·ti·lo·pe [anti'lo:pə] *f* (-; -n) antelope

An·ti·mi·li·ta'ris·mus *m* antimilitarism

An·ti·mon ['antimo:n] *n* (-s; *no pl.*) ⚗ antimony

An·ti·pa·thie [antipa'ti:] *f* (-; -n) antipathy (***gegen*** towards, to), dislike (of, for)

An·ti·po·de [anti'po:də] *m* (-n; -n) antipode

'an·tip·pen F *v/t. and v/i.* (*sep.*, h) tap, touch lightly; *fig.* touch (on); *fig.* ***bei j-m ~, ob*** sound s.o. out as to whether

An·ti·qua [an'ti:kva] *f* (-; *no pl.*) *typ.* roman (type)

An·ti·quar [anti'kva:ɐ] *m* (-s; -e) **1.** second-hand (*or* antiquarian) bookseller; **2.** → ***Antiquitätenhändler***; **An·ti·qua·ri·at** [antikva'rĭa:t] *n* (-[e]s; -e) **1.** second-hand (*or* antiquarian) bookshop; **2.** *no pl.* second-hand (*or* antiquarian) book trade; **an·ti·qua·risch** [anti'kva:rɪʃ] *adj.* second-hand; antiquarian; ***et. ~ bekommen*** get (*or* buy) s.th. second-hand

an·ti·quiert [anti'kvi:ɐt] *adj.* antiquated

An·ti·qui·tät [antikvi'tɛ:t] *f* (-; -en) antique

An·ti·qui'tä·ten|händ·ler *m* antique dealer; **~la·den** *m* antique shop; **~samm·ler** *m* antique collector

An·ti·se'mit *m* (-en; -en) anti-Semite; **an·ti·se'mi·tisch** *adj.* anti-Semitic; **An·ti·se·mi'tis·mus** *m* (-; *no pl.*) anti-Semitism

an·ti'sep·tisch *adj.* antiseptic

An·ti'sta·tik·tuch *n* antistatic cloth

an·ti'sta·tisch *adj.* antistatic

An·ti'ter·ror|ein·heit *f* anti-terrorist squad; **~ge·set·ze** *pl.* anti-terrorist legislation *sg.*

An·ti'the·se *f* antithesis; **an·ti·the·tisch** [anti'te:tɪʃ] *adj.* antithetical

An·ti·trans·pi·rant [antitranspi'rant] *n* (-s; -e, -s) antiperspirant

An·ti·zi·pa·ti·on [antitsypa'tsĭo:n] *f* (-; -en) anticipation; **an·ti·zi·pie·ren** [antitsy'pi:rən] *v/t.* (h) anticipate

an·ti'zy·klisch *adj.* anticyclical

An·ti·zy'klo·ne *f* (-; -n) anticyclone

Ant·litz ['antlɪts] *n* (-es; -e) face, *formal*: countenance

Ant·onym [anto'ny:m] *n* (-s; -e) antonym (***zu*** *dat.* of)

An·trag ['antra:k] *m* (-[e]s; Anträge ['antrɛːɡə]) **1.** application (***auf*** *acc.* for); *parl.* motion; bill; ⚖ petition; ***e-n ~ stellen auf*** *acc.* file an application for, *parl.* propose a motion for, ⚖ petition for; → ***durchbringen***; **2.** ***j-m e-n ~ machen*** propose to s.o.; **'an·tra·gen** (*irr.*, *sep.*, h, → ***tragen***) **I.** *v/t.*: ***j-m et. ~*** offer s.o. s.th.; **II.** *v/refl.*: ***sich ~ zu*** *inf.* offer to *inf*

'An·trags·for·mu|lar *n* application form

'An·trag·stel·ler [-ʃtɛlɐ] *m* (-s; -) applicant; ⚖ petitioner; *parl.* mover

'an·trai|nie·ren *v/t.* (*sep.*, h): ***j-m (sich) Ausdauer ~*** build up s.o.'s (one's) stamina; ***e-m Hund Gehorsam ~*** teach a dog obedience, teach (*or* train) a dog to be obedient (*or* to follow orders); ***j-m Höflichkeit ~*** teach s.o. some manners

'an·tref·fen *v/t.* (*irr.*, *sep.*, h, → ***treffen***) find; catch; meet, come across

'an·trei·ben (*irr.*, *sep.*, → ***treiben***) **I.** *v/t.* (h) **1.** drive; *fig.* urge *s.o.* on; ***j-n zur Arbeit ~*** make s.o. work; ***Eifersucht hat ihn dazu angetrieben*** it was jealousy that made him do it, he did it out of jealousy; **2.** *mot.*, ⚙ drive; **3.** wash ashore; **II.** *v/i.* (sn) be washed ashore;

'An·trei·ber *m* (-s; -) slave driver

'an·tre·ten (*irr.*, *sep.*, → ***treten***) **I.** *v/i.* (sn) **1.** line up; F *fig.* report (***bei*** to *the boss etc.*); **2.** *sport etc.*: enter (***bei, zu*** *dat.* for), participate (in); (*a.* ***zum Kampf ~***) compete (***gegen*** *acc.* with, against) (*a. w.s.*); ***~ gegen*** *a.* challenge; **3.** *sport*: accelerate; **II.** *v/t.* (h) **4.** ***die Arbeit (den Dienst) ~*** report for work (duty); ***sein Amt ~*** take up office; ***das Studium ~*** take up one's studies, start (at) university, (*a.* ***ein Studium ~***) start studying; ***e-e Erbschaft ~*** enter on (*or* come into) an inheritance; ⚖ ***e-e Strafe ~*** begin serving a sentence; ***e-e Reise ~*** set out (*or* off) on a journey; **5.** start up *motorbike*

'An·trieb *m* (-[e]s; -e) **1.** impetus, *a. psych.* urge; motive; incentive; ***e-r Sache (j-m) neuen ~ geben*** give s.th. a boost (give s.o. the motivation he *or* she needs); ***aus eigenem ~*** of one's own accord, F off one's own bat; **2.** ⚙ drive, propulsion; → ***Raketenantrieb***

'An·triebs|ach·se *f* driving axle; **~ag·gre|gat** *n* engine unit, prime mover; **~kraft** *f* motive power, driving force; **~lei·stung** *f* driving power; **~rad** *n* driving gear; **~rie·men** *m* drive belt; **~schwä·che** *f psych.* lack of drive; **~stu·fe** *f rocket*: propulsion stage; **~wel·le** *f* drive shaft

'an·trin·ken *v/t.* (*irr.*, *sep.*, h, → ***trinken***): ***sich e-n Rausch*** (F ***einen***) ***~*** get drunk (F tight); ***sich Mut ~*** give o.s. Dutch courage; → ***angetrunken*** II

'An·tritt *m* (-[e]s; *no pl.*) **1.** start *of a journey*; taking up *of office*; accession (*gen.* to *an inheritance etc.*); *pol.* coming into power; ***bei ~ der Reise*** when we *etc.* set out (*or* off) on the journey; ***beim ~ s-s Amtes*** when he took up office; **2.** *sport*: acceleration

'An·tritts|be·such *m* first visit; ***heute macht X s-n ~*** today X will be presenting his credentials (***bei*** *dat.* to); **~re·de** *f* inaugural address; *parl.* maiden speech; **2schnell** *adj. sport*: quick off the mark; **~vor·le·sung** *f* inaugural lecture

'an·trock·nen *v/i.* (*sep.*, sn) begin to dry

'an·tun *v/t.* (*irr.*, *sep.*, h, → ***tun***) **1.** ***j-m et. ~*** do s.th. to s.o.; ***j-m Gewalt ~*** do violence to s.o., rape s.o.; ***er würde niemandem etwas ~*** he wouldn't hurt (*or* harm) a fly; ***das darfst du mir nicht ~*** you can't do that to me; ***sich etwas ~*** lay hands upon o.s.; → ***Zwang***; **2.** ***es j-m ~*** take s.o.'s fancy; ***sie hat's ihm angetan*** he's quite taken by her

an·tur·nen ['antœrnən] F *v/t.* (*sep.*, h) F turn *s.o.* on; *a.* get *s.o.* high

Ant·wort ['antvɔrt] *f* (-; -en) answer, reply; *fig.* response (*all* ***auf*** *acc.* to); ***als ~ auf*** *acc.* in answer to; ***er ist um keine ~ verlegen, er weiß auf alles e-e ~*** he's got an answer for everything; ***keine ~ ist auch e-e ~*** *iro.* enough said; ***um ~ wird gebeten*** RSVP; → ***schuldig*** 2; **'ant·wor·ten** *v/t. and v/i.* (h) answer (***j-m*** s.o.), reply (to s.o.); retort; respond (to); ***~ auf*** *acc.* answer s.th., reply to s.th.; ***was hat sie geantwortet?*** what did she say (to that)?

'Ant·wort|kar·te *f* reply card; **~schein** *m* (international) reply coupon

'an·ver·trau·en *v/t.* (*sep.*, h): ***j-m et. ~*** entrust s.o. with s.th., place s.th. in s.o.'s hands; *fig.* ***j-m ein Geheimnis*** *etc.* ***~*** confide a secret *etc.* to s.o.; **'an·ver·traut I.** *p.p. of* ***anvertrauen***; **II.** *adj.* entrusted; ***die ihm ~en Aufgaben*** the tasks he has been entrusted with

'an·vi|sie·ren *v/t.* (*sep.*, h) take aim at; *fig.* aim for; ***für den Frühling hatten wir Malta anvisiert*** we were planning to go to Malta in (the) spring

'an·wach·sen *v/i.* (*irr.*, *sep.*, sn, → ***wachsen***) **1.** 🌱 take root; grow on (to ***an*** *dat.*); **2.** grow, increase, *a. river*: rise; *work, interest*: accumulate; ***~ auf*** *acc.* run up to

An·walt ['anvalt] *m* (-[e]s; Anwälte ['anvɛltə]) **1.** ⚖ lawyer, solicitor, *Am.* attorney; *Brit.* barrister; counsel (***des Angeklagten*** for the defen|ce [*Am.* -se]); ***e-n ~ nehmen*** get a solicitor (*Am.* an attorney); **2.** *fig.* champion (***e-r Sache*** of a cause); **'An·walt·schaft** *f* (-; -en) legal profession; *the* bar; **'An·walts·kam·mer** *f* Bar Council (*Am.* Association)

'An·wand·lung *f* (-; -en) fit; (sudden) impulse; ***in e-r ~ von Schwäche*** in a weak moment; ***in e-r ~ von Großzügigkeit*** in a fit of generosity; ***aus e-r ~ heraus*** on a sudden impulse

'an·wär·men *v/t.* (*sep.*, h) warm up (*a. mot.*); take the chill off

'An·wär·ter *m* (-s; -) candidate (***auf*** *acc.* for); *sport*: *a.* contender (for)

An·wart·schaft ['anvartʃaft] *f* (-; -en) **1.** ⚖ ***~ auf Leistungen*** right to (future) benefits; **2.** ***e-e gewisse (die) ~ auf ein Amt haben*** be a prospective (the number one) candidate for a post

'an·wa·schen *v/t.* (*irr.*, *sep.*, h, → ***waschen***) wash ashore

'an·we·hen (*sep.*) **I.** *v/t.* (h) **1.** ***j-n ~*** blow at s.o., *scent*: waft towards s.o.; ***e-e leichte Brise wehte uns an*** there was a gentle breeze; **2.** *fig.* ***j-n ~*** *sadness etc.*: come over s.o., *memory*: come back to s.o.; **3.** ***~ an*** *acc.* drift up to, blow up to *the door etc.*; **II.** *v/i.* (sn): ***~ an*** *acc.* drift up to, be blown up to

'an·wei·sen *v/t.* (*irr.*, *sep.*, h, → ***weisen***) **1.** ***j-n ~ zu*** *inf.* give s.o. instructions to *inf.*, tell (*or* ask) s.o. to *inf.*; ***angewiesen sein zu*** *inf.* have instructions to *inf.*; **2.** ***j-n ~*** give s.o. directions, show s.o. what to do; **3.** assign, allot; ***j-m e-n Platz ~*** show s.o. to his (*or* her) place (*or* seat); → ***angewiesen*** II; **4.** ✝ remit, transfer (*dat.* to); **'An·wei·sung** *f* (-; -en) instruction(s *pl.*); order; assignment, allotment; ♆ remittance, transfer; *computer*: statement; ***auf ~ von*** (*or gen.*) on the instructions of; ***strenge ~ haben zu*** *inf.* have strict instructions to *inf.*; F ***~(en) des Chefs (Arztes)!*** F boss's (doctor's) orders!

an·wend·bar ['anvɛntba:ɐ] *adj.* applicable (***auf*** *acc.* to); practicable; ***leicht ~*** easy to apply; **'An·wend·bar·keit** *f* (-; *no pl.*) applicability; practicability

'an·wen·den *v/t.* (*irr., sep.*, h, → ***wenden***) apply (***auf*** *acc.* to); use (***bei*** for); make use of; ***et. gut*** (*or* ***nutzbringend***) ~ make good use of s.th., put s.th. to good use; ***Gewalt*** ~ use (*or* resort to) force; → ***angewandt*** II; **'An·wen·dung** *f* (-; -en) application; use; ***unter ~ von*** (*or gen.*) (by) using, (by) resorting to

'An·wen·dungs|bei·spiel *n* example of use; **~be·reich** *m*, **~ge·biet** *n* field of application; **~mög·lich·keit** *f* applicability, possible use(s *pl.*)

'an·wer·ben *v/t.* (*irr., sep.*, h, → ***werben***) recruit (*a.* ⚔)

'an·wer·fen (*irr., sep.*, h, → ***werfen***) **I.** *v/i. sport*: have the first throw; **II.** *v/t. mot.* start (up); △ roughcast

'An·we·sen *n* (-s; -) property, estate

an·we·send ['anve:zənt] *adj.* present (***bei*** *dat.* at); ***bei et. ~ sein*** *a.* attend s.th.; ***er war nicht ~*** a) he wasn't there, b) F he was away with the fairies; ***die 2en*** those present; **'An·we·sen·heit** *f* (-; *no pl.*) presence (***bei*** *dat.* at); *ped. etc.*: attendance; ***in ~ von*** (*or gen.*) in the presence of; **'An·we·sen·heits·li·ste** *f* attendance list; *ped.* register

an·wi·dern ['anvi:dɐn] *v/t.* → ***anekeln***

'an·win·keln *v/t.* (*sep.*, h) bend

An·woh·ner ['anvo:nɐ] *m* (-s; -) resident; ***nur für ~*** (for) residents only

'An·wurf *m* (-[e]s; ⸚e) *sport*: first throw, throw-off; *fig.* accusation

'an·wur·zeln *v/i.* (*sep.*, sn) **1.** ⚘ take root; **2.** → ***angewurzelt*** II

'An·zahl *f* (-; *no pl.*) number; ***e-e große ~ von*** (*or gen.*) a large number of

'an·zah·len *v/t.* (*sep.*, h) **1.** make a down payment of 100 dollars *etc.* (***für*** for, on); **2.** make a down payment on (*or* for); **'An·zah·lung** *f* (-; -en) deposit; down payment, (first) instal(l)ment

'an·zap·fen *v/t.* (*sep.*, h) *a.* ⚙, ⚡, *teleph.* tap; F ***j-n ~*** a) tap s.o. (***um*** for *50 dollars etc.*), b) take some blood from s.o.

'An·zei·chen *n* (-s; -) sign, indication; ⚕ symptom; ***alle ~ sprechen dafür, daß*** everything seems to indicate that

An·zei·ge ['antsaɪgə] *f* (-; -n) **1.** announcement; *adm.* advice; **2.** ⚖ information; → ***erstatten*; 3.** advertisement, ad, *Brit. a.* advert; **4.** ⚙ indication; reading; **5.** *computer*: display; **'an·zei·gen** *v/t.* (*sep.*, h) **1.** notify (***j-m et.*** s.o. of s.th.), announce (s.th. to s.o.); ♆ advise (s.o. of s.th.); **2.** indicate; → ***angezeigt*** II; **3.** *computer*: display; **4.** ⚖ report *s.th.* (*dat.* to *the police etc.*); bring a charge against *s.o.*; report *s.o.* to the police

'An·zei·gen... *in cpds.* → ***Werbe...***; **~ab‚tei·lung** *f* advertising department; **~blatt** *n* free paper; **~schluß** *m* deadline; *a.* closing date; **~teil** *m* advertisements *pl.*, advertisement section, F ads *pl.*

'an·zei·ge·pflich·tig *adj.* notifiable

'An·zei·ger *m* (-s; -) **1.** ⚙ indicator; **2.** a) gazette, b) free paper

'An·zei·ge·ta·fel *f sport*: scoreboard

an·zet·teln ['antsɛtəln] *v/t.* (*sep.*, h) hatch *a plot*, instigate, F engineer; ***e-e Verschwörung ~ gegen*** plot against; ***das hat er alles angezettelt*** it's all his doing

'an·zie·hen (*irr., sep.*, h, → ***ziehen***) **I.** *v/t.* **1.** draw up *knee, leg*; stretch; apply *brake*; tighten *screw etc.*; draw in *reins*; **2.** put on *dress, coat etc.*; dress *s.o.*; **3.** absorb, take up *moisture etc.*; *phys.* attract (*a. fig.*); ♆ draw *capital*; ***ungleiche Pole ziehen sich an*** *a. fig.* opposite poles attract; ***ich fühlte mich von ihm angezogen*** I felt attracted to him; **II.** *v/i.* **4.** pull; **5.** *car, horse*: pull away; **6.** *chess etc.*: move first; ***Weiß zieht an*** white to play; **7.** ♆ *prices etc.*: advance; **III.** *v/refl.*: ***sich ~*** get dressed, dress; ***sich fürs Theater ~*** get dressed up for the theat|re (*Am. a.* -er); **'an·zie·hend** *fig. adj.* engaging, charming; attractive; **'Anzie·hung** *f* (-; -en) *a. phys.* attraction

'An·zie·hungs|kraft *f* **1.** *phys.* force of attraction; *moon etc.*: pull; *earth*: gravitational force, power of gravitation; **2.** *fig.* attraction, appeal; ***e-e starke ~ ausüben auf j-n*** have a strong attraction for s.o.; **~punkt** *m* draw

'an·zi·schen (*sep.*) **I.** *v/t.* (h) hiss at; *fig.* snarl at; F *fig.* ***sich einen ~*** F get a bit merry; **II.** F *v/i.* (sn) (*a.* ***angezischt kommen***) F come whizzing along

an·zockeln ['antsɔkəln] (*sep.* -k·k-) F *v/i.* (sn) (*a.* ***angezockelt kommen***) F roll up

'An·zucht *f* (-; *no pl.*) ⚘ growing, cultivation

An·zug ['antsu:k] *m* (-[e]s; Anzüge ['antsy:gə]) **1.** suit; ***im ~ erscheinen*** turn up in a suit (and tie); **2.** approach, advance; ***im ~ sein*** be on the advance; *storm*: be brewing, be coming up; **3.** *chess*: opening (*or* first) move; **4.** *mot.* pull

an·züg·lich ['antsy:klɪç] *adj.* suggestive *remark*; risqué *joke*, F near the knuckle; salacious *smile*; ***~ werden*** get personal; **'An·züg·lich·keit** *f* (-; -en) **1.** *no pl.* suggestiveness; **2.** suggestive remark

'An·zugs·ver·mö·gen *n mot.* pull

'an·zün·den *v/t.* (*sep.*, h) light; *a.* light up *pipe, cigar*; set fire to; **'An·zün·der** *m* (-s; -) lighter

'an·zwei·feln *v/t.* (*sep.*, h) doubt; (call in) question, dispute

'an·zwit·schern F (*sep.*) **I.** *v/i.* (sn) (*a.* ***angezwitschert kommen***) F roll up, come toddling along; **II.** *v/t.* (h) → ***andudeln***

Äo·nen [ɛ'o:nən] *pl.* (a)eons

Aor·ta [a'ɔrta] *f* (-; -ten) *anat.* aorta; **A'or·ten·klap·pe** *f* aortic valve

Apa·na·ge [apa'na:ʒə] *f* (-; -n) allowance

apart [a'part] *adj.* striking, unusual; stylish

Apart·heid [a'pa:ɐthaɪt] *f* (-; *no pl.*) apartheid; **~po·li‚tik** *f* policy of apartheid, apartheid policy (*or* politics *pl.*)

A'part·ho‚tel *n* apartment hotel, aparthotel

Apart·ment [a'partmənt] *n* (-s; -s) flatlet; one-room (*Am.* efficiency) apartment, *Brit. a.* one-room flat, studio flat; **~haus** *n* block of flats, block of one-room (*Am.* efficiency) apartments

Apa·thie [apa'ti:] *f* (-; *no pl.*) apathy; *psych.* listlessness; **apa·thisch** [a'pa:tɪʃ] *adj.* apathetic(ally *adv.*); *psych.* listless

Aper·çu [apɛr'sy:] *n* (-s; -s) witticism

Ape·ri·tif [aperi'ti:f] *m* (-s; -s) aperitif

Ap·fel ['apfəl] *m* (-s; Äpfel ['ɛpfəl]) apple; *fig.* ***in den sauren ~ beißen*** grasp the nettle; ***der ~ fällt nicht weit vom Stamm*** like father like son; ***für e-n ~ und ein Ei*** for a song, ***bekommen:*** *a.* dirt cheap, for next to nothing; **~baum** *m* apple tree; **~blü·te** *f* apple blossom; **~kern** *m* pip; **~ku·chen** *m* apple flan (*Am.* cake); **~most** *m* **1.** → ***Apfelsaft*; 2.** cider; **~mus** *n* apple purée; apple sauce; **~saft** *m* apple juice; **~scha·le** *f* apple skin (*or* peel); **~schim·mel** *m* dapple grey (*Am.* gray); **~schor·le** *f* apple-juice spritzer

Ap·fel·si·ne [apfəl'zi:nə] *f* (-; -n) orange

Ap·fel'si·nen|baum *m* orange tree; **~blü·te** *f* orange blossom; **~saft** *m* orange juice; **~scha·le** *f* orange peel; **~schei·be** *f* orange slice, slice of orange

'Ap·fel|stru·del *m* apple strudel; **~tor·te** *f* apple tart; **~wein** *m* (*Am.* hard) cider

Apho·ris·mus [afo'rɪsmʊs] *m* (-; -men) aphorism; **apho·ri·stisch** [afo'rɪstɪʃ] *adj.* aphoristic(ally *adv.*)

Aphro·di·sia·kum [afrodi'zi:akʊm] *n* (-s; -ka) aphrodisiac

Aplomb [a'plõ:] *m* (-s; *no pl.*) aplomb, self-confidence

apo·dik·tisch [apo'dɪktɪʃ] *adj.* apodictic(ally *adv.*); *w.s.* dogmatic(ally *adv.*)

Apo·gä·um [apo'gɛ:ʊm] *n* (-s; -gäen) apogee

Apo·ka·lyp·se [apoka'lʏpsə] *f* (-; -n) apocalypse; **apo·ka·lyp·tisch** [apoka'lʏptɪʃ] *adj.* apocalyptic; ***die 2en Reiter*** the Four Horsemen of the Apocalypse

'apo‚li·tisch *adj.* apolitical

Apo·lo·get [apolo'ge:t] *m* (-en; -en) apologist; **Apo·lo·ge·tik** [apolo'ge:tɪk] *f* (-; -en) **1.** apology, apologia; **2.** *no pl.* apologetics *pl.*; **apo·lo·ge·tisch** [apolo'ge:tɪʃ] *adj.* apologetic(ally *adv.*); **Apo·lo·gie** [apolo'gi:] *f* (-; -n) apology, apologia

Apo·stel [a'pɔstəl] *m* (-s; -) apostle (*a. fig.*); **~ge·schich·te** *f*: ***die ~*** Acts *pl.*, the Acts of the Apostles *pl.*

a po·ste·rio·ri [apɔste'rĭo:ri] *adv. and adj.* a posteriori

apo·sto·lisch [apɔs'to:lɪʃ] *adj.* apostolic; ***das 2e Glaubensbekenntnis*** the Apostles' Creed; *R.C.* ***der 2e Stuhl*** the Apostolic See

Apo·stroph [apo'stro:f] *m* (-s; -e) apostrophe; **apo·stro·phie·ren** [apostro'fi:rən] *v/t.* (h) apostrophize (*a. fig.*)

Apo·the·ke [apo'te:kə] *f* (-; -n) chemist's (shop), *Am.* pharmacy, drugstore

Apo'the·ken|hel·fe·rin *f* chemist's (*Am.* pharmacist's) assistant; **2pflich·tig** *adj.* obtainable in a chemist's shop (*Am.* in a pharmacy) only

Apo·the·ker [apo'te:kɐ] *m* (-s; -), **Apo·the·ke·rin** [apo'te:kərɪn] *f* (-; -nen) (dispensing) chemist, pharmacist, *Am.* druggist

Apo·the·ker|ge·wicht *n* apothecaries' weight; **~preis** F *m* extortionate price; ***die haben ja ~e!*** F you pay through the nose in that place

Ap·pa·rat [apa'ra:t] *m* (-[e]s; -e) **1.** apparatus; device, appliance; machine; *a. iro.*: gadget; instrument; **2.** *biol.* apparatus; **3.** F radio; *TV* set; *phot.* camera; *teleph.* phone, extension; ***am ~!*** speaking; ***am ~ bleiben*** hold the line; ***an den ~ gehen*** (go to) answer *or* pick up the phone; ***es geht keiner an den ~*** nobody's answering; **4.** *fig.* organization, apparatus; *a. political, party etc.* machine; **5.** F *fig.* a) F whopper; b) F (great) hulk; **6.** (***kritischer***) ~ critical apparatus

Ap·pa'ra·te·me·di,zin *f* high-tech(nology) medicine

Ap·pa·rat·schick [apa'ratʃɪk] *m* (-s; -s) apparatchik

Ap·pa·ra·tur [apara'tu:ɐ] *f* (-; -en) equipment, apparatus; machinery

Ap·par·te·ment [apartə'mã:] *n* (-s; -s) **1.** → ***Apartment***; **2.** *hotel*: suite

Ap·pell [a'pɛl] *m* (-s; -e) ⚔ roll call; *fig.* appeal (***an*** *acc.* to); **ap·pel·lie·ren** [apɛ'li:rən] *v/i.* (h): ~ ***an*** *acc.* appeal to; ***an j-n ~ zu*** *inf. a.* call on s.o. to *inf.*

Ap·pen·dix [a'pɛndɪks] *m* (-; -dizes [-ditse:s]) *anat.* appendix (*a. fig.*); **Ap·pen·di·zi·tis** [apɛndi'tsi:tɪs] *f* (-; -zitiden [-tsi'ti:dən]) appendicitis

Ap·pe·tit [ape'ti:t] *m* (-[e]s; -e) appetite (*a. fig.*) (***auf*** *acc.* for); ***~ haben auf*** *acc.* feel like *some chocolate etc.*; ***j-m ~ machen*** give s.o. an appetite; ***es macht ~*** it really gives you an appetite; ***j-m den ~ verderben*** spoil s.o.'s appetite, *fig.* put s.o. off; ***es verdirbt den ~*** it spoils your appetite; ***den ~ verlieren*** lose one's appetite; ***ich hätte richtig ~ auf ...*** I could just fancy ...; ***guten ~!*** bon appetit!, F *hum.* enjoy!; **2an·re·gend** *adj.* appetizing; ***~es Mittel*** appetite stimulant; **~hap·pen** *m* canapé; **~hem·mer** *m* appetite suppressant

ap·pe'tit·lich *adj.* appetizing; *fig.* attractive; *fig.* ***nicht besonders ~*** not very inviting

Ap·pe'tit·lo·sig·keit *f* (-; *no pl.*) loss of appetite

Ap·pe'tit·züg·ler [-tsy:glɐ] *m* (-s; -) appetite suppressant

ap·plau·die·ren [aplaʊ'di:rən] *v/i.* (h) applaud (*dat. s.o.*); **Ap·plaus** [a'plaʊs] *m* (-es; *no pl.*) applause; → ***Beifall***

Ap·pli·ka·ti·on [aplika'tsi̯o:n] *f* (-; -en) **1.** application; **2.** **~en** trimmings; **Ap·pli·ka·tor** [apli'ka:tɔr] *m* (-s; -en [-ka'to:rən]) applicator; **ap·pli·zie·ren** [apli'tsi:rən] *v/t.* (h) sew on; administer; apply; *fig.* ~ ***auf*** *acc.* apply to; ***es ist auf die Praxis nicht zu ~*** it doesn't work in practi|ce (*Am.* -se)

ap·por·tie·ren [apɔr'ti:rən] *v/t.* (h) retrieve, fetch

Ap·po·si·ti·on [apozi'tsi̯o:n] *f* (-; -en) apposition; ***~ zu et. sein*** be in apposition to s.th.

ap·pre·tie·ren [apre'ti:rən] *v/t.* (h), **Ap·pre·tur** [apre'tu:ɐ] *f* (-; -en) finish

Ap·pro·ba·ti·on [aproba'tsi̯o:n] *f* (-; -en) ⚕ licen|ce (*Am.* -se) to practi|se (*Am.* -ce) medicine; **ap·pro·biert** [apro'bi:ɐt] *adj.* qualified *doctor etc.*

ap·pro·xi·ma·tiv [aprɔksima'ti:f] *adj.* approximate

Après-Ski [aprɛ'ʃi:] *n* (-; *no pl.*) après-ski

Apri·ko·se [apri'ko:zə] *f* (-; -n) apricot

April [a'prɪl] *m* (-[s]; -e) April; ***im ~*** in April; ***j-n in den ~ schicken*** make an April fool of s.o.; ***~, ~!*** April fool!; **~schau·er** *m* April shower; **~scherz** *m* April-fool joke; *fig.* ***das ist wohl ein ~!*** is this some kind of practical joke?; **~wet·ter** *n* April showers *pl.*; ***das ist richtiges ~*** it's like April showers

a prio'ri [a: pri'o:ri] *adv. and adj.* a priori

apro·pos [apro'po:] *adv.* **1.** by the way; **2.** talking about ...

Ap·sis ['apsɪs] *f* (-; Apsiden [ap'si:dən]) apse

Aquä·dukt [akvɛ'dʊkt] *m* (-[e]s; -e) aqueduct

Aqua·kul,tur ['a:kva-] *f* (-; -en) aquaculture

aqua·ma·rin [akvama'ri:n] *adj.*, **Aqua·ma'rin** *m* (-s; -e) aquamarine

Aqua·naut [akva'naʊt] *m* (-en; -en) aquanaut

Aqua·pla·ning [akva'pla:nɪŋ] *n* (-[s]; *no pl.*) *mot.* aquaplaning

Aqua·rell [akva'rɛl] *n* (-s; -e) watercolo(u)r; **~far·be** *f* watercolo(u)r; **~ma·ler** *m* watercolo(u)rist; **~ma·le,rei** *f* watercolo(u)r painting

Aqua·ri·um [a'kva:ri̯ʊm] *n* (-s; -rien [-ri̯ən]) aquarium

Äqua·tor [ɛ'kva:to:ɐ] *m* (-s; -en [ɛkva'to:rən]) equator; ***den ~ überqueren*** cross the line; **~tau·fe** *f* crossing-the-line ceremony

äqui·va·lent [ɛkviva'lɛnt] **I.** *adj.* equivalent; **II.** **2** *n* (-[e]s; -e) **1.** recompense; **2.** equivalent

Ar [a:ɐ] *n* (-s; -e ['a:rə]) are

Ära ['ɛ:ra] *f* (-; Ären ['ɛ:rən]) era

Ara·ber ['arabɐ] *m* (-s; -) Arab (*a. horse*); Arabian; **Ara·be·rin** ['arabərɪn] *f* (-; -nen) **1.** Arab woman; **2.** Arabian woman

Ara·bes·ke [ara'bɛskə] *f* (-; -n) arabesque

ara·bisch [a'ra:bɪʃ] **I.** *adj.* Arab *League, States, custom etc.*; Arabian *nights, coffee etc.*; Arabic *numerals, language, literature etc.*; ***die 2e Halbinsel*** (***Wüste***) the Arabian Peninsula (Desert); **II.** **2** *n* (-[s]) *ling.* Arabic

Ar·beit ['arbaɪt] *f* (-; -en) **1.** a) work; b) hard work; ***geistige ~*** brainwork; ***an*** (*or* ***bei***) ***der ~*** at work; ***an die ~ gehen, sich an die ~ machen*** start work, set to work; ***ich hab' mit dem Garten viel ~*** the garden's a lot of work; ***et. in ~ haben*** be working on s.th.; ***ganze*** (*or* ***gründliche***) ***~ leisten*** do a good job (*a. fig.*); ***et. in ~ geben*** have s.th. done (*or* made); ***erst die ~, dann das Vergnügen!*** business before pleasure; *iro.* ***er hat die ~ nicht erfunden*** F he's a born skiver; ***immer nur halbe ~ machen*** never do things (*or* finish things off) properly; → ***getan***; **2.** *no pl.* trouble; effort; ***ich hoffe, es macht Ihnen nicht zu viel ~*** I hope it's not too much trouble for you; **3.** *no pl.* work, employment; ***~ haben*** have a job; ***ohne ~*** unemployed, out of work, jobless; ***~ suchen*** look for a job, *formal*: seek employment; ***zur*** (F ***auf***) ***~ gehen*** go to work; **4.** (piece of) work; *univ. etc.* paper, treatise; ***künstlerische ~*** work of art; **5.** *no pl. pol.* labo(u)r; ***Tag der ~*** Labo(u)r Day; **6.** *phys.* work; **7.** → ***Doktor-, Klassen-, Schularbeit***

ar·bei·ten ['arbaɪtən] (h) **I.** *v/i.* **1.** work; ***~ an*** *dat.* be working on; ***bei j-m ~*** work for s.o.; ***mit e-r Firma*** (***geschäftlich***) ***~*** deal with, do business with; *fig.* ***die Zeit arbeitet für*** (***gegen***) ***uns*** we've got time on our side (against us); ***man sah, wie es in ihm arbeitete*** you could almost see it being churned around inside him; **2.** ⚚ work (***mit Gewinn*** at a profit); ***sein Geld ~ lassen*** invest *one's money*; **3.** ⚙ work, operate, run; **4.** *physiol.* work, function; **5.** *wood etc.*: expand and contract; *dough*: rise; *wine etc.*: work; **II.** *v/t.* **6.** make; **III.** *v/refl.*: ***sich durch den Schnee*** (***e-n Roman***) ***~*** work one's way through *or* plough (*Am.* plow) through the snow (a novel); → ***Tod***; **IV.** *v/impers.*: ***hier arbeitet es sich schlecht*** it's difficult to work here

Ar·bei·ter ['arbaɪtɐ] *m* (-s; -) worker (*a. zo.*); blue-collar worker; labo(u)rer; → (***an***)***gelernt*** II; ***die ~ a.*** the working classes; **~amei·se** *f* worker ant; **~auf·stand** *m* workers' revolt; **~be·we·gung** *f hist.* Labo(u)r movement; **~dich·tung** *f* working-class literature; **~fa,mi·lie** *f* working-class family; **2feind·lich** *adj.* anti-labo(u)r; **~fra·ge** *f* labo(u)r question; **~füh·rer** *m* labo(u)r leader; **~ge·werk·schaft** *f* trade (*Am.* labor) union

Ar·bei·te·rin ['arbaɪtərɪn] *f* (-; -nen) **1.** (female) worker; **2.** *zo.* worker bee; worker ant

'Ar·bei·ter|ju·gend *f* young workers *pl.*; **~kind** *n* working-class boy (*or* girl), *pl.* working-class children (F kids); **~klas·se** *f* working class(es *pl.*); **~lied** *n* workers' song; **~mi·li,eu** *n* working-class background (*or* environment); ***aus dem ~ stammen*** come from a working-class background; **~par,tei** *f* workers' party

'Ar·bei·ter·schaft *f* (-; *no pl.*) labo(u)r force, workforce

'Ar·bei·ter|sied·lung *f* working-class estate; **~stadt** *f* working-class town; **~stand** *m* working class(es *pl.*); **~vier·tel** *n* working-class area; **~wohl·fahrt** *f* workers' welfare association

'Ar·beit·ge·ber *m* (-s; -) employer; **~an·teil** *m social security*: employer's contribution; **~ver·band** *m* employers' association

'Ar·beit·neh·mer *m* (-s; -) employee; **~an·teil** *m social security*: employee's contribution; **~frei·be·trag** *m* earned-income allowance; **~ver·tre·tung** *f* employee representatives *pl.*

'Ar·beits·ab·lauf *m* flow of work; sequence of operations

'ar·beit·sam *adj.* industrious, hardworking

'Ar·beits|amt *n* employment office; **~an·fall** *m* **1.** workload; **2.** F ***e-n ~ bekommen*** F have a working fit; **~an·ge·bot** *n* vacancies *pl.*; **~an·tritt** *m*: ***bei*** (***vor***) ***~*** on (before) taking up work (*or* one's job); **~an·zug** *m* work(ing) clothes *pl.*; overalls *pl.*; **~auf·fas·sung** *f* attitude to (-wards) work; **~auf·trag** *m* job order; **~auf·wand** *m* amount of work involved (***für*** in); ***et. mit großem ~ erreichen*** (have to) put a lot of work into s.th.; ***das lohnt den ~ nicht*** it's not worth the effort (involved); **2auf·wen·dig** *adj.* labo(u)r-intensive; complicated; ***~ sein*** *a.* be a lot of work; **~aus·fall** *m* loss of working hours; **~aus·schuß** *m* working committee, study group; **~be·din·gun·gen** *pl.* working (⚙ operating) conditions; **~be·la·stung** *f* work pressure; pressures *pl.* of work; **~be·reich** *m* scope (of work); ⚙ range of operation

'Ar·beits·be·schaf·fung *f* job creation

'Ar·beits·be·schaf·fungs|maß·nah·men *pl.* job-creating (*or* job-generating) measures; **~pro,gramm** *n* job-creation scheme

'Ar·beits|be·schei·ni·gung *f* certificate of employment; **~be·such** *m* working visit; **~be·wer·tung** *f* job evaluation; **~bie·ne** *f* **1.** *zo.* worker bee; **2.** *fig.* busy bee; *a.* busy Lizzie; **~blatt** *n* worksheet; ***elektronisches ~*** spreadsheet; **~büh·ne** *f* working platform; **~dis·zi,plin** *f* job discipline; **~ei·fer** *m* eagerness to work, zeal; **~ein·kom·men** *n* earned income; **~ein·spa·rung** *f* saving on working hours; **~ein·stel·lung** *f* **1.** work stoppage; shutdown; strike, walkout; **2.** → ***Arbeitsauffassung***; **~ent·frem·dung** *f* alienation from work; **~er·laub·nis** *f* work permit; **~er·leich·te·rung** *f*: ***e-e ~ darstellen*** (***für j-n***) save (s.o.) a lot of work; **~er·spar·nis** *f* labo(u)r saving; **~es·sen** *n* working lunch (*or* dinner); **~ethos** *n* work ethic

'ar·beits·fä·hig *adj.* fit for work; *pol.* ***~e Mehrheit*** working majority

'Ar·beits|feld *n* scope of work (*or* activity); **~fie·ber** *n* working fever; **~flä·che** *f* work surface

'ar·beits·frei *adj.*: ***~er Tag*** day off, public (*Am. a.* legal) holiday; ***~er Vormittag*** (***Nachmittag***) morning (afternoon) off; ***Freitag ist ein ~er Tag*** there's no work on Friday

'Ar·beits|frie·den *m* industrial peace; **~gang** *m* work cycle; ***in einem ~*** in one process (F go); **~ge·biet** *n* → ***Arbeitsfeld***; **~ge·mein·schaft** *f* **1.** ✝ joint venture; **2.** work(ing) group; syndicate; **3.** → ***Arbeitsgruppe***; **~ge·neh·mi·gung** *f* work permit; **~ge·richt** *n* industrial tribunal, *Am.* labor court; **~ge·setz** *n* labo(u)r law; **~ge·setz·ge·bung** *f* labo(u)r legislation; **~grund·la·ge** *f* working basis; **~grup·pe** *f* (working) team; *ped.* study group; **~hil·fe** *f* working aid; **~hy·gi̦e·ne** *f* hygiene at the workplace; **~hy·po̦the·se** *f* working hypothesis

'ar·beits·in·ten̦siv *adj.* labo(u)r-intensive

'Ar·beits·kampf *m* labo(u)r dispute; **~maß·nah·men** *pl.* industrial action *sg.*

'Ar·beits|kit·tel *m* overall; **~klei·dung** *f* work(ing) clothes *pl.*; **~kli·ma** *n* work climate, working atmosphere; **~kluft** *f* F work togs *pl.*; **~kol̦le·ge** *m* colleague (from work), F workmate; **~ko·sten** *pl.* labo(u)r cost *sg.*

'Ar·beits·kraft *f* **1.** capacity for work; **2.** worker; employee; *pl. coll.* manpower *sg.*; *the* workforce *sg.*; ***billige Arbeitskräfte*** cheap labo(u)r

'Ar·beits·kräf·te|ab·bau *m* reduction (*or* cuts *pl.*) in manpower; **~man·gel** *m* manpower shortage

'Ar·beits|kreis *m* working (*ped.* study) group; **~la·ger** *n* labo(u)r camp; **~le·ben** *n* working life; **~lei·stung** *f* efficiency; ⚙ *a.* performance; output; **~lohn** *m* wage(s *pl.*), pay

'ar·beits·los *adj.* unemployed, out of work, jobless; ***die ~en Jugendlichen*** the young jobless (*pl.*); **'Ar·beits·lo·se** *m, f* (-n; -n) unemployed person; *pl. coll. the* unemployed (*pl.*), *the* jobless (*pl.*)

'Ar·beits·lo·sen|geld *n* unemployment benefit; ***~ beziehen*** be on the dole; **~heer** *n* jobless (*or* unemployed) masses *pl.*; **~hil·fe** *f* unemployment assistance; **~quo·te** *f* unemployment rate; **~un·ter̦stüt·zung** *f* unemployment benefit; **~ver·si·che·rung** *f* unemployment insurance; **~zahl** *f* unemployment (*or* jobless) figures *pl.*

'Ar·beits·lo·sig·keit *f* (-; *no pl.*) unemployment

'Ar·beits|man·gel *m* shortage of work; **~markt** *m* labo(u)r (*or* job) market; ***Lage auf dem ~*** job situation; **~ma·̦schi·ne** *f* **1.** machine; **2.** *fig.* workhorse; **~ma·te·ri̦al** *n* working material; **~me·di̦zin** *f* industrial medicine; **~me̦tho·de** *f* working method; **~mi̦ni·ster** *m* employment (*Am.* labor) minister, minister for employment (*Am.* labor); *in GB*: Secretary of State for Employment, Employment Secretary; *in the USA*: Secretary of Labor; **~mi·ni̦ste·ri·um** *n* department of employment (*Am.* labor); *in GB*: Department of Employment (*in the USA*: Labor); **~mo̦dell** *n* working model; **~mög·lich·kei·ten** *pl.* job opportunities; **~mo̦ral** *f* (working) morale; **~mo·ti·va·ti̦on** *f* motivation to work; **~nach·weis** *m* **1.** employment agency; **2.** job placement; **~nie·der·le·gung** *f* strike, walkout, stoppage; **~norm** *f* work norm; target; **~ord·nung** *f* work regulations (*Am.* rules) *pl.*; **~pa̦pier** *n* working paper; **~pa̦pie·re** *pl.* working papers; **~pau·se** *f* break; **~pen·sum** *n* → ***Pensum***; **~pferd** *n* workhorse (*a. fig.*); **~plan** *m* work schedule

'Ar·beits·platz *m* workplace; *computer*: workstation; place of work; job; ***freier ~*** vacancy; ***Diskriminierung am ~*** discrimination at work; ***Sicherheit am ~*** workplace safety; ***Sicherheit des ~es*** job security; ***die Arbeitsplätze sichern*** safeguard employment; **~be·schaf·fung** *f* job creation; **~be·schaf·fungs·maß·nah·men** *pl.* job-generating (*or* job-creating) measures, job-creation scheme *sg.*; **~be·schrei·bung** *f* job specification; **~ga·ran̦tie** *f* job protection; **~ge·stal·tung** *f* workplace design; **~stu·die** *f* workplace study; **~tei·lung** *f* job sharing

'Ar·beits|pro·be *f* sample of one's work; **~pro̦zeß** *m* work process; ***j-n in den ~ eingliedern*** integrate s.o. into working life; **~psy·cho̦lo·ge** *m* industrial psychologist; **~psy·cho·lo̦gie** *f* industrial psychology; **~raum** *m* workroom; **~recht** *n* industrial (*Am.* labor) law

'ar·beits·reich *adj.* busy

'Ar·beits·re̦ser·ve *f* manpower (*or* labo[u]r) reserve, human resources *pl.*

'ar·beits·scheu I. *adj.* work-shy; **II.** 2 *f* aversion to work; **'Ar·beits·scheue** *m, f* (-n; -n) shirker, F skiver

'Ar·beits·schutz *m* industrial safety; **~ge·setz** *n* industrial safety act; *in GB*: Factories Act

'Ar·beits|sieg *m sport*: uninspired victory; **~sit·zung** *f* working session; **~skla·ve** *m* work slave

'ar·beits·spa·rend *adj.* labo(u)r-saving

'Ar·beits|spei·cher *m computer*: main memory; **~stab** *m* (working) team; **~stät·te** *f* → ***Arbeitsplatz***; **~stel·le** *f* **1.** job; **2.** place of work; **~streit** *m* labo(u)r dispute; **~stu·die** *f* time (and motion) study; **~stun·den** *pl.* working hours; ✝ manhours

'Ar·beits·su·che *f*: (***auf ~ sein*** be) job-hunting; **'Ar·beit(s)·su·chen·de** *m, f* (-n; -n) job-seeker

'Ar·beits·sucht *f* (-; *no pl.*) F workaholism; **'ar·beits·süch·tig** *adj.*: ***~ sein*** F be a workaholic; **'Ar·beits·süch·ti·ge** *m, f* (-n; -n) F workaholic

'Ar·beits|tag *m* working day, workday; **~takt** *m mot.* power stroke; **~tei·lung** *f* division of labo(u)r; **~the·ra̦pie** *f* work therapy; **~tier** *n* **1.** work(ing) animal; **2.** F *fig.* F workhorse; **~ti·tel** *m* working title

'ar·beits·un·fä·hig *adj.* unfit for work; disabled; **'Ar·beits·un·fä·hig·keit** *f* (-; *no pl.*) unfitness for work; disablement

'Ar·beits|un·fall *m* work accident (*or* injury); **~ur·laub** *m* working vacation; **~ver·fah·ren** *n* working method, technique; **~ver·hält·nis** *n* **1.** employer-employee relationship; **2.** ***im ~ stehen bei*** be employed by (*or* with); **3.** *pl.* working conditions; **~ver·mitt·lung** *f* employment agency; **~ver·trag** *m* employment contract; **~ver·wei·ge·rung** *f* refusal to work; **~vor·gang** *m* working procedure; ⚙ operation; **~wei·se** *f* working method; ⚙ functioning; **~welt** *f* world of employment

'ar·beits·wil·lig *adj.* willing to work

'Ar·beits|wis·sen·schaf·ten *pl.* work sciences; **~wo·che** *f* working week; **~wo·chen·en·de** *n* working weekend

'Ar·beits·wut *f* work mania; **'ar·beits·wü·tig** F *adj.* F work-crazy

'Ar·beits·zeit *f* **1.** working hours *pl.*; **2.** ⚙ operating time; **3.** production time; **~ver·kür·zung** *f* reduction in working hours

'Ar·beits|zeug *n* tools *pl.*; **~zeug·nis** *n* reference; **~zim·mer** *n* study; **~zu·frie·den·heit** *f* job satisfaction

Ar·bi·tra·ge [arbi'tra:ʒə] *f* (-; -n) ✝ arbitrage

ar·bi·trär [arbi'trɛ:ʁ] *adj.* arbitrary

ar·cha·isch [ar'ça:ɪʃ] *adj.* archaic; **Ar·cha·is·mus** [arça'ɪsmʊs] *m* (-; -men) archaism

Ar·chäo·lo·ge [arçɛo'lo:gə] *m* (-n; -n) arch(a)eologist; **Ar·chäo·lo·gie** [arçɛolo'gi:] *f* (-; *no pl.*) arch(a)eology; **ar·chäo·lo·gisch** [arçɛo'lo:gɪʃ] *adj.* arch(a)eological

Ar·che ['arçə] *f* (-; -n) ark; ***die ~ Noah*** Noah's ark

Ar·che·typ [arçə'ty:p] *m* (-s; -en) archetype; **ar·che·ty·pisch** [arçə'ty:pɪʃ] *adj.* archetypal

Ar·chi·pel [arçi'pe:l] *m* (-s; -e) archipelago

Ar·chi·tekt [arçi'tɛkt] *m* (-en; -en) architect; **ar·chi·tek·to·nisch** [arçitɛk'to:nɪʃ] *adj.* architectural

Ar·chi·tek·tur [arçitɛk'tu:ʁ] *f* (-; -en) architecture; **~bü̦ro** *n* architect's office

Ar·chiv [ar'çi:f] *n* (-s; -e [-və]) archives *pl.*; **Ar·chi·var** [arçi'va:ʁ] *m* (-s; -e) archivist

Ar'chiv|auf·nah·men *pl. TV etc.* library pictures; **~bild** *n phot.* library photo(graph); **~ex·em̦plar** *n* archive copy, ✝ file copy

ar·chi·vie·ren [arçi'vi:rən] *v/t.* (h) put into (the) archives

Ar'chiv·ma·te·ri̦al *n* archive material

Are·al [are'a:l] *n* (-s; -e) area

Are·na [a're:na] *f* (-; -nen) arena (*a. fig.*); ring

arg [ark] **I.** *adj.* bad; wicked, evil; → ***schlimm***; ***~e Enttäuschung*** great disappointment; ***sein ärgster Feind*** his worst enemy; ***das ist*** (***doch***) ***zu ~*** that's too much; ***im ~en liegen*** be in a bad way; **II.** *adv.* badly, severely; F terribly; F ***das ist ~ wenig*** F that's not a lot; ***j-n ~ mitnehmen*** (really) take it out of s.o.

Ar·gen·ti·nier [argɛn'ti:nĭɐ] *m* (-s; -), **Ar·gen·ti·nie·rin** [argɛn'ti:nĭərɪn] *f* (-; -nen) Argentine; **ar·gen·ti·nisch** [argɛn'ti:nɪʃ] *adj.* Argentine, Argentinian

Är·ger ['ɛrgɐ] *m* (-s; *no pl.*) trouble, F strife, *a.* hassle; annoyance, irritation (***über*** *acc.* at *s.th.*, with *s.o.*); anger; ***j-m***

~ ***machen*** cause s.o. trouble; ***das gibt*** ~ there'll be trouble; **'är·ger·lich** *adj.* annoyed, cross (***auf*** *acc.*, ***über*** *acc.* at, about *s.th.*, with *s.o.*); annoying; ~***e Sache*** nuisance; ***das ist*** ~ that's annoying, that's a (real) nuisance; **'är·gern** (h) **I.** *v/t.* annoy; tease; ***j-n bis aufs Blut*** ~ F make s.o. wild; **II.** *v/refl.*: ***sich*** ~ be (*or* get) annoyed (***über*** *acc.* at, about *s.th.*, with *s.o.*); ***ärgere dich nicht*** don't get annoyed (*or* upset); ***sich zu Tode*** ~ F be (*or* get) really mad; F ***ich könnte mich krank*** ~ F I could kick myself; → ***grün*** I, ***schwarz*** I; **'Är·ger·nis** *n* (-ses; -se) nuisance; offen|se (*Brit.* -ce); ***die Ärgernisse des täglichen Lebens*** the (little) upsets of daily life; ⚖ ***öffentliches*** ~ public nuisance; ~ ***erregen*** cause offen|ce (*Am.* -se)

'Arg·list *f* (-; *no pl.*) deceitfulness, guile; ⚖ malice, malicious intent; **'arg·li·stig** *adj.* deceitful; ⚖ fraudulent; ⚖ ~***e Täuschung*** wil(l)ful deceit

'arg·los *adj.* guileless; artless, innocent; unsuspecting; **'Arg·lo·sig·keit** *f* (-; *no pl.*) guilelessness, lack of guile; innocence; unawareness

Ar·gu·ment [argu'mɛnt] *n* (-[e]s; -e) argument; ***ein schwerwiegendes*** ~ ***dafür*** (***dagegen***) a strong argument in favo(u)r (against); ***es ist ein*** ~ ***für ...*** it's a case for...; **Ar·gu·men·ta·ti·on** [argumɛnta'tsĭo:n] *f* (-; -en) argumentation; ***das ist e-e*** (***keine***) ***stichhaltige*** ~ you've got a point there (you can't argue like that); **ar·gu·men·ta·tiv** [argumɛnta'ti:f] *adj.* argumentative; **ar·gu·men·tie·ren** [argumɛn'ti:rən] *v/i.* (h) argue, reason; ***...,*** (***so***) ***wird argumentiert*** ..., so the argument goes

Ar·gus·au·gen ['argʊs-] *pl.* eagle-eyes; ***et. mit*** ~ ***beobachten*** watch s.th. like a hawk

Arg·wohn ['arkvo:n] *m* (-[e]s; *no pl.*) suspicion, mistrust (***gegen*** of); ~ ***erregen*** arouse suspicion; ~ ***hegen*** be suspicious (***gegen*** of), ***gegen***: *a.* suspect *s.o. or s.th.*; **arg·wöh·nen** ['arkvø:nən] *v/t.* (ge-, h) suspect; **arg·wöh·nisch** ['arkvø:nɪʃ] *adj.* suspicious, distrustful (***gegen*** *acc.* of)

Arie ['a:rĭə] *f* (-; -n) ♪ aria

Ari·er ['a:rĭɐ] *m* (-s; -), **Arie·rin** ['a:rĭərɪn] *f* (-; -nen), **arisch** ['a:rɪʃ] *adj.* Arian, Aryan

Ari·sto·krat [arɪsto'kra:t] *m* (-en; -en) aristocrat; **Ari·sto·kra·tie** [arɪstokra'ti:] *f* (-; -n) aristocracy; **ari·sto·kra·tisch** [arɪsto'kra:tɪʃ] *adj.* aristocratic; ~***es Auftreten*** *etc.* patrician bearing *etc.*

Arith·me·tik [arɪt'me:tɪk] *f* (-; *no pl.*) arithmetic; **arith·me·tisch** [arɪt'me:tɪʃ] *adj.* arithmetical

Ar·ka·de [ar'ka:də] *f* (-; -n) *a. pl.* arcade

ark·tisch ['arktɪʃ] *adj.* arctic (*a. fig.*)

arm [arm] *adj.* poor (***an*** *dat.* in); ~ ***an*** *dat. a.* lacking in; ~ ***an Vitaminen*** low on vitamins; ~***er Kerl*** F poor bloke; ***um 100 Mark ärmer sein*** be 100 marks worse off; ~ ***dran sein*** have nothing to laugh about; F ***das ist ja nicht wie bei*** ~***en Leuten*** F we do have such things

Arm [arm] *m* (-[e]s; -e) arm; sleeve; *zo.* tentacle; *geogr.* tributary; branch *of candelabra*; ***der*** ~ ***des Gesetzes*** the arm of the law; ***in die*** ~***e nehmen*** hug, embrace; ***auf den*** ~ ***nehmen*** a) pick up, b) carry; c) *fig.* pull *s.o.'s* leg; *fig.* ***j-m unter die*** ~***e greifen*** help s.o. out; ***j-n mit offenen*** ~***en empfangen*** welcome s.o. with open arms; ***j-m in die*** ~***e laufen*** bump (*or* run) into s.o.; ***j-m in den*** ~ ***fallen*** hold s.o. back, stop s.o.; ***sich e-r Sache in die*** ~***e werfen*** launch into s.th. with a vengeance; ***j-n e-r Sache in die*** ~***e treiben*** drive s.o. to s.th.; ***e-n langen*** ~ ***haben*** have a lot of pull; ***den längeren*** ~ ***haben*** have more pull

Ar·ma·tu·ren [arma'tu:rən] *pl.* **1.** *bathroom etc.*: fittings; **2.** *mot. etc.* instruments, controls; ~**brett** *n* dashboard

'Arm·band *n* (-[e]s; ⸚er) bracelet; watchstrap; ~**uhr** *f* wristwatch

'Arm|beu·ge *f* **1.** crook of one's arm, inside of one's elbow; **2.** *sport*: arm bend; ~**bin·de** *f* armband; ⚕ sling; ~**brust** *f* (-; -e, ⸚e) crossbow; ~**drücken** (*sep.* -k·k-) *n* Indian (*Am. a.* arm) wrestling

Ar·me ['armə] *m, f* (-n; -n) poor man (woman); ***die*** ~***n*** the poor (*pl.*); ***der*** ~***!*** poor thing (*or* fellow)

Ar·mee [ar'me:] *f* (-; -n) army; *fig. a.* masses *pl.*; *fig.* ***e-e*** ~ ***von Ameisen*** (***Arbeitslosen***) an army of ants (masses of unemployed)

Är·mel ['ɛrməl] *m* (-s; -) sleeve; *fig.* ***et. aus dem*** ~ ***schütteln*** pull s.th. out of a hat, come up with s.th. just like that; give an off-the-cuff answer (*or* speech *etc.*); ~**auf·schlag** *m* cuff; ~**brett** *n* sleeve board

Ar·me'leu·te... *in cpds.* poor man's

'är·mel·los *adj.* sleeveless

'Ar·men|an·walt *m* ⚖ poor litigant's counsel; ~**haus** *n hist. and fig.* poorhouse

Ar·me·ni·er [ar'me:nĭɐ] *m* (-s; -), **Ar·me·nie·rin** [ar'me:nĭərɪn] *f* (-; -nen), **ar·me·nisch** [ar'me:nɪʃ] *adj.*, **Ar'me·nisch** *n* (-) *ling.* Armenian

'Ar·men|recht *n* ⚖ right to legal aid, forma pauperis; ~**vier·tel** *n* poor part of town; *w.s.* slums *pl.*

Ar·me'sün·der·mie·ne *f* hangdog look

'Arm|ge·lenk *n* elbow joint; ~**höh·le** *f* armpit

ar·mie·ren [ar'mi:rən] *v/t.* (h) reinforce; **Ar'mie·rung** *f* (-; -en) reinforcement

...armig [-armɪç] ...-armed, ...-branched

'Arm|län·ge *f* arm's length; *fig.* ***j-n auf*** ~ ***entfernt halten*** keep s.o. at arm's length; ~**leh·ne** *f* armrest; ~**leuch·ter** *m* **1.** candelabra; **2.** F *fig.* F twit, dope

ärm·lich ['ɛrmlɪç] *adj.* poor; shabby (-looking); *fig.* poor, paltry, meag|re (*Am.* -er); wretched, miserable

'Arm|loch *n* **1.** armhole; **2.** F *fig. sl.* swine; ~**man·schet·te** *f* ⚕ inflatable cuff; ~**mus·kel** *m* arm muscle; biceps; ~**reif** *m* bangle; ~**schie·ne** *f* ⚕ splint; ~**schlin·ge** *f* sling

'arm·se·lig *adj.* **1.** → **ärmlich**; **2.** *contp.* pathetic

'Arm|ses·sel *m* armchair, easy chair; ~**stüt·ze** *f* armrest

Ar·mut ['armu:t] *f* (-; *no pl.*) **1.** poverty; destitution; ***äußerste*** ~ extreme poverty; ***in*** ~ ***geraten*** be reduced to poverty; **2.** *fig.* poverty (***an*** *dat.* of); lack, dearth (of); ***geistige*** ~ intellectual poverty; **'Ar·muts·zeug·nis** *fig. n* sad reflection; ***das ist ein*** ~ *a.* F that's a bad show; ***erschreckendes*** ~ damning indictment; ***sich ein*** ~ ***ausstellen*** shame o.s.

Ar·ni·ka ['arnika] *f* (-; -s) ⚘ arnica

Aro·ma [a'ro:ma] *n* (-s; -men) fragrance; flavo(u)r; essence; **aro'ma·tisch** **I.** *adj.* aromatic; **II.** *adv.*: ***et.*** ~ ***verfeinern*** round off the flavo(u)r (of s.th.); **aro·ma·ti·sie·ren** [aromati'zi:rən] *v/t.* (h) flavo(u)r

Ar·peg·gio [ar'pɛdʒĭo] *n* (-s; -s, -gien [-dʒĭən]) arpeggio

Ar·rak ['arak] *m* (-s; -e, -s) arra(c)k

Ar·ran·ge·ment [arãʒə'mã:] *n* (-s; -s) **1.** *a.* ♪ arrangement; **2.** agreement; ***ein*** ~ ***treffen*** come to an arrangement (*or* agreement); **3.** ⚚ package deal; ***in*** ~***s*** as package deals; **Ar·ran·geur** [arã'ʒø:ɐ] *m* (-s; -e) arranger; **ar·ran·gie·ren** [arã'ʒi:rən] (h) **I.** *v/t.* arrange; **II.** *v/refl.*: ***sich*** ~ come to an arrangement

Ar·rest [a'rɛst] *m* (-[e]s; -e) **1.** detention (*a. ped.*), confinement; ***mit*** ~ ***bestrafen*** put in confinement; **2.** ⚖ seizure, impounding

ar·re·tie·ren [are'ti:rən] *v/t.* (h) ⚙ arrest, stop, lock

Ar·rhyth·mie [arʏt'mi:] *f* (-; -n) ⚕ arrhythmia, irregular heart rate; **ar·rhyth·misch** [a'rʏtmɪʃ] *adj.* arrhythmical

ar·ri·viert [ari'vi:ɐt] *adj.* successful; *contp.* upstart ...; **Ar·ri'vier·te** *m, f* (-n; -n) successful (*or* established) politician (*or* artist *etc.*); *contp.* parvenu, upstart; ***er gehört jetzt zu den*** ~***n*** he's made it

ar·ro·gant [aro'gant] *adj.* arrogant; **Ar·ro·ganz** [aro'gants] *f* (-; *no pl.*) arrogance

Arsch [arʃ] V *m* (-[e]s; Ärsche ['ɛrʃə]) V arse, *Am.* V ass; ***am*** ~ ***der Welt*** F at the back of beyond, F out in the sticks (*Am. a.* boondocks); ***j-m in den*** ~ ***kriechen*** F suck up to s.o.; ***er*** (***es***) ***ist im*** ~ he's (it's) had it; ***leck mich am*** ~***!*** *sl.* get stuffed, V bugger it; ~**backe** (*sep.* -k·k-) V *f* buttock; ~**ficker** (*sep.* -k·k-) V *m* V arse bandit; ~**gei·ge** V *f* V bastard; ~**krie·cher** V *m* V arse-licker; ~**loch** V *n* V arse-hole; *a.* V bastard; ~**tritt** V *m*: ***j-m e-n*** ~ ***geben*** V give s.o. a kick in the arse; ~**-und-Tit·ten-Pres·se** V *f* V tits-and-ass (*or* tits-and-bums) press (*or* magazines *pl.*)

Ar·sen [ar'ze:n] *n* (-s; *no pl.*) arsenic

Ar·se·nal [arze'na:l] *n* (-s; -e) **1.** arsenal; weaponry, (weapons) stockpile, armo(u)ry; **2.** *fig.* repository; battery

ar'sen·hal·tig *adj.* arsenic ...; ~ ***sein*** contain arsenic; **ar·se·nig** [ar'ze:nɪç] *adj.*: ~***e Säure*** arsenic acid; **Ar'sen·ver·gif·tung** *f* arsenic poisoning

Art [a:ɐt] *f* (-; -en) **1.** *no pl.* way, manner; method; ***auf die***(***se***) ~ (in) this way; ***auf irgendeine*** ~***, auf die eine oder andere*** ~ somehow or other; ***auf s-e*** ~ in his way; ***nach der*** ~ *gen.* along the lines of; ***in der*** ~ ***Rembrandts*** (***Haydns***) in the style of Rembrandt (Haydn); ***auf ruhige*** ~ quietly; ***er hat e-e angenehme*** ~ he has a nice way, he's very pleasant, ***zu lachen***: he has a pleasant laugh; ***das ist eigentlich nicht s-e*** ~ that's not like him (at all); ***das ist nun mal s-e*** ~ that's the way he is; **2.** *no pl.* nature, kind; (***von***) ***dieser*** ~ of this nature (*or* kind); **3.** *no pl.* nature; ***gewinnende*** ~ winning way; ***es ist nicht s-e*** ~ ***zu*** *inf.* he's not the sort to *inf.*; ***einzig in s-r*** ~ unique; **4.** *no pl.* behavio(u)r, manners *pl.*; ***das ist*** (***doch***) ***keine*** ~***!*** that's no way to behave; **5.** kind, sort, type; style; ***Geräte aller*** ~ *a.* tools of every description; ***e-e ...*** a kind (*or* sort, type) of ...; *iro.* ***e-e*** ~ ***Künstler***

an artist of sorts; **6.** *biol.* species; race; *fig.* ***er ist vollkommen aus der ~ geschlagen*** he's not like anyone else in the family

Ar·te·fakt [artə'fakt] *n* (-[e]s; -e) artifact, artefact

'**art·ei·gen** *adj.* characteristic, true to type

ar·ten ['aːɐtən] *v/i* (sn).: ***nach j-m ~*** take after s.o.; → ***geartet*** II

'**Ar·ten·ge·mein·schaft** *f* biological community

'**ar·ten·ge·recht** *adj.*: ***~e Tierhaltung*** keeping animals in their natural environment

'**ar·ten·reich** *adj.* ♣ *etc.*: very varied, with a large number of species; *area*: with a rich animal and plant life (*or* flora and fauna); '**Ar·ten·reich·tum** *m* (-s; *no pl.*) rich animal and plant life, rich flora and fauna; 🕮 biodiversity

'**Ar·ten|schutz** *m* protection of endangered species; **~viel·falt** *f* → ***Artenreichtum***

'**Art·er·hal·tung** *f* preservation of the species

Ar·te·rie [ar'teːrĭə] *f* (-; -n) artery; **Ar'te·ri·en·ver·kal·kung** *f*, **Ar·te·rio·skle·ro·se** [arterĭoskle'roːzə] *f* (-; -n) hardening of the arteries, ⚕ arteriosclerosis

'**art·fremd** *adj.* alien, foreign

'**Art·ge·nos·se** *m* member of the same species

'**art|ge·recht** *adj.* → ***artengerecht***; **~gleich** *adj.*: ***~ sein*** belong to the same species; ***sie sind ~*** they're the same species

Ar·thri·tis [ar'triːtɪs] *f* (-; -itiden [artri'tiːdən]) ⚕ arthritis

Ar·thro·se [ar'troːzə] *f* (-; -n) ⚕ arthrosis

ar·ti·fi·zi·ell [artifi'tsĭɛl] *adj.* artificial

ar·tig ['artɪç] *adj.* well-behaved, good; ***sei ~!*** be good!, be a good boy (*or* girl)!; '**Ar·tig·keit** *f* (-; *no pl.*) good behavio(u)r; politeness

Ar·ti·kel [ar'tiːkəl] *m* (-s; -) *a. ling. and* ⚖ article; ✝ *a.* item, commodity

Ar·ti·ku·la·ti·on [artikula'tsĭoːn] *f* (-; -en) articulation; **Ar·ti·ku·la·ti'ons·ver·mö·gen** *n* powers *pl.* of articulation; **ar·ti·ku·lie·ren** [artiku'liːrən] (h) **I.** *v/t.* express, put into words; articulate; **II.** *v/refl.*: ***sich ~*** express o.s.

Ar·til·le·rie [artɪlə'riː] *f* (-; -n) artillery; **~be·schuß** *m*, **~feu·er** *n* artillery fire

Ar·til·le·rist [artɪlə'rɪst] *m* (-en; -en) artilleryman, gunner

Ar·ti·schocke (*sep.* -k·k-) *f* (-; -n) artichoke

Ar·ti'schocken|bo·den *m* artichoke base; **~herz** *n* artichoke heart

Ar·tist [ar'tɪst] *m* (-en; -en), **Ar·ti·stin** [ar'tɪstɪn] *f* (-; -nen) (variety) artist, acrobat, *Am. a.* performer; **Ar·ti·stik** [ar'tɪstɪk] *f* (-; *no pl.*) **1.** acrobatics *pl.* **2.** skill; **ar·ti·stisch** [ar'tɪstɪʃ] *adj.* **1.** acrobatic(ally *adv.*); **2.** skil(l)ful

Ar·to·thek [arto'teːk] *f* (-; -en) picture lending gallery

'**art|spe͵zi·fisch** *adj.* characteristic of (*or* specific to) the species; **~ver·schie·den** *adj.* **1.** ***~ sein*** belong to a different species; ***sie sind ~*** they're different species; **2.** completely different; **~ver·wandt** *adj.* related, kindred ...

Arz·nei [arts'naɪ] *f* (-; -en) medicine, medicament, drug; remedy; **~buch** *n* pharmacopoeia; **~kun·de** *f* (-; *no pl.*) pharmaceutics *pl.*

Arz'nei·mit·tel *n* → ***Arznei***; **~for·schung** *f* pharmaceutical(s) research; **~in·du͵strie** *f* pharmaceutical industry; **~͵miß·brauch** *m* drug abuse

Arz'nei·schrank *m* medicine cabinet

Arzt [aːɐtst] *m* (-es; Ärzte ['ɛːɐrtstə]) doctor, *Am. and formal*: physician; ***praktischer ~*** general practitioner; **~be·ruf** *m* medical profession; ***der ~*** *w.s.* a doctor's life, being a doctor

'**Ärz·te|kam·mer** *f* medical association; **~mu·ster** *n* drug sample

'**Ärz·te·schaft** *f* (-; *no pl.*) medical profession

'**Ärz·te|schwem·me** *f* glut (*or* surfeit) of doctors; **~ver·tre·ter** *m* pharmaceutical representative

'**Arzt·hel·fe·rin** *f* (-; -nen) (doctor's) assistant *or* receptionist

Ärz·tin ['ɛːɐtstɪn] *f* (-; -nen) (lady) doctor *or* physician

'**Arzt·ko·sten** *pl.* doctor's (*or* medical) fees

ärzt·lich ['ɛːɐtstlɪç] *adj.* medical; ***in ~er Behandlung*** under medical care; ***~e Hilfe*** medical assistance; → ***Attest***

'**Arzt|pra·xis** *f* medical practice, *Brit. a.* (doctor's) surgery; **~rech·nung** *f* doctor's bill; **~ro͵man** *m* hospital romance; **~wahl** *f*: ***freie ~*** right to go to the doctor of one's choice (*or* to choose one's own doctor)

As[1] [as] *n* (Asses; Asse) **1.** ace (*a.* F *fig. person*); **2.** *tennis*: (clean) ace; *golf*: hole in one

As[2] [as] *n* (-; -) ♪ A flat

As·best [as'bɛst] *m* (-[e]s; -e) asbestos; **~an·zug** *m* asbestos suit

As·be·sto·se [asbɛs'toːzə] *f* (-; -n) ⚕ asbestosis

As'best|plat·te *f* asbestos mat; **~sa͵nie·rung** *f* asbestos abatement

As'best·staub *m* asbestos particles *pl.*; **~lun·ge** *f* ⚕ asbestosis

As'best·ze͵ment *m* asbestos cement

'**asch·blond** *adj.* ash blonde

Asche ['aʃə] *f* (-; -n) ash, *usu.* ashes *pl.*; ***glühende ~*** embers *pl.*; *fig.* ***sich ~ aufs Haupt streuen*** put on (*or* wear) sackcloth and ashes

'**Asch·ei·mer** *m* → ***Mülleimer***

Aschen|bahn ['aʃən-] *f* cinder track; *mot.* dirt track; **~be·cher** *m* ashtray

Aschenbrö·del ['aʃənbrøːdəl] *n* → ***Aschenputtel***; **~da·sein** *n* → ***Aschenputteldasein***

Aschen·platz *m tennis*: ash court

Aschen·put·tel ['aʃənpʊtəl] *n* (-s; -) Cinderella (*a. fig.*); **~da·sein** *n*: ***ein ~ führen*** lead a Cinderella-like existence

Ascher ['aʃɐ] F *m* (-s; -) ashtray

Ascher'mitt·woch *m* Ash Wednesday

'**asch|fahl** *adj.* ashen; **~grau** *adj.* ash-grey (*Am.* -gray)

As·cor·bin·säu·re [askɔr'biːn-] *f* (-; *no pl.*) ⚗ ascorbic acid

'**A-Sei·te** *f* A side

äsen ['ɛːzən] *v/i.* (h) graze

Asep·sis [a'zɛpsɪs] *f* (-; *no pl.*) asepsis; **asep·tisch** [a'zɛptɪʃ] *adj.* aseptic

'**ase·xu͵al**, '**ase·xu͵ell** *adj. biol.*, ⚕ asexual

Asiat [a'zĭaːt] *m* (-en; -en), **Asia'tin** [a'zĭaːtɪn] *f* (-; -nen) Asian; **asia·tisch** [a'zĭaːtɪʃ] *adj.* Asian; *a.* Asiatic *people etc.*; **Asia·ti·ka** [a'zĭaːtika] *pl.* Oriental art *sg.* (*or* antiquities)

As·ke·se [as'keːzə] *f* (-; *no pl.*) asceticism; **As·ket** [as'keːt] *m* (-en; -en) ascetic; **as·ke·tisch** [as'keːtɪʃ] *adj.* ascetic(ally *adv.*)

'**aso·zi͵al** *adj.* antisocial; '**Aso·zi͵a·le** *m, f* (-n; -n) antisocial; dropout; *pl. a.* antisocial elements

Aspekt [as'pɛkt] *m* (-[e]s; -e) aspect (*a. ling.*); ***unter diesem ~ betrachtet*** seen from this angle (*or* point of view)

As·phalt [as'falt] *m* (-s; -e) asphalt; **as·phal·tie·ren** [asfal'tiːrən] *v/t.* (h) (surface with) asphalt

As'phalt|ma·ler *m* pavement artist; **~ma·le͵rei** *f* pavement art; **~platz** *m tennis*: asphalt court; **~stra·ße** *f* asphalt road

Aspik [as'piːk] *m* (-s; -e) aspic; ***Aal in ~*** jellied eel

Aspi·rant [aspi'rant] *m* (-en; -en) candidate

aspi·rie·ren [aspi'riːrən] *v/t.* (h) *ling.* aspirate

aß [aːs] *pret. of* ***essen***

As·se·ku·ranz [aseku'rants] *f* (-; -en) insurance

As·sel ['asəl] *f* (-; -n) woodlouse

As·sem·bler [ə'sɛmblə] *m* (-s; -) *computer*: assembler; **~spra·che** *f* assembler language

As·ser·vat [asɛr'vaːt] *n* (-[e]s; -e) exhibit; **As·ser'va·ten·kam·mer** *f* exhibit room

As·ses·sor [a'sɛsɔr] *m* (-s; -en [asɛ'soːrən]), **As·ses·so·rin** [asɛ'soːrɪn] *f* (-; -nen) **1.** *civil servant who has completed his/her second state examination*; **2.** ⚖ assistant judge

As·si·mi·la·ti·on [asimila'tsĭoːn] *f* (-; -en) assimilation; **as·si·mi·lie·ren** [asimi'liːrən] *v/t.* (h) assimilate

As·si·stent [asɪs'tɛnt] *m* (-en; -en), **As·si'sten·tin** *f* (-; -nen) assistant

As·si·stenz [asɪs'tɛnts] *f* (-; -en) assistance; ***unter ~ von*** with the assistance of; **~arzt** *m* houseman, *Am.* intern

as·si·stie·ren [asɪs'tiːrən] *v/i.* (h) assist (***bei*** *dat.* in)

As·so·zia·ti·on [asotsĭa'tsĭoːn] *f* (-; -en) association; ✝ partnership; **as·so·zia·tiv** [asotsĭa'tiːf] *adj.* associative; **as·so·zi·ie·ren** [asotsi'iːrən] (h) **I.** *v/t.* associate; **II.** *v/refl.*: ***sich ~*** *pol.* associate (o.s.) (***mit*** *dat.* with); ✝ enter into a partnership (with)

Ast [ast] *m* (-[e]s; Äste ['ɛstə]) **1.** branch, *esp. lit.* bough; knot; *fig.* ***den ~ absägen, auf dem man sitzt*** saw off one's own branch, dig one's own grave; ***auf dem absteigenden ~ sein*** be going downhill; ***er ist auf dem aufsteigenden ~*** things are looking up for him, F he's on the up and up; **2.** F hump; → ***lachen*** I

as·ten ['astən] F *v/t.* (h) lug (along *or* up *etc.*)

As·ter ['astɐ] *f* (-; -n) ♣ aster

Asthe·nie [aste'niː] *f* (-; -n) ⚕ debility, asthenia; **Asthe·ni·ker** [as'teːnikɐ] *m* (-s; -) asthenic (person)

Äs·thet [ɛs'teːt] *m* (-en; -en) (a)esthete; **Äs·the·tik** [ɛs'teːtɪk] *f* (-; -en) **1.** (a)esthetics *pl.*; **2.** *no pl.* a) beauty, (a)esthetic appeal (*gen.* of); (a)esthetic; b) (a)esthetic sense; **äs·the·tisch** [ɛs'teːtɪʃ] *adj.* (a)esthetic(ally *adv.*)

Asth·ma ['astma] *n* (-s; *no pl.*) ⚕ asthma; **Asth·ma·ti·ker** [ast'maːtikɐ] *m* (-s; -), **asth·ma·tisch** [ast'maːtɪʃ] *adj.* asthmatic

astig·ma·tisch [astɪ'gmaːtɪʃ] *adj.* astigmatic

'Ast·loch *n* knothole
Astral·leib [as'tra:l-] *m* **1.** astral body; **2.** F *iro.* divine frame
'ast·rein F *fig. adj.* **1.** above-board; ***die Sache ist nicht ganz ~*** there's something fishy about the business; **2.** F great, fantastic
Astro·lo·ge [astro'lo:gə] *m* (-n; -n) astrologer; **Astro·lo·gie** [astrolo'gi:] *f* (-; *no pl.*) astrology; **astro·lo·gisch** [astro'lo:gɪʃ] *adj.* astrological
Astro·naut [astro'naʊt] *m* (-en; -en) astronaut; **Astro·nau·tik** [astro'naʊtɪk] *f* astronautics *pl.*
Astro·nom [astro'no:m] *m* (-en; -en) astronomer; **Astro·no·mie** [astrono'mi:] *f* (-; *no pl.*) astronomy; **astro·no·misch** [astro'no:mɪʃ] *adj.* astronomic(al) (*a. fig.*)
Astro·phy'sik [astro-] *f* astrophysics *pl.*; **Astro'phy·si·ker** *m* astrophysicist
'Ast·werk *n* (-[e]s; *no pl.*) branches *pl*
ASU ['a:zu] *f* → ***Abgassonderuntersuchung***
Asyl [a'zy:l] *n* (-s; -e) **1.** place of refuge, sanctuary; **2.** home; **3.** *pol.* asylum; ***um (politisches) ~ bitten*** ask for (political) asylum; **Asy·lant** [azy'lant] *m* (-en; -en) → ***Asylbewerber***; **Asy'lan·ten·wohn·heim** *n* asylum-seekers' hostel
Asyl|be·wer·ber [a'zy:l-] *m* asylum-seeker, (political) refugee; **~ge·wäh·rung** *f* granting of asylum; **~recht** *n* **1.** right of asylum; **2.** asylum laws *pl.*
Asym·me·trie [azʏme'tri:] *f* (-; -n) asymmetry, lack of symmetry; **asym·me·trisch** [azʏ'me:trɪʃ] *adj.* asymmetrical
asyn·chron ['azʏnkro:n] *adj.* asynchronous
As·zen·dent [astsɛn'dɛnt] *m* (-en; -en) ascendant
Ata·vis·mus [ata'vɪsmʊs] *m* (-; -men) atavism; **ata·vi·stisch** [ata'vɪstɪʃ] *adj.* atavistic
Ate·lier [ate'li̯e:] *n* (-s; -s) studio; **~auf·nah·me** *f* studio shot; **~ka·me·ra** *f* studio camera; **~se·kre,tä·rin** *f* continuity girl, script girl; **~woh·nung** *f* studio flat (*Am.* apartment); loft
Atem ['a:təm] *m* (-s; *no pl.*) breath; breathing; ***außer ~*** out of breath; ***~ holen*** take a breath, *fig.* (*a.* ***~ schöpfen***) get one's breath back; ***den ~ anhalten*** hold one's breath; ***mit angehaltenem ~*** with bated breath; ***im selben ~*** in the same breath; ***außer ~ kommen*** get out of breath; ***wieder zu ~ kommen*** *a. fig.* get one's breath back; *fig.* ***j-n in ~ halten*** keep s.o. on his *or* her toes (*or* on tenterhooks); ***den längeren ~ haben*** have more staying power; ***das verschlug ihm den ~*** his jaw just dropped; ***ihnen geht der ~ aus*** they're running dry (*or* out of resources)
'atem·be·rau·bend *fig. adj.* breathtaking
'Atem|be·schwer·den *pl.* difficulty *sg.* in breathing; ***~ haben*** have difficulty breathing; **~fre,quenz** *f* respiratory rate; **~ge·rät** *n* breathing apparatus; ⚕ respirator; **~gym,na·stik** *f* breathing exercises *pl.*; **~ho·len** *n* breathing; **~läh·mung** *f* respiratory standstill; **~loch** *n wale*: blowhole
'atem·los *adj.* breathless (*a. fig.*); out of breath; **'Atem·lo·sig·keit** *f* (-; *no pl.*) breathlessness
'Atem|mas·ke *f* breathing mask; **~not** *f* (-; *no pl.*) shortness of breath; ***an ~ leiden*** have difficulty breathing; **~pau·se** *f* F breather; ***e-e ~ einlegen (gewähren)*** take (give *s.o.*) a breather; **~schutz·ge·rät** *n* breathing apparatus; **~still·stand** *m* respiratory standstill; **~tech·nik** *f* breathing technique; **~übun·gen** *pl.* breathing exercises; **~we·ge** *pl.* respiratory tract *sg.*; **~zen·trum** *n* respiratory cent|re (*Am.* -er); **~zug** *m* breath; ***bis zum letzten ~*** to the last gasp; ***den letzten ~ tun*** breathe one's last; ***in e-m ~*** in one breath; ***im nächsten ~*** the next moment
Ätha·nol [ɛta'no:l] *n* (-s; *no pl.*) ethyl alcohol, ethanol
Athe·is·mus [ate'ɪsmʊs] *m* (-; *no pl.*) atheism; **Athe·ist** [ate'ɪst] *m* (-en; -en) atheist; **athe·istisch** [ate'ɪstɪʃ] *adj.* atheistic(ally *adv.*)
Athe·ner [a'te:nɐ] *m* (-s; -) Athenian
Äther ['ɛ:tɐ] *m* (-s; *no pl.*) *phys. and* ⚗ ether; *radio*: air (waves *pl.*); ***über den ~*** over the air
äthe·risch [ɛ'te:rɪʃ] *adj.* ethereal (*a. fig.*); ***~e Öle*** essential oils
Äther|krieg *m* war of the airwaves; **~nar,ko·se** *f* etherization
Äthio·pier [ɛ'ti̯o:pi̯ɐ] *m* (-s; -), **Äthio·pie·rin** [ɛ'ti̯o:pi̯ərɪn] *f* (-; -nen), **äthio·pisch** [ɛ'ti̯o:pɪʃ] *adj.* Ethiopian
Ath·let [at'le:t] *m* (-en; -en) athlete; **ath·le·tisch** [at'le:tɪʃ] *adj.* athletic
Äthyl [ɛ'ty:l] *n* (-s; *no pl.*) ⚗ ethyl; **~al·ko·hol** *m* ethyl alcohol
Äthy·len [ɛty'le:n] *n* (-s; *no pl.*) ⚗ ethylene
At·lant [at'lant] *m* (-en; -en) △ atlas, male caryatid
At·lan·tik·pakt [at'lantɪk-] *m* Atlantic Treaty
at·lan·tisch [at'lantɪʃ] *adj.* Atlantic; ***der ♀e Ozean*** the Atlantic (Ocean)
At·las¹ ['atlas] *m* (-, -sses; Atlanten [at'lantən]) **1.** atlas; **2.** *no pl. anat.* atlas
'At·las² *m* (-, -ses; -se) satin
at·men ['a:tmən] (h) **I.** *v/i. and v/t.* breathe; **II.** ♀ *n* (-s) breathing
At·mo·sphä·re [atmɔ'sfɛ:rə] *f* (-; -n) atmosphere (*a. fig.*)
At·mo'sphä·ren|druck *m* atmospheric pressure; **~,über·druck** *m* (atmospheric) excess pressure
at·mo·sphä·risch [atmɔ'sfɛ:rɪʃ] *adj.* atmospheric(ally *adv.*); ***~e Störungen*** *radio*: static, atmospheric disturbance
At·mung ['a:tmʊŋ] *f* (-; *no pl.*) breathing; ***künstliche ~*** artificial respiration
'at·mungs·ak,tiv *adj.* cellular, breathing ...
'At·mungs|or,gan *n* respiratory organ; ***Erkrankungen der ~e*** respiratory diseases; **~zen·trum** *n* respiratory cent|re (*Am.* -er)
Atoll [a'tɔl] *n* (-s; -e) atoll
Atom [a'to:m] *n* (-s; -e) atom; **~an·griff** *m* nuclear attack; **~an·trieb** *m* atomic propulsion
ato·mar [ato'ma:ɐ] *adj.* atomic, nuclear; ***~e Streitkräfte*** nuclear powers
Atom|bau [a'to:m-] *m* (-[e]s; *no pl.*) atomic structure; **♀be·trie·ben** *adj.* nuclear-powered; **~bom·be** *f* atom (*or* atomic) bomb, A-bomb; **~bun·ker** *m* atomic (*or* nuclear) shelter; **~bu·sen** *hum. m* F big boobs *pl.*; **~ei** F *n* atomic pile
Atom·ener,gie [a'to:m-] *f* atomic (*or* nuclear) energy; **~kom·mis·si,on** *f* Atomic Energy Commission
Atom|ex·plo·si,on [a'to:m-] *f* atomic (*or* nuclear) explosion; **~for·scher** *m* nuclear scientist; **~for·schung** *f* nuclear research; **~geg·ner** *m* anti-nuclear protester; **♀ge·trie·ben** *adj.* nuclear-powered; **~ge·wicht** *n* atomic weight; **~hül·le** *f* atomic shell; **~in·du,strie** *f* nuclear industry
ato·mi·sie·ren [atomi'zi:rən] *v/t.* (h) atomize
Atom|kern [a'to:m-] *m* atomic nucleus; **~kraft** *f* (-; *no pl.*) atomic (*or* nuclear) power; **~kraft·werk** *n* nuclear power station; **~krieg** *m* atomic (*or* nuclear) war(fare); **~macht** *f* nuclear power; **~mas·se** *f* atomic mass; **~me·di,zin** *f* nuclear medicine; **~mei·ler** *m* (nuclear) reactor, atomic pile
Atom·müll [a'to:m-] *m* nuclear waste
Atom·müll·la·ge·rung [a'to:m-] *f* nuclear waste disposal
Atom·müll·de·po,nie [a'to:m-] *f* nuclear waste disposal site
Atom|phy,sik [a'to:m-] *f* nuclear physics *pl.*; **~,phy·si·ker** *m* nuclear physicist; **~pilz** *m* mushroom cloud; **~ra,ke·te** *f* nuclear missile; **~re,ak·tor** *m* nuclear reactor; **~spal·tung** *f* nuclear fission; **~sperr·ver·trag** *m* non-proliferation treaty; **~spreng·kopf** *m* nuclear warhead; **~spreng·kör·per** *m* nuclear explosive; **~stopp** *m* nuclear ban; **~streit·macht** *f* nuclear power
Atom·test·stopp [a'to:m-] *m* (nuclear) test ban; **~ab·kom·men** *n* test ban treaty
Atom|tod [a'to:m-] *m* nuclear death; **~-U-Boot** *n* nuclear(-powered) submarine; **~uhr** *f* atomic clock; **~ver·such** *m* nuclear test
Atom·waf·fe [a'to:m-] *f* atomic (*or* nuclear) weapon; **atom·waf·fen·frei** *adj.* nuclear-free; **Atom·waf·fen·geg·ner** *m* anti-nuclear protester
Atom|wirt·schaft [a'to:m-] *f* nuclear industry; **~wis·sen·schaft** *f* (-; *no pl.*) (*a.* ***die ~***) nuclear science; **~wis·sen·schaft·ler** *m* nuclear scientist; **~zeit·al·ter** *n* nuclear age; **~zer·fall** *m* atomic disintegration; **~ziel** *n* nuclear target
ato·nal ['atona:l] *adj.* ♪ atonal
'ato·xisch *adj.* non-toxic
Atri·um·haus ['a:triʊm-] *n* atrium house (*or* building)
Atro·phie [atro'fi:] *f* (-; -n), **atro·phie·ren** [atro'fi:rən] *v/i.* atrophy
ätsch [ɛ:tʃ] *int.* **1.** see!; **2.** serves you right!
At·ta·ché [ata'ʃe] *m* (-s; -s) attaché
At·tacke (*sep.* -k·k-) *f* (-; -n) attack (*a.* ⚕ *and fig.*) (***gegen*** on); **at·tackie·ren** (*sep.* -k·k-) *v/t. and v/i.* (h) attack (*a. fig.*), charge
At·ten·tat ['atənta:t, atɛn'ta:t] *n* (-[e]s; -e) assassination attempt (***auf*** *acc.* on), attempted assassination; assassination; ***~ auf j-n*** attempt on s.o.'s life; ***ein ~ auf j-n verüben*** make an attempt on s.o.'s life, assassinate s.o.; F *fig.* ***ich habe ein ~ auf dich vor*** F I've got a big favo(u)r to ask of you (*or* a job lined up for you); **At·ten·tä·ter** ['atəntɛ:tɐ; atɛn'tɛ:tɐ] *m* (-s; -) assassin
At·test [a'tɛst] *n* (-[e]s; -e): (***ärztliches ~*** medical *or* doctor's) certificate; **at·te·stie·ren** [atɛs'ti:rən] *v/t.* (h) certify
At·trak·ti·on [atrak'tsi̯o:n] *f* (-; -en) attraction; *a.* draw; ✝ winner; **at·trak·tiv** [atrak'ti:f] *adj.* attractive; **At·trak·ti·vi·tät** [atraktivi'tɛ:t] *f* (-; *no pl.*) attractiveness; attraction; *w.s. a.* desirability

At·trap·pe [a'trapə] *f* (-; -n) dummy, ✝ *a.* display package; ⚙ mock-up; *fig.* ***das ist alles nur*** ~ it's all show
At·tri·but [atri'bu:t] *n* (-[e]s; -e) attribute; characteristic; *ling.* attribute, (attributive) adjunct; **at·tri·bu·tiv** [atribu'ti:f] *adj.* attributive
atü [a'ty:] → ***Atmosphärenüberdruck***
'**aty·pisch** *adj.* atypical
'**Ätz·al**ˌ**ka·li** *n* caustic alkali
ät·zen ['ɛtsən] *v/t.* (h) corrode, eat into; etch; ⚕ cauterize; '**ät·zend** *adj.* **1.** caustic, corrosive; **2.** *fig.* caustic, vitriolic; **3.** *fig. sl.* (really) crappy; **(*das ist*) *echt*** ~ *sl.* it's the pits
'**Ätz·na·tron** *n* caustic soda
Ät·zung ['ɛtsʊŋ] *f* (-; -en) **1.** corrosion; ⚕ cauterization; **2.** etching
au [aʊ] *int.* **1.** ouch!; **2.** ~ ***ja!*** oh yes!
Au·ber·gi·ne [obɛr'ʒi:nə] *f* (-; -n) aubergine, *Am. a.* eggplant
auch [aʊx] *cj. and adv.* a) also; too; as well; b) even; c) really; ***wenn*** ~ even if; *ich glaube es* - ***ich*** ~ so do I; ***ich kann es nicht - ich*** ~ ***nicht*** I can't do it - nor (*or* neither) can I, I can't either; ***nicht nur ..., sondern*** ~ not only ..., but also; ***sowohl ... als*** ~ ***...*** both ... and ..., ... as well as ...; ***wo*** ~ **(*immer*)** wherever; ***wenn*** ~ so?; ***wer es*** ~ ***sei*** whoever it is; ***was er dir*** ~ ***sagt*** whatever he says; ***mag er*** ~ ***noch so unfreundlich sein*** however unpleasant he is (*or* may be); ***so sehr ich*** ~ ***bedaure*** much as I regret; ***ohne*** ~ ***nur zu fragen*** without even (*or* so much as) asking; ***du bist aber*** ~ ***stur*** F talk about stubborn; ***das kommt*** ~ ***noch*** a) that's still to come, b) we'll cross that bridge when we get to it; ***da können wir*** ~ ***zu Hause bleiben*** we may as well stay at home; *ich gebe dir das Buch,* ***nun lies es aber*** ~ mind you read it though; ***wirst du es*** ~ **(*wirklich*)** ***tun?*** are you really going to do it?; ***ist es*** ~ ***wahr?*** is it really true?; ***haben Sie ihn*** ~ **(*wirklich*)** ***gesehen?*** are you sure you saw him?; ***er hat ja*** ~ ***schwer gearbeitet*** he has been working hard(, after all); ***das hab' ich*** ~ ***nicht gesagt*** that's not what I said(, is it?); F ***so sieht er*** ~ ***aus*** he looks it, *a.* he looks the sort; ***so ist es*** ~ absolutely, that's (exactly) it
Au·di·enz [aʊ'dĭɛnts] *f* (-; -en) audience (***bei*** with); ~ ***halten*** hold an audience; ***in*** ~ ***von j-m empfangen werden*** be given an audience by s.o.
Au·di·max [aʊdi'maks] F *n* (-; *no pl.*) main auditorium
Au·dio·me·ter [aʊdĭo'me:tɐ] *n* (-s; -) ⚕ audiometer; **Au·dio·me·trie** [aʊdĭome'tri:] *f* (-; *no pl.*) audiometry
au·dio·vi·su·ell [aʊdĭovi'zŭɛl] *adj.* audio-visual
Au·di·to·ri·um [aʊdi'to:rĭʊm] *n* (-s; -rien [-rĭən]) **1.** auditorium, lecture hall; ~ ***maximum*** → ***Audimax;*** **2.** audience
Aue ['aʊə] *f* (-; -n) (rich) pasture; meadow
Au·er|hahn ['aʊɐ-] *m* capercaillie, wood grouse; **~hen·ne** *f*, **~huhn** *n* capercaillie (hen), wood grouse; **~ochs** *m* aurochs
auf [aʊf] **I.** *prp.* **1.** *with dat.*: on; in; at; by; ~ ***dem Tisch*** on the table; ~ ***der Welt*** in the world; ***nirgends*** ~ ***der Welt*** nowhere in the (whole wide) world; ~ ***der Ausstellung*** **(*Post*)** at the exhibition (post office); ~ ***e-r Party*** **(*Schule, Universität*)** at a party (school, university); ~ ***dem Markt*** at the market; ~ ***der Straße*** in (*Am. a.* on) the street, on the road; ~ ***Malta*** in Malta; ~ ***der Insel*** on the island; ~ ***dem Rücken*** on one's back; ~ ***s-r Seite*** at (*or* by) his side, on his side; ~ ***Seite 15*** on page 15; ~ ***s-m Zimmer*** in his room; ~ **(*in*)*direktem Wege*** (in)directly; ~ ***Reisen*** travel(l)ing, on a trip; **(*et.*)** ~ ***der Geige*** *etc.* ***spielen*** play (s.th. on) the violin *etc.*; ***das Wort endet*** ~ ***t*** the word ends with (*or* in) a t; *fig.* ~ ***der Stelle*** on the spot; **2.** *with acc.*: on; onto; in; at; to; towards (*a.* ~ ***... zu***); up; ~ ***den Tisch*** on the table; ~ ***englisch*** in English; ~ ***e-e Entfernung von*** at a distance of; ~ ***die Erde fallen*** fall (on)to the ground; ~ ***die Post*** *etc.* ***gehen*** go to the post office *etc.*; ~ ***sein Zimmer gehen*** go to one's room; ***es geht*** ~ ***neun*** **(*Uhr*)** it's getting on for nine; ~ ***Jahre hinaus*** for years to come; ~ ***Monate*** **(*hinaus*)** ***ausgebucht*** booked (*or* sold) out (for) months ahead; ***Monat*** ~ ***Monat verging*** months went by; ~ ***ewig*** for ever (and ever); ***er kam um 6,*** ~ ***die Minute genau*** he came at 6 o'clock on the dot; ***er geht*** ~ ***die Siebzig zu*** he's getting on for seventy; ***es hat was*** ~ ***sich*** there's something to it; ***es hat nichts*** ~ ***sich, daß ...*** the fact that ... doesn't mean anything; ***das Gerücht hat nichts*** ~ ***sich*** there's nothing in (*or* to) the rumo(u)r; ***ich frage mich, was es mit ...*** ~ ***sich hat*** I wonder what's behind ...; → ***bis*** 6, ***Bitte, Gefahr, Vorschlag;*** **II.** *adv.* up, upwards; open; → ***aufhaben, aufsein;*** ~ ***und ab gehen*** walk up and down (*or* to and fro); ***sich*** ~ ***und davon machen*** clear off; **III.** *cj.*: ~ ***daß*** (in order) that; ~ ***daß nicht*** lest *he should get angry etc.*; **IV.** *int.*: ~***!*** (get) up!; let's get going!; come on!; F ~ ***geht's!*** F let's go!; **V.** ♀ *n*: ***das*** ~ ***und Ab des Lebens*** the ups and downs of life
'**auf·ar·bei·ten** *v/t.* (*sep.*, h) **1.** get through, get *s.th.* out of the way; clear *a backlog*; ***ich muß noch viel*** ~ I have a lot to catch up on; **2.** use up; **3.** F do up *upholstery etc.*; **4.** get a solid grounding in; consolidate; **5.** digest; come to terms with
'**auf·at·men** *v/i.* (*sep.*, h) draw a deep breath; *fig.* heave a sigh of relief; *fig.* ***wieder*** ~ **(*können*)** recover, revive
'**auf·backen** (*sep.* -k·k-) *v/t.* (*sep.*, h) crisp up
auf·bah·ren ['aʊfba:rən] *v/t.* (*sep.*, -ge-, h) lay out
'**Auf·bau** *m* (-[e]s; -ten) **1.** *no pl.* erection; *fig.* building up; rebuilding; **2.** *no pl.* ⚙ assembly; **3.** *no pl. fig.* structure; composition; **4.** (car) body
'**auf·bau·en** (*sep.*, h) **I.** *v/t.* **1.** put up, build; set (*or* put) up *stall etc.*; put up *tent*; ***wieder*** ~ rebuild; **2.** ⚙ assemble; **3.** arrange; **4.** *fig.* structure; **5.** set up, found *business etc.*; build up *organization etc.*; *fig.* ~ ***auf*** *dat.* build on; **6.** ***j-n*** ~ a) build s.o. up, b) give s.o. a pep talk; **7.** ***sich e-e Existenz*** ~ set o.s. up in life; **II.** *v/refl.*: **8.** ***sich*** ~ build up (*a. fig.*); **9.** ***sich*** ~ ***auf*** *dat.* a) be made up of; b) *theory etc.*: be based on; **10.** ***er baute sich vor mir auf*** he planted himself in front of me
'**Auf·bau·kost** *f* convalescent diet
'**auf·bäu·men** *v/refl.* (*sep.*, h): ***sich*** ~ *horse*: rear (up); ✔ buck; *person*: writhe (***unter*** *dat.* under); *fig.* rebel (***gegen*** against); ***sich vor Schmerzen*** ~ writhe in pain (*or* agony)
'**Auf·bau·prä·pa**ˌ**rat** *n* regenerative preparation
'**auf·bau·schen** *v/t.* (*sep.*, h) **1.** (*a. v/refl.* ***sich*** ~) swell (out); **2.** *fig.* exaggerate, play up
'**Auf·bau|spiel** *n sport*: buildup; **~stu·di·um** *n* postgraduate course (*or* studies *pl.*)
'**Auf·bau·ten** *pl. of* ***Aufbau;*** ⚠, ⚓ superstructure *sg.*; *film*: set *sg.*
'**Auf·bau·trai·ning** *n* stamina training
'**auf·be·geh·ren** *v/i.* (*sep.*, h): ~ ***gegen*** *acc.* rebel against
'**auf·be·hal·ten** *v/t.* (*irr.*, *sep.*, h, → ***behalten***)**:** ***den Hut*** *etc.* ~ keep one's hat *etc.* on; F ***die Augen*** ~ F keep one's eyes peeled
'**auf·bei·ßen** *v/t.* (*irr.*, *sep.*, h, → ***beißen***) bite open; crack *nut* with one's teeth; bite
'**auf·be·kom·men** *v/t.* (*irr.*, *sep.*, h, → ***bekommen***) **1.** get *door, window etc.* open; get *knot* undone; **2.** *ped.* be given, get; ***viel*** ~ get a lot of homework; ***wir haben heute nichts*** ~ we haven't got (*or* didn't get) any homework today; **3.** F finish, eat up
'**auf·be·rei·ten** *v/t.* (*sep.*, h) **1.** process; **2.** *a. computer*: edit *text, data etc.*; '**Auf·be·rei·tung** *f* (-; -en) **1.** processing; **2.** editing
'**Auf·be·rei·tungs·an·la·ge** *f* processing plant
'**auf·bes·sern** *v/t.* (*sep.*, h) improve; increase *salary*; F ***j-n*** ~ give s.o. a rise (*Am.* raise); '**Auf·bes·se·rung** *f* (-; -en) improvement; (salary) increase, *Am.* raise (in salary)
'**auf·be·wah·ren** *v/t.* (*sep.*, h) keep; **(*sich*) *et.*** ~ ***lassen*** deposit s.th. in a safe place; '**Auf·be·wah·rung** *f*: (-; *no pl.*) **(*sichere*** ~**)** safekeeping; ***j-m et. zur*** ~ ***geben*** leave s.th. with s.o. (for safekeeping)
'**Auf·be·wah·rungs·ort** *m*: ***sicherer*** ~ safe place (to keep s.th.)
'**auf·bie·ten** *v/t.* (*irr.*, *sep.*, h, → ***bieten***) mobilize *troops*; *fig.* muster, summon (up) *energy, courage etc.*; ***alles*** ~ do one's utmost; ***alle Kräfte*** ~ muster up all one's strength; ***s-n*** **(*ganzen*)** ***Einfluß*** ~ bring (all) one's influence to bear; '**Auf·bie·tung** *f* (-; *no pl.*) ⚔ mobilization; *fig.* exertion; ***unter*** ~ ***aller Kräfte*** with all one's might
'**auf·bin·den** *v/t.* (*irr.*, *sep.*, h, → ***binden***) **1.** untie, undo; **2.** F *fig.* ***sich*** *e-e Verpflichtung etc.* ~ get landed with (*doing*) *s.th.*; F ***j-m etwas*** (*or* ***e-n Bären***) ~ F take s.o. for a ride
'**auf·blä·hen** (*sep.*, h) **I.** *v/t.* blow out, puff up; *fig.* inflate; → ***aufgebläht*** II; **II.** *v/refl.*: ***sich*** ~ balloon; *sail*: fill, belly out; *fig.* → ***aufblasen*** II
'**auf·blas·bar** *adj.* inflatable; '**auf·bla·sen** (*irr.*, *sep.*, h, → ***blasen***) **I.** *v/t.* blow up, inflate; **II.** *fig. v/refl.*: ***sich*** ~ puff o.s. up; → ***aufgeblasen*** II
'**auf·blät·tern** *v/t.* (*sep.*, h) open (up)
'**auf·blei·ben** *v/i.* (*irr.*, *sep.*, sn, → ***bleiben***) **1.** stay open; **2.** stay up (***lange*** late)
'**auf·blen·den** (*sep.*, h) **I.** *v/t. film*: fade in; turn *floodlights etc.* on full beam; **II.** *v/i. mot.* turn the headlights on full beam; *phot.* open (the lens) up
'**auf·blicken** (*sep.* -k·k-) *v/i.* (*sep.*, h) look up (*fig.* ***zu j-m*** to s.o.)
'**auf·blit·zen** *v/i.* (*sep.*, sn) **1.** flash; **2.** *fig.* **(*in*)** ***j-m*** ~ *thought*: flash through s.o.'s mind

'auf·blü·hen *v/i.* (*sep.*, sn) blossom, open; *fig. girl*: blossom out; *business etc.*: begin to flourish (*or* prosper)

'auf·bocken (*sep.* -k·k-) *v/t.* (*sep.*, h) *mot.* jack up

'auf·boh·ren *v/t.* (*sep.*, h) bore; drill

'auf·bra·ten *v/t.* (*irr.*, *sep.*, h, → **braten**) fry up

'auf·brau·chen *v/t.* (*sep.*, h) use up

'auf·brau·sen *v/i.* (*sep.*, sn) **1.** *drink*: fizz; *sea*: surge; **2.** *fig.* fly off the handle; ***Beifall (Gelächter) brauste auf*** there was a surge of applause (a roar of laughter); **'auf·brau·send** *fig. adj.* quick-tempered

'auf·bre·chen (*irr.*, *sep.*, → **brechen**) **I.** *v/t.* (h) **1.** break open, force *lock*, *door etc.*; open *letter etc.*; **II.** *v/i.* (sn) **2.** *buds etc.*: open; ⚕ *boil etc.*: (burst) open; *sheet of ice*, *ground etc.*: crack; **3.** leave, set off (**nach** *dat.* for)

'auf·brin·gen *v/t.* (*irr.*, *sep.*, h, → **bringen**) **1.** get *door*, *window etc.* open; get *knot* undone; **2.** find; raise *money*; meet *costs*; summon up, muster *energy*, *courage etc.*; **3.** start *fashion*, *rumo(u)r etc.*; **4.** *fig.* make *s.o.* angry, F get *s.o.'s* goat; ***j-n ~ gegen*** *acc.* set s.o. against; → ***aufgebracht*** II

'Auf·bruch *m* (-[e]s; ⸚e) departure (**nach, zu** for); *fig. pol.* awakening; ***im ~ sein*** just be getting ready to go (*or* leave); ***zum ~ drängen*** be keen to get going; **'Auf·bruchs·stim·mung** *f*: ***es herrschte ~*** a) everyone was getting ready to go, b) *pol. etc.* there was the sense of a new era about to dawn

'auf·brü·hen *v/t.* (*sep.*, h) make; *a.* brew *tea*

'auf·brum·men F *v/t.* (*sep.*, h): ***j-m e-e*** *Strafe etc.* ~ F land s.o. with

'auf·bü·geln *v/t.* (*sep.*, h) iron, press

auf·bür·den ['aʊfbʏrdən] *v/t.* (*sep.*, h): ***j-m et. ~*** saddle s.o. with s.th.; ***j-m e-e Last ~*** place a burden on s.o.('s shoulders)

'auf·decken (*sep.* -k·k-) (*sep.*, h) **I.** *v/t.* **1.** uncover; ***das Bett ~*** turn the bedclothes down; **2.** *fig.* expose, reveal; **3.** put on *tablecloth etc.*; **II.** *v/i.* lay the table

'Auf·deckung (*sep.* -k·k-) *f* (-; -en) disclosure, bringing *s.th.* out into the open; **'Auf·deckungs·jour·na,lis·mus** *m* investigative journalism

'auf·don·nern F *v/refl.* (*sep.*, h): ***sich ~*** F get (all) dolled up

'auf·drän·gen (*sep.*, h) **I.** *v/t.*: ***j-m et. ~*** force s.th. on s.o.; ***j-m e-e Meinung ~*** force an opinion down s.o.'s throat; **II.** *v/refl.*: ***sich ~*** *idea etc.*: suggest itself; ***sich j-m ~*** force o.s. on s.o.; ***ich will mich nicht ~*** I don't want to intrude

'auf·dre·hen (*sep.*, h) **I.** *v/t.* **1.** ***die Haare ~*** put curlers in one's hair, put one's hair in curlers; **2.** turn on *tap etc.*; loosen, unscrew; screw on *lid*; **3.** turn up *radio etc.*; **4.** → ***aufgedreht*** II; **II.** F *v/i.* F step on it; *mot.* F step on the gas; *sport*: open up

'auf·dring·lich *adj.* obtrusive, importunate, F pushy; intrusive *question*; loud, showy *colo(u)rs*; obtrusive, strong, overpowering *scent*; ***diese ~en Leute!*** these people just won't go away; **'Auf·dring·lich·keit** *f* (-; *no pl.*) obtrusivenes, importunity, F pushiness; strong (*or* overpowering) smell *of scent*; loudness *of colo(u)rs*

auf·drö·seln ['aʊfdrøzəln] F *v/t.* (*sep.*, h) undo; unravel (*a. fig.*), take apart; *fig.* break down, analy|se (*Am.* -ze) *sentence etc.*

'Auf·druck *m* (-[e]s; -e) *typ.* imprint; company name; **'auf·drucken** (*sep.* -k·k-) *v/t.* (*sep.*, h) print (**auf** *acc.* on)

'auf·drücken (*sep.* -k·k-) *v/t.* (*sep.*, h) **1.** press (*or* push) open; **2.** (*a.* **~ auf** *acc.*) put *a stamp* on

auf·ein'an·der *adv.* a) on top of each other; b) against each other; c) one after the other, one by one; ***~ losgehen*** go for each other; ***~ abgestimmt*** coordinated, matching *colo(u)rs*; **~bei·ßen** *v/t.* (*irr.*, *sep.*, h, → ***beißen***): ***die Zähne ~*** press one's teeth together, grit one's teeth

Auf·ein'an·der·fol·ge *f* (-; *no pl.*) succession; series, round *of events*; ***in rascher ~*** in rapid (*or* quick) succession; **auf·ein'an·der·fol·gen** *v/i.* (*sep.*, sn) follow each other; ***im Abstand von fünf Minuten ~*** occur (*bus etc.*: run) every five minutes; **auf·ein'an·der·fol·gend** *adj.* successive, consecutive; ***während drei ~er Tage*** *a.* for three days running

auf·ein'an·der|häu·fen *v/t.* (*sep.*, h) pile up; **~het·zen** *v/t.* (*sep.*, h) set *dogs etc.* at each other; **~lie·gen** *v/i.* (*irr.*, *sep.*, h, → ***liegen***) lie on top of each other; lie in a pile; **~pral·len** *v/i* (*sep.*, sn), **~sto·ßen** *v/i.* (*irr.*, *sep.*, sn, → ***stoßen***) collide, crash; *fig.* clash

Auf·ent·halt ['aʊfˀɛnthalt] *m* (-[e]s; -e) **1.** stay; **2.** place of residence; **3.** 🚆 stop; ✈ stopover; ***ohne ~*** nonstop *train etc.*; ***wie lange haben wir hier ~?*** how long do we stop here?; ***wir hatten zwei Stunden ~*** we had a two-hour wait

'Auf·ent·halts|be·rech·ti·gung *f* unlimited right to residence; **~dau·er** *f* (duration of) stay; **~ge·neh·mi·gung** *f* residence permit; **~ort** *m* place of residence; ***momentaner ~ unbekannt*** (present) whereabouts unknown; **~raum** *m* lounge; *ped. etc.*: common room

'auf·er·le·gen *v/t.* (*sep.*, h) impose (***j-m*** on s.o.); ***j-m Schweigen ~*** constrain s.o. to silence; ***j-m Verantwortung ~*** place responsibility on s.o.('s shoulders); ***sich Entbehrungen ~*** make sacrifices; ***sich Zwang ~*** exercise (some) self-restraint

'auf·er·ste·hen *v/i.* (*irr.*, *sep.*, sn, → ***erstehen***) rise from the dead; *fig.* rise from the ashes; **'Auf·er·ste·hung** *f* (-; -en) resurrection

'auf·es·sen *v/t.* (*irr.*, *sep.*, h, → ***essen***) eat up, finish

'auf·fä·chern (*sep.*, h) **I.** *v/t.* fan out; *fig.* break down (**in** *acc.* into); **II.** *v/refl.*: ***sich ~*** fan out

'auf·fä·deln *v/t.* (*sep.*, h) thread (**auf** *acc.* onto)

'auf·fah·ren (*irr.*, *sep.*, → ***fahren***) **I.** *v/i.* (sn) **1.** drive up, pull up; **2.** **~ auf** *acc.* crash into, *a.* ⚓ ram; **3.** *mot.* (**zu**) **dicht ~** tailgate; **4.** (give a) start, jump; flare up; **5.** *window etc.*: fly (*or* burst) open; **II.** *v/t.* (h) **6.** ⚔ bring up, deploy; → ***Geschütz;*** **7.** *gastr.* bring on, serve (up); **8.** churn up

'Auf·fahrt *f* (-; -en) **1.** drive(way *Am.*); **2.** slip road, *Am.* (entrance) ramp; **3.** arrival

'Auf·fahr·un·fall *m* rear-end collision

'auf·fal·len *v/i.* (*irr.*, *sep.*, sn, → ***fallen***) **1.** be conspicuous, attract attention; ***j-m ~*** strike s.o., *n.s.* catch s.o.'s eye; ***er fiel unangenehm auf*** he made a bad impression; ***es fällt nicht auf*** nobody will notice; ***mir ist es gar nicht aufgefallen*** I never noticed; ***nicht ~ wollen*** keep one's head down, keep a low profile; **2.** **~ auf** *acc.* fall on(to), hit; **'auf·fal·lend I.** *adj.* noticeable; striking *beauty*, *appearance etc.*; ***~es Benehmen*** odd behavio(u)r; **II.** *adv.*: ***sich ~ ähnlich sein*** have a striking resemblance, be remarkably alike; **'auf·fäl·lig** *adj.* conspicuous; loud, F flashy *clothes*, *colo(u)rs etc.*

'auf·fal·ten (*sep.*, h) **I.** *v/t.* open up, unfold; **II.** *v/refl.*: ***sich ~*** open up; *geol.* fold upwards

'Auf·fang·becken (*sep.* -k·k-) *fig. n* rallying point

'auf·fan·gen *v/t.* (*irr.*, *sep.*, h, → ***fangen***) catch; collect *liquid*; pick up *radio signals etc.*; cushion *shock*, *fall etc.*; parry *blow etc.*; ✈ pull out (of a dive); cushion (the impact of)

'Auf·fang·la·ger *n* transit (*or* reception) camp

'auf·fas·sen (*sep.*, h) **I.** *v/t.* **1.** understand, grasp; **2.** interpret, understand; take (**als** as); ***falsch ~*** misunderstand, misinterpret; **II.** *v/i.*: ***leicht (schwer) ~*** be quick (slow) on the uptake

'Auf·fas·sung *f* (-; -en) **1.** interpretation; **2.** opinion, view; ***nach m-r ~*** as I see it; ***die ~ vertreten, daß*** take the view that; **3.** → ***Auffassungsgabe***

'Auf·fas·sungs|ga·be *f* perceptive faculty, intellectual grasp; **~sa·che** *f*: ***das ist ~*** that's a matter of opinion

auf·find·bar ['aʊffɪntbaːɐ] *adj.*: ***nicht ~*** not to be found; **'auf·fin·den** *v/t.* (*irr.*, *sep.*, h, → ***finden***) find, *a.* trace *s.o.*; ***tot aufgefunden werden*** be found dead

'auf·fi·schen *v/t.* (*sep.*, h) fish out of the water; *fig.* pick up

'auf·flackern (*sep.* -k·k-) *v/i.* (*sep.*, sn) flicker; *fig.* flare up

'auf·flam·men *v/i.* (*sep.*, sn) flare up (*a. fig.*); burst into flames; *match*: light up

'auf·flie·gen *v/i.* (*irr.*, *sep.*, sn, → ***fliegen***) **1.** fly up; *bird*: *a.* soar up; *door etc.*: fly open; **2.** *fig.* blow up (*a.* **~ *lassen***); be exposed; *gang of criminals*: be smashed

'auf·for·dern *v/t.* (*sep.*, h) call on *s.o.* (**zu** *inf.* to *inf.*); ask, request; order; urge, exhort; encourage; invite, ask (*all* to *inf.*); ***zum Kampf ~*** challenge to a fight; ***j-n (zum Tanz) ~*** ask s.o. for a (*or* the next) dance; **'Auf·for·de·rung** *f* (-; -en) call; request; order; exhortation; invitation; challenge

'auf·for·sten *v/t.* (*sep.*, h) reafforest, *Am.* reforest; **'Auf·for·stung** *f* (-; -en) reafforestation, *Am.* reforestation

'auf·fres·sen *v/t.* (*irr.*, *sep.*, h, → ***fressen***) eat up; devour; F ***er wird dich schon nicht ~*** he won't eat you; *fig.* ***mit den Augen ~*** devour *s.o.*, *s.th.* with one's eyes; ***die Arbeit frißt mich auf*** I'm drowning in work; ***der Chef wird uns ~*** F the boss will kill us

'auf·fri·schen *v/t.* (*sep.*, h) freshen up (*a.* ***sich ~*** *and v/i. wind*); touch up *colo(u)rs etc.*; replenish *stock*; refresh *one's memory*; brush up *one's English etc.*; revive *acquaintance etc.*

'Auf·fri·schungs|imp·fung *f* booster (vaccine); **~kurs** *m* refresher course

auf·führ·bar ['aʊffyːɐbaːɐ] *adj.* stageable; ***das Stück ist nicht ~*** *a.* the play can't be performed (*or* put on the stage); **'auf·füh·ren** (*sep.*, h) **I.** *v/t.* **1.** *thea. etc.* perform; **2.** list; ***einzeln ~*** specify, *Am.* itemize; **3.** ⚖ produce *witness*; **II.** *v/refl.*:

sich (**schlecht**) ~ behave (badly); '**Auf·füh·rung** *f* (-; -en) *thea.* performance; *film*: showing; '**Auf·füh·rungs·recht** *n thea.* performing rights *pl.*

'**auf·fül·len** *v/t.* (*sep.*, h) fill up; top up; replenish; restock

'**auf·fut·tern** F *v/t.* (*sep.*, h) F devour

'**Auf·ga·be** *f* (-; -n) **1.** job, assignment; duty; *ped.* exercise; *a. pl.* homework; **e-e ~ lösen** solve a problem; **er machte es sich zur ~ zu** *inf.* he made it his business to *inf.*; **es ist nicht m-e ~** it's not my job (*or* responsibility); **2.** posting, *Am.* mailing; registration, *Am.* checking *of baggage*; sending *of telegram(me)*; placing *of order, advert etc.*; **3.** giving up *one's flat, business etc.*; *sport*: dropping out *of a race etc.*; **er wurde zur ~ gezwungen** he was forced to drop out; **4.** *volleyball*: service

'**auf·ga·beln** F *v/t.* (*sep.*, h) F pick up

'**Auf·ga·ben|be·reich** *m* (area of) responsibility; **das gehört nicht zu m-m ~** that's not my job (*or* responsibility); **~heft** *n* homework book; **~stel·lung** *f* terms *pl.* of reference; **~ver·tei·lung** *f* allocation of duties (*or* tasks); dividing up of responsibilities; sharing of tasks

'**Auf·ga·be|ort** *m* place of posting (*esp. Am.* mailing); **~schein** *m* (luggage) receipt, *Am.* baggage check; **~stem·pel** *m* postmark

'**Auf·ga,lopp** *m* (-s; -s) trial gallop; *fig.* curtain raiser

'**Auf·gang** *m* (-[e]s; ⸚e) **1.** ascent; *ast. a.* rising; **2.** staircase, stairs *pl.*

'**auf·ge·ben** (*irr.*, *sep.*, h, → **geben**) **I.** *v/t.* **1.** deliver; post, *Am.* mail; register, *Am.* check *baggage etc.*; send *telegram(me)*; place *order etc.*; place *an ad* (in the newspaper); **2.** ask *a riddle*; set *a task etc.*; **sie gibt immer sehr viel auf** she always sets a lot of homework; **3.** give up; *a.* abandon *hope etc.*; ⚕ give up (hope for) *s.o.*; ⚖ relinquish *claim etc.*; leave *one's job*; **es ~ zu** *inf.* give up *ger.*; **das Trinken** *etc.* **~** give up (*or* stop) drinking *etc.*; **es** (*or* **den Kampf, das Spiel**) **~** → 4; **II.** *v/i.* **4.** give up; *boxing and fig.*: throw in the towel; *runner*: drop out; **5.** *volleyball*: serve

'**auf·ge·bläht I.** *p.p.of* **aufblähen**; **II.** *adj.* ⚕ distended; *fig.* inflated; † bloated *currency*

'**auf·ge·bla·sen I.** *p.p. of* **aufblasen**; **II.** *fig. adj.* conceited, self-important, puffed up; **so ein ~er Kerl!** F what a pompous ass; '**Auf·ge·bla·sen·heit** *f* (-; *no pl.*) conceitedness

'**Auf·ge·bot** *n* (-[e]s; -e) **1.** official wedding notice, *in GB*: (publishing the) banns *pl.*; **2.** array; crowd; **3.** *sport*: pool (of players); **polizeiliches** *etc.* **~** police *etc.* contingent; **mit starkem ~ erscheinen** turn out in full force; **4. das beste** (**stärkste**) **~** *sport*: the best (strongest) side; **letztes ~** last-ditch stand

'**auf·ge·bracht I.** *p.p. of* **aufbringen**; **II.** *adj.* angry, F mad (**gegen** with; **über** *acc.* at, about)

'**auf·ge·don·nert I.** *p.p. of* **aufdonnern**; **II.** F *adj.* all dressed up, F dolled up, dressed to the nines

'**auf·ge·dreht** F **I.** *p.p. of* **aufdrehen**; **II.** *adj.* in high spirits; (too) wound up; **III.** *adv. talk etc.*: excitedly

'**auf·ge·dun·sen** *adj.* bloated; puffy, puffed-up ..., *pred.* puffed up

'**auf·ge·hen** *v/i.* (*irr.*, *sep.*, sn, → **gehen**) **1.** *sun etc.*, *a. dough*: rise; *curtain*: *a.* go up; *seed etc.*: come up; **2.** *bud etc.*: open; *knot etc.*: come undone; *seam*: come open; ⚕ *boil etc.*: burst; **3.** 𝔄 divide exactly; *fig.* **diesmal ging s-e Rechnung nicht auf** he got his calculations wrong this time; **die Geschichte geht auf** there are no loose ends in the story; **4. ~ in** *dat.* be totally wrapped up in *one's work etc.*; **5. in e-m anderen Volk ~** be assimilated by another people; **6. j-m ~** become clear to s.o.; **plötzlich ging es mir auf** *a.* suddenly everything fell into place; → **Licht**

'**auf·ge·ho·ben I.** *p.p. of* **aufheben**; **II.** *adj.*: **gut ~ sein** be in good hands

auf·gei·len ['aʊfgaɪlən] (*sep.*, h) V **I.** *v/t.* F turn *s.o.* on (*a. fig.*), get *s.o.* worked up; **II.** *v/refl.*: **sich ~ an** *dat.* F be turned on by, get o.s. worked up with; *fig.* F go potty over *s.th.*, F get a kick out of *s.th.*

'**auf·ge·klärt I.** *p.p. of* **aufklären**; **II.** *adj.* **1.** enlightened, well-informed; **2. ist sie schon ~?** does she know the facts of life?, has she had any sex education?; '**Auf·ge·klärt·heit** *f* (-; *no pl.*) enlightened attitude

'**auf·ge·knöpft I.** *p.p. of* **aufknöpfen**; **II.** F *adj.* F chatty

'**auf·ge·kratzt I.** *p.p.of* **aufkratzen**; **II.** F *adj.* F chirpy, *Am.* F chipper

'**Auf·geld** *n* (-[e]s; -er) † premium, agio; surcharge

'**auf·ge·legt I.** *p.p. of* **auflegen**; **II.** *pred. adj.*: **zu et. ~ sein** feel like (doing) s.th.; **ich bin heute nicht dazu ~** I'm not in the mood for it today; **gut** (**schlecht**) **~** in a good (bad) mood

'**auf·ge·lockert** (*sep.* -k·k-) **I.** *p.p. of* **auflockern**; **II.** *adj.* **1.** *fig.* relaxed *mood, atmosphere etc.*; **2.** *meteor.* **~e Bewölkung** broken overcast; **3.** ⚠ dispersed *development*

'**auf·ge·löst I.** *p.p. of* **auflösen**; **II.** *adj.* **1.** loose *hair*; *fig.* untidy, F all over the place; **2.** *fig.* beside o.s.; **in Verzweiflung ~** absolutely desperate; **in Kummer ~** sick with worry; **er war in Tränen ~** he was crying his eyes (*or* heart) out, he was all tears

'**auf·ge·rauht I.** *p.p. of* **aufrauhen**; **II.** *adj.* roughened

'**auf·ge·räumt I.** *p.p. of* **aufräumen**; **II.** *fig. adj.* jovial

'**auf·ge·regt I.** *p.p. of* **aufregen**; **II.** *adj.* excited; nervous; upset

'**auf·ge·schlos·sen I.** *p.p. of* **aufschließen**; **II.** *fig. adj.* open (*dat. or* **für** to); open-minded, broad-minded; '**Auf·ge·schlos·sen·heit** *f* (-; *no pl.*) open-mindedness

'**auf·ge·schmis·sen** F *pred. adj.*: **~ sein** be stuck, F be in a fix

'**auf·ge·schos·sen I.** *p.p. of* **aufschießen**; **II.** *adj.* lanky

'**auf·ge·schwemmt I.** *p.p. of* **aufschwemmen**; **II.** *adj.* bloated, swollen; puffed-up ..., *pred.* puffed up

'**auf·ge·setzt I.** *p.p. of* **aufsetzen**; **II.** *adj.* **1. ~e Tasche** patch pocket; **2.** *fig.* put-on..., *pred.* put on; artificial

'**auf·ge·sprun·gen I.** *p.p. of* **aufspringen**; **II.** *adj.* chapped *lips etc.*

'**auf·ge·staut I.** *p.p. of* **aufstauen**; **II.** *adj.* pent-up *anger, rage etc.*

'**auf·ge·stülpt I.** *p.p. of* **aufstülpen**; **II.** *adj.*: **~e Nase** snub nose

'**auf·ge·ta·kelt I.** *p.p. of* **auftakeln**; **II.** F *adj.* F dolled up, dressed to kill

'**auf·ge·trie·ben I.** *p.p. of* **auftreiben**; **II.** *adj.* bloated

'**auf·ge·weckt I.** *p.p. of* **aufwecken**; **II.** *adj. fig.* very bright

'**auf·ge·wor·fen I.** *p.p. of* **aufwerfen**; **II.** *adj.* pouting *lips*

'**auf·ge·wühlt I.** *p.p. of* **aufwühlen**; **II.** *adj.* **1. ~e See** stormy sea(s); **2.** *fig.* **ganz ~ sein** be all churned up inside

'**auf·ge·zehrt I.** *p.p. of* **aufzehren**; **II.** *adj. fig.* completely spent, burnt out

'**auf·gie·ßen** *v/t.* (*irr.*, *sep.*, h, → **gießen**) pour (**auf** *acc.* on); *gastr.* add water *etc.* to; pour water on, *w.s.* make *tea*

'**auf·glie·dern** *v/t.* (*sep.*, h) split up; classify; *ling.* analy|se (*Am.* -ze) *sentence*; 𝔄 break down *figures*; '**Auf·glie·de·rung** *f* (-; -en) classification; analysis; breakdown

'**auf·glü·hen** *v/i.* (*sep.*, h) (begin to) glow

'**auf·gra·ben** *v/t.* (*irr.*, *sep.*, h, → **graben**) excavate; dig up

'**auf·grei·fen** *v/t.* (*irr.*, *sep.*, h, → **greifen**) **1.** pick *s.o.* up; **2.** *fig.* take up *subject*; *a.* come back to *s.th.*

auf'grund *prp.* (*gen.*) on account of

'**Auf·guß** *m* (-sses; ⸚sse) infusion; **zweiter ~** second brew; *fig.* **schlechter ~** poor imitation; **~beu·tel** *m* teabag

'**auf·ha·ben** (*irr.*, *sep.*, h, → **haben**) **I.** *v/t.* **1.** have on, be wearing; **2.** have open; **immer ~** keep open (all the time); **3.** have to do; **viel** (**wenig**) **~** have a lot of (very little) homework; **was haben wir** (**für morgen**) **auf?** what's for homework (what's our homework for tomorrow)?; **4.** F have finished; **II.** F *v/i.*: **das Geschäft** *etc.* **hat auf** the shop *etc.* is open

'**auf·hacken** (*sep.* -k·k-) *v/t.* (*sep.*, h) break up; break open

'**auf·ha·ken** *v/t.* (*sep.*, h) undo

auf·hal·sen ['aʊfhalzən] F *v/t.* (*sep.*, h): **j-m et. ~** saddle (F lump) s.o. with s.th.; **sich et. ~** get (o.s.)saddled with s.th., F get lumped with s.th.

'**auf·hal·ten** (*irr.*, *sep.*, h, → **halten**) **I.** *v/t.* **1.** hold open; **j-m die Tür ~** hold the door open for s.o.; **2.** stop; *fig.* check; ward off; delay; hold *s.o., s.th.* up; **ich werde Sie nicht lange ~** this will only take a minute; **ich will Sie nicht länger ~** don't let me keep you; **II.** *v/refl.* **3. sich ~** stay; **sich viel im Freien** (**in Bibliotheken** *etc.*) **~** spend a lot of time outside (in libraries *etc.*); **4.** *fig.* **sich ~ bei** (*or* **mit**) spend (*or* waste) one's time on

'**auf·hän·gen** (*sep.*, h) **I.** *v/t.* **1.** hang (up) (**an** *dat.* on); ⚙ suspend (from); **2. j-n ~** hang s.o.; **3.** *fig.* **j-m et. ~** fob s.th. off on s.o., saddle s.o. with s.th.; **j-m e-e Lüge** (**ein Märchen**) **~** tell s.o. lies (stories); **wer hat dir das aufgehängt?** who told you that (nonsense)?; **4. den Hörer ~** put the phone down, hang up; **5.** *fig.* **et. ~ an** *dat.* use *s.th.* as a peg to hang s.th. on; **II.** *v/i.* **6.** put the phone down, hang up; **III.** *v/refl.* **7. sich ~** hang o.s.; **8.** F **häng dich auf** hang your coat (*or* jacket) up; '**Auf·hän·ger** *m* (-s; -) **1.** tab; **2.** *fig.* peg (**für e-e Geschichte** *etc.* to hang a story *etc.* on), F gimmick; '**Auf·hän·gung** *f* (-; -en) *mot.* suspension

'**auf·hau·en** (*irr.*, *sep.*, → **hauen**) **I.** F *v/i.* (sn): **~ auf** *dat. or acc.* hit *the floor etc.*; **II.** *v/t.* (h) a) break up *ice etc.*; b) F cut *one's knee etc.*

'**auf·häu·fen** *v/t. and v/refl.* (**sich ~**) (*sep.*, h) pile up; accumulate; amass

'auf·he·ben (*irr., sep.*, h, → ***heben***) **I.** *v/t.* **1.** pick up; **2.** lift (up); raise *one's hand etc.*; help *s.o.* up; **3.** keep, F hold onto; → ***aufgehoben*** II; **4.** close *meeting etc.*; call off *strike etc.*; raise *siege*; lift *ban etc.*; abolish; annul *marriage*; ⚖ repeal, abrogate *law*; rescind, reverse *sentence etc.*; → ***Tafel***; **5.** compensate, offset; cancel, neutralize; ***sich gegenseitig*** ~ cancel each other out; **II.** ♀ *n*: ***viel ~s machen von*** make a big thing out of; ***ohne großes*** ~ quietly, without any fuss; **'Auf·he·bung** *f* (-; -en) calling off *of strike etc.*; lifting *of ban etc.*; ⚖ annulment, repeal *of law etc.*; reversal *of sentence*

auf·hei·tern ['aʊfhaɪtɐn] (*sep.*, h) **I.** *v/t.* cheer *s.o.* up; **II.** *v/refl.*: ***sich*** ~ *meteor.* clear up, *sky*: clear, *a. face*: brighten; **'Auf·hei·te·rung** *f* (-; -en) **1.** *no pl.* cheering up; **2.** *meteor.* ***~en*** sunny spells

'auf·hei·zen (*sep.*, h) **I.** *v/t.* **1.** heat (up); **2.** *fig.* stir up, *a.* ✝ stoke up *inflation*; **II.** *v/refl.*: ***sich*** ~ heat up

auf·hel·len ['aʊfhɛlən] (*sep.*, h) **I.** *v/t.* **1.** lighten, make *s.th.* lighter; *phot.* light(en) up *shadows*; **2.** *fig.* shed light on, clear up; **II.** *v/refl.*: ***sich*** ~ **3.** brighten; *sky*: brighten up, clear; **4.** *fig.* be cleared up; **III.** *v/i. phot.* light(en) up the shadows; **'Auf·hel·ler** *m* (-s; -) **1.** *phot.* fill-in lamp; **2.** *textil.* whitener; *paper*: brightening agent

'auf·het·zen *v/t.* (*sep.*, h) stir *s.o.* up (***gegen*** against); ***zu et.*** ~ incite (*or* get) *s.o.* to do s.th.; **'Auf·het·zer** *m* (-s; -) agitator; **'Auf·het·zung** *f* (-; -en) agitation

'auf·heu·len *v/i.* (*sep.*, h) (give a) howl; *mot.* roar; *siren*: begin to wail; ***den Motor ~ lassen*** rev up the engine

'auf·ho·len (*sep.*, h) **I.** *v/t.* make up (for) *lost time etc.*; catch up with (*or* on); **II.** *v/i.* catch up; 🚂 make up the delay; ✝ *prices etc.*: pick up; *exchange rates*: rally

'auf·hor·chen *v/i.* (*sep.*, h) prick (up) one's ears; *esp. fig.* sit up and take notice

'auf·hö·ren *v/i.* (*sep.*, h) stop; (come to an) end; ~ ***zu*** *inf.* stop *ger.*, *Am. a.* quit *ger.*; ***ohne aufzuhören*** continuously, nonstop; F ***da hört (sich) doch alles auf!*** that really is the limit (F takes the biscuit); ***hör auf damit!*** stop it!, *sl.* cut it out!

'auf·jauch·zen *v/i.* (*sep.*, h) shout for joy

'auf·ju·beln *v/i.* (*sep.*, h) give a shout of triumph

'auf·kan·ten (*sep.*, h) **I.** *v/t.* tilt; upend; carve *skis*; **II.** *v/i. skiing*: carve

'Auf·kauf *m* (-[e]s; ⸚e) ✝ buy-up, takeover, buyout; **'auf·kau·fen** *v/t.* (*sep.*, h) buy up (*or* out), take over; **'Auf·käu·fer** *m* (-s; -) buyer, purchaser

'auf·kei·men *v/i.* (*sep.*, sn) germinate; sprout; *fig.* begin to grow (*or* blossom), burgeon; **'auf·kei·mend** *fig. adj.* growing; burgeoning

'auf·klapp·bar *adj.* hinged; folding *seat etc.*; ***~es Verdeck*** folding roof; **'auf·klap·pen** *v/t.* (*sep.*, h) open *folding chair etc.*, pull down *seat*; turn up *collar etc.*

auf·kla·ren ['aʊfkla:rən] *v/i.* (*sep.*, h) clear (up), brighten up

'auf·klä·ren (*sep.*, h) **I.** *v/t.* **1.** clear up *misunderstanding, crime etc.*; **2.** inform *s.o.* (***über*** *acc.* of), enlighten *s.o.* (about); explain the facts of life to *s.o.*, *ped. a.* give *s.o.* sex education; **3.** ⚔ (*a. v/i.*) reconnoit|re (*Am.* -er), scout; **II.** *v/refl.*: ***sich*** ~ **4.** *meteor.* clear (up), brighten up; **5.** *fig.* be cleared up, be solved; **Auf·klä·rer** ['aʊfklɛ:rɐ] *m* (-s; -) ⚔ → ***Aufklärungsflugzeug***; **'Auf·klä·rung** *f* (-; -en) **1.** *meteor.* clearing (up); **2.** *no pl. fig.* a) clearing up, solving; b) enlightenment; c) clarification; ***sexuelle*** ~ sex education; ~ ***verlangen*** demand an explanation (***über*** *acc.* of); ***zur ~ e-r Sache (des Rätsels*** *etc.*) ***beitragen*** throw light on s.th. (on the matter); ***an der ~ e-s Verbrechens*** *etc.* ***arbeiten*** be trying to solve (*or* clear up) a crime *etc.*; **3.** ⚔ reconnaissance; **4.** *no pl. hist. the* Enlightenment

'Auf·klä·rungs|buch *n* sex education book; **~film** *m* sex education film; **~flugzeug** *n* reconnaissance plane, air scout; **~kam,pa·gne** *f* education campaign; **~quo·te** *f* clear-up rate; **~sa·tel,lit** *m* observation satellite; **~schrift** *f* informative pamphlet; **~,un·ter·richt** *m* sex education (classes *pl.*); **~zeit·al·ter** *n* Age of Enlightenment

'Auf·kle·be·a,dres·se *f* (gummed) address label; **'auf·kle·ben** *v/t.* (*sep.*, h) stick on; glue on; *a.* put on *stamp*; **'Auf·kle·ber** *m* (-s; -) sticker; *formal*: adhesive label; *mot.* bumper sticker

'auf·knacken (*sep.* -k·k-) *v/t.* (*sep.*, h) **1.** crack *nut*; **2.** F crack *safe*, break into *a car*

'auf·knal·len F (*sep.*) **I.** *v/t.* (h) **1.** slam *s.th.* down (***auf*** *acc.* on); **2.** fling open; **3.** ***j-m Hausaufgaben*** ~ pile homework on s.o.; **II.** *v/i.* (sn): ***mit dem Kopf*** ~ land on one's head, ***auf*** *dat. or acc.*: bang one's head on (*or* against)

'auf·knöp·fen *v/t.* (*sep.*, h) unbutton

'auf·kno·ten *v/t.* (*sep.*, h) undo, untie

'auf·knüp·fen *v/t.* (*sep.*, h) **1.** untie, undo; **2.** hang *s.o.*, F string *s.o.* up

'auf·ko·chen *v/i. and v/t.* (*sep.*, h) boil (up); ***et.*** ~ (***lassen***) bring s.th. to the boil

'auf·kom·men (*irr.*, *sep.*, sn, → ***kommen***) **I.** *v/i.* **1.** arise (*a. idea, suspicion etc.*); come into fashion; *rumo(u)r*: start; *thunderstorm*: come up; *wind*: spring up; ***Zweifel (Mißtrauen) ~ lassen*** give rise to doubt (suspicion); ***um keine Zweifel ~ zu lassen*** to make things absolutely clear; ***Mißtrauen kam (Zweifel kamen) in ihm auf*** he began to suspect (to be niggled by doubts); **2.** ~ ***gegen*** assert o.s. against; ***er läßt niemanden neben sich*** ~ he won't stand for any competition; **3.** ~ ***für*** *acc.* answer (*or* be responsible) for, pay for, pay *the costs*, compensate for *damage etc.*; **4.** *fig.* get out, leak (out); **5.** get up (off the ground *or* floor); **6.** land, *ball etc.*: *a.* hit the ground; **7.** *runner etc.*: catch up; **8.** ⚓ appear on the horizon; **II.** ♀ *n* (-s) **1.** revenue; **2.** *in cpds. usu.* amount *of*; → ***Verkehrsaufkommen***

'auf·krat·zen (*sep.*, h) **I.** *v/t.* **1.** scratch (open); **2.** *fig.* ***j-n*** ~ cheer s.o. up; → ***aufgekratzt*** II; **II.** *v/refl.*: ***sich*** ~ scratch o.s. sore

'auf·krem·peln *v/t.* (*sep.*, h) turn up *trousers*; roll up *sleeves*

'auf·kreu·zen F *fig. v/i.* (*sep.*, sn) turn up, show up

'auf·krie·gen F *v/t.* → ***aufbekommen***

'auf·kün·di·gen *v/t.* (*sep.*, h) → ***kündigen***; ***j-m den Gehorsam*** ~ refuse to obey s.o. any longer; ***j-m die Freundschaft*** ~ break (up) with s.o.

'auf·la·chen *v/i.* (*sep.*, h) laugh out loud; ***spöttisch*** *etc.* ~ give a sneering *etc.* laugh

auf·lad·bar ['aʊfla:tba:ɐ] *adj.* ⚡ rechargeable; **'auf·la·den** (*irr.*, *sep.*, h, → ***laden***) **I.** *v/t.* load (***auf*** *acc.* onto); *mot. and* ⚡ charge; *computer*: boot up; *fig.* ***j-m et.*** ~ load s.o. with s.th.; ***sich et.*** ~ get o.s. loaded with s.th.; **II.** *v/refl.*: ***sich*** ~ ⚡ be (re)charged; **'Auf·la·der** *m* (-s; -) loader, packer; **'Auf·la·dung** *f* (-; -en) ⚡ **1.** charging; **2.** charge

'Auf·la·ge *f* (-; -n) **1.** edition *of book*; print run, circulation *of paper etc.*; **2.** condition; ***et. zur ~ machen*** make s.th. a condition (***j-m*** for s.o.); **3.** overlay; **'Auf·la·gen·hö·he** *f* print run; circulation; **'auf·la·gen·stark** *adj.* high-circulation *paper*

'auf·las·sen *v/t.* (*irr.*, *sep.*, h, → ***lassen***) **1.** leave (*or* keep) open; **2.** let *s.o.* stay up; **3.** ⚖ convey; **'Auf·las·sung** *f* (-; -en) ⚖ conveyance

'auf·lau·ern *v/i.* (*sep.*, h): ***j-m*** ~ lie in wait for s.o., waylay s.o. (*both a. fig.*)

'Auf·lauf *m* (-[e]s; Aufläufe) **1.** crowd; tumult; ⚖ unlawful assembly; **2.** *potato etc.* bake; **'auf·lau·fen** (*irr.*, *sep.*, sn, → ***laufen***) **I.** *v/i.* **1.** *capital*: accumulate; *interest*: accrue; **2.** *river etc.*: rise; **3.** ⚓ run aground; **4.** *esp. sport*: run into s.o.; ***j-n ~ lassen*** *sport*: obstruct s.o.; F *fig.* put s.o. in his (*or* her) place; **II.** *v/t.*: ***sich die Füße*** ~ walk (*or* run) one's feet sore; **'Auf·lauf·form** *f* oven dish

'auf·le·ben *v/i.* (*sep.*, sn) come to life again (*a.* ***wieder*** ~); *discussion etc.*: come to life, *a. traffic etc.*: liven up; *hatred etc.*: be stirred up; *traditions*: be revived; ***wieder ~ lassen*** revive

'auf·lecken (*sep.* -k·k-) *v/t.* (*sep.*, h) lick (*cat*: lap) up

'Auf·le·ge·ma,trat·ze *f* overlay (mattress)

'auf·le·gen (*sep.*, h) **I.** *v/t.* **1.** put on *coal, tablecloth, record etc.*; rest *gun* (***auf*** *dat.* on); *teleph.* ***den Hörer*** ~ put the phone down, hang up; **2.** publish, print; ***wieder*** ~ reprint; **3.** ***j-m et.*** ~ burden s.o. with s.th.; **II.** *v/i. teleph.* put the phone down, hang up

'auf·leh·nen (*sep.*, h) **I.** *v/t.*: (*a.* ***sich***) ~ ***auf*** *acc.* lean (*or* rest) on *or* against; **II.** *fig. v/refl.*: ***sich ~ gegen*** oppose, rebel against; **'Auf·leh·nung** *f* (-; -en) opposition, resistance; revolt

'auf·le·sen *v/t.* (*irr.*, *sep.*, h, → ***lesen***) pick up (*a. fig.*)

'auf·leuch·ten *v/i.* (*sep.*, h) light up (*a. eyes*); *face*: *a.* brighten up; *lightning etc.*: flash

'auf·lich·ten *lit.* (*sep.*, h) **I.** *v/t.* **1.** thin out *forest*; **2.** make *a room* lighter; **3.** *fig.* shed light on, clear up *mystery etc.*; **II.** *v/refl.*: ***sich*** ~ **4.** *sky*: brighten up, clear; **5.** *fig.* become clear

'auf·lie·gen (*irr.*, *sep*, h, → ***liegen***) **I.** *v/i.* **1.** lie (***auf*** *dat.* on), rest (on); *record*: be on the turntable; *tablecloth*: be on the table; *receiver*: be on the hook; ***der Deckel liegt nicht richtig auf*** the lid isn't on properly; **2.** *magazines etc.*: be available (for reference *or* to the public); *list of candidates*: be available for inspection, F be out; **3.** ⚓ be laid up; **II.** *v/refl.*: ***sich*** ~ get bedsores

'auf·li·sten *v/t.* (*sep.*, h) make a list of, list; **'Auf·li·stung** *f* (-; -en) **1.** listing; **2.** list

'auf·lockern (*sep.* -k·k-) (*sep.*, h) **I.** *v/t.* **1.**

↗ dig up, loosen *the soil*; plump up *cushion*; **2.** *fig.* relax *atmosphere etc.*; liven up *party, lecture etc.*; relieve, break up *the monotony*; **II.** *v/refl.*: **sich ~ 3.** *clouds*: break up, disperse; → **Bewölkung; 4.** *fig. atmosphere*: relax, become relaxed, ease up; *lecture etc.*: liven up; **5.** *sport*: loosen up; → **aufgelockert** II; **'Auf·locke·rung** (*sep.* -k·k-) *f* (-; -en) **1.** digging up, loosening (*gen.* of *the soil*); **2.** *meteor.* breaking up *of clouds*; **3.** *fig.* livening up; **zur ~ der Stimmung** (*or* **Atmosphäre**) **beitragen** liven things up (a bit)

'auf·lo·dern *v/i.* (*sep.*, sn) flare up (*a. fig.*)

'auf·lös·bar *adj.* 𝔄 solvable; ⚗ *and fig.* soluble; ⚖ dissolvable; **'auf·lö·sen** (*sep.*, h) **I.** *v/t.* **1.** ⚗ *etc.* dissolve; **2.** cancel *contract etc.*; break off *engagement*; annul *marriage*; break off (*or* up) *meeting etc.*; break up, disperse *crowd*; close down *shop, store etc.*; wind up *business etc.*; close *account*; dissolve *parliament*; **3.** let down *one's hair*; → **aufgelöst** 1; **4.** solve *riddle, equation etc.*; 𝔄 remove, take away *brackets*; *fig.* clear up *contradiction etc.*; **5.** ♪ resolve; cancel *accidental*; **II.** *v/refl.*: **sich ~ 6.** ⚗ *etc.* dissolve; **7.** *fog, clouds*: disperse, disappear; *crowd*: break up, disperse; *meeting*: break up; **der Stau hat sich aufgelöst** traffic is back to normal; **8. sich ~ in** *acc.* turn into; **sich in nichts ~** disappear into thin air, *hopes etc.*: come to nothing, *plans etc.*: F go up in smoke; **die Spannung löste sich in Gelächter auf** the tension dissolved into laughter; → **aufgelöst** 2; **'Auf·lö·sung** *f* (-; -en) **1.** ⚗ *etc.* dissolving; **2.** fragmentation, disintegration; **3.** dispersal *of fog etc.*; **4.** ⚖ cancel(l)ation, cancel(l)ing; breaking off *of engagement*; annulment *of marriage*; ☤ closing down *of shop etc.*; winding up *of business etc.*; closing *of account*; *parl.* dissolution, dissolving; **5.** solution (*gen.* to); 𝔄 solution (of *equation*), removal *of brackets*; **6.** ♪ resolution; cancel(l)ation, cancel(l)ing *of accidental*; **7.** *opt., phot.* resolution; *TV a.* definition; **8. in e-m Zustand völliger ~** completely beside o.s.

'Auf·lö·sungs|er·schei·nun·gen *pl.* signs of disintegration; **~proˌzeß** *m* process of disintegration; **~ver·mö·gen** *n* **1.** *opt., phot.* resolution; *TV* number of lines, line rate; **2.** ⚗ solvent power; **~zei·chen** *n* ♪ natural

'auf·ma·chen (*sep.*, h) **I.** *v/t.* **1.** open; → **Auge** 1, **Ohr;** unlock; undo *knot, tie, dress*; unlace; unbutton; put up *umbrella etc.*; **2.** F open *an account*; open up, set up *a business*; **3.** make up, do; design; *fig.* **groß ~** go to town on; **II.** *v/i.* **4.** open; **5.** answer the door; **es hat keiner aufgemacht** *a.* nobody came to the door; **III.** *v/refl.*: **6. sich ~** set out (*or* off), F take off (**nach** *dat.* for); **7. sich ~, et. zu tun** make the effort to do s.th.; **'Auf·ma·cher** F *m* (-s; -) front-page story; **'Auf·ma·chung** *f* (-; -en) **1.** presentation, packaging, F getup; **2.** layout; **3.** F outfit, getup

'Auf·marsch *m* (-[e]s; ⸚e) **1.** marching up; march; rally; parade, march-past; **2.** (military) buildup; **'auf·marˌschie·ren** *v/i.* (*sep.*, sn) **1.** march up; F **als Zeuge ~** appear as witness; **2.** ⚔ mass

'auf·mer·ken *v/i.* (*sep.*, h) pay attention (**auf** *acc.* to); → **aufhorchen; auf·merk·sam** ['aʊfmɛrkza:m] **I.** *adj.* **1.** attentive (**auf** *acc.* to); **~ sein** *ped. etc.* pay attention; **j-n ~ machen auf** *acc.* call (*or* draw) s.o.'s attention to, point *s.th.* out to s.o.; **auf et. ~ werden** become aware of s.th., notice s.th.; **2.** attentive; considerate; **das war sehr ~ von ihr** that was very thoughtful of her; **danke, sehr ~!** thank you, that's very kind (of you); **II.** *adv.*: **~ verfolgen** follow closely; **~ zuhören** listen attentively; **'Auf·merk·sam·keit** *f* (-; -en) **1.** *no pl.* attention; **~ erregen** attract attention; **s-e ~ richten auf** focus one's attention on; **~ schenken** *dat.* pay attention to *s.o. or s.th.*; **j-s ~ entgehen** escape s.o.'s attention (*or* notice); **2.** *no pl.* attentiveness; **3.** little present

auf·mö·beln ['aʊfmø:bəln] F *v/t.* (*sep.*, h) F do up; F buck up, F pep up; polish up

'auf·monˌtie·ren *v/t.* (*sep.*, h) mount (**auf** *acc.* onto), attach (to)

'auf·mot·zen F (*sep.*, h) **I.** *v/i.*: **~ gegen** kick against, be up in arms about; **II.** *v/t.* F do up; F hype up; **III.** *v/refl.*: **sich ~** F get (o.s.) tarted up

'auf·mucken (*sep.* -k·k-), **'auf·muck·sen** F *v/i.* (*sep.*, h) be up in arms (**gegen** *acc.* against *s.th.*); **~ gegen** *acc. a.* kick against

auf·mun·tern ['aʊfmʊntɐn] *v/t.* (*sep.*, -ge-, h) encourage *s.o.* (**zu et.** to do s.th.); cheer *s.o.* up; *coffee etc.*: F pep *s.o.* up, get *s.o.* going; **Auf·mun·te·rung** ['aʊfmʊntərʊŋ] *f* (-; -en) encouragement; cheering up

auf·müp·fig ['aʊfmʏpfɪç] F *adj.* rebellious; **'Auf·müp·fig·keit** F *f* (-; *no pl.*) rebelliousness, rebellious attitude

'auf·nä·hen *v/t.* (*sep.*, h) sew on(to **auf** *acc.*)

Auf·nah·me ['aʊfna:mə] *f* (-; -n) **1.** *no pl.* taking up *of work etc.*; establishment *of relations etc.*; start *of talks etc.*; **2.** *no pl.* intake *of food*; assimilation (*a. fig. of knowledge etc.*); *fig.* taking in *of impressions etc.*; **3.** *no pl.* integration (**in** *acc.* within), incorporation (into); inclusion (in); admission ([in]to); **~ finden** be admitted (**bei** [in]to); **4.** admission (**in** *acc.* into *hospital etc.*); **5.** *no pl.* reception (*a. fig.*); **j-m e-e freundliche ~ bereiten** give s.o. a warm welcome; *fig.* **e-e herzliche** (**kühle**) **~ finden** be warmly received (meet with a cool reception); **6.** *no pl.* ☤ taking in, borrowing *of capital*; raising *of a fund etc.*; **7.** drawing up *of minutes*; **8.** a) *film*: shooting; shot, take; b) taking (a picture); photo(graph), shot; c) recording; **Achtung ~!** *film*: action, camera!; **~an·trag** *m* membership application, application for admission; **e-n ~ stellen** apply for membership (*or* admission); **~be·din·gun·gen** *pl.* terms of admission; **≈be·reit** *adj.* **1.** *camera*: ready to shoot; **2.** *fig.* receptive (**für** *acc.* to); **≈fä·hig** *adj. fig.* receptive (**für** *acc.* to); **abends bin ich nicht mehr ~** I can't take anything in any more in the evenings; **~ge·bühr** *f* admission fee; **~kopf** *m* recording head; **~lei·ter** *m* a) *film*: production (*TV* floor) manager; b) recording (*or* studio) manager; **~prü·fung** *f* entrance exam(ination); **~stu·dio** *n* (recording) studio; **~ta·ste** *f* record button; **~tech·nik** *f* **1.** recording method; **2.** *phot., film*: shooting technique; **~wa·gen** *m* recording van; **~zeit** *f* recording time

'auf·neh·men *v/t.* (*irr., sep.*, h, → **nehmen**) **1.** pick up *load etc., fig. trail etc.*; **2.** take in *food etc.*; assimilate (*both a. fig.*); grasp; **3.** include (**in** *acc.* in), incorporate (in); admit (to); **4.** receive (*a. fig.*); **j-n freundlich ~** give s.o. a warm welcome; *fig.* **begeistert ~** welcome with open arms; **unterschiedlich aufgenommen werden** *film etc.*: get mixed reviews; *e-e schlimme Nachricht etc.* **gut ~** take *s.th.* well; **5.** hold, take; **6.** accommodate; **7.** take up *job etc.*; start, open up *negotiations etc.*; enter into *relations*, establish *contacts*; **den Kampf ~** start fighting, **mit j-m:** take s.o. on; **sie kann es mit jedem ~** she can take anyone on; **beim Kochen kann er es mit jedem ~** he's hard to beat when it comes to cooking; **8.** borrow *money*; *a.* take up *capital*; take out *a loan*; **9.** take down *the facts etc.*; write (*or* take [down]) *the minutes*; take *a dictation, telegram(me)*; **ins Protokoll ~** record in the minutes; **10.** a) photograph, take a picture (*or* photo[graph]) of; b) shoot *film*; c) record, tape; **wo ist das Bild aufgenommen?** where was this picture (*or* photo) taken?, where did you take this picture (*or* photo)?

'Auf·neh·mer *m* (-s; -) floor cloth

'auf·noˌtie·ren *v/t.* (*sep.*, h) make a note of, jot down

'auf·nö·ti·gen *v/t.* (*sep.*, h): **j-m et. ~** force s.th. on s.o.

auf·ok·troy·ie·ren ['aʊfɔktrŏaji:rən] *v/t.* (*sep.*, h): **j-m et. ~** force (*or* impose) s.th. on s.o.

'auf·op·fern *v/t.* (*sep.*, h) sacrifice (**sich** o.s.) (**für** *or dat.* for); **'auf·op·fernd** *adj.* self-sacrificing; **'Auf·op·fe·rung** *f* (-; -en) self-sacrifice; **'auf·op·fe·rungs·voll** *adj.* self-sacrificing

'auf·päp·peln *v/t.* (*sep.*, h) feed up; get *s.o.* on his (*or* her) feet again

'auf·pas·sen *v/i.* (*sep.*, h) pay attention; take care; **~ auf** *acc.* take care of, look after, keep an eye on; **paß auf!** look out!, watch out!; **paß** (**mal**) **auf!** a) watch this, b) listen; **Auf·pas·ser** ['aʊfpasɐ] *m* (-s; -) F watchdog; spy; lookout

'auf·peit·schen (*sep.*, h) **I.** *v/t.* **1.** whip up; **2.** *wind*: lash *the waves*, churn up *the sea*; **3.** *fig.* get *s.o.* going; **II.** *fig. v/refl.*: **sich ~ mit** get o.s. going with, get high on

auf·pep·pen ['aʊfpɛpən] F *v/t.* (*sep.*, h) F pep up

'auf·pflan·zen (*sep.*, h) **I.** *v/t.* ⚔ fix *bayonet*; **II.** F *v/refl.*: **sich vor j-m ~** plant o.s. in front of s.o.

'auf·pfrop·fen *v/t.* (*sep.*, h) graft (**auf** *acc.* onto); *fig.* impose (on); **es wirkt wie aufgepfropft** it doesn't fit in with the rest of it

'auf·picken (*sep.* -k·k-) *v/t.* (*sep.*, h) peck up

'auf·plat·zen *v/i.* (*sep.*, sn) burst; *wound*: open; *skin*: chap

'auf·plu·stern *v/refl.* (*sep.*, h): **sich ~** ruffle its feathers; F *fig.* F act the big shot

'auf·poˌlie·ren *v/t.* (*sep.*, h) polish up; F *fig. a.* refurbish; F brush up

Auf·prall ['aʊfpral] *m* (-[e]s; -e) impact; **'auf·pral·len** *v/i.* (*sep.*, sn): **~ auf** *dat. or acc.* hit, crash into (*or* against *or* onto *the floor etc.*)

'Auf·preis *m* (-es; -e) ☤ extra charge; **ge-**

gen e-n ~ von tausend Mark for an extra thousand marks, for a thousand marks extra

ˈ**auf·proˌbie·ren** *v/t.* (*sep.*, h) try on

ˈ**auf·pum·pen** (*sep.*, h) **I.** *v/t.* blow up; **II.** F *fig. v/refl.*: ***sich ~*** act important, F act big

ˈ**auf·put·schen** (*sep.*, h) **I.** *v/t.* **1.** stir up *the masses*; **2.** *coffee etc.*: get *s.o.* going, F buck *s.o.* up; *drugs*: get *s.o.* high; **II.** *v/refl.*: ***sich ~*** get o.s. going, F buck o.s. up; get high (***mit*** *dat.* on *drugs*); ˈ**Auf·putsch·mit·tel** *n* stimulant; *a.* F pep pill; *sport*: *a. pl.* dope

ˈ**auf·put·zen** F (*sep.*, h) **I.** *v/t.* hype up; **II.** *v/refl.*: ***sich ~*** F get dolled up

ˈ**auf·quel·len** (*irr.*, *sep.*, → ***quellen***) **I.** *v/i.* (sn) *pulses*: swell; *dough*: rise; *face*: swell (up); *fig. tears etc.*: well up; **II.** *v/t.* (h) soak

ˈ**auf·raf·fen** *v/refl.* (*sep.*, h): ***sich ~*** struggle to one's feet, *fig.* pull o.s. together; *fig.* ***sich zu et. ~*** bring o.s. to do s.th.; ***ich kann mich dazu einfach nicht ~*** I just can't be bothered

ˈ**auf·ra·gen** *v/i.* (*sep.*, h) rise, loom (up)

ˈ**auf·rap·peln** F *v/refl.* (*sep.*, h): ***sich ~*** **1.** → ***aufraffen***; **2.** get back on one's feet again

ˈ**auf·rau·chen** *v/t.* (*sep.*, h) finish (off) *cigarette etc.*: get through, smoke *whole pack*

ˈ**auf·rau·hen** *v/t.* (*sep.*, h) roughen

ˈ**auf·räu·men** (*sep.*, h) **I.** *v/t.* **1.** tidy up; **2.** tidy away, put away; **II.** *v/i.* **3.** tidy up; **4.** *fig.* make a clean sweep; wreak havoc (***unter*** *dat.* among); ***~ mit*** get rid of, do away with; put an end to; ***mit der Vergangenheit ~*** make a clean break with the past; ˈ**Auf·räu·mungs·ar·bei·ten** *pl.* clearing work *sg.*

ˈ**auf·rech·nen** *v/t.* (*sep.*, h): ***j-m et. ~*** charge s.o. for s.th.; ***et. gegen et. ~*** set s.th. off (*or* offset s.th.) against s.th.; ***die Kosten gegeneinander ~*** balance the costs out against each other

ˈ**auf·recht** *adj.* **1.** *a. adv.* upright, erect; ***~ sitzen*** sit up; ***~ stehen*** stand erect; **2.** *fig.* upright, honest

ˈ**auf·recht·er·hal·ten** *v/t.* (*irr.*, *sep.*, h, → ***erhalten***) maintain, perpetuate; stand by, adhere to; keep up, keep *a contact* going; ˈ**Auf·recht·er·hal·tung** *f* (-; *no pl.*) maintenance; adherence (*gen.* to)

ˈ**auf·re·gen** (*sep.*, h) **I.** *v/t.* excite, get *s.o.* excited; worry, upset; annoy; ***er regt mich auf*** he gets on my nerves; **II.** *v/refl.*: ***sich ~*** get worked up (***über*** *acc.* about); ˈ**auf·re·gend** *adj.* exciting; upsetting; F tremendous; F ***nicht sehr ~*** F nothing to write home about; ˈ**Auf·re·gung** *f* (-; -en) excitement; upset; nervousness; ***kein Grund zur ~*** it's nothing to worry about; ***nur keine ~!*** don't get into a state, don't panic!

ˈ**auf·rei·ben** (*irr.*, *sep.*, h, → ***reiben***) **I.** *v/t.* **1.** rub *s.th.* sore, chafe; **2.** wear away; *fig.* exhaust, wear out; **II.** *fig. v/refl.*: ***sich ~*** wear o.s. out; ˈ**auf·rei·bend** *adj.* exhausting; ennervating

ˈ**auf·rei·hen** *v/t.* (*sep.*, h) put *things* in a row, line up (*a.* ***sich ~***); thread *beads etc.*

ˈ**auf·rei·ßen** (*irr.*, *sep.*, → ***reißen***) **I.** *v/t.* (h) **1.** tear open *package etc.*; tear *seam etc.*; tear up *road etc.*; *fig.* ***die Abwehr ~*** *sport*: rip open the defen|ce (*Am.* -se); ***alte Wunden ~*** open up old wounds; **2.** fling open *door etc.*; F *fig.* ***er riß die Augen auf*** his eyes nearly popped out of his head; → ***Maul*** 2; **3.** △ draw an elevation of; **4.** give a rough idea of *a problem etc.*; **5.** F get o.s., F land o.s. *a job etc.*; F pick up *a girl etc.*; **II.** *v/i.* (sn) **6.** *seam, bag etc.*: burst, split open; *skin*: chap; *wood*: crack; **7.** *clouds*: break up; **8.** F *phot.* open up; ˈ**Auf·rei·ßer** *m* (-s; -) **1.** *wrestling*: turnover; **2.** F womanizer

ˈ**auf·rei·zen** *v/t.* (*sep.*, h) **1.** stimulate, excite; F turn *s.o.* on; **2.** stir up; ˈ**auf·rei·zend** *adj.* provocative

ˈ**auf·rich·ten** (*sep.*, h) **I.** *v/t.* **1.** put up, erect; **2.** help *s.o.* up; sit *s.o.* up *in bed*; straighten up; **3.** *fig.* set *s.o.* up; **II.** *v/refl.*: ***sich ~*** **4.** get up; sit up *in bed*; straighten up; **5.** *fig.* pick o.s. up; ***sich an j-m ~*** a) lean on s.o., b) find s.o. very supportive

ˈ**auf·rich·tig** **I.** *adj.* sincere; honest; open; **II.** *adv.*: ***es tut mir ~ leid*** I really am sorry; ˈ**Auf·rich·tig·keit** *f* (-; *no pl.*) sincerity; honesty; frankness

ˈ**auf·rie·geln** *v/t.* (*sep.*, h) unbolt, open

ˈ**Auf·riß** *m* (-sses; -sse) △ elevation; front elevation (*or* view); *fig.* outline

ˈ**auf·rit·zen** *v/t.* (*sep.*, h) slit open; scratch

ˈ**auf·rol·len** *v/t.* (*sep.*, h) **1.** a) roll up; wind up; b) unroll; unfurl *flag etc.*; ***sich die Haare ~*** put curlers in one's hair, put one's hair in curlers; **2.** *fig.* go into; ***e-n Prozeß wieder*** (*or* ***neu***) ***~*** reopen a trial

ˈ**auf·rü·cken** (*sep.* -k·k-) *v/i.* (*sep.*, sn) a) move up; b) be promoted (***in e-e höhere Stellung*** to a higher position)

ˈ**Auf·ruf** *m* (-[e]s; -e) summons, appeal; ✈, *computer*: call; ✈ ***letzter ~*** last call; ˈ**auf·ru·fen** (*irr.*, *sep.*, h, → ***rufen***) **I.** *v/t.* call up (*a.* ⚔ *and computer*); *ped.* call on; ⚖ call *witness etc.*; *fig.* ***j-n ~ zu*** *inf.* call (up)on s.o. to *inf.*; **II.** *v/i.*: ***~ zu*** appeal for; ***zum Streik ~*** call a strike

Auf·ruhr [ˈaʊfruːɐ] *m* (-[e]s; -e) commotion, turmoil (*a. fig.*); riot, tumult; uprising, revolt; *fig.* conflict; ***in ~*** in a state of turmoil (*a. fig.*), up in arms; ***öffentlicher ~*** public clamo(u)r

ˈ**auf·rüh·ren** *v/t.* (*sep.*, h) stir up (*a. fig.*); *fig.* dig up *memory, story etc.*

Auf·rüh·rer [ˈaʊfryːrɐ] *m* (-s;-) rebel; *pol.* agitator; **auf·rüh·re·risch** [ˈaʊfryːrərɪʃ] *adj.* rebellious; inflammatory *speech etc.*

ˈ**auf·run·den** *v/t.* (*sep.*, h) round up (***auf*** *acc.* to)

ˈ**auf·rü·sten** *v/t. and v/i.* (*sep.*, h) ⚔ (re)arm; ˈ**Auf·rü·stung** *f* (-; -en) (military) buildup; (re)armament

ˈ**auf·rüt·teln** *v/t.* (*sep.*, h) **1.** shake *s.o.* awake; **2.** *fig.* shake *s.o.* up; ***~ aus*** *dat.* rouse from

ˈ**auf·sa·gen** *v/t.* (*sep.*, h) **1.** recite; **2.** *lit.* ***j-m die Freundschaft ~*** break with s.o.

ˈ**auf·sam·meln** *v/t.* (*sep.*, h) pick up (*a.* F *s.o.*)

auf·säs·sig [ˈaʊfzɛsɪç] *adj.* rebellious, refractory

ˈ**Auf·satz** *m* (-es; ⸚e) **1.** essay, *ped. a.* composition; paper; article; **2.** top (part); **3.** *golf*: tee; **~the·ma** *n* essay topic

ˈ**auf·sau·gen** *v/t.* (*sep.*, h) **1.** soak up; 🌿 absorb; **2.** *fig.* assimilate, absorb

ˈ**auf·schau·en** *v/i.* (*sep.*, h) look up (***zu*** *dat.* at, *fig.* to); glance up

ˈ**auf·schau·keln** (*sep.*, h) **I.** *v/t.* *phys.* build up, amplify; *fig.* ***sich gegenseitig ~*** get each other going; **II.** *fig. v/refl.*: ***sich ~*** build up, mount

ˈ**auf·schäu·men** *v/i.* (*sep.*, sn) froth up; *fig.* (***vor Wut***) ***~*** foam (with rage)

ˈ**auf·scheu·chen** *v/t.* (*sep.*, h) startle; frighten away; disturb; *fig.* rouse *s.o.* (***aus*** *dat.* from); *fig.* ***~ aus*** (*dat.*) *a.* shake out of

ˈ**auf·scheu·ern** *v/t.* (*sep.*, h) rub *one's skin* sore, chafe; ***sich die Haut ~*** rub o.s. sore, chafe o.s.

ˈ**auf·schich·ten** *v/t.* (*sep.*, h) stack up, pile up; *geol.* stratify

auf·schieb·bar [ˈaʊfʃiːpbaːɐ] *adj.* postponable; ***es ist*** (***nicht***) ***~*** it can('t) be postponed; ˈ**auf·schie·ben** *v/t.* (*irr.*, *sep.*, h, → ***schieben***) **1.** push open; **2.** *fig.* postpone, put off (***auf*** *acc.*, ***bis*** until, till); delay; ***er schiebt es immer wieder auf*** he keeps putting it off; ***aufgeschoben ist nicht aufgehoben*** we'll make up for it (another time)

ˈ**auf·schie·ßen** *v/i.* (*irr.*, *sep.*, sn, → ***schießen***) ✂ shoot up (*a. fig.*); *flames*: *a.* leap up; → ***aufgeschossen*** II

ˈ**Auf·schlag** *m* (-[e]s; ⸚e) **1.** a) cuff; b) turn-up, *Am.* cuff; c) lapel; **2.** impact; ***dumpfer ~*** thud; **3.** ✝ markup; **4.** *tennis*: a) service, b) serve; ˈ**Auf·schlag·ball** *m* service; ˈ**auf·schla·gen** (*irr.*, *sep.*, h, → ***schlagen***) **I.** *v/i.* **1.** (sn) ***~ auf*** *dat. or acc.* hit; **2.** *tennis*: serve; **3.** ✝ *goods*: go up (in price); *shopkeeper*: raise the price; **II.** *v/t.* **4.** break open; crack *egg*; cut *one's knee etc.*; **5.** open *one's eyes, a book etc.*; ***Seite 3 ~*** turn to page 3; **6.** *tennis*: serve *ball*; **7.** pitch *tent*; set up *camp*; take up *residence*; **8.** increase, raise *price*; **9.** *knitting*: cast on *stitches*; ˈ**Auf·schlag·feld** *n tennis*: service court

ˈ**auf·schlie·ßen** (*irr.*, *sep.*, h, → ***schließen***) **I.** *v/t.* **1.** unlock, open; **2.** → ***erschließen***; **II.** *v/i.* **3.** open up, open the door *etc.*; **4.** *sport*: move up; ***~ zu*** catch up with; **III.** *v/refl.*: ***sich j-m ~*** open one's heart to s.o., confide in s.o.

ˈ**auf·schlit·zen** *v/t.* (*sep.*, h) slit; slit open *envelope etc.*; slash *tires etc.*

ˈ**auf·schluch·zen** *v/i.* (*sep.*, h) give a loud sob

ˈ**Auf·schluß** *m* (-sses; ⸚sse) insight(s *pl.*) (***über*** *acc.* into); (***j-m***) ***über et. ~ geben*** inform s.o. about s.th., explain s.th. to s.o.; ***sich ~ verschaffen über*** *acc.* inform o.s. about, gain an (*or* some) insight into

auf·schlüs·seln [ˈaʊfʃlʏsəln] *v/t.* (*sep.*, h) break down (***nach*** into); classify (according to); ˈ**Auf·schlüs·se·lung** [ˈaʊfʃlʏsəlʊŋ] *f* (-; -en) breaking down; breakdown; categorization

ˈ**auf·schluß·reich** *adj.* informative; *w.s.* revealing; ***das war sehr ~*** *a.* that was very interesting

ˈ**auf·schmie·ren** *v/t.* (*sep.*, h) **1.** spread (on), put on; daub on; **2.** F scribble down

ˈ**auf·schnal·len** *v/t.* (*sep.*, h) **1.** strap on(to ***auf*** *acc.*); **2.** unstrap; undo, unbuckle

ˈ**auf·schnap·pen** (*sep.*) **I.** *v/t.* (h) catch; F *fig.* pick up; **II.** *v/i.* (sn) snap (*or* spring) open

ˈ**auf·schnei·den** (*irr.*, *sep.*, h, → ***schneiden***) **I.** *v/t.* cut open; *gastr.* cut up; slice; ✂ open; *a.* lance *boil etc.*; **II.** *v/i.* boast, show off; F lay it on thick; ˈ**Auf·schnei·der** *m* (-s; -) show-off; ***das ist ein ~*** F he really lays it on thick (*or* with a trowel)

ˈ**Auf·schnitt** *m* (-[e]s; *no pl.*) cold cuts *pl.*; **~plat·te** *f* (plate of) cold cuts *pl*

ˈ**auf·schnü·ren** *v/t.* (*sep.*, h) untie; undo; unlace

'auf·schram·men *v/t.* (*sep.*, h) graze
'auf·schrau·ben *v/t.* (*sep.*, h) **1.** screw on(to ***auf*** *acc.*); **2.** unscrew
'auf·schrecken (*sep.* -k·k-) (*sep.*) **I.** *v/t.* (h) startle; rouse (***aus*** *dat.* from); **II.** *v/i.* (sn) give a start, jump; ***aus dem Schlaf ~*** wake up with a start
'Auf·schrei *m* (-[e]s; -e) cry; scream; shriek; *fig.* outcry (***gegen*** against)
'auf·schrei·ben *v/t.* (*irr.*, *sep.*, h, → ***schreiben***) write down; make a note of; ***j-n ~*** *police*: take down s.o.'s particulars (*or* car number); ***ich bin dreimal wegen falschen Parkens aufgeschrieben worden*** I've had three parking tickets
'auf·schrei·en *v/i.* (*irr.*, *sep.*, h, → ***schreien***) cry out; (give a) scream; ***vor Schmerz ~*** cry out with pain
'Auf·schrift *f* (-; -en) lettering, writing; name; label; inscription
'Auf·schub *m* (-[e]s; ⸚e) deferment; delay; ***ohne ~*** without delay; ***die Sache duldet keinen ~*** the matter is extremely urgent (*formal*: brooks no further delay); ***j-m e-n ~ gewähren*** give (*or* grant) s.o. an extension
'auf·schür·fen *v/t.* (*sep.*, h): ***sich die Haut ~*** graze o.s. (*or* one's skin)
'auf·schüt·teln *v/t.* (*sep.*, h) shake up; *a.* plump up *cushion*
'auf·schüt·ten *v/t.* (*sep.*, h) pile up; scatter; throw up, raise *dam etc.*; *geol.* deposit; **'Auf·schüt·tung** *f* (-; -en) earth bank; *geol.* deposit
'auf·schwat·zen F *v/t.* (*sep.*, h): ***j-m et. ~*** talk s.o. into (buying) s.th.
'auf·schwei·ßen *v/t.* (*sep.*, h) **1.** weld on(to ***auf*** *acc.*); **2.** weld open
'auf·schwel·len *v/i.* (*irr.*, *sep.*, sn, → ***schwellen***) swell (up)
'auf·schwem·men *v/t.* (*sep.*, h) bloat; → ***aufgeschwemmt*** II
'auf·schwin·deln *v/t.* (*sep.*, h): ***j-m et. ~*** trick s.o. into buying s.th.
'auf·schwin·gen *v/refl.* (*irr.*, *sep.*, h, → ***schwingen***): ***sich ~*** *bird*: soar (up); *fig.* ***sich zu et. ~*** bring o.s. to do s.th.; ***sich zum besten Schüler der Klasse (zum Direktor) ~*** work one's way up to the top of the class (to the position of director); ***sich zum Moralprediger ~*** set o.s. up as (*or* appoint o.s.) a moralizer
'Auf·schwung *m* (-[e]s; ⸚e) **1.** *gym.* upward circle; **2.** *fig.* impetus; progress; ⚚ upturn, upswing; ***neuen ~ geben*** *dat.* give fresh impetus to; ⚚ ***e-n ~ nehmen*** see (*or* experience) a revival
'auf·se·hen I. *v/i.* (*irr.*, *sep.*, h, → ***sehen***) look up (*fig.* ***zu j-m*** to s.o.); **II.** ♀ *n* (-s): ***~ erregen, für ~ sorgen*** cause (quite) a stir (*or* sensation); ***ohne ~*** discreetly, quietly; ***um ~ zu vermeiden*** to avoid attracting attention, to avoid (any) publicity; **'auf·se·hen·er·re·gend** *adj.* sensational *news, discovery etc.*; outrageous, extravagant *hairstyle, dress etc.*; controversial, provocative *idea, speech etc.*; ***~ sein*** *a.* cause (quite) a stir; ***es war e-e ~e Rede*** *a.* it was a speech that made everyone sit up and think
'Auf·se·her *m* (-s; -), **'Auf·se·he·rin** *f* (-; -nen) attendant; prison officer, guard
'auf·sein *v/i.* (*irr.*, *sep.*, sn, → ***sein***) **1.** be up; **2.** be open
'auf·set·zen (*sep.*, h) **I.** *v/t.* **1.** put on *hat, glasses etc., a. fig. expression, smile etc.*; put *pot etc.* on the stove; ***Wasser ~*** put some water on to boil; → ***aufgesetzt*** II, ***Dämpfer, Glanzlicht, Horn*** 1, ***Krone*** 2; **2.** draft *speech, letter, contract etc.*, *ped. a.* make a draft of; **II.** *v/refl.*: ***sich ~*** sit up; **III.** *v/i.* ✈ touch down, *a. sport*: land; **'Auf·set·zer** *m* (-s; -) *sport*: awkward bouncing shot
'auf·seuf·zen *v/i.* (*sep.*, h): (***tief***) ***~*** heave a (deep) sigh
'Auf·sicht *f* (-; -en) **1.** *no pl.* supervision; ***die ~ führen*** be in charge (***über*** *acc.* of); ***unter ~ stehen*** be under supervision (*or* surveillance), *prisoner*: be in custody; **2.** supervisor, person in charge; **'auf·sicht·füh·rend** *adj.* supervisory; *teacher etc.* in charge
'Auf·sichts|be·am·te *m* (-n; -n) supervisor; guard; 🚂 stationmaster; **~be·hör·de** *f* board of control, inspectorate; **~per·so͵nal** *n* supervisory staff; prison wardens *pl.*; **~pflicht** *f* (-; *no pl.*) responsibility
'Auf·sichts·rat *m* ⚚ **1.** supervisory board; board of directors; **2.** member of the supervisory board (*or* board of directors); **'Auf·sichts·rats·vor·sit·zen·de** *m, f* (-n; -n) chairman (*f a.* chairwoman) of the board
'auf·sit·zen *v/i.* (*irr.*, *sep.*, h, → ***sitzen***) **1.** sit up *in bed etc.*; **2.** stay up (late); **3.** get on, mount *horse, motorbike etc.*; **4.** ⚙ rest (***auf*** *dat.* on); **5.** F *fig.* be taken in (*dat.* by); F ***j-n ~ lassen*** let s.o. down; F stand s.o. up
'auf·spal·ten *v/t. and v/refl.* (***sich ~***) (*sep.*, h) split; **'Auf·spal·tung** *f* (-; -en) splitting; ⚛ fission; *fig.* split
'auf·span·nen *v/t.* (*sep.*, h) stretch; put up *tent, umbrella*; open up, spread out *safety sheet etc.*
'auf·spa·ren *v/t.* (*sep.*, h) save (up); ***sparen wir uns die Überraschung auf*** let's keep it a surprise
'auf·spei·chern *v/t.* (*sep.*, h) store up; hoard; *fig.* bottle up (inside)
'auf·sper·ren *v/t.* (*sep.*, h) unlock; open wide; *fig.* ***er sperrte Mund und Nase auf*** his jaw dropped
'auf·spie·len (*sep.*, h) **I.** *v/t.* strike up *a tune*; **II.** *v/i.* play; **III.** *v/refl.*: ***sich ~*** throw one's weight around, F act the big shot; ***sich als Held*** *etc.* ***~*** play the hero *etc.*
'auf·spie·ßen *v/t.* (*sep.*, h) **1.** spear; gore; impale; skewer *meat*; spike *olive etc.*; mount *butterfly etc.*; ***~ auf*** *acc.* mount on(to), pin on(to); **2.** *fig.* pillory
'auf·split·tern (*sep.*) **I.** *v/t.* (h) *and v/i.* (sn) splinter; **II.** *fig. v/refl.* (h): ***sich ~*** split up, splinter
'auf·spren·gen *v/t.* (*sep.*, h) force open; blast open
'auf·sprin·gen *v/i.* (*irr.*, *sep.*, sn, → ***springen***) **1.** jump up, leap up; land; *ball*: bounce; ***auf e-n Zug ~*** jump onto a train; **2.** *skin, lips*: crack, chap; *buds*: burst; *button*: pop open; **3.** *door etc.*: fly (*or* burst) open; *lid etc.*: burst open; *lock*: spring open
'auf·sprit·zen (*sep.*) **I.** *v/t.* (h) spray on *paint*; **II.** *v/i.* (sn) spray (*or* spurt) into the air
'auf·sprü·hen (*sep.*, h) **I.** *v/t.* (*a.* ***~ auf*** *acc.*) spray on; **II.** *v/i.* shoot up
'Auf·sprung *m* (-[e]s; ⸚e) *esp. sport*: landing
'auf·spu·len *v/t.* (*sep.*, h) wind up, wind onto a spool
'auf·spü·ren *v/t.* (*sep.*, h) **1.** track (*or* hunt) down *game etc.*; **2.** *fig.* track down; unearth *secret etc.*
'auf·sta·cheln *v/t.* (*sep.*, h) stir up; ***j-n zu et. ~*** goad s.o. into (doing) s.th
'auf·stamp·fen *v/i.* (*sep.*, h) stamp one's foot (*or* feet), stamp on the ground
'Auf·stand *m* (-[e]s; ⸚e) revolt, rebellion, uprising; **auf·stän·disch** ['aʊfʃtɛndɪʃ] *adj.* rebellious, insurgent; **'Auf·stän·di·sche** *m* (-n; -n) rebel, insurgent
'auf·sta·peln *v/t.* (*sep.*, h) pile (*or* stack) up
'auf·stau·en (*sep.*, h) **I.** *v/t.* dam up; *fig.* bottle up (inside); **II.** *v/refl.*: ***sich ~*** collect; *fig.* build up, be bottled up; → ***aufgestaut*** II
'auf·ste·chen *v/t.* (*irr.*, *sep.*, h, → ***stechen***) pierce; ⚕ lance *boil etc.*
'auf·stecken (*sep.* -k·k-) *v/t.* (*sep.*, h) **1.** put on (*a.* ***~ auf*** *acc.*); pin (***auf*** *acc.* on[to]); pin up *hem*; put up *curtain, one's hair*; **2.** F chuck in
'auf·ste·hen *v/i.* (*irr.*, *sep.*, sn, → ***stehen***) **1.** stand up, get up; ***vor j-m ~*** give s.o. one's seat, stand (*or* get) up for s.o.; ***vom Tisch ~*** get up from (*or* leave) the table; **2.** stand (*or* be) open; **3.** *fig.* revolt, ***gegen***: *a.* rise up against
'auf·stei·gen *v/i.* (*irr.*, *sep.*, sn, → ***steigen***) **1.** rise, go up; *mountaineering*: climb (*a.* ***~ auf*** *acc.*); ✈ take off, become airborne, climb; *bird*: soar; **2.** get on, mount *horse, bicycle etc.*; **3.** *fig.* be promoted (*a. sport*); **4.** *fig.* arise; well up; be roused; ***ein Gedanke stieg in mir auf*** a thought struck me; **'auf·stei·gend** *adj.*: ***in ~er Reihenfolge*** in ascending order; → ***Tendenz***; **'Auf·stei·ger** *m* (-s; -) a) *sport*: (newly-)promoted team; b) social climber; c) chart climber; ***~ des Jahres*** man of the year
'auf·stel·len (*sep.*, h) **I.** *v/t.* set up; erect, put up *monument etc.*; ⚔ line up; post *guard etc.*; deploy *rockets etc.*; put on *water to boil etc.*; set *trap*; put forward, field *candidate*; *sport*: set up *record etc.*; pick *team*; lay down *law etc.*; propose *theory*; A̸ state, pose *problem*; form, set up *equation*; draw up *list, table, balance sheet*; ***e-e Behauptung ~*** make an assertion, claim (*or* maintain) s.th.; **II.** *v/refl.*: ***sich ~*** take one's stand; get into line; ⚔ fall in; **'Auf·stel·lung** *f* (-; -en) setting up; ⚙ installation; ⚔ deployment, emplacement *of rockets etc.*; arrangement, ⚔ formation; *a. sport*: line-up; list; table; nomination; drawing up *of balance sheet etc.*
'auf·stem·men *v/t.* (*sep.*, h) prise (*or* prize, *Am.* pry) open
Auf·stieg ['aʊfʃtiːk] *m* (-[e]s; -e [-ʃtiːgə]) ascent; ✈ takeoff, climb(ing); *fig.* rise; ascent, advancement; *sport*: promotion; ***~ zum Ruhm*** rise to fame
'Auf·stiegs|chan·cen *pl.*, **~mög·lich·kei·ten** *pl.* promotion prospects; *sport*: chances of being promoted; ***Stelle ohne ~*** dead-end job
'auf·stö·bern *v/t.* (*sep.*, h) rouse *animal etc.*; *fig.* hunt down; unearth
auf·stocken (*sep.* -k·k-) *v/t.* (*sep.*, h) **1.** ⌂ raise; add a stor(e)y to; **2.** ⚚ increase *capital*; top up; stock up on
'auf·stöh·nen *v/i.* (*sep.*, h) give a (loud) groan
'auf·sto·ßen (*irr.*, *sep.*, h, → ***stoßen***) **I.** *v/t.* **1.** push open *door etc.*; **2.** ***et. ~ auf*** *acc.* bang s.th. on(to) *s.th.*; ***sich den***

Kopf *etc.* ~ cut one's head; **II.** *v/i.* **3.** ~ **auf** *acc.* hit; **4.** burp; **j-m** ~ repeat on s.o., *fig.* strike s.o., hit s.o.; → **sauer** I

'**auf·stre·bend** *adj.* soaring; *fig.* aspiring; up-and-coming, *esp. Am.* upcoming

'**auf·strei·chen** *v/t.* (*irr.*, *sep.*, h, → **streichen**) apply *paint etc.* (**auf** *acc.* to); spread *butter etc.* (on); '**Auf·strich** *m* (-[e]s; -e) **1.** → **Brotaufstrich**; **2.** upstroke (*a.* ♪)

'**auf·stül·pen** *v/t.* (*sep.*, h) F pop on *hat etc.*; turn up *collar, brim etc.*; **die Lippen** ~ pout; → **aufgestülpt** II

'**auf·stüt·zen** (*sep.*, h) **I.** *v/t.* prop up; **II.** *v/refl.*: **sich** ~ prop o.s. up, **auf** *dat. or acc.*: *a.* lean on

'**auf·su·chen** *v/t.* (*sep.*, h) visit, call on; look up; (go and) see *one's doctor etc.*; go to *the toilet etc.*

'**auf·ta·feln** (*sep.*, h) **I.** *v/t.* serve (up); **II.** *v/i.* give a huge spread

'**auf·ta·keln** (*sep.*, h) **I.** *v/t.* ⚓ rig up; **II.** F *fig. v/refl.*: **sich** ~ F get rigged (*contp.* tarted) up; → **aufgetakelt** II

'**Auf·takt** *m* (-[e]s; -e) ♪ upbeat; *fig.* prelude, F lead-up; start, F send-off; curtain-raiser; **zum** ~ **des Festivals** to start the festival off, to launch the festival, to get the festival under way

'**auf·tan·ken** *v/t. and v/i.* (*sep.*, h) fill up; ✈ refuel

'**auf·tau·chen** *v/i.* (*sep.*, sn) **1.** come up, emerge; *submarine*: surface; **2.** *fig.* turn up; *question etc.*: come up, *esp. problem etc.*: *a.* crop up

'**auf·tau·en** *v/i.* (*sep.*, sn) **1.** *a. v/t.* (h) thaw; *mot.*, *gastr.* defrost; **2.** *fig.* thaw, come out of one's shell

'**auf·tei·len** *v/t.* (*sep.*, h) divide (up), split up; distribute; divide, partition *room*; parcel out *land*; '**Auf·tei·lung** *f* (-; -en) division; distribution

auf·ti·schen ['aʊftɪʃən] *v/t.* (*sep.*, h) serve, *a. fig.* F dish up

Auf·trag ['aʊftra:k] *m* (-[e]s; Aufträge ['aʊftrɛ:gə]) **1.** assignment; ⚕ order; contract; directions *pl.*, instructions *pl.*; mission; **im** ~ **von** (*or gen.*) on behalf of; **ich komme im** ~ **von** I have been sent by; **im** ~ (*abbr.* **i.A.**) pp, p.p. (= per procurationem); **et. bei j-m in** ~ **geben** commission s.o. to do s.th.; ⚕ place an order with s.o. for s.th.; **2.** job; purpose, mission; **die Kirche hat den** ~ **zu** *inf.* it's the job of the Church (*or* the Church's job) to *inf.*; **3.** *no pl.* application *of paint etc.*; '**auf·tra·gen** (*irr.*, *sep.*, h, → **tragen**) **I.** *v/t.* **1.** serve (up) *dishes*; apply *paint, make-up etc.*; **2.** wear out *clothes*; **3. j-m et.** ~ assign s.o. with s.th.; **er trug mir Grüße an dich auf** he asked me to give you his regards; **II.** *v/i.* **4.** *pullover etc.*: be bulky; **5.** F *fig.* **dick** ~ F lay it on thick (*or* with a trowel)

'**Auf·trag·ge·ber** *m* (-s; -) customer, client; *art*: patron

'**Auf·trags|ar·beit** *f* commissioned work; ~**be·stän·de** *pl.* backlog *sg.* of orders; ~**be·stä·ti·gung** *f* confirmation (*or* acknowledg[e]ment) of order; ~**buch** *n* order book; ~**ein·gang** *m* **1.** incoming orders *pl.*; **2.** intake of orders; ~**er·tei·lung** *f* placing of orders; award; ~**for·mu·lar** *n* order form (*Am.* blank)

'**auf·trags·ge·mäß** *adv.* as per order

'**Auf·trags|la·ge** *f* orders situation; **die** ~ **ist gut** the order books are well filled; ~**pol·ster** *n* full order books *pl.*; ~**rück·gang** *m* drop in orders; ~**werk** *n* commissioned work (*or* piece)

'**auf·tref·fen** *v/i.* (*irr.*, *sep.*, sn, → **treffen**): ~ **auf** *dat.* hit

'**auf·trei·ben** *v/t.* (*irr.*, *sep.*, h, → **treiben**) **1.** F get hold of; **2.** swell; → **aufgetrieben** II; **3.** swirl up; **4.** force *s.o.* up

'**auf·tren·nen** *v/t.* (*sep.*, h) undo, rip open *seam etc.*; undo, unravel *knitting*

'**auf·tre·ten** (*irr.*, *sep.*, → **treten**) **I.** *v/i.* (sn) **1.** step, tread; **vorsichtig** ~ tread carefully (*or* softly); **ich kann mit dem linken Fuß nicht** ~ I can't stand on my left foot; **2.** *thea.* appear (on stage); *a. musician etc.*: perform; **zum ersten Mal** ~ *a. fig.* make one's debut; **3.** appear; **öffentlich** ~ appear in public; **als Zeuge** ~ appear as witness; ~ **gegen** oppose; **4.** occur; *difficulties*, *problems etc.*: crop up; *doubts etc.*: arise; **5.** occur, be found; **6.** act, conduct o.s.; **II.** *v/t.* (h) **7.** kick open *door etc.*; tread open *chestnut etc.*; **III.** ♀ *n* (-s) **8.** appearance; occurrence, *a.* ⚕ incidence; **9.** manner; **er hat ein sehr selbstsicheres** ~ *a.* he comes across as very self-confident; **10.** *thea.* performance

'**Auf·trieb** *m* (-[e]s; *no pl.*) **1.** *phys.* buoyancy; ✈ lift; **2.** *fig.* impetus, stimulus, F boost; **neuen** ~ **geben** *dat.* give fresh impetus to; **j-m wieder** ~ **geben** get s.o. going again; **ich hab' heute überhaupt keinen** ~ I can't bring myself to do anything today

'**Auf·tritt** *m* (-[e]s; -e) *a. thea.* appearance; scene (*a. fig. quarrel*); entry

'**auf·trump·fen** *fig. v/i.* (*sep.*, h) **1.** play one's trumps; **2.** F come on strong; **gegen j-n** ~ F do the strong man act on s.o.

'**auf·tun** (*irr.*, *sep.*, h, → **tun**) **I.** *v/t.* **1.** *lit.* open; **2.** *dial.* put on *hat, glasses etc.*; **3. sich et.** ~ help o.s. to s.th., take s.th.; **j-m et.** ~ give s.o. (a helping of) s.th.; **4.** F find, discover, F dig up; **II.** *v/refl.*: **sich** ~ open (up); *fig.* open up (**vor** *dat.* before)

'**auf·tup·fen** *v/t.* (*sep.*, h) dab off

'**auf·tür·men** (*sep.*, h) **I.** *v/t.* pile up; **II.** *v/refl.*: **sich** ~ *dirty dishes*, *fig. work etc.*: pile up

'**auf·wa·chen** *v/i.* (*sep.*, sn) *a. fig.* wake up (**aus** *dat.* from); come round; *fig.* **er ist endlich aufgewacht** he's finally woken up to the truth (*or* to reality)

'**auf·wach·sen** *v/i.* (*irr.*, *sep.*, sn, → **wachsen**) grow up

'**auf·wal·len** *v/i.* (*sep.*, sn) bubble up; boil up; *fig.* surge up (**in j-m** inside s.o.); '**Auf·wal·lung** *f* (-; -en) surge; *fig. a.* fit

'**auf·wal·zen** *v/t.* (*sep.*, h) roll on

Auf·wand ['aʊfvant] *m* (-[e]s; *no pl.*) a) cost, expense; effort; b) luxury, extravagance; **mit e-m** ~ **von ...** at a cost of ...; **der** ~ **an Zeit** (**Kraft** *etc.*) the time (energy *etc.*) involved; **der** ~ **lohnt sich nicht** it's not worth the effort; **unnützer** ~ waste of (time and) energy, waste (of money); **großen** ~ **treiben** live in grand style; '**Auf·wands·ent·schä·di·gung** *f* expense allowance

'**auf·wär·men** (*sep.*, h) **I.** *v/t.* warm up; *fig.* rehash; **II.** *v/refl.*: **sich** ~ warm o.s. up; *sport and fig.* warm up

'**Auf·wärm|pha·se** *f* warm-up phase; ~**übun·gen** *pl.* warm(ing)-up exercises

'**Auf·war·te·frau** *f* cleaning lady

'**auf·war·ten** *v/i.* (*sep.*, h) **1.** *fig.* ~ **mit** come up with, offer; **2.** *gastr.* ~ **mit** serve

auf·wärts ['aʊfvɛrts] *adv.* upward(s); uphill; **den Fluß** ~ upstream, upriver; *fig.* **mit ihm** (**dem Geschäft**) **geht es** ~ things are looking up for him (business is looking up); ♀**be·we·gung** *f*, ♀**ent·wick·lung** *f* upward trend; ♀**ha·ken** *m boxing*: uppercut; ♀**trend** *m* upward trend, upswing

'**Auf·war·tung** *f*: **j-m s-e** ~ **machen** pay one's respects to s.o.

Auf·wasch ['aʊfvaʃ] *m* (-[e]s; *no pl.*) **1.** dirty dishes *pl.*; **2.** washing-up; **den** ~ **machen** → **aufwaschen**; *fig.* **in einem** ~ in one go; '**auf·wa·schen** *v/i.* (*irr.*, *sep.*, h, → **waschen**) do the dishes (*or* washing-up)

'**auf·wecken** (*sep.* -k·k-) *v/t.* (*sep.*, h) wake (up)

'**auf·wei·chen** (*sep.*) **I.** *v/t.* (h) soak; make *the ground* soggy; melt; *fig.* undermine; **II.** *v/i.* (sn) soak; *ground*: become soggy

'**auf·wei·sen** *v/t.* (*irr.*, *sep.*, h, → **weisen**) show; boast; have; **etwas** (**nichts**) **aufzuweisen haben** have something (nothing) to show (for o.s.)

'**auf·wen·den** *v/t.* (*sep.*, h) spend (**für** *acc.* on); *a.* devote *time etc.* (to); *a.* expend *energy etc.* (on); (**viel**) **Mühe** ~ take (great) pains (**auf** *acc.* over); **viel Geld** ~ go to great expense; '**auf·wen·dig** *adj.* costly, expensive; extravagant; ~**e Inszenierung** lavish production; '**Auf·wen·dun·gen** *pl.* expenditure *sg.*, expense *sg.*, expenses

'**auf·wer·fen** (*irr.*, *sep.*, h, → **werfen**) **I.** *v/t.* throw up *dam, soil etc.*; throw open; *fig.* raise *question etc.*; ~ **auf** *acc.* throw on(to); **II.** *v/refl.*: **sich zu et.** ~ set o.s. up as s.th., appoint o.s. s.th.; **sich zum Richter** ~ appoint o.s. as judge

'**auf·wer·ten** *v/t.* (*sep.*, h) revalue, upvalue; *fig.* upgrade; '**Auf·wer·tung** *f* (-; -en) revaluation, upvaluation; *fig.* upgrading

'**auf·wickeln** (*sep.* -k·k-) *v/t.* (*sep.*, h) **1.** wind up (*a. film*); **sich die Haare** ~ put one's hair in curlers; **2.** unwind; unwrap;

'**Auf·wickel·spu·le** *f film*: take-up spool (*or* reel)

auf·wie·geln ['aʊfvi:gəln] *v/t.* (*sep.*, h) stir up

'**auf·wie·gen** *fig. v/t.* (*irr.*, *sep.*, h, → **wiegen**) compensate for, make up for, offset, balance out

Auf·wieg·ler ['aʊfvi:glɐ] *m* (-s; -) agitator; **auf·wieg·le·risch** ['aʊfvi:glərɪʃ] *adj.* seditious; inflammatory

'**Auf·wind** *m* (-[e]s; -e) ✈ upward (*or* anabatic) wind; *fig.* **im** ~ **sein** be on the up and up; **j-m** (**neuen**) ~ **geben** get s.o. going (again), give s.o. an impetus (fresh impetus)

'**auf·wir·beln** *v/t.* (*sep.*, h) whirl up, swirl up; raise *dust*; *fig.* **viel Staub** ~ kick up a lot of dust, cause quite a stir

'**auf·wi·schen** *v/t.* (*sep.*, h) wipe up; wipe, mop *floor*

'**auf·wüh·len** *v/t.* (*sep.*, h) **1.** throw up *soil*; churn up *water, sea*; **2.** *fig.* **j-n** ~ stir s.o. up; → **aufgewühlt** II

'**auf·zäh·len** *v/t.* (*sep.*, h) enumerate; name, tell; list; '**Auf·zäh·lung** *f* (-; -en) enumeration; list

'**auf·zeh·ren** (*sep.*, h) **I.** *v/t.* eat up; *fig.* use up; spend; sap *energy*; drain, exhaust *s.o.*; → **aufgezehrt** II; **II.** *v/refl.*: **er zehrt sich vor Sorgen auf** he's eaten up with worry, his worries are eating away at him '**auf·zeich·nen** *v/t.* (*sep.*, h) draw, sketch; write down; record, tape; '**Auf·zeich·nung** *f* (-; -en) **1.** recording; **2.** **~en** notes; papers, documents; ***sich ~en machen*** make (*or* take) notes

'**auf·zei·gen** *v/t.* (*sep.*, h) show; demonstrate; point out

'**auf·zie·hen** (*irr.*, *sep.*, → **ziehen**) **I.** *v/t.* (h) **1.** draw up, pull up; hoist *flag*, *sail*; open *curtains*; *thea.* raise *curtain*; weigh *anchor*; (pull) open *drawer*; **2.** wind up *clock*, *toy etc.*; ***zum*** ⚘ clockwork *mouse etc.*; **3.** mount *photo etc.*; put on *strings*, *tires etc.*; *fig.* **andere Saiten ~** change one's tune; **4.** bring up, raise *child*, rear, raise *animal*; **5.** organize; arrange *party etc.*; set up *business etc.*; **6.** ***j-n ~*** F wind s.o. up, pull s.o.'s leg; tease s.o. (***wegen*** about); **II.** *v/i.* (sn) **7.** *thunderstorm*: come up; *clouds*: gather; **8.** ⚔ march up; *guard*: come on duty

'**Auf·zucht** *f* (-; *no pl.*) breeding, rearing

'**Auf·zug** *m* (-[e]s; ⸚e) **1.** lift, *Am.* elevator; **2.** parade; procession; **3.** F outfit; **4.** *thea.* act; **5.** *gym.* pull-up; '**Auf·zugs·schacht** *m* lift (*Am.* elevator) shaft

'**auf·zwin·gen** (*irr.*, *sep.*, h, → **zwingen**) **I.** *v/t.*: ***j-m et. ~*** force (*or* foist) s.th. on s.o., force s.o. into (doing) s.th.; **II.** *v/refl.*: ***sich j-m ~*** *idea etc.*: impinge (on s.o.)

Aug·ap·fel ['aʊkʔapfəl] *m* (-s; ⸚) eyeball; ***wie s-n ~ hüten*** guard with one's life

Au·ge ['aʊgə] *n* (-s; -n) **1.** eye; ***gute*** (***schlechte***) ***~n haben*** have good (bad) eyesight; ***die ~n aufmachen*** keep one's eyes open; ***im ~ behalten*** keep an eye on, *fig.* bear in mind; ***im ~ haben*** have in mind; ***ein ~ haben auf*** *acc.* have one's eye on; ***mit eigenen ~n*** with one's own eyes; ***ich hab's mit eigenen ~n gesehen*** *a.* it happened before my very eyes; ***unter j-s ~n*** before s.o.'s very eyes; ***unter vier ~n*** in private; ***Gespräch unter vier ~n*** private conversation; ***vor aller ~n*** in front of everyone, in full view (of everyone); ***wo hast du d-e ~n?, hast du keine ~n im Kopf?*** are you blind?; ***da blieb kein ~ trocken*** *a. iro.* there wasn't a dry eye in the place; ***mit e-m lachenden und e-m weinenden ~*** with mixed feelings; ***das ~ des Gesetzes*** the (sharp) eye of the law; ***aus den ~, aus dem Sinn*** out of sight, out of mind; ***vor et. die ~n verschließen*** refuse to see s.th.; ***vor m-m geistigen ~*** in my mind's eye; ***in m-n ~n*** as I see it; ***etwas fürs ~*** a feast for the eyes; ***nur fürs ~*** just for show; ***soweit das ~ reicht*** as far as the eye can see; ***j-m in die ~n sehen*** look into s.o.'s eyes; ***sieh mir mal in die ~n*** look at me; ***er konnte mir nicht in die ~n sehen*** he couldn't look me in the eye; ***j-m unter die ~n treten können*** be able to look s.o. in the face; ***den Tatsachen ins ~ sehen*** face (up to) the facts; ***~ in ~*** face to face (***mit*** with); ***aus den ~n verlieren*** lose sight of, *fig.* lose touch with; ***nicht aus den ~n lassen*** not to let *s.o. or s.th.* out of one's sight; (***e-m***) ***ins ~ springen*** catch one's eye, hit one in the eye; ***e-m in die ~n stechen*** a) take one's fancy, b) glare at one; ***ein ~ zudrücken*** turn a blind eye (***bei*** to); ***er wird große ~n machen!*** he's in for a surprise; ***er hat große ~n gemacht!*** you should have seen his face; ***s-e ~n sind größer als sein Magen*** his eyes are bigger than his stomach; ***sie haben sich die ~n aus dem Kopf geschaut*** F they just goggled, their eyes were popping out of their heads; ***sich die ~n aus dem Kopf weinen*** cry one's eyes out; ***etwas im ~ haben*** have something in one's eye, *fig.* have one's eye on s.th.; ***sie hat ihre ~n überall*** she's got eyes like a hawk; ***ich kann m-e ~n nicht überall haben*** I can't keep track of everything; ***vier ~n sehen mehr als zwei*** two pairs of eyes are better than one; ***ich hab' doch hinten keine ~n*** I haven't got eyes in the back of my head; ***ins ~ fassen*** consider; ***ins ~ gefaßt haben*** be considering, be planning; ***j-m*** (***schöne***) ***~n machen*** make eyes at s.o.; ***er hat kein***(***e***) ***~***(***n***) ***dafür*** he hasn't got an eye for that; ***j-m die ~n öffnen*** enlighten s.o., open s.o.'s eyes to the truth, be an eye-opener (for s.o.); ***mir gingen plötzlich die ~n auf*** suddenly I saw the light; ***kein ~ zutun*** not to sleep a wink (all night); ***et. mit anderen ~n ansehen*** see s.th. in a different light; ***sich et. vor ~n halten*** keep s.th. in mind; ***j-m et. vor ~n führen*** make s.th. clear to s.o.; ***das hätte leicht ins ~ gehen können*** that was close (*or* a close one), it could easily have backfired; ***geh mir aus den ~n!*** get out of my sight!; ***~ um ~***(***, Zahn um Zahn***) an eye for an eye(, a tooth for a tooth); → ***blau*** 1, ***blind*** 1, ***bloß*** 1, ***Dorn, Faust, trauen***[1] I, ***verderben*** I; **2.** *playing card, dice*: pip; ⚘, *zo. and fig.* eye; **3.** globule of fat

'**Au·gen|ab·stand** *m* distance between the (*or* one's) eyes, 📖 interocular distance; **~arzt** *m* eye specialist, 📖 ophthalmologist; **~auf·schlag** *m* blink; **~aus·wi·sche,rei** *f* (-; *no pl.*) eyewash; **~bad** *n* eye bath; **~bin·de** *f* eye bandage

'**Au·gen·blick** *m* moment; (***einen***) ***~!*** one moment (*or* just a minute), please; ***im ~*** at the moment; ***für den ~*** for the time being; ***im letzten ~*** at the last minute, *a.* just in time; ***im ersten ~*** for a moment; ***im richtigen ~*** at the right moment; ***in diesem ~*** at this moment (in time); ***ich erwarte ihn jeden ~*** he should be here any minute, I'm expecting him any minute; ***alle ~e*** constantly; ***in dem ~, als ich ihn sah*** the moment I saw him; → *a.* ***Moment***[1]; '**au·gen·blick·lich** **I.** *adj.* immediate; present; ***die ~e Lage*** the situation at present (*or* at the moment); **II.** *adv.* at the moment, just now; immediately

'**Au·gen·blicks|er·folg** *m* short-lived (*or* fleeting) success; **~mensch** *m* spontaneous person; **~stim·mung** *f*: ***aus e-r ~ heraus*** on the spur of the moment

'**Au·gen·braue** *f* eyebrow; '**Au·gen·brau·en·stift** *m* eyebrow pencil

'**Au·gen·druck** *m* (-[e]s; *no pl.*) intraocular pressure

'**au·gen·fäl·lig** *adj.* conspicuous; striking; obvious

'**Au·gen|fält·chen** *pl.* wrinkles around the eyes; **~far·be** *f* colo(u)r of s.o.'s eyes; ***was hat er für e-e ~?*** what colo(u)r are his eyes?; **~feh·ler** *m* eye defect; **~flim·mern** *n* spots *pl.* before one's eyes; **~heil·kun·de** *f* ophthalmology; **~hö·he** *f*: ***in ~*** at eye level; **~hö·hle** *f* eye socket, 📖 orbit(al cavity); **~klap·pe** *f* eye patch; **~kli·nik** *f* eye clinic; **~krank·heit** *f* eye disease; eye complaint; **~lei·den** *n* eye complaint; ***ein ~ haben*** *a.* have something wrong with one's eyes; **~licht** *n* (-[e]s; *no pl.*) eyesight; ***das ~ verlieren*** *a.* lose the sight of one's eyes; **~lid** *n* eyelid; **~maß** *n* (-es; *no pl.*) sense of distance; ***et. nach ~ einschätzen*** guess (at) the distance of s.th.; ***nach ~ würde ich sagen ...*** at a glance I'd say ...; ***ein gutes ~ haben*** have a good eye for distances, *fig.* be good at sizing things up; *fig.* ***Politik mit ~*** policy of moderation; **~mensch** *m* visual person; **~merk** *n*: ***sein ~ richten auf*** turn one's attention to; **~mus·kel** *m* eye muscle; **~nerv** *m* optic nerve; **~paar** *n* pair of eyes; **~pfle·ge** *f* **1.** eyecare; **2.** F ***~ machen*** F get a bit of shuteye; **~pul·ver** F *n* microscopic print; ***das ist ja das reinste ~*** you'd go blind trying to read that; **~rand** *m* **1.** rim of the (*or* one's) eye; ***gerötete Augenränder*** red-rimmed eyes; **2.** *pl.* → **~rin·ge** *pl.* rings under one's eyes; **~sal·be** *f* eye ointment; **~schein** *m* (-[e]s; *no pl.*) **1.** appearance; ***dem ~ nach*** to all appearances; ***der ~ trügt*** appearances are deceptive, don't be (*or* we mustn't be) deceived by appearances; **2.** examination, inspection; ⚖ (judicial) inspection; ***in ~ nehmen*** examine, inspect, take a close look at; **~schirm** *m* eyeshade; **~schmaus** *m* feast for the eyes; **~spie·gel** *m* ophthalmoscope; **~spra·che** *f* visual communication, F eye talk; **~täu·schung** *f* optical illusion; **~trop·fen** *pl.* eye drops; **~wei·de** *f* feast for the eyes; **~wim·per** *f* eyelash; **~win·kel** *m* corner of the (*or* one's) eye; ***j-n*** (***et.***) ***aus den ~n beobachten*** watch s.o. (s.th.) out of the corner of one's eye; **~wi·sche,rei** *f* (-; *no pl.*) eyewash; **~zahl** *f* number (of points); **~zahn** *m* eye-tooth

'**Au·gen·zeu·ge** *m* eye-witness; '**Au·gen·zeu·gen·be·richt** *m* eye-witness account

'**Au·gen·zwin·kern** *n* wink(ing); '**au·gen·zwin·kernd** *adv.* with a wink; with a twinkle in one's eye

Au·gi·as·stall [aʊ'giːas-] *m* Augean stables *pl.*

...äugig [-ɔʏgɪç] ...-eyed

Au·gur [aʊ'guːɐ] *m* (-s, -en; -en [aʊ'guːrən]) *pol.* pundit

Au·gust[1] [aʊ'gʊst] *m* (-[e]s; -e) August; ***im ~*** in August

Au·gust[2] ['aʊgʊst] *m*: ***dummer ~*** clown, *contp.* idiot

Au·gu·sti·ner [aʊgʊs'tiːnɐ-] *m* (-s; -), **~mönch** *m* Augustinian (monk), *Brit. a.* Austin friar; **~or·den** *m* Augustininan order

Auk·ti·on [aʊk'tsĭoːn] *f* (-; -en) auction; ***in die ~ geben*** put up for auction; ***zur ~ kommen*** be auctioned, come under the hammer; **Auk·tio·na·tor** [aʊktsĭo'naːtoːɐ] *m* (-s; -en [-na'toːrən]) auctioneer; **auk·tio·nie·ren** [aʊktsĭo'niːrən] *v/t.* (h) auction; **Auk·ti'ons·haus** *n* auctioneers *pl.*

Au·la ['aʊla] *f* (-; -s, Aulen) assembly hall, *Am.* auditorium

Au-pair-Mäd·chen [o'pɛːrmɛːtçən] *n* (-s; -) au pair (girl)

Au·ra ['aʊra] *f* (-; *no pl.*) *ast.*, ⚕ *and fig.* aura

Au·re·ole [aure'oːlə] *f* (-; -n) *ast.* aureole, halo, ring

aus [aʊs] **I.** *prp.* (*dat.*) out of; from; of; ***~ dem Fenster*** out of (*Am. a.* out) the window; ***~ e-m Glas trinken*** drink out of (*or* from) a glass; ~ **Holz** made of wood, wooden ...; **j-d ~ der Nachbarschaft** somebody from the neighbo(u)rhood; ~ **Berlin** from Berlin; ~ **Angst** (**Mitleid, Achtung**) out of fear (pity, respect); ~ **Angst vor** for fear of; ~ **Liebe** for love; ~ **zuverlässiger Quelle** on good authority; ~ **diesem Grund** for this reason; ~ **der Zeit Cromwells** from the time of Cromwell; ~ **dem Rokoko** from the rococo period; ~ **der Zeitung** from the newspaper; ~ **dem Englischen** from (the) English, **übersetzt**: translated from the English (original); ~ **dem Projekt ist nichts geworden** nothing came of the project; ~ **sich selbst heraus** of one's own accord; → **Erfahrung, Haß, Prinzip**; **II.** *adv.* → **aussein**; ~! *sport*: out!; **Licht** ~! lights out!; ~, **basta!** that's (*or* that was) that, and that's that, I don't want to hear another word; **von Zypern** ~ from Cyprus, *besuchen wir einige andere Länder*: using Cyprus as a base; **von mir** ~ I don't mind, I'm not bothered; **von mir ~ könnt ihr gehen** you can go as far as I'm concerned; → **an** 7, **ein²**, **Traum**; **III.** ♀ *n* (-; *no pl.*) *sport*: **im** (*or* **ins**) ~ out

'**aus·ar·bei·ten** (*sep.*, h) **I.** *v/t.* draw up *plan etc.*; complete; finish; **II.** *v/refl.*: **sich** (**körperlich**) ~ work out; '**Aus·ar·bei·tung** *f* (-; -en) drawing up; completion

'**aus·ar·ten** *v/i.* (*sep.*, sn) **1.** ~ **in** *acc.* turn into; **2.** go too far

'**aus·at·men** *v/i. and v/t.* (*sep.*, h) breathe out; 🕮 exhale; '**Aus·at·mung** *f* (-; -en) exhalation

'**aus·backen** (*sep.* -k·k-) *v/t.* (*sep.*, h) deep-fry

'**aus·ba·den** *fig. v/t.* (*sep.*, h) carry the can for, F take the rap for; **die Sache** ~ (**müssen**) (have to) carry the can (F take the rap)

'**aus·bag·gern** *v/t.* (*sep.*, h) dig out, excavate; dredge out *canal etc.*; dredge up *mud etc.*

'**aus·ba·lan,cie·ren** *v/t.* (*sep.*, h) balance (out); *fig.* balance out; *fig.* **gegeneinander** ~ balance out (*or* off) against each other

aus·bal·do·wern ['aʊsbaldoːvɐn] F *v/t.* (*sep.*, h) F nose out, *sl.* suss out

'**Aus·bau** *m* (-[e]s; *no pl.*) **1.** ⚠ completion; extension; **2.** *fig.* development, improvement; **3.** ⚙ removal; '**aus·bau·en** *v/t.* (*sep.*, h) **1.** ⚠ finish; extend; convert *attic etc.*; **2.** *fig.* develop, improve; **die Führung** ~ *sport*: increase one's lead; **3.** ⚙ remove; '**aus·bau·fä·hig** *adj.* capable of development; *job* with good prospects

'**Aus·bau|strecke** (*sep.* -k·k-) *f mot.* (motorway) extension; ~**woh·nung** *f* extension flat, *Brit. a.* F granny annexe

'**aus·be·din·gen** *v/t.* (*irr.*, *sep.*, h, → **bedingen**): **sich et.** ~ insist on s.th.; **sich** ~, **daß** stipulate that, make it a condition that

'**aus·bei·ßen** *v/t.* (*irr.*, *sep.*, h, → **beißen**): **sich e-n Zahn** ~ break a tooth (**an** *dat.* on); *fig.* **sich die Zähne an et.** ~ find s.th. a tough nut to crack

'**aus·bes·sern** *v/t.* (*sep.*, h) mend, repair; correct; touch up *painting etc.*; '**Aus·bes·se·rung** *f* (-; -en) correction; repair; '**Aus·bes·se·rungs·ar·bei·ten** *pl.* repairs, repair work *sg.*; '**aus·bes·se·rungs·be·dürf·tig** *adj.* in need of repair

'**aus·be·to,nie·ren** *v/t.* (*sep.*, h) concrete (*s.th.* over)

'**aus·beu·len** (*sep.*, h) **I.** *v/t.* **1. du hast d-e Hose ganz ausgebeult** your trousers have gone all baggy; → **ausgebeult** II; **2.** ⚙ *mot.* beat out; **II.** *v/refl.*: **sich** ~ go baggy

'**Aus·beu·te** *f* (-; *no pl.*) gain(s *pl.*), profit; yield, output (*a.* ⚙ *and* ⚒); *fig.* results *pl.*; *fig.* **die ~ war gering** nothing much came out of it; **e-e reiche** ~ rich pickings; **aus·beu·ten** ['aʊsbɔʏtən] *v/t.* (*sep.*, h) exploit; **Aus·beu·ter** ['aʊsbɔʏtɐ] *m* (-s; -) slave-driver; **aus·beu·te·risch** ['aʊsbɔʏtərɪʃ] *adj.* exploitative; **Aus·beu·tung** ['aʊsbɔʏtʊŋ] *f* (-; *no pl.*) exploitation

'**aus·be·zah·len** *v/t.* (*sep.*, h) pay out; pay *s.o.* off

'**aus·bil·den** (*sep.*, h) **I.** *v/t.* **1.** educate; instruct, train; ⚔ train, drill; *sport*: train, coach; **2.** develop; **II.** *v/refl.*: **sich** ~ (*a.* **sich ~ lassen**) train; study (**zu** to be); **sich ~ in** *dat.* learn (something) about; → **ausgebildet** II; **Aus·bil·der** ['aʊsbɪldɐ] *m* (-s; -) instructor (*a.* ⚔); '**Aus·bil·dung** *f* (-; -en) **1.** training; *univ.* education; **2.** development

'**Aus·bil·dungs|bei·hil·fe** *f* grant, *Am. a.* tuition aid; ~**be·ruf** *m* qualified job; ~**dau·er** *f* training (*or* qualification) period; **die ~ für e-n Ingenieur beträgt sechs Jahre** *a.* it takes six years to become an engineer; ~**för·de·rung** *f* **1.** a) promotion of vocational training, b) educational advancement; **2.** grant(s *pl.*); ~**ko·sten** *pl.* cost *sg.* of studying (*or* of a period of training, of a traineeship); ~**la·ger** *n* training camp; ~**mög·lich·kei·ten** *pl.* training opportunities; opportunities for studying; ~**platz** *m* traineeship; apprenticeship; ~**zeit** *f* → **Ausbildungsdauer**

'**aus·bit·ten** *v/t.* (*irr.*, *sep.*, h, → **bitten**): **sich et.** ~ ask for s.th.; expect s.th.

'**aus·bla·sen** *v/t.* (*irr.*, *sep.*, h, → **blasen**) blow out

'**aus·blei·ben** (*irr.*, *sep.*, sn, → **bleiben**) **I.** *v/i.* not to take place; *rain*: not to come; *pulse etc.*: stop; not to come (*or* turn up); stay away; **es konnte nicht** ~, **daß** it was inevitable that; **die Periode blieb bei ihr aus** she missed her period; **II.** ♀ *n* (-s) absence; non-payment; ⚖ default

'**aus·blei·chen** (*irr.*, *sep.*, → **bleichen**) **I.** *v/t.* (h) bleach; **II.** *v/i.* (sn) bleach, fade

'**aus·blen·den** (*sep.*, h) **I.** *v/t.* fade out; **II.** *v/refl.*: **sich** ~ go off the air, leave the (*or* a) broadcast

'**Aus·blick** *m* (-[e]s; -e) view (**auf** *acc.* of); *fig.* forward look (at), outlook (for), prospects *pl.* (for)

'**aus·blü·hen** *v/i.* (*sep.*, h) **1.** ⚘ **ausgeblüht haben** be finished; **2.** ⚗, *min.* effloresce

'**aus·blu·ten** *v/i.* (*sep.*, h) **1.** stop bleeding; ~ **lassen** allow *wound* to bleed; bleed *animal*; **2.** *fig.* be bled white; → **ausgeblutet** II

'**aus·boh·ren** *v/t.* (*sep.*, h) **1.** drill (out); **2.** drill *tooth*

'**aus·bom·ben** *v/t.* (*sep.*, h) bomb out

aus·boo·ten ['aʊsboːtən] *v/t.* (*sep.*, h) **1.** ⚓ take ashore; **2.** *fig.* oust, get rid of

'**aus·bor·gen** *v/t.* (*sep.*, h): **sich et.** ~ borrow s.th.; **j-m et.** ~ lend s.o. s.th., lend s.th. (out) to s.o.

'**aus·bre·chen** (*irr.*, *sep.*, → **brechen**) **I.** *v/t.* (h) break out (*or* off); quarry out; **II.** *v/i.* (sn) *volcano*: erupt; *fire, war, epidemic etc.*: break out; *prisoner*: break out (**aus** *dat.* of), escape (from); *fig.*, *a. sport*: break away (from); *horse*: bolt; *car*: swerve; **in Schweiß** ~ break out in a sweat; **in Beifall** ~ break into applause; **in Gelächter** (**Tränen**) ~ burst out laughing (crying); '**Aus·bre·cher** *m* (-s; -) escaped convict

'**aus·brei·ten** (*sep.*, h) **I.** *v/t.* **1.** spread (out); **2.** *fig.* extend; expand; **II.** *v/refl.*: **sich** ~ **3.** spread, stretch (out), extend (*all* **auf** *acc.* to); **4.** F spread o.s. out; **mußt du dich so ~?** do you have to take up so much room?; **5.** *fire, rumo(u)r, epidemic etc.*: spread (**auf** *acc.* to); **sich ~ auf** *acc. fighting etc.*: *a.* spill over into; **6.** go into detail, **über** *acc.*: enlarge on *a subject etc.*; '**Aus·breit·ung** *f* (-; *no pl.*) spreading; extension; expansion

'**aus·bren·nen** (*irr.*, *sep.*, → **brennen**) **I.** *v/t.* (h) **1.** burn out; ⚕ cauterize; **II.** *v/i.* (sn) **2.** burn (itself) out, go out; **3.** *building etc.*: be burnt out, be gutted; be scorched; → **ausgebrannt** II

'**aus·brin·gen** *v/t.* (*irr.*, *sep.*, h, → **bringen**) **1.** lower, launch *boat*; drop *anchor*; **2.** sow; spread *manure etc.*; **3. e-n Trinkspruch ~ auf** *acc.* propose a toast to; **4.** *typ.* space out

'**Aus·bruch** *m* (-[e]s; ⸚e) outbreak *of war, of an epidemic etc.*; eruption *of volcano*; escape, breakout *of prisoners*; *fig.* (*emotional*) outburst; **zum ~ kommen** break out, *fig. a.* erupt, explode; '**aus·bruch·si·cher** *adj.* escape-proof; '**Aus·bruchs·ver·such** *m* escape attempt

'**aus·brü·ten** *v/t.* (*sep.*, h) **1.** hatch out; incubate; **2.** *fig.* hatch *plan, plot etc.*; F be coming down with *flu etc.*

'**Aus·buch·tung** *f* (-; -en) projection; ⚙ *a.* protrusion; *geogr.* indentation

'**aus·bud·deln** F *v/t.* (*sep.*, h) dig up

'**aus·bü·geln** *v/t.* (*sep.*, h) iron out (*a.* F *fig.*)

'**aus·bu·hen** *v/t.* (*sep.*, h) boo

'**Aus·bund** *m* (-[e]s; *no pl.*) model (**an** *dat.*, **von** of); **ein ~ an Tugend** a paragon of virtue; **ein ~ von Bosheit** a real villain

aus·bür·gern ['aʊsbʏrgɐn] *v/t.* (*sep.*, h) denaturalize; **Aus·bür·ge·rung** ['aʊsbʏrgərʊŋ] *f* (-; -en) expatriation

'**aus·bür·sten** *v/t.* (*sep.*, h) brush; brush down *coat etc.*; brush out *stain etc.*

aus·bü·xen ['aʊsbʏksən] F *v/i.* (*sep.*, sn) run away (from home); F do a bunk

'**aus·checken** (*sep.* -k·k-) *v/i.* (*sep.*, h) check out (**aus** *dat.* of)

'**Aus·dau·er** *f* (-; *no pl.*) staying power; perseverance; tenacity; patience; stamina; '**Aus·dau·er·gren·ze** *f* (physical) limit; '**aus·dau·ernd I.** *adj.* persevering; enduring; tenacious; tireless; **II.** *adv.*: ~ **lernen können** be able to study for long stretches; '**Aus·dau·er·trai·ning** *n* stamina training

'**aus·dehn·bar** *adj.* ⚙ extensible; ✝ expansible; '**aus·deh·nen** (*sep.*, h) **I.** *v/t.* a) stretch; *fig.* extend (**auf** *acc.* to); *phys.*, ⚙ *and fig.* expand; b) extend, prolong; → **ausgedehnt** II; **II.** *v/refl.*: **sich** ~ a) spread; expand; b) extend, stretch (out); c) last, extend, *contp.* drag on; **sich rasch ~ über** *acc. a.* sweep across; '**Aus·deh·nung** *f* (-, -en) extension (*a. phys.*), expansion, spread; extent, scope, range

'aus·den·ken *v/t.* (*irr.*, *sep.*, h, → **denken**): **sich** *et.* ~ think *s.th.* up, come up with; work out; dream up; **es ist nicht auszudenken** it doesn't bear thinking about, it's too dreadful to think about, the mind boggles (at the thought); **da mußt du dir schon was anderes ~** you don't think I'm going to buy that(, do you?)

'aus·deu·ten *v/t.* (*sep.*, h) interpret; **falsch ~** misinterpret

'aus·die·nen *v/i.* (*sep.*, h): **ausgedient haben** have retired; F have had its day

'aus·dis·ku,tie·ren *v/t.* (*sep.*, h) F thrash out

'aus·dör·ren (*sep.*) **I.** *v/i.* (sn) dry up; become parched; **m-e Kehle ist wie ausgedörrt** my throat's absolutely parched; **II.** *v/t.* (h) dry up, parch

'aus·dre·hen *v/t.* (*sep.*, h) turn off; switch off

'Aus·druck¹ *m* (-[e]s; ¨e) **1.** *no pl.* expression; **~ geben** (*or* **verleihen**) (*dat.*) put into words, express; **zum ~ bringen** express, voice; **zum ~ kommen** be expressed; **der Erwartung ~ geben, daß** express the hope that; **ohne jeden ~** in a deadpan tone; **er hat mit viel ~ gesprochen** he put a lot of expression into it (*or* his speech *etc.*); → **Ausdrucksweise; 2.** expression, phrase; word, term; **ärgerlich? - das ist gar kein ~** angry is not the word

'Aus·druck² *m* (-[e]s; -e) *computer*: printout

'aus·drucken (*sep.* -k·k-) *v/t.* (*sep.*, h) print; *computer*: print out; print in full

'aus·drücken (*sep.* -k·k-) (*sep.*, h) **I.** *v/t.* **1.** squeeze; squeeze *s.th.* out (**aus** *dat.* of); stub out *cigarette etc*; **2.** express, put into words; **anders ausgedrückt** in other words, to put it another way; **einfach ausgedrückt** to put it simply (*or* in simple terms); **3.** express, show; **II.** *v/refl.*: **sich ~** express o.s.; be revealed;

aus·drück·lich ['aʊsdrʏklɪç] **I.** *adj.* express; explicit; strict *order*; **II.** *adv.* expressly; specially

'Aus·drucks·kraft *f* (-; *no pl.*) expressiveness

'aus·drucks·los *adj.* expressionless; blank *look etc.*; **~es Gesicht** poker face

'aus·drucks·stark *adj.* very expressive

'Aus·drucks|tanz *m* character dance; **~ver·mö·gen** *n* ability to express o.s., powers *pl.* of expression, articulatory powers *pl.*

'aus·drucks·voll *adj.* (very) expressive; meaningful *look etc.*

'Aus·drucks·wei·se *f* way of expressing o.s.; style; *w.s.* language

aus·dün·nen ['aʊsdʏnən] *v/t.* (*sep.*, h) thin out

'aus·dun·sten, 'aus·dün·sten (*sep.*, h) **I.** *v/t.* give off; **II.** *v/i.* evaporate; transpire (*a.* ♣), perspire; **'Aus·dun·stung** *f*, **'Aus·dün·stung** *f* (-; -en) emanation; evaporation; perspiration

aus·ein'an·der *adv.* apart; separated; **et. ~ schreiben** write s.th. as two words; **weit ~ liegen** a) be a long way away from each other, b) be years (*or* decades *etc.*) apart; **weit ~ stehen** *eyes*: be wide-set, *lines*: have big gaps (between them); **sie sind nicht weit ~** they're quite close in age, there's not much between them; **sie sind drei Jahre ~** they're three years apart, there are three years between them; **~ setzen** separate, make *the children* sit apart; **~ sein** have split up; **~be·kom·men** *v/t.* (*irr.*, *sep.*, h, → **bekommen**) get *s.th.* apart; **~bie·gen** *v/t.* (*irr.*, *sep.*, h, → **biegen**) bend *s.th.* apart; **~bre·chen** (*irr.*, *sep.*, → **brechen**) **I.** *v/t.* (h) break (up), break in two; **II.** *v/i.* (sn) break (apart); *fig.* break up; **~brin·gen** *v/t.* (*irr.*, *sep.*, h, → **bringen**) separate, split up; get *s.th.* apart; **~di·vi,die·ren** *v/t.* (*sep.*, h) **1.** break down *bill etc.*; **2.** *fig.* draw a clear dividing line between *opinions etc.*; **3.** *fig.* drive a wedge between *people*; **~fah·ren** *fig.* *v/i.* (*irr.*, *sep.*, sn, → **fahren**) jump (*or* jerk) apart; **~fal·len** *v/i.* (*irr.*, *sep.*, sn, → **fallen**) fall apart (*or* to pieces); disintegrate; **~fal·ten** *v/t.* (*sep.*, h) unfold, *a.* spread out *map etc.*, *a.* open up *newspaper etc.*; **~flie·hen** *v/i.* (*irr.*, *sep.*, sn, → **fliehen**) scatter (in all directions); **~ge·hen** *v/i.* (*irr.*, *sep.*, sn, → **gehen**) **1.** say goodbye; *crowd*: break up, disperse; **2.** *lovers, friends etc.*: split up, break up, go one's separate ways; **3.** *friendship, marriage*: break up; *engagement*: be broken off; **4.** *lines, paths etc.*: diverge; **5.** *opinions*: be divided; **6.** F fill out; **~hal·ten** *fig.* *v/t.* (*irr.*, *sep.*, h, → **halten**) distinguish (between); tell *things* apart; **~klaf·fen** *v/i.* (*sep.*, h) gape; *fig.* *opinions etc.*: differ enormously; **~kla·mü·sern** [-kla,myːzɐn] F *v/t.* (*sep.*, h) **1.** sort out; **2. j-m et. ~** spell s.th. out to s.o.; **~krie·gen** F *v/t.* (*sep.*, h) get *s.th.* apart; **~lau·fen** *v/i.* (*irr.*, *sep.*, sn, → **laufen**) **1.** *lines, paths*: diverge; **2.** *paint etc.*: run; **3.** go one's separate ways; **~le·ben** *v/refl.* (*sep.*, h): **sich ~** drift apart; **~neh·men** *v/t.* (*irr.*, *sep.*, h, → **nehmen**) take apart (*a.* F *fig.*); **~rei·ßen** *v/t.* (*irr.*, *sep.*, h, → **reißen**) tear apart

aus·ein'an·der·set·zen (*sep.*, h) **I.** *v/t.* explain (*dat.* to); **II.** *v/refl.*: **sich mit j-m ~** argue with s.o., F have it out with s.o.; **sich mit** *e-m Problem etc.* **~** go into, tackle, grapple with *a problem etc.*; **Aus·ein'an·der·set·zung** *f* (-; -en) **1.** analysis (**mit** of); *a.* attempt to come to terms *with a problem*; **2.** discussion; argument; *esp. pol.* dispute, confrontation, conflict; clash(es *pl.*); → **bewaffnet, blutig** 2

aus·ein'an·der|spren·gen *v/t.* (*sep.*, h) blow up; *fig.* disperse, scatter *crowd etc.*; **~trei·ben** (*irr.*, *sep.*, → **treiben**) **I.** *v/i.* (sn) drift apart; **II.** *v/t.* (h) scatter; **~zie·hen** (*irr.*, *sep.*, h, → **ziehen**) **I.** *v/t.* pull apart; stretch; **II.** *v/refl.*: **sich ~** string out

'aus·er·ko·ren *adj.* chosen

'aus·er·le·sen I. *v/t.* → **ausersehen; II.** *adj.* choice; select

'aus·er·se·hen *v/t.* (*irr.*, *sep.*, h, → **ersehen**) choose, select (**für, zu** for); designate (for *an office etc.*)

'aus·er·wäh·len *v/t.* (*sep.*, h) choose; **'aus·er·wählt** *adj.*: **das ~e Volk** the Chosen People; **die Ձen** the elect, the chosen few; F **s-e Ձe** F his number one girl; F **ihr Ձer** F her number one man

'aus·es·sen (*irr.*, *sep.*, h, → **essen**) **I.** *v/t.* eat up; empty, eat *one's plate* clean; **II.** *v/i.* finish eating

'aus·fä·deln (*sep.*, h) **I.** *v/i.* *mot.* filter out (**aus** *dat.* of), get into the exit lane; **II.** *v/refl.*: **sich aus** *e-m Bündnis etc.* **~** weave one's way out of an alliance *etc.*

'aus·fahr·bar *adj.* ⚙ telescopic; extendible; **'aus·fah·ren** (*irr.*, *sep.*, → **fahren**) **I.** *v/i.* (sn) **1.** go for a drive; **2.** 🚂 pull out; ⚓ put to sea; **3.** ⚒ come up, leave the pit; **4. aus j-m ~** *evil spirit etc.*: leave s.o.('s body); **II.** *v/t.* (h) **5.** take *s.o.* out for a drive (*or* walk); **6.** deliver; **7.** ✈ lower *undercarriage*; pull out, extend *antenna etc.*; **8.** *mot.* run *the engine* up to top speed; utilize *plant etc.* to capacity; **9.** round *bend*; **10.** rut *path, road etc.*; **'Aus·fah·rer** *m* (-s; -) delivery man; **'Aus·fahrt** *f* (-; -en) **1.** exit, driveway; **2.** drive, ride; **3.** *a.* ⚓ departure; **4.** ⚒ ascent

'Aus·fall *m* (-[e]s; ¨e) **1.** loss; **2.** cancellation *of lessons etc.*; **3.** absence; dropping out; **4.** ⚙ failure, breakdown; **5.** F *sport*: **ein glatter ~** F a dead loss; **6.** *fencing*: pass, thrust, *a.* *gym.* lunge; **7.** ⚔ sally, sortie; **8.** *fig.* invective, abuse; **~bürg·schaft** *f* (-; -en) ✝ deficiency guarantee

'aus·fal·len *v/i.* (*irr.*, *sep.*, sn, → **fallen**) **1.** *teeth, hair*: fall out; **2.** be cancelled, be called off; **die Schule fällt heute aus** (there's) no school today; **3.** ⚙ break down; **bei uns ist der Strom ausgefallen** we've had a power cut; **4. zu kurz ~** *dress etc.*: be too short; **die Rockmode fällt kürzer aus** hemlines are going up; **gut** (**schlecht**) **~** turn out well (badly), *examination etc.*: go well (badly); **wie ist die Prüfung ausgefallen?** how did you do in the exam?

'aus·fäl·len *v/t.* (*sep.*, h) ⚗ precipitate

'aus·fal·lend, 'aus·fäl·lig *adj.* offensive; **~ werden** get personal

'Aus·fall·quo·te *f* ✝ failure rate; *univ. etc.*: dropout rate

'Aus·fall(s)·er·schei·nung *f* ⚕ deficiency symptom

'aus·fall·si·cher *adj.* failsafe

'Aus·fall(s)·tor *fig.* *n* gateway

'Aus·fall|stra·ße *f* arterial road; **~win·kel** *m* angle of reflection; **~zeit** *f* ✝ down time; *insurance*: excluded period

'aus·fech·ten *v/t.* (*irr.*, *sep.*, h, → **fechten**) fight out; **mit j-m e-n Streit ~** F have it out with s.o.

'aus·fe·gen *v/t.* (*sep.*, h) sweep out

'aus·fei·len *v/t.* (*sep.*, h) file, smooth down; *fig.* polish, add the finishing touches to

'aus·fer·ti·gen *v/t.* (*sep.*, h) issue; ⚖ execute *deed etc.*; make out *bill etc.*; **'Aus·fer·ti·gung** *f* (-; -en) issuing; ⚖ execution; (certified) copy; **in doppelter ~** in duplicate; **schicken Sie den Antrag in dreifacher ~** send three copies of the application

'aus·fet·ten *v/t.* (*sep.*, h) grease *baking tin*

'aus·fil·tern *v/t.* (*sep.*, h) filter out

'aus·fin·dig *adv.*: **~ machen** find; trace

'aus·flie·gen (*irr.*, *sep.*, → **fliegen**) **I.** *v/i.* (sn) fly away; *bird*: leave the nest; F *fig.* **sie sind alle ausgeflogen** they're all out, there's nobody at home, *hum.* they've fled; **II.** *v/t.* (h) ✈ fly out

'aus·flie·ßen *v/i.* (*irr.*, *sep.*, sn, → **fließen**) run out, leak

aus·flip·pen ['aʊsflɪpən] F *v/i.* (*sep.*, sn) *sl.* freak out; *sl.* flip one's lid; → **ausgeflippt** II

'Aus·flucht *f* (-; Ausflüchte ['aʊsflʏçtə]) excuse; **Ausflüchte machen** make excuses, prevaricate; **keine Ausflüchte!** I don't want (to hear) any excuses

'Aus·flug *m* (-[e]s; ¨e) excursion (*a.* *fig.*), outing, trip; **e-n ~ machen** go on a trip;

Aus·flüg·ler ['aʊsfly:glɐ] *m* (-s; -) day tripper
'**Aus·flugs|damp·fer** *m* pleasure steamer; **~ort** *m* popular place for outings; *a.* beauty spot; **~ver·kehr** *m* **1.** weekend traffic; **2.** (bank) holiday traffic
'**Aus·fluß** *m* (-sses; ⸚sse) **1.** outflow; discharge; **2.** outlet; **3.** *fig.* product *of one's imagination etc.*; **~rohr** *n* discharge (*or* drainage) pipe
'**aus·for·men** (*sep.*, h) **I.** *v/t.* form, shape; **II.** *v/refl.*: **sich ~** form, take shape
'**aus·for·mu,lie·ren** *v/t.* (*sep.*, h) formulate (properly); ***ich muß es noch ~*** I still have to work out how to put it (properly)
'**Aus·for·mung** *f* (-; -en) form, shape
'**aus·for·schen** *v/t.* (*sep.*, h) **1.** seek out, find; *fig.* find out about *s.o.'s plans etc.*; get to the bottom of *s.th.*; **2. *j-n ~*** sound s.o. out (***über*** *acc.* on, about)
'**aus·fra·gen** *v/t.* (*sep.*, h) question, quiz; sound *s.o.* out; grill, F interrogate
'**aus·fran·sen** *v/i.* (*sep.*, sn) fray
'**aus·fres·sen** *v/t.* (*irr.*, *sep.*, h, → ***fressen***) **1.** *animal*: eat *s.th.* clean; suck out *egg*; F *person*: lick *s.th.* clean; **2.** *fig.* erode, wear away; **3.** F ***er hat wieder etwas ausgefressen*** he's been up to something (*or* his tricks, no good) again
'**Aus·fuhr** *f* (-; -en) ✝ **1.** *no pl.* export(ing); **2.** exports *pl.*; **~ar,ti·kel** *m* export(ed) article
'**aus·führ·bar** *adj.* **1.** practicable, feasible, workable; ***nicht ~*** impracticable, not feasible; **2.** ✝ exportable; '**Aus·führ·bar·keit** *f* (-; *no pl.*) practicability, feasibility
'**Aus·fuhr|be·schrän·kung** *f* export restriction; **~be·stim·mun·gen** *pl.* export regulations; **~be·wil·li·gung** *f* export licen|ce (*Am.* -se)
'**aus·füh·ren** *v/t.* (*sep.*, h) **1.** take *s.o.* out; take *a dog* for a walk; *hum.* ***e-n Mantel*** *etc.* **~** take a coat *etc.* for a walk; *hum.* ***j-m et. ~*** F swipe s.th. from s.o.; **2.** ✝ export; **3.** carry out *work, repairs etc.*; *a.* put *plan* into effect, execute *order, painting, dance step etc.*; realize *project etc.*; carry out, conduct *experiments etc.*; commit *crime*; perform *operation etc.*; do, paint *in oils etc.*; take *penalty kick*; ***diese Kirche ist von X ausgeführt*** this church was built by (*or* is the work of) X; **4.** explain; *a.* elaborate on; '**aus·füh·rend** *adj.* executive; '**Aus·füh·ren·de** *m, f* (-n; -n) soloist; singer; *pl.* performers; ***Sie hörten Ravels Streichquartett in F-Dur - die Ausführenden waren ...*** that was Ravel's string quartet in F major, performed by ...
'**Aus·fuhr|ge·neh·mi·gung** *f* export licen|ce (*Am.* -se); **~gü·ter** *pl.* exports; **~ha·fen** *m* port of exit; **~land** *n* exporting country
aus·führ·lich ['aʊsfy:rlɪç] **I.** *adj.* detailed; in-depth ...; long; comprehensive, full; ***~e Berichterstattung*** in-depth (*or* extended) coverage; ***könnten Sie etwas ~er sein?*** could you be more precise (*or* go into more detail)?; **II.** *adv.* in detail; in depth; ***sehr ~*** at great length, in great detail; ***~er*** in greater detail; '**Aus·führ·lich·keit** *f* (-; *no pl.*) detail(ed nature); comprehensiveness; ***et. in aller ~ beschreiben*** describe s.th. (down) to the last detail
'**Aus·fuhr|li·ste** *f* export list; **~prä·mie** *f* export bounty; **~quo·te** *f* export quota; **~sper·re** *f* export embargo
'**Aus·füh·rung** *f* (-; -en) **1.** *no pl.* carrying out, implementation; *a.* execution *of work, plan, order etc.*; realization *of project etc.*; perpetration *of crime*; ♪ performance; ⚠ construction; completion; ***zur ~ gelangen*** be carried out (*or* performed, built *etc.*); **2.** design; style; version; model; workmanship, quality; finish; **3.** exposition; ***~en*** comments, remarks, *pol. etc.* statement *sg.*, speech *sg.* (***zu*** *dat.*, ***über*** *acc.* on); '**Aus·füh·rungs·zeit** *f computer*: execution time
'**Aus·fuhr|ver·bot** *n* ban on exports; **~zoll** *m* export duty
'**aus·fül·len** *v/t.* (*sep.*, h) **1.** fill; fill in; **2.** fill in (*esp. Am.* out) *check, form etc.*, complete *form*; do, *a.* complete *crossword puzzle*; **3.** *fig.* fill; ***s-n Posten gewissenhaft ~*** do (*or* carry out) one's job very conscientiously; **4.** take up *time, space etc.*; ***die Sitzung füllte den ganzen Vormittag aus*** the meeting took up (*or* went on) the whole morning; **5. *die Abende mit Lesen ~*** spend the evenings reading; **6.** *fig.* ***j-n ~*** a) occupy s.o. completely, take up all (of) s.o.'s time, b) completely absorb s.o., c) fulfil(l) s.o.; ***sein Beruf füllt ihn ganz (nicht) aus*** his job fulfil(l)s him completely (doesn't fulfil[l] him, doesn't give him enough satisfaction)
'**aus·füt·tern** *v/t.* (*sep.*, h) line (*a.* ⚙)
'**Aus·ga·be** *f* (-; -n) **1.** *no pl.* handing out; distribution; **2.** edition; copy; issue, number; ***die letzte ~ der Tagesschau*** the late news headlines; **3.** *no pl.* issue *of stamps, shares, loan etc.*; **4.** expense, expenditure; *pl. a.* spending *sg.*; cost (*sg.*); **5.** *computer*: output; **7.** counter; desk; office; **~da,tei** *f computer*: output file; **~kurs** *m* ✝ issue price
'**Aus·ga·ben|buch** *n* accounts book; **~kür·zung** *f* expenditure cut, cut in expenditure
'**Aus·ga·be·stel·le** *f* issuing office
'**Aus·gang** *m* (-[e]s; ⸚e) **1.** way out, exit; ✈ (departure) gate; **2.** *no pl.* beginning; ***s-n ~ nehmen von*** start with; **3.** day (*or* afternoon, evening) off; ⚔ ***~ haben*** be on pass; ***mein erster ~ seit langem*** the first time I've been out for a long time; **4.** *pl.* outgoings; outgoing mail *sg.*; outgoing stocks; **5.** *no pl.* end; close; ending; outcome, upshot; ***tragischer ~*** tragic end(ing) *or* outcome; ***glücklicher ~*** happy end(ing); ***Unfall mit tödlichem ~*** fatal accident; ***e-n guten ~ nehmen*** turn out well (*or* all right, *Am.* alright) in the end; ***am ~ des Mittelalters*** at the end (*or* close) of the Middle Ages
'**Aus·gangs|ba·sis** *f* starting point; **~la·ge** *f* situation (*or* position) at the outset; initial situation; **~lei·stung** *f* ⚡ output; **~ma·te·ri,al** *n* source (*or* raw) material; **~po·si·ti,on** *f* starting position; point of departure; **~punkt** *m a. fig.* starting point, point of departure; **~si,gnal** *n* ⚡ output signal; **~sper·re** *f* curfew; ***e-e ~ verhängen über*** *acc.* impose a curfew on, put *a country etc.* under curfew; → ***nächtlich***; **~spra·che** *f* source language; **~stel·lung** *f* starting position; ⚔ line of departure; **~stoff** *m* basic material; **~stu·fe** *f* ⚡ output stage; *amplifier*: power stage; **~tür** *f* exit; **~,wi·der·stand** *m* ⚡ output resistance
'**aus·ge·ben** (*irr.*, *sep.*, h, → ***geben***) **I.** *v/t.* **1.** spend *money* (***für*** *acc.* on); hand out *baggage, food etc.*; deal *cards*; issue *order, shares, banknotes etc.*; *computer*: output, display, print out; ***wir haben (nicht) viel dafür ausgegeben*** we spent a lot of money on it (it wasn't very expensive); ***so viel wollte ich nicht ~*** I wasn't planning on spending that much; ***Geld mit vollen Händen ~*** F spend money like it's going out of style; F ***ich geb' dir einen aus*** let me buy (*or* get) you a drink; ***ich geb' einen aus*** this one's on me; **2. *die Wäsche ~*** take one's washing to the laundry; **3. *~ als*** pass *s.o. or s.th.* off as; **II.** *v/refl.*: **4. *sich ~ als*** (*or* ***für***) pass o.s. off as, pose as; ***er gibt sich als Computerexperte aus*** *a.* he tries to make himself out to be a computer expert; **5. *sich völlig ~*** drive o.s. to the limit
'**aus·ge·beult I.** *p.p. of* **ausbeulen**; **II.** *adj.* baggy *trousers etc.*
'**aus·ge·bil·det I.** *p.p. of* **ausbilden**; **II.** *adj.* trained; qualified; skilled *worker*
'**aus·ge·blu·tet I.** *p.p. of* **ausbluten**; **II.** *adj.*: ***~ sein*** have been bled white; ***er ist völlig ~*** *a.* he hasn't got a penny to his name
'**aus·ge·bombt I.** *p.p. of* **ausbomben**; **II.** *adj.* bombed-out
'**aus·ge·brannt I.** *p.p. of* **ausbrennen**; **II.** *adj.* burnt-out; gutted
'**aus·ge·bucht I.** *p.p. of* **ausbuchen**; **II.** *adj.* booked-out ..., *pred.* booked out; fully booked; ***auf Monate ~*** booked out for months ahead
aus·ge·bufft ['aʊsgəbʊft] F *adj.* F fly; ***ein ~er Profi*** F a real pro
'**Aus·ge·burt** *fig. f* (-; -en) **1.** monstrosity; excrescence; ***e-e ~ ihrer Phantasie*** a vile product of her imagination; **2. *er ist e-e ~ von Haß*** he's hatred incarnate
'**aus·ge·dehnt I.** *p.p. of* **ausdehnen**; **II.** *adj.* extensive (*a. fig.*); long; *fig.* ***weit ~*** far-flung; ***er genießt ein ~es Frühstück*** he likes to take his time over breakfast
'**aus·ge·drückt** *p.p. of* **ausdrücken**
'**aus·ge·fah·ren I.** *p.p. of* **ausfahren**; **II.** *adj.* rutted *path, road*; ***~e Spuren*** ruts; *fig.* ***sich auf ~en Gleisen bewegen*** keep to the beaten track
'**aus·ge·fal·len I.** *p.p. of* **ausfallen**; **II.** *adj.* unusual, F off-beat; *contp.* strange, weird; ***~e Größe*** odd size
'**aus·ge·feilt I.** *p.p. of* **ausfeilen**; **II.** *fig. adj.* polished
'**aus·ge·flippt** F **I.** *p.p. of* **ausflippen**; **II.** *adj.* F freaky; ***ein ~er Typ*** a real (*or* a bit of a) freak; '**Aus·ge·flipp·te** *m, f* (-n; -n) F freak
aus·ge·fuchst ['aʊsgəfʊkst] *adj.* sly
'**aus·ge·gli·chen I.** *p.p. of* **ausgleichen**; **II.** *adj.* well-balanced, well-adjusted; balanced *personality*; equable *climate*; ✝ balanced, settled; *sport*: balanced-out *match*; ***ein ~er Mensch*** a well-balanced person (*or* personality); '**Aus·ge·gli·chen·heit** *f* (-; *no pl.*) balance, harmony; equanimity; equability
aus·ge·go·ren ['aʊsgəgo:rən] *adj.* fully fermented *wine*; *fig.* mature, fully worked (*or* thought) out; ***der Plan ist noch nicht ~*** the plan is still in gestation
'**Aus·geh·an·zug** *m one's* best suit (*or* Sunday best), F *one's* glad rags *pl*
'**aus·ge·hen** *v/i.* (*irr.*, *sep.*, sn, → ***gehen***) **1.** go out (*a. in the evenings*); ***mein Vater ist ausgegangen*** my father's out (*or*

isn't in); ***sie gehen oft zum Essen aus*** they eat out a lot; ***sie gehen wenig aus*** they hardly ever go out, they don't go out much; **2.** ***gut*** *etc.* ~ turn out well *etc.*; ***unentschieden*** ~ end in a draw; ***der Film geht gut*** (***tragisch***) ***aus*** the film has a happy ending (tragic ending, the film ends tragically *or* in tragedy); **3.** *money, supplies etc.*: run out; run low; ***uns ging das Geld*** (***der Gesprächsstoff***) ***aus*** we ran out of money (things to say to each other); ***ihm ging die Luft*** (*or* ***der Atem***, F ***die Puste***) ***aus*** he ran out of breath (*fig.* steam); **4.** *light, fire etc.*: go out; **5.** *one's hair*: fall out; ***ihm gehen die Haare aus*** *a.* he's losing his hair; **6.** ~ ***von*** start from (*or* at); *fig.* take *s.th.* as a starting point; *fig.* ***bei e-r Entscheidung*** *etc.* ***von et.*** ~ base a decision *etc.* on s.th.; ***wenn wir davon*** ~, ***daß*** on the assumption that; ***ich gehe davon aus, daß*** I'm assuming that, I'm working on the assumption that; ***die Sache ging von ihm aus*** it was his idea; ***der Plan ging von der Regierung aus*** the government initiated the plan; **7.** ***von ihm geht e-e Ruhe*** (***Begeisterungsfähigkeit***) ***aus*** he radiates calm (enthusiasm); **8.** (***straf***)***frei*** ~ go unprosecuted (*or* unpunished), F get off scot-free; ***leer*** ~ come away empty-handed, end up with nothing; **9.** ~ ***auf*** *acc.* be after, be out for, seek; **10.** ~ ***auf*** *acc. word etc.*: end in (*or* with); **'aus·ge·hend** *adj.* ending; late; ***im*** ~***en 19. Jahrhundert*** towards the end of the 19th century

'aus·ge·höhlt I. *p.p. of* ***aushöhlen***; II. *adj.* hollow

'aus·ge·hun·gert I. *p.p. of* ***aushungern***; II. *adj.* half-starved; F *a.* starving to death

'Aus·geh|uni,form *f* dress uniform; ~**ver·bot** *n* ⚔ confinement to barracks; *w.s.* curfew

'aus·ge·klü·gelt I. *p.p. of* ***ausklügeln***; II. *adj.* ingenious, clever; elaborate, *w.s.* sophisticated

'aus·ge·kocht I. *p.p. of* ***auskochen***; II. F *adj.*: ***ein*** ~***er Betrüger*** a dirty cheat to the core; ***er ist ein ganz*** ~***er*** he's a sly one

'aus·ge·las·sen I. *p.p. of* ***auslassen***; II. *adj.* **1.** exuberant *mood etc.*; lively, boisterous *child etc.*; wild *party etc.*; **2.** ~***e Butter*** clarified butter; **'Aus·ge·las·sen·heit** *f* (-; *no pl.*) exuberance, high spirits *pl.*

'aus·ge·la·stet I. *p.p. of* ***auslasten***; II. *adj.* **1.** *machine etc.*: running to capacity, working at full capacity; **2.** (***nicht***) ***voll*** ~ ***sein*** be fully stretched (have too much time on one's hands)

aus·ge·laugt ['aʊsgəlaʊkt] I. *p.p. of* ***auslaugen***; II. *adj.* **1.** *geol.* eroded; **2.** *fig.* drained, washed-out

'aus·ge·legt *p.p. of* ***auslegen***

'aus·ge·lei·ert I. *p.p. of* ***ausleiern***; II. *adj.* **1.** worn; worn-out ..., *pred.* worn out; **2.** *fig.* well-worn, hackneyed *phrases etc.*

'aus·ge·lie·fert I. *p.p. of* ***ausliefern***; II. *adj.*: ***j-m*** ~ ***sein*** be at s.o.'s mercy; ***du bist denen*** ~ F they've got you over a barrel; ***e-r Sache hilflos*** ~ ***sein*** be helpless in the face of s.th.

'aus·ge·macht I. *p.p. of* ***ausmachen***; II. *adj.* **1.** settled; ~***e Sache*** foregone conclusion; **2.** absolute, out-and-out, consummate *fool, crook etc.*; full-blown *scandal etc.*; ***ein*** ~***er Unsinn*** absolute nonsense

'aus·ge·mer·gelt I. *p.p. of* ***ausmergeln***; II. *adj.* drained; emaciated *face, body etc.*; exhausted *soil*

'aus·ge·nom·men I. *p.p. of* ***ausnehmen***; II. *prp.* except (for), apart from, with the exception of; ***alle***, ~ ***ihn*** all except (for) him, everyone apart from him, all but him; ***Anwesende*** ~ present company excepted; III. *cj.* (*a.* ~, ***wenn***) unless; ~, ***daß*** except that

'aus·ge·prägt I. *p.p. of* ***ausprägen***; II. *adj.* distinct, marked, pronounced; prominent *chin etc.*; very distinct *profile*; ~***e Neigung zu*** strong tendency towards; ~***e Vorliebe für*** penchant for; ~***er Sinn für Humor*** *etc.* strongly developed sense of humo(u)r *etc.*; ~***e Persönlichkeit*** distinct (*or* forceful, colo[u]rful) personality

'aus·ge·pumpt I. *p.p. of* ***auspumpen***; II. F *adj.* F done, *Am.* F pooped

'aus·ge·rech·net I. *p.p. of* ***ausrechnen***; II. *adv.*: ~ ***er*** he (*or* him) of all people; ~ ***heute*** today of all days; ~ ***wenn ich nicht zu Hause bin*** just when I'm out; ***warum mußte es*** ~ ***mir passieren?*** why did it have to happen to me (of all people)?; ~ ***jetzt muß sie auftauchen*** she would have to turn up (right) now (*or* now of all times)

'aus·ge·reift I. *p.p. of* ***ausreifen***; II. *adj.* completely ripe; mature (*a. wine, cheese, a. fig.*); ⚙ fully developed *design, method etc.*; **'Aus·ge·reift·heit** *f* (-; *no pl.*) ⚙ (degree of) sophistication

'aus·ge·rich·tet I. *p.p. of* ***ausrichten***; II. *adj.*: ~ ***auf*** *acc.* aimed at, geared towards

'aus·ge·ruht I. *p.p. of* ***ausruhen***; II. *adj.* (well) rested; ***du siehst ganz*** ~ ***aus*** *a.* you look as if you've had a good rest

'aus·ge·schla·fen I. *p.p. of* ***ausschlafen***; II. *adj.* (*a.* ***gut*** ~) well rested; ***du bist ja überhaupt nicht*** ~ you haven't had enough sleep

'aus·ge·schlos·sen I. *p.p. of* ***ausschließen***; II. *pred. adj. and int.* impossible(!), out of the question(!)

'aus·ge·schnit·ten I. *p.p. of* ***ausschneiden***; II. *adj.* low-cut; ***tief*** ~ very low-cut

aus·ge·sorgt ['aʊsgəzɔrkt] *p.p. of* ***aussorgen***: F ~ ***haben*** F be sitting pretty; ***sie hat für den Rest ihres Lebens*** ~ she won't have to worry about money for the rest of her days

'aus·ge·spro·chen I. *p.p. of* ***aussprechen***; II. *adj.* distinct, marked; decided; ***das ist*** ~***es Pech*** that really is bad luck; III. *adv.* really; typically *British etc.*

'aus·ge·stal·ten *v/t.* (*sep.*, h) develop; organize

'aus·ge·stat·tet *p.p. of* ***ausstatten***

'aus·ge·stellt I. *p.p. of* ***ausstellen***; II. *adj.*: ~***e Hosen*** (~***er Rock***) flared trousers (skirt)

'aus·ge·stor·ben I. *p.p. of* ***aussterben***; II. *adj.* **1.** ♀, *zo.* extinct; **2.** *fig.* deserted; ***wie*** ~ ***wirken*** be like a ghost town

'Aus·ge·sto·ße·ne *m, f* (-n; -n) outcast

'aus·ge·sucht I. *p.p. of* ***aussuchen***; II. *adj.* exquisite, choice; extreme *politeness etc.*; select *gathering etc.*

'aus·ge·tre·ten I. *p.p. of* ***austreten***; II. *adj.* well-worn; *fig.* ~***e Pfade gehen*** keep to the beaten track

'aus·ge·trock·net *p.p. of* ***austrocknen***

'aus·ge·tüf·telt I. *p.p. of* ***austüfteln***; II. *adj.* carefully (*or* cleverly) worked out, *w.s.* elaborate

'aus·ge·wach·sen I. *p.p. of* ***auswachsen***; II. *adj.* **1.** fully grown, full-grown; fully developed; **2.** F *fig.* fully fledged, full-fledged *teacher etc.*; full-blown *scandal etc.*; ***ein*** ~***er Unsinn*** absolute nonsense, complete and utter nonsense

'aus·ge·wählt I. *p.p. of* ***auswählen***; II. *adj.* **1.** well-chosen, nicely chosen; **2.** ~***e Gedichte*** selected poems (***von*** by); ~***e Werke*** selected works

'aus·ge·wa·schen I. *p.p. of* ***auswaschen***; II. *adj.* washed-out ..., *pred.* washed out; faded *jeans etc.*

'Aus·ge·wie·se·ne *m, f* (-n; -n) expellee

'aus·ge·wo·gen I. *p.p. of* ***auswiegen***; II. *adj.* (well-)balanced; **'Aus·ge·wo·gen·heit** *f* (-; *no pl.*) balance, (well-)balanced nature

'aus·ge·zehrt I. *p.p. of* ***auszehren***; II. *adj.* emaciated; haggard, cadaverous

'aus·ge·zeich·net I. *p.p. of* ***auszeichnen***; II. *adj.* excellent; III. *adv.* very well; ***er kann*** ~ ***kochen*** *a.* he's an excellent cook; ***danke, mir geht's*** ~ I'm doing just fine, thanks

aus·gie·big ['aʊsgiːbɪç] I. *adj.* big *lunch etc.*; long *walk etc.*; extensive *research etc.*; II. *adv.* in detail; for a long time; ~ ***essen*** have a big meal (*or* lunch *etc.*), have plenty to eat; ~ ***spazierengehen*** go for a long walk, go for a lot of walks

'aus·gie·ßen *v/t.* (*irr.*, *sep.*, h, → ***gießen***) **1.** pour out; empty; **2.** ⚙ fill

'Aus·gleich *m* (-[e]s; -e) **1.** balance; *a.* ⚙ compensation; adjustment; ***als*** (*or* ***zum***) ~ ***für*** to compensate for; **2.** † balancing, settlement *of accounts*; **3.** *sport*: equalizer; ***den*** ~ ***erzielen*** equalize; **'aus·glei·chen** (*irr.*, *sep.*, h, → ***gleichen***) I. *v/t.* **1.** balance; level out; adjust; compensate (for) (*a.* ⚙), make up for; offset; ~***de Gerechtigkeit*** poetic justice; **2.** † balance, settle *accounts*; II. *v/i. sport*: equalize

'Aus·gleichs|ab·ga·be *f* ⚖ countervailing duty; ~**fonds** *m* † equalization fund; ~**ge·trie·be** *n mot.* differential (gear); ~**gym,na·stik** *f* remedial exercises *pl.*; ~**sport** *m* recreational sport; ~**tor** *n*, ~**tref·fer** *m* equalizer

'aus·glei·ten *v/i.* → ***ausrutschen***

'aus·glie·dern *v/t.* (*sep.*, h) sift out; † hive off

'aus·gra·ben (*irr.*, *sep.*, h, → ***graben***) I. *v/t.* dig up; excavate; *fig.* unearth; dig out; dredge up; II. *v/i.* dig; **'Aus·gra·bung** *f* (-; -en) **1.** excavation; ~***en*** *a.* dig; **2.** → ***Ausgrabungsfund***

'Aus·gra·bungs|fund *m* arch(a)eological find; ~**ort** *m* excavation site

'aus·gren·zen *v/t.* (*sep.*, h) leave aside, ignore; exclude (***aus*** *dat.* from)

Aus·guck ['aʊsgʊk] *m* (-s; -e) ⚓ lookout; crow's nest

'Aus·guß *m* (-sses; ˵sse) sink; drain

'aus·ha·ben F (*irr.*, *sep.*, h, → ***haben***) I. *v/t.* **1.** have (taken) off; ***hast du die Schuhe aus?*** have you taken (*or* got) your shoes off?, did you take your shoes off?; **2.** have finished *one's book etc.*; II. *v/i.*: ***wann hast du heute aus?*** when do you finish (school *etc.*) *or* get off today?

'aus·hacken (*sep.* -k·k-) *v/t.* (*sep.*, h) ⚒ hoe up; gouge out *eyes etc.*

'aus·ha·ken (*sep.*, h) I. *v/t.* unhook; II.

v/i. (*a. v/refl.*: **sich ~**) come unhooked; F *fig.* **da hakt's bei mir aus** F I just don't get it; F **bei ihm hat's ausgehakt** F he's flipped

'aus·hal·ten (*irr.*, *sep.*, h, → **halten**) **I.** *v/t.* **1.** put up with, endure, stand, take; bear up under; stand up to; ⚙ tolerate, take; **nicht zum ≈** unbearable; **ich halt's nicht mehr aus** I can't stand (*or* take) it any longer, I can't take any more of this; **ich halt's hier nicht mehr aus** I can't stand this place any longer, I've (just) got to get out of this place; **ich weiß nicht, wie sie es ~ zu** *inf.* I don't know how they can stand *ger.*; **hält er's bis zur nächsten Raststätte aus?** can he hold out (*or* will he last out) till the next service station?; F **das hältste ja im Kopf nicht aus** F it's enough to drive you round the bend; **2.** *contp.* keep *mistress, lover etc.*; **II.** *v/i.* hold out; **er hält nirgends lange aus** he never lasts long in any place

'aus·han·deln *v/t.* (*sep.*, h) negotiate; **endlich haben wir e-n Preis ausgehandelt** we finally agreed on a price

aus·hän·di·gen ['aʊshɛndɪgən] *v/t.* (*sep.*, h) hand over

'Aus·hang *m* (-[e]s; ⸚e) notice

'Aus·hän·ge·bo·gen *m typ.* advance (*or* specimen) sheet

'aus·hän·gen (*sep.*, h) **I.** *v/t.* **1.** put up *advertisement etc.*; **2.** take *s.th.* off its hinges; unhook; **II.** *v/refl.*: **sich ~** *dress etc*: smooth out; **III.** *v/i.* be (up) on the notice board; **die Listen hängen aus** *a.* the lists are up (*or* out)

'Aus·hän·ge·schild *n* sign; *fig.* advertisement (**für** for)

'aus·har·ren *v/i.* (*sep.*, h) hold out

'aus·här·ten *v/t.* (*sep.*, h) ⚙ harden, age

'aus·hau·chen *v/t.* (*sep.*, h) breathe out; *fig.* **sein Leben ~** breathe one's last

'aus·hau·en *v/t.* (*sep.*, h) **1.** cut out, hew out; chisel out, carve out; **2.** clear *forest*

aus·häu·sig ['aʊshɔyzɪç] *adj.* out (and about), out of the house

'aus·he·ben *v/t.* (*irr.*, *sep.*, h, → **heben**) **1.** dig up; excavate; **2.** → **aushängen** 2; **3.** *fig.* raid; round up

'aus·hecken (*sep.* -k·k-) F *v/t.* (*sep.*, h) F cook up

'aus·hei·len *v/i.* (*sep.*, sn) heal up; *illness*: be completely cured

'aus·hel·fen *v/i.* (*irr.*, *sep.*, h, → **helfen**): (**[bei] j-m**) ~ help (s.o.) out

'Aus·hil·fe *f* (-; -n) temporary help; stand-in; F temp

'Aus·hilfs|kraft *f* casual worker; **~leh·rer** *m* stand-in teacher; **~per·so,nal** *n* temporary staff

'aus·hilfs·wei·se *adv.* temporarily; **~ (bei j-m) arbeiten** *a.* help (s.o.) out

'aus·höh·len *v/t.* (*sep.*, h) **1.** hollow out; *geol.* erode; scoop out; **2.** *fig.* undermine, erode; drain *s.o.* (of all strength)

'aus·ho·len (*sep.*, h) **I.** *v/i.* raise one's hand *to hit s.o.*; swing one's arm back *to throw s.th.*; get ready to hit s.o. (*or* throw s.th.); **mit weit ~den Schritten** with great strides; *fig.* (**weit**) ~ go a long way back; **etwas ~** go back a bit; **II.** *v/t.* → **aushorchen**

'aus·hor·chen *v/t.* (*sep.*, h) sound *s.o.* out

'Aus·hub *m* (-[e]s; *no pl.*) excavation; earth

aus·hül·sen ['aʊshʏlzən] *v/t.* (*sep.*, h) shell *peas etc.*

'aus·hun·gern *v/t.* (*sep.*, h) starve; starve out *city etc.*; → **ausgehungert** II

'aus·hu·sten (*sep.*, h) **I.** *v/t.* cough up; **II.** *v/refl.*: **sich ~** have a good cough; **hast du dich jetzt ausgehustet?** have you finished coughing?

aus·ixen ['aʊsˀɪksən] *v/t.* (*sep.*, h) cross out, ex out

'aus·jä·ten *v/t.* (*sep.*, h) pull up; weed

'aus·kal·ku,lie·ren *v/t.* (*sep.*, h) work out, calculate

'aus·käm·men *v/t.* (*sep.*, h) comb out

'aus·kämp·fen *v/t.* (*sep.*, h) fight *s.th.* out

'aus·keh·ren *v/t.* (*sep.*, h) sweep (out)

'aus·kei·len *v/i.* (*sep.*, h) *horse*: lash out, kick; *person*: lash out in all directions

'aus·kei·men *v/i.* (*sep.*, h) germinate

'aus·ken·nen *v/refl.* (*irr.*, *sep.*, h, → **kennen**): **sich ~ in** *dat.* know one's way around *a place*; *fig.* know all about *s.th.*; **er kennt sich aus** he knows what's what; **ich kenne mich nicht mehr aus** I'm at a complete loss

aus·ker·nen ['aʊskɛrnən] *v/t.* (*sep.*, h) stone *cherries etc.*; pip *apples etc.*; seed *grapes etc.*; *a.* take the stones (*or* pips, seeds) out of

'aus·kip·pen *v/t.* (*sep.*, h) tip out; pour out (*or* away); empty

'aus·klam·mern *v/t.* (*sep.*, h) **1.** 𝔄 factor out; **2.** *fig.* leave aside, ignore

aus·kla·mü·sern ['aʊsklamyːzərn] F *v/t.* (*sep.*, h) figure (*or* work, puzzle) out

'Aus·klang *m* (-[e]s; *no pl.*) ♪ end (*a. fig.*); *fig.* **zum ~ des Abends** to end (*or* finish off) the evening

'aus·klapp·bar *adj.* folding; **'aus·klap·pen** *v/t.* (*sep.*, h) fold out

'aus·klau·ben F *v/t.* (*sep.*, h) pick out; sort out; **et. aus et. ~** pick s.th. out of s.th.

'aus·klei·den (*sep.*, h) **I.** *v/t.* line; **II.** *v/refl.*: **sich ~** undress; **'Aus·klei·dung** *f* (-; -en) lining, surfacing

'aus·klin·gen *v/i.* (*irr.*, *sep.*, sn, → **klingen**) die away; *fig.* come to an end; end (**in** *dat.* with)

aus·klin·ken ['aʊsklɪŋkən] *v/t.* (*sep.*, h) ⚙ disengage, trip, *a.* ✈ release

'aus·klop·fen *v/t.* (*sep.*, h) beat *carpet etc.*; dust (down) *clothes*; knock out *pipe*; **et. aus et. ~** beat (*or* knock) s.th. out of s.th.

aus·klü·geln ['aʊsklyːgəln] *v/t.* (*sep.*, -ge-, h) work out; → **ausgeklügelt** II

'aus·knei·fen F *v/i.* (*irr.*, *sep.*, sn, → **kneifen**) F do a bunk

'aus·knip·sen F *v/t.* (*sep.*, h) ⚡ switch off

'aus·kno·beln *v/t.* (*sep.*, h) **1.** throw dice for; **2.** F *fig.* figure *s.th.* out

'aus·knöpf·bar *adj.*: **~es (Innen)Futter** detachable lining (*or* liner)

'aus·ko·chen *v/t.* (*sep.*, h) boil; ⚕ sterilize; *fig.* hatch *plan etc.*; → **ausgekocht** II

'aus·kom·men I. *v/i.* (*irr.*, *sep.*, sn, → **kommen**) **1. ~ mit** *dat.* make do with, manage with; **mit s-m Geld ~** make both ends meet; **~ ohne** *acc.* manage without, *a.* do without *s.th.*; **er kommt ohne sie nicht aus** *a.* he can't live (*or* survive) without her; **2.** (**gut**) **mit j-m ~** get on (fine *or* well) with s.o.; **II.** ≈ *n* (-s; *no pl.*) **3.** livelihood; **sein ~ haben** make a (decent) living; **4. es ist kein ~ mit ihm** you just can't get along with him, he's impossible to get along with; **aus·kömm·lich** ['aʊskœmlɪç] **I.** *adj.* reasonable; **II.** *adv.*: **~ leben** live reasonably well

'aus·kop·peln *v/t.* (*sep.*, h) take (*or* lift) *song* from an album; **'Aus·kop·pe·lung** *f*, **'Aus·kopp·lung** *f* (-; -en) cut, follow-up single

'aus·ko·sten *v/t.* (*sep.*, h) savo(u)r, enjoy to the full; *iro.* **ich habe es ausgekostet** I've had my fill of it

'aus·kot·zen V (*sep.*, h) **I.** *v/t.* *sl.* throw up; **II.** *v/refl.*: **sich ~** *sl.* throw up; *fig.* let everything out; *fig.* **sich bei j-m ~** unload (one's problems) to s.o.

'aus·kra·men *v/t.* (*sep.*, h) dig out; pull everything out of *a drawer etc.*; *fig.* dig up *memories, old stories*

'aus·krat·zen *v/t.* (*sep.*, h) scratch out; scrape out (*a.* ⚕)

'aus·krie·chen *v/i.* (*irr.*, *sep.*, sn, → **kriechen**) hatch

'aus·ku·geln *v/t.* (*sep.*, h): **sich den Arm ~** dislocate one's arm

'aus·küh·len *v/i.* (*sep.*, sn) cool (down)

'aus·kund·schaf·ten *v/t.* (*sep.*, h) find out; track down; spy out

Aus·kunft ['aʊskʊnft] *f* (-; Auskünfte ['aʊskʏnftə]) **1.** information; **nähere ~** (further) details *pl.*; **2.** *teleph.* directory enquiries *pl.* (*Am.* assistance, information); **3.** → **Auskunftsbüro, -schalter; Aus·kunf·tei** [aʊskʊnf'taɪ] *f* (-; -en) credit inquiry agency

'Aus·kunfts|be·am·te *m* (-n; -n) information clerk; **~bü,ro** *n* inquiry (*or* information) office; **~per,son** *f* informant; **~pflicht** *f* (-; *no pl.*) duty to disclose information; **~schal·ter** *m* information (desk), inquiries *pl.*, enquiries *pl.*; **~stel·le** *f* **1.** → **Auskunftsbüro**; **2.** → **Auskunftsschalter**

'aus·kup·peln *v/i.* (*sep.*, h) *mot.* disengage the clutch, declutch

'aus·ku,rie·ren (*sep.*, h) **I.** *v/t.* cure (completely); **II.** *v/refl.*: **du solltest dich richtig ~** you should take a proper break until you're really fit again; you should get it out of your system

'aus·la·chen *v/t.* (*sep.*, h) laugh at

'Aus·la·de·ha·fen *m* port of discharge

'aus·la·den (*irr.*, *sep.*, h, → **laden**) **I.** *v/t.* **1.** unload; ⚓ disembark *passengers*; **2.** F disinvite, tell *s.o.* not to come; **II.** *v/i.* ⟁ jut out; **'aus·la·dend** *adj.* **1.** very wide, overhanging *roof etc.*; sweeping *branches*; **2.** *fig.* elaborate; sweeping, expansive

'Aus·la·de·stel·le *f* unloading point; ⚓ wharf

'Aus·la·ge *f* (-; -n) **1.** window display, goods *pl.* on display; **2.** *pl.* expenses

'aus·la·gern *v/t.* (*sep.*, h) outhouse; ⚔ evacuate; ✝ take out of the warehouse

'Aus·land *n* (-[e]s; *no pl.*): **ins ~, im ~** abroad; **aus dem ~** from abroad; **Waren aus dem ~** foreign goods, goods from abroad; **Handel mit dem ~** foreign trade; **Kontakte mit dem ~** foreign ties, ties abroad; **Meinungen aus dem ~** foreign opinion(s), opinion(s) abroad; **fürs ~ bestimmte Waren** goods destined for export, export goods

Aus·län·der ['aʊslɛndɐ] *m* (-s; -) foreigner; ⚖ alien; **~amt** *n* aliens' registration office; **~an·teil** *m* proportion (*or* percentage) of foreigners (*or* foreign pupils *etc.*); **≈feind·lich** *adj.* hostile to foreigners, xenophobic; **sie sind sehr ~** *a.* they hate foreigners; **~feind·lich·keit** *f* (-; *no pl.*) hostility to foreigners, xenophobia

Aus·län·de·rin ['aʊslɛndərɪn] *f* (-; -nen) foreigner; ⚖ alien
aus·län·disch ['aʊslɛndɪʃ] *adj.* foreign; ✝ *a.* external; ⚖ alien; **~e Besucher** visitors from abroad, international visitors
'**Aus·lands|ab,tei·lung** *f* ✝ export (*or* foreign sales) department; **~an·lei·he** *f* external loan; **~auf·ent·halt** *m* visit (*or* stay) abroad; **~auf·trag** *m* export order; **~bank** *f* (-; -en) foreign bank; **~be·tei·li·gung** *f* foreign investment; **~be·zie·hun·gen** *pl.* foreign relations; **~brief** *m* letter going abroad, *pl. a.* letters abroad; **~deut·sche** *m, f* (-n; -n) German national living abroad, German expatriate; **~dienst** *m* foreign service; **~flug** *m* international flight; **~ge·schäft** *n* export (*or* import) business, export-import business; **~ge·spräch** *n teleph.* international call; **~hil·fe** *f* foreign aid; **~in·ve·sti·ti,on** *f* foreign investment; **~ka·pi,tal** *n* foreign capital; **~kor·re·spon,dent** *m* foreign correspondent; **~kran·ken·schein** *m health insurance document for abroad*; **~pres·se** *f* international press; **~rei·se** *f* trip abroad; *pol., sport etc.*: foreign tour; **~schul·den** *pl.* foreign (*or* external) debt *sg.*; **~schutz·brief** *m mot. all-in protection package for motorists abroad*; **~sen·der** *m* foreign station; **~stu·di·um** *n* course of studies abroad; **ein ~ kann sehr teuer sein** studying abroad can be very expensive; **~tour,nee** *f* foreign tour; **~ver·mö·gen** *n* external assets *pl.*; **~ver·schul·dung** *f* foreign (*or* external) debt; **~ver·tre·tung** *f* ✝ agency abroad; *pol.* diplomatic mission
'**aus·lan·gen** F *v/i.* (*sep.*, h) **1.** get ready to hit s.o.; **2.** be enough; **das langt noch für e-e Woche aus** *a.* that'll last for another week
'**Aus·laß** *m* (-lasses; -lässe) outlet
'**aus·las·sen** (*irr., sep.*, h, → **lassen**) **I.** *v/t.* **1.** leave out, omit *word etc.*; skip; miss *an opportunity etc.*; miss (*or* leave) *s.o.* out; **2.** let out *water etc.*; **3.** melt *butter etc.*; render *fat*; **4.** let out *seams*; **5.** F leave *the light etc.* off; **6. s-e Wut** *etc.* **an j-m ~** take one's anger *etc.* out on s.o.; **II.** *v/refl.*: **sich ~ über** *acc.* talk about, hold forth on; **sie ließ sich sehr positiv** (**negativ**) **darüber aus** she was very positive (negative) about it; **er ließ sich nicht weiter aus** he didn't say any more about it; '**Aus·las·sung** *f* (-; -en) **1.** omission; **2.** remark(s *pl.*)
'**Aus·las·sungs|punk·te** *pl.* three dots, omission marks; **~zei·chen** *n* apostrophe
'**aus·la·sten** *v/t.* ⚙ use to capacity; *fig.* **der Haushalt lastet mich voll** (**nicht**) **aus** I've got plenty on my hands with the household (I need to be doing something else apart from the household); → **ausgelastet** II
'**aus·lat·schen** F *v/t.* (*sep.*, h) wear out
'**Aus·lauf** *m* (-[e]s; ⸚e) **1.** outlet, drain; **2.** *no pl. fig.* space to run about in; exercise; **3.** *skiing*: runout; '**aus·lau·fen** (*irr., sep.*, sn, → **laufen**) **I.** *v/i.* **1.** *liquid*: run out; *a. tank etc.*: leak; **2.** ⚓ sail; **3.** *sport, a. engine*: run out; **4.** *paint*: run; **5.** end, come to an end; *contract etc.*: expire; run out; *model, line*: be discontinued; be phased out; **~ lassen** phase out; **es wird für uns schlecht ~** it's going to turn out (*or* end up) badly for us; **6. ~ in** *acc.* end in, taper (in)to, narrow into; **II.** *v/refl.*: **sich ~** get some exercise; '**Aus·läu·fer** *m* (-s; -) **1.** *geogr.* foothills *pl.*; **2.** *meteor.* fringe(s *pl.*); **3.** *earthquake*: coda; **4.** ✿ runner; '**Aus·lauf·mo,dell** *n* discontinued (*or* phaseout) model *or* line
'**aus·lau·gen** *v/t.* (*sep.*, h) exhaust; *fig.* drain *s.o.* (of every ounce of strength); → **ausgelaugt** II; '**Aus·lau·gung** *f* (-; -en) exhaustion (**des Bodens** of the soil)
'**Aus·laut** *m* (-[e]s; -e) *ling.* final sound; **im ~** at the end of a (*or* the) word
'**aus·le·ben** (*sep.*, h) **I.** *v/t.* live out; let (*or* act) out; realize *one's talent etc.*; apply; **II.** *v/refl.*: **sich ~** enjoy life; F live it up
'**aus·lecken** (*sep.* -k·k-) *v/t.* (*sep.*, h) lick out (*or* clean)
'**aus·lee·ren** *v/t.* (*sep.*, h) empty; drain
aus·leg·bar ['aʊsleːkbaːɐ] *adj.* interpretable; **der Text ist so oder so ~** there are two ways of interpreting the text, the text can be interpreted in two ways; **es ist nur so ~** that's the only possible interpretation; '**aus·le·gen** *v/t.* (*sep.*, h) **1.** lay *cable, mines etc.*; put out *nets*; put down *bait, poison etc.*; sow; plant, set *potatoes*; **2.** (put on) display; put out *lists etc.*; **ausgelegt** on display; **öffentlich ausgelegt** *a.* on view to the public; **3.** cover *floor*; line *drawer etc.*; **mit e-m Teppich ~** carpet, *a.* put a carpet down on *the floor* (*or* in *a room*); **4.** inlay; **5.** advance; **et. für j-n ~** lend s.o. s.th., pay s.th. for s.o.; **6.** interpret; **falsch ~** misinterpret; (**j-m**) **et. als Eitelkeit** *etc.* **~** put s.th. down to (s.o.'s) vanity *etc.*; **7.** design; **ausgelegt für** designed to produce, designed to do *100 mph etc.*; *der Saal* **ist für 2000 ausgelegt** is designed to seat 2000
'**Aus·le·ger** *m* (-s; -) ⚙ jib; ⚓ outrigger; **~boot** *n* outrigger
'**Aus·le·ge·wa·re** *f* **1.** floor coverings *pl.*; **2.** wall-to-wall carpeting
'**Aus·le·gung** *f* (-; -en) interpretation; *eccl.* exegesis; '**Aus·le·gungs·fra·ge** *f*: **das ist e-e ~** it all depends which way you look at it
'**aus·lei·ern** *v/t.* (*sep.*, h) *and v/i.* (sn) wear out; → **ausgeleiert** II
'**Aus·leih·bib·lio,thek** *f* lending library; '**Aus·lei·he** *f* (-; -n) **1.** *no pl.* lending; **2.** issuing desk (*or* counter); '**aus·lei·hen** *v/t.* (*irr., sep.*, h, → **leihen**) lend (out), *esp. Am.* loan; **sich et. ~** borrow s.th.; '**Aus·leih·frist** *f* lending period; **die ~ beträgt drei Wochen** books may be borrowed for (a period of) up to three weeks
'**aus·ler·nen** *v/i.* (*sep.*, h) finish one's training; **man lernt nie aus** you live and learn
'**Aus·le·se** *f* (-; -n) **1.** *no pl.* choice, selection; **natürliche ~** natural selection; **e-e strenge ~ treffen** make a careful selection; **2.** elite, *the* crème de la crème, *the* cream of the crop; **3.** *gastr.* auslese; *wine from selected grapes*; **4.** anthology; **5.** *computer*: readout; '**aus·le·sen** *v/t.* (*irr., sep.*, h, → **lesen**) **1.** select, choose, pick out; **2.** read (to the end), finish; '**Aus·le·se·ver·fah·ren** *n* selection process
'**aus·leuch·ten** *v/t.* (*sep*, h) *a. fig.* illuminate; *thea. etc. a.* floodlight
'**aus·lie·fern** *v/t.* (*sep.*, h) hand *s.o., s.th.* over (**an** *acc.* to); ✝ deliver; ⚖ surrender; *pol.* extradite; → **ausgeliefert** II; '**Aus·lie·fe·rung** *f* (-; -en) ✝ delivery; ⚖ surrender; handing over, *pol. a.* extradition
'**Aus·lie·fe·rungs|ab·kom·men** *n* extradition treaty; **~an·trag** *m* request for extradition; **~la·ger** *n* ✝ supply depot; **~ver·trag** *m* extradition treaty
'**aus·lie·gen** *v/i.* (*irr., sep.*, h, → **liegen**) be on display; be available; **... liegen zur Einsichtnahme aus** ... may be viewed
'**Aus·li·nie** *f* **1.** *soccer etc.*: touchline; byline, goal line; **2.** *tennis*: sideline, base line
'**aus·lo·ben** *v/t.* (*sep.*, h) ⚖ offer as a reward
'**aus·löf·feln** *v/t.* (*sep.*, h) scrape *s.th.* clean; spoon up; *fig.* → **Suppe**
'**aus·lö·schen** *v/t.* (*sep.*, h) **1.** put out *light etc.*; *a.* extinguish *fire etc.*; **2.** rub out, *a.* erase *writing*; efface *inscription*; wipe out *traces etc.*; **3.** *fig.* wipe out *people etc.*; obliterate *memories etc.*
'**Aus·lö·se|he·bel** *m* release lever; **~im,puls** *m* ⚡ trigger pulse; **~knopf** *m* release button; **~me·cha,nis·mus** *m* ⚕, *psych.* release mechanism; ⚙ *a.* trigger mechanism
'**aus·lo·sen** *v/t.* (*sep.*, h) draw lots for
'**aus·lö·sen** *v/t.* (*sep.*, h) **1.** *phot.*, ⚙ release; trigger off *alarm etc.*; **2.** set off *chemical reaction etc.*; **3.** *fig.* trigger off, spark off *war, strike etc.*; **4.** *fig.* bring on *illness etc.*; **5.** *fig.* cause, touch off; arouse; **großen Beifall ~** draw loud applause; **es löste allgemeine Heiterkeit aus** it gave everyone a (good) laugh, *lit.* it caused great mirth; '**Aus·lö·ser** *m* (-s; -) **1.** ⚙ release; *phot.* shutter release; **2.** *fig.* cause; **der ~ war** what triggered (or set) it off was, what brought it on was
'**Aus·lo·sung** *f* (-; -en) draw(ing of lots)
'**aus·lo·ten** *v/t.* (*sep.*, h) **1.** ⚓ sound; △ plumb, level; **2.** *fig.* plumb the depths of; explore the ins and outs of *a problem etc.*
'**aus·lüf·ten** *v/t.* (*sep.*, h) air
'**aus·ma·chen** *v/t.* (*sep.*, h) **1.** put out *fire, light etc.*; *a.* stub out *one's cigarette*; turn off, switch off *radio etc.*; **2.** make out; **ich kann nichts ~** I can't see a thing; **3.** arrange; **e-n Termin ~** arrange *or* fix a time (*or* date, time and date), make an appointment (**bei** *dat.* with); **der Termin ist fest ausgemacht** the date's definite (*or* firmly fixed); **zur ausgemachten Stunde** at the agreed time; **an der ausgemachten Stelle** at the agreed place; **4.** settle; **das müssen sie unter sich ~** they'll have to sort (*or* fight) it out between themselves; **et. mit sich selbst ~** settle s.th. with one's own conscience; **et. im Guten ~** settle s.th. in good grace; **5.** make up, constitute; **6.** come to; **ein Vermögen ~** cost a fortune; **7. es macht viel aus** it makes a big difference, *a.* it matters a lot (*or* a great deal); **das macht nichts aus** it doesn't matter; **macht es Ihnen etwas aus, wenn ich Klavier spiele?** do you mind if I play the piano?, would you mind if I played the piano?; **macht es dir was aus, daß ich später komme?** do you mind my (*or* me) coming late?; **das macht mir nichts aus** I don't mind, I don't care; **die Kälte macht ihm nichts aus** the cold doesn't bother him
'**aus·ma·len** *v/t.* (*sep.*, h) colo(u)r; paint; *fig.* depict; embroider; *fig.* **sich et. ~** picture s.th. (to o.s.), imagine s.th.

'aus·ma·nö,vrie·ren *v/t.* (*sep.*, h) outmanoeuvre, *Am.* outmaneuver; outsmart; **'Aus·ma·nö,vrie·rung** *f* (-; *no pl.*) outmanoeuvring, *Am.* outmaneuvering

'Aus·maß *n* (-es; -e) size, dimensions *pl.*; *fig.* extent, magnitude; ***mit den ~en von*** (*or gen.*) the size of, *fig.* on the scale of; *fig.* ***in großem ~*** to a great extent; ***Reformen in großem ~*** wide-scale reforms; ***ein erstaunliches ~ an*** an astounding degree of; ***erschreckende ~e annehmen*** assume (*or* take on) alarming proportions; ***das ~ der Katastrophe ist noch nicht bekannt*** the extent of the damage caused by the disaster is not yet known

'aus·mei·ßeln *v/t.* (*sep.*, h) carve out

aus·mer·geln ['aʊsmɛrgəln] *v/t.* (*sep.*, h) drain; exhaust; → ***ausgemergelt*** II

aus·mer·zen ['aʊsmɛrtsən] *v/t.* (*sep.*, h) weed out *mistakes etc.*; *fig.* blot out, wipe (*or* stamp) out

'aus·mes·sen *v/t.* (*irr.*, *sep.*, h, → ***messen***) measure (out)

'aus·mi·sten (*sep.*, h) **I.** *v/t.* muck (*or* clean) out *stable etc.*; *fig.* clear out; ***Bücher*** (***Briefe*** *etc.*) ~ clear out old books (old letters *etc.*); **II.** *fig. v/i.* have a clearing-out session

'aus·mu·stern *v/t.* (*sep.*, h) **1.** sort out; **2.** ⚔ discharge (as unfit); exempt (from military service)

Aus·nah·me ['aʊsna:mə] *f* (-; -n) exception; ***mit ~ von*** (*or gen.*) except (for), excepting, with the exception of; ***e-e ~ bilden*** be an exception; (***bei j-m***) ***e-e ~ machen*** make an exception (in s.o.'s case); ***die ~ bestätigt die Regel*** the exception proves the rule; ***e-e ~ von der Regel*** an exception to the rule; **~be·stim·mung** *f* exception clause; **~er·schei·nung** *f* exception; ***dieser Spieler ist e-e absolute ~*** this player is one in a million; **~fall** *m* special case, exception; ***in Ausnahmefällen*** in special (*or* exceptional) circumstances; **~ge·neh·mi·gung** *f* exemption; **~ge·richt** *n* extraordinary court; **~mensch** *m* exceptional person; **~re·ge·lung** *f* exemption; **~si·tua·ti,on** *f* **1.** unusual situation; **2.** exceptional case; **~zu·stand** *m* **1.** state of emergency; ***den ~ verhängen*** declare a state of emergency; **2.** exception; ***es ist ein ~ a.*** it's not always like this

'aus·nahms·los I. *adv.* without exception; unanimously; ***~ alle*** all of them, without exception; every single one of them; **II.** *adj.* unanimous

'aus·nahms·wei·se *adv.* exceptionally, by way of exception; for once, just this once; *iro.* as it's you

'aus·neh·men (*irr.*, *sep.*, h, → ***nehmen***) **I.** *v/t.* **1.** gut *fish etc.*; draw *poultry*; rob *nest*; **2.** F *fig.* F fleece *s.o.*; **3.** except, exclude; → ***ausgenommen*** II; **II.** *v/refl.*: ***sich ~*** look *good, strange etc.*; **'aus·neh·mend I.** *adj.* exceptional; ***von ~er Schönheit*** exceptionally beautiful, *a woman* of exceptional beauty; **II.** *adv.* exceptionally, extremely

'aus·nüch·tern *v/i. and v/t.* (*sep.*, h) sober up; **'Aus·nüch·te·rungs·zel·le** *f* drying-out cell

'aus·nut·zen, 'aus·nüt·zen *v/t.* (*sep.*, h) use, make use of; make the most of; *a. b.s.* take advantage of; exploit

'aus·packen (*sep.* -k·k-) (*sep.*, h) **I.** *v/t.* unpack; unwrap; **II.** F *fig. v/i.* F talk, blab; ***pack aus!*** F come on, out with it (*or* spit it out)

'aus·par·ken *v/i.* (*sep.*, h) get out of a parking space (*Am.* lot)

'aus·peit·schen *v/t.* (*sep.*, h) whip

'aus·pen·nen F *v/i. and v/refl.* (***sich ~***) (*sep.*, h) have a good long sleep (*or* a good lie-in)

'aus·pfei·fen *v/t.* (*irr.*, *sep.*, h, → ***pfeifen***) boo (at); *thea. a.* boo off the stage

Au·spi·zi·en [aʊs'pi:tsĭən] *pl*: ***unter den ~ von*** under the auspices (*or* aegis) of; ***das Projekt steht unter guten*** (***schlechten***) ~ it augurs well (badly) for the project

'aus·plap·pern F *v/t.* (*sep.*, h) F blab out

'aus·plau·dern (*sep.*, h) **I.** *v/t.* let (F blab) out; **II.** *v/refl.*: ***sich ~*** have a good old chat (F natter, chinwag)

'aus·plün·dern *v/t.* (*sep.*, h) **1.** loot, ransack; **2.** exploit *resources*; bleed *country etc.* (white); **3.** F clean out *the till etc.*; raid *the fridge etc.*; **4.** rob *s.o.*; F fleece *s.o.*

'aus·pol·stern *v/t.* (*sep.*, h) pad (out)

'aus·po,sau·nen F *v/t.* (*sep.*, h) F broadcast

aus·pow·ern[1] ['aʊspo:vɐn] *v/t.* (*sep.*, h) impoverish

aus·pow·ern[2] ['aʊspaʊɐn] F *v/t.* (*sep.*, h) F elbow out

'aus·prä·gen (*sep.*, h) **I.** *v/t.* **1.** coin, mint; stamp; **II.** *v/refl.* **2.** ***sich ~*** develop, take shape; → ***ausgeprägt*** II; **3.** ***sich ~ in*** *dat.* be reflected in, find its expression in; ***Angst*** (***Haß***) ***prägte sich in ihrem Gesicht aus*** fear was written into her face (hatred was stamped on her face); *s-e Krankheit* ***hatte sich in s-m Gesicht ausgeprägt*** had left its mark (*or* stamp) on his face

'aus·prei·sen *v/t.* (*sep.*, h) price; put a price tag on

'aus·pres·sen *v/t.* (*sep.*, h) press out, squeeze out; squeeze

'aus·pro,bie·ren *v/t.* (*sep.*, h) try (out), test

Aus·puff ['aʊspʊf] *m* (-[e]s; -e) *mot.* exhaust; **~ga·se** *pl.* exhaust fumes; **~klap·pe** *f* exhaust valve; **~rohr** *n* exhaust pipe; **~topf** *m* silencer, *Am.* muffler

'aus·pum·pen *v/t.* (*sep.*, h) pump out; F *fig.* F grill *s.o.*

'aus·punk·ten *v/t.* (*sep.*, h) *boxing*: beat on points, outpoint; *fig.* cut out

'aus·pu·sten *v/t.* (*sep.*, h) blow out

'aus·put·zen (*sep.*, h) **I.** *v/t.* **1.** clean out; **2.** prune; **II.** *v/i. soccer*: sweep up at the back; **'Aus·put·zer** *m* (-s; -) *soccer*: sweeper-up

'aus·quar,tie·ren *v/t.* (*sep.*, h) move *s.o.* out; turn *s.o.* out

'aus·quat·schen F (*sep.*, h) **I.** *v/t.* F blab out; **II.** *v/refl.*: ***sich ~*** F have a good old natter (*or* chinwag)

'aus·quet·schen *v/t.* (*sep.*, h) **1.** → ***auspressen***; **2.** F *fig.* F grill *s.o.*

'aus·ra,die·ren *v/t.* (*sep.*, h) rub out, erase; *fig.* wipe out, eradicate

'aus·ran,gie·ren *v/t.* (*sep.*, h) **1.** sort out; throw out, get rid of; ⚙ scrap; **2.** 🚂 shunt out

'aus·ra,sie·ren *v/t.* (*sep.*, h) shave

'aus·ra·sten *v/i.* (*sep.*, sn) **1.** ⚙ disengage, be released; **2.** *sl. fig.* flip

'aus·rau·ben *v/t.* (*sep.*, h) rob; ransack

'aus·rau·chen *v/t.* (*sep.*, h): ***s-e Pfeife*** *etc.* ~ finish one's pipe *etc.*

'aus·räu·chern *v/t.* (*sep.*, h) fumigate; smoke out

'aus·rau·fen *v/t.* (*sep.*, h): ***sich die Haare ~*** tear one's hair out; ***ich könnte mir die Haare ~!*** I could kick myself!

'aus·räu·men *v/t.* (*sep.*, h) **1.** clear out (*a.* F *b.s.*); **2.** ⚕ purge; **3.** *fig.* clear up

'aus·rech·nen *v/t.* (*sep.*, h) work out (*a. fig.*); calculate; ***sich*** *et.* ~ guess, figure out; ***ich rechne mir gute Chancen aus*** I reckon (*or* think) I've got a good chance

'aus·recken (*sep.* -k·k-) (*sep.*, h) **I.** *v/t.* stretch; ***sich den Hals ~ nach*** *dat.* crane one's neck to see; **II.** *v/refl.*: ***sich ~*** stretch out (***nach*** *dat.* to reach)

'Aus·re·de *f* (-; -n) excuse; **'aus·re·den** (*sep.*, h) **I.** *v/i.* finish speaking; ***j-n ~ lassen*** let s.o. finish (speaking), hear s.o. out; ***lassen Sie mich ~*** let me finish; ***j-n nicht ~ lassen*** cut s.o. short; **II.** *v/t.*: ***j-m et. ~*** talk s.o. out of s.th.; **III.** *v/refl.*: ***sich bei j-m ~*** unburden o.s. to s.o.

'aus·reg·nen *v/impers.* (*sep.*, h): ***es hat*** (***sich***) ***ausgeregnet*** that's the end of the rain now (*or* for a while)

'aus·rei·ben *v/t.* (*irr.*, *sep.*, h, → ***reiben***) wipe out; ***sich die Augen ~*** rub one's eyes

'aus·rei·chen *v/i.* (*sep.*, h) be enough; last *a week etc.*; ***m-e Kenntnisse reichen nicht aus*** I don't know enough; ***s-e Ausbildung reicht für die Stelle nicht aus*** his training isn't (quite) adequate for the job; **'aus·rei·chend** *adj.* enough, sufficient; *ped.* D

'aus·rei·fen *v/i.* (*sep.*, sn) ripen; *cheese, wine*: *a.* mature, age; → ***ausgereift*** II

'Aus·rei·se *f* (-; -n) departure; ***bei der ~*** on leaving the country; **~er·laub·nis** *f* exit permit

'aus·rei·sen *v/i.* (*sep.*, sn) leave (the country)

'Aus·rei·se|sper·re *f* ban on exit visas, ban on leaving the country; **~vi·sum** *n* exit visa

'aus·rei·ßen (*irr.*, *sep.*, → ***reißen***) **I.** *v/t.* (h) **1.** tear out; pull up; ***ich fühle mich, als könnte ich Bäume ~*** I feel up to anything; F *fig.* ***dafür reiß' ich mir kein Bein aus*** I'm not going to kill myself (for that); **II.** *v/i.* (sn) **2.** *seam etc.*: split; *button etc.*: come off; **3.** F do a bunk; run away *from home*; **4.** *sport*: break away (from the field); **'Aus·rei·ßer** *m* (-s; -) **1.** runaway (*a. phys.*); **2.** *sport*: breakaway; **3.** F *fig.* F one-off

'aus·rei·ten (*irr.*, *sep.*, → ***reiten***) **I.** *v/i.* (sn) ride out (on horseback); **II.** *v/t.* (h) exercise *horse*

'aus·rei·zen *v/t.* (*sep.*, h) **1.** ***s-e Karten ~*** make the most of one's hand; **2.** *fig.* thrash out; ***das Thema ist ausgereizt*** that subject has been exhausted (F flogged to death)

aus·ren·ken ['aʊsrɛŋkən] *v/t.* (*sep.*, h): ***sich den Arm*** *etc.* ~ dislocate one's arm *etc.*; *fig.* ***sich*** (***fast***) ***den Hals ~ nach et.*** crane one's neck to see s.th., F nearly pull a muscle trying to see s.th.

'aus·rich·ten (*sep.*, h) **I.** *v/t.* **1.** straighten; align; adjust; *fig.* adjust (***nach*** *dat.* to); bring *s.o.* into line (with); → ***ausgerichtet*** II; **2.** achieve; ***nichts ~*** get nowhere; ***das wird nicht viel ~*** that won't make much (*or* any) difference; ***damit richtet er nichts aus*** that won't get him anywhere; **3.** pass *message etc.* on (***j-m*** to *s.o.*); ***könntest du ihm das ~?*** could you tell him (that)?; ***ich werd's ~*** I'll tell him *etc.*, I'll pass it on; ***richten Sie ihm Grüße*** (***von mir***) ***aus*** give him my regards; ***kann ich etwas ~?*** can I take a message?; **4.** organize; host; **II.** *v/refl.*: ⚔ ***sich ~*** fall in; **'Aus·rich·ter** *m* (-s; -) *sport*: organizer; host; **'Aus·rich·tung** *f* (-; *no pl.*) **1.** adjustment; alignment (*both a. fig.*); **2.** *sport etc.*: organization; hosting

'Aus·ritt *m* (-[e]s; -e) ride

'aus·ro·den *v/t.* (*sep.*, h) **1.** uproot, pull up *tree etc.*; **2.** clear *forest*

'aus·rol·len (*sep.*) **I.** *v/t.* (h) roll out *carpet, dough etc.*; run out *cable etc.*; **II.** *v/i.* (sn) come to a standstill; ✈ *a.* taxi to a halt

aus·rot·ten ['aʊsrɔtən] *v/t.* (*sep.*, h) pull up *weeds*; wipe out (*a. fig.*); *fig.* stamp out; **'Aus·rot·tung** *f* (-; -en) wiping out; *fig. a.* genocide

'aus·rücken (*sep.* -k·k-) (*sep.*) **I.** *v/i.* (sn) **1.** ⚔, *police etc.*: move out; *fire brigade*: go out on call; **2.** F do a bunk; run away *from home*; **II.** *v/t.* (h) ⚙ disengage; *a.* shift *clutch etc*

'Aus·ruf *m* (-[e]s; -e) cry; exclamation; *ling.* interjection; **'aus·ru·fen** *v/t.* (*irr.*, *sep.*, h, → ***rufen***) **1.** cry, shout; call out *s.o.'s name etc.*; ***j-n ~ lassen*** page s.o.; ***et. ~ lassen*** have s.th. announced; **2.** proclaim; call *strike*; ***j-n ~ als*** (***or zu***) proclaim s.o. *king etc.*; ***den Notstand ~*** declare a state of emergency; **'Aus·ru·fe·zei·chen** *n* exclamation mark; **'Aus·ru·fung** *f* (-; -en) proclamation; call *of strike*

'aus·ru·hen (*sep.*, h) **I.** *v/i. and v/refl.* (***sich ~***) (have a) rest; → ***ausgeruht*** II, ***Lorbeer*** 4; **II.** *v/t.*: ***die Beine*** *etc.* ~ rest one's legs *etc.*, give one's legs *etc.* a rest

'aus·rup·fen *v/t.* (*sep.*, h) pull out; pluck out

'aus·rü·sten *v/t.* (*sep.*, h) fit out (*a.* ⚙), equip, *a.* arm (***mit*** *dat.* with; ***für*** *acc.* for); *fig.* equip (with); ~ ***mit*** *a.* supply with; **'Aus·rü·stung** *f* (-; -en) *sport etc.*: gear; ⚔ equipment (*a.* ⚙), kit

'aus·rut·schen *v/i.* (*sep.*, sn) slip (***auf*** *dat.* on); *mot.* skid; *fig.* step out of line; **'Aus·rut·scher** *fig. m* (-s; -) faux pas, gaffe, blunder

'Aus·saat *f* (-; -en) **1.** *no pl.* sowing; **2.** seed; **'aus·sä·en** *v/t.* (*sep.*, h) sow; *fig.* sow the seeds of

'Aus·sa·ge *f* (-; -n) **1.** statement; *ling.* predicate; *art etc.*: message; ***nach ~ von*** (*or gen.*) according to; **2.** ⚖ testimony, evidence (*a. pl.*); ***e-e ~ machen*** → ***aussagen*** 2; ***die ~ verweigern*** refuse to give evidence; ***hier steht ~ gegen ~*** it's his word against hers *etc.*; ***aufgrund der ~ von*** on the evidence of

'Aus·sa·ge·kraft *f* (-; *no pl.*) expressiveness; validity; **'aus·sa·ge·kräf·tig** *adj.* expressive; *statistics etc.*: sound, convincing

'aus·sa·gen (*sep.*, h) **I.** *v/t.* state, declare, say; *painting etc*: have *s.th.* to say; **II.** *v/i.* ⚖ testify, give evidence (***gegen*** *acc.* against)

'aus·sä·gen *v/t.* (*sep.*, h) saw out

'Aus·sa·ge|satz *m ling.* clause of statement; **~ver·wei·ge·rung** *f* ⚖ refusal to testify (*or* give evidence)

'Aus·satz *m* (-es; *no pl.*) leprosy; **aus·sät·zig** ['aʊszɛtsɪç] *adj.* leprous; **Aus·sät·zi·ge** ['aʊszɛtsɪgə] *m, f* (-n; -n) leper (*a. fig.*)

'aus·sau·fen *v/t.* (*irr.*, *sep.*, h, → ***saufen***) *animal*: drink up; empty; *sl. person*: F guzzle *all the beer etc.*; finish off, drain *bottle etc.*

'aus·sau·gen *v/t.* (*sep.*, h) suck out; suck; *fig.* suck dry; (*a.* ***bis aufs Blut ~***) bleed *s.o.* white

'aus·scha·ben *v/t.* (*sep.*, h) scrape out (*a.* ⚕); scoop out; **'Aus·scha·bung** *f* (-; -en) ⚕ (womb) scrape

aus·schach·ten ['aʊsʃaxtən] *v/t.* (*sep.*, h) dig up; dig out; sink *shaft, well etc.*

'Aus·schalt·au·to,ma·tik *f* automatic shutoff

'aus·schal·ten *v/t.* (*sep.*, h) **1.** switch off; **2.** *fig.* dismiss *doubts etc.*; avoid *mistake etc.*; put *rival etc.* out of the running, get rid of *s.o.*; *esp. sport*: eliminate *s.o.*; inactivate *parliament etc.*; **'Aus·schal·ter** *m* (-s; -) ⚡ circuit breaker; **'Aus·schal·tung** *f* (-; -en) **1.** ⚡ disconnection; **2.** *esp. sport*: elimination

Aus·schank ['aʊsʃaŋk] *m* (-[e]s; Ausschänke ['aʊsʃɛŋkə]) **1.** *no pl.* sale of alcoholic drinks; ~ ***von Bier*** *etc.* sale of beer *etc.*; **2.** pub, *Am.* bar; **3.** bar, counter; **~er·laub·nis** *f* licen|ce (*Am.* -se) (to sell alcoholic drinks)

'Aus·schau *f*: ~ ***halten*** keep a lookout, ***nach*** *dat.*: look out for, be on (*or* keep) a lookout for, F keep one's eyes peeled for, look around for *a job etc.*; **'aus·schau·en** *v/i.* (*sep.*, h) **1.** ~ ***nach*** *dat.* look out for, look around for *a job etc.*; **2.** *dial.* → ***aussehen***

'aus·schau·feln *v/t.* (*sep.*, h) dig out

'aus·schei·den (*irr.*, *sep.*, → ***scheiden***) **I.** *v/t.* (h) **1.** *physiol.* excrete; pass *water*; secrete; expel; **2.** sort out; get rid of; **II.** *v/i.* (sn) **3.** ~ ***aus*** *dat.* retire from *office*, leave *firm, government etc.*; ***aus s-m Amt ~*** *pol.* withdraw from office; ***als Kabinettsminister ~*** leave one's post as cabinet minister (*or* one's cabinet post); **4.** *sport*: be eliminated (***aus*** *dat.* from), drop out (of); **5.** have to be ruled out; *person*: not to be eligible; ***sie scheidet von vornherein aus*** *a.* she can't be considered; **III.** ~ *n* (-s): ***nach s-m ~ aus der Firma*** (***dem Amt***) after leaving the company (withdrawing from office); **'aus·schei·dend** *adj. pol. etc.* departing; **'Aus·schei·dung** *f* (-; -en) **1.** *no pl. physiol.* excretion; passing; secretion; expulsion; **2.** *physiol.* excreted matter; excrement; *pl.* excreta (*pl.*); *a. pl.* discharge; **3.** *sport*: → ***Ausscheidungskampf***

'Aus·schei·dungs|kampf *m sport*: qualifying contest; **~or,gan** *n* excretory organ; **~pro,dukt** *n* waste product; **~run·de** *f sport*: qualifying round; **~spiel** *n sport*: qualifying match

'aus·schel·ten *v/t.* (*irr.*, *sep.*, h, → ***schelten***) scold

'aus·schen·ken *v/t.* (*sep.*, h) **1.** pour out; **2.** sell

'aus·sche·ren *v/i.* (*sep.*, sn) swerve to the right (*or* left); pull out; *fig.* go one's own way; *fig.* ~ ***aus*** *dat.* pull out of *an alliance etc.*, leave *a party etc.*

'aus·schicken (*sep.* -k·k-) *v/t.* → ***aussenden***

aus·schif·fen ['aʊsʃɪfən] *v/t.* (*sep.*, h) put ashore; unload

'aus·schil·dern *v/t.* (*sep.*, h) signpost

'aus·schimp·fen *v/t.* (*sep.*, h) give *s.o.* a telling-off (F wigging)

'aus·schlach·ten *v/t.* (*sep.*, h) **1.** cut up; **2.** F ⚙ cannibalize; **3.** *fig.* exploit, make *political etc.* capital out of; quarry *s.th.* for information *etc.*

'aus·schla·fen (*irr.*, *sep.*, h, → ***schlafen***) **I.** *v/i. and v/refl.* (***sich ~***) get a good night's sleep; have a lie-in; → ***ausgeschlafen*** II; **II.** *v/t*: (***s-n Rausch*** *etc.*) ~ sleep (it) off

'Aus·schlag *m* (-[e]s; ⸚e) **1.** ⚕ rash; ***e-n ~ bekommen*** break out in a rash (*or* in spots); **2.** deflection *of a needle*; swing *of a pendulum*; **3.** *fig.* ***den ~ geben*** decide the issue, clinch matters, tip the balance; ***den ~ geben für*** decide, ***j-n***: tip the scales in s.o.'s favo(u)r; ***er gab den ~ für unseren Sieg*** without him we would have lost; **'aus·schla·gen** (*irr.*, *sep.*, h, → ***schlagen***) **I.** *v/t.* **1.** knock out; → ***Faß***; **2.** turn down; **3.** ⚖ disclaim; **II.** *v/i.* **4.** *horse*: kick out; *person*: hit out (in all directions); **5.** *needle*: deflect; *scales*: turn; *pendulum*: swing; **6.** ♣ sprout, bud; *trees*: come into leaf; **'aus·schlag·ge·bend** *adj.* decisive; ~ ***sein*** *a.* be the deciding factor; ***das war*** (***für ihn***) ~ that tipped the scales (in his favo[u]r); ***das ist für mich nicht ~*** that doesn't weigh with me; **~e *Stimme*** casting vote; **'Aus·schla·gung** *f* (-; -en) ⚖ disclaimer

'aus·schlie·ßen (*irr.*, *sep.*, h, → ***schließen***) **I.** *v/t.* **1.** lock *s.o.* out; bar *s.o.* (***aus*** *dat.* from); expel (from *a party etc.*); *sport*: disqualify *or* suspend (from); (***aus der Gesellschaft*** *or* ***Gemeinschaft***) ~ ostracize; **2.** rule out, preclude; ***jeden Zweifel ~*** remove all (*or* any trace of) doubt; → ***ausgeschlossen*** II; **3.** exclude; **4.** ***sich*** (***gegenseitig***) ~ be mutually exclusive; **II.** *v/refl.*: ***sich ~*** exclude o.s. (***von*** from); **'aus·schließ·lich I.** *adj.* (*and adv.*) exclusive(ly), sole(ly); ~ ***für Mitglieder*** (for) members only; ***er interessiert sich ~ für*** all he's interested in is, he's only interested in; **II.** *prp.* (*gen.*) excluding, exclusive of; **'Aus·schließ·lich·keit** *f* (-; *no pl.*) exclusiveness; **'Aus·schlie·ßung** *f* (-; -en) exclusion; lockout; → ***Ausschluß***

'aus·schlüp·fen *v/i.* (*sep.*, sn) *zo.* hatch out

'aus·schlür·fen *v/t.* (*sep.*, h) slurp

'Aus·schluß *m* (-sses; ⸚sse) exclusion; expulsion; *sport*: disqualification, suspension; ***unter ~ der Öffentlichkeit*** ⚖ in camera, behind closed doors

'aus·schmie·ren *v/t.* (*sep.*, h) **1.** grease *baking tin etc.*; **2.** ⚙ lubricate; grease; oil; **3.** F *fig.* F put one over on *s.o.*

'aus·schmücken (*sep.* -k·k-) *v/t.* (*sep.*, h) decorate; *fig.* embroider, embellish; **'Aus·schmückung** (*sep.* -k·k-) *f* (-; -en) decoration; *fig.* embellishment

'aus·schnap·pen *v/i.* (*sep.*, sn) **1.** *door*: click open; *lock*: snap open; **2.** F *fig.* F snap out of it

'aus·schnau·fen *dial. v/i.* (*sep.*, h) **1.** get one's breath back; **2.** F take a breather

'aus·schnei·den *v/t.* (*irr.*, *sep.*, h, → ***schneiden***) cut out; prune

'Aus·schnitt *m* (-[e]s; -e) **1.** neck, *w.s.* neckline; **2.** cutting, clipping; **3.** 𝔄 sector; **4.** *fig.* part; detail *of painting etc.*; extract *of book*; excerpt *of film, concert etc.*; **~e** highlights (***aus*** *dat.* of, from); ***ich habe es nur in ~en gesehen*** I only saw parts of it

'aus·schnüf·feln F *v/t.* (*sep.*, h) F nose out

'aus·schöp·fen *v/t.* (*sep.*, h) scoop out; *fig.* exhaust *subject etc.*

'aus·schrau·ben *v/t.* (*sep.*, h) unscrew; *a.* take out *bulb etc.*

'aus·schrei·ben *v/t.* (*irr.*, *sep.*, h, → **schreiben**) **1.** write out (in full); **2.** make (*or* write) out (**j-m** to s.o.); **j-m ein Rezept** *etc.* ~ write s.o. a prescription *etc.*; **3.** announce; advertise *a post*; offer *a reward*; impose *taxes*; † put *s.th.* out to tender; **Wahlen** ~ call elections, *in GB*: *a.* go to the country; **'Aus·schrei·bung** *f* (-; -en) advertisement; † tender, call for tenders; *sport*: invitation to a competition

'aus·schrei·en (*irr.*, *sep.*, h, → **schreien**) **I.** *v/t.* shout out; F *fig.* **sich die Kehle** ~ F scream one's head off; **II.** *v/refl.*: **sich** ~ have a good scream; stop screaming

'aus·schrei·ten *v/i.* (*irr.*, *sep.*, sn, → **schreiten**) step out, stride (out); **'Aus·schrei·tun·gen** *pl.* rioting *sg.*, riot *sg.*, riots, violent clashes; **es kam zu** ~ there was rioting, there were violent clashes

'Aus·schuß *m* (-sses; ¨sse) **1.** committee; **2.** waste; → **Ausschußware**; **3.** exit wound; **~mit·glied** *n* committee member; **~sit·zung** *f* committee meeting; **~wa·re** *f* rejects *pl.*

'aus·schüt·teln *v/t.* (*sep.*, h) shake out

'aus·schüt·ten *v/t.* (*sep.*, h) **1.** pour out; spill; empty out, dump; **2.** empty; *fig.* **sein Herz** ~ pour one's heart out; → **Lachen**; **'Aus·schüt·tung** *f* (-; -en) † distribution *of dividends*

'aus·schwär·men *v/i.* (*sep.*, sn) swarm out; *fig.* scatter (to the four winds)

'aus·schwat·zen (*sep.*, h) **I.** *v/t.* F blab out; **II.** *v/refl.*: **sich** ~ have a good old chat

'aus·schwe·feln *v/t.* (*sep.*, h) sulphurize, *Am.* sulfurize; fumigate (with sulphur [*Am.* sulfur])

'aus·schwei·fen *v/i.* (*sep.*, sn) **1.** go to extremes; lead a dissolute life; **2.** go off at a tangent; **'aus·schwei·fend** *adj.* excessive; wild *imagination*; dissolute, licentious *life*; **'Aus·schwei·fung** *f* (-; -en) excess; **wüste ~en** wild excesses; **e-e ~ der Phantasie** a product of s.o.'s wild imagination

'aus·schwei·gen *v/refl.* (*irr.*, *sep.*, h, → **schweigen**): **sich** ~ remain silent (**über** *acc.* on), refuse to speak (about), refuse to comment (on)

'aus·schwen·ken (*sep.*, h) **I.** *v/t.* swill out; rinse; **II.** *v/i. crane etc.*: swivel, swing out; *trailer etc.*: veer round, veer to the left (*or* right)

'aus·schwit·zen *v/t.* (*sep.*, h) sweat (out); sweat out *a cold etc.*

'aus·se·hen (*irr.*, *sep.*, h, → **sehen**) **I.** *v/i.* look; **gut** ~ a) be good-looking, b) look well; **schlecht** ~ look ill; **du siehst schlecht aus** *a.* you don't look very well; F **wie siehst du denn aus?** what happened to you?; F **er sah vielleicht aus!** he looked a real sight; you should have seen him; **wie sieht er aus?** what does he look like?; **es sieht (ganz) danach aus** it (certainly) looks like it; F **er sieht ganz danach aus** he looks the sort; F **sehe ich danach aus?** what do you take me for?; **es sieht nach Regen aus** it looks like rain (*or* as if it's going to rain); F **so siehst du aus!** that's what you think; **wie sieht's bei dir aus?** a) how are things?, b) how about you?; **wie sieht's (damit) aus?** what's the verdict?; **II.** ~ *n* (-s) appearance, looks *pl.*; **dem ~ nach** judging by appearances; **man sollte nicht nach dem ~ urteilen** one shouldn't judge (*or* go) by appearances

'aus·sein F *v/i.* (*irr.*, *sep.*, sn, → **sein**) **1.** be over; **damit ist es (jetzt) aus** it's all over now, that's the end of that; **mit unserem Urlaub ist es jetzt aus** that's the end of our holiday, so much for our holiday; **es ist aus mit ihm** he's had it, F it's curtains for him; **mit ihm ist es aus** I'm (*or* she's) not going out with him any more, I've (*or* she's) finished with him; **zwischen den beiden ist es aus** they've split up, they've finished with each other, they're not going out with each other any more; **mit m-r Geduld ist es jetzt aus** I've had enough, there's a limit to what you can take; **2.** be (switched) off, *light*: *a.* be out; **3.** *fire*: be out, have gone out; **4.** *sport*: be out; **5.** be out; **ich war gestern mit ihm aus** I was (*or* went) out with him yesterday; **6.** ~ **auf** *acc.* be out for *s.th.*, be out to get *s.th.*

au·ßen ['aʊsən] *adv.* outside; **von** ~ from (the) outside; **nach ~ dringen** get out, *a. fig.* leak out, *sound etc.*: get through to the outside; **dringt die Musik nach ~?** can you hear the music through the walls?; *fig.* **nach ~ hin** outwardly, on the outside (*or* surface); **nach ~ hin erscheint sie sehr höflich** *a.* she has a veneer of politeness

'Au·ßen|an,ten·ne *f* outdoor aerial (*or* antenna); **~ar·bei·ten** *pl.* outside work *sg.*; **~auf·nah·me** *f phot.* outdoor shot; *film*: location shot; **~bahn** *f sport*: outside lane; **~be·zirk** *m* outlying area (*or* suburb); **~e** *a.* outskirts; **~bord·mo·tor** *m* outboard motor

'aus·sen·den *v/t.* (*irr.*, *sep.*, h, → **senden**) send out; transmit

'Au·ßen·dienst *m* field service; **im** ~ in the field; **~mit·ar·bei·ter** *m* field representative; *pl. a.* outdoor staff *sg.*; ~ **sein** *a.* work in the field

'Au·ßen|han·del *m* foreign trade; **~li·nie** *f sport*: boundary line, *n.s.* sideline; **~ma·ße** *pl.* outside measurements; **~mi,ni·ster** *m* foreign minister (*or* secretary); *in GB*: Foreign Secretary; *in the USA*: Secretary of State; **~mi·ni,ste·ri·um** *n* foreign ministry; *in GB*: Foreign and Commonwealth Office; *in the USA*: State Department; **~po·li,tik** *f* foreign affairs *pl.*; foreign policy; **~po,li·tisch** *adj.* foreign-policy ...; international; **~er Sprecher** spokesman on foreign affairs; **~sei·te** *f* outside

Au·ßen·sei·ter ['aʊsənzaɪtɐ] *m* (-s; -) *sport and fig.*: outsider; **gesellschaftlicher** ~ social misfit, *pl. a. the* fringes of society; **~po·si·ti,on** *f* fringe existence; **in e-e ~ geraten** end up on the fringes; **e-e gesellschaftliche ~ einnehmen** be socially out on the fringes; **~rol·le** *f* role of an *or* the outsider (*or* [the] outsiders); **in e-e ~ gedrängt werden** be pushed onto the sidelines, be marginalized

'Au·ßen|ski *m* outside ski; **~soh·le** *f* outer sole, outsole; **~spie·gel** *m* wing mirror; **~stän·de** *pl.* † outstanding accounts, accounts receivable; **~ste·hen·de** *m, f* (-n; -n) outsider; outside observer, observer on the outside; **~stel·le** *f* branch office; **~stür·mer** *m* winger; **linker** ~ outside left; **~ta·sche** *f* outside pocket; **~tem·pe·ra,tur** *f* outdoor temperature(s *pl.*); **~toi,let·te** *f* outside toilet; **~über,tra·gung** *f* outside broadcast; **~ver·tei·di·ger** *m* full-back; **~vier·tel** *n* suburb; **in e-m ~ leben** live in (one of) the suburbs; **~wand** *f* outer wall; **~welt** *f* outside world; **von der ~ abgeschnitten** *a.* cut off from the world around; **~win·kel** *m* external angle; **~wirt·schaft** *f* foreign trade

au·ßer ['aʊsɐ] **I.** *prp.* (*dat.*) **1.** out of; → **Betrieb** 3, **Dienst** 4, **Frage**; ~ **sich sein** be beside o.s. (**vor** *dat.* with); ~ **sich geraten** lose control over o.s., F flip one's lid; **2.** apart from, *esp. Am.* aside from; except (for); **3.** besides, in addition to; **II.** *cj.*: ~ **(wenn)** unless; ~ **daß** except that, apart from the fact that

äu·ßer ['ɔʏsɐ] *adj.* **1.** outer, outside *wall, layer, pressure etc.*; external *injury, circumstances, pressure, danger etc.*; *a. pressure, danger etc.*: from outside; *similarity, impression*: on the surface; **~er Rahmen** setting (*gen.* for); **~e Erscheinung** → **Äußere** 2; **2.** †, *pol.* foreign

Au·ßer'acht·las·sung *f* (-; *no pl.*) neglect (*gen.* of)

'au·ßer|be·ruf·lich *adj.* private; **~be·trieb·lich** *adj.* external

'au·ßer·dem *adv.* **1.** as well, in addition; *er besitzt e-e Hotelkette* **und ~ (noch) e-e Fluggesellschaft** and an airline as well, plus (*or* as well as) an airline, and an airline on top of it; ~ **gibt es was zu essen** and there'll be something to eat too (*or* as well); **2.** and anyway, and apart from that (*or* anything), *a.* and on top of that

'au·ßer·dienst·lich *adj.* unofficial; ⚔ off-duty ...

äußere(r, -s) ['ɔʏsərə; 'ɔʏsərɐ; 'ɔʏsərəs] *adj.* → **äußer**

'Äu·ße·re *n* (-n; *no pl.*) **1.** outside; **2.** (outward) appearance; externals *pl.*; **nach dem ~n urteilen** go by appearances

'au·ßer|ehe·lich *adj.* illegitimate; **~er Verkehr** extramarital intercourse (*or* sex); **~eu·ro,pä·isch** *adj.* non-European; **~fahr·plan·mä·ßig** *adj.* special *train etc.*; **~ge·richt·lich** *adj.* out-of-court *settlement etc.*; **~ge·setz·lich** *adj.* extralegal; **~ge·wöhn·lich I.** *adj.* unusual; exceptional, remarkable *achievement etc.*; **das ist für ihn ~** that's not typical of him (*or* like him) at all; **II.** *adv.* extremely, exceptionally; ~ **gut** *a.* exceptional, outstanding

'au·ßer·halb I. *prp.* (*gen.*) outside; beyond (*a. fig.*); ~ **der Arbeitszeit (Geschäftszeit)** out of working hours (business *or* office hours); ~ **der Legalität** beyond the law; **es ist ~ m-r Reichweite** a) it doesn't fall within my range of duties, b) it's beyond my range (*or* scope); **II.** *adv.* out of town

Au·ßer'haus·ver·kauf *m* takeaway(s *pl.*)

'au·ßer·ir·disch *adj.* extraterrestrial; **~es Wesen** *a.* being from outer space, alien (from outer space)

Au·ßer'kraft·set·zung *f* (-; *no pl.*) annulment; ⚖ repeal; suspension

'äu·ßer·lich I. *adj.* **1.** external; surface *wound*; ⚕ **nur zur ~en Anwendung** for external use only; **2.** *fig.* on the surface; superficial; **II.** *adv.* **3.** on the outside (*or* surface); **4.** *fig.* outwardly, on the surface; ***rein ~ betrachtet*** on the surface; **'Äu·ßer·lich·keit** *f* (-; -en) **1.** (outward) appearance, externals *pl.*; **2.** *fig.* formality; minor detail

äu·ßern ['ɔʏsɐn] (*sep.*, h) **I.** *v/t.* **1.** express, voice *suspicion, disapproval etc.*; ***s-e Meinung ~*** put one's point of view; **2.** show, express; **II.** *v/refl.*: ***sich ~*** **3.** say something (***über*** *acc.*, ***zu*** *dat.* about); say what one thinks (about), give one's opinion (on); ***sich ~ über*** *acc.* comment on, make a statement on; ***sich kritisch*** (***lobend***) ***~ über*** *acc.* criticize (praise), be critical about (be full of praise for); **4.** show; ***die Krankheit äußert sich in ...*** the symptoms of the disease are ...

'au·ßer|or·dent·lich I. *adj.* **1.** extraordinary; exceptional; remarkable; **2.** special, extraordinary; ***~e Ausgaben*** extras; ***~es Gericht*** special court; ***~er Professor*** reader, senior lecturer, *Am.* associate professor; **II.** *adv.* exceptionally; ***ich bedaure es ~*** I very much regret it; ***es freut mich ~*** I'm very pleased indeed; **~par·la·men,ta·risch** *adj.* extraparliamentary; **~plan·mä·ßig** *adj.* additional; supernumerary *civil servant*; unbudgeted *funds*; 🚂 *etc.*: special, unscheduled *service etc.*; **~schu·lisch** *adj.* private; ***~e Erziehung*** non-formal education; **~sinn·lich** *adj.*: ***~e Wahrnehmung*** extrasensory perception, ESP

äu·ßerst ['ɔʏsɐst] **I.** *adj.* **1.** outermost; furthest, ... furthest away; remotest; ***im ~en Norden*** in the far (*or* extreme) north; **2.** latest possible; ***das ist der ~e Termin*** *a.* that's the latest deadline possible; **3.** lowest possible *price etc.*; ***das ist der ~e Preis*** I can't go any lower than that; **4.** extreme; ***im ~en Fall*** if the worst comes to the worst; ***mit ~er Konzentration*** with the utmost concentration; ***mit ~er Kraft*** by a supreme effort, *drive etc.*: (at) full speed; ***von ~er Wichtigkeit*** extremely important, of the utmost importance; **II.** *adv.* extremely; ***~ verwirrend*** *a.* confusing to the extreme

au·ßer·stan·de ['aʊsɐʃtandə] *pred. adj.*: ***~ sein zu*** *inf.* be unable to *inf.*, be incapable of *ger.*; ***ich fühle mich ~, es zu tun*** *a.* I can't possibly do it

'Äu·ßer·ste *n* (-n; *no pl.*) *the* limit; *the* maximum, *the* most; *the* worst; ***es bis zum ~n treiben*** push things to the limit; ***zum ~n entschlossen*** prepared to go to any lengths; ***sein ~s tun*** do one's utmost; ***auf das ~ gefaßt*** prepared for the worst

'äu·ßer·sten·falls *adv.* **1.** at (the) most, at best, at the outside; **2.** at worst, if the worst comes to the worst

'au·ßer·ta,rif·lich *adj.* outside the agreed scale; ***~e Leistungen*** fringe benefits

Äu·ße·rung ['ɔʏsərʊŋ] *f* (-; -en) **1.** remark, comment; statement; ***unbedachte ~*** careless remark; ***sich jeder ~ enthalten*** refuse to comment; **2.** expression, sign

'aus·set·zen (*sep.*, h) **I.** *v/t.* **1.** abandon; maroon; **2.** release *wild animals, fish*; **3.** expose (*dat.* to); **4.** offer *reward etc.*; put *a price on s.o.'s head*; **5.** interrupt; ⚖ suspend *sentence, judgement*; **6.** ***etwas ~*** (*or* ***auszusetzen haben***) ***an*** *dat.* object to; ***was ist daran auszusetzen?*** what's wrong with it?; ***er hat immer etwas auszusetzen*** he's never satisfied, ***an*** *dat.*: he never stops criticizing; ***er hat dauernd an mir was auszusetzen*** he's always getting on at me about something (or other); ***ich habe nichts daran auszusetzen*** I have no objections, I have nothing against it, I have no complaints (about it); **II.** *v/i.* stop, break off; *heart, pulse*: miss a beat, be irregular, stop (beating); *engine*: stall; take a rest; *games*: miss a turn; ***e-n Tag ~*** take a day off; ***mit*** *et.* ***~*** stop *work(ing), taking the pill etc.*; **III.** *v/refl.*: ***sich ~*** expose o.s. (*dat.* to), *a.* lay o.s. open (to *criticism, ridicule etc.*); **'Aus·set·zung** *f* (-; -en) **1.** abandonment; **2.** exposure (*dat.* to *heat, cold etc.*); **3.** offer *of a reward etc.*; **4.** ⚖ suspension

'Aus·sicht *f* (-; -en) **1.** view (***auf*** *acc.* of); ***ein Zimmer mit ~ aufs Meer*** a room overlooking the sea (*or* with seaview); ***hier oben ist e-e schöne ~*** there's a lovely view from up here; ***j-m die ~ versperren*** obstruct s.o.'s view; **2.** *fig.* prospect(s *pl.*), chance (***auf*** *acc.* of); ***politische ~en*** political outlook; ***weitere ~en*** *meteor.* further outlook; ***~en haben auf*** *acc.* be in the running (*or* in line) for; ***~en haben zu*** *inf.* have a chance of *ger.*; ***er hat nicht die geringste ~ zu*** *inf.* he hasn't got (*or* doesn't stand) a chance of *ger.*; ***in ~ sein*** be coming up; ***in ~ stellen*** promise, hold out the prospect of; ***in ~ haben*** have *s.th.* in prospect; ***e-e neue Stelle in ~ haben*** have the possibility of getting a new job; *iro.* ***das sind ja schöne ~en!*** that's a fine lookout

'aus·sichts·los *adj.* hopeless; ***~!*** *a.* no chance; ***es ist ein ~es Vorhaben*** it's a hopeless venture, it's doomed to fail(ure); ***es ist ~, es zu versuchen*** there's no point in even trying; **'Aus·sichts·lo·sig·keit** *f* (-; *no pl.*) hopelessness, futility

'Aus·sichts|punkt *m* lookout (*or* vantage) point; **⁀reich** *adj.* promising; ***es ist ein ~er Posten*** the job has good prospects; **~stra·ße** *f* scenic road (*or* route); **~turm** *m* observation tower; **~wa·gen** *m* 🚂 observation car

'aus·sickern (*sep.* -k·k-) *v/i.* (*sep.*, sn) seep out; trickle out

'aus·sie·ben *v/t.* (*sep.*, h) **1.** sift out; ⚡ filter (out); **2.** *fig.* sift (*or* weed) out

'aus·sie·deln *v/t.* (*sep.*, h) resettle; evacuate; **'Aus·sied·ler** *m* (-s; -) emigrant, *a.* refugee; *a.* ethnic German (emigrant); **'Aus·sied·lung** *f* (-; -en) resettlement; forced migration

'aus·sit·zen *v/t.* (*irr., sep.*, h, → ***sitzen***) **1.** hatch; **2.** wear *s.th.* out of shape; **3.** *fig.* wait out

aus·söh·nen ['aʊszøːnən] *v/t. and v/refl.* (*sep.*, h): ***j-n*** (***sich***) ***~ mit et.*** *or* ***j-m*** reconcile s.o. (o.s.) to s.th. *or* with s.o.; ***sich ~ mit*** *a.* make one's peace with; **'Aus·söh·nung** *f* (-; -en) reconciliation

'aus·son·dern *v/t.* (*sep.*, h) sort out

'aus·sor·gen *v/i.* → ***ausgesorgt***

'aus·sor,tie·ren *v/t.* (*sep.*, h) sort out

'aus·spach·teln *v/t.* (*sep.*, h) plaster up

'aus·spä·hen (*sep.*, h) **I.** *v/t.* spy out; **II.** *v/i.*: ***~ nach*** *dat.* look out for

'aus·span·nen (*sep.*, h) **I.** *v/t.* **1.** stretch; spread (out); **2.** unharness *horses*; unyoke *oxen*; unhitch *cart etc.*; **3.** *fig.* ***j-m et. ~*** talk s.o. into giving one s.th.; wheedle s.th. out of s.o.; ***j-m die Freundin ~*** take s.o.'s girlfriend away (from him), F pinch s.o.'s girlfriend; **II.** *v/i.* relax, F take it easy

'aus·spa·ren *v/t.* (*sep.*, h) **1.** leave free; **2.** *fig.* leave out; **'Aus·spa·rung** *f* (-; -en) **1.** empty space; **2.** ⚙ recess

'aus·spei·en *v/t. and v/i.* (*irr., sep.*, h, → ***speien***) spit out; *fig.* spew (out), belch

'aus·sper·ren *v/t.* (*sep.*, h) lock out (*a. workers*); ***sich ~*** lock o.s. out; **'Aus·sper·rung** *f* (-; -en) lockout

'aus·spie·len (*sep.*, h) **I.** *v/t.* **1.** play, lead; *fig.* → ***Trumpf***; **2.** *sport*: a) play for *a cup etc.*, b) outplay *competitor*; **3.** ***es wird ein Gewinn von drei Millionen ausgespielt*** there are three million marks *etc.* to be won; **4.** *fig.* ***j-n gegen j-n ~*** play s.o. off against s.o.; **5.** bring to bear; **II.** *v/i.* **6.** *fig.* ***er hat ausgespielt*** F he's through (*or* done for); ***der hat bei mir ausgespielt*** F I'm through with him; **7.** *card games*: lead; ***wer spielt aus?*** whose lead (is it)?; **'Aus·spie·lung** *f* (-; -en) draw(ing of lots)

'aus·spin·nen *fig. v/t.* (*irr., sep.*, h, → ***spinnen***) spin out

'aus·spio,nie·ren *v/t.* (*sep.*, h) spy out; spy on *s.o.*

'Aus·spra·che *f* (-; -n) **1.** *no pl.* pronunciation; articulation; ***das ist die falsche ~*** that's not the right pronunciation, that's not how you pronounce (*or* say) it; F ***die haben aber e-e komische ~!*** what a funny accent they've got, F don't they speak funny?; F ***hast du e-e feuchte ~!*** F say it, don't spray it; **2.** discussion, *a. parl.* debate; ***offene ~*** heart-to-heart talk; **~re·gel** *f* pronunciation rule; *pl. a.* rules of pronunciation; **~wör·ter·buch** *n* pronouncing dictionary

'aus·sprech·bar *adj.*: ***schwer ~*** hard to pronounce; ***nicht ~*** unpronounceable; *fig.* unspeakable; **'aus·spre·chen** (*irr., sep.*, h, → ***sprechen***) **I.** *v/t.* **1.** pronounce; say; articulate; ***nicht ausgesprochen werden*** *ling.* be silent (*or* mute), *w.s.* remain unspoken; **2.** finish; **3.** express (*dat.* to), voice; ⚖ pronounce, pass *sentence*; *der Regierung* ***das Vertrauen ~*** *parl.* pass a vote of confidence (*dat.* in); **II.** *v/refl.*: ***sich ~*** **4.** express one's views (***über*** *acc.* on); ***sich für*** (***gegen***) *et.* ***~*** speak out (*or* come out, declare o.s.) in favo(u)r of (against), support (reject); **5.** unbosom o.s., F unload o.s.; ***sich*** (***mit j-m***) ***~*** have it out (with s.o.); ***sprich dich nur aus!*** get it off your chest, F spit it out; → ***ausgesprochen*** II; **III.** *v/i.* finish (speaking); ***laß ihn doch ~!*** let him finish

'aus·sprit·zen (*sep.*) **I.** *v/t.* (h) **1.** squirt out; ejaculate; **2.** ⚕ syringe; **II.** *v/i.* (sn) squirt out

'Aus·spruch *m* (-[e]s; ⸚e) utterance; remark; saying

'aus·spucken (*sep.* -k·k-) (*sep.*, h) **I.** *v/t.* spit out (*a. fig.*); bring up, *sl.* spew up; F *fig.* F cough up; F churn out; **II.** *v/i.* spit; ***vor j-m ~*** spit at s.o.'s feet, *fig.* spit on s.o.

'aus·spü·len *v/t.* (*sep.*, h) **1.** rinse; rinse out; ⚕ wash (out); **2.** *geol.* erode; wash away

'aus·staf,fie·ren *v/t.* (*sep.*, h) fit out; trim; dress *s.o.* up, F rig *s.o.* out

'Aus·stand *m* (-[e]s; ⸚e) **1.** strike; ***in den ~ treten*** go on strike; **2.** *pl.* ✝ outstanding accounts; **3.** ***s-n ~ geben*** have a leaving (*or* going-away) party

'aus·stan·zen *v/t.* (*sep.*, h) punch out

aus·stat·ten ['aʊsʃtatən] *v/t.* (*sep.*, h) fit out; supply; furnish; *typ.* get up; ***mit Personal*** **~** staff; *fig.* **~ *mit*** endow with, vest with; ***e-e Praxis mit Teppichböden*** **~** have a surgery fitted with carpets, have carpets laid (*or* put) in a surgery; ***der Wagen ist sehr gut ausgestattet*** the car's got all the trimmings; **'Aus·stat·tung** *f* (-; -en) equipment; fittings *pl.*; furnishings *pl.*; design; *thea.* sets and costumes *pl.*; *typ.* getup

'Aus·stat·tungs|film *m* (screen) spectacular; **~stück** *n thea.* spectacular (play *or* show)

'aus·ste·chen *v/t.* (*irr.*, *sep.*, h, → ***stechen***) **1.** dig *trench*; cut (out) *peat etc.*; *gastr.* cut out *pastry*; core *apple*; put out, poke out *eyes*; **2.** *fig.* outdo; cut out *rival etc.*; **'Aus·stech·form** *f* pastry cutter

'aus·ste·hen (*irr.*, *sep.*, h, → ***stehen***) **I.** *v/t.* put up with, suffer; ***es ist ausgestanden*** it's all over, we've *etc.* made it; ***ich kann ihn (es) nicht*** **~** I can't stand him (it); **II.** *v/i. decision etc.*: be pending; *payment*: be outstanding; *money*: be owing; *consignment*: be overdue; ***s-e Antwort steht noch aus*** we're still waiting for his answer, he has yet to give us an answer

'aus·stei·gen *v/i.* (*irr.*, *sep.*, sn, → ***steigen***) **1.** get out (***aus*** *dat.* of), get off (***aus*** *dat. a train, bus etc.*), *formal*: alight (from); ✈ F bale out; **2.** F *fig.* drop out (***aus*** *dat.* of); back out (of); ***aus der Kernenergie*** **~** back (*or* opt) out of the nuclear energy program(me); **'Aus·stei·ger** F *m* (-s; -) F dropout

aus·stei·nen ['aʊsʃtaɪnən] *v/t.* (*sep.*, h) stone

'aus·stel·len *v/t.* (*sep.*, h) **1.** show, display; exhibit; **2.** issue *passport etc.* (*dat.* for *s.o.*); make out *bill, check etc.* (to *s.o.*); write out *prescription, receipt etc.*; ***j-m ein Rezept*** **~** write (*or* give) s.o. a prescription; **3.** F switch off, turn off; **4.** → ***ausgestellt*** II; **Aus·stel·ler** ['aʊsʃtɛlɐ] *m* (-s; -) a) issuer; b) exhibitor

'Aus·stell·fen·ster *n mot.* quarterlight, *Am.* vent window

'Aus·stel·lung *f* (-; -en) **1.** exhibition, *Am.* exhibit; **2.** display *of goods etc.*; **3.** issue *of passport etc.*

'Aus·stel·lungs|da·tum *n* date of issue; **~flä·che** *f* exhibition space; **~ge·län·de** *n* exhibition site; **~hal·le** *f* exhibition hall; **~ka·ta͵log** *m* exhibition catalog(ue); **~ob͵jekt** *n* exhibit; **~ort** *m* place of issue; **~raum** *m* showroom; **~stand** *m* exhibition stand; **~stück** *n* exhibit; **~tag** *m* date of issue

'aus·stem·men *v/i.* (*sep.*, h) *skiing*: stem

'aus·stem·peln *v/i.* (*sep.*, h) clock out

'Aus·ster·be·etat F *m*: ***auf dem*** **~** ***stehen*** be on the way out; ***auf den*** **~** ***setzen*** write off

'aus·ster·ben *v/i.* (*irr.*, *sep.*, sn, → ***sterben***) die out (*a. fig.*); *zo. a.* become extinct; → ***ausgestorben*** II

'Aus·steu·er *f* (-; -n) trousseau; dowry

'aus·steu·ern (*sep.*, h) **I.** *v/i.* (*and v/t.*) ⚡, *radio etc.*: modulate; control the recording level (of); ***du hast zu stark ausgesteuert*** the recording level was too high; **II.** *v/t.* give *s.o.* a dowry; **'Aus·steue·rung** *f* (-; -en) ⚡, *radio etc.*: modulation; level control

'Aus·steu·er·ver·si·che·rung *f* endowment insurance

Aus·stieg ['aʊsʃtiːk] *m* (-[e]s; -e) **1.** exit; **2.** **~ *aus der Kernenergie*** withdrawal from (*or* opting out of) the nuclear energy program(me); ***sie fordern den*** **~** ***aus der Kernenergie*** they want the government to back out of the nuclear energy program(me)

'aus·stop·fen *v/t.* (*sep.*, h) stuff; pad

'Aus·stoß *m* (-es; *no pl.*) ⚒ output; **'aus·sto·ßen** *v/t.* (*irr.*, *sep.*, h, → ***stoßen***) **1.** push (*or* knock) out; **2.** expel (***aus*** *dat.* from); exile (from); (***aus der Gesellschaft***) **~** ostracize; **3.** expel *air*; give off *steam etc.*; send out *clouds of smoke etc.*; **4.** ⚒ turn out, produce; **5.** utter *swearword etc.*; give *a yell etc.*; heave *a sigh*; **'Aus·sto·ßung** *f* (-; -en) expulsion (*a. physiol.*); *fig.* ostracism

'aus·strah·len (*sep.*, h) **I.** *v/t.* **1.** *phys.* radiate, emit; *radio, TV*: broadcast; ***ausgestrahlt werden*** *a.* take the air; **2.** *fig.* radiate; exude; ***er strahlt Ruhe auf s-e Umgebung aus*** he has a calming effect on people; ***das Bild strahlt Ruhe (Harmonie) aus*** the picture gives you a great sense of calm (harmony); **3.** illuminate; **II.** *v/i.* **4.** radiate (*a. fig.*); **5.** *pain*: spread (***in*** *acc.* to); ***in die Beine*** **~** spread down one's legs; **'Aus·strah·lung** *f* (-; -en) **1.** *phys.* radiation (*a. fig.*), emission; *radio, TV*: transmission; **2.** *fig.* personality, personal magnetism, charisma; ***von ihm geht e-e starke*** **~** ***aus*** he has tremendous personal magnetism; **'Aus·strah·lungs·kraft** *fig. f* → ***Ausstrahlung*** 2

'aus·strecken (*sep.* -k·k-) (*sep.*, h) **I.** *v/t.* stretch out; put out *feelers*; stretch; ***die Hand*** **~** ***nach*** *dat.* reach out for; ***mit ausgestreckten Armen*** with outstretched arms; **II.** *v/refl.*: ***sich*** **~** a) stretch (o.s.) out; b) stretch (o.s.)

'aus·strei·chen *v/t.* (*irr.*, *sep.*, h, → ***streichen***) **1.** cross out; **2.** smooth down; **3.** ⚙ a) fill up, point; b) paint

'aus·streu·en *v/t.* (*sep.*, h) scatter; *a. fig.* spread *rumo(u)r etc.*

'aus·strö·men (*sep.*) **I.** *v/i.* (sn) **1.** *liquid*: gush out (***aus*** *dat.* of); *gas, steam*: escape (from); **~ *von*** *light, heat*: emanate from; **2.** *fig.* radiate (***aus*** *dat.* from); **3.** *crowd etc.*: ***ein- und*** **~** pour in and out; **II.** *v/t.* (h) **4.** radiate, emit *heat etc.*; give off *scent etc.*; **5.** *fig.* radiate, exude

'aus·stu͵die·ren F *v/i.* (*sep.*, h) finish one's degree, finish studying; ***ich will erst einmal*** **~** *a.* I want to get my degree first

'aus·su·chen *v/t.* (*sep.*, h) **1.** pick, choose; ***suchen Sie sich was aus*** take your pick; → ***ausgesucht*** II; **2.** sort (out)

'aus·ta͵rie·ren *v/t.* (*sep.*, h) balance; *fig.* balance out

'Aus·tausch *m* (-[e]s; *no pl.*) exchange; *sport*: substitution; ⚙ replacement; ***im*** **~** ***gegen*** in exchange for; **~ak·ti͵on** *f* new-for-old campaign

'aus·tausch·bar *adj.* interchangeable; **'Aus·tausch·bar·keit** *f* (-; *no pl.*) interchangeability

'Aus·tausch·do͵zent *m* exchange lecturer

'aus·tau·schen *v/t.* (*sep.*, h) exchange (***gegen*** *acc.* for); interchange; F swap; ***A gegen B*** **~** replace A by B, substitute B for A; ***Blicke*** **~** exchange looks, look at each other; ***Erfahrungen*** **~** compare notes; ***Erinnerungen*** **~** reminisce (about the past); ***Beleidigungen*** **~** trade insults

'Aus·tausch|leh·rer *m* exchange teacher; **~mo·tor** *m* reconditioned engine; **~pro͵fes·sor** *m* exchange professor; **~pro͵gramm** *n* exchange program(me); **~schü·ler** *m* exchange pupil (*Am.* student); **~spie·ler** *m sport*: substitute; **~stu͵dent** *m* exchange student

'aus·tei·len (*sep.*, h) **I.** *v/t.* hand out, distribute (***an*** *acc.* to; ***unter*** *dat.* among); share out (among); give *orders*; serve *food*; deal *cards, blows*; ***mit vollen Händen*** **~** be very lavish with; **II.** *v/i. card game*: deal; ***wer teilt aus?*** who's dealing, whose deal is it?; F ***er kann nicht nur einstecken, sondern auch*** **~** he can give as good as he gets; **'Aus·tei·lung** *f* (-; -en) distribution

Au·ster ['aʊstɐ] *f* (-; -n) oyster

'Au·stern|bank *f* (-; ⸚e) oyster bed; **~fi·scher** *m zo.* oyster catcher; **~fi·sche͵rei** *f* oyster fishing; **~pilz** *m* oyster mushroom; **~scha·le** *f* oyster shell; **~zucht** *f* oyster culture; oyster farm

'aus·te·sten *v/t.* (*sep.*, h) test; *computer*: debug *program*

'aus·til·gen *v/t.* (*sep.*, h) wipe out; eradicate (*a. fig.*), get rid of; *fig.* blot out *memory etc.*

'aus·to·ben *v/refl.* (*sep.*, h): ***sich*** **~** have one's fling; sow one's wild oats; have a good romp; *fig.* let one's anger *etc.* out; *storm*: spend itself

Aus·trag ['aʊstraːk] *m* (-[e]s; *no pl.*) **1.** settlement *of dispute etc.*; ***zum*** **~** ***bringen*** settle; ***zum*** **~** ***kommen*** be settled; **2.** *dial.* ***im*** **~** ***leben*** have retired from active life

'aus·tra·gen (*irr.*, *sep.*, h, → ***tragen***) **I.** *v/t.* **1.** 📯 deliver; **2.** ⚕ carry to term; ***sie will das Kind*** **~** she wants to have the child (*or* baby); **3.** argue out; settle *dispute etc.*; **4.** *sport*: hold *contest etc.*; **5.** take (*or* cross) *a name* off the list; **II.** *v/refl.*: ***sich*** **~** **6.** take one's name off the list; **7.** sign out; **'Aus·trä·ger** *m* (-s; -) delivery man (*or* boy); newspaper man (*or* boy)

'Aus·tra·gung *f*: ***die*** **~** ***des Spiels findet hier statt*** the game will be held here; **'Aus·tra·gungs·ort** *m* venue

Au·stral·asier [aʊs'traːlʔaːzĭɐ] *m* (-s; -), **au·stral·asisch** [aʊs'traːlʔaːzɪʃ] *adj.* Australasian

Au·stra·li·er [aʊs'traːlĭɐ] *m* (-s; -), **Au·stra·lie·rin** [aʊs'traːlĭərɪn] *f* (-; -nen), **au·stra·lisch** [aʊs'traːlɪʃ] *adj.* Australian

Au·stra·lo·pi·the·kus [aʊstralo'piːtekʊs] *m* (-; *no pl.*) Australopithecus

'aus·trai͵niert *adj.* fighting fit

'aus·träu·men (*sep.*, h) **I.** *v/i.*: ***er hat ausgeträumt*** he's come down to earth again; **II.** *v/t.*: ***der Traum ist ausgeträumt*** it was nice while it lasted

'aus·trei·ben (*irr.*, *sep.*, h, → ***treiben***) **I.** *v/t.* **1.** drive out; exorci|se (*a. Am.* -ze), cast out *evil spirit etc.*; **2.** F *fig.* ***j-m et.*** **~** F cure s.o. of s.th.; **II.** *v/i.* ⚘ sprout; **'Aus·trei·bung** *f* (-; -en) expulsion (*a.* ⚕); exorcism; **'Aus·trei·bungs·pha·se** *f* expulsive stage (of labo[u]r)

'aus·tre·ten (*irr.*, *sep.*, → ***treten***) **I.** *v/t.* (h) **1.** stamp out *fire etc.*; **2.** wear out *shoes*; break in *new shoes*; **3.** wear down *steps etc.*; tread *path*; → ***ausgetreten*** II; **II.** *v/i.* (sn) **4.** *steam, gas*: escape; *liquid*: come out; **5.** **~ *aus*** *dat.* leave *club etc.*; *a.*

resign from *a party*; leave, pull out of *an alliance etc.*; **6.** F go and spend a penny, *Am.* go to the bathroom; ***ich muß mal*** ~ *a.* I must disappear for a minute, F nature calls

Au·stria·zis·mus [aʊstriaˈtsɪsmʊs] *m* (-; -men) *ling.* Austriacism

ˈaus·trick·sen F *v/t.* (*sep.*, h) outsmart, outwit

ˈaus·trin·ken (*irr., sep.*, h, → ***trinken***) **I.** *v/t.* drink up, finish; empty; **II.** *v/i.* drink up, finish one's beer (*or* coffee *etc.*); finish the bottle *etc*

ˈAus·tritt *m* (-[e]s; -e) **1.** resignation (***aus*** *dat.* from *a party etc.*); withdrawal (from *a club etc.*); ***sein ~ aus der Kirche hat viele schockiert*** many people were shocked when he left the church; ***s-n ~ erklären*** hand in one's resignation, announce (*or* say) that one is leaving the church *etc.*; **2.** ⚙ escape *of gas, steam etc.*; **ˈAus·tritts·er·klä·rung** *f* (letter of) resignation; notice of withdrawal; ***s-e ~ kam überraschend*** his announcement that he is (*or* was) going to resign (*or* leave the church *etc.*) came as a surprise

ˈaus·trock·nen (*sep.*) **I.** *v/t.* (h) dry; dry up, parch *soil, throat*; drain *swamp, river etc.*; season *wood*; **II.** *v/i.* (sn) dry up; *new building etc.*: dry out; *skin*: go (*or* become) dry; ***m-e Kehle ist ausgetrocknet*** my throat is parched

ˈaus·trom·pe·ten *v/t.* (*sep.*, h) broadcast

ˈaus·tüf·teln F *v/t.* (*sep.*, h) work out (carefully); → ***ausgetüftelt*** II

ˈaus·üben *v/t.* (*sep.*, h) **1.** carry out *a trade, a profession, an office, one's duties etc.*, have *a profession*; practi|se (*Am.* -ce) *law, medicine etc.*; pursue *a career*; carry out, be involved in *an acitivity*; hold *an office*; perform *one's duties*; ***den Beruf des Musikers*** (***Künstlers***) ~ be a professional (*or* practi|sing [*Am.* -cing]) musician (artist); **2.** exercise *power, one's right etc.*; exert *influence* (***auf*** *acc.* on); have *an effect etc.* (on); use *pressure etc.* (on), apply (to); → ***Druck***[1] 3; ***e-n Reiz ~ auf*** *acc.* hold an attraction for; **ˈAus·übung** *f* (-; *no pl.*) **1.** ***die ~ e-s Berufs*** having (*or* carrying out) a profession; ***in ~ s-s Dienstes*** in the line of duty; **2.** exercise; exertion; use, application

aus·ufern [ˈaʊsʔuːfɐn] *v/i.* (*sep.*, sn) *town*: (begin to) sprawl; *fig. conflict etc.*: escalate; *discussion etc.*: get out of control

ˈAus·ver·kauf *m* (-[e]s; ⸚e) **1.** (clearance) sale; ***im*** ~ *buy* at the sales; **2.** *fig. pol. etc.* sellout; **ˈaus·ver·kau·fen** *v/t.* (*sep.*, h) sell off; **ˈAus·ver·kaufs·wa·re** *f* sale goods *pl.*; **ˈaus·ver·kauft** *adj.* sold out (*a. thea. etc.*); ***die Größe ist ~*** *a.* we've (*or* they've) sold out of that size, that size is out of stock at the moment; ***~es Konzert*** sellout concert; ***~es Haus*** packed house; ***vor ~em Haus*** (***Stadion***) ***spielen*** play to a full *or* packed house (in front of a capacity crowd)

ˈaus·wach·sen (*irr., sep.*, → ***wachsen***) **I.** *v/i.* (sn) **1.** → ***ausgewachsen*** II; **2.** ❦ go to seed; **3.** F ***es ist ja zum*** ≗! F it's enough to drive you up the wall; **II.** *v/refl.* (h) **4.** ***sich ~ zu*** *dat.* grow into; *fig. a.* develop into; **5.** ***sich*** ~ disappear (*or* sort itself out) in time

ˈAus·wahl *f* (-; *no pl.*) **1.** choice, selection (*gen. or* ***an*** *dat.* of); ✝ range; *market research*: sample; ***e-e kleine*** ~ a small selection; ***e-e große*** ~ a large *or* wide choice (*or* selection); ***e-e riesige*** ~ a vast choice (*or* selection); ***e-e ~ aus*** *dat.* a selection from; ***die ~ ist nicht besonders gut*** there isn't much choice; ***e-e ~ treffen*** choose (***aus*** *dat.*, ***unter*** *dat.* from); ***e-e sorgfältige ~ treffen*** make a careful choice (*or* selection); ***zur ~*** *hundreds of books etc.* to choose from; **2.** → ***Auswahlmannschaft***; **ˈaus·wäh·len** *v/t.* (*sep.*, h) choose, pick, select (***aus*** *dat.* from); *a.* pick out; → ***ausgewählt*** II

ˈAus·wahl|gre·mi·um *n* selection board; **~mann·schaft** *f sport*: select team; **~mög·lich·keit** *f* choice; ***es sind nicht viele ~en*** there isn't much choice, there aren't many alternatives; **~prin·zip** *n* selection principle; **~sen·dung** *f* ✝ consignment on approval; **~ver·fah·ren** *n* selection procedure

ˈaus·wal·zen *v/t.* (*sep.*, h) ⚙ roll out; *fig.* (***breit***) ~ make a big thing out of, go to town on, drag out (endlessly)

ˈAus·wan·de·rer *m* (-s; -) emigrant; **ˈaus·wan·dern** *v/i.* (*sep.*, sn) emigrate; migrate; **ˈAus·wan·de·rung** *f* (-; -en) emigration; migration; *fig.* exodus

aus·wär·tig [ˈaʊsvɛrtɪç] *adj.* outside ..., from outside; in (*or* from) another town; *pol.* foreign; ***das ≗e Amt*** → ***Außenministerium***; ***~e Angelegenheiten*** foreign affairs; ***~e Studenten*** non-local (and foreign) students

aus·wärts [ˈaʊsvɛrts] *adv.* outwards; out, away (from home); out of town; in another town; ~ ***essen*** *etc.* eat *etc.* out; ~ ***spielen*** *sport*: play away from home

ˈAus·wärts·spiel *n sport*: away match

ˈaus·wa·schen *v/t.* (*irr., sep.*, h, → ***waschen***) wash out; ⚕ bathe; *geol.* erode

ˈaus·wech·sel·bar *adj.* interchangeable; replaceable; **ˈaus·wech·seln** (*sep*, h) **I.** *v/t.* exchange (***gegen*** for); replace (by); interchange (*all a.* ⚙); change *wheel, battery etc.*; *sport*: substitute *a player*; ***die Batterien*** *etc.* ~ *a.* put new batteries *etc.* in; *fig.* ***wie ausgewechselt*** (like) a different person; **II.** *v/i. sport*: make a substitution; **ˈAus·wech·sel·spie·ler** *m* substitute; **ˈAus·wech·se·lung** *f* (-; -en) exchange; replacement; *sport*: substitution

ˈAus·weg *m* (-[e]s; -e) way out (***aus*** *dat.* of); ***letzter*** ~ last resort; ***es gibt sonst keinen ~*** *a.* there's no other solution

ˈaus·weg·los *adj.* hopeless; **ˈAusweg·lo·sig·keit** *f* (-; *no pl.*) hopelessness

ˈaus·wei·chen *v/i.* (*irr., sep.*, sn, → ***weichen***) **1.** make way (*dat.* for), get out of the way (of); ***e-m Fußgänger*** *etc.* ~ avoid hitting a pedestrian *etc.*; ***e-m Schlag*** *etc.* ~ dodge a blow *etc.*; ***nach rechts*** (***links***) ~ swerve to the right (left); ***ich konnte ihm gerade noch ~*** *driver*: I just missed him, I just managed to swerve out of the way in time, *pedestrian*: he just missed me, I just managed to jump out of the way in time; **2.** *fig.* be evasive; ***j-m*** (***e-r Sache***) ~ avoid s.o. (s.th.); ***e-m Thema ~*** *a.* talk round a subject; ***e-r Entscheidung*** ~ avoid making a decision; ***er weicht m-n Fragen aus*** he won't answer my questions; **3.** ~ ***auf*** *acc.* switch to; *a.* take *a different road etc.* (instead); fall back on; **ˈaus·wei·chend** *adj.*: ***~e Antwort*** evasive answer

ˈAus·weich|flug·ha·fen *m* alternate airport; **~ma·nö·ver** *n* **1.** *mot.* swerve to avoid hitting s.o. (*or* s.th.); ***das war ein geschicktes*** ~ that was a nice bit of dodging (*or* piece of driving); **2.** *fig. a. pl.* evasive action; ***s-e Antwort war ein reines*** ~ he was just trying to avoid the issue with his answer; **~mög·lich·keit** *f* way out; **~stel·le** *f mot.* passing point; 🚃 siding

ˈaus·wei·den *v/t.* (*sep.*, h) **1.** gut; **2.** *fig.* exploit

ˈaus·wei·nen (*sep.*, h) **I.** *v/refl.*: ***sich*** ~ have a good cry, ***bei j-m***: cry on s.o.'s shoulder; **II.** *v/t.*: ***sich die Augen*** ~ cry one's eyes out

Aus·weis [ˈaʊsvaɪs] *m* (-es; -e) identity card, ID (card); membership (*or* admission *etc.*) card; *w.s.* pass, permit; passport; ***den*** (*or* ***j-s***) ~ ***verlangen*** ask for identification; **ˈaus·wei·sen** (*irr., sep.*, h, → ***weisen***) **I.** *v/t.* **1.** expel, deport (***aus*** *dat.* from); **2.** ✝ show (on the books); **3.** ***j-n ~ als*** identify s.o. as, *fig.* prove s.o. to be; **II.** *v/refl.*: ***sich*** ~ identify o.s., prove one's identity; *fig.* ***sich ~ als*** prove o.s. (to be) *an expert etc.*

ˈAus·weis|fäl·schung *f* forging of IDs; **~kar·te** *f* → ***Ausweis***; **~kon·trol·le** *f* ID check; **~le·ser** *m computer*: badge reader; **~pa·pie·re** *pl.* (identification *or* ID) papers

ˈAus·wei·sung *f* (-; -en) expulsion; deportation; ⚖ eviction; **ˈAus·wei·sungs·be·fehl** *m* deportation (*or* expulsion) order

ˈaus·wei·ten (*sep.*, h) **I.** *v/t.* extend (***zu*** *dat.* into); stretch *shoes, gloves*; *fig.* extend (to); **II.** *v/refl.*: ***sich*** ~ expand; *pullover etc.*: stretch; *fig. organization etc.*: expand, grow; *conflict*: spread; ***sich ~ zu*** *dat.* grow (*or* develop) into; *conflict*: *a.* escalate into; **ˈAus·wei·tung** *f* (-; -en) extension; expansion; spreading; escalation

ˈaus·wen·dig *adv.*: ~ ***lernen*** (***können***) learn (know) by heart; ~ ***spielen*** play from memory; ***et. in- und ~ kennen*** know s.th. inside out, know s.th. like the back of one's hand

ˈaus·wer·fen *v/t.* (*irr., sep.*, h, → ***werfen***) **1.** throw out; cast *anchor, net etc.*; **2.** spew up *lava*; ⚕ cough up *phlegm, blood*; ⚙ eject, throw up; turn out; **3.** allocate, set aside *sum of money*; pay out *premium, dividend*; ***e-n Gewinn von ... ~*** *lottery etc.*: pay ... in prize money; **4.** dig *trench etc.*

ˈaus·wer·ten *v/t.* (*sep.*, h) **1.** evaluate (*a.* ℞), analy|se (*Am.* -ze); *a.* interpret *statistics*; **2.** utilize, make (full) use of, exploit; **ˈAus·wer·tung** *f* (-; -en) evaluation (*a.* ℞), analysis; *a.* interpretation *of statistics*; utilization, exploitation

ˈaus·wet·zen *fig. v/t.* (*sep.*, h) → ***Scharte***

ˈaus·wickeln (*sep.* -k·k-) *v/t.* (*sep.*, h) **1.** unwrap; **2.** ***ein Kind*** ~ take a baby's nappies off

ˈaus·wie·gen *v/t.* (*irr., sep.*, h, → ***wiegen***) weigh out (*a. sport*); → ***ausgewogen*** II

ˈaus·wir·ken *v/refl.* (*sep.*, h): ***sich*** ~ have an effect (***auf*** *acc.* on), have its effect, make itself felt; ***sich ~ auf*** *acc. a.* affect; ***sich*** (***un***)***günstig ~ auf*** *acc.* have a positive (a negative, an adverse) effect on; **ˈAus·wir·kung** *f* (-; -en) effect (***auf*** *acc.* on); consequence(s *pl.*) (for); implication(s *pl.*) (for); repercussions *pl.* (on, *a.* in *the north etc.*); outcome, result(s *pl.*);

diplomatische *etc.* **~*en*** *a.* diplomatic *etc.* fallout
'aus·wi·schen *v/t.* (*sep.*, h) wipe (*or* clean) out; wipe out (*or* off); ***sich die Augen*** ~ rub one's eyes; F *fig.* ***j-m eins*** ~ F get s.o.; ***dem werd' ich anständig eins*** ~ F I'm going to get him good and proper
'aus·wit·tern (*sep.*) **I.** *v/i.* (sn) *geol.* wear away; ⚗ effloresce; *Holz* ~ ***lassen*** season; **II.** *v/t.* (h) season
'aus·wrin·gen *v/t.* (*irr.*, *sep.*, h, → ***wringen***) wring out
Aus·wuchs ['aʊsvuːks] *m* (-es; Auswüchse ['aʊsvyːksə]) **1.** ⚕ growth; deformity; hump; **2.** *fig.* negative spin-off; *pl.* excesses; ***das ist ein*** ~ ***s-r krankhaften Phantasie*** it's a product of his sick imagination
'aus·wuch·ten *v/t.* (*sep.*, h) (counter)balance *wheels*
'Aus·wurf *m* (-[e]s; *no pl.*) **1.** ⚙ ejection; **2.** ⚕ sputum; ***blutigen*** ~ ***haben*** be coughing up blood; **3.** *fig.* ~ (***der Menschheit***) scum (of the earth), *the* dregs of society
'aus·wür·feln *v/t.* (*sep.*, h) throw dice for; ***laß uns*** ~, ***wer fahren muß*** let's throw dice to see (*or* decide) who is to drive
'aus·zah·len (*sep.*, h) **I.** *v/t.* pay (out); pay in cash; pay off *workers*, *creditors etc.*; buy out *business partner*; **II.** *fig.* *v/refl.*: ***sich*** ~ pay off; ***das zahlt sich aus*** it pays (off in the end); ***es zahlt sich nicht aus*** it doesn't pay, it's not worth it (*or* the effort *etc.*)
'aus·zäh·len *v/t.* (*sep.*, h) **1.** count (out); count *votes*; **2.** count out *boxer*; **3.** *children's game*: count out; **'Aus·zähl·reim** *m* (-[e]s; -e) counting-out rhyme
'Aus·zah·lung *f* (-; -en) **1.** payment; paying off *of workers*, *creditors etc.*; buying out *of business partner*; **2.** payment; payoff
'aus·zeh·ren *v/t.* (*sep.*, h): ***j-n*** ~ drain s.o., drain s.o. of all his *or* her strength (*or* of every ounce of strength); ***ein Land*** ~ drain a country of all its resources, bleed a country white; → ***ausgezehrt*** II; **'Aus·zeh·rung** *f* (-; *no pl.*) emaciation
'aus·zeich·nen (*sep.*, h) **I.** *v/t.* **1.** label; price, put a price tag on; **2.** distinguish; ***Ausdauer zeichnet sie aus*** she's known for her (powers of) stamina; ***die reiche Auswahl an Fisch zeichnet den See aus*** the lake is known (*or* noted) for its great variety of fish; ***was dieses Buch auszeichnet*** what distinguishes this book, what sets this book apart from others, what is so special about this book; **3.** hono(u)r; ***j-n mit e-m Preis*** *etc.* ~ award a prize *etc.* to s.o.; ***mit Orden*** ~ decorate; ***der Film wurde in Cannes ausgezeichnet*** the film received a Cannes award; ***X, ein mehrfach ausgezeichneter Musiker*** X, winner of several music prizes; **4.** *typ.* mark up; **II.** *v/refl.*: ***sich*** ~ distinguish o.s., excel (***als*** as; ***durch*** *acc.* by; ***in*** *dat.* at, in); **'Aus·zeich·nung** *f* (-; -en) **1.** ✝ label(l)ing; pricing; **2.** a) hono(u)ring; b) (mark of) distinction, hono(u)r; decoration, medal; award, prize; ***mit*** ~ ***bestehen*** pass with distinction, get a distinction; **3.** *typ.* markup, display
'Aus·zeit *f* (-; -en) *sport*: time out
'aus·zieh·bar *adj.* extendible; pull-out ...; telescopic; **'aus·zie·hen** (*irr.*, *sep.*, → ***ziehen***) **I.** *v/t.* (h) **1.** pull out (*a. table*, *antenna etc.*); **2.** take off *coat etc.*; undress *s.o.*; F *fig.* fleece *s.o.*; **3.** ⚗ *and* ⚗ extract (***aus*** *dat.* from); **II.** *v/i.* (sn) **4.** move; ~ ***aus*** *dat.* move out of; **5.** set out (*or* off); ***zum Kampf*** ~ set out to battle; **III.** *v/refl.*: ***sich*** ~ get undressed; take one's clothes off
'Aus·zieh|fe·der *f* drawing pen; **~lei·ter** *f* extension ladder; **~plat·te** *f* leaf; **~tisch** *m* pull-out table; **~tu·sche** *f* drawing ink
'aus·zir·keln *v/t.* (*sep*, h) mark out with compasses; *fig.* figure out
'aus·zi·schen *v/t.* (*sep.*, h) *thea.* hiss (at)
Aus·zu·bil·den·de ['aʊstsuːbɪldəndə] *m*, *f* (-n; -n) trainee
Aus·zug ['aʊstsuːk] *m* (-[e]s; Auszüge ['aʊstsyːgə]) **1.** move (***aus*** *dat.* from); **2.** departure (***aus*** *dat.* from); march (out of); procession (out of); ⚔, *pol.* pullout (from); *a. fig.* exodus (from); **3.** ⚗ extraction; extract, essence; **4.** extract, excerpt (***aus*** *dat.* from); **5.** statement (of account)
'Aus·zugs·mehl *n* superfine flour
'aus·zugs·wei·se *adv.* in parts; ***et.*** ~ ***vorlesen*** read extracts from s.th
'aus·zup·fen *v/t.* (*sep.*, h) pluck out; ***sich die Augenbrauen*** ~ pluck one's eyebrows
aut·ark [aʊ'tark] *adj.* self-sufficient; **Aut·ar·kie** [aʊtar'kiː] *f* (-; -n) (economic) self-sufficiency, autarky, autarchy
au·then·tisch [aʊ'tɛntɪʃ] *adj.* authentic(ally *adv.*); genuine; ***von*** **~*er Seite*** on good authority; **Au·then·ti·zi·tät** [aʊtɛntitsi'tɛːt] *f* (-; *no pl.*) authenticity
Au·tis·mus [aʊ'tɪsmʊs] *m* (-; *no pl.*) ⚕ autism; **au·ti·stisch** [aʊ'tɪstɪʃ] *adj.* autistic
Au·to ['aʊto] *n* (-s; -s) car, *esp. Am.* auto(mobile); F motor; ~ ***fahren*** drive (a car); ***mit dem*** (*or* ***im***) ~ ***fahren*** go by car; ***ich bin mit dem*** ~ ***da*** I've come by car, I've got my car with me; → ***mitnehmen*** 1; **~ab·ga·se** *pl.* car exhaust fumes; **~an,ten·ne** *f* car aerial (*esp. Am.* antenna); **~apo,the·ke** *f* (driver's) first-aid kit; **~at·las** *m* road atlas; **~auf·kle·ber** *m* bumper sticker; **~aus·stel·lung** *f* motor (*Am.* automobile) show
'Au·to·bahn *f* (-; -en) motorway; *Am.* highway; *in Germany etc.*: autobahn; **~aus·fahrt** *f* motorway *etc.* exit; **~drei·eck** *n* motorway *etc.* junction; **~ge·bühr** *f* motorway *etc.* toll; *Am.* turnpike toll; **~klee·blatt** *n* cloverleaf junction; **~kreuz** *n* motorway *etc.* intersection; **~netz** *n* motorway *etc.* network; **~rast·stät·te** *f* motorway *etc.* service area; **~zu·brin·ger** *m* feeder road
Au·to·bio·gra·phie [aʊtobiogra'fiː] *f* (-; -n) autobiography; **au·to·bio·gra·phisch** [aʊtobio'graːfɪʃ] *adj.* autobiographical
'Au·to|bom·be *f* car bomb; **~bril·le** *f*: (***e-e*** ~ a pair of) driving glasses *pl.*; **~bü·che,rei** *f* mobile library; **~bus(...)** → ***Bus(...)***
au·to·chthon [aʊtɔx'toːn] *adj.* autochthonous
Au·to·di·dakt [aʊtodi'dakt] *m* (-en; -en) self-taught (*or* self-educated) person; **au·to·di'dak·tisch** [-tɪʃ] *adj.* autodidactic(ally *adv.*)
'Au·to|dieb *m* car thief; **~dieb·stahl** *m* car theft; **~elek·tri·ker** *m* car electrician
Au·to·ero·tik [aʊto'ʔe'roːtɪk] *f* (-; *no pl.*) autoeroticism; **au·to·ero·tisch** [aʊto-ʔe'roːtɪʃ] *adj.* autoerotic
'Au·to|fa,brik *f* car (*esp. Am.* automobile) factory; **~fa·bri,kant** *m* car (*esp. Am.* automobile) manufacturer; **~fäh·re** *f* car ferry; **~fah·rer** *m* motorist, driver; **~fahrt** *f* drive; **~fal·le** *f* speed trap
Au·to·fo·cus·ka·me·ra [aʊto'foːkʊs-] *f* autofocus camera
'au·to·frei *adj.* car-free *day*, *zone etc.*
'Au·to·fried·hof F *m* car dump, breaker's yard
au·to·gen [aʊto'geːn] *adj. psych.* autogenic; **~es *Training*** autogenic training, relaxation exercises
Au·to·gramm [aʊto'gram] *n* (-[e]s; -e) autograph; **~e *geben*** sign autographs; **~jä·ger** *m* autograph hunter; **~stun·de** *f* autograph session; ***e-e*** ~ ***geben*** have an autograph session, sign autographs
'Au·to|händ·ler *m* car dealer; **~hand·schu·he** *pl.* driving gloves; **~haus** *n* car dealer; **~,her·stel·ler** *m* car (*esp. Am.* automobile) manufacturer(s *pl.*); **~hu·pe** *f* (car) horn; **~in·du,strie** *f* car (*or* automobile, *Am. a.* automotive) industry; **~kar·te** *f* road map; **~kenn·zei·chen** *n* car registration (*Am.* license) number; ***wissen Sie noch das*** ~? *a.* can you remember the number of the car?; **~ki·no** *n* drive-in (cinema); **~knacker** (*sep.* -k·k-) F *m* (-s; -) car burglar; **~ko,lon·ne** *f* line of cars; convoy
Au·to·krat [aʊto'kraːt] *m* (-en; -en) autocrat; **Au·to·kra·tie** [aʊtokra'tiː] *f* (-; -n) autocracy; **au·to·kra·tisch** [aʊto'kraːtɪʃ] *adj.* autocratic(ally *adv.*)
'Au·to|lack *m* paint; **~le·der** *n* chamois (leather); **~mar·der** F *m* car burglar; **~mar·ke** *f* make (of car), marque
Au·to·mat [aʊto'maːt] *m* (-en; -en) **1.** machine; **2.** vending machine; juke box; slot machine
Au·to'ma·ten|knacker (*sep.* -k·k-) F *m* (-s; -) slot machine burglar; **~packung** (*sep.* -k·k-) *f* vending pack; **~re·stau,rant** *n* automat
Au·to·ma·tik [aʊto'maːtɪk] *f* (-; -en) automation, automatic system; automatic mechanism; *mot.* automatic transmission; *radio*: automatic tuning; **~gurt** *m* *mot.* (inertia) reel seatbelt; **~,ka·me·ra** *f* automatic camera, F point and shoot camera
Au·to·ma·ti·on [aʊtoma'tsi̯oːn] *f* (-; *no pl.*) automation
au·to·ma·tisch [aʊto'maːtɪʃ] *adj.* automatic(ally *adv.*), *fig. a.* mechanical push-button ...
au·to·ma·ti·sie·ren [aʊtomati'ziːrən] *v/t.* (h) automate; **Au·to·ma·ti'sie·rung** *f* (-; -en) automation
Au·to·ma·tis·mus [aʊtoma'tɪsmʊs] *m* (-; -men) automatism
'Au·to|me,cha·ni·ker *m* car (*or* motor) mechanic; **~mi,nu·te** *f*: ***nur fünf*** **~*n von hier entfernt*** only five minutes (away) by car (*or* in the car)
Au·to·mo·bil [aʊtomo'biːl] *n* (-s; -e), **~...** *in cpds.* → ***Auto(...)***; **~klub** *m* automobile association; **~sa,lon** *m* motor (*Am.* automobile) show
'Au·to·mo,dell *n* **1.** model; **2.** model car
au·to·nom [aʊto'noːm] *adj.* autonomous (*a. fig.*), self-governing; self-contained *system*, *unit etc.*; **Au·to·no·mie** [aʊto-no'miː] *f* (-; -n) autonomy

'Au·to·num·mer *f* registration (*Am.* license) number
'Au·to·pi,lot *m* ✈ autopilot
Au·top·sie [aʊtɔ'psiː] *f* (-; -n) autopsy, post-mortem
Au·tor ['aʊtoːɐ] *m* (-s; -en [aʊ'toːrən]) author, writer
'Au·to|ra·dio *n* car radio; **~rei·fen** *m* (car) tyre (*Am.* tire); **~rei·se·zug** *m* motorail train
Au'to·ren|ex·em,plar *n* author's copy; **~le·sung** *f* author's reading
'Au·to|ren·nen *n* car race; **~renn·sport** *m* motor racing
'Au·to·re·pa·ra,tur *f* car repair; **~werk·statt** *f* garage, car repair shop
Au·to·rin [aʊ'toːrɪn] *f* (-; -nen) author, writer
au·to·ri·sie·ren [aʊtori'ziːrən] *v/t.* (h) authorize
au·to·ri·tär [aʊtori'tɛːɐ] *adj.* authoritarian; very strict *parents etc.*; ***~e Erziehung*** authoritarian upbringing
Au·to·ri·tät [aʊtori'tɛːt] *f* (-; -en) **1.** *no pl.* authority; **2.** authority (***auf dem Gebiet*** *gen.* on), expert (on)
au·to·ri·ta·tiv [aʊtorita'tiːf] *adj.* authoritative
au·to·ri'täts·gläu·big *adj.*: ***~ sein*** have blind faith in authority
'Au·tor·schaft *f* (-; *no pl.*) authorship
'Au·to|sa,lon *m* → ***Automobilsalon***; **~schad·stof·fe** *pl.* car emissions; **~schal·ter** *m* drive-up counter; *a.* drive-in till; **~schlan·ge** *f* line of cars; **~schlos·ser** *m* panel beater; **~schlüs·sel** *m* car key; **~schup·pen** *m* car shed; **~skoo·ter** *m* dodgem (*or* bumper) car; ***~ fahren*** go on the dodgems (*or* bumper cars); **~sport** *m* motor sport; **~stopp** *m* hitchhiking; ***per ~ fahren*** hitchhike; **~stun·de** *f*: ***sechs ~n entfernt*** six hours' (*or* a six-hour) drive away (*or* from here), six hours by (*or* in the) car
Au·to·sug·ge·sti'on *f* (-; *no pl.*) autosuggestion
'Au·to|te·le,fon *n* carphone; **~trans,por·ter** *m* car transporter; **~un·fall** *m* car accident, car crash; **~ver·kehr** *m* road traffic; **~ver·leih** *m*, **~ver·mie·tung** *f* car hire, *a. Am.* car rental; **~ver·si·che·rung** *f* car insurance; **~wasch·an·la·ge** *f* car wash; **~werk·statt** *f* garage, car repair shop; **~wrack** *n* wrecked car
'Au·to·zoom *m phot.* automatic zoom
'Au·to|zu·be·hör *n* car accessories *pl.*; ✝ car components *pl.*; **~zu,sam·men·stoß** *m* car crash, collision
autsch [aʊtʃ] *int.* ouch!
au·weia [aʊ'vaɪa] *int.* oh no!
Avan·cen [a'vɑ̃ːsən] *pl*: ***j-m ~ machen*** make approaches to s.o.
avan·cie·ren [avɑ̃'siːrən] *v/i.* (sn) be promoted; ***~ zu*** *dat. a.* rise (*or* advance) to the position (*or* post) of
Avant·gar·de [avɑ̃'gardə] *f* (-; -n) avant-garde; **Avant·gar·dis·mus** [avɑ̃gar'dɪsmʊs] *m* (-; *no pl.*) avant-gardism; **Avant·gar·dist** [avɑ̃gar'dɪst] *m* (-en; -en) avant-gardist; **avant·gar·di·stisch** [avɑ̃gar'dɪstɪʃ] *adj.* avant-garde
Aver·si·on [avɛr'zĭoːn] *f* (-; -en) aversion (***gegen*** *acc.* to); ***er hat (irgendwelche) ~en gegen mich*** he doesn't like me (for some reason)
Avio·nik [a'vĭoːnɪk] *f* (-; *no pl.*) avionics *pl.*
Avis [a'viː] *m, n* (-; -) notice, notification; **avi·sie·ren** [avi'ziːrən] *v/t.* (h): ***j-m j-n (et.) ~*** notify s.o. of s.o.'s arrival (of s.th.)
Avit·ami·no·se [avitami'noːzə] *f* (-; -n) ⚕ vitamin deficiency disease, 🕮 avitaminosis
Avo·ca·do [avo'kaːdo] *f* (-; -s), **Avo·ka·to** [avo'kaːto] *f* (-; -s) avocado
Axi·om [a'ksĭoːm] *n* (-s; -e) axiom; **axio·ma·tisch** [aksĭo'maːtɪʃ] *adj.* axiomatic(ally *adv.*)
Axt [akst] *f* (-; Äxte ['ɛkstə]) axe, *Am.* ax; ***mit der ~ erschlagen*** axe (*Am.* ax) to death, kill with an axe (*Am.* ax); *fig.* ***sich wie die ~ im Wald benehmen*** behave like a boor (*or* savage); ***die ~ an die Wurzel(n) legen*** strike at the root; ***die ~ im Haus erspart den Zimmermann*** do it yourself
Aza·lee [atsa'leːə] *f* (-; -n) ⚘ azalea
Aze·tat → ***Acetat***
Aze·ton → ***Aceton***
Aze·ty·len → ***Acetylen***
Az·te·ke [ats'teːkə] *m* (-n; -n) *hist.* Aztec; **Az'te·ken·reich** *n* Aztec Empire; **az·te·kisch** [ats'teːkɪʃ] *adj.* Aztec, Aztecan
Azu·bi [a'tsuːbi] F *m* (-s; -s), *f* (-; -s) trainee
Azur [a'tsuːɐ] *m* (-s; *no pl.*) azure, sky blue; **ᛟblau** *adj.* azure, sky-blue
azy·klisch ['atsyːklɪʃ] *adj.* acyclic(ally *adv.*); irregular

B

B, b [beː] *n* (-; -) B, b; ♪ B flat; ♪ flat
bab·beln [ˈbabəln] (h) **I.** *v/i.* babble; **II.** *v/t.* (*a.* ***dummes Zeug*** *~*) babble; ***was babbelt er?*** what's he babbling on about?
Ba·bel [ˈbaːbəl] *n* (-s; *no pl.*) *bibl.* Babel; *fig.* Babylon; → ***Turm, Turmbau***
Ba·by [ˈbeːbi] *n* (-s; -s) baby; ***sie bekommt ein*** *~* she's expecting (*or* going to have) a baby; → ***Bord;*** **~ar·ti·kel** *pl.* baby goods (*or* accessories); baby department *sg.*; **~aus·stat·tung** *f* layette; **~boom** *m* baby boom; **~fla·sche** *f* baby's bottle; **~jahr** *n* (one year's) maternity leave; **~lift** *m skiing*: baby lift
ba·by·lo·nisch [babyˈloːnɪʃ] *adj.* Babylonian; ***~e Sprachverwirrung*** *bibl.* Confusion of Tongues (at Babel); *fig.* babel, confusion of tongues
ˈ**Ba·by·nah·rung** *f* baby food
ba·by·sit·ten [ˈbeːbizɪtən] *v/i.* (*only inf.*) babysit; **Ba·by·sit·ter** [ˈbeːbizɪtɐ] *m* (-s; -) babysitter; **Ba·by·sit·ting** [ˈbeːbizɪtɪŋ] *n* (-[s]; *no pl.*) babysitting
ˈ**Ba·by|speck** F *m a. fig.* F puppy fat; **~spra·che** *f* baby talk; **~strich** F *m* child prostitution; **~-ˈTra·ge·ta·sche** *f* carrycot; Moses basket; **~wä·sche** *f* babies' clothes *pl.*
Bac·cha·nal [baxaˈnaːl] *n* (-s; -lien [-lĭən]) bacchanal
Bach [bax] *m* (-[e]s; Bäche [ˈbɛçə]) stream; brook; *fig.* ***Bäche von Schweiß*** (***Tränen***) ***flossen ihr übers Gesicht*** the sweat was pouring (the tears were streaming) down her face; F *fig.* ***den ~ hinuntergehen*** F go up in smoke
Ba·che [ˈbaxə] *f* (-; -n) (wild) sow
ˈ**Bach|fo·rel·le** *f* (-; -n) brook trout; **~stel·ze** *f* (-; -n) wagtail
ˈ**Back·blech** *n* (-[e]s; -e) baking tray
Back·bord [ˈbakbɔrt] ⚓ **I.** *n* (-[e]s; -e [-bɔrdə]) port (side); ***nach*** *~* to port; **II.** ⚓ *adv.* to port; **~mo·tor** *m* port engine
ˈ**Back·buch** *n* baking book
Backe [ˈbakə] (*sep.* -k·k-) *f* (-; -n) **1.** cheek; ***mit vollen ~n kauen*** (*or* ***essen***) stuff one's mouth full; *dial.* ***au ~!*** oh no!; **2.** *on gun*: cheek piece; *on ski*: toe piece; **3.** ⚙ jaw; shoe
backen [ˈbakən] (*sep.* -k·k-) (bäckt, *a.* backt, backte, *obs.* buk, gebacken, h) **I.** *v/t.* **1.** bake; *dial.* fry; **II.** *v/i.* **2.** bake; **3.** stick
ˈ**Backen|bart** (*sep.* -k·k-) *m* sideburns *pl.*; **~brem·se** *f* **1.** *mot.* shoe brake; **2.** F ***die ~ ziehen*** land on one's backside; **~kno·chen** *m* cheekbone; **~ta·sche** *f zo.* (cheek) pouch; **~zahn** *m* molar
Bäcker [ˈbɛkɐ] (*sep.* -k·k-) *m* (-s; -) baker; **Bäcke·rei** [bɛkəˈraɪ] (*sep.* -k·k-) *f* (-; -en) **1.** baker's (shop), bakery; **2.** *no pl.* baking; **3.** *no pl.* baker's trade; **4.** *esp. Austrian* (biscuits and) pastries *pl.*
ˈ**Bäcker|la·den** (*sep.* -k·k-) *m* → ***Bäkkerei*** 1; **~lehr·ling** *m* apprentice (*or* trainee) baker; **~mei·ster** *m* master baker
ˈ**back·fer·tig** *adj.* oven-ready
ˈ**Back|fett** *n* cooking fat; shortening; **~fisch** *m* **1.** fried fish; **2.** *fig. obs.* (young) teenager, teenage girl; **~form** *f* baking tin, *Am.* bake pan
Back·ground [ˈbɛkgraʊnt] *m* (-s; -s) **1.** background; **2.** ♪ background music; backing
ˈ**Back|hähn·chen** *dial. n* fried chicken; **~huhn** *dial. n* fried chicken; **~obst** *n* dried fruit
ˈ**Back·ofen** *m* oven; **~hit·ze** F *f* sweltering heat; ***das ist e-e ~!*** it's sweltering
ˈ**Back|pfei·fe** F *f* (-; -n) F clout (*or* clip) round the ears; **~pflau·me** *f* prune; **~pul·ver** *n* baking powder; **~re·zept** *n* baking recipe; **~röh·re** *f* oven
ˈ**Back·stein** *m* brick; **~bau** *m* (-[e]s; -ten) brick building; **~go·tik** *f* brick Gothic
ˈ**Back|teig** *m* dough; batter; **~wa·ren** *pl.* bread, cakes and pastries
Bad [baːt] *n* (-[e]s; Bäder [ˈbɛːdɐ]) **1.** bath (*a.* ⚕ *and* ⚗); ***ein ~ nehmen*** have (*or* take) a bath; *fig.* ***~ in der Menge*** walkabout; ***ein ~ in der Menge nehmen*** go on a walkabout; → ***Kind;*** **2.** swim; ***ein ~ nehmen*** go for a swim (F dip); **3.** → a) ***Badezimmer,*** b) ***Badeanstalt,*** c) ***Badeort***
Ba·de|an·stalt [ˈbaːdə-] *f* swimming pool, *formal*: swimming baths *pl.*; **~an·zug** *m* swimsuit; **~gast** *m* bather; **~ge·le·gen·heit** *f* place to swim; ***gibt es dort e-e ~?*** *a.* can you go swimming there?; **~hand·tuch** *n* bath towel; **~hau·be** *f* bathing cap; **~ho·se** *f*: (***e-e ~*** a pair of) (swimming) trunks *pl.*; **~kap·pe** *f* bathing cap; **~man·tel** *m* bathrobe; **~mat·te** *f* bath mat; **~mei·ster** *m* pool attendant
ba·den [ˈbaːdən] (h) **I.** *v/i.* **1.** have (*or* take) a bath, bathe; **2.** swim; ***~ gehen*** go swimming, go for a swim; F *fig.* F come a cropper; **II.** *v/t.* bath, *Am.* bathe; → ***heiß*** II; **III.** *v/refl.*: ***sich ~*** → **1;** *fig.* bask (***in*** *dat.* in), revel (in)
Ba·de·ner [ˈbaːdənɐ] *m* (-s; -) man from Baden; ***~ sein*** *a.* come from Baden; **Ba·de·ne·rin** [ˈbaːdənərɪn] *f* (-; -nen) woman from Baden
ˈ**Ba·de·ni·xe** *f* bathing beauty (*or* belle)
Ba·den·ser [baˈdɛnzɐ] *m* (-s; -) → ***Badener***
ba·den-würt·tem·ber·gisch [ˈbaːdən-ˈvʏrtəmbɛrgɪʃ] *adj.* Baden-Württemberg ..., from Baden-Württemberg
ˈ**Ba·de|ofen** *m* bathroom boiler; **~öl** *n* bath oil; **~ort** *m* **1.** seaside resort; **2.** health resort; **~sa·chen** *pl.* swimming things; **~sai·son** *f* swimming season; **~salz** *n* bath salts *pl.*; **~schu·he** *f* beach shoes; **~strand** *m* (bathing) beach; **~ther·mo·me·ter** *n* bath thermometer; **~tuch** *n* bath towel; **~ur·laub** *m* holiday at the seaside; ***~ machen*** spend one's holiday at the seaside; **~wan·ne** *f* bath (-tub); **~was·ser** *n* bathwater; **~wet·ter** *n* weather for the beach; sunbathing weather; **~zeug** *n* swimming things *pl.*
ˈ**Ba·de·zim·mer** *n* bathroom; **~schrank** *m* bathroom cabinet
ˈ**Ba·de·zu·satz** *m* bath essence (*or* product)
baff [baf] F *adj.*: ***da war ich aber ~*** I was floored, my jaw just dropped; ***da bist du ~, was?*** you weren't expecting that, were you?
Ba·ga·ge [baˈgaːʒə] *contp. f* (-; -n) F rabble, shower; ***die ganze ~!*** F the whole lot of them
Ba·gaˈtell|be·trag *m* petty (*or* insignificant) sum; **~de·likt** *n* petty (*or* minor) offen|ce (*Am.* -se)
Ba·ga·tel·le [bagaˈtɛlə] *f* (-; -n) **1.** trifle; **2.** ♪ bagatelle; **ba·ga·tel·li·sie·ren** [bagatɛliˈziːrən] *v/t.* (h) play down, minimize
Ba·gaˈtell|sa·che *f* minor affair; ⚖ petty case; **~scha·den** *m* superficial damage; **~ver·let·zung** *f* minor (*or* superficial) injury
Bag·ger [ˈbagɐ] *m* (-s; -) excavator; dredge(r)
bag·gern [ˈbagɐn] *v/i. and v/t.* (h) excavate; dredge
ˈ**Bag·ger·see** *m* flooded gravel pit
Ba·guette [baˈgɛt] *f* (-; -n) French stick
bäh [bɛː] *int.* **1.** *sheep*: baa!; **2.** ha, ha!; **3.** ugh!; **bä·hen** [ˈbɛːən] *v/i.* (h) bleat, baa
Bahn [baːn] *f* (-; -en) **1.** way, path; *fig.* ***die ~ ist frei*** the road is clear; ***freie ~ haben*** have the go-ahead (to do what one likes); ***du hast freie ~*** it's all yours; ***sich ~ brechen*** win through, *idea etc.*: gain acceptance; forge ahead; ***e-r Sache ~ brechen*** pioneer s.th., blaze the trail for s.th.; ***auf die schiefe ~ geraten*** go astray, stray off the straight and narrow; ***in die richtige ~ lenken*** direct into the right channels; ***sich in den gewohnten ~en bewegen*** move along the same old track, *contp.* be stuck in the same old rut; keep to the well-trodden paths; ***auf ähnlichen ~en*** along similar lines; ***j-n aus der ~ werfen*** throw s.o. off his (*or* her) track, leave s.o. floundering; **2.** lane (*a. sport*); **3.** trajectory; *ast.* course; orbit (*a. phys.*); path *of a comet*; **4.** *sport*: track; (*ice-skating*) rink; (*bowling*) alley; **5.** railway, *Am.* railroad; train; tram, *Am.* streetcar, trolley; ***mit der ~*** by train, 🚂 by rail; (***mit der***) ***~ fahren*** travel by train

(*or* on trains); ***ich fahre gern (mit der) ~*** *a.* I like going on the train; ***bei der ~ arbeiten*** work for the railway (*Am.* railroad); ***j-n zur ~ bringen*** take s.o. to the station, see s.o. off (at the station); ***j-n von der ~ abholen*** (go and) meet s.o. at the station; ***in der ~*** on the train; **6.** (*paper, plastic*) web; width *of cloth*; gore; **7.** ⚙ face *of hammer, anvil etc.*; **8.** ⚙ track

Bahn... → *a.* ***Eisenbahn...***; **~an·ge·stell·te** *m, f* (-n; -n) railway (*Am.* railroad) employee; **~an·schluß** *m* rail connection; **~ar·bei·ter** *m* railway (*Am.* railroad) worker; **~be·am·te** *m* railway (*Am.* railroad) official

'bahn·bre·chend I. *adj.* pioneering, pioneer ..., trailblazing; revolutionary, epoch-making *invention, discovery etc.*; **II.** *adv.*: **~ *wirken*** be pioneering, blaze the trail; **'Bahn·bre·cher** *m* (-s; -) pioneer, trailblazer

'Bahn·damm *m* railway (*Am.* railroad) embankment

bah·nen ['ba:nən] *v/t.* (h): ***(sich) e-n Weg ~*** clear a path (for o.s.), ***durch** acc.*: fight (*or* force) one's way through; *fig.* ***den Weg ~*** pave the way (*dat.* for); ***j-m den Weg zum Erfolg ~*** put s.o. on the road (*or* path) to success

'Bahn|fahrt *f* train journey (*or* ride); rail journey; **~fracht** *f* rail freight; **≈frei** *adv.* ☨ carriage paid; **~ge·län·de** *n* railway (*Am.* railroad) area *or* complex; **~gleis** *n* railway (*Am.* railroad) track

'Bahn·hof *m* (-[e]s; ⸚e) **1.** (railway, *Am.* railroad) station; ***auf dem ~*** at the station; **2.** F *fig.* ***großer ~*** red carpet treatment; ***j-n mit großem ~ empfangen*** roll out the red carpet for s.o., give s.o. the red carpet treatment; ***es gab e-n großen ~*** they had the red carpets out; F ***ich verstehe immer nur ~*** F I don't know what he's *etc.* on about, it's all double dutch to me

'Bahn·hofs|buch·hand·lung *f* station bookshop (*Am.* bookstore); **~hal·le** *f* (station) concourse, main concourse (of a station); **~nä·he** *f*: ***in ~*** near the station; **~re·stau,rant** *n* station restaurant; **~uhr** *f* station clock; **~vier·tel** *n* (seedy) area around the main station; **~vor·ste·her** *m* stationmaster

'Bahn|kör·per *m* permanent way, roadbed; **≈la·gernd** *adv.* to be called for at the station; **~lie·fe·rung** *f* rail consignment; **~li·nie** *f* railway (line), *Am.* railroad (line); **~po·li,zei** *f* station police; **~rei·se** *f* train (*or* rail) journey; **~schran·ke** *f* (grade crossing) barrier; **~schwel·le** *f* sleeper, *Am.* tie; **~sta·ti,on** *f* railway (*Am.* railroad) station *or* stop

'Bahn·steig *m* platform; **~kar·te** *obs. f* platform ticket

'Bahn|strecke (*sep.* -k·k-) *f* (railway) track, line; **~trans,port** *m* rail transport; **~über,füh·rung** *f* railway bridge, *Am.* railroad overpass; **~,über·gang** *m* level (*Am.* grade) crossing; **~un·ter,füh·rung** *f* railway (*Am.* railroad) underpass; **~ver·bin·dung** *f* rail connection; **~wär·ter** *m* **1.** level crossing attendant; **2.** → ***Streckenwärter***

Bah·re ['ba:rə] *f* (-; -n) stretcher; bier; → ***Wiege***

Bai [baɪ] *f* (-; -en) bay

Bai·ser [bɛ'ze:] *n* (-s; -s) meringue

Bais·se ['bɛ:sə] *f* (-; -n) ☨ slump, bear market, fall (in prices), sharp drop in prices; ***auf ~ spekulieren*** speculate for a fall, sell short; **~ge·schäft** *n* bear transaction, *a. pl.* short selling; **~spe·ku,lant** *m* bear; **~spe·ku·la·ti,on** *f* bear(ish) speculation; **~stim·mung** *f* bearish mood

Bais·sier [bɛ'sje:] *m* (-s; -s) ☨ bear

Ba·jo·nett [bajo'nɛt] *n* (-[e]s; -e) bayonet; **~fas·sung** *f* ⚡ bayonet socket; **~ver·schluß** *m* ⚙ bayonet joint (*phot.* mount)

Ba·ke ['ba:kə] *f* (-; -n) beacon; *surv.* marking pole

Bak·ka·rat ['bakara(t); baka'ra] *n* (-s; *no pl.*) baccarat

Bak·schisch ['bakʃɪʃ] *n* (-es; -e) baksheesh; ***j-m ein ~ geben*** give s.o. baksheesh, *fig.* grease s.o.'s palm

Bak·te·rie [bak'te:rĭə] *f* (-; -n) bacterium (*pl.* bacteria), germ; **bak·te·ri·ell** [bakte'rĭɛl] *adj.* bacterial; ***~e Infektion*** bacteria(l) infection

bak'te·ri·en|feind·lich *adj.* germ-killing ..., bactericidal; **≈for·schung** *f* bacteriology, bacteriological research; **~frei** *adj.* germ-free, free of bacteria; **≈ko·lo,nie** *f* bacterial colony; **≈krieg** *m* biological (*or* germ) warfare; **≈kul,tur** *f* (bacteria[l]) culture; **≈stamm** *m* strain (of bacteria); **~tö·tend** *adj.* bactericidal, germ-killing ...; **≈trä·ger** *m* germ-carrier; **≈zucht** *f* growing of bacteria; bacteria culture

Bak·te·rio·lo·ge [bakterĭo'lo:gə] *m* (-n; -n) bacteriologist; **Bak·te·rio·lo·gie** [bakterĭolo'gi:] *f* (-; *no pl.*) bacteriology; **bak·te·rio·lo·gisch** [bakterĭo'lo:gɪʃ] *adj.* bacteriological

Ba·lan·ce [ba'lã:s(ə)] *f* (-; *no pl.*) balance; **~akt** *m a. fig.* balancing act; **~reg·ler** *m* balance control

ba·lan·cie·ren [balã'si:rən] *v/t.* (h) *and v/i.* (sn) balance

Ba·lan'cier·stan·ge *f* (balancing) pole

bald [balt] *adv.* **1.** soon; **~ *darauf*** soon *or* shortly after(wards); **~ *ist dein Geburtstag*** it's (*or* it'll be) your birthday soon; ***das wird's so ~ nicht wieder geben*** we won't see the likes of that again in a hurry; ***wird's ~?*** how much longer are you going to take?; ***ich hab's ~*** I'm nearly ready, I won't be a minute; ***wirst du ~ ruhig sein!*** 'will you be quiet; ***bis ~!*** see you soon!, be seeing you!; **~ *will er,* ~ *will er nicht*** one minute he wants to, the next (minute) he doesn't; **2.** F almost, nearly; ***ich hätte ~ was gesagt*** I almost said something, I was on the point of saying something

Bal·da·chin ['baldaxi:n] *m* (-s; -e) canopy

Bäl·de ['bɛldə] *f*: ***in ~*** soon, before long

bal·dig ['baldɪç] *adj.* speedy; ***auf ein ~es Wiedersehen*** hope to see you again soon; **bal·digst** ['baldɪçst] *adv.* as soon as possible

'bald'mög·lichst I. *adj.* earliest (*or* soonest) possible; ***zum ~en Zeitpunkt*** → **II.** *adv.* as soon as possible

Bal·dri·an ['baldria:n] *m* (-s; *no pl.*) valerian; **~trop·fen** *pl.* valerian *sg.* (drops)

Balg¹ [balk] *m* (-[e]s; Bälge ['bɛlgə]) **1.** skin, hide; **2.** *organ, a. phot.*: bellows *pl.*; **3.** F paunch

Balg² [balk] *n* (-[e]s; Bälger ['bɛlgɐ]) F brat

Bal·gen ['balgən] *m* (-s; -) *phot.* bellows *pl.*

bal·gen *v/refl.* (h): ***sich ~*** scuffle, tussle, F scrap (***um*** *acc.* over); **Bal·ge·rei** [balgə'raɪ] *f* (-; -en) scuffle, tussle, F scrap (***um*** *acc.* for, over)

Bal·ken ['balkən] *m* (-s; -) **1.** ⚠ beam; rafter; joist; girder; F ***lügen, daß sich die ~ biegen*** F lie through one's teeth; **2.** → ***Schwebebalken***; **3.** ♪ crossbar; **4.** *TV* bar; **~decke** (*sep.* -k·k-) *f* timbered ceiling; **~dia,gramm** *n* bar graph; **~,über·schrift** *f* banner headline; **~waa- ge** *f* beam scales *pl.*; **~werk** *n* (-[e]s; *no pl.*) timbering

Bal·kon [bal'kɔŋ; bal'kõ:] *m* (-s; -s, -e [bal'ko:nə]) **1.** balcony; **2.** *thea.* dress circle, *Am.* balcony; **~pflan·ze** *f* outdoor (potted) plant; **~tür** *f* balcony door, French window(s *pl.*)

Ball¹ [bal] *m* (-[e]s; Bälle ['bɛlə]) ball; ***am ~ sein*** *sport*: have the ball, be in possession of the ball; *fig.* ***er ist am ~*** a) it's his turn, the ball's in his court, b) he's very involved, c) he's on the ball; ***am ~ bleiben*** *sport*: hold onto the ball, *fig.* keep at it, ***bei j-m***: keep up with s.o., keep in the running with s.o.; → ***zuspielen***

Ball² [bal] *m* (-[e]s; Bälle ['bɛlə]) ball, dance; ***auf e-m ~*** at a ball; ***auf e-n ~ gehen*** go to a ball

'Ball·ab·ga·be *f* (-; -n) *sport*: pass

Bal·la·de [ba'la:də] *f* (-; -n) ballad; **Bal'la·den·sän·ger** *m* balladeer

'Ball·an·nah·me *f* (-; -n) stopping and controlling the ball; bringing down the ball

Bal·last [ba'last; 'balast] *m* (-[e]s; -e) ballast; *fig.* burden; deadwood; handicap; **~ *abwerfen*** dump ballast, *fig.* shed some ballast; *fig.* ***er ist nur ~*** he's just an encumbrance

Bal'last·stof·fe *pl.* roughage *sg.*; fiber, *Brit.* fibre *sg.*; **bal'last·stoff·reich** *adj.*: ***~e Nahrung*** high-fib|re (*Am.* -er) food(s) *or* diet; food(s) with plenty of roughage

'Ball|be·herr·schung *f* ball control; **~be·sitz** *m*: ***im ~ sein*** have (the) possession, have the (*or* be in) possession of the ball

bal·len ['balən] (h) **I.** *v/t.* **1.** make into a ball; screw up; **2.** clench *one's fist*; **II.** *v/refl.*: ***sich ~*** **3.** form into a ball (*or* balls); **4.** *clouds, people etc.*: gather; *fig. problems etc.*: mount, build up, pile up; ***sich ~ um*** *acc.* build up around, cluster around, move in on; → ***geballt*** II

'Bal·len *m* (-s; -) **1.** *anat.* ball of one's *or* the foot (*or* hand); **2.** ☨ bale; *paper*: ten reams *pl.*; **~pres·se** *f* baling press

'bal·len·wei·se *adv.* by the bale, in bales

Bal·le·ri·na [balə'ri:na] *f* (-; -nen) ballerina

Bal·ler·mann ['balɐman] F *m* (-[e]s; -männer [-mɛnɐ]) gun, *sl.* rod

bal·lern ['balɐn] (h) F **I.** *v/i.* bang (away) (*a. soccer*); **~ *an*** *acc.* hammer away at; **II.** *v/t.* hurl; *soccer*: bang

Bal·lett [ba'lɛt] *n* (-[e]s; -e) ballet; ballet company; ***beim ~ sein*** be with the ballet, *n.s.* be a ballet dancer; ***zum ~ gehen*** join a ballet company, *n.s.* become a ballet dancer

Bal'lettän·zer(in *f*) *m* (*sep.* -tt·t-) ballet dancer

Bal'lett|mei·ster *m* ballet master; **~mei·ste·rin** *f* ballet mistress; **~mu,sik** *f* ballet music; **~rat·te** F *f* ballet girl; budding young ballerina; **~röck·chen** *n* tutu;

~schuh *m* ballet shoe; **~schu·le** *f* ballet school; **~trup·pe** *f* ballet company
'ball·för·mig *adj.* ball-shaped, spherical
'Ball·füh·rung *f sport*: ball control
Bal·li·stik [ba'lɪstɪk] *f* (-; *no pl.*) ballistics *pl.*; **Bal·li·sti·ker** [ba'lɪstikɐ] *m* (-s; -) ballistics expert; **bal·li·stisch** [ba'lɪstɪʃ] *adj.* ballistic(ally *adv.*)
'Ball·jun·ge *m tennis*: ball boy
'Ball·kleid *n* ball dress
'Ball|künst·ler *m sport*: wizard with the ball; **~mäd·chen** *n tennis*: ball girl
Bal·lon [ba'lɔŋ; ba'lõ:] *m* (-s; -s, -e [ba'lo:nə]) **1.** balloon; **2.** carboy; demijohn; **3.** F noddle; ***er hat so e-n ~ gekriegt*** he went bright red; **~fah·rer** *m* balloonist; **~fahrt** *f* balloon ride (*or* trip); **~ka,the·ter** *m* ⚕ balloon catheter; **~rei·fen** *m* balloon tyre (*Am.* tire), F doughnut; **~son·de** *f* balloon probe
'Ball·saal *m* ballroom
'Ball|spiel *n* ball game; **~tech·nik** *f* ball control; **~trai·ning** *n* training with the ball
Bal·lung ['balʊŋ] *f* (-; -en) agglomeration; *fig.* concentration, buildup
'Bal·lungs|ge·biet *n*, **~raum** *m* conurbation; (industrial) belt; *contp.* congested area; **~zen·trum** *n* hub of a conurbation; population cent|re (*Am.* -er); cent|re (*Am.* -er) of industry
'Ball|wech·sel *m tennis*: rally; **~wurf·ma,schi·ne** *f* ball thrower
Bal·sam ['balza:m] *m* (-s; -e) *a. fig.* balm; *fig.* ***das ist ~ für m-e Seele*** *esp. iro.* it soothes my troubled soul; ***j-m ~ auf die Wunde träufeln*** pour balm on s.o.'s wounds; **bal·sa·mie·ren** [balza'mi:rən] *v/t.* (h) embalm; **bal·sa·misch** [bal'za:mɪʃ] *adj.* balsamic; *a.* balmy *fragrance*; soothing
Bal·te ['baltə] *m* (-n; -n) person from the Baltic; ***die ~n*** the Baltic peoples; **bal·tisch** ['baltɪʃ] *adj.* Baltic; ***die ≈en Länder*** the Baltic Nations
Ba·lu·stra·de [balʊs'tra:də] *f* (-; -n) balustrade
Balz [balts] *f* (-; -en) *zo.* courtship; mating; mating season; **bal·zen** ['baltsən] *v/i.* (h) court, call; mate
'Balz|ruf *m* mating call; **~ver·hal·ten** *n* mating (*or* courtship) display *or* behavio(u)r; **~zeit** *f* mating season
Bam·bus ['bambʊs] *m* (-[ses]; -se) bamboo; **~rohr** *n* bamboo (cane); **~spros·sen** *pl.* bamboo sprouts (*or* shoots); **~stab** *m* (bamboo) cane; **~vor·hang** *m* **1.** bamboo curtain; **2.** *fig. pol.* Bamboo Curtain
Bam·mel ['baməl] F *m* → ***Schiß*** 2
bam·meln ['baməln] F *dial. v/i.* (h) dangle
ba·nal [ba'na:l] *adj.* trite, banal; run-of-the-mill ...; very straightforward, F too simple to be true; ***ins ≈e ziehen*** reduce to the banal; **ba·na·li·sie·ren** [banali'zi:rən] *v/t.* (h) trivialize; **Ba·na·li·tät** [banali'tɛ:t] *f* (-; -en) **1.** *no pl.* banality, triteness, banal nature (*gen.* of); **2.** trite (*or* banal) remark
Ba·na·ne [ba'na:nə] *f* (-; -n) banana
Ba'na·nen|buch·se *f* ⚡ banana jack; **~damp·fer** *m a. fig.* banana boat; **~re·pu,blik** F *f* F banana republic; **~scha·le** *f* banana skin (*or* peel); **~stau·de** *f* banana tree; **~stecker** (*sep.* -k·k-) *m* ⚡ banana plug
Ba·nau·se [ba'naʊzə] *m* (-n; -n) ignoramus; philistine; **Ba'nau·sen·tum** *n* (-s; *no pl.*) cultural illiteracy; philistinism
band [bant] *pret. of* ***binden***
Band¹ [bant] *n* (-[e]s; Bänder ['bɛndɐ]) **1.** tape; (*apron etc.*) string; (*hat*) band; (*typewriter etc.*) ribbon; ***auf ~ aufnehmen*** tape, record; ***hast du's auf ~?*** have you got a tape of it?; ***auf ~ sprechen*** speak onto (a) tape, ***et.***: record s.th. onto (a) tape, tape s.th.; ***auf ~ diktieren*** dictate onto (a) tape; **2.** △ tie, bond; **3.** ⚙ metal strip; (conveyor) belt; assembly (*or* production) line; *fig.* ***am laufenden ~*** one after the other, nonstop; ***wir hatten Schwierigkeiten am laufenden ~*** there were no end of problems, it was just one problem after another; ***er macht das am laufenden ~*** he does it more or less nonstop, *contp. a.* he (just) keeps on doing it; **4.** *anat.* ligament; **5.** *radio*: (wave)band; **6.** *fig.* bond(s *pl.*), ties *pl.*; ***das ~ der Ehe*** the bond of marriage; ***familiäre ~e*** family ties; ***das ~ der Liebe (Freundschaft)*** the bonds of love (the ties *or* bond of friendship); **7.** *lit.* **~e** bonds, fetters
Band² *m* (-[e]s; Bände ['bɛndə]) volume; F ***das spricht Bände*** that speaks volumes (F mouthfuls); ***darüber könnte man Bände schreiben*** that would fill volumes
Band³ [bɛnt] *f* (-; -s) ♪ band
Ban·da·ge [ban'da:ʒə] *f* (-; -n) bandage; ***j-m e-e ~ anlegen*** put a bandage on s.o., bandage s.o. up; *fig.* ***mit harten ~n kämpfen*** F go at it hammer and tongs (*or* with a vengeance); **ban·da·gie·ren** [banda'ʒi:rən] *v/t.* (h) bandage (up), put a bandage on
'Band|ar,chiv *n* tape library (*or* archive); **~auf·nah·me** *f*, **~auf·zeich·nung** *f* tape recording; **~brei·te** *f radio*: frequency range, bandwidth; *statistics*: spread; *stock exchange*: fluctuation margin; *fig.* range; spectrum
Ban·de¹ ['bandə] *f* (-; -n) **1.** gang *of criminals*, ring; **2.** F *contp.* F shower; ***~ von ...*** F bunch of ...; ***die ganze ~*** the whole lot (of them); ***e-e saubere ~!*** a fine (*or* nice) lot!; ***das ist e-e ausgelassene ~!*** they're a lively lot (*or* bunch)
'Ban·de² *f* (-; -n) **1.** *billiards, bowling*: cushion; **2.** *ice hockey etc.*: boards *pl*
'Ban·den·chef *m* gang leader (*or* boss), ringleader
'Band·end·ab·schal·tung *f* automatic shut-off
'Ban·den|füh·rer *m* → ***Bandenchef***; **~krieg** *m* gang war(fare); **~mit·glied** *n* member of a (*or* the) gang
'Ban·den·wer·bung *f* touchline (*or* perimeter board) advertising
'Ban·den·we·sen *n* (-s; *no pl.*) gangs *pl.*; gangland
Bän·der·deh·nung ['bɛndɐ-] *f* ⚕ stretched (*or* pulled) ligament
Ban·de·ro·le [bandə'ro:lə] *f* (-; -n) **1.** revenue stamp; band *of cigar*; **2.** *art*: scroll
Bän·der|riß ['bɛndɐ-] *m* ⚕ torn ligament; **~zer·rung** *f* ⚕ stretched (*or* pulled) ligament
'Band|fil·ter *m radio*: band(-pass) filter; **~för·de·rer** *m* belt conveyor; **~ge·rät** *n* reel-to-reel (tape recorder); **~ge·schwin·dig·keit** *f* tape speed; *a.* recording speed
bän·di·gen ['bɛndɪgən] *v/t.* (h) tame; break in *horse*; *fig.* restrain, (bring under) control, harness; (get *or* keep under) control; **Bän·di·ger** ['bɛndɪgɐ] *m* (-s; -) tamer; **Bän·di·gung** ['bɛndɪgʊŋ] *f* (-; *no pl.*) taming; *fig.* control; harnessing
Ban·dit [ban'di:t] *m* (-en; -en) bandit; *fig.* F crook; **Ban'di·ten·we·sen** *n* (-s; *no pl.*) banditry
'Band|ke,ra·mik *f* band ceramics *pl.*; **~maß** *n* measuring tape; **~mon,ta·ge** *f* line assembly; **~nu·deln** *pl.* tagliatelle, ribbon noodles; **~rau·schen** *n* tape noise (*or* hiss); **~riß** *m* tape break; **~sä·ge** *f* band saw; **~sa,lat** F *m* chewed-up tape, F spaghetti
'Band·schei·be *f anat.* (intervertebral) disc
'Band·schei·ben|scha·den *m* ⚕ damaged disc; **~vor·fall** *m* slipped disc
'Band·sor·ten·schal·ter *m* tape select(or) switch
'Band·spei·cher *m computer*: magnetic tape storage
'Band·wurm *m* tapeworm; **~satz** F *fig. m* endless sentence
ban·ge ['baŋə] *adj. pred.* anxious (***um*** *acc.* about); worried (about); ***ihm ist ~ (vor*** *dat.*) *a.* he's afraid (*or* scared, frightened) (of); ***j-m ~ machen*** frighten s.o.; ***~ Ahnung*** foreboding, awful feeling; ***~s Gefühl*** uneasy feeling; ***e-e ~ Stunde*** an hour of anxious waiting (*or* suspense *etc.*); ***e-e ~ Sekunde (lang)*** for one dreadful (*or* awful) moment; F ***~ machen gilt nicht!*** a) you can't scare me, b) don't be such a coward; **'Ban·ge** *f*: ***keine ~!*** don't (you) worry; ***keine ~, wir schaffen das schon!*** *a.* we'll manage it, no fears; **ban·gen** ['baŋən] *v/i. and v/refl.* (h): ***(sich) ~ um*** *acc.* be worried about; ***um sein Leben ~*** fear for one's life; ***mir bangt es vor ...*** I'm frightened (*or* scared) of *or* about, I'm afraid of
Ban·jo ['banjo] *n* (-s; -s) banjo
Bank¹ [baŋk] *f* (-; Bänke ['bɛŋkə]) **1.** bench, seat; desk; pew; ***in der vordersten ~*** in the front row; F ***durch die ~*** right down the line, every one of them, F the whole lot (of them); ***et. auf die lange ~ schieben*** put s.th. off, shelve s.th. for the time being; ***vor leeren Bänken spielen*** play before an empty house; ***vor leeren Bänken predigen*** preach to an empty church, *fig.* talk to the wind; **2.** ⚙ (work)bench; → ***Drehbank, Hobelbank***; **3.** *geol.* layer, bed, stratum; → ***Sandbank***
Bank² *f* (-; -en) **1.** ⚚ bank; *Geld* ***auf der ~*** in the bank; ***auf die ~ gehen*** go to the bank; *Konto* ***bei der ~*** at (*or* with) the bank; ***bei e-r ~ sein*** work for a bank; **2.** *gambling*: bank; ***die ~ halten*** hold the bank; ***die ~ sprengen*** break the bank; **~an·ge·stell·te** *m, f* (-n; -n) bank employee; ***~(r) sein*** *a.* work for a bank; **~an·lei·he** *f* bank loan; **~an·wei·sung** *f* banker's order; **~au·to,mat** *m* cash dispenser (F machine), autoteller; *formal*: automated teller machine, ATM; F hole in the wall; **~dar·le·hen** *n* bank loan; **~di,rek·tor** *m* bank manager; **~ein·bruch** *m* bank raid (*or* robbery), raid on a bank, break-in at a bank; **~ein·la·ge** *f* (bank) deposit
Bän·kel|lied ['bɛŋkəl-] *n* (street) ballad; **~sän·ger** *m hist.* roving minstrel; balladeer
'Ban·ken|auf·sicht *f* bank supervision; **~kon,sor·ti·um** *n* banking syndicate, bank group

Ban·ker ['bɛŋkɐ] *m* (-s; -) banker; *w.s.* financier
Ban·kett [baŋ'kɛt] *n* (-[e]s; -e) **1.** banquet; ***auf e-m ~*** at a banquet; ***ein ~ geben*** hold (*or* throw) a banquet; **2.** *road*: shoulder; ⚠ base course; ***~ nicht befahrbar*** soft shoulder
Ban·ket·te [baŋ'kɛtə] *f* (-; -n) *road*: shoulder
'**Bank·fach** *n* (-[e]s; -fächer) **1.** *no pl.* banking (business); **2.** safe(-deposit) box
'**bank·fä·hig** *adj.* bankable, eligible, negotiable; '**Bank·fä·hig·keit** *f* (-; *no pl.*) bankability, eligibility, negotiability
'**Bank|fi·li,ale** *f* branch bank; **~ge·bäu·de** *n* bank; **~ge·heim·nis** *n* banking secrecy; **~ge·schäft** *n* banking transaction; **~ge·sell·schaft** *f* banking corporation; **~ge·wer·be** *n* (-s; *no pl.*) banking industry; **~gut·ha·ben** *n* bank balance; cash in the bank; **~hal·ter** *m gambling*: banker; **~haus** *n* banking house
Ban·kier [baŋ'kje:] *m* (-s; -s) banker; *w.s.* financier
'**Bank|kauf·frau** *f*, **~kauf·mann** *m* (qualified) bank employee; **~kon·to** *n* bank account; **~kon,zern** *m* banking group; **~krach** *m* bank crash; **~kre,dit** *m* bank loan; **~krei·se** *pl.* banking circles, *the* banking community *sg.*; **~kun·de** *m* bank customer; **~leh·re** *f* (-; *no pl.*) bank traineeship; **~leit·zahl** *f* ✝ bank code; **~no·te** *f* (bank) note, *Am.* (bank) bill
'**Bank·no·ten|aus·ga·be** *f* note issue; **~fäl·schung** *f* forgery of bank notes
'**Bank|pro·vi·si,on** *f* banking commission; **~ra·te** *f* official discount rate; **~raub** *m* bank robbery; **~räu·ber** *m* bank robber; **~recht** *n* banking laws *pl.*; **~re,ser·ven** *pl.* bank reserves
Bank·rott [baŋ'krɔt] **I.** *m* (-[e]s; -e) bankruptcy (*a. fig.*); (business) failure; ***den ~ erklären*** file for bankruptcy; ***~ machen*** go bankrupt, F go bust; ***vor dem ~ stehen*** face (*or* be on the verge of) bankruptcy; *fig.* ***es bedeutete den politischen*** (***wirtschaftlichen***) ***~*** it spelt out political bankruptcy (the complete breakdown of the economy); **II.** 2 *adj.* **1.** bankrupt; F (stony) broke; ***~ gehen*** go bankrupt; ***j-n ~ machen*** drive s.o. bankrupt, bankrupt s.o.; ***sich*** (***für***) ***~ erklären*** declare o.s. bankrupt, file for bankruptcy; **2.** *fig.* bankrupt; ***innerlich ~*** crushed, devastated; **Bank'rott·er·klä·rung** *f a. fig.* declaration of bankruptcy; **Bank·rot·teur** [baŋkrɔ'tø:ɐ] *m* (-s; -e [-'tø:rə]) bankrupt; bankrupt firm
'**Bank|sal·do** *m* bank balance; **~schal·ter** *m* (bank) counter *or* window; **~scheck** *m* banker's cheque (*Am.* check); **~schließ·fach** *n* safe(-deposit box); **~spe·sen** *pl.* bank(ing) charges; **~tre,sor** *m* bank('s) vault; **~,über·fall** *m* bank raid (*or* robbery), raid on a bank; **~über,wei·sung** *f* bank transfer; **~ver·bin·dung** *f* **1.** bank account; **2.** correspondent *of a bank*; **~ver·kehr** *m* banking business, interbank dealings *pl.*; **~we·sen** *n* (-s; *no pl.*) (world of) banking; **~wirt·schaft** *f* (-; *no pl.*) banking industry
Bann [ban] *m* (-[e]s; -e) **1.** *hist.* banishment; *eccl.* excommunication; ***in den ~ tun, mit dem ~ belegen*** banish, outlaw, *eccl.* excommunicate, *fig.* ostracize, ✝ boycott; **2.** *fig.* charm, spell; ***unter dem ~ stehen von*** (*or gen.*) be (*or* have come) under the spell *or* sway of, be spellbound by, be under the spell of, *b.s.* be in the grip of; ***in j-s ~ geraten*** come under s.o.'s spell; ***in den ~ der Musik*** *etc.* ***geraten*** be enthralled (*or* spellbound) by the music *etc.*; ***in den ~ von Alkohol geraten*** become a slave to alcohol (*or* the demon drink); ***in ~ schlagen*** captivate, spellbind; ***in ~ halten*** have *s.o.* spellbound; ***endlich war der ~ gebrochen*** the ice had broken at last; **ban·nen** ['banən] *v/t.* (h) **1.** banish (*a. fig.*); avert, ward off *danger etc.*; exorcize, cast out *evil spirit*; *eccl.* excommunicate; **2.** *fig.* captivate, transfix, spellbind; → ***gebannt*** II; **3.** ***et. auf den Film*** (***das Band*** *etc.*) ***~*** capture s.th. on film (tape *etc.*)
Ban·ner ['banɐ] *n* (-s; -) banner (*a. fig.*), standard; **~trä·ger** *m* (-s; -) standard-bearer (*a. fig.*)
'**Bann|fluch** *m hist.* excommunication; ***j-n mit dem ~ belegen*** excommunicate s.o.; **~kreis** *fig. m* sphere of influence, spell; ***in j-s ~ geraten*** come under s.o.'s sway (*or* spell); **~mei·le** *f* **1.** *hist.* precincts *pl.*; **2.** *pol.* neutral zone
Ban·tam·ge·wicht ['bantam-] *n* (-[e]s; *no pl.*), '**Ban·tam·ge·wicht·ler** [-gəvɪçtlɐ] *m* (-s; -) *sport*: bantamweight
'**Ban·tam·huhn** *n* bantam
Ban·tu ['bantu] *m* (-[s]; -[s]) Bantu; **~spra·che** *f* Bantu language; **~volk** *n* Bantu people (*or* tribe)
Bap·tist [bap'tɪst] *m* (-en; -en) baptist
Bap·ti·ste·ri·um [baptɪs'te:rĭʊm] *n* (-s; -rien [-rĭən]) baptistry
bap·ti·stisch [bap'tɪstɪʃ] *adj.* Baptist
bar [ba:ɐ] *adj.* **1.** ***~es Geld*** (ready) cash; (***in***) ***~ bezahlen*** pay cash; ***gegen ~*** for cash; ***zahlen Sie ~ oder mit Scheck?*** is it cash or cheque (*Am.* check)?; **2.** pure *gold*; → ***Münze***; *contp. a.* downright; ***~er Unsinn*** sheer (*or* utter) nonsense; **3.** (*gen.*) devoid of, lacking in; ***~ jeglichen Gefühls*** totally lacking (in) any feeling; **4.** *obs.* ***~en Hauptes*** bareheaded
Bar[1] [ba:ɐ] *f* (-; -s) bar; nightclub; drinks cabinet; ***in e-e ~ gehen*** go to a bar; ***an der ~*** at the bar
Bar[2] [ba:ɐ] *n* (-s; -s) *phys.* bar
Bär [bɛ:ɐ] *m* (-en; -en) **1.** bear; ***schlafen wie ein ~*** sleep like a log; → ***aufbinden***; **2.** *ast.* ***der Große*** (***Kleine***) ***~*** the Great (Little) Bear, Ursa Major (Minor), F the Big (Little) Dipper
'**Bar|ab·fin·dung** *f* cash settlement; **~ab·he·bung** *f* cash withdrawal
Ba·racke (*sep.* -k·k-) *f* (-; -n) hut; *esp. contp.* shack; ***elende ~*** hovel
Ba'racken|la·ger (*sep.* -k·k-) *n* hut camp; **~sied·lung** *f* shantytown, slums *pl.*
'**Bar|aus·ga·ben** *pl.* cash expenditure *sg.*; **~aus·la·gen** *pl.* cash outlays (*or* outlay *sg.*); **~aus·schüt·tung** *f* cash dividend; **~aus·zah·lung** *f* cash payment
Bar·bar [bar'ba:ɐ] *m* (-en; -en [bar'ba:rən]) barbarian (*a. fig. contp.*); **Bar·ba·rei** [barba'raɪ] *f* (-; -en) barbarism, savagery; barbarity, savage act; **Bar·ba·ren·tum** *n* (-s; *no pl.*) barbarism; **bar·ba·risch** [bar'ba:rɪʃ] **I.** *adj.* barbaric, barbarous (*a. fig. contp.*); barbarian *tribe etc.*; *fig.* savage, cruel; brutal; F dreadful; F ***ich habe e-n ~en Hunger*** I'm ravenous, I could eat a horse; **II.** *adv.*: ***sich ~ benehmen*** behave like a barbarian (*or* barbarians); F ***~ stinken*** *etc.* F smell *etc.* something awful; **bar·ba·ri·sie·ren** [barbari'zi:rən] *v/t.* (h) barbarize
Bar·be ['barbə] *f* (-; -n) *zo.* barbel
bär·bei·ßig ['bɛ:ɐbaɪsɪç] *adj.* surly
'**Bar|be·stand** *m* cash in hand; cash reserve(s *pl.*); **~be·trag** *m* cash sum; **~be·zü·ge** *pl.* remuneration *sg.* in cash
Bar·bi·tu·rat [barbitu'ra:t] *n* (-s; -e) barbiturate
Bar·bi·tur·säu·re [barbi'tu:ɐ-] *f* barbituric acid
bar·bu·sig ['ba:rbu:zɪç] *adj.* bare-bosomed, topless
'**Bar·da·me** *f* barmaid
Bar·de ['bardə] *m* (-n; -n) *hist. and iro.* bard
'**Bar|de,pot** *n* cash deposit; **~di·vi,den·de** *f* cash dividend (*or* bonus); **~ein·gän·ge** *pl.* cash receipts; **~ein·la·ge** *f* cash deposit; **~ein·nah·men** *pl.* cash receipts
'**Bä·ren·dienst** *m*: ***j-m e-n ~ erweisen*** do s.o. a bad turn; ***da hast du mir e-n ~ geleistet!*** *iro.* that was a great help
'**Bä·ren·fell** *n* bearskin; **~müt·ze** *f* bearskin (hat); *Brit.* ⚔ bearskin (cap), busby
'**bä·ren·haft** *adj.* lumbering; ***~e Gestalt*** (great) hulk
'**Bä·ren|hatz** *f* bear-baiting; **~haut** *f* bearskin; *fig.* ***auf der ~ liegen*** laze around, have a lazy time of it
'**Bä·ren|hun·ger** *m*: ***ich habe e-n ~*** I'm ravenous, I could eat a horse; **~jagd** *f* bear-baiting, bear-hunting, bear hunt; **~kraft** *f a. pl. the* strength of a horse; Herculean strength; ***e-e ~*** (*or* ***Bärenkräfte***) ***haben*** *a.* be as strong as an ox; **~na,tur** *f the* constitution of a horse
'**bä·ren·stark** *adj.* **1.** (as) strong as an ox; **2.** F *fig.* F great, *pred. a.* brill
'**Bar|er·lös** *m*, **~er·trag** *m* cash (*or* net) proceeds *pl.*
Ba·rett [ba'rɛt] *n* (-[e]s; -e) beret; biretta, cap
'**bar·fuß** **I.** *adj.* barefoot(ed); **II.** *adv.* barefoot; ***~ herumlaufen*** *a.* run around with nothing on one's feet; '**Bar·fuß·arzt** *m* barefoot doctor; **bar·fü·ßig** ['ba:ɐfy:sɪç] *adj.* barefoot(ed)
barg [bark] *pret. of* ***bergen***
'**Bar·geld** *n* cash; '**bar·geld·los** *adj.* cashless; ***~er Zahlungsverkehr*** (payment by) money transfer; ***~er Einkauf*** cashless shopping
bar·häup·tig ['ba:ɐhɔyptɪç] *adj.* bareheaded; *a. adv.* without a hat on
'**Bar·hocker** (*sep.* -k·k-) *m* bar stool
Bä·rin ['bɛ:rɪn] *f* (-; -nen) she-bear
Ba·ri·ton ['ba:ritɔn] *m* (-; -e [-to:nə]) baritone (*a. singer*); ***den ~ singen*** sing baritone, be the baritone
Bar·kas·se [bar'kasə] *f* (-; -n) ⚓ (motor) launch
'**Bar·kauf** *m* cash purchase
Bar·ke ['barkə] *f* (-; -n) ⚓ rowing boat; *poet.* barque
'**Bar·kee·per** ['ba:ɐki:pɐ] *m* (-s; -) barman, bartender
'**Bar·kre,dit** *m* cash credit
Bär·lapp ['bɛ:ɐlap] *m* (-s; -e) ⚘ club moss
'**Bar·lei·stung** *f* cash payment
barm·her·zig [barm'hɛrtsɪç] *adj.* compassionate, kind-hearted; charitable; merciful (***gegen*** *acc.* to[wards]); ***~ sein gegen*** (*or* ***mit*** *dat.*) *a.* have mercy on; → ***Samariter***; **Barm'her·zig·keit** *f* (-; *no pl.*) compassion; charity; mercy

'Bar·mit·tel *pl.* cash *sg.*, cash resources
'Bar·mi·xer *m* barman, bartender
ba·rock [ba'rɔk] **I.** *adj.* baroque (*a. fig.*), Baroque; **II.** ♀ *m, n* (-s; *no pl.*) **1.** Baroque (period, era, age); **2.** baroque *or* Baroque (style)
Ba·ro·me·ter [baro'me:tɐ] *n* (-s; -) barometer (*a. fig.* **für** *acc.* of); ***das ~ steht hoch*** (***tief***) the barometer is high (low); *fig.* ***das ~ steht auf Sturm*** there's a storm brewing; **~stand** *m* barometer reading; barometric pressure; ***den ~ ablesen*** read the barometer; **~sturz** *m* sudden drop in (atmospheric) pressure
Ba·ron [ba'ro:n] *m* (-s; -e) baron; **Ba·ro·nes·se** [baro'nɛsə] *f* (-; -n), **Ba·ro·nin** [ba'ro:nɪn] *f* (-; -nen) baroness
'Bar|preis *m* cash price; **~re,ser·ven** *pl.* cash reserves
Bar·ras ['baras] F *m*: ***beim ~*** in the army, *a.* doing one's national service; ***er muß zum ~*** he's got his conscription papers, he's been called up (for national service)
Bar·ren ['barən] *m* (-s; -) **1.** bar, ingot; *pl. a.* bullion *sg.*; **2.** *gym.* parallel bars *pl.*; **~gold** *n* gold bullion
Bar·rie·re [ba'rĭe:rə] *f* (-; -n) barrier (*a. fig.*)
Bar·ri·ka·de [bari'ka:də] *f* (-; -n) barricade; ***auf die ~n steigen*** (*or* ***gehen***) *a. fig.* mount the barricades (***für*** *acc.* for); **Bar·ri'ka·den·kämp·fe** *pl.* street battles (*or* fighting *sg.*)
Barsch [ba:ɐʃ] *m* (-es; -e) *zo.* perch
barsch *adj.* gruff, brusque (***gegen*** *acc.* towards), short (with); ***~e Antwort*** gruff (*or* curt) reply
'Bar·schaft *f* (-; *no pl.*) ready money, F cash; ***m-e ganze ~ beläuft sich auf*** *acc.* ***...*** I have on me a total of ..
'Bar·scheck *m* cash cheque (*Am.* check)
'Barsch·heit *f* (-; *no pl.*) gruffness, brusqueness; gruff (*or* brusque) manner
barst [barst] *pret. of* ***bersten***
Bart [ba:ɐt] *m* (-[e]s; Bärte ['bɛ:ɐtə]) **1.** beard; *zo.* whiskers *pl.*; *ein Mann* ***mit ~*** with a beard; ***e-n ~ tragen*** have (*or* sport) a beard; ***sich e-n ~ stehenlassen*** grow a beard; *fig.* ***in den ~ brummen*** mumble to o.s.; ***j-m um den ~ gehen*** F soft-soap s.o.; F ***das hat ja so e-n ~!*** F that's as old as the hills; F ***der ~ ist ab!*** that's done it; **2.** bit, ward; **~flech·te** *f* **1.** ⚕ shaving rash; **2.** ♣ beardmoss; **~haar** *n* **1.** hair from s.o.'s beard; **2.** *pl.* beard
bär·tig ['bɛ:ɐtɪç] *adj.* bearded
'bart·los *adj.* clean-shaven
'Bart|stop·peln *pl.* stubble *sg.*; **~trä·ger** *m*: ***~ sein*** have a beard; **~wuchs** *m*: ***er hat e-n starken*** (***schwachen***) ***~*** he has a strong (slow) growth of beard, he has to shave a lot (he doesn't have to shave very often)
'Bar|über,wei·sung *f* cash transfer; **~ver·gü·tung** *f* cash imbursement; **~ver·kauf** *m* cash sale; **~ver·mö·gen** *n* cash assets *pl.*; **~wert** *m* cash value
'Bar·zah·lung *f* cash payment; (***Verkauf***) ***nur gegen ~*** cash terms only; **'Bar·zah·lungs·ra,batt** *m* cash discount
ba·sal [ba'za:l] *adj.* basal
Ba·salt [ba'zalt] *m* (-[e]s; -e) basalt
Ba'sal·wert *m* basal value
Ba·sar [ba'za:ɐ] *m* (-s; -e [ba'za:rə]) bazaar
Ba·se[1] ['ba:zə] *obs. f* (-; -n) (female) cousin
Ba·se[2] ['ba:zə] *f* (-; -n) ⚗ base
Ba·se·dow·sche Krank·heit ['ba:zədo:ʃə] *f* (*no pl.*) Basedow's disease; F protruding eyes *pl.*
ba·sie·ren [ba'zi:rən] *v/i.* (h): ***~ auf*** *dat.* be based on; *theory etc.*: *a.* be founded on
Ba·si·li·ka [ba'zi:lika] *f* (-; -ken) basilica
Ba·si·li·kum [ba'zi:likʊm] *n* (-s; *no pl.*) ♣ basil
Ba·si·lisk [bazi'lɪsk] *m* (-en; -en) basilisk
Ba·sis ['ba:zɪs] *f* (-; Basen ['ba:zən]) △, ⚗, ⚔ base; *fig.* basis, foundation; *pol.* grassroots *pl.*; rank and file; ***auf breiter ~*** on a broad basis; ***auf gesunder ~*** on a sound basis; ***auf gleicher ~*** on equal terms, on an equal footing; ***auf solider ~*** on a solid (*or* firm) footing; ***auf der ~ von ... beruhen*** be founded on ...; **~ar·beit** *f* constituency-level work
ba·sisch ['ba:zɪʃ] *adj.* ⚗ basic; **ein~** monobasic; **zwei~** dibasic
'Ba·sis|de·mo·kra,tie *f* grassroots democracy; **~ein·kom·men** *n* basic income; **~la·ger** *n* base camp; **~wis·sen** *n* basics *pl.*; **~zins** *m* base interest rate
Bas·ke ['baskə] *m* (-n; -n) Basque; **'Bas·ken·müt·ze** *f* beret
Bas·ket·ball ['ba:skətbal] *m* (-[e]s; *as a game no pl.*) basketball
bas·kisch ['baskɪʃ] *adj.* Basque
Bas·re·li·ef ['barelĭɛf] *n* (-s; -s) bas-relief
baß [bas] *obs. adv.*: ***~ erstaunt*** most surprised
Baß [bas] *m* (Basses; Bässe ['bɛsə]) ♪ **1.** bass (voice); **2.** bass (singer); **3.** bass (part); **4.** double bass; bass (guitar); **~an·he·bung** *f* bass lift; **~,ba·ri·ton** *m* bass baritone; **~be·glei·tung** *f* bass accompaniment; **~gei·ge** *f* double bass; **~gi,tar·re** *f* bass guitar
Bas·sin [ba'sɛ̃:] *n* (-s; -s) **1.** tank; **2.** pool
Bas·sist [ba'sɪst] *m* (-en; -en) **1.** bass (singer); **2.** (double) bass player
'Baß|kla·ri,net·te *f* bass clarinet; **~par,tie** *f* bass (part); **~reg·ler** *m* bass control; **~schlüs·sel** *m* bass clef; **~stim·me** *f* → ***Baß*** 1, 3
Bast [bast] *m* (-[e]s; *no pl.*) **1.** raffia; **2.** ♣ bast, phloem; **3.** *zo.* velvet
ba·sta ['basta] *int.* that's enough (of that)!; ***und damit ~!*** and that's that!
Ba·stard ['bastart] *m* (-[e]s; -e [-tardə]) **1.** ♣ hybrid; **2.** *zo.* crossbreed; mongrel; ***ein ~ zwischen ... und ...*** a cross between a ... and a ...; **ba·star·die·ren** [bastar'di:rən] *v/t.* (h) hybridize
Ba·stei [bas'taɪ] *f* (-; -en) bastion
'Ba·stel·ar·beit *f* handicraft(s *pl.*); F making things
ba·steln ['bastəln] (h) **I.** *v/t.* **1.** make; **II.** *v/i.* **2.** do handicrafts; ***er bastelt gern*** he likes to do things with his hands (*or* make things); ***mit Holz*** (***Papier*** *etc.*) ***~*** make things out of wood (paper *etc.*); **3.** ***~ an*** *dat.* tinker around with; **III.** ♀ *n* (-s; *no pl.*) handicrafts *pl.*; F making things
Ba·sti·on [bas'tĭo:n] *f* (-; -en) *a. fig.* bastion, bulwark
Bast·ler ['bastlɐ] *m*: ***er ist ein leidenschaftlicher*** (***guter***) ***~*** he loves to make things (he's good at making things *or* doing things with his hands)
'Bast·sei·de *f* raw silk
bat [ba:t] *pret. of* ***bitten***
Ba·tail·lon [batal'jo:n] *n* (-s; -e) battalion
Ba·tail'lons|chef *m*, **~füh·rer** *m* battalion leader
Ba·tik ['ba:tɪk] *m* (-; -en), *f* (-; -en) batik
Ba·tist [ba'tɪst] *m* (-[e]s; -e) cambric, batiste
Bat·te·rie [batə'ri:] *f* (-; -n) **1.** battery; ***mit ~ betreiben*** run on batteries (*or* a battery); **2.** ⚔ battery; **3.** F *fig.* battery, array *of bottles etc.*; **~an·zei·ger** *m* battery meter; **~be·trieb** *m* battery operation; ***mit ~*** → ♀**be·trie·ben** *adj.* battery-operated; **~fach** *n* battery compartment; **~ge·rät** *n* battery-operated device; ***es ist ein ~*** *a.* it runs on batteries; **~huhn** *n* battery hen; **~la·de·ge·rät** *n* battery charger; **~span·nung** *f* voltage; **~uhr** *f* battery watch (*or* clock)
Bat·zen ['batsən] *m* (-s; -) **1.** clump; **2.** F ***es hat e-n ~ Geld gekostet*** F it put me back a few bob; ***sie verdient e-n ~ Geld*** F she's raking it in; ***das ist ein ~ Geld*** F that's a tidy (little) sum
Bau [baʊ] *m* (-[e]s; Bauten ['baʊtən]) **1.** *no pl.* construction; ***im ~*** under construction, being built; **2.** building; ***Bauten*** *film*: setting *sg.*; **3.** *no pl.* ⚙ design, structure; **4.** → ***Baugewerbe; er ist beim ~, er arbeitet auf dem ~*** he's a building worker, he's in the building trade; F *fig.* ***er ist vom ~*** he's an expert; **5.** → ***Baustelle***; **6.** (*pl.* Baue) *zo.* earth, den; burrow; lodge; **7.** *no pl. sl.* ⚔ guardhouse; ***fünf Tage ~*** five days in the guardhouse; **8.** *no pl.* build; **~ab·schnitt** *m* construction (*or* building) stage; **~amt** *n* building authorities *pl.*; **~an·lei·tung** *f* construction manual; **~ar·bei·ten** *pl.* construction work *sg.*; roadworks; **~ar·bei·ter** *m* building (*or* construction) worker, labo(u)rer on a building site, F hard hat; **~art** *f* style (of construction); ⚙ design; type, model; **~auf·sichts·be·hör·de** *f* construction supervising body; **~be·ginn** *m* start of construction (work); **~be·hör·de** *f* building authority; **~be·wil·li·gung** *f* planning permission; **~bio·lo,gie** *f* organic architecture; **~boom** *m* building (*or* construction) boom
Bauch [baʊx] *m* (-[e]s; Bäuche ['bɔʏçə]) stomach, F tummy; *anat.* abdomen; paunch, pot-belly; *fig.* bulge, (*ship's etc.*) belly; ***auf dem ~ liegen*** lie on one's stomach, lie face down; ***mit vollem*** (***leerem***) ***~*** on a full (on an empty) stomach; ***ich hab' seit heute morgen nichts im ~*** I haven't eaten a thing since this morning; *fig.* ***sich den ~ halten vor Lachen*** split one's sides laughing, F roll with laughter; ***auf den ~ fallen*** F fall flat on one's face; ***vor j-m auf dem ~ kriechen*** crawl (F toady up) to s.o.; ***ich hab' mir die Füße*** (*or* ***Beine***) ***in den ~ gestanden*** I stood till I dropped; ***ich hab' e-e Wut im ~*** I'm ready to explode; F ***aus dem ~ heraus reagieren*** act on instinct; ***ich hab' aus dem ~ heraus reagiert*** *a.* F it was a gut reaction; F ***aus dem hohlen ~*** *talk etc.* F off the top of one's head; F ***es geht*** (***direkt***) ***in den ~*** F it really hits you; → ***Loch***; **~an·satz** *m* beginnings *pl.* of a paunch, F bit of a spare tyre (*Am.* tire); **~at·mung** *f* abdominal breathing; **~bin·de** *f* **1.** ⚕ abdominal bandage; **2.** band; **~decke** (*sep.* -k·k-) *f anat.* abdominal wall
'Bauch·fell *n* peritoneum; **~ent·zün·dung** *f* peritonitis
'Bauch·flos·se *f* ventral fin
'Bauch·höh·le *f* abdominal cavity; **'Bauch·höh·len·schwan·ger·schaft** *f* extra-uterine pregnancy
bau·chig ['baʊxɪç] *adj.* bulbous

'Bauch|klat·scher F *m* (-s; -) F belly flop; **~knöpf·chen** F *n* F belly button; **~la·den** F *m* vendor's tray; **~lan·dung** *f* F belly landing; *a.* F belly flop; ***e-e ~ machen*** land on one's belly, do a belly landing (*or* F belly flop), *fig.* F fall flat on one's face; **~mus·keln** *pl.*, **~mus·ku·laˌtur** *f* stomach muscles (*pl.*); **~na·bel** *m* navel; **≈pin·seln** F *v/t.* → ***gebauchpinselt***; **~re·de·kunst** *f* (-; *no pl.*) (art of) ventriloquism; **~red·ner** *m* (-s; -) ventriloquist; **~schmer·zen** *pl.* stomach-ache *sg.*; ***~ haben*** have a stomach-ache; **~schuß** *m* stomach wound; **~spei·chel·drü·se** *f* pancreas; **~tanz** *m* belly dance (*or* dancing); **~tän·ze·rin** *f* belly dancer; **~ta·sche** *f zo.* pouch; **~weh** F *n* (-s; *no pl.*) → ***Bauchschmerzen***

'Bau|denk·mal *n* historic (architectural) monument; **~eleˌment** *n* **1.** construction element; **2.** architectural element (*or* component)

bau·en ['baʊən] (h) **I.** *v/t.* **1.** build; erect; **2.** make, build, ⚙ *a.* construct; **3.** F *fig.* take *an exam*; ***e-n Unfall ~*** have an accident; → ***Mist*** 3; **4.** *fig.* ***s-e Hoffnungen*** *etc.* ***~ auf*** *acc.* base one's hopes *etc.* on; **II.** *v/i.* **5.** build; build a house; ***~ an*** *dat.* work on; **6.** *fig.* ***~ auf*** *acc.* count on, depend on

Bau·er[1] ['baʊɐ] *m* (-n; -n) **1.** farmer; **2.** *contp.* peasant; **3.** *chess*: pawn; *card game*: jack

Bau·er[2] ['baʊɐ] *n* (-s; -) (bird)cage

Bäu·er·chen ['bɔʏɐçən] F *n*: ***ein ~ machen*** *baby*: F do (*or* bring up) its windies

Bäue·rin ['bɔʏərɪn] *f* (-; -nen) **1.** (woman) farmer; **2.** farmer's wife

bäu·er·lich ['bɔʏɐlɪç] *adj.* rural; rustic

'Bau·ern|brot *n* (coarse) brown bread; **~bur·sche** *m* country lad; **~dorf** *n* farming village

'Bau·ern·fang *m*: ***auf ~ ausgehen*** F go out on the con game; **'Bau·ern·fän·ger** *m* (-s; -) F con man; **Bau·ern·fän·ge·rei** [-fɛŋə'raɪ] *f* (-; *no pl.*) F con (game)

'Bau·ern|früh·stück *n fried potatoes, ham and scrambled eggs*; **~gut** *n* farm(-stead); **~haus** *n* farmhouse; **~hoch·zeit** *f* country wedding; **~hof** *m* farm; **~krieg** *m hist.* Peasants' War; *in England*: Peasants' Revolt; **~lüm·mel** *m* country yokel, *Am.* F lick; **~mäd·chen** *n* country girl; **~magd** *f* farmgirl; **~mö·bel** *pl.* rustic furniture *sg.*; **~re·gel** *f* (piece of) country lore; *pl.* country lore *sg.*; **~schläue** *f* cunning, shrewdness; **~stand** *m* farmers *pl.*; *esp. hist.* peasantry; **~stu·be** *f* **1.** room in a farmhouse; **2.** rustic(-style) room; **~thea·ter** [-teˌaːtɐ] *n* rural folk theat|re (*Am. a.* -er)

'Bau|er·war·tungs·land *n* development site; **~fach** *n* (-[e]s; *no pl.*) **1.** architecture; **2.** building trade; **~fach·mann** *m* construction expert

'bau·fäl·lig *adj.* dilapidated, ramshackle; **'Bau·fäl·lig·keit** *f* (-; *no pl.*) dilapidated state; (state of) dilapidation

'Bau|fi·nanˌzie·rung *f* construction financing; financing of the (*or* a) building project; **~fir·ma** *f* construction company, (firm of) builders and contractors *pl.*; **~flucht** *f* alignment; **~füh·rer** *m* site manager; **~füh·rung** *f* site management; **~ge·län·de** *n* development area (*or* site); building site; **~ge·neh·mi·gung** *f* planning permission; **~ge·nos·sen·schaft** *f* cooperative building association; **~ge·rüst** *n* scaffolding; **~ge·sell·schaft** *f* construction company; **~ge·wer·be** *n* building trade; **~gru·be** *f* excavation (pit); **~grund** *m* **1.** development site; **2.** → **~grund·stück** *n* site, (building) plot; **~grup·pe** *f* ⚙ assembly; **~hand·werk** *n* building trade

'Bau·herr *m* builder-owner; (property) developer; **'Bau·her·ren·moˌdell** *n* builder's (*or* builder-owner) model

'Bau|holz *n* (building) timber; **~hüt·te** *f* builders' hut; **~in·duˌstrie** *f* building (*or* construction) industry; **~in·ge·niˌeur** *m* civil engineer; **~jahr** *n* construction year; ***~ 1990*** 1990 model; ***der Wagen*** *etc.* ***ist ~ 53*** it's a 1953 model

'Bau·ka·sten *m* box of bricks; construction kit (*or* set); **~prinˌzip** *n* modular (assembly) concept; **~syˌstem** *n* modular (assembly) system

'Bau·klotz *m* building brick; F ***da staunt man Bauklötze(r)*** it's absolutely amazing

'Bau·ko·sten *pl.* building costs; *w.s.* production costs; **~zu·schuß** *m* building subsidy

'Bau|kran *m* construction crane; **~kunst** *f* (-; *no pl.*) architecture; **≈künst·le·risch** *adj.* architectural; **~land** *n* (-[e]s; *no pl.*) development area; **~lei·ter** *m* site manager; **~lei·tung** *f* site management

'bau·lich *adj.* architectural; structural; ***in gutem*** (***schlechtem***) ***~en Zustand*** in good (bad) repair; ***~e Sünde*** architectural eyesore, unsightly development, F blot on the landscape, carbuncle

'Bau·lich·kei·ten *pl.* buildings, architecture *sg.*

'Bau|lö·we F *m* property giant; **~lücke** (*sep.* -k·k-) *f* (-; -n) vacant lot, empty site

Baum [baʊm] *m* (-[e]s; Bäume ['bɔʏmə]) tree; *fig.* ***der ~ der Erkenntnis*** the tree of knowledge; ***es ist dafür gesorgt, daß die Bäume nicht in den Himmel wachsen*** there's a limit to everything(, I suppose); ***zwischen ~ und Borke stekken*** be between the devil and the deep blue sea; F ***es ist, um auf die Bäume zu klettern*** it's enough to drive you up the wall; → ***ausreißen*** 1

'Bau|markt *m* **1.** ⚚ property market; **2.** DIY store; **~maˌschi·nen** *pl.* construction equipment *sg.*; **~maß·nah·men** *pl.* building operations; **~ma·te·riˌal** *n* building material(s *pl.*)

'Baum|be·stand *m* stock of trees, tree population; **~blü·te** *f* **1.** blossoming of a tree; **2.** flowering season

Bäum·chen ['bɔʏmçən] *n* (-s; -) small (*or* little) tree

'Baum|chirˌurg *m* tree surgeon; **~chir·urˌgie** *f* tree surgery

'Bau·mei·ster *m* (-s; -) **1.** master builder; **2.** *a. fig.* architect

bau·meln ['baʊməln] *v/i.* (h) **1.** dangle, swing (**an** *dat.* from); ***mit den Beinen ~*** dangle one's legs; **2.** F swing

bäu·men ['bɔʏmən] *v/t. and v/refl.* (**sich** ~) → ***aufbäumen***

'Baum|farn *m* ⚘ treefern; **~fäu·le** *f* dry rot; **~flech·te** *f* ⚘ lichen, tree moss; **~fre·vel** *m* wil(l)ful damaging of trees; **~gar·ten** *m* orchard; **~gren·ze** *f* treeline, timberline; **~grup·pe** *f* clump of trees; **~haus** *n* tree-house; **~hecke** (*sep.* -k·k-) *f* hedge of trees; **≈hoch** *adj.* (as) tall as a tree (*or* trees); **~kro·ne** *f* treetop; **~ku·chen** *m* pyramid cake; **≈lang** *adj.* giant ...; *pred.* (as) tall as a lamppost; **~läu·fer** *m zo.* (tree) creeper

'baum·los *adj.* treeless

'Baum|mar·der *m* pine marten; **~pflan·zung** *f* tree nursery; **≈reich** *adj.* densely wooded; **~rie·se** *m* giant tree; **~rin·de** *f* bark (of a *or* the tree); **~sche·re** *f*: (***e-e*** ~ a pair of) pruning shears *pl.*; **~schu·le** *f* (tree) nursery; **~schwamm** *m* ⚘ agaric; **~stamm** *m* (tree) trunk; log; **≈stark** *adj.* (as) strong as an ox; **~ster·ben** *n* dying (off) of trees (*or* forests), forest deaths *pl.*; **~stumpf** *m* (tree) stump; **~stüt·ze** *f* tree prop; **~wip·fel** *m* treetop

'Baum·wol·le *f* (-; *no pl.*) cotton; **'baum·wol·len** *adj.* cotton

'Baum·woll|garn *n* (sewing) cotton; **~hemd** *n* (100%) cotton shirt; **~in·duˌstrie** *f* cotton industry; **~pflan·zer** *m* (-s; -) cotton planter; **~pflücker** (*sep.* -k·k-) *m* (-s; -) cotton picker; **~planˌta·ge** *f* cotton plantation; **~spin·neˌrei** *f* cotton mill; **~stau·de** *f* cotton plant; **~stoff** *m* cotton; **~strauch** *m* cotton plant

'Baum·wur·zel *f* tree root

'Bau|norm *f* building standard(s *pl.*); **~obˌjekt** *n* building (*or* construction) project; **~ord·nung** *f* building regulations *pl.*; **~plan** *m* architect's plan; ⚙ blueprint; **~pla·nung** *f* project planning; **~platz** *m* site, (building) plot; **~preis** *m* building costs *pl.*; **~proˌgramm** *n* building (*or* construction) program(me); **~proˌjekt** *n* building (*or* construction) project; **~rat** *m* government building surveyor; **~recht** *n* (-[e]s; *no pl.*) building regulations *pl.*; **≈reif** *adj.* ⚙ developed; △ ready for building; **~re·zes·siˌon** *f* slump in the building (*or* construction) industry; **~rui·ne** *f* half-finished (*or* abandoned) building; **~saiˌson** *f* building season; **~satz** *m* construction kit

Bausch [baʊʃ] *m* (-es; Bäusche ['bɔʏʃə]) wad, ball; *fig.* ***in ~ und Bogen*** lock, stock and barrel; **'Bausch·är·mel** *pl.* puff sleeves; **bau·schen** ['baʊʃən] (h) **I.** *v/i. and v/refl.* (**sich** ~) billow; **II.** *v/t.* puff out; swell; **bau·schig** ['baʊʃɪç] *adj.* puffed out

'Bau|schlos·ser *m* building fitter; **~schutt** *m* rubble (from a building site); **~sek·tor** *m* building sector

'bau·spa·ren *v/i.* (*only inf.*) save with a building society; **'Bau·spa·rer** *m* (-s; -) building society investor; **'Bau·spar·kas·se** *f* building society; **'Bau·spar·ver·trag** *m* building society savings agreement

'Bau·sta·tik *f* architectural statics *pl.*; **'bau·sta·tisch** *adj.* statical; ***~e Berechnung*** stress analysis

'Bau|stein *m* brick (*a. toy*); stone; *fig.* element, component; important contribution; **~stel·le** *f* building site; roadworks *pl.*; **~stil** *m* (architectural) style; **~stoff** *m* **1.** building material; **2.** *biol.* nutrient; **~stopp** *m* building freeze; ***e-n ~ anordnen*** halt building (works); **~subˌstanz** *f* structural fabric; architectural fabric (*or* core) *of a town etc.*; **~tä·tig·keit** *f* building (activity)

'Bau·tech·nik *f* constructional engineering; building technique; **'Bau·tech·ni·ker** *m* constructional engineer; **'bau·tech·nisch** *adj.* constructional

'Bau·teil *n* (-[e]s; -e) component (part)

'Bau·ten *pl.* buildings

'Bau|trä·ger *m* (-s; -) (property) developer(s *pl.*); **~un·ter,neh·men** *n* **1.** building contractors *pl.*, (property) developers *pl.*; **2.** building project; **~un·ter,neh·mer** *m* building contractor, (property) developer; **~ver·bot** *n* building ban; **~ver·trag** *m* building contract; **~vor·ha·ben** *n* building (*or* construction) project; **~vor·schrif·ten** *pl.* building regulations; **~wei·se** *f* **1.** construction (method); **2.** style (of architecture); **~werk** *n* building; **~we·sen** *n* (-s; *no pl.*) **1.** civil engineering; **2.** architecture; **~wirt·schaft** *f* (-; *no pl.*) building (*or* construction) industry; **~wut** *f* building craze

Bau·xit [baʊ'ksiːt] *n* (-s; -e) *min.* bauxite

'Bau|zaun *m* hoarding; **~zeich·ner** *m* architectural draughtsman (*Am.* draftsman); **~zeich·nung** *f* construction plan; architect's plan (*or* drawing); **~zeit** *f* construction time; **~zu·schuß** *m* building subsidy

Bay·er ['baɪɐ] *m* (-n; -n), **Baye·rin** ['baɪərɪn] *f* (-; -nen) Bavarian; **bay(e)·risch** ['baɪ(ə)rɪʃ] *adj.* Bavarian; ***der Bayerische Wald*** the Bavarian Forest

Ba·zar [ba'tsaːɐ] *m* (-s; -e [ba'tsaːrə]) bazaar

Ba·zil·le [ba'tsɪlə] F *f* (-; -n) germ

Ba'zil·len|stamm *m* strain of bacilli; **~trä·ger** *m* (-s; -) (germ) carrier

Ba·zil·lus [ba'tsɪlʊs] *m* (-; -len) germ; 🕮 bacillus (*pl.* bacilli)

be·ab·sich·ti·gen [bə'ʔapzɪçtɪgən] *v/t.* (h) intend (**zu** *inf.* to *inf.*, *ger.*); plan (to *inf.* or on *ger.*); ***es war beabsichtigt*** it was intentional, he *etc.* did it on purpose (*or* meant it); ***es war nicht beabsichtigt*** it wasn't intentional, I *etc.* didn't mean to (do it); ***was hast du damit beabsichtigt?*** what were you trying to do (*or* achieve) (by that)?; **be'ab·sich·tigt** *adj.* **1.** intended; ***die ~e Wirkung*** the desired effect; ***die ~e Wirkung blieb aus*** *drug etc.*: it didn't have the desired effect, the effect didn't come off; **2.** intentional, deliberate

be'ach·ten *v/t.* (h) pay attention to; note; follow, keep to *instructions, rules etc.*, observe *law*; bear in mind, take into account; ***nicht ~*** take no notice of, ignore; *a.* disregard *s.o.'s advice etc.*; not to notice, miss; ***bitte zu ~*** please note; ***man muß dabei ~, daß*** you've got to be aware (*or* remember) that; *die Ereignisse etc.* ***wurden kaum beachtet*** were scarcely noticed, aroused little attention, passed by without notice; **be'ach·tens·wert** *adj.* noteworthy; ***e-e ~e Leistung*** *a.* quite an achievement; **be·acht·lich** [bə'ʔaxtlɪç] **I.** *adj.* considerable; sizeable; remarkable; serious; formidable; ***er hat ein ~es Talent*** he has considerable talent; ***das war e-e ~e Leistung*** that was quite an achievement (*or* some feat); ***~!*** F pretty good!; **II.** *adv.*: ***~ steigen*** climb sharply; **Be'ach·tung** *f* (-; *no pl.*) attention; consideration; observance; ***~ finden*** be taken note of; ***keine ~ finden*** be ignored, *achievement etc.*: remain unacknowledged; **(*keine*) *~ schenken*** *dat.* pay (no) attention to; ***~ verdienen*** be worthy of note; ***unter ~ von*** (*or gen.*) with ... in mind, in compliance with, following *s.o.'s advice etc.*

be'ackern (*sep.* -k·k-) *v/t.* (h) **1.** plough, *Am.* plow; **2.** *fig.* work through

Be·am·te [bə'ʔamtə] *m* (-n; -n) official; (*police, customs*) officer; government official, civil servant; F employee

Be'am·ten|an·wär·ter *m* civil service applicant; **~ap·pa,rat** *m* civil service machinery; **~be·lei·di·gung** *f*: (***wegen ~*** for) insulting an official (*or* a police officer); **~be·ste·chung** *f* bribery of an official (*or* officials); **~deutsch** *n contp.* officialese

be'am·ten·haft *adj.* bureaucratic

Be'am·ten·lauf·bahn *f* civil service career

Be'am·ten·tum *n* (-s; *no pl.*) civil servants *pl.*; *contp.* officialdom

Be·am·tin [bə'ʔamtɪn] *f* (-; -nen) → ***Beamte***

be'äng·sti·gen *v/t.* (h) worry, get *s.o.* worried; **be'äng·sti·gend** *adj.* frightening, alarming; **Be'äng·sti·gung** *f* (-; -en) worry, concern; fear; alarm

be·an·spru·chen [bə'ʔanʃprʊxən] *v/t.* (h) claim, lay claim to; demand, require, call for; take up *time, space*; use, make use of, avail o.s. of; preoccupy, absorb; strain, be (*or* put) a strain on, tax; ⚙ stress, strain; ***stark ~*** be (*or* put) a heavy strain on *s.th.*; keep *s.o.* very busy, take up a lot of *s.o.'s* time (and energy), make heavy demands on *s.o.('s* time); preoccupy *s.o.* greatly; **be'an·sprucht** *adj.*: ***stark ~*** very (*or* extremely) busy; ***sie ist zur Zeit stark ~*** *a.* she's got a lot on her plate at the moment; **Be'an·spru·chung** *f* (-; -en) claim (*gen.* on); demand (on); use; strain, ⚙ *a.* stress, load; ***~ durch die Arbeit*** *etc. the* demands of work *etc.*; ⚙ ***für starke*** (*or* ***hohe***) ***~*** for heavy-duty service, heavy-duty *materials etc.*, for hard wear; ***für normale ~*** for normal service; ***unter normaler ~*** under normal (working) conditions

be·an·stan·den [bə'ʔanʃtandən] *v/t.* (h) complain about; query; criticize; object to; ***was ich an ihm*** (***daran***) ***zu ~ habe*** what I don't like about him (it), the thing I have against him (it); ***ich habe nichts daran zu ~*** I can't see anything wrong with it; ***das einzige, was ich daran zu ~ habe*** the only criticism (*or* objection) I have; **Be'an·stan·dung** *f* (-; -en) complaint (***an*** *dat.* about); query (about); criticism (of, about); objection (to)

be·an·tra·gen [bə'ʔantraːgən] *v/t.* (h) apply for, put in an application for; ⚖, *parl.* move for; propose; ***~ zu*** *inf. parl.* move that *s.th. be done*; propose that *s.th. be done*; **Be'an·tra·gung** *f* (-; -en) application; motion; proposal

be·ant·wort·bar [bə'ʔantvɔrtbaːɐ] *adj.* answerable; **be'ant·wor·ten** *v/t.* (h) answer (***mit*** *dat.* with) (*a. fig.*), reply to; ***mit ja*** (***nein***) ***~*** answer yes (no); **Be'ant·wor·tung** *f* (-; -en) answer, reply; answering; ***in ~*** *gen.* in answer (*or* reply) to

be'ar·bei·ten *v/t.* (h) **1.** ⛏ work, cultivate; **2.** ⚙ work, *a.* dress *leather*; machine; treat; **3.** work on *a subject etc.*; *a.* deal with *a case etc.*; **4.** edit, revise *book*; *thea.* adapt; ♪ arrange; **5.** *fig.* ***j-n ~*** work on s.o.; **6.** F *fig.* ***j-n ~*** F give s.o. a working over; **Be'ar·bei·ter** *m* (-s; -) **1.** person in charge (*or* dealing with) the case *etc.*; **2.** editor; adapter; ♪ arranger; **Be'ar·bei·tung** *f* (-; -en) **1.** ⛏ working, cultivation; **2.** ⚙ working; treatment; **3.** treatment; processing; **4.** revision, revised edition; *thea.* adaptation; *esp.* ♪ arrangement; **Be'ar·bei·tungs·ge·bühr** *f* handling charge; (bank) service charge

be'arg·wöh·nen *v/t.* (h) be suspicious of; **Be'arg·wöh·nung** *f* (-; -en) suspicion (*gen.* of, towards)

be'at·men *v/t.* (h) give *s.o.* artificial respiration; **Be'at·mung** *f*: (-; -en) (***künstliche ~***) artificial respiration; **Be'at·mungs·ge·rät** *n* respirator

be·auf·sich·ti·gen [bə'ʔaʊfzɪçtɪgən] *v/t.* (h) supervise; look after; ***die Kinder bei ihren Hausaufgaben ~*** supervise the children's homework; **Be'auf·sich·ti·gung** *f* (-;-en) supervision

be'auf·tra·gen *v/t.* (h) **1.** ***j-n ~, et. zu tun*** ask (*or* instruct, commission) s.o. to do s.th.; ***wer hat Sie dazu beauftragt?*** on whose instructions are you doing this?, F who told you to do this?; **2.** ***j-n mit e-m Fall*** *etc.* ***~*** put s.o. in charge of a case *etc.*; **Be·auf·trag·te** [bə'ʔaʊftraːktə] *m, f* (-n; -n) (authorized) representative; delegate; **Be'auf·tra·gung** *f* (-; -en) instructions *pl.* (***zu*** *inf.* to *inf.*); authorization

be·äu·ge(l)n [bə'ʔɔʏgə(l)n] *v/t.* (h) have a good look at; *a.* ogle at *s.o.*

be·au·gen·schei·ni·gen [bə'ʔaʊgənʃaɪnɪgən] *v/t.* (h) *usu. iro.* have a close look at

be·bau·bar [bə'baʊbaːɐ] *adj.* developable; **be'bau·en** *v/t.* (h) **1.** ⛏ cultivate; **2.** build on; **be'baut** *adj.*: ***~es Gebiet*** (***or Gelände***) built-up area; **Be'bau·ung** *f* (-; -en) **1.** ⛏ cultivation; **2.** development

Be'bau·ungs|dich·te *f* building density; **~plan** *m* building (*or* development) plan

be·ben ['beːbən] **I.** *v/i.* (h) shake, tremble (*a. voice etc.*) (***vor*** *dat.* with); vibrate; **II.** ♀ *n* (-s; -) trembling; vibration(s *pl.*); *geol.* tremor, (earth)quake

be·bil·dern [bə'bɪldɐn] *v/t.* (h) illustrate; **Be·bil·de·rung** [bə'bɪldərʊŋ] *f* (-; -en) illustrations *pl.*

be·brillt [bə'brɪlt] *adj.* spectacled

be'brü·ten *v/t.* (h) **1.** incubate, sit on *eggs*; **2.** F *fig.* brood over

Be·cher ['bɛçɐ] *m* (-s; -) **1.** glass, tumbler; beaker; mug; (*paper*) cup, tub; *hist.* cup, goblet; F *fig.* ***er hat zu tief in den ~ geschaut*** F he's had one too many (*or* one over the eight); **2.** ❀ cup, calix; **~glas** *n* ⚗ beaker

be·chern ['bɛçɐn] F *v/i. and v/t.* (h) F tipple; ***einen ~*** have a (bit of a) tipple

be·cir·cen [bə'tsɪrtsən] F *v/t.* (h) bewitch

Becken ['bɛkən] (*sep.* -k·k-) *n* (-s; -) **1.** basin (*a.* ⚙, *geol. and harbo[u]r*); sink; (*toilet*) bowl; (*swimming*) pool; **2.** *anat.* pelvis; **3.** ♪ cymbal; **~bruch** *m* ⚕ fractured pelvis; **~gurt** *m* lap seatbelt; **~kno·chen** *m* pelvic bone; **~stüt·ze** *f* pelvic (*or* lumbar) support; **~ver·let·zung** *f* pelvic injury

Beck·mes·ser ['bɛkmɛsɐ] *fig. m* (-s; -) faultfinder, carping critic; **Beck·mes·se·rei** [bɛkmɛsə'raɪ] *f* (-; -en) carping, faultfinding

be·da·chen [bə'daxən] *v/t.* (h) roof (over); put a roof on

be·dacht [bə'daxt] *adj.* careful; ***~ auf*** *acc.* intent (*or* keen) on *s.th. or ger.*; ***darauf ~ sein zu*** *inf. a.* be anxious to *inf.*; ***darauf ~ sein, nett zu sein*** *etc.* make a point of being friendly *etc*

Be'dacht *m*: ***mit ~*** with deliberation, circumspectly, carefully, with great care; ***ohne ~*** without thinking, rashly, without pausing to think, carelessly

be·däch·tig [bəˈdɛçtɪç] **I.** *adj.* careful; circumspect; slow, measured; **II.** *adv.* with deliberation; slowly, deliberately; **Beˈdäch·tig·keit** *f* (-; *no pl.*) care; circumspection; deliberation

be·dacht·sam [bəˈdaxtza:m] *adj. and adv.* → ***bedächtig***; **Beˈdacht·sam·keit** *f* (-; *no pl.*) → ***Bedächtigkeit***

Beˈda·chung *f* (-; -en) roof(ing); **~en** ⚙ roofing, roofs

beˈdan·ken *v/refl.* (h): ***sich ~*** say thank you, *formal*: express one's thanks (***bei j-m*** to s.o.); ***sich bei j-m ~*** *a.* thank s.o. (***für*** *acc.* for); *iro.* ***dafür bedanke ich mich*** no thank you very much

Be·darf [bəˈdarf] *m* (-[e]s; *no pl.*) need (***an*** *dat.* for); ☤ demand (for); requirements *pl.*; supply (of); ***bei ~*** if required (*or* necessary); ***(je) nach ~*** as the need arises, as required; ***für den ~*** *gen.* for *s.o. or s.th.*; ***für den eigenen ~*** for oneself, for one's personal requirements; ***Dinge für den täglichen (häuslichen) ~*** everyday (household) essentials; ***~ haben an*** *dat.* need; ***den ~ decken*** meet the demand; ***s-n ~ decken*** keep oneself in good supply; *iro.* ***mein ~ (an*** *dat.*) ***ist gedeckt*** I've had my fill (of); F ***kein ~!*** no thank you (very much)

Beˈdarfs|am·pel *f* pelican crossing; **~ana͵ly·se** *f* ☤ demand analysis; **~ar͵ti·kel** *m* commodity; *pl. a.* consumer goods; **~deckung** (*sep.* -k·k-) *f* supply of needs; **~fall** *m*: ***im ~*** in case of need, if required; whenever required (*or* necessary); **~gü·ter** *pl.* consumer goods; **~hal·te·stel·le** *f* request stop; **~len·kung** *f* consumption control; creation of needs; **~lücke** (*sep.* -k·k-) *f* unsatisfied demand; **2ori·en͵tiert** *adj.* demand-oriented; **~weckung** (*sep.* -k·k-) *f* (-; *no pl.*) creation of needs

be·dau·er·lich [bəˈdaʊɐlɪç] *adj.* regrettable, unfortunate; ***es ist sehr ~*** it's a great pity; **beˈdau·er·li·cher·wei·se** *adv.* unfortunately, regrettably; I regret to have to say (that)

beˈdau·ern (h) **I.** *v/t.* regret; feel sorry for *s.o.*; ***(es) ~, et. tun zu müssen*** regret having (*or* to have) to do s.th.; ***(es) ~, et. getan zu haben*** regret having done s.th.; ***ich habe es immer bedauert*** I've regretted it ever since; ***ich bedauere sehr, daß*** a) I very much regret that, b) I'm very sorry that; ***wir ~, sagen zu müssen*** we regret to (have to) say; ***so sehr ich es (auch) bedauere*** much as I regret it; ***er ist zu ~*** you can't help feeling (*or* you have to feel) sorry for him; ***er läßt sich gern ~*** he likes everyone to feel sorry for him, he craves pity; **II.** *v/i.*: ***bedaure!*** sorry!, F very sorry and all that; **III.** 2 *n* (-s; *no pl.*) regret (***über*** *acc.* at); pity (***mit*** *dat.* for); ***zu m-m (großen) ~*** (much) to my regret

beˈdau·erns·wert, beˈdau·erns·wür·dig *adj.* **1.** pitiable; **2.** → ***bedauerlich***

beˈdecken (*sep.* -k·k-) (h) **I.** *v/t.* cover (up); **II.** *v/refl.*: ***sich ~*** cover o.s.; *sky*: cloud over; **beˈdeckt** *adj.* overcast; ***teils ~*** partly cloudy; *fig.* ***sich ~ halten*** play one's cards close to one's chest; **Beˈdeckung** (*sep.* -k·k-) *f* (-; -en) covering

beˈden·ken (bedachte, bedacht, h) **I.** *v/t.* **1.** consider; think *s.th.* over; bear in mind, *a.* take into account; ***wenn man es recht bedenkt*** when you think about it; ***ich gebe dir nur zu ~, daß*** I'd just like to point out that (*or* make you aware [of the fact] that); **2.** ***j-n mit et. ~*** give s.o. s.th., *formal*: bestow s.th. on s.o.; ***j-n mit Applaus ~*** acknowledge s.o. with applause; *die Rede etc.* ***wurde mit heftigem Applaus bedacht*** was greeted with loud applause; ***j-n in s-m Testament ~*** remember s.o. in one's will; **II.** *v/refl.*: ***sich ~*** think it over; ***ohne mich*** *etc.* ***lange zu ~*** without much further thought; **III.** 2 *n* (-s; -) doubt; objection; scruple, *pl. a.* qualms; reservation, misgiving; ***~ haben*** (*or* ***hegen***) have one's doubts (*or* reservations), have scruples *or* reservations (***zu*** *inf.* about doing); ***~ anmelden*** raise objections; ***ich habe da m-e ~*** I have my doubts (about it), I'm not so sure (about it); ***sie hat ~, ob sie ihm das Geld leihen soll*** she has some (*or* certain) misgivings about lending him the money; ***j-m die ~ nehmen*** allay s.o.'s doubts; ***keine ~ haben*** have no reservations (***wegen*** *gen.* about; ***zu*** *inf.* about *ger.*); ***ohne ~*** without hesitation, without thinking twice (about it), without giving it a second thought

beˈden·ken·los **I.** *adj.* unscrupulous; **II.** *adv.* without thinking; without hesitation, without thinking twice, *formal*: without demur; without reservation; without scruple

be·denk·lich [bəˈdɛŋklɪç] *adj.* **1.** dubious, questionable; **2.** alarming; critical, serious; risky; ***das ist höchst ~*** *a.* that is cause for alarm; ***der Himmel sieht ~ aus*** the sky looks threatening; **3.** doubtful, sceptical, *Am.* skeptical; worried; ***ein ~es Gesicht machen*** look sceptical (*Am.* skeptical), look worried; ***j-n ~ stimmen*** have s.o. doubting (*or* worried); **Beˈdenk·lich·keit** *f* (-; *no pl.*) **1.** questionable nature, dubiousness; **2.** serious (*or* alarming) nature (*gen.* of), seriousness

Beˈdenk·zeit *f* (-; *no pl.*) time to think it over (*or* think about it); ***ich gebe dir bis morgen ~*** I'll give you till tomorrow

be·dep·pert [bəˈdɛpɐt] F *adj.* baffled; sheepish; crestfallen

beˈdeu·ten *v/t.* (h) **1.** mean; stand for; *j-s Name etc.* ***bedeutet etwas*** means (*or* stands for) something; ***was soll das denn ~!, was hat das zu ~!*** what's the idea?, what's the meaning of this?; ***es hat nichts zu ~*** a) it doesn't mean a thing, b) it doesn't matter; ***das hat was zu ~!*** that says something; ***das bedeutet nichts Gutes*** that's a bad sign, that augurs badly, that's rather ominous; ***das bedeutet für mich, daß ich es noch mal machen muß*** it means I'll have to do it again; ***es bedeutet e-e erhöhte Gefahr*** it means (*or* implies, comes down to) an increased risk; **2.** ***j-m viel (nichts) ~*** mean a lot (nothing) to s.o.; ***sie bedeutet mir alles*** she's (*or* she means) everything *or* the world to me; **3.** ***j-m et. ~*** indicate s.th. to s.o.; ***j-m ~, daß*** give s.o. to understand that

beˈdeu·tend **I.** *adj.* important, major, significant; considerable; leading, prominent; outstanding; remarkable; distinguished; ***~e Fortschritte machen*** make significant (*or* major) progress, forge ahead; ***das ist ein ~er Schritt vorwärts*** that's a great (*or* significant, major) step forward; **II.** *adv.* *improve etc.* a great deal, markedly; ***~ besser*** *etc.* much (*or* a great deal) better *etc.*

be·deut·sam [bəˈdɔʏtza:m] **I.** *adj.* **1.** significant, important; **2.** knowing, meaningful *look, smile etc.*; **II.** *adv.* knowingly; ***j-n ~ anblicken (anlächeln)*** *a.* give s.o. a knowing look (smile); ***j-m ~ zuzwinkern*** *a.* give s.o. a knowing wink; **Beˈdeut·sam·keit** *f* (-; *no pl.*) significance, importance

Beˈdeu·tung *f* (-; -en) **1.** meaning; sense; **2.** *no pl.* importance; import, implications *pl.*; ***von ~ sein*** be important, be significant, be relevant (***für*** *acc.* to); ***nichts von ~*** nothing important, nothing worth mentioning; ***ein Mann von ~*** a man of some standing

Beˈdeu·tungs|er·wei·te·rung *f ling.* extension of meaning; **~feld** *n ling.* semantic field

beˈdeu·tungs·gleich *adj.* identical in meaning; ***die Wörter sind ~*** *a.* the words have the same meaning (*or* mean the same)

beˈdeu·tungs·los *adj.* unimportant, insignificant; meaningless; **Beˈdeu·tungs·lo·sig·keit** *f* (-; *no pl.*) insignificance; meaninglessness

beˈdeu·tungs·schwer *adj.* fraught with significance; momentous

Beˈdeu·tungs|ver·en·gung *f ling.* narrowing of meaning; **~ver·schie·bung** *f ling.* shift in meaning, semantic shift

beˈdeu·tungs·voll *adj.* **1.** significant; **2.** meaningful; knowing; ***~es Schweigen*** pregnant silence

Beˈdeu·tungs·wan·del *m ling.* semantic change

beˈdie·nen (h) **I.** *v/t.* **1.** serve (*a. customer*), wait on *s.o.*; F *sport*: pass (the ball) to *s.o.*; ***gut bedient werden*** get good service; ***dort wird man immer freundlich bedient*** the service is very friendly there; ***werden Sie schon bedient?*** can I help you?, are you being served?; ***ich bin damit gut bedient*** it's serving me well, F it's doing a good job; ***damit wärst du schlecht bedient*** it's not the right thing for you, I don't think it would help you; ***damit wärst du besser bedient*** you'd be better off with that (one); *iro.* ***ich bin bedient!*** I've had enough; **2.** ⚙ work, operate; **II.** *v/i.* **3.** serve; ***wer bedient an diesem Tisch?*** who's serving (at) this table?; **4.** *card game*: follow suit; **III.** *v/refl.* **5.** ***sich ~*** help o.s.; ***bedien dich! (bedient euch!)*** help yourself (yourselves), F tuck in; **6.** ***sich e-r Sache ~*** use s.th., make use of s.th., avail o.s. of s.th.

Beˈdie·ner·ober·flä·che *f computer*: user interface

Be·dien·ste·te [bəˈdi:nstətə] *m, f* (-n; -n) **1.** employee (in public service); **2.** *obs.* servant; *pl. a.* household staff (*pl.*)

Beˈdie·nung *f* (-; -en) **1.** *no pl.* service; ***die ~ ist hier sehr prompt*** the service is very fast here, you get fast service here; **2.** waiter (*f* waitress); **3.** *no pl.* ⚙ operation; **4.** service (charge)

Beˈdie·nungs|an·lei·tung *f* instructions *pl.* for use, ⚙ *a.* operating instructions *pl.*; instruction manual; **~auf·schlag** *m* service charge; **~feh·ler** *m* operating error

beˈdie·nungs·freund·lich *adj.* user-friendly; **Beˈdie·nungs·freund·lich·keit** *f* (-; *no pl.*) user-friendliness; serviceability

Be'die·nungs|geld *n* service charge; **~hand·buch** *n* instruction manual; **~he·bel** *m* control lever; **~kom͵fort** *m* operational ease, easy operation; **~per·so͵nal** *n* operating staff; **~pult** *n* operating panel; electric switches *pl.*; **~schal·ter** *m* control switch; **~ta·fel** *f* control panel; **~vor·schrif·ten** *pl.* operating instructions; **~zu·schlag** *m* service charge

be·din·gen [bə'dıŋən] *v/t.* (h) cause, give rise to; determine; require, call for; presuppose; ***das bedingt ...*** it would imply ...; ***sich gegenseitig ~*** be mutually conditional; ***bedingt werden durch*** be caused by, go back to; **be'dingt I.** *adj.* **1.** conditional; qualified; ***~er Reflex*** conditioned reflex; ***~ durch*** *acc.* (*or* ***von*** *dat.*) conditional on, dependent on, contingent (up)on; ***~ sein durch*** *acc. a.* be determined by; ***es ist psychisch ~*** it's psychological, F it's all in the mind; **2.** ⚖ conditional; ***~er Straferlaß*** suspended sentence; **II.** *adv.* **3.** partly; in a sense; up to a point; **4.** under certain circumstances; with some reservations; ***~ tauglich*** fit for limited service; **Be'dingt·heit** *f* (-; *no pl.*) dependence (***durch*** *acc.* on); conditional nature (*gen.* of); limitation(s *pl.*), limited nature (of); cause

Be'din·gung *f* (-; -en) condition; prerequisite; ***~en*** ✝ terms; conditions; circumstances; ***~en stellen*** make stipulations; ***zur ~ machen*** make it a condition; ***unter der ~, daß*** on condition that, provided (that); **(*nur*) *unter einer ~*** on one condition (only); ***unter diesen ~en*** under these circumstances; ***unter keiner ~*** on no account, under no circumstances; ***daran ist die ~ geknüpft, daß er ...*** it is conditional on his *ger.*; ***er knüpfte daran die ~, daß wir ...*** he made it conditional on our *ger.*; ✝ ***zu günstigen ~en*** on easy terms

Be'din·gungs·form *f ling.* conditional

be'din·gungs·los I. *adj.* unconditional; unreserved; unquestioning; ***~es Vertrauen*** implicit trust; ***~e Zustimmung*** unqualified consent; **II.** *adv.* unconditionally; ***j-m ~ vertrauen*** have implicit trust in s.o.; ***~ akzeptieren*** accept without reservation; **Be'din·gungs·lo·sig·keit** *f* (-; *no pl.*) unconditional nature (*gen.* of); wholeheartedness; complete lack of reservation

Be'din·gungs·satz *m* conditional clause

be'drän·gen *v/t.* (h) press *s.o.* (hard), harry; pester, plague *with requests etc.*; harass; *sport*: hustle, challenge; molest; worry; **Be·dräng·nis** [bə'drɛŋnıs] *f* (-; -se) (very) difficult situation, distress; ***in ~ sein*** *a.* be in great difficulty, be in financial (*or* dire) straits; ***in ~ geraten*** get (o.s.) into difficulties

be'dro·hen *v/t.* (h) threaten; ***ihr Leben ist bedroht*** her life is in danger (*or* threatened); ***j-n mit dem Tod ~*** threaten to kill s.o.; **be·droh·lich** [bə'dro:lıç] **I.** *adj.* menacing; precarious *situation etc.*; alarming *proportions etc.*; ominous; ***in ~e Nähe rücken*** come (*or* get) dangerously *or* threateningly close; ***~e Ausmaße annehmen*** take on alarming proportions; **II.** *adv.* threateningly; ***sich ~ auswirken auf*** *acc.* (begin to) threaten; ***~ nahe*** dangerously (*or* threateningly) close; ***... hat sich ~ verschlechtert*** (***ist ~ angestiegen***) there's been an alarming deterioration (increase) in ...; **be'droht** *adj.*: (***vom Aussterben***) ***~e Tierarten*** *etc.* threatened species *etc*; **Be'dro·hung** *f* (-; -en) threat (***für*** *acc. or gen.* to); menace (to); ⚖ ***tätliche ~*** threatening behavio(u)r, criminal assault; ***unter ständiger ~ leben*** live under constant threat

be'drucken (*sep.* -k·k-) *v/t.* (h) print; **be'druckt** *adj.* printed; ***mit Blumen ~*** floral-print ...

be'drücken (*sep.* -k·k-) *v/t.* (h) oppress; depress, get *s.o.* down; **be'drückend** *adj.* oppressive; depressing; **be'drückt** *adj.* down in the dumps, depressed; **Be'drückt·heit** *f* (- *no pl.*) dejection; **Be'drückung** (*sep.* -k·k-) *f* (-; -en) oppression; dejection

be'dür·fen *v/i.* (bedarf, bedurfte, bedurft, h) need; take; ***es bedurfte all s-r Kraft*** it took all his strength; ***es bedurfte keiner Beweise*** no evidence was necessary; ***es bedarf ...*** (*gen.*) ... is (are) required; ***es bedarf nur eines Wortes*** (***von Ihnen***) just say the word; ***es hätte nur eines Wortes*** (***von Ihnen***) ***bedurft*** you should have said so, it would have taken no more than a word from you

Be·dürf·nis [bə'dʏrfnıs] *n* (-ses; -se) need (***nach*** *dat.* for); requirement; ✝ demand; urge (***zu*** *inf.* to *inf.*), desire, wish (***nach*** *dat.* for; ***zu*** *inf.* to *inf.*); ***es ist ihm ein ~ zu*** *inf.* he would like to *inf.*; ***ich hatte das*** (***dringende***) ***~ zu*** *inf.* I felt an urge (an urgent need) to *inf.*; ***sein ~ verrichten*** relieve o.s.; F ***ich habe ein großes ~ nach Schlaf*** F I'm desperate for some sleep; **~an·stalt** *f* public convenience, *Am.* comfort station

be'dürf·nis·los *adj.*: ***er ist ~*** he doesn't need much, *w.s.* he's very undemanding, he's very modest; **Be'dürf·nis·lo·sig·keit** *f* (-; *no pl.*) making do with what one has; undemandingness; modest requirements *pl.*

be'dürf·tig *adj.* needy, poor; in need (*gen.* of); **Be'dürf·tig·keit** *f* (-; *no pl.*) want, neediness; poverty

be·du·selt [bə'du:zəlt] F *adj.* F a) slightly sozzled; b) punch-drunk, dazed, F in a bit of a daze; dizzy; ***ich fühle mich ~*** *a.* my head's spinning

Beef·steak ['bi:fste:k] *n* (-s; -s) **1.** steak; **2.** (*a.* ***deutsches ~***) beefburger

be'eh·ren (h) **I.** *v/t.* hono(u)r; **II.** *v/refl.*: ***sich ~ zu*** *inf.* have the hono(u)r of *ger.*

be·ei·den [bə'ʔaıdən] *v/t.* (h) swear to

be·ei·di·gen [bə'ʔaıdıgən] *v/t.* swear to; **be·ei·digt** [bə'ʔaıdıçt] *adj.*: ⚖ ***~e Aussage*** sworn evidence; ***~er Sachverständiger*** (accredited) expert; **Be'ei·di·gung** *f* (-; -en) affirmation by oath

be'ei·len *v/refl.* (h): ***sich ~*** hurry; ***sich mit e-r Sache ~*** hurry up with s.th.; ***beeil dich!*** hurry up!, F get a move on!; ***du brauchst dich nicht zu ~*** there's no hurry (*or* rush), take your time; ***sich ~ zu*** *inf.* hasten to *inf.*, quickly *do s.th.*; **Be'ei·lung** *f*: ***~*** (***bitte***)***!*** F get a move on(, will you)!

be·ein·drucken [bə'ʔaındrʊkən] (*sep.*, -k·k-) *v/t.* (h) impress; ***er war sehr beeindruckt*** *a.* it *etc.* made quite an impression on him; **be'ein·druckend** *adj.* impressive

be'ein·fluß·bar *adj.*: ***sehr*** (*or* ***leicht***) ***~*** easily influenced (*or* swayed); **be·ein·flus·sen** [bə'ʔaınflʊsən] *v/t.* (h) influence; affect, have an effect on; ***negativ*** (***positiv***) ***~*** have a bad (good) influence (*or* effect) on; ***er läßt sich nicht ~*** he won't be swayed; **Be'ein·flus·sung** *f* (-; -en) influencing; influence

be·ein·träch·ti·gen [bə'ʔaıntrɛçtıgən] *v/t.* (h) interfere with; encroach on *s.o.'s rights etc.*; impede; affect, have a negative effect on; mar, spoil; lessen, detract from; ***es beeinträchtigte keineswegs den Wert*** (***s-n Erfolg, ihre gute Laune***) it in no way detracted from the value (his success, their good mood); **Be'ein·träch·ti·gung** *f* (-; -en) interference (*gen.* with); encroachment (on); impeding (of); negative (*or* adverse) effect (on); reduction (in); diminution (of); → ***beeinträchtigen***

Be·el·ze·bub [be'ɛltsəbu:p] *m* → ***Teufel***

be'en·den, be'en·di·gen *v/t.* (h) end; bring to an end (*or* a close); finish; complete *work etc.*; terminate *contract etc.*; close, wind up, conclude *speech etc.*; **Be'en·dung, Be'en·di·gung** *f* (-; *no pl.*) ending; completion; termination; conclusion, close

be·en·gen [bə'ʔɛŋən] *v/t.* (h) cramp; *dress etc.*: be too tight for, *collar*: *a.* F choke; *fig.* cramp, restrict, oppress; **be'en·gend** *adj.* oppressive; **be'engt** *adj.* cramped; ***in ~en Verhältnissen leben*** live in cramped (*or* confined) conditions; ***sich ~ fühlen*** feel cramped, *fig.* feel stifled; **Be'engt·heit** *f* (-; *no pl.*) cramped conditions *pl.*; restrictiveness; ***ein Gefühl der ~ haben*** feel stifled; **Be'en·gung** *f* (-; -en) restriction

be'er·ben *v/t.* (h): ***j-n ~*** be s.o.'s heir

be·er·di·gen [bə'ʔe:ɐdıgən] *v/t.* (h) bury; **Be'er·di·gung** *f* (-; -en) burial; funeral; F *fig.* ***auf der falschen ~ sein*** a) have come to the wrong place, b) be a square peg in a round hole, c) F be barking up the wrong tree

Be'er·di·gungs|got·tes·dienst *m* funeral service; **~in·sti͵tut** *n* undertaker's; *formal*: funeral home (*or* parlor); funeral directors *pl.*; **~ko·sten** *pl.* funeral expenses

Bee·re ['be:rə] *f* (-; -n) berry; ***~n sammeln*** go berry-picking

'Bee·ren|aus·le·se *f* beerenauslese; *quality wine made from selected grapes*; **~frucht** *f* berry; **~obst** *n* soft fruits *pl.*; **~wein** *m* berry wine; **~zeit** *f* berry-picking season

Beet [be:t] *n* (-[e]s; -e) bed; patch

Bee·te ['be:tə] *f* (-; -n): ***rote ~*** beetroot

be·fä·hi·gen [bə'fɛ:ıgən] *v/t.* (h) enable *to do*; qualify (***für*** *acc.*, ***zu*** *dat.* for); **be·fä·higt** [bə'fɛ:ıçt] *adj.* capable (***zu*** *inf.* of *ger.*), competent (enough) (to *inf.*); qualified (***zu*** *dat.* for *an office etc.*); ***zu e-r Aufgabe*** *etc.* ***~ sein*** be capable of handling a task *etc.*, be able to cope with a task *etc.*; **Be'fä·hi·gung** *f* (-; -en) ability; aptitude, talent; qualifications *pl.*; **Be'fä·hi·gungs·nach·weis** *m* proof of qualification

be·fahl [bə'fa:l] *pret. of* ***befehlen***

be'fahr·bar *adj.* passable; ⚓ navigable; ***nicht ~*** not open to traffic, ⚓ unnavigable; → ***Bankett*** 2, ***Seitenstreifen***; **Be'fahr·bar·keit** *f* (-; *no pl.*) trafficability, practicability; (road) conditions *pl.*; ⚓ navigability; **be'fah·ren** (befuhr, befahren, h) **I.** *v/t.* drive on; use *a road*; cover *distance, bus etc.*: serve *a route*; **II.** *adj.*: (***sehr*** *or* ***stark ~***) busy; ***wenig*** (*or*

kaum) ~ (very) quiet, uncrowded; ***die Strecke ist kaum*** ~ *a.* hardly anyone uses that (part of the) road

Be'fall *m* (-[e]s; *no pl.*) attack; **be'fal·len** (befiel, befallen, h) **I.** *v/t.* attack (*a.* ⚘); *pests*: *a.* infest; ~ ***werden von*** *dat.* be seized by (*or* with); be overcome by *fatigue etc.*, be laid low by (*or* with) *influenza etc.*, *lit.* be struck down by (*or* with); be infested by (*or* with) *pests etc.*; **II.** *adj.*: ***von Insekten*** ~ insect-ridden, insect-infested; ***von Fieber*** ~ fever-stricken

be'fand *pret. of* ***befinden***

be'fan·gen *adj.* **1.** inhibited, shy, self-conscious, embarrassed; **2.** *a.* ⚖ bias(s)ed; ~ ***sein in*** *dat.* be caught up in, be blinded by; ***in e-m Irrtum*** ~ ***sein*** labo(u)r under a delusion; **Be'fan·gen·heit** *f* (-; *no pl.*) **1.** shyness, self-consciousness, inhibition(s *pl.*), embarrassment; **2.** *a.* ⚖ bias, prejudice

be'fas·sen *v/refl.* (h): ***sich*** ~ ***mit*** concern o.s. with; deal with *matter*, *problem etc.*; work on *a subject*; look into; ***damit kann ich mich jetzt nicht*** ~ I haven't got time for that now

be·feh·den [bə'fe:dən] *v/t.* (h) be having a feud with; ***sich*** ~ be feuding, be having a feud

Be·fehl [bə'fe:l] *m* (-[e]s; -e) **1.** order; ~ ***zum Angriff*** order to attack; ***auf*** ~ ***von*** (*or gen.*) on the orders of, by order of; ***auf*** ~ ***handeln*** act on orders; ***auf höheren*** ~ on orders from above; ***bis auf weiteren*** ~ till further orders; ***den*** ~ ***haben zu*** *inf.* have (*or* be under orders) to *inf.*; ~ ***ist*** ~*!* orders are orders; ***zu*** ~*!* yes, sir!; **2.** command; ***den*** ~ ***haben*** (***übernehmen***) ***über*** *acc.* be in (take) command of; **be'feh·len** (befahl, befohlen, h) **I.** *v/t.* order, give the order for, ⚔ *a.* give the command to *attack etc.*; ***j-m et.*** ~ order s.o. to do s.th.; ***Schweigen*** ~ order silence; ***Gehorsam*** ~ order s.o. (*or* everybody) to obey; ***von dir lasse ich mir nichts*** ~ I won't be ordered about by you; **II.** *v/i.* give the orders; ***j-m*** ~ ***zu*** *inf.* order s.o. to *inf.*; ~ ***über*** *acc.* be in command of, have *s.th.* at (*or* under) one's command; **III.** *lit.* *v/refl.*: ***sich*** ~ command o.s. (*dat.* to, into the hands of); **be·feh·le·risch** [bə'fe:lərɪʃ] *adj.* imperious, F bossy; **be·feh·li·gen** [bə'fe:lɪgən] *v/t.* (h) command, be in command of

Be'fehls|aus·ga·be *f* briefing; ~**be·reich** *m* (area of) command; ~**da,tei** *f computer*: command file; ~**emp·fän·ger** *m* **1.** recipient of an order; ***wer war der*** ~*?* who received the order?; **2.** *fig.* apparatchik; ~**form** *f ling.* imperative; ~**ge·walt** *f* command, authority

Be'fehls·ha·ber [-ha:bɐ] *m* (-s; -) commander(-in-chief); **be'fehls·ha·be·risch** [-ha:bərɪʃ] *adj.* → ***befehlerisch***

Be'fehls|ket·te *f* chain of command; ~**not·stand** *m* compulsion to obey orders; ***unter*** ~ ***handeln*** act under (binding) orders; ~**satz** *m ling.* imperative clause; ~**spra·che** *f computer*: command language; ~**ton** *m* (-[e]s; *no pl.*) commanding tone (of voice); ~**ver·wei·ge·rung** *f* refusal to obey orders; ≈**wid·rig** *adj. and adv.* contrary to orders

be'fe·sti·gen *v/t.* (h) **1.** fix (***an*** *dat.* onto), attach (to), fasten ([on]to); stick (onto); **2.** surface, pave *road etc.*; **3.** reinforce *wall, dam etc.*; **4.** ⚔ fortify; **5.** *fig.* secure, consolidate; cement; **Be'fe·sti·gung** *f* (-; -en) fixing, attaching, fastening; sticking; surfacing; reinforcement; ⚔ fortification; *fig.* securing, consolidation; cementing

Be'fe·sti·gungs|an·la·ge *f* defen|ces (*Am.* -ses) *pl.*; ~**gür·tel** *m* ring of defen|ces (*Am.* -ses) *or* fortifications

be·feuch·ten [bə'fɔʏçtən] *v/t.* (h) moisten; *a.* lick *stamp*; wet; sprinkle, dampen *ironing*; **Be'feuch·tung** *f* (-; *no pl.*) moistening; wetting; dampening

be'feu·ern *v/t.* (h) **1.** ✈, ⚓ mark with beacons; **2.** fuel; **3.** bombard (*a. fig.*); **4.** *fig.* spur *s.o.* on

be·fie·dert [bə'fi:dɐt] *adj.* feathered; **Be'fie·de·rung** *f* (-; -en) feathers *pl.*, plumage

be'fiel *pret. of* ***befallen***

be'fin·den (befand, befunden, h) **I.** *v/refl.* **1.** ***sich*** ~ be; *building etc.*: *a.* be located; **2.** ***wie befindet er sich?*** how is he?; ***sich gut*** ~ be (*or* feel) fine; ***sich in gutem Zustand*** ~ be in good shape (*or* condition); **3.** ***sich im Irrtum*** ~ be mistaken; **II.** *v/t.* **4.** ***et. für gut*** *etc.* ~ think s.th. is good *etc.*, consider s.th. to be good *etc.*; → ***schuldig*** 1; **III.** *v/i.* **5.** decide; **IV.** ≈ *n* (-s; *no pl.*) **6.** (state of) health; ***wie ist sein*** ~*?* how is he (feeling)?; **7.** ***nach m-m*** ~ in my view, as I see it; **be·find·lich** [bə'fɪntlɪç] *adj.*: ***die im Museum*** ~***en Skulpturen*** the sculptures (contained) in the museum; ***die im Hauptgebäude*** ~***en Abteilungen*** the departments (located *or* to be found) in the main building

be'fin·gern F *v/t.* (h) finger

be'flag·gen *v/t.* (h) decorate with flags, put flags out on, line *street etc.* with flags; **be·flaggt** [bə'flakt] *adj.* flag-decked; flag-lined *street etc.*; **Be'flag·gung** *f* (-; -en) decorating (*or* lining) with flags; flags *pl.*

be'flecken (*sep.* -k·k-) *v/t.* (h) stain, soil; *fig.* tarnish, sully; ***mit Blut befleckt*** bloodstained

be·flei·ßi·gen [bə'flaɪsɪgən] *v/refl.* (h): ***sich*** ~ ***zu*** *inf.* take pains to *inf.*, endeavo(u)r to *inf.*; ***sich e-r Sache*** ~ apply o.s. to (the task of doing) s.th.; ***er befleißigt sich e-r deutlichen Sprechweise*** he's very careful with his enunciation

be'flie·gen *v/t.* (beflog, beflogen, h) fly

be·flis·sen [bə'flɪsən] *adj.* assiduous, very keen; ~ ***sein zu*** *inf.*, ***sich*** ~ ***zeigen zu*** *inf.* (always) be eager to *inf.*, go out of one's way to *inf.*; **Be'flis·sen·heit** *f* (-; *no pl.*) assiduousness, keenness

be'flog *pret. of* ***befliegen***

be·flo·gen [bə'flo:gən] *p.p. of* ***befliegen***

be·flü·geln [bə'fly:gəln] *v/t.* (h) inspire *s.o.*; fire, *lit.* give wing to *s.o.'s imagination etc.*; ***j-s Schritte*** ~ quicken s.o.'s pace, *lit.* lend wings to s.o.'s feet; **be'flü·gelt** *adj.* winged; *fig.* ***mit*** ~***en Schritten*** on winged feet

be·foh·len [bə'fo:lən] *p.p. of* ***befehlen***

be'fol·gen *v/t.* (h) follow; observe, comply with; keep to, stick to, *formal*: abide by; ***nicht*** ~ *a.* ignore; **Be'fol·gung** *f* (-; *no pl.*) following (*gen.* of), compliance (with); observance (of)

be'för·dern *v/t.* (h) **1.** transport, carry, take, *formal*: convey; send, ✝ *a.* ship, forward; → ***Jenseits, hinausbefördern***; **2.** promote *s.o.* (***zu*** *dat.* to, to the position [⚔ rank] of); **3.** → ***fördern***; **Be'för·de·rung** *f* (-; -en) **1.** transportation, *formal*: conveyance; sending, ✝ *a.* shipping, forwarding; shipment; **2.** promotion (***zu*** *dat.* to, to the position [⚔ rank] of); **3.** → ***Förderung***

Be'för·de·rungs|art *f* mode of transport(ation) *or* conveyance; ~**aus·sich·ten** *pl.* promotion prospects, chances (*or* prospects) of promotion; ~**be·din·gun·gen** *pl.* terms of transport; ~**ko·sten** *pl.* transportation costs; ~**mit·tel** *n* (means of) transport(ation); ~**steu·er** *f* transport tax; ~**ta,rif** *m* transport(ation) charges *pl.*

be·frach·ten [bə'fraxtən] *v/t.* (h) load (*a. fig.*); **Be'frach·ter** *m* (-s; -) ✝ consignor, shipper; **Be'frach·tung** *f* (-; -en) loading

be·frackt [bə'frakt] *adj.* in tails, wearing tails

be'fra·gen *v/t.* (h) ask (***über*** *acc.* about; ***um*** *acc.* for); question (about); consult (***wegen*** *gen.*, ***in*** *dat.* about, on), ask *s.o.'s* opinion, turn to *s.o.*; **Be'fra·ger** *m* (-s; -) interviewer; **Be·frag·te** [bə'fra:ktə] *m, f* (-n; -n) person asked, interviewee; *statistics*: respondent; ***die*** ~***n*** *a.* those asked, the people asked (*or* interviewed); **Be'fra·gung** *f* (-; -en) questioning; interview; public opinion poll; *pol.* referendum

be'frei·en (h) **I.** *v/t.* **1.** free, liberate; set *s.o.* free; rescue; *adm.* exempt (***von*** *dat.* from); release (from *obligation etc.*); relieve (from *duty, worry etc.*); excuse (from *school etc.*); rid (of); **2.** ~ ***aus*** *dat.* get *s.o.* out of, extricate *s.o.* from; ***et. von s-r Verpackung*** ~ unwrap s.th., unpack s.th., take the wrapping off s.th.; **3.** ***et. vom Rost*** *etc.* ~ take the rust *etc.* off s.th., get rid of the rust *etc.* on s.th.; ***et. vom Schmutz*** *etc.* ~ clean (the dirt *etc.* off) s.th., get rid of the dirt *etc.* on (*or* in) s.th.; **II.** *v/refl.*: ***sich*** ~ free o.s. (***von*** *dat.* of); extricate o.s. (***aus*** *dat.* from); ***sich*** ~ ***von*** *dat. a.* get rid of, rid o.s. of; shake off; **be'frei·end** *fig. adj.* liberating; ~***es Gelächter*** relieved laughter; **Be'frei·er** *m* (-s; -) liberator; **Be'frei·ung** *f* (-; *no pl.*) setting free; liberation; rescue; exemption; release (*all* ***von*** *dat.* from); relieving (of)

Be'frei·ungs|be·we·gung *f* liberation movement; ~**kampf** *m* fight for independence (*or* liberation); ~**klau·sel** *f* escape clause; ~**krieg** *m* war of independence (*or* liberation); ~**theo·lo,gie** *f* liberation theology; ~**ver·such** *m* **1.** rescue attempt; **2.** attempt to escape, attempted flight (*or* escape)

be·frem·den [bə'frɛmdən] (h) **I.** *v/t.* take *s.o.* aback; strike *s.o.* as strange; ***es hat mich befremdet*** *a.* I found it quite disconcerting; **II.** ≈ *n* (-s; *no pl.*) astonishment (***über*** *acc.* at); ***ich habe mit*** ~ ***festgestellt*** I was quite disconcerted to realize; ***ihr Verhalten löste allgemeines*** ~ ***aus*** everyone was taken aback by her behavio(u)r; **be'frem·dend, be·fremd·lich** [bə'frɛmtlɪç] *adj.* strange; disconcerting; **Be'frem·dung** *f* (-; *no pl.*) → ***Befremden***

be·freun·den [bə'frɔʏndən] *v/refl.* (h): ***sich mit j-m*** ~ make friends with s.o.; ***sich*** (***miteinander***) ~ become friends; ***sich mit et.*** ~ get used to (the idea of) s.th.; **be'freun·det** *adj.*: (***miteinander***) ~ ***sein*** be friends; ~***er Staat*** friendly nation; ***ein*** ~***er Arzt*** a doctor friend of mine *etc.*; ***eng*** ~ ***sein*** be good (*or* close) friends; ***wir sind mit ihnen*** ~ they're friends of ours; ***ich bin mit ihr*** ~ she's a friend (of mine), we're friends; ***sind sie mit irgendwelchen Nachbarn ~?*** are they friendly with any of the neighbo(u)rs?

be·frie·den [bə'fri:dən] *v/t.* (h) bring peace to; **Be'frie·dung** *f* (-; *no pl.*) establishment of peace (*gen.* in)

be·frie·di·gen [bə'fri:dıgən] (h) **I.** *v/t.* satisfy (*a. sexually*); *a.* please *s.o.*; satisfy, gratify *s.o.'s curiosity, desire etc.*; meet, come up to *s.o.'s expectations etc.*; pay off *creditor*; ***schwer zu ~ sein*** be hard to please; ***die Arbeit befriedigt mich nicht*** I'm not getting enough satisfaction out of my work; **II.** *v/i.* be satisfactory; *work etc.*: give *s.o.* (enough) satisfaction; **III.** *v/refl.*: ***sich*** (***selbst***) ~ masturbate; **be'frie·di·gend** *adj.* satisfactory (*a. ped.*); **be·frie·digt** [bə'fri:dıçt] *adj.* satisfied, pleased; **Be'frie·di·gung** *f* (-; *no pl.*) satisfaction (*a.* ⚖, ✝ *and physiol.*); gratification

be'fri·sten *v/t.* (h) set (*or* place, put) a time limit on; ***auf eine Woche*** ~ limit to one week, set (*or* place, put) a limit of one week on; **be'fri·stet I.** *adj.* limited (in time); ***~e Einlagen*** time deposits; **II.** *adv.* for a limited (*or* fixed) period; **Be'fri·stung** *f* (-; -en) (setting of a) time limit (***auf*** *acc.* of *10 days etc.*)

be'fruch·ten *v/t.* (h) fertilize; pollinate; *fig.* stimulate, be (very) fruitful for; **be'fruch·tend** *fig.* **I.** *adj.* fruitful, stimulating; **II.** *adv.*: ***sich ~ auswirken, ~ wirken*** prove very fruitful (***auf*** *acc.* for), have a stimulating effect (on); **Be'fruch·tung** *f* (-; -en) **1.** fertilization; pollination; ***künstliche*** ~ artificial insemination; **2.** *fig.* stimulation; ***gegenseitige*** ~ cross-fertilization

be·fu·gen [bə'fu:gən] *v/t.* (h) authorize, give *s.o.* permission (*or* the authority); **Be·fug·nis** [bə'fu:knıs] *f* (-; -se) *a. pl.* authority, power(s *pl.*); ***j-m ~ erteilen*** authorize s.o. (***zu*** *inf.* to *inf.*); **be·fugt** [bə'fu:kt] *adj.* authorized, entitled (***zu*** *inf.* to *inf.*); ***zur Unterschrift*** (***Ausführung, Festnahme*** *etc.*) ~ authorized to sign (carry *s.th.* out, arrest *s.o. etc.*); ***er ist dazu nicht*** ~ *a.* he has no authority (*or* right) to do so

be'füh·len *v/t.* (h) feel

be'fum·meln F *v/t.* (h) finger, touch; F paw, *sl.* feel up, *sl.* touch up

Be'fund *m* (-es; -e) findings *pl.*, *a.* ⚕ results *pl.*; ⚕ ***ohne*** ~ negative

be·fun·den [bə'fʊndən] *p.p. of* ***befinden***

be'fürch·ten *v/t.* (h) fear, expect; be afraid of; suspect; ***wir ~ das Schlimmste*** we're prepared for the worst; ***es ist zu ~, daß*** it is feared that; ***... sind nicht zu*** ~ there's no danger (*or* risk) of ...; ***das ist nicht zu*** ~ there's no fear (*or* danger) of that; **Be'fürch·tung** *f* (-; -en) fear; misgivings *pl.*, apprehensions *pl.*; ***ich habe die ~, daß*** I fear (that), F I have a funny feeling that

be·für·wor·ten [bə'fy:ɐvɔrtən] *v/t.* (h) recommend, advocate; endorse; support, back; **Be'für·wor·ter** *m* (-s; -) supporter (*gen.* of), backer (of), advocate (of); believer (in); ***ein entschiedener*** ~ a staunch supporter (*or* advocate) (*gen.* of); **Be'für·wor·tung** *f* (-; -en) recommendation, advocacy; endorsement; support, backing

be'gab *pret. of* ***begeben***

be·gabt [bə'ga:pt] *adj.* talented, gifted; ***~ sein für*** *acc.* have a gift for; → ***vielseitig*** II; **Be'gab·ten·för·de·rung** *f* scholarship system; (*provision of*) *scholarships for outstanding pupils or students*; **Be·ga·bung** [bə'ga:bʊŋ] *f* (-; -en) **1.** gift, talent; ***es ist e-e*** ~ *a.* he (*or* she) was born with it; ***sie hat e-e ~ zum Klavierspielen*** (***Organisieren***) she's got a talent for (playing) the piano (she's got a talent for organizing things, she's got organizational talent); **2.** talent, (very) gifted person; **Be'ga·bungs·re‚ser·ve** *f* untapped educational potential

be'gaf·fen F *v/t.* (h) gape (F gawk) at

be·gann [bə'gan] *pret. of* ***beginnen***

be·gat·ten [bə'gatən] *v/t.* (h) *zo.* mate (*or* copulate) with; ***sich*** ~ mate, copulate; **Be'gat·tung** *f* (-; -en) mating, copulation

be'gau·nern F *v/t.* (h) cheat, F con (***um*** *acc.* out of *money etc.*)

be·geb·bar [bə'ge:pba:ɐ] *adj.* ✝ transferable; negotiable; **be'ge·ben** (begab, begeben, h) **I.** *v/refl.* **1.** ***sich ~ nach*** *dat.* (*or* ***zu*** *dat.*) go to, proceed to, ***zu j-m:*** *a.* join s.o.; ***sich an die Arbeit*** ~ set to work; ***sich auf die Reise*** ~ set out (on one's journey); ***sich unter j-s Schutz*** (*or* ***Obhut***) ~ place o.s. under s.o.'s protection; ***sich in ärztliche Behandlung*** ~ seek medical treatment, see a doctor; → ***Gefahr, Ruhe***; **2.** ***sich*** ~ happen, occur; *lit.* ***es begab sich, daß*** it came to pass that; **3.** ***sich*** ~ (*gen.*) forfeit, forgo *an opportunity etc.*; *esp.* ⚖ waive, renounce *right, privilege etc.*; **II.** *v/t.* ✝ transfer; negotiate; **Be'ge·ben·heit** *f* (-; -en) occurrence, event, incident; ***der Geschichte*** (***dem Roman***) ***liegt e-e wahre ~ zugrunde*** the story is based on a true incident *or* on fact (the novel is based on a true incident *or* story)

be·geg·nen [bə'ge:gnən] *v/i.* (sn) **1.** meet, bump into *s.o.*, come across *s.th.*; ***sich*** (*or* ***einander***) ~ meet, bump into each other; *fig.* ***ihre Blicke begegneten sich*** their eyes met; **2.** *fig.* meet with, come up against, have to face up to *difficulties, problems etc.*; confront, face; counter; combat (*a. illness*); check; ***e-r Gefahr*** *etc.* ***mit et.*** ~ *a.* respond to a danger *etc.* with s.th. (*or* by *ger.*); **3.** ***mir ist das schon einmal begegnet*** it's happened to me before, I've experienced it before; ***das Schlimmste, was dir ~ kann*** the worst that can happen to you; **4.** treat, behave *very coolly etc.* towards; **5.** be found (***bei*** *dat.* in), come up (in); ***dieser Stil*** *etc.* ***begegnet ebenfalls in ...*** *a.* this style *etc.* is also to be found in (*or* can also be found in, also appears in), you also come across this style *etc.* in; **Be'geg·nung** *f* (-; -en) meeting, encounter; *sport*: match; **Be'geg·nungs·stät·te** *f* meeting place, social cent|re (*Am.* -er)

be·geh·bar [bə'ge:ba:ɐ] *adj.* **1.** passable; ***ist es ~?*** can you walk on (*or* along) it?; **2.** ***~er Schrank*** walk-in closet (*or* cupboard); **be'ge·hen** *v/t.* (beging, begangen, h) **1.** walk on (*or* along); use; inspect; **2.** celebrate; observe *holiday*; **3.** make *mistake etc.*; commit *crime etc.*; → ***Selbstmord***

be·geh·ren [bə'ge:rən] (h) **I.** *v/t.* desire; crave for; demand; → ***Herz***; **II.** ♀ *n* (-s; *no pl.*) desire; **be'geh·rens·wert** *adj.* desirable; **be·gehr·lich** [bə'ge:ɐlıç] *adj.* covetous; **be'gehrt** *adj.* (much) sought-after, (very) popular; *pred. a.* very much in demand; coveted

Be'ge·hung *f* (-; *no pl.*) celebration; observance *of a holiday*

be·gei·stern [bə'gaıstɐn] (h) **I.** *v/t.* inspire, fill with enthusiasm; delight (***durch*** *acc.* with); ***j-n für et.*** ~ get s.o. interested in (*or* enthusiastic about) s.th.; ***sie ist für nichts zu*** ~ you can't get her interested in anything; **II.** *v/refl.*: ***sich ~ für*** *acc.* get enthusiastic about s.th., be very much interested in (*or* very keen on) s.th.; ***sich ~ an*** *dat.* get very enthusiastic (F all excited) about s.th., *w.s.* think s.th. is wonderful; ***ich kann mich dafür nicht*** ~ I can't work up any enthusiasm for it, it just doesn't appeal to me (F grab me); **be'gei·sternd** *adj.* inspiring, rousing; **be'gei·stert I.** *adj.* enthusiastic; keen; passionate; ***ein ~er Jazzanhänger*** *etc.* a great jazz fan *etc.*; *in cpds.* ***...~*** ...-mad, F ...-crazy, *pred.* mad about ..., F crazy about ...; ***er war ~ von dem Plan*** he was all for (*or* very enthusiastic about) the project, ***dem Konzert:*** he thought the concert was marvel(l)ous; ***sie waren*** ~ they were quite taken (***von*** *dat.* with); **II.** *adv.* enthusiastically, with (great) enthusiasm; ***~ aufnehmen*** give a warm (*or* rapturous) welcome to; ***~ mitmachen*** join in wholeheartedly; **Be'gei·ste·rung** *f* (-; *no pl.*) enthusiasm (***für*** *acc.* for, about); ***mit*** ~ enthusiastically, with (great) enthusiasm; ***in ~ geraten*** get all enthusiastic *or* excited (***über*** *acc.* about), go into raptures (about); ***ohne*** (***rechte***) ~ without much enthusiasm, halfheartedly; **be'gei·ste·rungs·fä·hig** *adj.*: ***er ist sehr*** (***nicht***) ~ he can get very enthusiastic about things (you can't get him excited about anything)

Be'gei·ste·rungs|sturm *m* storm of enthusiasm; *pl.* storms of applause, rapturous applause *sg.*; **~tau·mel** *m* frenzy of enthusiasm

Be·gier·de [bə'gi:ɐdə] *f* (-; -n) desire, appetite (***nach*** *dat.* for); desire, lust; **be'gie·rig I.** *adj.* eager (***nach*** *dat.* for), *contp.* greedy (for); greedy, lustful; ***~ zu erfahren*** eager (*or* keen) to find out; **II.** *adv.*: ***~ lauschen*** listen intently (*dat.* to)

be'gie·ßen *v/t.* (begoß, begossen, h) **1.** pour water *etc.* over (*or* on); ⚘ water; *gastr.* baste; → ***Pudel***; **2.** F drink to, celebrate (with a drink); ***das müssen wir ~, das muß begossen werden*** *a.* that calls for a drink

be'ging *pret. of* ***begehen***

Be·ginn [bə'gın] *m* (-[e]s; *no pl.*) beginning, start; *formal*: commencement; ***zu ~*** *a.* at the outset; ***seit*** ~ since the beginning (*gen.* of); ***gleich zu*** ~ right at the outset; ***mit ~*** *gen.* at the start of, when ... starts (*or* begins); ***~ der Vorstellung: 19.30*** performance starts at 7.30 p.m.; **be·ginnen** [bə'gınən] *v/t. and v/i.* (begann, begonnen, h) begin, start; *formal*: commence; ***mit der Arbeit*** *etc.* ~ start work *etc.*, get down to work *etc.*; ***die Rede begann mit ...*** the speech started off with ..., he *etc.* opened the speech with ...; **be'gin·nend** *adj. formal*: incipient; ***der ~e Schneefall*** *etc.* the first of the snow *etc.*

be·glau·bi·gen [bə'glaʊbıgən] *v/t.* (h) certify; *pol.* accredit (***bei*** *dat.* to); ***nota-***

riell** ~ **lassen have *s.th.* notarized; **be·glau·bigt** [bəˈglaʊbɪçt] *adj.* certified; *pol.* accredited; ***~e Abschrift*** certified copy, a true copy; **Beˈglau·bi·gung** *f* (-; -en) certification; *pol.* accreditation; **Beˈglau·bi·gungs·schrei·ben** *n* credentials *pl*

beˈglei·chen *v/t.* (beglich, beglichen, h) ✝ pay, settle; **Beˈglei·chung** *f* (-; *no pl.*) settlement, payment

Beˈgleit|brief *m* covering letter; **~buch** *n* TV tie-in; **~do·kuˌmen·te** *pl.* accompanying documents

beˈglei·ten *v/t.* (h) walk along with, *a.* ♪ *and fig.* accompany; *a.* ⚔, ⚓, *mot.* escort; ***begleitet von*** accompanied by (*a.* ♪), fraught with *danger etc.*; ***von Erfolg begleitet*** very successful; ***j-n zur Bahn*** ~ see s.o. off (at the station); ***j-n zu e-m Konzert*** ~ take s.o. to a concert, go to a concert with s.o.; ***j-n nach Hause*** ~ take (*or* walk) s.o. home; **beˈglei·tend** *adj.* accompanying; ***~e Umstände*** attendant circumstances; **Be·glei·ter** [bəˈglaɪtɐ] *m* (-s; -) companion; attendant (*gen.* to, of); escort; ♪ accompanist; → ***ständig*** I

Beˈgleit|er·schei·nung *f* concomitant; ⚕ side effect; ***es ist e-e*** ~ ***von*** *a.* it goes with; ***das sind so die ~en des Alters*** F they're all signs of old age, it's all part (and parcel) of growing old; **~fahr·zeug** *n* escort vehicle; **~flug·zeug** *n* escort plane; **~in·struˌment** *n* ♪ accompanying instrument; **~ma·te·riˌal** *n* backup material(s *pl.*); **~muˌsik** *f* incidental (*or* background) music; *fig.* accompaniment; **~perˌson** *f* escort; **~per·soˌnal** *n* (personal) escort; **~schein** *m* dispatch note; **~schiff** *n* escort vessel; **~schrei·ben** *n* covering letter; **~schutz** *m* escort; **~stim·me** *f* ♪ supporting voice; **~text** *m* accompanying text; **~umˌstän·de** *pl.* surrounding (*or* attendant) circumstances

Beˈglei·tung *f* (-; -en) **1.** company; entourage; escort; ***in*** ~ ***von*** (*or gen.*) accompanied by; ***in*** ~ ***e-s Mannes*** (***e-r Frau***) in male (female) company, with a man (woman); ***ohne*** ~ alone, unaccompanied; ***in*** ~ ***sein*** be with someone; **2.** ♪ accompaniment

Beˈgleit·zet·tel *m* accompanying note; ✝ dispatch note

beˈglich *pret. of* ***begleichen***

be·gli·chen [bəˈglɪçən] *p.p. of* ***begleichen***

beˈglot·zen F *v/t.* (h) F gawk at, goggle at

beˈglücken (*sep.* -k·k-) *v/t.* (h) make *s.o.* happy; *esp. iro.* delight; *iro.* ***sie hat uns mit ihrer Anwesenheit beglückt*** she hono(u)red us with her presence; **beˈglückend** (*sep.* -k·k-) *adj.* heartening, exhilarating; **beˈglückt** *adj.* (very) happy (***über*** *acc.* about), F thrilled (with); ***~es Lächeln*** blissful smile; **Beˈglücktheit** *f* (-; *no pl.*) (sheer) happiness, bliss; **Beˈglückung** (*sep.* -k·k-) *f* (-; -en) **1.** making *s.o.* happy; **2.** happiness, bliss

beˈglück·wün·schen *v/t.* (h) congratulate (***zu*** *dat.* on); ***wir möchten dich zur bestandenen Prüfung*** ~ we'd like to congratulate you on passing your exam; **Beˈglück·wün·schung** *f* (-; -en) congratulations *pl*

be·gna·det [bəˈgna:dət] *adj.* exceptionally (*or* highly) gifted; ~ ***sein mit*** be endowed with, have the extraordinary gift of *being able to* ...

be·gna·di·gen [bəˈgna:dɪgən] *v/t.* (h) pardon, reprieve; **Beˈgna·di·gung** *f* (-; -en) pardon; *pol.* amnesty

Beˈgna·di·gungs|ge·such *n* petition for pardon; **~recht** *n* right of pardon

be·gnü·gen [bəˈgny:gən] *v/refl.* (h): ***sich*** ~ ***mit*** *dat.* make do with, be satisfied (*or* content) with, content o.s. with

Be·go·nie [beˈgo:nĭə] *f* (-; -n) ⚘ begonia

be·gon·nen [bəˈgɔnən] *p.p. of* ***beginnen***

be·gön·nern [bəˈgœnɐn] *v/t.* (h) *contp.* patronize

beˈgoß *pret. of* ***begießen***

be·gos·sen [bəˈgɔsən] **I.** *p.p. of* ***begießen***; **II.** *adj.* → ***Pudel***

beˈgra·ben *v/t.* (begrub, begraben, h) bury (*a. fig. hopes*); *fig.* give up, abandon *plan etc.*; *fig.* ***e-n Streit*** ~ bury the hatchet

Be·gräb·nis [bəˈgrɛ:pnɪs] *n* (-ses; -se) burial; funeral; **~fei·er** *f*, **~fei·er·lich·kei·ten** *pl.* funeral (ceremony) *sg.*; *formal*: obsequies; **~ko·sten** *pl.* funeral expenses; **~stät·te** *f* place of burial; burial site

be·gra·di·gen [bəˈgra:dɪgən] *v/t.* (h) straighten; regulate *river etc.*; *fig.* straighten out; **Beˈgra·di·gung** *f* (-; -en) straightening; regulation; *fig.* straightening out

beˈgrei·fen (begriff, begriffen, h) **I.** *v/t.* understand; grasp; ***es ist nicht zu*** ~ *a.* I can't make it out; ***hast du das endlich begriffen?*** have you got that into your head?; **II.** *v/i.* understand, F catch on; ***schnell*** (***langsam***) ~ be quick (slow) on the uptake; **be·greif·lich** [bəˈgraɪflɪç] *adj.* understandable; ***j-m et.*** ~ ***machen*** make s.th. clear to s.o.; ***leicht*** (***schwer***) ~ easy (hard) to understand; **beˈgreif·li·cher·wei·se** *adv.* understandably (enough)

be·grenz·bar [bəˈgrɛntsba:ɐ] *adj.* limitable; ***ist es ~?*** can it be limited?; **beˈgren·zen** *v/t.* (h) **1.** mark off; form the boundary of; **2.** *fig.* limit, restrict (***auf*** *acc.* to); **beˈgrenzt I.** *adj.* restricted; limited; ***eng*** (*or* ***genau***) ~ clearly defined; ***es ist zeitlich nicht*** ~ there's no time limit (on it), it's open-ended; **II.** *adv.* (*a.* ***zeitlich*** ~) for a limited period; ~ ***verfügbar*** in limited supply; ~ ***haltbar*** perishable, short-life *goods etc.*; **Beˈgrenzt·heit** *f* (-; *no pl.*) restrictions *pl.* (*gen.* of *or* on); limitations *pl.* (of), narrowness, narrow-mindedness; **Beˈgren·zung** *f* (-; -en) **1.** boundary, perimeter; demarcation; **2.** restriction, limitation

Beˈgren·zungs·licht *n mot.* sidelight, *Am.* parking light

be·griff [bəˈgrɪf] *pret. of* ***begreifen***

Beˈgriff *m* (-[e]s; -e) **1.** idea, concept, notion; ***sich e-n*** ~ ***machen von*** form (*or* get) an idea of, imagine; ***du machst dir keinen ~!*** you have no idea; ***ist dir das ein ~?*** does that mean anything to you?; ***das geht über m-e ~e*** that's beyond me; ***für m-e ~e*** a) as I see it, if you ask me, b) for me, as far as I'm concerned; F ***schwer von*** ~ slow on the uptake, F a bit dense; **2.** term, expression; ***fester*** ~ common expression, household word; **3.** household name; ***ein*** ~ ***in der Modewelt*** *etc.* a big name in fashion *etc.*; ***ein*** ~ (***für Qualität***) a byword for quality; **4.** ***im*** ~ ***sein zu*** *inf.* be about to *inf.*, be on the point of *ger.*

be·grif·fen [bəˈgrɪfən] **I.** *p.p. of* ***begreifen***; **II.** *adj.*: ~ ***sein in*** *dat.* be in the process of (doing) s.th.; ***im Anmarsch*** ~ approaching; ***im Fortgehen*** ~ about to leave; ***im Entstehen*** ~ ***sein*** be forming; ***e-e im Entstehen ~e Organisation*** an organization that is just forming, *formal*: a nascent organization; ***in der Entwicklung*** ~ ***sein*** be developing, be (in the process of) being developed; ***im Wachstum*** ~ ***sein*** be in the process of growth

beˈgriff·lich I. *adj.* conceptual; notional; ***~es Denken*** abstract thinking; **II.** *adv.*: ~ ***erfassen*** conceptualize

Beˈgriffs|be·stim·mung *f* definition; **~bil·dung** *f* forming of concepts; **~in·halt** *m* (ideal) content; *phls.* connotation; **~merk·mal** *n* conceptual characteristic

beˈgriffs·stut·zig *adj.* dense, slow (on the uptake); **Beˈgriffs·stut·zig·keit** *f* (-; *no pl.*) denseness, slowness

Beˈgriffs|syˌstem *n* system of concepts; **~ver·mö·gen** *n* grasp, capacity to understand; ***über j-s*** ~ ***hinausgehen*** be beyond s.o.'s grasp; **~ver·wir·rung** *f* **1.** confusion of ideas (*or* terms); **2.** confused (*or* muddled) thinking

beˈgrub *pret. of* ***begraben***

beˈgrün·den *v/t.* (h) **1.** found, establish; set up *business etc.*; *fig.* establish *s.o.'s reputation etc.*; lay the foundations for (*or* of) *s.o.'s happiness etc.*; **2.** give reasons for, explain; justify, back up; ***er begründete es damit, daß*** he explained (*or* justified) it by the fact that; ***durch nichts zu*** ~ completely unfounded (*or* unjustified); **Beˈgrün·der** *m* (-s; -) founder; **beˈgrün·det** *adj.* valid, justified, well-founded; reasonable; ***nicht*** ~ unfounded, unjustified; ***~er Einwand*** reasonable (*or* valid) objection; ***es besteht ~e Hoffnung*** there is cause for hope; ~ ***liegen in*** *dat.* go back to, be rooted in; ***die Arbeitslosigkeit liegt in der politischen Mißwirtschaft*** ~ political mismanagement is the root cause of unemployment; **Beˈgrün·dung** *f* (-; -en) **1.** founding, establishment; setting up; **2.** reason(s *pl.*); explanation; argument; justification; ***mit der*** ~, ***daß*** on the grounds that; ***ohne jede*** ~ without giving any reasons (*or* explanation); ***als*** (*or* ***zur***) ~ ***von*** (*or gen.*) by way of explaining, as an explanation *or* justification of (*or* for)

beˈgrü·nen (h) **I.** *v/t.* plant with grass (*or* trees, bushes *etc.*), plant over *s.th.*; **II.** *v/refl.*: ***sich*** ~ turn green; ***die Bäume*** ~ ***sich*** *a.* the leaves are coming out on the trees; **beˈgrünt** *adj.* green; planted with grass (*or* trees, bushes *etc.*); ***~e Flächen*** green areas (*or* spaces); **Beˈgrü·nung** *f* (-; *no pl.*) planting of grass (*or* trees *etc.*) (*gen.* on); greenery

beˈgrü·ßen *v/t.* (h) greet; *formal*: receive *visitor etc.*; welcome (*a. fig.*); *fig.* applaud; ***das wäre zu*** ~ that would be very welcome, that would be a welcome development (*or* improvement *etc.*); ***es ist zu ~, daß*** we (*or* I) welcome the fact that, we are (*or* I am) pleased to see that; **beˈgrü·ßens·wert** *adj.* welcome; **Beˈgrü·ßung** *f* (-; -en) greeting; reception, welcome

Beˈgrü·ßungs|an·spra·che *f* welcoming speech; **~schluck** *m* welcoming drink; **~wor·te** *pl.* words of welcome

beˈgucken (*sep.* -k·k-) (h) **I.** *v/t.* have a good look at; **II.** *v/refl.*: ***sich*** ~ *a.* eye o.s. *in the mirror etc.*

be·gün·sti·gen [bəˈɡʏnstɪɡən] *v/t.* (h) favo(u)r; help *s.th.* (along), further; **Be·gün·stig·te** [bəˈɡʏnstɪçtə] *m,f* (-n; -n) ⚖ beneficiary; **Beˈgün·sti·gung** *f* (-; -en) preferential treatment, favo(u)ritism; furtherance; ⚖ aiding and abetting

beˈgut·ach·ten *v/t.* (h) give an (expert's) opinion on; examine; F have a (close) look at; ***et. ~ lassen*** get an expert's opinion on s.th., F get the experts to have a look at s.th.; **Beˈgut·ach·ter** *m* (-s; -) expert; appraiser; **Beˈgut·ach·tung** *f* (-; -en) **1.** examination; appraisal; **2.** → ***Gutachten***

be·gü·tert [bəˈɡyːtɐt] *adj.* wealthy, well-to-do

beˈhaa·ren *v/refl.* (h): ***sich ~*** grow hairs; become hairy; **beˈhaart** *adj.* hairy; *formal*: hirsute; ***stark ~*** covered in hair, very hairy; **Beˈhaa·rung** *f* (-; -en) hairs *pl.*

be·hä·big [bəˈhɛːbɪç] *adj.* sedate; phlegmatic; portly; **Beˈhä·big·keit** *f* (-; *no pl.*) sedateness; phlegmatic nature; portliness

be·haf·tet [bəˈhaftət] *adj.*: ***mit Fehlern ~*** flawed; ***mit Problemen ~*** fraught with problems; ***mit negativen Konnotationen ~*** negatively loaded, ***sein:*** *a.* have negative connotations; ***mit e-m negativen Beigeschmack ~*** marred by (*or* tainted with) negative associations; ***mit e-m Makel ~ sein*** be tainted, bear a stigma; ***mit e-m schlechten Ruf ~ sein*** have (*or* be burdened with) a bad reputation; ***mit Schuldgefühlen ~*** guilt-ridden; ***mit e-m unangenehmen Geruch*** *etc.* ***~ sein*** have an unpleasant smell *etc.* about it

be·ha·gen [bəˈhaːɡən] **I.** *v/i.* (h) suit *s.o.*; ***das behagt mir (ganz und gar) nicht*** I don't like it (one bit); **II.** ♀ *n* (-s; *no pl.*) comfort, ease; pleasure, relish; contentment; ***mit ~*** with relish; **be·hag·lich** [bəˈhaːklɪç] **I.** *adj.* comfortable; cosy, homey, homely contented *smile etc.*; **II.** *adv.* comfortably; contentedly; **Beˈhag·lich·keit** *f* (-; *no pl.*) comfort; cosiness, homeliness, *Am.* homeyness

beˈhal·ten *v/t.* (behielt, behalten, h) keep; hold onto; maintain; retain; remember; ♧ carry; ***recht ~*** be right (in the end); ***et. für sich ~*** keep s.th. to o.s.; ***behalt das für dich!*** *a.* F keep that under your hat; ***er kann nichts für sich ~*** *a.* F he's a blabbermouth; *Nahrung* ***bei sich ~*** keep down; ***er hat s-n Humor ~*** he hasn't lost his sense of humo(u)r; ***s-e gute Laune ~*** keep up one's good spirits; ***die Nerven ~*** keep cool

Be·häl·ter [bəˈhɛltɐ] *m* (-s; -) container (*a.* ⛟), *formal*: receptacle; box; tank; ***hast du dafür e-n ~?*** have you got something to put it in?

Be·hält·nis [bəˈhɛltnɪs] *n* (-ses; -se) receptacle

be·häm·mert [bəˈhɛmɐt] F *adj.* F nuts; F dumb

beˈhan·deln *v/t.* (h) treat (*a.* ⚕, ⚙); deal with *problem, subject etc.*); *ped. etc.*: go through, F do; handle *s.o.*; ***e-e Wunde mit et. ~*** treat a wound with s.th., put s.th. on a wound; **Beˈhand·lung** *f* (-; -en) treatment; handling; ***in (ärztlicher) ~ sein*** be receiving medical treatment

Beˈhand·lungs|ko·sten *pl.* treatment (*or* medical) costs, cost *sg.* of treatment; ***~meˌtho·de*** *f*, ***~wei·se*** *f* (method of) treatment; ***~zim·mer*** *n* ⚕ surgery, consulting room, *Am.* (doctor's) office

Beˈhang *m* (-[e]s; ¨e) hangings *pl.*; decoration(s *pl.*)

be·han·gen [bəˈhaŋən] *adj.* laden (***mit*** *dat.* with); *Christmas tree*: *a.* decorated, decked (with); decorated, *lit.* bedecked (with *flowers*); draped (with *jewelry*)

beˈhän·gen *v/t.* (h) hang, drape (***mit*** *dat.* with); decorate (with); F *contp.* ***sich ~ mit*** drape o.s. with, cover o.s. in

beˈhar·ren *v/i.* (h): ***~ auf*** *dat. or* ***bei*** *dat.* insist on, stick to *one's opinion etc.*, persist in *one's belief etc.*; ***darauf ~, daß*** insist that; **be·harr·lich** [bəˈharlɪç] **I.** *adj.* persevering; dogged; unwavering; persistent, importunate; stubborn; **II.** *adv.*: ***~ dabei bleiben, daß, ~ darauf bestehen, daß*** insist that; ***er bleibt ~ dabei, daß*** *a.* he 'will insist that; ***sich ~ weigern*** doggedly (*or* stubbornly) refuse; ***~ schweigen*** refuse to speak (*or* say anything), maintain a dogged silence; **Beˈharr·lich·keit** *f* (-; *no pl.*) perseverance; doggedness, tenacity; unwaveringness; persistence; stubbornness; **Beˈhar·rung** *f* (-; *no pl.*) **1.** insistence (***auf*** *dat.* on); **2.** *phys.* inertia

Beˈhar·rungs|ver·mö·gen *n phys.* inertia; ***~zu·stand*** *m* state of equilibrium (*or* inertia)

beˈhau·en *v/t.* (h) hew

be·haup·ten [bəˈhaʊptən] (h) **I.** *v/t.* **1.** claim, maintain, say; argue; *formal*: assert, allege; ***~ zu*** *inf.* claim to *inf.*, maintain (*or* say) that ...; ***j-m gegenüber ~, daß*** tell s.o. that; ***steif und fest ~, daß*** insist (*or* swear) that; ***Sie wollen also tatsächlich ~, daß ...*** are you trying to tell me that ...?, do you mean to say that ...?; ***es wird von ihm behauptet, daß*** he is said to *inf.*, it is said (*or* they say) that he; **2.** maintain; ***das Feld ~*** stand one's ground; **II.** *v/refl.*: ***sich ~*** assert o.s.; hold one's own, stand one's ground; *esp.* ⚔ prevail; *sport*: come out on top; ♱ *exchange rates, prices*: remain firm; ***sich ~ gegen*** *acc. a.* stand up against; ***sich in s-r Stellung ~*** maintain one's position; **Beˈhaup·tung** *f* (-; -en) **1.** claim, assertion; *formal*: contention; allegation; ***s-e ~en*** what he says, the claims *etc.* he makes; ***ihre ~, sie hätte es schon bezahlt, ist nicht richtig*** what she says about having paid for it isn't true; ***die ~, er würde zurücktreten, ist nicht richtig*** what people say about him (*or* his) resigning isn't true; ***ich bleibe bei m-r ~, daß*** I still say (*or* maintain) that; ***er bleibt bei s-r ~, daß*** *a.* he still insists that; ***wie kommst du zu dieser ~?*** what makes you say that?; **2.** *no pl.* maintenance; defen|ce (*Am.* -se)

Be·hau·sung [bəˈhaʊzʊŋ] *f* (-; -en) **1.** *a. pl.* accommodation; **2.** dwelling, home; **3.** providing accommodation (for people)

beˈhe·ben *v/t.* (behob, behoben, h) repair *damage etc.*; get rid of; remedy, redress *abuses*; **Beˈhe·bung** *f* (-; *no pl.*) repair; removal; redressal

be·hei·ma·tet [bəˈhaɪmaːtət] *adj.* resident; ***~ sein in*** *dat.* come from, *zo. a.* be at home in, be native to; ***er (es) ist in X ~*** *a.* his (its) home is (in) X

beˈheiz·bar *adj.* heatable; ***nicht ~*** unheatable; ***~e Heckscheibe*** heated rear window; **beˈhei·zen** *v/t.* (h) heat

Be·helf [bəˈhɛlf] *m* (-[e]s; -e) makeshift; **beˈhel·fen** *v/refl.* (behalf, beholfen, h): ***sich ~*** manage, get by, ***mit:*** make do with; ***sich ohne et. ~*** do without s.th.

Beˈhelfs... *in cpds.* makeshift; emergency; temporary, stopgap; ***~aus·fahrt*** *f* temporary exit; emergency exit; ***~lan·de·bahn*** *f* makeshift (*or* emergency) runway

beˈhelfs·mä·ßig **I.** *adj.* makeshift; emergency ...; temporary, stopgap ...; **II.** *adv.* as a makeshift; for the time being, as a stopgap; ***~ eingerichtet*** *a.* F thrown together

Beˈhelfs|maß·nah·men *pl.* stopgap measures; ***~ˌun·ter·kunft*** *f* temporary (*or* emergency) accommodation

beˈhelfs·wei·se *adv.*: ***der Raum dient ~ als Küche*** the room serves as a makeshift kitchen (when needed)

be·hel·li·gen [bəˈhɛlɪɡən] *v/t.* (h) bother, trouble, pester, annoy; **Beˈhel·li·gung** *f* (-; -en) *a. pl.* pestering; ***er mit s-n dauernden ~en!*** he never stops pestering (you)

be·hend [bəˈhɛnt], **be·hen·de** [bəˈhɛndə] *adj.* nimble, agile; dext(e)rous; **Be·hen·dig·keit** [bəˈhɛndɪçkaɪt] *f* (-; *no pl.*) agility; dexterity

be·her·ber·gen [bəˈhɛrbɛrɡən] *v/t.* (h) **1.** put up, accommodate; **2.** *fig.* harbo(u)r

beˈherr·schen (h) **I.** *v/t.* **1.** *pol. etc.* rule (over), govern; *fig.* dominate; *a.* rule (over), hold sway over, F run *family, firm etc.*; *fig.* ***es beherrscht sein ganzes Denken*** it governs (*or* dominates, determines) his whole way of thinking; **2.** *fig.* control, be in control of, have *s.th.* under control; control, dominate *the market etc.*; (keep under) control; ***den Luftraum ~*** control airspace, have air supremacy; **3.** know *one's trade*; have complete command of *s.th.*; have a good command of, speak *a language* (fluently); **4.** command, dominate, tower (*or* soar) above; **5.** ***alte Eichen ~ die Landschaft*** the landscape is dominated by ancient oaks; **II.** *v/refl.*: ***sich ~*** control o.s., restrain o.s.; ***ich mußte mich ~*** *a.* I had to pull myself together (***um nicht zu*** *inf.* so as not to *inf.*, so that I wouldn't *do s.th.*); ***sie kann sich nicht ~*** *a.* she just can't hold back, she has a quick temper; F ***ich kann mich ~!*** F you'll be lucky!; **beˈherr·schend** *adj.* dominating; ***~es Thema der Verhandlungen war*** topic number one (*or* the leading topic) at the talks was; **Beˈherr·scher** *m* (-s; -) ruler; **beˈherrscht** *adj.* restrained, disciplined; **Beˈherrscht·heit** *f* (-; *no pl.*) self-restraint, self-possession; **Beˈherr·schung** *f* (-; *no pl.*) **1.** *pol. etc.* rule (*gen.* over); **2.** *fig.* control (*gen.* of, over); self-control; mastery (*gen.* of); command (of); ***die ~ verlieren*** lose control, lose one's self-control (F cool)

be·her·zi·gen [bəˈhɛrtsɪɡən] *v/t.* (h) take to heart, heed; follow; **beˈher·zi·gens·wert** *adj.* worth heeding; **Beˈher·zi·gung** *f* (-; *no pl.*) heeding (*gen.* of)

be·herzt [bəˈhɛrtst] *adj.* courageous, brave, plucky; determined; **Beˈherzt·heit** *f* (-; *no pl.*) courage, bravery, pluck; determination

beˈhe·xen *v/t.* (h) bewitch; put a spell on

be·hilf·lich [bəˈhɪlflɪç] *adj.*: ***j-m ~ sein*** help s.o. (***bei*** *dat.* with), *formal*: assist s.o. (with, in *ger.*); ***darf ich Ihnen ~ sein?*** can I help you?, allow me

be'hin·dern *v/t.* (h) hinder, impede (***bei*** *dat.* in); *a.* obstruct *view, traffic etc.*; *a.* be (*or* get) in the way

be'hin·dert *adj.* ⚕ handicapped, disabled; ***geistig ~*** mentally handicapped; **Be'hin·der·te** *m, f* (-n; -n) handicapped (*or* disabled) person

Be'hin·der·ten|aus·weis *m* disabled pass; **𝔖ge·recht** *adj.* suitable for the handicapped (*or* for wheelchairs); *building*: *a.* with wheelchair access; **~toi,let·te** *f* disabled toilet

Be'hin·de·rung *f* (-; -en) **1.** hindrance, impediment; **2.** ⚕ handicap; ***geistige ~*** mental handicap; ***e-e geistige ~ haben*** be mentally handicapped (*or* retarded); **3.** *sport*: obstruction

Be'hin·de·rungs·wett·be·werb *m* ✝ restraint of competition

Be·hör·de [bə'hø:ɐdə] *f* (-; -n) (public) authority; administrative body; ***die ~n*** the authorities; ***er ist auf der ~*** he's at the town hall

Be'hör·den|ap·pa,rat *m* administrative machinery; *contp.* bureaucratic machine, bureaucracy; **~spra·che** *f* officialese; **~weg** *m*: (***den ~ gehen*** go through the) official channels *pl.*

be·hörd·lich [bə'hø:ɐtlıç] **I.** *adj.* official, government ...; **II.** *adv.* officially; ***~ genehmigen lassen*** get official approval for; ***~ genehmigt*** officially authorized; ***~ anerkannt*** officially recognized

be'hü·ten *v/t.* (h) look after; protect (***vor*** *dat.* from); (***Gott***) ***behüte!*** God forbid!, perish the thought!; ***behütete Kindheit*** sheltered upbringing

be·hut·sam [bə'hu:tza:m] **I.** *adj.* cautious; gentle; **II.** *adv.*: ***~ umgehen mit*** *dat.* handle with care, be gentle on *s.o.*; **Be'hut·sam·keit** *f* (-; *no pl.*) caution; gentleness

bei [baı] *prp.* (*dat.*) **1.** ***~ Berlin*** near Berlin; ***~m Rathaus*** (just) near *or* by the town hall, at the town hall; ***die Schlacht ~ Waterloo*** the Battle of Waterloo; ***~m Metzger*** at the butcher's; ***~ m-n Eltern*** at my parents' (place); ***~ ihr zu Hause*** in her house, at her place; ***~ Schmidt*** c/o (= care of) Schmidt; ***er arbeitet*** (***or ist***) ***~ der Post*** (***Bahn***) he works for the post office (railway, *Am.* railroad); ***sie ist ~m Fernsehen*** she works for (the) TV; ***ich habe kein Geld ~ mir*** I have no money on me; ***er hatte s-n Hund ~ sich*** he had his dog with him; ***Stunden nehmen ~*** have lessons with *s.o.*; ***~ welchem Arzt bist du?*** which doctor do you go to?, *Brit. a.* who's your GP?; ***~ Schiller steht*** in one of Schiller's works it says, Schiller says; ***das ist oft so ~ Kindern*** that's nothing unusual with children, *contp.* children are like that; ***~ den Römern gab es*** the Romans had; **2.** ***~ m-r Ankunft*** when I arrived, on my arrival; ***~ Tagesanbruch*** at dawn; ***~ Nacht*** at night; ***~ Tag*** during the daytime, by day; ***~ schönem Wetter*** when the weather is fine; ***~m Lesen der Zeitung fiel mir auf*** while (*or* when) I was reading the paper it struck me; ***~ der Arbeit*** at work; ***er ist ~m Essen*** he's having his dinner (*or* lunch); ***~ e-m Unfall*** in an accident; ***~m Unterricht*** during a (*or* the) lesson; ***~ e-m Glas Wein*** over a glass of wine; ***~ Strafe von*** under penalty of; ***~ guter Gesundheit*** in good health; ***~ offenem Fenster*** with the window open; **3.** ***~ der Hand*** *etc.* ***fassen*** take *s.o.* by the hand *etc.*; ***j-n ~m Namen nennen*** call s.o. by (his *or* her) name; **4.** among; ***~ den alten Fotos*** among the old photos; **5.** ***~ Alkohol muß ich aufpassen*** I have to be careful with alcohol; ***~ Geldfragen muß ich passen*** when it comes to (questions of) money, I have to pass; ***~ Männern hat sie Pech*** she's unlucky with men; **6.** ***~ d-m Gehalt!*** (you) with your salary!; ***~ m-m Gehalt kann ich mir das nicht leisten*** I can't afford that on (*or* with) my salary; ***~ d-r Erkältung solltest du nicht rausgehen*** you should stay in with your cold (*or* with that cold of yours); ***~ 50 Mark pro Stunde*** at 50 marks an hour; ***~ so vielen Schwierigkeiten*** considering all the difficulties; ***~ Lage der Dinge*** (with) matters *or* things being as they are; ***~ all s-r Mühe*** for all his effort; **7.** ***schwören ~*** swear by; ***~ Gott!*** by God!; **8.** ***~ weitem*** by far

'bei·be·hal·ten *v/t.* (*irr.*, *sep.*, h, → ***behalten***) keep, retain, maintain; stick to *habit etc.*; keep up *tradition etc.*; carry on in *a direction*, keep to *one's pace etc.*; **'Bei·be·hal·tung** *f* (-; *no pl.*) upholding; ***unter ~ von*** (*or gen.*) while maintaining

'bei·bie·gen F *v/t.* (*irr.*, *sep.*, h, → ***biegen***): ***j-m et. ~*** break it (*or* s.th.) to s.o. gently

'Bei·blatt *n* insert

'Bei·boot *n* dinghy

'bei·brin·gen *v/t.* (*irr.*, *sep.*, h, → ***bringen***) **1.** ***j-m et. ~*** teach s.o. s.th.; make s.th. clear to s.o., get s.th. across to s.o.; tell s.o. s.th., break s.th. to s.o.; F ***dir werd' ich's schon noch ~!*** F I'll show you what's what!; **2.** inflict *wound, losses etc.* (*dat.* on); **3.** produce, come up with

Beich·te ['baıçtə] *f* (-; -n) confession; ***die ~ ablegen*** confess; ***j-m die ~ abnehmen*** hear s.o.'s confession, confess s.o.; **beich·ten** ['baıçtən] *v/t. and v/i.* (h) confess (***bei*** *dat.* to); *fig.* ***ich muß dir etwas ~*** I've got something to confess (to you), I've got a confession to make (to you), *a.* F I've got to get something off my chest

'Beicht|ge·heim·nis *n* seal of confession; **~spie·gel** *m* penitential; **~stuhl** *m* confessional (box); **~va·ter** *m* (father) confessor

beid·ar·mig ['baıtˀarmıç] *adj.* *sport*: two-handed

beid·bei·nig ['baıtbaınıç] *adj.* *sport*: two-footed

bei·de ['baıdə] *indef. pron.* both; the two; either (*sg.*); ***m-e ~n Brüder*** both my brothers, my two brothers; ***wir ~*** both of us, the two of us; ***alle ~*** both of them; ***in ~n Fällen*** in both cases, in either case; ***kein(e)s*** *or* ***keine(r) von ~n*** neither (of them *or* of the two); ***zu ~n Seiten*** on both sides, on either side; ***~ sind angekommen*** both of them have arrived, they've both arrived; *tennis*: ***15 ~*** 15 all; → ***Bein***

'bei·de·mal *adv.* both times

bei·der·lei ['baıdɐlaı] *adj.* (of) both kinds; ***~ Geschlechts*** of either sex

bei·der·sei·tig ['baıdɐzaıtıç] *adj.* **1.** on both sides; **2.** mutual; ***in ~em Einvernehmen*** by mutual agreement; ***zur ~en Zufriedenheit*** to the satisfaction of both sides; **3.** *pol. etc.* bilateral, two-sided; **bei·der·seits** ['baıdɐzaıts] **I.** *prp.* on both sides (*gen.* of), on either side (of); **II.** *adv.* on both sides

bei·des ['baıdəs] *pron.* both (of them); ***ich mag ~ nicht*** I don't like either (of them)

beid·hän·dig ['baıthɛndıç] *adj.* ambidextrous; *sport*: two-handed

'bei·dre·hen *v/t. and v/i.* (*sep.*, h) ⚓ heave to

beid·sei·tig ['baıtzaıtıç] *adj.* → ***beiderseitig***

bei·ein'an·der *adv.* together; (***dicht***) ***~*** next to each other; **~blei·ben** *v/i.* (*irr.*, *sep.*, sn, → ***bleiben***) stay (F stick) together; **~ha·ben** *v/t.* (*irr.*, *sep.*, h, → ***haben***) have *s.th.* together; have *a sum* (ready); F ***er hat nicht alle beieinander*** F he's not all there, he must have a screw loose somewhere; F ***du hast wohl nicht alle beieinander?*** have you gone mad (F gone off your nut)?; **~hal·ten** *v/t.* (*irr.*, *sep.*, h, → ***halten***) keep together; **~sein** **I.** F *v/i.* (*irr.*, *sep.*, sn, → ***sein***): ***gut ~*** be in good shape; ***er ist nicht gut beieinander*** he's not (too) well; **II.** 𝔖 *n* (-s; *no pl.*) (***gemütliches ~*** cosy, *Am.* cozy) get-together; ***das ~*** being together (with s.o. *or* people)

'Bei·fah·rer *m* (-s; -) (front-seat) passenger; co-driver (*a. sport*), F driver's mate; pillion rider; **~sitz** *m* front passenger seat; pillion (seat)

'Bei·fall *m* (-[e]s; *no pl.*) applause, clapping; (loud) cheers *pl.*; *fig.* approval; ***~ ernten*** (***or finden***) meet with approval, draw applause; ***~ spenden*** applaud (***j-m*** s.o.); **𝔖hei·schend** **I.** *adj.* eager for applause; **II.** *adv.*: ***sich ~ umsehen*** look around for applause

'bei·fäl·lig **I.** *adj.* approving; ***~es Lächeln*** smile of approval; **II.** *adv.* approvingly; ***~ nicken*** nod (in) approval; ***et. ~ aufnehmen*** welcome s.th.

'Bei·fall·klat·schen *n* (-s; *no pl.*) applause, clapping

'Bei·falls|be·kun·dung *f* (-; -en), **~be·zei·gung** *f* (-; -en) show of approval; **~klat·schen** *n* → ***Beifallklatschen***; **~kund·ge·bung** *f* show of approval; **~ruf** *m* cheer(s *pl.*); **~sturm** *m* thunderous (*or* rapturous) applause, storms *pl.* of applause

'Bei·film *m* supporting film

'bei·fü·gen *v/t.* (*sep.*, h) add (*dat.* to); enclose, include (with *a letter etc.*); **'Bei·fü·gung** *f* (-; -en) **1.** *no pl.* addition (*gen.* of); ***unter ~ von*** (*or gen.*) (by) adding, enclosing; **2.** *ling.* attribute

'Bei·fuß *m* (-es; *no pl.*) ♣ mugwort

'Bei·ga·be *f* (-; -n) **1.** addition; *gastr.* ***unter ~ von*** adding; **2.** extra; **3.** burial offering

beige [be:ʃ] *adj.*, 𝔖 *n* (-; -) beige

'bei·ge·ben (*irr.*, *sep.*, h, → ***geben***) **I.** *v/t.* add (*dat.* to); ***j-m j-n*** *als Berater etc.* ***~*** assign s.o. to s.o.; **II.** *v/i.*: F ***klein ~*** F climb down

'beige·far·ben *adj.* beige(-colo[u]red)

'Bei·ge·ord·ne·te *m, f* (-n; -n) assistant; *pol.* town council(l)or

'Bei·ge·schmack *m* (-[e]s; *no pl.*) (unpleasant) taste; ***e-n ~ haben von*** *a.* smack of (*a. fig.*); ***bitterer*** *etc.* ***~*** slightly bitter *etc.* taste; ***e-n unangenehmen ~ haben*** *a. fig.* have an unpleasant taste (to it), *fig.* have a negative connotation

'Bei·heft *n* (-[e]s; -e) supplement; accompanying notes *pl.*

'bei·hef·ten *v/t.* (*sep.*, h): **et.** ~ attach (*or* staple) s.th. (*dat.* to *s.th.*)

'Bei·hil·fe *f* (-; -n) **1.** subsidy, grant; **2.** ⚖ aiding and abetting; ~ **leisten** aid and abet (**j-m** s.o.); ~ **zum Mord** complicity in murder

'bei·ho·len *v/t.* (*sep.*, h) ⚓ take in *sail*

'Bei·klang *m* (-[e]s; ⁼e) *a. fig.* overtone(s *pl.*)

'bei·kom·men *v/i.* (*irr.*, *sep.*, sn, → **kommen**) **1. j-m** ~ get at s.o., *fig. a.* get the better of s.o.; get hold of s.o.; **ihm ist nicht beizukommen** there's no getting at him; **mit Argumenten ist ihr nicht beizukommen** she's deaf to argument; **2. e-r Sache** ~ cope with s.th., get to grips with s.th., get to the root of s.th.

'Bei·kost *f* (-; *no pl.*) supplementary food

Beil [bail] *n* (-[e]s; -e) hatchet; chopper; axe, *Am.* ax

'Bei·la·ge *f* (-; -n) **1.** supplement; insert; **2.** *gastr.* garnishings *pl.*; side dish; **Fleisch mit** ~ meat and vegetables; **was gibt es als ~?** what does it come with?, what is it served with?; **es gibt Reis als** ~ there's rice with it, it comes with rice

'bei·läu·fig I. *adj.* casual; **~e Bemerkung** passing remark; **II.** *adv.* casually; ~ **erwähnen** *etc.* mention *etc.* in passing

'bei·le·gen *v/t.* (*sep.*, h) **1.** add (*dat.* to); enclose, include (with *a letter etc.*); **2.** confer *title etc.* (*dat.* on), give *name*; **sich** *e-n Titel etc.* ~ assume, take on; **e-r Sache Wert** (*or* **Bedeutung**) ~ attach (great) importance to s.th.; **3.** settle; **Meinungsverschiedenheiten** ~ settle the (*or* one's) differences; **'Bei·le·gung** *f* (-; -en) settlement, reconciliation; **friedliche** ~ peaceful settlement

bei·lei·be [bai'laibə] *adv.*: ~ **nicht!** certainly not, F not by a long shot; **es war** ~ **kein Spaß!** it was no picnic, I can tell you; **er ist** ~ **kein Kenner, aber** he's far from being (*or* he's hardly) a connoisseur, but; **sie ist** ~ **nicht kritisch, aber** she's far from (being) critical, but

'Bei·leid *n* (-s; *no pl.*) condolences *pl.*, sympathy; **j-m sein** ~ **aussprechen** offer s.o. one's condolences; **j-m sein** ~ **bekunden** express one's sympathy (to s.o.); → **herzlich** I

'Bei·leids|be·such *m* visit of condolence; **~be·zei·gung** *f* (-; -en) condolences *pl.*; **von ~en bitten wir abzusehen** no cards or flowers please; **~kar·te** *f* condolence (*or* sympathy) card; **~schrei·ben** *n* letter of condolence; **~te·le·ˌgramm** *n* sympathy telegram

'bei·lie·gen *v/i.* (*irr.*, *sep.*, h, → **liegen**) be enclosed (with *a letter etc.*), be attached (to); **'bei·lie·gend** *adj. and adv.* enclosed; ~ **übersenden wir Ihnen** enclosed please find, we are enclosing, we enclose

'bei·men·gen *v/t.* → **beimischen**

'bei·mes·sen *v/t.* (*irr.*, *sep.*, h, → **messen**): **e-r Sache Bedeutung** (*or* **Wert**) ~ attach (great) importance to s.th.; **ich messe der Sache keinen großen Wert bei** I don't attach any great importance to the matter, I don't see it as being terribly important

'bei·mi·schen *v/t.* (*sep.*, h): **e-r Sache et.** ~ mix s.th. with s.th.; add s.th. to s.th.; **'Bei·mi·schung** *f* (-; -en) admixture; *fig. a.* touch, tinge; **unter** ~ **von** while (*or* by) adding

Bein [bain] *n* (-[e]s; -e) leg; **ich konnte mich nicht mehr auf den ~en halten** I could hardly stand on my (own two) feet; **das geht in die ~e!** you really feel it in your legs, it goes for your legs; **j-m ein** ~ **stellen** *a. fig.* trip s.o. up; **schon auf den ~en sein** be up and about; **ich muß mich auf die ~e machen** I must be making tracks; **dauernd auf den ~en sein** always be on the go; **j-m auf die ~e helfen** help s.o. up, help s.o. onto his (*or* her) feet, *fig.* set s.o. up, get s.th. going; **wir werden dich bald wieder auf die ~e bringen!** we'll have you back on your feet (*or* running around) again in no time; **schwach auf den ~en sein** be a bit shaky (*or* wobbly); *fig.* **auf schwachen ~en stehen** be shaky, be a shaky affair; **auf eigenen ~en stehen** stand on one's own two feet; **mit beiden ~en im Leben stehen** have both feet firmly on the ground; **die ~e in die Hand nehmen** shoot off, **müssen:** F have to stir one's stumps, have to step on it; **j-m ~e machen** get s.o. moving; **es hat ~e bekommen** it seems to have just walked off; **die ganze Stadt war auf den ~en** the whole town had turned out; **alles, was ~e hat** anyone and everyone, the whole population; → **ausreißen** 1, **Bauch, Grab, Klotz, Knüppel, link**

'bei·na·he *adv.* almost, nearly; very nearly; **er hätte ~ gewonnen** *a.* he came very close to winning

'Bei·na·he·zu·sam·men·stoß *m* near miss, near collision; ✈ *a.* airmiss

'Bei·na·me *m* (-ns; -n) epithet; nickname

'bein·am·puˌtiert *adj.* with an amputated leg; with both legs amputated; **er ist** ~ *a.* he's had a leg (*or* both legs) amputated; **'Bein·am·puˌtier·te** *m, f* (-n; -n) person (*or* man, woman) with an amputated leg (*or* with both legs amputated)

'Bein|ar·beit *f* footwork; *swimming*: legwork; **~bruch** *m* fractured (*or* broken) leg; *fig.* **das ist doch kein ~!** it's not the end of the world; **~frei·heit** *f* (-; *no pl.*) legroom; room to stretch one's legs

be·in·hal·ten [bə'ʔinhaltən] *v/t.* (h) contain; say; imply

'bein'hart *adj.* (as) hard as rock (*or* stone)

'Bein|haus *n* charnel house; **~proˌthe·se** *f* artificial leg; **~schie·ne** *f* **1.** ✱ splint; **2.** → **~schüt·zer** *m* shin pad

'bei·ord·nen *v/t.* (*sep.*, h) **1. j-m j-n** ~ assign s.o. to s.o.; **2.** *ling.* coordinate

'bei·packen (*sep.* -k·k-) *v/t.* (*sep.*, h): **e-r Sache et.** ~ enclose (*or* include) s.th. with (*or* in) s.th.

'Bei·pack·zet·tel *m* (✱ patient) package insert, ✱ *a.* PPI; F blurb

'bei·pflich·ten ['baipfliçtən] *v/i.* (*sep.*, h): **j-m** (**e-r Sache**) ~ agree with s.o. (s.th.) (**in** *dat.* on); **'bei·pflich·tend** *adj.* approving

'Bei·proˌgramm *n* supporting program(me)

'Bei·rat *m* (-[e]s; ⁼e) advisory board

be'ir·ren *v/t.* (h) disconcert; put *s.o.* off; **er läßt sich durch nichts** ~ he won't be put off

bei·sam·men [bai'zamən] *adv.* together; **gute Nacht ~!** goodnight everyone (*or* all); **~ha·ben** *v/t.* (*irr.*, *sep.*, h, → **haben**): **s-e Gedanken** ~ have one's wits about one; F **er hat nicht alle beisammen** F he's not all there, he must have a screw loose somewhere; **~sein I.** F *v/i.* (*irr.*, *sep.*, sn, → **sein**): **er ist schlecht beisammen** he's not (too) well; **II.** ♀ *n* (-s; *no pl.*): **geselliges** ~ (social) get-together

'Bei·satz *m ling.* apposition

'Bei·schlaf *m* (-[e]s; *no pl.*) sexual intercourse

'Bei·sein *n* (-s; *no pl.*) presence; **im** ~ **von** (*or gen.*) in the presence of, in front of; **in j-s** ~ in s.o.'s presence, in front of s.o.; **im** ~ **anderer** with others present

bei'sei·te *adv.* aside (*a. thea.*); **Spaß ~!** seriously now; ~ **gehen** step aside; ~ **legen** put aside, *a.* set aside, F stash away *money*; put down (*or* aside) *book, glasses etc.*; ~ **schaffen** remove, get rid of, *a.* F bump *s.o.* off; ~ **lassen** leave aside, ignore, disregard

'bei·set·zen *v/t.* (*sep.*, h) **1.** bury; *lit.* lay to rest; **mit militärischen Ehren** ~ lay to rest with (full) military hono(u)rs; **2.** ⚓ set *sail*; **'Bei·set·zung** *f* (-; -en) burial; funeral; **'Bei·set·zungs·fei·er·lich·kei·ten** *pl.* funeral ceremony *sg.*; obsequies

'Bei·sitz *m* (-es; *no pl.*) **1.** seat (on a committee *etc.*); **2.** assessorship; **'bei·sit·zen** *v/i.* (*irr.*, *sep.*, h, → **sitzen**): **e-m Ausschuß** ~ sit on a committee; **Bei·sit·zer** ['baizitsɐ] *m* (-s; -) **1.** member (of a committee *etc.*); **2.** assessor; **3.** observer, co-examiner

'Bei·spiel *n* (-[e]s; -e) example (**für** *acc.* of); model; **warnendes** (*or* **abschreckendes**) ~ warning; **praktisches** ~ concrete example; **zum** ~ for instance, for example (*abbr.* e.g.); **wie zum ~ ...** (such as) ..., for example; **~e anführen** give examples; **ein** ~ **geben** set an example; **sich ein** ~ **nehmen an** *dat.* take *s.o. or s.th.* as an example, take a leaf out of *s.o.'s* book; **mit gutem** ~ **vorangehen** set an (*or* a good) example; **ohne** ~ → **beispiellos; mit ~en belegen** give examples of (*or* to support); **es soll uns ein** ~ **sein** let it be a lesson (*or* an example) to us all

'bei·spiel·ge·bend *adj.* exemplary; ~ **sein** (*or* **wirken**) serve as (*or* be) an example

'bei·spiel·haft I. *adj.* exemplary; model ...; **II.** *adv.*: **sich** ~ **benehmen** behave impeccably; ~ **vorangehen** set a positive example

'bei·spiel·hal·ber [-halbɐ] *adv.* by way of example; for example, for instance

'bei·spiel·los *adj.* unequal(l)ed, unparalleled; matchless, peerless; unprecedented, unheard-of; **'Bei·spiel·lo·sig·keit** *f* (-; *no pl.*) uniqueness

'Bei·spiel·satz *m* example (sentence)

'bei·spiels·wei·se *adv.* for example, for instance; **ein** ~ **oft angewandter Trick** one trick, for example, that is often used

'bei·sprin·gen *v/i.* (*irr.*, *sep.*, sn, → **springen**): **j-m** ~ come (*or* rush) to s.o.'s aid; help s.o. out

bei·ßen ['baisən] (biß, gebissen, h) **I.** *v/t.* **1.** *a. insect*: bite; **j-n ins Bein** ~ bite s.o.'s leg; **das kann man ja kaum ~!** it's as hard as rock, you can hardly get your teeth into it; F **nichts zu ~ haben** not to have a bite to eat; *iro.* **er wird dich schon nicht** ~ he won't bite (*or* eat) you; → **Hund** 2; **II.** *v/i.* **2.** *a. insect and fish*: bite; ~ **in** *acc.* bite (into); ~ **auf** *acc.* bite on; ~ **nach** *dat.* snap at; → **Apfel, Granit, Gras; 3.** bite, burn, sting; **III.** *v/refl.*: **4. sich** ~ bite o.s.; **sich auf die Zunge** (**Lippe**) ~ bite one's tongue (lip);

→ ***Hintern***; **5.** *fig.* ***sich*** ~ clash; **'bei·ßend** *adj.* biting *wind*; sharp, acrid *smell*; sharp *pain*; *fig.* biting, caustic, acrid, acerbic *remark etc.*, *a.* mordant *criticism*
Bei·ßer·chen ['baisɐçən] F *n* (-s; -) F toothy-peg
'Beiß|korb *m* → ***Maulkorb***; **~ring** *m* teething ring; **~zan·ge** *f* **1.** (***e-e*** ~ a pair of) pliers *pl.*; **2.** F shrew, *sl.* bitch
'Bei·stand *m* (-[e]s; ⸚e) **1.** *no pl.* help, support, assistance; ***j-m*** ~ ***leisten*** → ***beistehen***; **2.** ⚖ legal adviser, counsel
'Bei·stands|kre,dit *m* standby credit; **~pakt** *m pol.* mutual assistance pact
'bei·ste·hen *v/i.* (*irr.*, *sep.*, h, → ***stehen***): ***j-m*** ~ help s.o., stand by s.o., give s.o. one's support; ***Gott steh' mir bei!*** God help me; → ***Rat*** 1
'Bei·stell|mö·bel *pl.* occasional furniture *sg.*; **~tisch** *m* side table
'bei·steu·ern *v/t. and v/i.* (*sep.*, h) contribute (**zu** *dat.* to), F chip *s.th.* in
'bei·stim·men *v/i.* (*sep.*, h): ***j-m*** (***e-r Sache***) ~ agree with s.o. (s.th.)
'Bei·strich *m* (-[e]s; -e) comma
Bei·tel ['baitəl] *m* (-s; -) ⚙ chisel; gouge
Bei·trag ['baitra:k] *m* (-[e]s; Beiträge ['baitrɛ:gə]) **1.** contribution (*a. fig.*); ***e-n*** ~ ***leisten*** contribute (**zu** *dat.* to), make a contribution (to); **2.** subscription (fee); **3.** article (**von** *dat.* by), *esp. pl. a.* contributions (by, from); **'bei·tra·gen** *v/t. and v/i.* (*irr.*, *sep.*, h, → ***tragen***) contribute (**zu** *dat.* to); help, **zu** *inf.*: *a.* serve to *inf.*; ***das trägt nur dazu bei zu*** *inf.* it will only help (*or* serve) to *inf.*; ***sein Teil*** (***dazu***) ~ contribute one's share, F do one's bit (**um zu** *inf.* towards *ger.*), play one's (*or* its) part (in *ger.*); ***viel dazu*** ~, ***um zu*** *inf. a.* go a long way towards *ger.*
'Bei·trags|be·mes·sungs·gren·ze *f* income threshold; **~er·hö·hung** *f* increase in contributions, increased contributions *pl.*; **⁀frei** *adj.* non-contributory; **~frei·heit** *f* (-; *no pl.*) exemption from contributions; **⁀pflich·tig** *adj.* liable to contributions; **~rück·er·stat·tung** *f* contribution refund
'bei·trei·ben *v/t.* (*irr.*, *sep.*, h, → ***treiben***) collect *taxes etc.*; recover *debts*, sue for
'bei·tre·ten *v/i.* (*irr.*, *sep.*, sn, → ***treten***) join, become a member of; *a.* enter (into); enter into *an agreement etc.*; **'Bei·tritt** *m* (-[e]s; -e) joining (**zu** *dat.* of *a party etc.*); entry (into *an alliance etc.*), membership (of)
'Bei·tritts|er·klä·rung *f* application for membership; **~ver·hand·lun·gen** *pl.* membership talks (*or* negotiations); **~ver·trag** *m* accession treaty
'Bei·wa·gen *m* sidecar; **~fah·rer** *m* sidecar passenger; **~ma,schi·ne** *f* motorcycle combination
'Bei·werk *n* (-[e]s; *no pl.*) trimmings *pl.*, F *contp.* frills *pl.*; accessories *pl.*
'bei·woh·nen *v/i.* (*sep.*, h): ***e-r Sache*** ~ be present at s.th.; witness s.th
'Bei·wort *n* (-[e]s; ⸚er) epithet
Bei·ze¹ ['baitsə] *f* (-; -n) **1.** ⚗ corrosive; ⚕ dressing; *wood*: stain; *dyeing*: mordant; *tanning*: bate; *tobacco*: sauce; *gastr.* marinade; ⚕ caustic; **2.** *no pl.* corrosion etching; *wood*: staining
'Bei·ze² *f* (-; -n) hawking, falconry
bei·zei·ten [bai'tsaitən] *adv.* in good time; ***du solltest dich*** ~ ***darum kümmern*** you'd better not leave it too long, you'd better see to it soon
bei·zen¹ ['baitsən] *v/t.* (h) ⚗ corrode; stain *wood*; bate *skins*; *dyeing*: (steep in) mordant; *metall.* pickle, dip; sauce *tobacco*; ⚕ dress; *gastr.* marinade; ⚕ cauterize
'bei·zen² *v/t. and v/i.* (h) hawk
'bei·zie·hen *v/t.* (*irr.*, *sep.*, h, → ***ziehen***) call in, consult; **Bei'zie·hung** *f* (-; *no pl.*) consultation, consulting
'Beiz·jagd *f* → ***Beize²***
'Beiz·mit·tel *n* → ***Beize¹*** 1
be·ja·hen [bə'ja:ən] *v/t.* (h) **1.** answer (*or* say) yes to; *formal*: answer *a question* in the affirmative; **2.** see *s.th.* positively (*or* as positive); ***das Leben*** ~ have a positive outlook on life; ***die Zukunft*** ~ feel positive about the future; **be'ja·hend I.** *adj.* **1.** affirmative; **2.** positive, affirmative; optimistic; **II.** *adv.* **3.** in the affirmative; **4.** positively, affirmatively; optimistically, with optimism
be·jahrt [bə'ja:ɐt] *adj.* old, advanced in years; **Be'jahrt·heit** *f* (-; *no pl.*) advanced age
Be'ja·hung *f* (-; -en) **1.** affirmation; **2.** affirmation; ~ ***des Lebens*** positive outlook on life
be'jam·mern *v/t.* (h) lament, *lit.* bemoan; **be'jam·merns·wert, be'jam·merns·wür·dig** *adj.* lamentable
be'ju·beln *v/t.* (h) (loudly) acclaim, *a.* cheer *s.o.*; rejoice at *s.th.*
be'kam *pret. of* ***bekommen***
be'kämp·fen *v/t.* (h) fight (against); combat; fight *a fire*; fight, control *pests*; **Be'kämp·fung** *f* (-; *no pl.*) fight, struggle (*gen.*, **von** *dat.* against); (*pest*) control
be·kannt [bə'kant] **I.** *p.p. of* ***bekennen***; **II.** *adj.* known (*dat.* to); well-known (***wegen*** *gen.* for), *b.s.* notorious; **~e *Gesichter*** familiar faces; ***mit j-m*** ~ ***sein*** (***werden***) know (get to know) s.o., be (become) acquainted with s.o.; ~ ***sein mit*** *dat.* be familiar with *s.th.*; ***j-n mit j-m*** (***et.***) ~ ***machen*** introduce s.o. to s.o. (s.th.); ***sich mit et.*** ~ ***machen*** get to know s.th., familiarize o.s. with s.th.; ***et. als*** ~ ***voraussetzen*** assume that s.th. is known; ***das ist mir*** ~ I know that, I'm aware of that; ***soviel mir*** ~ ***ist*** as far as I know (*or* I'm aware); ***das Wort ist mir*** ~ I've come across the word, I've heard (*or* seen) the word used; ***er kommt mir*** ~ ***vor*** I think I've seen him (*or* his face) before; ***es kommt mir*** ~ ***vor*** it looks (*or* sounds *etc.*) familiar; *iro.* ***die Geschichte kommt mir*** ~ ***vor*** I think I've heard that one before; ***es ist allgemein*** ~ it is generally known, it's a generally-known fact; ***dafür*** ~ ***sein, daß*** have a reputation for *ger.*, *b.s. a.* be notorious for *ger.*
Be'kann·te *m, f* (-n; -n) friend; acquaintance; boyfriend (*f* girlfriend); ***ein*** **~r *von mir*** a friend of mine, someone I know; ***er ist ein guter*** **~r** I know him quite well; **Be'kann·ten·kreis** *m* circle of friends; ***e-n großen*** ~ ***haben*** have a lot (*or* plenty) of friends, have a wide circle of friends; ***einer aus ihrem*** ~ one of her friends, somebody she knows
be·kann·ter·ma·ßen [bə'kantɐ'ma:sən] *adv.* → ***bekanntlich***
Be'kannt·ga·be *f* (-; *no pl.*) announcement; **be'kannt·ge·ben** *v/t.* (*irr.*, *sep.*, h, → ***geben***) announce; make *s.th.* public; ***sie wollen es nicht*** ~ they don't want to say (*or* disclose) anything
Be'kannt·heits·grad *m* (-[e]s; *no pl.*) (degree of) familiarity; ~ ***e-r Person*** extent of s.o.'s fame; ***der*** ~ ***ist*** (***nicht***) ***sehr hoch*** it's *etc.* (not) very widely known
be'kannt·lich *adv.* as everybody knows
be'kannt·ma·chen *v/t.* (*sep.*, h): ***et.*** ~ announce s.th., make s.th. known; → ***bekannt***; **Be'kannt·ma·chung** *f* (-; -en) **1.** announcement; *pol. a.* communiqué; **2.** announcement, notice
Be'kannt·schaft *f* (-; -en) **1.** *no pl.* familiarity; ***j-s*** ~ ***machen*** get to know s.o., meet s.o.; ~ ***schließen mit j-m*** (***et.***) make s.o.'s acquaintance (get to know s.th., become familiar with s.th.); ***bei näherer*** ~ on closer acquaintance; **2.** circle of friends; **~s·an·zei·ge** *f* personal ad; *pl. a.* personal column *sg.*
be'kannt·wer·den *v/i.* (*irr.*, *sep.*, sn, → ***werden***) become known; become public; get out, leak out; ***es ist bekanntgeworden, daß*** we've been informed that, news has come in that (*or* of ...)
be'keh·ren (h) **I.** *v/t.* convert (**zu** *dat.* to); bring *s.o.* round (to); *w.s.* reclaim *defector, sinner etc.*; **II.** *v/refl.*: ***sich*** ~ become converted, **zu** *dat.*: *a.* become a convert to; *a.* turn *Catholic etc.*; **Be'keh·rer** *m* (-s; -) proselytizer; **Be'kehr·te** *m, f* (-n; -n) convert; **Be'keh·rung** *f* (-; -en) conversion; *w.s.* reclamation
be'ken·nen (bekannte, bekannt, h) **I.** *v/t.* confess (to); ~, ***et. getan zu haben*** confess to having done s.th.; **II.** *v/refl.*: ***sich*** ~ ***zu*** *dat.* confess (to), admit (*or* claim) responsibility for *a bomb attempt etc.*; profess; stand by, stand up for *s.o.*; → ***Farbe, schuldig*** 1
Be'ken·ner *m* (-s; -) supporter (*gen.* of); **~brief** *m* (written) responsibility claim, letter claiming responsibility; **~mut** *m* courage of one's conviction(s)
Be'kennt·nis *n* (-ses; -se) **1.** confession; ***ein*** ~ ***ablegen*** make a confession, confess; **2.** *eccl.*, *pol. etc.* creed; **3.** *a. pol.* (public) avowal (**zu** *dat.* of), profession of loyalty (to); ~ ***zum Glauben*** profession (*or* confession) of faith; **4.** denomination; **~frei·heit** *f* (-; *no pl.*) freedom of religion (*or* belief); **~schu·le** *f* denominational school
be'kla·gen (h) **I.** *v/t.* lament, grieve; ***es sind tausende von*** (***keine***) ***Menschenleben zu*** ~ the death toll runs into thousands (there are no casualties); **II.** *v/refl.*: ***sich*** ~ complain (**über** *acc.* about); ***ich kann mich nicht*** ~ I can't complain, I have no complaints, F I mustn't grumble; **be'kla·gens·wert** *adj.* **1.** lamentable, sad; pitiable; **2.** ***in e-m*** **~en *Zustand*** in a sorry state
be·klagt [bə'kla:kt] *adj.* ⚖ defendant; **~e *Partei*** → **Be'klag·te** *m, f* (-n; -n) defendant
be'klat·schen *v/t.* (h) applaud
be'klau·en F *v/t.* (h): ***j-n*** ~ steal (s.th.) from s.o.
be'kle·ben *v/t.* (h) stick s.th. onto; ***mit Bildern*** ~ stick pictures all over, cover with pictures
be'kleckern (*sep.* -k·k-) (h) **I.** *v/t.* mess up; spill s.th. on; drop s.th. on; splash (*or* get) paint on; spatter *one's shirt etc.* (with s.th.); **II.** *v/refl.*: ***sich*** ~ spill *or* drop s.th. on one's tie (*or* blouse *etc.*), mess up one's tie *etc.*; ***du hast dich mit Tinte bekleckert*** *a.* you've got ink on (*or* all over) your shirt *etc.*; F *fig.* ***du hast dich nicht gerade mit Ruhm beklek-***

kert you haven't exactly covered yourself with glory

be'klei·den *v/t.* (h) **1.** dress; **2.** hold *post, office etc.*; **be'klei·det** *adj.* dressed (***mit*** *dat.* in); ~ ***mit*** *a.* wearing; ***leicht*** ~ lightly dressed, in light dress; ***spärlich*** ~ scantily clad; **Be'klei·dung** *f* (-; -en) clothing, clothes *pl.*

Be'klei·dungs|ge·gen·stän·de *pl.* (articles of) clothing *sg.*; **~in·du,strie** *f* clothing industry; **~vor·schrif·ten** *pl.* dress regulations

be'klem·men *v/t.* (h) make *s.o.* (feel) uneasy, oppress; **be'klem·mend** *adj.* oppressive, suffocating, stifling (*all a. fig.*); *fig.* ***~es Gefühl*** uneasy feeling; ***~es Schweigen*** embarrassed silence; **Be'klem·mung** *f* (-; -en) **1.** suffocating feeling; **2.** *fig.* feeling of unease, sense of anxiety, oppressive feeling; **be·klom·men** [bə'klɔmən] *adj.* anxious, uneasy; ***~es Gefühl*** *a.* feeling of anxiety; **Be'klom·men·heit** *f* (-; *no pl.*) uneasiness, anxiety

be·kloppt [bə'klɔpt] F *adj.* F crazy, *pred.* F nuts; ***so was 2es!*** what a crazy thing to do (*or* happen *etc.*)

be·knackt [bə'knakt] F *adj.* **1.** F crazy; *pred.* F nuts, off one's rocker; **2.** F rotten, stupid

be'knien *v/t.* (h) beg *s.o.* (***zu*** *inf.* to *inf.*), F go on at *s.o.* (to *inf.*)

be'ko·chen *v/t.* (h) cook for *s.o.*

be'kom·men (bekam, bekommen, h) **I.** *v/t.* get; be given, receive; catch *train, bus etc.*; ***ein Kind*** ~ have a baby; *zo.* ***Junge*** ~ have pups *etc.*; ***Zähne*** ~ cut one's teeth; ***e-n Bauch*** ~ develop a paunch; ***Hunger*** (***Durst***) ~ get hungry (thirsty); ***das bekommt man überall*** you can get that anywhere; ~ ***Sie schon?*** are you being served?; ***was*** ~ ***Sie?*** how much is that (*or* does that come to)?; ***et. geschenkt*** ~ get a present, be given s.th. as a present; ***hast du noch Karten*** ~? did you manage to get tickets?; ***zu sehen*** ~ get to see; ***es mit der Angst*** ~ get scared, F get the wind up; **II.** *v/i.*: ***j-m*** (***gut***) ~ agree with s.o.; ***j-m nicht*** (*or* ***schlecht***) ~ disagree with s.o.; ***es bekommt ihm gut*** (***ausgezeichnet***) it's doing him (the world of) good; ***es bekommt ihm überhaupt nicht*** it doesn't agree with him at all; ***wohl bekomm's!*** cheers!, *iro.* the best of luck (to you)

be·kömm·lich [bə'kœmlɪç] *adj.* easily digestible, easy on the stomach; light; *drug*: innocuous, with (next to) no side effects; (very) agreeable; ***schwer*** ~ hard on the stomach (*or* digestion), heavy

be·kö·sti·gen [bə'kœstɪgən] (h) **I.** *v/t.* feed, cook for; **II.** *v/refl.*: ***sich selbst*** ~ cook (*or* cater) for o.s.; **Be'kö·sti·gung** *f* (-; *no pl.*) **1.** food; **2.** catering (*gen.*, ***von*** *dat.* for), feeding (*s.o.*)

be'kräf·ti·gen *v/t.* (h) support, corroborate, *w.s.* reinforce, endorse, confirm (***durch*** *acc.* with, by *ger.*); **Be'kräf·ti·gung** *f* (-; -en) support(ing); corroboration; reinforcement; endorsement; confirmation; ***zur*** ~ *gen.* in support (*or* corroboration) of

be'kreu·zi·gen *v/refl.* (h): ***sich*** ~ cross o.s., make the sign of the cross

be'krie·gen *v/t.* (h) wage war against; ***sich*** ~ be at war with one another

be'krit·teln *v/t.* (h) criticize, find fault with; **Be'krit·te·lung** *f* (-, -en) criticism (*gen.* of), carping (at), finding fault (with)

be'krit·zeln *v/t.* (h) scribble on

be'küm·mern *v/t.* (h) worry; ***das bekümmert ihn gar nicht*** it doesn't worry (*or* bother) him in the slightest; ***das braucht Sie nicht zu*** ~ you needn't worry about that; **be'küm·mert** *adj.* worried, anxious *look etc*

be·kun·den [bə'kʊndən] (h) **I.** *v/t.* **1.** show, display; ***Interesse*** ~ show *or* display (some) interest; **2.** state, declare; ⚖ testify; **II.** *v/refl.*: ***sich*** ~ reveal itself; **Be'kun·dung** *f* (-; -en) **1.** show, display, manifestation; **2.** declaration, avowal

be'lä·cheln *v/t.* (h) smile (condescendingly *etc.*) at

be'la·chen *v/t.* (h) laugh at

be'la·den I. *v/t.* (belud, beladen, h) load (up); *fig.* load *s.o.* down *with work etc.*; burden *s.o. with problems etc.*; **II.** *adj.*: ~ ***mit*** *dat.* loaded with, *table etc.*: *a.* piled up with; *fig.* weighed down with *work etc.* (*or* by *problems etc.*), burdened with *problems etc.*

Be·lag [bə'la:k] *m* (-[e]s; Beläge [bə'lɛ:gə]) coat(ing); layer; *a. mot.* lining; (*floor etc.*) covering; (*road*) surface; base, (running) surface *of ski*; ⚕ coating; plaque, tartar; *gastr.* topping, spread, (sandwich) filling

be'la·gern *v/t.* (h) besiege; *fig. a.* throng, crowd (round); **Be·la·ge·rer** [bə'la:gərɐ] *m* (-s; -) besieger; **Be'la·ge·rung** *f* (-; -en) siege; **Be'la·ge·rungs·zu·stand** *m*: (***im*** ~ in a) state of siege, (under) siege; ***den*** ~ ***über e-e Stadt verhängen*** put a city under siege, lay siege to a city

Be·lang [bə'laŋ] *m* (-[e]s; -e) **1.** ***~e*** concerns, issues, affairs; interests; ***öffentliche ~e*** public issues, matters of public concern (*or* interest); **2.** ***von*** ~ of importance (***für*** *acc.* to), relevant (to); ***ohne*** ~ unimportant (***für*** *acc.* for), of no consequence *or* importance (to), irrelevant (to), immaterial (to)

be'lan·gen *v/t.* (h) ⚖ sue, prosecute

be'lang·los *adj.* unimportant, insignificant; irrelevant; **Be'lang·lo·sig·keit** *f* (-; -en) **1.** *no pl.* insignificance; irrelevance; **2.** insignificant matter, triviality, irrelevancy, F piddling little thing; *pl. a.* trivia; **3.** *pl.* trivial talk *sg.*, F insignificant twaddle *sg.*

be'las·sen *v/t.* (beließen, belassen, h) leave *s.th.* (as it is); ***et. an s-m Platz*** ~ leave s.th. where it is; ***j-n in dem Glauben*** ~, ***daß*** let s.o. go on thinking (*or* believing) that; ***es dabei*** ~ leave it at that; ***alles beim alten*** ~ leave things as they are; ***wir wollen es dabei*** ~ let's leave it at that

be'last·bar *adj.* **1.** ⚙ loadable; ~ ***bis*** with a maximum loading capacity of; **2.** ~ ***sein*** be able to cope with a heavy workload, be able to work under pressure, be able to take some strain (*or* pressure); ***er ist nicht*** ~ he can't take any kind of pressure (*or* strain); **Be'last·bar·keit** *f* (-; *no pl.*) **1.** ⚙ loading capacity; ⚡ power rating; power-handling capacity; **2.** ability to cope with pressure (*or* strain); ***bis zur Grenze der*** ~ to breaking point

be'la·sten (h) **I.** *v/t.* **1.** load (*a.* ⚙, ⚡); ⚙ stress; weight (*a. ski*); **2.** ☤ ***j-n*** (***j-s Konto***) ~ debit s.o. (s.o.'s account) (***mit*** *dat.* with); **3.** ***j-n finanziell*** (***stark***) ~ be a (heavy) financial burden on s.o., present a (heavy) financial strain on s.o.; **4.** encumber, mortgage; **5.** ⚖ incriminate; **6.** pollute, contaminate, add to the pollution of *the environment*; **7.** ⚕ strain; exert; **8.** *a. fig.* strain, put a strain on; ***stark*** ~ put a heavy strain on; ***j-n*** (***stark***) ~ put s.o. under (a lot of) pressure, give s.o. a heavy workload; ***j-n*** (***sehr***) ~ a) be a (great) strain on s.o.; b) be a (big) worry for s.o., give s.o. a (really) bad conscience; ***es belastet mich*** (***allmählich***) *a.* it's getting to me; **II.** *v/refl.*: ***sich*** ~ ***mit*** *dat.* burden (*or* saddle) o.s. with; ***damit kann ich mich nicht*** ~ *a.* I haven't got time for that sort of thing; **be'la·stend** *adj.* **1.** ⚖ incriminating; **2.** ~ ***sein*** be a strain; **be'la·stet** *adj.* **1.** (***voll***) ~ (fully) loaded; **2.** encumbered; **3.** (***stark***) ~ under a (heavy) financial strain; **4.** ⚕ under strain, overworked, overtaxed; **5.** *a. fig.* under strain; under pressure; (***stark***) ~ ***mit*** *dat.* under (great) strain *or* pressure from, weighed down with *problems etc.*; **6.** polluted, contaminated *environment*; **7.** ***erblich*** ~ ***sein*** suffer from a hereditary disease

be·lä·sti·gen [bə'lɛstɪgən] *v/t.* (h) pester, annoy; molest; trouble, bother (***mit*** *dat.* with *questions, requests etc.*); **Be'lä·sti·gung** *f* (-; -en) *a. pl.* pestering; molestation

Be'la·stung *f* (-; -en) **1.** ⚙, ⚡ load, stress; ***zulässige*** ~ maximum permissible load, safe load; **2.** ☤ charge, debit; **3.** (financial) burden (*gen.* on); **4.** encumbrance, mortgage; **5.** ⚖ incrimination; **6.** pollution, contamination (***für*** *acc.* of *the environment etc.*); **7.** ⚕ strain (***für*** *acc.* on); exertion; ***unter*** ~ under exertion; **8.** *a. fig.* strain, burden (***für*** *acc.* on); ***e-e starke*** ~ a great (*or* real) strain; **9.** ***erbliche*** ~ hereditary disease

Be'la·stungs|fä·hig·keit *f* → ***Belastbarkeit***; **~gren·ze** *f* **1.** maximum load; **2.** *fig.* limit(s *pl.*) of what s.o. can take; ***ich habe m-e*** ~ ***erreicht*** I can't take any more, F I've had just about all I can take; **~ma·te·ri,al** *n* ⚖ incriminating evidence; **~pro·be** *f* **1.** ⚙ load test; **2.** *fig.* test (of endurance); **~spit·ze** *f* peak load; **~zeu·ge** *m* witness for the prosecution

be·lau·ben [bə'laʊbən] *v/refl.* (h): ***sich*** ~ come into leaf; **be·laubt** [bə'laʊpt] *adj.* leafy; in leaf

be'lau·ern *v/t.* (h) lie in wait for; *w.s.* watch *s.o.* closely; spy on

be'lau·fen *v/refl.* (belief, belaufen, h): ***sich*** ~ ***auf*** *acc.* amount to, run up to, total

be'lau·schen *v/t.* (h) **1.** eavesdrop on; **2.** watch, observe

be'le·ben (h) **I.** *v/t.* liven up, get (*or* put) some life into; stimulate, get *s.th.* going; *drink etc.*: revive *s.o.*, get *s.o. or s.th.* going (again), F buck up; invigorate; brighten up; ***neu*** ~ put new life into; → ***wiederbeleben***; **II.** *v/refl.*: ***sich*** ~ liven up; *street etc.*: come to life; *face*: brighten up; **be'le·bend** *adj.* stimulating, invigorating; refreshing *drink etc.*; **be·lebt** [bə'le:pt] *adj.* lively; animated *a. talk etc.*; busy, bustling; ☤ brisk; **Be'lebt·heit** *f* (-; *no pl.*) hustle and bustle (*gen.* of), bustling life (of); **Be'le·bung** *f* (-; *no pl.*) livening up; stimulation

Be'le·bungs|mit·tel *n* tonic, restorative,

F pick-me-up; **~ver·such** *m* resuscitation attempt
be'lecken (*sep.* -k·k-) *v/t.* (h) lick; *fig.* ***sie scheinen von der Kultur kaum beleckt zu sein*** civilization seems to have passed them by
Be·leg [bə'le:k] *m* (-[e]s; -e [bə'le:gə]) **1.** record; *a. pl.* proof, evidence; receipt; **2.** example (***für*** *acc.* of); reference
Be'leg·bett *n* private bed (*allotted to a specific practitioner*)
be'le·gen (h) **I.** *v/t.* **1.** cover; line *a. brakes*; coat; ***mit Fliesen*** ~ tile; ***mit Teppichboden*** ~ carpet; **2.** *gastr.* ~ ***mit*** *dat.* put *s.th.* on; **3.** occupy *room etc.*; ***mit j-m*** ~ put s.o. in(to); **4.** sign up for, register for, enrol(l) for; **5.** book, reserve; **6.** ***den ersten*** (***zweiten*** *etc.*) ***Platz*** ~ *sport*: take first (second *etc.*) place, come first (second *etc.*); **7.** *fig.* ~ ***mit*** *dat.* impose *s.th.* on; **8.** give evidence for, substantiate, back up, prove; verify; give (*or* quote) a reference for; **9.** *zo.* cover; **II.** *v/refl.*: ***sich*** ~ get covered (***mit*** *dat.* with), form a layer of; ⚘ fur; *voice*: get husky; → ***belegt*** II
Be'leg·ex·em,plar *n* specimen copy; *a.* author's copy
Be'leg·schaft *f* (-; -en) personnel, workforce; employees *pl.*; staff; **Be'leg·schafts·ak·tie** *f* employee share (*pl. a.* stock *sg.*)
Be'leg|schein *m* voucher; receipt; **~sta·ti,on** *f* private wing (*allotted to a specific practitioner*); **~stel·le** *f* reference
be·legt [bə'le:kt] **I.** *p.p. of* ***belegen***; **II.** *adj.* **1.** *tongue*: coated, furred; *voice*: husky; **2.** *seat, room*: taken, occupied; full (up); **3.** *teleph.* engaged, *Am.* busy; **4.** ***~es Brot*** (open) sandwich; ***~es Brötchen*** filled roll; **5.** ~ ***sein bei*** *dat.* occur in; ***es ist nirgends*** ~ there's no evidence for it
be'leh·ren *v/t.* (h) teach, instruct; inform (***über*** *acc.* of); ***sich*** ~ ***lassen*** a) take some advice, b) listen to reason; → ***Bessere***; **be'leh·rend** *adj.* **1.** instructive; **2.** *contp.* schoolmasterly, schoolmarmish; **Be'leh·rung** *f* (-; -en) instruction; advice; *contp.* ***ständige ~en*** constant lecturing (*or* preaching)
be·leibt [bə'laipt] *adj.* stout, portly; **Be'leibt·heit** *f* (-; *no pl.*) stoutness, portliness
be·lei·di·gen [bə'laidɪgən] *v/t.* (h) offend (*a. fig. the eye, s.o.'s feelings etc.*); hurt; insult; ⚖ slander, libel; ***ich wollte dich nicht*** ~ *a.* I didn't mean any offen|ce (*Am.* -se); **be'lei·di·gend** *adj.* offensive; insulting; ⚖ slanderous, libel(l)ous; ~ ***werden*** start insulting s.o.; **be·lei·digt** [bə'laidɪçt] *adj.* offended, F miffed; ***ein ~es Gesicht machen*** look hurt (*or* offended); ***zutiefst*** ~ deeply offended, *esp. iro.* mortally wounded; F ***die ~e Leberwurst spielen*** be (*or* go off) in a huff, sulk (in a corner somewhere); **Be'lei·di·gung** *f* (-; -en) insult; ⚖ slander, libel; ***als*** ~ ***empfinden*** take offen|ce (*Am.* -se) at, consider *s.th.* an offen|ce (*Am.* -se); ***sich gegenseitig ~en an den Kopf werfen*** trade insults; **Be'lei·di·gungs·kla·ge** *f* libel suit
be·lem·mert [bə'lɛmɐt] F *adj.* **1.** sheepish; **2.** F rotten, stupid
be'le·sen *adj.* well-read; **Be'le·sen·heit** *f* (-; *no pl.*) (wide) knowledge of literature; ***ich staune über s-e*** ~ I'm amazed at how well-read he is (*or* at how much he's read)
be'leuch·ten *v/t.* (h) **1.** light (up), illuminate; **2.** *fig.* examine, take a look at; ***kritisch*** (***genauer***) ~ take a critical (closer) look at; ***von allen Seiten*** ~ examine (*or* look at) *s.th.* from every angle; **Be'leuch·ter** *m* (-s; -) lighting technician; **be'leuch·tet** *adj.* lit (up), illuminated; ***gut*** (***schlecht***) ~ well-lit (badly lit); **Be'leuch·tung** *f* (-; -en) **1.** lighting; light(s *pl.*); **2.** *fig.* investigation
Be'leuch·tungs|an·la·ge *f* lighting (system); **~kör·per** *m* light, lamp; lighting fixture
be·leum·det [bə'lɔymdət], **be·leu·mun·det** [bə'lɔymʊndət] *adj.*: ***gut*** (***schlecht***) ~ held in good (bad) repute
Bel·gier ['bɛlgĭɐ] *m* (-s; -), **Bel·gie·rin** ['bɛlgĭərɪn] *f* (-; -nen), **bel·gisch** ['bɛlgɪʃ] *adj.* Belgian
be'lich·ten *v/t. and v/i.* (h) *phot.* expose; **Be'lich·tung** *f* (-; -en) exposure
Be'lich·tungs|au·to,ma·tik *f* automatic exposure (control); **~mes·ser** *m* light meter; **~spiel·raum** *m* (exposure) latitude; **~steue·rung** *f* automatic exposure (control); **~zeit** *f* exposure (time)
be'lie·ben (h) **I.** *v/t. esp. iro.*: ~ ***zu*** *inf.* deign to *inf.*; ***Sie*** ~ ***wohl zu scherzen?*** you 'are joking, of course; **II.** *v/i.*: ***wie es Ihnen beliebt*** as you wish; ***tu ganz, was dir beliebt*** do as you like, suit yourself; *hum.* ***wie beliebt?*** what say?; **III.** ♀ *n* (-s; *no pl.*) pleasure; discretion; ***nach*** ~ at will, *a.* ***ganz nach*** ~ (just) as you like (*or* one likes *etc.*); ***es steht in Ihrem*** ~ it's (entirely) up to you (***zu*** *inf.* to *inf.*)
be·lie·big [bə'li:bɪç] **I.** *adj.* any (... you like); ***jeder ~e*** anyone; ***die Anordnung ist*** ~ they can be arranged any way (you like); **II.** *adv.* just as you like (*or* one likes *etc.*); ~ ***viele*** as many as you like; ~ ***lang*** as long as you like
be·liebt [bə'li:pt] *adj.* popular (***bei*** *dat.* with); (very much) in demand (among); ***sich bei j-m*** ~ ***machen*** (try and) get into s.o.'s good books, *contp.* F suck up to s.o.; **Be'liebt·heit** *f* (-; *no pl.*) popularity (***bei*** *dat.* among); ***sich e-r großen*** ~ ***erfreuen*** be very popular, enjoy great popularity
Be'liebt·heits|grad *m* popularity (rating); **~ska·la** *f* popularity scale
be'lief *pret. of* ***belaufen***
be'lie·fern *v/t.* (h) supply (***mit*** *dat.* with); **Be'lie·fe·rung** *f* (-; -en) supply (***von j-m mit et.*** of s.th. to s.o.)
be'ließ *pret. of* ***belassen***
Bel·la·don·na [bɛla'dɔna] *f* (-; -nen) ⚘ belladonna (*a.* ⚕), deadly nightshade
bel·len ['bɛlən] *v/t. and v/i.* (h) bark (*a. fig.*)
Bel·le·trist [bɛle'trɪst] *m* (-en; -en) writer of fiction, fiction writer; **Bel·le·tri·stik** [bɛle'trɪstɪk] *f* (-; *no pl.*) (poetry and) fiction; *n.s.* belles lettres (*sg.*); **bel·le·tri·stisch** [bɛle'trɪstɪʃ] *adj.* fiction ...; *w.s.* literary *journal etc.*; ***~e Werke*** works of (poetry and) fiction
be·lo·bi·gen [bə'lo:bɪgən] *v/t.* (h) praise, commend; **Be'lo·bi·gung** *f* (-; -en) praise, commendation
be'log *pret. of* ***belügen***
be·lo·gen [bə'lo:gən] *p.p. of* ***belügen***
be'loh·nen *v/t.* (h) reward (*a. fig.*), give *s.o.* a reward; ***mit et. belohnt werden*** get a reward of, *a. fig.* be rewarded with; **Be'loh·nung** *f* (-; -en) reward; ***als*** (*or* ***zur***) ~ as a reward (***für*** *acc.* for), in return (for); ***e-e*** ~ (***in Höhe von ...***) ***aussetzen*** offer a reward (of ...)
be'lud *pret. of* ***beladen***
be'lüf·ten *v/t.* (h) ventilate; aerate; **be'lüf·tet** *adj.*: ***gut*** (***schlecht***) ~ well-ventilated (poorly ventilated); **Be'lüf·tung** *f* (-; -en) ventilation; aeration
Be'lüf·tungs|an·la·ge *f* ventilating system; **~rohr** *n* air pipe; **~ven,til** *n* air-bleed valve
be'lü·gen (belog, belogen, h) **I.** *v/t.* lie to, tell *s.o.* a lie (*or* lies); **II.** *v/refl.*: ***sich selbst*** ~ delude o.s., deceive o.s
be·lu·sti·gen [bə'lʊstɪgən] (h) **I.** *v/t.* amuse; entertain; **II.** *v/refl.*: ***sich*** ~ a) amuse o.s., b) be amused (***über*** *acc.* by); ***sich damit*** ~ ***zu*** *inf.* amuse o.s. by *ger.*; **be'lu·sti·gend** *adj.* amusing, funny; **be·lu·stigt** [bə'lʊstɪçt] **I.** *adj.* amused; **II.** *adv.*: ~ ***schmunzeln*** smile in amusement; **Be'lu·sti·gung** *f* (-; -en) amusement; entertainment; ***zur großen*** ~ *gen.* much to the amusement of; ***zur allgemeinen*** ~ to everybody's amusement
be·mäch·ti·gen [bə'mɛçtɪgən] *v/refl.* (h): ***sich*** ~ (*gen.*) seize *s.o., a. fig.* take hold of *s.o.*; *a.* take possession of *s.th.*; usurp *power*; *fig.* ***Furcht bemächtigte sich seiner*** he was seized with fear, fear took hold of him
be'mä·keln *v/t.* (h) criticize, find fault with; **Be'mä·ke·lung** *f* (-; -en) criticism (*gen.* of), criticizing (*s.th.*)
be'ma·len (h) **I.** *v/t.* paint; **II.** *v/refl.*: F ***sich*** ~ F paint one's face, put one's face on
be·män·geln [bə'mɛŋəln] *v/t.* (h) criticize, find fault with; ***ich habe nichts zu*** ~ I have no criticisms (*or* complaints); **Be'män·ge·lung** *f* (-; -en) criticism (*gen.* of)
be·mannt [bə'mant] *adj.* manned (***mit*** *dat.* by)
be·män·teln [bə'mɛntəln] *v/t.* (h) disguise, cover up; gloss over
be'maß *pret. of* ***bemessen***
be'merk·bar *adj.* noticeable; ***sich*** ~ ***machen*** draw (*or* attract) attention to o.s., show, become apparent, make itself felt; ***die Anstrengung machte sich bei ihm*** (***allmählich***) ~ the strain began to tell on him; ***es ist kaum*** ~ you can hardly tell (*or* notice); **be'mer·ken** *v/t.* (h) **1.** notice, become aware of; *formal*: note; see; realize; ***ich bemerkte sie zu spät*** I saw her too late; ***ich habe es sehr wohl bemerkt!*** it hasn't (*or* hadn't) escaped my notice; **2.** say, remark, *formal*: note, observe; mention; ~, ***daß*** *a.* make the point that; ***einiges zu*** ~ ***haben*** have a few comments (*or* remarks) to make; ***haben Sie*** (***dazu***) ***et. zu*** ~***?*** would you like to comment?, do you have any comments to make?; ***nebenbei bemerkt*** by the way, incidentally; **be'mer·kens·wert I.** *adj.* remarkable (***wegen*** *gen.* for); noteworthy (for); **II.** *adv.*: ~ ***überzeugend*** *etc.* remarkably convincing *etc.*; **Be'mer·kung** *f* (-; -en) remark (***über*** *acc.* on, about); comment (on); *a.* note; annotation; ***~en machen über*** *acc.* remark (*or* comment) on, make remarks about, make comments on; ***was soll diese ~?*** what's that (remark) supposed to mean?
be'mes·sen (bemaß, bemessen, h) **I.** *v/t.*

calculate; time; rate; fix *price, sentence etc.*; *fig.* measure (**nach** *dat.* by); → **knapp** II; **II.** *v/refl.*: **sich ~ nach** be calculated (*or* measured) by *or* according to; **III.** *adj.* limited; → **knapp** II; **Be'mes·sung** *f* (-; -en) calculation; rating; assessment

Be'mes·sungs|grund·la·ge *f* basis for assessment; **~zeit·raum** *m* income year

be·mit·lei·den [bəˈmɪtlaɪdən] *v/t.* (h) feel sorry for, pity; **be'mit·lei·dens·wert** *adj.* pitiable, wretched; ***er ist schon ~*** you have to feel sorry for him; **Be'mit·lei·dung** *f* (-; *no pl.*) sympathy (*gen.* for); ***d-e ~ hilft mir nicht*** *a.* your feeling sorry for me doesn't help

be·mit·telt [bəˈmɪtəlt] *adj.* well-off; well-to-do

be'mo·geln F *v/t* (h).: ***j-n ~*** cheat s.o

be·moost [bəˈmoːst] *adj.*: F ***~es Haupt*** eternal student; old man, F wrinkly

be'mü·hen (h) **I.** *v/t.* trouble (**mit** *dat.* with; **um** *acc.* for); call in; **II.** *v/refl.*: **sich ~** go to a lot of trouble *or* effort (**zu** *inf.* to *inf.*), make an effort, try (hard); **sich ~ um** *acc.* try to get, court *s.o.('s favo[u]r)*; (try to) help *s.o., w.s.* look after *s.o.*; ***~ Sie sich nicht!*** don't go to any trouble; ***sich für j-n ~*** try to help s.o., *n.s.* put in a good word for s.o.; **sich ~ zu** (*dat. or* **nach** *dat.*) go all the way to; ***sich zu j-m ~*** take the trouble to go and see s.o.; **be'müht** *adj.* **1. ~ *sein zu*** *inf.* take care to *inf.*, be at pains to *inf.*, be anxious to *inf.*; **2.** labo(u)red; forced; unnatural, artificial; **Be'mü·hung** *f* (-; -en) effort(s *pl.*) (**um** *acc.* towards); trouble; ***alle s-e ~en waren umsonst*** he went to all that trouble (*or* effort) for nothing; ***danke für Ihre ~en*** thank you for (all) your help

be·mü·ßigt [bəˈmyːsɪçt] *adj.*: ***sich ~ fühlen zu*** *inf.* feel obliged (*or* duty bound) to *inf.*

be·mut·tern [bəˈmʊtɐn] *v/t.* (h) mother; *w.s. a.* nanny; **Be·mut·te·rung** [bəˈmʊtərʊŋ] *f* (-; *no pl.*) mothering; ***ich halte ihre ~ nicht mehr aus*** I can't stand her mothering me like that any more

be·nach·bart [bəˈnaxbaːɐt] *adj.* neighbo(u)ring; *fig.* related

be·nach·rich·ti·gen [bəˈnaːxrɪçtɪgən] *v/t.* (h) inform, notify (**von** *dat.* of), let *s.o.* know (about); † advise; **Be'nach·rich·ti·gung** *f* (-; -en) notification; † advice; ***e-e schriftliche ~*** written notification; ***die ~ der Betroffenen erfolgte unverzüglich*** all persons concerned were immediately notified

be·nach·tei·li·gen [bəˈnaːxtaɪlɪgən] *v/t.* (h) put *s.o.* at a disadvantage; discriminate against; **be·nach·tei·ligt** [bəˈnaːxtaɪlɪçt] *adj.* at a disadvantage, disadvantaged, underprivileged; **Be'nach·tei·lig·te** *m, f* (-n; -n) disadvantaged person; ***die ~n*** the disadvantaged, the underprivileged; **Be'nach·tei·li·gung** *f* (-; -en) **1.** discrimination (*gen.* against); **2.** handicap, disadvantage

be'nahm *pret. of* **benehmen**

be·nannt [bəˈnant] *p.p. of* **benennen**

be'nann·te *pret. of* **benennen**

be·ne·beln [bəˈneːbəln] *v/t.* (h) befuddle; make *s.o.* dop(e)y; **be'ne·belt** F *adj.* (be)fuddled; F dop(e)y; F slightly tiddly

Be·ne·dik·ti·ner [benedɪkˈtiːnɐ] *m* (-s; -) **1.** Benedictine (monk); **2.** *gastr.* Benedictine; **~or·den** *m* Benedictine order, Order of St Benedict; **~re·gel** *f* Benedictine Rule

Be·ne·fiz|kon,zert [beneˈfiːts-] *n* charity concert; **~spiel** *n* charity fixture, benefit match; **~vor·stel·lung** *f* charity performance

be'neh·men I. *v/refl.* (benahm, benommen, h) **1. *sich ~*** behave (***gegenüber*** towards); **2. *sich schlecht ~*** behave badly, misbehave; ***sich gut ~*** behave (oneself), behave well; ***er hat sich unmöglich benommen*** he was impossible, he behaved abysmally; **II.** ♀ *n* (-s; *no pl.*) **3.** behavio(u)r, conduct; (good *or* bad) manners *pl.*; ***er hat kein ~*** he has no manners, he doesn't know how to behave; **4.** *adm.* **im ~ mit** *dat.* in agreement with; ***sich mit j-m ins ~ setzen*** get in touch with s.o., confer with s.o., consult s.o.

be'nei·den *v/t.* (h) envy (***j-n um et.*** s.o. s.th.); ***sie beneidet mich um m-e neue Wohnung*** *a.* she's envious of my new flat (*Am.* apartment); ***ich beneide dich um d-e Geduld*** I envy your patience, I wish I had your patience; ***er ist nicht zu ~*** I wouldn't like to be in his shoes, he's not to be envied; ***er ist zu ~*** lucky man; **be'nei·dens·wert** *adj.* enviable

be'nen·nen *v/t.* (benannte, benannt, h) name (**nach** *dat.* after, for), call; fix *date etc.*; nominate *candidate etc.*; call (as a witness); ***neu ~*** rename; ***sie wird nach ihrer Tante benannt*** she's named (*or* called) after (*Am.* for) her aunt; **Be'nen·nung** *f* (-; -en) naming; name; nomenclature; ✝ title; ***falsche ~*** misnomer

be'net·zen *v/t.* (h) moisten; sprinkle

Ben·ga·le [bɛŋˈgaːlə] *m* (-n; -n) Bengali; **ben·ga·lisch** [bɛŋˈgaːlɪʃ] *adj.* Bengali; ***~e Beleuchtung*** Bengal lights

Ben·gel [ˈbɛŋl] *m* (-s; -) rascal, scamp

Be·nimm [bəˈnɪm] F *m* (-s; *no pl.*) manners *pl.*; ***er hat keinen ~*** he has no manners, he doesn't know how to behave (himself)

Ben·ja·min [ˈbɛnjamiːn] *fig. m* (-s; -e) *the* youngest, *the* baby

be·nom·men [bəˈnɔmən] **I.** *p.p. of* **benehmen**; **II.** *adj.* dazed, F dop(e)y; **Be'nom·men·heit** *f* (-; *no pl.*) dazed feeling, F dopiness

be·no·ten [bəˈnoːtən] *v/t.* (h) mark, *Am.* grade

be'nö·ti·gen *v/t.* (h) need; ***dringend ~*** badly need, need *s.th.* urgently, be badly in need of, be in urgent need of; **be·nö·tigt** [bəˈnøːtɪçt] *adj.* required

Be'no·tung *f* (-; -en) **1.** marking, *Am.* grading; **2.** marks *pl.*, *esp. Am.* grades *pl.*

be·num·mern [bəˈnʊmɐn] *v/t.* (h) number

be'nutz·bar *adj.* usable; passable

be'nut·zen, be'nüt·zen *v/t.* (h) use, make use of; take, go by *bus, train etc.*; → ***Gelegenheit***

Be'nut·zer *m* (-s; -) user; borrower, member, visitor; **~be·darf** *m* user needs *pl.*; **♀freund·lich** *adj.* user-friendly; **~freund·lich·keit** *f* (-; *no pl.*) user-friendliness; ⚙ *a.* ease of operation; **~kreis** *m* users *pl.*

be'nutzt, be'nützt *adj.* used; ***es ist ~*** it's been used

Be'nut·zung, Be'nüt·zung (-; *no pl.*) *f* use; **mit** (*or* **unter**) **~ von** *dat.* by using, with the aid of

Be'nut·zungs|ge·bühr *f* charge, fee; **~recht** *n* right to use, use

Ben·zin [bɛnˈtsiːn] *n* (-s; -e) *mot.* petrol, *Am.* gas(oline); lighter fuel; ⚗ benzine; **~bom·be** *f* petrol (*Am.* gasoline) bomb; **~ein·sprit·zung** *f mot.* fuel injection

Ben·zi·ner [bɛnˈtsiːnɐ] F *m* (-s; -) petrol-driven (*Am.* gasoline-driven) car

Ben'zin|feu·er·zeug *n* fuel lighter; **~fres·ser** F *m* (-s; -) *mot.* F fuel-guzzler, gas-guzzler; **~gut·schein** *m* petrol (*Am.* gas) coupon; **~ka,ni·ster** *m* jerry can

Ben'zin·ko·sten *pl.* petrol (*Am.* gas) costs, fuel costs; **~be·tei·li·gung** *f*: ***~!*** share petrol (*Am.* gas) costs

Ben'zin|lei·tung *f* fuel pipe; **~mo·tor** *m* petrol (*Am.* gasoline) engine; **~preis** *m a. pl.* cost of petrol (*Am.* gas), petrol (*Am.* gas) prices *pl.*; **~pum·pe** *f* fuel pump; **~tank** *m* petrol (*Am.* gas) tank, fuel tank; **~uhr** *f* petrol (*or* fuel) ga(u)ge, *Am.* gas (*or* fuel) gage; **~ver·brauch** *m* fuel consumption

Ben·zoe [ˈbɛntsoe] *f* (-; *no pl.*) benzoin; **~säu·re** *f* (-; *no pl.*) benzoic acid

Ben·zol [bɛnˈtsoːl] *n* (-s; -e) benzol(e)

be·ob·ach·ten [bəˈʔoːbaxtən] *v/t.* (h) **1.** watch, *a.* ⚕ *and police*: observe; scan; track; ***j-n ~ bei*** *dat.* watch s.o. *doing s.th.*; **2.** see; ***ich beobachtete, wie sie das Haus verließ*** I saw her leave (*or* leaving) the house; **3.** notice; ***ich beobachtete, wie sie immer apathischer wurde*** I noticed her getting (*or* how she got) more and more listless

Be·ob·ach·ter [bəˈʔoːbaxtɐ] *m* (-s; -) observer (*a. pol.*, ⚔ *etc.*); onlooker; **~sta·tus** *m* observer status; ***bei e-r Konferenz*** *etc.* ***~ haben*** take part in a conference *etc.* as an observer

Be'ob·ach·tung *f* (-; -en) observation; ***unter ~ stehen*** be under observation

Be'ob·ach·tungs|flug·zeug *n* observation plane; **~ga·be** *f* (-; *no pl.*) powers *pl.* of observation; ***e-e gute ~ besitzen*** be very observant; **~po·sten** *m* lookout (man); **~sa·tel,lit** *m* observation satellite; **~sta·ti,on** *f* **1.** ⚕ observation ward; **2.** tracking station; **~zeit·raum** *m* period of observation

be'or·dern *v/t.* (h) order (**nach** *dat.* [to go] to), send (to); summon (**zu** *dat.* to); send away (to)

be'packen (*sep.* -k·k-) *v/t.* (h) load (up)

be'pflan·zen *v/t.* (h) plant; ***mit Bäumen*** *etc.* **~** *a.* plant trees *etc.* on (*or* along *etc.*)

be'pfla·stern *v/t.* (h) pave

be'pin·keln F *v/t.* (h) F pee on

be'pin·seln *v/t.* (h) paint over, *a. gastr.* brush (over); ⚕ paint; ***mit Fett ~*** grease

be'quat·schen F *v/t.* (h) **1.** F thrash out; **2. *j-n ~*** talk s.o. into doing s.th., get s.o. round to s.th.

be·quem [bəˈkveːm] **I.** *adj.* **1.** comfortable; cosy, cozy; **2.** easy; cushy *job*; ***es ~ haben*** have an easy time of it; **3.** convenient (*a. fig. excuse etc.*); handy; ***fürs Einkaufen ist es sehr ~*** it's very convenient for shopping (*or* the shops); **4. *~e Lösung*** easy way out; **5.** comfort-loving, indolent, lazy; ***er ist zu ~, um zu*** *inf.* he just can't be bothered to *inf.*, he's too lazy to *inf.*; ***es sich ~ machen*** make o.s. at home, *fig.* take the easy way out; **II.** *adv.* **6. *hier sitzt man sehr ~*** this is a very comfortable armchair (*or* sofa *etc.*);

7. easily; **be·que·men** [bəˈkveːmən] *v/refl.* (h): ***sich zu e-r Antwort** etc.* ~ deign to give an answer *etc.*; ***sich dazu ~, et. zu tun*** take the trouble to do s.th.; **Beˈquem·lich·keit** *f* (-; -en) **1.** comfort, ease; **2.** *no pl.* indolence; laziness; ***et. aus ~ nicht tun*** be too lazy to do s.th.; **3.** convenience, *pl. a.* amenities

be·rannt [bəˈrant] *p.p. of* ***berennen***

be·rann·te *pret. of* ***berennen***

be·rap·pen [bəˈrapən] F *v/t.* (h) F cough up, fork out

beˈra·ten (beriet, beraten, h) **I.** *v/t.* **1.** advise *s.o.*, give *s.o.* (some) advice (***bei*** *dat.* on); ***sich ~ lassen von*** *dat.* consult *s.o.*; ***ich habe mich von ihm ~ lassen*** *a.* I asked him for his advice; ***gut (schlecht) ~ sein zu*** *inf.* be well-advised (ill-advised) to *inf.*; **2.** discuss *s.th.*; **II.** *v/i.* deliberate (***über*** *acc.* on); **III.** *v/refl.*: ***sich mit j-m ~*** consult (*or* confer) with s.o. (***über*** *acc.* on), ***über et.***: *a.* discuss s.th. with s.o.; **beˈra·tend I.** *adj.* advisory, consultative; ***in ~er Funktion*** in an advisory capacity; **II.** *adv.* in an advisory capacity, as an adviser; ***j-m ~ beistehen*** act as s.o.'s adviser

Be·ra·ter [bəˈraːtɐ] *m* (-s; -) adviser, consultant; ***enger ~*** aide; **~fir·ma** *f* firm of consultants, consulting firm; **~funk·tiˌon** *f* advisory function; **~gre·mi·um** *n* advisory body; **~ho·noˌrar** *n* consulting fee; **~po·sten** *m* consultative post; **~stab** *m* team of advisers, F think tank; **~stel·lung** *f* consultative post

be·rat·schla·gen [bəˈraːtʃlaːgən] *v/i.* → ***beraten*** II, III

Beˈra·tung *f* (-; -en) **1.** discussion; consultation; *formal*: conferral; *parl.* deliberation; ***sich zur ~ zurückziehen*** adjourn for (further) consultation; **2.** advice; **3.** advisory service; **4.** → ***Beratungsgespräch***

Beˈra·tungs|aus·schuß *m* advisory committee; **~ge·spräch** *n* consultation; **~ko·sten** *pl.* consultation fee *sg.* (*or* fees); **~orˌgan** *n* advisory body; **~stel·le** *f* advice cent|re (*Am.* -er); **~un·terˌneh·men** *n* consulting firm

beˈrau·ben *v/t.* (h) **1.** rob *s.o.* (*gen.* of); divest *s.o.* (of *a right etc.*); **2.** *fig.* deprive, rob (*gen.* of); **3.** ***sich*** *e-r Sache* ~ deprive o.s. of; **be·raubt** [bəˈraʊpt] *adj.* deprived (*gen.* of); *lit.* bereft (of); ***aller Macht*** *etc.* ~ ***sein*** *a. lit.* be shorn of all power *etc.*; **Beˈrau·bung** *f* (-; -en) robbing (*gen.* of); deprivation (of)

beˈrau·schen (h) **I.** *v/t.* make *s.o.* drunk, *a. fig. scent etc.*: intoxicate; *fig. power etc.*: go to one's head; **II.** *v/refl.*: ***sich ~*** get drunk; *fig.* ***sich ~ an*** *dat.* go into raptures over, F get high on; **beˈrau·schend I.** *adj.* intoxicating; alcoholic; *fig.* heady, intoxicating; breathtaking *beauty*; F *iro.* ***nicht gerade ~*** F nothing to shout (*or* write home) about; **II.** *adv.*: ***~ wirken*** have an intoxicating effect (***auf*** *acc.* on); **beˈrauscht** *adj.* drunk (***von*** *dat.* with); *fig. a.* heady (with)

be·re·chen·bar [bəˈrɛçənbaːɐ] *adj.* calculable; **beˈrech·nen** *v/t.* (h) calculate (*a. fig.*), F figure out; estimate (***auf*** *acc.* at); ✝ invoice, quote; ***j-m et. ~*** charge s.o. for s.th.; ***j-m zuviel ~*** *a.* overcharge s.o.; ***j-m et. mit 50 DM ~*** charge s.o. 50 marks for s.th.; *fig.* ***darauf berechnet sein zu*** *inf.* be calculated to *inf.*; **beˈrech·nend** *fig. adj.* calculating; **Beˈrech·nung** *f* (-; -en) **1.** calculation; figure(s *pl.*); estimate; ✝ charge, invoicing, debit, quotation; **2.** *no pl. fig.* calculation; ***mit ~*** with deliberation; ***bei ihr ist alles ~*** it's all a question of calculation with her

be·rech·ti·gen [bəˈrɛçtɪgən] (h) **I.** *v/t.* entitle (***zu*** to *s.th. or inf.*); authorize (to *inf.*); **II.** *v/i.*: ***zu et. ~*** entitle *s.o.* to (do) s.th., authorize *s.o.* to do s.th.; ***zu der Annahme (Hoffnung) ~, daß*** warrant the assumption (hope) that; ***zu Hoffnungen ~*** give cause for hope, be promising; **be·rech·tigt** [bəˈrɛçtɪçt] *adj.* **1.** entitled (***zu*** to *s.th. or inf.*), allowed (to *inf.*); authorized (to *inf.*); legitimate *claim etc.*; **2.** legitimate, justified, justifiable *cause, reason, demand etc.*; ***es ist vollkommen ~, wenn er fragt*** *etc.* he's perfectly justified in asking *etc.*, he has every reason to ask *etc.*; **beˈrech·tig·terˈwei·se** *adv.* rightly, (quite) legitimately; (and) rightly so; **Beˈrech·ti·gung** *f* (-; *no pl.*) right (***zu*** *inf.* to *inf.*); authorization (to *inf.*); power, authority (to *inf.*); legitimacy, justification; ***die ~ haben zu*** *inf.* have the right to *inf.*, be authorized to *inf.*; **Beˈrech·ti·gungs·schein** *m* permit

beˈre·den (h) **I.** *v/t.* **1.** talk *s.th.* over, discuss; ***ich muß mit dir et. ~*** there's s.th. I've got to talk to you about; **2.** persuade *s.o.*; ***j-n ~ zu*** *inf.* talk s.o. into *ger.*; **3.** talk (*or* gossip) about; **II.** *v/refl.*: ***sich mit j-m ~*** talk to s.o. (***über*** *acc.* about), ***über et.***: *a.* talk s.th. over with s.o., discuss s.th. with s.o.

be·red·sam [bəˈreːtzaːm] *adj.* eloquent; talkative; **Beˈred·sam·keit** *f* (-; *no pl.*) eloquence; talkativeness

be·redt [bəˈreːt] *adj.* eloquent (*a. fig. silence etc.*); **Beˈredt·heit** *f* (-; *no pl.*) eloquence

Beˈreich *m* (-[e]s; -e) **1.** area; ***militärischer ~*** military zone (*or* area); ***im ~ der Stadt*** (with)in the town; **2.** *fig.* range; field, sphere, area; *w.s.* sphere (of influence *or* action), *formal*: ambit; ***im ~ des Möglichen*** within the bounds of possibility

be·rei·chern [bəˈraɪçɐn] (h) **I.** *v/t.* enrich; expand, increase; ***e-e Bibliothek um einige wertvolle Bände ~*** add some valuable books to a library's collection; ***es hat mich sehr bereichert*** I gained (*or* learned) a lot from it; **II.** *v/refl.*: ***sich ~*** get rich (***an*** *dat.* on), *contp. a.* F line one's pockets, feather one's nest; ***sich ~ an*** *dat. a.* make money out of; ***sich ~ auf Kosten anderer*** get rich at the expense of others; **Beˈrei·che·rung** *f* (-; *no pl.*) enrichment; expansion (*gen.* of), increase (in); personal enrichment; ***zur ~*** *gen. a.* to add to; ***es war e-e große ~ für mich*** I gained (*or* learned) a lot from it

be·rei·fen [bəˈraɪfən] *v/t.* (h) *mot.* put tyres (*Am.* tires) on

be·reift [bəˈraɪft] *adj.* covered with (hoar)frost, frost-covered

Beˈrei·fung *f* (-; -en) *mot.* tyres *pl.*, *Am.* tires *pl.*

beˈrei·ni·gen *v/t.* (h) **1.** settle *argument etc.*; clear up *misunderstanding etc.*; iron out *problem, difficulties etc.*; **2.** settle *an account*; validate *securities*; adjust, correct *figures etc.*; **Beˈrei·ni·gung** *f* (-; -en) settlement; clearing up; validation; adjustment, correction

beˈrei·sen *v/t.* (h) **1.** tour, travel around (*or* through); **2.** ✝ cover, F do *district etc.*

be·reit [bəˈraɪt] *adj.* ready (***zu et.*** for s.th., ***zu*** *inf.* to *inf.*); prepared, willing (to *inf.*); ***zur Abfahrt ~*** ready to leave; ✝ ***wir sind gern ~ zu*** *inf.* we shall be pleased to *inf.*; ***zu allem ~*** game for anything, prepared to try (*or* risk) anything; ***sich ~ erklären zu*** *inf.* agree to *inf.*, volunteer to *inf.*; ***sich ~ halten*** stand by (at the ready); ***sich ~ machen*** get ready (***zu*** *dat.* for)

be·rei·ten [bəˈraɪtən] *v/t.* (h) **1.** prepare, get *s.th.* ready; make *some tea etc.*; **2.** *fig.* cause; ***j-m Kopfschmerzen*** *etc.* ~ *a.* give s.o. a headache *etc.*; → ***Empfang*** 2, ***Ende, Freude***

beˈreit|ge·stellt *adj.*: ***~e Gelder*** *etc.* available funds *etc.*, funds *etc.* provided; **~hal·ten** *v/t.* (*irr., sep.*, h, → ***halten***) have *s.th.* ready; **~le·gen** *v/t.* (*sep.*, h) lay out, get *s.th.* ready; **~lie·gen** *v/i.* (*irr., sep.*, h, → ***liegen***) be ready, be laid out (ready); **~ma·chen** *v/t.* (*sep.*, h) get *s.th.* ready, prepare *s.th.*

be·reits [bəˈraɪts] *adv.* **1.** already; ***ich habe ~ drei*** I've got three already, I've already got three; ***er schläft ~ seit zwei Stunden*** he's been asleep for two hours (already); ***~ morgen*** tomorrow (already); ***~ vor zehn Jahren hatte er es*** he already had it ten years ago; ***das gab es ~ vor 50 Jahren*** that was (already) around fifty years ago; **2.** even; ***~ fünf Tropfen können tödlich wirken*** even five drops (*or* five drops alone) can be lethal

Beˈreit·schaft *f* (-; -en) **1.** *no pl.* readiness; willingness; ***in ~ sein*** (*or* ***stehen***) → ***bereitstehen***; ***in ~ haben*** (*or* ***halten***) have *s.th.* (at the) ready; **2.** *no pl.* ⚙ standby mode; **3.** (*police*) squad

Beˈreit·schafts|arzt *m* duty doctor; **~dienst** *m* **1.** standby duty; ***~ haben*** be on standby, *doctor*: *a.* be on call; *pharmacy*: be open all night; **2.** riot squad; **~kreˌdit** *m* standby credit; **~po·liˌzei** *f* riot squad; **~ta·sche** *f phot.* camera case (*or* holdall); **~ta·ste** *f* standby button

beˈreit·ste·hen *v/i.* (*irr., sep.*, h, → ***stehen***) be ready; be available; *police etc.*: stand by, be on standby

beˈreit·stel·len *v/t.* (*sep.*, h) make available; provide, supply; allocate, earmark *funds*; ⚔ marshal; **Beˈreit·stel·lung** *f* (-; *no pl.*) supply, provision; allocation, earmarking *of funds*; ⚔ (final) assembly

Beˈrei·tung *f* (-; *no pl.*) preparation

beˈreit·wil·lig I. *adj.* willing; eager; obliging; **II.** *adv.*: ***er bot uns ~ s-e Hilfe an*** he didn't hesitate to offer his help, he obligingly offered his help; **Beˈreit·wil·lig·keit** *f* (-; *no pl.*) willingness; readiness (to oblige); ***mit großer ~*** with alacrity

beˈren·nen *v/t.* (berannte, berannt, h) storm, attack

beˈreu·en *v/t.* (h) regret (*having done*) *s.th.*; ***ich bereue gar nichts*** I have no regrets (about anything)

Berg [bɛrk] *m* (-[e]s; -e [ˈbɛrgə]) **1.** mountain; hill; ***in die ~e fahren*** drive (up in)to the mountains; ***über ~ und Tal*** over hill and dale; **2.** *fig.* ***~e von*** *dat.* F piles of, heaps of, a huge pile of, a mountain of; ***~e versetzen*** move mountains; ***j-m goldene ~e versprechen*** promise s.o. the moon; ***über den ~ sein*** be out of the wood(s), be over the worst; ***mit et. nicht hinterm ~ halten*** make no bones about s.th., not to beat about (*or* around) the bush with s.th.; ***mit et. hin-***

term ~ halten keep quiet about s.th., not to come forward with s.th.; ***über alle ~e sein*** be over the hills and far away, be miles away; ***zu ~e stehen*** *hair*: stand on end
berg·ab [bɛrk'ʔap] *adv.* downhill (*a. fig.*); *fig.* ***mit ihm geht es ~*** things are going downhill with him; → ***rapide*** II; **berg·ab·wärts** [bɛrk'ʔapvɛrts] *adv.* downhill; down the mountain
'Berg·aka·de,mie *f* mining academy
Ber·ga·mot·te [bɛrga'mɔtə] *f* (-; -n) bergamot; **Ber·ga'mott·öl** *n* bergamot oil (*or* essence)
berg·an [bɛrk'ʔan] *adv.* uphill; up the mountain
'Berg·ar·bei·ter *m* miner
berg·auf [bɛrk'ʔaʊf] *adv.* uphill; *fig.* ***es geht wieder ~*** things are looking up (***mit*** *dat.* for); **berg·auf·wärts** [bɛrk'ʔaʊfvɛrts] *adv.* uphill
'Berg·bahn *f* mountain (*or* cable) railway
'Berg·bau *m* (-[e]s; *no pl.*) mining (industry); **~in·ge·ni,eur** *m* mining engineer
'Berg·be·woh·ner *m* (-s; -) mountain dweller, *pl. a.* mountain people
ber·gen ['bɛrgən] *v/t.* (barg, geborgen, h) **1.** rescue; recover; ⚓ salvage; take in *sails*; **2.** hold, contain; involve *danger etc.*; conceal, hide
'ber·ge·ver·set·zend *adj.*: ***~er Glaube*** faith that can move mountains
'ber·ge·wei·se F *adv.*: ***~ Antworten*** *etc.* ***bekommen*** F get piles of (*or* an avalanche of) replies *etc.*
Berg|fried ['bɛrkfri:t] *m* (-[e]s; -e [-fri:də]) *hist.* keep; **~füh·rer** *m* mountain guide; **~gip·fel** *m* mountain top, summit; **~grat** *m* (mountain) ridge
ber·gig ['bɛrgɪç] *adj.* mountainous; hilly; ***e-e ~e Gegend*** *a.* mountainous (*or* hill) country
'Berg|kamm *m* (mountain) crest; **~ket·te** *f* mountain range; **2krank** *adj.*: ***~ sein*** have (*or* be suffering from) mountain sickness; **~krank·heit** *f* mountain sickness; **~kri,stall** *m* rock crystal; **~land** *n* mountainous country; **~land·schaft** *f* mountain(ous) landscape, mountain scenery
'Berg·mann *m* (-[e]s; -leute) ⚒ miner; **berg·män·nisch** ['bɛrkmɛnɪʃ] *adj.* miners' ..., mining ...
'Berg|mas,siv *n* massif; **~not** *f*: ***in ~ geraten*** get into difficulty up in the mountains; ***aus ~ retten*** rescue *s.o.* from the mountainside; **~paß** *m* mountain pass; **~pre·digt** *f bibl.* Sermon on the Mount; **~ret·tungs·dienst** *m* → ***Bergwacht***; **~rutsch** *m* landslide; **~salz** *n* rock salt; **~sat·tel** *m* saddle; **~schu·he** *pl.* mountain(eering) boots; **~see** *m* mountain lake; **~ski** *m* upper ski; **~spit·ze** *f* mountain peak, tip of a (*or* the) mountain; summit; **~sta·ti,on** *f* top terminal
'Berg·stei·gen *n* (-s; *no pl.*) mountaineering; **'Berg·stei·ger** *m* (-s; -) mountain climber, mountaineer
'Berg|stie·fel *pl.* mountain(eering) boots; **~stra·ße** *f* mountain road; **~tour** *f* mountain hike
'Berg-und-'Tal-Bahn *f* roller coaster, *Brit. a.* big dipper
'Ber·gung *f* (-; -en) **1.** rescue; **2.** recovery; ⚓ salvage
'Ber·gungs|ak·ti,on *f* **1.** rescue operation; **2.** ⚓ salvage operation; **~ar·bei·ten** *pl.* **1.** rescue work *sg.*; **2.** ⚓ salvage operation(s); **~dienst** *m* recovery (⚓ salvage) service; **~fahr·zeug** *n* **1.** rescue (✈ crash) vehicle; **2.** ⚓ salvage vessel; **~flot·te** *f* salvage fleet; **~hub·schrau·ber** *m* rescue helicopter; **~kom,man·do** *n* → ***Bergungsmannschaft***; **~ko·sten** *pl.* **1.** rescue costs; **2.** ⚓ salvage costs; **~mann·schaft** *f* **1.** rescue team; **2.** ⚓ salvage party; **~schiff** *n* salvage vessel; **~trupp** *m* → ***Bergungsmannschaft***; **~ver·such** *m* **1.** rescue attempt; **2.** ⚓ salvage attempt (*or* bid)
'Berg|volk *n* mountain tribe (*or* people [*sg.*]); **~wacht** *f* mountain rescue service (*or* team); **~wand** *f* rock face; **~wan·de·rung** *f* mountain hike; **~werk** *n* mine; **~we·sen** *n* (-s; *no pl.*) mining
Be·richt [bə'rɪçt] *m* (-[e]s; -e) report (***über*** *acc.* on); account (of); commentary; bulletin; ***~ erstatten*** (give a) report (***über*** *acc.* on; ***j-m*** to s.o.); ***nach ~en*** *gen.* according to reports by; ***~ zur Lage*** account of the situation; ***~ zur Lage der Nation*** State of the Nation message (*or* speech); **be'rich·ten** (h) **I.** *v/t.* report; tell, *formal*: relate; ***j-m et. ~*** inform s.o. of s.th., report s.th. to s.o., tell s.o. about s.th.; ***wie berichtet*** as reported; **II.** *v/i.* report (***über*** *acc.* on), give a report (on); ***ausführlich ~*** give a detailed account (***über*** *acc.* of); ***j-m über et. ~*** tell s.o. about s.th.; ***du hast mir noch gar nicht über die Party berichtet*** you haven't told me about the party yet
Be'richt·er·stat·ter [-ɛɐʃtatɐ] *m* (-s; -) **1.** reporter, (foreign) correspondent; *radio, TV*: commentator; **2.** ⚖ *etc.* referee; **Be'richt·er·stat·tung** *f* (-; *no pl.*) **1.** reporting, coverage; **2.** report; *radio, TV*: *a.* commentary
be·rich·ti·gen [bə'rɪçtɪgən] (h) **I.** *v/t.* correct; *formal*: rectify; *parl.*, ⚖ amend; ⚙ correct, adjust (*a.* ☤); *pol.* rectify; **II.** *v/refl.*: ***sich ~*** correct o.s.; **Be'rich·ti·gung** *f* (-; -en) correction; rectification; amendment; adjustment
Be'rich·ti·gungs|an·zei·ge *f* notice of error; **~kon·to** *n* ☤ suspense account; **~wert** *m* correction value
Be'richts|jahr *n* ☤ year under review; **~pe·rio·de** *f*, **~zeit·raum** *m* period under review
be'rie·chen *v/t.* (beroch, berochen, h) **1.** smell (at), sniff at; **2.** F *fig.* ***j-n*** (***sich*** *or* ***einander***) ***~*** size s.o. (one another) up, have a good look at s.o. (one another)
be'rief *pret. of* ***berufen***
be'rie·seln *v/t.* (h) **1.** irrigate, water; sprinkle; **2.** *fig.* ***mit Musik*** *etc.* ***~*** expose *s.o.* to an endless flow of music *etc.*; **Be'rie·se·lung** *f* (-; *no pl.*) **1.** irrigation; sprinkling; **2.** *fig.* constant exposure (***mit*** *dat.* to); → ***Musikberieselung***; **Be'rie·se·lungs·an·la·ge** *f* sprinkler system
be'riet *pret. of* ***beraten***
be·rit·ten [bə'rɪtən] *adj.* mounted, on horseback
Ber·li·ner[1] [bɛr'li:nɐ] **I.** *m* (-s; -), **Ber·li·ne·rin** [bɛr'li:nərɪn] *f* (-; -nen) Berliner; **II.** *adj.* (of) Berlin; *hist.* ***die ~ Mauer*** the Berlin Wall
Ber'li·ner[2] *m* (-s; -) doughnut
ber·li·nern [bɛr'li:nɐn] *v/i.* (h) speak the Berlin dialect
Bern·har·di·ner [bɛrnhar'di:nɐ] *m* (-s;-) St Bernard (dog)
Bern·stein ['bɛrnʃtaɪn] *m* (-[e]s; *no pl.*) amber; **2far·ben** *adj.* amber(-colo[u]red)
be'roch *pret. of* ***beriechen***
be·ro·chen [bə'rɔxən] *p.p. of* ***beriechen***
Ber·ser·ker [bɛr'zɛrkɐ] *m* (-s; -) **1.** madman; ***wie ein ~ toben*** go berserk; **2.** *hist.* berserk(er)
ber·sten ['bɛrstən] *v/i.* (barst, geborsten, sn) burst (*fig.* ***vor*** *dat.* with); *ice, glass etc*: crack; explode; ***zum 2 voll*** full to bursting (***von*** *dat.* with), F jampacked (with), chock-a-block (with)
be·rüch·tigt [bə'rʏçtɪçt] *adj.* notorious (***wegen*** *gen.* for); infamous
be'rücken (*sep.* -k·k-) *lit.* *v/t.* (h) enchant, bewitch; **be'rückend** *adj.* enchanting; ravishing *beauty*
be·rück·sich·ti·gen [bə'rʏkzɪçtɪgən] *v/t.* (h) consider, take into consideration; bear *s.th.* in mind, reflect *changes etc.*; allow for; take into account; ***überhaupt nicht ~*** *a.* disregard, ignore; **Be'rück·sich·ti·gung** *f* (-; *no pl.*) consideration; ***unter ~*** *gen.* considering; ***unter ~ aller Vorschriften*** subject to all regulations; ***unter ~ von Verzögerungen*** allowing for delay(s); ***ohne ~*** *gen.* regardless of
Be'ruf *m* (-[e]s; -e) job, occupation; profession; trade; business; line; career; ***e-n ~ ergreifen*** take up a career (*or* profession); ***was ist er von ~?*** what does he do (for a living)?; ***er ist Lehrer von ~*** he's a teacher (by profession); ***ich glaube, ich bin im falschen ~*** I think I'm in the wrong (kind of) job; ***~ und Haushalt*** work and the home; → ***ausüben, nachgehen*** 2
be'ru·fen (berief, berufen, h) **I.** *v/t.* **1.** ***j-n zu e-m Amt ~*** appoint s.o. to; ***j-n zum Vorsitzenden ~*** appoint s.o. chairman; ***j-n auf e-n Lehrstuhl ~*** offer s.o. a chair (at university); ***nach Berlin ~ werden*** be called to Berlin; **2.** F ***ich will es nicht ~*** touch wood, I don't want to put the kiss of death on it; **II.** *v/refl.*: ***sich ~ auf*** *acc.* cite, quote, refer to, mention *s.o.'s* name; ***sich darauf ~, daß*** plead that; ***darf ich mich auf Sie ~?*** may I mention your name (*or* quote you)?; **III.** *adj.* called; qualified, competent; ***aus ~em Munde*** from a reliable source, F straight from the horse's mouth; ***~ sein*** (***sich ~ fühlen***) ***zu*** *inf.* be (feel) competent enough *or* qualified to *inf.*, have (feel one has) a mission to *inf.*; ***ich fühlte mich*** (***nicht***) ***~ einzugreifen*** I felt called upon (I didn't feel it was for me) to intervene; ***zum Priester*** *etc.* ***~ sein*** have a calling to be a priest (*or* to the priesthood) *etc.*; ***zur Malerei*** *etc.* ***~ sein*** have a vocation for painting *etc.*; ***sich zu*** (***etwas***) ***Höherem ~ fühlen*** feel one is destined for higher things
be'ruf·lich **I.** *adj.* professional; work ...; vocational; ***~er Ärger*** *etc.* trouble *etc.* at work; ***~e Aussichten*** job (*or* career) prospects; ***~e Eignung*** suitability for a (*or* the) job *or* career; ***~er Werdegang*** career path; → ***Fortbildung***; **II.** *adv.* as far as work (*or* one's job, career, profession) is concerned; ***~ unterwegs*** away on business; ***sich ~ fortbilden*** do further (vocational) training; ***was machen Sie ~?*** what do you do (for a living)?, what's your line of work?
Be'rufs|an·fän·ger *m* first-time employee; **~aus·bil·dung** *f* vocational (*or* professional) training; **~aus·sich·ten** *pl.*

career prospects; **~be·am·te** *m* career civil servant
be'rufs·be·dingt I. *adj.* occupational, work-related, job-related; **II.** *adv.* for work (*or* professional) reasons
Be'rufs|be·ra·ter *m* careers adviser, job counsel(l)or; **~be·ra·tung** *f* careers guidance; **~be·ra·tungs·stel·le** *f* careers guidance office; **~be·zeich·nung** *f* job title (*or* designation)
be'rufs·be·zo·gen *adj.* job-related
Be'rufs|bild *n* job profile; **~chan·cen** *pl.* job (*or* career) prospects; **~er·fah·rung** *f* (work) experience; **~ethik** *f* professional ethics *pl.*; **~ethos** *n* professional ethics *pl.*; **~fach·schu·le** *f* vocational college; **~feu·er·wehr** *f* fire service (*Am.* department); **~fo·to,graf** *m* professional photographer; **~ge·heim·nis** *n* **1.** professional (*or* trade) secret; **2.** professional secrecy (*or* discretion); ***das ~ wahren*** (***verletzen***) maintain (violate) professional secrecy; **~ge·nos·sen·schaft** *f* professional (*or* trade) association; **~grup·pe** *f* professional group; **~heer** *n* professional (*or* regular) army; **~klei·dung** *f* work(ing) clothes *pl.*; **~krank·heit** *f* occupational (*or* industrial) disease; **~le·ben** *n* professional (*or* active) life; ***im ~ stehen*** work, be active in a job
be'rufs·mä·ßig I. *adj.* professional; **II.** *adv.* professionally, as a profession
Be'rufs|po,li·ti·ker *m* professional (*or* career) politician; **~rich·ter** *m* professional judge; **~ri·si·ko** *n* occupational hazard; **~schu·le** *f* vocational school; **~sol,dat** *m* regular (soldier); **~spie·ler** *m* professional (player); **~sport·ler** *m* professional (sportsman); **~stand** *m* profession, professional group; ***~ der Juristen*** legal profession
be'rufs·tä·tig *adj.* working ...; (*adm.* gainfully) employed; ***~ sein*** (go to) work, have a job; ***~e Mütter*** working mothers; ***nicht mehr ~*** no longer employed; **Be'rufs·tä·ti·ge** *m, f* (-n; -n) employed person; **Be'rufs·tä·tig·keit** *f* (-; *no pl.*) employment; job
Be'rufs,um·schu·lung *f* (-; -en) (vocational) retraining
be'rufs·un·fä·hig *adj.* unable to work; **Be'rufs·un·fä·hig·keit** *f* (-; *no pl.*) inability to work; occupational disability; **Be'rufs·un·fä·hig·keits·ren·te** *f* disability pension
Be'rufs|un·fall *m* workplace accident; **~ver·band** *m* professional association; **~ver·bot** *n* disqualification from a profession (*pol.* from public service); ⚖ (professional) disbarment; ***mit ~ belegt werden*** be disqualified from one's profession (*pol.* from public service), ⚖ be disbarred; **~ver·bre·cher** *m* professional criminal; **~ver·kehr** *m* **1.** rush-hour traffic; **2.** weekday traffic; **~wahl** *f* choosing a career, *one's* choice of career; **~wech·sel** *m* change of job (*or* profession); switching jobs (*or* professions, careers); **~ziel** *n* planned career; professional aim; **~zweig** *m* line of work
Be'ru·fung *f* (-; -en) **1.** calling, vocation (***zu et.*** for s.th., to [be] s.th.); ***die ~ zum Schriftsteller fühlen*** feel a calling to be a writer, feel (that) one's vocation is writing; **2.** *univ.* appointment; ***e-e ~ erhalten*** *a.* be offered a chair (***an*** *dat.* at); **3.** reference; ***unter ~ auf*** *acc.* with reference to; **4.** ⚖ appeal; ***in die ~ gehen, ~ einlegen*** (file an) appeal (***gegen*** *acc.* against)
Be'ru·fungs|an·trag *m* petition for appeal; **~ge·richt** *n*, **~in,stanz** *f* court of appeal, appellate court; **~klä·ge** *f* appeal; **~klä·ger** *m* appealer, party appealing; **~ver·fah·ren** *n* appeal proceedings *pl*
be'ru·hen *v/i.* (h) **1.** ***~ auf*** *dat.* be based on, be founded on; stem from, go back to; ***es beruht auf e-m Mißverständnis*** it was (all) a misunderstanding; F ***das beruht auf Gegenseitigkeit*** the feeling is mutual; **2.** ***et. auf sich ~ lassen*** let s.th. rest; ***lassen wir die Sache auf sich ~*** let's leave it at that; ***wir können das nicht auf sich ~ lassen*** we'll have to do something about it
be·ru·hi·gen [bə'ruːɪgən] (h) **I.** *v/t.* calm (down); reassure; ease *one's conscience*; calm, soothe *one's nerves*; relax; ***da bin ich*** (***aber***) ***beruhigt*** that's all right (*Am.* alright) then, that's a relief, thank goodness; ***seien Sie beruhigt!*** there's no need to worry; **II.** *v/refl.*: ***sich ~*** calm down; *situation*: quieten down; *storm, wind*: die down; *sea, waves*: calm down; **III.** *v/i.*: ***das beruhigt*** that'll calm you down (*or* relax you); **be'ru·hi·gend I.** *adj.* **1.** comforting, reassuring; **2.** relaxing; **3.** ⚕ sedative; **II.** *adv.*: ***~ wirken auf*** *acc.* have a calming (*or* relaxing) effect on; **Be'ru·hi·gung** *f* (-; *no pl.*) calming (down); reassurance; easing; soothing; calming down, stabilization; ***zur ~ der Gemüter*** to set people's minds at rest; ***zu unserer großen ~*** much to our relief; ***ich brauche etwas zur ~*** I need something to calm me down
Be'ru·hi·gungs|mit·tel *n* sedative, tranquil(l)izer; **~pil·le** *f* sedative (tablet *or* pill), tranquil(l)izer; **~sprit·ze** *f* sedative (shot), tranquil(l)izer
be·rühmt [bə'ryːmt] *adj.* famous (***wegen*** *gen.*, ***für*** *acc.* for); celebrated (for), renowned (for); F ***nicht ~*** F nothing to shout about; **be'rühmt-be'rüch·tigt** *adj.* notorious, infamous (***wegen*** *gen.* for); **Be'rühmt·heit** *f* (-; -en) **1.** *no pl.* fame, renown; ***~ erlangen*** rise to fame; ***zu trauriger ~ gelangen*** gain a doubtful reputation, achieve tragic fame; **2.** celebrity, big name
be'rüh·ren *v/t.* (h) **1.** touch; graze; ***sich*** (*or* ***einander***) ***~*** touch, *fig.* meet; ***er berührte sein Essen gar nicht*** he didn't touch his food; **2.** *fig.* touch on *subject etc.*; **3.** touch *s.o.* (to the quick), move, have an effect on *s.o.*; ***das berührt mich*** (***überhaupt***) ***nicht*** that doesn't concern me (in the slightest); ***es hat mich seltsam berührt*** it touched me in a strange way, it had a strange effect on me; ***ich war*** (***un***)***angenehm berührt*** I was pleased (I didn't like it); → ***peinlich*** 3
Be'rüh·rung *f* (-; -en) **1.** touch; contact; ***körperliche ~*** bodily (*or* physical) contact; ***in ~ kommen mit*** *dat.* come into contact with, touch; ***bei der leisesten ~*** at the slightest touch; **2.** *fig.* contact; ***in ~ bleiben*** keep in touch; ***in ~ kommen mit*** *dat.* be introduced to, come across
Be'rüh·rungs|angst *f* fear of physical contact; *fig.* ***unter ~ leiden*** be afraid of people; **~li·nie** *f* ⩤ tangent; **~punkt** *m* point of contact (*a. fig.*); ⩤ tangential point; *fig. pl.* common ground *sg.*
be'sab·bern F (h) **I.** *v/t.* dribble (*or* F slobber) all over *s.th.*; **II.** *v/refl.*: ***sich ~*** dribble, F slobber
be'sä·en *v/t.* (h) sow; → ***besät***
be'sa·gen *v/t.* (h) say; mean; ***das besagt noch gar nichts*** that doesn't mean (*or* prove) a thing; ***das besagt nicht, daß*** it doesn't mean (to say) that; ***was besagt das schon?*** what does that prove?; **besagt** [bə'zaːkt] *adj.* said, *esp.* ⚖ *the* aforementioned
be'sah *pret. of* ***besehen***
be·sa·men [bə'zaːmən] *v/t.* (h) **1.** inseminate; **2.** ⚘ pollinate; **Be'samung** *f* (-; -en) **1.** (***künstliche ~*** artificial) insemination; **2.** ⚘ pollination
be·sänf·ti·gen [bə'zɛnftɪgən] (h) **I.** *v/t.* appease; calm (down); **II.** *v/refl.*: ***sich ~*** calm down; **Be'sänf·ti·gung** *f* (-; *no pl.*) appeasement; calming (down)
be'sang *pret. of* ***besingen***
be'sann *pret. of* ***besinnen***
be'saß *pret. of* ***besitzen***
be·sät [bə'zɛːt] *adj.*: ***~ mit*** *dat.* covered (*or* strewn) with
Be'satz *m* (-es; ⸚e) trimming(s *pl.*)
Be'sat·zung *f* (-; -en) **1.** ⚔ a) occupying (*or* occupational) forces *pl.*, b) garrison; **2.** ⚓, ✈ crew
Be'sat·zungs|ar,mee *f* occupying army (*or* forces *pl.*), occupational forces *pl.*; **~macht** *f* occupying power; **~mit·glied** *n* crew member; **~re,gime** *n* occupation regime; **~streit·kräf·te** *pl.*, **~trup·pen** *pl.* occupying (*or* occupational) forces; **~zo·ne** *f* occupied zone
be'sau·fen F *v/refl.* (besoff, besoffen, h): ***sich ~*** F get plastered (*sl.* sloshed); **Be·säuf·nis** [bə'zɔʏfnɪs] F *n* (-ses; -se) F booze-up
be·säu·selt [bə'zɔʏzəlt] F *adj.* F slightly sozzled
be'schä·di·gen *v/t.* (h) damage; **Be'schä·di·gung** *f* (-; -en) **1.** damaging; **2.** *a. pl.* damage (*gen.* to)
be'schaf·fen[1] *v/t.* (h) get, *formal*: procure; F get hold of *s.th.* (***j-m*** for s.o.); find *a job, an apartment etc*
be'schaf·fen[2] *adj.*: ***gut*** (***schlecht***) ***~*** in a good (bad) state; ***wie ist die Straße ~?*** what (kind of) state is the road in?; ***so ~, daß*** made in such a way that; *fig.* ***wie ist es mit ... ~?*** what about ...?; ***die Sache ist so ~*** it's like this, the situation is this (*or* is as follows); **Be'schaf·fen·heit** *f* (-; *no pl.*) **1.** state, condition; quality; nature; structure; ***weiche*** (***rohe*** *etc.*) ***~*** softness (roughness *etc.*); **2.** (physical) constitution; (psychological) makeup
Be'schaf·fung *f* (-; *no pl.*) procurement, provision
be·schäf·ti·gen [bə'ʃɛftɪgən] (h) **I.** *v/t.* **1.** keep *s.o.* busy, occupy *s.o.*; find *s.o.* something to do; **2.** employ; give *s.o.* a job; ***wieviele Leute beschäftigt er?*** how many people has he got working for him?, how many employees has he got?; **3.** occupy, absorb; preoccupy; ***es beschäftigt mich ständig*** I can't get it out of my mind; **II.** *v/refl.*: ***sich ~ mit*** *dat.* be busy with; look after; work at (*or* on); deal with; spend (a lot of) time with; ***er beschäftigt sich nie mit den Kindern*** he never has time for the children; ***ich muß mich mal mit was anderem ~*** I must concentrate on something else for a change; **be·schäf·tigt** [bə'ʃɛftɪçt] *adj.* **1.** busy (***mit*** *dat.* with); ***damit ~ sein, et. zu tun*** be busy doing s.th. (*or* with s.th.);

mit Briefeschreiben ~ sein be busy writing letters; ***mit etwas anderem ~ sein*** be busy with (*or* doing) something else *or* other things, have something else (*or* other things) to do; **2.** ***~ sein bei*** *dat.* work for, have a job with (*or* at), be employed with (*or* at); **Be'schäf·tig·te** *m, f* (-n; -n) employee; ***Zahl der ~n*** number of persons employed; **Be'schäf·ti·gung** *f* (-; -en) **1.** something to do; activity; ***e-e*** (***keine***) ***~ haben*** have something (nothing) to do; ***das ist e-e nützliche ~*** that's something useful (to be doing); ***das ist doch keine ~ für dich*** you don't want to be doing that kind of thing; **2.** employment; job; employment; activity; ***ohne ~*** unemployed; **3.** treatment (***mit*** *dat.* of *a subject etc.*), preoccupation (with *a problem etc.*)

Be'schäf·ti·gungs·la·ge *f* employment situation

be'schäf·ti·gungs·los *adj.* unemployed, out of work

Be'schäf·ti·gungs|nach·weis *m* proof of employment; **~ni͵veau** *n* level of employment; **~po·li͵tik** *f* employment (*or* manpower) policy *or* policies *pl.*; **~po·ten·ti͵al** *n* manpower reserves *pl.*; **~pro͵gramm** *n* work scheme, job creation scheme; **~struk͵tur** *f* pattern of employment; **~the·ra͵peut** *m* occupational therapist; **~the·ra͵pie** *f* occupational therapy; **~ver·hält·nis** *n* employment; employed status; ***in was für e-m ~ stehen Sie?*** what type of employment are you in?

be'schä·men *v/t.* (h) (put to) shame; embarrass; **be'schä·mend I.** *adj.* shameful, disgraceful; ***es ist ~*** *a.* it's a disgrace; ***es ist ein ~es Gefühl*** it makes you feel ashamed; ***für j-n ~ sein*** *a.* put s.o. to shame; **II.** *adv.* shamefully; embarrassingly; **be'schämt I.** *adj.* ashamed; embarrassed; **II.** *adv.*: ***~ die Augen senken*** look down in shame (*or* with embarrassment); **Be'schä·mung** *f* (-; *no pl.*) shame; humiliation; ***zu m-r ~*** I'm ashamed to say (that)

be·schat·ten [bə'ʃatən] *v/t.* (h) **1.** shade; *fig.* overshadow, cast a shadow over (*or* on); **2.** *fig.* shadow, tail; **Be·schat·ter** [bə'ʃatɐ] *m* (-s; -) shadow; **Be'schat·tung** *fig. f* (-; *no pl.*) shadowing, tailing

be'schau·en *v/t.* (h) (have a) look at; examine; *adm.* inspect

be·schau·lich [bə'ʃaʊlɪç] *adj.* leisurely; quiet, peaceful; contemplative, meditative; ***ein ~es Dasein führen*** lead a quiet (, contemplative) life; ***~er Typ*** inward-looking person (*or* type); **Be'schau·lich·keit** *f* (-; *no pl.*) leisureliness; peace and quiet; contemplativeness; contemplation

Be·scheid [bə'ʃaɪt] *m* (-[e]s; -e [bə'ʃaɪdə]) answer, reply; notification; ***~ bekommen*** be told, be informed; ***j-m ~ geben*** let s.o. know (***über*** *acc.* about); ***~ wissen*** know, F be in the picture (***über*** *acc.* about), know about things (*or* how things work *etc.*); ***über j-n ~ wissen*** *a.* know all about s.o.; ***auf e-m Gebiet ~ wissen*** know (one's way around in) a subject; ***in e-r Sache genau ~ wissen*** know all the ins and outs of s.th.; ***weißt du mit diesem Computer ~?*** do you know how this computer works?; ***ich weiß überhaupt nicht ~*** I've no idea (how it works *etc.*); ***ich weiß überhaupt nicht mehr ~*** I don't know what's going on any more; ***er weiß dort ~*** he knows his way around there; ***Sie brauchen nur m-n Namen zu nennen, dann weiß er schon ~*** just mention my name and he'll know (*or* he'll be in the picture); ***ich weiß ~!*** *a. iro.* I know all about it; F ***j-m gehörig ~ sagen*** (*or* ***stoßen***) give s.o. a piece of one's mind

be'schei·den[1] **I.** *adj.* **1.** modest; unassuming; undemanding; simple; ***~es Auftreten*** unassuming presence; ***~e Mittel*** modest means; ***mit ~en Mitteln*** *et. aufbauen etc.*: *a.* on a shoestring; ***sie ist ein ~er Esser*** she eats very little; ***aus ~en Anfängen*** from humble (*or* small) beginnings; ***e-e ~e Frage: ...*** would it be unreasonable to ask ...; **2.** meag|re (*Am.* -er), very modest; **3.** F awful; **II.** *adv.*: ***sehr ~ leben*** get by on very little, live modestly, lead a frugal existence; ***etwas ~er leben müssen*** have to get by on less (*or* tighten one's belt)

be'schei·den[2] (beschied, beschieden, h) **I.** *v/refl.* **1.** ***sich ~*** make do with what one has got; ***sich ~ mit*** *dat.* be content (*or* satisfied) with, content o.s. with, make do with; **II.** *v/t.* **2.** ***es war ihm nicht beschieden zu*** *inf.* it wasn't given to him to *inf.*, he wasn't destined (*or* meant) to *inf.*; ***ihm war kein Erfolg*** *etc.* ***beschieden*** he wasn't destined to succeed *etc.*; ***es war ihm nicht beschieden*** it wasn't (meant) to be; **3.** *esp.* ⚖ notify, advise

Be'schei·den·heit *f* (-; *no pl.*) modesty; *s.o.'s* unassuming nature; simplicity; humbleness, lowliness; ***falsche ~*** false modesty; ***bei aller ~*** with all due modesty; ***aus lauter ~ hat er nicht gefragt*** he was too modest to ask

be'schei·nen *v/t.* (beschien, beschienen, h) shine on, light up; ***von der Sonne*** (***vom Mond***) ***beschienen*** sunlit (moonlit), bathed in sunlight (moonlight)

be·schei·ni·gen [bə'ʃaɪnɪgən] *v/t.* (h) certify; authenticate; confirm (in writing); *w.s.* confirm, vouch for *s.th.*; ***den Empfang ~*** acknowledge receipt of, give a receipt for; ***hiermit wird bescheinigt, daß*** this is to certify that; ***das muß ich mir ~ lassen*** I'll have to get that in writing; ***könnten Sie mir ~, daß*** could you give me something in writing stating that, could I have written confirmation that; ***sich gegenseitig Unfähigkeit*** *etc.* ***~*** accuse each other of incompetence *etc.*; **Be'schei·ni·gung** *f* (-; -en) (written) confirmation, statement; something in writing; certificate; receipt

be'schei·ßen *sl. v/t.* (beschiß, beschissen, h) *sl.* do (***um*** *acc.* out of), F rip off

be'schen·ken *v/t.* (h): ***j-n ~*** give s.o. a present (*or* presents), ***mit et.:*** give s.o. s.th. (as a present); ***reich ~*** shower *s.o.* with presents, ***mit Büchern*** *etc.*: shower *s.o.* with books *etc.*

be·sche·ren [bə'ʃeːrən] *v/t.* (h): ***j-m et. ~*** give s.o. s.th.; *fig.* bring s.o. s.th., bless s.o. with s.th.; ***was hat dir das Christkind beschert?*** what did Santa Claus bring you?; **Be'sche·rung** *f* (-; -en) opening of (Christmas) presents; *iro.* F ***e-e schöne ~!*** a fine mess that is, we're in a fine mess now; ***da haben wir die ~!*** that's it, there we are, what did I say?

be·scheu·ert [bə'ʃɔʏɐt] F *adj.* **1.** F cracked, *pred. a.* F nuts; ***er ist ~*** *a.* F he's gone off his nut; ***ich bin doch nicht ~!*** I'm not that stupid; **2.** stupid, F crazy *idea, plan, situation etc.*

be'schich·ten *v/t.* (h) coat; **be'schich·tet** *adj.* coated; **Be'schich·tung** *f* (-; -en) coat(ing)

be'schicken (*sep.* -k·k-) *v/t.* (h) **1.** ⚙ load, charge; **2.** a) send representatives *etc.* to, b) send exhibits *etc.* to

be·schickern [bə'ʃɪkɐn] (*sep.* -k·k) F *v/refl.* (h): ***sich ~*** F get tiddly; **be'schickert** F *adj.* F tiddly, slightly sozzled

be'schied *pret. of* **bescheiden**[2]

be·schie·den [bə'ʃiːdən] *p.p. of* **bescheiden**[2]

be'schien *pret. of* **bescheinen**

be·schie·nen [bə'ʃiːnən] *p.p. of* **bescheinen**

be'schie·ßen *v/t.* (beschoß, beschossen, h) fire at; ⚔ bombard (*a. phys. and fig.*), shell; **Be'schie·ßung** *f* (-; -en) ⚔ bombardment, shelling

be'schil·dern *v/t.* (h) **1.** signpost; mark (up) *the route*; **2.** ✝ label; **Be'schil·de·rung** *f* (-; -en) **1.** signposting; signposts *pl.*; **2.** ✝ label(l)ing

be'schimp·fen *v/t.* (h) call *s.o.* names; insult; swear at *s.o.*; ***j-n als Lügner*** *etc.* ***~*** call s.o. a liar *etc.*; **Be'schimp·fung** *f* (-; -en) *a. pl.* abuse; insult(s *pl.*)

be·schir·men [bə'ʃɪrmən] *v/t.* (h) protect; shield; **Be'schir·mung** *f* (-; *no pl.*) protection

be'schiß *pret. of* **bescheißen**

Be'schiß *sl. m* (-sses; *no pl.*) swindle, F rip-off

be·schis·sen [bə'ʃɪsən] V **I.** *p.p. of* **bescheißen**; **II.** *adj.* F lousy, rotten, *sl.* bloody awful; **III.** *adv.*: ***mir geht's ~*** F a) I feel lousy *etc.*, b) things are pretty lousy (at the moment)

be'schla·fen F *v/t.* (beschlief, beschlafen, h) sleep with

Be'schlag *m* (-[e]s; ⸚e) **1.** ⚙ (*usu. pl.*) metal fitting(s *pl.*); clasp; shoes *pl.*; **2.** *min.*, ⚒ efflorescence, bloom; film; condensation; **3.** ***in ~ nehmen*** reserve, F bag *seats etc.*; *fig.* monopolize; **be'schla·gen** (beschlug, beschlagen) **I.** *v/t.* (h) **1.** put metal fittings on *door etc.*; cover, line; stud; **2.** shoe *horse*; **3.** steam up; **II.** *v/i.* (sn) *and v/refl.* ***sich ~*** (h) *mirror etc.*: steam up; *walls*: sweat; *metal*: oxidize, tarnish; go mo(u)ldy; **III.** *adj.* **1.** steamed up *window etc.*; **2.** ***sehr ~ sein in*** *dat.* be well up in; ***wenig ~ sein in*** *dat.* know very little about, be ignorant about; **Be'schla·gen·heit** *f* (-; *no pl.*) (sound) knowledge (***in*** *dat.* of)

Be·schlag·nah·me [bə'ʃlaːknaːmə] *f* → ***Beschlagnahmung***; **be·schlag·nah·men** [bə'ʃlaːknaːmən] *v/t.* (h) seize; confiscate; *fig.* ***j-n ~*** monopolize s.o., *work etc.*: *a.* take up all of s.o.'s time; ***von et. beschlagnahmt sein*** be completely tied up with s.th.; **Be'schlag·nah·mung** *f* (-; -en) seizure; confiscation; requisition(ing); sequestration

be'schlei·chen *fig. v/t.* (beschlich, beschlichen, h) *fear etc.*: steal *or* creep over (*or* up on *s.o.*)

be·schleu·ni·gen [bə'ʃlɔʏnɪgən] (h) **I.** *v/t.* accelerate (*a. mot., phys.*); speed up; ***die Schritte ~*** quicken one's pace; ***das Tempo ~*** speed up; **II.** *v/refl.*: ***sich ~*** speed up; gather speed; *mot.* accelerate; *pulse*: go faster; **III.** *v/i. mot.* accelerate;

er beschleunigt von 0 auf 100 km/h in 10 Sekunden it goes from 0 to 60 mph in 10 seconds; **Be·schleu·ni·ger** [bəˈʃlɔynɪgɐ] *m* (-s; -) *mot., phys.* accelerator; **Beˈschleu·ni·gung** *f* (-; -en) acceleration (*a. phys.*); speeding up

Beˈschleu·ni·gungs|spur *f* acceleration lane; **~ver·mö·gen** *n mot.* acceleration

beˈschlich *pret. of* ***beschleichen***

be·schli·chen [bəˈʃlɪçən] *p.p. of* ***beschleichen***

beˈschlief *pret. of* ***beschlafen***

beˈschlie·ßen *v/t.* (beschloß, beschlossen, h) **1.** decide (***zu*** *inf.* to *inf.*); make up one's mind (to *inf.*); resolve (to *inf.*); *parl.* vote; ***e-n Antrag ~*** carry a motion, pass a resolution; **2.** end, settle; **be·schlossen** [bəˈʃlɔsən] **I.** *p.p. of* ***beschließen***; **II** *adj.* agreed, settled; ***es ist (e-e) ~e Sache, daß*** it's definite that, ***er geht:*** *a.* he's definitely going; **III.** *obs. p.p.*: ***~ sein in*** *dat.* be contained (with)in *s.th.*; ***darin liegt das ganze Dilemma ~*** that more or less sums up the dilemma

Beˈschluß *m* (-sses; ⸚sse) decision; resolution; *parl.* ***e-n ~ fassen*** pass a resolution

beˈschluß·fä·hig *adj.* quorate; ***~ sein*** constitute a quorum; **Beˈschluß·fä·hig·keit** *f* (-; *no pl.*) quorum; ***~ haben*** constitute a quorum

Beˈschluß|fas·sung *f* (-; *no pl.*) passing of a resolution; **~orˌgan** *n* decision-making body; **Ȣreif** *adj.* ready to be voted on, ready for the vote

beˈschluß·un·fä·hig *adj.* inquorate; ***die Versammlung ist ~*** there is no quorum; **Beˈschluß·un·fä·hig·keit** *f* (-; *no pl.*) absence of quorum

beˈschmie·ren (h) **I.** *v/t.* **1.** get *s.th.* dirty, smear paint *etc.* on *s.th.*; **2.** scrawl on; smear all over *a wall etc.*, smear s.th. on (*or* all over), daub *a wall etc.* with s.th.; ***e-e Mauer mit Graffiti ~*** *a.* paint (*or* spray) graffiti on a wall; **3.** ***Brot mit Butter*** *etc.* **~** put (*or* spread) butter *etc.* on bread; **4.** grease; **II.** *v/refl.*: ***sich ~*** get o.s. dirty, smear paint *etc.* on one's clothes *etc.*, get ink *etc.* all over o.s.

beˈschmut·zen *v/t.* (h) **1.** dirty, get *s.th.* dirty, soil; **2.** *fig.* soil, sully, *lit.* besmirch; → ***Nest***

beˈschnei·den *v/t.* (beschnitt, beschnitten, h) trim; prune; cut; ⚕ circumcise; *fig.* trim, cut (down); pare down, whittle down; → ***Flügel***; **Beˈschnei·dung** *f* (-; -en) trimming; pruning; cutting; ⚕ circumcision; *fig.* curtailment (*gen.* of), cutting down (on)

beˈschnüf·feln, beˈschnup·pern *v/t.* (h) sniff (at); ***sich (gegenseitig) ~*** *dogs etc.*: have a (good) sniff at each other, *fig.* size each other up, have a good look at each other; *fig.* ***alles ~*** stick one's nose into everything

be·schö·ni·gen [bəˈʃøːnɪgən] *v/t.* (h) whitewash; gloss over; palliate; **beˈschö·ni·gend I.** *adj.* palliative; *ling.* euphemistic; ***~er Ausdruck*** euphemism; **II.** *adv.* euphemistically; ***..., fügte er ~ hinzu*** he added in an attempt to gloss over the matter; **Beˈschö·ni·gung** *f* (-; -en) whitewashing; glossing over; palliation; ***ohne ~*** (quite) plainly, without mincing one's words

beˈschoß *pret. of* ***beschießen***

be·schos·sen [bəˈʃɔsən] *p.p. of* ***beschießen***

be·schrän·ken [bəˈʃrɛŋkən] (h) **I.** *v/t.* limit, restrict (***auf*** *acc.* to); curb; **II.** *v/refl.*: ***sich ~*** limit o.s., restrict o.s., confine o.s. (***auf*** *acc.* to); ***sich darauf ~ zu*** *inf.* confine o.s. to *ger.*; **beˈschränkt I.** *adj.* **1.** limited, restricted (***auf*** *acc.* to); ***~e Mittel*** limited means (*or* resources); ***in ~en Verhältnissen leben*** live in cramped (*or* confined) conditions; → ***Haftung*** 2; **2.** dense, dim; *formal*: obtuse; **3.** narrow-minded; ***~e Ansichten*** narrow(-minded) views, blinkered outlook; ***e-n ~en Horizont haben*** have very narrow horizons; **II.** *adv.*: ***~ lieferbar*** (*or* ***verfügbar***) in limited supply

be·schrankt [bəˈʃraŋkt] *adj.*: ***~er Bahnübergang*** level (*Am.* grade) crossing

Beˈschränkt·heit *f* (-; *no pl.*) **1.** limitedness; **2.** denseness, stupidity; *formal*: obtuseness; **3.** narrow-mindedness

Beˈschrän·kung *f* (-; -en) limitation, restriction (***auf*** *acc.* to); restrictive measure; restraint (*gen.* on); *pl. economic, financial etc.* restrictions, cuts

beˈschrei·ben *v/t.* (beschrieb, beschrieben, h) **1.** ✍ describe; **2.** describe; depict, portray; ***es ist nicht zu ~*** you can't describe it, it's indescribable, it's beyond description; ***et. genau ~*** describe s.th. in detail, give a detailed description of s.th.; ***könnten Sie es etwas näher ~?*** could you describe it in more detail?, could you be a bit more precise?; **3.** write on; **Beˈschrei·bung** *f* (-; -en) description; depiction, portrayal; account; ***kurze ~*** outline, ***der Ereignisse:*** *a.* rundown of events; → ***spotten***

beˈschrei·en F *v/t.* (beschrie, beschrieen, h): ***ich will es nicht ~*** touch wood, I don't want to put the kiss of death on it

beˈschrei·ten *v/t.* (beschritt, beschritten, h) walk on; *fig.* ***neue Wege ~*** tread new paths, F try a new tack; → ***Rechtsweg***

beˈschrieb *pret. of* ***beschreiben***

be·schrie·ben [bəˈʃriːbən] *p.p. of* ***beschreiben***

be·schrif·ten [bəˈʃrɪftən] *v/t.* (h) write on; address; label; caption, add a caption to; inscribe, put an inscription on; **Beˈschrif·tung** *f* (-; -en) writing, lettering; address; label, label(l)ing; caption; inscription

beˈschritt *pret. of* ***beschreiten***

be·schrit·ten [bəˈʃrɪtən] *p.p. of* ***beschreiten***

be·schul·di·gen [bəˈʃʊldɪgən] *v/t.* (h) accuse (*gen.* of); ⚖ *a.* charge (with); **Be·schul·dig·te** [bəˈʃʊldɪçtə] *m, f* (-n; -n) (supposed) culprit; *a.* ⚖ alleged offender; ⚖ *a.* accused, defendant; **Beˈschul·di·gung** *f* (-; -en) accusation; ⚖ *a.* charge

beˈschum·meln F *v/t.* (h): ***j-n ~*** F diddle s.o. (***um*** *acc.* out of), cheat

Beˈschuß *m* (-sses; *no pl.*) shelling, bombardment; ***unter ~ geraten*** come under fire (*fig. a.* attack) (***wegen*** *gen.* for); ***unter ~ stehen*** *a. fig.* be under fire (*or* attack); ***unter ~ nehmen*** fire at, *fig.* attack

beˈschüt·ten *v/t.* (h): ***mit Wasser*** *etc.* **~** pour (*or* throw) water *etc.* on; ***mit Kies*** *etc.* **~** spread gravel *etc.* on

beˈschüt·zen *v/t.* (h) protect, shield (***vor*** *dat.*, ***gegen*** *acc.* from); ***ich werde dich schon ~!*** I'll protect (*or* look after) you, I'll see that you come to no harm; **Beˈschüt·zer** *m* (-s; -) guardian; patron; *eccl.* patron (saint); F friend and protector; *euphem.* pimp; ***~ des Glaubens*** protector (*or* guardian) of the faith

beˈschwat·zen *v/t.* (h) **1.** talk *s.o.* round (***zu*** *dat.* to); ***j-n zu et. ~*** *a.* talk s.o. into (doing) s.th.; **2.** chat about

Be·schwer·de [bəˈʃveːɐdə] *f* (-; -n) **1.** complaint (***über*** *acc.* about); ⚖ appeal; grievance; ***~ führen gegen*** *acc.* lodge a complaint against (***bei*** *dat.* with); **2.** *pl.* F *aches and pains*; problems (***mit*** *dat.* with), trouble *sg.* (with); pain *sg.*; ***die ~n des Alters*** the infirmities (F aches and pains) of old age; ***~n beim Atmen (bei der Verdauung) haben*** have trouble breathing (have problems digesting *or* with one's digestion); ***m-e Beine machen mir immer noch ~n*** I'm still having problems (*or* trouble) with my legs, my legs are still causing me problems (*or* trouble); **3.** *a. pl.* discomfort, strain; ***j-m ~n machen*** cause s.o. great discomfort (*or* a lot of trouble), be a (great) strain on s.o.; **~aus·schuß** *m* grievance board (*or* committee); **~brief** *m* (letter of) complaint, written complaint; **~buch** *n* complaints book

beˈschwer·de·frei *adj.* a) free of pain; b) fully recovered; ***~ sein*** *a.* have (*or* feel) no pain; ***ich bin seit längerem ~*** I've had no problems (*or* pain) for a while now

Beˈschwer·de|füh·rer *m* complainant; **~punkt** *m* grievance, (subject of) complaint

be·schwe·ren [bəˈʃveːrən] (h) **I.** *v/refl.*: ***sich ~*** complain (***über*** *acc.* about; ***bei*** *dat.* to); ***ich möchte mich ~*** I have a complaint (to make), I'd like to make a complaint; ***du kannst dich doch überhaupt nicht ~*** you can't complain, you have no cause for complaint (*or* to complain); **II.** *v/t.* weigh(t) down; *fig.* weigh down

beˈschwer·lich *adj.* hard, arduous; troublesome, *pred.* a nuisance; inconvenient; tiring; **Beˈschwer·lich·keit** *f* (-; -en) trouble, troublesomeness; inconvenience

Be·schwer·nis [bəˈʃveːɐnɪs] *f* (-; -se) complaint, trouble; hardship

be·schwich·ti·gen [bəˈʃvɪçtɪgən] *v/t.* (h) appease (*a. pol.*); calm down; ease; set at rest, allay *anger, fear etc.*; **~d** calming, emollient; **Beˈschwich·ti·gung** *f* (-; -en) appeasement; calming down; easing; **Beˈschwich·ti·gungs·po·liˌtik** *f* policy of appeasement

beˈschwin·deln *v/t.* (h) lie to *s.o.*, tell *s.o.* a lie (*or* lies), F tell *s.o.* a fib (*or* fibs)

beˈschwin·gen *v/t.* (h) get *s.o.* going; cheer, elate; **beˈschwingt I.** *adj.* buoyant, elated; lively, lilting *tune etc.*; ***~en Schrittes*** with a spring (*or* bounce) in one's step, *lit.* with winged steps; **II.** *adv.* buoyantly, in buoyant mood; with a spring (*or* bounce) in one's step; **Beˈschwingt·heit** *f* (-; *no pl.*) buoyancy; elation, elatedness; liveliness

be·schwipst [bəˈʃvɪpst] F *adj.* F tiddly, tipsy, slightly sozzled

beˈschwö·ren *v/t.* (beschwor, beschworen, h) **1.** swear to; ***ich könnte (nicht) ~, daß*** I could(n't) swear (that); **2.** implore, beseech *s.o.*; **3.** conjure up (*spirits, a. fig. memories etc.*), invoke; exorci|ce (*a. Am.* -ze); charm *snakes*; **beˈschwö·rend I.** *adj.* imploring, beseeching *look etc.*; **II.** *adv.*: ***j-n ~ ansehen*** give s.o. an imploring look; **Be'schwö·rung** *f* (-; -en) **1.** oath; **2.** entreaty; **3.** invocation; exorcism; **Be'schwö·rungs·for·mel** *f* incantation

be·see·len [bə'ze:lən] *v/t.* (h) inspire, buoy up; bring *s.th.* to life; **be'seelt** *adj.* soulful, inspired; animate

be'se·hen *v/t.* (besah, besehen, h) (*a.* ***sich et.*** ~) (have a) look at; examine

be·sei·ti·gen [bə'zaitıgən] *v/t.* (h) move out of the way, remove; dispose of, get rid of, throw away; do away with, put an end to; redress, remedy *abuse etc.*; repair *damage etc.*; get rid of *s.o.*, F bump *s.o.* off; **Be'sei·ti·gung** *f* (-; *no pl.*) removal; disposal; redressment; repair

be·se·li·gen [bə'ze:lıgən] *v/t.* (h) make *s.o.* happy, fill *s.o.* with bliss; **be'se·li·gend** *adj.* blissful; **be·se·ligt** [bə'ze:lıçt] *adj.* blissful

Be·sen ['be:zən] *m* (-s; -) **1.** broom, brush; ***Schaufel und*** ~ brush and pan; *fig.* ***neue*** ~ ***kehren gut*** a new broom sweeps clean; F ***ich fresse e-n*** ~, ***wenn*** I'll eat my hat if; **2.** F *contp.* F old bag; **&rein** *adj.* well-swept, *pred. a.* swept clean; **~schrank** *m* broom cupboard; **~stiel** *m* broomstick; F ***steif wie ein*** ~ (as) stiff as a poker

be·ses·sen [bə'zɛsən] **I.** *p.p. of* **besitzen; II.** *adj.* **1.** obsessed (***von*** *dat.* with), possessed (by); frantic; passionate; **2.** possessed (***von*** *dat.* by); ***wie*** ~ like a maniac; **Be'ses·se·ne** *m, f* (-n; -n) maniac; **Be'ses·sen·heit** *f* (-; *no pl.*) obsession; fanatical zeal

be'set·zen *v/t.* (h) **1.** take, occupy *seat etc.*; **2.** occupy *territory etc.*; ⚔ take; **3.** occupy; block *road etc.*; ***ein Haus*** ~ squat (in a house); **4.** fill *office, post etc.*; ***mit j-m*** ~ put s.o. in *a position etc.*; **5.** *thea. etc.* cast; ***neu*** ~ recast; ***die Rollen e-s Stückes*** ~ cast a play; **6.** ♪ score (***mit*** *dat.* for); **7.** set (***mit*** *dat.* with *rubies etc.*); trim (with *lace etc.*); **8.** stock (***mit*** *dat.* with *trout etc.*), *a.* populate (with *deer*); **be'setzt** *adj.* **1.** occupied (*a.* ⚔, *pol.*); *seat*: taken; *bus etc.*: full (up); ~ ***halten*** hold *a building* occupied, occupy; ***die ~en Gebiete im Westjordanland*** the occupied territories in the West Bank; **2.** *teleph.* engaged, *Am.* busy; ***unsere Telefone sind bis 22 Uhr*** ~ our telephones will be manned (*or* the lines will be open) until 10 p.m.; **3.** ~ ***mit*** *dat. committee etc.*: made up of; **4.** ♪ ***das Orchester ist mit fünf Violinen*** ~ the orchestra has five violins, there are five violins in the orchestra; ***das Stück ist mit fünf Violinen*** ~ the piece is scored for five violins; **5.** ***mit Edelsteinen*** *etc.* ~ set with jewels *etc.*, jewel-studded *etc.*; ***mit Pailletten*** ~ sequined; ***mit Spitzen*** *etc.* ~ trimmed with lace *etc.*

Be'setzt·zei·chen *n teleph.* engaged tone (*or* signal), *esp. Am.* busy signal

Be'set·zung *f* (-; -en) **1.** occupation; **2.** occupation; squatting; **3.** filling (*gen.* of *position etc.*); **4.** members *pl.*; **5.** *sport*: entrants *pl.*; **6.** *thea.* a) cast, b) casting; **7.** ♪ instruments *pl.*; players *pl.*; ***in großer*** (*or* ***voller***) ~ ***spielen*** play with a full orchestra *or* band; ***in kleiner*** ~ ***spielen*** play with a small orchestra (*or* band, ensemble); **Be'set·zungs·li·ste** *f* cast (list)

be·sich·ti·gen [bə'zıçtıgən] *v/t.* (h) **1.** have a look at, *formal*: view; *a.* visit *sights etc.*; *a.* go round, tour; ***zu*** ~ ***sein*** be on view, be open to the public; **2.** inspect; *a.* tour, go round *a plant etc.*; **Be'sich·ti·gung** *f* (-; -en) **1.** visit (*gen.* to); *a.* tour (of *museum etc.*); look (at), *formal*: viewing (of); **2.** inspection (*gen.* of); *a.* tour (of, around *a plant etc.*)

Be'sich·ti·gungs|fahrt *f* sightseeing tour; **~zei·ten** *pl.* hours of opening

be'sie·deln *v/t.* (h) **1.** settle in; colonize; populate; **2.** settle *an area etc.*; **be'sie·delt** *adj.* settled *area etc.*; populated (***von*** *dat.* by); ***dicht*** (***dünn***) ~ densely (sparsely) populated; **Be'sie·de·lung** *f* (-; -en) settlement; colonization; *w.s.* population; **Be'sie·de·lungs·dich·te** *f* population density

be'sie·geln *v/t.* (h) **1.** seal; ***damit war ihr Schicksal besiegelt*** that sealed her fate, her fate was sealed; **2.** confirm; seal; ***mit Blut*** ~ seal in blood; ***mit Handschlag*** ~ shake hands on; **Be'sie·ge·lung** *f* (-; *no pl.*) confirmation

be'sie·gen *v/t.* (h) *a. sport, pol. etc.*: defeat, F beat; ⚔ *a.* conquer; *fig.* overcome, *lit.* conquer; **Be·sieg·te** [bə'zi:ktə] *m, f* (-n; -n) defeated person, *a. sport*: loser

be'sin·gen *v/t.* (besang, besungen, h) **1.** celebrate, sing of; sing to; **2.** *fig.* extol, sing the praises of; **3.** record (songs on *tape etc.*)

be'sin·nen *v/refl.* (besann, besonnen, h): ***sich*** ~ reflect, think; think about things, F do a bit of thinking; collect o.s.; come to one's senses; ***sich*** ~ ***auf*** *acc.* recall, remember; ***sich anders*** ~ change one's mind; ***sich e-s Besseren*** ~ think better of it; ***wenn ich mich recht besinne*** if I remember rightly; ***ohne sich lange zu*** ~ without thinking twice

be'sinn·lich *adj.* contemplative; thought-provoking *story etc.*; → **heiter-besinnlich; Be'sinn·lich·keit** *f* (-; *no pl.*) contemplativeness; contemplation

Be'sin·nung *f* (-; *no pl.*) **1.** consciousness; ***die*** ~ ***verlieren*** lose consciousness; (***wieder***) ***zur*** ~ ***kommen*** regain consciousness, come round; **2.** senses *pl.*; ***die*** ~ ***verlieren*** lose one's head; ***du bist wohl nicht bei*** ~**!** you must be out of your (F tiny little) mind; (***wieder***) ***zur*** ~ ***kommen*** come to one's senses; ***j-n*** (***wieder***) ***zur*** ~ ***bringen*** bring s.o. back to his (*or* her) senses, make s.o. listen to reason; **3.** reflection, contemplation; meditation; ***man kommt überhaupt nicht zur*** ~ you don't get time to think; **Be'sin·nungs·auf·satz** *m ped.* discursive essay

be'sin·nungs·los *adj.* **1.** ⚕ unconscious; **2.** *fig.* blind, uncontrolled, *formal*: insensate; ~ ***vor Wut*** raging (*or* blind) with fury *or* anger; ~ ***vor Angst*** out of one's mind with fear; **Be'sin·nungs·lo·sig·keit** *f* (-; *no pl.*) ⚕ unconsciousness

Be'sitz *m* (-es; *no pl.*) ownership, possession (***an*** *dat.*, ***von*** *dat.*, *gen.* of); possession(s *pl.*); property; ***privater*** ~ private(ly owned) property; ***staatlicher*** ~ state(-owned) property; ***im*** ~ ***sein von*** *dat.* be in possession of; ***im vollen*** ~ ***s-r geistigen Kräfte sein*** be in full possession of one's mental faculties; ***in*** ~ ***nehmen***, ~ ***ergreifen von*** *dat.* take possession of, *fig.* ***von j-m***: take hold of s.o.; ***in den*** ~ ***e-r Sache gelangen*** come into possession of s.th.; **~an·spruch** *m* claim for possession; **&an·zei·gend** *adj.*: *ling.* ***~es Fürwort*** possessive pronoun

be'sit·zen *v/t.* (besaß, besessen, h) have, own, *formal*: possess; have, hold, be in possession of *documents etc.*; have *talent etc.*; **be'sit·zend** *adj.*: ***die ~en Klassen*** the propertied classes; **Be·sit·zer** [bə'zıtsɐ] *m* (-s; -) owner; proprietor; holder *of documents etc.*; ***er ist stolzer*** ~ ***e-r Wohnung*** he's the proud owner of a flat (*Am.* an apartment); ***den*** ~ ***wechseln*** change hands

Be'sitz·er·grei·fung *f* (-; *no pl.*) taking possession (***von*** *dat.* of); seizure; usurpation

Be'sit·zer·stolz *m* pride of possession (*or* ownership)

Be'sitz·gier *f* acquisitiveness, (material) greed

be'sitz·los *adj.* unpropertied; dispossessed; **Be'sitz·lo·se** *m, f* (-n; -n) unpropertied (*or* dispossessed) person; ***die ~n*** the unpropertied (*or* dispossessed), F the have-nots

Be'sitz·stand *m* (-[e]s; *no pl.*) ownership; ✝ assets *pl.*

Be'sitz·tum *n* (-[e]s; -tümer [-ty:mɐ]) possession, *a. pl.* property

Be'sitz·über,tra·gung *f* transfer of property

Be'sit·zung *f* (-; -en) estate

Be'sitz·ur·kun·de *f* title deed

be·sof·fen [bə'zɔfən] F *adj.* F plastered, *sl.* stoned, sloshed; ***da muß ich*** ~ ***gewesen sein*** I must have been drunk; **Be'sof·fe·ne** F *m, f* (-n; -n) drunk; **Be'sof·fen·heit** F *f* (-; *no pl.*) drunkenness

be·soh·len [bə'zo:lən] *v/t.* (h) sole; ***neu*** ~ resole; (***neu***) ~ ***lassen*** have *shoes etc.* (re)soled

be·sol·den [bə'zɔldən] *v/t.* (h) pay; **be'sol·det** *adj.* salaried; **Be'sol·dung** *f* (-; -en) salary; ⚔ pay; **Be'sol·dungs·grup·pe** *f* salary bracket

be·son·der [bə'zɔndɐ] *adj.* special; particular, specific; very special, exceptional; separate; ***dazu brauchst du e-e ~e Ausbildung*** you need special qualifications for that; ***ein ~er Fall*** a special case; ***in diesem ~en Fall*** in this particular case; ***gibt es e-n ~en Grund?*** is there any particular reason?; ***suchst du e-n ~en Stil?*** are you looking for a particular style?; ***es ist mir e-e ~e Freude zu*** *inf.* it gives me great pleasure to *inf.*; **~e Merkmale** special features; **Be·son·de·re** [bə'zɔndərə] *n* (-n; *no pl.*): ***etwas ~s*** something special; ***nichts ~s*** nothing unusual, *a. contp.* nothing special, F no great shakes; nothing in particular; ***im &n*** in particular, above all; ***das*** ~ ***daran ist*** what is so special about it is; **Be'son·der·heit** *f* (-; -en) **1.** specific feature (*or* characteristic), peculiarity; quirk, foible; ***es ist e-e*** ~ ***von ihm*** it's one of his (little) quirks *or* foibles; ***die*** ~ ***daran war*** what was so unusual (*or* remarkable) about it was; **2.** ⚙ special feature; **be·son·ders** [bə'zɔndɐs] *adv.* **1.** particularly, in particular, (e)specially; above all; ***dieser gefällt mir*** ~ I specially (*or* particularly) like this one; **2.** particularly, (e)specially; exceptionally; ~ ***viel(e)*** (a lot) more than usual; ***es waren*** ~ ***viele Leute da*** there were a lot more people (there) than usual; **3.** specially, expressly; ~ ***erwähnen*** give special mention to; **4.** *gefällt es dir? -* ***nicht*** ~ not particularly; F ***es ist***

nicht ~ it's nothing special; F ***es geht ihm nicht*** ~ he's not too well, he's feeling a bit under the weather; **5.** separately; *treat* as a separate item

be·son·nen [bəˈzɔnən] **I.** *p.p. of* ***besinnen***; **II.** *adj.* sensible, level-headed; circumspect; prudent; calm; **Beˈson·nen·heit** *f* (-; *no pl.*) level-headedness; composure

beˈsor·gen *v/t.* (h) **1.** get (***j-m et.*** s.o. s.th.); *formal*: provide (s.o. with s.th.); F get hold of (s.th. for s.o.); ***sich et.*** ~ get (*or* buy) s.th., F borrow s.th.; ***ich habe einiges zu*** ~ I've got a bit of shopping to do; F ***ihm werd' ich's*** ~ F I'll sort him out; **2.** see to, look after; F ***wird besorgt!*** F will do!; ***die Auswahl der Stücke besorgte ...*** the pieces were chosen (*or* compiled) by ...; ***was du heute kannst*** ~, ***das verschiebe nicht auf morgen*** never put off till tomorrow what you can do today

Be·sorg·nis [bəˈzɔrknɪs] *f* (-; -se) concern, anxiety (***um*** *acc.* for; ***über*** *acc.* about, at); ~ ***erregen*** cause concern; ***es besteht kein Grund zur*** ~ there's no cause for concern, there's no need to worry; **beˈsorg·nis·er·re·gend** *adj.* worrying, alarming; ~ ***sein*** *a.* be causing (great) concern

be·sorgt [bəˈzɔrkt] *adj.* **1.** worried, concerned (***um*** *acc.*, ***wegen*** *gen.* about); **2.** ~ ***um*** *acc.* concerned for (*or* about); **3.** concerned, anxious (***zu*** *inf.* to *inf.*); **Beˈsorgt·heit** *f* (-; *no pl.*) **1.** concern, worry, worries *pl.* (***um*** *acc.*, ***wegen*** *gen.* about); **2.** concern, solicitousness (***um*** *acc.* for)

Beˈsor·gung *f* (-; -en) **1.** *no pl.* getting (hold of) (*gen.* s.th.); buying (s.th.); ***die*** ~ ***von Karten ist sehr schwierig*** *a.* it's very difficult to get hold of tickets; **2.** ~***en machen*** go shopping; ***ich muß noch ein paar*** ~***en machen*** I've still got some shopping to do (*or* a few things to buy *or* get); **3.** *no pl.* dealing with (*gen.* s.th.); management *of affairs etc.*

beˈspan·nen *v/t.* (h) **1.** (*a.* ***mit Saiten*** ~) string; ***neu*** ~ restring; **2.** cover; **3.** ***mit Pferden*** ~ hitch up; **Beˈspan·nung** *f* (-; -en) **1.** strings *pl.*; **2.** cover

be·spickt [bəˈʃpɪkt] *fig. adj.*: ~ ***mit*** *dat.* studded with, bristling with

beˈspie·geln (h) **I.** *v/refl.*: ***sich*** ~ look at o.s. in the (*or* a) mirror, *fig.* preen o.s.; **II.** *v/t.* depict, portray

beˈspiel·bar *adj.*: ***nicht*** ~ *sport*: unplayable; **beˈspie·len** *v/t.* (h) **1.** record *or* tape (s.th.) on, record; **2.** *thea.* perform in *a town* (*or on a stage etc.*); **beˈspielt** *adj.* (pre)recorded

beˈspit·zeln *v/t.* (h) spy on *s.o.*; **Beˈspit·ze·lung** *f* (-; -en) spying (*gen.* on)

beˈspöt·teln *v/t.* (h) make fun of; **Beˈspöt·te·lung** *f* (-; -en) mocking, mockery

beˈsprang *pret. of* ***bespringen***

beˈspre·chen (besprach, besprochen, h) **I.** *v/t.* **1.** discuss, talk *s.th.* over; **2.** review *book, film etc.*; **3.** record s.th. on *tape etc.*; **II.** *v/refl.*: ***sich mit j-m*** ~ discuss the matter with s.o., talk things over with s.o.; **Beˈspre·chung** *f* (-; -en) **1.** discussion; **2.** meeting, conference; ***in e-r*** ~ ***sein*** be having a meeting (*or* conference), be at a meeting; **3.** review, write-up; **Beˈspre·chungs·ex·emˌplar** *n* review copy

beˈspren·gen *v/t.* (h) sprinkle; dampen *ironing*; spray *road etc.*

beˈsprin·gen *v/t.* (besprang, besprungen, h) *zo.* cover, mount

beˈsprit·zen *v/t.* (h) splash, spatter

be·spro·chen [bəˈʃprɔxən] *p.p. of* ***besprechen***

beˈsprü·hen *v/t.* (h) spray

be·sprun·gen [bəˈʃprʊŋən] *p.p. of* ***bespringen***

beˈspucken (*sep.* -k·k-) *v/t.* (h) spit at (*or* on)

bes·ser [ˈbɛsɐ] *adj., adv.* better (***als*** than); ***ein*** ~***es Geschäft*** *etc.* a good (*or* an upmarket) shop *etc.*; ***e-e*** ~***e Tippse*** *etc.* a glorified typist *etc.*; ***in*** ~***en Kreisen verkehren*** move in high(er) circles; → ***Hälfte***; ***um so*** ~ so much the better, that's even better; *iro.* ***das wäre ja noch*** ~***!*** that would be really great; ~ ***als gar nichts*** better than nothing(, I suppose); ~ ***gesagt*** or rather; ~ ***ist*** ~ just to be on the safe side; ~ ***werden*** improve, get better; ***es*** ~ ***wissen*** know better; ***es*** ~ ***machen als j-d*** do better than s.o., go one up on s.o.; ***es geht ihm heute*** ~ he's feeling better today; ***es geht*** (***wirtschaftlich*** *etc.*) ~ things are looking up; ***du kannst es*** ~ ***als er*** you're better at it than him (*or* he is); ***er ist*** ~ ***dran als ich*** he's better off than me; ***es ist*** ~, ***wenn wir gehen, gehen wir*** ~ I think we should go, I think (*or* perhaps) we'd better go; ***du tätest*** ~ ***daran zu gehen*** *a.* you'd do well to go; → ***Ruf*** 4; **Bes·se·re** [ˈbɛsərə] *n* (-n) something better; ***j-n e-s*** ~***n belehren*** set s.o. right, *w.s.* open s.o.'s eyes; → ***besinnen***; ***ich habe*** ~***s zu tun*** I've got more important things to do; ***sie meint, sie sei etwas*** ~***s*** she thinks she's somebody special; ***e-e Wende zum*** ~***n*** a change for the better

ˈbes·ser·ge·stellt *adj.* better-off

bes·sern [ˈbɛsɐn] (h) **I.** *v/t.* improve; reform *s.o.*; **II.** *v/refl.*: ***sich*** ~ improve, get better; *meteor. a.* brighten up; *fig.* mend one's ways; ***er hat sich nicht gebessert*** he hasn't changed, he's still the same (as ever)

ˈBes·ser·stel·lung *f* (-; -en) (financial, social *etc.*) betterment

Bes·se·rung [ˈbɛsərʊŋ] *f* (-; -en) improvement; change for the better; *a.* ⚕ recovery; ***auf dem Wege der*** ~ ***sein*** be recovering, be on the road to recovery; ***gute*** ~***!*** I hope you feel better soon, *on cards*: get well soon!; → ***Weg***

Bes·ser·wis·ser [ˈbɛsɐvɪsɐ] *m* (-s; -) F know-(it-)all, smart aleck; **Bes·ser·wis·se·rei** [bɛsɐvɪsəˈraɪ] *f* (-; *no pl.*) F know-it-all attitude; ***der mit s-r*** ~ he thinks he knows it all; **bes·ser·wis·se·risch** [ˈbɛsɐvɪsərɪʃ] *adj.* F know-(it-)all ...

best [bɛst] *adj., adv.* best; ***am*** ~***en*** best; ***am*** ~***en bleibst du da*** the best thing would be for you to stay here, it would be best for you to stay here; ***im*** ~***en Falle*** at best; ***im*** ~***en Alter*** in the prime of life; ***bei*** ~***er Gesundheit*** in the best of health; ***in*** ~***em Zustand*** in perfect (*or* mint) condition; ***mit den*** ~***en Wünschen*** with all good wishes; ***es steht mit ihr nicht zum*** ~***en*** things aren't looking too good for her; ***zum*** ~***en geben*** tell; sing; ***er gab e-e Geschichte*** (***ein Lied***) ***zum*** ~***en*** *a.* he recited a little story (he gave us a little song *or* ditty); ***j-n zum*** ~***en haben*** pull s.o.'s leg, have s.o. on; ***aufs*** ~***e geregelt*** all taken care of; → ***Familie, Kraft*** 1, ***Seite, Stück, Weg, Wille(n), Wissen***

beˈstach *pret. of* ***bestechen***

beˈstahl *pret. of* ***bestehlen***

be·stal·len [bəˈʃtalən] *v/t.* (h): ***j-n*** ~ ***zu*** *dat.* appoint s.o. *judge etc.*; **Beˈstal·lung** *f* (-; -en) appointment

Beˈstand *m* (-[e]s; ¨e) **1.** *no pl.* (continued) existence; survival; duration; ***von*** ~ ***sein***, ~ ***haben*** be lasting, last; ***von kurzem*** ~ ***sein*** be short-lived; ***es ist nicht von*** ~ it won't last; **2.** *a. pl.* stock, supplies *pl.*; holdings *pl.*; *tree etc.* population; cash in hand, liquid assets *pl.*; ~ ***aufnehmen*** *a. fig.* take stock; → ***eisern***

beˈstand *pret. of* ***bestehen***

be·stan·den[1] [bəˈʃtandən] **I.** *p.p. of* ***bestehen***; **II.** *adj.*: ***nach*** ~***er Prüfung*** after passing the exam; ***j-m zur*** ~***en Prüfung gratulieren*** congratulate s.o. on passing his (*or* her) exam

beˈstan·den[2] *adj.*: ***mit Bäumen*** ~ covered in trees, tree-covered ...; lined with trees, tree-lined *avenue*

beˈstän·dig **I.** *adj.* **1.** permanent; lasting; continual, constant, incessant; continuous; **2.** steady, stable (*a.* ✝); *meteor.* settled; **3.** persevering; **4.** resistant (***gegen*** *acc.* to); fast *colo(u)r*; **II.** *adv.* constantly, continually; **Beˈstän·dig·keit** *f* (-; *no pl.*) permanence; lasting nature (*or* quality); stability; resistance (***gegen*** *acc.* to); perseverance

Beˈstands|auf·nah·me *f* (-; -n) *a. fig.* stocktaking; ~ ***machen*** take stock; ~**er·wei·te·rung** *f* expansion of a collection; ~**ka·taˌlog** *m* catalog(ue) of holdings; ~**li·ste** *f* inventory, stock list; ~**ver·zeich·nis** *n* inventory

Beˈstand·teil *m* component, part, constituent (part); element; feature; ***et. in s-e*** ~***e zerlegen*** take s.th. apart (*or* to pieces); ***sich in s-e*** ~***e auflösen*** disintegrate, F *w.s.* F fall apart

beˈstär·ken *v/t.* (h) encourage; confirm (***in*** *dat.* in); reinforce, strengthen; ***j-n in s-r Meinung*** ~ confirm s.o.'s opinion, back s.o. up; ***es hat mich in m-m Entschluß bestärkt*** it made me all the more determined, *formal*: it strengthened my resolve; **Beˈstär·kung** *f* (-; *no pl.*) encouragement; confirmation; reinforcement, strengthening

be·stä·ti·gen [bəˈʃtɛːtɪgən] (h) **I.** *v/t.* confirm; back up; bear out, corroborate; certify; ✝ acknowledge (receipt of); ***j-n im Amt*** ~ confirm s.o. in office; ***er sah sich in s-r Annahme*** (***Meinung***) ***bestätigt*** he was borne out in his assumption (his opinion was confirmed); ***ich kann das nur*** ~ I can support that fully, I couldn't agree with you more; **II.** *v/refl.*: ***sich*** ~ be confirmed, be borne out, prove (to be) correct *or* true; ***mein Verdacht hat sich nicht bestätigt*** my suspicion proved (*or* turned out) to be wrong *or* unjustified; **Beˈstä·ti·gung** *f* (-; -en) **1.** confirmation; corroboration; ***s-e*** ~ ***finden*** be confirmed (*or* borne out, corroborated) (***in*** *dat.* by); **2.** written confirmation; certificate; **Beˈstä·ti·gungs·schrei·ben** *n* letter of confirmation

be·stat·ten [bəˈʃtatən] *v/t.* (h) bury; *formal*: inter; **Beˈstat·tung** *f* (-; -en) burial; *formal*: interment

Beˈstat·tungs|in·stiˌtut *n* undertaker's; *formal*: funeral directors *pl.*; *Am.* funeral home (*or* parlor); ~**ko·sten** *pl.* funeral expenses

be'stäu·ben *v/t.* (h) **1.** dust (*a. gastr.*), spray; **2.** ♀ pollinate; **Be'stäu·bung** *f* (-; -en) **1.** dusting; **2.** ♀ pollination
be'stau·nen *v/t.* (h) look at *s.o.*, *s.th.* in amazement, gape at; marvel at
'best|aus·ge·stat·tet *adj.* best-equipped; **~be·kannt** *adj.* best-known; **~be·zahlt** *adj.* best-paid
Be·ste ['bɛstə] *n* (-n; *no pl.*) the best; ***das ~, die ~n*** *a.* F the pick of the bunch; ***sein ~s tun*** (*or* ***geben***) do one's (level) best; ***ich werde mein ~s tun*** *a.* I'll do what I can; ***das ~ herausholen*** (*or* ***draus machen***) make the best of it (*or* of a bad job)
be'ste·chen (bestach, bestochen, h) **I.** *v/t.* **1.** bribe; ***j-n ~*** *a.* F grease s.o.'s palm; ***sich ~ lassen*** take bribes, be open to bribery; **2.** *fig.* captivate (***durch*** *acc.* with); **II.** *v/i.* be impressive (*or* captivating), impress (*or* captivate) people (***durch*** *acc.* with); **be'ste·chend I.** *adj.* fascinating; ***~es Lächeln*** winning (*or* charming) smile; ***~es Angebot*** tempting offer; ***~e Leistung*** brilliant performance; **II.** *adv.*: ***~ einfach*** deceptively simple
be·stech·lich [bə'ʃtɛçlɪç] *adj.* corruptible, open to bribery; **Be'stech·lich·keit** *f* (-; *no pl.*) corruptibility
Be'ste·chung *f* (-; -en) bribery; ***aktive*** (***passive***) ~ offering (taking) of bribes *or* a bribe
Be'ste·chungs|af,fä·re *f* corruption scandal; **~geld** *n*, **~sum·me** *f* bribe (money); **~ver·such** *m* attempted bribery
Be·steck [bə'ʃtɛk] *n* (-[e]s; -e) **1.** knife, fork and spoon; *coll. or* **~e** cutlery, silverware; ***sechsteiliges ~*** six-piece set (of cutlery); **2.** (***chirurgisches ~***) surgical) instruments *pl.*; **3.** ⚓ ship's position, reckoning; ***das ~ nehmen*** take the ship's position; **~ka·sten** *m* cutlery box
be'ste·hen (bestand, bestanden, h) **I.** *v/t.* **1.** pass, F get through *an exam etc.*; stand *or* pass *the test*; ***die Prüfung*** (***Probe***) ***nicht ~*** fail the exam (test); **2.** come through, survive; **II.** *v/i.* **3.** exist, be; continue, last; remain, survive, have survived; ***es besteht*** (***bestehen***) ***...*** *a.* there is (are) ...; ***es besteht die Gefahr, daß sich das Feuer ausbreitet*** there's a danger of the fire spreading; **4.** ***~ aus*** *dat.* be made (up) of, *a. w.s.* consist of, comprise; **5.** ***~ in*** *dat.* consist in, be; ***das Problem besteht darin, daß*** (***darin zu*** *inf.*) the problem is that (is *ger.*); ***der Unterschied besteht darin, daß*** the difference is (*or* lies in the fact) that; ***die Besonderheit besteht darin, daß*** what is so special (about it) is (the fact) that; **6.** ***~ auf*** *dat.* insist (up)on; ***darauf ~, et. zu tun*** insist on doing s.th.; ***darauf ~, daß et. getan wird*** insist on s.th. being done; ***ich bestehe darauf*** (***, daß er kommt***) I insist (that he comes, *formal*: on his coming); ***ich bestehe nicht darauf*** I'm not insisting, *a.* you don't have to; **7.** stand one's ground, hold one's own (***gegen*** *acc.* against); **8.** pass, F get through; **III.** ♀ *n* (-s; *no pl.*) **9.** existence; ***seit ~ unserer Firma*** ever since our firm was founded; ***seit ~ der Regierung*** ever since the government came into power; ***das 50jährige ~ feiern*** celebrate the fiftieth anniversary *of s.th.*; **10.** (***j-s***) ***~ auf*** *dat.* (s.o.'s) insistence on; **11.** passing; **be'ste·hen·blei·ben** *v/i.* (*irr.*, *sep.*, sn, → ***bleiben***) continue (to exist); *danger etc.*: remain; remain valid, (still) hold good; **be'ste·hend** *adj.* existing; present, current; prevailing; extant
be'steh·len *v/t.* (bestahl, bestohlen, h) steal from; rob; ***bestohlen werden*** have s.th. stolen, be robbed
be'stei·gen *v/t.* (bestieg, bestiegen, h) climb (up); mount, get onto *horse, bicycle etc.*; get on *bus, train etc.*, get into *a car*, board *a ship*; ascend (to *the throne*); ***e-n Turm ~*** climb up to the top of a tower; **Be'stei·gung** *f* (-; -en) ascent; accession *to the throne*
Be'stell|block *m* order pad; **~buch** *n* ✝ order book
be'stel·len *v/t.* (h) **1.** order; book, *a. Am.* reserve *seat, room etc.*; subscribe to *a paper*; F ***wie bestellt und nicht abgeholt*** like a lost soul, F all dressed up and no place to go; **2.** (***zu sich ~***) ask *s.o.* to come (and see one), send for *s.o.*; **3.** give *s.o. a message*; ***j-m etwas ~ lassen*** send s.o. a message, pass a message on to s.o.; ***bestell ihr bitte ...*** would you tell her ...; ***bestell ihm e-n schönen Gruß von mir*** give him my regards; F ***er hat nichts zu ~*** he doesn't have much (of a) say; **4.** ⚘ cultivate; ***das Feld ~*** *a.* till the ground; → ***Haus*** 1; **5.** ⚖ appoint; ***j-n zum Vormund*** *etc.* ~ appoint s.o. guardian *etc.*; **6.** ***es ist gut*** (***schlecht***) ***um j-n*** *or* ***et. bestellt*** things are looking good (aren't looking too good) for s.o. *or* s.th.; **Be·stel·ler** [bə'ʃtɛlɐ] *m* (-s; -) customer; buyer
Be'stell·for·mu,lar *n* order form
Be'stelli·ste *f* (*sep.* -ll·l-) order list
Be'stell|kar·te *f* order card; **~num·mer** *f* order number; **~pra·xis** *f* appointments-only surgery, surgery with an appointments system; **~schein** *m* order form
Be'stel·lung *f* (-; -en) **1.** order; ***auf ~ anfertigen*** make to order; ***e-e ~ aufgeben*** place an order (***bei*** *dat.* with); **2.** booking, *Am. a.* reservation; **3.** delivery; message; **4.** ⚘ cultivation; **5.** appointment
Be'stell·zet·tel *m* order form (*or* slip)
be·sten·falls ['bɛstən'fals] *adv.* at best; at most; at the earliest
be·stens ['bɛstəns] *adv.* extremely (*or* very) well; ***ihm geht's ~*** *a.* he's fine; (***ich***) ***danke ~!*** thank you very much (indeed), *iro.* thanks but no thanks
be'steu·ern *v/t.* (h) tax; **Be'steue·rung** *f* (-; -en) taxation
'Best·form *f sport*: top condition
'best|ge·haßt F *adj.* most hated; **~ge·klei·det** *adj.* best-dressed
be·stia·lisch [bɛs'tĭa:lɪʃ] **I.** *adj.* brutal; F unbearable *heat etc.*; ***es ist e-e ~e Hitze*** *etc. a. sl.* it's hot *etc.* as hell; **II.** F *adv.* dreadfully; ***~ kalt*** *a. sl.* cold as hell; ***es tut ~ weh*** *sl.* it hurts like hell; ***es stinkt ~*** F it smells something awful, *sl.* it stinks like hell; **Be·stia·li·tät** [bɛstĭali'tɛ:t] *f* (-; -en) **1.** *no pl.* bestiality; **2.** atrocity
be'sticken (*sep.* -k·k-) *v/t.* (h) embroider
Be·stie ['bɛstĭə] *f* (-; -n) beast; *fig. a.* brute
be'stieg *pret. of* **besteigen**
be·stie·gen [bə'ʃti:gən] *p.p. of* **besteigen**
be·stimm·bar [bə'ʃtɪmba:ɐ] *adj.* determinable; **be'stim·men** *v/t. and v/i.* (h) **1.** determine, decide; fix *date, price etc.*; **2.** decide; give the orders (for); ***wer bestimmt hier?*** who gives the orders around here?; ***du hast hier nichts zu ~*** F who asked you for your opinion?; **3.** determine, control; **4.** characterize; **5.** choose; ***~ zu*** *dat.* (*or* ***für*** *acc.*) intend *s.th.* for, intend *s.o.* to be, *a.* allocate *funds* for, set *s.th.* aside for; **6.** induce (***zu*** *inf.* to *inf.*); persuade (to *inf.*); ***sich von et. ~ lassen*** (let o.s.) be influenced by s.th., *w.s.* let s.th. get the better of one; **7.** ascertain, *a.* ♣, ⚗, *phys.* determine; define; **8.** ***~ über*** *acc.* have at one's disposal; ***über sein Geld*** (***s-e Zeit***) ***~*** decide how to spend one's money (what to do with one's time); ***über s-e Angelegenheiten ~*** decide one's affairs for oneself; ***er ist alt genug, um über sich selbst zu ~*** he's old enough to look after himself (*or* to run his own life); **be'stim·mend** *adj.* determining, decisive; *ling.* determinative
be·stimmt [bə'ʃtɪmt] **I.** *adj.* **1.** certain *time, number etc.*; particular, specific *plan, intention etc.*; **2.** determined; firm, resolute; **3.** ***~ sein für*** *acc.* be meant for; ***füreinander ~ sein*** be meant for each other; **4.** ***~ sein zu*** *dat.* be destined for (*or* to be), *a.* be fated to *inf.*; ***zu Höherem ~ sein*** be destined for higher (F bigger and better) things; ***es war ihm vom Schicksal ~ zu*** *inf.* he was destined by fate to *inf.*; **5.** *ling.* ***~er Artikel*** definite article; **II.** *adv.* **6.** definitely; ***ich komme*** (***mache es***) ***ganz ~*** I'm definitely coming (I'll definitely do it, I promise I'll do it); ***machst du es auch ganz ~?*** can I rely on you to do it?, do you promise to do it?; *war er es wirklich?* - ***ganz ~*** no question about it; ***~ wissen, daß*** know for sure that; ***er kommt ~*** he's sure to come; ***ich hab's ~ nicht gemacht*** I really didn't do it; honestly, it wasn't me; **7.** probably; ***er hat ~ den Bus verpaßt*** *a.* he must have missed the bus, F I bet he missed the bus; **8.** firmly, decidedly; **Be'stimm·te** *n* (-n; *no pl.*): ***etwas ~s*** something (*or* anything) particular (*or* specific, special); **Be'stimmt·heit** *f* (-; *no pl.*) **1.** firmness; determination; force; ***mit ~*** confidently, emphatically; categorically; **2.** certainty; ***ich kann es nicht mit ~ sagen*** I can't say for certain (*or* with certainty); ***mit ~ wissen*** know for certain
Be'stim·mung *f* (-; -en) **1.** *no pl.* fixing (*gen.* of *a date etc.*); determination (of, *a. phys.*, ♣ *etc.*), decision (on); **2.** regulation, rule; **3.** *no pl.* (intended) purpose; **4.** definition; ***nähere ~*** closer definition, qualification; **5.** *ling.* qualification; ***adverbiale ~*** adverbial element; **6.** *no pl.* a) calling; b) destiny
Be'stim·mungs|bahn·hof *m* station of destination; **~flug·ha·fen** *m* airport of destination
be'stim·mungs·ge·mäß *adj. and adv.* as directed, as agreed
Be'stim·mungs|grö·ße *f* ♣, *phys.* defining quantity; **~ha·fen** *m* port of destination; **~ort** *m* destination; **~wort** *n ling.* determinative element
'Best|lei·stung *f* **1.** best performance; **2.** (*a.* ***persönliche ~***) personal best (*or* record); ***die persönliche ~ übertreffen*** beat one's personal best; **~mar·ke** *f sport*: record
'best'mög·lich *adj.* best possible; optimum
be·sto·chen [bə'ʃtɔxən] *p.p. of* **bestechen**

be'stra·fen *v/t.* (h) *a.* ⚖ punish (***wegen*** *gen.*, ***für*** *acc.* for; ***mit*** *dat.* with); ⚖ sentence (***mit*** *dat.* to); fine; ⚖ ***bestraft werden mit*** *offense etc.*: be punishable by; ***Zuwiderhandlungen werden bestraft*** violations will be prosecuted; **Be'stra·fung** *f* (-; -en) punishment; penalty

be'strah·len *v/t.* (h) shine on; light up, illuminate; *phys.* irradiate; ⚕ give *s.o.* ray treatment; **Be'strah·lung** *f* (-; -en) *phys.* irradiation; ⚕ ray treatment

Be'stre·ben *n* (-s; *no pl.*) endeavo(u)r, effort; ***es ist sein ~ zu*** *inf.* he is endeavo(u)ring to *inf.*; ***in dem ~ zu*** *inf.* in an attempt (*or* endeavo[u]r) to *inf.*, while trying to *inf.*; **be·strebt** [bə'ʃtreːpt] *pred. adj.*: ***~ sein zu*** *inf.* endeavo(u)r to *inf.*, be anxious to *inf.*; **Be'stre·bung** *f* (-; -en) endeavo(u)r, attempt, effort(s *pl.*)

be'strei·chen *v/t.* (bestrich, bestrichen, h) **1.** ***et. mit et.*** **~** spread s.th. on s.th.; ***mit Farbe*** **~** paint, give *s.th.* a coat of paint; ***mit Butter*** **~** butter; ***mit Fett*** **~** grease; ***mit Öl*** **~** oil; **2.** ***mit Gewehrfeuer*** **~** spray with machine-gun fire

be'strei·ken *v/t.* (h) go out on (*or* be on) strike against; **be'streikt** *adj.* strike-bound; affected by a strike (*or* strikes); **Be'strei·kung** *f* (-; -en) strike(s *pl.*) (*gen.* against)

be'streit·bar *adj.* open to question, contestable, disputable; **be'strei·ten** *v/t.* (bestritt, bestritten, h) **1.** contest, dispute, challenge; deny; ***es läßt sich nicht ~, daß*** there's no denying that; → ***energisch*** II; **2.** bear, pay, meet *the costs*; pay for, finance; **3.** fill *the program*; hold, carry out *contest etc.*; ***sie bestritt die Unterhaltung allein*** she did all the talking, she (more or less) monopolized the conversation; **Be'strei·tung** *f* (-; *no pl.*) **1.** challenge, contestation, disputation; **2.** payment, financing; ***zur ~ der Unkosten*** (in order) to meet the costs

be'streu·en *v/t.* (h) strew (***mit*** *dat.* with); *gastr.* dredge *or* dust *or* sprinkle (with)

be'strich *pret. of* ***bestreichen***

be·stri·chen [bə'ʃtrɪçən] *p.p. of* ***bestreichen***

be'stricken (*sep.* -k·k-) *v/t.* (h) **1.** charm, bewitch; **2.** F ***die ganze Familie ~*** knit for the whole family; **be'strickend** *adj.* charming, captivating

be'stritt *pret. of* ***bestreiten***

be·strit·ten [bə'ʃtrɪtən] *p.p. of* ***bestreiten***

Best·sel·ler ['bɛstzɛlɐ] *m* (-s; -) bestseller; **~au·tor** *m* bestselling author; **~li·ste** *f* bestseller list, list of bestsellers; **2ver·däch·tig** *adj.*: ***das Buch ist ~*** the book has the makings of a bestseller, the book looks as if it might well become a bestseller

be·stücken [bə'ʃtʏkən] (*sep.* -k·k-) *v/t.* (h) arm (with guns); *w.s.* equip (***mit*** *dat.* with); **be'stückt** *adj.* **1.** ***~ mit*** *dat.* equipped with; **2.** ✝ ***gut ~*** well-stocked; ***mit et. gut ~ sein*** *a.* have a wide range of s.th.

be·stuh·len [bə'ʃtuːlən] *v/t.* (h) put seating in, provide with seats (*or* seating); **Be'stuh·lung** *f* (-; -en) seating; seats *pl*

be'stür·men *v/t.* (h) storm; *fig.* urge, implore; bombard, assail (***mit*** *dat.* with *questions, requests etc.*)

be'stür·zen *v/t.* (h) dismay, shock, stun; **be'stürzt I.** *adj.* dismayed (***über*** *acc.* at), completely taken aback (by), shocked (by), stunned (at); ***ein ~es Gesicht machen*** look dismayed (*or* aghast); **II.** *adv.* in dismay; ***~ dastehen*** stand aghast; **Be'stür·zung** *f* (-; *no pl.*) dismay (***über*** *acc.* at); shock (at); ***große ~ auslösen*** cause great shock, shock everybody; ***ihr Tod löste große ~ aus*** *a.* everybody was shocked by her death

'Best|wert *m* optimum (value); **~zeit** *f* best (*or* record) time; ***persönliche ~*** personal record

Be·such [bə'zuːx] *m* (-[e]s; -e) **1.** visit (***bei*** *dat.*, ***in*** *dat.*, *gen.* to); call; stay; ***bei j-m auf*** (*or* ***zu***) ***~ sein*** be visiting s.o.; ***e-n ~ bei j-m machen, j-m e-n ~ abstatten*** pay s.o. a visit, go and see s.o.; ***m-e Schwester kommt zu ~*** my sister's coming to see me (*or* us); ***es ist e-n ~ wert*** it's worth seeing (*or* visiting); ***dies ist mein erster ~ in Rom*** this is my first visit (*or* trip) to Rome; ✝ ***wir danken für Ihren ~*** thank you for your custom; **2.** *no pl.*; *ped. etc.* attendance (*gen.* at); ***nach dem ~ der Universität*** after attending (*or* going to) university; **3.** *no pl.*; visitor(s *pl.*); ***wir haben ~*** we've got a visitor (*or* visitors); ***hoher ~*** a) an important guest, b) important visitors; ***sie hat immer viel ~*** she always has a lot of visitors; **be'su·chen** *v/t.* (h) **1.** go and see *s.o.*; pay *s.o.* a visit, visit; call on *s.o.*; go to *the movies etc.*; **2.** go to *school, classes etc.*; *formal*: attend; take *a course etc.*

Be'su·cher *m* (-s; -) visitor (*gen.* to); guest; *formal*: patron; **~re,kord** *m* record number of visitors, record attendance; **~rit·ze** F *f*: ***du kommst in die ~*** F you can be piggy-in-the-middle (in the double bed); **~schar** *f* crowd of visitors; **~strom** *m* stream of visitors; ***der ~ hielt den ganzen Vormittag an*** there was a steady stream of visitors throughout the morning; **~zahl** *f* number of visitors; attendance figures *pl.*; ***durchschnittliche ~*** average attendance

Be'suchs|er·laub·nis *f* **1.** permission to visit; visitor's permit; **2.** permission to receive visitors; **~recht** *n* ⚖ visiting rights *pl.*; **~tag** *m* visiting day; **~zeit** *f* visiting hours *pl.*; **~zim·mer** *n* visitors' room

be'sucht *adj.*: ***gut ~*** well-attended, much-frequented; *w.s.* popular; ***schlecht ~*** poorly attended, half-empty

be'su·deln *v/t.* (h) dirty, soil; *fig.* stain, sully, *lit.* besmirch; defile; **Be'su·de·lung** *f* (-; -en) defilement

be·sun·gen [bə'zʊŋən] *p.p. of* ***besingen***

Be·ta·blocker ['beːtablɔkɐ] (*sep.* -k·k-) *m* (-s; -) ⚕ beta blocker

be·tagt [bə'taːkt] *adj.* old, advanced in years; *lit.* aged

be'tan·ken *v/t.* (h) refuel, tank up

'Be·ta·re,zep·tor *m* ⚕ beta receptor

be'ta·sten *v/t.* (h) touch; feel, ⚕ *a.* palpate

'Be·ta|strah·len *pl.* beta rays; **~strah·lung** *f* beta radiation; **~teil·chen** *n* beta particle

be'tä·ti·gen (h) **I.** *v/t.* ⚙ operate, work; switch on, turn on; press, push *button, switch etc.*, turn; get *s.th.* going (*or* working), set *s.th.* in motion; apply *brake*; control; **II.** *v/refl.*: ***sich ~*** be active, busy o.s., work, F potter around; ***sich ~ als*** act as, work as; ***sich politisch ~*** be active (*or* involved) in politics; ***sich sportlich ~*** do sport(s); ***sich schriftstellerisch ~*** write; **Be'tä·ti·gung** *f* (-; -en) **1.** activity; work; something (*or* things) to do; job; ***körperliche ~*** physical exercise; **2.** *no pl.* ⚙ operation

Be'tä·ti·gungs|drang *m* urge to be doing something; **~feld** *n* field (of activity), sphere of activity; *s.o.'s* sphere of action, field of operation; *w.s.* outlet

be·tat·schen [bə'tatʃən] F *v/t.* (h) F paw; ***hör auf, die Schallplatten zu ~!*** get your dirty paws (*or* mitts) off those records!

be·täu·ben [bə'tɔʏbən] *v/t.* (h) deafen; stun, *a. fig.* daze; ⚕ an(a)esthetize, give *s.o.* an an(a)esthetic; deaden *nerve etc.*, kill *pain etc.*; numb, suppress *the hunger pangs*; *fig.* intoxicate; blunt, dull; stifle; ***s-n Kummer mit Alkohol ~*** drown one's sorrows (in alcohol); **be'täu·bend** *adj.* deafening *noise etc.*; intoxicating *scent etc.*; **be·täubt** [bə'tɔʏpt] *adj.*: (***wie***) **~** dazed, stunned; in a daze; **Be'täu·bung** *f* (-; -en) **1.** daze; stupor; **2.** ⚕ an(a)esthetization, (***örtliche ~*** local) anaesthetic (*Am.* anesthesia)

Be'täu·bungs·mit·tel *n* an(a)esthetic; **~ge·setz** *n* drug law

'Bet·bru·der *contp. m* F holy Joe; F Saint ...

Be·te ['beːtə] *f* (-; -n) ⚘ beet; ***rote ~*** beetroot

be·tei·li·gen [bə'taɪlɪgən] (h) **I.** *v/t.*: ***j-n ~*** give s.o. a share (***an*** *dat.* in); **II.** *v/refl.*: ***sich ~ an*** (*dat. or* ***bei*** *dat.*) take part (*or* participate) in; contribute to; cooperate in; ***beteiligt sein an*** *dat.* be involved in; have a share in (*a.* ✝); be a party to; ✝ share in *profits*; **Be·tei·lig·te** [bə'taɪlɪçtə] *m, f* (-n; -n) person concerned (*or* involved); ✝ partner; party (***an*** *dat.* to); *pl. a.* those involved; **Be'tei·li·gung** *f* (-; -en) **1.** participation (***an*** *dat.* in), involvement (in); **2.** attendance (***an*** *dat.*, ***bei*** *dat.* at); (*voter*) turnout; **3.** ✝ share, interest (***an*** *dat.* in); investment; holdings *pl.*; partnership

Be'tei·li·gungs|ge·sell·schaft *f* holding company; **~ge·winn** *m* investment earnings *pl.*; **~ka·pi,tal** *n* investment capital

Be·tel ['beːtəl] *m* (-s; *no pl.*) betel; **~nuß** *f* betel nut

be·ten ['beːtən] (h) **I.** *v/i.* pray (***um*** *acc.* for); say a prayer; say one's prayers; say grace; **II.** *v/t.*: ***das Vaterunser ~*** say the Lord's Prayer

be·teu·ern [bə'tɔʏɐn] *v/t.* (h) protest (***s-e Unschuld*** one's innocence); swear to; (solemnly) vow; **Be'teue·rung** *f* (-; -en) protestation; solemn declaration

be'tex·ten *v/t.* (h) write the words (*or* lyrics) to

be·ti·teln [bə'tiːtəln] *v/t.* (h) give a title to, name; find (*or* decide on) a title for; call, address *s.o.* as; ***wie soll man ihn ~?*** what are you supposed to call him?, how are you supposed to address him?

Be·ton [be'tɔŋ] *m* (-s; -s, -e) concrete; ***aus ~*** made of concrete, concrete ...; **~bau** *m* (-[e]s; -ten) concrete structure (*or* building); **~bau·wei·se** *f* concrete construction; **~bun·ker** *contp. m* → ***Betonklotz*** 2

be·to·nen [bə'toːnən] *v/t.* (h) **1.** *ling.*, ♪ stress; ***wie wird das Wort betont?*** how is that word stressed?, where does the stress come in that word?; ***falsch ~*** stress wrong(ly), put the wrong stress on; **2.** stress, emphasize, underline, underscore; ***besonders ~*** place particular emphasis on; ***man kann es nicht genug ~*** it can't be emphasized (strongly) enough; ***wobei ich „sauber" betone*** 'clean' being the operative word; **3.** emphasize, bring out

be·to·nie·ren [beto'ni:rən] (h) **I.** *v/t.* concrete; *fig.* firm up; **II.** *v/i. soccer*: stonewall

Be'ton|klotz *m* **1.** concrete block; **2.** *contp.* concrete pile, (concrete) box; **~kopf** F *m pol.* hardliner; **~mau·er** *f* concrete wall; **~misch·ma,schi·ne** *f* cement mixer; **~pfei·ler** *m* concrete pillar; **~si·lo** *contp. m, n* concrete pile, tower block

be·tont [bə'to:nt] **I.** *adj.* **1.** *ling.* stressed; **2.** *fig.* emphatic, deliberate; ***mit ~er Höflichkeit (Gleichgültigkeit)*** with studied politeness (unconcern); **II.** *adv.* emphatically, deliberately; ***~ einfach*** markedly simple; ***~ gleichgültig (uninteressiert*** *etc.*) a) pointedly indifferent (uninterested *etc.*), b) with pointed *or* studied indifference (with a pointed lack of interest *etc.*)

Be'to·nung *f* (-; -en) **1.** *ling.* stress, emphasis; ***die ~ liegt auf der zweiten Silbe*** the stress is on the second syllable; **2.** *fig.* emphasis, stress; ***die ~ legen auf*** *acc.* stress, emphasize, place the emphasis on; ***die ~ liegt auf*** *dat.* the emphasis is on; ***mit der ~ auf „bald"*** 'soon' being the operative word; **Be'to·nungs·zei·chen** *n ling.* stress mark; ♪ accent mark

Be'ton·wü·ste *contp. f* concrete jungle

be·tö·ren [bə'tø:rən] *v/t.* (h) beguile, turn *s.o.'s* head; **be'tö·rend** *adj.* beguiling, seductive

Be·tracht [bə'traxt] *m*: ***außer ~ lassen*** disregard, leave out of consideration; ***außer ~ bleiben*** be disregarded, be left out of consideration, not to be taken into account; ***in ~ kommen*** be a possibility (*or* consideration); ***nicht in ~ kommen*** be out of the question; ***in ~ ziehen*** take into consideration (*or* account); ***wenn man ... in ~ zieht*** considering ...

be'trach·ten *v/t.* (h) look at; *fig. a.* view; ***~ als*** look (up)on as, consider (to be); ***et. als s-e Pflicht ~*** see s.th. as one's duty, consider (*formal*: deem) s.th. one's duty; ***genau(er) betrachtet*** on closer examination (*or* inspection), strictly speaking; **Be·trach·ter** [bə'traxtɐ] *m* (-s; -) **1.** viewer; *a. fig.* observer; ***links vom Standpunkt des ~s aus*** to the left as you're facing the building *etc.*; **2.** → ***Diabetrachter***

be·trächt·lich [bə'trɛçtlıç] **I.** *adj.* considerable, substantial, siz(e)able; heavy *losses etc.*; **II.** *adv.* considerably, a great deal *faster etc.*

Be'trach·tung *f* (-; -en) viewing (*gen.* of); contemplation (of); consideration (of); ***bei näherer ~*** on closer inspection (*or* examination), on reflection; ***~en anstellen über*** *acc.* reflect on; ***in ~en versunken*** lost (*or* wrapped up) in thought; **Be'trach·tungs·wei·se** *f* (-; -n) approach (*gen.* to), view (of)

be'traf *pret. of* ***betreffen***

Be·trag [bə'tra:k] *m* (-[e]s; Beträge [bə'trɛ:gə]) amount, sum; total; figure; ***im ~ von*** *dat.* to the amount of

be'tra·gen (betrug, betragen, h) **I.** *v/t.* amount to, come to; be; **II.** *v/refl.*: ***sich ~*** behave (o.s.); ***sich anständig ~*** behave (properly *or* well); **III.** 2 *n* (-s; *no pl.*) behavio(u)r, conduct

be'trank *pret. of* ***betrinken***

be'trat *pret. of* ***betreten***[1]

be'trau·en *v/t.* (h): ***j-n ~ mit*** *dat.* entrust s.o. with; ***j-n damit ~ zu*** *inf.* entrust s.o. with (the task of) *ger.*

be'trau·ern *v/t.* (h) mourn (over)

be'träu·feln *v/t.* (h): ***~ mit*** *dat.* put a few drops of *s.th.* on; ***mit Wasser ~*** *a.* sprinkle a few drops of water on; ***mit Zitrone ~*** squeeze a few drops (*or* a bit) of lemon (juice) on

Be·treff [bə'trɛf] *m* (-[e]s; -e) ✝ reference; *letterhead*: (*Betr.*) Re; **be'tref·fen** *v/t.* (betraf, betroffen, h) **1.** concern; ***was mich betrifft*** as for me, as far as I'm concerned; ***was das betrifft*** as far as that is concerned (*or* goes), as for that; → ***betroffen*** 2; **2.** affect (deeply); → ***betroffen*** 1; **3.** *lit.* befall; ***betroffen werden von*** fall victim to, *country etc.*: be ravaged by; → ***betroffen*** 3; **be'tref·fend** *adj.* **1.** concerning, regarding; **2.** ... concerned, in question; **3.** respective; **4.** relevant; **Be'tref·fen·de** *m, f* (-n; -n) person concerned, person in question; F *the* man himself, *the* lady herself; ***die ~n*** *a.* those concerned; **be·treffs** [bə'trɛfs] *prp.* (*gen.*) as for, regarding, as far as ... is (*or* are) concerned; ✝ *a.* re

be'trei·ben (betrieb, betrieben, h) **I.** *v/t.* **1.** pursue, take part in; play, go in for *sports, politics etc.*; be involved in; ***sein Studium ~*** pursue one's studies; **2.** carry out *a trade*; **3.** run *a factory etc.*; **4.** ⚙ run, operate; **II.** 2 *n* (-s; *no pl.*): ***auf j-s ~*** at s.o.'s instigation; **Be'trei·ber** *m* (-s; -), **Be'trei·ber·fir·ma** *f* (-; -firmen) operator, operating company

be'tre·ten[1] (betrat, betreten, h) **I.** *v/t.* step (*or* walk) on; set foot on; enter, walk (*or* step, come) into, set foot in; ***die Bühne ~*** walk on stage, come (*or* walk) onto the stage; **II.** 2 *n* (-s; *no pl.*): ***~ verboten!*** a) keep off!, no trespassing!, b) no entrance

be'tre·ten[2] **I.** *adj.* embarrassed, sheepish *look, smile etc.*; ***es herrschte ~es Schweigen*** there was an awkward silence; **II.** *adv.* sheepishly; ***~ dreinschauen*** look rather sheepish; ***~ schweigen*** be too embarrassed to say anything, *formal*: maintain an embarrassed silence; **Be'tre·ten·heit** *f* (-; *no pl.*) embarrassment, (feeling of) awkwardness

be·treu·en [bə'trɔyən] *v/t.* (h) look after; see to, attend to; *sport*: coach; ✝ serve *district etc.*; be in charge of, be responsible for; ***gut betreut werden*** be well looked after; **Be·treu·er** [bə'trɔyɐ] *m* (-s; -) person in charge; someone who looks after s.o. (*or* s.th.); *sport*: doctor, physio; **Be'treu·ung** *f* (-; *no pl.*) looking after (*gen. s.o., s.th.*); ***medizinische ~*** medical care; ***soziale ~*** (social) welfare; ***mit der ~ von ... beauftragt sein*** be in charge of; ***du bist für die ~ dieser Gruppe zuständig*** you're responsible for (looking after) this group

Be·trieb [bə'tri:p] *m* (-[e]s; -e [bə'tri:bə]) **1.** business, firm, company; factory, works *pl.*; ***im ~ sein*** *a.* be at work, be at the office; ***in den ~ gehen*** *a.* go to work, go to the office; **2.** *no pl.* running, management; **3.** *no pl.* operation, running; ***in ~*** working, in operation, ⚙ *a.* running; ***außer ~*** not working, *a.* out of order; ***außer ~ setzen*** stop, switch off, put out of action; ***in ~ nehmen*** ⚙ start running, put into operation, put into service, *w.s.* open; **4.** *no pl.* activity; (hustle and) bustle; heavy traffic; ***wir hatten heute viel ~*** we were very busy today; ***hier ist immer viel ~*** there's always a lot going on around here, it's always full in here; **5.** *no pl.* F *contp.* business, F caboodle; ***bald schmeiß' ich den ganzen ~ hin*** F I'm going to chuck it all (*or* the whole business) in before long; **6.** F ***den ganzen ~ aufhalten*** hold everything up; **be'trieb·lich** *adj.* internal; company ...; ***~e Ausbildung*** in-house training; ***~e Altersversorgung*** employee pension scheme

Be'triebs·ab·lauf *m* (operational) procedure

be·trieb·sam [bə'tri:pza:m] *adj.* active, busy; bustling; **Be'trieb·sam·keit** *f* (-; *no pl.*) activity; bustle

Be'triebs|an·ge·hö·ri·ge *m, f* (-n; -n) (company) employee; *pl. a.* (company) personnel; **~an·la·ge** *f* plant; **~an·lei·tung** *f*, **~an·wei·sung** *f* operating instructions *pl.*; **~art** *f computer*: (operating) mode; **~arzt** *m* works (*or* company) doctor; **~auf·nah·me** *f* startup, putting into operation (*or* on stream); **~aus·flug** *m* (annual) office outing; **~aus·stat·tung** *f* equipment; technology

be'triebs·be·reit *adj.* operational

Be'triebs·be·sich·ti·gung *f* tour of a (*or* the) factory *or* plant

be'triebs·blind *adj.* (professionally) blinkered; ***~ sein*** *a.* be wearing professional blinkers; **Be'triebs·blind·heit** *f* professional blinkers *pl.*

be'triebs·ei·gen *adj.* company-owned, company ...

be'triebs·fä·hig *adj.* in (good) working condition

Be'triebs|fe·ri·en *pl.* company holiday *sg.*; ***~ von ... bis ...*** closed for holidays from ... till ...; ***~ haben*** be (*or* have) closed down (over the holidays); **~fest** *n* annual do, company do; office party

be'triebs·fremd *adj.* outside ..., external; ***~e Person*** outsider

Be'triebs|füh·rung *f* (business *or* works) management; **~ge·heim·nis** *n* trade secret; **~in·ge,nieur** *m* production engineer

be'triebs·in,tern **I.** *adj.* internal; in-house ..., (intra-)company ...; **II.** *adv.*: ***~ regeln*** settle *s.th.* within the company

Be'triebs|ka·pa·zi,tät *f* **1.** works capacity; **2.** operating capacity; **~ka·pi,tal** *n* working (*or* business) capital; **~kli·ma** *n* work climate, working atmosphere; **~ko·sten** *pl.* running costs; **~kran·ken·kas·se** *f* company health insurance fund; **~lei·ter** *m* (works, factory, plant) manager; **~lei·tung** *f* (works, factory, plant) management; **~netz·ge·rät** *n* operating power pack; **~nu·del** F *f the* life and soul of the department (*or* office), F resident comedian; **~ob·mann** *m* works steward; **~per·so,nal** *n* (company *or* factory) staff; **~prak·ti·kum** *n* industrial placement; *pl. a.* industrial training *sg.*; **~prü·fung** *f* (company) audit; **~psy·cho,lo·ge** *m* industrial psychologist; **~psy·cho·lo,gie** *f* industrial psychology

Be'triebs·rat *m* (-[e]s; -räte) **1.** works council; **2.** member of the works council; **Be'triebs·rats·vor·sit·zen·de** *m, f* (-n; -n) works council chairman (*or* chairperson)

Be'triebs|ren·te *f* company pension; **~schal·ter** *m* operating switch; **~schluß**

m closing hours *pl.*; ***nach*** ~ after hours, after work
be'triebs•si•cher *adj.* safe (to operate); reliable (in service); **Be'triebs•si•cher•heit** *f* (-; *no pl.*) **1.** operational safety; **2.** works security
Be'triebs|so•zio•lo,gie *f* industrial sociology; **~span•nung** *f* operating voltage; **~stille•gung** (*sep.* -ll·l-) *f* shutdown, (plant) closure; **~stö•rung** *f* stoppage; ⚙ breakdown; **~sy,stem** *n computer*: operating system; **~treue** *f* company loyalty, loyalty to the company (*or* firm); **~un•fall** *m* workplace (*or* industrial) accident; **~ver•fas•sung** *f* industrial-relations scheme; **~ver•samm•lung** *f* works meeting
Be'triebs•wirt *m* graduate in business management; MBA (= Master of Business Administration); **Be'triebs•wirt•schaft** *f* → ***Betriebswirtschaftslehre***; **be'triebs•wirt•schaft•lich** *adj.* economic; management ...; administrative; **Be'triebs•wirt•schafts•leh•re** *f* business administration *or* economics *pl.*
Be'triebs•zu•ge•hö•rig•keit *f* employment (with a company); period of employment; ***nach zehnjähriger*** ~ after ten years(' employment) with the company, after working for the company for ten years
be'trin•ken *v/refl.* (betrank, betrunken, h): ***sich*** ~ get drunk
be•trof•fen [bə'trɔfən] **I.** *p.p. of* **betreffen**; **II.** *adj.* **1.** (completely) taken aback; shocked *a. silence etc.*; *adv.* ~ ***schweigen*** be too shocked to speak; **2.** affected (***von*** *dat.* by); ***die 2en*** those concerned (*or* affected); **3.** affected (***von*** *dat.* by), hit (by); ***am schwersten*** ~ worst affected (*or* hit); ***von der Hungersnot*** (***Flutkatastrophe*** *etc.*) ~ famine-stricken (flood-stricken *etc.*); **Be'trof•fen•heit** *f* (-; *no pl.*) dismay, shock
be'trog *pret. of* **betrügen**
be•tro•gen [bə'tro:gən] **I.** *p.p. of* **betrügen**; **II.** *adj.* cheated; deceived; ***~er Ehemann*** cuckold; ***in s-n Hoffnungen ~ sein*** have had one's hopes dashed (*or* frustrated); **Be'tro•ge•ne** *m, f* (-n; -n): ***der*** (***die***) ~ ***sein*** be the dupe
be'trü•ben *v/t.* (h) sadden; grieve, distress; **be•trüb•lich** [bə'try:plıç] *adj.* sad, saddening; distressing; **be'trüb•li•cher•wei•se** *adv.* unfortunately (enough); sadly; **Be•trüb•nis** [bə'try:pnıs] *f* (-; -se) sadness; distress; ***zu unserer*** ~ (much) to our regret (*or* distress); **be•trübt** [bə'try:pt] *adj.* sad (***über*** *acc.* about, at), distressed (about, at); **Be'trübt•heit** *f* (-; *no pl.*) sadness; grief, distress
Be•trug [bə'tru:k] *m* (-[e]s; *no pl.*) fraud (*a.* ⚖), swindle; deception; ***das ist ja ~!*** that's fraud, that's a swindle; **be'trü•gen** (betrog, betrogen, h) **I.** *v/t.* cheat, swindle; ⚖ defraud; be unfaithful to, deceive, F two-time; ***j-n ~ um*** *acc.* cheat (F do) s.o. out of *s.th.*; ***in s-n Hoffnungen betrogen werden*** have (*or* see) one's hopes dashed; → **betrogen**; **II.** *v/i.* cheat; be a swindler (*or* cheat); **III.** *v/refl.*: ***sich*** ~ deceive (*or* delude) o.s.; **Be•trü•ger** [bə'try:gɐ] *m* (-s; -) swindler, cheat, fraud, F con man; **Be•trü•ge•rei** [bətry:gə'raı] *f* (-; -en) cheating; ⚖ fraud(ulence); **be'trü•ge•risch I.** *adj.* deceitful; ⚖ fraudulent; ⚖ ***in ~er Absicht*** with intent to defraud; ***durch ~e Mittel*** by fraudulent means; **II.** *adv.* fraudulently, by fraud
be'trug *pret. of* **betragen**
be•trun•ken [bə'trʊŋkən] **I.** *p.p. of* **betrinken**; **II.** *adj.* drunk; drunken *driver etc.*; *formal*: intoxicated, inebriated; ⚖ ***in ~em Zustand*** under the influence of alcohol; **II.** *adv.* drunk, in a drunken state, in a state of drunkenness; **Be'trun•ke•ne** *m, f* (-n; -n) drunk; **Be'trun•ken•heit** *f* (-; *no pl.*) drunkenness
Bet•schwe•ster ['be:t-] *contp. f* F churchy type, pious Annie; F Saint ...
Bett [bɛt] *n* (-[e]s; -en) bed (*a. geol.*); duvet; ***im*** ~ in bed; ***ins ~ gehen*** go to bed, F turn in; ***j-n zu ~ bringen*** put s.o. to bed; ***ab ins ~!*** off to bed (with you)!; ***ich komme*** (***or finde***) ***morgens nicht aus dem*** ~ I can't get up (*or* get out of bed) in the mornings; ***das ~ hüten*** (***müssen***) be laid up (***wegen*** *gen.* with), be bedridden (with, by); ***die ~en lüften*** air the bedclothes; F ***mit j-m ins ~ gehen*** F go to bed with s.o.; *fig.* ***sich ins gemachte ~ legen*** climb into a feathered nest; → ***finden*** III; **~be•zug** *m* duvet cover; **~couch** *f* bed-settee; **~decke** (*sep.* -k·k-) *f* blanket; quilt; bedspread
bet•tel•arm ['bɛtəlˀarm] *adj.* desperately poor, poverty-stricken; **Bet•te•lei** [bɛtə'laı] *f* (-; -en) **1.** begging; **2.** F pleading; **'Bet•tel•mönch** *m* mendicant (friar); **bet•teln** ['bɛtəln] *v/i.* (h) **1.** beg (***um*** *acc.* for); ~ ***gehen*** go begging; **2.** beg (***um*** *acc.* for); ***er bettelte so lange, bis ich ja sagte*** he pestered me (*or* went on at me) until I said yes; ***sie bettelten, daß sie reindurften*** they begged me *etc.* to let them in; **'Bet•tel•or•den** *m* mendicant order; **'Bet•tel•stab** *m*: ***j-n an den ~ bringen*** reduce s.o. to poverty (*or* beggary, penury)
bet•ten ['bɛtən] (h) **I.** *v/t.* bed; lay (down), bed down; *fig.* ***j-n in Watte*** ~ wrap (*or* keep) s.o. in cotton wool; ***j-n zur letzten Ruhe*** ~ lay s.o. to rest; **II.** *v/refl.*: ***wie man sich bettet, so liegt man*** as you make your bed, so you must lie in it; he's made his bed, let him lie in it; you've made your bed, now lie in it
'Bet•ten|ma•chen *n* (-s; *no pl.*) making (the) beds; ***beim ~ sein*** be making the beds; **~man•gel** *m* (-s; *no pl.*) *a* shortage of beds; **~zahl** *f* bedspace, number of beds
'Bet•tep•pich *m* prayer mat (*or* rug)
'Bett|fe•der *f* **1.** bedspring; **2.** **~n** duvet feathers; **~ge•schich•te** *f* **1.** amorous escapade; **2.** kiss and tell story; **~ge•stell** *n* bedstead; **~häs•chen** F *n sl. a* bit of all right (*Am.* alright); **~hup•ferl** [-hʊpfɐl] *dial. n* (-s; -) **1.** bedtime treat; chocolate on one's pillow; **2.** → ***Betthäschen***; **~jäck•chen** *n*, **~jacke** (*sep.* -k·k-) *f* bed jacket; **~kan•te** *f* edge of the bed; **~ka•sten** *m* bedding box
bett•lä•ge•rig ['bɛtlɛ:gərıç] *adj.* laid up, bedridden; *formal*: confined to bed
'Bett|la•ken *n* sheet; **~lek,tü•re** *f* bedtime reading; ***es eignet sich nicht als*** ~ it's not exactly bedtime reading
Bett•ler ['bɛtlɐ] *m* (-s; -) beggar
'Bett•näs•sen *n* (-s; *no pl.*) ⚕ bed-wetting; **Bett•näs•ser** ['bɛtnɛsɐ] *m* (-s; -) bed-wetter
'Bett|pfan•ne *f* bedpan; **2reif** *adj.* ready for bed, F ready to hit the sack (*Am.* hay); **~ru•he** *f* rest in bed, bed rest; ***der Arzt hat mir ~ verordnet*** the doctor told me to stay in bed; **~schwe•re** *f*: F ***die nötige ~ haben*** be ready to fall into bed; **~sze•ne** *f* bedroom scene
'Bettuch *n* (*sep.* -tt·t-) sheet
'Bett|vor•le•ger *m* bedside rug; **~wä•sche** *f* bed linen, sheets (and covers) *pl.*; **~zeug** *n* bedclothes *pl.*, bedding
be•tucht [bə'tu:xt] F *adj.* F well-heeled
be•tu•lich [bə'tu:lıç] *adj.* overattentive, fussy
be'tup•fen *v/t.* (h) dab, ⚕ swab
Beu•ge ['bɔʏgə] *f* (-; -n) bend (*a. sport and anat.*)
'Beu•ge•haft *f* ⚖ coercive detention
'Beu•ge•mus•kel *m* flexor (muscle)
beu•gen ['bɔʏgən] (h) **I.** *v/t.* **1.** bend; bow; incline *one's head*; → **gebeugt**; **2.** *phys.* deflect, diffract; **3.** ***das Recht*** ~ pervert justice; **4.** *ling.* inflect; decline *substantive, adjective*; conjugate *verb*; **II.** *v/refl.*: ***sich*** ~ **5.** bend; ***sich ~ über*** *acc.* bend over *s.th.*; ***sich aus dem Fenster*** ~ lean out of (*Am. a.* out) the window; ***sich nach vorn*** ~ lean forward; **6.** *fig.* bow, yield, submit (*dat.* to); ***sich dem Schicksal*** ~ bow (*or* submit) to one's fate; **'Beu•gung** *f* (-; -en) **1.** bending; **2.** *phys.* diffraction; **3.** *ling.* inflection; **'Beu•gungs•win•kel** *m phys.* diffraction angle
Beu•le ['bɔʏlə] *f* (-; -n) bump, swelling; dent; bulge; ***dicke*** ~ big bump, F great big lump
'Beu•len•pest *f* bubonic plague
be•un•ru•hi•gen [bəˀʊnru:ıgən] (h) **I.** *v/t.* worry, get *s.o.* worried; alarm; ***es beunruhigt mich*** *a.* I feel uneasy (*or* nervous) about it; **II.** *v/refl.*: ***sich*** ~ worry, be worried (***über*** *acc.* about); **be'un•ru•hi- gend** *adj.* unsettling, worrying, disconcerting; disturbing, alarming; **Be'un•ru•hi•gung** *f* (-; -en) uneasiness, anxiety; worry
be•ur•kun•den [bəˀu:ɐkʊndən] *v/t.* (h) record; certify; register *birth etc.*; **Be'ur•kun•dung** *f* (-; -en) registration; certification
be•ur•lau•ben [bəˀu:ɐlaʊbən] *v/t.* (h) give *s.o.* time off (⚔ leave); grant *s.o.* a sabbatical; suspend (from office); ***sich ~ lassen*** a) ask for time off, apply for a sabbatical, b) take (some) time off, go on (*or* take a) sabbatical; ***sich eine Woche ~ lassen*** a) ask for a week's leave (*or* a week off), b) take a week's leave (*or* a week off); **Be'ur•lau•bung** *f* (-; -en) time off; ⚔ leave; sabbatical; suspension (from office)
be'ur•tei•len *v/t.* (h) judge (***nach*** *dat.* by); rate, assess, ga(u)ge (on, according to); review; ***falsch*** ~ misjudge; ***et. gut ~ können*** be a good judge of s.th.; ***nicht daß ich das ~ könnte*** not that I'm any judge, but who am I to judge?; ***wie hat er das Buch beurteilt?*** what did he say about the book?, what was his review of the book like?; ***wie ~ Sie die Lage?*** what's your view of the situation?; ***wie soll ich das ~?*** how am I supposed to know (*or* tell, judge)?; ***das kannst du doch nicht*** ~ how do you know?, how can you tell?; **Be'ur•tei•lung** *f* (-; -en) judg(e)ment (*gen.* of, on); assessment (of); confidential report (on); review, write-up (of)
Beu•te ['bɔʏtə] *f* (-; *no pl.*) booty; loot, haul; spoils *pl. of war*; *hunt.* bag; *zo.* prey, quarry; *fig.* prey (*gen.* to), victim

(of); ***zur ~ fallen*** *dat.* fall into the hands of, *fig.* fall victim to; ***reiche*** (*or* ***fette***) *~ a. fig.* rich pickings; ***reiche ~ machen*** make a big haul; ***(e-e) leichte ~*** a sitting duck

Beu·tel ['bɔytəl] *m* (-s; -) **1.** bag; (*tobacco*) pouch; F *fig.* ***tief in den ~ greifen*** (*or* ***langen***) ***müssen*** F have to dig deep into one's pockets; F ***j-m ein Loch in den ~ reißen*** F burn a big hole in s.o.'s pocket; F ***der ~ ist leer*** F there's no money left in the till; **2.** *zo.* pouch

beu·teln ['bɔytəln] *v/t.* (h) shake; *fig.* ***vom Schicksal*** (***Leben***) ***gebeutelt werden*** be knocked about by fate (life's vicissitudes)

'Beu·tel·rat·te *f* opossum

'Beu·tel·schnei·der *m* (-s; -) F shark, rip-off artist; **Beu·tel·schnei·de'rei** *f* (-; -en) F *a* rip-off

'Beu·tel·tier *n* marsupial

'Beu·te|stück *n* piece of booty, F piece of the loot; **~tier** *n* prey, quarry

be·völ·kern [bə'fœlkɐn] (h) **I.** *v/t.* **1.** populate; inhabit; *fig.* fill, crowd; **2.** settle; **II.** *v/refl.*: ***sich ~*** become inhabited; *fig.* be filling up (with people), become crowded; → ***dicht*** 4, 6; **Be·völ·ke·rung** [bə'fœlkərʊŋ] *f* (-; -en) population; inhabitants *pl.*; *the* people *pl.*; ***die ganze ~ a.*** the whole country; ***die ~ Moskaus*** the people of Moscow, Moscow's inhabitants, the population of Moscow

Be'völ·ke·rungs|ab·nah·me *f* population decrease, decrease in population; **~ab·wan·de·rung** *f* (mass) exodus; **~be·we·gung** *f* population movement; **~dich·te** *f* population density; **~ex·plo·si,on** *f* population explosion; **~grup·pe** *f* section (*or* segment) of the population; **~po·li,tik** *f* population (*or* demographic) policy; **2po,li·tisch** *adj.* demographic(ally *adv.*); **~pro,gno·se** *f* population (*or* demographic) forecast *or* projection; **~py·ra,mi·de** *f* age pyramid; **~rück·gang** *m* decline in population; **~schicht** *f* social stratum (*or* class); **~stand** *m* population; **~sta,ti·stik** *f* population statistics *pl.*; **~struk,tur** *f* population structure; **~,über·schuß** *m* overspill; **~wachs·tum** *n* growth in population; **~zahl** *f* population figures *pl.*; total population; **~zu·nah·me** *f* population growth (*or* increase); **~zu,sam·men·set·zung** *f* demographics *pl.*; **~zu·wachs** *m* → ***Bevölkerungszunahme***

be·voll·mäch·ti·gen [bə'fɔlmɛçtɪgən] *v/t.* (h) authorize (***zu*** *inf.* to *inf.*); ⚖ give *s.o.* power of attorney; **Be·voll·mäch·tig·te** [bə'fɔlmɛçtɪçtə] *m, f* (-n; -n) authorized person (⚖ representative); *pol.* plenipotentiary; **Be'voll·mäch·ti·gung** *f* (-; -en) authorization; authority, power; ⚖ power of attorney

be·vor [bə'foːɐ] *cj.* before; ***nicht ~*** not before, not until; ***sag nichts, ~ er kommt*** don't say anything until he comes; ***ich tu' nichts, ~ er mir nicht Bescheid sagt*** I'm not doing anything until he lets me know; ***wir können nicht gehen, ~ du nicht abgeschlossen hast*** we can't go unless you lock the door (*or* before you've locked the door)

be·vor·mun·den [bə'foːɐmʊndən] *v/t.* (h) tell *s.o.* what to do (all the time), treat *s.o.* like a child; *pol. etc.* patronize; ***j-n geistig ~*** make up s.o.'s mind for him (*or* her); ***ich laß' mich nicht von dir ~ a.*** I'm not going to let you run my life for me; **be'vor·mun·dend** *adj.* patronizing; *pol.* paternalistic; **Be'vor·mun·dung** *f*: ***~ durch den Staat*** paternalism, patronage by the state; ***ich verbitte mir jede ~*** I won't be treated like a child, I won't have my decisions made for me; ***ich habe ihre dauernde ~ satt*** I'm fed up of her telling me what to do all the time

be·vor·rech·ten [bə'foːɐrɛçtən] *v/t.* → **be·vor·rech·ti·gen** [bə'foːɐrɛçtɪgən] *v/t.* (h) grant privileges to; ⚖, ✝ give preference to; **be·vor·rech·tigt** [bə'foːɐrɛçtɪçt] *adj.* privileged; ⚖ preferential *claim etc.*; **Be'vor·rech·ti·gung** *f* (-; -en) privileges *pl.* (*gen.* granted to); preferential treatment

be·vor·schus·sen [bə'foːɐʃʊsən] *v/t.* (h) give *s.o.* an advance, advance money to *s.o.* (***für*** *acc.* on *s.th.*); **Be'vor·schus·sung** *f* (-; -en) advance

be'vor·ste·hen *v/i.* (*irr., sep.*, h, → ***stehen***) be approaching; lie ahead; *danger*: be imminent; be in store for, await *s.o.*; ***ihm steht e-e große Enttäuschung bevor*** he's in for a big disappointment; ***das Schlimmste steht noch bevor*** the worst is yet (*or* still) to come; *iro.* ***das steht uns noch bevor*** we've still got that to look forward to; ***s-e Entlassung stand bevor*** he was about to be dismissed; **be'vor·ste·hend** *adj.* forthcoming, approaching, upcoming; next; *pleasures etc.* to come; impending *danger etc.*

be·vor·zu·gen [bə'foːɐtsuːgən] *v/t.* (h) prefer (***vor*** *dat.* to); favo(u)r (above); give preferential treatment to; give preference to; give priority to; ⚖ privilege; ***hier wird keiner bevorzugt*** everyone is treated equally here, there's no favo(u)ritism around here; **be·vor·zugt** [bə'foːɐtsuːkt] **I.** *adj.* preferred; favo(u)rite; popular; ***~e Behandlung*** preferential treatment; ***~e Stellung*** privileged position; ***~e Lage*** prime location; **II.** *adv.*: ***~ behandeln*** → ***bevorzugen***; **Be'vor·zu·gung** *f* (-; -en) preference (***j-s*** given to s.o.); preferential *or* priority treatment (of s.o.)

be'wa·chen *v/t.* (h) guard; watch over; *sport*: mark; ***bewacht werden von*** *sport*: be marked (*or* shadowed) by; **Be·wa·cher** [bə'vaxɐ] *m* (-s; -) guard; shadow; *hum.* watchdog; *sport*: marker

be'wach·sen *adj.*: ***~ mit*** *dat.* covered with (*or* in), overgrown (with); ***mit Moos ~ a.*** moss-covered ...

be·wacht [bə'vaxt] *adj.* guarded; ***streng ~*** closely (*or* heavily) guarded; ***~er Parkplatz*** supervised car park

Be·wa·chung [bə'vaxʊŋ] *f* (-; -en) guarding; surveillance; *sport*: marking; guard(s *pl.*), escort; ***unter ~ stellen*** (***halten***) put (keep) under guard

be·waff·nen [bə'vafnən] *v/t.* (h) arm (***sich*** o.s.) (*a. fig.*); **be'waff·net** *adj.* armed (***mit*** *dat.* with) (*a. fig.*); ***~e Auseinandersetzung*** armed struggle; **Be'waff·nung** *f* (-; -en) arming; arms *pl.*, weapons *pl.*

be'wah·ren (h) **I.** *v/t.* **1.** keep, preserve; retain; ***er hat s-n Humor bewahrt*** he's kept (*or* he hasn't lost) his sense of humo(u)r; ***j-m ein gutes Andenken ~*** keep s.o. in fond remembrance; ***et.*** (***j-n***) ***in guter Erinnerung ~*** have happy memories of s.th. (s.o.); → ***Fassung*** 3; **2.** ***~ vor*** *dat.* protect (*or* keep) *s.o.* from; *a.* save *s.o.* from; ***j-n vor e-r Dummheit ~*** stop s.o. (from) doing something stupid; (***Gott***) ***bewahre!*** God forbid!; **II.** *v/refl.*: ***sich ~*** survive, be preserved; ***es hat sich bis zum heutigen Tag bewahrt*** it survives (*or* has survived) to this day

be'wäh·ren *v/refl.* (h): ***sich ~*** prove o.s. (*or* itself), prove one's (*or* its) worth; prove a success, prove successful; hold good; stand the test of time; ***sich bestens ~*** give a (very) good account of o.s. (*or* itself), do a good (*or* an excellent) job; ***sich ~ als*** prove (to be) a good *teacher, remedy etc.*; ***sich nicht ~*** prove a failure

be·wahr·hei·ten [bə'vaːɐhaɪtən] *v/refl.* (h): ***sich ~*** prove (to be) true; *hopes, fears etc.*: be confirmed, prove to be right (*or* justified); come true

be·währt [bə'vɛːɐt] *adj.* well-tried, tried and tested; reliable; effective; capable, experienced; ***~es Mittel*** proven (*or* old, *iro.* ancient) remedy, *a.* ***~e Methode*** proven method; ***~er Grundsatz*** established principle; ***unter ihrer ~en Führung*** under her excellent guidance, in her capable hands; **Be'währt·heit** *f* (-; *no pl.*) reliability, proven effectiveness (*or* worth)

Be'wah·rung *f* (-; *no pl.*) preservation (***vor*** *dat.* from)

Be'wäh·rung *f* (-; -en) **1.** demonstration of one's *or* its worth (*or* reliability); ***bei ~*** on qualifying, provided it (*or* he *etc.*) proves reliable; ***die ~ bestehen*** pass the test; **2.** ⚖ (release on) probation; ***zwei Jahre Gefängnis mit*** (***ohne***) ***~*** a suspended (an unconditional) sentence of two years; ***e-e Strafe zur ~ aussetzen*** suspend a sentence

Be'wäh·rungs|frist *f* ⚖ (period of) probation; **~hel·fer** *m* probation officer; **~pro·be** *f* (acid) test

be·wal·det [bə'valdət] *adj.* wooded; tree-covered; **Be'wal·dung** *f* (-; -en) **1.** woods *pl.*, woodland, forests *pl.*; **2.** afforestation

be·wäl·ti·gen [bə'vɛltɪgən] *v/t.* (h) cope with, manage; come to grips with *a problem etc.*; cope with, overcome *difficulties etc.*; assimilate, absorb, F digest; conquer *mountain etc.*; cover *distance etc.*; come to terms with *the past etc.*; **Be'wäl·ti·gung** *f* (-; -en) coping with *one's work etc.*; assimilation; coming to terms with *the past etc.*

be·wan·dert [bə'vandɐt] *adj.*: (***gut***) ***~ in*** *dat.* well up in, well versed in; ***sie ist in Wirtschaft gut ~ a.*** she knows her (way around in) economics; ***da bin ich nicht sehr gut ~*** I'm not very well up in that, I don't know very much about that

Be·wandt·nis [bə'vantnɪs] *f*: ***damit hat es folgende ~*** the matter is as follows; ***das hat e-e ganz andere ~*** it's completely different; ***damit hat es e-e besondere ~*** a) you have to know the background (to it), b) it's a strange thing; ***was hat es eigentlich mit ... für e-e ~?*** what's the story behind ...?; ***das hat s-e eigene ~*** *hum.* (and) thereby hangs a tale

be'warb *pret. of* **bewerben**

be'warf *pret. of* **bewerfen**

be'wäs·sern *v/t.* (h) irrigate; **Be'wäs·se·rung** *f* (-; -en) irrigation

Be'wäs·se·rungs|an·la·ge *f* irrigation plant; **~gra·ben** *m* irrigation channel (*or* ditch); **~ka͵nal** *m* irrigation channel; **~pum·pe** *f* irrigation pump

be·we·gen¹ [bəˈveːgən] (h) **I.** *v/t.* **1.** move; F shift; ***ich kann m-n linken Arm nicht ~*** *a.* I have no movement in my left arm; ***es läßt sich nicht von der Stelle ~*** it won't budge; **2.** stir; **3.** ⚙ *and fig.* set *s.th.* in motion; drive; **4.** *fig.* move, touch; (pre)occupy, *problem etc.*: *a.* bother *s.o.*; **5.** exercise *a horse*; **II.** *v/refl.*: ***sich ~*** **6.** move; stir; *flag, sail etc.*: flap; **7.** get (some) exercise; ***du mußt dich mehr ~*** you need (to get) more exercise; ***er bewegt sich diese Tage kaum*** *a.* he hardly gets out of the house these days; **8.** *fig.* ***sich in Politikerkreisen*** *etc.* ***~*** move in political *etc.* circles; **9.** *fig.* ***sich in e-e Richtung ~*** *thoughts etc.*: tend in a (certain) direction; **10.** *die Kosten* ***~ sich zwischen ... und ...*** range between ... and ...; **be'we·gen²** *v/t.* (bewog, bewogen, h): ***j-n ~ zu*** *inf.* get (*or* bring) s.o. to *inf.*; ***was hat ihn (wohl) dazu bewogen?*** (I wonder) what made him do it?; ***sich zu et. ~ lassen*** (allow o.s. to) be persuaded to do s.th.; ***sich nicht ~ lassen*** stand firm, remain adamant, F refuse to budge; ***es konnte ihn nichts dazu ~ zu*** *inf.* wild horses couldn't make him *inf.*; → ***bewogen***; **be'we·gend** *adj.* **1.** (*a.* ***sich ~***) moving; **2.** *fig.* moving, touching; stirring *speech*

Be·weg·grund [bəˈveːk-] *m* motive; consideration; ***aus moralischen*** *etc.* ***Beweggründen*** out of moral *etc.* considerations; ***der tiefere ~ war ...*** the real motive was ..., what was at the back of it was ...

be·weg·lich [bəˈveːklıç] *adj.* **1.** movable (*a. holiday*), mobile; agile; ⚙ flexible, *mot. etc.* manoeuvrable, *Am.* maneuverable; ***~e Teile*** moving parts; ⚖ ***~e Sachen*** movables; ***schwer ~*** hard to move; ***geistig ~*** mentally agile, F on the ball, with it; ***mit e-m Auto ist man ~er*** you can get around more easily (*or* you're more mobile) with a car; ***ohne Gepäck ist man ~er*** you're freer to move (*or* you can move around better) without luggage; **2.** flexible, adaptable; **Be'weg·lich·keit** *f* (-; *no pl.*) mobility; flexibility (*a. fig.*); agility; *mot. etc.* manoeuvrability, *Am.* maneuverability; ***geistige ~*** mental agility

be·wegt [bəˈveːkt] *adj.* **1.** rough; heavy *seas*; **2.** *fig.* exciting, *a.* eventful *days etc.*; turbulent, stirring, troubled; ***wir leben in ~en Zeiten*** these are exciting (*or* turbulent) times; **3.** animated (*a. discussion*); ***et. mit ~en Worten schildern*** give a dramatic account of s.th.; **4.** moved, touched; choked, trembling (with emotion); ***mit ~er Stimme*** in a choked (*or* trembling) voice

Be'we·gung *f* (-; -en) **1.** movement, motion (*a. phys.*); move; gesture; ***in ~*** moving, ⚙ *a.* in motion, *fig.* astir, on the move; ***in ~ bringen*** get *s.o., s.th.* moving; ***et. in ~ setzen*** start s.th. (*a. fig.*), set s.th. in motion; ***in ~ geraten, sich in ~ setzen*** start to move, ⚙ *a.* start (working), *fig.* get going; ***et. in ~ halten*** keep s.th. moving *or* going; *fig.* ***(ein bißchen) ~ bringen in*** *acc.* liven *s.th.* up, get *s.th.* going, stir up; ***keine falsche ~!*** don't move!; → ***Hebel***; **2.** exercise; ***du brauchst mehr ~*** you need (to get) more exercise; ***~ an der frischen Luft*** fresh air and exercise; **3.** *pol. etc.* movement; **4.** emotion

Be'we·gungs|ab·lauf *m* motions *pl.*; **~drang** *m* **1.** motor activity; **2.** ⚕ hyperkinesia; **~ener͵gie** *f* kinetic energy; **~frei·heit** *f* (-; *no pl.*) **1.** room to move, elbowroom; **2.** *fig.* personal freedom, freedom of action; latitude

be'we·gungs·los I. *adj.* motionless, completely still; **II.** *adv.*: ***~ daliegen*** lie there motionless (*or* without moving); **Be'we·gungs·lo·sig·keit** *f* (-; *no pl.*) immobility

Be'we·gungs|man·gel *m* (-s; *no pl.*) lack of (*or* too little) exercise; ***Sie leiden an ~*** you don't get enough exercise; **~nerv** *m* motor nerve; **~stö·rung** *f* motor disturbance; **~stu·die** *f* motion study; **~the·ra͵pie** *f* therapeutic exercises *pl.*, kinetotherapy

be'we·gungs·un·fä·hig *adj.* unable to move, immobilized; **Be'we·gungs·un·fä·hig·keit** *f* (-; *no pl.*) inability to move, immobility

be·weibt [bəˈvaıpt] *hum. adj.* F hitched up (with a woman)

be·weih·räu·chern [bəˈvaırɔyçərn] *fig. v/t.* (h) adulate *s.o.*; praise *s.o., s.th.* to the skies (*or* to high heaven), eulogize; ***sich selbst ~*** sing one's own praises; **Be'weih·räu·che·rung** *f* (-; -en) adulation; eulogizing

be'wei·nen *v/t.* (h) mourn (for *or* over); **Be'wei·nung** *f* (-; -en) mourning; *art*: ***die ~ Christi*** the Lamentation (of Christ)

Be·weis [bəˈvaıs] *m* (-es; -e) proof (***für*** *acc.* of), evidence (of); ⚖ *a. pl.* proof; (piece of) evidence, sign, indication; ***als*** (*or* ***zum***) ***~*** as proof *or* evidence (***für*** *acc., gen.* of), in evidence (of), ***für*** *acc.*: *a.* to prove *s.th.*; ***als ~, daß*** to prove (*or* show) that; ***als ~ ihrer Zuneigung*** as a token of her affection; ***ein ~ von Unfähigkeit*** a show of incompetence; ***den ~ erbringen*** furnish proof, provide (⚖ produce) evidence (***für*** *acc.* of), ***für*** *acc.*: *a.* prove; ***et. unter ~ stellen*** prove s.th.; ***bis zum ~ des Gegenteils*** until there is proof to the contrary; → ***mangels***; **~auf·nah·me** *f* hearing of evidence

be'weis·bar *adj.* provable; **be'wei·sen** *v/t.* (bewies, bewiesen, h) **1.** prove (***j-m et.*** s.th. to s.o.); be evidence of; ***man konnte ihm s-e Schuld nicht ~*** they couldn't prove that he was guilty; ***~, daß man recht hat*** prove o.s. right; ***das beweist zur Genüge, daß*** it's ample proof (*or* evidence) that, it proves beyond doubt that; ***das beweist noch gar nichts*** that doesn't prove a thing; ***das mußt du mir erst (einmal) ~!*** I'd like to see you prove it; **2.** show; display

Be'weis|füh·rung *f* argumentation, line of argument (*or* reasoning); ⚖ giving of evidence; → ***lückenlos***; **~grund** *m* argument; **~ket·te** *f* chain of evidence; → ***lückenlos***

Be'weis·kraft *f* (-; *no pl.*) conclusiveness, cogency, strength; **be'weis·kräf·tig** *adj.* conclusive, cogent

Be'weis|last *f* (-; *no pl.*) ⚖ burden of proof, onus; ***ihm obliegt die ~*** the burden of proof lies with him; **~ma·te·ri͵al** *n* (body of) evidence; ***aufgrund des ~s*** on the evidence (available); **~mit·tel** *n* (piece of) evidence; *pl.* evidence *sg.* (***für*** *acc.* of); **~not** *f* (-; *no pl.*) lack of evidence; ***in ~ sein*** have no evidence (to bring forward)

Be'weis·pflicht *f* → ***Beweislast***; **be'weis·pflich·tig** *adj.*: ***er ist ~*** the burden of proof lies with him

Be'weis|si·che·rung *f* perpetuation of evidence; **~stück** *n* (piece of) evidence; ⚖ exhibit

be'wen·den (*only inf.*) **I.** *v/i.*: ***es dabei ~ lassen*** leave it at that; ***sie ließen es bei e-r Verwarnung ~*** they decided to let him *etc.* off (*or* go) with a warning, they decided a warning would be enough; **II.** ♀ *n* (-s; *no pl.*): ***damit hatte es sein ~*** that was the end of that (*or* the matter)

be'wer·ben *v/refl.* (bewarb, beworben, h): ***sich ~*** apply (***um*** *acc.* for); ***sich ~ um*** *acc.* stand for, *esp. Am.* run for *presidency etc.*; *a. party*: contend for; compete (*or* contend) for; ***er hat sich bei X beworben*** he's applied to X (for a job); **Be·wer·ber** [bəˈvɛrbɐ] *m* (-s; -) applicant; candidate; ✝ bidder, competitor; *sport*: entrant, competitor; **Be'wer·bung** *f* (-; -en) application (***um*** *acc.* for); ***es gingen über 100 ~en ein*** we *etc.* had (*or* there were) over a hundred applications (*or* applicants)

Be'wer·bungs|bo·gen *m*, **~for·mu͵lar** *n* application form; **~schrei·ben** *n* (letter of) application; **~͵un·ter·la·gen** *pl.* application *sg.*, application papers; CV and references

be'wer·fen *v/t.* (bewarf, beworfen, h) **1.** ***j-n mit et. ~*** throw s.th. at s.o.; pelt s.o. with s.th.; greet s.o. with s.th.; **2.** ⚠ plaster, rough-cast

be·werk·stel·li·gen [bəˈvɛrkʃtɛlıgən] *v/t.* (h) manage; ***~, daß j-d ...*** arrange for s.o. to ...

be'wer·ten *v/t.* (h) assess (***nach*** *dat.* by, according to); judge (by); ✝ value (***auf*** *acc.* at); ***~ als*** judge *s.o. or s.th.* to be, see *s.o. or s.th.* as; ***zu hoch (niedrig) ~*** overrate (underrate); *der Sprung* ***wurde mit 7 Punkten bewertet*** scored 7 points; ***e-n Aufsatz mit der Note 2 (mit e-r guten Note) ~*** give an essay a B (a good mark [*esp. Am.* grade]); **Be'wer·tung** *f* (-; -en) assessment; *ped.* mark(s *pl.*), *esp. Am.* grade(s *pl.*); *sport*: scoring, score(s *pl.*); ✝ valuation

be'wies *pret. of* ***beweisen***

be·wie·sen [bəˈviːzən] *p.p. of* ***beweisen***

be·wil·li·gen [bəˈvılıgən] *v/t.* (h) allow (***j-m et.*** s.o. s.th.); grant *funds etc.*; *parl.* sanction; consent to; **Be'wil·li·gung** *f* (-; -en) approval; permission; granting *of funds etc.*

be·will·komm·nen [bəˈvılkɔmnən] *v/t.* (h) welcome

be'wir·ken *v/t.* (h) bring *s.th.* about, cause; give rise to, result in; achieve; ***~, daß j-d et. tut*** get s.o. to do s.th.; ***das Gegenteil ~*** produce (*or* have) the opposite effect; ***es hat einiges (nicht viel) bewirkt*** it achieved quite a lot (it didn't achieve much *or* have much of an effect); ***was willst du damit ~?*** what do you hope to achieve by that?

be·wir·ten [bəˈvırtən] *v/t.* (h) feed (***mit*** *dat.* with, on); cater for; ***bewirtet werden mit*** *dat.* be offered *s.th.*, *lit.* be regaled with *s.th.*

be'wirt·schaf·ten *v/t.* (h) **1.** 🌾 cultivate, work; run *an estate etc.*; **2.** ✝ ration;

be'wirt·schaf·tet *adj. mountain hut*: open (to the public); **Be'wirt·schaf·tung** *f* (-; -en) **1.** ⚒ cultivation; running *an estate etc.*; **2.** ✝ rationing
Be'wir·tung *f* (-; -en) catering (*gen.* for); food and service; ***vielen Dank für die ~!*** thank you for looking after (F feeding) us *etc.* so well, *formal*: thank you for your hospitality; **Be'wir·tungs·ko·sten** *pl.* entertainment expenses
be'wit·zeln *v/t.* (h) make fun of, crack jokes about
be·wog [bə'vo:k] *pret. of* **bewegen²**
be·wo·gen [bə'vo:gən] *p.p. of* **bewegen²**: ***sich*** (***nicht***) ***~ fühlen zu*** *inf.* feel prompted to *inf.* (not to feel inclined to *inf.*)
be·wohn·bar [bə'vo:nba:ɐ] *adj.* (in)habitable; **Be'wohn·bar·keit** *f* (-; *no pl.*) habitability; **be'woh·nen** *v/t.* (h) live in, occupy; inhabit; **Be·woh·ner** [bə'vo:nɐ] *m* (-s; -) occupant; tenant; inhabitant; **Be'woh·ner·schaft** *f* (-; -en) inhabitants *pl.*, residents *pl.*; occupants *pl.*; **be'wohnt** *adj.* inhabited; occupied; ***das Haus ist ~*** *a.* somebody lives (*or* people live) in the house, there's somebody (*or* there are people) living in the house; ***das Haus ist nicht ~*** the house is empty (*or* vacant, unoccupied), nobody lives (*or* there's nobody living) in the house
be·wöl·ken [bə'vœlkən] *v/refl.* (h): ***sich ~*** get cloudy, cloud over, become overcast; *fig. face etc.*: darken; **be'wölkt** *adj.* cloudy; overcast; *fig.* dark, gloomy; *meteor.* ***leicht*** (***stark***) ***~*** scattered (heavy) cloud; ***~ bis bedeckt*** cloudy, becoming overcast; **Be'wöl·kung** *f* (-; *no pl.*) clouds *pl.*; clouding over; ***starke ~*** heavy cloud cover; ***leichte ~*** scattered cloud; ***zunehmende ~*** increasing cloudiness; ***vereinzelte ~*** scattered cloud; ***wechselnde ~*** variable cloud; ***auflockernde ~*** heavy cloud to begin with, breaking up later
Be'wöl·kungs|auf·locke·rung *f*, **~rück·gang** *m* cloud dispersal; **~ver·dich·tung** *f*, **~zu·nah·me** *f* increasing cloud (-iness)
Be·wuchs [bə'vu:ks] *m* (-es; *no pl.*) vegetation (*gen.* on); plant life
Be·wun·de·rer [bə'vʊndərɐ] *m* (-s; -) admirer; **be'wun·dern** *v/t.* (h) **1.** admire (***wegen*** *gen.* for); ***ich bewundere ihn wegen s-r Ausdauer*** *a.* I admire his perseverance; **2.** go and see, *usu. iro.* go to admire; ***wir haben bei der Ausstellung Ihre Skulpturen bewundert*** we very much enjoyed (seeing) your sculptures at the exhibition; **be'wun·derns·wert, be'wun·derns·wür·dig** *adj.* admirable; **Be'wun·de·rung** *f* (-; *no pl.*) admiration
Be·wurf [bə'vʊrf] *m* (-[e]s; ⁻e) ⚠ facing; rough cast
be·wußt [bə'vʊst] **I.** *adj.* **1.** conscious (*gen.* of); *in cpds. usu.* ...-conscious (*i.e.* ***gesundheitsbewußt*** health-conscious); ***sich*** *e-r Sache* ***~ sein*** be aware (*or* conscious) of; ***sich*** *e-r Sache* ***~ werden*** realize, become aware of (the fact that), wake up to the fact that; ***erst dann wurde mir ~, daß*** *a.* only then did it dawn on me that; ***er war sich der Situation vollkommen ~*** he knew exactly what was going on; ***er war sich dessen nicht mehr ~*** he couldn't remember; ***ich bin mir dessen völlig ~*** I'm quite (*or* perfectly) aware of that (*or* the fact); **2.** aware; ***seiner selbst ~*** self-aware; **3.** deliberate, conscious; calculated; **4.** said, ... in question; *the* agreed *hour etc.*; **II.** *adv.* **5.** consciously; with full awareness; ***~ wahrnehmen*** (consciously) register; ***er hat es nicht ~ miterlebt*** he was too young (*or* ill, drunk *etc.*) to know what was going on; ***das habe ich gar nicht ~ mitbekommen*** I (must have) missed that; ***~ leben*** live life to the full; **6.** deliberately, consciously, wittingly; ***er hat ~ gelogen*** *a.* he knew he was lying, it was a calculated lie
be'wußt·los *adj.* unconscious; ***~ werden*** lose consciousness, faint, F black out; ***~ zusammenbrechen*** collapse onto the floor (*or* ground) unconscious, faint; ***j-n ~ schlagen*** knock s.o. unconscious; **Be'wußt·lo·se** *m, f* (-n; -n) unconscious person (F body); ***da liegt ein ~r*** there's somebody lying there unconscious; **Be'wußt·lo·sig·keit** *f* unconsciousness; coma; ***in tiefer ~*** in a deep state of unconsciousness, in a coma; ***aus s-r ~ erwachen*** come round (again), regain consciousness; *fig.* ***bis zur ~*** ad nauseam; ***er hat mich bis zur ~ ausgefragt*** he drove me mad with all his questions
be'wußt·ma·chen *v/t.* (*sep.*, h): ***j-m et. ~*** make s.o. realize s.th., open s.o.'s eyes to s.th., bring s.th. home to s.o.; ***j-m ~, daß*** make s.o. realize that, open s.o.'s eyes to the fact that, bring home to s.o. the fact that; ***j-m et. bewußter machen*** heighten s.o.'s awareness of s.th.; ***sich et. ~*** make s.th. clear to o.s., F keep telling o.s. s.th.
Be'wußt·sein *n* (-s; *no pl.*) **1.** consciousness; ***bei*** (***vollem***) ***~*** (fully) conscious; ***das ~ verlieren*** lose consciousness, faint; ***j-n zu***(***m***) ***~ bringen*** bring s.o. round (again); ***wieder zu***(***m***) ***~ kommen*** regain consciousness, come round (again); **2.** *a. psych.* awareness, consciousness; realization; ***j-m et. zum ~ bringen*** → ***bewußtmachen***; ***es kam mir zu***(***m***) ***~, daß*** I realized that, I became aware (of the fact) that, it occurred to me that, it dawned on me that; ***sie tat es mit vollem ~*** she was fully aware of (*or* she knew exactly) what she was doing; ***im ~ zu*** *inf.*, ***im ~, daß*** conscious of *ger.*, aware of the fact that; **3.** sense *of duty, responsibility etc.*; **4.** *national, religious etc.* awareness, consciousness
Be'wußt·seins|bil·dung *f* raising of (people's) awareness; **~ebe·ne** *f* plane of consciousness; **2er·wei·ternd** *adj.* mind-expanding, consciousness-raising; **~er·wei·te·rung** *f* heightening of (one's *or* people's) awareness; **~schwel·le** *f* threshold of consciousness; **~spal·tung** *f* schizophrenia; split personality; **~strom** *m* stream of consciousness; **~trü·bung** *f* clouded awareness; **~ver·än·de·rung** *f* change in awareness (*or* outlook); **~zu·stand** *m* state of consciousness
Be'wußt·wer·dung *f* (-; *no pl.*) (growing) realization *or* awareness
be'zahl·bar *adj.* payable; ***es war nicht ~*** we *etc.* couldn't afford it (*or* pay for it); ***es war gerade noch ~*** we *etc.* just about managed to pay for it; **be'zah·len** (h) **I.** *v/t.* pay; pay for *s.th.*; pay (off), settle *debts etc.*; ***das kann ich nicht ~*** I can't afford (*or* pay for) that, that's beyond my means(, I'm afraid); ***das ist doch nicht zu ~*** who can afford that?; ***dafür bezahlt werden, daß*** get (*or* be) paid for *ger.*; ***er hat mir die Reise bezahlt*** he paid for my holiday; *fig.* ***das ist nicht mit Geld zu ~*** it's priceless, no amount of money could buy that; ***et. teuer ~*** pay dearly for s.th.; **II.** *v/i.* pay; ***kann ich ~?*** can I have the bill (*Am.* check), please?; **be'zahlt** *adj.* **1.** paid for; **2.** ***~e Kräfte*** paid employees; ***~er Urlaub*** paid leave; **3.** ***sich ~ machen*** pay (off); ***es macht sich ~ zu*** *inf.* it pays to *inf.*; ***es hat sich ~ gemacht*** it paid off, it was worth it; **Be'zah·lung** *f* (-; *no pl.*) payment; fee; pay; salary; wages *pl.*; ***gegen ~*** for money, for a fee (F price)
be'zäh·men (h) **I.** *v/t.* **1.** curb, restrain, control; **2.** *lit.* tame; **II.** *v/refl.*: ***sich ~*** control o.s., restrain o.s.; **Be'zäh·mung** *f* (-; *no pl.*) **1.** restraint, control; **2.** *lit.* taming
be'zau·bern *fig. v/t.* (h) charm, captivate, bewitch (***durch*** *acc.* with); **be'zau·bernd** *adj.* charming, delightful
be·zecht [bə'tsɛçt] *adj.* drunk, F tiddly
be'zeich·nen *v/t.* (h) **1.** call (*a.* ***~ als***), describe (***als*** as); ***wie bezeichnet man ...?*** what do you call ...?, what's the name for ...?; ***wie würdest du das ~?*** what would you call that?, how would you describe that?; ***es wird verschieden bezeichnet*** it has several names (*or* descriptions), it's referred to in various ways; ***j-n als ... ~*** call s.o. a ..., refer to s.o. as a ...; ***er wird als intolerant bezeichnet*** he's said to be intolerant, he's described as (being) intolerant; ***es wurde als große Blamage bezeichnet*** it was described (*or* put down) as a big disgrace; **2.** describe, refer to; stand for; mean; **3.** mark; indicate; **be'zeich·nend** *adj.* **1.** characteristic, typical (***für*** *acc.* of); ***es ist ~ für s-n Egoismus, daß*** it's a reflection of his selfishness that; **2.** significant; revealing; ***es ist ~, daß sie die Sitzung aufgeschoben hat*** it says something for her to have postponed the meeting; **be'zeich·nen·der'wei·se** *adv.* **1.** typically (enough); **2.** significantly; **Be'zeich·nung** *f* (-; -en) name, term, *formal*: designation; ***falsche ~*** misnomer, wrong description; ***es hat verschiedene ~en*** it has several names, it's referred to by various names; **Be'zeich·nungs·sy,stem** *n* nomenclature
be'zei·gen *v/t.* (h) show, express; grant; ***j-m Achtung ~*** show respect to(wards) s.o., treat s.o. with respect; ***j-m Ehre ~*** pay hono(u)r to s.o.; **Be'zei·gung** *f* (-; -en) show (*gen.* of), display (of)
be'zeu·gen *v/t.* (h) **1.** ⚖ *and fig.* testify (to); vouch for; certify; ***die Siedlung ist*** (***sicher***) ***bezeugt*** there is (firm) evidence for (*or* of) the settlement's existence, the settlement is known to have existed; ***das Wort ist für das 19. Jahrhundert bezeugt*** the word is recorded in the 19th century; **2.** → ***bezeigen***; **Be'zeu·gung** *f* (-; -en) **1.** testimony; **2.** → ***Bezeigung***
be·zich·ti·gen [bə'tsɪçtɪgən] *v/t.* (h) accuse (*gen.* of); ***j-n ~, et. getan zu haben*** accuse s.o. of doing (*or* having done) s.th.; **Be'zich·ti·gung** *f* (-; -en) accusation
be'zieh·bar *adj.* **1.** ready for occupation (*or* occupancy); **2.** ✝ obtainable (***über*** *acc.* through); **3.** *fig.* referable (***auf*** *acc.* to); **be'zie·hen** (bezog, bezogen, h) **I.**

v/t. **1.** cover *armchair etc.*; put clean sheets on; string *guitar etc.*; **2.** move into; **3.** ✝ get, buy; take, subscribe to *a paper etc.*; receive *salary etc.*; get (hold of) *informations etc.*; ~ **aus** *dat. a.* draw from; **4.** ~ **auf** *acc.* relate to, apply to; **er bezog es auf sich** he took it personally; **5. e-n klaren Standpunkt** ~ take a (firm) stand; **II.** *v/refl.* **6. sich** ~ *sky*: cloud over, become overcast; **7. sich** ~ **auf** *acc.* refer to, relate to, concern, apply to; **wir** ~ **uns auf Ihr Schreiben vom ...** with reference to your letter of ...(, we ...);
Be·zie·her [bəˈtsiːɐ] *m* (-s; -) subscriber (*gen.* to); ✝ importer; customer; **Beˈziehung** *f* (-; -en) **1.** relation (**zu** *dat.* to), relationship (with, to); connection (with, to); **wechselseitige** ~ interrelationship; **in (direkter)** ~ **stehen** be (directly) connected *or* linked (**zu** *dat.* with, to), **zu** *dat.*: *a.* have a (direct) relation to; **in** ~ **bringen** relate (**zu** *dat.* to), see (*or* establish) a link between; **2. in dieser** ~ from that point of view, in that respect, in this connection; **in mancher** ~ in some ways (*or* respects); **in gewisser** ~ in a way; **in jeder** ~ in every way (*or* respect); **in** ~ **auf** *acc.* with regard to, as far as ... goes (*or* is concerned); **in politischer** ~ politically (speaking), in political terms; **in wirtschaftlicher** ~ (seen) in economic terms *or* from an economic point of view; **3.** relationship (**zu** *dat.* with, to); affair; connections *pl.* (with, to); contact (with), contacts *pl.* (with, to); **menschliche (diplomatische)** ~**en** human (diplomatic) relations; **wirtschaftliche** ~**en** economic relations (*or* contacts); **in guten** ~**en stehen zu** be on good terms with; **gute** ~**en haben** have good (*or* the right) connections, F know the right people; **du brauchst** ~**en** you need connections, F you've got to know the right people; **er hat es durch** ~**en bekommen** he got it through contacts; → **spielen** 7; **4.** relationship (**zu** *dat.* to); affinity (for, to); feeling (for); understanding (of); appreciation (for, of); **ich habe keine** ~ **zur Musik** *a.* I can't relate to music, music doesn't mean anything (*or* means nothing) to me; **ich habe keine** ~ **zu ihm** I can't relate to him, I feel no affinity for (*or* towards) him, I can't warm to him
Beˈzie·hungs·ki·ste F *f* relationship, F (romantic) set-up
beˈzie·hungs·los *adj.* unconnected, without any connection, (completely) unrelated; ~ **nebeneinanderstehen** *a.* bear no relationship to one another; **Beˈzie·hungs·lo·sig·keit** *f* (-; *no pl.*) unconnectedness, lack of (any) connection (**zu** *dat.* with, to)
beˈzie·hungs·reich, beˈzie·hungs·voll *adj.* allusive; suggestive
Beˈzie·hungs·satz *m ling.* relative clause
beˈzie·hungs·wei·se *adv.* **1.** (either ...) or (..., as the case may be); **2.** or rather, that's to say; **3.** respectively; **zwei Bücher in englischer** ~ **deutscher Sprache** two books in English and German respectively
Beˈzie·hungs·wort *n ling.* antecedent
be·zif·fer·bar [bəˈtsɪfɐbaːɐ] *adj.* quantifiable; **nicht** ~ unquantifiable; **be·zif·fern** [bəˈtsɪfɐn] *v/t.* (h) number; estimate (**auf** *acc.* at); **sich** ~ **auf** *acc.* amount to, come to; **beˈzif·fert** *adj.*: ♪ ~**er Baß** figured bass; **Be·zif·fe·rung** [bəˈtsɪfərʊŋ] *f* (-; -en) numbering
Be·zirk [bəˈtsɪrk] *m* (-[e]s; -e) district; borough; ward; *Am.* precinct; *fig.* → **Bereich** 2
Beˈzirks... *in cpds.* district ..., regional; ~**parˌtei·tag** *m* regional party conference
be·zir·zen F *v/t.* → **becircen**
beˈzog *pret. of* **beziehen**
be·zo·gen [bəˈtsoːgən] *p.p. of* **beziehen**
Beˈzo·ge·ne *m, f* (-n; -n) drawee
Be·zug [bəˈtsuːk] *m* (-[e]s; ⸚e [bəˈtsyːgə]) **1.** cover; cushion cover, pillowcase, pillow slip; **2.** *no pl.* buying; subscription (*gen.* to); drawing (of *a pension etc.*); **bei** ~ **von** *25 Stück* on orders of; **3.** *pl.* income *sg.*, earnings; **4.** *fig.* reference; **mit** (*or* **unter**) ~ **auf** *acc.* with reference to; **in** ≈ **auf** as far as ... goes (*or* is concerned); ~ **nehmen auf** *acc.* refer to; **5.** *fig.* connection (**zu** *dat.* with, to); **der** ~ **war mir nicht ganz klar** *a.* I wasn't quite sure how it *or* they related (*or* what the connection was); **6.** *fig.* relationship (**zu** *dat.* to)
be·züg·lich [bəˈtsyːklɪç] **I.** *prp.* (*gen.*) **1.** regarding, concerning; ~ **Ihres Schreibens** with reference to your letter; **II.** *adj.* **2.** ~**es Fürwort** relative pronoun; **3.** ~ **auf** *acc.* relating to, relative to; **der darauf** ~**e Brief** the letter relating to (*or* concerning) that
Beˈzug·nah·me *f* (-; *no pl.*): **unter** ~ **auf** *acc.* with reference to, **unser Telefongespräch vom ...:** *a.* following our telephone conversation of ...
Beˈzugs|ak·ti·en *pl.* preemptive shares; ~**be·din·gun·gen** *pl.* terms of sale; ≈**be·rech·tigt** *adj.* entitled to draw *a pension etc.*; ~**be·rech·tig·te** *m, f* (-n; -n) beneficiary; ≈**fer·tig** *adj.* ready for occupation (*or* occupancy); ~**grö·ße** *f* standard for comparison; ~**perˌson** *f* attachment figure; *psych.* role model; psychological parent; **s-e einzige** ~ **ist ...** the only person he can relate (*or* look up) to is ...; ~**preis** *m* purchase price; subscription (price); ~**punkt** *m* reference point, point of reference; benchmark; ~**quel·le** *f* supply source; ~**recht** *n* subscription right; **mit (ohne)** ~ cum (ex) rights; ~**stoff** *m* covering; ~**syˌstem** *n* frame of reference; ~**wert** *m* reference value; ~**wort** *n ling.* antecedent
be·zu·schus·sen [bəˈtsuːʃʊsən] *v/t.* (h) subsidize
beˈzwang *pret. of* **bezwingen**
be·zwecken [bəˈtsvɛkən] (*sep.* -k·k-) *v/t.* (h) aim at (bringing about); have *s.th.* in mind; have as its object; **was bezweckt er mit s-m Besuch?** what's the aim (*or* object) of his visit?; **was bezweckst du damit?** what do you hope (*or* are you trying) to achieve by that?
beˈzwei·feln *v/t.* (h) doubt; question; **ich bezweifle das** I doubt it, I have my doubts (about it)
beˈzwin·gen *v/t.* (bezwang, bezwungen, h) defeat; overcome *difficulties etc.*; control, get the better of; subdue; conquer; **Be·zwin·ger** [bəˈtsvɪŋɐ] *m* (-s; -) conqueror; **Beˈzwin·gung** *f* (-; *no pl.*) defeat; conquest; control, mastery
BH [beːˈhaː] F *m* (-[s]; -[s]) bra
bi [biː] F *adj.* F AC/DC, bi
Bi·ath·lon [ˈbiːatlɔn] *n* (-s; -s) biathlon
bib·bern [ˈbɪbɐn] F *v/i.* (h) tremble (**vor** *dat.* with); shiver (with)
Bi·bel [ˈbiːbəl] *f* (-; -n) Bible; *fig.* bible; ~**aus·le·gung** *f* **1.** biblical exegesis; **2.** interpretation of the Bible; ~**druck·paˌpier** *n* Bible paper; ~**ex·ege·se** *f* biblical exegesis; ≈**fest** *adj.*: ~ **sein** know one's Bible; ~**for·scher** *m* biblical scholar; ~**for·schung** *f* biblical scholarship; ~**kom·menˌtar** *m* Bible commentary; ~**kon·korˌdanz** *f* concordance of (*or* to) the Bible, Bible concordance; ~**le·xi·kon** *n* biblical encyclop(a)edia; ~**spruch** *m* biblical saying; verse from the Bible; ~**stel·le** *f* passage in (*or* from) the Bible; verse from the Bible; ~**stun·de** *f a. pl.* Bible study; ~**überˌset·zung** *f* translation of the Bible, Bible translation; ~**wort** *n* biblical saying (*or* quotation), quotation from the Bible
Bi·ber [ˈbiːbɐ] *m* (-s; -) beaver; ~**bau** *m* (-[e]s; -e) beaver's lodge; ~**pelz** *m* beaver (fur); ~**rat·te** *f* nutria; ~**schwanz** *m* **1.** *zo.* beaver's tail; **2.** ⚠ flat tile
Bi·blio·graph [biblioˈgraːf] *m* (-en; -en) bibliographer; **Bi·blio·gra·phie** [bibliograˈfiː] *f* (-; -n) bibliography (**zu** *dat.* of); **bi·blio·gra·phisch** [biblioˈgraːfɪʃ] *adj.* bibliographical
Bi·blio·ma·nie [bibliomaˈniː] *f* (-; *no pl.*) bibliomania
bi·blio·phil [biblioˈfiːl] *adj.* bibliophile; ~**e Ausgabe** fine edition; ~**es Antiquariat** antiquarian bookseller's; *antiquarian bookshop selling rare editions*; **Bi·blioˈphi·le** *m, f* (-n; -n) bibliophile
Bi·blio·thek [biblioˈteːk] *f* (-; -en) library; **Bi·blio·the·kar** [biblioteˈkaːɐ] *m* (-s; -e), **Bi·blio·the·ka·rin** [biblioteˈkaːrɪn] *f* (-; -nen) librarian
Bi·blioˈtheks|aus·ga·be *f* library edition; ~**ex·emˌplar** *n* library copy; ~**ge·bäu·de** *n* library (building); ~**we·sen** *n* (-s; *no pl.*) librarianship; → ~**wis·sen·schaft** *f* library science
bi·blisch [ˈbiːblɪʃ] *adj.* biblical, scriptural; ~**e Geschichte** story from the Bible; *fig.* **das** ~**e Alter von ... erreichen** live to the ripe old age of ...
Bi·det [biˈdeː] *n* (-s; -s) bidet
bie·der [ˈbiːdɐ] *adj.* honest, upright; simple
ˈBie·der·mann *m* (-[e]s; -männer) honest man (*or* citizen); *contp.* petty bourgeois
Bie·der·mei·er [ˈbiːdɐmaɪɐ] *n* (-s; *no pl.*) Biedermeier (period *or* style); ~**zeit** *f* (-; *no pl.*) Biedermeier period
bieg·bar [ˈbiːkbaːɐ] *adj.* flexible, pliable
ˈBie·ge·fe·stig·keit *f* (-; *no pl.*) bending strength
bie·gen (bog, gebogen, h) **I.** *v/t.* bend; curve; camber; **II.** *v/refl.*: **sich** ~ bend; **III.** *v/i.* (sn): **nach links (rechts)** ~ turn left (right); **um e-e Ecke** ~ turn (round) a corner; **IV.** ≈ *n*: **auf** ~ **oder Brechen** F come hell or high water
bieg·sam [ˈbiːkzaːm] *adj.* pliable (*a. fig.*), flexible; supple, lithe; *fig.* malleable, pliant; **ˈBieg·sam·keit** *f* (-; *no pl.*) pliability (*a. fig.*), flexibility; suppleness; *fig.* malleability
Bie·gung [ˈbiːgʊŋ] *f* (-; -en) bend; curve; curvature; **e-e** ~ **machen** curve
Bie·ne [ˈbiːnə] *f* (-; -n) **1.** bee; **männliche** ~ drone; *fig.* **fleißig wie e-e** ~ (as) busy as a bee; **2.** F girl, *sl.* chick
ˈBie·nen|fleiß *m* industriousness; *formal*: sedulousness; ≈**flei·ßig** *adj.* very hard-working (*or* industrious); ~**gift** *n* bee poison; ~**haus** *n* apiary; ~**ho·nig** *m* honey; ~**kö·ni·gin** *f* queen bee; ~**korb** *m* beehive; ~**schwarm** *m* swarm of bees;

~staat *m* colony of bees; **~stich** *m* **1.** bee sting; **2.** *almond-covered cake filled with cream or custard*; **~stock** *m* beehive; *fig.* ***da wimmelt es wie im ~*** it's swarming with people; **~wa·be** *f* honeycomb; **~wachs** *n* beeswax; **~zucht** *f* beekeeping; *formal*: apiculture; **~züch·ter** *m* beekeeper, apiarist

Bier [biːɐ] *n* (-[e]s; -e) beer; ***helles ~*** lager, *Am. a.* light beer; ***dunkles ~*** brown ale, *Am.* dark beer; ***~ vom Faß*** draught (*Am.* draft) beer; ***zwei ~ bitte!*** two beers, please; F *fig.* ***das ist nicht mein ~!*** F that's not my pigeon; **~baß** F *m* deep bass (voice); **~bauch** *m* beer belly, paunch, F beer gut; **~brau·er** *m* brewer; **~braue'rei** *f* brewery; **~deckel** (*sep.* -k·k-) *m* beer mat, *esp. Am.* (beer) coaster; **~do·se** *f* beer can; **~ei·fer** F *m* grim-faced zeal, dogged determination

'bier·ernst F **I.** *adj.* deadly serious; **II.** ♀ *m* (-es; *no pl.*) deadly seriousness

'Bier|fah·ne F *f* beery breath; ***e-e ~ haben*** smell of beer; **~faß** *n* beer barrel; **~filz** *m* → ***Bierdeckel***; **~fla·sche** *f* beer bottle; **~gar·ten** *m* beer garden; **~glas** *n* beer glass; **~hahn** *m* beer tap; **~he·fe** *f* brewer's yeast; **~ka·sten** *m* beer crate (*Am.* case); **~kel·ler** *m* **1.** beer cellar, bierkeller; **2.** beer cellar; **~krug** *m* tankard; beer mug, (beer) stein; **~lau·ne** *f* jolly mood, high spirits *pl.*; **~lei·che** F *f* drunk, F drunken heap; ***am Schluß gab es e-e Menge ~n*** there were quite a few drunks littered about the place at the end; **~rei·se** F *f* F pub crawl; ***auf e-e ~ gehen*** go (off) on a pub crawl; **~ru·he** F *f* unflappability; ***sich nicht aus s-r ~ bringen lassen*** remain unflappable; **~sei·del** *n* beer mug, (beer) stein; **~zelt** *n* beer tent

Bie·se ['biːzə] *f* (-; -n) **1.** tuck; **2.** *a. pl.* piping

Biest [biːst] *n* (-[e]s; -er) beast; F *fig.* F brat; *sl.* swine; F cow; ***freches ~*** F cheeky brat, F cheeky cow; ***faules ~*** F lazy brat, *sl.* lazy sod

bie·ten (bot, geboten, h) **I.** *v/t.* offer (***j-m et.*** s.o. s.th.); present *view, difficulties etc.*; afford, give; show; ✝ bid; ***mehr*** (***weniger***) ***~ als*** outbid (underbid); ***im Kino*** *etc.* ***geboten werden*** be on at the cinema (*esp. Am.* movies) *etc.*; ***was hast du uns heute zu ~?*** *a. iro.* what have you got to offer us today?, what have you got lined up for us today?; ***j-m Hilfe*** (***Trost***) ***~*** help (comfort) s.o.; ***wer bietet mehr?*** *auction*: any more bids?; ***bis zu DM 50000 ~*** go as high as 50000 marks; ***das läßt er sich nicht ~*** he won't stand for that; ***das solltest du dir nicht ~ lassen*** I wouldn't stand for it if I were you; ***und das läßt du dir einfach ~?*** and you just sit back and take it?; **II.** *v/refl.*: ***sich ~*** *opportunity etc.*: come up, present itself; ***es bot sich ihr e-e traumhafte*** (***grauenvolle***) ***Szene*** a wonderful scene unfolded before her eyes (she was met with a scene of horror); **Bie·ter** ['biːtɐ] *m* (-s; -) bidder

bi·fo·kal [bifo'kaːl] *adj.* bifocal; ♀**bril·le** *f*: (***e-e ~*** a pair of) bifocals *pl.*, bifocal glasses *pl.*

Bi·ga·mie [biga'miː] *f* (-; -n) bigamy; **Bi·ga·mist** [biga'mɪst] *m* (-en; -en) bigamist

bi·gott [bi'gɔt] *adj.* (over)sanctimonious; self-righteous, F holier-than-thou; hypocritical; **Bi·got·te·rie** [bigɔtə'riː] *f* (-; *no pl.*) (over)sanctimoniousness; self-righteousness; hypocrisy

Bi·ki·ni [bi'kiːni] *m* (-s; -s) bikini

bi·kon·kav [bikɔn'kaːf] *adj.* biconcave

bi·kon·vex [bikɔn'vɛks] *adj.* biconvex

Bi·lanz [bi'lants] *f* (-; -en) balance; balance sheet; *fig.* result, outcome; stocktaking; survey; ***e-e ~ aufstellen*** draw up (*or* make out) a balance sheet; ***die ~ ziehen*** strike the balance, *fig.* take stock (***aus*** *dat.* of); *fig.* ***~ ziehen*** take stock of one's life; ***traurige ~*** sad outcome, tragic toll; **~buch** *n* balance sheet book; **~buch·hal·ter** *m* accountant; **~de,likt** *n* accounting fraud, *a. pl.* F cooking (*or* juggling) the books

bi·lan·zie·ren [bilan'tsiːrən] (h) **I.** *v/i.* **1.** make out a balance sheet; **2.** show in the balance sheet; **II.** *v/t.* balance *accounts*

Bi'lanz|jahr *n* financial (*or* fiscal) year; **~po·sten** *m* balance sheet item; **~prü·fer** *m* auditor; **~prü·fung** *f* balance sheet audit; **~sum·me** *f* balance sheet total; **~ver·schleie·rung** *f* window-dressing, F cooking the books; **~wert** *m* balance sheet value

bi·la·te·ral ['biːlateraːl] *adj.* bilateral

Bild [bɪlt] *n* (-[e]s; -er ['bɪldɐ]) picture (*a. phot., TV and fig.*); image (*a. TV*); painting, portrait; photo; illustration; *thea. etc.* scene; *in the credits*: Camera; *fig.* sight; idea; image; description, portrait; *rhet.* metaphor, simile; ***~ der Zerstörung*** (***des Grauens***) scene of destruction (horror); ***ein ~ von e-m Mädchen*** a lovely girl; ***im ~e sein*** be in the picture; ***jetzt bin ich im ~e*** now I get the picture, F now I get it, I'm with you now; ***j-n ins ~ setzen*** put s.o. in the picture (***über*** *acc.* about), ***über*** *acc.*: *a.* fill s.o. in on; ***ein falsches ~ bekommen*** get the wrong idea (*or* impression, picture); ***sich ein ~ machen*** form an impression (in one's mind) (***von*** *dat.* of); ***sich ein ~ machen von*** *a.* visualize, see *s.th.* for o.s.; ***sich ein falsches*** (***zu optimistisches*** *etc.*) ***~ machen von*** *dat.* see *s.th.* in the wrong light (too optimistically *etc.*); ***du machst dir kein ~*** you have no idea; → ***düster*** I; **~ab·ta·stung** *f TV* scanning; **~ar,chiv** *n* photo (*or* picture) library; **~auf·lö·sung** *f* definition, (picture) resolution; **~aus·fall** *m TV* picture loss; **~aus·schnitt** *m* detail; **~band** *m* (-[e]s; ⸚e) illustrated book; **~bei·la·ge** *f* colo(u)r supplement; **~be·richt** *m* picture story; **~brei·te** *f* picture width; **~do·ku,ment** *n* documentary photo (*or* drawing, film, footage *etc.*); **~do·ku·men·ta·ti,on** *f* picture (*or* photo, film *etc.*) documentary; **~ein·stel·lung** *f* (image) focus(s)ing; **~ele,ment** *n TV etc.* pixel, picture element

bil·den ['bɪldən] (h) **I.** *v/t.* **1.** form; shape, mo(u)ld (*all a. fig.*); make; *typ.* make (up); *ling.* coin; ***sich e-e Meinung ~*** form an opinion; **2.** create; establish, set up; form *a government*; **3.** form, develop; **4.** form, constitute, make up, comprise, be; ***e-e Ausnahme ~*** be an exception; ***die Regel ~*** be the rule; **5.** educate, cultivate; → ***gebildet*** II; **II.** *v/i.* **6.** broaden the mind; ***Reisen bildet*** *a.* there's nothing like travel for broadening the mind; **III.** *v/refl.*: ***sich ~*** **7.** form, ⚕ *tumo(u)r etc.*: grow, develop; **8.** educate o.s., F get some culture; *w.s.* broaden one's horizons; **'bil·dend** *adj.* **1.** educational; **2.** ***~e Künste*** fine arts

Bil·der|at·las ['bɪldɐ-] *m* picture atlas; **~bo·gen** *m art*: illustrated broadsheet; **~buch** *n* picture book; ***Schottland wie aus dem ~*** a picture-book Scotland

Bil·der·buch... ['bɪldɐ-] *in cpds.* F *fig.* perfect ...; model ...; *a. sport*: textbook ..., copybook ...; **~ehe·mann** *m a* model husband, *the* perfect husband; **~hoch·zeit** *f* fairytale wedding; **~land·schaft** *f* storybook landscape; **~lan·dung** *f* textbook landing; **~som·mer** *m* perfect summer; **~wet·ter** *n* perfect (*or* glorious, unbelievable) weather

Bil·der|chro·nik ['bɪldɐ-] *f* illustrated (*or* picture) chronicle; **~ga·le,rie** *f* picture gallery; **~ge·schich·te** *f* picture story; comic strip, strip cartoon; **~rah·men** *m* picture frame; **~rät·sel** *n* picture puzzle

bil·der·reich ['bɪldɐ-] *adj.* richly illustrated; *ling.* rich in imagery

Bil·der|schrift ['bɪldɐ-] *f* pictographic system; hieroglyphics *pl.*; **~spra·che** *f* imagery (and metaphor); **~streit** *m hist.* iconoclastic controversy

Bil·der·sturm ['bɪldɐ-] *m hist.* iconoclasm; iconoclastic movement; **'Bil·der·stür·mer** *m a. fig.* iconoclast; **bil·der·stür·me·risch** ['bɪldɐʃtʏrmərɪʃ] *fig. adj.* iconoclastic

'Bild|fang *m video*: frame hold; **~feld** *n* field of vision; *TV* a) picture screen, b) frame; **~flä·che** *f TV* image area; *film*: screen; F *fig.* ***von der ~ verschwinden*** disappear from the scene, F do a vanishing trick; ***er ist wie von der ~ verschwunden*** he seems to have vanished into thin air; ***auf der ~ erscheinen*** (suddenly) appear on the scene, suddenly appear from nowhere; **~fol·ge** *f* picture sequence; *TV* picture frequency

'bild·haft **I.** *adj.* **1.** visual; **2.** *ling.* rich in imagery; **3.** vivid, graphic *description etc.*; **II.** *adv.*: ***et. ~ beschreiben*** give a vivid (*or* graphic) description of s.th.; ***sich et. ~ vorstellen*** (try and) visualize s.th., conjure s.th. up in one's mind; **Bild·haf·tig·keit** ['bɪlthaftɪçkaɪt] *f* (-; *no pl.*) **1.** *ling.* rich imagery (*gen.* of, in); **2.** vividness, graphic nature (*gen.* of)

'Bild·hau·er *m* (-s; -) sculptor; **'Bild·hau·er·ate·lier** *n* sculptor's studio; **Bild·haue'rei** *f* (-; *no pl.*), **'Bild·hau·er·kunst** *f* sculpture; **'Bild·hau·er·werk·statt** *f* sculptor's workshop (*or* studio)

'Bild·hel·lig·keit *f* (-; *no pl.*) *TV* (image) brightness

'bild'hübsch *adj.* lovely(-looking); beautiful, lovely

'Bild|idee *f* idea for a (*or* the) picture *or* painting; ***die ~ kam von ...*** *a.* the picture (*or* painting) was inspired by ...; **~journa,list** *m* photojournalist; **~kom·po·si·ti,on** *f* composition of a (*or* the) picture *or* painting

'bild·lich **I.** *adj.* pictorial, graphic; visual; ***~e Umsetzung*** visualization; ***~er Ausdruck*** figurative expression, metaphor (-ical expression); **II.** *adv.*: ***~ gesprochen*** figuratively speaking; ***sich et. ~ vorstellen*** → ***bildhaft*** II

'Bild|ma·te·ri,al *n* illustrations *pl.*; photos *pl.*; **~nach·weis** *m* acknowledg(e)ment; *pl.* photo credits

bild·ne·risch ['bɪltnərɪʃ] *adj.* **1.** artistic; *w.s.* creative; ***~e Darstellung*** artistic representation; **2.** sculptural

Bild·nis ['bɪltnɪs] *n* (-ses; -se) portrait; effigy, head *of coin*

'**Bild|plat·te** *f TV* video disc; **~plat·ten·spie·ler** *m* video disc player; **~qua·li,tät** *f TV* picture quality; **~re·por,ta·ge** *f* picture story; *TV* film documentary; **~röh·re** *f TV* tube, picture (*or* cathode ray) tube; **~schär·fe** *f* definition, sharpness

'**Bild·schirm** *m* screen; *computer*: *a.* display, monitor; F TV, F *the* box; **~an·zei·ge** *f* monitor (*or* screen) display; **~ar·beits·platz** *m* workstation; **~auf·lö·sung** *f* screen resolution; **~ge·rät** *n* visual display unit; **~ka·pa·zi,tät** *f* display capacity; **~kar·te** *f* graphics card (*or* adapter); **~mas·ke** *f* screen mask; **~sei·te** *f* screen page; **~text** *m* viewdata

'**Bild·schnit·zer** *m* (-s; -) (wood) carver; **Bild·schnit·ze'rei** *f* (-; -en) (wood) carving

'**bild'schön** *adj.* beautiful; ***es ist ~*** *a.* it's a dream

'**Bild|sei·te** *f* **1.** *typ.* picture page; **2.** face, obverse *of coin*; **~se·rie** *f* picture series; **~si,gnal** *n* picture signal; **~stel·le** *f* picture (*or* film) library; **~stö·rung** *f* (TV) interference; **~su·cher** *m phot.* viewfinder; **~such·lauf** *m video*: picture search; ***~ rückwärts*** review; ***~ vorwärts*** cue; **~sym,bol** *n* pictogram; *computer*: icon; **~ta·fel** *f* plate; **~te·le,fon** *n* videophone; **~tep·pich** *m* tapestry; **~text** *m* caption; **~über,tra·gung** *f* picture transmission

Bil·dung ['bɪldʊŋ] *f* (-; -en) **1.** education; learning, erudition; culture; ***~ haben*** be educated, be cultured; ***ein Mensch mit ~*** an educated (*or* a cultured) person; ***er hat überhaupt keine ~*** he's completely uneducated (*or* uncultured), he's got no education (*or* culture); **2.** *biol.* formation; development; **3.** creation, formation; establishment; setting up *of a committee etc.*; **4.** *ling.* coinage; forming *of a sentence etc.*; **5.** *ling.* form

'**Bil·dungs|an·stalt** *f* educational establishment; **⁀be·flis·sen** *adj.* eager to learn, eager for knowledge; **~bür·ger·tum** *n the* educated classes *pl.*; **~chan·cen** *pl.* educational opportunities; ***gleiche ~*** equal opportunities in education; **~drang** *m* → ***Bildungseifer***; **~dün·kel** *m* intellectual snobbery (*or* conceit); **~ei·fer** *m* desire for education; **⁀eif·rig** *adj.* → ***bildungsbeflissen***; **~ein·rich·tung** *f* educational institution; **~fa,brik** F *f* educational mill

'**bil·dungs·fä·hig** *adj.* educable; '**Bil·dungs·fä·hig·keit** *f* educability

'**bil·dungs·feind·lich** *adj.* anti-education; *a.* (educationally) retrogressive *policy*

'**Bil·dungs|gang** *m* education, educational background; **~ge·we·be** *n anat.* formative tissue; **~grad** *m* educational level; **~hun·ger** *m* thirst for knowledge (*or* education); **⁀hung·rig** *adj.* hungry for knowledge, education-hungry; **~lü·cke** (*sep.* -k·k-) *f* gap in one's knowledge; **~mi,ni·ster** *m* education minister, minister for education; *in GB*: Secretary of State for Education, Education Secretary; *in the USA*: Secretary of Education; **~mi·ni,ste·ri·um** *n* ministry of education, education ministry; *in GB*: Department of Education and Science; *in the USA*: Department of Education; **~mo·no,pol** *n* monopoly on education; ***das ~ haben*** *a.* control education; **~ni,veau** *n* (level of) education, educational standard(s *pl.*); **~not·stand** *m* education crisis; **~po·li,tik** *f* educational policy; **⁀po,li·tisch** *adj.* educational, education policy ...; **~re,form** *f* educational reform; **~rei·se** *f* educational trip; **~ro,man** *m* novel of education, Bildungsroman; **~stand** *m* level of education; **~stät·te** *f* educational institution; **~stu·fe** *f* educational level; **~sy,stem** *n* education system; **~ur·laub** *m* educational leave; **~weg** *m* **1.** education; **2.** ***zweiter ~*** evening classes *pl.* (*with a view to obtaining school or university qualifications*); ***auf dem zweiten ~*** through evening classes; **~we·sen** *n* (-s; *no pl.*) education; **~zen·trum** *n* educational cent|re (*Am.* -er)

'**Bild|,un·ter·schrift** *f* caption; **~wand** *f* projection screen; **~wand·ler** *m opt.* image converter; **~win·kel** *m* angle of vision; **~wör·ter·buch** *n* picture dictionary; **~zäh·ler** *m phot.* frame counter; **~zei·le** *f TV* (scanning) line

Bil·har·zio·se [bɪlhar'tsi̯oːzə] *f* (-; -n) bilharzia

Bil·lard ['bɪljart] *n* (-s- -e [-də]) billiards (*sg.*); **~ball** *m*, **~ku·gel** *f* billiard ball; **~saal** *m* billiard room, *Am.* poolroom; **~stock** *m* (billiard) cue; **~tisch** *m* billiard table

bil·lig ['bɪlɪç] **I.** *adj.* **1.** cheap, inexpensive; low *price*; ***ein ~er Kauf*** a bargain; **2.** *fig.* cheap; lame, poor *excuse*, *advice etc.*; ***~er Trost*** small consolation; **3.** just; fair; → ***recht*** I; **II.** *adv. produce etc.*: cheaply; ***et. ~ bekommen*** (***verkaufen***) get (sell) s.th. cheap(ly); ***~ wegkommen*** get off cheaply (*fig.* lightly); ***~ abzugeben!*** cheap sale; ***Schallplatten ~ abzugeben!*** cheap records; **⁀an·ge·bot** *n* cut-price offer

bil·li·gen ['bɪlɪgən] *v/t.* (h) approve of; *formal*: sanction; endorse; *adm.* approve; '**bil·li·gend** *adj.* approving(ly *adv.*)

'**Bil·lig|flag·ge** *f* ⚓ flag of convenience; **~flug** *m* cheap flight; **~flug·prei·se** *pl.* cut-price (air) fares; **~im,por·te** *pl.* cut-price imports

'**Bil·lig·keit** *f* (-; *no pl.*) **1.** cheapness; **2.** *fig.* cheapness; justness; fairness, equity

'**Bil·lig·ko,pie** *f* cheap imitation

'**Bil·lig·lohn·land** *n* low-wage country

'**Bil·lig|preis** *m* low price; **~rei·se** *f* cheap holiday; *pl. coll. a.* cut-price travel *sg.*

'**Bil·li·gung** *f* (-; *no pl.*) approval, approbation; endorsement; ***j-s ~ finden*** meet with s.o.'s approval

Bil·li·on [bɪ'li̯oːn] *f* (-; -en) (10^{12}) trillion, million million, *Brit. obs.* billion; **Bil·li'on·stel** [-stəl] *n* (-s; -) trillionth, million millionth, *Brit. obs.* billionth

Bim·bam[1] ['bɪm'bam] *n* (-s; *no pl.*) ding-dong

'**Bim'bam**[2] F *m*: (***du***) ***heiliger ~!*** F crikey!, Gordon Bennett!, *sl.* hell's bells!

bim·meln ['bɪməln] F *v/i.* (h) ring; ***es hat gebimmelt*** there's s.o. at the door

bim·sen ['bɪmzən] *v/t.* (h) **1.** (rub with) pumice; **2.** F ⚔ drill hard, put *recruits etc.* through their paces; **3.** F beat up; **4.** F swot up, mug up

Bims·stein ['bɪms-] *m* pumice (stone)

bi·när [bi'nɛːɐ] *adj.* ⚗, *phys. etc.* binary; **⁀code** *m computer*: binary code; **⁀sy,stem** *n* binary system; **⁀zahl** *f* binary number; **⁀zei·chen** *n* binary digit; bit

Bin·de ['bɪndə] *f* (-; -n) ⚕ bandage; sling; sanitary towel (*Am.* napkin); necktie; armband; blindfold; ***den Arm in e-r ~ tragen*** have one's arm in a sling; F (***sich***) ***e-n hinter die ~ gießen*** F have a tipple, hoist one

'**Bin·de·ge·we·be** *n anat.* connective tissue; '**Bin·de·ge·webs·ent·zün·dung** *f* fibrositis

'**Bin·de·glied** *n* (connecting) link, connection; *fig.* ***fehlendes ~*** missing link

'**Bin·de·haut** *f anat.* conjunctiva; **~ent·zün·dung** *f* conjunctivitis

'**Bin·de·mit·tel** *n* **1.** ⚙ bonding agent; **2.** *gastr.* thickening

bin·den ['bɪndən] (band, gebunden, h) **I.** *v/t.* **1.** *a. fig.* tie (**an** *acc.* to); *fig.* ***j-n an sich ~*** tie s.o. to o.s.; ***j-n an Händen und Füßen ~*** bind s.o. hand and foot; ***mich bindet nichts an diesen Ort*** I have no real ties to this place; **2.** tie (up); tie *knot*; tie (a knot in); make; ***Rosen zu e-m Strauß ~*** tie roses into a bouquet, make a bouquet of roses; **3.** *typ.* bind; ***zum ⁀ geben*** have *a book* bound; **4.** ⚗ bind; *a. phys.* absorb *heat*; **5.** ⚙ bond, cement; **6.** *gastr.* thicken, bind; **7.** ♪ tie; slur; **8.** *ling.* link; **9.** ⚘ tie up *funds etc.*; fix *prices*; **10.** bind, commit *s.o.*; tie *s.o.* down (**an** *acc.* to); → ***gebunden*** II; **II.** *v/i.* **11.** bind; **12.** *gastr.* bind, thicken; **13.** *glue*: stick; *cement etc.*: harden, set; *plastics*: bond; **14.** *fig.* create a bond; **III.** *v/refl.*: ***sich ~*** commit o.s., tie o.s. down (**an** *acc.* to); bind o.s. (to); *contp.* get tied down; ***sie will sich noch nicht ~*** *a.* she doesn't want to commit herself yet; '**bin·dend** *fig. adj.* binding (**für** *acc.* upon)

'**Bin·de|strich** *m* hyphen; ***hat es e-n ~?*** has it got a hyphen?, is it hyphenated?; **~wort** *n* conjunction

Bind·fa·den ['bɪnt-] *m*: (***ein ~*** a piece of *or* some) string; *fig.* ***es regnet Bindfäden*** it's pouring, F it's coming down in buckets

Bin·dung ['bɪndʊŋ] *f* (-; -en) **1.** (close) relationship (**zu** with, to); bond (**an** *acc.* with), *a. pol.* ties *pl.* (to, with); attachment (to *s.th.*); **2.** commitment, obligation; ***e-e ~*** (*or* ***~en***) ***eingehen*** commit o.s., tie o.s. down (**mit** *dat.* to); ***ohne ~en*** without (any) obligation(s), unattached; **3.** *ski*: binding; **4.** ⚗, *phys.*, ⚙ bond(ing); **5.** *a. biol.* linkage; **6.** *phys.* absorption; fusion; **7.** ♪ ligature

'**Bin·dungs·angst** *f* fear of getting too involved (with anyone)

bin·dungs·fä·hig *adj.*: (***nicht ~*** in)capable of having a (personal) relationship

bin·nen ['bɪnən] *prp.* (*dat.*) within; ***~ kurzem*** before long, within a short space of time

'**bin·nen·deutsch** **I.** *adj.* ⚘ internal, domestic (German); **II.** ⁀ *n* German (as) spoken in Germany, F German German

'**Bin·nen|fi·sche,rei** *f* freshwater fishing; **~ge·wäs·ser** *pl.* inland waters; **~ha·fen** *m* inland (*or* river) port; **~han·del** *m* domestic trade

'**Bin·nen·land** *n* interior, inland area; ***im ~*** inland; '**bin·nen·län·disch** [-lɛndɪʃ] *adj.* inland ...

'**Bin·nen|markt** *m* home (*or* domestic) market; *EC*: internal market; **~meer** *n* inland sea; **~reim** *m* internal rhyme; **~schiffahrt** (*sep.* -ff·f-) *f* inland navigation; **~see** *m* inland lake; **~staat** *m* inland (*or* landlocked) state *or* country; **~ver·kehr** *m* inland traffic; **~wan·de-**

rung *f* internal migration; **~was·ser·stra·ße** *f* inland waterway; **~wirt·schaft** *f* (-; *no pl.*) domestic economy; **~zoll** *m* inland duty

Bi·nom [bi'noːm] *n* (-s; -e), **bi·no·misch** [bi'noːmɪʃ] *adj.* ℞ binomial

Bin·se ['bɪnzə] *f* (-; -n) ♣ rush; F *fig.* ***in die ~n gehen*** *plan etc.*: F go up in smoke, *apparatus etc.*: F give up the ghost, conk out

'Bin·sen·weis·heit *f* (-; -en) truism, commonplace, platitude

Bio ['biːo] F *f* (-; *no pl.*) biology

bio·ak·tiv [bioˀak'tiːf] *adj.* biological

Bio·ar·chi·tek'tur [bio-] *f* bio-architecture

Bio·che'mie [bio-] *f* biochemistry; **Bio·'che·mi·ker** *m* biochemist; **bio'che·misch** *adj.* biochemical

bio·dy'na·misch [bio-] *adj.* biodynamic

Bio·ener'ge·tik [bio-] *f* bioenergetics *pl.*

Bio'ethik [bio-] *f* bioethics *pl.*

Bio·gas ['biːo-] *n* biogas, *a.* methane

bio·gen [bio'geːn] *adj.* biogenic

Bio·ge'ne·se [bio-] *f* biogenesis; **Bio·ge'ne·tik** *f* biogenetics *pl.*; **bio·ge'ne·tisch** *adj.* biogenetic(ally *adv.*)

Bio·graph [bio'graːf] *m* (-en; -en) biographer; **Bio·gra·phie** [biogra'fiː] *f* (-; -n) biography; **bio·gra·phisch** [bio'graːfɪʃ] *adj.* biographical

Bio·kost ['biːo-] *f* organic food

Bio·la·den ['biːo-] *m* whole food shop

Bio·lo·ge [bio'loːgə] *m* (-n; -n) biologist; **Bio·lo·gie** [biolo'giː] *f* (-; *no pl.*) biology; **bio·lo·gisch** [bio'loːgɪʃ] **I.** *adj.* biological (*a. fig.*); ***~er Anbau*** organic farming (*or* gardening); ***~e Waffen*** biological weapons; **II.** *adv.*: ***~ abbaubar*** biodegradable; **bio'lo·gisch-dy'na·misch** *adj.* organic, biological

Bio·mas·se ['biːo-] *m* biomass

Bio·me·trie [biome'triː] *f* (-; *no pl.*) biometry, biometrics *pl.*; **bio·me·trisch** [bio'meːtrɪʃ] *adj.* biometric

Bio·nik [bi'oːnɪk] *f* (-; *no pl.*) bionics *pl.*; **bio·nisch** [bi'oːnɪʃ] *adj.* bionic

Bio·phy'sik [bio-] *f* biophysics *pl.*; **Bio'phy·si·ker** *m* biophysicist

Bi·op·sie [biɔ'psiː] *f* (-; -n) biopsy

Bio·rhyth·mus ['biːo-] *m* biorhythm

Bio'sphä·re [bio-] *f* (-; *no pl.*) biosphere

Bio'tech·nik [bio-] *f* biotechnology, bioengineering

Bio·top [bio'toːp] *n* (-s; -e) biotope

Bio·wis·sen·schaft ['biːo-] *f* life science, bioscience; **'Bio·wis·sen·schaft·ler** *m* bioscientist; **'bio·wis·sen·schaft·lich** *adj.* bioscientific

bi·po·lar [bipo'laːɐ] *adj.* bipolar; **Bi·po·la·ri·tät** [bipolari'tɛːt] *f* (-; *no pl.*) bipolarity

Bir·ke ['bɪrkə] *f* (-; -n) birch (tree)

'Bir·ken|al,lee *f* avenue of birches; **~hain** *m* birch grove; **~holz** *n* birch (-wood); **~ru·te** *f* birch rod; **~wald** *m* birch(wood) forest, birch wood; **~was·ser** *n* hair lotion (*made from birch sap*)

Birk·hahn ['bɪrk-] *m* black cock; **'Birk·huhn** *n* black grouse

Bir·ma·ne [bɪr'maːnə] *m* (-n; -n), **Bir·ma·nin** [bɪr'maːnɪn] *f* (-; -nen), **bir·ma·nisch** [bɪr'maːnɪʃ] *adj.* Burmese

Birn·baum ['bɪrn-] *m* pear tree

Bir·ne ['bɪrnə] *f* (-; -n) **1.** pear; pear tree; F *fig.* F noddle, nut; F *fig.* ***e-e weiche ~ haben*** be (going) soft in the head; **2.** (electric) (light) bulb

'Bir·nen|fas·sung *f* ⚡ **1.** light-bulb socket; **2.** thread (of the *or* a light bulb); **2för·mig** *adj.* pear-shaped; **~saft** *m* pear juice

bis [bɪs] **I.** *prp.* (*acc.*) **1.** till, until; ***~ heute*** so far, to date, to this day; ***~ jetzt*** up to now; so far; ***~ jetzt noch nicht*** not (as) yet; ***ich habe ~ jetzt nichts gehört*** I haven't heard anything yet (*or* so far); ***~ dahin*** until then, in the meantime; ***~ auf weiteres*** for the present; ***~ in die Nacht*** into the night; ***~ zum späten Nachmittag*** till late in the afternoon; ***~ vor einigen Jahren*** until a few years ago; ***~ zum Ende*** (right) to the end; ***~ wann*** *wird es dauern?* how long ...?; ***in der Zeit vom ... ~ ...*** between ... and ...; ***~ morgen (bald)!*** see you tomorrow (soon); ***~ dann!*** see you then (*or* later); **2.** by; by the time *he gets back etc.*; ***es muß ~ Freitag eingereicht werden*** it has to be handed in by Friday; ***~ wann ist es fertig?*** when will it be ready by?; ***~ Ende April*** by the end of April; ***alle ~ ... eingegangenen Bewerbungen*** all applications received by (*or* before) ...; ***er hätte ~ jetzt dasein müssen*** he should have been here by now; ***~ dahin*** *werden wir fertig sein etc.* by then, by that time; **3.** to, up to, as far as; ***~ hierher*** up to here; ***~ dahin*** as far as that (*or* there); ***~ wohin?*** how far?; ***~ ans Knie*** up to one's knees, *skirt*: down to the knee; ***von hier ~ New York*** from here to New York; ***~ vor das Haus fahren*** drive up to the front door of the house, drive (right) up to the house; ***wie weit ist es noch ~ nach Innsbruck?*** how far is it to Innsbruck?, how far have we got to go (before we get) to Innsbruck?; ***er folgte mir bis ins Hotelfoyer*** he followed me (right) into the hotel foyer (*or* as far as the hotel foyer); → ***hier*** 1, ***oben*** *etc.*; **4. *7 ~ 10 Tage*** from 7 to 10 days, between 7 and 10 days; ***5 ~ 6 Wagen*** 5 to 6 cars; ***~ zu*** *100 Mann* up to ..., as many as ...; ***~ zu ... hoch*** up to ..., as high as ...; ***~ 20 zählen*** count (up) to 20; ***~ auf das letzte Stück*** down to the last bit (*or* piece); **5.** ***~ aufs höchste*** to the utmost; ***~ ins kleinste*** down to the last detail; ***~ zur Tollkühnheit*** to the point of rashness; → ***Bewußtlosigkeit***; **6.** ***~ auf*** *acc.* except, with the exception of; ***alle ~ auf einen*** all except (*or* but) one; ***~ auf drei sind alle gekommen*** all except three have come; → ***letzt*** I; **II.** *cj.* till, until; by the time; ***es wird e-e Zeitlang dauern, ~ er es merkt*** it will take a while for him to find out (*or* before he finds out); ***er kommt nicht, ~ ich ihn rufe*** he won't come until (*or* unless) I call him; ***du gehst nicht, ~ du aufgeräumt hast*** you're not going until (*or* before) you've tidied up

Bi·sam ['biːzam] *m* (-s; -s) *zo.* musk; musquash *or* muskrat (fur); **~rat·te** *f* muskrat

Bi·schof ['bɪʃɔf] *m* (-s; Bischöfe ['bɪʃœfə]) bishop; **bi·schöf·lich** ['bɪʃœflɪç] *adj.* episcopal

'Bi·schofs|amt *n* episcopate, bishopric; **~kon·fe,renz** *f* bishops' conference; **~müt·ze** *f* mit|re (*Am.* -er); **~sitz** *m* episcopal see; **~stab** *m* crosier, crozier; **~syn,ode** *f* episcopal synod, synod of bishops

Bi·se·xua·li·tät [bizɛksŭali'tɛːt] *f* (-; *no pl.*) bisexuality; **bi·se·xu·ell** [bizɛ'ksŭɛl] *adj.* bisexual

bis·her [bɪs'heːɐ] *adv.* up to now, so far; ***~ (noch) nicht*** not (as) yet; ***wie ~*** as before, as always; ***das ~ beste Ergebnis*** the best result so far; **bis·he·rig** [bɪs'heːrɪç] *adj.* ... so far, ... up to now, ... up till (*or* until) now; ...; present ...; past, previous *experience*; ***der ~e Minister*** *etc.* the outgoing minister *etc.*; ***die ~en Ereignisse*** events so far

Bis·kuit [bɪs'kviːt] *n, m* (-[e]s; -s, -e) (fatless) sponge; **~bo·den** *m* flan base; **~rol·le** *f* Swiss roll

bis'lang *adv.* → ***bisher***

Bi·son ['biːzɔn] *m* (-s; -s) *zo.* bison

biß [bɪs] *pret. of* ***beißen***

Biß *m* (Bisses; Bisse) bite (*a.* ⚒ *and fig.*); *fig.* ***sie spielten mit (ohne) ~*** they played with a lot of fight (there was no fight in their play)

biß·chen ['bɪsçən] **I.** *adj.*: ***ein ~*** a (little) bit of; a little; a drop of; ***ein kleines ~*** a tiny bit, just a little (bit); ***das ~ Geld, das sie hat*** what little money she has; ***wegen dem ~ Dreck hat sie sich aufgeregt?*** she got upset about a bit of dirt?; **II.** *adv.*: ***ein ~*** a bit; slightly; ***kein ~ müde*** not (in) the least bit tired; ***ein ~ viel*** a bit (too) much; ***das ist ein ~ zuviel verlangt*** that's asking a bit much; ***wenn du ein ~ wartest*** if you wait a while (F hang on a bit); ***ein ~ schneller!*** a bit faster, F get a move on!; **III.** *su.* a (little) bit; a little; ***kein ~*** not a bit; F ***ach du liebes ~!*** goodness (me)!, good grief!

Bis·sen ['bɪsən] *m* (-s; -) **1.** bite (***von*** *dat.* of); morsel; titbit, *Am.* tidbit; ***ich brachte keinen ~ hinunter*** I couldn't eat a thing; ***er rührte keinen ~ an*** he didn't touch (*or* eat) a thing; *fig.* ***mir blieb der ~ im Hals stecken*** I nearly choked; ***sich den letzten ~ vom Mund absparen*** stint o.s.; **2.** bite, snack

bis·sig ['bɪsɪç] *adj.* **1.** vicious *dog*; ***der Hund ist (nicht) ~*** *a.* the dog bites (doesn't bite); ***Vorsicht, ~er Hund!*** beware of the dog; **2.** *fig.* cutting, caustic, mordant *remark etc.*; scathing *criticism*; snappy *person*; **'Bis·sig·keit** *f* (-; -en) **1.** acerbity; **2.** *no pl.* sharpness *of a remark etc.*; *s.o.'s* snappiness

'Biß·wun·de *f* bite

Bis·tum ['bɪstuːm] *n* (-s; Bistümer ['bɪstyːmɐ] *eccl.* bishopric, diocese

bis·wei·len [bɪs'vaɪlən] *adv.* at times; from time to time, occasionally

Bit [bɪt] *n* (-[s]; -[s]) *computer*: bit; **~dich·te** *f* bit density; **~ra·te** *f* bit rate

Bitt·brief ['bɪt-] *m* petition

Bit·te ['bɪtə] *f* (-; -n) request; petition (*a. eccl.*); ***dringende ~*** urgent appeal (*or* plea) (***an*** *acc.* to); ***e-e ~ an j-n richten*** request s.th. of s.o., appeal to s.o.; ***auf m-e ~*** at my request; ***ich habe e-e (große) ~ an Sie*** I want to ask you a (big) favo(u)r; ***ich habe nur die eine ~*** I have just one request

'bit·te *adv.* **1.** please; ***~, gib mir die Zeitung*** would you pass me the paper, please; **2.** *Darf ich mal?* - ***(aber) ~!*** of course, certainly, F go ahead; *formal*: by all means, please do; **3.** ***(aber) ~!*** that's all right (*Am.* alright), not at all, *esp. Am.* that's okay, F no problem; **4.** ***wie ~?*** sorry(, what did you say)?, pardon?, *formal*: I beg your pardon?; **5.** ***~!*** there you are, F there you go; **6.** there you are; **7.**

(**na**) ~! what did I say?, didn't I tell you?; **8.** ~! a) come in, please; b) after you, go ahead; **9.** ~! *film*: action!

bit·ten ['bɪtən] *v/t. and v/i.* (bat, gebeten, h) ask (**j-n um et.** s.o. for s.th.); request (s.th. of s.o.); beg; implore, beseech; **j-n ~ um** *acc.* trouble s.o. for *s.th.*; ~ **für** *acc.* intercede for; **dürfte ich Sie ~** could I ask you (**zu** *inf.* to *inf.*), would you mind (*ger.*); **es wird gebeten, daß** it is requested that; **... werden gebeten zu** *inf.* ... are asked (*or* requested) to *inf.*; → **dringend** II; **er läßt sich nicht** (**erst**) **lange ~** he doesn't have to be asked twice; **j-n zu sich ~** ask s.o. to come and see one (*or* to come into the office *etc.*); **Herr X läßt ~** Mr X would like to see you now; **wenn ich ~ darf** if you don't mind; **darf ich ~?** a) would you come this way, please?, b) may I have this dance?, c) dinner is served; **ich bitte dich!** please!; **aber ich bitte dich,** *das ist doch selbstverständlich, unmöglich etc.* oh, come on; **darum möchte ich aber auch ~** (*or* **gebeten haben**) I should jolly well hope so; **ich bitte darum** if you wouldn't mind; (**aber**) **ich bitte Sie!** (well,) really!; **da muß ich doch sehr ~!** I beg your pardon!; **darf ich um Ihren Namen ~?** would you mind telling me your name?; **'bit·tend** *adj.* pleading, beseeching

bit·ter ['bɪtɐ] **I.** *adj.* bitter (*a. fig.*); ~ **schmecken** taste bitter, have a bitter taste; *fig.* **e-n ~en Nachgeschmack hinterlassen** leave a sour aftertaste (*or* taste in one's mouth); **j-m ~e Vorwürfe machen** reproach s.o. bitterly; **es ist mein ~er Ernst** I (really) mean it; **bis zum ~en Ende** right to the bitter end; **das ist ~** that's hard (F tough); **~e Tränen weinen** weep bitterly; **II.** *fig. adv.* bitterly; **et. ~ nötig haben** need s.th. badly, be in desperate (*or* dire) need of s.th.; **sich ~ beklagen** complain bitterly; **es hat sich ~ gerächt** I *etc.* had to pay dearly for it

'bit·ter|'bö·se *adj.* furious, F livid; wicked; **~r Brief** nasty letter; **~'ernst** *adj.* dead serious; **es ist mir ~** (**damit**)**!** I'm serious, I mean it, I'm dead serious (about it); **~'kalt** *adj.* bitter(ly) cold

'Bit·ter·keit *f* (-; *no pl.*) bitterness (*a. fig.*)

'bit·ter·lich *adv.*: ~ **weinen** weep bitterly

'Bit·ter·man·del·öl *n gastr.* bitter almond oil

'Bit·ter·nis *f* (-; -se) bitterness

'Bit·ter·scho·ko,la·de *f* plain chocolate

'bit·ter'schwer *adj.* desperately hard; **der Abschied war ~** it was terrible saying goodbye

'Bit·ter·stoff *m* bitter constituent

'bit·ter'süß *adj. a. fig.* bittersweet

'Bit·ter·wur·zel *f* ♣ gentian root

'Bitt|ge·such *n*, **~schrift** *f* petition; **~stel·ler** ['bɪtʃtɛlɐ] *m* (-s; -) petitioner

Bi·tu·men [bi'tu:mən] *n* (-s; -) bitumen

Bi·wak ['bi:vak] *n* (-s; -s), **bi·wa·kie·ren** [biva'ki:rən] *v/i.* (h) bivouac

bi·zarr [bi'tsar] *adj.* bizarre, strange

Bi·zeps ['bi:tsɛps] *m* (-es; -e) biceps

Bla·bla [bla'bla:] F *n* (-[s]; *no pl.*) F twaddle, hot air, blah

Black·out ['blɛkʔaʊt] *m* (-[s]; -s) **1.** (mental) blackout; **ich hatte e-n ~** my mind went completely blank (*or* was a complete blank), I had a (mental) blackout; **2.** (temporary *or* mental) blackout; temporary lapse; **3.** ⚕ blackout; **e-n ~ haben** *a.* black out

blä·hen ['blɛ:ən] (h) **I.** *v/i.*: *Zwiebeln etc.* ~ give you wind; **II.** *v/t.* swell out; **III.** *v/refl.*: **sich ~** fill out; *fig.* puff o.s. up; **'Blä·hun·gen** *pl.* wind *sg.*, *formal*: flatulence *sg.*

bla·ma·bel [bla'ma:bəl] *adj.* disgraceful, shaming; embarrassing, humiliating; **Bla·ma·ge** [bla'ma:ʒə] *f* (-; -n) disgrace; **es war e-e ~** it was embarrassing; **es war e-e** (**große**) **~ für ihn** he made a (real) fool of himself; **bla·mie·ren** [bla'mi:rən] (h) **I.** *v/t.* show *s.o.* up; make a fool of *s.o.*; **II.** *v/refl.*: **sich ~** show o.s. up; make a fool of o.s.

blan·chie·ren [blã'ʃi:rən] *v/t.* (h) *gastr.* blanch

blank [blaŋk] *adj.* **1.** shiny, shining; polished; shiny (with wear); **et. ~ putzen** polish (*or* clean) s.th. till it shines, put a good shine on s.th.; **2.** bare; naked; **3.** *fig.* pure, sheer *nonsense, envy etc.*; **die ~e Wahrheit** the plain (*lit.* unvarnished) truth; **4.** F broke

blan·ko ['blaŋko] ✝ **I.** *adj.* blank; **II.** *adv.* in blank; ~ **verkaufen** sell short; **℞for·mu,lar** *n* blank (form); **℞kre,dit** *m* blank (*or* open) credit; **℞scheck** *m* blank cheque (*Am.* check); *fig.* **ein ~** carte blanche; **℞,un·ter·schrift** *f* blank signature; **℞,voll·macht** *f* full discretionary power(s *pl.*); *fig.* carte blanche

'Blank·vers *m* blank verse

Bläs·chen ['blɛ:sçən] *n* (-s; -) **1.** *anat.*, ♣ vesicle; **2.** ⚕ (small) blister; pustule; **~aus·schlag** *m* blistery rash, blisters *pl.*

Bla·se ['bla:zə] *f* (-; -n) **1.** bubble; ⚕ blister; ⚙ *a.* flaw; **sich ~n laufen** get blisters on one's feet from walking; **~n werfen** (*or* **ziehen**) blister, *gastr.* get frothy; **2.** *anat.* bladder; F **er hat's mit der ~** he's got bladder trouble, F he's having trouble with his waterworks; **3.** ⚒ still; **4.** balloon, (speech) bubble; **5.** F *contp.* F crowd, lot, shower

'Bla·se·balg *m* bellows *pl.*

bla·sen ['bla:zən] (blies, geblasen, h) **I.** *v/t.* **1.** blow; ♪ *a.* play; F *fig.* **dem werd' ich was ~!** F he's got another thing coming; → **Marsch¹**, **Trübsal**; **2.** V **j-m e-n ~** *sl.* suck s.o. off, do a blow job on s.o.; **II.** *v/i.* blow; **es bläst ganz schön** there's quite a wind (going)

'Bla·sen|aus·schlag *m* blistery rash, blisters *pl.*; **~bil·dung** *f* ⚕, ⚙ blistering; **~ent·zün·dung** *f* cystitis, bladder infection; **℞för·mig** *adj.* bubble-shaped; **~lei·den** *n* bladder complaint; **~spie·ge·lung** *f* cystoscopy; **~stein** *m* bladder stone

Blä·ser ['blɛ:zɐ] *m* (-s; -) **1.** ♪ wind player; **die ~** the wind (section); **2.** ⚙ blower; fan; **~en,sem·ble** *n* wind ensemble; **~ok,tett** *n* wind octet

bla·siert [bla'zi:ɐt] *adj.* smug; **Bla'siert·heit** *f* (-; *no pl.*) smugness

'Blas|in·stru,ment *n* wind instrument; **~ka,pel·le** *f* brass band; **~mu,sik** *f* music for brass band; *am Sonntag* **gibt es ~** a brass band will be playing; **magst du ~?** do you like brass bands?

Blas·phe·mie [blasfe'mi:] *f* (-; -n) blasphemy; **blas·phe·misch** [blas'fe:mɪʃ] *adj.* blasphemous

'Blas·rohr *n* **1.** blowpipe; **2.** peashooter

blaß [blas] *adj.* pale (**vor** *dat.* with); pallid; pale *colo(u)r etc.*; *fig.* colo(u)rless; **blasses Gesicht** pale face, pale (*or* pallid) complexion; **ganz ~ aussehen** look pale and wan; *fig.* **~ vor Neid** green with envy; **der blasse Neid** sheer (*or* pure) envy; **blasse Erinnerung** dim recollection; **blasse Hoffnung** faint hope; → **Ahnung, Schimmer** 2; **'blaß·blau** *adj.* pale blue; **Bläs·se** ['blɛsə] *f* (-; *no pl.*) paleness, pallor; **'blaß·grün** *adj.* pale green

Bläß·huhn ['blɛs-] *n* coot

bläß·lich ['blɛslɪç] *adj.* slightly pale

Blatt [blat] *n* (-[e]s; Blätter ['blɛtɐ]) **1.** ♣ leaf; petal; sepal; *fig.* **kein ~ vor den Mund nehmen** not to mince matters (*or* one's words); **2.** leaf; page; sheet; **500 ~ Papier** 500 sheets of paper; ♪ **vom ~ spielen** (*or* **singen**) sightread; **et. vom ~ spielen** (**singen**) *a.* play (sing) s.th. at sight; *fig.* **das steht auf e-m anderen ~** a) that's a completely different matter, b) F that's another story; **das ~ hat sich gewendet** the tide has turned; → **unbeschrieben**; **3.** (news)paper; **4.** *art*: print; drawing; engraving; **5.** card; hand; **6.** ⚙ plate, lamina, foil; blade (*a.* ✈); **7.** ♪ reed

Blätt·chen ['blɛtçən] *n* (-s; -) **1.** *anat.*, ♣, ⚒ lamella; ⚙ membrane; **2.** slip (of paper); **3.** local newspaper (F rag); **4.** ♪ → **Blatt** 7

blät·te·rig ['blɛtərɪç] *adj.* leafy; *gastr.* flaky; *in cpds.* ...-leaved

blät·tern ['blɛtɐn] (h) **I.** *v/i.* **1. in e-m Buch** (**Fotoalbum**) ~ leaf through a book (have a look at a photo album); **2.** → **abblättern**; **II.** *v/t.* → **hinblättern**

Blät·ter|pilz ['blɛtɐ-] *m* agaric; **~teig** *m* flaky (*or* puff) pastry; **~wald** *hum. m the* press; **es rauscht im** (**deutschen**) ~ the (German) press is in a flurry

'Blatt|fe·der *f* ⚙ leaf spring; **℞för·mig** *adj.* leaf-shaped; **~ge·mü·se** *n* leafy vegetables *pl.*; **~gold** *n* gold leaf; **~grün** *n* ♣ chlorophyll; **~knos·pe** *f* leaf bud; **~laus** *f* greenfly, aphid

'blatt·los *adj.* leafless; bare

'Blatt|pflan·ze *f* foliage (*or* leafy) plant; **~sä·ge** *f* pad saw; **~sa,lat** *m* green salad; **~schuß** *m hunt.* chest shot; **~sil·ber** *n* silver leaf; **~werk** *n* foliage

blau [blaʊ] **I.** *adj.* **1.** blue; **~es Auge** black eye; **~er Fleck** bruise; **er hatte überall ~e Flecke** he was black and blue; **du hast ~e Lippen bekommen** your lips have gone blue; **im Gesicht ~ anlaufen** go blue in the face; *fig.* **mit e-m ~en Auge davonkommen** get off lightly; **~es Blut in s-n Adern haben** be blue-blooded; **~er Brief** a) (letter of) dismissal, F marching orders, *Am.* F pink slip, b) *ped.* (letter of) warning; **der ℞e Reiter** *art*: the Blue Rider, the Blaue Reiter; → **Forelle, Wunder**; **2.** F plastered, *sl.* tight; **total ~** *sl.* blotto; **II.** **℞** *n* (-s; *no pl.*) blue (colo[u]r); **das ~e vom Himmel herunterlügen** F lie through one's teeth, lie like a trooper; **ins ~e hinein reden** prattle (on); **j-m das ~e vom Himmel versprechen** promise s.o. the moon; **Fahrt ins ~e** jaunt (through the countryside), mystery tour; **Schuß ins ~e** random shot

'blau·äu·gig [-ɔʏgɪç] *adj.* blue-eyed; *fig.* starry-eyed, dewy-eyed, naive

'Blau·bee·re *f* bilberry, *Am.* blueberry

'blau·blü·tig [-bly:tɪç] *adj.* blue-blooded

'Blaue F *m* (-n; -n) hundred mark note (*Am.* bill)

Bläue ['blɔʏə] *f* (-; *no pl.*) blue(ness)
'**Blau|fel·chen** [-fɛlçən] *m* (-s; -) *zo.* powan; **~fich·te** *f* blue spruce; **~fil·ter** *m, n phot.* blue filter; **~fuchs** *m* Arctic fox
'**blau·grau** *adj.* blue-grey (*Am.* -gray), bluish-grey (*Am.* -gray)
'**blau·grün** *adj.* blue-green, bluish-green
'**Blau·helm** *m* blue beret
'**Blau·kraut** *dial. n* red cabbage
bläu·lich ['blɔʏlıç] *adj.* bluish
'**Blau·licht** *n* flashing light(s *pl.*); ***mit ~*** with (its *or* their) light(s) flashing; ***mit ~ ins Krankenhaus gebracht werden*** be rushed to hospital (in an ambulance)
'**blau·ma·chen** F *v/i.* (*sep.*, h) F skip work (*or* classes *etc.*), *Brit. a.* skive (off), skive off work *etc.*; ***er macht heute blau*** he's skiving (off) today, he's skived off today
'**Blau|mei·se** *f* blue tit; **~pa,pier** *n* blue carbon paper; **~pau·se** *f* blueprint
'**blau·rot** *adj.* purple
'**Blau·säu·re** *f* ⚗ prussic acid
'**Blau·schim·mel·kä·se** *m* blue cheese
'**blau·schwarz** *adj.* blue-black, bluish-black
'**Blau·stich** *m phot.* blue cast; **blau·sti·chig** ['blaʊʃtıçıç] *adj.*: ***~ sein*** have a blue cast
'**Blau|strumpf** *fig. m* bluestocking; **~tan·ne** *f* blue spruce; **~wal** *m* blue whale
Bla·zer ['ble:zɐ] *m* (-s; -) blazer
Blech [blɛç] *n* (-[e]s; -e) **1.** metal, tin; ⚙ a) sheet metal; b) metal sheet; *mot.* bodywork; ***ein Eimer*** *etc.* ***aus ~*** a metal bucket *etc.*; ***das ist doch bloß ~*** that's just cheap (*or* ordinary) metal; F *fig.* ***aufs ~ hauen*** F blow one's horn; **2.** baking tray; **3.** ♪ brass; **4.** F *fig.* rubbish, *Am.* garbage; ***red doch nicht so'n ~!*** don't talk such rubbish (F rot, *Am.* garbage); **~blä·ser** *m* brass player; ***die ~*** the brass (section); **~blas·in·stru,ment** *n* brass instrument; **~büch·se** *f*, **~do·se** *f* **1.** tin (can), *esp. Am.* can; **2.** tin, (metal) box; **~ei·mer** *m* metal bucket
ble·chen ['blɛçən] F (h) **I.** *v/t.* F fork out, cough up; **II.** *v/i.* F foot the bill
ble·chern ['blɛçɐn] *adj.* **1.** tin ...; **2.** tinny *sound etc.*; hollow
'**Blech|hüt·te** *f* corrugated iron hut; **~in·stru,ment** *n* ♪ brass instrument; **~ka,ni·ster** *m* (metal) canister; **~kan·ne** *f* tin can; **~la,wi·ne** F *f* endless stream of traffic, F endless convoy of tin; **~napf** *m* tin bowl; **~schach·tel** *f* tin, (metal) box; **~scha·den** *m mot.* bodywork damage; ***es gab nur ~*** it was just a bump, *w.s.* nobody got hurt; **~sche·re** *f*: (***e-e*** ~ a pair of) metal shears *pl.*; **~schüs·sel** *f* tin (*or* aluminium, *Am.* aluminum) bowl; **~trom·mel** *f* tin drum
blecken ['blɛkən] (*sep.* -k·k-) *v/t.* (h): ***die Zähne ~*** show one's teeth; *zo.* bare its teeth
Blei [blaı] *n* (-[e]s; *no pl.*) **1.** lead; ***aus ~*** lead ..., made of lead; *fig.* (***schwer***) ***wie ~*** like lead, like a lead (*or* dead) weight, leaden; ***es liegt mir wie ~ in den Gliedern*** I feel like a lead weight; **2.** → ***Senkblei***; **3.** *hunt.* shot; bullet; '**blei·arm** *adj.* low-lead ...
Blei·be ['blaıbə] F *f* (-; -n) place to stay; *a.* F crash pad; (***k***)***eine ~ haben*** have somewhere (nowhere) to stay
blei·ben ['blaıbən] (blieb, geblieben, sn) **I.** *v/i.* **1.** stay; ***zu Hause ~*** stay in, stay at home; ***im Bett ~*** stay in bed; ***draußen ~*** stay out; ***hinten ~*** be left behind; ***zum Essen ~*** stay for dinner; F ***und wo bleibe ich?*** what about me?, and where do I come into it?; ***wir müssen*** (***selber***) ***sehen, wo wir ~*** we'll just have to fend for ourselves (F do our own thing); F ***sieh zu, wo du bleibst!*** F you're on your own, kid!; (***im Krieg*** *etc.*) ~ fall, be killed (***bei*** *dat.* at); → ***Ball, Leib***; **2.** ***~ bei*** *dat.* keep to, stick to, stand by; ***bei der Wahrheit ~*** stick to the truth; ***ich bleibe dabei*** I'm not going to change my mind, ***daß***: I still think (*or* maintain *etc.*) that; ***ich bleibe*** (***lieber***) ***beim Bier*** (I think) I'll stick to beer, thanks; → ***Sache, Stange, Takt*** 1, ***treu*** I; **3.** remain, stay, continue (to be), keep; ***an*** (***aus***) ~ stay *or* be kept on (off); ***geschlossen*** (***trocken,*** *meteor.* ***kalt***) ~ stay closed (dry, cold); ***gesund ~*** stay (*or* keep) healthy; ***bleib gesund!*** mind how you go, now; ***unbestraft*** (***unentdeckt***) ~ go unpunished (undiscovered); ***ungenannt*** (***anonym***) ~ remain unnamed (anonymous); ***er bleibt immer nett*** he's always very pleasant; ***für sich ~*** keep to o.s.; ***das bleibt unter uns!*** that's between you and me, F keep that under your hat; ***~ Sie*** (***doch***) ***sitzen!*** don't get up, please; ***bleib doch sitzen!*** can't you sit still (for one minute)?; ***bleib***(***, wo du bist***)***!*** stay where you are!, don't move!; ***bleib, wie du bist*** stay the way you are; → ***Leben, ruhig*** I; **4.** be left, remain; ***uns bleibt nicht mehr viel Zeit*** we haven't got (*or* there isn't) much time left; ***mir bleibt keine*** (***andere***) ***Wahl*** I have no choice (***als zu*** *inf.* but to *inf.*); → ***vorbehalten*** II; **5.** ***wo bleibt er denn?*** what's taking him (so long)?, where's he got to?; ***wo bist du so lange geblieben?*** where've you been all this time?, what took you so long?; **II.** *v/impers.*: ***es bleibt dabei!*** that's final (*or* settled) then; ***und dabei bleibt es!*** and that's that, and that's final; ***dabei wird es nicht ~*** that won't be the end of it (*or* the last we'll *etc.* hear of it), matters won't rest there; ***es bleibt nur noch wenig zu tun*** there isn't much left to be done; ***bleibt nur noch zu hoffen, daß*** we can only hope (that), (well,) let's hope (that); → ***abwarten*** I, ***überlassen***; '**blei·bend** *adj.* lasting, permanent *damage etc.*; ***~er Eindruck*** lasting impression; ***~e Erinnerung*** (***Werte***) lasting memory (values)
'**blei·ben·las·sen** *v/t.* (*irr.*, *sep.*, h, → ***lassen***) a) not to do *s.th.*, b) stop (*doing*) *s.th.*; ***laß das bleiben!*** stop it!; ***das wirst du schön ~!*** you'll do nothing of the sort!; ***laß es lieber bleiben*** (better) leave it; ***dann laß es eben bleiben*** don't, then; nobody's forcing you; ***er kann es nicht ~*** he won't stop (doing it); ***das Rauchen*** (***Trinken*** *etc.*) ~ stop (F quit) smoking (drinking *etc.*)
bleich [blaıç] *adj.* pale (***vor*** *dat.* with), pallid, wan; ***ganz ~*** *a.* (as) white as a sheet, *lit.* pale as death; **Blei·che** ['blaıçə] *f* (-; -n) **1.** *no pl.* paleness, pallor; **2.** bleach; **blei·chen** ['blaıçən] (h) **I.** *v/t.* bleach; **II.** *v/i.* bleach; fade; '**Bleich·ge·sicht** *n* paleface; '**Bleich·heit** *f* (-; *no pl.*) paleness, pallor; '**Bleich·mit·tel** *n* bleach(ing agent); '**Bleich·sel·le·rie** *m* celery (stalks *pl.*)
blei·ern ['blaıɐn] *adj.* lead; *fig.* leaden; *fig.* ***~e Schwere*** leaden feeling
'**Blei·erz** *n* lead ore
'**Blei·far·be** *f* lead paint; '**blei·far·ben** *adj.* lead-colo(u)red; leaden
'**blei·frei I.** *adj.* unleaded, lead-free; **II.** *adv.*: ***~ tanken*** fill up with unleaded petrol (*Am.* gas); ***kann man dort ~ tanken?*** have they got unleaded petrol (*Am.* gas)?
'**Blei|ge·halt** *m* lead content; **~glas** *n* lead glass
'**blei·grau** *adj.* lead-colo(u)red
blei·hal·tig ['blaıhaltıç] *adj.* containing lead; ***~ sein*** contain lead
'**Blei|hüt·te** *f* lead refining plant; **~kon·zen·tra·ti,on** *f* lead concentration; **~kri,stall** *n* lead crystal; **~ku·gel** *f* lead bullet; **~rohr** *n* lead pipe; **~satz** *m* hot metal type; **~schür·ze** *f* lead apron
'**blei'schwer** *adj.* like lead, like a lead weight
'**Blei·sol,dat** *m* tin soldier
'**Blei·stift** *m* pencil; **~ab·satz** *m* stiletto heel; **~spit·zer** *m* pencil sharpener; **~zeich·nung** *f* pencil drawing
'**Blei·ver·gif·tung** *f* lead poisoning
'**blei·ver·glast** *adj.* leaded *window*
'**blei·ver·seucht** *adj.* lead-polluted
Blen·de ['blɛndə] *f* (-; -n) **1.** screen; ⚔ shield; *mot.* (sun) visor; **2.** *phot.* a) diaphragm, b) aperture, c) f-stop; (***bei***) ***~ 8*** (at) f-8; **3.** ⚠ transom; blind arch (*or* door *etc.*); **4.** facing
blen·den ['blɛndən] (h) **I.** *v/t.* **1.** blind, dazzle; ***du blendest mich!*** *a.* you're shining it (*or* the torch *etc.*) right into my eyes; **2.** ***j-n ~*** blind s.o., gouge s.o.'s eyes out; **3.** *fig.* deceive, delude, blind; take *s.o.* in; **II.** *v/i.* dazzle, be dazzling; ***das blendet aber!*** that light's strong (*or* too strong for my eyes); **III.** ♀ *n* (-s; *no pl.*) *mot. etc.* glare
'**Blen·den·au·to,ma·tik** *f phot.* automatic aperture (control)
'**blen·dend I.** *adj.* **1.** dazzling; **2.** *fig.* brilliant, dazzling; ***~es Aussehen*** stunning good looks; ***~ aussehen*** a) look great, b) be extremely good-looking (*or* attractive); **II.** *fig. adv.* brilliantly, dazzlingly; ***sich ~ amüsieren*** have a great time; ***sich ~ verstehen, ~ miteinander auskommen*** get along brilliantly (F just great, like a house on fire); ***es geht ihr ~*** she's getting along just fine; *iro.* ***es geht ihm nicht gerade ~*** he could be doing worse(, I suppose)
'**blen·dend'weiß** *adj.* dazzling white
'**Blen·den|ein·stel·lung** *f* aperture setting; **~öff·nung** *f* aperture; **~ska·la** *f* aperture ring; **~vor·wahl** *f* aperture priority; **~zahl** *f* f-stop, f-number
Blen·der ['blɛndɐ] *fig. m* (-s; -) fake, phoney; ***er ist ein richtiger ~*** *a.* he's all show
blend·frei ['blɛnt-] *adj.* anti-glare ..., anti-dazzle ..., non-dazzling
Blend|gra,na·te ['blɛnt-] *f* stun grenade; **~rah·men** *m* **1.** window frame; **2.** *art*: canvas stretcher
Blend·schutz ['blɛnt-] *m* glare shield; **~schei·be** *f* anti-glare screen
Blend·stein ['blɛnt-] *m* facing stone
'**Blen·dung** *f* (-; -en) **1.** blinding; *mot.* dazzle, glare; **2.** *fig.* deception
Blend|werk ['blɛnt-] *n* deception; illusion; tricks *pl.*, trickery; ***es ist alles ~*** *a.* it's all a fake; **~zaun** *m* anti-dazzle barrier
Bles·se ['blɛsə] *f* (-; -n) blaze
Bles·sur [blɛ'su:ɐ] *obs. f* (-; -en) wound;

leichte ~en superficial wounds, F a few scratches
bleu [blø:] *adj.*, **Bleu** *n* (-s; -) (pale) blue
Blick [blɪk] *m* (-[e]s; -e) **1.** look (***auf*** *acc.* at); gaze; eye(s *pl.*); look (in one's eyes), eyes *pl.*; ***flüchtiger ~*** (quick) glance; ***e-n kurzen ~ werfen auf*** *acc.* have a quick look at, cast a quick glance at (*or* over); ***sein ~ fiel auf*** *acc.* his eye(s) *or* gaze fell on; ***s-n*** (*or* ***den***) ***~ richten auf*** *acc.* look at (*or* towards, in the direction of), *lit.* cast one's eye(s) on (*or* in the direction of); ***den ~ heben*** (***senken***) look up (down), raise one's eyes (cast one's eyes down, lower one's gaze); ***den ~ wenden von*** *dat.* look away from, turn one's eyes away from; ***er wandte den ~ nicht von ...*** he wouldn't take his eyes off ...; ***soweit der ~ reicht*** as far as the eye can see; ***wenn ~e töten könnten*** if looks could kill; ***der böse ~*** the evil eye; ***auf den ersten ~*** at first sight (*or* glance), when you first look at it (*or* see it); ***Liebe auf den ersten ~*** love at first sight; ***das sieht man doch auf den ersten ~*** you can see that straightaway (F with half an eye); ***erst auf den zweiten ~ ...*** it's only when you look at it again that ...; ***e-n ~ werfen auf*** *acc.* have (*or* take) a look at; ***j-m e-n ~ zuwerfen*** give s.o. a look; → ***durchbohren, finster*** I, ***starr*** 1; **2.** view (***auf*** *acc.* of); ***mit ~ auf*** *acc.* with a view of, overlooking *the lake etc.*; **3.** *fig.* eye(s *pl.*); outlook, horizon(s *pl.*); ***e-n*** (***guten***) ***~ haben für*** have an (a good) eye for; ***dafür hat er keinen ~*** he has no eyes for (*or* he just doesn't see) that kind of thing; ***j-m den ~ für et. verstellen*** (***trüben***) distort (cloud) s.o.'s view of s.th. (*or* outlook on s.th.); **blicken** ['blɪkən] (*sep.* -k·k-) (h) **I.** *v/i.* look (***auf*** *acc.* at; ***in*** *acc.* into); ***das läßt tief ~*** that's very revealing; *fig.* ***durch die Wolken*** *etc.* ***~*** peep through the clouds *etc.*; **II.** *v/t.*: ***sich ~ lassen*** show up, *a.* put in an appearance, drop in (***bei*** *dat.* on), drop by (at); ***er läßt sich nicht mehr ~*** you never see him (any more) these days; ***sobald er sich ~ läßt*** as soon as he shows (*or* turns) up; ***laß dich nicht mehr ~!*** don't you ever show your face around here again!
'**Blick|fang** *m* eyecatcher; ***es soll als ~ dienen*** it's meant to catch people's eyes (*or* to be eyecatching); **~feld** *n* field of vision (*a. fig.*); *fig.* (***mehr und mehr***) ***ins ~ der Öffentlichkeit rücken*** (increasingly) become the focus of public attention; **~kon,takt** *m* eye contact; ***~ mit j-m aufnehmen*** (***suchen***) (try to) catch s.o.'s eye; **~punkt** *m* **1.** *opt.* visual focus; **2.** *fig.* ***im ~*** (***der Öffentlichkeit***) ***stehen*** be the focus of (public) attention, be in the limelight (be very much in the public eye); **3.** *fig.* → ***Blickwinkel*** 2; **~richtung** *f* line of vision; *fig. a.* direction; **~wech·sel** *m* exchange of glances; *fig.* change of view; **~wei·te** *f* range of vision; **~win·kel** *m* **1.** angle of view; **2.** *fig.* point of view, perspective; ***es kommt auf den ~ an*** it depends which angle you look at it from; ***aus dem ~*** *gen.* from the point of view (*or* perspective) of; ***aus diesem ~*** seen from this angle (*or* point of view, perspective)
blieb [bli:p] *pret. of* ***bleiben***
blies [bli:s] *pret. of* ***blasen***
blind [blɪnt] **I.** *adj.* **1.** blind (*a. fig.*, ***gegen*** *acc.*, ***für*** *acc.* to; ***vor*** *dat.* with); ***auf einem Auge ~*** blind in one eye; F ***bist du ~?*** are you blind?, haven't you got eyes in your head?; *fig.* ***~er Glaube*** blind faith; ***~es Vertrauen*** blind (*or* implicit) trust; ***der ~e Zufall*** blind (*or* pure) chance; ***~e Gewalt*** uncontrolled violence; ***j-n ~ machen*** blind s.o., blindfold s.o. (***gegen*** *acc.* to); ***Liebe macht ~*** love is blind; → ***Alarm, Eifer, Passagier***; **2.** cloudy *mirror etc.*; tarnished *metal*; dull *wine*; **3.** ⚠, ⚙ blind; invisible, concealed *seam*; **4.** ⚔ blank *cartridge*; **II.** *adv.* **5.** blind; ***~ fliegen*** fly blind; ***~*** (***maschine***)***schreiben*** touch-type; ***et. ~ machen können*** be able to do s.th. blindfolded (*or* with one's eyes closed); **6.** *believe, trust etc.* blindly, implicitly; **7.** → ***blindlings***
'**Blind|an·flug** *m* blind approach; **~band** *m* (-[e]s; ⸚e) dummy; **~bo·den** *m* ⚠ dead floor
'**Blind·darm** *m* **1.** appendix; ***mir haben sie mit 14 den ~ entfernt*** I had my appendix taken out when I was 14; **2.** c(a)ecum; **~ent·zün·dung** *f* appendicitis; **~ope·ra·ti,on** *f* appendectomy; ***sich e-r ~ unterziehen*** *a.* have one's appendix (taken) out
Blin·de·kuh ['blɪndəku:] *no art.* blind man's buff
Blin·den|heim ['blɪndən-] *n* home for the blind; **~hund** *m* guide dog; **~schrift** *f* braille; **~schu·le** *f* school for the blind; **~stock** *m* white stick, (blind person's) cane
Blin·de ['blɪndə] *m, f* (-n; -n) blind man (woman), blind person; ***die ~n*** the blind (*pl.*); ***das sieht doch ein ~r!*** anyone can see that; ***unter den ~n ist der Einäugige König*** in the country of the blind the one-eyed man is king
'**Blind|fen·ster** *n* blind window; **~flug** *m* blind flight; *pl. a.* blind flying *sg.*; **~gänger** [-gɛŋɐ] *m* (-s; -) **1.** ⚔ dud; **2.** F *fig.* F dead loss
'**blind·ge·bo·ren** *adj.* blind from birth; ***ein ~es Kind*** (***ein 2er***) a child (someone) who was born blind (*or* who has been blind from birth)
'**blind·gläu·big** **I.** *adj.* (utterly) credulous; **II.** *adv.* unquestioningly; blindly
'**Blind·heit** *f* (-; *no pl.*) blindness (***gegenüber*** *dat.* to) (*a. fig.*); *fig.* ***er ist mit ~ geschlagen*** he must be blind (not to see it)
'**Blind·lan·dung** *f* instrument (*or* blind) landing
blind·lings ['blɪntlɪŋs] *adv.* blindly; ***~ in sein Verderben rennen*** rush headlong into disaster
'**Blind|pro·be** *f gastr.* blind tasting; **~schlei·che** *f zo.* blindworm; **~schreiben** *n* (-s; *no pl.*) touch typing; **~spiel** *n* (game of) blindfold chess; **~start** *m* blind takeoff; **~ver·such** *m* ⚕, *psych.* blind test
'**blind·wü·tig** [-vy:tɪç] **I.** *adj.* blind with rage; **II.** *adv.* in a blind rage (*or* fury); ***~ um sich schlagen*** lash out wildly (in all directions)
blin·ken ['blɪŋkən] *v/i.* (h) sparkle; twinkle; flash; (*a. v/t.*) (flash a) signal; **Blinker** ['blɪŋkɐ] *m* (-s; -) **1.** *mot.* indicator, *Am.* blinker; **2.** *angling*: spoon bait
'**Blink|feu·er** *n* flashing light(s *pl.*); **~leuch·te** *f mot.* indicator, *Am.* blinker
'**Blink·licht** *n* flashing light(s *pl.*); *a.* beacon; **~an·la·ge** *f* warning light(s *pl.*)
'**Blink·zei·chen** *n* **1.** flashing signal; ***ein ~ geben*** flash a signal; **2.** *mot.* indicator (*or* passing) signal
blin·zeln ['blɪntsəln] *v/i.* (h) (*a.* ***mit den Augen ~***) blink; wink; ***in die Sonne ~*** squint against the sun (*or* in the bright sun)
Blitz [blɪts] *m* (-es; -e) **1.** lightning; flash (of lightning); ***der ~ schlug in den Turm ein*** the tower was struck by lightning; ***vom ~ getroffen werden*** be struck by lightning; *fig.* ***wie vom ~ getroffen*** stunned, thunderstruck; ***wie der ~*** like (a flash of) lightning; like (*or* in) a flash; F ***wie ein geölter ~*** like greased lightning; ***wie ein ~ aus heiterem Himmel*** like a bolt from (*or* out of) the blue; ***wie ein ~ einschlagen*** *news etc.*: take everyone by surprise, come like a bomb; **2.** F *phot.* flash; ***ohne ~ kann ich hier nicht fotografieren*** I can't take anything here without a flash, I need a flash here; **~ablei·ter** *m* (-s; -) lightning conductor (*or* rod); *fig.* ***j-n als ~ benutzen*** F take it out on s.o.; **~ak·ti,on** *f* lightning operation
'**blitz·ar·tig** **I.** *adj.* lightning *speed etc.*; **II.** *adv.* like (a flash of) lightning; like (*or* in) a flash
'**Blitz|auf·nah·me** *f phot.* flash shot; **~be·such** *m* lightning (*or* flying) visit; **~bir·ne** *f* flashbulb
'**blitz'blank** *adj.* spotless, F squeaky clean
'**Blitz·ein·schlag** *m* lightning (strike); ***man sah den ~*** you could see the lightning strike (*or* striking the tree *etc.*); ***beim ~*** when the lightning struck
blit·zen ['blɪtsən] (h) **I.** *v/i.* **1.** *impers.* ***es blitzt*** there's lightning; ***es blitzte*** there was (a flash of) lightning; ***es blitzt und donnert*** there's thunder and lightning; F *fig.* ***bei dir blitzt es*** F Charlie's dead; **2.** *fig.* flash; sparkle; **3.** *phot.* flash; ***hat es geblitzt?*** *a.* did the flash work?; **II.** *v/t.* **4.** take (*or* photograph) *s.th.* with a flash; ***hast du's geblitzt?*** did you use a flash?; **5.** *mot.* ***ich wurde gestern geblitzt*** I was caught speeding yesterday
Blit·zer ['blɪtsɐ] F *m* (-s; -) streaker
Blit·zes·schnel·le ['blɪtsəs-] *f*: ***in ~*** quick as a flash, at lightning speed
'**Blitz·ge·rät** *n phot.* flashlight, flash(gun)
'**blitz·ge·scheit** *adj.* very bright; ***er ist ~*** *a.* he's a bright spark
'**Blitz|ge·spräch** *n teleph.* lightning call; **~kar·rie·re** *f* lightning career; meteoric rise; **~kon,takt** *m* flash socket; **~krieg** *m* blitzkrieg; **~lam·pe** *f* flashbulb
'**Blitz·licht** *n phot.* flashlight, flash(gun); (***et.***) ***mit ~ fotografieren*** use a flash (for s.th.); **~auf·nah·me** *f* flash shot
'**Blitz·rei·se** *f* whirlwind tour (***nach*** *dat.* to; ***durch*** *acc.* of)
'**blitz'sau·ber** *adj.* spotless, F squeaky clean
'**Blitz·schlag** *m* lightning (strike)
'**blitz'schnell** **I.** *adj.* as quick as lightning, lightning ..., split-second ...; **II.** *adv.* quick as a flash, like a flash (*or* shot); *respond etc.*: instantaneously; ***es verbreitete sich ~*** it spread like wildfire
'**Blitz|schuh** *m phot.* hot shoe; **~schutz** *m* ⚡ lightning protection; lightning arrester; **~start** *m* lightning (*or* jump) start; **~strahl** *m* streak of lightning; **~,um·fra·ge** *f* snap opinion poll; **~vi,si·te** *f* lightning (*or* flying) visit; **~wür·fel** *m phot.* flash cube
Block [blɔk] *m* (-[e]s; Blöcke ['blœkə]) **1.**

block *of wood etc.*; boulder; bar *of soap, chocolate etc.*; *metall.* ingot, pig; **2.** block of flats; block (of houses); ***sie wohnen im gleichen ~*** a) they live in the same building (*or* block of flats), b) they live on the same block; **3.** writing pad, notepad; scribbling block; book *of tickets*; block *of stamps etc.*; **4.** *parl.*, *pol.*, ✝ bloc; ***e-n ~ bilden, sich zu e-m ~ zusammenschließen*** form a bloc

Blocka·de [blɔ'ka:də] (*sep.* -k·k-) *f* (-; -n) **1.** blockade; ***die ~ brechen*** run the blockade; → ***aufheben*** 4; **2.** *typ.* turned letter(s *pl.*), black; **~bre·cher** *m* blockade-runner; **~zu·stand** *m* state of blockade

'Block|bil·dung *f pol.* forming of blocs (*or* a bloc); **~buch·sta·be** *m* block letter

blocken ['blɔkən] (*sep.* -k·k-) *v/t.* (h) *sport and* ⚽ block

'Block·flö·te *f* recorder

'block·frei *adj. pol.* nonaligned; ***~e Staaten*** nonaligned countries (*or* nations); **'Block·frei·heit** *f* (-; *no pl.*) nonalignment; nonaligned status

'Block|haus *n*, **~hüt·te** *f* log cabin

blockie·ren [blɔ'ki:rən] (*sep.* -k·k-) (h) **I.** *v/t.* block, obstruct; clog (up); lock *wheels*; ⚙ jam; **II.** *v/i.* lock; ⚙ jam; **Blockie·rung** [blɔ'ki:rʊŋ] (*sep.* -k·k-) *f* (-; -en) blocking; obstruction

'Block|par͵tei·en *pl.* party bloc *sg.*; **~satz** *m typ.* justified (*or* flush) setting, flush (*or* justified) left and right margins *pl.*; **~scho·ko͵la·de** *f* cooking chocolate; **~schrift** *f* block letters (*or* capitals) *pl.*; **~staat** *m* aligned *or* bloc country (*or* state, nation)

blöd [blø:t] → ***blöde***

blö·de ['blø:də] **I.** *adj.* **1.** stupid, F thick, *esp. Am.* F dumb; silly; ***er ist ~*** *a.* he's an idiot; ***~r Kerl*** idiot; *sl.* bastard (*a.* ***~r Hund***); ***~ Frage*** stupid (F dumb) question; **2.** F stupid; embarrassing; awkward; ***diese ~ Tür!*** F this damn door!; ***~ Angelegenheit*** stupid situation; ***so was 2s!*** how stupid!, what a (F damn) nuisance; ***das 2 daran*** the stupid thing about it; ***das war ein ~s Gefühl*** it wasn't a very pleasant feeling; **3.** *obs. and* ⚕ feeble-minded; ***~ sein*** *a.* be an imbecile; **II.** *adv.*: ***~ daherreden*** talk a lot of nonsense (*or* rubbish); ***~ grinsen*** give a stupid grin; ***grins nicht so ~!*** take that silly grin off your face; ***sich ~ anstellen*** a) be hopeless, b) act stupid; ***stell dich nicht so ~ an!*** a) F stop being so dop(e)y, snap out of it, b) F stop acting the goat, stop acting so stupid

Blö·de·lei [blø:də'laɪ] *f* (-; -en) nonsense; silly joke; clowning about; **blö·deln** ['blø:dəln] *v/i.* (h) talk nonsense; crack (silly) jokes; clown about

Blö·di·an ['blø:dĭa:n] F *m* (-s; -e) idiot, F blockhead

Blöd·mann ['blø:tman] F *m* (-[e]s; -männer [-mɛnɐ]) **1.** idiot; **2.** *sl.* bastard

Blöd·sinn ['blø:tzɪn] *m* (-[e]s; *no pl.*) rubbish; nonsense; ***mach keinen ~!*** a) don't be silly!, b) watch what you do now; **blöd·sin·nig** ['blø:tzɪnɪç] F *adj.* stupid, idiotic

blö·ken ['blø:kən] *v/i.* (h) low; bleat

blond [blɔnt] *adj.* blond(e), fair(-haired); **Blon·de** ['blɔndə] *f* (-n; -n) **1.** blonde (woman); **2.** F pale beer; **'blond·ge·färbt** *adj.* dyed blond(e) *hair*; **'blond·ge·lockt** *adj.* with blond(e) curls; ***~es Haar*** blond(e), curly hair, curly blond(e) hair; **blon·die·ren** [blɔn'di:rən] *v/t.* (h) dye *one's hair* blond(e), bleach; **Blon·di·ne** [blɔn'di:nə] *f* (-; -n) blonde

bloß [blo:s] **I.** *adj.* **1.** bare, naked; ***mit ~en Füßen*** barefoot, *a. adv.* barefooted; ***mit ~en Händen*** with one's bare hands; ***mit dem ~en Auge*** with the naked eye; ***im ~en Hemd*** in just a shirt; **2.** nothing but, mere, just; ***~e Worte*** empty words; ***das ist ~es Gerede*** that's just (empty) talk; ***der ~e Gedanke*** the mere thought (of it); **II.** *adv.* just, only; *what, how, who etc.* on earth; ***es war ~ ein bißchen kalt*** it was just a bit cold(, that's all); ***er wird sich ~ aufregen*** he'll just (*or* only) get upset; ***was hat er ~?*** I wonder (*or* I'd love to know) what's wrong with him; ***wie machst du das ~?*** how on earth do you do it?; ***hätte ich's ~ nicht gemacht!*** I wish (*or* if only) I hadn't done it; *soll ich's ihm sagen?* - ***~ nicht!*** (goodness,) no!, don't you dare!; ***laß ihn ~ nicht raus!*** don't let him out, whatever you do, don't you dare let him out!; ***~ jetzt nicht!*** not now, 'please!; ***sag ~ ...!*** don't say ..., don't tell me ...

Blö·ße ['blø:sə] *f* (-; -n) **1.** nakedness; **2.** *fig.* giveaway; *esp. sport*: opening; ***sich e-e ~ geben*** leave o.s. wide open, give o.s. away, expose o.s.; **3.** clearing; **4.** ⚙ smoothed skin

'bloß·le·gen *v/t.* (*sep.*, h) uncover, expose, lay bare (*all a. fig.*)

'bloß·stel·len *v/t.* (*sep.*, h): ***j-n (sich) ~*** show s.o. (o.s.) up, make a fool of s.o. (o.s.); **'Bloß·stel·lung** *f* (-; *no pl.*) showing up, exposure; ***aus Angst vor e-r ~*** for fear of losing face

Blou·son [blu'zõ:] *n*, *m* (-[s]; -s) bomber (*or* flying) jacket

blub·bern ['blʊbɐn] *v/i.* (h) **1.** bubble (away); **2.** mumble

Bluff [blʊf] *m* (-s; -s), **bluf·fen** ['blʊfən] *v/i. and v/t.* (h) bluff

blü·hen ['bly:ən] *v/i.* (h) blossom, flower (*a. fig.*); be in bloom (*or* blossom); *fig.* prosper, thrive; ***im verborgenen ~*** blossom in obscurity; ***wer weiß, was uns noch blüht*** who knows what's in store for us (*or* what we're in for); ***es kann dir noch ~, daß*** don't be surprised if; ***das kann uns auch ~*** we're not immune (either); F ***... dann blüht dir was!*** F ... you'll be in for it!; **'blü·hend** *adj.* flowering; flourishing, thriving; *fig.* healthy *look*; glowing, radiant *health*; vivid *imagination*; ***~er Unsinn*** complete (*or* utter) nonsense; ***e-n ~en Handel treiben*** do a roaring trade (***mit*** *dat.* in); ***wie das ~e Leben aussehen*** be the picture of health; ***im ~en Alter von*** at the early age of

Blu·me ['blu:mə] *f* (-; -n) **1.** flower; *fig.* ***durch die ~*** in as many words; ***j-m durch die ~ sagen, daß*** *a.* hint to s.o. that, try to tell s.o. that; ***laßt ~ sprechen*** say it with flowers; **2.** bouquet *of wine*; froth, head *of beer*; **3.** *hunt.* tail, brush

'Blu·men|aus·stel·lung *f* flower show; **~beet** *n* flowerbed; **~draht** *m* florist's wire; **~er·de** *f* garden mo(u)ld; **~fen·ster** *n* **1.** flower window; **2.** window with (*or* full of) flowers; **~gar·ten** *m* flower garden; **~ge·stell** *n* flower stand; **~händ·ler** *m* florist; **~hand·lung** *f* flower shop, florist's; **~ka·sten** *m* window box; **~kelch** *m* ⚘ calyx; **~kis·sen** *n* frog

'Blu·men·kohl *m* cauliflower; **~ohr** *n* cauliflower ear

Blu·men|la·den *m* flower shop, florist's; **~meer** *n* sea (*or* riot) of flowers; **~mu·ster** *n* floral design

'blu·men·reich *fig. adj.* flowery

'Blu·men|scha·le *f* flower bowl; **~schmuck** *m* flower arrangement(s *pl.*), floral decoration(s *pl.*), flowers *pl.*; **~spen·de** *f* flowers *pl.*; **~spra·che** *f* language of flowers; **~stand** *m* flower stall; **~stän·der** *m* flower stand; **~staub** *m* flower pollen; **~sten·gel** *m*, **~stiel** *m* flower stalk; **~stock** *m* flowering (pot) plant; **~strauß** *m* bunch of flowers, bouquet; ***j-m e-n ~ schenken*** give s.o. (some) flowers; **~stück** *n art*: flower piece

'Blu·men·topf *m* flowerpot; F *fig.* ***damit kannst du keinen ~ gewinnen*** that won't get you very far; **~er·de** *f* potting compost

Blu·men|va·se *f* vase; **~zucht** *f* flower-growing; **~züch·ter** *m* flower-grower; **~zwie·bel** *f* (flower) bulb

blü·me·rant [blymə'rant] F *adj.*: ***mir ist ganz ~ (zumute)*** I feel queasy (*or* queer)

blu·mig ['blu:mɪç] *adj.* flowery (*a. fig.*); *wine*: *a.* with a fine bouquet

Blu·se ['blu:zə] *f* (-; -n) blouse

Blut [blu:t] *n* (-[e]s; *no pl.*) **1.** blood; ***das ~ stieg ihm zu Kopf*** the blood rushed to his head; *der Sekt etc.* ***geht ins ~*** goes (straight) to your head; *fig. die Musik etc.* ***geht ins ~*** gets into your bloodstream; ***sich mit ~ bespritzen*** get o.s. bloody; ***in s-m ~ liegen*** be covered in blood, be lying in a pool of blood; ***ich kann kein ~ sehen*** I can't stand the sight of blood; ***et. im ~ haben*** have s.th. in one's bloodstream (*fig.* blood); *fig.* ***es liegt ihm im ~*** it's in his blood; ***heißes ~ haben*** be hot-blooded; ***j-n bis aufs ~ ärgern*** *etc.* get s.o.'s blood up; ***ihm stockte*** (*or* ***erstarrte, gefror***) ***das ~ in den Adern*** his blood froze; ***das wird böses ~ machen*** that'll stir up bad feeling; ***~ und Wasser schwitzen*** sweat blood; ***er hat ~ geleckt*** he's tasted blood; ***an ihren Händen klebt ~*** she's got blood on her hands; ***ruhig ~!*** take it easy!, don't get excited!, *sl.* cool it!; **2.** *fig.* ***junges ~*** young blood; **~ader** *f* vein; **~͵al·ko·hol(ge·halt)** *m* blood alcohol level; **~an·drang** *m* congestion

'blut·arm *adj.* **1.** ⚕ an(a)emic; **2.** *fig.* (utterly) destitute, penniless; **'Blut·ar·mut** *f* ⚕ an(a)emia

'Blut|bad *n* bloodbath, massacre; ***ein ~ anrichten*** carry out a massacre, cause a bloodbath; **~bahn** *f* bloodstream; **~bank** *f* (-; -en) blood bank

'blut|be·fleckt *adj.* bloodstained; **~be·schmiert** *adj.* bloodstained, bloody; **~be·spritzt** *adj.* blood-spattered

'Blut·bild *n* blood count (*or* picture)

'blut·bil·dend I. *adj.* blood-forming; **II.** *adv.*: ***~ wirken*** help to form blood; **'Blut·bil·dung** *f* formation of blood

'Blut|bla·se *f* ⚕ blood blister; **~bu·che** *f* ⚘ copper beech

'Blut·druck *m* (-[e]s; *no pl.*) blood pressure; ***bei j-m den ~ messen*** take s.o.'s blood pressure; **2er·hö·hend** *adj.* hypertensive; **~mes·ser** *m* blood-pressure meter (*or* ga[u]ge), 📖 sphygmomanometer; **~mes·sung** *f* (taking a) blood pres-

sure reading; **2sen·kend** *adj.* hypotensive
'**Blut·drü·se** *f* endocrine gland
'**blut·dür·stig** [-dʏrstɪç] *adj.* bloodthirsty
Blü·te ['bly:tə] *f* (-; -n) **1.** flower, blossom, bloom; flowering time; *fig.* height, *a.* heyday *of power, a fashion etc.*; cream, elite; ✝ time of prosperity; *hist., art:* flowering, height; ***in (voller) ~ stehen*** be in (full) bloom (*or* flower, blossom); *fig.* ***die ~ der Jugend*** the flower of youth; ***in der ~ s-r Jugend (Jahre)*** in the prime of youth (life); ***seltsame ~n treiben*** come up with some strange things (*or* effects); ***zur ~ gelangen*** come to fruition; ***s-e ~ erleben*** flourish, reach its peak; have its heyday; ***zu neuer ~ gelangen*** experience a revival, *w.s.* reach new heights; **2.** → ***Stilblüte***; **3.** F dud
'**Blut·egel** *m* leech
blu·ten ['blu:tən] *v/i.* **1.** bleed (***aus*** *dat.* from, *a.* out of *the mouth*); *fig.* ***mir blutet das Herz, wenn ich sehe, wie ...*** my heart bleeds to see ...; ***~den Herzens*** with a heavy heart; **2.** F *fig.* F cough up; ***wir haben dafür schwer ~ müssen*** F it cost us enough; ***j-n ~ lassen*** bleed s.o. white
'**Blü·ten|blatt** *n* petal; **~bo·den** *m* receptacle; **~ho·nig** *m* honey (made from blossoms and flowers); **~kelch** *m* calyx; **~knos·pe** *f* flower bud; **~kro·ne** *f* corolla; **~le·se** *fig. f* anthology; *iro.* collection of howlers
'**blü·ten·los** *adj.* flowerless
'**Blü·ten|meer** *n* sea of blossom; **~stand** *m* inflorescence; **~staub** *m* pollen; **~stiel** *m* pedicel
'**Blut·ent·nah·me** *f* (taking of a) blood sample; ***bei j-m e-e ~ vornehmen*** take s.o.'s blood, take a blood sample from s.o.
'**blü·ten·tra·gend** *adj.* blossoming, 🕮 floriferous
'**blü·ten'weiß** *adj.* snow-white
'**Blü·ten·zweig** *m* spray
Blu·ter ['blu:tɐ] *m* (-s; -) ⚕ h(a)emophiliac
'**Blut·er·guß** *m* h(a)ematoma; bruise
'**Blu·ter·krank·heit** *f* h(a)emophilia
'**Blut·er·satz** *m* blood substitute, artificial blood
'**Blü·te·zeit** *f* → ***Blüte*** 1
'**Blut·farb·stoff** *m* h(a)emoglobin
'**Blut·fett** *n* blood lipids *pl.*; **~wer·te** *pl.* blood lipid concentration *sg.*
'**Blut|fleck** *m* bloodstain; **~ge·fäß** *n* blood vessel; **~ge·rinn·sel** *n* blood clot
'**Blut·ge·rin·nung** *f* (blood) clotting *or* coagulation; '**Blut·ge·rin·nungs·zeit** *f* (blood) coagulation time
'**Blut·grup·pe** *f* blood group; ***j-s ~ bestimmen*** determine s.o.'s blood group, type s.o.'s blood; ***die ~ A haben*** be (*or* belong to) blood group A; ***welche ~ haben Sie?*** which blood group are you (*or* do you belong to)?; '**Blut·grup·pen·be·stim·mung** *f* blood typing
'**Blut|hoch·druck** *m* high blood pressure, hypertension; ***an ~ leiden*** have high blood pressure; **~hund** *m* bloodhound
blu·tig ['blu:tɪç] *adj.* **1.** bloody; bloodstained; bleeding *wound*; ***j-m die Nase ~ schlagen*** give s.o. a bloody nose; ***sich die Köpfe ~ schlagen*** have a real go at each other; ***sich e-n ~en Kopf holen*** get o.s. a bloody nose; ***sich die Hände ~ machen*** get one's hands (all) bloody; ***du bist ja ganz ~!*** you're covered in blood!; ***e-n ~en Urin haben*** be passing blood (with one's urine); **2.** *fig.* bloody; ***~e Szene*** bloody sight (*or* scene), *film:* bloody scene, scene full of blood (and violence), F blood and guts scene; ***~e Unruhen*** violent unrest, violence and bloodshed; ***es kam zu ~en Zwischenfällen*** (*or* ***Auseinandersetzungen***) there were bloody clashes (***zwischen*** *dat.* between); **3.** *gastr.* rare; **4.** *fig.* ***~er Anfänger*** absolute beginner, F raw recruit, greenhorn; ***~er Laie*** complete layman; ***es ist mein ~er Ernst*** I'm dead serious, F (and) I bloody well mean it
'**blut'jung** *adj.* very young; ***ich war ~, als a.*** F I was just a kid when
'**Blut|kon͵ser·ve** *f* unit of (stored) blood; **~kör·per·chen** *n* blood corpuscle; ***weißes ~*** leucocyte; ***rotes ~*** erythrocyte; **~krank·heit** *f* blood disease; **~krebs** *m* leuk(a)emia; **~kreis·lauf** *m* (blood) circulation; **~la·che** *f* pool of blood
'**blut·leer** *adj.* bloodless (*a. fig.*); an(a)emic(-looking); '**Blut·lee·re** *f* hypox(a)emia; ***ich hatte e-e plötzliche ~ im Kopf*** the blood suddenly just went (*or* drained) from my head
'**blut·los** *adj.* bloodless (*a. fig.*)
'**Blut|man·gel** *m* blood deficiency; **~op·fer** *n* **1.** blood sacrifice; **2.** *fig.* human sacrifice; ***dem Land wurden hohe ~ abverlangt*** the blood toll for the nation was great, the scale of human sacrifice for the nation was vast; **~oran·ge** *f* blood orange; **~plas·ma** *n* blood plasma; **~plätt·chen** *n* platelet; **~pro·be** *f* blood test; blood sample; ⚖ blood (alcohol) test; ***bei j-m e-e ~ machen*** take s.o.'s blood, take a blood sample from s.o.; **~pfropf** *m* blood clot; **~ra·che** *f* (bloody) vendetta; **~rausch** *m* bloodlust
'**blut·rei·ni·gend** *adj.* blood-cleansing; '**Blut·rei·ni·gung** *f* cleansing (*or* purification) of the bloodstream; '**Blut·rei·ni·gungs·tee** *m* blood-cleansing tea
'**blut'rot** *adj.* blood-red, (dark) crimson
blut·rün·stig ['blu:trʏnstɪç] *adj.* bloodthirsty; *w.s.* bloody; gory, F blood and guts *story, film etc.*
'**Blut·sau·ger** *m* bloodsucker (*a. fig.*)
'**Bluts·bru·der** *m* blood brother; '**Bluts·brü·der·schaft** *f* blood brotherhood; ***miteinander ~ schließen*** become blood brothers
'**Blut·schan·de** *f* incest; '**blut·schän·de·risch** [-ʃɛndərɪʃ] *adj.* incestuous
'**Blut|schuld** *f* (-; *no pl.*) blood guilt; **~sen·kung** *f* blood sedimentation; **~se·rum** *n* blood serum
'**Blut·spen·de** *f* blood donation; ***zur ~ gehen*** go to give blood; ***die Bevölkerung zur ~ aufrufen*** appeal for blood (donations); '**Blut·spen·der** *m* blood donor; '**Blut·spen·der·aus·weis** *m* blood donor card
'**Blut|spie·gel** *m* blood level; **~spur** *f* **1.** trail of blood; **2.** trace of blood, *a.* bloodstain; **~stau·ung** *f* congestion; **~stein** *m min.* h(a)ematite
'**blut·stil·lend** *adj.* (*a.* ***~es Mittel***) styptic
'**Blut|strahl** *m* **1.** spurt of blood; **2.** spurting blood; **~strom** *m* flow of blood
'**Bluts·trop·fen** *m* drop of blood
'**Blut·sturz** *m* ⚕ h(a)emorrhage
'**bluts·ver·wandt** *adj.* related by blood (***mit*** *dat.* to); '**Bluts·ver·wand·te** *m, f* (-n; -n) blood relation; ⚖ ***der nächste ~*** the next of kin; '**Bluts·ver·wandt·schaft** *f* blood relationship, kinship
'**Blut|tat** *f* bloody deed; ***e-e ~ begehen*** commit (an act of) murder; **~trans·fu·si͵on** *f* blood transfusion
'**blut·trie·fend** *adj.* dripping with blood
'**blut·über͵strömt** *adj.* covered in blood
'**Blut·über͵tra·gung** *f* blood transfusion
Blu·tung ['blu:tʊŋ] *f* (-; -en) bleeding, h(a)emorrhage; ***starke ~(en)*** heavy bleeding (*or* flow)
'**blut·un·ter͵lau·fen** *adj.* bloodshot
'**Blut·un·ter͵su·chung** *f* blood test
'**Blut·ver·dün·nung** *f* h(a)emodilution, thinning of the blood; '**Blutver·dün·nungs·mit·tel** *n* anticoagulant
'**Blut|ver·gie·ßen** *n* (-s; *no pl.*) bloodshed; **~ver·gif·tung** *f* ⚕ blood poisoning; **~ver·lust** *m* loss of blood; blood loss
'**blut·ver·schmiert** *adj.* bloodied, bloodstained
'**blut·voll** *fig. adj.* full-blooded
'**Blut|wä·sche** *f* (blood) dialysis; **~wurst** *f* black pudding, *Am.* blood sausage; **~zoll** *m* (death) toll, toll of lives; ***e-n schweren ~ fordern*** take a heavy toll (of lives)
'**Blut·zucker** (*sep.* -k·k-) *m* blood sugar; F ***mein ~ ist zu niedrig*** my blood sugar has dropped; **~spie·gel** *m* blood sugar level
Bö [bø:] *f* (-; -en) squall, gust; ✈ bump
Boa ['bo:a] *f* (-; -s) **1.** *zo.* boa (constrictor); **2.** boa
Bob [bɔp] *m* (-s; -s) bob(sleigh); **~bahn** *f* bobsleigh run; **~fah·ren** *n* bobsleighing; **~fah·rer** *m* bobber; **~mann·schaft** *f* bob(sleigh) team; **~mei·ster·schaft** *f* bob(sleigh) championship(s *pl.*); **~ren·nen** *n* bob(sleigh) race (*or* racing); **~schlit·ten** *m* bob(sleigh)
Bock [bɔk] *m* (-[e]s; Böcke ['bœkə]) **1.** he-goat, billy goat; ram; buck; (roe-) buck; F *fig.* ***sturer ~*** F stubborn old so-and-so; (***geiler***) ***alter ~*** F (randy) old goat; F ***ein steifer ~ sein*** F be (as) stiff as a poker; F ***e-n ~ schießen*** F boob, F drop a clanger; ***den ~ zum Gärtner machen*** set the fox to keep the geese; F ***et. aus ~ tun*** do s.th. for the fun of it; *sl.* ***ich hab' keinen ~ (drauf)*** *sl.* it doesn't really grab me; **2.** stand; jack; **3.** *gym.* buck; ***~ springen*** a) vault over the buck, b) (play) leapfrog; **4.** bock (beer)
'**bock·bei·nig** [-baɪnɪç] F *adj.* stubborn
'**Bock·bier** *n* bock (beer)
bocken ['bɔkən] (*sep.* -k·k-) *v/i.* (h) buck (*a.* F *mot.*); *fig.* be stubborn; sulk
bockig ['bɔkɪç] (*sep.* -k·k-) *adj.* **1.** stubborn; **2.** sulky; '**Bockig·keit** (*sep.* -k·k-) *f* (-; *no pl.*) **1.** stubbornness; **2.** sulking; sulkiness
'**Bock·lei·ter** *f* stepladder
'**Bock·mist** F *m sl.* crap, *Am. sl.* bullshit
'**Bocks·beu·tel** *m* **1.** bocksbeutel (*or* Franconian) wine; **2.** bocksbeutel
'**Bocks·horn** *n*: *fig.* ***sich ins ~ jagen lassen*** let o.s. be intimidated (*or* put off); ***laß dich von ihm nicht ins ~ jagen!*** *a.* don't let him put you off
'**Bock·sprin·gen** *n* **1.** leapfrog; **2.** → '**Bock·sprung** *m* buck vaulting; *fig.* ***Bocksprünge machen*** cut capers
'**Bock·wurst** *f* (fat) frankfurter
Bo·den ['bo:dən] *m* (-s; Böden ['bø:dən]) **1.** ground; soil; floor; bottom; *fig.* basis; ***auf britischem ~*** on British soil;

heiliger ~ holy (*or* consecrated) ground; ***doppelter ~*** false bottom; ***zu ~ stürzen*** fall to the ground (*or* floor); ***die Augen zu ~ schlagen*** cast one's eyes down (to the ground); ***fester ~*** firm ground; ***festen ~ unter den Füßen haben*** be standing on firm ground, be on terra firma; ***(festen) ~ fassen*** get a (firm) footing *or* foothold, *fig.* find one's feet, *idea etc.*: take hold (*or* root); *fig.* ***sich auf festem (unsicherem) ~ bewegen*** be on safe ground (be standing on shaky ground); ***den ~ für et. bereiten*** prepare the ground for s.th.; F ***am ~ zerstören*** (completely) demolish; F ***am ~ zerstört*** a) (completely) devastated, b) completely drained (F washed out); ***~ gewinnen (verlieren)*** gain (lose) ground; ***~ zurückgewinnen*** make up for lost ground; ***den ~ unter den Füßen verlieren*** lose one's footing, *fig.* get out of one's depth, be thrown off balance; *fig.* ***j-m den ~ unter den Füßen wegziehen*** pull the rug out from under s.o.; *e-m Argument etc.* ***den ~ entziehen*** knock the bottom out of; ***sich auf gefährlichem ~ bewegen*** be treading on slippery ground; ***sich auf den ~ der Tatsachen stellen*** be realistic, look at things realistically, take a realistic view (of things); ***auf dem ~ der Tatsachen bleiben*** stick (*or* keep) to the facts; ***den ~ der Tatsachen verlassen*** get away from (*or* forget) the facts; ***der ~ wurde ihm zu heiß, der ~ brannte ihm unter den Füßen*** things got too hot for him; ***ich hätte (vor Scham or Verlegenheit) im ~ versinken können*** (I was so ashamed *or* embarrassed,) I wished the ground would open up and swallow me; ***zu ~ drücken*** crush, overwhelm; ***aus dem ~ schießen*** mushroom (up); → ***Faß, fruchtbar, Grund*** 1, ***stampfen*** II; **2.** loft, attic; hayloft; **~ab·stand** *m mot.* (ground) clearance; **~ab·wehr** *f* ⚔ ground defen|ce (*Am.* -se); **~be·lag** *m* floor covering; **~be·schaf·fen·heit** *f* **1.** surface conditions *pl.*; **2.** ⚒ properties *pl.* of the soil; **~-'Bo·den-Ra‚ke·te** *f* ⚔ surface-to-surface missile; **~de·to·na·ti‚on** *f* groundburst; **~dienst** *m* ✈ ground services *pl.*; **~er·he·bung** *f* elevation; **~ero·si‚on** *f* soil erosion; **~er·schlie·ßung** *f* soil development; **~er·trag** *m* crop yield; **~fal·te** *f* furrow; **~feuch·tig·keit** *f* humidity of the soil; **~flä·che** *f* ⚒ acreage; △ groundspace; *a.* ⚙ floor space; **~frei·heit** *f mot.* (ground) clearance; **~frost** *m* ground frost; **~fund** *m* arch(a)eological find; **~ge·fecht** *n* ground battle; *a. pl.* ground combat (*or* fighting)

'bo·den·ge·stützt *adj.*: ***~e Rakete*** *etc.*: ground-launched missile *etc.*

'Bo·den|gym‚na·stik *f* floor exercises *pl.*; **~haf·tung** *f mot.* (road) holding; **~hö·he** *f* ground level; **~iso‚lie·rung** *f* floor insulation; **~kampf** *m* → ***Bodengefecht***; **~kon‚trol·le** *f*, **~kon‚troll·sta·ti‚on** *f* ✈ ground control

'Bo·den·kre‚dit *m* mortgage credit; **~an·stalt** *f* land mortgage bank

'bo·den·los *adj.* bottomless; *fig.* incredible; *fig.* ***das war e-e ~e Frechheit!*** what an incredible cheek (*or* nerve)

'Bo·den|-'Luft-Ra‚ke·te *f* ground-to-air missile; **~mar‚kie·run·gen** *pl.* markings; **~mat·te** *f* floor mat; **~nä·he** *f*: ***(in ~*** at) ground level, ✈ zero altitude; **~nähr·stoff** *m* soil nutrient; **~ne·bel** *m* ground fog; **~nut·zung** *f* cultivation (of the soil); **~per·so‚nal** *n* ✈ ground staff, ground crew; **~plat·te** *f* ⚙ base plate; **~pro·be** *f* soil sample; **~re‚form** *f* land reform; **~ren·te** *f* ground rent; **~satz** *m* deposit; sediment; **~schät·ze** *pl.* mineral resources; ***reich an ~n sein*** be rich in (*or* have rich) mineral resources; **~schutz** *m* soil conservation; **~sen·ke** *f* depression, hollow; **~sicht** *f* ✈ ground contact; **~spe·ku‚lant** *m* land jobber; **~spe·ku·la·ti‚on** *f* land speculation

'bo·den·stän·dig *adj.* native, indigenous; *industries etc.*: rooted to the soil; rooted to one's native soil; **'Bo·den·stän·dig·keit** *f* (-; *no pl.*) rootedness to one's native soil

'Bo·den|sta·ti‚on *f* ✈ ground control; *satellite etc.*: tracking (*or* earth) station; **~ste·war·deß** *f* ground hostess; **~streit·kräf·te** *pl.* ground forces; **~tur·nen** *n* floor exercises *pl.*; **~un·ter‚su·chung** *f* soil test (*or* analysis); **~ver·seu·chung** *f* contamination of the soil; soil pollution

Bo·dy·buil·ding ['bɔdibɪldɪŋ] *n* (-s; *no pl.*) body-building; ***~ machen*** do (*or* go to) body-building

bog [bo:k] *pret. of* ***biegen***

Bo·gen ['bo:gən] *m* (-s; Bögen ['bø:gən]) **1.** curve; bend; ⚡, ⚡, *ast.* arc; camber; *skiing*: turn; *figure skating*: curve, circle; ***e-n weiten ~ beschreiben*** describe a wide arc; ***e-n ~ machen*** *road, river etc.*: go into (F do) a bend, ***um*** *acc.*: go (*or* curve) around, F do a bend around; ***e-n großen ~ fahren*** go the long way round; *fig.* ***e-n großen ~ machen um*** *acc.* steer clear of, give *s.o. or s.th.* a wide berth; ***in hohem ~*** *throw, fly etc.* in a high arc; F *fig.* ***in hohem ~ rausfliegen*** F be turned (*or* thrown, kicked) out on one's ear; F ***er hat den ~ raus*** F he's got the hang of it, ***bei*** *dat.*: F he's a dab hand at (*ger.*); **2.** △ arch; **3.** bow; *fig.* ***den ~ überspannen*** overstep the mark, overdo it; push one's luck too far; **4.** ♪ bow; **5.** sheet (of paper), piece of paper; sheet; (printed) sheet; sheet (of stamps); **~brücke** (*sep.* -k·k-) *f* arched bridge; **~fen·ster** *n* arched window; **ꝛför·mig** *adj.* arched, arch-shaped; **~füh·rung** *f* ♪ bowing (technique); **~gang** *m* arcade; archway; **~lam·pe** *f* arc lamp; **~pfei·ler** △ *m* flying buttress; **~schie·ßen** *n* archery; **~schüt·ze** *m* archer; **~seh·ne** *f* bowstring; **~strich** *m* ♪ stroke of the bow; *w.s.* bowing (technique); **~tech·nik** *f* ♪ bowing technique; **~wei·te** *f* span (of an *or* the arch)

Bo·heme [bo'e:m] *f* (-; *no pl.*) bohemian world; **Bo·he·mi·en** [boe'mjɛ̃:] *m* (-s; -s) Bohemian

Boh·le ['bo:lə] *f* (-; -n) plank

Böh·me ['bø:mə] *m* (-n; -n), **Böh·min** ['bø:mɪn] *f* (-; -nen), **böh·misch** ['bø:mɪʃ] *adj.* Bohemian; *fig.* ***das sind böhmische Dörfer für mich*** it's all Greek to me

Boh·ne *f* (-; -n) bean; broad bean; ***grüne ~n*** French (*or* string, runner) beans; ***weiße ~n*** haricot beans; *fig.* ***nicht die ~ wert*** not worth a fig (*or* cent); F ***nicht die ~!*** not a bit!; F ***es kümmert ihn nicht die ~*** F he doesn't care two hoots about it; F ***er versteht nicht die ~ davon*** he doesn't know the first thing about it

'Boh·nen|kaf‚fee *m* fresh (*or* filtered, real) coffee; **~kraut** *n* savo(u)ry; **~ran·ke** *f* beanstalk; **~sa‚lat** *m* (French) bean salad; **~spros·se** *f* bean sprout; **~stan·ge** *f* beanpole (*a.* F *fig.*); **~stroh:** F ***dumm wie ~*** F as thick as two short planks

Boh·ner ['bo:nɐ] *m* (-s; -), **'Boh·ner·be·sen** *m* floor polisher; **'Boh·ner·ma‚schi·ne** *f* electric floor polisher; **boh·nern** ['bo:nɐn] (h) **I.** *v/t.* polish, wax; **II.** *v/i.* polish (*or* wax) the floor(s); **'Boh·ner·wachs** *n* floor polish

'Bohr·ar·bei·ten *pl.* drilling (work) *sg.*

boh·ren ['bo:rən] (h) **I.** *v/t.* **1.** ⚙, ⚒ drill; sink *well etc.*; drive *tunnel etc.*; ***ein Loch ~*** drill a hole (***in*** *acc.* into); *e-n Pfahl etc.* ***in den Boden ~*** drive (*or* sink) into the ground; *ein Messer or Schwert etc.* ***in j-n ~*** plunge (*or* sink) into s.o.; ***ein Schiff in den Grund ~*** send a ship to the bottom; F ***er hat mir zwei Zähne gebohrt*** I had to have two fillings; **II.** *v/i.* **2.** ⚙, ⚒ drill (***nach*** *dat.* for); **3.** ***in der Nase ~*** pick one's nose; **4.** *fig.* probe (***in*** *acc.* into); **5.** *fig.* ***in j-m ~*** *pain, envy, ambition etc.*: gnaw at s.o., *fear etc.*: torment s.o.; **6.** persist, F go on and on; ***er bohrt*** *a.* he's very persistent, he'll go on and on at you; ***so lange ~, bis j-d et. tut*** pester s.o. into doing s.th., F go on and on at s.o. until he (*or* she) does s.th. (*od.* gives in); **III.** *v/refl.*: ***sich ~ in*** *acc.* (***durch*** *acc. etc.*) bore (its way) into (through *etc.*); ***sich ~ in*** *acc.* get into, get stuck in; **'boh·rend** *adj.* piercing, penetrating *look etc.*; gnawing *pain etc.*; penetrating, probing *question etc.*

Boh·rer ['bo:rɐ] *m* (-s; -) ⚙, ⚒ drill; gimlet

'Bohr|in·sel *f* drilling rig; oilrig; **~kopf** *m* drilling head; **~loch** *n* drill hole; bore hole; **~ma‚schi·ne** *f* ⚙ drill; **~mei·ßel** *m* boring tool, cutter; **~scha‚blo·ne** *f* drilling template; **~turm** *m* (drilling) derrick

Boh·rung ['bo:rʊŋ] *f* (-; -en) drilling; (drilled) hole; *mot.* bore

'Bohr·ver·such *m* trial drilling

bö·ig ['bø:ɪç] *adj.* gusty; ✈ F bumpy

Boi·ler ['bɔylɐ] *m* (-s; -) ⚙ boiler; water heater, *Brit. a.* geyser

Bo·je [bo:jə] *f* (-; -n) buoy

Bo·lid [bo'li:t] *m* (-s, -en; -e, -en [bo'li:dən]) **1.** *ast.* fireball, bolide; **2.** *mot.* racer

Bo·li·de [bo'li:də] *m* (-n; -n) → ***Bolid*** 2

Bo·li·via·ner [boli'vĭa:nɐ] *m* (-s; -), **Bo·li·via·ne·rin** [boli'vĭa:nərɪn] *f* (-; -nen), **bo·li·via·nisch** [boli'vĭa:nɪʃ] *adj.* Bolivian

Böl·ler ['bœlɐ] *m* (-s; -) saluting gun; **böl·lern** ['bœlɐn] *v/i.* (h) fire (a salute); **'Böl·ler·schuß** *m* gun salute

Bol·ler·wa·gen ['bɔlɐ-] *dial. m* (wooden) cart (*Am. a.* wagon)

Boll·werk ['bɔlvɛrk] *n* (-[e]s; -e) ⚔ *and fig.* bulwark

Bol·sche·wik [bɔlʃe'vi:k] *m* (-en; -i) Bolshevik; **Bol·sche·wis·mus** [bɔlʃe'vɪsmʊs] *m* (-; *no pl.*) Bolshevism; **Bol·sche·wist** [bɔlʃe'vɪst] *m* (-en; -en), **bol·sche·wi·stisch** [bɔlʃe'vɪstɪʃ] *adj.* Bolshevist

Bol·zen ['bɔltsən] *m* (-s; -) **1.** ⚙ bolt; pin; **2.** *hist.* bolt

'bol·zen F (h) **I.** *v/i. soccer*: kick around; **II.** *v/t.* F boot

'bol·zen·ge'ra·de *adj.* (as) straight as a poker

Bolz·platz [bɔlts-] *m* playing field

Bom·bar·de·ment [bɔmbardə'mã:] *n*

(-s; -s) bombardment (*a. phys. and fig.*); bombing; ⚔ shelling; **bom·bar·die·ren** [bɔmbarˈdiːrən] *v/t.* (h) bomb, bombard; ⚔ *a.* shell; *fig.* pelt (**mit** *dat.* with); bombard, assail (with *questions etc.*); **Bom·barˈdie·rung** *f* (-; -en) → ***Bombardement***

bom·ba·stisch [bɔmˈbastɪʃ] *adj.* bombastic(ally *adv.*)

Bom·be [ˈbɔmbə] *f* (-; -n) **1.** bomb; *fig.* ***wie e-e ~ einschlagen*** *news etc.*: come like a bomb; ***die ~ ist geplatzt*** the cat's out of the bag; → ***abwerfen***; **2.** *soccer*: rocket, rasper

ˈBom·ben... F *in cpds. often* tremendous; **~alarm** *m* bomb alert; **~an·griff** *m* bomb attack, air raid; **~an·schlag** *m* **1.** bomb attack; **2.** → **~at·ten͵tat** *n* bomb attempt; **~be·set·zung** F *f thea., film*: star cast; **~dro·hung** *f* bomb threat; **~er·folg** F *m* tremendous (*or* huge) success; *thea.* box-office hit; (*record*) F smash hit; **~ex·plo·si͵on** *f* bomb explosion; **²fest I.** *adj.* bombproof; **II.** F *fig. adv.*: ~ ***überzeugt*** *etc.* F dead sure *etc.*; ***das steht ~*** F that's a dead cert; **~flug·zeug** *n* bomber (aircraft); **~form** F *f*: ***in ~ sein*** be in great shape; **~ge·halt** F *n* F fantastic salary; **~geld** F *n*: ***ein ~ verdienen*** F earn a packet; **~ge·schäft** F *n* roaring business; ***ein ~ machen*** do a roaring trade; **~hit·ze** F *f* sweltering heat; **~la·ge** F *f* prime location, F plum site; **~last** *f* bomb load; **~le·ger** [-leːgɐ] *m* (-s; -) bomber, bomb planter; ***der ~*** *a.* the man (*or* person) who planted the bomb; **~nacht** *f* night of bombing; **~preis** F *m* **1.** rockbottom price; ***zu e-m ~*** *a.* for next to nothing; **2.** top price; F incredible price; **~rol·le** F *f thea.* dream part; **~sa·che** F *f* F knockout; **~scha·den** *m* air-raid damage; **~schuß** F *m* F cracking shot; **~schüt·ze** *m* ⚔ bombardier; **²si·cher** *adj.* **1.** bombproof; **2.** F surefire; ***es ist e-e ~e Sache*** F it's a dead cert; **~split·ter** *m* bomb splinter; **~stel·lung** F *f* F plum job, fantastic job; **~stim·mung** F *f* F terrific (*or* tremendous) atmosphere; **~ter·ror** *m* terrorist bombing(s *pl.*) *or* attacks *pl.*; **~trich·ter** *m* bomb crater, crater left by a (*or* the) bomb

Bom·ber [ˈbɔmbɐ] *m* (-s; -) ✈ bomber (*a.* F *fig. sport*); **~ge·schwa·der** *n* bomber group (*Am.* wing)

bom·big [ˈbɔmbɪç] F **I.** *adj.* F great, terrific; **II.** *adv.*: ~ ***verdienen*** F earn a packet

Bon [bɔŋ, bõː] *m* (-s; -s) voucher; receipt

Bon·bon [bɔŋˈbɔŋ, bõˈbõː] *m, n* (-s; -s) sweet, *Am. a. pl.* candy; **bonˈbon·far·ben, bonˈbon·far·big** *adj.* sickly pink (*or* yellow *etc.*)

bon·gen [ˈbɔŋən] *v/t.* (h) ring up; → ***gebongt*** II

Bon·go [ˈbɔŋgo] *n* (-[s]; -s), *f* (-; -s), **~trom·mel** *f* bongo (drum), bongos *pl.*; ***mit X auf der ~*** with X on bongos

Bo·ni·fi·ka·ti·on [bonifikaˈtsi̯oːn] *f* (-; -en) allowance; bonus

Bo·ni·tät [boniˈtɛːt] *f* (-; -en) **1.** ✝ *credit standing*, creditworthiness; **2.** ✝ quality; **3.** ⚒ quality of the soil

Bon·mot [bõˈmoː] *n* (-s; -s) witty remark, witticism

Bon·sai [ˈbɔnzaɪ] *n* (-s; -) bonsai; **~baum** *m* bonsai (tree)

Bo·nus [ˈboːnʊs] *m* (-[ses]; -[se]) ✝ **1.** bonus, premium; **2.** special dividend

Bon·ze [ˈbɔntsə] *m* (-n; -n) **1.** F bigwig; ***die ~n der Partei*** the party bigwigs; ***die ~n der Wirtschaft*** the tycoons of industry; **2.** F big shot; **3.** *buddhism*: bonze; **ˈBon·zen·tum** F *n* (-s; *no pl.*), **ˈBon·zen·wirt·schaft** F *f* (-; *no pl.*) F boss rule

Boom [buːm] *m* (-s; -s) ✝ boom

Boot [boːt] *n* (-[e]s; -e) boat; ~ ***fahren*** go boating; *fig.* ***wir sitzen alle im gleichen ~*** we're all in the same boat

boo·ten [ˈbuːtən] *v/t. and v/i.* (h) *computer*: boot (up)

ˈBoots|an·hän·ger *m* boat trailer; **~bau** *m* (-[e]s; *no pl.*) boat building; **~bau·er** *m* (-s; -) boat builder; **~be·sat·zung** *f* (boat's *or* ship's) crew; **~fahrt** *f* boat trip (*or* ride); **~füh·rer** *m sport*: coxswain; **~ha·fen** *m* marina; **~haus** *n* boathouse; **~mann** *m* (-[e]s; -leute) boatswain; ⚔ petty officer; **~ren·nen** *n* boat race; **~steg** *m* landing stage; **~ver·leih** *m* boat hire; boats for hire; **~werft** *f* boatyard

Bor [boːɐ] *n* (-s; *no pl.*) ⚗ boron

Bo·rax [ˈboːraks] *m* (-[es]; *no pl.*) ⚗ borax; **~säu·re** *f* bor(ac)ic acid

Bord[1] [bɔrt] *m* (-[e]s; -e) ⚓, ✈: ***an ~*** on board, aboard; ***an ~ e-s Schiffes*** (***Flugzeugs***) ***gehen*** board a ship (plane); ***an ~ gehen*** ⚓ go aboard, board ship, ✈ board (the aircraft); ***von ~ gehen*** ⚓ disembark, ✈ leave the aircraft; ***an ~ nehmen*** ⚓ take aboard, ✈ take onto the plane; ***über ~ gehen*** fall overboard; ***über ~ werfen*** throw overboard (*a. fig.*), ⚓ jettison; ***Mann über ~!*** man overboard!; ***wir begrüßen Sie an ~ unserer Maschine*** (***unseres Schiffes***) we welcome you aboard our aircraft (ship)

Bord[2] *n* (-[e]s; -e) shelf

ˈBord|buch *n* log book; **~case** *n, m* flight case; **~com͵pu·ter** *m* ✈ on-board computer, *mot. a.* dashboard computer

bor·deaux [bɔrˈdoː] *adj.*, **Borˈdeaux**[1] *n* (-; *no pl.*) burgundy, claret

Borˈdeaux[2] *m* (-; - [bɔrˈdoːs]), **~wein** *m* claret, Bordeaux (wine)

ˈbord·ei·gen *adj.* on-board ...

ˈBord·elek͵tro·nik *f* avionics *pl.*

Bor·dell [bɔrˈdɛl] *n* (-s; -e) brothel; **~vier·tel** *n* red-light district; **~wir·tin** *f* madam

ˈBord|funk *m* ⚓ ship's radio; ✈ aircraft radio equipment; **~fun·ker** *m* radio operator; **~ge·päck** *n* hand luggage (*or* baggage), *esp. Am.* carry-on (baggage); **~in·ge͵nieur** *m* flight engineer; **~͵ka·me·ra** *f* on-board camera; **~kan·te** *f* curb, *Brit.* kerb; **~kar·te** *f* boarding pass; **~ki·no** *n* **1.** in-flight movies *pl.*; **2.** ship's cinema; **~kof·fer** *m* flight case; **~kran** *m* ⚓ deck crane; **~kü·che** *f* galley; **~me͵cha·ni·ker** *m* flight mechanic; **~per·so͵nal** *n* flight crew; **~pro͵gramm** *n* in-flight entertainment program(me); **~͵ra·dar** *n* airborne radar; **~sen·der** *m* airborne transmitter; **~stein**(**kan·te** *f*) *m* kerb, *Am.* curb; **~ta·sche** *f* flight bag, *esp. Am.* carry-on (bag); **~te·le͵fon** *n* interphone; **~un·ter͵hal·tung** *f* in-flight entertainment

Bor·dü·re [bɔrˈdyːrə] *f* (-; -n) border, trimming

ˈBord|ver·pfle·gung *f* in-flight meals *pl.* (*or* catering, fare), F meals *pl.* on the plane; **~waf·fen** *pl.* aircraft weapons; tank armament *sg*

bor·gen [ˈbɔrgən] *v/t.* (h) **1.** ***sich et. ~*** borrow s.th.; *fig. a.* lift s.th.; ***es ist nur geborgt*** I've *etc.* just borrowed it; **2.** lend (out), *esp. Am.* loan (out); ***j-m et. ~*** lend s.o. s.th., lend s.th. (out) to s.o., *esp. Am.* loan s.o. s.th., loan s.th. (out) to s.o.

Bor·ke [ˈbɔrkə] *f* (-; -n) bark; crust (*a.* ⚕)

ˈBor·ken|flech·te *f* ⚕ ringworm; **~kä·fer** *m* bark beetle

bor·niert [bɔrˈniːɐt] *adj.* **1.** narrow-minded; **2.** dense; **Borˈniert·heit** *f* (-; *no pl.*) **1.** narrow-mindedness; **2.** denseness

Bor·retsch [ˈbɔrɛtʃ] *m* (-[e]s; *no pl.*) ✿, *gastr.* borage

ˈBor|sal·be *f* boric acid ointment; **~säu·re** *f* bor(ac)ic acid

Borschtsch [bɔrʃtʃ] *m* (-; *no pl.*) *gastr.* borscht

Bör·se [ˈbœrzə] *f* (-; -n) **1.** ✝ stock exchange (*or* market); money market; ***Frankfurter*** (***Pariser*** *etc.*) ~ *a.* Frankfurt (Paris *etc.*) bourse; ***an der ~*** on the stock exchange (*or* market); **2.** *obs.* purse, wallet; **3.** *boxing*: purse

ˈBör·sen|be·ginn *m* opening of the stock market; ***bei ~*** when the stock market opened (*or* opens); **~be·richt** *m* stock market report; **~er·öff·nung** *f* → ***Börsenbeginn***; **²fä·hig** *adj.* **1.** listed; **2.** marketable; **²gän·gig** *adj.* → ***börsenfähig*** 2; **~ge·schäft** *n* stock market transaction; bargain; **~han·del** *m* stock exchange trading; **~͵in·dex** *m* stock exchange index; **~krach** *m* (stock market) crash, stock market collapse, collapse of the stock market; **~kurs** *m* market price (*or* rate), quotation; **~mak·ler** *m* stockbroker; **~nach·rich·ten** *pl.* financial news (*or* report) *sg.*; **~no͵tie·rung** *f* quotation; **~ord·nung** *f* stock exchange regulations *pl.*; **~pa͵pie·re** *pl.* listed securities; **~preis** *m* market price (*or* rate), quotation; **~schluß** *m* close of the stock market; ***bei ~*** when the stock market closed (*or* closes); **~schwan·kun·gen** *pl.* stock market fluctuations; **~spe·ku͵lant** *m* stock exchange speculator; **~spe·ku·la·ti͵on** *f* speculation on the stock market; playing the stock market; **~spra·che** *f* stock exchange jargon; **~ter͵min·ge·schäft** *n*, **~ter͵min·han·del** *m* trading in futures; **~tip** *m* market tip; **~ver·kehr** *m* stock market transactions *pl.*; **~wert** *m* market value; **~zei·tung** *f* financial paper; **~zet·tel** *m* stock list

Bör·sia·ner [bœrˈzi̯aːnɐ] *m* (-s; -) broker, F operator; speculator

Bor·ste [ˈbɔrstə] *f* (-; -n) bristle

ˈBor·sten|be·sen *m* coarse broom; **~kopf** *m* spike; **~pin·sel** *m* bristle brush; **~tier** *n* pig; *pl. coll.* swine *sg.*; **~vieh** *n* → ***Borstentier***

bor·stig [ˈbɔrstɪç] *adj.* bristly; F *fig.* gruff; **ˈBor·stig·keit** *f* (-; *no pl.*) gruffness

Bor·te [ˈbɔrtə] *f* (-; -n) border; braid, trimming; galloon

bös [bøːs] *adj.* → ***böse***

ˈbös·ar·tig *adj.* **1.** malicious, nasty; *zo.* vicious; **2.** ⚕ malignant *growth etc.*; *a.* pernicious *disease*; **ˈBös·ar·tig·keit** *f* (-; *no pl.*) **1.** spitefulness; *zo.* vicious nature; **2.** ⚕ malignancy; pernicious nature *of a disease*

Bö·schung [ˈbœʃʊŋ] *f* (-; -en) embankment; *geol.* scarp, escarpment

bö·se [ˈbøːzə] **I.** *adj.* **1.** bad; evil, wicked; spiteful; naughty; **2.** unpleasant, bad; nasty; ~ ***Erkältung*** nasty (F rotten) cold; ~ ***Krankheit*** nasty (*or* very unpleasant) illness; ~ ***Verletzung*** nasty cut (*or* wound); ~ ***Folgen*** dire consequences;

e-e ~ Sache a nasty business; ***~ Überraschung*** nasty surprise; ***es sieht ~ aus*** things don't look too good, things look (F pretty) bad; ***ein ~s Ende nehmen*** come to a bad end; ***e-e ~ Wende nehmen*** take a nasty turn; ***im ~n auseinandergehen*** part on bad terms; → ***Blick*** 1, ***Blut*** 1; **3.** F ⚕ bad, sore; **4.** angry, cross, F mad (***über*** *acc.* about); ***j-m*** (*or* ***auf j-n***) ***~ sein*** be angry (*or* cross) with s.o., F be mad at s.o.; ***~ werden*** get angry *etc.*; **II.** *adv.* **5.** badly *etc.*; → I; ***ich habe es nicht ~ gemeint*** I didn't mean any harm; **6.** ***~ enden*** come to a bad end; ***sich ganz ~ irren*** make a fatal (*or* very bad) mistake; ***sich ganz ~ verirren*** (*or* ***verlaufen***) get hopelessly lost; **7.** ***j-n ~ ansehen*** scowl at s.o., give s.o. a black look; **'Bö·se**[1] *m*, *f* (-n; -n) bad person, bad boy (girl); ***die ~n*** *film etc.*: F the baddies; ***der ~*** the Evil One, the Devil; **'Bö·se** *n* (-n; *no pl.*) evil; harm; ***~s tun*** do evil; ***j-m*** (***etwas***) ***~s antun*** do s.o. harm, do s.th. to hurt s.o.; ***~s im Sinn haben*** be up to no good; ***~s reden über*** *acc.* speak ill of; → ***ahnen***

'Bö·se·wicht *m* (-[e]s; -er) villain, rogue (*both a. fig., iro.*)

bos·haft ['bo:shaft] *adj.* malicious, nasty; **Bos·haf·tig·keit** ['bo:shaftıçkaıt] *f* (-; *no pl.*) maliciousness, malicious nature; *lit.* wickedness

Bos·heit ['bo:shaıt] *f* (-; -en) **1.** *no pl.* malice; ***aus ~*** out of spite; **2.** nasty remark; ***so e-e ~!*** what a nasty thing to do (*or* say)

Boß [bɔs] F *m* (Bosses; Bosse) F boss; (*party etc.*) leader

bos·seln ['bɔsəln] F *v/i.* (h): ***~ an*** *dat.* tinker *or* fiddle (around *or* about) with, *fig.* tinker with *a problem etc.*, doctor *s.th.*

'bös·wil·lig I. *adj.* malicious; ⚖ *a.* wil(l)ful; ⚖ ***in ~er Absicht*** with malice aforethought, with malicious intent; **II.** *adv.* out of spite; ⚖ with malice aforethought, with malicious intent; **'Bös·wil·lig·keit** *f* (-; *no pl.*) malevolence, ill-will; ⚖ wil(l)fulness

bot [bo:t] *pret. of* ***bieten***

Bo·ta·nik [bo'ta:nık] *f* (-; *no pl.*) botany; **Bo·ta·ni·ker** [bo'ta:nikɐ] *m* (-s; -) botanist; **bo·ta·nisch** [bo'ta:nıʃ] *adj.* botanic(al); ***~er Garten*** botanical gardens

Bo·te ['bo:tə] *m* (-n; -n) messenger; errand boy, *Am.* F gofer; emissary; courier; *fig.* apostle; herald, harbinger

Bo·ten|dienst *m* **1.** courier service; **2.** ***~e leisten*** run errands; **~gang** *m* errand; ***Botengänge machen*** run errands

Bot·schaft *f* (-; -en) **1.** message (***an*** *acc.* to) (*a. fig.*); news (*sg.*); → ***froh***; **2.** *pol.* embassy

Bot·schaf·ter ['bo:tʃaftɐ] *m* (-s; -) ambassador (***in*** *dat.* to *Spain etc.*, in *Madrid etc.*); **~ebe·ne** *f*: ***auf ~*** at ambassadorial level; **~kon·fe,renz** *f* ambassadors' conference

'Bot·schafts|be·set·zung *f* occupation of the (*or* an) embassy; **~ge·bäu·de** *n* embassy (building); **~ge·län·de** *n* embassy grounds *pl.* (*or* compound); ***auf dem ~*** in the embassy grounds

Bött·cher ['bœtçɐ] *m* (-s; -) cooper

Bot·tich ['bɔtıç] *m* (-s; -e) tub, vat

Bouil·lon [bʊl'jɔŋ] *f* (-; -s) consommé, clear soup; **~wür·fel** *m* stock cube

Bou·le·vard [bulə'va:ɐ] *m* (-s; -s) boulevard; **~blatt** *n* popular newspaper, tabloid; **~pres·se** *f* popular (*contp.* gutter) press; **~stück** *n* light comedy; **~thea·ter** *n* **1.** light comedy; **2.** comedy theat|re (*Am. a.* -er); **~zei·tung** *f* popular newspaper, tabloid

bour·geois [bʊr'ʒo̯a] **I.** *adj.* bourgeois (*a. contp.*), middle-class; **II.** 𝔖 *m* (-; -) bourgeois; **Bour·geoi·sie** [bʊrʒo̯a'zi:] *f* (-; -n) bourgeoisie, middle classes *pl.*

Bou·tique [bu'ti:k] *f* (-; -en) boutique

Bow·le ['bo:lə] *f* (-; -n) **1.** (cold) punch; ***die ~ ansetzen*** make the punch; **2.** punchbowl

bow·len ['bo:lən] *v/i.* (h) bowl

Bow·ling ['bo:lıŋ] *n* (-s; *no pl.*) **1.** bowling; **2.** bowls (*sg.*); **~bahn** *f* bowling alley; **~platz** *m* bowling green

Box [bɔks] *f* (-; -en) **1.** box; **2.** parking space; **3.** *motor racing*: pit; **4.** speaker; **5.** box camera

Box·calf ['bɔkskalf] *n* (-s; *no pl.*) boxcalf

Bo·xe ['bɔksə] *f* (-; -n) → ***Box*** 1

bo·xen ['bɔksən] (h) **I.** *v/i.* fight; *sport*: box; **II.** *v/t.* hit; **III.** *v/refl.*: ***sich*** (***mit j-m***) ***~*** have a fight (with s.o.); *fig.* ***sich ~ durch*** *acc.* fight one's way through; **IV.** 𝔖 *n* (-s; *no pl.*) boxing

Bo·xer ['bɔksɐ] *m* (-s; -) **1.** boxer, fighter; **2.** *zo.* boxer; **~na·se** *f* boxer's nose; **~shorts** *pl.* boxer shorts, boxers

'Box·hand·schuh *m* boxing glove

Box·kalf → ***Boxcalf***

'Box|kampf *m* boxing match, fight; **~ring** *m* boxing ring; **~sport** *m* boxing

Boy·kott [bɔy'kɔt] *m* (-[e]s; -s, -e) boycott; ***den ~ verhängen über*** *acc.* boycott; **~dro·hung** *f* threat of a boycott; **~er·klä·rung** *f* announcement of a boycott

boy·kot·tie·ren [bɔyko'ti:rən] *v/t.* (h) boycott

brach[1] [bra:x] *pret. of* ***brechen***

brach[2] *adj.* fallow; **𝔖feld** *n* fallow land (*or* field)

Bra·chi·al·ge·walt [bra'xi̯a:l-] *f*: (***mit ~*** by) (sheer) brute force

'Brach·land *n* fallow (land)

'brach·le·gen *v/t.* (*sep.*, h) leave fallow; **'brach·lie·gen** *v/i.* (*irr., sep.*, h, → ***liegen***) lie fallow; *fig.* go to waste; **'brach·lie·gend** *adj.* fallow

brach·te ['braxtə] *pret. of* ***bringen***

brackig ['brakıç] (*sep.* -k·k-) *adj.* brackish; **Brack·was·ser** ['brak-] *n* brackish water

Brah·ma·ne [bra'ma:nə] *m* (-n; -n), **brah·ma·nisch** [bra'ma:nıʃ] *adj.* Brahmin

Braille·schrift ['bra:jəʃrıft] *f* (-; *no pl.*) braille

Bran·che ['brã:ʃə] *f* (-; -n) ✝ **1.** industrial sector; **2.** line of business

'Bran·chen|adreß·buch *n* classified directory; **~blatt** *n* trade journal; **~er·fah·rung** *f* experience in the trade; **𝔖fremd** *adj.* new to the trade; **~kennt·nis** *f* knowledge of the trade; **𝔖kun·dig** *adj.* experienced in the trade; **𝔖üb·lich** *adj.* customary (in the trade); **~ver·zeich·nis** *n* classified directory, F *the* yellow pages *pl.*

Brand [brant] *m* (-[e]s; Brände ['brɛndə]) **1.** fire, blaze; ***in ~*** (***stehen*** be) on fire, (be) in flames; ***in ~ geraten*** catch fire; ***in ~ stecken*** set fire to, set on fire, kindle *firewood etc.*, light *one's pipe etc.*; **2.** F ***e-n riesigen ~ haben*** F be parched, be dying of thirst; **3.** ⚘ blight, mildew; **4.** ⚕ gangrene; **5.** ⚙ firing

'brand·ak·tu'ell *adj.* up-to-the-minute *news, issue etc.*; *announcement etc.* hot off the press; the very latest *fashion etc.*; the latest *hit etc.*

'Brand|an·schlag *m* arson attack; ***e-n ~ verüben auf*** *acc.* set fire to; **~be·kämp·fung** *f* fire fighting; **~bla·se** *f* (burn) blister; **~bom·be** *f* fire (*or* incendiary) bomb; **~brief** F *m* **1.** urgent reminder; **2.** urgent request; **~di,rek·tor** *m* fire chief

'brand'ei·lig *adj.* extremely urgent; ***er hat's wieder ~*** he's in a terrible hurry as usual, *a.* it's all terribly urgent as usual

'Brand·ei·sen *n* branding iron

bran·den ['brandən] *v/i.* (sn) surge (***gegen*** *acc.* against); ***~ gegen*** *acc. a.* break on (*or* against)

Bran·den·bur·ger ['brandənbʊrgɐ] *m* (-s; -) man from Brandenburg; ***~ sein*** *usu.* come (*or* be) from Brandenburg; **bran·den·bur·gisch** ['brandənbʊrgıʃ] *adj.* Brandenburg ..., from Brandenburg

'Brand|fackel (*sep.* -k·k-) *f* firebrand (*a. fig.*); **~fleck** *m* burn (mark); **~ge·fahr** *f* risk of fire (breaking out), fire risk; ***e-e ~ darstellen*** be a fire hazard (*or* risk); **~ge·ruch** *m* smell of burning; *gastr.* burnt smell; **~ge·schoß** *n* fire shell

'brand'heiß *adj.* the very latest *news, announcement etc.* hot off the press

'Brand|herd *m* source *or* focus of (the) fire; *fig.* trouble spot; **~ka·ta,stro·phe** *f* fire disaster; **~mal** *n* brand; *fig.* stigma

brand·mar·ken ['brantmarkən] *v/t.* (h) *a. fig.* brand; **'Brand·mar·kung** *f* (-; -en) *a. fig.* branding

'Brand|mau·er *f* fire wall; **~nar·be** *f* burn scar, scar from a burn

'brand'neu *adj.* brand-new

'Brand|op·fer *n* **1.** fire victim; **2.** burnt offering; **~re·de** *f* inflammatory speech; **~sal·be** *f* burn ointment; **~scha·den** *m* fire damage

brand·schat·zen ['brantʃatsən] *v/t. and v/i.* (h) pillage, plunder; **'Brand·schat·zung** *f* (-; -en) pillage

'Brand·schnei·se *f* fire lane

'Brand·schutz *m* fire prevention; **~be·auf·trag·te** *m* (-n; -n) fire prevention officer

'Brand|soh·le *f* insole; **~spur** *f* trace of a (*or* the) fire; **~stät·te** *f* scene of the fire; **~stel·le** *f* **1.** scene of the fire; **2.** → ***Brandfleck***; **~stif·ter** *m* arsonist, fire-raiser; **~stif·tung** *f* arson; **~teig** *m* choux pastry mixture

Bran·dung ['brandʊŋ] *f* (-; *no pl.*) surf; surge, wave; **'Bran·dungs·wel·le** *f* breaker

'Brand|ur·sa·che *f* cause of the fire; **~ver·hü·tung** *f* fire prevention; **~wa·che** *f* firewatch; fireguard; **~wun·de** *f* burn; scald; **~zei·chen** *n* brand

brann·te ['brantə] *pret. of* ***brennen***

Brannt·kalk ['brant-] *m* burnt lime

'Brannt·wein *m* brandy; spirits *pl.*; **~bren·ner** *m* distiller; **~bren·ne,rei** *f* **1.** distillery; **2.** distilling; **~mo·no,pol** *n* alcohol (*or* spirits) monopoly; **~steu·er** *f* spirits duty

Bra·si·lia·ner [brazi'li̯a:nɐ] *m* (-s; -), **Bra·si·lia·ne·rin** [brazi'li̯a:nərın] *f* (-; -nen), **bra·si·lia·nisch** [brazi'li̯a:nıʃ] *adj.* Brazilian

Bras·se ['brasə] *f* (-; -n) *zo.* bream

Brat·ap·fel ['bra:t-] *m* baked apple

bra·ten (briet, gebraten, h) **I.** *v/t.* (*and v/i.*) roast; grill; fry; ***am Spieß ~*** roast on a spit; → ***gebraten*** II; **II.** F *v/i.* F roast *or* bake (in the sun)

'**Bra·ten** *m* (-s; -) roast; joint; ***kalter*** ~ cold meat; *fig.* ***fetter*** ~ fine catch; ***den*** ~ ***riechen*** smell a rat; **~duft** *m* smell of roasting; **~fett** *n* dripping; **~saft** *m* **1.** juice from the meat; **2.** → **~so·ße** *f* gravy

Brä·ter ['brɛːtɐ] *m* (-s; -) roasting pan

'**brat·fer·tig** *adj.* oven-ready

'**Brat|fett** *n* cooking fat; **~fisch** *m* fried fish; **~fo·lie** *f* tin foil; **~häh·chen** *n* → ***Brathuhn***; **~he·ring** *m* grilled (and pickled) herring; **~huhn** *n*, **~hühn·chen** *n* roast (*or* grilled, broiled) chicken; broiler; **~kar,tof·feln** *pl.* fried potatoes; **~ofen** *m* oven; **~pfan·ne** *f* frying pan; **~röh·re** *f* oven; **~rost** *m* grill

Brat·sche ['braːtʃə] *f* (-; -n) ♪ viola; **Brat·scher** ['braːtʃɐ] *m* (-s; -), **Brat·schist** [bra'tʃɪst] *m* (-en; -en) viola player

'**Brat|spieß** *m* spit; **~wurst** *f* fried (*or* grilled) sausage

Brauch [braʊx] *m* (-[e]s; Bräuche ['brɔʏçə]) custom; practi|ce (*Am. a.* -se); ***herkömmlicher*** ~ tradition; ***es ist hier der*** ~ (***, daß die Männer ...***) it's the custom (*or* it's customary) around here (for the men to ...); ***es ist bei uns so*** ~ that's the way we've always done it, it's the custom with us; ***so wie es der*** ~ ***will*** as custom has it; ***nach altem*** ~ according to tradition (*or* custom), *do s.th.* the traditional way; ***es kommt außer*** ~ it's falling into disuse, *w.s.* people don't do it (so much) any more

'**brauch·bar** *adj.* **1.** useful; usable; practicable; **2.** F useful, decent, not bad; '**Brauch·bar·keit** *f* (-; *no pl.*) usefulness; usability; practicability

brau·chen ['braʊxən] (h) **I.** *v/t.* need; require; take *esp. time, energy etc.*; use, make use of; ***Sie*** ~ ***den Vierer(bus)*** you need (to take) the number four (bus); ***wozu brauchst du es?*** what do you need it for?; ***wie lange wird er*** ~***?*** how long will it take him?; ***ich brauche zwei Stunden, um zu*** *inf.* it takes me two hours to *inf.*; ***das braucht (seine) Zeit*** it takes time; ***ich könnte ein paar Helfer*** ~ I could do with some help (*or* a few people to help me); F ***ich kann es nicht*** ~***, wenn er ständig anruft*** I can't do without him ringing up all the time; **II.** *v/aux.* need, have to; ***du brauchst (es) mir nicht zu sagen*** you don't have to tell me; ***er brauchte nicht zu kommen*** he didn't have to come; ***er hätte nicht zu kommen*** ~ he needn't have come; ***du brauchst es nur zu sagen*** just say the word; ***du brauchst keine Angst zu haben*** there's no need to be scared; ***du brauchst nicht gleich in die Luft zu gehen*** there's no need to lose your temper; ***es braucht wohl nicht gesagt zu werden, daß*** I don't suppose there's any need to stress that

'**Brauch·tum** *n* (-*s*; *no pl.*) customs *pl.*, tradition(s *pl.*)

'**Brauch·was·ser** *n* industrial water

Braue ['braʊə] *f* (-; -n) (eye)brow; ***die*** **~*n*** ***hochziehen*** raise one's eyebrows (*or* an eyebrow)

brau·en ['braʊən] (h) **I.** *v/t.* brew; make *tea etc.*; **II.** *fig. v/i.* be brewing; **Brau·er** ['braʊɐ] *m* (-s; -) brewer; **Braue·rei** [braʊə'raɪ] *f* (-; -en) brewery; '**Brau·haus** *n* brewery

braun [braʊn] **I.** *adj.* brown; tanned; **~*e*** ***Butter*** browned (*or* fried) butter; **~*es*** ***Pferd*** bay; ~ ***werden*** get a tan, go brown; ***schnell*** ~ ***werden*** tan easily (*or* quickly), go brown quickly; ***du bist aber*** ~ ***geworden!*** you're very brown, you've got quite a tan; **II.** ♀ *n* (-s; -) brown

'**braun·äu·gig** [-ɔʏgɪç] *adj.* brown-eyed

'**Braun·bär** *m* brown bear

Bräu·ne ['brɔʏnə] *f* (-; *no pl.*) brown(ness); (sun)tan; '**bräu·nen I.** *v/i.* (sn) *and v/refl.* (***sich*** ~) (h) get brown; get a tan; **II.** *v/t.* (h) brown; tan

'**Braun·fäu·le** *f* blight

'**braun|ge·brannt** *adj.* tanned, bronzed; **~haa·rig** *adj.* brown-haired

'**Braun·koh·le** *f* brown (*Am.* soft) coal, lignite

bräun·lich ['brɔʏnlɪç] *adj.* brownish

Braun·sche Röh·re ['braʊnʃə] *f* ⚙ cathode-ray tube

'**Bräu·nungs|ka,bi·ne** *f* tanning booth; **~stu·dio** *n* solarium, *Am.* tanning salon

Brau·se ['braʊzə] *f* (-; -n) **1.** → ***Brauselimonade***; **2.** sprinkler, nozzle; **3.** shower; ***sich unter die*** ~ ***stellen*** have (*or* take) a shower; **~bad** *n* shower (bath); **~li·mo,na·de** *f* fizzy drink, *Brit. a.* lemonade

brau·sen ['braʊzən] **I.** *v/i.* **1.** (h) roar; boom; rage; ***mir braust es in den Ohren*** my ears are buzzing; **2.** (sn) F *fig.* zoom, *car etc.*: *a.* roar; ***um die Ecke*** ~ come (*or* go) zooming round the corner; **3.** (sn) F *fig.* ~ ***durch*** *acc.* whisk (F whizz, *Am.* whiz) through *a report etc.*; **4.** (h) have (*or* take) a shower; **II.** *v/t.* (h) spray, shower; '**brau·send** *adj.*: **~*er Beifall*** thunderous applause

Brau·se|pul·ver *n* sherbet; **~ta,blet·te** *f* effervescent tablet

Braut [braʊt] *f* (-; Bräute ['brɔʏtə]) **1.** bride; **2.** fiancée, F intended; **3.** F girl; *sl.* bird; **~el·tern** *pl.* parents of the bride, bride's parents; **~füh·rer** *m man who gives away the bride*; **~ge·mach** *n esp. iro.* nuptial chamber

Bräu·ti·gam ['brɔʏtɪgam] *m* (-s; -e) **1.** (bride)groom; **2.** fiancé

'**Braut|jung·fer** *f* bridesmaid; **~kleid** *n* wedding dress; **~kranz** *m* bridal wreath; **~leu·te** *pl.* bride and groom; **~mut·ter** *f* mother of the bride, bride's mother; **~paar** *n* **1.** bride and (bride)groom; **2.** engaged couple; **~schau** *f*: F ***auf*** ~ ***gehen*** look for a wife; **~schlei·er** *m* bridal veil; **~strauß** *m* bridal bouquet; **~va·ter** *m* father of the bride, bride's father

'**Brau·we·sen** *n* (-s; *no pl.*) brewing industry

brav [braːf] *adj.* **1.** well-behaved, good; ***sei schön*** ~***!*** be good now; ***sei*** ~ ***und geh ins Bett!*** go to bed like a good boy (*or* girl); **2.** good, honest (and upright), upright; ***e-e*** **~*e*** ***Leistung*** a good attempt; *adv.* ***er hat sich*** ~ ***geschlagen*** he tried hard, he did his best; **3.** F very conventional, ordinary; plain

bra·vo ['braːvo] *int.* well done!; *thea. etc.* bravo!; '**Bra·vo** *n* (-s; -s), '**Bra·vo·ruf** *m* bravo, *pl. a.* cheers

Bra·vour [bra'vuːɐ] *f* (-; *no pl.*) **1.** spirit; ***mit*** ~ brilliantly; **2.** ♪ bravura; **3.** bravery; **~arie** *f* ♪ bravura aria; **~lei·stung** *f* → ***Bravourstück***

bra·vou·rös [bravu'røːs] *adj.* courageous, bold; ♪ brilliant, bravura ...

Bra'vour·stück *n* **1.** daring feat; **2.** ♪ bravura

brech·bar ['brɛç-] *adj.* breakable

'**Brech|boh·ne** *f* French bean; **~durch·fall** *m* ⚕ diarrh(o)ea with vomiting; **~ei·sen** *n* crowbar

bre·chen ['brɛçən] (brach, gebrochen) **I.** *v/t.* (h) **1.** break (*a. fig. oath, record, silence, pride etc.*; *a.* quarry *stones*; *phys.* refract; F ⚕ vomit, bring up; (***sich***) ***den Arm*** ~ break one's arm; **2.** *fig.* break, violate *law, contract etc.*; run *the blockade*; break, crush *resistance*; ***die Ehe*** ~ commit adultery; F ***zum*** ♀ ***voll*** packed, F jampacked, chock-a-block; → ***Blokkade*** 1, ***Eis, Genick, Herz, Knie, Zaun***; → ***gebrochen*** II; **II.** *v/i.* (sn) **3.** break (*a. voice*); *fig.* break down; F ⚕ be sick, vomit; ~ ***aus*** *dat.* burst out of, *tears*: pour from; ~ ***durch*** *acc.* break (*or* crash) through; F ***ich muß*** ~ I'm going to be sick; **4.** *fig.* ~ ***mit*** *dat.* break with *s.o.*, break *a habit*; **III.** *v/refl.*: ***sich*** ~ (h) **5.** *waves*: break; ***sich*** ~ ***an*** *dat.* break on (*or* against), crash against; **6.** *phys.* refract; '**bre·chend I.** *adj. opt.* refractive; **II.** *adv.*: F ~ ***voll*** crammed, packed, F jampacked, chock-a-block; **Bre·cher** ['brɛçɐ] *m* (-s; -) **1.** breaker; **2.** ⚙ crusher, breaker

'**Brech|kraft** *f* (-; *no pl.*) *opt.* refractive power; **~mit·tel** *n* **1.** ⚕ emetic; **2.** F ***er (es) ist ein echtes*** ~ *sl.* he's (it's) enough to make you want to puke; **~reiz** *m* (feeling of) nausea; ***e-n*** ~ ***verursachen*** *a.* make one feel sick; **~stan·ge** *f* crowbar

'**Bre·chung** *f* (-; -en) *opt.* refraction; *ling.* fracture; ♪ arpeggio

'**Bre·chungs|pris·ma** *n* refraction prism; **~win·kel** *m* refracting angle

Bre·douil·le [bre'dʊljə] F *f*: ***in der*** ~ ***sein*** F be in a fix, be in a bit of a mess; ***in die*** ~ ***geraten*** get (o.s.) into a fix (*or* a bit of a mess)

Brei [braɪ] *m* (-[e]s; -e) pudding; porridge; *Am.* mush; pap, *contp. a.* mush; ***zu*** ~ ***kochen*** cook to a pulp; F *fig.* ***j-n zu*** ~ ***schlagen*** beat s.o. to a pulp; ***um den heißen*** ~ ***herumreden*** beat about (*or* around) the bush; F ***j-m*** ~ ***ums Maul schmieren*** F butter s.o. up; → ***Katze*** 1, ***Koch***; **brei·ig** ['braɪɪç] *adj.* mushy

breit [braɪt] **I.** *adj.* **1.** wide, broad; square *chin, shoulders etc.*; large, wide; ***120 Zentimeter*** ~ 120 centimet|res (*Am.* -ers) wide (*or* across); ~ ***drücken*** flatten (out), press *s.th.* flat; *et.* **~*er machen***, *a.* **~*er werden*** widen; **2.** *fig.* **~*es Angebot*** wide (*or* broad) range; **~*e Grundlage*** broad basis; **~*es Echo*** wide echo; **~*es Grinsen*** broad grin; ***die*** **~*e Masse*** the masses; ***die*** **~*e Öffentlichkeit*** the public at large; **~*e Schichten der Bevölkerung*** wide (*or* broad) sections of society; **~*es Interesse*** widespread interest; → ***breitmachen***; **II.** *adv.* **3.** broadly; ~ ***gebaut*** broadly (*or* squarely) built; ***et.*** ~ ***erzählen*** give a longwinded account of s.th.; → ***groß*** II, ***weit*** II; **4.** ♪ largo; **~an·ge·legt** *fig. adj.* wide-ranging; expansive

'**Breit·band...** *in cpds. usu.* broadband, wide-band ...; *pharm. etc.* broad-spectrum *antibiotic etc.*; **~ab·stim·mung** *f radio*: broad tuning; **~emp·fän·ger** *m* broadband receiver; **~laut·spre·cher** *m* full-range loudspeaker

'**breit·bei·nig** [-baɪnɪç] *adj. and adv.* with legs apart; ~ ***stehen auf*** *dat.* straddle *s.th.*

Brei·te ['braɪtə] *f* (-; -n) width; breadth; ⚓

beam; *ast.*, *geogr.* latitude; *fig.* breadth, scope, range; *contp.* longwindedness; ***es hat e-e ~ von sechs Metern*** it is six met|res (*Am.* -ers) wide; ***der ~ nach*** breadthwise; ***in die ~ gehen*** a) put on weight, F spread out, b) *fig.* be (*or* get) very longwinded, ramble; *geogr.* ***in diesen ~n*** in these latitudes; → ***episch;*** **brei·ten** ['braɪtən] (h) **I.** *v/t.*: ~ ***über*** *acc.* spread *s.th.* on (*or* over); **II.** *v/refl.*: ***sich ~*** spread (out), stretch (out); *fig.* spread
'Brei·ten|grad *m* (degree of) latitude; ***der 30. ~*** the 30th parallel; ***in diesen ~en*** in these latitudes, *fig. a.* in these spheres, in this part of the world; **~kreis** *m* parallel (of latitude); **~sport** *m* mass sport(s *pl.*); **~wir·kung** *f* effectiveness; ***mit großer ~*** *film etc.* with wide (*or* popular, mass) appeal, *measures, innovations etc.* with far-reaching (*or* wide-reaching) effects
'breit|ge·fä·chert *adj.* wide(-ranging); diversified; **~hüf·tig** [-hʏftɪç] *adj.* broad-hipped; **~ma·chen** F *v/refl.*: ***sich ~*** (*sep.*, h) **1.** *fear etc.*: spread; **2.** spread o.s. out, *fig.* throw one's weight around; **~schla·gen** F *v/t.* (*irr.*, *sep.*, h, → ***schlagen***): ***j-n ~*** talk s.o. round, ***zu et.***: talk s.o. into (doing) s.th.; ***sich ~ lassen*** give in, allow o.s. to be swayed (*or* persuaded); **~schul(·)t(e)·rig** [-ʃʊlt(ə)rɪç] *adj.* broadshouldered
'Breit·sei·te *f* (-; -n) ⚓ *and fig.* broadside; ***e-e ~ abfeuern gegen*** *acc. a. fig.* deliver a broadside against
'Breit·spek·trum... ⚕ *in cpds.* broad-spectrum ...
'breit|spu·rig [-ʃpuːrɪç] *adj.* **1.** 🚂 broad-ga(u)ge; **2.** F *fig.* bumptious, full of o.s.; **~tre·ten** *fig. v/t.* (*irr.*, *sep.*, h, → ***treten***) spin out; → **~wal·zen** F *v/t.* (*sep.*, h) F thrash to death
'Breit·wand *f film*: wide screen; **~film** *m* wide-screen film
Brems... [brɛms-] *in cpds. usu.* brake ...; **~ab·stand** *m* braking distance; **~an·lage** *f* brake system; **~backe** (*sep.* -k·k-) *f* brake shoe; **~be·lag** *m* brake lining; ***den ~ erneuern*** reline the brakes
Brem·se¹ ['brɛmzə] *f* (-; -n) *mot.* brake; ***auf die ~ treten*** (F ***steigen***) step on (F slam on) the brake(s); ***die ~ betätigen*** apply (*or* put on) the brakes
'Brem·se² *f* (-; -n) *zo.* horsefly
brem·sen ['brɛmzən] (h) **I.** *v/t.* **1.** brake; cushion *a fall*; **2.** *fig.* check, curb; slow down; F ***j-n ~*** slow s.o. down, hold s.o. back; F ***er war nicht zu ~*** there was no holding him (back); **II.** *v/i.* **3.** brake, apply (*or* put on) the brakes; **4.** *fig.* act as a brake, slow things down; F *person*: slow down, ease up; F cut down on things; F ***mit et. ~*** cut down on s.th.; **III.** *v/refl.*: ***sich ~*** restrain o.s., hold (o.s.) back
'Brem·sen|pla·ge *f* plague of horseflies; **~stich** *m* horsefly bite
Brem·ser ['brɛmzɐ] *m* (-s; -) brakeman
'Brems·fall·schirm *m* brake parachute
'Brems·flüs·sig·keit *f* brake fluid; **'Brems·flüs·sig·keits·an·zei·ger** *m* brake fluid indicator
'Brems|he·bel *m* brake lever; **~keil** *m* chock; **~klap·pe** *f* ✈ brake flap; **~klotz** *m* brake block, ✈ (wheel) chock
'Brems·kraft *f* braking power; **~verstär·ker** *m* brake booster
'Brems|last *f phys.* brakeload; **~lei·stung** *f* braking power; **~leuch·te** *f*, **~licht** *n* stop light, brake light; **~pe͵dal** *n* brake pedal; **~pro·be** *f* brake test; ***e-e ~ machen lassen*** have one's brakes tested; **~ra͵ke·te** *f* retro-rocket; **~schei·be** *f* brake disc; **~schluß·leuch·te** *f* stop and tail lamp; **~schuh** *m* brake shoe; **~soh·le** *f* brake pad; **~spur** *f* skid mark(s *pl.*); **~trom·mel** *f* brake drum
'Brem·sung *f* (-; -en) braking (effect)
'Brems|ver·zö·ge·rung *f* brake retardation; **~vor·rich·tung** *f* brake mechanism; **~weg** *m* braking distance; **~wir·kung** *f* braking action; **~zeit** *f* braking time; **~zy͵lin·der** *m* brake cylinder
brenn·bar ['brɛn-] *adj.* combustible; (in-)flammable; **'Brenn·bar·keit** *f* (-; *no pl.*) combustibility; (in)flammability
'Brenn·ele͵ment *n* fuel element
bren·nen ['brɛnən] (brannte, gebrannt, h) **I.** *v/t.* burn; singe; distil(l); roast; ⚙ fire; bake *bricks*; ***ein Loch ~ in*** *acc.* burn a hole in(to) *s.th.*; **II.** *v/i.* burn (*a. fig.*); *house etc.*: *a.* be on fire; *light etc.*: *a.* be on; *fig. nettle, acid, skin etc.*: sting, *wound etc.*: *a.* smart; *feet etc.*: be sore, hurt; *eyes*: sting, burn, smart, be sore; *gastr.* be hot; ***es brennt*** there's something burning; ***es brennt!*** fire!; ***die Sonne brennt auf die Haut*** the sun's scorching hot; ***das Licht ~ lassen*** leave the light on; *fig.* ***vor Ungeduld*** *etc.* ~ be burning with impatience *etc.*; F ***darauf ~ zu*** *inf.* be dying (*or* itching) to *inf.*; F ***wo brennt's?*** F where's the fire?; **III.** ♀ *n* (-s; *no pl.*) burning; distillation; ⚕ soreness, itchiness; **'bren·nend I.** *adj.* burning (*a. fig.*); *a. house etc.* on fire; ⚕ caustic; *fig.* burning, scorching, searing *heat*; **II.** *adv.*: ***es interessiert ihn ~*** he's desperately interested (to know); ***es interessiert mich ~, ob*** I'm dying to know if;
Bren·ner ['brɛnɐ] *m* (-s; -) **1.** distiller; **2.** ⚙ burner; **Bren·ne·rei** [brɛnə'raɪ] *f* (-; -en) distillery
Bren·nes·sel (*sep.* -nn·n-) *f* (-; -n) nettle
'Brenn|glas *n* burning glass; **~holz** *n* firewood; **~kam·mer** *f* combustion chamber; **~kol·ben** *m* still; **~ma·te·ri͵al** *n* fuel; ***kann man das als ~ verwenden?*** can that be used for heating?; **~ofen** *m* kiln; *metall.* furnace; **~öl** *n* fuel oil; **~punkt** *m phys. and fig.* focus, focal point; ***in den ~ rücken*** a) bring into focus, *fig. a.* focus attention on, b) pass into focus, *fig.* become the focus of attention; *fig.* ***im ~ des (öffentlichen) Interesses stehen*** be the focus of (public) attention; **~sche·re** *f*: (***e-e ~*** a pair of) curling tongs *pl.*; **~schluß** *m rocket*: burnout; **~schnei·der** *m* oxyacetylene cutter; **~spi·ri·tus** *m* methylated spirits *pl.*; **~stab** *m* fuel rod
'Brenn·stoff *m* fuel; **~ele͵ment** *n* fuel element
'Brenn|wei·te *f opt.* focal length (*or* distance); **~wert** *m* calorific value
brenz·lig ['brɛntslɪç] *adj.* **1.** F *fig.* dangerous; ***es wird mir zu ~*** F things are getting too hot for me; **2.** *obs.* burnt *smell etc.*
Bre·sche ['brɛʃə] *f* (-; -n) breach; ***e-e ~ schlagen*** *a. fig.* clear the way; ***e-e ~ schlagen in*** *acc. a. fig.* breach; *fig.* ***in die ~ springen*** step (*or* throw o.s.) into the breach
Bre·to·ne [bre'toːnə] *m* (-n; -n), **bre·to·nisch** [bre'toːnɪʃ] *adj.* Breton
Brett [brɛt] *n* (-[e]s; -er ['brɛtɐ]) board; plank; shelf; tray; *sport*: springboard; F **~er** F boards; *thea.* ***die ~er(, die die Welt bedeuten)*** the stage; ***mit ~ern belegen*** board; ***mit ~ern vernageln*** (*or* ***einzäunen***) board up; F *fig.* ***ich hatte plötzlich ein ~ vorm Kopf*** my mind went blank; → ***schwarz*** I, ***Stein*** 1
Bret·ter|bo·den ['brɛtɐ-] *m* wooden floor; **~bu·de** *f* wooden hut, shack; (market) stall; **~tür** *f* plank door; **~ver·klei·dung** *f* wood panel(l)ing; **~ver·schlag** *m* **1.** wooden partition; **2.** wooden shed; **~wand** *f* boarding; wooden partition; **~zaun** *m* wooden fence
'Brett·spiel *n* board game
Bre·vier [bre'viːɐ] *n* (-s; -e) **1.** *eccl.* breviary; **2.** guide (*gen.* to)
Bre·vis ['breːvɪs] *f* (-; -ves [-vɛs]) ♪ breve
Bre·zel ['breːtsəl] *f* (-; -n) pretzel
Brief [briːf] *m* (-[e]s; -e) letter; F a few lines *pl.*; *bibl. and iro.* epistle; **~e** *a.* correspondence *sg.*; → ***blau*** 1, ***offen*** I; *fig.* ***darauf gebe ich Ihnen ~ und Siegel*** I give you my word (on it), you can take my word for it; **~ab·la·ge** *f* letter file; **~an·fang** *m* opening (of a *or* the letter); **~be·schwe·rer** *m* paperweight; **~block** *m* writing pad; **~bo·gen** *m* sheet (*or* piece) of writing paper; **~bom·be** *f* letter bomb; **~druck·sa·che** *f a. pl.* printed matter; **~ein·wurf** *m* letterbox, *Am.* mailbox; slot; **~fach** *n* pigeonhole; **~form** *f*: ***in ~*** in letter form, by letter; **~freund** *m* penfriend, pen pal; **~ge·heim·nis** *n* privacy of correspondence; **~kar·te** *f* letter card
'Brief·ka·sten *m* **1.** letterbox, postbox, *Am.* mailbox; **2.** letters page; *a.* letters from our readers; **3.** suggestion box; **4.** ***toter ~*** dead letter box; **~fir·ma** *f* F letterbox company; **~on·kel** F *m* F agony uncle; **~tan·te** F *f* F agony aunt, *esp. Am.* sob sister
'Brief|klam·mer *f* paper clip; **~kon͵takt** *m* written contact; ***in ~ stehen mit*** correspond with, write to; **~kopf** *m* letterhead; **~korb** *m* letter tray; **~kurs** *m* ✝ selling rate
'brief·lich I. *adj.* written, in writing; ***~e Anfrage*** letter of enquiry (*or* inquiry); ***~er Verkehr*** correspondence; **II.** *adv.* in writing; ***~ verkehren mit*** correspond with; ***(miteinander) ~ verkehren*** correspond; ***er teilte uns ~ mit, daß*** *a.* he sent us a letter to the effect that
'Brief|map·pe *f* portfolio; **~mar·ke** *f* (postage) stamp
'Brief·mar·ken|al·bum *n* stamp album; **~au·to͵mat** *m* stamp machine; **~block** *m* block of stamps; **~bo·gen** *m* sheet of stamps; **~händ·ler** *m* stamp dealer; **~heft·chen** *n* book of stamps; **~samm·ler** *m* stamp collector, philatelist; **~samm·lung** *f* stamp collection; **~se·rie** *f* stamp issue
'Brief|mu·ster *n* specimen letter; **~öff·ner** *m* paper knife, letter opener; **~pa͵pier** *n* notepaper, writing paper; **~por·to** *n* letter rate; **~post** *f* letter post, *Am.* first-class mail; **~ro͵man** *m* epistolary novel; **~schal·ter** *m* (letter) counter; **~schluß** *m* close (of a letter); ***ein geeigneter ~*** *a.* an appropriate way of signing off; **~schrei·ber** *m* letter writer, correspondent; **~schul·den** *pl.* unanswered letters; ***s-e ~ erledigen*** answer (*or* write) some letters, catch up on one's correspondence; **~sen·dung** *f* → ***Briefpost;*** **~ta·sche** *f* wallet, *Am. a.* pocketbook; **~tau·be** *f* carrier pigeon; **~te·le-**

ˌ**gramm** *n* letter telegram; **~trä·ger** *m* postman, *Am. a.* mailman; **~trä·ge·rin** *f* postwoman; **~ˌum·schlag** *m* envelope; **~ver·kehr** *m* correspondence; **~waa·ge** *f* letter scale(s *pl.*); **~wahl** *f pol.* postal vote, absentee ballot; **~wäh·ler** *m* absentee voter; **~wech·sel** *m* correspondence; **mit j-m in ~ stehen** (**treten**) be corresponding (take up correspondence) with s.o.; (**miteinander**) **in ~ stehen** correspond

Bries [bri:s] *n* (-es; -e) **1.** *zo.* thymus (gland); **2.** *gastr.* sweetbread

briet [bri:t] *pret. of* **braten**

Bri·ga·de [briˈga:də] *f* (-; -n) brigade

Brigg [brɪg] *f* (-; -s) ⚓ brig

Bri·kett [briˈkɛt] *n* (-s; -s) briquette

bril·lant [brɪlˈjant] *adj.* brilliant; excellent

Brilˈlant *m* (-en; -en) (cut) diamond; **~feu·er·werk** *n* cascade

Bril·lan·ti·ne [brɪljanˈti:nə] *f* (-; -n) brilliantine

Brilˈlant|ring *m* diamond ring; **~schliff** *m* brilliant cut; **~schmuck** *m* diamond jewellery (*esp. Am.* jewelry); **~su·cher** *m phot.* brilliant viewfinder

Bril·lanz [brɪlˈjants] *f* (-; *no pl.*) *a. phot.* brilliance

Bril·le [ˈbrɪlə] *f* (-; -n) **1.** (**e-e ~** a pair of) glasses *pl.*, spectacles *pl.*, F specs *pl.*; goggles *pl.*; **e-e ~ tragen** wear glasses; *fig.* **et. durch e-e schwarze ~ betrachten** take a gloomy view of s.th.; → **rosa** (**-rot**); **2.** toilet seat

ˈ**Bril·len|bü·gel** *m* ear piece, *Am.* temple; **~etui** *n*, **~fut·teˌral** *n* spectacle case; **~fas·sung** *f*, **~ge·stell** *n* spectacle frame; **~glas** *n* glass, lens; **~ket·te** *f* spectacle chain; **~schlan·ge** *f* **1.** *zo.* spectacled cobra; **2.** F *fig.* F four-eyes *pl.*; **~trä·ger** *m* spectacle wearer; **~ sein** wear glasses (*or* spectacles)

bril·lie·ren [brɪlˈji:rən] *v/i.* (h) be brilliant; **als Redner** *etc.* **~** a) prove (to be) a brilliant speaker *etc.*, b) be a brilliant speaker *etc.*; **~ mit** *dat.* impress everybody with, show off (with), display *one's knowledge etc.*; **er brillierte mit e-r Chopin-Etude** he gave a brilliant rendering of a Chopin etude; **er brillierte mit e-r Stegreifrede** he gave a brilliant off-the-cuff speech

Brim·bo·ri·um [brɪmˈbo:rĭʊm] F *n* (-s; *no pl.*) fuss, F to-do; **ein riesiges ~ machen um** *acc.* make a great big fuss about (*or* over)

brin·gen [ˈbrɪŋən] *v/t.* (brachte, gebracht, h) **1.** bring; get, fetch; **2.** take, carry; put; **bring es ins Haus** take (*or* put) it inside; **er wurde ins Krankenhaus gebracht** he was taken to (*Am.* the) hospital; **ich brachte ihm Pralinen** I took him some chocolates; **3.** take, see (**j-n zur Bahn** s.o. to the station; **nach Hause** home); **4.** cause; bring; **das bringt nur Ärger** that'll cause nothing but trouble; *das Mittel* **brachte ihm keine Linderung** brought (*or* gave) him no relief; F **das bringt nichts** that won't get you *etc.* anywhere, that's no use; **was bringt das?** what's the point; F **das bringt's** F that'll do the trick; **5.** bring in; **Zinsen ~** bear (*or* yield) interest; **6.** show *film etc.*; *thea.* bring, stage; ♪ perform, play, sing; *newspaper etc.*: bring; **was bringt das 1. Programm heute abend?** what's on channel one this evening?; **die letzte Ausgabe brachte ...** the last issue had ...; **7.** F do, manage; **es ~** F make it, F pull it off; **ich bring's nicht** I (just) can't do it; **8.** *with adv.*: **es dahin ~, daß** manage to *inf.*; **j-n dahin** (*or* **dazu**) **~, daß** bring s.o. to *inf.*, make s.o. *inf.*; → **weit** II; **9.** *with prp.*: **j-n** (**et.**) **~ in** *acc.* (**aus** *dat.*) get s.o. (s.th.) into (out of); **ich bring' das Ding nicht in die Schachtel** I can't get the thing into the box; **ich bring' den Schmutz nicht von den Schuhen** I can't get the dirt off these shoes; *fig.* **an sich ~** acquire; take possession of; **du bringst mich auf etwas** now that you mention it; **es** (**bis**) **auf achtzig Jahre ~** live to be eighty; **er brachte es auf acht Punkte** he managed eight points; **es bis zum Major** *etc.* **~** make it to major *etc.*; **es zu etwas** (**nichts**) **~** go far (get nowhere); → **hinter**[1]; **j-n ins Gefängnis ~** F land s.o. in jail; **mit sich ~** involve, require; **die Umstände ~ es mit sich** it's inevitable under the circumstances; **e-e Pflanze über den Winter ~** get a plant through the winter; **ich kann es nicht über mich** (*or* **übers Herz**) **~** I can't bring myself to do it; **j-n um et. ~** deprive s.o. of s.th., F do s.o. out of s.th.; **er ist nicht vom Fleck zu ~** he won't budge; **j-n in Aufregung ~** get s.o. (all) excited; → **Abwechslung, Ausdruck** 1, **Bewußtsein** 1, 2

bri·sant [briˈzant] *adj.* **1.** highly explosive; **2.** *fig.* highly charged, explosive *issue etc.*; volatile *situation*; **politisch ~** politically charged; **Bri·sanz** [briˈzants] *f* (-; *no pl.*) **1.** explosive effect; **2.** *fig.* explosiveness; volatile nature *of a problem etc*

Bri·se [ˈbri:zə] *f* (-; -n) (light) wind; **steife ~** strong breeze

Bri·te [ˈbrɪtə] *m* (-n; -n), **Bri·tin** [ˈbrɪtɪn] *f* (-; -nen) British man (woman), Briton; **die Briten** the British (*pl.*); **bri·tisch** [ˈbrɪtɪʃ] *adj.* British; **die Ωen Inseln** the British Isles; **~es Englisch** British (F English) English; **Bri·ti·zis·mus** [britiˈtsɪsmʊs] *m* (-; -men) Briticism

Bröck·chen [ˈbrœkçən] *n* (-s; -) bit; ˈ**bröck·chen·wei·se** *adv.* bit by bit

bröcke·lig [ˈbrœkəlɪç] (*sep.* -k·k-) *adj.* crumbly; crumbling; brittle; **bröckeln** [ˈbrœkəln] (*sep.* -k·k-) *v/i.* (sn) crumble; *paint*: flake (**von** *dat.* off)

Brocken [ˈbrɔkən] (*sep.* -k·k-) *m* (-s; -) piece, bit; morsel; lump, chunk; *fig. pl.* snatches *of conversation etc.*, scraps *of English etc.*; F *fig.* **ein ~ von Mann** F a (great) hulk of a man; F **das war ein harter ~** F that was tough (going); F **fetter ~** F big haul, F brilliant deal; **e-n fetten ~ an Land ziehen** F make a big haul; **das ist ein fetter ~!** *a. fig.* F that's a humdinger; ˈ**brocken·wei·se** (*sep.* -k·k-) *adv.* bit by bit; *tell etc.* by fits and starts

bro·deln [ˈbro:dəln] *v/i.* (h) **1.** bubble (*a. lava etc.*), simmer; **2.** *fig.* seethe; **es brodelt im Volk** there's growing unrest among the people; **es brodelte in ihm** (**vor Zorn**) he was seething with rage

Bro·kat [broˈka:t] *m* (-[e]s; -e) brocade

Brok·ko·li [ˈbrɔkoli] *pl.* broccoli

Brom [bro:m] *n* (-s; *no pl.*) ⚗ bromine

Brom·bee·re [ˈbrɔmbe:rə] *f* (-; -n) blackberry

ˈ**Brom·beer|ge·strüpp** *n*: (**im ~** among the) blackberry bushes *pl.*; **~mar·meˌla·de** *f* blackberry jam; **~strauch** *m* blackberry bush

Bro·mid [broˈmi:t] *n* (-[e]s; -e [broˈmi:də]) ⚗ bromide

ˈ**Brom|ka·li·um** *n* potassium bromide; **~säu·re** *f* bromic acid; **~sil·ber** *n* silver bromide; **~sil·ber·paˌpier** *n phot.* bromide paper

Bron·chi·al|asth·ma [brɔnˈçĭa:l-] *n* bronchial asthma; **~kaˌtarrh** *m* bronchial catarrh; **~spie·ge·lung** *f* bronchoscopy; **~tee** *m* bronchial tea

Bron·chien [ˈbrɔnçĭən] *pl.* bronchial tubes, bronchi; **Bron·chi·tis** [brɔnˈçi:tɪs] *f* (-; *no pl.*) bronchitis

Bron·ze [ˈbrõ:sə] *f* (-; -n) **1.** *no pl.* bronze; **2.** (*paint*) bronze

ˈ**Bron·ze·far·be** *f* bronze; ˈ**bron·ze·far·ben,** ˈ**bron·ze·far·big** *adj.* bronze (-colo[u]red)

ˈ**Bron·ze|guß** *m* **1.** bronze casting; **2.** (cast) bronze; **~meˌdail·le** *f* bronze medal

bron·zen [ˈbrõ:sən] *adj.* (of) bronze

ˈ**Bron·ze|pla·stik** *f* bronze figure (*or* statue); **~zeit** *f* (-; *no pl.*) Bronze Age

Bro·sa·me [ˈbro:za:mə] *f* (-; -n) *usu. fig.* crumb

Bro·sche [ˈbrɔʃə] *f* (-; -n) brooch

bro·schiert [brɔˈʃi:ɐt] *adj.* paperback; in wrappers

Bro·schü·re [brɔˈʃy:rə] *f* (-; -n) pamphlet; brochure; leaflet

Brö·sel [ˈbrø:zəl] *m* crumb; **brö·se·lig** [ˈbrø:zəlɪç] *adj.* crumbly; **brö·seln** [ˈbrø:zəln] *v/t.* (h) *and v/i.* (sn) crumble

Brot [bro:t] *n* (-[e]s; -e) bread (*a. eccl.*); loaf (of bread); sandwich; *fig.* living, livelihood; **zwei ~e** two loaves of bread; **e-e Scheibe ~** a slice of bread; *fig.* **sein ~ verdienen** earn one's daily bread, make (*or* earn) a living; **sein ~ hart** (*or* **schwer**) **verdienen müssen** have to work hard for a living; **der Mensch lebt nicht vom ~ allein** man does not live by bread alone; → **Butterbrot, täglich** I; **~auf·strich** *m* something to spread on one's bread; **Quark** *etc.* **eignet sich als ~** (**ist ein schmackhafter ~**) quark *etc.* makes a good spread (tastes good on bread); **er nimmt nur Butter** (**Marmelade**) **als ~** he only has butter (jam) on his bread; **~be·lag** *m* sandwich topping; **~be·ruf** *m* bread and butter job

Bröt·chen [ˈbrø:tçən] *n* (-s; -) roll; F *fig.* **s-e ~ verdienen** F earn one's bread and butter; F **kleine**(**re**) **~ backen müssen** have to make do with what one has (have to cut down on things); **~ge·ber** F *fig. m* (-s; -) employer, F boss

ˈ**Brot|ein·heit** *f* bread unit; **~er·werb** *m* (earning a) living; **zum** (*or* **als**) **~** for a living; **~frucht** *f* breadfruit; **~ge·trei·de** *n* bread grain, *coll.* bread cereals *pl.*; **~ka·sten** *m* bread bin (*or* box); **~korb** *m* bread basket; *fig.* **j-m den ~ höher hängen** a) put s.o. on short rations, b) cut s.o.'s income; **~kru·me** *f* (bread)crumb; **~kru·ste** *f* crust (of bread); **~laib** *m* loaf of bread

ˈ**brot·los** *fig. adj.* jobless; unprofitable; **j-n ~ machen** take the bread out of s.o.'s mouth; **~ werden** lose one's job; **es ist e-e ~e Kunst** there's no money in it; **... ist e-e ~e Kunst** there's no money (to be earned) in ...

ˈ**Brot|maˌschi·ne** *f* bread slicer; **~mes·ser** *n* breadknife; **~neid** *m* professional jealousy; **~ra·tiˌon** *f* bread rations *pl.*; **~rin·de** *f* (bread)crust; **~schei·be** *f* slice (*or* piece) of bread; **~schnei·de·ma-**

ˌ**schi·ne** *f* bread slicer; **~stu·di·um** *n* utilitarian degree; **~teig** *m* dough; **~ver·die·ner** *m* breadwinner; **~zeit** *dial. f* break (for a bite to eat); snack; **~ *machen*** have a snack (*or* a bite to eat)

brr [br] *int.* **1.** whoa!; **2.** ugh!

Bruch [brʊx] *m* (-[e]s; Brüche ['brʏçə]) **1.** breaking; ***zu ~ gehen*** break, be broken; **2.** ⚕ fracture; rupture, hernia; ⚙ break, fracture; ✈ crash; ✈ ***~ machen*** crash (-land); ***ein Auto zu ~ fahren*** smash (up) a car; **3.** breakage; wreckage; scrap; **4.** ℞ fraction; **5.** *fig.* breach *of peace, a promise etc.*; ⚖ violation; infringement; breaking-off (*gen.* of), rupture (in); ***~ mit der Vergangenheit*** (clean) break with the past; F ***in die Brüche gehen*** *plans etc.*: come to nothing, *marriage etc.*: break up; ***es kam zum ~ zwischen ihnen*** (***beiden Ländern***) they broke up (the two countries broke off relations); **6.** F *contp.* junk, rubbish; **7.** *geol.* fault; **~band** *n* (-[e]s; ⸗er) ⚕ truss; **~bu·de** F *f* **1.** rundown place; F dump; **2.** *fig. sl.* lousy joint

'**bruch·fest** *adj.* unbreakable

'**Bruch·flä·che** *f* fractured surface, fracture

brü·chig ['brʏçɪç] *adj.* **1.** fragile; brittle, *a.* cracked *leather*; crumbly; crumbling; broken; **~ *werden*** begin to crumble, start to get cracks; **2.** *fig.* cracked *voice*; shaky *argument etc*

'**bruch·lan·den** *v/i.* (*only inf. and p.p.*, -ge-, sn) crash-land; '**Bruch·lan·dung** *f* crash landing; *fig.* ***e-e ~ machen*** fall flat on one's face (***mit*** *dat.* with)

'**Bruch|ope·ra·tiˌon** *f* ⚕ hernia operation; **~rech·nung** *f* fractions *pl.*; **~scha·den** *m* breakage; **~scho·koˌla·de** *f* broken chocolate

'**bruch·si·cher** *adj.* breakproof, unbreakable

'**Bruch|stein** *m* quarrystone; **~stel·le** *f* crack, break; ⚕ point of fracture; **~strich** *m* ℞ (horizontal) line

'**Bruch·stück** *n* fragment (*a. fig.*); **~e** snatches *of conversation etc.*; '**bruch·stück·haft I.** *adj.* fragmentary; **II.** *adv.* in fragments, fragmentarily; ***ich habe es nur ~ mitbekommen*** I only caught snatches of it

'**Bruch|teil** *m* fraction; ***im ~ e-r Sekunde*** in a fraction of a second; **~zahl** *f* fraction

Brücke ['brʏkə] (*sep.* -k·k-) *f* (-; -n) bridge (*a.* ⚓, *gym.*, ⚕, ⚡); rug; *anat.* pons; *fig.* link (**zu** *dat.* with); ***schwimmende ~*** pontoon bridge; ***e-e ~ schlagen über*** *acc.* build a bridge across; *fig.* ***~n schlagen*** forge links (***zwischen*** *dat.* between), ***zwischen*** *dat.*: *a.* breach the gap between, bring together, create a common bond between; ***alle ~n hinter sich abbrechen*** burn one's bridges (behind one); ***j-m goldene ~n bauen*** bend over backwards to make it easy for s.o.

'**Brücken|bau** (*sep.* -k·k-) *m* (-[e]s; -ten) bridge building; **~bau·er** *m* (-s; -) bridge-builder (*a. fig.*); **~bo·gen** *m* arch (of a *or* the bridge); **~ge·län·der** *n* bridge railing; parapet; **~kopf** *m* ⚔ *and fig.* bridgehead; **~pfei·ler** *m* bridge pier; **~schlag** *m* building of a bridge; *fig.* breaching of the gap (***zwischen*** *dat.* between); **~steg** *m* footbridge; **~waa·ge** *f* platform scale; **~zoll** *m* bridge toll

Bru·der ['bruːdɐ] *m* (-s; Brüder ['bryːdɐ]) brother (*a. eccl.*, *pl.* brethren); monk; F guy; F ***unter Brüdern*** between friends

Brü·der·chen ['bryːdɐçən] *n* (-s; -) little brother

'**Bru·der|herz** *hum. n* dear brother; brother dear; **~krieg** *m* fratricidal war(fare)

brü·der·lich ['bryːdɐlɪç] **I.** *adj.* brotherly; **II.** *adv.* like brothers; **~ *teilen*** share and share alike; '**Brü·der·lich·keit** *f* (-; *no pl.*) brotherliness

'**Bru·der|lie·be** *f* brotherly love; **~mord** *m* fratricide; **~mör·der** *m* fratricide

'**Bru·der·schaft** *f* (-; -en) *eccl.* brotherhood, society

'**Brü·der·schaft** *f* (-; -en) brotherhood; **~ *trinken*** *agree to use the familiar 'du' form of address*

'**Bru·der|volk** *n* cousins *pl.*; ***unser ~ in Afrika*** our African cousins; **~zwist** *m* fraternal strife

Brü·he ['bryːə] *f* (-; -n) *gastr.* broth; stock; *contp.* F dishwater, slop; F *fig.* bilge water; F ***mir läuft die ~ runter*** F I'm sweating like a pig

brü·hen ['bryːən] *v/t.* (h) **1.** *gastr.* scald; blanch; **2.** soak

'**brüh|'heiß** *adj.* boiling hot, scalding (hot); **~'warm** *fig.* **I.** *adj. news etc.* hot off the press; **II.** *adv.*: ***j-m et. ~ wiedererzählen*** run off to tell s.o. s.th. straightaway; ***er hat's mir ~ weitererzählt*** *a.* he couldn't wait to tell me

'**Brüh|wür·fel** *m* stock cube; **~wurst** *f sausage for heating in simmering water*

Brüll·af·fe ['brʏl-] *m* **1.** *zo.* howling monkey; **2.** F *contp.* F screaming idiot

brül·len ['brʏlən] (h) **I.** *v/i.* roar (*a. fig. gun, engine etc.*); *cattle*: bellow; low; *person*: shout, scream, howl, shout and scream; ***vor Lachen*** (***Schmerz***) **~** roar with laughter (scream with pain); **II.** ♀ *n* (-s; *no pl.*) roar; F ***er*** (***es***) ***ist zum ~*** F he's (it's) a (real) scream

Brumm|bär ['brʊm-] *fig. m* grumbler, F grouch; **~baß** *m* growling bass

brum·meln ['brʊməln] (h) **I.** *v/i.* mutter *or* mumble (away *or* into one's beard); **II.** *v/t.* mumble, mutter

brum·men ['brʊmən] (h) **I.** *v/i. and v/t. zo.* growl; hum, buzz; *engine*: drone; *loudspeaker etc.*: hum; *fig.* growl, grumble (***über*** *acc.* about), mutter; F do time; ***mir brummt der Kopf*** my head's throbbing; **II.** ♀ *n* → ***Brummton***; **Brum·mer** ['brʊmɐ] F *m* (-s; -) **1.** bluebottle; bumblebee; **2.** heavy lorry (*esp. Am.* truck), juggernaut; **3.** F (real) whopper; **brum·mig** ['brʊmɪç] *adj.* F grumpy

'**Brumm|krei·sel** *m* humming top; **~schä·del** F *m* throbbing headache; hangover; **~ton** *m* ⚡ low(-pitched) hum, humming noise

brü·nett [bry'nɛt] *adj.*, **Brü·net·te** [bry'nɛtə] *f* (-; -n) brunette

Brunft [brʊnft] *f* (-; Brünfte ['brʏnftə]), **brunf·ten** ['brʊnftən] *v/i.* (h) rut; '**Brunft·zeit** *f* rutting season

Brun·nen ['brʊnən] *m* (-s; -) **1.** well; spring; fountain (*a. fig.*); ⚕ mineral spring, (mineral) waters *pl.*; *fig.* ***den ~*** (***erst***) ***zudecken, wenn das Kind hineingefallen ist*** lock the stable door after the horse has bolted; ***da war das Kind schon im ~*** the damage had already been done; **2.** *gastr.* mineral water; **~an·la·ge** *f* fountain; ♀**frisch** *adj.* straight from the well (*or* spring); **~es *Wasser*** *a.* fresh spring (*or* mountain) water; **~kres·se** *f* watercress; **~kur** *f* mineral water cure; ***e-e ~ machen*** *a.* take the waters; **~ver·gif·tung** *fig. f* calumny; **~was·ser** *n* well water

Brunst [brʊnst] *f* (-; Brünste ['brʏnstə]) **1.** *zo.* rut(ting), heat; **2.** rutting season; **brün·stig** ['brʏnstɪç] *adj. zo.* rutting, *female* on heat

brüsk [brʏsk] **I.** *adj.* brusque, curt; **II.** *adv.*: ***j-n ~ abfertigen*** give s.o. short shrift; **brüs·kie·ren** [brʏs'kiːrən] *v/t.* (h) snub; **Brüs'kie·rung** *f* (-; -en) snub(bing)

Brust [brʊst] *f* (-; Brüste ['brʏstə]) **1.** breast; chest, *anat.* thorax; breast(s *pl.*); bust; *gastr.* → ***Bruststück*** 1; *fig.* breast, bosom, heart; ***e-m Baby die ~ geben*** feed (*or* nurse) a baby, *lit.* put a baby to one's breast; F ***es auf der ~ haben*** have chest trouble; ***schwach auf der ~ sein*** have a weak chest, F *fig.* F be hard up, ***in*** *dat.*: F not to be very well up in *a subjetc etc.*; ***sich in die ~ werfen*** give o.s. airs, strut around; F (***sich***) ***j-n an die ~ nehmen*** F have a heart to heart with s.o.; F ***e-n zur ~ nehmen*** a) F have a quickie, b) F have one over the eight; → ***Pistole, voll*** I; **2.** *sport*: breaststroke

'**Brust-an-'Brust-'Ren·nen** *n* neck-and-neck race, photo finish

'**Brust|at·mung** *f* thoracic breathing; **~bein** *n* breastbone, sternum; wishbone; **~beu·tel** *m* money bag (*worn around the neck*); **~bild** *n* head-and-shoulders portrait; **~brei·te** *f sport*: ***um ~ gewinnen*** win by inches; ***j-n um e-e ~ schlagen*** pip s.o. at the post; **~drü·se** *f anat.* mammary gland

brü·sten ['brʏstən] *v/refl.* (h): ***sich ~*** boast (***mit*** *dat.* about)

'**Brust·fell** *n anat.* pleura; **~ent·zün·dung** *f* pleurisy

'**Brust|flos·se** *f* pectoral fin; **~haar** *n* chest hair; ***er hat noch kein ~*** *a.* he hasn't got any hairs on his chest yet; ♀**hoch** *adj.* chest-high; **~höh·le** *f* thoracic cavity; **~ka·sten** *m*, **~korb** *m* rib cage, thorax; **~kind** *n* breastfed child; **~krebs** *m* breast cancer; **~la·ge** *f sport*: prone position; **~lei·den** *n* chest complaint (*or* trouble); **~mus·kel** *m* chest (📖 pectoral) muscle; **~pla·stik** *f* cosmetic breast surgery, 📖 mammoplasty; **~reˌgi·ster** *n* ♪ chest register; **~schmerz** *m* pain in the chest, *pl. a.* chest pain(s); **~schwim·men** *n* breaststroke; **~stim·me** *f* ♪ chest voice; **~stück** *n* **1.** *gastr.* brisket, breast; **2.** *zo.* thorax; **~ta·sche** *f* breast pocket; inside pocket; ♀**tief I.** *adj.* chest-deep; **II.** *adv. a.* up to one's chest *in water etc.*; **~ton** *m* ♪ chest note; *fig.* ***im ~ der Überzeugung*** with deep conviction; **~ˌum·fang** *m* chest measurement; bust (measurement)

Brü·stung ['brʏstʊŋ] *f* (-; -en) balustrade; breast

'**Brust|ver·let·zung** *f* chest injury; **~war·ze** *f* nipple, 📖 papilla; **~wehr** *f* parapet; **~wei·te** *f* chest measurement; bust (measurement)

Brut [bruːt] *f* (-; -en) **1.** brooding; hatching; ***in der ~ sein*** be hatching; **2.** brood (*a.* F *fig.*); spawn; *contp.* F shower, rabble

bru·tal [bru'taːl] **I.** *adj.* **1.** brutal; violent; cruel; ***mit ~er Gewalt*** with (sheer) brute force; **2.** tough, hard; ***~e Enttäuschung*** tough blow; ***~e Tatsachen*** cold (*or* hard, brutal) facts; **~e Offenheit** brutal openness; **das war ~!** that was tough (*or* hard), F that was a bit stiff; **II.** *adv.*: **~ mißhandeln** violently abuse; **bru·ta·li·sie·ren** [brutali'zi:rən] *v/t.* (h) brutalize; **Bru·ta·li'sie·rung** *f* (-; *no pl.*) brutalization; **Bru·ta·li·tät** [brutali'tɛ:t] *f* (-; -en) **1.** *no pl.* brutality; **2.** violence; **Bru·ta·lo** [bru'ta:lo] F *m* (-s; -s) **1.** (big) brute, F (real) rambo; **2.** F blood and guts film *etc.*; F video nasty

'**Brut|ap·pa,rat** *m* incubator; **~ei** *n* **1.** egg for hatching; **2.** rotten egg

brü·ten ['bry:tən] (h) **I.** *v/i.* **1.** brood, hatch, sit; **2.** *fig.* brood (**über** *dat.* over); **3.** *fig.* brood (**über** *acc.* on, over); **II.** *v/t.* **4.** *phys.* breed; **5.** *fig.* → **ausbrüten** 2; '**brü·tend** *adj.*: **~e Hitze** sweltering heat; '**brü·tend'heiß** *adj.* sweltering (hot); **Brü·ter** ['bry:tɐ] *m* (-s; -) *phys.* breeder; **schneller ~** fast breeder (reactor)

'**Brut|hen·ne** *f* sitting hen; **~hit·ze** *f* sweltering (*or* stifling) heat; **~ka·sten** *m* ⚕ incubator; **~platz** *m* breeding place; spawning ground; **~re,ak·tor** *m* breeder (reactor); **~schrank** *m* incubator; **~stät·te** *f* **1.** → **Brutplatz; 2.** *fig.* breeding ground (*gen.* for), hotbed (of)

brut·to ['bruto] *adv.* ✝ gross; **~ für netto** gross for net; **DM 50000 ~ bekommen** earn (*or* get) 50000 marks before tax, gross 50000 marks

'**Brut·to|be·trag** *m* gross amount; **~ein·kom·men** *n* gross income (*or* earnings *pl.*); **~er·trag** *m* gross return; **~ge·halt** *n* gross salary; **~ge·wicht** *n* gross weight; **~ge·winn** *m* gross profit; **~ge·winn·span·ne** *f* gross margin; **~lohn** *m* gross pay; **~preis** *m* gross price; **~pro·duk·ti,on** *f* gross output; **~re,gi·ster·ton·ne** *f* (*abbr.* **BRT**) gross register ton (*abbr.* GRT); **~so·zi,al·pro,dukt** *n* gross national product (*abbr.* GNP); **~ver·dienst** *m* gross earnings *pl.*

'**Brut·zeit** *f* hatching time

brut·zeln ['brutsəln] F (h) **I.** *v/t.* fry; **II.** *v/i.* sizzle

BTX [be:te:'ɪks] → **Bildschirmtext**

Bub [bu:p] *dial.* *m* (-en; -en ['bu:bən]) boy

Bu·be ['bu:bə] *m* (-n; -n) jack

Bu·bi ['bu:bi] F *m* (-s; -s) **1.** F sonny, my lad; **2.** *contp.* F squirt; **~kopf** *m* urchin cut

Buch [bu:x] *n* (-[e]s; Bücher ['by:çɐ]) book (*a. fig.*); script; volume; ✝ book, *pl. a.* records; **das ~ der Bücher** the Book of Books; ✝ **~ führen** keep accounts, do (the) bookkeeping; **~ führen über** *acc.* keep a record of; **zu ~e schlagen** show favo(u)rably in the books, *fig.* make a difference; **er redet wie ein ~** he never stops talking, F he could talk the hind legs off a donkey; **ein ..., wie es im ~e steht** a perfect example of a ...., F your archetypal ...; **er ist ein Künstler (Engländer), wie er im ~e steht** *a.* he's the classic artist (he's as English as they come); **ein ~ mit sieben Siegeln** a closed book; **er ist für mich ein offenes ~** I can read him like a book, *a.* I know exactly how his mind works; → **golden, Mose(s)**; **~aus·stel·lung** *f* book exhibition; **~be·spre·chung** *f* book review; **~be·stän·de** *pl.* stock(s) of books, collection *sg.* of books

'**Buch·bin·der** *m* (-s; -) bookbinder; **Buch·bin·de'rei** *f* (-; -en) **1.** bookbinder's (shop); bookbinding department, bookbinder's; **2.** *no pl.* bookbinding

'**Buch·deckel** (*sep.* -k·k-) *m* (book) cover

'**Buch·druck** *m* (-[e]s; *no pl.*) printing; '**Buch·drucker** (*sep.* -k·k-) *m* printer; **Buch·drucke'rei** (*sep.* -k·k-) *f* **1.** printer's; (printing) press; **2.** *no pl.* printing; '**Buch·drucker·kunst** (*sep.* -k·k-) *f* (-; *no pl.*) (art of) printing

Bu·che ['bu:xə] *f* (-; -n) beech (tree); **Buch·ecker** ['bu:xʔɛkɐ] (*sep.* -k·k) *f* (-; -n) beechnut

'**Buch·ein·band** *m* binding, cover

bu·chen[1] ['bu:xən] (h) **I.** *v/t.* **1.** book, reserve; **2.** ✝ enter in the books; *fig.* put down, F notch up (**als** as *a success etc.*); **II.** *v/i.* book; make a reservation; **hast du schon gebucht?** have you booked (yet)?, have you made a reservation (yet)?; **haben Sie gebucht?** have you got a reservation?

'**bu·chen**[2] *adj.* beech(wood) ..., made of beech(wood)

'**Bu·chen·wald** *m* beech(wood) forest

Bü·cher|aus·wahl ['by:çɐ-] *f* choice (*or* selection) of books; **~be·darf** *m* **1.** demand for books; **2.** book requirements *pl.*; **~bord** *n*, **~brett** *n* bookshelf

Bü·che·rei [by:çə'raɪ] *f* (-; -en) library

Bü·cher|etat ['by:çɐ-] *m* book allowance (*or* budget); **~freund** *m* booklover; **~ge·stell** *n* bookrack, bookstand; **~gut·schein** *m* book token; **~kun·de** *f* bibliology; **~markt** *m* book market; **~narr** *m* book fanatic, F real bookworm; **~re,gal** *n* bookshelf; **~rei·he** *f* **1.** row of books; **2.** series (of books); **~samm·lung** *f* collection of books; **~schrank** *m* bookcase; **~sen·dung** *f* **1.** book post; printed papers at reduced rates; **2.** parcel (*Am.* package) of books; **~stän·der** *m* bookstand; **~stüt·ze** *f* bookend, book support; **~ver·bren·nung** *f* burning of books; **~ver·zeich·nis** *n* **1.** book catalog(ue), list of books; **2.** bibliography; **~wand** *f* **1.** wall of books; **2.** wall-to-wall bookshelves *pl.*; **~weis·heit** *f* bookish knowledge; **~wurm** *m* bookworm (*a. fig.*)

'**Buch|fink** *m* chaffinch; **~form** *f*: **in ~** in book form, as a book; **~for,mat** *n* book format (*or* size); **~füh·rung** *f* bookkeeping, accounting, accountancy; **einfache (doppelte) ~** single-entry (double-entry) bookkeeping; **~ge·mein·schaft** *f* book club; **~ge·schenk** *n* book gift; **~ge·schich·te** *f* history of books (*or* printing); **~ge·wer·be** *n* book trade; (book) publishing

'**Buch·hal·ter** *m* (-s; -) accountant; **buch·hal·te·risch** ['bu:xhaltərɪʃ] *adj.* accounting ...., accounts ...., bookkeeping ....; '**Buch·hal·tung** *f* **1.** → **Buchführung; 2.** accounts department

'**Buch·han·del** *m* book (*or* publishing) trade; '**Buch·händ·ler** *m* bookseller; *pl. coll. a.* bookshops, *esp. Am.* bookstores; '**Buch·hand·lung** *f* bookshop, *esp. Am.* bookstore

'**Buch|hül·le** *f* dustjacket; book wrapper; **~klub** *m* book club; **~kri,tik** *f* book review; **~,kri·ti·ker** *m* book critic; **~la·den** *m* → **Buchhandlung; ~ma·cher** *m* bookmaker, F bookie; **~ma·le,rei** *f* **1.** *art*: book illumination; **2.** *coll.* illuminated manuscripts *pl.*; **~mes·se** *f* book fair; **~prü·fer** *m* auditor; **~prü·fung** *f* audit; **~rei·he** *f* series (of books); **~rücken** (*sep.* -k·k-) *m* spine

Buchs·baum ['bʊks-] *m* (-[e]s; ⸚e) box (tree); **~holz** *n* boxwood

'**Buch|schmuck** *m* book decoration (*or* ornamentation); **~schnitt** *m* book edge

Buch·se ['bʊksə] *f* (-; -n) ⚡ jack; ⚙ bush(ing); sleeve; liner

Büch·se ['bʏksə] *f* (-; -n) **1.** tin, *esp. Am.* can; box; **e-e ~ Erbsen** *etc.* a can of peas *etc.*; → **Pandora; 2.** gun, rifle

'**Büch·sen|fleisch** *n* tinned (*esp. Am.* canned) meat; **~ma·cher** *m* gunsmith; **~milch** *f* tinned (*or* evaporated, *Am.* canned) milk; **~öff·ner** *m* can-opener, *Brit. a.* tin-opener

Buch·sta·be ['bu:xʃta:bə] *m* (-n; -n) letter; character; **großer ~** capital (letter), *typ.* uppercase letter; **kleiner ~** small (*typ.* lowercase) letter; **auf den ~n genau** to the letter; **nach dem ~n des Gesetzes** according to the letter of the law; **am ~n kleben** take s.th. (*or* things) very literally; F **setz dich auf deine vier ~n** F plonk yourself down, take a pew; '**Buch·sta·ben·blind·heit** *f* dyslexia, word-blindness; '**buch·sta·ben·ge·treu** **I.** *adj.* literal; **II.** *adv. repeat etc.* word for word, verbatim

Buch·sta·bier·al·pha,bet [bu:xʃta'bi:ɐ-] *n* phonetic alphabet; **buch·sta·bie·ren** [bu:xʃta'bi:rən] **I.** *v/t.* (h) spell (out); spell out; **falsch ~** misspell; **II.** ♀ *n* (-s; *no pl.*) spelling

buch·stäb·lich ['bu:xʃtɛ:plɪç] **I.** *adj.* literal (*a. fig.*); **II.** *adv.* literally (*a. fig.*); **~ nichts** *a.* absolutely nothing

'**Buch·stüt·ze** *f* bookend, book support

Bucht [bʊxt] *f* (-; -en) bay, inlet

'**Buch|ti·tel** *m* (book) title; **~,um·schlag** *m* dustjacket

Bu·chung ['bu:xʊŋ] *f* (-; -en) **1.** booking, reservation; **2.** ✝ booking; entry

'**Bu·chungs|be·leg** *m* voucher; **~be·stä·ti·gung** *f* confirmation (of booking); **~feh·ler** *m* false entry

'**Buch·ver·lag** *m* book publisher(s *pl.*) *or* publisher's

'**Buch·wei·zen** *m* buckwheat

'**Buch|wert** *m* book value; **~wis·sen** *n* bookish knowledge; **~zei·chen** *n* **1.** bookmark(er); **2.** ex libris

Buckel ['bʊkəl] (*sep.* -k·k-) *m* (-s; -) **1.** hump; hunchback; stoop, round shoulders *pl.*; **e-n ~ machen** stoop, arch one's shoulders; *cat*: arch its back; F *fig.* **sich e-n ~ lachen** F crease up (laughing), split one's sides laughing; **2.** F back; F *fig.* **e-n breiten ~ haben** F have a thick skin; F **e-e Menge (genug) auf dem ~ haben** F have a lot (plenty) on one's plate; F **... Jahre auf dem ~ haben** F have notched up ... years; F **er hat schon etliche Jahre auf dem ~** F he's been around for a while (*or* a bit); F **du kannst mir den ~ runterrutschen!** F you know what you can do; F **j-m den ~ voll lügen** F tell s.o. a pack of lies; **3.** hillock, knoll; bump; *skiing*: mogul; boss; knob; **bucke·lig** ['bʊkəlɪç] (*sep.* -k·k-) *adj.* **1.** hunchbacked; F *fig.* **sich ~ lachen** F crease up (laughing), split one's sides laughing; **2.** hilly *terrain etc.*; F bumpy *road etc.*; **Bucke·li·ge** ['bʊkəlɪgə] (*sep.* -k·k-) *m*, *f* (-n; -n) hunchback

'**Buckel|pi·ste** *f* mogul field; **~rind** *n* zebu; **~wal** *m* humpback whale

bücken ['bʏkən] (*sep.* -k·k-) *v/refl.* (h):

sich ~ bend over; ***sich ~ nach*** *dat.* bend down *or* stoop (to pick *s.th.* up)

buck·lig ['bʊklɪç] *adj.*, **Buck·li·ge** ['bʊklɪgə] *m, f* → ***buckelig, Buckelige***

Bück·ling ['bʏklɪŋ] *m* (-s; -e) **1.** *gastr.* smoked herring; **2.** F bow

Bud·del ['bʊdəl] F *dial. f* (-; -n) bottle

bud·deln ['bʊdəln] F (h) **I.** *v/i.* dig; dig about (*or* play) in the sand; **II.** *v/t.* dig

Bud·dhis·mus [bʊ'dɪsmʊs] *m* (-; *no pl.*) Buddhism; **Bud·dhist** [bʊ'dɪst] *m* (-en; -en), **bud·dhi·stisch** [bʊ'dɪstɪʃ] *adj.* Buddhist

Bu·de [bu:də] *f* (-; -n) **1.** kiosk; stall; **2.** *contp.* F place, *sl.* joint; F digs *pl.*; F place, pad; ***die ~ zumachen*** shut up shop; ***j-m die ~ einrennen*** keep pestering s.o. (***mit*** *dat.* with); ***er rennt mir bald die ~ ein*** he just won't leave me in peace; ***j-m auf die ~ rücken*** F crash in on s.o.; → ***Kopf*** 5, ***Leben, sturmfrei***

Bud·get [bʏ'dʒe:] *n* (-s; -s) *a. parl.* budget; **~aus·gleich** *m* balancing of the budget; **~aus·schuß** *m* budget committee; **~be·ra·tung** *f* budget(ary) debate, debate on the budget; **~ent·wurf** *m*, **~vor·la·ge** *f* budget proposals *pl.*

Bü·fett [by'fɛt] *n* (-[e]s; -s, -e) **1.** sideboard; **2.** counter; **3.** *gastr.* buffet; ***kaltes ~*** cold buffet; ***kaltes und warmes ~*** hot and cold buffet (*or* dishes); **Bü'fett·da·me** *f*, **Bü'fett·frau** *f the* lady behind the counter; **Bü·fet·tier** [byfɛ'tĭe:] *m* (-s; -s) barman

Büf·fel ['bʏfəl] *m* (-s; -) buffalo; F *fig.* lout, oaf

Büf·fe·lei [bʏfə'laɪ] F *f* (-; -en) F swotting

'Büf·fel|her·de *f* herd of buffalo (*or* buffalo[e]s); **~le·der** *n* buffalo skin

büf·feln ['bʏfəln] F (h) **I.** *v/i.* F swot, cram; ***~ für*** *acc. a.* swot up for; **II.** *v/t.* F swot (up on)

Buf·fet [bʏ'fe:] *n* (-s; -s) → ***Büfett***

Bug [bu:k] *m* (-[e]s; -e ['bu:gə]) **1.** ⚓ bow; ✈ nose; → ***Schuß***; **2.** *zo. and gastr.* shoulder

Bü·gel ['by:gəl] *m* (-s; -) hanger; stirrup; ear piece, *Am.* temple; handle; clamp; ⚡ bow, ⚙ *a.* frame; harness; trigger guard; **~brett** *n* ironing board; **~ei·sen** *n* iron; **~fal·te** *f* crease; **2frei** *adj.* drip-dry, non-iron ...; wash and wear; **~ma,schi·ne** *f* ironer

bü·geln ['by:gəln] (h) **I.** *v/t.* iron; press; **II.** *v/i.* iron, do the (*or* some) ironing

'Bü·gel|sä·ge *f* hacksaw; **~ver·schluß** *m* swing top; **~wä·sche** *f* ironing

'Bug·kan·zel *f* ✈ cockpit, flight deck

'bug·la·stig *adj.* nose-heavy

Bug·sier·boot [bʊ'ksi:ɐ-] *n* tug(boat); **bug·sie·ren** [bʊ'ksi:rən] *v/t.* (h) tow, tug; *fig.* steer, manoeuvre, *Am.* maneuver; **Bug·sie·rer** [bʊ'ksi:rɐ] *m* (-s; -), **Bug'sier·schlep·per** *m* tug(boat)

'Bug·wel·le *f* bow wave

buh [bu:] **I.** *int.* boo!; **II.** 2 F *n* (-s; -s) boo; *pl.* booing *sg.*; **bu·hen** ['bu:ən] F *v/i.* (h) boo

buh·len ['bu:lən] *v/i.* (h): ***~ um*** *acc.* court *s.th.*, woo *s.th.*; ***um j-s Gunst ~*** curry favo(u)r with s.o., court s.o.'s favo(u)r; **Buh·le·rei** [bu:lə'raɪ] *contp. f* (-; *no pl.*) courting (***um*** *acc.* for); **buh·le·risch** ['bu:lərɪʃ] *adj.* fawning ...

'Buh·mann F *m* (-[e]s; -männer) bogeyman (*a. fig.*)

Buh·ne ['bu:nə] *f* breakwater, groyne, *Am.* groin

Büh·ne ['by:nə] *f* (-; -n) **1.** stage; theat|re (*Am.* -er); ***auf der ~*** on stage; ***hinter der ~*** backstage (*a. fig.*); ***auf die ~ bringen*** stage, produce; ***auf der ~ stehen*** *a. fig.* be on stage; ***auf offener ~*** on the open stage, *fig.* for everyone (*or* all) to see; ***über die ~ gehen*** be put on stage, be staged, *fig.* go off (***glatt*** smoothly); *fig.* ***et. über die ~ bringen*** get s.th. out of the way; ***wir haben es gut über die ~ gebracht*** we managed (it) quite well; ***von der ~ abtreten*** take one's last curtain call; ***von der politischen*** *etc.* ***~ abtreten*** bow out of politics *etc.*, quit the political *etc.* scene; → ***betreten***[1] I; **2.** *a.* ⚙ platform

'Büh·nen|an·wei·sung *f* stage direction; **~ar·bei·ter** *m* stage hand; **~auf·füh·rung** *f* stage performance; **~aus·spra·che** *f* standard diction; **~aus·stat·tung** *f* set(s *pl.*); **~be·ar·bei·tung** *f* stage adaptation; dramatization; **~be·leuch·tung** *f* stage lighting

'Büh·nen·bild *n* (stage) set, stage setting; **'Büh·nen·bild·ner** [-bɪldnɐ] *m* (-s; -) stage designer

'Büh·nen|de·ko·ra·ti,on *f* set(s *pl.*); **~ef,fekt** *m* stage effect; **~ein·gang** *m* stage entrance; **~er·fah·rung** *f* experience of the stage, theatrical experience; **~er·folg** *m* box-office success; **~fas·sung** *f* stage version

'büh·nen·ge·recht *adj.* stageworthy

'Büh·nen|held *m* stage hero; **~him·mel** *m* cyclorama; **~künst·ler** *m* stage artist; **~lauf·bahn** *f* stage career; **~lei·ter** *m* stage manager; **~ma·ler** *m* scene painter; **~ma·le,rei** *f* scene painting; **~ma·nu,skript** *n* (stage) script

'büh·nen·mä·ßig *adj.* stage-like

'Büh·nen|mei·ster *m* stage manager; **~mu,sik** *f* incidental music; **~na·me** *m* stage name; **~raum** *m* stage area; **~rech·te** *pl.* stage rights

'büh·nen·reif *adj.* ready for the stage; ***s-e Nachahmung des Chefs ist ~*** he could go on stage with his impersonation of the boss

'Büh·nen·stück *n* play

'Büh·nen·tech·nik *f* stage technique; **'Büh·nen·tech·ni·ker** *m* stage technician; **'büh·nen·tech·nisch** *adj.* stage ...; ***~e Anweisungen*** stage directions

'Büh·nen|vor·hang *m* curtain; **~werk** *n* drama, play

'büh·nen·wirk·sam *adj.* stageworthy; (theatrically) effective; **'Büh·nen·wirk·sam·keit** *f* stageworthiness; (theatrical) effectiveness; **'Büh·nen·wir·kung** *f* stage (*or* theatrical) effect, effect on stage

'Buh·ru·fe *pl.* booing *sg.*, boos

buk [bu:k] *obs. pret. of* ***backen***

Bu·kett [bu'kɛt] *n* (-s; -s, -e) **1.** bouquet; **2.** bouquet, nose *of wine*; **bu'kett·reich** *adj.*: ***~ sein*** *wine*: have a full bouquet (*or* nose)

bu·ko·lisch [bu'ko:lɪʃ] *adj.* bucolic

'Bu·let·te [bu'lɛtə] *f* (-; -n) meatball; F ***ran an die ~n!*** F let's go (for it)!

Bul·ga·re [bʊl'ga:rə] *m* (-n; -n), **Bul·ga·rin** [bʊl'ga:rɪn] *f* (-; -nen), **bul·ga·risch** [bʊl'ga:rɪʃ] *adj.* Bulgarian

Bu·li·mie [buli'mi:] *f* (-; *no pl.*) ⚕ bulimia

Bull·au·ge ['bʊl-] *n* (-s; -n) porthole

Bull·dog·ge ['bʊl-] *f* (-; -n) bulldog

Bull·do·zer ['bʊldo:zɐ] *m* (-s; -) bulldozer

Bul·le[1] ['bʊlə] *m* (-n; -n) **1.** *zo.* bull; **2.** F *fig.* F gorilla, heavyweight; **3.** F screw (*sl.*); ***die ~n*** *sl.* the fuzz (*pl.*)

'Bul·le[2] *f* (-; -n) **1.** seal; **2.** (***päpstliche ~*** papal) bull

'Bul·len·hit·ze F *f* scorching (*or* sweltering) heat; ***heute ist aber e-e ~*** it's absolutely sweltering today

bul·lern ['bʊlɐn] F *v/i.* (h) bang (***an*** *acc.* on; ***gegen*** *acc.* against, on); rumble; bubble (away); *stove:* roar

Bul·le·tin [bʏl'tɛ̃:] *n* (-s; -s) bulletin

bul·lig ['bʊlɪç] *adj.* **1.** beefy, hefty; **2.** F scorching, sweltering *heat*

bum(m) [bʊm] *int.* bang!, boom!

Bu·me·rang ['bu:məraŋ] *m* (-s; -e) boomerang (*a. fig.*); *fig.* ***sich als ~ erweisen*** have a boomerang effect, backfire, ***für j-n:*** *a.* come back at s.o.; **~ef,fekt** *m* boomerang effect

Bum·mel ['bʊməl] F *m* (-s; -) **1.** stroll, walk; ***e-n ~ machen*** go for (*or* take) a walk; **2.** pub crawl; ***e-n ~ machen*** go on a pub crawl

Bum·me·lant [bʊmə'lant] F *m* (-en; -en) → ***Bummler*** 2, 3; **Bum·me'lan·ten·tum** *n* (-s; *no pl.*) absenteeism; → **Bum·me·lei** [bʊmə'laɪ] *f* (-; *no pl.*) dawdling; idling (around); **bum·me·lig** ['bʊməlɪç] *adj.* slow; dawdling ...; **bum·meln** ['bʊməln] *v/i.* **1.** (sn) stroll; go for a stroll; **2.** (h) mess around; dawdle; **3.** ***~ gehen*** F have a night out on the tiles

'Bum·mel|streik *m* go-slow, *Am.* slow-down; work-to-rule; **~stu·di·um** *n* never-ending studies *pl.*; **~zug** *m* slow train

Bumm·ler ['bʊmlɐ] *m* (-s; -) **1.** stroller; **2.** dawdler, slowcoach, *Am.* slowpoke; **3.** idler

bums [bʊms] **I.** *int.* bang!; **II.** 2 *m* (-es; -e) bang, thud; **bum·sen** ['bʊmzən] (h) **I.** *v/i.* **1.** bang, bump (***gegen*** *acc.* against); ***plötzlich bumste es*** suddenly there was a loud crash(ing sound); F *mot.* ***es hat gebumst*** there's been a crash (*or* an accident); F ***an der Ecke bumst es dauernd*** they're always having accidents at that corner; **2.** *sl.* have it away, bonk; ***mit j-m ~*** *sl.* have it off (*or* away) with s.o.; **II.** *sl. v/t. sl.* bonk, bang; **'Bums·lo,kal** F *n* F (low) dive

Bund[1] [bʊnt] *n* (-[e]s; -e [-də]) bundle; bunch; truss

Bund[2] *m* (-[e]s; Bünde ['bʏndə]) **1.** bond; **2.** agreement; ***im ~e mit*** together with, in association with; **3.** ***mit j-m im ~e stehen*** be in league with s.o.; **4.** *pol.* alliance; federation, league; union; ***ein ~ zweier Länder*** an alliance between two nations; ***e-n ~ schließen mit*** *dat.* enter into an alliance with; ***im ~ stehen mit*** *dat.* be allied to (*or* with); ***der ~*** a) the Federal Government, b) F the army; F ***beim ~*** in the army; F ***er muß zum ~*** he's got to do his national service; ***~ und Länder*** the Federal Government and the Länder (*or* Laender); **5.** *bibl.* covenant

Bund[3] *m* (-[e]s; -e [-də]) waistband

Bün·del ['bʏndəl] *n* (-s; -) **1.** bundle (*a. fig.*); sheaf; ✝ package, parcel; *fig.* ***sein ~ schnüren*** pack one's bags; ***jeder hat sein ~ zu tragen*** everyone has his (*or* their) cross to bear; **2.** *phys.* bundle, pencil, beam; **3.** *anat.* fascicle; **'bün·deln** *v/t.* (h) bundle up; ⚡ bunch; *phys., opt.* focus; **'bün·del·wei·se** *adv.* in bundles

Bun·des... ['bʊndəs-] *in cpds.* federal, Federal ...; **~amt** *n* Federal Agency *or*

Office (***für*** *acc.* for); → ***Verfassungsschutz***; **~an·lei·he** *f* government bond; **~an·stalt** *f*: ~ ***für Arbeit*** Federal Labo(u)r Office; **~an·walt** *m* Chief Federal Prosecutor; **~an·zei·ger** *m* Federal Gazette; **~ar·beits·ge·richt** *n* Federal Labo(u)r Court; **~au·to·bahn** *f* autobahn; motorway, *Am.* highway; **~bahn** *f* Federal Railway(s *pl.*); **~bank** *f* (-; *no pl.*) (*a.* ***Deutsche*** ~) German Central Bank; **~be·hör·de** *f* federal authority; **~bür·ger** *m* German citizen, citizen of the Federal Republic

'bun·des·deutsch *adj.* (German) Federal ...; **'Bun·des·deut·sche** *m, f* (-n; -n) → ***Bundesbürger***

'Bun·des|ebe·ne *f*: ***auf*** ~ on a national (*or* federal) level; ***auf Bundes- und Länderebene*** on a federal and state level; **2ei·gen** *adj.* national, federal; **~fi,nanz·hof** *m* Federal Fiscal Court; **~fo·rum** *n* civic forum; **~ge·biet** *n*: ***im gesamten*** (***über das gesamte***) ~ throughout (across the whole of) Germany; **~ge·richt** *n* federal court; **~ge·richts·hof** *m* Federal High Court; **~grenz·schutz** *m* Federal Border Guard; **~haupt·stadt** *f* federal capital; **~haus** *n* (-es; *no pl.*) Federal Parliament buildings *pl.*; **~haus·halt** *m* federal budget; **~heer** *n* (Austrian) armed forces *pl.*; **~ka·bi,nett** *n* (German) federal cabinet; **~kanz·ler** *m* **1.** German (*or* Federal) Chancellor; **2.** Austrian (*or* Federal) Chancellor; **3.** *Switzerland*: Chancellor of the Confederation; **~kanz·ler·amt** *n* Federal Chancellery; **~kar,tell·amt** *n* Federal Cartel Office; **~kri·mi,nal·amt** *n* Federal Bureau of Criminal Investigation; **~la·de** *f* *bibl.* Ark of the Covenant; **~land** *n* (federal) state, land, Land; ***die neuen*** (***die alten***) ***Bundesländer*** the newly-formed German (the old West German) states; ***das neue*** ~ ***Sachsen-Anhalt*** *etc.* the newly-formed German state of Sachsen-Anhalt *etc.*; **~li·ga** *f*: (***erste, zweite*** ~ First, Second) Division; **~mi,ni·ster** *m* minister (***für*** *acc.* of, for); → ***Finanzminister, Postminister*** *etc.*; **~mi·ni,ste·ri·um** *n* ministry (***für*** *acc.* of); **~mit·tel** *pl.* federal funds; **~nach·rich·ten·dienst** *m* Federal Intelligence Service; **~post** *f* Federal Post Office; **~prä·si,dent** *m* **1.** German (*or* Federal) President; **2.** Austrian (*or* Federal) President; **3.** *Switzerland*: President of the Confederation; **~prä·si·di,al·amt** *n* Office of the Federal President; **~pres·se·amt** *n* Federal Information Agency; **~rat** *m* *parl.* **1.** *FRG and Austria*: Bundesrat, Upper House (of the German [Austrian] Parliament); **2.** *Switzerland*: Bundesrat, Executive Federal Council; **3.** *Austria, Switzerland*: member of the Bundesrat; **2recht·lich** *adj. and adv.* under federal law; **~re,gie·rung** *f* Federal Government; **~re·pu,blik** *f*: ~ ***Deutschland*** Federal Republic of Germany; ~ ***Österreich*** Federal Republic of Austria; **~rich·ter** *m* Federal High Court judge; **~so·zi,al·ge·richt** *n* Federal Social Court

'Bun·des·staat *m* federal state; (con)federation; **'bun·des·staat·lich** *adj.* federal

'Bun·des|stra·ße *f* major road; **~tag** *m* (-[e]s; *no pl.*) **1.** Bundestag, Lower House (of the German Parliament); **2.** *hist.* Diet of the German Confederation

'Bun·des·tags|ab·ge·ord·ne·te *m, f* (-n; -n) member of the Bundestag; **~de,bat·te** *f* debate of the Bundestag; **~frak·ti,on** *f* group in the Bundestag; **~mit·glied** *n* member of the Bundestag; **~prä·si,dent** *m* speaker of the Bundestag, parliamentary speaker; **~wahl** *f* parliamentary elections *pl*

'Bun·des|trai·ner *m* national team manager; **~ver·dienst·kreuz** *n* Order of Merit (of the Federal Republic of Germany); **~ver·fas·sung** *f* federal constitution; **~ver·fas·sungs·ge·richt** *n* Federal Constitutional Court; **~ver·samm·lung** *f* Federal Assembly; **~ver·wal·tungs·ge·richt** *n* Federal Administrative Court; **~wehr** *f* (-; *no pl.*) (German) armed forces *pl*

'bun·des·weit *adj. and adv.* nationwide

'Bund·fal·te *f* tuck; **'Bund·fal·ten·ho·se** *f*: (**e-e** ~ a pair of) pleated trousers *pl*

'Bund·ho·se *f*: (**e-e** ~ a pair of) knickerbockers *pl*

bün·dig ['bʏndɪç] *adj.* **1.** conclusive; concise, terse; precise; **2.** ⚙ flush; level

Bünd·nis ['bʏntnɪs] *n* (-ses; -se) alliance; → ***Bund***[2] 4; agreement; **2frei** *adj.* nonaligned; **~part·ner** *m* ally; **~po·li,tik** *f* policy of alliances; **~sy,stem** *n* system of alliances

'Bund·wei·te *f* waist (measurement)

Bun·ga·low ['bʊŋgalo] *m* (-s; -s) bungalow

Bun·ker ['bʊŋkɐ] *m* (-s; -) **1.** air-raid shelter; **2.** ⚔ dugout; **3.** (*coal etc.*) bunker; **4.** *golf*: bunker; **5.** *sl.* clink, *Am. sl.* slammer; **'bun·kern** *v/t.* (h) **1.** bunker; **2.** F stash away

Bun·sen·bren·ner ['bʊnzən-] *m* (-s; -) Bunsen burner

bunt [bʊnt] **I.** *adj.* colo(u)red; colo(u)rful (*a. fig.*), bright, multicolo(u)red; spotted; *fig.* mixed, motley; varied; *contp.* confused; ***~er Abend*** evening of entertainment; ***~es Durcheinander*** chaos; ***~e Menge*** motley crowd; ***~e Reihe machen*** seat (the) men and women alternately; F ***das wird mir doch zu ~!*** I've had enough!; → ***Hund*** 2; **II.** *adv.* in different colo(u)rs; ***et. ~ bemalen*** paint s.th. in different (*or* all sorts of) colo(u)rs; ~ ***durcheinander*** in a complete jumble; ***das geht ~ durcheinander*** there's no system in it, it goes all over the place; F ***es ging ~ zu*** F things were pretty lively; F ***er treibt es zu ~*** he takes things too far, he overdoes it; **~be·malt** *adj.* brightly colo(u)red, multi-colo(u)red, painted in (all sorts of) different colo(u)rs; **2druck** *m* (-[e]s; -e) **1.** *no pl.* colo(u)r printing; **2.** colo(u)r print; **2film** *m* colo(u)r film; **~ge·fie·dert** *adj.* with brightly-colo(u)red feathers; **~ge·mischt** *adj.* motley ..., mixed, assorted; **~ge·mu·stert** *adj.* brightly patterned; **~ka,riert** *adj.* with colo(u)r checks; **2me,tall** *n* non-ferrous metal; **2pa,pier** *n* colo(u)red paper; **2sand·stein** *m* new red sandstone; **~scheckig** (*sep.* -k·k-) *adj.* spotted; piebald; **~schil·lernd** *adj.* iridescent; **2specht** *m* spotted woodpecker; **2stift** *m* crayon, colo(u)red pencil; **2wä·sche** *f* colo(u)reds *pl*

Bür·de ['bʏrdə] *f* (-; -n) burden (*a. fig.*), (heavy) load; *fig.* ***j-m e-e ~ auferlegen*** place a (heavy) burden on s.o.; ***e-e ~ auf sich nehmen*** take on a (heavy) burden

Bu·re ['buːrə] *m* (-n; -n) Boer; **'Bu·ren·krieg** *m hist.* Boer War

Bü·ret·te [by'rɛtə] *f* (-; -n) burette

Burg [bʊrk] *f* (-; -en ['bʊrgən]) castle; fortress, citadel (*both a. fig.*); ***die ~en und Schlösser Frankreichs*** (***am Rhein***) the castles of France (along the Rhine)

Bür·ge ['bʏrgə] *m* (-n; -n) ⚖ guarantor (*a. fig.*), surety; reference; ***e-n ~n stellen*** offer bail; **'bür·gen** *v/i.* (h) **1.** ~ ***für*** *acc.* vouch for, guarantee, answer for *s.th.*; ***der Name bürgt für Qualität*** the name guarantees quality, it's (*or* the make *etc.*) is a byword for quality; **2.** ⚖ ~ ***für*** *acc.* go bail for, stand surety for *s.o*

Bür·ger ['bʏrgɐ] *m* (-s; -) **1.** citizen; *w.s. a.* member of society; resident, inhabitant; ***braver ~*** upright citizen (*or* member of society); ***friedlicher ~*** peaceful citizen; **2.** middle-class citizen, member of the middle classes; bourgeois; **3.** *hist.* burgher, freeman; **~in·itia,ti·ve** *f* **1.** citizens' (action) group, civic action group; **2.** civic action

'Bür·ger·krieg *m* civil war; **'bür·ger·kriegs·ähn·lich** *adj.*: ***~e Zustände*** internal conflict; ***in Nordirland herrschen ~e Zustände*** *a.* Northern Ireland is virtually in a state of civil war

'bür·ger·lich *adj.* **1.** *a.* ⚖ civil; civilian; ***~es Recht*** civil law; ***~e Pflichten*** civil (*or* civic) duties; ***2es Gesetzbuch*** (German) Civil Code; **2.** middle-class, *contp.* bourgeois; ***er führt ein sehr ~es Leben*** he has a very bourgeois lifestyle; **3.** untitled; **4.** plain, simple; ***~e Küche*** home cooking; **'Bür·ger·li·che** *m, f* (-n; -n) commoner; **'bür·ger·lich-'recht·lich** *adj.* civil-law ...; under civil law

'Bür·ger·mei·ster *m* (-s; -) mayor

'bür·ger·nah *adj.* grass-roots *politics etc*

'Bür·ger·pflicht *f* civil (*or* civic) duty

'Bür·ger·recht *n* civil rights *pl.*; **'Bür·ger·recht·ler** [-rɛçtlɐ] *m* (-s; -) civil rights campaigner (*or* activist); **'Bür·ger·rechts·be·we·gung** *f* civil rights movement

'Bür·ger|schreck *m* anti-establishment figure; **~sinn** *m* public spirit; **~stand** *m* (-[e]s; *no pl.*) *the* middle classes *pl.*; bourgeoisie; **~steig** *m* pavement, *Am.* sidewalk

'Bür·ger·tum *n* → ***Bürgerstand***

'Bür·ger·ver·samm·lung *f* town meeting

'Burg|frie·de *m* **1.** *hist.* (area of) jurisdiction; **2.** *fig.* truce (*a. pol.*); ***~n schließen*** make a truce; **~gra·ben** *m* moat; **~graf** *m* burgrave; **~grä·fin** *f* burgrave's wife; **~herr** *m* lord (*or* governor) of the castle, castellan; **~her·rin** *f* lady of the castle; **~rui·ne** *f* ruined castle, castle ruins *pl*

Bürg·schaft ['bʏrkʃaft] *f* (-; -en) surety, *a. fig.* guarantee; ⚖ bail; ~ ***leisten, die ~ übernehmen*** stand surety, ⚖ go bail, *defendant*: give bail, ***für e-n Wechsel*** *etc.*: guarantee a bill *etc.*; ***gegen ~ freilassen*** release on bail

'Bürg·schafts|er·klä·rung *f* declaration of surety; **~lei·stung** *f* surety

Bur·gun·der [bʊr'gʊndɐ] *m* (-s; -) **1.** *a. hist.* Burgundian; **2.** → **Bur'gun·der·wein** *m* Burgundy (wine); **bur·gun·disch** [bʊr'gʊndɪʃ] *adj.* Burgundian

'Burg|ver·lies *n* dungeon; **~vogt** *m* castellan

bur·lesk [bʊr'lɛsk] *adj.* burlesque, farcical; **Bur'les·ke** *f* (-; -n) burlesque, farce

Bü·ro [by'roː] *n* (-s; -s) office; **~an·ge·stell·te** *m, f* (-n; -n) office employee;

white-collar worker; **~ar·beit** *f* **1.** office work; **2.** desk work; **~au·to·ma·ti̦on** *f* office automation; **~be·darf** *m* office supplies *pl.*; **~block** *m* office complex; **~ein·rich·tung** *f* office equipment; **~elek̦tro·nik** *f* office automation; **~ge·bäu·de** *n* office building (*or* block); **~ge·hil·fe** *m*, **~ge·hil·fin** *f* office junior, clerical assistant; **~hengst** F *m* F pen pusher; **~hoch·haus** *n* high-rise office block (*or* building), commercial tower; **~kauf·frau** *f*, **~kauf·mann** *m* trained clerical worker; **~klam·mer** *f* paper clip; **~kom·mu·ni·ka·ti̦on** *f* office communication; **~kraft** *f* office worker; **~kram** F *m* F odd jobs *pl.*, odd bits of paperwork *pl*

Bü·ro·krat [byro'kra:t] *m* (-en; -en) bureaucrat; **Bü·ro·kra·tie** [byrokra'ti:] *f* (-; -n) **1.** *no pl.* bureaucracy; officialdom; **2.** red tape, red-tapism; **bü·ro·kra·tisch** [byro'kra:tɪʃ] *adj.* bureaucratic(ally *adv.*); **bü·ro·kra·ti·sie·ren** [byrokrati'zi:rən] *v/t.* (h) bureaucratize; **Bü·ro·kra·ti'sie·rung** *f* (-; *no pl.*) bureaucratization; **Bü·ro·kra·tis·mus** [byrokra'tɪsmʊs] *m* → ***Bürokratie*** 2

Bü'ro|land·schaft *f* landscaped office; **~ma̦schi·nen** *pl.* (electronic) office equipment *sg.*; **~ma·te·ri̦al** *n* office supplies *pl.*, stationery; **~mensch** F *m* F pen pusher; **~mö·bel** *pl.* office furniture *sg.*; **~per·so̦nal** *n* office staff, office workers (*or* employees) *pl.*; **~schluß** *m* (office) closing time; ***nach ~*** after office hours; ***um 17 Uhr haben wir ~*** we leave the office (*or* stop work) at five o'clock; **~stun·den** *pl.* office hours *pl.*; **~tä·tig·keit** *f* office work; **~zeit** *f* office hours *pl.*

Bürsch·chen ['bʏrʃçən] F *n* (-s; -) F my lad, sonny; ***paß bloß auf, ~!*** you'd better watch it, my lad (*or* sonny); ***freches ~*** F cheeky (little) so-and-so

Bur·sche ['bʊrʃə] *m* (-n; -n) lad; guy; ***das ist ein übler ~*** F he's a nasty sort

'Bur·schen·schaft *f* (-; -en) (student) fraternity, student league

bur·schi·kos [bʊrʃi'ko:s] *adj.* boyish; jaunty; careless

Bür·ste ['bʏrstə] *f* (-; -n) brush (*a.* ⚙, ⚡); F crew cut; **'bür·sten** *v/t.* (h) brush; ***sich die Haare ~*** brush one's hair; ***sich die Zähne ~*** brush (*or* clean) one's teeth

'Bür·sten|bin·der *m*: F ***saufen wie ein ~*** drink like a fish; **~schnitt** *m* crew cut

Bür·zel ['bʏrtsəl] *m* (-s; -) *zo.* rump; *gastr.* parson's nose; *hunt.* tail

Bus [bʊs] *m* (Busses; Busse) bus; coach; ***mit dem ~ fahren*** go by bus, take the bus; **~bahn·hof** *m* (bus) terminal, bus (*or* coach) station

Busch [bʊʃ] *m* (-[e]s; Büsche ['bʏʃə]) **1.** bush; shrub; copse, thicket, *Am.* brush; F *fig.* ***da ist etwas im ~*** (I'm sure) they're up to something, there's something brewing; ***auf den ~ klopfen*** stretch out one's feelers, ***bei j-m:*** sound s.o. out; ***hinterm ~ halten mit*** *dat.* keep quiet about; ***sich (seitwärts) in die Büsche schlagen*** sneak away; **2.** bunch; **3.** *geogr.* bush; F jungle; **~boh·ne** *f* dwarf (*Am.* bush) bean

Bü·schel ['bʏʃəl] *n* (-s; -) bunch; bundle; tuft *of hair etc.*, *zo. a.* crest; *phys.*, ✎ pencil; **'bü·schel·wei·se** *adv.*: ***er verlor ~ Haare*** his hair was coming out in handfuls

'Busch|feu·er *n* bushfire; **~hemd** *n* bush jacket

bu·schig ['bʊʃɪç] *adj.* bushy

'Busch|mann *m* (-[e]s; -männer) bushman; **~mes·ser** *n* machete; **~ro·se** *f* polyantha (rose), bushrose; **~trom·meln** F *fig. pl.* F bush telegraphy *sg.*; ***et. über die ~ erfahren*** hear s.th. on the bush telegraph; **~wald** *m* scrub; **~wind·rös·chen** *n* wood anemone

Bu·sen ['bu:zən] *m* (-s; -) **1.** breasts *pl.*; bust, chest; *lit.* bosom (*a. fig.*); *fig.* breast, heart; ***voller ~*** big breasts (*or* bust, chest); *fig.* ***am ~ der Natur*** in nature's bosom; ***ein Geheimnis (e-n Haß) in s-m ~ nähren*** cherish a secret (harbo[u]r hatred in one's heart); **2.** bodice; **~freund** *m* bosom friend, F bosom buddy

'Bus|fah·rer *m* bus driver; **~fahr·plan** *m* bus timetable, *esp. Am.* bus schedule; **~fahrt** *f* bus ride; coachride, coach tour (***durch*** *acc.* of, through); **~geld** *n* bus fare; **~hal·te·stel·le** *f* bus stop; **~la·dung** *f* busload *of tourists etc.*; **~li·nie** *f* bus route; ***die ~ 8*** bus number 8, the number 8 (bus)

Bus·sard ['bʊsart] *m* (-[e]s; -e ['bʊsardə]) buzzard

Bu·ße ['bu:sə] *f* (-; -n) **1.** penance; repentance; atonement, expiation; ***~ tun*** do penance, ***für*** *acc.* atone (*w.s.* make amends) for; **2.** penalty; fine; **bü·ßen** ['by:sən] (h) **I.** *v/t.* **1.** pay for; *fig. a.* suffer for; *fig.* ***er büßte es mit s-m Leben*** he paid for it with his life, he sacrificed his life for it; ***das sollst du mir ~*** you'll pay for that, I'll make you pay for that; **2.** *eccl.* atone for; repent of; **II.** *v/i.* **3.** ***~ für*** *acc.* pay for; *fig. a.* suffer for; *fig.* ***dafür habe ich schwer ~ müssen*** I had to pay dearly for it; **4.** *eccl.* do penance; repent

Bü·ßer ['by:sɐ] *m* (-s; -) penitent; **~ge·wand** *n* penitential robe; **~hemd** *n* hair shirt

'buß·fer·tig *adj.* repentant

'Buß·geld *n* fine; ***zu e-m ~ in Höhe von ... verurteilt werden*** be sentenced to a fine of ..., be fined ...; **~be·scheid** *m* penalty notice; **~ka·ta̦log** *m* list of (traffic offen|ce, *Am.* -se) penalties; **~ver·fah·ren** *n* fining system

'Buß·got·tes·dienst *m* penitential service

Bus·si ['bʊsi] *dial. n* (-s; -s) kiss

'Bus·spur *f* bus lane

'Buß- und 'Bet·tag *m day of prayer and repentance*

Bü·ste ['by:stə] *f* (-; -n) bust

'Bü·sten·hal·ter *m* bra; *formal*: brassiere

'Bus·ver·bin·dung *f* bus connection (*or* service)

Bu·tan [bu'ta:n] *n* (-s; -e) ⚗ butane

Butt [bʊt] *m* (-[e]s; -e) flounder

Büt·ten|pa̦pier ['bʏtən-] *n* deckle-edge(d) paper; **~rand** *m* deckle edge; **~re·de** *f* carnival speech; **~red·ner** *m* carnival orator

But·ter ['bʊtɐ] *f* (-; *no pl.*) butter; ***mit ~ bestreichen*** butter, spread butter on; *fig.* ***er gönnt ihr nicht die ~ auf dem Brot*** he begrudges her every little thing; F ***mir ist fast die ~ vom Brot gefallen*** F I nearly fell off my chair; ***er läßt sich die ~ nicht vom Brot nehmen*** he can stick up for (*or* look after) himself; F ***alles in ~*** everything's just fine (F hunky-dory), F couldn't be better; **~berg** *m* butter mountain; **~blu·me** *f* buttercup

'But·ter·brot *n* (piece *or* slice of) bread and butter, *Brit. a.* F butty; F *fig.* ***j-m et. aufs ~ schmieren*** F rub s.th. under s.o.'s nose, rub s.th. (*or* it) in; ***für ein ~*** *buy etc.* for a song, *work* for peanuts; **~pa̦pier** *n* greaseproof paper

'But·ter·creme *f* buttercream; **~tor·te** *f* buttercream cake

'But·ter|do·se *f* butter dish; **~fahrt** F *f* duty-free cruise; **~ge·bäck** *n* rich biscuits (*Am.* cookies) *pl.*; **~kä·se** *m* mild, full-fat cheese; **~keks** *m* rich tea biscuit; **~ku·gel** *f* pat of butter; **~mes·ser** *n* butter knife; **~milch** *f* buttermilk

but·tern ['bʊtɐn] (h) **I.** *v/t.* **1.** butter; grease (with butter); **2.** F *fig.* ***Geld ~ in*** *acc.* pour (F sink) money into s.th.; **II.** *v/i.* make butter

'But·ter|schmalz *n* clarified butter; **~sei·te** F *fig. f*: ***die ~ des Lebens*** the sunny side of life; **2weich** *adj.* **1.** *gastr.* lovely and soft (*or* tender); ***die Karotten sind ~*** *a.* the carrots just melt on your tongue; **2.** *fig.* soft; **3.** *fig. sport*: delicate

But·ze·mann ['bʊtsəman] F *m* (-[e]s; -männer) bogeyman

But·zen·schei·be ['bʊtsən-] *f* bull's eye (pane)

By·pass ['baɪpa:s] *m* (-es; -es, -pässe [-pɛsə]) bypass; **~ope·ra·ti̦on** *f* bypass operation (*or* surgery)

Byte [baɪt] *n* (-s; -s) byte

by·zan·ti·nisch [bytsan'ti:nɪʃ] *adj.* Byzantine; ***~e Zeitrechnung*** Byzantine calendar; **By·zan·ti·ni·stik** [bytsanti'nɪstɪk] *f* (-; *no pl.*) Byzantine studies *pl.*

C

C, c [tse:] *n* (-; -) C, c; ♪ C; ♪ ***das hohe C*** top C

Ca·bo·chon [kabɔ'ʃõ:] *m* (-s; -s) **1.** cabochon; **2.** → **~schliff** *m* cabochon

Ca·brio(let) *n* → ***Kabrio(let)***

Cache-Spei·cher ['kaʃ-] *m* *computer*: cache memory

Cad·mi·um *n* → ***Kadmium***

Ca·fé [ka'fe:] *n* (-s; -s) café; ***ins ~ gehen*** go to a (*or* the) café

Ca·fe·te·ria [kafetə'ri:a] *f* (-; -s) snack bar, cafeteria

Call·boy ['kɔ:lbɔy] *m* (-s; -s) call boy; **Call·girl** ['kɔ:lgø:ɐl] *n* (-s; -s) call girl

cam·pen ['kɛmpən] *v/i.* (h) camp, go camping; **Cam·per** ['kɛmpɐ] *m* (-s; -) **1.** camper; **2.** → ***Campingbus***

Cam·ping ['kɛmpɪŋ] *n* (-s; *no pl.*) camping; **~aus·rü·stung** *f* camping equipment; **~bett** *n* camp bed; **~bus** *m* camper (van); **~füh·rer** *m* camping guide; **~platz** *m* camping site, campsite; **~stuhl** *m* folding chair; **~tisch** *m* folding table; **~ur·laub** *m* camping holiday; ***~ machen*** go on a camping holiday, go camping

Ca·nail·le *f* → ***Kanaille***

Cap·puc·ci·no [kapʊ'tʃi:no] *m* (-[s]; -s) cappuccino

Car·toon [kar'tu:n] *m, n* (-[s]; -s) **1.** cartoon; **2.** comic (*or* cartoon) strip

Ca·sa·no·va [kaza'no:va] *fig. m* (-[s]; -s) Casanova, Don Juan

Ca·se·in *n* → ***Kasein***

Cas·set·te *f* → ***Kassette***

Cas·set·ten... → ***Kassetten...***

cat·chen ['kɛtʃən] *v/i.* (h) do all-in wrestling; **Cat·cher** ['kɛtʃɐ] *m* (-s; -) all-in wrestler

CB-Funk [tse:'be:fʊŋk] *m* (-s; *no pl.*) CB radio, citizens' band radio

CD [tse:'de:] *f* (-; -s), **~-Plat·te** *f* CD, compact disc; **~-ROM** CD-ROM; **~-Spie·ler** *m* CD player; **~-Vi·deo** *n* **1.** CD video, CDV; **2.** compact video disc, CDV

Cel·list [tʃɛ'lɪst] *m* (-en; -en) cellist, cello player; **Cel·lo** ['tʃɛlo] *n* (-s; -s, Celli ['tʃɛli]) cello

Cel·lo·phan [tsɛlo'fa:n] (*TM*) *n* (-s; *no pl.*) cellophane (*TM*)

Cel·si·us ['tsɛlzĭʊs] centigrade, Celsius; ***... Grad ~*** ... degrees centigrade (*or* Celsius); **~ska·la** *f* Celsius (*or* centigrade) scale; **~ther·mo,me·ter** *n* centigrade (*or* Celsius) thermometer

Cem·ba·list [tʃɛmba'lɪst] *m* (-en; -en) harpsichordist, harpsichord player; **Cem·ba·lo** ['tʃɛmbalo] *n* (-s; -s, -li) harpsichord

Ces [tsɛs] *n* (-; -) ♪ C flat

Cey·lo·ne·se [tsailo'ne:zə] *m* (-n; -n), **Cey·lo'ne·sin** *f* (-; -nen) Ceylonese; **cey·lo'ne·sisch** *adj.* Ceylonese; Ceylon ...

Chaise·longue [ʃɛzə'lɔŋ] *f* (-; -en [-'lɔŋən]) chaise longue, divan

Cha·let [ʃa'le:] *n* (-s; -s) chalet

Cha·mä·le·on [ka'mɛ:leɔn] *n* (-s; -s) chameleon (*a. fig.*)

cha·mois [ʃa'mŏa] **I.** *adj.* buff(-colo[u]red); **II.** ♀ *n* → **♀le·der** *n* chamois (leather)

Cham·pa·gner [ʃam'panjɐ] *m* (-s; -) champagne; **cham'pa·gner·far·ben** *adj.* champagne(-colo[u]red); **Cham'pa·gner·glas** *n* champagne glass

Cham·pi·gnon ['ʃampɪnjɔŋ] *m* (-s; -s) button mushroom

Cham·pi·on ['tʃɛmpĭən] *m* (-s; -s) champion(s *pl.*); ***der ~ im Speerwerfen*** the javelin champion, the champion javelin-thrower

Chan·ce ['ʃã:sə] *f* (-; -n) chance (***zu*** *inf.* to *inf.*, of *ger.*); opportunity (to *inf.*); *pl.* prospects; ***geringe ~n*** a slim chance; *dieser Beruf hat* ***gute ~n*** good prospects; ***nicht die geringste ~*** not a chance; ***bei j-m ~n haben*** stand a chance with s.o.; ***sich ~n ausrechnen*** fancy one's chances; ***die ~n stehen gut*** the odds are in our *etc.* favo(u)r, *w.s.* the prospects are good, things look (quite) hopeful; ***die ~n stehen gleich*** it's fifty-fifty; ***s-e ~ wahrnehmen*** seize the opportunity; ***s-e ~ verpassen*** miss one's chance, miss the boat; F ***keine ~!*** F no way, not a chance; **'Chan·cen·gleich·heit** *f* (-; *no pl.*) equal opportunities *pl.*; **'chan·cen·los** *adj.*: ***die Mannschaft ist ~*** the team's got no chance; **'chan·cen·reich** *adj.*: ***~e Aussichten*** good prospects (for the future); ***~er Beruf*** *etc.* job *etc.* with good prospects

chan·gie·ren [ʃã'ʒi:rən] *v/i.* (h) iridesce, shimmer

Chan·son [ʃã'sõ:] *n* (-s; -s) chanson; political song

Cha·os ['ka:ɔs] *n* (-; *no pl.*) chaos; ***hier herrscht ja das reinste ~*** it's absolutely chaotic (*or* sheer bedlam) in this place; **Cha·ot** [ka'o:t] *m* (-en; -en) **1.** *pol.* (young) radical; *pl. a.* lunatic fringe (*or* element) *sg.*; **2.** completely disorganized person; ***er ist ein absoluter ~*** he just can't get himself organized properly (F get his act together); **chao·tisch** [ka'o:tɪʃ] **I.** *adj.* chaotic; ***~e Zustände*** chaos, chaotic situation; **II.** *adv.*: ***es ging ziemlich ~ zu*** F it was pretty chaotic

Cha·rak·ter [ka'raktɐ] *m* (-s; -e [karak'te:rə]) **1.** *no pl.* character; (strength of) character, (moral) backbone; personality; nature; ***ein Mann von ~*** a man of character; ***ein Mensch mit ~ hätte ...*** anyone with a bit of character (*or* backbone) would have ...; ***sie hat ~*** she's got (real) character; ***sie hat keinen ~*** she's got no character (*or* backbone), F she's a spineless jellyfish; ***~ beweisen*** show some character (*or* backbone); ***vom ~ her*** as far as his *etc.* character goes, *w.s.* personalitywise; *Gespräche* ***vertraulichen ~s*** of a confidential nature; **2.** personality; character; **~an·la·ge** *f* disposition; **~bild** *n* **1.** character sketch (*or* study); **2.** character, personality

cha'rak·ter·bil·dend *adj.* character-forming, character-mo(u)lding; **Cha'rak·ter·bil·dung** *f* (-; *no pl.*) **1.** character (*or* personality) development; **2.** character-mo(u)lding

Cha'rak·ter|dar·stel·ler *m thea.* character actor; **~ei·gen·schaft** *f* (personality *or* personal) trait; **~feh·ler** *m* (character) weakness, flaw in one's character, character (*or* personality) flaw

cha'rak·ter·fest *adj.* of strong character, stable; **Cha'rak·ter·fe·stig·keit** *f* strength of character

cha·rak·te·ri·sie·ren [karakteri'zi:rən] *v/t.* (h) **1.** describe; depict; sum up; **2.** mark; be typical of *s.o.*; ***charakterisiert sein durch*** be marked by; ***es wird durch folgendes charakterisiert*** *a.* it has the following characteristics; **Cha·rak·te·ri'sie·rung** *f* (-; -en) characterization; description; summary; **Cha·rak·te·ri·stik** [karakte'rɪstɪk] *f* (-; -en) **1.** characterization; **2.** A, ⚙ characteristic; **Cha·rak·te·ri·sti·kum** [karakte'rɪstikʊm] *n* (-s; -ka) characteristic feature; **cha·rak·te·ri·stisch** [karakte'rɪstɪʃ] *adj.* characteristic, typical (***für*** *acc.* of); ***~e Eigenschaft*** characteristic (feature)

Cha'rak·ter|ko,mö·die *f thea.* comedy of character; **~kopf** *m* striking (*or* interesting) face; ***e-n ~ haben*** *a.* have striking features

cha'rak·ter·lich **I.** *adj.* character ..., in (one's) character; personal; ***~e Schwäche*** weakness in character, character flaw; **II.** *adv.* in character; ***sich ~ verändern*** change in character, change one's personality; ***er hat sich ~ vollkommen geändert*** *a.* he's a completely different person (*or* personality); ***j-n ~ einschätzen*** assess s.o.'s character

cha'rak·ter·los *adj.* **1.** unprincipled; condemnable; **2.** *fig.* colo(u)rless, bland; (totally) lacking in personality; **Cha'rak·ter·lo·sig·keit** *f* (-; *no pl.*) **1.** lack of character; **2.** blandness

Cha'rak·ter|rol·le *f thea.* character part; **~schil·de·rung** *f* characterization

cha'rak·ter·schwach *adj.* weak(-charactered); weak-willed; **Cha'rak·ter·schwä·che** *f* weakness (of character); character flaw

Cha'rak·ter·schwein F *n* low character; *sl.* rat, swine, *esp. Am.* (rat)fink
cha'rak·ter·stark *adj.* → ***charakterfest;*** **Cha'rak·ter·stär·ke** *f* strength of character; strength, strong point
Cha'rak·ter|stück *n* character play (♪ piece); **~stu·die** *f* character study
cha'rak·ter·voll *adj.* full of character; interesting, striking *features etc.*; *man etc.* of character
Cha'rak·ter·zug *m* (personality *or* personal) trait
Char·ge ['ʃarʒə] *f* (-; -n) **1.** *thea.* supporting part; **2.** *metall.* charge, heat; **3.** ⚔ rank; ***die ~n*** the non-commissioned ranks, the NCOs
Cha·ris·ma ['ça:rɪsma] *n* (-s; -men [ça'rɪsmən]) charisma; **cha·ris·ma·tisch** [çarɪs'ma:tɪʃ] *adj.* charismatic
char·mant [ʃar'mant] **I.** *adj.* charming; **II.** *adv.*: ***~ lächeln*** give a charming smile; **Charme** [ʃarm] *m* (-s; *no pl.*) charm; personality; ***s-n (ganzen) ~ spielen lassen*** F turn on the old charm; **Char·meur** [ʃar'mø:ɐ] *m* (-s; -s, -e [-'mø:rə]) charmer
Char·ta ['karta] *f* (-; -s) *pol.* charter; ***die ~ der Vereinten Nationen*** the United Nations Charter
Char·ter ['tʃartɐ] *m* (-s; -s) charter; **~flug** *m* charter flight; **~ge·sell·schaft** *f* charter company; **~ma,schi·ne** *f* charter plane
char·tern ['tʃartɐn] *v/t.* (h) charter, hire
'Char·ter·ver·kehr *m* charter flights *pl.*
Charts [tʃa:rts] F *pl.* charts; ***in die ~ kommen*** get into the charts
Chas·sis [ʃa'si:] *n* (-; - [ʃa'si:z]) *mot., radio etc.*: chassis
Chauf·feur [ʃɔ'fø:ɐ] *m* (-s; -e [ʃɔ'fø:rə]) driver, chauffeur
Chaus·see [ʃɔ'se:] *obs. f* (-; -n) country road
Chau·vi ['ʃo:vi] F *m* (-s; -s) male chauvinist (pig F), F MCP; **Chau·vi·nis·mus** [ʃovi'nɪsmʊs] *m* (-; *no pl.*) **1.** chauvinism, jingoism; **2.** male chauvinism; **Chau·vi·nist** [ʃovi'nɪst] *m* (-en; -en) **1.** chauvinist; **2.** male chauvinist; **chau·vi'ni·stisch** *adj.* chauvinist(ic)
Check [tʃɛk] *m* (-s; -s) *ice hockey*: check; **checken** ['tʃɛkən] (*sep.* -k·k-) *v/t.* (h) **1.** check; **2.** F get; ***hast du's endlich gecheckt?*** F have you got that into your thick head now?; **3.** *sport*: check, barge (*a. v/i.*); **'Check·li·ste** *f* check list
Chef [ʃɛf] *m* (-s; -s) **1.** head *of the company, department etc.*; boss, *formal*: supervisor, *s.o.'s* superior; F ***~!*** *sl.* guv, chief; ***wer ist hier der ~?*** who's in charge around here?; ***ich möchte mit dem ~ sprechen*** I'd like to speak to the manager; F ***den ~ markieren*** act as if one owns the place; **2.** *gastr.* chef; **~arzt** *m* senior consultant, *Am.* chief of staff; **~be·ra·ter** *m* chief (*or* senior) adviser; **~de·le·,gier·te** *m, f* (-n; -n) head of the delegation; **~di·ri,gent** *m* principal conductor; **~eta·ge** *f* executive floor; **~ideo,lo·ge** *m* chief ideologist
Che·fin ['ʃɛfɪn] *f* (-; -nen) **1.** → ***Chef;*** **2.** F *the* boss's wife
'Chef|kell·ner *m* head waiter; **~koch** *m* chef; **~pi,lot** *m* (flight) captain; **~re·dak,teur** *m* editor (in chief); **~sa·che** *f*: ***et. zur ~ erklären*** give top priority to s.th.; **~se·kre,tä·rin** *f* personal assistant, PA; **~ses·sel** *m*: F *fig.* ***es auf den ~ abgesehen haben*** have one's eye on the boss's job; **~trai·ner** *m* manager, coach; **~,un·ter·händ·ler** *m* chief negotiator; **~vi,si·te** *f* ⚕ consultant's round
Che·mie [çe'mi:] *f* (-; *no pl.*) **1.** chemistry; ***(an)organische ~*** (in)organic chemistry; **2.** chemicals industry; **~an·la·ge** *f* chemical (processing) plant; **~fa·ser** *f* man-made fib|re (*Am.* -er); **~gi,gant** *m* chemical giant; **~in·du,strie** *f* chemicals industry; **~kon,zern** *m* chemicals group; **~un·ter,neh·men** *n* chemicals company
Che·mi·ka·li·en [çemi'ka:lĭən] *pl.* chemicals
Che·mi·ker ['çe:mikɐ] *m* (-s; -), **Che·mi·ke·rin** ['çe:mikərɪn] *f* (-; -nen) chemist
che·misch ['çe:mɪʃ] **I.** *adj.* chemical; ***~e Erzeugnisse*** chemicals; ***~e Reinigung*** a) dry cleaning, b) dry cleaner's; ***~e Wirkung*** chemical action; → ***Keule*** 3; **II.** *adv.*: ***et. ~ reinigen lassen*** have s.th. dry-cleaned, take s.th. to the dry cleaner's
Che·mo'tech·nik [çemo-] *f* chemical engineering; **Che·mo'tech·ni·ker** *m* laboratory technician
Che·mo·the·ra'pie [çemo-] *f* ⚕ chemotherapy
Che·rub ['çe:rʊp] *m* (-s; -rubim [-rubi:m]) *bibl.* cherub (*pl.* cherubim)
chic *adj.*, **Chic** *m* → ***schick, Schick***
Chi·co·rée [ʃiko're] *m* (-s; *no pl.*) ⚘ chicory, *Am.* endive(s *pl.*)
Chif·fon ['ʃɪfõ] *m* (-s; -s) chiffon
Chif·fre ['ʃɪfrə] *f* (-; -n) cipher, code; box number; ***Zuschriften unter ~ 360*** replies to box no. 360; **~an·zei·ge** *f* box number advertisement, blind ad; **~num·mer** *f* box number
chif·frie·ren [ʃɪ'fri:rən] *v/t.* (h) (en)code
Chi·le·ne [tʃi'le:nə] *m* (-n; -n), **Chi·le·nin** [tʃi'le:nɪn] *f* (-; -nen), **chi·le·nisch** [tʃi'le:nɪʃ] *adj.* Chilean
Chi·li ['tʃi:li] *m* (-s; *no pl.*) chil(l)i; **~pul·ver** *n* chil(l)i powder; **~sau·ce** *f* chil(l)i sauce
Chi·mä·re [çi'mɛ:rə] *f* (-; -n) *myth., fig.,* ⚘ chimera
Chi·na|kohl ['çi:na-] *m* Chinese cabbage (*or* leaves *pl.*); **~re·stau,rant** *n* Chinese restaurant; **~rin·de** *f* chinchona bark
Chin·chil·la [tʃɪn'tʃɪla] **1.** *f* (-; -s) *zo.* chinchilla; **2.** *n, m* (-s; -s) chinchilla
Chi·ne·se [çi'ne:zə] *m* (-n; -n) **1.** Chinese; **2.** F Chinese restaurant; ***zum ~n gehen*** F go to a Chinese; ***in der Nähe ist ein ~*** F there's a Chinese place near here; **Chi'ne·sen·vier·tel** *n* (*a.* ***das ~***) Chinatown; **Chi·ne·sin** [çi'ne:zɪn] *f* (-; -nen) Chinese (woman); **chi·ne·sisch** [çi'ne:zɪʃ] **I.** *adj.* Chinese; ***die ℒe Mauer*** the Great Wall of China, the Chinese Wall; **II.** ℒ *n* (-en) Chinese; *fig.* ***das ist ~ für mich*** that's all Greek (*or* that's Chinese) to me
Chi·nin [çi'ni:n] *n* (-s; *no pl.*) quinine
Chi·noi·se·rie [ʃinŏazə'ri:] *f* (-; -n) *art*: chinoiserie
Chintz [tʃɪnts] *m* (-[es]; -e) chintz
Chip [tʃɪp] *m* (-s; -s) **1.** chip; **2.** *pl. gastr.* (potato) crisps, *Am.* potato chips; **3.** *computer*: chip
Chi·ro·mant [çiro'mant] *m* (-en; -en) chiromancer; **Chi·ro·man·tie** [çiroman'ti:] *f* (-; *no pl.*) chiromancy
Chi·ro·prak·tik [çiro'praktɪk] *f* (-; *no pl.*) ⚕ chiropractic; **Chi·ro'prak·ti·ker** *m* (-s; -) chiropractor
Chir·urg [çi'rʊrk] *m* (-en; -en [-gən]) surgeon; **Chir·ur·gie** [çirʊr'gi:] *f* (-; -n) **1.** *no pl.* surgery; **2.** surgical ward; ***in der ~ liegen*** *a.* be in surgery; **chir·ur·gisch** [çi'rʊrgɪʃ] *adj.* surgical; ***ein ~er Eingriff*** surgery (*a. pl.*), an operation; ***e-n ~en Eingriff vornehmen*** operate (***bei*** *dat.* on), carry out surgery (on)
Chi·tin [çi'ti:n] *n* (-s; *no pl.*) chitin; **~pan·zer** *m* exoskeleton
Chlor [klo:ɐ] *n* (-s; *no pl.*) ⚗ chlorine; **chlo·ren** ['klo:rən] *v/t.* (h) chlorinate; **'Chlor·gas** *n* chloric gas; **'chlor·hal·tig** [-haltɪç] *adj.* chlorinated; **Chlo·rid** [klo'ri:t] *n* (-[e]s; -e [-də]) chloride; **chlo·rie·ren** [klo'ri:rən] *v/t.* (h) chlorinate
Chlo·ro·form [kloro'fɔrm] *n* (-s; *no pl.*) chloroform; **chlo·ro·for·mie·ren** [klorofɔr'mi:rən] *v/t.* (h) chloroform
Chlo·ro·phyll [kloro'fʏl] *n* (-s; *no pl.*) ⚘ chlorophyll
'Chlor·was·ser·stoff *m* hydrogen chloride
Choke [tʃo:k] *m* (-s; -s) *mot.* choke
Cho·le·ra ['ko:lera] *f* (-; *no pl.*) ⚕ cholera; **~aus·bruch** *m* outbreak of cholera; **~epi·de,mie** *f* cholera epidemic; **~schutz·imp·fung** *f* cholera inoculation; **~ver·dacht** *m* suspected cholera; ***in ~ stehen*** be a suspected cholera case, be a cholera suspect; **~ver·däch·ti·ge** *m, f* (-n; -n) cholera suspect
Cho·le·ri·ker [ko'le:rikɐ] *m* (-s; -) choleric type; **cho·le·risch** [ko'le:rɪʃ] *adj.* choleric
Cho·le·ste·rin [çolɛste'ri:n] *n* (-s; *no pl.*) cholesterol; **ℒarm** *adj.* low-cholesterol ..., *pred.* low in cholesterol; **ℒreich** *adj.* high-cholesterol ..., *pred.* high in cholesterol; **~spie·gel** *m* cholesterol level
Chor[1] [ko:ɐ] *m* (-[e]s; Chöre ['kø:rə]) **1.** choir; **2.** ♪, *thea.* chorus; *fig.* ***im ~*** in chorus, all together; **3.** ♪ section
Chor[2] *m* (-[e]s; -e) ⛪ choir, chancel
Cho·ral [ko'ra:l] *m* (-s; Choräle [ko'rɛ:lə]) chorale, hymn; Gregorian chant; plainsong
'Chor·amt *n* choir office
Cho·reo·graph [koreo'gra:f] *m* (-en; -en) choreographer; **Cho·reo·gra·phie** [koreogra'fi:] *f* (-; -n) choreography; **cho·reo·gra·phie·ren** [koreogra'fi:rən] *v/t. and v/i.* (h) choreograph; **cho·reo·gra·phisch** [koreo'gra:fɪʃ] choreographic(ally *adv.*)
'Chor|gang *m* choir aisle; **~ge·bet** *n* canonical hour(s *pl.*); **~ge·sang** *m* **1.** *coll.* choral music; **2.** singing of a (*or* the) choir; **~ge·stühl** *n* (choir) stalls *pl.*; **~hemd** *n* surplice, rochet; **~herr** *m* canon; **~kna·be** *m* choirboy; **~kon,zert** *n* choral concert; **~lei·ter** *m* choirmaster, choir director; **~mu,sik** *f* choral music; **~sän·ger** *m* member of a (*or* the) choir, chorister; **~stuhl** *m* (choir) stall
Cho·se ['ʃo:zə] F *f* (-; -n) **1.** business; ***die ganze ~ hinschmeißen*** F chuck the whole thing; **2.** F stuff
Chow-Chow [tʃau'tʃaʊ] *m* (-s; -s) chow (chow)
Christ [krɪst] *m* (-en; -en) Christian
Christ... *in cpds.* → *a.* ***Weihnachts...***
'Christ·baum *m* Christmas tree; **~schmuck** *m* Christmas tree decorations *pl.*
'Christ·de·mo,krat *m* (-en; -en) Christian Democrat; **'christ·de·mo,kra·tisch** *adj.* Christian Democrat

'Chri·sten|ge·mein·de *f* **1.** Christian community; **2.** ~ ***der Frühzeit*** early Christian church; **~glau·be(n)** *m the* Christian faith

'Chri·sten·heit *f*: ***die*** ~ Christendom, the Christian world; ***die gesamte*** ~ the whole of Christendom, the entire Christian world

'Chri·sten·pflicht *f one's* duty as a Christian

'Chri·sten·tum *n*: ***das*** ~ Christianity

'Chri·sten·ver·fol·gung *f* persecution of (the) Christians

chri·stia·ni·sie·ren [krıstĭani'zi:rən] *v/t.* (h) convert to Christianity; **Chri·stia·ni'sie·rung** *f* (-; *no pl.*) christianization, conversion *of a country etc.* to Christianity

Chri·stin ['krıstın] *f* (-; -nen) Christian

'Christ·kind *n*: ***das*** ~ a) the infant Jesus; (the) baby Jesus, b) Father Christmas, Santa Claus; **'Christ·kindl·markt** *m* Christmas market

'christ·lich I. *adj.* Christian; **(*die*)** ~***e Nächstenliebe*** Christian charity, love for one's fellow man; **II.** *adv.* like a Christian; F ~ ***teilen*** share (s.th.) out evenly; **~-de·mo'kra·tisch** *adj.* Christian Democrat; **2*e Union*** Christian Democratic Party

'Christ|mes·se *f* midnight mass; **~met·te** [-mɛtə] *f* (-; -n) *R.C.* midnight mass (*or* service); **~ro·se** *f* Christmas rose; **~stol·len** *m* stollen (cake)

Chri·stus ['krıstʊs] *m* (Christi ['krısti]; *no pl.*) Christ; ***vor Christi Geburt*** **(*v.Chr.*)** before Christ (*abbr.* BC); ***nach Christi Geburt*** **(*n.Chr.*)** Anno Domini (*abbr.* AD); **~bild** *n* image of Christ; crucifix; **~dorn** *m* ⚘ Christ's thorn; **~fi͵gur** *f* figure (*or* statue) of Christ; **~kopf** *m art*: head (*or* portrait) of Christ

Chrom [kro:m] *n* (-s; *no pl.*) chrome; ⚗ *a.* chromium

Chro·ma·tik [kro'ma:tık] *f* (-; *no pl.*) ♪, *opt.* chromatics *pl.*; **chro·ma·tisch** [kro'ma:tıʃ] *adj.* chromatic(ally *adv.*); ~***e Tonleiter*** chromatic scale

'chrom|blit·zend *adj.* gleaming (with metal); **~gelb** *adj.* chrome yellow; **~grün** *adj.* viridian (*or* chrome) green

'Chrom·le·der *n* chrome leather

Chro·mo·som [kromo'zo:m] *n* (-s; -en) chromosome; **Chro·mo'so·men·zahl** *f* chromosome number

Chro·mo·sphä·re [kromo'sfɛ:rə] *f* (-; *no pl.*) chromosphere

Chro·nik ['kro:nık] *f* (-; -en) chronicle; *bibl.* ***das* 1. (2.) *Buch der*** ~ the 1st (2nd) Book of Chronicles, Chronicles I (II); ***die Bücher der*** ~ (the Books of) Chronicles, Chronicles I and II; ***in e-r*** ~ ***aufzeichnen*** chronicle

chro·nisch ['kro:nıʃ] *adj.* ⚕ *and fig.* chronic(ally *adv.*)

Chro·nist [kro'nıst] *m* (-en; -en) chronicler

Chro·no·lo·gie [kronolo'gi:] *f* (-; *no pl.*) chronology; ***die*** ~ ***der Ereignisse*** *a.* the sequence of events; **chro·no·lo·gisch** [krono'lo:gıʃ] *adj.* chronological; ***in*** ~***er Folge*** in chronological order, chronologically

Chro·no·me·ter [krono'me:tɐ] *n* (-s; -) chronometer

Chrys·an·the·me [kryzan'te:mə] *f* (-; -n) ⚘ chrysanthemum

Chry·so·lith [çryzo'li:t] *m* (-s, -en; -e[n]) *min.* chrysolite

Chuz·pe ['xʊtspə] F *f* (-; *no pl.*) F chutzpah

ciao [tʃaʊ] *int.* bye!, see you!

Ci·ne·ast [sine'ast] *m* (-en; -en) **1.** film-maker; **2.** movie buff

cir·ca ['tsırka] *adv.* about, approximately

Cir·cu·lus vi·tio·sus ['tsırkulʊs vi'tsĭo:zʊs] *m* (- -; Circuli vitiosi [-li -zi]) vicious circle

Cis [tsıs] *n* (-; -) ♪ C sharp

Ci·ty ['sıti] *f* (-; -s) town centre, *Am.* downtown (business center); **~nä·he** *f*: ***in*** ~ central(ly)

Clan [kla:n] *m* (-s; -s) *a. iro.* clan

Claque [klak(ə)] *f* (-; *no pl.*) claque; **Cla·queur** [kla'kø:ɐ] *m* (-s; -e [kla'kø:rə]) claqueur

clean [kli:n] F *adj.* F clean, off drugs

Clea·ring ['kli:rıŋ] *n* (-s; -s) ✝ clearing; **~haus** *n* clearing house; **~ver·kehr** *m* clearing (transactions *pl.*)

cle·ver ['klɛvɐ] *adj.* smart, clever

Clinch [klıntʃ] *m* (-[e]s; *no pl.*) *boxing*: clinch; *fig.* ***im*** ~ ***sein mit*** be at loggerheads with

Cli·que ['klıkə] *f* (-; -n) clique, coterie, F crowd; *pol. a.* faction; **'Cli·quen·wirt·schaft** *f* (-; *no pl.*) cliquism

Clou [klu:] *m* (-s; -s) main attraction, high spot; climax; point; ***jetzt kommt der*** ~**!** wait for this

Clown [klaʊn] *m* (-s; -s) clown

Club *m* → ***Klub***

Co·ca ['ko:ka] *f* → ***Cola***

Cocker·spa·ni·el ['kɔkɐ-] (*sep.* -k·k-) *m* cocker spaniel

Cock·pit ['kɔkpıt] *n* (-s; -s) cockpit; ✈ *a.* flight deck

Cock·tail ['kɔkte:l] *m* (-s; -s) **1.** cocktail; **2.** cocktail party; **~kleid** *n* cocktail dress; **~par·ty** *f* cocktail party; **~to͵ma·te** *f* cherry tomato

Co·da *f* → ***Koda***

Code *m* → ***Kode***

Co·de·in *n* → ***Kodein***

co·die·ren *v/t.* → ***kodieren***; **Co·die·rung** *f* → ***Kodierung***

Co·gnac ['kɔnjak] *m* (-s; -s) cognac; **'co·gnac·far·ben** *adj.* cognac(-colo[u]red)

Co·itus *m* → ***Koitus***

Co·la ['ko:la] *f* (-; -), *n* (-[s]; *no pl.*) coke (*TM*); ***zwei*** ~ two cokes; **~nuß** *f* cola nut

Col·la·ge [kɔ'la:ʒə] *f* (-; -n) collage

Col·lie ['kɔli] *m* (-s; -s) collie

Col·lier *n* → ***Kollier***

Come·back [kam'bɛk] *n* (-[s]; -s) comeback; ***ein*** ~ ***erleben*** **(*starten*)** make (stage) a comeback

Co·mic ['kɔmık] *m* (-s; -s) **1.** comic (*or* cartoon) strip; **2.** → **~heft** *n* comic; **~strip** *m* → ***Comic*** 1

Com·mu·ni·qué *n* → ***Kommuniqué***

Com·pact Disc [kɔm'paktdısk] *f* (-; -s) compact disc

Com·pu·ter [kɔm'pju:tɐ] *m* (-s; -) computer; **~aus·druck** *m* computer printout; **~be·fehl** *m* computer command; **~blitz** *m phot.* computer(ized) flash (-gun), dedicated flash; **~brief** *m* personalized computer letter; **~dia͵gno·stik** *f* computer diagnostics *pl.*; **~er·fah·rung** *f* computer experience; **~fahn·dung** *f* computer-aided search(es *pl.*); **~fir·ma** *f* computer firm (*or* company); **~ge·ne·ra·ti͵on** *f* generation of computers, computer generation; **2ge·recht** *adj.* computer-compatible; **2ge·steu·ert** *adj.* computer-controlled; **2ge·stützt** *adj.* computer-aided, computerized; **~gra·fik** *f* computer graphics *pl.*; **~͵her·stel·ler** *m* computer manufacturer(s *pl.*)

com·pu·te·ri·sie·ren [kɔmpjutəri'zi:rən] *v/t.* (h) computerize

Com'pu·ter|kri·mi·na·li͵tät *f* computer crime; **2les·bar** *adj.* machine-readable; **~lin͵gui·stik** *f* computer linguistics *pl.*; **~͵miß·brauch** *m* computer abuse; **~pro͵gramm** *n* computer program; **~satz** *m typ.* computer typesetting; **~spiel** *n* computer game; **~to·mo·gra͵phie** *f* ⚕ computer tomography; **2un·ter͵stützt** *adj.* computer-aided; **~vi·rus** *n, m* computer virus; **~wis·sen·schaft** *f* computer science

Con·fé·rence [kõfe'rã:s] *f* (-; *no pl.*) presentation; ***die*** ~ ***haben bei e-r Veranstaltung*** *etc.* present (*or* emcee, *Brit. a.* compere) a show *etc.*; **Con·fé·ren·cier** [kõferã'sje:] *m* (-s; -s) compere, emcee, MC

Con·nais·seur [kɔnɛ'sø:ɐ] *m* (-s; -s) connoisseur

Con·tai·ner [kɔn'te:nɐ] *m* (-s; -) **1.** container; **2.** skip; **~bahn·hof** *m*, **~ha·fen** *m* container terminal; **~schiff** *n* container ship

Con·ter·gan·kind [kɔntɛr'ga:n-] *n* thalidomide baby (*or* child, victim)

co·ram pu·bli·co ['ko:ram 'pu:bliko] *adv.* in public, publicly

Cord *m* → ***Kord***

Cor·ner ['ko:ɐnɐ] *Austrian m sport*: corner

Cor·ni·chon [korni'ʃõ:] *n* (-s; -s) cocktail gherkin

Cor·pus ['kɔrpʊs] *n* (-; Korpora ['kɔrpora]) **1.** ⚕ corpus, body; **2.** *ling.* corpus; **3.** ~ ***delicti*** corpus delicti

Cor·ti·son [kɔrti'zo:n] *n* (-s; -e) cortisone

Couch [kaʊtʃ] *f* (-; -[e]s) sofa, couch; **~gar·ni͵tur** *f* three-piece suite; **~tisch** *m* coffee table

Cou·leur [ku'lø:ɐ] *f* (-; -s) *pol. etc.* complexion; ***jeder*** ~ *a.* of every shade and colo(u)r

Count·down ['kaʊnt'daʊn] *m, n* (-[s]; -s) countdown; ***der*** ~ ***läuft*** we're into the final countdown

Coup [ku:] *m* (-s; -s) coup; ***e-n*** ~ ***landen*** pull off a coup

Cou·pé [ku'pe:] *n* (-s; -s) **1.** *mot.* coupé; **2.** *obs. or Austrian* 🚂 compartment

Cou·pon [ku'põ:] *m* (-s; -s) **1.** coupon, voucher; (interest) coupon, dividend warrant; counterfoil; **2.** *textil.* length (of material)

Cou·ra·ge [ku'ra:ʒə] *f* (-; *no pl.*) courage, pluck; ~ ***zeigen*** show some courage (*or* pluck, F bottle); F ***Angst vor der eigenen*** ~ ***kriegen*** F get the wind up; **cou·ra·giert** [kura'ʒi:ɐt] *adj.* bold, F plucky

Cour·ta·ge [kur'ta:ʒə] *f* (-; -n) ✝ brokerage

Cou·sin [ku'zɛ̃:] *m* (-s; -s) (male) cousin; **Cou·si·ne** [ku'zi:nə] *f* (-; -n) (female) cousin

Cou·tu·rier [kuty'rĭe:] *m* (-s; -s) couturier, fashion designer

Co·ver ['kavɐ] *n* (-s; -s) **1.** (front) cover, front page; **2.** cover, sleeve

Crack[1] [krɛk] *m* (-s; -s) *tennis etc.* ace; crack tennis player *etc.*

Crack[2] *n* (-s; *no pl.*) crack

Cracker ['krɛkɐ] (*sep.* -k·k-) *m* (-s; -) **1.** *gastr.* cracker; **2.** banger, firecracker

Cre·do ['kre:do] *n* (-s; -s) *eccl.* credo; *fig.* creed
Creme [kre:m] *f* (-; -s) cream; *gastr.* crème; *fig.* ***die ~ der Gesellschaft*** the crème de la crème; **'creme·far·ben** *adj.* cream(-colo[u]red)
'Creme|schnit·te *f* cream slice; **~spei·se** *f* crème; **~tor·te** *f* cream gateau
cre·mig ['kre:mɪç] *adj.* creamy
Crêpe¹ [krɛp] *f* (-; -s) *gastr.* crêpe, pancake
Crêpe² *m* (-; -s) (*a.* ***~ de Chine***) crêpe (de Chine)
Crew [kru:] *f* (-; -s) crew
Crois·sant [krõa'sã:] *n* (-s; -s) croissant
Cro·ma·gnon·mensch [kroma'ɲõ-] *m* Cro-Magnon man
Crou·pier [kru'pie:] *m* (-s; -s) croupier
Crux [krʊks] *f* (-; *no pl.*) **1.** ***man hat schon s-e ~ mit ihm*** he certainly doesn't make life easy; ***man muß s-e ~ tragen*** we all have our little crosses to bear; **2.** ***die ~ dabei ist*** the crux of the matter is
c.t. ['tse:'te:] *adv.* (= ***cum tempore***): ***14 Uhr ~*** 2.15 p.m.; ***~ oder s.t.?*** quarter past or sharp?
cum [kʊm] *prp.*: ***~ grano salis*** with a pinch of salt
cum tem·po·re *adv.* → ***c.t.***
Cup [kap] *m* (-s; -s) *sport*: cup; **~fi͵na·le** *n* cup final
Cur·ri·cu·lum [kʊ'ri:kulʊm] *n* (-s; -la) curriculum
Cur·ry ['kari, 'kœri] *m, n* (-s; -s) **1.** curry; **2.** curry powder; **~sau·ce** *f*, **~so·ße** *f* curry sauce; **~wurst** *f* curried, grilled sausage
Cur·sor ['kœrsɐ] *m* (-s; -s) cursor; **~steue·rung** *f* cursor control
Cut·ter ['katɐ] *m* (-s; -), **Cut·te·rin** ['katərɪn] *f* (-; -nen) *film etc.*: cutter
Cy·an... → ***Zyan...***
Cy·cla·mat [tsykla'ma:t] *n* (-s; -e) cyclamate

D

D, d [de:] *n* (-; -) D, d; ♪ D

da [da:] **I.** *adv.* **1.** a) there; **~, *wo*** where; **~ *oben*** (***unten***) up (down) there; **~ *draußen*, ~ *hinaus*** out there; **~ *drinnen*, ~ *hinein*** in there; **~ *drüben*, ~ *hinüber*** over there; ***hier und* ~** here and there; ***den*** (***das***) **~** that one; ***der*** (***die***) **~** that man (woman) over there; ***der*** (***die***) **~ *war's*** it was him (her), b) here; **~ *bin ich*** here I am; ***ich bin gleich wieder* ~** I'll be back in a minute; **~** (***hast du's***)***!*** there you are; **2. *sieh* ~*!*** look (at that)!, *iro.* lo and behold!; **3. *als* ~ *sind*** for instance, such as; ***als ich ihn sah*, ~ *lachte er*** when I saw him he laughed; ***es gibt Leute, die* ~ *glauben*** there are people who believe; ***was* ~ *kommen mag*** whatever happens; **4.** then, at that time; **~ *erst*** only then; ***von* ~ *an*** from then on, since then; ***hier und* ~** now and then; **~ *gab es noch keinen Strom*** there was no electricity in those days; **5.** there, under the circumstances; ***was läßt sich* ~ *machen?*** what can be done about it?; **~ *irren Sie sich*** you're mistaken there; **~ *wäre ich*** (***doch***) ***dumm*** I would be stupid to do so; **~ *fragt man sich wirklich, warum*** it really makes you wonder why; **~ *kann man nichts machen*** what can you do about it?, there's not much you can do about it; **II.** *cj.* **6.** as, when, while; ***in dem Augenblick*, ~ *er ...*** the moment he ...; **7.** as, since, because; **~ *ja*, ~ *doch*** seeing (as); **~ *ich keine Nachricht erhalten hatte, ging ich weg*** not having received any news, I left; **8. ~ *aber*, ~ *jedoch*** but since; since ..., however

'da·be·hal·ten *v/t.* (*irr.*, *sep.*, h, → ***behalten***) hold onto; ***sie behielten ihn gleich da*** they kept him in

da'bei *pron. adv.* **1.** with it; near-by, close by; ***ein Haus mit Garten* ~** a house with a garden; **2.** about (*or* going) to *do s.th.*, on the point of *doing s.th.*; ***ich war gerade* ~ *zu packen*** I was just packing; **3.** at the same time, while doing so; ***sie strickt und liest* ~** she knits and reads at the same time; ***er aß und sah mich* ~ *fragend an*** while he ate, he looked at me questioningly; **4.** besides; ***sie ist hübsch und* ~ *auch noch klug*** *a.* she's attractive and intelligent into the bargain; **5.** nevertheless, yet, for all that, at the same time; ***und* ~ *ist er doch schon alt*** and he's an old man, after all; ***er ist streng und* ~ *sehr fair*** he's strict but very fair; **6. *er schenkte es mir*, ~ *hatte ich es gar nicht verlangt*** he gave it to me although I hadn't even asked for it; **~ *hätten wir gewinnen können*** to think we could have won; **~ *macht man sich gar keinen Begriff, wie schwierig es ist*** but people have no idea how hard it is; **7.** a) on the occasion, then; b) as a result; **~ *kam es zu e-r heftigen Auseinandersetzung*** this gave rise to (*or* resulted in) a heated argument; ***es kommt nichts* ~ *heraus*** it's no use, it's not worth it; **~ *dürfen wir nicht vergessen*** here we must not forget; **~ *fällt mir ein*** talking of which; ***alle* ~ *entstehenden Kosten*** all resulting costs; **8. *ich bleibe* ~** I'm not changing my mind; ***und ich bleibe* ~, *in X ist es am schönsten*** I'm still convinced X is the most beautiful place in the world; ***du kommst mit, und* ~ *bleibt's*** you're coming with us, and that's that; **~ *blieb's*** (and) that was the end of that; ***ich dachte mir nichts Böses* ~** I meant no harm; ***ich dachte mir nichts* ~** I thought nothing of it; ***sich nichts* ~ *denken zu*** *inf.* think nothing of *ger.*; ***was hast du dir eigentlich* ~ *gedacht?*** what on earth made you do (*or* say *etc.*) that?; ***ich finde nichts* ~** I don't see any harm in it; ***man könnte verrückt werden* ~** it's enough to drive you mad; ***was ist schon* ~*?*** so what?; ***was ist schon dabei, wenn ...?*** what difference does it make if ...?; ***mir ist gar nicht wohl* ~** I don't feel too good about it; ***lassen wir es* ~** let's leave it at that

da'bei|blei·ben *v/i.* (*irr.*, *sep.*, sn, → ***bleiben***) keep (*or* stick) to it; **~ha·ben** *v/t.* (*irr.*, *sep.*, h, → ***haben***)**:** ***er hat keinen Schirm dabei*** he didn't bring his umbrella; ***ich hab' kein Geld dabei*** I haven't got any money on me; ***niemand wollte ihn* ~** nobody wanted him to come (*or* to be in on it); **~sein** *v/i.* (*irr.*, *sep.*, sn, → ***sein***) be there; take part (in it); see it; ***darf ich* ~*?*** can I come too?, can I join in?; ***ich bin dabei!*** (you can) count me in; ***er muß immer* ~** he's got to be in on everything; ***es war ziemlich viel Glück dabei*** I was *etc.* pretty lucky there; ***dabeizusein ist alles*** it's taking part that counts; **~ste·hen** *v/i.* (*irr.*, *sep.*, h, → ***stehen***) stand by watching; happen to be there

'da·blei·ben *v/i.* (*irr.*, *sep.*, sn, → ***bleiben***) stay; ***bleib doch noch ein bißchen da*** can't you stay a bit longer?; *ped.* **~ *müssen*** be kept in

da ca·po [da 'ka:po] **I.** *adv.* ♪ da capo; **II.** *int. thea.* encore!; **~ *rufen*** call for an encore

Da·ca·po *n* → ***Dakapo***

Dach [dax] *n* (-[e]s; Dächer ['dɛçɐ]) roof; *mot. a.* top; ***ein* ~ *über dem Kopf haben*** have a roof over one's head; ***sie wohnen alle unter einem* ~** they all live under the same roof; ***unterm* ~ *wohnen*** live under the roof; ***unter* ~ *und Fach*** under cover; *contract etc.*: all settled, F in the bag; ***unter* ~ *und Fach bringen*** shelter, *fig.* get *s.th.* settled, get *s.th.* out of the way; F ***eins aufs* ~ *kriegen*** F get a clip round the ears, get a real ticking-off; F ***j-m aufs* ~ *steigen*** F come down on s.o. like a ton of bricks, give s.o. hell; **~an,ten·ne** *f* roof aerial (*or* antenna); **~bal·ken** *m* roof beam, rafter; **~be·griff** *m* blanket (*or* umbrella) term; **~bo·den** *m* loft; **~decker** (*sep.* -k·k-) *m* (-s; -) roofer; tiler; slater; **~fen·ster** *n* **1.** dormer (window); **2.** skylight; **~first** *m* (roof) ridge

'dach·för·mig *adj.* roof-shaped

'Dach|gar·ten *m* roof garden; **~gau·be** [-gaʊbə] *f*, **~gau·pe** [-gaʊpə] *f* dormer; **~ge·päck·trä·ger** *m mot.* roofrack

'Dach·ge·schoß *n* top floor; ***im* ~** in the attic, on the top floor; ***im* ~ *wohnen*** *a.* live under the roof; **~woh·nung** *f* attic flat, *Am.* (converted) loft

'Dach|ge·sell·schaft *f* ✝ holding company; **~gie·bel** *m* gable; **~iso,lie·rung** *f* roof insulation; **~kam·mer** *f* attic, garret; **~land·schaft** *f* roofscape; **~lu·ke** *f* skylight; **~or·ga·ni·sa·ti,on** *f* umbrella organization; **~pap·pe** *f* roofing felt; **~rin·ne** *f* gutter

Dachs [daks] *m* (-es; -e) badger; *fig.* F (***junger***) **~** F little squirt; F ***wie ein* ~ *schlafen*** sleep like a log

'Dach|sat·tel *m* (roof) ridge; **~scha·den** *m* roof damage; F *fig.* ***e-n* ~ *haben*** F have lost one's marbles; **~schie·fer** *m* roofing slate

'Dachs·hund *m* dachshund

'Dach|spar·ren *m* rafter; **~stu·be** *f* attic, garret; **~stuhl** *m* roof timbering

dach·te ['daxtə] *pret. of* ***denken***

'Dach|ter,ras·se *f* roof terrace; **~trau·fe** *f* gutter; **~ver·band** *m* umbrella organization; **~vie·rung** *f* roof crossing; **~woh·nung** *f* attic flat, *Am.* (converted) loft; **~zie·gel** *m* (roofing) tile

Dackel ['dakəl] (*sep.* -k·k-) *m* (-s; -) **1.** dachshund; **2.** F idiot, fool, dimwit; **~bei·ne** F *pl.* F (short) bandy legs

Da·da ['dada] *m* (-[s]; *no pl.*) Dada; **Da·da·is·mus** [dada'ɪsmʊs] *m* (-; *no pl.*) Dadaism; **Da·da·ist** [dada'ɪst] *m* (-en; -en) Dadaist; **da·dai·stisch** [dada'ɪstɪʃ] *adj.* Dadaistic(ally *adv.*), Dadaist

da'durch I. *pron. adv.* **1.** through (it, there *etc.*); that way; **2.** because of that, that's how (*or* why); **II.** *cj.* **3. ~, *daß*** because, due to the fact that; **~, *daß er uns geholfen hat*** *a.* thanks to his help; **4. ~, *daß*** by *ger.*; **~, *daß er hart arbeitete*** by working hard

da'für I. *pron. adv.* **1.** for it, for them, for that, for this; **2.** in return; **3. ~ *sein*** be for it, be in favo(u)r of it, *voting*: be in favo(u)r; **~ *sein, et. zu tun*** be for doing s.th.; ***ich bin ganz* ~** I'm all in favo(u)r;

es läßt sich vieles ~ und dagegen sagen it has its pros and cons; ***alles spricht ~, daß*** all the evidence seems to indicate that, it looks very much as if; **4.** ***~ ist er ja da*** that's what he's there for (after all), that's his job, isn't it?; **II.** *cj.* **5.** ***~, daß*** for *ger.*; ***er wurde ~ bestraft, daß er gelogen hatte*** he was punished for telling lies; ***~ sorgen, daß*** see to it that; **6.** *er ist blind*, ***hat aber ~ ein sehr gutes Gehör*** but has extremely good ears; ***er ist reich, ~ aber sehr krank*** he's rich but very sick; **7.** F *er müßte es wissen*, ***~ ist er ja Lehrer*** after all, he's a teacher(, isn't he?); **2hal·ten** *n*: ***nach m-m ~*** as I see it; **~kön·nen** *v/t.* (*irr.*, *sep.*, h, → ***können***): ***er kann nichts dafür*** it's not his fault, he can't help it; **~ste·hen** *v/i.* (*irr.*, *sep.*, *h*, → ***stehen***) *esp. Austrian*: ***es steht nicht dafür*** it's not worth it

da'ge·gen I. *pron. adv.* **1.** against it (*or* them); ***s-e Gründe ~*** his objections to it; ***~ sein*** be against (*or* opposed to) it, *voting*: be against; ***er sprach sich entschieden ~ aus*** he strongly opposed it; ***haben Sie etwas ~, wenn ich rauche?*** do you mind if I smoke?; ***wenn Sie nichts ~ haben*** if you don't mind (*a. iro.*); ***ich habe nichts ~*** I don't mind; ***~ hilft nichts*** there's nothing you can do about it; **2.** in return *or* exchange (for it); **3.** in comparison, by contrast; *unsere Qualität* ***ist nichts ~*** can't compare; **II.** *cj.* **4.** on the other hand, however; **5.** but then; whereas, whilst, while; **~hal·ten** *v/t.* (*irr.*, *sep.*, h, → ***halten***) hold *s.th.* against it (*or* them); *fig.* compare (with it); argue; **~han·deln** *v/i.* (*sep.*, h) act against it; **~set·zen** *v/t.* (*sep.*, h): ***s-e Meinung*** *etc.* ~ put forward one's own opinion *etc.*; **~spre·chen** *v/i.* (*irr.*, *sep.*, h, → ***sprechen***): ***was spricht dagegen, daß wir ...?*** why shouldn't we ...?; ***alles spricht dagegen (,daß es geschehen wird)*** the odds are (stacked) against it; ***alles spricht dagegen, daß er das Verbrechen begangen hat*** all the evidence points against his having committed the crime; **~stel·len** *v/refl.* (*sep.*, h): ***sich ~*** oppose it; **~stem·men** *v/refl.* (*sep.*, h): ***sich ~*** fight it; **~wir·ken** *v/i.* (*sep.*, h) take action against it

'Da·ge·we·se·ne *n*: ***das übertrifft alles ~*** that beats everything (*or* it all, them all)

da'heim I. *adv.* at home, in; back home; ***~ ist ~*** there's no place like home; ***bei mir ~*** at my place; ***wo sind Sie ~?*** where do you come from?, where's home for you?; *fig.* ***er ist in dieser Materie ~*** he's at home in this field; **II. 2** *n* (-s; *no pl.*) home

da'her I. *adv.* from there; *fig.* that's why, that's the reason for; ***~ (stammt) die ganze Verwirrung*** hence the confusion; ***~ kam es, daß*** that's why (*or* how); **II.** *cj.* that's why, and so; and so, as a result; **~ge·lau·fen** *adj.*: ***~er Kerl*** F bum; ***jeder ~e Kerl*** any Tom, Dick or Harry; **~kom·men** *v/i.* (*irr.*, *sep.*, sn, → ***kommen***) come along; **~re·den** *v/i. and v/t.* (*sep.*, h): ***dumm (dummes Zeug, Unsinn) ~*** talk nonsense

da'hin *adv.* **1.** there; ***das gehört nicht ~*** that doesn't belong there; **2.** ***bis ~*** until then, till then; ***hoffentlich bist du bis ~ fertig*** I hope you'll be finished by then (*or* by that time); **3.** ***m-e Meinung geht ~, daß*** I tend to think that; → ***dahingehend***; **4.** ***es ~ bringen, daß jemand ...*** bring s.o. to the point where he *will ...*; ***ist es ~ gekommen?*** has it come to that?; **5.** ***~ sein*** a) be past, be over; b) have passed away, be dead; c) be broken, F have had it; ***sein guter Ruf ist ~*** he's lost his good reputation, *iro.* so much for his reputation

da·hin'auf *adv.* up there

da·hin'aus *adv.* out there, out that way

da'hin|be·we·gen *v/refl.* (*sep.*, h): ***sich ~*** move along; **~däm·mern** *v/i.* (*sep.*, h): ***er dämmert nur noch dahin*** he's just vegetating (away); **~ei·len** *v/i.* (*sep.*, sn) hurry along; *fig. time*: fly

da·hin'ein *adv.* in there

da'hin|fah·ren *v/i.* (*irr.*, *sep.*, sn, → ***fahren***) drive (*or* ride) along; **~flie·gen** *v/i.* (*irr.*, *sep.*, sn, → ***fliegen***) fly along; *fig. time*: fly; **~flie·ßen** *v/i.* (*irr.*, *sep.*, sn, → ***fließen***) flow along; *fig. years etc.*: pass by

da·hin'ge·gen *cj.* on the other hand

da'hin·ge·hen *v/i.* (*irr.*, *sep.*, sn, → ***gehen***) go along; *fig. time*: pass; *euphem.* pass away

'da·hin·ge·hend *adv.*: ***~, daß*** to the effect that; ***sie haben sich ~ geäußert, daß*** what they said was (more or less) that, what it boiled down to was that; ***man hat sich ~ geeinigt, daß*** it was agreed that; ***sich ~ äußern, daß*** say that

da'hin|ge·stellt *adj.*: ***es ~ sein lassen, ob*** leave it open as to whether; ***das sei ~*** who knows?; ***es bleibt ~*** it remains to be seen; ***es sei ~, ob er es war*** let's leave aside the question of whether it was him or not; **~krie·chen** *v/i.* (*irr.*, *sep.*, sn, → ***kriechen***) creep (*or* crawl) along; *fig. time*: drag (on), *years*: drag by (slowly); **~le·ben** *v/i.* (*sep.*, h) live (from day to day); ***nur so ~*** while away one's days; **~plät·schern** *v/i.* (*sep.*, sn): *conversation*: meander along; *music*: tinkle away (in the background); **~schei·den** *v/i.* (*irr.*, *sep.*, sn, → ***scheiden***) pass away; **~schlei·chen** → ***dahinkriechen***; **~schlep·pen** *v/refl.* (*sep.*, h): ***sich ~*** drag o.s. along; *fig.* drag (on); **~schmel·zen** *v/i.* (*irr.*, *sep.*, sn, → ***schmelzen***) melt away, *fig. a.* dwindle away; **~schwin·den** *v/i.* (*irr.*, *sep.*, sn, → ***schwinden***) dwindle away; *fig.* waste away, pine away; *beauty*: fade; **~sie·chen** *v/i.* (*sep.*, sn) languish; **~sie·chend** *fig. adj.* ailing

da'hin·ten *adv.* back there

da'hin·ter *pron. adv.* behind it (*or* them); at the back; *fig.* behind it; ***es ist was ~*** there's something in it; ***es ist nichts ~*** there's nothing to it; **~'her** F *adv.*: ***(sehr) ~ sein*** a) be after it, b) be doing all one can; ***~ sein, daß*** *or* ***zu*** *inf.* make a point of *ger.*; **~klem·men** F *v/refl.* (*sep.*, h), **~knien** F *v/refl.* (*sep.*, h) → ***dahintermachen***; **~kom·men** F *v/i.* (*irr.*, *sep.*, sn, → ***kommen***) a) get to the bottom of it; find out (about it); b) F get it; **~ma·chen** F *v/refl.* (*sep.*, h), **~set·zen** F *v/refl.* (*sep.*, h): ***sich ~*** put one's back into it; **~stek·ken** (*sep.* -k·k-) *fig. v/i.* (*sep.*, h) be behind (*or* at the bottom of) it; ***da muß etwas ~*** there's more to it than meets the eye; **~ste·hen** *fig. v/i.* (*irr.*, *sep.*, h, → ***stehen***) be behind it; be backing it (up)

da·hin'un·ter *adv.* down there

da'hin|ve·ge,tie·ren *v/i.* (*sep.*, h) vegetate (away); **~wel·ken** *v/i.* (*sep.*, sn) wither away; **~zie·hen** (*irr.*, *sep.*, → ***ziehen***) **I.** *v/i.* (sn) move along; *clouds*: drift past; **II.** *v/refl.* (h): ***sich ~*** a) go on and on; b) stretch (out) for miles

Dah·lie ['da:liə] *f* (-; -n) ♀ dahlia

Da·ka·po [da'ka:po] *n* (-s; -s) encore; **~ruf** *m* (call for an) encore

'da·las·sen *v/t.* (*irr.*, *sep.*, h, → ***lassen***) leave there (*or* behind)

'da·lie·gen *v/i.* (*irr.*, *sep.*, h, → ***liegen***) lie there

dal·li ['dali] F *adv.*: ***aber ein bißchen ~!*** F and make it snappy!

Dal·ma·ti·ner [dalma'ti:nɐ] *m* (-s; -) *zo.* dalmatian

da·ma·lig ['da:ma:lıç] *adj.* then, of (*or* at) that time; ***der ~e Besitzer*** the then owner; ***sein ~es Versprechen*** the promise he made then

da·mals ['da:ma:ls] *adv.* then, at that time; in those days, F back then; ***~, als*** (at the time) when; (in the days) when; ***schon ~*** even then, even at that time; ***Aufnahmen von ~*** photos from that time; ***Ereignisse von ~*** events of the time; ***Geschichten von ~*** stories from that time (*or* from those years)

Da·mast [da'mast] *m* (-[e]s; -e), **da'ma·sten** *adj.* damask

Da·me ['da:mə] *f* (-; -n) **1.** lady; *dancing*: partner; ***„Damen"*** "Ladies"; ***e-e echte ~*** a real lady; ***ganz ~ sein*** be every inch a lady; ***die große (*** *or* ***feine) ~ spielen*** play the lady; ***~ des Hauses*** hostess; ***m-e ~n und Herren!*** ladies and gentlemen; **2.** draughts *pl.*, *Am.* checkers *pl.*; **3.** king; *chess and card games*: queen; **~brett** *n* draughtboard, *Am.* checkerboard

'Da·men|bart *m* facial hair; **~be·glei·tung** *f*: ***in ~*** in female company, with a woman; **~be·such** *m* lady visitor(s *pl.*); **~bin·de** *f* sanitary towel (*Am.* napkin); **~dop·pel** *n tennis etc.*: women's doubles *pl.*; **~ein·zel** *n tennis etc.*: women's singles *pl.*; **~fahr·rad** *n* ladies' bicycle; **~fri,seur** *m* ladies' hairdresser (*or* hairdresser's); **~fuß·ball** *m* women's football (*or* soccer); **~gar·de,ro·be** *f* ladies' changing room; **~ge·sell·schaft** *f* **1.** ladies-only party, F hen party; **2.** → ***Damenbegleitung***; **~grö·ße** *f* ladies' size

'da·men·haft I. *adj.* ladylike; **II.** *adv.*: ***sich ~ benehmen*** behave like a lady (*or* in a ladylike way)

'Da·men|ho·se *f*: ***(e-e ~*** a pair of) ladies' trousers (*Am.* pants) *pl.*; **~hut** *m* ladies' hat; **~klei·dung** *f* ladies' wear; **~kränz·chen** *n* ladies' afternoon; ***sie gehört zu unserem ~*** she's one of the ladies' afternoon crowd; **~mann·schaft** *f* women's team; **~mo·de** *f* ladies' fashions *pl.*; **~ober·be·klei·dung** *f* ladies' wear; **~rad** *n* ladies' bicycle (F bike); **~sa,lon** *m* ladies' hairdresser's; **~schirm** *m* ladies' umbrella; **~schnei·der** *m* ladies' tailor; **~toi,let·te** *f* ladies' toilet (*Am.* room), *the* ladies *pl.*; **~,un·ter·wä·sche** *f* ladies' underwear; lingerie; **~wahl** *f* ladies' choice; **~welt** *f* (-; *no pl.*) *the* ladies *pl.*

'Da·me|spiel *n* draughts *pl.*, *Am.* checkers *pl.*; **~stein** *m* draughtsman, *Am.* checker

Dam·hirsch ['dam-] *m* fallow buck

da·mit [da'mıt; 'da:mıt] **I.** *pron. adv.* with it (*or* them), with that (*or* those); by *or* with it (*or* that), *pl.* with them (*or* those); (and) so; as a result, (and) so; with that, with these words; ***her ~!*** give it to me, hand it over; ***weg ~!*** take (*or* put) it away; ***was will er ~ sagen?*** what's he trying to say?; ***was soll ich ~?*** what am I supposed to do with it?; ***wie steht's*** (*or* ***wär's***) ***~?*** how about it?; ***wir sind ~ einverstanden*** we have no objections; ***~ wirst du nichts erreichen*** that won't get you anywhere; ***~ kann man niemanden überzeugen*** that won't convince anybody; ***er fing ~ an, daß er*** he began by *ger.*; ***~ war es aus*** that was the end (of it); ***~ soll nicht gesagt sein, daß*** that doesn't mean that; ***~ war alles wieder beim alten*** things were back to where we started; **II.** *cj.* so that, in order to *inf.*, so as to *inf.*; ***~ nicht*** so as not to *inf.*; for fear that *s.o. or s.th. might* ...; ***~ er nicht kommt*** so that he doesn't come

däm·lich ['dɛːmlɪç] F *adj.* stupid, idiotic(ally *adv.*); '**Däm·lich·keit** F *f* (-; -en) **1.** *no pl.* silliness; **2.** silly prank, *pl. a.* nonsense *sg.*

Damm [dam] *m* (-[e]s; Dämme ['dɛmə]) **1.** dam; sea wall, dike; 🚂 *etc.* embankment; *fig.* barrier; F *fig.* ***wieder auf dem ~ sein*** F be fighting fit again; F ***nicht ganz auf dem ~ sein*** F be (feeling) a bit under the weather; F ***j-n wieder auf den ~ bringen*** get s.o.(up) on his (*or* her) feet again; **2.** *dial.* street, road; ***über den ~ gehen*** cross the road (*or* street); **3.** *anat.* perineum; **~bruch** *m* bursting of a dam, breach in a dam

däm·men ['dɛmən] *v/t.* (h) dam up; ⚙ insulate; *fig.* check, curb

däm·me·rig ['dɛmərɪç] *adj.* dim (*a. fig.*), *lit.* crepuscular; dimly lit, twilit

'**Däm·mer·licht** *n* (-[e]s; *no pl.*) twilight; *w.s.* dim light

däm·mern ['dɛmɐn] (h) **I.** *v/impers.* **1.** ***es dämmert*** a) it's getting light, b) it's getting dark; *fig.* ***langsam dämmert's bei ihm*** it's beginning to get through to him, *iro. a.* he's getting there; **II.** *v/i.* **2.** ***der Morgen dämmert*** day is breaking; ***der Abend dämmert*** night is falling; **3.** *fig.* ***vor sich hin ~*** doze, ⚕ be very dop(e)y

'**Däm·mer|schein** *m* → ***Dämmerlicht***; **~schlaf** *m* light sleep, doze; ⚕ twilight sleep; **~schop·pen** *m* sundowner; **~stun·de** *f* twilight hour

Däm·me·rung ['dɛmərʊŋ] *f* (-; -en) **1.** dawn; ***bei ~*** at dawn, at daybreak; **2.** twilight, dusk; ***in der ~*** at dusk, at nightfall

'**Däm·mer·zu·stand** *m* ⚕ semiconscious state; *w.s.* daze

'**Dämm·plat·te** *f* ⚙ insulating board, softboard

dämm·rig ['dɛmrɪç] → ***dämmerig***

'**Damm|riß** *m* ⚕ perineal tear; **~schnitt** *m* ⚕ episiotomy

'**Däm·mung** *f* (-; -en) ⚙ insulation

'**Damm·weg** *m* causeway

Da·mo·kles·schwert ['daːmoklɛs-] *fig. n* sword of Damocles; ***wie ein ~ über j-m hängen*** (*or* ***schweben***) hang over s.o. like a sword of Damocles

Dä·mon ['dɛːmɔn] *m* (-s; -en [dɛ'moːnən]) demon, evil spirit; **dä·mo·nisch** [dɛ'moːnɪʃ] *adj.* demoniacal; *w.s. a.* demonic

Dampf [dampf] *m* (-[e]s; Dämpfe ['dɛmpfə]) steam; *phys.* vapo(u)r; smoke; (***chemische***) ***Dämpfe*** fumes; ***~ ablassen*** ⚙ blow off steam, F *fig.* let off steam; F *fig.* ***aus dem Projekt*** *etc.* ***ist der ~ raus*** F the project *etc.* has run out of steam; F ***~ dahinter setzen*** F speed things up a bit; F ***j-m ~ machen*** F give s.o. a kick in the pants; **~an·trieb** *m* steam drive; **~bad** *n* steam bath

'**dampf·be·trie·ben** *adj.* steampowered

'**Dampf|boot** *n* steamboat; **~bü·gel·ei·sen** *n* steam iron; **~druck** *m* (-[e]s; ⁼e) ⚙ steam pressure

damp·fen ['dampfən] *v/i.* (h) steam; smoke (*a.* F *person*); fume; 🚂 puff; ***die Suppe dampft*** the soup is steaming (*or* piping) hot

dämp·fen ['dɛmpfən] *v/t.* (h) **1.** steam; a) steam-iron, b) press *trousers etc.* with a damp cloth; *gastr.* steam, stew; **2.** muffle *sound etc.*; ♪ mute; subdue, soften *colo(u)r, light*; ⚡ attenuate; cushion, absorb *impact etc.*; ✈ stabilize; lower *one's voice*; *fig.* put a damper on; subdue; suppress; → ***gedämpft***; **3.** ✝ curb, slow down *rise in prices etc.*

Damp·fer ['dampfɐ] *m* (-s; -) steamer, steamship; F *fig.* ***auf dem falschen ~ sein*** be on the wrong track

Dämp·fer ['dɛmpfɐ] *m* (-s; -) damper (*a. fig.*); ♪ *a.* mute; ⚡ baffle; *fig.* ***j-m*** (***e-r Sache***) ***e-n ~ aufsetzen*** put a damper on s.o. (s.th.); ***e-n ~ bekommen*** *enthusiasm etc.*: be dampened, F get a rap over the knuckles

'**Dampf|ham·mer** *m* steam hammer; **~hei·zung** *f* steam heating

damp·fig ['dampfɪç] *adj.* steamy

'**Dampf|kes·sel** *m* boiler; **~koch·topf** *m* pressure cooker; **~kraft** *f* (-; *no pl.*) steam power; **~kraft·werk** *n* steam power station; **~lok** *f*, **~lo·ko·mo,ti·ve** *f* steam engine; **~ma,schi·ne** *f* steam engine; **~nu·del** *f* sweet yeast dumpling; **~roß** *hum. n* iron horse; **~schiff** *n* steamship (*abbr.* SS), steamer; **~strahl** *m* steam jet; **~topf** *m* pressure cooker; **~tur,bi·ne** *f* steam turbine

Dämp·fung ['dɛmpfʊŋ] *f* (-; -en) steaming *etc.*; *phys.* loss; ⚡ attenuation; '**Dämp·fungs·kreis** *m* ⚡ attenuation circuit

'**Dampf·wal·ze** *f* steamroller

da·nach [da'naːx; 'daːnaːx] *pron. adv.* after that (*or* it), *pl.* after them; then, afterwards; later on; according to it (*or* that); accordingly; ***ich sehnte mich ~ zu*** *inf.* I longed to *inf.*; ***ich fragte ihn ~*** I asked him about it; *iro.* ***er sieht ganz ~ aus*** he looks the sort; ***er ist nicht der Typ ~*** he's not that sort of person; ***mir ist nicht ~*** I don't feel like it; ***wenn es ~ ginge, was ...*** if it was (*or* were) a matter *or* case of what ...; ***wenn es ~ ginge*** if that was what counted; ***es sieht*** (***ganz***) ***~ aus, als ob*** it looks as though

Dä·ne ['dɛːnə] *m* (-n; -n) Dane

da'ne·ben *pron. adv.* beside it (*or* them), next to it (*or* them); in addition; at the same time; beside it (*or* him *etc.*), in comparison; off the mark; ***das Zimmer ~*** the room next door; ***rechts*** (***links***) ***~*** a) to the right (left) (of it), b) on his *etc.* right (left); ***direkt ~*** right next to it; ***~!*** missed!; F ***total ~!*** *a. fig.* F way out!; *fig.* ***weit ~*** wide of (F way off) the mark; **~be·neh·men** F *v/refl.* (*irr.*, *sep.*, h, → ***benehmen***): ***sich ~*** show o.s. up, step out of line; ***du hast dich natürlich mal wieder danebenbenommen*** *a.* F can't take you anywhere, can we?; **~ge·hen** *v/i.* (*irr.*, *sep.*, sn, → ***gehen***) *shot etc.*: miss, be off target, *soccer etc.*: *a.* go wide; *fig.* be wide of the mark, *plan etc.*: misfire; **~grei·fen** *v/i.* (*irr.*, *sep.*, h, → ***greifen***) miss; ♪ play a (few) wrong note(s); F *fig.* F be way out; **~hau·en** *v/i.* (*sep.*, h) miss; F *fig.* F be way out; **~lie·gen** F *v/i.* (*irr.*, *sep.*, h, → ***liegen***): ***weit ~*** F be way off the mark (***mit*** *dat.* with); **~schie·ßen** *v/i.* (*irr.*, *sep.*, h, → ***schießen***), **~schla·gen** *v/i.* (*irr.*, *sep.*, h, → ***schlagen***), **~tref·fen** *v/i.* (*irr.*, *sep.*, h, → ***treffen***) miss

da'nie·der·lie·gen *v/i.* (*irr.*, *sep.*, h, → ***liegen***) *trade etc.*: be stagnating; ⚕ be laid low (***an*** *dat.* with)

Da·ni·el ['daːnieːl] *m bibl.* Daniel; ***~ in der Löwengrube*** Daniel in the lion's den

Dä·nin ['dɛːnɪn] *f* (-; -nen) Dane, Danish woman; **dä·nisch** ['dɛːnɪʃ] *adj.*, '**Dä·nisch** *n* (-en) *ling.* Danish

dank [daŋk] *prp.* (*gen. or dat.*) thanks to (*a. iro.*)

Dank *m* (-[e]s; *no pl.*) thanks *pl.*; gratitude; reward; ***vielen*** (*or* ***besten, schönen***) ***~!*** many thanks, thank you very much; ***mit ~*** with thanks; ***mit ~ zurück*** returned with thanks, F thanks for the loan; ***j-m ~ sagen*** thank s.o.; ***j-m ~ schulden, j-m zu ~ verpflichtet sein*** be deeply indebted to s.o.; ***keinen ~ erwarten*** not to expect any thanks; ***ist das der ~ für m-e Mühe?*** is that all I get for the trouble I went to?; *iro.* ***das ist nun der ~ dafür*** that's gratitude for you; ***zum ~ für s-e Dienste*** in recognition of his services; ***zum*** (*or* ***als***) ***~ dafür, daß Sie ihm geholfen haben*** in appreciation of your help

'**dank·bar** *adj.* grateful, appreciative; worthwhile, rewarding *task etc.*; hard-wearing *material etc.*; ***ich wäre Ihnen ~, wenn*** I'd be much obliged if (*a. iro.*), I'd appreciate it if; *iro.* ***ich wäre Ihnen sehr ~, wenn Sie sich um Ihre eigenen Angelegenheiten kümmern würden*** *a.* I'll thank you to mind your own business; ***man muß für alles ~ sein*** you have to be thankful for small mercies (*or* for every little thing); '**Dank·bar·keit** *f* (-; *no pl.*) gratitude; ***aus ~ für*** *acc.* out of gratitude for

'**Dank·brief** *m* letter of thanks, F thank-you letter

dan·ken ['daŋkən] (h) **I.** *v/i.* thank (***j-m für*** *acc.* s.o. for); ***kurz ~*** say a brief thanks; ***er läßt ~*** he says thank you; (***j-m***) ***~*** return the (s.o.'s) greeting; ***ich weiß nicht, wie ich Ihnen ~ soll*** I don't know how to thank you; ***danke*** (***schön***)***!*** (many) thanks, thank you (very much); ***danke***(***, ja***)***!*** thank you; ***danke***(***, nein***)***!*** no, thank you; no, thanks; ***danke der Nachfrage*** nice of you to ask, *iro. a.* so kind of you to ask; F ***mir geht's danke*** F can't complain; ***nichts zu ~!*** you're welcome, not at all; *iro.* ***na, ich danke!*** no thanks, I can do without it; **II.** *v/t.*: ***j-m et. ~*** a) owe s.th. to s.o.; b) reward s.o. for s.th.; ***ihm ~ wir, daß*** we owe it to him that, it's due (*or* thanks) to him that; ***wie kann ich dir das jemals ~?*** how can I ever thank you?; '**dan·kend** *adv.* with thanks; ***Betrag ~ erhalten*** amount gratefully received

'**dan·kens·wert** *adj.* **1.** commendable; **2.** rewarding *task etc.*; '**dan·kens·wer·ter'wei·se** *adv.* kindly (enough)

'**Dan·kes|be·zei·gung** *f* (expression of) thanks *pl.*, token of one's gratitude; **~brief** *m* → ***Dankbrief***

'Dan·ke·schön *n* (-s; *no pl.*) thankyou; word of thanks; ***als (kleines) ~*** as a (small) token of my *etc.* thanks

'Dan·kes·wort *n* (-[e]s; -e) *a. pl.* word of thanks

'Dank|ge·bet *n* thanksgiving (prayer); **~got·tes·dienst** *m* thanksgiving service; **~sa·gung** [-za:gʊŋ] *f* (-; -en) **1.** expression of thanks; **2.** acknowledg(e)ment *of a letter of condolence*; **3.** *eccl.* thanksgiving; **~schrei·ben** *n* letter of thanks

dann [dan] *adv.* then; after that, afterwards; in that case, then; so; ***wer (wo, wie*** *etc.*) ***~?*** who (where, how *etc.*) else then?; ***wenn er es nicht weiß, wer ~?*** if he doesn't know, who does?; ***~ und ~*** at such and such a time; ***~ und wann*** now and then; ***was geschah ~?*** what happened then (*or* next)?; ***~ eben nicht!*** all right (*Am.* alright), forget it!; ***wenn du mich brauchst, ~ sag mir Bescheid*** if you need me, just let me know; ***~ kommst du also?*** so you 'are coming (then)?

dan·nen ['danən] *obs. adv.*: ***von ~*** away, off

dar'an *pron. adv.* at (*or* in, on, onto, to) that *or* it; ***~ befestigen*** attach to it; ***~ glauben*** believe in it; ***~ leiden*** suffer from it; ***komm nicht ~!*** don't touch it!, keep away from it!; ***nahe ~*** nearby; *fig.* ***nahe ~ sein zu*** *inf.* be on the point of *ger.*, come close to *ger.*; ***ich war nahe ~, ihn zu schlagen*** I nearly hit him; ***~ kann man sehen, wie*** *etc.* that goes to show how *etc.*; ***im Anschluß ~*** following that, after that; ***~ schloß sich e-e Rede (an)*** that was followed by a speech; → ***glauben*** II, ***liegen*** I, ***Schuld*** 1; **~ge·hen** *v/i.* (*irr.*, *sep.*, sn, → ***gehen***) get down to it; ***~ zu*** *inf.* get down to *ger.*; **~hal·ten** *v/refl.* (*irr.*, *sep.*, h, → ***halten***): ***sich ~*** → ***dranhalten***; **~ma·chen** F *v/refl.* (*sep.*, h): ***sich ~*** → ***darangehen***; **~set·zen** (*sep.*, h) **I.** *v/t.* risk; *fig.* ***alles ~, um zu*** *inf.* do everything in one's power to *inf.*; **II.** *v/refl.*: ***sich ~*** **1.** F get cracking; **2.** → ***darangehen***

dar·auf [da'raʊf; 'da:raʊf] *pron. adv.* **1.** on it (*or* them); on top of it (*or* them); **2.** after that, then, *lit.* thereupon; next; ***bald ~*** soon after (that); ***gleich ~*** immediately afterwards; ***am Tag (or tags) ~*** the day after, the next day; ***zwei Jahre ~*** two years later (*or* on); **3.** *fig.* on it (*or* that); ***mein Wort ~*** my word on it; ***er arbeitete ~ hin zu*** *inf.* he was working towards (*or* on) *ger.*; → ***ankommen*** 5, ***kommen*** 2; **~fol·gend** *adj.* following, subsequent

dar·auf·hin [daraʊf'hɪn] *adv.* **1.** after that, then; whereupon; **2.** as a result; **3.** in reply; ***~ sagte er a.*** ..., to which he replied; **4.** ***et. ~ untersuchen, ob*** examine s.th. to see if

dar·aus [da'raʊs; 'da:raʊs] *pron. adv.* from *or* out of it (*or* them); ***~ kann man schließen*** one may conclude from that; ***~ wird nichts werden*** a) nothing will come of it, b) we (*or* you) can forget about that; ***~ wird nichts!*** F nothing doing!; ***was ist ~ geworden?*** what happened to it?, what's become of it?; ***ich mache mir nichts ~*** a) it doesn't bother me, b) I'm not that keen on it

dar·ben ['darbən] *v/i.* (h) live in want; suffer privations

dar·bie·ten ['da:ɐ-] (*irr.*, *sep.*, h, → ***bieten***) **I.** *v/t.* offer (*dat.* to); present; perform, play; **II.** *v/refl.*: ***sich ~*** present itself; arise; **'Dar·bie·tung** *f* (-; -en) presentation; *thea. etc.* performance; number, act

dar·brin·gen ['da:ɐ-] *v/t.* (*irr.*, *sep.*, h, → ***bringen***) present (*dat.* to), give (to); offer, make *sacrifice etc.* (to); give *s.o. an ovation etc.*

dar·ein [da'raɪn; 'da:raɪn] *pron. adv.* in(to) it (*or* them); ***sich ~ ergeben (or fügen)*** → **~fin·den** *v/refl.* (*irr.*, *sep.*, h, → ***finden***): ***sich ~*** come to terms with it, resign o.s. to the fact, put up with it; ***sich ~ zu*** *inf.* come to terms with *ger.*, resign o.s. to *ger.*, put up with *ger.*; **~mi·schen** *v/refl.* (*sep.*, h): ***sich ~*** interfere; **~re·den** *v/i.* → ***dreinreden***

dar·in [da'rɪn; 'da:rɪn] *pron. adv.* **1.** in it (*or* them); in there; ***was ist ~?*** what's inside?; ***da ist ... ~*** there's ... in it, it contains ...; *fig.* ***die Schwierigkeit liegt ~, daß*** the difficulty is that; **2.** in this respect; ***~ irren Sie sich*** there you are mistaken; ***~ kann ich Ihnen nicht zustimmen*** I can't agree with you there; ***es unterscheidet sich von anderen ~, daß*** it distinguishes itself from others in that; **3.** at it (*or* that); ***~ ist er gut*** he's good at it (*or* that); ***er kennt sich ~ gut aus*** he knows a lot about it

dar·le·gen ['da:ɐ-] *v/t.* (*sep.*, h) present; explain; state; ***s-e Position ~*** set out one's position; **'Dar·le·gung** *f* (-; -en) presentation; explanation, exposition

Dar·le·hen ['da:ɐle:ən] *n* (-s; -) loan; ***ein ~ aufnehmen (geben)*** take up (grant) a loan

'Dar·le·hens|be·din·gun·gen *pl.* terms of a (*or* the) loan; **~ge·ber** *m* (-s; -) lender; **~kas·se** *f* (mutual) loan society, *Am.* credit corporation; **~neh·mer** *m* (-s; -) borrower; **~zin·sen** *pl.* interest *sg.* on loans

Darm [darm] *m* (-[e]s; Därme ['dɛrmə]) **1.** *anat.* intestine, bowels *pl.*; **2.** *gastr.* skin; **~aus·gang** *m* anus; **~ent·lee·rung** *f* evacuation of the bowels; **~ent·zün·dung** *f* enteritis; **~flo·ra** *f* intestinal flora; **~grip·pe** *f* gastroenteritis; **~ko·lik** *f* abdominal (*or* intestinal) colic; **~krebs** *m* cancer of the intestine; **~sai·te** *f* catgut (string); **~spie·ge·lung** *f* enteroscopy; **~tä·tig·keit** *f* (-; *no pl.*) bowel movement; **~träg·heit** *f* constipation; **~ver·schluß** *m* intestinal occlusion; **~wand** *f* wall of the intestine, intestinal wall

dar·rei·chen ['da:ɐ-] *v/t.* (*sep.*, h): ***j-m et. ~*** hand s.o. s.th., offer s.o. s.th.; ⚕ *and eccl.* administer s.th. to s.o.; **'Dar·rei·chungs·form** *f* presentation; ⚕ (form of) administration

dar·ren ['darən] *v/t.* (h) kiln-dry; **'Darr·ofen** *m* kiln

dar·stell·bar ['da:ɐʃtɛlba:ɐ] *adj.* **1.** ***es ist in Worten (numerisch, auf der Leinwand) nicht ~*** it can't be described in words (expressed in numbers, portrayed on the screen); **2.** *thea.* actable; **'dar·stel·len** (*sep.*, h) **I.** *v/t.* **1.** describe; present *facts etc.*; ***falsch ~*** misrepresent; ***negativ ~*** portray in a negative light; **2.** show, depict, portray; ***was soll dieses Bild ~?*** what is this picture supposed to represent?; **3.** be, represent; ***was stellt das eigentlich dar?*** what is it supposed to be?; ***was stellt dieses Zeichen dar?*** what does this symbol stand for (*or* represent)?; ***dieses Ereignis stellt e-n großen Fortschritt dar*** this event is a major step forward; *fig.* ***er stellt etwas dar*** he's somebody; **4.** *thea.* act *or* play (the part of); **5.** represent; ✍ describe; outline, sketch; ***in e-m Diagramm ~*** draw a graph of; **6.** ⚗ prepare, synthesize, produce; **II.** *v/refl.*: ***sich ~*** present itself, appear; present o.s., ***als:*** show o.s. to be; **'dar·stel·lend** *adj.*: ***~e Geometrie*** descriptive geometry; ***~e Künste*** a) interpretative arts, b) plastic arts; **Dar·stel·ler** ['da:ɐʃtɛlɐ] *m* (-s; -) actor, performer; ***der Darsteller des Faust*** the actor playing (the part of) Faust; **Dar·stel·le·rin** ['da:ɐʃtɛlərɪn] *f* (-; -nen) actress, performer; **dar·stel·le·risch** ['da:ɐʃtɛlərɪʃ] **I.** *adj.* acting, theatrical; ***s-e ~e Leistung*** his performance; **II.** *adv.*: ***~ war der Film wenig überzeugend*** the acting in the film wasn't very convincing; **'Dar·stel·lung** *f* (-; -en) **1.** description, portrayal; account; presentation *of facts etc.*; ***falsche ~*** misrepresentation; **2.** representation; interpretation; **3.** *thea.* a) interpretation, acting; b) production; **4.** ⚗ preparation

'Dar·stel·lungs|kraft *f* powers *pl.* of interpretation; descriptive powers *pl.*; **~kunst** *f* art of interpretation; *thea.* acting ability; **~ob|jekt** *n* object; **~wei·se** *f* style

dar·tun ['da:ɐtu:n] *v/t.* (*sep.*, h) show, demonstrate; set out

dar·über [da'ry:bɐ; 'da:ry:bɐ] *pron. adv.* **1.** over it (*or* them); over that; above it *etc.*; across it *etc.*; ***das Zimmer ~*** the room above; ***mit e-m Dach*** *etc.* ***~*** with a roof *etc.* on top; *fig.* ***es geht nichts ~*** there's nothing like it; **2.** in the meantime; ***ich bin ~ eingeschlafen*** I fell asleep over it; ***~ werden Jahre vergehen*** that will take years; **3.** *fig.* about that (*or* it); on that (*or* it); ***ich freue mich ~, daß*** I'm glad (that); ***~ vergaß er s-e Probleme*** it took his mind off his problems; ***~ wird morgen verhandelt*** we'll *etc.* be discussing that tomorrow; ***~ läßt sich streiten*** that's a matter of opinion, that's a debatable point; **4.** ***~ hinaus*** beyond it, past it; *fig.* in addition, on top of it, beyond that; **5.** more; **6.** ***wir sind ~ hinweg*** we've got over it; ***er beklagt sich ~, daß er unfair behandelt worden sei*** he complains of having been treated unfairly; **~brei·ten** *v/t.* (*sep.*, h) spread over it; **~fah·ren** *v/i.* (*irr.*, *sep.*, sn, → ***fahren***): ***mit der Hand ~*** run one's hand over it; ***mit e-m Staubtuch ~*** go over it with a duster; **~lie·gen** *fig. v/i.* (*irr.*, *sep.*, h, → ***liegen***) be higher; ***weit ~*** be much higher; **~ma·chen** F *v/refl.* (*sep.*, h): ***sich ~*** F get on with it; *sl.* get stuck in(to it); **~schrei·ben** *v/t.* (*irr.*, *sep.*, h, → ***schreiben***) write over it; write *name etc.* at the top; **~ste·hen** *fig. v/i.* (*irr.*, *sep.*, h, → ***stehen***) be above that (*or* such things)

dar·um [da'rʊm; 'da:rʊm] *pron. adv.* **1.** around it (*or* them); around there; **2.** *fig.* about that; ***j-n ~ bitten zu*** *inf.* ask s.o. to *inf.*; ***~ geht es gar nicht*** that's not the point; ***er kümmert sich nicht ~*** he doesn't care (about it); ***es handelt sich ~ festzustellen*** it's a matter of finding out; ***ich gäbe was (viel) ~ zu wissen*** I wouldn't mind knowing (I'd love to know); **3.** that's why; ***ich habe es ~***

getan, weil the reason I did it was because; *warum? - ~!* because!
dar·un·ter [da'rʊntɐ; 'da:rʊntɐ] *pron. adv.* **1.** under it (*or* them); under there; underneath; further down; **2.** among them; including; ***mitten*** ~ right in the middle (of it *or* them); **3.** less; ***20 Dollar und*** ~ 20 dollars and under (*or* less); **4.** *fig.* → ***leiden, daß*** suffer from *ger.*; ***er leidet sehr*** ~ he's taking it hard; ***sie leidet ~, daß sie nicht mehr arbeitet*** not having a job is getting her down; ***was verstehst du ~?*** what do you understand by it?; ~ ***kann ich mir nichts vorstellen*** it doesn't mean a thing to me; **~blei·ben** *v/i.* (*irr., sep.*, sn, → ***bleiben***) be lower; ***die Ergebnisse*** *etc.* ***blieben darunter*** the results *etc.* didn't reach the required (*or* expected) level; **~fal·len** *fig. v/i.* (*irr., sep.*, sn, → ***fallen***) be included; be covered by it; **~he·ben** *v/t.* (*irr., sep.*, h, → ***heben***) *gastr.* fold in; **~lie·gen** *fig. v/i.* (*irr., sep.*, h, → ***liegen***) be lower; ***weit*** ~ be much lower; ***er liegt mit s-n Leistungen darunter*** he doesn't come up to this level; **~mi·schen** (*sep.*, h) **I.** *v/t.* add, mix *s.th.* into it; **II.** *v/refl.*: ***sich*** ~ mix with them (*or* the crowd *etc.*); **~schrei·ben** *v/t.* (*irr., sep.*, h, → ***schreiben***) write at the bottom; **~set·zen** *v/t.* (*sep.*, h) put at the bottom; ***s-e Unterschrift*** ~ sign (it), sign at the bottom; **~zie·hen** *v/t.* (*irr., sep.*, h, → ***ziehen***) put on as well, put on underneath
das [das] → ***der***
'da·sein I. *v/i.* (*irr., sep.*, sn, → ***sein***) **1.** be there; ***ist jemand da?*** is there anybody there?; ***wenn Sie schon da sind*** while you're here; ***ist noch Brot da?*** is there any bread left?; ***es ist keine Milch mehr da*** we've run out of milk; ***Geld ist dazu da, daß man es ausgibt*** money is there to be spent; ***ich bin gleich wieder da*** I'll be back in a second; ***noch nie dagewesen*** unheard-of, unprecedented; ***so etwas ist noch nie dagewesen*** that's never happened before; **2.** ***jetzt ist er wieder da*** he's come round again; **3.** (***wieder***) ***voll*** ~ be (back) in top form; **4.** ***er ist nur für sie da*** he's only got time for her, *w.s.* he lives for her; ***ich bin immer für dich da*** I'll always be around when you need me; **II.** 𝔖 *n* (-s; *no pl.*) **1.** existence, life; → ***Kampf***; **2.** presence
'Da·seins|be·rech·ti·gung *f* right to exist; raison d'être; **~form** *f* way of life; **~kampf** *m* struggle for existence (*or* survival)
da'selbst *adv.* there, in that very place; *in books etc.*: ibidem; ***wohnhaft*** ~ residing at said place
'da·sit·zen *v/i.* (*irr., sep.*, h, → ***sitzen***) sit there; F *fig.* ***ohne Geld*** ~ be left without a penny (to one's name)
das·je·ni·ge → ***derjenige***
daß [das] *cj.* that; ***so*** ~ so that; ***es sei denn***, ~ unless; ***ohne*** ~ without *ger.*; ***er weiß, ~ es wahr ist*** he knows it's true; ***er entschuldigte sich, ~ er zu spät kam*** he apologized for being late; ***entschuldigen Sie, ~ ich Sie störe*** sorry to disturb you; ***es ist nett, ~ du anrufst*** it's nice of you to ring; ***kaum, ~ er e-n Blick darauf warf*** he hardly gave it a look; ~ ***du mir ja nichts anrührst!*** don't go and touch anything, now; ~ ***du ja kommst!*** you had better be there!; ~ ***ich es bloß nicht vergesse!*** I hope I don't forget it, I'd better not forget it; ~ ***er so was sagen konnte!*** how could he say such a thing?; ***nicht, ~ ich wüßte*** not that I know of; ***nicht, ~ es etwas ausmachte*** not that it mattered; ***es sind zwei Jahre, ~ ich ihn nicht gesehen habe*** it's two years now since I saw him
das·sel·be → ***derselbe***
'da·ste·hen *v/i.* (*irr., sep.*, h, → ***stehen***) stand (there); *fig.* ***ganz allein*** ~ be left all on one's own; F ***dumm*** ~ be left looking the fool; ***gut*** ~ be doing all right (*Am.* alright), *w.s.* be in a good position; ***mit leeren Händen*** ~ be left without a penny (to one's name); ***wie stehe ich nun da!*** and where does that leave me?, F I look a right idiot (now); ***wie stehe ich nun vor m-n Kollegen da!*** and what am I going to say to my colleagues (now)?, and how am I going to face my colleagues (now)?
Da·tei [da'taɪ] *f* (-; -en) (data) file
Da·ten ['da:tən] *pl.* data, facts; particulars, personal data; ***technische*** ~ specifications; **~bank** *f* data bank (*or* base); **~er·fas·sung** *f* data acquisition; **~er·he·bung** *f* survey
'Da·ten·fluß *m* data flow; **~plan** *m* data flowchart
'Da·ten|ˌmiß·brauch *m* data abuse; **~netz** *n* data network; **~satz** *m* record
'Da·ten·schutz *m* data protection; **~be·auf·trag·te** *m, f* (-n; -n) data protection registrar (*Am.* commissioner); **~ge·setz** *n* data protection law
'Da·ten|si·cher·heit *f* data security; **~sicht·ge·rät** *n* visual display unit, VDU; **~spei·cher** *m* data memory (*or* storage); **~tech·nik** *f* data systems technology; **~trä·ger** *m* data medium (*or* carrier); **~tyˌpi·stin** *f* (-; -nen) data typist; **~überˌtra·gung** *f* data transfer; **~ver·ar·bei·tung** *f* data processing
da·tier·bar [da'ti:ɐba:ɐ] *adj.*: *die Funde* ***sind nicht genau*** ~ cannot be dated exactly; **da·tie·ren** [da:'ti:rən] (h) **I.** *v/t.* date; **II.** *v/i.*: ~ ***von*** date from (*or* back to); ***der Brief datiert vom 2. Mai*** the letter is dated May 2nd
Da·tiv ['da:ti:f] *m* (-s; -e ['da:ti:və]) *ling.* dative (case); **~obˌjekt** *n* indirect object
da·to ['da:to] *adv.*: ***bis*** ~ up to now, to date
Dat·tel ['datəl] *f* (-; -n) date; **~baum** *m*, **~pal·me** *f* date palm
Da·tum ['da:tʊm] *n* (-s; Daten ['da:tən]) date; ***heutigen ~s*** of today; ***ohne*** ~ undated; ***welches ~ haben wir heute?*** what's the date today?; ***der Brief trägt das ~ vom 2. Mai*** the letter is dated May 2nd; ***neueren ~s*** recent
'Da·tums|an·ga·be *f* date; ***ohne*** ~ undated; **~gren·ze** *f* (international) date line
'Da·tum(s)·stem·pel *m* **1.** date stamp; **2.** dater
Dau·be ['daʊbə] *f* (-; -n) stave
Dau·er ['daʊɐ] *f* (-; *no pl.*) duration; period (of time), *esp.* ✝, ⚖ term; length; ***auf die*** ~ in the long run; ***auf die ~ wird es unerträglich*** it becomes unbearable after a time; ***sie können auf die ~ nicht so weitermachen*** they can't go on like that forever; ***das ist keine Lösung auf ~*** that's no long-term solution; ***für die ~ von*** for a period of; ***für die ~ unseres Aufenthalts*** for the course (*or* duration) of our stay; ***von ~ sein*** last; ***von kurzer ~ sein*** be short-lived; ***während der ~ unseres Aufenthalts*** during (the course of) our stay; **~ar·beits·lo·sig·keit** *f* long-term unemployment; **~auf·trag** *m* ✝ standing order; ***et. per ~ überweisen*** pay s.th. by standing order; **~aus·stel·lung** *f* permanent exhibition; **~be·an·spru·chung** *f* constant (⚙ endurance) stress; **~be·hand·lung** *f* prolonged treatment; **~be·hin·de·rung** *f* permanent disability; **~be·la·stung** *f* constant strain (*or* stress), ⚙ constant load; **~be·schäf·ti·gung** *f* ✝ permanent employment; ***e-e ~ suchen*** look for a permanent job; **~be·trieb** *m* continuous operation; **~be·zie·hung** *f* long-term (*or* permanent) relationship; **~bren·ner** *m* **1.** ⚙ slow-combustion stove; **2.** F *fig.* long-running success; **3.** F long-running issue; **4.** F long kiss; **~ein·rich·tung** *f a. fig.* permanent institution; ***zu e-r ~ werden*** become a permanent institution; **~er·folg** *m* lasting success; **~flug** *m* long-haul flight; **~frost** *m* permafrost; **~frost·gren·ze** *f* permafrost line; **~gast** *m* permanent resident; F ***er ist bei uns ~*** F he's a permanent fixture here; **~ge·schwin·dig·keit** *f* cruising speed
'dau·er·haft I. *adj.* durable, lasting *a. fig. peace etc.*; long-term ...; fast *colo(u)r*; hard-wearing *material etc.*; solid *building etc.*; **~e** (***Konsum***)***Güter*** (consumer) durables; **II.** *adv.*: ~ ***gearbeitet*** made to last; **'Dau·er·haf·tig·keit** *f* (-; *no pl.*) durability
'Dau·er|in·sti·tu·tiˌon *f* → ***Dauereinrichtung***; **~kaˌlen·der** *m* perpetual calendar; **~kar·te** *f* season ticket; **~kun·de** *m* regular customer; **~kund·schaft** *f* regular customers *pl.*; **~lauf** *m* long-distance run(ning); ***im*** ~ at a jog; **~lei·stung** *f* long-term performance; ⚙ continuous output; **~lö·sung** *f* long-term solution; **~lut·scher** *m* lollipop; **~mie·ter** *m* permanent tenant
dau·ern¹ ['daʊɐn] *v/i.* (h) last; take; ***es wird lange ~, bis er kommt*** it'll be a long time before he comes; ***es wird nicht lange ~, dann ...*** it won't be long before ...; ***das dauert mir zu lange*** a) it's taking too long for my liking, b) that's too long for me; ***wie lange dauert das noch?*** how much longer is that going to take?; F ***das dauert aber!*** F it doesn't half take a long time
'dau·ern² *lit. v/t.* (h): ***er dauert mich*** I feel sorry for him
'dau·ernd I. *adj.* lasting, permanent; durable; constant; incessant; **II.** *adv.*: ***er lachte*** ~ he kept laughing; ***unterbrich mich nicht ~!*** stop interrupting me (all the time)!; ~ ***ist was los*** there's always something going on
'Dau·er|par·ker *m* long-term parker; **~re·ge·lung** *f* permanent arrangement; **~re·gen** *m* continuous rain; **~scha·den** *m* ⚕ permanent damage; ***er hat Dauerschäden davongetragen*** he's suffered permanent damage; **~schlaf** *m* prolonged sleep; **~stel·lung** *f* permanent post; **~test** *m* endurance test; **~ton** *m* continuous tone; **~vi·sum** *n* permanent visa; **~wel·le** *f* perm; ***sich e-e ~ machen lassen*** get one's hair permed, get a perm; **~wir·kung** *f* lasting effect; **~wurst** *f* hard smoked sausage; **~zu·stand** *m* permanent condition (*or* state of affairs);

zu e-m ~ werden become permanent (*or* a permanent state of affairs)
Däum·chen ['dɔʏmçən] *n* (-s; -): *a. fig.* ~ ***drehen*** twiddle one's thumbs
Dau·men ['daʊmən] *m* (-s; -) thumb; *fig.* ***j-m die ~ halten*** (*or* ***drücken***) keep one's fingers crossed (for s.o.); *a. fig.* (***die***) ~ ***drehen*** twiddle one's thumbs; *fig.* ***den ~ auf et. halten*** keep tabs on s.th.; ***et. über den ~ peilen*** make a rough guess at s.th.; ***über den ~ (gepeilt)*** at a rough guess; **~ab·druck** *m* thumbprint; **~brei·te** *f*: ***um ~*** by about an inch; **~ki·no** *n* flip-book; **~lut·schen** *n* (-s) thumb-sucking; **~lut·scher** *m* thumb-sucker; **~na·gel** *m* thumbnail; **~re͵gi·ster** *n* thumb index; **~schrau·be** *f hist.* thumbscrew; *fig.* ***j-m ~n anlegen*** put the screws on s.o.
Däum·ling ['dɔʏmlɪŋ] *m* (-s; -e) **1.** thumbstall; thumb; **2.** Tom Thumb
Dau·ne ['daʊnə] *f* (-; -n) downy feather; *pl.* down *sg.*; **'Dau·nen·ano·rak** *m* quilted anorak; **'Dau·nen·decke** *f* eiderdown; **'dau·nen·weich** *adj.* downy
Da·vids·stern ['da:fɪts-] *m* Star of David
da·von [da'fɔn; 'da:fɔn] *pron. adv.* of it (*or* them); from it (*or* them), from there; away; about it, of it; ***was habe ich ~?*** what do I get out of it?; ***das kommt ~!*** what did you expect?; ***~ wird man müde*** it makes you tired; ***~ leben*** live off it; **~ei·len** *v/i.* (*sep.*, sn) hurry away; **~fah·ren** *v/i.* (*irr.*, *sep.*, sn, → ***fahren***) drive (*or* ride) off *or* away; ***mir ist der Bus davongefahren*** I just missed the bus; **~flie·gen** *v/i.* (*irr.*, *sep.*, sn, → ***fliegen***) fly off (*or* away); **~ja·gen** *v/t.* (*sep.*, h) chase away; **~kom·men** *v/i.* (*irr.*, *sep.*, sn, → ***kommen***) get away, escape; (*a.* ***mit dem Leben ~***) escape, survive; ***~ mit*** *dat.* escape (*or* get away) with *minor injuries etc.*; get away (*or* off) with *a fine etc.*; ***wir sind noch einmal davongekommen*** it was a close shave; → ***blau*** 1, ***Schreck*** 1; **~las·sen** *v/t.* (*irr.*, *sep.*, h, → ***lassen***): → ***Finger***; **~lau·fen** *v/i.* (*irr.*, *sep.*, sn, → ***laufen***) run away (***j-m*** from s.o.); *fig. prices etc.*: get out of control (*or* hand); ***ihm ist die Freundin davongelaufen*** his girlfriend (got up and) left him; ***es ist zum ♀!*** it's enough to make you weep; **~ma·chen** *v/refl.* (*sep.*, h): ***sich ~*** make off; **~schlei·chen** *v/i.* (*irr.*, *sep.*, sn, → ***schleichen***) *and v/refl.* (***sich ~***) (h) → **~steh·len** *v/refl.* (*irr.*, *sep.*, h, → ***stehlen***): ***sich ~*** sneak off (*or* away); **~tra·gen** *v/t.* (*irr.*, *sep.*, h, → ***tragen***) carry off; *fig.* come away with, *formal*: sustain *injuries etc.*; get, catch, F end up with *a cold etc.*; → ***Sieg***; **~zie·hen** *v/i.* (*irr.*, *sep.*, sn, → ***ziehen***) march off; F *sport*: pull away (***j-m*** from s.o.)
da·vor [da'fo:ɐ; 'da:fo:ɐ] *pron. adv.* before *or* in front of it (*or* them); beforehand; before that; ***e-e Stunde ~*** an hour earlier; *fig.* ***er fürchtet sich ~*** he's afraid of it
da·zu [da'tsu:; 'da:tsu:] *pron. adv.* to it (*or* them); for it (*or* that); about it (*or* that); besides, in addition; ***noch ~*** on top of it (*or* that); ***er ist zu dumm ~*** he's too stupid for that; ***~ gehört Zeit*** it takes time; ***es gehört schon einiges ~ zu*** *inf.* it takes quite a lot to *inf.*; ***wie kamst du dazu zu*** *inf.* how did you come to *inf.* (*or* to be *doing*)?; ***wie bist du ~ gekommen?*** how did you get hold of it?; ***wie ist es ~ gekommen?*** how did it happen?; ***ich kam nie ~*** I never got round to it, ***zu*** *inf.*: I never got round to *ger.*; ***wie komme ich ~?*** why should I?; ***~ ist er da*** that's what he's there for, that's his job; ***~ hast du's doch*** that's what you've got it for (*or* it's there for), isn't it?; **~ge·ben** *v/t.* (*irr.*, *sep.*, h, → ***geben***) add; ***j-m et. ~*** give s.o. s.th. towards it
da'zu·ge·hö·ren *v/i.* (*sep.*, h) belong to it (*or* them); be part of it; belong; *fig.* ***das gehört mit ~*** that's part (and parcel) of it; ***es gehört schon einiges ~*** F it takes a fair bit (***zu*** *inf.* to *inf.*); **da'zu·ge·hö·rig** *adj.* belonging to it (*or* them); appropriate; ***der ~e Deckel*** *a.* the lid that goes with it
da'zu|kom·men *v/i. irr.*, *sep.*, sn, → ***kommen***) **1.** come along; join them (*or* us *etc.*); ***er kam gerade dazu, als*** he arrived just as; **2.** be added; ***kommt noch was dazu?*** is there anything else?; ***dazu kommt noch, daß*** in addition, it has to be added that; **~kön·nen** *v/t.* (*irr.*, *sep.*, h, → ***können***) → ***dafürkönnen***; **~ler·nen** *v/t.* (*and v/i.*) (*sep.*, h) learn (something new); ***schon wieder etwas dazugelernt!*** you live and learn!; ***er hat nichts dazugelernt*** he'll never learn
da·zu·mal ['da:tsuma:l] *adv.* → ***Anno***
da'zu·tun I. *v/t.* (*irr.*, *sep.*, h, → ***tun***) add; **II.** ♀ *n*: ***ohne sein ~*** without any help from him
da'zwi·schen *pron. adv.* between (them), in between; among them; in between; **~fah·ren** *v/i.* (*irr.*, *sep.*, sn, → ***fahren***) step in; butt in; **~fra·gen** *v/i.* (*sep.*, h): ***darf ich mal kurz ~?*** could I ask a quick question before you (*or* we) go on?; **~fun·ken** F *v/i.* (*sep.*, h) **1.** interfere (***j-m*** with s.o.'s plans *etc.*); F put a spoke in the wheel; **2.** butt in; **~ge·ra·ten** *v/i.* (*irr.*, *sep.*, sn, → ***geraten***) **1.** ***mit den Fingern*** *etc.* ~ get one's fingers *etc.* caught; **2.** *fig.* get involved; ***irgendwie bin ich ~*** somehow I managed to get myself involved; **~kom·men** *v/i.* (*irr.*, *sep.*, sn, → ***kommen***): ***wenn nichts dazwischenkommt*** if all goes well; ***es*** (*or* ***mir*** *etc.*) ***ist etwas dazwischengekommen*** s.th.'s cropped up; **~lie·gend** *adj.* intervening; **~re·den** *v/i.* (*sep.*, h) interrupt (***j-m*** s.o.), butt in; **~ru·fen** (*irr.*, *sep.*, h, → ***rufen***) **I.** *v/t.* shout *s.th.* (in between); **II.** *v/i.* interrupt a speech *etc.* with shouts, shout; **~tre·ten** *fig. v/i.* (*irr.*, *sep.*, sn, → ***treten***) interfere; step in; **~wer·fen** (*irr.*, *sep.*, h, → ***werfen***) **I.** *fig. v/t.* throw in *a question etc.*; **II.** *v/refl.*: ***sich ~*** jump in, try and break up the fight
dea·len ['di:lən] F *v/i.* (h) push drugs; **Dea·ler** ['di:lɐ] *m* (-s; -) drug dealer, F pusher
De·ba·kel [de'ba:kəl] *n* (-s; -) débâcle, debacle
De·bat·te [de'batə] *f* (-; -n) debate (*a. parl.*), discussion (***über*** *acc.* on); ***zur ~ stehen*** be up for discussion; ***zur ~ stellen*** put *s.th.* forward for discussion, moot *a point*; ***das steht hier nicht zur ~*** that's not the issue here
de·bat·tie·ren [deba'ti:rən] (h) **I.** *v/t.* debate, discuss; **II.** *v/i.* debate; ***über et. ~*** debate (*or* discuss) s.th.
De·bet ['de:bɛt] *n* (-s; -s) ☨ debit; **~sal·do** *m* balance due
De·bi·li·tät [debili'tɛ:t] *f* (-; *no pl.*) ⚕ debility
de·bi·tie·ren [debi'ti:rən] *v/t.* (h) ☨ charge, debit; ***j-m e-n Betrag ~*** charge a sum to s.o.'s account, debit s.o. with a sum
De·bi·to·ren [debi'to:rən] *pl.* ☨ accounts receivable
De·büt [de'by:] *n* (-s; -s) debut, début; ***sein ~ geben*** → ***debütieren***; **De·bü·tant** [deby'tant] *m* (-en; -en) débutant; **De·bü'tan·tin** *f* (-; -nen) débutante; **de·bü·tie·ren** [deby'ti:rən] *v/i.* (h) make one's debut *or* début (***als*** as)
De·chant [dɛ'çant] *m* (-en; -en) *eccl.* dean
de·chif·frie·ren [deʃɪ'fri:rən] *v/t.* (h) decipher, decode
Deck [dɛk] *n* (-[e]s; -s) ⚓ *etc.* deck; (*parking*) level; ***an*** (*or* ***auf***) ~ on deck; ***alle Mann an ~!*** all hands on deck!; ***unter ~*** below deck; **~adres·se** *f*, **~an·schrift** *f* cover address; **~an·strich** *m* top coat; **~auf·bau·ten** *pl.* ⚓ superstructure *sg.*; **~bett** *n* duvet, *Brit. a.* continental quilt; **~blatt** *n* **1.** wrapper; **2.** ⚘ bract; **3.** correction sheet; overlay
Decke ['dɛkə] (*sep.* -k·k-) *f* (-; -n) blanket; (bed)cover; tablecloth; ⚠ ceiling; surface (*a.* ⚙); lining; layer, coat; F *fig.* (***vor Freude***) (***bis***) ***an die ~ springen*** jump for joy; ***an die ~ gehen*** F hit the roof; ***sich nach der ~ strecken*** cut one's coat according to one's cloth; ***unter einer ~ stecken mit*** *dat.* be hand in glove (*or* be in league, F in cahoots) with
Deckel ['dɛkəl] (*sep.* -k·k-) *m* (-s; -) cover; lid (*a.* F *hat*), top; ⚘, *zo.* operculum; F ***eins auf den ~ kriegen*** F get a clip round the ears, get a real ticking-off
decken ['dɛkən] (*sep.* -k·k-) (h) **I.** *v/t.* **1.** cover; roof, tile, slate; ***den Tisch ~*** lay (*or* set) the table; ***es ist für vier Personen gedeckt*** the table's laid (*or* set) for four; **2.** put, spread (***über*** *acc.* over); **3.** shield, *a.* ⚔, *chess etc.*: cover, protect (*all a.* ***sich*** o.s.); **4.** cover up for; **5.** *sport*: mark, *esp. Am.* cover; *boxing*: guard (***sich*** o.s.); **6.** ☨ a) cover *costs etc.*, b) reimburse *expenses etc.*, c) meet *the demand etc.*, cover *check*, *damage etc.*; → ***Bedarf***; **7.** *zo.* cover; **II.** *v/i.* **8.** *paint etc.*: cover; **9.** *sport*: mark, *esp. Am.* cover; *boxing*: cover (up); **III.** *v/refl.*: ***sich ~*** **10.** → **3, 5**; **11.** *figures, statements etc.*: correspond, tally; be identical; **12.** ⩚ coincide, be congruent
'Decken|bal·ken (*sep.* -k·k-) *m* ceiling beam; **~be·leuch·tung** *f* ceiling lamp(s *pl.*); **~ge·mäl·de** *n* ceiling fresco; **~lampe** *f*, **~leuch·te** *f* ceiling lamp
'Deck|far·be *f* body colo(u)r; **~man·tel** *m* cover; ***unter dem ~*** *gen.* under the cloak of; **~na·me** *m* alias; pseudonym, pen name, nom de plume; code name; **~pas·sa͵gier** *m* deck passenger; **~plat·te** *f* cover plate; covering slab
Deckung ['dɛkʊŋ] (*sep.* -k·k) *f* (-; -en) **1.** covering; *a.* ⚔ cover, shelter; camouflage; *sport*: a) marking, *Am.* covering, b) defen|ce (*Am.* -se); *boxing*: guard; *chess etc.*: cover, guard; ***in ~ gehen*** take cover (***vor*** *dat.* from); ⚔ (***in*** *or* ***volle***) ***~!*** take cover!; **2.** ☨ cover; reimbursement; payment; security; backing; funds *pl.*; ***zur ~ der Nachfrage*** (***Unkosten***) to meet the demand (to cover the costs); **3.** correspondence; **4.** ⩚ coincidence, congruence
'Deckungs·feh·ler *m sport*: case of bad marking (*esp. Am.* covering)
'deckungs·gleich *adj.* **1.** identical; **2.** ⩚

congruent; '**Deckungs·gleich·heit** *f a.* ⚘ congruence
'**Deckungs|ka·pi,tal** *n* covering funds *pl.*; **~klau·sel** *f* cover clause
'**deckungs·los** *adj.* uncovered; **~*es Gelände*** open ground
'**Deckungs|loch** F *n*, **~lücke** F *f* hole in the budget; **~mit·tel** *pl.* covering funds; **~spie·ler** *m sport*: defender; **~sum·me** *f* sum insured
'**Deck|weiß** *n* whitener; **~wort** *n* code word
De·duk·ti·on [dedʊk'tsĭo:n] *f* (-; -en) deduction; **de·duk·tiv** [dedʊk'ti:f] *adj.* deductive; **de·du·zie·ren** [dedu'tsi:rən] *v/t.* (h) deduce (**aus** *dat.* from)
de facto [de: 'fakto] *adv.* de facto; **De-'fac·to-...** de facto ...
De·fä·tis·mus [defɛ'tɪsmʊs] *m* (-; *no pl.*) defeatism; **De·fä·tist** [defɛ'tɪst] *m* (-en; -en), **de·fä·ti·stisch** [defɛ'tɪstɪʃ] *adj.* defeatist
de·fekt [de'fɛkt] **I.** *adj.* faulty; damaged; **II.** ≈ *m* (-[e]s; -e) fault; *psych.*, ⚕ defect, deficiency; ***e-n ~ haben*** ⚙ be faulty
de·fen·siv [defɛn'zi:f] **I.** *adj.* defensive; **II.** *adv.*: ***sich ~ verhalten*** be on the defensive; **De·fen'siv·bünd·nis** *n* defen|ce (*Am.* -se) alliance; **De·fen·si·ve** [defɛn-'zi:və] *f* (-; -n) defensive; ***in der ~*** on the defensive; ***in die ~ drängen*** force onto the defensive; **De·fen'siv·krieg** *m* defensive war(fare); **De·fen'siv·spiel** *n sport*: defensive play
De·fi·bril·la·tor [defibrɪ'la:to:ɐ] *m* (-s; -en [-la'to:rən]) ⚕ defibrillator
de·fi·lie·ren [defi'li:rən] *v/i.* (h *and* sn) march past
de·fi·nie·ren [defi'ni:rən] *v/t.* (h) define; ***neu ~*** redefine; **De·fi·ni·ti·on** [defini-'tsĭo:n] *f* (-; -en) definition; **de·fi·ni·tiv** [defini'ti:f] **I.** *adj.* definite, positive; definitive, final; **II.** *adv.*: ***et. ~ entscheiden*** make a final decision on s.th.; ***~ feststehen*** be absolutely final; ***das kann ich Ihnen ~ sagen*** I can tell you that for certain; ***~ zusagen*** give one's word
De·fi·zit ['de:fitsɪt] *n* (-s; -e) ✝ deficit; **de·fi·zi·tär** [defitsi'tɛ:ɐ] *adj.* in deficit, deficit *budget etc.*; '**De·fi·zit·fi·nan,zie·rung** *f* deficit spending
De·fla·ti·on [defla'tsĭo:n] *f* (-; -en) deflation; **de·fla·tio·när** [deflatsĭo'nɛ:ɐ] *adj.*, **de·fla·tio·ni·stisch** [deflatsĭo'nɪstɪʃ] *adj.* deflationary; **De·fla·ti'ons·po·li,tik** *f* deflationary policy; **de·fla·to·risch** [defla'to:rɪʃ] *adj.* deflationary
De·flo·ra·ti·on [deflora'tsĭo:n] *f* (-; -en) defloration; **de·flo·rie·ren** [deflo'ri:rən] *v/t.* (h) deflower
De·for·ma·ti·on [defɔrma'tsĭo:n] *f* (-; -en) deformity; **de·for·mie·ren** [defɔr'mi:rən] *v/t.* (h) deform
def·tig ['dɛftɪç] *adj.* coarse *joke etc.*, near the knuckle; solid *food*, *material etc.*; sharp *blow etc.*; steep *prices*
De·gen ['de:gən] *m* (-s; -) sword, *fencing*: épée
De·ge·ne·ra·ti·on [degenera'tsĭo:n] *f* (-; -en) degeneration; **de·ge·ne·rie·ren** [degene'ri:rən] *v/i.* (sn) degenerate (**zu** *dat.* into); **de·ge·ne·riert** [degene'ri:ɐt] *adj.* degenerate; effete
'**De·gen|fech·ten** *n* épée fencing; **~fech·ter** *m* épéeist
de·gra·die·ren [degra'di:rən] *v/t.* (h) ⚔ demote (**zu** *dat.* to the rank of); *fig.* degrade (**zu** *dat.* to); **De·gra'die·rung** *f* (-; -en) demotion; *fig.* degradation
dehn·bar ['de:nba:ɐ] *adj.* flexible, elastic; *phys.* expansible; malleable; *fig.* **~*er Begriff*** *etc.* elastic term *etc.*; ***der Vokal ist ~*** can be lengthened; '**Dehn·bar·keit** *f* (-; *no pl.*) elasticity; expansibility; malleability; **deh·nen** ['de:nən] (h) **I.** *v/t.* stretch (*a. fig.*); lengthen *vowel*; drawl *word*; hold *a note*; *Gespräch etc.* ***in die Länge ~*** spin out, drag out; → ***gedehnt*** II; **II.** *v/refl.*: ***sich ~*** stretch (o.s.); *clothing*: stretch; *phys.* expand; *geogr.* extend, stretch out; ***sich in die Länge ~*** *conversation etc.*: drag on; '**Deh·nung** *f* (-; -en) stretch(ing); *phys.* expansion; *ling.* lengthening
de·hy·drie·ren [dehy'dri:rən] *v/t.* (h) ⚗ dehydrate; **De·hy'drie·rung** *f* (-; -en) dehydration
Deich [daɪç] *m* (-[e]s; -e) dike; embankment, *Am.* levee; **~bruch** *m* a) bursting of a dike, b) breach in a dike
Deich·sel ['daɪksəl] *f* (-; -n) pole; thills *pl.*; drawbar; '**deich·seln** F *v/t.* (h) manage; ***ich werde das schon ~*** I'll see to it all right (*Am.* alright), F I'll wangle it somehow
dein [daɪn] **I.** *poss. pron.* **1.** *adj.* your; ***e-s ~er Bücher*** one of your books; ***e-r ~er Freunde*** a friend of yours, one of your friends; **2.** *su.* yours; ***~er, ~e, ~(e)s, der (die, das) ~(ig)e*** yours; **II.** *pers. pron.* (*gen. of du*) of you; ***ich werde ~(er) gedenken*** I shall remember you
dei·ner ['daɪnɐ] → ***dein*** II
dei·ner·seits ['daɪnɐzaɪts] *adv.* for (*or* on) your part
dei·nes·glei·chen ['daɪnəs'glaɪçən] *pron.* people like yourself; *contp.* the likes of you, your sort
dei·net|hal·ben ['daɪnət'halbən] *obs. adv.* → **~we·gen** *adv.* **1.** a) because of you, on your account; b) because of you, for your sake; **2.** on your behalf; **~wil·len** *adv.*: (**um**) ~ a) for your sake; b) on your behalf
dei·ni·ge ['daɪnɪgə] → ***dein*** 2
De·is·mus [de'ɪsmʊs] *m* (-; *no pl.*) deism; **dei·stisch** [de'ɪstɪʃ] *adj.* deistic
Dé·jà-vu-Er·leb·nis [deʒa'vy:-] *n psych.* déjà vu
de ju·re [de 'ju:rə] *adv.* de jure; **De-'ju·re-...** de jure ...
De·ka·de [de'ka:də] *f* (-; -n) (period of) ten days (*or* ten weeks, ten months) *pl.*; decade
de·ka·dent [deka'dɛnt] *adj.* decadent; **De·ka·denz** [deka'dɛnts] *f* (-; *no pl.*) decadence; **De·ka'denz·er·schei·nung** *f* sign of decadence
De·kan [de'ka:n] *m* (-s; -e) *univ. and R.C.* dean; *Protestant*: superintendent; **De·ka·nat** [deka'na:t] *n* (-s; -e) **1.** *univ.* dean's office; **2.** *R.C.* deanery; *Protestant*: superintendent's district
de·kan·tie·ren [dekan'ti:rən] *v/t.* (h) ⚗ decant *a. wine*
De·kla·ma·ti·on [deklama'tsĭo:n] *f* (-; -en) declamation; *fig. a.* harangue; **De·kla·ma·tor** [dekla'ma:to:ɐ] *m* (-s; -en [-ma'to:rən]) declaimer; **de·kla·ma·to·risch** [deklama'to:rɪʃ] *adj.* declamatory; **de·kla·mie·ren** [dekla'mi:rən] *v/t. and v/i.* (h) declaim, F spout
De·kla·ra·ti·on [deklara'tsĭo:n] *f* (-; -en) declaration; **de·kla·rie·ren** [dekla'ri:rən] *v/t.* (h) declare
de·klas·sie·ren [dekla'si:rən] *v/t.* (h) degrade (**zu** *dat.* to); *sport*: outclass
De·kli·na·ti·on [deklina'tsĭo:n] *f* (-; -en) *ling.* declension; *ast.*, *phys.* declination; **de·kli·nier·bar** [dekli'ni:ɐba:ɐ] *adj.* declinable; **de·kli·nie·ren** [dekli'ni:rən] *v/t.* (h) decline
De·kol·le·té [dekɔl'te:] *n* (-s; -s) low neckline; ***tiefes ~*** plunging neckline; **de·kol·le·tiert** [dekɔl'ti:ɐt] *adj.* low-cut, décolleté; ***tief ~*** very low-cut, F *hum.* rather revealing
De·kor [de'ko:ɐ] *m*, *n* (-s; -s, -e [de'ko:rə]) decoration; *thea.* décor, scenery, set; **De·ko·ra·teur** [dekora'tø:ɐ] *m* (-s; -e [-'tø:rə]) (painter and) decorator; window dresser; *thea.* a) scene painter, b) set designer; **De·ko·ra·ti·on** [dekora'tsĭo:n] *f* (-; -en) decoration; window display; *thea.* set(s *pl.*); **de·ko·ra·tiv** [dekora'ti:f] *adj.* decorative; **de·ko·rie·ren** [deko'ri:rən] *v/t.* (h) decorate; dress *shop window*
De·kret [de'kre:t] *n* (-[e]s; -e) decree
De·le·ga·ti·on [delega'tsĭo:n] *f* (-; -en) delegation
De·le·ga·ti'ons|chef *m* head of the *or* a delegation; **~mit·glied** *n* member of the *or* a delegation
de·le·gie·ren [dele'gi:rən] *v/t.* (h) delegate; **De·le·gier·te** [dele'gi:ɐtə] *m*, *f* (-n; -n) delegate
de·li·kat [deli'ka:t] *adj.* **1.** delicious, exquisite; **2.** delicate, ticklish; **3.** tactful, discreet; **De·li·ka·tes·se** [delika'tɛsə] *f* (-; -n) **1.** delicacy; **2.** tact(fulness), discretion; **De·li·ka'tes·sen·la·den** *m* delicatessen, F deli
De·likt [de'lɪkt] *n* offen|ce (*Am.* -se)
De·lin·quent [delɪŋ'kvɛnt] *m* (-en; -en) offender
De·li·ri·um [de'li:rĭʊm] *n* (-s; -en [-'li:rĭən]) delirium; ***im ~ liegen*** (***or sein***) be delirious; ***~ tremens*** delirium tremens, DT's
Del·le ['dɛlə] *f* (-; -n) **1.** dent; **2.** *geogr.* depression
Del·phin¹ [dɛl'fi:n] *m* (-s; -e) *zo.* dolphin
Del'phin² *n sport* → **~schwim·men** *n*, **~stil** *m* butterfly (stroke)
Del·ta ['dɛlta] *n* (-s; -s, Delten) *geogr.* delta; **~flü·gel** *m* delta wing; **~mus·kel** *m anat.* deltoid (muscle)
dem [de:m] *art.* (*dat. sg. of der, das*) to *the*; *rel. pron.*: to whom, to which; ***an ~ und ~ Ort*** at such and such a place; ***nach ~, was ich gehört habe*** from what I've heard; ***wenn ~ so ist*** if that is the case; ***wie ~ auch sei*** be that as it may
Dem·ago·ge [dema'go:gə] *m* (-n; -n) demagogue; **Dem·ago·gie** [demago'gi:] *f* (-; -n) demagogy; **dem·ago·gisch** [dema'go:gɪʃ] *adj.* demagogic(ally *adv.*)
De·mar·ka·ti·ons·li·nie [demarka'tsĭo:ns-] *f* demarcation line
de·mas·kie·ren [demas'ki:rən] (h) **I.** *v/t.* unmask; *fig. a.* expose; *fig.* ***~ als*** expose as; **II.** *v/refl.*: ***sich ~*** unmask o.s.; *fig. a.* drop one's mask, reveal one's true identity
De·men·ti [de'mɛnti] *n* (-s; -s) (official) denial, disclaimer; **de·men·tie·ren** [demɛn'ti:rən] *v/t.* (h) deny, disclaim
'**dem·ent·spre·chend** **I.** *adj.* corresponding; *pred.* as expected; **II.** *adv.* accordingly
'**dem·ge·gen,über** *adv.* **1.** compared with this; **2.** on the other hand
'**dem·ge·mäß** *adj. and adv.* → ***dementsprechend***
de·mi·li·ta·ri·sie·ren [demilitari'zi:rən]

v/t. (h) demilitarize; **De·mi·li·ta·ri'sie·rung** *f* (-; -en) demilitarization

De·mis·si·on [demɪ'sĭo:n] *f* (-; -en) resignation; ***s-e ~ einreichen*** hand in one's resignation

'dem'nach *adv.* **1.** thus, so; **2.** according to that

'dem'nächst *adv.* soon, before long; ***~ stattfindend*** *etc.* forthcoming; ***~ im Kino*** *etc.* coming shortly (*or* soon)

De·mo ['de:mo] F *f* (-; -s) F demo

de·mo·bi·li·sie·ren [demobili'zi:rən] *v/t. and v/i.* (h) demobilize; **De·mo·bi·li'sie·rung** *f* (-; -en) demobilization

'De·mo|cas͵set·te *f* demonstration cassette, F demo tape; **~dis͵ket·te** *f computer*: demonstration diskette, F demo disk

De·mo·du·la·ti·on [demodula'tsĭo:n] *f* (-; -en) ⚡ demodulation; **De·mo·du·la·tor** [demodu'la:to:ɐ] *m* (-s; -en [-la'to:rən]) demodulator; **de·mo·du·lie·ren** [demodu'li:rən] *v/t.* (h) demodulate

De·mo·graph [demo'gra:f] *m* (-en; -en) demographer; **De·mo·gra·phie** [demogra'fi:] *f* (-; -n) demography; **de·mo·gra·phisch** [demo'gra:fɪʃ] *adj.* demographic(ally *adv.*), population ...

De·mo·krat [demo'kra:t] *m* (-en; -en) democrat; **De·mo·kra·tie** [demokra'ti:] *f* (-; -n) democracy; **de·mo·kra·tisch** [demo'kra:tɪʃ] *adj.* democratic(ally *adv.*); **de·mo·kra·ti·sie·ren** [demokrati'zi:rən] *v/t.* (h) democratize; **De·mo·kra·ti'sie·rung** *f* (-; -en) democratization; **De·mo·kra·ti'sie·rungs·pro͵zeß** *m* process of democratization, democratic process

de·mo·lie·ren [demo'li:rən] *v/t.* (h) damage; wreck (*a.* F *car etc.*), vandalize

De·mon·strant [demɔn'strant] *m* (-en; -en) demonstrator

De·mon·stra·ti·on [demɔnstra'tsĭo:n] *f* (-; -en) **1.** demonstration; **2.** demonstration, show; **3.** demonstration; ***zur ~*** *gen.* to demonstrate (*or* illustrate) *s.th.*

De·mon·stra·ti'ons|flug *m* demonstration flight; **~recht** *n* right to demonstrate; **~ver·bot** *n* ban on demonstrations; **~zug** *m* **1.** demonstrators *pl.*; **2.** demonstration, protest march

de·mon·stra·tiv [demɔnstra'ti:f] **I.** *adj.* **1.** graphic; **2.** ostentatious; pointed; **3.** *ling.* demonstrative; **II.** *adv.* ostentatiously; in protest; ***~ den Saal verlassen*** walk out (in protest)

de·mon·strie·ren [demɔn'stri:rən] *v/t. and v/i.* (h) demonstrate

De·mon·ta·ge [demɔn'ta:ʒə] *f* (-; -n) dismantling; **de·mon·tie·ren** [demɔn'ti:rən] *v/t.* (h) dismantle; take apart; *fig.* break down; chip away at *s.o.'s reputation etc.*

de·mo·ra·li·sie·ren [demorali'zi:rən] *v/t.* (h) demoralize; **De·mo·ra·li'sie·rung** *f* (-; -en) demoralization

De·mo·sko·pie [demosko'pi:] *f* (-; -n) public opinion research; **de·mo·sko·pisch** [demo'sko:pɪʃ] *adj.*: ***~e Umfrage*** (public) opinion poll; ***~es Institut*** public opinion research institute

de·mo·ti·vie·ren [demoti'vi:rən] (h) **I.** *v/t.* put *s.o.* off, demotivate; **II.** *v/i.*: ***zuviel Schreibarbeit demotiviert*** too much paperwork really puts you off

De·mut ['de:mu:t] *f* (-; *no pl.*) humility; **de·mü·tig** ['de:my:tɪç] *adj.* humble; submissive; **de·mü·ti·gen** ['de:my:tɪgən] (h) **I.** *v/t.* humiliate; **II.** *v/refl.*: ***sich ~*** humble o.s.; grovel; **'de·mü·ti·gend** *adj.* humiliating; **De·mü·ti·gung** ['de:my:tɪgʊŋ] *f* (-; -en) humiliation; **'de·muts·voll** *adv.* → ***demütig***

dem·zu·fol·ge ['de:mtsu'fɔlgə] *adv.* **1.** accordingly; **2.** consequently

den [de:n] → ***der***

de·na·tu·rie·ren [denatu'ri:rən] (h) **I.** *v/t.* denature; **II.** *v/i.* degenerate (**zu** *dat.* into)

de·nen ['de:nən] → ***der***

Denk|an·satz ['dɛŋk-] *m* approach; **~an·stoß** *m*: ***ein ~*** cause (*or* food) for thought; ***j-m e-n ~ geben*** *a.* set s.o. thinking; ***das war für mich der ~*** that was what gave me the idea; **~ar·beit** *f* mental effort; **~art** *f* way of thinking; mentality; **~auf·ga·be** *f* brainteaser

denk·bar ['dɛŋkba:ɐ] **I.** *adj.* conceivable, possible; **II.** *adv.*: ***in der ~ kürzesten Zeit*** in the shortest possible time; ***das ist ~ einfach*** it's the easiest thing in the world

den·ken ['dɛŋkən] **I.** *v/t. and v/i.* (dachte, gedacht, h) think; reflect; reason; imagine; ***sich*** *et.* ***~*** imagine; ***~ an*** *acc.* a) think of, b) remember, c) have in mind, think of; ***ans Heiraten ~*** think of marrying; ***es gibt e-m zu ~*** it makes you think; ***~ Sie nur!*** just imagine!; ***ich denke schon*** I (should) think so; ***ich dachte schon!*** I was going to say; ***ich dachte schon, du wolltest nicht mitkommen*** I was beginning to think (*or* for a minute I thought) you didn't want to come; ***wer hätte das gedacht!*** who would have thought it; ***das habe ich mir gedacht*** I thought as much; ***das hätte ich von ihr gar nicht gedacht*** I didn't think (*or* wouldn't have thought) she was capable; ***das hast du dir so gedacht!*** → ***denkste*** 1; ***das kann ich mir ~*** I can well imagine; ***das hättest du dir ~ können*** you should have known that; ***ich denke nicht daran!*** I wouldn't dream of it; ***er denkt daran zu*** *inf.* he's thinking of *ger.*; ***er denkt gar nicht daran zu*** *inf.* he has no intention of *ger.*; ***denk daran!*** don't forget!; ***es war für dich gedacht*** it was meant for you; ***~ über*** *acc.* think about; ***wie denkst du darüber?*** what do you think about (*or* of) it?, how do you see it?; ***wo ~ Sie hin?*** what are you thinking of?; ***solange ich ~ kann*** as long as I can remember; F ***den Wein mußt du dir ~*** you'll just have to imagine (*or* pretend) there's wine; → ***dabei*** 8; **II.** ℒ *n* (-s) thinking, thought; reasoning; way of thinking; F ***das ~ soll man den Pferden überlassen*** F don't think too hard, you might hurt yourself (*or* pull a muscle); **'den·kend** *adj.* thinking; rational

Den·ker ['dɛŋkɐ] *m* (-s; -) thinker; ***großer ~*** great thinker (*or* mind); **den·ke·risch** ['dɛŋkərɪʃ] *adj.* intellectual; **'Den·ker·stirn** *f* lofty brow

'denk·fä·hig *adj.* intelligent, rational, capable of (logical *or* rational) thinking; **'Denk·fä·hig·keit** *f* (-; *no pl.*) intelligence, mental capabilities *pl.*

'denk·faul *adj.* mentally lazy; ***~ sein*** have a lazy brain

'Denk|feh·ler *m* logical flaw, mistake in one's reasoning; ***das war dein ~*** that's where you went wrong; **~ge·wohn·heit** *f* (habitual) way of thinking; **~hil·fe** *f* clue

Denk·mal ['dɛŋkma:l] *n* (-s; -mäler [-mɛ:lɐ]) monument (*gen.* to); memorial (to); statue (of); ***j-m ein ~ setzen*** put up (*fig.* create) a monument to s.o.; *fig.* ***sich ein ~ setzen*** F do one's bit for posterity; **~pfle·ge** *f* preservation of historic buildings and monuments; **~schutz** *m* protection of historic buildings and monuments; ***unter ~ stehen*** *building*: be listed, *monument*: be scheduled, *tree etc.*: be protected; ***unter ~ stellen*** put a preservation order on, *a.* list *a building*, *a.* schedule *a monument*; **~schüt·zer** *m* preservationist

'Denk|mo͵dell *n* working model; **~mu·ster** *n* thought pattern; **~pau·se** *f* pause for reflection; **~pro͵zeß** *m* thought process; **~rich·tung** *f* line of thought (*or* thinking), school of thought; **~scha͵blo·ne** *f s.o.'s* way of thinking; **~schrift** *f* memorandum; **~sport** *m* brainteaser(s *pl.*); **~spruch** *m* **1.** maxim; **2.** aphorism

denk·ste ['dɛŋkstə] F *int.* **1.** that's what you think; **2.** F no way!; **3.** no such luck

'Denk·übung *f* brainteaser, logic problem

'Den·kungs·art *f* → ***Denkart***

'Denk|ver·mö·gen *n* intellectual capacity; **~wei·se** *f* → ***Denkart***

'denk·wür·dig *adj.* memorable (***wegen*** *gen.* for); ***ein ~er Tag*** *a.* a day to be remembered

'Denk·zet·tel *fig. m* lesson; ***j-m e-n ~ geben*** (*or* ***verpassen***) teach s.o. a lesson; ***das wird für ihn auf lange Sicht ein ~ sein*** that's something he won't forget about in a hurry

denn [dɛn] **I.** *cj.* **1.** because; since; **2.** than; ***mehr ~ je*** more than ever; **3. *es sei ~*** unless; **II.** *adv.* ***was sollen wir ~ machen?*** what are we supposed to do then?; ***wo ~?*** where?; ***wo war es ~?*** where was it (then)?; ***ist er ~ so arm?*** is he really that poor?; ***was ~?*** what?; ***wieso ~?*** why?; ***was ist ~?*** what's up?, what (is it)?; ***wo bleibt er ~ nur?*** where on earth is he?

den·noch ['dɛnɔx] *adv. and cj.* (yet ...) still, nevertheless; ***er wollte es ~ machen*** (yet) he still wanted to do it, he wanted to do it nevertheless

Den·si·tät [dɛnzi'tɛ:t] *f* (-; *no pl.*) *phys.* density

den·tal [dɛn'ta:l] **I.** *adj.* dental; **II.** ℒ *m* (-s; -e) → **ℒlaut** *m ling.* dental

de·nu·klea·ri·sie·ren [denukleari'zi:rən] *v/t.* denuclearize; **De·nu·klea·ri'sie·rung** *f* (-; -en) denuclearization

De·nun·zi·ant [denʊn'tsĭant] *m* (-en; -en) informer; **de·nun·zie·ren** [denʊn'tsi:rən] *v/t.* (h) inform on; ***j-n bei der Polizei ~*** *a.* report s.o. to the police

De·odo·rant [deˀodo'rant] *n* (-s; -s) deodorant

Deo|rol·ler ['de:o-] *m* roll-on (deodorant); **~spray** *m, n* deodorant spray

De·pen·dance [depɑ̃'dɑ̃:s] *f* (-; -n) **1.** ✝ branch; **2.** △ annex(e)

De·pi·la·ti·on [depila'tsĭo:n] *f* (-; -en) ✱ depilation; **de·pi·lie·ren** [depi'li:rən] *v/t.* (h) depilate

de·pla·ciert [depla'si:ɐt] *adj.* out of place, *a.* misplaced *remark etc.*

De·po·nie [depo'ni:] *f* (-; -n) **1.** refuse tip, waste disposal site, landfill site; **2. *wilde ~*** uncontrolled (*or* indiscriminate) dumping; **3.** *fig.* dumping ground; **de·po·nie·ren** [depo'ni:rən] *v/t.* (h) deposit, leave

De·por·ta·ti·on [depɔrta'tsĭo:n] *f* (-; -en) deportation; **de·por·tie·ren** [depɔr'ti:rən] *v/t.* (h) deport; **De·por·tier·te** [depɔr'ti:ɐtə] *m, f* (-n; -n) deported person, deportee

De·po·si·ten [depo'zi:tən] *pl.* ✝ deposits; **~bank** *f* (-; -en) deposit bank; **~gel·der** *pl.* deposits; **~ge·schäft** *n* deposit banking; **~kon·to** *n* deposit account

De·pot [de'po:] *n* (-s; -s) depot (*a.* ⚔ *and* 💉); ✝ deposit; securities account; warehouse; **~bi·blio͵thek** *f* deposit library; **~ef͵fekt** *m pharm.* controlled sustained release; **~prä·pa͵rat** *n pharm.* depot preparation; **~schein** *m* ✝ deposit receipt; **~wir·kung** *f* → ***Depoteffekt***

Depp [dɛp] *m* (-en; -en) idiot, F twit

De·pres·si·on [deprɛ'sĭo:n] *f* (-; -en) depression; ***an*** (*or* ***unter***) ***~en leiden*** suffer from depression(s); **de·pres·siv** [deprɛ'si:f] *adj.*: ***in e-r ~en Stimmung sein*** be depressed; ***~ sein*** a) suffer from depression, be depressive, b) be depressed

de·pri·mie·ren [depri'mi:rən] *v/t.* (h) get *s.o.* down, depress; **de·pri'mie·rend** *adj.* depressing; ***es ist ~*** *a.* it gets you down; **de·pri·miert** [depri'mi:ɐt] *adj.* down in the dumps, depressed

De·pri·va·ti·on [depriva'tsĭo:n] *f* (-; -en) *psych.* deprivation

De·pu·tat [depu'ta:t] *n* (-[e]s; -e) **1.** ✝ payment in kind; **2.** *ped.* teaching load

De·pu·ta·ti·on [deputa'tsĭo:n] *f* (-; -en) delegation; **de·pu·tie·ren** [depu'ti:rən] *v/t.* (h) delegate; **De·pu·tier·te** [depu'ti:ɐtə] *m, f* (-n; -n) delegate

der [de:ɐ] *m*, **die** [di:] *f*, **das** [das] *n*, **die** *pl.* **I.** *art.* the; ***der arme Peter*** poor Peter; ***die Königin Elisabeth*** Queen Elizabeth; ***der Hyde Park*** Hyde Park; ***die Chemie*** chemistry; ***das Fernsehen*** television; ***ich wusch mir das Gesicht*** I washed my face; ***zwei Dollar das Kilo*** two dollars a kilo; **II.** *dem. pron.* that (one), this (one); he, she, it; *pl.* these, those, they, them; ***der Mann hier*** this man; ***der*** (*or* ***die***) ***mit der Brille*** the one with the glasses; ***nimm den hier*** take this one; ***sind das Ihre Bücher?*** are those your books?; ***das, was er sagt*** what he says; ***das waren Chinesen*** they were Chinese; ***zu der und der Zeit*** at such and such a time; ***der und baden gehen?*** you won't catch him going swimming; **III.** *rel. pron.* who, which, that; ***das Mädchen, mit dem*** (***mit dessen Vater***) ***ich sprach*** the girl (whose father) I spoke to; ***das Material, dessen Eigenschaften ...*** the material, whose properties (*or* the properties of which) ...; ***der Bezirk, der e-n Teil von X bildet*** the district forming part of X; ***er war der erste, der es erfuhr*** he was the first to know; ***jeder, der ...*** anyone who ...

de·ran·giert [derã'ʒi:ɐt] *adj.* untidy, *a.* dishevel(l)ed, mussed up

der·art ['de:ɐ'ʔa:ɐt] *adv.* so, ... like that, so much, to such an extent; ***er hat ~ geschrien, daß*** he screamed so much (*or* loud) that; ***die Folgen waren ~, daß*** the consequences were such that; **der·ar·tig** ['de:ɐ'ʔa:ɐtɪç] **I.** *adj.* such; ***e-e ~e Politik*** such a policy, a policy such as this; ***ein ~er Fehler*** a mistake like that; ***es war e-e ~e Kälte*** it was so cold; **II.** *adv.* → ***derart***

derb [dɛrp] *adj.* rough, coarse (*a. fig. language etc.*); tough; *fig.* earthy; crude *joke etc.*; **'Derb·heit** *f* (-; -en) **1.** *no pl.* coarse behavio(u)r; **2.** ***~en*** a) crude jokes, b) crude remarks

der·einst ['de:ɐ'ʔaɪnst] *adv.* some day, one day

de·re(n)t·we·gen ['de:rə(n)t've:gən] *adv.* for her (*or* their) sake; ***die Frau, ~ er s-e Frau verließ*** the woman for whom he left his wife; ***die Couch, ~ er gekommen war*** the settee for which he had come

de·re(n)t·wil·len ['de:rə(n)t'vɪlən] *adv.*: (***um***) ***~*** → ***dere(n)twegen***

'der·ge·stalt *adv.* a) in such a way, b) to such an extent; ***~ bewaffnet*** *etc.* thus armed *etc.*

'der'glei·chen *pron. and adj.* such, like that, of that kind; *su.* the like, such a thing, something like that; ***nichts ~*** no such thing, nothing of the kind; ***und ~*** (***mehr***), ***u. dgl.*** and the like, and so forth; ***er tat nicht ~*** he just didn't react

De·ri·vat [deri'va:t] *n* (-[e]s; -e) ⚗, *ling.* derivative

'der-, 'die-, 'das·je·ni·ge [-je:nɪgə] *dem. pron.* the one; that one; ***derjenige, der*** (*or* ***welcher***), ***diejenige, die*** (*or* ***welche***) the one who; ***diejenigen, die*** (*or* ***welche***) those who; the ones who

der·lei ['de:ɐ'laɪ] *pron. and adj.* → ***dergleichen***

der·ma·ßen ['de:ɐ'ma:sən] *adv.* → ***derart***

Der·ma·to·lo·ge [dɛrmato'lo:gə] *m* (-n; -n) dermatologist, skin specialist; **Der·ma·to·lo·gie** [dɛrmatolo'gi:] *f* (-; *no pl.*) dermatology; **der·ma·to·lo·gisch** [dɛrmato'lo:gɪʃ] *adj.* dermatological

der-, die-, das·sel·be [-'zɛlbə] *dem. pron.* the same; ***derselbe, dieselbe*** the same person; ***ein und dieselbe Person*** one and the same person; ***ziemlich dasselbe*** much the same (thing); ***auf dieselbe Weise wie*** the same (way) as; ***jedesmal dasselbe!*** it's the same (old) thing every time; ***dasselbe nochmal!*** (the) same again, please; ***es kommt auf dasselbe heraus*** it comes to the same thing

der·weil ['de:ɐ'vaɪl] **I.** *cj.* while, whilst; **II.** *adv.* meanwhile

Der·wisch ['dɛrvɪʃ] *m* (-[e]s; -e): (***tanzender ~*** whirling) dervish

der·zeit ['de:ɐ'tsaɪt] *adv.* at present, at the moment; **der·zei·tig** ['de:ɐ'tsaɪtɪç] *adj.* **1.** present, current; **2.** then, ... at the time

Des [dɛs] *n* (-; -) ♪ D flat

des·ak·ti'vie·ren [dɛs-] *v/t.* (h) ⚗ inactivate

De·sa·ster [de'zastɐ] *n* (-s; -) disaster; ***mit e-m ~ enden*** end disastrously (*or* in disaster)

de·sen·si·bi·li'sie·ren [de-] *v/t.* (h) 💉, *phot.* desensitize (***gegenüber*** *dat.* to); harden *s.o.* (to); **De·sen·si·bi·li'sie·rung** *f* (-; -en) desensitization

De·ser·teur [dezɛr'tø:ɐ] *m* (-s; -e [-'tø:rə]) deserter; **de·ser·tie·ren** [dezɛr'ti:rən] *v/i.* (sn) desert (***von*** *dat.* from); ***zum Feind ~*** run over to the enemy

des·glei·chen ['dɛs'glaɪçən] **I.** *pron.* likewise, the same; *ich stand auf* ***und mein Freund tat ~*** and so did my friend; **II.** *cj.* likewise, similarly

des·halb ['dɛs'halp] *adv. and cj.* that's why, so, *formal*: therefore; ***~ mußt du nicht gleich weinen*** there's no need to cry; ***die Lage ist ~ nicht besser*** that doesn't mean to say things have improved; ***er ist ~ keineswegs gesünder*** he isn't any the healthier for it; ***~, weil*** because; ***er tat es gerade ~*** that's precisely why he did it; ***ich tue es schon ~ nicht, weil*** I'm not going to do it for the simple reason that

De·sign [di'zaɪn] *n* (-s; -s) design; **De·si·gner** [di'zaɪnɐ] *m* (-s; -) designer

de·si·gniert [dezɪ'gni:ɐt] *adj.* ... designate

des·il·lu·sio·nie·ren [dɛsʔɪluzĭo'ni:rən] *v/t.* (h) disillusion

Des·in·fek·ti·on [dɛsʔɪnfɛk'tsĭo:n] *f* (-; -en) disinfection; **Des·in·fek·ti'ons·mit·tel** *n* disinfectant; antiseptic; **des·in·fi·zie·ren** [dɛsʔɪnfi'tsi:rən] *v/t.* (h) disinfect; **des·in·fi'zie·rend** *adj.* disinfectant; ***e-e ~e Wirkung haben*** act as a disinfectant

Des·in·for·ma·ti·on [dɛsʔɪnfɔrma'tsĭo:n] *f* (-; -en) disinformation

Des·in·te·gra·ti·on [dɛsʔɪntegra'tsĭo:n] *f* (-; -en) disintegration

Des·in·ter·es·se [dɛsʔɪntə'rɛsə] *n* (-s; *no pl.*) indifference (***an*** *dat.* to, towards), apathy (towards); **des·in·ter·es·siert** ['dɛsʔɪntərɛ͵si:ɐt] *adj.* uninterested (***an*** *dat.* in), indifferent (to, towards)

de·skrip·tiv [deskrɪp'ti:f] *adj.* descriptive

Des·odo·rant [dɛsʔodo'rant] *n* (-s; -s) deodorant

de·so·lat [dezo'la:t] *adj.* wretched, desperate *state etc.*; pitiable *sight*

Des·or·ga·ni·sa·ti·on [dɛsʔorganiza'tsĭo:n] *f* (-; -en) **1.** breakdown of order; **2.** lack of organization; state of disarray; chaos

des·ori·en·tiert [dɛsʔorĭen'ti:ɐt] *adj.* disorient(at)ed; confused; ***er ist völlig ~*** *a.* he doesn't know where he's going; **Des·ori·en'tie·rung** *f* (-; *no pl.*) disorientation

de·spek·tier·lich [despɛk'ti:ɐlɪç] *adj.* disrespectful, contemptuous

de·spe·rat [dɛspe'ra:t] *adj.* desperate

Des·pot [dɛs'po:t] *m* (-en; -en) despot; **des·po·tisch** [dɛs'po:tɪʃ] *adj.* despotic(ally *adv.*); **Des·po·tis·mus** [dɛspo'tɪsmʊs] *m* (-; *no pl.*) despotism

des·sen ['dɛsən] **I.** *rel. pron.* whose; of which; **II.** *poss. pron.*: ***mein Bekannter und ~ Frau*** my friend and his wife; **III.** *dem. pron.*: ***~ bin ich sicher*** I'm absolutely certain about that; ***ist er sich ~ bewußt?*** is he aware of it?; **des·sent·we·gen** ['dɛsənt've:gən] *adv.* for his sake; ***das Mädchen, ~ er s-e Frau verließ*** the girl for whom he left his wife; ***der Stuhl, ~ er gekommen war*** the chair for which he had come; **des·sent·wil·len** ['dɛsənt'vɪlən] *adv.*: (***um***) ***~*** → ***dessentwegen***; **des·sen·un·ge·ach·tet** ['dɛsənʔʊngə'ʔaxtət] *cj.* notwithstanding (that), nevertheless, all the same

Des·sert [dɛ'se:ɐ] *n* (-s; -s) dessert; ***als*** (*or* ***zum***) ***~*** for dessert; **~löf·fel** *m* dessert-spoon; **~tel·ler** *m* dessert plate; **~wein** *m* dessert wine

Des·sin [dɛ'sɛ̃:] *n* (-s; -s) design, pattern

de·sta·bi·li·sie·ren [destabili'zi:rən] *v/t.* (h) destabilize; **De·sta·bi·li'sie·rung** *f* (-; -en) destabilization

De·stil·lat [dɛstɪ'la:t] *n* (-[e]s; -e) ⚗ distillate; **De·stil·la·ti·on** [dɛstɪla'tsĭo:n] *f* (-; -en) distillation; **de·stil·lie·ren** [dɛstɪ'li:rən] *v/t.* (h) distil(l); **De·stil·lier·kol·ben** [dɛstɪ'li:ɐ-] *m* distillation (*or* distilling) flask

de·sto ['dɛsto] *adv. and cj.* (all) the; **~ *besser*** a) so much the better, b) the better *he plays etc.*; **~ *weniger*** the less; ***je mehr, ~ besser*** the more the better
De·struk·ti·on [destrʊk'tsĭo:n] *f* (-; -en) destruction; **de·struk·tiv** [destrʊk'ti:f] *adj.* destructive
'des'we·gen *adv. and cj.* → ***deshalb***
De·tail [de'taɪ, de'ta:j] *n* (-s; -s) detail; ***die kleinen ~s*** the finer points, the fine details; ***ins ~ gehen*** go into detail; ***bis ins kleinste ~*** (down) to the last detail; → ***Teufel***; **~be·richt** *m* detailed report; **~fra·ge** *f* **1.** penetrating question; **2.** matter of detail; **~kennt·nis·se** *pl.* detailed knowledge *sg.*
de·tail·lie·ren [deta'ji:rən] *v/t.* (h) specify; ***kannst du es ein wenig ~?*** can you be more specific (*or* give some details)?; **de·tail·liert** [deta'ji:ɐt] *adj.* detailed
de'tail·reich *adj.* (very) detailed
De·tail|schil·de·rung *f* detailed account; **~zeich·nung** *f* detail drawing
De·tek·tei [detɛk'taɪ] *f* (-; -en) detective agency, private investigators *pl.*
De·tek·tiv [detɛk'ti:f] *m* (-s; -e [-ti:və]) (private) detective; **~bü·ro** *n* → ***Detektei***; **~ro·man** *m* detective story (*or* novel); *pl. coll. a.* detective fiction *sg.*
De·tek·tor [de'tɛktoɐ] *m* (-s; -en [-'to:rən]) *radio*: detector
De·to·na·ti·on [detona'tsĭo:n] *f* (-; -en) detonation
De·to·na·ti'ons|druck *m* force of the blast; **~wel·le** *f* blast
de·to·nie·ren [deto'ni:rən] *v/i.* (sn) detonate
Deut [dɔʏt] *m*: ***keinen ~ wert*** not worth a penny; ***er kümmerte sich keinen ~ darum*** he didn't care a hoot about it; (***um***) ***keinen ~ besser*** not the slightest bit better
'deut·bar *adj.* interpretable; explainable; ***es ist nicht anders ~*** it can't be explained (*or* interpreted) any other way
deu·teln ['dɔʏtəln] *v/i.* (h): ***daran gibt es nichts zu ~*** there are no two ways about it
deu·ten ['dɔʏtən] (h) **I.** *v/i.* **1.** (***mit dem Finger***) **~ *auf*** *acc.* point to, point at *s.o.*; **2.** *fig.* **~ *auf*** *acc.* point to, indicate, suggest; point to(wards); **II.** *v/t.* interpret; explain; ***falsch ~*** misinterpret
'deut·lich I. *adj.* clear, distinct; intelligible; legible; plain; blunt, plain(spoken); noticeable; **~*er Wink*** broad hint; ***et. ~ machen*** make s.th. clear (*or* plain) (*dat.* to), ***j-m***: *a.* explain s.th. to s.o., *w.s.* drive s.th. home to s.o.; ***sehr ~ werden*** not to pull any punches, ***j-m gegenüber***: F talk turkey with s.o.; ***muß ich noch ~er werden?*** am I making myself understood?; ***e-e ~e Sprache sprechen*** a) not to mince matters (*or* one's words), ***mit j-m***: F talk turkey with s.o., b) *fig.* speak volumes; **II.** *adv.*: **~ *besser*** much better; ***um es ganz ~ zu sagen*** to put it quite bluntly, not to put too fine a point on it; ***habe ich mich ~ genug ausgedrückt?*** have I made myself understood?; **'Deut·lich·keit** *f* (-; -en) **1.** *no pl.* clearness, distinctness *etc.*; → ***deutlich*** I; ***et. mit aller ~ sagen*** put s.th. quite bluntly; ***an ~ nichts zu wünschen übriglassen*** leave no room for doubt; **2.** ***j-m ein paar ~en sagen*** tell s.o. a few home truths
deutsch [dɔʏtʃ] **I.** *adj.* German; **~ *reden*** talk (in) German, *fig.* not to mince matters (*or* one's words); ***jetzt reden wir mal ~ miteinander*** it's about time we had a word with each other; **II. ≈** *n* (-en) German, the German language; *fig.* ***auf gut deutsch*** (***gesagt***) in plain English
'Deutsch·ame·ri·ka·ner *m*, **'deutsch·ame·ri·ka·nisch** *adj.* German-American
'deutsch-'deutsch *adj. hist.* German-German, East-West German
Deut·sche ['dɔʏtʃə] *m, f* (-n; -n) German; ***sie ist ~*** she's (a) German
'deutsch·feind·lich *adj.* anti-German
'Deutsch·land|bild *n* image of the Germans; **~fra·ge** *f hist.* German question; **~lied** *n* German national anthem
'deutsch·spra·chig [-ʃpra:xɪç] *adj.* **1.** German-language *magazine etc.*; ***die ~e Literatur*** German literature; **2.** → **'deutsch·spre·chend** *adj.* German-speaking
'deutsch·stäm·mig [-ʃtɛmɪç] *adj.* ethnic German, of German origin; **'Deutsch·stäm·mi·ge** [-ʃtɛmɪgə] *m, f* (-n; -n) ethnic German
'Deutsch·un·ter·richt *m* **1.** teaching of German; **2.** German lesson(s *pl.*) *or* class(es *pl.*)
Deu·tung ['dɔʏtʊŋ] *f* (-; -en) interpretation; explanation; ***falsche ~*** misinterpretation
De·vi·se [de'vi:zə] *f* (-; -n) motto; ***als oberste ~ gilt: Ruhe bewahren*** the most important thing is to keep calm
De'vi·sen *pl.* ✝ foreign exchange (*or* currency) *sg.*; **~ab·kom·men** *n* foreign exchange agreement; **~be·schrän·kun·gen** *pl.* foreign exchange restrictions; **~be·stim·mun·gen** *pl.* currency regulations; **~be·wirt·schaf·tung** *f* foreign exchange control; **~bör·se** *f* foreign exchange market; **~brin·ger** *m* currency (*or* foreign exchange) earner; **~ein·nah·men** *pl.* currency receipts; **~han·del** *m* foreign exchange trading; **~kon·trol·le** *f* (foreign) exchange control; **~kurs** *m* rate of exchange; **~mak·ler** *m* (foreign) exchange broker; **~markt** *m* (foreign) exchange market; **~po·li·tik** *f* foreign exchange policy; **~schmug·gel** *m* currency smuggling; **~sper·re** *f* exchange embargo; **~ver·kehr** *m* foreign exchange transactions *pl.*
de·vot [de'vo:t] *contp. adj.* servile
De·zem·ber [de'tsɛmbɐ] *m* (-[s]; -) December; ***im ~*** in December
de·zent [de'tsɛnt] *adj.* discreet, unobtrusive; soft *light, colo(u)r, music etc.*; tasteful *clothes etc.*
de·zen·tra·li·sie·ren [detsɛntrali'zi:rən] *v/t.* (h) decentralize; **De·zen·tra·li'sie·rung** *f* (-; -en) decentralization; **De·zen·tra·li'sie·rungs·po·li·tik** *f* policy of decentralization (*or* devolution)
De·zer·nat [detsɛr'na:t] *n* (-[e]s; -e) department; → ***Morddezernat, Rauschgiftdezernat***
De·zi·bel [detsi'bɛl] *n* (-s; -) decibel
de·zi·diert [detsi'di:ɐt] **I.** *adj.* firm; **II.** *adv.* decidedly
de·zi·mal [detsi'ma:l] *adj.* decimal; **≈bruch** *m* decimal
De·zi·ma·le [detsi'ma:lə] *f* (-[n]; -n) decimal (place)
De·zi'mal|kom·ma *n* decimal point; **~rech·nung** *f* decimals *pl.*; **~stel·le** *f* decimal (place); **~sy·stem** *n* decimal system; metric system; ***auf das ~ umstellen*** decimalize *a monetary system*, go decimal; **~wäh·rung** *f* decimal currency; **~zahl** *f* decimal
De·zi·me [de'tsi:mə] *f* (-; -n) ♪ tenth
De·zi·me·ter [detsi'me:tɐ] *m, n* (-s; -) decimet|re (*Am.* -er)
de·zi·mie·ren [detsi'mi:rən] *v/t.* (h) decimate; **De·zi'mie·rung** *f* (-; -en) decimation
Dia ['di:a] *n* (-s; -s) *phot.* slide; **~*s machen*** take slides
Dia·be·tes [dia'be:tɛs] *m* (-; *no pl.*) ⚕ diabetes; **Dia·be·ti·ker** [dia'be:tikɐ] *m* (-s; -) diabetic; ***er ist ~*** he's (a) diabetic; **Dia'be·ti·ker·kost** *f* diabetic food; **dia·be·tisch** [dia'be:tɪʃ] *adj.* diabetic
'Dia·be·trach·ter *m* slide viewer
dia·bo·lisch [dia'bo:lɪʃ] *adj.* devilish
Dia·do·chen·kämp·fe [dia'dɔxən-] *pl.* battle *sg.* for the succession
'Dia·film *m* slide film
Dia·gno·se [dia'gno:zə] *f* (-; -n) diagnosis; ***e-e ~ stellen*** make a diagnosis; ***die ~ lautet ...*** the diagnosis is ...; **Dia·gno·sti·ker** [dia'gnɔstikɐ] *m* (-s; -) diagnostician; **dia·gno·stisch** [dia'gnɔstɪʃ] *adj.* diagnostic(ally *adv.*); **dia·gno·sti·zie·ren** [diagnɔsti'tsi:rən] *v/t. and v/i.* (h): ***e-e*** (*or* ***auf***) ***Lungenentzündung ~*** diagnose pneumonia; ***e-e Krankheit ~ als*** diagnose an illness as
dia·go·nal [diago'na:l] *adj.*, **Dia·go·na·le** [diago'na:lə] *f* (-; -n) diagonal
Dia·go'nal|paß *m sport*: diagonal ball; **~rei·fen** *m mot.* cross-ply (tyre, *Am.* tire), *Am. a.* bias-ply (tire)
Dia·gramm [dia'gram] *n* (-s; -e) graph; **~pa·pier** *n* graph paper
Dia·kon [dia'ko:n] *m* (-s, -en; -e[n]), **Dia·ko·nin** [dia'ko:nɪn] *f* (-; -nen) deacon; **Dia·ko·nis·se** [diako'nɪsə] *f* (-; -n) deaconess
dia·kri·tisch [dia'kri:tɪʃ] *adj.*: **~*es Zeichen*** diacritic(al mark)
Dia·lekt [dia'lɛkt] *m* (-[e]s; -e) dialect; **~ *sprechen*** speak (a) dialect; **dia·lek·tal** [dialɛk'ta:l] *adj.* dialectal
Dia'lekt|aus·druck *m* dialect word (*or* expression); **~dich·ter** *m* dialect poet; **~dich·tung** *f* dialect poetry; **~for·scher** *m* dialectician, dialectologist; **~for·schung** *f* dialectology
dia'lekt·frei *adv.*: **~ *sprechen*** speak standard English *etc.*
Dia·lek·tik [dia'lɛktɪk] *f* (-; *no pl.*) *phls.* dialectics *pl.*; **Dia·lek·ti·ker** [dia'lɛktikɐ] *m* (-s; -) dialectician; **dia·lek·tisch** [dia'lɛktɪʃ] *adj.* dialectical; **~*er Materialismus*** dialectical materialism
Dia·log [dia'lo:k] *m* (-[e]s; -e [dia'lo:gə]) dialogue, *Am. a.* dialog; *fig. a.* discourse
dia'log·be·reit *adj.*: *pol.* **~ *sein*** be willing to negotiate (*or* have talks); **Dia'log·be·reit·schaft** *f* willingness to negotiate (*or* have talks), openness for talks
dia'log·fä·hig *adj.* **1.** open to communication; **2.** → ***dialogbereit***; **3.** *computer*: interactive; **Dia'log·fä·hig·keit** *f* → ***Dialogbereitschaft***
Dia'log·form *f*: ***in ~*** in dialogue (form)
Dia·ly·se [dia'ly:zə] *f* (-; -n) ⚗, ⚕ dialysis
'Dia·ma·ga·zin *n* slide tray
Dia·mant [dia'mant] *m* (-en; -en) **1.** diamond; **2.** stylus; **≈be·setzt** *adj.* diamond-studded
dia·man·ten [dia'mantən] *adj.* diamond ...; **~*e Hochzeit*** diamond wedding

dia'man·ten|be·setzt *adj.* → ***diamantbesetzt***; **꞉kol,lier** *n* diamond necklace; **꞉schmuck** *m* diamond jewellery (*esp. Am.* jewelry), diamonds *pl.*, F ice

Dia'mant|kol,lier *n* → ***Diamantenkollier***; **~ring** *m* diamond ring; **~schlei·fer** *m* diamond cutter; **~schmuck** *m* → ***Diamantenschmuck***

Dia·me·ter [dia'me:tɐ] *m* (-s; -) ⩓ diameter; **dia·me·tral** [diame'tra:l] **I.** *adj.* diametric(al); *fig.* diametrically opposed; ***in ~em Gegensatz stehen*** be diametrically opposed (**zu** *dat.* to); **II.** *fig. adv.* **~ *entgegengesetzt*** diametrically opposed (*dat.* to); **dia·me·trisch** [dia'me:trɪʃ] *adj.* diametric(al)

Dia|po·si·tiv [diapozi'ti:f] *n* (-s; -e [-'ti:və]) *phot.* transparency, slide; **~pro,jek·tor** *m* slide projector; **~rähm·chen** *n*, **~rahmen** *m* slide frame

Di·ät [di'ɛ:t] **I.** *f* (-; -en) (special) diet; **~ *halten*** be on (*or* keep to) a diet; ***e-e ~ machen*** be (*or* go) on a diet; ***j-m e-e ~ verordnen,*** F ***j-n auf ~ setzen*** put s.o. on a diet; **II.** ꞉ *adv.*: **~ *kochen*** cook according to a diet; ***streng ~ leben*** keep to (*or* follow) a strict diet

Diä·ten [di'ɛ:tən] *pl. parl.* emoluments *pl.*, parliamentary pay

Diä·te·tik [diɛ'te:tɪk] *f* (-; -en) dietetics *pl.*; **diä·te·tisch** [diɛ'te:tɪʃ] *adj.* dietary

Di'ät|kost *f* dietary food; **~kur** *f* diet cure

Dia·to·nik [dia'to:nɪk] *f* (-; *no pl.*) ♪ diatonicism; **dia·to·nisch** [dia'to:nɪʃ] *adj.* diatonic(ally *adv.*)

'Dia·vor·trag *m* slide talk (*or* show)

dich [dɪç] **I.** *pers. pron.* (*acc. of du*) you; **II.** *refl. pron.* yourself; *after prp.*: you; *often untranslated*: ***beruhige ~!*** calm down

dicht [dɪçt] **I.** *adj.* **1.** dense *wood etc.*, thick (*fog, hair etc.*); heavy *traffic*; tightly packed (*a. program*); compact *style*; ***in ~er Folge*** in quick succession; **2.** a) watertight, b) airtight; ***nicht mehr ~ sein*** leak, be leaky; F *fig.* ***er ist nicht ganz ~*** F he's got a screw loose; **3.** F closed, shut; **II.** *adv.* **4. ~ *an*** (*or* ***bei***) close to; **~ *dabeistehen*** stand close by; **~ *gefolgt von*** *dat.* closely followed by; **~ *hinter j-m hersein*** be hot on s.o.'s heels; **~ *bevölkert*** densely populated; **~ *gedrängt*** tightly packed; → ***auffahren*** 3; **5. ~ *bevorstehen*** be imminent; **6. ~ *schließen*** shut tight(ly), *door*: shut tight (*or* properly); **~be·haart** *adj.* (very) hairy, *formal*: hirsute; **~be·sie·delt** *adj.*, **~be·völ·kert** *adj.* densely populated

Dich·te ['dɪçtə] *f* (-; *rare* -n) **1.** density, thickness; **2.** specific gravity

dich·ten¹ ['dɪçtən] (h) **I.** *v/t.* write; **II.** *v/i.* write poetry (*or* plays, novels *etc.*)

'dich·ten² *v/t.* (h) ⚙ seal; flush; lute; ⚓ ca(u)lk

Dich·ter ['dɪçtɐ] *m* (-s; -), **Dich·te·rin** ['dɪçtərɪn] *f* (-; -nen) poet; author, writer; **dich·te·risch** ['dɪçtərɪʃ] *adj.* **1.** poetic(ally *adv.*); **2.** literary; **~e *Freiheit*** poetic licen|ce (*Am.* -se); **'Dich·ter·le·sung** *f* (author's) reading; ***e-e ~ halten*** read from one's own works; **Dich·ter·ling** ['dɪçtɐlɪŋ] *contp. m* (-s; -e) poetaster

'dicht·ge·drängt *adj.* tightly packed

'dicht·hal·ten F *v/i.* (*irr.*, *sep.*, h, → ***halten***) keep mum, F keep one's mouth shut

'Dicht·heit *f* (-; *no pl.*) → ***Dichte*** 1

'Dicht·kunst *f* (-; *no pl.*) poetry

'dicht·ma·chen F (*sep.*, h) **I.** *v/t.* **1.** a) close (*or* shut up) (for the night), b) close down; ***j-m das Restaurant ~*** close down s.o.'s restaurant; **II.** *v/i.* **2.** a) close, shut, b) close down, F put up the shutters; **3.** *sport*: (***hinten***) **~** put up a defensive barrier

Dich·tung¹ ['dɪçtʊŋ] *f* (-; -en) **1.** *no pl.* literature; **2.** *no pl.* poetry; **3.** a) work(s *pl.*), writing(s *pl.*), b) poetry, poetic works *pl.*; **4.** poem; work (of literature); ***sinfonische ~*** symphonic poem; **5.** F ***das ist doch reine ~!*** F that's a lot of old fairytales, he's *etc.* made it all up

'Dich·tung² *f* (-; -en) ⚙ seal; packing; gasket; washer; lute; ⚓ ca(u)lking

'Dich·tungs|ma·te·ri,al *n* sealing compound; sealant; **~ring** *m*, **~schei·be** *f* sealing ring; washer, gasket

dick [dɪk] **I.** *adj.* thick (*a. gastr.*); big; swollen; fat; F (F great) big ..., *sl.* whopping great ...; F ***mach dich nicht so ~!*** do you have to spread (yourself) out like that?; F ***mit j-m durch ~ und dünn gehen*** stick by s.o. through thick and thin; F ***ein ~es Lob ernten*** be praised to the skies; F ***hier ist*** (*or* ***herrscht***) **~*e Luft*** a) there's something in the air, b) feelings are running high; ***sie sind ~e Freunde*** F they're (as) thick as thieves, they're very thick; → ***Ei*** 1, ***Ende, Fell, Hund*** 2; **II.** *adv.*: **~ *mit Staub bedeckt*** thick with dust; ***sich ~ anziehen*** wrap up well; F **~ *befreundet sein*** F be very thick (***mit*** *dat.* with); F *j-n or et.* **~ *haben*** (***kriegen***) F be (get) sick and tired of; → ***auftragen*** 5

'Dick·bauch *m* fat belly, paunch; **dick·bäu·chig** ['dɪkbɔʏçɪç] *adj.* fat-bellied

'Dick·darm *m* colon

Dicke¹ ['dɪkə] (*sep.* -k·k-) *f* (-; -n) thickness; diameter

'Dicke² (*sep.* -k·k-) *m*, *f* (-n; -n), **Dickerchen** ['dɪkɐçən] (*sep.* -k·k-) F *n* (-s; -) F fatty, chubby cheeks, podge

dick·fel·lig ['dɪkfɛlɪç] *adj.* thick-skinned

'dick·flüs·sig *adj.* syrupy; 🕮 *and* ⚙ viscous

Dick·häu·ter ['dɪkhɔʏtɐ] *m* (-s; -) *zo.* pachyderm

Dickicht ['dɪkɪçt] (*sep.* -k·k-) *n* (-[e]s; -e) thicket; *fig.* labyrinth, jungle

'Dick·kopf F *m*: ***ein ~ sein, e-n ~ haben*** be pigheaded (*or* stubborn); ***so ein ~!*** he's so pigheaded, how stubborn can you get; ***s-n ~ aufsetzen*** put on one's pigheaded act; **dick·köp·fig** ['dɪkkœpfɪç] F *adj.* pigheaded, stubborn

dick·lei·big ['dɪklaɪbɪç] *adj.* corpulent, obese; *euphem.* portly, stout

'dick·lich *adj.* slightly plump, a bit on the plump side

'Dick|ma·cher *m* (-s; -) fattener; *pl. a.* fattening food *sg.* (*or* foods); ***das ist ein ~*** *a.* that's very fattening; **~milch** *f* soured milk; **~schä·del** F *m* → ***Dickkopf***

'dick·tun F **I.** *v/refl.* (*irr.*, *sep.*, h, → ***tun***): ***sich ~*** act big; **II.** *v/i.*: **~ *mit*** *dat.* show off with

'Dick·wanst F *contp. m* F tub of lard, fat slob, fatso

Di·dak·tik [di'daktɪk] *f* (-; *no pl.*) didactics *pl.*; **di·dak·tisch** [di'daktɪʃ] *adj.* didactic(ally *adv.*)

die [di:] → ***der***

Dieb [di:p] *m* (-[e]s; -e ['di:bə]) thief; burglar; ***haltet den ~!*** stop, thief!

Die·bes|ban·de ['di:bəs-] *f* gang of thieves; **~gut** *n* stolen goods *pl.*; **꞉si·cher** *adj.* theftproof; burglarproof; ***et. ~ aufbewahren*** keep s.th. in a safe place (*or* under lock and key)

die·bisch ['di:bɪʃ] **I.** *adj.* **1.** thieving; → ***Elster***; **2.** *fig.* malicious, fiendish; **II.** *adv.*: ***sich ~ freuen*** secretly rejoice (***über*** *acc.* at)

Dieb·stahl ['di:pʃta:l] *m* (-[e]s; -stähle [-ʃtɛ:lə]) theft, ⚖ larceny; ***geistiger ~*** plagiarism; **꞉si·cher** *adj.* → ***diebessicher***; **~si·che·rung** *f mot.* anti-theft device; **~ver·si·che·rung** *f* theft insurance

Die·le ['di:lə] *f* (-; -n) **1.** (floor)board, plank; **2.** hall

die·nen ['di:nən] *v/i.* (h) **1** serve (***j-m*** s.o.; ***als*** as); ***dazu ~ zu*** *inf.* serve to *inf.*; ***es dient dazu zu*** *inf.* *a.* it's for *ger.*; ***e-r Sache ~*** help (*or* contribute to) s.th.; ***es dient e-m guten Zweck*** it's all for a good purpose; ***damit ist mir nicht gedient*** that doesn't help me at all; ***mit 20 Mark wäre mir schon gedient*** 20 marks would do me; ***womit kann ich ~?*** what can I do for you?; ***wozu soll das ~?*** what's that (meant) for?, what's that supposed to achieve?; **2.** ⚔ serve one's time; ***15 Monate ~*** do 15 months' service; ***bei der Marine ~*** serve in the Navy

Die·ner ['di:nɐ] *m* (-s; -) **1.** servant (*a. fig.*); **2.** bow; ***e-n ~ machen*** (make a) bow, ***vor*** *dat.*: bow to (*or* before); **3.** ***stummer ~*** dumb waiter; **Die·ne·rin** ['di:nərɪn] *f* (-; -nen) maid; *fig.* handmaid(en); **die·nern** ['di:nɐn] *v/i.* (h) bow and scrape (***vor*** *dat.* to); **'Die·ner·schaft** *f* (-; *no pl.*) servants *pl.*, domestics *pl.*

dien·lich ['di:nlɪç] *adj.* useful, helpful (*dat.* to); expedient; ***e-r Sache ~ sein*** further s.th.; ***es war mir sehr ~*** it was of great help to me

Dienst [di:nst] *m* (-[e]s; -e) **1.** service (***an*** *dat.* to); ***sich in den ~ e-r*** *Sache* ***stellen*** offer one's services to; F (***das ist***) **~ *am Kunden*** (that's) all part of the service, madam (*or* sir); **2.** service; ***j-m e-n guten ~ leisten*** do s.o. a good turn; ***j-m gute ~e leisten*** serve s.o. well, stand s.o. in good stead, be a great help (to s.o.); ***j-m e-n schlechten ~ erweisen*** do s.o. a disservice (*or* bad turn); **3.** service; ***in*** (***außer***) **~ *stellen*** put in (out of) service (*or* commission); ***die Beine versagten ihm den ~*** his legs gave way; ***j-m zu ~en stehen*** be at s.o.'s command; **4.** *no pl.* civil service; ***außer ~*** retired, in retirement; ***den ~ quittieren*** resign; → ***öffentlich*** I; **5.** *no pl.* duty (*a.* ⚔); (***nicht***) ***im ~*** on (off) duty; ⚔ ***im aktiven ~*** on active duty; *hum.* ***Torschütze vom ~*** goal machine; ***in Ausübung des ~es, im ~*** in the line of duty; **~ *haben,* ~ *tun*** be on duty; ***ich habe heute lange ~*** I'm working late today; **~ *ist ~, und Schnaps ist Schnaps*** never mix business with pleasure; → ***Vorschrift***; **6.** *no pl.* work; ***im ~*** *gen.* ***stehen*** work for, *contp.* be in the pay of; ***in den ~*** *gen.* ***treten*** start work with; ***in ~ nehmen*** take on, *esp. Am.* hire; **~ab,teil** *n* 🚂 guard's (*Am.* conductor's) compartment

Diens·tag ['di:nsta:k] *m* (-[e]s; -e) Tuesday; (***am***) **~** on Tuesday; **'diens·tags** *adv.* on Tuesday(s)

'Dienst·al·ter *n* length of service; ***nach ~*** according to seniority

'dienst·äl·test *adj.* most senior; **'Dienst-**

äl·te·ste *m, f* (-n; -n) senior member of staff
'Dienst|an·tritt *m*: **bei ~** on taking up one's post; **~auf·fas·sung** *f* workethic; **~aus·weis** *m* identity (*or* ID) card, pass
'dienst·bar *adj.* subservient (*dat.* to); F *hum.* **~er Geist** helpful soul
'dienst·be·flis·sen *adj.* zealous; officious
'Dienst|be·ginn *m*: **~ ist 8 Uhr** work starts at 8 o'clock; **bei ~** when starting work; **~be·reich** *m* area of responsibility, competence
'dienst·be·reit *adj.* **1.** obliging; **2.** *doctor etc.*: on call; *pharmacy*: open; **~er Arzt** *a.* duty doctor; **'Dienst·be·reit·schaft** *f* **1.** obligingness; **2.** standby duty; **~ haben** be on standby, *doctor*: *a.* be on call, *pharmacy*: be open
'Dienst·bo·te *obs. m* (-n; -n) domestic (servant)
'Dienst·ei·fer *m* zeal; officiousness; **'dienst·eif·rig** *adj.* → **dienstbeflissen**
'dienst|fä·hig *adj.* → **diensttauglich**; **~frei** *adj.*: **~ haben** be off (duty); **~er Tag** day off; **heute ist mein ~er Tag** it's my day off today
'Dienst|gang *m* business errand; **e-n ~ machen** do a business errand; **auf e-m ~ sein** be out on business; **~ge·brauch** *m*: **nur für den ~** for official use only; **~ge·heim·nis** *n* **1.** trade secret; **2.** official secrecy; **~ge·schäf·te** *pl.* business *sg.*; **~ge·spräch** *n* **1.** business call; **2.** official call; **~grad** *m* rank; *Am.* grade, ⚓ rating
'dienst·ha·bend *adj.* duty ..., ... on duty
'Dienst|jah·re *pl.* years of service; **~klei·dung** *f* working clothes *pl.*; uniform; **~lei·stung** *f* service (rendered); *pl.* ✝ services
'Dienst·lei·stungs|abend *m* late-night shopping; **~ge·sell·schaft** *f* service-orient(at)ed society; **~ge·wer·be** *n* service industries *pl.*; **~sek·tor** *m* services sector
'dienst·lich I. *adj.* official; **~ werden** take on an official tone; **II.** *adv.*: **~ unterwegs sein** be away on business; **er ist ~ verhindert** he's tied up with business (matters)
'Dienst|mäd·chen *n* maid, home help; **~mar·ke** *f* identity disc; **~ord·nung** *f* regulations *pl.*; **~per·so,nal** *n* (*hotel etc.*) staff, domestic staff; **~pflicht** *f* (official) duty; **~plan** *m* duty roster; **~pro,gramm** *n computer*: utility program; **~rang** *m* → **Dienstgrad**; **~rei·se** *f* business trip; **e-e ~ machen** go away on business, *a.* **auf ~ sein** be away on business; **~schluß** *m*: **nach ~** after (office) hours; **~stel·le** *f* department; office; **~stun·den** *pl.* (office) hours
'dienst|taug·lich *adj. esp.* ⚔ fit for service (*or* duty); **~tu·end** *adj.* → **diensthabend**; **~un·fä·hig** *adj.*, **~un·taug·lich** *adj.* not fit for service (⚔ *a.* duty)
'Dienst|ver·ge·hen *n* → **Disziplinarvergehen**; **~ver·hält·nis** *n* employment; **~ver·trag** *m* contract of employment; **~vor·schrift** *f* regulation(s *pl.*); **~waf·fe** *f* service weapon; **~wa·gen** *m* **1.** company car; **2.** *pol. etc.*: official car; **3.** ⚔ staff car; **~weg** *m*: **auf dem ~** through the official channels
'dienst·wid·rig I. *adj.*: **~es Verhalten** breaking of the regulations; **wegen ~en Verhaltens** for breaking (*or* going against) the regulations; **II.** *adv.*: **sich ~ verhalten** go against the regulations
'Dienst|woh·nung *f* **1.** company flat (*Am.* apartment), company house; **2.** army *etc.* flat (*Am.* apartment), army *etc.* house; **3.** flat (*or Am.* apartment, house) provided by the post office *etc.*; **~zeit** *f* **1.** working hours *pl.*; **2.** ⚔ term of service
dies·be·züg·lich ['di:sbətsy:klɪç] *adj. and adv.* concerning this, in this connection; **e-e ~e Erklärung** a statement on the matter
Die·sel ['di:zəl] F *m* (-[s]; -) diesel, *Brit. a.* derv; **~an·trieb** *m* diesel drive; **mit ~** diesel-driven; **2elek·trisch** *adj.* diesel-electric(ally *adv.*); **~kraft·stoff** *m* diesel fuel; **~mo·tor** *m* diesel engine; **~öl** *n* diesel oil
die·ser ['di:zɐ], **die·se** ['di:zə], **dies** [di:s], **die·ses** ['di:zəs], **'die·se** *pl. dem. pron.* **1.** *adj.* this, that; *pl.* these, those; **dies alles** all this; **dieser Tage** a) the other day, b) soon; **diese Ihre Bemerkung** this remark of yours; **2.** *su.* this (*or* that) one; he, she; *pl.* these, those; the latter; **dieser ist es** this is the one; **dieser war es** *a.* it was him; **diese sind es** these are the ones; **dies sind m-e Schwestern** these are my sisters; **wir sprachen über dieses und jenes** we talked about this, that and the other; **ich muß noch dieses und jenes einkaufen** (**erledigen**) I still have a few bits and pieces to buy (a few things to do *or* to sort out)
die·sig ['di:zɪç] *adj.* hazy
dies·jäh·rig ['di:sjɛ:rɪç] *adj.*: **der** (**die, das**) **~e ...** this year's ...
dies·mal ['di:sma:l] *adv.* this time; for once; **dies·ma·lig** ['di:sma:lɪç] *adj.*: **sein ~er Auftritt war ein voller Erfolg** his performance this time was a complete success
dies·sei·tig ['di:szaɪtɪç] *adj.* **1. das ~e Ufer** this side of the river (*or* lake); **2.** *fig.* worldly; **das ~e Leben** life on earth; **dies·seits** ['di:szaɪts] **I.** *prp.* (*gen.*) (on) this side of; **II.** 2 *n* (-; *no pl.*): **das ~** this life, life on earth; **im ~** in this life
Diet·rich ['di:trɪç] *m* (-s; -e) skeleton key
die'weil *obs.* **I.** *cj.* a) while; b) because, since; **II.** *adv.* meanwhile
dif·fa·mie·ren [dɪfa'mi:rən] *v/t.* (h) slander; **dif·fa'mie·rend** *adj.* defamatory; **Dif·fa'mie·rung** *f* (-; -en) defamation, slander(ing)
Dif·fe·ren·ti·al [dɪfərɛn'tsĭa:l] *n* (-s; -e) 𝔄 differential; *mot.* → **~ge·trie·be** *n* differential (gear); **~glei·chung** *f* differential equation; **~rech·nung** *f* differential calculus
Dif·fe·renz [dɪfə'rɛnts] *f* (-; -en) **1.** difference; balance; surplus, F *the* rest; **2.** *usu. pl.* difference(s) of opinion
dif·fe·ren·zie·ren [dɪfərɛn'tsi:rən] (h) **I.** *v/t.* distinguish (*or* make a distinction) between; distinguish; elaborate, develop; **II.** *v/i.* make distinctions, differentiate; **III.** *v/refl.*: **sich ~** become more and more sophisticated; diversify; **dif·fe·ren·ziert** [dɪfərɛn'tsi:ɐt] *adj.* sophisticated; discriminating, refined
dif·fe·rie·ren [dɪfə'ri:rən] *v/i.* (h) differ, vary (**um** *acc.* by)
dif·fi·zil [dɪfi'tsi:l] *adj.* difficult; hard to please; tricky, delicate; meticulous
dif'fus [dɪ'fu:s] *adj.* **1.** diffuse, diffused, scattered; **2.** *fig.* vague, foggy, hazy
Di·ge·stif [diʒɛs'ti:f] *m* (-s; -s) digestivo
di·gi·tal [digi'ta:l] *adj.* digital
Di·gi'tal|-Ana'log-'Um·set·zer *m*, **~-Ana'log-'Wand·ler** *m* digital-analog converter; **~an·zei·ge** *f* digital display; **~auf·nah·me** *f*, **~auf·zeich·nung** *f* digital recording
Di·gi·ta·lis [digi'ta:lɪs] *n* (-; *no pl.*) *pharm.* digitalis
di·gi·ta·li·sie·ren [digitali'zi:rən] *v/t.* (h) digitize
Di·gi'tal|rech·ner *m* digital computer; **~tech·nik** *f* digital technology; **~uhr** *f* digital clock (*or* watch)
Dik·tat [dɪk'ta:t] *n* (-[e]s; -e) **1.** dictation; **ein ~ aufnehmen** take a dictation; **2.** dictates *pl.*, *pol. a.* diktat
Dik·ta·tor [dɪk'ta:to:ɐ] *m* (-s; -en [-ta'to:rən]) dictator; **dik·ta·to·risch** [dɪkta'to:rɪʃ] *adj.* dictatorial; **Dik·ta·tur** [dɪkta'tu:ɐ] *f* (-; -en [-'tu:rən]) dictatorship
dik·tie·ren [dɪk'ti:rən] *v/t. and v/i.* (h) dictate (*a. fig.*); **j-m e-n Brief ~** dictate a letter to s.o.; **Dik·tier·ge·rät** [dɪk'ti:ɐ-] *n* dictating machine
Di·lem·ma [di'lɛma] *n* (-s; -s) dilemma, F fix; **sich in e-m ~ befinden** be in a dilemma (*or* fix)
Di·let·tant [dilɛ'tant] *m* (-en; -en) *esp. contp.* dilettante, amateur; **di·let'tan·tisch** *adj.* amateurish, dilettante ...; **Di·let·tan·tis·mus** [dilɛtan'tɪsmʊs] *m* (-; *no pl.*) dilettantism
Dill [dɪl] *m* (-[e]s; -e) ✿ dill
Di·men·si·on [dimɛn'zĭo:n] *f* (-; -en) **1.** dimension; **2.** *pl.* dimensions, size *sg.*; **3.** *fig. pl.* dimensions; proportions, extent *sg.*; **gigantische ~en annehmen** assume vast proportions; **di·men·sio·nal** [dimɛnzĭo'na:l] *adj.* dim; **di·men·sio·nie·ren** [dimɛnzĭo'ni:rən] *v/t.* (h) dimension
di·mi·nu·tiv [diminu'ti:f] *adj.*, 2 *n* (-s; -e [-'ti:və]) *ling.* diminutive
DIN [di:n, dɪn] **1.** German Institute for Standardization; **2.** German Industrial Standard; **~ A4** A4; **~ A4 Papier** A4 (-sized) paper
Di·ner [di'ne:] *n* (-s; -s) dinner (party); banquet
Ding [dɪŋ] *n* (-[e]s) **1.** (*pl.* -e) thing, object; **vor allen ~en** above all; **das ist ein ~ der Unmöglichkeit** that's absolutely impossible, that's completely out of the question; **gut ~ will Weile haben** Rome wasn't built in a day; **guter ~e** cheerful; **aller guten ~e sind drei** a) all good things come in threes, b) third time lucky; → **Name**; **2. ~e** *pl.* things, matters; (**so,**) **wie die ~e liegen** (*or* **stehen**) as matters stand; **das geht nicht mit rechten ~en zu** F there's something fishy about it; **wie ich die ~e sehe** as I see it; **über den ~en stehen** be above it all; → **Lage** 2; **3.** (*pl.* -er) F thing; **armes** (**dummes**) **~** poor (silly) thing; **4.** (*pl.* -er) F **ein ~ drehen** *sl.* pull a job
'ding·fest *adj.*: **j-n ~ machen** arrest s.o.; put s.o. behind bars
'ding·lich *adj.* real (*a.* ⚖)
Dings [dɪŋs], **'Dings·da, 'Dings·bums** F **1.** *n* (-; *no pl.*) thing, F what-d'you-call-it, what's-its-name; **2.** *m, f* (-; *no pl.*) F what's-his-(her-)name, thingumajig
di·nie·ren [di'ni:rən] *v/i.* (h) dine (**bei** *dat.* at)
DIN-Norm ['di:n-, 'dɪn-] *f* German Industrial Standard
Di·no·sau·ri·er [dino'zaʊrĭɐ] *m* (-s; -) dinosaur
Di·o·de [di'ʔo:də] *f* (-; -n) ⚡ diode

Di·op·trie [diɔp'triː] *f* (-; -n) *opt.* diopter
Di·oxin [diɔ'ksiːn] *n* (-s; -e) dioxin
Di·oxyd ['diːʔɔksyːt] *n* (-s; -e [-syːdə]) ⚗ dioxide
Di·öze·se [diø'tseːzə] *f* (-; -n) *eccl.* diocese
Diph·the·rie [dɪfte'riː] *f* (-; -n) ⚕ diphtheria
Diph·thong [dɪf'tɔŋ] *m* (-s; -e) *ling.* diphthong
Di·plom [di'ploːm] *n* (-s; -e) diploma, degree; *in cpds.* qualified; **~ar·beit** *f* dissertation (submitted for a diploma)
Di·plo·mat [diplo'maːt] *m* (-en; -en) diplomat (*a. fig.*)
Di·plo'ma·ten|ge·päck *n* diplomatic bag(s *pl.*); **~kof·fer** *m* executive briefcase, attaché case; **~lauf·bahn** *f* diplomatic career; **~vier·tel** *n* diplomatic quarter
Di·plo·ma·tie [diploma'tiː] *f* (-; *no pl.*) diplomacy (*a. fig.*); **di·plo·ma·tisch** [diplo'maːtɪʃ] *adj.* diplomatic(ally *adv.*) (*a. fig.*); ***~es Korps*** diplomatic corps; ***~e Vertretung*** diplomatic mission; ***die ~en Beziehungen abbrechen zu*** *dat.* break off diplomatic relations with
di·plo·miert [diplo'miːɐt] *adj.* qualified
Di'plom·in·ge,nieur *m* qualified engineer; engineering graduate
Di'plom·kauf·mann *m* business graduate; MBA (= Master of Business Administration); ***er ist ~ a.*** he's got a business degree
Di·pol ['diːpoːl] *m* (-s; -e) ⚡ dipole; **~an,ten·ne** *f* dipole (aerial *or* antenna)
dir [diːɐ] *pers. pron.* (*dat. of du*) (to) you; (*a.* **~ *selbst***) yourself; ***ich werde es ~ erklären*** I'll explain it to you; ***nach ~!*** after you; ***wasch ~ die Hände*** (go and) wash your hands
di·rekt [di'rɛkt] **I.** *adj.* **1.** direct; ***~er Zug nach*** *dat.* through train to; **2.** direct, immediate; firsthand *information etc.*; **3.** straight *question, answer etc.*; direct *manner etc.*; **4.** absolute; ***~er Wahnsinn*** *a.* sheer madness; **5.** *ling.* ***~e Rede*** direct speech; **II.** *adv.* **6.** direct(ly), straight; ***es landete ~ vor m-n Füßen*** it landed right in front of my feet; → ***Nase*** 1; **7.** directly, immediately, at once; ***~ am Bahnhof*** right at the station; ***~ nach dem Essen*** right (*or* straight) after dinner; ***~ gegenüber*** directly opposite; **8.** pointblank, straight to s.o.'s face; **9.** F absolutely, really, just; ***das war mir ~ peinlich*** it was actually quite embarrassing, I felt quite embarrassed; ***es tut mir ~ leid*** I'm really sorry; **10.** ***nicht ~ falsch*** not exactly (*or* really) wrong; *hat er das gesagt?* - ***nicht ~(, aber ...)*** not in so many words(, but ...); ***man müßte es ~ mal versuchen*** one really ought to try it out; **11.** *radio, TV*: live
Di'rekt·flug *m* ✈ direct flight
Di'rekt·heit *f* (-; *no pl.*) directness
Di·rek·ti·on [dirɛk'tsǐoːn] *f* (-; -en) **1.** *no pl.* management; **2.** board of directors, (board of) management; **3.** manager's office; **4.** head office
Di·rek·ti'ons|as·si,stent *m* assistant manager; **~se·kre,tä·rin** *f* personal assistant
Di·rek·ti·ve [dirɛk'tiːvə] *f* (-; -n) instruction(s *pl.*), directive
Di'rekt·man,dat *n* direct mandate
Di·rek·tor [di'rɛktoːɐ] *m* (-s; -en [-'toːrən]) manager; (*zoo*) director; headmaster, *Am.* principal; **Di·rek·to·rat** [dirɛkto'raːt] *n* (-[e]s; -e) **1.** directorship; **2.** headmaster's (*Am.* principal's) office; **Di·rek·to·rin** [dirɛk'toːrɪn] *f* (-; -nen) manageress; director; headmistress, *Am.* principal; **Di·rek·to·ri·um** [dirɛk'toːrǐʊm] *n* (-s; -ien [rǐən]) board of directors; ✝ management committee; board of supervisors
Di'rekt|paß *m sport*: first-time pass; **~schuß** *m sport*: volley (shot); **~sen·dung** *f*, **~über,tra·gung** *f radio, TV*: live broadcast; **~ver·hand·lun·gen** *pl.* face-to-face negotiations; **~wahl** *f* **1.** direct elections *pl.*; **2.** *teleph.* direct dial(l)ing; **~wer·bung** *f* direct advertising
Di·ri·gent [diri'gɛnt] *m* (-en; -en) conductor, *Am. a.* director; *das waren die Wiener Philharmoniker* ***unter dem ~en*** conducted by, directed by
Di·ri'gen·ten|po·di·um *n* (conductor's) rostrum; **~pult** *n* (conductor's) desk; **~stab** *m* (conductor's) baton
di·ri·gie·ren [diri'giːrən] *v/t.* (h) direct; ♪ conduct; **Di·ri·gis·mus** [diri'gɪsmʊs] *m* (-; *no pl.*) *pol.*, ✝ dirigisme; **di·ri·gi·stisch** [diri'gɪstɪʃ] *adj.* dirigiste
Dirndl ['dɪrndl] *n* (-s; -), **~kleid** *n* dirndl
Dir·ne ['dɪrnə] *f* (-; -n) prostitute
Dis [dɪs] *n* (-; -) ♪ D sharp
Dis·agio [dɪs'ʔaːdʒo] *n* (-s; -s) ✝ discount
Disc·jockey ['dɪsk-] (*sep.* -k·k-) *m* (-s; -s) disc jockey, F DJ, deejay
Dis·co ['dɪsko] F *f* (-; -s) F disco
Dis·count... [dɪs'kaʊnt-] discount *shop, store, price etc.*, cut-price *shop, articles*
Dis·har·mo'nie [dɪs-] *f* (-; -n) ♪ dissonance, discord, *fig. a.* disharmony (*gen.* between); **dis·har·mo'nie·ren** *v/i.* (h) ♪ be discordant (*or* dissonant); *fig.* clash; *fig.* ***die beiden ~ grundsätzlich*** those two just don't get on (together); **dis·har'mo·nisch** *adj.* ♪ discordant, dissonant, *fig. a.* disharmonious; clashing *colo(u)rs*
Dis·ket·te [dɪs'kɛtə] *f* (-; -n) diskette, floppy (disk); **Dis'ket·ten·lauf·werk** *n* disk drive
Disk·jockey *m* → ***Discjockey***
Dis·kont [dɪs'kɔnt] *m* (-s; -e) ✝ discount; discount rate; **2fä·hig** *adj.* discountable, eligible (for discount)
Dis'kont·ge·schäf(·)t(e *pl.*) *n* discounting (business *sg.*)
dis·kon·tie·ren [dɪskɔn'tiːrən] *v/t.* (h) discount
dis·kon·ti·nu·ier·lich [dɪskɔntinu'iːɐlɪç] *adj.* intermittent
Dis'kont|po·li,tik *f* discount policy; **~satz** *m* discount rate
Dis·ko·thek [dɪsko'teːk] *f* (-; -en) discotheque
dis·kre·di·tie·ren [dɪskredi'tiːrən] *v/t.* (h) (bring into) discredit
Dis·kre·panz [dɪskre'pants] *f* (-; -en) discrepancy
dis·kret [dɪs'kreːt] *adj.* **1.** discreet; ***j-m ein ~es Zeichen geben*** give s.o. a subtle hint; **2.** unobtrusive; **3.** ⚛ discrete; **Dis·kre·ti·on** [dɪskre'tsǐoːn] *f* discretion, secrecy; ***~ Ehrensache!*** discretion guaranteed; ***strengste ~ wahren*** be absolutely discreet about it
dis·kri·mi·nie·ren [dɪskrimi'niːrən] *v/t.* (h) discriminate against (***wegen*** *gen.* on account of); **dis·kri·mi'nie·rend** *adj.* discriminating, discriminatory; **Dis·kri·mi'nie·rung** *f* (-; -en) discrimination (*gen.* against); → ***Arbeitsplatz***; **Dis·kri·mi'nie·rungs·ver·bot** *n* ban on discrimination
Dis·kurs [dɪs'kʊrs] *m* (-es; -e [-'kʊrzə]) discourse; treatise; **dis·kur·siv** [dɪskʊr'ziːf] *adj.* discursive
Dis·kus ['dɪskʊs] *m* (-[ses]; -se, Disken) **1.** *sport*: discus; **2.** *anat., zo.,* ⚘ disc
Dis·kus·si·on [dɪskʊ'sǐoːn] *f* (-; -en) discussion (***um*** *acc.* on, about), debate (on); ***zur ~ stehen*** be on the agenda; ***das steht nicht zur ~*** that's not what we're here to discuss; ***und ich will keine ~*** and I don't want any arguments
Dis·kus·si'ons|bei·trag *m* contribution to the discussion; ***danke für Ihren ~*** thank you for taking part in the discussion; **2be·reit** *adj.* open to discussion; **~grund·la·ge** *f* basis for discussion; **~lei·ter** *m* (panel) chairman; ***~ war ...*** *a.* chairing the discussion (*or* debate) was ...; **~part·ner** *m* partner in discussion; *pol.* negotiating partner; **~run·de** *f* **1.** discussion group; **2.** round of discussions; **~teil·neh·mer** *m* participant; *TV etc.*: panel(l)ist, member of the panel, guest; **~the·ma** *n* subject for discussion; **~ver·an·stal·tung** *f* forum
'Dis·kus|wer·fen *n* discus (throwing); **~wer·fer** *m* discus thrower; **~wurf** *m* **1.** *no pl.* discus (throwing); **2.** discus throw
dis·ku·ta·bel [dɪsku'taːbəl] *adj.* worth discussing; **dis·ku·tie·ren** [dɪsku'tiːrən] (h) **I.** *v/t.* discuss; **II.** *v/i.* have a discussion; **~ *über*** *acc.* discuss, have a discussion about; ***darüber läßt sich (durchaus) ~*** we can talk about it; ***ich hab' keine Lust, mit dir zu ~*** I don't want to argue with you
dis·pen·sie·ren [dɪspɛn'ziːrən] *v/t.* (h) **1.** exempt (***von*** *dat.* from); **2.** *pharm.* dispense
Dis·po·nent [dɪspo'nɛnt] *m* (-en; -en) ✝ managing clerk; **dis·po·ni·bel** [dɪspo'niːbəl] *adj.* available; **dis·po·nie·ren** [dɪspo'niːrən] (h) **I.** *v/i.* **1.** make arrangements, plan (ahead); ***anders ~*** make other arrangements; **2.** **~ *über*** *acc.* a) have at one's disposal, b) do what one likes with; **3.** ✝ place orders; **II.** *v/t.* allot (***für*** *acc.* to); **dis·po·niert** [dɪspo'niːɐt] *adj.*: ***gut (schlecht) ~ sein*** be in good (bad) form; ⚕ ***~ sein für*** *acc.* (*or* ***zu*** *dat.*) be prone to
Dis·po·si·ti·on [dɪspozi'tsǐoːn] *f* (-; -en) **1.** ⚕ proneness (***für*** *acc.*, ***zu*** *dat.* to); ***e-e ~ haben für*** (*or* ***zu***) be prone to; **2.** *usu. pl.* arrangements; plans; instructions; ***(s-e) ~en treffen für*** *acc.* (*or* ***zu*** *dat.*) make arrangements for; **3.** outline, plan; **4.** ***zu j-s ~ stehen*** be at s.o.'s disposal; **Dis·po·si·ti'ons·kre,dit** *m* ✝ drawing credit
Dis·put [dɪs'puːt] *m* (-[e]s; -e) dispute, argument; **Dis·pu·ta·ti·on** [dɪsputa'tsǐoːn] *f* (-; -en) controversy, debate; **dis·pu·tie·ren** [dɪspu'tiːrən] *v/i.* (h) **1.** dispute (***über*** *acc.* [on *or* about] *s.th.*), debate ([on] *s.th.*), argue (about *s.th.*); **2.** argue, quarrel
Dis·qua·li·fi·ka·ti·on [dɪskvalifika'tsǐoːn] *f* (-; -en) disqualification; **dis·qua·li·fi·zie·ren** [dɪskvalifi'tsiːrən] (h) **I.** *v/t.* disqualify (***wegen*** *gen.* for); **II.** *v/refl.*: ***sich ~*** lose one's (*or* all) credibility (***als*** as)
Dis·ser·ta·ti·on [dɪsɛrta'tsǐoːn] *f* (-; -en) (doctoral) thesis
Dis·si·dent [dɪsi'dɛnt] *m* (-en; -en) dissident

Dis·si'den·ten|be·we·gung *f* dissident movement; **~grup·pe** *f* group of dissidents

Dis·so·nanz [dɪso'nants] *f* (-; -en) ♪ dissonance; *fig. a. pl.* (note of) discord

Di·stanz [dɪs'tants] *f* (-; -en) **1.** distance (*a. sport*); ***das Rennen geht über e-e ~ von 100 km*** *sport*: the race covers a distance of 100 km; ***der Kampf ging über die volle ~*** *boxing*: the fight went the distance; **2.** *fig.* distance; detachment; ***~ halten*** keep one's distance (***j-m gegenüber*** from s.o.); ***auf ~ gehen*** back off, start cooling the relationship; ***et. mit ~ betrachten*** take a detached view of s.th.; ***et. aus der ~ beurteilen*** judge s.th. with the necessary distance (*or* detachment); ***~ gewinnen zu*** *dat.* get a bit of distance to; **di·stan·zie·ren** [dɪstan'tsiːrən] (h) **I.** *v/refl.*: ***sich ~*** dissociate o.s. (***von*** *dat.* from); **II.** *v/t. sport*: leave *s.o.* trailing (***um*** *acc.* by), outdistance; beat; **di·stan·ziert** [dɪstan'tsiːɐt] *adj.* reserved, *contp.* aloof; **Di·stan'ziert·heit** *f* (-; *no pl.*) reserve, *contp.* aloofness

Di·stel ['dɪstəl] *f* (-; -n) ⚘ thistle

Di·sti·chon ['dɪstɪçɔn] *n* (-s; -chen) [-çən]) distich

di·stin·guiert [dɪstɪŋ'giːɐt] *adj.* distinguished

Di·strikt [dɪs'trɪkt] *m* (-[e]s; -e) district

Dis·zi·plin [dɪstsi'pliːn] *f* (-; -en) **1.** *no pl.* discipline; ***~ halten*** (*or* ***wahren***) be disciplined, maintain discipline; ***hier herrscht ~*** things are very disciplined around here; **2.** *sport etc.*: discipline

Dis·zi·pli·nar|ge·richt [dɪstsipli'naːɐ-] *n* disciplinary court; **~ge·walt** *f* disciplinary power(s *pl.*)

dis·zi·pli·na·risch [dɪstsipli'naːrɪʃ] **I.** *adj.* disciplinary; **II.** *adv.*: ***~ vorgehen*** take disciplinary action (***gegen*** *acc.* against)

Dis·zi·pli'nar|maß·nah·me *f* disciplinary measure; **~recht** *n* (-[e]s; *no pl.*) disciplinary law; **~ver·fah·ren** *n* disciplinary proceedings *pl.*; **~ver·ge·hen** *n* disciplinary offen|ce (*Am.* -se)

dis·zi·pli·nie·ren [dɪstsipli'niːrən] (h) **I.** *v/t.* discipline; **II.** *v/refl.*: ***sich ~*** discipline o.s.; **dis·zi·pli·niert** [dɪstsipli'niːɐt] **I.** *adj.* disciplined; **II.** *adv.*: ***sich ~ verhalten*** be (very) disciplined

dis·zi'plin·los *adj.* undisciplined; **Dis·zi'plin·lo·sig·keit** *f* (-; *no pl.*) lack of discipline

Di·va ['diːva] *f* (-; -s, Diven ['diːvən]) diva, star

Di·ver·genz [divɛr'gɛnts] *f* (-; -en) divergence (*a. fig.*); **di·ver·gie·ren** [divɛr'giːrən] *v/i.* (h) diverge (***von*** *dat.* from); **di·ver'gie·rend** *adj.* divergent

di·vers [di'vɛrs] *adj.* various; **Di·ver·ses** [di'vɛrzəs] *no art.* various things *pl.*; *esp.* ☤ sundries *pl.*; Miscellaneous

di·ver·si·fi·zie·ren [divɛrzifi'tsiːrən] *v/t.* (h) ☤ diversify; **Di·ver·si·fi'zie·rung** *f* (-; -en) diversification

Di·vi·dend [divi'dɛnt] *m* (-en; -en [-'dɛndən]) ⩲ dividend

Di·vi·den·de [divi'dɛndə] *f* (-; -n) ☤ dividend; dividend rate

Di·vi'den·den|aus·schüt·tung *f* ☤ dividend distribution; **~schein** *m* dividend coupon

di·vi·die·ren [divi'diːrən] *v/t.* (h) divide (***durch*** *acc.* by); **Di·vi·si·on** [divi'zioːn] *f* (-; -en) ⩲, ⚔ division; **Di·vi·sor** [di'viːzoːɐ] *m* (-s; -en [divi'zoːrən]) ⩲ divisor

Di·wan ['diːvaːn] *m* (-s; -e) **1.** divan, ottoman; **2.** *hist.* divan

Do·ber·mann(pin·scher) ['doːbɐman-] *m* Doberman (pinscher)

doch [dɔx] *cj. and adv.* but, however; yet, still; all the same, nevertheless; after all; surely; you know ...; ***setzen Sie sich ~*** do sit down; ***sei ~ mal still!*** be quiet, will you; *willst du nicht? - ~!* yes, I do; ***er kam also ~?*** then he did come after all?; ***nicht ~!*** don't!, stop it!; ***du weißt ~, daß*** a) you know (that) ..., don't you?, b) surely you know (that); ***du kommst ~?*** you will come, won't you?; ***wo er ~ genau wußte*** knowing very well; ***ich hab's ~ gewußt*** I knew it; ***er ist ~ nicht (etwa) krank?*** he isn't ill, is he?; ***das kann ~ nicht dein Ernst sein?*** you're not serious, are you?; ***wenn er ~ käme*** if only he would come; ***hättest du das ~ gleich gesagt*** why didn't you tell me straightaway?; ***das ist ~ Peter da drüben*** look, there's Peter over there

Docht [dɔxt] *m* (-[e]s; -e) wick

Dock [dɔk] *n* (-s; -s) ⚓ dock(s *pl.*), dockyard; ***auf ~ legen*** (put into) dock; **'Dock·ar·bei·ter** *m* docker, dockworker; **docken** ['dɔkən] (*sep.* -k·k-) *v/t. and v/i.* (h) ⚓ *and space travel*: dock

Do·ge ['doːʒə] *m* (-n; -n) *hist.* doge

Dog·ge ['dɔgə] *f* (-; -n): (***englische***) ***~*** mastiff; ***dänische*** (*or* ***deutsche***) ***~*** Great Dane

Dog·ma ['dɔgma] *n* (-s; -men) dogma; ***et. zum ~ erheben*** make s.th. into a dogma; **Dog·ma·tik** [dɔg'maːtɪk] *f* (-; -en) dogmatics *pl.*; *contp.* dogmatism; **Dog·ma·ti·ker** [dɔg'maːtikɐ] *m* (-s; -) dogmatist; **dog·ma·tisch** [dɔg'maːtɪʃ] *adj.* dogmatic(ally *adv.*); **dog·ma·ti·sie·ren** [dɔgmati'ziːrən] *v/t.* (h) dogmatize; **Dog·ma·tis·mus** [dɔgma'tɪsmʊs] *m* (-; *no pl.*) dogmatism

Doh·le ['doːlə] *f* (-; -n) jackdaw

Dok·tor ['dɔktoːɐ] *m* (-s; -en [dɔk'toːrən]) **1.** (*abbr.* ***Dr.***) *univ.* doctor; ***den*** (*or* ***s-n***) ***~ machen*** do one's doctorate (*or* PhD); ***Herr (Frau) ~*** ⚕ doctor, Dr. *Schubert etc.*; ***Herr (Frau) Dr. Schubert*** Dr Schubert; **2.** F doctor; **3.** F ***~ spielen*** play doctors and nurses; **Dok·to·rand** [dɔkto'rant] *m* (-en; -en [-'randən]) doctoral candidate

'Dok·tor|ar·beit *f* (doctoral *or* PhD) thesis; ***das wäre ein Thema für e-e ~*** somebody ought to write a thesis on that; **~fra·ge** F *fig. f* (really) tricky question; **~grad** *m*, **~hut** F *m* doctor's degree; ***den ~ erwerben*** do (*or* get) one's doctorate; **~prü·fung** *f* viva (voce); **~ti·tel** *m* a) doctorate, b) doctor's title; ***den ~ führen*** a) have a doctorate, b) call o.s. doctor; **~va·ter** *m* supervisor; **~wür·de** *f* doctorate; ***die ~ erlangen*** get (*or* obtain) one's doctorate

Dok·trin [dɔk'triːn] *f* (-; -en) doctrine

dok·tri·när [dɔktri'nɛːɐ] *adj.*, ♀ *m* (-s; -e) doctrinaire

Do·ku·ment [doku'mɛnt] *n* (-[e]s; -e) **1.** document; *adm.* record (*both a. fig.*); **2.** *fig.* ***ein ~*** proof (*gen.* of), evidence (of)

Do·ku·men·tar|be·richt [dokumɛn'taːɐ-] *m* documentary report; **~film** *m* documentary (film)

do·ku·men·ta·risch [dokumɛn'taːrɪʃ] **I.** *adj.* documentary; **II.** *adv.*: ***et. ~ belegen*** provide documentary evidence of s.th.; ***~ belegt*** documented

Do·ku·men'tar|sen·dung *f* documentary (program[me]); **~spiel** *n* documentary drama, docudrama

Do·ku·men·ta·ti·on [dokumɛnta'tsioːn] *f* (-; -en) documentation; *fig. a.* demonstration; **do·ku·men·tie·ren** [dokumɛn'tiːrən] (h) **I.** *v/t.* document; *fig.* show, demonstrate; **II.** *v/refl.*: ***sich ~*** be shown, be revealed

Dolch [dɔlç] *m* (-[e]s; -e) dagger

'Dolch·stoß *m* dagger thrust; *fig.* (*a.* ***~ von hinten***) stab in the back; **~le,gen·de** *f hist.* stab-in-the-back legend

Dol·de ['dɔldə] *f* (-; -n) ⚘ umbel

doll [dɔl] F *adj.* → ***toll***

Dol·lar ['dɔlar] *m* (-[s]; -s) dollar; **~kurs** *m* value of the dollar; ***der ~ ist gestiegen*** *a.* the dollar has gone up (in value); **~zei·chen** *n* dollar sign

Dol·le ['dɔlə] *f* (-; -n) ⚓ tholepin

Dol·metsch ['dɔlmɛtʃ] *m* (-[e]s; -e) **1.** *Austrian* interpreter; **2.** *fig.* spokesman; **dol·met·schen** ['dɔlmɛtʃən] (h) **I.** *v/i.* interpret, act as interpreter (***j-m*** for s.o.); **II.** *v/t.* interpret; ***e-e Rede ins Englische ~*** translate a speech into English

Dol·met·scher ['dɔlmɛtʃɐ] *m* (-s; -) interpreter; **~in·sti,tut** *n*, **~schu·le** *f* school for interpreters

Dom [doːm] *m* (-[e]s; -e) **1.** cathedral; **2.** ⚠, ⚙, *geol.* dome, cupola

Do·mä·ne [do'mɛːnə] *f* (-; -n) domain, estate; *fig.* sphere

do·me·sti·zie·ren [domɛsti'tsiːrən] *v/t.* (h) domesticate

'Dom·herr *m* canon

do·mi·nant [domi'nant] *adj.* dominant; **Do·mi'nant·ak,kord** *m* ♪ dominant chord; **Do·mi·nan·te** [domi'nantə] *f* (-; -n) ♪ dominant; *fig.* dominant feature; **Do·mi·nanz** [domi'nants] *f* (-; -en) dominance; **do·mi·nie·ren** [domi'niːrən] (h) **I.** *v/i.* dominate; have the upper hand; predominate, be predominant; **II.** *v/t.* dominate; **do·mi'nie·rend** *adj.* dominant, dominating

Do·mi·ni·ka·ner [domini'kaːnɐ] *m* (-s; -) Dominican (friar); **Do·mi·ni·ka·ne·rin** [domini'kaːnərɪn] *f* (-; -nen) Dominican (nun); **Do·mi·ni'ka·ner·or·den** *m* Dominican Order, Order of St Dominic

Do·mi·no ['doːmino] **1.** *m* (-s; -s) domino; **2.** *n* (-s; -s) dominoes *pl.*; **~mas·ke** *f* → ***Domino*** 1; **~spiel** *n* → ***Domino*** 2; **~stein** *m* domino

Do·mi·zil [domi'tsiːl] *n* (-s; -e) domicile (*a.* ☤); **do·mi·zi·lie·ren** [domitsi'liːrən] *v/t.* (h) ☤ domicile *bill*; **Do·mi'zil·wech·sel** *m* ☤ domiciled bill

'Dom|ka,pi·tel *n* chapter; **~pfaff** [-pfaf] *m* (-en, -s; -en) *zo.* bullfinch

Domp·teur [dɔmp'tøːɐ] *m* (-s; -e [-'tøːrə]), **Domp·teu·se** [dɔmp'tøːzə] *f* (-; -n) (animal) trainer

Dö·ner·ke·bab [dønɛrke'bap] *m* (-s; -s) doner kebab

Don·ner ['dɔnɐ] *m* (-s; -) thunder (*a. fig.*); ***wie vom ~ gerührt*** thunderstruck; **'Don·ner·keil** *m* **1.** *myth.* thunderbolt; **2.** F *int.* heavens!, my word!; **don·nern** ['dɔnɐn] **I.** *v/i.* **1.** (h) thunder; *fig. a.* roar; ***an die Tür ~*** hammer *or* pound (away) at the door; ***mit der Faust auf den Tisch ~*** bang one's fist on the table; **2.** (sn) thunder; ***zu Boden ~*** crash (on)to the floor (*or* ground); ***gegen e-e Mauer ~*** crash (*or* smash) into a wall; **II.** F *v/t.* (h) fling; slam; ***e-e gedonnert kriegen*** F get a belt round the ears; '**don·nernd** *adj.* thundering, roaring; thunderous *applause*; **~es Gelächter** roars of laughter; '**Don·ner·schlag** *m* clap of thunder, thunderclap; **es traf ihn wie ein ~** it came like a bombshell (to him)

Don·ners·tag ['dɔnɐsta:k] *m* (-[e]s; -e) Thursday; (**am**) ~ on Thursday; '**don·ners·tags** *adv.* on Thursday(s)

'**Don·ner|stim·me** *f* thundering voice; **mit ~ brüllen** thunder; **~wet·ter** F **I.** *n* (-s; -) **1. ein ~ ging auf ihn nieder** F he got a real roasting; **wenn er heimkommt, gibt** (*or* **setzt**) **es ein ~** F he'll be in for it when he gets home; **II.** *int.* **2.** F (well) blow me!, blimey!; **3. zum ~!** damn it!; **warum** (**wer** *etc.*) **zum ~?** *sl.* why (who *etc.*) the hell?

doof [do:f] F *adj.* stupid; boring; **dieses ~e Fenster schließt nicht richtig** I can't get this stupid window to shut properly; **Doo·fi** ['do:fi] F *m* (-s; -s) F dumbo

do·pen ['do:pən, 'dɔpən] (h) **I.** *v/t.* dope; **II.** *v/refl.*: **sich ~** take dope; **Do·ping** ['do:pɪŋ, 'dɔpɪŋ] *n* (-s; -s) doping; '**Do·ping·kon,trol·le** *f* dope test

Dop·pel ['dɔpəl] *n* (-s; -) **1.** duplicate; **2.** *tennis etc.*: doubles *pl.*; doubles team; **gemischtes ~** mixed doubles *pl.*; **~ad·ler** *m* double eagle; **~agent** *m* double agent; **~b** *n* ♪ double flat (sign); **~be·deu·tung** *f* double meaning; **~be·la·stung** *f* double load; **~be·le·gung** *f* double occupancy; **~be·lich·tung** *f* *phot.* double exposure; **~be·rei·fung** *f* twin tyres (*Am.* tires) *pl.*; **~be·steue·rung** *f* double taxation; **~bett** *n* double bed; **~blind·ver·such** *m* double-blind trial (*or* test); **~bo·den** *m* false bottom

'**dop·pel·bö·dig** [-bø:dɪç] *fig. adj.* ambiguous; **~e Moral** double standards *pl.*; '**Dop·pel·bö·dig·keit** *f* (-; *no pl.*) ambiguity; double standards *pl.*

'**Dop·pel·decker** [-dɛkɐ] (*sep.* -k·k-) *m* (-s; -) biplane; F double-decker

'**dop·pel·deu·tig** [-dɔʏtɪç] *adj.* ambiguous; suggestive; '**Dop·pel·deu·tig·keit** *f* (-; -en) **1.** *no pl.* ambiguity; suggestiveness; **2.** ambiguous (*or* suggestive) remark

'**Dop·pel|ehe** *f* bigamy; **e-e ~ führen** have (*or* live with) two wives *or* husbands; **~er·folg** *m* double victory (*or* success); **~feh·ler** *m* *tennis*: double fault; **~fen·ster** *n* double(-glazed) window; *pl. coll. a.* double glazing *sg.*; **~flin·te** *f* double-barrel(l)ed gun; **~gän·ger** [-gɛŋɐ] *m* (-s; -) double, lookalike; **~gan·ze** *f* (-n; -n), **~ganz·no·te** *f* ♪ breve; **2glei·sig** [-glaɪzɪç] *adj.* → **zweigleisig**; **~griff** *m* ♪ double stop

'**Dop·pel·haus** *n* pair of semis; **~hälf·te** *f* semi-detached house, F semi

'**Dop·pel|hoch·zeit** *f* double wedding; **~kinn** *n* double chin; **~klin·ge** *f*: **Rasierer mit ~** twin-bladed razor; **~kon,zert** *n* double concerto; **~kreuz** *n* ♪ double sharp (sign); **2läu·fig** *adj.* double-barrel(l)ed; **~laut** *m* *ling.* diphthong; **~le·ben** *n* double life; **~mo,ral** *f* double standards *pl.*; **~mord** *m* double murder; **~na·me** *m* double-barel(l)ed name; double name; **~packung** (*sep.* -k·k-) *f* double pack; **~paß** *m* *soccer*: one-two; **~por,trät** *n* double portrait; **~punkt** *m* colon; **~rahm·kä·se** *m* full-fat cheese; **~rei·fen** *m* twin tyre (*Am.* tire); **2rei·hig** [-raɪɪç] *adj.* double-breasted; **~rol·le** *f* *thea. and fig.* double role; **2sei·tig** [-zaɪtɪç] **I.** *adj.* double-page *spread*; *textil.* reversible; ⚘ double; **~e Lungenentzündung** double pneumonia; **II.** *adv.* on both sides; → **gelähmt**; **~sieg** *m* double victory

'**Dop·pel·sinn** *m* double meaning, ambiguity; '**dop·pel·sin·nig** *adj.* ambiguous

'**Dop·pel|spiel** *fig. n* double dealing; **ein ~ mit j-m treiben** F double-cross s.o., two-time s.o.; **~spül·becken** (*sep.* -k·k-) *n* double-bowl kitchen sink; **~staats·an·ge·hö·rig·keit** *f* dual nationality; **~steck·do·se** *f* ⚡ two-socket outlet; **~stecker** (*sep.* -k·k-) *m* (-s; -) ⚡ double plug; two-way adapter; **2stöckig** [-ʃtœkɪç] (*sep.* -k·k-) *adj.* two-stor(e)y ..., *pred.* two-storeyed, *Am.* two-storied; *motorway etc.*: two-tiered, two-tier ...; F **~er Whisky** double whisky; **~strich** *m* ♪ double bar

dop·pelt ['dɔpəlt] **I.** *adj.* double (*a. whisky etc.*); **den ~en Preis** double the price; **~er Lohn** double-time payment; **~es Übel** twin evils; *et.* **~ haben** have two (copies) of; → **Ausfertigung, Boden** 1, **Buchführung, Moral** 1, **Spiel** 1, **Staatsangehörigkeit**; **II.** *adv.* double; twice; *with adj.*: doubly; **~ sehen** see double; **~ schmerzlich** doubly painful; **~ so alt wie ich** twice my age; **~ so lang** twice as long; **~ so groß** twice the size; **~ soviel** twice as much, double the amount (*or* price *etc.*); F **et. ~ und dreifach sichern** make absolutely sure; F **es j-m ~ und dreifach heimzahlen** F pay s.o. back with a vengeance; F **~ gemoppelt** tautologous; → **nähen** I; '**Dop·pel·te 1.** *n* (-n; *no pl.*) double; twice as much (*or* many); **das ~ des Betrags** double the amount; **2.** F *m* (-n; -n) double whisky *etc.*; '**dop·pelt·koh·len·sau·er** *adj.*: ⚗ **doppeltkohlensaures Natron** bicarbonate of soda

'**Dop·pel|tür** *f* double door(s *pl.*); **~ver·die·ner** *m* **1.** double wage-earner; **2.** *pl.* dual-income couple *sg.*; **~ver·dienst** *m* dual income; **~ver·ga·ser** *m* dual carburet(t)or; **~ver·gla·sung** *f* double glazing; **~vor·stel·lung** *f* double bill; double feature; **~wäh·rung** *f* ✝ bimetallism; **2zei·lig** [-tsaɪlɪç] *adv.*: **~ getippt** double-paced; **~zim·mer** *n* double room; twin-bedded room

'**dop·pel·zün·gig** [-tsʏŋɪç] *adj.* two--faced; ambiguous *remark etc.*; '**Dop·pel·zün·gig·keit** *f* (-; -en) **1.** *no pl.* two--facedness; ambiguity; **2.** ambiguous remark

Dopp·ler·ef,fekt ['dɔplɐ-] *m* *phys.* Doppler effect

Dorf [dɔrf] *n* (-[e]s; Dörfer ['dœrfɐ]) village; **auf dem ~ wohnen** live in a village; **er stammt vom ~** he's from the country; **die Welt ist ein ~** it's a small world; *contp.* **das ist ja hier ein richtiges ~** this place is so provincial; **~be·woh·ner** *m* villager

Dörf·chen ['dœrfçən] *n* (-s; -) little village; hamlet

'**Dorf·ju·gend** *f* young people (*or* youngsters) *pl.* in the village

dörf·lich ['dœrflɪç] *adj.* village *life etc.*; rustic

'**Dorf|pfar·rer** *m* country vicar; **~platz** *m* village green; **~schen·ke** *f*, **~wirts·haus** *n* village inn

Dorn [dɔrn] *m* (-[e]s; -en) thorn (*a. fig.*); prickle, ⚘ spine; *a. sport*: spike; tongue; ⚙ pin, bolt; *fig.* **er ist ihr ein ~ im Auge** he's a thorn in her side (*or* flesh); **~busch** *m* thornbush; *bibl.* **der brennende ~** the burning bush

Dor·nen|ge·strüpp ['dɔrnən-] *n* thornbushes *pl.*, brambles *pl.*; **~hecke** (*sep.* -k·k-) *f* prickly hedge, hedge of thorns; **~kro·ne** *f* crown of thorns; **2reich** *fig. adj.*, **2voll** *adj.* hard, difficult

'**Dorn|fort·satz** *m* *anat.* spinous process; **~hai** *m* dogfish

dor·nig ['dɔrnɪç] *adj.* thorny (*a. fig.*), prickly

Dorn·rös·chen ['dɔrnrø:sçən] *n* (-s; *no pl.*) Sleeping Beauty; **~schlaf** *m*: **im ~ liegen** be in (a state of) hibernation; **aus s-m ~ erwachen** come out of one's long hibernation

dör·ren ['dœrən] **I.** *v/t.* (h) dry, desiccate; kiln-dry; **II.** *v/i.* (sn) dry (up)

Dörr|fleisch ['dœr-] *n* dried meat; **~obst** *n* dried fruit; **~pflau·me** *f* prune

Dorsch [dɔrʃ] *m* (-[e]s; -e) cod, *Am. a.* codfish

dort [dɔrt] *adv.* there; **~ drüben** over there; **von ~** → **~'her** *adv.*: (**von**) **~** from there; **~'hin** *adv.* **1.** there; **2.** that way; **~hin'auf** *adv.* up there; **~hin'aus** *adv.* out there; F *fig.* **bis ~** F incredibly ...; **bis ~ arbeiten** F work like crazy; **~hin'ein** *adv.* in there; **~hin'un·ter** *adv.* down there

dor·tig ['dɔrtɪç] *adj.*: **die ~en Verhältnisse** the conditions there

dort·zu·lan·de ['dɔrttsulandə] *adv.* there, in those parts

Do·se ['do:zə] *f* (-; -n) box; tin, can; ⚡ box

dö·sen ['dø:zən] F *v/i.* (h) doze; (**vor sich hin**) **~** daydream; **ein bißchen ~** have a little doze

'**Do·sen|bier** *n* canned beer; **~fleisch** *n*, **~milch** *f*, **~öff·ner** *m* → **Büchsenfleisch** *etc.*

do·sie·ren [do'zi:rən] *v/t.* (h) measure out; *fig.* mete out, dispense; **richtig ~** *pharm.* give (*or* take) the right dose of; **Do'sie·rung** *f* (-; -en) dosage, dose

dö·sig ['dø:zɪç] F *adj.* **1.** dozy, sleepy; **2.** F dop(e)y

Do·sis ['do:zɪs] *f* (-; Dosen ['do:zən]) dose (*a. fig.*), dosage; *fig.* touch, dash

Dos·sier [dɔ'sje:] *n* (-s; -s) file

do·tiert [do'ti:ɐt] *adj.*: **gut ~ sein** be well paid; **die Stellung ist mit 5000 Mark ~** the monthly salary for the post is 5000 marks; **das Turnier ist mit 300 000 Mark ~** the total prize money for the tournament is 300 000 marks; **die Auszeichnung ist mit 25 000 Mark ~** the award includes prize money of 25 000 marks

Dot·ter ['dɔtɐ] *m, n* (-s; -) (egg) yolk; **~blu·me** *f* marsh marigold; **2gelb** *adj.* deep yellow

dou·beln ['du:bəln] *v/t.* (h): **j-n ~** *film*: be (*or* act as) s.o.'s stuntman *or* stuntwoman (*or* double); **er mußte in dieser Szene gedoubelt werden** they had to bring in a stuntman (*or* double) for that scene; **Dou·ble** ['du:bəl] *n* (-s; -s) **1.** *film*: stuntman, stuntwoman, double; **2.** ♪ double; **3.** double, lookalike; **4.** *sport*: double; **das ~ schaffen** do the double

Dou·blet·te *f* → **Dublette**

Do·zent [do'tsɛnt] *m* (-en; -en) (university) lecturer; *Am.* assistant professor; **do·zie·ren** [do'tsi:rən] *v/i.* (h) lecture (**über**

acc. on) (*a. fig.*); ***er doziert an e-r Universität*** he's a university lecturer

Dra·che ['draxə] *m* (-n; -n) dragon

Dra·chen ['draxən] *m* (-s; -) **1.** kite; ***e-n ~ steigen lassen*** fly a kite; **2.** hang glider; **3.** *fig.* shrew, F battleaxe; **~flie·ger** *m* hang glider; **~saat** *lit. f* seeds *pl.* of discord, dragon's teeth *pl.*

Dra·gee *n*, **Dra·gée** [dra'ʒe:] *n* (-s; -s) (sugar)coated tablet, dragee

Draht [dra:t] *m* (-[e]s; Drähte ['drɛ:tə]) wire; *fig.* line; *pol.* ***heißer ~*** hot line; ***direkter ~*** direct line (***zu*** *dat.* to); F ***auf ~ sein*** F be on the ball; **~aus·lö·ser** *m phot.* cable release; **~bür·ste** *f* wire brush; **~esel** F *hum. m* F pushbike; F boneshaker; **~funk** *m radio:* wired broadcasting; **~git·ter** *n* wire netting; **~glas** *n* wire(d) glass

'Draht·haar|dackel (*sep.* -k·k-) *m* wirehair(ed dachshund); **~ter·ri·er** *m* wirehair(ed terrier)

drah·tig ['dra:tıç] *adj.* wiry

'draht·los *adj.* wireless, radio ...; ***~es Telefon*** cordless phone; ***~e Fernbedienung*** infrared remote control

'Draht|pup·pe *f* marionette; **~sai·te** *f* wire string; **~sche·re** *f* wire cutter(s *pl.*); ***e-e ~*** a pair of wirecutters, a wirecutter

'Draht·seil *n* wire rope, (wire) cable; tightrope; → ***Nerv;*** **~akt** *m* tightrope (*or* high-wire) act; *fig.* razor-edge affair; *fig.* ***das Ganze ist ein ziemlicher ~*** we're *etc.* balancing on a razor edge; **~bahn** *f* cable railway; **~künst·ler** *m* tightrope artist

'Draht|sieb *n* wire sieve; **~zan·ge** *f* wire cutter; **~zaun** *m* wire fence; **~zie·her** [-tsi:ɐ] *fig. m* (-s; -) wirepuller; *pol.* powerbroker

Drai·na·ge [drɛ'na:ʒə] *f* (-; -n) *a.* ⚒ drainage; **drai·nie·ren** [drɛ'ni:rən] *v/t.* (h) drain

dra·ko·nisch [dra'ko:nıʃ] *adj.* draconian

drall [dral] **I.** *adj.* buxom; full, plump; **II.** **2** *m* (-[e]s; -e) *textil.* twist; spin *of a ball*

Dra·ma ['dra:ma] *n* (-s; -men) drama (*a. fig.*); play; *fig.* ***mach kein ~ draus*** don't make a big thing out of it; **Dra·ma·tik** [dra'ma:tık] *f* (- *no pl.*) **1.** drama; **2.** *fig.* (high) drama, excitement; **Dra·ma·ti·ker** [dra'ma:tikɐ] *m* (-s; -) dramatist, playwright; **dra·ma·tisch** [dra'ma:tıʃ] *adj.* dramatic(ally *adv.*) (*a. fig.*); **dra·ma·ti·sie·ren** [dramati'zi:rən] *v/t.* (h) adapt for the stage; *fig.* dramatize; **Dra·ma·turg** [drama'tʊrk] *m* (-en; -en [-'tʊrgən]) script editor, dramaturg(e); **dra·ma·tur·gisch** [drama'tʊrgıʃ] *adj.* dramaturgical

dran [dran] F *pron. adv.* **1.** ***an ihm*** (***an dem Hühnchen***) ***ist nichts ~*** F he's (the chicken's) all skin and bones; ***es ist etwas*** (***nichts***) ***~*** there's something in it (nothing to it); ***früh*** (***spät***) ***~ sein*** be early (late); ***er ist gut ~*** F he's got it good, he's doing all right (*Am.* alright); ***er ist schlecht*** (*or* ***übel***) ***~*** he's in a bad way, F he's scraping the barrel; ***wie ist er mit Kleidung ~?*** F how's he doing (*or* fixed) for clothes?; ***ich weiß nie, wie ich mit ihr ~ bin*** I never know where I stand with her; **2.** ***wer ist ~?*** whose turn is it?; ***ich bin ~*** it's my turn; *fig.* ***jetzt ist er aber ~*** F he's really copped it now; → ***glauben*** II; **~blei·ben** F *v/i.* (*irr.*, *sep.*, sn, → ***bleiben***) stay on; stick; *fig.* ***an et. ~*** keep at it; ***an j-m ~*** keep on at s.o.; *teleph.* ***bleib dran!*** hang on

drang [draŋ] *pret. of* ***dringen***

Drang *m* (-[e]s; *no pl.*) **1.** urge, wish, desire, need (***nach*** *dat.*, ***zu*** *dat.* for; ***zu*** *inf.* to *inf.*); ***~ nach Freiheit*** urge for freedom; ***~ zum Lügen*** urge (*or* compulsion) to tell lies; ***e-n ~ zum Lügen haben*** *a.* be a compulsive liar; ***e-n ~ nach Höherem haben*** aspire to higher things; **2.** pressure; ***im ~ der Ereignisse*** under the pressure of events

Drän·ge·lei [drɛŋə'laı] F *f* (-; -en) pushing and shoving, jostling; **drän·geln** ['drɛŋəln] F (h) **I.** *v/i. and v/refl.* (***sich ~***) push, jostle, F shove; ***sich nach vorn ~*** push (*or* elbow) one's way to the front; jump the queue (*Am.* line); **II.** *v/t.* push, jostle, F shove; *fig.* pester

drän·gen ['drɛŋən] (h) **I.** *v/t.* **1.** push; ***j-n zur Seite ~*** push s.o. aside (*or* out of the way); → ***Defensive, Ecke, Hintergrund;*** **2.** press (***zu tun*** into doing), urge (to do), pressurize (into doing); rush; ***ich lasse mich nicht ~*** I'm not going to let anyone (*or* them *etc.*) rush me; ***ich möchte Sie nicht ~*** I don't mean to put pressure on you; **3.** ***es drängte mich zu*** *inf.* I felt (*or* had) the urge to *inf.*, I felt I ought to (*or* had to) *inf.*, I felt compelled to *inf.*, I felt obliged to *inf.*; **II.** *v/i.* **4.** push (and shove); ***nach vorn ~*** push one's way forward (*or* to the front); ***zum Eingang ~*** push its *or* their way (*or* crowd) towards the entrance; ***alles drängte ins Freie*** everyone wanted to get out into the open; ***alles drängt nach München*** (***zum Stadion***) everyone seems to be moving to Munich (to be converging on *or* making their way to the stadium); ***~ in*** *acc.* flood into; **5.** be urgent; ***die Zeit drängt*** time's running short; **6.** ***~ auf*** *acc.* press for; ***darauf ~, daß j-d et. tut*** press (for) s.o. to do s.th.; ***darauf ~, daß et. getan wird*** press for s.th. to be done; ***darauf ~, daß sich j-d entscheidet*** press (for) s.o. to make a decision, press s.o. for a decision; → ***Aufbruch;*** **III.** *v/refl.:* ***sich ~*** **7.** push (and shove); → *a.* **4;** ***sich um j-n ~*** crowd (a)round s.o.; ***die Leute ~ sich auf den Straßen*** people are crowding the streets, the streets are crowded with people; **8.** *fig.* ***sich ~ nach*** *dat.* be keen on; ***die Leute ~ sich danach, bei uns zu arbeiten*** people are queuing up to work for us; **IV.** **2** *n* (-s) pushing and shoving; *fig.* urging; insistence; *fig.* ***auf ~ der Regierung*** on the government's urging (*or* insistence); ***ich habe es auf sein ~ hin getan*** he persuaded (*or* forced) me to do it

Drang·sal ['draŋza:l] *f* (-; -e) distress, hardship; **drang·sa·lie·ren** [draŋza'li:rən] *v/t.* (h) pester, plague; pick on

'dran|hal·ten F *v/refl.* (*irr.*, *sep.*, h, → ***halten***): ***sich ~*** hurry up, F get a move on; put one's back into it (*or* the job), keep at it; **~hän·gen** F (*irr.*, *sep.*, h, → ***hängen***) **I.** *v/t.* F tag on; **II.** *fig. v/refl.:* ***sich ~*** tag along; jump on the bandwagon; **~kom·men** F *v/i.* (*irr.*, *sep.*, sn, → ***kommen***) **1.** get at it, reach it; **2.** *ped.* be called; ***ich komme jetzt dran*** it's my turn, I'm next; ***wer kommt dran?*** who's next?; ***das kommt nächste Woche dran*** we'll be doing that next week; **~krie·gen** F *v/t.* (*sep.*, h) **1.** get *s.o.* to do it; **2.** fool *s.o.*; **~ma·chen** F *v/refl.* (*sep.*, h): ***sich ~*** get down to it; **~neh·men** F *v/t.* (*irr.*, *sep.*, h, → ***nehmen***) **1.** take *patient*; see to, serve *customer*; **2.** *ped.* ask *a pupil*; **3.** *b.s.* → ***rannehmen***

dra·pie·ren [dra'pi:rən] *v/t.* (h) drape (***mit*** *dat.* with)

dra·stisch ['drastıʃ] *adj.* drastic(ally *adv.*); *adv.* ***~ kürzen*** slash

drauf [draʊf] F *pron. adv.* **1.** → ***darauf;*** **2.** ***et.*** (***gut***) ***~ haben*** have s.th. at one's fingertips, F have s.th. off pat; ***technisch hat er nichts ~*** F he hasn't got a clue about technical things; ***sie hat was ~*** she's really good, *a.* F she knows her stuff, she's in top form; ***gut ~ sein*** F be on the ball, feel good; **3.** ***~ und dran sein zu*** *inf.* be on the point of *ger.*, be about to *inf.*; ***ich war ~ und dran, ihn zu schlagen*** I (very) nearly hit him; **~be·kom·men** F *v/i.* (*irr.*, *sep.*, h, → ***bekommen***) → ***draufkriegen***

Drauf·gän·ger ['draʊfgɛŋɐ] *m* (-s; -) **1.** daredevil; **2.** go-getter; **drauf·gän·ge·risch** ['draʊfgɛŋərıʃ] *adj.* **1.** daredevil ..., reckless; **2.** go-getting; **'Drauf·gän·ger·tum** *n* (-s; *no pl.*) **1.** recklessness; **2.** aggressiveness

'drauf|ge·ben F *v/t.* (*irr.*, *sep.*, h, → ***geben***): ***j-m eins ~*** F belt s.o. one, give s.o. a belt round the ears; **~ge·hen** F *v/i.* (*irr.*, *sep.*, sn, → ***gehen***) a) be used (up), be lost; *money:* be used up, F go down the drain; b) F go to pot; c) be killed, *sl.* snuff it; **~kom·men** F *v/i.* (*irr.*, *sep.*, sn, → ***kommen***): ***ich bin einfach nicht draufgekommen*** it just didn't occur to me; ***ich komm' nicht drauf*** I can't think of it; ***j-m ~*** find s.o. out; **~krie·gen** F *v/t.* (*sep.*, h): ***eins ~*** F get a belt round the ears; F get a (real) roasting

drauf'los|ar·bei·ten F *v/i.* (*sep.*, h) F get cracking; **~ge·hen** F *v/i.* (*irr.*, *sep.*, sn, → ***gehen***) F go at it; make straight for it; **~re·den** F *v/i.* (*sep.*, h) F start rattling away; **~schie·ßen** F *v/i.* (*irr.*, *sep.*, h, → ***schießen***) start shooting wildly; **~schimp·fen** F *v/i.* (*sep.*, h) F let rip; **~schla·gen** F *v/i.* (*irr.*, *sep.*, h, → ***schlagen***) let fly

'drauf|ma·chen F *v/t.* (*sep.*, h): ***einen ~*** F have (*or* go on) a binge; **2sicht** *f* top view; **~sto·ßen** F *v/t.* (*irr.*, *sep.*, h, → ***stoßen***): ***j-n ~*** point it out to s.o., *iro.* spell it out (to s.o.), F rub s.o.'s nose in it; **~zah·len** F (*sep.*, h) **I.** *v/t.* pay an extra *20 marks etc.*; **II.** *v/i.* (*a.* ***ganz schön ~***) F make a bad deal (on it); *fig.* lose out

draus [draʊs] F *pron. adv.* → ***daraus***

drau·ßen ['draʊsən] *adv.* outside; in the open; ***da ~*** out there

drech·seln ['drɛksəln] *v/t.* (h) **1.** turn *s.th.* on the lathe; **2.** *fig.* turn *s.th.* out; **Drechs·ler** ['drɛkslɐ] *m* (-s; -) wood turner

Dreck [drɛk] F *m* (-[e]s; *no pl.*) dirt, muck, filth; *fig.* rubbish, *esp. Am.* garbage; *fig.* ***hast du ~ in den Ohren?*** it's time you washed your ears out; ***ganz schön im ~ sitzen*** F be in a fine (*or* real) mess; ***j-n wie den letzten ~ behandeln*** treat s.o. like dirt (*or* muck); ***mit ~ bewerfen*** sling mud at; ***durch den ~ ziehen*** drag through the mud (*or* mire); ***wir sind aus dem ärgsten*** (*or* ***gröbsten, schlimmsten***) ***~ heraus*** the worst (of it) is behind us, we're out of the wood(s); ***er kümmert sich e-n ~ darum*** F he doesn't care a damn; ***das geht dich e-n ~ an!*** that's

none of your (F bloody) business; ***du verstehst e-n ~ davon*** you don't know the first thing about it; ***sich wegen jedem ~ beschweren*** complain about every little (F piddling) thing; ***~ am Stekken haben*** have a skeleton in the cupboard, have blotted one's copybook; ***sie haben alle ~ am Stecken*** *a.* not one of them has got a clean record (*or* slate), not one of them is innocent; **~ar·beit** F *f* dirty work (*a. fig.*); **~fleck** F *m* dirty mark
dreckig ['drɛkɪç] (*sep.* -k·k-) F **I.** *adj.* dirty, filthy (*both a. fig.*); *fig.* dirty, nasty; **II.** *adv.*: ***es geht ihm ~*** a) F he's going through a bad patch, b) he's not in the best of health, he's in a pretty bad state
'Dreck|loch *contp. n* pigsty, F hole; **~nest** *contp. n* dump, F hole; **~sack** *contp. m sl.* swine; **~sau** *contp. f* (dirty) pig; *sl.* swine; **~schleu·der** *contp. f* F nasty piece (*or* bit) of work; ***e-e ~ sein*** *a.* have a wicked tongue; **~schwein** *contp. n* → ***Drecksau***
'Drecks·kerl *contp. m* → ***Drecksack***
'Dreck·spatz F *m* F mucky pup
'Drecks·zeug F *n* rubbish, *esp. Am.* garbage
'Dreck|wet·ter F *n* filthy weather; **~zeug** *n* → ***Dreckszeug***
Dreh [dre:] *m* (-s; -s) turn; F trick; ***jetzt hab' ich den ~ heraus*** (*or* ***weg***) now I've got the hang of it; F (***so***) ***um den ~*** round about then; ***sagen wir sechs Uhr oder so um den ~*** *a.* F let's say sixish; *20 Mark* ***oder so um den ~*** or so, or thereabouts; **~ach·se** *f* axis of rotation; **~ar·bei·ten** *pl. film*: shooting *sg.*; ***bei den ~ sein*** be on set; **~bank** *f* (-; ⸚e) lathe
'dreh·bar *adj.* revolving; rotating; swivel ...
'Dreh|be·we·gung *f* rotation; turn; **~blei·stift** *m* propelling pencil; **~bol·zen** *m* pivot pin; **~brücke** (*sep.* -k·k-) *f* swing bridge
'Dreh·buch *n* script, screenplay; **~au·tor** *m* screenwriter, scriptwriter
'Dreh·büh·ne *f* revolving stage
dre·hen ['dre:ən] (h) **I.** *v/t.* **1.** turn (*a.* ⚙); *fig.* ***man kann es ~ und wenden(, wie man will), wie man es auch dreht und wendet*** whichever way you look at it; **2.** twist (*a. fig.*); **3.** rotate; swivel; **4.** ***sich e-e Zigarette ~*** roll a cigarette; **5.** ***durch den*** (***Fleisch***)***Wolf ~*** grind, put through the grinder (*or* mincer); **6.** shoot *film etc.*; **7.** F *fig.* ***es ~*** F wangle it; → ***Ding*** 4; **II.** *v/i.* **8.** turn; **9.** ***~ an*** *dat.* turn; F *fig.* fiddle with; **III.** *v/refl.*: ***sich ~*** **10.** turn, go round, spin round; *die Erde* ***dreht sich um ihre Achse*** (***um die Sonne***) rotates on its axis (revolves around the sun); ***mir dreht sich alles*** my head's spinning; *fig.* ***sich ~ und winden*** hedge; **11.** *wind*: shift, veer (round); **12.** *fig.* ***sich ~ um*** *acc.* revolve round; ***alles drehte sich um ihn*** he was the cent|re (*Am.* -er) of attraction; **13.** F *fig.* ***sich ~ um*** *acc.* be about, concern; ***es dreht sich darum, ob*** it's a question (*or* matter) of whether; ***worum dreht es sich?*** what's it all about?; *das Gespräch* ***drehte sich um Steuern*** was about taxes
Dre·her ['dre:ɐ] *m* (-s; -) ⚙ turner
'Dreh|er·laub·nis *f* filming permission; **~feld** *n* ⚡ rotating field; **~flü·gel·flug·zeug** *n*, **~flüg·ler** ['dre:fly:glɐ] *m* (-s; -) rotorplane; **~ge·schwin·dig·keit** *f* speed (of rotation), rotating speed; **~kar͵tei** *f* rotary file; **~knopf** *m* knob; **~kol·ben·mo·tor** *m* rotary piston engine; **~kraft** *f* torque; **~kran** *m* swing crane; **~kreuz** *n* turnstile; **~lei·er** *f* hurdy-gurdy; **~ma͵schi·ne** *f* lathe; **~mo͵ment** *n* torque; **~or·gel** *f* barrel organ; **~ort** *m* location; **~pau·se** *f* break in shooting; **~punkt** *m* ⚙ fulcrum; *fig.* ***Dreh- und Angelpunkt*** pivot; **~re·stau͵rant** *n* revolving restaurant; **~schal·ter** *m* ⚡ rotary switch; **~schei·be** *f* **1.** turntable; potter's wheel; *teleph. etc.* dial; **2.** *fig.* hub, nerve cent|re (*Am.* -er); **~strom** *m* ⚡ three-phase current; **~stuhl** *m* swivel chair; **~tag** *m film*: shooting day; ***am dritten ~*** on the third day of shooting; **~tür** *f* revolving door
Dre·hung ['dre:ʊŋ] *f* (-; -en) turn; rotation (***um*** *acc.* on); revolution (round); spin; twist
'Dreh·wurm *m*: F *fig.* ***den ~ haben*** feel dizzy (*or* giddy)
'Dreh·zahl *f* ⚙ speed, revolutions *pl.* per minute (rpm); **~mes·ser** *m* revolution counter; *mot.* rev counter, *Am.* tachometer
'Dreh·zeit *f film*: shooting time
drei [draɪ] **I.** *adj.* three; ***ehe man bis ~ zählen konnte*** before you could say Jack Robinson; ***er sieht aus, als ob er nicht bis ~ zählen könnte*** a) he looks as if butter wouldn't melt in his mouth, b) F he looks a right idiot; → ***Ding*** 1; **II.** ⁲ *f* (-; -en) three; *ped.* C; (*bus etc.*) (number) three; ***e-e ~ schreiben*** get a C
'Drei·ach·ser ['draɪʔaksɐ] *m* (-s; -) *mot.* six-wheeler
Drei'ach·tel·takt *m* ♪: (***im ~*** in) three-eight time
Drei|ak·ter ['draɪʔaktɐ] *m* (-s; -) *thea.* three-act play; **⁲bän·dig** ['draɪbɛndɪç] *adj.* three-volume ..., in three volumes; **⁲bei·nig** ['draɪbaɪnɪç] *adj.* three-legged
'Drei·bett·zim·mer *n* three-bed room
'drei·di·men·sio·nal ['draɪdimɛnzĭona:l] *adj.* three-dimensional
'Drei·eck *n* (-[e]s; -e) triangle; **'Drei·eck·ge·schäft** *n* ✝ three-way deal; **'drei·eckig** (*sep.* -k·k-) *adj.* triangular; **'Drei·eck·schal·tung** *f* ⚡ delta connection; **'Drei·ecks·ge·schich·te** *f a* case of the eternal triangle; **'Drei·ecks·ver·hält·nis** *n* love triangle, ménage à trois; ***ein ~ haben*** run a ménage à trois
'drei·ein'halb *adj.* three and a half
Drei'ei·nig·keit *f* (-; *no pl.*) Trinity
Drei·er ['draɪɐ] *m* (-s; -) **1.** → ***Drei***; **2.** ***e-n ~ haben*** *lotto*: have (got) three right; **3.** *figure skating etc.*: figure (of) three; **4.** F ***flotter ~*** F threesome, three-way deal
drei·er·lei ['draɪɐ'laɪ] *adj.* three (different) kinds of; *su.* three things
'Drei·er·takt *m* triple time
drei·fach ['draɪfax] **I.** *adj.* triple; ***in ~er Ausfertigung*** in triplicate; ***et. in ~er Ausfertigung schicken*** send three copies of s.th.; ***die ~e Menge*** three times the amount; ***~er Sieger*** three-time winner (*or* champion); **II.** *adv.* three times; **'Drei·fa·che** *n* (-n): ***das ~*** three times as much; three times the amount; ***um ein ~s steigen*** triple, rise (*or* go up) threefold
Drei'fal·tig·keit *f* (-; *no pl.*) Trinity; **Drei'fal·tig·keits·fest** *n* Trinity Sunday
Drei'far·ben·druck *m* (-[e]s; -e) three-colo(u)r print(ing); **'drei·far·big** *adj.* three-colo(u)red
'Drei·gang·schal·tung *f bicycle*: three-speed gears *pl.*
'Drei|ge·spann *n* three-horse carriage; *fig.* trio, threesome; **~ge·stirn** *fig. n* triumvirate; **⁲ge·teilt** *adj.* divided into three parts; three-part *article etc.*
Drei'gro·schen·heft *n esp. Brit.* penny dreadful, *Am.* dime novel
'drei'hun·dert *adj.* three hundred
'drei·jäh·rig ['draɪjɛ:rɪç] *adj.* **1.** three-year-old ...; **2.** three year ...; ***ein ~es ...*** *a.* three years of ...; **'Drei·jäh·ri·ge** ['draɪjɛ:rɪgə] *m, f* (-n; -n) three-year-old
'Drei·kampf *m sport*: triathlon
'drei·ka·rä·tig [-karɛ:tɪç] *adj.* three-carat ...
Drei'kä·se·hoch F *m* (-s; -[s]) F titch
'Drei·klang ♪ *m* triad
Drei'kö·nigs·fest *n*: ***das ~*** Epiphany
'drei·köp·fig [-kœpfɪç] *adj. family etc.* of three
'drei·la·gig [-la:gɪç] *adj.* three-ply
Drei'län·der·eck *n* triangle (*where three countries meet*)
Drei'mäch·te·ab·kom·men *n pol.* three-power (*or* tripartite) agreement
'drei·mal *adv.* three times; **'drei·ma·lig** [-ma:lɪç] *adj.*: ***nach ~er Wiederholung*** after repeating it three times, after three repetitions (*or* repeats); ***nach ~em Klingeln*** after I *etc.* had rung three times; ***nach ~em Versuch*** after three attempts, after the third attempt
Drei·ma·ster ['draɪmastɐ] *m* (-s; -) ⚓ three-master
Drei'mei·len·zo·ne *f* ⚓, ⚖ three-mile limit
'drei·mo·na·tig [-mona:tɪç] *adj.* **1.** three-month-old *baby etc.*; **2.** three-month ...; ***nach e-m ~en Englandaufenthalt*** after three months (*or* a three-month stay) in England; **'drei·mo·nat·lich** **I.** *adj.* three-monthly ..., quarterly; **II.** *adv.* every three months
drein [draɪn] F *pron. adv.* → ***darein***; **~blicken** (*sep.* -k·k-) F *v/i.* (*sep.*, h) look *happy, sad etc.*; **~re·den** F *v/i.* (*sep.*, h) **1.** interrupt, butt in; ***j-m ~*** butt into s.o.'s conversation; **2.** interfere (***bei*** *dat.* with; ***in*** *acc.* in); ***er läßt sich in s-e Arbeit nicht*** (*or* ***von niemandem***) ***~*** he won't let anyone tell him what to do; **~schau·en** F *v/i.* (*sep.*, h) → ***dreinblikken***; **~schla·gen** F *v/i.* (*irr.*, *sep.*, h, → ***schlagen***) join in the fight; ***mit den Fäusten ~*** use one's fists
Drei·par'tei·en·sy͵stem *n* three-party system
'drei|pha·sig [-fa:zɪç] *adj.* ⚡ three-phase ...; **~po·lig** [-po:lɪç] *adj.* three-pole ...
'Drei·punkt|gurt *m mot.* three-point belt; **~lan·dung** *f* ✈ three-point landing
'Drei|rad *n* tricycle; **~satz** *m* (-es; *no pl.*), **~satz·rech·nung** *f* ⩚ rule of three; **⁲sei·tig** [-zaɪtɪç] *adj.* **1.** three-sided, ⩚ *a.* trilateral; **2.** three-page ...; **⁲sil·big** [-zɪlbɪç] *adj.* three-syllable ...; **~spitz** *m* (-es; -e) tricorn(e), three-cornered hat; **⁲spra·chig** [-ʃpra:xɪç] *adj.* trilingual; ***~ sein*** *a.* speak three languages fluently, be fluent in three languages; **~sprung** *m* triple jump; **⁲spu·rig** [-ʃpu:rɪç] *adj.* three-lane ...
drei·ßig ['draɪsɪç] *adj.* thirty; ***~ beide*** *tennis*: thirty all; ***in den ~er Jahren*** in the thirties; ***er ist in den ⁲ern*** he's in his thirties; **Drei·ßi·ger** ['draɪsɪgɐ] *m* (-s; -) man in his thirties; F thirtysomething;

Drei·ßi·ge·rin ['draɪsɪgərɪn] *f* (-; -nen) woman in her thirties; **'drei·ßig·jäh·rig** [-jɛːrɪç] *adj.*: ***der* 2*e Krieg*** the Thirty Years' War; **'drei·ßigst** *adj.* thirtieth; ***sie hat heute ihren* 2*en*** she's thirty today, it's her thirtieth birthday today

dreist [draɪst] *adj.* bold as brass; cheeky, impudent; brazen *lie etc.*

'drei·stel·lig [-ʃtɛlɪç] *adj.* three-digit *figure etc.*

Drei'ster·ne|ho,tel *n* three-star hotel; **~koch** *m* five-star chef; **~re·stau,rant** *n* five-star restaurant

Drei·stig·keit ['draɪstɪçkaɪt] *f* (-; -en) **1.** *no pl.* boldness, audacity; impudence; **2.** impudent remark

'drei|stim·mig [-ʃtɪmɪç] ♪ **I.** *adj.* three-part ...; **II.** *adv.*: ~ ***singen*** sing in three-part harmony; **~stöckig** [-ʃtœkɪç] (*sep.* -k·k-) *adj.* three-stor(e)y ...

Drei'stu·fen|plan *m* three-stage plan; **~ra,ke·te** *f* three-stage rocket (*or* missile)

'drei·stu·fig [-ʃtuːfɪç] *adj.* three-stage ...

'drei|stün·dig [-ʃtʏndɪç] *adj.* three-hour(-long) ...; 2**'ta·ge·bart** F *m* F designer stubble; **~tä·gig** [-tɛːgɪç] *adj.* **1.** three-day(-long) ...; **2.** three-day-old ...; **~tei·lig** [-taɪlɪç] *adj.* three-part ..., tripartite ..., in three parts; three-piece *suit etc.*

'drei'vier·tel I. *adj.*: ***in e-r ~ Stunde*** in three quarters of an hour, in 45 minutes; ***~ der Bevölkerung*** three quarters of the population; **II.** *adv.*: ~ ***voll*** three-quarters full

Drei'vier·tel·mehr·heit *f* three-quarter majority

'Drei·vier·tel'stun·de *f* three quarters of an hour, 45 minutes *pl.*

Drei'vier·tel·takt *m* ♪: (***im*** ~ in) three-four time

'Drei·weg·box *f* three-way speaker; **Drei'we·ge·ka·ta·ly,sa·tor** *m mot.* three-way catalyst (*or* catalytic converter); **'Drei·weg·laut·spre·cher** *m* three-way loudspeaker

'drei|wer·tig [-veːɐtɪç] *adj.* ⚗ trivalent; **~wö·chig** [-vœçɪç] *adj.* **1.** three-week ...; **2.** three-week-old ...

'Drei·zack *m* (-s; -e) **1.** trident; **2.** ⚘ arrow grass

'drei·zehn *adj.* thirteen; **'drei·zehnt** *adj.* thirteenth; **'Drei·zehn·tel** *n* (-s; -) thirteenth (part)

Drei'zim·mer·woh·nung *f* two-bedroom(ed) flat (*Am.* apartment)

Dre·sche ['drɛʃə] F *f* (-; *no pl.*): ***~ bekommen*** get a good hiding; **dre·schen** ['drɛʃən] (drosch, gedroschen, h) **I.** *v/t.* thresh; F bang *ball etc.*; → ***grün*** I, ***Phrase, Stroh, windelweich***; **II.** *v/i.* thresh; F ***auf die Tasten*** ~ hammer (*or* pound) away at the piano (*or* typewriter *etc.*); **'Dresch·fle·gel** *m* flail; **'Dresch·ma,schi·ne** *f* threshing machine

Dreß [drɛs] *m* (Dresses; Dresse) *sport*: outfit, *esp. Brit. soccer*: strip

Dres·seur [drɛ'søːɐ] *m* (-s; -e [-'søːrə]) (animal) trainer; **dres·sie·ren** [drɛ'siːrən] *v/t.* (h) train; break in; *fig.* drill; ⚙ finish; *gastr.* truss (up); **dres·siert** [drɛ'siːɐt] *adj.* trained; performing *seal etc.*; ***der Hund ist auf den Mann*** ~ he's been trained as an attack dog

Dres·sing ['drɛsɪŋ] *n* (-s; -s) **1.** (*salad*) dressing; **2.** stuffing, *Am. a.* dressing

Dress·man ['drɛsmən] *m* (-s; -men) male model (*a. euphem.*)

Dres·sur [drɛ'suːɐ] *f* (-; -en [-'suːrən]) training; *sport*: → **~rei·ten** *n* dressage

drib·beln ['drɪbəln] *v/i.* (h) *sport*: dribble (the ball); **Dribb·ling** ['drɪblɪŋ] *n* (-s; -s) dribble

Drill [drɪl] *m* (-[e]s; *no pl.*) ⚔ drill (*a. fig.*); **'Drill·boh·rer** *m* drill; **dril·len** ['drɪlən] *v/t.* (h) **1.** ⚔ drill (*a. fig.*); coach; **2.** ⚙ twist; **3.** drill (*a.* ⚒)

Dril·lich ['drɪlɪç] *m* (-s; -e) drill; **~an·zug** *m* overalls *pl.*

Dril·ling ['drɪlɪŋ] *m* (-s; -e) triplet

drin [drɪn] F *pron. adv.* **1.** → ***darin***; **2.** *fig.* ***das ist nicht ~!*** that's not on; ***das ist bei mir nicht*** ~ that's out of the question for me, you can count me out on that; ***mehr war nicht*** ~ that was the best I *etc.* could do; ***es ist noch alles*** ~ anything's possible

drin·gen ['drɪŋən] *v/i.* (drang, gedrungen, sn) **1.** ~ ***durch*** *acc.* force one's way (*or* break) through; *light, bullet etc.*: penetrate, pierce; *water etc.*: leak (*or* seep) through; **2.** ~ ***aus*** *dat.* come out of; *crowd*: surge out of; *sound*: come from; ***aus der Küche drang lautes Gelächter*** you could hear loud laughter coming from the kitchen; **3.** ~ ***in*** *acc.* penetrate (into); force one's way into; ***in die Öffentlichkeit*** ~ leak out; **4.** ~ ***bis zu*** *dat.* reach, get as far as; **5.** ~ ***auf*** *acc.* press for, urge; ***darauf ~, daß et. getan wird*** press for s.th. to be done; **6.** ~ ***in*** *acc.* press *s.o.*, ***mit Bitten***: plead with *s.o.*, ***mit Fragen***: press *s.o.* with questions; ***er drang nicht weiter in sie*** he didn't press the point (any further); **'drin·gend I.** *adj.* urgent; priority ...; imminent *danger*; → ***Bedürfnis, Bitte***; **II.** *adv.* urgently; ~ ***notwendig*** absolutely essential; ~ ***brauchen*** desperately need, need *s.th.* very badly (*or* urgently); ***j-m ~ raten, et. zu tun*** urge (*or* strongly advise) s.o. to do s.th.; ***j-m ~ davon abraten, et. zu tun*** urge s.o. not to do s.th., strongly advise s.o. against doing s.th.; ***ich rate Ihnen ~ davon ab*** I would urge (*or* strongly advise) you not to (do it), I would strongly advise you against it; ***... werden ~ gebeten zu inf.*** ... are urged (*or* urgently requested) to *inf.*, ***sich umgehend zum Flugsteig 19 zu begeben***: ... are requested to proceed to gate 19 immediately; → ***verdächtig***

dring·lich ['drɪŋlɪç] *adj.* urgent; ***~es Problem*** pressing issue (*or* problem); **'Dring·lich·keit** *f* (-; *no pl.*) urgency; priority

'Dring·lich·keits|an·trag *m* emergency motion; **~de,bat·te** *f* emergency debate; **~li·ste** *f* priority list; **~stu·fe** *f* priority (class); ***höchste*** ~ top priority

drin·nen ['drɪnən] *adv.* inside; indoors

dritt [drɪt] **I.** *adj.* third; ***~es Kapitel*** chapter three; ***am ~en April*** on the third of April, on April the third, *Am.* on April third; ***3. April*** 3rd April, April 3(rd); *pol.* ***~e Welt*** Third World; ***die ~en Zähne*** dentures, F (one's) false teeth; **II.** *adv.*: ***wir waren zu*** ~ there were three of us; ***sie gingen zu ~ hin*** three of them went; **'dritt·äl·test** *adj.* third eldest; **'dritt·best** *adj.* third best; **Drit·te** ['drɪtə] *m, f* (-n; -n) **1.** (the) third; *w.s.* another person; ⚖ third party; ***Heinrich III.*** Henry III (= Henry the Third); ***heute ist der*** ~ it's the third today; ***im Beisein ~r*** in front of others (*or* other people); ***der ~ im Bunde*** the third member of the trio (F league), F number three (in the trio); ⚖ ***Rechte ~r*** third-party rights; **2.** third (best); ***er wurde*** ~ he came third; ***sie erreichte das Ziel als*** ~ she came in (*or* finished) third

'Dritt·ehe *f* third marriage

drit·tel ['drɪtəl] **I.** *adj.*: ***e-e ~ Sekunde*** a third of a second; **II.** 2 *n* (-s; -) third; ***zwei*** ~ two thirds

drit·tens ['drɪtəns] *adv.* third(ly)

Drit·te-'Welt-La·den *m* third world shop

'dritt|klas·sig [-klasɪç] *adj.* third-class ...; *fig.* third-rate ...; 2**land** *n* third country; *EC*: non-member country; **~letzt** *adj.* third last; ***das ~e Haus*** the third house from the end; **~ran·gig** [-raŋɪç] *adj.* third-rate ...

dro·ben ['droːbən] *adv.* up there; upstairs

Dro·ge ['droːgə] *f* (-; -n) drug

'dro·gen|ab·hän·gig *adj.* addicted to drugs; ***~ sein*** be a drug addict; 2**ab·hän·gi·ge** *m, f* (-n; -n) drug addict; 2**ab·hän·gig·keit** *f* drug addiction; 2**be·ra·tungs·stel·le** *f* drugs advice cent|re (*Am.* -er); 2**boss** *m* drugs baron; 2**fahn·der** *m* narcotics agent, *sl.* narco; **~ge·fähr·det** *adj.* drug-risk *group etc.*; 2**han·del** *m* drug trafficking; 2**händ·ler** *m* drug trafficker (*or* dealer); 2**,miß·brauch** *m* drug abuse; 2**sucht** *f*, **~süch·tig** *adj. etc.* → ***Drogenabhängigkeit, drogenabhängig*** *etc.*; 2**sze·ne** *f* drug scene; 2**to·te** *m, f* (-n; -n) drug victim; ***die Zahl der ~n*** the number of deaths caused by drugs (*or* drug overdose)

Dro·ge·rie [drogə'riː] *f* (-; -n) chemist's (shop), *Am.* drugstore; **Dro·gist** [dro-'gɪst] *m* (-en; -en) chemist, *Am.* druggist

Droh·brief ['droː-] *m* threatening letter; *pl. a.* hate mail *sg.*

dro·hen ['droːən] *v/i.* (h) **1.** threaten (***zu*** *inf.* to *inf.*); ***er drohte*** (***ihm*** *etc.*) ***mit der Polizei*** he threatened to call the police; ***sie drohte ihm, ihn anzuzeigen, sie drohte ihm mit e-r Anzeige*** she threatened to report him to the police; ***j-m mit der Faust*** (***dem Finger***) ~ shake one's fist (finger) at s.o.; **2.** threaten, approach; ***er weiß noch nicht, was ihm droht*** he doesn't know what's in store for him (*or* what he's in for) yet; ***ihm droht e-e Gefängnisstrafe*** if he's unlucky he could get a prison sentence; ***der Wirtschaft droht der Kollaps*** the economy is threatened with (*or* is on the brink of) collapse; **3.** *fig.* ~ ***zu*** *inf.* threaten to *inf.*, be in danger of *ger.*; ***es drohte zu regnen*** it looked like rain; **'dro·hend** *adj.* threatening, menacing; imminent, impending

Droh·ne ['droːnə] *f* (-; -n) drone, *fig. a.* parasite

dröh·nen ['drøːnən] *v/i.* (h) *engine, machine etc.*: drone, roar; *voice*: drone, boom; *footsteps*: ring; *room etc.*: ring, echo (***von*** *dat.* with); *thunder, guns etc.*: rumble, boom; ***die Musik dröhnt mir in den Ohren*** the music's ringing in my ears; ***mir dröhnt der Kopf*** my head's pounding (*or* throbbing) (***von*** *dat.* with); **'dröh·nend I.** *adj.*: ***~es Gelächter*** roars *pl.* of laughter; **II.** *adv.*: ~ ***lachen*** roar with laughter

'Droh·nen·da·sein *n*: ***ein ~ führen*** lead the life of a parasite

Dro·hung ['droːʊŋ] *f* (-; -en) threat; intimidation; ***~en ausstoßen*** make threaten-

ing remarks, utter threats; ***e-e ~ wahr machen*** carry out a threat; ***unter ~en*** amid threats; → ***leer*** I
drol·lig ['drɔlıç] *adj.* funny; cute
Dro·me·dar [drome'daːɐ] *n* (-s; -e [-'daːrə]) dromedary
Drops [drɔps] *pl.*: ***saure ~*** acid drops
drosch [drɔʃ] *pret. of* ***dreschen***
Drosch·ke ['drɔʃkə] *f* (-; -n) **1.** *hist.* cab; **2.** *mot. obs.* taxi, cab
Dros·sel¹ ['drɔsəl] *f* (-; -n) *zo.* thrush
'**Dros·sel²** *f* (-; -n) **1.** ⚙ throttle; **2.** ⚡ choke; '**Dros·sel·klap·pe** *f* ⚙ throttle valve; **dros·seln** ['drɔsəln] *v/t.* (h) **1.** ⚙ throttle, choke (*a.* ⚡); slow down; **2.** *fig.* curb, cut (down); '**Dros·sel·spu·le** *f* ⚡ choke coil; '**Dros·sel·ven,til** *n* ⚙ throttle valve
drü·ben ['dryːbən] *adv.* **1.** over there; on the other side (of the lake *etc.*); across the road, over the way; ~ ***(im anderen Gebäude)*** over in the other building; **2.** *hist.* (*in the GDR*) in East Germany; ***sie kamen von ~*** they came from East Germany; **3.** over in America (*or* the States), *esp. Am.* stateside
drü·ber ['dryːbɐ] *pron. adv.* → ***darüber***
Druck¹ [drʊk] *m* (-[e]s; Drücke ['drʏkə]) **1.** pressure (*a.* ⚙, *meteor.*); *phys.* compression, thrust, load, stress; blast; ***ein ~ auf den Knopf genügt*** just press the button; **2.** *no pl.* ⚕ tension; tight feeling; **3.** *no pl. fig.* pressure; stress; burden; ***(e-n) ~ auf j-n ausüben, j-n unter ~ setzen*** put s.o. under pressure, F put the screws on s.o.; ***~ machen hinter*** *acc.* speed up; ***ziemlich im ~ sein*** be under quite a bit of pressure
Druck² *m* (-[e]s; -e) **1.** *no pl.* a) printing; b) print, type; ***in ~ geben*** send to press; ***in ~ gehen*** go to press; ***im ~ sein*** be in (the) press; **2.** edition; *art*: print; **3.** *textil.* print
'**Druck|ab·fall** *m* drop in pressure; **~an·stieg** *m* increase (*or* rise) in pressure; **~an·zug** *m* ✈ pressure suit; **~blei·stift** *m* drop-action pencil; **~buch·sta·be** *m* block letter; ***in ~n schreiben*** print
Drü·cke·ber·ger ['drʏkəbɛrgɐ] (*sep.* -k·k-) F *m* (-s; -) shirker, *Brit. a.* F skiver
'**druck·emp·find·lich** *adj.* ⚕ tender, sore to the touch; easily bruised; easily crushed; ***diese Stelle ist ~*** ⚕ this part hurts when you touch (*or* press on) it
drucken ['drʊkən] (*sep.* -k·k-) *v/t.* (h) print; ***~ lassen*** have *s.th.* printed, publish; → ***gedruckt***
drücken ['drʏkən] (*sep.* -k·k-) (h) **I.** *v/t.* **1.** press; squeeze; squash; push; ***breit*** (*or* ***flach***) ~ flatten; ***j-m die Hand ~*** shake hands with s.o., shake (*or* squeeze) s.o.'s hand; ***j-m et. in die Hand ~*** give (*or* hand) s.o. s.th., slip s.th. into s.o.'s hand; ***j-n an sich ~*** give s.o. a hug, hold s.o. tight; *sl.* ***sich eins*** (*or* ***e-e***) ~ *sl.* shoot (some heroin *etc.*) up; → ***Daumen, Schulbank, Wand***; **2.** *backpack etc.*: hurt; *shoes etc.*: pinch; **3.** *fig.* worry, depress; *responsibility etc.*: weigh (heavily) on; **4.** ✝ bring (*or* force) down *prices etc.*; **5.** lower *standards etc.*; better *record* (***um*** *acc.* by); ***er drückte den Rekord um zwei Sekunden*** *a.* he took two seconds off the record; **6.** ***die Stimmung ~*** put a damper on things, ***j-m***: depress s.o.; **7.** ✈ nose down; **II.** *v/refl.* **8.** ***sich in e-e Ecke ~*** huddle into a corner; ***sich an j-n ~*** cuddle up to s.o.; **9.** F ***sich (heimlich) aus dem Saal ~*** sneak out of the hall; ***sich ~*** shirk, *Brit. a.* F skive (off); F chicken out; ***sich ~ vor*** *dat.* get out of *s.th.*, shirk, *Brit. a.* F skive; chicken out of; ***er drückt sich mal wieder*** he's shirking again, *Brit. a.* F he's on the skive again; ***er drückt sich dauernd*** he somehow always manages to get out of it (*or* things); **III.** *v/i.* **10.** press; ***~ auf*** *acc.* press (on), press, push *button etc.*; → ***Tube*** 1; **11.** *backpack etc.*: hurt; *shoes etc.*: pinch, be too tight; **12.** *sl.* shoot (some heroin) up; '**drückend** (*sep.* -k·k-) *adj. meteor.* close; oppressive *heat*; *fig.* ***~e Überlegenheit*** overwhelming superiority
Drucker ['drʊkɐ] (*sep.* -k·k-) *m* (-s; -) printer
Drücker ['drʏkɐ] (*sep.* -k·k-) *m* (-s; -) (push)button; latch; ⚙ trigger; F *fig.* ***am ~ sitzen*** be at the controls; F ***auf den letzten ~*** at the last minute
Drucke·rei [drʊkə'raı] (*sep.* -k·k-) *f* (-; -en) printers *pl.*
'**Druck·er·laub·nis** *f* permission to print, imprimatur
'**Drucker|pres·se** *f* (printing) press; **~schwär·ze** *f* newsprint, printing (*or* printer's) ink; **~zei·chen** *n* printer's mark
'**Druck|er·zeug·nis** *n* publication; **⁀fä·hig** *adj.* printable; *fig.* ***s-e Antwort war nicht ~*** his answer wasn't printable (*or* fit to be printed); **~far·be** *f* printing (*or* printer's) ink; **~fe·der** *f* compression spring; **~feh·ler** *m* misprint, printing error; **⁀fer·tig** *adj.* ready for (the) press; ***~es Manuskript*** fair copy; **⁀fest** *adj.* pressure-proof; ✈ pressurized; **⁀frisch** *adj.* fresh from the press; **~ge·neh·mi·gung** *f* → ***Druckerlaubnis***; **~in·du,strie** *f* printing industry; **~ka,bi·ne** *f* pressurized (*or* pressure) cabin; **~knopf** *m* ⚙ (push)button; press stud, *esp. Brit.* F popper, *Am.* snap fastener; **~kos·ten** *pl.* printing costs; **~last** *f* ⚙ load
'**Druck·luft** *f* compressed air; **~...** *in cpds. usu.* pneumatic ...; **~brem·se** *f* air brake
'**Druck|mes·ser** *m* ⚙ pressure ga(u)ge; **~mit·tel** *fig. n* lever; ***~ anwenden*** apply pressure, F put the screws on; **~plat·te** *f* plate; **~po·sten** F *m* cushy job (F number); **~pum·pe** *f* pressure pump; **⁀reif** *adj.* **1.** → ***druckfertig***; **2.** *fig.* ***s-e Reden sind ~*** he ought to have his speeches published; **~sa·che(n** *pl.*) *f* printed matter, *Am. a.* second-class (matter); **~schrift** *f* **1.** block letters *pl.*; *typ.* print, type; ***in ~ schreiben*** print; ***bitte in ~ ausfüllen*** please write in capital letters; **2.** publication, pamphlet
druck·sen ['drʊksən] F *v/i.* (h) hum and haw
'**Druck|stel·le** *f* ⚕ tender spot, bruise; **~stock** *m typ.* printing plate; **~ta·ste** *f* (push)button; **~ver·band** *m* ⚕ compression bandage; **~ver·fah·ren** *n* printing process; **~was·ser·re,ak·tor** *m* pressurized water reactor; **~wel·le** *f* blast, shock wave
Drui·de [dru'iːdə] *m* (-n; -n) Druid
drum [drʊm] **I.** *pron. adv.* → ***darum***; **II.** ⁀ *n*: ***das ganze ~ und Dran*** all the little things; ***mit allem ~ und Dran*** with all the trimmings
drun·ten ['drʊntən] *adv.* down there; downstairs
drun·ter ['drʊntɐ] **I.** *pron. adv.* → ***darunter***; **II.** *adv.*: ***es ging alles ~ und drüber*** it was absolutely chaotic
Dru·se¹ ['druːzə] *f* (-; -n) *min.* druse
'**Dru·se²** *m* (-n; -n) *Islam*: Druse, Druze
Drü·se ['dryːzə] *f* (-; -n) gland
'**Drü·sen|fie·ber** *n* glandular fever; **~schwel·lung** *f* swelling of the glands; **~tä·tig·keit** *f* glandular activity
Dschun·gel ['dʒʊŋəl] *m* (-s; -) jungle (*a. fig.*); **~fie·ber** *n* jungle fever; **~krieg** *m* jungle warfare; **~pfad** *m* path through the jungle
Dschun·ke ['dʒʊŋkə] *f* (-; -n) junk
du [duː] **I.** *pers. pron.* you; ***bist ~ es?*** is that you?; ***~, komm mal her*** come here a minute, will you?; ***auf ~ und ~ stehen*** be good friends; ***per ~ sein*** say 'du' to each other, be on first-name terms (***mit j-m*** with s.o.); ***zu j-m ~ sagen*** → ***duzen***; **II.** ⁀ *n* (-[s]; -[s]): ***er hat mir das ~ angeboten*** he suggested we drop the polite form of address (*or* use the familiar form of address, use the familiar 'du')
du·al [du'aːl] *adj.* ⚡, *computer*: binary; **Dua·lis·mus** [dua'lısmʊs] *m* (-; *no pl.*) dualism; **dua·li·stisch** [dua'lıstıʃ] *adj.* dualistic(ally *adv.*)
Du'al|sy,stem *n* ⚡, *computer*: binary system; **~zahl** *f* ⚡, *computer*: binary number
Dü·bel ['dyːbəl] *m* (-s; -) rawl plug, dowel; '**dü·beln** *v/t.* (h) rawlplug (***an*** *acc.* to *the wall*)
du·bi·os [du'bĭoːs] *adj.* dubious; **Du·bio·sa** [du'bĭoːza] *pl.*, **Du·bio·sen** [du'bĭoːzən] *pl.* doubtful debts
Du·blee [du'bleː] *n* (-s; -s) rolled gold; ***... aus ~*** gold-plated ...
Du·blet·te [du'blɛtə] *f* (-; -n) **1.** double, F swap; **2.** *boxing*: double blow
ducken ['dʊkən] (*sep.* -k·k-) (h) **I.** *v/t.* duck; *fig.* put *s.o.* down; **II.** *v/refl.*: ***sich ~*** duck; *fig.* knuckle under (***vor*** *dat.* to)
Duck·mäu·ser ['dʊkmɔyzɐ] *m* (-s; -) coward, F spineless jellyfish; yes-man; **Duck·mäu·se·rei** [dʊkmɔyzə'raı] *f* (-; *no pl.*) submissiveness; **duck·mäu·se·risch** ['dʊkmɔyzərıʃ] *adj.* submissive, servile, cringing
Du·de·lei [duːdə'laı] F *f* (-; -en) tootling; droning; **du·deln** ['duːdəln] F *v/i.* (h) *radio etc.*: drone (on); ***~ auf*** *dat.* tootle away on
Du·del·sack ['duːdəlzak] *m* bagpipes *pl.*; **~pfei·fer** *m* (bag)piper
Du·ell [du'ɛl] *n* (-s; -e) duel (***auf Pistolen*** with pistols); **Du·el·lant** [duɛ'lant] *m* (-en; -en) duellist; **du·el·lie·ren** [duɛ'liːrən] *v/t. and v/refl.* (***sich ~***) (h) fight a duel (***mit*** *dat.* with)
Du·ett [du'ɛt] *n* (-[e]s; -e) ♪ duet; ***im ~ singen*** sing a duet
Duft [dʊft] *m* (-[e]s; Düfte ['dʏftə]) (pleasant) smell; scent, fragrance
duf·te ['dʊftə] F *adj.* F great
duf·ten ['dʊftən] *v/i.* (h) smell (***nach*** *dat.* of); smell good; ***hier duftet es aber!*** what a nice smell!, *iro.* F what a pong!; ***hier duftet es nach ...*** I can smell ...; '**duf·tend** *adj.* nice-(*or* sweet-)smelling; fragrant
'**Duft·hauch** *m* breath, waft
duf·tig ['dʊftıç] *adj.* **1.** fragrant; scented; **2.** airy
'**Duft|kis·sen** *n* sachet; **~mar·ke** *f zo.* scent mark; **~no·te** *f* scent; **~pro·be** *f* perfume sample; **~stoff** *m* scent; **~wol·ke** *f* cloud of perfume

Du·ka·ten [du'ka:tən] *m* (-s; -) *hist.* ducat; **~esel** F *m*, **~schei·ßer** V *m*: ***ich bin doch kein ~*** I'm not made of money(, you know)
dul·den ['dʊldən] *v/t.* (h) endure, suffer; tolerate, condone, shut one's eyes to; put up with, stand for; ***er ist hier nur geduldet*** he's only here on sufferance; ***ich dulde es nicht*** I won't have it; → ***Aufschub, Widerspruch***
Dul·der ['dʊldɐ] *m* (-s; -) patient sufferer, martyr; **~mie·ne** *f* martyred expression
duld·sam ['dʊltza:m] *adj.* tolerant (***gegen*** *acc.*, ***gegenüber*** *dat.* of); indulgent (to), forbearing; **'Duld·sam·keit** *f* (-; *no pl.*) tolerance (***gegen*** *acc.*, ***gegenüber*** *dat.* of), forbearance
Dul·dung ['dʊldʊŋ] *f* (-; *no pl.*) toleration; → ***stillschweigend*** I
dumm [dʊm] **I.** *adj.* stupid; silly; foolish; awkward; clumsy; ***j-n wie e-n ~en Jungen behandeln*** treat s.o. like a child; ***e-e ~e Sache*** an awkward business; ***~es Zeug!*** rubbish!; ***~es Zeug reden*** talk nonsense; ***sich ~ stellen*** act the fool; ***er ist nicht (so) ~*** he's no fool; F ***er ist dümmer, als die Polizei erlaubt*** F he's as thick as two short planks; ***zu ~!, wie ~!*** what a nuisance; ***schließlich wurde es mir zu ~*** in the end I got tired of the whole business; ***das war ~ von mir*** how stupid of me; ***willst du mich für ~ verkaufen?*** you must think I'm stupid; ***schön ~ wärst du*** you'd be a fool; F ***mir ist ganz ~ im Kopf*** I feel really weird; F ***sich ~ und dämlich reden*** talk o.s. silly; F ***sich ~ und dämlich verdienen*** F be raking it in; **II.** *adv.*: ***sich ~ anstellen*** be stupid, do s.th. stupid; ***wer ~ fragt, bekommt ~e Antworten*** ask a silly question(, get a silly answer); → ***daherreden, dastehen, Wäsche***; **'Dumm·chen** *n* → ***Dummerchen***; **Dum·me** ['dʊmə] *m, f* (-n; -n) fool, F mug; ***der ~ sein*** be left holding the baby; ***e-n ~n findet man immer*** there are plenty of mugs around; **Dum·me'jun·gen·streich** *m* silly prank; **Dum·mer·chen** ['dʊmɐçən] F *n* (-s; -) F silly (billy); **'dum·mer'wei·se** *adv.* **1.** stupidly; ***ich habe ~ zugesagt*** I was stupid enough to say yes; **2.** unfortunately; **'Dumm·heit** *f* (-; -en) **1.** *no pl.* stupidity; ignorance; F ***vor ~ brüllen*** F be as thick as two short planks; ***gegen ~ ist kein Kraut gewachsen*** some people are born that way; **2.** stupid thing to do; ***e-e ~ begehen*** do s.th. stupid; ***so e-e ~!*** what a stupid thing to do; ***mach keine ~en!*** don't do anything stupid, *w.s.* no funny tricks!; ***er hat nur ~en im Kopf*** he's always up to something; **'Dumm·kopf** *m* idiot; ***er ist kein ~*** he's no fool; **dümm·lich** ['dʏmlɪç] *adj.* silly
dumpf [dʊmpf] *adj.* **1.** dull, muffled; ***~er Aufprall*** *etc.* thud; **2.** sultry, close; muggy; **3.** stuffy; mo(u)ldy, musty; **4.** dull *pain*; **5.** gloomy *atmosphere etc.*; **6.** vague *suspicion etc.*; **dumpf·ig** ['dʊmpfɪç] *adj.* musty; dank
Dum·ping ['dampɪŋ] *n* (-s; *no pl.*) dumping; **~preis** *m* dumping price
Dü·ne ['dy:nə] *f* (-; -n) dune; **'Dü·nen·fel·der** *pl.* sand dunes
Dung [dʊŋ] *m* (-[e]s; *no pl.*) manure, dung
Dün·ge·mit·tel ['dʏŋə-] *n* → ***Dünger***; **dün·gen** ['dʏŋən] *v/t.* (h) manure, dung; fertilize; **Dün·ger** ['dʏŋɐ] *m* (-s; -) manure, dung; fertilizer
'Dung|gru·be *f* manure pit; **~hau·fen** *m* manure heap
Dün·gung ['dʏŋʊŋ] *f* (-; -en) manuring; fertilizing
dun·kel ['dʊŋkəl] **I.** *adj.* dark (*a. fig.*); deep *voice*; *fig.* gloomy; mysterious; vague, dim *memories etc.*; shady *dealings etc.*; ***~ werden*** get dark; ***~ machen*** darken; ***dunkles Bier*** dark beer; ***im 2n*** in the dark; *fig.* ***j-n im ~n lassen*** keep (*or* leave) s.o. in the dark; ***das liegt noch im ~n*** a) that's still a mystery, b) that remains to be seen; ***im ~n tappen*** grope in the dark; **II.** 2 *n* (-s; *no pl.*) *the* dark, darkness (*a. fig.*); *fig.* mystery; ***das ~ um et. aufhellen*** (*or* ***lichten***) shed light on s.th.
Dün·kel ['dʏŋkəl] *m* (-s; *no pl.*) arrogance; ***er hat e-n akademischen ~*** he thinks he's something special because he's got a degree
'dun·kel|blau *adj.* dark blue; **~blond** *adj.* light brown; **~braun** *adj.* dark brown; **~far·ben** *adj.*, **~far·big** *adj.* dark (-colo[u]red); **~ge·klei·det** *adj.* dressed in dark colo(u)rs (*or* clothes); **~haa·rig** *adj.* dark-haired
'dün·kel·haft *adj.* arrogant, conceited
'dun·kel·häu·tig [-hɔʏtɪç] *adj.* dark(-skinned); swarthy
'Dun·kel·heit *f* (-; *no pl.*) darkness; → ***Einbruch*** 4
'Dun·kel|kam·mer *f phot.* darkroom; **2rot** *adj.* dark red; **~zif·fer** *f* number of unreported cases (*or* crimes, victims); **~zo·ne** *f* twilight zone
dün·ken ['dʏŋkən] *lit.* (h) **I.** *v/impers.*: ***es dünkt mich*** (*or* ***mir***), ***mir*** (*or* ***mich***) ***dünkt*** it seems to me, *obs. or iro.* methinks; **II.** *v/refl.*: ***sich sehr schlau*** *etc.* ~ think one is very clever *etc.*
dünn [dʏn] **I.** *adj.* thin; fine; lightweight *paper*; watery, watered down; rarefied; *fig.* weak; flimsy; ***~er werden*** lose weight; ***er ist sehr ~ geworden*** he's gone really thin; *fig.* ***sich ~ machen*** make room, squeeze up, F breathe in; **II.** *adv.*: ***~ besiedelt*** sparsely populated; *fig.* ***~ gesät*** scarce, few and far between; **~be·sie·delt** *adj.* sparsely populated
'Dünn·darm *m* small intestine
'Dünn·druck·pa,pier *n* India paper
dün·ne·ma·chen ['dʏnə-] F *v/refl.* → ***dünnmachen***
'dünn|flüs·sig *adj.* watery; light, thin-bodied *oil*; **~ge·sät** *fig. adj.* rare, scarce; **~häu·tig** [-hɔʏtɪç] *fig. adj.* very sensitive (*or* delicate)
'Dünn·heit *f* (-; *no pl.*) thinness
'dünn|ma·chen F *v/refl.* (*sep.*, h): ***sich ~*** F make o.s. scarce; **2pfiff** F *m* (-[e]s; *no pl.*) F *the* runs *pl.*; **2säu·re** *f* ⚗ dilute acid; sewage sludge; **2säu·re·ver·klap·pung** *f* dumping of dilute acid (*or* sewage sludge); **2schiß** V *m* (-sses; *no pl.*) V *the* shits *pl.*
Dunst [dʊnst] *m* (-es; Dünste ['dʏnstə]) vapo(u)r, steam; smoke; fumes *pl.*; haze, mist; F *fig.* ***j-m e-n blauen ~ vormachen*** throw dust in s.o.'s eyes; ***er hat keinen*** (***blassen***) ***~ davon*** F he hasn't the foggiest (idea) about it
dün·sten ['dʏnstən] *v/t. and v/i.* (h) steam
'Dunst·glocke *f* blanket of smog
dun·stig ['dʊnstɪç] *adj.* hazy, misty
'Dunst|kreis *fig. m* sphere of influence; **~schlei·er** *m* haze
Dü·nung ['dy:nʊŋ] *f* (-; -en) ⚓ swell
Duo ['du:o] *n* (-s; -s) ♪ duo
Duo·de·zi·mal·sy,stem [duodetsi'ma:l-] *n* ⩓ duodecimal system
Duo·de·zi·me [duo'de:tsimə] *f* (-; -n) ♪ twelfth
dü·pie·ren [dy'pi:rən] *v/t.* (h) dupe
Du·plex... ['du:plɛks-] *in cpds* ⚡, ⚙, *computer*: duplex ...
Du·pli·kat [dupli'ka:t] *n* (-[e]s; -e) duplicate; copy; *art*: replica
Du·pli·zi·tät [duplitsi'tɛ:t] *f* (-; -en): ***die ~ der Ereignisse*** strange parallel (*or* coincidence)
Dur [du:ɐ] *n* (-; *no pl.*) ♪ major (key); ***A-~*** A major; **~ak·kord** *m* major chord
durch [dʊrç] **I.** *prp.* (*acc.*) **1.** *a. fig.* through; across; ***~ ganz England*** all over England; **2.** through, by, by means of; **3.** because of; **4.** through(out), during; ***das ganze Jahr ~*** the whole year (long); ***den ganzen Tag ~*** all day (long); **II.** *adv.* **5.** ***~ und ~*** completely, ... through and through; to the core; ***ein Politiker ~ und ~*** a dyed-in-the-wool politician; ***ein Gentleman ~ und ~*** a gentleman born and bred; ***~ und ~ naß*** soaked to the skin, drenched; **6.** ***es ist acht Uhr ~*** it's past (*or* gone) eight o'clock; **~ackern** (*sep.* -k·k-) F *fig. v/t.* (*a. v/refl.*: ***sich ~ durch*** *acc.*) (h) plough (*Am.* plow) through *s.th.*; **~ar·bei·ten** (*sep.*, h) **I.** *v/t.* work through *s.th.*; go through *s.th.* thoroughly; work out (in detail); ***die ganze Nacht ~*** work through the night (without a break); **II.** *v/refl.*: ***sich ~ durch*** *acc.* fight one's way through, plough (*Am.* plow) through (*a. fig.*); *fig.* work one's way through; **III.** *v/i.* work through without a break, work nonstop; **~at·men** *v/i.* (h) breathe deeply; ***tief ~*** *a.* take deep breaths
durch'aus *adv.* thoroughly; absolutely; quite; ***~!*** absolutely; ***~ nicht*** not at all, not in the least; ***~ nicht arm*** far from poor, not in the least bit poor; ***sie ist ~ nicht zufrieden*** she's not satisfied in the least; ***~ möglich*** quite possible; ***ich bin ~ Ihrer Meinung*** I absolutely agree, I couldn't agree with you more; ***wenn du es ~ willst*** if you absolutely must, if you insist
'durch·bei·ßen (*irr.*, *sep.*, h, → ***beißen***) **I.** *v/t.* bite through *s.th.*, bite *s.th.* in two; **II.** F *fig. v/refl.*: ***sich ~*** struggle through; **durch'bei·ßen** *v/t.* (durchbiß, durchbissen, h) bite through *s.th.*
'durch|be·kom·men *v/t.* (*irr.*, *sep.*, h, → ***bekommen***) **1.** (*a.* ***~ durch***) get *s.th.* through (*a. fig.*); **2.** pull *s.o.* through; **~beu·teln** F *v/t.* (*sep.*, h) give *s.o.* a shaking; **~bie·gen** (*irr.*, *sep.*, h, → ***biegen***) **I.** *v/t.* bend back; **II.** *v/refl.*: ***sich ~*** bend, sag; **~blät·tern** *v/t.* (*sep.*, h) leaf (*or* thumb, F flick) through *s.th.*
'Durch·blick *m* (-[e]s; -e) **1.** view (***auf*** *acc.*, ***in*** *acc.* of); **2.** F *fig.* ***sich den nötigen ~ verschaffen*** find out what's what; (***den nötigen***) ***~ haben*** know what's going on; ***er hat überhaupt keinen ~*** he has no idea what's going on; **'durch·blik·ken** *v/i.* (*sep.*, h) **1.** (*a.* ***~ durch*** *acc.*) look through; *fig.* ***et. ~ lassen*** hint at, intimate *that*; ***~ lassen, daß*** hint (at the fact) that, intimate that; **2.** F *fig.* ***ich blick' da nicht durch*** F I don't get it; ***da***

blick' ich nicht mehr durch I'm lost; ***blickst du bei dem Film durch?*** F d'you know what the film is on about?

durch'blu·ten *v/t.* (*insep.*, *no* -ge-, h) supply with blood; ***das Gehirn ist gut*** (***schlecht***) ***durchblutet*** the blood flow (*or* circulation) in the brain is good (bad); ***durchblutete Haut*** live skin; **Durch'blu·tung** *f* (-; *no pl.*) blood flow, circulation (*gen.* *or* ***in*** *dat.* in); **Durch'blu·tungs·stö·rung** *f* circulatory problem

durch'boh·ren *v/t.* (*insep.*, *no* -ge-, h) pierce; stab; run through; perforate; *fig.* ***j-n mit Blicken*** ~ look daggers at s.o.; **'durch·boh·ren** (*sep.*, -ge-, h) **I.** *v/t.* drill through *s.th.*; **II.** *v/refl.*: ***sich*** ~ bore one's way through; **durch'boh·rend** *adj.* piercing *look etc.*

'durch|bo·xen (*sep.*, -ge-, h) F **I.** *fig.* *v/t.* push *s.th.* through; **II.** *v/refl.*: ***sich*** ~ battle one's way through; *fig.* struggle through; **~bra·ten** *v/t.* (*irr.*, *sep.*, h, → ***braten***) cook well; → ***durchgebraten***

'durch·bre·chen (*irr.*, *sep.*, → ***brechen***) **I.** *v/t.* (h) **1.** break *s.th.* (in two), snap; **2.** break through; ***ein Fenster*** ~ put a window in a (*or* the) wall; **II.** *v/i.* (sn) **3.** break (in two); **4.** collapse; **5.** fall through *the ice*; **6.** come out; *teeth*, *sun*: come through; **7.** ⚕ burst; **durch'bre·chen** *v/t.* (durchbrach, durchbrochen, h) break through *s.th.*; run *the blockade*; *fig.* break *rule etc.*

'durch|bren·nen (*irr.*, *sep.*, → ***brennen***) **I.** *v/t.* (h) **1.** burn a hole in; **II.** *v/i.* (sn) **2.** *bulb*: burn out; *fuse*: blow; **3.** F *fig.* run away; make off *with the money*, elope; F do a bunk; ***mit dem Geld*** ~ *a.* F take the money and run; → ***Sicherung*** 1; **~brin·gen** (*irr.*, *sep.*, h, → ***bringen***) **I.** *v/t.* get *s.th.* *or s.o.* through; pull *s.o.* through; support, feed; squander; **II.** *v/refl.*: ***sich*** ~ make (both) ends meet, scrape through

'Durch·bruch *m* (-[e]s; ⸚e) **1.** ⚔ *and sport*: breakthrough; bursting *of a dam*, *boil etc.*; gap, opening; cutting *of teeth*; **2.** *fig.* breakthrough; ***ihm ist der*** ~ ***gelungen, er hat den*** ~ ***geschafft*** he finally made the breakthrough (*or* made it); ***zum*** ~ ***kommen*** show, become apparent, *idea*: gain acceptance; ***e-r Idee zum*** ~ ***verhelfen*** help to get an idea accepted

'durch·checken *v/t.* (*sep.*, h) **1.** check through *s.th.*; **2.** check *one's luggage* through; **3.** F ⚕ ***sich*** ~ ***lassen*** have a complete checkup

durch·dacht [-'daxt] *adj.*: (***gut***) ~ well thought-out; **durch'den·ken** *v/t.* (durchdachte, durchdacht, h) think *s.th.* through; think *s.th.* over, give *s.th.* some thought

'durch|dis·ku,tie·ren *v/t.* (*sep.*, h) talk *s.th.* through; ***gründlich*** ~ discuss from every angle, F thrash out; **~drän·gen** *v/refl.* (*sep.*, h): ***sich*** ~ (***durch*** *acc.*) push one's way through; **~dre·hen** (*sep.*, h) **I.** *v/t.* **1.** *gastr.* mince, put through the grinder (*or* mincer); **II.** *v/i.* **2.** *wheels*: spin; **3.** F *fig.* F crack up; panic, F go into a flat panic

'durch·drin·gen *v/i.* (*irr.*, *sep.*, sn, → ***dringen***) **1.** (*a.* ~ ***durch*** *acc.*) get through; seep through; *fig. news etc.*: get out, leak (out); *fig.* ~ ***zu*** *dat.* reach, get to *s.o.*; **2.** *fig.* succeed (***mit*** *dat.* with); ***mit et.*** ~ *a.* get s.th. accepted; **durch'drin·gen** *v/t.* (durchdrang, durchdrungen, h) penetrate; *fig.* fathom, grasp; pervade, permeate; ***er durchdrang mich mit s-m Blick*** his look went right through me; → ***durchdrungen***; **'durch·drin·gend** *adj.* penetrating, piercing; biting *cold, wind etc.*; piercing, shrill *voice*; keen, penetrating *mind*

'durch·drücken *v/t.* (*sep.*, h) (*a.* ~ ***durch*** *acc.*) force (*or* squeeze) through; straighten *one's knees*; stretch *one's back*; *fig.* → ***durchsetzen***; **'Durch·drück·packung** *f* bubble pack; *pl. coll.* bubble packaging *sg.*

durch·drun·gen [-'drʊŋən] *adj.* filled, inspired, *lit.* suffused (***von*** *dat.* with); ~ ***von*** *dat.* steeped in

'durch·dür·fen F *v/i.* (*irr.*, *sep.*, h, → ***dürfen***) (*a.* ~ ***durch*** *acc.*) be allowed through; ***darf ich mal durch?*** excuse me

durch'ei·len *v/t.* (*insep.*, *no* -ge-, h) rush through (*a. fig.*); rush across; **'durch·ei·len** *v/i.* (*sep.*, sn) rush through

durch·ein'an·der **I.** *adj.*: ~ ***sein*** be in a mess; ***ganz*** ~ ***sein*** be totally confused, be all mixed up; **II.** *adv.*: ***alles*** ~ ***essen*** eat everything as it comes; **III.** ♀ *n* (-s; *no pl.*) mess, muddle; confusion, chaos; **~brin·gen** *v/t.* (*irr.*, *sep.*, h, → ***bringen***) **1.** → ***durcheinanderwerfen***; **2.** *fig.* get *s.o.* all flustered; **~ge·ra·ten** *v/i.* (*irr.*, *sep.*, sn, → ***geraten***), **~kom·men** F *v/i.* (*irr.*, *sep.*, sn, → ***kommen***) get mixed up (*a. fig.*); **~re·den** *v/i.* (*sep.*, h) **1.** talk all at the same time; **2.** F say strange things, F rave; **~wer·fen** *v/t.* (*irr.*, *sep.*, h, → ***werfen***) jumble up; *fig.* mix up

'durch·ex·er,zie·ren *v/t.* (*sep.*, *no* -ge-, h) go through *s.th.*; practi|se (*Am.* -ce)

'durch·fä·deln *v/t.* (*sep.*, h) thread; ***e-n Faden durch Perlen*** ~ thread pearls onto a string, string pearls

'durch·fah·ren *v/i.* (*irr.*, *sep.*, sn, → ***fahren***) (*a.* ~ ***durch*** *acc.*) pass (*or* go, *mot. a.* drive, ⚓ sail) through; ***bis X*** ~ drive *etc.* nonstop to X; ***der Zug fährt in X durch*** the train doesn't stop in X; → ***Rot***; **durch'fah·ren** *v/t.* (durchfuhr, durchfahren, h) go (*or* pass, *mot. a.* drive) through; go *etc.* across; drive; *fig.* ***der Gedanke durchfuhr mich, daß*** it suddenly struck (*or* hit) me that; ***ein Schreck*** *etc.* ***durchfuhr ihn*** he was suddenly hit by a shock *etc.*

'Durch·fahrt *f* (-; -en) **1.** *no pl.* passage; ~ ***verboten!*** no through road, no thoroughfare; **2.** way; ***die*** ~ ***zur Kirche*** the road leading up to the church; **3.** → ***Durchreise***; **'Durch·fahrts·stra·ße** *f* through road

'Durch·fall *m* (-[e]s; ⸚e) **1.** ⚕ diarrh(o)ea; **2.** *fig.* failure, *thea. etc.* F flop

'durch·fal·len (*irr.*, *sep.*, sn, → ***fallen***) **I.** *v/i.* **1.** (*a.* ~ ***durch*** *acc.*) fall through; **2.** fail, F flunk *the exam*; be defeated, be beaten *in an election etc.*; *thea. etc.* F be a flop; *proposal etc.*: be turned down; ~ ***lassen*** fail; ***im Examen*** ~ fail (F flunk) the *or* one's exam; **durch'fal·len** *v/t.* (durchfiel, durchfallen, h) fall through

'Durch·fall·quo·te *f* failure rate

'durch|fech·ten (*irr.*, *sep.*, h, → ***fechten***) **I.** *v/t.* fight *s.th.* through; **II.** *v/refl.*: ***sich*** ~ fight one's way through; **~fei·ern** *v/i.* (*a.* *v/t.*: ***die Nacht*** ~) (*sep.*, h) celebrate all night, make a night of it; ***wir haben durchgefeiert*** *a.* the party went on all night; **~fin·den** *v/refl.* (*irr.*, *sep.*, h, → ***finden***): ***sich*** ~ (***durch*** *acc.*) find one's way through; ***sich nicht mehr*** ~ be lost

durch'flech·ten *v/t.* (durchflocht, durchflochten, h) intertwine (***mit*** *dat.* with)

durch'flie·gen *v/t.* (durchflog, durchflogen, h) **1.** fly through; fly, cover *distance*; **2.** *fig.* skim through *s.th.*; **'durch·flie·gen** *v/i.* (*irr.*, *sep.*, sn, → ***fliegen***) **1.** (*a.* ~ ***durch*** *acc.*) fly through; ✈ fly nonstop (***bis*** [***zu***] *dat.* to); **2.** F flunk (the *or* one's exam)

'durch·flie·ßen *v/i.* (*irr.*, *sep.*, sn, → ***fließen***), **durch'flie·ßen** *v/t.* (durchfloß, durchflossen, h) flow (*or* run) through

'Durch|flug *m* (-[e]s; ⸚e) flight (***durch*** *acc.* through); (air) transit; **~fluß** *m* (-sses; ⸚sse) flow; ⚙ opening

durch'flu·ten *v/t.* (*insep.*, *no* -ge-, h) flow through; *fig.* flood

durch'for·schen *v/t.*(*insep.*, *no* -ge-, h) investigate; scrutinize; explore; search; comb through; **Durch'for·schung** *f* (-; -en) investigation; scrutiny; exploration; search(ing)

durch·for·sten [-'fɔrstən] *v/t.* (*insep.*, *no* -ge-, h) **1.** thin (out); **2.** *fig.* comb (*or* sift) through *s.th.*

'durch|fra·gen *v/refl.* (*sep.*, h): ***sich*** ~ ask one's way (***nach*** *dat.*, ***zu*** *dat.* to); **~fres·sen** (*irr.*, *sep.*, h, → ***fressen***) **I.** *v/t.* **1.** *a.* 🐛 eat through (*a.* ***sich*** ~ ***durch*** *acc.*); **II.** *v/refl.*: ***sich*** ~ **2.** *worm etc.*: eat its way through; **3.** F ***sich*** ~ ***bei*** (*dat.*) F sponge off; **4.** ***sich*** ~ ***durch*** *acc.* plough (*Am.* plow) through *s.th.*, wade through *s.th.*

durch·fro·ren [-'fro:rən] *adj.* (*a.* ***ganz*** *or* ***völlig*** ~) frozen to the bone

Durch·fuhr ['dʊrçfu:ɐ] *f* (-; -en [-fu:rən]) ☤ transit

'durch·führ·bar *adj.* practicable, feasible; **'Durch·führ·bar·keit** *f* (-; *no pl.*) practicability, feasibility; **'Durch·führ·bar·keits·stu·die** *f* feasibility study; **'durch·füh·ren** *v/t.* (*sep.*, h) **1.** (*a.* ~ ***durch*** *acc.*) lead (*or* take) through *or* across; take through (*or* round); **2.** (*a.* ~ ***durch*** *acc.*) pass through; **3.** *fig.* carry out; go ahead with; carry *s.th.* through; realize *project etc.*; enforce *law*; **'Durch·füh·rung** *f* (-; -en) realization; ⚖ enforcement

'Durch·fuhr|ver·bot *n* ☤ transit embargo; **~zoll** *m* transit duty

durch·furcht [dʊrç'fʊrçt] *adj.* lined; **~e Stirn** lined forehead, *lit.* furrowed brow

'durch·füttern *v/t.* (*sep.*, h) feed, support; ***sich von j-m*** ~ ***lassen*** live off s.o.

'Durch·ga·be *f* (-; -n) → ***Durchsage***

'Durch·gang *m* (-[e]s; ⸚e) passage(way); ☤, *ast.* transit; *sport*: round; heat; ~ ***verboten!*** no through road, no thoroughfare, private (road); **'durch·gän·gig** **I.** *adj.* general; uniform; **II.** *adv.* generally; throughout

'Durch·gangs|bahn·hof *m* through station; **~la·ger** *n* transit camp; **~sta·di·um** *n* transitional stage; **~stra·ße** *f* through road; **~ton** *m* ♪ passing note; **~ver·kehr** *m* through traffic; ☤ transit trade; **~zoll** *m* transit duty

'durch·ge·ben *v/t.* (*irr.*, *sep.*, h, → ***geben***) pass on, *radio*: announce

'durch·ge·bra·ten **I.** *p.p. of* ***durchbraten***; **II.** *adj.* well-done; ***es ist noch nicht*** ~ it isn't done (properly) yet

'durch·ge·fro·ren → ***durchfroren***

'durch·ge·hen (*irr.*, *sep.*, sn, → ***gehen***) **I.** *v/i.* **1.** (*a.* ~ ***durch*** *acc.*) go (*or* walk) through, pass (through); *fig.* go through;

2. (*a.* ~ ***durch*** *acc.*) go through; **3.** run away, *lovers*: elope; *horse*: bolt; *fig.* ***s-e Phantasie*** *etc.* ***geht manchmal mit ihm durch*** sometimes his imagination *etc.* just runs wild; ***sein Temperament ging mit ihm durch*** he got carried away; **4.** *motion etc.*: be accepted; *bill etc.*: be passed; **5.** pass; ***et.*** ~ ***lassen*** let s.th. pass; ***j-m et.*** ~ ***lassen*** let s.o. get away with s.th.; **II.** *v/t.* go through (*or* over) *document etc.*; **'durch·ge·hend I.** *adj.* **1.** through *train etc.*; continuous *a.* ⚙ *operation etc.*; **II.** *adv.* **2.** generally; **3.** continuously; ~ ***geöffnet*** open all day; ~ ***von 9 - 18.30 geöffnet*** open 9 a.m. - 6.30 p.m.; ~ ***arbeiten*** work through; ~ ***Einlaß*** nonstop admission; **4.** throughout

durch·gei·stigt [dʊrç'gaɪstɪçt] *adj.* (very) cerebral

'durch|ge·knöpft *adj.* button-through *dress etc.*; **~ge·schwitzt** *adj.* sweaty, soaked with sweat; **~ge·stal·tet** *adj.* (*a.* ***gut*** ~) worked out to the last detail; **~ge·stylt** [-gəʃtaɪlt] *adj.* carefully styled; ***ein ~er Yuppie*** a yuppie from head to toe; **~gra·ben** *v/refl.* (*irr.*, *sep.*, h, → ***graben***): ***sich*** ~ (***durch*** *acc.*) dig (*or* burrow) one's way through

'durch·grei·fen *v/i.* (*irr.*, *sep.*, h, → ***greifen***) **1.** (*a.* ~ ***durch*** *acc.*) reach through; **2.** *fig.* take (tough) action, F do something; ***hart*** ~ ***bei*** *dat.* crack down on, take tough action (*or* a tough line) against; **'durch·grei·fend** *adj.* drastic; radical, sweeping

'durch·ha·ben F *v/t.* (*irr.*, *sep.*, h, → ***haben***): ***hast du das Buch schon durch?*** have you finished the book?

'durch·hal·ten (*irr.*, *sep.*, h, → ***halten***) **I.** *v/i.* hold out, F stick it out; ***du mußt*** ~ *a.* you mustn't give up, *esp. Am.* F hang in there; **II.** *v/t.* keep *s.th.* up; *a.* stand *the pace*; **'Durch·hal·te·ver·mö·gen** *n* staying power

'durch·hän·gen *v/i.* (*irr.*, *sep.*, h, → ***hängen²***) **1.** sag; **2.** F *fig.* have (*or* be going through) a low; ***laß dich nicht so*** ~ come on, get a grip of yourself; **'Durch·hän·ger** F *m* (-s; -) F low; ***e-n*** ~ ***haben*** have (*or* be going through) a low

'durch|hau·en (*sep.*, h) **I.** *v/t.* **1.** (hieb *or* F haute durch) chop in two; split; **2.** (haute durch) F give *s.o.* a thrashing; **II.** *v/refl.* (hieb *or* F haute durch): ***sich*** ~ (***durch*** *acc.*) hack one's way through; **~he·cheln** F *v/t.* (*sep.*, h) gossip about; **~hei·zen** (*sep.*, h) **I.** *v/t.* heat properly; **II.** *v/i.* keep the heating on night and day; **~hel·fen** (*irr.*, *sep.*, h, → ***helfen***) **I.** *v/i.* (*a.* ~ ***durch*** *acc.*) help *s.o.* through; **II.** *v/refl.*: ***sich*** ~ get by, manage; **~hö·ren** *v/t.* (*sep.*, h) **1.** hear (through the wall *etc.*); **2.** ~, ***daß*** be able to tell that; **~hun·gern** *v/refl.* (*sep.*, h): ***sich*** ~ (***durch*** *acc.*) have to survive (*a war etc.*) on very little; ***wir haben uns durch den Krieg durchgehungert*** *a.* we had very little (*or* virtually nothing) to eat during the war

'durch·ja·gen (*sep.*) **I.** *v/i.* (sn) (*a.* ~ ***durch*** *acc.*) race (*or* tear) through; **II.** *v/t.* (h) rush through (*a. fig.*); **durch'ja·gen** *v/t.* (*insep.*, *no* -ge-, h) chase through (*or* across)

'durch·käm·men *v/t.* (*sep.*, h) **1.** comb out *hair*; **2.** *fig.* comb (***nach*** *dat.* for); **durch'käm·men** *v/t.* (*insep.*, *no* -ge-, h) comb (***nach*** *dat.* for)

'durch|kämp·fen (*sep.*, h) **I.** *v/t.* fight *s.th.* through; **II.** *v/refl.*: ***sich*** ~ fight one's way through (*a.* ***sich*** ~ ***durch*** *acc.*) (*a. fig.*); *fig.* → ***durchringen***; **~kau·en** *v/t.* (*sep.*, h) chew well; *fig.* go over *s.th.* again and again; **~klin·gen** *v/i.* (*irr.*, *sep.*, h, → ***klingen***) sound through; *fig.* ***es klang etwas Neid durch*** you could detect a tinge of envy; **~knal·len** F *v/i.* (*sep.*, sn) blow; **~kne·ten** *v/t.* (*sep.*, h) knead (thoroughly); knead *muscles*; **~kom·men** *v/i.* (*irr.*, *sep.*, sn, → ***kommen***) (*a.* ~ ***durch*** *acc.*) come through (*a. fig.*); (manage to) get through (*a. teleph.*); *sun*: break through; make it; pass *the exam*; *patient*: pull through; ~ ***mit*** *dat.* get *s.th.* through, *fig.* get away with; ***mit et.*** ~ get by with; ***damit kommst du*** (***bei ihm***) ***nicht durch*** that won't work (that won't cut any ice with him); **~kom·po,niert** *adj.* ♪ through composed; **~kön·nen** F *v/i.* (*irr.*, *sep.*, h, → ***können***) (*a.* ~ ***durch*** *acc.*) be able to get through; **~kon·stru,iert** *adj.* carefully designed

durch'kreu·zen *v/t.* (*insep.*, *no* -ge-, h) cross; *fig.* thwart, frustrate; **'durch·kreu·zen** *v/t.* (*sep.*, h) cross out

'durch·krie·chen *v/i.* (*irr.*, *sep.*, sn, → ***kriechen***) (*a.* ~ ***durch*** *acc.*) crawl through

'durch·krie·gen F *v/t.* (*sep.*, h) → ***durchbekommen***

Durch·laß ['dʊrçlas] *m* (-lasses; -lässe [-lɛsə]) passage(way); opening, gap; ***j-m*** ~ ***gewähren*** let s.o. pass (*or* through); **'durch·las·sen** *v/t.* (*irr.*, *sep.*, h, → ***lassen***) (*a.* ~ ***durch*** *acc.*) let *s.o. or s.th.* pass (*or* through); pass; let *the light* through; ***Wasser*** ~ leak; F ***et.*** ~ let s.th. pass; F ***j-m et.*** ~ let s.o. get away with s.th.; **'durch·läs·sig** *adj.* pervious (***für*** *acc.* to); porous; leaky; translucent; **'Durch·läs·sig·keit** *f* (-; *no pl.*) perviousness; porosity; leakiness; translucence

Durch·laucht ['dʊrçlaʊxt] *f*: (***Euer*** ~ Your) Highness (*or* Grace)

durch'lau·fen *v/t.* (durchlief, durchlaufen, h) **1.** run through; cover *distance*; ⚙, *phys.* travel through; **2.** *fig.* pass through; *rumo(u)r etc.*: spread all over *town etc.*; ***ein Schauder durchlief ihn*** he shuddered, a shiver ran down his spine

'durch·lau·fen (*irr.*, *sep.*, → ***laufen***) **I.** *v/i.* (sn) (*a.* ~ ***durch*** *acc.*) run through; rush through; ⚙, ✝ pass through; **II.** *v/t.* (h) go through *a pair of shoes*; ***sich die Füße*** ~ walk one's feet off; **'durch·lau·fend** *adj.* continuous (*a.* ⚙); ✝ transitory; **'Durch·lauf·er·hit·zer** *m* (-s; -) instant(aneous) water heater

'durch·la,vie·ren *v/refl.* (*sep.*, h): ***sich*** ~ F wangle one's way through

durch'le·ben *v/t.* (*insep.*, *no* -ge-, h) go (*or* live) through, experience; (***im Geiste***) ***noch einmal*** ~ relive

'durch|lei·ten *v/t.* (*sep.*, h) (*a.* ~ ***durch*** *acc.*) lead through; **~le·sen** *v/t.* (*irr.*, *sep.*, h, → ***lesen***) read through

'durch·leuch·ten *v/i.* (*sep.*, h) (*a.* ~ ***durch*** *acc.*) shine through; *fig. a.* show; **durch'leuch·ten** *v/t.* (*insep.*, *no* -ge-, h) ⚕ x-ray, screen; ✈ *etc.* x-ray, put through the scanner; test *eggs*; *fig.* investigate (***auf*** *acc.* [***... hin***] for), probe into *s.o.'s past etc.*

Durch'leuch·tung *f* (-; -en) ⚕ x-ray, fluoroscopic examination; **Durch'leuch·tungs·ge·rät** *n* ✈ *etc.*: (x-ray) scanner

'durch·lie·gen *v/refl.* (*irr.*, *sep.*, h, → ***liegen***): ***sich*** ~ get bedsores

durch'lö·chern *v/t.* (*insep.*, *no* -ge-, h) make holes in; pierce; riddle with bullets; F *fig.* shoot holes in; **durch'lö·chert** *adj.* full of holes, F holy ...; riddled with bullets; ***völlig*** ~ *a.* riddled with holes

'durch·lot·sen *v/t.* (*sep.*, h) (*a.* ~ ***durch*** *acc.*) pilot (*or* guide) through

'durch·lüf·ten *v/t.* (*sep.*, h) air, give *s.th.* a good airing; **durch'lüf·ten** *v/t.* (*insep.*, no -ge-, h) **1.** → ***'durchlüften***; **2.** ventilate; aerate

'durch·ma·chen (*sep.*, h) **I.** *v/t.* go through; undergo; ***er hat einiges durchgemacht*** he's been through a lot, he hasn't had an easy time of it; **II.** *v/i.* carry on; (*a.* ***die ganze Nacht*** ~) make a night of it

'Durch·marsch *m* (-[e]s; ⸚e) **1.** march through; **2.** *no pl.* F *the* runs *pl.*; **'durch·mar,schie·ren** *v/i.* (*sep.*, sn) (*a.* ~ ***durch*** *acc.*) march through

durch'mes·sen *v/t.* (durchmaß, durchmessen, h): ***er durchmaß das Zimmer*** he paced the floor; **'Durch·mes·ser** *m* (-s; -) diameter; ***e-n*** ~ ***von drei Metern haben*** be three met|res (*Am.* -ers) in diameter

'durch·mi·schen *v/t.* (*sep.*, h) mix thoroughly; **durch'mi·schen** *v/t.* (*insep.*, *no* -ge-, h) mix (***mit*** *dat.* with)

'durch|mo·geln F *v/refl.* (*sep.*, h): ***sich*** ~ wangle one's way through; cheat; **~müs·sen** F *v/i.* (*irr.*, *sep.*, h, → ***müssen***) (*a.* ~ ***durch*** *acc.*) have to get (*or* go) through; *fig.* ***da muß ich*** (***einfach***) ***durch*** I've (just) got to get through it somehow, I've got to ride this one out

durch·näßt [dʊrç'nɛst] *adj.* soaked, drenched, soaked to the skin

'durch|neh·men *v/t.* (*irr.*, *sep.*, h, → ***nehmen***) go through, do; **~nu·me,rie·ren** *v/t.* (*sep.*, *no* -ge-, h) number all the way through; **~or·ga·ni,siert** *adj.* (*a.* ***gut*** ~) well-organized; **~pau·sen** *v/t.* (*sep.*, h) trace; **~peit·schen** *v/t.* (*sep.*, h) **1.** give *s.o.* a whipping; **2.** *fig.* rush *s.th.* through; **~prü·fen** *v/t.* (*sep.*, h) give *s.th.* a thorough check

durch'que·ren *v/t.* (*insep.*, *no* -ge-, h) cross

'durch·quet·schen (*sep.*, h) **I.** *v/t.* (*a.* ~ ***durch*** *acc.*) squeeze *s.th.* through; **II.** *v/refl.*: ***sich*** ~ (***durch*** *acc.*) squeeze through

'durch·ra·sen *v/i.* (*sep.*, sn) (*a.* ~ ***durch*** *acc.*) race (*or* tear, shoot) through; **durch'ra·sen** *v/t.* (*insep.*, *no* -ge-, h) race (*or* tear, shoot) through

'durch|ras·seln F *v/i.* (*sep.*, sn), **~rau·schen** F *v/i.* (*sep.*, sn) F flunk; **~rech·nen** *v/t.* (*sep.*, h) make an estimate of; go over, check; **~reg·nen** *v/impers.* (*sep.*, h): ***hier regnet es durch*** the rain's coming through; **~rei·ben** *v/t.* (*irr.*, *sep.*, h, → ***reiben***) wear through (*a.* ***sich*** ~)

Durch·rei·che ['dʊrçraɪçə] *f* (-; -n) hatch; **'durch·rei·chen** *v/t.* (*sep.*, h) pass (*or* hand) *s.th.* through

'Durch·rei·se *f*: ***auf der*** ~ (***durch*** *acc.*) on one's way through; ***wir sind nur auf der*** ~ we're just passing through; **durch'rei·sen** *v/t.* (*insep.*, *no* -ge-, h) travel through; travel around; **'durch·rei·sen** *v/i.* (*sep.*, sn) (*a.* ~ ***durch*** *acc.*) pass through; **'Durch·rei·sen·de** *m, f* (-n; -n)

travel(l)er, *Am. a.* transient; ✈ transit (🚂 through) passenger; **'Durch·rei·se·vi·sum** *n* transit visa
'durch·rei·ßen (*irr.*, *sep.*, → **reißen**) **I.** *v/t.* (h) tear (in two); **II.** *v/i.* (sn) tear, get torn; snap
'durch·rei·ten *v/i.* (*irr.*, *sep.*, sn, → **reiten**) (*a.* ~ **durch** *acc.*) ride through; **durch'rei·ten** *v/t.* (durchritt, durchritten, h) ride through
'durch·ren·nen *v/i.* (*irr.*, *sep.*, sn, → **rennen**) (*a.* ~ **durch** *acc.*) run through
'durch·rie·seln *v/i.* (*sep.*, sn) (*a.* ~ **durch** *acc.*) trickle through; **durch'rie·seln** *v/t.* (*insep.*, *no* -ge-, h): ***es durchrieselte ihn kalt*** a cold shiver ran down his spine
'durch|rin·gen *v/refl.* (*irr.*, *sep.*, h, → **ringen**): ***sich (dazu)*** ~, ***et. zu tun*** finally make up one's mind to do s.th.; ***sich zu e-m Entschluß*** ~ force o.s. to make a decision; **~ro·sten** *v/i.* (*sep.*, sn) rust through; **~rüh·ren** *v/t.* (*sep.*, h) stir (*or* mix) thoroughly; **~rut·schen** *v/i.* (*sep.*, sn) (*a.* ~ **durch** *acc.*) slip through (*a. fig.*); *fig.* F scrape through *the exam*; ***sie ist bei der Prüfung durchgerutscht*** she (just about) scraped through the exam; **~rüt·teln** *v/t.* (*sep.*, h) shake about; **~sacken** (*sep.* -k·k-) *v/i.* (*sep.*, sn) ✈ stall, pancake
Durch·sa·ge ['dʊrçza:gə] *f* (-; -n) announcement; *radio*: (news) flash; ~ ***der Polizei*** police message; **'durch·sa·gen** *v/t.* (*sep.*, h) *radio*: announce; pass *s.th.* on
'durch·sä·gen *v/t.* (*sep.*, h) saw through (*or* in two)
durch'schau·bar *adj.* obvious, transparent; ***schwer*** ~ inscrutable, enigmatic; ***er ist leicht*** ~ you can read him like a book
'durch·schau·en *v/i.* (*sep.*, h) (*a.* ~ **durch** *acc.*) look through; ***man kann durch die Fenster kaum*** ~ you can hardly see through the windows; **durch'schau·en** *v/t.* (*insep.*, *no* -ge-, h) see through; understand
'durch·schei·nen *v/i.* (*irr.*, *sep.*, h, → **scheinen**) (*a.* ~ **durch** *acc.*) shine through (*a. fig.*); *writing etc.*: show through; **'durch·schei·nend** *adj.* translucent
'durch·scheu·ern *v/t.* (*sep.*, h) wear through (*a.* ***sich*** ~); ***sich die Haut*** ~ rub one's skin off, chafe one's skin
'durch·schie·ßen *v/i.* (*irr.*, *sep.*, h, → **schießen**) (*a.* ~ **durch** *acc.*) shoot through; **durch'schie·ßen** *v/t.* (durchschoß, durchschossen, h) **1.** shoot through *s.th.*; **2.** *typ.* space (out); **3.** interleave
'durch|schim·mern *v/i.* (*sep.*, h) (*a.* ~ **durch** *acc.*) shimmer through; *writing etc.*: come through; **~schla·fen** *v/i.* (*irr.*, *sep.*, h, → **schlafen**) sleep through
'Durch·schlag *m* (-[e]s; ⸗e) **1.** (carbon) copy; **2.** colander, strainer; **3.** ⚙ punch; **4.** *mot.* puncture; **5.** ⚡ disruptive discharge, *Am.* puncture; blowout
durch'schla·gen *v/t.* (durchschlug, durchschlagen, h) go through
'durch·schla·gen (*irr.*, *sep.*, → **schlagen**) **I.** *v/t.* (h) **1.** break *s.th.* in two; **2.** ***ein Loch durch*** *et.* ~ make a hole in; **3.** *gastr.* pass *s.th.* through a strainer; **II.** *v/i.* **4.** (sn) (*a.* ~ **durch** *acc.*) *humidity etc.*: come through, *colo(u)r*: *a.* show through; **5.** (sn) *genes etc.*: come through; ***bei ihm schlägt die Mutter durch*** he takes after his mother's side; **6.** (sn) have an effect (***auf*** *acc.* on); **7.** (h) ⚕ go straight through (***bei j-m*** s.o.); **8.** (sn) ⚡ blow; **III.** *v/refl.*: ***sich*** ~ (h) fight one's way through (*a.* ***sich*** ~ ***durch*** *acc.*); *fig.* get by (***mit*** *dat.* on); ***sich mühsam*** ~ have a hard time of it; **'durch·schla·gend** *adj.* conclusive, irrefutable *evidence etc.*; sweeping *success etc.*
'Durch·schlag·pa,pier *n* carbon paper
'Durch·schlags·kraft *f* striking force; *fig.* force *of an argument etc.*
'durch|schlän·geln *v/refl.* (*sep.*, h): ***sich*** ~ (***durch*** *acc.*) *river etc.*: wind (its way) through; *person*: weave one's way through; *fig.* muddle through; **~schlei·chen** *v/refl.* (*irr.*, *sep.*, sn, → **schleichen**): ***sich*** ~ (***durch*** *acc.*) sneak through; **~schleu·sen** *v/t.* (*sep.*, h) **1.** pass *a ship etc.* through a lock; **2.** *fig.* (*a.* ~ **durch** *acc.*) guide *s.o. or s.th.* through; hustle *s.o.* through, smuggle *s.o. or s.th.* through; **~schlüp·fen** *v/i.* (*sep.*, sn) (*a.* ~ **durch** *acc.*) slip through; **~schmecken** (*sep.*, h) **I.** *v/t.* taste; **II.** *v/i.*: ***der Senf schmeckte durch*** you could taste the mustard (quite strongly); **~schmug·geln** (*sep.*, h) **I.** *v/t.* (*a.* ~ **durch** *acc.*) smuggle through; **II.** *v/refl.*: ***sich*** ~ (***durch*** *acc.*) sneak through
'durch·schnei·den *v/t.* (*irr.*, *sep.*, h, → **schneiden**) cut (in two); **durch'schnei·den** *v/t.* (durchschnitt, durchschnitten, h) **1.** → **'durchschneiden; 2.** cut through *s.th.*; intersect; cross; plough (*Am.* plow) through *the waves etc.*
'Durch·schnitt *m* (-[e]s; -e) **1.** average; ***im*** ~ on average; ***über*** (***unter***) ***dem*** ~ ***liegen*** be above (below) average; ***im*** ~ ***erzielen*** *etc.* average; ***er ist guter*** ~ he's not a bad player *etc.*; **2.** section; **'durch·schnitt·lich I.** *adj.* average; ordinary; average, *contp.* mediocre; F fair to middling; **II.** *adv.* on (an) average; ~ ***leisten*** *etc.* average; ***er arbeitet*** ~ ***zehn Stunden am Tag*** he works an average of ten hours a day, he works ten hours a day, on average
'Durch·schnitts... *in cpds. usu.* average; **~al·ter** *n* average age; **~bür·ger** *m* average citizen; ***der*** ~ the (F your) average citizen, the man in the street, F Mr Average; **~ein·kom·men** *n* average income; **~ge·schwin·dig·keit** *f* average speed; **~ge·sicht** *n* nondescript face; **~lei·stung** *f* average performance; **~mensch** *m* ordinary person, *the* man in the street; **~no·te** *f* average mark (*esp. Am.* grade); **~typ** F *m* F ordinary sort of person; **~wert** *m* average (value); **~zeit** *f* average time (it takes)
durch'schnüf·feln *v/t.* (*insep.*, *no* -ge-, h) snoop (*or* nose) around in
'Durch·schrei·be·block *m* carbon-copy pad; **'durch·schrei·ben** *v/t.* (*irr.*, *sep.*, h, → **schreiben**) make a (carbon) copy of
'durch·schrei·ten *v/i.* (*irr.*, *sep.*, sn, → **schreiten**) (*a.* ~ **durch** *acc.*) walk through (*or* across), stride through; **durch'schrei·ten** *v/t.* (durchschritt, durchschritten, h) walk through (*or* across), stride through
'Durch·schrift *f* (-; -en) (carbon) copy
'Durch·schuß *m* (-sses; ⸗sse) **1.** penetration wound; ***das war ein*** (***glatter***) ~ ***durch den Arm*** the shot went right through his (*or* her) arm; **2.** *typ.* space; **3.** *textil.* woof
'durch·schüt·teln *v/t.* (*sep.*, h) shake thoroughly; shake *s.o.* about
'durch·schwim·men *v/i.* (*irr.*, *sep.*, sn, → **schwimmen**) (*a.* ~ **durch** *acc.*) swim (*or* float) through (*or* across); **durch'schwim·men** *v/t.* (durchschwamm, durchschwommen, h) swim through (*or* across), cross; swim *a distance*
'durch·schwit·zen *v/t.* (*sep.*, h): ***ich habe mein Hemd durchgeschwitzt, mein Hemd ist durchgeschwitzt*** my shirt's soaked (*or* soaking, drenched) with sweat
durch'se·geln *v/t.* (*insep.*, *no* -ge-, h) sail (across), cross; **'durch·se·geln** *v/i.* (*sep.*, sn) **1.** sail through; **2.** F flunk (it); ***er ist in der Prüfung durchgesegelt*** he flunked the exam
'durch·se·hen (*irr.*, *sep.*, h, → **sehen**) **I.** *v/i.* (*a.* ~ **durch** *acc.*) see (*or* look) through; **II.** *v/t.* look (*or* go) through, go over, check
'durch·sein F *v/i.* (*irr.*, *sep.*, sn, → **sein**) **1.** be worn through; ***die Hose ist durch*** *a.* F these trousers have had it; **2.** ~ ***mit*** *dat.* have finished, *a.* have finished with (*or* reading) *a book etc.*; **3.** *motion etc.*: be (*or* have got) through; **4.** be out of the wood(s); be over the worst; **5.** have made it, be through; **6.** *gastr.* be done; *cheese*: be ripe; **7.** ***er ist bei mir unten durch*** I'm through with him; **8.** ***es ist drei*** (***Uhr***) ***durch*** it's past (*or* gone) three
'durch·set·zen¹ (*sep.*, h) **I.** *v/t.* get *s.th.* through (*or* accepted); push *s.th.* through; ***s-e Meinung*** ~ get (the) others to agree; ***s-n Kopf*** (*or* ***Willen***) ~ have one's way; **II.** *v/refl.*: ***sich*** ~ get one's way; assert o.s.; prevail; *idea etc.*: catch on, gain acceptance (***bei*** *dat.* with); *goods*: catch on, sell; ***sich*** ~ ***gegen*** *acc.* come out on top against (*a. sport*), prevail over, overcome *resistance etc.*; ***sie kann sich bei den Kindern nicht*** ~ the children always get their own way with her, she has no control over the children; ***du mußt lernen, dich durchzusetzen*** you've got to assert yourself more, you've got to be more self-assertive (*or* forceful)
durch'set·zen² *v/t.* (*insep.*, *no* -ge-, h) intersperse, interlard (***mit*** *dat.* with); infiltrate (with)
'Durch·set·zungs|kraft *f*, **~ver·mö·gen** *n* (powers *pl.* of) self-assertion; ***er hat nicht genügend*** ~ he isn't forceful enough
durch·seu·chen [-'zɔʏçən] *v/t.* (*insep.*, *no* -ge-, h) contaminate; **Durch'seu·chung** *f* (-; -en) contamination
'Durch·sicht *f* (-; *no pl.*) checking; ***bei*** ~ *gen.* on (*or* while) looking through (*or* checking) *s.th.*
durch·sich·tig ['dʊrçzɪçtɪç] *adj.* transparent (*a. fig.*), see-through; translucent; *fig.* obvious; **'Durch·sich·tig·keit** *f* (-; *no pl.*) transparency (*a. fig.*); translucence, translucent quality
'durch·sickern *v/i.* (*sep.*, sn) (*a.* ~ **durch** *acc.*) seep (*or* trickle) through; *fig.* filter through, leak out; ~ ***bis*** *a.* filter (*or* trickle) down to
'durch·sie·ben *v/t.* (*sep.*, h) sift (*a. fig.*); **durch·siebt** [dʊrç'zi:pt] *adj.* riddled with bullets
'durch|spie·len (*sep.*, h) **I.** *v/t.* **1.** ♪ play

s.th. right through; go through; **II.** *v/i.* **2.** *sport*: play a through ball; **3.** *sport*: a) last the whole match *etc.*, b) go through the whole season (*or* tournament *etc.*) *with the same team etc.*; **III.** *v/refl.*: ***sich ~*** *sport*: weave one's way through; **~spre·chen** *v/t.* (*irr., sep.,* h, → ***sprechen***) talk *s.th.* over, discuss; **~spü·len** *v/t.* (*sep.,* h) **1.** rinse thoroughly; **2.** ⚕ (*a.* ***gut ~***) flush; **~star·ten** *v/i.* (*sep.,* sn) ✈ reaccelerate for a new landing approach; *mot.* rev up

'durch·ste·chen *v/i.* (*irr., sep.,* h, → ***ste·chen***): ***~ durch*** *acc.* pierce; ***mit e-r Nadel ~*** stick (*or* pass) a needle through; **durch'ste·chen** *v/t.* (durchstach, durchstochen, h) pierce; prick; cut

'durch|stecken *v/t.* (*sep.,* h) (*a.* ***~ durch*** *acc.*) pass (*or* put) through; **~ste·hen** *v/t.* (*irr., sep.,* h, → ***stehen***) get through, F stick *s.th.* out

durch'stö·bern *v/t.* (*insep., no* -ge-, h), **'durch·stö·bern** *v/t.* (*sep.,* h) rummage through *s.th.* (***nach*** *dat.* for)

'durch·sto·ßen (*irr., sep.,* → ***stoßen***) **I.** *v/i.* (sn) *a.* ⚔ *and sport*: break through; **II.** *v/t.* (h) (*a.* ***~ durch*** *acc.*) push through; **durch'sto·ßen** *v/t.* (durchstieß, durchstoßen, h) pierce; ⚔, ✈ break through *the clouds*

'durch·strei·chen *v/t.* (*irr., sep.,* h, → ***streichen***) cross out

'durch·strö·men *v/i.* (*sep.,* sn) (*a.* ***~ durch*** *acc.*) flow (*or* run) through; **durch'strö·men** *v/t.* (*insep., no* -ge-, h) flow (*or* run) through; *fig.* ***ein Gefühl der Zufriedenheit durchströmte ihn*** he was filled with a great sense of satisfaction

durch'su·chen *v/t.* (*insep., no* -ge-, h) search (***nach*** *dat.* for); **Durch'su·chung** *f* (-; -en) search; **Durch'su·chungs·be·fehl** *m* search warrant

durch'tan·zen *v/t.* (*insep., no* -ge-, h) ***die ganze Nacht ~*** dance the night away; **'durch·tan·zen** *v/i.* (*sep.,* h) dance nonstop; ***~ bis*** dance (away) until (*or* till)

'durch·ta·sten *v/refl.* (*sep.,*h): ***sich ~*** (***durch*** *acc.*) grope one's way through

'durch·trai,niert *adj.* well-trained; supple, athletic

durch'trän·ken *v/t.* (*insep., no* -ge-, h) soak (***mit*** *dat.* in); *lit. fig.* ***durchtränkt von*** suffused with

'durch·tren·nen *v/t.* (*sep.,* h), **durch'tren·nen** *v/t.* (*insep., no* -ge-, h) tear (in two); cut (in two); sever

'durch·tre·ten *v/t.* (*irr., sep.,* h, → ***treten***) **1.** wear out; **2.** *mot.* floor *pedal*; kick *starter*

durch·trie·ben [dʊrç'tri:bən] *adj.* sly; ***das ist ein ~er Kerl*** he's a sly one

'durch·wa·chen *v/t.* (*sep.,* h): (***die Nacht***) ~ be (*or* lie, stay) awake all night, ***bei j-m:*** stay by s.o.'s bedside (*or* stay up with s.o.) all night; ***ich habe die Nacht durchgewacht*** *a.* I didn't sleep a wink (*or* get a wink of sleep) all night

'durch·wach·sen *v/i.* (*irr., sep.,* sn, → ***wachsen***) (*a.* ***~ durch*** *acc.*) grow through

durch'wach·sen *adj.* marbled *meat*; streaky *bacon*; F *fig.* F so-so, fair to middling; *meteor.* up and down

'Durch·wahl *f* (-; *no pl.*) *teleph.* direct dial(l)ing; **'durch·wäh·len** *v/i.* (*sep.,* h) dial through (*or* direct); *Am.* direct dial

'durch·wan·dern *v/i.* (*sep.,* sn) (*a.* ***~ durch*** *acc.*) walk (*or* hike) through; do (*or* go on) a walking *or* hiking tour through; **durch'wan·dern** *v/t.* (*insep., no* -ge-, h) walk (*or* hike) through; do (*or* go on) a walking *or* hiking tour through

durch'wär·men *v/t.* (*insep., no* -ge-, h) warm *s.o. or s.th.* up

'durch·wa·ten *v/i.* (*sep.,* sn) (*a.* ***~ durch*** *acc.*) wade through; **durch'wa·ten** *v/t.* (*insep., no* -ge-, h) wade through

durch'we·ben *v/t.* (*insep., no* -ge-, h) interweave (*a. fig.*)

'durch·weg *adv.* entirely; ***sie waren ~ defekt*** they were all faulty, every one of them was faulty

durch'wei·chen *v/t.* (*insep., no* -ge-, h) soften; soak; **durch·weicht** [dʊrç'vaɪçt] *adj.* soaked; soggy

'durch·win·den *v/refl.* (*irr., sep.,* h, → ***winden***): ***sich ~*** (***durch*** *acc.*) wind its way through; weave one's way through; (manage to) get round *difficulties etc.*

'durch·win·ken *v/t.* (*sep.,* h) wave *s.o.* through

'durch·wüh·len (*sep.,* h) **I.** *v/t.* → ***durch'wühlen***; **II.** *v/refl.*: ***sich ~ durch*** *acc.* burrow (one's *or* its way) through; *fig.* plough (*Am.* plow) through; **durch'wüh·len** *v/t.* (*insep., no* -ge-, h) dig up, root up; rummage through

durch|wursch·teln ['dʊrçvʊrʃtəln] F *v/refl.* (*sep.,* h): ***sich ~*** muddle through, ***durch*** *acc.*: muddle one's way through *s.th.*; **~zäh·len** *v/t.* (*sep.,* h) count (up); **~zeich·nen** *v/t.* (*sep.,* h) trace

'durch·zie·hen (*irr., sep.,* → ***ziehen***) **I.** *v/t.* (h) (*a.* ***~ durch*** *acc.*) pull *s.th.* through; carry *s.th.* through (to the end); **II.** *v/i.* (sn) (*a.* ***~ durch*** *acc.*) pass through; *gastr.* ***~ lassen*** steep; **III.** *v/refl.*: ***sich ~*** (***durch*** *acc.*) go right through; *motif etc.*: run all the way through; **durch'zie·hen** *v/t.* (durchzog, durchzogen, h) pass through; *a. motif etc.*: run through

durch'zucken *v/t.* (*insep., no* -ge-, h) *lightning*: flash across *the sky*; *fig. pain etc.*: shoot through; *idea, thought etc.*: flash through *s.o.'s mind*

'Durch·zug *m* (-[e]s; ⁓e) **1.** *no pl.* draught, *Am.* draft; ***~ machen*** air the room *etc.* through; F *fig.* ***auf ~ schalten*** F switch off; **2.** passage *of birds*; ⚔ march through

'durch·zwän·gen (*sep.,* h) **I.** *v/t.* (*a.* ***~ durch*** *acc.*) force (*or* squeeze) through; **II.** *v/refl.*: ***sich ~*** (***durch*** *acc.*) squeeze (o.s.) through

dür·fen ['dʏrfən] *v/i.* (darf, durfte, gedurft, h) **1.** be allowed to *inf.*; ***darf ich rausgehen?*** can (*or* may) I go out?; ***nein, du darfst nicht*** no you can't, no you may not; ***er darf*** (***durfte***) ***nicht raus*** he's not (he wasn't) allowed out; ***ich darf keinen Alkohol trinken*** I'm not allowed (to drink) any alcohol; **2.** ***du darfst den Hund nicht anfassen*** you mustn't touch the dog, don't touch the dog; ***wir ~ den Bus nicht verpassen*** we mustn't miss the bus; ***so etwas darfst du nicht sagen*** you mustn't (*or* shouldn't) say things like that; ***das darfst du doch nicht*** you shouldn't do (things like) that; ***das hättest du nicht sagen ~*** you shouldn't have said that; ***das darf keiner erfahren*** nobody's to know, nobody must find out; **3.** ***wenn man es so nennen darf*** if one can call it that; ***du darfst stolz auf ihn sein*** you can be proud of him; ***du darfst es mir glauben*** you can take my word for it; **4.** ***das dürfte der Neue sein*** that must be the new teacher *etc.*; ***es dürfte bald zu Ende sein*** it should be finished soon; ***das dürfte die beste Lösung sein*** that's probably (*or* that seems to be, I think that's) the best solution; **5.** ***darf ich?*** may I?; ***was darf's sein?*** what can I do for you?, what would you like (to drink)?, F *hum.* what's your poison?; ***ich darf mich jetzt verabschieden*** I'm afraid I've got to go now; → ***bitten***

durf·te ['dʊrftə] *pret. of* ***dürfen***

dürf·tig ['dʏrftɪç] *adj.* poor; humble; meag|re (*Am.* -er); scanty, *a.* skimpy *clothes*; weak, flimsy *argument etc.*; feeble *excuse etc.*

dürr [dʏr] *adj.* dry; arid, barren; thin, skinny; scrawny *neck*; spindly *legs*; ***in ~en Worten*** in sober terms; **Dür·re** ['dʏrə] *f* (-; -n) **1.** *no pl.* dryness; aridity; **2.** drought; **'Dür·re·pe·ri,ode** *f* period of drought

Durst [dʊrst] *m* (-[e]s; *no pl.*) thirst (***nach*** *dat.* for) (*a. fig.*); ***~ bekommen*** (***haben***) get (be) thirsty; ***das macht ~*** it makes you thirsty; ***Gartenarbeit macht ~*** gardening is thirsty work; ***hab' ich e-n ~!*** I'm dying of thirst; F ***einen über den ~ getrunken haben*** have had one too many (F one over the eight); **dur·sten** ['dʊrstən] *v/i.* (h) be thirsty; ***~ müssen*** go thirsty; *fig.* ***~ nach*** *dat.* thirst (*or* be thirsting) for; **dur·stig** ['dʊrstɪç] *adj.* thirsty

'durst·lö·schend, 'durst·stil·lend *adj.* thirst-quenching

'Durst·strecke (*sep.* -k·k-) *fig.* *f* (-; -n) long hard haul

'Dur|ton·art *f* ♪ major key; **~ton·lei·ter** *f* ♪ major scale

Dusch·bad ['dʊʃ-, 'du:ʃ-] *n* shower-bath

Du·sche ['dʊʃə, 'du:ʃə] *f* (-; -n) shower; ***e-e ~ nehmen*** have (*or* take) a shower; ***unter der ~*** in the shower; *fig.* ***das war e-e kalte ~ für ihn*** that brought him down to earth with a bump; **du·schen** ['dʊʃən, 'du:ʃən] (h) **I.** *v/i.* (*a. v/refl.*: ***sich ~***) have (*or* take) a shower; **II.** *v/t.* give *s.o.* a shower; shower down

'Dusch|gel ['dʊʃ-, 'du:ʃ-] *n* shower gel; **~ge·le·gen·heit** *f* shower facilities *pl.*; **~hau·be** *f* shower cap; **~ka,bi·ne** *f* shower (cubicle); **~kopf** *m* shower head; **~raum** *m* shower room, showers *pl.*; **~vor·hang** *m* shower curtain

Dü·se ['dy:zə] *f* (-; -n) ⚙ nozzle; jet

Du·sel ['du:zəl] F *m* (-s; *no pl.*) luck; ***~ haben*** be in luck, be lucky; ***da haben wir noch einmal ~ gehabt*** that was lucky, that was close

du·se·lig ['du:zəlɪç] F *adj.* F dop(e)y; ***mir ist ganz ~*** (***im Kopf***) I feel really dop(e)y

'Dü·sen|an·trieb *m* jet propulsion; ***mit ~*** → ***düsengetrieben***; **~bom·ber** *m* jet bomber; **~flug·zeug** *n* jet aircraft, jet (plane)

'dü·sen·ge·trie·ben *adj.* jet-propelled

'Dü·sen|jä·ger *m* jet fighter; **~trieb·werk** *n* jet engine; **~zeit·al·ter** *n* jet age

Dus·sel ['dʊsəl] F *m* (-s; -) F dope, twit, dumbo

dü·ster ['dy:stɐ] **I.** *adj.* dark, gloomy; dim; somb|re (*Am.* -er); dismal; ominous; sinister; shady; ***~e Gedanken*** black thoughts; ***~e Prognose*** gloomy prediction; ***~es Schweigen*** gloomy silence;

~e Stimmung a) gloomy atmosphere, b) grim mood; ***ein ~es Bild von et. zeichnen*** (*or* ***entwerfen***) paint a black picture of s.th.; **II.** *adv.*: ***es sieht ~ aus*** things are looking grim

'Dü·ster·heit *f* (-; *no pl.*), **'Dü·ster·keit** *f* (-; *no pl.*) gloom(iness)

Dut·zend ['dʊtsənt] *n* (-s; -e [-də]) dozen; ***ein*** (***zwei***) ***~ Eier*** a (two) dozen eggs; ***~e von Leuten*** dozens of people; ***sie kamen in*** (*or* ***zu***) ***~en*** dozens (of them) came; ***~ge·sicht*** *n* nondescript face

'dut·zend·mal *adv* dozens of times

'Dut·zend|mensch *m* nonentity; ***~wa·re*** *contp. f* cheap stuff

'dut·zend·wei·se *adv.* by the dozen

du·zen ['duːtsən] *v/t.* (h) say 'du' to *s.o.*, be on first-name terms with *s.o.*

Duz·freund ['duːts-] *m* good friend; ***sie sind ~e*** *a.* F they're good mates (*or* pals)

Dy·na·mik [dy'naːmɪk] *f* (-; *no pl.*) *phys.*, ♪ dynamics *pl.*; *fig.* dynamic force; dynamism, (tremendous) drive; **dy·na·misch** [dy'naːmɪʃ] *adj.* dynamic(ally *adv.*) (*a. fig.*); *fig.* index-linked *pension etc.*

Dy·na·mit [dyna'miːt] *n* (-s; *no pl.*) dynamite

Dy·na·mo [dy'naːmo, 'dyːnamo] *m* (-s; -s), ***~ma,schi·ne*** *f* dynamo, *Am.* generator

Dy·na·stie [dynas'tiː] *f* (-; -n) dynasty

Dys·to·nie [dʏsto'niː] *f* (-; -n) ⚕ dystonia; ***vegetative ~*** neurodystonia

D-Zug ['deː'tsuːk] *m* express, fast train

E

E, e [eː] *n* (-; -) E, e; ♪ E

Eau| de Co·lo·gne ['oː də ko'lɔnjə] *n* (- - -; Eaux - - ['oː]) eau de Cologne; **~ de toi·lette** ['oː də tŏa'lɛt] *n* (- - -; Eaux - - ['oː]) eau de toilette, toilet water

Eb·be ['ɛbə] *f* (-; -n) low tide; ***~ und Flut*** high tide and low tide; ***es ist ~*** the tide's out, it's low tide; F *fig.* ***in m-m Geldbeutel ist ~*** I'm a bit hard up at the moment

eben ['eːbən] **I.** *adj.* **1.** even, level; smooth; **II.** *adv.* **2.** just (now); ***~ erst*** only just; ***ich wollte ~ gehen*** I was just about (*or* going) to leave; **3.** just, exactly; ***~ das wollte ich sagen*** that's just what I was going to say; ***~!*** exactly; (***das ist es ja***) ***~!*** that's it, that's what I've been trying to say all along; ***~ nicht!*** no - that's the whole point; **4.** ***ja, ~!*** that's right; **5.** ***~ noch*** only just; **6.** just; ***er will ~ nicht*** he doesn't want to - it's as simple as that; ***ich weiß es ~ nicht*** I just don't know; ***er ist ~ müde*** he's tired, that's all; ***es taugt ~ nichts*** I told you it was no good; ***dann ~ nicht!*** all right (*Am.* alright), nobody's forcing you; ***da kann man ~ nichts machen*** well, it can't be helped; ***er ist ~ der Bessere*** he's better - there's no denying it; ***dann komme ich ~ nicht*** well, I'll just not come, then; ***das ist ~ so*** well, that's how it is; **7.** *iro.* ***nicht ~ klug*** *etc.* not exactly clever *etc.*

'Eben·bild *n* image; ***das ~ s-s Vaters*** the spitting image (*or* spit and image) of his father

'eben·bür·tig [-bʏrtɪç] *adj.* equal, of equal rank (*or* quality); ***j-m ~ sein*** be on a level (*or* par) with s.o.; ***sie ist ihm an Intelligenz ~*** she's every bit as intelligent as he is; ***ein ~er Nachfolger*** a worthy successor; **'Eben·bür·tig·keit** *f* (-; *no pl.*) equality

'eben'da *adv.* just there; ibidem (*abbr.* ibid.)

'eben'der, 'eben'die, 'eben'das(selbe) **I.** *dem. pron.* that very one, the very same; **II.** *adj.* that very ...

'eben'des·we·gen *adv.* that's precisely why; that's exactly why I did it *etc.*

Ebe·ne ['eːbənə] *f* (-; -n) *geogr.* plain; ⩓ plane; ⚙ plane surface; *fig.* level; ⩓ ***schiefe ~*** inclined plane; *fig.* ***auf die schiefe ~ geraten*** go off the straight and narrow; ***auf staatlicher*** (***politischer***) ***~*** at government (on a political) level; ***auf höchster ~*** at the highest level, (right) at the top; ***Gespräche auf höchster ~*** top-level talks; ***auf gleicher ~ liegen mit*** *dat.* be on a level (*or* par) with

'eben·er·dig [-eːɐdɪç] *adj.* ground-level ..., at ground level

'eben·falls *adv.* likewise, also; ... too, ... as well; ***~ nicht*** (***kein***) not ... either; ***danke, ~!*** you too

'Eben·heit *f* (-; *no pl.*) evenness; smoothness

'Eben·holz *n* ebony

'Eben·maß *n* (-es; *no pl.*) harmony, symmetry, regularity; shapeliness; **'eben·mä·ßig** *adj.* regular; well-proportioned; shapely; **'Eben·mä·ßig·keit** *f* → ***Ebenmaß***

'eben·so *adv.* **1.** just as; ***es ist ~ voll wie gestern*** it's (just) as full as it was yesterday; ***er ist ~ fleißig wie hilfreich*** he's as hard-working as he is helpful; **2.** (in) the same way; ***ich reagierte ~*** *a.* my reaction was the same; ***in Europa ~ wie in Amerika*** in Europe and America alike; **3.** → ***ebenfalls, auch***; ***~gern, ~gut*** *adv. etc.* → ***genausogern, genausogut*** *etc.*

Eber ['eːbɐ] *m* (-s; -) (wild) boar; → ***angestochen***

'Eber·esche *f* ⚘ mountain ash, rowan (tree)

eb·nen ['eːbnən] *v/t.* (h) level (off *or* out); *fig.* → ***Weg***

echauf·fie·ren [eʃɔ'fiːrən] *v/refl.* (h): ***sich ~*** get all excited (*or* worked up, hot and bothered) (***über*** *acc.* about); **echauffiert** [eʃɔ'fiːɐt] *adj.* (all) hot and bothered, (all) worked up (***über*** *acc.* about)

Echo ['ɛço] *n* (-s; -s) **1.** echo; ***ein ~ geben*** (*or* ***zurückwerfen***) echo; **2.** *fig.* response (***auf*** *acc.* to), echo; ***ein begeistertes ~ finden*** go down well, meet with an overwhelming response, be welcomed with open arms; ***es fand kein ~*** there was no response (*or* support) (***bei*** *dat.* from); ***ein weltweites ~ hervorrufen*** a) be hailed throughout the world, b) have worldwide repercussions

'Echo·lot *n* sonar

Ech·se ['ɛksə] *f* (-; -n) **1.** saurian; **2.** → ***Eidechse***

echt [ɛçt] **I.** *adj.* real *gold, leather etc.*; genuine *painting etc.*; authentic *document etc.*; fast *colo(u)r*; natural *colo(u)r of hair*; *fig.* real; ⩓ ***~er Bruch*** proper fraction; *das Gemälde etc.* ***ist nicht ~*** *a.* is a forgery; ***für ~ erklären*** authenticate; ***ein ~er Engländer*** a real (*or* true) Englishman, an Englishman born and bred; ***~e Gefühle*** genuine feelings; ***e-e ~e Atmosphäre erzielen*** get the genuine (*or* real) feel *of the place etc.*; ***ein ~er Verlust*** a real (*or* great) loss; **II.** *adv.* really; F ***das ist ~ Paul!*** that's Paul all over; F ***das war ~ gut!*** it was really good; **'Echtheit** *f* (-; *no pl.*) genuineness; authenticity; ***die ~ von et. überprüfen*** check whether s.th. is genuine (*or* authentic)

'Echt·zeit *f computer*: real time; ***~ver·ar·bei·tung*** *f* real-time processing

Eck|ball ['ɛk-] *m sport*: corner; **~bank** *f* (-; ⸚e) corner seat(ing unit); **~da·ten** *pl.* key features

Ecke ['ɛkə] (*sep.* -k·k-) *f* (-; -n) corner (*a. sport*); piece; F *fig.* F corner (of town, of the country, of the world); F *fig.* F stretch; ***an der ~*** at (*or* on) the corner; ***~ Weinstraße*** at (*or* on) the corner of Weinstraße; ***gleich um die ~*** just (a)round the corner; F *fig.* ***j-n um die ~ bringen*** F bump s.o. off; ***in die ~ drängen*** corner, *fig.* push *s.o.* into the background; ***ich bin um fünf ~n mit ihm verwandt*** I'm a distant relation of his; ***es fehlt an allen ~n und Enden*** we're *etc.* short on everything; ***das ist noch e-e ganze ~*** F that's still a fair way to go; ***er ist ein Mann mit ~n und Kanten*** he rubs people up the wrong way; ***dem traue ich nicht um die ~*** I wouldn't trust him as far as I could throw him; ***die ~n*** (***und Kanten***) ***abschleifen*** smooth away the rough edges

'Ecken·ste·her F *m* (-s; -) F loafer

Eck|fen·ster ['ɛk-] *n* corner window; **~haus** *n* corner house

eckig ['ɛkɪç] (*sep.* -k·k-) *adj.* rectangular *table etc.*; angular *body*, square *chin etc.*; *fig.* awkward, stiff; rough; → ***Klammer***

...eckig *adj.* ...-cornered; ⩓ ...angular

Eck|la·den ['ɛk-] *m* corner shop; **~lohn** *m* basic wage; **~pfei·ler** *m* corner pillar; *fig.* cornerstone; **~platz** *m* corner seat; **~schrank** *m* corner cupboard; **~stein** *m* cornerstone (*a. fig.*); **~stoß** *m soccer*: corner kick; **~wert** *m* benchmark figure; **~zahn** *m* eyetooth, canine; **~zim·mer** *n* corner room; **~zins** *m* basic interest rate, base rate, *Am.* prime rate

Ecu [e'kyː] *m* (-s; -s) ecu, ECU

Ecua·do·ria·ner [ekŭado'riaːnɐ] *m* (-s; -), **Ecua·do·ria·ne·rin** [ekŭado'riaːnərɪn] *f* (-; -nen), **ecua·do·ria·nisch** [ekŭado'riaːnɪʃ] *adj.* Ecuadorian

edel ['eːdəl] *adj.* noble; fine *quality, wine etc.*; precious *metal*; → ***Tropfen***

'Edel|fäu·le *f wine*: noble rot; *cheese*: mo(u)ld; **~frau** *f hist.* noblewoman; **~gas** *n* noble gas; **~holz** *n* precious wood; **~ka͵sta·nie** *f* sweet chestnut; **~kitsch** *contp. m* glorified (*or* elevated) kitsch; **~kna·be** *m hist.* page, squire; **~kri·mi** *m* high-class thriller; **~mann** *m* (-[e]s; -leute) *hist.* nobleman; **~me͵tall** *n* precious metal

'Edel·mut *m* (-[e]s; *no pl.*) noble-mindedness, magnanimity; **'edel·mü·tig** [-myːtɪç] *adj.* noble-minded, magnanimous

'Edel|nut·te F *f* F high-class tart; **~pilz·kä·se** *m* blue-veined cheese; **~stahl** *m* high-grade steel; **~stein** *m* precious stone; jewel, gem(stone); ♀**süß** *adj.*: ***~er Paprika*** sweet paprika; **~tan·ne** *f* silver fir; **~weiß** *n* (-[es]; -e) ⚘ edelweiss; **~wild** *n* red deer

Eden ['eːdən] *n* (-[s], *no pl.*): *bibl.* (***der***

Garten ~ the Garden of) Eden; *fig.* Eden
edie·ren [e'di:rən] *v/t.* (h) **1.** edit; be the editor of; **2.** publish
Edikt [e'dɪkt] *n* (-[e]s; -e) edict
edi·tie·ren [edi'ti:rən] *v/t.* (h) *computer*: edit; **Edi·tier·funk·ti̦on** [edi'ti:ɐ-] *f* editing function
Edi·ti·on [edi'tsi̯o:n] *f* (-; -en) edition; publication
Edi·tor ['e:dito:ɐ] *m* (-s; -en [edi'to:rən]) *computer*: editor
Ed·le *m, f* (-n; -n) → ***Edelfrau, Edelmann***
EDV [e:de:'faʊ] *f* (-; *no pl.*) (electronic) data processing
EEG [e:e:'ge:] *n* (-s; -s) ⚕ EEG
Efeu ['e:fɔʏ] *m* (-s; *no pl.*) ivy; **≈be·wach·sen** *adj.* covered in ivy; *lit.* ivy-clad
Eff·eff [ɛf'ɛf] F *n*: ***et. aus dem ~ können*** be able to do s.th. blindfolded; ***et. aus dem ~ kennen*** know s.th. inside out (*or* like the back of one's hand)
Ef·fekt [ɛ'fɛkt] *m* (-[e]s; -e) effect; *thea. etc.* (special) effect; ⚙ *a.* efficiency; result; ***auf ~ angelegt*** calculated for effect; **~be·leuch·tung** *f film etc.*: effect lighting
Ef'fek·ten *pl.* † stocks and bonds; **~bör·se** *f* stock exchange, bourse; **~han·del** *m* trading in stock; **~händ·ler** *m* stock dealer; **~mak·ler** *m* stockbroker; **~markt** *m* stock market
Ef·fekt·ha·sche·rei [ɛˌfɛkthaʃə'raɪ] *f* (-; -en) showing off, sensationalism; claptrap; ***billige ~*** cheap showmanship; ***bei ihm ist es bloß ~*** *a.* he's just out for show
ef·fek·tiv [ɛfɛk'ti:f] **I.** *adj.* actual; † *a.* effective; ***~e Verzinsung*** net yield; **II.** *adv.* really, literally; definitely
Ef·fek'tiv|ge·schäft *n* spot market transactions *pl.*; **~ko·sten** *pl.* actual cost *sg.*; **~lei·stung** *f* ⚙ effective output; **~lohn** *m* actual earnings *pl.*
ef'fekt·voll *adj.* effective
ef·fe·mi·niert [ɛfemi'ni:ɐt] *adj.* effeminate
ef·fi·zi·ent [ɛfi'tsi̯ɛnt] *adj.* efficient; effective; **Ef·fi·zi·enz** [ɛfi'tsi̯ɛnts] *f* (-; *no pl.*) efficiency; effectiveness
EG [e:'ge:] *f* (-; *no pl.*) EC, European Community
egal [e'ga:l] F *adj.* **1.** *pred.* ***das ist ganz ~*** it doesn't matter, it doesn't make any difference; ***das ist mir (ganz) ~*** I don't mind, it doesn't matter (*or* make any difference) to me, I couldn't care less, why should I care, F I don't give (*or* couldn't give) a damn; ***ihr ist alles ~*** she doesn't care about anything; ***ganz ~ wo (warum, wer, was)*** no matter where (why, who, what), I don't care where (why, who, what); **2.** identical; ***~ sein*** be the same; **3.** even; **ega·li·sie·ren** [egali'zi:rən] *v/t.* (h) equal
E'G-Bei·hil·fe *f* EC subsidy
Egel ['e:gəl] *m* (-s; -) *zo.* leech
Eger·ling ['e:gɐlɪŋ] *m* (-s; -e) chestnut (*or* brown cap) mushroom
Eg·ge ['ɛgə] *f* (-; -n), **eg·gen** ['ɛgən] *v/t.* (h) harrow
E'G|-Gip·fel *m* EC summit; **~-kon̦form** *adj. and adv.* in line with EC provisions; **~-Land** *n* EC country; **~-Mit·glied(s·land)** *n* member of the EC, EC member (state *or* nation); **~-Norm** *f* EC standard
Ego ['e:go] *n* (-s; *no pl.*) ego
Ego·is·mus [ego'ɪsmʊs] *m* (-; *no pl.*) selfishness, ego(t)ism; **Ego·ist** [ego'ɪst] *m* (-en; -en) selfish person, ego(t)ist; **egoi·stisch** [ego'ɪstɪʃ] *adj.* selfish, ego(t)istical
ego·man [ego'ma:n] *adj.* self-obsessed, (completely) obsessed with o.s.; ***~ sein*** *a.* be an egomaniac; **Ego·ma·nie** [egoma'ni:] *f* (-; *no pl.*) egomania
'Ego·trip F *m*: ***auf dem ~ sein*** F be on an ego trip
Ego·zen·tri·ker [ego'tsɛntrikɐ] *m* (-s; -) self-centred (*Am.* -centered) person, egocentric (person); **ego·zen·trisch** [ego'tsɛntrɪʃ] *adj.* self-centred (*Am.* -centered), egocentric
E'G|-Staat *m* EC state (*or* country); **~-weit** *adj. and adv.* EC-wide
eh [e:] **I.** *adv.* **1.** F anyway, anyhow; ***er weiß es ~ schon*** *a.* he knows already; **2.** ***das ist seit ~ und je so*** it's always been like that, it's been like that ever since I can remember; ***es ist wie ~ und je*** it's the same as ever; ***er ist optimistisch wie ~ und je*** he's as optimistic as ever; **II.** F *int.*: ***~?*** eh?, huh?; **III.** F *cj.* → ***ehe***
ehe ['e:ə] *cj.* before; ***nicht ~*** not until, not before; ***~ er mir das Zimmer ruiniert, renoviere ich es selber*** rather than let him ruin the room, I'll do it up myself
Ehe ['e:ə] *f* (-; -n) marriage (*a. fig.*); married life; ***aus erster ~*** by one's first marriage, by one's first husband (*or* wife); ***e-e glückliche ~ führen*** be happily married; ***sie hat zwei Kinder mit in die ~ gebracht*** she's got two children from a previous marriage; ***er ist in zweiter ~ verheiratet mit ...*** his second wife is ...; ***j-m die ~ versprechen*** promise to marry s.o.; ***die*** (*or* ***e-e***) ***~ schließen*** get married (***mit*** *dat.* to); ***in den Stand der (heiligen) ~ (ein)treten*** enter into holy matrimony; → ***brechen*** 2
'ehe·ähn·lich *adj.*: ***sie leben in e-m ~en Verhältnis*** they live together as man and wife
'Ehe·an·bah·nung *f* → ***Heiratsvermittlung***; **'Ehe·an·bah·nungs·in·sti̦tut** *n* → ***Heiratsinstitut***
'Ehe·be·ra·ter *m* (-s; -) marriage guidance counsel(l)or; **'Ehe·be·ra·tung** *f* (-; -en) **1.** marriage guidance (counsel[l]ing); **2.** → **'Ehe·be·ra·tungs·stel·le** *f* marriage guidance bureau
'Ehe·bett *n* **1.** marriage bed; **2.** double bed
'Ehe·bre·cher [-brɛçɐ] *m* (-s; -) adulterer; **'Ehe·bre·che·rin** [-brɛçərɪn] *f* (-; -nen) adulteress; **'ehe·bre·che·risch** [-brɛçərɪʃ] *adj.* adulterous; **'Ehe·bruch** *m* (-[e]s; ⸚e) adultery; ***~ begehen*** commit adultery
'Ehe·bünd·nis *n* (bonds *pl.* of) marriage
'ehe'dem *adv.* formerly
'Ehe·frau *f* (-; -en) **1.** wife; **2.** married woman, *pl. a.* wives
'Ehe·gat·te *m*, **'Ehe·gat·tin** *f* ⚖ spouse; ***beide Ehegatten*** (both) husband and wife; **'Ehe·gat·ten·split·ting** *n* independent taxation of husbands and wives
'Ehe|glück *n* married (*or* wedded) bliss; **~hin·der·nis** *n* impediment to marriage; **~joch** *hum. n* yoke of marriage; **~kan·di̦dat** F *m* prospective husband (*or* wife); husband-(*or* wife-)to-be; **~kon̦flikt** *m* marital conflict (*or* dispute); **~krach** F *m* marital row(s *pl.*); **~krieg** *m* marital feud; **~kri·se** *f* marital crisis; **~krüp·pel** F *m* victim of marriage (*or* married life); **~le·ben** *n* married life; **~leu·te** *pl.* married couple *sg.*; ***(die) ~ Miller*** Mr and Mrs Miller
'ehe·lich I. *adj.* marital; legitimate *child*; ***die ~e Gemeinschaft*** marriage, married life, *formal*: matrimony; ***~e Rechte*** conjugal rights; **II.** *adv.*: ***das Kind ist ~ geboren*** he's (she's) a legitimate child, *formal*: the child was born in wedlock; **ehe·li·chen** ['e:əlɪçən] *v/t.* (h) marry; **'Ehe·lich·keit** *f* (-; *no pl.*) legitimacy
'ehe·los *adj.* unmarried; *eccl.* celibate; **'Ehe·lo·sig·keit** *f* (-; *no pl.*) unmarried state; celibacy; ***die ~*** *a.* not being married
ehe·ma·lig ['e:əma:lɪç] *adj.* former, ex-..., *esp. Am. a.* one-time; old; late; *lit.* quondam; ***die ~e Sakristei*** *etc. a.* what used to be the vestry *etc.*; ***die ~e Fleet Street*** *etc. a.* Fleet Street *etc.* as it was; **ehe·mals** ['e:əma:ls] *adv.* formerly; ***es war ~ ein(e) ...*** *a.* it used to be a ...
'Ehe|mann *m* (-[e]s; ⸚er) **1.** husband; **2.** married man, *pl. a.* husbands; **≈mü·de** *adj.* tired of married life; **≈mün·dig** *adj.* of marriageable age; **~paar** *n* married couple; ***(das) ~ Peters*** Mr and Mrs Peters; **~part·ner** *m* husband; wife; ***der ~*** *a.* the husband or wife; ***beide ~*** both partners in marriage, (both) the husband and the wife
eher ['e:ɐ] *adv.* **1.** earlier, sooner; ***~ als*** *a.* before; ***je ~, desto lieber*** the sooner the better; ***ich konnte leider nicht ~ kommen*** I'm afraid I couldn't make it any earlier; **2.** rather; more; more likely; ***~ würde ich ...*** I'd rather (*or* sooner) ...; ***das läßt sich schon ~ hören*** that sounds more like it; ***es ist ~ grün als blau*** it's more green than blue, it's more on the green side; ***er hätte es ~ geschafft*** he would have been more likely to manage it; ***man sollte ~ annehmen*** you'd think, you would have thought; → ***Kamel***
'Ehe|recht *n* (-[e]s; *no pl.*) matrimonial law; **~ring** *m* wedding ring
ehern ['e:ɐn] *adj.* brass; *fig.* firm, unshak(e)able; iron *will, law etc.*; bold, brazen
'Ehe|schei·dung *f* divorce; **≈scheu** *adj.* not keen on marriage (*or* getting married); **~schlie·ßung** *f* **1.** marriage; **2.** → ***Trauung***
ehest ['e:əst] **I.** *adj.* earliest, first; **II.** *adv.*: ***am ~en*** (the) soonest, (the) earliest, first; *fig.* best, most easily; most of all; most likely; ***am ~en würde ich noch nach England ziehen*** if I had to choose, I'd probably go to England; ***am ~en würde ich wohl die braunen Stiefel nehmen*** (for lack of anything better,) I suppose I'll have to take the brown boots; ***am ~en finden wir ihn in der Bibliothek*** he's most likely to be in the library, the library is the likeliest place he'll be; ***er kann uns am ~en helfen*** if anyone can help us, it's him; ***so geht es wohl am ~en*** that's probably the best way
'Ehe·stand *m* (-[e]s; *no pl.*) married state
ehe·stens ['e:əstəns] *adv.*: (***~ Montag*** Monday) at the earliest
'Ehe|stif·ter *m* matchmaker; **~streit** *m* marital row(s *pl.*); marriage (*or* marital) dispute
'Ehe·ver·mitt·ler *m* → ***Heiratsvermittler***; **'Ehe·ver·mitt·lung** *f* → ***Heiratsvermittlung***; **'Ehe·ver·mitt·lungs·in·sti̦tut** *n* → ***Heiratsinstitut***

ˈ**Ehe|ver·spre·chen** *n*: ***j-m das ~ geben*** promise to marry s.o.; ***Bruch des ~s*** breach of promise; **~ver·trag** *m* marriage contract

Ehr·ab·schnei·der [ˈeːɐ-] *m* (-s; -) slanderer, calumniator

ˈ**ehr·bar** *adj.* upright, upstanding, respectable

ˈ**Ehr·be·griff** *m* code of hono(u)r

Eh·re [ˈeːrə] *f* (-; -n) hono(u)r; sense of hono(u)r; self-respect, pride; reputation; glory; ***es ist mir e-e (große) ~*** it is an (a great) hono(u)r for me; ***es sich zur ~ anrechnen*** consider it an hono(u)r; ***damit kannst du keine ~ einlegen*** that won't gain you any credit (***bei j-m*** with s.o., in s.o.'s eyes); ***j-m die letzte ~ erweisen*** pay one's last respects to s.o.; ***j-m (keine) ~ machen*** be a (no) credit to s.o.; ***j-m zur ~ gereichen*** do s.o. credit; ***es gereicht ihm zur ~*** it is to his credit; ***~ wem ~ gebührt*** credit where credit is due; ***zu hohen ~n gelangen, es zu hohen ~n bringen*** achieve (great) eminence; ***j-n bei s-r ~ packen*** appeal to s.o.'s sense of hono(u)r; ***in ~n halten*** (hold in) hono(u)r; ***in ~n gehalten*** revered; ***wieder zu ~n kommen*** come back into favo(u)r; ***keine ~ im Leib haben*** have no sense of hono(u)r; ***um der Wahrheit die ~ zu geben*** to be quite honest; ***mit wem habe ich die ~?*** *often iro.* to whom have I the pleasure of speaking?; ***ihm zu ~n*** in his hono(u)r; ***zu s-r ~ muß gesagt werden, daß*** in his defen|ce (*Am.* -se) it ought to be said that; ***er fühlte sich dadurch in s-r ~ gekränkt*** it hurt (*or* pricked) his pride, he felt rather piqued by it; ***zu ~n des Tages*** in hono(u)r of the day; ***zur ~ Gottes*** to the glory of God

eh·ren [ˈeːrən] *v/t.* (h) **1.** hono(u)r; ***sich geehrt fühlen*** be (*or* feel) hono(u)red; ***Ihr Vertrauen ehrt mich*** your confidence flatters me; **2.** ***mit e-r Medaille geehrt werden*** be presented with a medal; **3.** do *s.o.* credit; **4.** respect

ˈ**Eh·ren·amt** *n* honorary post; ˈ**eh·ren·amt·lich I.** *adj.* honorary, voluntary; ***~er Helfer*** voluntary worker, volunteer; **II.** *adv.* in an honorary capacity

ˈ**Eh·ren|be·zei·gung** *f* (-; -en), **~be·zeu·gung** *f* (-; -en) ⚔ salute; **~bür·ger** *m* freeman; ***er wurde zum ~ der Stadt ernannt*** he was given the freedom (*or* he was made freeman) of the city

ˈ**eh·rend** *adj.*: ***j-m ein ~es Andenken bewahren*** hono(u)r s.o.'s memory

ˈ**Eh·ren·dok·tor** *m* **1.** honorary doctor; **2.** honorary doctorate; **~ti·tel** *m*, **~wür·de** *f* honorary doctorate; ***ihm wurde die Ehrendoktorwürde der Universität München verliehen*** he was given an honorary doctorate by the University of Munich

ˈ**Eh·ren|er·klä·rung** *f* public apology; ***e-e ~ abgeben*** make a public apology; **~for·ma·tiˌon** *f* guard of hono(u)r; **~gast** *m* guest of hono(u)r; guest celebrity; **~ge·leit** *n* escort; ***j-m das ~ geben*** escort s.o.

ˈ**Eh·ren·ge·richt** *n* disciplinary court; ˈ**eh·ren·ge·richt·lich** *adj.* disciplinary

ˈ**eh·ren·haft** *adj.* respectable; upright; ˈ**Eh·ren·haf·tig·keit** *f* (-; *no pl.*) respectability; uprightness

ˈ**eh·ren·hal·ber** [-halbɐ] *adv.*: *univ.* ***Doktor ~*** honorary doctor, *formal*: doctor honoris causa; ***j-m den Titel ... ~ verleihen*** give s.o. the honorary title of ...

ˈ**Eh·ren|kar·te** *f* complimentary ticket; **~ko·dex** *m* code of hono(u)r; **~kom·paˌnie** *f* ⚔ guard of hono(u)r; **~le·giˌon** *f* Legion of Hono(u)r; **~mal** *n* monument (***für*** *acc.* to); ⚔ memorial (to); **~mann** *m* (-[e]s; ⸗er) man of hono(u)r; **~mit·glied** *n* honorary member; **~pflicht** *f*: ***es für s-e ~ halten, et. zu tun*** be duty bound to do s.th.; **~platz** *m* place (*or* seat) of hono(u)r; ***e-m Bild*** *etc.* ***den ~ geben*** give a picture *etc.* pride of place; **~prä·siˌdent** *m* honorary president

ˈ**Eh·ren·preis**[1] *m* (-es; -e) **1.** prize; **2.** *iro.* consolation prize

ˈ**Eh·ren·preis**[2] *n, m* (-es; -) ⚘ speedwell, veronica

ˈ**Eh·ren|rech·te** *pl.*: ***bürgerliche ~*** civil rights; **~ret·tung** *f* vindication (of s.o.'s hono[u]r); ***zu s-r ~ muß gesagt werden, daß*** in his defen|ce (*Am.* -se) it ought to be said that

ˈ**eh·ren·rüh·rig** *adj.* defamatory

ˈ**Eh·ren|run·de** *f sport*: lap of hono(u)r; ***e-e ~ drehen*** do a lap of hono(u)r, F *fig. ped.* have to repeat a year; **~sa·che** *f* matter of hono(u)r; ***das ist doch ~!*** that goes without saying; F ***~!*** you can count on me; **~sal·ve** *f* (gun) salute; **~schuld** *f* debt of hono(u)r; **~tag** *m* great day; **~ti·tel** *m* honorary title; **~tor** *n*, **~tref·fer** *m* consolation goal; **~triˌbü·ne** *f* VIP lounge

ˈ**eh·ren·voll** *adj.* hono(u)rable; glorious

ˈ**Eh·ren·wa·che** *f* **1.** guard of hono(u)r; **2.** (***~ halten*** be on) sentry duty

ˈ**eh·ren·wert** *adj.* respectable

ˈ**Eh·ren·wort** *n* (-[e]s; -e) word of hono(u)r; ***~!*** I promise (you), cross my heart, I swear, honest to God, *Brit. a. iro.* F scout's (*or* guide's) honour; ***sein ~ geben*** give one's word; ˈ**eh·ren·wört·lich I.** *adj.* solemn; ***er gab uns s-e ~e Zusage*** he gave us his word; **II.** *adv.* solemnly; ***er versprach uns ~ zu kommen*** he gave us his word that he would come

ˈ**Eh·ren·zei·chen** *n* decoration

ehr·er·bie·tig [ˈeːɐʔɛɐbiːtɪç] *adj.* respectful, deferential (***gegen*** *acc.* towards); ˈ**Ehr·er·bie·tung** *f* (-; *no pl.*) deference, reverence; ***aus ~ gegen*** *acc.* in (*or* out of) deference to(wards)

ˈ**Ehr·furcht** *f* (-; *no pl.*) respect (***vor*** *dat.* for), awe (of); *iro.* ***in ~ erstarren, vor ~ erschauern*** be awestruck, F nearly die of awe; ˈ**ehr·furcht·ge·bie·tend** *adj.* awe-inspiring; **ehr·fürch·tig** [ˈeːɐfʏrçtɪç] **I.** *adj.* respectful, reverential; awed *silence*; **II.** *adv.*: ***~ lauschen*** listen in awe; ˈ**Ehr·furchts·be·zei·gung** *f* (-; -en) mark of respect; ˈ**ehr·furchts·los** *adj.* disrespectful, irreverent; ˈ**ehr·furchts·voll** *adj.* reverential

ˈ**Ehr·ge·fühl** *n* (-[e]s; *no pl.*) sense of hono(u)r; self-respect; pride

Ehr·geiz [ˈeːɐgaɪts] *m* (-es; *no pl.*) ambition; ***vor lauter ~*** driven (*or* fired) by ambition; ***sie macht es aus ~*** she does it out of ambition (*or* because she's ambitious); **ehr·gei·zig** [ˈeːɐgaɪtsɪç] *adj.* ambitious; *a.* high-flown *plans etc.*

ehr·lich [ˈeːɐlɪç] **I.** *adj.* honest; fair, *pred.* above board; sincere; genuine; open, frank; ***~e Absichten*** hono(u)rable intentions; *pol.* ***~er Makler*** honest broker; ***~ währt am längsten*** honesty is the best policy; ***sei mal ganz ~*** be honest; ***seien wir ~*** let's face it, let's be honest (with ourselves); **II.** *adv.* fairly; really; honestly; ***~ spielen*** play fair; ***~ gesagt*** to tell you the truth, to be absolutely honest; ***soll ich dir ~ m-e Meinung sagen?*** do you want my honest opinion?; ***mal ganz ~ - hat er das gesagt?*** seriously now, did he say that?; ***sie haben sich ~ bemüht*** they really tried (hard); F ***es war ~ gut*** it was really good; ***er meint es ~*** he means well; ***ich mein's ~ mit dir*** I'm only thinking of your own good; ˈ**ehr·li·cher·wei·se** *adv.*: ***er hat es ~ zugegeben*** he was honest enough to admit it; ***ich muß ~ sagen*** in all honesty (*or* to be quite honest) I have to say *or* admit; ˈ**Ehr·lich·keit** *f* (-; *no pl.*) honesty; openness

ˈ**ehr·los** *adj.* disreputable, disgraceful; ˈ**Ehr·lo·sig·keit** *f* (-; *no pl.*) disreputable (*or* disgraceful) nature *of a deed etc.*; disreputable (*or* disgraceful) behavio(u)r

ˈ**Ehr·sucht** *f* (-; *no pl.*) overambitiousness; ˈ**ehr·süch·tig** *adj.* overambitious

Eh·rung [ˈeːrʊŋ] *f* (-; -en) hono(u)r (*gen.* conferred on *s.o.*); tribute (to); hono(u)ring (of); paying tribute (to); presentation ceremony (for)

ˈ**Ehr·ver·lust** *m*: ***e-n ~ erleiden*** suffer a disgrace

Ehr·wür·den [ˈeːɐvʏrdən] *no art.* Reverend; ***Seine ~ ...*** the Reverend (*abbr.* Rev.) ...; ˈ**ehr·wür·dig** *adj.* venerable; *eccl.* reverend; ˈ**Ehr·wür·dig·keit** *f* (-; *no pl.*) venerableness

Ei [aɪ] *n* (-[e]s; Eier [ˈaɪɐ]) **1.** egg; *physiol.* ovum; *fig.* ***das ist das ~ des Kolumbus!*** that's it(, why didn't I *or* we think of that before?), that's the answer (*or* solution) we've all been looking for; ***wie auf ~ern gehen*** tread carefully; ***wie ein ~ dem andern gleichen*** be as like as two peas (in a pod); ***wie ein rohes ~ behandeln*** handle *s.o.* with kid gloves; ***kümmere dich nicht um ungelegte ~er*** you can worry about that when the time comes, we'll cross that bridge when we get to it; ***wie aus dem ~ gepellt*** very smart, ***aussehen***: *a.* look as if one has just stepped out of a fashion catalog(ue); F ***das ist ein dickes ~!*** F that's a bit thick; **2.** ***~er*** F marks; *Brit.* F quid; *Am.* F bucks; ***3000 ~er*** *a.* F three grand; **3.** ***~er*** V balls, *esp. Am.* V nuts

ei [aɪ] *int.* **1.** oh!; ***~, ~!*** *iro.* well fancy that!; ***~, wer kommt denn da?*** look who's here!; **2.** ***~ machen*** stroke the dog (*or* teddy *etc.*); ***mach ~!*** nice doggy *etc.*

Ei·be [ˈaɪbə] *f* (-; -n) ⚘ yew (tree)

ˈ**Ei·be·fruch·tung** *f* fertilization

ˈ**Ei·ben·holz** *n* yew

Eich·amt [ˈaɪç-] *n in GB*: Office of Weights and Measures; *in the USA*: Bureau of Standards

Ei·che [ˈaɪçə] *f* (-; -n) oak (tree); oak

Ei·chel [ˈaɪçəl] *f* (-; -n) **1.** ⚘ acorn; **2.** *anat.* glans (penis); **~hä·her** *m* jay

ei·chen [ˈaɪçən] *v/t.* (h) adjust; calibrate

ˈ**Ei·chen|blatt** *n* oak leaf; **~holz** *n* oak; **~laub** *n* oak leaves *pl.*

ˈ**Eich·ge·wicht** *n* standard weight

ˈ**Eich|hörn·chen** *n* squirrel; → ***mühsam*** II; **~kätz·chen** *n* squirrel

ˈ**Eich|maß** *n* standard (measure); **~stab** *m* ga(u)ging rod; **~stem·pel** *m* verification stamp

Ei·chung ['aɪçʊŋ] *f* (-; -en) adjustment; calibration

Eid [aɪt] *m* (-[e]s; -e ['aɪdə]) oath; ***an ~es Statt*** in lieu of an oath; ***e-n ~ ablegen*** (*or* ***leisten***) take an oath, ***auf die Bibel:*** swear by the Bible; ***j-m e-n ~ abnehmen*** administer an oath to s.o.; ***unter ~ aussagen*** testify on oath; ***unter ~ stehen*** be under oath

'Eid·bruch *m* breach (*or* breaking) of an oath; **'eid·brü·chig** *adj.*: **~ *werden*** break one's oath

Ei·dech·se ['aɪdɛksə] *f* (-; -n) lizard; **'Ei·dech·sen·le·der** *n* lizard-skin; ***... aus ~*** lizard-skin ...

Ei·der|dau·nen ['aɪdɐ-] *pl.* eider down; **~en·te** *f*, **~gans** *f* eider (duck)

Ei·des|for·mel ['aɪdəs-] *f* (wording of an) oath; **~lei·stung** *f* taking of an oath; ***die ~ verweigern*** refuse to take an oath

'ei·des·statt·lich *adj.* in lieu of an oath; ***e-e ~e Erklärung abgeben*** make a declaration in lieu of an oath

'Eid·ge·nos·se *m* **1.** confederate; **2.** Swiss (citizen); **'Eid·ge·nos·sen·schaft** *f* (-; *no pl.*) **1.** confederation; **2.** ***die Schweizer ~*** the Swiss Confederation, Switzerland; **eid·ge·nös·sisch** ['aɪtgənœsɪʃ] *adj.* **1.** confederate; **2.** Swiss

'eid·lich I. *adj.* sworn; **~*e Aussage*** sworn statement, affidavit; ***e-e ~e Erklärung abgeben*** swear an affidavit; **II.** *adv.* on (*or* under) oath

'Ei·dot·ter *m, n* (egg) yolk, yolk of an egg

Ei·er|auf·lauf ['aɪɐ-] *m* souffle; **~be·cher** *m* egg cup; **~frucht** *f* aubergine, *esp. Am.* eggplant; **~ge·richt** *n* egg dish; **~ko·cher** *m* egg boiler; **~kopf** F *m* **1.** egg--shaped head; **2.** F egghead, boffin; **3.** F blockhead, numskull; **~ku·chen** *m* pancake; **~lau·fen** *n* egg-and-spoon race

'ei·er·le·gend *adj. biol.* egg-laying, oviparous

'Ei·er|li͵kör *m* advocaat; **~löf·fel** *m* egg spoon

ei·ern ['aɪɐn] F *v/i.* (h) F be wonky

'Ei·er|nu·deln *pl.* (egg) noodles; **~pfann·ku·chen** *m* pancake; **~pflau·me** *f* egg plum; **~punsch** *m* eggnog; **~sa͵lat** *m* egg salad

'Ei·er·scha·le *f* eggshell; F *fig.* ***er hat noch ~n hinter den Ohren*** F he's still wet behind the ears; **'ei·er·scha·len·far·ben** *adj.* eggshell(-colo[u]red); **'Ei·er·scha·len·por·zel͵lan** *n* eggshell china (*or* porcelain)

'Ei·er|schnei·der *m* egg slicer; **~spei·se** *f* egg dish; *Austrian.* scrambled egg(s *pl.*)

'Ei·er·stock *m anat.* ovary; **~ent·zün·dung** *f* inflammation of the ovaries

'Ei·er|tanz *fig. m*: ***e-n ~ aufführen*** perform a skil(l)ful balancing act; ***der ~ der Regierung um die Steuerreform*** the government's shilly-shallying about the tax reform; **~uhr** *f* egg timer; **~wär·mer** [-vɛrmɐ] *m* (-s; -) egg cosy

Ei·fer ['aɪfɐ] *m* (-s; *no pl.*) keenness, eagerness, zeal, fervo(u)r; enthusiasm; ***voller ~*** full of enthusiasm, with great fervo(u)r; ***blinder ~*** blind zeal; ***sich mit ~ ans Werk machen*** set to work with a will (*or* vengeance); ***im ~ des Gefechts*** in the heat of the moment; → ***missionarisch*** I; **Ei·fe·rer** ['aɪfərɐ] *m* (-s; -) fanatic; **ei·fern** ['aɪfɐn] *v/i.* (h) **1. ~ *nach*** *dat.* strive for; **2. ~ *für*** *acc.* campaign for; **~ *gegen*** *acc.* a) campaign against, b) rail against; **3. *mit j-m um et.* ~** vie with s.o. for s.th.

'Ei·fer·sucht *f* (-; *no pl.*) jealousy (***auf*** *acc.* of); **Ei·fer·süch·te·lei** [aɪfɐzyçtə'laɪ] *f* (-; -en) petty jealousy; **'ei·fer·süch·tig I.** *adj.* jealous (***auf*** *acc.* of); **II.** *adv.*: **~ *über et. wachen*** guard s.th. jealously

'Ei·fer·suchts|sze·ne *f* jealous scene; (dramatic) display of jealousy; **~tat** *f* act of jealousy

ei·för·mig ['aɪfœrmɪç] *adj.* egg-shaped, oval

eif·rig ['aɪfrɪç] **I.** *adj.* keen; enthusiastic(ally *adv.*); hard-working, diligent; busy; officious, fussy; **II.** *adv.*: **~ *lernen*** (***arbeiten***) study (work) hard; **~ *die Kirche besuchen*** *etc.* go to church *etc.* regularly (*or* as often as one can); **~ *bemüht sein zu*** *inf.* be anxious to *inf.*

'Ei·gelb *n* (-[e]s; -e) (egg) yolk, yolk of an egg; ***vier ~*** four egg yolks

ei·gen ['aɪgən] *adj.* **1.** *one's* own, of one's own; *in cpds.* ...-owned (*e.g.* ***staats~*** state-owned); **~*e Ansichten*** personal views; ***darüber habe ich m-e ~en Ansichten*** I have my own (personal) views on that; ***ein ~es Zimmer*** a room of one's own; ***er braucht ein ~es Zimmer*** *a.* he needs a room to himself (*or* his own room); ***Zimmer mit ~em Bad*** room with a private bath (*or* an en suite bathroom); ***mit ~em Eingang*** with a separate entrance; ***für den ~en Bedarf*** for personal use; ***sich zu ~ machen*** make *s.th.* one's own, adopt *view etc.*; → ***Antrieb*** 1, ***Faust, Fleisch, Herr*** 2; **2.** special (*dat.* to); particular (to), characteristic (of), specific (to); inherent (in); ***mit dem ihm ~en Sarkasmus*** with his characteristic sarcasm; **3.** particular (***in*** *dat.* about), fussy (about); **4.** strange

'Ei·gen·an·trieb *m*: ⚙ ***mit ~*** self-propelled, self-powered

Ei·gen·art ['aɪgənʔaːɐt] *f* (-; -en) **1.** characteristic feature, peculiarity, peculiar characteristic; foible, idiosyncrasy; **2.** distinctiveness, specific *or* special character (*or* nature); ***die ~ s-r Musik besteht in*** *a.* his music is characterized by, the special quality of his music lies in; **ei·gen·ar·tig** ['aɪgənʔaːɐtɪç] *adj.* strange; **ei·gen·ar·ti·ger·wei·se** ['aɪgənʔaːɐtɪgɐ'vaɪzə] *adv.* strangely (*or* oddly) enough; **'Ei·gen·ar·tig·keit** *f* (-; -en) **1.** *no pl.* strangeness; **2.** odd behavio(u)r

'Ei·gen|bau *m*: ***es ist ~*** it's homemade (*or* homegrown); F ***Marke ~*** F *real ale etc.* a la Jones *etc.*; **~be·darf** *m one's* personal needs *pl.*; domestic requirements *pl.*; **~be·richt** *m* correspondent's report, report from one's own correspondent

'Ei·gen·blut·be·hand·lung *f* auto-h(a)emotherapy

'Ei·gen·bräu [-brɔʏ] *m* (-[e]s; -s, -e) home brew

'Ei·gen·bröt·ler [-brøːtlɐ] *m* (-s; -) **1.** loner; ***er ist ein ziemlicher ~*** he's a bit of a loner, he keeps very much to himself; **2.** eccentric; **'ei·gen·bröt·le·risch** [-brøːtlərɪʃ] *adj.* **1.** solitary; **2.** eccentric

'Ei·gen|dün·kel *m* self-conceit; **~dy͵na·mik** *fig. f* momentum (of its own); ***e-e*** (***gewisse***) **~ *entwickeln*** develop a life (*or* momentum) of its own; **~fi·nan͵zie·rung** *f* self-financing; **~fre͵quenz** *f* natural frequency; **2ge·nutzt** *adj.* owner--occupied *flat etc.*

'ei·gen·ge·setz·lich *adj.* autonomous; self-contained; **'Ei·gen·ge·setz·lich·keit** *f* autonomy; inherent order; order of its (*or* one's) own; ***e-e gewisse ~ entwickeln*** create an order of its (*or* one's) own

'Ei·gen·ge·wicht *n* ⚙ dead weight; ✝ net weight; *phys.* specific weight

'ei·gen·hän·dig [-hɛndɪç] **I.** *adj.* personal; ⚖ **~*es Delikt*** personal crime; **~*es Testament*** holographic will; ***es muß Ihre ~e Unterschrift sein*** it has to be signed by you personally; **II.** *adv.* personally; oneself, on one's own, without any (outside) help; *build etc.* with one's own two hands; **~ *übergeben*** deliver personally

'Ei·gen·heim *n* house *or* home (of one's own), one's own house (*or* home)

'Ei·gen·heit *f* (-; -en) → ***Eigenart***

'Ei·gen|in·itia͵ti·ve *f* **1.** initiative (of one's own); ***ohne jede ~ sein*** *a.* be completely unresourceful; **2. *es ist e-e ~ von ihm*** it was his own idea, he came up with it (*or* the idea) himself; **~in·ter͵es·se** *n* vested interest, *contp.* self-interest; ***aus ~*** out of self-interest, to serve one's own interests; **~ka·pi͵tal** *n* ✝ capital resources *pl.*; **~le·ben** *n one's* own way of life, *a* life of one's own; ***ein ~ führen*** *a.* live one's own life, be independent, be an individual (in one's own right); **~lie·be** *f* love of self; *psych.* narcissism; **~lob** *n* self-adulation; **~ *stinkt!*** *iro.* I love me, who do you love?

'ei·gen·mäch·tig I. *adj.* high-handed; unauthorized; independent; **II.** *adv.* high-handedly, without anyone's permission, without instructions from anyone, F just like that; ***et. ~ entscheiden*** decide s.th. for oneself; **~ *handeln*** act on one's own authority, take the law into one's own hands; **'Ei·gen·mäch·tig·keit** *f* (-; -en) **1.** *no pl.* high-handedness; **2.** unauthorized act

'Ei·gen|mit·tel *pl. one's* own resources (*or* funds, capital *sg.*); ***aus ~n finanzieren*** finance with one's own resources *etc.*; **~na·me** *m* proper name (*or* noun)

'Ei·gen·nutz [-nʊts] *m* (-es; *no pl.*) self-interest, selfishness; desire for personal advancement; **'ei·gen·nüt·zig** [-nʏtsɪç] *adj.* selfish

'Ei·gen|nut·zung *f* owner-occupation; **~pro·duk·ti͵on** *f* own-label record; *TV Channel Four etc.* production

ei·gens ['aɪgəns] *adv.* specially; specifically, expressly; **~ *für dich*** *a.* just for you; ***ich bin ~ wegen dir gekommen*** *a.* I came for your sake

'Ei·gen·schaft *f* (-; -en) quality; (distinctive) feature, characteristic; *phys.*, ⚗ property; nature; peculiarity; ***gute*** (***schlechte***) **~*en*** good (bad) points *or* habits, positive (negative) traits, advantages (disadvantages, drawbacks); ***in s-r ~ als*** in his capacity of (*or* as), acting as; **'Ei·gen·schafts·wort** *n* (-[e]s; ⸚er) adjective

'Ei·gen·sinn *m* (-[e]s; *no pl.*) stubbornness; **'ei·gen·sin·nig** *adj.* stubborn, headstrong; **~ *sein*** *a.* have a will of one's own

'ei·gen·staat·lich *adj.* sovereign; **'Ei·gen·staat·lich·keit** *f* sovereignty

'ei·gen·stän·dig *adj.* independent; **'Ei·gen·stän·dig·keit** *f* (-; *no pl.*) independence

ei·gent·lich ['aɪgəntlɪç] **I.** *adj.* actual, real; true *motives*; specific; essential; **~*e***

Ursache root cause; ***im ~en Sinne (des Wortes)*** in the true sense (of the word); **II.** *adv.* actually; really; strictly speaking; by rights; actually; anyway; ***~ nicht*** not really; ***~ kann ich ihn nicht ausstehen*** to be honest (*or* to tell you the truth), I can't stand him; ***was wollen Sie ~?*** what do you want anyway?; ***wie spät ist es ~?*** what time is it(, by the way)?; ***~ ist er ganz vernünftig*** a) he's actually quite sensible, b) I suppose he's quite sensible, really; ***was ist ~ passiert?*** what actually (*or* exactly) happened?; ***~ heißt er Manfred*** his real name's Manfred; ***~ wollte ich früher hier sein*** I was (actually) hoping to be here earlier

'Ei·gen·tor *n sport*: *an* own goal (*a. fig.*); ***ein ~ schießen*** *a. fig.* score an own goal

Ei·gen·tum ['aɪgəntuːm] *n* (-s; *no pl.*) property; ⚖ ownership (***an*** *dat.* of); → ***geistig*** I; ***es ist mein ~*** *a.* it belongs to me; **Ei·gen·tü·mer** ['aɪgəntyːmɐ] *m* (-s; -) owner; proprietor; **'Ei·gen·tü·mer·schaft** *f* (-; *no pl.*) ownership; proprietorship

ei·gen·tüm·lich ['aɪgəntyːmlɪç] **I.** *adj.* peculiar (*dat.* to), characteristic (of); strange; ***mit der ihm ~en Ironie*** with his characteristic irony, in his (typically) ironic way; **II.** *adv.*: ***j-n ~ berühren*** have a curious effect on s.o.; **'ei·gen·tüm·li·cher'wei·se** *adv.* strangely (*or* oddly) enough; **'Ei·gen·tüm·lich·keit** *f* (-; -en) **1.** *no pl.* peculiarity; **2.** peculiarity, characteristic; peculiar habit

'Ei·gen·tums|de,likt *n* property offen|ce (*Am.* -se); **~er·werb** *m* acquisition of property; **~recht** *n* **1.** ownership (***an*** *dat.* of); **2.** ownership law(s *pl.*); **~über,tra·gung** *f* transfer of ownership; **~ur·kun·de** *f* title deed; **~woh·nung** *f* (owner-occupied) flat, *Am.* apartment, condominium, F condo; ***sie haben e-e ~*** *a.* they own a flat (*Am.* an apartment), they've got a flat (*Am.* an apartment) of their own

'ei·gen·ver·ant·wort·lich I. *adj.* independent; **II.** *adv.* on one's own authority; ***er muß ~ handeln*** he must act as he sees fit

'Ei·gen|ver·brauch *m* private consumption; **~wär·me** *f* body temperature; *phys.* specific heat; **~wer·bung** *f* self-advertising (*or* -publicity); ***~ treiben*** promote o.s.; **~,wi·der·stand** *m* ⚡ inherent resistance; **~wert** *m* intrinsic value

'ei·gen·wil·lig *adj.* **1.** very individual, unusual; **2.** wayward; headstrong, *contp.* obstinate

eig·nen ['aɪgnən] *v/refl.* (h): ***sich ~*** be suitable (***für*** *acc.* for), be suited (***für*** *acc.* for; ***als*** as; ***zu*** *dat.* as, for); ***sich schlecht ~*** be unsuitable; ***sich hervorragend ~ für*** be ideal for (*or* as); ***es eignet sich gut als Geschenk*** it makes (*or* would make) a good present; ***die Äpfel ~ sich gut zum Kochen*** they're good cooking apples, these apples are ideal for cooking; ***er würde sich als Lehrer (nicht) ~*** he'd make *or* be a good teacher (he's not cut out for teaching); ***er (das Holz*** *etc.*) ***eignet sich überhaupt nicht*** *a.* he just isn't the right kind of person (it's the wrong kind of wood *etc.*); **Eig·nung** ['aɪgnʊŋ] *f* (-; *no pl.*) suitability (***für*** *acc.* for; ***zu*** *dat.* as, for), aptitude (***für*** *acc.* for); ***keine ~ haben für*** show no aptitude for, have no talent for

'Eig·nungs|prü·fung *f*, **~test** *m* aptitude test

Ei·land ['aɪlant] *lit. n* (-[e]s; -e ['aɪlandə]) island, *lit.* isle

'Eil|auf·trag ['aɪl-] *m* rush order; **~bo·te** *m*: ***durch ~n*** express, *Am.* (by) special delivery; **~brief** *m* express letter, *Am.* special delivery (letter); ***als ~ schicken*** send *a letter* express

Ei·le ['aɪlə] *f* (-; *no pl.*) hurry, rush; ***in ~ sein*** be in a hurry; ***in der ~*** *habe ich es übersehen etc.* in the (general) rush; ***in größter ~*** in a great rush (*or* hurry); ***damit hat es keine ~*** there's no hurry (for it), there's no (great) rush; ***j-n zur ~ antreiben*** hurry s.o. up; ***in aller ~*** hurriedly; ***ein paar Zeilen in aller ~*** just a quick note, a few hurried lines

'Ei·lei·ter *m anat.* Fallopian tube

ei·len ['aɪlən] *v/i.* (sn) a) hurry; rush; b) be urgent; ***es eilt nicht, damit eilt es nicht*** there's no hurry (for it), there's no (great) rush; ***eilt!*** urgent; ***eile mit Weile!*** more haste, less speed; → ***Hilfe***; **ei·lends** ['aɪlənts] *adv.* hastily, in haste

eil·fer·tig ['aɪl-] *adj.* rash, (over)hasty; zealous; **'Eil·fer·tig·keit** *f* (-; *no pl.*) rashness, hastiness; zealousness

'Eil|fracht *f* express (*Am.* fast) freight; **~ge·bühr** *f* express delivery charge; **~gut** *n* express (*Am.* fast) freight; ***per*** *or* ***als ~ schicken*** send *s.th.* express (freight) (*Am.* fast freight)

ei·lig ['aɪlɪç] *adj.* hurried; urgent; ***es ~ haben*** be in a hurry (*or* rush); ***ich hab's mit dem Brief nicht sehr ~*** I'm in no hurry for the letter to be done; ***wohin so ~?*** what's the hurry?, where are you off to in such a hurry?; **'ei·ligst** *adv.* in a great hurry; as quickly as possible

'Eil|marsch *m* speed (*or* forced) march; **~pa,ket** *n* express parcel; **~schritt** *m*: ***im ~*** at a face pace, ***vorbeirauschen***: breeze past; **~tem·po** *n*: ***im ~*** in double quick time; **~ver·fah·ren** *n* ⚖ summary proceeding(s *pl.*); *fig.* ***im ~ durchnehmen*** rush through *s.th.*; ***im ~ herstellen*** *etc.* rush *s.th.* off; **~zug** *m* fast train

Ei·mer ['aɪmɐ] *m* (-s; -) bucket, *esp. Am.* pail; ***ein ~ Wasser*** a bucket(ful) of water; ***es gießt wie aus ~n*** F it's coming down in buckets; F *fig. mein Auto, die Uhr etc.* ***ist im ~*** F has had it; ***ihre Ehe ist im ~*** F their marriage is in tatters; ***damit sind unsere Pläne im ~*** F bang go our plans; **'ei·mer·wei·se** *adv.* in bucketfuls; by the bucket(ful)

ein[1] [aɪn] **I.** *adj.* one; ***~ für allemal*** once and for all; ***~ und derselbe Mann*** one and the same person; ***an ~ und demselben Tag*** on the very same day; ***er ist ihr ~ und alles*** he means the world to her; **II.** *indef. art.* a, an; ***~es Tages*** one day; *die Beredsamkeit etc.* ***~es X*** of a man like X; ***das konnte nur ~ Nero behaupten*** only somebody like Nero could say that; ***~ (gewisser) Herr Braun*** a (certain) Mr Braun; **III.** *indef. pron.*: ***~er*** one, one thing; ***~er m-r Freunde*** a friend of mine; ***~er von beiden*** one (or other) of them; ***~er nach dem andern*** one after the other, ***bitte!***: *a.* one at a time, please!; ***die ~en sagen*** some (people) say; ***das tut ~em gut*** that does you good; ***du bist ja ~er!*** you're a fine one!; → *a.* ***eins***

ein[2] [aɪn] *adv.* **1.** ⚡ *etc.* on; ***~ - aus*** on - off; **2.** ***~ und aus gehen*** come and go, ***bei j-m***: be a frequent visitor of s.o. (*or* at s.o.'s place); ***ich weiß nicht mehr ~ noch aus*** I'm at my wit's end

ein|ach·sig ['aɪnˀaksɪç] *adj. mot.* single-axle ..., two-wheel ..., *a. pred.* two-wheeled; **~ad·rig** ['aɪnˀaːdrɪç] *adj.* ⚡ single-wire ...

Ein·ak·ter ['aɪnˀaktɐ] *m* (-s; -) *thea.* one-act play

ein·an·der [aɪ'nandɐ] *adv.* each other, one another; ***sie sind ~ im Weg*** they are in each other's way

'ein·ar·bei·ten (*sep.*, h) **I.** *v/t.* **1.** show *s.o.* the ropes; **2.** work in; add; **3.** make up for, work in; **II.** *v/refl.*: ***sich ~*** familiarize o.s. with the work (*or* subject *etc.*), get to know the ropes; ***sich ~ in*** *acc. a.* get into; ***sich schnell in e-e neue Stelle ~*** settle into a new job very quickly; **'Ein·ar·bei·tungs·zeit** *f* settling-in period

ein·ar·mig ['aɪnˀarmɪç] **I.** *adj.* one-armed; ***er ist ~*** he's only got one arm; ***ein ~er Mann*** *a.* a man with (just) one arm; **II.** *adv.* with one arm

ein·äschern ['aɪnˀɛʃɐn] *v/t.* (h) burn to ashes; cremate; **Ein·äsche·rung** ['aɪnˀɛʃərʊŋ] *f* (-; -en) cremation

'ein·at·men (*sep.*, h) **I.** *v/t.* breathe in, inhale; **II.** *v/i.* breathe in; ***tief ~*** take a deep breath (*or* deep breaths); **'Ein·at·mung** *f* (-; *no pl.*) inhalation; inhaling

ein·äu·gig ['aɪnˀɔʏgɪç] *adj.* **1.** one-eyed; ***er ist ~*** *a.* he's only got one eye; ***unter den Blinden ist der Ɛe König*** in the country of the blind, the one-eyed man is king; **2.** ***~e Spiegelreflexkamera*** single-lens reflex (camera), SLR

'Ein·bahn|stra·ße *f* one-way street; **~ver·kehr** *m* one-way traffic

'ein·bal·sa,mie·ren *v/t.* (h) embalm

'Ein·band *m* (-[e]s; ⸚e) binding; cover

ein·bän·dig ['aɪnbɛndɪç] *adj.* one-volume ..., single-volume ...; in one volume

'Ein·bau *m* (-[e]s; -ten) **1.** *no pl.* installation, fitting; **2.** fitting; **'ein·bau·en** *v/t.* (*sep.*, h) **1.** install (***in*** *acc.* into); fit *s.th.* in(to) fit *engine*; **2.** *fig.* work in; **'Ein·bau·kü·che** *f* fitted kitchen

'Ein·baum *m* dugout (canoe)

'Ein·bau|mö·bel *pl.* fitted furniture *sg.*; **~schrank** *m* built-in *or* fitted cupboard(s *pl.*) (*or* wardrobe, *Am.* closet)

'ein·be·grei·fen *v/t.* (*irr.*, *sep.*, h, → ***begreifen***) (*a.* ***mit ~***) include; **'ein·be·grif·fen** *adj.* included (***in*** *dat.* in)

'ein·be·hal·ten *v/t.* (*irr.*, *sep.*, h, → ***behalten***) withhold, keep, F hold onto; deduct; **'Ein·be·hal·tung** *f* (-; -en) deduction; ***unter ~ von*** after deducting

ein·bei·nig ['aɪnbaɪnɪç] *adj.* one-legged; ***er ist ~*** he's only got one leg; ***ein ~er Mann*** *a.* a man with (just) one leg

'ein·be·ru·fen *v/t.* (*irr.*, *sep.*, h, → ***berufen***) **1.** call; *parl.* summon, convene; **2.** ⚔ call up (***zu*** *dat.* for), *Am.* draft (into); **'Ein·be·ru·fe·ne** *m* (-n; -n) conscript, *Am.* draftee; **'Ein·be·ru·fung** *f* (-; -en) **1.** calling; *parl.* summoning, convening; **2.** ⚔ conscription, *Am.* draft

'Ein·be·ru·fungs|be·fehl *m*, **~be·scheid** *m* ⚔ call-up orders *pl.*, *Am.* draft papers *pl.*

'ein·be·to,nie·ren *v/t.* (*sep.*, h) embed in concrete

'ein·bet·ten *v/t.* (*sep.*, h) embed (***in*** *acc.* in) (*a.* ⚙); wrap (***in*** *acc.* in[to])

'Ein·bett|ka,bi·ne *f* single-berth cabin, stateroom; **~zim·mer** *n* single room

'ein·beu·len *v/t.* (*sep.*, h) dent

'ein·be·zie·hen *v/t.* (*irr.*, *sep.*, h, → **beziehen**) include (**in** *acc.* in); incorporate (into); ∼ **in** *acc. a.* cover; **'Ein·be·zie·hung** *f* (-; *no pl.*) inclusion (**in** *acc.* in), incorporation (into)

'ein·bie·gen (*irr.*, *sep.*, → **biegen**) **I.** *v/t.* (h) bend in(wards); **II.** *v/i.* (sn): ∼ **in** *acc.* turn into; **links** ∼ turn left

'ein·bil·den *v/t.* (*sep.*, h): **sich** ∼ imagine; think; **er bildet sich ein, beliebt zu sein** he thinks (*or* likes to think) he's popular; **sich steif und fest** ∼**, daß** be (firmly) convinced that; **das bildest du dir nur ein** you're (just) imagining it (*or* things); **bilde dir ja nicht ein, daß** you needn't (for one minute) think that, don't go running away with the idea that; **was bildest du dir eigentlich ein?** what on earth has got into you?, what on earth do you think you're doing?; **darauf brauchst du dir nichts einzubilden** that's nothing to be proud of (F to write home about); **bilde dir doch nichts ein!** don't fool (F kid) yourself; **ich bilde mir nicht ein, ein Genie zu sein** I don't pretend (*or* claim) to be a genius; **er bildet sich auf s-n Erfolg was ein** his success has gone to his head; **bilde dir ja nicht zuviel ein!** don't let it go to your head(, now); **darauf kannst du dir was** ∼ that's something to be proud of; → **eingebildet**; **'Ein·bil·dung** *f* (-; -en) **1.** *no pl.* **das ist reine** ∼ you're (*or* he's *etc.*) imagining things, it's all in the mind; **nur in j-s** ∼ **existieren** be a figment of s.o.'s imagination; **2.** illusion; **3.** *no pl.* conceitedness

'Ein·bil·dungs|ga·be *f* (-; *no pl.*), ∼**kraft** *f* (-; *no pl.*), ∼**ver·mö·gen** *n* (-s; *no pl.*) (powers *pl.* of) imagination

'ein·bin·den *v/t.* (*irr.*, *sep.*, h, → **binden**) **1.** tie up (**in** *acc.* in); bind *book*; ⚕ bandage; **2.** integrate (**in** *acc.* into); **'Ein·bin·dung** *f* (-; -en) integration (**in** *acc.* into), involvement (in)

'ein·bla·sen *v/t.* (*irr.*, *sep.*, h, → **blasen**) blow in(to **in** *acc.*); *fig.* **j-m et.** ∼ put s.th. into s.o.'s head

'Ein·blatt(druck *m*) *n* broadsheet

'ein·blen·den (*sep.*, h) **I.** *v/t.* fade in; dub in(to **in** *acc.*); superimpose (**in** *acc.* on); slot in; **II.** *v/refl.*: **sich** ∼ **in** *acc.* join, go over to; **sich** ∼ join (*or* go over to) the other studio *or* one's crew at Wembley Stadium *etc.*; **'Ein·blen·dung** *f* (-; -en) fade-in; insert

ein·bleu·en ['aɪnblɔyən] F *v/t.* (*sep.*, h): **j-m et.** ∼ drum s.th. into s.o.('s head), get s.th. into s.o.'s (F thick) head

'Ein·blick *m* (-[e]s; -e) **1.** look (**in** *acc.* at); insight (into); **e-n gewissen** ∼ **haben** have some idea (**in** *acc.* of, about); ∼ **gewinnen, sich** (**e-n**) ∼ **verschaffen** get some sort of idea, get a general idea (**in** *acc.* of), **in** *acc.*: *a.* get (*or* gain) an insight into; **j-m** ∼ **gewähren in** *acc.* allow s.o. access to; **2.** view (**in** *acc.* of)

ein·boo·ten ['aɪnbo:tən] *v/t. and v/refl.* (**sich** ∼) (*sep.*, h) embark

'ein·bre·chen (*irr.*, *sep.*, → **brechen**) **I.** *v/i.* (sn) **1.** break in(to **in** *acc.*); ∼ **in** *acc. a.* burgle; **bei ihm wurde eingebrochen** his house (*or* flat, *Am.* apartment) was burgled (*esp. Am.* burglarized), he had burglars, he was burgled; **2.** collapse, cave in; break (*or* go) through the ice; *fig.* suffer a severe defeat (*or* setback); **3.** ⚔ ∼ **in** *acc.* invade *a country*; **4.** *winter etc.*: set in; **bei** ∼**der Dunkelheit** at nightfall; **II.** *v/t.* (h) break down

'Ein·bre·cher *m* (-s; -) burglar; ∼**ban·de** *f* gang of burglars

Ein·bren·ne ['aɪnbrɛnə] *f* (-; -n) *gastr.* roux; **'ein·bren·nen** *v/t.* (*irr.*, *sep.*, h, → **brennen**) **1.** burn in(to **in** *acc.*); *e-m Tier* **ein Zeichen** ∼ brand; **2.** *gastr.* brown; thicken with roux

'ein·brin·gen (*irr.*, *sep.*, h, → **bringen**) **I.** *v/t.* **1.** bring in; ✝ *a.* yield, net; fetch *price*; *a. fig.* contribute (**in** *acc.* to); **j-m et.** ∼ earn s.o. s.th.; **das bringt nichts ein** it doesn't pay; **es bringt mir ... ein** it gets me ...; **2.** make up (for) *lost time etc.*; *typ.* get in *word, line etc.*; **3.** *parl.* **e-e Gesetzesvorlage** ∼ introduce a bill; ⚖ **e-e Klage** ∼ file an action; **II.** *v/refl.*: **sich** ∼ put a lot of time (and energy) into it

'ein·brocken (*sep.* -k·k-) *v/t.* (*sep.*, h) **1. et.** ∼ **in** *acc.* crumble s.th. into *the soup etc.*; **2.** *fig.* **j-m** (**sich**) **etwas** (**Schönes**) ∼ get s.o. (o.s.) into a real fix; **das hast du dir selbst eingebrockt** it's your own fault

'Ein·bruch *m* (-[e]s; ⸚e) **1.** burglary; **e-n** ∼ **verüben in** *acc.* break into; **2.** ⚔ invasion (**in** *acc.* of); **3.** collapse; **4. bei** ∼ **der Dunkelheit** at nightfall; **bei** ∼ **der Kälte** when the cold (weather) sets in; **5.** severe defeat (*or* setback); **6.** ✝ slump

'Ein·bruch(s)|dieb·stahl *m* burglary; ∼**ge·fahr** *f* **1. es besteht** ∼ the roof *etc.* is in danger of collapsing; the ice is dangerously thin (in places); **2.** likelihood of a burglary (*or* of being burgled); ≗**si·cher** *adj.* burglar-proof; ∼**ver·si·che·rung** *f* burglary insurance; ∼**ver·such** *m*: (**wegen** ∼ for) attempted burglary; ∼**werk·zeug** *n* housebreaking tool; **sie haben die** ∼**e gefunden** they found the instruments he *etc.* used to (try and) break in

ein·buch·ten ['aɪnbʊxtən] *v/t.* (*sep.*, h) **1.** indent; **2.** F → **einlochen** 2; **'Ein·buch·tung** *f* (-; -en) **1.** indentation; **2.** *geol.* bay, inlet

'ein·bud·deln (*sep.*, h) F **I.** *v/t.* bury; **II.** *v/refl.*: **sich** ∼ dig o.s. in(to **in** *acc.*)

ein·bür·gern ['aɪnbʏrgɐn] (*sep.*, h) **I.** *v/t.* naturalize; **sich** ∼ **lassen** become naturalized; **II.** *fig. v/refl.*: **sich** ∼ take root; establish itself; come into use; **sich in e-r Sprache** ∼ *a.* find its (*or* their) way into a language; **es hat sich so eingebürgert** it's become a habit (**bei** *dat.* with), it's become the done thing (**,daß man ...** to *inf.*), **daß er auf die Kinder aufpaßt:** it became a habit for him to (*or* a fixed pattern that he should) look after the children; **'Ein·bür·ge·rung** *f* (-; -en) **1.** naturalization; **2.** *fig.* establishment

'Ein·bür·ge·rungs|an·trag *m* application (*or* petition) for naturalization; **e-n** ∼ **stellen** apply for naturalization; ∼**ur·kun·de** *f* certificate of naturalization

'Ein·bu·ße *f* (-; -n) loss (**an** *dat.* of); **unter** ∼ *gen.* at the cost of; **schwere** ∼**n erleiden** suffer heavy losses; **'ein·bü·ßen** (*sep.*, h) **I.** *v/t.* lose; forfeit; **II.** *v/i.*: ∼ **an** *dat.* lose (some of)

'ein·checken (*sep.* -k·k-) **I.** *v/t. and v/i.* (*sep.*, h) check in; **II.** ≗ *n* (-s) checking in, check-in; **beim** ∼ as I was *etc.* checking in; **das** ∼ **dauert immer furchtbar lange** it always takes ages to check in

ein·cre·men ['aɪnkre:mən] *v/t.* (*sep.*, h) (*a.* **sich** ∼) put some cream on; **sich die Hände** ∼ put some handcream on; **die Schuhe** ∼ put (the) polish on the shoes

'ein·däm·men *v/t.* (h) dam up; *fig.* stem; check; get under control; curb, control; *esp. pol.* contain

'ein·däm·mern *v/i.* (*sep.*, sn) doze off

'Ein·däm·mungs·po·liˌ**tik** *f* policy of containment

'ein·damp·fen *v/t.* (*sep.*, h) ⚗ evaporate, boil *s.th.* down

'ein·decken (*sep.* -k·k-) (*sep.*, h) **I.** *v/t.* cover (up); *fig.* shower; *fig.* **j-n mit Fragen** ∼ bombard s.o. with questions; **II.** *v/refl.*: **sich** ∼ stock up (**mit** *dat.* on); **sich gut** ∼ **mit** *dat.* stock up on plenty of, lay in a good supply of

Ein·decker ['aɪndɛkɐ] (*sep.* -k·k-) *m* (-s; -) ✈ monoplane

ein·dei·chen ['aɪndaɪçən] *v/t.* (*sep.*, h) dyke, dike

ein·del·len ['aɪndɛlən] F *v/t.* (*sep.*, h) dent

ein·deu·tig ['aɪndɔʏtɪç] **I.** *adj.* clear, obvious, straightforward; unambiguous, unequivocal; unmistakable; indisputable *evidence etc.*; clear, undisputed *winner, victory etc.*; **II.** *adv.* clearly; definitely; unambiguously; obviously; **es ist** ∼ **s-e Schuld** it was clearly his fault, there's no doubt that it was his fault; **j-m** ∼ **zu verstehen geben, daß** make it quite clear to s.o. that, make no bones about the fact that; ∼ **Stellung beziehen** take an unequivocal stand (**zu** *dat.* on)

ein·deut·schen ['aɪndɔʏtʃən] *v/t.* (*sep.*, h) Germanize; **'Ein·deut·schung** *f* (-; *no pl.*) Germanization

'ein·dicken (*sep.* -k·k-) *v/t.* (*sep.*, h) *and v/i.* (*sep.*, sn) thicken

'ein·di·men·sioˌ**nal** *adj.* one-dimensional

'ein·dö·sen F *v/i.* (*sep.*, sn) doze off, F nod off

'ein·drän·gen (*sep.*, h) **I.** *v/refl.*: **sich** ∼ push one's way in; *fig.* intrude (**bei** *dat.* on); interfere (with); **II.** *v/i.*: **auf j-n** ∼ *memories etc.*: crowd in on s.o.

'ein·dre·hen *v/t.* (*sep.*, h) screw in; **sich die Haare** ∼ put curlers in one's hair, put one's hair in curlers

'ein·dre·schen F **I.** *v/i.* (*irr.*, *sep.*, h, → **dreschen**): ∼ **auf** *acc.* beat; **II.** ≗ *n* (-s): (**das**) ∼ **auf die Gewerkschaften** *etc.* union-bashing *etc.*

'ein·dril·len *v/t.* (*sep.*, h): **j-m et.** ∼ drill s.th. into s.o.

'ein·drin·gen *v/i.* (*irr.*, *sep.*, sn, → **dringen**) **1.** get in(to **in** *acc.*); seep in(to); force one's way in(to); ∼ **in** *acc.* penetrate (*a.* ⚔ *and fig.*), pierce; invade; *fig.* make inroads into (*or* on); *idea etc.*: *a.* find its way into, become established in; *fig.* **bei j-m** (*or* **in j-n**) ∼ register with s.o.; **2.** ∼ **in** *acc.* go into, comprehend, fathom; **3.** ∼ **auf** *acc.* close in on *s.o.*, *fig.* press *s.o.*, crowd in on *s.o.*

'ein·dring·lich **I.** *adj.* urgent *request, warning etc.*; forceful *speech etc.*; **II.** *adv.*: **aufs** ∼**ste** (most) urgently; **ich rate Ihnen aufs** ∼**ste ab** I strongly advise you against it, I urge you not to do it; **Sie werden** ∼**st gewarnt, nicht zu** *inf.* you are urgently warned not to *inf.* (*or* against *ger.*); **'Ein·dring·lich·keit** *f* (-; *no pl.*) urgency

Ein·dring·ling ['aɪndrɪŋlɪŋ] *m* (-s; -e) intruder; invader

'Ein·druck *m* (-[e]s; ⸚e) **1.** impression; ∼

machen auf *acc.* impress, make an impression on; ***es hat keinen ~ auf mich gemacht*** it didn't impress me at all, it didn't make the slightest impression on me; ***er macht e-n intelligenten ~*** he seems to be quite intelligent, he gives the impression of being quite intelligent; ***e-n schlechten ~ machen*** make a bad impression (***auf*** *acc.* on); ***den ~ erwecken, daß*** give (s.o.) the impression that; ***ich habe den ~, daß*** I have (*or* get) the impression (that), I have a feeling (that); ***ich werde den ~ nicht los, daß*** I can't help thinking (that), I have the distinct feeling (that); ***welchen ~ haben Sie von ihm?*** what's your impression of him?, what do you think of him?; → ***erwehren, schinden*** 3; **2.** imprint, impression

'ein·drü·cken (*sep.* -k·k-) (*sep.*, h) **I.** *v/t.* break; smash; force, break down *door etc.*; flatten; crush; dent; **II.** *v/refl.*: ***sich ~*** *a. fig.* make (*or* leave) an impression (***in*** *acc.* in)

'ein·drucks·voll *adj.* impressive

'ein·dü·beln *v/t.* (*sep.*, h) rawlplug *s.th.* into the wall

'ein·du·seln F *v/i.* (*sep.*, sn) doze off, F nod off

ei·ne ['aɪnə] → ***ein¹***

'ein·eb·nen *v/t.* (*sep.*, h) level (off); *fig.* level out

'Ein·ehe *f* monogamy

ein·ei·ig ['aɪnˀaɪɪç] *adj.*: ***~e Zwillinge*** identical twins

'ein·ein'halb *adj.* one and a half

ein·en·gen ['aɪnˀɛŋən] *v/t.* (*sep.*, h) narrow down, limit; restrict, hem *s.o.* in, constrict; ***j-n ~*** *a.* F cramp s.o.'s style; **Ein·en·gung** ['aɪnˀɛŋʊŋ] *f* (-; -en) limitation; restriction

ei·ner ['aɪnɐ] **I.** *pron.* someone, somebody; → *a.* ***ein¹*** III; **II.** ♀ *m* (-s; -) **1.** ⩓ unit, digit; **2.** single (sculler)

ei·ner·lei ['aɪnɐ'laɪ] **I.** *adj.* **1.** *pred.* ***das ist mir ~*** it's all the same to me; **2.** the same; the same sort (*or* kind) of; **II.** ♀ *n* (-s; *no pl.*) monotony; ***das ~ des Alltags*** the daily grind (*or* rut)

ei·ner·seits ['aɪnɐ'zaɪts] *adv.* on the one hand

ein·fach ['aɪnfax] **I.** *adj.* **1.** easy, simple; ***~ zu verstehen*** easy to understand (*or* follow); ***es ist ~ zu verstehen, warum*** you can understand (*or* see) why; ***das ist gar nicht so ~*** it's not so easy, it's not as easy as it looks; ***nichts ~er (als das)!*** no problem at all; **2.** single; ***~e Fahrkarte*** single (ticket), *Am.* one-way ticket; ***X ~, bitte*** a single to X, please, *Am.* X one way, please; **3.** simple; ***~er Bruch*** ⚕ simple fracture; → ***Buchführung, Mehrheit***; **4.** simple, plain; modest; ordinary; **II.** *adv.* easily *etc.*; ***das ist ~ toll*** that's really great; ***das ist ~ e-e Unverschämtheit*** it's a downright cheek; ***zu ~ darstellen*** (***dargestellt***) oversimplify (oversimplified); ***es ist ~ unglaublich*** it's just incredible; ***die Sache ist ~ die, daß*** it's like this ...; ***er ist ~ gegangen*** he just got up and left; **'Ein·fach·heit** *f* (-; *no pl.*) simplicity; plainness; ***der ~ halber*** to simplify matters

'ein·fä·deln (*sep.*, h) **I.** *v/t.* **1.** thread; **2.** *fig.* arrange, fix up; go about *s.th. or ger.*; **II.** *v/refl.*: *mot.* ***sich ~*** merge, filter in; ***sich links*** (***rechts***) ***~*** filter left (right); **III.** *v/i. skiing*: straddle a gate

'ein·fah·ren (*irr.*, *sep.*, → ***fahren***) **I.** *v/i.* (sn) **1.** drive in(to ***in*** *acc.*); arrive; *train*: *a.* come in, pull in; **II.** *v/t.* (h) **2.** run in *a car etc.*; **3.** retract *landing gear*; **4.** drive into; knock down; **5.** bring in *hay etc.*; **III.** *v/refl.*: ***sich ~*** become a habit (***bei*** *dat.* with); ***es hat sich bei uns so eingefahren, daß*** *a.* we just got into the habit of *ger.*; **'Ein·fahrt** *f* (-; -en) **1.** entrance; drive; ***~ freihalten!*** keep clear; ***keine ~!*** no entry; **2.** *no pl.* 🚂 entry; ***Vorsicht bei der ~*** please stand back; **3.** access road

'Ein·fall *m* (-[e]s; ⸚e) **1.** idea (***et. zu tun*** of doing s.th.); ***er hatte den plötzlichen ~ zu*** *inf.* he had (*or* took) a sudden notion to *inf.*; **2.** ⚔ invasion (***in*** *acc.* of), raid (on); **3.** *phys.* incidence; **'ein·fal·len** *v/i.* (*irr.*, *sep.*, sn, → ***fallen***) **1.** ***mir fällt gerade ein*** it has just occurred to me; I've just remembered; ***mir fällt nichts Besseres ein*** I can't think of anything better; ***da mußt du dir schon was Besseres ~ lassen*** you'll have to do better than that; ***ihm fällt immer was ein*** he always comes up with (*or* thinks of) something, he's never at a loss for ideas (*or* an excuse *etc.*); ***es fällt mir im Moment nicht ein*** I can't think of it right now; ***es wird mir schon wieder ~*** it'll come back to me (eventually); ***es fiel mir in letzter Minute ein*** I remembered just in time; ***zu dem Thema fällt mir nichts mehr ein*** I can't think of anything else to say on the subject; ***dazu fällt mir gar nichts ein*** my mind's a blank (on that); ***ich werde mir schon was ~ lassen*** I'll think of something; ***was fällt dir ein?*** a) what do you think you're doing?, b) you must be joking!; ***wie's ihm gerade einfällt*** just as the mood takes him; ***wo's mir gerade einfällt*** while I think of it; F ***fällt mir gar nicht ein!*** who do you think I am?, you must be joking!; → ***Traum***; **2.** ⚔ ***~ in*** *acc.* invade *a country*; **3.** *light*: enter, come in(to ***in*** *acc.*); **4.** ♪ enter; join in; **5.** butt in (***in*** *acc.* on *the conversation*); **6.** collapse, cave in; *fig. a.* sink in

'ein·falls·los *adj.* unimaginative; boring

'ein·falls·reich I. *adj.* full of ideas, original; resourceful; **II.** *adv.* imaginatively; with plenty of imagination; **'Ein·falls·reich·tum** *m* (-s; *no pl.*) imaginativeness; wealth of ideas; resourcefulness; ***dieser ~!*** *a.* where does he *etc.* get all these ideas from?

'Ein·falls·win·kel *m* angle of incidence

Ein·falt ['aɪnfalt] *f* (-; *no pl.*) naivety; simple-mindedness; **ein·fäl·tig** ['aɪnfɛltɪç] *adj.* naive; simple-minded; stupid, F dumb; **'Ein·falts·pin·sel** F *m* F nincompoop, numskull

Ein·fa'mi·li·en·haus *n* detached house

'ein·fan·gen *v/t.* (*irr.*, *sep.*, h, → ***fangen***) catch; *fig.* capture

'ein·fär·ben *v/t.* (*sep.*, h) dye

'ein·far·big *adj.* plain, self-colo(u)red; *phot.*, *typ.* monochrome; ***~ streichen*** paint *s.th.* one colo(u)r, paint *s.th.* all the same colo(u)r; ***~ gestalten*** design *s.th.* in one (basic) colo(u)r

'ein·fas·sen *v/t.* (*sep.*, h) enclose; fence in; line; trim; frame; set; **'Ein·fas·sung** *f* (-; -en) enclosure; lining; edge, border; trim(ming); frame; setting

'ein·fet·ten *v/t.* (*sep.*, h) grease; oil; ⚙ *a.* lubricate; rub (some) cream into; soften *shoes* up with dubbin

'ein·fin·den *v/refl.* (*irr.*, *sep.*, h, → ***finden***): ***sich ~*** arrive, F turn up; assemble, gather

'ein·flech·ten *v/t.* (*irr.*, *sep.*, h, → ***flechten***) **1.** weave in(to ***in*** *acc.*); plait; **2.** *fig.* work in(to ***in*** *acc.*); mention in passing; ***~, daß*** *a.* throw in that

'ein·flie·gen (*irr.*, *sep.*, → ***fliegen***) **I.** *v/i.* (sn) **1.** fly in(to ***in*** *acc.*); ***~ in*** *acc. a.* enter; **2.** approach; **II.** *v/t.* (h) **3.** fly in; **4.** test-fly

'ein·flie·ßen *v/i.* (*irr.*, *sep.*, sn, → ***fließen***) flow in(to ***in*** *acc.*); *meteor.* enter; ***nach Schottland*** *etc.* ***~*** enter (into) Scotland *etc.*; *fig.* ***et. ~ lassen*** slip s.th. in; let s.th. be known; ***~ lassen, daß*** let it be known that; ***er hat es gesprächsweise ~ lassen*** he slipped it into the conversation

'ein·flö·ßen *v/t.* (*sep.*, h) **1.** ***j-m et. ~*** give s.o. s.th., make s.o. drink s.th.; **2.** *fig.* command; ***j-m et. ~*** instil(l) s.th. into s.o.; ***j-m Respekt*** (***Vertrauen***) ***~*** teach s.o. a bit of respect (win *or* gain s.o.'s confidence); ***j-m Respekt eingeflößt haben*** *a.* command s.o.'s respect

'Ein·flug *m* (-[e]s; ⸚e) flight (***in*** *acc.* into); entry (of); **~schnei·se** *f* approach corridor

'Ein·fluß *m* (-sses; ⸚sse) influence (***auf*** *acc.* on, over *s.o.*); *pol. a.* clout; power (over); effect (on); ***ein Mann von (großem) ~*** a (highly) influential man; ***~ haben auf*** *acc.* influence, affect; ***e-n schlechten ~ haben auf*** *acc.* be a bad influence on; ***unter j-s ~ stehen*** (***geraten***) be (fall) under s.o.'s sway; ***s-n ~ geltend machen*** bring one's influence to bear (***bei*** *dat.*, ***auf*** *acc.* on); ***es entzieht sich m-m ~*** it's beyond my control, I have no influence on the matter; **~be·reich** *m* sphere of influence; **~nah·me** [-na:mə] *f* (-; *no pl.*) influencing control; ***wegen versuchter ~ auf*** *acc.* for attempting to influence; **♀reich** *adj.* influential; powerful; **~sphä·re** *f* → ***Einflußbereich***

'ein·flü·stern *v/t.* (*sep.*, h): ***j-m et. ~*** whisper (*fig.* insinuate) s.th. to s.o.

'ein·for·dern *v/t.* (*sep.*, h) demand (payment of); recall, demand the return of

ein·för·mig ['aɪnfœrmɪç] *adj.* uniform; monotonous; **'Ein·för·mig·keit** *f* (-; *no pl.*) uniformity; monotony

'ein·fres·sen *v/refl.* (*irr.*, *sep.*, h, → ***fressen***): ***sich ~ in*** *acc.* eat into

Ein·frie·dung ['aɪnfri:dʊŋ] *f* (-; -en) enclosure

'ein·frie·ren (*irr.*, *sep.*, → ***frieren***) **I.** *v/i.* (sn) **1.** *pipes etc.*: freeze (up); ⚓ become icebound; **2.** *fig. negotiations etc.*: reach (a) deadlock; **3.** *fig. smile etc.*: freeze; **4.** *fig. conversation etc.*: dry up; **II.** *v/t.* (h) **5.** *gastr.* (deep-)freeze; **6.** ⚚ (*a.* ***~ lassen***) freeze *capital*

'ein·fü·gen (*sep.*, h) **I.** *v/t.* add (***in*** *acc.* to); fit in(to ***in*** *acc.*); **II.** *v/refl.*: ***sich ~*** fit in (well); adapt (***in*** *acc.* to); **'Ein·fü·ge·ta·ste** *f computer*: insert key; **'Ein·fü·gung** *f* (-; -en) **1.** adding; **2.** addition

'ein·füh·len *v/refl.* (*sep.*, h): ***sich ~ in*** *acc.* empathize with, ***j-n:*** *a.* put o.s. in s.o.'s position, ***et.:*** *a.* get into the spirit of s.th.; **ein·fühl·sam** ['aɪnfy:lza:m] *adj.* sensitive; understanding

'Ein·füh·lungs|ga·be *f* (-; *no pl.*), **~ver·mö·gen** *n* (-s; *no pl.*) sensitivity; (powers *pl.* of) empathy; intuitive understanding

Ein·fuhr ['aɪnfu:ɐ] *f* (-; -en) **1.** *no pl.* importing; **2.** imports *pl.*; **~ar'ti·kel** *m* imported article, (foreign) import; *pl.* imports; **~be·schrän·kun·gen** *pl.* import restrictions; **~be·stim·mun·gen** *pl.* import regulations; **~be·wil·li·gung** *f* import licen|ce (*Am.* -se)

'ein·füh·ren *v/t.* (*sep.*, h) **1.** introduce (***in*** *acc.* into); establish, set up; F ***das wollen wir gar nicht erst*** ~ we're not going to start anything like that; **2.** ✝ import; **3.** introduce *s.o.* (***in*** *acc.* into, ***bei j-m*** to s.o.); initiate *or* inaugurate *s.o.* (***in*** *acc.* into); **4.** insert *s.th.* (***in*** *acc.* into); feed *s.th.* in(to)

'Ein·fuhr|er·laub·nis *f*, **~ge·neh·mi·gung** *f* import licen|ce (*Am.* -se); **~ha·fen** *m* port of entry; **~han·del** *m* import trade; **~land** *n* importing country; **~li͵zenz** *f* import licen|ce (*Am.* -se); **~quo·te** *f* import quota; **~sper·re** *f*, **~stopp** *m* import ban

'Ein·füh·rung *f* (-; -en) **1.** *no pl.* introduction; establishment; importation; initiation, inauguration; insertion; **2.** introduction (***in*** *acc.* to)

'Ein·füh·rungs|an·ge·bot *n* introductory offer; **~kurs** *m* introductory (*or* beginner's) course; **~preis** *m* introductory price

'Ein·fuhr|ver·bot *n* import ban; **~wa·ren** *pl.* imported goods, imports; **~zoll** *m* import duty

'ein·fül·len *v/t.* (*sep.*, h) pour in(to ***in*** *acc.*); bottle; ~ ***in*** *acc.* fill (*or* put) into; ***Kartoffeln*** *etc.* ***in Säcke*** ~ *a.* fill (the) sacks with potatoes

'Ein·füll·stut·zen *m mot.* filler neck

'Ein·ga·be *f* (-; -n) **1.** application (***an*** *acc.* to; ***um*** *acc.* for); ***e-e*** ~ ***machen*** file a petition, apply (***um*** *acc.* for); **2.** *computer*: input; ***nach*** ~ *gen.* after entering; **3.** ⚕ administering (*gen.* of); **~da͵tei** *f* input file; **~feh·ler** *m* input error; **~mas·ke** *f* input mask; **~ta·ste** *f* enter (*or* return) key

'Ein·gang *m* (-[e]s; ¨e) **1.** entrance, way in; ***kein*** ~**!** no entrance, no entry; **2.** *no pl.* entry (***in*** *acc.* into); access (***zu*** *dat.* to); *fig.* ~ ***finden*** become established; come into fashion; ~ ***finden in*** *acc.* be accepted into *a circle etc.*; ***j-m*** ~ ***gewähren*** give s.o. access (***zu*** *dat.* to); ***sich*** ~ ***verschaffen in*** gain admission to; **3.** ✝ arrival *of goods etc.*; receipt; ***Eingänge*** goods (*or* payments) received; receipts; ***„Eingänge"*** In; ***bei*** (*or* ***nach***) ~ on receipt; **4.** *no pl.* beginning; ***zu*** ~ at the beginning; **5.** introduction; **6.** *anat.* inlet; **7.** ⚡, *electron.* source, input

'ein·gän·gig I. *adj.*: (***leicht*** ~) comprehensible, easy to grasp (*or* understand); catchy *tune*; **II.** *adv.*: ~ ***erläutern*** explain in simple terms

ein·gangs ['aɪngaŋs] **I.** *adv.* at the beginning (*or* outset); by way of introduction; ~ ***erwähnt*** above(-mentioned); ***wie*** ~ ***erwähnt*** as mentioned above; **II.** *prp.* at the beginning of

'Ein·gangs|be·stä·ti·gung *f* acknowledg(e)ment of receipt; **~da·tum** *n* date of receipt; value date; **~for·mel** *f* preamble; introduction; **~hal·le** *f* entrance hall, foyer; **~por͵tal** *n* portal; **~si͵gnal** *n* ⚡ input signal; **~span·nung** *f* ⚡ input voltage; **~stem·pel** *m* date stamp; **~strom** *m* ⚡ input current; **~stu·fe** *f tuner*: input stage; **~tor** *n* (entrance) gate; **~tür** *f* entrance; **~ver·merk** *m* file mark

'ein·ge·baut *adj.* built-in

'ein·ge·ben *v/t.* (*irr.*, *sep.*, h, → ***geben***) **1.** give, administer (*dat.* to); **2.** *computer*: feed, enter, input (***in*** *acc.* into); **3.** ***j-m e-n Gedanken*** ~ give s.o. an idea

'ein·ge·bet·tet *adj.* embedded (***in*** *acc.* in); ~ ***zwischen Bergen*** (***Wäldern*** *etc.*) tucked away (*or* nestling) between mountains (among woods and trees *etc.*)

'ein·ge·beult *adj.* dented

'ein·ge·bil·det *adj.* **1.** arrogant, full of o.s., conceited; ***er ist auf s-n Doktortitel*** (***s-e neue Stelle***) ***furchtbar*** ~ his PhD *or* doctorate (his new job) has gone to his head completely; **2.** imaginary

'ein·ge·bo·ren *adj.* **1.** native; **2.** innate; **'Ein·ge·bo·re·ne** *m, f* (-n; -n) native; aborigine

Ein·ge·bung ['aɪnge:bʊŋ] *f* (-; -en): (***e-e göttliche*** divine) inspiration; impulse; brainwave; ***e-r plötzlichen*** ~ ***folgend*** on (an) impulse

ein·ge·bür·gert ['aɪngəbʏrgɐt] *adj.* naturalized

'ein·ge·deckt *adj.*: ***gut*** ~ ***sein*** be well stocked, ***mit*** *dat.*: *a.* have plenty of, ***mit Arbeit***: have plenty of work to do (*or* to be getting on with)

ein·ge·denk ['aɪngədɛŋk] *pred. adj.* mindful (*gen.* of); ***e-r Sache*** ~ ***sein*** (***bleiben***) bear (keep) s.th. in mind, remember s.th.

ein·ge·deutscht ['aɪngədɔʏtʃt] *adj.* Germanized

'ein·ge·fah·ren I. *p.p. of* ***einfahren***; **II.** *adj.* **1.** *mot.* run-in, broken-in; **2.** *fig.* ingrained; ***das ist bei ihr vollkommen*** ~ it's become second nature to her, it's second nature with (*or* for) her; ***sich in*** ~***en Gleisen bewegen*** keep to well-trodden paths, stay in the same old groove

'ein·ge·fal·len I. *p.p. of* ***einfallen***; **II.** *adj.* dilapidated *building etc.*; haggard *face*; hollow, sunken *cheeks etc.*

ein·ge·fleischt ['aɪngəflaɪʃt] *adj.* inveterate, ingrained, hardened; deep-rooted; ~***er Junggeselle*** confirmed bachelor

'ein·ge·fro·ren I. *p.p. of* ***einfrieren***; **II.** *adj.* frozen (*a. fig. capital etc.*); icebound

'ein·ge·führt *adj.* **1.** imported; ♀ exotic; **2.** ✝ well-established *firm etc.*

'ein·ge·hen (*irr.*, *sep.*, sn, → ***gehen***) **I.** *v/i.* **1.** ✝ come in, arrive; **2.** ~ ***in*** *acc.* enter; → ***Geschichte*** 2; **3.** F ***es will ihm nicht*** ~ he can't grasp it, ***daß***: he can't accept (the fact) that, he can't come to terms with the fact that; **4.** ~ ***auf*** *acc.* show an interest in; deal with; go into; go along with; accept; ***auf j-n*** ~ respond to s.o., listen to s.o., humo(u)r s.o.; ***auf die Frage*** *gen.* ~ *a.* address the issue of; ***näher*** ~ ***auf*** *acc.* elaborate on, expand on, amplify; (***überhaupt***) ***nicht*** ~ ***auf*** *acc. a.* ignore (completely); **5.** shrink; **6.** *animal, plant*: die (***an*** *dat.* of), perish (***bei*** *dat.* in *a fire etc.*); *firm, newspaper etc.*: F fold up; F ***dabei*** (***bei der Hitze***) ***geht man ja ein!*** F it's enough to finish you off; **7.** F come a cropper (***bei*** *dat.* with); **II.** *v/t.* **8.** enter into *marriage, a contract*; ***e-n Vergleich*** ~ come to an arrangement, ***mit*** *Gläubigern*: compound with; ***ein Risiko*** ~ take a chance; ***e-e Wette*** ~ make a bet; **9.** ⚗ form *compound*; undergo *reaction*; **'ein·ge·hend I.** *adj.* **1.** ✝ incoming; **2.** detailed; full *report etc.*; thorough; in-depth *story, article etc.*; careful; **II.** *adv.* in detail; thoroughly; in depth; carefully; ***sich*** ~ ***mit et. auseinandersetzen*** (***befassen*** *etc.*) *a.* look at s.th. from every angle

'ein·ge·hüllt *adj.*: ~ ***in*** *acc.* wrapped up in; *fig.* ***in Nebel*** *etc.* ~ enveloped (*or* shrouded) in fog *etc.*

'ein·ge·keilt *adj.* wedged in

'ein·ge·kerbt *adj.* scalloped

'ein·ge·klam·mert *adj.* in brackets, *esp. Am.* in parentheses; bracketed off

'ein·ge·klemmt *adj.* stuck; trapped *nerve*; strangulated *hernia*

'ein·ge·knif·fen I. *p.p. of* ***einkneifen***; **II.** *adj.* → ***einkneifen***

'ein·ge·la·den I. *p.p. of* ***einladen***; **II.** *adj.* invited; ***nur für*** ~***e Gäste*** invited guests only; ***ich bin nicht*** ~ I'm not (*or* I wasn't) invited

'ein·ge·la·gert *adj.* in storage

'ein·ge·las·sen I. *p.p. of* ***einlassen***; **II.** *adj.* ⚙ sunk; *jewel*: set

'ein·ge·legt *adj.* **1.** inlaid; ~***e Arbeit*** inlay (*or* inlaid) work; **2.** *gastr.* pickled; marinated; ~***e Gurke*** pickled cucumber, *Am.* pickle

'ein·ge·lei·tet *adj.*: ~***e Maßnahmen*** adopted measures

'Ein·ge·mach·te *n* (-n; *no pl.*) preserves *pl.*; preserved fruit; pickles *pl.*; F *fig.* ***jetzt geht's ans*** ~ F we're really scraping the barrel now

'ein·ge·mau·ert *adj.* walled (in)

ein·ge·mein·den ['aɪngəmaɪndən] *v/t.* (*sep.*, h) incorporate; **'Ein·ge·mein·dung** *f* (-; -en) incorporation

ein·ge·mot·tet ['aɪngəmɔtət] *adj.* mothballed

'ein·ge·nom·men I. *p.p. of* ***einnehmen***; **II.** *adj.* **1.** (***sehr***) ~ ***sein von*** *dat.* be (quite) taken with; **2.** ***von sich selbst*** ~ ***sein*** be full of o.s.; **3.** ~ ***sein für*** (***gegen***) *acc.* be bias(s)ed *or* prejudiced towards (against); **'Ein·ge·nom·men·heit** *f* (-; *no pl.*) **1.** bias, prejudice; **2.** conceitedness

'ein·ge·pfercht *adj.* cooped up

'ein·ge·rahmt *adj.* framed; *fig.* ~ ***von*** *dat.* framed by; ***sie war von ihren Söhnen*** ~ *a.* she had her sons sitting (*or* standing) on either side (of her)

'ein·ge·rech·net *adj.*: **...** (***nicht***) ~ (not) including ..., *w.s.* (not) taking into account ...; ***alles*** ~ including everything, *w.s.* all in all

'ein·ge·rich·tet *adj.* furnished *flat etc.*; fully-equipped *kitchen etc.*; ***sie sind nett*** ~ they've got a nice flat *etc.*

'ein·ge·ritzt *adj.* carved; ~ ***in*** *acc. a.* scratched into (the surface of)

'ein·ge·ro·stet *adj.* rusty (*a. fig.*), stiff (*or* jammed) with rust

'ein·ge·rückt *adj. typ.* indented

'ein·ge·säumt *adj.*: ~ ***mit*** (*or* ***von***) *dat.* bordered (*or* skirted) by; ***ein mit Bäumen*** ~***er Weg*** a tree-lined path

'ein·ge·schal·tet *adj.* (switched) on

ein·ge·schlech·tig ['aɪngəʃlɛçtɪç] *adj.* ♀ unisexual

'ein·ge·schlos·sen I. *p.p. of* ***einschließen***; **II.** *adj.* **1.** locked in; **2.** included; ***im Preis*** ~ included in the price; ***es ist im Preis alles*** ~ *a.* the price is all-inclusive

'ein·ge·schnappt F *adj.* F miffed, in a huff; ***er ist leicht*** ~ you have to watch what you say to him

'ein·ge·schneit *adj.* snowed-in ..., *pred.* snowed in

ein·ge·schos·sig ['aɪngəʃɔsɪç] *adj.* one-stor(e)y ...

'ein·ge·schränkt *adj.* limited, restricted;

sich* ∼ *fühlen feel restricted (*or* inhibited)

'ein·ge·schrie·ben I. *p.p. of* ***einschreiben***; **II.** *adj.* registered *letter*

'ein·ge·schüch·tert *adj.* frightened; too scared to say (*or* do *etc.*) anything

'ein·ge·schwo·ren *adj.* confirmed; committed; ∼ ***sein auf*** *acc.* swear by

'ein·ge·ses·sen *adj.* old-established

'ein·ge·spielt *adj.*: ***gut* (*aufeinander*)** ∼ ***sein*** work well together, make a good team; ***sie sind ein* ∼*es Team*** *a.* they're a well-established (*or* well-coordinated) team, they've been working (*or* playing *etc.*) together for years

'ein·ge·sprengt *adj.*: ***mit* ∼*en* ...** interspersed with ..., scattered with ...

'ein·ge·stan·de·ner'ma·ßen *adv.* admittedly; **'Ein·ge·ständ·nis** *n* (-ses; -se) admission, confession

'ein·ge·staubt *adj.* very dusty, covered in dust

'ein·ge·ste·hen *v/t.* (*irr.*, *sep.*, h, → ***gestehen***) admit; ***sie hat die Tat eingestanden*** she admitted to having done it

'ein·ge·stellt *adj.*: ∼ ***sein gegen*** *acc.* be opposed to, be against; ∼ ***auf*** *acc.* prepared for; keyed (*or* geared) to; ***sozial*** ∼ socially-minded; ***materialistisch*** ∼ very materialistic; ***sehr fortschrittlich*** ∼ ***sein*** be very progressive (in one's views), have very progressive views; ***wie ist er politisch* ∼?** what are his political leanings?

'ein·ge·stimmt *adj.*: *fig.* ***aufeinander*** ∼ ***sein*** be attuned to one another, form a harmonious pair *etc.*

'ein·ge·tra·gen I. *p.p. of* ***eintragen***; **II.** *adj.* ✝ registered

'ein·ge·trof·fen I. *p.p. of* ***eintreffen***; **II.** *adj.*: ***„frisch* ∼"** *goods*: just in

'ein·ge·wach·sen I. *p.p. of* ***einwachsen***[1]; **II.** *adj.*: ∼***er Zehennagel*** ingrown toenail

'ein·ge·wan·dert *adj.* immigrant *families etc.*; **'Ein·ge·wan·der·te** *m, f* (-n; -n) immigrant

Ein·ge·wei·de ['aɪngəvaɪdə] *pl.* insides, F innards, 📖 viscera; intestines, guts

'ein·ge·weiht *adj.*: ∼ ***sein*** be in the know, F be in on it; **'Ein·ge·weih·te** *m, f* (-n; -n) insider; ***die* ∼*n*** *a.* those in the know

'ein·ge·wöh·nen *v/refl.* (*sep.*, h): ***sich*** ∼ get used to one's new surroundings, settle in; ***sich* ∼ *in*** *acc.* get used to; **'Ein·ge·wöh·nungs·zeit** *f* settling-in period

'ein·ge·wur·zelt *adj.* deep-rooted

'ein·ge·zwängt *adj.* **1.** ∼ ***in*** *acc.* packed (F jammed) into; **2.** *fig.* straitjacketed; ***sich*** ∼ ***fühlen*** *a.* feel (very) restricted

'ein·gie·ßen *v/t.* (*irr.*, *sep.*, h, → ***gießen***) pour in(to ***in*** *acc.*); pour; ⚙ *a.* cast (into)

'ein·gip·sen *v/t.* (*sep.*, h) **1.** ⚕ put in plaster, put a (plaster) cast on; **2.** ⚙ plaster in

ein·glei·sig ['aɪnglaɪzɪç] **I.** *adj.* single-track ..., *pred.* single-tracked; **II.** *adv.*: ∼ ***denken*** take a very narrow view of things

'ein·glie·dern (*sep.*, h) **I.** *v/t.* integrate (***in*** *acc.* into); classify (into); assign (to); annex (to); **II.** *v/refl.*: ***sich*** ∼ adapt o.s. (***in*** *acc.* to), ***in*** *acc.*: *a.* become a part of; **'Ein·glie·de·rung** *f* (-; -en) integration; classification; annexation; adaptation

'ein·gra·ben (*irr.*, *sep.*, h, → ***graben***) **I.** *v/t.* bury; plant; drive in(to the ground); **II.** *v/refl.*: ***sich*** ∼ dig o.s. (*zo.* itself) in(to ***in*** *acc.*); *bullet etc.*: embed itself (in); *fig.* engrave itself (***ins Gedächtnis*** in one's memory)

'ein·gra͵vie·ren *v/t.* (*sep.*, h) engrave (***in*** *acc.* on)

'ein·grei·fen (*irr.*, *sep.*, h, → ***greifen***) **I.** *v/i.* **1.** step in, intervene (***in*** *acc.* in); interfere (in); *esp.* ⚖ encroach (on); ∼ ***in*** *acc.* cut in on *a debate etc.*; **2.** ⚙ move into gear (***in*** *acc.* with); **II.** ℒ *n* (-s) intervention; **'ein·grei·fend** *adj.* crucial; far-reaching; **'Ein·greif·trup·pe** *f* task force; ***schnelle*** ∼ rapid deployment (*or* reaction) force

'ein·gren·zen *v/t.* (*sep.*, h) **1.** enclose; **2.** *fig.* limit (***auf*** *acc.* to), narrow down (to)

'Ein·griff *m* (-[e]s; -e) **1.** *a. pl.* intervention (***in*** *acc.* in); *a. pl.* interference (in); *esp.* ⚖ encroachment (on); **2.** ⚕ (***kleiner*** ∼ minor) operation; ***e-n*** ∼ ***vornehmen*** operate (***bei*** *dat.* on), perform an operation (on); ***unerlaubter*** ∼ illegal abortion

'ein·grup͵pie·ren *v/t.* (*sep.*, h) group (***in*** *acc.* into)

'ein·hacken (*sep.* -k·k-) *v/i.* (*sep.*, h): ∼ ***auf*** *acc.* hack (away) at; *bird*: peck at; *fig.* keep on at *s.o.*

'ein·ha·geln *v/i.* (*sep.*, sn): *fig.* ∼ ***auf*** *acc.* rain down on

'ein·ha·ken (*sep.*, h) **I.** *v/t.* hook (***in*** *acc.* into), fasten; fasten back *shutters*; **II.** *v/refl.*: ***sich bei j-m*** ∼ take s.o.'s arm; **III.** *fig. v/i.* cut in (***bei*** *dat.* on); ***hier möchte ich mal*** ∼ if I could just take up that point

'Ein·halt *m*: ***e-r Sache* ∼ *gebieten*** call a halt to s.th., put a stop to s.th.; check s.th.; **'ein·hal·ten** (*irr.*, *sep.*, h, → ***halten***) **I.** *v/t.* keep to; stick to; *a.* keep *promise*; meet; ***den Kurs*** ∼ keep going in the same direction; **II.** *lit. v/i.*: ***mit*** (*or* ***im***) ***Lesen*** *etc.* ∼ stop reading *etc.*; **'Ein·hal·tung** *f* (-; *no pl.*) adherence (*gen.* to); compliance (with)

'ein·häm·mern *v/t.* (*sep.*, h) **1.** → ***einschlagen*** 1; **2.** *fig.* ***j-m et.*** ∼ drum s.th. into s.o.

'ein·han·deln *v/t.* (*sep.*, h) buy; ***et.*** ∼ ***gegen*** (*or* ***für***) *acc.* swap s.th. for; *fig.* ***sich et.*** ∼ land o.s. (with) s.th.; ***damit handelst du dir garantiert Ärger ein*** that's asking for trouble

ein·hän·dig ['aɪnhɛndɪç] **I.** *adj.* one-handed; **II.** *adv. a.* with (only) one hand

ein·hän·di·gen ['aɪnhɛndɪgən] *v/t.* (*sep.*, h) hand over (*dat.* to); hand in (to)

'ein·hän·gen (*sep.*, h) **I.** *v/t.* put *door etc.* on its hinges; **II.** *v/i. teleph.* hang up, *Brit. a.* ring off; **III.** *v/refl.*: ***sich bei j-m*** ∼ take s.o.'s arm

'ein·hau·chen *v/t.* (*sep.*, h): *fig. j-m or e-r Sache* ***neues Leben*** ∼ breathe new life into

'ein·hau·en (*irr.*, *sep.*, h, → ***hauen***) **I.** *v/t.* **1.** → ***einschlagen*** 1, 2; **2.** carve *inscription etc.* (***in*** *acc.* into); **II.** *v/i.* → ***einschlagen*** 9

'ein·hef·ten *v/t.* (*sep.*, h) **1.** file; **2.** tack in

'ein·hei·misch *adj.* local, native, *a.* ♣, *zo.* indigenous; ✝ domestic; ∼***e Agrarprodukte*** home-grown produce; ∼***e Mannschaft*** home team; **'Ein·hei·mi·sche** *m, f* (-n; -n): ***die* ∼*n*** the people (who live) here (*or* there), the locals; ***ein* ∼*r*** one of the locals

ein·heim·sen ['aɪnhaɪmzən] F *v/t.* (*sep.*, h) pocket, F rake in; take

'Ein·hei·rat *f*: ∼ ***in*** *acc.* marriage into *a family etc.*; **'ein·hei·ra·ten** *v/i.* (*sep.*, h): ∼ ***in*** *acc.* marry into

Ein·heit ['aɪnhaɪt] *f* (-; -en) **1.** unity; *thea.* ***die drei* ∼*en*** the three unities; ***e-e*** ∼ ***bilden*** form a (unified) whole; *hist.* ***Tag der deutschen*** ∼ German Unity Day; **2.** uniformity; **3.** unit (*a. teleph.*); **4.** ⚔ unit; **'ein·heit·lich I.** *adj.* uniform; homogeneous; standardized; consistent *method etc.*; ∼***e Front*** united front; ***ein* ∼*es Vorgehen*** concerted action; **II.** *adv.* uniformly *etc.*; → ***I***; ∼ ***gekleidet*** wearing (*or* dressed in) the same clothes, (dressed) in uniform; ∼ ***vorgehen*** take concerted action, act in unison; **'Ein·heit·lich·keit** *f* (; *no pl.*) uniformity; homogeneity; consistency; unity; uniformity

'Ein·heits|be·stre·bun·gen *pl.* unitary tendencies; *pol. a.* efforts towards (*or* striving for) political union; ∼**front** *f* united front; ∼**ge·bühr** *f* flat (*or* standard) rate; ∼**ge·dan·ke** *m* idea of unity; ∼**ge·werk·schaft** *f* unified trade (*Am.* labor) union; ∼**ge·wicht** *n* standard weight; ∼**grö·ße** *f* standard size; ∼**klei·dung** *f* uniform(s *pl.*); ∼**kurs** *m* ✝ standard quotation; ∼**li·ste** *f pol.* single list (*Am.* ticket); ∼**par͵tei** *f* united party; ***es gibt nur eine*** ∼ there's only one (central) party; ∼**preis** *m* ✝ standard price; flat rate; ∼**staat** *m* centralized state; ∼**steu·er** *f* flat-rate tax

'ein·hei·zen (*sep.*, h) **I.** *v/i.* **1.** light the fire; turn the heating on; **2.** F *fig.* ***j-m*** ∼ F give s.o. a good going over; **II.** *v/t.* warm up; put on *stove*

ein·hel·lig ['aɪnhɛlɪç] *adj.* unanimous; **'Ein·hel·lig·keit** *f* (-; *no pl.*) unanimity

ein'her... *in cpds.* ... along; ∼**ge·hen** *v/i.* (*irr.*, *sep.*, sn, → ***gehen***) **1.** walk along; come walking along; **2.** ∼ ***mit*** *dat.* accompany; ***Arbeitslosigkeit geht mit Konjunkturrückgang einher*** unemployment is a concomitant of (F goes hand in hand with) economic decline; ∼**schrei·ten** *v/i.* (*irr.*, *sep.*, sn, → ***schreiten***) stride along; come striding along; ∼**stol͵zie·ren** *v/i.* (*sep.*, sn) strut along; come strutting along

'ein·ho·len (*sep.*, h) **I.** *v/t.* **1.** catch up with *s.o.*, *a car etc.*; make up for *lost time etc.*; ***e-n Rückstand*** ∼ catch up with one's arrears (*or* work); **2.** get; obtain *permission etc.*; F buy; ***Rat*** ∼ seek advice (***bei*** *dat.* from), ***bei j-m***: *a.* consult s.o.; **3.** ⚓ strike *sail*; lower *flag*; haul in *rope etc.*; **II.** *v/i.*: F ∼ ***gehen*** go shopping

'Ein·horn *n* (-[e]s; ∸er) unicorn

'ein·hül·len (*sep.*, h) **I.** *v/t.* wrap (up) (***in*** *acc.* in), cover (with); ⚙ encase (in); → ***eingehüllt***; **II.** *v/refl.*: ***sich*** ∼ wrap o.s. up (***in*** *acc.* in), ***in*** *e-e Decke*: *a.* F snuggle into

'ein'hun·dert *adj.* a hundred, *Am.* one hundred

ei·nig[1] ['aɪnɪç] *adj.* **1.** ∼ ***sein mit*** *dat.* be in agreement with; (***sich***) ∼ ***werden*** come to an agreement (***über*** *acc.* about); ***sich nicht*** ∼ ***sein*** disagree, differ (***über*** *acc.* on); ***die Fachwelt ist sich* ∼ *darüber, daß*** the experts are agreed that; ***man ist sich noch nicht* ∼ *darüber, was*** (***wie*** *etc.*) there's still some disagreement as to what (how *etc.*); ***er ist sich selbst nicht* ∼, *was er tun soll*** he can't make up his mind; **2.** united

'ei·nig[2] **I.** *indef. pron.* **1.** ∼***e*** a few; several; **2.** ∼***es*** a) something, a few things; b) quite a bit, a fair amount (F bit); quite a few things; ∼***es an ...*** *dat.* quite a bit of

..., quite a few ...; ***es gäbe noch ~es zu tun*** there's (still) plenty to do (*or* to be getting on with); ***dazu möchte ich noch ~es sagen*** I'd just like to make a few comments on that; ***ich könnte dir ~es erzählen*** I could tell you a thing or two; ***dazu gehört schon ~es*** it takes a fair bit of courage (*or* nerve *etc.*); **II.** *adj.* **3.** ***~e*** a few; several; **4.** quite a bit of; quite a few; some *hope etc.*; ***es wird noch ~e Zeit dauern*** it'll take a while yet; ***~es Aufsehen erregen*** cause quite a stir; **5.** some; ***~e 20 Jahre*** some 20 years, 20 years or so

ein·igeln ['aɪnʔi:gəln] *v/refl.* (*sep.*, h): ***sich ~*** **1.** curl up (into a ball); **2.** *fig.* go into hiding, shut o.s. off from the (rest of the) world, withdraw into one's shell

ei·ni·ge·mal ['aɪnɪgəma:l] *adv.* several times

ei·ni·gen ['aɪnɪgən] (h) **I.** *v/refl.*: ***sich ~*** agree (***über*** *acc.*, ***auf*** *acc.* on); *esp. pol.* reach (an) agreement *or* a settlement (on); ***sich ~ auf*** *acc. a.* settle on; ***sich auf e-n Kompromiß ~*** reach (*or* come to) a compromise; ***wir müssen uns irgendwie ~*** we'll have to come to some sort of agreement (*or* settlement); **II.** *v/t.* unite; reconcile

ei·ni·ger·ma·ßen ['aɪnɪgɐ'ma:sən] *adv.* quite, fairly, reasonably; quite well, fairly well; to some extent; ***es geht ihm ~*** he's not doing too badly; ***~ Bescheid wissen*** have a fairly good idea (***über*** *acc.* of)

'ei·nig·ge·hen F *v/i.* (*irr.*, *sep.*, sn, → ***gehen***) agree (***mit*** *dat.* with; ***in*** *dat.* about, on)

'Ei·nig·keit *f* (-; *no pl.*) unity; agreement, consensus (***über*** *acc.* on, about); ***es herrschte ~ darüber, daß*** everybody agreed that; ***es herrscht noch keine ~ darüber, was*** (***wo*** *etc.*) there's still some disagreement as to what (how *etc.*)

Ei·ni·gung ['aɪnɪgʊŋ] *f* (-; -en) **1.** agreement, settlement; ***~ erzielen*** reach (an) agreement, reach a settlement, reach an accord (***über*** *acc.* on), ***über*** *acc.*: *a.* reach accord on; **2.** unification

'Ei·ni·gungs|be·stre·bun·gen *pl.* unification movement *sg.*; **~ver·such** *m* attempt at reconciliation

'ein·imp·fen *v/t.* (*sep.*, h) **1.** ***j-m et. ~*** instil(l) *s.th.* into s.o.; indoctrinate s.o. with; drum *s.th.* into s.o.; **2.** ⚕ ***j-m ein Serum ~*** give s.o. a vaccination, vaccinate s.o., inoculate s.o.

'ein·ja·gen *v/t.* (*sep.*, h): ***j-m e-n Schrekken ~*** give s.o. a fright, frighten s.o., give s.o. quite a turn; ***hast du mir e-n Schrecken eingejagt!*** F you frightened me out of my wits, I nearly jumped out of my skin

ein·jäh·rig ['aɪnjɛ:rɪç] *adj.* **1.** one-year-old ...; **2.** year-long ..., one-year ...; **3.** ⚘ annual; **Ein·jäh·ri·ge** ['aɪnjɛ:rɪgə] *m, f* (-n; -n) one-year-old (child *or* baby)

'ein·kal·ku·lie·ren *v/t.* (*sep.*, h) take into account, allow for; include

ein·kap·seln ['aɪnkapsəln] *fig.* *v/refl.* (*sep.*, h): ***sich ~*** withdraw into one's shell, shut o.s. off (from the world)

ein·ka·rä·tig ['aɪnkarɛ:tɪç] *adj.* one-carat ...

'ein·kas·sie·ren *v/t.* (*sep.*, h) **1.** collect; **2.** F *fig.* F pocket, swipe; **3.** F *fig.* F collar

'Ein·kauf *m* (-[e]s; ⸚e) **1.** purchase; ✝ purchasing; *pl.* shopping; ***Einkäufe machen*** go shopping; ***ich muß noch einige Einkäufe machen*** I've still got some shopping to do; **2.** *no pl.* purchasing (department); **'ein·kau·fen** (*sep.*, h) **I.** *v/t.* buy; ✝ *a.* purchase; **II.** *v/i.*: ***~*** (***gehen***) go shopping; **III.** *v/refl.*: ✝ ***sich ~ in*** *acc.* buy shares in, buy into; **'Ein·käu·fer** *m* (-s; -) ✝ buyer

'Ein·kaufs|ab·tei·lung *f* purchasing department; **~bum·mel** *m*: ***e-n ~ machen*** have a look around the shops; **~korb** *m* shopping basket; **~li·ste** *f* shopping list; **~netz** *n* shopping net, string bag; **~preis** *m* purchase price; ***zum ~*** at cost price; **~ta·sche** *f* shopping bag; **~wa·gen** *m* (supermarket) trolley, *Am.* shopping cart; **~zen·trum** *n* shopping cent|re (*Am.* -er), *Am. a.* shopping mall; hypermarket; **~zet·tel** *m* shopping list

Ein·kehr ['aɪnke:ɐ] *f* (-; *no pl.*): ***innere ~*** reflection, meditation, F soul-searching; **'ein·keh·ren** *v/i.* (*sep.*, sn) **1.** stop for a bite to eat; ***in e-m Gasthof ~*** *a.* stop (off) at an inn; **2.** *fig.* come (***bei*** *dat.* to)

ein·kei·len ['aɪnkaɪlən] *v/t.* (*sep.*, h) *a. fig.* wedge in

ein·kel·lern ['aɪnkɛlɐn] *v/t.* (*sep.*, h) store in the cellar, cellar

'ein·ker·ben *v/t.* (*sep.*, h) **1.** put a notch (*or* notches) in; **2.** notch (***in*** *acc.* into); carve (into); **'Ein·ker·bung** *f* (-; -en) notch

ein·ker·kern ['aɪnkɛrkɐn] *v/t.* (*sep.*, h) throw into prison, incarcerate

ein·kes·seln ['aɪnkɛsəln] *v/t.* (*sep.*, h) ⚔ encircle, surround, trap; **'Ein·kes·se·lung** *f* (-; -en) ⚔ encirclement

'ein·kla·gen *v/t.* (*sep.*, h): ***et. bei j-m ~*** sue s.o. for s.th.

'ein·klam·mern *v/t.* (*sep.*, h) put in brackets (*or* parentheses); **'Ein·klam·me·rung** *f* (-; -en) bracketing; brackets *pl.* (*gen.* around)

'Ein·klang *m* (-[e]s; *no pl.*) **1.** ♪ unison; **2.** *fig.* accord, harmony, unison, concord; ***in ~ bringen*** bring in line, harmonize, reconcile; ***in ~ mit*** *dat.* in line with; ***in ~ stehen*** be compatible, be in accord (***mit*** *dat.* with); ***miteinander in ~ stehen*** *facts etc.*: tally; ***nicht im ~ stehen*** be incompatible

'ein·kle·ben *v/t.* (*sep.*, h) stick in(to ***in*** *acc.*)

'ein·klei·den *v/t.* (*sep.*, h) **1.** fit out; ⚔ *a.* kit out; ***neu ~*** buy new clothes for; ***ich mußte ihn ganz neu ~*** I had to buy him a whole new set of clothes; **2.** *fig.* couch (***in*** *acc.* in)

'ein·klem·men *v/t.* (*sep.*, h) wedge in; ⚙ clamp; (*a.* ***sich*** *et.* ***~***) get *s.th.* caught (***in der Tür*** in the door); → ***eingeklemmt***

'ein·klin·ken (*sep.*) **I.** *v/t.* (h) shut *the door* properly; hitch up (***an*** *dat.* to); **II.** *v/i.* (sn) click shut; click in

'ein·knei·fen *v/t.* (*irr.*, *sep.*, h, → ***kneifen***) pull in; ***die Lippen ~*** press one's lips together; ***den Schwanz ~*** put its tail between its legs; ***mit eingekniffenem Schwanz abziehen*** slink off with its (*a. fig.* one's) tail between its (one's) legs

'ein·knicken (*sep.* -k·k-) (*sep.*) **I.** *v/t.* (h) bend; break, snap; crease; **II.** *v/i.* (sn) bend; break, snap; *knees*: give way; ***mit dem Fuß ~*** go over on one's ankle; ***ich bin mit dem Knie eingeknickt*** my knee (just) gave way

'ein·knöpf·bar *adj.* button-in ...; **'ein·knöp·fen** *v/t.* (*sep.*, h) button in

'ein·ko·chen *v/t.* (*sep.*, h) boil down, thicken (*both a. v/i.*); preserve; make *jam*

'ein·kom·men *v/i.* (*irr.*, *sep.*, sn, → ***kommen***): ***~ um*** *acc.* apply for *s.th.* (***bei*** *dat.* to *s.o.*)

'Ein·kom·men *n* (-s; -) income, earnings *pl.*; revenue

'Ein·kom·mens|grup·pe *f*, **~schicht** *f* income bracket; **⁓schwach** low-income ...; **⁓stark** *adj.* high-income ...

'Ein·kom·men(s)·steu·er *f* income tax; **~er·klä·rung** *f* income-tax return; ***s-e ~ abgeben*** file one's income-tax return; **~ge·setz** *n* income-tax law(s *pl.*); **⁓pflich·tig** *adj.* liable to (pay) income tax

'ein·köp·fen *v/t. and v/i.* (*sep.*, h) *soccer*: head (the ball) in

'ein·kral·len *v/refl.* (*sep.*, h): ***sich ~*** dig its claws (*or* one's nails) in(to ***in*** *acc.*)

'ein·krat·zen *v/t.* (*sep.*, h): ***et. ~ in*** *acc.* scratch s.th. into (*or* onto)

'ein·krei·sen *v/t.* (*sep.*, h) **1.** surround; ⚔ *a.* encircle (*a. fig. pol.*); **2.** put a ring round; **3.** *fig.* narrow down; **'Ein·krei·sung** *f* (-; -en) encirclement; *fig.* narrowing down; **'Ein·krei·sungs·po·li·tik** *f* policy of encirclement

'ein·kre·men *v/t. and v/refl.* → ***eincremen***

'ein·krie·gen F (*sep.*, h) **I.** *v/t.* catch up with; **II.** *v/refl.*: ***wir konnten uns vor Lachen nicht mehr ~*** F we were rolling about

Ein·künf·te ['aɪnkʏnftə] *pl.* income *sg.*, earnings; revenue *sg.*

'ein·kup·peln *v/i.* (*sep.*, h) *mot.* let in (*or* engage) the clutch

'ein·ku·scheln F *v/refl.*: ***sich ~*** (*sep.*, h) F snuggle up (***in*** *acc.* inside)

'ein·la·den (*irr.*, *sep.*, h, → ***laden***) **I.** *v/t.* **1.** invite *or* ask *s.o.* round (*or* to dinner *etc.*); ask *or* take *s.o.* (out) to a concert *etc.*; buy (F stand) s.o. a drink *etc.*; ***ich bin heute abend eingeladen*** I've been invited out tonight; ***wir haben Freunde eingeladen*** we're having friends round; ***ich lad' dich ein*** a) let me treat you (***zu*** *dat.* to *a beer etc.*), b) it's on me; **2.** load; **II.** *v/i.*: ***zu Mißbrauch*** *etc.* ***~*** invite abuse *etc.*; ***zum Verweilen*** *etc.* ***~*** be (*or* look) very inviting; **'ein·la·dend** *adj.* inviting; tempting; delicious(-looking); **'Ein·la·dung** *f* (-; -en) invitation; ***auf ~ von*** (*or gen.*) at *s.o.'s* invitation

'Ein·la·dungs|kar·te *f* invitation card; **~schrei·ben** *n* letter of invitation

'Ein·la·ge *f* (-; -n) **1.** enclosure; insert; **2.** (arch) support; insole; **3.** padding; stiffener; **4.** temporary filling; **5.** *gastr.* garnish; **6.** ✝ contribution, investment; deposit; **7.** *thea.* interlude; **8.** ⚙ insertion

'ein·la·gern (*sep.*, h) **I.** *v/t.* store; put into storage; → ***eingelagert***; **II.** *v/refl.*: ***sich ~*** settle (***in*** *acc.* in[to]), be(come) deposited (in); **'Ein·la·ge·rung** *f* (-; -en) **1.** storage; **2.** *geol.*, ⚕ deposit

ein·la·gig ['aɪnla:gɪç] *adj.* one-ply

Ein·laß ['aɪnlas] *m* (Einlasses; Einlässe ['aɪnlɛsə]) **1.** *no pl.* admittance (***zu*** *dat.* to); ***~ ab 17 Uhr*** doors open at 5 p.m.; → ***gewähren***; **2.** ⚙ intake

'ein·las·sen (*irr.*, *sep.*, h, → ***lassen***) **I.** *v/t.* **1.** let *s.o.* in; **2.** run *water etc.* (***in*** *acc.* into), let in(to); **3.** set (***in*** *acc.* in); **4.** ⚙ insert; fit in; **II.** *v/refl.* **5.** ***sich ~ auf*** *acc.* let o.s. in for, get involved in, go into *a question etc.*, agree to *a proposal etc.*; ***laß dich nicht darauf ein!*** don't get involved, keep out of it, *n.s.* don't let them talk you into it; ***da hab' ich mich auf was Schönes eingelassen!*** I've really let myself in for something there; **6. *sich ~ mit*** *dat.* a) get involved with, *contp. a.* get in with; b) get involved in an argument (*or* a fight) with

'Ein·laß|kar·te *f* admission ticket; **~ven·til** *n* intake valve

'Ein·lauf *m* (-[e]s; ⸚e) **1.** *sport*: finish; **2.** ⚕ enema; ***j-m e-n ~ machen*** give s.o. an enema; **'ein·lau·fen** (*irr., sep.,* → ***laufen***) **I.** *v/i.* (sn) **1.** come in, arrive; ⚓ put in(to ***in*** *acc.*); **2.** *water*: run (in); **3.** shrink; ***nicht ~d*** non-shrink; **II.** *v/t.* (h) wear in *shoes*; **III.** *v/refl.* (h): ***sich ~*** *sport*: warm up; *fig.* get going

'ein·läu·ten *v/t.* (*sep.*, h) ring in

'ein·le·ben *v/refl.* (*sep.*, h): ***sich ~*** settle in(to ***in*** *acc.*); *fig.* ***sich ~ in*** *acc.* project o.s. into *a situation etc.*

'Ein·le·ge·ar·beit *f* inlaid work, intarsia

'ein·le·gen *v/t.* (*sep.*, h) **1.** put in, insert; enclose; **2.** *mot.* ***den zweiten Gang ~*** change (*or* shift) into second gear; **3.** ***e-e Pause ~*** have a break; ***Überstunden ~*** work (*or* put in some, do some) overtime; ***e-e Gedenkminute ~*** observe a minute's silence; **4.** *gastr.* pickle; marinate; → ***eingelegt*** 2; **5.** ***mit*** *Elfenbein etc.* ~ inlay with; → ***eingelegt*** 1; **6.** lodge, file; → ***Berufung*** 4, ***Ehre, Veto, Wort***

'Ein·le·ge·soh·le *f* insole

'ein·lei·ten *v/t.* (*sep.*, h) **1.** start, begin; initiate; implement, introduce (*a. ling.*); *fig.* mark the beginning of, usher in; write a preface (*or* an introduction) to *a book etc.*; ***e-n Prozeß ~*** go to court (***gegen*** *acc.* with); → ***eingeleitet***; **2.** ⚕ induce; **3.** dump (*in acc.* into *a river, the sea etc.*); **'ein·lei·tend I.** *adj.* introductory, opening, preliminary; ***sie sagte ein paar ~e Worte*** she gave a few words of introduction, she said a few introductory words, she made a few introductory remarks; **II.** *adv.* by way of introduction; ***~ möchte ich sagen ...*** *a.* may I start by saying ...; **'Ein·lei·tung** *f* (-; -en) introduction (*a.* ♪) (***in*** *acc.* to); opening; preface (*gen.* to); ⚖ preamble (*gen. or* ***zu*** *dat.* to); **'Ein·lei·tungs·ka,pi·tel** *n* introductory chapter

'ein·len·ken *v/i.* (*sep.*, h) **1.** *mot.* ***~ in*** *acc.* turn into; **2.** *fig.* relent; soften one's tone

'ein·le·sen (*irr., sep.,* h, → ***lesen***) **I.** *v/refl.*: ***sich ~ in*** *acc.* get into, read one's way into; **II.** *v/t.*: ***Daten ~*** *computer*: read data in

'ein·leuch·ten *v/i.* (*sep.*, h) make sense (***j-m*** to s.o.); ***es leuchtet ein*** *a.* it stands to reason, it's obvious why; ***es leuchtet mir nicht ein, daß*** I don't see why (*or* how); **'ein·leuch·tend** *adj.* (quite) clear, quite plain; obvious; convincing, cogent; ***~ sein*** *a.* make sense, stand to reason; ***aus ~en Gründen*** for obvious reasons

'ein·lie·fern *v/t.* (*sep.*, h) deliver; take *s.o.* (***in*** *acc.* to); admit *s.o.* (to *hospital etc.*); put *s.o.* (into *prison etc.*); ***er wurde ins Gefängnis eingeliefert*** *a.* he was committed (*or* placed in prison); **'Ein·lie·fe·rung** *f* (-; -en) delivery; admission (***in*** *acc.* to *hospital etc.*); committal (to *prison etc.*); **'Ein·lie·fe·rungs·schein** *m* postal receipt

Ein·lie·ger·woh·nung ['aɪnliːgɐ-] *f* F granny annexe

'ein·lo·chen *v/t.* (*sep.*, h) **1.** *golf*: putt; **2.** F clap *s.o.* in jail, put *s.o.* in clink (*Am.* in the slammer)

'ein·lo,gie·ren (*sep.*, h) **I.** *v/t.* put *s.o.* up (***bei*** *dat.* at); **II.** *v/refl.*: ***sich ~*** take up lodgings (***bei*** *dat.* at, with)

'ein·lö·sen *v/t.* (*sep.*, h) redeem; use up *voucher*; cash, hono(u)r *check*; hand in *prescription*; *fig.* keep, make good *one's promise*; **'Ein·lö·sung** *f* (-; -en) redemption; cashing; hono(u)ring

'ein·lul·len *v/t.* (*sep.*, h) lull to sleep; *fig.* lull into a false sense of security

'ein·ma·chen *v/t.* (*sep.*, h) preserve, can; bottle; pickle

'Ein·mach|glas *n* preserving (*Am.* canning) jar; **~zucker** (*sep.* -k·k-) *m* preserving sugar

'ein·mal *adv.* **1.** once; ***~ eins ist eins*** once one is one; ***~ im Jahr*** once a year; ***~ und nie wieder*** never again; ***noch ~*** once more, one more time; ***versuch's noch ~*** *a.* have another go; ***noch ~ soviel*** twice as much; ***noch ~ so alt*** (***wie er*** *etc.*) twice his *etc.* age; *iro.* ***~ dies, ~ jenes*** it's something different every time; ***~ sagst du ja, dann sagst du nein*** *a.* first it's yes, then it's no; ***auf ~*** a) suddenly; b) at the same time; c) in one go; ***~ zählt nicht*** once (*or* one) doesn't count; **2.** once; ***das war ~*** that's all in the past; ***es war ~*** once upon a time there was; ***haben Sie schon ~ ...?*** have you ever ...?; ***es ist nicht mehr das, was es ~ war*** it's not the same as it used to be, it isn't what it used to be; **3.** one day, some day (or other); ***wenn du ~ groß bist*** when you grow up, when you're a big boy (*or* girl); **4.** later on (some time); **5.** before; ***ich war (schon) ~ da*** I've been there before, I was there once; **6.** ***nicht ~*** not even, not so much as; ***er hat mich nicht ~ angesehen*** he didn't even (deign to) look at me; **7.** ***ich bin nun ~ so*** I can't help it; ***er ist nun ~ so*** *a.* that's just the way he is, he's like that; ***es ist nun ~ so*** that's the way it is, F c'est la vie; **8.** ***erst ~*** first; **9.** for a change; **10.** ***hör ~!*** listen; ***sei endlich ~ ruhig!*** be quiet, will you!, how many times do I have to tell you to be quiet!; **11.** ***stell dir ~ vor*** just imagine, can you imagine

Ein·mal·eins [aɪnmaːl'aɪns] *n* (-; *no pl.*) **1.** (multiplication) tables *pl.*; ***das kleine (große) ~*** the (*or* one's) tables up to (over) ten; ***das ~ aufsagen*** say one's tables; **2.** *fig.* ***das ~*** the basics, the fundamentals

'Ein·mal·hand·tuch *n* paper towel

ein·ma·lig ['aɪnmaːlɪç] **I.** *adj.* **1.** single ..., one-off ...; once-in-a-lifetime *purchase*; ***es ist e-e ~e Anschaffung*** *a.* you only buy that sort of thing once in your life; ***es ist e-e ~e Ausgabe*** it's the only extant copy, it's the only copy that has come down to us; **2.** unique, one-off *chance*; **3.** brilliant, F fantastic; **II.** *adv.*: ***~ schön*** absolutely beautiful; ***~ gut*** brilliant; **'Ein·ma·lig·keit** *f* (; *no pl.*) uniqueness

'Ein·mal·sprit·ze *f* disposable syringe

'Ein·mann... *in cpds.* one-man ...; **~betrieb** *m* one-man business (F show); **~bus** *m* driver-only bus

Ein'mark·stück *n* one-mark piece

'Ein·marsch *m* (-[e]s; ⸚e) marching in; invasion; ***beim ~ der Truppen*** when the troops invaded; **'ein·mar,schie·ren** *v/i.* (*sep.*, sn) march in(to ***in*** *acc.*), (*a.* ***~ in*** *acc.*) enter; invade

'ein·mas,sie·ren *v/t.* (*sep.*, h) rub in (gently); ***~ in*** *acc.* rub (gently) into

'ein·mau·ern *v/t.* (*sep.*, h) wall in, immure; fix (*or* embed) in a wall

'ein·mei·ßeln *v/t.* (*sep.*, h) chisel (***in*** *acc.* into)

'ein·mie·ten *v/refl.* (*sep.*, h): ***sich ~*** take a room (***bei*** *dat.* at)

'ein·mi·schen (*sep.*, h) **I.** *v/t.* mix *s.th.* in(to ***in*** *acc.*), add (to); **II.** *v/refl.*: ***sich ~*** interfere (***in*** *acc.* in, with), meddle (in, with), poke one's nose in(to); ***sich in ein Gespräch ~*** join in (*or* F butt in on) a conversation; ***misch dich lieber nicht ein*** don't get involved; ***misch dich da nicht ein!*** (you) just keep out of it; **'Ein·mi·schung** *f* (-; -en) interference; *esp. pol.* involvement, intervention

ein·mo·na·tig ['aɪnmoːnatɪç] *adj.* **1.** one-month-old *baby*; **2.** one-month ..., four-week ...; ***nach e-m ~en Englandaufenthalt*** after a month (*or* four weeks) in England

'ein·mon,tie·ren *v/t.* (*sep.*, h) instal(l), fit in(to ***in*** *acc.*)

ein·mo·to·rig ['aɪnmotoːrɪç] *adj.* single-engined

ein·mot·ten ['aɪnmɔtən] *v/t.* (*sep.*, h) put in mothballs; mothball *ship, tank etc.*; *fig.* lock away, mothball

ein·mum·men ['aɪnmʊmən] (*sep.*, h) **I.** *v/t.* wrap *s.o.* up; **II.** *v/refl.*: ***sich ~*** wrap o.s. up, get wrapped up

'ein·mün·den *v/i.* (*sep.*, sn): ***~ in*** *acc.* flow into; join, lead into; **'Ein·mün·dung** *f* (-; -en) mouth, estuary; junction

ein·mü·tig ['aɪnmyːtɪç] **I.** *adj.* unanimous; **II.** *adv.* unanimously; ***et. ~ tun*** be unanimous in doing s.th.; ***~ der Meinung sein, daß*** be unanimous that; **'Ein·mü·tig·keit** *f* (-; *no pl.*) unanimity

'ein·nä·hen *v/t.* (*sep.*, h) sew in(to ***in*** *acc.*); take in

Ein·nah·me ['aɪnnaːmə] *f* (-; -n) **1.** *no pl.* taking; ***vor ~ des Mittels*** before taking the medicine; **2.** *no pl.* ⚔ capture; occupation; **3.** *pl.* ✝ receipts; proceeds; earnings; income, revenue; **~quel·le** *f* source of income (*or* revenue)

ein·ne·beln ['aɪnneːbəln] (*sep.*, h) **I.** *v/t.* **1.** put a smoke screen up around *s.th.*; F *fig.* F smoke up *a room etc.*; F smoke out; **II.** *v/refl.* **2.** ***sich ~*** put up a smoke screen; **3.** ***es nebelt sich ein*** it's getting foggy, the fog seems to be settling

'ein·neh·men *v/t.* (*irr., sep.,* h, → ***nehmen***) **1.** take *medicine etc.*; have *a meal etc.*; **2.** take in; earn; **3.** ⚔ capture; occupy; **4.** take up *space etc.*; **5.** take (up); ***s-n Platz ~*** take one's seat; **6.** take (up); hold; ***die Stellung e-s Chefberaters ~*** take up the position of chief adviser; **7.** take up, adopt; ***den Standpunkt ~, daß*** take the view that; **8.** *fig.* ***j-n (für sich) ~*** win s.o. over, charm s.o.; ***j-n gegen sich ~*** set s.o. against o.s.; ***das nimmt mich für ihn ein*** I find that quite endearing, *w.s.* that does him credit; ***das nahm die Leute gegen ihn ein*** it didn't do much for his popularity; → ***eingenommen*** II; **'ein·neh·mend** *adj.* winning, engaging, fetching; ***er hat ein ~es Wesen*** he has a very engaging personality; F *iro.* he just can't get enough

'ein·nicken (*sep.* -k·k-) F *v/i.* (*sep.*, sn) F nod off, drop off

'ein·ni·sten *v/refl.* (*sep.*, h): **sich ~ 1.** (build one's) nest (**in** *acc. or dat.* in); **2.** lodge itself, get lodged, settle (**in** *acc. or dat.* in); **sich bei j-m ~** F park o.s. on s.o., *fig. idea etc.*: take hold of s.o.
'Ein·öde *f* (-; -n) wilderness
'ein·ölen *v/t.* (*sep.*, h) oil; rub (some) oil into
'ein·ord·nen (*sep.*, h) **I.** *v/t.* **1.** sort out (and put in their proper place); file (away); **~ in** *acc.* sort into; **~ nach** *dat.* arrange according to; **alphabetisch ~** enter alphabetically (*or* in alphabetical order); **2.** classify; **3.** place; date; **4.** put *s.o.* down as a certain type; **II.** *v/refl.*: **sich ~ 5.** adjust o.s. (**in** *acc. to*), fall into line; **6.** fit in(to **in** *acc.*); **7.** *mot.* get in lane; **sich rechts** (**links**) **~** get into the right (left) lane
'ein·packen (*sep.* -k·k-) (*sep.*, h) **I.** *v/t.* pack (up); wrap up; do up; **II.** *v/i.* pack; F *fig.* **da können wir ~** we might as well pack up and leave; F **gegen ihn kann ich gleich ~** *a.* F I haven't got a cat's chance in hell against him; **III.** *v/refl.*: **sich** (**warm**) **~** wrap (o.s.) up (warmly)
'ein·par·ken *v/i.* (*sep.*, h) park; **rück-wärts ~** back into a parking space; **hier müßtest du gerade noch ~ können** *a.* you should just be able to slot in here
Ein·par'tei·en... *in cpds.* one-party ...
'ein·pas·sen (*sep.*, h) **I.** *v/t.* fit in(to **in** *acc.*); **II.** *v/refl.*: **sich ~** adjust (**in** *acc.* to); **sich überall ~ können** (be able to) fit in anywhere
'ein·pau·ken F *v/t.* (*sep.*, h) F swot (*or* bone, mug) up on
Ein·peit·scher ['aınpaıtʃɐ] *m* (-s; -) *parl.* (party) whip
'ein·pen·deln *v/refl.* (*sep.*, h): **sich ~** level out (**auf** *acc.* at)
'ein·pen·nen F *v/i.* (*sep.*, sn) F nod off
Ein·per'so·nen·haus·halt *m* one-person (*or* single-person) household
'ein·pfer·chen *v/t.* (*sep.*, h) **1.** pen up; **2.** *fig.* coop up; **~ in** *acc. a.* crowd into, herd into; → **eingepfercht**
'ein·pflan·zen *v/t.* (*sep.*, h) plant; ⚕ implant; **j-m e-e fremde Niere ~** give s.o. a kidney transplant; *fig.* **j-m et. ~** instil(l) s.th. in s.o.('s mind)
Ein'pha·sen... *in cpds.*, **ein·pha·sig** ['aınfa:zıç] *adj.* ⚡ single-phase ...
'ein·pin·seln *v/t.* (*sep.*, h) ⚕ paint (**mit** *dat.* with); **mit Jod** *etc.* **~** put (*or* dab) iodine *etc.* on
'ein·pla·nen *v/t.* (*sep.*, h) include (in the plan), plan; allow for; F **das hatten wir nicht eingeplant** we weren't planning on that
'ein·pö·keln *v/t.* (*sep.*, h) salt
ein·po·lig ['aınpo:lıç] *adj.* ⚡ single-pole ...; one-pin *plug etc.*
'ein·prä·gen (*sep.*, h) **I.** *v/t.* **1.** imprint, stamp (**in** *acc.* on); **2.** *fig.* **j-m et. ~** impress s.th. (up)on s.o.; **sich** *et.* **~** remember, memorize; **II.** *v/refl.*: **sich j-m ~** stick in s.o.'s mind, make an (*or* a lasting) impression on s.o.; **sich leicht ~** be easy to remember, be catchy; **es hat sich bei mir tief eingeprägt** it's stamped itself on my mind; **ein·präg·sam** ['aınprɛ:kza:m] *adj.* easy to remember, memorable; catchy; **'Ein·präg·sam·keit** *f* (-; *no pl.*) memorableness; catchiness
'ein·prü·geln I. *v/i.* (*sep.*, h): **~ auf** *acc.* beat, F bash; **II.** ♀ *n* (-s): (**das**) **~ auf die Gewerkschaften** *etc.* union-bashing *etc.*
'ein·pu·dern *v/t.* (*sep.*, h) powder
'ein·pum·pen *v/t.* (*sep.*, h) pump *s.th.* in(to **in** *acc.*)
ein·pup·pen ['aınpʊpən] *v/refl.*: **sich ~** (*sep.*, h) *zo.* change into a pupa
'ein·quar,tie·ren (*sep.*, h) **I.** *v/t.* ⚔ billet (**bei** *dat.* on); put *s.o.* up (**bei j-m** at s.o.'s place); **II.** *v/refl.*: **sich ~ bei** *dat.* move in with; **ich habe mich bei m-m Bruder einquartiert** *a.* I'm staying with my brother; **'Ein·quar,tie·rung** *f* (-; -en) ⚔ billeting
'ein·quet·schen *v/t.* (*sep.*, h): **j-m den Finger** *etc.* **~** jam s.o.'s finger *etc.* (**in der Tür** in the door); **sich den Finger ~** get one's finger stuck (*or* jammed)
'ein·rah·men *v/t.* (*sep.*, h) frame; → **eingerahmt**
'ein·ram·men *v/t.* (*sep.*, h) ram in(to **in** *acc.*); drive in(to)
'ein·ran,gie·ren *v/t.* (*sep.*, h) **1. ~ in** *acc.* manoeuvre into; **2.** rank, put, place; **gesellschaftlich höher einrangiert werden** rank higher on the social scale, have a higher social standing
'ein·ra·sten *v/i.* (*sep.*, sn) click into place; ⚙ engage
'ein·räu·men *v/t.* (*sep.*, h) **1.** put the furniture in *a room*; put (the) things in *a closet etc.*; **2.** put (*or* clear) away; **3.** grant; concede (*dat.* to); ⚖ grant, allow *a credit etc.*; **e-r Sache den Vorrang ~** give precedence to s.th.; **4.** concede, admit, acknowledge (**daß** that); **'ein·räu·mend** *adj. ling.* concessive; **'Ein·räu·mungs·satz** *m ling.* concessive clause
'ein·rech·nen *v/t.* (*sep.*, h) include; allow for, take into acocunt; → **eingerechnet**
'Ein·re·de *f* (-; -n) objection; ⚖ plea; (**e-e**) **~ erheben** raise an objection, enter a plea
'ein·re·den (*sep.*, h) **I.** *v/t.*: **j-m et. ~** talk s.o. into (believing) s.th.; **j-m ~, daß** persuade s.o. that; **wer hat dir das eingeredet?** who told you that nonsense?, who put that (idea) into your head?; **sich et. ~** talk o.s. into s.th.; **das lasse ich mir nicht ~** they'll *etc.* have a hard time getting me to believe that; **das redest du dir** (**doch**) **nur ein!** you're imagining it; **II.** *v/i.*: **auf j-n ~** talk to s.o.; keep (*or* go) on at s.o.
'ein·reg·nen (*sep.*, h) **I.** *v/refl.*: **es regnet sich ein** the rain is settling in; **II.** *v/i.*: *fig.* **Ehren** *etc.* **regneten auf ihn ein** he was showered with hono(u)rs (*or* tributes) *etc.*
'Ein·rei·be·mit·tel *n* → **Einreibungsmittel**; **'ein·rei·ben** (*irr.*, *sep.*, h, → **reiben**) **I.** *v/t.* rub in(to **in** *acc.*); put on (**in** *acc. one's face etc.*); *die Haut etc.* **mit et. ~** rub s.th. on (*or* into); **II.** *v/refl.*: **sich ~ mit** *dat.* put *s.th.* on, rub *s.th.* in; **'Ein·rei·bungs·mit·tel** *n* liniment; ointment
'ein·rei·chen *v/t.* (*sep.*, h) send in, hand in; submit; ⚖ **e-e Klage ~** file (*or* bring) an action; → **Scheidung** 2
'ein·rei·hen (*sep.*, h) **I.** *v/t.* class, classify; *fig.* **j-n ~ unter** *acc.* rank s.o. with (*or* among); **eingereiht werden unter** *acc. a.* be counted among; **II.** *v/refl.*: **sich ~** take one's place (**in** *acc.* among), get in line; **sich ~ in** *acc. a.* join
Ein·rei·her ['aınraıɐ] *m* (-s; -) single-breasted suit; **ein·rei·hig** ['aınraıç] *adj.* single-breasted *suit etc.*
'Ein·rei·se *f* (-; -n) entry (**in** *acc.*, **nach** *dat.* into); **bei der ~** on arrival, **in** *acc.*: *a.* when entering; **j-m die ~ verweigern** refuse s.o. entry (*or* admission); **~be·din·gun·gen** *pl.* conditions of entry; **~er·laub·nis** *f*, **~ge·neh·mi·gung** *f* entry permit
'ein·rei·sen *v/i.* (*sep.*, sn) enter the country; **~ in** *acc.* (*or* **nach** *dat.*) enter
'Ein·rei·se|ver·bot *n*: **~ haben** have been refused entry *or* admission (to the country), not to be allowed to enter the country; **~vi·sum** *n* entry visa
'ein·rei·ßen (*irr.*, *sep.*, → **reißen**) **I.** *v/t.* (h) **1.** tear; **2.** pull down; **II.** *v/i.* (sn) **3.** tear; **eingerissen sein** have a tear, be (slightly) torn; **4.** F *fig.* (start to) spread, take hold; **das dürfen wir gar nicht erst ~ lassen** we'd better put a stop to that before it starts
'ein·rei·ten (*irr.*, *sep.*, → **reiten**) **I.** *v/t.* (h) break in *a horse*; **II.** *v/i.* (sn) ride in(to **in** *acc.*), enter on horseback
ein·ren·ken ['aınrɛŋkən] (*sep.*, h) **I.** *v/t.* ⚕ set; *fig.* put *s.th.* right, straighten out; **II.** *fig. v/refl.*: **sich ~** sort (*or* straighten) itself out
'ein·ren·nen *v/t.* (*irr.*, *sep.*, h, → **rennen**) break down (*or* open); **sich den Schädel am Schrank ~** run into the cupboard (and hurt one's head), bang one's head against the cupboard; *fig.* **offene Türen ~** preach to the converted; → **Bude** 2
'ein·rich·ten (*sep.*, h) **I.** *v/t.* **1.** furnish, F do up *room etc.*; fit out *kitchen etc.*; install, set up, put up; **~ in** *dat. a.* put *s.th.* in(to); **er hat sein Zimmer nett eingerichtet** he's done his room up very nicely; **2.** ⚙ adjust; ⚕ set; **3.** establish; set up; found; build; **4.** arrange (for); **es ~, daß** see to it that; **wenn du es ~ kannst** if you can (manage); **et. ~ nach** *dat.* arrange s.th. according to (*or* around); **kannst du es irgendwie ~, daß ...** can you possibly arrange things so that ..., **daß er kommt?**: *a.* is there any way you can get him to come?; **ich werde es so ~, daß ich um vier gehen kann** *a.* I'll work things out so that I can leave at four; **das wird sich schon ~ lassen** we'll see to that(, don't worry); **II.** *v/refl.*: **sich ~ 5.** furnish one's flat *etc.*, F do one's flat *etc.* up; *w.s.* settle in; **sich neu ~** refurnish one's flat *etc.*, buy new furniture; **du hast dich nett eingerichtet** *a.* you've got a nice place; **wie hat er sich eingerichtet?** *a.* what's his flat *etc.* like?; → **häuslich** II; **6.** a) make ends meet; b) adapt, F make the most of it; **7. sich ~ auf** *acc.* prepare for, get ready for, make arrangements for; be prepared for; **auf so etwas sind** (**waren**) **wir nicht eingerichtet** we're not geared to that sort of thing (we weren't prepared for anything like that); **'Ein·rich·tung** *f* (-; -en) **1.** set-up; furniture; fittings *pl.*; installation; **~en** facilities, equipment; **2.** ⚙ adjustment; **3.** *no pl.* setting up; arrangement, organization; **4.** institution; *w.s.* facility; **5. ständige ~** permanent fixture
'Ein·rich·tungs|ge·gen·stän·de *pl.* fixtures; **~haus** *n* furniture store (*or* showrooms *pl.*)
'Ein·riß *m* tear; ⚕ laceration
'ein·rit·zen *v/t.* (*sep.*, h) **1.** carve; **~ in** *acc. a.* scratch into (the surface of), scratch onto; **2.** scratch *one's skin*
'ein·rol·len (*sep.*) **I.** *v/t.* (h) roll up; **sich**

die Haare ~ put one's hair in curlers; **II.** *v/i.* (sn) 🚗 come in; **III.** *v/refl.*: ***sich*** ~ (h) curl up; *zo. a.* curl itself up, curl up into a ball

ˈein·ro·sten *v/i.* (*sep.*, sn) **1.** get rusty; get stiff with rust; **2.** F *fig.* get rusty; get stiff (from lack of use); stagnate, vegetate; ***m-e Knochen sind ziemlich eingerostet*** *a.* F I think my joints need oiling, my joints are a bit creaky; → ***eingerostet***

ˈein·rücken (*sep.* -k·k-) (*sep.*) **I.** *v/t.* (h) **1.** *typ.* indent; **2.** put *an ad* in *a newspaper*; **II.** *v/i.* (sn) **3.** move (*or* march) in(to ***in*** *acc.*), (*a.* ~ ***in*** *acc.*) enter; **4.** ⚔ report for duty; **ˈEin·rückung** (*sep.* -k·k-) *f* (-; -en) **1.** *typ.* indentation; **2.** ⚔ entry (***in*** *acc.* into); invasion (of)

ˈein·rüh·ren *v/t.* (*sep.*, h) stir in(to ***in*** *acc.*)

eins [aɪns] **I.** *adj.* **1.** one; ***um*** ~ at one (o'clock); **2.** *pred.* ~ ***sein*** (*or* ***werden***) ***mit j-m*** agree with s.o.; ***wir sind uns*** ~ ***darüber, daß*** we agree that; **3.** *pred.* ***es ist mir alles*** ~ I couldn't care less; **II.** *pron.* **4.** one thing; ~ ***gefällt mir nicht*** there's one thing I don't like about it; ***noch*** ~ another one; ~ ***wollte ich dir noch sagen*** another thing (I wanted to say); ***es kam*** ~ ***zum andern*** one thing led to another; ~ ***nach dem andern!*** one after the other; ***j-m*** ~ ***versetzen*** land s.o. one; **5.** ***es kommt alles auf*** ~ ***heraus*** it all boils (*or* comes) down to the same thing; **III.** ♀ *f* (-; -en) one; *ped.* A; (*bus etc.*) (number) one; ***e-e*** ~ ***schreiben*** get an A; ~ ***komma Null*** a straight A, the highest mark possible

ein·sacken[1] [ˈaɪnzakən] (*sep.* -k·k-) *v/t.* (*sep.*, h) **1.** sack, put in sacks; **2.** F *fig.* F rake in

ˈein·sacken[2] *v/i.* (*sep.*, sn) sag; sink; ~ ***in*** *acc.* sink into

ˈein·sa·gen (*sep.*, h) **I.** *v/t.*: ***j-m et.*** ~ whisper s.th. to s.o.; **II.** *v/i.*: ***j-m*** ~ prompt s.o.

ˈein·sal·ben *v/t.* (*sep.*, h) put some ointment (*or* cream) on

ˈein·sal·zen *v/t.* (*sep.*, h) salt

ein·sam [ˈaɪnzaːm] *adj.* **1.** lonely; secluded; ***sich*** ~ ***fühlen*** *a.* feel (very) isolated; **2.** lonely, isolated, secluded *house etc.*; empty, deserted *beach, road etc.*; ~***e Insel*** lonely (*or* uninhabited) island, desert island; **3.** solitary, lone *tree etc.*; lonely; **4.** F ~***e Spitze*** (*or* ***Klasse***) ***sein*** F be brilliant; **ˈEin·sam·keit** *f* (-; *no pl.*) loneliness; seclusion; isolation

ˈein·sam·meln *v/t.* (*sep.*, h) gather; pick up; collect *money etc.*

ˈEin·satz *m* (-es; ⸚e) **1.** insert; (extension) leaf *of table*; *fashion*: inset; (*filter*) element; **2.** stake (*a. fig.*); deposit; *fig.* share; **3.** ♪ entry; **4.** *no pl.* risk; ***unter*** ~ ***s-s Lebens*** at the risk of one's life; **5.** *no pl.* effort, hard work; dedication; commitment; ***unter*** ~ ***aller Kräfte*** by a supreme effort; ***beide Seiten haben mit vollem*** ~ ***gekämpft*** it was an all-out battle; **6.** *no pl.* employment, use; **7.** ⚔ deployment, mission, sortie; intervention; ***im*** ~ ***sein*** be on duty, ⚔ be in action; ***zum*** ~ ***bringen*** use, send in *troops*; ***zum*** ~ ***kommen*** (*or* ***gelangen***) be used, *troops etc.*: be sent in, *player*: come on; ~***be·fehl*** *m* ⚔ combat order

ˈein·satz·be·reit *adj.* **1.** ready for duty (⚔ action), operational; ***sich*** ~ ***halten*** stand by; **2.** willing, keen; devoted; **3.** daring; **4.** ⚙ operational, ready for use; ***et.*** ~ ***halten*** have s.th. ready; **ˈEin·satz·be·reit·schaft** *f* (-; *no pl.*) **1.** readiness for duty (⚔ action); **2.** willingness; devotedness; **3.** daringness; **4.** ⚙ readiness for use

ˈein·satz·fä·hig *adj.* operational; available; *sport*: fit (to play); ***voll*** ~ fully operational, *sport*: a hundred per cent (*or* percent) fit; **ˈEin·satz·fä·hig·keit** *f* (-; *no pl.*) utilizability; *sport*: fitness (to play)

ˈEin·satz·fahr·zeug *n* emergency vehicle

ˈEin·satz·freu·de *f* (-; *no pl.*) keenness; **ˈein·satz·freu·dig** *adj.* keen; ~ ***sein*** *sport*: put a lot into the game

ˈEin·satz|ge·biet *n* ⚔ operational area; *w.s.* field; ~**grup·pe** *f*, ~**komˌman·do** *n* task force; ~**lei·ter** *m* group leader; person in charge of operations; ~**ort** *m* **1.** place of action; **2.** posting; ~**trup·pe** *f* task force; ~**wa·gen** *m* **1.** relief *or* extra bus (*or* tram); **2.** police car (*or* van)

ˈein·sau·gen (*sep.*, h) **I.** *v/t.* soak up; suck in; *fig.* draw in; → ***Muttermilch***; **II.** *v/refl.*: ***sich*** ~ soak up (*or* in)

ˈein·säu·men *v/t.* (*sep.*, h) **1.** hem; **2.** border; → ***eingesäumt***

ˈein·schal·ten (*sep.*, h) **I.** *v/t.* **1.** switch (*or* turn) on; start *engine*; *TV*, *radio*: tune into, put on, switch on; *TV* ***das 1. Programm eingeschaltet haben*** *a.* have switched onto channel 1, F have it on channel 1; **2.** add, insert, *formal*: interpolate; ***e-e Pause*** ~ have a break; **3.** call *s.o.* in; **II.** *v/refl.*: ***sich*** ~ **4.** step in, intervene; ***sich in ein Gespräch*** ~ join in (on) a conversation; **5.** ⚡, ⚙ switch itself on

ˈEin·schalt|he·bel *m* starting lever; ~**quo·te** *f TV*, *radio*: ratings *pl.*; *TV a.* viewing figures *pl.*; ***die höchste*** ~ the top ratings; ~**ta·ste** *f* switch, on button, power button

ˈEin·schal·tung *f* (-; -en) **1.** switching on; ***bei der*** ~ when switching on; **2.** *ling.* interpolation; **3.** involvement (*gen.* of)

ˈEin·schalt·zeit *f* preset time

ˈein·schär·fen *v/t.* (*sep.*, h): ***j-m*** ~ ***zu*** *inf.* urge s.o. to *inf.*, warn s.o. to *inf.*; ***j-m*** ~, ***daß*** impress (up)on s.o. that; ***j-m Gehorsam*** *etc.* ~ inculcate (a sense of) obedience *etc.* in s.o., F drum obedience *etc.* into s.o.

ˈein·schar·ren (*sep.*, h) **I.** *v/t.* bury; quickly bury *s.o.*; **II.** *v/refl.*: ***sich*** ~ *zo.* burrow (itself) (***in*** *acc.* into)

ˈein·schät·zen *v/t.* (*sep.*, h) estimate, assess (***auf*** *acc.* at); rate, assess; judge, assess, size up *situation etc.*; ***falsch*** ~ misjudge; ***richtig*** ~ get *s.th.* right, be right about; ~ ***als*** see *s.o. or s.th.* as; ***wie schätzen Sie die Lage ein?*** what's your view of the situation?, how do you see (*or* view) the situation?; ***das ist schwer einzuschätzen*** it's hard to say; **ˈEin·schät·zung** *f* (-; -en) **1.** assessment, judg(e)ment; ***nach m-r*** ~ the way I see it; **2.** estimate

ˈein·schen·ken *v/t.* (*sep.*, h) pour (out); ***j-m*** (***ein Glas***) ***Wein*** ~ pour s.o. some (a glass of) wine; → ***Wein***

ˈein·sche·ren *v/i.* (*sep.*, sn) *mot.* cut in (***vor*** *dat.* on)

ˈein·schicken (*sep.* -k·k-) *v/t.* (*sep.*, h) send (in) (***an*** *acc.* to)

ˈein·schie·ben *v/t.* (*irr.*, *sep.*, h, → ***schieben***) push (*or* slide) in; *fig.* add, insert; fit *or* slot *s.o.*, *s.th.* in(to ***in*** *acc.*); **Ein·schieb·sel** [ˈainʃiːpsəl] *n* (-s; -) insertion; interpolation; **ˈEin·schie·bung** *f* (-; -en) addition, insertion; interpolation

ˈein·schie·ßen (*irr.*, *sep.*, h, → ***schießen***) **I.** *v/t.* **1.** shoot through; shoot out, smash *windows etc.*; **2.** break in *weapon*; **3.** *soccer*: drive *the ball* home; **4.** *fig.* contribute *money* (***in*** *acc.* to), invest (in); ~ ***in*** *acc. a.* F sink into; **II.** *v/refl.*: **5.** ***sich*** ~ get one's range; ***sich*** ~ ***auf*** *acc. a. fig.* zero (*or* home) in on; *fig.* ***die Zeitungen haben sich auf ihn eingeschossen*** *a.* F the papers are having a real go at him; **III.** *v/i.* **6.** *sport*: score; ***zum 2:0*** ~ score to make it 2-0 (= two-nil); **7.** (sn) rush in; *mother's milk*: come in

ˈein·schif·fen (*sep.*, h) **I.** *v/t.* embark, ship; **II.** *v/refl.*: ***sich*** ~ embark (***nach*** *dat.* for), board the ship; **ˈEin·schif·fung** *f* (-; -en) embarkation

ˈein·schla·fen *v/i.* (*irr.*, *sep.*, sn, → ***schlafen***) **1.** fall asleep, go to sleep, F drop off; ***ich konnte letzte Nacht nicht*** ~ I couldn't get to sleep last night; ***wieder*** ~ go (*or* get) back to sleep; **2.** go to sleep; ***mir ist der rechte Arm eingeschlafen*** *a.* I've got pins and needles in my right arm; **3.** *euphem.* pass away; **4.** *correspondence, conversation etc.*: peter out, F fizzle out; *friendship*: cool off; *tradition etc.*: die out

ein·schlä·fern [ˈaɪnʃlɛːfɐn] *v/t.* (*sep.*, h) **1.** put (*or* send) to sleep; **2.** ⚕ put to sleep; **3.** put down *an animal*, put *an animal* to sleep; **4.** *fig.* salve; lull *s.o.* into a false sense of security; **ˈein·schlä·fernd I.** *adj.* ⚕ *and fig.* soporific; **II.** *adv.*: *die Musik etc.* ***wirkt*** ~ sends you to sleep

ˈEin·schlag *m* (-[e]s; ⸚e) **1.** impact; impact mark; ***beim*** ~ ***des Blitzes*** when the lightning struck; **2.** *fig.* touch, element; ***er hat e-n türkischen*** ~ he's got some Turkish (blood) in him; ***er hat e-n kriminellen*** ~ he's a bit of a crook; ***ein*** ~ ***ins Exotische*** an exotic touch, a touch of the exotic; **3.** *mot.* lock; **4.** tuck, fold; **5.** *textil.* weft, woof; **ˈein·schla·gen** (*irr.*, *sep.*, h, → ***schlagen***) **I.** *v/t.* **1.** hammer in(to ***in*** *acc.*); **2.** smash; break; ***j-m den Schädel*** (***die Zähne***) ~ smash s.o.'s head in (knock s.o.'s teeth out); **3.** wrap up (***in*** *acc.* in); **4.** ***e-n Weg*** ~ take a path, *fig. a.* tread a path, adopt a course; ***e-e Laufbahn*** ~ take up (*or* pursue) a career; → ***Richtung***; **5.** tuck in; **6.** *mot.* turn; ***das Steuer nach rechts*** ~ pull the steering wheel over to the right; **II.** *v/i.* **7.** *bullet etc.*: hit; *lightning*: strike; *fig.* be a big hit, F go down a bomb; ***es schlug in der Kirche ein*** the church was struck by lightning; → ***Blitz*** 1, ***Bombe*** 1; **8.** shake on it; **9.** ~ ***auf*** *acc.* thrash away at

ein·schlä·gig [ˈaɪnʃlɛːgɪç] **I.** *adj.* relevant, appropriate; ***ein*** ~***es Beispiel*** a case in point; ***in allen*** ~***en Geschäften zu finden*** available at all stockists (*or* at your local dealer's); **II.** *adv.*: ***er ist*** ~ ***vorbestraft*** he's been previously convicted for the same (*or* for a similar) offen|ce (*Am.* -se)

ˈein·schlei·chen *v/refl.* (*irr.*, *sep.*, h, → ***schleichen***): ***sich*** ~ creep (*or* sneak) in(to ***in*** *acc.*); *fig. mistake*: creep in(to); *fig.* ***sich in j-s Vertrauen*** ~ worm one's way into s.o.'s confidence

ˈein·schlei·fen (*irr.*, *sep.*, h, → ***schleifen***) **I.** *v/t.* **1.** grind; engrave, cut (***in*** *acc.* into); **2.** ⚡ loop in; **II.** *v/refl.*: ***sich*** ~

behavio(u)r etc.: become a habit, become ingrained, *habit*: take root

'ein·schlep·pen *v/t.* (*sep.*, h) **1.** ⚓ tow in(to **in** *acc.*); **2.** ⚕ bring in(to **in** *acc.*, **nach** *dat.*), introduce (to, into); **3.** F drag along; F have *people* in tow

'ein·schleu·sen *fig. v/t.* (*sep.*, h) infiltrate (**in** *acc.* into); smuggle in(to)

'ein·schlie·ßen *v/t.* (*irr.*, *sep.*, h, → **schließen**) **1.** lock up; ~ **in** *acc. or dat.* lock (up) in, lock into; **2.** enclose; surround, encircle; **3.** *fig.* include; ***j-n in sein Gebet*** ~ remember (*or* include) s.o. in one's prayers; **'ein·schließ·lich** *adv. and prp.* (*gen.*) including, inclusive of; ***bis ~ Seite 7*** up to and including page 7; ***vom 1. bis ~ 4. Mai*** from the 1st to the 4th of May inclusive(ly), *Am.* (from) the 1st through 4th of May; ***von Montag bis ~ Mittwoch*** from Monday to Wednesday inclusive(ly), *Am.* Monday through Wednesday; ***bis ~ Freitag*** up to and including Friday

'ein·schlum·mern *v/i.* (*sep.*, sn) doze off; *fig.* peter out; *euphem.* ***friedlich*** ~ pass away, die peacefully

'Ein·schluß *m* (-sses; ⸚sse) **1.** *geol.* inclusion; **2. *unter*** (*or* ***mit***) ~ ***von*** (*or gen.*) including, with the inclusion of

'ein·schmei·cheln *v/refl.* (*sep.*, h): ***sich bei j-m*** ~ play up to s.o., butter s.o. up; **'ein·schmei·chelnd** *adj.* soft, melodious *tune etc.*, silky *voice*; **'Ein·schmei(·)ch(e)·lung** *f* (-; -en) ingratiation

'ein·schmei·ßen F *v/t.* (*irr.*, *sep.*, h, → **schmeißen**) **1.** smash *window etc.*; **2.** post, *Am.* mail; F throw in; **3.** insert, put in *coin*

'ein·schmel·zen *v/t.* (*irr.*, *sep.*, h, → **schmelzen**) *and v/i.* (sn) melt (down)

'ein·schmie·ren (*sep.*, h) **I.** *v/t.* rub in, put on, rub on; ⚙ grease, lubricate; ~ **in** *acc.* rub into (*or* on), put on; ***die Hände etc.*** ~ put (some) cream on one's hands *etc.*, rub (some) cream into one's hands *etc.*; **II.** *v/refl.*: ***sich*** ~ rub (*or* put) some cream on, rub some oil in

'ein·schmug·geln (*sep.*, h) **I.** *v/t.* smuggle in(to **in** *acc.*); **II.** *v/refl.*: ***sich*** ~ smuggle one's way in(to **in** *acc.*), F sneak in(to)

'ein·schnap·pen *v/i.* (*sep.*, sn) **1.** *lock etc.*: snap shut; *door*: click shut; click into place; **2.** F go into a huff; → ***eingeschnappt***

'ein·schnei·den (*irr.*, *sep.*, h, → **schneiden**) **I.** *v/t.* cut (into); carve (**in** *acc.* into); ***j-m den Hals*** *etc.* ~ cut into s.o.'s neck *etc.*; **II.** *v/i.* cut, pinch; ~ **in** *acc.* cut into, pinch; **'ein·schnei·dend** *fig. adj.* incisive, drastic; radical, major; far-reaching, wide-reaching; ***von ~er Bedeutung*** of far-(*or* wide-)reaching significance; ***~e Wirkungen haben*** have far-reaching effects (***auf*** *acc.* on)

'ein·schnei·dig *adj.* one-edged, single-edged

'Ein·schnitt *m* (-[e]s; -e) **1.** cut; ⚕ *a.* incision; **2.** notch; **3.** cleft; **4.** *fig.* crucial (*or* decisive) event; turning point; break

'ein·schnit·zen *v/t.* (*sep.*, h) carve (**in** *acc.* into)

'ein·schnü·ren *v/t.* (*sep.*, h) tie up; strangle; *sport*: pin down; ***der Gürtel schnürt mich ein*** this belt is far too tight, F I can hardly breathe with this belt on; ***diese Socken schnüren mir die Beine ein*** these socks are cutting off my circulation; *fig.* ***es schnürte ihm die Kehle ein*** it choked him, it brought a lump to his throat

ein·schrän·ken ['aɪnʃrɛŋkən] (*sep.*, h) **I.** *v/t.* limit, restrict (***auf*** *acc.* to); cut (down) *expenditure etc.*, cut down on *smoking etc.*; reduce *size*, *production etc.*; qualify *remark etc.*; → ***eingeschränkt***; **II.** *v/refl.*: ***sich*** ~ cut down (on things), economize; ***sich ~ müssen*** *a.* F have to tighten one's belt; **'ein·schrän·kend I.** *adj.* qualifying; *ling.* restrictive; **II.** *adv.*: ***dazu muß ich ~ hinzufügen*** I should qualify that by saying; **'Ein·schrän·kung** *f* (-; -en) restriction (*gen.* of); cut (in); qualification (of); ***ohne ~ sagen*** *etc.*: without reservation; ***mit der ~, daß*** with the (one) reservation that; ***~en*** cuts; ***~en vornehmen*** make cuts, **in** *dat.*: *a.* cut down on; ***e-e ~ der Ausgaben*** a cut in expenditure

'Ein·schrän·kungs|klau·sel *f* restrictive clause; **~maß·nah·men** *pl.* restrictive measures; ⚚ austerity measures

'ein·schrau·ben *v/t.* (*sep.*, h) screw in(to **in** *acc.*)

'Ein·schrei·be|brief *m* registered letter; **~ge·bühr** *f* registration fee

'ein·schrei·ben (*irr.*, *sep.*, h, → **schreiben**) **I.** *v/t.* enter; enrol(l); ***e-n Brief ~ lassen*** have a letter registered; ***sich ~ lassen*** → **II.** *v/refl.*: ***sich*** ~ sign up; *univ.* register, *Am.* enrol(l); **III.** ♀ *n* (-s; -): ***per ~ schicken*** send *s.th.* registered (*or* by registered mail); ***~!*** Registered; **'Ein·schrei·bung** *f* (-; -en) signing up; *univ.* registration, *Am.* enrollment

'ein·schrei·ten *v/i.* (*irr.*, *sep.*, sn, → **schreiten**) intervene, step in; ~ ***gegen*** *acc.* take action against; ***energisch ~ gegen*** *acc.* take drastic measures against, clamp down on

'ein·schrum·peln F *v/i.* (*sep.*, sn) shrivel (up)

'ein·schrump·fen *v/i.* (*sep.*, sn) shrivel (up); F shrink; *supplies etc.*: dwindle

'Ein·schub *m* (-[e]s; ⸚e) **1.** insertion; **2.** ⚙ plug-in unit

'ein·schüch·tern *v/t.* (*sep.*, h) intimidate, frighten; cow; browbeat; ***laß dich von ihm nicht*** ~ don't be intimidated by him; **'Ein·schüch·te·rung** *f* (-; -en) intimidation; browbeating

'Ein·schüch·te·rungs|po·li,tik *f*, **~tak·tik** *f* scare tactics *pl.*; **~ver·such** *m* attempt to intimidate s.o.; *pol.* scare tactics *pl.*

'ein·schu·len *v/t.* (*sep.*, h) send to school; ***eingeschult werden*** start school; **'Ein·schu·lung** *f* (-; -en) **1.** enrol(l)ment; **2.** first day at school

'Ein·schuß *m* (-sses; ⸚sse) **1.** hit; bullet hole; ⚕ bullet wound; **2.** *sport*: shot (into the goal); **3.** ⚚ capital invested; margin; **4.** *textil.* woof, weft; **♀be·reit** *adj. sport*: F ready to pop the ball home; **~stel·le** *f* point of entry; ***hier ist die ~*** *a.* this is where the bullet entered

'ein·schüt·ten *v/t.* (*sep.*, h) pour in(to **in** *acc.*)

'ein·schwär·zen *v/t.* (*sep.*, h) blacken; *typ.* ink

'ein·schwat·zen (*sep.*, h) **I.** *v/i.*: ***auf j-n*** ~ go on and on; **II.** *v/t.*: ***j-m et.*** ~ talk s.o. into (believing) s.th.

'ein·schwei·ßen *v/t.* (*sep.*, h) **1.** ~ **in** *acc.* weld into; **2.** shrink-wrap

'ein·schwen·ken (*sep.*) **I.** *v/i.* (sn) turn (**in** *acc.* into); ***nach links*** ~ turn (to the) left; *fig.* ~ ***auf*** *acc.* switch to, fall in line with; ***auf e-n neuen Kurs*** ~ change course; **II.** *v/t.* (h) swivel *s.th.* into position; ~ **in** *acc.* swivel into

'ein·seg·nen *v/t.* (*sep.*, h) consecrate, bless; confirm; **'Ein·seg·nung** *f* (-; -en) consecration, blessing; confirmation

'ein·se·hen (*irr.*, *sep.*, h, → **sehen**) **I.** *v/t.* **1.** have a look at; ***die Dokumente dürfen eingesehen werden*** the documents may be viewed (*or* consulted); **2.** *fig.* see; realize; appreciate; ***das sehe ich nicht ein*** I don't see why; ***er will es einfach nicht*** ~ he just won't accept it (*or* see it that way); ***e-n Fehler*** ~ recognize one's mistake; **II.** ♀ *n*: ***ein ~ haben*** show some consideration (*or* understanding); be reasonable; be lenient, show some lenience; F ***das Wetter hatte ein ~ mit uns*** the weather was kind to us

'ein·sei·fen *v/t.* (*sep.*, h) **1.** soap; lather; ***j-n*** ~ lather s.o.'s face; **2.** F *fig.* F con, take *s.o.* for a ride

'Ein·sei·ten·band *n radio*: single sideband, SSB

ein·sei·tig ['aɪnzaɪtɪç] **I.** *adj.* one-sided; *fig. a.* lopsided; *pol.*, ⚖, ⚕ unilateral; ⚕ *a.* on one side; partial, bias(s)ed; exclusive; unbalanced; ***~e Ernährung*** unbalanced diet; ***e-e ~e Lungenentzündung*** single pneumonia; → ***Lähmung***; **II.** *adv. pol.*, ⚖ unilaterally; ***et. ~ darstellen*** give a (very) one-sided view of s.th.; ~ ***begabt***, ~ ***veranlagt*** one-sided; ***er ist nur ~ interessiert*** his interest is very one-sided, he's only interested in one side of it; → ***gelähmt***; **'Ein·sei·tig·keit** *f* (-; *no pl.*) one-sidedness; partiality, bias

'ein·sen·den *v/t.* (*irr.*, *sep.*, h, → **senden**) send in; **'Ein·sen·der** *m* (-s; -) sender; contributor; **'Ein·sen·de·schluß** *m* closing date (for entries); **'Ein·sen·dung** *f* (-; -en) sending in; entry; letter, reply

'ein·sen·ken *v/t.* (*sep.*, h) sink (*or* let) in; ⚒ set; **'Ein·sen·kung** *f* (-; -en) depression

Ein·ser ['aɪnzɐ] F *m* (-s; -) → ***Eins***

'ein·set·zen (*sep.*, h) **I.** *v/t.* **1.** put in; insert; enter (**in** *acc.* into); **2.** set up; **3.** use, employ; apply; *fig.* bring into play; **4.** ⚔ put into action; call in; **5.** bet; ***sein Leben*** ~ risk one's life (***für*** *acc.* for), put one's life at stake (for); **6.** appoint (**in** *acc.* to *an office*); ***als Bevollmächtigten*** (***Erben*** *etc.*) ~ appoint s.o. representative (heir *etc.*); **II.** *v/refl.* **7. *sich*** (***voll***) ~ do one's utmost, F go all out; ***sich ~ für*** *acc.* support, speak up for, champion *a cause*; *w.s.* do what one can for, do one's best to help; ***sich für et. voll ~*** *a.* put everything one has got into s.th.; ***sich*** (***bei j-m***) ***für j-n*** ~ put in a good word for s.o. (with s.o.), *formal*: intercede (with s.o.) on s.o.'s behalf; **III.** *v/i.* **8.** ♪ come in; **9.** start (off); set in; **'Ein·set·zung** *f* (-; -en) insertion; appointment

'Ein·sicht *f* (-; -en) **1.** examination (***in Akten*** of records); ~ ***nehmen in*** *acc.* examine, take a look at; ***j-m ~ gewähren in*** *acc.* allow s.o. to look at; **2.** *fig.* understanding; ***zur ~ kommen*** listen to reason; ***gegen s-e bessere ~*** against one's better judg(e)ment; **3.** *fig.* insight; ***zur ~ kommen, daß*** realize that; **ein·sich·tig** ['aɪnzɪçtɪç] *adj.* **1.** reasonable;

understanding; **2.** cogent; **'Ein·sicht·nah·me** [-na:mə] *f* (-; -n): (***zur*** ~ for) inspection; ***nach*** ~ on sight; **'ein·sichts·los** *adj.* unreasonable; lacking in understanding; **'ein·sichts·voll** *adj.* understanding; reasonable

'ein·sickern (*sep.* -k·k-) *v/i.* (*sep.*, sn) seep *or* trickle in(to ***in*** *acc.*); *fig.* trickle in(to); *spies etc.*: infiltrate (into)

Ein·sie·de·lei [aɪnzi:də'laɪ] *f* (-; -en) **1.** hermitage; **2.** (life of) solitude; **'Ein·sied·ler** *m* (-s; -) *a. fig.* hermit, recluse; **ein·sied·le·risch** ['aɪnzi:dlərɪʃ] *adj.* hermit-like, *lit.* anchoritic; *w.s.* solitary

'Ein·sied·ler|krebs *m zo.* hermit crab; **~le·ben** *n* hermit's life, life of a hermit; ***ein ~ führen*** lead the life of a hermit (*or* a hermit's life), live like a hermit

ein·sil·big ['aɪnzɪlbɪç] *adj.* **1.** monosyllabic; ***~es Wort*** monosyllable; **2.** *fig.* taciturn; curt, short; ***~e Antworten geben*** answer in monosyllables; **'Ein·sil·big·keit** *fig. f* (-; *no pl.*) taciturnity; curtness

'ein·sin·ken *v/i.* (*irr.*, *sep.*, sn, → ***sinken***) sink in(to ***in*** *acc.*); *ground etc.*: subside, cave in

'ein·sit·zen *v/i.* (*irr.*, *sep.*, h, → ***sitzen***) ⚖ serve a sentence

Ein·sit·zer ['aɪnzɪtsɐ] *m* (-s; -) single-seater

'ein·sor,tie·ren *v/t.* (*sep.*, h) sort (***in*** *acc.* into)

'ein·span·nen *v/t.* (*sep.*, h) **1.** ⚙ clamp; put *sheet of paper* in(to the typewriter *etc.*); load, put in *film*; **2.** harness *horse*; F *fig.* ***j-n*** ~ rope s.o. in, ***zu et.:*** rope s.o. into doing s.th.

Ein·spän·ner ['aɪnʃpɛnɐ] *m* (-s; -) **1.** one-horse carriage; **2.** *Austrian*; *glass of black coffee with cream topping*

'ein·spa·ren *v/t.* (*sep.*, h) save; **'Ein·spa·rung** *f* (-; -en) saving(s *pl.*)

'ein·spei·chern *v/t.* (*sep.*, h) **1.** *computer*: store; **2.** *fig.* store (up) in one's memory

'ein·spei·sen *v/t.* (*sep.*, h) ⚙ feed (***in*** *acc.* into, *dat.* to)

'ein·sper·ren *v/t.* (*sep.*, h) lock up; put behind bars; put in a cage, cage

'ein·spie·len (*sep.*, h) **I.** *v/refl.*: ***sich*** ~ **1.** *a. sport*: warm up; *fig.* get going (properly); ***es hat sich gut eingespielt*** it's going (very) well; ***sich auf e-m Instrument*** ~ get the feel of (*or* get used to) an instrument; **2.** ⚙ balance out; **3.** ***sich aufeinander*** ~ learn to work *etc.* together, get used to one another; ***sie sind gut aufeinander eingespielt*** they make a good team; **II.** *v/t.* **4.** ♪ break in *violin etc.*; **5.** record; **6.** bring in; **'Ein·spiel·er·geb·nis·se** *pl.* box-office returns; **'Ein·spie·lung** *f* (-; -en) recording (***von*** *dat.* by)

'ein·spin·nen (*irr.*, *sep.*, h, → ***spinnen***) **I.** *v/refl.*: ***sich*** ~ **1.** *zo.* cocoon itself; **2.** *fig.* cocoon (*or* seclude) o.s.; ***eingesponnen in*** *acc.* wrapped up in, (deeply) absorbed in; **II.** *v/t. zo.* spin a web around

ein·spra·chig ['aɪnʃpra:xɪç] *adj.* monolingual

'ein·spren·gen *v/t.* (*sep.*, h) sprinkle; → ***eingesprengt***; **Ein·spreng·sel** ['aɪnʃprɛŋzəl] *n* (-s; -) insert, insertion; isolated element

'ein·sprin·gen *v/i.* (*irr.*, *sep.*, sn, → ***springen***) **1.** *fig.* step in(to the breach), help out, F chip in; ***für j-n*** ~ step (*or* stand) in for s.o.; **2.** ⚙ click (into place), catch, snap; **3.** △ recede; **'ein·sprin·gend** *adj.* **1.** △ recessed, set back; **2.** A ***~er Winkel*** reentrant angle

'Ein·spritz·dü·se *f mot.* injection nozzle; jet

'ein·sprit·zen *v/t.* (*sep.*, h) inject (***in*** *acc.* into); ***j-m et.*** ~ give s.o. an injection of s.th., inject s.o. with s.th.

'Ein·spritz|mo·tor *m* fuel injection engine; **~pum·pe** *f mot.* (fuel) injection pump

'Ein·spruch *m* (-[e]s; ⸚e) *a.* ⚖ objection (***gegen*** *acc.* to); ⚖ appeal (against); *patent law*: opposition (to); ~ ***erheben*** raise an objection (***gegen*** *acc.* to), object (to), ⚖ (file an) appeal (against); **'Ein·spruchs·recht** *n* right to appeal; *pol.* (power of) veto

ein·spu·rig ['aɪnʃpu:rɪç] *adj.* 🚂 single-track ..., *pred.* single-tracked; single-lane *road*

'Eins·sein *n* (-s; *no pl.*) oneness, unity (***mit*** *dat.* with)

einst [aɪnst] *adv.* **1.** once; ***... ~ und jetzt*** ... past and present, ... then and now; ***das England von ~*** the England of days past (*or* of former days), England as it once was; **2.** one day, some day

'ein·stamp·fen *v/t.* (*sep.*, h) press; stamp down; pulp *books etc.*

'Ein·stand *m* (-[e]s; ⸚e) **1.** *tennis*: deuce; **2.** first day (in a new job *etc.*); ***s-n ~ feiern*** celebrate the start of one's new job; ***s-n ~ geben*** *a. sport*: make one's debut (*or* début)

'ein·stan·zen *v/t.* (*sep.*, h) stamp in(to ***in*** *acc.*)

'ein·stau·ben *v/t.* (*sep.*, h) dust; → ***eingestaubt***

'ein·ste·chen (*irr.*, *sep.*, h, → ***stechen***) **I.** *v/t.* prick, pierce; stick *needle* in(to ***in*** *acc.*); insert (in); ⚙ cut; engrave (into); **II.** *v/i.*: ***mit e-r Nadel*** *etc.* ***~ in*** *acc.* stick a needle *etc.* into; ~ ***auf*** *acc.* stab away at *s.o.*

'ein·stecken (*sep.* -k·k-) *v/t.* (*sep.*, h) put in, F stick in; put in one's pocket (*or* bag *etc.*); F pop into the letterbox; take; F pocket (*a. fig.*); *fig.* swallow; take *blow*; ***steck's schnell ein!*** put it away quick!; F *fig.* ***er kann viel ~*** he can take a lot (of punishment); F ***er hat schwer ~ müssen*** he took quite a beating; F ***viel ~ müssen*** F have to take a lot of stick; F ***den steckst du leicht ein*** you can beat him with your hands tied; **'Ein·steck·tuch** *n* breast-pocket handkerchief

'ein·ste·hen *v/i.* (*irr.*, *sep.*, h, → ***stehen***): ***~ für*** *acc.* answer for, take responsibility for, vouch for; stand by, stick by; ***für s-e Überzeugung ~*** have the courage of one's convictions; ***ich stehe dafür ein, daß*** I guarantee (you) that

'ein·stei·gen *v/i.* (*irr.*, *sep.*, sn, → ***steigen***) get in(to ***in*** *acc.*); (*a.* ***~ in*** *acc.*) get on *a bus, train, plane etc.*; climb in(to); ***alle(s) ~!*** all aboard!; ***steigt ein!*** jump in!; *fig.* ***~ in*** *acc.* join, get into, go into *politics*; ***mit e-r hohen Summe in et. ~*** invest (F sink) a large sum of money in (into) s.th.; F ***hart ~*** *sport*: F go for it; **'Ein·stei·ger** *m* (-s; -) newcomer (***in*** *acc.* to)

ein·stell·bar ['aɪnʃtɛlba:ɐ] *adj.* adjustable; **'ein·stel·len** (*sep.*, h) **I.** *v/t.* **1.** put in(to ***in*** *acc.*); store; put in the garage, put away; **2.** take on, hire; **3.** ⚙ set; tune *radio* in(to ***auf*** *acc.*); *TV* switch (to); *opt.* focus; *phot.* ***auf e-e größere Blende ~*** use a bigger aperture, open up the aperture; **4.** stop; discontinue; ⚖ suspend *proceedings*, drop *the case*; ✕ ***das Feuer ~*** stop shooting (*or* firing); ***die Feindseligkeiten ~*** cease (*or* end) hostilities; **5.** *fig.* adjust, adapt (***auf*** *acc.* to); focus (on); **6.** *sport*: equal *a record*; **II.** *v/refl.* **7.** ***sich ~*** appear, turn up; *fig.* set in; *difficulties etc.*: arise; ensue, make themselves felt; ***sich wieder ~*** come back (again); **8.** ***sich ~ auf*** *acc.* adapt *or* adjust (o.s. *or* itself) to, prepare (o.s.) for, get ready for, F gear (o.s.) up for, be prepared for; ***sich geistig ~ auf*** *acc.* get into the right frame of mind for, F gear o.s. up mentally for; ***sich (voll und) ganz ~ auf*** *acc.* a) focus all one's attention on, b) adjust one's whole lifestyle (*or* way of thinking) to; ***du mußt dich darauf ~*** you'll have to get used to it (*or* learn to accept it); → ***eingestellt***

ein·stel·lig ['aɪnʃtɛlɪç] *adj.* one-digit *number*; one-place *decimal*

'Ein·stell|knopf *m* control (knob); **~platz** *m* parking space; **~schrau·be** *f* set screw

'Ein·stel·lung *f* (-; -en) **1.** employment; **2.** ⚙ adjustment, setting; timing; *opt.*, *phot.* focus([s]ing); *film*: angle, *w.s.* shot; **3.** discontinuance; stoppage; suspension *of payments*; ⚖ stay, discontinuance *of proceedings*; dismissal *of action*; ***~ der Feindseligkeiten*** suspension (*or* cessation) of hostilities; **4.** attitude (***zu*** *dat.* to[wards]), approach (to); outlook (on *life*); ***politische ~*** political views *pl.* (*or* outlook); ***was ist denn das für e-e ~?*** what kind of (an) attitude is that?; ***das ist e-e Frage der ~*** → ***Einstellungsfrage***

'Ein·stel·lungs|än·de·rung *f* change of (*or* in) approach *or* attitude; **~fra·ge** *f*: ***das ist e-e ~*** it depends on how (*or* the way) you look at things; **~ge·spräch** *n* (job) interview; **~stopp** *m* freeze on further recruitment

'Ein·stich *m* (-[e]s; -e) prick; ***der ~ hat weh getan*** it hurt when he (*or* she) put the needle in

Ein·stieg ['aɪnʃti:k] *m* (-[e]s; -e [-ʃti:gə]) **1.** entrance, way in; **2.** ***beim ~*** while getting in; ***der ~ war schwierig*** it was difficult getting (*or* to get) in; *fig.* it was hard at the start (*or* beginning); *fig.* ***der ~ in ein solches Thema ist nicht einfach*** it's not easy getting into that kind of subject; ***der ~ ins Berufsleben*** starting (*or* embarking on) a career; ***der ~ in e-e neue Stelle*** starting (*or* settling [down]) into, getting into) a new job; **~lu·ke** *f* (access) hatch

'Ein·stiegs·dro·ge *f* gateway drug

ein·stig ['aɪnstɪç] *adj.* former, *formal*: erstwhile; F one-time *president etc.*

'ein·stim·men (*sep.*, h) **I.** *v/i.* **1.** ♪ join in; **2.** *fig.* join in *the applause etc.*; agree (***in*** *acc.* to); **II.** *v/t.* **3.** ♪ tune (up) *instrument*; **4.** *fig.* get *s.o.* into the right mood (***auf*** *acc.* for); **III.** *fig. v/refl.*: ***sich ~*** get into the right mood (***auf*** *acc.* for)

ein·stim·mig ['aɪnʃtɪmɪç] **I.** *adj.* **1.** unanimous; **2.** ♪ for one voice; **II.** *adv.* **3.** unanimously, to a man; **4.** ♪ *sing etc.* in unison; **'Ein·stim·mig·keit** *f* (-; *no pl.*) unanimity, consensus; ***~ erzielen*** come to an agreement, reach a consensus (***über*** *acc.* on)

einst·ma·lig ['aɪnstma:lɪç] *adj.* → ***einstig***; **einst·mals** ['aɪnstma:ls] → ***einst***

ein·stöckig ['aınʃtœkıç] (*sep.* -k·k-) *adj.* one-stor(e)y ...
'ein·stöp·seln *v/t.* (*sep.*, h) put in, plug in
'ein·sto·ßen *v/t.* (*irr.*, *sep.*, h, → ***stoßen***) push in; smash (in) *windows etc.*; break down *door etc.*
'ein·strah·len (*sep.*, h) **I.** *v/i.* shine (***in*** *acc.* into; ***auf*** *acc.* on); **II.** *v/t.* radiate (***auf*** *acc.* onto); **'Ein·strah·lung** *f* (-; -en) radiation
'ein·strei·chen *v/t.* (*irr.*, *sep.*, h, → ***streichen***) **1.** ***mit Gips*** *etc.* ~ fill *s.th.* with plaster *etc.*; ***mit Farbe*** ~ paint, give *s.th.* a coat of paint; **2.** cut *text etc.* down (to size); **3.** F rake in *money etc.*; F pocket
'ein·streu·en *v/t.* (*sep.*, h) **1.** sprinkle in(to ***in*** *acc.*); **2.** *fig.* put in(to ***in*** *acc.*), slip in(to); ***Zitate*** *etc.* ***in et.*** ~ intersperse s.th. with quotations
'ein·strö·men *v/i.* (*sep.*, sn) pour in(to ***in*** *acc.*); come in(to), stream in(to); *fig.* pour in(to), stream in(to)
'ein·stuˌdie·ren *v/t.* (*sep.*, h) learn (by heart); rehearse; **'Ein·stuˌdie·rung** *f* (-; -en) *thea.* production
'ein·stu·fen *v/t.* (*sep.*, h) class; assess; ~ ***in*** *acc.* put in(to *tax bracket etc.*); ***hoch*** (***niedrig***) ~ rate high (low); ***j-n falsch*** ~ assess s.o. wrongly, misjudge s.o.('s capabilities)
ein·stu·fig ['aınʃtu:fıç] *adj.* ⚙ single-stage ...
Ein·stu·fung ['aınʃtu:fʊŋ] *f* (-; -en) classification; rating; **'Ein·stu·fungs·prü·fung** *f* placement test
ein·stün·dig ['aınʃtʏndıç] *adj.* one--hour(-long) ...
'ein·stür·men *v/i.* (*sep.*, sn): ~ ***auf*** *acc.* rush at, *a.* ⚔ charge; *fig.* ***auf j-n*** ~ assail s.o. (*a. fig.*)
'Ein·sturz *m* (-es; ⸚e) collapse; ***dem*** ~ ***nahe*** about to collapse; ***vom*** ~ ***bedroht*** in danger of collapsing; ***zum*** ~ ***bringen*** cause *s.th.* to collapse (*or* cave in); **'ein·stür·zen** *v/i.* (*sep.*, sn) cave in; *fig.* ~ ***auf*** *acc.* assail; **'Ein·sturz·ge·fahr** *f*: „~!" danger - building unsafe; ***es ist wegen*** ~ ***geschlossen*** it's closed because it's unsafe
einst·wei·len ['aınst'vaılən] *adv.* meanwhile, in the meantime; for the time being; **einst·wei·lig** ['aınst'vaılıç] *adj.* temporary, provisional, interim ...; ⚖ ~***e Verfügung*** interim order, injunction
ein·tä·gig ['aıntɛ:gıç] *adj.* **1.** one-day ...; **2.** *zo.*, ⚘, ⚕ ephemeral
'Ein·tags·flie·ge *f* **1.** *fig.* nine days' wonder; flash in the pan; **2.** *zo.* dayfly, ephemera
'ein·ta·sten *v/t.* (*sep.*, h) *computer*: key in
'ein·tau·chen (*sep.*) **I.** *v/t.* (h) dip in(to ***in*** *acc.*); **II.** *v/i.* (sn) dive in(to ***in*** *acc.*)
'Ein·tausch *m*: ***im*** ~ ***für*** (*or* ***gegen***) *acc.* in exchange for; **'ein·tau·schen** *v/t.* (*sep.*, h) exchange (***gegen*** *acc.* for)
'ein'tau·send *adj.* a (*or* one) thousand
'ein·tei·len *v/t.* (*sep.*, h) divide (up) (***in*** *acc.* into); arrange (***in*** *acc.* in; ***nach*** *dat.* according to); organize *one's time*; ***sein Geld richtig*** ~ budget; ***zur Wache*** ~ put on guard duty
ein·tei·lig ['aıntaılıç] *adj.* one-piece ...
'Ein·tei·lung *f* (-; -en) division; arrangement; plan, schedule; budgeting
ein·tö·nig ['aıntø:nıç] **I.** *adj.* monotonous; humdrum, dull; **II.** *adv.*: ~ ***vorlesen*** read out in a monotonous tone (of voice); **'Ein·tö·nig·keit** *f* (-; *no pl.*) monotony
'Ein·topf(ge·richt *n*) *m* stew
Ein·tracht ['aıntraxt] *f* (-; *no pl.*) harmony, concord; unity; ***völlige*** ~ complete (*or* perfect) harmony; ***in*** ~ ***leben*** live in harmony; **ein·träch·tig** ['aıntrɛçtıç] *adj.* harmonious; peaceful
Ein·trag ['aıntra:k] *m* (-[e]s; Einträge ['aıntrɛ:gə]) **1.** entry, item; **2.** *fig.* ***e-r Sache*** ~ ***tun*** harm; **'ein·tra·gen** (*irr.*, *ssep.*, h, → ***tragen***) **I.** *v/t.* **1.** put down (***in*** *acc.* on *a list etc.*); enter (into); *adm.* register (***bei*** *dat.* with); enrol(l) (in); → ***eingetragen*** II; **2.** bring in; net; *fig.* ***j-m et.*** ~ earn s.o. s.th.; *fig.* ***es trug ihm den Haß s-r Kollegen ein*** *a.* it incurred his colleagues' hatred; **II.** *v/refl.*: ***sich*** ~ put one's name down (on the list), *a.* sign up; **ein·träg·lich** ['aıntrɛ:klıç] *adj.* profitable, lucrative; **'Ein·tra·gung** *f* (-; -en) entry; *adm.* registration; item
'ein·trän·ken *v/t.* (*sep.*, h) **1.** soak; **2.** F *fig.* ***dem werd' ich's*** ~**!** I'll make him pay for it
'ein·träu·feln *v/t.* (*sep.*, h) **1.** ***et.*** ~ ***in*** *acc.* put some drops in; **2.** *fig.* instil(l) (***in*** *acc.* into)
'ein·tref·fen *v/i.* (*irr.*, *sep.*, sn, → ***treffen***) **1.** arrive, come, get here (*or* there); → ***eingetroffen*** II; **2.** happen; prove true; ***es ist alles so eingetroffen, wie er es voraussagte*** it all happened just as he had predicted
'ein·trei·ben *v/t.* (*irr.*, *sep.*, h, → ***treiben***) **1.** drive home; **2.** collect *debts*; **3.** drive in *nail etc.*
'ein·tre·ten (*irr.*, *sep*, sn, → ***treten***) **I.** *v/i.* **1.** go in(to ***in*** *acc.*), come in(to), (*a.* ~ ***in*** *acc.*) enter; **2.** *fig.* ~ ***in*** *acc.* take up *office etc.*; enter *the war*, join *firm*, *club etc.*; enter into *negotiations*, go into *politics*; ***in ein Kloster*** ~ enter (*or* go into) a monastery *or* convent; **3.** happen, take place, occur; arise; *dusk*, *silence*: fall; *meteor.* set in; *death*: occur; ***der Tod trat auf der Stelle ein*** death was instantaneous; ***es ist noch keine Besserung eingetreten*** there has been no improvement as yet; **4.** ***für j-n*** ~ stand (*or* speak) up for s.o., intervene on s.o.'s behalf; → ***einspringen*** 1; ***für et.*** ~ speak out in favo(u)r of s.th., support s.th., give s.th. one's full backing; plead for; **II.** *v/t.* **5.** stamp in(to the ground); tread *crumbs etc.* in(to the carpet); **6.** kick down *the door etc.*; **7.** ***sich et.*** ~ run (*or* get) s.th. into one's foot; **III.** ∼ *n* (-s) → ***Eintritt***
ein·trich·tern ['aıntrıçtɐn] *v/t.* (*sep.*, h): *fig.* ***j-m et.*** ~ drum s.th. into s.o.'s head
Ein·tritt *m* (-[e]s; -e) **1.** entry (***in*** *acc.* into); entrance (into); „~ ***verboten!***" no admittance; **2.** *fig.* entry (***in*** *acc.* into); ~ ***in e-e Firma*** (***Partei***) joining a company (party); ***nach s-m*** ~ ***in die Partei*** *etc.* after he had joined the party *etc.*; **3.** beginning, start; *meteor.*, ⚕ *etc.*: onset; ***nach*** ~ ***der Dunkelheit*** after dark; **4.** occurrence; **5.** admission; ~ ***frei*** admission free; ***was verlangen sie für den*** ~**?** what do they charge for admission?; **6.** → ***Eintrittsgebühr, Eintrittsgeld***
'Ein·tritts|ge·bühr *f*, ~**geld** *n* admission fee; *sport*: gate money; ~**kar·te** *f* (admission) ticket
'ein·trock·nen *v/i.* (*sep.*, sn) dry up; shrivel up
'ein·trom·meln *v/i.* (*sep.*, h) **1.** *fig.* ***j-m et.*** ~ drum s.th. into s.o.('s head); **2.** ~ ***auf*** *acc.* pound (*or* hit, F bash) away at
'ein·tröp·feln *v/t.* → ***einträufeln***
'ein·trü·ben *v/refl.* (*sep.*, h): ***sich*** ~ *meteor.* become overcast
'ein·tru·deln F *v/i.* (*sep.*, sn) F shuffle in
'ein·üben *v/t.* (*sep.*, h) (*a.* ***sich et.*** ~) practi|se (*Am.* -ce)
ein·ver·lei·ben ['aınfɛɐlaıbən] *v/t.* (verleibte ein, einverleibt, h) **1.** add (*dat. or* ***in*** *acc.* to); annex(e) (to); **2.** F ***sich et.*** ~ F stow (*or* put) away; **'Ein·ver·lei·bung** *f* (-; -en) annexation
Ein·ver·neh·men ['aınfɛɐne:mən] *n* (-s; *no pl.*) agreement, understanding; ***in gutem*** ~ on good (*or* friendly) terms; ***im*** ~ ***mit*** *dat.* after consultation with, in agreement with; ***im gegenseitigen*** ~ by mutual agreement; ***sich mit j-m ins*** ~ ***setzen*** come to an understanding (*or* agreement) with s.o.; **ein·ver·nehm·lich** ['aınfɛɐne:mlıç] **I.** *adj.* amicable; **II.** *adv.* amicably, by mutual agreement
'ein·ver·stan·den *adj.*: ~ ***sein*** (***mit*** *dat.*), ***sich*** ~ ***erklären*** (***mit*** *dat.*) agree (to), be agreed, approve (of); ***damit*** ~ ***sein, daß j-d et. tut*** agree to (*or* approve of) s.o.('s) doing s.th.; ***damit*** ~ ***sein zu*** *inf.* agree to *inf.*; ***damit bin ich ganz und gar nicht*** ~ a) I disagree totally (*or* entirely), b) I don't approve at all, I don't like it at all; ***er ist mit allem*** ~ he has no objections, he doesn't mind one way or another; ***ich bin damit*** ~ it's all right (*Am.* alright) with me; ~**!** okay, all right, *Am.* alright; F it's a deal
'Ein·ver·ständ·nis *n* (-ses; *no pl.*) **1.** consent (***zu*** *dat.* to), approval (of); ***sein*** ~ ***geben*** (give one's) consent (***zu*** *dat.* to); **2.** ***geheimes*** ~ tacit understanding, *esp.* ⚖ collusion, connivance; ~**er·klä·rung** *f* (declaration of) consent
'ein·wach·sen[1] *v/i.* (*irr.*, *sep.*, sn, → ***wachsen***) *nail*: grow in(to ***in*** *acc.*); → ***eingewachsen*** II
'ein·wach·sen[2] *v/t.* (*sep.*, h) wax
Ein·wand ['aınvant] *m* (-[e]s; Einwände ['aınvɛndə]) objection (***gegen*** *acc.* to); ***e-n*** ~ ***vorbringen*** raise an objection
'Ein·wan·de·rer *m* (-s; -) immigrant; incomer; **'ein·wan·dern** *v/i.* (*sep.*, sn) immigrate (***in*** *acc.* to); **'Ein·wan·de·rung** *f* (-; -en) immigration
'Ein·wan·de·rungs|be·hör·de *f* immigration authorities *pl.*; ~**er·laub·nis** *f* immigration permit; ~**po·liˌtik** *f* immigration policy; ~**quo·te** *f* immigration quota; ~**strom** *m* flow (*or* influx) of immigrants; ~**ver·bot** *n* ban on immigration
'ein·wand·frei **I.** *adj.* perfect, flawless; impeccable; incontestable; *gastr.* good, fresh; ***es ist alles*** ~ everything's perfect (*or* in perfect condition); ***er spricht ein*** ~***es Englisch*** his English is perfect, he speaks perfect (*or* flawless) English; **II.** *adv.*: ~ ***der Beste*** undoubtedly the best; ***sich*** ~ ***benehmen*** behave impeccably; ~ ***funktionieren*** work perfectly, be in perfect working order, *fig.* work out perfectly, go perfectly; ~ ***beweisen*** prove beyond doubt; ***es steht*** ~ ***fest*** it's indisputable, ***daß:*** there's no question that
ein·wärts ['aınvɛrts] *adv.* inward(s)
'ein·we·ben *v/t.* (*sep.*, h) *a. fig.* work in(to ***in*** *acc.*)
'ein·wech·seln *v/t.* (*sep.*, h) **1.** (ex)change; cash; **2.** *sport*: bring on
'ein·wecken (*sep.* -k·k-) *v/t.* (*sep.*, h) pre-

serve, *Am. a.* can; bottle; pickle; '**Ein·weck·glas** *n* preserving (*Am.* canning) jar

Ein·weg|fla·sche ['aınve:k-] *f* non-returnable bottle; **~packung** (*sep.* -k·k-) *f* throwaway pack; **~ra·sie·rer** [-ra,zi:rɐ] *m* (-s; -) disposable razor; **~schei·be** *f* one-way glass; **~spie·gel** *m* two-way mirror; **~sprit·ze** *f* disposable syringe

'**ein·wei·chen** *v/t.* (*sep.*, h) soak

'**ein·wei·hen** *v/t.* (*sep.*, h) **1.** open; *eccl.* consecrate; F christen; ***s-e Wohnung ~*** have a housewarming (*or* flatwarming) party; **2.** ***~ in** acc.* initiate into; ***j-n in ein Geheimnis ~*** let s.o. into a secret; → ***eingeweiht, Eingeweihte***; '**Ein·wei·hung** *f* (-; -en) (formal) opening; *eccl.* consecration

'**Ein·wei·hungs|fei·er** *f* opening ceremony; housewarming (*or* flatwarming) party; **~re·de** *f* inaugural address

'**ein·wei·sen** *v/t.* (*irr.*, *sep.*, h, → ***weisen***) **1.** ***~ in** acc.* admit to *hospital, a home etc.*; ***in e-e Anstalt ~*** institutionalize; **2.** ***j-n in e-e Aufgabe ~*** show s.o. what to do; ***j-n in s-e neue Stelle ~*** introduce s.o. to his (*or* her) new job, F show s.o. the ropes; **3.** instal(l) (***in** acc.* in), inaugurate (into *office etc.*); **4.** *mot.* direct (***in** acc.* into); **Ein·wei·ser** ['aınvaızɐ] *m* (-s; -) ✈ marshal(l)er; '**Ein·wei·sung** *f* (-; -en) **1.** admittance (***in** acc.* to *hospital, a home etc.*); **2.** introduction (***in** acc.* to); induction course; **3.** induction, inauguration *into office etc.*

'**ein·wen·den** *v/t.* (*irr.*, *sep.*, h, → ***wenden***): ***~, daß*** object (*or* argue) that; ***er wandte (dagegen) ein, daß*** *a.* he raised (*or* made) the objection that; ***dagegen läßt sich ~, daß*** it could be objected that; ***ich habe nichts dagegen einzuwenden*** I have no objections; ***es läßt sich nichts dagegen ~*** there's nothing to be said against it; ***sie hat immer irgend etwas einzuwenden*** she always finds something to object to (*or* complain about); ***wenn niemand etwas einzuwenden hat*** if there are no objections (from anyone); '**Ein·wen·dung** *f* (-; -en) objection (***gegen** acc.* to); ***~en erheben gegen** acc.* raise objections to

'**ein·wer·fen** (*irr.*, *sep.*, h, → ***werfen***) **I.** *v/t.* **1.** throw in; post, *Am.* mail, F pop into the letterbox (*or* mailbox); insert, put in *coin etc.*; *fig.* throw in *remark etc.*; **2.** smash, break; **II.** *v/i.* **3.** *sport*: throw in; **4.** *fig.* ***~, daß*** object (*or* argue) that

ein·wer·tig ['aınve:ɐtıç] *adj.* ⚗ monovalent; '**Ein·wer·tig·keit** *f* (-; *no pl.*) monovalence

'**ein·wickeln** (*sep.* -k·k-) *v/t.* (*sep.*, h) **1.** wrap up (***in** acc.* in); **2.** F *fig.* take in, fool; F soft-soap; ***laß dich nicht von ihm ~*** don't be taken in by him, don't fall for his line; '**Ein·wickel·pa,pier** *n* wrapping paper

'**ein·wie·gen** *v/t.* (*sep.*, h) **1.** rock *s.o.* to sleep; **2.** *fig.* lull

ein·wil·li·gen ['aınvılıgən] *v/i.* (willigte ein, eingewilligt, h) agree (***in** acc.* to); consent (to); '**Ein·wil·li·gung** *f* (-; -en) approval; consent; ***s-e ~ zu et. geben*** consent to s.th.

'**ein·win·ken** *v/t.* (*sep.*, h) *mot.* wave (***in** acc.* into); ✈ marshal

'**ein·wir·ken** *v/i.* (*sep.*, h): ***~ auf** acc.* have an effect on; affect; influence; work on *s.o.*; ***et. ~ lassen*** let s.th. take effect (***auf** acc.* on), let s.th. work itself in(to), *fig.* (*a.* ***auf sich ~ lassen***) let s.th. sink in; *Creme etc.* ***fünf Minuten ~ lassen*** leave on for five minutes; ***versuchen, auf j-n einzuwirken*** *a.* try and talk to s.o.; '**Ein·wir·kung** *f* (-; -en) effect (***auf** acc.* on); *pharm. etc.*: effects *pl.* (on); *a. pl.* influence (on)

'**Ein·wir·kungs|be·reich** *m*, **~sphä·re** *f* sphere of influence; ***in j-s ~ geraten*** come under s.o.'s spell

ein·wö·chig ['aınvœçıç] *adj.* **1.** week-long ..., one-week ...; **2.** week-old ...

Ein·woh·ner ['aınvo:nɐ] *m* (-s; -) inhabitant; resident; '**Ein·woh·ner·mel·de·amt** *n* residents' registration office; '**Ein·woh·ner·schaft** *f* (-; -en) inhabitants *pl.*, population; '**Ein·woh·ner·zahl** *f* (total) population, number of inhabitants

'**Ein·wurf** *m* (-[e]s; ⸚e) **1.** *soccer*: throw in; **2.** insertion; ***nach ~ der Münze*** after inserting the coin; **3.** slot; opening, slit; **4.** *fig.* objection

'**ein·wur·zeln** *v/i.* (*sep.*, sn) *and v/refl.* (***sich ~***) (h) take root; *fig.* put down (one's) roots, settle down; → ***eingewurzelt***

'**Ein·zahl** *f* (-; *no pl.*) *ling.* singular

'**ein·zah·len** *v/t.* (*sep.*, h) pay in; deposit (***in** acc.* at); ***auf ein Konto ~*** pay *s.th.* into an account, deposit *s.th.* in an account; '**Ein·zah·lung** *f* (-; -en) payment; deposit; instal(l)ment; '**Ein·zah·lungs·schein** *m* pay(ing)-in slip, *Am.* deposit slip

ein·zäu·nen ['aıntsɔʏnən] *v/t.* (*sep.*, h) fence in; '**Ein·zäu·nung** *f* (-; -en) enclosure; fence

'**ein·zeich·nen** *v/t.* (*sep.*, h) draw in, sketch in; mark (***in** acc. or dat.*, ***auf** dat.* on); ***die Stadt ist nicht eingezeichnet*** the town isn't on the map

ein·zei·lig ['aıntsaılıç] *adj.* one-line ...; (*a. adv.* ***~ geschrieben***) single-spaced

Ein·zel ['aıntsəl] *n* (-s; -) *tennis etc.*: singles *pl.*

'**Ein·zel|ab,teil** *n* separate compartment; **~ak·ti,on** *f* act of an individual; ***es war e-e ~*** *a.* he (*or* she) acted alone; **~an·fer·ti·gung** *f*: ***es ist e-e ~*** I *etc.* had it specially made, it was custom-built; **~an·trieb** *m* ⚙ separate drive; **~auf·hän·gung** *f mot.* independent suspension; **~auf·stel·lung** *f* itemized list; **~aus·ga·be** *f* separate edition; **~aus·stel·ler** *m* individual exhibitor; **~bei·spiel** *n* isolated case; **~be·ra·tung** *f*: *parl.* ***in ~ eintreten*** go into committee; **~bett** *n* single bed

'**Ein·zel·bild** *n video*: (single) frame; **~ta·ste** *f* frame button

'**Ein·zel|dar·stel·lung** *f* individual study; monograph; **~dis·zi,plin** *f sport*: individual event; **~er·schei·nung** *f* isolated instance; **~ex·em,plar** *n* rare *or* unique specimen (*or* copy); **~fahr·kar·te** *f* single-trip (*or* one-trip) ticket; **~fall** *m* isolated case; **~fir·ma** *f* one-man business; **~fra·ge** *f* individual question; detailed question

'**Ein·zel·gän·ger** [-gɛŋɐ] *m* (-s; -) loner, F lone wolf; *esp. pol.* maverick; rogue elephant *etc.*; '**ein·zel·gän·ge·risch** [-gɛŋərıʃ] *adj.* solitary, lone ...

'**Ein·zel|ge·spräch** *n* one-to-one conversation; **~haft** *f* solitary confinement

'**Ein·zel·han·del** *m* (-s; *no pl.*) retail trade; '**Ein·zel·han·dels·ge·schäft** *n* retail shop; '**Ein·zel·han·dels·preis** *m* retail price; '**Ein·zel·händ·ler** *m* (-s; -) retailer

'**Ein·zel|haus** *n* detached house; **~haus·halt** *m* one-person household; **~heft** *n* individual (*or* single) issue

'**Ein·zel·heit** *f* (-; -en) detail; ***nähere ~en*** further details; ***ausführliche ~en*** full particulars; ***bis in alle ~en*** down to the last detail; ***auf ~en eingehen*** go into detail (*or* particulars); ***ich will nicht auf alle ~en eingehen*** I don't want to bore you with all the details; ***er kennt die ~en*** he knows all the details, he knows the ins and outs

'**Ein·zel|in·itia,ti·ve** *f* individual initiative; **~in·ter,es·sen** *pl.* individual (*or* personal) interests; **~ka,bi·ne** *f* single cabin; **~kampf** *m* ⚔ single combat, hand-to-hand fighting; F ✈ dogfight; *sport*: individual competition; **~kind** *n an* only child; **~ko·sten** *pl.* itemized costs; **~kre,dit** *m* personal loan

Ein·zel·ler ['aıntsɛlɐ] *m* (-s; -) protozoon, protozoan, monad; **ein·zel·lig** ['aıntsɛlıç] *adj.* single-cell ..., *pred. a.* single-celled; 🕮 monocellular

ein·zeln ['aıntsəln] **I.** *adj.* **1.** single; individual; separate; isolated; particular; ***jedes ~e Stück*** each individual piece, every single piece; ***die ~en Mitgliedsstaaten*** the individual (*or* various) member states; ***et. in s-e ~en Teile zerlegen*** take s.th. apart (*or* to pieces); **2.** odd *shoe, glove etc.*; **3.** ***~e*** some, one or two, isolated ...; ***es gab ~e Proteste*** *a.* there were protests here and there; **II.** *indef. pron.*: ***der ~e*** the individual; ***jeder ~e*** every single person (*or* one), every one of them; ***~es*** some (things, points *etc.*); ***im ~en*** a) in detail, b) in particular; ***im ~en geht es um folgende Fragen*** we are concerned specifically with the following questions; ***ins ~e gehen*** go into detail; **III.** *adv.* individually; separately; one by one, one at a time; ***~ angeben*** specify

'**Ein·zel|paar** *n* odd pair; **~packung** *f* single pack; **~per,son** *f* single person; unaccompanied person; ***für e-e ~*** for one person (only); **~rad·auf·hän·gung** *f mot.* independent suspension; **~rei·sen·de** *m, f* (-n; -n) lone (*or* individual) travel(l)er; **~schick·sal** *n* personal tragedy; **~spiel** *n tennis*: singles *pl.*, singles match; **⁓ste·hend** *adj.* isolated; *pl. a.* scattered; **~stück** *n* **1.** odd piece; **2.** unique specimen; **~tä·ter** *m* lone operator; **~teil** *n* (component) part; **~,un·ter·richt** *m* private lessons *pl.*, coaching; **~ver·packung** *f* individual packaging; **~wahl** *f* uninominal voting; **~we·sen** *n* individual (being); **~zel·le** *f* **1.** solitary cell; **2.** *biol.* single cell

'**Ein·zel·zim·mer** *n* single room; **~zu·schlag** *m* single-room supplement

ein·zieh·bar ['aıntsi:ba:ɐ] *adj.* ⚙ retractable; ♆ collectible; ⚖ seizable; '**ein·zie·hen** (*irr.*, *sep.*, → ***ziehen***) **I.** *v/t.* (h) **1.** pull in *stomach*; draw in *claws*; ⚙, ✈ retract; hand down *flag*; take in *sails*; haul in, pull in *fishing nets*; thread; ***den Kopf ~*** duck; ***den Bauch ~*** *a.* F breathe in; **2.** put in; put up *wall*; **3.** draw in, breathe in, inhale; absorb, soak in (*or* up); **4.** *typ.* indent; **5.** ⚔ call up, *Am.* draft; **6.** ⚖ seize, confiscate; ♆ collect; cash; withdraw (from circulation); **7.** ***Erkundigungen ~*** make inquiries *or* enquiries (***über*** *acc.* about, into); **II.** *v/i.* (sn) **8.** move in; **9.** *troops*: march in; ~ ***in*** *acc.* enter, march into, arrive in *town*; ***in den Bundestag*** ~ take up one's seat in the Bundestag; **10.** soak in, be absorbed, be soaked up; **11.** *fig.* arrive; **12.** *fig.* take over, set in; **'Ein·zie·hung** *f* (-; -en) **1.** ⚔ conscription, *Am.* drafting; **2.** ⚖ confiscation, seizure; ✝ collection; **3.** withdrawal

ein·zig ['aɪntsɪç] **I.** *adj.* only; ***mein ~er Freund*** my (one and) only friend; ***mein ~er Gedanke*** my one thought; ***ein ~es Buch*** (just) one book; ***kein ~es Auto*** not a single car; ***kein ~es Wort*** not a word (F peep); ***sein ~er Halt*** his sole support; ***ein ~es Mal*** (just) once; ***nicht ein ~es Mal*** not once; ***sie hat keinen ~en Fehler gemacht*** she didn't make one (*or* a single) mistake; ***sein Leben war e-e ~e Flucht*** his life was one big escape; → ***einzigartig*** I; **II.** *adv.* only, (*a.* ~ ***und allein***) solely; ~ ***dastehen*** be unique (*or* unequal[l]ed), stand alone; ***das ~ Richtige*** (*or* ***Wahre***) the only answer (*or* solution, thing to do *etc.*); ***das ~ Richtige für dich wäre*** what you need is; ***das ~ Gute daran*** the only good (*or* positive) thing about it; ***das ~ Vernünftige wäre*** the only sensible thing to do is (*or* would be); ***es hängt ~ und allein davon ab, ob*** it depends entirely on whether; **III.** *indef. pron.*: ***der ~e, die ~e*** the only one, the only person, the one person; ***das ~e*** the only thing, the one thing; ***ein ~er*** just one (person *etc.*), one single (*or* solitary) person; ***kein ~er*** not (a single) one; ***das ~e wäre zu*** *inf.* the only thing would be to *inf.*

ein·zig·ar·tig ['aɪntsɪçʔa:ɐtɪç] **I.** *adj.* unique; unequal(l)ed *achievement*; unparalleled *beauty*; tremendous; **II.** *adv.*: ~ ***schön*** *a. w.s.* wonderful; **'Ein·zig·ar·tig·keit** *f* (-; *no pl.*) uniqueness

Ein'zim·mer·ap·par·te,ment *n* one-room (*Am. a.* efficiency) apartment; *Brit. a.* bedsit(ter)

Ein·zug ['aɪntsu:k] *m* (-[e]s; ⸚e [-tsy:gə]) **1.** moving in; **2.** entry (***in*** *acc.* into); ⚔ march(ing) in; **3.** *fig.* arrival, *lit.* advent; (***s-n***) ~ ***halten*** make its arrival; arrive (F on the scene); **4.** *typ.* indentation; **5.** → ***Einziehung***

'Ein·zugs|be·reich *m* → ***Einzugsgebiet***; **~er·mäch·ti·gung** *f* direct-debit mandate; **~ge·biet** *n* *geogr.*, ✝, *ped.* catchment area; hinterland, *n.s.* commuter belt

'ein·zwän·gen (*sep.*, h) **I.** *v/t.* squeeze in, F jam in; *fig.* constrain, straitjacket; → ***eingezwängt***; **II.** *v/refl.*: ***sich*** ~ ***in*** *acc.* squeeze (o.s.) into

'Ei·pul·ver *n* dried egg

Eis[1] [aɪs] *n* (-es; *no pl.*) ice; *gastr.* ice cream; ***im ~ eingeschlossen*** icebound; ***Whisky*** *etc.* ***mit*** ~ Scotch *etc.* on the rocks; ***auf ~ legen*** *a. fig.* put on ice; *fig.* ***das ~ brechen*** break the ice; → ***Glatteis***

Eis[2] ['e:ɪs] *n* (-; -) ♪ E sharp

'Eis|bahn *f* ice-skating rink; **~bär** *m* polar bear; **~be·cher** *m* **1.** sundae; **2.** (ice-cream) tub; **2be·deckt** *adj.* ice-capped; **~bein** *n* *gastr.* pickled knuckle of pork; **~berg** *m* iceberg; → ***Spitze***[1] 1; **~beu·tel** *m* ice bag; **~bil·dung** *f* ice formation; **~blink** *m* iceblink; **~block** *m* block of ice; **~blu·men** *pl.* frostwork *sg.*; **~bom·be** *f* *gastr.* bombe glacée; **~bre·cher** *m* icebreaker; **~ca·fé** *n* ice-cream parlo(u)r

'Ei·schnee *m* beaten egg white

'Eis|creme *f* ice cream; **~decke** *f* sheet of ice; **~die·le** *f* ice-cream parlo(u)r

Ei·sen ['aɪzən] *n* (-s; -) iron (*a.* ⚙, *golf and pharm.*); horseshoe; ***altes*** ~ scrap iron; *fig.* ***zum alten ~ werfen*** throw on the scrapheap; ***zum alten ~ gehören*** be past it, have had one's day; ***ein heißes ~*** a tricky affair (*or* business); ***ein heißes ~ anfassen*** a) tread on thin ice, b) grasp the nettle; ***zwei*** (*or* ***mehrere, noch ein***) ~ ***im Feuer haben*** have more than one string to one's bow (*or* iron in the fire); (***man muß***) ***das ~ schmieden, solange es heiß ist*** strike while the iron is hot, make hay while the sun shines

'Ei·sen·bahn *f* (-; -en) railway, *Am.* railroad; train; ***mit der ~*** by rail, by train; → ***Bahn*** 5; F ***es ist höchste ~*** it's high time we got going *etc.*; **~brücke** *f* railway (*Am.* railroad) bridge

Ei·sen·bah·ner ['aɪzənba:nɐ] *m* (-s; -) railwayman, *Am.* railroadman; **~streik** *m* rail strike

'Eis·en·bahn|kno·ten·punkt *m* (railway, *Am.* railroad) junction; **~netz** *n* railway (*Am.* railroad) network; **~schaff·ner** *m* guard, conductor; **~sta·ti,on** *f* railway (*Am.* railroad) station; **~tun·nel** *m* railway (*Am.* railroad) tunnel; **~un·glück** *n* railway (*Am.* railroad) accident; **~wa·gen** *m* railway carriage, coach, *Am.* railroad car; **~zug** *m* train

'Ei·sen|band *n* steel band; iron hoop; **~berg·werk** *n* iron mine; **~be·schlag** *m* iron mounting(s *pl.*); **~blech** *n* sheet iron; **~draht** *m* steel wire; **~erz** *n* iron ore; **~ge·halt** *m* iron content; **~gie·ße,rei** *f* iron foundry; **~glanz** *m* h(a)ematite; **~guß** *m* (-sses; *no pl.*) iron casting; cast iron

'ei·sen·hal·tig [-haltɪç] *adj.* **1.** ~ ***sein*** contain iron; ~***e Diät*** diet with plenty of iron; **2.** *min.* ferruginous

'Ei·sen|hut *m* ⚘ monk's-hood, aconite; **~hüt·te** *f*, **~hüt·ten·werk** *n* ironworks *pl.*; **~in·du,strie** *f* iron industry; **~ket·te** *f* iron chain; **~man·gel** *m* *physiol.* iron deficiency; **~oxyd** *n* ferric oxide; **~prä·pa,rat** *n* iron preparation; iron tablets *pl.*; **~rost** *m* (-[e]s; -e) iron grating; **~spä·ne** *pl.* iron filings; **~stan·ge** *f* iron (*or* steel) rod

'Ei·sen·wa·ren *pl.* ironware *sg.*, hardware *sg.*; **~händ·ler** *m* ironmonger, hardware dealer; **~hand·lung** *f* ironmonger's, hardware shop (*Am.* store)

'Ei·sen·zeit *f* (-; *no pl.*) Iron Age

ei·sern ['aɪzɐn] **I.** *adj.* iron (*a. fig. discipline, law, will etc.*), ... of iron (*a. fig.*); adamant, hard; firm; rigorous; ***~er Bestand*** emergency (*or* iron) rations; ***zum ~en Bestand gehören*** be a stock item in the repertoire (*or* collection *etc.*); ***~e Gesundheit*** cast-iron constitution; ***mit ~em Griff*** with a grip of iron (*or* steel); ***mit ~er Faust niederschlagen*** crush *revolt etc.*; ***ein Tyrann mit ~er Faust*** a heavy-handed tyrant; ***mit ~er Hand herrschen*** rule with a rod of iron; ***~e Hochzeit*** seventieth (*or* seventy-fifth) wedding anniversary; ***mit ~er Miene*** with a stony expression; ***~e Nerven*** nerves of steel; ***~e Regel*** hard and fast rule; ***~e Reserve*** emergency reserves; ***mit ~er Ruhe*** with imperturbable calm; ***mit ~er Stirn*** brazenly; → ***Jungfrau*** 1, ***Kanzler, Kreuz*** I, ***Lunge, Ration, Vorhang***; **II.** *adv.* firmly; unyieldingly, rigidly; resolutely, unswervingly, with iron determination; ~ ***lernen*** (***üben*** *etc.*) study (practi|se [*Am.* -ce] *etc.*) hard; ~ ***festhalten an*** *dat.* hold on rigidly to *a principle etc.*; ~ ***durchhalten*** keep going to the (bitter) end; ***sich ~ behaupten*** sit tight; (***aber***) ~! F you bet!

Ei·ses·käl·te ['aɪzəs-] *f* icy cold

'Eis|fa,brik *f* ice factory; **~fach** *n* freezing compartment; **~flä·che** *f* **1.** icy (*or* frozen) surface; ice cover; **2.** expanse of ice; **2frei** *adj.* free of ice, ice-free; **2ge·kühlt** *adj.* cold, chilled; **~glas** *n* frosted glass; **~glät·te** *f* icy roads *pl.*; **2grau** *adj.* hoary; **~gren·ze** *f* glacial boundary; **~hei·li·gen** *pl.*: ***die*** ~ the Ice Saints

'Eis·hockey (*sep.* -k·k-) *n* ice hockey, *Am. a.* hockey; **~schlä·ger** *m* ice-hockey (*Am. a.* hockey) stick; **~spie·ler** *m* ice-hockey (*Am. a.* hockey) player

ei·sig ['aɪzɪç] **I.** *adj. a. fig.* icy; *fig.* ***~er Blick*** icy (*or* cold) stare; ***~es Schweigen*** an icy (*or* frosty) silence; **II.** *adv.*: ~ ***kalt*** ice-cold, icy cold; *fig.* ***j-n ~ anblicken*** (***empfangen***) give s.o. an icy stare (welcome *or* reception)

'Eis|kaf·fee *m* iced coffee; **2kalt I.** *adj.* ice-cold; *fig.* icy; cold (as ice); **II.** *adv.*: *fig.* ***dabei überlief es mich*** ~ it sent shivers down my spine; ***et. ~ tun*** do s.th. without turning a hair; ***j-n ~ umbringen*** kill s.o. in cold blood; ~ ***rechnen*** be a cold calculator; **~kap·pe** *f* polar (ice-) cap; **~kel·ler** *m* cold room (*or* store); *fig.* icebox; **~krem** *f* ice cream; **~kri,stall** *m* ice crystal; **~kü·bel** *m* ice bucket

'Eis·kunst·lauf *m* (-[e]s; *no pl.*) figure skating; **'Eis·kunst·läu·fer** *m*, **'Eis·kunst·läu·fe·rin** *f* figure skater

'Eis·lauf *m* (-[e]s; *no pl.*) ice-skating; **'eis·lau·fen** *v/i.* (*irr.*, *sep.*, sn, → ***laufen***) ice-skate; **'Eis·läu·fer** *m*, **'Eis·läu·fe·rin** *f* ice-skater

'Eis|mann *m* (-[e]s; ⸚er) ice-cream man; **~ma,schi·ne** *f* ice(-cream) maker; **~mas·se** *f* **1.** mass of ice; **2.** ice floe; **~meer** *n* polar sea; ***Nördliches*** (***Südliches***) ~ Arctic (Antarctic) Ocean; **~pa,last** *m* ice stadium; ice-skating rink; **~pickel** (*sep.* -k·k-) *m* ice pick, ice axe (*Am.* ax); **~plat·te** *f* sheet of ice; **~prinz** *m* prince on ice; **~prin,zes·sin** *f* princess on ice

'Ei·sprung *m* *physiol.* ovulation

'Eis|re,vue *f* ice show; **~sa,lat** *m* iceberg lettuce; **~schicht** *f* layer of ice; **~schie·ßen** *n* curling

'Eis·schnellauf (*sep.* -ll·l) *m* (-[e]s; *no pl.*) speed skating; **'Eis·schnelläufer** (*sep.* -ll·l-) *m* (-s; -) speed skater

'Eis|scho·ko,la·de *f* iced chocolate; **~schol·le** *f* ice floe; **~schrank** *m* fridge, refrigerator; **~sport** *m* ice sports *pl.*; **~sta·di·on** *n* ice stadium

'Eis·stock *m* curling stone; **~schie·ßen** *n* curling

'Eis|sturm·vo·gel *m* fulmar; **~tanz** *m*, **~tan·zen** *n* ice-dancing; **~tor·te** *f* ice-cream gateau; **~trei·ben** *n* ice drift; **~tü·te** *f* ice-cream cone; **~,um·schlag** *m* ice pack; **~ver·käu·fer** *m* ice-cream seller; **~vo·gel** *m* kingfisher; **~was·ser** *n* iced water; **~wein** *m* eiswein; *very sweet wine made from frostbitten grapes*; **~wol·le** *f* eis (*or* ice) wool

'Eis·wür·fel *m* ice cube; **~scha·le** *f* ice-cube tray
'Eis|wü·ste *f* frozen waste(s *pl.*); **~zap·fen** *m* icicle
'Eis·zeit *f* ice age; *fig.* ***es herrscht ~ zwischen ...*** relations have cooled off dramatically between ...; **'eis·zeit·lich** *adj.* ice-age ..., glacial
ei·tel ['aɪtəl] *adj.* **1.** vain; conceited; **2.** vain; futile; ***eitles Gerede*** idle talk; ***eitle Hoffnung*** vain hope; ***eitle Versprechungen*** empty promises; **'Ei·tel·keit** *f* (-; -en) **1.** vanity; ***verletzte ~*** wounded vanity; **2.** vanity, futility
Ei·ter ['aɪtɐ] *m* (-s; *no pl.*) ⚕ pus; **~beu·le** *f* abscess, boil; **~bläs·chen** *n* pustule; **~er·re·ger** *m* pyogenic organism; **~herd** *m* suppurative focus
ei·tern ['aɪtɐn] *v/i.* (h) fester, suppurate
'Ei·ter|pfropf *m* core (of a boil *etc.*); head (of a spot *or* pimple); **~pickel** (*sep.* -k·k-) *m* spot, pimple
Ei·te·rung ['aɪtərʊŋ] *f* (-; -en) suppuration
ei·trig ['aɪtrɪç] *adj.* suppurating *wound etc.*
'Ei·weiß *n* (-es; -e) white of an egg, 🕮 albumen; *biol.*, ⚗ protein; *gastr.* ***drei ~*** the whites of three eggs; ***pflanzliches*** (***tierisches***) ~ vegetable (animal) protein; **&arm** *adj.* low in protein, low-protein *diet etc.*; **~be·darf** *m* protein requirement; **~ge·halt** *m* protein content; **&hal·tig** [-haltɪç] *adj.* 🕮 albuminous; ***~ sein*** contain protein; **~kon·zen͵trat** *n* protein concentrate; **~kör·per** *m* protein; **~man·gel** *m* protein deficiency; **&reich** *adj.* rich in protein, high-protein *diet etc.*; **~stoff** *m* protein
'Ei·zel·le *f* egg cell, ovum
Eja·ku·lat [ejaku'la:t] *n* ([e]s; -e) ejaculated semen; **Eja·ku·la·ti·on** [ejakula'tsĭo:n] *f* (-; -en) ejaculation; **eja·ku·lie·ren** [ejaku'li:rən] *v/t. and v/i.* (h) ejaculate
Ekel¹ ['e:kəl] *m* (-s; *no pl.*) revulsion (***vor*** *dat.* at), disgust (at); ***~ empfinden*** (*or* ***e-n ~ haben***) ***vor*** → ***ekeln; es ist mir ein ~*** I loathe it, F I can't stomach (*or* stand) it; ***Spinnen sind mir ein ~*** I can't stand spiders, F spiders give me the creeps; ***sich vor ~ abwenden*** look away in disgust; ***ich mußte mich vor ~ abwenden*** *a.* F I couldn't stomach the sight
'Ekel² F *n* (-s; -) obnoxious (*or* repulsive) person; F pain in the neck; ***du ~!*** F you rotter, you rotten old so-and-so
'ekel·er·re·gend *adj.* disgusting; revolting, repulsive
'Ekel·ge·fühl *n* (feeling of) revulsion
'ekel·haft, eke·lig ['e:kəlɪç] **I.** *adj.* revolting, disgusting; F *fig.* nasty; **II.** *adv.*: ***~ kalt*** F rotten cold
ekeln ['e:kəln] *v/refl. and v/impers.* (h): ***es ekelt mich*** (*or* ***mich ekelt, ich ekle mich***) ***davor*** I'm revolted by it, it gives me the shivers (F creeps), ***vor ihm:*** F he gives me the creeps
EKG ['e:ka:'ge:] *n* (-s; -s) ⚕ ECG, *Am.* EKG
Eklat [e'kla:] *m* (-s; -s) **1.** scandal; confrontation, row; ***es wird zu e-m ~ kommen*** there'll be (a) scandal (*or* a row); **2.** ***mit ~*** spectacularly, splendidly; ***mit ~ durchfallen*** fail miserably; **ekla·tant** [ekla'tant] *adj.* **1.** striking *example etc.*; *contp.* blatant, glaring, flagrant; **2.** spectacular, sensational; ***~er Vorfall*** sensation
Ek·lek·ti·ker [ɛk'lɛktikɐ] *m* (-s; -) eclectic; **ek·lek·tisch** [ɛk'lɛktɪʃ] *adj.* eclectic; **Ek·lek·ti·zis·mus** [ɛklɛkti'tsɪsmʊs] *m* (-; *no pl.*) eclecticism
ek·lig ['e:klɪç] *adj.* → ***ekelig***
Ek·lip·se [ɛk'lɪpsə] *f* (-; -n) eclipse; **ek·lip·tisch** [ɛk'lɪptɪʃ] *adj.* ecliptic(al)
Ek·lo·ge [ɛk'lo:gə] *f* (-; -n) eclogue
Ek·sta·se [ɛk'sta:zə] *f* (-; -n) ecstasy; ***in ~ geraten*** go into ecstasies *or* raptures (***über*** *acc.* over), get carried away; ***j-n in ~ versetzen*** send s.o. into ecstasies (*or* raptures); **ek·sta·tisch** [ɛk'sta:tɪʃ] *adj.* ecstatic(ally *adv.*)
Ek·zem [ɛk'tse:m] *n* (-s; -e) ⚕ eczema
Ela·bo·rat [elabo'ra:t] *contp. n* (-[e]s; -e) piece of hack writing
Elan [e'la:n] *m* (-s; *no pl.*) vigo(u)r; ***sich mit ~ an die Arbeit machen*** set to work with alacrity; ***sie haben ohne ~ gespielt*** they didn't put much life into the (*or* their) game
Ela·stik [e'lastɪk] *f* (-; -en) elastic; **~bin·de** *f* elastic bandage
ela·stisch [e'lastɪʃ] *adj.* elastic(ally *adv.*) (*a. fig.*); springy; ⚙, *mot. and fig.* flexible; *fig.* ***~er Gang*** springy (*or* elastic) gait; ***er kam mit ~en Schritten daher*** he came bouncing along; **Ela·sti·zi·tät** [elastitsi'tɛ:t] *f* (-; *no pl.*) elasticity; springiness; flexibility
Elch [ɛlç] *m* (-[e]s; -e) elk; moose
Ele·fant [ele'fant] *m* (-en; -en) elephant; F *fig.* ***sich wie ein ~ im Porzellanladen benehmen*** tread on everyone's toes; → ***Mücke***
Ele'fan·ten|ba·by *n* baby elephant; **~bul·le** *m* male (*or* bull) elephant; **~ge·dächt·nis** *n* memory like an elephant; **~gras** *n* elephant grass; **~haut** F *fig. f* thick skin; **~hoch·zeit** F *f* ✝ F jumbo (*or* giant) merger; **~kuh** *f* female (*or* cow) elephant; **~rüs·sel** *m* elephant's trunk
Ele·fan·tia·sis [elefan'ti:azɪs] *f* (-; -tiasen [-'tĭa:zən]) ⚕ elephantiasis
ele·gant [ele'gant] **I.** *adj.* elegant (*a. fig.*), smart; *fig.* ***auf ~e Weise*** elegantly; **II.** *adv.*: ***sich ~ aus der Affäre ziehen*** F get out of it nicely; **Ele·ganz** [ele'gants] *f* (-; *no pl.*) elegance
Ele·gie [ele'gi:] *f* (-; -n) elegy; **ele·gisch** [e'le:gɪʃ] *adj.* elegiac; *fig. a.* melancholy
Elek·tra·kom͵plex [e'lɛktra-] *m psych.* Electra complex
elek·tri·fi·zie·ren [elɛktrifi'tsi:rən] *v/t.* (h) electrify; **Elek·tri·fi'zie·rung** *f* (-; -en) electrification
Elek·trik [e'lɛktrɪk] *f* (-; -en) electricity; electrical system (*or* equipment); **Elek·tri·ker** [e'lɛktrikɐ] *m* (-s; -) electrician; **elek·trisch** [e'lɛktrɪʃ] **I.** *adj.* electric(al); ***~e Energie*** electrical energy; ***~er Schlag*** electric shock; ***~er Strom*** electric current; ***~er Stuhl*** electric chair; **II.** *adv.*: ***~ geladen*** (***gesteuert*** *etc.*) electrically charged (control[l]ed *etc.*); ***~ beleuchten*** (***heizen*** *etc.*) light (heat *etc.*) with *or* by electricity; ***~ betrieben sein*** be run on electricity
elek·tri·sie·ren [elɛktri'zi:rən] *v/t.* (h) electrify (*a. fig.*); ***sich ~*** get (*or* give o.s.) an electric shock; **elek·tri·siert** [elɛktri'zi:ɐt] *adj.* electrified; ***er sprang wie ~ auf*** he jumped up as if he'd been given an electrical charge; **Elek·tri'sie·rung** *f* (-; -en) electrification
Elek·tri·zi·tät [elɛktritsi'tɛ:t] *f* (-; *no pl.*) electricity; (electric) current
Elek·tri·zi'täts|ver·sor·gung *f* electricity (*or* power) supply; **~werk** *n* (electric) power station; **~zäh·ler** *m* electricity metre
Elek·tro·aku·stik [elɛktroʔa'kʊstɪk] *f* (-; *no pl.*) electroacoustics *pl.*; **elek·tro·aku·stisch** [elɛktroʔa'kʊstɪʃ] *adj.* electroacoustic(al)
Elek·tro·ana'ly·se [elɛktro-] *f* electroanalysis
Elek·tro|an·trieb [e'lɛktro-] *m* electric drive; **~au·to** *n* electric car; **~boh·rer** *m* electric drill; **~bus** *m* electric bus
Elek·tro·che'mie *f* electrochemistry
Elek·tro·de [elɛk'tro:də] *f* (-; -n) electrode; ***negative ~*** negative electrode, cathode; ***positive ~*** positive electrode, anode
Elek·tro|dy'na·mik *f* electrodynamics *pl.*; **~-En·ze·pha·lo'gramm** *n* ⚕ electroencephalogram, EEG
Elek·tro|fahr·zeug [e'lɛktro-] *n* electric vehicle; **~ge·rät** *n* electrical appliance; *pl. a.* electrical equipment *sg.*; **~ge·schäft** *n* electrical shop (*Am.* store); **~gi͵tar·re** *f* electric guitar; **~herd** *m* electric cooker; **~in·du͵strie** *f* electrical industry; **~in·ge·ni͵eur** *m* electrical engineer; **~in·stal·la͵teur** *m* electrician; **~kar·dio͵gramm** *n* ⚕ electrocardiogram, ECG, *Am.* EKG; **~lo·ko·mo͵ti·ve** *f* electric locomotive
Elek·tro·ly·se [elɛktro'ly:zə] *f* (-; -n) electrolysis; **Elek·tro·lyt** [elɛktro'ly:t] *m* (-s, -en; -e) electrolyte; **elek·tro·ly·tisch** [elɛktro'ly:tɪʃ] *adj.* electrolytic; **Elek·tro'lyt·kon·den͵sa·tor** *m* ⚡ electrolytic capacitor
Elek·tro·ma'gnet *m* electromagnet; **elek·tro·ma'gne·tisch** *adj.* electromagnetic(ally *adv.*)
elek·tro·me'cha·nisch *adj.* electromechanical
Elek·tro·mo·tor [e'lɛktro-] *m* (electric) motor
Elek·tron ['e:lɛktrɔn] *n* (-s; -en [elɛk'tro:nən]) electron
Elek'tro·nen|blitz(ge·rät *n*) *m phot.* electronic flash(gun); **~ge·hirn** *n* electronic brain; **~hül·le** *f* electron shell; **~ka·me·ra** *f* electronic camera; **~mi·kro͵skop** *n* electron microscope; **~rech·ner** *m* computer; **~röh·re** *f* electronic valve (*Am.* tube)
Elek·tro·nik [elɛk'tro:nɪk] *f* (-; *no pl.*) **1.** electronics *pl.*; **2.** electronic system; **~in·du͵strie** *f* electronics industry; **~spiel·zeug** *n* electronic toys *pl.*
elek·tro·nisch [elɛk'tro:nɪʃ] *adj.* electronic(ally *adv.*); ***~e Datenverarbeitung*** electronic data processing
Elek·tro|ofen [e'lɛktro-] *m* ⚙ electric furnace; electric stove; **~or·gel** *f* electric organ
Elek·tro·phy'sik *f* electrophysics *pl.*
Elek·tro·ra·sie·rer [e'lɛktrorazi:rɐ] *m* (-s; -) electric razor
Elek·tro·schock [e'lɛktro-] *m* ⚕ electroshock; **~the·ra͵pie** *f* electroshock treatment (*or* therapy)
Elek·tro·schwei·ßen [e'lɛktro-] *n* electronic welding
Elek·tro·skop [elɛktro'sko:p] *n* (-s; -e) electroscope
Elek·tro·stab [e'lɛktro-] *m* electric(-shock) baton
elek·tro'sta·tisch *adj.* electrostatic(ally *adv.*)
Elek·tro'tech·nik *f* (-; *no pl.*) electrical

engineering; **Elek·tro'tech·ni·ker** *m* (-s; -) electrical engineer; **elek·tro'tech·nisch** *adj.* electrotechnical; electrical
Elek·tro·the·ra'pie *f* electrotherapy
Elek·tro·zaun [e'lɛktro-] *m* electric fence
Ele·ment [ele'mɛnt] *n* (-[e]s; -e) **1.** *phys.*, ⚕, ⚗, ⚙ *etc.* element; ⚡ *a.* cell, battery; *fig.* ***unliebsame*** (***kriminelle*** *etc.*) **~*e*** undesirable (criminal *etc.*) elements; ***in s-m ~ sein*** be in one's element; **2.** *pl.* elements, rudiments; **3. *die ~e*** the elements
ele·men·tar [elemɛn'taːɐ] *adj.* **1.** elemental; **2.** elementary, basic; ***~er Fehler*** fundamental (*or* basic) mistake *or* flaw; **3.** elementary, primary
Ele·men'tar|be·griff *m* fundamental idea; **~buch** *n* primer; **~geist** *m myth.* elemental spirit; **~kennt·nis·se** *pl.* rudiments; **~la·dung** *f* elementary charge; **~stoff** *m* element, elementary matter; **~stu·fe** *f* elementary grade
Ele·men'tar·teil·chen *n* elementary particle; **~phy,sik** *f* particle physics *pl.*
Ele·men'tar,un·ter·richt *m* elementary instruction
Elend ['eːlɛnt] *n* (-s; *no pl.*) misery; (dire *or* abject) poverty; ***ins ~ geraten*** be reduced to poverty; ***soziales ~*** social hardship; ***aus tiefstem ~*** from the depths of misery; ***ins ~ stürzen*** (***or bringen***) plunge into poverty (and distress); ***wie das leibhaftige ~ aussehen*** F look like death warmed up, look like a corpse; F ***es ist ein ~ mit ihm*** F he's a hopeless case; F ***langes ~*** F beanpole; F ***da kriegt man das heulende ~*** F it's enough to make you weep; → ***Häufchen*** 2
elend I. *adj.* miserable, wretched; poverty-stricken; pitiable; terrible; ***~e Hütte*** (*or* ***Baracke***) hovel; ***in ~en Verhältnissen leben*** live in wretched conditions; ***ein ~es Leben führen*** live a life of misery; ***~ aussehen*** look dreadful; ***sich ~ fühlen*** feel terrible (*or* wretched, F rotten); **II.** *adv.* miserably; dreadfully; ***~ zugrunde gehen*** come to a wretched end; ***~ verhungern*** die of slow (and painful) starvation; F ***es tut ~ weh*** *sl.* it hurts like hell; F ***es ist ~ kalt*** F it's absolutely freezing; **elen·dig·lich** ['eːlɛndɪklɪç] *adv.* → ***elend*** II
'Elends|quar,tier *n* hovel; **~vier·tel** *n* slum(s *pl.*)
Ele·ve [e'leːvə] *m* (-n; -n), **Ele·vin** [e'leːvɪn] *f* (-; -nen) *thea. etc.* student
elf [ɛlf] *adj.* eleven
Elf[1] *f* (-; -en) eleven; (*bus etc.*) (number) eleven; *soccer*: team, eleven
Elf[2] *m* (-en; -en), **El·fe** ['ɛlfə] *f* (-; -n) elf
El·fen·bein ['ɛlfənbaɪn] *n* (-[e]s; *no pl.*) ivory; **el·fen·bei·nern** ['ɛlfənbaɪnɐn] *adj.* ivory; **'el·fen·bein·far·big** *adj.* ivory(-colo[u]red)
'El·fen·bein|schnit·ze,rei *f* ivory carving; ivory; **~turm** *fig. m* (-[e]s; *no pl.*) ivory tower; ***im ~ leben*** live in an ivory tower
'el·fen·haft *adj.* elfin
'El·fen|kö·nig *m* king of the elves; **~kö·ni·gin** *f* fairy queen; **~reich** *n* kingdom of the elves, elfland; **~rei·gen** *m* dance of the elves
El·fer ['ɛlfɐ] F *m* (-s; -) *soccer*: penalty kick
Elf'me·ter *m* (-s; -) *soccer*: penalty kick; **~schie·ßen** *n* penalty shootout; **~tor** *n* penalty goal
elft [ɛlft] *adj.* eleventh; **Elf·tel** ['ɛlftəl] *n* (-s; -) eleventh (part)
eli·mi·nie·ren [elimi'niːrən] *v/t.* (h) eliminate; **Eli·mi'nie·rung** *f* (-; -en) elimination
eli·tär [eli'tɛːɐ] *adj.* elitist
Eli·te [e'liːtə] *f* (-; -n) elite; **~den·ken** *n* elitism; **~schu·le** *f* F magnet school; **~trup·pe** *f* crack regiment (*pl. a.* troops)
Eli·xier [elɪ'ksiːɐ] *n* (-s; -e) (magic) potion
Ell·bo·gen ['ɛlboːgən] *m* elbow; ***sich mit den ~ e-n Weg bahnen durch*** *acc.* elbow one's way through; *fig.* ***s-e ~ gebrauchen*** use one's elbows; **~frei·heit** *f* (-; *no pl.*) *a. fig.* elbowroom, room to move; **~ge·lenk** *n* elbow joint; **~ge·sell·schaft** *f* dog-eat-dog society; rat race; **~mensch** *m* pushy type, F ruthless go-getter; **~tak·tik** *f* pushiness
El·le ['ɛlə] *f* (-; -n) **1.** *obs.* ell; *fig.* ***alles mit der gleichen ~ messen*** measure everything by the same yardstick; **2.** *anat.* ulna; **'el·len·lang** *adj.* **1.** endless; **2.** really tall
El·lip·se [ɛ'lɪpsə] *f* (-; -n) ⚕ ellipse; *ling.* ellipsis; **el·lip·tisch** [ɛ'lɪptɪʃ] *adj.* elliptical
Elms·feu·er [ɛlms-] *n* St Elmo's fire
Elo·ge [e'loːʒə] *f* (-; -n) eulogy (***auf*** *acc.* to)
E-Lok ['eːlɔk] *f* (-; -s) electric locomotive
elo·quent [elo'kvɛnt] *adj.* eloquent; **Elo·quenz** [elo'kvɛnts] *f* (-; *no pl.*) eloquence
El·säs·ser ['ɛlzɛsɐ] *m* (-s; -), **El·säs·se·rin** ['ɛlzɛsərɪn] *f* (-; -nen) Alsatian; ***Elsässer(in) sein*** *a.* be (*or* come) from (the) Alsace; **el·säs·sisch** ['ɛlzɛsɪʃ] *adj.* Alsatian, Alsace ...; ***~e Weine*** wines from the Alsace, Alsace wines; **el·saß·-loth·rin·gisch** ['ɛlzas'loːtrɪŋɪʃ] *adj.* Alsace-Lorraine ..., of (*or* from) Alsace-Lorraine
El·ster ['ɛlstɐ] *f* (-; -n) magpie; *fig.* ***er ist e-e diebische ~*** he'll steal anything that isn't nailed down; ***geschwätzig wie e-e ~ sein*** F be a real chatterbox
el·ter·lich ['ɛltɐlɪç] *adj.* parental; parents' ...; ***die ~en Pflichten*** one's duties as a parent, one's parental duties; ⚖ ***~e Gewalt*** parental authority
El·tern ['ɛltɐn] *pl.* parents; F ***nicht von schlechten ~*** F not bad at all; **~abend** *m* parent-teacher meeting; **~bei·rat** *m* parents' council; **~haus** *n* **1.** *one's* parents' house; **2.** home; ***aus gutem ~ stammen*** come from a good family (*or* home), have a good family background; **~in·itia,ti·ve** *f* parents' action group, parent pressure group; **~lie·be** *f* parental love
'el·tern·los *adj.* orphan ..., orphaned
'El·tern·pflicht *f* parental duty; ***die ~en*** *a.* one's duties as a parent
'El·tern·schaft *f* (-; -en) **1.** *no pl.* parenthood; **2.** parents *pl.*
'El·tern|schlaf·zim·mer *n* parents' (*or* master) bedroom; **~sprech·stun·de** *f* teacher's consultation period, surgery (for parents); **~sprech·tag** *m* open day; **~teil** *m* parent; **~ver·samm·lung** *f* parents' meeting
Email [e'maɪ, e'maːj] *n* (-s; -s) enamel; **~ar·beit** *f* enamel work; **~lack** *m* enamel varnish
Email·le [e'maljə] *f* (-; -n) → ***Email***
email·lie·ren [ema(l)'jiːrən] *v/t.* (h) enamel
Email·ma·le,rei *f* enamel painting
Eman·ze [e'mantsə] F *f* (-; -n) F women's libber; **Eman·zi·pa·ti·on** [emantsipa'tsi̯oːn] *f* (-; -en) emancipation; ***die ~ der Frau*** women's liberation (F lib); **eman·zi·pa·to·risch** [emantsipa'toːrɪʃ] *adj.* emancipatory; **eman·zi·pie·ren** [emantsi'piːrən] (h) **I.** *v/t.* emancipate; **II.** *v/refl.*: ***sich ~*** become emancipated
Em·bar·go [ɛm'bargo] *n* (-s; -s) embargo; ***ein ~ verhängen über*** *acc.* place (*or* impose) an embargo on
Em·blem [ɛm'bleːm] *n* (-s; -e) emblem; symbol; **Em·ble·ma·tik** [ɛmble'maːtɪk] *f* (-; *no pl.*) emblematics *pl.*; **em·ble·ma·tisch** [ɛmble'maːtɪʃ] *adj.* emblematic(ally *adv.*)
Em·bo·lie [ɛmbo'liː] *f* (-; -n) ⚕ embolism
Em·bryo ['ɛmbryo] *m* (-s; -s) embryo; **Em·bryo·lo·gie** [ɛmbryolo'giː] *f* (-; *no pl.*) embryology; **em·bryo·nal** [ɛmbryo'naːl] *adj.* embryonic, embryo ...; *fig.* ***noch im ~en Zustand*** still in embryo
emen·die·ren [emɛn'diːrən] *v/t.* (h) emend
eme·ri·tie·ren [emeri'tiːrən] *v/t.* (h) *univ.* retire, give *s.o.* emeritus status; **eme·ri·tiert** [emeri'tiːɐt] *adj.* retired; ***~er Professor*** retired (*or* emeritus) professor, professor emeritus; **Eme·ri·tus** [e'meːritʊs] **I.** *m* (-; -ti) emeritus professor; **II.** ♀ *adj.*: ***Professor ~*** emeritus professor
Eme·ti·kum [e'meːtikʊm] *n* (-s; -ka) emetic
Emi·grant [emi'grant] *m* (-en; -en) emigrant; émigré; **Emi'gran·ten·li·te·ra,tur** *f* émigré literature; **Emi'gran·ten·schick·sal** *n one's* fate as an exile (*or* émigré); **Emi'gran·ten·tum** *n* (-s; *no pl.*) émigré existence; life in exile, life as an exile (*or* émigré); **Emi·gra·ti·on** [emigra'tsi̯oːn] *f* (-; -en) emigration; ***in der*** (***die***) ***~*** in(to) exile; **emi·grie·ren** [emi'griːrən] *v/i.* (sn) emigrate
emi·nent [emi'nɛnt] **I.** *adj.*: ***~e Begabung*** outstanding talent; ***von ~er Wichtigkeit*** of the utmost importance; **II.** *adv.* exceptionally, extremely, *formal*: most; ***~ gefährlich*** extremely dangerous, dangerous in the extreme; **Emi·nenz** [emi'nɛnts] *f* (-; -en) **1.** *no pl.*: ***Seine ~*** His Eminence; **2. *Graue ~*** eminence grise, grey (*Am.* gray) eminence
Emir ['eːmɪr, e'miːɐ] *m* (-s; -e [-iːrə]) emir; **Emi·rat** [emi'raːt] *n* (-[e]s; -e) emirate
Emis·si·on [emɪ'si̯oːn] *f* (-; -en) **1.** *phys.* emission; **2.** ✝ issue
Emis·si'ons|bank *f* (-; -en) ✝ bank of issue; **~grenz·wer·te** *pl.* emission standards; **~schutz** *m* emission control; **~schutz·ge·setz** *n* anti-pollution law (*pl. a.* legislation *sg.*)
Emit·ter [e'mɪtɐ] *m* (-s; -) *electron.* emitter
emit·tie·ren [emɪ'tiːrən] *v/t.* (h) **1.** ✝ issue; **2.** *phys.*, *electron.* emit
Em·men·ta·ler ['ɛməntaːlɐ] *m* (-s; -) Emmental(er) (cheese), Swiss cheese
Emo·ti·on [emo'tsi̯oːn] *f* (-; -en) emotion; ***von ~en erfüllt*** full of emotion; **emo·tio·nal** [emotsi̯o'naːl], **emo·tio·nell** [emotsi̯o'nɛl] *adj.* emotional; **emo·tio·na·li·sie·ren** [emotsi̯onali'ziːrən] *v/t.* (h) emotionalize; **Emo·tio·na·li·tät** [emotsi̯onali'tɛːt] *f* (-; *no pl.*) emotionality; **emo·ti'ons·frei** *adj.* free of emotion; **emo·ti'ons·ge·la·den** *adj.* emotive, highly-charged *issue etc.*; very emotional, highly-charged *atmosphere etc.*; **emo·ti'ons·los** *adj.* unemotional
Em·pa·thie [ɛmpa'tiː] *f* (-; *no pl.*) *psych.* empathy
emp·fahl [ɛm'pfaːl] *pret. of* ***empfehlen***

emp·fand [ɛm'pfant] *pret. of* ***empfinden***
Emp·fang [ɛm'pfaŋ] *m* (-[e]s; Empfänge [ɛm'pfɛŋə]) **1.** *no pl.* receipt; ***nach*** (*or* ***bei***) ~ on receipt, on delivery (***von*** *or gen.* of); ***in ~ nehmen*** receive, † take delivery of, meet *s.o.*; **2.** *no pl.* reception, welcome; ***j-m e-n begeisterten*** (***kühlen***) ~ ***bereiten*** give s.o. an enthusiastic (a cool) reception; **3.** reception; ***e-n ~ geben*** hold a reception; **4.** *radio etc.*: reception; **5.** reception (desk); **emp·fan·gen** [ɛm'pfaŋən] (empfing, empfangen, h) **I.** *v/t.* **1.** receive; welcome, meet, *formal*: receive; see; accept; *radio etc.*: receive, get (***auf*** *dat.* on); ***j-n mit Jubel*** *etc.* ~ greet s.o. with cheers *etc.*; **2.** conceive *a child*; **II.** *v/i.* **3.** conceive; **4.** see (*or* receive) visitors; ***er empfängt heute nicht*** he's not seeing (*or* receiving) any visitors today; **Emp·fän·ger** [ɛm'pfɛŋɐ] *m* (-s; -) **1.** receiver, recipient; consignee; addressee; **2.** *radio*: receiver, tuner
emp·fäng·lich [ɛm'pfɛŋlɪç] *adj.* **1.** receptive, responsive (***für*** *acc.* to); impressionable; ~ ***für*** *acc. a.* open to; **2.** ⚕ susceptible (***für*** *acc.* to); ~ ***für*** *acc. a.* prone to; **Emp'fäng·lich·keit** *f* (-; *-no pl.*) **1.** receptivity (***für*** *acc.* for); impressionableness; **2.** ⚕ susceptibility (***für*** *acc.* to), proneness (to)
Emp·fäng·nis [ɛm'pfɛŋnɪs] *f* (-; *no pl.*) conception; **2ver·hü·tend** *adj.* (*a.* ***~es Mittel***) contraceptive; **~ver·hü·tung** *f* contraception; **~ver·hü·tungs·mit·tel** *n* contraceptive
Emp'fangs|an,ten·ne *f* receiving aerial (*or* antenna); **2be·rech·tigt** *adj.* authorized to receive goods *etc.*; **~be·reich** *m radio*: **1.** reception area; **2.** frequency range; **~be·schei·ni·gung** *f* receipt; **~be·stä·ti·gung** *f* acknowledg(e)ment of receipt; **~be·trieb** *m computer*: receive mode; **~chef** *m* reception (*Am.* room) clerk; **~da·me** *f* receptionist; **~ge·rät** *n* receiver; **~hal·le** *f* foyer; **~ko·mi,tee** *n* reception committee; **~la·ger** *n* reception cent|re (*Am.* -er); **~loch** *n radio*: blind spot; **~raum** *m* reception room; **~saal** *m* reception hall; **~schein** *m* receipt; **~stö·rung** *f radio*: *a. pl.* interference; static; **~zim·mer** *n* reception room
emp·feh·len [ɛm'pfe:lən] (empfahl, empfohlen, h) **I.** *v/t.* **1.** recommend; ***j-m et. wärmstens*** ~ warmly recommend s.th. to s.o.; ***nicht zu*** ~ not to be recommended; ***... ist sehr zu*** ~ I can highly (*or* warmly) recommend ...; **2.** ~ ***Sie mich*** *Ihrer Frau*: give my regards to; **II.** *v/refl.*: ***sich*** ~ **3.** recommend itself, suggest itself; ***der Tee empfiehlt sich bei ...*** the tea is recommended for ...; *Qualität etc.* ***empfiehlt sich selbst*** is its own recommendation; ***es empfiehlt sich zu*** *inf.* it is advisable to *inf.*; **4.** offer one's services (***als*** as); **5.** take one's leave; **emp'feh·lens·wert** *adj.* recommendable; advisable; **Emp'feh·lung** *f* (-; -en) recommendation; ***auf*** ~ (***von j-m***) on (s.o.'s) recommendation; ***gute ~en haben*** have good references; ***m-e besten ~en an*** *acc.* give my regards to; **Emp'feh·lungs·schrei·ben** *n* letter of recommendation (*or* introduction)
emp·fin·den [ɛm'pfɪndən] (empfand, empfunden, h) **I.** *v/t.* feel (*a. v/i.* ***mit*** for); ***Mitleid ~ für*** *a.* have sympathy for; ***et. als lästig*** *etc.* ~ find s.th. a nuisance *etc.*; ***nichts ~ für*** *acc.* feel nothing for, have no feelings for; ***was empfindest du dabei?*** what kind of feeling do you have (*or* does it give you)?; **II.** *v/refl.*: ***sich ~ als*** see (*or* regard) o.s. as; **III.** 2 *n* (-s) feeling; opinion; sense; ***nach m-m*** ~ the way I see it; ***für mein*** ~ for me, as far as I'm concerned; ***ihr gesundes ~ sagt ihr*** her intuitive feeling tells her; ***er hat kein ~ dafür*** he has no appreciation for it
emp·find·lich [ɛm'pfɪntlɪç] **I.** *adj.* **1.** sensitive (*a. phot.*, ⚙) (***gegen*** *acc.* to); tender, sore; ***~e Stelle*** sensitive (*or* tender, sore) spot; **2.** (very) sensitive (***gegen*** *acc.* about), easily offended, touchy (about); **3.** delicate; **4.** severe *losses etc.*; **II.** *adv.* severely, badly; ~ ***kalt*** bitter(ly) cold; ***j-n ~ treffen*** *remark etc.*: hit home, cut s.o. to the quick; **Emp'find·lich·keit** *f* (-; *no pl.*) **1.** sensitiveness; tenderness, soreness; touchiness; **2.** *phot.* speed; ***was für e-e ~ hat der Film?*** what speed is the film?
emp·find·sam [ɛm'pfɪntza:m] *adj.* sensitive; sentimental; **Emp'find·sam·keit** *f* (-; *no pl.*) sensitivity; sentimentality
Emp'fin·dung [ɛm'pfɪndʊŋ] *f* (-; -en) sensation; perception; *w.s.* feeling, sense; ***die ~ des Schmerzes*** *etc.* the sensation of pain *etc.*; **emp'fin·dungs·los** *adj.* insensitive (***für*** *acc.*, ***gegen*** *acc.* to); *contp. a.* unfeeling; numb
Emp'fin·dungs|nerv *m* sensory nerve; **~ver·mö·gen** *n* (-s; *no pl.*) sensitivity; **~wort** *n* (-[e]s; ⸚er) *ling.* interjection
emp'fing *pret. of* ***empfangen***
emp·foh·len [ɛm'pfo:lən] **I.** *p.p. of* ***empfehlen***; **II.** *adj.* recommended
emp·fun·den [ɛm'pfʊndən] *p.p. of* ***empfinden***
Em·pha·se [ɛm'fa:zə] *f* (-; -n) emphasis; **em·pha·tisch** [ɛm'fa:tɪʃ] *adj.* emphatic(ally *adv.*)
Em·phy·sem [ɛmfy'ze:m] *n* (-s; -e) ⚕ emphysema
Em·pi·rie [ɛmpi'ri:] *f* (-; *no pl.*), **Em·pi·rik** [ɛm'pi:rɪk] *f* (-; *no pl.*) empiricism; **Em·pi·ri·ker** [ɛm'pi:rikɐ] *m* (-s; -) empiricist; **em·pi·risch** [ɛm'pi:rɪʃ] *adj.* empirical
em·por [ɛm'po:ɐ] *adv.* up, upward(s); **~ar·bei·ten** *v/refl.* (*sep.*, h): ***sich*** ~ work one's way up; **~blicken** (*sep.* -k·k-) *v/i.* (*sep.*, h) look up (***zu*** *dat.* at, *fig.* to)
Em·po·re [ɛm'po:rə] *f* (-; -n) △ gallery
em·pö·ren [ɛm'pø:rən] (h) **I.** *v/t.* **1.** outrage; insult; shock, scandalize; **II.** *v/refl.*: ***sich*** ~ **2.** be outraged (***über*** *acc.* at), express (one's) outrage (at); **3.** rebel, rise up (in arms); **em'pö·rend** *adj.* outrageous; shocking, scandalous; **em·pö·re·risch** [ɛm'pø:rərɪʃ] *adj.* rebellious, insurgent; inflammatory *speech etc.*
em'por·he·ben *v/t.* (*irr.*, *sep.*, h, → ***heben***) lift, raise
em'por·kom·men *v/i.* (*irr.*, *sep.*, sn, → ***kommen***) **1.** get up; **2.** *fig.* get on in life; ***in der Gesellschaft*** ~ climb up the social ladder; **Em'por·kömm·ling** [-kœmlɪŋ] *m* (-s; -e) upstart, parvenu
em'por|ra·gen *v/i.* (*sep.*, h): ~ ***über*** *acc.* tower (*or* loom) above; ~ ***aus*** *dat.* loom up from (*or* out of); **~schie·ßen** *v/i.* (*irr.*, *sep.*, sn, → ***schießen***) shoot up (*a. fig.*); *jet of water*: gush up; *fig.* jump up; mushroom; **~schnel·len** *v/i.* (*sep.*, sn) † *prices etc.*: soar; **~schwin·gen** *v/refl.* (*irr.*, *sep.*, h, → ***schwingen***): ***sich*** ~ swing o.s. up; *bird*: soar; *fig.* rise (***zu*** *dat.* to); *fig.* ***sich zu großen künstlerischen Leistungen*** ~ rise to great artistic heights; **~stei·gen** (*irr.*, *sep.*, sn, → ***steigen***) **I.** *v/i.* rise; **II.** *v/t.* climb (*a. fig.*); **~stre·ben** *v/i.* (*sep.*, sn) strive upwards; soar (upwards); *fig.* ~ ***zu*** *dat.* aspire to
em·pört [ɛm'pø:ɐt] *adj.* shocked; indignant; angry; **Em·pö·rung** [ɛm'pø:rʊŋ] *f* (-; -en) **1.** *no pl.* indignation; outrage; shock and resentment; **2.** *obs.* revolt
em·sig ['ɛmzɪç] *adj.* busy; industrious, hardworking; eager, keen; **'Em·sig·keit** *f* (-; *no pl.*) bustle; industry; zeal
Emu ['e:mu] *m* (-s; -s) emu
Emul·ga·tor [emʊl'ga:to:ɐ] *m* (-s; -en [-ga'to:rən]) emulsifier
Emul·si·on [emʊl'zio:n] *f* (-; -en) emulsion
'E-Mu,sik *f* serious (*or* classical) music
en bloc [ã'blɔk] *adv.* † en bloc, *a. fig.* wholesale
End|ab·neh·mer ['ɛnt-] *m* (-s; -) † end user; **~ab·rech·nung** *f* final account; **~ab·schal·tung** *f* (-; -en): ***automatische*** ~ automatic tape shut-off; **~bahn·hof** *m* terminus; **~be·trag** *m* (sum) total; **~bo·gen** *m typ.* end (*or* back) matter; **~buch·sta·be** *m* last (*or* final) letter; **~drei·ßi·ger** *m* man in his late thirties; ***ein ~ sein*** *a.* be in one's late thirties
En·de ['ɛndə] *n* (-s; -n) end; close; *film etc.*: ending; result, outcome; ***~!*** over!; ~ ***Januar*** at the end of January; ~ ***der dreißiger Jahre*** in the late thirties; ***er ist ~ zwanzig*** he's in his late twenties; ***am*** ~ a) in the end, b) after all, eventually, c) in the long run, d) maybe; ***am ~ mußten wir hinlaufen*** we ended (F wound) up having to walk there; *fig.* ***ich bin am*** ~ I'm finished, F I've had it; ***der Wagen ist*** (***ziemlich***) ***am*** ~ the car's (just about) had it; ***bis zum bitteren*** ~ to the bitter end; ***letzten ~s*** after all; in the end, at the end of the day, when all is said and done; *e-r Sache* ***ein ~ machen*** (*or* ***bereiten***) put an end to; ***zu ~ führen*** finish, see *s.th.* through; ***zu ~ gehen*** a) → ***enden,*** b) *supplies etc.*: run short; ***zu ~ sein*** be over; ***zu ~ lesen*** finish (reading); ***zu ~ schreiben*** finish (writing); *et.* ***zu ~ denken*** think out; ***alles hat einmal ein*** ~ there's an end to everything; ***das muß ein ~ haben*** (*or* ***nehmen***) it's got to stop; ***es nimmt kein*** ~ it just goes on and on; ***ein schlimmes*** (*or* ***böses***) ***~ nehmen*** come to a bad end; ***mit dir wird es noch ein schlimmes ~ nehmen*** you'll come to a bad end; ***und damit ~!*** and that's that!; ***er findet kein*** ~ he can't stop; ~ ***gut, alles gut*** all's well that ends well; ***das dicke ~ kommt nach*** the worst is yet to come; *die Arbeit* ***geht ihrem ~ entgegen*** is nearing completion; ***es geht mit ihm zu*** ~ he's going fast; ***es ist noch ein gutes ~ bis dahin*** it's a long way off yet; ***ohne daß ein ~ abzusehen wäre*** with no end in sight; ***das bedeutet das ~ von*** (*or gen.*) that spells the end (*or* demise) of; ***das ~ vom Lied war*** the end of the story was, F the upshot of it was; F ***am ~ der Welt wohnen*** F live at the back of beyond; → ***Latein, Weisheit***
End·ef,fekt ['ɛnt-] *m*: ***im*** ~ in the final analysis; in the end
en·de·misch [ɛn'de:mɪʃ] *adj.* ⚕ endemic
en·den ['ɛndən] *v/i.* (h) (come to an) end, draw to a close; finish, stop; ~ ***in*** *dat.* end (F wind) up in; ~ ***mit*** *dat.* end (up) with,

end in; *ling.* ~ ***auf*** *acc.* end with; ***schlimm*** (*or* ***böse***) ~ come to a bad end; ***es endete damit, daß*** the outcome (*or* result, F upshot) was that, ***er ging:*** *a.* it ended (up) with him leaving; ***nicht ~ wollend*** unending

End|er·geb·nis ['ɛnt-] *n* final result (*a. sport and* ℛ); **~er·zeug·nis** *n* end product; **~fünf·zi·ger** *m* man in his late fifties; ***ein ~ sein*** *a.* be in one's late fifties

end·gül·tig ['ɛntgʏltɪç] **I.** *adj.* final; conclusive; ***~ machen*** finalize; **II.** *adv.* finally; for good; once and for all; ***das steht ~ fest*** that's (for) definite; ***damit ist es ~ aus*** that's over for good; ***damit ist die Sache ~ entschieden*** that settles the matter once and for all; **'End·gül·tig·keit** *f* (-; *no pl.*) finality

End|hal·te·stel·le ['ɛnt-] *f* terminus; **~haus** *n* end-of-terrace house; ***wir wohnen im ~*** we live at the end of the row

en·di·gen ['ɛndɪgən] *v/i.* → ***enden***

En·di·vie [ɛn'diːvĭə] *f* (-; -n) ⚘ endive

End|kampf ['ɛnt-] *m* **1.** *sport*: final; **2.** ⚔ final phase of fighting, final struggle; **~kon·so,nant** *m* final consonant

End·la·ger ['ɛnt-] *n* final disposal site; **'end·la·gern** *v/t.* (*only inf. and p.p.*, h) dispose of *s.th.* permanently; **'End·la·ger·stät·te** *f* final disposal site; **'End·la·ge·rung** *f* final disposal

End·lauf ['ɛnt-] *m sport*: final (heat)

end·lich ['ɛntlɪç] **I.** *adv.* **1.** finally, at (long) last; ***~ doch*** after all; ***hör ~ auf!*** stop it, will you!; ***na ~!*** at last!, *iro.* about time too!; ***bist du ~ fertig?*** *iro.* have you quite finished?; ***das solltest du ~ wissen*** you should know that by now; **II.** *adj.* **2.** final, ultimate; **3.** limited; **4.** *phls. and* ℛ finite; **'End·lich·keit** *f* (-; *no pl.*) finiteness, finite nature (*gen.* of)

end·los ['ɛntloːs] **I.** *adj.* endless, never-ending, unending; interminable; *a. fig.* infinite, boundless; ⚙ continuous; ***bis ins 2e*** ad infinitum; **II.** *adv.* endlessly; ***es zog sich ~ hin*** it went on forever; ***vor ~ langer Zeit*** ages and ages ago, a long, long time ago, back at the beginning of time; **'End·lo·sig·keit** *f* (-; *no pl.*) endlessness

'End·los|pa,pier *n* fan-fold paper; **~schlei·fe** *f* (infinite) loop

End|lö·sung ['ɛnt-] *f pol. hist.* Final Solution; **~mar·ke** *f* end-of-tape marker; **~mon,ta·ge** *f* ⚙ final assembly; **~num·mer** *f* final digit

en·do·gen [ɛndo'geːn] *adj.* endogenous

en·do·krin [ɛndo'kriːn] *adj.* endocrine

en·do·morph [ɛndo'mɔrf] *adj.* endomorphic

En·dor·phin [ɛndɔr'fiːn] *n* (-s; -e) endorphin

En·do·skop [ɛndo'skoːp] *n* (-s; -e) endoscope; **En·do·sko·pie** [ɛndosko'piː] *f* (-; -n) endoscopy

End|pha·se ['ɛnt-] *f* final stage; **~preis** *m* retail price; **~pro,dukt** *n* end (*or* final, finished) product; **~punkt** *m* end; *fig.* ***an e-m ~ angelangt sein*** have come to an end (***in*** *dat.* in); **~reim** *m* end rhyme; **~re·sul,tat** *n* final result; **~run·de** *f sport*: final(s *pl.*); **~sech·zi·ger** *m* man in his sixties; ***ein ~ sein*** *a.* be in one's late sixties; **~sieb·zi·ger** *m* man in his late seventies; ***ein ~ sein*** *a.* be in one's late seventies; **~sil·be** *f* final syllable; **~spiel** *n* **1.** *sport*: final(s *pl.*); ***ins ~ einziehen*** go to the finals; **2.** *chess*: end game; **~spurt** *m* final spurt (*a. fig.*), finish; *fig. a.* final burst; **~sta·di·um** *n* final stage(s *pl.*); ***im ~*** in the final stages; ⚕ ***Krebs im ~*** terminal cancer; **~sta·ti,on** *f* terminus; *fig.* end of the road; ***~! Alles aussteigen bitte!*** all change please!; **~stück** *n* end (piece); **~stu·fe** *f* **1.** ⚡ output stage; → ***Endverstärker***; **2.** *rocket*: final stage; **~sum·me** *f* (sum) total

En·dung ['ɛndʊŋ] *f* (-; -en) *ling.* ending

End|ur·sa·che ['ɛnt-] *f* final cause; **~urteil** *n* final judg(e)ment; **~ver·brauch** *m* final consumption; **~ver·brau·cher** *m* end user; **~ver·stär·ker** *m* power amplifier; **~vier·zi·ger** *m* man in his late forties; ***ein ~ sein*** *a.* be in one's late forties; **~vo,kal** *m* final vowel

End·zeit ['ɛnt-] *f bibl.* last days *pl.*; **'end·zeit·lich** *adj.* eschatological; **'End·zeit·stim·mung** *f* doomsday atmosphere

End|ziel ['ɛnt-] *n* final objective, ultimate goal; **~zif·fer** *f* last (*or* final) digit; **~zu·stand** *m* final state; **~zwan·zi·ger** *m* young man in his late twenties; ***ein ~ sein*** *a.* be in one's late twenties; **~zweck** *m* final purpose

Ener·ge·tik [enɛr'geːtɪk] *f* (-; *no pl.*) *phys.* energetics *pl.*; **ener·ge·tisch** [enɛr'geːtɪʃ] *adj.* energetical

Ener·gie [enɛr'giː] *f* (-; -n) **1.** *phys.* energy, ⚡ *a.* power; **2.** *no pl. fig.* energy, drive; **2arm** *adj.* **1.** low-energy ..., low in energy; **2.** low in energy resources; **~auf·wand** *m* (amount of) energy involved; ***der ~ lohnt (sich) nicht*** it's not worth the effort involved; **~be·auf·trag·te** *m* energy commissioner; **~be·darf** *m* energy requirement(s *pl.*) *or* demand; **2be·wußt** *adj.* energy-conscious; **~bün·del** *fig. n* bundle of energy, live wire; **~ein·heit** *f* unit of energy; **~ein·spa·rung** *f a. pl.* conservation of energy; energy saving; **2ge·la·den** *fig. adj.* bursting with energy; **~ge·win·nung** *f* energy production; **~haus·halt** *m physiol.* energy balance; **~kri·se** *f* energy crisis

ener'gie·los *adj.* lacking in energy, listless; ***~ sein*** *a.* have no energy; **Ener'gie·lo·sig·keit** *f* (-; *no pl.*) lack of energy, listlessness

Ener'gie|po·li,tik *f* energy policy; **~quel·le** *f* **1.** source of energy; **2.** ⚡ *etc.* power source; **2reich** *adj.* **1.** high-energy ..., high in energy; **2.** energy-rich ..., rich in energy resources; **~re,ser·ven** *pl.* energy reserves; spare energy *sg.*

Ener'gie·spa·ren *n* conservation of energy; energy saving; **ener'gie·spa·rend** *adj.* energy-saving, power-saving; **Ener'gie·spar·pro,gramm** *n* energy-saving program(me)

Ener'gie|spen·der *m* energy booster; **~trä·ger** *m* source of energy; **~ver·brauch** *m* energy consumption; **~ver·schwen·dung** *f* waste of energy; **~ver·sor·gung** *f* energy supply; **~wirt·schaft** *f* energy (*or* power-supply) industry

ener·gisch [e'nɛrgɪʃ] **I.** *adj.* energetic; forceful *personality etc.*; brisk; firm, vigorous *measures etc.*; vehement *protest etc.*; ***~ werden*** put one's foot down, ***j-m gegenüber:*** get tough with s.o.; ***ein ~es Wort mit j-m reden*** have a word with s.o., give s.o. a good talking-to; **II.** *adv.* energetically; forcefully; vigorously; vehemently; ***~ vorgehen*** take firm measures *or* action (***gegen*** *acc.* against); ***~ bestreiten*** firmly (*or* vehemently) deny; ***~ vorantreiben*** push (*or* drive) forward

eng [ɛŋ] **I.** *adj.* narrow (*a. fig.*); cramped; crowded; small; tight *dress etc.*; *fig.* close *friend(ship) etc.*; ***~ an*** *dat.* close to; ***~e Kurve*** tight corner; ***in ~en Verhältnissen leben*** live in cramped conditions; ***auf ~stem Raum*** crowded together; ***es ist sehr ~ in der Küche*** *a.* there's not much room to move in the kitchen; ***es ist bei uns etwas ~*** we're a bit cramped for space; ***~er machen*** tighten, take in; ***die Hose ist mir zu ~ geworden*** these trousers don't fit (me) any more; *fig.* ***im ~sten Kreis*** with (the family and) a few close friends; ***im ~sten Kreis der Familie*** with the close family members; ***die ~ere Familie*** the immediate family; → ***Sinn, Wahl*** 1; **II.** *adv.* narrowly; tightly; closely; ***~ anliegen*** fit tightly, be a tight fit; ***~ beieinander*** (*or* ***nebeneinander***) close together; ***~ zusammengedrängt*** crowded (*or* huddled) together; *fig.* ***~ befreundet sein*** be close friends; ***~ verbunden sein*** be closely connected; ***er sieht die Sache sehr ~*** he takes a very narrow view of the matter; ***du darfst es nicht so ~ sehen*** a) you mustn't take such a narrow view, b) you mustn't take it so seriously; ***sich ~ an die Vorschriften halten*** stick closely to the rules

En·ga·ge·ment [ãgaʒə'mãː] *n* (-s; -s) **1.** commitment, involvement; ***ein stärkeres ~*** greater involvement, stronger commitment; **2.** *thea. etc.* engagement;

en·ga·gie·ren [ãga'ʒiːrən] (h) **I.** *v/t.* employ, take on; engage; **II.** *v/refl.*: ***sich ~*** get (*or* be) involved (***in*** *dat.* in); ***sich ~ für*** *acc.* be very involved (*or* active) in, do a lot (*or* a great deal) for; **en·ga·giert** [ãga'ʒiːɐt] *adj.* committed; ***sehr ~ sein*** *a.* be very involved (***bei*** *dat.* with, in); ***politisch ~*** politically involved (*or* active); **En·ga'giert·heit** *f* (-; *no pl.*) commitment

'eng|an·lie·gend *adj.* tight(-fitting); **~be·druckt** *adj.* closely printed; **~be·freun·det** *adj.* close; **~be·grenzt** *adj.* narrow, restricted; **~be·schrie·ben** *adj.* closely written; **~brü·stig** [-brʏstɪç] *adj.* narrow-chested

En·ge ['ɛŋə] *f* (-; -n) **1.** *no pl.* narrowness (*a. fig.*); cramped (*or* claustrophobic) conditions *pl.*; tightness; *fig.* ***in die ~ treiben*** drive into a corner; ***in die ~ getrieben*** with one's back to the wall; **2.** narrow passage, *a. fig.* bottleneck; **3.** *geogr.* strait(s *pl.*)

En·gel ['ɛŋəl] *m* (-s; -) angel; ***guter*** (*or* ***rettender***) ~ guardian angel; ***gefallener ~*** fallen angel; ***~ des Lichts*** (***Todes***) angel of light (death); F ***die ~ im Himmel singen hören*** see stars; ***du bist ein ~!*** you're an angel (*or* a real dear)!; ***er ist auch nicht gerade ein ~*** he's not exactly an angel himself; **'En·gel·chen** *n* (-s; -) little angel; **'en·gel·haft** *adj.* angelic(ally *adv.*)

'En·gel|ma·cher *m* (-s; -) backstreet abortionist; **~schar** *f* host of angels

'En·gels|chor *m* choir of angels; **~ge·duld** *f* endless (*or* infinite) patience, *the* patience of Job; **~mie·ne** *f* innocent look; **~zun·ge** *f*: ***mit ~n reden*** use all one's powers of persuasion, *lit.* speak honeyed words; ***mit ~n auf j-n einreden*** do everything in one's power to persuade s.o.

En·ger·ling ['ɛŋɐlɪŋ] *m* (-s; -e) white (*or* cockchafer) grub
'**eng·her·zig** *adj.* small-minded; '**Eng·her·zig·keit** *f* (-; *no pl.*) small-mindedness
Eng·län·der ['ɛŋlɛndɐ] *m* (-s; -) **1.** Englishman; ***die*** ~ the English (*pl.*); ***er ist*** ~ he's English, he's an Englishman; **2.** ⚙ wrench; **Eng·län·de·rin** ['ɛŋlɛndərɪn] *f* (-; -nen) Englishwoman; ***sie ist*** ~ she's English
eng·lisch[1] ['ɛŋlɪʃ] **I.** *adj.* English; *w.s.* British; ***die*** ~***e Kirche*** the Church of England, the Anglican church; **II.** *adv.*: *gastr.* ~ (***gebraten***) rare; **III.** 2 *n* (-en) English, the English language; ***auf englisch*** in English; ***aus dem*** ~***en*** from (the) English
'**eng·lisch**[2] *adj.*: ***der*** 2***e Gruß*** *eccl.*, *art*: the Angelic Salutation
'**Eng·lisch|horn** *n* ♪ cor anglais; 2**spra·chig** [-ʃpraːxɪç] *adj.* **1.** English-language ...; ~***e Literatur*** English literature; **2.** → 2**spre·chend** *adj.* English-speaking; ~ˌ**un·ter·richt** *m* **1.** teaching of English; **2.** English lesson(s *pl.*) *or* class(es *pl.*)
eng·ma·schig ['ɛŋmaʃɪç] *adj.* fine-meshed; *fig.* close-meshed; *soccer etc.*: close
'**Eng·paß** *m* **1.** (narrow) pass; **2.** *fig.* bottleneck (***in*** *dat.* in), squeeze (in); shortage (of); ***Engpässe in der Produktion*** a production bottleneck; ***Fernseher sind ein*** ~ there's a bottleneck in the supply of television sets, television sets are in short supply
en gros [ã'gro] *adv.* wholesale
eng·stir·nig ['ɛŋʃtɪrnɪç] *adj.* narrow-minded; '**Eng·stir·nig·keit** *f* (-; *no pl.*) narrow-mindedness, tunnel vision
'**eng|umˌgrenzt** *adj.* narrowly defined; ~**umˌschlun·gen** *adj.* in close embrace, locked in embrace; ***ein*** ~***es Paar*** *a.* an embracing couple; ~**ver·bün·det** *adj.* closely allied; ~**zei·lig** [-tsaɪlɪç] *adj.* narrow-spaced; (*a. adv.* ~ ***getippt***) single-spaced
En·kel ['ɛŋkəl] *m* (-s; -) grandchild; grandson; *w.s.* descendant; **En·ke·lin** ['ɛŋkəlɪn] *f* (-; -nen) granddaughter
'**En·kel|kind** *n* grandchild; ~**sohn** *m* grandson; ~**toch·ter** *f* granddaughter
En·kla·ve [ɛn'klaːvə] *f* (-; -n) enclave
en masse [ã'mas] *adv.* en masse
en mi·nia·ture [ãminja'tyːr] *adv.* in miniature
enorm [e'nɔrm] **I.** *adj.* vast, huge; *fig.* tremendous; **II.** *adv.*: ~ ***hoch*** *etc.* enormously (*or* immensely) tall *etc.*; ***die Preise sind*** ~ ***gestiegen*** prices have shot up; ~ ***viel Geld*** vast (*or* huge) amounts of money
en pas·sant [ãpa'sãː] *adv.* in passing
En·quete [ã'keːt(ə)] *f* (-; -n) *pol.* inquiry; ~**kom·mis·siˌon** *f* commission of inquiry
En·sem·ble [ã'sãːbl] *n* (-s; -s) ♪ ensemble; *thea. a.* company; cast
ent'ar·ten *v/i.* (sn) degenerate, become degenerate; **ent'ar·tet** *adj.* degenerate; *fig. a.* decadent; *hist.* ~***e Kunst*** degenerate art; **Ent'ar·tung** *f* (-; -en) degeneration
ent'äu·ßern *v/refl.* (h): ***sich*** *e-r Sache* ~ a) relinquish, b) dispose of, divest o.s. of
ent·beh·ren [ɛnt'beːrən] (h) **I.** *v/t.* **1.** do (*or* live) without; spare; ***könntest du den Computer ein paar Stunden*** ~? could you do (*or* manage) without the computer for a few hours?; **2.** miss; **II.** *v/i.*: *e-r Sache* ~ be without, lack; ***die Beschuldigung entbehrt jeder Grundlage*** the charge is entirely unfounded; ***das entbehrt nicht e-r gewissen Ironie*** it's not without its irony; **ent·behr·lich** [ɛnt'beːɐlɪç] *adj.* dispensable; non-essential; **Ent'behr·lich·keit** *f* (-; *no pl.*) dispensability; superfluousness; **Ent'beh·rung** *f* (-; -en) privation, want, deprivation; **ent'beh·rungs·reich** *adj.* full of privation; ***ein*** ~***es Leben*** *a.* a life of want
ent'bin·den (entband, entbunden, h) **I.** *v/t.* **1.** release, excuse (***von*** *dat.* from); **2.** ⚖ set free; **3.** ⚕ deliver (***von*** *dat.* of); ***entbunden werden von*** *dat.* give birth to; **II.** *v/i.* ⚕ be confined; **Ent'bin·dung** *f* (-; -en) **1.** *no pl.* release (***von*** *dat.* from); **2.** ⚕ delivery
Ent'bin·dungs|pfle·ger *m* male midwife; ~**sta·tiˌon** *f* maternity ward
ent'blät·tern (h) **I.** *v/t.* strip of leaves; **II.** *v/refl.*: ***sich*** ~ shed its leaves; F *fig.* strip, shed one's clothes, F peel one's clothes off
ent·blö·den [ɛnt'bløːdən] *v/refl.* (h): ***sich nicht*** ~ ***zu*** *inf.* have the cheek to *inf.*
ent·blö·ßen [ɛnt'bløːsən] (h) **I.** *v/t.* bare, expose; uncover; *fig.* lay bare; *fig.* ***j-n e-r Sache*** ~ denude s.o. of s.th.; **II.** *v/refl.*: ***sich*** ~ take one's clothes off; *fig.* ***sich*** *e-r Sache* ~ divest o.s. of; **ent'blößt** *adj.* bare; *fig.* destitute, stripped (*gen.* of); ~***en Hauptes*** bareheaded; **Ent'blö·ßung** *f* (-; -en) baring, exposing; uncovering; *fig.* exposure
ent'bren·nen *v/i.* (entbrannte, entbrannt, sn) *fight*: break out, *a. temper etc.*: flare up; ***in Haß entbrannt*** burning with hate; ***in Liebe für j-n*** ~ fall passionately in love with s.o.
ent·bü·ro·kra·ti'sie·ren *v/t.* (h) deregulate; **Ent·bü·ro·kra·ti'sie·rung** *f* (-; *no pl.*) deregulation
Ent·chen ['ɛntçən] *n* (-s; -) duckling, little duck
ent'decken (*sep.* -k·k-) *v/t.* (h) **1.** discover; find out; see, spot; detect, spot *mistake etc.*; ***zufällig*** ~ stumble (up)on; **2.** ***j-m et.*** ~ reveal (*or* disclose) s.th. to s.o.
Ent·decker [ɛnt'dɛkɐ] (*sep.* -k·k-) *m* (-s; -) discoverer; explorer; ~**freu·de** *f* joy(s *pl.*) of discovery; ~**stolz** *m* pride of discovery
Ent'deckung (*sep.* -k·k-) *f* (-; -en) discovery; ***m-e neueste*** ~ my latest discovery
Ent'deckungs|rei·se *f* voyage of discovery; expedition; F *fig.* ***auf*** ~ ***gehen*** (go out and) explore one's surroundings; ~**rei·sen·de** *m*, *f* (-n; -n) explorer; discoverer; ~**zeit·al·ter** *n* age of discovery
En·te ['ɛntə] *f* (-; -n) **1.** duck; ***junge*** ~ duckling; F *fig.* ***schwimmen wie e-e bleierne*** ~ F swim like a brick; → ***lahm*** 3; **2.** canard, hoax; **3.** F *mot.* deux chevaux, 2CV; **4.** ⚕ (bed) urinal
ent'eh·ren *v/t.* (h) dishono(u)r, disgrace; degrade; *obs.* violate; **ent'eh·rend** *adj.* disgraceful; degrading; **Ent'eh·rung** *f* (-; -en) dishono(u)r(ing); degradation
ent'eig·nen *v/t.* (h) expropriate; dispossess; **Ent'eig·nung** *f* (-; -en) expropriation; dispossession
ent'ei·len *lit. v/i.* (sn) hasten away; *time*: fly past
ent·ei·sen [ɛnt'ʔaɪzən] *v/t.* (enteiste, enteist, h) clear of ice; *mot.* defrost; ✈ de-ice; **Ent'ei·sung** *f* (-; -en) *mot.* defrosting; ✈ de-icing; **Ent'ei·sungs·an·la·ge** *f mot.* defroster; ✈ de-icing system
En·te·le·chie [ɛntelɛ'çiː] *f* (-; -n) *phls.* entelechy
'**En·ten|bra·ten** *m* roast duck; ~**ei** *n* duck's egg; ~**grüt·ze** *f* ♣ duckweed; ~**jagd** *f* duck shooting; ~**kü·ken** *n* duckling; ~**schna·bel** *m* duck's bill
En·tente [ã'tãːt(ə)] *f* (-; -n) *pol.* entente; *hist.* ~ ***cordiale*** entente (cordiale); ***Große*** (***Kleine***) ~ Great (Little) Entente
'**En·ten·teich** *m* duck pond
ent'er·ben *v/t.* (h) disinherit; **ent·erbt** [ɛnt'ʔɛrpt] *adj*: ***die*** 2***en*** the disinherited (*pl.*); **Ent'er·bung** *f* (-, -en) disinheriting
En·te·rich ['ɛntərɪç] *m* (-s; -e) drake
en·tern ['ɛntɐn] *v/t.* (h) board *a ship*
ent·fa·chen [ɛnt'faxən] *v/t.* (entfachte, entfacht, h) kindle (*a. fig.*), *fig.* rouse; whip up; provoke, spark off *a discussion etc.*
ent'fah·ren *v/i.* (entfuhr, entfahren, sn): ***ihm entfuhr ein Seufzer*** *etc.* he let out a sigh *etc.*
ent'fal·len *v/i.* (entfiel, entfallen, sn) **1.** ***der Name ist mir*** ~ the name escapes me, I forget the name, I can't think of the name; **2.** be cancel(l)ed, be dropped, be omitted, be left out; be inapplicable; ***entfällt*** not applicable (*abbr.* N/A); **3.** ***auf j-n*** ~ *share etc.*: fall to s.o.; ***auf jeden*** ~ ***10 Mark*** each person pays (*or* gets) 10 marks
ent'fal·ten (h) **I.** *v/t.* **1.** unfold; spread out; unroll, roll out; **2.** *fig.* develop (***zu*** *dat.* into); display; **II.** *v/refl.*: ***sich*** ~ **3.** *blossom etc.*: open up; *feathers*: open out, fan out; *parachute*: open (up); *flag*: unfurl; **4.** *fig.* develop (***zu*** *dat.* into); ***sich kreativ*** ~ develop one's creative abilities; ***hier kann man sich frei*** ~ there's plenty of room for (personal) development here; **5.** *fig.* display itself, *lit.* unfurl; **Ent'fal·tung** *fig. f* (-; *no pl.*) **1.** development; ***zur*** ~ ***kommen*** (be able to) develop, blossom, *talent, potential etc.*: *a.* be realized; **2.** display; **Ent'fal·tungs·mög·lich·kei·ten** *pl.* opportunities for development
ent'fär·ben *v/t.* (h) take the colo(u)r (*or* dye) out of; bleach; **Ent'fär·bung** *f* (-; *no pl.*) removal of the dye (*gen.* from); **Ent'fär·bungs·mit·tel** *n* dye remover; bleaching agent
ent·fer·nen [ɛnt'fɛrnən] (entfernte, entfernt, h) **I.** *v/t.* remove (*a. stain*), take away; clear away; ~ ***von*** *dat.* take off, cross off *a list etc.*; ***j-n aus dem Amt*** ~ remove s.o. from office; **II.** *v/refl.*: ***sich*** ~ go away, leave, take o.s. off; withdraw; (gradually) disappear; *fig.* deviate (***von*** *dat.* from *a subject etc.*); distance o.s. (from); become estranged (from *s.o.*); *fig.* ***sich*** (***voneinander***) ~ drift apart;
ent'fernt **I.** *adj.* **1.** remote, distant; ***e-e Meile von X*** ~ a mile away from X; ***zwei Meilen voneinander*** ~ two miles apart; **2.** *fig.* remote, faint, vague *recollection etc.*; ~***e Verwandte*** distant relations (*or* relatives); ***weit*** ~***!*** far from it, F way out; ***weit*** ~ ***davon zu*** *inf.* far from *ger.*; ***ich bin weit davon*** ~ ***zu*** *inf.* I haven't the slightest intention of *ger.*; **II.** *adv.* **3.** far away; **4.** *fig.* ~ ***verwandt*** distantly related; ***nicht im*** ~***esten*** not in the least; ***ich habe nicht im*** ~***esten daran gedacht***

zu *inf.* I never even dreamed of *ger.*, it never occurred to me to *inf.*; **ich hätte nicht im ~esten geglaubt, daß** I wouldn't have dreamed that, I didn't have the slightest idea that; **Ent'fer·nung** *f* (-; -en) **1.** distance; range; **in e-r ~ von** *dat.* at a distance of; **aus der ~** from (*or* at) a distance; **aus einiger ~** from a distance; **aus kurzer ~** at short (*or* close) range; **aus großer ~** at long range; **2.** *no pl.* removal; **3.** *no pl.* dismissal; **~ aus dem Amt** *a.* removal from office

Ent'fer·nungs|mes·ser *m phot.* rangefinder; **~ring** *m phot.* focus(s)ing ring; **~ska·la** *f phot.* focus(s)ing scale

ent'fes·seln *v/t.* (h) provoke, unleash, touch off, trigger (off); **ent'fes·selt** *adj.* raging *elements etc.*; **Ent'fes·se·lungs·künst·ler** *m* escape artist

ent'fet·ten *v/t.* (h) remove the grease (*or* fat) from; **Ent'fet·tungs·kur** *f* slimming diet

ent'fiel *pret. of* **entfallen**

ent·flamm·bar [ɛnt'flambaːɐ] *adj. a.* ⚙ flammable, *Brit. a.* inflammable; **ent'flam·men I.** *v/t.* (h) **1.** *fig.* rouse, stir up; **II.** *v/i.* (sn) **2.** *fig.* be aroused (*or* kindled), flare up, break out; **3.** ⚙ ignite; flash; **III.** *v/refl.* (h): *fig.* **sich ~ an** *dat.* be aroused by

ent'flech·ten *v/t.* (entflocht, entflochten, h) **1.** *a. fig.* disentangle; **2.** ✝ decartelize

ent'flie·gen *v/i.* (entflog, entflogen, sn) fly away (*dat.* from); **dem Käfig ~** escape from its cage; **„blauer Papagei entflogen"** escaped: blue parrot

ent'flie·hen *v/i.* (entfloh, entflohen, sn) **1.** escape (*dat.* from); flee ([from] *s.th., s.o.*); *fig.* **dem Schicksal ~** escape one's fate; **dem Alltag ~** escape from (*or* flee) everyday reality; **dem Lärm ~** escape (from) the noise; **2.** *fig.* slip away, fly past

ent·frem·den [ɛnt'frɛmdən] (h) **I.** *v/t.* alienate (*dat.* from); **et. s-m Zweck ~** put s.th. to an unintended use; **II.** *v/refl.*: **sich (gegenseitig) ~** become estranged; **sich j-m ~** become estranged from s.o., become a stranger to s.o.; **Ent'frem·dung** *f* (-; *no pl.*) estrangement, alienation

ent'fro·sten *v/t.* (h) defrost; **Ent·fro·ster** [ɛnt'frɔstɐ] *m* (-s; -) *mot.* defroster

ent'fuhr *pret. of* **entfahren**

ent'füh·ren *v/t.* (h) kidnap, abduct; ✈ hijack, *esp. Am. a.* skyjack; F *fig.* run away with *s.th.*; **Ent'füh·rer** *m* (-s; -) kidnapper; ✈ hijacker, *esp. Am. a.* skyjacker; **Ent'füh·rung** *f* (-; -en) kidnapping, abduction; ✈ hijacking, *esp. Am. a.* skyjacking

ent·gan·gen [ɛnt'gaŋən] *p.p. of* **entgehen**

ent'ge·gen I. *prp.* (*dat.*) contrary to, against; **~ allen Erwartungen** contrary to all expectations; **~ s-n Anweisungen** *a.* in defiance of his instructions; **II.** *adv.* towards; against *the wind etc.*; **~ar·bei·ten** *v/i.* (*sep.*, h) work against, counteract; **~blicken** (*sep.* -k·k-) *v/i.* (*sep.*, h) → **entgegensehen; ~brin·gen** *v/t.* (*irr.*, *sep.*, h, → **bringen**): **j-m et. ~** bring s.th. to s.o.; *fig.* **j-m** *ein Gefühl etc.* **~** show *s.th.* for s.o.; *e-r Sache* **Interesse** *etc.* **~** show an (*or* some) interest *etc.* in; **~ei·len** *v/i.* (*sep.*, sn) rush towards (*a. fig.*), rush to meet *s.o.*; *fig.* rush headlong into *disaster etc.*; **~fah·ren** *v/i.* (*irr.*, *sep.*, sn, → **fahren**): **j-m ~** drive out to meet s.o.; **~fie·bern** *v/i.* (*sep.*, h): **e-r Sache ~** feverishly await s.th.; **~ge·hen** *v/i.* (*irr.*, *sep.*, sn, → **gehen**) walk towards, go to meet *s.o.*; *fig.* approach; face *danger, fate etc.*; be heading for *disaster etc.*; *fig.* **dem Ende ~** be drawing to(wards) a close

ent'ge·gen·ge·setzt I. *adj.* opposite; contradictory, opposing, conflicting; **s-e Meinung ist Ihrer völlig ~** his opinion completely contradicts yours (*or* is completely opposed to yours); **II.** *adv.*: **genau ~ handeln** do the exact opposite, do exactly the opposite

ent'ge·gen|hal·ten *v/t.* (*irr.*, *sep.*, h, → **halten**) **1. j-m et. ~** hold s.th. out to s.o.; **2.** *fig.* say *s.th.* in answer *or* reply (*dat.* to); **j-m et. ~** point s.th. out to s.o.; **dem hielt er entgegen, daß** he countered (*or* objected) that; **~han·deln** *v/i.* (*sep.*, h) act against (*dat. s.th.*)

ent'ge·gen·kom·men I. *v/i.* (*irr.*, *sep.*, sn, → **kommen**) come towards, come to meet *s.o.*; *fig.* make concessions towards, oblige *s.o.*; comply with *s.o.'s requests etc.*; **j-m auf halbem Wege ~** *a. fig.* meet s.o. halfway; *fig.* **j-m sehr ~** be very convenient for s.o., suit s.o. fine, (*a.* **j-s Vorstellungen ~**) fit in well with s.o.'s plans (*or* ideas); **II.** ♀ *n* (-s) **1.** obligingness, complaisance; **2.** concession(s *pl.*); **ent'ge·gen·kom·mend** *adj.* **1.** *fig.* obliging, accommodating, complaisant; **2.** oncoming *traffic*; **ent'ge·gen·kom·men·der'wei·se** *adv.* **1.** obligingly; **2.** as a (*or* by way of) concession

ent'ge·gen·lau·fen *v/i.* (*irr.*, *sep.*, sn, → **laufen**) **1.** run towards, run to meet *s.o.*; **2.** *fig.* go against, run counter to *one's plans etc.*

Ent'ge·gen·nah·me [-naːmə] *f* (-; *no pl.*) acceptance; **bei ~** *gen.* on receipt of; **ent'ge·gen·neh·men** *v/t.* (*irr.*, *sep.*, h, → **nehmen**) accept, take; **et. dankend ~** gratefully accept s.th., accept s.th. with thanks

ent'ge·gen|schau·en *v/i.* (*sep.*, h) → **entgegensehen; ~schla·gen** *fig. v/i.* (*irr.*, *sep.*, h, → **schlagen**): **j-m ~** go out to s.o.; **~se·hen** *v/i.* (*irr.*, *sep.*, h, → **sehen**) await, look forward to; face *danger etc.*; **~set·zen** (*sep.*, h) **I.** *v/t.* **1.** → **entgegenhalten** 2; **2. e-m Argument** *etc.* **et. ~** counter an argument *etc.* with s.th.; **Widerstand** *etc.* **~** put up a resistance, offer (some) resistance (*dat.* to); **dem habe ich nichts entgegenzusetzen** I can't think of any arguments against, F it sounds fine to me; **II.** *v/refl.*: **sich e-r Sache ~** oppose s.th.

ent'ge·gen·ste·hen *v/i.* (*irr.*, *sep.*, h, → **stehen**) **1.** stand in the way of; **2.** conflict with; **dem steht nichts entgegen** there's nothing to be said against that; **ent'ge·gen·ste·hend** *adj.* contradictory, conflicting

ent'ge·gen|stel·len (*sep.*, h) **I.** *v/t.* **1. j-m et. ~** set s.th. against s.o.; **2.** → **entgegensetzen; II.** *fig. v/refl.*: **sich** *j-m or e-r Sache* **~** oppose, resist; **~stem·men** *fig. v/refl.* (*sep.*, h): **sich e-r Sache ~** set o.s. against s.th., resist s.th. (with all one's might); **~strecken** (*sep.* -k·k-) *v/t.* (*sep.*, h): **j-m et. ~** hold s.th. out towards s.o.; **~tre·ten** *v/i.* (*irr.*, *sep.*, sn, → **treten**) **1.** (*dat.*) walk towards, go up to *s.o.*; **2.** *fig.* **j-m ~** present itself to s.o.; **3.** (*dat.*) oppose; take steps against *s.th.*; face *danger etc.*; counter *threats etc.*; contradict, speak out against *rumo(u)rs etc.*; **~wir·ken** *v/i.* (*sep.*, h) counteract, fight

ent·geg·nen [ɛnt'geːgnən] *v/t. and v/i.* (entgegnete, entgegnet, h) reply; retort; **Ent'geg·nung** *f* (-; -en) reply (**auf** *acc.* to); retort

ent'ge·hen *v/i.* (entging, entgangen, sn) **1.** escape *death etc.*; **e-r Strafe (dem Gesetz) ~** evade punishment (the law); **knapp e-m Attentat** *etc.* **~** narrowly escape assassination *etc.*; **2.** *fig.* **j-m ~** escape s.o.('s notice); **es kann ihm doch nicht ~, daß** he can't fail to notice that; **ihm entging nichts** he didn't miss a thing; **3.** *fig.* **sich et. ~ lassen** miss s.th., let s.th. slip; **er ließ sich die Gelegenheit nicht ~** he seized (F grabbed) the opportunity; **sie läßt sich nichts ~** she takes everything she can get

ent·gei·stert [ɛnt'gaɪstɐt] *adj. and adv.* aghast, dumbfounded, flabbergasted; horrified; **was siehst du mich so ~ an?** why do you look so surprised (*or* shocked)?

Ent·gelt [ɛnt'gɛlt] *n* (-[e]s; -e) remuneration; fee; reward; **gegen ~** subject to payment; **als ~ für** *acc.* in return for; **ent'gel·ten** *v/t.* (entgalt, entgolten, h): **j-m et. ~** pay s.o. for s.th., repay s.o. for s.th.; **j-n et. ~ lassen** make s.o. pay for s.th.; **ent·gelt·lich** [ɛnt'gɛltlɪç] *adj. and adv.* against payment

ent'gif·ten *v/t.* (h) **1.** detoxify; decontaminate, scrub *gases*; **2.** *fig.* **die Atmosphäre ~** clear the air; **Ent'gif·tung** *f* (-; *no pl.*) detoxification; decontamination; **Ent'gif·tungs·an·la·ge** *f* detoxification plant

ent'ging *pret. of* **entgehen**

ent·glei·sen [ɛnt'glaɪzən] *v/i.* (sn) **1.** be derailed, jump the track; **2.** *fig.* commit a faux pas; overstep the mark; **moralisch ~** stray off the straight and narrow; **3.** *fig.* get off the track; **Ent'glei·sung** *f* (-; -en) **1.** derailment; **2.** *fig.* faux pas, gaffe

ent'glei·ten *v/i.* (entglitt, entglitten, sn) **1. j-m ~** slip out of s.o.'s hand(s); **2.** *fig.* **j-m ~** slip out of s.o.'s control, *child etc.*: drift away from s.o.; **es entgleitet mir** I'm losing my grip on it (*or* my hold over it)

ent·gra·ten [ɛnt'graːtən] *v/t.* (entgratete, entgratet, h) ⚙ deburr

ent·grä·ten [ɛnt'grɛːtən] *v/t.* (entgrätete, entgrätet, h) bone, fillet

ent'haa·ren *v/t.* (h) depilate; **Ent'haa·rungs·creme** *f* depilatory (cream)

ent'hal·ten (enthielt, enthalten, h) **I.** *v/t.* contain; hold; comprise; **mit ~ sein in** *dat.* be included in; **3 ist in 12 viermal ~** three goes into twelve four times; **II.** *v/refl.*: **sich ~** *gen.* abstain from, refrain from (*ger.*); *parl.* **sich der Stimme ~** abstain; **ich konnte micht nicht ~ zu** *inf.* I couldn't restrain myself from *ger.*; **ent·halt·sam** [ɛnt'haltzaːm] *adj.* abstemious; moderate, temperate; continent; **Ent'halt·sam·keit** *f* (-; *no pl.*) abstinence; moderation; continence; **vollkommene ~** total abstinence, teetotalism; **Ent'hal·tung** *f* (-; -en) **1.** *no pl.* abstention, continence; **2.** *pol.* abstention

ent'här·ten *v/t.* (h) soften; **Ent'här·tungs·mit·tel** *n* (water) softener

ent·haup·ten [ɛnt'haʊptən] *v/t.* (enthauptete, enthauptet, h) behead, decapitate; **Ent'haup·tung** *f* (-; -en) decapitation; execution

ent'häu·ten *v/t.* (h) **1.** skin, flay; **2.** skin, peel
ent'he·ben *v/t.* (enthob, enthoben, h) relieve of; release (*or* exempt) from *duty etc.*; remove from *office*; ***j-n der Mühe ~*** save (*or* spare) s.o. the trouble; ***j-n vorläufig s-s Amtes ~*** suspend s.o. from office; **Ent'he·bung** *f* (-; -en) release (***von*** *dat.* from); ~ ***vom Amt*** dismissal (*or* removal) from office
ent·hei·li·gen *v/t.* desecrate; **Ent·hei·li·gung** *f* desecration
ent·hem·men I. *v/t.* disinhibit, help *s.o.* lose his (*or* her) inhibitions; **II.** *v/i.* have a disinhibiting effect; **ent·hem·mend I.** *adj.* disinhibitory; **II.** *adv.*: ~ ***wirken*** have a disinhibiting effect (***auf*** *acc.* on); **ent·hemmt** *adj.* free of inhibitions, disinhibited; **Ent·hem·mung** *f* breaking down of (*s.o.'s*) inhibitions
ent'hielt *pret. of* ***enthalten***
ent'hob *pret. of* ***entheben***
ent·ho·ben [ɛnt'ho:bən] *p.p. of* ***entheben***
ent'hül·len (h) **I.** *v/t.* **1.** unveil; show; **2.** *fig.* reveal; bring to light; unmask; **II.** *v/refl.*: ***sich ~*** **3.** F peel off one's clothes; **4.** *fig.* reveal o.s.; **5.** be revealed *or* disclosed (*dat.* to); **Ent'hül·lung** *f* (-; -en) **1.** unveiling; **2.** *fig.* disclosure (*gen.* of); unmasking (of); **3.** *pl.* revelations (***über*** *acc.* about), disclosures (about)
Ent'hül·lungs|jour·na,lis·mus *m* investigative journalism; **~jour·na,list** *m* investigative journalist
ent·hül·sen [ɛnt'hʏlzən] *v/t.* (enthülste, enthülst, h) husk; shell, hull
En·thu·si·as·mus [ɛntu'zĭasmʊs] *m* (-; *no pl.*) enthusiasm; **En·thu·si·ast** [ɛntu'zĭast] *m* (-en; -en) enthusiast, F fan; **en·thu·sia·stisch** [ɛntu'zĭastɪʃ] *adj.* enthusiastic(ally *adv.*)
ent·jung·fern [ɛnt'jʊŋfɐn] *v/t.* (entjungferte, entjungfert, h) deflower; **Ent'jung·fe·rung** *f* (-; -en) deflowering
ent'kal·ken *v/t.* (h) descale, delime; **Ent·kal·ker** [ɛnt'kalkɐ] *m* (-s; -) descaler
ent'kam *pret. of* ***entkommen***
ent'kei·men (h) **I.** *v/i.* **1.** germinate, sprout; **2.** *fig.* spring from; **II.** *v/t.* sterilize; disinfect
ent·ker·nen [ɛnt'kɛrnən] *v/t.* (entkernte, entkernt, h) stone; core; seed
ent'klei·den (h) **I.** *v/t.* **1.** undress; take *s.o.'s* clothes off; **2.** *fig.* divest of, strip of; **II.** *v/refl.*: ***sich ~*** undress, get undressed, take one's clothes off, *formal*: remove (all) one's clothes
ent·kof·fei·niert [ɛntkɔfei'ni:ɐt] *adj.* decaffeinated; ***~er Kaffee*** *a.* F decaf
ent·ko·lo·nia·li'sie·ren *v/t.* (h) decolonialize; **Ent·ko·lo·nia·li'sie·rung** *f* (-; -en) decolonialization
ent'kom·men I. *v/i.* (entkam, entkommen, sn) escape (*dat.* from), get away (from); → ***knapp*** I; **II.** 2 *n* (-s) escape; ***da gibt es kein ~*** there's no escaping
ent'kop·peln *v/t.* (h) uncouple; *radio*: decouple
ent·kor·ken [ɛnt'kɔrkən] *v/t.* (entkorkte, entkorkt, h) uncork
ent·kräf·ten [ɛnt'krɛftən] *v/t.* (entkräftete, entkräftet, h) **1.** weaken, enfeeble, debilitate; enervate; exhaust; **2.** ⚖ invalidate, refute; **Ent'kräf·tung** *f* (-; -en) **1.** weakening, enfeeblement, debilitation; **2.** ⚖ invalidation; refutation
ent'kramp·fen (h) **I.** *v/t.* **1.** relax *muscles etc.*; **II.** *v/refl.*: ***sich ~*** **2.** relax; **3.** *fig.* ease; **Ent'kramp·fung** *f* (-; -en) **1.** relaxation; **2.** *fig.* easing
ent'la·den (entlud, entladen, h) **I.** *v/t.* **1.** unload (*a. rifle etc.*), dump; ⚡ discharge; **2.** *fig.* give vent to *one's anger etc.*; **II.** *v/refl.*: ***sich ~*** **3.** ⚡ discharge; *thunderstorm*: break; *weapon*: go off; **4.** *fig. tension*: be released; *anger etc.*: break out, erupt; ***sein Zorn entlud sich über uns*** he took his anger out on us; **Ent'la·dung** *f* (-; -en) **1.** unloading; dumping; discharge; **2.** *fig.* release; eruption
ent'lang *adv. and prp.* (*acc.*) along; ***die Küste*** (***den Wald*** *etc.*) ~ along the coast (the woods *etc.*); ***die Straße ~*** along the street (*or* road), *walk etc.*: *a.* up (*or* down) the street *or* road; ***die ganze Straße ~*** all the way up (*or* down) the street *or* road, all along the street (*or* road); ***hier ~, bitte!*** this way, please; **~ge·hen** *etc. v/t.* (*a. v/i.*: ***~ an*** *dat.*) (*irr.*, *sep.*, sn, → ***gehen***) go (*or* walk) *etc.* along
ent·lar·ven [ɛnt'larfən] (entlarvte, entlarvt, h) **I.** *v/t.* unmask, expose, F debunk; **II.** *v/refl.*: ***sich ~ als*** turn out to be; **Ent'lar·vung** *f* (-; -en) unmasking, exposure
ent'las·sen *v/t.* (entließ, entlassen, h) discharge (***aus*** *dat.* from); release; dismiss, F fire, give *s.o.* the sack; make redundant; pension off; ⚔ disband; ***aus der Schule ~ werden*** a) leave school, b) be expelled (from school); ***j-n aus e-r Verpflichtung ~*** release (*or* free) s.o. from an obligation; → ***fristlos***; **Ent'las·sung** *f* (-; -en) dismissal; discharge; release; pensioning off; ⚔ disbanding; ***s-e ~ einreichen*** hand in one's notice (*or* resignation), *formal*: tender one's resignation
Ent'las·sungs|ge·such *n* (letter of) resignation; **~grund** *m* grounds *pl.* for dismissal; **~pa,pie·re** *pl.* ⚔ discharge papers, F marching orders, *Am.* F walking papers, pink slip *sg.*; **~schrei·ben** *n* letter of dismissal
ent'la·sten *v/t.* (h) **1.** relieve *s.o.* (***von*** *dat.* of), ease the burden (*or* workload *etc.*) of *s.o.*; take some of the strain off *s.o.*; make life easier for *s.o.*; **2.** ease *the traffic load*; relieve the congestion in *an area*; **3.** ⚖ clear *s.o.* of a charge, exonerate *s.o.*; **4.** ✝ credit *account*; discharge *debtor*; **5.** *skiing*: unweight; **ent'la·stend** *adj.* ⚖ exonerating; **Ent'la·stung** *f* (-; -en) **1.** relief of the strain (*gen.* on), easing the burden *etc.* (of, on); **2.** ⚖ exoneration
Ent'la·stungs|be·weis *m*, **~ma·te·ri,al** *n* ⚖ evidence for the defen|ce (*Am.* -se); **~stra·ße** *f* relief road; **~ven,til** *n* ⚙ safety (*or* relief) valve; **~zeu·ge** *m* witness for the defen|ce (*Am.* -se); **~zug** *m* relief train
ent·lau·ben [ɛnt'laʊbən] (entlaubte, entlaubt, h) **I.** *v/t.* strip of its leaves; defoliate; **II.** *v/refl.*: ***sich ~*** shed its leaves; **ent·laubt** [ɛnt'laʊpt] *adj.* bare, leafless; **Ent'lau·bung** *f* (-; -en) defoliation; **Ent'lau·bungs·mit·tel** *n* defoliant
ent'lau·fen (entlief, entlaufen, sn) **I.** *v/i.* run away (*dat.* from); **II.** *adj.* runaway *child etc.*; escaped *prisoner*; **„Siamkatze ~"** lost: Siamese cat; missing: Siamese cat
ent'lau·sen *v/t.* (h) delouse
ent·le·di·gen [ɛnt'le:dɪgən] *v/refl.* (entledigte, entledigt, h): ***sich ~*** (*gen.*) get rid of; take off, remove *coat etc.*; *fig.* carry out *task etc.*; fulfil(l) *obligation etc.*; **Ent'le·di·gung** *f* (-; *no pl.*) fulfil(l)ment; release, exemption
ent'lee·ren (h) **I.** *v/t.* empty; *phys. and physiol.* evacuate; **II.** *v/refl.*: ***sich ~*** empty one's bowels; **Ent'lee·rung** *f* (-; -en) emptying; *phys. and physiol.* evacuation
ent·le·gen [ɛnt'le:gən] *adj.* remote; out-of-the-way; *fig.* strange *idea etc.*
ent·leh·nen [ɛnt'le:nən] *v/t.* (h) borrow (***aus*** *dat.* from); **Ent'leh·nung** *f* (-; -en) borrowing (***aus*** *dat.* from)
ent'lei·hen *v/t.* (entlieh, entliehen, h) borrow; **Ent·lei·her** [ɛnt'laɪɐ] *m* (-s; -) borrower; **Ent'lei·hung** *f* (-; -en) borrowing
Ent·lein ['ɛntlaɪn] *n* (-s; -) duckling; *fig.* ***häßliches ~*** ugly duckling
ent'lief *pret. of* ***entlaufen***
ent'ließ *pret. of* ***entlassen***
ent'lo·ben *v/refl.* (h): ***sich ~*** break off one's engagement; **Ent'lo·bung** *f* (-; -en) breaking off of an (*or* one's) engagement, F *hum.* disengagement
ent'locken (*sep.* -k·k-) *v/t.* (h): ***e-r Sache et. ~*** draw s.th. out of s.th.; ***j-m et. ~*** coax s.th. out of s.o.; ***j-m ein Geständnis*** (***Geheimnis***) ~ get s.o. to admit s.th. (worm a secret out of s.o.)
ent'loh·nen *v/t.* (h) pay; **Ent'loh·nung** *f* (-; -en) pay, payment
ent'lud *pret. of* ***entladen***
ent'lüf·ten *v/t.* (h) air; ⚗ de-aerate; bleed *brake*; **Ent'lüf·ter** *m* (-s; -) ventilator; *mot.* bleeder; air vent; **Ent'lüf·tung** *f* (-; *no pl.*) ventilation; ⚗ de-aeration
Ent'lüf·tungs|an·la·ge *f* ventilation system; **~rohr** *n mot.* vent pipe; **~ven,til** *n* ventilation valve; *mot.*, ⚙ bleeder valve
ent·mach·ten [ɛnt'maxtən] *v/t.* (entmachtete, entmachtet, h) strip *s.o.* of (political) power (*or* of all power[s]), topple *s.o.* from power, take all power(s) away from *s.o.*; **Ent'mach·tung** *f* (-; *no pl.*) loss of power; toppling (*gen.* of); dethronement; ***nach ihrer ~*** after being toppled (*or* dethroned) (***durch*** *acc.* by, at the hands of)
ent·ma·gne·ti'sie·ren *v/t.* (h) demagnetize
ent·man·nen [ɛnt'manən] *v/t.* (entmannte, entmannt, h) castrate; **Ent'man·nung** *f* (-; *no pl.*) castration, *a. fig.* emasculation
ent·ma·te·ria·li'sie·ren *v/t.* (h) dematerialize
ent·mensch·li·chen [ɛnt'mɛnʃlɪçən] *v/t.* (entmenschlichte, entmenschlicht, h) dehumanize; **ent'mensch·licht** *adj.* inhuman; **Ent·mensch·li·chung** *f* (-; *no pl.*) dehumanization
ent·mi·li·ta·ri'sie·ren *v/t.* (h) demilitarize; **ent·mi·li·ta·ri·siert** [ɛntmilitari'zi:ɐt] *adj.* demilitarized; **Ent·mi·li·ta·ri'sie·rung** *f* (-; *no pl.*) demilitarization
ent·mi·nen [ɛnt'mi:nən] *v/t.* (entminte, entmint, h) ⚔ clear of mines
ent·mün·di·gen [ɛnt'mʏndɪgən] *v/t.* (entmündigte, entmündigt, h) (legally) incapacitate; **ent·mün·digt** [ɛnt'mʏndɪçt] *adj.* (legally) incapacitated; **Ent'mün·di·gung** *f* (-; *no pl.*) (legal) incapacitation; interdiction
ent·mu·ti·gen [ɛnt'mu:tɪgən] *v/t.* (entmutigte, entmutigt, h) discourage, dishearten; ***laß dich nicht ~!*** don't be put off, don't let them put you off, don't lose heart; **ent'mu·ti·gend** *adj.* discouraging, disheartening; **ent·mu·tigt** [ɛnt-

'mu:tɪçt] *adj.* disheartened, dispirited; **Ent'mu·ti·gung** *f* (-; -en) disheartenment; ***tiefe*** ~ despondency
ent·my·sti·fi'zie·ren *v/t.* (h) demystify, F debunk; **Ent·my·sti·fi'zie·rung** *f* (-; -en) demystification, F debunking
ent·my·tho·lo·gi'sie·ren *v/t.* (h) demythologize; **Ent·my·tho·lo·gi'sie·rung** *f* (-; -en) demythologization
Ent·nah·me [ɛnt'na:mə] *f* (-; -n) taking *of blood, of a sample etc.*; ✝ withdrawal
ent·na·zi·fi·zie·ren [ɛntnatsifi'tsi:rən] *v/t.* (entnazifizierte, entnazifiziert, h) denazify; **Ent·na·zi·fi'zie·rung** *f* (-; -en) denazification
ent'neh·men *v/t.* (entnahm, entnommen, h) **1.** take (*dat.* from, out of); borrow (from), quote (from); **2.** *fig.* learn (*dat.* from); take it (from); gather (from), infer (from); ***ich entnehme Ihrem Schreiben, daß*** I infer from your letter that; **(*aus*) *s-n Worten war zu* ~, *daß*** from what he said it seemed that; ***s-n Ausführungen war nicht zu* ~, *ob*** it wasn't clear from what he said whether; ***aus ihrer Ansprache war nicht viel zu*** ~ there wasn't much to be gleaned from her address; ***ich entnehme Ihren Worten, daß Sie ...*** I take it that you ...
ent'ner·ven *v/t.* (h) enervate; ***j-n*** ~ fray s.o.'s nerves; **ent'ner·vend** *adj.* enervating, nerve-racking; **ent·nervt** [ɛnt'nɛrft] *adj.* enervated; ***ich bin völlig*** ~ my nerves are shot
En·to·blast [ɛnto'blast] *n* (-[e]s; -e) *biol.* endoblast
En·to·derm [ɛnto'dɛrm] *n* (-[e]s; -e) *biol.* endoderm
En·to·mo·lo·ge [ɛntomo'lo:gə] *m* (-n; -n) entomologist; **En·to·mo·lo·gie** [ɛntomolo'gi:] *f* (-; *no pl.*) entomology; **en·to·mo·lo·gisch** [ɛntomo'lo:gɪʃ] *adj.* entomological
ent·per·sön·li·chen [ɛntpɛr'zø:nlɪçən] *v/t.* (entpersönlichte, entpersönlicht, h) depersonalize
ent·po·li·ti'sie·ren *v/t.* (h) depoliticize; **Ent·po·li·ti'sie·rung** *f* (-; *no pl.*) depoliticization
ent·pri·va·ti'sie·ren *v/t.* (h) deprivatize, nationalize; **Ent·pri·va·ti'sie·rung** *f* (-; *no pl.*) deprivatization, nationalization
ent·pup·pen [ɛnt'pʊpən] *v/refl.* (entpuppte, entpuppt, h) **1.** ***sich*** ~ ***als*** turn out to be; *iro.* ***er hat sich ganz schön entpuppt*** he's (finally) shown himself in his true colo(u)rs; **2.** *zo.* ***sich*** ~ emerge from its cocoon
ent'rah·men *v/t.* (h) skim; separate the cream from *the milk*; **ent·rahmt** [ɛnt'ra:mt] *adj.*: ~***e Milch*** skimmed milk
ent'rang *pret. of* ***entringen***
ent'rann *pret. of* ***entrinnen***
ent'rät·seln *v/t.* (h) solve; decipher; ***ein Geheimnis*** ~ *a.* unravel a mystery
ent·rech·ten [ɛnt'rɛçtən] *v/t.* (entrechtete, entrechtet, h): ***j-n*** ~ deprive s.o. of his (*or* her) rights; **Ent'rech·tung** *f* (-; -en) deprivation of rights
En·tre·cote [ãtrə'ko:t] *n* (-[s]; -s) *gastr.* entrecote, rib of beef
ent'rei·ßen *v/t.* (entriß, entrissen, h): ***j-m et.*** ~ *a. fig.* snatch s.th. from s.o.; ***j-n den Flammen*** *etc.* ~ rescue s.o. from the flames *etc.*; ***j-n dem Tod*** ~ snatch s.o. from the jaws of death; ***j-m den Sieg*** ~ snatch victory from s.o.
ent'rich·ten *v/t.* (h) **1.** pay; **2.** *fig.* ***j-m s-n Tribut*** ~ pay (one's) tribute to s.o.; **Ent'rich·tung** *f* (-; *no pl.*) payment (*gen.* of)
ent'rie·geln *v/t.* (h) unlock, release; **Ent'rie·ge·lung** *f* (-; -en) unlocking, release
ent'rin·gen (entrang, entrungen, h) **I.** *v/t.*: ***j-m et.*** ~ wrench (*a. fig.* wrest) s.th. from s.o.; **II.** *v/refl.*: ***sich j-m etc.*** ~ break away from
ent'rin·nen I. *v/i.* (entrann, entronnen, sn) escape, get away (*dat.* from); **II.** ♀ *n* (-s) escape; ***es gibt kein*** ~ there's no escaping (***vor*** *dat. s.th.*)
ent'riß *pret. of* ***entreißen***
ent·ris·sen [ɛnt'rɪsən] *p.p. of* ***entreißen***
ent'rol·len (h) **I.** *v/t.* unroll; unfurl; **II.** *fig. v/refl.*: ***sich*** ~ unfold
ent·ro·man·ti'sie·ren *v/t.* (h) deromanticize; **Ent·ro·man·ti'sie·rung** *f* (-; -en) deromanticization
ent'ro·sten *v/t.* (h) remove the rust from; **Ent'ro·stung** *f* (-; *no pl.*) removal of (the) rust, rust removal
ent'rücken (*sep.* -k·k-) *v/t.* (h) carry away, transport (*dat.* from; ***nach*** *dat.* to); *fig.* enrapture, entrance; *bibl.* translate; **ent'rückt** *adj.* rapt, entranced; **Ent'rückt·heit** *f* (-; *no pl.*) state of rapture (*or* ecstasy); **Ent'rückung** (*sep.* -k·k-) *f* (-; *no pl.*) (state of) rapture *or* ecstasy; *bibl.* translation
ent·rüm·peln [ɛnt'rʏmpəln] *v/t.* (entrümpelte, entrümpelt, h) clear out; *fig.* clean up; **Ent'rüm·pe·lung** *f* (-; *no pl.*) clearing out; *fig.* clean-up
ent·run·gen [ɛnt'rʊŋən] *p.p. of* ***entringen***
ent'rü·sten (h) **I.** *v/t.* fill *s.o.* with indignation; anger, incense; shock; **II.** *v/refl.*: ***sich*** ~ become (*or* be) very indignant (***über*** *acc.* at *s.th.*, with *s.o.*), get (*or* be) angry (at, with); be up in arms (over, about); be shocked (at); **ent'rü·stet** *adj.* indignant; angry, furious; shocked; up in arms; **Ent'rü·stung** *f* (-; *no pl.*) (shock and) indignation (***über*** *acc.* at); anger (at); **Ent'rü·stungs·sturm** *m* storm of indignation
ent·saf·ten [ɛnt'zaftən] *v/t.* (entsaftete, entsaftet, h) extract the juice from; squeeze *lemon etc.*; **Ent·saf·ter** [ɛnt'zaftɐ] *m* (-s; -) juice extractor, *Am.* juicer
ent·sa·gen *v/i.* (h) (*dat.*) renounce; give up; ***der Welt*** ~ *a.* turn one's back on the world, renounce all worldly things; ***dem Thron*** ~ abdicate (from the throne); **Ent·sa·gung** *f* (-; *no pl.*) renunciation (*gen.* of); self-denial; **ent'sa·gungs·reich** *adj. life etc.* full of privation; **ent'sa·gungs·voll** *adj. life etc.* full of privation; self-denying; resigned *look etc.*; ***ein*** ~***es Leben*** *a.* a life of self-denial; ***es ist ein*** ~***er Beruf*** it's a career (*or* job) requiring a great deal of self-denial (*or* self-sacrifice)
ent'sal·zen *v/t.* (h) desalinate; **Ent'sal·zung** *f* (-; *no pl.*) desalination; **Ent'sal·zungs·an·la·ge** *f* desalination plant
ent'sann *pret. of* ***entsinnen***
Ent'satz [ɛnt'zats] *m* (-es; *no pl.*) relief (troops *or* forces *pl.*)
ent'säu·ern *v/t.* (h) de-acidify; **Ent'säue·rung** *f* (-; *no pl.*) de-acidification
ent'schä·di·gen (h) **I.** *v/t.*: ~ ***für*** *acc.* compensate for *loss etc.*; remunerate for *services rendered*; reimburse for *expenses etc.*; *fig.* compensate for, make up for; **II.** *v/refl.*: ***sich*** ~ recoup (*or* make good) one's losses; *fig.* compensate, make up for it, ***für*** *acc.*: compensate for, make up for; **Ent'schä·di·gung** *f* (-; -en) compensation (*a. fig.*); remuneration; reimbursement; *fig.* ~ ***erhalten*** gain redress
Ent'schä·di·gungs|an·spruch *m* claim for compensation; ~**kla·ge** *f* action for damages; ~**sum·me** *f* amount of compensation, damages *pl.*, indemnity
ent'schär·fen (h) **I.** *v/t.* **1.** ⚔ defuse; deactivate; **2.** *fig.* defuse; take the edge off; take the offensive parts out of, *Brit. a.* bowdlerize; **II.** *fig. v/refl.*: ***sich*** ~ ease, lose its tension
Ent·scheid [ɛnt'ʃaɪt] *m* (-[e]s; -e [-də]) decision, ruling, decree; **ent'schei·den** (entschied, entschieden, h) **I.** *v/t.* **1.** decide; settle; ⚖ *a.* rule; ***damit war die Sache entschieden*** that settled it; ***das mußt du*** ~ that's up to you; ⚖ ***der Fall ist noch nicht entschieden*** the case is still pending; **II.** *v/i.* **2.** be decisive; ~ ***über*** *acc.* decide (on) *s.th.*, determine; ⚖ ***es wurde gegen ihn entschieden*** he lost the case; **III.** *v/refl.*: ***sich*** ~ **3.** decide, make up one's mind; ***sich*** ~ ***zu*** *inf.* decide to *inf.*, decide on *ger.*; ***sich für et.*** ~ decide on s.th.; ***wir haben uns entschieden, nicht hinzugehen*** we('ve) decided not to go (*or* against going); **4.** be decided, be settled; **ent'schei·dend I.** *adj.* decisive (***für*** *acc.* for, in); crucial; critical *moment etc.*; fatal *mistake etc.*; vital *problem etc.*; fundamental *changes etc.*; ***der*** ~***e Faktor*** the deciding factor; ~***e Stimme*** casting vote; ***das*** ♀***e*** the most important thing, the key factor; **II.** *adv.* decisively; ***et.*** ~ ***ändern*** bring about fundamental changes in s.th.; ~ ***zu et. beitragen*** be instrumental in bringing s.th. about; **Ent'schei·dung** *f* (-; -en) decision (***über*** *acc.* on); ⚖ *a.* ruling; verdict; ***e-e*** ~ ***treffen*** (*or* ***fällen***) make (*or* come to) a decision, decide; ***die*** ~ ***fällt mir schwer*** I can't decide, I'm finding it hard to decide; ***zur*** ~ ***kommen*** come up for decision, be decided; ***um die*** ~ ***spielen*** *sport*: play (*or* be) in the final
Ent'schei·dungs|be·fug·nis *f* competence; ~**frei·heit** *f* freedom of choice; ♀**freu·dig** *adj.* quick to make decisions; not afraid of making (*or* to make) decisions; ~**grund** *m* decisive factor; ~**kampf** *m* decisive battle; *fig.* showdown; *sport*: decisive match; ~**merk·mal** *n* criterion; ~**mög·lich·keit** *f* possibility, possible decision; ~**pro,zeß** *m* decision-making process; ~**schlacht** *f* decisive battle; ♀**schwer** *adj.* momentous; ~**spiel** *n sport*: deciding match, decider; final; ~**stun·de** *f* moment of truth; ~**trä·ger** *m* decision-maker; ***politischer*** ~ policy-maker
ent·schie·den [ɛnt'ʃi:dən] **I.** *p.p. of* ***entscheiden***; **II.** *adj.* determined, resolute; decided; emphatic(ally *adv.*); unquestionable; peremptory, authoritative; ***ein*** ~***er Gegner von*** (*or gen.*) a declared opponent (*or* enemy) of; **II.** *adv.* firmly, resolutely; definitely, without (a) doubt, decidedly; (***ganz***) ~ ***bestreiten*** firmly (*or* vehemently) dispute; (***ganz***) ~ ***zurückweisen*** categorically (*or* flatly) deny; (***ganz***) ~ ***ablehnen*** flatly refuse; ~ ***zu wenig*** *etc. a.* much too little *etc.*; ***sich*** ~ ***aussprechen für*** (***gegen***) *acc.* come out strongly in favo(u)r of (against);

Ent'schie·den·heit *f* (-; *no pl.*) determination, resoluteness; ***mit*** (***aller***) ~ categorically; ***mit*** (***aller***) ~ ***ablehnen*** flatly refuse

ent·schlacken [ɛnt'ʃlakən] (*sep.* -k·k-) *v/t.* (h) **1.** ⚙ remove the cinders (*or* slag) from; **2.** ⚕ purify; purge; ***den Körper*** ~ *a.* flush one's body through, get rid of all the poisons in one's body (*or* bloodstream); **Ent'schlackung** (*sep.* -k·k-) *f* (-; *no pl.*) ⚕ purification; purging, purge

ent'schla·fen *v/i.* (entschlief, entschlafen, sn) **1.** fall asleep; **2.** *euphem.* (***sanft***) ~ pass away (peacefully)

ent·schlei·ern [ɛnt'ʃlaɪɐn] (h) **I.** *v/t.* **1.** unveil, take *s.o.'s* veil off; **2.** *fig.* reveal, disclose, unveil; **II.** *v/refl.*: ***sich*** ~ take off one's veil, unveil (o.s.); **Ent'schleie·rung** *f* (-; *no pl.*) *a. fig.* unveiling

ent'schlie·ßen *v/refl.* (entschloß, entschlossen, h): ***sich*** ~ decide (***zu*** *dat.*, ***für*** *acc.* on; ***zu*** *inf.* to *inf.*); make up one's mind (to *inf.*); ***sich anders*** ~ change one's mind; ***ich weiß nicht, wozu ich mich*** ~ ***soll*** I don't know what to decide; ***er kann sich zu nichts*** ~ he (just) can't make up his mind; **Ent'schlie·ßung** *f* (-; -en) *esp. pol.* resolution; **Ent'schlie·ßungs·an·trag** *m pol.* proposal for a resolution

ent·schlos·sen [ɛnt'ʃlɔsən] **I.** *p.p. of* ***entschließen***; **II.** *adj.* determined; resolute; ***zu allem*** ~ prepared to go to any length(s); ***e-n*** ~***en Eindruck machen*** seem very determined, have an air of determination (about one); ***e-e*** ~***e Haltung annehmen*** take a firm stand (***in*** *dat.* on); **II.** *adv.* resolutely; with determination; ***kurz*** ~ without a moment's hesitation, suddenly, out of the blue, on the spur of the moment; ***e-r Sache*** ~ ***ins Auge sehen*** face up to s.th. squarely; **Ent'schlos·sen·heit** *f* (-; *no pl.*) determination, resolution, resoluteness

ent'schlüp·fen *v/i.* (sn) slip away, escape (*dat.* from); ***j-m*** ~ *a.* give s.o. the slip; *fig. word*: slip out

Ent'schluß *m* (-sses; ⸚sse) decision; ***e-n*** ~ ***fassen, zu e-m*** ~ ***kommen*** make (*or* reach) a decision, make up one's mind; ***zu dem*** ~ ***kommen zu*** *inf.* make up one's mind (*or* decide) to *inf.*; ***es ist sein fester*** ~ ***zu*** *inf.* he firmly intends to *inf.*; ***aus eigenem*** ~ on one's own initiative, F off one's own bat

ent·schlüs·seln [ɛnt'ʃlʏsəln] *v/t.* (entschlüsselte, entschlüsselt, h) decipher; decode; **Ent'schlüs·se·lung** *f* (-; *no pl.*) decipherment, deciphering; decoding

ent'schluß·fä·hig *adj.* capable of deciding; **ent'schluß·freu·dig** *adj.* quick to make decisions, not afraid of making (*or* to make) decisions; enterprising; **Ent'schluß·kraft** *f* (-; *no pl.*) determination

ent·schuld·bar [ɛnt'ʃʊltbaːɐ] *adj.* excusable, pardonable; **ent·schul·di·gen** [ɛnt'ʃʊldɪgən] (entschuldigte, entschuldigt, h) **I.** *v/t.* excuse; ***sich*** ~ ***lassen*** excuse o.s. *or* apologize (for not coming *etc.*), send an excuse (*or* apology); ***j-n*** ~ ***lassen*** ask for s.o. to be excused; ***Herr X läßt sich*** ~ Mr X sends his apologies (*or* regrets), Mr X regrets he cannot attend (*or* be present); ~ ***Sie, daß ich nicht gekommen bin*** I'm sorry I didn't come, please forgive me for not coming; ~ ***Sie die Störung!*** sorry to bother (*or* disturb) you; ~ ***Sie die Unordnung!*** (please) excuse the mess; **II.** *v/i.*: ~ ***Sie!, entschuldige!*** sorry, *Am.* excuse me; **III.** *v/refl.*: ***sich*** ~ a) apologize, say (one is) sorry; b) excuse o.s.; ***sich bei j-m*** ~ apologize *or* say sorry (to s.o.) (***wegen*** *gen.* for, about); ***ich habe mich bei ihm entschuldigt*** *a.* I told him I was sorry; ***ich entschuldigte mich, daß ich es vergessen hatte*** I apologized for having forgotten (it); ***du brauchst dich nicht zu*** ~ don't (*or* no need to) apologize; **ent'schul·di·gend I.** *adj.* apologetic; **II.** *adv.* apologetically; ***fügte er*** ~ ***hinzu*** *a.* he added by way of apology; **Ent'schul·di·gung** *f* (-; -en) apology; excuse; *ped.* note; ~***!*** sorry, *Am.* excuse me; ~, *darf ich mal vorbei?* excuse me, ...; ***als*** (*or* ***zur***) ~ ***für*** *acc.* a) by way of apology for, b) as an excuse (*or* explanation) for, to excuse; ***als*** ~ ***dienen für*** *acc.* serve as a pretext for; ***dafür gibt es keine*** ~ there's no excuse for it; ***es muß zu ihrer*** ~ ***gesagt werden*** it has to be said in her defen|ce (*Am.* -se); ***ich bitte Sie vielmals um*** ~ I do apologize (***wegen*** *gen.* for, about); ***ich bitte tausendmal um*** ~ *iro.* a thousand pardons

Ent'schul·di·gungs|grund *m* excuse; ~**schrei·ben** *n* (letter of) apology, written apology; ~**zet·tel** *m ped.* note, written excuse

ent'schwe·feln *v/t.* (h) desulphurize, *Am.* desulfurize; **Ent'schwe·fe·lung** *f* (-; -en) desulphurization, *Am.* desulfurization

ent'schwin·den *v/i.* (entschwand, entschwunden, sn) disappear, vanish (***in*** *acc.* into); ***im Dunkeln*** ~ vanish into the dark (*or* night); ***dem Gedächtnis*** ~ slip (*or* escape) one's memory

ent·seelt [ɛnt'zeːlt] *adj. a. fig.* dead, lifeless

ent'sen·den *v/t.* (h) send, dispatch

ent·set·zen [ɛnt'zɛtsən] (h) **I.** *v/t.* **1.** appal(l), shock; horrify; **2.** ⚔ relieve; **II.** *v/refl.*: ***sich*** ~ be horrified (*or* appalled) (***über*** *acc.* at), be shocked (at); **III.** ♀ *n* (-s) horror, dismay; ***mit*** ~ ***vernahmen wir*** we were shocked to hear (*or* learn); **Ent'set·zens·schrei** *m* cry of horror; **ent·setz·lich** [ɛnt'zɛtslɪç] **I.** *adj.* dreadful, terrible, appalling; shocking; **II.** *adv.* dreadfully, terribly; F ~ ***langweilig*** F deadly boring; F ~ ***dumm*** F incredibly thick; **ent'setzt** *adj.* appalled, shocked, horrified (*all* ***über*** *acc.* at, by); aghast (at); ~***er Blick*** look of (absolute) horror; ***ein*** ~***es Gesicht machen*** look shocked (*or* horrified)

ent·seu·chen [ɛnt'zɔʏçən] *v/t.* (h) decontaminate; **Ent'seu·chung** *f* (-; -en) decontamination; **Ent'seu·chungs·an·la·ge** *f* decontamination plant

ent'si·chern *v/t.* (h) release the safety catch of, cock; **ent'si·chert** *adj.*: ~ ***sein*** have the safety catch off

ent'sie·geln *v/t.* (h) unseal

ent'sin·nen *v/refl.* (entsann, entsonnen, h): ***sich*** ~ recall, recollect, remember (*gen. s.o., s.th.*); ***wenn ich mich recht entsinne*** if I remember rightly; ***ich entsinne mich, daß er das sagte*** I remember him saying it

ent'sor·gen *v/t.* (h) dispose of (*radioactive*) *waste etc.*; clean (up), decontaminate; clean up *city etc.*; **Ent'sor·gung** *f* (-; *no pl.*) (waste) disposal; cleaning (up), decontamination; cleaning up *of city etc.*

Ent'sor·gungs|an·la·ge *f* waste disposal plant; ~**fir·ma** *f* waste disposal company; *n.s.* atomic waste disposer; ~**zen·trum** *n* waste disposal plant

ent'span·nen (h) **I.** *v/refl.*: ***sich*** ~ **1.** *person*: relax, unwind; *muscles etc.*: relax, slacken, loosen up; ***man kann sich dabei gut*** ~ it helps you relax, it's good for relaxing; **2.** *fig. situation etc.*: ease (up), cool off, calm down; *relationship*: become more relaxed, lose its tension; **II.** *v/t.* **3.** relax, slacken, loosen up *muscles etc.*; relax, have a relaxing effect on *s.o.*; ***das entspannt die Nerven*** that will soothe your nerves; **4.** slacken *rope etc.*; unbend; unstress, reduce the surface tension of; **5.** *fig.* ease (up); **III.** *v/i.* be relaxing, have a relaxing effect; **Ent'span·nung** *f* (-; *no pl.*) **1.** relaxation, rest; **2.** ⚕ easing; *pol.* easing of tension, detente

Ent'span·nungs|ge·spräch *n pol.* conciliatory talks *pl.*; ~**li·te·ra,tur** *f* light reading; ~**po·li,tik** *f* policy of detente; ~**pro,zeß** *m pol.* process of detente; ~**übung** *f* relaxation exercise

ent·spie·gelt [ɛnt'ʃpiːgəlt] *adj.*: ~***es Objektiv*** (***Glas***) coated lens (glass)

ent'spin·nen *v/refl.* (entspann, entsponnen, h): ***sich*** ~ arise, develop (***aus*** from); (*folgen*) ensue (from)

ent'sprang *pret. of* ***entspringen***

ent'spre·chen *v/i.* (entsprach, entsprochen, h) **1.** correspond to (*or* with); fit, agree with; be equivalent to; tally (*or* tie up) with; **2.** fulfil(l); meet, come (*or* live) up to; comply with; ***nicht*** ~ *dat.* fall short of, fail to meet *expectations etc.*; **ent'spre·chend I.** *adj.* corresponding (*dat.* to); appropriate (to), adequate (to); equivalent (to); necessary (for, to); analogous (to); proportionate (to), commensurate (with); respective; appropriate, competent; ~***es Gehalt*** commensurate salary; ***der*** ~***e französische Ausdruck*** the French equivalent; *das Essen war miserabel* ***und der Wein war*** ~ and so was the wine, and the wine was no better; **II.** *adv.* correspondingly *etc.*; ***er verhielt sich*** ~ he acted accordingly; ~ ***hat er geantwortet*** he gave a fitting reply; *dicke Arme* ***und*** ~ ***dicke Beine*** and legs to match; **III.** *prp.* (*dat.*) according to; in compliance with; ***sich s-m Alter*** ~ ***benehmen*** act one's age, *formal*: act in a manner befitting one's age; *wie geht es ihr?* - ***den Umständen*** ~ as well as one might expect under the circumstances; *wie ist die Stimmung?* - ***den Umständen*** ~ as one might expect under the circumstances; **Ent'spre·chung** *f* (-; -en) **1.** correspondence (***mit*** *dat.* with, to); **2.** equivalent (*a. ling.*); counterpart; analogy; parallel

ent'sprie·ßen *v/i.* (entsproß, entsprossen, sn) spring from (*or* out of); *fig.* → ***entstammen***

ent'sprin·gen *v/i.* (entsprang, entsprungen, sn) **1.** *river*: rise, have its source (*dat. or* ***in*** *dat.* in, at); spring (from); **2.** *fig.* spring *or* arise, come (*dat. or* ***aus*** *dat.* from); originate (from *or* in); **3.** escape (*dat. or* ***aus*** *dat.* from); **4.** → ***entstammen***

ent·staat·li·chen [ɛnt'ʃtaːtlɪçən] *v/t.* (entstaatlichte, entstaatlicht, h) denationalize; *eccl.* disestablish; **Ent'staat·li·chung** *f* (-; -en) denationalization; *eccl.* disestablishment

ent·sta·li·ni·sie·ren [ɛntʃtalini'ziːrən] *v/t.* (entstalinisierte, entstalinisiert, h) *pol.* destalinize; **Ent·sta·li·ni'sie·rung** *f* (-; *no pl.*) destalinization
ent'stam·men *v/i.* (h) **1.** descend from, be descended from; come from; have grown up in; **2.** come from, originate from (*or* in), derive from, go back to
ent'stau·ben *v/t.* (h) dust, remove the dust from
ent'ste·hen (entstand, entstanden, sn) **I.** *v/i.* come into being; *nation*: *a.* be born; emerge (**aus** *dat.* from), develop (from), *difficulties etc.*: arise (from); be made (from), be created (from); be built; be written; ⚠ spring up, develop, grow; ~ **durch** *acc.* result from, be caused by, be a result of; ~ **aus** *dat.* grow out of; **aus der Situation entstand ...** *a.* the situation gave rise to (*or* led to, brought about) ...; **die Idee entstand aus** the idea stems from (*or* goes back to); **als die Welt entstand** when the world began (*or* came into being); **daraus ~de Kosten** (any) costs arising from it; **II.** ♀ *n* (-s) → **Entstehung; im ~ begriffen** developing, ... in the making; *formal*: incipient (*a.* ⚕); emergent *nation*; ⚗ nascent; **Ent'ste·hung** *f* (-; *no pl.*) emergence, development; origin, beginning; birth
Ent'ste·hungs|ge·schich·te *f* history of the origin(s) (*gen.* of); genesis; *bibl.* Genesis; **s-e ~** *a.* the story of how it came into being, the history of its beginnings; **die ~ der Menschheit** the evolution of man (*or* the human race); **~ort** *m* place of origin, home; **~zeit** *f* period (*or* date) of origin; **die ~ dieser Vase liegt in der Frührenaissance** this vase dates (*or* goes) back to the early Renaissance, this vase originated in the early Renaissance
ent'stei·gen *v/i.* (entstieg, entstiegen, sn) **1.** emerge from, get out of, step out of, alight from; **2.** *fig.* rise (up) from
ent·stei·nen [ɛnt'ʃtaɪnən] *v/t.* (entsteinte, entsteint, h) stone
ent'stel·len *v/t.* (h) **1.** disfigure; mar, spoil; **~de Narbe** disfiguring scar; **2.** *fig.* twist, distort, misrepresent *facts etc.*; garble *report etc.*; **ent'stellt** *adj.* **1.** disfigured, deformed; marred, spoilt; *fig.* **vor Wut (Schmerz)** ~*face* distorted with rage (contorted with pain); **2.** *fig.* distorted; garbled; **Ent'stel·lung** *f* (-; -en) disfigurement; marring; distortion, misrepresentation; garbled account
ent'stö·ren *v/t.* (h) ⚡ radio-shield, screen; fit *engine etc.* with a suppressor; *teleph.* clear; **Ent'stö·rer** *m* (-s; -) (interference) suppressor; **ent·stört** [ɛnt'ʃtøːɐt] *adj.* noise-suppressed; interference-free; **Ent'stö·rung** *f* (-; -en) interference suppression; anti-jamming; *mot.* shielding
Ent'stö·rungs|dienst *m*, **~stel·le** *f* *teleph.* fault-clearing service; **die Entstörungsstelle anrufen** call the engineers
ent'strah·len *v/t.* (h) decontaminate; **Ent'strah·lung** *f* (-; *no pl.*) decontamination
ent'strö·men *v/i.* (sn) flow (*or* pour, gush) out (*dat.* of); *gas etc.*: escape (from), come out (of)
ent·ta·bui'sie·ren *v/t.* (h) remove the taboo(s) from; remove the taboo value from, destigmatize
ent'tar·nen *v/t.* (h) unmask; **e-n Spion ~** *a.* F blow a spy's cover; **Ent'tar·nung** *f* (-; -en) unmasking, exposure
ent'täu·schen (h) **I.** *v/t.* disappoint; let *s.o.* down; **enttäuscht werden** suffer a disappointment; **angenehm enttäuscht werden** be pleasantly surprised; **der Film hat mich tief enttäuscht** the film was a big disappointment for me, I was really disappointed with the film; **II.** *v/i.* be disappointing, be a disappointment (*or* letdown); **ent'täuscht I.** *adj.* **1.** disappointed (**über** *acc.* at, about; **von** *dat.* with); **er ist ~ von dir** *a.* he feels let down by you; **2.** disenchanted, disillusioned; **II.** *adv.* disappointed(ly), in disappointment; **Ent'täu·schung** *f* (-; -en) disappointment, letdown; **es war e-e einzige ~** it was one big disappointment (*or* letdown); **ent'täu·schungs·reich** *adj.* full of disappointment
ent'thro·nen *v/t.* (h) dethrone (*a. fig.*), depose, oust from the throne; **Ent'thro·nung** *f* (-; -en) dethronement
ent·völ·kern [ɛnt'fœlkɐn] *v/t.* (entvölkerte, entvölkert, h) depopulate; **ent·völ·kert** [ɛnt'fœlkɐt] *adj.* depopulated; deserted; **Ent·völ·ke·rung** [ɛnt'fœlkərʊŋ] *f* (-; -en) depopulation
ent'wach·sen *v/i.* (entwuchs, entwachsen, sn) **1.** outgrow, grow out of; **2.** grow out of, come up out of
ent·waff·nen [ɛnt'vafnən] *v/t.* (entwaffnete, entwaffnet, h) disarm (*a. fig.*); **ent'waff·nend** *fig. adj.* disarming; **von ~er Ehrlichkeit** *etc.* disarmingly honest *etc.*; **Ent'waff·nung** *f* (-; *no pl.*) disarming
ent'wand *pret. of* **entwinden**
ent'warf *pret. of* **entwerfen**
ent'war·nen *v/i.* (h) give the all clear; **Ent'war·nung** *f* (-; -en) all clear (signal)
ent'wäs·sern *v/t.* (h) drain; **Ent'wäs·se·rung** *f* (-; -en) draining; *coll.* drainage; ⚗, ⚕ dehydration
Ent'wäs·se·rungs|an·la·ge *f* drainage system; **~gra·ben** *m* drainage ditch (*or* channel); **~ka͵nal** *m* drainage canal
ent'we·der *cj.*: **~ ... oder** either ... or; **~ oder!** take it or leave it; **~ alles oder gar nichts** it's all or nothing; **Ent'we·der-Oder** *n*: **hier gibt es nur ein ~** you've *etc.* got to decide one way or the other, it's one or the other
ent'wei·chen *v/i.* (entwich, entwichen, sn) **1.** escape (*dat. or* **aus** *dat.* from); **2.** *gas etc.*: escape, leak (*dat. or* **aus** *dat.* from)
ent'wei·hen *v/t.* (h) desecrate; profane; **Ent'wei·hung** *f* (-; *no pl.*) desecration; profanation
ent'wen·den *v/t.* (h) purloin, steal, pilfer, *euphem.* remove; embezzle; **Ent'wendung** *f* (-; -en) purloining, theft, *euphem.* removal; embezzlement
ent'wer·fen *v/t.* (entwarf, entworfen, h) **1.** sketch, outline; **2.** draw up, draft; **3.** design; **4.** *fig.* draw; **ein Bild ~ von** (*or* *gen.*) *a.* depict, portray; **Ent'wer·fer** *m* (-s; -) designer
ent'wer·ten *v/t.* (h) **1.** devaluate; cancel *stamp, ticket etc.*; **entwertet werden** *a.* fall in value, lose its value; **2.** *fig.* devalue, devaluate; debase; **Ent·wer·ter** [ɛnt'vɛrtɐ] *m* (-s; -) ticket-cancel(l)ing machine; **Ent'wer·tung** *f* (-; -en) **1.** devaluation; cancellation; **2.** *fig.* devaluing, devaluation; debasement
ent'wich *pret. of* **entweichen**
ent·wi·chen [ɛnt'vɪçən] *p.p. of* **entweichen**
ent'wickeln (*sep.* -k·k-) (h) **I.** *v/t.* develop (*a.* ⚙, ⚡, *phot.*, *phys.*, ⚕); generate, produce *heat etc.*; acquire, develop *taste etc.* (**für** *acc.* for); build up *an appetite*; display, show *some initiative etc.*; develop, evolve *theory etc.*; **II.** *v/refl.*: **sich ~** develop (**aus** *dat.* from; **zu** *dat.* into); grow (into); progress; *gas etc.*: form, arise; take shape; **sich gut ~** *w.s.* be shaping up (well); **daraus entwickelte sich e-e Krise** a crisis ensued (*or* grew out of it), it gave rise to a crisis
Ent'wick·ler *m* (-s; -) *phot.* developer; **~bad** *n* developing bath; **~scha·le** *f* developing dish
Ent'wick·lung *f* (-; -en) development; *a.* *biol.* evolution; *a.* generation, buildup *of heat etc.*; ⚙ *a.* research; *phot. a.* developing, *film and* ✝ *a.* processing; trend; **in der ~ sein** be developing, be growing, *method etc.*: be at the development stage; **zur ~ bringen** develop; → **zukünftig** I
Ent'wick·lungs|ab·lauf *m* development, evolution; **~ab͵tei·lung** *f* (research and) development department; **~al·ter** *n* **1.** developmental age; mental age; physical age; **2.** adolescence; **~dienst** *m* overseas development (*or* aid) service; *Am.* Peace Corps, *Brit.* Voluntary Service Overseas, VSO
ent'wick·lungs·fä·hig *adj.* capable of development; progressive; promising; *biol.* viable; **Ent'wick·lungs·fä·hig·keit** *f* capacity for development, potential (for development); *biol.* viability
Ent'wick·lungs|feh·ler *m* malformation; **~gang** *m* development, *a. biol.* evolution; **~ge·biet** *n* development area
Ent'wick·lungs·ge·schich·te *f* history; *biol.* (history of) evolution, 🕮 biogenesis; phylogeny, ontogeny; **die ~ der Menschheit** a) *biol.* the history of evolution, the evolution of man, b) the history of mankind (*or* civilization); **ent'wick·lungs·ge·schicht·lich I.** *adj.* historical; *biol.* biogenetic; **II.** *adv.* historically; *biol.* biogenetically; **~ gesehen** (seen) from a historical (*or* an evolutionary) point of view
Ent'wick·lungs·hel·fer *m* development aid worker (*or* volunteer); *Brit.* VSO worker, *Am.* Peace Corps worker
ent'wick·lungs·hem·mend *adj.* growth-inhibiting *hormone etc.*; **Ent'wick·lungs·hem·mer** *m* (-s; -) growth inhibitor
Ent'wick·lungs|hil·fe *f pol.* aid to developing countries, foreign aid; **~jah·re** *pl.* adolescence, puberty; **~land** *n* developing nation (*or* country); **die Entwicklungsländer** the developing world; **~leh·re** *f* theory of evolution; **~mög·lich·keit** *f* possibility (of development), (development) potential; **~ni͵veau** *n* level of development; **~pa͵pier** *n* photographic paper; **~pha·se** *f* development stage (*or* phase), stage of development; **~po·li͵tik** *f* third world aid policy; **~pro͵gramm** *n* development program(me) *or* plan; **~pro͵zeß** *m* (process of) development, development process; **~raum** *m* → **Entwicklungsgebiet; ~ro͵man** *m* novel of education, Bildungsroman; **~sta·di·um** *n* → **Entwicklungsstufe; ~stö·rung** *f* developmental disturbance (*or* disorder); **~stu·fe** *f* stage of development; **~zeit** *f* **1.** period of devel-

opment; **2.** adolescence; **3.** ⚕ incubation period; **4.** *phot.* developing time

·**ent'win·den** (entwand, entwunden, h) **I.** *v/t.*: ***j-m et.*** ~ wrest s.th. from s.o.; **II.** *v/refl.*: ***sich*** ~ extricate o.s. (***aus*** *dat.* from)

ent·wir·ren [ɛnt'vɪrən] *v/t.* (entwirrte, entwirrt, h) disentangle, unravel (*both a. fig.*); **Ent'wir·rung** *f* (-; *no pl.*) disentanglement, unravel(l)ing (*both a. fig.*)

ent'wi·schen *v/i.* (sn) slip away (*dat.* from); escape (from); ***j-m*** ~ *a.* give s.o. the slip

ent·wöh·nen [ɛnt'vø:nən] *v/t.* (entwöhnte, entwöhnt, h) **1.** ***j-n*** ~ cure s.o. (*gen.* of), break s.o. of the habit (of); ***j-n dem Alkohol*** ~ wean s.o. from alcohol, F get s.o. off alcohol; ***j-n von Drogen*** ~ F get s.o. off drugs; **2.** wean *a baby*; **II.** *v/refl.*: ***sich e-r Sache*** ~ give s.th. up, F kick the drugs (*or* alcohol *etc.*) habit, come off drugs (*or* alcohol *etc.*); **Ent'wöh·nung** *f* (-; *no pl.*) **1.** withdrawal *of drugs etc.*; **2.** weaning *of a baby*; **Ent'wöh·nungs·kur** *f* withdrawal treatment

ent·wor·fen [ɛnt'vɔrfən] *p.p. of* ***entwerfen***

ent'wuchs *pret. of* ***entwachsen***

ent'wür·di·gen (h) **I.** *v/t.* degrade, debase; disgrace; **II.** *v/refl.*: ***sich*** ~ degrade o.s., debase o.s.; disgrace o.s.; **ent'wür·di·gend** *adj.* degrading; disgraceful; **Ent'wür·di·gung** *f* (-; -en) degradation, debasement

Ent'wurf *m* (-[e]s; ⸚e) **1.** sketch, study; model; outline, draft; *parl.* bill; ***erster*** ~ rough draft; **2.** ⚙ *etc.* design, plan, blueprint (***für*** *acc. or gen.* of); ***im*** ~ ***sein*** be in (*or* at) the planning stage

ent'wur·zeln *v/t.* (h) uproot (*a. fig.*); **ent'wur·zelt** *adj.* uprooted (*a. fig.*); **Ent'wur·ze·lung** *f* (-; -en) uprooting (*a. fig.*)

ent'zau·bern *v/t.* (h) **1.** break the spell on, free *s.o. or s.th.* from a (*or* the) magic spell; **2.** *fig.* break the spell of, take the magic away from; ***entzaubert werden*** lose its magic (*or* spell)

ent'zer·ren *v/t.* (h) **1.** ⚡ correct; *phot.* rectify; **2.** *fig.* rectify, set straight, straighten out; **Ent·zer·rer** [ɛnt'tsɛrɐ] *m* (-s; -) ⚡ equalizer; *radio*: distortion corrector; **Ent'zer·rung** *f* (-; -en) **1.** *radio*: distortion correction; *phot.* rectification; **2.** *fig.* rectification, straightening out

ent'zie·hen (entzog, entzogen, h) **I.** *v/t.* **1.** ***j-m et.*** ~ take s.th. away from s.o.; deprive s.o. of s.th.; withdraw s.o.'s permission *etc.*; ***j-m den Führerschein*** ~ take s.o.'s driving licence (*Am.* driver's license) away, disqualify s.o. from driving; ***j-m den Alkohol*** ~ stop (*or* prevent) s.o. from drinking; ***j-m s-e Befugnisse*** ~ strip s.o. of his (*or* her) powers; ***j-m das Wort*** ~ *esp. pol.* impose silence on s.o.; ***et. j-s Zugriff*** ~ put s.th. out of s.o.'s reach; ***j-n j-s Einfluß*** ~ remove s.o. from s.o.'s sphere of influence; **2.** ⚗ extract; ***Kohlensäure*** (***Sauerstoff***) ~ (*dat.*) decarbonate (deoxygenize); *dem Körper* ***Wärme*** ~ take heat (away) from; **II.** *v/refl.*: ***sich*** ~ (*dat.*) avoid; escape; free o.s. (*or* itself) from; escape, evade *punishment etc.*; evade, F dodge *duty etc.*; elude *pursuers etc., a. fig. definition etc.*; ***sich dem Gericht*** ~ flee from justice; ***sich j-s Blicken*** ~ hide from s.o., disappear (from s.o.'s view, from sight); ***es entzieht sich m-r Beurteilung*** I'm in no position to judge (that), I'm no judge of that; → ***Kenntnis*** 1; **Ent'zie·hung** *f* (-; -en) withdrawal (*a.* ⚕); denial; prohibition; ⚗ extraction; ~ ***des Wahlrechts*** disfranchisement; ⚖ ***zeitweilige*** ~ suspension

Ent'zie·hungs|an·stalt *f* (drug) detoxification cent|re (*Am.* -er), drying-out cent|re (*Am.* -er); **~kur** *f* withdrawal treatment

Ent·zif·fe·rer [ɛnt'tsɪfərɐ] *m* (-s; -) cryptanalyst; **ent·zif·fern** [ɛnt'tsɪfɐn] *v/t.* (entzifferte, entziffert, h) decipher; make out; decode; break the key of; puzzle (*or* work) out; **Ent·zif·fe·rung** [ɛnt'tsɪfərʊŋ] *f* (-; -en) decipherment; decoding

ent'zücken (*sep.* -k·k-) **I.** *v/t.* (h) charm, delight; **II.** ♀ *n* (-s) → ***Entzückung;*** **ent'zückend** *adj.* charming, delightful; lovely; **ent'zückt** *adj.* delighted, thrilled (***über*** *accc.* at; ***von*** *dat.* with); ***er war ganz*** ~ he was absolutely delighted, F he was thrilled to bits; **Ent'zückung** (*sep.* -k·k-) *f* (-; -en) delight; ecstasy; ***in*** ~ ***geraten*** go into raptures (***über*** *acc.* over); ***in*** ~ ***versetzen*** send into raptures

Ent'zug *m* (-[e]s; *no pl.*) → ***Entziehung***

Ent'zugs|blu·tung *f* withdrawal bleeding; **~er·schei·nun·gen** *pl.* withdrawal symptoms

ent·zünd·bar [ɛnt'tsʏntba:ɐ] *adj.* **1.** inflammable; *Am. and* ⚙ *a.* flammable; **2.** *fig.* easily excited; **ent'zün·den** (h) **I.** *v/refl.*: ***sich*** ~ **1.** catch fire; *fuel*: ignite; **2.** ⚕ become inflamed; **3.** *fig.* be roused (***an*** *dat.* by); be sparked off (by); be inflamed (by); **II.** *v/t.* **4.** light; **5.** *fig.* arouse; **ent'zün·det** *adj.* ⚕ inflamed; red; **ent·zünd·lich** [ɛnt'tsʏntlɪç] *adj.* **1.** inflammable; **2.** ⚕ inflammatory; **Ent'zün·dung** *f* (-; -en) ⚕ inflammation; **ent·'zün·dungs·hem·mend** *adj.* ⚕ anti-inflammatory; 📖 antiphlogistic; **Ent'zün·dungs·herd** *m* ⚕ focus of inflammation

ent·zwei [ɛnt'tsvaɪ] *adv.* broken (in two), in pieces; torn (apart); **~bre·chen** *v/t.* (*irr.*, *sep.*, h, → ***brechen***) *and v/i.* (sn) break in two; come apart

ent·zwei·en [ɛnt'tsvaɪən] (entzweite, entzweit, h) **I.** *v/t.* divide, separate; ***er versuchte, sie zu*** ~ he tried to turn them against each other; **II.** *v/refl.*: ***sich*** ~ fall out (***mit*** *dat.* with)

ent'zwei|ge·hen *v/i.* (*irr.*, *sep.*, sn, → ***gehen***) **1.** break (in two); come apart; **2.** *fig.* break up, go to pieces; **~rei·ßen** (*irr.*, *sep.*, → ***reißen***) **I.** *v/t.* (h) tear in two; tear up; **II.** *v/i.* (sn) tear; **~schla·gen** *v/t.* (*irr.*, *sep.*, h, → ***schlagen***) smash to pieces; **~schnei·den** *v/t.* (*irr.*, *sep.*, h, → ***schneiden***) cut in two; cut into pieces, cut up

Ent·zwei·ung [ɛnt'tsvaɪʊŋ] *f* (-; -en) division, split, rupture

En·ze·pha·li·tis [ɛntsefa'li:tɪs] *f* (-; -litiden [-li'ti:dən]) ⚕ encephalitis

En·zi·an ['ɛntsĭa:n] *m* (-s; -e) **1.** 🌿 gentian; **2.** *spirit distilled from the roots of yellow gentian*

En·zy·kli·ka [ɛn'tsy:klika] *f* (-; -ken) encyclical

En·zy·klo·pä·die [ɛntsyklopɛ'di:] *f* (-; -n) encyclop(a)edia; **en·zy·klo·pä·disch** [ɛntsyklo'pɛ:dɪʃ] *adj.* encyclop(a)edic; **En·zy·klo·pä·dist** [ɛntsyklopɛ'dɪst] *m* (-en; -en) encyclop(a)edist

En·zym [ɛn'tsy:m] *n* (-s; -e) *biol.* enzyme

eo ip·so ['e:o 'ɪpso] *adv.* ipso facto

eph·emer [efe'me:ɐ] *adj.* ephemeral

Ephe·ser ['e:fezɐ] *m* (-s; -) *hist.* Ephesian; ***Brief an die*** ~ → **~brief** *m*: *bibl.* ***der*** ~ the (*or* St Paul's) Epistle to the Ephesians, Ephesians *pl.*

Epi·de·mie [epide'mi:] *f* (-; -n) epidemic (disease); **Epi·de·mio·lo·ge** [epidemĭo-'lo:gə] *m* (-n; -n) epidemiologist; **Epi·de·mio·lo·gie** [epidemĭolo'gi:] *f* (-; *no pl.*) epidemiology; **epi·de·misch** [epi'de:-mɪʃ] *adj.* epidemic; **~e *Ausmaße*** (*or* ***Formen***) ***annehmen*** take on (*or* reach) epidemic proportions

Epi·der·mis [epi'dɛrmɪs] *f* (-; -men) epidermis

Epi·glot·tis [epi'glɔtɪs] *f* (-; -tiden [-glɔ-'ti:dən]) epiglottis

Epi·go·ne [epi'go:nə] *m* (-n; -n) epigone; imitator; **epi'go·nen·haft** *adj.* epigonous; **Epi'go·nen·tum** *n* (-s; *no pl.*) epigonism

Epi·gramm [epi'gram] *n* (-s; -e) **1.** epigraph; **2.** epigram; **Epi·gram·ma·ti·ker** [epigra'ma(:)tikɐ] *m* (-s; -) epigrammist, epigrammatist; **epi·gram·ma·tisch** [epigra'ma(:)tɪʃ] *adj.* epigrammatic(ally *adv.*)

Epik ['e:pɪk] *f* (-; *no pl.*) **1.** epic poetry; **2.** narrative literature; **Epi·ker** ['e:pikɐ] *m* (-s; -) **1.** epic poet; **2.** narrative author

Epi·ku·re·er [epiku're:ɐ] *m* (-s; -), **epi·ku·re·isch** [epiku're:ɪʃ] *adj.* **1.** *hist.* Epicurean; **2.** *fig.* epicurean

Epi·lep·sie [epilɛ'psi:] *f* (-; *no pl.*) epilepsy; **Epi·lep·ti·ker** [epi'lɛptikɐ] *m* (-s; -) epileptic; **epi·lep·tisch** [epi'lɛptɪʃ] *adj.* epileptic; **~er *Anfall*** epileptic fit (📖 seizure)

Epi·log [epi'lo:k] *m* (-s; -e [-gə]) epilog(ue)

episch ['e:pɪʃ] *adj.* epic; **~e *Dichtung*** *coll.* epic literature, epic narrative (*or* poem); **~e *Breite*** epic breadth; F *fig.* ***et. in ~er Breite erzählen*** make an epic out of s.th., F give s.o. the whole saga

epi·sko·pal [epɪsko'pa:l] *adj.* episcopal; **Epi·sko·pat** [epɪsko'pa:t] *n* (-[e]s; -e) *eccl.* episcopate

Epi·so·de [epi'zo:də] *f* (-; -n) episode (*a.* ♪); **epi'so·den·haft, epi·so·disch** [epi-'zo:dɪʃ] *adj.* episodic(ally *adv.*)

Epi·stel [e'pɪstəl] *f* (-; -n) epistle

Epi·ste·mo·lo·gie [epɪstemolo'gi:] *f* (-; *no pl.*) *phls.* epistemology

Epi·taph [epi'ta:f] *n* (-s; -e) **1.** epitaph; **2.** memorial slab

Epi·thel [epi'te:l] *n* (-s; -e) *biol.* epithelium

Epi·zen·trum [epi'tsɛntrʊm] *n* (-s; -tren) epicent|re (*Am.* -er)

epo·chal [epɔ'xa:l] *adj.* epoch-making; revolutionary *discovery etc.*; landmark *decision etc.*; sensational; **Epo·che** [e'pɔxə] *f* (-; -n) era, age, epoch; ~ ***machen*** have a profound (*or* revolutionary) impact; usher in a new age; **epo·che·ma·chend** *adj.* epoch-making; revolutionary; sensational

Epo·nym [epo'ny:m] *n* (-s; -e) eponym

Epos ['e:pɔs] *n* (-; Epen ['e:pən]) epic (poem); epos

Equi·pa·ge [ek(v)i'pa:ʒə] *obs. f* (-; -n) **1.** carriage (and horses *pl.*); **2.** ⚓ ship's crew

er [e:ɐ] **I.** *pers. pron.* he; it; ~ ***ist es*** it's him; **II.** ♀ *m* (-; -s) **1.** ***es ist ein*** ~ *a. zo.* it's a he; **2.** *on towels etc.*: his

er'ach·ten (h) **I.** *v/t.* consider, think, *for-*

mal: judge, deem; ***et. für unnötig ~*** consider s.th. unnecessary; ***es als s-e Pflicht ~ zu*** *inf.* consider it (*or* see it as) one's duty to *inf.*; **II.** ℒ *n* (-s) opinion, judg(e)ment; ***m-s ~s*** in my opinion, as I see it; ***m-s ~s war es ein Fehler*** *a.* I regard it as (*or* consider it) a mistake, I feel it was a mistake; ***nach s-m ~*** *a.* he takes the view that

er'ar·bei·ten *v/t.* (h) (*a.* ***sich*** *dat.* ~) work (hard) for; acquire, gather; *ped.* cover; compile, develop

Erb|adel ['ɛrp-] *m* hereditary nobility; **~an·la·ge** *f* genes *pl.*, genetic make-up (*or* endowment); ⚕ hereditary disposition; **~an·spruch** *m* hereditary title, claim to an inheritance; **~an·teil** *m* → ***Erbteil***

er·bar·men [ɛɐ'barmən] (erbarmte, erbarmt, h) **I.** *v/refl.*: ***sich j-s ~*** take (*or* have) pity on s.o.; *eccl.* ***Herr, erbarme Dich unser*** Lord, have mercy upon us; **II.** *v/t.* move *s.o.* to pity; **III.** ℒ *n* (-s) pity, compassion; ***er kennt kein ~*** he's merciless; ***zum ~*** pitiful; appalling; miserable; **er'bar·mens·wert, er'bar·mens·wür·dig** *adj.* pitiful, wretched; **er·bärm·lich** [ɛɐ'bɛrmlɪç] **I.** *adj. a. contp.* wretched, pitiful; *a. contp.* miserable, wretched; paltry; mean; ***in e-m ~en Zustand*** in a wretched state; **II.** *adv.* terribly, dreadfully; ***~ wenig*** precious little; **Er'bärm·lich·keit** *f* (-; *no pl.*) misery; wretchedness; deplorable nature; **Er'bar·mung** *f* (-; *no pl.*) pity, mercy; **er'bar·mungs·los** *adj.* merciless; **Er'bar·mungs·lo·sig·keit** *f* (-; *no pl.*) mercilessness; **er'bar·mungs·voll** *adj.* compassionate; full of pity

er'bat *pret. of* ***erbitten***

er'bau·en (h) **I.** *v/t.* **1.** build, construct; **2.** *fig.* edify; F ***er war nicht besonders erbaut davon*** F he wasn't exactly over the moon about it; **II.** *v/refl.*: ***sich ~ an*** *dat.* find great pleasure in, be uplifted by; **Er'bau·er** *m* (-s; -) architect, builder; founder; **er'bau·lich** *adj.* edifying (*a. iro.*), elevating; devotional

Erb·aus·ein,an·der·set·zung ['ɛrp-] *f* division of an estate

Er'bau·ung *f* (-; *no pl.*) **1.** construction, erection; **2.** *fig.* edification

Er'bau·ungs|li·te·ra,tur *f* devotional literature; **~schrift** *f* religious (*or* devotional) tract

Erb·bau·recht ['ɛrp-] *n* inheritable (*or* hereditary) building rights *pl.*

erb·be·rech·tigt ['ɛrp-] *adj.* entitled to inherit; **'Erb·be·rech·tig·te** *m* (-n; -n) (legitimate) heir

Er·be¹ ['ɛrbə] *m* (-n; -n) heir, successor (*both a. fig.*), ***e-s Vermögens:*** to an estate; beneficiary; legatee; heir apparent; ***alleiniger ~*** sole heir; ***gesetzlicher ~*** legal heir, heir-at-law; ***mutmaßlicher ~*** heir presumptive; ***rechtmäßiger ~*** legal (*or* lawful, right) heir; ***j-n zum ~n einsetzen*** make s.o. one's heir; → ***lachend***

'Er·be² *n* (-s; *no pl.*) inheritance; *fig.* heritage, legacy

er'be·ben *v/i.* (sn) *a. fig.* shake, tremble (***vor*** *dat.* with; ***bei*** *dat.* at); ***et. ~ lassen*** make s.th. shake (*or* tremble)

erb·ei·gen ['ɛrp-] *adj.* inherited; **'Erb·ei·gen·schaft** *f* hereditary trait; **'Erb·ei·gen·tum** *n* (-s; ⸚er) **1.** inheritance; **2.** family estate

er·ben ['ɛrbən] (h) **I.** *v/t.* inherit (*a. fig.*); come into; F *fig.* get; *fig.* ***das hat er von der Mutter geerbt*** he's got that from his mother; F ***hier ist nichts zu ~*** F there's nothing doing here; **II.** *v/i.* inherit, come into an inheritance

'Er·ben·ge·mein·schaft *f* community of heirs

er'be·ten *p.p. of* ***erbitten***

er'bet·teln *v/t.* (h) (*a.* ***sich*** *dat.* ~) get *s.th.* by begging; *contp.* scrounge, cadge *s.th.* (***von*** *dat.* off); wheedle *s.th.* (out of)

er·beu·ten [ɛɐ'bɔʏtən] *v/t.* (erbeutete, erbeutet, h) **1.** get away with; **2.** seize, *esp.* ⚔ *a.* capture; **3.** F *fig.* carry off, manage to get *prize etc.*; **Er'beu·tung** *f* (-; *no pl.*) capture

Erb|fak·tor ['ɛrp-] *m* gene; **~feh·ler** *m* hereditary defect; **~feind** *m* sworn (*or* traditional, age-old) enemy; **~feind·schaft** *f* traditional (*or* longstanding) enmity

Erb·fol·ge ['ɛrp-] *f* succession; **~krieg** *m* war of succession

Erb|for·schung ['ɛrp-] *f* genetics *pl.*, genetic research; **~gut** *n* (-[e]s; ⸚er) **1.** *no pl. biol.* genetic make-up; **2.** a) ⚖ inheritance, b) ⚖ estate

er'bie·ten *v/refl.* (erbot, erboten, h): ***sich ~ zu*** *inf.* offer (*or* volunteer) to *inf.*

Er·bin ['ɛrbɪn] *f* (-; -nen) heiress; → ***Erbe¹***

er'bit·ten *v/t.* (erbat, erbeten, h) (*a.* ***sich*** *dat.* ~) ask for, request

er·bit·tern [ɛɐ'bɪtɐn] (erbitterte, erbittert, h) **I.** *v/t.* **1.** anger, enrage; **2.** make *s.o.* (feel) very bitter, embitter; **II.** *v/refl.*: ***sich ~*** **3.** get angry (***über*** *acc.* about), get upset (about, over); **4.** become embittered *or* bitter (***über*** *acc.* about); **er'bit·tert I.** *adj.* **1.** embittered (***über*** *acc.* at, by), bitter (about); resentful (about); **2.** bitter *enemy etc.*; fierce *struggle etc.*; stubborn; ***~en Widerstand leisten*** fight back fiercely, put up a fierce resistance; **II.** *adv.*: ***et. ~ bekämpfen*** fight s.th. tooth and nail; **Er'bit·te·rung** *f* (-; *no pl.*) bitterness; embitterment

erb·krank ['ɛrp-] *adj.* suffering from a hereditary disease; **'Erb·krank·heit** *f* hereditary disease

er·blas·sen [ɛɐ'blasən] *v/i.* (erblaßte, erblaßt, sn) go (*or* turn, grow) pale, go (*or* turn) white

Erb·las·ser ['ɛrplasɐ] *m* (-s; -), **Erb·las·se·rin** ['ɛrplasərɪn] *f* (-; -nen) *the* deceased; testator, *f* testatrix

Erb·last ['ɛrp-] *f* burden of the past; ***die ~ der Nazizeit*** the burden of the (*or* their, our) Nazi past

er'blei·chen *v/i.* → ***erblassen***

erb·lich ['ɛrplɪç] **I.** *adj.* hereditary; inheritable *title etc.*; **II.** *adv.*: ***er ist ~ belastet*** ⚕ it's a hereditary disease, it runs in the family; **'Erb·lich·keit** *f* (-; *no pl.*) hereditary character (*or* nature)

er'blicken (*sep.* -k·k-) *v/t.* (h) see; catch sight of; F clap eyes on; *fig.* ***in j-m s-n Feind*** *etc.* ~ see s.o. as one's enemy *etc.*

er·blin·den [ɛɐ'blɪndən] *v/i.* (erblindete, erblindet, sn) **1.** go blind, lose one's sight; ***auf einem Auge ~*** go blind in one eye, lose the sight of one eye; **2.** *glass etc.*: (grow) dull; **Er'blin·dung** *f* (-; -en) loss of (one's) sight; blindness

er'blü·hen *v/i.* (sn) blossom (*a. fig.*), open (out); *fig.* ***~ zu*** *dat.* blossom into

Erb|mas·se ['ɛrp-] *f* **1.** estate; **2.** *biol.* genetic make-up; **~on·kel** *m* rich uncle

er·bo·sen [ɛɐ'bo:zən] (erboste, erbost, h) **I.** *v/t.* anger, infuriate; **II.** *v/refl.*: ***sich ~*** get angry (***über*** *acc.* at); **er'bost** *adj.* angry (***über*** *acc.* about *s.th.*, with *s.o.*)

er'bot *pret. of* ***erbieten***

er·bo·ten [ɛɐ'bo:tən] *p.p. of* ***erbieten***

er·bö·tig [ɛɐ'bø:tɪç] *adj.*: ***sich ~ machen zu*** *inf.* offer (*or* volunteer) to *inf.*

Erb·pacht ['ɛrp-] *f* hereditary leasehold

er'bre·chen (erbrach, erbrochen, h) **I.** *v/t.* **1.** ⚕ vomit, bring up; **2.** break open; *a.* force *a door*; open *letter etc.*; **II.** *v/i. and v/refl.* (***sich*** ~) vomit, be sick; **III.** ℒ *n* (-s) ⚕ vomiting; F *fig.* ***bis zum ~*** ad nauseam

Erb·recht ['ɛrp-] *n* (-[e]s; -e) **1.** *no pl.* law of succession; **2.** right of succession, hereditary title

er'brin·gen *v/t.* (erbrachte, erbracht, h) produce, provide, *a.* furnish *proof etc.*; bring, yield *profit etc.*; ***Leistungen ~*** produce results, F come up with the goods

Erb·schä·di·gung ['ɛrp-] *f* genetic defect

Erb·schaft ['ɛrpʃaft] *f* (-; -en) inheritance; → ***antreten*** 4

'Erb·schafts|an·spruch *m* claim to an inheritance; **~schwin·del** *m* inheritance fraud; **~steu·er** *f* inheritance tax

Erb·schein ['ɛrp-] *m* certificate of heirship

Erb·schlei·cher ['ɛrp-] *m* (-s; -) legacy hunter; **,Erb·schlei·che'rei** *f* (-; *no pl.*) legacy hunting

Erb·se ['ɛrpsə] *f* (-; -n) pea; ***wie die Prinzessin auf der ~*** like the princess and the pea

'Erb·sen|brei *m* pureed peas *pl.*, *Brit. a.* pease pudding; **ℒgroß** *adj.* ... the size of a pea; **~pü,ree** *n* → ***Erbsenbrei***; **~scho·te** *f* pea pod; **~sup·pe** *f* pea soup

'Erb·sen·zäh·ler *m* **1.** pedant; **2.** miser; **,Erb·sen·zäh·le'rei** *f* (-; *no pl.*) **1.** F nit-picking; **2.** miserliness

Erb|sprung ['ɛrp-] *m biol.* saltation; **~strei·tig·keit** *f* inheritance dispute; quarrel over a will; **~stück** *n* heirloom; **~sub,stanz** *f* genes *pl.*; **~sün·de** *f* original sin; **~tan·te** *f* rich aunt; **~teil** *n* share of the inheritance; **~tei·lung** *f* division of an estate; **~übel** *n* hereditary evil; **~ver·trag** *m* testamentary contract; **~ver·zicht** *m* renunciation of inheritance rights

Erd·ach·se ['e:ɐt-] *f* earth's axis

er·dacht [ɛɐ'daxt] **I.** *p.p. of* ***erdenken***; **II.** *adj.* imaginary, invented, fictitious; made-up ..., *pred.* made up; **er'dach·te** *pret. of* ***erdenken***

Erd|an·zie·hung ['e:ɐt-] *f* earth's pull; **~ap·fel** *dial. m* potato; **~ar·bei·ten** *pl.* excavation work *sg.*, excavations; **~at·mo,sphä·re** *f* (earth's) atmosphere; **~bahn** *f* earth's orbit; **~ball** *m* (-[e]s; *no pl.*) globe; *w.s.* earth

Erd·be·ben ['e:ɐt-] *n* earthquake; ***schweres ~*** heavy (*or* strong, bad) earthquake; ***das ~ von San Francisco*** *etc.* the San Francisco *etc.* earthquake, the earthquake in San Francisco *etc.*; ***bei e-m ~ umkommen*** die in an earthquake; ***bei e-m ~*** *würde* ... in the event of an earthquake, if an earthquake struck (*or* were to strike); **~ge·biet** *n* **1.** earthquake area; **2.** area hit by the (*or* an) earthquake; **~herd** *m* focus of the (*or* an) earthquake, seismic focus; **~kun·de** *f* seismology; **~mes·ser** *m* seismograph; **~schutz** *m* earthquake protection; **ℒ-si·cher** *adj.* earthquake-proof; **~war·te**

f seismographical station; **~wel·le** *f* seismic wave

Erd·bee·re ['e:ɐtbe:rə] *f* (-; -n) strawberry; **'erd·beer·far·ben** *adj.* strawberry(-colo[u]red)

'Erd·beer|mar·me,la·de *f* strawberry jam; **~sekt** *m* strawberry champagne; **~tor·te** *f* strawberry cake (*or* gateau)

Erd|be·stat·tung ['e:ɐt-] *f* burial; *formal*: interment; **~be·völ·ke·rung** *f* population of the earth, earth's population; **~be·we·gung** *f* **1.** *ast.* motion of the earth; **2.** ⚙ earth movement; **~be·woh·ner** *m* inhabitant of the earth; F *hum.* F earthling; **~bo·den** *m* ground, earth; ***dem ~ gleichmachen*** raze (to the ground); ***vom ~ verschwinden*** disappear from the face of the earth; ***es war wie vom ~ verschluckt*** it was as if the earth had swallowed it up, it had just vanished (into thin air)

Er·de ['e:ɐdə] *f* (-; -n) **1.** earth, soil; ***zu ~ werden*** turn to dust; *eccl.* **~ zu ~, Staub zu Staub** ashes to ashes, dust to dust; ***in fremder (geweihter) ~ ruhen*** rest in foreign (consecrated) soil; **2.** *no pl.* ground; ***über der ~*** above ground; ***unter der ~*** underground; ***auf die*** (*or* ***zur***) ***~ fallen*** fall to the ground; ***auf nackter ~, auf der nackten ~*** on the bare ground; *fig.* ***j-n unter die ~ bringen*** be the death of s.o.; → ***Fuß*** 1; **3.** *no pl.* (planet) earth; ***auf der ganzen ~*** all over the world, the world over; ***auf ~n*** on earth, here below; **4.** *no pl.* floor; **5.** ⚡ (*a.* ***an ~ legen***) earth, *Am.* ground

er·den ['e:ɐdən] *v/t.* (h) ⚡ earth, *Am.* ground

'Er·den|bür·ger *m* mortal; ***ein neuer kleiner ~*** a new addition (*or* another little addition) to the human race; **~glück** *n* earthly happiness

er'den·ken *v/t.* (erdachte, erdacht, h) think up; invent; → ***erdacht*** II; **er·denk·lich** [ɛɐ'dɛŋklıç] *adj.* imaginable, conceivable, possible; ***auf jede ~e Weise*** (in) every possible (*or* imaginable, conceivable) way, every way imaginable; ***sich alle ~e Mühe geben, alles 2e tun*** do one's utmost (***um zu*** *inf.* to *inf.*)

'Er·den|le·ben *n* earthly life, life on earth; **~wurm** *m* sorry mortal

Erd|er·schüt·te·rung ['e:ɐt-] *f* earth tremor; **~er·wär·mung** *f* global warming; **2far·ben** *adj.* earth-colo[u]red; **~fer·kel** *n* aardvark, anteater; **2fern** far from the earth; **~fer·ne** *f ast.* apogee; **~gas** *n* natural gas; **2ge·bo·ren** *poet. adj.* earthborn, mortal; **2ge·bun·den** *adj.* earthly; **~geist** *m* **1.** earth spirit; **2.** gnome; **~ge·ruch** *m* earthy smell

Erd·ge·schich·te ['e:ɐt-] *f* (-; *no pl.*) history of the earth; geology; **'erd·ge·schicht·lich** *adj.* geological

Erd|ge·schoß ['e:ɐt-] *n*: (***im*** on the) ground (*Am.* first) floor; **~hälf·te** *f* hemisphere; **~hau·fen** *m* heap of earth, small mound of earth; **~hü·gel** *m* mound

er'dich·ten *v/t.* (h) make up, think up, invent; *contp. a.* fabricate; **er'dich·tet** *adj.* made-up ..., *pred.* made up; ***es ist ~ a.*** it's a fabrication; **Er'dich·tung** *f* (-; -en) invention; fabrication

er·dig ['e:ɐdıç] *adj.* earthy

Erd|in·ne·re ['e:ɐt-] *n* interior of the earth; **~ka·bel** *n* underground cable; **~kar·te** *f* map of the world; **~kern** *m* earth's core; **~klum·pen** *m* clod of earth; **~kreis** *m*: ***der ganze ~*** the whole world; ***auf dem ganzen ~*** all over the world, the world over; **~kru·me** *f* topsoil; **~krüm·mung** *f* curvature of the earth; **~kru·ste** *f* earth's crust; **~ku·gel** *f* globe; *w.s.* earth

Erd·kun·de ['e:ɐt-] *f* (-; *no pl.*) geography; **erd·kund·lich** ['e:ɐtkʊndlıç] *adj.* geographic(al)

Erd|lei·ter ['e:ɐt-] *m* ⚡ earth (*Am.* ground) wire; **~lei·tung** *f* **1.** ⚡ earth (*Am.* ground) wire; **2.** ⚙ underground pipe(line); **~loch** *n* hole (in the ground); ⚔ foxhole; **~ma·gne,tis·mus** *m* geomagnetism; **~man·tel** *m* earth's mantle; **~mas·sen** *pl.* masses of earth, earth masses; **~mes·sung** *f* geodesy

Erd·nuß ['e:ɐt-] *f* ♣ peanut; **~but·ter** *f* peanut butter; **~öl** *n* peanut oil

Erd·ober·flä·che ['e:ɐt-] *f* earth's surface, surface of the earth

Erd·öl ['e:ɐtˀø:l] *n* (crude) oil, petroleum

er·dol·chen [ɛɐ'dɔlçən] *v/t.* (erdolchte, erdolcht, h) stab to death

'Erd·öl|er·zeu·ger *m* oil producer, oil-producing nation; **~er·zeug·nis** *n* oil product; **~feld** *n* oilfield; **2för·dernd** *adj.*: **~e *Länder*** (*or* ***Staaten***) oil-producing countries (*or* nations); **~för·de·rung** *f* oil production; **~ge·sell·schaft** *f* oil company; **2im·por,tie·rend** *adj.*: **~e *Länder*** (*or* ***Staaten***) oil-importing countries; **~kri·se** *f* oil crisis; **~mi,ni·ster** *m* oil minister; **~prei·se** *pl.* oil prices, price *sg.* of oil; **~pro,dukt** *n* oil product; **2pro·du,zie·rend** *adj.* → ***erdölfördernd***; **~raf·fi·ne,rie** *f* oil refinery; **~ver·brauch** *m* oil consumption; **~,vor·kom·men** *pl.* sources of oil, oilfields

Erd|pol ['e:ɐt-] *m* pole (of the earth); **~pro·be** *f* soil sample; **~reich** *n* earth, soil

er·drei·sten [ɛɐ'draıstən] *v/refl.* (erdreistete, erdreistet, h) : ***sich ~ zu*** *inf.* dare to *inf.*; have the cheek (*or* nerve) to *inf.*

Erd·rin·de ['e:ɐt-] *f* earth's crust

er'dröh·nen *v/i.* (h) boom, roar, resound (***von*** *dat.* with)

er'dros·seln *v/t.* (h) strangle; *fig.* smother; **Er'dros·se·lung** *f* (-; *no pl.*) strangulation

'Erd·ro·ta·ti,on *f* → ***Erdumdrehung***

er'drücken (*sep.* -k·k-) *v/t.* (h) crush (to death); *fig.* overwhelm; weigh down; *furniture etc.*: swamp *a room etc.*; ***von Arbeit fast erdrückt*** snowed under (*or* swamped) with work; **er'drückend** *adj. fig.* oppressive; **~e *Beweise*** overwhelming (*or* incontrovertible) evidence; **~e *Mehrheit*** overwhelming majority

Erd·rutsch ['e:ɐt-] *m a. fig. pol.* landslide; **'erd·rutsch·ar·tig** *adj.*: *pol.* **~e *Verluste*** devastating losses; **'Erd·rutsch·sieg** *m pol.* landslide victory

Erd|sa·tel,lit ['e:ɐt-] *m ast. and* ⚙ earth satellite; **~schat·ten** *m* earth's shadow; **~schicht** *f* layer of the earth; stratum; subsoil; **~schol·le** *f* clod of earth; *fig.* soil; **~sicht** *f* ✈ ground visibility; **~spal·te** *f* fissure; **~sta·ti,on** *f* ground control; **~stoß** *m* tremor; seismic shock, earthshock; **~strah·lung** *f* ground radiation; **~sturz** *m* landslide; **~teil** *m* continent; **~tra,bant** *m* earth satellite

er'dul·den *v/t.* (h) bear, endure, *lit.* suffer; **Er'dul·dung** *f* (-; *no pl.*) endurance

Erd|um,dre·hung ['e:ɐt-] *f* earth's rotation; rotation of the earth; **~,um·fang** *m* earth's circumference, circumference of the earth; **~um,krei·sung** *f* orbit around the earth; **~,um·lauf** *m*: **~ *um die Sonne*** revolution of the earth around the sun; **~,um·lauf·bahn** *f* (earth) orbit; ***in die ~ schießen*** send into orbit; **~um,se·ge·lung** *f* (-; -en) circumnavigation of the earth, voyage around the world

Er·dung ['e:ɐdʊŋ] *f* (-; -en) ⚡ earth(ing), *Am.* ground(ing); **'Er·dungs·draht** *m* earth (*Am.* ground) wire

erd·ver·bun·den ['e:ɐt-] *adj.* rooted to the soil; bound up with nature

Erd|wall ['e:ɐt-] *m* earthwork; **~zeit·al·ter** *n* geological era

er'ei·fern *v/refl.* (h): ***sich ~*** get worked up (***über*** *acc.* about); ***sich ~ gegen*** *acc.* lash out against

er·eig·nen [ɛɐˀaıgnən] *v/refl.* (h): ***sich ~*** happen, take place, occur; ***es hat sich nichts Ungewöhnliches ereignet*** nothing much happened; **Er·eig·nis** [ɛɐˀaıgnıs] *n* (-ses; -se) event; incident; sensation; ***freudiges ~*** happy event; **er'eig·nis·los** *adj.* uneventful; **er'eig·nis·reich** *adj.* very eventful; exciting

er'ei·len *lit. v/t.* (h) catch up with, *lit.* overtake; *lit.* befall; *news etc.*: reach; ***das Schicksal hat ihn ereilt*** fate caught up with him; ***der Tod hat ihn ereilt*** death caught up with (*or* overtook) him; ***der Tod hat ihn in ... ereilt*** he met his death in ...

Erek·ti·on [erɛk'tsĭo:n] *f* (-; -en) erection

Ere·mit [ere'mi:t] *m* (-en; -en) hermit; **Ere'mi·ten·da·sein** *n* life of a hermit

er'er·ben *v/t.* (h) inherit (***von*** *dat.* from); **er·erbt** [ɛɐˀɛrpt] *adj.* inherited; *biol.* hereditary

er'fah·ren¹ (erfuhr, erfahren, h) **I.** *v/t.* **1.** hear (about); be told (about); find out (about); discover; ***ich habe nichts davon ~*** *a.* nobody told me anything (*or* about it); ***sie hat es durch die Zeitung ~*** she read about it in the newspaper(s); ***ich habe es nur durch Zufall ~*** I only found out by chance; **2.** experience; suffer; get; **II.** *v/i.*: **~ *von*** *dat.* get to know about, hear about (*or* that ...)

er'fah·ren² **I.** *p.p. of* ***erfahren¹***; **II.** *adj.* experienced; well versed (***in*** *dat.* in); ***er ist sehr ~*** *a.* he's got a lot of experience; ***er ist in diesen Dingen sehr ~*** *a.* he's an old hand at that sort of thing; **Er'fah·ren·heit** *f* (-; *no pl.*) experience

Er·fah·rung [ɛɐ'fa:rʊŋ] *f* (-; -en) **1.** experience; ***technische ~*** *a.* know-how; ***aus*** (***eigener***) **~** from (one's personal) experience; **~*(en) sammeln*** (*or* ***machen***) gain (*or* pick up) experience; ***durch ~ klug werden*** learn the hard way; ***die ~ machen, daß*** find that; ***ich mußte die traurige ~ machen, daß*** sadly, I found that; ***schlechte ~en machen*** have problems *or* trouble (***mit*** *dat.* with), fare badly (with); ***gute ~en machen*** have no problems *or* trouble at all (***mit*** *dat.* with), fare very well (with); ***wir haben bisher mit dem Wagen nur gute ~en gemacht*** we've had absolutely no trouble with the car so far; ***die ~ hat gezeigt*** (*or* ***gelehrt***), ***daß*** (past) experience has shown that; ***da bin ich wieder um e-e ~ reicher*** you learn something new every day, I'll just have to put it down to experience, that's another lesson; **2.** ***in ~ bringen*** learn, find out

Er'fah·rungs|aus·tausch *m* exchange of views; ***sich zu e-m ~ treffen*** get together (in order) to compare notes; **~be·reich** *m* scope (of experience); **~be·richt** *m* ✝ progress report

er'fah·rungs·ge·mäß *adv.* experience has shown (*or* shows) that, we know from experience that

Er'fah·rungs|sa·che *f*: ***das ist ~*** it's just a question of experience; **~schatz** *m* store (*or* wealth) of experience; sum total of one's experience; **~tat·sa·che** *f* well-known (*or* well-established) fact; **~ur·teil** *n* empirical judg(e)ment; **~wert** *m* experience (*or* practical) value; *pl.* experience *sg.*

er'fand *pret. of* ***erfinden***

er'faß·bar *adj.* **1.** recordable; *statistics*: ascertainable; **2.** cognizable; **er'fas·sen** *v/t.* (h) **1.** seize, grasp; *car*: hit *s.o.*; *current etc.*: sweep away; ***von den Rädern erfaßt werden*** be caught under the wheels; ***von e-m Auto erfaßt werden*** be hit (*or* knocked down, run over) by a car; *fig.* ***von Furcht*** *etc.* ***erfaßt werden*** be seized with fear *etc.*; **2.** *fig.* grasp; realize; **3.** register, record; collect *data*; ***erfaßt sein*** be on file; ***wir sind vermutlich erfaßt*** *a.* F they've probably got us down on their files; **4.** *fig.* include; cover; **5.** compose *text*; **Er'fas·sung** *f* (-; -en) *adm.* registration

er'fech·ten *v/t.* (erfocht, erfochten, h) gain; win

er'fin·den *v/t.* (erfand, erfunden, h) invent; make up; → ***erfunden***; **Er'fin·der** *m* (-s; -) inventor; ***der ~*** *gen. a.* the man (*or* woman) who invented ...; **Er'fin·der·geist** *m* (-[e]s; *no pl.*) inventiveness; **er'fin·de·risch** *adj.* inventive; imaginative; creative; resourceful; → ***Not***; **Er'fin·dung** *f* (-; -en) **1.** invention; idea; ***e-e ~ machen*** invent something; ***m-e neueste ~*** my latest invention; **2.** invention, fabrication; ***das ist reine ~*** *a.* he's *etc.* made it all up; **Er'fin·dungs·ga·be** *f* (-; *no pl.*) inventive talent (*or* genius); imagination; **er'fin·dungs·reich** *adj.* inventive; **Er'fin·dungs·reich·tum** *m* (-s; *no pl.*) inventiveness

er'fle·hen *v/t.* (h) implore; ***j-s Hilfe ~*** *a.* implore (*or* beseech) s.o. to help one

er'focht *pret. of* ***erfechten***

er·foch·ten [ɛɐ'fɔxtən] *p.p. of* ***erfechten***

Er·folg [ɛɐ'fɔlk] *m* (-[e]s; -e) success; result, outcome; consequence, upshot; effect; achievement; ***großer ~*** great success; ***guter ~*** good result; ***~ haben*** succeed, be successful; ***hattest du ~?*** *a.* did you get what you wanted?; ***keinen ~ haben*** be unsuccessful, fail; ***mit dem ~, daß*** with the result that; ***er hatte keinerlei ~ bei ihr*** he didn't get anywhere with her; ***er hat bei den Frauen*** (***keinen***) ***~*** he's (not) very successful with women; ***von ~ gekrönt*** crowned with success; ***mit ~ bestanden*** passed

er'fol·gen *v/i.* (sn) follow; happen, take place, occur; ***~ nach*** *dat. a.* come after; ***es ist noch keine Antwort erfolgt*** we haven't had a (*or* any) reply yet; ***die Zahlung muß sofort ~*** payment must be made immediately

Er,folg·ha·sche·rei [-haʃə'rai] *f* (-; *no pl.*) success-seeking, pursuit of success, chasing after success (F fame and fortune)

er'folg·los *adj.* unsuccessful; fruitless; ineffective; ***ein ~es Bemühen*** a fruitless enterprise; *die Bemühungen etc.* ***blieben ~*** *a.* were to no avail; **Er'folg·lo·sig·keit** *f* (-; *no pl.*) failure; ineffectiveness

er'folg·reich **I.** *adj.* successful; **II.** *adv.*: ***e-e Prüfung ~ bestehen*** pass an exam

Er'folgs|aus·sich·ten *pl.* chances of success; **~au·tor** *m* best-selling author; **~be·tei·li·gung** *f* ✝ profit-sharing; **~bi,lanz** *f* list of successes; **~buch** *n* best-selling book (*or* work); **~chan·ce** *f* chance (of winning *etc.*); **~den·ken** *n* positive thinking; **~er·leb·nis** *n* sense of achievement; ***jeder braucht mal ein ~*** everyone needs a lift now and again; **~film** *m* box-office hit (*or* success); film success; **~ge·heim·nis** *n* secret behind s.o.'s success; **~ho·no,rar** *n* contingent fee; **~kur·ve** *f* success spiral (*or* cycle); **~lei·ter** *f* ladder of success; **~mel·dung** *f* good news; news of s.o.'s success; **~mensch** *m* success-seeker, F go-getter; **~quo·te** *f* success rate; **~re,zept** *n* recipe for success; **~schla·ger** *m* (top) hit, hit success; **2si·cher** *adj.* certain *or* sure of success (*or* to succeed); **~streß** *m* → ***Erfolgszwang***; **~wel·le** *f* wave of success; **~zwang** *m*: ***unter ~ stehen*** be under pressure to succeed (*or* do well)

er'folg·ver·spre·chend *adj.* promising

er·for·der·lich [ɛɐ'fɔrdɐlɪç] *adj.* necessary; required; ***unbedingt ~*** essential; ***falls ~*** if required; ***~ machen*** require, necessitate; ***die ~en Maßnahmen ergreifen*** take the necessary steps; **er'for·dern** *v/t.* (h) require, demand, call for; necessitate; take *time, patience, courage etc.*; **Er·for·der·nis** [ɛɐ'fɔrdɐnɪs] *n* (-ses; -se) requirement, demand; prerequisite

er'for·schen *v/t.* (h) **1.** inquire into, investigate; study, research (into); do research on; explore; **2.** ***sein Gewissen ~*** search one's conscience, F do a bit of soul-searching; **Er'for·scher** *m* (-s; -) explorer; **Er'for·schung** *f* (-; *no pl.*) investigation (*gen.* of, into); research (into); exploration (of)

er'fra·gen *v/t.* (h) ask (for); ***zu ~ bei*** *dat.* apply to

er·fre·chen [ɛɐ'frɛçən] *v/refl.* (erfrechte, erfrecht, h): ***sich ~ zu*** *inf.* have the audacity to *inf.*

er'freu·en (h) **I.** *v/t.* please; *formal*: give *s.o.* pleasure; F give *s.o.* a thrill; ***j-s Herz ~*** *lit.* gladden s.o.'s heart; **II.** *v/refl.*: ***sich ~ an*** *dat.* enjoy, *formal*: take pleasure in; ***sich e-r Sache ~*** enjoy s.th.; ***sich großer Beliebtheit ~*** be very popular, enjoy great popularity; → ***erfreut***; **er·freu·lich** [ɛɐ'frɔʏlɪç] **I.** *adj.* pleasing; good, welcome *news etc.*; encouraging, heartening; ***das ist ja sehr ~*** that's good to hear; **II.** *adv.*: ***es waren ~ wenig Leute da*** we were *etc.* pleased to find so few people there; ***es sind ~ wenig Unfälle passiert*** we are pleased to report that there were relatively few accidents; ***ich habe ~ viel geschafft*** I'm pleased at how much I managed to get done; ***das 2e daran*** the nice thing about it; ***es gibt wenig 2es zu berichten*** the news isn't very good, I'm afraid; **er'freu·li·cher·'wei·se** *adv.* fortunately, happily; ***~ hat es geklappt*** I'm glad to say it worked; ***~ hat sie sich gebessert*** we're *etc.* glad to see she's improved; **er'freut** *adj.* pleased (***über*** *acc.* at, about), delighted (with, about, at); ***hoch ~*** (absolutely) delighted; ***ein ~es Gesicht machen*** look pleased; ***..., sagte sie ~*** ..., she said delightedly; *obs.* ***sehr ~*** pleased to meet you

er'frie·ren (erfror, erfroren) **I.** *v/i.* (sn) freeze to death; ⚘ be killed by frost; ***ihm sind zwei Finger erfroren*** he lost two fingers through frostbite; ***mir sind die Finger erfroren*** my fingers were frozen to the bone; **II.** *v/t.* (h): ***er hat sich zwei Finger erfroren*** he got frostbite on two fingers; **Er·frie·rung** [ɛɐ'friːrʊŋ] *f* (-; -en) *a. pl.* frostbite (***an*** *dat.* on); ***~en erleiden*** get frostbite, get frostbitten; **Er'frie·rungs·tod** *m*: ***den ~ sterben*** die from exposure (📖 of hypothermia), freeze to death

er'fri·schen (h) **I.** *v/t.* refresh; revive; **II.** *v/refl.*: ***sich ~*** a) refresh o.s., take some refreshment; b) freshen up; c) cool o.s. (down); **er'fri·schend** *adj.* refreshing (*a. fig.*); *fig.* ***von ~er Offenheit*** refreshingly frank; **Er·fri·schung** [ɛɐ'frɪʃʊŋ] *f* (-; -en) refreshment; ***e-e ~*** (*or* ***~en***) ***zu sich nehmen*** have (*or* take) some refreshment

Er'fri·schungs|ge·tränk *n* **1.** soft drink; **2.** cool drink; **~raum** *m* refreshment room; **~tuch** *n* moist (*or* moistened) tissue

er'fror *pret. of* ***erfrieren***

er·fro·ren [ɛɐ'froːrən] *p.p. of* ***erfrieren***

er'fuhr *pret. of* ***erfahren***[1]

er'fül·len (h) **I.** *v/t.* **1.** *a. fig.* fill (***mit*** *dat.* with); **2.** fulfil(l) *task, request etc.*; meet *demand, condition etc.*; grant *wish etc.*; meet, come up to *expectations etc.*; carry out *duty etc.*; keep *promise etc.*; serve *a purpose*; ***das Auto erfüllt noch s-n Zweck*** the car still serves its purpose (*or* does its job); **3.** ***s-e Arbeit erfüllt ihn*** he finds his work very satisfying; **II.** *v/refl.*: ***sich ~*** come true; **er'füllt** *adj.*: ***~ von*** *dat.* filled with, full of, bubbling over with; ***~ von dem Wunsch zu*** *inf.* filled with (*or* possessed by) the desire to *inf.*; ***ein ~es Leben*** a full (and active) life; ***ein ~er Traum*** a dream come true, the fulfil(l)ment of a dream; ***nicht ~e Forderungen*** *etc.* unmet demands *etc.*; **Er'fül·lung** *f* (-; *no pl.*) fulfil(l)ment; ***in ~ gehen*** come true, be fulfilled; **Er'fül·lungs·ort** *m* ✝ place of fulfil(l)ment

er·fun·den [ɛɐ'fʊndən] **I.** *p.p. of* ***erfinden***; **II.** *adj.* imaginary, fictitious; ***das ist alles ~*** he's *etc.* made it all up, it's pure fabrication

Erg [ɛrk] *n* (-s; -) *phys.* erg

er'gab *pret. of* ***ergeben***[1]

er·gan·gen [ɛɐ'gaŋən] *p.p. of* ***ergehen***[1]

er·gän·zen [ɛɐ'gɛntsən] *v/t.* (ergänzte, ergänzt, h) complement; complete; supplement; add; replenish *stocks*; make up *sum*; restore; ***sich*** (*or* ***einander***) ***~*** complement one another, be complementary; ***sie ~ sich hervorragend*** they make the perfect (man-and-wife) team; **er'gän·zend** **I.** *adj.* complementary; supplementary; additional; integral; *ling.* completive *clause*; **II.** *adv.*: ***~ möchte ich noch hinzufügen, daß*** I would just like to add that; ***~ muß noch gesagt werden, daß*** it must be added that; **Er·gän·zung** [ɛɐ'gɛntsʊŋ] *f* (-; -en) **1.** completion; supplementation; addition; ***zur ~*** *gen.* to add to, to supplement, in addition to; **2.** complement (*a. ling.*, ♪); supplement; addition; ⚖ amendment

Er'gän·zungs|ab·ga·be *f* supplemental income tax; **~band** *m* (-[e]s; ⸚e) supplement(ary volume); **~far·be** *f* complementary colo(u)r; **~fra·ge** *f* follow-up question; **~haus·halt** *m* supplementary budget; **~ma·te·ri|al** *n* supplementary material; **~wort** *n* (-[e]s; ⸚er) *ling.* supplementary word

er·gat·tern [ɛɐ'gatɐn] F *v/t.* (ergatterte, ergattert, h) (*a.* **sich** *dat.* ~) (manage to) get hold of

er'gau·nern *v/t.* (h): (**sich**) **et.** ~ get s.th. in some racket (or other), **bei j-m:** swindle s.o. out of s.th.

er'ge·ben[1] (ergab, ergeben, h) **I.** *v/t.* **1.** result in; come to, make; yield; **2.** show, establish, prove; **es hat nichts ~** *a.* nothing came of it; **es ergibt keinen Sinn** it doesn't make sense; **II.** *v/refl.*: **3. sich ~** arise, crop up; **es ergab sich e-e Diskussion** a discussion ensued, it led to a discussion; **sich ~ aus** *dat.* result (*or* arise) from; **daraus ergibt sich, daß** it follows that; **es ergab sich, daß** it turned out that; **es hat sich so ~** it happened to work out like that, **daß:** it so happened that; as it turned out,...; **4. sich ~** ⚔ *and w.s.* surrender (*dat.* to); devote o.s. to *s.th.*; *b.s.* take to (*doing*) *s.th.*; **sich ~ in** *acc.* resign o.s. to, surrender to

er'ge·ben[2] **I.** *p.p. of* **ergeben**[1]; **II.** *adj.* devoted (*dat.* to); loyal (to); resigned (to); **dem Laster** (**dem Trunk**) ~ a slave to vice (drink); **~er Diener** obedient servant; **Er'ge·ben·heit** *f* (-; *no pl.*) devotion; loyalty; resignation

Er·geb·nis [ɛɐ'geːpnɪs] *n* (-ses; -se) result (*a. sport etc.*), outcome; result, consequence(s *pl.*); score; findings *pl.*; results *pl.*; answer; conclusion; **zu dem ~ kommen** (*or* **gelangen**), **daß** come to (*or* arrive at) the conclusion that; **zu keinem ~ gelangen** *talks etc.*: (turn out to) be unsuccessful; **das richtige ~ lautet** the correct answer is; **er'geb·nis·los** *adj.* without result; unsuccessful; **~ bleiben** remain unsuccessful, lead nowhere, fail

Er·ge·bung [ɛɐ'geːbʊŋ] *f* (-; *no pl.*) **1.** surrender; **2.** resignation, submission; **er'ge·bungs·voll** *adj.* submissive

er'ge·hen (erging, ergangen) **I.** *v/i.* (sn) **1.** *order etc.*: be issued (**an** *acc.* to); *law*: come out; be sent (to); ⚖ *sentence etc.*: be passed; **~ lassen** issue; send (**an** *acc.* to), extend (to); ⚖ pass *resolution etc.*; **es erging e-e Aufforderung an die Mitglieder zu** *inf.* the members were called (*or* summoned) to *inf.*; **es erging an sie ein Ruf an die Universität London** she was offered a chair at London University; **2. et. über sich ~ lassen** (patiently) endure, submit to; **II.** *v/refl.* (h) **3. sich ~ über** *acc.* hold forth on *a subject etc.*; **4. sich ~ in** *dat.* indulge in; pour forth *abuse etc.*; **5.** *lit.* **sich ~** take a walk (*or* stroll); **III.** *v/impers.* (sn): **es ist ihm schlecht ergangen** he had a bad (*or* rough) time of it; **es ist mir gut ergangen** I fared (*or* things went) very well, **bei m-n Großeltern:** I was well looked-after by my grandparents; **wie ist es dir ergangen?** how did you fare?, how did it go?; **mir ist's genauso ergangen** it was the same with me, I had the same experience; **IV.** ♀ *n* (-s) → **Befinden**

er·gie·big [ɛɐ'giːbɪç] *adj.* economical; fertile; rich (**an** *dat.* in); profitable, lucrative; *fig.* useful, productive, fruitful *talks etc.*; broad, endless *subject*; ⚒ high-yield; **der Tee ist sehr ~** this tea goes a long way; **Er'gie·big·keit** *f* (-; *no pl.*) economy; fertility; richness; lucrativeness; usefulness; breadth; ⚒ yield

er'gie·ßen (ergoß, ergossen, h) **I.** *v/refl.*: **sich ~ in** (**auf, über**) *acc.* flow *or* pour into (onto, over); **sich ~ in** *acc. river*: flow (*or* empty) into; **II.** *v/t.* pour (**in** *acc.* into; **auf** *acc.* onto; **über** *acc.* over)

er'glän·zen *v/i.* (sn) (begin to) shine *or* gleam

er'glü·hen *v/i.* (sn) (begin to) glow, *lit.* catch (*or* be on) fire; *fig. face*: glow, blush, go red; *fig.* **~ vor** *dat. a.* flush with *pride etc.*; *w.s.* be flushed with *enthusiasm*

er·go ['ɛrgo] *cj.* ergo, therefore

Er·go·no·mie [ɛrgono'miː] *f* (-; *no pl.*) ergonomics *pl.*, human engineering; **er·go·no·misch** [ɛrgo'noːmɪʃ] *adj.* ergonomic(ally *adv.*)

er'goß *pret. of* **ergießen**

er·gos·sen [ɛɐ'gɔsən] *p.p. of* **ergießen**

er·göt·zen [ɛɐ'gœtsən] (ergötzte, ergötzt, h) **I.** *v/t.* amuse, entertain; delight; **II.** *v/refl.*: **sich ~ an** *dat.* enjoy; be amused by; revel in; feast one's eyes on; gloat at; **III.** ♀ *n* (-s): **zu j-s ~** to s.o.'s delight; **er·götz·lich** [ɛɐ'gœtslɪç] *adj.* delightful; amusing, funny

er'grau·en *v/i.* (sn) turn grey (*Am.* gray)

er'grei·fen *v/t.* (ergriff, ergriffen, h) **1.** seize, grasp; **2.** seize, catch, F get hold of; **3.** *fig.* take; **das Wort ~** begin to speak; → **Beruf, Besitz, Gelegenheit, Initiative** 1; **4.** *fig.* move; overcome; seize; **von Angst** *etc.* **ergriffen werden** be seized (*or* gripped) with fear *etc.*; **er'grei·fend** *adj.* moving, stirring; heart-rending; **Er'grei·fung** *f* (-; *no pl.*) capture; arrest

er·grif·fen [ɛɐ'grɪfən] **I.** *p.p. of* **ergreifen**; **II.** *adj. and adv.* deeply moved (**von** *dat.* by); shaken (by); **mit ~er Stimme** in a trembling voice; **sie schwiegen ~** they were moved to silence; **von Panik ~** panic-stricken, seized with panic; **von Trauer ~** grief-stricken, overcome with grief; **Er'grif·fen·heit** *f* (-; *no pl.*) emotion; **in tiefer ~** deeply moved (*or* touched)

er'grün·den *v/t.* (h) get to the bottom of; fathom (out); find out, determine; **Er'grün·dung** *f* (-; *no pl.*) explanation (*gen.* for); solving

Er'guß *m* (Ergusses; Ergüsse) **1.** discharge (*a. physiol.*); contusion; emission, ejaculation; **2.** *fig.* effusion, outburst, *pl. a.* outpourings; flood, torrent

er'ha·ben *adj.* **1.** raised, elevated; **~e Arbeit** embossed (*or* raised) work; **2.** *fig.* grand, magnificent; lofty, noble, sublime; **~ über** *acc.* above (*doing*) *s.th.*, superior to; **über alles Lob ~** beyond all praise; **über jeden Tadel** (**Verdacht**) ~ beyond reproach (above suspicion); **Er'ha·ben·heit** *f* (-; *no pl.*) grandeur; loftiness; superiority

Er'halt *m* (-[e]s; *no pl.*) *adm.* receipt

er'hal·ten[1] (erhielt, erhalten, h) **I.** *v/t.* **1.** get, receive; obtain; be awarded, be given *a prize etc.*; **2.** keep; preserve, conserve; maintain, keep up *tradition etc.*; maintain, preserve *peace*; save; keep, support *one's family*; **j-n am Leben ~** keep s.o. alive; **j-n bei guter Laune** (**Gesundheit**) **~** keep s.o. in a good mood (in good health); **sich s-n Optimismus ~** keep up one's optimism, stay optimistic; **erhalt dir d-n Humor!** keep (*or* don't lose) your sense of humo(u)r; *iro.* **Gott erhalte dir d-e kindliche Unschuld!** blessed are the innocent; **II.** *v/refl.*: **sich ~** survive; **sich am Leben ~** stay alive, survive; **sich gesund ~** stay (*or* keep) healthy; **sich bei guter Laune ~** keep up the good mood, keep one's spirits up; **sich ~ von** *dat.* subsist on

er'hal·ten[2] **I.** *p.p. of* **erhalten**[1]; **II.** *adj.*: **gut** (**schlecht**) ~ in good (bad) condition; *iro.* **er ist noch gut ~** F he's still in pretty good shape; **~ bleiben** survive; **er bleibt uns noch ~** he'll be around for some time yet, *euphem.* he's been spared; **noch ~ sein** remain, be left

Er'hal·ter *m* (-s; -) preserver; supporter; **er·hält·lich** [ɛɐ'hɛltlɪç] *adj.* obtainable, available; **schwer ~** hard to get hold of (*or* come by); **Er'hal·tung** *f* (- *no pl.*) preservation; conservation; upkeep; **etwas für die ~ s-r Gesundheit tun** do something for one's health

Er'hal·tungs|ko·sten *pl.* maintenance costs, cost *sg.* of upkeep; **~zu·stand** *m* condition; **wie ist der ~?** what kind of condition is it in?

er'hän·gen *v/t.* (h) hang (**sich** o.s.); **erhängt werden** be hanged; (**der**) **Tod durch** ♀ death by hanging; **j-n zum Tod durch** ♀ **verurteilen** sentence s.o. to be hanged

er'här·ten (h) **I.** *v/t.* **1.** ⚙ harden, set; **2.** *fig.* bear out, confirm, corroborate, substantiate; **erhärtet werden durch** *acc.* be borne out *etc.* by; **II.** *fig. v/refl.*: **sich ~** be corroborated, be substantiated, **durch** *acc.*: *a.* be borne out by; **III.** *v/i.* *cement etc.*: harden, set; *lava*: solidify; **Er'här·tung** *f* (-; *no pl.*) **1.** ⚙ hardening, setting; **2.** *fig.* corroboration, substantiation

er'ha·schen *v/t.* (h) catch; pick up; **schnell noch ~** grab; **e-n flüchtigen Blick von et. ~** catch a (fleeting) glimpse of s.th.

er'he·ben (erhob, erhoben, h) **I.** *v/t.* **1.** raise (*a. fig.*) , lift (up); → **Anspruch, Klage** 3, **Protest**; **2.** elevate, promote; **zum König** *etc.* **erhoben werden** be made king *etc.*; **in den Adelsstand erhoben werden** *in England*: be given a peerage, be knighted; *hist.* be raised to the nobility; **3.** *fig.* **~ zu** *dat.* make *a system* of, adopt as; **4.** impose *taxes*; charge *fee*; **5.** ⩤ raise; **ins Quadrat ~** square; **zur dritten Potenz ~** cube; **6.** *fig.* elevate; ennoble; **II.** *v/refl.*: **sich ~** get up, *formal*: rise (to one's feet); ✈ rise, *a. bird*: soar (up); *wind etc.*: come up; *fig. question, doubt, difficulties etc.*: arise; *people*: rise up (**gegen** *acc.* against); **sich ~ über** *acc.* rise (*or* tower) above, *fig.* rise above, look down on *s.o.*; **es erhob sich ein lauter Protest** there was (*or* this gave rise to) loud protest; **e-e Stimme erhob sich** somebody spoke, F a voice piped up, **aus der Menge:** a voice could be heard (F a voice piped up) from among the crowd; **er·he·bend** *fig. adj.* edifying; exalting

er·heb·lich [ɛɐ'heːplɪç] **I.** *adj.* considerable; important; relevant (**für** *acc.*, **in** *dat.* to); **II.** *adv.* considerably; **~ besser** much better; **~ größer** (**teurer** *etc.*) much (*or* a great deal) bigger (more ex-

pensive *etc.*); **Er'heb·lich·keit** *f* (-; *no pl.*) importance; relevance (**für** *acc.*, **in** *acc.* to)
Er'he·bung *f* (-; -en) **1.** *geol.* elevation, rise (in the ground), *w.s.* hill(ock); **2.** *fig.* elevation, promotion (**in** *acc.* to *the rank of*); **3.** ✝ levy; charge; **4.** ℞ involution; **~ ins Quadrat** squaring; **~ in die dritte Potenz** cubing; **5.** inquiry; **6.** survey; **~en** statistics; census; **7.** uprising, popular revolt; **8.** *fig.* edification
er'hei·schen *v/t.* (h) demand; **Respekt ~** command respect
er·hei·tern [ɛɐ'haɪtɐn] (erheiterte, erheitert, h) **I.** *v/t.* amuse; cheer up; **II.** *v/refl.*: **sich ~** *face*: brighten, light up, *sky*: brighten up; **sich ~ über** *acc.* be amused by; **Er·hei·te·rung** [ɛɐ'haɪtərʊŋ] *f* (-; *no pl.*) amusement; **zur allgemeinen ~** to everyone's amusement
er·hel·len [ɛɐ'hɛlən] (erhellte, erhellt, h) **I.** *v/t.* **1.** light up, illuminate; **2.** *fig.* shed (*or* throw) light (up)on; **II.** *v/refl.*: **sich ~ 3.** brighten; *face*: *a.* light up; **4.** *fig. problem etc.*: be cleared up; **III.** *v/i.*: *lit.* **daraus erhellt, daß** from this it appears that, this would indicate that; **Er'hel·lung** *f* (-; *no pl.*) illumination; brightening
er·hit·zen [ɛɐ'hɪtsən] (erhitzte, erhitzt, h) **I.** *v/t.* **1.** heat (up); pasteurize; **2.** *fig.* rouse; fire; **II.** *v/refl.*: **sich ~ 3.** get hot; **4.** *fig. discussion*: become heated; *passions*: be roused; get worked up (*or* excited, all hot and bothered) (**über** *dat.* about); **die Gemüter erhitzten sich** feelings were running high; **er'hitzt** *adj.* **1.** hot, flushed; **2.** *fig.* heated *debate etc.*; worked up, hot and bothered; **~e Gemüter** raised tempers; **Er'hit·zung** *f* (-; *no pl.*) **1.** heating (up); **2.** *fig.* agitation, excitement
er'hob *pret. of* **erheben**
er·ho·ben [ɛɐ'ho:bən] *p.p. of* **erheben**
er'hof·fen *v/t.* (h) (*a.* **sich** *dat.* **~**) hope for; expect (**von** *dat.* of); **er'hofft** *adj.* hoped-for
er·hö·hen [ɛɐ'hø:ən] (erhöhte, erhöht, h) **I.** *v/t.* **1.** raise; ♪ *a.* sharpen (**um e-n Halbton** by half a tone); **2.** raise, put up, F hike *price*; raise *temperature*, *blood pressure*; increase (**auf** *acc.* to; **um** *acc.* by); improve (by); enhance, heighten *tension*, *effect etc.*; promote; **II.** *v/refl.*: **sich ~** increase (**auf** *acc.* to; **um** *acc.* by); *price etc.*: *a.* go up; *temperature etc.*: rise, go up; *tension etc.*: heighten; **er'höht** *adj.* **1.** raised, elevated; **2.** increased *prices*; heightened *tension etc.*; **~e Temperatur haben** have (*or* be running) a temperature; **mit ~er Aufmerksamkeit fahren** drive more carefully; **Er'hö·hung** *f* (-; -en) **1.** raising; ♪ *a.* sharpening (**um** *acc.* by); **2.** *geol.* elevation; hill(ock); **3.** increase; improvement; enhancement; heightening; (*pay*) rise, *Am.* raise; increase, rise (*gen.* in *prices*)
Er'hö·hungs|win·kel *m* angle of elevation; **~zei·chen** *n* ♪ sharp (sign)
er'ho·len *v/refl.*: **sich ~** (h) **1.** recover (*a. fig.*), recuperate; (take a) rest; relax; have a (good) rest; **sich vom Schreck** *etc.* **~** get over (*or* recover from) the shock *etc.*; **2.** ✝ recover, rally; pick up, be on the rebound; **er·hol·sam** [ɛɐ'ho:lza:m] *adj.* restful, relaxing; **ich wünsche Ihnen e-n ~en Urlaub** *a.* I hope you come back from your holiday refreshed; **Er'hol·sam·keit** *f* (-; *no pl.*) relaxing (*or* recuperative) effect; **er'holt** *adj.* rested; F fighting fit (again); **du siehst gut ~ aus** *a.* you look your old self again; **Er·ho·lung** [ɛɐ'ho:lʊŋ] *f* (-; *no pl.*) **1.** recovery, recuperation; rest, relaxation; recreation; convalescence; **wir fahren zur ~ hin** we're going there for a rest (*or* to relax); **gute ~!** have a good rest; **2.** ✝ recovery, rally; **3.** holiday, *Am.* vacation
Er'ho·lungs|auf·ent·halt *m* holiday, *Am.* vacation; **≗be·dürf·tig** *adj.* in need of a rest (*or* holiday, *Am.* vacation); **~ge·biet** *n* recreation area; beauty spot; **~heim** *n* rest home; **~kur** *f* rest cure; **~ort** *m* (health *or* holiday) resort; **~pau·se** *f* rest, breather; **~rei·se** *f* holiday trip, pleasure trip; **~ur·laub** *m* holiday, *Am.* vacation; ⚕ convalescent leave; **~wert** *m* recreational value; **~zen·trum** *n* recreation park
er'hö·ren *v/t.* (h) **1.** hear, answer *prayer*; grant *petition etc.*; **2. j-n ~** a) hear (*or* answer) s.o.'s prayers; b) give in to s.o.; **Er·hö·rung** [ɛɐ'hø:rʊŋ] *f*: **die ~ e-s Gebets** the answering of a prayer
eri·gie·ren [eri'gi:rən] *v/i.* (sn) *physiol.* become erect; **eri·giert** [eri'gi:ɐt] *adj.* erect
Eri·ka ['e:rika] *f* (-; -s) ♣ heather
er·in·ner·lich [ɛɐ'ʔɪnɐlɪç] *adj.*: **soviel mir ~ ist** as far as I can recall (*or* recollect); **das ist mir noch gut ~** I can remember it well, I can remember (*or* recall) it quite clearly; **erin·nern** [ɛɐ'ʔɪnɐn] (erinnerte, erinnert, h) **I.** *v/t.*: **j-n ~ an** *acc.* remind s.o. of, put s.o. in mind of; **j-n daran ~, et. zu tun** remind s.o. to do s.th.; **könntest du mich daran ~?** could you remind me (*or* give me a reminder)?; **II.** *v/refl.*: **sich ~** remember (*gen. or* **an** *acc. s.th.*, *s.o.*); **sich ~** *gen.* (*or* **an** *acc.*) *a.* recall, recollect, think back to, call to mind; **wenn ich mich recht erinnere** if I remember rightly; **soviel ich mich ~ kann** as far as I can remember (*or* recall); **jetzt erinnere ich mich vage** it's slowly coming back to me now; **III.** *v/i.*: **~ an** *acc.* be reminiscent of, remind one of; **es erinnert stark an Goethe** it's strongly suggestive of Goethe; **er erinnert an s-n Onkel** he has a strong resemblance to his uncle, he reminds me (*or* one) of his uncle; **ich erinnere (nur) an** *acc.* **...** I recall ... (suffice it to recall ...); **Er·in·ne·rung** [ɛɐ'ʔɪnərʊŋ] *f* (-; -en) memory, recollection; memento, keepsake; **~en** reminiscences; memoirs; **in guter (schlechter) ~ haben** have fond (unpleasant) memories of; **ich habe keine ~ daran** I can't remember it at all; **zur ~ an** *acc.* in memory (*or* remembrance) of; **als ~ an** *acc.* as a memento of
Er'in·ne·rungs|lücke *f* gap in one's memory; **~schrei·ben** *n* reminder; **~ta·fel** *f* memorial tablet; **~ver·mö·gen** *n* (-s; *no pl.*) memory, powers *pl.* of recollection; **~wert** *m* sentimental value
Erin·nyen [e'rɪnyən] *pl. myth.* Furies, Erin(n)yes
er'ja·gen *v/t.* (h) **1.** catch; **2.** *fig.* hunt down
er·kal·ten [ɛɐ'kaltən] *v/i.* (erkaltete, erkaltet, sn) **1.** *lava etc.*: cool (down), *gastr. a.* get cold; *corpse*: get (*or* grow) cold; **2.** *fig.* cool off; *heart*: turn to stone
er·käl·ten [ɛɐ'kɛltən] (erkältete, erkältet, h) **I.** *v/refl.*: **sich ~** catch (a) cold (**beim Skifahren** *etc.* skiing *etc.*); **II.** *v/t.*: **sich die Blase** *etc.* **~** catch a chill in one's bladder *etc.*; **er'käl·tet** *adj.*: **~ sein** have a cold; **stark ~ sein** have a bad (*or* heavy) cold; **ich bin furchtbar ~** I've got a rotten cold (F a stinker of a cold); **Er'käl·tung** *f* (-; -en) cold; **leichte (starke) ~** slight (bad, heavy) cold; **Er'käl·tungs·krank·hei·ten** *pl.* colds and flu
er'kämp·fen *v/t.* (h) fight for; *sport*: win; **et. hart ~ müssen** have to really fight for s.th., have to struggle to attain s.th.
er'kau·fen *v/t.* (h) **1.** *fig.* buy; **et. teuer ~ müssen** (have to) pay a high price for s.th.; **die Freiheit mit s-r Ehre ~** pay for one's freedom with one's hono(u)r, sacrifice one's hono(u)r for one's freedom; **2.** bribe
er·kenn·bar [ɛɐ'kɛnba:ɐ] *adj.* recognizable; perceptible, discernible; *phls.* cognizable; *in der Ferne* **war die Stadt deutlich ~** you could clearly make out the town; **ohne ~en Grund** for no apparent reason; **er'ken·nen** (erkannte, erkannt, h) **I.** *v/t.* recognize (**an** *dat.* by); make out, see, read; detect; identify; ⚕ diagnose; realize, see, *formal*: recognize; see through; **man erkennt ihn an s-m Akzent** *a.* his accent gives him away; **ich habe dich mit der Brille kaum erkannt** I hardly recognized you in those glasses; **~ lassen** show, reveal, suggest; **zu ~ geben** indicate, give to understand; **sich zu ~ geben** disclose one's identity, *fig.* come out into the open; ⚖ **j-n für schuldig ~** find s.o. guilty; **II.** *v/i.*: ⚖ **in e-r Sache ~** decide in a matter; ⚖ **~ auf** *acc.* impose *s.th.*
er'kennt·lich *adj.* **1.** perceptible; clear; obvious; **2. sich (j-m) ~ zeigen** show one's appreciation (**für** *acc.* for, of); **Er'kennt·lich·keit** *f* (-; -en) **1.** *no pl.* gratitude, appreciation; **2.** token of one's (*or* s.o.'s) appreciation
Er'kennt·nis *f* (-; -se) knowledge (*a. pl.*); perception; realization; understanding; *phls.* cognition; *a. pl.* idea; discovery, finding; *pl.* findings; **neueste ~se** *the* latest findings; **zu der ~ gelangen, daß** (come to) realize that; **der Baum der ~** the tree of knowledge; **~drang** *m* thirst for knowledge; **~kri,tik** *f phls.* epistemology; **≗reich** *adj.* informative, instructive; eye-opening; **~stand** *m* level of knowledge; **≗theo,re·tisch** *adj.* epistemological; **~theo,rie** *f* epistemology; **~ver·mö·gen** *n* (-s; *no pl.*) cognitive faculties *pl.*
Er'ken·nung *f* (-; *no pl.*) recognition; identification
Er'ken·nungs|dienst *m* (police) records department; **~mar·ke** *f* identity disc; **~me·lo,die** *f* signature tune; **~wort** *n* password; **~zei·chen** *n* **1. als ~ werde ich e-e rote Fliege tragen** you'll recognize me by my red bow tie; **2.** ⚕ symptom; **3.** badge; **4.** ✈ markings *pl.*; **5.** *radio*: station identification signal
Er·ker ['ɛrkɐ] *m* (-s; -) oriel; **~fen·ster** *n* oriel window
er'klang *pret. of* **erklingen**
er·klär·bar [ɛɐ'klɛ:ɐba:ɐ] *adj.* explainable (**durch** *acc.* by); **es ist ~ durch** *acc. a.* it can be explained by; **er'klä·ren** (h) **I.** *v/t.* **1.** explain (**j-m** to s.o.); define; illustrate; account for, explain; **~ Sie mir bitte, warum** could you tell me why; **ich**

kann es mir nicht ~ I don't understand it, it's a mystery to me; **2.** declare, state; pronounce; express; ***für gesund*** ~ pronounce *s.o.* healthy; → ***Rücktritt*** 1; **II.** *v/refl.* **3.** ***das erklärt sich daraus, daß*** that is to be (*or* can be) explained by the fact that; ***das erklärt sich von selbst*** that is self-explanatory; ***so erklärt es sich, wie*** this explains how; ***dadurch erklärt sich*** that explains, that accounts for; **4.** ***sich*** ~ explain o.s.; **5.** ***sich*** ~ ***für (gegen)*** *acc.* declare o.s. for (against); **6.** ***sich (für) bankrott*** *etc.* ~ declare o.s. bankrupt *etc.*; ***sich einverstanden*** ~ declare o.s. in agreement; ***sich mit et. zufrieden*** ~ express one's satisfaction with s.th.; **er'klä·rend** *adj.* explanatory; **er·klär·lich** [ɛɐ'klɛːɐlɪç] *adj.* **1.** → ***erklärbar***; **2.** understandable; evident, obvious; ***es ist mir nicht*** ~ I can't understand it, it's a mystery to me; ***aus*** ~***en Gründen*** → **er'klär·li·cher'wei·se** *adv.* understandably, for obvious reasons; **er'klärt** *adj.* declared, professed, avowed; ~***es Ziel,*** ~***e Zielsetzung*** stated objective, declared aim; ***sein*** ~***es Ziel ist es zu*** *inf.* it is his stated objective (*or* declared aim) to *inf.*; **Er'klä·rung** *f* (-; -en) explanation (*gen. or* ***für*** *acc.* of, for); reasons *pl.*; definition; declaration, statement (*a. pol.*); ***das ist die*** ~ ***für*** *acc.* that explains, that is the explanation for; ***zur*** ~ *gen.* by way of explaining, as an explanation for; ***e-e*** ~ ***abgeben*** *a. pol.* make a statement (***zu*** *dat.* on); **er'klä·rungs·be·dürf·tig** *adj.* in need of (an) explanation; **Er'klä·rungs·ver·such** *m* attempt at explanation (*or* to explain s.th.)

er·kleck·lich [ɛɐ'klɛklɪç] *adj.* considerable, hefty; ***e-e*** ~***e Summe*** *a.* a tidy sum

er'klet·tern *v/t.* (h) climb (up)

er'klim·men *v/t.* (erklomm, erklommen, h) climb (up to); *fig.* reach

er'klin·gen *v/i.* (erklang, erklungen, sn) sound, ring out; ***Gelächter erklang*** you could hear the sound of laughter; ***ein Lied*** ~ ***lassen*** strike up a tune (*or* song)

er·klü·geln [ɛɐ'klyːgəln] *v/t.* (erklügelte, erklügelt, h) think up (*or* out)

er·ko·ren [ɛɐ'koːrən] *adj.* chosen (***zu*** *dat.* for, as), select ...

er'kran·ken *v/i.* (sn) fall ill *or* sick (***an*** *dat.* with); ~ ***an*** *dat. a.* get, come down with; ***erkrankt sein an*** *dat.* have, F be laid up with; **Er'kran·kung** *f* (-; -en) illness, sickness; disease; **Er'kran·kungs·fall** *m*: ***im*** ~ in case of (*or* in the event of) illness

er·küh·nen [ɛɐ'kyːnən] *v/refl.* (erkühnte, erkühnt, h): ***sich*** ~ ***zu*** *inf.* have the audacity to *inf.*, *formal*: make bold to *inf.*

er·kun·den [ɛɐ'kʊndən] *v/t.* (erkundete, erkundet, h) **1.** explore; ⚔ reconnoit|re (*Am.* -er); **2.** discover, find out; investigate, scout out

er·kun·di·gen [ɛɐ'kʊndɪgən] *v/refl.* (erkundigte, erkundigt, h): ***sich*** ~ inquire *or* enquire (***über*** *acc.* about), ask (about); make inquiries (*or* enquiries); ***sich*** ~ ***nach*** *dat.* ask *the way, the time*; inquire (*or* enquire) after *s.o.('s health)*; ask for *a book etc.*; ***ich werde mich*** ~ *a.* I'll try and find out; ***hast du dich erkundigt, wann ...?*** did you find out when ...?; **Er·kun·di·gung** [ɛɐ'kʊndɪgʊŋ] *f* (-; -en) inquiry, enquiry; ~***en einziehen*** (*or* ***einholen***) make inquiries *or* enquiries (***über*** *acc.* about)

Er·kun·dung [ɛɐ'kʊndʊŋ] *f* (-; -en) **1.** exploration; ⚔ reconnaissance; **2.** finding out *of facts etc.*

Er'kun·dungs|fahrt *f* exploratory mission; ⚔ reconnaissance trip (*or* mission); ~**flug** *m* ⚔ reconnaissance flight

er·kün·stelt [ɛɐ'kʏnstəlt] *adj.* a) affected, b) feigned, c) forced

er'la·ben *obs.* (h) **I.** *v/t.* restore; **II.** *fig. v/refl.*: ***sich*** ~ ***an*** *dat.* feast on; ***wir erlabten uns an dem Anblick*** (*gen.*) we drank in the view (of), we feasted our eyes on the view (of)

er'lah·men *v/i.* (sn) **1.** tire, grow weary; **2.** *fig.* slacken (*a.* ✝); *interest etc.*: flag

er·lan·gen [ɛɐ'laŋən] *v/t.* (h) **1.** gain; **2.** attain; reach; → ***Geltung***; **Er·lan·gung** [ɛɐ'laŋʊŋ] *f* (-; *no pl.*) attainment; ***nach*** ~ *gen.* after gaining (*or* attaining) *s.th.*

Er·laß [ɛɐ'las] *m* (Erlasses; Erlässe [ɛɐ'lɛsə]) **1.** decree, edict; law; **2.** *no pl.* dispensation, exemption (*gen.* from); remission *of sentence*; **3.** *no pl.* issuing, ⚖ enactment; **er'las·sen** *v/t.* (erließ, erlassen, h) **1.** remit *sentence etc.*; ***j-m e-e*** *Verpflichtung* ~ release s.o. from, let s.o. off; **2.** waive; **3.** issue; publish; ⚖ enact; **Er·las·sung** [ɛɐ'lasʊŋ] *f* (-; *no pl.*) → ***Erlaß*** 2

er·lau·ben [ɛɐ'laubən] *v/t.* (h) allow; *formal*: permit (***j-m et.*** s.o. to do s.th.); *fig.* permit *no delay etc.*; ***j-m*** ~, ***et. zu tun*** *a.* give s.o. permission to do s.th.; ***ich erlaube nicht, daß sie mit dem Motorrad fahren*** I won't allow them to go (*or* I won't have them going) by motorbike, I refuse to let them go by motorbike; ***wenn es das Wetter erlaubt*** weather permitting; ***sich*** ~ ***zu*** *inf.* take the liberty of *ger.*, *b.s. a.* dare (to) *inf.*; ***sich et.*** ~ treat o.s. to s.th.; ***sich Frechheiten*** ~ take liberties; ***er kann sich das*** ~ *w.s.* he can get away with it; ***was sich die Leute*** ~***!*** what a nerve some people have; ***ich kann mir nicht*** ~ ***zu*** *inf.* I can't afford to *inf.*; ***ich kann mir kein weiteres Stück Kuchen*** ~ I can't afford to eat another piece of cake; ***ich habe mir nur e-n kleinen Scherz erlaubt*** I was just having a little joke (*or* a bit of fun); ~ ***Sie?*** may I?; ~ ***Sie, daß ich etwas früher gehe?*** would you mind if I left a bit early?; ***wenn Sie*** ~ if you don't mind; ~ ***Sie mal!, was*** ~ ***Sie sich?*** what do you think you're doing?, who do you think you are?; → ***erlaubt***

Er·laub·nis [ɛɐ'laupnɪs] *f* (-; -se) permission; authority; ***behördliche*** ~ permit, licen|ce (*Am.* -se); ***j-n um*** ~ ***bitten*** ask s.o.'s (*or* s.o. for) permission (***et. zu tun*** to do s.th.); ***die*** ~ ***erhalten zu*** *inf.* be given permission to *inf.*; ***ich habe es mit s-r*** ~ ***getan*** he gave me permission to do so, I did it on his authority; ~**schein** *m* permit, licen|ce (*Am.* -se)

er·laubt [ɛɐ'laupt] *adj.* permitted, allowed; *a.* permissible; ***ist es*** ~ ***zu*** *inf.*? can one ...?, is it permissible to *inf.*?; ***das ist nicht*** ~ that's not allowed, F that's a no-no; ***Rauchen ist hier nicht*** ~ smoking is not allowed here, there's no smoking here; ***es ist alles*** ~ you can do what you want (*or* whatever you like), anything goes (around here); ***innerhalb der Grenzen des*** 2***en*** within the accepted limits

er·laucht [ɛɐ'lauxt] *adj.* illustrious; ~***e Versammlung*** (*or* ***Gesellschaft***) illustrious circle (of guests *etc.*)

er·läu·tern [ɛɐ'lɔʏtɐn] *v/t.* (h) explain (***j-m*** to s.o.); ***durch Beispiele*** ~ illustrate; ***könntest du mir*** ~, ***wie ...?*** could you explain to me (*or* show me) how ...?; **er'läu·ternd I.** *adj.* explanatory; illustrative; **II.** *adv.*: ~ ***hinzufügen*** add by way of explanation; **Er·läu·te·rung** [ɛɐ'lɔʏtərʊŋ] *f* (-; -en) explanation; (explanatory) note, annotation; ***mit*** ~***en versehen*** annotated

Er·le ['ɛrlə] *f* (-; -n) ✿ alder

er'le·ben *v/t.* (h) a) experience; *b.s. a.* go through, b) live to see, c) see, witness, d) have *a nice holiday, fun etc.*; ***sechs Auflagen*** ~ run into six editions; ***er hat viel erlebt*** a) he's seen a lot of the world, b) he's been through a lot; ***ich habe etwas Seltsames erlebt*** I had a strange (*or* weird) experience; ***ich habe es oft erlebt(, daß)*** I've often seen it happen (that); ***wir werden es ja*** ~***!*** we'll see!; ***das möchte ich*** ~***!*** I'd like to see that, I'll believe that when I see it; ***ich habe nie erlebt, daß er ...*** I've never known him to *inf.*; ***hat man so etwas schon erlebt!*** F have you ever seen (*or* heard) the likes of that?; ***das muß man einfach erlebt haben*** a) you've got to see it to believe it, b) you've got to have been through it yourself; F ***na, du kannst was*** ~***!*** you just wait!; F ***die kann was*** ~***!*** F she's in for it, F she won't know what's hit her; F ***sonst kannst du was*** ~***!*** or else!

Er'le·bens·fall *m*: ***im*** ~ in case of survival

Er·leb·nis [ɛɐ'leːpnɪs] *n* (-ses; -se) experience; event; adventure; ***ein großes*** ~ a tremendous experience; ***das war ein*** ~***!*** that was quite an experience (*or* quite something); ***das schönste*** ~ ***war*** the nicest experience (*or* thing I experienced) was; ~**auf·satz** *m* composition

Er'leb·nis·hun·ger *m* thirst for adventure; **er'leb·nis·hung·rig** *adj.* thirsty for adventure

er'leb·nis·reich *adj.* eventful, exciting

er·lebt [ɛɐ'leːpt] *adj.* real-life ..., true; ~***e Rede*** interior monolog(ue)

er·le·di·gen [ɛɐ'leːdɪgən] (erledigte, erledigt, h) **I.** *v/t.* **1.** finish (off); do, deal with, take care of, see to; get through with, get *s.th.* out of the way; settle; carry out; dispense with; ***Einkäufe*** ~ go shopping, do the (*or* some) shopping; ***ich habe in der Stadt einiges zu*** ~ I have a few things to do (*or* see to) in town; ***würden Sie das für mich*** ~***?*** would you do that for me?; **2.** F ***j-n*** ~ F finish s.o. off, *a.* wear s.o. out, *a.* ruin s.o., *a.* F do s.o. in; **II.** *v/refl.*: ***sich von selbst*** ~ take care of itself; ***die Sache hat sich inzwischen erledigt*** that's been taken care of now; ***damit*** ~ ***sich die übrigen Punkte*** that takes care of the remaining points; **er·le·digt** [ɛɐ'leːdɪçt] *adj.* **1.** finished; done; settled; ***das wäre*** ~ that's that; ***das ist für mich*** ~ that's all over and done with as far as I'm concerned; F ***du bist für mich*** ~ F I'm through with you; **2.** F a) F whacked, bushed; b) F done for, finished; ***ich bin*** ~ *a.* F I've had it; **Er·le·di·gung** [ɛɐ'leːdɪgʊŋ] *f* (-; -en) **1.** *no pl.* handling, dealing with; settlement; ***für die sofortige*** ~ ***e-r Sache sorgen*** see to it that s.th. is done immediately; ***zur umgehenden*** ~ for immediate attention; **2.** ***einige*** ~***en in der Stadt haben*** have a few things to do (*or* see to) in town

er'le·gen[1] *p.p. of* **erliegen**
er'le·gen[2] *v/t.* (h) shoot *animal*
er·leich·tern [ɛɐ'laɪçtɐn] (erleichterte, erleichtert, h) **I.** *v/t.* **1.** make easier; ease *the burden*, lighten *the load*; relieve, ease *pain etc.*; ***sich das Herz ~*** unburden one's heart; ***das erleichtert vieles*** that makes things a lot easier; ***das erleichtert mir m-e Aufgabe nicht*** that doesn't make my task any easier; F ***j-n um*** *s-e Brieftasche etc.* ~ F relieve s.o. of; **II.** *v/refl.*: ***sich ~*** **2.** unburden o.s.; **3.** F shed a few clothes; **4.** relieve o.s.; **er'leich·tert I.** *adj.* relieved; **II.** *adv.*: ~ ***aufatmen*** breathe (*or* heave) a sigh of relief; **Er·leich·te·rung** [ɛɐ'laɪçtərʊŋ] *f* (-; -en) **1.** *no pl.* relief; ~ ***verschaffen*** give relief; ***zur ~ der Schmerzen*** to relieve (*or* ease) the pain; ***zu m-r (großen) ~*** (much) to my relief; **2.** help; ***es stellt e-e große ~ dar*** it makes things much easier
er'lei·den *v/t.* (erlitt, erlitten, h) suffer; go through; sustain *injury, loss etc.*; ***den Tod ~*** die, *lit.* meet one's death
er'lern·bar *adj.* learnable; ***es ist ~*** it can be learnt, you can learn it; ***leicht (schwer) ~*** easy (hard) to learn *or* pick up; **er'ler·nen** *v/t.* (h) learn
er'le·sen *adj.* select, choice; exquisite; ***ein ~er Kreis*** a select circle; ***ein ~er Geschmack*** exquisite taste
er'leuch·ten *v/t.* (h) **1.** light up, illuminate; **2.** F *fig.* enlighten; **Er'leuch·tung** *f* (-; -en) F enlightenment; inspiration, F brainwave; ***plötzlich kam die ~*** suddenly inspiration came (*or* struck)
er'lie·gen I. *v/i.* (erlag, erlegen, sn) give in (*dat.* to), succumb (to); be defeated (by); die (of *or* from); fall victim (to); **II.** ≈ *n*: ***zum ~ kommen*** grind to a halt; ***zum ~ bringen*** bring to a standstill, paralyze
er·lischt [ɛɐ'lɪʃt] *pres. of* **erlöschen**
er'litt *pret. of* **erleiden**
er·lit·ten [ɛɐ'lɪtən] *p.p. of* **erleiden**
Erl·kö·nig ['ɛrl-] *m* **1.** erl-king; **2.** F *mot.* mystery model
er'log *pret. of* **erlügen**
er·lo·gen [ɛɐ'lo:gən] **I.** *p.p. of* **erlügen; II.** *adj.* not true; made-up ..., *pred.* made up; ***das ist ~*** that's a lie; ***das ist von Anfang bis Ende ~*** there's not a word of truth in it, F it's a pack of lies; → ***erstunken***
Er·lös [ɛɐ'lø:s] *m* (-es; -e [-zə]) proceeds *pl.*; net profit(s *pl.*)
er·losch [ɛɐ'lɔʃ] *pret. of* **erlöschen**
er·lo·schen [ɛɐ'lɔʃən] **I.** *p.p. of* **erlöschen; II.** *adj.* **1.** extinct (*a. volcano*); defunct; **2.** ⚖ expired; defunct; **3.** *fig.* dead
er'lö·schen (erlischt, erlosch, erloschen, sn) **I.** *v/i.* **1.** go out; *volcano*: become extinct; **2.** *contract etc.*: expire; **3.** *name etc.*: die out; **4.** *fig. eyes*: grow dim; *life*: be extinguished; *passion*: die; ***mit ~der Stimme*** with a failing voice; **II.** ≈ *n* (-s) extinction; ⚖ expiry; ***zum ~ bringen*** extinguish
er'lö·sen *v/t.* (h) release, free; rescue; *eccl.* save, redeem; **er'lö·send** *adj.*: *fig.* ***das war ein ~es Gefühl*** what a relief that was; ***er sprach endlich das ~e Wort*** he finally put us *etc.* out of our *etc.* misery; **Er·lö·ser** [ɛɐ'lø:zɐ] *m* (-s; -) liberator; rescuer; *eccl.* Savio(u)r, Redeemer; **er'löst I.** *adj.* relieved; ***wie ~ sein, sich wie ~ fühlen*** experience a great feeling of release (*or* relief); ***er ist ~*** his sufferings are over; **II.** *adv.*: ~ ***aufatmen*** breathe (*or* heave) a sigh of relief; **Er'lö·sung** *f* (-; *no pl.*) release; relief; *eccl.* redemption, salvation
er'lü·gen *v/t.* (erlog, erlogen, h) make up; → ***erlogen*** II
er·mäch·ti·gen [ɛɐ'mɛçtɪgən] *v/t.* (ermächtigte, ermächtigt, h) authorize; ***j-n zu et.*** ~ authorize s.o. to do s.th., give s.o. (official) permission to do s.th.; **Er'mäch·ti·gung** *f* (-; -en) authorization; authority; warrant; **Er'mäch·ti·gungs·ge·setz** *n* **1.** enabling act; **2.** *hist.* Enabling Act (of 1933)
er'mah·nen *v/t.* (h) admonish, exhort (***j-n zur Vorsicht*** *etc.* s.o. to be careful *etc.*); urge; caution, warn, *sport*: give *s.o.* a warning; **Er'mah·nung** *f* (-; -en) admonition, exhortation; warning (*a. sport*); rebuke
er'man·geln *lit. v/i.* (h) lack (*gen. s.th.*), be lacking (in *s.th.*); **Er'man·ge·lung** *lit. f*: ***in ~*** *gen.* for want (*or* lack) of, in the absence of; ***in ~ e-s Besseren*** for want (*or* lack) of anything better
er·man·nen [ɛɐ'manən] *v/refl.* (ermannte, ermannt, h): ***sich ~*** take heart; pull o.s. together
er'maß *pret. of* **ermessen**
er'mä·ßi·gen (h) **I.** *v/t.* reduce, lower, cut; **II.** *v/refl.*: ***sich ~*** come down (in price), *price*: be reduced, be cut (***auf*** *acc.* to; ***um*** *acc.* by); **er·mä·ßigt** [ɛɐ'mɛ:sɪçt] *adj.* reduced; ***~e Preise*** reduced prices, *tickets etc.*: *a.* reduced rates; **Er'mä·ßi·gung** *f* (-; -en) reduction, cut (***von*** *dat.* of); ***mit e-r ~ von 15%, mit 15% ~*** at a reduction (*or* discount) of 15 per cent (*or* percent)
er·mat·ten [ɛɐ'matən] (ermattete, ermattet) **I.** *v/t.* (h) tire (out); wear out; **II.** *v/i.* (sn) tire; slacken; *interest etc.*: flag; **er'mat·tet** *adj.* tired; worn-out ..., *pred.* worn out; weary, jaded; **Er'mat·tung** *f* (-; *no pl.*) fatigue, weariness
er'mes·sen I. *v/t.* (ermaß, ermessen, h) assess, ga(u)ge; judge; consider; realize, understand, appreciate, conceive; imagine; infer, conclude (***aus*** *dat.* from); **II.** ≈ *n* (-s) judg(e)ment; discretion; ***nach m-m ~*** as I see it, in my opinion (*or* estimation); ***nach eigenem ~ handeln*** act as one sees fit; ***das steht nicht in s-m ~*** that's not within his discretion, that's not for him to decide; ***ich stelle es in Ihr ~*** I leave it to you (*or* your discretion); ***das liegt ganz in Ihrem ~*** *a.* it's entirely up to you; ***nach bestem ~*** to the best of one's judg(e)ment; ***nach menschlichem ~*** as far as is humanly possible to tell, in all probability
Er'mes·sens|fra·ge *f* matter of opinion; **~frei·heit** *f* (-; *no pl.*) powers *pl.* of discretion; **~spiel·raum** *m* latitude
er·mit·teln [ɛɐ'mɪtəln] (ermittelte, ermittelt, h) **I.** *v/t.* find out, ascertain, establish; locate, *a. teleph.* trace; determine; ***j-s Identität ~*** identify s.o.; **II.** *v/i.* investigate, carry out investigations (***gegen*** *acc.* concerning *s.o.*), hold an inquiry (***in*** *dat.* into); ***in e-m Fall ~*** investigate a case; **Er'mitt·lung** *f* (-; -en) **1.** establishment; determination; ***~en*** findings; **2.** investigation, inquiry (*gen. or* ***in*** *dat.* into; ***über*** *acc.* about); ***~en anstellen über*** *acc.* make inquiries (*or* enquiries) about, investigate
Er'mitt·lungs|aus·schuß *m* fact-finding committee; **~be·am·te** *m* investigator; **~be·hör·de** *f* investigating agency; **~rich·ter** *m* investigating magistrate; **~ver·fah·ren** *n* ⚖ preliminary proceedings *pl.*, judicial inquiry; ***das ~ einstellen*** drop the charge
er·mög·li·chen [ɛɐ'mø:klɪçən] *v/t.* (ermöglichte, ermöglicht, h) make possible; enable (***et.*** s.th. [to be done *etc.*]); allow; ***j-m ~, et. zu tun*** make it possible for (*or* enable) s.o. to do s.th.; ***j-m das Studium ~*** make it possible for (*or* enable) s.o. to study; ***den Bau e-s Flughafens ~*** make it possible to build an airport, enable an airport to be built; ***wenn es sich ~ läßt*** if it can be arranged, if it is at all possible; **Er'mög·li·chung** *f*: ***zur ~*** *gen.* to make *s.th.* possible, to enable *s.th.* to be done *etc.*
er'mor·den *v/t.* (h) murder; assassinate; **Er·mor·de·te** [ɛɐ'mɔrdətə] *m, f* (-n; -n) (murder) victim; **Er'mor·dung** *f* (-; -en) murder; assassination
er·mü·den [ɛɐ'my:dən] (ermüdete, ermüdet) **I.** *v/t.* (h) tire, wear *s.o.* out; **II.** *v/i.* (sn) tire, get tired; **er'mü·dend** *adj.* tiring; **er'mü·det** *adj.* tired; **Er'mü·dung** *f* (-; *no pl.*) tiredness, *a.* ⚙ fatigue
Er'mü·dungs|er·schei·nung *f* sign of tiredness (*or a.* ⚙ fatigue); **~gren·ze** *f* ⚙ fatigue limit; **~zu·stand** *m* state of tiredness
er·mun·tern [ɛɐ'mʊntɐn] *v/t.* (ermunterte, ermuntert, h) encourage (***zu*** *inf.* to *inf.*); cheer up; get *s.o.* going (again); **er'mun·ternd** *adj.* encouraging; *words* of encouragement; **Er·mun·te·rung** [ɛɐ'mʊntərʊŋ] *f* (-; *no pl.*) encouragement; cheering up; ***zu d-r ~*** (just) to cheer you up
er·mu·ti·gen [ɛɐ'mu:tɪgən] *v/t.* (ermutigte, ermutigt, h) encourage (***zu*** *inf.* to *inf.*); give *s.o.* courage, ***zu*** *inf.*: give *s.o.* the courage to *inf.*; **er'mu·ti·gend** *adj.* encouraging, reassuring; ***~e Worte*** *a.* words of encouragement; **Er'mu·ti·gung** *f* (- *no pl.*) encouragement; ***zu s-r ~*** to encourage him
er'näh·ren (h) **I.** *v/t.* feed, nourish; support, keep; ***gut ernährt*** well fed; ***schlecht ernährt*** malnourished; **II.** *v/refl.*: ***sich ~*** live (***von*** *dat.* on); *fig.* make a living (by *ger.*); *fig.* ***davon kann ich mich kaum ~*** I can hardly survive (*or* get by) on that; **Er·näh·rer** [ɛɐ'nɛ:rɐ] *m* (-s; -) earner, breadwinner; **Er'näh·rung** *f* (-; *no pl.*) feeding; food, *esp.* ⚕ nutrition; *vegetarian etc.* diet; ***schlechte ~*** poor diet, malnutrition
Er'näh·rungs|be·ra·ter *m* nutrition consultant; **≈be·wußt** *adj.* nutrition-conscious; **~fach·mann** *m* nutrition expert, nutritionist, dietician; **~feh·ler** *m* wrong eating habit; *pl. a.* false (*or* wrong) diet *sg.*; **~ge·wohn·heit** *f* eating habit; **~in·du,strie** *f* food industry; **~krank·heit** *f* nutritional disease; **~kun·de** *f* dietetics *pl.*; **~la·ge** *f* food situation; **~leh·re** *f* dietetics *pl.*; **~stö·rung** *f* nutritional disorder, ⚕ dystrophy; **~wei·se** *f* **1.** eating habits *pl.*; **2.** nutrition, *vegetarian etc.* diet; **~wis·sen·schaft** *f* dietetics *pl.*, nutritional science; **~wis·sen·schaft·ler** *m* dietician
er'nen·nen *v/t.* (ernannte, ernannt, h) appoint; ***er wurde zum Vorsitzenden ernannt*** he was appointed (*or* made, elected) chairman; **Er'nen·nung** *f* (-; -en)

appointment; ***s-e ~ zum Konsul*** his appointment as (*or* to the post of) consul; **Er'nen·nungs·ur·kun·de** *f* letter of appointment

Er'neue·rer *m* (-s; -) reviver; revitaliser; ***der ~ dieser Bewegung*** *a.* the man who brought this movement back to life; **er·neu·ern** [ɛɐ'nɔʏɐn] (erneuerte, erneuert, h) **I.** *v/t.* renew (*a.* ⚙); renovate; repair, mend; restore; replace; repeat; revive; **II.** *v/refl.*: ***sich ~*** a) *contract etc.*: be renewed; b) regenerate; **Er'neue·rung** *f* (-; -en) renewal; renovation; repair; restoration; replacement; revival; **er·neut** [ɛɐ'nɔʏt] **I.** *adj.* renewed, new; repeated, fresh *attempt etc.*; ***~e Kämpfe*** renewed fighting; **II.** *adv.* once more, (once) again

er·nied·ri·gen [ɛɐ'ni:drɪgən] (erniedrigte, erniedrigt, h) **I.** *v/t.* **1.** degrade; humiliate; **2.** lower; **3.** ♪ flatten; **II.** *v/refl.*: ***sich ~*** degrade o.s., ***et. zu tun***: lower o.s. (*or* stoop) to do s.th.; **er'nied·ri·gend** *adj.* humiliating, degrading, demeaning; **Er'nied·ri·gung** *f* (-; -en) **1.** degradation; humiliation; **2.** ♪ flattening; **3.** lowering

Ernst [ɛrnst] **I.** *m* (-[e]s; *no pl.*) seriousness, earnest; earnestness; gravity; severity; solemnity; ***der ~ des Lebens*** the serious side of life; ***es beginnt wieder der ~ des Lebens*** life begins in earnest again, F it's back to the grindstone (again); ***allen ~es*** in all seriousness; ***ich meine es im ~*** I (really) mean it, I'm serious; ***es ist mein voller ~*** F I'm dead serious; ***ist das Ihr ~?*** are you serious?; ***wollen Sie im ~*** (*or* ***allen ~es***) ***behaupten ...?*** do you really mean to say ...?; ***im ~?*** seriously?, F you're kidding; ***ganz im ~!*** seriously, though; no, seriously (now); ***das kann doch nicht dein ~ sein!*** you're not serious, are you?, F you're joking, of course; ***~ machen mit*** *dat.* go through with *a plan, project etc.*, carry out *threat etc.*; ***aus e-m Scherz wurde plötzlich ~*** the joke suddenly turned serious; **II.** ♀ *adj.* serious; grave; solemn; severe; ***~e Musik*** serious music; ***~es Gesicht*** serious expression (*or* face), straight face; ***~ bleiben*** keep a straight face; ***jetzt wird's ~!*** this is where the hard part begins, this is where we get down to serious business; **III.** *adv.* seriously *etc.*; ***et.*** (***j-n***) ***~ nehmen*** take s.th. (s.o.) seriously; ***du darfst die Dinge nicht so ~ nehmen*** you mustn't take things so seriously; ***ich meine es ~*** I'm serious (***mit*** *dat.* about), I mean it, I'm not joking; ***das war nicht ~ gemeint*** he was *etc.* only joking, it was (said) tongue-in-cheek; ***es steht ~ um*** *acc.* things aren't looking too good for

'Ernst·fall *m* emergency; ***im ~*** a) in case of emergency, b) if the worst comes to the worst, c) ⚔ in the event of a war; ***auf den ~ vorbereitet*** prepared for an (*or* any) emergency

'ernst·ge·meint *adj.* serious, genuine, seriously (*or* sincerely) meant

'ernst·haft I. *adj.* serious; ***ich mache mir ~e Sorgen um ihn*** I'm really worried about him; ***ich muß mit dir ein ~es Wort reden*** I must have a little talk with you; **II.** *adv.* seriously; ***~ krank*** seriously ill; ***~ erkranken*** come down with a serious illness; ***~ besorgt*** genuinely (*or* seriously) worried; **'Ernst·haf·tig·keit** *f* (-; *no pl.*) seriousness, serious nature (*gen.* of)

'ernst·lich I. *adj.* serious; **II.** *adv.* seriously

'ernst·zu·neh·mend *adj.* serious; ***ein ~er Gegner*** *etc.* a force to be reckoned with

Ern·te ['ɛrntə] *f* (-; -n) harvest (*a. fig.*); crop; ***~ar·beit*** *f* harvest(ing); ***~aus·fall*** *m* crop failure; ***~dank·fest*** *n* harvest festival; ♀**frisch** *adj.* farm-fresh, garden-fresh

ern·ten ['ɛrntən] (h) **I.** *v/t.* **1.** harvest, reap; pick; F pick (the apples *etc.* from); **2.** *fig.* earn, win; ***Dank ~*** earn thanks; ***Undank ~*** get nothing but ingratitude; ***Spott ~*** earn (o.s.) ridicule, be(come) a laughing stock; ***Lohn ~*** reap a reward (*or* rewards); ***die Früchte s-r Arbeit ~*** reap the rewards of one's labo(u)r; **II.** *v/i.* **3.** harvest; **4.** *fig.* ***~, wo man nicht gesät hat*** reap where one has not sown

'Ern·te|schä·den *pl.* crop damage *sg.*; ***~zeit*** *f* harvest (time)

er'nüch·tern *v/t.* (ernüchterte, ernüchtert, h) sober up; *fig.* bring *s.o.* down to earth again; **er'nüch·ternd I.** *adj.* sobering; **II.** *adv.*: ***~ auf j-n wirken*** have a sobering effect on s.o.; **Er·nüch·te·rung** [ɛɐ'nʏçtərʊŋ] *f* (-, -en) sobering-up; *fig.* disillusionment; disappointment; ***er braucht ein paar ~en*** he needs a bit of sobering-up

Er·obe·rer [ɛɐ'ʔo:bərɐ] *m* (-s; -) conqueror; **er·obern** [ɛɐ'ʔo:bɐn] *v/t.* (eroberte, erobert, h) conquer (*a. fig.*); ⚔ capture, take; ***im Sturm ~*** *a. fig.* take by storm; *fig.* ***sich*** *et.* ***~*** manage to get hold of, *a.* F manage to grab; ***sich den ersten Platz ~*** *sport*: gain (*or* win) first place; **Er·obe·rung** [ɛɐ'ʔo:bərʊŋ] *f* (-; -en) conquest (*a. fig.*); capture; *fig.* ***e-e ~ machen*** make a conquest; ***auf ~en aus sein*** F be out for the kill

Er'obe·rungs|feld·zug *m* warring campaign, campaign of conquest; ***~krieg*** *m* war of conquest

er'öff·nen (h) **I.** *v/t.* **1.** open, inaugurate; open up, start, set up *a business*; open, start off *discussion etc.*; ***das Feuer ~*** open fire; ***das*** (*or* ***ein***) ***Konkursverfahren ~*** institute bankruptcy proceedings; **2.** open (up) *prospects etc.* (***j-m*** for s.o.), offer (s.o.); **3.** ***j-m et. ~*** disclose s.th. to s.o., inform s.o. of s.th.; **II.** *v/i.* **4.** ✝ open; **5.** *chess*: open; **III.** *v/refl.* **6.** ***sich ~*** *opportunity etc.*: present itself; **7.** ***sich j-m ~*** take s.o. into one's confidence; **Er'öff·nung** *f* (-; -en) **1.** opening (*a. chess*); inauguration; **2.** disclosure

Er'öff·nungs|an·ge·bot *n* introductory offer; ***~an·spra·che*** *f* inaugural address; ***~be·schluß*** *m* ⚖ order to proceed; bankruptcy order; ***~bi͵lanz*** *f* ✝ opening balance sheet; ***~fei·er*** *f* opening ceremony; ***~kampf*** *m boxing*: opening bout; ***~kurs*** *m* ✝ opening quotation; ***~me͵nü*** *n computer*: start menu; ***~sit·zung*** *f* introductory meeting; *parl.* opening session

ero·gen [ero'ge:n] *adj.* erogenous; ***~e Zone*** erogenous zone

er·ör·tern [ɛɐ'œrtɐn] *v/t.* (erörterte, erörtert, h) discuss; ***ausführlich ~*** discuss in detail, F thrash out; **Er'ör·te·rung** [ɛɐ'œrtərʊŋ] *f* (-; -en) **1.** discussion; **2.** *ped.* (discursive) essay

Eros ['e:rɔs] *m* (-; *no pl.*) *myth. and fig.* Eros

Ero·si·on [ero'zĭo:n] *f* (-; -en) erosion; **Ero·si'ons·schä·den** *pl.* damage *sg.* caused by erosion

Ero·tik [e'ro:tɪk] *f* (-; *no pl.*) sensuality, eroticism; sexuality; sex; Eros; **Ero·ti·ka** [e'ro:tika] *pl.* erotica; erotic literature *sg.*; **ero·tisch** [e'ro:tɪʃ] *adj.* sensual, erotic; sexual; ***~es Dreieck*** love triangle; **ero·ti·sie·ren** [eroti'zi:rən] *v/t.* (h) eroticize; **Ero·ti'sie·rung** *f* (-; *no pl.*) eroticization

er·picht [ɛɐ'pɪçt] *adj.*: ***~ auf*** *acc.* very (F dead) keen on (*or* to get *etc.*); ***darauf ~ sein zu*** *inf.* be bent on *ger.*, F be desperate to *inf.*

er'pres·sen *v/t.* (h) blackmail *s.o.* (***mit*** *dat.* over; ***zu*** *inf.* into *ger.*); extort *s.th.* (***von*** *dat.* from); ***von j-m e-e Unterschrift*** (***ein Zugeständnis*** *etc.*) ***~*** blackmail s.o. into signing s.th. (making a concession *etc.*)

Er·pres·ser [ɛɐ'prɛsɐ] *m* (-s; -) blackmailer; ***~ban·de*** *f* gang of blackmailers; ***~brief*** *m* blackmail letter

er·pres·se·risch [ɛɐ'prɛsərɪʃ] *adj.* extortionate; blackmailing ...; ***in ~er Absicht*** with a view to blackmail(ing s.o.)

Er'pres·sung *f* (-; -en) blackmail, blackmailing; extortion

Er'pres·sungs|fall *m* blackmail case; ***~ver·such*** *m* blackmail attempt; attempted blackmail

er'pro·ben *v/t.* (h) try (out), test; put to the test; **er·probt** [ɛɐ'pro:pt] *adj.* well-tried, tried and tested; experienced; reliable; ***klinisch ~*** clinically tested; ***nach ~er Manier*** in the tried and tested fashion (*or* manner); **Er'pro·bung** *f* (-; -en) trial, test

Er'pro·bungs|flug *m* test flight; ***~ge·län·de*** *n* test range

er·quicken [ɛɐ'kvɪkən] (*sep.* -k·k-) *v/t.* (erquickte, erquickt, h) refresh (***sich*** o.s.); revive; **er'quickend** *adj.* refreshing; **er·quick·lich** [ɛɐ'kvɪklɪç] *adj.* pleasant; uplifting; edifying; *iro.* ***wenig ~*** not exactly edifying; **Er'quickung** *f* (-; -en) refreshment

er'rang *pret. of* ***erringen***

Er·ra·ta [ɛ'ra:ta] *pl. of* ***Erratum***

er'ra·ten *v/t.* (erriet, erraten, h) guess; ***du hast es ~!*** you've guessed (right)

er·ra·tisch [ɛ'ra:tɪʃ] *adj.* erratic(ally *adv.*); ***~er Block*** erratic (block)

Er·ra·tum [ɛ'ra:tʊm] *n* (-s; -ta) erratum

er'rech·nen *v/t.* (h) work out, calculate; ***sich s-e Chancen*** *etc.* ***~*** work out one's chances *etc.* (for oneself)

er·reg·bar [ɛɐ're:kba:ɐ] *adj.* excitable (*a.* ⚡); irritable; (over)sensitive, touchy; ***er ist leicht ~*** *a.* he gets upset (*or* angry) easily; **Er'reg·bar·keit** *f* (-; *no pl.*) excitability; irritability; oversensitiveness; **er're·gen** (h) **I.** *v/t.* **1.** excite, get *s.o.* excited, *a. sexually*: arouse; irritate; infuriate; ***die Gemüter ~*** cause quite a stir, get people's blood up; **2.** cause; provoke; arouse, stir up; ***j-s Abscheu*** *etc.* ***~*** fill s.o. with disgust *etc.*; **3.** ⚡ excite, energize; **II.** *v/refl.*: ***sich ~*** get excited; get all worked up (***über*** *acc.* about); get angry; → ***erregt***; **er're·gend** *adj.* exciting; *sexually*: *a.* F on-turning; ⚕ ***~es Mittel*** stimulant

Er·re·ger [ɛɐ're:gɐ] *m* (-s; -) **1.** cause; **2.** ⚡ exciter; **3.** ⚕ pathogen, agent, virus; germ; ***~stamm*** *m* strain of virus, virus strain

er·regt [ɛɐ'reːkt] **I.** *adj.* **1.** excited, agitated; *sexually*: excited, aroused; heated *debate etc.*; turbulent *times*; ***in ~em Zustand*** in a state of excitement (*or* sexual arousement); **2.** ⚡ excited, energized; **II.** *adv.*: ***es ging ~ zu*** a) feelings ran high; b) there was quite a stir (*or* commotion); **Er'regt·heit** *f* (-; *no pl.*) excitement

Er're·gung *f* (-; -en) **1.** (state of) excitement, agitation; anger; **2.** provocation *of anger etc.*; *physiol.* stimulation; *sexual*: arousal; ⚡ excitation; ⚖ ***wegen ~ öffentlichen Ärgernisses*** for creating a public disturbance; **Er're·gungs·zu·stand** *m* state of excitement; emotional state

er·reich·bar [ɛɐ'raɪçbaːɐ] *adj.* **1.** (*a.* ***in ~er Nähe***) within reach; accessible; ***leicht ~ sein*** be within easy reach, be easy to get to; ***schwer ~ sein*** be hard to get to, not to be within easy reach; ***zu Fuß (mit dem Wagen) leicht ~*** within easy walking (driving) distance; **2.** *fig.* attainable, within (one's) reach; **3.** available, there; ***er ist nie ~*** you just can't get hold of him; ***ich bin telefonisch ~*** I'm on the phone, ***von ... bis ...***: you can reach me (*or* get in touch with me) by phone between ... and ...; **er'rei·chen** *v/t.* (h) **1.** reach; arrive at, get to; make (it to *or* as far as); ***von der Bahn leicht zu ~*** within easy reach of the station; **2.** catch *bus, train etc.*, make *one's connection*; catch up with; ***der Brief erreichte ihn nicht mehr*** the letter didn't get to him in time; **3.** ***j-n (telefonisch) ~*** get hold of s.o. (on the phone); ***zu ~*** → ***erreichbar*** 3; **4.** *fig.* achieve; reach; obtain, get; equal, match; come up to; ***ein hohes Alter ~*** live to a ripe old age; ***etwas ~*** get somewhere, get results, be successful; ***hast du (bei ihm) etwas erreicht?*** did you get anywhere (with him)?; ***ich habe nichts erreicht*** I didn't get anywhere, I got nowhere; ***ich erreichte, daß ...*** I managed to *inf.*; ***so wirst du nichts ~*** that won't get you anywhere; → ***Höhepunkt, Klassenziel, Ziel***; **Er'rei·chung** *f* (-; *no pl.*) **1.** ***bei (nach) ~ von*** *dat.* on (after) reaching *or* arriving at (*or* in); **2.** *fig.* attainment; ***nach ~ des 50. Lebensjahres*** on reaching the age of 50

er'ret·ten *v/t.* (h) save, rescue (***von*** *dat.*, ***aus*** *dat.* from); **Er'ret·ter** *m* (-s; -) rescuer; *eccl.* → ***Erlöser***; **Er'ret·tung** *f* (-; -en) rescue; *eccl.* → ***Erlösung***

er'rich·ten *v/t.* (h) **1.** put up, erect, build; *fig.* put up, set up, erect; **2.** *fig.* found, *esp.* ⚖ set up; draw up *last will and testament*; **Er'rich·tung** *f* (-; *no pl.*) **1.** building; erection; **2.** *fig.* founding; establishment

er'riet *pret. of* ***erraten***

er'rin·gen *v/t.* (errang, errungen, h) gain, win; ***den Sieg ~*** gain victory, win; ***e-n Erfolg ~*** be successful, F notch up a success; **Er'rin·gung** *f* (-; *no pl.*) achievement; → ***Errungenschaft***

er'rö·ten I. *v/i.* (sn) blush, go red; flush (***vor*** *dat.* with; ***über*** *acc.* at); **II.** 2 *n* (-s) blush(ing); ***j-n zum ~ bringen*** make s.o. blush (*or* go red)

er·run·gen [ɛɐ'rʊŋən] **I.** *p.p. of* ***erringen***; **II.** *adj.*: ***hart ~*** hard-won, hard-earned; **Er'run·gen·schaft** *f* (-; -en) **1.** achievement; feat; ***~en der Technik*** technological achievements (*or* advances); ***technische ~en*** technical gadgets; ***die neuesten technischen ~en*** the latest technology; **2.** acquisition; ***m-e neueste ~*** my latest acquisition

er'sann *pret. of* ***ersinnen***

Er·satz [ɛɐ'zats] *m* (-es; *no pl.*) **1.** substitute; replacement; ⚔ replacements *pl.*; **2.** compensation; indemnification; damages *pl.*; reparation; restitution; ***als ~ für*** *acc.* by way of compensation for; in exchange (*or* return) for; ***~ leisten für*** *acc.* compensate (*or* make amends) for; ***~ schaffen*** find a replacement (*or* replacements); **~an·spruch** *m* claim for compensation; **~bank** *f* (-; ¨e) *sport*: substitutes' bench; **~be·frie·di·gung** *f psych.* vicarious satisfaction, F compensation; **~bril·le** *f* spare pair of glasses (*or* spectacles); **~dienst** *m* alternative (*or* community) service (for conscientious objectors); ***~ leisten*** do alternative (*or* community) service (***als*** as); **~dro·ge** *f* substitute drug; **~fah·rer** *m* substitute driver; **~geld** *n* token money; **~hand·lung** *f psych.* (act of) compensation; **~kaf·fee** *m* coffee substitute, ersatz coffee; **~kas·se** *f* health insurance; **~lei·stung** *f* compensation; damages *pl.*

er'satz·los *adv.*: ***~ streichen*** freeze

Er'satz|mann *m* substitute (*a. sport*), replacement; **~mi·ne** *f* refill; **~mit·tel** *n* substitute, surrogate; *esp. contp.* ersatz

Er'satz·pflicht *f* liability (for damages); **er'satz·pflich·tig** *adj.* liable for damages

Er'satz|rad *n mot.* spare wheel; **~rei·fen** *m* spare tyre (*Am.* tire); **~re·li·gi,on** *f* ersatz religion; **~spie·ler** *m sport*: substitute; **~stück** *n* → ***Ersatzteil***

Er'satz·teil *n* ⚙ replacement part; spare (part); **~chir·ur,gie** *f* spare part surgery; **~la·ger** *n* spare parts store

Er'satz·wa·gen *m* replacement car

er'satz·wei·se *adv.* as a substitute; as an alternative

er'sau·fen *v/i.* (ersoff, ersoffen, sn) **1.** F drown; **2.** *engine etc.*: flood

er·säu·fen [ɛɐ'zɔʏfən] *v/t.* (ersäufte, ersäuft, h) drown; F *fig.* ***s-e Sorgen im Alkohol ~*** drown one's sorrows in drink

er'schaf·fen *v/t.* (erschuf, erschaffen, h) create, make; **Er·schaf·fer** [ɛɐ'ʃafɐ] *m* (-s; -) creator; **Er'schaf·fung** *f* (-; *no pl.*) creation

er'schal·len *v/i.* (sn) ring out; resound, echo

er'schau·dern *v/i.* (sn) shudder (with horror); ***~ vor Angst*** *etc.* shudder with fear *etc.*; ***bei dem Gedanken ~, daß*** shudder at the thought that (*or* of *s.o. ger.*)

er'schau·ern *v/i.* (sn) tremble, shiver; thrill (*all* ***vor*** *dat.* with; ***über*** *acc.* at)

er'schei·nen I. *v/i.* (erschien, erschienen, sn) **1.** appear (***j-m*** to s.o.); come (***zu*** *dat.* to), turn up (at); put in an appearance; ***vor Gericht ~*** appear in court; ***nicht erschienen sein*** be absent; ***sie ist schon ein paarmal im Fernsehen erschienen*** *a.* she's made a few appearances on TV (*or* a few TV appearances); **2.** appear, present itself (***in e-m anderen Licht*** in a different light); be mentioned; seem, look (***j-m*** to s.o.); ***es erscheint mir merkwürdig*** it strikes me as (rather) strange; ***es erscheint ratsam*** it would seem (*or* appear) advisable; ***sie erscheint heute gelassener*** *etc.* she seems *or* appears (to be) more relaxed *etc.* today; **3.** come out, *book*: *a.* be published, appear; ***soeben erschienen*** just published, just out; ***erstmals bei X erschienen*** first published by X; **II.** 2 *n* (-s) **1.** appearance; attendance; ***um pünktliches ~ wird gebeten*** you are kindly requested to attend punctually; ***wir danken für Ihr zahlreiches ~*** we appreciate that so many of you have (been able to) come; **2.** publication; ***im ~ begriffen*** forthcoming

Er·schei·nung [ɛɐ'ʃaɪnʊŋ] *f* (-; -en) **1.** phenomenon; occurrence; indication (*gen.* of), sign (of), ⚕ *a.* symptom (of); ***das ist e-e ganz normale ~*** *a.* that's perfectly normal, that's nothing out of the ordinary; **2.** appearance; ***in ~ treten*** appear, *fig. a.* emerge, make itself felt; ***stark (kaum) in ~ treten*** be very much in evidence (be hardly noticeable); ***er tritt kaum in ~*** he keeps very much in the background; **3.** apparition; vision; spect|re (*Am.* -er), phantom; ***e-e ~ haben*** a) have a vision, b) see a ghost (*or* an apparition); **4.** *eccl.* manifestation; **5.** figure; ***e-e glänzende*** (*or* ***imposante***) ***~ sein*** cut a fine figure; ***sie ist e-e sympathische ~*** she comes across as very friendly (*or* likeable); **6.** outward appearance; ***von der ~ her*** outwardly; ***ihrer (äußeren) ~ nach*** to look at her, judging by her (outward) appearance

Er'schei·nungs|bild *n* **1.** appearance, look; **2.** ⚕ manifestation; **3.** *biol.* phenotype; **~da·tum** *n* date (*or* day) of publication, publication date; **~form** *f* **1.** (outward) form; **2.** ⚕ manifestation; **3.** *biol.* phenotype; **~jahr** *n* year of publication; **~ort** *m* place of publication; **~tag** *m* day (*or* date) of publication; **~wei·se** *f* publication dates *pl.*; ***~: wöchentlich*** published (*or* appearing) weekly; **~welt** *f* physical world

er'schien *pret. of* ***erscheinen***

er·schie·nen [ɛɐ'ʃiːnən] *p.p. of* ***erscheinen***

er'schie·ßen (erschoß, erschossen, h) **I.** *v/t.* shoot (dead), shoot and kill; ***~ lassen*** have *s.o.* shot; **II.** *v/refl.*: ***sich ~*** shoot o.s.; **Er'schie·ßung** *f* (-; -en) shooting; execution (by firing squad); **Er'schie·ßungs·kom,man·do** *n* firing squad

er·schlaf·fen [ɛɐ'ʃlafən] *v/i.* (erschlaffte, erschlafft, sn) **1.** go limp; *muscles*: grow tired, slacken; *skin*: (begin to) sag, become (*or* get, go) flabby; **2.** tire, get (*or* grow) tired; ***er erschlaffte in der letzten Runde*** his strength failed him in the last round; **3.** *fig.* (begin to) flag

Er'schlaf·fung *f* (-; *no pl.*) **1.** tiring; (sudden) limpness; slackening *of muscles*; flabbiness *of skin*; **2.** (sudden) tiredness; **3.** *fig.* flagging (*gen.* of), drop (in)

er'schla·gen I. *v/t.* (erschlug, erschlagen, h) kill; ***er wurde vom Blitz ~*** he was struck (dead) by lightning; **II.** F *adj.*: ***wie ~*** a) F flabbergasted; b) F whacked, bushed, out for the count

er'schlei·chen *v/t.* (erschlich, erschlichen, h) obtain by devious means; ***sich j-s Gunst ~*** worm o.s. into s.o.'s favo(u)r

er'schlie·ßen (erschloß, erschlossen, h) **I.** *v/t.* **1.** open, make accessible; open up *market etc.*; develop; tap, exploit *resources*; **2.** infer (***von*** *dat.* from); *ling.* reconstruct (from), derive (from); **3.** (*offenbaren*) disclose; **II.** *v/refl.*: ***sich j-m ~*** *secret*, *meaning etc.*: be revealed to s.o.; *opportunities*: open up before s.o.; (*a.* ***j-m sein Herz*** ~) open one's heart to s.o.; **Er'schlie·ßung** *f* (-; -en) opening (up), development; tapping, exploitation; *ling.* reconstruction, derivation

er'schlug *pret. of* ***erschlagen***

er'schmei·cheln *v/t.* (h) (*a.* ***sich*** *et.* ~) get *s.th.* by flattery; ***sich et. von j-m*** ~ wheedle s.th. out of s.o.

er'schöp·fen (h) **I.** *v/t.* **1.** wear out, exhaust; **2.** deplete, exhaust *supplies, resources etc.*; **3.** *fig.* exhaust; F flog *subject etc.* to death; **II.** *v/refl.*: ***sich*** ~ **4.** wear o.s. out; **5.** *opportunities*: be exhausted; *subject*: *a.* F be flogged to death; ***sich*** ~ ***in*** *dat. activity, talent etc.*: be limited to, not to go beyond; ***die Diskussion erschöpfte sich in leerem Geschwätz*** the discussion fizzled out into superficial chitchat; **6.** *supplies, resources etc.*: be (-come) depleted; *soil*: *a.* be worked to death; **er'schöp·fend I.** *adj.* **1.** exhausting; **2.** exhaustive; **II.** *adv.*: ***ein Thema*** ~ ***behandeln*** treat a topic exhaustively, look at a topic from every (possible) angle; **er'schöpft** *adj.* exhausted (***von*** *dat.* by); *battery*: run-down; **Er'schöp·fung** *f* (-; *no pl.*) exhaustion; ***bis zur*** ~ to the point of exhaustion; ***vor*** ~ ***umfallen*** collapse with (*or* from) exhaustion

Er'schöp·fungs|tod *m* death from exhaustion; **~zu·stand** *m* (state of) exhaustion

er'schoß *pret. of* ***erschießen***

er·schos·sen [ɛɐ'ʃɔsən] **I.** *p.p. of* ***erschießen***; **II.** F *adj.* F whacked, bushed; ***ich bin*** ~ *a.* F I've had it

er'schrecken (*sep.* -k·k-) (erschrickt, erschrak, erschrocken) **I.** *v/t.* (h) frighten, scare; startle, give *s.o.* a shock; ***j-n zu Tode*** ~ frighten s.o. out of his (*or* her) wits, frighten s.o. to death; ***du hast mich zu Tode erschreckt*** *a.* you gave me the fright of my life, I nearly jumped out of my skin; **II.** *v/i.* (sn) get a fright (*or* shock); jump, start; ~ ***über*** *acc.* be startled (*or* shocked) by; ***bin ich erschrokken!*** what a fright I got (*or* you gave me); ***er erschrickt beim leisesten Geräusch*** the slightest noise frightens him, he jumps at the slightest noise; **III.** *v/refl.* (h): ***sich*** ~ get a fright; jump, start; ***sich zu Tode*** ~ get the fright of one's life, be frightened out of one's wits; ***er hat sich ganz schön erschrocken*** he got quite a fright, it gave him quite a fright (*od.* scare); **IV.** ≈ *n* (-s) fright, scare; **er'schreckend I.** *adj.* alarming, frightening; dreadful, terrible; appalling, horrific; **II.** *adv.*: ~ ***wenige*** *etc.* alarmingly few *etc.*; ~ ***viel(e)*** an alarming amount (number) of; ***sie haben*** ~ ***wenig gewußt*** *a.* their knowledge was alarmingly restricted

er·schrocken [ɛɐ'ʃrɔkən] (*sep.* -k·k-) **I.** *p.p. of* ***erschrecken***; **II.** *adj.* startled; taken aback; ***ich war ganz*** ~ I got (*or* it gave me) quite a fright *or* scare; ***er war zu Tode*** ~ he got (*or* it gave him) the fright of his life; **III.** *adv.* in (*or* with) fright; ~ ***zusammenfahren*** (*or* ***auffahren***) jump, start; ~ ***aus dem Schlaf hochfahren*** wake up with a start

er'schuf *pret. of* ***erschaffen***

er·schüt·tern [ɛɐ'ʃʏtɐn] *v/t.* (erschütterte, erschüttert, h) **1.** shake; **2.** *fig.* shake; shock (deeply), shake (up); move deeply; ***j-n in s-m Glauben*** ~ shake s.o.'s faith; ***das kann mich nicht*** ~ that leaves me cold; ***sich durch nichts*** ~ ***lassen*** be completely unflappable; ***ihn kann nichts mehr*** ~ he's seen (*or* been through) it all; **er'schüt·ternd** *adj.* shocking, devastating; deeply moving; **er'schüt·tert** *adj.* shocked, devastated; (completely) shaken up; shattered (*all* ***von*** *dat.* by); **Er·schüt·te·rung** [ɛɐ'ʃʏtərʊŋ] *f* (-; -en) **1.** vibration, tremor, shock(wave); **2.** ⚙ vibration; **3.** ⚕ concussion; **4.** *fig.* shock; shockwave; ~ ***auslösen bei*** *dat.* be a shock for, shock, send a shock(wave) through; ***sie konnte vor*** ~ ***nichts sagen*** she was too shocked to speak; ***zur*** ~ ***des Systems*** *etc.* ***führen*** rock (*or* shake) the system *etc.*; **er'schüt·te·rungs·fest** *adj.* shockproof; **er'schüt·te·rungs·frei** *adj.* ⚙ free from vibration(s), shock-absorbent

er·schwe·ren [ɛɐ'ʃveːrən] *v/t.* (erschwerte, erschwert, h) make (more) difficult, complicate, bedevil, compound; impede, hamper; seriously interfere with; **er'schwe·rend I.** *adj.*: ⚖ ~***e Umstände*** aggravating circumstances; **II.** *adv.*: ~ ***tritt hinzu, daß*** to aggravate the situation

Er·schwer·nis [ɛɐ'ʃveːɐnɪs] *f* (-; -se) (added) difficulty *or* burden; impediment, obstacle; **~zu·la·ge** *f* hardship allowance

er·schwert [ɛɐ'ʃveːɐt] *adj.* more difficult, harder; **Er'schwe·rung** *f* (-; -en) complication; ***e-e*** ~ *gen.* ***bedeuten*** make *s.th.* more difficult

er'schwin·deln *v/t.* (h) obtain by fraud (*or* dishonest means); **(*sich*) *et. von j-m*** ~ swindle s.th. out of s.o.

er·schwing·lich [ɛɐ'ʃvɪŋlɪç] *adj.* within s.o.'s means; ***zu*** ~***en Preisen*** at reasonable prices; ***das ist für uns nicht*** ~ we can't afford it; ***Mieten, die für jeden*** ~ ***sind*** rents that everyone can afford, rents within everyone's means

er'se·hen *v/t.* (ersah, ersehen, h) see; *et.* ~ ***aus*** *dat.* see (*or* understand) from; gather from; ***daraus ist zu*** ~, ***daß*** this shows (*or* indicates) that; ***daraus ist nicht zu*** ~, ***ob*** it doesn't indicate (*or* tell you) whether

er'seh·nen *v/t.* (h) long for, yearn for; **er'sehnt** *adj.* longed-for

er·setz·bar [ɛɐ'zɛtsbaːɐ] *adj.* replaceable (*a.* ⚙); reparable *damage*; recoverable *loss*; **er'set·zen** *v/t.* (h) replace (***durch*** *acc.* by, with *s.th.*); *a.* take the place of *s.o.*; compensate for *loss etc.*; reimburse (***j-m*** s.o. *for expenses*); ***A durch B*** ~ replace A by (*or* with) B, substitute B for A; ***den Schaden ersetzt bekommen*** get paid (*formal*: receive compensation) for the damage; ***... ist nicht zu*** ~ ... is irreplaceable, ... cannot be replaced; ***sie ersetzte ihnen die Eltern*** she was father and mother to them; **Er'set·zung** *f* (-; -en) replacement; compensation; reimbursement

er'sicht·lich *adj.* apparent, evident (***aus*** *dat.* from); clear; ***klar*** ~ obvious, clearly evident (*or* apparent); ***ohne*** ~***en Grund*** for no apparent reason; ***daraus wird*** ~, ***daß*** this shows (*or* indicates) that, thus it appears that; ***aus Ihrem Schreiben ist*** (*or* ***wird***) ~, ***daß*** from your letter it would appear that; ***wie aus ...*** ~ ***ist*** as can be seen from ...

er'sin·nen *v/t.* (ersann, ersonnen, h) think up, dream up; invent

er'soff *pret. of* ***ersaufen***

er·sof·fen [ɛɐ'zɔfən] *p.p. of* ***ersaufen***

er'spä·hen *v/t.* (h) catch sight of, spot; *lit.* espy

er'spa·ren *v/t.* (h) (*a.* ***sich*** *dat. et.* ~) save; ***j-m Arbeit*** (***Kosten*** *etc.*) ~ save s.o. work (money *etc.*); ***j-m e-e Demütigung*** *etc.* ~ spare s.o. a humiliation *etc.*; ***um dir unnötige Erklärungen zu*** ~ so as not to bother you with unnecessary explanations; ***erspare dir d-e Bemerkungen*** just keep your remarks to yourself; ***das wird uns nicht erspart bleiben*** there's no getting round it; ***mir*** (***ihm***) ***bleibt aber auch nichts erspart*** why does everything have to happen to me (he really seems to get one bad break after another); **Er·spar·nis** [ɛɐ'ʃpaːɐnɪs] *f* (-; -se) saving(s *pl.*); ~***se*** savings; **er'spart** *adj.*: ~***es Geld*** savings; ***vom*** ≈***en leben*** live off one's savings

er·sprieß·lich [ɛɐ'ʃpriːslɪç] *adj.* fruitful; beneficial (*dat.* to)

erst [eːɐst] **I.** *adv.* **1.** (at) first; first; only, not until (*or* till), not before; (***eben***) ~ just; ~ ***als*** only when; ~ ***als er anrief, wurde mir klar*** it was only when he rang up that I realized; ~ ***dann*** only then, not until (*or* till) then; ~ ***einmal*** first; ***wir müssen*** ~ ***einmal aufräumen*** *a.* we've got to tidy up before we do anything else; ~ ***jetzt*** only now, not until (*or* till) now; ~ ***jetzt wissen wir*** only now do we know, not until (*or* till) now did we know; ~ ***nach der Vorstellung*** not until (*or* till) after the performance; ***ich muß*** ~ ***m-n Chef fragen*** I'll have to ask my boss first; ***ich habe sie*** ~ ***letzte Woche gesehen*** I only saw her last week, it was only last week (that) I saw her; ***dann kann er es ja*** ~ ***recht tun*** all the more reason (for him) to do so; ***jetzt zeig' ich's ihr*** ~ ***recht!*** now I'm really going to show her; ***das macht es*** ~ ***recht schlimm*** that makes it even worse; ***was glaubst du, wie mir*** ~ ***zumute ist?*** how do you think 'I feel?; ***wäre er*** ~ ***hier!*** if only he were here; ***wenn du*** ~ ***so alt bist wie ich*** when you get to my age; ***wenn wir*** ~ ***reich sind*** when (*or* once) we're rich, wait till we're rich, *then we'll* ...; ***wenn du ihn*** ~ ***siehst!*** (just) wait till you see him; **2.** only, just; ***ich habe*** ~ ***zwei Antworten bekommen*** I've only had two replies (so far); **II.** *adj.* first; ~***es Kapitel*** chapter one; ***am*** ~***en Mai*** on the first of May, on May the first; ***1. Mai*** 1st May, May 1(st); ≈***e Hilfe*** first aid; ~***e Qualität*** prime quality; ~***e beste*** → ***erstbest***; ***er war der*** ~***e, der ...*** he was the first to *inf.*; ***sie ging als*** ~***e durchs Ziel*** she finished first; ***aus*** ~***er Ehe*** from one's first marriage, by one's first wife (*or* husband); ***fürs*** ~***e*** for the moment, for the time being; → ***Mal***[1]; ***zum*** ~***en, zum zweiten, zum dritten!*** *auction*: going, going, gone!; → ***Hand, Linie*** 1, ***Stelle*** 1, ***Stock*** 4

er'stach *pret. of* ***erstechen***

er'stand *pret. of* ***erstehen***[1] *and* ***erstehen***[2]

er·stan·den [ɛɐ'ʃtandən] *p.p. of* ***erstehen***[1] *and* ***erstehen***[2]

er'starb *pret. of* ***ersterben***

er·star·ken [ɛɐ'ʃtarkən] *v/i.* (erstarkte, erstarkt, sn) grow strong(er), gain strength

er'star·ren *v/i.* (sn) **1.** grow stiff, stiffen; go numb; ⚗ *etc.* solidify, *oil, grease*: *a.* congeal; **2.** *fig.* freeze; *face*: turn to stone; *habits etc.*: become rigid; *tradition etc.*: ossify; ***vor Angst ~*** freeze (with fear *or* terror), be paralyzed with fear; ***j-s Blut ~ lassen*** make s.o.'s blood run cold; **er'starrt** *adj.* **1.** stiff; numb; **2.** *fig.* paralyzed; rigid; ossified; ***vor Ehrfurcht ~*** awestruck; **Er'star·rung** *f* (-; *no pl.*) **1.** stiffness; numbness; ⚗ solidification, congealing; **2.** *fig.* paralysis; rigidity; **Er'star·rungs·punkt** *m* congealing (*or* solidification) point *or* temperature

er'stat·ten [ɛɐ'ʃtatən] *v/t.* (erstattete, erstattet, h) **1.** reimburse, refund (***j-m*** s.o. *for expenses etc.*); **2.** ***Anzeige ~ gegen*** *acc.* report *s.o.* to the police; → ***Bericht;*** **Er'stat·tung** *f* (-; -en) reimbursement, refund(ing)

'erst·auf·füh·ren *v/t.* (*only inf. and p.p.* erstaufgeführt, h) perform (in public) for the first time, give the first public performance of, première; **'Erst·auf·füh·rung** *f* (-; -en) *thea., film*: première; *film*: first run

er'stau·nen I. *v/t.* (h) astonish, astound, amaze; *news etc.*: cause astonishment (*or* amazement), astonish (*or* amaze) everyone; **II.** *v/i.* (sn) be astonished, be astounded, be amazed; **III.** ♀ *n* (-s) astonishment, amazement; ***in ~ (ver)setzen*** → **I;** ***(sehr) zu m-m ~*** (much) to my astonishment; **er·staun·lich** [ɛɐ'ʃtaunlɪç] *adj.* astonishing, astounding, amazing; remarkable; unbelievable, incredible; **er'staun·li·cher'wei·se** *adv.* astonishingly, to my *etc.* surprise, amazingly, to my *etc.* amazement; **er'staunt** *adj.* astonished, astounded, amazed (***über*** *acc.* at)

'Erst|aus·fer·ti·gung *f* original (copy); **~aus·füh·rung** *f* prototype; **~aus·ga·be** *f* first edition; **~aus·stat·tung** *f* **1.** basic equipment (*or* kit); **2.** layette; **~aus·strah·lung** *f TV etc.* first broadcast

'erst'best I. *adj.* first; any old; ***er fragte das ~e Kind*** he asked the first child he saw (*or* he happened to see, that came along); ***kauf doch nicht einfach das ~e Auto*** don't go and buy just any old car; ***das ~e Hotel*** the first hotel you *etc.* (happen to) find *or* stumble across; **II.** *su.*: ***der (die) ~e*** just anyone; the first person (*or* man, woman) to come along

'Erst|be·stei·gung *f* first ascent; **~druck** *m* (-[e]s; -e) first edition

Er·ste ['eːɐstə] *m, f* (-n; -n) (the) first; ***er war ~r*** he was (*or* came) first; ***er ist ~r (der Klasse)*** he's top of the class; ***Karl I.*** Charles I (= Charles the First); ***heute ist der ~*** it's the first (of the month) today

er'ste·chen *v/t.* (erstach, erstochen, h) stab (to death)

'Erst·ehe *f* first marriage

er'ste·hen[1] *v/i.* (erstand, erstanden, sn) arise, result (***aus*** *dat.* from); *lit.* rise up (from); ***daraus können uns Unannehmlichkeiten ~*** it could cause us trouble

er'ste·hen[2] *v/t.* (erstand, erstanden, h) buy (o.s.), get; **Er'ste·hung** *f* (-; *no pl.*) acquisition

er'stei·gen *v/t.* (erstieg, erstiegen, h) climb, ascend; climb (up to); *fig.* rise to; climb, move up

er'stei·gern *v/t.* (h) buy at an auction; F *fig.* ***wo hast du denn das ersteigert?*** F where did you get hold of that?

Er'stei·gung *f* (-; -en) ascent, climbing

'Er·ste(r)-'Klas·se|-Ab'teil *n* first-class compartment; **~-Wa·gen** *m* first-class carriage (*or* car)

er'stel·len *v/t.* (h) **1.** provide; **2.** draw up *plan etc.*; **3.** build, construct

'er·ste·mal *adv.*: ***das ~*** the first time; ***beim erstenmal*** the first time, *a.* straightaway; ***zum erstenmal*** for the first time; ***ich bin zum erstenmal hier*** this is the first time I've been here, this is my first visit here; ***ich sehe ihn zum erstenmal*** I've never seen (*or* set eyes on) him before; ***das sehe ich zum erstenmal*** *a.* I've never noticed that before; ***das höre ich zum erstenmal*** that's the first I hear (*or* I've heard) of it, that's news to me

er·stens ['eːɐstəns] *adv.* first(ly), first of all; to start with; for a start

er·ste·re ['eːɐstərə] *pron. and adj. the* former; ***der (die, das) erstere ...*** the former ...

er'ster·ben *v/i.* (erstarb, erstorben, sn) *sound*: die (*or* fade) away; *smile*: fade; ***das Lächeln erstarb auf s-n Lippen*** the smile faded (*or* disappeared) from his lips; *fig.* ***vor Ehrfurcht ~*** be awestruck

'Erst·er·folg *m* first success; beginner's success

'erst·ge·bo·ren *adj.* firstborn; **'Erst·ge·burt** *f* **1.** firstborn (child); **2.** → **'Erst·ge·burts·recht** *n* birthright, ⚖ (right of) primogeniture

'erst·ge·nannt *adj.* first-mentioned, first-named; former

er·sticken [ɛɐ'ʃtɪkən] (*sep.* -k·k-) (erstickte, erstickt) **I.** *v/t.* (h) **1.** suffocate; choke; **2.** smother, put out *fire*; **3.** *fig.* suppress; smother, stifle *sound, laughter etc.*; suppress, quell *revolt etc.*; → ***Keim;*** **II.** *v/i.* (sn) **4.** suffocate (***an*** *dat.* from), be suffocated (by); ***an e-r Gräte etc.***: choke (to death) on; ***vor Hitze ~*** suffocate from the heat; **5.** *fig.* ***vor Lachen*** *etc.* ***~*** choke with laughter *etc.*; ***in Arbeit ~*** be snowed under with work, be drowning in work; ***mit erstickter Stimme*** in a choked voice; **III.** ♀ *n* (-s) suffocation, 🕮 asphyxiation; ***zum ~*** stifling, suffocating *air etc.*; ***zum ~ heiß*** stifling hot; **er'stickend** *adj.* stifling, suffocating; **Er'stickung** (*sep.* -k·k-) *f* (-; *no pl.*) suffocation, 🕮 asphyxiation

Er'stickungs|an·fall *m* choking fit; **~ge·fahr** *f* danger of suffocation; **~tod** *m*: ***den ~ sterben*** die of suffocation (🕮 asphyxiation)

er'stieg *pret. of* ***ersteigen***

er·stie·gen [ɛɐ'ʃtiːgən] *p.p. of* ***ersteigen***

'Erst·in,stanz *f* (court of) first instance

'erst·klas·sig [-klasɪç] *adj.* first-class, first-rate; *sport*: *a.* top-class, F crack ..., ace ...; ⚜ top-quality...

'Erst·kläß·ler [-klɛslɐ] *m* (-s; -) first-year (primary) pupil, *Am.* firstgrader

'Erst·kom·mu·ni,on *f* first Communion

'erst·lich *adv.* → ***erstens***

Erst·ling ['eːɐstlɪŋ] *m* (-s; -e) **1.** first work; **2.** firstborn child

'Erst·lings|aus·stat·tung *f* layette; **~film** *m* debut film; **~plat·te** *f* debut album; **~ro,man** *m* first novel; **~ver·such** *m* first attempt; **~werk** *n* first work

erst·ma·lig ['eːɐstmaːlɪç] **I.** *adj.* first; **II.** *adv.* → **erst·mals** ['eːɐstmaːls] *adv.* for the first time, first; ***es erschien ~ 1990*** it first appeared (*or* it appeared for the first time) in 1990

'Erst·mel·dung *f* exclusive report (*or* story), scoop

er·stor·ben [ɛɐ'ʃtɔrbən] *p.p. of* ***ersterben***

er'strah·len *v/i.* (sn) shine; sparkle, glitter

'erst·ran·gig [-raŋɪç] *adj.* first-rate; top-priority *problem, question etc.*

er'stre·ben *v/t.* (h) aim for; strive after; desire, covet; **er'stre·bens·wert** *adj.* desirable, worthwhile

er'strecken (*sep.* -k·k-) *v/refl.* (h) **1.** ***sich ~*** extend, stretch (***bis zu*** to, as far as; ***über*** *acc.* across, over); **2.** ***sich ~ über*** *acc.* cover *or* span (a period of); ***sich über Jahrzehnte ~*** cover (*or* span) several decades; **3.** ***sich ~ auf*** *acc.* concern, apply to; include

'Erst|schlag *m* first strike; **~se,me·ster** *n* new student; *esp. Am.* freshman, F fresher; **~stim·me** *f pol.* first vote

'Erst·tags|brief *m* first-day cover; **~stem·pel** *m* first-day stamp

'Erst·tä·ter *m* first-time offender

er·stun·ken [ɛɐ'ʃtʊŋkən]: F ***das ist ~ und erlogen*** F that's a dirty lie (*or* a pack of lies)

'Erst|wa·gen *m* first car; **~wäh·ler** *m* first-time voter; **~zu·las·sung** *f* first registration

er'stür·men *v/t.* (h) (take by) storm; **Er'stür·mung** *f* (-; -en) storming

er'su·chen (h) **I.** *v/t.*: ***j-n ~ zu*** *inf.* ask (*or* urgently request, implore) s.o. to *inf.*; ***j-n um et. ~*** request s.th. from s.o.; **II.** *v/i.*: ***um et. ~*** request s.th.; **III.** ♀ *n* (-s) request; ***auf sein ~ hin*** at his request

er'tap·pen (h) **I.** *v/t.* catch (***bei*** *dat.* at); ***j-n beim Stehlen ~*** catch s.o. stealing; ***laß dich nicht ~*** mind you don't get caught; → ***Tat;*** **II.** *v/refl.*: ***sich dabei ~, et. zu tun*** catch o.s. doing s.th.; ***sich bei dem Gedanken ~, daß*** catch o.s. thinking that

er'ta·sten *v/t.* (h) feel (the shape of); grope one's way towards

er'tei·len *v/t.* (h) give (***j-m*** [to] s.o.); confer *right etc.* (*dat.* on); grant *patent* (to); → ***Abfuhr, Vollmacht;*** **Er'tei·lung** *f* (-; -en) granting; conferral

er'tö·nen *v/i.* (sn) sound; ***plötzlich ertönte Musik*** suddenly music could be heard, suddenly there was music in the air; ***~ von*** *dat.* resound (*or* echo) with

er'tö·ten *v/t.* (h) stifle

Er·trag [ɛɐ'traːk] *m* (-[e]s; Erträge [ɛɐ'trɛːgə]) yield; ⚒ *etc.* output; ⚜ proceeds *pl.*, returns *pl.*, profit(s *pl.*) (***aus*** *dat.* from); *fig.* fruits *pl.*, results *pl.*

er'tra·gen *v/t.* (ertrug, ertragen, h) bear (*a. sight, thought etc.*), endure; tolerate, put up with; ***wie kannst du es ~?*** *a.* how can you stand it?; ***nicht zu ~*** → ***unerträglich***

er·träg·lich [ɛɐ'trɛːklɪç] **I.** *adj.* bearable; tolerable; **II.** *adv.* tolerably well

er'trag|los *adj.* unproductive; ⚜ unprofitable; **~reich** *adj.* productive; ⚜ profitable

er'trags·arm *adj.* low-yield

er'trag(s)·fä·hig *adj.* productive; ⚜ profit-bearing; **Er'trag(s)·fä·hig·keit** *f* productivity; ⚜ earning potential (*or* capacity)

Er'trags|kraft *f* earning power (*or* poten-

tial); **~la·ge** *f* profit situation; **~steu·er** *f* profits tax; **~wert** *m* earning power
er'trank *pret. of* ***ertrinken***
er'trän·ken *v/t.* (h) drown (**sich** o.s.)
er'träu·men *v/t.* (h) (*a.* **sich** *dat.* ~) dream of; imagine; **er'träumt** *adj.* dreamed-of; imaginary; ***nie*** ~ undreamt-of
er'trin·ken I. *v/i.* (ertrank, ertrunken, sn) drown, be drowned; **II.** ♀ *n* (-s): (***Tod durch*** ~ death by) drowning; **Er'trin·ken·de** *m, f* (-n; -n) drowning man (*f* woman)
er'trot·zen *v/t.* (h): (**sich**) ***et.*** ~ get s.th. through sheer stubbornness, stubbornly insist until one gets s.th.
er'trug *pret. of* ***ertragen***
er·tüch·ti·gen [ɛɐ'tʏçtɪgən] *v/t.* (ertüchtigte, ertüchtigt, h) get *s.o.* in shape; toughen *s.o.* up; **Er'tüch·ti·gung** *f* (-; *no pl.*) physical training (*or* fitness)
er·üb·ri·gen [ɛɐ'ʔy:brɪgən] (erübrigte, erübrigt, h) **I.** *v/t.* save, put aside; spare; ***können Sie zehn Mark (fünf Minuten) ~?*** can you spare ten marks (five minutes)?; **II.** *v/refl.*: **sich** ~ be unnecessary, be superfluous; ***es hat sich erübrigt*** it's been solved, F forget it; ***es dürfte sich*** ~ it will hardly be necessary; ***jedes weitere Wort erübrigt sich*** there's nothing more to be said
eru·ie·ren [eru'i:rən] *v/t.* (h) find out, determine
Erup·ti·on [erʊp'tsĭo:n] *f* (-; -en) *geol. and* ⚕ eruption; **erup·tiv** [erʊp'ti:f] *adj.* eruptive
er'wa·chen I. *v/i.* (sn) wake up (*a. fig.*), *formal*: awake, awaken (*all* **aus** *dat.* from); *fig. day*: dawn; *memories, interests etc.*: be awakened; *suspicion etc.*: be aroused; *fig.* ***zu neuem Leben*** ~ revive, come to life again; → ***Bewußtlosigkeit;*** **II.** ♀ *n* (-s): (*fig.* ***trauriges, unsanftes*** ~ sad, rude) awakening
er'wach·sen¹ *v/i.* (erwuchs, erwachsen, sn) arise (**aus** *dat.* from); ~ **aus** *dat.* accrue (*or* result) from; ***daraus können Ihnen Unannehmlichkeiten*** ~ it may cause you trouble
er'wach·sen² I. *p.p. of* ***erwachsen¹***; **II.** *adj.* grown-up, adult; fully-grown; of age; ***~er Mensch*** grown-up; ***er ist ein ~er Mensch*** he's old enough to know what he's doing; ***sehr*** ~ ***sein*** be very grown-up for one's age; **Er'wach·se·ne** *m, f* (-n; -n) grown-up, adult; ***nur für*** ~ (for) adults only
Er'wach·se·nen|bil·dung *f* adult (*or* further) education; **~tau·fe** *f* adult baptism
er'wä·gen *v/t.* (erwog, erwogen, h) consider, think *s.th.* over; take into account; ***~, et. zu tun*** consider doing s.th.; ***die Vor- und Nachteile*** ~ weigh up the pros and cons (*or* advantages and disadvantages); ***es wird ernsthaft erwogen*** it's under serious consideration; **er'wä·gens·wert** *adj.* worth considering; **Er'wä·gung** *f* (-; -en) consideration; ***in*** ~ ***ziehen*** take into consideration, consider; contemplate, consider (*ger.*); ***~en anstellen, ob*** consider whether
er'wäh·len *v/t.* (h) choose; elect; ***j-n zum Parlamentssprecher*** *etc.* ~ elect s.o. (as) parliamentary speaker *etc.*; **Er'wähl·te** *m, f* (-n; -n) → ***auserwählt***
er'wäh·nen *v/t.* (h) mention; ***nebenbei*** ~ mention in passing; ***j-n namentlich*** ~ mention s.o. by name, mention s.o.'s name; ***du wurdest namentlich erwähnt*** your name was mentioned; ***ich wurde überhaupt nicht erwähnt*** I didn't even get a mention; **er'wäh·nens·wert** *adj.* worth mentioning; worthy of note; **Er'wäh·nung** *f* (-; -en) mention (*gen.* of), reference (to)
er'wan·dern *v/t.* (h): (**sich**) ***ein Gebiet*** ~ discover (*or* get to know) an area on foot
er'warb *pret. of* ***erwerben***
er'wär·men (h) **I.** *v/t.* warm *or* heat (up); *fig.* ***j-n für et.*** ~ get s.o. interested in s.th.; **II.** *v/refl.*: **sich** ~ warm up, heat up (***auf*** *acc.* to), get warm, warm o.s. (up); *fig.* ***sich*** ~ ***für*** *acc.* warm to, get to like; **Er'wär·mung** *f* (-; *no pl.*) warming up, heating up; ~ ***der Erdatmosphäre*** global warming
er'war·ten I. *v/t.* (h) (*a.* **sich** *dat.* ~) expect; wait for; (*a.* **sich** *dat.* ~) hope for; ***er kann es kaum ~(, daß s-e Eltern zurückkommen)*** he can hardly wait (for his parents to get back); ***es ist zu*** ~ it's to be expected; ***wie zu*** ~ as (was to be) expected; ***ich erwarte von dir, daß du ...*** I expect you to *inf.*; ***es wird erwartet, daß sie zusagen*** they are expected to agree, it is expected that they will agree; ***so was habe ich gar nicht erwartet*** I wasn't expecting (*or* I didn't expect) anything like that; ***wenn er wüßte, was ihn erwartet*** if he knew what is in store for him; ***das war mehr, als er erwartet hatte*** that was more than he had bargained for; ***von ihm kann man noch allerhand*** ~ he's somebody to watch; ***von ihm kann man nichts*** ~ you can't expect anything of him (*or* him to do anything), F he's hopeless; → ***Kind;*** **II.** ♀ *n* (-s): ***wider*** ~ contrary to all expectation(s); **Er'war·tung** *f* (-; -en) **1.** expectation (*gen.* of); anticipation (of), expectancy (of); hope(s *pl.*) (for); ***voller*** ~ → ***erwartungsvoll; in*** ~ *gen.* in anticipation of; **2.** *pl.* hopes; ***in j-n große ~en setzen*** place great hopes in s.o., expect a great deal of s.o.; ***hochgeschraubte ~en*** high hopes (*or* expectations); ***die ~en herabsetzen*** lower one's expectations (*or* sights); ***du hast m-e ~en enttäuscht*** you disappoint me, I expected you to do better than that; ***entgegen allen ~en*** against all expectations, against the odds; **er'war·tungs·froh I.** *adj.* expectant; **II.** *adv.* expectantly; *lit.* in joyful anticipation; **er'war·tungs·ge·mäß** *adv.* as expected
Er'war·tungs|hal·tung *f* expectations *pl.*; **~ho·ri͵zont** *m* horizon of expectations
er'war·tungs·voll *adj. and adv.* full of expectation, expectant(ly); ***in ~er Haltung*** in a state of expectancy
er'wecken (*sep.* -k·k-) *v/t.* (h) **1.** → ***wekken*** I; **2.** ***wieder zum Leben*** ~ revive *s.o. or s.th.*; ***von den Toten*** ~ raise from the dead; **3.** *fig.* arouse *curiosity, interest, etc.*; *a.* awaken, stir up *emotions etc.*; bring back, stir up *memories etc.*; raise *hope*; inspire *confidence*; ***bei j-m den Glauben ~, daß*** make s.o. believe that; → ***Anschein, Eindruck*** 1; **4.** *eccl.* convert; **Er'weckung** *f fig.* arousal; awakening, stirring up; raising
er'weh·ren *v/refl.* (h): **sich** ~ ward off; resist; ***sich der Tränen*** ~ hold back one's (*or* the) tears; ***sich nicht ~ können*** *gen.* be helpless against, be unable to resist (*ger.*); ***ich konnte mich des Lachens nicht*** ~ I couldn't help (*or* stop myself from) laughing; ***man konnte sich des Eindrucks nicht ~, daß*** you couldn't help feeling (that)
er'wei·chen *v/t.* (h) soften (up); *fig.* soften, mollify *s.o.*; move, touch *s.o.*; *fig.* ***sich*** ~ ***lassen*** relent, yield, give in; **Er'wei·chung** *f* (-; *no pl.*) softening; *fig. a.* mollification
Er·weis [ɛɐ'vaɪs] *m* (-es; -e) proof; ***den*** ~ ***bringen, daß*** prove that, furnish proof (*or* evidence) that; **er'wei·sen** (erwies, erwiesen, h) **I.** *v/t.* **1.** prove, show, demonstrate, establish; ***es ist erwiesen, daß*** it has been proved *etc.* that; **2.** do *s.o. a service etc.*; grant *s.o. a favo(u)r*; show *respect etc.*; **II.** *v/refl.*: **3.** ***sich*** ~ ***als*** turn out (to be), prove (to be), *a.* prove o.s. (to be); ***es erwies sich, daß*** it turned out that; **4.** ***sich j-m gegenüber dankbar*** ~ show one's gratitude to (*or* towards) s.o.
er·wei·tern [ɛɐ'vaɪtɐn] (erweiterte, erweitert, h) **I.** *v/t.* widen *road etc.*; extend *building etc.*; enlarge *book*; let out *skirt etc.*; *fig.* extend *sphere of influence etc.*; broaden *one's knowledge*; ℞ reduce to higher terms; ***s-e Spanischkenntnisse*** ~ improve one's Spanish; → ***Horizont;*** **II.** *v/refl.*: **sich** ~ *road etc.*: widen; *pupil, blood vessels*: dilate; *heart*: become enlarged; *fig. knowledge*: increase; *term*: take on a wider meaning; **er'wei·tert** *adj.* enlarged *etc.*; → ***erweitern; ~e Berichterstattung*** extended coverage; *ling.* ***~er Satz*** compound sentence; ***~er Infinitiv*** extended infinitive; **Er·wei·te·rung** [ɛɐ'vaɪtərʊŋ] *f* (-; -en) widening; extension; enlargement; broadening; ⚕ dilation; **Er'wei·te·rungs·bau** *m* annex(e), extension (wing); **er'wei·te·rungs·fä·hig** *adj.* capable of being enlarged (*or* extended), expansible; ***es ist*** ~ *a.* it can be enlarged (*or* extended, expanded)
Er·werb [ɛɐ'vɛrp] *m* (-[e]s; *no pl.*) acquisition; purchase; earnings *pl.*; living; ***s-m*** ~ ***nachgehen*** earn one's living; **er'werben** *v/t.* (erwarb, erworben, h) acquire (*a. fig. knowledge etc.*); purchase; earn; *fig.* win *fame, s.o.'s respect etc.*; ***sich sein Brot*** ~ earn one's *od.* a living; ***sich Reichtum*** ~ gain riches; ***sich ein Vermögen*** ~ make a fortune; ***sich um die Organisation*** *etc.* ***große Verdienste*** ~ serve the organization *etc.* well, do great service for the organization *etc.*; **er'werb·lich** *adj.* for sale
er'werbs|be·hin·dert, ~be·schränkt *adj.* partially disabled
er'werbs·fä·hig *adj.* capable of work; fit for work; ***~es Alter*** employable (*or* working) age; **Er'werbs·fä·hig·keit** *f* (-; *no pl.*) ability to work
Er'werbs·le·ben *n* working life
er'werbs·los *adj.* unemployed; **Er'werbs·lo·se** *m, f* (-n; -n) unemployed person; ***die ~n*** the unemployed (*pl.*); **Er'werbs·lo·sen·quo·te** *f* level of unemployment
Er'werbs|min·de·rung *f* reduction in earning capacity; **~quel·le** *f* source of income; **~sinn** *m* (-[e]s; *no pl.*) business sense (*or* acumen)
er'werbs·tä·tig *adj.* gainfully employed; ***~e Bevölkerung*** *a.* economically active population; **Er'werbs·tä·ti·ge** *m, f* (-n; -n) employed person; ***die ~n*** the employed population (*sg.*); ***die Zahl der ~n***

the number of employed; **Er'werbs·tä·tig·keit** *f* gainful employment

Er'werbs·trieb *m* acquisitive urge

er'werbs·un·fä·hig *adj.* incapable of work; unfit for work; **Er'werbs·un·fä·hig·keit** *f* incapacity to work

Er'werbs|ur·kun·de *f* ⚖ title deed; **~zweig** *m* branch of industry; line (of business)

Er'wer·bung *f* (-; -en) acquisition

er·wi·dern [ɛɐ'vi:dɐn] *v/t.* (erwiderte, erwidert, h) return *visit etc.*, *a.* ⚔ *fire*; reciprocate; (*a. v/i.*) reply, answer (**auf** *acc.* to), retort; ***auf m-e Frage erwiderte er ...*** in reply to my question he said ...; ***er wußte nicht, was er darauf ~ sollte*** he didn't know what to say to that; **Er'wi·de·rung** *f* (-; -en) **1.** reciprocation; ***in ~*** *gen.* in reply to; ***keine ~ finden*** *love*: be (left) unrequited; **2.** reply, answer; retort; **3.** ⚔ ***flexible ~*** flexible response

er'wies *pret. of* **erweisen**

er·wie·sen [ɛɐ'vi:zən] **I.** *p.p. of* **erweisen; II.** *adj.* proved; ***e-e ~e Tatsache*** an established fact; **er·wie·se·ner·ma·ßen** [ɛɐ'vi:zənɐ'ma:sən] *adv.* as has been proved (*or* shown, demonstrated, established); demonstrably; ***es erscheint ~ nur im Winter*** it has been proved to appear only in winter; ***sie war ~ dabei*** she is proved to have been present

er'wir·ken *v/t.* (h) achieve, bring about; secure, succeed in getting; obtain, secure *permission etc.*

er'wirt·schaf·ten *v/t.* (h) gain (by good management), make

er'wi·schen F *v/t.* (h) catch, get (*both a.* ⚡); *a.* make *bus, train etc.*; get hold of; ***sich ~ lassen*** get caught; ***ihn hat's erwischt*** a) F he's been laid low, b) F he's come a cropper, c) F he's got it in the neck, d) F he's smitten, e) F he's had it

er'wog *pret. of* **erwägen**

er·wo·gen [ɛɐ'vo:gən] *p.p. of* **erwägen**

er·wor·ben [ɛɐ'vɔrbən] *p.p. of* **erwerben**

er·wünscht [ɛɐ'vʏnʃt] *adj.* desired; welcome; desirable; ***du bist hier nicht ~*** you're not wanted around here; ***Computerkenntnisse ~, aber nicht Bedingung*** computer skills an asset, not essential

er'wür·gen I. *v/t.* (h) strangle; **II.** ♀ *n* (-s) → **Er'wür·gung** *f* (-; *no pl.*) strangling, strangulation

Ery·thro·zyt [erytro'tsy:t] *m* (-en; -en) *physiol.* erythrocyte, red (blood) cell; **Ery·thro'zy·ten·zäh·lung** *f* red cell count

Erz [e:ɐts; ɛrts] *n* ore; **~ader** *f* vein of ore

er·zäh·len [ɛɐ'tsɛ:lən] (erzählte, erzählt, h) **I.** *v/t.* tell; recount; narrate; ***man hat mir erzählt*** I've been told; ***was hat er erzählt?*** what did he (have to) say?; ***sie kann was ~!*** she's got a few stories (*or* tales) to tell; ***komm, erzähl uns was!*** so what's new?; ***man erzählt sich*** they say; ***er erzählt nur noch Unsinn*** he talks a lot of nonsense; ***erzähl doch keinen Unsinn!*** F who are you trying to kid?, don't talk such nonsense; F ***das kannst du mir nicht ~!, das kannst du d-r Großmutter ~!*** F pull the other one; F ***wem ~ Sie das!*** F you're telling me; F ***dem werd' ich was ~!*** F I'll tell him a thing or two; **II.** *v/i.* tell a story (*or* stories); ***~ von*** *dat.* tell s.o. about, *lit.* tell of; ***er soll niemandem davon ~*** he's not to tell (*or* breathe a word to) anyone about it; ***er erzählte, daß*** he told us *etc.* that, he said that; ***er kann gut ~*** he's a good storyteller; **III.** ♀ *n* (-s) storytelling; narration; ***die Kunst des ~s*** the art of storytelling (*or* narrative); **er'zäh·lend** *adj.* narrative *style etc.*; **er'zäh·lens·wert** *adj.* worth telling; ***e-e ~e Geschichte*** *a.* a good story; **Er·zäh·ler** [ɛɐ'tsɛ:lɐ] *m* (-s; -) narrator; storyteller; raconteur; narrative writer; **er·zäh·le·risch** [ɛɐ'tsɛ:lərɪʃ] *adj.* narrative; ***~es Talent besitzen*** be a good storyteller; **er'zähl·freu·dig** *adj.* communicative

Er'zähl|kunst *f* (-; *no pl.*) narrative (art), art of narrative; ***ein Meister der ~*** a master of narrative (*or* of [the] narrative art); **~per·spek,ti·ve** *f* narrative perspective; **~tech·nik** *f* narrative technique; **~ton** *m* narrative style; style of storytelling

Er·zäh·lung [ɛɐ'tsɛ:lʊŋ] *f* (-; -en) **1.** telling; narration; **2.** story; **3.** account; **4.** *lit.* (short) story; tale; **5.** *coll.* fiction

'Erz·berg·werk *n* ore mine

'Erz·bi·schof *m* archbishop; **'erz·bi·schöf·lich** *adj.* archiepiscopal; **'Erz·bis·tum** *n*, **'Erz·di·öze·se** *f* archbishopric, archdiocese

'Erz·en·gel *m* archangel

er'zeu·gen *v/t.* (h) produce, ⚘ *a.* grow, ⚙ *a.* make; *phys.*, ⚗ generate; *fig.* cause, bring about; create, generate, engender

Er·zeu·ger [ɛɐ'tsɔʏgɐ] *m* (-s; -) **1.** father, *iro.* procreator; **2.** producer, ⚙ *a.* manufacturer, ⚘ *a.* grower; **~land** *n* country of origin

Er·zeug·nis [ɛɐ'tsɔʏknɪs] *n* (-ses; -se) product; ⚘ *usu. pl.* produce (*sg.*); *fig.* creation, *iro.* brainchild; product *of imagination etc.*; ***eigenes ~*** my *etc.* own make (*or* brand)

Er'zeu·gung *f* (-; -en) production, ⚙ *a.* manufacture; *phys.*, ⚗ generation; *fig.* creation; **Er'zeu·gungs·ko·sten** *pl.* production costs

'Erz·feind *m* arch-enemy; ***der ~*** Satan; **'Erz·feind·schaft** *f* archrivalry

'Erz·gau·ner *m* F (real) crook

'Erz|ge·win·nung *f* ore production; **~gie·ße,rei** *f* (metal) foundry; **~gru·be** *f* (ore) mine, pit

'erz·hal·tig *adj.* ore-bearing

'Erz·ha·lun·ke *m* F (real) crook

'Erz·her·zog *m* archduke; **'Erz·her·zo·gin** *f* archduchess; **'Erz·her·zog·tum** *n* archduchy

'Erz·hüt·te *f* smelting works *pl.*

er·zieh·bar [ɛɐ'tsi:ba:ɐ] *adj.* educable; ***schwer ~es Kind*** problem child; **er'zie·hen** *v/t.* (erzog, erzogen, h) bring up, raise; educate; ***j-n ~ zu*** *dat.* bring up (*or* train) s.o. to be; ***j-n zu e-m selbständigen Menschen ~*** bring s.o. up to be an independent person; ***j-n zur Sparsamkeit ~*** bring s.o. up (*or* teach s.o.) to be economical; ***er wurde streng erzogen*** he had a strict upbringing; → ***erzogen;*** **Er·zie·her** [ɛɐ'tsi:ɐ] *m* (-s; -) educator; teacher; tutor; **Er·zie·he·rin** [ɛɐ'tsi:ərɪn] *f* (-; -nen) (qualified) kindergarten teacher; governess; **er·zie·he·risch** [ɛɐ'tsi:ərɪʃ] **I.** *adj.* educational; ***~e Probleme (Fragen)*** problems (questions) of upbringing; **II.** *adv.*: ***j-n ~ beeinflussen*** have an educational effect on s.o.; ***das ist ~ ganz falsch*** F you're never going to teach them *etc.* that way; **Er'zie·hung** *f* (-; *no pl.*) upbringing; education; training; breeding, manners *pl.*; ***er hat e-e gute ~ genossen*** he had a good upbringing; ***falsche ~*** the wrong (*or* a bad) upbringing; ***ihr fehlt jede ~*** she's got no upbringing (*or* manners)

Er'zie·hungs|an·stalt *f* approved school, *Am.* reformatory, reform school; **~bei·hil·fe** *f* educational grant; **~be·ra·tung** *f* child guidance (service); **~be·rech·tig·te** *m, f* (-n; -n) **1.** parent; **2.** legal guardian; **~feh·ler** *pl.* wrong upbringing *sg.* (*gen.* on the part of); **~ur·laub** *m* maternity (*or* paternity) leave; **~we·sen** *n* (-s; *no pl.*) **1.** education; **2.** educational system; **~wis·sen·schaft** *f* educational science

er'zie·len *v/t.* (h) achieve, attain, get; produce, come up with *results etc.*; score; make; fetch *prize etc.*; reach, come to *an understanding etc.*; have *an effect*; ***als Reingewinn ~*** clear, net; ***Einigung ~*** reach (an) agreement (**über** *acc.* on)

er'zit·tern *v/i.* (sn) tremble, shake (**vor** *dat.* with)

'Erz·ka·tho,lik *m*, **'erz·ka,tho·lisch** *adj.* ultra-Catholic

'erz·kon·ser·va·tiv *adj.* ultra-conservative; *in GB*: *a.* true-blue ...; ***~ sein*** *in GB*: *a.* be a true blue; **'Erz·kon·ser·va·ti·ve** *m, f* (-n; -n) dyed-in-the-wool conservative; *in GB*: *a.* true blue

'Erz|lüg·ner *m* chronic liar; **~lump** F *m* real scoundrel

er·zo·gen [ɛɐ'tso:gən] **I.** *p.p. of* **erziehen; II.** *adj.*: ***er ist gut (schlecht) ~*** he's very well-mannered (he's got no manners at all)

'erz·re·ak·tio,när *adj.* ultra-reactionary

'Erz|ri,va·le *m* archrival; **~schur·ke** F *m* real scoundrel; **~ty,rann** *m* archtyrant, archdespot

er'zür·nen *lit.* (h) **I.** *v/t.* anger, enrage; **II.** *v/refl.*: ***sich ~*** get angry (**über** *acc.* at, about)

'Erz·va·ter *m* patriarch

'Erz·vor·kom·men *n* ore deposit(s *pl.*)

er'zwin·gen *v/t.* (erzwang, erzwungen, h) force, get *s.th.* by force; enforce (*a. obedience etc.*); ***e-e Entscheidung ~*** force an issue; ***Liebe läßt sich nicht ~*** you can't force love; ***ein Geständnis von j-m ~*** force a confession out of s.o.; **er·zwun·gen** [ɛɐ'tsvʊŋən] **I.** *p.p. of* **erzwingen; II.** *adj.* forced; put-on; **er'zwun·ge·ner'ma·ßen** *adv.* under pressure

es [ɛs] *pers. pron.* **1.** it, *zo. a.* he (*f* she); ⚓, *mot.* it, *a.* she; *impers.* ***~ schneit*** it's snowing; ***~ ist kalt*** it's cold; ***~ wurde getanzt*** they *etc.* danced; *wer ist der Junge?* - ***~ ist mein Bruder*** he's my brother; *wer sind diese Mädchen?* - ***~ sind m-e Schwestern*** they're my sisters; *wer hat angerufen?* - ***~ war mein Chef*** it was my boss; ***ich bin's*** it's me; ***sie sind ~*** it's them; ***~ war keiner da*** there was nobody there, nobody was there; ***~ war einmal ein König*** once upon a time there was a king; ***~ gibt zu viele Probleme*** there are too many problems; ***~ wird erzählt*** they say; ***~ heißt in der Bibel*** it says in the Bible; **2.** it; ***ich nahm ~*** I took it; ***ich halte es für leichtsinnig zu*** *inf.* I think it would be careless to *inf.*; ***da hast du's*** what did I say?; ***ich weiß ~*** I know; ***ich bin ~ leid, ich habe ~ satt*** I'm (sick and) tired of it; **3.** *er ist reich,* ***ich bin ~ auch*** so am I; ***ich hoffe ~*** I hope so; ***er hat ~ mir gesagt*** he told me so; *er sagte, ich sollte gehen,* ***und ich tat ~*** so I did, and I did so; *bist du bereit? -* ***ja, ich bin ~*** yes, I am; ***ich kann ~*** I can (do it); ***ich will ~*** I want to; ***ich will ~ versuchen*** I'll (give it a) try

Es¹ *n* (-; *no pl.*) *psych.* id

Es² *n* (-; -) ♪ E flat

Es·cha·to·lo·gie [ɛsçatoloˈgiː] *f* (-; *no pl.*) *eccl.* eschatology; **es·cha·to·lo·gisch** [ɛsçatoˈloːgɪʃ] *adj.* eschatological

Esche [ˈɛʃə] *f* (-; -n) ash (tree); **ˈeschen** *adj.* ash; **ˈEschen·holz** *n* ash(wood)

Esel [ˈeːzəl] *m* (-s; -) **1.** donkey, ass; ***männlicher ~*** he-ass, jackass; ***störrisch wie ein ~*** (as) stubborn as a mule; ***ein ~ schimpft den andern Langohr*** it's the pot calling the kettle black; ***wenn man den ~ nennt, kommt er schon gerannt*** talk (*or* speak) of the devil; **2.** F twit; ***alter ~*** old fool; ***ich ~!*** what an idiot I am, how stupid can you get; **Ese·lin** [ˈeːzəlɪn] *f* (-; -nen) she-ass

Esels|brücke *f* mnemonic (aid); ***ich muß mir e-e ~ bauen*** I've got to have something that will help me remember; **~ohr** *n* turned-down corner; ***Buch mit ~en*** dog-eared book

Es·ka·la·ti·on [ɛskalaˈtsi̯oːn] *f* (-; -en) *pol. and* ⚔ escalation; **es·ka·lie·ren** [ɛskaˈliːrən] (h) **I.** *v/i.* escalate; **II.** *v/t.* step up

Es·ka·pa·de [ɛskaˈpaːdə] *f* (-; -n) escapade

Es·ka·pis·mus [ɛskaˈpɪsmʊs] *m* (-; *no pl.*) escapism; **es·ka·pi·stisch** [ɛskaˈpɪstɪʃ] *adj.* escapist

Es·ki·mo [ˈɛskimo] *m* (-s; -s) Eskimo

Es·kor·te [ɛsˈkɔrtə] *f* (-; -n) escort; *a.* motorcade; **es·kor·tie·ren** [ɛskɔrˈtiːrən] *v/t.* (h) escort

Eso·te·rik [ezoˈteːrɪk] *f* (-; *no pl.*) **1.** esoteric arts *pl.*; **2.** esotericism; **3.** *w.s.* New Age (movement); **eso·te·risch** [ezoˈteːrɪʃ] *adj.* esoteric

Es·pe [ˈɛspə] *f* (-; -n) ♣ aspen; **ˈEs·pen·laub** *n*: ***wie ~ zittern*** tremble like a leaf

Es·pe·ran·to [ɛspeˈranto] *n* (-[s]; *no pl.*) Esperanto

Es·pla·na·de [ɛsplaˈnaːdə] *f* (-; -n) esplanade

Es·pres·so [ɛsˈprɛso] *m* (-[s]; -s, -si) espresso (*pl.* espressos); **~au·toˌmat** *m* espresso machine; **~bar** *f* espresso place; **~maˌschi·ne** *f* espresso machine

Es·prit [ɛsˈpriː] *m* (-s; *no pl.*) wit; ***ein Mann mit*** (*or* ***von***) **~** a (man of) wit

Eß·ap·fel [ˈɛs-] *m* eating apple, eater

Es·say [ˈɛse] *m, n* (-s; -s) essay; **Es·say·ist** [ɛseˈɪst] *m* (-en; -en) essayist; **Es·sayi·stik** [ɛseˈɪstɪk] *f* (-; *no pl.*) **1.** (*the* art of) essay writing; **2.** essayistic writings *pl.*; **es·sayi·stisch** [ɛseˈɪstɪʃ] *adj.* essayistic

eß·bar [ˈɛsbaːɐ] *adj.* eatable; edible; ***~er Pilz*** (edible) mushroom

Eß·be·steck [ˈɛs-] *n* cutlery (set)

Es·se [ˈɛsə] *f* (-; -n) **1.** chimney; **2.** forge

Eß·ecke [ˈɛs-] *f* dining area

es·sen [ˈɛsən] **I.** *v/t. and v/i.* (aß, gegessen, h) eat; ***zu Mittag*** (***Abend***) **~** have lunch (dinner); ***viel ~*** eat a lot, be a big eater; ***warm*** (***kalt***) **~** have a hot (cold) meal; ***er ißt nie warm*** he never has a hot meal; ***was gibt es zu ~?*** what's for dinner (*or* lunch)?, what are we having for dinner (*or* lunch)?; ***wir können gleich ~*** dinner (*or* lunch) will be ready in a minute; ***hast du schon gegessen?*** have you eaten yet?, have you had your dinner (*or* lunch) yet?; *et.* ***gern ~*** like; ***s-n Teller leer ~*** clean one's plate; ***im Restaurant ~*** eat out, eat at a restaurant; ***man ißt dort ganz gut*** the food is quite good there; ***ich geh' zu m-r Schwester ~*** I'm eating (*or* having a meal) at my sister's; → ***Abend, auswärts, satt*** *etc.*; **II.** ≈ *n* (-s) eating; food; dish; meal; dinner; ***~ und Trinken*** food and drink; ***wir sind gerade beim ~*** we're just having dinner (*or* lunch), we're at the table; ***j-n zum ~ einladen*** invite s.o. for a meal (*or* to dinner, lunch); ***zum ~ bleiben*** stay for dinner (*or* lunch); ***et. vor*** (***nach***) ***dem ~ einnehmen*** take s.th. before (after) meals

ˈEs·sen(s)·aus·ga·be *f*: ***~ von 12-14 Uhr*** meals served from 12 p.m - 2 p.m

ˈEs·sens·ge·ruch *m* smell of food (*or* cooking)

ˈEs·sen(s)·mar·ke *f* meal ticket, *Brit. a.* lunch(eon) voucher

ˈEs·sens|zeit *f* a) lunchtime, lunch hour, b) dinnertime; **~zu·schuß** *m* lunch allowance

es·sen·ti·ell [ɛsɛnˈtsi̯ɛl] *adj.* essential (*a.* ⚗, *biol.*); ***von ~er Bedeutung*** of paramount importance

Es·senz [ɛˈsɛnts] *f* (-; -en) essence (*a. fig.*)

Es·ser [ˈɛsɐ] *m* (-s; -): ***starker*** (***schwacher***) **~** big (poor, bad) eater; **Es·se·rei** [ɛsəˈraɪ] *f* (-; *no pl.*) eating; ***diese dauernde ~!*** all this eating (*or* food)!, we *etc.* seem to do nothing but eat

Eß|ge·schirr [ˈɛs-] *n* crockery; dinner service; **~ge·wohn·hei·ten** *pl.* eating habits; **~gier** *f* greed, gluttony; **~grup·pe** *f* dining set, dining table and chairs *pl.*

Es·sig [ˈɛsɪç] *m* (-s; -e) vinegar; F *fig.* ***damit ist es ~*** F it's all off; **~esˌsenz** *f* vinegar essence; **~ester** *m* ethyl acetate; **~fla·sche** *f* vinegar bottle; **~gur·ke** *f* pickled cucumber, (pickled) gherkin, *Am.* pickle; **≈sau·er** *adj.* acetic; → ***Tonerde***; **~säu·re** *f* acetic acid; **~-und-Öl-Stän·der** *m* cruet stand

Eß|kaˌsta·nie [ˈɛs-] *f* (sweet) chestnut; **~korb** *m* hamper; **~löf·fel** *m* tablespoon; ***zwei*** (***gestrichene***) **~** two (level) tablespoons(ful); **~lust** *f* appetite; **~ni·sche** *f* dining alcove, dinette; **~obst** *n* eating fruit; **~stäb·chen** *pl.* chopsticks; **~sucht** *f* craving for food; **~tisch** *m* dining table; **~wa·ren** *pl.* food *sg.*; ✝ foodstuffs; **~zim·mer** *n* dining room

Esta·blish·ment [ɪsˈtæblɪʃmənt] *n* (-s; -s) *the* establishment, *the* Establishment

Este [ˈeːstə] *m* (-n; -n) Estonian

Ester [ˈɛstɐ] *m* (-s; -) ⚗ ester

Estin [ˈeːstɪn] (-; -nen) *f*, **est·nisch** [ˈeːstnɪʃ] *adj.* Estonian

Estra·gon [ˈɛstragɔn] *m* (-s; *no pl.*) tarragon

Est·rich [ˈɛstrɪç] *m* (-s; -e) stone floor

eta·blie·ren [etaˈbliːrən] *v/refl.* (h): ***sich ~*** establish o.s. (*or* itself), become established; set o.s. up, start a business; settle in; ***sich ~ als*** set o.s. up as

Eta·blis·se·ment [etablɪsəˈmãː] *n* (-s; -s) **1.** (business) establishment; **2.** establishment; **3.** ***ein gepflegtes ~*** a clean place; **4.** place, establishment

Eta·ge [eˈtaːʒə] *f* (-; -n) floor, stor(e)y; ***auf*** (*or* ***in***) ***der ersten ~*** on the first (*Am.* second) floor; ***auf welcher ~ wohnst du?*** which floor do you live on (*or* are you on)?

Eta·gen·bett *n* bunk bed(s *pl.*)

eta·gen·för·mig [-fœrmɪç] *adj.* terraced, tiered, (arranged) in tiers

Eta·gen|hei·zung *f* single-stor(e)y heating (system); **~kell·ner** *m* floor waiter; **~woh·nung** *f* flat, *Am.* apartment

Etap·pe [eˈtapə] *f* (-; -n) **1.** stage, *sport: a.* leg; ***~ des Lebens*** stage in life, phase of life; **2.** ⚔ communication zone; base

Etap·pen|sieg *m* stage win (*or* victory); **~sie·ger** *m* stage winner

etap·pen·wei·se I. *adv.* in stages, step by step, F bit by bit; **II.** *adj.* step-by-step ...

Etat [eˈtaː] *m* (-s; -s) **1.** ✝, *pol.* budget; estimates *pl.*; ***das ist nicht im ~ vorgesehen*** that hasn't been budgeted for; **2.** ⚔ establishment; **~aus·gleich** *m* balancing (of) the budget; **~be·ra·tung** *f* budget discussion; **~ent·wurf** *m* budget proposals *pl.*; **~jahr** *n* fiscal (*or* financial) year; **~kür·zung** *f* cut in the budget, budget cut

etat·mä·ßig *adj.* budgetary; permanent; regular

Etat|po·sten *m* budget(ary) item; **~überˌschrei·tung** *f* spending in excess of the budget

ete·pe·te·te [eːtəpeˈteːtə] F *adj.* **1.** F la-di-da; **2.** fussy; **3.** squeamish

Ethik [ˈeːtɪk] *f* (-; *no pl.*) ethics *pl.*; **Ethi·ker** [ˈeːtikɐ] *m* (-s; -) moral philosopher; **ethisch** [ˈeːtɪʃ] *adj.* ethical; ***~e Frage*** ethical question, question of ethics; ***aus ~en Gründen ablehnen*** reject on ethical grounds

eth·nisch [ˈɛtnɪʃ] *adj.* ethnic(ally *adv.*)

Eth·no·graph [ɛtnoˈgraːf] *m* (-en; -en) ethnographer; **Eth·no·gra·phie** [ɛtnograˈfiː] *f* (-; *no pl.*) ethnography; **eth·no·gra·phisch** [ɛtnoˈgraːfɪʃ] *adj.* ethnographic(ally *adv.*)

Eth·no·lo·ge [ɛtnoˈloːgə] *m* (-n; -n) ethnologist; **Eth·no·lo·gie** [ɛtnoloˈgiː] *f* (-; *no pl.*) ethnology

Etho·lo·ge [etoˈloːgə] *m* (-n; -n) ethologist; **Etho·lo·gie** [etoloˈgiː] *f* (-; *no pl.*) ethology; **etho·lo·gisch** [etoˈloːgɪʃ] *adj.* ethological

Ethos [ˈeːtɔs] *n* (-; *no pl.*) ethos; *w.s.* ethics *pl.*

Eti·kett [etiˈkɛt] *n* (-[e]s; -e) label; price tag; ***auf dem ~ steht*** it says on the label, the label says; *fig.* ***mit e-m ~ versehen*** label

Eti·ket·te [etiˈkɛtə] *f* (-; *no pl.*) etiquette, convention(s *pl.*); ***Verstoß gegen die ~*** breach of etiquette; ***es ist gegen die ~ zu*** *inf.* it's bad form to *inf.*

Etiˈket·ten·schwin·del *m* **1.** bogus claim(s *pl.*), fraudulent label(l)ing; **2.** *fig.* (a) fraud; ***das ist ja der reinste ~*** they ought to be done under the Trades Descriptions Act; **eti·ket·tie·ren** [etikɛˈtiːrən] *v/t.* (h) put a label on; price-tag; *fig.* label; *fig.* ***j-n als Betrüger ~*** label s.o. a cheat

et·li·che [ˈɛtlɪçə] *indef. pron. pl.* a number of, quite a few; ***~ tausend Mark*** several thousand marks; ***~ Millionen*** several million(s); **~s** (*sg.*) a number of things (*pl.*), a thing or two; **ˈet·li·che·mal** *adv.* quite a few times, a number of times

Etrus·ker [eˈtrʊskɐ] *m* (-s; -), **Etrus·ke·rin** [eˈtrʊskərɪn] *f* (-; -nen), **etrus·kisch** [eˈtrʊskɪʃ] *adj.*, **Etrus·kisch** *n* (-en) *ling.* Etruscan

Etü·de [eˈtyːdə] *f* (-; -n) ♪ etude

Etui [ɛtˈviː] *n* (-s; -s) case

et·wa [ˈɛtva] *adv.* **1.** *a.* ***in ~*** about, approximately, F around; ... or so, ... or thereabouts; **in ~fertig etc.**: more or less; **wann ~?** approximately when?, F around what time?; **2.** a) by any chance, possibly; b) for instance, for example, (let's) say; **war sie ~ da?** was she there, then?; **du warst doch nicht ~ da?** you weren't there, were you?, don't tell me you were there; **nicht ~, daß** not that *it mattered etc.*; **ist das ~ besser?** is that any better?; **du glaubt doch nicht ~ ...?** surely you don't think ...?

et·wa·ig ['ɛtvaıç] *adj.* any; possible; **~e Schwierigkeiten** any difficulties (that might arise)

et·was ['ɛtvas] **I.** *indef. pron.* something; anything; **~ Merkwürdiges** something strange, a strange thing; **~ anderes** something (*or* anything) else; **ohne ~ zu sagen** without a word; **so ~ habe ich noch nie gehört** I've never heard anything like it; **so ~ kommt schon vor** that kind of thing does happen; **aus ihm wird ~** he'll go a long way; **das ist immerhin ~** that's something, at least; F **die haben ~ miteinander** there's something going on between them; **die Sache hat ~ für sich** there's something to be said for it; **er versteht ~ davon** he knows a thing or two about it; **er hat ~ Gelehrtes an sich** there's something of the scholar about him; **II.** *adj.* some; any; a little; a bit of; **ich brauche ~ Geld** I need some (*or* a bit of) money; **~ Englisch** a little English; **hab ~ Geduld** be patient; **III.** *adv.* a bit, a little; **IV.** ≈ *n*: **das gewisse ~** that certain something; **so ein kleines ~** such a little thing

Ety·mo·lo·ge [etymo'lo:gə] *m* (-n; -n) etymologist; **Ety·mo·lo·gie** [etymolo'gi:] *f* (-; *no pl.*) etymology; **ety·mo·lo·gisch** [etymo'lo:gıʃ] *adj.* etymological

euch [ɔʏç] **I.** *pers. pron.* (*dat. and acc. of ihr*) (to) you; for you; **bei ~** with you; at your place; **ich hab's ~ gesagt** (**gegeben**) I told you (I gave it to you, I gave you it); **wie geht's ~?** how are you?; **II.** *refl. pron.* yourselves; *after prp.*: you; **setzt ~!** sit down; **bedient ~!** help yourselves

Eu·cha·ri·stie [ɔʏçarıs'ti:] *f* (-; -n): **die ~** the Eucharist; **~fei·er** *f* Eucharistic mass

eu·cha·ri·stisch [ɔʏça'rıstıʃ] *adj.* Eucharistic

eu·er ['ɔʏɐ] **I.** *poss. pron.* **1.** *adj.* your; ≈ **Ehren** (**Gnaden**) Your Hono(u)r (Grace); ≈ **Robert** Yours, Robert; **2.** *su.* yours; **~er, ~e, ~es, eurer, eure, eures, der** (**die, das**) **eu(e)re** yours; **II.** *pers. pron.* (*gen. of ihr*) of you

Eu·ge·nik [ɔʏ'ge:nık] *f* (-; *no pl.*) eugenics *pl.*; **eu·ge·nisch** [ɔʏ'ge:nıʃ] *adj.* eugenic(ally *adv.*)

Eu·ka·lyp·tus [ɔʏka'lʏptʊs] *m* (-; -, -ten) eucalyptus; **~baum** *m* eucalyptus tree; **~bon,bon** *n*, *m* eucalyptus sweet (*Am.* candy); **~öl** *n* eucalyptus oil

eu·kli·disch [ɔʏ'kli:dıʃ] *adj.* Euclidean

Eu·le ['ɔʏlə] *f* (-; -n) owl; *fig.* **~n nach Athen tragen** carry coals to Newcastle; **das hieße ~n nach Athen tragen** that would be carrying coals to Newcastle

Eu·len·spie·ge'lei *f* (-; -en) prank

Eu·nuch [ɔʏ'nu:x] *m* (-en; -en) eunuch; **eu'nu·chen·haft** *adj.* eunuch-like; **Eu'nu·chen·stim·me** *f* high-pitched (F squeaky) voice

Eu·phe·mis·mus [ɔʏfe'mısmʊs] *m* (-; -men) euphemism; **eu·phe·mi·stisch** [ɔʏfe'mıstıʃ] **I.** *adj.* euphemistic; **II.** *adv.* euphemistically; **~ ausgedrückt** put euphemistically

Eu·pho·rie [ɔʏfo'ri:] *f* (-; *no pl.*) ⚕ *and fig.* euphoria; **eu·pho·risch** [ɔʏ'fo:rıʃ] *adj.* euphoric(ally *adv.*)

Eu·ra·si·er [ɔʏ'ra:zĭɐ] *m* (-s; -), **Eu·ra·sie·rin** [ɔʏ'ra:zĭərın] *f* (-; -nen), **eu·ra·sisch** [ɔʏ'ra:zıʃ] *adj.* Eurasian

eu·re ['ɔʏrə] → **euer**

eu·rer·seits ['ɔʏrɐzaıts] *adv.* for (*or* on) your part

eu·res·glei·chen ['ɔʏrəs'glaıçən] *pron.* people like yourselves, *contp.* F the likes of you, your sort

eu·ret·hal·ben ['ɔʏrət'halbən] *obs. adv.* → **'eu·ret'we·gen** *adv.* **1.** a) because of you, *a.* on your account, *a.* for your sake(s); **2.** on your behalf; **'eu·ret'wil·len** *adv.*: (**um**) **~** for your sake(s); on your behalf

Eu·rhyth·mie [ɔʏrʏt'mi:] *f* (-; *no pl.*) eur(h)ythmics *pl.*; ⚕ eurhythmia

eu·rig ['ɔʏrıç] → **euer** II

Eu·ro|dol·lar ['ɔʏro-] *m* Eurodollar; **~geld·markt** *m* Euro-currency market

Eu·ro·kom·mu'nis·mus [ɔʏro-] *m* Eurocommunism; **Eu·ro·kom·mu'nist** *m* Eurocommunist

Eu·ro·krat [ɔʏro'kra:t] *m* (-en; -en) Eurocrat; **eu·ro·kra·tisch** [ɔʏro'kra:tıʃ] *adj.* Eurocratic

Eu·ro·pä·er [ɔʏro'pɛ:ɐ] *m* (-s; -) European; **eu·ro·pä·isch** [ɔʏro'pɛ:ıʃ] *adj.* European; ≈**e Gemeinschaft** European Community; ≈**er Gerichtshof** European Court of Justice, **für Menschenrechte:** European Court of Human Rights; ≈**es Parlament** European Parliament; → **Menschenrechtskommission**; **eu·ro·päi·sie·ren** [ɔʏropɛi'zi:rən] *v/t.* (h) Europeanize; **Eu·ro·päi'sie·rung** *f* (-; *no pl.*) Europeanization

Eu'ro·pa|mei·ster *m* European champion (*or* champions *pl.*); **~mei·ster·schaft** *f* European championships *pl.*; **~par·la,ment** *n* European Parliament; **~par·la·men,ta·ri·er** *m* Euro-MP; **~po,kal** *m* (*a.* **~ der Landesmeister**) European Cup; **~ der Pokalsieger** European Cup Winners' Cup; **~po·li,tik** *f* Europolitics *pl.*

Eu'ro·pa·rat *m* Council of Europe; **Eu'ro·pa·rats·sit·zung** *f* Council of Europe meeting

Eu'ro·pa·re,kord *m* European record

Eu'ro·pa·wah·len *pl.* Euro-elections

eu'ro·pa·weit **I.** *adj.* cross-Europe ..., Europe-wide; **II.** *adv.* Europe-wide, all over (*or* throughout) Europe

Eu·ro·scheck ['ɔʏro-] *m* Eurocheque; **~kar·te** *f* Eurocheque card

Eu·ro·vi·si·on [ɔʏrovi'zĭo:n] *f* (-; *no pl.*) *TV* Eurovision; **Eu·ro·vi·si'ons·sen·dung** *f* Eurovision broadcast

Eu·sta·chisch [ɔʏs'taxıʃ] *adj.*: *anat.* **~e Röhre** Eustachian tube

Eu·ter ['ɔʏtɐ] *n* (-s; -) udder

Eu·tha·na·sie [ɔʏtana'zi:] *f* (-; *no pl.*) euthanasia, mercy killing

eva·ku·ie·ren [evaku'i:rən] *v/t.* (h) evacuate (*a.* ⚕ *and phys.*); **Eva·ku'ie·rung** *f* (-; -en) evacuation

evan·ge·lisch [evaŋ'ge:lıʃ] *adj.* Protestant; **~-lutherisch** Lutheran; **~-reformiert** Reformed; **evan·ge·li·sie·ren** [evaŋgeli'zi:rən] *v/t.* (h) evangelize, convert to the Gospel; **Evan·ge·list** [evaŋge'lıst] *m* (-en; -en) evangelist; **Evan·ge·li·um** [evaŋ'ge:lĭʊm] *n* (-s; -lien) *bibl.* Gospel; *fig.* gospel; *fig.* **was s-e Schwester sagt, ist für ihn das ~** what his sister says is gospel to him

Evas·ko,stüm ['e:fas-, 'e:vas-] F *n*: **im ~** in the nude, F in one's birthday suit

Even·tua·li·tät [evɛntŭali'tɛ:t] *f* (-; -en) eventuality; **even·tu·ell** [evɛn'tŭɛl] **I.** *adj.* possible; any; **~e Beschwerden** any complaints (that might arise); **II.** *adv.* possibly; if necessary; should the occasion arise; *kommst du mit? -* **~** I might; **ich würde es ~ nehmen** I might (well) take it, I might consider taking it

evi·dent [evi'dɛnt] *adj.* obvious, clear; self-evident; **Evi·denz** [evi'dɛnts] *f* (-; *no pl.*) evident nature, obviousness (*gen.* of)

Evo·lu·ti·on [evolu'tsĭo:n] *f* (-; -en) evolution; **evo·lu·tio·när** [evolutsĭo'nɛ:ɐ] *adj.* evolutionary

Evo·lu·ti'ons|leh·re *f*, **~theo,rie** *f* Theory of Evolution

E-Werk *n* power station

EWG|-Land [e:ve:'ge:-] *n hist.* EEC country; **~-Mit·glied(s·staat** *m*) *n hist.* member of the EEC, EEC member state (*or* nation)

ewig ['e:vıç] **I.** *adj.* eternal; everlasting, perpetual *happiness, peace etc.*, *a.* undying *love, loyalty etc.*; endless; F eternal, constant, incessant; **der ~e Jude** the Wandering Jew; **die ~e Jugend** eternal youth; **das ~e Leben** eternal life, immortality; **~e Liebe** (**Treue**) **schwören** pledge one's eternal *or* undying love (loyalty); **~er Schnee** perennial snowfield; **die ≈e Stadt** (*Rome*) the Eternal City; F **~er Student** perennial student; **der ~e Verlierer** the perennial loser (*or* underdog); **seit ~en Zeiten** from (*or* since) time immemorial, F for ages; **~er Zweifler** *etc.* arch-sceptic (*Am.* -skeptic) *etc.*; **du mit d-r ~en Meckerei** *etc.* you never stop, do you?; **II.** *adv.* forever, eternally; **auf immer und ~** for ever and ever; **es ist ~ schade** it's just too bad; F **~** (**lange**) for ages; **ich habe dich ~** (**lange**) **nicht mehr gesehen** I haven't seen you for ages; **es dauert ~** it's taking ages; **er jammert ~** he never stops moaning; **Ewi·ge¹** ['e:vıgə] *m* (-n): **der ~** the Eternal, the Everlasting; **'Ewi·ge²** *n*: **das ~** the eternal; **'Ewig·ge·stri·ge** [-'gɛstrıgə] *m*, *f* (-n; -n) diehard; **'Ewig·keit** *f* (-; -en) eternity; **bis in alle ~** to the end of time; **in die ~ eingehen** pass into eternity; F **es ist e-e ~ her, seit** it's (*or* it's been) ages since; **ich wartete e-e ~** I waited for ages; **ewig·lich** ['e:vıklıç] *lit. adv.* eternally, for evermore

ex [ɛks] F *adv.* **1. ~ trinken** empty one's glass (in one go); **~!** F bottoms up!; **2.** all over; **3. ~ sein** F have had it

Ex... *in cpds.* ex-..., former ...

ex·akt [ɛ'ksakt] *adj.* precise, accurate; exact *translation*; scrupulous, *contp.* pernickety; **die ~en Wissenschaften** the exact sciences; **Ex'akt·heit** *f* (-; *no pl.*) precision, accuracy; exactitude; scrupulousness

ex·al·tiert [ɛksal'ti:ɐt] *adj.* **1.** (over-)excited; **2.** effusive; **Ex·al'tiert·heit** *f* (-; *no pl.*) **1.** (over-)excitement; **2.** effusion, effusiveness

Ex·amen [ɛ'ksa:mən] *n* (-s; Examina [ɛ'ksa:mina]) examination, exam; **~ ma-**

chen take one's exams (*or* finals); **Ex·amens·ar·beit** *f* extended essay

'Ex·dik,ta·tor *m* former dictator

Ex·ege·se [ɛkse'ge:zə] *f* (-; -n) exegesis; **Ex·eget** [ɛkse'ge:t] *m* (-en; -en) exegete; **Ex·ege·tik** [ɛkse'ge:tɪk] *f* exegetics *pl.*

exe·ku·tie·ren [ɛkseku'ti:rən] *v/t.* (h) execute; **Exe·ku·ti·on** [ɛkseku'tsĭo:n] *f* (-; -en) execution; **Exe·ku·ti'ons·be·fehl** *m* execution order

exe·ku·tiv [ɛkseku'ti:f] *adj.* executive; **Exe·ku'tiv·aus·schuß** *m pol.* executive committee; ☤ executive board; **Exe·ku·ti·ve** [ɛkseku'ti:və] *f* (-; -n) executive; **Exe·ku'tiv·ge·walt** *f* executive power(s *pl.*)

Ex·em·pel [ɛ'ksɛmpəl] *n* (-s; -) example; exemplum; ***die Probe aufs ~ machen*** put it to the test; → ***statuieren***

Ex·em·plar [ɛksɛm'pla:ʁ] *n* specimen; copy; issue; sample; **ex·em·pla·risch** [ɛksɛm'pla:rɪʃ] **I.** *adj.* exemplary; **II.** *adv.*: ***j-n ~ bestrafen*** make an example of s.o.

ex·er·zie·ren [ɛksɛr'tsi:rən] (h) **I.** *v/i.* ⚔ drill; **II.** *v/t.* ⚔ drill *s.o.*; practi|se (*Am.* -ce) *s.th.*; go through *s.th.*; **Ex·er·zier·platz** [ɛksɛr'tsi:ʁ-] *m* parade ground

Ex·er·zi·ti·en [ɛksɛr'tsi:tsĭən] *pl. eccl.* spiritual exercises

Ex·hi·bi·tio·nis·mus [ɛkshibitsĭo'nɪsmʊs] *m* (-; *no pl.*) exhibitionism; ⚖ indecent exposure; **Ex·hi·bi·tio·nist** [ɛkshibitsĭo'nɪst] *m* (-en; -en) exhibitionist, F flasher; **ex·hi·bi·tio·ni·stisch** [ɛkshibitsĭo'nɪstɪʃ] *adj.* exhibitionist

ex·hu·mie·ren [ɛkshu'mi:rən] *v/t.* (h) exhume; **Ex·hu'mie·rung** *f* (-; -en) exhumation

Exil [ɛ'ksi:l] *n* (-s; -e) exile; place of exile; ***im ~*** in exile; ***im ~ lebende Person*** exile, émigré; ***im südamerikanischen ~ leben*** live in exile (*or* as an exile) in South America; ***ins ~ gehen*** go into exile; ***ins ~ schicken*** exile; **~da·sein** *n* life in exile (*or* as an exile); **~deut·sche** *m, f etc.* German *etc.* exile (*or* émigré), exiled German *etc.*

exi·lie·ren [ɛksi'li:rən] *v/t.* (h) exile, send into exile

Exil|land *n* country (*or* place) of exile; **~li·te·ra,tur** *f* exilic (*or* émigré) literature; **~po,li·ti·ker** *m* exiled politician, statesman in exile; **~re,gie·rung** *f* government in exile; **~schrift·stel·ler** *m* exiled (*or* émigré) writer, writer in exile

exi·stent [ɛksɪs'tɛnt] *adj.* existent; ***~ sein*** exist; ***für ihn war das Problem einfach nicht ~*** as far as he was concerned the problem did not exist (*or* was non-existent)

Exi·sten·tia·lis·mus [ɛksɪstɛntsĭa'lɪsmʊs] *m* (-; *no pl.*) existentialism; **Exi·sten·tia·list** [ɛksɪstɛntsĭa'lɪst] *m* (-en; -en), **exi·sten·tia·li·stisch** [ɛksɪstɛntsĭa'lɪstɪʃ] *adj.* existentialist

exi·sten·ti·ell [ɛksɪstɛn'tsĭɛl] *adj.* **1.** existential; **2.** ***von ~er Bedeutung*** vitally important

Exi·stenz [ɛksɪs'tɛnts] *f* (-; -en) **1.** *no pl.* existence; life; living; ***sichere ~*** secure living; → ***aufbauen*** 7; **2.** *contp.* character; → ***verkracht***; **~angst** *f* **1.** fear for one's livelihood; **2.** *psych.* existential fear, angst; **≈be·rech·tigt** *adj.*: ***~ sein*** have the right to exist; **~be·rech·ti·gung** *f* (-; *no pl.*) right to exist; raison d'être; **≈fä·hig** *adj.* able to exist; ☤ *etc.* viable; **~kampf** *m* struggle for survival; **~mi·ni·mum** *n* subsistence level; ***knapp über dem ~ leben*** live on the poverty line (*or* breadline); **~mit·tel** *n* means *pl.* of existence

exi·stie·ren [ɛksɪs'ti:rən] *v/i.* (h) **1.** exist, be; be extant; ***davon ~ nur zwei*** there are only two of them (in existence *or* to be found); ***nur wenige ~ noch*** only a few have survived, there are only a few left; **2.** exist, live (***von*** *dat.* on)

Exi·tus ['ɛksitʊs] *m* (-; *no pl.*) ⚕ exitus, death

'Ex·kanz·ler *m* former chancellor (*or* prime minister)

Ex·kla·ve [ɛks'kla:və] *f* (-; -n) exclave

ex·klu·siv [ɛksklu'zi:f] *adj.* exclusive; ***~er Kreis*** select circle (*or* group)

Ex·klu'siv·be·richt *m* exclusive (story), scoop

ex·klu·si·ve [ɛksklu'zi:və] *prp.* (*gen.*) *and adv.* exclusive of, excluding, not counting, not including

Ex·klu'siv·in·ter·view *n* exclusive interview

Ex·klu·si·vi·tät [ɛkskluzivi'tɛ:t] *f* (-; *no pl.*) exclusiveness

Ex·klu'siv|mel·dung *f* scoop; **~rech·te** *pl.* sole (*or* exclusive) rights; **~ver·trag** *m* exclusive contract (*or* agreement)

Ex·kom·mu·ni·ka·ti·on [ɛkskɔmunika'tsĭo:n] *f* (-; -en) excommunication; **ex·kom·mu·ni·zie·ren** [ɛkskɔmuni'tsi:rən] *v/t.* (h) excommunicate

Ex·kre·men·te [ɛkskre'mɛntə] *pl.* excrement *sg.*

Ex·kret [ɛks'kre:t] *n* (-[e]s; -e), **Ex·kre·ti·on** [ɛkskre'tsĭo:n] *f* (-; -en) *physiol.* excretion

ex·kul·pie·ren [ɛkskʊl'pi:rən] *v/t.* (h) exculpate

Ex·kurs ['ɛkskʊrs] *m* (-es; -e) **1.** digression (***in*** *acc.* into); **2.** excursus

Ex·kur·si·on [ɛkskʊr'zĭo:n] *f* (-; -en) excursion, field trip

Ex·li·bris [ɛks'li:bri:s] *n* (-; -) ex libris, bookplate

ex·ma·tri·ku·lie·ren [ɛksmatriku'li:rən] (h) **I.** *v/refl.*: ***sich ~*** take one's name off the (university) register; **II.** *v/t.*: ***j-n ~*** take s.o.'s name off the (university) register

'Ex·mei·ster *m* former champion

'Ex·mi,ni·ster *m* former (government) minister

Ex·odus ['ɛksodʊs] *m* (-; *no pl.*) **1.** *bibl.* Exodus; **2.** *fig.* (mass) exodus

exo·gen [ɛkso'ge:n] *adj.* **1.** *biol.* exogenous; **2.** extraneous

Exo·karp [ɛkso'karp] *n* (-s; -e) ✿ exocarp

ex·or·bi·tant [ɛksɔrbi'tant] *adj.* excessive; exorbitant

Ex·or·zis·mus [ɛksɔr'tsɪsmʊs] *m* (-; -men) exorcism; **Ex·or·zist** [ɛksɔr'tsɪst] *m* (-en; -en) exorcist

Exot [ɛ'kso:t] *m* (-en; -en), **Ex·ote** [ɛ'kso:tə] *m* (-n; -n) **1.** stranger from a faraway place; F *fig.* flamboyant character; **2.** exotic animal; exotic (*or* tropical) plant; **3.** F exotic (car); **4.** F ☤ *pl.* unlisted papers; **exo·tisch** [ɛ'kso:tɪʃ] *adj.* exotic; tropical

Ex·pan·der [ɛks'pandɐ] *m* (-s; -) (chest) expander

ex·pan·die·ren [ɛkspan'di:rən] *v/i. and v/t.* (h) expand; **ex·pan'die·rend** *adj.* expanding, growing; **Ex·pan·si·on** [ɛkspan'zĭo:n] *f* (-; -en) expansion; **ex·pan·sio·ni·stisch** [ɛkspanzĭo'nɪstɪʃ] *adj. pol.* expansionist

Ex·pan·si'ons|be·stre·bun·gen *pl.*, **~drang** *m* expansionist tendencies *pl.*; **~kurs** *m*: ***auf ~ sein*** be on an expansion course; **~po·li,tik** *f* expansionism; **~ra·te** *f* rate of growth

ex·pan·siv [ɛkspan'zi:f] *adj. pol.* expansionary

ex·pe·die·ren [ɛkspe'di:rən] *v/t.* (h) dispatch, forward; F whisk *s.o.* off

Ex·pe·di·ti·on [ɛkspedi'tsĭo:n] *f* (-; -en) **1.** expedition; **2.** ☤ a) dispatch, forwarding, b) forwarding department; **3.** *obs.* (military) expedition

Ex·pe·di·ti'ons|korps *n* ⚔ expeditionary force; **~teil·neh·mer** *m* member of an (*or* the) expedition

Ex·pe·ri·ment [ɛksperi'mɛnt] *n* (-[e]s; -e) experiment; **ex·pe·ri·men·tal** [ɛksperimɛn'ta:l] *adj.* experimental

Ex·pe·ri·men'tal|phy,sik *f* experimental physics *pl.*; **~thea·ter** *n* experimental theat|re (*Am. a.* -er)

ex·pe·ri·men·tell [ɛksperimɛn'tɛl] *adj.* experimental

Ex·pe·ri·men'tier·büh·ne *f* experimental stage (*or* theat|re [*Am. a.* -er])

ex·pe·ri·men·tie·ren [ɛksperimɛn'ti:rən] *v/i.* (h) experiment (***an*** *dat.* on); **ex·pe·ri·men'tier·freu·dig** *adj.*: ***er ist sehr ~*** he likes to experiment (*or* try new things out)

Ex·pe·ri·men'tier|sta·di·um *n*: (***im ~*** in an) experimental state; **~thea·ter** *n* experimental theat|re (*Am. a.* -er)

Ex·per·te [ɛks'pɛrtə] *m* (-n; -n) expert; F pundit; ***die ~n*** the pundits

Ex'per·ten|gre·mi·um *n* panel of experts, brains trust; **~kon·fe,renz** *f* brains trust; **~kreis** *m*: ***in ~en heißt es(, daß)*** according to the experts; **~man·gel** *m* shortage of experts; **~team** *n* team of experts; **~wis·sen** *n* expert knowledge

Ex·per·ti·se [ɛkspɛr'ti:zə] *f* (-; -n) expertise, expert('s) opinion

ex·pli·zit [ɛkspli'tsi:t] **I.** *adj.* explicit; **II.** *adv.* explicitly; ***sie hat es nicht ~ gesagt*** *a.* she didn't say it in so many words

ex·plo·die·ren [ɛksplo'di:rən] *v/i.* (sn) explode (*a. fig.*); *fig. prices etc.*: *a.* go through the roof; *fig. person*: *a.* hit the roof; **Ex·plo·si·on** [ɛksplo'zĭo:n] *f* (-; -en) explosion (*a. fig.*); *fig.* flare-up; ***zur ~ bringen*** explode, detonate; **ex·plo·si'ons·ar·tig** *adj.* like an explosion; explosive *growth etc.*; ***~er Preisanstieg*** price explosion; ***~e Inflation*** runaway inflation; ***~es Bevölkerungswachstum*** population explosion

Ex·plo·si'ons|druck *m* (pressure of the) blast; **~ge·fahr** *f* danger of explosion; **~kraft** *f* explosive force; **~kra·ter** *m* bomb crater; *geol.* crater; **~mo·tor** *m* internal combustion engine; **≈si·cher** *adj.* explosion-proof; **~wel·le** *f* blast (wave)

ex·plo·siv [ɛksplo'zi:f] *adj.* explosive (*a. fig.*); *fig.* volatile; *fig.* ***~er Preisanstieg*** (***Kostenanstieg***) *a.* price (cost) explosion; **≈stoff** *m* explosive(s *pl.*)

Ex·po·nat [ɛkspo'na:t] *n* (-[e]s; -e) exhibit

Ex·po·nent [ɛkspo'nɛnt] *m* (-en; -en) 𝔄 exponent (*a. fig.*); *fig.* representative

Ex·po·nen·ti·al|funk·ti,on [ɛksponɛn'tsĭa:l-] *f* exponential function; **~glei·chung** *f* exponential equation; **~kur·ve** *f* exponential curve

ex·po·nen·ti·ell [ɛksponɛn'tsi̯ɛl] *adj.* (*and adv.*) exponential(ly)
ex·po·nie·ren [ɛkspo'ni:rən] (h) **I.** *v/t.* expose (*dat.* to); **II.** *v/refl.*: ***sich*** ~ expose o.s. (*dat.* to)
Ex·port [ɛks'pɔrt] *m* (-[e]s; -e) **1.** *no pl.* exportation, export(ing); **2.** exports *pl.*; **~ab͵tei·lung** *f* export department; **~ar͵ti·kel** *m* export article (*or* item), *pl. a.* exports; **~aus·füh·rung** *f* ⚙ export model; **~be·schrän·kun·gen** *pl.* export restraints
Ex·por·teur [ɛkspɔr'tø:ʁ] *m* (-s; -e) exporter
Ex'port|fir·ma *f* export(ing) firm (*or* company, business); **~ge·schäft** *n* **1.** → ***Exportfirma***; **2.** export transaction; **3.** → ***Exporthandel***; **~gü·ter** *pl.* exports, export(ed) goods; **~han·del** *m* export trade
ex·por·tie·ren [ɛkspɔr'ti:rən] *v/t.* (h) export (***nach*** *dat.* to)
Ex'port|in·du͵strie *f* export industry; **~kauf·mann** *m* export salesman; **~land** *n* exporting country; country of destination; **~lei·ter** *m* export manager; **~quo·te** *f* export share; **~͵über·schuß** *m* export surplus; **~wa·re** *f* export(ed) articles *pl.*
Ex·po·sé [ɛkspo'ze:] *n* (-s; -s) exposé; plan; outline of the plot
Ex·po·si·ti·on [ɛkspozi'tsi̯o:n] *f* (-; -en) exposition
'Ex·prä·si͵dent *m* former president; ~ ***Reagan*** (the) former US president (Mr) Ronald Reagan
'Ex·pre·mier·mi͵ni·ster *m* former prime minister
ex·preß [ɛks'prɛs] *adv.*: ~ ***schicken*** send express (*Am.* by special delivery)
Ex'preß|brief *m* → ***Eilbrief***; **~fahr·stuhl** *m* high-speed lift; **~gut** *n* express goods *pl.*
Ex·pres·sio·nis·mus [ɛksprɛsi̯o'nɪsmʊs] *m* (-; *no pl.*) Expressionism; **Ex·pres·sio·nist** [ɛksprɛsi̯o'nɪst] *m* (-en; -en) Expressionist; **ex·pres·sio·ni·stisch** [ɛksprɛsi̯o'nɪstɪʃ] *adj.* expressionist(ic); *art*: Expressionist
ex·pres·siv [ɛksprɛ'si:f] *adj.* expressive
Ex'preß·lift *m* high-speed lift
ex·qui·sit [ɛkskvi'zi:t] *adj.* exquisite, choice ...
ex tem·po·re [ɛks 'tɛmpore] *adv.* off the cuff; ~ ***sprechen*** *a.* ad lib, improvise; **Ex'tem·po·re** *n* (-s; -s) improvisation, ad lib; **ex·tem·po·rie·ren** [ɛkstɛmpo'ri:rən] *v/t. and v/i.* improvise, ad lib
ex·ten·siv [ɛkstɛn'zi:f] *adj.* extensive
Ex·te·rieur [ɛkste'ri̯ø:ʁ] *n* (-s; -s, -e [-rə]) exterior
ex·tern [ɛks'tɛrn] *adj.* external; outside; **~er Schüler** day pupil
ex·ter·ri·to·ri·al [ɛkstɛrito'ri̯a:l] *adj.* extraterritorial
ex·tra ['ɛkstra] **I.** *adj.* extra; **II.** *adv.* separately; extra; specially; on purpose; ~ ***für dich*** just (*or* specially) for you; ***ich habe es*** ~ ***mitgebracht*** I brought it specially; **III.** ♀ *n* (-s; -s) (optional) extra, option
'Ex·tra|aus·stat·tung *f mot.* optional extras *pl.*, options *pl.*; **~blatt** *n* supplement; extra
'ex·tra·fein *adj.* extra-fine
ex·tra·hie·ren [ɛkstra'hi:rən] *v/t.* (h) extract
'Ex·tra·klas·se F *f*: ***ein Film*** (***Wagen***) ***der*** ~ a first-rate film (a top-line model); ***das ist*** ~ F that's great
ex·tra·kor·po·ral [ɛkstrakɔrpo'ra:l] *adj.*: **~e Befruchtung** in vitro fertilization
Ex·trakt [ɛks'trakt] *m* (-[e]s; -e) extract
Ex·trak·ti·on [ɛkstrak'tsi̯o:n] *f* (-; -en) extraction
Ex·tra·or·di·na·ri·us [ɛkstraɔrdi'na:ri̯ʊs] *m univ.* associate professor
'Ex·tra·tour F *f* something special (*or* extra)
ex·tra·va·gant [ɛkstrava'gant] *adj.* outré; flamboyant; **Ex·tra·va·ganz** [ɛkstrava'gants] *f* (-; -en) flamboyance, flamboyant nature (*gen.* of)
ex·tra·ver·tiert [ɛkstravɛr'ti:ʁt] *adj.* (*a.* **~e Person**) extrovert; **Ex·tra·ver'tiert·heit** *f* (-; *no pl.*) extroversion, extrovert nature (*gen.* of)
'Ex·tra·wurst F *f* special treatment; ***ich kann dir nicht immer e-e*** ~ ***braten*** F you can't have everything with jam on it, you know; ***sie will immer e-e*** ~ ***gebraten haben*** she wants everything with jam on it
ex·trem [ɛks'tre:m] **I.** *adj.* extreme; *pol. a.* radical; ***er ist ein bißchen*** ~ *a.* he tends to go to extremes, he takes things a bit too far; **II.** *adv.* extremely, F incredibly; ~ ***kalt*** *a.* freezing cold; **III.** ♀ *n* (-s; -e) extreme; ***bis zum*** ~ to the extreme; ***von einem*** ~ ***ins andere fallen*** go from one extreme to the other; **Ex'trem·fall** *m*: (***im*** ~ in an) extreme case
Ex·tre·mis·mus [ɛkstre'mɪsmʊs] *m* (-; -men) extremism; **Ex·tre·mist** [ɛkstre'mɪst] *m* (-en; -en) extremist; **Ex·tre'mi·sten·grup·pe** *f* extremist group, group of extremists; **ex·tre·mi·stisch** [ɛkstre'mɪstɪʃ] *adj.* extremist
Ex·tre·mi·tä·ten [ɛkstremi'tɛ:tən] *pl.* extremities
Ex'trem·si·tua·ti͵on *f* extreme situation
ex·tro·ver·tiert [ɛkstrovɛr'ti:ʁt] *adj.* → ***extravertiert***
ex·zel·lent [ɛktsɛ'lɛnt] *adj.* excellent; exquisite; ***er ist ein*** **~er Kenner** *gen.* he's an expert in, he has an excellent knowledge of
Ex·zel·lenz [ɛktsɛ'lɛnts] *f*: ***Eure*** (***Seine***) ~ your (his) Excellency
Ex·zen·tri·ker [ɛks'tsɛntrikʁ] *m* (-s; -) eccentric; **ex·zen·trisch** [ɛks'tsɛntrɪʃ] *adj.* **1.** eccentric; **2.** ♞, ⚙ eccentric, off-cent|re (*Am.* -er); **Ex·zen·tri·zi·tät** [ɛkstsɛntritsi'tɛ:t] *f* (-; -en) **1.** a) *no pl.* eccentricity; b) **~en** eccentric behavio(u)r; **2.** ♞ eccentricity; ⚙ *a.* off-cent|re (*Am.* -er) position
ex·zer·pie·ren [ɛkstsɛr'pi:rən] *v/t.* (h) extract; excerpt, make extracts from *a book etc.*; **Ex·zerpt** [ɛks'tsɛrpt] *n* (-[e]s; -e) extract
Ex·zeß [ɛks'tsɛs] *m* (-sses; -sse) **1.** excess; ***et. bis zum*** ~ ***treiben*** go to extremes with s.th.; ***bis zum*** ~ ad nauseam; **2. *es kam zu wilden Exzessen*** there were violent incidents; **ex·zes·siv** [ɛkstsɛ'si:f] **I.** *adj.* excessive; exaggerated; **II.** *adv.* excessively, to excess; ***et.*** ~ ***betreiben*** go to extremes with s.th.

F

F, f [ɛf] *n* (-; -) F, f; ♪ F; → *Schema*

Fa·bel [ˈfaːbəl] *f* (-; -n) fable (*a. fig.*); plot, story; *fig.* tall story; ***das gehört ins Reich der*** ~ that's pure fabrication; **~dich·ter** *m* writer of fables; **~ge·stalt** *f* **1.** figure from a fable; **2.** → *Fabelwesen*
1

ˈfa·bel·haft I. *adj.* fantastic, wonderful; **II.** *adv.* fantastically, wonderfully; ***es hat*** ~ ***geklappt*** it worked out fantastic(ally) *or* super; ***du hast*** ~ ***gekocht*** it was a wonderful meal

ˈFa·bel|tier *n* fabulous (*or* mythical) beast *or* creature; **~welt** *f* **1.** world of fable; **2.** fantasy (*or* fairytale) world; **~we·sen** *n* **1.** mythical figure (*or* creature); **2.** → *Fabeltier*

Fa·brik [faˈbriːk] *f* (-; -en) factory; works *pl.*; **~an·la·ge** *f* (manufacturing) plant

Fa·bri·kant [fabriˈkant] *m* (-en; -en) factory owner; manufacturer

Faˈbrik|ar·beit *f* **1.** factory work; **2.** → *Fabrikware*; **~ar·bei·ter** *m* factory worker

Fa·bri·kat [fabriˈkaːt] *n* (-[e]s; -e) **1.** make; brand; **2.** product

Fa·bri·ka·ti·on [fabrikaˈtsi̯oːn] *f* (-; -en) production; ***in*** (***die***) ~ ***geben*** put *s.th.* into production

Fa·bri·ka·tiˈons|feh·ler *m* (factory) flaw *or* defect; **~ge·heim·nis** *n* industrial secret; **~ko·sten** *pl.* production costs (*or* cost *sg.*); **~num·mer** *f* serial number; **~zweig** *m* line of production

Faˈbrik|be·sit·zer *m* factory owner; **~diˌrek·tor** *m* works manager; **≈fer·tig** *adj.* prefabricated; **≈frisch** *adj.* ... straight from the factory; ~ ***sein*** *a.* have come straight from the factory; **~ge·bäu·de** *n* factory building; **~ge·län·de** *n* factory site; **~hal·le** *f* factory building; **≈neu** *adj.* brand-new; **~num·mer** *f* serial number; **~preis** *m* factory price; price ex works; **~schiff** *n* factory ship; **~schorn·stein** *m* factory chimney; (industrial) smoke stack; **~stadt** *f* manufacturing town; **~wa·re** *f* manufactured article (*coll.* goods *pl.*)

fa·bri·zie·ren [fabriˈtsiːrən] F *v/t.* (h) **1.** cobble together; concoct; **2.** get up to

fa·bu·lie·ren [fabuˈliːrən] (h) **I.** *v/i.* tell stories; **II.** *v/t.* tell

Fa·cet·te [faˈsɛtə] *f* (-; -n) facet (*a. fig.*); **faˈcet·ten·ar·tig** *adj.* facet(t)ed; **Faˈcet·ten·au·ge** *n zo.* compound eye; **faˈcet·ten·reich** *adj.* many-facet(t)ed; **Faˈcet·ten·schliff** *m* facet(t)ing, facets *pl.*; ***Rubin mit*** ~ facet(t)ed ruby

Fach [fax] *n* (-[e]s; Fächer [ˈfɛçɐ]) **1.** compartment; pigeonhole; shelf; **2.** subject; field; job; line (of business); ***er ist vom*** ~ he's an expert; ***Musiker vom*** ~ professional musician; ***sein*** ~ ***verstehen*** know one's job (F stuff); ***das ist*** (***nicht***) ***mein*** ~ that's right up my street (that's not my line)

...fach *in cpds.* ...fold; ... times; → *dreifach, zweifach*

ˈFach|aka·deˌmie *f* technical (*or* vocational) college; **~ar·beit** *f* **1.** skilled work; **2.** paper

ˈFach·ar·bei·ter *m* skilled worker; *pl.* skilled labo(u)r *sg.*; **~brief** *m* skilled worker's certificate

ˈFach·arzt *m* (medical) specialist (***für*** *acc.* in); **ˈfach·ärzt·lich** *adj.* (*adv.* by a) specialist

ˈFach|aus·bil·dung *f* special(ized) *or* professional training; **~aus·druck** *m* technical term; ***medizinischer*** ~ medical term; **~aus·schuß** *m* committee of experts; **~be·ra·ter** *m* technical adviser, consultant; **~be·reich** *m* **1.** faculty, *Am.* department, school; **2.** → *Fachgebiet*; **~blatt** *n* (professional *or* specialist) journal, periodical; **~buch** *n* specialist book (*pl. a.* literature *sg.*); ***medizinisches*** *etc.* ~ medical *etc.* book; **~chiˌne·sisch** F *n* (technical) jargon, F gobbledygook

fä·cheln [ˈfɛçəln] (h) **I.** *v/t.* fan; *wind:* waft against (*or* through); **II.** *v/i. leaves etc.*: flutter; *breeze:* waft (***über*** *acc.* through)

Fä·cher [ˈfɛçɐ] *m* (-s; -) fan; *fig.* array; **~anˌten·ne** *f* fan aerial (*or* antenna); **≈ar·tig, ≈för·mig** [-fœrmɪç] **I.** *adj.* fan-shaped, fan-like; **II.** *adv.*: ***sich*** ~ ***ausbreiten*** (*or* ***verteilen*** *etc.*) fan out; **~kom·bi·na·tiˌon** *f* combination of studies

fä·chern [ˈfɛçɐn] *v/t. and v/refl.* (***sich*** ~) (h) fan out

ˈFach|fra·ge *f* technical question; question for the experts; **~frau** *f* expert (***in*** *dat.* in, at; ***für*** *acc.* on), specialist (in); authority (on); **≈fremd** *adj.* **1.** unrelated (to one's field); **2.** unqualified; **~ge·biet** *n* (special) field; **~ge·lehr·te** *m, f* (-n; -n) expert, specialist; **≈ge·mäß, ≈ge·recht** *adj.* skilled, professional; **~ge·schäft** *n* specialist shop (*Am.* store); **~ge·spräch** *n*: ***das*** (*or* ***ein***) ~ shop talk (*a. pl.*); **~han·del** *m* specialized trade (*or* dealers *pl.*); **~händ·ler** *m* specialist dealer; **~hoch·schu·le** *f* advanced technical college; **~idiˌot** *m* narrow specialist; **~in·geˌnieur** *m* specialist engineer; **~jarˌgon** *m* (technical) jargon; **~ju·ry** *f* panel of experts; **~kennt·nis(se** *pl.*) *f* knowledge (of the *or* a subject); specialist knowledge; expertise; ***Fachkenntnisse erwerben*** *a.* gain some background knowledge; ***mir fehlen die Fachkenntnisse*** I haven't got the expertise; ***sie hat sehr gute*** ~ she knows a lot about the subject; **~kolˌle·ge** *m* colleague (in the field); **~kom·peˌtenz** *f* professional competence; expertise; **~konˌgreß** *m* specialist (*or* trade) conference; **~kräf·te** *pl.* skilled labo(u)r *sg.*; qualified personnel *sg.*; **~kreis** *m*: ***in*** ~***en*** among the experts; ***in*** ~***en heißt es*** the experts say (*or* claim); ***in medizinischen*** ~***en*** in medical circles; **≈kun·dig** *adj.* competent; expert; skilled; **~leh·rer** *m* (subject) teacher; (***er ist***) ~ ***für Englisch*** (he's an) English teacher; **~leu·te** *pl.* experts

ˈfach·lich I. *adj.* professional, specialized; ~***es Können*** competence *or* ability (in a *or* the field); **II.** *adv.*: ~ ***qualifiziert*** (*or* ***ausgebildet***) trained, qualified; ***sich*** ~ ***weiterbilden*** do further training, extend one's qualifications (in a *or* the field)

ˈFach·li·te·raˌtur *f* specialized literature

ˈFach·mann *m* (-[e]s; -leute) expert (***in*** *dat.* in, at; ***für*** *acc.* on), specialist (in); authority (on); **ˈfach·män·nisch** [-mɛnɪʃ] *adj.* expert, specialist ...; professional; ~***es Auge*** expert's eye; ~***es Urteil*** expert opinion; ***unter der*** ~***en Leitung von*** under the expert guidance of

ˈFach|mes·se *f* trade fair; **~ober·schu·le** *f* technical college; **~per·soˌnal** *n* qualified personnel; **~pres·se** *f* trade press; **~rich·tung** *f* field (of study)

ˈFach·schaft *f* (-; -en) **1.** professional association; **2.** *univ.* students *pl.* of a department; student representatives *pl.*

ˈFach·schu·le *f* technical college

Fach·sim·pe·lei [faxzɪmpəˈlaɪ] *f* (-; -en) shop talk; **fach·sim·peln** [ˈfaxzɪmpəln] *v/i.* (fachsimpelte, gefachsimpelt, h) talk shop

ˈfach·speˌzi·fisch *adj.* specialist ...

ˈFach|spra·che *f* technical language (*or* jargon); specialist terminology; ***juristische*** ~ legal jargon (*or* terminology); ***in der juristischen*** ~ ***heißt es*** the legal term is; **≈sprach·lich I.** *adj.* specialized, technical; ~***er Ausdruck*** technical term; **II.** *adv.* ~ ***ausgedrückt*** (to put it) in technical terms; **~stu·di·um** *n* degree; **~text** *m* specialist paper (*or* article *etc.*); ***medizinischer*** ~ medical paper *etc.*; **~überˌset·zer** *m* specialist (*or* technical) translator; ***er ist*** ~ ***für Medizin*** he specializes in medical translation(s); **~überˌset·zung** *f* specialist (*or* technical) translation; **~ver·band** *m* trade association; professional association; **~welt** *f*: (***in der*** ~ among the) experts *pl.*; ***die*** ~ ***behauptet*** experts claim

ˈFach·werk *n* (-[e]s; *no pl.*) half-timbering; **~bau** *m* **1.** half-timbered (*or* timber-framed) house; **2.** half-timbering; **~bau·wei·se** *f* → *Fachwerkbau* 2; **~haus** *n* half-timbered (*or* timber-framed) house

ˈFach|wis·sen *n* → *Fachkenntnis*(*se*); **~wör·ter·buch** *n* specialized (*or* special-

ist) dictionary; **~zeit·schrift** *f* (professional *or* specialist) journal, periodical; trade journal
Fackel ['fakəl] (*sep.* -k·k-) *f* (-; -n) torch; **'fackeln** (*sep.* -k·k-) F *fig. v/i.* (h) dither, F shilly-shally; ***los, nicht lange ~!*** stop dithering; come on, get on with it; ***er fackelte nicht lange*** he didn't waste any time
'Fackel|schein *m* torchlight; **~trä·ger** *m* torchbearer; **~zug** *m* torchlight procession
fad [fa:t], **fa·de** ['fa:də] *adj.* tasteless, insipid; stale; flat *beer*; dull *colo(u)r*; *fig.* dull, boring; ***fade schmecken*** have no taste; *fig.* ***fader Kerl*** bore; ***e-e fade Sache*** F a (real) drag
fä·deln ['fɛ:dəln] *v/t.* (h) thread
Fa·den ['fa:dən] *m* (-s; Fäden ['fɛ:dən]) thread (*a. fig.*); ✠ stitch; ⚡, ⚙ filament; *a. fig.*: string; ✠ ***die Fäden ziehen*** take out (*or* remove) the stitches; *fig.* ***der rote ~*** the central thread; ***den ~ verlieren*** lose one's thread; ***den ~ wiederaufnehmen*** pick up the thread; ***es hing an e-m (seidenen) ~*** it was hanging by a thread; ***er hatte keinen trockenen ~ am Leib*** he was soaked to the skin; ***sie ließ keinen guten ~ an ihm*** she tore him to shreds, she didn't have a good word to say about him; ***die Fäden laufen in s-r Hand zusammen*** he's in control of everything, he's at the controls; ***er hat die Fäden fest in der Hand*** he's got a tight grip on things; **~hef·tung** *f typ.* (thread) sewing; **~kreuz** *n opt.* reticule, *a. computer*: crosshairs *pl.*; *fig.* ***im ~ haben*** have *s.o. or s.th.* in one's sights; **~nu·deln** *pl.* vermicelli *pl.*
'fa·den·schei·nig [-ʃaɪnɪç] *adj.* **1.** flimsy, weak *excuse etc.*; **2.** shabby, threadbare
'Fa·den·wurm *m* threadworm, 📖 nematode
'Fad·heit *f* (-; *no pl.*) tastelessness; staleness; *fig.* dullness
Fa·gott [fa'gɔt] *n* (-[e]s; -e) ♪ bassoon; **Fa·got·tist** [fagɔ'tɪst] *m* (-en; -en) bassoonist
fä·hig ['fɛ:ɪç] *adj.* capable (**zu *et.*** of s.th.; **zu** *inf.* of *ger.*), able (to *inf.*); capable; talented; ***er ist ein ~er Kopf*** he's a clever man; ***er ist zu allem ~*** he's capable of anything, he'll stop at nothing, *criminal etc.*: he's desperate; **'Fä·hig·keit** *f* (-; -en) ability; capability; talent; capacity; ***bei d-n ~en*** with your ability; ***sie hat die ~ zur dauerhaften Konzentration*** she has the ability (*or* she's able) to concentrate for long periods of time
fahl [fa:l] *adj.* pale (and wan), wan; **'fahl·gelb** *adj.* pale yellow; **'Fahl·heit** *f* (-; *no pl.*) paleness, wanness
Fähn·chen ['fɛ:nçən] *n* (-s; -) **1.** (little) flag; pennant; *sport*: marker; *fig.* ***sein ~nach dem Wind drehen*** swim with the tide; **2.** F cheap, flimsy dress, F rag
fahn·den ['fa:ndən] *v/i.* (h): **~ *nach*** *dat.* search for; **Fahn·der** ['fa:ndɐ] *m* (-s; -) investigator; **Fahn·dung** ['fa:ndʊŋ] *f* (-; -en) search
'Fahn·dungs|ak·ti,on *f* (police) search; **~fo·to** *n* police portrait, F mugshot; **~li·ste** *f* wanted persons list; ***auf der ~ stehen*** be wanted by the police; **~stel·le** *f* tracing and search department
Fah·ne ['fa:nə] *f* (-; -n) **1.** flag; *esp. fig.* banner; ⚔, ⚓ colo(u)rs *pl.*; *fig.* ***die ~ hochhalten*** keep the flag flying; → ***fliegend***; **2.** F ***e-e ~ haben*** smell of drink, reek of alcohol; **3.** *typ.* (galley) proof
'Fah·nen|ab·zug *m typ.* galley (proof); **~eid** *m* oath of allegiance
'Fah·nen·flucht *f* desertion; **'fah·nen·flüch·tig** *adj.*: **~ *sein*** be a deserter; **~ *werden*** desert; **'Fah·nen·flüch·ti·ge** *m* (-n; -n) deserter
'Fah·nen|kor·rek,tur *f typ.* proofreading of galleys; **~mast** *m*, **~stan·ge** *f* flagpole; **~trä·ger** *m* standard-bearer (*a. fig.*); **~tuch** *n* bunting
Fähn·rich ['fɛ:nrɪç] *m* (-s; -e) ⚔ cadet; ⚓ **~ *zur See*** midshipman
Fahr·aus·weis ['fa:ɐ-] *m* ticket
Fahr·bahn ['fa:ɐ-] *f* (-; -en) road, carriageway; lane; **~mar,kie·rung** *f* lane markings *pl.*; **~rand** *m* edge of the road; (hard) shoulder; ***fahren Sie am äußersten rechten ~*** keep to the edge of the inside lane (*Am.* to the extreme right)
fahr·bar ['fa:ɐba:ɐ] *adj.* mobile, travel(l)ing *library etc.*; *bed etc.* on wheels; movable *stage*; → ***Untersatz***
fahr·be·reit ['fa:ɐ-] *adj.* in running order; ready to start; **'Fahr·be·reit·schaft** *f* (-; -en) car pool
Fähr·boot ['fɛ:ɐ-] *n* ferryboat
Fäh·re ['fɛ:rə] *f* (-; -n) ferry
Fahr·ei·gen·schaf·ten ['fa:ɐ-] *pl.* road performance *sg.*
fah·ren (fuhr, gefahren) **I.** *v/i.* (sn) a) go (***mit*** *dat.* by); *esp. mot.*: drive; ride *bicycle etc.*; ⚓ sail; run; b) leave, go; c) be moving; ***rechts ~!*** keep to the right; ***an den Straßenrand ~*** pull over to the side; ***sie fährt gut (schlecht)*** she's a good (not a very good) driver; ***nach Köln fährt man sieben Stunden*** it's a seven-hour drive to Cologne, 🚂 it's a seven-hour train journey to Cologne, it's seven hours on the train to Cologne; *das Boot, der Zug* ***fährt zweimal am Tag*** runs (*or* goes) twice a day; ***mit der Bahn ~*** go by train; ***erster Klasse ~*** go first class; ***mit dem Bus ~*** go (*or* travel) by bus, take a (*or* the) bus; ***über e-n Fluß (Platz*** *etc.*) **~** cross a river (square *etc.*); ***mit der Hand ~ über*** *acc.* run one's hand over; **~ *in*** *acc. bullet, knife etc.*: go into; *fig.* ***gut (schlecht) ~ bei*** *dat.* do well (badly) by *s.th.*; ***er ist sehr gut (schlecht) dabei gefahren*** he did very well (badly) out of it; ***was ist in ihn gefahren?*** what's got into him?; ***plötzlich fuhr mir der Gedanke durch den Kopf, daß*** it suddenly occurred to me that; ***der Schreck fuhr ihm durch alle Glieder*** he froze with terror; F ***einen ~ lassen*** F let off; → ***Boot, Haut***; **II.** *v/t.* (h) drive; ride *bicycle etc.*; ⚓ sail; row; take, drive, transport; cover, travel *distance etc.*; run, do *race*; make, clock *time*; *computer*: run *program*; ***auf den Grund ~*** run aground; ***das Auto fährt 120 km/h*** the car does 120 kph; ***auf dieser Straße fährt es sich gut*** this is a good road to drive on; **'fah·rend** *adj.* moving; travel(l)ing, itinerant; **~*er Ritter*** knight errant; **~*es Volk*** vagrants
Fah·ren·heit ['fa:rənhaɪt] *n* (-; *no pl.*) (***30 Grad ~*** 30 degrees) Fahrenheit; **~ska·la** *f* Fahrenheit scale
'fah·ren·las·sen F *v/t.* (*irr.*, *sep.*, fahrengelassen, h, → ***lassen***) give up, abandon
Fah·rer ['fa:rɐ] *m* (-s; -) driver; chauffeur; motorcyclist; cyclist
Fah·re·rei [fa:rə'raɪ] *f* (-; *no pl.*) driving (*or* travel[l]ing) (around); ***diese ~!*** all this driving (*or* travel[l]ing)
'Fah·rer|flucht *f* hit-and-run offen|ce (*Am.* -se); **~ *begehen*** flee from the scene of the accident, ⚖ commit a hit-and-run offen|ce (*Am.* -se); **~haus** *n* driver's cab
fah·re·risch ['fa:rərɪʃ] *adj.*: **~*es Können*** driving skill(s)
'Fah·rer·ka,bi·ne *f* driver's cab
Fahr·er·laub·nis ['fa:ɐ-] *f* driving licence, *Am.* driver's license
'Fah·rer|sitz *m* driver's seat; **~tür** *f* driver's door
Fahr·gast ['fa:ɐ-] *m* passenger; **~raum** *m* passenger area; **~schiff** *n* passenger ship
Fahr·ge·fühl ['fa:ɐ-] *n* (-[e]s; *no pl.*) driving experience; driving skill; ***das ist ein ~!*** that's what I call driving
Fahr·geld ['fa:ɐ-] *n* fare; **~zu·schuß** *m* travel allowance
Fahr|ge·le·gen·heit ['fa:ɐ-] *f* means of transport(ation); **~ge·mein·schaft** *f* car pool, *pl. a.* car sharing *sg.*, *Am.* ride sharing *sg.*; **~ge·schwin·dig·keit** *f* speed
Fahr·ge·stell ['fa:ɐ-] *n* **1.** *mot.* chassis; ✈ undercarriage; **2.** F *fig.* F pins *pl.*; **~num·mer** *f* chassis number
fah·rig ['fa:rɪç] *adj.* erratic; nervous; uncontrolled; inattentive; ***er ist furchtbar ~*** he can't concentrate on anything
Fahr·kar·te ['fa:ɐ-] *f* ticket; ***e-e ~ lösen*** buy a ticket (***nach*** *dat.* to)
'Fahr·kar·ten|aus·ga·be *f* ticket office; **~au·to,mat** *m* ticket machine; **~ent·wer·ter** *m* ticket-cancel(l)ing machine; **~kon,trol·le** *f* ticket inspection; **~kon·trol,leur** *m* ticket inspector; **~schal·ter** *m* ticket office
Fahr·kom,fort ['fa:ɐ-] *m mot.* ride comfort
Fahr·ko·sten ['fa:ɐ-] *pl.* travel(l)ing (*or* travel) costs; **~zu·schuß** *m* travel(l)ing allowance
Fahr·kunst ['fa:ɐ-] *f a. pl.* driving skill
fahr·läs·sig ['fa:ɐlɛsɪç] *adj.* careless, *a.* ⚖ negligent, reckless; **~*e Tötung*** (involuntary) manslaughter, *Am.* negligent homicide; **'Fahr·läs·sig·keit** *f* (-; *no pl.*) carelessness, *a.* ⚖ negligence, recklessness; ***grobe ~*** gross negligence
Fahr|leh·rer ['fa:ɐ-] *m* driving instructor; **~lei·stung** *f* road performance
Fähr|leu·te ['fɛ:ɐ-] *pl.* ferrymen, ferry workers; **~mann** *m* ferryman
Fahr·plan ['fa:ɐ-] *m* timetable (*a. fig.*), *esp. Am.* schedule; ***du kannst nicht nach dem ~ gehen*** you can't rely on the timetable (*or* schedule); **~än·de·rung** *f* change in (the) timetable (*or* schedule); **≈mä·ßig I.** *adj.* scheduled; **II.** *adv.* on time, according to schedule; ***der Zug fährt ~ ab (kommt ~ an) um 12 Uhr*** the train is scheduled to leave (is due) at 12 o'clock
Fahr·pra·xis ['fa:ɐ-] *f* (-; *no pl.*) driving experience; experience behind the wheel
Fahr·preis ['fa:ɐ-] *m* fare; **~er·hö·hung** *f* fare increase, increase in fares; **~er·mä·ßi·gung** *f* fare discount
Fahr·prü·fung ['fa:ɐ-] *f* driving test
Fahr·rad ['fa:ɐra:t] *n* bicycle, F bike; **~fah·rer** *m* cyclist; **~ket·te** *f* bicycle chain; **~lam·pe** *f* bicycle lamp; **~pum·pe** *f* bicycle pump; **~rei·fen** *m* bicycle tyre (*Am* tire); **~schlauch** *m* inner tube; **~stän·der** *m* bicycle stand; **~tour** *f* bicycle (*or* cycling) tour; **~weg** *m* cycle path
Fahr·rin·ne ['fa:ɐ-] *f* shipping lane

Fahr·schein ['faːɐ-] *m* ticket; **~ent·wer·ter** *m* ticket-cancel(l)ing machine; **~heft** *n* book of tickets

Fahr|schu·le ['faːɐ-] *f* driving school; **~schü·ler** *m* **1.** learner (driver); **2.** *ped.* non-local pupil; **~si·cher·heit** *f* (-; *no pl.*) road safety; (safe) driving; **~spaß** *m* driving pleasure; **~spur** *f* lane; **~strecke** *f* **1.** route; **2.** distance ([to be] covered); **~strei·fen** *m* lane; **~stuhl** *m* lift, *Am.* elevator; ***mit dem ~ fahren*** take the lift (*Am.* elevator); **~stun·de** *f* driving lesson

Fahrt [faːɐt] *f* (-; -en) **1.** *mot.* drive, ride; journey, trip; outing; *skiing*: run; ***gute ~!*** have a good trip; ***e-e ~ nach Rom machen*** make (*or* go on) a trip to Rome; ***während der ~*** *nicht aus dem Fenster lehnen etc.* while the train (*or* bus *etc.*) is in motion (*or* moving); ***auf der ~ nach X*** on the way to X; ***jetzt habe ich freie ~*** the road's clear now, *fig.* there's nothing to stop me now; → ***Blau***; **2.** speed; ***~ aufnehmen*** pick up (speed); ***in voller ~*** (at) full speed; ***in ~ kommen*** get under way, F *fig.* get going; *fig.* ***in ~ bringen*** get *s.o. or s.th.* going; ***in ~ sein*** be in full swing, be going it strong, F be going wild

fahr·taug·lich ['faːɐ-] *adj.* → ***fahrtüchtig***; **'Fahr·taug·lich·keit** *f* → ***Fahrtüchtigkeit***

'Fahrt|aus·weis *m* ticket; **~dau·er** *f* length of the trip; ***die ~ beträgt etwa drei Stunden*** it will take approximately three hours (to get there)

Fähr·te ['fɛːɐtə] *f* (-; -n) trail (*a. fig.*); *fig.* ***j-n von der ~ abbringen*** throw s.o. off the scent; ***auf der richtigen*** (***falschen***) ***~ sein*** be on the right (wrong) track

Fahr·tech·nik ['faːɐ-] *f* driving technique

'Fahr·ten|buch *n mot.* logbook; **~mes·ser** *n* hunting knife; **~schrei·ber** *m* tachograph

'Fahrt|ko·sten *pl.* **1.** → ***Fahrkosten***; **2.** fare; **~rich·tung** *f* direction; 🚂 ***in ~ fahren*** (*or* ***sitzen***) sit facing the engine, ride forwards; ***mit dem Rücken zur ~ fahren*** (*or* ***sitzen***) sit with one's back to the engine, ride backwards

fahr·tüch·tig ['faːɐ-] *adj. mot.* roadworthy; fit to drive; **'Fahr·tüch·tig·keit** *f mot.* roadworthiness; suitability for driving (*or* as a driver)

'Fahrt|un·ter,bre·chung *f* stop, *Am. a.* stopover; **~wind** *m* airstream

fahr·un·taug·lich ['faːɐ-] *adj.* → ***fahruntüchtig***; **'Fahr·un·taug·lich·keit** *f* → ***Fahruntüchtigkeit***

fahr·un·tüch·tig ['faːɐ-] *adj. mot.* not roadworthy; unfit to drive; **'Fahr·un·tüch·tig·keit** *f* (-; *no pl.*) *mot.* unroadworthiness; unsuitability for driving (*or* as a driver)

Fahr|ver·bot ['faːɐ-] *n* **1.** suspension of *s.o.'s* driving licence (*Am.* driver's license); ***ein ~ erhalten*** be banned from driving; **2.** ban on driving; ***Lastwagen haben sonntags*** (***auf der Autobahn***) ***~*** lorries (*or* trucks) aren't allowed on the roads (aren't allowed to use the autobahn) on Sundays; **~ver·hal·ten** *n* **1.** behavio(u)r behind the wheel; **2.** *mot.* road behavio(u)r; **~was·ser** *n* **1.** waterway; **2.** *fig.* element; ***im richtigen*** (*or* ***in s-m***) ***~ sein*** be in one's element; ***in ein politisches ~ geraten*** take a political turn; ***in j-s ~ geraten*** (***schwimmen***) come (be) under s.o.'s spell; **~wei·se** *f* (way of) driving; ***bei d-r ~*** the way you drive; **~werk** *n mot.* chassis; ✈ landing gear, undercarriage; **~wind** *m* **1.** ⚓ behind wind; **2.** → ***Fahrtwind***; **~zeit** *f* (running) time; → ***Fahrtdauer***

Fahr·zeug ['faːɐtsɔʏk] *n* (-[e]s; -e [-tsɔʏgə]) vehicle; ⚓ vessel; ***gesperrt für ~e aller Art*** closed to all traffic; **~auf·kom·men** *n* traffic volume; ***hohes ~*** heavy traffic; **~brief** *m* (vehicle) registration document; **~füh·rer** *m* driver of a vehicle; **~hal·ter** *m* vehicle owner; **~ko,lon·ne** *f* line of vehicles; motorcade; **~pa,pie·re** *pl.* car documents; **~park** *m mot.* fleet of cars; 🚂 rolling stock; **~schein** *m* (vehicle) registration papers *pl.*; **~ver·kehr** *m*: ***für den ~ gesperrt*** closed to all traffic

Fai·ble ['fɛːbəl] *n* (-s; -s) weakness; soft spot

fair [fɛːɐ] **I.** *adj.* fair; **II.** *adv.*: ***~ spielen*** play fair; **Fair·neß** ['fɛːɐnɛs] *f* (-; *no pl.*) fairness

Fait ac·com·pli [fɛtakõ'pli] *n* (- -; -s -s [fɛz-]) fait accompli; ***j-n vor ein ~ stellen*** present s.o. with a fait accompli

fä·kal [fɛ'kaːl] *adj.* f(a)ecal; **Fä·ka·li·en** [fɛ'kaːlĭən] *pl.* f(a)eces

Fa·kir ['faːkiːɐ] *m* (-s; -e) fakir

Fak·si·mi·le [fak'ziːmile] *n* (-s; -s) facsimile; **~aus·ga·be** *f* facsimile edition; **~über,tra·gung** *f* facsimile transmission; **~,un·ter·schrift** *f* facsimile signature

Fakt [fakt] *n, m* (-[e]s; -en) fact; **'Fak·ten·wis·sen** *n* factual knowledge

fak·tisch ['faktɪʃ] **I.** *adj.* actual, effective; **II.** *adv.* in fact, in reality; virtually; ***~ unmöglich*** practically impossible

Fak·tor ['faktoːɐ] *m* (-s; -en [fak'toːrən]) factor (*a.* 𝔄, *biol.*); **Fak'to·ren·ana·,ly·se** *f* factor analysis

Fak·to·tum [fak'toːtʊm] *n* (-s; -s) factotum

Fak·tum ['faktʊm] *n* (-s; -ten) fact; *pl.* facts, data

fak·tu·rie·ren [faktu'riːrən] *v/t.* (h) ⚕ invoice

Fa·kul·tät [fakʊl'tɛːt] *f* (-; -en) *univ.* faculty, *Am.* department, school

fa·kul·ta·tiv [fakʊlta'tiːf] *adj.* optional

Fal·ke ['falkə] *m* (-n; -n) falcon; *hunt. and fig. pol. a.* hawk; ***Augen wie ein ~ haben*** have eyes like a hawk

Fal·ken|au·ge *fig. n* eagle-eye; **~bei·ze** *f*, **~jagd** *f* falconry

Falk·ner ['falknɐ] *m* (-s; -) falconer

Fall [fal] *m* (-[e]s; Fälle ['fɛlə]) **1.** fall; descent; drop; *fig.* downfall, *pol. a.* overthrow, collapse; ⚔ fall, surrender; ⚕ fall, drop, slump; *phys.* ***freier ~*** free fall; ***sich bei e-m ~ verletzen*** be hurt in a fall; ***zu ~ bringen*** cause *s.o.* to fall, *a. pol.* bring down, *a. fig.* trip up; thwart *plans etc.*, defeat *bill etc.*; ***zu ~ kommen*** fall, *fig.* founder, come to grief, be defeated *etc.*; **2.** case (*a. ling.*, ⚕, ⚖); matter, affair; instance; occurrence; ***der ~ Graf*** the case of Graf; ***ein ~ von Typhus*** a typhoid case, a case of typhoid; ***in den meisten Fällen*** in most cases; ***im besten*** (*or* ***günstigsten***) ***~*** at best; ***im schlimmsten ~*** at worst; ***im ~e e-s ~es*** if the worst comes to the worst; ***auf alle Fälle, auf jeden ~*** anyway, definitely; ***laß den Schlüssel auf alle Fälle*** (*or* ***in jedem ~***) ***da*** whatever you do, leave the key behind; ***für alle Fälle*** just in case, to be on the safe side; ***auf keinen ~*** on no account, under no circumstances, definitely not; ***sag es ihm auf keinen ~*** don't tell him whatever you do; ***für den*** (*or* ***im***) ***~, daß*** in case *he should come*; ***gesetzt den ~*** suppose, supposing, let's assume; ***in diesem ~*** in that (*or* this) case; ***das ist von ~ zu ~ verschieden*** that varies from case to case; ***das muß man von ~ zu ~ entscheiden*** *a.* you have to decide each case on its merits; ***wenn der ~ zutrifft, wenn das der ~ ist*** if that is the case; ***wenn der ~ zutrifft*** (*or* ***wenn es der Fall ist***)***, daß er*** if this is a case of his (*or* him) *ger.*; ***der ~ liegt so*** the situation is as follows; F ***klarer ~!*** F (oh,) sure!; ***das ist*** (***nicht***) ***ganz mein ~*** that's right up my street (not exactly my cup of tea); ***er ist genau*** (***nicht ganz***) ***mein ~*** he's just (not exactly) my type; ***das ist auch bei ihm der ~*** it's the same with him; → ***hoffnungslos***; **~ap·fel** *m* windfall; **~beil** *n* guillotine; **~bei·spiel** *n* case study; **~be·schleu·ni·gung** *f* gravitational acceleration; **~be·schrei·bung** *f* ⚕ case description; **~bir·ne** *f* demolition (*or* wrecking, drop) ball; **~brücke** *f* drawbridge

Fal·le ['falə] *f* (-; -n) trap (*a. fig.*); snare; pit; ***mit e-r ~ fangen*** *a.* trap; ***in e-e ~ gehen*** (*or* ***geraten***) be (*or* get) caught in a trap, *fig.* walk into a trap; *fig.* ***j-m in die ~ gehen*** walk right into s.o.'s trap; ***er ist in die ~ gegangen*** *a.* he took the bait; ***e-e ~ stellen*** set a trap (***j-m*** for s.o.); ***in der ~ sitzen*** be caught in a trap; F ***in die ~ gehen*** F hit the sack (*esp. Am.* hay)

fal·len ['falən] **I.** *v/i.* (fiel, gefallen, sn) fall, drop; go down; fall (down); ⚔ fall, be taken; *soldier*: fall, be killed (in action); *barometer*: fall, be falling; *look etc.*: fall (***auf*** *acc.* on), *light*: *a.* come (***durch*** *acc.* through); ♪ descend, fall; *goal*: be scored; *decision*: be made; *remark*: fall, be heard; *holiday etc.*: fall (***auf*** *acc.* on); ***~ in*** *acc.*, ***~ unter*** *acc.* come under; ***~ an*** *acc. inheritance etc.*: fall (*or* go) to *s.o.*, devolve on *s.o.*; ***durch e-e Prüfung ~*** fail an exam; ***in e-n tiefen Schlaf ~*** fall into a deep sleep; ***~ lassen*** drop; ***heute nacht sind 30 Zentimeter Schnee gefallen*** there was 30 centimet|res (*Am.* -ers) of snowfall last night; ***die Entscheidung fiel*** (***zwei Tore fielen***) *in der zweiten Halbzeit*: the match was decided (there were two goals); ***es fielen drei Schüsse*** there were three shots, three shots were fired; ***auch sein Name fiel*** his name was also mentioned; ***es fielen harte Worte*** there were harsh words; → ***Extrem, Hand, Nerven, Ohnmacht*** 1; **II.** ♀ *n* (-s) fall(ing)

fäl·len ['fɛlən] *v/t.* (h) cut (*or* chop) down; ⚗ precipitate; 𝔄 ***das Lot ~*** drop a perpendicular; ⚖ ***ein Urteil ~*** pass sentence (***über*** *acc.* on), *a. fig.* pass judg(e)ment (on); → ***Entscheidung***

'fal·len·las·sen *fig. v/t.* (*irr.*, *sep.*, h, → ***lassen***) drop; (casually) drop, let drop *a remark*; ***darüber hat er kein Wort ~*** he didn't say a word about it

'Fal·len·stel·ler *m* (-s; -) trapper

'Fall|ge·schich·te *f* case history; **~ge·schwin·dig·keit** *f phys.* rate of fall; **~ge·setz** *n phys.* law of falling bodies; **~gru·be** *f* pit, *a. fig.* trap; **~ham·mer** *m* drop forge (*or* hammer); **~hö·he** *f* **1.** *phys.*

height of fall; **2.** ⚙ height of drop; **~holz** *n* fallen wood

fal·lie·ren [fa'li:rən] *v/i.* (h) ⚕ go bankrupt

fäl·lig ['fɛlɪç] *adj.* due; payable; ~ ***werden*** a) become due (*or* payable), b) expire; ~ ***zum 31. Mai*** payable by May 31; ***längst*** ~ long overdue; ***der Haarschnitt war aber längst*** ~ *a.* it was high time (*or* about time) you *etc.* had that haircut; F ***der Mantel ist mal wieder*** ~ I think this coat is due for the cleaner's again; ***du bist mal wieder*** ~ I think it's your turn (again); F ***jetzt ist er*** **~!** F he's asked for it now; F ***morgen ist er*** **~!** F I'll be after him tomorrow; **'Fäl·lig·keit** *f* (-; -en) ⚕ maturity; **'Fäl·lig·keits·tag** *m* maturity (date)

'Falli·nie (*sep.* -ll·l-) *f skiing*: fall line

'Fall·obst *n* windfall

Fall·out ['fɔ:lˀaʊt] *m* (-s; -s) (radioactive) fall-out

'Fall|recht *n* ⚖ case law; **~rohr** *n* drainpipe; **~rück·zie·her** *m soccer*: overhead kick

falls [fals] *cj.* if; in case; ~ ***sie kommt*** if she comes, if she should come, if she happens to come; ~ ***er nicht erscheinen sollte*** *a.* in the event that he should not turn up

'Fall·schirm *m* parachute; ***den*** ~ ***öffnen*** open up one's parachute; **~ab·sprung** *m* parachute jump (*or* descent); **~ab·wurf** *m* airdrop; **~gurt** *m* parachute harness; **~jä·ger** *m* paratrooper; **~sprin·gen** *n* parachuting, parachute jumping; *sport*: skydiving; **~sprin·ger** *m* parachutist; *sport*: skydiver; **~trup·pen** *pl.* parachute troops, paratroops

'Fall|strick *fig. m* trap, snare; ***j-m*** **~*e legen*** set a trap for s.o.; **~stu·die** *f* case study; **~trep·pe** *f* foldaway stairs *pl.*; **~tür** *f* trapdoor

Fäl·lung ['fɛlʊŋ] *f* (-; -en) ⚗ precipitation; **'Fäl·lungs·mit·tel** *n* precipitant

'fall·wei·se *adv.* from case to case

'Fall·wind *m* down wind

falsch [falʃ] **I.** *adj.* **1.** wrong, ♪ *a.* false; untrue; **~*e Bezeichnung*** misnomer; **~*e Darstellung*** misrepresentation; ***ein*** **~*es Wort*** a word out of place; ***da bist du an den*** **℞*en geraten*** you've come to the wrong place (*or* person) for that; → ***Kehle*** 1; **2.** false; forged, counterfeit; **~*er Name*** false (*or* fictitious) name; ***unter*** **~*em Namen*** under a false name; **~*e Rippe*** floating rib; **3.** false, two-faced; insincere; ***er ist ein ganz*** **~*er Typ*** he's so false; **~*er Prophet*** false prophet; → ***Schlange*** 1, ***Vorspiegelung*; 4.** false *shame, modesty etc.*; misplaced; **II.** *adv.* wrong(ly); the wrong way; ~ ***abbiegen*** take the wrong turning; ***et.*** ~ ***anpacken*** go about s.th. the wrong way; ~ ***antworten*** give the wrong answer, get the answer wrong, answer wrong; ***et.*** ~ ***beantworten*** answer s.th. wrong, give the wrong answer to s.th.; ~ ***auffassen*** misunderstand, get *s.th.* wrong; ~ ***aussagen*** make a false statement; ~ ***aussprechen*** pronounce wrong(ly), mispronounce; ~ ***gehen*** *watch*: be wrong; ~ ***liegen*** lie funny, *fig.* be wrong, be on the wrong track; ~ ***herum*** → ***verkehrt*; *da liegst du*** ~ you're wrong on (*or* about) that; ***er macht alles*** ~ he can't do a thing right; ~ ***schreiben*** misspell, spell wrong(ly); ~ ***singen*** sing out of tune (*or* off-key); ~ ***spielen*** ♪ play a (*or* the) wrong note, hit the wrong key; *teleph.* ~ ***verbunden*** sorry, wrong number; ***ich glaube, Sie sind*** ~ ***verbunden*** I think you've got the wrong number; ***et.*** (***j-n***) ~ ***verstehen*** get s.th. (s.o.) wrong; ***et.*** ~ ***wiedergeben*** misquote s.th.; **III.** ℞ *m*: ***ohne*** ~ guileless

'Falsch|aus·sa·ge *f* ⚖ false statement; **~eid** *m* false oath

fäl·schen ['fɛlʃən] *v/t.* (h) fake; forge; counterfeit; ⚕ tamper with, F doctor *the accounts*, cook *the books*; *w.s.* falsify *s.th.*

Fäl·scher ['fɛlʃɐ] *m* (-s; -) forger, counterfeiter; **~ban·de** *f* gang of forgers

'Falsch|fah·rer *m* wrong-way driver; **~geld** *n* counterfeit money

'Falsch·heit *f* (-; *no pl.*) falseness; two-facedness

fälsch·lich ['fɛlʃlɪç] *adv.* wrongly; → **'fälsch·li·cher'wei·se** *adv.* by mistake, erroneously

'Falsch·mel·dung *f* false report; hoax, canard

'Falsch·mün·zer [-mʏntsɐ] *m* (-s; -) forger; **Falsch·mün·ze·rei** [-mʏntsə'raɪ] *f* (-; *no pl.*) forgery, counterfeiting

'Falsch|par·ken *n* illegal parking; **~par·ker** [-parkɐ] *m* (-s; -) **1.** parking offender; ***diese*** **~!** these people who park their cars all over the place; **2.** wrongly-parked car, F offending car; **~schrei·bung** *f* misspelling; misspelt word; **℞spie·len** *v/i.* (*sep.*, h) cheat; **~spie·ler** *m* cheat

Fäl·schung ['fɛlʃʊŋ] *f* (-; -en) **1.** forging, counterfeiting; **2.** fake, forgery; **'fäl·schungs·si·cher** *adj.* forgery-proof, counterfeit-proof

Fal·sett [fal'zɛt] *n* (-[e]s; *no pl.*) ♪ falsetto; **~stim·me** *f* falsetto voice

Fal·si·fi·kat [falzifi'ka:t] *n* (-[e]s; -e) fake, forgery; **fal·si·fi·zie·ren** [falzifi'tsi:rən] *v/t.* (h) falsify; **Fal·si·fi'zie·rung** *f* (-; -en) falsification

falt·bar ['faltba:ɐ] *adj.* folding ...; collapsible; ***ist es*** **~?** can it be folded up (*or* together)?

'Falt|blatt *n* leaflet; **~boot** *n* folding canoe

Fält·chen ['fɛltçən] *n* (-s; -) crease; (tiny) wrinkle

Fal·te ['faltə] *f* (-; -n) fold; pleat; crease; wrinkle; **~*n werfen*** fall in folds, pucker; ***die Stirn in*** **~*n ziehen*** knit one's brow, frown

fäl·teln ['fɛltəln] *v/t.* (h) pleat; fold

fal·ten ['faltən] (h) **I.** *v/t.* fold; fold up; ***die Hände*** ~ fold one's hands; ***mit gefalteten Händen*** hands folded; ***die Stirn*** ~ knit one's brow, frown; **II.** *v/refl.*: ***sich*** ~ wrinkle, crease

'Fal·ten|bil·dung *f* **1.** wrinkling; **2.** *geol.* plication; **℞frei** *adj. textil.* non-crumple, non-crease; **~ge·bir·ge** *n* folded mountains *pl.*; **℞los** *adj.* smooth, unlined *face etc.*; **~rock** *m* pleated skirt; **~wurf** *m art*: drapery

Fal·ter ['faltɐ] *m* (-s; -) butterfly; moth

fal·tig ['faltɪç] *adj.* creased; wrinkled

'Falt|kar,ton *m* collapsible cardboard box; **~pro,spekt** *m* leaflet; **~schach·tel** *f* → ***Faltkarton*; ~tür** *f* folding door

Falz [falts] *m* (-es; -e) fold; ⚙ welt, edge; seam; rabbet; groove, notch; mount, hinge; **fal·zen** ['faltsən] *v/t.* (h) fold; ⚙ rabbet; groove; welt

Fa·ma ['fa:ma] *f* (-; *no pl.*) rumo(u)r

fa·mi·li·är [fami'liɛ:ɐ] *adj.* **1.** family *affairs etc.*; ***aus*** **~*en Gründen*** for personal reasons; **2.** familiar; informal; **3.** *ling.* familiar, colloquial; **~*er Ausdruck*** colloquialism

Fa·mi·lie [fa'mi:lĭə] *f* (-; -n) family (*a. ling.*, *zo.*, ♣); (***die***) ~ ***Miller*** the Miller family, the Millers; ***e-e*** ~ ***gründen*** start a family; ~ ***haben*** have a family, have children; ***sechsköpfige*** ~ family of six; ***es liegt in der*** ~ it runs in the family; ***das kommt in den besten*** **~*n vor*** it happens to the best of us

Fa'mi·li·en|ähn·lich·keit *f* family likeness; **~an·ge·hö·ri·ge** *m, f* (-n; -n) member of the family; close relative; *adm.* dependant; **~an·ge·le·gen·heit** *f* family affair; **~aus·flug** *m* family outing; **~be·sitz** *m* family estate; **~be·trieb** *m* family business; **~fei·er** *f*, **~fest** *n* family celebration; **~for·schung** *f* genealogy; **~fo·to** *n* family portrait; **℞freund·lich** *adj.* family *hotel etc.*; ***das Restaurant ist*** ~ *a.* the restaurant welcomes families (*or* children); **~ge·heim·nis** *n* family secret; **~ge·richt** *n* **1.** ⚖ family court; **2.** F → ***Familienrat*; ~glück** *n* domestic bliss; **~grab** *n* family grave; **~kreis** *m* family circle; ***der engste*** ~ the immediate family, the next of kin; ***das Begräbnis findet im engsten*** ~ ***statt*** only the closest members of the family will be attending the funeral, *in obituary*: private funeral; **~le·ben** *n* family life; **~mit·glied** *n* member of the family, family member; *adm.* dependant; **~na·me** *m* surname, last name; **~ober·haupt** *n* head of the family; **~pak·kung** (-k·k-) *f* family pack; **~pla·nung** *f* family planning; **~rat** *m* family council (*or* tribunal); **~recht** *n* (-[e]s; *no pl.*) ⚖ family law; **~ro,man** *m* roman fleuve; **~sinn** *m* (-[e]s; *no pl.*) sense of family; **~sitz** *m* family home (*or* residence); **~stand** *m* (-[e]s; *no pl.*) marital status; **~streit** *m* family argument (*or* row); **~stück** *n* (family) heirloom; **~tra·di·ti,on** *f* family tradition; **~tref·fen** *n* family get-together (F *iro.* affair); family reunion; **~,un·ter·halt** *m* upkeep of the family; **~va·ter** *m* **1.** head of the family; **2.** family man; **~ver·hält·nis·se** *pl.* family set-up (*or* background) *sg.*; **~wa·gen** *m* family car; **~zu·la·ge** *f* family allowance; **~zu,sam·men·füh·rung** *f* family reunification; **~zu·wachs** *m* new arrival (to the family); ***sie bekommen*** ~ *a.* they're expecting an addition to the family

fa·mos [fa'mo:s] F *obs. adj.* F *obs.* capital

Fa·mu·la·tur [famula'tu:ɐ] *f* (-; -en) (period of) medical training, *Am.* internship; **fa·mu·lie·ren** [famu'li:rən] *v/i.* (h) do one's medical training (*Am.* internship)

Fan [fɛn] F *m* (-s; -s) fan

Fa·nal [fa'na:l] *n* (-s; -e) beacon; *fig.* signal

Fa·na·ti·ker [fa'na:tikɐ] *m* (-s; -) fanatic; **fa·na·tisch** [fa'na:tɪʃ] *adj.* fanatic(al); **Fa·na·tis·mus** [fana'tɪsmʊs] *m* (-; *no pl.*) fanaticism

'Fan·club *m* fan club

fand [fant] *pret. of* ***finden***

Fan·fa·re [fan'fa:rə] *f* (-; -n) fanfare; flourish of trumpets; **Fan'fa·ren·stoß** *m* fanfare, blast of trumpets

Fang [faŋ] *m* (-[e]s; Fänge ['fɛŋə]) **1.** catch, haul (*both a. fig.*); ***auf*** ~ ***ausgehen*** (***ausfahren***) go hunting (fishing); ***e-n guten*** ~ ***machen*** make a good catch (*or* haul), take home a good (*or* rich) haul, *fig.* make a big haul; *fig.* ***das war ein guter***

~ that was a real bargain; ***mit ihm haben wir e-n guten ~ gemacht*** he was a good catch, we couldn't have made a better catch; **2.** *zo.* claw; fang; tusk; *fig.* ***j-n (et.) in den Fängen haben*** have s.o. (s.th.) in one's clutches; ***wenn ich ihn erst in den Fängen habe*** once I get hold of him (*or* lay my fingers on him); **~arm** *m zo.* tentacle

fan·gen ['faŋən] (fing, gefangen, h) **I.** *v/t.* catch; *fig.* trap; captivate; ***sich ~ lassen*** get caught; ***Feuer ~*** catch fire, *fig.* be bitten (***für*** *acc.* by, with), be smitten; ***für die kommunistische Idee Feuer ~*** be bitten by the Communist bug; F ***eine ~*** F cop one, cop it; → ***gefangen*** II; **II.** *v/refl.*: ***sich ~*** a) *an dat.*: be (*or* get) caught; b) catch o.s.; *fig.* ***sich (wieder) ~*** get a grip on o.s. (again), get to grips with o.s. (again), ⚕ come round; ***ich fang' mich schon wieder*** I'll be all right (*Am.* alright) (in a minute); **III.** ♀ *n* (-s; *no pl.*) catch, *Am.* tag

Fän·ger ['fɛŋɐ] *m* (-s; -) catcher

'Fang|fra·ge *f* trick question; **♀frisch** *adj.* fresh-caught; **~ge·bie·te** *pl.* fishing grounds; **~lei·ne** *f* **1.** ⚓ painter; **2.** rigging line; **~netz** *n* net; ✈ arrester net; *fig.* snare

Fan·go ['faŋo] *m* (-s; *no pl.*) fango; **~bad** *n* mud bath; **~packung** (-k·k-) *f* mudpack, fango pack

'Fang|plät·ze *pl.* fishing grounds; **~quo·te** *f* fishing quota; **~zahn** *m zo.* fang

'Fan|klub *m* fan club; **~post** *f* fan mail; fan letter

Fa·ra·day·kä·fig ['færədı-] *m*, **Fa·ra·day·scher Kä·fig** *m phys.* Faraday cage

Farb|ab·stim·mung ['farp-] *f* colo(u)r scheme; **~ab·zug** *m* colo(u)r print; **~an·strich** *m* coat of paint; **~auf·nah·me** *f* colo(u)r photo (*or* print); **~band** *n* (-[e]s; ⸚er) typewriter ribbon; **~bei·la·ge** *f* colo(u)r supplement; **~beu·tel** *m* paint bomb; **~bild** *n* colo(u)r photo (*or* print); **~bild·schirm** *m* colo(u)r screen; **~druck** *m* (-[e]s; -e) **1.** *no pl.* colo(u)r printing; **2.** colo(u)r print

Far·be ['farbə] *f* (-; -n) colo(u)r, *a.* shade, *a.* complexion; paint; dye; *typ.* (printer's) ink; *card game*: suit; ***was für e-e ~ hat es?*** what colo(u)r is it?; ***~ bekommen*** get some colo(u)r into one's cheeks, get a tan; ***du hast richtig ~ bekommen*** a) you're looking really healthy, b) you've got yourself a nice tan; ***~ verlieren*** go pale; ***~ bekennen*** *fig.* declare o.s., come down on one or other side of the fence; *card game*: follow suit; *fig.* ***et. in den herrlichsten (or glühendsten) ~n ausmalen*** paint in glowing colo(u)rs, paint a glowing portrait (*or* picture) of s.th.; ***e-r Sache ~ verleihen*** add (*or* lend) colo(u)r to s.th.

farb|echt ['farp-] *adj.* colo(u)rfast; *phot.* orthochromatic; **♀ef'fekt** *m* colo(u)r effect; **~emp·find·lich** *adj.* colo(u)r-sensitive

fär·ben ['fɛrbən] (h) **I.** *v/t.* dye *hair, fabric etc.*; stain *glass, paper*; tint; *fig.* colo(u)r; ***sich die Haare ~ (lassen)*** dye one's hair (have one's hair dyed); ***sich die Haare schwarz ~ (lassen)*** dye one's hair black; → ***gefärbt*** II; **II.** *v/refl.*: ***sich ~*** colo(u)r; *leaves*: change colo(u)r; ***sich rot ~*** turn red

'far·ben·blind *adj.* colo(u)r-blind; **'Far·ben·blind·heit** *f* colo(u)r-blindness

'Far·ben|bre·chung *f* colo(u)r refraction; **~druck** *m* (-[e]s; -e) **1.** *no pl.* colo(u)r printing; **2.** colo(u)r print; **♀freu·dig, ♀froh** *adj.* colo(u)rful; **~ge·schäft** *n* paint shop (*or* store); **~in·du'strie** *f* paint industry; **~leh·re** *f phys.* theory of colo(u)rs, chromatics *pl.*; **~or·gie** *f* riot of colo(u)r

'Far·ben·pracht *f* rich colo(u)ring; blaze of colo(u)r; **'far·ben·präch·tig** *adj.* colo(u)rful; richly colo(u)red

'Far·ben|spiel *n* play of colo(u)r; **~sym'bo·lik** *f* colo(u)r symbolism

Fär·ber ['fɛrbɐ] *m* (-s; -) dyer; **Fär·be·rei** [fɛrbə'raı] *f* (-; -en) **1.** dyeworks *pl.*; **2.** *no pl.* dyer's trade

Farb·fern·se·hen ['farp-] *n* colo(u)r television (*or* TV); **'Farb·fern·se·her** *m*, **'Farb·fern·seh·ge·rät** *n* colo(u)r television (*or* TV); colo(u)r set

Farb|film ['farp-] *m* colo(u)r film; **~fil·ter** *m, n phot.* colo(u)r filter; **~fleck** *m* paint mark; stain; **~fo·to** *n* colo(u)r photo (*or* print); **~fo·to·gra'fie** *f* **1.** colo(u)r photography; **2.** *colo(u)r photograph*; **~ge·bung** *f* (-; -en) colo(u)ring; colo(u)r scheme

far·big ['farbıç] *adj.* colo(u)red; *fig.* colo(u)rful; **Far·bi·ge** ['farbıgə] *m, f* (-n; -n) non-white; black; *in South Africa*: (Cape) Colo(u)red; **'Far·big·keit** *f* (-; *no pl.*) colo(u)r, colo(u)rfulness

Farb|ka·sten ['farp-] *m* paintbox; **~kis·sen** *n* ink pad; **~klecks** *m* blob (*or* spot) of paint; *fig.* spot (*or* dash) of colo(u)r; *fig.* ***es ist ein netter ~*** it adds a nice bit of colo(u)r; **~kom·po·si·ti'on** *f* colo(u)r composition (*or* scheme); **~kon'trast** *m* (colo[u]r) contrast; **~ko'pie** *f* colo(u)r copy; **~kör·per** *m* pigment (*a. biol.*)

Farb·kor·rek'tur ['farp-] *f* colo(u)r adjustment (*or* correction); **~fil·ter** *m, n* colo(u)r correction filter

farb·kräf·tig ['farp-] *adj.* (very) colo(u)rful; ***du brauchst was ♀es*** you need some strong colo(u)rs

farb·lich ['farplıç] **I.** *adj.* colo(u)r ..., in colo(u)r; **II.** *adv.* in colo(u)r; colo(u)rwise, as far as the colo(u)rs go; ***~ (aufeinander) abstimmen*** match the colo(u)rs of

farb·los ['farplo:s] *adj.* colo(u)rless (*a. fig.*); pale; *fig.* ***er ist völlig ~*** he has no personality; **'Farb·lo·sig·keit** *f* (-; *no pl.*) colo(u)rlessness (*a. fig.*); *fig. a.* lack of personality

Farb·mo·ni·tor ['farp-] *m* colo(u)r monitor (*or* screen)

Farb·ne·ga·tiv ['farp-] *n* colo(u)r negative; **~film** *m* colo(u)r film

Farb|nu·an·ce ['farp-] *f* shade (of colo[u]r); **~pa'pier** *n* colo(u)r paper; **~pho·to** *n* → ***Farbfoto***; **~pho·to·gra'phie** *f* → ***Farbfotografie***; **~sät·ti·gung** *f* colo(u)r saturation; **~schat'tie·rung** *f* shade (of colo[u]r), hue; **~schicht** *f* layer of paint; coat of paint; **~ska·la** *f* colo(u)r range; **~skiz·ze** *f* colo(u)r sketch; **~stich** *m* colo(u)r cast; **~stift** *m* colo(u)red pencil (*or* pen), crayon; ***grüner ~*** green pencil (*or* crayon, pen); **~stoff** *m* **1.** → ***Farbkörper***; **2.** dye; *gastr., a. pl.* colo(u)ring; ***ohne ~e*** contains no (artificial) colo(u)ring; **~ta·fel** *f* **1.** colo(u)r plate; **2.** colo(u)r chart; **~tem·pe·ra'tur** *f* colo(u)r temperature; **~ton** *m* tone; hue; tint; shade; ***im ~ zusammenpassen*** match; **~tup·fer** *m* dab (*or* spot) of paint; *fig.* spot of colo(u)r

Fär·bung ['fɛrbʊŋ] *f* (-; -en) colo(u)ring (*a. fig.*); hue; *fig. pol.* bias

Farb|wal·ze ['farp-] *f* ink(ing) roller; **~'wie·der·ga·be** *f* colo(u)r rendering, colo(u)rs *pl.*; **~zu'sam·men·stel·lung** *f* colo(u)r combination (*or* scheme)

Far·ce ['farsə] *f* (-; -n) **1.** *thea.* burlesque, *a. fig.* farce; **2.** *gastr.* stuffing; **'far·cen·haft** *adj.* farcical; **far·cie·ren** [far'si:rən] *v/t.* (h) *gastr.* stuff

Fa·rin·zucker [fa'ri:n-] *m* brown sugar

Farm [farm] *f* (-; -en) farm; **Far·mer** ['farmɐ] *m* (-s; -) farmer

Farn [farn] *m* (-[e]s; -e), **~kraut** *n* ⚘ fern

Fär·se ['fɛrzə] *f* (-; -n) young cow, heifer

Fa·san [fa'za:n] *m* (-s; -e) pheasant; **Fa'sa·nen·jagd** *f* **1.** pheasant shooting; **2.** pheasant shoot (*or* hunt)

fa·schie·ren [fa'ʃi:rən] *dial. v/t.* (h) mince, put through the mincer; **Fa·schier·te** [fa'ʃi:ɐtə] *n* (-n; *no pl.*) mincemeat, mince(d meat)

Fa·sching ['faʃıŋ] *m* (-s; *no pl.*) carnival, Fasching

'Fa·schings... carnival ..., Fasching ...; **~diens·tag** *m* Shrove Tuesday, F Pancake Day; *Am.* Mardi Gras

Fa·schis·mus [fa'ʃısmʊs] *m* (-; *no pl.*) fascism; **Fa·schist** [fa'ʃıst] *m* (-en; -en), **fa·schi·stisch** [fa'ʃıstıʃ] *adj.* fascist; **fa·schi·sto·id** [faʃısto'i:d] *adj.* protofascist

Fa·se·lei [fazə'laı] F *f* (-; -en) drivel; **Fa·sel·feh·ler** ['fa:zəl-] F *m* careless mistake (*or* slip); **fa·se·lig** ['fa:zəlıç] F *adj.* scatterbrained; **fa·seln** ['fa:zəln] F *v/i.* (h) (talk) drivel

Fa·ser ['fa:zɐ] *f* (-; -n) *anat.*, ⚘ fibre (*Am.* fiber); thread; string; grain; *fig.* ***mit jeder ~ m-s Herzens*** with every fibre (*Am.* fiber) of my heart; **fa·se·rig** ['fa:zərıç] *adj.* fibrous; *gastr.* stringy; frayed; **fa·sern** ['fa:zɐn] *v/i.* (h) fray; **'fa·ser'nackt** *adj.* stark naked, *pred.* F starkers

'Fa·ser|op·tik *f* fibre (*Am.* fiber) optics *pl.*; **~pflan·ze** *f* fibre (*Am.* fiber) plant; **~plat·te** *f* fibreboard, *Am.* fiberboard

Fa·se·rung ['fa:zərʊŋ] *f* (-; *no pl.*) fraying; ⚙ grain

Fas·ler ['fa:zlɐ] F *m* (-s; -) drivel(l)er, F blether; ***er ist ein richtiger ~*** *a.* he just goes on and on

Faß [fas] *n* (Fasses; Fässer ['fɛsɐ]) barrel; keg; vat, tub; ***ein ~ Bier*** a barrel (*or* keg) of beer; ***Bier vom ~*** → ***Faßbier***; *fig.* ***~ ohne Boden*** bottomless pit; ***das ist ein ~ ohne Boden*** *a.* it's never-ending, it just goes on and on, you could go on talking about that all night; ***das schlägt dem ~ den Boden aus!*** that's the last straw, F that takes the biscuit; F ***ein ~ aufmachen*** have a fling (F binge); → ***überlaufen***[1] 1

Fas·sa·de [fa'sa:də] *f* (-; -n) façade, front (*both a. fig.*)

Fas'sa·den|be·leuch·tung *f* **1.** floodlighting; **2.** floodlit building(s *pl.*); **~klet·te·rer** *m* cat burglar; **~ma·le'rei** *f* façade painting

faß·bar ['fasba:ɐ] *adj.* tangible; comprehensible; ***schwer ~*** hard to comprehend

'Faß·bier *n* draught (*Am.* draft) beer

fas·sen (h) **I.** *v/t.* **1.** take hold of, grasp; hold; seize; catch, arrest *criminal etc.*; ***j-n am Kragen ~*** grab s.o. by the collar; ***j-n an (or bei) der Hand ~*** take s.o. by the hand, take s.o.'s hand; ***j-n am Arm ~***

take s.o.'s arm; ***zu ~ kriegen*** get hold of; ***faß ihn!*** *to a dog*: get him!; **2.** ⚙ mount *in silver etc.*; set *gem*; **3.** hold; seat; **4.** contain; *fig.* ***in sich*** ~ include; **5.** put, formulate; ***in Worte*** ~ put into words; ***das läßt sich nicht in Worte*** ~ *a.* it can't be described; **6.** *fig.* grasp, understand; believe; ***nicht zu*** ~ unbelievable, incredible; ***das ist kaum zu*** ~ *a.* it's hard to believe; **7.** *fig.* ***e-n Gedanken*** ~ form an idea; ***ich konnte keinen klaren Gedanken*** ~ I couldn't think straight; → ***Abneigung, Beschluß, Entschluß, Fuß***; **II.** *v/i.* **8.** ~ ***an*** *acc.* touch; ~ ***in*** (***auf***) *acc.* put one's hand in (on); ***sich an*** *die Stirn etc.* ~ put one's hand to; ***da kann man sich nur noch an den Kopf*** ~ it really makes you wonder; **9.** ⚙ grip; **III.** *v/refl.* **10.** ***sich*** ~ regain one's composure, pull o.s. together; ***er konnte sich vor Glück kaum*** ~ he was beside himself with joy; → ***gefaßt***; **11.** ***sich kurz*** ~ be brief; ***fasse dich kurz!*** make it brief; → ***Geduld***

faß·lich ['faslıç] *adj.*: ***leicht*** (***schwer***) ~ easy (hard) to understand

Fas·son [fa'sõ:] *f* (-; -s) shape; cut; trim; *fig.* ***nach s-r eigenen*** ~ after one's own fashion; ***jeder muß nach s-r eigenen*** ~ ***glücklich werden*** everyone has to look to his own salvation

'Faß·rei·fen *m* (barrel) hoop

Fas·sung ['fasʊŋ] *f* (-; -en) **1.** (*spectacle*) frame; ⚡ socket; ⚙ setting; **2.** version; ***in der vorliegenden*** ~ in its present form; **3.** *no pl.* composure; equanimity; ***aus der*** ~ ***bringen*** put out, F throw; ***sie ist durch nichts aus der*** ~ ***zu bringen*** she's unflappable; ***die*** ~ ***bewahren*** maintain one's composure, F keep cool; ***nach*** (*or* ***um***) ~ ***ringen*** a) try to regain one's composure, b) try not to lose one's temper; ***die*** ~ ***verlieren*** lose one's composure, lose one's temper (F cool); ***er war ganz außer*** ~ he was completely beside himself

'Fas·sungs·kraft *f* powers *pl.* of comprehension, (mental) capacity

'fas·sungs·los **I.** *adj.* stunned; speechless; perplexed, bewildered; **II.** *adv.*: ***er sah mich*** ~ ***an*** he looked at me in amazement (*or* disbelief), he just gaped at me; **'Fas·sungs·lo·sig·keit** *f* (-; *no pl.*) shock; bewilderment

'Fas·sungs·ver·mö·gen *n* (-s; *no pl.*) **1.** capacity; **2.** *fig.* (mental) capacity; ***das übersteigt mein*** ~ that's beyond me, that's above my head

fast [fast] *adv.* almost; nearly; ~ ***nichts*** next to nothing; ~ ***nie*** hardly ever; ~ ***keine*** hardly any; ***in*** ~ ***allen Fällen*** in almost every case; ***ich hätte*** ~ ***geglaubt, daß*** I could almost have sworn (that); F ~ ***hätte ich ihn rausgeschmissen*** I very nearly kicked him out, I was on the point of kicking him out; F ***wir haben's*** ~ we're almost there, we've almost (*or* nearly) finished

fa·sten ['fastən] **I.** *v/i.* (h) fast; go on a fast; **II.** 2 *n* (-s) fast(ing); ***das*** ~ ***unterbrechen*** break one's fast

'Fa·sten|kur *f* starvation cure; **~tag** *m* **1.** fast (day), day of fasting; **2.** ⚕ fasting day; **~zeit** *f* **1.** *eccl.* ***die*** ~ Lent; **2.** fasting period

'Fast·nacht *f* (-; *no pl.*) Shrove Tuesday, *Am.* Mardi Gras; carnival, Fasching; **'Fast·nachts...** → ***Faschings...***

Fas·zi·na·ti·on [fastsina'tsio:n] *f* (-; *no pl.*) fascination; ***e-e*** ~ ***ausüben auf*** *acc.* hold a great fascination for; **fas·zi·nie·ren** [fastsi'ni:rən] *v/t.* (h) fascinate; **Fas·zi·no·sum** [fastsi'no:zʊm] *n* (-s; *no pl.*) fascinating (*or* amazing) phenomenon

fa·tal [fa'ta:l] *adj.* fateful; disastrous, fatal; awkward; annoying; **Fa·ta·lis·mus** [fata'lısmʊs] *m* (-; *no pl.*) fatalism; **Fa·ta·list** [fata'lıst] *m* (-en; -en) fatalist; **fa·ta·li·stisch** [fata'lıstıʃ] *adj.* fatalist(ic)

Fa·ta Mor·ga·na ['fa:ta mɔr'ga:na] *f* (- -; -s, - -nen) mirage, *a. fig.* fata morgana

Fatz·ke ['fatskə] F *m* (-n, -s; -n, -s) F poser, *sl.* arrogant swine

fau·chen ['faʊxən] *v/i.* (h) hiss, *tiger etc.*: snarl (*both a. fig.*)

faul [faʊl] *adj.* **1.** rotten, bad; *fish, meat*: *a. pred.* off; putrid; **2.** lazy, idle; F **~es Aas** a) *sl.* lazy sod (*or* bitch), b) F *hum.* lazybones (*sg.*); *adv.* ~ ***herumliegen*** laze around (*or* about); → ***Haut***; **3.** *fig.* rotten; hollow *compromise*; shady; **~er Kunde** shady customer; **~e Sache** fishy business; **~er Witz** bad joke; ***an der Sache*** (*or* ***Geschichte***) ***ist etwas*** ~ there's something fishy about it

'Faul·baum *m* ♣ black alder, alder buckthorn; **~rin·de** *f pharm.* buckthorn bark

Fäu·le ['fɔʏlə] *f* (-; *no pl.*) **1.** rot; **2.** → ***Fäulnis***

fau·len ['faʊlən] *v/i.* (h, sn) go bad, rot; *tooth etc.*: *a.* decay

fau·len·zen ['faʊlɛntsən] *v/i.* (h) laze around; *contp.* be lazy, do nothing; **Fau·len·zer** ['faʊlɛntsɐ] *m* (-s; -) lazybones (*sg.*); *contp.* lazy person, idler, F layabout; **Fau·len·ze·rei** [faʊlɛntsə'raı] *f* (-; *no pl.*) laziness; lazy life

'Faul·gas *n* sewer gas

'Faul·heit *f* (-; *no pl.*) laziness; F ***vor*** ~ ***stinken*** be bone idle

fau·lig ['faʊlıç] *adj.* rotten; rotting; mo(u)ldy

Fäul·nis ['fɔʏlnıs] *f* (-; *no pl.*) rottenness; putrefaction; ⚕ sepsis; caries; *fig.* decay; ***in*** ~ ***übergehen*** (begin to) rot; **2er·re·gend** *adj.* putrefactive; ⚕ septic; **~er·re·ger** *m* putrefactive agent; **2hem·mend** *adj.* ⚕ antiseptic(ally *adv.*); **~pro,zeß** *m* process of decay

'Faul·pelz F *m* F lazybones (*sg.*)

'Faul·tier *n zo.* sloth; F *fig.* lazy person

Faun [faʊn] *m* (-[e]s; -e) faun

Fau·na ['faʊna] *f* (-; Faunen) fauna

Faust [faʊst] *f* (-; Fäuste ['fɔʏstə]) fist; ***die*** ~ ***ballen*** clench one's fist; ***j-m die*** ~ ***zeigen, j-m mit der*** ~ ***drohen*** raise one's fist at s.o.; ***mit der bloßen*** (*or* ***blanken***) ~ with one's bare fist(s); ***mit der*** ~ ***auf den Tisch hauen*** bang one's fist on the table, *fig.* put one's foot down; *fig.* ***auf eigene*** ~ on one's own initiative, F off one's own bat; ***die*** ~ ***im Nacken spüren*** really feel the pressure; ***das paßt wie die*** ~ ***aufs Auge*** a) it goes together like chalk and cheese, b) it's a perfect fit (*or* match); → ***eisern*** I

Fäust·chen ['fɔʏstçən] *n* (-s; -): *fig.* ***sich ins*** ~ ***lachen*** have a good chuckle, laugh up one's sleeve

'faust'dick **I.** *adj.* as big as your fist; *fig.* ***e-e*** **~e** ***Lüge*** F a whopping great lie, a whopper; ***er hat es*** ~ ***hinter den Ohren*** he's as sly as they come; **II.** *fig. adv.*: ~ ***auftragen*** F lay it on thick (*or* with a trowel); ~ ***lügen*** F lie through one's teeth

Fäu·stel ['fɔʏstəl] *m* (-s; -) ⚒ mallet

fau·sten ['faʊstən] *v/t. and v/i.* (h) *sport*: punch (the ball)

'Faust|feu·er·waf·fe *f* hand gun; **2groß** *adj.* as big as your fist; **~hand·schuh** *m* mitten

Fäust·ling ['fɔʏstlıŋ] *m* (-s; -e) mitten

'Faust|pfand *n* pledge; security; *fig.* lever; **~recht** *fig. n* (-[e]s; *no pl.*) jungle law; ***dort gilt das*** ~ it's dog eat dog in (*or* out) there; **~re·gel** *f*: (***als*** ~ as a) general rule; **~schlag** *m* punch; **~skiz·ze** *f* rough sketch

Faux·pas [fo'pa] *m* (- [-pa(s)]; - [-pas]) (social) blunder, faux pas, gaffe; ***e-n*** ~ ***begehen*** make a blunder, commit a faux pas (*or* gaffe)

fa·vo·ri·sie·ren [favori'zi:rən] *v/t.* (h) favo(u)r; *sport*: fancy; favo(u)ritise *child*; **fa·vo·ri·siert** [favori'zi:ɐt] *adj.* *sport*: strongly fancied; ~ ***sein*** be (a *or* the) favo(u)rite, be (the) favo(u)rites; **Fa·vo·rit** [favo'ri:t] *m* (-en; -en) *a. sport*: favo(u)rite (***auf*** *e-n Titel* for); *pol.* front runner; ***klarer*** ~ clear favo(u)rite; ***hoher*** (***todsicherer***) ~ hot (odds-on) favo(u)rite; **Fa·vo'ri·ten·rol·le** *f* role as favo(u)rite

Fax [faks] *n* (-; -[e]) **1.** fax; **2.** fax (machine); **fa·xen** ['faksən] *v/t. and v/i.* (h) fax; ***j-m et.*** ~ fax s.th. (through) to s.o.

'Fa·xen *pl.* **1.** ~ ***machen*** (*or* ***schneiden***) pull faces; **2.** nonsense *sg.*; ***laß die*** **~!** stop acting the goat; **~ma·cher** *m* (-s; -) clown

'Fax-Mit·tei·lung *f* fax message

Fa·yence [fa'jã:s] *f* (-; -n) faïence

Fa·zit ['fa:tsıt] *n* (-s; -s) (net) result, upshot, F bottom line; ***das*** ~ ***ziehen*** sum up, consider the results (***aus*** *dat.* of); ***das*** ~ ***aus et. ziehen*** *a.* sum s.th. up; **~:** to sum up, F what it boils down to is (that); ***sein*** **~:** his conclusion is (that)

FCKW [ɛftse:ka've:] *m* (-[s]; -s) CFC, chlorofluorocarbon; **~frei** *adj.* CFC-free

Fe·bru·ar ['fe:brua:ɐ] *m* (-[s]; *no pl.*) February; ***im*** ~ in February

Fecht·bo·den ['fɛçt-] *m* fencing hall

fech·ten ['fɛçtən] **I.** *v/i.* (focht, gefochten, h) **1.** fence; *a. fig.* fight; **2.** F scrounge; **II.** 2 *n* (-s) fencing; **Fech·ter** ['fɛçtɐ] *m* (-s; -) fencer

'Fecht|hand·schuh *m* fencing glove; **~kunst** *f* (art of) fencing; **~sport** *m* fencing; **~tur,nier** *n* fencing tournament

Fe·der ['fe:dɐ] *f* (-; -n) feather; quill (feather); plume; pen, nib; quill; ⚙ spring; *fig.* ***sich mit fremden*** **~n** ***schmücken*** take the credit (for what s.o. else has done); **~n** ***lassen müssen*** lose a few feathers; ***zur*** ~ ***greifen*** put pen to paper; *ein Roman etc.* ***aus s-r*** ~ written (*or* penned) by him; F ***noch in den*** **~n** ***liegen*** still be in bed; F **~n** ***haben*** F be scared stiff (***vor*** *dat.* of, about), *sl.* have the wind up (about); **~an·trieb** *m* ⚙ spring drive

'Fe·der·ball *m* **1.** shuttlecock; **2.** *no pl.* badminton; **~schlä·ger** *m* badminton racket (*or* racquet)

'Fe·der|bett *n* duvet, continental quilt; **~busch** *m* **1.** *zo.* tuft; **2.** plume; **~fuch·ser** [-fʊksɐ] *m* (-s; -) **1.** pedant; **2.** pen-pusher; **2füh·rend** *adj.* leading ...; responsible; **~füh·rung** *f*: ***unter*** (***der***) ~ ***von ...*** (*or gen.*) with ... responsible (*or* in charge); **~ge·wicht** *n* (-[e]s; *no pl.*), **~ge·wicht·ler** [-gəvıçtlɐ] *m* (-s; -) featherweight; **~hal·ter** *m* fountain pen; **~hut** *m* feathered hat (*or* cap), plumed hat

fe·de·rig ['fe:dərɪç] *adj.* feathery
'Fe·der·ka·sten *m* pencil box
'Fe·der·kern·ma,trat·ze *f* spring interior (*Am.* innerspring) mattress
'Fe·der|kiel *m* quill; **~kis·sen** *n* feather pillow; **~kleid** *lit. n* plumage; **2'leicht** *adj.* (as) light as a feather; **~le·sen** *n* (-s): *fig.* ***nicht viel ~s machen mit*** make short work of, give *s.o.* short shrift; ***ohne viel ~(s)*** unceremoniously, without much ado; **~mäpp·chen** *n* pencil case; **~mes·ser** *n* penknife
fe·dern ['fe:dɐn] (h) **I.** *v/i.* **1.** be springy; give; bounce; **2.** *gym.* flex; **3.** *a. v/refl.* (***sich ~***) *zo.* mo(u)lt, lose its feathers; **II.** *v/t.* fit with springs; ⚙ spring-load; ***gut gefedert sein*** be well-sprung, *mot.* have good suspension; **'fe·dernd** *adj.* springy; ***~er Gang*** springy (*or* bouncy) gait
'Fe·der|nel·ke *f* feathered pink; **~schloß** *n* spring lock; **~schmuck** *m zo.* plumage; headdress; **~stab** *m mot.* torsion bar; **~strich** *m* stroke of the pen (*a. fig.*)
Fe·de·rung ['fe:dərʊŋ] *f* (-; -en) springs *pl.*; *mot.* suspension
'Fe·der|vieh *n* poultry; **~waa·ge** *f* spring scale; **~wei·ße** *m* (-n; -n) (fermenting) new wine; **~werk** *n* spring mechanism; **~wild** *n* wildfowl, game birds *pl.*; **~wisch** *m* feather duster; **~wölk·chen** *n* fluffy (*or* fleecy) cloud; **~wol·ke** *f meteor.* cirrus (cloud); **~zeich·nung** *f* pen-and-ink drawing; **~zir·kel** *m*: (***ein ~*** a pair of) spring dividers *pl.*
Fee [fe:] *f* (-; -n ['fe:ən]) fairy; ***gute ~*** fairy godmother; ***böse ~*** wicked fairy
Feed·back ['fi:dbɛk] *n* (-s; -s) feedback, reaction(s *pl.*)
Fee·ling ['fi:lɪŋ] F *n* (-s; -s) feeling, sensation; ***es ist ein tolles ~*** *a.* F it feels great
feen·haft *adj.* fairylike; *fig.* magic(al)
'Feen|kö·ni·gin *f* fairy queen; **~reich** *n* fairy kingdom; ***das ~*** *a.* Fairyland
Fe·ge·feu·er ['fe:gə-] *n*: ***das ~*** purgatory
fe·gen ['fe:gən] **I.** *v/t.* (h) sweep (*a. fig.*); ***das Geweih ~*** fray its antlers; → ***Tisch***; **II.** *v/i.* (sn) sweep (*a. fig.*), *wind*: *a.* rush
Feh [fe:] *n* (-[e]s; -e) squirrel (fur)
Feh·de ['fe:də] *f* (-; -n) feud (*a. fig.*); ***in ~ liegen mit*** *dat.* be at war with; **~hand·schuh** *m*: ***den ~ hinwerfen*** (***aufheben***) throw down (pick up) the gauntlet
fehl [fe:l] *adv.* → ***Platz*** 3
Fehl·an·zei·ge ['fe:l-] *f* **1.** (***war***) ~ F nothing doing; no such luck; **2.** ⚙ instrument error
fehl·bar ['fe:lba:ɐ] *adj.* fallible; **'Fehl·bar·keit** *f* (-; *no pl.*) fallibility
Fehl|be·die·nung ['fe:l-] *f* operating error; **~be·set·zung** *f thea.* miscasting; miscast actor (*or* actress); *sport etc.*: *the* wrong man (*or* woman) for the job; **~be·stand** *m* deficiency; **~be·trag** *m* deficit, shortfall; **~be·zeich·nung** *f* misnomer; **~bil·dung** *f biol. etc.* malformation; **~bit·te** *f*: ***e-e ~ tun*** meet with a refusal; **~deu·tung** *f* misinterpretation; **~dia·,gno·se** *f* ⚕ wrong diagnosis; diagnostic error; ***e-e ~ stellen*** make a wrong diagnosis (*or* diagnostic error), diagnose wrong; **~ein·schät·zung** *f* misinterpretation; misjudg(e)ment; **~ein·stel·lung** *f* **1.** *psych.* maladjustment; **2.** misconception; **3.** ⚙ *etc.* incorrect focus(s)ing
feh·len ['fe:lən] **I.** *v/i.* (h) **1.** be absent (***in der Schule***, ***bei*** *e-r Sitzung etc.* from); ***er hat gefehlt*** *a.* he didn't turn up; ***er hat e-e Woche gefehlt*** he was absent for a week; **2.** be missing; ***bei dir fehlt ein Knopf*** you've lost a button, there's a button missing from (*or* on) your coat *etc.*; ***ihm ~ zwei Zähne*** he has two teeth missing; ***du hast uns sehr gefehlt*** we really missed you; **3.** be lacking; ***mir fehlt ...*** I need ..., I haven't got (any *or* enough) ...; ***es fehlt an ...*** there's (*or* there are) no ..., there isn't (*or* there aren't) enough ..., there's a lack of ...; ***uns fehlt das nötige Geld, es fehlt uns am nötigen Geld*** we haven't got the money; ***es ~ uns immer noch einige Leute*** we still need a few people; ***ihr fehlten noch DM 50*** she was short of 50 marks, she needed another 50 marks; ***es an nichts ~ lassen*** spare no pains (*or* expense); ***es fehlt ihm an nichts*** he's got everything he wants; ***es fehlte an jeder Zusammenarbeit*** there was no cooperation whatsoever; ***das fehlte gerade noch!*** that's all we *etc.* need(ed); ***wo fehlt's denn?*** what's the trouble?; ***fehlt Ihnen etwas?*** are you all right (*Am.* alright)?; ***es fehlte nicht viel, und er wäre daran gestorben*** he very nearly died of it; ***an mir soll's nicht ~*** (well,) I'll do what I can; ***daran soll's nicht ~*** that's no problem; ***dazu fehlt noch viel*** that's still a long way off, he's *etc.* still got a long way to go before he *etc.* can do that; ***mir ~ die Worte*** words fail me; → ***Ecke***; **4.** miss; *fig.* ***weit gefehlt!*** he *etc.* couldn't be more wrong; **II.** 2 *n* (-s) **5.** absence (***bei*** *dat.*, ***in*** *dat.* from); absenteeism; **6.** lack, absence; **'feh·lend** *adj.* missing; ✝ outstanding
'Fehl|ent·schei·dung *f* mistake; *sport*: wrong decision; ***e-e ~ treffen*** make a mistake (*or* wrong decision); **~ent·wick·lung** *f* ✝ undesirable trend; ⚕ malformation
Feh·ler ['fe:lɐ] *m* (-s; -) mistake; ⚙ fault, flaw, defect; *sport*: fault; *computer*: error, bug; *fig.* flaw, blemish; fault, weakness, shortcoming; drawback; ***kleiner ~*** ✝ slight flaw, *fig.* minor flaw; ***e-n ~ machen*** a) make a mistake, b) make a wrong move, put one's foot in it; ***jeder hat s-e ~*** nobody's perfect, we all have our little failings; ***in den ~ verfallen zu*** *inf.*, ***den ~ begehen zu*** *inf.* make the mistake of *ger.*; ***das hat den ~, daß*** the drawback (*or* the trouble with it) is that; ***das hat nur den ~, daß*** the only snag (*or* problem) is that; **~an·zei·ge** *f computer*: error display; **~be·sei·ti·gung** *f computer*: debugging
'feh·ler·frei *adj.* perfect; correct; flawless
'Feh·ler·gren·ze *f* margin of error; ⚙ tolerance
'feh·ler·haft *adj.* faulty, flawed, defective; incorrect; *essay etc.* full of mistakes; ***~e Stelle*** flaw
'Feh·ler·kor·rek,tur *f computer*: error correction; *CD-player*: *a.* error concealment
'feh·ler·los *adj.* → ***fehlerfrei***
'Feh·ler·mel·dung *f computer*: error message
'Fehl·er·näh·rung *f* wrong nutrition; bad eating habits *pl.*
'Feh·ler|quel·le *f* source of error (⚙ trouble); **~quo·te** *f* error rate; **~su·che** *f* ⚙ troubleshooting; **~ver·zeich·nis** *n* errata *pl.*
Fehl|funk·ti,on ['fe:l-] *f* ⚕ *etc.* malfunctioning; **~ge·burt** *f* miscarriage; **2ge·hen** *v/i.* (*irr.*, *sep.*, sn, → ***gehen***) *a. fig.* go wrong; ***gehe ich fehl in der Annahme ...?*** am I mistaken in assuming ...?; **2ge·lei·tet** *fig. adj.* misguided; **~griff** *m* mistake; wrong (*or* bad) choice; ***e-n ~ tun*** make a mistake, make a wrong (*or* bad) choice; **~hal·tung** *f* **1.** bad posture; **2.** *psych.* abnormal attitude; **~hand·lung** *f* slip, lapse; **~in·for·ma·ti,on** *f* (*a.* ***e-e ~***) wrong (*or* misleading) information; **~in·ter·pre·ta·ti,on** *f* misinterpretation; wrong interpretation; **2in·ter·pre,tie·ren** *v/t.* (*sep.*, h) misconstrue; **~in·ve·sti·ti,on** *f* bad investment; **~kal·ku·la·ti,on** *f* miscalculation; **~kauf** *m* bad buy; **~kon·struk·ti,on** *f* **1.** faulty design; ***diese Überführung ist e-e ~*** this overpass is badly designed; **2.** F piece of junk; **~lei·stung** *f*: (***Freudsche ~*** Freudian) slip; **2lei·ten** *v/t.* (*sep.*, h) misdirect; *fig.* lead *s.o.* astray; → ***fehlgeleitet***; **~mel·dung** *f* → ***Fehlanzeige*** 1; **~men·ge** *f* shortage, shortfall; **~paß** *m sport*: bad pass; **~pla·nung** *f* bad planning; **~pro,gno·se** *f* wrong prediction
Fehl·schlag ['fe:l-] *m* miss; *fig.* failure; disappointment; setback; **'fehl·schla·gen** *v/i.* (*irr.*, *sep.*, sn, → ***schlagen***) miss; *fig.* go wrong; come to nothing
Fehl|schluß ['fe:l-] *m* fallacy; **~schuß** *m* miss; **~spe·ku·la·ti,on** *f*: (***e-e ~*** *a.* a piece of) bad speculation; *fig.* (a) wrong assumption, wrong thinking; **~start** *m* false start; ✈ *a.* unsuccessful takeoff attempt; *sport*: ***e-n ~ verursachen*** jump the gun
fehl·tre·ten ['fe:l-] *v/i.* (*irr.*, *sep.*, sn, → ***treten***) lose one's footing; *fig.* commit a faux pas; **'Fehl·tritt** *m* slip; *fig.* faux pas, lapse, aberration; ***ein ~, und ...*** *a.* one foot wrong and ... (*a. fig.*)
Fehl|ur·teil ['fe:l-] *n* misjudg(e)ment; ⚖ judicial error; **~ver·hal·ten** *n* abnormal behavio(u)r; lapse; **~zeit** *f* time debit
fehl·zün·den ['fe:l-] *v/i.* (*sep.*, h) *mot.* backfire; **'Fehl·zün·dung** *f mot.* backfire; F *fig.* wrong reaction; *mot.* ***~en haben*** backfire; F *fig.* ***das war bei ihm bestimmt e-e ~*** F he must have got the wrong end of the stick
Fei·er ['faɪɐ] *f* (-; -n) celebration; party; ceremony; ***e-e ~ abhalten*** (*or* ***begehen***) have (*or* hold) a celebration; ***zur ~ des Tages*** to mark the occasion
'Fei·er·abend *m* **1.** ***~ machen*** finish (work), F knock off (work); *shop*: close; ***nach ~*** after work; F *fig.* ***jetzt ist aber ~!*** that's enough now!; **2.** evening; ***schönen ~!*** have a nice evening
'fei·er·lich I. *adj.* solemn; ceremonious; F ***das ist*** (***schon***) ***nicht mehr ~*** F it's no joke; **II.** *adv.*: ***~ begehen*** celebrate; ***~ versprechen*** solemnly promise, ***daß***: *a.* make a solemn promise that; **'Fei·er·lich·keit** *f* (-, -en) **1.** *no pl.* solemnity; ceremoniousness; pomp; ***in*** (*or* ***mit***) ***aller ~*** with all due ceremony; **2.** *a. pl.* ceremony
fei·ern ['faɪɐn] (h) **I.** *v/t.* celebrate; keep, observe; commemorate; ***das muß gefeiert werden*** that calls for a celebration; → ***gefeiert***; **II.** *v/i.* celebrate; have a party; F take it easy; F ***~ müssen*** be laid off
'Fei·er|schicht *f* idle shift; ***e-e ~ einlegen*** drop a shift; **~stun·de** *f* ceremony; celebration

'Fei·er·tag *m*: (**gesetzlicher ~** public *or* bank, *Am. a.* legal) holiday; *eccl.* religious holiday; **'fei·er·tags** *adv.*: **sonn- und ~** on Sundays and public (*or* bank) holidays
feig [faɪk], **fei·ge** ['faɪgə] *adj.* cowardly, F yellow, lily-livered; **sei doch nicht so ~!** don't be such a coward; **er ist viel zu ~, um zu** *inf.* he's too much of a coward to *inf.*
Fei·ge ['faɪgə] *f* (-; -n) fig
'Fei·gen|baum *m* fig tree; **~blatt** *n* fig leaf (*a. fig.*)
Feig·heit ['faɪkhaɪt] *f* (-; *no pl.*) cowardice, cowardliness
Feig·ling ['faɪklɪŋ] *m* (-s; -e) coward
feil·bie·ten ['faɪl-] *v/t.* (*irr.*, *sep.*, h, → **bieten**) offer *s.th.* for sale; *contp.* prostitute (**sich** o.s.)
Fei·le ['faɪlə] *f* (-; -n) file; *fig.* finish; *fig.* **die letzte ~ legen an** add the finishing touches to; **'fei·len** (h) **I.** *v/t.* file; **II.** *fig. v/i.*: **~ an** *dat.* polish (up)
feil·schen ['faɪlʃən] *v/i.* (h) haggle (**um** *acc.* over)
fein [faɪn] **I.** *adj.* a) fine; delicate; minute, b) graceful; refined; elegant, smart, c) fine(-quality), choice; excellent, d) accurate, precise; subtle; fine, sensitive; keen; **ein ~es Ohr haben für** *acc.* have a fine ear for; **~es Gebäck** fancy biscuits; **~er Regen** (light) drizzle; **~e Nase** sensitive nose, keen (*or* good) sense of smell, *fig.* good nose; **der ~e Ton** good form; **~er Unterschied** fine (*or* subtle) distinction; **~er Beobachter** keen (*or* shrewd) observer; **die ~e Küche** haute cuisine; **ein ~es Gesicht haben** have very fine features; *iro.* **ein ~er Herr** F a (real) toff; **die ~en Leute** F the nobs; **das 2ste vom 2sten** the very best, the best that money can buy; **das ist schon e-e ~e Sache** you can do worse than that; *iro.* **du bist mir ein ~er Freund** a fine friend you are; **ich bin dir wohl nicht ~ genug** I'm not good enough for you, then, am I?; → **feinmachen**; **II.** *adv.* finely; well, nicely; **~ schmecken** taste good; **das hast du ~ gemacht!** good boy (*or* girl); **er ist ~ heraus** F he's sitting pretty; **III.** *int.*: good!
'Fein|ab·stim·mung *f* fine tuning (*a. fig.*); *TV a.* fine adjustment; **~ar·beit** *f* precision work; *fig.* fine tuning; *fig.* **die ~ machen** *a.* add the finishing touches; **~bäcke'rei** *f* patisserie; **~blech** *n* sheet metal
Feind [faɪnt] **I.** *m* (-[e]s; -e [-də]) enemy (*a.* ⚔); *lit.* foe; adversary; rival; **Freund und ~** friend and foe; **sich ~e machen** make enemies; **sich j-n zum ~ machen** antagonize s.o., make an enemy of s.o.; **ein ~ sein von** (*or gen.*) → **II.** 2 *pred. adj.*: *dat.* **~ sein** be opposed to, be against, be an enemy of; hate, loathe; **~be·rüh·rung** *f* ⚔ contact with the enemy; **~bild** *n*: **ein ~ aufbauen von** make a bogeyman out of
Fein·des·hand ['faɪndəs-] *f*: **in ~ geraten** fall into enemy hands
'feind·lich I. *adj.* **1.** ⚔ hostile, enemy *fire, lines etc.*; **~e Truppen** enemy forces; **2.** hostile, antagonistic, unfriendly (**gegen** *acc.* to[wards]); **II.** *adv.*: **~ gesinnt** hostile (*dat.* to[wards]); **~ eingestellt gegen** opposed to; **'Feind·lich·keit** *f* (-; *no pl.*) animosity, hostility
'Feind·schaft *f* (-; -en) enmity, hostility; antagonism; ranco(u)r; hatred; ill will; feud, quarrel; **persönliche ~** personal animosity (*or* enmity)
feind·se·lig ['faɪntzeːlɪç] *adj.* hostile (**gegen** *acc.* to[wards]); malevolent; **'Feind·se·lig·keit** *f* (-; -en) **1.** *no pl.* hostility; malevolence; **2.** ⚔ **die ~en eröffnen** start (*or* open) hostilities; **die ~en einstellen** suspend hostilities
'Feind·staat *m* enemy state; **'Feind·staa·ten·klau·sel** *f* enemy state clause
'Fein·ein·stel·lung *f* fine adjustment
'fein·füh·lig [-fyːlɪç] *adj.* sensitive; tactful; **'Fein·ge·fühl** *n* sensitiveness; tact, delicacy
'fein·ge·hackt *adj.* finely chopped
'Fein·ge·halt *m* standard; **'Fein·ge·halts·stem·pel** *m* hallmark
'fein|ge·mah·len *adj.* finely ground, fine-ground; **~ge·schnit·ten** *adj.* **1.** finely cut (*or* sliced); **2.** fine-featured; **~es Gesicht** *a.* face with (very) fine features; **~ge·spon·nen** *adj.* finely spun, *a. fig.* fine-spun; **~glied·rig** [-gliːdrɪç] *adj.* slender, gracefully built; **2gold** *n* fine (*or* refined) gold
'Fein·heit *f* (-; -en) **1.** *no pl.* fineness; delicacy; grace(fulness); refinement, elegance; tact; subtlety, finesse; quality; workmanship; *textil.* size, grist; **2. die ~en** the finer points, the niceties, the subtleties; **die letzten ~en** the final touches
'fein|hö·rig *adj.*: **~ sein** have a very sensitive ear; **~kör·nig** *adj.* fine-grained; *phot.* fine-grain; **2korn** *n* fine sight; *phot.* fine grain
'Fein·kost *f* delicatessen *pl.*; **~la·den** *m* delicatessen shop
'fein·ma·chen *v/refl.* (*sep.*, h): **sich ~** get dressed up, dress up; put on one's best clothes; **er hat sich aber feingemacht!** he looks very smart
'fein·ma·schig [-maʃɪç] *adj.* fine-meshed
'Fein·meˌcha·nik *f* precision mechanics *pl.*; **'Fein·meˌcha·ni·ker** *m* precision mechanic
'fein·poˌliert *adj.* highly finished
'Fein·schliff *m* **1.** ⚙ a) finishing; b) finish; **2.** *fig.* a) finish, b) sophistication
'Fein·schmecker [-ʃmɛkɐ] (*sep.* -k·k-) *m* (-s; -) gourmet; **~loˌkal** *n* gourmet restaurant
'Fein|schnitt *m* fine cut *tobacco*; **~sei·fe** *f* good soap; **~sil·ber** *n* fine (*or* refined) silver
'fein·sin·nig *adj.* sensitive; subtle *humo(u)r etc.*; **'Fein·sin·nig·keit** *f* (-; *no pl.*) sensitivity; subtlety
Feinst|be·ar·bei·tung ['faɪnst-] *f* superfinish(ing); **~ein·stel·lung** *f* micrometer adjustment
'Fein|strukˌtur *f phys.* microstructure; **2ver·teilt** *adj.* finely spread; **~waa·ge** *f* precision balance; **~wä·sche** *f* delicate fabrics *pl.*; **~wasch·mit·tel** *n* gentle washing powder; **~zucker** *m* refined sugar
feist [faɪst] *adj.* fat, stout
fei·xen ['faɪksən] F *v/i.* (h) smirk
Feld [fɛlt] *n* (-[e]s; -er ['fɛldɐ]) field (*a.* ⚔, ⚒, *phys.*, *TV*, *her.*, *psych.*, *computer*, *sport and fig.*); △ panel, coffer; square; **auf freiem ~** in the open; **das ~ anführen** *sport*: lead the field; **des ~es verwiesen werden** *sport*: be sent off; *fig.* **ein weites ~** a vast area; **es steht ein weites ~ offen für** (*or dat.*) a) there's considerable scope for, b) there are plenty of (*or* endless) possibilities for; **das ~ behaupten** stand one's ground; **das ~ räumen** beat a retreat; **aus dem ~(e) schlagen** defeat; **j-m das ~ überlassen** leave the field to s.o., clear the way for s.o.; **ins ~ führen** put forward, advance *an argument*; **zu ~e ziehen gegen** *acc.* campaign (*or* crusade) against; (**noch**) **weit im ~e** a long way off; **er hat freies ~** he has free reign; → **bestellen** 4; **~ar·beit** *f* **1.** ↗ work(ing) in the fields; **2.** fieldwork; **~ar·bei·ter** *m* agricultural labo(u)rer; **~bett** *n* campbed; **~blu·me** *f* wild flower
feld'ein·wärts *adv.* across the fields
'Feld·elek·tron *n* field electron
'Fel·der·wirt·schaft *f* crop rotation
'Feld|fla·sche *f* water bottle, canteen; **~for·schung** *f* field research, fieldwork; **~früch·te** *pl.* field crops; **~got·tes·dienst** *m* camp service; **~heer** *n* field forces *pl.*
'Feld·herr *m* general; strategist; **'Feld·herrn·blick** *m* authoritative air
'Feld|hockey *n* field hockey; **~huhn** *n* grey (*Am.* gray) partridge; **~jä·ger** *m* military policeman; *pl.* military police (*pl.*), MPs; **~kü·che** *f* field kitchen; **~la·ger** *n* bivouac, (military) camp; **~laˌzaˌrett** *n* casualty clearing station, *Am.* evacuation hospital; **~ler·che** *f* skylark; **~mar·schall** *m* field marshal; *NATO*: five-star general; **~maus** *f* field vole; **~mes·ser** *m* (-s; -) surveyor
'Feld·post *f* forces' mail (service); **~brief** *m* letter from (*or* to) the front
'Feld|saˌlat *m* lamb's lettuce, corn salad; **~spat** [-ʃpaːt] *m* (-[e]s; -e) *min.* feldspar; **~stär·ke** *f phys.* field strength; **~ste·cher** [-ʃtɛçɐ] *m* (-s; -): (**ein ~** a pair of) binoculars *pl. or* field glasses *pl.*; **~stein** *m* fieldstone; erratic block; boundary stone; **~stu·die** *f* field study; **~stuhl** *m* camp stool; **~te·leˌfon** *n* field telephone; **~theoˌrie** *f phys.* field theory; **2überˌle·gen** *adj.*: **~ sein** *sport*: see more of the ball; **~ver·such** *m* field test; **~ver·weis** *m*: **sich e-n ~ einhandeln** be sent off
'Feld-'Wald-und-'Wie·sen-... F common-or-garden ..., run-of-the-mill ...
'Feld·we·bel [-veːbəl] *m* (-s; -) sergeant; F *contp.* F sergeant major; **~ton** *m*: **im ~** in a sergeant major voice
'Feld|weg *m* country lane; **~zug** *m* ⚔ campaign (*a. fig.*), expedition; **e-n ~ führen gegen** *acc.* conduct (*or* go on) a military campaign against, *fig.* wage a campaign against, campaign (*or* crusade) against
Fel·ge ['fɛlgə] *f* (-; -n) **1.** ⚙, *mot.* rim; **2.** *gym.* circle; **'Fel·gen·brem·se** *f* calliper brake
Fell [fɛl] *n* (-[e]s; -e) *zo.* coat; hide, skin (*a.* ♪ *and* F *fig.*); pelt; fur; **das ~ abziehen** *dat.* skin; F *fig.* **ein dickes ~ haben** have a thick skin; **j-m das ~ über die Ohren ziehen** pull the wool over s.o.'s eyes; **s-e ~e davonschwimmen sehen** see one's hopes dashed, (have to) wave goodbye to one's plans *etc.*; → **gerben, jucken** I; **~jacke** *f* sheepskin jacket
Fels [fɛls] *m* (-en; -en ['fɛlzən]) rock (*a. fig.*); *fig.* pillar; **wie ein ~ in der Brandung** (as) steady (*or* firm) as a rock, like the Rock of Gibraltar; **~ab·hang** *m* precipice; **~block** *m*, **~brocken** *m* boulder, (piece of) rock
Fel·sen ['fɛlzən] *m* (-s; -) rock; crag; cliff;

℮fest I. *adj.* (as) steady as a rock; steadfast, unshak(e)able, unwavering; **II.** *adv.*: ***ich bin ~ davon überzeugt*** I'm firmly (*or* absolutely) convinced of it; ***sich ~ auf j-n verlassen*** rely on s.o. totally, absolutely rely on s.o.; **~klip·pe** *f* cliff; **~kü·ste** *f* rocky coast(line); **~riff** *n* reef

'Fels|for·ma·ti,on *f* rock formation; **~grat** *m* rocky ridge

fel·sig ['fɛlzɪç] *adj.* rocky

'Fels|mas,siv *n* **1.** huge rock; **2.** mountain; **~spal·te** *f* crevice; **~vor·sprung** *m* ledge; **~wand** *f* rockface; wall of rock; **~zeich·nung** *f* rock drawing

Fe·me ['fe:mə] *f* (-; -n), **Fem·ge·richt** *n* **1.** *hist.* vehmgericht; **2.** kangaroo court

fe·mi·nin [femi'ni:n] *adj.* feminine (*a. ling.*); *contp.* effeminate; **Fe·mi·nis·mus** [femi'nɪsmʊs] *m* (-; *no pl.*) feminism; **Fe·mi·nist** [femi'nɪst] *m* (-en; -en), **Fe·mi'ni·stin** *f* (-; -nen) feminist; **fe·mi·ni·stisch** [femi'nɪstɪʃ] *adj.* feminist

Fen·chel ['fɛnçəl] *m* (-s; *no pl.*) fennel; **~tee** *m* fennel tea

Fen·der ['fɛndɐ] *m* (-s; -) ⚓ fender

Fen·ster ['fɛnstɐ] *n* (-s; -) window (*a. envelope and computer*); shop window; ⚒ (glass) frame; *fig. pol.* gate (**nach** *dat.* to); ***zum ~ hinausschauen*** look out of (*Am. a.* out) the window; *fig.* ***sein Geld zum ~ hinauswerfen*** throw one's money away; ***es ist, als wenn ich zum ~ hinausredete*** it's like talking to a brick wall; F ***er ist weg vom ~*** F he's had his chips; **~bank** *f* (-; ⸚e) **1.** window seat; **2.** → **~brett** *n* windowsill; **~brief,um·schlag** *m* window envelope; **~flü·gel** *m* casement; **~git·ter** *n* (window) grille; **~glas** *n* window glass; **~he·ber** *m mot.*: ***elektrische ~*** electric (*or* power) windows; **~kitt** *m* putty; **~kur·bel** *f mot.* window winder; **~la·den** *m* shutter; **~le·der** *n* chamois (leather)

fen·sterln ['fɛnstɐln] *dial. v/i.* (h) *sneak into one's girlfriend's room through the window at night with the help of a ladder*

'Fen·ster|platz *m* window seat; **~put·zer** *m* window cleaner; **~rah·men** *m* window frame; **~ro·se** *f* ⚠ rose window; **~schei·be** *f* windowpane; **~sims** *m, n* windowsill, window ledge; **~spie·gel** *m* window mirror; **~sturz** *m* **1.** lintel; **2.** *hist.* defenestration; **~tech·nik** *f computer*: windowing technique; **~tür** *f* French window; **~,um·schlag** *m* window envelope

Fe·ri·en ['fe:rĭən] *pl.* holidays; *esp.* ⚖, *univ. or Am.* vacation *sg., Brit. univ. a.* F vac; *parl.* recess *sg.*; ***die großen ~*** the long vacation; ***~ haben*** be on holiday (*Am.* vacation); ***wann habt ihr ~?*** when are (*or* when do you have) your holidays?, *Am.* when is (*or* when do you have) your vacation?; ***~ machen*** go on holiday (*Am.* vacation); **~aus·tausch** *m* holiday exchange; **~be·ginn** *m* beginning of the holidays (*Am.* vacation); **~dorf** *n* holiday village; **~en·de** *n* end of the holidays (*Am.* vacation); **~haus** *n* holiday (*Am.* vacation) home; **~job** *m* holiday (*Am.* vacation) job; *a.* summer job; **~kurs** *m* vacation course, *a.* summer course; **~la·ger** *n* holiday camp; summer camp; ***ins ~ fahren*** go to a holiday camp, go to summer camp; **~ort** *m* holiday resort; **~pa·ra,dies** *n* holidaymaker's paradise; **~rei·se** *f* holiday (*Am.* vacation) trip; **~rei·sen·de** *m, f* (-n; -n) holidaymaker; *Am.* vacationist, vacationer; **~woh·nung** *f* holiday apartment; **~zeit** *f* holiday (*Am.* vacation) period; **~ziel** *n* vacation spot; tourist destination

Fer·kel ['fɛrkəl] *n* (-s; -) young pig, piglet; *fig.* pig, F mucky pup; *sl.* filthy swine; **Fer·ke·lei** [fɛrkə'laɪ] *f* (-; -en) obscenity; dirty remark; **'fer·keln** *v/i.* (h) **1.** *zo.* farrow, litter; **2.** *fig.* a) make a mess, behave like a pig, b) talk smut

Fer·ma·te [fɛr'ma:tə] *f* (-; -n) ♪ pause, hold, fermata

Fer·ment [fɛr'mɛnt] *n* (-[e]s; -e) ferment, enzyme; **Fer·men·ta·ti·on** [fɛrmɛnta'tsĭo:n] *f* (-; -en) fermentation; **fer·men·tie·ren** [fɛrmɛn'ti:rən] *v/t. and v/i.* (h) ferment

fern [fɛrn] **I.** *adj.* far (*a. adv.*); far off, distant; *days etc.* long past; ***~e Gegenden*** (*or* ***Länder***) faraway places; ***der ℮e Osten*** the Far East; ***von ~*** from (*or* at) a distance (*a. fig.*), *lit.* from afar; ***ich sah ihn von ~ kommen*** I could see him coming in the distance; ***in nicht*** (***allzu***) ***~er Zukunft*** in the not too distant future; ***in ~er Vergangenheit*** a long, long time ago; ***das sei ~ von mir!*** I wouldn't dream of it; → ***nah*** 1; **II.** *prp.* far (away) from

fern'ab *adv.* far away

'Fern|ab·fra·ge *f teleph.* remote pickup (*or* interrogation); **~ab·fra·ger** *m teleph.* tone pad; **~amt** *n teleph.* long-distance exchange; **~auf·klä·rung** *f* ⚔ long-range reconnaissance; **~auf·nah·me** *f* long-distance shot; **~aus·lö·ser** *m phot.* cable release; **~be·die·nung** *f* remote control; **℮blei·ben** *v/i.* (*irr., sep.*, sn, → ***bleiben***) not to come *or* go (**von** *dat. or dat.* to), *ped. etc.* be absent (from), stay away (from); ***~ von*** *dat. a.* not to attend *a meeting etc.*; **~blick** *m* vista, view into the distance; **~bril·le** *f*: (***e-e ~*** a pair of) distance glasses *pl.*; **~dia,gno·se** *f* ⚕ absentee diagnosis

Fer·ne ['fɛrnə] *f* (-; *no pl.*) distance; ***aus der ~*** from a distance (*a. fig.*); ***in der ~ verschwinden*** disappear in(to) the distance (*or* out of view), fade out of sight; ***es zieht ihn wieder in die ~*** he's got wanderlust again; *fig.* (***noch***) ***in weiter ~*** (still) a long way off

'Fern·emp·fang *m radio*: long-range reception

fer·ner ['fɛrnɐ] **I.** *adj.* further; **II.** *adv.* further(more); besides, moreover; on top of that, and then; ***~ liefen*** *sport*: also ran; F *fig.* ***er erschien unter ~ liefen*** he was among the also-rans

'fer·ner·hin *adv.* for the (*or* in) future, henceforth; ***auch ~ tun*** continue to do

'Fern|fah·rer *m* long-distance lorry driver, *Am.* long-haul truck driver; **~fahrt** *f* long-distance trip; long haul; **~flug** *m* long-distance (*or* long-haul) flight; **~funk** *m* long-range transmission; **℮ge·lenkt** *adj.* → ***ferngesteuert***; **~ge·spräch** *n* long-distance call; **℮ge·steu·ert** *adj.* remote-controlled, remote control ...; ✈ pilotless; ***~es Geschoß*** guided missile; **~glas** *n*: (***ein ~*** a pair of) binoculars *pl.*

'fern·hal·ten (*irr., sep.*, h, → ***halten***) **I.** *v/t.* keep away (**von** *dat.* from); ***j-n von sich ~*** keep s.o. at a distance (*or* at arm's length); ***et. von j-m ~*** keep s.th. from s.o., protect s.o. from s.th.; **II.** *v/refl.*: ***sich ~*** keep away (**von** *dat.* from), steer clear (of)

'Fern|hei·zung *f* district heating (plant); **~ka·bel** *n* long-distance cable; **~ko,pie·rer** *m* facsimile (*or* fax) machine; telecopier; **~kurs** *m* correspondence course; **~la·ster** F *m*, **~last·wa·gen** *m* long-distance lorry, *Am.* long-haul truck; **~lei·he** [-laɪə] *f* (-; -n) inter-library loan (system); **~lei·tung** *f teleph.* long-distance line; ⚡ transmission line; ⚙ pipeline

'fern·len·ken *v/t.* (*sep.*, h) operate (*or* guide) by remote control; **'Fern·len·kung** *f* remote control; **'Fern·lenk·waf·fe** *f* guided weapon (*or* missile)

'Fern·licht *n* (-[e]s; *no pl.*) *mot.* full (*or* high) beam (position)

'fern·lie·gen *v/i.* (*irr., sep.*, h, → ***liegen***): ***es liegt mir fern zu*** *inf.* far be it from me to *inf.*; ***es lag ihm fern zu*** *inf.* he had no intention of *ger.*; ***nichts lag mir ferner*** nothing was further from my mind, I wouldn't have dreamt of it

'Fern·mel·de|amt *n* telephone exchange; **~ge·büh·ren** *pl.* telephone charges; **~sa·tel,lit** *m* communications satellite; **~tech·nik** *f* (tele)communications *pl.*; **~turm** *m* radio and TV tower; **~we·sen** *n* (-s; *no pl.*) telecommunications *pl.*

'fern·münd·lich I. *adj.* telephone ...; **II.** *adv.* by telephone

'Fern'ost..., 'fern'öst·lich *adj.* Far Eastern

'Fern|rei·se *f* long-distance (*or* long-haul) holiday; **~rohr** *n* telescope; **~ruf** *m* telephone call; Telephone (*abbr.* Tel.); **~schach** *n* correspondence chess; **~schrei·ben** *n* telex; **~schrei·ber** *m* telex machine

'fern·schrift·lich I. *adj.* telex *message etc.*; **II.** *adv.* by telex

'Fern·schuß *m soccer*: long-range shot

'Fern·seh... *in cpds.* television ..., TV *aerial, camera, channel, interview, satellite, studio etc.*; **~an·sa·ger** *m* television *or* TV presenter (*a. Am.* announcer); **~an·spra·che** *f* television (*or* televised) address; **~an·stalt** *f* television company; **~an,ten·ne** *f* television *or* TV aerial (*or* antenna); **~ap·pa,rat** *m* → ***Fernsehgerät***; **~auf·tritt** *m* television (*or* TV) appearance; **~bild** *n* television image (*or* picture); **~de,bat·te** *f* television debate; **~dis·kus·si,on** *f* (TV) panel discussion; **~emp·fang** *m* TV reception

'Fern·se·hen I. *n* (-s) television, TV; ***im ~*** on television; **II.** ℮ *v/i.* (*irr., sep.*, h, → ***sehen***) watch television (*or* TV)

'Fern·se·her F *m* (-s; -) **1.** TV (set); **2.** TV viewer

'Fern·seh|fas·sung *f* television (*or* TV) adaptation; **~film** *m* TV film, film made for television, TV version; **~ge·büh·ren** *pl.* television licen|ce (*Am.* -se) fee *sg.*; **~ge·rät** *n* television (set), TV (set); **~ge·sell·schaft** *f* television (*or* TV) company; **~jour·na,list** *m* television (*or* TV) journalist; **~kom·men,tar** *m* television (*or* TV) commentary; **~kom·men,ta·tor** *m* television (*or* TV) commentator; **~norm** *f* TV standard; **~pro,gramm** *n* **1.** television (*or* TV) program(me); **2.** TV guide; **~pu·bli·kum** *n* television audience; **~re,por·ter** *m* television (*or* TV) reporter; **~röh·re** *f* television tube; **~sa·tel,lit** *m* TV (*or* television) satellite;

~schirm *m* (television) screen; **~sender** *m* **1.** television transmitter; **2.** television (broadcasting) station; **3.** television channel; **~sen·dung** *f* (television *or* TV) program(me); **~se·rie** *f* television (*or* TV) series; **~spiel** *n*, **~stück** *n* television (*or* TV) play; **~spot** *m* TV ad; **~stu·dio** *n* television (*or* TV) studio(s *pl.*); **~tech·ni·ker** *m* television engineer; **~teil·neh·mer** *m* television viewer; **~tru·he** *f* TV cabinet; **~turm** *m* television (*or* TV) tower; **~über·tra·gung** *f* television (*or* TV) broadcast; **~un·ter·hal·tung** *f* television (*or* TV) entertainment; **~wer·bung** *f* **1.** television (*or* TV) advertising *or* commercials *pl.*; **2.** TV commercial (*or* ad, *Brit. a.* advert); **~zeit·schrift** *f* TV guide; **~zim·mer** *n* TV room; **~zu·schau·er** *m* (television *or* TV) viewer; *pl. a.* television (*or* TV) audience *sg.*

'Fern·sicht *f* (-; *no pl.*) **1.** view; **2.** *meteor.* visibility

'Fern·sprech|amt *n* telephone exchange; **~an·schluß** *m* telephone connection; **~auf·trags·dienst** *m* answering service; **~au·to·mat** *m* pay phone; **~buch** *n* telephone directory, phone book

'Fern·spre·cher *m* (-s; -) telephone, phone; ***öffentlicher ~*** public telephone

'Fern·sprech|ge·büh·ren *pl.* telephone charges; **~lei·tung** *f* telephone line; **~netz** *n* telephone network; **~num·mer** *f* telephone number; **~teil·neh·mer** *m* telephone subscriber; **~ver·kehr** *m* telephone communications *pl.*

'fern·ste·hen *v/i.* (*irr.*, *sep.*, h, → ***stehen***): ***j-m ~*** have no (real) contact with s.o., have no (real) relationship with s.o.; ***e-r Sache ~*** have nothing to do with s.th.

'fern·steu·ern *v/t.* (*sep.*, h) operate by remote control; **'Fern·steue·rung** *f* remote control

'Fern|stra·ße *f* major road; motorway, *Am.* freeway, interstate (highway); **~stu·di·um** *n* **1.** (degree by) correspondence course; **2.** distance learning; **~tou·ris·mus** *m* long-haul holidays *pl.*; **~trans·port** *m* long-distance (*or* long-haul) transport; **~trau·ung** *f* marriage by proxy; **~uni·ver·si·tät** *f* distance learning institute, *in GB*: *the* Open University; **~un·ter·richt** *m* correspondence course(s *pl.*)

'Fern·ver·kehr *m* long-distance traffic; **'Fern·ver·kehrs·stra·ße** *f* → ***Fernstraße***

'Fern|waf·fe *f* long-range weapon; **~wahl** *f teleph.* direct dial(l)ing; **~wär·me** *f* district heating; **~weh** *n* wanderlust, F itchy feet; **~wir·kung** *f* **1.** *phys.* long-distance effect; **2.** ⚙ remote action; **3.** *psych.* telepathy; **4.** *fig.* long-range (*or* long-term) effect; **~ziel** *n* long-term objective; **~zug** *m* long-distance train; **~zün·dung** *f* remote-control(l)ed ignition

Fer·se ['fɛrzə] *f* (-; -n) heel (*a. of stocking etc.*); *fig. j-m or e-r Sache* (***dicht***) ***auf den ~n folgen*** follow (hot *or* hard) on the heels of; ***j-m auf den ~n sein*** be hard on s.o.'s heels

'Fer·sen|bein *n* heel bone; **~geld** *n*: ***~ geben*** take to one's heels, turn tail; **~schub** *m* heel push; **~sitz** *m* squat

fer·tig ['fɛrtɪç] *adj.* **1.** ready; ***ich bin gleich ~*** I'll be ready (*or* with you) in a minute; (***Achtung,***) ***~, los!*** *sport*: ready, steady, go!; **2.** finished, done; ***fix und ~*** all ready; → *a.* **4**; ***~ sein mit*** *dat.* have finished with, have finished *book, letter etc.*; ***bist du mit dem Putzen ~?*** have you finished (with the) cleaning?; ***~ werden mit*** *dat.* finish, get through *s.th.*, *fig.* cope with, get over *s.th.*, be able to handle (*or* take); ***man wird*** (***damit***) ***nie ~*** there's no end to it, it's never-ending; *fig.* ***mit ihm werd' ich schon ~*** I can (*or* know how to) handle him; ***soll er damit ~ werden*** that's his problem; ***damit mußt du allein ~ werden*** nobody can help you there, you're on your own there, I'm afraid; ***ohne*** *j-n or et.* ***~ werden*** get along (*or* manage) quite well without; ***er wurde nie damit ~, daß sie ihn verlassen hatte*** (***daß ihm gekündigt wurde***) he never got over her leaving him (being fired); ***und damit ~!*** and that's that!; ***mit ihm bin ich ~!*** I'm through (*or* I've finished) with him; **3.** ✝ finished; ⚙ prefabricated; off-the-peg *clothes*; *gastr.* pre-cooked; ready-to-serve ...; **4.** F *fig.* (*a.* ***fix und ~***) shattered, F bushed; done for; ***der ist ~!*** F he's had it; → ***fertigmachen*** 2, ***Nerv***; **5.** F *fig.* speechless, *pred.* F floored; ***da war ich*** (***aber***) ***~!*** F that really floored me

'Fer·tig|bau *m* (-[e]s; -ten) **1.** prefabricated building, F prefab; **2.** *no pl.* → **~bau·wei·se** *f* prefabricated construction; ***in ~*** prefabricated

'fer·tig|be·kom·men *v/t.* (*irr.*, *sep.*, h, → ***bekommen***) → ***fertigbringen***; **≗be·ton** *m* ready-mixed concrete; **~brin·gen** *v/t.* (*irr.*, *sep.*, h, → ***bringen***) finish, get *s.th.* done; manage, bring *s.th.* off; *w.s.* do; ***es ~ zu*** *inf.* manage to *inf.*; ***ich brachte es nicht fertig*** I couldn't do it, I couldn't bring myself to do it; F ***er brachte es fertig, sie rauszuschmeißen*** he actually threw her out; ***wie bringt jemand so etwas fertig?*** how can anyone do a thing like that?; *contp.* ***er bringt es*** (***glatt***) ***fertig*** I wouldn't put it past him; ***das bringst nur du fertig*** that's just like you(, isn't it?), it couldn't have been anyone else

fer·ti·gen ['fɛrtɪgən] *v/t.* (h) make, produce, manufacture

'Fer·tig|er·zeug·nis *n*, **~fa·bri·kat** *n* finished product (*pl. a.* goods); **≗ge·packt** *adj.* prepacked; **~ge·richt** *n* ready-to-serve meal; **≗ge·schnit·ten** *adj.* pre-cut; **~haus** *n* prefabricated house, F prefab

'Fer·tig·keit *f* (-; -en) **1.** *no pl.* skill; talent; proficiency (***in*** *dat.* in); fluency; **2.** **~en** practi|ce (*Am. a.* -se)

'Fer·tig·klei·dung *f* ready-to-wear (*or* off-the-peg) clothes *pl.*

'fer·tig|krie·gen F *v/t.* (*sep.*, h) → ***fertigbringen***; **~le·sen** *v/t.* (*irr.*, *sep.*, h, → ***lesen***) finish (reading); **~ma·chen** *v/t.* (*sep.*, h) **1.** a) finish (off); b) get *s.o. or s.th.* ready; **2.** F (*a.* ***fix und fertig machen***) take it out of *s.o.*, finish (off), get *s.o.* down; ruin, wipe out; F tear *s.o.* to pieces (*or* shreds); F really tear a strip off *s.o.*; F slam; F give *s.o.* a (real) clobbering; *sport*: F clobber; F finish *s.o.* off, do *s.o.* in; ***die Sache macht mich langsam fertig*** F it's starting to get to me; ***er macht mich fertig*** he's getting me down, F he's driving me spare

'Fer·tig|me·nü *n* ready-to-serve meal; **~mon·ta·ge** *f* final assembly; **~nah·rung** *f* convenience food(s *pl.*); **~pro·dukt** *n* finished product

'fer·tig·stel·len *v/t.* (*sep.*, h) finish, complete; **'Fer·tig·stel·lung** *f* (-; *no pl.*) completion

'Fer·tig·teil *n* prefabricated part; finished part

Fer·ti·gung ['fɛrtɪgʊŋ] *f* (-; *no pl.*) manufacture, production

'Fer·ti·gungs|be·reich *m* ✝ manufacturing sector; **~be·trieb** *m* production plant; factory; **~stra·ße** *f* production (*or* assembly) line; **~tech·nik** *f* production engineering

'Fer·tig·wa·ren *pl.* finished products

Fes[1] [fɛs] *n* (-; -) ♪ F flat

Fes[2] [fe:s] *m* (-es; -e ['fe:zə]) fez

fesch [fɛʃ] F *adj.* smart; dashing; ***~er Kerl*** dashing young man, smart lad

Fes·sel[1] ['fɛsəl] *f* (-; -n) rope; chain; *fig.* fetters *pl.*, shackles *pl.*; ***j-m ~n anlegen*** put s.o. in chains, handcuff s.o.; *fig.* ***die ~n abschütteln*** (***sprengen***) shake off (break out of) one's chains; ***et. als ~ empfinden*** feel tied down by s.th.

'Fes·sel[2] *f* (-; -n) *anat.* ankle; *zo.* pastern, fetlock

'Fes·sel·bal·lon *m* captive balloon

'Fes·sel·ge·lenk *n zo.* pastern, fetlock, hock

fes·seln ['fɛsəln] *v/t.* (h) **1.** tie up, put *s.o.* in chains, handcuff; *fig.* fetter; ***j-n an Händen und Füßen ~*** tie s.o.'s hands and feet; *fig.* ***j-n an sich ~*** tie s.o. to one; → ***gefesselt*** 1; **2.** *fig.* captivate, enthral(l); catch *s.o.'s attention, eye etc.*; ***das Buch hat mich gefesselt*** I found the book quite gripping; → ***gefesselt*** 2; **'fes·selnd I.** *adj.* captivating, fascinating; arresting; absorbing, riveting; gripping; **II.** *adv.*: ***~ schreiben*** *or* ***erzählen*** (***können***) be a captivating writer *or* storyteller

fest [fɛst] **I.** *adj.* firm (*a. fig. decision etc.*); solid (*a. food*); hard; strong; sturdy, good *pair of shoes*; fixed, rigid, ⚙ stationary; surfaced *road*; firmly fixed, tight *screw etc.*; fixed (*a. fig. date etc.*); tight; *fig.* permanent *post, job etc.*, steady (*a. boyfriend etc.*); fixed *abode*; close *friendship*; firm, binding *agreement etc.*; set *phrase*; heavy *blow etc.*; firm, unshak(e)able; ✝ steady, firm *market etc.*; fixed *income, salary, prices etc.*; hard, stable *currency*; regular *customers*; deep *sleep*; ***~er Bestandteil*** integral part; ***~er Gewahrsam*** safe custody; *phys.* ***~er Körper*** solid (body); ***ohne ~en Wohnsitz*** of no fixed abode; ***~ werden*** harden, solidify, *cement etc.*: set; ***~er machen*** (*or* ***ziehen***) tighten; ***in Geschichte ist er*** (***nicht sehr***) ***~*** he knows his history (F he's not too hot on history); ***ich hatte die ~e Absicht zu*** *inf.* I had every intention of *ger.*; → ***Boden*** 1, ***Fuß*** 1, ***Hand***; **II.** *adv.* firmly *etc.*; → ***I***; ***~ anbringen*** fix (*or* attach) securely (***an*** *dat.* to); *Geld* ***~ anlegen*** tie up; ***~ angestellt*** permanently employed, ***sein:*** *a.* have a permanent post (*or* job); ***~ beharren auf*** *dat.* insist on; (***steif und***) ***~ behaupten*** (absolutely) insist; ***ich hab's ihm ~ versprochen*** I can't go back on my promise; ***ich bin ~ davon überzeugt, daß*** I'm absolutely convinced (*or* positive) that; ***es ist ~ abgemacht*** it's definite; ***ich bin ~ entschlossen zu*** *inf.* I'm determined to *inf.*; ***sie sind ~ be-***

freundet they're (very) good friends, they're going steady; F ***(immer) ~e!*** a) F let him (*or* her) have it!, b) F go at it!
Fest [fɛst] *n* (-[e]s; -e) celebration; festivities *pl.*; party; banquet; fete; *eccl.* feast, festival; F treat; ***frohes ~!*** Merry Christmas!; ***ein ~ geben*** have (*or* throw) a party, have (*or* hold) a reception; ***ein ~ feiern*** have (*or* throw) a party, (*a.* ***ein ~ begehen***) celebrate, have a celebration, *eccl.* hold (*or* celebrate) a feast; F ***es ist ein wahres ~ zu*** *inf.* it's a real treat to *inf.*; ***man muß die ~e feiern, wie sie fallen*** it's not every day you get a chance to celebrate, F any excuse for a celebration, *fig.* you've got to take your chances; **~akt** *m* ceremony
'**fest|an·ge·legt** *adj.* ✝ tied-up, *pred.* tied up; **~an·ge·stellt** *adj.* permanently employed
'**Fest|an·spra·che** *f* → ***Festrede***; **~auf·füh·rung** *f* gala performance
'**Fest|auf·trag** *m* ✝ firm order; **2bei·ßen** *v/refl.* (*irr.*, *sep.*, h, → ***beißen***) **1.** ***der Hund biß sich an ihrem Bein fest*** (***hatte sich an ihrem Bein festgebissen***) the dog sank its teeth into her leg (wouldn't let go of her leg); **2.** *fig.* ***sich an e-m Problem*** *etc.* **~** become totally absorbed by (F get bogged down with) a problem *etc.*; ***er hat sich an der Idee festgebissen*** he's obsessed with (*or* by) the idea
'**Fest·be·leuch·tung** *f* illuminations *pl.*, (Christmas *etc.*) lights *pl.*; lighting
'**fest|be·sol·det** *adj.* salaried; **~bin·den** *v/t.* (*irr.*, *sep.*, h, → ***binden***) tie up; tether; **~ *an*** *dat.* tie to; **~blei·ben** *v/i.* (*irr.*, *sep.*, sn, → ***bleiben***) remain (*or* stand) firm; stick to one's decision (*or* promise *etc.*); **2brenn·stoff** *m* solid fuel; **~dre·hen** *v/t.* (*sep.*, h) tighten
fe·ste ['fɛstə] F *adv.* → ***fest*** II
'**Fest·es·sen** *n* dinner, banquet
'**fest|fah·ren** (*irr.*, *sep.*, → ***fahren***) **I.** *v/t.* (h) ⚓ run *a ship* aground; *mot.* get *a car* stuck; **II.** *v/i.* (sn) *and v/refl.*: ***sich ~*** (h) get stuck (*a. fig.*); *fig. negotiations etc.*: come to a standstill, reach (a) deadlock; → ***festgefahren*** II; **~fres·sen** *v/refl.* (*irr.*, *sep.*, h, → ***fressen***): ***sich ~*** get stuck, ⚙ *a.* jam; ***sich ~ in*** *dat.* rust into; *fig. idea etc.*: take hold of; **~frie·ren** *v/i.* (*irr.*, *sep.*, sn, → ***frieren***) freeze; **~ *an*** *dat.* freeze to; **~ge·fah·ren I.** *p.p. of* ***festfahren***; **II.** *fig. adj.* rigid, inflexible *habits etc.*; fixed *opinion etc.*; **~ge·fügt** *adj.* firmly established
'**Fest·ge·halt** *n* fixed salary
'**fest·ge·klemmt** *adj.* jammed, stuck; **~ *sein*** *a.* have got stuck
'**Fest·ge·la·ge** *n* feast
'**Fest·geld** *n* fixed term deposits *pl.*
'**fest|ge·schrie·ben I.** *p.p. of* ***festschreiben***; **II.** *adj.* legally established (*or* anchored); sanctioned; ***das ist gesetzlich ~*** *a.* that's (the) law; **~ *in*** *dat.* enshrined in *the constitution etc.*; **~ge·wur·zelt** *adj.* deep-rooted
'**Fest|got·tes·dienst** *m* special service; **~hal·le** *f* hall, auditorium
'**fest|hal·ten** (*irr.*, *sep.*, h, → ***halten***) **I.** *v/t.* hold onto; stop; detain; buttonhole; withhold, hold back; *fig.* record; get a photo of, get *s.o.*, *s.th.* on film; ***et. schriftlich ~*** put s.th. down in writing; ***das wollen wir mal ~*** let there be no doubt about that, I'd like to make that quite clear; (***nur***) ***um das mal festzuhalten ...*** just for the record ...; **II.** *fig. v/i.*: **~ *an*** *dat.* stick to, cling to; **III.** *v/refl.*: ***sich ~*** hold on(to ***an*** *dat.*); ***sich*** (***krampfhaft***) **~ *an*** *dat.* clutch (at), *a. fig.* cling to; F *fig.* ***halt dich fest!*** F hold tight (while I tell you this), wait for this; **~hän·gen** *v/i.* (*irr.*, *sep.*, h, → ***hängen²***) be stuck (*a. fig.*); **~ *an*** *dat.* be caught in (*or* on), have got (o.s.) caught in (*or* on)
fe·sti·gen ['fɛstɪgən] (h) **I.** *v/t.* strengthen; consolidate; stabilize *currency etc.*; *fig.* secure; **II.** *v/refl.*: ***sich ~*** harden, solidify; *currency etc.*: firm; *fig.* strengthen, grow stronger
Fe·stig·keit ['fɛstɪçkaɪt] *f* (-; *no pl.*) *phys.*, ⚙ strength, resistance; stability; ✝ firmness (*a. fig.*), steadiness; stability *of a currency*; *fig.* steadfastness
Fe·sti·gung ['fɛstɪgʊŋ] *f* (-; *no pl.*) strengthening; consolidation; stabilization
Fe·sti·val ['fɛstivəl, 'fɛstival] *n* (-s; -s) festival; **~ver·an·stal·ter** *m* festival organizer
Fe·sti·vi·tät [fɛstivi'tɛːt] *hum. f* (-; -en) festivities *pl.*
'**fest|kei·len** *v/t.* (*sep.*, h) *a. fig.* wedge in; **~klam·mern** (*sep.*, h) **I.** *v/t.* clip on; peg on; ⚙ clamp on; **II.** *v/refl.*: ***sich ~ an*** *dat.* clutch (at), *a. fig.* cling to; **~kle·ben** (*sep.*, h) **I.** *v/i.* stick (***an*** *dat.* to); **II.** *v/t.* stick (***an*** *dat.* to), glue (to); **~klem·men** (*sep.*, h) **I.** *v/t.* clamp; → ***festgeklemmt***; **II.** *v/i. and v/refl.* (***sich ~***) jam, get jammed, get stuck
'**Fest·kom·ma** *n* fixed point
'**Fest·kon,zert** *n* gala concert
'**Fest·kör·per** *m* solid; **~phy,sik** *f* solid state physics *pl.*
'**Fest·ko·sten** *pl.* fixed costs
'**fest·kral·len** *v/refl.* (*sep.*, h): ***sich ~ an*** *dat.* a) dig its claws into, b) cling to
'**Fest·kurs** *m* ✝ fixed quotation
'**Fest·land** *n* (-[e]s; ⸚er) **1.** mainland; **2.** *no pl.* land; '**fest·län·disch** [-lɛndɪʃ] *adj.* mainland; continental; '**Fest·land(s)·sockel** *m* continental shelf
'**fest·le·gen** (*sep.*, h) **I.** *v/t.* **1.** → ***festsetzen*** 1; **2.** lay down *rules etc.*; **3.** ⚓ plot *the course*; **4.** ✝ lock up *capital etc.*; **5.** *fig.* ***j-n ~*** pin (*or* nail) s.o. down (***auf*** *acc.* on), *thea. etc.* typecast s.o. (as); **II.** *v/refl.*: ***sich ~*** commit o.s. (***auf*** *acc.* to); ***ich möchte mich noch nicht ~*** *a.* I'd like to leave that open for the time being; '**Fest·le·gung** *f* (-; -en) **1.** → ***Festsetzung***; **2.** commitment (***auf*** *acc.* to); '**Fest·le·gungs·frist** *f* fixed period of investment
'**fest·lich I.** *adj.* festive; solemn; splendid; dressy; **II.** *adv.*: **~ *begehen*** celebrate; **~ *bewirten*** entertain lavishly; '**Fest·lich·keit** *f* (-; -en) **1.** festivity; **2.** *no pl.* festive atmosphere
'**fest|lie·gen** *v/i.* (*irr.*, *sep.*, h, → ***liegen***) **1.** *date etc.*: be fixed, be settled; **2.** *capital*: be tied up; **2lohn** *m* fixed wage; **~ma·chen** (*sep.*, h) **I.** *v/t.* fix, attach (***an*** *dat.* to); ⚓ moor; *fig.* fix, settle; **II.** *v/i.* ⚓ moor
'**Fest·mahl** *n* banquet
·**fest·na·geln** *v/t.* (*sep.*, h) **1.** nail down; **~ *an*** *dat.* nail to; **2.** *fig.* nail down (***auf*** *acc.* to)
'**Fest·nah·me** [-naːmə] *f* (-; -n) arrest; '**fest·neh·men** *v/t.* (*irr.*, *sep.*, h, → ***nehmen***) (put under) arrest
'**Fest·ob·jek,tiv** *n* fixed lens
'**Fest·ord·ner** *m* steward
'**Fest|plat·te** *f computer*: hard disk; **~preis** *m* fixed price
'**Fest·pro,gramm** *n* program(me) of events
'**Fest·punkt** *m* fixed point, base
'**Fest|re·de** *f* (ceremonial) address; **~red·ner** *m* speaker; ***unser ~*** our speaker on this occasion; **~saal** *m* banqueting hall
'**fest|schnal·len** *v/t.* (*sep.*, h) → ***anschnallen*** I; **~schnü·ren** *v/t.* (*sep.*, h) tie up; **~schrau·ben** *v/t.* (*sep.*, h) screw on (*or* down); **~schrei·ben** *v/t.* (*irr.*, *sep.*, h, → ***schreiben***) codify; sanction; → ***festgeschrieben***
'**Fest·schrift** *f* commemorative volume; festschrift
'**fest·set·zen** (*sep.*, h) **I.** *v/t.* **1.** settle; regulate; prescribe; lay down; fix, set *date etc.* (***auf*** *acc.* for); fix *salary, price etc.* (at); assess; agree on; **2.** arrest, take *s.o.* into custody; put *s.o.* in prison; **II.** *v/refl.*: ***sich ~*** *dirt etc.*: settle, collect; *person*: settle (*a.* ⚕ *disease*); *fig. idea etc.*: become firmly fixed in s.o.'s mind; '**Fest·set·zung** *f* (-; *no pl.*) settling; laying down; fixing; assessment; agreement; imprisonment
'**fest·sit·zen** *v/i.* (*irr.*, *sep.*, h, → ***sitzen***) be stuck (*a. fig.*); ⚓ be stranded (*a.* F *person*), be icebound, be snowbound; *der Schmutz etc.* ***sitzt fest*** won't come off
'**Fest·spei·cher** *m computer*: read-only memory, ROM
'**Fest·spiel** *n* festival performance; **~e** festival; festspiele; **~thea·ter** *n* festival theat|re (*Am. a.* -er); **~wo·che** *f a. pl.* festival, festspiele *pl.*
'**fest·stecken** (*sep.*, h) **I.** *v/t.* pin (***an*** *dat.* [on]to); pin up; **II.** *v/i.* be (*or* have got) stuck
'**fest·ste·hen** *v/i.* (*irr.*, *sep.*, h, → ***stehen***) be fixed; be certain; ***eins steht fest, fest steht, daß*** one thing's for certain; '**fest·ste·hend** *adj.* ⚙ fixed, stationary; still; *fig.* established *fact, tradition etc.*; set *phrase*
'**fest·stell·bar** *adj.* **1.** ascertainable; noticeable; identifiable; ***schwer ~*** hard to ascertain; **2.** ⚙ lockable
'**Fest·stell·brem·se** *f mot.* parking brake
'**fest·stel·len** *v/t.* (*sep.*, h) **1.** find out, discover, ascertain; establish; ⚕ diagnose; determine; assess; locate; see, notice; observe; realize; note; **2.** state; **3.** ⚙ lock
'**Fest·stell|schrau·be** *f* set screw; **~ta·ste** *f* shift lock
'**Fest·stel·lung** *f* (-; -en) discovery; establishment; ascertainment; assessment; locating; ⚖ *etc.* finding(s *pl.*); realization; observation
'**Fest·stel·lungs|be·scheid** *m* ⚖ notice of assessment; **~kla·ge** *f* action for declaratory judg(e)ment
'**Fest·stim·mung** *f* celebratory mood; festive mood (*or* atmosphere)
'**Fest·stoff** *m* solid matter; **~ra,ke·te** *f* solid fuel rocket
'**Fest·ta·fel** *f* (banquet) table
'**Fest·tag** *m* holiday; *eccl.* religious holiday; red-letter day; '**fest·täg·lich** *adj.* festive; '**Fest·tags·stim·mung** *f* celebratory *or* festive mood (*or* atmosphere)
'**fest·tre·ten** *v/t.* (*irr.*, *sep.*, h, → ***treten***) tread down; F ***das tritt sich fest!*** F it's good for the carpet
'**fest·um,ris·sen** *fig. adj.* clear-cut, clearly defined

Fe·stung ['fɛstʊŋ] *f* (-; -en) fortress (*a. fig.*); castle; citadel; fort; *fig.* stronghold
'Fe·stungs|an·la·gen *pl.* fortifications; **~gra·ben** *m* moat; **~krieg** *m* siege warfare; **~stadt** *f* fortress town; **~wall** *m* rampart
'Fest·ver·an·stal·tung *f* **1.** event; (official) celebrations *pl.*; festivities *pl.*; **2.** gala performance
'fest|ver·drah·tet *adj. electron.* hardwired; **~ver·wur·zelt** *adj.* ✿ deeply rooted; *fig. a.* deep-rooted, ingrained; **~verzins·lich** *adj.* fixed-interest (bearing); **~e *Anlagepapiere*** investment bonds; **~wach·sen** *v/i.* (*irr., sep.*, sn, → ***wachsen***) **1.** **~ *an dat.*** grow onto; **2.** ⚕ take; **~ *an dat.*** adhere to
'Fest·wert *m* standard value; *phys.*, ∡ constant, coefficient; **~spei·cher** *m computer*: read-only memory, ROM
'Fest|wie·se *f* fairground; **~wo·che** *f a. pl.* festival
'fest·wur·zeln *v/i.* (*sep.*, sn) take root; *fig. a.* establish itself (*or* themselves); → ***festgewurzelt***
'Fest·zelt *n* marquee
'fest·zie·hen *v/t.* (*irr., sep.*, h, → ***ziehen***) tighten
'Fest·zug *m* procession
Fe·te ['fe:tə] F *f* (-; -n) party, F do; ***e-e* ~ *feiern*** (*or* ***veranstalten***) have a party (*or* do)
Fe·tisch ['fe:tɪʃ] *m* (-[e]s; -e) fetish; ***et. zum ~ machen*** make a fetish (out) of s.th.; **Fe·ti·schis·mus** [feti'ʃɪsmʊs] *m* (-; *no pl.*) fetishism; **Fe·ti·schist** [feti'ʃɪst] *m* (-en; -en) fetishist
fett [fɛt] **I.** *adj.* fat; greasy, fatty *food*; rich *milk etc.*; oily; 🚗, ⚙ rich *mixture*; *typ.* bold, heavy *type*; *fig.* fat *years etc.*; **~ *machen*** fatten; **~*er Bissen*** juicy morsel; *fig.* **~*e Zeiten*** times of plenty; ***davon wird man nicht* ~** you (*or* we *etc.*) won't get fat on that; → ***Brocken*; II.** *adv.*: **~ *essen*** eat a lot of fatty food(s); **~ *kochen*** use a lot of fat (in one's cooking)
Fett [fɛt] *n* (-[e]s; -e) **1.** fat; lard; dripping; shortening; ⚙ grease; **~ *ansetzen*** put on weight; **2.** F *fig.* ***er hat sein ~ abgekriegt*** he got what was coming to him; ***j-m sein ~ geben*** F let s.o. have it; **~ab·bau** *m* breakdown of (body) fats; **~ab·la·ge·rung** *f* deposit of fats, adiposis; fatty deposit; **~an·satz** *m* **1.** first signs *pl.* of a spare tyre (*Am.* tire), beginnings *pl.* of a paunch; **2.** ***zu ~ neigen*** put on weight easily; **≈arm** *adj.* low-fat, *pred.* low in fat; **~ *sein*** *a.* have a low fat content; **~au·ge** *n* blob (*or* globule) of fat
'fett·bäu·chig [-bɔʏçɪç] *adj.* fat-bellied
'Fett|be·darf *m* fat requirement; **~creme** *f* rich oil-based cream; **~de͵pot** *n* fatty deposit; **~druck** *m* (-[e]s; -e) *typ.* bold(-faced) *or* heavy type; **~drü·se** *f* sebacious gland; **~em·bo͵lie** *f* fat embolism
fet·ten ['fɛtən] (h) **I.** *v/t.* grease, lubricate; **II.** *v/i.* be greasy; ***schnell* ~** *hair*: get very greasy
'Fett|film *m* greasy film; **~fleck** *m* grease mark (*or* spot); **≈frei I.** *adj.* fat-free, *a.* non-fat *diet*; **II.** *adv.*: **~ *kochen*** cook without fats; **≈ge·druckt** *adj.* boldface ..., in bold type (*or* print); **~ge·halt** *m* fat content; **~ge·we·be** *n* fatty tissue; **≈glän·zend** *adj.* greasy, shiny
'fett·hal·tig [-haltɪç] *adj.* containing fat, fatty; oil-based, oily *cream*
'Fett·heit *f* (-; *no pl.*) fatness
'Fett·herz *n* fatty heart
fet·tig ['fɛtɪç] *adj.* fat(ty); greasy; oily *cream*; **'Fet·tig·keit** *f* (-; *no pl.*) **1.** fatness; **2.** greasiness
'Fett|kloß F *contp. m* F tub of lard; **~le·ber** *f* ⚕ fatty liver
'fett·lei·big [-laɪbɪç] *adj.* obese; **'Fett·lei·big·keit** *f* (-; *no pl.*) obesity
'fett·lö·send *adj.* grease-cutting; **'fett·lös·lich** *adj.* fat-soluble
'Fett|näpf·chen *n*: *fig.* ***ins ~ treten*** put one's foot in it; ***er tritt dauernd ins ~*** he's always putting his foot in it, F he suffers from foot-in-mouth disease; **~pa͵pier** *n* greaseproof (*Am.* waxed) paper; **~pol·ster** *n* fatty tissue; *a. pl.* F flab; *fig.* buffer stocks *pl.*; **~pres·se** *f mot.* grease gun; **≈reich** *adj.* high-fat, *pred.* high in fat; fatty, rich; **~ *sein*** *a.* have a high fat content; **~sack** F *contp. m* F barrel, tub of lard; **~sal·be** *f* greasy ointment; **~sau** *sl. f sl.* fat slob; **~säu·re** *f* fatty acid; **~schicht** *f* layer of fat; **~stift** *m* **1.** ⚙ grease pencil; **2.** chapstick
'Fett·sucht *f* (-; *no pl.*) ⚕ obesity, adiposity; **'fett·süch·tig** *adj.*: **~ *sein*** suffer from obesity
'fett·trie·fend *adj.* dripping with fat (*or* grease)
'Fett|wanst *m* a) paunch, b) F barrel, tub of lard; **~zel·le** *f* fat (*or* adipose) cell
Fe·tus ['fe:tʊs] *m* (-[ses]; -se, Feten ['fe:tən]) *biol.* f(o)etus
Fet·zen ['fɛtsən] *m* (-s; -) scrap; shred *of material*, rag; wisp *of smoke*; F *fig.* rag; F *pl.* snatches *of conversation etc.*; ***in* ~** in shreds, in tatters; ***in ~ reißen*** tear to shreds; F ***daß die ~ fliegen*** F like crazy
fet·zen ['fɛtsən] **I.** F *v/i.* (sn) **1.** tear; **2. *daß es nur so fetzt*** F like crazy; **3. *das fetzt!*** F it's really great; **II.** *v/t.* (h) tear; ***in Stücke* ~** tear to shreds
feucht [fɔʏçt] *adj.* damp; moist; humid; clammy, dank; *fig.* watery *grave etc.*; **~*e Hitze*** humidity, damp (*or* humid) heat; **~*e Hände*** sweaty palms; ***er hatte*** (***bekam***) **~*e Augen*** his eyes were (became) moist; → ***Kehricht*; Feuch·te** ['fɔʏçtə] *f* (-; *no pl.*) damp(ness)
'feucht-'fröh·lich F *adj.* (very) merry; ***wir hatten e-n* ~*en Abend*** F we had a merry time of it, we had a bit of a booze-up
Feuch·tig·keit ['fɔʏçtɪçkaɪt] *f* (-; *no pl.*) damp(ness); moisture; humidity; ***vor ~ schützen!*** keep in a dry place, keep dry
'Feuch·tig·keits|an·zei·ger *m* hygrometer; **≈an·zie·hend** *adj.* hygroscopic; **≈be·stän·dig** *adj.* moisture-proof; damp-proof; **~creme** *f* moisturizing cream; **~ge·halt** *m* moisture content; **~grad** *m* degree of moisture; humidity; **~iso͵lie·rung** *f* damp-proofing; **~mas·ke** *f* moisturizing mask; **~mes·ser** *m* hygrometer
'feucht|kalt *adj.* clammy, dank; *meteor.* cold and damp; **~warm** *adj.* humid
feu·dal [fɔʏ'da:l] *adj.* a) *hist., pol.* feudal; aristocratic, b) F classy; grand
Feu'dal|herr *m* feudal lord; **~herr·schaft** *f* feudalism, feudal rule
Feu·da·lis·mus [fɔʏda'lɪsmʊs] *m* (-; *no pl.*) feudalism, feudal system; **feu·da·li·stisch** [fɔʏda'lɪstɪʃ] *adj.* feudalistic
Feu·er ['fɔʏɐ] *n* (-s; -) **1.** fire; **~ *legen an acc. or dat.*** (*or* ***in dat.***) set fire to; ***auf offenem* ~ *kochen*** cook over a fire; ***j-m ~ geben*** give s.o. a light; *fig.* ***durchs ~ gehen für*** *acc.* go through fire and water for; ***mit dem ~ spielen*** play with fire; ***das Spiel aus dem ~ reißen*** *sport*: snatch victory from the jaws of defeat; ***zwischen zwei ~ geraten sein*** be caught between the devil and the deep blue sea; F ***j-m ~ unter dem Hintern machen*** a) F give s.o. a kick in the backside, b) F give s.o. hell; ***mit ~ und Schwert*** with fire and sword; → ***anmachen*** 3, ***auslöschen*** 1, ***Eisen, fangen*** I; **2.** ⚓ beacon; **3.** ⚔ fire; ***das ~ eröffnen*** open fire; ***im ~ stehen*** be under fire; **~!** fire!; **4.** *fig.* a) fire, sparkle, b) fire, fervo(u)r; spirit, c) *gastr.* body, vigo(u)r *of wine*; **~ *und Flamme sein*** be all for it, ***für*** *acc.*: be all for *s.o. or s.th.*; ***in ~ geraten*** get quite excited (***über*** *acc.* about)
'Feu·er·alarm *m* fire alarm; **~übung** *f* fire drill
'Feu·er|an·be·ter *m* fire worshipper; **~an·zün·der** *m* firelighter; **~ball** *m phys.* fireball; *lit.* ball of fire; **~be·fehl** *m* ⚔ order to (open) fire; **~be·kämp·fung** *f* fire fighting
'feu·er·be·stän·dig *adj.* fire-resistant, fireproof
'Feu·er|be·stat·tung *f* cremation; **~boh·ne** *f* ✿ scarlet runner; **~ei·fer** *m* zeal; ***mit* ~** with great zeal; **~ein·stel·lung** *f* ⚔ **1.** cessation of hostilities; **2.** ceasefire; **~er·öff·nung** *f* ⚔ opening of fire; **≈fest** *adj.* fireproof, fire-resistant; heat-resistant; incombustible; **~fres·ser** *m* fire-eater; **~ge·fahr** *f* fire risk; danger of fire (breaking out); **≈ge·fähr·lich** *adj.* (in-)flammable; **~ge·fecht** *n* ⚔ gun battle; **~geist** *m* **1.** fire spirit; **2.** *fig.* fiery spirit; **~ha·ken** *m* poker; **≈hem·mend** *adj.* flame-retardant; **~lei·ter** *f* fire ladder (*or* escape); **~li·nie** *f* ⚔ firing line; **~lösch·boot** *n* fire boat (*or* tug); **~lö·scher** *m* fire extinguisher
'Feu·er·lösch|fahr·zeug *n* fire engine; **~ge·rät** *n* fire extinguisher; *pl.* fire-fighting equipment; **~übung** *f* fire drill
'Feu·er|meer *n* sea of flames; **~mel·der** *m* fire alarm
feu·ern ['fɔʏɐn] (h) **I.** *v/i.* **1.** make (*or* light) a fire; ***mit Holz*** (***Kohlen***) **~** burn wood (coal); **2.** ⚔ fire (***auf*** *acc.* at); **II.** *v/t.* **3.** *a.* ⚔ fire; **4.** F *fig.* fling; **5.** F fire, F give *s.o.* the sack; **6.** F ***j-m eine* ~** F land s.o. one
'Feu·er|nel·ke *f* ✿ scarlet lychnis; **~pau·se** *f* ⚔ pause in (the) fighting; **~pro·be** *f* **1.** *hist.* ordeal by fire; **2.** *fig.* acid test; **~rad** *n* Catherine wheel; **~ri·si·ko** *n* fire hazard (*or* risk); **≈rot** *adj.* blazing red; **~ *werden*** turn crimson, go bright red; **~sa·la͵man·der** *m* spotted salamander; **~säu·le** *f* pillar of fire
'Feu·ers·brunst *f* blaze, conflagration
'Feu·er|scha·den *m* damage caused by fire; ***gegen ~ versichert*** insured against fire; **~schein** *m* glow of the fire; ⚔ sky glow; **~schiff** *n* lightship; **~schirm** *m* fire screen; fireguard; **~schlucker** (*sep.* -k·k-) *m* fire-eater; **~schutz** *m* fire prevention; ⚔ covering fire; **≈si·cher** *adj.* fireproof; **≈spei·end** *adj.*: **~*er Vulkan*** volcano spewing (*or* belching) flames *or* fire; **~sprit·ze** *f* fire extinguisher; **~stät·te** *f* fireplace; **~stein** *m* flint; **~stel·le** *f* (site of an) open hearth; scene of a (*or* the) fire; **~stel·lung** *f* ⚔ firing position; **~stoß** *m* burst of fire; **~strahl** *m* jet of fire; backblast; **~tau·fe** *f* baptism of fire;

die ~ erhalten (***bestehen***) have (come through) one's baptism of fire; **~teu·fel** F *m* F firebug; **~tod** *m*: ***den ~ sterben*** be burnt to death; **~ton** *m* fireclay; **~trep·pe** *f* fire escape; **~tür** *f* fire door; **~ˌüber·fall** *m* ⚔ surprise fire (*or* attack)

Feue·rung ['fɔʏərʊŋ] *f* (-; *no pl.*) a) heating; firing, b) fuel

'Feu·er|un·terˌstüt·zung *f* ⚔ fire support; **~ver·hü·tung** *f* fire prevention; **~ver·si·che·rung** *f* fire insurance; **2ver·zinkt** *adj.* hot-galvanized; **~vor·hang** *m thea.* fire curtain; ⚔ fire screen; **~wa·che** *f* fire station; **~waf·fe** *f* firearm, gun; **~was·ser** F *n* F firewater

'Feu·er·wehr *f* (-; -en) fire brigade, *Am.* fire department; F ***wie die ~*** like a flash, ***fahren***: F drive like the clappers (*or* like a bomb); **~au·to** *n* fire engine; **~helm** *m* fireman's helmet; **~mann** *m* fireman, fire fighter

'Feu·er·werk *n* fireworks *pl.*; *fig.* pyrotechnics *pl.*; **'Feu·er·werks·kör·per** *m* firework

'Feu·er·zan·ge *f* tongs *pl.*; **'Feu·er·zan·gen·bow·le** *f* burnt punch

'Feu·er·zei·chen *n* fire signal; ⚓ beacon

'Feu·er·zeug *n* (-[e]s; -e) (cigarette) lighter; **~benˌzin** *n* lighter fluid

'Feu·er|zo·ne *f* ⚔ zone of fire; **~zug** *m* flue

Feuil·le·ton [fœjə'tõ:] *n* (-s; -s) **1.** feature (*or* arts) pages *pl.*; **2.** feature (article); **Feuil·le·to·nist** [fœjəto'nɪst] *m* (-en; -en) feature writer, feuilletonist(e); **feuil·le·to·nis·tisch** [fœjəto'nɪstɪʃ] *adj.* **1.** *contp.* facile; **2. ~*er Beitrag*** article for the feature pages; **Feuil·le'ton·re·dakˌteur** *m* features editor; **Feuil·le'ton·teil** *m* feature (*or* arts) section *or* pages *pl.*

feu·rig ['fɔʏrɪç] *adj.* fiery (*a. fig.*); sparkling *jewel*; *fig.* flashing, burning *eyes etc.*; rich *wine*; impassioned *speech*; ***~er Liebhaber*** passionate (*or* fiery) lover

Fez[1] [fe:ts, fe:s] → ***Fes***

Fez[2] [fe:ts] F *m*: ***~ machen*** fool around; ***aus ~*** F for kicks

Fia·ker ['fiakɐ] *m* (-s; -) **1.** cab; **2.** coachman

Fi·as·ko ['fiasko] *n* (-s; -s) fiasco; flop; ***mit e-m ~ enden*** end in fiasco

Fi·bel[1] ['fi:bəl] *f* (-; -n) primer

'Fi·bel[2] *f* (-; -n) *hist.* fibula, brooch

Fi·ber ['fi:bɐ] *f* fibre (*Am.* fiber); **~glas** *n* fibreglass, *Am.* fiberglass

Fi·bril·le [fi'brɪlə] *f* (-; -n) *anat.*, *bot.* fibril

Fich·te ['fɪçtə] *f* (-; -n) spruce, *a.* pine (tree)

'Fich·ten|holz *n* deal; **~na·del** *f* pine needle

ficken ['fɪkən] (*sep.* -k·k-) V *v/i. and v/t.* (h) V screw, fuck; **Ficker** ['fɪkɐ] (*sep.* -k·k-) V *contp. m* (-s; -) V motherfucker; **ficke·rig** ['fɪkərɪç] (*sep.* -k·k-) *adj.* **1.** *dial.* fidgety; **2.** V randy (*sl.*), horny (*sl.*)

fi·del [fi'de:l] *adj.* cheerful; ***er ist ganz ~*** *a.* F he's quite chirpy (*Am.* chipper)

Fie·ber ['fi:bɐ] *n* (-s; *no pl.*) fever (*a. fig.*); (high) temperature; ***~ haben*** have (*or* be running) a temperature; ***leichtes*** (***hohes***) ***~*** a slight (a high) temperature; ***... Grad ~ haben*** have a temperature of ... (degrees); (***bei j-m***) ***~ messen*** take s.o.'s temperature; *fig.* ***im ~ der Begeisterung*** swept away by enthusiasm; **~an·fall** *m* attack of fever; ***e-n ~ bekommen*** come down with a temperature; **~bläs·chen** *n* fever blister; **~flecken** *pl.* fever spots; **2frei** *adj.*: ***sie ist jetzt ~*** her temperature's back to normal again

'fie·ber·haft *adj.* feverish (*a. fig.*); ***~e Suche*** mad (*or* frantic) search; **'Fie·ber·haf·tig·keit** *f* (-; *no pl.*) feverishness; *fig. a.* feverish activity

'Fie·ber|kur·ve *f* temperature curve; **~mes·ser** *m* thermometer; **~mit·tel** *n* antipyretic

fie·bern ['fi:bɐn] *v/i.* (h) have (*or* be running) a temperature; be delirious, be raving; *fig.* be feverish (***vor*** *dat.* with), be in a fever (of); *fig.* ***~ nach*** *dat.* crave (for); **'fie·bernd** *adj.* feverish (*fig.* ***vor*** *dat.* with)

'Fie·ber|phan·taˌsie *f* (feverish) ravings *pl.*; ***~n haben, in ~n liegen*** be delirious (with fever), be raving; **~rin·de** *f* Peruvian bark; **~schau·er** *m* feverish shivering, shivering fit; **2sen·kend I.** *adj.* antipyretic; **II.** *adv.*: ***das wirkt ~*** that'll bring your *etc.* temperature down; **~taˌbel·le** *f* temperature chart; **~ther·moˌme·ter** *n* (clinical) thermometer; **~traum** *m* feverish dream; **~wahn** *m* delirium; ***im ~ sein*** be delirious (with fever), be raving

fieb·rig ['fi:brɪç] *adj.* feverish (*a. fig.*)

Fie·del ['fi:dəl] *f* (-; -n), **'fie·deln** *v/i. and v/t.* (h) fiddle; **Fied·ler** ['fi:dlɐ] *m* (-s; -) fiddler

fiel [fi:l] *pret. of* ***fallen***

fies [fi:s] F **I.** *adj.* nasty, horrible; **II.** *adv.*: ***das schmeckt ja ~!*** it tastes horrible (*or* revolting); **Fies·ling** ['fi:slɪŋ] F *m* (-s; -e) F nasty piece of work, *sl.* swine, bastard, ratfink

fif·ty-fif·ty ['fɪftɪ'fɪftɪ] F **1. *machen wir ~*** let's go halves (on it), let's go fifty-fifty, let's split it down the middle; **2. *es steht ~*** it's fifty-fifty, there's a fifty-fifty chance

Fight [faɪt] F *m* (-s; -s) fight, battle; **figh·ten** ['faɪtən] F *v/i.* (h) fight, put up a fight

Fi·gur [fi'gu:ɐ] *f* (-; -en [fi'gu:rən]) **1.** figure; build; ***auf s-e ~ achten*** watch one's weight; ***e-e gute*** (***schlechte***) ***~ machen*** cut a fine (poor) figure; **2.** *lit.*, *film*: figure, character; ***komische ~*** a) figure of fun, b) strange character; **3.** a) *chess*: piece, *pl. a.* chessmen, b) *art*: figure, statue, figurine; **4.** ⩘ a) figure, b) diagram; **5.** figure of speech

fi·gu·ra·tiv [figura'ti:f] *adj. ling.* figurative; ***in der ~en Bedeutung*** in the figurative sense

Fi'gu·ren|lau·fen *n* figure skating; **~tanz** *m* figure dance

fi·gu·rie·ren [figu'ri:rən] *v/i.* (h) figure (***als*** as)

Fi·gu·ri·ne [figu'ri:nə] *f* (-; -n) figurine

fi·gür·lich [fi'gy:ɐlɪç] *adj.* **1.** *art*: figured; **2.** *ling.* figurative

Fik·ti·on [fɪk'tsio:n] *f* (-; -en) myth; *a. lit.* fiction; **fik·tiv** [fɪk'ti:f] *adj.* fictitious

Fi·let [fi'le:] *n* (-s; -s) **1.** fillet, *Am. a.* filet; breast *of chicken etc.*; **2.** → ***Filetsteak***

Fi'let·ar·beit *f* netting

fi·le·tie·ren [file'ti:rən] *v/t.* (h) *gastr.* fillet, *Am.* filet

Fi'let|steak *n* fillet steak; **~stück** *n* piece of sirloin

Fi·li·al·be·trieb [fi'lia:l-] *m* branch

Fi·lia·le [fi'lia:lə] *f* (-; -n) **1.** branch (office), subsidiary; **2.** branch; **3.** → ***Filialgeschäft***

Fi·li'al|ge·schäft *n* branch (store *or* shop), outlet; **~lei·ter** *m* branch manager

Fi·li·gran [fili'gra:n] *n* (-s; -e), **~ar·beit** *f* filigree (work)

Fi·li·pi·no [fili'pi:no] *m* (-s; -s) Filipino

Fi·li·us ['fi:lius] F *m*: ***mein*** (*or* ***sein*** *etc.*) ~ F junior

Film [fɪlm] *m* (-[e]s; -e) **1.** *phot.* film; **2.** film, *esp. Am. a.* movie; *the* cinema, *esp. Am. the* movies *pl.*; the film (*Am.* motion picture) industry; ***e-n ~ drehen*** shoot (*or* make) a film, ***von et.***: film s.th.; ***beim ~ sein*** a) be in the film (*esp. Am. a.* movie) business, b) be a film (*esp. Am. a.* movie) actor (*f* actress); **3.** film; **~arˌchiv** *n* film library (*or* archives *pl.*); **~ateˌlier** *n* film studio; **~auf·nah·me** *f* a) shooting (of a film); b) shot, take; **~aus·schnitt** *m* film clip; **~au·tor** *m* screenwriter; **~bau·ten** *pl.* film sets; **~be·ar·bei·tung** *f* film (*or* screen) adaptation; **~be·richt** *m* film report; **~be·wer·tungs·stel·le** *f* film assessment board; **~dar·stel·ler** *m* → ***Filmschauspieler***; **~deˌbüt** *n* screen debut; **~di·va** *f* film (*esp. Am. a.* movie) star, screen goddess

'Fil·me·ma·cher *m* (-s; -) film (*esp. Am. a.* movie) maker

'Film·emp·find·lich·keit *f phot.* film speed

fil·men ['fɪlmən] (h) **I.** *v/t.* film, shoot; **II.** *v/i.* film, make a film; be on location

'Film|ent·wick·lung *f* (film) processing; **~fas·sung** *f* film (*or* screen, *Am. a.* movie) version; **~fe·sti·val** *n*, **~fest·spie·le** *pl.* film festival (*sg.*); **~freun·de** *pl.* film (*or* movie) buffs, cinemagoers; **~ge·län·de** *n* studio lot; location; **~ge·sell·schaft** *f* film (*Am.* motion picture) company; **~grö·ße** *f* film (*esp. Am. a.* movie) star; **~held** *m* screen hero; **~ˌher·stel·ler** *m* film producer; **~in·duˌstrie** *f* film (*Am.* motion picture) industry

fil·misch ['fɪlmɪʃ] *adj.* cinematic(ally *adv.*)

'Film|ka·me·ra *f* movie (*or* cine) camera; **~karˌrie·re** *f* film (*or* screen, *esp. Am. a.* movie) career; **~ko·mi·ker** *m* screen comedian; **~koˌmö·die** *f* (film) comedy; **~kom·poˌnist** *m* film music composer; **~koˌpie** *f* (film) copy *or* print; **~kriˌtik** *f* film review; **~kri·ti·ker** *m* film critic; **~kunst** *f* (-; *no pl.*) cinematography; **~kunst·thea·ter** *n* repertory cinema; **~lein·wand** *f* screen; **~leu·te** *pl.* film (*esp. Am. a.* movie) people; **~ma·nu·ˌskript** *n* film script; **~muˌsik** *f* **1.** film music; **2.** soundtrack, music to the film; **~preis** *m* film (*or* screen, *Am. a.* movie) award; **~pro·duk·tiˌon** *f* film production; **~pro·duˌzent** *m* (film) producer; **~proˌjek·tor** *m* film (*esp. Am. a.* movie) projector; **~prüf·stel·le** *f* film censorship board; **~pu·bli·kum** *n* **1.** cinemagoers *pl.*; **2.** audience; **~rech·te** *pl.* film (*or* screen, *esp. Am. a.* movie) rights; **~re·gisˌseur** *m* film (*esp. Am. a.* movie) director; **~reˌkla·me** *f* screen advertising; **~re·porˌta·ge** *f* screen documentary; **~riß** *m* film tear; F *fig.* ***ich hatte e-n ~*** I had a (mental) blackout, my mind (just) went blank; **~rol·le** *f* film part (*or* role); **~schau·spie·ler** *m* film (*or* screen, *esp. Am. a.* movie) actor; **~spu·le** *f* film spool (*or* reel); **~stadt** *f* **1.** cardboard town; **2.** film (*esp. Am.* movie) capital; **~star** *m* film (*esp. Am. a.* movie) star; **~stern·chen** *n* starlet; **~strei·fen** *m* reel; **~stu·dio** *n* film studio(s *pl.*); **~thea·ter** *n* cinema, *Am.* movie theat|er (*or* -re); **~transˌport·he·bel** *m* film advance lever; **~ver·leih** *m* a) film distribution; b) film distributors *pl.*; **~ver·siˌon** *f* film (*or* screen, *Am. a.* movie) version; **~vor·füh·rer** *m* projectionist; **~vor·führ·raum** *m* projection room; **~vor·füh·rung** *f* **1.** film; **2.** showing (of a film); **~vor·füh·rungs·raum** *m* projection room; **~vor·schau** *f* a) preview; b) trailer; c) forthcoming films *pl.*; **~vor·spann** *m* opening credits *pl.*, titles *pl.*; **~vor·stel·lung** *f* **1.** performance; **2.** film (*esp. Am. a.* movie) show; **~welt** *f* (-; *no pl.*): ***die*** ~ the film world, filmland, *Am.* F *a.* movieland; **~wer·bung** *f* → ***Filmreklame***; **~wirt·schaft** *f* film (*Am.* motion picture) industry; **~zeit·schrift** *f* film (*Am. a.* movie) magazine

Fi·lou [fi'lu:] F *m* (-s; -s) rogue

Fil·ter ['fɪltɐ] *m, n* (-s; -) filter; ***Zigarette mit*** ~ filter(-tipped) cigarette; ***Zigarette ohne*** ~ plain cigarette; **~an·la·ge** *f* filtration plant; **~ge·rät** *n* filter; **~kaf·fee** *m* filter (*or* fresh, real) coffee; **~koh·le** *f* filtering charcoal; **~mund·stück** *n* filter tip

fil·tern ['fɪltɐn] *v/t.* (h) filter; percolate

'Fil·ter|pa,pier *n* filter paper; **~tuch** *n* straining cloth; **~tü·te** *f* filter, paper cone, *pl. a.* filter paper *sg.*; **~zi·ga,ret·te** *f* filter(-tipped) cigarette

Fil·trat [fɪl'tra:t] *n* (-[e]s; -e) filtrate; **fil·trie·ren** [fɪl'tri:rən] *v/t.* (h) filter

Filz [fɪlts] *m* (-es; -e) **1.** felt; **2.** F felt hat; **3.** F tangle; **4.** → ***Filzokratie***

fil·zen ['fɪltsən] (h) **I.** *v/t.* **1.** felt; **2.** F frisk; **II.** *v/i. wool*: felt

'Filz·hut *m* felt hat; trilby, *Am.* fedora

fil·zig ['fɪltsɪç] *adj.* matted; ⚘ downy

'Filz·laus *f* crab louse

Fil·zo·kra·tie [fɪltsokra'ti:] F *f* (-; -n) cronyism

'Filz|pan,tof·fel *m* slipper; **~schrei·ber** *m* → ***Filzstift***; **~soh·le** *f* felt sole; **~stie·fel** *m* felt boot; **~stift** *m* felt(-tip) pen, felt tip; **~,un·ter·la·ge** *f* felt pad

Fim·mel ['fɪməl] F *m* (-s; -) craze; ***e-n ~ haben*** F be nuts; ***er hat den Fußballfimmel*** he's mad about football, he's football-mad

Fi·na·le [fi'na:lə] *n* (-s; -[s]) **1.** ♪ finale; **2.** *sport*: final (round), finals *pl.*

Fi'nal|satz *m ling.* final clause; **~spiel** *n* final (round), finals *pl.*

Fi·nanz [fi'nants] *f* (-; *no pl.*) finance; financial world; **~ab,tei·lung** *f* finance department; **~adel** *m* plutocracy; **~amt** *n* inland revenue (office), *Am.* internal revenue service; F taxman; **~aus·gleich** *m* financial adjustment; **~aus·schuß** *m* finance committee; **~be·amte** *m* revenue officer; **~be·darf** *m* financial requirements *pl.*; **~be·hör·de** *f* fiscal (*or* tax) authority; **~be·richt** *m* financial report; **~blatt** *n* financial newspaper; **~buch·hal·ter** *m* financial accountant; **~buch·hal·tung** *f* financial accounting

Fi·nan·zen [fi'nantsən] *pl.* **1.** finances; **2.** F money *sg.*, funds; ***wie steht es mit d-n ~?*** how are you off for money?, how's your money situation?; ***mit m-n ~ steht es nicht gut*** I'm hard up for money (F cash)

Fi'nanz|ge,nie *n* financial wizard; **~ge·richt** *n* tax (*or* fiscal) court; **~ge·schäft** *n* financing; investment banking; *pl.* financial affairs; **~grö·ße** *f* financial giant; **~grup·pe** *f* group of financiers; **~hil·fe** *f* financial aid

fi·nan·zi·ell [finan'tsǐɛl] **I.** *adj.* financial; ***~e Krise*** *a.* cash(-flow) crisis; ***in ~er Hinsicht*** financially; **II.** *adv.* financially; ***~ gut*** (***schlecht***) ***gestellt sein*** be well (badly) off (financially)

Fi·nan·zier [finan'tsǐe:] *m* (-s; -s) financier; **fi·nan·zie·ren** [finan'tsi:rən] *v/t.* (h) finance; subsidize, *Am. a.* bankroll; sponsor; **Fi·nan'zie·rung** *f* (-; -en) financing

Fi·nan'zie·rungs|ge·sell·schaft *f* finance company; **~ko·sten** *pl.* financing expenses; ***~ für et.*** cost of financing s.th.; **~mit·tel** *pl.* funds; **~po·li,tik** *f* financial policy

Fi'nanz|im,pe·ri·um *n* financial empire; **~in·sti,tut** *n* financial institution; **~jahr** *n* fiscal (*or* financial) year; **2kräf·tig** *adj.* financially strong; **~kri·se** *f* financial crisis; **~la·ge** *f* financial situation (*or* position); ***die ~ ist schlecht*** (*or* ***kritisch***) funds are low; **~loch** *n* fiscal gap; **~mann** *m* financier; **~mi,ni·ster** *m* minister of finance, finance minister; *in GB*: Chancellor of the Exchequer; *in the USA*: Secretary of the Treasury; **~mi·ni,ste·ri·um** *n* ministry of finance, finance ministry; *in GB*: Treasury; *in the USA*: Treasury Department; **~pla·nung** *f* budgetary planning; **~po·li,tik** *f* financial (*or* fiscal) policy; **2po,li·tisch** *adj.* fiscal, financial; **~rie·se** *m* financial giant; **~schul·den** *pl.* corporate debt *sg.*, borrowings; **2schwach** *adj.* financially weak; **~sprit·ze** F *f* F cash injection, (fiscal) shot in the arm; **2tech·nisch** *adj.* financial, fiscal; **~teil** *m* financial page(s *pl.*); **~ver·wal·tung** *f* financial administration; fiscal authority; **~welt** *f* (-; *no pl.*) financial world (*or* circles *pl.*); **~we·sen** *n*: ***das*** ~ (the world of) finance, public finance; **~wirt·schaft** *f* financial management; **2wirt·schaft·lich** *adj.* financial; **~wis·sen·schaft** *f* public finance

Fin·del·kind ['fɪndəl-] *n* foundling

fin·den (fand, gefunden, h) **I.** *v/t.* find; discover, come across; → ***Beifall, Gefallen²; Trost ~ in*** *dat.* find comfort in; ***wir fanden ihn bei der Arbeit*** we found him at work; ***ich finde keine Worte*** I'm lost for words; ***ich finde es gut*** (***schlecht***) a) I (don't) like it, b) I (don't) think it's a good idea; ***ich finde, daß*** I think (*or* feel) (that); ***~ Sie nicht?*** don't you think so?; ***wie ~ Sie das Buch?*** how do you like (*or* what do you think of) the book?; ***ich weiß nicht, was sie an ihm findet*** I don't know what she sees in him; ***ich kann nichts dabei ~*** I don't see any harm in it, ***daß er ...:*** I can't see any harm in him (*or* his) *ger.*; **II.** *v/refl.*: ***sich ~*** be found; find o.s. (***umzingelt*** *etc.* surrounded *etc.*); *sport etc.*: get into one's stride; *die Pflanze etc.* ***findet sich nur im*** *Gebirge etc.* is only to be found; ***sich ~ in*** *acc.* resign (*or* reconcile) o.s. to, get used to; ***es fand sich keinerlei Hinweis*** *etc.* there were no clues *etc.* (at all *or* to be found); ***es fand sich, daß*** it turned out that; ***es wird sich ~*** we'll see, wait and see; ***das wird sich schon alles ~*** it'll work out (*or* sort itself out) somehow; ***es fanden sich nur wenige Freiwillige*** there were only a few volunteers; **III.** *v/i.*: ***~ nach*** (*or* ***zu***) *dat.* find one's way *home* (to *God etc.*); ***zur Musik ~*** discover music, develop an appreciation for music; ***er findet nicht aus dem Bett*** he just can't get (*or* drag himself) out of bed; ***sie fand nicht zum Zahnarzt*** she (just) couldn't bring herself to go to the dentist

Fin·der ['fɪndɐ] *m* (-s; -) finder; ***der ehrliche ~*** a) anyone finding (and returning) the wallet *etc.*, b) the person who found the wallet *etc.*; **~lohn** *m* finder's reward

fin·dig ['fɪndɪç] *adj.* clever; **'Fin·dig·keit** *f* (-; *no pl.*) resourcefulness; cleverness

Find·ling ['fɪntlɪŋ] *m* (-s; -e) **1.** foundling; **2.** *geol.* boulder, erratic block

Fi·nes·se [fi'nɛsə] *f* (-; -n) finesse; *pl.* tricks; ***mit sämtlichen ~n arbeiten*** use all the tricks of the trade; *Auto etc.* ***mit allen ~n*** with all the trimmings

fing [fɪŋ] *pret. of* ***fangen***

Fin·ger ['fɪŋɐ] *m* (-s; -) finger; ***mit dem ~ auf j-n zeigen*** point at (*or* to) s.o., *fig.* point one's finger at s.o.; ***sich die ~ verbrennen*** burn one's fingers (*a. fig.*); ***sich in den ~ schneiden*** cut one's finger, *fig.* make a big mistake; ***j-m auf die ~ klopfen*** rap s.o.'s knuckles; ***laß die ~ davon!*** hands off!, don't touch!, *fig.* don't you get involved; *fig.* ***die kannst du dir an den ~n abzählen*** you can count them on the fingers of one hand; ***et. in*** (*or* ***zwischen***) ***die ~ bekommen*** get hold of s.th.; (***sich***) ***aus den ~n saugen*** make up; ***j-m auf die ~ sehen*** keep a sharp eye on s.o.; ***j-n um den kleinen ~ wickeln*** twist s.o. round one's little finger; ***et. im kleinen ~ haben*** have s.th. at one's fingertips; ***das macht er mit dem kleinen ~*** he can do that with his hands tied; ***keinen ~ rühren*** (*or* ***krümmen, krumm machen***) not to lift a finger; ***er hat keinen ~ gerührt*** *etc.* he never once lifted a finger (to help); ***j-m durch die ~ schlüpfen*** slip through s.o.'s fingers (*or* clutches), *criminal etc.*: *a.* give s.o. the slip; ***s-e ~ im Spiel*** (F ***drin***) ***haben*** have a hand in it; ***er hat überall s-e ~ im Spiel*** (F ***drin***) he's got a finger in every pie; ***sie würde sich die ~ danach lecken*** she'd give her right arm for it; ***gibt man ihm den kleinen ~, nimmt er gleich die ganze Hand*** give him an inch, and he'll take a yard; → ***abzählen***; **~ab·druck** *m* fingerprint; ***Fingerabdrücke*** (***von j-m***) ***nehmen*** take (s.o.'s) fingerprints

'fin·ger·breit I. *adj.* inch-wide ..., *pred.* an inch wide; **II.** *adv.* an inch wide; **III.** 2 *m* (-; -) inch; ***zwei ~*** two inches; ***keinen ~ nachgeben*** not to budge (*or* give) an inch

'fin·ger·dick *adj.* as thick as your finger; *adv.* ***et. ~ auftragen*** spread s.th. thickly

'Fin·ger·druck *m*: ***ein ~ genügt, und die Maschine läuft*** you just press the button and the machine starts

'Fin·ger·far·be *f* fingerpaint

'fin·ger·fer·tig *adj.* dext(e)rous; **'Fin·ger·fer·tig·keit** *f* (-; *no pl.*) dexterity; skill

'fin·ger·för·mig [-fœrmɪç] *adj.* finger-shaped

'Fin·ger|ge·lenk *n*, **~glied** *n* finger joint; **~hand·schuh** *m* glove; **~hut** *m* **1.** thimble; ***ein ~ voll*** a thimbleful (of); **2.** ⚘ foxglove, digitalis; **~kup·pe** *f* fingertip

'Fin·ger·ling *m* (-s; -e) fingerstall

fin·gern ['fɪŋɐn] *v/i.* (h): ***~ an*** *dat.* finger, fumble around on (*or* at); ***~ nach*** *dat.* fumble for

'Fin·ger|na·gel *m* fingernail; **~ring** *m* ring; **~satz** *m* ♪ fingering; **~scha·le** *f* finger bowl

'Fin·ger·spit·ze *f* fingertip; *fig.* ***bis zu***

den ~n down to one's fingertips; **'Fin·ger·spit·zen·ge·fühl** *n* instinct, flair; tact; ***dazu braucht man ~*** you've got to have the right feel for it
'Fin·ger|spra·che *f* finger language; **~übung** *f* finger exercise; **~zeig** [-tsaɪk] *m* (-s; -e) pointer, hint; ***ein ~ Gottes*** a sign (from above)
fin·gie·ren [fɪŋ'giːrən] *v/t.* (h) fake; fabricate; **fin·giert** [fɪŋ'giːɐt] *adj.* fake ..., faked; made-up, fictitious, invented
fi·nit [fi'niːt] *adj. ling.* finite
Fink [fɪŋk] *m* (-en; -en) finch
Fin·ne¹ ['fɪnə] *f* (-; -n) fin
'Fin·ne² *f* (-; -n) **1.** *zo.* bladder worm; **2.** ⚕ pimple
'Fin·ne³ *m* (-n; -n), **Fin·nin** ['fɪnɪn] *f* (-; -nen) Finn; **fin·nisch** ['fɪnɪʃ] *adj.* Finnish; **Finn·lan·di·sie·rung** [fɪnlandi'ziːrʊŋ] *f* (-; *no pl.*) *pol.* Finlandization
Finn·wal ['fɪn-] *m* finback
fin·ster ['fɪnstɐ] **I.** *adj.* dark; gloomy (*both a. fig.*); *fig.* ominous; stern; grim; sinister, evil; F shady; ***es wird ~*** it's getting dark; ***im 2n*** in the dark; *fig.* ***im ~n tappen*** grope in the dark; ***~er Blick*** black look; ***es sieht ~ aus*** things aren't looking too good, the outlook is pretty dim (*or* grim); F ***ein ~er Typ*** F a shady customer; F ***es geht zu wie im ~sten Mittelalter*** it's just like (being back in) the Middle Ages; **II.** *adv.*: ***j-n ~ ansehen*** glower at s.o.; **'Fin·ster·nis** *f* (-; -se) darkness, obscurity (*a. fig.*); *ast.* eclipse; ***die Mächte der ~*** the powers of darkness (*or* evil); **'Fin·ster·ling** *m* (-s; -e) **1.** obscurantist; **2.** F shady customer
Fin·te ['fɪntə] *f* (-; -n) trick; *sport*: feint; **'fin·ten·reich** *adj.* crafty
Fir·le·fanz ['fɪrləfants] *m* (-es; *no pl.*) **1.** rubbish; fancy bits *pl.*; **2.** nonsense; ***~ treiben*** fool around
firm [fɪrm] *adj.*: ***~ sein in dat.*** be well up in, be good at
Fir·ma ['fɪrma] *f* (-; -men) a) firm, company; b) company name; ***die ~ Wellington*** Wellingtons; ***(An) ~ X*** Messrs X; The X Company
Fir·ma·ment [fɪrma'mɛnt] *n* (-[e]s; *no pl.*) heavens *pl.*
Fir·men|be·zeich·nung ['fɪrmən-] *f* company name; **~chef** *m* head of the company (*or* firm), F company chief; **2ei·gen** *adj.* company-owned; **~ge·schich·te** *f* company (*or* corporate) history; **~in·ha·ber** *m* owner (of a *or* the company); **~lei·tung** *f* management; **~look** *m* corporate identity (*or* face, image); **~na·me** *m* company name; **~schild** *n* company sign (*or* name), facia; ⚙ nameplate; contractor's nameplate; **~schutz** *m* protection of registered company names; **~sitz** *m* (company) headquarters *pl.*; **~spre·cher** *m* company spokesman (*or* spokesperson); **~stem·pel** *m* company stamp; **~ver·zeich·nis** *n* trade directory; **~wa·gen** *m* company car; **~wert** *m* goodwill; **~zei·chen** *n* logo
fir·mie·ren [fɪr'miːrən] *v/i.* (h): ***~ als*** (*or* ***mit*** *dat.*, ***unter dem Namen***) trade under the name of
Firm·ling ['fɪrmlɪŋ] *m* (-s; -e) confirmand; **Fir·mung** *f* confirmation
Firn [fɪrn] *m* (-[e]s; *no pl.*) corn snow
Fir·nis ['fɪrnɪs] *m* (-ses; -se) varnish; *fig.* veneer; **fir·nis·sen** ['fɪrnɪsən] *v/t.* (h) varnish
'Firn·schnee *m* corn snow
First [fɪrst] *m* (-[e]s; -e) ridge; ⚒ roof; **~bal·ken** *m* ridge beam
Fis [fɪs] *n* (-; -) ♪ F sharp
Fisch [fɪʃ] *m* (-[e]s; -e) **1.** fish; *pl. usu.* fish (*pl.*); F *fig.* ***großer*** (*or* ***dicker***) ***~*** big fish; ***kleine ~e*** a) peanuts, b) small fry; ***das sind kleine ~e*** F that's no big deal; ***faule ~e*** lame excuses, tall stories; ***gesund*** (***und munter***) ***wie ein ~ im Wasser*** (as) fit as a fiddle; ***weder ~ noch Fleisch*** neither fish nor fowl; F ***die ~e füttern*** F feed the fishes; → ***stumm***; **2.** *pl. ast.* Pisces *sg.*; ***ein ~ sein*** be (a) Pisces, be a Piscean; **~ad·ler** *m* osprey; **~au·ge** *n phot.* fisheye lens; **~bein** *n* whalebone; **~be·stand** *m* fish stocks *pl.* (*or* population); **~be·steck** *n coll.* fish knives and forks *pl.*; **~blut** *n*: *fig.* ***~ in den Adern haben*** be (as) cold as a fish; **~brut** *f* fry *pl.*; **~damp·fer** *m* trawler
fi·schen ['fɪʃən] **I.** *v/t. and v/i.* (h) fish (***nach*** *dat.* for) (*a.* F *fig.*); *fig.* ***im trüben ~*** fish in troubled waters; F ***sich j-n ~*** hook (o.s.) s.o.; **II.** 2 *n* (-s) fishing
Fi·scher ['fɪʃɐ] *m* (-s; -) fisherman; **~boot** *n* fishing boat; **~dorf** *n* fishing village
Fi·sche·rei [fɪʃə'raɪ] *f* (-; *no pl.*) fishing; fishing industry; **~ab·kom·men** *n* fisheries agreement; **~flot·te** *f* fishing fleet; **~ha·fen** *m* fishing port; **~po·li,tik** *f* fisheries policy
'Fi·scher·netz *n* fishing net
'Fisch·fa,brik·schiff *n* factory ship
'Fisch·fang *m* (-[e]s; *no pl.*) fishing; **~ge·biet** *n* fishing grounds *pl.*
'Fisch|fi,let *n* fish fillet; **~flos·se** *f* fin; **~fri·ka,del·le** *f* fishcake; **~ga·bel** *f* fish fork; **~ge·richt** *n* fish (dish); **~ge·ruch** *m* fishy smell, smell of fish; **~ge·schäft** *n* fishmonger('s), *Am.* fish dealer
'Fisch·grä·te *f* fishbone; **'Fisch·grä·ten·mu·ster** *n* herringbone (pattern)
'Fisch|händ·ler *m* fishmonger, *Am.* fish dealer; fish merchant; **~haut** *f* fish skin
fi·schig ['fɪʃɪç] *adj.* fishy
'Fisch|kö·der *m* bait; **~kon,ser·ve(n** *pl.*) *f* tinned (*Am.* canned) fish; **~kun·de** *f* ichthyology; **~kut·ter** *m* (fishing) trawler; **~laich** *m* (fish) spawn; **~markt** *m* fishmarket; **~mehl** *n* fish meal; **~mes·ser** *n* fish knife; **~ot·ter** *m* otter; **~rei·her** *m* heron; **~ro·gen** *m* roe; **~schup·pe** *f* scale; **~schwarm** *m* shoal (of fish); **~stäb·chen** *n* fish finger; **~ster·ben** *n* fish kill; **~sup·pe** *f* fish soup; **~teich** *m* fishpond; **~ver·gif·tung** *f* fish poisoning; **~weib** *contp. n* fishwife; **~wil·de,rei** *f* fish poaching; **~wirt·schaft** *f* fishing industry; **~zucht** *f* fish farming; **~züch·ter** *m* fish farmer; **~zug** *m* catch, haul (*both a. fig.*); *fig.* ***ein guter ~*** a big haul
Fi·si·ma·ten·ten [fizima'tɛntən] F *pl.* fuss *sg.*; trouble *sg.*; excuses; nonsense *sg.*; ***mach keine ~!*** a) stop making such a fuss, b) enough of that nonsense
fis·ka·lisch [fɪs'kaːlɪʃ] *adj.* fiscal; **Fis·kus** ['fɪskʊs] *m* (-; *no pl.*) **1.** tax authorities *pl.*; treasury; **2.** government; *in GB*: *a. the* Crown
Fis·sur [fɪ'suːɐ] *f* (-; -en) ⚕ fissure; crack
Fi·stel ['fɪstəl] *f* (-; -n) ⚕ fistula; **~stim·me** *f* ♪ falsetto; *contp.* falsetto (F squeaky) voice
fit [fɪt] *adj.* fit; ***~ in*** *dat.* well up in *a subjetc etc.*; ***nicht sehr ~ in*** *dat.* F not too hot on; ***geistig ~*** on the ball
Fit·neß ['fɪtnɛs] *f* (-; *no pl.*) physical fitness; **~cen·ter** *n* health club, fitness cent|re (*Am.* -er), gym; **~raum** *m* exercise room; **~trai·ning** *n*: ***~ machen*** go for workouts in the gym
Fit·tich ['fɪtɪç] *m* (-[e]s; -e) wing, pinion; *fig.* ***j-n unter s-e ~e nehmen*** take s.o. under one's wing
fix [fɪks] **I.** *adj.* **1.** fixed *salary, prices etc.*; → ***Fixkosten***; *fig.* ***~e Idee*** obsession; ***das ist so e-e ~e Idee von ihm*** he's got a thing about it; **2.** F quick (***in*** *dat.* at); **3.** F smart, sharp; **4.** F ***~ und fertig*** → ***fertig*** 2, 4; **II.** F *adv.* quickly, in a flash; ***mach ~!, jetzt aber ~!*** F get a move on, make it snappy
fi·xen ['fɪksən] *v/i.* (h) **1.** ♰ sell a bear, sell short; **2.** *sl.* shoot, *sl.* mainline; **Fi·xer** ['fɪksɐ] *m* (-s; -) **1.** ♰ bear; **2.** *sl.* mainliner, *sl.* junkie
'Fix·fo·kus·ob·jek,tiv *n* fixed-focus lens
Fi·xier·bad [fɪ'ksiːɐ-] *n phot.* fixer
fi·xier·bar [fɪ'ksiːɐbaːɐ] *adj.* determinable; **fi·xie·ren** [fɪ'ksiːrən] (h) **I.** *v/t.* **1.** *a. phot.* fix; **2.** record, (*a.* ***schriftlich ~***) put down in writing; → ***festsetzen*** 1; **3.** a) stare at, b) focus on; **II.** *v/refl. psych.*: ***sich ~ auf*** *acc.* fixate on
Fi·xier|mit·tel [fɪ'ksiːɐ-] *n* fixative; *phot.* fixer; **~salz** *n* hypo; fixer
fi·xiert [fɪ'ksiːɐt] *adj.*: ***~ auf*** *acc.* fixated on; *psych.* ***auf s-e Mutter ~ sein*** have a mother fixation; **Fi·xie·rung** [fɪ'ksiːrʊŋ] *f* (-; -en) **1.** fixing (*a. phot.*); **2.** *psych.* fixation (***auf*** *acc.* on); *fig. a.* obsession (with)
'Fix|ko·sten *pl.* standing expenses; **~punkt** *m* point of reference; *opt.* point of focus; *fig.* focal point; **~stern** *m* fixed star
Fi·xum ['fɪksʊm] *n* (-s; Fixa ['fɪksa]) basic salary
Fjord [fjɔrt] *m* (-[e]s; -e ['fjɔrdə]) fiord, fjord
FKK [ɛfkaː'kaː] → ***Freikörperkultur***; **~Ge·län·de** *n* nudist camp
FKKler [ɛfkaː'kaːlɐ] *m* (-s; -) naturist
FK'K|-Strand *m* nudist beach; **~Ur·laub** *m* naturist holiday
flach [flax] **I.** *adj.* flat; level, even; Ⱥ plane; shallow *water*; low; flat-bottomed *boat*; *fig.* shallow, superficial; ***~e Brust*** flat chest; ***mit der ~en Hand*** with the flat of one's hand; ***auf dem ~en Land*** (out) in the country; ***~ machen*** level (off); ***~ werden*** flatten (out), level (off); **II.** *adv.*: ***~ liegen*** lie flat; ***sich ~ hinlegen*** lie down flat; ***~ schlafen*** sleep without a pillow; ***~ spielen*** *soccer*: keep the ball on the ground; ***~ über et. fliegen*** (***hinwegstreichen*** *etc.*) fly (skim *etc.*) low over s.th.; ***~ atmen*** breathe shallow(ly), take shallow breaths
'Flach·bau *m* (-[e]s; -ten) low building
'flach·brü·stig [-brʏstɪç] *adj.* flat-chested
'Flach|dach *n* flat roof; **~druck** *m* (-[e]s; *no pl.*) flatbed printing
Flä·che ['flɛçə] *f* (-; -n) **1.** surface; Ⱥ plane; face *of crystal*; facet *of diamond etc.*; **2.** expanse; area; space; △ floorspace
'Flach·ei·sen *n* flat iron
'Flä·chen|aus·deh·nung *f* area; **~be·rech·nung** *f* Ⱥ planimetry; **~blitz** *m* sheet lightning; **~bom·bar·de,ment** *n* saturation (*or* carpet) bombing; **~brand** *m* extensive fire; **2deckend** (*sep.* -k·k-) *adj.* exhaustive; ***~er Polizeieinsatz*** *etc.* saturation policing *etc.*; ***~es Bombardement*** saturation (*or* carpet) bombing;

~fahn·dung *f* dragnet operation; **~maß** *n* surface measurement; **~mes·ser** *m* ⚙ planimeter; **~mes·sung** *f* planimetry; **~nut·zungs·plan** *m* zoning (*or* land development) plan; **~sa,nie·rung** *f* area rehabilitation; **~win·kel** *m* ⟁ plane (*or* interfacial) angle

'flach|fal·len F *v/i.* (*irr.*, *sep.*, sn, → ***fallen***) fall through; **2fei·le** *f* flat file; **~gedrückt** *adj.* flat(tened down); **2glas** *n* flat (*or* sheet) glass; **2hang** *m* gentle slope

'Flach·heit *f* (-; *no pl.*) flatness; *fig.* shallowness, superficiality

flä·chig ['flɛçıç] *adj.* flat; two-dimensional

'Flach|ka·bel *n* ⚡ flat cable; **~kopf** F *contp. m* F blockhead; **~kü·ste** *f* flat coast (*or* shore)

'Flach·land *n* (-[e]s; *no pl.*) plain, lowland, flat country; **'Flach·län·der** [-lɛndɐ] *m* (-s; -) lowlander

'flach|le·gen F (*sep.*, h) **I.** *v/refl.*: ***sich*** (***eine Weile***) ~ lie down for a bit; **II.** *v/t.* bring *s.o.* down; **~lie·gen** F *v/i.* (*irr.*, *sep.*, h, → ***liegen***) F be laid up (in bed)

'Flach|mann F *m* (-[e]s; ⸚er) hip flask; **~mei·ßel** *m* flat chisel; **~paß** *m soccer*: low pass; **~re·li,ef** *n* bas-relief

Flachs[1] [flaks] *m* (-es; *no pl.*) ⚘ flax

Flachs[2] F *fig. m* (-es; *no pl.*) nonsense; ***hör auf mit dem*** ~ F stop kidding (around); ***mal ganz ohne*** ~ seriously though

'flachs·blond *adj.* flaxen

'Flach·schuß *m soccer*: low ball

flach·sen ['flaksən] F *v/i.* (h) F be kidding; joke around

'flachs·far·ben *adj.* flaxen

Flach|stahl *m* flat steel; **~stecker** *m* ⚡ tab; **~zan·ge** *f*: (***e-e*** ~ a pair of) flat(-nose) pliers *pl.*

flackern ['flakɐn] (*sep.* -k·k-) **I.** *v/i.* (h) flicker (*a. eyes*), *candle*: *a.* gutter; **II.** 2 *n* (-s) flicker(ing)

Fla·den ['fla:dən] *m* (-s; -) pancake; flat cake; → ***Kuhfladen;*** **~brot** *n* flat bread (*or* loaf); pita (bread)

Fla·gel·lant [flagɛ'lant] *m* (-en; -en) *eccl. and psych.* flagellant; **Fla·gel·la·ti·on** [flagɛla'tsĭo:n] *f* (-; *no pl.*) flagellation

Fla·geo·lett [flaʒo'lɛt] *n* (-s; -s, e) ♪ harmonic

Flag·ge ['flagə] *f* (-; -n) flag; ***die*** ~ ***hissen*** (*or* ***aufziehen***) hoist the flag; ***die*** ~ ***einholen*** lower the flag; ***die britische*** ~ the Union Jack; ***die amerikanische*** ~ the Stars and Stripes; ***unter fremder*** ~ (***fahren*** *or* ***segeln***) (sail) under a foreign flag; *fig.* ***unter falscher*** ~ under false colo(u)rs; ~ ***zeigen*** make a stand; **'flaggen** (h) **I.** *v/i.* fly a flag (*or* flags); *person*: hoist a flag; **II.** *v/t.* flag *a message*, signal (with flags)

'Flag·gen|mast *m* flagpole; **~tuch** *n* bunting; **~zei·chen** *n* ⚓ flag signal

Flagg·schiff ['flag-] *n a. fig.* flagship

fla·grant [fla'grant] *adj.* flagrant

Flair [flɛ:ɐ] *n* (-s; *no pl.*) aura; atmosphere; charm

Flak [flak] *f* (-; -) ⚔ **1.** anti-aircraft gun; **2.** anti-aircraft artillery; **~artil·le,rie** *f* → ***Flak*** 2; **~feu·er** *n* flak, anti-aircraft fire

Fla·kon [fla'kõ:] *m* (-s; -s) small bottle

flam·bie·ren [flam'bi:rən] *v/t.* (h) flambé; **flam·biert** [flam'bi:ɐt] *adj.* flambé(e), *pl.*: flambé(e)s; **~es Steak** steak flambé

Fla·me ['fla:mə] *m* (-n; -n) Fleming; *coll. the* Flemish; **Flä·min** ['flɛ:mın] *f* (-; -nen) Flemish woman, Fleming

Fla·min·go [fla'mıŋgo] *m* (-s; -s) flamingo

flä·misch ['flɛ:mıʃ] *adj.* Flemish

Flam·me ['flamə] *f* (-; -n) flame (*a. fig.*); ***in*** **~*n*** in flames, blazing; ***in*** **~*n aufgehen*** go up in flames; ***in*** **~*n ausbrechen*** burst into flames; ***auf kleiner*** ~ ***kochen*** cook on a low heat, *fig.* make do with very little, ***müssen:*** *fig.* have to get by on (*or* make do with) very little; → ***Feuer*** 4

flam·men ['flamən] *lit. v/i.* (h) blaze; *fig. face etc.*: burn; **'flam·mend** *fig.* **I.** *adj.* fiery; stirring *appeal*; **II.** *adv.*: ~ ***rot*** fiery (*or* flaming) red

'Flam·men|meer *n* sea of flames; **~schwert** *n* flaming sword; **~tod** *m*: ***den*** ~ ***erleiden*** be burnt to death; **~wer·fer** *m* ⚔ flame-thrower

Fla·nell [fla'nɛl] *m* (-s; -e) flannel; **Fla'nell·an·zug** *m* flannel suit; **fla'nel·len** *adj.* (made of) flannel; **Fla'nell·ho·se** *f*: (***e-e*** ~ a pair of) flannel trousers *pl.*, flannels *pl.*

fla·nie·ren [fla'ni:rən] *v/i.* (h *or* sn) stroll, saunter

Flan·ke ['flaŋkə] *f* (-; -n) flank (*a. geol.*, ⟁, ⚙, ⚔); side, *soccer*: *a.* wing; cross; **'flan·ken** (h) *sport* **I.** *v/t.* cross; **II.** *v/i.* cross the ball

'Flan·ken|an·griff *m* ⚔ flank attack; **~ball** *m sport*: cross

flan·kie·ren [flaŋ'ki:rən] *v/t.* (h) flank; ✝, *pol.* **~de Maßnahmen** supporting measures

Flansch [flanʃ] *m* (-[e]s; -e), **'flan·schen** *v/t.* (h) ⚙ flange

Flaps [flaps] F *m* (-es; -e) whippersnapper; lout; **flap·sig** ['flapsıç] F *adj.* boorish, uncouth

Fläsch·chen ['flɛʃçən] *n* (-s; -) small bottle; *pharm.* phial; (*baby's*) bottle

Fla·sche ['flaʃə] *f* (-; -n) bottle; (*baby's*) bottle; ⚙ cylinder; F *fig.* F dummy; ***e-e*** ~ ***Wein*** a bottle of wine; ***bei e-r*** ~ ***Wein*** *besprechen etc.*: over a bottle of wine; ***in*** **~*n füllen*** bottle; ***e-m Kind die*** ~ ***geben*** give a baby its bottle; ***es kriegt noch die*** ~ it's still on the bottle; ***zur*** ~ ***greifen*** take to (F hit) the bottle

'Fla·schen|auf·schrift *f* (bottle) label; **~bat·te,rie** F *f* (whole) array *or* battery of bottles; **~bier** *n* bottled beer; **~bür·ste** *f* bottle brush; **~eti,kett** *n* (bottle) label; label on the bottle; **~gä·rung** *f* fermentation in the bottle; **~gas** *n* bottled gas; **~ge·stell** *n* bottle rack; **2grün** *adj.* bottle green; **~hals** *m* neck of a bottle; *fig.* bottleneck; **~kind** *n* bottle-fed baby; **~kür·bis** *m* bottle gourd; **~milch** *f* bottled milk; **~öff·ner** *m* bottle opener; **~pfand** *n* deposit (on a *or* the bottle); **~post** *f* bottle post; message in a bottle; **~ver·schluß** *m* bottle top; **~wär·mer** *m* bottle warmer; **~wein** *m* bottled wine

'fla·schen·wei·se *adv.* by the bottle

'Fla·schen·zug *m* ⚙ (block and) tackle, F pulley

Flat·ter ['flatɐ] F *f*: ***die*** ~ ***machen*** F hop it

'Flat·ter·geist *m* flighty character

'flat·ter·haft *adj.* flighty; fickle

'Flat·ter·mann F *m* (-[e]s; ⸚er) **1.** F chook, bird; **2.** ***e-n*** ~ ***haben*** F be scared stiff, be quaking in one's boots

flat·tern ['flatɐn] *v/i.* (h) flutter (*a.* ⚙ *and fig.*); flap its wings; *sail etc.*: flap (in the wind); *hands*: tremble; *hair*: stream; *wheels*: wobble; *skis*: chatter; *fig.* ***mir flatterte heute e-e Einladung auf den Tisch*** an invitation landed on my desk today

'Flat·ter·satz *m typ.* unjustified margin(s *pl.*), ragged right

flau [flaʊ] *adj.* queasy; weak, faint; listless; *phot.* flat *negative*; ✝ slack; *fig.* dull, flat; ***mir ist*** (*or* ***wird***) ***ganz*** ~ (***im Magen***) I feel queasy; **'Flau·heit** *f* (-; *no pl.*) queasiness; faintness; listlessness; dullness; slackness

Flaum [flaʊm] *m* (-[e]s; *no pl.*) **1.** *zo.* down; **2.** a) baby (*or* downy) hair; b) down, F fuzz, *sl.* bumfluff; **3.** ⚘ down, fur; **~bart** *m* downy moustache, *sl.* (a bit of) bumfluff; **~fe·der** *f* down(y) feather

flau·mig ['flaʊmıç] *adj.* downy; fluffy

Flausch [flaʊʃ] *m* (-[e]s; -e) fleece; **flau·schig** ['flaʊʃıç] *adj.* fleecy

Flau·sen ['flaʊzən] F *pl.* nonsense *sg.*, silly ideas; ***er hat nur*** ~ ***im Kopf*** he's got nothing but nonsense in his head, he's full of nonsense; ***j-m*** ~ ***in den Kopf setzen*** put ideas into s.o.'s head; ***dem werd' ich die*** ~ ***austreiben*** I'll knock all that nonsense out of his head; ***mach keine*** ~! I don't want any (of your) nonsense

Flau·te ['flaʊtə] *f* (-; -n) lull; *fig.* ✝ slack period; ***in der Bauindustrie herrscht*** ~ the building industry is going through a slack period

Flech·te[1] ['flɛçtə] *f* (-; -n) ⚘ lichen; ⚕ eczema

'Flech·te[2] *f* (-; -n) braid; **flech·ten** ['flɛçtən] (flocht, geflochten, h) **I.** *v/t.* plait *hair*; bind *wreath etc.*; weave *basket etc.*; twist *rope*; **II.** *v/refl.*: ***sich*** ~ twine, wind (***um*** *acc.* round); **'Flecht·werk** *n* wickerwork

Fleck [flɛk] *m* (-[e]s; -e) **1.** spot, stain; **2.** a) *zo.* spot, patch; b) ⚕ mark, bruise; c) *fig.* blemish, blot; **3.** spot, place; ***ein schöner*** ~ a nice (little) spot; ***am falschen*** ~ in the wrong place; ***sich nicht vom*** ~ ***rühren*** not to budge; ***rühren Sie sich nicht vom*** ~! don't (you) move; ***ich krieg' den Schrank nicht vom*** ~ I can't budge this cupboard; ***ich komm' nicht vom*** ~ a) I can't move, b) I can't get about, c) *fig.* I'm not getting anywhere, I'm getting nowhere; *fig.* ***er hat das Herz auf dem rechten*** ~ his heart's in the right place; ***vom*** ~ ***weg*** on the spot

Fleck·chen ['flɛkçən] *n* (-s; -) **1.** speck; **2.** spot; ***ein schönes*** ~ ***Erde*** a beautiful spot (*or* corner of the earth)

flecken ['flɛkən] (*sep.* -k·k-) *v/i.* (h) a) stain, b) stain very easily

Flecken ['flɛkən] (*sep.* -k·k-) *m* (-s; -) → ***Fleck;*** **~ent·fer·ner** [-ɛntfɛrnɐ] *m* (-s; -) stain remover

'flecken·los (*sep.* -k·k-) *adj.* spotless; *fig. a.* unimpeachable

'Flecken·was·ser *n* stain remover

Fleckerl·tep·pich ['flɛkɐl-] (*sep.* -k·k-) *dial. m* rag rug

'Fleck·fie·ber *n* ⚕ (epidemic) typhus

fleckig ['flɛkıç] (*sep.* -k·k-) *adj.* spotted; blotchy *skin*; stained; ~ ***machen,*** ~ ***werden*** stain; ~ ***sein*** *fruit*: have spots

'Fleck|ty·phus *m* ⚕ (epidemic) typhus; **~vieh** *n* spotted cattle

fled·dern ['flɛdɐn] *v/t.* (h) plunder, rob

Fle·der·maus ['fle:dɐ-] *f* bat

Fle·gel ['fle:gəl] *m* (-s; -) **1.** lout; **2.** flail; **~al·ter** *n* → ***Flegeljahre***

Fle·ge·lei [fle:gə'laı] *f* (-; -en) loutish behavio(u)r

'fle·gel·haft *adj.* loutish

'Fle·gel·jah·re *pl.*: ***in den*** **~*n sein*** be at an awkward age

fle·geln ['fle:gəln] *v/refl.* (h): ***sich ~*** sprawl (about), loll about

fle·hen ['fle:ən] **I.** *v/i.* (h) beg (***um*** *acc.* for); ***bei j-m um Hilfe ~*** implore (*or* beg) s.o. to help one; ***zu Gott ~*** pray to God; **II.** ♀ *n* (-s) supplication, entreaty; **'fle·hend, fle·hent·lich** ['fle:əntlıç] **I.** *adj.* imploring, beseeching *look etc.*; ***~e Bitte*** urgent plea; ***~es Gebet*** fervent prayer; **II.** *adv.* imploringly *etc.*; ***j-n ~ bitten*** → ***flehen***

Fleisch [flaıʃ] *n gastr.* meat; ⚕, ♣ flesh; *fig. the* flesh; ⚕ ***wildes ~*** proud flesh; ***in ~ und Blut*** in the flesh; ***das eigene ~ und Blut*** one's own flesh and blood; *fig.* ***(j-m) in ~ und Blut übergehen*** become second nature (to s.o.); ***sich ins eigene ~ schneiden*** a) dig one's own grave, b) cut off one's nose to spite one's face; ***vom ~ fallen*** go thin; *bibl.* ***~ werden*** be made flesh; ***den Weg allen ~es gehen*** go the way of all flesh; → ***Fisch*** 1; **~ab,tei·lung** *f* meat department; **~be·schau** *f* meat inspection; F *hum.* body-watching; **~be·schau·er** *m* meat inspector; **~brü·he** *f* consommé; (beef) stock

Flei·scher ['flaıʃɐ] *m* (-s; -) butcher; **Flei·sche·rei** [flaıʃə'raı] *f* (-; -en) → ***Fleischerladen***

'Flei·scher|la·den *m* butcher's shop, *Am.* meat market; **~mes·ser** *n* butcher's knife

'Fleisch·ex,trakt *m usu.* beef extract

'fleisch·far·ben, 'fleisch·far·big *adj.* flesh-colo(u)red, fleshy pink

'Fleisch·fon,due *n* meat fondu(e)

'fleisch·fres·send *adj.* carnivorous; ***~es Tier, ~e Pflanze*** *a.* carnivore; **'Fleisch·fres·ser** *m* carnivore

'Fleisch|gang *m gastr.* meat course; **~ge·richt** *n* meat dish

flei·schig ['flaıʃıç] *adj.* fleshy

'Fleisch|klop·fer *m* mallet; **~kloß** *m* meatball; **~kon,ser·ven** *pl.* tinned (*esp. Am.* canned) meat *sg.*

'fleisch·lich *adj.* carnal

'fleisch·los I. *adj.* **1.** ***~e Kost*** vegetarian diet (*or* meals, food); ***~er Tag*** meatless day; **2.** emaciated, skinny; **II.** *adv.*: ***sich ~ ernähren*** eat no meat

'Fleisch|ma·de *f* maggot; **~ma,schi·ne** *f* mincer; **~mes·ser** *n* carving knife; **~nah·rung** *f* meat(s *pl.*); meat diet; **~pa,ste·te** *f* meat pie; **~saft** *m* gravy; **~to,ma·te** *f* beef tomato; **~ton** *m art*: flesh tint; **~topf** *m* saucepan; *fig.* ***sich nach den Fleischtöpfen Ägyptens zurücksehnen*** long for the fleshpots of Egypt; **~ver·gif·tung** *f* meat poisoning; **~wa·ren** *pl.* a) meat products; b) meat department *sg.*

Fleisch|wolf *m* mincer; **~wun·de** *f* flesh wound; **~zart·ma·cher** *m gastr.* (meat) tenderizer

Fleiß [flaıs] *m* (-es; *no pl.*) diligence; hard work; ***viel ~ verwenden auf*** *acc.* take great pains over; ***ohne ~ kein Preis*** no pains, no gains, F you don't get nowt for nowt; F ***mit ~*** on purpose; ***ich hab's nicht mit ~ getan*** *a.* I didn't mean (to do) it; **~ar·beit** *f* hard work; ***das war e-e reine ~*** she *etc.* managed to do it by sheer hard work

flei·ßig ['flaısıç] **I.** *adj.* diligent, hard-working; busy; frequent, regular *visitor etc.*; ♀***es Lieschen*** busy Lizzie; **II.** *adv.* diligently *etc.*; F a lot; hard; ***~ studieren*** study hard; ***~ spazierengehen*** do a lot of walking

flek·tier·bar [flɛk'ti:ɐba:ɐ] *adj.* inflectional; **flek·tie·ren** [flɛk'ti:rən] *v/t.* (h) inflect

flen·nen ['flɛnən] F *v/i.* (h) howl

flet·schen ['flɛtʃən] *v/t.* (h): ***die Zähne ~*** show (*or* flash) one's teeth, snarl; *zo.* bare its teeth, snarl

fle·xi·bel [flɛ'ksi:bəl] *adj.* flexible; ***flexible Arbeitszeit*** flextime, flexible working hours; ***flexibler Wechselkurs*** floating exchange rate; **Fle·xi·bi·li·tät** [flɛksibili'tɛ:t] *f* (-; *no pl.*) flexibility

Fle·xi·on [flɛ'ksĭo:n] *f* (-; -en) *ling.* inflection

Fle·xi'ons|en·dung *f* inflectional ending; **~leh·re** *f* accidence; **~sy,stem** *n* inflectional system

Fle·xor ['flɛkso:ɐ] *m* (-s; -en [flɛ'kso:rən]) *anat.* flexor (muscle)

Flick·ar·beit ['flık-] *f a. contp.* patchwork

flicken ['flıkən] (*sep.* -k·k-) *v/t.* (h) mend; F *fig.* patch up; *fig.* ***j-m et. am Zeug ~*** try to give s.o. a bad name

Flicken ['flıkən] (*sep.* -k·k-) *m* (-s; -) patch; **~tep·pich** *m* rag rug

Flicke·rei [flıkə'raı] (*sep.* -k·k) *f* (-; -en) mending

Flick·flack ['flıkflak] *m* (-s; -s) *gym.* backflip

'Flick·schu·ster *fig. m* bungler

'Flick|werk *fig. n* (-[e]s; *no pl.*) patch-up job, F botch(-up); **~wort** *n* filler; **~zeug** *n* a) sewing kit, b) repair kit

Flie·der ['fli:dɐ] *m* (-s; -) **1.** lilac; **2.** *dial.* elder; **~bee·re** *dial. f* elderberry; ♀**far·ben** *adj.* lilac; **~strauch** *m* lilac; **~strauß** *m* bunch of lilacs

Flie·ge ['fli:gə] *f* (-; -n) **1.** fly; *fig.* ***er tut keiner ~ was zuleide*** he wouldn't hurt a fly; ***ihn stört (sogar) die ~ an der Wand*** you're afraid to breathe when he's around; ***wie die ~n sterben*** (*or* ***umfallen***) go down like flies; ***zwei ~n mit einer Klappe schlagen*** kill two birds with one stone; F ***die*** (*or* ***e-e***) ***~ machen*** F hop it, scarper; → ***Not;*** **2.** bow tie; **3.** shadow

flie·gen ['fli:gən] (flog, geflogen) **I.** *v/i.* (sn) **1.** fly; ✈ fly, go by air; ***~ lassen*** fly *a kite*; ***wie lange fliegt man nach New York?*** how long is the flight to New York?; F ***ich kann doch nicht ~*** I haven't got wings; → ***Luft;*** **2.** *flag etc.*: flutter; *hair*: stream; **3.** *fig.* fly, rush; *hands*: flutter; *pulse*: race; *lit.* ***ein Lächeln flog über ihr Gesicht*** a smile flitted across her face; **4.** F be thrown; land; fall (***von*** *dat.* off, from); ***die Schultaschen ~ einfach in die Ecke*** the schoolbags just get thrown (F slung) into the corner; ***in den Mülleimer ~*** land (*or* end up) in the dustbin (*Am.* garbage can); **5.** F *fig.* a) be fired, F get the sack; b) be kicked out (***aus*** *dat.* of *school, one's flat etc.*); c) F flunk (it); **6.** F *fig.* ***~ auf*** *acc.* F really go for; **II.** *v/t.* (h) fly; *a.* cover *a distance*; *a.* do *a curve*; **III.** ♀ *n* (-s) flying; aviation; **'flie·gend** *adj.* flying; *zo.* ***~er Hund*** flying fox; ***~er Teppich*** magic carpet; ***~e Untertasse*** flying saucer, UFO; ✈ ***~es Personal*** flight crew; ***~er Händler*** hawker; ***~e Blätter*** loose leaves; ⚕ ***~e Hitze*** hot flushes; ⚙ ***~e Achse*** floating axle; *fig.* ***mit ~en Fahnen überlaufen*** go running to the other side; ***mit ~en Fahnen untergehen*** go down fighting

'Flie·gen|dreck *m* flies' droppings *pl.*; **~fän·ger** *m* flypaper; **~fen·ster** *n* (fly)screen; **~ge·wicht** *n*, **~ge·wicht·ler** [-gəvıçtlɐ] *m* (-s; -) *boxing*: flyweight; **~git·ter** *n* **1.** wire mesh; **2.** fly (*or* insect) screen; **~klap·pe** *f*, **~klat·sche** *f* fly swatter; **~netz** *n* fly net; **~pilz** *m* ♣ toadstool; **~schwarm** *m* swarm of flies; **~spray** *m, n* fly spray

Flie·ger ['fli:gɐ] *m* (-s; -) **1.** ⚔ *Brit.* aircraftman 2nd class, *Am.* airman basic; **2.** *zo.* flyer, flier; **3.** F → ***Flugzeug;*** **4.** *cycling*: sprinter; *horse racing*: flyer; **~ab·wehr** *f* anti-aircraft (*or* air) defen|ce (*Am.* -se); *in cpds.* anti-aircraft ...; **~ab·zei·chen** *n* wings *pl.*; **~alarm** *m* air-raid warning; **~an·griff** *m* air raid, air attack; F blitz; **~bom·be** *f* aircraft bomb

Flie·ge·rei [fli:gə'raı] F *f* (-; *no pl.*) flying

'Flie·ger·horst *m* air base

flie·ge·risch ['fli:gərıʃ] *adj.* flying, aviation ..., aeronautic(al)

'Flie·ger|jacke *f* bomber jacket; **~krank·heit** *f* aviation sickness; **~of·fi,zier** *m* air force officer; **~schu·le** *f* flying school; **~spra·che** *f* airman's slang; **~staf·fel** *f* flying squadron; **~-'Such·ak·ti,on** *f* aerial search

flie·hen ['fli:ən] (floh, geflohen) **I.** *v/i.* (sn) flee, run away (***vor*** *dat.*, ***aus*** *dat.* from); escape; ***zu j-m ~*** flee to s.o., take refuge with s.o.; **II.** *v/t.* (h) avoid, shun; **'flie·hend** *adj.* fleeing, fugitive; receding *chin, forehead etc.*

'Flieh·kraft *f* (-; *no pl.*) *phys.* centrifugal force

Flie·se ['fli:zə] *f* (-; -n) (wall *or* floor) tile; ***mit ~n auslegen*** → **'flie·sen** *v/t.* (h) tile

'Flie·sen|bo·den *m* tiled floor; **~le·ger** [-le:gɐ] *m* (-s; -) tiler

Fließ·ar·beit ['fli:s-] *f* assembly-line work

'Fließ·band *n* (-[e]s; ⸚er) assembly (*or* production) line; conveyor belt; **~ar·beit** *f* assembly-line work; **~ar·bei·ter** *m* assembly-line worker; **~fer·ti·gung** *f* assembly-line production

flie·ßen ['fli:sən] *v/i.* (floß, geflossen, sn) flow, *river, water etc.*: *a.* run; pour, stream; *fig.* flow (easily); ***~ in*** *acc. river*: flow (*or* run) into, *fig. capital etc.*: flow into, be pumped into; *fig.* ***alles fließt*** everything is in (a state of) flux; ***es ist viel Blut geflossen*** there was a lot of bloodshed; ***es wird Blut ~*** blood will flow, there will be bloodshed; **'flie·ßend I.** *adj.* flowing; *fig.* fluid; fluent; ***~es Wasser*** running water; ***~ Kalt- u. Warmwasser*** hot and cold running water; ***~er Verkehr*** moving traffic; *fig.* ***in ~em Englisch*** in fluent English; ***die Grenzen*** (*or* ***Übergänge***) ***sind ~*** there's no clear(-cut) dividing line *or* difference (***zwischen*** *dat.* between); **II.** *adv.* fluently; ***sie spricht ~ Deutsch*** she speaks fluent German

'Fließ|heck *n mot.* fastback; **~kom·ma** *n* floating point; **~pa,pier** *n* blotting paper; **~text** *m computer*: continuous text; **~was·ser** *n* running water

Flim·mer ['flımɐ] *m* (-s; *no pl.*) shimmer; *fig.* glitter; **~epi,thel** *n anat.* ciliated epithelium

'flim·mer·frei *adj.* flicker-free

flim·me·rig ['flımərıç] *adj.* flickering

'Flim·mer·ki·ste F *f* F (goggle) box, *Am.* tube

flim·mern ['flımɐn] *v/i.* (h) shimmer; *stars*: twinkle; *TV etc.*: flicker; ***mir flimmert's vor den Augen*** everything's dancing in front of my eyes

flink [flıŋk] *adj.* quick, agile; alert; ***er ist ~***

wie ein Wiesel F he's a real speedy Gonzalez
Flin·te ['flɪntə] *f* (-; -n) gun, shotgun; *fig.* ***die ~ ins Korn werfen*** give up, throw in the towel
Flip·per(au·to͵mat) ['flɪpɐ-] *m* pinball machine; **flip·pern** ['flɪpɐn] *v/i.* (h) play pinball
flip·pig ['flɪpɪç] F *adj.* **1.** excited; **2.** flighty
flir·ren ['flɪrən] *v/i.* (h) **1.** whirr, *Am.* whir; buzz; **2.** shimmer
Flirt [flœrt, flø:ɐt] *m* (-s; -s) a) flirt(ing); b) flirt; **'flir·ten** *v/i.* (h) flirt (around)
Flitt·chen ['flɪtçən] F *n* (-s; -) *sl.* floozie, (bit of a) tart
Flit·ter ['flɪtɐ] *m* (-s; -) **1.** *coll.* sequins *pl.*; **2.** *no pl. fig.* glitter; tinsel; **~gold** *n* tinsel
flit·tern ['flɪtɐn] F *v/i.* (h) honeymoon; **'Flit·ter·wo·chen** *pl.*: (***die*** ~ *usu.* one's) honeymoon *sg.*
Flitz·bo·gen ['flɪts-] *m* bow (and arrow); *fig.* ***ich bin gespannt wie ein*** ~ I can't wait to find out *etc.*
flit·zen ['flɪtsən] F *v/i.* (sn) **1.** flit, F scoot; *mot.* shoot; **2.** flit, F beat it; **Flit·zer** ['flɪtsɐ] F *m* (-s; -) *mot.* nippy little car, runabout (car)
floa·ten ['flo:tən] *v/t. and v/i.* (h) ⚕ float; **Floa·ting** ['flo:tɪŋ] *n* (-s; *no pl.*) floating
flocht [flɔxt] *pret. of* ***flechten***
Flocke ['flɔkə] (*sep.* -k·k) *f* (-; -n) flake; flock; ball of fluff; **'flocken** (*sep.* -k·k-) *v/i.* (h) flake; fuzz; **flockig** ['flɔkɪç] (*sep.* -k·k-) *adj.* fluffy
flog [flo:k] *pret. of* ***fliegen***
floh [flo:] *pret. of* ***fliehen***
Floh [flo:] *m* (-[e]s; Flöhe ['flø:ə]) flea; *fig.* ***j-m e-n ~ ins Ohr setzen*** put ideas into s.o.'s head; F ***er hört die Flöhe husten*** → ***Gras***; **~hüp·fen** *n* tiddlywinks (*sg.*); **~ki·no** F *n* fleapit; **~markt** F *m* flea market; **~stich** *m* fleabite; **~zir·kus** *m* flea circus
flö·hen ['flø:ən] (h) **I.** *v/t.* deflea, pick *a dog's etc.* fleas; **II.** *v/refl.*: ***sich*** ~ deflea o.s. (*or* itself), get rid of *or* pick one's (*or* its) fleas
Flo·men ['flo:mən] *m* (-s; *no pl.*) lard
Flop [flɔp] F *m* (-s; -s) flop; ***sich zum ~ entwickeln*** turn out (to be) a flop
Flop·py ['flɔpi] *f* (-; -s) *computer*: floppy (disk), diskette
Flor[1] [flo:ɐ] *m* (-s; *no pl.*) bloom; mass of flowers (*or* blossoms); *fig.* bevy
Flor[2] [flo:ɐ] *m* (-s; -e) a) pile, b) gauze, c) crepe (band)
Flor·a ['flo:ra] *f* (-; Floren) flora; ***~ u. Fauna*** flora and fauna, the animal and plant world
flo·ral [flo'ra:l] *adj.* floral
Flo·rett [flo'rɛt] *n* (-s; -e) foil; **~fech·ten** *n* foil fencing; **~sei·de** *f* floss (silk)
flo·rie·ren [flo'ri:rən] *v/i.* (h) flourish, prosper, thrive, boom; **flo'rie·rend** *adj.*: ***ein ~es Geschäft*** a flourishing (*or* thriving) business, ***treiben mit*** *dat.*: do a roaring trade with
Flo·rist [flo'rɪst] *m* (-en; -en) florist
Flos·kel ['flɔskəl] *f* (-; -n) meaningless phrase, *pl. a.* (empty) words; **'flos·kel·haft** *adj.* meaningless; stereotyped; ***ein ~er Ausdruck*** *a.* just a phrase
floß [flɔs] *pret. of* ***fließen***
Floß [flo:s] *n* (-es; Flöße ['flø:sə]) raft
Flos·se ['flɔsə] *f* (-; -n) *zo.* fin; flipper (*a. sport*); ✈ stabilizer fin; F a) F paw; b) F trotter
flö·ßen ['flø:sən] *v/t. and v/i.* (h) float
Flos·sen·fü·ßer ['flɔsənfy:sɐ] *m* (-s; -) *zo.* pinniped; pygopod
Flö·ßer ['flø:sɐ] *m* (-s; -) raftsman
Flö·te ['flø:tə] *f* (-; -n) **1.** ♪ a) flute, b) recorder; ***~ spielen*** play the flute; **2.** champagne flute; **3.** *card game*: flush
flö·ten ['flø:tən] *v/t. and v/i.* (h) play the flute (*or* recorder); *bird*: sing; F *fig.* say *s.th.* in a honeyed voice; **~ge·hen** F *v/i.* (*irr.*, *sep.*, sn, → ***gehen***) go by the board; F go down the drain; F go for a burton; ***m-e Hoffnungen*** (***die neuen Gläser***) ***sind flötengegangen*** that's put paid to my hopes (to the new glasses)
'Flö·ten·ton *m* note of a flute; ***Flötentöne*** *the* sound of a flute (*or* flutes); F *fig.* ***j-m*** (***die***) ***Flötentöne beibringen*** show s.o. what's what
Flö·tist [flø'tɪst] *m* (-en; -en) flute-player, flautist
flott [flɔt] **I.** *adj.* **1.** a) fast; lively, b) smooth; ⚕ ***~er Absatz*** brisk trading; **2.** smart; **3.** ⚓ ***~ sein*** be afloat; **II.** *adv.* **4.** a) fast, b) smoothly, without a hitch; ♪ ***~ spielen*** play very lively music; ***~ leben*** lead a fast life; ***es geht ihm ~ von der Hand*** he's very fast (at it); ***es geht ~ voran*** things are getting on nicely; ***das Geschäft geht ~*** business is doing well; ***~ geschrieben*** (***gemacht*** *etc.*) punchy; **5.** smartly; **~be·kom·men** *v/t.* (*irr.*, *sep.*, h, → ***bekommen***) set afloat; get *a car etc.* going (again); get *a company etc.* back on its feet (again)
Flot·te ['flɔtə] *f* (-; -n) ⚓ fleet
'Flot·ten|ab·kom·men *n* naval agreement; **~chef** *m* fleet commander; **~ma͵nö·ver** *pl.* naval manoeuvres (*Am.* maneuvers); **~stütz·punkt** *m* naval base; **~ver·band** *m* naval formation
'flott·ge·hend *adj.* brisk, lively *trading*
Flot·til·le [flɔ'tɪljə] *f* (-; -n) ⚓ flotilla
'flott|krie·gen F *v/t.* (*sep.*, h), **~ma·chen** *v/t.* (*sep.*, h) → ***flottbekommen***
'flott'weg F *adv.* quickly; nonstop
Flöz [flø:ts] *m* (-es; -e) *geol. and* ⚒ seam
Fluch [flu:x] *m* (-[e]s; Flüche ['fly:çə]) curse (*a. fig.*); swearword; ***unter e-m ~ stehen*** be under a curse; ***mit e-m ~ belegen*** put a curse on; ***zum ~ für die Menschheit werden*** become the curse of mankind; **flu·chen** ['flu:xən] *v/i.* (h) curse; swear; ***~ auf*** *acc.* curse; ***~ wie ein Landsknecht*** (*or* ***Fuhrknecht***) swear like a trooper
Flucht [flʊxt] *f* (-; -en) **1.** *no pl.* flight (***vor*** *dat.* from); *a. psych.* escape; ***auf der ~*** a) while fleeing, b) while attempting to escape, on the run; ***die ~ ergreifen*** → ***flüchten***; ***in die ~ schlagen*** put to flight; ***das ist die ~ vor der Verantwortung*** that's trying to evade responsibility; ***er versuchte es mit der ~ in den Alkohol*** he tried alcohol (*or* he turned to drink) as an escape; ***die ~ in die Öffentlichkeit*** *etc.* ***antreten*** resort to publicity *etc.*; ***die ~ nach vorn antreten*** take the bull by the horns; ***wir müssen die ~ nach vorn antreten*** *a.* attack is the best means of defen|ce (*Am.* -se); **2.** ⚕ flight *of capital etc.*; **3.** suite *of rooms*; flight *of stairs*; **4.** ⚠, ⚙ straight line
'flucht·ar·tig **I.** *adj.* hasty, hurried; **II.** *adv.* in a hurry; ***~ verlassen*** leave *a place* in a hurry, make a quick getaway from, beat a hasty retreat from; ***~ davonrennen***, F ***~ abhauen*** beat a hasty retreat, F scarper
'Flucht|au·to *n* getaway car; **~be·we·gung** *f* tide of refugees
flüch·ten ['flʏçtən] (sn) **I.** *v/i.* flee (***vor*** *dat.* from); run away; escape (*a. fig.*); **II.** *v/refl.*: ***sich ~*** flee; ***sich zu j-m ~*** take refuge with s.o.; ***sich ~ in*** *acc.* take shelter in; *fig.* ***sich in et. ~*** resort to s.th., turn to s.th. as a means of escape
'Flucht|ge·fahr *f* ⚖ danger of absconding; **~hel·fer** *m pol.* escape agent; F people smuggler; **~hil·fe** *f* escape aid
flüch·tig ['flʏçtɪç] **I.** *adj.* **1.** a) quick; b) superficial; careless *work*, cursory *glance*; c) vague, hazy; fleeting *moment etc.*; ***~e Bekanntschaft*** (***Bemerkung***) passing acquaintance (remark); (***j-m***) ***e-n ~en Besuch machen*** briefly drop in (on s.o.); ***~er Eindruck*** fleeting impression; ***~er Einblick*** glimpse (***in*** *acc.* of); **2.** escaped, fugitive; ⚖ ***~ werden*** abscond; ***~er Schuldner*** F fly-by-night; **3.** ⚗ volatile; **II.** *adv.* quickly *etc.*; → **I**; ***~ bemerken*** (*or* ***erwähnen***) mention in passing; ***~ durchlesen*** skim over; ***~ bekannt sein mit j-m*** vaguely know s.o.; **Flüch·ti·ge** ['flʏçtɪgə] *m, f* (-n; -n) fugitive, runaway; **'Flüch·tig·keit** *f* (-; *no pl.*) **1.** transitoriness, fleetingness; **2.** ⚗ volatility
'Flüch·tig·keits·feh·ler *m* careless mistake, slip
'Flucht·ka·pi͵tal *n* flight capital
Flücht·ling ['flʏçtlɪŋ] *m* (-s; -e) refugee
'Flücht·lings|la·ger *n* refugee camp; **~strom** *m* stream (*or* influx) of refugees; **~wel·le** *f* tide of refugees
'Flucht|li·nie *f* ⚠ alignment; *opt.* vanishing line; **~punkt** *m opt.* vanishing point; **~ver·dacht** *m*: ⚖ ***es besteht ~*** the prisoner is likely to try and escape; **~ver·such** *m* escape (*or* breakout) attempt, attempted escape; ***e-n ~ unternehmen*** attempt to escape (*or* break out); **~wa·gen** *m* getaway car; **~weg** *m* escape route
'Fluch·wort *n* (-[e]s; ⁻er) swearword
Flug [flu:k] *m* (-[e]s; Flüge ['fly:gə]) flight; *zo.* ***im ~*** in flight; *fig.* (***wie***) ***im ~(e)*** very quickly; ***die Woche verging wie im ~(e)*** *a.* the week just flew by (*or* went by just like that, went by in no time); **~ab·fer·ti·gung** *f* handling of flights; **~ab·kom·men** *n* air agreement; **~ab·wehr** *f* air defen|ce (*Am.* -se); *in cpds.* anti-aircraft ...; **~angst** *f* fear of flying; **~asche** *f* flue ash; **~bahn** *f* trajectory; ✈ flight path; **~ball** *m sport*: volley; **~be·glei·ter** *m* flight attendant; **~ben͵zin** *n* aviation fuel (*Am. a.* gasoline); **~be·reich** *m* flying range; **&be·reit** *adj.* ready for takeoff; **~be·trieb** *m* air traffic; **~blatt** *n* leaflet; *hist.* broadsheet; **~da·ten·schrei·ber** *m* flight recorder, black box; **~dau·er** *f* flying time; **~dra·che** *m zo.* flying dragon; **~ei·gen·schaf·ten** *pl.* ✈ flying characteristics
Flü·gel ['fly:gəl] *m* (-s; -) **1.** wing (*a.* ⚠, *pol.*, *sport*); (*propeller*, *ventilator*) blade; sail *of a windmill*; ⚘ wing, side petal; *anat.* lobe; door; panel *of an altarpiece*; ⚔ flank; ***mit den ~n schlagen*** flap (*or* beat) its wings; *fig.* ***die ~ hängenlassen*** a) lose heart, b) be down in the mouth; ***j-m die ~ beschneiden*** (*or* ***stutzen***) clip s.o.'s wings; ***auf den ~n der Phantasie*** on the wings of fantasy; **2.** ♪ grand piano; **~al͵tar** *m* winged altarpiece; ***dreiteiliger ~*** triptych; **~fen·ster** *n* casement window; **&för·mig** [-fœrmɪç] *adj.*

wing-shaped; **~horn** *n* ♪ flugelhorn; **~kampf** *m pol.* factional dispute (*a. pl.* fighting); **2lahm** *adj.* **1.** *zo.* broken-winged, *a.* lame *duck*; **~er Vogel** *a.* bird with a broken wing; **2.** *fig.* dejected; weary; ***er ist ~*** *a.* the fizz has gone out of him

'flü·gel·los *adj.* wingless

'Flü·gel|mut·ter *f* ⚙ wing nut; **~schlag** *m* flapping (*or* beating) of wings; **~schrau·be** *f* ⚙ wing screw; **~spann·wei·te** *f* wingspan; **~spit·ze** *f* wing tip; **~stür·mer** *m sport*: winger; **~tür** *f* double door(s *pl.*)

'Flug|ent·fer·nung *f* flying distance; **~er·fah·rung** *f* flying experience; **2fä·hig** *adj. zo.* able to fly; ✈ airworthy; **~feld** *n* airfield

'Flug·gast *m* (air) passenger; **~ab·fer·ti·gung** *f* **1.** passenger clearance; **2.** check-in desk

flüg·ge ['flʏgə] *adj.* fully fledged; ***~ werden*** *zo.* fledge, *fig.* begin to stand on one's own two feet

'Flug|ge·rät *n coll.* (military) aircraft; **~ge·schwin·dig·keit** *f* flying speed; **~ge·sell·schaft** *f* airline (company), carrier

'Flug·ha·fen *m* airport; **~be·reich** *m* airport area; ***im ~*** *a.* near (*or* around) the airport; **~bus** *m* airport shuttle bus; **~ge·bühr** *f a. pl.* airport tax; **~ge·län·de** *n* airport; **~ho,tel** *n* airport hotel; **~nä·he** *f*: ***in ~*** near the (*or* an) airport; **~po·li,zei** *f* airport security *sg.*; **~re·stau,rant** *n* airport restaurant; **~ver·wal·tung** *f* airport authorities *pl.*

'Flug|hal·le *f* hangar; **~hö·he** *f* ✈ (flying) altitude; **~in·ge,nieur** *m* flight engineer; **~ka·pi,tän** *m* (flight) captain; **~kar·te** *f* **1.** (air) ticket; **2.** aeronautical chart; **2klar** *adj.* ready for takeoff; **~kom,fort** *m* in-flight amenities *pl.* (*or* service); **~kör·per** *m* projectile; **~lärm** *m* aircraft noise, *the* sound of aircraft taking off and landing; **~leh·rer** *m* flying instructor; **~lei·ter** *m* air traffic control(l)er; **~lei·tung** *f* air traffic control; **~li·nie** *f* **1.** airline (company), carrier; **2.** (air) route; **3.** flight path; **~lot·se** *m* air traffic control(l)er; **~num·mer** *f* flight number; **~ob,jekt** *n*: ***unbekanntes ~*** unidentified flying object, UFO; **~pas·sa,gier** *m* (air) passenger; **~per·so,nal** *n* crew; **~plan** *m* (flight) schedule, timetable; **~platz** *m* airfield, airport; **~pra·xis** *f* flying experience; **~preis** *m* (air) fare; **~prü·fung** *f* flying test; **~rei·se** *f* journey by air; **~rei·sen·de** *m, f* (-n; -n) air travel(l)er; (air) passenger; **~re·ser,vie·rung** *f* flight reservation

flugs [flu:ks] *obs. adv.* swiftly; at once, instantly

'Flug|sand *m* drifting (*or* windborne) sand; **~schal·ter** *m* flight desk; **~schan·ze** *f* (ski) jump; **~schau** *f* air show; **~schein** *m* **1.** (air *or* flight) ticket; **2.** pilot's licen|ce (*Am.* -se); **~schnei·se** *f* approach corridor; **~schrei·ber** *m* flight recorder, black box; **~schrift** *f* leaflet, pamphlet; **~si·cher·heit** *f* air safety; **~si·che·rung** *f* air traffic control; **~si·mu,la·tor** *m* flight simulator; **~sport** *m* (sport) flying; **~steig** *m* jetway, airgate; **~strecke** *f* a) (air) route, b) distance flown (*or* covered); leg; **~stun·de** *f* **1.** flying hour; **2.** ***nach zwei ~n waren wir da*** we arrived after a two-hour flight, we were there in two hours; **3.** flying lesson; **~stütz·punkt** *m* airbase; **2taug·lich** *adj.* fit to fly; ✈ airworthy; **~tech·nik** *f* aeronautics *pl.*; ⚙ aircraft engineering; flying technique; **~tech·ni·ker** *m* aeronautical engineer; **2tech·nisch** *adj.* aeronautical; **~ticket** *n* (air *or* flight) ticket; **2tüch·tig** *adj.* airworthy; **~über,wa·chung** *f* air traffic control; **~ver·bin·dung** *f* air connection; ***gibt es e-e (direkte) ~?*** can you fly there? (is there a direct flight?); **~ver·bot** *n* ban on flying; grounding order; ***~ erhalten*** be grounded; **~ver·kehr** *m* air traffic; air services *pl.*; **~ver·such** *m* attempt to fly; ✈ flight test; **~we·sen** *n* (-s; *no pl.*) aviation, aeronautics *pl.*, flying; **~wet·ter** *n* flying weather; **~wet·ter·dienst** *m* aviation weather service; **~zeit** *f* flying time; ***wie ist die ~ nach X?*** how long is the flight to X?

'Flug·zeug *n* (-[e]s; -e) (aero)plane, *Am.* (air)plane; *a. pl. coll.* aircraft; **~ab·sturz** *m* air (*or* plane) crash; **~ab·wehr** *f* anti-aircraft defen|ce (*Am.* -se); **~bau** *m* (-[e]s; *no pl.*) aircraft construction; **~be·sat·zung** *f* (air *or* flight) crew; **~ent·füh·rer** *m* hijacker, *esp. Am. a.* skyjacker; **~ent·füh·rung** *f* hijacking, *esp. Am. a.* skyjacking; **~füh·rer** *m* pilot; **~hal·le** *f* hangar; **~in·du,strie** *f* aircraft industry; **~ka·ta,stro·phe** *f* air(line) disaster; **~kon·struk,teur** *m* aircraft designer; **~mo,dell** *n* model aeroplane (*Am.* airplane); **~trä·ger** *m* aircraft carrier; **~un·glück** *n* air (*or* plane) crash, air(line) disaster; **~wrack** *n* wreck of an (*or* the) aeroplane (*Am.* airplane), wrecked plane; aircraft wreck

'Flug·ziel *n* destination

Flui·dum ['flu:idʊm] *n* (-s; -da) fluid; *fig.* aura, air

Fluk·tua·ti·on [flʊktŭa'tsĭo:n] *f* (-; -en) fluctuation; turnover; **fluk·tu·ie·ren** [flʊktu'i:rən] *v/i.* (h) fluctuate; ***~de Preise*** price fluctuations, fluctuations in price

Flun·der ['flʊndɐ] *f* (-; -n) flounder

Flun·ke·rei [flʊŋkə'rai] F *f* (-; -en) **1.** story, *coll.* stories *pl.*; **2.** *no pl.* storytelling; bragging; **flun·kern** ['flʊŋkɐn] F *v/i.* (h) tell stories (*or* fibs); brag

Flunsch [flʊnʃ] *dial. m* (-[e]s; -e): ***e-n ~ ziehen*** pull a face

Flu·or ['flu:o:ɐ] *n* (-s; *no pl.*) fluorine; fluoride; **Flu·or·chlor·koh·len·was·ser·stoff** *m* chlorofluorocarbon, CFC

Fluo·res·zenz [fluorɛs'tsɛnts] *f* (-; *no pl.*) fluorescence; **fluo·res·zie·ren** [fluorɛs'tsi:rən] *v/i.* (h) fluoresce; **fluo·res'zie·rend** *adj.* fluorescent

Fluo·rid [fluo'ri:t] *n* (-[e]s; -e [-də]) fluoride

Fluo·ro·skop [fluoro'sko:p] *n* (-s; -e) ⚕ fluoroscope

Flu·or|säu·re *f* fluoric acid; **~was·ser·stoff** *m* hydrogen fluoride

Flur[1] [flu:ɐ] *m* (-[e]s; -e) hall; corridor; ***auf dem ~*** in the corridor

Flur[2] *f* (-; -en) open fields *pl.*; village land(s *pl.*); ***durch Wald und ~*** through fields and meadows; *fig.* ***allein auf weiter ~ sein*** be on one's own, be all alone (with no-one to turn to); ***da bist du allein auf weiter ~*** *a.* F you'll be going it alone; **~be·rei·ni·gung** *f* land consolidation; *fig.* settling of disputes, smoothing over of difficulties; **~na·me** *m* field name; **~scha·den** *m a. pl.* crop damage

Fluß [flʊs] *m* (Flusses; Flüsse ['flʏsə]) **1.** river; stream, *Am. a.* creek; **2.** *no pl.* flow(ing); *fig.* flow *of traffic etc.*; *fig.* ***im ~*** in (a state of) flux; ***et. in ~ bringen*** get s.th. going (*or* under way); ***in ~ kommen*** get going, get under way, get into its stride; **2'ab·wärts** *adv.* down the river, downriver, downstream; **~arm** *m* arm of a (*or* the) river; **2'auf·wärts** *adv.* up the river, upriver, upstream; **~bau** *m* (-[e]s; *no pl.*) river engineering; **~bett** *n* riverbed

Flüß·chen ['flʏsçən] *n* (-s; -) (little) stream, *Am.* creek

'Fluß|damp·fer *m* riverboat; **~dia·,gramm** *n* flowchart; **~fisch** *m* river fish; **~ge·biet** *n* river basin; **~ha·fen** *m* river port

flüs·sig ['flʏsɪç] **I.** *adj.* liquid; molten, melted; ⚜ liquid, available *capital etc.*; *fig.* fluent, flowing *style etc.*; ♪ smooth; ***~ machen, ~ werden*** liquefy, melt; → ***flüssigmachen***; **II.** *adv.* in liquid form; *fig.* fluently; *run etc.*: smoothly; *fig.* ***sich ~ lesen*** read well

'Flüs·sig|ei *n* liquid egg; **~gas** *n* liquid gas

'Flüs·sig·keit *f* (-; -en) **1.** liquid; ***viel ~ zu sich nehmen*** drink plenty of liquids; **2.** *no pl.* liquidity; *fig.* fluency, flow; ♪ smoothness

'Flüs·sig·keits|brem·se *f mot.* hydraulic brake; **~grad** *m* liquidity; ⚗ viscosity; **~maß** *n* liquid measure

'Flüs·sig·kri,stall·an·zei·ge *f* liquid crystal display, LCD

'flüs·sig·ma·chen *v/t.* (*sep.*, h) ⚜ mobilize

'Fluß|in·sel *f* river island; **~krebs** *m* (freshwater) crayfish, *Am. a.* crawfish; **~land·schaft** *f* **1.** river country; **2.** countryside (*or* terrain) through which a (*or* the) river flows; **3.** *art*: riverscape; **~lauf** *m* course of a (*or* the) river; **~mün·dung** *f* mouth (of a *or* the river), estuary; **~netz** *n* river network (*or* system); **~nie·der·ung** *f* river plain; **~pferd** *n* hippopotamus; **~re·gu,lie·rung** *f* river control; **~säu·re** *f* ⚗ hydrofluoric acid; **~schiff** *n* riverboat; **~schiffahrt** (*sep.* -ff·f-) *f* river navigation (*or* traffic); **~spat** *m* fluorite, fluorspar; **~tal** *n* river valley; **~ufer** *n* riverbank, riverside; **~ver·lauf** *m* course of a (*or* the) river; **~ver·schmut·zung** *f* river pollution

Flü·ster|ga·le,rie ['flʏstɐ-] *f* whispering gallery; **~kam,pa·gne** *f* whispering campaign

flü·stern ['flʏstɐn] (h) **I.** *v/i.* (speak in a) whisper; ***du brauchst nicht zu ~*** there's no need to whisper; **II.** *v/t.* whisper; ***j-m et. (ins Ohr) ~*** whisper s.th. to s.o. (into s.o.'s ear); *fig.* F ***dem werd' ich was ~*** I'll tell him a thing or two; F ***das kann ich dir ~!*** you can take it from me; **III. 2** *n* (-s) whisper(ing); ***ein ~*** a whisper, (some) whispering

'Flü·ster|pa,ro·le *f* whispered word (*or* message); **~pro·pa,gan·da** *f* subversive propaganda; **~stim·me** *f*: ***mit ~*** → **~ton** *m*: ***im ~*** in a whisper; **~tü·te** F *f* megaphone; **~witz** *m* underground joke

Flut [flu:t] *f* (-; -en) **1.** *no pl.* (high) tide; ***die ~ kommt (geht)*** the tide is coming in (going out); ***es ist ~*** the tide is in; **2.** *usu. pl.* waves *pl.*; waters *pl.*; flood (*a. fig. of tears*); **3.** *fig.* (great) crowd, hordes *pl. of people etc.*; tide *of fugitives*; torrent, stream *of words etc.*; flood, avalanche *of written protests etc.*; **mit e-r ~ von Zuschriften überschüttet werden** be inundated with letters; **e-e ~ von Schimpfwörtern ergoß sich über ihn** a torrent of abuse rained down on him; **'flu·ten I.** *v/i.* (sn) surge, *a. light*: stream, pour; *fig. crowd etc.*: pour, *a. traffic*: stream; **II.** *v/t.* (h) flood

'Flut|gren·ze *f* high water mark; **~ha·fen** *m* tidal harbo(u)r; **~ka·ta,stro·phe** *f* flood disaster

'Flut·licht *n* (-[e]s; *no pl.*) floodlights *pl.*; **bei ~** under floodlight; **~an·la·ge** *f* floodlights *pl.*, floodlighting

'Flut·li·nie *f* high water mark

flut·schen ['flʊtʃən] F *v/i.* **1.** (sn) slip; **es ist mir aus der Hand geflutscht** *a.* F it just sort of fell; **2.** (h) *fig. work etc.*: go very well; **es flutscht nur so** it's (*or* things are) going like clockwork; **es flutscht nicht recht** it's hard going

'Flut·wel·le *f* tidal wave

focht [fɔxt] *pret. of* **fechten**

Fock [fɔk] *f* (-; -en), **~mast** *m* foremast; **~se·gel** *n* foresail

Fö·de·ra·lis·mus [fødera'lɪsmʊs] *m* (-; *no pl.*) federalism; **fö·de·ra·li·stisch** [fødera'lɪstɪʃ] *adj.* federalistic; federal; **Fö·de·ra·ti·on** [fødera'tsĭo:n] *f* (-; -en) (con-) federation, confederacy; **fö·de·ra·tiv** [fødera'ti:f] *adj.* federative, federal

Foh·len ['fo:lən] *n* (-s; -) foal; colt; filly; **'foh·len** *v/i.* (h) foal

Föhn [fø:n] *m* (-[e]s; *no pl.*) foehn, föhn; **bei ~** when there's foehn (*or* föhn); **heute haben wir ~** it's foehn (*or* föhn) today; **föh·nig** ['fø:nɪç] *adj.* foehn ..., föhn ...; **'Föhn·wet·ter** *n* foehn (*or* föhn) weather

Föh·re *f* pine (tree)

Fo·kus ['fo:kʊs] *m* (-; -se), **fo·kus·sie·ren** [fokʊ'si:rən] *v/t.* (h) *phys.*, ✱ focus

Fol·ge ['fɔlgə] *f* (-; -n) **1.** sequence, succession; order; → **zwanglos; in der ~** subsequently; **in rascher ~** in rapid succession; **2.** series; instal(l)ment; *TV*: part, sequel; number, issue; *novel, film etc.* **in mehreren ~n** in instal(l)ments; **3.** result, consequence, effect; aftermath; ✱ aftereffect; *phls.* corollary; ⩗ sequence; **(üble) ~n haben** have (unpleasant) consequences; **die ~n tragen** bear the consequences; **ohne ~n bleiben** have no consequences; **es blieb ohne ~n** *a.* there were no consequences; **die ~n blieben nicht aus** it wasn't without (its) consequences; **zur ~ haben** result in, lead to; **als ~ davon** as a result; **die ~ war, daß** the outcome (F upshot) was that; **sie starb an den ~n des Unfalls** she died as a result of the accident; **~ leisten** *dat.* grant; → **folgen** 6; **~er·schei·nung** *f* consequence; ✱ aftereffect; **~ko·sten** *pl.*, **~la·sten** *pl.* follow-up costs

fol·gen ['fɔlgən] *v/i.* (sn) **1.** follow (*a. fig.*); **der Rede folgte ein Empfang** the speech was followed by a reception; **ein Unglück folgte dem andern** it was one disaster after the other; **j-m auf Schritt und Tritt ~** dog s.o.'s footsteps; **Brief folgt** letter will follow; **weitere Einzelheiten ~** further details to come; **es folgt ...** we now have ..., and now ...; **wie folgt** as follows; **... lautet wie folgt** ... reads as follows; *fig.* **können Sie ~?** do you follow me?; **ich kann Ihnen da(rin) nicht ~** I can't agree with you there; **mit dem Finger ~** trace *s.th.* with one's finger; → **Fortsetzung; 2.** succeed, follow *s.o.*; **3.** follow, come after *s.o.*; **auf Platz 3 folgt ...** in third place we have ..., third is (*or* are) ...; **4.** follow, ensue (**aus** *dat.* from); **daraus folgt, daß** it follows (from this) that; **5.** follow; **j-s Beispiel ~** follow s.o.'s example; **j-s Rat ~** follow (*or* take) s.o.'s advice; **s-m Gefühl ~** a) do what one's heart tells one, b) do what one feels is best; **6.** obey *an order*; comply with, carry out *order, request etc.*; accept *an invitation*; **(j-m) aufs Wort ~** a) obey (s.o.) instantly, b) obey (s.o.) to the letter; **7.** F obey; **nicht ~** disobey; **er folgt nicht** he (just) won't listen; **'fol·gend** *adj.* following; ensuing; subsequent; next; **am ~en Tag** the next (*or* following) day, the day after; **im ~en** in the following; **es handelt sich um ~es** the matter is as follows, F what it's (all) about is this; **dazu möchte ich ~es sagen** may I just make the following point (*or* make one thing clear), the way I see it is; **fol·gen·der·ma·ßen** ['fɔlgəndɐ'ma:sən] *adv.* as follows

'fol·gen·los *adj.* without consequences; **es blieb ~** there were no consequences

'fol·gen·reich *adj.* momentous; far-reaching

'fol·gen·schwer *adj.* momentous; grave; far-reaching

'fol·ge·rich·tig I. *adj.* logical; consistent; **II.** *adv.*: **~ denken** think logically (*or* along logical lines); **'Fol·ge·rich·tig·keit** *f* (-; *no pl.*) (logical) consistency

fol·gern ['fɔlgɐn] *v/t.* (h) conclude (**aus** *dat.* from), deduce (*s.th.* from); **Fol·ge·rung** ['fɔlgərʊŋ] *f* (-; -en) conclusion; **e-e ~ ziehen** draw a conclusion (**aus** *dat.* from); **daraus ergibt sich die ~, daß** from this it follows (*or* one may conclude) that

'Fol·ge|satz *m ling.* consecutive clause; ⩗, *phls.* corollary; **~scha·den** *m* ⚖ consequential damage

'fol·ge·wid·rig *adj.* illogical; inconsistent; **'Fol·ge·wid·rig·keit** *f* (-; *no pl.*) inconsistency

'Fol·ge|wir·kung *f* consequence; *pl. a.* impact *sg.*; **e-e ~ war** one of the consequences (it had) was ...; **~zeit** *f* period following

folg·lich ['fɔlklɪç] *cj.* therefore; so

folg·sam ['fɔlkza:m] *adj.* obedient; submissive; good; **'Folg·sam·keit** *f* (-; *no pl.*) obedience; submissiveness

Fo·li·ant [fo'lĭant] *m* (-en; -en) folio; large tome

Fo·lie ['fo:lĭə] *f* (-; -n) foil; cling film, *Am.* plastic wrap; *fig.* **als ~ dienen** serve as a foil (*dat.* to)

'Fo·li·en|kar,tof·fel *f* jacket potato (baked in alumin[i]um foil); **~ver·packt** *adj.* alumin(i)um-wrapped; cling-wrapped, *Am.* plastic-wrapped

Fo·lio ['fo:lĭo] *n* (-s; Folien ['fo:lĭən]), **~blatt** *n*, **~for,mat** *n* folio

Folk·lo·re [fɔlk'lo:rə] *f* (-; *no pl.*) folklore; traditional (Brazilian *etc.*) music, folkloric music, folk (music); folk culture; **Folk'lo·re·abend** *m* evening of traditional music and dance; **folk·lo·ri·stisch** [fɔlklo'rɪstɪʃ] *adj.* ♪ traditional, folk(loric); traditional, ethnic *dress*; **~e Elemente** *a.* folk elements; **~er Abend** → **Folkloreabend**

Fol·li·kel [fɔ'li:kəl] *m* (-s; -) *physiol.* follicle; **~sprung** *m* ovulation

Fol·säu·re ['fo:l-] *f* folic acid

Fol·ter ['fɔltɐ] *f* (-; -n) torture (*a. fig.*); rack; *fig.* **es war e-e ~** it was torture (*or* sheer agony); **j-n auf die ~ spannen** keep s.o. in suspense (*or* on tenterhooks); **~bank** *f* (-; ⸚e) rack; **~in·stru,ment** *n* instrument of torture; **~kam·mer** *f* torture chamber; **~knecht** *m* torturer; **der General mit s-n ~en** the general and his henchmen; **~me,tho·de** *f* method of torture

fol·tern ['fɔltɐn] *v/t.* (h) torture; *fig. a.* torment

'Fol·ter·qua·len *pl.* agony *sg.*; *fig.* **~ erleiden** go through absolute agony

Fol·te·rung ['fɔltərʊŋ] *f* (-; -en) torture (*a. fig.*), torturing

'Fol·ter·werk·zeug *n* instrument of torture

Fön [fø:n] *TM m* (-[e]s; -e) hair drier

Fond [fõ:] *m* (-s; -s) **1.** background; **2.** *mot.* back (of the car); **im ~** *a.* on the back seat; **3.** basis, foundation; **4.** *gastr.* meat juice, juice from the meat

Fon·dant [fõ'dã:] *m*, *n* (-s; -s) fondant

Fonds [fõ:] *m* (- [fõ:(s)]; -s [fõ:s]) ✝ fund (*a. fig.*); funds *pl.*, capital; government stocks *pl.*

Fon·due [fõ'dy:] *n* (-s; -), *f* (-; -s) *gastr.* fondu(e)

fö·nen ['fø:nən] *v/t.* (h) (blow-)dry

Fon·tä·ne [fɔn'tɛ:nə] *f* (-; -n) fountain; jet of water

Fon·ta·nel·le [fɔnta'nɛlə] *f* (-; -n) *anat.* fontanel(le)

fop·pen ['fɔpən] *v/t.* (h) pull *s.o.'s* leg, F kid; fool; **Fop·pe·rei** [fɔpə'raɪ] *f* (-; -en) leg-pulling

for·cie·ren [fɔr'si:rən] *v/t.* (h) force; F squeeze out; **for·ciert** [fɔr'si:ɐt] *adj.* forced

För·de ['fœrdə] *f* (-; -n) firth, narrow inlet

För·der|an·la·ge ['fœrdɐ-] *f* conveyor (system); **~band** *n* conveyor belt

För·de·rer ['fœrdərɐ] *m* (-s; -) promoter, sponsor; supporter; patron

För·der|ge·rät ['fœrdɐ-] *n* conveyor; **~gut** *n* material to be transported; **~korb** *m* (pit) cage; **~kreis** *m*: **~ für ...** society for the promotion of ...; **~kurs** *m ped.* special class; *pl. a.* special tuition *sg.*; **~lei·stung** *f* ⚙ output, yield

för·der·lich ['fœrdɐlɪç] *adj.* conducive (*dat.* to); beneficial (to); useful (for, to); effective; *e-r Sache* **~ sein** *a.* help, promote, contribute to

För·der·men·ge ['fœrdɐ-] *f* output

for·dern ['fɔrdɐn] *v/t.* (h) **1.** demand (**von j-m** of s.o.); call for; ⚖ claim; ask for *price*; *fig.* claim *victims etc.*; **zuviel ~** be too demanding; **du forderst zuviel** you're asking too much (of me); *fig.* **hunderte von Todesopfern ~** claim hundreds of lives; **2. j-n ~** stretch s.o., take it out of s.o., *sport*: push (*or* stretch) s.o. to the limit; **(richtig) gefordert werden** be faced with a (real) challenge; **der Job fordert ihn nicht** the job's too easy for him, he needs a more challenging job; **3. zum Duell ~** challenge to a duel; **vor Gericht ~** summon before a court

för·dern ['fœrdɐn] *v/t.* (h) **1.** encourage, promote; support; cultivate, foster; help, be good for *s.th.*; patronize, *esp. Am. a.* sponsor; **2.** ⚙ a) produce, b) convey, transport, c) feed; → **zutage** 1; **'för·dernd** *adj.*: **~es Mitglied** supporting member

ˈfor·dernd *adj.* expectant *look etc.*; imperious
För·der|preis [ˈfœrdɐ-] *m* (literary *etc.*) award; **~schacht** *m* ⚒ mine shaft; **~stufe** *f* → **Orientierungsstufe**
For·de·rung [ˈfɔrdərʊŋ] *f* (-; -en) demand (**nach** *dat.* for; **an** *acc.* on); call (for); ⚖ claim (for); ✝ charge; exaction *of fees etc.*; **~en stellen** make demands; **die ~ stellen, daß** demand (*or* insist) that; ✝ **e-e ~ haben an** *acc.* have a claim against (*or* on); **ausstehende ~en** outstanding debts, accounts receivable
För·de·rung [ˈfœrdərʊŋ] *f* (-; *no pl.*) **1.** promotion; support; cultivation; patronage, sponsorship; **2.** a) ⚒ extraction; (*oil*) production; output, b) ⚙ conveyance, c) ⚙ supply
ˈFör·de·rungs|maß·nah·men *pl.* incentive measures; **~mit·tel** *pl.* development funds; **~pro͵gramm** *n* development program(me); **2wür·dig** *adj.* worthy of promotion (*or* sponsorship); **~ sein** *a.* deserve to be promoted (*or* sponsored)
ˈFör·der·wa·gen *m* (mine) car; tub
Fo·rel·le [foˈrɛlə] *f* (-; -n) trout; *gastr.* **~ blau** truite bleu
Foˈrel·len|teich *m* trout pond; **~zucht** *f* **1.** trout farming; **2.** trout nursery
fo·ren·sisch [foˈrɛnzɪʃ] *adj.* forensic(ally *adv.*)
For·ke [ˈfɔrkə] *f* (-; -n) pitchfork
Form [fɔrm] *f* (-; -en) **1.** form (*a. biol.*, ♪, *phys.*), *ling. a.* voice; **2.** form, shape; *dat.* **~ geben** lend shape to; **s-e ~ behalten** keep its shape; **aus der ~ geraten** (*or* **kommen**) get out of shape; **(feste) ~(en) annehmen** (begin to) take shape; **in ~ von** (*or gen.*) in the form of (*a. fig.*); **die ~ e-s Halbmonds** *etc.* **haben** be in the shape of a crescent *etc.*, be shaped like a crescent *etc.*; **3.** form, shape, outline; *fashion*: style, cut; *esp.* ⚙ design, styling; **weibliche ~en** F curves; **4.** model; **5.** ⚙ mo(u)ld, die; **6.** a) tin, b) pastry cutter; **7.** *fig.* form, way; **in höflicher ~** politely; **8.** formality, form; **der ~ halber** pro forma, as a matter of form; **in aller ~** formally, solemnly; **sich in aller ~ entschuldigen** make a formal apology; **9.** good form; **10.** convention(s *pl.*), etiquette; **der ~ halber** to keep up appearances; **die ~ wahren** observe the proprieties, F stick to the rules; **11.** *pl.* manners; **12.** *sport*: condition, shape, *a. w.s.* form; **in (guter) ~** in good form (*sport*: *a.* shape, condition); **in bester ~** in top form; **nicht in ~** off form, not in form; **in ~ bleiben, sich in ~ halten** keep in form (*sport*: *a.* shape); **in ~ kommen** get into shape; **j-n in ~ bringen** get s.o. into shape
for·mal [fɔrˈmaːl] **I.** *adj.* formal; **in ~er Hinsicht** formally, from a formal point of view; ⚖ **~er Einwand** technical objection; **II.** *adv.* formally; **~ und inhaltlich** in form and content
Form·al·de·hyd [ˈfɔrmʔaldehyːt] *n* (-s; *no pl.*) formaldehyde
For·ma·lie [fɔrˈmaːlĭə] *f* (-; -n) formality
For·ma·lin [fɔrmaˈliːn] *TM n* (-s; *no pl.*) ⚗ formalin
for·ma·li·sie·ren [fɔrmaliˈziːrən] *v/t.* (h) formalize; **For·ma·lis·mus** [fɔrmaˈlɪsmʊs] *m* (-; -men) formalism; **For·ma·list** [fɔrmaˈlɪst] *m* (-en; -en) formalist; **for·ma·li·stisch** [fɔrmaˈlɪstɪʃ] *adj.* formalist(ic); **For·ma·li·tät** [fɔrmaliˈtɛːt] *f* (-; -en) formality
For·mat [fɔrˈmaːt] *n* (-[e]s; -e) **1.** format, size; **2.** *fig.* stature, calib|re (*Am.* -er); **er hat kein ~** he hasn't got the personality it takes; **ein Mann (e-e Frau) von ~** a man (woman) of stature (*or* substance); **ein Musiker von internationalem ~** a musician of international standing (*or* stature)
for·ma·tie·ren [fɔrmaˈtiːrən] *v/t.* (h) *computer*: format; **for·ma·tiert** [fɔrmaˈtiːɐt] *adj.* formatted; **For·maˈtie·rung** *f* (-; *no pl.*) formatting
For·ma·ti·ons|flug [fɔrmaˈtsĭoːns-] *m* formation flying (*or* flight); **~tanz** *m* formation dancing
for·ma·tiv [fɔrmaˈtiːf] *adj.* formative
ˈform·bar *adj. metall. and fig.* malleable
ˈform·be·stän·dig *adj.* shape-retaining; *synthetics*: dimensionally stable; **~ sein** *a.* keep its shape
ˈForm|blatt *n* form; **~brief** *m* form letter
For·mel [ˈfɔrməl] *f* (-; -n) **1.** formula; **auf e-e ~ bringen** bring down to a simple formula; **2.** (set) phrase
ˈFor·mel-1|-Fah·rer *m* Formula-one racing driver; **~-Ren·nen** *n* Formula-one racing (*or* race); **~-Wa·gen** *m* Formula-one racing car
ˈfor·mel·haft *adj.* stereotyped
for·mell [fɔrˈmɛl] **I.** *adj.* formal; **sehr ~ sein** *a.* stand on ceremony; **II.** *adv.* a) formally, b) as a matter of form; **~ leitet sie das Projekt** officially she's in charge of the project
ˈFor·mel·wa·gen *m* formula car
for·men [ˈfɔrmən] *v/t.* (h) form, shape (*both a.* **sich ~**) (**aus** *dat.* out of, from; **zu** *dat.* into); ⚙ mo(u)ld, shape; *fig.* form *s.o., idea, sentence etc., a.* mo(u)ld *s.o.('s character)*
ˈFor·men|leh·re *f* **1.** morphology, accidence; **2.** ♪ theory of musical forms; **~reich·tum** *m* (-s; *no pl.*) (great *or* rich) variety of forms, multitude of forms
For·mer [ˈfɔrmɐ] *m* (-s; -) mo(u)lder
ˈForm|feh·ler *m* irregularity; ⚖ formal defect; faux pas; **~fra·ge** *f* question of form; **~ge·bung** [-geːbʊŋ] *f* (-; -en) ⚙ styling, design; **2ge·recht** *adj.* correct; ⚖ in proper form; **~ge·stal·ter** *m* designer; **~ge·stal·tung** *f* styling, design
for·mie·ren [fɔrˈmiːrən] *v/t. and v/refl.* (**sich ~**) (h) form; ⚔ line up
förm·lich [ˈfœrmlɪç] **I.** *adj.* **1.** formal; ceremonious; punctilious; **2.** F regular; **II.** *adv.* **3.** formally; **4.** literally; really; **ˈFörm·lich·keit** *f* (-; -en) **1.** *no pl.* formality; **2.** formality; **keine ~en!** we don't stand on ceremony around here
ˈform·los *adj.* **1.** shapeless, amorphous; **2.** informal; **3.** ⚖ informal, formless; **ˈForm·lo·sig·keit** *f* (-; *no pl.*) **1.** shapelessness; **2.** informality
ˈForm·sa·che *f* matter of form; (**e-e reine ~** a mere) formality
ˈform·schön *adj.* ⚙ beautifully designed, very stylish; **ˈForm·schön·heit** *f* (a)esthetic design
ˈForm·tief *n sport*: **ein ~ haben** be off form
For·mu·lar [fɔrmuˈlaːɐ] *n* (-s; -e) form
for·mu·lie·ren [fɔrmuˈliːrən] *v/t.* (h) formulate, word; express, put into words; **neu ~** rephrase, reword; **knapp ~** sum *s.th.* up in a few words (*or* briefly); **ich weiß nicht, wie ich es ~ soll** I don't know how to put it; **das hast du treffend formuliert** I couldn't have put it better myself; (*a. v/i.*) **wenn ich (es) mal so ~ darf** if I may put it like that; **Forˈmu·lie·rung** *f* (-; -en) formulation; wording, phrasing
For·mung [ˈfɔrmʊŋ] *f* (-; *no pl.*) formation; forming, shaping
ˈForm·ver·än·de·rung *f* change in (*or* of) form; modification
ˈform·voll͵en·det *adj.* a) perfectly shaped, finished, b) perfect, immaculate, flawless
ˈform·wid·rig *adj.* **1.** irregular; **2.** offensive; **ˈForm·wid·rig·keit** *f* **1.** irregularity; **2.** breach of form (*or* etiquette)
forsch [fɔrʃ] F **I.** *adj.* very get up and go; brash; **II.** *adv.*: **~ auftreten** have a very self-confident manner
for·schen [ˈfɔrʃən] *v/i.* (h) **1.** do research (**auf dem Gebiet** *gen.* on, in the field of); **~ in** *dat.* search in (*or* through), investigate; **2. ~ nach** *dat.* search for; **nach den Ursachen braucht man nicht lange zu ~** you don't have to look far to find the reasons; **ˈfor·schend** *adj.* searching *look*; questioning, inquiring
For·scher [ˈfɔrʃɐ] *m* (-s; -) researcher; scientist; explorer; **~drang** *m* intellectual curiosity; **~geist** *m* intellectual curiosity, inquiring mind; **sie ist ein ~** she likes to get to the bottom of things
ˈForsch·heit F *f* (-; *no pl.*) brashness; dash, F pep, go
For·schung [ˈfɔrʃʊŋ] *f* (-; -en) **1.** *a. pl.* research (work); **~en betreiben** do research (work); **~ u. Entwicklung** research and development, RD; **2.** *coll.* researchers *pl.*, scientists *pl.*
ˈFor·schungs|ar·beit *f* research work; **~auf·trag** *m* research assignment; **~be·reich** *m* field of research; **~be·richt** *m* research report; **~er·geb·nis** *n* result(s *pl.*) of the research; **~frei·jahr** *n* sabbatical; **ein ~ haben** be on sabbatical; **~ge·biet** *n* field of research; **~ge·gen·stand** *m* object of research; **~in·sti͵tut** *n* research institute; **~la·bor** *n*, **~la·bo·ra·to·ri·um** *n* research lab(oratory); **~pro͵gramm** *n* research program(me); **~pro͵jekt** *n* research project; **~re͵ak·tor** *m* research reactor; **~rei·se** *f* **1.** expedition; **2.** research trip; **~rei·sen·de** *m* explorer; **~sa·tel͵lit** *m* research satellite; **~schiff** *n* research vessel; **~se͵me·ster** *n* (half-year) sabbatical; **ein ~ haben** be on sabbatical; **~sta·ti͵on** *f* research station; **~sti͵pen·di·um** *n* (-s; -en) research scholarship (*or* grant, fellowship); **~ur·laub** *m* sabbatical; **im ~ sein** be on sabbatical; **~vor·ha·ben** *n* research project; **~zen·trum** *n* research cent|re (*Am.* -er)
Forst [fɔrst] *m* (-[e]s; -e) forest; **~amt** *n* forestry office
För·ster [ˈfœrstɐ] *m* (-s; -) forester
ˈForst|fach *n* forestry; **~fre·vel** *m* infringement of forest laws; **~re͵vier** *n* forest district; **~ver·wal·tung** *f* forestry commission; **~we·sen** *n* (-s; *no pl.*) forestry; **~wirt** *m* forestry engineer; **~wirt·schaft** *f* forestry; **2wirt·schaft·lich** *adj.* forest *property etc.*; **~wis·sen·schaft** *f* forestry
Fort [foːɐ] *n* (-s; -s) fort
fort [fɔrt] *adv.* **1.** away, gone; **sie sind schon ~** they've already left (*or* gone); **2.** gone; **der Wagen ist ~** the car is (*or* has) gone; **3. und so ~** and so on (*or* forth); **in einem ~** continuously, without interruption (*or* stopping); **er redete in**

einem ~ a. he wouldn't stop talking, F he just went on and on

fort'an *adv.* henceforth, from now on

'Fort·be·stand *m* (-[e]s; *no pl.*) continued existence, continuance; survival; **'fort·be·ste·hen I.** *v/i.* (*irr., sep.*, h, → ***beste-hen***) continue (to exist), survive; live on; **II.** 2 *n* (-s) → ***Fortbestand***

'fort·be·we·gen (*sep.*, h) **I.** *v/t.* move (away); **II.** *v/refl.*: ***sich ~*** move; *mot.* move (along); walk; ***sich nur mit Mühe ~ können*** have great difficulty walking; **'Fort·be·we·gung** *f* (-; *no pl.*) movement, (loco)motion

'fort·bil·den (*sep.*, h) **I.** *v/t.*: ***j-n ~*** further s.o.'s education; give s.o. further (vocational) training; **II.** *v/refl.*: ***sich ~*** further one's education; do evening classes; do a course *in s.th.*; ***sich*** (***beruflich***) ***~*** do further (vocational) training; **'Fort·bil·dung** *f* continuing education; (***beruf-liche***) ***~*** further (vocational) training; **'Fort·bil·dungs·kurs** *m* (further training) course

'fort·blei·ben I. *v/i.* (*irr., sep.*, sn, → ***blei-ben***) stay away; **II.** 2 *n* (-s) absence

'fort·brin·gen *v/t.* (*irr., sep.*, h, → ***brin-gen***) a) take away, b) move

'Fort·dau·er *f* continuation; **'fort·dau-ern** *v/i.* (*sep.*, h) continue, last; **'fort-dau·ernd I.** *adj.* lasting; continuous; recurrent; **II.** *adv.* continuously

'fort·dür·fen *v/i.* (*irr., sep.*, h, → ***dürfen***) be allowed to go (*or* leave)

for·te ['fɔrtə] *adv.*, 2 *n* (-s; -s, -ti) ♪ forte

'fort|ei·len *v/i.* (*sep.*, sn) hurry away; **~ent·wickeln** *v/t.* (*sep.*, h) → ***weiter-entwickeln*** I; **~fah·ren** *v/i.* (*irr., sep.*, sn, → ***fahren***) **1.** a) leave, go away, *mot. a.* drive off (*or* away), b) go off for the day, c) go off on a trip (*or* on holiday); **2.** continue, carry on; ***~ zu*** *inf.* continue *ger.* (*or* to *inf.*), carry (*or* go, keep) on *ger.*; ***mit s-r Erzählung ~*** continue (with) *or* resume one's story; ***fahren Sie fort!*** go on; **~fal·len** *v/i.* (*irr., sep.*, sn, → ***fallen***) → ***wegfallen***; **~flie·gen** *v/i.* (*irr., sep.*, sn, → ***fliegen***) fly away (*or* off)

'fort·füh·ren *v/t.* (*sep.*, h) **1.** lead away; **2.** go on with, continue; carry on *business etc.*; **'Fort·füh·rung** *f* (-; *no pl.*) continuation

'Fort·gang *m* (-[e]s; *no pl.*) **1.** a) progress; further development, b) continuation; ***s-n ~ nehmen*** progress; **2.** *lit.* departure; **'fort·ge·hen** *v/i.* (*irr., sep.*, sn, → ***gehen***) **1.** go (away), leave; **2.** go on

'fort·ge·schrit·ten I. *p.p. of* ***fortschrei-ten***; **II.** *adj.* advanced; ***Kurs für 2e*** advanced course; ***in e-m ~en Stadium*** at an advanced stage; ***Krebs im ~en Sta-dium*** terminal cancer; ***in e-m ~en Alter sein*** be fairly advanced in years; ***zu ~er Stunde*** at a very late hour, in the small (*or* wee) hours

'fort·ge·setzt I. *adj.* continued; **II.** *adv.* continually

'fort·ja·gen *v/t.* (*sep.*, h) chase away; F kick *s.o.* out

'fort·kom·men I. *v/i.* (*irr., sep.*, sn, → ***kommen***) **1.** get away; ***mach, daß du fortkommst!*** get out of here; **2.** *fig.* get on; **II.** 2 *n* (-s) **3.** progress; **4.** advancement; ***berufliches ~*** career, professional advancement

'fort·las·sen *v/t.* (*irr., sep.*, h, → ***lassen***) **1.** let *s.o.* go; **2.** leave out

'fort·lau·fen *v/i.* (*irr., sep.*, sn, → ***laufen***) **1.** run away ([***vor***] ***j-m*** from s.o.); **2.** continue; **'fort·lau·fend I.** *adj.* continuous, running; **II.** *adv.* continuously; ***~ numeriert*** numbered consecutively

'fort·le·ben I. *v/i.* (*sep.*, h) live on; **II.** 2 *n* (-s) survival

'fort|ma·chen F *v/refl.* (*sep.*, h): ***sich ~*** F clear off; **~müs·sen** *v/i.* (*irr., sep.*, h, → ***müssen***) have to go; ***das muß fort*** it's got to go, we've got to get rid of it

'fort·pflan·zen (*sep.*, h) **I.** *v/t. biol.* propagate, reproduce; *phys.* transmit; *fig.* spread; **II.** *v/refl.*: ***sich ~*** *biol.* multiply, reproduce; *phys.* be transmitted, travel; *fig.* spread, be passed on; **'Fort·pflan-zung** *f* (-; *no pl.*) *biol.* reproduction; *phys.* transmission; *fig.* spread(ing), propagation

'fort·pflan·zungs|fä·hig *adj.* capable of reproduction; **2or,gan** *n* reproductive organ; **2trieb** *m* reproductive drive (*or* instinct)

'fort|rei·sen *v/i.* (*sep.*, h) go away; **~rei-ßen** *v/t.* (*irr., sep.*, h, → ***reißen***) **1.** (*a.* ***mit sich ~***) sweep away; **2.** *fig.* → ***hinrei-ßen*** 2; **~ren·nen** *v/i.* (*irr., sep.*, sn, → ***rennen***) run away (*or* off); ***~ vor*** *dat.* run away from *s.o. or s.th.*, run out on *s.o.*

'Fort·satz *m* (-es; ⸚e) *anat.* process; appendix; eminence

'fort|schaf·fen *v/t.* (*sep.*, h) → ***wegschaf-fen***; **~sche·ren** F *v/refl.* (*sep.*, h): ***scher dich fort!*** F get lost; **~schicken** *v/t.* (*sep.*, h) send away; F send *s.o.* packing; **~schlep·pen** (*sep.*, h) **I.** *v/t.* drag away; **II.** *v/refl.*: ***sich ~*** drag o.s. along; *fig.* drag (on)

'fort·schrei·ten *fig.* **I.** *v/i.* (*irr., sep.*, sn, → ***schreiten***) progress; *time*: march on; *ep-idemic etc.*: spread; **II.** 2 *n* (-s) progress; **'fort·schrei·tend** *adj.* progressive

'Fort·schritt *m* (-[e]s; -e) progress, headway; improvement; ***~e machen*** make progress (*or* headway), get on (*or* ahead); ***große ~e machen*** make great strides, forge ahead; **Fort·schritt·ler** ['fɔrtʃrɪtlɐ] *m* (-s; -) progressive; **fort·schritt·lich** ['fɔrtʃrɪtlɪç] *adj.* progressive; (very) modern, up-to-date ..., *pred.* up to date

'Fort·schritts|fa,na·ti·ker *m* fanatical progressive; **2feind·lich** *adj.* reactionary, Luddite; **~glau·be** *m* belief in progress

'fort·seh·nen *v/refl.* (*sep.*, h): ***sich ~*** long to be somewhere else (*or* to escape)

'fort·set·zen *v/t.* (*sep.*, h) continue (*a.* ***sich ~***), *a.* resume, take *s.th.* up again; **'Fort·set·zung** *f* (-; -en) **1.** *no pl.* a) continuation, b) resumption; **2.** sequel; part, instal(l)ment, *TV*, *radio*: *a.* episode; ***in ~en*** (***erscheinend***) serialized; ***~ folgt*** to be continued; ***~ von Seite 2*** continued from page two; **'Fort·set·zungs·ro-,man** *m* serialized novel

'fort|steh·len *v/refl.* (*irr., sep.*, h, → ***steh-len***): ***sich ~*** sneak away (*or* off); **~tra-gen** *v/t.* (*irr., sep.*, h, → ***tragen***) carry away; **~trei·ben** (*irr., sep.*, → ***treiben***) **I.** *v/t.* (h) **1.** drive away; **2.** *fig.* carry on (with), go on with; **II.** *v/i.* (sn) drift away

For·tu·na [fɔr'tuːna] *f* (-; *no pl.*) fortune, luck; Dame Fortune, F Lady Luck; ***~ war ihr hold*** fortune (*or* Dame Fortune) smiled on her

'fort·wa·gen *v/refl.* (*sep.*, h): ***sich ~*** dare to go away (*or* leave)

'fort·wäh·rend I. *adj.* continual, constant; continuous, incessant; **II.** *adv.* continually *etc.*; → ***I***; all the time; ***er ruft ~ an*** he keeps (*or* won't stop) ringing up

'fort·wer·fen *v/t.* (*irr., sep.*, h, → ***werfen***) throw away

'fort·wir·ken I. *v/i.* (*sep.*, h) continue to have an effect (*or* take effect) (***in*** *dat.* on, among); continue to make itself felt (in, among); **II.** 2 *n* (-s) continued *or* continuing effect (*or* influence)

'Fort·zah·lung *f* continued payment

'fort·zie·hen *v/i.* (*irr., sep.*, sn, → ***ziehen***) move (away)

Fo·rum ['foːrʊm] *n* (-s; Foren ['foːrən]) **1.** a) forum, b) platform; **2.** panel discussion

fos·sil [fɔ'siːl] **I.** *adj.* fossil ..., fossilized; **II.** 2 *n* (-s; Fossilien [fɔ'siːliən]) fossil

Fo·to[1] ['foːto] *n* (-s; -s) photo(graph), shot, F snap

'Fo·to[2] F *m* (-s; -s) camera

'Fo·to|al·bum *n* photo(graph) album; **~ap·pa,rat** *m* camera; **~ar,chiv** *n* photo library (*or* archives *pl.*); **~ar,ti·kel** *pl.* photographic equipment *sg.*, cameras and accessories; **~aus·rü·stung** *f* photo(graphic) equipment, camera(s) and lenses *pl.*; **~aus·stel·lung** *f* photo (-graphic) exhibition; **~ecken** *pl.* adhesive corners

Fo·to·graf [foto'graːf] *m* (-en; -en), **Fo·to-gra·fin** *f* (-; -nen) photographer

Fo·to·gra·fie [fotogra'fiː] *f* (-; -n) **1.** *no pl.* photography; **2.** photograph, picture; portrait

fo·to·gra·fie·ren [fotogra'fiːrən] (h) **I.** *v/t.* take (*or* get) a photo(graph) *or* picture of, get a shot of; ***sich ~ lassen*** have one's *or* a photo(graph) *or* picture taken; ***er läßt sich gut ~*** he's very photogenic; **II.** *v/i.* take photographs (*or* pictures); ***er fotografiert gern*** he's a keen photographer; ***ich fotografiere nicht mehr*** I've stopped taking photographs, I've given up photography; **III.** 2 *n* (-s) photography; taking of photographs; ***~ verboten*** no photographs

fo·to·gra·fisch [foto'graːfɪʃ] *adj.* photographic(ally *adv.*); ***~es Gedächtnis*** photographic memory

'Fo·to·jour·na,lis·mus *m* photojournalism

Fo·to·ko'pie [foto-] *f* photocopy; **fo·to-ko'pie·ren** (h) **I.** *v/t.* (photo)copy; **II.** *v/i.* photocopy; ***er fotokopiert gerade*** he's just doing some photocopying; **Fo·to·ko'pie·rer** *m*, **Fo·to·ko'pier·ge-rät** *n* photocopier

Fo·to|la,bor ['foːto-] *n* photographic lab(oratory), photo lab(oratory); developers *pl.*; **~ma·te·ri,al** *n* photo(graphic) materials *pl.*; **~mo,dell** *n* (photographic) model; **~mon,ta·ge** *f* photomontage; **~rea,lis·mus** *m* photorealism; **~re-por,ta·ge** *f* photo reportage; **~re,por-ter** *m* photojournalist; **~sa·chen** F *pl.* camera(s) and lenses, photographic equipment *sg.*; **~sa,fa·ri** *f* photo safari; **~satz** *m* photocomposition; **2scheu** *adj.* camera-shy; **~stu·dio** *n* photo(graphic) studio (*or* atelier); **~ta·sche** *f* camera holdall; **~ter,min** *m* photocall

Fo·to·thek [foto'teːk] *f* (-; -en) photo library

Fo·to|wett·be·werb ['foːto-] *m* photo(graphic) competition; **~zeit·schrift** *f* photo magazine; **~zel·le** *f* photo(electric) cell

Fö·tus ['føːtʊs] *m* (-[ses]; -se) f(o)etus

Fot·ze ['fɔtsə] V *f* (-; -n) V cunt
Foul [faʊl] *n* (-s; -s) foul; **~elf·me·ter** *m* penalty (kick)
fou·len ['faʊlən] *v/t. and v/i.* (h) foul
Fox·ter·ri·er ['fɔks-] *m* fox terrier
Fox·trott ['fɔkstrɔt] *m* (-s; -e, -s) foxtrot; *~ **tanzen*** do the foxtrot
Foy·er [fŏa'je:] *n* (-s; -s) foyer (*a. thea. etc.*), entrance hall, *esp. Am.* lobby (*a. thea. etc.*)
Fracht [fraxt] *f* (-; -en) **1.** load, freight; ⚓ cargo; air freight; **2.** carriage, *Am.* freight(age), ⚓ freightage; **~brief** *m* consignment note, *Am.* freight bill; **~dampfer** *m* cargo ship, freighter
Frach·ter ['fraxtɐ] *m* (-s; -) **1.** freighter; **2.** → ***Frachtflugzeug***
'**Fracht|flug·zeug** *n* cargo (*or* freight) plane, (air) freighter; **≈frei** *adj.* carriage paid, *Am.* freight prepaid; **~füh·rer** *m* carrier; **~ge·bühr** *f*, **~geld** *n* carriage, *Am.* freight (charge); **~gut** *n* freight; ⚓ cargo; ***als ~*** by goods (*Am.* freight) train; **~ko·sten** *pl.* freight charges; **~raum** *m* **1.** cargo hold; **2.** freight capacity; **~schiff** *n* cargo ship, freighter; **~sen·dung** *f* consignment; **~stück** *n* package; **~ta,rif** *m* freight rates *pl.*; **~ver·kehr** *m* freight traffic; **~ver·si·che·rung** *f* freight (*or* cargo) insurance
Frack [frak] *m* (-[e]s; Fräcke ['frɛkə]) tails *pl.*, tailcoat; ***im ~*** in evening dress, in tails; **~hemd** *n* dress shirt; **~zwang** *m* evening dress; ***es herrscht ~*** tails are compulsory
Fra·ge ['fra:gə] *f* (-; -n) a) question (***zu*** *dat.* about, on); query; inquiry, enquiry, b) matter, question, c) problem; ***(j-m) e-e ~ stellen*** ask (s.o.) a question; ***ich habe mal e-e ~*** can I ask you something?; ***es war nur e-e ~*** I was only asking; ***das steht außer ~, das ist überhaupt keine ~*** there's no question about that; ***in ~ kommen*** be a possibility, ***für e-e Stelle etc.***: be considered for, be under consideration for *a job etc.*; ***er kommt nicht in ~*** he's not the right man (for the job *etc.*), he's out of the question; ***das kommt nicht in ~*** that's out of the question; ***in ~ kommend*** possible, eligible; ***in ~ stellen*** a) (call into) question, query, challenge, b) jeopardize, make *s.th.* uncertain; ***die ~ ist, ob*** (***wie*** *etc.*) ... the question *or* point is whether (how *etc.*) ...; ***das ist e-e ~ der Zeit*** that's a matter (*or* question) of time; ***das ist e-e andere ~*** that's a different matter; ***das ist eben die ~*** that is the question, that's just the point; ***das ist noch sehr die ~*** that's anybody's guess; ***was soll diese ~?*** what kind of question is that?, what are you getting at?; ***das ist gar keine ~*** there's no question about it, that's been decided (*or* settled); ***gar keine ~!*** of course; you don't have to ask; ***ohne ~*** undoubtedly; ***so e-e ~!*** what a question, what a thing to ask; **~bo·gen** *m* questionnaire, form; **~form** *f ling.* interrogative form; **~für·wort** *n* interrogative (pronoun)
fra·gen ['fra:gən] (h) **I.** *v/t. and v/i.* ask; question, query; inquire (***nach*** *dat.* about, after *s.o.*); ***(j-n) etwas ~*** ask (s.o.) a question; ***(j-n) ~ nach*** *dat.* ask (s.o.) for; ***j-n nach s-m Namen*** (***dem Weg*** *etc.*) ***~*** ask s.o. his (*or* her) name (the way *etc.*); ***j-n um Rat ~*** ask s.o.'s advice; ***viel ~*** ask a lot of questions; ***gern ~*** like to ask questions; ***ich wollte ~, ob*** I was wondering if (*or* whether), I wanted to ask if (*or* whether); ***niemand fragt nach mir*** nobody bothers about me; ***wenn ich ~ darf*** if I may ask; ***da fragst du mich zuviel*** (I'm afraid) I can't tell you that, I don't know about that; ***frag lieber nicht!*** don't ask; let's talk about something else, shall we?; ***man wird ja wohl noch ~ dürfen*** sorry I asked; ***frag nicht so dumm!*** don't ask such silly (*or* stupid) questions; ***da fragst du noch?*** how can you even ask (such a thing)?, you've got a nerve; ***≈ kostet nichts*** there's no harm in asking; → ***gefragt***; **II.** *v/refl.*: ***sich ~*** wonder; ***ich frage mich, wie er es schafft*** *a.* I'd like to know how he does it; ***ich frage mich, warum*** I (just) wonder why, I can't help wondering why; ***da fragt man sich doch!*** F I ask you; ***es fragt sich, ob*** (***wann*** *etc.*) it's a question of whether (when *etc.*), the question is whether (when *etc.*); '**fragend** *adj.* questioning, inquiring; *ling.* interrogative
'**Fra·gen|ka·ta,log** *m* package of questions; ***ein ganzer ~*** *a.* a long list of questions; **~kom,plex** *m* (problem) area; topic, subject; ***der ganze ~ um*** *acc.* the whole array of questions concerning
Fra·ger ['fra:gɐ] *m* (-s; -) questioner; ***er ist ein lästiger ~*** he's always (*or* he won't stop) asking questions
Fra·ge·rei [fra:gə'raɪ] *f* (-; -en) questions *pl.*; ***hör auf mit d-r ~*** I wish you'd stop asking all these questions (*or* pestering me with your questions)
'**Fra·ge|satz** *m ling.* interrogative sentence (*or* clause), question; **~stel·lung** *f* **1.** question; ***das ist e-e falsche ~*** the question has to be put differently; **2.** question, problem; **~stun·de** *f parl.* (*in GB*: Prime Minister's) question time; **~-und-'Ant·wort-Spiel** *n* quiz, *a. fig.* question-and-answer game; **~wort** *n* (-[e]s; ⸚er) *ling.* interrogative; **~zei·chen** *n* question mark; *fig.* query; *fig.* ***et. mit e-m (großen) ~ versehen*** put a (big) question mark behind s.th.
frag·lich ['fra:klɪç] *adj.* **1.** doubtful; **2.** ... in question; ***an dem ~en Tag*** on that particular day, on the day in question; '**Frag·lich·keit** *f* (-; *no pl.*) doubtfulness; uncertainty
frag·los ['fra:klo:s] *adv.* undoubtedly
Frag·ment [fra'gmɛnt] *n* (-[e]s; -e) fragment; **frag·men·ta·risch** [fragmɛn'ta:rɪʃ] **I.** *adj.* fragmentary; **II.** *adv.* in fragmentary form; **Frag·men·ta·ti·on** [fragmɛnta'tsĭo:n] *f* (-; -en) fragmentation; **frag·men·tie·ren** [fragmɛn'ti:rən] *v/t.* (h) fragment, break up (into fragments)
frag·wür·dig [fra:kvʏrdɪç] *adj.* questionable; dubious; **~es Subjekt** shady character; '**Frag·wür·dig·keit** *f* (-; *no pl.*) dubious nature, dubiousness; shadiness
Frak·ti·on [frak'tsĭo:n] *f* (-; -en) **1.** *parl.* parliamentary party; faction; **2.** ⚗ fraction; **frak·tio·nie·ren** [fraktsĭo'ni:rən] *v/t.* (h) ⚗ fractionate
Frak·ti'ons|aus·schuß *m* party committee; **~be·schluß** *m* party resolution; **~dis·zi,plin** *f* party discipline; **~füh·rer** *m* party leader, *Am.* floor leader; **≈los** *adj.* independent; **~mit·glied** *n* party member; **~sit·zung** *f* party meeting; **~vor·sit·zen·de** *m, f* (-n; -n) party leader, *Am.* floor leader; **~zwang** *m* party discipline; ***unter ~ stehen*** be under the party whip
Frak·tur [frak'tu:ɐ] *f* (-; -en [-rən]) **1.** *typ.* Gothic (type), Gothic black letter; F *fig.* ***mit j-m ~ reden*** tell s.o. what's what, *esp. Am.* F talk turkey with s.o.; **2.** ⚕ fracture
Franc [frã:] *m* (-; -s [frã:]) franc
frank [fraŋk] *adv.*: ***~ und frei*** quite frankly, openly
Fran·ke ['fraŋkə] *m* (-n; -n) **1.** *hist.* Frank; **2.** Franconian
Fran·ken ['fraŋkən] *m* (-s; -) (Swiss) franc
Frank·fur·ter ['fraŋkfʊrtɐ] *f* (-; -) (*a.* ***~ Würstchen***) frankfurter; ***ein Paar ~*** two frankfurters
fran·kie·ren [fraŋ'ki:rən] *v/t.* (h) stamp; frank; **Fran'kier·ma,schi·ne** *f* franking machine; **fran·kiert** [fraŋ'ki:ɐt] *adj.* **1.** ***~ sein*** have a stamp (*or* stamps) on it; ***der Brief ist nicht ausreichend ~*** they didn't put enough stamps on the letter; **2.** ✝ (*a.* ***ausreichend ~***) prepaid, post paid
frän·kisch ['frɛŋkɪʃ] *adj.* **1.** *hist.* Frankish, Franconian; *hist.* ***das ~e Reich*** the Frankish Empire (*or* Kingdom), the Kingdom of the Franks; **2.** Franconian
fran·ko ['fraŋko] *adv.* prepaid, post paid
'**Fran·ko·ka,na·di·er** *m* French Canadian; '**fran·ko·ka,na·disch** *adj.* French-Canadian
fran·ko·phil [fraŋko'fi:l] *adj.*, **Fran·ko'phi·le** *m, f* (-n; -n) Francophile
fran·ko·phon [fraŋko'fo:n] *adj.*, **Fran·ko'pho·ne** *m, f* (-n; -n) Francophone
Fran·se ['franzə] *f* (-; -n) fringe; (loose) thread; **~n** fringe, *Am.* bangs; *contp.* strands of hair; ***in ~n sein*** be in shreds (*or* tatters); '**fran·sen** *v/i.* (h) fray; **fransig** ['franzɪç] *adj.* a) fringed, b) frayed; F ***sich den Mund ~ reden*** talk till one is blue in the face
Franz·brannt·wein ['frants-] *m* (-[e]s; *no pl.*) rubbing alcohol
Fran·zis·ka·ner [frantsɪs'ka:nɐ] *m* (-s; -) Franciscan (friar); **Fran·zis·ka·ne·rin** [frantsɪs'ka:nərɪn] *f* (-; -nen) Franciscan (nun); **Fran·zis'ka·ner·or·den** *m* Franciscan Order, Order of St Francis
Fran·zo·se [fran'tso:zə] *m* (-n; -n) **1.** Frenchman; ***die ~n*** the French (*pl.*); ***er ist ~*** he's French; **2.** ⚙ monkey wrench;
Fran·zö·sin [fran'tsø:zɪn] *f* (-; -nen) Frenchwoman; ***sie ist ~*** she's French;
fran·zö·sisch [fran'tsø:zɪʃ] **I.** *adj.* French; ***~es Bett*** (double) divan; ***die ~e Küche*** French cuisine; ***die ~e Schweiz*** French-speaking Switzerland; **II.** *adv.*: ***sich ~ empfehlen*** take French leave;
fran·zö(si)sie·ren [frantsø(zi)'zi:rən] *v/t.* (h) Gallicize, gallicize; *esp. contp.* Frenchify
frap·pant [fra'pant] *adj.* striking; **frap·pie·ren** [fra'pi:rən] *v/t.* (h) astonish, take *s.o.* aback; **frap'pie·rend** *adj.* amazing, astonishing, remarkable; ***~e Ähnlichkeit*** striking resemblance
Frä·se ['frɛ:zə] *f* (-; -n) **1.** milling machine; shaper; **2.** ⚒ rotary hoe; '**frä·sen** *v/t. and v/i.* (h) mill; shape
'**Fräs|kopf** *m* milling head; **~ma,schi·ne** *f* milling machine
fraß [fra:s] *pret. of* ***fressen***
Fraß [fra:s] *m* (-es; *no pl.*) **1.** F *contp.* F muck, swill; **2.** feed; *fig.* food (*gen.* for); ***et. e-m Tier zum ~ vorwerfen*** throw

s.th. to an animal; **3.** damage; ✱ caries; ⚙, ⚗ corrosion

Fra·ter ['fraːtɐ] *m* (-s; Fratres ['fraːtreːs]) *R.C.* Brother

fra·ter·ni·sie·ren [fratɛrni'ziːrən] *v/i.* (h) fraternize; **Fra·ter·ni'sie·rung** *f* (-; *no pl.*) fraternization

Fratz [frats] *m* (-es; -e) little monkey, F *contp.* brat; ***niedlicher*** (*or* ***süßer***) ~ cute little thing

Frat·ze ['fratsə] *f* (-; -n) a) grimace, b) F (ugly *or* grotesque) face; ***so e-e ~!*** what a face!; ***widerliche*** ~ F ugly mug; ***~n schneiden*** pull faces; **'frat·zen·haft** *adj.* grotesque

Frau [frau] *f* (-; -en) a) woman; *statistics*: female, b) lady, c) wife, d) Mrs, Ms, *obs.* Miss, e) F girl; ***~ Doktor*** Doctor; ***wie geht es Ihrer ~?*** how's Mrs X?, how's the wife (F missus)?; ***Ihre ~ Mutter*** your mother; *eccl.* ***Unsere Liebe ~*** Our (Blessed) Lady; ***~ und Kinder haben*** have a wife and children (F kids); ***zur ~ nehmen*** marry; **'Frau·chen** *n* (-s; -) little old lady, F old biddy; ***mein ~*** my dear wife, F my old woman; ***komm zu ~!*** *to a dog*: come to Mummy!

'Frau·en|ar·beit *f* **1.** *a* woman's job, women's jobs *pl.*, women's labo(u)r; ***das ist keine ~!*** that's no job for a woman, that's a man's job; **2.** women's aid; ***ich interessiere mich für ~*** I'd like to do something to help women (*or* the women's cause); **~arzt** *m* gyn(a)ecologist, F gyny; **~be·auf·trag·te** [-bə'ʔaufːtraːktə] *f* (-n; -n) women's representative; **~be·ruf** *m* female profession; **~be·we·gung** *f*: ***die ~*** women's lib(eration), the women's liberation movement; **~chor** *m* (all-)female choir; **~feind** *m* woman-hater, misogynist; **≈feind·lich** *adj.* anti-women; woman-hating ...; *formal*: misogynous; ***das Konzept ist ~*** *a.* the concept is directed against women; **~fuß·ball** *m* women's football (*Am.* soccer); **~ge·fäng·nis** *n* women's prison; **~grup·pe** *f* **1.** group of women; **2.** women's group (*or* association)

'frau·en·haft *adj.* feminine

'Frau·en|haus *n* women's refuge (*Am.* shelter); **~heil·kun·de** *f* gyn(a)ecology; **~held** *m* lady-killer; **~herr·schaft** *f* matriarchal rule; female domination; matriarchy; **~kli·nik** *f* gyn(a)ecological hospital (*or* clinic); **~klo·ster** *n* convent; **~krank·heit** *f*, **~lei·den** *n* gyn(a)ecological disorder (*or* problem); **~lieb·ling** *m* favo(u)rite among the ladies; **~li·te·ra,tur** *f* women's literature; feminist writing(s *pl.*) *or* literature; **~rech·te** *pl.* women's rights; **~recht·le·rin** [-rɛçtlərɪn] *f* (-; -nen) feminist, F women's libber; **~rol·le** *f thea.* female part; **~schuh** *m* ♣ lady's slipper; **~sport** *m* women's sport(s *pl.*); **~sta·ti,on** *f* women's ward; **~stim·me** *f* woman's (♪ female) voice; **~stimm·recht** *n* votes *pl.* for women, women's suffrage; **~treff** F *m* women's meeting place, F female hangout; **~,über·schuß** *m* surplus of women; **~zeit·schrift** *f* women's magazine; **~zim·mer** *n usu. contp.* female, woman; daughter of Eve; ***unverschämtes ~*** F brazen hussy

Fräu·lein ['frɔylaɪn] *n* (-s; -) a) (young) lady, b) Miss, c) governess, d) sales girl, e) waitress; ***~!*** excuse me; ***Ihr ~ Tochter*** your daughter; *teleph.* ***~ vom Amt*** operator

'frau·lich *adj.* feminine; womanly; **'Frau·lich·keit** *f* (-; *no pl.*) femininity; womanliness, womanly quality (*or* qualities *pl.*)

frech [frɛç] **I.** *adj.* cheeky, *esp. Am.* fresh; daring; brazen; saucy; ***zuletzt wurde sie noch ~*** then she started getting cheeky (*esp. Am.* fresh); F ***der ist ~ wie Oskar*** F he's a cheeky little brat; **II.** *adv.*: F ***j-m ~ kommen*** get cheeky (*esp. Am.* fresh) with s.o.; ***~ grinsen*** give a cheeky grin; ***er hat es ~ geleugnet*** he had the nerve to deny it; **'Frech·dachs** F *m* F cheeky (little) monkey; **'Frech·heit** *f* (-; -en) **1.** *no pl.* cheek; ***so e-e ~!*** what a cheek (*or* nerve), of all the cheek (*or* nerve); ***die ~ haben zu*** *inf.* have the cheek (*or* nerve, *formal*: temerity) to *inf.*; **2.** ***sich*** (***j-m gegenüber***) ***~en erlauben*** start getting cheeky (*esp. Am.* fresh) (with s.o.)

Fre·gat·te [fre'gatə] *f* (-; -n) frigate

frei [fraɪ] **I.** *adj.* a) free (***von*** *dat.* from, of), *a.* independent; exempt (from *taxes etc.*); freelance *journalist etc.*, b) free (*a. phys.*), unrestrained; ⚗ uncombined; *teleph.* vacant *line*; vacant, open *post etc.*; open *field, sky etc.*; clear *road etc.*; *sport*: unmarked; blank *page etc.*, c) open, free and easy *manner etc.*; unattached; liberal, d) ✝ free (of charge); ✉ prepaid, post paid; ***~er Beruf*** independent profession; ***~er Eintritt*** admission free (***für*** *acc.* to); ***die ~en Künste*** the liberal arts; ***ein ~er Mensch*** a free agent; ***~er Mitarbeiter*** freelance(r); ***~er Nachmittag*** afternoon off; ***~e Stadt*** free city; ***~e Stelle*** vacancy; ***~e Wahl*** free choice; ***≈e Demokratische Partei*** Free Democratic Party; ***„Zimmer ~"*** room to let (*Am.* rent); ***im ~en Handel*** in the shops; ***~er Markt*** open market, *stock exchange*: unofficial market; ***~e Marktwirtschaft*** free market economy; ***(die) ~e Wirtschaft*** free enterprise; ***im ≈en, unter ~em Himmel*** in the open (air); ***~ werden*** *energy etc.*: be released; *fig.* ***~er werden*** loosen up; ***~ machen*** clear *the path etc.*; ***den Oberkörper ~ machen*** strip to the waist; *fig.* ***sich ~ machen von*** *dat.* free o.s. of, get out of, get rid of; ***„~ ab 15"*** 15 (= no admission to persons under 15 years); → ***Fuß, Hand, Stück***; → *a.* ***freibekommen, freihaben, freilaufen, freimachen, freinehmen***; **II.** *adv.* freely *etc.*; ***~ sprechen*** a) speak openly, b) ad-lib, speak without notes; ***~ erfunden*** (entirely) fictitious; ***das hat er ~ erfunden*** he made that up; ***~ nach*** (***e-m Stück von***) ***X*** freely adapted from the play by X; ***~ heraus*** frankly, point-blank; ***Lieferung ~ Haus*** no delivery charge; ***~ an Bord*** free on board (*abbr.* f.o.b.); ***~ finanziert*** privately financed; ***~ assoziativ*** in free association

'Frei|bad *n* open-air (*or* outdoor) swimming pool; **~bal,lon** *m* free balloon; **~bank** *f* (-; *no pl.*) cheap meat counter

'frei·be·kom·men (*irr.*, *sep.*, h, → ***bekommen***) **I.** *v/t.* **1.** get *a day etc.* off; **2.** get *s.o., one's hands etc.* free; ***j-n ~*** get s.o. free, obtain s.o.'s release; **II.** *v/i.* get the day *etc.* off

Frei·be·ruf·ler ['fraɪbəruːflɐ] *m* (-s; -) freelance(r), self-employed person; ***~ sein*** be a freelance(r), be freelance (*or* self-employed); **'frei·be·ruf·lich I.** *adj.* freelance, self-employed; *solicitor, doctor*: *a. adv.* in private practi|ce (*Am. a.* -se); **II.** *adv.*: ***~ tätig sein*** *a.* work (as a) freelance

'Frei·be·trag *m* tax allowance

Frei·beu·ter ['fraɪbɔytɐ] *m* (-s; -) buccaneer; *fig.* shark

'frei|be·weg·lich *adj.* ⚙ freely moving, mobile; **≈bier** *n* free beer; **~blei·bend** *adj. and adv.* ✝ subject to being sold; **~bo·xen** *fig. v/t.* (*sep.*, h) bail *s.o.* out; **≈brief** *m* charter; *fig.* privilege (***für*** *acc.* to *inf.*); right (to *inf.*); excuse (for *s.th.*, to *inf.*); *fig.* ***j-m e-n ~ ausstellen*** give s.o. carte blanche (to do s.th.)

'Frei·de·mo,krat *m* Free Democrat, Liberal

'Frei·den·ker *m* (-s; -) freethinker; **frei·den·ke·risch** ['fraɪdɛŋkərɪʃ] *adj.* freethinking

Freie[1] ['fraɪə] *n* (-n; *no pl.*) *the* open air; ***im ~n*** in the open (air), outside; ***Spiele im ~n*** outdoor games; ***im ~n übernachten*** camp out

Freie[2] *m, f* (-n; -n) freeborn citizen

Frei·er ['fraɪɐ] *m* (-s; -) **1.** (*a prostitute's*) client; **2.** *obs.* suitor; **'Frei·ers·fü·ße** *pl.*: ***auf ~n gehen*** be looking for a wife, be courting

'Frei|ex·em,plar *n* free copy; **~fahr·schein** *m* free ticket; **~fahrt** *f* free ride; **~flug** *m* ✈ free flight; **~frau** *f*, **~fräu·lein** *n* baroness; **~ga·be** *f* (-; *no pl.*) release; ✝ floating; ✈ clearance

Frei·gän·ger ['fraɪgɛŋɐ] *m* (-s; -) day release prisoner; ***~ sein*** *a.* be on day release

'frei·ge·ben (*irr.*, *sep.*, h, → ***geben***) **I.** *v/t.* release; ✈ clear; ✝ float; ***für den Verkehr ~*** open to traffic; ***zur Veröffentlichung ~*** release for publication; **II.** *v/i.*: ***j-m ~*** let s.o. off, give s.o. the day *etc.* off; ***sich ~ lassen*** get time (*or* the day *etc.*) off

frei·ge·big ['fraɪgeːbɪç] *adj.* generous; **'Frei·ge·big·keit** *f* (-; *no pl.*) generosity, largesse, *Am.* largess

'frei·ge·bo·ren *adj.* freeborn

'Frei|ge·he·ge *n* open-air enclosure; **~geist** *m* (-[e]s; -er) freethinker; **≈ge·legt** *adj.* exposed; **~ge·päck** *n* baggage allowance

frei·gie·big ['fraɪgiːbɪç] *adj.* → ***freigebig***

'Frei·gren·ze *f* tax exemption limit

'frei·ha·ben *v/i.* (*irr.*, *sep.*, h, → ***haben***) be off, have the day *etc.* off; ***freitags habe ich ~*** Friday's my day off; ***sie hat heute frei*** a) she's off today, b) it's her day off today

'Frei·ha·fen *m* free port

'frei·hal·ten (*irr.*, *sep.*, h, → ***halten***) **I.** *v/t.* **1.** keep, save *seat etc.*; keep *road* clear; keep open *offer etc.*; ***„Eingang ~!"*** do not block entrance; **2.** treat, pay for *s.o.*; **3.** ***~ von*** *dat.* keep *s.th.* free of, keep *s.th.* clear of; ***j-n von Erkältungen*** *etc.* ***~*** keep s.o. free (*or* protect s.o.) from colds *etc.*, keep colds *etc.* away from s.o.; **II.** *v/refl.*: ***sich ~*** keep o.s. free (***für*** *acc.* for), ***von*** *dat.*: ward off, avoid

'Frei·hand·bü·che,rei *f* open access (*Am.* open stack) library

'Frei·han·del *m* free trade

'Frei·han·dels|ab·kom·men *n* free trade agreement; **~zo·ne** *f* free trade area

frei·hän·dig ['fraɪhɛndɪç] *adj. and adv. cycle etc.* with no hands; *shoot* offhand *or* without support; *draw etc.* freehand; ⚖ privately; ✝ direct *sale*; ***~er Verkauf*** over-the-counter trade *of stocks etc.*

'Frei·hand·zeich·nung *f* freehand drawing

'frei·hän·gend *adj.* ⚙ freely suspended
'Frei·heit *f* (-; -en) **1.** *no pl.* freedom, liberty; ✝ exemption; scope, latitude; independence; ***dichterische ~*** poetic licen|ce (*Am.* -se); ***in ~ sein*** be free; ***in ~ setzen*** release, set *an animal* free; ***die ~ haben zu*** *inf.* be free to *inf.*; ***sich die ~ (heraus)nehmen zu*** *inf.* take the liberty of *ger.* (*or* to *inf.*); **2.** privilege, liberty; ***sich ~en erlauben*** take liberties (***gegenüber*** *dat.* with); ***j-m volle ~ gewähren*** give s.o. carte blanche (***zu*** *inf.* to *inf.*); **'frei·heit·lich** *adj.* free; liberal
'Frei·heits|be·rau·bung *f* unlawful detention (*or* imprisonment); **~be·schrän·kung** *f* restriction of personal liberty; **~be·we·gung** *f* freedom movement; **~drang** *m* desire for independence (*or* freedom); love of liberty; **~ent·zug** *m* imprisonment; **~kampf** *m* struggle for freedom (*or* [political] independence); revolt; **~kämp·fer** *m* freedom fighter; **~krieg** *m* war of liberation (*or* independence); **~lie·be** *f* love of liberty; **2lie·bend** *adj.* freedom-loving; **~sta·tue** *f* Statue of Liberty; **~stra·fe** *f* ⚖ prison sentence; ***zu e-r ~ von fünf Jahren verurteilt werden*** be sentenced to five years' imprisonment
frei·her'aus *adv.* openly, straight out
'Frei·herr *m* baron; **'Frei·her·rin** *f* baroness
'frei·kämp·fen (*sep.*, h) **I.** *v/t.* (fight to) free; **II.** *v/refl.*: ***sich ~*** a) fight o.s. free, b) fight (*or* battle) one's way out (***aus*** *dat.* of)
'Frei·kar·te *f* free ticket, *thea. etc. a.* complimentary ticket
'Frei·kauf *m* ransom; **'frei·kau·fen** (*sep.*, h) **I.** *v/t.*: ***j-n ~*** pay for s.o.'s release, pay a ransom to have s.o. released; **II.** *v/refl.*: ***sich ~*** pay for one's release (*or* freedom); *fig.* buy a clear conscience
'Frei·kir·che *f* free church; **'frei·kirch·lich** *adj.* free-church ...
'frei·kom·men *v/i.* (*irr.*, *sep.*, sn, → ***kommen***) get free; get away; ⚖ be released; be acquitted
'Frei·kör·per·kul,tur *f* naturism, nudism
'frei·krie·gen F *v/t.* (*sep.*, h) → ***freibekommen***
'Frei·land·ge·mü·se *n* outdoor vegetables *pl.*
'frei·las·sen *v/t.* (*irr.*, *sep.*, h, → ***lassen***) release, set *s.o.* free; ⚖ ***gegen Kaution ~*** release on bail; **'Frei·las·sung** *f* (-; -en) release
'Frei·lauf *m* freewheel; ***im ~ fahren*** freewheel, coast
'frei|lau·fen *v/refl.* (*irr.*, *sep.*, h, → ***laufen***): ***sich ~*** *sport*: get into space; **~lau·fend** *adj.*: ***~e Hühner*** free-range hens; ***Eier von ~en Hühnern*** free-range eggs; **~le·bend** *adj.*: ***~e Tiere*** wildlife, animals living in the wild (*or* out of captivity); **2le·gen** *v/t.* (*sep.*, h) lay open, expose; uncover
'Frei·lei·tung *f* ⚡ overhead (transmission) line
frei·lich ['frailɪç] *adv.* of course; admittedly; though; ***er hat es ~ geleugnet*** of course he denied it, though he 'did deny it(, of course); ***ja ~!*** of course!; F what do you think?
'Frei·licht|büh·ne *f* open-air theat|re (*Am. a.* -er); **~ki·no** *n* open-air cinema; **~kon,zert** *n* open-air concert; **~ma·le,rei** *f* plein air painting; **~mu,se·um** *n* open-air museum; **~thea·ter** *n* open-air theat|re (*Am. a.* -er)
'frei·lie·gen *v/i.* (*irr.*, *sep.*, h, → ***liegen***) lie exposed (*or* uncovered, open)
'Frei·los *n* free (lottery) ticket; *sport*: bye
'Frei·luft... *in cpds.* open-air ..., outdoor ...
'frei·ma·chen (*sep.*, h) **I.** *v/t.* ✉ stamp; **II.** *v/i.* take time off; ***e-n Tag ~*** take a day off; **III.** *v/refl.*: ***sich ~*** a) take time off, b) undresss, get undressed; ***sich e-n Tag ~*** take a day off
'Frei·mau·rer *m* (-s; -) freemason; **Frei·mau·re·rei** [fraimaʊrə'rai] *f* (-; *no pl.*) freemasonry; **frei·mau·re·risch** ['fraimaʊrərɪʃ] *adj.* masonic; **'Frei·mau·rer·lo·ge** *f* freemasons' (*or* masonic) lodge
frei·mü·tig ['fraimy:tɪç] *adj.* candid, open; **'Frei·mü·tig·keit** *f* (-; *no pl.*) cando(u)r, openness
'frei·neh·men *v/t.* (*irr.*, *sep.*, h, → ***nehmen***): ***(sich) e-n Tag ~*** take a day off
'Frei|pla·stik *f* free-standing sculpture; **~platz** *m ped.* free place; *thea.* free seat
'frei·pres·sen *v/t.* (*sep.*, h): ***j-n ~*** obtain s.o.'s release
'Frei·raum *m* (-[e]s; ⁼e) *a. pl.* (personal) freedom; room to manoeuvre (*Am.* maneuver); scope for development; ***sich Freiräume schaffen*** allow o.s. room for personal development
'frei|re·li·gi,ös *adj.* non-denominational; **~schaf·fend I.** *adj.* freelance; **II.** *adv.*: ***~ tätig sein*** work (as a) freelance, be a freelance(r)
'Frei·schär·ler ['fraiʃɛ:ɐlɐ] *m* (-s; -) guer(r)illa; *hist.* irregular
'frei|schie·ßen *v/refl.* (*irr.*, *sep.*, h, → ***schießen***): ***sich ~*** shoot one's way out (*or* to the door *etc.*); **~schwe·bend** *adj.* freely suspended; **~schwim·men** *v/refl.* (*irr.*, *sep.*, h, → ***schwimmen***): ***sich ~*** **1.** *pass one's 15-minute swimming test*; **2.** F *fig.* learn to stand on one's own two feet, F make the break; **~set·zen** *v/t.* (sep., h) ⚗, *phys. and fig.* release; lay off *workers*, make redundant; **~sin·nig** *adj.* liberal(-minded); **~spie·len** (*sep.*, h) **I.** *v/refl.*: ***sich ~*** *sport*: get into space; **II.** *v/t.* get *a player* in the clear
'frei·spre·chen *v/t.* (*irr.*, *sep.*, h, → ***sprechen***) **1.** ⚖ acquit (***von*** *dat.* of); exonerate (from); clear (of); *eccl.* absolve (from); **2.** release *apprentice* from his (*or* her) articles; **'Frei·spre·chung** *f* (-; -en) **1.** exoneration; ⚖ → ***Freispruch***; *eccl.* absolution; **2.** release from his (*or* her) articles; **'Frei·spruch** *m* (-[e]s; ⁼e) ⚖ acquittal; verdict of not guilty
'Frei·staat *m* free state; republic; ***der ~ Bayern*** (***Sachsen***) the Free State of Bavaria (Saxony)
'frei·ste·hen *v/i.* (*irr.*, *sep.*, h, → ***stehen***) **1.** be unoccupied, be empty; **2.** *sport*: be unmarked; **3.** ***j-m ~*** be up to s.o.; ***es steht Ihnen frei zu*** *inf.* it's up to you whether you want to *inf.*; **'frei·ste·hend** *adj.* a) empty, b) detached *house*, c) *sport*: unmarked
'frei·stel·len (*sep.*, h) **I.** *v/t.* **1.** exempt, release *s.o.* (***von*** *dat.* from) (*a.* ⚔); **2.** ***j-m et. ~*** leave s.th. (up) to s.o.; ***freigestellt*** optional; ***es ist ihm freigestellt zu*** *inf.* he's free to *inf.*; **II.** *v/refl.*: ***sich ~*** *sport*: run clear; **'Frei·stel·lung** *f* (-; -en) exemption; release
'Frei·stil *m* (-[e]s; *no pl.*) *sport*: freestyle; **~rin·gen** *n* freestyle wrestling; **~schwim·men** *n* freestyle swimming
'Frei|stoß *m soccer*: free kick; **~stun·de** *f ped.* free period
'Frei·tag *m* (-s; -e) Friday; (***am***) **~** on Friday; **'frei·tags** *adv.* on Friday(s)
'Frei|tod *m* suicide; ***in den ~ gehen, den ~ wählen*** commit suicide, take one's own life; **2tra·gend** *adj.* ⚙ cantilever ..., self-supporting; floating *axle*; **~trep·pe** *f* steps *pl.* (*gen.* of, in front of, leading up to); **~übun·gen** *pl.* exercises; **~,um·schlag** *m* stamped addressed envelope, prepaid envelope; **~ver·merk** *m* ✝ prepaid notice
frei'weg F *adv.* straight out
'Frei·wild *n* unprotected (*fig.* fair) game
'frei·wil·lig I. *adj.* voluntary; spontaneous; ✝ ***~e Leistung*** ex gratia payment; **II.** *adv. a.* of one's own free will; ***sich ~ melden*** volunteer (***zu*** *dat.* for); **Frei·wil·li·ge** ['fraivɪlɪgə] *m*, *f* (-n; -n) volunteer
'Frei|wurf *m sport*: free throw; **~zei·chen** *n teleph.* dial(l)ing tone
'Frei·zeit *f* (-; *no pl.*) free (*or* leisure) time; **~an·ge·bot** *n* leisure amenities *pl.*; cultural and entertainment facilities *pl.*; ***ein großes ~ haben*** *a.* offer a lot of leisure amenities; **~be·schäf·ti·gung** *f* leisure-time activity (*or* activities *pl.*); **~ge·sell·schaft** *f* leisure(-oriented) society; **~ge·stal·tung** *f* leisure-time activities *pl.*; ***die richtige ~ ist sehr wichtig*** it's important to organize one's leisure time properly; **~in·du,strie** *f* leisure industry; **~klei·dung** *f* leisurewear; **~park** *m* leisure park; **~pro,blem** *n* problem of how to fill one's free time; **~wert** *m* (-[e]s; *no pl.*) recreational assets *pl.*; ***mit hohem ~*** with a wide range of leisure facilities; **~zen·trum** *n* leisure cent|re (*Am.* -er)
'frei·zü·gig *adj.* **1.** a) generous, liberal, b) free, permissive, *film etc.*: explicit; ✝ unrestricted; **2.** free to move; **'Frei·zü·gig·keit** *f* (-; *no pl.*) **1.** a) generosity, b) permissiveness; **2.** freedom of movement
fremd [frɛmt] *adj.* strange; foreign; exotic; outside ...; ***~e Leute*** strangers; ***~e Sitten*** foreign (*or* strange) customs; ***~e Länder*** foreign (*or* exotic) countries; ***~e Sprachen*** foreign languages; ***~es Organ*** transplanted organ; ***~e Hilfe*** outside help; ***in ~en Händen*** in strange hands; ***unter ~em Namen*** under an assumed name, incognito; ***ich bin hier*** (***selbst***) **~** I'm a stranger here (myself); ***sich ~ fühlen*** feel like a stranger, feel very strange; ***er ist mir ~*** he's a stranger to me, I don't know him (at all); ***er ist mir nicht ~*** he's no stranger to me, I know him (well); ***das ist mir*** (***nicht***) **~** that's (nothing) new to me; ***das ist mir alles noch sehr ~*** it's all still too new to me; ***sich*** (*or* ***einander***) ***~ werden*** grow apart, become strangers; ***nicht für ~e Ohren bestimmt*** for your ears only; ***misch dich nicht in ~e Angelegenheiten*** don't go poking your nose into other people's business; ***sie tat so ~*** she was very distant (*or* shy); ***s-e Stimme klang ganz ~*** his voice sounded very strange (*or* different); ***das ist ihm ganz ~*** that's completely alien to him
'Fremd·ar·bei·ter *obs. m* foreign worker
'fremd·ar·tig *adj.* foreign; strange; *a. fig.* exotic; **'Fremd·ar·tig·keit** *f* (-; *no pl.*) foreignness, strangeness; exoticism
'Fremd|be·fruch·tung *f* ⚘ cross-fertiliza-

tion; **~be·stäu·bung** *f* cross-pollination

Frem·de¹ ['frɛmdə] *f* (-; *no pl.*): **die ~** foreign parts *pl.*; **in die (der) ~** away from home, abroad

'Frem·de² *m, f* (-n; -n) stranger; foreigner; tourist; **er ist mir kein ~r** he's no stranger to me

frem·deln ['frɛmdəln] *v/i.* (h) be shy (with strangers); **er fremdelt sehr** he doesn't take to strangers very easily

'Frem·den|bett *n* (guest) bed; **~buch** *n* visitors' book

'frem·den·feind·lich *adj.* xenophobic, hostile to foreigners; **die Leute hier sind sehr ~** *a.* they don't like foreigners around here; **'Frem·den·feind·lich·keit** *f* (-; *no pl.*) xenophobia, hostility towards foreigners

'Frem·den|füh·rer *m* (tourist) guide; **~haß** *m* xenophobia, hatred of foreigners; **~heim** *n* guest house; **~in·du,strie** *f* tourist industry; **~le·gi,on** *f* Foreign Legion; **~le·gio,när** *m* (Foreign) Legionnaire

'Frem·den·ver·kehr *m* tourism

'Frem·den·ver·kehrs|amt *n*, **~ver·ein** *m* tourist association (*or* board)

'Frem·den·zim·mer *n* room (to let, *Am.* to rent)

'Fremd|fi·nan,zie·rung *f* outside financing; **≈ge·hen** F *v/i.* (*irr.*, *sep.*, sn, → **gehen**) F two-time; be unfaithful (to one's husband *or* wife, boyfriend *or* girlfriend); go out with another man *or* woman; **~herr·schaft** *f* (-; *no pl.*) foreign rule; **~ka·pi,tal** *n* borrowed capital; **~kör·per** *m* **1.** *biol.* foreign body; **2.** *fig.* alien element; odd man out; **wie ein ~ wirken** be (completely) out of place

'fremd·län·disch [-lɛndɪʃ] *adj.* foreign; *w.s.* exotic

Fremd·ling ['frɛmtlɪŋ] *lit. m* (-s; -e) stranger, alien

'Fremd·spra·che *f* foreign language

'Fremd·spra·chen|kennt·nis·se *pl.* foreign language ability *sg.*, knowledge *sg.* of foreign languages; foreign languages; **~kor·re·spon,dent** *m* foreign language correspondent; **~se·kre,tä·rin** *f* bilingual secretary; **~,un·ter·richt** *m* foreign language teaching; **~wör·ter·buch** *n* foreign language dictionary

'fremd·spra·chig [-ʃpraːxɪç] *adj.* **1.** foreign-speaking ...; **2.** foreign-language ...; **~er Unterricht** teaching (*or* tuition) in the foreign (*or* target) language

'fremd·sprach·lich *adj.* foreign-language *teaching, texts etc.*

'Fremd|stoff *m* foreign substance; **~wäh·rung** *f* foreign currency

'Fremd·wort *n* (-[e]s; ⸚er) foreign word; *fig.* **das ist für ihn ein ~** he doesn't know what it means; **'Fremd·wör·ter·buch** *n* dictionary of foreign loan words

fre·ne·tisch [fre'neːtɪʃ] *adj.* frenzied; *a.* wild *applause*

fre·quen·tie·ren [frekvɛn'tiːrən] *v/t.* (h) frequent; **stark frequentiert** very popular *pub etc.*; *das Museum* **wird stark frequentiert** has a lot of visitors

Fre·quenz [fre'kvɛnts] *f* (-; -en) **1.** a) *phys.* frequency, b) ⚕ (pulse) rate; **2.** a) number of visitors, b) traffic (density); **~be·reich** *m* frequency range; **~re·ge·lung** *f* frequency control; **~ska·la** *f* tuning dial; **~ver·schie·bung** *f* frequency shift; **~ver·tei·lung** *f* frequency allocation; **~wei·che** *f* frequency separator; crossover network

Fres·ke ['frɛskə] *f* (-; -n) fresco

Fres·ken|ge·mäl·de ['frɛskən-] *n* fresco (painting); **~ma·ler** *m* fresco painter; **~ma·le,rei** *f* fresco (painting)

Fres·ko ['frɛsko] *n* (-s; Fresken ['frɛskən]) fresco

Fres·sa·li·en [frɛ'saːliən] F *pl.* F grub *sg.*, *sl.* nosh *sg.*

Freß·beu·tel ['frɛs-] *m* **1.** nosebag; **2.** F nosh bag (*sl.*)

Fres·se ['frɛsə] V *f* (-; -n) *sl.* mug; **halt die ~!** *sl.* shut your face; **ich hau' dir gleich in die ~!** *sl.* I'll put your face out of joint if you don't watch it

fres·sen ['frɛsən] (fraß, gefressen, h) **I.** *v/t.* **1.** eat, *zo. a.* devour; V scoff (F), F stuff o.s. with; feed on; *fig.* F devour *book*; F gobble up *money etc.*; F eat up, F guzzle *petrol etc.*; **e-m Tier ... zu ~ geben** feed an animal on ...; **e-m Tier et. zu ~ geben** give an animal s.th. to eat; *fig.* **j-n arm ~** eat s.o. out of house and home; **ihn frißt der Neid** he's eaten up (*or* consumed) with envy; F **er wird dich schon nicht ~!** he won't bite you; F **friß mich nicht gleich!** there's no need to bite my head off; F **den (das) habe ich gefressen** I can't stand him (it); F **er hat's gefressen** F a) the penny's dropped, b) he fell for it; F **er hat's immer noch nicht gefressen** F he still hasn't got it into his thick skull; **da heißt's ~ oder gefressen werden** it's (a case of) dog eat dog; → **Besen** 1, **Narr**; **II.** *v/refl.* **2. sich ~ in** *acc. a.* ⚒ eat into; **III.** *v/i.* **3.** eat; V gobble, eat like a pig; **er ißt nicht, er frißt** he eats like a pig; *fig.* **j-m aus der Hand ~** eat out of s.o.'s hand; **4.** *fig.* **~ an** *dat.* eat away at; **IV.** ≈ *n* (-s) food; V **das ist ein ungenießbares ~** F how is anybody expected to eat this muck?; **~ und Saufen** eating and drinking; F **sie ist zum ~ (süß)** I could eat her alive; **das ist ein gefundenes ~ für ihn** that's just what he was waiting for

Fres·ser ['frɛsɐ] *m* (-s; -) **1.** *zo.* feeder; **2.** F glutton; **Fres·se·rei** [frɛsə'raɪ] V *f* (-; -en) **1.** F guzzling; **2.** → **Freßgelage**

'Freß·ge·la·ge F *n* F blowout, *sl.* great nosh-up

'Freß·gier *f* voracity; *contp.* gluttony, greed(iness); ⚕ b(o)ulimia; **'freß·gie·rig** *adj.* voracious; *contp.* greedy, gluttonous

'Freß|korb F *m* (food) hamper; **~lust** *f* (-; *no pl.*) *zo.* appetite; **~napf** *m* a) (feeding) bowl, b) seed dish; **~pa,ket** F *n* food parcel; **~sack** F *m* glutton; **~sucht** *f* (-; *no pl.*) → **Freßgier**; **~tem·pel** F *m* gourmet temple

Frett·chen ['frɛtçən] *n* (-s; -) ferret

Freu·de ['frɔʏdə] *f* (-; -n) **1.** *no pl.* joy (**über** *acc.* at); pleasure; delight; **~ haben** (*or* **finden**) **an** enjoy *s.th.*; **er hat viel ~ daran** it gives him a lot of pleasure; **j-m ~ machen** (*or* **bereiten**) give s.o. pleasure, make s.o. happy; **es macht mir (keine) ~** I (don't) enjoy it, **zu** *inf.*: I (don't) enjoy *ger.*; **ich wollte ihr e-e kleine ~ machen** I wanted to do something nice (for her); **Freud und Leid** joy and sorrow; **in Freud und Leid** through thick and thin, in good times and bad; **s-e einzige ~** his only pleasure (in life); **die Malerei ist s-e einzige ~** *a.* he lives for his painting; **j-m die ~ verderben** spoil it for s.o.; **vor ~ weinen** weep for (*or* with) joy; **außer sich vor ~** overjoyed; **es war e-e ~ zu** *inf.* it was a pleasure to *inf.*; **das war e-e ~!** it was a real joy; **zu m-r großen ~** much to my pleasure; **es war keine reine ~** F it was no picnic (*or* fun and games), it wasn't exactly (great) fun; → **geteilt**; **2.** *iro.* **die kleinen ~n des Alltags** the little things that are sent to try us

Freu·den... ['frɔʏdən-] *in cpds usu.* ... of joy; **~bot·schaft** *f* good news, *lit. and hum.* glad tidings *pl.*; **~fest** *n* (joyful) celebration(s *pl.*); **~feu·er** *n* bonfire; **~ge·schrei** *n* shouts *pl.* of joy; cheers *pl.*, cheering; **~haus** *n* brothel, *iro.* house of ill repute; **~mäd·chen** *n* prostitute; **≈reich** *adj.* joyful; **~er Tag** *a.* day of rejoicing (*or* joy), day full of joy; **~schrei** *m* cry of joy; **e-n ~ ausstoßen** shout for joy; **~sprung** *m*: **e-n ~ machen** jump for joy; **~tag** *m* day of rejoicing; day to be remembered; **~tanz** *m*: **e-n ~ aufführen** dance a jig, dance for joy; **~tau·mel** *m*: **in e-n ~ geraten** go into ecstasies; **~trä·nen** *pl.* tears of joy

'freu·de|strah·lend *adj.* beaming (with joy *or* happiness); **~trun·ken** *lit. adj.* delirious with joy, deliriously happy, ecstatic

Freu·dia·ner [frɔʏ'dĭaːnɐ] *m* (-s; -) Freudian, follower (*or* adherent) of Freud; **freu·dia·nisch** [frɔʏ'dĭaːnɪʃ] *adj.* Freudian

freu·dig ['frɔʏdɪç] **I.** *adj.* a) happy; cheerful, b) enthusiastic, keen, c) joyful; **~es Ereignis** happy event; **~e Nachricht** good news; **~e Überraschung** wonderful surprise; **II.** *adv.* happily *etc.*; → **I**; **~ erregt** very excited; **j-n ~ begrüßen** give s.o. a cheerful hello (*or* warm welcome), be happy to see s.o.; **'Freu·dig·keit** *f* (-; *no pl.*) happiness, joy

freud·los ['frɔʏtloːs] *adj.* miserable, bleak, cheerless; **ein ~es Dasein fristen** lead a miserable life

Freudsch [frɔʏtʃ] *adj.* Freudian; **~er Fehler** Freudian slip

freud·voll ['frɔʏtfɔl] *adj.* joyful, full of joy

freu·en (h) **I.** *v/refl.*: **sich ~** be glad, be pleased (**über** *acc.* about, with *a present etc.*); **sie hat sich über d-n Besuch gefreut** she was glad (*or* pleased) that you visited her; **sich riesig ~** F be over the moon; **sich an et. ~** get a lot of pleasure out of s.th.; **sich s-s Lebens ~** enjoy life (to the full); **sich ~ auf** *acc.* look forward to; **sich darauf ~ zu** *inf.* look forward to *ger.*; **sich zu früh ~** rejoice too soon; **freu dich nicht zu früh!** *a.* don't start celebrating too soon; **II.** *v/t.* please; **das freut mich sehr** I'm glad to hear that; **III.** *v/impers.*: **es freut mich, Sie zu sehen** nice to see you; **es würde mich ~, wenn** I'd be very pleased if; **freut mich!** how d'you do

Freund [frɔʏnt] *m* (-[e]s; -e ['frɔʏndə]) friend, *fig. a.* patron; boyfriend; **~ und Feind** friend and foe; **j-m ein guter ~ sein** be a good friend to s.o.; **sich j-n zum ~ machen** make a friend of s.o.; **j-n zum ~ haben** have a friend in s.o.; **e-n guten ~ an j-m haben** have a good friend in s.o.; **ein ~ in der Not** a friend in need; **dadurch hat sie sich viele ~e gemacht** it won (*or* made) her a lot of friends; **gut ~ sein mit** be good friends with; **der beste ~ des Menschen** a man's best friend; *fig.* **~ der Musik** *etc.* music lover *etc.*; **ein ~ sein von** *dat.* be fond of; ***kein ~ sein von*** *dat.* be averse to, be no fan of; ***er ist kein ~ von vielen Worten*** he's not a man of many words, he's not one for talking much; → ***dick***

'Freund·chen *n*: *iro.* ***hör mal, ~*** listen to me, chum (*or* my lad)

Freun·des·kreis ['frɔyndəs-] *m* (circle of) friends *pl.*; ***e-n großen ~ haben*** have a lot of friends; ***im engsten ~ feiern*** celebrate with a few good friends (*or* with one's close[st] friends)

Freun·din ['frɔyndɪn] *f* (-; -nen) friend, *fig. a.* patron; girlfriend

'freund·lich I. *adj.* friendly (***gegen*** *acc.* to[wards]), *a.* pleasant; obliging; affable; *meteor.* pleasant, mild *climate*; *fig.* cheerful *room etc.*; ✝ favo(u)rable, cheerful; ***das macht das Zimmer ~er*** it brightens up the room; ***sehr ~!*** very kind of you; ***mit ~er Genehmigung*** *gen.* by courtesy of; ***seien Sie so ~ zu*** *inf.* would you be good enough to *inf.?*; → ***Gruß***; **II.** *adv.*: ***j-n ~ empfangen*** give s.o. a warm welcome; ***j-m (e-r Sache) ~ gesinnt sein*** be well-disposed towards s.o. (s.th.); *pol.* ***~ gesinnt*** friendly; **'freund·li·cher'wei·se** *adv.* (very) kindly; **'Freund·lich·keit** *f* (-; -en) **1.** *no pl.* friendliness; pleasantness; obligingness; affability; ***würden Sie die ~ haben zu*** *inf.?* would you be kind enough to *inf.?*; ***j-m e-e ~ erweisen*** do s.o. a favo(u)r; **2.** ***j-m ein paar ~en sagen*** say a few nice words to s.o., *iro.* tell s.o. what's what

'freund·los *adj.* friendless, without friends

'Freund·schaft *f* (-; -en) friendship; ***~ schließen mit*** make friends with; ***aus ~*** because we're *etc.* friends; ***in aller ~*** in all friendliness; ***da hört die ~ auf*** my friendship doesn't extend that far, we're not that good friends; **'freund·schaft·lich I.** *adj.* friendly, amicable; ***auf ~em Fuße stehen mit j-m*** be on friendly terms with s.o.; **II.** *adv.*: ***~ gesinnt gegen*** *acc.* well-disposed towards; ***~ auseinandergehen*** part as friends, part on friendly (*or* amicable) terms

'Freund·schafts|ban·de *pl.* ties of friendship; **~be·such** *m pol.* goodwill visit; **~be·zei·gung** *f* token of one's friendship; **~dienst** *m* good turn; ***j-m e-n ~ erweisen*** do s.o. a good turn; **~pakt** *m* friendship pact; **~preis** *m* special price, F mate's rate; **~spiel** *n sport*: friendly (game); **~ver·trag** *m* treaty of friendship

Fre·vel ['fre:fəl] *m* (-s; -) *eccl.* sacrilege; blasphemy; *a. fig.* crime, outrage (***an*** *dat.*, ***gegen*** *acc.* against); wantonness; wickedness, iniquity; **'fre·vel·haft** *adj.* sacrilegious; outrageous; wanton; wicked; **'fre·veln** *v/i.* (h) commit an outrage (*or* crime); ***~ an*** *dat.* (*or* ***gegen*** *acc.*) trespass against *the law etc.*, *eccl.* commit sacrilege (*or* blasphemy) against; **'Fre·vel·tat** *f* outrage, crime; **Frev·ler** ['fre:flɐ] *m* (-s; -) evil-doer, transgressor, offender; *eccl.* blasphemer; **frev·le·risch** ['fre:flərɪʃ] *adj.* → ***frevelhaft***

Frie·de ['fri:də] *m* (-ns; -n) → ***Frieden***

Frie·den ['fri:dən] *m* (-s; -) *a. pol.* peace; *pol.* peace treaty; (time of) peace, peacetime; *fig.* harmony; tranquil(l)ity, peace of mind; ***~ schließen*** make peace; ***den ~ bewahren*** keep the peace; ***s-n ~ machen mit*** *dat.* make one's peace with; ***laß mich in ~!*** leave me alone; ***laß mich mit dem Unsinn in ~!*** leave me alone (*or* go away) with that nonsense (of yours); ***er gibt mir keinen ~*** he gives me no peace, he won't leave me in peace; ***dem ~ traue ich nicht*** things are too quiet to be true, things are suspiciously quiet; ***um des lieben ~s willen*** for the sake of peace (and quiet); ***(er) ruhe in ~*** (may he) rest in peace

'Frie·dens... *in cpds.* ... of peace, peace ...; **~an·ge·bot** *n* peace offer; **~apo·stel** F *m* prophet of peace; *w.s.* peace campaigner; **~ap͵pell** *m* call for peace; **~be·din·gun·gen** *pl.* peace terms, terms of peace; **~be·mü·hun·gen** *pl.* peace effort *sg.*, attempt to bring about a peace settlement; **~be·reit·schaft** *f* (-; *no pl.*) desire for peace; **~be·we·gung** *f* peace movement; **~bre·cher** *m* peacebreaker; **~bruch** *m* ⚖ breach (*pol.* violation) of the peace; **~for·mel** *f* peace formula; **~for·schung** *f* peace studies *pl.*; **~ga·ran͵tie** *f* guarantee of peace; guaranteed peace; **~ge·sprä·che** *pl.* peace talks; **~in·itia͵ti·ve** *f* peace initiative (*or* move); **~kon·fe͵renz** *f* peace conference; **~kund·ge·bung** *f* peace rally; **~lie·be** *f* love of peace; **~marsch** *m* peace march; **~mis·si͵on** *f* peace mission; **~no͵bel·preis** *m* Nobel Peace Prize; **~pfei·fe** *f* peace-pipe; ***die ~ rauchen*** smoke the pipe of peace; **~po·li͵tik** *f* peace politics *pl.*; **~preis** *m* peace prize (*or* award); **~rich·ter** *m* lay magistrate; *in GB and the USA*: justice of the peace; **~schluß** *m* conclusion of a (*or* the) peace treaty; **~si·che·rung** *f* securing (*or* preservation) of peace; peacekeeping (measures *pl.*); ***~ im Nahen Osten*** *a.* bringing about peace (*or* a peace settlement) in the Middle East; **~stär·ke** *f* ⚔ peacetime strength; **~stif·ter** *m* peacemaker; **~stö·rer** *m* disturber of the peace; **~sym͵bol** *n* symbol of peace; **~tau·be** *f* dove of peace; **~trup·pe** *f* peacekeeping force; **~ver·hand·lun·gen** *pl.* peace negotiations (*or* talks); **~ver·trag** *m* peace treaty; **~wil·le** *m* desire for peace; **~zei·ten** *pl.* times of peace, peacetime *sg.*

fried·fer·tig ['fri:t-] *adj.* peaceable; *zo.* gentle, docile

Fried·hof ['fri:t-] *m* cemetery, graveyard; ***auf welchem ~ liegt er (begraben)?*** which cemetery is he buried in?

fried·lich ['fri:t-] *adj.* peaceful; congenial; *zo.* gentle; ***j-n ~ stimmen*** pacify s.o.; ***auf ~em Wege*** by peaceful means, ***lösen:*** find a peaceful solution to (*or* for) *s.th.*; F ***sei ~*** a) be quiet, b) F take it easy, *sl.* cool it; **'Fried·lich·keit** *f* (-; *no pl.*) peacefulness

fried·lie·bend ['fri:t-] *adj.* peaceloving

frie·ren ['fri:rən] *v/i.* (fror, gefroren, sn) *and v/impers.* (h) freeze; ***mich friert, es friert mich*** I'm freezing (*or* frozen); ***mich friert an den Füßen*** I've got cold feet, my feet are cold (*or* freezing); ***es friert*** it's freezing; ***heute nacht wird es ~*** temperatures will be (*or* will drop to) below freezing tonight; → ***gefroren*** II

Fries [fri:s] *m* (-es; -e ['fri:zə]) ⚠ *and textil.* frieze

Frie·se ['fri:zə] *m* (-n; -n), **Frie·sin** ['fri:zɪn] *f* (-; -nen), **frie·sisch** ['fri:zɪʃ] *adj.*, **'Frie·sisch** *n* (-en) *ling.* Frisian; **'Frie·sen·nerz** F *m* oilskin jacket

fri·gi·de [fri'gi:də] *adj.* frigid; **Fri·gi·di·tät** [frigidi'tɛ:t] *f* (-; *no pl.*) frigidity

Fri·ka·del·le [frika'dɛlə] *f* (-; -n) meatball, *Am.* (ham)burger

Fri·kas·see [frika'se:] *n* (-s; -s), **fri·kas·sie·ren** [frika'si:rən] *v/t.* (h) fricassee

Frik·ti·on [frɪk'tsi̯o:n] *f* (-; -en) friction

frisch [frɪʃ] **I.** *adj.* fresh, fresh-laid, freshly laid, new-laid; clean (*a. sheet of paper etc.*); fresh, new; *fig.* recent; bright *colo(u)r*; *meteor.* cool, chilly; ***~ und munter*** wide awake, F bright-eyed and bushy-tailed; ***mit ~er Kraft*** refreshed, with renewed strength; ***sich ~ machen*** freshen up; ***noch in ~er Erinnerung*** fresh in my *etc.* mind; ***~er werden*** *wind*: freshen; → ***Luft, Tat***; **II.** *adv.* a) freshly *etc.*; → ***I***, b) again; ***~ geschnitten*** freshly cut, fresh-cut *flowers etc.*; ***~ gewaschen*** a) clean, just washed, b) (nice and) clean; ***~ gereinigt*** straight from the dry cleaners; ***~ gelegt*** → ***frisch*** I; ***~ gestrichen*** newly painted; ***~ gestrichen!*** wet (*Am.* fresh) paint; ***~ rasiert*** clean-shaven; ***~ verheiratet*** newly-wed *couple*; ***das Bett ~ beziehen*** put clean sheets on the bed

Fri·sche ['frɪʃə] *f* (-; *no pl.*) freshness; *meteor.* coolness, chill(iness); *fig.* briskness, liveliness, vigo(u)r; ***geistige ~*** mental alertness, alert (*or* lively) mind; ***in alter ~*** as alive and well as ever, *work etc.* with renewed vigo(u)r

'Frisch·ei *n* fresh (*or* fresh-laid, freshly laid, new-laid) egg

fri·schen ['frɪʃən] *v/t.* (h) *metall.* refine

'Frisch·fleisch *n* fresh meat

'frisch·ge·backen *adj.* fresh from the oven; F ***~er Ehemann*** newly-wed husband; F ***~er Lehrer*** *etc.* F fledgling teacher *etc.*

'Frisch|ge·mü·se *n* fresh vegetables *pl.*; **~ge·wicht** *n* fresh weight

'Frisch·hal·te|beu·tel *m* polythene bag; **~fo·lie** *f* cling film, *Am.* plastic wrap

'Frisch·hal·tung *f* (-; *no pl.*) preservation; refrigeration, cold storage

'Frisch·kä·se *m* cream cheese

Frisch·ling ['frɪʃlɪŋ] *m* (-s; -e) young wild boar; *fig.* greenhorn

'Frisch·luft *f* fresh air; **~fa͵na·ti·ker** *m* fresh-air fiend; **~hei·zung** *f mot.* fresh-air heating system; **~mas·sen** *pl.* fresh air mass *sg.*; **~schnei·se** *f* fresh air corridor

'Frisch|milch *f* fresh milk; **~obst** *n* fresh fruit

'Frisch·wa·ren *pl.* fresh produce *sg.*; perishables; **~ab͵tei·lung** *f* produce section

'Frisch·was·ser *n* fresh water; **~ver·sor·gung** *f* supply of fresh water, fresh water supplies *pl.*

'Frisch·zel·le *f* living cell; **'Frisch·zel·len·the·ra͵pie** *f* living cell therapy

Fri·seur [fri'zø:ɐ] *m* (-s; -e [-'zø:rə]) hairdresser, barber; **~la·den** *m*, **~sa͵lon** *m* hairdresser's shop, barbershop

Fri·seu·se [fri'zø:zə] *f* (-; -n) hairdresser

fri·sie·ren [fri'zi:rən] (h) **I.** *v/t.* **1.** ***j-n ~*** do s.o.'s hair; **2.** F *fig.* F doctor *the accounts*, cook *the books*; *mot.* F soup up; **II.** *v/refl.*: ***sich ~*** do one's hair; **Fri'sier·sa͵lon** *m* hairdressing salon; **fri·siert** [fri'zi:ɐt] F *adj. mot. etc.* F souped up, hyped up; **Fri'sier·tisch** *m* dressing table, dresser

Frist [frɪst] *f* (-; -en) a) (fixed) period of time, b) deadline, c) extension, ✝ respite, ⚖ reprieve; ⚖, ✝ ***drei Tage ~*** three days' grace; ***innerhalb e-r ~ von zehn***

Tagen within a ten-day period; ***in kürzester*** ~ at (very) short notice; ***äußerste*** ~ final date (*or* deadline); ***e-e*** ~ ***einhalten*** meet a deadline; **(*j-m*) *e-e*** ~ ***gewähren*** give s.o. *three days' etc.* grace; ***e-e*** ~ ***setzen*** fix a deadline; ***die*** ~ ***ist abgelaufen*** the deadline (*or* period) has expired, *fig.* your *etc.* time is up, F time's up

fri·sten ['frɪstən] *v/t.* (h) ***ein kümmerliches Dasein*** (*or* ***Leben***) ~ eke out a miserable existence (***mit*** *dat.* with, by *doing s.th.*); ***sein Leben*** (*or* ***Dasein***) ~ get by somehow, live as best one can

'frist·ge·mäß, 'frist·ge·recht *adj. and adv.* in time, within the agreed time limit

'frist·los *adj. and adv.* without notice; ~***e Entlassung*** dismissal without notice; ~ ***entlassen werden*** be dismissed without notice, be fired on the spot

'Frist|über,schrei·tung *f* failure to meet the deadline; ~**ver·län·ge·rung** *f* extension (of the deadline), deadline extension; ~**ver·säum·nis** *n* ⚖ default

Fri·sur [fri'zu:ɐ] *f* (-; -en [-'zu:rən]) hairstyle; haircut

Fri·teu·se [fri'tø:zə] *f* (-; -n) chip pan, deep fat fryer, *Am.* deep fryer

Frit·ten ['frɪtən] F *pl.* chips, *Am.* fries

fri·vol [fri'vo:l] *adj.* frivolous, flippant; suggestive *remark etc.*; **Fri·vo·li·tät** [frivoli'tɛ:t] *f* (-; -en) **1.** *no pl.* frivolity, flippancy, levity; indecency; **2.** suggestive remark

froh [fro:] *adj.* glad (***über*** *acc.* about); cheerful; ~***en Mutes*** cheerfully; ~***es Ereignis*** happy event; ***e-e*** ~***e Nachricht*** good news (*sg.*); *eccl.* ***die*** ~***e Botschaft*** the Gospel; ***er ist s-s Lebens nicht mehr*** ~ ***geworden*** he never got over it; ***sei*** ~, ***daß du nicht dabei warst*** be thankful (*or* glad) you weren't there; ***bin ich*** ~, ***daß das vorbei ist!*** *a.* what a relief that that's over; → ***Ostern, Weihnachten*** I

'froh·ge·mut *adj.* cheerful

fröh·lich ['frø:lɪç] **I.** *adj.* cheerful, happy; merry; ~ ***Weihnachten*** I; ***j-n*** ~ ***stimmen*** put s.o. in a good mood; **II.** *adv.* blithely, merrily; **'Fröh·lich·keit** *f* (-; *no pl.*) cheerfulness; high spirits *pl.*

froh·locken [fro'lɔkən] (*sep.* -k·k-) **I.** *v/i.* (h) rejoice (***über*** *acc.* at), be jubilant (at); gloat (over); **II.** ♀ *n* (-s) jubilation; gloating; **froh'lockend** *adj.* jubilant, exultant

'Froh|na,tur *f*: ***e-e*** ~ ***haben*** (*or* ***sein***) be a cheerful person (*or* type); ~**sinn** *m* (-[e]s; *no pl.*) cheerfulness

fromm [frɔm] *adj.* a) pious, devout, b) gentle, meek (as a lamb), *horse*: quiet, steady; ~***e Lüge*** white lie; ~***er Betrug*** pious fraud; ~***es Getue*** sanctimoniousness; ***ein*** ~***er Wunsch*** wishful thinking

Fröm·me·lei [frœmə'laɪ] *f* (-; *no pl.*) sanctimoniousness; **fröm·meln** ['frœməln] *v/i.* (h) be sanctimonious, F put on one's pious act; **'fröm·melnd** *adj.* sanctimonious

Fröm·mig·keit ['frœmɪçkaɪt] *f* (-; *no pl.*) piety

Fron [fro:n] *f* (-; -en), ~**ar·beit** *f*, ~**dienst** *m hist.* soc(c)age, statute labo(u)r; *fig.* drudgery; ***Frondienste leisten*** (*dat. or* ***für*** *acc.*) → ***fronen***

fro·nen ['fro:nən] *v/i.* (h) perform statute labo(u)r (*dat.* for); *fig.* slave away (for)

frö·nen ['frø:nən] *v/i.* (h) indulge in; gratify; ***s-n Leidenschaften*** ~ let one's passions run wild; ***dem Alkohol*** ~ a) be a heavy drinker, *iro.* enjoy one's drink, b) imbibe, F have a bit of a booze-up

Fron'leich·nam *m* Corpus Christi

Front [frɔnt] *f* (-; -en) △, *meteor. and fig.* front; ⚔ front (line); ***an der*** ~ at the front; ***hinter der*** ~ behind the lines; ***die feindliche*** ~ enemy lines; ***an der vordersten*** ~ ***stehen*** be in the front line; ***an zwei*** ~***en kämpfen*** *a. fig.* fight on two fronts; *fig.* ~ ***machen gegen*** *acc.* make a stand against, resist; ***klare*** ~***en schaffen*** make a clear stand, make one's position clear; ***in*** ~ ***gehen*** *sport*: take the lead; ***in*** ~ ***liegen*** be in the lead; → ***abstecken*** 2, ***geschlossen*** I, ***verhärten***

fron·tal [frɔn'ta:l] **I.** *adj.* head-on, frontal ...; **II.** *adv.* head on

Fron'tal|an·griff *m* frontal attack; ~,**un·ter·richt** *m* class teaching, F chalk and talk; ~**zu,sam·men·stoß** *m* head-on collision

'Front|an·sicht *f* front(al) view; ~**an·trieb** *m mot.* front-wheel drive; ~**be·richt** *m* ⚔ front-line report; ~**dienst** *m* ⚔ combat duty; ~**ein·satz** *m* ⚔ action at the front

'Fron·ten|sy,stem *n meteor.* frontal system; ~**ver·här·tung** *f* hardening of fronts (*or* positions)

Fron·ti·spiz [frɔnti'spi:ts] *n* (-es; -e) △, *typ.* frontispiece

'Front|kämp·fer *m* a) front-line soldier, b) ex-serviceman, *Am.* veteran; ~**la·der** *m video etc.*: front loader; ~**li·nie** *f* ⚔ front line; ~**schei·be** *f mot.* windscreen, *Am.* windshield; ~**spoi·ler** *m mot.* front spoiler; ~**staa·ten** *pl.* frontline states; ~**stadt** *f* front-line city; ~**ur·laub** *m* ⚔ leave from the front; ~**wech·sel** *fig. m* about-face, about-turn, volte-face; ***e-n*** ~ ***vornehmen*** do an about-turn; ~**zu·la·ge** *f* ⚔ combat pay

fror [fro:ɐ] *pret. of* ***frieren***

Frosch [frɔʃ] *m* (-[e]s; Frösche ['frœʃə]) a) *zo.* frog, b) squib, c) ♪ frog, heel; F *fig.* ***sei kein*** ~***!*** don't be a spoilsport; ***e-n*** ~ ***im Hals haben*** have a frog in one's throat; ~**au·gen** F *pl.* bulging eyes; ~**hüp·fen** *n* leapfrog; ~**laich** *m* frogspawn; ~**mann** *m* (-[e]s; ⸗er) frogman; ~**per·spek,ti·ve** *f* worm's eye view, *film*: *a.* tilt shot; ***aus der*** ~ ***sehen*** have a worm's eye view of; ~**schen·kel** *pl. gastr.* frog's legs; ~**teich** *m* frog pond; ~**test** *m* ⚕ frog test

Frost [frɔst] *m* (-[e]s; Fröste ['frœstə]) frost; ⚕ *the* shivers *pl.*; ***bei*** ~ when there's frost, in frosty weather; ***bei schwerem*** ~ in heavy frost; ~ ***abbekommen*** get a touch of frost; ♀**be·stän·dig** *adj.* frost-resistant; ~**beu·le** *f* chilblain; ~**ein·bruch** *m* sudden frost

frö·steln ['frœstəln] **I.** *v/i. and v/impers.* (h) shiver (with cold); shudder; ***mich fröstelt*** I feel shivery; ***da fröstelt's einen ja*** (***bei dem Gedanken***) it makes you shudder (to think of it); **II.** ♀ *n* (-s) shivering

'frost·emp·find·lich *adj.* sensitive to frost

fro·sten ['frɔstən] *v/t.* (h) freeze

'frost·frei *adj.* free of frost, frost-free

'Frost|ge·fahr *f* danger of frost; ~**gren·ze** *f* frost line

fro·stig ['frɔstɪç] *adj.* frosty; *fig. a.* icy; **'Fro·stig·keit** *fig. f* (-; *no pl.*) frostiness, iciness

'frost·klar *adj.*: ~***e Nacht*** clear, frosty night

'Frost|pe·rio·de *f* spell of frost; ~**scha·den** *m* frost damage; ~**schutz·mit·tel** *n mot.* antifreeze; ♀**si·cher** *adj.* frost-resistant; *place*: free of frost; ~**wet·ter** *n* frosty weather

Frot·tee [frɔ'te:] *n, m* (-s; -s) (terry) towel(l)ing, terry(cloth); ~**ba·de·man·tel** *m* terry(cloth) bathrobe; ~**bettuch** *n* (*sep.* -tt·t-) terry(cloth) sheet; ~**hand·tuch** *n* (fleecy) towel; ~**socken** *pl.* terry(cloth) socks

frot·tie·ren [frɔ'ti:rən] *v/t.* (h) rub down; rub (with a towel); **Frot'tier(hand)tuch** *n* (fleecy) towel

Frot·ze·lei [frɔtsə'laɪ] F *f* (-; -en) *a. pl.* teasing; ***hör auf mit der*** ~***!*** stop teasing; **frot·zeln** ['frɔtsəln] F (h) **I.** *v/t.* tease, make fun of; **II.** *v/i.*: ~ ***über*** *acc.* make fun of, F take the mickey out of

Frucht [frʊxt] *f* (-; Früchte ['frʏçtə]) **1.** ⚘ *a. pl.* fruit ; *fig. pl.* fruit *sg.*, fruits, result *sg.*, results; ***Früchte tragen*** bear fruit, *fig. a.* come to fruition; *fig.* ***die Früchte s-r Arbeit*** the fruits of one's labo(u)r, ***genießen:*** reap the rewards of one's labo(u)r; *bibl.* ***an ihren Früchten sollt ihr sie erkennen*** by their fruits ye shall know them; → ***verboten***; **2.** ⚕ f(o)etus

'frucht·bar *adj. biol.* fertile; *fig.* fruitful; prolific *writer*; ***nicht*** ~ infertile, *fig.* unfruitful; ⚕ ~***e Tage*** fertile period; *fig.* ***auf*** ~***en Boden fallen*** fall on fertile ground; **'Frucht·bar·keit** *f* (-; *no pl.*) fertility; *fig.* fruitfulness

'Frucht·bar·keits|gott *m*, ~**göt·tin** *f* fertility god (goddess *f*)

'Frucht|be·cher *m* **1.** *gastr.* fruit sundae; **2.** ⚘ cup; ~**bla·se** *f* ⚕ amniotic sac; ~**bon,bon** *m, n* fruit drop

'frucht·brin·gend *adj.* fruitful

Frücht·chen ['frʏçtçən] F *iro. n* (-s; -) troublemaker; F (little) scamp

Früch·te|brot ['frʏçtə-] *n* fruit loaf; ~**cock·tail** *m* fruit cocktail

'Frucht·eis *n* fruit-flavo(u)red ice cream

fruch·ten ['frʊxtən] *fig. v/i.* (h) be of use; have an effect; ***es hat nichts gefruchtet*** it was fruitless (*or* no use)

'Frucht|fleisch *n* flesh; ~**fol·ge** *f* ⚒ crop rotation; ~**hül·le** *f* ⚘ pericarp; ~**hül·se** *f* ⚘ pod

fruch·tig ['frʊxtɪç] *adj.* fruity

'Frucht|jo·ghurt *m* fruit yoghurt; ~**kap·sel** *f* ⚘ capsule; ~**kno·ten** *m* ⚘ ovary

'frucht·los *fig. adj.* fruitless, futile

'Frucht|mark *n* fruit pulp; ~**pres·se** *f* juicer; ~**saft** *m* fruit juice; ~**sa,lat** *m* fruit salad; ~**säu·re** *f* fruit acid

'Frucht·was·ser *n physiol.* amniotic fluid, F *the* waters *pl.*; ~**punk·ti,on** *f* ⚕ amniocentesis

'Frucht·zucker *m* fruit sugar, fructose

Fruc·to·se [frʊk'to:zə] *f* (-; *no pl.*) fructose

fru·gal [fru'ga:l] *adj.* frugal; **Fru·ga·li·tät** [frugali'tɛ:t] *f* (-; *no pl.*) frugality

früh [fry:] **I.** *adj.* early; ***ein*** ~***er van Gogh*** an early van Gogh (*or* work of van Gogh's); ***am*** ~***en Morgen*** early (*or* first thing) in the morning; ***am*** ~***en Nachmittag*** (***Abend***) early in the afternoon (evening), in the early afternoon (evening), early afternoon (evening); → ***früher, frühest***; **II.** *adv.* early; at an early age; early on, at an early stage; ***heute*** ~ this morning; ~ ***um fünf, um fünf Uhr*** ~ at five (o'clock) in the morning; (***schon***) ~ early on; ~ ***genug*** soon enough; ***von*** ~ ***bis spät*** from morning till night; ~ ***auf-***

stehen get up early, be an early riser; ~ ***sterben*** die prematurely (*or* young, before one's time); ***zu ~ kommen*** be early

'Früh|an,ti·ke *f*: ***die ~*** early antiquity; **~ap·fel** *m* early apple

'früh·auf *adv.*: ***von ~*** from an early age

'Früh|auf·ste·her *m* (-s; -) early riser (F bird); **~aus·ga·be** *f* first edition; **~beet** *n* cold frame; **~be·ga·bung** *f* **1.** ***er zeigte e-e ~*** his talent surfaced very early; **2.** very talented child; ***sie ist e-e ~*** *a.* she's extremely talented for her age

Früh·chen ['fry:çən] F *n* (-s; -) premature baby, F early arrival

'früh·christ·lich *adj.* early Christian

'Früh|dia,gno·se *f* early diagnosis; **~dienst** *m* early shift; ***~ haben*** be on early shift

Frü·he ['fry:ə] *f* (-; *no pl.*) (early) morning; ***in aller ~*** early (*or* first thing) in the morning

frü·her ['fry:ɐ] **I.** *adj.* earlier; former, previous; past; older; ***~e Fassung*** earlier version; ***der ~e Besitzer*** the previous owner; ***in ~en Zeiten*** in the past; ***die ~e DDR*** former East Germany; **II.** *adv.* earlier; sooner; in the past; ***~, als ...*** in the old days when ...; ***~ oder später*** sooner or later; ***~ habe ich geraucht*** I used to smoke; ***~ habe ich nie geraucht*** I never used to smoke (in the past); ***hast du ~ wirklich geraucht?*** did you really use to smoke?; ***warst du ~ wirklich Rennfahrer?*** did you really use to be a racing driver?; ***ich hab' noch m-e ganzen Bücher von ~*** I've still got all my old books (from university *etc.*); ***ich kenne ihn von ~*** I know him from a long way back (F from way back); ***es ist alles noch wie ~*** nothing has changed

'Früh·er·ken·nung *f* ⚕ early detection (*or* diagnosis)

frü·hest ['fry:əst] *adj.* earliest; ***in ~er Kindheit*** at a very early age; **frü·hestens** ['fry:əstəns] *adv.* at the earliest, not before; ***~ am Sonntag*** (on) Sunday at the earliest, not before Sunday; ***das Haus ist ~ in e-m Jahr fertig*** it will take at least a year to build (*or* finish) the house

'frü·hest·mög·lich I. *adj. the* earliest possible *date etc.*; ***zum ~en Zeitpunkt*** → **II.** *adv.* as soon as possible, as soon as you *etc.* can

'Früh·ge·burt *f* **1.** premature birth; **2.** premature baby

'Früh·ge·schich·te *f*: ***die ~*** early history; ***die ~ der Menschheit*** the early history of man(kind); ***in der ~ der Menschheit*** *a.* in the early days of man(kind); **'früh·ge·schicht·lich** *adj.* early, ancient; ancient history ...

'Früh|got·tes·dienst *m* morning service; **~herbst** *m* early autumn (*Am. a.* fall)

'Früh·jahr *n* spring; ***im ~*** in (the) spring

'Früh·jahrs|kol·lek·ti,on *f* spring collection; **~mes·se** *f* spring fair; **~mo·de** *f* spring fashions *pl.*; **~mü·dig·keit** *f* springtime lethargy (*or* tiredness); **~putz** *m* spring cleaning

'Früh·ka·pi·ta,lis·mus *m* (*a.* ***Zeit des ~***) early age (*or* days *pl.*) of capitalism

'Früh·kar,tof·feln *pl.* new potatoes

'früh·kind·lich *adj.* infant ...

'Früh·kul,tur *f* early civilization; ***die chinesische ~*** early Chinese society (*or* civilization)

Früh·ling ['fry:lɪŋ] *m* (-s; -e) spring(time) (*a. fig.*); ***im ~*** in (the) spring; ***es riecht nach ~*** spring is in the air, you can smell the spring air; *fig.* ***e-n zweiten ~ erleben*** go through a second youth

'Früh·lings|an·fang *m*, **~be·ginn** *m* beginning of spring; first day of spring; early spring; **~blu·me** *f* spring flower; **~ge·füh·le** *pl.*: ***~e haben*** be feeling frisky

'früh·lings·haft *adj.* springlike, spring ...

'Früh·lings|luft *f* spring air; **~rol·le** *f* *gastr.* spring roll; **~tag** *m* spring day; ***an e-m schönen ~*** one fine day in spring; **~wet·ter** *n* spring weather; **~zeit** *f* springtime

'Früh|mensch *m*: ***der ~*** early man; **~mes·se** *f* morning service; **~met·te** *f* matins *pl.*; **~mit·tel·al·ter** *n* early Middle Ages *pl.*

früh'mor·gens *adv.* early in the morning

'Früh·nach·rich·ten *pl.* early morning news (bulletin) *sg.*

'Früh·ne·bel *m* early morning fog; **~felder** *pl.* early morning fog patches (*or* fog *sg.* in places)

'Früh·obst *n* early fruit, primeurs *pl.*

'Früh·pen·sio,nie·rung *f* early retirement

'früh·reif *adj.* **1.** precocious; **2.** ⚘ early-maturing; **'Früh·rei·fe** *f* **1.** precociousness; **2.** ⚘ early maturity

'Früh|ren·te *f* early retirement; ***in ~ gehen*** take (*or* go into) early retirement; **~rent·ner** *m* early leaver; ***er ist ~*** *a.* he took (*or* went into) early retirement; **~schicht** *f* early shift; ***~ haben*** be on early shift; **~schop·pen** *m* pre-lunch drink(s *pl.*), *Brit. a.* midday pint; **~sommer** *m* early summer; **~sport** *m* early morning exercises *pl.*, F *one's* daily dozen *pl.*; **~sta·di·um** *n*: (***im ~*** at an) early stage

'Früh·stück *n* (-[e]s; -e) breakfast; ***zweites ~*** mid-morning snack, *Brit. a.* elevenses *pl.*; ***Zimmer mit ~*** bed and breakfast; **früh·stücken** ['fry:ʃtʏkən] (*sep.* -k·k-) (h) **I.** *v/i.* have (one's) breakfast, breakfast; **II.** *v/t.* have *s.th.* for breakfast

'Früh·stücks|bü,fett *n* breakfast buffet; **~fern·se·hen** *n* breakfast TV; **~fleisch** *n* luncheon meat; **~ge·schirr** *n* breakfast dishes (*or* plates) *pl.*; **~pau·se** *f* morning break; **~speck** *m* bacon; **~tisch** *m*: (***am ~*** at the) breakfast table; **~zim·mer** *n* breakfast room

'Früh|warn·sy,stem *n* early warning system; **~werk** *n* early work(s *pl.*); *a. coll.* early writings *pl.*; **~zeit** *f* **1.** early period; **2.** (***in der ~*** in) prehistoric times *pl.*; **2zei·tig I.** *adj.* untimely, premature; **II.** *adv.* early, in good time; **~zug** *m* early train; **~zün·dung** *f mot.* pre-ignition

Frust [frʊst] F *m* (-[e]s; *no pl.*) *sl.* grind; ***hab' ich e-n ~!*** F am I cheesed off (*sl.* pissed off); ***so ein ~!*** *sl.* what a drag (*or* pain, grind); ***nichts als ~!*** F it's like banging your head off a brick wall; **Frustra·ti·on** [frʊstra'tsi̯o:n] *f* (-; -en) frustration; ***e-e ~ erleben*** be frustrated, have a frustrating time (of it); **fru·strieren** [frʊs'tri:rən] *v/t.* (h) frustrate; get on *s.o.'s* nerves, F drive *s.o.* mad; get *s.o.* down

Fuchs [fʊks] *m* (-es; Füchse ['fʏksə]) **1.** fox; *fig.* ***alter ~*** cunning old devil; F ***wo sich ~ und Hase gute Nacht sagen*** F at the back of beyond, out in the sticks (*Am. a.* boondocks); **2.** → ***Fuchspelz***; **3.** *zo.* sorrel; **4.** *zo.* ***Großer ~*** large tortoiseshell; ***Kleiner ~*** painted lady; **~bau** *m* (-[e]s; -e) fox's den, earth

fuch·sen ['fʊksən] F (h) **I.** *v/t.* rile, F get to *s.o.*; **II.** *v/refl.*: ***sich ~ über*** *acc.* be riled about

Fuch·sie ['fʊksi̯ə] *f* (-; -n) ⚘ fuchsia

fuch·sig ['fʊksɪç] *adj.* **1.** ginger; **2.** F *fig.* mad

Füch·sin ['fʏksɪn] *f* (-; -nen) vixen

'Fuchs|jagd *f* fox hunt(ing); **~pelz** *m* fox (fur); **2rot** *adj.* ginger; **~schwanz** *m* **1.** *zo.* foxtail, fox brush; **2.** ⚘ a) amaranth, b) love-lies-bleeding; **3.** ⚙ handsaw

'fuchs'teu·fels'wild F *adj.* F (hopping) mad, wild

Fuch·tel ['fʊxtəl] F *f*: ***j-n unter s-r ~ haben*** have s.o. under one's thumb; **'fuchteln** *v/i.* (h): ***~ mit*** *dat.* wave *s.th.* around; brandish; ***mit den Händen ~*** gesticulate wildly

fuch·tig ['fʊxtɪç] F *adj.* F (hopping) mad, wild

Fug [fu:k]: ***mit ~ und Recht*** rightly, with good reason; ***sie behauptet mit ~ und Recht*** she justly claims, she is justified in claiming (*or* saying); ***er tat es mit ~ und Recht*** he had every reason to do so

Fu·ge[1] ['fu:gə] *f* (-; -n) ♪ fugue

'Fu·ge[2] *f* (-; -n) ⚙ joint; interstice; ***aus den ~n geraten*** fall apart, *fig.* be thrown out of joint; *fig.* ***in allen ~n krachen*** be coming apart at the seams; **fu·gen** ['fu:gən] *v/t.* (h) joint; point up

fü·gen ['fy:gən] (h) **I.** *v/t.* **1.** → ***an-, hinzu-, zusammenfügen***; **2.** *fig.* decree; **II.** *v/refl.* **3.** ***sich ~ in*** *acc.* fit in well with; *fig.* ***sich ~ an*** *acc.* follow on from; ***eines fügte sich ans andere*** one thing followed (*or* led to) another; **4.** ***sich ~*** *dat.* (*or* ***in*** *acc.*) submit to; resign o.s. to; **III.** *v/impers.*: ***es fügt sich*** it so happens

füg·lich ['fy:klɪç] *adv.* rightly, justifiably

füg·sam ['fy:kza:m] *adj.* obedient; compliant; **'Füg·sam·keit** *f* (-; *no pl.*) obedience; compliance

Fü·gung ['fy:gʊŋ] *f* (-; -en) (act of) providence; coincidence; fate; ***durch e-e glückliche ~*** by a lucky coincidence; ***e-e merkwürdige ~ des Schicksals*** a (strange) twist of fate

fühl·bar ['fy:lba:ɐ] *adj.* **1.** noticeable; considerable, appreciable; ***~er Verlust*** serious loss; ***sich ~ machen*** make itself felt; **2.** tangible; **füh·len** ['fy:lən] (h) **I.** *v/t.* **1.** feel, *a.* sense; **2.** feel; **II.** *v/i.* **3.** feel; ***mit j-m ~*** feel with s.o.; **4.** ***~ nach*** *dat.* feel (*or* grope) for; **III.** *v/refl.*: ***sich glücklich*** *etc.* ***~*** feel happy *etc.*; ***sich ~ als*** see o.s. as; F ***er fühlt sich aber!*** F he doesn't half fancy himself; **'füh·lend** *adj.* feeling *heart etc.*, sympathetic; **Füh·ler** ['fy:lɐ] *m* (-s; -) *zo.* feeler, antenna, tentacle; ⚙ sensor, probe; ***die ~ ausstrecken*** *snail:* put out its horns, *fig.* put out (one's) feelers; **Füh·lung** ['fy:lʊŋ] *f* (-; *no pl.*) contact; ***~ haben (verlieren) mit*** *dat.* be in (lose) touch with; ***~ (auf)nehmen mit*** *dat.* contact, get in touch with; **'Füh·lung·nah·me** *f* (-; -n) initial (*or* first) contact

fuhr [fu:ɐ] *pret. of* ***fahren***

Fuh·re ['fu:rə] *f* (-; -n) **1.** loaded cart; **2.** (lorry)load, *esp. Am.* (truck)load; cart (-load)

füh·ren ['fy:rən] (h) **I.** *v/t.* **1.** lead (***nach*** *dat.*, ***zu*** *dat.* to), *a.* take, *a.* usher; guide *s.o.*, escort *s.o.*; ⚔, *sport:* lead; ***j-n in ein Zimmer ~*** show (*or* lead, usher) s.o. into a room; ***was führt dich her?*** what brings you here?; ***zum Mund ~*** raise to one's lips; ***ein Leben ~*** lead (*or* live) a life; ***sie ~ e-e gute Ehe*** they're happily married, they have a good (husband-and-wife) relationship; ***er führt den Ball gut*** *soccer*: he's got good ball control; → ***Gespräch, Krieg, Schild²*** 1; **2.** carry; ***bei sich ~*** have on one; **3.** drive; **4.** ⚙ handle, guide; **5.** be in charge of; hold *an office*; head, lead *a revolt etc.*; ✝ keep *the books*; manage, run *a business etc.*; ♪ conduct; **6.** bear, go by (*or* under) *the name of*; hold *a title*; have *on one's coat of arms*; ***den Titel ... ~*** be entitled ...; **7.** ✝ stock, sell, have; **8.** strike *a blow*; **9.** use *language*; **10.** ⚡ carry, conduct; **II.** *v/i.* **11.** lead (***nach*** *dat.*, ***zu*** *dat.* to), *sport*: *a.* be in the lead; ***mit zwei Toren ~*** be two goals ahead, have a two-goal lead; ***mit 3:1 ~*** be 3-1 up, ***gegen X:*** lead X by 3-1; ***die Straße führt nach X*** this road leads to X; ***das Tal führt in e-e Bucht*** the valley opens into a bay; *fig.* ***~ zu*** *dat.* lead to, end in, result in; ***das führt zu nichts*** that won't get us *etc.* anywhere; ***das führt zu weit*** that's (*or* that would be) going too far; **III.** *v/refl.*: ***sich ~*** conduct o.s., *esp. ped.* behave (o.s.); ***sich gut ~*** behave; **'füh·rend** *adj.* leading, *a.* senior, top-ranking *politician etc.*, *a.* prominent *artist etc.*; ***~er Politiker (Unternehmer)*** *a.* political (business) leader; ***~e Position*** senior position; ***~ sein*** lead, rank in first place; ***e-e ~e Rolle spielen*** play a key role, hold a key position

Füh·rer ['fy:rɐ] *m* (-s; -) **1.** a) leader, ⚔ *a.* commander, head, *sport*: captain, b) guide; **2.** *mot. etc.* driver; ✈ pilot; ⚙ operator; **3.** guide (***für*** *acc.*, ***durch*** *acc.* to), guidebook (on); **4.** *hist.* ***der ~*** the Fuehrer; **~haus** *n mot.* driver's cab

'füh·rer·los *adj.* without a leader (*or* guide *etc.*), leaderless; *mot.* driverless; ✈ unpiloted, pilotless

'Füh·rer|na,tur *f*, **~per,sön·lich·keit** *f* born (*or* natural) leader; **~rol·le** *f* role of (a) leader

'Füh·rer·schaft *f* (-; *no pl.*) leadership; *coll. the* leaders *pl.*

'Füh·rer·schein *m mot.* driving licence, *Am.* driver's license; ***s-n ~ machen*** take (*or* do) one's driving test; **~ent·zug** *m* suspension of one's driving licence (*Am.* driver's license); ***zu e-m Jahr ~ verurteilt werden*** be banned from driving for a year

'Füh·rer·stel·lung *f* (position of) leadership

Fuhr|mann ['fu:ɐ-] *m* (-[e]s; -leute) **1.** carter; **2.** coachman; **3.** *ast.* Auriga, *the* Charioteer; **~park** *m* car pool, fleet (of cars *or* vehicles)

Füh·rung ['fy:rʊŋ] *f* (-; -en) **1.** *no pl.* a) guidance, direction; *pol. etc.* leadership; ⚔ command; ✝ management; ⚙ guiding, b) *the* leaders *pl.*; ***unter der ~ von*** headed by, under the direction (*or* leadership, ⚔ command) of; ***die ~ übernehmen*** take charge, take over; → *a.* **5**; ***die ~ an sich reißen*** seize control; **2.** (guided) tour; **3.** *no pl.* conduct *of negotiations etc.*; **4.** *no pl.* conduct, behavio(u)r; ***gute ~*** good conduct; **5.** *no pl. sport and fig.*: lead; ***in ~ gehen, die ~ übernehmen*** take the lead; ***in ~ sein*** be in the lead; ***in ~ bleiben*** keep the lead, stay in front; ***er hat sie in ~ gebracht*** he's given them the lead; **6.** *no pl.* use *of a title*

'Füh·rungs|an·spruch *m* claim to (the) leadership; ***s-n ~ anmelden*** make a bid for (the) leadership; **~auf·ga·be** *f* executive function; **~ei·gen·schaf·ten** *pl.* leadership qualities; **~gre·mi·um** *n*, **~grup·pe** *f* management committee; **~kampf** *m* struggle for (the) leadership; **~kraft** *f* ✝ executive; *pl.* executive personnel (*pl.*); *pl. pol.* leaders; **~krei·se** *pl.* leadership (ranks) *sg.*; ***in ~n*** among the leadership; **~kri·se** *f* crisis of leadership; **~nach·wuchs** *m pol.* future leaders *pl.*; ✝ future executives *pl.*; **~nut** *f* ⚙ guide slot; **~po·si·ti,on** *f* **1.** position of leadership; **2.** top position; **~ril·le** *f* ⚙ groove; **~rol·le** *f* **1.** leading role; **2.** leadership role; **~schicht** *f* ruling class(es *pl.*); **~schie·ne** *f* ⚙ guide rail; **~schwä·che** *f* weak leadership; **~spit·ze** *f* top echelons *pl.* (✝ management, executives *pl.*); **~stab** *m* ⚔ command; ✝ top executive team; **~stil** *m* style of leadership; ✝ managerial style; **~struk,tur** *f* ✝ management structure; **~tref·fer** *m sport*: ***den ~ erzielen*** put one's team into the lead; **~wech·sel** *m* change in leadership; **~zeug·nis** *n* (*a.* ***polizeiliches ~***) certificate of (good) conduct (*or* no conviction)

'Fuhr|un·ter,neh·men *n* haulage company; **~un·ter,neh·mer** *m* haulage contractor

'Fuhr·werk *n* (-[e]s; -e) horsedrawn vehicle, carriage; cart; **'fuhr·wer·ken** F *v/i.* (h) bustle (*or* bang) around; ***mit et. ~*** brandish s.th.

Fül·le ['fʏlə] *f* (-; *no pl.*) fullness (*a. fig.*); wealth, abundance; stoutness; richness, sonority; ***Essen*** *etc.* ***war in ~ vorhanden*** there was plenty of food *etc.*; ***zur ~ neigen*** be a bit on the stout side; → ***Hülle***

fül·len ['fʏlən] (h) **I.** *v/t.* fill (*a. tooth*); *gastr.* stuff; ***den Eimer mit Wasser ~*** fill the bucket up with water; ***in Flaschen ~*** bottle; ***Wein in Fässer ~*** fill wine into casks; ***bis zum Rand ~*** fill (right) up; ***der Bericht füllte 15 Seiten*** the report took up 15 pages; → ***gefüllt***; **II.** *v/refl.*: ***sich ~*** fill; ***der Saal füllte sich schnell*** the hall filled up very quickly

Fül·len ['fʏlən] *n* (-s; -) *zo.* foal; colt; filly

Fül·ler ['fʏlɐ] *m* (-s; -) (fountain) pen

'Füll(fe·der)hal·ter *m* fountain pen

'Füll·horn *n* horn of plenty, cornucopia

fül·lig ['fʏlɪç] *adj.* full, *a.* ample *figure*; stout *person*

'Füll|mas·se *f* filling compound; **~ma·te·ri,al** *n*, **~mit·tel** *n* filler

Füll·sel ['fʏlzəl] *n* (-s; -) filler; *a. fig.* padding; *gastr.* filling, stuffing

Fül·lung ['fʏlʊŋ] *f* (-; -en) **1.** filling (*a.* ⚕); *gastr.* stuffing; cent|re (*Am.* -er) *of chocolate etc.*; **2.** padding

'Füll·wort *n* (-[e]s; ¨er) filler

ful·mi·nant [fʊlmi'nant] *adj.* brilliant

Fum·mel ['fʊməl] F *contp. m* (-s; -) F rag

fum·meln ['fʊməln] F *v/i.* (h) **1.** fiddle around (***an*** *dat.* with); fumble around; **2.** F grope; ***mit j-m ~*** *sl.* feel s.o. up

Fund [fʊnt] *m* (-[e]s; -e ['fʊndə]) a) finding, discovery, b) find; ***e-n ~ machen*** make a find (*or* discovery)

Fun·da·ment [fʊnda'mɛnt] *n* (-[e]s; -e) △ foundations *pl.*; *fig.* foundation, basis; ***bis auf die ~e zerstört werden*** be razed (to the ground); *fig.* ***das ~ legen für*** *acc.* lay the foundations for (*or* of); ***ein gutes ~*** a solid foundation (*or* grounding); ***auf e-m festen ~ stehen*** be on a firm footing; ***in s-n ~en erschüttern*** destroy the (very) foundations *or* roots of

fun·da·men·tal [fʊndamɛn'ta:l] **I.** *adj.* fundamental, basic; ***~er Irrtum*** grave mistake; ***von ~er Bedeutung*** crucially important; **II.** *adv.*: ***~ voneinander abweichen*** be fundamentally different (*or* opposed); **Fun·da·men·ta·lis·mus** [fʊndamɛnta'lɪsmʊs] *m* (-; *no pl.*) fundamentalism; **Fun·da·men·ta·list** [fʊndamɛnta'lɪst] *m* (-en; -en) fundamentalist; **fun·da·men·ta·li·stisch** [fʊndamɛnta'lɪstɪʃ] *adj.* fundamentalist

fun·da·men·tie·ren [fʊndamɛn'ti:rən] *v/t.* (h) lay the foundations of

'Fund|bü,ro *n* lost property office; *sign*: *a.* lost and found; **~ge·gen·stand** *m* → ***Fundsache***; **~gru·be** *fig. f* goldmine; treasure chest; ✝ bargain offers *pl.*

Fun·di ['fʊndi] F *m* (-s; -s) *pol.* radical Green

fun·die·ren [fʊn'di:rən] *v/t.* (h) **1.** substantiate; **2.** ✝ fund, consolidate; **fundiert** [fʊn'di:ɐt] *adj.* **1.** sound *knowledge etc.*; well-founded, well-grounded; ***wissenschaftlich ~*** well-founded, backed up by research; **2.** ✝ funded; ***(gut) ~*** solid, sound *business etc.*

fün·dig ['fʏndɪç] *adj.*: ***~ werden*** strike gold (*or* oil *etc.*), *a. w.s.* make a strike, strike it lucky; *w.s. a.* find s.th.; ***bist du ~ geworden?*** did you find anything?, did you have any luck?

'Fund|ort *m* place where s.th. was found; *arch(a)eology etc.*: site of the discovery *etc.*; **~sa·che** *f* lost article, piece of lost property; *pl.* lost property *sg.*; **~stät·te** *f* *arch(a)eology*: site (of the discovery); **~un·ter,schla·gung** *f* unlawful keeping of lost property

Fun·dus ['fʊndʊs] *m* (-; -) **1.** store *of knowledge etc.*; **2.** *thea.* general equipment

fünf [fʏnf] **I.** *adj.* five; *fig.* ***~ vor zwölf*** at the eleventh hour; ***es ist ~ vor zwölf*** time is running out fast, it's almost high noon; ***s-e ~ Sinne beisammenhaben (zusammennehmen)*** have one's wits about one (collect *or* gather one's wits); ***alle ~e gerade sein lassen*** stretch a point; ***du mußt ~e gerade sein lassen*** you mustn't be so critical, you must take a more relaxed view of things; **II.** ♀ *f* (-; -en) five; *ped.* E; *bus etc.* (number) five; *ped.* ***e-e ~ schreiben*** get an E

'Fünf·ak·ter [-aktɐ] *m* (-s; -) *thea.* five-act play

'fünf·bän·dig [-bɛndɪç] *adj.* five-volume ..., in five volumes

'Fünf·eck *n* pentagon; **'fünf·eckig** *adj.* pentagonal

Fün·fer ['fʏnfɐ] F *m* (-s; -) **1.** five-pfennig piece; **2.** → ***Fünf***

fün·fer·lei ['fʏnfɐlaɪ] *adj.* five (different) kinds of; *su.* five things

'fünf·fach *adj.* fivefold; ***die ~e Menge*** five times the amount; ***~er Sieger*** five-time winner (*or* champion)

'fünf'hun·dert *adj.* five hundred

Fünf'jah·res·plan *m* five-year plan

'fünf·jäh·rig [-jɛ:rɪç] *adj.* **1.** five-year-old ...; **2.** five-year ...; ***ein ~es ...*** *a.* five years of ...; **'Fünf·jäh·ri·ge** [-jɛ:rɪgə] *m, f* (-n; -n) five-year-old

'Fünf·kampf *m* pentathlon

'fünf|ka·rä·tig [-karɛ:tɪç] *adj.* five-carat

...; **~köp·fig** [-kœpfɪç] *adj. family etc.* of five; **~e Delegation** *a.* five-member (*or* five-man) delegation
Fünf·lin·ge [ˈfʏnflɪŋə] *pl.* quintuplets, F quins
ˈfünf·mal *adv.* five times
Fünfˈmark·stück *n* five-mark piece
Fünf·proˈzent|hür·de *f parl.* five per cent (*or* percent) hurdle (*or* threshold); **~klau·sel** *f* five per cent (*or* percent) clause
ˈfünf·sei·tig [-zaɪtɪç] *adj.* pentagonal
ˈfünf·stel·lig [-ʃtɛlɪç] *adj.* five-digit *figure etc.*
Fünfˈster·ne·hoˌtel *n* five-star hotel
ˈfünf|stöckig [-ʃtœkɪç] (*sep.* -k·k-) *adj.* five-stor(e)y ...; **~stün·dig** [-ʃtʏndɪç] *adj.* five-hour(-long) ...
fünft [fʏnft] **I.** *adj.* fifth; **~es Kapitel** chapter five; **am ~en Mai** on the fifth of May, on May the fifth; **5. Mai** 5th May, May 5(th); → **Kolonne, Rad; II.** *adv.*: **wir waren zu ~** there were five of us; **wir gingen zu ~ hin** five of us went there
Fünfˈta·ge·wo·che *f* five-day working week
ˈfünf·tä·gig [-tɛːgɪç] *adj.* **1.** five-day(-long) ...; **2.** five-day-old
ˈfünfˈtau·send *adj.* five thousand
Fünf·te [ˈfʏnftə] *m, f* (-n; -n) (the) fifth; **er war (wurde) ~r** he was (came) fifth; **Georg V.** George V (= George the Fifth); **heute ist der ~** it's the fifth today
ˈfünf·tei·lig [-taɪlɪç] *adj.* five-part ..., in five parts
Fünf·tel [ˈfʏnftəl] *n* (-s; -) fifth
fünf·tens [ˈfʏnftəns] *adv.* fifth(ly), five, in fifth place
ˈFünf·uhr·tee *m* five-o'clock tea
ˈfünf·wö·chig [-vœçɪç] *adj.* **1.** five-week ...; **2.** five-week-old ...
ˈfünf·zehn *adj.* fifteen; **ˈfünf·zehnt** *adj.* fifteenth; **ˈFünf·zehn·tel** *n* (-s; -) fifteenth (part)
fünf·zig [ˈfʏnftsɪç] *adj.* fifty; **in den ~er Jahren** in the fifties; **sie ist in den Ձern** she's in her fifties; **Fünf·zi·ger**[1] [ˈfʏnftsɪgɐ] *m* (-s; -) fifty-mark note; **ˈFünf·zi·ger**[2] *m* (-s; -) man in his fifties; F fiftysomething; **Fünf·zi·ge·rin** [ˈfʏnftsɪgərɪn] *f* (-; -nen) woman in her fities, F fiftysomething; **Fünf·zigˈmark·schein** *m* fifty-mark note (*Am.* bill); **ˈfünf·zigst** *adj.* fiftieth; **er hat heute s-n Ձen** he's fifty today, it's his fiftieth birthday today
fun·gie·ren [fʊŋˈgiːrən] *v/i.* (h): **~ als** act as, serve as, function as
Funk [fʊŋk] *m* (-s; *no pl.*) radio; → *a.* **Radio, Rundfunk; ~amaˌteur** *m* radio ham; **~auf·klä·rung** *f* signal intelligence; **~aus·stel·lung** *f* radio (and TV) show; **~be·ar·bei·tung** *f* radio adaptation, adaptation for radio; **~bild** *n* radio picture
Fünk·chen [ˈfʏŋkçən] *fig. n* (-s; -) scrap, *a.* grain *of truth*, flicker *of hope*; **da ist kein ~ Wahrheit dran** there's not a scrap (*or* grain) of truth in it
Fun·ke [ˈfʊŋkə] *m* (-n; -n) spark, flash; *fig.* scrap, *a.* grain *of truth*, flicker *of hope*; **~n sprühen** send out sparks; **~n sprühten aus** *dat.* sparks were flying from (*or* out of); *fig.* **nicht e-n ~n (von** *dat.*) not a scrap (*or* bit) of; **der ~ ist übergesprungen** we (*or* they) clicked; **sie arbeiteten, daß die ~n flogen** they worked so fast you could see the sparks fly
fun·keln [ˈfʊŋkəln] *v/i.* (h) sparkle (*a. fig.*); glisten, glitter; *stars*: twinkle; *eyes*: flash
ˈfun·kelˈna·gelˈneu F *adj.* brand-new, F spanking new
ˈFunk·emp·fän·ger *m* radio receiver
fun·ken [ˈfʊŋkən] (h) **I.** *v/t.* send out, radio; **II.** F *fig. v/impers.*: **hat es bei ihm endlich gefunkt?** F has the penny finally dropped?; **es hat bei ihnen gefunkt** F they hit it off (from the word go), they clicked
Fun·ken [ˈfʊŋkən] *m* → **Funke; ~bil·dung** *f* sparking; **~flug** *m* flying sparks *pl.*; **~re·gen** *m* shower of sparks; **Ձsprü·hend** *adj.* **1. ~e Räder** wheels sending out sparks; **2.** *fig.* flashing *eyes*; heated *discussion*; scintillating *mind*; **~strecke** *f* spark gap
ˈfunk·ent·stört *adj.* suppressed; **ˈFunk·ent·stö·rung** *f* a) noise suppression, b) static screen
Fun·ker [ˈfʊŋkɐ] *m* (-s; -) radio operator
ˈFunk|ge·rät *n* transmitter; **~haus** *n* broadcasting studios *pl.*; **~kolˌleg** *n* educational broadcasts *pl.*, schools program(me)s *pl.*; **~konˌtakt** *m* radio contact; **~ haben** be in radio contact (**mit** *dat.* with); **~mel·dung** *f*, **~nach·richt** *f* radio message; **~of·fiˌzier** *m* signal officer; **~or·tung** *f* radio location; **~peil·ge·rät** *n* radio direction finder (*abbr.* RDF); **~pei·lung** *f* direction finding; **~ruf·emp·fän·ger** *m* bleeper; **~siˌgnal** *n* radio signal
ˈFunk·sprech|ge·rät *n* walkie-talkie; **~stun·de** *f* radio phone-in; **~ver·kehr** *m* radio telephony
ˈFunk|spruch *m* radio message; **~sta·tiˌon** *f*, **~stel·le** *f* radio station; **~stil·le** *f* radio silence, blackout; break in transmission; *fig.* silence; *fig.* **bei ihnen herrscht ~** they're not on speaking terms; **~stö·rung** *f* interference; jamming
ˈFunk·strei·fe *f* **1.** radio patrol; **2.** → **ˈFunk·strei·fen·wa·gen** *m* squad car
ˈFunk|ta·xi *n* radio cab; **~tech·nik** *f* radio engineering; **~tech·ni·ker** *m* radio engineer; **~te·leˌfon** *n* cellular phone
Funk·ti·on [fʊŋkˈtsi̯oːn] *f* (-; -en) **1.** function; ⚒ functioning; **außer ~** not working, not in operation, at a standstill; **außer ~ setzen** bring to a standstill; **in ~ treten** a) go into operation, b) take up one's duties, go into action; **dies hat die ~ zu** *inf.* this is supposed to *inf.*, this is for *ger.*; **was hat es für e-e ~?** what's it for?, what's it supposed to do?; **2.** position; **e-e hohe ~ ausüben** hold a key (*or* an important) position
funk·tio·nal [fʊŋktsi̯oˈnaːl] *adj.* functional; **Funk·tio·na·lis·mus** [fʊŋktsi̯onaˈlɪsmʊs] *m* (-; *no pl.*) functionalism
Funk·tio·när [fʊŋktsi̯oˈnɛːɐ] *m* (-s; -e) official; **hoher ~** top official, F top nob; **hohe ~e** *a.* (the) top brass
funk·tio·nell [fʊŋktsi̯oˈnɛl] *adj.* functional
funk·tio·nie·ren [fʊŋktsi̯oˈniːrən] *v/i.* (h) work, ⚙ *a.* function, be functioning; *der Apparat* **funktioniert nicht** doesn't work, is out of order; *fig.* **gut ~** go well
Funk·tiˈons|ab·lauf *m* operational sequence; **Ձfä·hig** *adj.* functioning, working, in working order; workable *system etc.*; **~stö·rung** *f* ⚒ malfunction; **~ta·ste** *f* function key
ˈFunk|turm *m* radio tower; **~ver·bin·dung** *f* radio contact; **~ver·kehr** *m* radio communication; **~wa·gen** *m* **1.** radio van; **2.** → **Funkstreifenwagen**
für [fyːɐ] **I.** *prp.* (*acc.*) a) for, *a.* in exchange (*or* return) for, *a.* in favo(u)r of, *a.* instead of, b) on behalf of *s.o.*; **Tag ~ Tag** day after day; **Schritt ~ Schritt** step by step; **~ mich** for my sake; **ich ~ m-e Person, ich ~ mein Teil** I myself; **~s erste** for the moment; **~ sich leben** live by o.s.; **er ist gern ~ sich (allein)** he likes to be on his own; **das ist e-e Sache ~ sich** a) that's another matter entirely, b) that's a different story; **das hat viel ~ sich** there's a lot to be said for it; **ich halte es ~ unklug** I don't think it's (*or* it would be) a good idea; **was ~ (ein)?** what (kind of)?; **II.** Ձ *n*: **das ~ und Wider** the pros and cons *pl.*
ˈFür·bit·te *f* intercession; **~ einlegen** intercede (**für** *acc.* for, on behalf of; **bei** *dat.* with); **Für·bit·ter** [ˈfyːɐbɪtɐ] *m* (-s; -) intercessor
Fur·che [ˈfʊrçə] *f* (-; -n) furrow (*a. anat. and fig.*); ⚙ groove; rut
Furcht [fʊrçt] *f* (-; *no pl.*) fear (**vor** *dat.* of), dread (of); **~ haben vor** *dat.* be afraid (*or* scared, frightened) of; **aus ~ vor** *dat.* because he's *etc.* afraid (*or* scared, frightened) of, for fear of *ger.*; **ohne ~ sein, keine ~ kennen** be fearless, know no fear; **j-m ~ einflößen** (*or* **einjagen**) frighten (*or* scare, terrify) s.o., put the fear of death into s.o.; **~ und Schrecken verbreiten** spread fear and terror, **in** *dat.*: *a.* terrorize; **zwischen ~ und Hoffnung schweben** be in a state of trepidation, live in fear and trepidation
ˈfurcht·bar I. *adj.* terrible, dreadful; **II.** *adv.* terribly, F *a.* dreadfully; **~ aufregend** really exciting; **~ nett** extremely nice; **das ist ~ nett von Ihnen** that's very kind of you; **es ist ~ einfach** F it's dead easy; **ich bin ~ erschrocken** I got such a (*or* a real) fright
ˈfurcht·ein·flö·ßend *adj.* frightening
fürch·ten [ˈfʏrçtən] (h) **I.** *v/t.* be afraid of, dread; **Gott ~** fear God; **ich fürchte, wir schaffen es nicht** I don't think we're (*or* I have a feeling we're not) going to make it; → **gefürchtet; II.** *v/i.*: **~ für** (*or* **um**) *acc.* fear for; **ich fürchte um sein Leben** I fear for his life; **III.** *v/refl.*: **sich ~** be frightened, be scared, be afraid (**vor** *dat.* of); **sich ~ vor** *dat.* be afraid of, dread; **sich (davor) ~ zu** *inf.* be afraid of *ger.*, be scared to *inf.*; **sich im Dunkeln ~** be afraid (*or* scared) of the dark; **IV.** Ձ *n* (-s): **j-n das ~ lehren** put the fear of God (*or* death) into s.o.; **da kann man das ~ lernen** it soon teaches you what fear is all about; **das ist ja zum ~** it's enough to frighten the life (*or* wits) out of you; **er sieht zum ~ aus** F he looks a (real) fright
fürch·ter·lich [ˈfʏrçtɐlɪç] *adj. and adv.* → **furchtbar**
ˈfurcht·er·re·gend *adj.* frightening, horrific
ˈfurcht·los *adj.* fearless, intrepid; **ˈFurcht·lo·sig·keit** *f* (-; *no pl.*) fearlessness
ˈfurcht·sam *adj.* timorous; **ˈFurcht·sam·keit** *f* (-; *no pl.*) timorousness
Fur·chung [ˈfʊrçʊŋ] *f* (-; -en) **1.** *biol.* cleavage; **2.** *geol.* striation
für·einˈan·der I. *adv.* for each other, for one another; **II.** Ձ *n* (-s; *no pl.*) concern for one another, mutual (care and) concern

Fu·rie ['fu:rĭə] *f* (-; -n) Fury; *fig.* virago; ***wie e-e ~*** like a madwoman

fu·ri·os [fu'rĭo:s] *adj.* a) passionate; rousing; brilliant, b) furious

Fur·nier [fʊr'ni:ɐ] *n* (-s; -e), **fur·nie·ren** [fʊr'ni:rən] *v/t.* (h) veneer

Fu·ro·re [fu'ro:rə] *f, n*: ***~ machen*** a) cause a sensation, cause (*or* create) quite a stir, b) be all the rage; ***er hat mit s-m Buch ~ gemacht*** his book caused quite a sensation (*or* stir)

'Für·sor·ge *f* (-; *no pl.*) care (***für*** *acc.* for), solicitude; ***ärztliche ~*** medical care; ***öffentliche ~*** public welfare; → ***Fürsorgeunterstützung; ~ein·rich·tung*** *f* welfare institution; ***~emp·fän·ger*** *m* social security beneficiary; ***~ sein*** be on social security

'Für·sor·ge·un·ter,stüt·zung *f* social security; ***von der ~ leben*** be (*or* live) on social security

für·sorg·lich ['fy:ɐzɔrklɪç] *adj.* thoughtful, considerate; solicitous

'Für·spra·che *f* (-; *no pl.*) intercession (***für*** *acc.* for, on behalf of; ***bei*** *dat.* with), plea; recommendation; mediation; ***für j-n ~ einlegen*** intercede on s.o.'s behalf, F put in a good word for s.o.; **'Für·spre·cher** *m* **1.** intercessor; mediator; **2.** *fig.* advocate

Fürst [fʏrst] *m* (-en; -en) prince (*a. fig.*); ruler; F ***leben wie ein ~*** live like a lord (*or* king); *bibl.* ***der ~ der Finsternis*** the Prince of Darkness

'Für·sten|ge·schlecht *n*, ***~haus*** *n* dynasty; ***~hof*** *m* royal court

'Für·sten·tum *n* (-s; -tümer [-ty:mɐ]) principality; ***das ~ Monaco*** the Principality of Monaco

'fürst·lich I. *adj.* princely; prince's ...; *fig.* splendid; lavish; sumptuous *meal*; generous *tip, salary etc.*, *a.* princely *sum*; **II.** *adv.*: ***~ leben*** live in grand style; ***j-n ~ belohnen*** reward s.o. royally; ***j-n ~ bewirten*** entertain s.o. lavishly, F lay on the works for s.o.

Furt [fʊrt] *f* (-; -en) ford

Fu·run·kel [fu'rʊŋkəl] *m, n* (-s; -) ⚕ boil

'Für·wort *n* (-[e]s; ⸚er) *ling.* pronoun

Furz [fʊrts] V *m* (-es; Fürze ['fʏrtsə]), **fur·zen** ['fʊrtsən] V *v/i.* (h) V fart

Fu·sel ['fu:zəl] F *m* (-s; -) F gutrot, rotgut

Fu·si·on [fu'zĭo:n] *f* (-; -en) **1.** ⚛ fusion; **2.** ✝ merger; amalgamation; takeover; **fu·sio·nie·ren** [fuzĭo'ni:rən] *v/i.* (h) ✝ merge; amalgamate

Fu·si'ons|ener,gie *f* fusion energy; ***~re,ak·tor*** *m* fusion reactor

Fuß [fu:s] *m* (-es; Füße ['fy:sə]) **1.** *anat.* foot (*pl.* feet); foot, bottom *of a page, mountain etc.*; base, pedestal *of a column etc.*; stem *of a glass*; stand *of a lamp etc.*; leg *of a table, chair etc.*; ***zu ~*** on foot; ***zu ~ gehen*** walk; ***zu ~ (bequem) erreichbar*** within (easy) walking distance; ***gut zu ~ sein*** be a good walker; ***bei ~!*** heel!; ***wir werden uns auf die Füße treten*** we'll be tripping over each other; ***(festen) ~ fassen*** get (*fig. a.* gain) a foothold, *fig. Sache*: *a.* catch on; ***auf dem ~e folgen*** *a. fig.* follow (hard) on the heels of; ***sich j-m zu Füßen werfen*** *a. fig.* throw o.s. at s.o.'s feet; *fig.* ***j-m zu Füßen liegen*** worship s.o.; ***wieder auf den Füßen sein*** be back on one's feet again; ***auf die Füße fallen*** fall on one's feet; ***auf freiem ~*** at large; ***j-n auf freien ~ setzen*** let s.o. go; ***auf eigenen Füßen stehen*** stand on one's own two feet; ***auf schwachen Füßen stehen*** stand on shaky ground; ***auf festen Füßen stehen*** be on a sound footing; ***mit beiden Füßen auf der Erde stehen*** have both feet firmly on the ground; ***auf großem ~ leben*** live in grand style (*or* on a grand scale); ***auf gutem (schlechtem) ~e stehen mit*** *dat.* be on good (bad) terms with; ***mit Füßen treten*** trample on; ***sein Glück mit Füßen treten*** cast away one's fortune; ***j-m auf die Füße treten*** tread on s.o.'s toes; ***kalte Füße bekommen*** get cold feet; ***rate mal, wer mir heute über die Füße gelaufen ist*** guess who I ran (*or* bumped) into today; F ***mein Taschenrechner hat Füße bekommen*** my calculator seems to have just walked off; → ***Grab, link*** 1; **2.** foot (= *30,48 cm*); ***zehn ~ lang*** ten feet long; ***ein zehn ~ langes Brett*** a ten-foot(-long) plank

'Fuß|ab·druck *m* footprint; ***~ab·strei·fer*** *m* doormat; ***~an·gel*** *f* mantrap; *fig.* trap; *fig.* ***j-m ~n legen*** set (up) traps for s.o.; ***~bad*** *n* footbath

'Fuß·ball *m* (-[e]s; ⸚e) **1.** *no pl.* football, *esp. Am.* soccer; ***amerikanischer ~*** American football, *Am.* football; **2.** football, *Am.* soccer ball; **'Fuß·ballän·der·spiel** (*sep.* -ll·l-) *n* international (football) match; **'Fuß·ball·bun·des·li·ga** *f* Bundesliga

'Fuß·bal·len *m anat.* ball of the (*or* one's) foot

Fuß·bal·ler ['fu:sbalɐ] F *m* (-s; -) footballer

'Fuß·ball|fan *m* football fan; ***~feld*** *n* football pitch; ***~klub*** *m* football club; ***~mann·schaft*** *f* football team; ***~na·tio,nal·mann·schaft*** *f* national football team (*or* side); ***~platz*** *m* football pitch; ***~pro·fi*** *m* professional football player; ***~schuh*** *m* football boot; ***~spiel*** *n* football match; ***~spie·ler*** *m* football player; ***~sta·di·on*** *n* football stadium; ***~star*** *m* football star; ***~team*** *n* football team; ***~to·to*** *m, n* football pools *pl.*, F *the* pools *pl.*; ***~trai·ner*** *m* football coach; ***~tur,nier*** *n* football tournament; ***~ver·band*** *m* football association; ***~ver·ein*** *m* football club; ***~welt·mei·ster*** *m* World Cup holders *pl.*; ***~welt·mei·ster·schaft*** *f* World Cup

'Fuß|bank *f* footstool; ***~be·klei·dung*** *f* socks and shoes *pl.*, footwear

'Fuß·bo·den *m* **1.** floor; **2.** → ***~belag*** *m* floor covering, flooring; ***~hei·zung*** *f* underfloor heating

'Fuß|breit *m*: ***er wollte keinen ~ weichen*** he refused to budge (*or* give) an inch; ***~brem·se*** *f* footbrake; ***~ei·sen*** *n* mantrap

Fus·sel ['fʊsəl] *f* (-; -n) (piece of) fluff; **fus·se·lig** ['fʊsəlɪç] *adj.* covered in fluff; F ***sich den Mund ~ reden*** talk till one is blue in the face; **'fus·seln** *v/i.* shed a lot of fluff, F mo(u)lt

fu·ßeln ['fu:səln], **fü·ßeln** ['fy:səln] F *v/i.* (h) F play footsie

fu·ßen ['fu:sən] *v/i.* (h): ***~ auf*** *dat.* be based (up)on, rest on

'Fuß·en·de *n* foot of the bed, bottom (of the bed)

'Fuß·fall *m* prostration; ***e-n ~ vor j-m tun*** throw o.s. at s.o.'s feet; **'fuß·fäl·lig** *fig. adv.* on bended knee

'Fuß·feh·ler *m sport*: foot fault

Fuß·gän·ger ['fu:sgɛŋɐ] *m* (-s; -) pedestrian; ***~am·pel*** *f* pedestrian lights *pl.*; ***~brücke*** *f* footbridge; ***~strom*** *m* stream of pedestrians; ***~über,füh·rung*** *f* (pedestrian) overpass; footbridge; ***~,über·gang*** *m*, ***~,über·weg*** *m* pedestrian crossing; ***~un·ter,füh·rung*** *f* (pedestrian) underpass, *Brit. a.* subway; ***~zo·ne*** *f* pedestrian precinct (*Am.* mall)

'Fuß|ge·her *Austrian m* pedestrian; ***~ge·lenk*** *n* ankle; ***~he·bel*** *m* pedal; **≈hoch** *adj.* ankle-deep; **≈kalt** *adj.*: ***dieses Zimmer ist ~*** I'm always cold around the feet in this room; ***~knö·chel*** *m* ankle; **≈krank** *adj.* **1.** footsore; **2.** ***~ sein*** have a foot disease; ***~lei·ste*** *f* skirting board

Füß·ling ['fy:slɪŋ] *m* (-s; -e) foot

'Fuß|marsch *m* (long) walk; ⚔ march; ***wir haben noch e-n langen ~ vor uns*** we've still got a long trek ahead; ***es ist ein ~ von drei Stunden*** it's a three-hour walk, it's three hours on foot; ***~mat·te*** *f* doormat; *mot.* car rug; ***~no·te*** *f* footnote; ***~pfad*** *m* footpath; ***~pfle·ge*** *f* pedicure, chiropody; care of the feet; ***~pfle·ger*** *m* pedicurist, *esp. Brit.* chiropodist; ***~pilz*** *m* ⚕ athlete's foot; ***~pu·der*** *m* foot powder; ***~punkt*** *m* ⩘ foot; *ast.* nadir; ***~ra·ste*** *f* footrest; ***~sack*** *m* foot muff; ***~schal·ter*** *m* pedal switch; ***~sche·mel*** *m* footstool; ***~schweiß*** *m usu.* sweaty feet *pl.*; ***~soh·le*** *f* sole (of the *or* one's foot); ***~sol,dat*** *m* foot soldier, infantryman; ***~spann*** *m* instep; ***~spit·ze*** *f*: ***auf den ~n gehen*** (walk on) tiptoe; ***auf den ~n stehen*** stand on tiptoe; ***~spray*** *m, n* foot spray; ***~sprung*** *m*: ***e-n ~ machen*** jump in feet first; ***~spur*** *f* footprint; track; ***~stap·fe*** *f* footstep; *fig.* ***in j-s ~n treten*** follow in s.o.'s footsteps; ***~stüt·ze*** *f* footrest; ⚕ arch support; **≈tief** *adj.* ankle-deep; ***~tritt*** *m* **1.** footstep, footfall; **2.** footprint; **3.** kick; ***j-m e-n ~ geben (or versetzen)*** give s.o. a kick, kick s.o.; *fig.* ***e-n ~ kriegen (or bekommen)*** F get the boot, be kicked (F turfed) out; ***~volk*** *n* **1.** ⚔ infantry; **2.** *fig.* rank and file *of a party etc.*; ***~wan·de·rung*** *f* hike, walking tour; ***~wa·schung*** *f* foot washing; ***~weg*** *m* **1.** footpath; **2.** ***ein ~ von einer Stunde*** an hour's walk, an hour on foot; **≈wund** *adj.* footsore; ***~wur·zel*** *f* tarsus

futsch [fʊtʃ] F *adj.* broken, smashed (up), *sl.* bust, kaput; ruined; gone; ***alles ~!*** F forget it

Fut·ter¹ ['fʊtɐ] *n* (-s; *no pl.*) feed, fodder; F grub, *esp. Am.* F chow; F ***gut im ~ stehen*** be well-fed

'Fut·ter² *n* (-s; *no pl.*) lining; ⚠ casing; ⚙ lining

Fut·te·ral [fʊtə'ra:l] *n* (-s; -e) case; cover

'Fut·ter|beu·tel *m* nosebag; ***~getrei·de*** *n* fodder cereals *pl.*; ***~häus·chen*** *n* (covered) bird table; ***~krip·pe*** *f* manger; *fig.* gravy train; *fig.* ***an der ~ sitzen*** be doing nicely for o.s.; ***~mit·tel*** *n* feed; fodder

fut·tern ['fʊtɐn] F (h) **I.** *v/t.* F dig into, scoff; **II.** *v/i.* F scoff, feed one's face

füt·tern¹ ['fʏtɐn] *v/t.* (h) feed; F ***j-n ~ mit*** *dat.* feed s.o. on, F stuff s.o. with

'füt·tern² *v/t.* (h) line (*a.* ⚙); pad

'Fut·ter|napf *m* feeding bowl; ***~neid*** *fig. m* (professional *or* social) envy *or* jealousy; envy of the have-nots; ***~pflan·ze*** *f* forage plant (*or* crop); ***~sack*** *m* nosebag; ***~sei·de*** *f* lining silk; ***~stel·le*** *f* feeding ground; **~stoff** *m* lining (material); **~trog** *m* feeding trough

Füt·te·rung ['fʏtərʊŋ] *f* (-; -en) feeding; *in a zoo*: feeding time

'**Fut·ter·ver·wer·ter** F *m*: ***ein guter ~ sein*** a) get by on very little (food), b) F put it on (*or* put on the pounds) very quickly; ***ein schlechter ~ sein*** a) F put away huge amounts (of food), b) never put on weight

Fu·tur [fu'tuːɐ] *n* (-s; -e) *ling*. future (tense) (*a.* = ***erstes ~***); ***zweites ~*** future perfect; **Fu·tu·ris·mus** [futu'rɪsmʊs] *m* (-; *no pl.*) futurism; **Fu·tu·rist** [futu'rɪst] *m* (-en; -en), **fu·tu·ri·stisch** [futu'rɪstɪʃ] *adj*. futurist; **Fu·tu·ro·lo·ge** [futuro'loːgə] *m* (-n; -n) futurologist; **Fu·tu·ro·lo·gie** [futurolo'giː] *f* (-; *no pl.*) futorology

G

G, g [geː] *n* (-; -) G, g; ♪ G
gab [gaːp] *pret. of* ***geben***
Ga·bar·dine ['gabardiːn] *m* (-s; -), *f* (-; -) gabardine
Ga·be ['gaːbə] *f* (-; -n) **1.** contribution (***an*** *acc.* to); donation; offering; gift, present; ***um e-e milde ~ bitten*** ask for alms; **2.** *fig.* gift, talent; F knack; ***die ~ haben zu*** *inf.* have a gift for *ger.*, F *iro. a.* have a (great) knack of *ger.*, be (very) good at *ger.*; **3.** ⚕ dose
Ga·bel ['gaːbəl] *f* (-; -n) fork (*a.* ⚘, *mot.*); ⚒ pitchfork; *teleph.* cradle; shafts *pl.*; **∽för·mig** [-fœrmɪç] *adj.* forked
ga·beln ['gaːbəln] (h) **I.** *v/t.* fork *s.th.* up; F *fig.* ***sich*** *j-n or et.* ~ F pick up; **II.** *v/refl.*: ***sich*** ~ fork (off *or* out)
'**Ga·bel·stap·ler** [-ʃtaːplɐ] *m* (-s; -) fork-lift truck
Ga·be·lung ['gaːbəlʊŋ] *f* (-; -en) fork (in the road *etc.*)
'**Ga·bel·zin·ke** *f* prong, tine
'**Ga·ben·tisch** *m* table with (the) presents
gackern ['gakɐn] (*sep.* -k·k-) *v/i.* (h) cluck; *fig.* gabble
gaf·fen ['gafən] *v/i.* (h) F gawk, gawp
Gaf·fer ['gafɐ] *m* (-s; -) F nosy parker
Gag [gɛk] *m* (-s; -s) gag; F gimmick; *pl. a.* special effects; ***da hat er sich wieder e-n ~ einfallen lassen*** he always comes up with something new; F ***der ~ war ...*** the thing was ...
Ga·ge ['gaːʒə] *f* (-; -n) fee
gäh·nen ['gɛːnən] **I.** *v/i.* (h) yawn; **II.** ∽ *n* (-s) yawn(ing); '**gäh·nend** *fig. adj.* yawning *chasm etc.*; ***~e Leere*** gaping void
Ga·la ['gaːla] *f* (-; *no pl.*) gala dress; F ***sich in ~ werfen*** F put on one's glad rags; **~abend** *m* gala night; **~auf·füh·rung** *f* gala performance; **~di·ner** *n* gala dinner, (gala) banquet; **~emp·fang** *m* formal reception; **~kon͵zert** *n* gala concert
ga·lak·tisch [ga'laktɪʃ] *adj.* galactic
Ga·lan [ga'laːn] F *m* (-s; -e) F Romeo; ***sie hat sich mit ihrem ~ verabredet*** *a.* F she's got a date with her man
ga·lant [ga'lant] *adj.* gallant; ***~es Abenteuer*** amorous escapade; **Ga·lan·te·rie** [galantə'riː] *f* (-; -n) gallantry
'**Ga·la|uni͵form** *f* full dress; **~vor·stel·lung** *f* gala performance
Ga·la·xie [gala'ksiː] *f* (-; -n) galaxy
Ga·la·xis [ga'laksɪs] *f* (-; -xien [gala'ksiːən]) Galaxy, Milky Way
Ga·lee·re [ga'leːrə] *f* (-; -n) galley
Ga'lee·ren|skla·ve *m*, **~sträf·ling** *m* galley slave
Ga·le·rie [galə'riː] *f* (-; -n) △, *thea. etc.* gallery; art gallery; F *fig.* ***e-e ganze ~ von*** F a whole battery of; **Ga·le·rist** [galə'rɪst] *m* (-en; -en) (art) gallery owner, art dealer, gallerist; ***er ist ~*** *a.* he owns (*or* runs) an art gallery
Gal·gen ['galgən] *m* (-s; -) **1.** gallows *pl.*; ***an den ~ bringen*** (***kommen***) send to (end up on) the gallows; **2.** (microphone) boom; **~frist** *f* reprieve; ***ich gebe dir eine Woche ~*** I'll give you a week's grace; **~hu͵mor** *m* gallows humo(u)r; **~strick** F *m*, **~vo·gel** F *m* good-for-nothing
Ga·li·ons·fi͵gur [ga'lĭoːns-] *f* figurehead
gä·lisch ['gɛːlɪʃ] *adj.*, ∽ *n* (-en) *ling.* Gaelic
Gall·ap·fel ['gal-] *m* oak apple
Gal·le ['galə] *f* (-; -n) **1.** *anat.* gall bladder; **2.** *physiol.* bile, *esp. zo.*, ⚘ gall; *fig.* bile, venom; *fig.* ***ihm kam die ~ hoch, ihm lief die ~ über*** his blood was up, he was seething; → ***Gift***
Gall·ei·che ['gal-] *f* gall oak
'**gal·len'bit·ter** *adj.* acrid; *fig. a.* caustic
'**Gal·len·bla·se** *f* gall bladder; '**Gal·len·bla·sen·ent·zün·dung** *f* inflammation of the gall bladder, 📖 cholecystitis
'**Gal·len|gang** *m* bile duct; **~ko·lik** *f* bilious colic; **~lei·den** *n* gall bladder complaint
'**Gal·len·stein** *m* gallstone; **~ope·ra·ti͵on** *f* gallstone operation
'**Gal·len·we·ge** *pl.* biliary tract *sg.*
Gal·lert ['galɐt, ga'lɛrt] *n* (-[e]s; *no pl.*) jelly; **∽ar·tig** *adj.* gelatinous, jelly-like; ***~e Masse*** gelatinous (*or* jelly-like) substance *or* mass
Gal·li·er ['galĭɐ] *m* (-s; -) *hist.* Gaul
gal·lig ['galɪç] *adj.* acrid *taste etc.*; bilious *humo(u)r etc.*; caustic *remark etc.*; biting *satire etc.*
gal·lisch ['galɪʃ] *adj.* Gallic, Gaulic, Gaulish
Gal·li·zis·mus [gali'tsɪsmʊs] *m* (-; -men) Gallicism
Gal·lo·ne [ga'loːnə] *f* (-; -n) (*in GB a.* Imperial) gallon (= *4,54 l*), (*in the USA a.* US) gallon (= *3,78 l*)
Ga·lopp [ga'lɔp] *m* (-s; *no pl.*) gallop; ***leichter ~*** canter; ***im ~*** at a gallop; ***in*** (***den***) ***~ fallen*** break into a gallop; *fig.* ***im ~ ankommen*** come galloping along; F *fig.* ***et. im ~ erledigen*** race (*or* gallop) through s.th.; **ga·lop·pie·ren** [galɔ'piːrən] *v/i.* (h, sn) gallop; **ga·lop'pie·rend** *fig. adj.* ⚕ galloping *consumption etc.*; ☤ *a.* runaway *inflation etc.*
Ga·lo·schen [ga'lɔʃən] *pl.* galoshes, overshoes, *Am. a.* rubbers
galt [galt] *pret. of* ***gelten***
gal·va·nisch [gal'vaːnɪʃ] *adj.* galvanic(ally *adv.*); ***~es Element*** galvanic cell; **Gal·va·ni·seur** [galvani'zøːɐ] *m* (-s; -e [-'zøːrə]) electroplater; **gal·va·ni·sie·ren** [galvani'ziːrən] *v/t.* (h) galvanize (*a.* ⚕), ⚙ *a.* electroplate; **Gal·va·ni'sie·rung** *f* (-; *no pl.*) galvanization, electroplating; **Gal·va·no·me·ter** [galvano'meːtɐ] *n* (-s; -) galvanometer
Ga·ma·sche [ga'maʃə] *f* (-; -n) gaiter, legging; spat; F *fig.* ***er hat ~n vor ihr*** F she puts the wind up him
Gam·be ['gambə] *f* (-; -n) ♪ viola da gamba, viol
Ga·met [ga'meːt] *m* (-en; -en) *biol.* gamete
Gam·ma|strah·len ['gama-] *pl.* gamma rays; **~strah·lung** *f* gamma radiation
Gam·me·lei [gamə'laɪ] F *f* (-; *no pl.*) loafing (F bumming, *Am.* F goofing) around;
gam·me·lig ['gaməlɪç] F *adj.* **1.** mo(u)ldy, rotten; **2.** scruffy; **gam·meln** ['gaməln] F *v/i.* (h) loaf (F bum) around, *Am.* F goof off (*or* around); **Gamm·ler** ['gamlɐ] F *m* (-s; -) F layabout
Gams [gams] *dial. f* (-; -[en]) chamois; **~bart** *m* tuft of chamois hair, F *hum.* shaving brush
Gang [gaŋ] *m* (-[e]s; Gänge ['gɛŋə]) **1.** *no pl.* walk, way *s.o.* walks, gait; *a. zo. and fig.* pace; **2.** walk; errand; way; ***auf dem ~ zu*** *dat.* on the (*or* one's) way to; ***e-n ~ machen*** go (*or* be) on an errand; ***Gänge besorgen*** run errands; ***e-n kleinen ~ machen*** take (*or* go for) a short walk; ***e-n ~ machen zu*** go to; *fig.* ***letzter ~*** last journey; ***das war ein schwerer ~*** that wasn't easy, that was no easy business (*or* matter); ***ihr erster ~ war*** the first thing she did was (to) *inf.*; **3.** *no pl.* course *of business, of events etc.*; ***s-n ~ gehen*** take its course; ***s-n gewohnten ~ gehen*** go (*or* carry) on as usual; **4.** *no pl.* ⚙ running, working; action; *fig.* movement, progress; ***e-n leisen ~ haben*** run quietly; ***in ~ bringen*** (*or* ***setzen***) start, put into operation, *fig.* get *s.th.* going, set *s.th.* in train; ***in ~ sein*** be running, *fig.* be under way; ***außer ~ setzen*** put out of operation; *a. fig.* ***in ~ halten*** (***kommen***) keep (get) going; *fig.* ***in vollem ~e*** in full swing; ***im ~e sein*** be afoot; ***es ist etwas im ~e*** *a.* there's something (fishy) going on; **5.** corridor; passage(way); ✈ *etc.* aisle; △ arcade; ⚙ walkway; duct; **6.** *gastr.* course; ***Essen mit drei Gängen*** three-course meal; **7.** ⚙ speed; *mot.* gear; ***erster ~*** first (*or* bottom) gear; ***zweiter ~*** second gear; ***den ~ wechseln*** change (*esp. Am.* shift) gears; ***den ~ herausnehmen*** change (*esp. Am.* shift) into neutral; ***den zweiten ~ einschalten, in den zweiten ~ gehen*** (*or* ***schalten***) change (*esp. Am.* shift) into second (gear); ***durch die Gänge jagen*** run through the gears; **8.** *anat.* duct, canal, passage
gang *adj.*: ***~ und gäbe sein*** be quite usual, be the usual thing; ***das ist*** (***hier***) ***~ und gäbe*** *a.* that's nothing unusual (around here)
'**Gang·art** *f* gait, walk, *horse:* pace; *fig.* approach; ***e-e andere ~ anschlagen*** change the (*or* one's) pace, *a.* ***e-e här-***

tere ~ anschlagen force the pace, *fig.* take a tougher line (***gegenüber*** *dat.* against)

'**gang·bar** *adj.* passable; *fig.* practicable, feasible, workable

Gän·gel·band ['gɛŋəl-] *n fig.*: ***am ~ führen*** (*or* ***halten***) → **gän·geln** ['gɛŋəln] *v/t.* (h) lead *s.o.* by the nose; keep *s.o.* tied to one's apron strings

'**Gang·he·bel** *m* gearstick, gear lever, *Am.* gearshift

gän·gig ['gɛŋıç] *adj.* **1.** current *expression etc.*; (very) common *method etc.*; ***die ~e Meinung*** the conventional wisdom; **2.** ✝ sal(e)able, marketable; fast-selling; ***~st*** best-selling; '**Gän·gig·keit** *f* (-; *no pl.*) **1.** currency; commonness; **2.** ✝ sal(e)ability, marketability

Gan·gli·en|kno·ten ['gaŋliən-] *m anat.* gangliar node; **~sy,stem** *n* gangliar system; **~zel·le** *f* ganglion cell

Gan·gli·on ['gaŋliɔn] *n* (-s; -ien [-liən]) ganglion; *pl.* ganglia

'**Gang·schal·tung** *f mot.* gearshift(ing)

Gang·ster ['gɛŋstɐ] *m* (-s; -) gangster; **~ban·de** *f* gang of criminals; **~boß** *m* gang boss, gangland leader; **~braut** *f sl.* moll; **~film** *m* gangster film; **~held** *m* gangster hero; **~me,tho·den** *pl.*: ***das sind ja ~!*** that's (almost) criminal

'**Gang·ster·tum** *n* (-s; *no pl.*) world of gangsters

Gang·way ['gæŋweı] *f* ✈ steps *pl.*; ⚓ gangway

Ga·no·ve [ga'no:və] F *m* (-n; -n) F crook, hoodlum; ***kleiner ~*** small-time crook; **Ga'no·ven·spra·che** *f* underworld slang, thieves' cant

Gans [gans] *f* (-; Gänse ['gɛnzə]) goose (*pl.* geese); ***junge ~*** gosling; *fig.* ***dumme ~*** stupid thing (*or* girl)

Gän·se|blüm·chen ['gɛnzə-] *n* daisy; **~bra·ten** *m* roast goose; **~fe·der** *f* **1.** goose feather; **2.** (goose) quill; **~füß·chen** *pl.* quotation marks, inverted commas; **~haut** *fig. f* goose pimples *pl.*; ***ich bekam e-e ~*** it sent shivers down my spine, F it gave me the creeps; **~kiel** *m* (goose) quill; **~klein** *n gastr.* goose giblets *pl.*

'**Gän·se·le·ber** *f* goose liver; **~pa,ste·te** *f* pâté de foie gras

'**Gän·se·marsch** *m*: ***im ~*** in single (*esp. Am.* Indian) file

Gän·se·rich ['gɛnzərıç] *m* (-s; -e) gander

'**Gän·se·schmalz** *n* goose dripping

ganz [gants] **I.** *adj.* **1.** whole; complete; ***~ Deutschland*** the whole (*or* all) of Germany; ***die ~e Stadt*** the whole town; ***über ~ Amerika*** all over America; ***in der ~en Welt*** all over the world; ***~e Länge*** total (*or* overall) length; ***~e Zahl*** whole number; ♪ ***~e Note*** semibreve, *Am.* whole note; ♪ ***~e Pause*** semibreve (*Am.* whole note) rest; ***~e Wochen an e-r Sache arbeiten*** be working on s.th. for weeks on end; ***von ~em Herzen*** with all my *etc.* heart; ***m-e ~en Schuhe*** all (of) my shoes; ***den ~en Morgen (Tag)*** all morning (day); ***die ~e Nacht (hindurch)*** all night long; ***die ~e Zeit*** all the time, the whole time; ***den ~en Goethe*** the whole (*or* all) of Goethe; **2.** in one piece, intact; ***wieder ~ machen*** mend; ***die Tasse ist noch ~*** *a.* the cup didn't break; **3.** F ***~e zwei Stunden*** a) (for) two solid hours, b) just two hours; ***es hat ~e fünf Minuten gedauert*** it didn't take more than five minutes, it was all over in five minutes; ***er hat mir ~e zehn Mark gegeben*** all he gave me was ten marks; ***es hat mich ~e 50 Mark gekostet*** it only cost me 50 marks; **II.** *adv.* a) completely, totally, b) quite, F pretty, c) very, really; ***~ gut*** quite good, F not bad; ***es hat mir ~ gut gefallen*** I quite liked (*or* enjoyed) it; ***~ schön viel*** quite a lot, F a fair bit; ***~ schön dreckig*** F pretty dirty; ***~ und gar nicht*** not at all; ***das ist was ~ anderes*** that's a completely different matter; ***nicht ~ dasselbe*** not quite the same thing; ***~ gewiß*** certainly, (oh,) definitely; ***~ naß*** wet through; ***(ich bin) ~ Ihrer Meinung*** I quite agree; ***das hatte ich ~ vergessen*** I'd completely forgotten (about that); ***er ist ~ der Vater*** he's just like his father, F he's a chip off the old block; ***nicht ~ zehn*** just under ten, F coming up for ten; ***ich würde es ~ gern machen, aber*** I'd like to, but; ***~ besonders, weil*** (e)specially since; ***im großen (und) ~en*** on the whole, all in all

'**Ganz|auf·nah·me** *f*, **~bild** *n* full-length portrait

Gan·ze ['gantsə] *n* (-n; *no pl.*) whole; total (amount); entirety; ***einheitliches ~s*** integral whole; ***das ~*** the whole thing; ***et. als ~s betrachten*** look at s.th. as a whole; ***aufs (große) ~ gesehen*** seen (*or* viewed) as a whole, all in all; ***aufs ~ gehen*** go all out, F go the whole hog; ***jetzt geht's ums ~*** it's all or nothing now

Gän·ze ['gɛntsə] *f*: ***zur ~*** completely, in full; ***in s-r ~*** in its entirety

'**Ganz·fo·to** *n* full-length portrait

'**Ganz·heit** *f* (-; *no pl.*) whole; ***in s-r ~*** as a whole, in its entirety; '**ganz·heit·lich I.** *adj.* comprehensive, all-embracing; *phls., psych.,* ⚕ *etc.* holistic; **II.** *adv.* comprehensively; *phls.,* ⚕ *etc.* holistically; ***~ betrachtet*** seen as a whole (*or* in its entirety)

'**Ganz·heits|me·di,zin** *f* holistic medicine; **~me,tho·de** *f* **1.** holistic method; **2.** *ped.* integrated curriculum; **~psy·cho·lo,gie** *f* holistic psychology; **~,un·ter·richt** *m ped.* **1.** integrated curriculum; **2.** → ***Ganzwortmethode***

'**ganz·jäh·rig** [-jɛ:rıç] **I.** *adj.* all-year ...; all-season *oil etc.*; **II.** *adv.* all year round

'**Ganz·kör·per·be·strah·lung** *f* whole body dose (of radiation)

'**Ganz·le·der** *n* (full) leather; ***in ~*** leatherbound; **~band** *m* leatherbound volume

'**Ganz·lei·nen** *n* full cloth (binding); ***in ~*** clothbound

gänz·lich ['gɛntslıç] **I.** *adj.* complete, total; **II.** *adv.* completely, totally, absolutely

'**Ganz|me,tall** *n* all-metal *construction etc.*; **~sei·de** *f* pure silk

'**ganz·sei·tig** [-zaıtıç] *adj.* full-page ...

'**ganz·tä·gig** [-tɛ:gıç] **I.** *adj.* all-day ...; full-time *employment etc.*; **II.** *adv.* all day, (for) the whole day; ***~ geöffnet*** open all day; ***~ beschäftigt sein*** have a full-time job

'**Ganz·tags|be·schäf·ti·gung** *f* full-time job; **~schu·le** *f* all-day school(ing)

'**Ganz·wort·me,tho·de** *f ped.* whole word method

'**ganz·zäh·lig** *adj.* ⅍ integer

gar [ga:ɐ] **I.** *adj. gastr.* done, cooked; ***nicht ~*** underdone; **II.** *adv.* even; perhaps; ***~ nicht*** not at all; ***~ nichts*** not a thing, nothing at all, absolutely nothing; ***~ keiner*** nobody at all; ***es hat ~ keinen Sinn*** it's no use (at all); ***es besteht ~ kein Zweifel*** there's no doubt whatsoever; ***~ nicht schlecht*** not bad at all; ***das ist ~ nichts gegen m-e Geschichte*** that's got nothing on my story; ***oder ~*** let alone; ***~ so*** so very; ***~ zu*** (a bit) too

Ga·ra·ge [ga'ra:ʒə] *f* (-; -n) garage

Ga'ra·gen|ein·fahrt *f* garage entrance; **~tor** *n* garage door

Ga·rant [ga'rant] *m* (-en; -en) guarantor

Ga·ran·tie [garan'ti:] *f* (-; -n) guarantee; ***es hat ein Jahr ~*** it's got a year's (*or* a one-year) guarantee; *fig.* ***dafür kann ich keine ~ übernehmen*** I can't make any guarantees; F ***er fällt unter ~ durch*** he's bound to fail, F he's just got to fail, there's no way he's going to pass; F ***sie hat's unter ~ vergessen*** she's bound to have forgotten, F I bet (you any money) she's forgotten; **~an·spruch** *m* ⚖ warranty claim; **~be·din·gun·gen** *pl.* terms of a (*or* the) guarantee; **~frist** *f* guarantee period

ga·ran·tie·ren [garan'ti:rən] *v/t.* (h) (*and v/i.* ***für*** *et.* ~) guarantee (*a. fig.*); ***garantiert echt*** guaranteed genuine; F ***sie kommt garantiert nicht*** F I bet (you) she won't come

Ga·ran'tie|schein *m* guarantee; **~zeit** *f* guarantee (period); ***die ~ ist abgelaufen*** the guarantee has run out

Gar·aus ['ga:ɐ?aʊs] *m*: ***j-m den ~ machen*** F finish (*or* bump) s.o. off; ***e-r Sache den ~ machen*** put paid to s.th.

Gar·be ['garbə] *f* (-; -n) 🌾 sheaf; ***in ~n binden*** bundle, tie up into sheaves

Gär·bot·tich ['gɛ:ɐ-] *m* fermenting vat

Gar·de ['gardə] *f* (-; -n) ⚔ *the* guards *pl.*; *fig.* ***er ist noch von der alten ~*** he's still one of the old school

Gar·de·nie [gar'de:nĭə] *f* (-; -n) ⚘ gardenia

'**Gar·de|of·fi,zier** *m* guards officer; **~re·gi,ment** *n* guards regiment

Gar·de·ro·be [gardə'ro:bə] *f* (-; -n) **1.** a) cloakroom, *Am. a.* checkroom; *thea. etc.* dressing room, b) coatrack, hall stand; ***et. an der ~ abgeben*** leave s.th. in the cloakroom (*Am.* checkroom); **2.** *no pl.* a) clothes *pl.*, wardrobe, b) hats and coats *pl.*; ***e-e große ~ haben*** have a lot of clothes (*or* a large wardrobe); ***für ~ wird nicht gehaftet*** we regret that the management cannot accept responsibility for losses due to theft

Gar·de'ro·ben|frau *f* cloakroom (*Am.* checkroom) attendant; **~mar·ke** *f*, **~num·mer** *f* cloakroom ticket, *Am.* check; **~stän·der** *m* coatrack, hall stand

Gar·de·ro·bie·re [gardəro'bĭe:rə] *f* (-; -n) → ***Garderobenfrau***

Gar·di·ne [gar'di:nə] *f* (-; -n) (net) curtain; *fig.* ***hinter schwedischen ~n*** behind bars; **Gar'di·nen·pre·digt** F *f* lecture, dressing down

Gar·dist [gar'dıst] *m* (-en; -en) guardsman

ga·ren ['ga:rən] *v/t.* (h) (*a. v/i.* ***~ lassen***) *gastr.* cook slowly

gä·ren ['gɛ:rən] *v/i.* (***gärte/gor, gegärt/gegoren, h u. sn***) ferment (*a.* ***~ lassen***); *fig.* be seething, fester; ***es gärte in ihm*** he was seething with hatred (*or* rage *etc.*); ***der Aufruhr gärt im Lande*** the country is seething with unrest (*or* revolt); ***es gärt im Volk*** there's growing unrest among the people

Gär·mit·tel ['gɛ:ɐ-] *n* ferment

Garn [garn] *n* (-[e]s; -e) thread; cotton; *fig.* ***(j-m) ins ~ gehen*** walk into the (s.o.'s) trap; ***ein ~ spinnen*** spin a yarn
Gar·ne·le [gar'ne:lə] *f* (-; -n) shrimp (*Am. a. pl.*), prawn
gar·ni [gar'ni:] *adj.* → ***Hotel***
gar·nie·ren [gar'ni:rən] *v/t.* (h) decorate; trim *a hat etc.*; *gastr.* garnish; **Gar'nie·rung** *f* (-; -en) decoration; trimmings *pl.*; *gastr.* garnish(ing)
Gar·ni·son [garni'zo:n] *f* (-; -en) garrison; **Gar·ni'sons·stadt** *f* garrison town
Gar·ni·tur [garni'tu:ɐ] *f* (-; -en) **1.** set; matching underwear; **2.** ⚔ full uniform; **3.** trimming(s *pl.*); **4.** *fig.* ***erste ~*** top rank(s), F top notcher(s); ***zweite (dritte) ~*** second- (third-)rater(s); ***Solisten der ersten ~*** top-class (F top-notch) soloists
'**Garn|knäu·el** *m, n* ball of thread; **~rol·le** *f* reel (of thread *or* cotton); **~spu·le** *f* spool, bobbin
Gär·pro͵zeß ['gɛ:ɐ-] *m* fermentation process, (process of) fermentation
gar·stig *adj.* nasty
Gär·stoff ['gɛ:ɐ-] *m* ferment
Gar·ten ['gartən] *m* (-s; Gärten ['gɛrtən]) garden; ***botanischer ~*** botanical gardens; ***zoologischer ~*** zoological gardens, zoo; *bibl.* ***der ~ Eden*** the Garden of Eden; **~an·la·ge** *f* (public) gardens *pl.*; **~ar·beit** *f* gardening; **~ar·chi͵tekt** *m* landscape gardener; **~bank** *f* (-; ⸚e) garden bench
'**Gar·ten·bau** *m* (-[e]s; *no pl.*) horticulture; *in cpds.* horticultural *show etc.*; **~in·ge͵nieur** *m* horticulturist
'**Gar·ten|beet** *n* flower (*or* vegetable) bed; **~fest** *n* garden party; **~ge·rä·te** *pl.* gardening tools; **~ge·wächs** *n* **1.** garden plant; **2.** *pl.* garden produce *sg.*; **~haus** *n* summer house; **~kräu·ter** *pl.* pot herbs; **~kres·se** *f* garden cress; **~lau·be** *f* arbo(u)r, bower; summer house; **~lo͵kal** *n* → ***Gartenwirtschaft***; **~mö·bel** *pl.* garden furniture *sg.*; **~schau** *f* horticultural show; garden festival; **~sche·re** *f*: (***e-e ~*** a pair of) pruning shears *pl.*; **~schlauch** *m* garden hose; **~stadt** *f* garden city; **~stuhl** *m* garden chair; **~wirt·schaft** *f* **1.** outdoor café (*or* restaurant); **2.** beer garden; **~zaun** *m* garden fence; **~zwerg** *m* (garden) gnome; F *fig.* ugly little thing, F horrible little squirt
Gärt·ner ['gɛrtnɐ] *m* (-s; -) gardener; **Gärt·ne·rei** [gɛrtnə'raɪ] *f* (-; -en) **1.** *no pl.* gardening; **2.** market garden, *Am.* truck farm; **Gärt·ne·rin** ['gɛrtnərɪn] *f* (-; -nen) gardener; '**Gärt·ne·rin·art** *f*: *gastr.* ***nach ~*** à la jardinière; **gärt·nern** ['gɛrtnɐn] *v/i.* (h) do gardening, work in the garden
Gä·rung ['gɛ:rʊŋ] *f* (-; -en) fermentation; *fig.* (state of) unrest
'**Gä·rungs|al·ko·hol** *m* ethyl alcohol; **~mit·tel** *n* ferment; **~pro͵zeß** *m* fermentation process, (process of) fermentation; **~zeit** *f* fermentation period
'**Gar·zeit** *f* cooking time
Gas [ga:s] *n* (-es; -e ['ga:zə]) gas; *mot.* ***~ geben*** step on the accelerator (F *and Am.* gas); ***gib ~!*** F step on it!; ***~ wegnehmen*** throttle down (*Am.* back); **~ab·le·ser** *m* gasman; **~an·zün·der** *m* gas lighter; **2ar·tig** *adj.* gaseous; **~be·häl·ter** *m* gas tank; **2be·heizt** *adj.* gas-fired, gas-heated; **~e *Wohnung*** house (*or* flat, *Am.* apartment) with gas heating; **~be·leuch·tung** *f* gas light(ing); **~bren·ner** *m* gas burner; **2dicht** *adj.* gasproof; **~druck** *m* (-[e]s; ⸚e) gas pressure; **~ent·wick·lung** *f*, **~er·zeu·gung** *f* gas production; **~ex·plo·si͵on** *f* gas explosion; **~fern·lei·tung** *f* long-distance gas pipe; **~feue·rung** *f* gas firing; **~feu·er·zeug** *n* gas lighter; **~flam·me** *f* gas flame; burner; **~fla·sche** *f* gas cylinder; **2för·mig** [-fœrmɪç] *adj.* gaseous; **2ge·füllt** *adj.* gas-filled, filled with gas; **2ge·kühlt** *adj.* gas-cooled; **~ge·misch** *n* gas(eous) mixture; **~ge·ruch** *m* smell of gas; **~ge·win·nung** *f* gas production; **~hahn** *m* gas tap; ***den ~ aufdrehen (abdrehen)*** turn the gas on (off)
'**gas·hal·tig** [-haltɪç] *adj.* gaseous
'**Gas|hebel** *m mot.* **1.** throttle control; **2.** → ***Gaspedal***; **~heiz·ofen** *m* gas fire; **~hei·zung** *f* gas heating; **~herd** *m* gas cooker (*or* stove, *Am. a.* range); **~kam·mer** *f* gas chamber; **~ko·cher** *m* camping stove; **~lam·pe** *f* gas lamp, gaslight; **~lei·tung** *f* gas pipe; **~licht** *n* gaslight; **~-Luft-Ge·misch** *n mot.* explosive mixture; **~mann** *m* gasman; **~mas·ke** *f* gas mask; **~ofen** *m* gas stove
Ga·so·me·ter [gazo'me:tɐ] *m* (-s; -) gasometer
'**Gas|pe͵dal** *n mot.* accelerator (pedal), *Am. a.* gas pedal; **~pi͵sto·le** *f* tear-gas pistol; **~rech·nung** *f* gas bill; **~rohr** *n* gas pipe
Gäß·chen ['gɛsçən] *n* (-s; -) (little) alleyway, narrow lane
Gas·se ['gasə] *f* (-; -n) narrow street, (narrow) lane; path; ***sich e-e ~ bahnen durch*** *acc.* force one's way through; *dial.* ***auf der ~*** in (*or* on) the street; → ***Hansdampf***
Gas·si ['gasi] F: ***(mit dem Hund) ~ gehen*** take the dog out (for a walk), F go walkies (with the dog); ***komm, wir gehen jetzt ~!*** F time for walkies!
Gast [gast] *m* (-[e]s; Gäste ['gɛstə]) guest; visitor; customer; *thea.* guest (performer *or* artist); *pl. sport*: away (*or* visiting) team *sg.*, F visitors *pl.*; ***er ist ein seltener ~*** he's a stranger in these parts; ***Gäste haben*** have visitors (*or* company); ***oft Gäste haben*** a) often have people to stay, b) do a lot of entertaining; ***wir haben heute abend Gäste*** we're having guests (*or* visitors) tonight, we're having some people round tonight; ***heute abend haben wir X zu ~*** *TV etc.* our guest tonight is X; ***heute bist du mein ~*** it's all on me (today); ***bei j-m zu ~ sein*** be staying with s.o.; ***j-n zu ~ bitten*** invite s.o., *formal*: request the pleasure of s.o.'s company; ***nur für Gäste*** for patrons only; *Vorstellung etc.* ***für geladene Gäste*** for an invited audience; **~ar·bei·ter** *m* foreign (*or* immigrant) worker; **~di·ri͵gent** *m* guest conductor; **~do͵zent** *m* guest (*or* visiting) lecturer
Gä·ste|bett ['gɛstə-] *n* guest (*or* spare) bed; **~buch** *n* visitors' book; **~hand·tuch** *n* guest towel; **~haus** *n* guest house; **~-WC** *n* guest toilet; **~zim·mer** *n* guest room; *hotel etc.*: lounge
'**gast·frei** *adj.* hospitable; '**Gast·frei·heit** *f* (-; *no pl.*) hospitality
'**gast·freund·lich I.** *adj.* hospitable; very friendly towards visitors (*or* tourists); **II.** *adv.*: ***j-n ~ empfangen*** give s.o. a warm welcome; ***wir wurden sehr ~ behandelt*** we were made to feel at home, we were treated very kindly; '**Gast·freund·lich·keit** *f* (-; *no pl.*) hospitality
'**Gast·freund·schaft** *f* (-; *no pl.*) hospitality
'**Gast·ge·ber** *m* (-s; -) host; *pl. sport*: home team *sg.*; '**Gast·ge·be·rin** [-ge:bərɪn] *f* (-; -nen) hostess
'**Gast|ge·schenk** *n* present (for the host[ess]); **~haus** *n*, **~hof** *m* restaurant; guesthouse; **~hö·rer** *m univ.* auditor
ga·stie·ren [gas'ti:rən] *v/i.* (h) give a guest performance, *esp. Am.* guest (***in*** *dat.* in; ***an*** *dat.* at); *w.s.* perform, give a performance; ***in Japan ~*** tour Japan
'**Gast|kon͵zert** *n* guest concert (*or* performance); **~land** *n* (-[e]s; ⸚er) host country
'**gast·lich** *adj.* **1.** hospitable; **2.** inviting; cosy, *Am.* homey; '**Gast·lich·keit** *f* (-; *no pl.*) **1.** hospitality; **2.** cosiness, *Am.* homeyness
'**Gast|mahl** *n* banquet; **~mann·schaft** *f sport*: visiting team; **~pro͵fes·sor** *m* visiting professor; **~recht** *n* (right of) hospitality; **~red·ner** *m* guest speaker
ga·strisch ['gastrɪʃ] *adj.* ⚕ gastric
Ga·stri·tis [gas'tri:tɪs] *f* (-; -tiden [gastri'ti:dən]) ⚕ gastritis
Ga·stro·en·te·ri·tis [gastroʔɛnte'ri:tɪs] *f* ⚕ gastroenteritis
'**Gast·rol·le** *f thea.* guest part; *fig.* ***e-e ~ geben*** pay a flying visit (***in*** *dat.* to), put in a brief appearance (at, in)
Ga·stro·nom [gastro'no:m] *m* (-en; -en) restaurateur, restaurant chef; **Ga·stro·no·mie** [gastrono'mi:] *f* (-; *no pl.*) **1.** catering trade; **2.** gastronomy; **ga·stro·no·misch** [gastro'no:mɪʃ] *adj.* **1.** catering *business etc.*; **2.** gastronomic(al)
'**Gast·spiel** *n* guest performance; *sport*: away game; *fig.* → ***Gastrolle***; **~rei·se** *f* tour (***in*** *acc.* of)
'**Gast·stät·te** *f* restaurant; '**Gast·stät·ten·ge·wer·be** *n* catering trade
'**Gas·tur͵bi·ne** *f* gas turbine
'**Gast|vor·le·sung** *f* guest lecture; **~vor·stel·lung** *f thea.* guest performance; *fig.* → ***Gastrolle***; **~vor·trag** *m* guest lecture
'**Gast·wirt** *m* landlord, proprietor; '**Gast·wir·tin** *f* landlady, proprietress; '**Gast·wirt·schaft** *f* → ***Gasthaus***
'**Gas|uhr** *f* gas meter; **~ver·gif·tung** *f* gas poisoning; **~werk** *n* gasworks *pl.*; **~wol·ke** *f* cloud of gas; **~zäh·ler** *m* gas meter
Gatt [gat] *n* (-[e]s; -en, -s) ⚓ **1.** stern; **2.** hole; scupper (hole)
Gat·te ['gatə] *m* (-n; -n) husband; ⚖ spouse; '**Gat·ten·wahl** *f zo.* choosing (*or* choice of) a mate
Gat·ter ['gatɐ] *n* (-s; -) gate (*a. electron.*); fence; **~sä·ge** *f* framesaw; **~tor** *n*, **~tür** *f* gate; fence
Gat·tin ['gatɪn] *f* (-; -nen) wife; ⚖ spouse; ***Ihre ~*** your wife, *formal*: Mrs X
Gat·tung ['gatʊŋ] *f* (-; -en) **1.** *zo.*, ⚘ genus, family, species; **2.** *art*: form; *literature*: genre; **3.** kind, type
'**Gat·tungs|be·griff** *m* generic term; **~na·me** *m* generic name; *ling.* collective (*or* common) noun
Gau [gaʊ] *m* (-[e]s; -e) district
GAU [gaʊ] *m* (-[s]; -s) maximum credible accident, MCA
Gau·di ['gaʊdi] F *f* (-; *no pl.*): ***das war e-e ~!*** F it was a (real) scream (*Am. a.* gas); ***nur zur ~*** just for fun (F kicks), just for the fun of it
Gau·kel·bild ['gaʊkəl-] *n* illusion, mirage; delusion
Gau·ke·lei [gaʊkə'laɪ] *f* (-; -en) delusion;

tricks *pl.*; **gau·keln** ['gaʊkəln] *v/i.* (sn) flutter (around)
'**Gau·kel|spiel** *n* delusion; ***ein ~ treiben mit*** *dat.* delude; **~werk** *n* delusion
Gauk·ler ['gaʊklɐ] *m* (-s; -) a) tumbler, clown, b) charlatan
Gaul [gaʊl] *m* (-[e]s; Gäule ['gɔʏlə]) horse; *contp.* nag; ***alter ~*** (old) jade; *fig.* ***e-m geschenkten ~ sieht man nicht ins Maul*** never look a gift horse in the mouth
'**Gau·lei·ter** *m hist.* gauleiter
Gau·men ['gaʊmən] *m* (-s; -) *a. fig.* palate; *fig.* ***e-n feinen ~ haben*** have a fine palate (*or* tongue, sense of taste); → ***gespalten***; **~freu·den** *pl.* culinary delights; **~kit·zel** *m*: ***jetzt gibt es e-n kleinen ~*** now for something to tickle your palate (*or* tastebuds); **~laut** *m* palatal; **~plat·te** *f* ⚕ upper plate; **~zäpf·chen** *n* uvula
Gau·ner ['gaʊnɐ] *m* (-s; -) crook, swindler; rascal; ***diese ~!*** what a bunch of crooks!; **~ban·de** *f* gang of crooks
Gau·ne·rei [gaʊnə'raɪ] *f* (-; -en) swindling, swindle, F con game; '**gau·nerhaft** *adj.* F crooked; **gau·nern** ['gaʊnɐn] *v/i.* (h) swindle
'**Gau·ner|spra·che** *f* underworld jargon, thieves' cant; **~streich** *m*, **~stück** *n* swindle, F con
Ga·ze ['ga:zə] *f* (-; -n) gauze (*a.* ⚕); ✝ gossamer; cheesecloth; ⚙ wire gauze; **~bin·de** *f* gauze bandage
Ga·zel·le [ga'tsɛlə] *f* (-; -n) gazelle
ge'ach·tet *adj.* respected; ***bei allen ~ sein*** have everyone's respect
Ge'äch·te·te *m, f* (-n; -n) outlaw
Ge'äch·ze *n* (-s; *no pl.*) groaning, groans *pl.*
Ge·äder [gə'ʔɛ:dɐ] *n* (-s; -) **1.** blood vessels *pl.*; **2.** veins *pl.*, veined structure; *in wood*: grain; **ge'ädert** *adj.* veined; marbled; grained *wood*; veiny *cheese*
ge'ar·tet *adj.* disposed; ***anders ~ sein*** be different; ***besonders ~*** special *case*; ***so ~, daß*** the kind of person *etc.* that *would, will etc.*
Ge·äst [gə'ʔɛst] *n* (-[e]s; *no pl.*) branches *pl.*
Ge·bäck [gə'bɛk] *n* (-[e]s; *no pl.*) (fancy) cakes *pl.*; biscuits *pl.*, *Am.* cookies *pl.*
ge'backen *p.p. of* **backen**
ge'ba·det *adj.* → ***Schweiß***
Ge·bälk [gə'bɛlk] *n* (-[e]s; *no pl.*) beams *pl.*; entablature; *fig.* ***es knistert im ~*** there's trouble brewing (*or* in the air)
ge'ballt I. *adj.* clenched *fist*; *fig.* concentrated; compact; ***~er Angriff*** concerted attack; → ***Ladung*** 1 3; **II.** *adv.*: ***~ auftreten*** *problems etc.*: come all at once, come thick and fast
ge'bannt *adj. and adv.* (*a.* ***wie ~***) fascinated, spellbound; ***~ zusehen*** *a.* be riveted; ***~ vor dem Fernseher sitzen*** be glued to the TV; ***wie ~ stehenbleiben*** stop dead in one's tracks
Ge·bär·de [gə'bɛ:ɐdə] *f* (-; -n) gesture; *fig.* air
ge·bär·den [gə'bɛ:ɐdən] *v/refl.* (h): ***sich ~*** behave, act (***wie*** like); ***sich wie toll ~*** behave (*or* act) like a madman
Ge'bär·den|dol·met·scher *m* sign language interpreter; **~spiel** *n* gestures *pl.*; pantomime (*a. fig.*); **~spra·che** *f* sign language; *thea.* mimicry
ge·bar [gə'ba:ɐ] *pret. of* **gebären**
Ge·ba·ren [gə'ba:rən] *n* (-s; *no pl.*) behavio(u)r, demeano(u)r; ✝ conduct
ge·bä·ren [gə'bɛ:rən] (gebar, geboren, h) **I.** *v/t.* give birth to; *fig.* breed, beget; ***geboren werden*** be born; ***ich wurde geboren am*** I was born on; *fig.* ***der Mann muß noch geboren werden*** that man hasn't been born yet; → ***geboren*** II; **II.** *v/i.* give birth; **ge·bär·fä·hig** [gə'bɛ:ɐ-] *adj.* capable of childbearing (*zo.* of giving birth); ***im ~en Alter*** of childbearing age; **ge'bär·freu·dig** *adj.* fertile; F *hum.* ***sie hat ein ~es Becken*** F she's broad in the beam
Ge·bär·mut·ter [gə'bɛ:ɐ-] *f* womb, uterus; **~hals** *m* neck of the uterus, 🕮 cervix uteri; **~krebs** *m* cervical cancer, cancer of the womb; **~sen·kung** *f* uterine descent; **~ˌvor·fall** *m* (uterine) prolapse
ge'bauch·pin·selt F *adj.*: ***sich ~ fühlen*** F be *or* feel (quite) tickled
Ge·bäu·de [gə'bɔʏdə] *n* (-s; -) building; *a. fig.* structure, edifice; **~flü·gel** *m* wing (of a *or* the building); **~komˌplex** *m* complex (of buildings), group of buildings; **~trakt** *m* part of a (*or* the) building; wing
ge'bauscht *adj.* puffed-out
ge'baut *adj.*: ***gut ~*** well-built (*a. iro.*); ***so wie er ~ ist, schafft er es leicht*** a man of his size won't have any problems
'**ge·be·freu·dig** *adj.* open-handed, (very) generous; '**Ge·be·freu·dig·keit** *f* (-; *no pl.*) open-handedness, generosity
Ge'bein *n* (-[e]s; -e) **1.** bones *pl.*; skeleton; **2.** *pl.* (mortal) remains; *eccl.* relics
Ge·bel·fer [gə'bɛlfɐ] *n* (-s; *no pl.*) yelping, yapping; *fig.* barking
Ge·bell [gə'bɛl] *n* (-[e]s; *no pl.*) barking; yapping
ge·ben ['ge:bən] (gab, gegeben, h) **I.** *v/t.* **1.** give (***j-m et.*** s.o. s.th., s.th. to s.o.); hand; *ped.* teach *subject etc*, set *a task etc*; ***j-m zu trinken*** (***essen***) ***~*** give s.o. s.th. to drink (eat); ***sich et. ~ lassen*** ask for s.th.; F ***ich gäbe was drum zu wissen*** I'd give anything to know; F ***es j-m ~*** let s.o. have it; → ***Anlaß, bedenken*** 1, ***Bescheid, Blöße*** 2, ***denken*** I; → ***gegeben*** II; **2.** give, grant; ✝ yield; **3.** give *a recital etc.*; *thea. etc.* perform, F do; show *a film etc.*; have, give *a party etc.*; ***was wird heute abend gegeben?*** what's on tonight?; ***das Stück wurde drei Monate lang gegeben*** the play ran (*or* was on) for three months; **4.** make *a good soup etc.*; make, leave *a stain etc.*; *fig.* ***das gibt keinen Sinn*** it doesn't make (any) sense; ***fünf mal sechs gibt dreißig*** five sixes are thirty, five times six is thirty; **5.** put; add; ***Salz in die Suppe ~*** put salt into (*or* add salt to) the soup; **6.** ***von sich ~*** ⚗ give off, emit; ⚕ bring up *one's food*; *fig.* make *a remark etc.*; give, let out *a scream etc.*; ***nichts als Unsinn von sich ~*** talk nothing but nonsense; → ***Ton*** 1; **7.** ***viel ~ auf*** *acc.* set great store by, think highly (*or* a lot) of *s.o.*; **II.** *v/i.* **8.** give (***mit vollen Händen*** freely); **9.** *card game*: deal; ***wer gibt?*** whose deal is it?; **10.** *tennis*: serve; **III.** *v/refl.*: ***sich ~*** **11.** act, behave; ***sich natürlich ~*** act naturally; **12.** *opportunity etc.*: arise, present itself; **13.** ease up; pass, blow over; *passion etc.*: *a.* cool (down); *pain*: let up, go away; *temperature*: go down; *fig.* come right; ***das gibt sich wieder*** *a.* it'll sort itself out; **14.** ***sich als Experte*** *etc.* ***~*** (try to) act the expert *etc.*, try to pass o.s. off as an expert *etc.*; **15.** ***sich in sein Schicksal ~*** give o.s. up to one's fate; → ***gefangen, geschlagen, verloren***; **IV.** *v/impers.* **16.** ***es gibt*** there is, there are; ***es gibt Leute, die ...*** some people ...; ***der beste Spieler, den es je gab*** the best player of all time; ***es gab viel zu tun*** there was a lot to do; ***es gab kein Entrinnen*** there was no escaping; ***das gibt Ärger*** there'll be trouble; ***was gibt's?*** what's up?; ***was gibt's Neues?*** what's new?; ***was gibt es zum Mittagessen?*** what's for lunch?; ***was es nicht alles gibt!*** you don't say; ***so was gibt es nicht*** there's no such thing; ***das gibt's nicht!*** a) that's out, b) you're joking, that can't be true; ***das gibt's nicht, daß sie noch aufgetaucht ist*** I don't (*or* can't) believe she actually turned up; ***gibt's den noch?*** is he still around?; ***da gibt's nichts!*** a) there's no doubt about that, and no mistake about it, b) and if it kills me; ***morgen gibt es Schnee*** it's going to snow (*or* there's going to be snow) tomorrow; ***heute wird's noch was ~*** a) I think we're in for something, b) there's trouble brewing (*or* in the air); F ***sei ruhig, sonst gibt's was!*** be quiet, or else!; **V.** ♀ *n* (-s) **17.** giving; ***es ist alles ein ~ und Nehmen*** it's all a matter of give and take; *bibl.* ***~ ist seliger denn Nehmen*** it is more blessed to give than to receive; **18.** *card game*: ***am ~ sein*** be dealing; ***er ist am ~*** it's his deal
ge·be·ne·deit [gəbene'daɪt] *adj.* blessed
Ge·ber ['ge:bɐ] *m* (-s; -) giver; *card game*: dealer; ⚡ pickup; *radio*: transmitter; ✝ ***~ und Nehmer*** (*pl.*) sellers and buyers; **~land** *n* (-[e]s; ⁼er) donor country; **~lau·ne** *f*: (***in ~ sein*** be in a) generous mood
Ge·bet [gə'be:t] *n* (-[e]s; -e) prayer; ***sein ~ verrichten*** say one's prayers; *fig.* ***j-n ins ~ nehmen*** give s.o. a good talking-to; **~buch** *n* prayer book
ge'be·ten *p.p. of* **bitten**
Ge'bets|müh·le *f* prayer wheel; **~rie·men** *m* phylactery; **~tep·pich** *m* prayer mat
Ge'bet·tel *n*: (***dauerndes ~*** constant) begging
ge·beugt [gə'bɔʏkt] *adj.*: ***vom Alter ~*** bowed (down) *or* bent with age; ***vom Kummer ~*** bowed down with grief
Ge·biet [gə'bi:t] *n* (-[e]s; -e) **1.** area; region; district, zone; territory; ***benachbarte ~e*** a) neighbo(u)ring territories, b) neighbo(u)ring countries; **2.** *fig.* field; area, sphere; ***auf politischem ~*** in the political field (*or* sphere); ***er ist Fachmann auf dem ~ der Kernspaltung*** he's an authority on (*or* in the field of) nuclear fission; ***ich kenne mich in dem ~ überhaupt nicht aus*** I don't know anything (*or* the first thing) about the subject; ***das ist nicht mein ~*** that's not my field (*or* line, F territory)
ge'bie·ten (gebot, geboten, h) **I.** *v/t.* require, call for; command *respect etc.*; impose *silence*; call for *peace etc.*; ***j-m ~, et. zu tun*** order (*or* instruct) s.o. to do s.th.; ***die Vernunft gebietet uns zu*** *inf.* reason demands of us that we ...; **II.** *v/i.*: ***~ über*** *acc.* a) control, hold sway over, b) rule (over), govern, c) have at one's disposal (*or* command); → ***geboten*** II; **Ge'bie·ter** *m* (-s; -) master, lord; ruler; → ***Herr***; **Ge·bie·te·rin** [gə'bi:tərɪn] *f* (-; -nen) mistress; ruler; **ge·bie·te·risch**

[gəˈbiːtərɪʃ] *adj.* imperious; peremptory; **~es Wesen** *a.* imperiousness

Geˈbiets|ab·tre·tung *f* cession of territory; **~en verlangen von** make territorial claims on; **~an·spruch** *m* territorial claim; **~ho·heit** *f* territorial sovereignty (*or* jurisdiction); **~kör·per·schaft** *f* territorial authority; **~lei·ter** *m* † regional manager; **~reˌform** *f* regional reorganization

geˈbiets·wei·se *adv.* regionally, locally; by (*or* according to) regions; **~ Regen** local showers, rain in places

Ge·bil·de [gəˈbɪldə] *n* (-s; -) a) thing, b) form, shape; structure, *a. geol.* formation, c) work, creation; product, d) †, ⚖ entity

geˈbil·det *adj.* educated; cultured; well-informed; well-read; **Geˈbil·de·te** *m, f* (-n; -n) educated person; **die ~n** the educated world (*or* classes), *w.s.* the intellectuals; *iro.* **das ist so ein ~r** he's one of those educated people

Geˈbim·mel *n* (-s; *no pl.*): (**dauerndes ~** continual) ringing

Geˈbin·de *n* (-s; -) **1.** bundle; spray; **2.** skein; **3.** △ truss; **4.** barrel, cask

Ge·bir·ge [gəˈbɪrgə] *n* (-s; -) mountains *pl.*; mountain range; **ge·bir·gig** [gəˈbɪrgɪç] *adj.* mountainous; **Ge·birg·ler** [gəˈbɪrklɐ] *m* (-s; -) mountain-dweller

Ge·birgs|aus·läu·fer [gəˈbɪrks-] *m* spur; **~bach** *m* mountain stream; (mountain) torrent; **~be·woh·ner** *m* mountain-dweller; **~blu·me** *f* mountain (*or* alpine) flower; **~dorf** *n* mountain village; **~ge·gend** *f* mountainous region; **~jä·ger** *m* ⚔ mountain infantryman; *pl.* mountain infantry *sg.*; **~ket·te** *f* mountain range; **~kli·ma** *n* mountain climate; **~land** *n* (-[e]s; ⸚er) mountain(ous) country; **~land·schaft** *f* **1.** *geogr.* mountainous region (*or* area); **2.** mountain scenery; **3.** *art*: mountain landscape; **~masˌsiv** *n* massif; **~paß** *m* mountain pass; **~stock** *m* massif; **~stra·ße** *f* mountain road (*or* route); **~tal** *n* mountain valley; **~trup·pen** *pl.* mountain troops; **~volk** *n* mountain people (*or* tribe); **~wand** *f* mountain face, rockface; **~zug** *m* mountain range

Geˈbiß *n* (-sses; -sse) a) (set of) teeth *pl.*, b) dentures *pl.*, (set of) false teeth *pl.*, c) bit; **ein scharfes ~** sharp teeth; **ein ~ tragen** wear dentures, have false teeth; **~ab·druck** *m* (dental) impression; **~trä·ger** *m*: **~ sein** wear dentures

ge·bis·sen [gəˈbɪsən] *p.p. of* **beißen**

Ge·blä·se [gəˈblɛːzə] *n* (-s; -) ⚙ fan, blower; *mot.* supercharger; airpipe; bellows *pl.*; **~mo·tor** *m* fan motor; supercharger engine; blast-injection engine

ge·bla·sen [gəˈblaːzən] *p.p. of* **blasen**

Ge·blö·del [gəˈbløːdəl] *n* (-s; *no pl.*) fooling around, larking about

ge·blümt [gəˈblyːmt] **I.** *adj.* floral; *fig.* flowery; **II.** *adv.*: **sich ~ ausdrücken** a) use flowery language, b) talk around things

Ge·blüt [gəˈblyːt] *n* (-[e]s; *no pl.*) blood; lineage; **von edlem ~** of noble blood (*or* birth)

geˈbo·gen I. *p.p. of* **biegen**; **II.** *adj.* bent, curved; hooked *nose*

geˈbongt *adj.*: F **ist ~** F will do

ge·bo·ren [gəˈboːrən] **I.** *p.p. of* **gebären**; **II.** *adj.* born; **er ist ein ~er Deutscher** (**Berliner**) he's German by birth (he was born in Berlin); **~e Schmidt** née Schmidt; **sie ist e-e ~e Schmidt** her maiden name is Schmidt; **~ sein zu** *dat.* be born to *s.th.* (*or* to be *or* to do *s.th.*), *a.* be cut out for *teaching, politics etc.*; **ein ~er Geschäftsmann** a born (*or* natural) businessman

ge·bor·gen [gəˈbɔrgən] **I.** *p.p. of* **bergen**; **II.** *adj.* safe, secure, safe and secure; **sie fühlt sich bei ihm ~** she feels very secure with him, he gives her a sense of security; **Geˈbor·gen·heit** *f* (-; *no pl.*) security; **die ~ des Elternhauses** the warmth and security of the home; **Geˈbor·gen·heits·ge·fühl** *n* sense of security

ge·bor·sten [gəˈbɔrstən] *p.p. of* **bersten**

ge·bot [gəˈboːt] *pret. of* **gebieten**

Ge·bot [gəˈboːt] *n* (-[e]s; -e) a) order, command; rule, b) requirement, necessity, c) *auction*: bid; **die Zehn ~e** the Ten Commandments; **ein ~ abgeben** make a bid; **dem ~ der Vernunft folgen** follow the dictates of reason; **es ist ein ~ der Vernunft, daß** reason demands that; **es ist ein ~ der Höflichkeit** *etc.* it's a matter of courtesy *etc.*; **... ist das ~ der Stunde, ... ist oberstes ~ ...** is top (*or* number one) priority, ... is urgently called for, ... is of paramount importance; **j-m zu ~e stehen** be at s.o.'s disposal; **zu ~e stehend** available; **mit allen zu ~e stehenden Mitteln** by fair means or foul, **versuchen zu** *inf.*: try every possible means to *inf.*, do one's utmost to *inf.*

ge·bo·ten [gəˈboːtən] **I.** *p.p. of* **bieten** *and* **gebieten**; **II.** *adj.* necessary; *pred.* called for; due; **dringend ~** (absolutely) imperative; **es ist Vorsicht ~** caution is called for, it would do good to exercise caution (*or* be cautious); F **da ist was ~** F there's something doing there

Geˈbots·schild *n* traffic sign (*giving an instruction*)

ge·bracht [gəˈbraxt] *p.p. of* **bringen**

ge·brannt [gəˈbrant] **I.** *p.p. of* **brennen**; **II.** *adj.* burnt; roasted *coffee etc.*; fired *ceramics*; → **Kind**

geˈbra·ten I. *p.p. of* **braten**; **II.** *adj.* fried; **Gebratenes** fried foods (F stuff)

Ge·bräu [gəˈbrɔʏ] *n* (-[e]s; -e) brew; *fig. a.* concoction

Geˈbrauch *m* (-[e]s; *no pl.*) use; application (*a. pharm.*, ✾); *ling.* usage; custom; practi|ce (*Am. a.* -se); **heilige Gebräuche** sacred rites; **von et. ~ machen** make use of s.th., use s.th.; **guten** (**schlechten**) **~ von et. machen** put s.th. to good (bad) use; **in ~ kommen** come into use; **im ~ sein** be in use, be used; **außer ~ kommen** pass out of use; **allgemein in ~** in common use; **der ~ s-s linken Arms** the use of his left arm; **zum äußeren** (**inneren**) **~** for external (internal) application *or* use; **zum persönlichen ~** for personal use; **vor ~ schütteln!** shake before use; **geˈbrau·chen** *v/t.* (h) use; *pharm.* take; **kannst du das ~?** can you make (any) use of that?; **s-n Verstand ~** use one's head (*or* brains); **ich könnte e-n Schirm** (**e-n Whisky**) **~** I could do with an umbrella (a Scotch); **das hätte ich ~ können** I could have done with that; **du wirst nicht mehr gebraucht** you can go now; **dich kann ich jetzt nicht ~** I haven't got time for you right now; **er** (**es**) **ist zu nichts zu ~** he's absolutely hopeless (it's useless)

ge·bräuch·lich [gəˈbrɔʏçlɪç] *adj.* common (*a. ling.*); normal; **nicht mehr ~** no longer used; outdated; **das ist hier nicht ~** it's not done (*or* they don't do that) around here; **~ werden** come into use; **Geˈbräuch·lich·keit** *f* (-; *no pl.*) *ling.* currency

Geˈbrauchs|an·lei·tung *f*, **~an·wei·sung** *f* directions *pl.* for use, instructions *pl.* (for use); **~arˌti·kel** *m* (basic) commodity; *pl. a.* consumer goods; **≈fä·hig** *adj.* usable; in working order; **~fahr·zeug** *n* utility vehicle; **≈fer·tig** *adj.* ready for use; **~ge·gen·stand** *m* → **Gebrauchsartikel**; **~gra·phik** *f* commercial art; **~gra·phi·ker** *m* commercial artist; **~gü·ter** *pl.* (consumer) durables; **~mö·bel** *pl.* utility furniture *sg.*; **~muˌsik** *f* functional music

Geˈbrauchs·mu·ster *n* patented design; **~schutz** *m* protection of patented designs

Geˈbrauchs|wert *m* practical value; **~zweck** *m* purpose, intended use

geˈbraucht *adj.* used, † *a.* second-hand; *a.* old *clothes*; **et. ~ kaufen** buy s.th. second-hand

Geˈbraucht·wa·gen *m* used (*or* second-hand) car; **~han·del** *m* used (*or* second-hand) car trade; **~händ·ler** *m* used (*or* second-hand) car dealer; **~markt** *m* used (*or* second-hand) car market

Geˈbraucht·wa·ren *pl.* second-hand goods; **~la·den** *m* second-hand shop

geˈbräunt *adj.* tanned; **tief ~** bronzed

Ge·bre·chen [gəˈbrɛçən] *n* (-s; -) (physical) disability *or* handicap; complaint, ailment; *fig.* shortcoming; **die ~ des Alters** the infirmities of old age

ge·brech·lich [gəˈbrɛçlɪç] *adj.* frail; **Geˈbrech·lich·keit** *f* (-; *no pl.*) frailty; infirmity

ge·bro·chen [gəˈbrɔxən] **I.** *p.p. of* **brechen**; **II.** *adj.* broken (*a. colo[u]rs, chord and fig.*); ✾ *a.* fractured; **mit ~er Stimme** in a broken voice; **mit ~em Herzen, ~en Herzens** broken-hearted, heartbroken; **an ~em Herzen sterben** die of a broken heart; **er** (**sie**) **ist ein ~er Mensch** he's a broken man (she's a broken woman); **~es Englisch** broken English; **~ weiß** off-white; **~es Verhältnis** fractured relationship; **sie haben ein ~es Verhältnis** (**zueinander**) they have a compromised relationship

Ge·brü·der [gəˈbryːdɐ] *pl.* brothers; † **~** (**Gebr.**) **Wolfram** Wolfram Brothers (*abbr.* Bros.)

Ge·brüll [gəˈbrʏl] *n* (-[e]s; *no pl.*) roaring; screaming; bellowing

Ge·brum·me [gəˈbrʊmə] *n* (-s; *no pl.*) (loud) hum(ming), (loud) humming sound; drone, droning

geˈbückt *adj.* stooping; **~ sein** *a.* be bending down

Ge·bühr [gəˈbyːɐ] *f* (-; -en) **1.** charge, fee; subscription; rate; postage; toll; *pl. radio, TV*: licen|ce (*Am.* -se) fee; ✉ **ermäßigte ~** reduced rate; **~ bezahlt** postage paid; **~ zahlt Empfänger** postage to be paid by addressee; **e-e ~ erheben** charge a fee, charge postage (*or* toll *etc.*); **e-e ~ von hundert Mark erheben** *a.* charge a hundred marks; **e-e ~ entrichten** pay a fee, pay postage (*or* toll *etc.*); **2.** **nach ~** duly, as s.o. deserves; **über ~** excessively, unduly

ge·büh·ren [gəˈbyːrən] (h) **I.** *v/i.*: **j-m ~** be due to s.o.; **es gebührt ihm** he deserves it, it's his due; ***gib ihm, was ihm gebührt*** give him his due; **II.** *obs. v/refl. impers.*: **sich ~** → ***gehören*** II

Ge'büh·ren|an·pas·sung *f* rate increase; **~an·sa·ge** *f*: ***Gespräch mit ~*** ADC call; **~an·zei·ger** *m* → ***Gebührenzähler***

ge·büh·rend [gə'by:rənt] **I.** *adj.* due, proper, fitting; ***j-m die ~e Achtung entgegenbringen*** treat s.o. with due respect; *iro.* ***in ~em Abstand*** at a respectful distance; **II.** *adv.* duly, properly, as is fitting; as befits the occasion

ge·büh·ren·der'ma·ßen [gə'by:rəndɐ'ma:sən], **ge'büh·ren·der'wei·se** *adv.* → ***gebührend*** II

Ge'büh·ren|ein·heit *f* unit; **~er·hö·hung** *f* increase in charges *etc.*; → **Gebühr;** rate increase; **~er·laß** *m* remission of fees

ge'büh·ren·frei *adj.* free of charge; **Ge'büh·ren·frei·heit** *f* (-; *no pl.*) exemption from charges

Ge'büh·ren|mar·ke *f* revenue stamp; **~ord·nung** *f* scale of fees (*or* charges); **2pflich·tig I.** *adj.* subject to charges; ***~e Straße*** toll road; ***~e Verwarnung*** ticket, fine; **II.** *adv.*: ***~ verwarnt werden*** get ticketed; **~satz** *m* rate; **~zäh·ler** *m teleph.* call-fee indicator

ge'bün·delt *adj.* bundled, *phys. a.* pencil(l)ed *rays*

ge·bun·den [gə'bʊndən] **I.** *p.p. of* ***binden*; II.** *adj.* **1.** *typ.* bound; hardcover; **2.** *fig.* tied (**an** *acc.* to); ***anderweitig ~ sein*** have already committed o.s., *formal*: be otherwise engaged, *euphem.* be already attached; ***vertraglich ~*** bound by contract; ***an e-n Ort ~ sein*** be tied to a (particular) place; ***sich an et. ~ fühlen*** feel committed to s.th.; ***ich fühle mich in keiner Weise ~*** I don't feel in any way obliged (*or* committed), I'm free to choose; ***mir sind die Hände ~*** my hands are tied; **3.** ✝ tied (up); blocked; earmarked *funds etc.*; controlled; **4.** ⚗ fixed (**an** *acc.* to), combined (with); *phys.* latent *heat*; **5.** ♪ tied, (*a. adv.*) legato; **6.** ***in ~er Rede*** in verse; **7.** *gastr.* thickened; **Ge'bun·den·heit** *f* (-; *no pl.*) a) commitment (**an** *acc.* to), b) dependence (on)

Ge·burt [gə'bu:ɐt] *f* (-; -en) **1.** birth (*a. fig.*); ⚕ (child)birth; delivery; parturition; ***bei der ~ ... wiegen*** weigh ... at birth, F weigh in at ...; ***s-e Frau starb bei der ~*** his wife died in childbirth; ***von ~ an*** from birth; ***Katholiken*** *etc.* ***von ~ an*** *a.* cradle Catholics *etc.*; F *fig.* ***es war e-e schwere ~*** F it was a tough job, it was tough going; **2.** birth, descent; ***er ist Deutscher von ~*** he's (a) German by birth

Ge'bur·ten|ab·stand *m* birth spacing; **~be·schrän·kung** *f* birth (*or* population) control; **~kon,trol·le** *f* birth control; **~ra·te** *f* birthrate; **~re·ge·lung** *f* birth control; **~rück·gang** *m* decline (*or* drop) in the birthrate; **2schwach** *adj.* low-birthrate *year etc.*; ***die ~en Jahrgänge*** *a.* F the baby-bust generation; **2stark** *adj.* high-birthrate *year etc.*; ***die ~en Jahrgänge*** *a.* F the baby boomer generation; **~,über·schuß** *m* excess of births over deaths; **~zif·fer** *f* birthrate

ge·bür·tig [gə'bʏrtɪç] *adj.*: ***er ist ~er Engländer*** he's English (*or* British) by birth

Ge'burts|adel *m* hereditary nobility; **~an·zei·ge** *f* a) birth announcement, b) registration of a (*or* the) birth; **~bei·hil·fe** *f* maternity benefit; **~da·tum** *n* date of birth; **~ein·lei·tung** *f* induction of labo(u)r; **~feh·ler** *m* congenital defect; **~ge·wicht** *n* weight at birth; **~haus** *n*: ***mein*** *etc.* **~** the house where I *etc.* was born; **~hel·fer** *m* male midwife; obstetrician; **~hel·fe·rin** *f* midwife; **~hil·fe** *f* obstetrics *pl.*; *n.s.* midwifery; ***~ leisten*** assist at a (*or* the) birth; **~jahr** *n* year of birth; **~jahr·gang** *m* cohort; **~land** *n* (-[e]s; ⁼er) native country; **~na·me** *m* birth name; maiden name; **~ort** *m* birthplace; ***~ und Geburtstag*** place and date of birth; **~schein** *m* birth certificate; **~stadt** *f* native town; **~stät·te** *f* birthplace; **~stun·de** *f* hour of birth; *fig.* birth; **~tag** *m* birthday; *adm.* date of birth; ***wann hast du ~?*** when's your birthday?; ***er hat heute ~*** it's his birthday today; (***ich***) ***gratuliere*** (*or* ***herzliche Glückwünsche***) ***zum ~*** many happy returns of the day; ***alles Gute zum ~*** *a.* happy birthday; ***was hast du zum ~ bekommen?*** what did you get for your birthday?; ***was wünschst du dir zum ~?*** what would you like for your birthday?

Ge'burts·tags|fei·er *f* birthday party; **~ge·schenk** *n* birthday present; **~kar·te** *f* birthday card; **~kind** *n* birthday boy (*or* girl); **~ku·chen** *m* birthday cake; **~wunsch** *m*: ***was hast du für Geburtstagswünsche?*** what would you like for your birthday?

Ge'burts|ur·kun·de *f* birth certificate; **~we·hen** *pl.* labo(u)r pains, labo(u)r *sg.*; **~zan·ge** *f* ⚕ forceps

Ge·büsch [gə'bʏʃ] *n* (-[e]s; -e) bushes *pl.*; thicket; underbrush, brushwood; ***sich ins ~ schlagen*** take to the bush (*or* brush, wilds)

Geck [gɛk] *m* (-en; -en) fop

ge·dacht [gə'daxt] **I.** *p.p. of* ***denken*; II.** *adj.* imagined, imaginary; assumed; ***~ als*** intended (*or* meant) as *or* to be; ***~ für*** *acc.* intended (*or* meant) for

Ge·dächt·nis [gə'dɛçtnɪs] *n* (-ses; *no pl.*) memory; ***aus dem ~*** from memory, by heart; ***sich et. ins ~ (zurück)rufen*** recall s.th., call s.th. to mind; ***zum ~ an*** *acc.* in memory of; ***ein ~ wie ein Sieb*** a memory like a sieve; ***wenn mich mein ~ nicht trügt*** if my memory serves me right; ***ich habe kein gutes ~ für Gesichter*** *etc.* I'm no good at remembering faces *etc.*; ***j-s ~ nachhelfen*** jog s.o.'s memory; ***wir haben unsere Methoden, Ihrem ~ nachzuhelfen*** we have ways of making you remember; **~fei·er** *f* **1.** commemoration; **2.** → **~got·tes·dienst** *m* memorial service; **~hil·fe** *f* mnemonic (aid); **~kir·che** *f* memorial church; **~kon,zert** *n* memorial concert; **~kraft** *f* (-; *no pl.*) memory; **~lücke** *f* lapse of memory; **~pro·to,koll** *n* minutes from memory; **~re·de** *f* commemorative address (*or* speech); **~schwä·che** *f* weak memory; ***an ~ leiden*** have a weak (*or* poor) memory; **~schwund** *m* loss of memory; **~stät·te** *f* memorial (site); **~stö·rung** *f a. pl.* partial amnesia; **~stüt·ze** *f* mnemonic (aid); **~test** *m* recall test; **~trai·ning** *n* memory training; **~übung** *f* memory training exercise; **~ver·lust** *m* amnesia, loss of memory

ge'dämpft *adj.* muffled *sound etc.*; subdued *voice, colo(u)r etc., a. fig. mood etc.*; ♪ *and fig.* muted; *phys.* damped; *gastr.* steamed; ***mit ~er Stimme*** in an undertone; *fig.* ***~er Optimismus*** guarded (*or* cautious) optimism

Ge·dan·ke [gə'daŋkə] *m* (-n; -n) thought (**an** *acc.* of); idea; notion; conjecture; thoughts *pl.*, view(s *pl.*) (**über** *acc.* on); ***der ~ der Demokratie*** the idea (*or* concept) of democracy; ***guter ~*** good idea; ***das ist ein (guter) ~!*** *a.* that's an (*or* the) idea; ***in ~n*** a) absent-mindedly, b) in spirit, c) in one's mind's eye; ***in ~n versunken*** (*or* ***vertieft***) lost in thought, F miles away; ***et. ganz in ~n tun*** do s.th. absent-mindedly; ***sie ist mit ihren ~n immer woanders*** she's always got her mind on other things; ***s-e ~n beisammenhaben*** (***beisammenhalten***) have (keep) one's wits about one; ***j-n auf andere ~n bringen*** get s.o.'s mind onto other things, take s.o.'s mind off things; ***j-n auf den ~n bringen zu*** *inf.* give s.o. the idea of *ger.*; ***er kam auf den ~n zu*** *inf.* he had the idea of *ger.*, it occurred to him to *inf.*; ***auf dumme ~n kommen*** get ideas; ***j-n auf dumme ~n bringen*** put ideas into s.o.'s head; ***ich will nicht, daß sie auf dumme ~n kommt*** I don't want her to get any (silly) ideas; ***j-s ~n lesen*** read s.o.'s mind; ***der ~, daß*** the thought of *s.o. or s.th. ger.* (*or* that); ***schon bei dem ~n, allein der ~*** (***daran***) just to think of it, just the thought of it; ***ich kann keinen klaren ~n fassen*** I can't think straight; ***sein einziger ~ war zu*** *inf.* his one thought was to *inf.*; ***sich ~n machen über*** *acc.* a) think about, wonder about, b) worry about, be worried about; ***mach dir keine ~n darüber*** don't worry about it, don't let it worry you; ***wie kommst du auf den ~n?*** what made you think of that?; ***das bringt mich auf e-n ~n*** that's (*or* you've *etc.*) just given me an idea; ***auf den ~n wäre ich nie gekommen*** I would never have thought of it, it would never have occurred to me; ***~n sind (zoll)frei*** you can think what you like, there's no harm in thinking; → ***spielen*** 6, ***tragen*** III

ge'dan·ken·arm *adj.* lacking in ideas; uninspired; **Ge'dan·ken·ar·mut** *f* lack of ideas

Ge'dan·ken|aus·tausch *m* exchange of ideas; ***sich zu e-m ~ treffen*** *pol.* get together for informal talks; **~blitz** *m* sudden inspiration, F brainwave; **~flug** *m* leap of the imagination; **~frei·heit** *f* (-; *no pl.*) freedom of thought; **~fül·le** *f* wealth of ideas; **~gang** *m* line of thought; **~ge·bäu·de** *n* system of thought; philosophy; **2leer** *adj.* devoid of (*or* lacking in) ideas; vacant, blank *look*; **~le·sen** *n* mind-reading; **~le·ser** *m* mind-reader

ge'dan·ken·los *adj.* thoughtless, inconsiderate; mechanical; absent-minded, *adv. a.* without thinking; **Ge'dan·ken·lo·sig·keit** *f* (-; -en) **1.** *no pl.* thoughtlessness; **2.** thoughtless act (*or* remark); ***so e-e ~!*** what a thoughtless thing to do (*or* say), how thoughtless (of her *etc.*)

Ge'dan·ken·ly·rik *f* contemplative (*or* reflective) poetry

ge'dan·ken·reich *adj.* full of ideas, very thoughtful; **Ge'dan·ken·reich·tum** *m* wealth of ideas

Ge'dan·ken|rich·tung *f* direction of thought; **2schnell** *adj. and adv.* (as)

quick as a flash; ≗**schwer** *adj.* a) deep, heavy, b) weighed down with thoughts; **~sprung** *m* mental leap; **~: ...** to take a leap - ...; ***das ist jetzt ein ~ von mir*** this has got nothing to do with what we're talking about, but; if I may change the subject briefly; **~stim·me** *f film, TV*: voice-over; **~strich** *m* dash; **~über₍tra·gung** *f* (-; *no pl.*) telepathy; ≗**ver·lo·ren** *adj.* lost in thought; ≗**voll** *adj.* pensive; **~welt** *f* (world of) ideas *pl.*

ge·dank·lich [gəˈdaŋklɪç] **I.** *adj.* intellectual; **II.** *adv.* intellectually; ***~ verarbeiten*** (mentally) digest

Ge·därm [gəˈdɛrm] *n* (-[e]s; -e) *usu. pl.* intestines (*pl.*), *zo.* entrails (*pl.*)

Ge·deck [gəˈdɛk] *n* (-[e]s; -e) **1.** cover; ***ein ~ auflegen*** set a place; **2.** set meal; **3.** cover charge

geˈdeckt *adj.* covered (*a.* ✝); laid *table*; *sport*: marked, shadowed (**von** *dat.* by); subdued *colo(u)rs*

geˈdehnt I. *adj.*: ***~e Sprechweise*** drawl; **II.** *adv.*: ***~ sprechen*** speak with a drawl, drawl (one's words)

Ge·deih [gəˈdaɪ] *m*: ***auf ~ und Verderb*** come what may; ***j-m auf ~ und Verderb ausgeliefert sein*** be completely at s.o.'s mercy; **ge·dei·hen** [gəˈdaɪən] **I.** *v/i.* (gedieh, gediehen, sn) **1.** thrive (*a. fig.*); grow; flourish (*a. fig.*); *fig.* prosper, progress (well), get on (well); ***die Sache ist nun so weit gediehen, daß*** the matter has now reached a point where; F ***wie weit bist du gediehen?*** how far have you got?; **II.** ≗ *n* (-s) prosperity; success; **ge·deih·lich** [gəˈdaɪlɪç] *adj.* **1.** profitable; **2.** fruitful, productive

Geˈdenk·aus·ga·be *f* commemorative issue

geˈden·ken (gedachte, gedacht, h) **I.** *v/i.* (*gen.*) a) think of; remember, recollect, b) bear in mind, c) mention, d) commemorate; ***e-r Sache nicht ~*** pass s.th. over in silence; **II.** *v/t.*: ***~ zu tun*** think of doing, intend (*or* propose) to do; *esp. iro.* ***was gedenkst du zu tun?*** what do you propose to do (about it)?; **III.** ≗ *n* (-s) memory; ***zum ~ an*** *acc.* in memory (*or* remembrance) of

Geˈdenk|fei·er *f* commemoration (ceremony); **~got·tes·dienst** *m* memorial service; **~mi₍nu·te** *f a* minute's silence (**für** *acc.* in memory of); → ***einlegen*** 3; **~mün·ze** *f* commemorative coin; **~re·de** *f* commemorative address; **~säu·le** *f* commemorative column; **~stät·te** *f* memorial (site); **~stein** *m* memorial (stone); **~stun·de** *f* hour of remembrance; **~ta·fel** *f* commemorative plaque; **~tag** *m* day of remembrance

Ge·dicht [gəˈdɪçt] *n* (-[e]s; -e) poem, *pl. a.* poetry *sg.*; F ***das Kleid*** *etc.* ***ist ein ~*** the dress *etc.* is a dream; **~band** *m* (-[e]s; ⸚e) book of poems (*or* poetry); **~form** *f* poetic form; ***in ~*** in verse; **~samm·lung** *f* collection of poems; anthology; **~zy·klus** *m* cycle of poems

ge·die·gen [gəˈdiːgən] *adj.* **1.** good-quality ...; solid (*a. fig.*); tasteful; *fig.* sound *knowledge etc.*; worthy, upright *person*; ***e-e ~e Arbeit*** *a. fig.* a solid piece of work; ***ihre Einrichtung ist ~*** her flat *etc.* has got class; **2.** F funny; ***das ist ~*** that's a good one

ge·dieh [gəˈdiː] *pret. of* ***gedeihen***

ge·die·hen [gəˈdiːən] *p.p. of* ***gedeihen***

Geˈdon·ner *n* (-s) thundering

Ge·döns [gəˈdøːns] F *n* (-es; *no pl.*) fuss; ***mach doch nicht so'n ~!*** don't make such a fuss (*or* hue and cry) about it

Ge·drän·ge [gəˈdrɛŋə] *n* (-s; *no pl.*) a) pushing (and shoving), b) crowd, F crush, c) rush (**nach** *dat.*, **um** *acc.* for), d) *rugby*: scrummage; *fig.* ***ins ~ kommen*** get into a (mad) rush; ***damit wir nicht ins ~ kommen*** so that we don't have to rush things (*or* don't get pushed for time)

Ge·drän·gel [gəˈdrɛŋəl] *n* (-s; *no pl.*) pushing (and shoving); ***laß doch das ~!*** stop pushing, will you?

geˈdrängt I. *adj.* **1.** crowded, packed; **2.** *fig.* concise, compact, terse; ***~e Übersicht*** condensed summary, F quick rundown; **II.** *adv. write etc.* concisely, tersely, in a concise (*or* terse) style; ***~ voll*** (F jam)packed

geˈdrech·selt *adj. fig.* stilted

Ge·dröh·ne [gəˈdrøːnə] *n* (-s; *no pl.*) droning; roaring

ge·dro·schen [gəˈdrɔʃən] *p.p. of* ***dreschen***

geˈdruckt *adj.* printed; *electron.* ***~e Schaltung*** printed circuit; F ***lügen wie ~*** F lie through one's teeth

geˈdrückt *adj.* depressed (*a.* ✝); ***in ~er Stimmung sein*** be down in the dumps; **Geˈdrückt·heit** *f* (-; *no pl.*) depressed feeling (*or* atmosphere)

ge·drun·gen [gəˈdrʊŋən] **I.** *p.p. of* ***dringen***; **II.** *adj.* stocky, thickset

Ge·du·del [gəˈduːdəl] *n* (-s; *no pl.*) tootling

Ge·duld [gəˈdʊlt] *f* (-; *no pl.*) patience; perseverance; (***nur***) ***~!*** patience, be patient, don't get impatient; ***~ haben mit*** *dat.* be patient with; ***die ~ verlieren*** lose (one's) patience; ***gleich verlier' ich die ~!*** my patience is wearing very thin, I'm beginning to lose my patience; ***jetzt reißt mir aber die ~!*** that's done it!; ***sich in ~ fassen*** have patience; ***j-s ~ auf die Probe stellen*** try s.o.'s patience; ***er war mit s-r ~ am Ende*** he was at the end of his tether; F ***mit ~ und Spucke*** (***fängt man e-e Mucke***) patience is a virtue; **geˈdul·den** *v/refl.*: ***sich ~*** (h) be patient; ***wenn Sie sich noch ein wenig ~ würden*** if you wouldn't mind waiting a moment; **ge·dul·dig** [gəˈdʊldɪç] *adj.* patient; ***~ wie ein Lamm*** meek as a lamb

Geˈdulds|ar·beit *f*: ***das ist reine ~*** it takes a lot of patience, you need a lot of patience to do that; **~fa·den** F *m*: ***mir riß der ~*** I lost my patience; **~pro·be** *f* test of one's patience; ***j-n auf e-e harte ~ stellen*** (really) put s.o.'s patience to the test, try s.o.'s patience hard; **~spiel** *n* game to test your nerve (*or* skill, wits); test of skill; *fig.* test of patience

ge·dun·gen [gəˈdʊŋən] *adj.* hired *killer etc.*

ge·dun·sen [gəˈdʊnzən] *adj.* bloated

ge·durft [gəˈdʊrft] *p.p. of* ***dürfen***

geˈehrt *adj.* hono(u)red; ***Sehr ~er Herr N.!*** Dear Mr N; ***Sehr ~e Herren!*** Dear Sirs; ***Sehr ~e Damen und Herren!*** Dear Sir or Madam, Dear Sir/Madam

geˈeicht *adj.* ⚙ calibrated, standardized; *fig.* ***darauf ist er ~*** he's an expert on that kind of thing, it's right up his street

geˈeig·net *adj.* **1.** suitable (**für** *acc.*, **zu** *dat.* for); right (for); ***~e Schritte*** appropriate action; ***gut ~*** just right; ***er ist nicht dafür ~*** he's not the right man (for it); ***er ist für s-n Job nicht ~*** he doesn't fit into his job properly; ***im ~en Augenblick*** at the right moment; ***sie ist als*** (*or* ***zur***) ***Lehrerin nicht ~*** she wasn't cut out to be a teacher; **2.** ***das ist*** (***eher***) ***~ zu*** *inf.* that's (more) likely to *inf.*

Geest [geːst] *f* (-; *no pl.*) geest; *North German coastal heathland*

Ge·fahr [gəˈfaːɐ] *f* (-; -en) [gəˈfaːrən]) danger (**für** *acc.* for, to); threat; risk; ***~ für die Gesundheit*** health hazard; ***auf eigene ~*** at one's own risk, on one's own responsibility; ***unter ~*** *gen.* (*or* ***zu*** *inf.*) at the risk of (*ger.*); ***außer ~*** out of danger, F out of the wood(s); ***auf die ~ hin zu*** *inf.* at the risk of *ger.*; ***ohne ~*** safely; ***in ~ sein zu*** *inf.* be in danger of *ger.*; ***~ laufen zu*** *inf.* *a.* run the risk of *ger.*, be liable to *inf.*; ***~ laufen, sich lächerlich zu machen*** invite ridicule; ***der ~ aussetzen*** expose to danger; ***in ~ bringen*** → ***gefährden***; ***sich in ~ begeben*** take a risk; ***es besteht keine ~*** there's no danger, it's perfectly safe; ***mit ~ verbunden sein*** involve a certain risk

geˈfahr·brin·gend *adj.* dangerous

ge·fähr·den [gəˈfɛːɐdən] *v/t.* (h) endanger; threaten; (put at) risk; jeopardize; compromise *one's reputation etc.*; ***j-s Leben ~*** put s.o.'s life at risk; **geˈfähr·det** *adj.* endangered, imperilled; *pred. a.* at risk; ***am meisten ~ sein*** run the highest risk, be in greatest danger, be particularly at risk; **Geˈfähr·dung** *f* (-; -en) **1.** *no pl.* endangering *etc.*; → ***gefährden***; **2.** danger, threat, menace (*gen.* to)

geˈfah·ren *p.p. of* ***fahren***

Ge·fah·ren|be·reich [gəˈfaːrən-] *m* danger zone; **~gren·ze** *f* danger limit; **~herd** *m* (constant) source of danger; *pol.* trouble spot; **~mo₍ment** *n* hazard; **~punkt** *m* danger spot; *fig.* critical point; **~quel·le** *f* **1.** safety hazard; **2.** → **~stel·le** *f* danger spot, (accident) black spot; **~stu·fe** *f* danger level; **~zo·ne** *f* danger zone; **~zu·la·ge** *f* danger money

ge·fähr·lich [gəˈfɛːɐlɪç] *adj.* dangerous; risky; critical, grave, serious; unsafe; ***~es Alter*** tricky age; ***sie kommt in ein ~es Alter*** she's getting to a tricky age; ***ein ~er Bursche*** F a dangerous customer; F ***der könnte mir ~ werden*** F I'll have to watch myself with him; F ***der sieht ja ~ aus!*** what a sight; → ***Spiel*** 1; **Geˈfähr·lich·keit** *f* (-; *no pl.*) danger; seriousness, gravity

geˈfahr·los *adj.* not dangerous; safe; harmless; ***es ist ~*** *a.* there's no danger; **Geˈfahr·lo·sig·keit** *f* (-; *no pl.*) safety; harmlessness

Ge·fährt [gəˈfɛːɐt] *n* (-[e]s; -e) vehicle

Ge·fähr·te [gəˈfɛːɐtə] *m* (-n; -n), **Ge·fähr·tin** [gəˈfɛːɐtɪn] *f* (-; -nen) companion

geˈfahr·voll *adj.* dangerous

Ge·fäl·le [gəˈfɛlə] *n* (-s; -) slope, incline, gradient (*a.* ⚒, ⚡, *phys.*), *esp. Am.* grade; (height of) fall; *fig.* differential(s *pl.*); ***„starkes ~!"*** steep slope; ***ein starkes ~ haben*** slope (down) steeply, drop sharply; → ***Lohngefälle, Nord-Süd-Gefälle, Zinsgefälle***

Geˈfal·len[1] *m* (-s; *no pl.*) favo(u)r; ***j-m e-n ~ tun*** do s.o. a favo(u)r; ***j-n um e-n ~ bitten*** ask a favo(u)r of s.o.; ***tu mir den ~ und ...*** do me a favo(u)r and ...(, will you?)

Geˈfal·len[2] *n* (-s; *no pl.*) pleasure; ***~ finden an*** *dat.* enjoy *s.th.*, like *s.o.*; ***~ daran finden zu*** *inf.* enjoy *ger.*, *formal*: take pleasure in *ger.*; ***ich finde kein ~ daran*** I don't enjoy it, I don't get anything out of it; ***mir zu ~*** for my sake, for me; ***j-m et. zu ~ tun*** do s.th. to please s.o.

ge'fal·len[1] *v/i.* (gefiel, gefallen, h) **1.** ***es gefällt mir*** I like it, ***sehr gut:*** I really like it, I like it a lot; ***er gefiel mir auf den ersten Blick*** I took to him straightaway; ***was mir daran (an ihr) gefällt*** what I like about it (her); ***solche Filme ~ der Masse*** films like that appeal to the masses; ***er gefällt mir nicht*** I don't like the look of him; ***hat dir das Konzert ~?*** did you enjoy the concert?; ***wie gefällt dir mein Hut?*** how d'you like my hat?; ***wie gefällt es Ihnen in X?*** how do you like X?; ***tu, was dir gefällt*** please yourself; ***er will allen ~*** he wants everybody to like him; **2.** ***sich et. ~ lassen*** put up with s.th.; ***das lasse ich mir nicht ~*** I'm not going to put up with it; ***er läßt sich alles (nichts) ~*** he lets people walk all over him (he won't let you get away with anything); ***das lasse ich mir ~!*** a) that's what I like to see (*or* hear)!, b) F now you're talking!; **3.** ***sich ~ in*** *dat.* enjoy *ger.*, take great pleasure in *ger.*; ***er gefällt sich in der Rolle des Märtyrers (Helden*** *etc.*) he likes to play *or* act the martyr (hero *etc.*), ***des Frauenhelden*** *etc.*: *a.* he fancies himself as a ladies' man *etc.*

ge'fal·len[2] **I.** *p.p. of* **fallen** *and* **gefallen**[1]; **II.** *adj.* fallen *angel, woman*; ⚔ killed in action, fallen; ***e-e ~e Größe*** a has-been; **Ge·fal·le·ne** [gə'faləna] *m* (-n; -n) soldier killed in the war; ***die ~n*** the (war) dead (*pl.*)

Ge'fal·le·nen|denk·mal *n* war memorial; **~fried·hof** *m* war cemetery

ge'fäl·lig *adj.* a) pleasant, pleasing, *a.* palatable *wine*, agreeable, b) obliging, complaisant; kind; ***j-m ~ sein*** oblige s.o., help s.o.; ***sich j-m ~ zeigen*** help s.o. (out), do s.o. a favo(u)r; ***sie war so ~, mir zu helfen*** she was kind enough to help out; ***etwas zu trinken ~?*** would you like something to drink?; *iro.* ***sonst noch was ~?*** anything else (while I'm at it)?; *iro.* ***wenn's ~ ist*** if you don't mind, of course; → ***gefälligst;*** **Ge'fäl·lig·keit** *f* (-; -en) **1.** *no pl.* obligingness; **2.** favo(u)r; **Ge'fäl·lig·keits·ver·trag** *m* accommodation agreement; **ge'fäl·ligst** *adv. iro.* if you don't mind; ***sei ~ still!*** be quiet, will you!; ***hör ~ zu(, wenn ich rede)!*** will you listen to me (when I'm talking)

Ge'fall·sucht *f* (-; *no pl.*) desire to please; **ge'fall·süch·tig** *adj.* anxious to please

ge'fan·gen I. *p.p. of* **fangen; II.** *adj.* caught; ⚔ captive; imprisoned, in prison; *fig.* captivated (**von** *dat.* by); ***sich ~ geben*** surrender; **Ge·fan·ge·ne** [gə'faŋənə] *m, f* (-n; -n) prisoner; convict

Ge'fan·ge·nen|aus·tausch *m* exchange of prisoners (of war); **~für·sor·ge** *f* prison welfare work; **~hil·fe** *f* prisoners' aid; **~hilfs·or·ga·ni·sa·ti͵on** *f* prisoners' aid society (*or* organization); **~la·ger** *n* prison camp; ⚔ prisoner-of-war (*abbr.* POW) camp; **~miß͵hand·lung** *f* mistreatment of prisoners

ge'fan·gen·hal·ten *v/t.* (*irr.*, *sep.*, h, → **halten**) keep (*or* hold) *s.o.* prisoner, keep *s.o.* imprisoned; keep *an animal* locked up, hold *an animal* captive; *fig.* hold *s.o.* under one's spell, have *s.o.* spellbound

Ge'fan·gen·nah·me [-naːmə] *f* (-; *no pl.*) arrest; ⚔ capture; **ge'fan·gen·neh·men** *v/t.* (*irr.*, *sep.*, h, → **nehmen**) arrest; ⚔ capture, take *s.o.* prisoner; *fig.* captivate, enthral(l); ***sich ~ lassen*** surrender, *fig.* be enthral(l)ed, be captivated (**von** *dat.* by); *fig.* ***sich von j-m ~ lassen*** come under s.o.'s spell

Ge'fan·gen·schaft *f* (-; *no pl.*) imprisonment; ⚔ *and zo.* captivity; ***in ~ geraten*** be taken prisoner, be captured; ***in ~ sein*** be a prisoner-of-war

ge'fan·gen·set·zen *v/t.* (*sep.*, h) put *s.o.* in prison, imprison

Ge·fäng·nis [gə'fɛŋnɪs] *n* (-ses; -se) prison, jail, *Brit. a.* gaol; ⚖ (term of) imprisonment; ***ins ~ kommen*** be sent (*or* go) to prison; F ***j-n ins ~ stecken*** put s.o. in prison, F lock s.o. up; ***fünf Jahre ~ bekommen*** get five years in prison, get five years' imprisonment; ***mit ~ bestraft werden*** a) be punishable by imprisonment, b) be sentenced to prison; **~arzt** *m* prison doctor; **~auf·se·her** *m* prison officer, *Am.* warder, guard; **~di͵rek·tor** *m* director of a prison, *Am.* warden; **~geist·li·che** *m* prison chaplain; **~haft** *f* detention (in prison); **~in·sas·se** *m* prison inmate; **~mau·er** *f* prison wall; **~re͵vol·te** *f* prison riot(s *pl.*); **~stra·fe** *f* ⚖ (term of) imprisonment; **~ver·wal·tung** *f* prison administration; **~wär·ter** *m* → ***Gefängnisaufseher;*** **~zel·le** *f* prison cell

ge·färbt [gə'fɛrpt] *adj.* **1.** dyed *hair*; *gastr.* artificially colo(u)red; ***~e Lebensmittel*** *a.* foods with artificial colo(u)ring; **2.** *fig.* tinged (**mit** *dat.* with); bias(s)ed; ***s-e Aussprache ist (italienisch) ~*** he has an (Italian) accent

Ge·fa·sel [gə'faːzəl] F *n* (-s; *no pl.*) F drivel

Ge·fäß [gə'fɛːs] *n* (-es; -e) receptacle; bowl; jar; *anat.*, ⚘ *and bibl. fig.* vessel; **~chir·ur͵gie** *f* vascular surgery; **~ent·zün·dung** *f* ⚕ vasculitis; **≗er·wei·ternd** *adj.* ⚕ vasodilatory; **~er·wei·te·rung** *f* ⚕ vasodilation; **~krank·heit** *f*, **~lei·den** *n* vascular disease

ge'faßt I. *adj.* calm, composed; ***~ sein auf*** *acc.* be prepared for; ***sich ~ machen auf*** *acc.* prepare for, brace o.s. for; F ***er kann sich auf etwas ~ machen*** F he's in for it now; F ***darauf kannst du dich ~ machen!*** F you can bet your bottom dollar on that; **II.** *adv.* calmly, with composure; **Ge'faßt·heit** *f* (-; *no pl.*) composure

ge'fäß|ver·en·gend *adj.* ⚕ vasoconstrictive; **≗ver·en·gung** *f* ⚕ vasoconstriction; **≗ver·schluß** *m* ⚕ vascular obstruction; **≗wand** *f* vascular wall

Ge·fecht [gə'fɛçt] *n* (-[e]s; -e) fight; skirmish; battle; action; *fig.* conflict; ***außer ~ setzen*** put out of action (*a. fig.*), *a.* silence *guns*; *fig.* *Argumente etc.* ***ins ~ führen*** advance; ***letztes ~*** last-ditch stand; → ***Hitze***

ge'fechts·be·reit *adj.* ready for combat (*or* action)

Ge'fechts|ein·heit *f* combat unit; **~kopf** *m*: **(*nuklearer* ~** nuclear) warhead; **~stär·ke** *f* fighting strength; **~tä·tig·keit** *f* combat activity; **~übung** *f* field exercise; **~ziel** *n* objective

ge'fei·ert *adj.* (highly) acclaimed, renowned, celebrated

ge·feit [gə'fait] *adj.*: ***~ gegen*** *acc.* immune to, safe from

ge'fes·selt *adj.* **1.** tied up, bound; in chains; handcuffed; *fig.* ***ans Bett ~*** confined to one's bed, bedridden; ***an den Rollstuhl ~*** wheelchair-bound; **2.** *fig.* fascinated, spellbound, entranced

ge·fe·stigt [gə'fɛstɪçt] *adj.* stable, firm

Ge·fie·der [gə'fiːdɐ] *n* (-s; -) plumage, feathers *pl.*; **ge'fie·dert** *adj.* feathered, feathery; ***unsere ~en Freunde*** our feathered friends

ge·fiel [gə'fiːl] *pret. of* **gefallen**

Ge·fil·de [gə'fɪldə] *n* (-s; -) **1.** *poet.* fields *pl.*; ***das ~ der Seligen*** the Elysian Fields; *iro.* ***in höheren ~n schweben*** be up in the clouds; **2.** *lit.* zone; ***heimatliche ~*** home ground; **3.** *fig.* realm

Ge·flat·ter [gə'flatɐ] *n* (-s; *no pl.*) fluttering

Ge·flecht [gə'flɛçt] *n* (-[e]s; -e) wickerwork; netting, mesh; *anat.* plexus; *fig.* web *of lies etc.*

ge·fleckt [gə'flɛkt] *adj.* spotted; speckled; mottled

Ge·flen·ne [gə'flɛnə] F *n* (-s; *no pl.*) howling

Ge·flim·mer [gə'flɪmɐ] *n* (-s; *no pl.*) flickering

ge·flis·sent·lich [gə'flɪsəntlɪç] **I.** *adj.* intentional, deliberate; **II.** *adv. a.* studiously

ge·floch·ten [gə'flɔxtn] *p.p. of* **flechten**

ge·flo·gen [gə'floːgn] *p.p. of* **fliegen**

ge·flo·hen [gə'floːən] *p.p. of* **fliehen**

ge·flos·sen [gə'flɔsn] *p.p. of* **fließen**

Ge'flü·gel *n* (-s; *no pl.*) poultry *sg.*; **~creme·sup·pe** *f* cream of fowl (*or* chicken) soup; **~farm** *f* poultry farm, chicken (*or* turkey *etc.*) farm; **~händ·ler** *m* poulterer; **~hand·lung** *f* poultry shop; **~klein** *n* (-s; *no pl.*) chicken (*or* turkey *etc.*) giblets *pl.*; **~le·ber** *f* chicken (*or* turkey *etc.*) liver(s *pl.*); **~sa͵lat** *m* chicken (*or* turkey *etc.*) salad; **~sche·re** *f*: **(*e-e* ~** a pair of) poultry shears *pl.*

ge·flü·gelt [gə'flyːgəlt] *adj.* winged; ***~es Wort*** saying

Ge'flü·gel|zucht *f* poultry farming, chicken (*or* turkey *etc.*) farming; **~züch·ter** *m* poultry farmer, chicken (*or* turkey *etc.*) farmer

Ge·flun·ker [gə'flʊŋkɐ] F *n* (-s; *no pl.*) a) fibbing, b) fibs *pl.*, lies *pl.*

Ge·flü·ster [gə'flʏstɐ] *n* (-s; *no pl.*) whispering

ge·foch·ten [gə'fɔxtən] *p.p. of* **fechten**

Ge'fol·ge *n* (-s; -) a) entourage; attendants *pl.*; escort, b) cortège, mourners *pl.*; *fig.* ***im ~ von*** (*or gen.*) in the wake of; ***et. im ~ haben*** bring s.th. in its wake; **Ge·folg·schaft** [gə'fɔlkʃaft] *f* (-; -en) followers *pl.*, following, adherents *pl.*; ***j-m ~ leisten*** show one's allegiance to s.o.; ***j-m die ~ verweigern*** refuse to be led by s.o., reject s.o. as a leader; ***j-m die ~ (auf)kündigen*** dissociate o.s. from s.o.; **Ge'folgs·leu·te** *pl.* → **Ge'folgs·mann** *m* (-[e]s; ⸚er, -leute) **1.** vassal; **2.** *pol. etc.* follower, supporter, acolyte, henchman

Ge'fra·ge *n* (-s; *no pl.*) (endless) questions *pl.*; ***hör auf mit dem ~*** I wish you'd stop asking all those questions; ***was soll das ~?*** what are you after (*or* getting at)?

ge·fragt [gə'fraːkt] *adj.*: **(*sehr*) ~** (very much) in demand; ***nicht mehr ~ sein*** *a.* have fallen out of favo(u)r; ***ein ~er Mann*** *a.* a popular man; ***Mut ist nicht ~*** courage is not called for (*or* appreciated)

ge·frä·ßig [gə'frɛːsɪç] *adj.* greedy; voracious; F ***es herrscht ~e Stille*** everyone's busy eating (*or* digesting); **Ge'frä·ßig·keit** *f* (-; *no pl.*) greediness; voracity

Ge·frei·te [gə'fraɪtə] *m* (-n; -n) ⚔ lance corporal, *Am.* private 1st class (Pfc.); ✈ aircraftman 1st class, *Am.* airman 3rd class

ge'fres·sen *p.p. of* ***fressen***

Ge·frier|an·la·ge [gə'friːɐ-] *f* refrigeration plant; **~beu·tel** *m* freezer bag; **~brand** *m* freezer burn

ge'frie·ren *v/i.* (gefror, gefroren, sn) (*a.* **~ *lassen***) freeze

Ge·frier|fach [gə'friːɐ-] *n* freezer, freezing compartment; **≈fest** *adj.* non-freezing; **~fleisch** *n* frozen meat; **≈ge·trock·net** *adj.* freeze-dried; **~gut** *n* (-[e]s; *no pl.*) → ***Gefrierkost***; **~ket·te** *f* cold chain; **~kom·bi·na·ti,on** *f* fridge-freezer; **~kost** *f* frozen food(s *pl.*); **~pro,duk·te** *pl.* frozen goods; **~punkt** *m*: (***auf dem ~*** at) freezing point; ***unter dem ~*** below zero, below freezing (point); ***auf den ~ sinken*** drop to zero; **~raum** *m* cold room; **~schrank** *m* (upright) freezer; **~schutz·mit·tel** *n* anti-freeze; **≈trock·nen** *v/t.* (*only inf. and p.p.* gefriergetrocknet) freeze-dry; **~trock·nung** *f* (-; *no pl.*) freeze-drying; **~tru·he** *f* deep-freeze, (chest) freezer

ge'fror *pret. of* ***gefrieren***

ge·fro·ren [gə'froːrən] **I.** *p.p. of* ***frieren*** *and* ***gefrieren***; **II.** *adj.* frozen; freezing(-cold), ice-cold *hands etc.*; *lake etc.*: frozen over; **Ge'fro·re·ne** *Austrian n* (-n; *no pl.*) ice cream

Ge·fü·ge [gə'fyːgə] *n* (-s; -) **1.** ⚠ structure; **2.** *fig.* structure; make-up; fabric; system; ***soziales ~*** social fabric; ***syntaktisches ~*** syntactic structure

ge·fü·gig [gə'fyːgɪç] *adj.* pliable; compliant, docile, submissive; (***sich***) ***j-n ~ machen*** bring s.o. to heel, make sure s.o. toes the line; ***er ist ihr ein ~es Werkzeug*** he's wax in her hands, she can do what she likes with him

Ge·fühl [gə'fyːl] *n* (-[e]s; -e) feeling; sense (***für*** *acc.* of); *physiol.* sensation; touch, *w.s.* feel; instinct, feel(ing), flair; ***~ der Kälte*** cold sensation; ***ich hab' kein ~ im Arm*** I can't feel anything in my arm, my arm's gone numb (*or* dead); ***~ für Anstand*** (***Proportionen, Recht und Unrecht***) sense of propriety (proportion, justice); ***mit gemischten ~en*** with mixed feelings; ***e-r Sache mit gemischten ~en gegenüberstehen*** have mixed feelings about s.th.; ***für mein ~, m-m ~ nach*** my feeling is that; I think (that); ***s-e ~e zur Schau tragen*** wear one's heart on one's sleeve; ***ich habe das ~, daß*** I have a feeling that; ***ich habe dabei ein ungutes ~*** I've got a funny feeling about it; ***von s-n ~en überwältigt*** overcome with emotion; ***das muß man mit ~ machen*** you've got to have the right touch; ***et. im ~ haben*** a) have a feeling (*or* instinct) for s.th., b) feel it in one's bones; F ***das ist das höchste der ~e*** a) F it's heaven, I can't describe the feeling, b) that's the (absolute) limit

ge·füh·lig [gə'fyːlɪç] *adj.* sentimental, mawkish

ge'fühl·los *adj.* numb; *a. fig.* insensitive (***gegen*** *acc.* to); *fig.* unfeeling, callous, heartless; **Ge'fühl·lo·sig·keit** *f* (-; -en) **1.** *no pl.* numbness; *fig.* heartlessness, cruelty; **2.** cruelty

Ge'fühls|an·wand·lung *f* fit of emotion; ***in e-r ~ a.*** suddenly overcome with emotion; **≈arm** *adj.* emotionally cold; ***er ist ~*** he's got no feelings; **~aus·bruch** *m* (emotional) outburst; **≈be·dingt** *adj.* emotional; **≈be·tont** *adj.* emotional; **~du·se·lei** [-duːzə'laɪ] *f* (-; *no pl.*) (sloppy) sentimentality; **≈du·se·lig** *adj.* sentimental, mawkish, sloppy; **≈ge·la·den** *adj.* (very) emotional, emotionally charged; *ling. a.* emotive; **≈kalt** *adj.* (emotionally) cold; **~käl·te** *f* emotional frigidity; **~le·ben** *n* emotional life

ge'fühls·mä·ßig I. *adj.* emotional; *w.s.* intuitive, instinctive; **II.** *adv.* emotionally *etc.*; by instinct

Ge'fühls|mensch *m* emotional person; **~nerv** *m* sensory nerve; **~re·gung** *f* emotion; ***keine ~ zeigen*** show no trace of emotion, show no emotion at all; **~sa·che** *f*: ***das ist ~*** it's a matter of feeling; **~ska·la** *f* range of emotions; **≈stark** *adj.* very emotional; **~tie·fe** *f* emotional depth; **~tu·be** F *f*: ***auf die ~ drücken*** F give s.o. a sob story; **~,um·schwung** *m* emotional about-turn; **~wär·me** *f* warmth; **~welt** *f* emotional world; **~wert** *m* emotional (*or* sentimental) value

ge'fühl·voll I. *adj.* full of feeling; sensitive; tender; emotional; sentimental; **II.** *adv.* feelingly *etc.*; *sing etc.* with feeling; F gently

ge·führt [gə'fyːɐt] *adj.*: ***~e Fahrt*** guided tour

ge'füllt *adj.* filled (***mit*** *dat.* with); full; *gastr.* ***~e Tomaten*** stuffed tomatoes

Ge·fum·mel [gə'fʊməl] F *n* (-s; *no pl.*) **1.** fiddling around; **2.** groping

ge·fun·den [gə'fʊndən] **I.** *p.p. of* ***finden***; **II.** *adj.* → ***Fressen***

ge'furcht *adj.* furrowed

ge'fürch·tet *adj.* feared, dreaded

ge·gan·gen [gə'gaŋən] *p.p. of* ***gehen***

ge'ge·ben I. *p.p. of* ***geben***; **II.** *adj.* given *temperature, facts etc.*; 𝔄 ***~e Größe*** given quantity; ***wenn wir es als ~ voraussetzen, daß*** taking (it) for granted that; ***unter den ~en Umständen*** under the circumstances; ***zu ~er Zeit*** a) when the occasion arises, b) at some future time; ***das ist das ~e*** it's the obvious thing; **ge·ge·be·nen·falls** [gə'geːbənən'fals] *adv.* a) should the occasion arise, b) if necessary, c) if applicable; **Ge'ge·ben·heit** *f* (-; -en) given fact; *pl.* circumstances, reality *sg.*

ge·gen ['geːgən] *prp.* (*acc.*) a) towards, b) against; ⚖, *sport*: versus (*abbr.* v.), c) about, around, d) *pharm.* for, e) compared with, f) in return for; ***~ die Tür klopfen*** knock at the door; ***~ die Wand lehnen*** (***stoßen***) lean (knock [o.s.]) against the wall; ***~ e-n Baum fahren*** drive (*or* crash) into a tree; ***et. ~ das Licht halten*** hold s.th. up to the light; ***ich wette zehn ~ eins*** I bet you ten to one; ***ich bin ~ den Vorschlag*** I don't agree with the proposal; ***et. eintauschen ~*** exchange s.th. for; ***freundlich*** (***grausam*** *etc.*) ***~*** kind (cruel *etc.*) to(wards); ***~ die Vernunft*** contrary to reason; ***~ Bezahlung*** for money (*or* payment); ***~ bar*** for cash

'Ge·gen|ak·ti,on *f* countermove; **~an·ge·bot** *n* counteroffer; **~an·griff** *m a. fig.* counterattack (*a.* ***e-n ~ führen gegen***); **~an·kla·ge** *f* countercharge; **~an·schlag** *m* counterattack; **~an·sicht** *f* opposing view; **~an·spruch** *m* counterclaim; **~an·trag** *m* countermotion; **~ant·wort** *f* reply, rejoinder; **~an·zei·ge** *f* ⚕ contraindication; **~ar·gu,ment** *n* counterargument; **~auf·trag** *m* counterorder; **~aus·sa·ge** *f* counterstatement; **~be·din·gung** *f* counterstipulation; ***zur ~ machen, daß*** stipulate in return that; **~be·fehl** *m* counterorder; **~be·haup·tung** *f* counterclaim; **~bei·spiel** *n* example to prove (*or* show) the opposite; **~be·mer·kung** *f* rejoinder; **~be·schul·di·gung** *f* countercharge; **~be·stre·bung** *f* countertendency; **~be·such** *m* return visit; ***j-m e-n ~ machen*** return s.o.'s visit; **~be·we·gung** *f* countermovement; ♪ contrary motion; **~be·weis** *m* proof to the contrary; ⚖ *a.* counterevidence; ***den ~ antreten*** provide evidence to the contrary, ***für*** *acc.* (*or* ***zu*** *dat.*): provide evidence against (*or* to counter) *s.th.*; **~bit·te** *f*: ***ich habe e-e ~*** could you do me a favo(u)r in return?; **~bu·chung** *f* ✝ cross entry

Ge·gend ['geːgənt] *f* (-; -en [-dən] **1.** a) area, part of town (*or* the country *etc.*), parts *pl.*, b) *no pl.* neighbo(u)rhood, vicinity; ***umliegende ~*** surroundings *pl.*, environs *pl.*; ***in der ~ von*** near, around, in the *Munich etc.* area; ***in unserer ~*** where we live; ***hier in der ~*** around here, in this area, in these parts; ***ungefähr in dieser ~*** somewhere around here; ***wenn Sie mal wieder in dieser ~ sind*** if ever you happen to be in these parts (*or* in this part of the country *etc.*) again; F ***durch die ~ laufen*** run around the place; F ***et. durch die ~ schmeißen*** throw s.th. around; F ***die ganze ~ kam*** everyone (from miles around) came, the whole village *etc.* came; F ***die ~ unsicher machen*** terrorize the neighbo(u)rhood; **2.** *no pl.* ⚕ region, area; ***die ~ um den Blinddarm*** (the area) around the appendix; **3.** *no pl.* direction

'Ge·gen|dar·stel·lung *f* correction; refutation; ***s-e ~*** his version; **~de·mon·stra·ti,on** *f* counterdemonstration; **~dienst** *m* favo(u)r in return, return favo(u)r; ***als ~*** in return; ***e-n ~ leisten*** return the favo(u)r, reciprocate; ***j-m e-n ~ leisten*** return s.o.'s favo(u)r, do s.o. a favo(u)r in return, do s.th. for s.o. in return; ***zu ~en*** (***jederzeit***) ***gern bereit*** (always) glad to reciprocate; **~druck** *m* (-[e]s; *no pl.*) counterpressure, back pressure; *fig.* resistance

ge·gen·ein'an·der I. *adv.* against (*or* towards) one another *or* each other; mutually; **II.** ≈ *n* (-s) antagonism; **~hal·ten** *v/t.* (*irr.*, *sep.*, h, → ***halten***) put side by side, *a.* compare; **~pral·len** *v/i.* (*sep.*, sn) run (*or* bump) into each other; hit each other, collide; **~stel·len** *v/t.* (*sep.*, h) put (*or* place) side by side, *a.* compare; **~sto·ßen** (*irr.*, *sep.*, → ***stoßen***) **I.** *v/i.* (sn) → ***gegeneinanderprallen***; **II.** *v/t.* (h) bang *things* together

'Ge·gen|ent·wurf *m* alternative concept, counterconcept (***zu*** *dat.* to); **~er·klä·rung** *f* counterstatement; **~fahr·bahn** *f* opposite lane; **~far·be** *f* complementary colo(u)r; **~for·de·rung** *f* counterdemand; ⚖ *etc.* counterclaim; **~fra·ge** *f*: ***erlauben Sie mir e-e ~*** if I may answer your question with another question, let me ask 'you something; **~fu·ge** *f* ♪ counterfugue; **~ge·ra·de** *f sport*: back straight, *esp. Am.* backstretch; **~ge·schenk** *n* present (given) in return; ***j-m ein ~ machen*** give s.o. a present in return; ***j-m et. als ~ überreichen*** give s.o. s.th. in return; **~ge·wicht** *n a. fig.* counterweight; *fig.* ***ein ~ bilden*** (*or* ***darstellen***) act as a counterbalance; ***das ~ halten*** *dat.*, ***ein ~ bilden zu*** *dat.* counterbalance; ***als ~ zu*** *dat.* to balance *s.th.*, to set *s.th.* off; **~gift** *n a. fig.* antidote (***gegen*** *acc.* to, against; ***für*** *acc.* for); **~grund** *m* counterargument, argument against (it); **~gut·ach·ten** *n* opposing opinion; **~kan·di͵dat** *m* opponent, rival; rival (*or* opposition) candidate; ***ohne ~*** unopposed, uncontested; **~kan·di·da͵tur** *f* counter-candidacy, rival candidacy; **~kla·ge** *f* ⚖ cross action; ***~ erheben*** (***gegen j-n***) file a cross action (against s.o.), countersue (*s.o.*); **~kraft** *f* counteracting force (*a. fig.*); **~kul͵tur** *f* counterculture; **~kurs** *m* opposite course (*a. fig.*); ***auf ~ gehen*** take the opposite course; **&läu·fig** *adj.* ⚙ counter-rotating; *fig.* opposite; ***~e Tendenz*** reversal; ***~er Zyklus*** anticyclical pattern; **~lei·stung** *f* return favo(u)r, quid pro quo; ***als ~*** in return (***für*** *acc.* for); **&len·ken** *v/i.* (*sep.*, h) → ***gegensteuern***; **&le·sen** *v/t.* (*irr.*, *sep.*, h, → ***lesen***) check; ***könntest du das bitte ~?*** could you check this to see that I haven't missed anything?

'Ge·gen·licht *n* (-[e]s; *no pl.*) back light(ing); contre jour; ***bei ~*** against the light; **~auf·nah·me** *f* contre-jour shot; **~blen·de** *f* lens hood

'Ge·gen|lie·be *f*: ***er fand keine ~*** a) his love remained unrequited, b) *fig.* his suggestion *etc.* didn't go down particularly well; **~maß·nah·me** *f* countermeasure; preventive measure; reprisal; ***~n ergreifen gegen*** *acc.* take steps against; **~mei·nung** *f* opposing view; **~mit·tel** *n a. fig.* remedy (***gegen*** *acc.* for); antidote (against); **~mut·ter** *f* ⚙ counternut; **~of·fen͵si·ve** *f* counteroffensive; **~papst** *m* antipope; **~par͵tei** *f* ⚖ opposing party, other side; *pol.* opposition; *sport*: opponents *pl.*; ***die ~ ergreifen*** take the other side; **~pol** *m* opposite pole; *fig.* counterpart; **~pro·be** *f* cross-check; *parl.* counter-verification; ***die ~ machen*** cross-check (***auf et.*** s.th.); **~pro·pa͵gan·da** *f* counterpropaganda; **~re·ak·ti͵on** *f* counter-reaction; backlash; **~rech·nung** *f* **1.** cross-checking; *fig.* ***ich muß erst die ~ machen*** I'll have to see what there is to lose; **2.** ✝ counterclaim, set-off; **~re·de** *f* (-; *no pl.*) a) reply, b) contradiction, objection; ***sie wechselten Rede und ~*** their conversation went to and fro; **~re·vo·lu·ti͵on** *f* counter-revolution; **~rich·tung** *f* opposite direction; ***Verkehr aus der ~*** oncoming traffic

'Ge·gen·satz *m* (-es; ⸚e) contrast (***zu*** *dat.* to, with); *the* opposite, *the* contrary (***von*** *dat.* of); *usu. pl.* differences *of opinion etc.*; ***im ~ zu*** *dat.* in contrast to (*or* with), unlike; ***im ~ dazu*** by contrast; ***e-n scharfen ~ bilden zu*** *dat.*, ***im scharfen ~ stehen zu*** *dat.* stand in (*or* form a) sharp contrast to, *opinion etc.*: be in sharp opposition to; ***Gegensätze ziehen sich an*** opposites (*or* opposite poles) attract; **'ge·gen·sätz·lich** [-zɛtslɪç] *adj.* opposite; contrary; opposing, antagonistic; ***~e Vorschriften*** conflicting regulations; **'Ge·gen·sätz·lich·keit** *f* (-; *no pl.*) oppositeness, opposing (*or* antithetical) nature (*gen.* of), polarity; antagonism

'Ge·gen|schlag *m* counterblow, *fig. a.* retaliation; ***e-n ~ tun*** counter, *fig. a.* retaliate; ***zum ~ ausholen*** *a. fig.* start to hit back; **~sei·te** *f* opposite (*or* other) side

ge·gen·sei·tig [-zaɪtɪç] **I.** *adj.* mutual, reciprocal; ***~e Abhängigkeit*** interdependence; ***~e Beziehung*** interrelation; correlation; ***~e Hilfe*** mutual help (*or* aid); ***~es Interesse*** mutual interest; **II.** *adv.*: ***sich ~ helfen*** *etc.* help *etc.* one another (*or* each other); **'Ge·gen·sei·tig·keit** *f* (-; *no pl.*) reciprocity, mutuality; ***Abkommen auf ~*** mutual agreement; ***auf ~ beruhen*** be mutual; ***es beruht ja schließlich auf ~*** you scratch my back and I'll scratch yours; *iro.* ***das beruht ganz auf ~*** (I can assure you) the feeling is mutual

'Ge·gen·sei·tig·keits|ab·kom·men *n* ✝ reciprocal trade agreement; **~klau·sel** *f* reciprocity clause; **~prin͵zip** *n* principle of reciprocity; **~ver·trag** *m pol.* bilateral agreement; mutual assistance treaty

'Ge·gen|sinn *m*: ***im ~*** in the opposite direction; **~spie·ler** *m* antagonist, *a. sport etc.*: opponent; **~spio͵na·ge** *f* counter-espionage, counterintelligence

'Ge·gen·sprech|an·la·ge *f* intercom system; **~ver·kehr** *m* duplex communication

'Ge·gen·stand *m* (-[e]s; ⸚e) a) object, thing, item, b) subject, topic, c) motif, theme; subject matter, d) matter, affair; issue; ***~ des Mitleids*** *etc.* object of pity *etc.*; ***~ des Spottes*** figure of fun; ***zum ~ haben*** deal (*or* be concerned) with

'ge·gen·stän·dig *adj.* ⚘ opposite

ge·gen·ständ·lich ['ge:gənʃtɛntlɪç] *adj.* concrete (*a. ling.*); graphic(ally *adv.*); *art*: representational

'ge·gen·stands·be·zo·gen *adj.* **1.** factual; **2.** *art*: representational

'ge·gen·stands·los *adj.* a) abstract, *art*: *a.* nonrepresentational, b) useless; meaningless, c) unnecessary, superfluous; irrelevant, immaterial; invalid; ***der Vertrag ist ~ geworden*** the contract is no longer valid; ***damit ist Ihre Frage ~ geworden*** that takes care of your question

'ge·gen·steu·ern *v/i.* (*sep.*, h) steer against it; *fig.* take countermeasures

'Ge·gen|stim·me *f* **1.** *parl.* dissenting vote, vote against; ***es gab fünf ~n*** *a.* there were five noes; ***ohne ~*** unanimously; **2.** objection; *usu. iro.* dissenting voice; **3.** ♪ counterpart; **~stoß** *m*: ***(e-n ~ führen*** make a) counterthrust; **~strom** *m* ⚡ countercurrent; **~strö·mung** *f* ⚡ countercurrent; *fig.* countermovement; **~stück** *n* **1.** counterpart; *art*: pendant; matching piece; **2.** opposite (***zu*** *dat.* of); ***er ist das genaue ~ zu s-m Vater*** he's the exact opposite of his father

'Ge·gen·teil *n* (-[e]s; *no pl.*) opposite (***von*** *dat.* of), reverse; (***ganz***) ***im ~*** on the contrary; oh no(, not at all); ***genau das ~*** the exact opposite, exactly the opposite; ***das ~ behaupten*** argue the converse; ***das ~ bewirken*** have the opposite effect, be counterproductive; ***et. ins ~ verkehren*** twist s.th. round (completely); ***dann schlug alles ins ~ um*** then there was a complete reversal (of events); **'ge·gen·tei·lig** [-taɪlɪç] *adj.* contrary, opposite; ***~e Behauptung*** contradictory claim; ***~er Meinung sein*** disagree; ***e-e ~e Wirkung haben*** have the opposite (*or* a paradoxical) effect

'Ge·gen|ter·ror *m* counter-terrorism; **~tor** *n*: *der Torwart* ***ist in den letzten vier Spielen ohne ~*** hasn't lost a goal in the last four matches

ge·gen'über I. *adv.* opposite, face to face; across the way (*or* street); ***sie saßen einander ~*** *a.* they sat facing one another; ***direkt ~*** right opposite; **II.** *prp.* (*dat.*) a) opposite, facing, b) *fig.* to(wards), c) compared with, as against, d) in contrast to, e) in view of, in the face of; ***Männern ~ verhält sie sich komisch*** she's funny with men; **III.** & *n* (-s; -) a) person opposite; vis-à-vis; *sport*: opponent; *pol. etc.* counterpart, opposite number, b) house opposite, c) *fig.* antithesis; **~lie·gen** *v/i.* (*irr.*, *sep.*, h, → ***liegen***) be opposite, face (*dat. s.th.*); **~d** ... opposite; **~se·hen** *v/refl.* (*irr.*, *sep.*, h, → ***sehen***): ***sich ~*** *dat.* be up against; **~ste·hen** *v/i.* (*irr.*, *sep.*, h, → ***stehen***): ***j-m ~*** face s.o. (*a. fig.*); ***sich*** (*or* ***einander***) ***~*** be facing each other, *fig.* be opponents, be enemies; *fig. e-r Sache* ***~*** a) be faced (*or* confronted) with, face, be up against, b) view, regard, look upon; ***e-r Sache kritisch*** (***skeptisch***) ***~*** take a critical (sceptical, *Am.* skeptical) view of s.th., view s.th. with criticism (scepticism, *Am.* skepticism); ***sich*** (*or* ***einander***) ***~de Meinungen*** conflicting opinions

ge·gen'über·stel·len *v/t.* (*sep.*, h) **1.** *fig.* ***j-n j-m ~*** confront s.o. with s.o., bring s.o. face to face with s.o.; **2.** ***et. e-r Sache ~*** put s.th. opposite s.th., *fig.* compare s.th. with s.th.; **Ge·gen'über·stel·lung** *f* (-; *no pl.*) **1.** *a.* ⚖ confrontation; **2.** identification parade, *Am.* line-up; **3.** comparison

ge·gen'über·tre·ten *v/i.* (*irr.*, *sep.*, sn, → ***treten***) *a. fig.* face; oppose (*dat. s.o., s.th.*)

'Ge·gen|͵un·ter·schrift *f* countersignature; **~ver·kehr** *m* oncoming (*or* contraflow) traffic; *sign*: two-way traffic; **~ver·such** *m* control test; **~vor·schlag** *m* alternative (suggestion); ***darf ich e-n ~ machen?*** *a.* may I suggest an alternative?

Ge·gen·wart ['ge:gənvart] *f* (-; *no pl.*) **1.** the present (time); ***der ~*** → ***gegenwärtig*** 2; **2.** presence; ***in der ~ von*** *dat.* in the presence of, with ... present (*or* around); ***in s-r ~*** when he's around (*or* there); **3.** *ling.* present (tense); **ge·gen·wär·tig** ['ge:gənvɛrtɪç] **I.** *adj.* **1.** present; prevailing; ***zum ~en Zeitpunkt*** at the moment, at present; **2.** present-day ..., contemporary, of our time, today's; **3.** present; **4.** ***es ist mir im Moment nicht ~*** I can't think of it right now, I forget; **II.** *adv.* **5.** at the moment; at present; *esp. Am.* at this moment in time; **6.** nowadays, these days, today

'ge·gen·warts|be·zo·gen *adj.* topical; modern; **~fern, ~fremd** *adj.* remote, unrealistic; out of touch

'Ge·gen·warts|kunst *f* contemporary art; **~li·te·ra͵tur** *f* contemporary literature; **&nah** *adj.* topical; **~nä·he** *f* topicality; relevance to the present; **~pro͵ble-**

me *pl.* present-day problems; **~spra·che** *f* present-day language (*or* speech)
'Ge·gen|wehr *f* (-; *no pl.*) defen|ce (*Am.* -se); resistance; **~ leisten** put up a defen|ce (*Am.* -se) *or* fight; **keine ~ leisten** offer no resistance; **~wert** *m* equivalent (value); **im ~ von** *dat.* to the equivalent value of; **~wind** *m* headwind; **wir haben ~** there's a headwind (blowing); **~win·kel** *m* opposite angle; **~wir·kung** *f* reaction (**auf** *acc.* to), countereffect; adverse reaction
'ge·gen·zeich·nen *v/i. and v/t.* (*sep.*, h) countersign; endorse; **'Ge·gen·zeich·nung** *f* (-; *no pl.*) countersignature
'Ge·gen|zeu·ge *m* counterwitness; **~zug** *m* **1.** *chess and fig.* countermove; **im ~ (zu** *dat.*) as a countermove (to), in reaction (to); **2.** train coming from the other direction
ge·ges·sen [gə'gɛsən] *p.p. of* **essen**
ge·gli·chen [gə'glıçən] *p.p. of* **gleichen**
ge'glie·dert *adj.* **1.** *anat.* jointed; **2.** ⚙, ⚠ **~e Bauweise** sectionalized design; **3.** *fig.* organized, planned; structured
ge·glit·ten [gə'glıtən] *p.p. of* **gleiten**
ge·glom·men [gə'glɔmən] *lit. p.p. of* **glimmen**
Geg·ner ['ge:gnɐ] *m* (-s; -) opponent (*a. sport*), antagonist; enemy, *lit.* foe; assailant; rival, competitor; opposing party, other side; **ein ~ sein** *gen.* (*or* **von** *dat.*) be against, strongly oppose; **sich j-n zum ~ machen** make an enemy of s.o., antagonize s.o.; **j-n zum ~ haben** have s.o. as a rival *etc.*, have to compete against s.o.; **geg·ne·risch** ['ge:gnərıʃ] *adj.* opposing, antagonistic; enemy ...; **die ~e Mannschaft** the opponents, the other side; **'Geg·ner·schaft** *f* (-; *no pl.*) **1.** opponents *pl.*, opposition; **2.** opposition, antagonism; rivalry
ge·gol·ten [gə'gɔltən] *p.p. of* **gelten**
ge·go·ren [gə'go:rən] *p.p. of* **gären**
ge·gos·sen [gə'gɔsən] *p.p. of* **gießen**
ge'gra·ben *p.p. of* **graben**
ge·grif·fen [gə'grıfən] *p.p. of* **greifen**
Ge·ha·be [gə'ha:bə] *n* (-s; *no pl.*) silly behavio(u)r, affectation; fuss
ge'ha·ben *v/refl.*: *usu. iro.* **gehab dich wohl!** farewell
ge·habt [gə'ha:pt] **I.** *p.p. of* **haben; II.** *adj.*: **(alles) wie ~** same as ever; **es ist alles wie ~** *a.* nothing's changed; **wie ~** as always, as usual; **das bleibt wie ~** that stays as it is
Ge·hack·te [gə'haktə] *n* (-n; *no pl.*) mincemeat, minced (*Am.* ground) meat; *Am. a.* hamburger
Ge·halt¹ [gə'halt] *m* (-[e]s; *no pl.*) **1.** content; substance; **geistiger ~** intellectual content; **2.** content, percentage, *a.* concentration (*all* **an** *dat.* of); *wine*: body; **~ an Öl** oil content
Ge'halt² *n* (-[e]s; Gehälter [gə'hɛltɐ]) salary, pay; **ein ~ beziehen** draw a salary; **mit vollem ~** on full pay
ge'hal·ten I. *p.p. of* **halten; II.** *adj.* **1. ~ sein zu** *inf.* be expected to *inf.*; **ich bin ~ zu** *inf.* I'm constrained (*or* under an obligation) to *inf.*; **2.** restrained, subdued
ge'halt·los *adj.* **1.** insubstantial *food*; *wine*: lacking body; **2.** *fig.* empty, lacking in substance; meaningless
Ge'halts|ab·rech·nung *f* pay slip; **~ab·stu·fung** *f* salary scale; **~ab·zug** *m* deduction from salary; **~an·glei·chung** *f* salary adjustment; **~an·sprü·che** *pl.* salary expectations; **~aus·zah·lung** *f* payment of salary (*or* salaries); **~emp·fän·ger** *m* salaried employee; **~er·hö·hung** *f* (pay) rise; salary increase; **~for·de·rung** *f* salary claim; **~fort·zah·lung** *f* continued payment of salary; **~gren·ze** *f* salary limit; **~grup·pe** *f*, **~klas·se** *f* salary bracket; **~kon·to** *n* salary account; **~kür·zung** *f* salary cut; **~li·ste** *f* payroll; **~strei·fen** *m* pay slip; **~stu·fe** *f* salary bracket; **~vor·schuß** *m* advance; **~zah·lung** *f* payment of salary; **~zu·la·ge** *f* bonus
ge'halt·voll *adj.* **1.** substantial, nourishing *food*; full-bodied *wine*; **2.** *fig. work etc.* of substance; profound
ge·han·di·kapt [gə'hɛndikɛpt] *adj.* handicapped
Ge·hän·ge [gə'hɛŋə] *n* (-s; -) **1.** festoon(s *pl.*); **2.** pendants *pl.*; ear drops *pl.*; **3.** *sl.* accoutrements *pl.*, (family) jewels *pl.*
ge·har·nischt [gə'harnıʃt] *adj.* **1.** withering *reply etc.*; **ein ~er Brief** a strongly-worded reply, F a nasty letter; **2.** (clad) in armo(u)r, armo(u)r-clad
ge·häs·sig [gə'hɛsıç] *adj.* spiteful; **Ge'häs·sig·keit** *f* (-; -en) **1.** *no pl.* spitefulness; **aus reiner ~** out of sheer spite; **2.** spiteful remark
ge'häuft I. *adj.* heaped; **ein ~er Teelöffel** one heaped teaspoonful; **II.** *adv.* frequently, at frequent intervals, repeatedly; **die Anschläge sind in letzter Zeit ~ vorgekommen** there's been a spate of attacks recently
Ge·häu·se [gə'hɔyzə] *n* (-s; -) casing, case; cabinet; *phot.* body; *zo.* (*snail*) shell, *a.* case, pericarp, (*apple*) core
'geh·be·hin·dert *adj.*: **sie ist ~** she can't walk properly
ge'hef·tet *adj. typ.* stitched, sewn
Ge·he·ge [gə'he:gə] *n* (-s; -) enclosure; pen; paddock, *Am.* corral; *a. fig.* preserve; *fig.* **j-m ins ~ kommen** F get under s.o.'s feet; **komm mir ja nicht ins ~!** just keep out of my way
ge·heim [gə'haım] *adj.* secret; confidential, private; hidden; clandestine, surreptitious; occult *doctrine etc.*; **im ~en** secretly (*a. fig.*), in secret; **~!** Restricted!; **streng ~** top secret
Ge'heim|ab·kom·men *n* secret agreement; **~agent** *m* secret agent; **~ak·te** *f* secret (*or* classified) document; *pl.* secret files; **~auf·trag** *m* secret mission; **~be·fehl** *m* secret order; **~bund** *m* secret society; **~dienst** *m* secret service; **~do·ku·ˌment** *n* secret document; **~fach** *n* secret drawer; hidden safe
ge'heim·hal·ten *v/t.* (*irr.*, *sep.*, h, → **hal·ten**) keep *s.th.* secret (F under wraps); hush *s.th.* up; **et. vor j-m ~** keep s.th. a secret from s.o.; **wir müssen es vor ihm ~** *a.* he mustn't find out (about it); **Ge'heim·hal·tung** *f* (-; *no pl.*) (observance of) secrecy; concealment; **zur ~ verpflichtet sein** be sworn to secrecy
Ge'heim·hal·tungs... *in cpds.* ⚔, *pol.* security *measures etc.*; **~pflicht** *f* (imposed) secrecy; **~stu·fe** *f* security classification (*or* grade); **die ~ e-s Dokuments aufhe·ben** declassify a document
Ge'heim|kon·to *n* **1.** secret account; **2.** numbered account; **~leh·re** *f* **1.** esoteric doctrine; **2.** occult doctrine; **~mit·tel** *n* secret remedy
Ge·heim·nis [gə'haımnıs] *n* (-ses; -se) secret; mystery; **ein (kein) ~ aus et. ma·chen** make a secret out of s.th. (make no secret of s.th.); **ein öffentliches** (*or* **of·fenes**) **~** an open secret; **die ~se der Physik** the mysteries of physics; F **das ist das ganze ~** that's all there is to it; **~krä·mer** [-krɛ:mɐ] *m*: **er ist ein richti·ger ~** a) he likes to make a mystery out of things, b) he likes to make out he knows things that other people don't; **~krä·me·rei** [-krɛ:mə'raı] *f*: **hör doch auf mit dieser ~** stop making such a big secret out of it; **~trä·ger** *m* bearer of official secrets; **~tu·er** [-tu:ɐ] *m* → **Geheimnis·krämer; ~tue·rei** [-tu:ə'raı] *f* → **Ge·heimniskrämerei; ~umˌwit·tert** *adj.* surrounded by mystery, mysterious; enigmatic; → **~um·wo·ben** [-ʊmˌvo:bən] *adj.* shrouded in mystery
ge'heim·nis·voll *adj.* mysterious; enigmatic; arcane; **tu nicht so ~!** don't be so secretive, don't make such a big secret out of it
Ge'heim|num·mer *f* secret number; *teleph.* ex-directory (*Am.* unlisted) number; **~or·ga·ni·sa·tiˌon** *f* secret organization; **~po·liˌzei** *f* secret police; **~po·liˌzist** *m* member of the secret police; **er ist ~** *a.* he's from the secret police
Ge'heim·rat *m hist.* privy councillor; **Ge'heim·rats·ecken** *pl.*: **er hat ~** his hair is receding at the temples, F he's got a widow's peak
Ge'heim|reˌzept *n* secret recipe; **~sa·che** *f* secret matter; *pol.*, ⚔ security matter; **~schrift** *f* secret code; **~sen·der** *m* secret transmitter; **~sit·zung** *f* secret meeting; **~spra·che** *f* secret language; *contp.* jargon; **~tin·te** *f* invisible ink; **~tip** F *m* F hot tip; *betting etc.*: insiders' tip; **dieser Ort ist mein ~** this is a place I don't like to tell everyone about; **~tür** *f* secret door; **~ver·steck** *n* secret hiding place; **~ver·trag** *m* secret treaty; **~waf·fe** *f* secret weapon; **~zah·lun·gen** *pl.* secret payments; **~zei·chen** *n* secret sign; code, cipher
Ge·heiß [gə'haıs] *n*: **auf j-s ~ (hin)** at s.o.'s behest
ge'hemmt *adj.* inhibited; self-conscious; shy; **~ sein** feel inhibited, be (*or* feel) self-conscious *or* shy; **Ge'hemmt·heit** *f* (-; *no pl.*) inhibition; self-consciousness, shyness
ge·hen ['ge:ən] **I.** *v/i.* (ging, gegangen, sn) **1.** (*a. v/t.*) **(zu Fuß) ~** walk, go (on foot); **schwimmen ~** go swimming; **j-n su·chen ~** (go and) look for s.o.; **mit j-m zum Bahnhof ~** see s.o. to the station; **mit** *e-m Freund, Mädchen* **~** go out with, *esp. Am.* go steady with; **~ als** a) work as, b) go as; **ganz in Weiß** *etc.* **~** wear white *etc.*, be all in white *etc.*; **2.** a) go, leave, *a.* resign *from office etc.*, b) *bus etc.*: go, run (**nach** *dat.*, **bis** to, as far as), *road etc.*: go, lead (to), c) go (**um** *acc.* round *the waist etc.*); **j-n ~ lassen** a) let s.o. go, b) let s.o. off; → *a.* **gehenlassen; er ist gegangen** he's (= he has) gone *or* left; F **er ist gegangen worden** F he was sacked (*or* fired); **er ist von uns gegan·gen** he has passed away; F *fig.* **(ach,) geh!** come on!, go on!; **geh mir doch mit d-n faulen Ausreden!** I don't want to hear any of your excuses; **3.** a) ⚙ go, work (*a. fig.*), b) *fig.* be possible, c) *fig.* be allowed; *die Uhr* **geht nicht** has stopped, is broken; *das Gedicht, Lied* **geht so** goes like this; **wie geht es Ihnen?, wie**

geht's? how are you?, how are you feeling?; F ***wie geht's, wie steht's?*** how are things?, how's life (with you)?, how's life treating you?; ***es geht*** a) not too bad(ly), (it) could be worse, b) I can manage, c) it works; ***es geht nicht*** a) it can't be done, it's impossible, F nothing doing, no way, b) it just won't do, c) it doesn't work; ***es wird schon ~*** it'll be all right (*Am.* alright); ***es geht auch so*** we can manage without (it); ***es geht (eben) nicht anders*** it can't be helped(, I'm afraid); ***mir ist es genauso gegangen*** it was the same with me, F same here; ***mir geht es genauso*** I feel exactly the same way, F same here; ***ihm ist es (auch) nicht besser gegangen*** he didn't do (*or* fare) any better; ***so geht es, wenn man*** *nicht aufpaßt etc.*: that's what comes of *ger.*; ***das geht nun schon seit Jahren so*** that's been going on for years; ***wie ~ die Geschäfte?*** how's business?; ***so geht's nicht!*** you can't just go about it like that; → *a.* ***gutgehen, schlechtgehen***; **4.** ✝ sell (***gut*** well), go (well); ***die Stiefel ~ überhaupt nicht*** nobody's buying (*or* interested in) the boots, the boots aren't selling at all; **5.** *bell*: ring, go; *doorbell*: ring; *radio*: be on; *pulse*: beat; *dough*: rise; *wind*: blow; **6.** ***~ bis an*** *acc.* go as far as, reach *or* come up (*or* down) to; *das Erbteil* ***ging an ihn*** went (*or* fell) to him; ***an die Arbeit ~*** get down to work; ***geh mir ja nicht an m-e Sachen*** don't you (dare) touch (*or* interfere with) my things; ***wenn's ans Trinken geht*** when it comes to drinking; ***~ auf*** *acc.* go (*or* climb) up to, climb onto, go out into; *das Fenster* ***geht auf die Straße (hinaus)*** looks out onto the street; ***es geht auf zehn*** it's getting on for ten; ***das geht auf dich*** that's meant for you; ***auf e-n Zentner ~ 50 Kilogramm*** 50 kilogram(me)s make a (metric) hundredweight; ***das geht auf die Leber*** *etc.* it's bad for your liver *etc.*, it takes its toll on your liver *etc.*; ***s-e Kritik ging dahin, daß*** his criticism was to the effect that, what his criticism boiled down to was that; ***~ durch*** *acc.* go (*or* pass) through, *fig.* run through; ***~ gegen*** *acc.* go against; ***~ in*** *acc.* a) go into, enter, b) go (*or* fit) in(to), c) *ped., thea. etc.* go to, d) *stairs*: lead (up *or* down) to, ⚡ lead into; *der Schaden* ***geht in die Millionen*** runs into millions; ***die Kämpfe ~ in den vierten Tag*** fighting has entered its fourth day; ***es ~ 200 Personen in den Saal*** the hall holds (*or* seats) two hundred people; ***in die Industrie ~*** go into industry; ***in sich ~*** do a bit of soul-searching; ***wie oft geht fünf in neunzig?*** how many times does five go into ninety?; ***~ nach*** *dat.* go by; *das Fenster* ***geht nach Norden*** faces (*or* looks) north; ***wenn es nach mir ginge*** if I had my way; ***~ über*** *acc.* go (*or* walk) over, cross *the street etc.*; *die Brücke* ***geht über e-e Schlucht*** spans (*or* goes over) a ravine; *der Zug etc.* ***geht über Berlin*** goes via Berlin; ***das geht ihm über alles*** it means everything to him; ***nichts geht über ...*** *acc.* there's nothing like ...; ***es geht ihm nur ums Geld*** he's just interested in the money; ***mir geht's nicht ums Geld*** it's not a question of money, I'm not interested in the money; ***es geht hier um ...*** *acc.* we're talking about (*or* looking at) ...; ***es geht um*** *acc.* *his life etc.* is at stake; ***worum geht es?*** what's the problem?; ***es geht darum zu*** *inf.* it's a question (*or* matter) of *ger.*; ***darum geht es hier (gar) nicht*** that's not the point; ***~ vor*** *dat. a. fig.* go before; ***vor sich ~*** happen; ***was geht hier vor sich?*** what's going on here?; ***zu j-m ~*** a) join s.o., b) go up to s.o., c) go and see s.o.; → ***Auge*** 1, ***Begriff*** 1, ***Bett, Bord, Grund*** 1; ***vonstatten, weit*** II; **II.** ♀ *n* (-s) **1.** *a. sport*: walking; ***das ~ fällt ihm schwer*** he finds it hard to walk; **2.** ⚙ ***zum ~ bringen*** get *s.th.* going; **~las·sen** *v/refl.* (*irr., sep.*, h, → ***lassen***): ***sich ~*** a) let o.s. go, b) lose one's temper

Ge·her ['ge:ɐ] *m* (-s; -) *sport*: walker

Ge'het·ze *n* (-s; *no pl.*) rush(ing); *w.s.* rat-race; ***ich kann dieses ~ nicht ausstehen*** I can't stand having to rush round like an idiot all the time; **ge'hetzt** *adj.* hunted (*a. fig.*); *fig.* harassed

ge·heu·er [gə'hɔʏɐ] *adj.*: ***nicht ~*** a) eerie, F creepy, spooky, scary, b) fishy, strange; dubious; ***es ist dort nicht ganz ~*** it's a funny place; ***mir ist dieser Ort nicht ~*** this place gives me the creeps; ***er (die Sache*** *etc.*) ***ist mir nicht ~*** I've got a funny feeling about him (it *etc.*); ***ihm war nicht ganz ~ zumute*** he felt very uneasy

Ge·heul [gə'hɔʏl] *n* (-[e]s; *no pl.*) howling, howls *pl.*; **Ge'heu·le** F *n* (-s; *no pl.*) howling; ***hör mit dem ~ auf!*** stop your howling now

ge'hext *adj.*: ***wie ~*** as if by magic; ***der Haushalt läuft wie ~*** the household seems to run itself

'geh·fä·hig *adj.* able to walk

'Geh|feh·ler *m* limp; **~gips** *m* walking cast

Ge'hil·fe *m* (-n; -n) assistant; someone to help out; shop assistant; clerk; journeyman; ⚖ accessory (before the fact); *contp.* henchman

Ge'hirn *n* (-[e]s; -e) brain; F *fig.* brain(s *pl.*), mind; **~...** *in cpds.* brain, cerebral, ... of the brain; **~akro,ba·tik** F *f* mental acrobatics (*or* gyrations) *pl.*; **♀am·pu,tiert** F *hum. adj.* F dead from the neck up; **~blu·tung** *f* brain (*or* cerebral) h(a)emorrhage; **~chir·urg** *m* brain surgeon; **~chir·ur,gie** *f* brain surgery; **~durch,blu·tung** *f* blood flow (*or* circulation) in the brain; ***es fördert die ~*** *a.* F it gets your brain cells working; **~er·schüt·te·rung** *f* concussion; ***e-e ~ haben*** have (*or* be suffering from) concussion; → ***schwer*** I; **~er·wei·chung** *f a. fig.* softening of the brain

Ge'hirn·haut *f* cerebral membrane; **~ent·zün·dung** *f* meningitis

Ge'hirn|ka·sten F *m* F skull; ***streng d-n ~ an!*** use your brains (F noddle)!; **~lap·pen** *m* lobe of the brain; **~nerv** *m* cranial nerve; **~quet·schung** *f* cerebral contusion; **~rin·de** *f* cerebral cortex; **~schlag** *m* stroke; **~schmalz** F *n* F (little) grey (*Am.* gray) cells *pl.*; ***dafür habe ich e-e Menge ~ verschwendet*** that cost me a few grey (*Am.* gray) cells; ***bei dir reicht wohl das ~ nicht aus*** F have you got sawdust between your ears?; **~schwund** *m* atrophy of the brain; **~tä·tig·keit** *f* cerebral activity; ***die ~ hat ausgesetzt*** the brain has stopped functioning; **~tod** *m* brain death; **~tu·mor** *m* brain tumo(u)r; **~ver·let·zung** *f* brain injury; **~wä·sche** *f* brainwashing; ***j-n e-r ~ unterziehen*** brainwash s.o.

'Geh·mi,nu·te *f*: ***es ist nur ein paar ~n von hier*** it's only a few minutes' walk away (*or* from here)

ge·ho·ben [gə'ho:bən] **I.** *p.p. of* ***heben***; **II.** *adj.* high, senior *official, post etc.*; *fig.* elevated *style*; ***~e Stimmung*** high spirits *pl.*; ***~e Ansprüche*** expensive tastes; ✝ ***Güter des ~en Bedarfs*** luxuries and semi-luxuries

Ge·höft [gə'hœft] *n* (-[e]s; -e) farm(stead)

ge·hol·fen [gə'hɔlfən] *p.p. of* ***helfen***

Ge·hölz [gə'hœlts] *n* (-es; -e) wood, copse; thicket

Ge·hör [gə'hø:ɐ] *n* (-[e]s; *no pl.*) (sense of) hearing; ears *pl.*; *fig.* ear; ⚖ hearing; ***feines (scharfes) ~*** sensitive (keen) ear; ***nach dem ~*** by ear; ***ein ~ haben für*** *acc.* have an ear for; ***j-m ~ schenken*** listen to what s.o. has to say; ***kein ~ schenken*** *dat.* turn a deaf ear to *s.th.*, refuse to listen to *s.o.*; ***(j-n) um ~ bitten*** request a hearing (from s.o.); ***~ finden*** get a hearing; ***sich ~ verschaffen*** make o.s. heard; ⚖ ***j-n ohne rechtliches ~ verurteilen*** sentence s.o. without a hearing; → ***absolut*** I; **~bil·dung** *f* aural training

ge'hor·chen *v/i.* (h): ***j-m (nicht) ~*** (dis-)obey s.o.; ***du mußt d-r Mutter ~*** you must do as your mother tells you; → ***Wort***

ge'hö·ren (h) **I.** *v/i.* belong to (*a. fig.*); ***~ zu*** *dat.* belong to, be part of, rank (*or* be) among; ***~ unter*** *acc.* come (*or* fall) under *a heading etc.*; ***wem gehört das Buch?*** whose book is this?, who does this book belong to?; ***gehört der Handschuh dir?*** is this your glove?; ***er gehört zu den besten Spielern*** he's one of the best players; ***die Sachen ~ in den Schrank*** these things go into the cupboard; ***das Fahrrad gehört nicht in die Wohnung!*** the flat is no place for a bike; ***es gehört zu s-r Arbeit*** it's part of his job; ***das gehört nicht zur Sache*** that's not relevant; ***er gehört nicht zu dieser Sorte*** he's not like that, he's not that sort of person; ***dazu gehört Geld*** you need money for that, ***Zeit:*** that kind of thing takes time; ***Mut:*** it takes a lot of courage; ***es gehört nicht viel dazu*** it doesn't take much; ***dazu gehört schon einiges*** a) that takes a lot of doing, b) you've got to be pretty cheeky to do that; ***du gehörst ins Bett*** you should be in bed; F ***er gehört tüchtig verprügelt*** what he wants is a good hiding; ***er gehört auf den Fußballplatz*** he ought to be playing football; **II.** *v/refl.*: ***das gehört sich nicht*** it's not done; ***so gehört es sich auch*** that's the way it should be; ***er weiß, was sich gehört*** he knows how to behave; ***wie es sich gehört*** properly; *ihr habt ja e-n tollen Wagen -* ***wie sich's gehört*** what do you expect?

Ge'hör|feh·ler *m* hearing defect; impaired hearing; **~gang** *m* auditory canal

ge'hö·rig **I.** *adj.* **1.** right, due, proper; necessary; ***mit dem ~en Respekt*** with due respect; **2.** F decent; ***e-e ~e Portion Kartoffelbrei*** a decent serving (F a good dollop) of mashed potatoes; ***dazu gehört e-e ~e Portion Frechheit*** that takes a fair bit of cheek; ***e-e ~e Tracht Prügel*** a good hiding; ***ein ~er Schluck*** a decent gulp (F swig); **3.** ***(zu) j-m (e-r Sache) ~ sein*** belong to s.o. (s.th.); ***(nicht) zur Sache ~*** (ir)relevant; **II.** *adv.* duly, properly; ***ich habe es ihm ~ gegeben*** F I really let him have it

Ge'hör·knö·chel·chen *n* (-s; -) *anat.* ossicle

Ge'hör·lei·den *n* hearing defect

ge'hör·los *adj.* deaf; **Ge'hör·lo·sen·schu·le** *f* school for the deaf; **Ge'hör·lo·sig·keit** *f* (-; *no pl.*) deafness

Ge·hörn [gə'hœrn] *n* (-[e]s; -e) horns *pl.*; antlers *pl.*

Ge'hör·nerv *m* auditory nerve

ge·hörnt [gə'hœrnt] *adj.* horned; F *fig.* **~er Ehemann** cuckold

Ge'hör·prü·fung *f* hearing test

ge·hor·sam [gə'ho:ɐza:m] **I.** *adj.* obedient (**gegen** *acc.* to); law-abiding *citizen*; submissive; **die Kinder sind sehr ~** the children always do as they're told; **II. ~** *m* (-s; *no pl.*) obedience (**gegen** *acc.*, **gegenüber** *dat.* to); **blinder ~** blind (*or* unquestioning) obedience; **j-m ~ leisten** obey s.o.; **j-m den ~ verweigern** disobey s.o., refuse to carry out s.o.'s orders; **sich bei j-m ~ verschaffen** force s.o. to obey; **Ge'hor·sams·ver·wei·ge·rung** *f* disobedience; ⚔ insubordination

Ge'hör|scha·den *m* hearing defect; impaired hearing; **~sinn** *m* sense of hearing; **~ver·lust** *m* loss of hearing

'Geh·rock *m* (-[e]s; ¨e) frock coat

Geh·rung ['ge:rʊŋ] *f* (-; -en) ⚙ mitre (*Am.* miter); bevel

'Geh·steig *m* (-[e]s; -e) pavement, *Am.* sidewalk

Ge·hu·del [gə'hu:dəl] F *n* (-s; *no pl.*) a) sloppiness, b) sloppy (*or* messy) piece of work

Ge'hu·pe *n* (-s; *no pl.*) honking (of car horns), tooting; blaring horns *pl.*

ge'hupft → **hupfen**

Ge·hu·ste [gə'hu:stə] *n* (-s; *no pl.*) (endless) coughing, F coughing and spluttering

'Geh·ver·such *m* attempt to walk; *fig.* **erste literarische ~e** first attempt to write, first literary effort

'Geh·weg *m* **1.** footpath; **2.** pavement, *Am.* sidewalk

Gei·er ['gaɪɐ] *m* (-s; -) vulture (*a. fig.*); F **hol's der ~!** F to hell with it!; F **weiß der ~!** God knows

Gei·fer ['gaɪfɐ] *m* (-s; *no pl.*) dribble, slaver; foam, froth; *fig.* venom, spite; **Gei·fe·rer** ['gaɪfərɐ] *m* (-s; -) vituperator; **'gei·fern** *v/i.* (h) dribble, slaver; **vor Wut ~** froth at the mouth; *fig.* **~ gegen** *acc.* rail at

Gei·ge ['gaɪgə] *f* (-; -n) violin; **~ spielen** play the violin; **(die) erste (zweite) ~ spielen** play first (second) violin, *fig.* play first (second) fiddle; **'gei·gen** (h) **I.** *v/i.* play the violin, F fiddle; **II.** *v/t.* play *s.th.* on the violin, F fiddle *a tune*; F *fig.* **es j-m ~** F tell s.o. what's what

'Gei·gen|bau *m* (-[e]s; *no pl.*) violin making; **~bau·er** *m* (-s; -) violin maker; **~bo·gen** *m* violin bow; **~harz** *n* rosin; **~ka·sten** *m* violin case; **~spiel** *n* (-[e]s; *no pl.*) violin playing; **~spie·ler** *m* violinist; **~stim·me** *f* violin part; **~strich** *m* stroke (of the bow)

Gei·ger ['gaɪgɐ] *m* (-s; -), **Gei·ge·rin** ['gaɪgərɪn] *f* (-; -nen) violinist

'Gei·ger·zäh·ler *m* Geiger counter

geil [gaɪl] *adj.* **1.** F randy, horny; lecherous; F **~er alter Bock** F randy (*or* dirty) old man, *sl.* lech; F *fig.* **~ sein auf** *acc.* a) F be crazy about, b) be burning to get, lust after (*or* for), *sl.* lech after; **2.** F brill (*sl.*), ace; **3.** rank, luxuriant *vegetation*

Gei·sel ['gaɪzəl] *f* (-; -n) hostage; **j-n als ~ nehmen** take s.o. hostage; **~be·frei·ung** *f* freeing (*or* release) of (the) hostages; **~dra·ma** *n* hostage drama (*or* crisis); kidnapping drama; **~gang·ster** *m* violent kidnapper; **~haft** *f* captivity as a hostage; **nach drei Jahren ~** *a.* after three years of being held hostage

'Gei·sel·nah·me [-na:mə] *f* (-; -n) taking of hostages (*or* a hostage); kidnapping; **'Gei·sel·neh·mer** [-ne:mɐ] *m* (-s; -) hostage-taker, kidnapper, captor

Gei·sha ['ge:ʃa] *f* (-; -s) geisha (girl)

Geiß [gaɪs] *f* (-; -en) (nanny) goat; doe; **~bock** *m* billy goat

Gei·ßel ['gaɪsəl] *f* (-; -n) **1.** whip; *fig.* scourge; **2.** *biol.* flagellum; **'gei·ßeln** *v/t.* (h) whip; *eccl.* flagellate (**sich** o.s.); *fig.* castigate (o.s.), chastise (o.s.); **'Gei·ßel·tier·chen** *n* flagellate; **'Gei·ße·lung** *f* (-; -en) flagellation; *fig.* castigation; severe condemnation

Geist[1] [gaɪst] *m* (-[e]s; *no pl.*) mind; intellect; wit; spirit; morale; **~ und Körper** mind and body, body and spirit; **der ~ des Christentums** the spirit of Christianity; **Mann von ~** man of wit; **der ~ ist willig, aber das Fleisch ist schwach** the spirit is willing but the flesh is weak; **im ~e** in one's mind's eye; **im ~e sah sie sich schon als Siegerin** she already imagined (*or* saw) herself as the winner; **wir werden im ~e bei euch sein** our thoughts will be with you; **in j-s ~e handeln** act in the spirit of s.o.; **daran sieht man, wes ~es Kind er ist** it says a lot about him; **sie ist ein unruhiger ~** she's a restless person, she can't sit still for one moment, F she's up and down like a yoyo; F **das geht mir auf den ~** F it really gets on my wick, it's driving me spare; F **der Wagen hat den ~ aufgegeben** F the car has given up the ghost, the car has conked out; → **scheiden** III

Geist[2] *m* (-[e]s; -er) **1.** spirit; ghost; apparition; **böser ~** evil spirit, demon; *eccl.* **der Böse ~** the Evil One; *fig.* **j-s guter ~** s.o.'s good genius; **hier geht ein ~ um** this place is haunted; **bist du denn von allen guten ~ern verlassen?** are you out of your (F tiny little) mind?; → **heilig; 2.** thinker; **ein großer ~** a great thinker

Gei·ster|bahn ['gaɪstɐ-] *f* ghost train; **~be·schwö·rer** *m* (-s; -) necromancer; exorcist; **~be·schwö·rung** *f* necromancy; exorcism; **~bild** *n* *TV* ghosting, F shadow(s *pl.*); **~er·schei·nung** *f* apparition; **~fah·rer** *m* wrong-way driver; **plötzlich kam uns ein ~ entgegen** suddenly a car was driving towards us in the wrong direction; **~ge·schich·te** *f* ghost story; **~glau·be** *m* belief in ghosts; superstition

'gei·ster·haft *adj.* ghostly, F spooky

'Gei·ster|hand *f*: **wie von ~** as if by magic; **~haus** *n* **1.** haunted house; **2.** *buddhism etc.*: spirit house

gei·stern ['gaɪstɐn] *fig.* *v/i.* (h, sn): **~ durch** *acc.* flit around; **~ über** *acc.* flit across; **die Idee geistert immer noch in ihren Köpfen** they still haven't managed to get that idea out of their heads

'Gei·ster|reich *n* realm of spirits; **~schiff** *n* phantom ship; **~schloß** *n* haunted castle; **~schrei·ber** *m* ghostwriter; **~stadt** *f* ghost town; **~stim·me** *f* spooky voice; *TV* voice-over; **~stun·de** *f* witching hour; **~welt** *f* realm (*or* world) of the supernatural; **~zug** *m* empty train

gei·stes·ab·we·send ['gaɪstəs-] **I.** *adj.* absent, distracted; **II.** *adv.* absent-mindedly; absently; **'Gei·stes·ab·we·sen·heit** *f* (-; *no pl.*) distractedness; absent-mindedness

'Gei·stes|an·stren·gung *f* mental effort; **~ar·beit** *f* brainwork; **~ar·bei·ter** *m* brainworker; **~bil·dung** *f* cultivation of the mind; **ein Mann von großer ~** a highly educated man; **~blitz** *m* flash of inspiration; F brainwave; **~frei·heit** *f* (-; *no pl.*) intellectual freedom; **~ga·ben** *pl.* intellectual gifts

'Gei·stes·ge·gen·wart *f* presence of mind; **'gei·stes·ge·gen·wär·tig** **I.** *adj.* alert, F on the ball; quick *a. answer, reaction etc.*; **II.** *adv.*: **~ riß er das Kind weg** he had the presence of mind to pull the child away

'Gei·stes·ge·schich·te *f* (-; *no pl.*) history of thought (*or* ideas); **die deutsche** *etc.* **~** the history of German *etc.* thought

'gei·stes·ge·stört *adj.* mentally disturbed; **'Gei·stes·ge·stör·te** *m, f* (-n; -n) mentally disturbed person; **'Gei·stes·ge·stört·heit** *f* (-; *no pl.*) mental imbalance (*or* derangement)

'Gei·stes|hal·tung *f* attitude, mentality; **~kräf·te** *pl.* mental faculties

'gei·stes·krank *adj.* mentally ill (*or* disordered); **'Gei·stes·kran·ke** *m, f* (-n; -n) mental patient; *pl. the* mentally ill (*pl.*); **'Gei·stes·krank·heit** *f* mental disease

'Gei·stes|le·ben *n* intellectual life; **~pro,dukt** *n* (intellectual) product, brainchild; **~rich·tung** *f* school of thought; **~schär·fe** *f* acuity of mind; keen intellect

'gei·stes·schwach *adj.* feebleminded; **'Gei·stes·schwä·che** *f* (-; *no pl.*) feeblemindedness

'Gei·stes|stö·rung *f* mental disorder; **~träg·heit** *f* mental sluggishness; **~ver·fas·sung** *f* frame of mind, (mental) state

'gei·stes·ver·wandt *adj.* congenial (**mit** *dat.* to), kindred ...; **~e Menschen** kindred spirits; **'Gei·stes·ver·wandt·schaft** *f* (spiritual) affinity

'Gei·stes·ver·wir·rung *f* confused state of mind

'Gei·stes·wis·sen·schaft *f* arts subject; **die ~en** the arts, the humanities; **'Gei·stes·wis·sen·schaft·ler** *m* (-s; -) a) arts scholar (F person, man), b) arts student; **'gei·stes·wis·sen·schaft·lich** *adj.* arts ...; *research etc.* in the arts *or* in the (field of) humanities

'Gei·stes|zer·rüt·tung *f* mental derangement, dementia; **~zu·stand** *m* (-[e]s; *no pl.*) mental state; **j-n auf s-n ~ (hin) untersuchen** give s.o. a mental examination; F **du solltest dich mal auf d-n ~ untersuchen lassen!** F you need your head testing (*or* tested)

gei·stig ['gaɪstɪç] **I.** *adj.* spiritual; intellectual, mental; **~e Entwicklung** spiritual (*or* intellectual) development; **~es Eigentum** intellectual property; → **Diebstahl; ~er Austausch** exchange of ideas; **~e Arbeit** → **Geistesarbeit; ~er Vater** spiritual father; F **~e Getränke** spirits, alcohol; → **Auge** 1; **II.** *adv.* mentally *etc.*; → **I; ~ anspruchsvoll** highbrow; **~ behindert** mentally handicapped; **~ aktiv sein** a) have an active mind, b) exercise one's mind, c) have a lot of intellectual pursuits; ***ich kann ~ nicht mehr folgen*** I'm lost, you've *etc.* lost me; '**Gei·stig·keit** *f* (-; *no pl.*) intellectuality; spirituality

'**gei·stig-'see·lisch** *adj.* mental and spiritual

'**geist·lich** *adj.* religious; ♪ *etc. a.* sacred; clerical; ecclesiastical; spiritual; ***~es Amt*** ministry; ***~er Orden*** religious order; → ***Stand*** 3; '**Geist·li·che** *m* (-n; -n) clergyman; minister; priest; ⚔ chaplain, padre; ***die ~n*** → '**Geist·lich·keit** *f* (-; *no pl.*) *the* clergy

'**geist·los** *adj.* dull; insipid, vapid; stupid; '**Geist·lo·sig·keit** *f* (-; -en) **1.** *no pl.* insipidity; **2.** banality, platitude

'**geist·reich** *adj.* witty, clever; ***e-e nicht gerade ~e Bemerkung*** not the most profound remark; '**geist·rei·cheln** [-raɪçəln] *v/i.* (h) try to be clever, display one's wit

'**geist|sprü·hend** *adj.* sparkling, scintillating; **~tö·tend** *adj.* deadly boring; mind-dulling, mind-numbing, F brainless; ***es war ~*** *a.* F it was a crushing bore; **~voll** *adj.* **1.** profound; **2.** → ***geistreich***

Geiz [gaɪts] *m* (-es; *no pl.*) stinginess, miserliness; ***aus lauter ~ macht er die Heizung nicht an*** he's too stingy to turn the heating on; **gei·zen** ['gaɪtsən] *v/i.* (h): ~ ***mit*** *dat.* be mean with; ***nicht ~ mit*** *dat.* be very generous with, not to stint (on); ***mit Worten ~*** be very sparing with words; ***mit s-r Zeit ~*** plan one's time very carefully; ***er geizt mit jeder Mark*** he turns every mark round in his pocket; '**Geiz·hals** *m* skinflint, (old) miser; **gei·zig** ['gaɪtsɪç] *adj.* stingy, tight-fisted, miserly; '**Geiz·kra·gen** *m* skinflint, (old) miser

Ge·jam·mer [gə'jamɐ] *n* (-s; *no pl.*) moaning, whining

Ge·jau·le [gə'jaʊlə] *n* (-s; *no pl.*) howling

Ge·joh·le [gə'jo:lə] *n* (-s; *no pl.*) shouting

ge'ka·chelt *adj.* tiled

ge·kannt [gə'kant] *p.p. of* ***kennen***

Ge·kei·fe [gə'kaɪfə] *n* (-s; *no pl.*) squawking

Ge·ki·cher [gə'kɪçɐ] *n* (-s; *no pl.*) giggling

Ge·kläff [gə'klɛf] *n* (-[e]s; *no pl.*) yapping, barking

Ge·klap·per [gə'klapɐ] *n* (-s; *no pl.*) rattling, clatter

Ge·klat·sche [gə'klatʃə] *n* (-s; *no pl.*) clapping; ***dieses ~ geht mir auf die Nerven*** I wish they wouldn't keep clapping

Ge·klim·per [gə'klɪmpɐ] *n* (-s; *no pl.*) tinkling

Ge'klin·gel *n* (-s; *no pl.*) ringing; *bells etc.*: tinkling, jingling

Ge·klirr [gə'klɪr] *n* (-[e]s; *no pl.*) tinkling; clattering *of dishes*; rattling *of chains*

ge·klom·men [gə'klɔmən] *p.p. of* ***klimmen***

Ge·klop·fe [gə'klɔpfə] *n* (-s; *no pl.*) knocking, banging

ge·klun·gen [gə'klʊŋən] *p.p. of* ***klingen***

Ge·knat·ter [gə'knatɐ] *n* (-s; *no pl.*) crackling; *mot.* put-put(ting)

ge·knickt [gə'knɪkt] *fig. adj.* crestfallen, crushed

ge·knif·fen [gə'knɪfən] *p.p. of* ***kneifen***

Ge·kni·ster [gə'knɪstɐ] *n* (-s; *no pl.*) crackling; rustling *of paper*

ge·knüp·pelt [gə'knʏpəlt] F *adv.*: ~ ***voll*** F jampacked, chock-a-block

Ge·knut·sche [gə'knu:tʃə] F *n* (-s; *no pl.*) necking

ge'kocht *adj.* boiled; cooked; ***~es Gemüse*** boiled (*or* cooked) vegetables; ***~es Obst*** stewed fruit

ge·konnt [gə'kɔnt] **I.** *p.p. of* ***können***; **II.** *adj.* skil(l)ful; masterly; ***das war ~!*** *a.* it was brilliant; **III.** *adv.*: ***das hat sie ~ gemacht*** *a.* she made an excellent job of it

ge'kop·pelt *adj.* linked (***an*** *acc.* to, with)

Ge'kra·kel *n* (-s; *no pl.*) scrawl; ***das ist ja ein furchtbares ~*** *a.* it looks as if a spider's walked all over it

ge'kränkt *adj.* hurt, offended (***über*** *acc.* at, by); injured *pride etc.*

ge'kräu·selt *adj.* curly *hair*; rippled *water*; gathered *skirt etc.*

Ge·kreisch [gə'kraɪʃ] *n* (-[e]s; *no pl.*) screeching, screaming

Ge·kreu·zig·te [gə'krɔʏtsɪçtə] *m* (-n; -n): *eccl.* ***der ~*** Christ on the cross, Christ crucified

Ge·krit·zel [gə'krɪtsəl] *n* (-s; *no pl.*) a) scrawling, scribbling, b) scrawl

ge·kro·chen [gə'krɔxən] *p.p. of* ***kriechen***

ge'krönt *adj.*: ***~e Häupter*** crowned heads; *fig.* ***von Erfolg ~*** crowned with success

ge'kröpft *adj.* ⚙ cranked, goosenecked; ⚠ angulate

Ge·krö·se [gə'krø:zə] *n* (-s; -) **1.** *gastr.* tripe; **2.** *anat.* mesentery

ge'krümmt I. *adj.* curved; hooked; bent; warped; **II.** *adv.*: ***sie geht ganz ~*** she's almost bent double

ge'kün·stelt *adj.* artificial, affected; stilted, contrived *style*; forced *smile*

Gel [ge:l] *n* (-s; -e) gel

Ge·la·ber [gə'la:bɐ] *n* (-s; *no pl.*) drivel

Ge·läch·ter [gə'lɛçtɐ] *n* (-s; *no pl.*) laughing, laughter; ***in schallendes ~ ausbrechen*** roar with laughter; ***j-n (et.) dem ~ preisgeben*** expose s.o. (s.th.) to ridicule, make s.o. a laughing stock, make s.o. the laughing stock (*gen.* of)

ge·lack·mei·ert [gə'lakmaɪɐt] F *adj.*: ***sich ~ fühlen*** feel one has been had (*or* conned); ***ich bin der ⁀e*** I've been had (*or* taken for a ride), F I'm the sucker (*or* mug)

ge'la·den I. *p.p. of* ***laden***; **II.** *adj.* **1.** loaded; ⚡ charged, live; F *fig.* fuming, F mad; F *fig.* ***auf j-n ~ sein*** F have it in for s.o.; ~ ***mit*** *dat.* brimming with; **2.** invited *guests*

Ge·la·ge [gə'la:gə] *n* (-s; -) feast; ***wildes ~*** wild carousal

ge'la·gert *fig. adj.*: ***anders ~*** different; ***das hängt davon ab, wie der Fall ~ ist*** that depends on the particular case; ***in besonders ~en Fällen*** in special cases

ge·lähmt [gə'lɛ:mt] *adj.* paralyzed (*fig.* ***vor*** *dat.* with); ***einseitig (doppelseitig) ~*** paralyzed on *or* down one side (both sides) of one's body, 🕮 hemiplegic (paraplegic); ***rechtsseitig (linksseitig) ~*** paralyzed on the right (left) *or* down one's right (left) side; *fig.* ***wie ~ dastehen*** stand rooted to the spot, stand transfixed; ***sie war vor Angst wie ~*** she was petrified (*or* paralyzed with fear)

Ge·län·de [gə'lɛndə] *n* (-s; -) area; ground, terrain; site; grounds *pl.*, complex; ***(ein) hügeliges ~*** hilly ground; ***(ein) offenes ~*** open country (*or* terrain); ***(ein) schwieriges ~*** difficult terrain; **~auf·nah·me** *f* topographical survey; aerial photograph; **~aus·bil·dung** *f* ⚔ field training; **~er·kun·dung** *f* ⚔ terrain reconnaissance; **~fahr·rad** *n* BMX bike, (BMX) fun bike; **~fahrt** *f* cross-country drive; **~fahr·zeug** *n* cross-country (*or* off-road) vehicle; all-wheel (*or* four-wheel) drive; **⁀gän·gig** *adj.* cross-country *vehicle etc.*; **~kar·te** *f* ground map; **~kun·de** *f* topography; **~lauf** *m* cross-country run (*or* race); **~läu·fer** *m* cross-country runner; **~marsch** *m* cross-country march

Ge·län·der [gə'lɛndɐ] *n* (-s; -) railing(s *pl.*); banister(s *pl.*)

Ge'län·de|rei·fen *m* cross-country tyre (*Am.* tire); **~sport** *m* field sports *pl.*; **~übung** *f* field exercise; **~wa·gen** *m* → ***Geländefahrzeug***

ge·lang [gə'laŋ] *pret. of* ***gelingen***

ge'lan·gen *v/i.* (sn): ~ ***an*** *acc.* (*or* ***nach*** *dat.*, ***zu*** *dat.*) reach, get to; ***zum Ziel ~*** reach (*or* arrive at) one's destination, *fig.* reach one's goal; ~ ***zu*** *dat.* gain *power etc.*, acquire *a fortune, great wealth etc.*, reach (*or* come to) *an agreement, an understanding*; ***zu Ehren ~*** make a name for o.s.; ***in j-s Hände ~*** get into s.o.'s hands; ***in den Besitz von et. ~*** come into the possession of s.th.; ***zu der Ansicht ~, daß*** come to the conclusion that, decide that; ***zum Abschluß ~*** be finished, be completed, come to an end; ***zur Aufführung ~*** be put on stage; ***zur Ausführung ~*** be carried out; → ***Erkenntnis, Macht, Schluß*** 2

ge·lang·weilt [gə'laŋvaɪlt] **I.** *adj.* bored; bored-looking *face*; *fig.* ***zu Tode ~*** bored to death (*or* tears); **II.** *adv.*: ***sie hörten ~ zu*** they listened, completely bored

ge'las·sen I. *p.p. of* ***lassen***; **II.** *adj.* calm; composed; cool; imperturbable; ~ ***bleiben*** keep (one's) cool; ***sich ~ geben*** act cool; F ***~er Typ*** F laid-back sort of guy; **III.** *adv.*: ***et. ~ hinnehmen*** take s.th. calmly, take s.th. in one's stride; ~ ***s-m Schicksal entgegensehen*** calmly await one's fate; **Ge'las·sen·heit** *f* (-; *no pl.*) calm(ness); composure; coolness; imperturbability

Ge·la·ti·ne [ʒela'ti:nə] *f* (-; *no pl.*) gelatin(e)

ge'lau·fen *p.p. of* ***laufen***

ge·läu·fig [gə'lɔʏfɪç] *adj.* **1.** familiar, common; ***das Wort ist mir (nicht) ~*** I've heard (of) the word, I know the word (I've never heard [of] the word, I don't know the word); **2.** fluent; **Ge·läu·fig·keit** *f* (-; *no pl.*) **1.** widespread use, currency; **2.** ease (***beim Spielen*** with which one plays)

ge·launt [gə'laʊnt] *adj.*: ***schlecht (gut) ~ sein*** be in a bad (good) mood; ***ich bin dazu nicht ~*** I'm not in the mood (for it), I don't feel like it; ***wie ist sie heute ~?*** what kind of mood is she in today?; *iro.* ***wie bist du wieder ~!*** in a bad mood, are we?

Ge·läut [gə'lɔʏt] *n* (-[e]s; -e) **1.** *no pl.* ringing (of bells); **2.** bells *pl.*, chime(s *pl.*)

ge'läu·tert *adj.* ⚙ refined; *fig.* purified, chastened

gelb [gɛlp] **I.** *adj.* yellow; *traffic light*: amber; sallow *complexion*; ***~e Seiten*** yellow pages; *fig. contp.* ***die ~e Gefahr*** the yellow peril; ~ ***vor Neid*** green with envy; → ***Karte***; **II.** ⁀ *n* (-s; -) yellow; ***bei ~ über die Kreuzung fahren*** cross when the lights are at (*or* on) amber; **~braun** *adj.* yellowish-brown, yellowy-brown

Gel·be ['gɛlbə] *n* (-n; *no pl.*) yolk *of an egg*;

F *fig.* ***das ist auch nicht gerade das ~ vom Ei*** that's not exactly brilliant either, is it?

'Gelb|fie·ber *n* yellow fever; **~fil·ter** *m, n phot.* yellow filter; **2grün** *adj.* yellowish-green, yellowy-green; **~kör·per** *m anat.* corpus luteum

'gelb·lich *adj.* yellowish, yellowy

'Gelb·licht *n* (-[e]s; *no pl.*) *traffic light*: amber

'Gelb·stich *m phot.* yellow cast; **'gelb·sti·chig** [-ʃtɪçɪç] *adj.*: ***~ sein*** have a yellow cast

'Gelb·sucht *f* (-; *no pl.*) ⚕ (yellow) jaundice; **'gelb·süch·tig** *adj.* jaundiced; ***~ sein*** have (yellow) jaundice

'Gelb·wurz *f* ⚘ turmeric

Geld [gɛlt] *n* (-es; -er ['gɛldɐ]) money, F cash, *sl.* brass; *pl.* money, funds; deposits; ***billiges ~*** easy money; ***teures ~*** hard-earned money; ***großes ~*** notes; ***kleines ~*** small change; ***~ zurück*** money back; F ***~ machen*** make money; F ***das große ~ machen*** make big money; ***zu ~ kommen*** a) get hold of some money, b) F strike (it) rich, hit the jackpot; ***wenn ich wieder bei ~ bin*** when I'm in the money (F black) again; ***~ spielt keine Rolle*** money is no object; ***er ist nur auf ~ aus*** all he (ever) thinks of is money; ***die wollen nur dein ~*** all they're after is your money; ***et. für sein ~ bekommen*** get one's money's worth; F ***rausgeschmissenes ~*** money down the drain; F ***sie hat ~ wie Heu*** F she's rolling in money (*or* it); F ***mit s-m ~ um sich schmeißen*** F spend one's money like it's going out of style; ***schade ums ~!*** what a waste of money; ***von dem bißchen ~ kann doch keiner leben*** how are you supposed to live on a pittance like that?; ***ins ~ gehen*** run into a lot of money; ***das geht ins ~*** *a.* F that's going to cost me *etc.* a pretty packet; ***es (er) ist für ~ nicht zu haben*** it's not for sale (you can't buy him); ***sie ist nicht mit ~ zu bezahlen*** she's worth her weight in gold, she's priceless; ***was machst du mit dem vielen ~?*** what do you do with all that money of yours?; ***zu ~ machen*** turn into cash; ***~ stinkt nicht*** money's money, money talks; ***~ regiert die Welt*** money makes the world go round; ***~ allein macht nicht glücklich*** money's not everything; ***nicht für ~ und gute Worte*** not for love or money; **~ab·fin·dung** *f* cash settlement; **~ab·fluß** *m* outflow of money; **~ab·wer·tung** *f* (currency) devaluation; **~adel** *m* moneyed aristocracy, plutocracy; **~an·ge·le·gen·heit** *f* money matter; **~an·la·ge** *f* investment; **~an·le·ger** *m* investor; **~an·lei·he** *f* loan; **~an·wei·sung** *f* money order; **~auf·wand** *m* expenditure(s *pl.*); **~auf·wer·tung** *f* (currency) revaluation; **~aus·ga·be** *f* expenditure, expense; **~aus·la·ge** *f* (financial) outlay; **~au·to·ˌmat** *m* cash dispenser (F machine), autoteller, automated teller machine, ATM; **~be·darf** *m* cash requirements *pl.*; ✝ currency demands *pl.*; **~be·stand** *m* monetary holdings *pl.* (*or* stock); **~be·trag** *m* amount, sum; **~beu·tel** *m* purse, *Am.* money purse; *fig.* ***(nicht) für jeden ~*** (not) within everybody's means *or* reach; **~bom·be** *f* night safe container; **~bu·ße** *f* fine; ***zu e-r ~ verurteilt werden*** be fined; **~din·ge** *pl.*: ***in ~n*** in money (*or* monetary) matters, when it's a question of money; **~ein·la·ge** *f* **1.** deposit; **2.** ✝ investment, capital invested; **~ein·nah·men** *pl.* receipts; **~ein·wurf** *m* (coin) slot; **~emp·fän·ger** *m* payee; **~ent·schä·di·gung** *f* compensation; **~ent·wer·tung** *f* inflation; **~er·werb** *m* moneymaking; ***zum ~*** to make money; ***auf ~ ausgehen*** (try to) earn a living; **~for·de·rung** *f* money due; outstanding debt; monetary claim; **~fra·ge** *f* financial matter; ***e-e (reine) ~*** (just) a question of money; **~ge·ber** *m* financial backer; *n.s.* sponsor; **~ge·schäft** *n* **1.** money transaction; **2.** banking (business); **~ge·schenk** *n* (gift of) money; donation

'Geld·gier *f* greed for money, avarice; **'geld·gie·rig** *adj.* greedy for money, obsessed with money

'Geld|hahn *m*: ***j-m den ~ zudrehen*** cut off s.o.'s money supply; ***e-m Institut*** *etc.* ***den ~ zudrehen*** axe an institute's *etc.* funds; **~hei·rat** *f* money match, marriage for money; **~herr·schaft** *f* plutocracy; **~hil·fe** *f* financial aid; **~in·stiˌtut** *n* financial institution; **~kasˌset·te** *f* cash box; **~klem·me** F *f*: ***in e-r ~ sein*** F be hard up (for cash), be in a tight spot (financially); **~knapp·heit** *f* shortage of money, F money crunch; **~kreis·lauf** *m* money circuit; **~kri·se** *f* monetary crisis; **~kurs** *m* buying rate; *stock exchange*: bid price; **~lei·stung** *f* payment; **~leu·te** F *pl.* **1.** financiers; **2.** rich people

'geld·lich *adj.* financial, monetary

'Geld|ma·che·rei [-maxəraɪ] F *f* (-; *no pl.*) moneymaking, money-spinning; **~macht** *f* financial power; **~mak·ler** *m* money broker; **~man·gel** *m* lack of money; **~mann** F *m* (-[e]s; -leute) **1.** financier; **2.** rich man; **~markt** *m* money market; **~men·ge** *f* ✝ money supply; **~mensch** F *m* **1.** money-minded (F money-mad) person; **2.** → ***Geldmann***; **~mit·tel** *pl.* means, funds, (financial) resources; **~mün·ze** *f* coin; **~not** *f* shortage of money; **~po·liˌtik** *f* monetary policy; **~prä·mie** *f* bonus; **~preis** *m sport*: cash prize; **~protz** F *m*: ***er ist ein ~*** he likes to flash his money around; **~quel·le** *f* source of money; **~reˌform** *f* monetary reform; **~reˌser·ve** *f* money reserve; **~rol·le** *f* roll of coins; **~rück·ga·be** *f* money back; **~sa·che** *f* money matter; **~sack** *m* **1.** moneybag; bag of money; **2.** F moneybags (*sg.*); **~samm·lung** *f* collection; **~satz** *m* money rate; **~schein** *m* (bank)note, *Am.* bill; **~schöp·fung** *f* creation of money

'Geld·schrank *m* safe; **~knacker** (-k·k-) F *m* F safecracker

'Geld|schuld *f* (money) debt; **~schwem·me** *f* glut of money; **~schwie·rig·kei·ten** *pl.* financial difficulties (*or* straits); **~sen·dung** *f* cash remittance; **~sor·gen** *pl.* money worries; **~sor·ten** *pl.* notes and coins; **~spen·de** *f* donation; **~sprit·ze** F *f* (fiscal) shot in the arm, cash injection; **~stra·fe** *f* fine; ***zu e-r ~ verurteilen*** fine; **~stück** *n* coin; **~sum·me** *f* sum (of money); **~ta·sche** *f* money bag; **~theoˌrie** *f* monetary theory; **~trans·ˌport** *m* transport(ing) of money; **~transˌpor·ter** *m* security van; **~ˌüber·hang** *m* ✝ money surplus; surplus money; **~über·ˌwei·sung** *f* remittance, (money) transfer; **~ˌum·lauf** *m* circulation of money; **~ˌum·satz** *m* turnover; **~ˌum·tausch** *m* currency exchange; **~un·terˌstüt·zung** *f* financial support; **~ver·die·nen** *n* moneymaking; earning a living; ***sich ans ~ machen*** start earning some money; **~ver·die·ner** *m* money-earner; **~ver·knap·pung** *f* monetary restraint; **~ver·le·gen·heit** *f*: ***in ~ sein*** be pushed for money; **~ver·lei·her** *m* moneylender; **~ver·lust** *m* financial loss; **~ver·mö·gen** *n* financial assets *pl.*; **~ver·mö·gens·wert** *m* financial asset; **~ver·schwen·dung** *f* **1.** waste of money; **2.** wasting of money; extravagance; **~voˌlu·men** *n* money supply; **~vor·rat** *m* funds *pl.*; cash reserve; cash in hand; ✝ supply of money; **~vor·schuß** *m* (cash) advance; **~wäh·rung** *f* currency; **~wasch·an·la·ge** *f* money laundry (*or* laundering outfit); **~wä·sche** *f* money laundering; **~wech·sel** *m* currency exchange; *sign*: Bureau de Change; **~wechs·ler** *m* (-s; -) moneychanger; **~wert** *m* cash value; ✝ value of (the) currency; **~we·sen** *n* (-s; *no pl.*) monetary system, finance; **~wirt·schaft** *f* money economy; **2wirt·schaft·lich** *adj.* monetary; **~wu·cher** *m* usury; **~zu·wachs·ra·te** *f* rate of money growth; **~zu·wen·dung** *f* **1.** allowance; **2.** appropriation of funds; **3.** → ***Geldgeschenk***

ge'leckt *adj.*: ***wie ~ aussehen*** be spick and span, F be squeaky clean; be all spruced up

Ge·lee [ʒe'leː] *n, m* (-s; -s) jelly

ge'le·gen I. *p.p. of* ***liegen***; **II.** *adj.* **1.** lying, situated, located; **2.** convenient, suitable; opportune; ***es kommt mir ganz ~*** a) that suits me just fine, b) that's just what I need; ***du kommst mir gerade ~*** you're just the person I wanted to see; ***ihm ist (sehr) daran ~ zu*** *inf.* he's keen (anxious) to *inf.*; ***es ist ihr sehr daran ~*** it's very important to her, it matters a lot to her, she sets great store by it; ***mir ist sehr daran ~, daß er es tut*** I'm very anxious *od.* keen for him to do it (*or* that he should do it); ***mir ist nichts daran ~*** I don't care one way or the other; ***was ist daran ~?*** what difference does it make?

Ge'le·gen·heit *f* (-; -en) opportunity, chance; occasion; ***bei ~*** a) some time, b) when I *etc.* get a chance; ***bei dieser ~ lernte ich ihn kennen*** that's when I got to know him; ***bei dieser ~ möchte ich ...*** I'd like to take this opportunity to *inf.*, ***bemerken*** *etc.*: in this connection I'd like to note *etc.*; ***bei der ersten ~*** at the first best opportunity; ***bei solchen ~en*** at such times; ***~ haben zu*** *inf.* have the opportunity (*or* chance) to *inf.*; ***die ~ ergreifen (or wahrnehmen, nutzen) zu*** *inf.* take the opportunity to *inf.*; ***die ~ ungenutzt verstreichen lassen*** pass up the opportunity; ***j-m ~ geben zu*** *inf.* give s.o. the opportunity to *inf.* (*or* of *ger.*), give s.o. a (*or* the) chance to *inf.*; ***es bot sich eine ~*** an opportunity came up (*or* presented itself); ***~ macht Diebe*** opportunity makes the thief; ***~ zum 3:0*** *sport*: chance to make it 3-0 (= three nil); → ***Schopf***

Ge'le·gen·heits|ar·beit *f* casual labo(u)r, F odd jobs *pl.*; **~ar·bei·ter** *m* casual labo(u)rer; **~dieb** *m* sneak thief; **~dieb·stahl** *m* casual theft; **~ge·dicht** *n* occasional poem; **~kauf** *m* bargain;

~käu·fer *m* chance buyer; **~rau·cher** *m* occasional smoker; ***er ist ~ a.*** he has the occasional cigarette; **~trin·ker** *m* occasional drinker

ge·le·gent·lich [gəˈleːgəntlɪç] **I.** *adj.* occasional; chance ...; casual; temporary; ***~e Anrufe*** the occasional (*or* odd) phone call; **II.** *adv.* a) occasionally, now and then, from time to time, b) when you get (*or* she gets *etc.*) a chance, b) some time; ***~ e-e Tasse Kaffee trinken*** have the occasional cup of coffee

ge·leh·rig [gəˈleːrɪç] *adj.* receptive; *zo.* docile; quick; **Geˈleh·rig·keit** *f* (-; *no pl.*) receptiveness; docility; quickness

Ge·lehr·sam·keit [gəˈleːɐzaːmkaɪt] *f* (-; *no pl.*) erudition, learning, scholarship

geˈlehrt I. *adj.* learned, erudite; scholarly; ***~e Abhandlung*** scholarly treatise; ***die ~e Welt*** the world of scholarship; **II.** *adv.*: F ***sich ~ ausdrücken*** F speak in tongues

Geˈlehr·te *m, f* (-n; -n) scholar; ***die ~n a.*** (the world of) scholarship *or* academe

Geˈlehr·ten|da·sein *n the* life of a scholar, scholarly existence; **~kreis** *m* scholarly circle, circle of scholars; *pl.* scholarly circles; ***in ~en a.*** among scholars; **~streit** *m* academic (*or* scholarly) dispute *or* debate; **~ver·ei·ni·gung** *f* scholarly society, society for intellectuals

Geˈlehrt·heit *f* → ***Gelehrsamkeit***

Ge·lei·er [gəˈlaɪɐ] *n* (-s; *no pl.*) (endless) droning

Ge·lei·se [gəˈlaɪzə] *n* (-s; -) → ***Gleis***

geˈlei·stet *adj.*: ***~e Arbeitsstunden*** hours worked (*or* put in); ***~e Zahlungen*** payments made

Ge·leit [gəˈlaɪt] *n* (-[e]s; *no pl.*) escort; ⚔ convoy; ***j-m das ~ geben*** escort s.o.; ***j-m freies*** (*or* ***sicheres***) ***~ geben*** give s.o. safe conduct; ***j-m das letzte ~ geben*** pay s.o. one's last respects; ***Zum ~*** Foreword; **~boot** *n* escort vessel; **~brief** *m* letter of safe conduct

geˈlei·ten *v/t.* (h) accompany; ⚔ escort; ***an die Tür ~*** see *s.o.* to the door

Geˈleit|fahr·zeug *n* escorting vehicle; ⚓ escort vessel; **~schutz** *m* escort; ***unter ~*** under escort, escorted; ***~ geben*** escort; **~wort** *n* (-[e]s; -e) foreword; **~zug** *m* ⚓, ⚔ convoy

Ge·lenk [gəˈlɛŋk] *n* (-[e]s; -e) *anat.* joint (*a.* ⚙), wrist, ankle; ⚘ articulation, joint; **~bus** *m* articulated bus; **~ent·zün·dung** *f* ⚕ synovitis; **~fahr·zeug** *n* articulated vehicle, *Brit. a.* F artic

ge·len·kig [gəˈlɛŋkɪç] *adj.* supple; agile; lithe, lissom; **Geˈlen·kig·keit** *f* (-; *no pl.*) suppleness; agility; litheness

Geˈlenk|kap·sel *f anat.* articular capsule; **~kopf** *m* **1.** ⚙ swivel head; **2.** *anat.* condyle; **~pfan·ne** *f anat.* socket; **~rheu·maˌtis·mus** *m* ⚕ rheumatoid arthritis; **~schmer·zen** *pl.* pains in one's joints; painful joints; **~schmie·re** *f physiol.* synovial fluid; **~stan·ge** *f* ⚙ toggle link

geˈlenkt *adj.* controlled; guided *missile etc.*; ***~e Wirtschaft*** planned economy

Geˈlenk|ver·bin·dung *f* ⚙ link joint; **~ver·stei·fung** *f* ⚕ stiffening of the joints; stiff joints *pl.*; **~wel·le** *f* ⚙ cardan shaft

geˈlernt *adj.* qualified, trained; skilled *worker*

geˈle·sen *p.p. of* ***lesen***

Ge·lieb·te [gəˈliːptə] *m, f* (-n; -n) **1.** lover, *f usu.* F mistress; **2.** *obs.* love, sweetheart

geˈlie·fert F *adj.*: ***~ sein*** F have had it, have had one's chips; ***wenn sie das erfährt, bin ich ~ a.*** F if she finds out she'll have my guts for garters

ge·lie·hen [gəˈliːən] *p.p. of* ***leihen***

ge·lie·ren [ʒeˈliːrən] *v/i.* (h) gel

Ge·lier|mit·tel [ʒeˈliːɐ-] *n* gelling agent; **~zucker** *m* preserving sugar

ge·lin·de [gəˈlɪndə] **I.** *adj.* mild (*a. fig.*); slow *fire*; moderate, slight; F ***~ Zweifel*** some doubt; ***mich packte e-e ~ Wut*** I got really angry; ***da packt einen ein ~s Grauen*** it sends shivers down your spine; **II.** *adv.*: ***~ gesagt*** to put it mildly

ge·lin·gen [gəˈlɪŋən] **I.** *v/i.* (gelang, gelungen, sn) succeed, be successful; ***es gelang ihm*** he managed (it), he succeeded, ***zu*** *inf.*: he managed to *inf.*, he succeeded in *ger.*; ***es gelang ihm nicht a.*** he failed (***zu*** *inf.* to *inf.*); ***es gelingt mir einfach nicht zu*** *inf.* I just don't seem to be able to *inf.*; ***ist dir der Auftrag gelungen?*** were you successful with the assignment?, did you manage all right (*Am.* alright) with the assignment?; ***m-e Fotos*** (***Aufsätze, Pläne***) ***~ nie*** my photos never turn out (my essays never turn out well, my plans never work out); *die Ausstellung etc.* ***gelang gut*** turned out well, was a success; ***das Badezimmer ist dir gut gelungen*** you've made a good job of (*or* done a good job on) the bathroom; ***der Kuchen ist mir nicht ganz gelungen*** the cake hasn't quite turned out as I'd hoped (*or* intended); → ***gelungen***; **II.** 2 *n* (-s) success; successful outcome; ***zum ~ e-r Sache beitragen*** help (*or* do one's bit) to make s.th. a success; ***gutes ~!*** (the) best of luck

ge·lit·ten [gəˈlɪtən] *p.p. of* ***leiden***

gell¹ [gɛl] *adj.* shrill, piercing

gell² *int.* → ***gelt***

gel·len [ˈgɛlən] *v/i.* (h) a) ring out, b) scream, c) ring (***von*** *dat.* with); ***mir ~ die Ohren, es gellt mir in den Ohren*** my ears are ringing; **ˈgel·lend** *adj.* shrill, piercing; ***~es Geschrei*** screaming, high-pitched screams

geˈlo·ben *v/t.* (h) solemnly promise (***j-m et.*** s.o. s.th.); vow, pledge; ***sich ~ zu*** *inf.* solemnly resolve to *inf.*; **Ge·löb·nis** [gəˈløːpnɪs] *n* (-ses; -se) (solemn) promise; pledge, vow; **ge·lobt** [gəˈloːpt] *adj.*: ***das 2e Land, a. fig. das ~e Land*** the Promised Land

geˈlockt *adj.*: ***~es Haar*** curly hair, curls

ge·lo·gen [gəˈloːgən] *p.p. of* ***lügen***

geˈlöst *fig. adj.* relaxed; ***er machte e-n ~en Eindruck*** he seemed very relaxed; **Geˈlöst·heit** *f* (-; *no pl.*) relaxed manner (*or* mood *etc.*)

gelt [gɛlt] *int.*: ***sie ist ziemlich reich, ~?*** she's quite rich, isn't she?; ***so was würdest du nicht machen, ~?*** you wouldn't do a thing like that, would you?; ***das hat dich überrascht, ~?*** I bet that surprised you

gel·ten [ˈgɛltən] *v/t. and v/i.* (galt, gegolten, h) a) be worth *two points etc.*, b) be valid, ⚖ be effective; *rule etc.*: apply, c) *mistake, goal etc.*: count; ***der Paß gilt nicht mehr*** the passport is invalid (*or* has run out); ***etwas ~*** carry weight; ***nicht viel ~*** not to count for much (***bei*** *dat.* with); ***wenig ~*** rate low; ***j-m ~*** *shot, reproach etc.*: be meant for s.o., *sympathy etc.*: be for s.o.; ***für*** (*or* ***als***) ***reich*** *etc.* ***~*** be considered to be rich *etc.*; ***~ für*** *acc.* apply to, go for; ***das gilt auch für dich*** the same goes for (*or* applies to) you too; ***~ lassen*** a) accept, allow, b) let *s.th.* pass (***als*** for); ***das will ich ~ lassen!*** I'll grant you that; ⚖ *in Zweifelsfällen* ***gilt die englische Fassung*** the English version shall prevail; ***was er sagt, gilt*** what he says goes, his word is the law; ***es gilt!, a. die Wette gilt!*** you're on!; ***das gilt nicht*** a) that's not allowed (*or* not fair), b) that doesn't count; ***jetzt gilt's!*** this is it; ***es gilt zu*** *inf.* it's a matter of *ger.*; ***es gilt e-n Versuch*** we should give it a try, it's worth a try; ***es gilt, rasch zu handeln*** we've got to act quickly, immediate action is called for; ***da galt kein Zaudern*** there was no time for hesitation; ***es galt unser Leben*** it was a matter of life and death; → ***Prophet***

ˈgel·tend *adj.* valid, ⚖ *a.* in effect; current *prices etc.*; accepted; prevailing *opinion etc.*; ***~ machen*** assert *claim, right etc.*, advance *argument etc.*; ***~ machen, daß*** argue that; ***wieder ~ machen*** reassert; ***als Entschuldigung ~ machen*** plead; ***sich ~ machen*** make itself felt, be felt; → ***Einfluß***; **ˈGel·tend·ma·chung** *f* (-; *no pl.*) assertion *of claim, right etc.*; exercise *of one's influence etc.*; advancing *of arguments etc.*

Gel·tung [ˈgɛltʊŋ] *f* (-; *no pl.*) a) value, importance, *a. s.o.'s* prestige, respect, recognition, b) ⚖ validity; ***~ haben*** ⚖ be valid; be accepted *or* recognized (***bei*** *dat.* by); carry (a great deal of) weight (***bei*** *dat.* with); ***zur ~ bringen*** a) bring *one's influence etc.* to bear, b) accentuate, bring out; ***zur ~ kommen*** a) (begin to) tell, be (*or* make itself) felt, *influence etc.*: come into play, b) stand out, be (very) effective, show to advantage; ***das Bild kommt dort nicht richtig zur ~*** the picture's in the wrong place (there); ***er kam in der Masse nicht zur ~*** he was swallowed up by the crowd; ***sich ~ verschaffen*** assert o.s., gain prestige (*or* importance); ***e-m Gesetz*** (***e-r Maßnahme*** *etc.*) ***~ verschaffen*** enforce a law (a measure *etc.*) (***bei*** *dat.* [up]on); ***e-r Ansicht*** *etc.* ***~ verschaffen*** get a view *etc.* (generally) accepted (***bei*** *dat.* by); ***~ erlangen*** gain acceptance (*or* recognition)

ˈGel·tungs|be·dürf·nis *n* → ***Geltungsdrang***; **~be·reich** *m* scope; area of applicability; ⚖ jurisdiction, scope, purview; ***in den ~ e-s Gesetzes fallen*** come within the purview of a law; **~dau·er** *f* (period of) validity; life *of a patent*; term *of a contract*; ***e-e ~ von ... haben*** be valid for ...; **~drang** *m*, **~trieb** *m* craving for recognition; ***e-n ~ haben*** crave recognition

Ge·lüb·de [gəˈlʏpdə] *n* (-s; -) vow; ***ein ~ ablegen*** take (*or* make) a vow

Geˈlump F *n* (-[e]s; *no pl.*) rubbish

ge·lun·gen [gəˈlʊŋən] **I.** *p.p. of* ***gelingen***; **II.** *adj.* **1.** very good, successful, *pred. a.* a success; effective; ***das Bild ist gut ~*** the picture has turned out well; **2.** F funny; ***das war ja ~!*** it was brilliant, F what a scream

Ge·lüst [gəˈlʏst] *n* (-[e]s; -e) craving (***nach*** *dat.* for); desire, appetite; **ge·lü·sten** [gəˈlʏstən] *v/impers.* (h) *usu. hum.*: ***es gelüstet mich*** (*or* ***mich gelüstet***) ***nach*** *dat.* I'm craving for; ***es gelüstet mich sehr zu*** *inf.* I'd love to *inf.*

Ge·mach [gəˈmaːx] *n* (-[e]s; Gemächer

[gəˈmɛːçɐ]) room, chamber; *hum.* ***sich in s-e Gemächer zurückziehen*** retire to (*or* withdraw into) one's closet

ge·mäch·lich [gəˈmɛːçlɪç] **I.** *adj.* leisurely, slow; ***~es Tempo*** leisurely (*or* relaxed) pace; ***~en Schrittes*** at a leisurely pace; **II.** *adv.* without any hurry, in one's own time; ***wir gingen ~ nach Hause*** *a.* we slowly strolled home

geˈmacht I. *p.p. of* **machen**: ***gut 2!*** well done!, good show!; **II.** *adj.* ***er ist ein ~er Mann*** he's got it made

Ge·mahl [gəˈmaːl] *m* (-[e]s; -e) husband; ***grüßen Sie Ihren Herrn ~*** say hello to Mr N from me

geˈmah·len *adj.* ground *coffee etc.*

Ge·mah·lin [gəˈmaːlɪn] *f* (-; -nen) wife, spouse; ***Ihre Frau ~*** Mrs N, your wife

geˈmah·nen *lit.* (h) **I.** *v/t.*: ***j-n ~ an*** *acc.* remind s.o. of; **II.** *v/i.*: ***~ an*** *acc.* recall, remind us (*or* them) of

Ge·mäl·de [gəˈmɛːldə] *n* (-s; -) painting; *fig.* portrait; **~aus·stel·lung** *f* exhibition of paintings, art exhibition; **~fäl·scher** *m* art forger; **~ga·le͵rie** *f* art (*or* picture) gallery; **~samm·lung** *f* collection of paintings, art collection

ge·ma·sert [gəˈmaːzɐt] *adj.* veined; grained; marbled

ge·mäß [gəˈmɛːs] **I.** *prp.* (*dat.*) according to, in accordance with; in compliance (*or* conformity) with; ***~ Ihren Anweisungen*** *a.* as you had instructed, ✝ *etc.* as per your instructions; **II.** *adj.* appropriate (*dat.* to), in keeping (with); suited (to); commensurate (with)

ge·mä·ßigt [gəˈmɛːsɪçt] *adj.* **1.** moderate; ***~e Politik*** policy of moderation; *pol.* ***die ~e Rechte (Linke)*** the center (*Brit.* centre) right (left); ***~er Optimismus*** guarded optimism; **2.** temperate *zone*; moderate *climate*; **Geˈmä·ßig·te** *m, f* (-n; -n) moderate; *in GB*: *a.* F wet

Ge·mäu·er [gəˈmɔʏɐ] *n* (-s; -) walls *pl.*; ***altes ~*** ruins

Ge·mecker [gəˈmɛkɐ] (*sep.* -k·k-) *n* (-s; *no pl.*) → ***Meckerei***

ge·mein [gəˈmaɪn] **I.** *adj.* **1.** a) mean, nasty (*a.* F *injury etc.*), F bitchy; snide *remark etc.*, b) vulgar; coarse; ***~er Kerl*** nasty guy; ***~e Lüge*** F rotten (*or* dirty, filthy) lie; ***~er Streich*** dirty trick; ***das 2e daran*** the nasty thing about it, the nasty part (of it); ***das ist ~!*** that's not fair, that's mean; ***wie kann man nur so ~ sein?*** how can anyone be so mean (*or* nasty, cruel)?; F *die Prüfung, das Interview etc.* ***war ~*** F was really tough, was a real stinker; **2.** common; public; ***der ~e Mann*** the man in the street; ***das ~e Volk*** the common people; ***das ~e Wohl*** the common good (*lit.* weal); ***für das ~e Wohl*** *a.* for the good (*or* benefit) of all; ⅌ ***~er Bruch*** vulgar fraction; **3.** ***et. ~ haben mit*** *dat.* have s.th. in common with; ***sie haben nichts miteinander ~*** they have nothing in common; ***das hat mit Nächstenliebe nichts ~*** that's got very little to do with brotherly love; ***sich ~ machen mit*** *dat.* start to have dealings with, F get chummy with; **4.** *zo.*, ♀ common; **II.** F *adv.*: ***~ kalt*** really (F rotten) cold; ***es tut ~ weh*** F it hurts like hell

Geˈmein·be·sitz *m* public property

Ge·mein·de [gəˈmaɪndə] *f* (-; -n) a) municipality; local authority; rural commune, b) *eccl.* parish; congregation, c) community; F ***auf die ~ gehen*** go to the town hall, *Am.* go to city hall; **~ab·ga·ben** *pl.* rates, *Am.* local taxes; **~amt** *n* local authority; **~be·trieb** *m* communal enterprise; **~be·zirk** *m* (municipal) district

geˈmein·de·ei·gen *adj.* municipal, communal(ly-owned)

Geˈmein·de|haus *n eccl.* parish hall; **~haus·halt** *m* municipal (*or* local government) budget; **~hel·fer** *m* parish worker; **~mit·glied** *n eccl.* parishioner, member of the parish; **~ord·nung** *f* municipal code; *Brit. a.* byelaws *pl.*; **~rat** *m* **1.** local council; **2.** municipal council(l)or; **~saal** *m eccl.* church (*or* parish) hall; **~schwe·ster** *f* district nurse; **~steu·er** *f* local tax; rates *pl.*

geˈmein·deutsch *adj.* standard German; ***das 2e*** standard German

Geˈmein·de|ver·tre·ter *m* local council(l)or; **~ver·tre·tung** *f* local council; **~ver·wal·tung** *f* local government; **~vor·stand** *m eccl.* **1.** parish council; **2.** chairman of a (*or* the) parish council; **~wahl** *f* local election(s *pl.*); **~zen·trum** *n* community cent|re (*Am.* -er)

Geˈmein|ei·gen·tum *n* common (*or* communal) property; **2ge·fähr·lich I.** *adj.* dangerous to the public, *pred. a.* a public danger, a danger to the public; ***~er Verbrecher*** dangerous criminal, *Am. a.* public enemy; **II.** *adv.*: ***~ handeln*** endanger the public safety; **~geist** *m* (-[e]s; *no pl.*) public spirit; **2gül·tig** *adj.* (generally) accepted, recognized; **~gut** *n* (-[e]s; *no pl.*) common property (*a. fig.*); *fig.* ***zum ~ (der Deutschen) gehören*** be part of our *etc.* common heritage (be part of Germany's heritage); ***zum ~ gehören*** be common knowledge

Geˈmein·heit *f* (-; -en) **1.** *no pl.* meanness, nastiness; ***aus ~*** out of (sheer) spite, just to be nasty; ***es war e-e ~ zu*** *inf.* it was really mean of him *etc.* to *inf.*; ***die ~ dabei*** the mean thing about it; **2.** ***so e-e ~*** what a nasty thing to do (*or* say, happen)

geˈmein·hin *adv.* commonly, generally

Geˈmein·ko·sten *pl.* overheads *pl.*

Geˈmein·nutz [-nʊts] *m* (-es; *no pl.*) *the* common good, *the* public interest; **geˈmein·nüt·zig** [-nʏtsɪç] *adj.* for the public welfare; charitable, welfare ...; cooperative; non-profit(-making); **Geˈmein·nüt·zig·keit** *f* (-; *no pl.*) charitable (*or* non-profit) status

Geˈmein·platz *m* commonplace, platitude

geˈmein·sam I. *adj.* common (*dat.* to); joint, mutual; joint, shared *account*; combined; ***~e Anstrengung*** concerted effort; ***~es Eigentum*** joint (*or* common) property; ***~e Eigentümer*** joint owners; ***~er Freund*** mutual friend; ***~e Überzeugung*** shared belief; ***~es Ziel*** common goal; ***2er Markt*** Common Market; ***allen ~*** common to all; ***vieles ~ haben*** have a lot in common; ***sie haben ein ~es Zimmer*** *etc.* they share a room *etc.*; → ***Nenner, Sache***; **II.** *adv.* together; jointly; ***~ vorgehen*** take joint action; **Geˈmein·sam·keit** *f* (-; -en) common interest; ***sie haben viele ~en*** they have a lot (of things) in common

Geˈmein·schaft *f* (-; -en) community (*a. pol.*); association (***mit*** *dat.* with); ***Europäische ~*** European Community; *eccl.* ***~ der Heiligen*** community of saints; ***in ~ mit*** *dat.* together (*or* jointly, in conjunction) with; ***in enger ~ leben*** live in close companionship (***mit*** *dat.* with), ***arbeiten***: work in close association (with); **geˈmein·schaft·lich** *adj. and adv.* → ***gemeinsam***

Geˈmein·schafts|ab·kom·men *n* ✝ joint venture agreement; **~ak·ti͵on** *f* cooperative action; **~an·la·gen** *pl.* communal installations; **~an·schluß** *m teleph.* party line; **~an͵ten·ne** *f* communal aerial (*or* antenna); **~ar·beit** *f* teamwork, joint effort; ***es ist in ~ entstanden*** it's the result of a joint effort; **~be·sitz** *m* a) joint ownership, b) joint property; **~fi·nan͵zie·rung** *f* group financing; **~ge·fühl** *n* sense of community; (sense of) solidarity; **~geist** *m* (-[e]s; *no pl.*) team spirit; public spirit; **~grab** *n* communal grave; **~haus·halt** *m EC*: Community budget; **~kas·se** *f* F kitty; **~kon·to** *n* joint account; **~kü·che** *f* communal (*or* shared) kitchen; canteen; **~kun·de** *f ped.* social studies *pl.*; **~le·ben** *n* communal living; **~pra·xis** *f* joint (*or* group) practice; **~pro·duk·ti͵on** *f* coproduction; **~pro͵gramm** *n TV, radio*: joint program(me); **~raum** *m* common room; **~sau·na** *f* mixed sauna; **~schu·le** *f* interdenominational school; **~sen·dung** *f* joint program(me); **~ver·pfle·gung** *f* canteen meals *pl.* (*or* food); **~wer·bung** *f* a) joint advertising, b) joint advertisement; **~zel·le** *f* communal cell

Geˈmein|schuld·ner *m* bankrupt; **~sinn** *m* (-[e]s; *no pl.*) public spirit; **~spra·che** *f* standard language; **2ver·ständ·lich I.** *adj.* generally intelligible; **II.** *adv.*: ***sich ~ ausdrücken*** express o.s. in a way that everyone can (*or* will) understand, express o.s. in plain English *etc.*; **~we·sen** *n* (-s; *no pl.*) community; polity; **~wirt·schaft** *f* social economy; **2wirt·schaft·lich** *adj.* non-profit; ***~er Nutzungsbetrieb*** public utilities *pl.*; **~wohl** *n* public welfare (*or* interest); *lit.* public (*or* common) weal

Geˈmen·ge *n* (-s; -) **1.** mixture; **2.** → ***Handgemenge***

Ge·meng·sel [gəˈmɛŋzəl] *n* (-s; -) mishmash

geˈmes·sen I. *p.p. of* **messen**; **II.** *adj.* measured (*a.* ♪); grave, solemn; dignified; ***~en Schrittes*** *lit.* at a measured pace; ***~en Schrittes dem Sarg folgen*** pace slowly behind the coffin; ***mit ~en Worten*** with well-considered words; ***~ an*** *dat.* compared with

Ge·met·zel [gəˈmɛtsəl] *n* (-s; -) bloodbath, carnage, slaughter; massacre

geˈmie·den [gəˈmiːdən] *p.p. of* **meiden**

Ge·misch [gəˈmɪʃ] *n* (-[e]s; -e) mixture (*a.* ⚗, *mot.*); *fig.* jumble; F *gastr.* F concoction

geˈmischt I. *adj.* mixed (*a. tennis*); assorted *biscuits etc.*; F *fig.* dubious; patchy; ***~e Gesellschaft*** mixed company; → ***Gefühl***; **II.** *adv.*: F ***es ging sehr ~ zu*** all sorts of things were going on; F ***jetzt wird's ~*** things are really happening now; F ***mir geht's ziemlich ~*** I'm not doing too well; **2bau·wei·se** *f* composite construction; **~wirt·schaft·lich** *adj.* mixed(-enterprise ...)

Gem·me [ˈgɛmə] *f* (-; -n) cameo

ge·mocht [gəˈmɔxt] *p.p. of* **mögen**

ge·mol·ken [gəˈmɔlkən] *p.p. of* **melken**

ge·mop·pelt [gə'mɔpəlt] F *adj.* → ***doppelt*** II
Ge·mot·ze [gə'mɔtsə] F *n* (-s; *no pl.*) moaning
Gems·bock ['gɛms-] *m* chamois buck; **Gem·se** ['gɛmzə] *f* (-; -n) chamois; **'Gems·le·der** *n* chamois (leather)
Ge·mun·kel [gə'mʊŋkəl] *n* (-s; *no pl.*) whisperings *pl.*; rumo(u)r(s *pl.*), gossip, talk
Ge·murk·se [gə'mʊrksə] F *n* (-s; *no pl.*) **1.** messing around; **2.** mess
Ge·mur·mel [gə'mʊrməl] *n* (-s; *no pl.*) murmuring; muttering, mumbling
Ge·mü·se [gə'my:zə] *n* (-s; -) vegetable; *coll.* vegetables *pl.*, greens *pl.*; F *fig.* ***junges*** ~ youngsters; **~(an)bau** *m* (-[e]s; *no pl.*) vegetable (✝ market) gardening, *Am.* truck farming; **~beet** *n* vegetable bed; **~ein·topf** *m* vegetable stew; **~gar·ten** *m* vegetable garden; **~gärt·ner** *m* market gardener, *Am.* truck farmer; **~gärt·ne͵rei** *f* market garden, *Am.* truck farm; **~händ·ler** *m* greengrocer; **~kon͵ser·ven** *pl.* tinned (*esp. Am.* canned) vegetables; **~la·den** *m* greengrocer's; **~markt** *m* vegetable market; **~pflan·ze** *f* vegetable; **~saft** *m* vegetable juice; **~stand** *m* vegetable stand; **~sup·pe** *f* vegetable soup
ge·mü·ßigt [gə'my:sɪçt] *adj.*: ***sich ~ sehen zu*** *inf.* feel compelled to *inf.*
ge·mußt [gə'mʊst] *p.p. of* ***müssen***
ge'mu·stert *adj.* patterned
Ge·müt [gə'my:t] *n* (-[e]s; -er) mind; feeling; soul (*a.* F *person*); heart; nature, disposition; *pl.* people; ***sonniges ~*** sunny disposition (*or* nature); ***das deutsche ~*** the German mentality (*or* soul); ***in s-m kindlichen ~*** in his childlike innocence, in his naive way; ***etwas fürs ~*** something for the soul; F ***sich et. zu ~e führen*** treat o.s. to (*or* indulge in) s.th.; ***es schlägt ihm aufs ~*** it's getting him down; ***die ~er bewegen*** (*or* ***erregen***) cause quite a stir, stir the blood; ***wenn sich die ~er wieder beruhigt haben*** when things have calmed down (again); → ***erhitzen***
ge·müt·lich [gə'my:tlɪç] **I.** *adj.* **1.** a) comfortable, F comfy; cosy, *Am.* cozy; pleasant, b) relaxed; leisurely; ***es sich ~ machen*** make o.s. at home, relax; *iro.* ***der macht sich's aber ~*** you'd think he owned the place; ***~es Beisammensein*** cosy (*Am.* cozy) get-together; ***jetzt beginnt der ~e Teil des Abends*** this is where the fun starts; ***jetzt wird's doch erst richtig ~*** the fun's only just started; **2.** quiet; ***e-e ~e Tasse Tee trinken*** have a nice (quiet) cup of tea; **3.** easygoing; **II.** *adv.* a) cozily *etc.*; → ***I***, b) in peace and quiet; ***(ganz) ~ et. tun*** take one's time doing (*or* over) s.th.; ***jetzt können wir (ganz) ~ e-n Kaffee trinken*** we've got plenty of time for a nice cup of coffee now; ***~ dasitzen*** sit and relax; ***~ durch die Stadt (nach Hause) schlendern*** saunter through town (slowly make one's way home); **Ge'müt·lich·keit** *f* (-; *no pl.*) a) cosiness, *Am.* coziness; cosy (*Am.* cozy) atmosphere; gemütlichkeit, b) leisureliness; ***in aller ~ et. tun*** take one's time doing (*or* over) s.th.; ***in aller ~ frühstücken*** have breakfast in peace, have a nice long(-drawn-out) breakfast; F ***da hört doch die ~ auf!*** that's the limit!
ge'müts·arm *adj.* lacking in feeling; cold
Ge'müts|art *f* disposition, temperament, nature; **~be·we·gung** *f* emotion; ***sie zeigte keine ~*** *a.* there was no trace of emotion in her face, she didn't flinch; **~er·re·gung** *f* agitation, excitement; *psych.* affect; ***die Nachricht löste bei ihm e-e heftige ~ aus*** the news gave him quite a turn, he reacted visibly to the news
ge'müts·krank *adj.* emotionally disturbed; depressed, depressive; F ***da wird man ja ~*** F it's enough to drive you insane; **Ge'müts·krank·heit** *f* emotional disorder; depression
Ge'müts|krüp·pel F *m* F emotional cripple; **~la·ge** *f* mood, frame of mind; **~le·ben** *n* emotional life; **~lei·den** *n* → ***Gemütskrankheit***; **~mensch** *m* good-natured (*or* imperturbable) person; *iro.* ***du bist ein ~!*** you've got a nerve; anything else?; **~re·gung** *f* emotion; **~ru·he** *f* composure, calmness; ***in aller ~*** with the greatest of calm; unhurriedly; calmly, as cool as you please; ***er trank in aller ~ sein Bier aus*** *a.* he took his time over his beer; **~ver·fas·sung** *f*, **~zu·stand** *m* frame of mind
ge'müt·voll *adj.* warmhearted; emotional
gen [gɛn] *lit. prp.* (*acc.*) to, toward(s); ***~ Osten*** eastward; ***~ Himmel*** heavenward
Gen [ge:n] *n* (-s; -e) *biol.* gene; **~ab·druck** *m* genetic (*or* DNA) fingerprint; **~än·de·rung** *f* gene mutation
ge·nannt [gə'nant] **I.** *p.p. of* ***nennen***; **II.** *adj.* (the) said, (the) above-mentioned
ge·narbt [gə'narpt] *adj.* grained *leather*; *a.* ⚕ pitted
ge·nas [gə'na:s] *pret. of* ***genesen***
ge·nau [gə'naʊ] **I.** *adj.* a) exact, accurate, ⚙ *a.* true, precise, b) strict, careful, thorough, meticulous, particular, c) detailed; ***die ~e Zeit*** the exact time; ***~er Bericht*** detailed account, full report; ***et. ⁀es*** s.th. definite; ***⁀eres*** further details *pl.*; ***weißt du ⁀eres?*** do you know any more about it?; **II.** *adv.* exactly *etc.*; → ***I***; ***~!*** exactly, that's it; ***stimmt ~!*** (you're) absolutely right; ***~ dasselbe*** (exactly) the same thing; ***~ das wollte ich auch sagen*** that's exactly (*or* just) what I was going to say; ***~ überlegt*** carefully considered; ***~ um 4 Uhr*** at exactly 4 o'clock, at 4 o'clock on the dot; ***~ in der Mitte*** right in the middle; ***~ der Mann, den wir brauchen*** just the man we want; ***~ aufpassen*** pay close attention, watch closely (*or* carefully); ***~ hinhören*** listen closely (*or* carefully); ***die Regeln ~ befolgen*** follow the rules closely; ***~ gehen*** *watch*: keep good time; ***~ kennen*** know inside out; ***~ passen*** be a perfect fit, ***j-m***: fit s.o. perfectly; ***ich weiß es ncch nicht ~*** I'm not sure yet; ***ich weiß es ~*** I know (for sure); ***merk dir das ~*** make sure you don't forget it; ***es ~ nehmen*** be very particular *or* strict (***mit*** *dat.* about); ***es mit der Disziplin (der Wahrheit*** *etc.*) ***~ nehmen*** be a stickler for discipline (the truth *etc.*); ***es mit der Etikette ~ nehmen*** stand on etiquette; ***du darfst es nicht so ~ nehmen*** a) you mustn't take it so seriously, b) you've got to stretch a point here and there; ***aufs ~este*** to a T; → ***genauso***
ge'nau·ge·nom·men *adv.* strictly speaking; actually
Ge'nau·ig·keit *f* (-; *no pl.*) a) accuracy; precision, b) strictness; care, meticulousness, c) *radio etc.* fidelity; ***mit ~*** accurately; **Ge'nau·ig·keits·grad** *m* ⚙ (degree of) accuracy
ge'nau·so *adv.* **1.** exactly (*or* just) the same (way); ***ich sehe es ~*** I see it the same way; ***ich denke darüber ~*** I feel the same way about it; **2.** just as *good etc.*; ***~ wie*** just like *his father etc.*; **~gern** *adv.*: ***er mag Äpfel ~*** he likes apples just as much; ***ich fahre ~ morgen*** I can just as easily go tomorrow; **~gut** *adv.* (just) as well; **~lan·ge** *adv.* just as long; **~oft** *adv.* just as often; **~viel** *adv. and pron.* just as much (*pl.* many); **~we·nig** *adv. and pron.* just as little; *a. pl.* no more (***wie*** than); ***es waren ~ da wie am Montag*** *a.* the numbers were just as low as on Monday
'Gen-Bank *f* (-; -en) gene bank
Gen·darm [ʒan'darm] *Austrian m* (-en; -en) policeman; **Gen·dar·me·rie** [ʒandarmə'ri:] *f* (-; -n) police station
Ge·nea·lo·ge [genea'lo:gə] *m* (-n; -n) genealogist; **Ge·nea·lo·gie** [genealo'gi:] *f* (-; -n) genealogy; **ge·nea·lo·gisch** [genea'lo:gɪʃ] *adj.* genealogical
ge·nehm [gə'ne:m] *adj.* convenient, agreeable (*dat.* to); ***wann es ihm ~ ist*** when it suits him
ge·neh·mi·gen [gə'ne:mɪgən] *v/t.* (h) approve; grant, give; agree (*or* consent) to; accept; ratify; ***amtlich genehmigt*** (officially) approved; ***er hat es mir genehmigt*** *a.* F he's okayed it; F ***sich et. ~*** treat o.s. to s.th.; F ***sich einen ~*** F have a wee drop; **Ge'neh·mi·gung** *f* (-; -en) approval (*gen.* of); granting (of); ratification; permission; authorization; *adm.* permit; ***mit freundlicher ~*** *gen.* (*or* ***von*** *dat.*) by courtesy of; ***j-m e-e ~ erteilen*** give s.o. permission (*or* authorization, ✝ *a.* licen|ce [*Am.* -se]); ***j-m die ~ erteilen zu*** *inf.* give s.o. permission to *inf.*, authorize s.o. to *inf.*; ***j-m die ~ verweigern*** refuse s.o. permission (***zu*** *inf.* to *inf.*)
Ge'neh·mi·gungs·pflicht *f* licen|ce (*Am.* -se) requirement; ***es besteht ~ für*** a licen|ce (*Am.* -se) is required for (*or* to *inf.*); **ge'neh·mi·gungs·pflich·tig** *adj.* subject to authorization; ***~ sein*** *a.* require official approval, ✝, *radio*, *TV etc.*: require a licen|ce (*Am.* -se)
ge'neigt *adj.* **1.** ***~ sein zu*** *inf.* feel inclined to *inf.*, feel like *ger.*; ***du scheinst dazu nicht sehr ~ zu sein*** you don't seem to be very keen (on it); ***ich bin dazu überhaupt nicht ~*** it's the last thing I feel like doing; **2.** *lit.* ***j-m ~ sein*** *formal*: be well-disposed towards s.o.; ***j-m ein ~es Ohr schenken*** lend s.o. a willing ear; ***~er Leser*** gentle reader; **3.** sloping
Ge·ne·ral [genə'ra:l] *m* (-s; Generäle [genə'rɛ:lə]) general; **~agent** *m* general agent; **~am·ne͵stie** *f* general amnesty; **~an·griff** *m* all-out attack; **~an·walt** *m* advocate general; **~baß** *m* (basso) continuo; **~be·voll·mäch·tig·te** *m*, *f* (-n; -n) *pol.* plenipotentiary; ✝ universal agent, general manager; **~bun·des·an·walt** *m* Chief Federal Prosecutor; **~de͵bat·te** *f* policy (review) debate; F *fig.* ***wir wollen keine ~ daraus machen*** we don't want a full-scale debate about it; **~di·rek·ti͵on** *f* executive board; **~di͵rek·tor** *m* general manager, chairman, *Am.* president; ***stellvertretender ~*** *Am.* executive vice president; **~gou·ver·neur** *m* gover-

nor general; **~in·spek‚teur** *m* ⚔ Chief of Staff (of the German Armed Forces); **~in·spek·ti‚on** *f* general inspection; **~in·ten‚dant** *m thea. etc.* director

ge·ne·ra·li·sie·ren [genərali'zi:rən] *v/t. and v/i.* (h) generalize; **Ge·ne·ra·li'sie·rung** *f* (-; -en) generalization

Ge·ne·ra·li·tät [genərali'tɛ:t] *f* (-; *no pl.*) ⚔ *the* generals *pl.*

Ge·ne'ral|klau·sel *f* blanket clause; **~kom‚man·do** *n* a) chief command, b) command headquarters *pl.*; **~kon·sul** *m* consul general; **~kon·su‚lat** *n* consulate general; **~leut·nant** *m* lieutenant general; ✈ *Brit.* air marshal; **~li·nie** *f* general policy; *pol.* party line; **~ma‚jor** *m* major general; ✈ *Brit.* air vice marshal; **~nen·ner** *m* & *and fig.* common denominator; ***auf e-n ~ bringen*** reduce to a common denominator, *fig. a.* bring *things* down to a common denominator; **~oberst** *m hist.* colonel general; **~pau·se** *f* ♪ tacit; **~pro·be** *f* (final) dress rehearsal; *thea. a.* full dress rehearsal; *fig.* dress rehearsal; **~se·kre‚tär** *m* secretary general

Ge·ne·ral'staats·an·walt *m* chief public prosecutor

Ge·ne'ral·stab *m* ⚔ general staff

Ge·ne'ral·stabs|chef *m* chief of staff; **~kar·te** *f* ordnance survey map; **~of·fi‚zier** *m* general staff officer

Ge·ne'ral·streik *m* general strike

ge·ne'ral·über‚ho·len *v/t.* (*only inf. and p.p.* generalüberholt, h) ⚙ (give *s.th.* a complete) overhaul; **Ge·ne'ral·über‚ho·lung** *f* major overhaul

Ge·ne'ral|un·ter‚su·chung *f* ⚕ general checkup; **~ver·samm·lung** *f* ✝ shareholders' meeting; *pol.* general assembly; **~ver·tre·ter** *m* general agent; **~ver·tre·tung** *f* general agency; **~voll·macht** *f* ⚖ full power of attorney

Ge·ne·ra·ti·on [genəra'tsĭo:n] *f* (-; -en) generation (*a. fig.*); ***die ~ unserer Eltern*** our parents' generation; ***Computer*** *etc.* ***der dritten ~*** third-generation computers *etc.*; ***seit ~en*** for generations

Ge·ne·ra·ti'ons|kon‚flikt *m* generation gap; **~pro‚blem** *n* **1.** generation gap; problems *pl.* between the generations; **2.** problem of (*or* specifically connected with) the younger *etc.* generation; **~‚un·ter·schied** *m* difference in generation; **~wech·sel** *m* **1.** ⚘ alternation in generations; **2.** ***es hat ein ~ stattgefunden*** a new generation has taken over

ge·ne·ra·tiv [genəra'ti:f] *adj.* **1.** ⚘ reproductive; **2.** ***~e Transformationsgrammatik*** generative transformational grammar

Ge·ne·ra·tor [genə'ra:to:ɐ] *m* (-s; -en [-ra'to:rən]) ⚡ generator, dynamo, alternator

ge·ne·rell [genə'rɛl] *adj.* general(ly *adv.*)

ge·ne·rie·ren [genə'ri:rən] *v/t.* (h) generate

ge·ne·risch [ge'ne:rɪʃ] *adj.* generic(ally *adv.*)

ge·ne·rös [genə'rø:s] *adj.* generous, liberal; magnanimous; **Ge·ne·ro·si·tät** [genərozi'tɛ:t] *f* (-; *no pl.*) generosity; magnanimity

ge'nervt F *adj.*: ***~ sein*** be at the end of one's tether; ***er ist zur Zeit ziemlich ~*** *a.* he's having a very trying time

Ge·ne·se [ge'ne:zə] *f* (-; -n) *biol. and fig.* genesis

ge·ne·sen [gə'ne:zən] *v/i.* (genas, genesen, sn) recover (***von*** *dat.* from), get well; **Ge·ne·sen·de** [gə'ne:zəndə] *m, f* (-n; -n) convalescent

Ge·ne·sis ['ge:nezɪs] *f* (-; *no pl.*) genesis; *bibl.* ***die ~*** Genesis

Ge·ne·sung [gə'ne:zʊŋ] *f* (-; -en) recovery, convalescence (***von*** *dat.* from)

Ge'ne·sungs|heim *n* convalescent home; **~pro‚zeß** *m* (process of) recovery; convalescence; **~ur·laub** *m* sick leave

Ge·ne·tik [ge'ne:tɪk] *f* (-; *no pl.*) genetics *pl.*; **Ge·ne·ti·ker** [ge'ne:tikɐ] *m* (-s; -) geneticist; **ge·ne·tisch** [ge'ne:tɪʃ] *adj.* genetic(ally *adv.*)

'Gen·fak·tor *m* unit factor

'Gen·for·schung *f* genetic research, genetics *pl.*

ge·nial [ge'nĭa:l] *adj.* ingenious, brilliant; ***e-e ~e Leistung*** the work of a genius; ***ein ~er Einfall*** a stroke of genius; ***ein ~er Mensch*** (*or* ***Kopf***) a genius; ***er ist ~, er hat e-e ~e Begabung*** he's a genius; ***er hat etwas 2es*** he has a touch of genius about him; **ge·nia·lisch** [ge'nĭa:lɪʃ] **I.** *adj.* brilliant; ***er hat ein ~es Talent*** he has a touch of genius; **II.** *adv.* with a touch of genius; **Ge·nia·li·tät** [genĭali'tɛ:t] *f* (- *no pl.*) genius; brilliance

Ge·nick [gə'nɪk] *n* (-[e]s; -e) (back of the) neck, nape (of the neck); ***steifes ~*** stiff neck; ***(sich) das ~ brechen*** break one's neck; *fig.* ***das brach ihm das ~*** that was his ruin (*or* undoing); ***du wirst dir noch mal das ~ brechen*** you'll get yourself into trouble one of these days; ***j-m im ~ sitzen*** be breathing down s.o.'s neck; **~bruch** *m* neck fracture; broken neck; **~schuß** *m* shot in the back of the neck

Ge·nie [ʒe'ni:] *n* (-s; -s) genius; ***sie hat ~*** she's a genius; ***er ist ein ~ im Kreuzworträtsellösen*** he's a genius at (*or* when it comes to) solving crossword puzzles; *iro.* ***er ist nicht gerade ein ~*** he's not exactly an Einstein; → ***verkannt***

ge·nie·ren [ʒe'ni:rən] (h) **I.** *v/refl.*: ***sich ~*** feel embarrassed *or* awkward (***vor*** *dat.* in front of, with ... there), be shy (with, in front of); ***ich geniere mich vor ihm*** *a.* he makes me feel awkward (*or* uncomfortable); ***sich ~, et. zu tun*** be too shy to do s.th.; ***~ Sie sich nicht*** make yourself at home, help yourself; ***du brauchst dich nicht zu ~*** no need to be shy (*or* prudish); ***er genierte sich nicht zu*** *inf.* he had the nerve to *inf.*; **II.** *v/t.* bother; embarrass; ***das geniert ihn nicht*** he doesn't mind, that doesn't bother him; **ge·nier·lich** [ʒe'ni:ɐlɪç] *adj.* **1.** awkward; embarrassing; ***es war ihm ~*** he felt awkward about it; **2.** shy, bashful

ge·nieß·bar [gə'ni:sba:ɐ] *adj.* eatable, edible; drinkable; F *fig.* enjoyable; readable; bearable; ***nicht ~*** → ***ungenießbar***; ***das Essen ist ja fast nicht ~*** F how are you supposed to eat this food?; **ge·nie·ßen** [gə'ni:sən] *v/t.* (genoß, genossen, h) a) enjoy (*a. fig. reputation etc.*), relish, savo(u)r (*a. fig.*); revel in, b) take, eat, drink; ***nicht zu ~*** → ***ungenießbar***; ***kaum zu ~*** (virtually) inedible; ***er genoß es zu*** *inf.* he enjoyed *ger.*; ***j-s Vertrauen ~*** be in s.o.'s confidence; ***e-e gute Erziehung ~*** receive a good education; *iro.* ***ich hab' die Armee gründlich genossen*** I've had enough (*or* just about all I can take) of the army; → ***Vorsicht***; **Ge·nie·ßer** [gə'ni:sɐ] *m* (-s; -) epicure; bon vivant; gourmet; ***er ist ein stiller ~*** he knows how to enjoy life in his own quiet way; **ge·nie·ße·risch** [gə'ni:sərɪʃ] **I.** *adj.* appreciative; **II.** *adv.* with (great) relish

Ge'nie·streich *m* stroke of genius; *iro. a.* bright idea, inspired blunder

ge·ni·tal [geni'ta:l] *adj.* genital; **Ge·ni'tal·be·reich** *m* genitals *pl.*; ***im ~*** around (*or* on) the genitals, in the genital area; **Ge·ni·ta·li·en** [geni'ta:lĭən] *pl.* genitals

Ge·ni·tiv ['ge:niti:f] *m* (-s; -e [-ti:və]) genitive; **~ob‚jekt** *n* genitive object

Ge·ni·us ['ge:nĭʊs] *m* (-; Genien ['ge:nĭən]) genius; ***guter ~*** guardian angel

'Gen|ma·ni·pu·la·ti‚on *f* genetic engineering; **~mar·ker** *m* gene marker; **~ma·te·ri‚al** *n* genetic material; **~mu·ta·ti‚on** *f* gene mutation

ge·nom·men [gə'nɔmən] *p.p. of* ***nehmen***

Ge·nör·gel [gə'nœrgəl] *n* (-s; *no pl.*) niggling, moaning

ge·normt [gə'nɔrmt] *adj.* standardized

ge·noß [gə'nɔs] *pret. of* ***genießen***

Ge·nos·se [gə'nɔsə] *m* (-n; -n) **1.** *pol.* comrade; ***liebe Genossinnen und ~n*** comrades; **2.** F mate; *contp.* ***Kruse und ~n*** Kruse and co., Kruse and his ilk; **3.** *obs.* companion; **4.** ✝ *obs.* ***Braun und ~n*** Braun and associates

ge·nos·sen [gə'nɔsən] *p.p. of* ***genießen***

Ge'nos·sen·schaft *f* (-; -en) association; ✝ cooperative (society); ***landwirtschaftliche ~*** farmers' cooperative; **Ge'nos·sen·schafts·bank** *f* (-; -en) cooperative bank

Ge·nos·sin [gə'nɔsɪn] *f* (-; -nen) → ***Genosse***

ge·nö·tigt [gə'nø:tɪçt] → ***nötigen***

Ge·no·typ [geno'ty:p] *m* (-s; -en) genotype; **ge·no·ty·pisch** [geno'ty:pɪʃ] *adj.* genotypic(al)

Ge·no·zid [geno'tsi:t] *m* (-[e]s; -e [-də]) genocide

Gen·re ['ʒã:rə] *n* (-s; -s) genre; **~bild** *n* genre painting; **~ma·ler** *m* genre painter; **~ma·le‚rei** *f* genre painting

'Gen|tech·nik *f* genetic engineering; **~tech·no·lo‚gie** *f* **1.** gene technology; **2.** → ***Gentechnik***

ge·nug [gə'nu:k] *adv. and adj.* enough; a sufficient amount (*or* number) of; ***das ist ~ für mich*** that's enough (*or* that'll do) for me; ***gut ~*** good enough; ***~ (davon)!*** enough (of that)!, that'll do!; ***ich hab' ~ davon*** I've had enough, I'm fed up; ***ich hab' ~*** I've had enough, F I've had it; ***das ist wenig ~*** it's precious little as it is; ***er kann nie ~ kriegen*** he just can't get enough; ***nicht ~ (damit), daß ich Überstunden mache, der Chef verlangt neuerdings Wochenendarbeit*** not only am I doing overtime, the boss wants me to work at the weekends as well; ***sag, wenn es ~ ist!*** say when; → ***betonen***

Ge·nü·ge [gə'ny:gə] *f only in* **1.** ***zur ~*** only too well; **2.** ***~ tun*** (*or* ***leisten***) *dat.* a) give *s.o.* satisfaction, b) → ***genügen*** 2

ge'nü·gen *v/i.* (h) **1.** be enough (*dat.* for); ***das genügt (mir)*** that's enough, that'll do for me; ***das genügt für eine Woche*** that'll do for a week; ***Anruf genügt!*** just give me (*or* us) a call; **2.** (*dat.*) come up to, meet *requirements etc.*; **ge'nü·gend** *adj.* a) enough, sufficient(ly *adv.*); plenty of, b) satisfactory; *ped.* fair

ge·nüg·sam [gə'ny:kza:m] *adj.* easily satisfied, easy to please; *a.* ⚘, *zo. etc.* undemanding; moderate, frugal; modest; ***er ist sehr ~*** *a.* he doesn't make many demands, he gets by on very little; **Ge'nüg·sam·keit** *f* (-; *no pl.*) modesty; frugality

ge'nug·tun *v/i.* (*irr.*, *sep.*, h, → **tun**) (*dat.*) satisfy, please *s.o.*; ***er kann sich nicht ~, es zu loben*** he can't praise it enough; **Ge'nug·tu·ung** *f* (-; *no pl.*) **1.** satisfaction (***für*** *acc.* for); ***~ leisten*** make amends (***für*** *acc.* for); ***~ verlangen*** demand satisfaction; **2.** satisfaction (***über*** *acc.* at); ***ich habe mit großer ~ vernommen, daß*** I was gratified to hear that, it gave me great satisfaction to hear that

Ge·nus ['ge:nʊs] *n* (-; Genera ['ge:nera]) **1.** *biol.* genus; **2.** *ling.* gender

Ge·nuß [gə'nʊs] *m* (-sses; Genüsse [gə'nʏsə]) **1.** consumption, eating, drinking; ***übermäßiger ~ von*** *dat.* too much *alcohol etc.*, too many *sweet things etc.*, overindulgence in; **2.** pleasure, delight; enjoyment; ***es war ein ~*** *a.* it was a (real) treat, I really enjoyed it; ***mit ~*** with relish; ***et. mit ~ essen (trinken, sehen, hören*** *etc.*) enjoy s.th.; **3.** ***in den ~ kommen*** (*gen. or* ***von*** *dat.*) get (the benefit of), *w.s.* be treated to; **~ak·tie** *f* bonus share; **2freu·dig** *adj.* pleasure-loving

ge·nüß·lich [gə'nʏslɪç] **I.** *adj.* voluptuous; pleasurable; **II.** *adv.* with (great) relish

Ge'nuß|mensch *m* pleasure-seeker, epicure; **~mit·tel** *n* semi-luxury; stimulant; **2reich** *adj.* enjoyable; **~schein** *m* ✝ participating certificate

Ge'nuß·sucht *f* (-; *no pl.*) hedonism; **ge'nuß·süch·tig** *adj.* hedonistic; sybaritic

ge'nuß·voll *adj. and adv.* → **genüßlich**

Geo·che'mie [geo-] *f* geochemistry

Geo·dä·sie [geodɛ'zi:] *f* (-; *no pl.*) geodesy; **Geo·dät** [geo'dɛ:t] *m* (-en; -en) geodesist; **geo·dä·tisch** [geo'dɛ:tɪʃ] *adj.* geodetic(al), geodesic(al)

Geo·drei·eck ['ge:o-] *n* set square

ge'öff·net *adj.* open; ***nur vormittags ~*** open mornings only; ***von 9 bis 18 h ~*** open 9 a.m. till 6. p.m.; ***bis wann haben sie ~?*** how long are they open till?; ***das Geschäft ist ab 9 h ~*** the shop opens at 9

Geo·graph [geo'gra:f] *m* (-en; -en) geographer; **Geo·gra·phie** [geogra'fi:] *f* (-; *no pl.*) geography; **geo·gra·phisch** [geo'gra:fɪʃ] *adj.* geographic(al)

Geo·lo·ge [geo'lo:gə] *m* (-n; -n) geologist; **Geo·lo·gie** [geolo'gi:] *f* (-; *no pl.*) geology; **geo·lo·gisch** [geo'lo:gɪʃ] *adj.* geologic(al)

ge'ölt → ***ölen***

Geo·ma·gne'tis·mus [geo-] *m* geomagnetism

Geo·me·trie [geome'tri:] *f* (-; *no pl.*) geometry; **geo·me·trisch** [geo'me:trɪʃ] *adj.* geometric(al)

Geo·phy'sik [geo-] *f* geophysics *pl.*; **Geo'phy·si·ker** *m* geophysicist

Geo·po·li'tik [geo-] *f* geopolitics *pl.*; **geo·po'li·tisch** *adj.* geopolitical

ge'ord·net *adj.* tidy, orderly; systematic; ***in ~en Verhältnissen leben*** a) live in well-ordered circumstances, b) have a steady income; ***aus ~en Verhältnissen stammen*** come from a perfectly respectable family (*or* background); → ***ordnen***

Geo'sphä·re [geo-] *f* (-; *no pl.*) geosphere

geo·sta·tio'när [geo-] *adj.* geostationary *satellite etc.*

Geo·wis·sen·schaf·ten ['ge:o-] *pl.* earth sciences

geo'zen·trisch [geo-] *adj.* geocentric(ally *adv.*)

Ge·päck [gə'pɛk] *n* (-[e]s; *no pl.*) luggage, *esp.* ✈ *and Am.* baggage; ***mit leichtem ~ reisen*** travel light; ***ich habe nie viel ~ dabei*** I never take much with me (when I'm travel[l]ing); **~ab·fer·ti·gung** *f* luggage (*or* baggage) counter; ✈ baggage check-in; **~an·nah·me** *f* luggage (*or* baggage) counter; **~auf·be·wah·rung** *f* left-luggage (office), *Am.* checkroom; **~aus·ga·be** *f* **1.** ✈ baggage claim; **2.** → ***Gepäckannahme***; **~er·mitt·lung** *f* baggage tracing; **~för·der·band** *n* baggage conveyor; **~iden·ti·fi,zie·rung** *f* baggage identification; **~kon,trol·le** *f* luggage (*or* baggage) check; **~netz** *n* luggage (*or* baggage) rack; **~raum** *m* luggage (*esp.* ✈ baggage) hold; *mot.* boot, *Am.* trunk; **~schal·ter** *m* → ***Gepäckannahme***; **~schein** *m* luggage ticket, *Am.* baggage check; **~schließ·fach** *n* luggage (*or* baggage) locker; **~stück** *n* piece *or* item of luggage (*or* baggage); **~trä·ger** *m* **1.** *bicycle*: carrier; *mot.* roofrack; **2.** porter; **~ver·si·che·rung** *f* luggage (*or* baggage) insurance; **~wa·gen** *m* luggage van, *Am.* baggage car

ge'panscht *adj.*: ***~er Wein*** adulterated wine

ge'pan·zert *adj.* **1.** *mot.* armo(u)red; **2.** *zo.* mailed; sclerodermic

Ge·pard ['ge:part] *m* (-s; -e [-də]) *zo.* cheetah

ge'pfef·fert F *adj.* steep *price etc.*, *a.* hefty *check etc.*; stiff *sentence etc.*; biting *criticism etc.*; tough *question, test etc.*; spicy *joke etc.*

Ge·pfei·fe [gə'pfaɪfə] *n* (-s; *no pl.*) (awful) whistling

ge·pfif·fen [gə'pfɪfən] *p.p. of* ***pfeifen***

ge'pflegt **I.** *adj.* very neat; well-looked--after; well-kept *garden etc.*, *a.* manicured *lawn*; select *wine*; *fig.* cultivated, refined *speech etc.*; ***er hat sehr ~e Hände*** *etc.* he takes good care of his hands *etc.*; **II.** *adv.*: ***sich ~ ausdrücken*** be well-spoken; ***sich ~ unterhalten*** have a good (*or* decent) conversation; ***dort kann man sehr ~ essen*** it's a very nice place to eat; **Ge'pflegt·heit** *f* (-; *no pl.*) **1.** (a) neat appearance; **2.** refinement *of speech etc.*

Ge·pflo·gen·heit [gə'pflo:gənhaɪt] *f* (-; -en) habit; custom; *esp.* ✝ practi|ce (*Am. a.* -se)

ge'pfropft *adv.*: F ***~ voll*** F jampacked, chock-a-block

ge·plagt [gə'pla:kt] *adj.*: ***~ von*** dogged by *difficulties etc.*, plagued by *pain etc.*; ***von Sorgen ~*** beset with worries; ***von Zweifeln ~*** racked with doubts; ***von der Hitze ~*** wilting under the heat; ***er ist ein ~er Mann*** F he's got a lot on his plate

Ge·plän·kel [gə'plɛŋkəl] *n* (-s; -) skirmish; *fig.* tit for tat, banter

Ge·plap·per [gə'plapɐ] *n* (-s; *no pl.*) *a. contp.* babbling

Ge·plärr [gə'plɛr] *n* (-[e]s; *no pl.*) (terrible) bawling

Ge·plät·scher [gə'plɛtʃɐ] *n* (-s; *no pl.*) **1.** babbling *of a brook etc.*; **2.** F *contp.* (shallow) chit-chat

ge'plät·tet F *adj.* F floored; ***er war ziemlich ~*** *a.* that floored him

Ge·plau·der [gə'plaʊdɐ] *n* (-s; *no pl.*) chat(ting); chit-chat

ge'pol·stert *adj.* **1.** upholstered *furniture*; padded *jacket etc.*; **2.** F *fig.* ***gut ~*** F well-padded

Ge·prä·ge [gə'prɛ:gə] *n* (-s; *no pl.*) **1.** impression, stamp; **2.** *fig.* character; look; ***sein ~ geben*** *dat.* leave one's stamp on *s.th.*

ge·prägt [gə'prɛ:kt] *adj.* → ***prägen***

Ge·prah·le [gə'pra:lə] *n* (-s; *no pl.*) boasting, F big talk

Ge·prän·ge [gə'prɛŋə] *n* (-s; *no pl.*) pomp, splendo(u)r

ge'preßt *adj.* pressed; squeezed; ***~er Orangensaft*** *a.* fresh(ly squeezed) orange juice; *fig.* ***mit ~er Stimme*** in a choked voice

ge·prie·sen [gə'pri:zən] *p.p. of* ***preisen***

ge'punk·tet *adj.* dotted; *dress etc.* with dots, polka-dot *dress etc.*

Ge·qua·ke [gə'kva:kə] *n* (-s; *no pl.*) croaking *of frogs*; quacking *of ducks*; *fig.* grizzling; F whing(e)ing; *radio etc.*: squawking

Ge·quä·ke [gə'kvɛ:kə] *n* (-s; *no pl.*) squawking

ge'quält *adj. fig.* pained, anguished *expression etc.*; forced *smile*

Ge'quas·sel [gə'kvasəl] F *n* (-s; *no pl.*), **Ge·quat·sche** [gə'kvatʃə] F *n* (-s; *no pl.*) blather(ing), F yak-yakking

Ge·quie·ke [gə'kvi:kə] *n* (-s; *no pl.*) squeaking

Ge·quiet·sche [gə'kvi:tʃə] *n* (-s; *no pl.*) squeaking; squealing *of tires etc.*; screeching *of brakes etc.*

ge'quol·len [gə'kvɔlən] *p.p. of* ***quellen***

ge·ra·de [gə'ra:də] **I.** *adj.* a) straight; erect, b) even *number*, c) *fig.* honest, upright; outspoken; ***in ~r Linie abstammen von*** *dat.* be a direct descendant of; **II.** *adv.* a) straight, b) just, exactly; ***das ist es ja ~*** that's just it, that's the point; ***~ gegenüber*** directly opposite; ***~ entgegengesetzt*** diametrically opposed; ***~ das Gegenteil*** the exact opposite; ***~ in dem Augenblick*** just then, at that very moment; ***ich bin ~ gekommen*** I've just arrived; ***sie wollte ~ gehen*** she was just about (*or* going) to leave; ***ich war ~ beim Lesen*** I was just reading, I was in the middle of reading; ***er ist ~ unterwegs*** he's out just (*or* right) now; ***könntest du ~ mal runterkommen?*** could you come down(stairs) for a minute?; ***ich war ~ dort*** I happened to be there (at the time); ***~ heute!*** today of all days; ***warum ~ heute?*** *a.* why does it have to be today?; ***~ im Winter*** *ist es am schlimmsten etc.*: in winter especially; ***daß ich ~ dich treffe!*** fancy bumping into you of all people!; ***warum ~ ich?*** why me (of all people)?; ***das hat mir ~ noch gefehlt*** that's all I needed; ***ich hab's ~ noch geschafft*** I only just made it; ***ich hab' ihn ~ noch erwischt*** I caught him just in time; ***das ging ~ noch gut*** that was close (*or* a close shave); ***wir haben ~ noch genug*** we've got just about enough; ***sie ist nicht ~ e-e Schönheit*** she's not exactly what you might call beautiful; ***das ist (nicht) ~ das Richtige*** that's just what we need (it's not quite what we're looking for); ***da wir ~ von Kindern sprechen*** speaking of children; ***~ zur rechten Zeit*** just in time (***um zu*** *inf.* to *inf.*), not a moment too soon, F in the nick of time; → ***recht*** II

Ge'ra·de *f* (-n; -n) ⩕ straight line; *sport*:

straight; → *Zielgerade; linke (rechte)* ~ *boxing*: straight left (right)

ge·ra·de'aus I. *adv.* straight on (*or* ahead); *fahren Sie (200 Meter)* ~ go straight on *or* ahead (for about 200 yards); *immer ~!* just keep going straight on (*or* ahead); **II.** *fig. pred. adj.* very outspoken

ge'ra·de|bie·gen *v/t.* (*irr., sep.,* h, → *biegen*) straighten; F *fig.* straighten *s.th.* out, put *s.th.* right; **~hal·ten** *v/refl.* (*irr., sep.,* h, → *halten*): *sich* ~ sit (up) straight, stand up straight

ge·ra·de·her'aus I. *adv.* straight out; bluntly, point-blank; **II.** *adj. pred.* open, outspoken

ge'ra·de|le·gen, ~ma·chen, ~rich·ten *v/t.* (*sep.,* h) straighten (out)

ge·rä·dert [gə'rɛːdɐt] F *adj.*: *(wie)* ~ absolutely shattered, F whacked

ge'ra·de·so *adv.* → *genauso, ebenso* 1

ge'ra·de·ste·hen *v/i.* (*irr., sep.,* h, → *stehen*) **1.** stand up straight; *ich konnte (vor Müdigkeit) kaum noch* ~ (I was so tired) I could hardly stand up *or* stand on my feet; **2.** *fig.* ~ *für acc.* answer for, take the responsibility for, stand up for

ge'ra·de·wegs [-veːks] *adv.* **1.** straight, directly; ~ *losgehen auf acc.* head straight for, make a beeline for, *fig.* get straight down to; **2.** straightaway

ge'ra·de·zu *adv.* **1.** → *geradeheraus;* **2.** virtually; almost; absolute(ly); really; *es machte* ~ *Spaß* we actually (*or* even) enjoyed it; *es wäre* ~ *ein Wunder* it would be nothing short of a miracle

Ge·rad·heit [gə'raːthaɪt] *f* (-; *no pl.*) **1.** straightness; **2.** *fig.* honesty, uprightness; outspokenness

ge·rad·li·nig [gə'raːtliːnɪç] **I.** *adj.* straight (*a. fig.*), ⩲ *a.* rectilinear; direct *descent*; **II.** *adv.* in a straight line; **Ge'rad·li·nig·keit** *f* (-; *no pl.*) straightness (*a. fig.*), ⩲ *a.* linearity

ge·ram·melt [gə'ramәlt] F *adv.*: ~ *voll* F jampacked, chock-a-block

Ge·ran·gel [gə'raŋəl] F *n* (-s; *no pl.*) wrangling, dispute, infighting (*um acc.* over), F free-for-all (for); scramble (for)

Ge·ra·nie [ge'raːnĭə] *f* (-; -n) ♣ geranium

ge·rann [gə'ran] *pret. of* *gerinnen*

ge·rannt [gə'rant] *p.p. of* *rennen*

Ge·rät [gə'rɛːt] *n* (-[e]s; -e) a) ⚙ device, gadget, instrument, tool, implement, *a. pl. coll.* apparatus, b) *radio, TV*: set, c) (*household*) appliance, d) *no pl.* equipment, outfit, e) *gym.* piece of apparatus, *coll. and pl.* apparatus (*sg.*); *er hat so viele ~e in s-m Zimmer* F he's got so many bits and pieces of equipment in his room

Ge'rä·te·me·di̦zin *f* high-tech(nology) medicine

ge·ra·ten¹ [gə'raːtən] *v/i.* (geriet, geraten, sn) **1.** turn out *well etc.*; *der Kuchen ist mir nicht* ~ hasn't turned out (properly); *die Suppe ist ein bißchen salzig* ~ the soup's a bit on the salty side; *j-m zum Vorteil* ~ turn out to s.o.'s advantage; *ihm gerät alles* everything turns out right with him; **2.** *nach j-m* ~ take after s.o.; *er gerät ganz nach s-m Vater* he really takes after his father, *b.s.* he's getting to be just like his father; **3.** get; ~ *an acc.* a) come by, get hold of, come across *s.th.*, b) meet, come across *s.o.*, *b.s.* fall foul of *s.o.*; *da sind Sie (bei mir) an den Falschen* ~ you've come to the wrong person, I'm afraid; F *wie bist du denn an den ~?* F where did you find him (*or* pick him up)?; *in j-s Hände* ~ fall into s.o.'s hands; *in Gefahr* ~ run into danger; ~ *in acc.* get caught in *a storm etc.*; *in e-n Stau* ~ get into (*or* get stuck in) a traffic jam; *in Besorgnis* ~ get worried; *unter ein Auto* ~ be (*or* get) run over by a car; *unter j-s Einfluß* ~ come under s.o.'s influence (*or* sway); → *Abweg, Adresse, außer* I, *Brand* 1, *Wut*

ge'ra·ten² I. *p.p. of* *raten¹* *and* *raten²* *and* *geraten¹*; **II.** *adj.* advisable; advantageous; *es scheint mir* ~ *zu inf.* I think it would be advisable to *inf.*, the best policy would seem to be to *inf.*; *ich halte es nicht gerade für* ~ *zu inf.* I don't really think it would be a good idea to *inf.*

Ge'rä·te|schup·pen *m* (tool)shed; **~stecker** *m* plug connector; **~tur·nen** *n* apparatus gymnastics *pl.*

Ge'ra·te·wohl *n*: *aufs* ~ at random, haphazardly; *es aufs* ~ *tun* take a chance (on it), do it on the off-chance; *sich aufs* ~ *bewerben* apply on the off-chance of getting a job

Ge'rät·schaf·ten *pl.* equipment *sg.*; tools; instruments

Ge'räu·cher·te *n* (-n; *no pl.*) smoked meat

Ge·rau·fe [gə'raʊfə] *n* (-s; *no pl.*) fighting, scuffling, F tussling

ge·raum [gə'raʊm] *adj.*: *(e-e) ~e Zeit* a fairly long time; *seit ~er Zeit* for quite a long time, for a while now

ge·räu·mig [gə'rɔʏmɪç] *adj.* spacious, roomy, large; **Ge'räu·mig·keit** *f* (-; *no pl.*) spaciousness

Ge·räusch [gə'rɔʏʃ] *n* (-[e]s; -e) noise, sound; *radio etc.*: noise; *pl. thea., Film*: sound effects; **~ar̦chiv** *n* sound effects library; **~arm** *adj.* quiet; soundproof; low-noise *cassette etc.*; **~däm·mend** *adj.* noise-reducing; **~dämp·fer** *m* noise suppressor; **~dämp·fung** *f* noise reduction

Ge'räu·sche·ma·cher *m film, radio*: foley, sound effects technician

ge'räusch·emp·find·lich *adj.* sensitive to noise

Ge'räusch·ku̦lis·se *f* background noise; *thea., film*: sound effects *pl.*

ge'räusch·los *adj.* silent, quiet (*a.* ⚙); **Ge'räusch·lo·sig·keit** *f* (-; *no pl.*) silence, quietness

Ge'räusch·min·de·rung *f* noise reduction

Ge'räusch·pe·gel *m* noise level; **~messer** *m* noise level detector (*or* meter)

ge'räusch·voll *adj.* noisy, loud; boisterous

ger·ben ['gɛrbən] *v/t.* (h) tan; *metall.* refine; *fig. j-m tüchtig das Fell* ~ give s.o. a good hiding; **Ger·ber** ['gɛrbɐ] *m* (-s; -) tanner; **Ger·be·rei** [gɛrbə'raɪ] *f* (-; -en) **1.** *no pl.* tanner's trade; **2.** tannery; **'Ger·ber·vier·tel** *n* tanners' quarter (*or* district); **Gerb·säu·re** ['gɛrp-] *f* tannic acid, tannin

ge'recht I. *adj.* a) just, fair; impartial, b) justified; (well-)deserved; just *punishment etc.*, c) good, righteous; *iro.* *~er Lohn* one's just deserts *pl.*; *~e Sache* good cause; *~er Zorn* righteous anger; ~ *werden dat.* do justice to *s.o. or s.th.* (*a. fig.*), meet *requirements etc.*, *a.* come up to *expectations etc.*, live up to *one's reputation etc.*; *e-r Aufgabe* ~ *werden* (be able to) cope with a task; *allen Seiten* ~ *werden* deal with all aspects *of a problem etc.*; *allen (Leuten)* ~ *werden* please everybody; **II.** *adv.*: *et.* ~ *teilen* share s.th. (out) properly, share s.th. out fairly; divide s.th. (up) fairly; **Ge'rechte** *m* (-n; -n) *bibl.* righteous man; *die ~n* the righteous (*pl.*); *den Schlaf des ~n schlafen* sleep the sleep of the just; **ge'rech·ter·wei·se** *adv.* justly; in fairness; **ge'recht·fer·tigt** [-fɛrtɪçt] *adj.* justified, justifiable

Ge·rech·tig·keit [gə'rɛçtɪçkaɪt] *f* (-; *no pl.*) a) justice; fairness, justness, b) legitimacy; ~ *walten lassen* be just; → *ausgleichen* 1

Ge'rech·tig·keits|fa̦na·ti·ker *m* (fanatical) stickler for justice; **~fim·mel** *m*: *e-n* ~ *haben* be obsessed with justice; **~gefühl** *n* sense of justice; **~lie·be** *f* love of justice, fair-mindedness; **~lie·bend** *adj.* fair-minded

Ge're·de *n* (-s; *no pl.*) talk; gossip; rumo(u)r(s *pl.*); *ins* ~ *kommen* get o.s. talked about; *sie ist ins* ~ *gekommen* people have started (*or* are) talking about her; *j-n ins* ~ *bringen* start people talking about s.o.; *dummes* ~ nonsense; *hör dir das* ~ *der Leute nicht an* don't listen to what people say (*or* are saying); → *leer* I

ge're·gelt *adj.* regular; orderly; ⚙ control(l)ed; *mot.* *~er Katalysator* three-way catalytic converter (*or* catalyst)

ge'rei·chen *v/i.* (h): *es gereicht ihm zur Ehre* it's a credit to his name; *es gereicht mir zur Freude* it gives me great pleasure; *es gereicht ihm zum Vorteil* it's to his advantage

ge'reift *adj.* ripe; *fig.* mature; *in ~en Jahren* at a mature (F ripe old) age

ge'reizt *adj.* irritated (*a.* ✱); irritable, edgy; tense, strained *atmosphere etc.*; **Ge'reizt·heit** *f* (-; *no pl.*) irritability

Ge·ren·ne [gə'rɛnə] *n* (-s; *no pl.*) running (around); ~ *nach dat.* rush for

Ge·ria·trie [gerĭa'triː] *f* (-; *no pl.*) ✱ geriatrics *pl.*; *in der* ~ *arbeiten* work in geriatrics; **ge·ria·trisch** [ge'rĭaːtrɪʃ] *adj.* geriatric

Ge·richt¹ [gə'rɪçt] *n* (-[e]s; -e) dish; meal; course

Ge'richt² n (-[e]s; -e) **1.** (law) court(s *pl.*); *ordentliches* ~ ordinary court (of law); ~ *(ab)halten* hold court, sit; *j-n vor* ~ *bringen* take s.o. to court; *vor* ~ *gehen* go to court; *vor* ~ *kommen* a) come before the court(s), b) go on trial; *vor* ~ *laden* summon before a (*or* the) court; *vor* ~ *stehen* be up for trial, be on trial; *vor* ~ *aussagen* testify before a (*or* the) court; *vor* ~ *vertreten* represent *s.o. or s.th.* in court; **2.** *no pl.* a) *usu. lit. and fig.* tribunal, b) *the* judges *pl.*, c) hearing, trial, d) jurisdiction; *eccl.* *Jüngstes* ~ Last Judg(e)ment; *Tag des (Jüngsten) ~s* Day of Judg(e)ment; *sich vor* ~ *verantworten* stand trial; *Hohes ~!* Your Lordship (*Am.* Your Honor), Members of the Jury; *fig.* *mit j-m scharf ins* ~ *gehen* take s.o. to task, haul s.o. over the coals; ~ *halten über acc.* sit in judg(e)ment on *s.o.*; **ge'richt·lich I.** *adj.* judicial, legal; court ..., of the court; *~e Medizin* forensic medicine; *~e Untersuchung* judicial inquiry; *~es Verfahren* legal proceedings; *~e Verfügung* court order; *~e Verfolgung* prosecution; **II.**

adv. judicially, legally; by order of the court; ***j-n ~ belangen, gegen j-n ~ vorgehen*** take legal action against s.o.; ***et. ~ austragen*** fight s.th. through the courts; ***~ vereidigt*** sworn *interpreter etc.*
Ge'richts|ak·ten *pl.* court records; **~arzt** *m* forensic pathologist; **≈ärzt·lich** *adj.* medico-legal; **~as,ses·sor** *m* junior barrister
Ge'richts·bar·keit *f* (-; *no pl.*) jurisdiction
Ge'richts|be·am·te *m* court official; **~be·fehl** *m* writ, court order; **~be·richt·er·stat·ter** *m* courtroom reporter; **~be·schluß** *m* court order, decree of the court; **~be·zirk** *m* court circuit, juridical district; **~die·ner** *m* (court) usher, *Am. a.* marshal; **~ent·schei·dung** *f* court decision, judicial ruling; **~fe·ri·en** *pl.* vacation *sg.*, *Am.* recess *sg.*; **~ge·bäu·de** *n* law court(s *pl.*), *Am.* courthouse; **~hof** *m* court of justice, law court; *usu. lit. or fig.* tribunal; ***Oberster ~*** supreme court; **~ko·sten** *pl.* legal costs; **~me·di,zin** *f* forensic medicine; **~me·di·,zi·ner** *m* forensic pathologist; **≈me·di,zi·nisch** *adj.* forensic; ***~e Untersuchung*** forensic tests; **≈no,to·risch** *adj.* known to the court(s); **~ord·nung** *f* rules *pl.* of the court; **~per,son** *f* member of the court; **~prä·si,dent** *m* presiding judge; **~re·fe·ren,dar** *m* junior lawyer; **~saal** *m* courtroom; **~schrei·ber** *m* clerk; **~sit·zung** *f* session, hearing; **~stand** *m* (legal) domicile; ***~: Berlin*** *a.* any disputes arising hereunder will be settled before a competent Berlin court of law; **~tag** *m* day of hearing; ***~ halten*** be in session; **~ur·teil** *n* verdict; judg(e)ment; sentence; **~ver·fah·ren** *n* a) court procedure, b) legal proceedings *pl.*, lawsuit; trial; ***ein ~ einleiten gegen*** *acc.* institute legal proceedings against; **~ver·fas·sung** *f* **1.** constitution of the courts; **2.** judiciary; **~ver·hand·lung** *f* (judicial) hearing; trial; **~voll·zie·her** *m* bailiff, *Am.* marshal; F ***du wirst bald den ~ im Haus haben*** F you'll have the bailiffs at your door before long; **~vor·sit·zen·de** *m, f* (-n; -n) presiding judge; **~weg** *m*: ***auf dem ~*** by legal action, through the courts; ***den ~ einschlagen*** take legal action; **~we·sen** *n* (-s; *no pl.*) judicial system, judiciary
ge·rie·ben [gə'ri:bən] **I.** *p.p. of* ***reiben***; **II.** F *adj.* sly; ***das ist ein ~er Kerl*** he's a sly one
Ge·rie·sel [gə'ri:zəl] *n* (-s; *no pl.*) trickling; soft fall *of snow*
ge·riet [gə'ri:t] *pret. of* ***geraten***
ge'rif·felt *adj.* grooved, fluted; ribbed; corrugated; serrated
ge·ring [gə'rɪŋ] **I.** *adj.* a) small *amount etc.*, little, *pl.* few; → ***geringer, geringst,*** b) insignificant, negligible, minor *amount etc.*; slight, little; modest; limited, c) inferior, poor, low *quality, price, income etc.*, modest *income, means etc.*; short *distance*; ***~e Chancen*** slim prospects; ***die Chancen sind ~*** *a.* there isn't much chance (*or* hope); ***~es Interesse*** little interest; ***~e Kenntnisse*** scant knowledge; ***e-e ~e Meinung haben von*** have a low opinion of, not to think much (*or* too highly) of; ***mit ~er Verspätung*** slightly late, 🚗 *etc.* with a slight delay; ***in ~er Höhe*** fairly low (down); ***in ~er Tiefe*** not too deep (down); ***nichts ≈es*** no small matter; ***um ein ~es*** a little *better etc.*; **II.** *adv.* a little; ***~ geschätzt*** at least, at a conservative estimate; ***zu ~ einschätzen*** a) underestimate, b) underrate
ge'ring·ach·ten *v/t.* (*sep.*, h) **1.** → ***geringschätzen***; **2.** place little value on, not to care (much) about; disregard *risk etc.*; **Ge'ring·ach·tung** *f* (-; *no pl.*) **1.** → ***Geringschätzung***; **2.** disregard (*gen.* of, for)
ge'rin·gelt *adj.* ringed *socks etc.*; striped, with stripes going across, F strip(e)y
ge·rin·ger [gə'rɪŋɐ] *adj.* a) smaller, b) less, c) lower, inferior *quality etc.*; ***in ~em Maße*** to a lesser extent; ***das ~e von zwei Übeln*** the lesser of two evils; ***nichts ≈es als*** nothing (*or* no) less than; ***kein ≈er als*** no less than; ..., no less
ge'ring·fü·gig [-fy:gɪç] **I.** *adj.* slight; negligible, insignificant; minor, marginal *difference etc.*; petty *crime*; **II.** *adv.* very slightly, marginally; **Ge'ring·fü·gig·keit** *f* (-; -en) **1.** *no pl.* insignificance, trivial nature; triviality; **2.** trifle, little thing
ge'ring·hal·tig [-haltɪç] *adj. min.* base, low-grade ...
ge'ring·schät·zen *v/t.* (*sep.*, h) have a low opinion of, not to think much (*or* very highly) of; *a.* hold *s.th.* cheap, set little store by *s.th.*; despise; ignore; **ge'ring·schät·zig** [-ʃɛtsɪç] **I.** *adj.* disdainful, contemptuous; deprecatory, disparaging; ***~e Geste*** dismissive gesture; **II.** *adv.* disdainfully *etc.*; ***j-n ~ behandeln*** treat s.o. with contempt; ***et. ~ abtun*** dismiss s.th.; **Ge'ring·schät·zig·keit** *f* (-; *no pl.*) disdain, contempt; deprecatory (*or* disparaging) manner; **Ge'ring·schät·zung** *f* (-; *no pl.*) contempt (*gen.* of, for), disdain (of, for); scant regard (for)
ge'ringst *adj.* least; slightest; minimum; smallest; ***nicht im ~en*** not in the least (*or* slightest); ***das interessiert mich nicht im ~en*** *a.* that doesn't interest me one bit; ***nicht das ≈e*** not a thing; ***die ~e Kleinigkeit*** the least little thing; ***bei der ~en Kleinigkeit*** at the drop of a hat; ***wir haben nicht die ~e Aussicht*** we haven't got the slightest chance (F the *or* a ghost of a chance); ***er hat nicht die ~e Ahnung*** he has no idea, he hasn't got the faintest (F foggiest) idea, *esp. contp.* F he hasn't got a clue; ***nicht den ~en Zweifel*** not the slightest doubt, not the shadow of a doubt; ***das ist m-e ~e Sorge*** that's the least of my worries; ***beim ~en Anzeichen*** *gen.* at the first sign of; **ge'ring·sten·falls** *adv.* at the very least; **ge'ringst·mög·lich** *adj.* least possible
ge'ring·wer·tig [-ve:ɐtɪç] *adj.* inferior, of inferior quality
ge'rin·nen *v/i.* (gerann, geronnen, sn) ⚗ coagulate, clot, congeal; *milk*: curdle; *fig.* ***ihm gerann das Blut in den Adern*** his blood ran cold; ***j-m das Blut in den Adern ~ lassen*** make s.o.'s blood curdle (*or* run cold)
Ge·rinn·sel [gə'rɪnzəl] *n* (-s; -) (blood)clot
Ge·rin·nung [gə'rɪnʊŋ] *f* (-; *no pl.*) coagulation; clotting
ge'rin·nungs|fä·hig *adj.* coagulable; **≈fak·tor** *m* coagulation (*or* clotting) factor; **~hem·mend** *adj.* anticoagulant; **≈mit·tel** *n* clotting agent, coagulant
Ge·rip·pe [gə'rɪpə] *n* (-s; -) skeleton (*a. fig.*); F bag of bones; △ framework, shell; *fig.* outline
ge·rippt [gə'rɪpt] *adj.* ribbed (*a.* ⚙); corded; △ fluted; laid *paper*
ge·ris·sen [gə'rɪsən] **I.** *p.p. of* ***reißen***; **II.** F *adj.* sly, crafty; ***ein ~er Geschäftsmann*** *etc.* a (shrewd,) calculating businessman *etc.*; ***ein ~er Bursche*** *a.* a shrewd operator
ge·rit·ten [gə'rɪtən] *p.p. of* ***reiten***
ge'ritzt F *adj.*: ***die Sache*** (*or* ***das***) ***ist ~*** that's settled, then
Ger·ma·ne [gɛr'ma:nə] *m* (-n; -n), **Ger·ma·nin** [gɛr'ma:nɪn] *f* (-; -nen) Teuton, ancient German; ***die alten Germanen*** *a.* the ancient Germanic peoples (*or* tribes); **ger·ma·nisch** [gɛr'ma:nɪʃ] *adj.* Germanic, Teutonic
Ger·ma·nis·mus [gɛrma'nɪsmʊs] *m* (-; -men) Germanism; **Ger·ma·nist** [gɛrma'nɪst] *m* (-en; -en) **1.** Germanist; **2.** student of German (language and literature), German student; **Ger·ma·ni·stik** [gɛrma'nɪstɪk] *f* (-; *no pl.*) German(ic) philology, German (studies *pl.*), German language and literature
gern [gɛrn], **ger·ne** ['gɛrnə] *adv.* gladly; willingly; ***~!*** of course, I'd love to; ***ich helfe ~*** I'll be glad to help; ***~ haben*** (*or* ***mögen***) like *s.o. or s.th., doing s.th.*, F be keen on (*ger.*); ***~ tun*** *a.* enjoy *ger.*; ***ich würde es ganz ~ tun*** I wouldn't mind (doing it); *nach dem Essen* ***ging er ~ spazieren*** he would go for a walk; ***er kommt ~ um diese Zeit*** he usually comes (*or* turns up) around this time; ***Erlen wachsen ~ am Fluß*** alders tend to grow (*or* are usually found) along riverbanks; ***... wird ~ gekauft*** sells well, is in demand; ***das glaube ich ~*** I can believe that; ***das kannst du ~ haben*** you're welcome to it; ***du kannst ~ kommen*** you're welcome to come; ***ich möchte ~ wissen*** I'd (really) like to know, I wonder; ***ich hätte ~ Herrn X gesprochen*** could I speak to Mr X, please?; ***du weißt, du bist bei uns immer ~ gesehen*** you know you're always welcome here; ***er (es) ist nicht ~ gesehen*** he's not welcome around here *etc.* (it's frowned [up]on); ***er sieht es nicht ~, wenn du ...*** he doesn't like you *ger.*; ***~ geschehen!*** you're welcome; ***das haben wir ~!*** *iro.* that's just great; F ***du kannst mich ~ haben!*** F you know what you can do; → ***Leben***
'Ger·ne·groß *m*: ***das ist so ein kleiner ~*** he likes to act the big shot
ge·ro·chen [gə'rɔxən] *p.p. of* ***riechen***
Ge·röll [gə'rœl] *n* (-[e]s; *no pl.*) gravel; pebbles *pl.*; boulders *pl.*; rubble, *geol.* debris, detritus; **~hal·de** *f* scree
ge·ron·nen [gə'rɔnən] *p.p. of* ***rinnen*** *and* ***gerinnen***
Ge·ron·to·lo·ge [gerɔnto'lo:gə] *m* (-n; -n) gerontologist; **Ge·ron·to·lo·gie** [gerɔntolo'gi:] *f* (-; *no pl.*) gerontology; **ge·ron·to·lo·gisch** [gerɔnto'lo:gɪʃ] *adj.* gerontological
ge'rö·tet *adj.* red(dened); ⚕ inflamed; → ***Augenrand***
Ger·ste ['gɛrstə] *f* (-; *no pl.*) barley
'Ger·sten|grau·pen *pl.* pearl barley *sg.*; **~korn** *n* **1.** barleycorn; **2.** ⚕ sty(e); **~saft** *hum. m* F juice of the barley, amber liquid
Ger·te ['gɛrtə] *f* (-; -n) switch; riding crop; **'ger·ten·schlank** *adj.* very slender, willowy
Ge·ruch [gə'rʊx] *m* (-[e]s; Gerüche

[gəˈrʏçə]) **1.** smell; scent, fragrance; ***übler*** ~ bad (*or* unpleasant) smell *or* odo(u)r, stench; → ***Körpergeruch, Mundgeruch***; **2.** → ***Geruchssinn***; **3.** *fig.* reputation; ***in dem*** ~ ***stehen zu*** *inf.* be said to *inf.*, have the reputation of *ger.*; ***in schlechtem*** ~ ***stehen*** be in bad odo(u)r (***bei*** *dat.* with); ***im*** ~ ***der Heiligkeit stehen*** have an odo(u)r of sanctity; **2frei** *adj.* odo(u)rless

geˈruch·los *adj.* odo(u)rless; inodorous *gas etc.*; unscented *soap etc.*; *die Blume* ***ist*** ~ has no scent

Geˈruchs|be·lä·sti·gung *f* offensive smell; **2emp·find·lich** *adj.* sensitive to smell; ~ ***sein*** *a.* have a sensitive nose; **~nerv** *m* olfactory nerve; **2neuˌtral** *adj.* unscented, fragrance-free; non-odiferous; **~sinn** *m* (-[e]s; *no pl.*) sense of smell; ***feiner*** ~ *a.* F good nose; **~stoff** *m* odorous substance

Ge·rücht [gəˈrʏçt] *n* (-[e]s; -e) rumo(u)r; ***es geht das*** ~, ***daß*** there's a rumo(u)r that, rumo(u)r has it that; F ***das halte ich für ein*** ~ I have my doubts about that, I don't believe that for one minute

Geˈrüch·te|kü·che *f* rumo(u)r factory (*or* mill); **~ma·cher** *m* (-s; -) rumo(u)r-monger

geˈruch·til·gend *adj.* deodorizing

geˈrücht·wei·se *adv.*: ~ ***verlautet, daß*** rumo(u)r has it that; ***ich habe es nur*** ~ ***gehört*** I only know it from hearsay, I heard it on the grapevine

geˈru·fen *p.p. of* ***rufen***

geˈru·hen *v/i.* (h): ~ ***zu*** *inf. esp. iro.* deign to *inf.*

ge·rührt [gəˈryːɐt] *fig. adj.* touched, moved; ***zutiefst*** ~ deeply moved (*or* touched); ***zu Tränen*** ~ moved to tears

ge·ruh·sam [gəˈruːzaːm] **I.** *adj.* quiet, peaceful; leisurely; **II.** *adv.*: ~ ***frühstükken*** have a leisurely breakfast

Ge·rüm·pel [gəˈrʏmpəl] *n* (-s; *no pl.*) junk

Ge·run·di·um [geˈrʊndiʊm] *n* (-s; -ien) *ling.* gerund

ge·run·gen [gəˈrʊŋən] *p.p. of* ***ringen***

Ge·rüst [gəˈrʏst] *n* (-[e]s; -e) scaffold(ing); trestle; truss; *a.* ⚙ stage, platform; *biol.* stroma, reticulum; *fig.* framework; outline *of novel etc.*; **~bau** *m* (-[e]s; *no pl.*) scaffolding; **~bau·er** *m* (-s; -) scaffolder

geˈrü·stet *fig. adj.* ready, prepared, *iro.* armed (***für*** *acc.* for); ***für den Kampf*** ~ ready for the fray (*or* to do battle)

Ges [gɛs] *n* (-; -) ♪ G flat

ge·sagt [gəˈzaːkt] *adj.*: ~, ***getan*** no sooner said than done

geˈsal·zen I. *p.p. of* ***salzen***; **II.** *adj.* salted; *fig.* steep *price etc.*, *a.* hefty *check etc.*; stiff *letter, reply etc.*; spicy *joke etc.*

geˈsam·melt *adj.*: **~e** ***Werke*** complete works

ge·samt [gəˈzamt] *adj.* whole, entire; all *his money etc.*; complete; total, overall *amount etc.*

Geˈsam·te *n* (-n; *no pl.*) *the* whole, *the* total; ***im*** **2*n*** all in all, all told; ***... beträgt im*** **2*n*** ... amounts to a total of, ... totals

Geˈsamt|ab·satz *m* ☤ total sales *pl.*; **~an·sicht** *f* general view; **~auf·kom·men** *n* total revenue; **~auf·la·ge** *f* a) total circulation, b) total number of copies published; **~auf·nah·me** *f* **1.** *film*: long shot; **2.** complete (*or* full-length) recording; **~aus·fall** *m* total failure; **~aus·ga·be** *f* complete edition (*or* works *pl.*); **~aus·ga·ben** *pl.* ☤ total expenditure *sg.*; **~be·darf** *m* total requirements *pl.*; **~be·stand** *m* total stock; **~be·trag** *m* total (amount), grand total, sum total; **~be·völ·ke·rung** *f* total population; **~bild** *n* overall picture; **2deutsch** *adj. pol.* all-German; **~ei·gen·tum** *n* joint property; **~ein·druck** *m* general impression; **~ein·kom·men** *n* total income; **~ein·nah·me** *f* total revenue; **~ent·wick·lung** *f* general trend; **~er·be** *m*, **~er·bin** *f* sole heir; **~er·lös** *m* total revenue; **~er·geb·nis** *n* overall result; **~er·trag** *m* total proceeds *pl.*; ⚒ total yield; **2eu·roˌpä·isch** *adj.* Europe-wide, European-wide, pan-European; **~flä·che** *f* total area; **~ge·wicht** *n* total weight

Geˈsamt·heit *f* (-; *no pl.*) totality; *the* whole; *the* entirety; ***in s-r*** ~ in its entirety

Geˈsamt|hoch·schu·le *f* polytechnic; **~hö·he** *f* total (*or* overall) height; **~ka·piˌtal** *n* total capital; **~ka·taˌlog** *m* union catalog(ue); **~konˌzept** *n*, **~kon·zep·tiˌon** *f* overall plan (*or* idea, design); master plan; **~ko·sten** *pl.* total cost *sg.*; **~kunst·werk** *n* total art work; **~la·ge** *f* general (*or* overall) situation; ***wirtschaftliche*** ~ state of the economy; **~län·ge** *f* overall length; **~lei·stung** *f* ☤ total output; *a.* ⚙ overall performance; **~no·te** *f ped.* overall mark (*or* grade); **~plan** *m* master plan; **~pla·nung** *f* overall planning; **~preis** *m* total price; **~pro·duk·tiˌon** *f* total output; **~rah·men** *m* overall framework; **~re·ge·lung** *f* general arrangement; ⚖ overall settlement; **~scha·den** *m* total loss; **~schuld** *f* joint liability (*or* debt); **~schuld·ner** *m* co-debtor; joint guarantor; **~schu·le** *f* (*a.* ***integrierte*** ~) comprehensive (school); **~sie·ger** *m* final winner; **~sum·me** *f* → ***Gesamtbetrag***; **~ti·tel** *m* overall (*or* general) title; **~ˌüber·blick** *m*, **~ˌüber·sicht** *f* overall idea (*or* picture); **~ˌum·satz** *m* total turnover; **~ˌun·ter·richt** *m ped.* integrated-curriculum teaching; **~ur·teil** *n* overall assessment (*or* rating); **~ver·ant·wor·tung** *f* overall responsibility; ***die*** ~ ***liegt bei*** *dat.* overall responsibility lies with; **~ver·band** *m* general association; **~ver·brauch** *m* total consumption; **~ver·mö·gen** *n* total assets *pl.*; **~ˌvoll·macht** *f* ⚖ joint power of attorney; **~werk** *n* complete works *pl.*; **~wert** *m* total value; ***im*** ~ ***von ...*** totalling ... (in value); **~wer·tung** *f* overall placing(s *pl.*); ***in der*** ~ ***führen*** have the overall lead; **~wet·ter·la·ge** *f* overall (weather) conditions *pl.* (*or* outlook); **~wir·kung** *f* general effect; **~wirt·schaft** *f* national (*or* overall) economy; **2wirt·schaft·lich I.** *adj.* national (*or* overall) economic ...; **II.** *adv.*: ~ ***gesehen*** seen from an overall economic point of view; **~zahl** *f* total number

ge·sandt [gəˈzant] *p.p. of* ***senden¹***

Ge·sand·te [gəˈzantə] *m* (-n; -n) *pol.* envoy; minister; ambassador; ***päpstlicher*** **~r** (papal) nuncio; **Geˈsandt·schaft** *f* (-; -en) **1.** legation; **2.** embassy

Ge·sang [gəˈzaŋ] *m* (-[e]s; Gesänge [gəˈzɛŋə]) **1.** *no pl.* singing; ♪ vocal music; voice; ~ ***studieren*** study voice (***bei*** *dat.* with); **2.** a) ♪ song, b) canto, book; **~buch** *n* songbook; *eccl.* hymnbook, hymnal

geˈsang·lich *adj.* singing ...; **~e** ***Begabung*** talent for singing, good voice; **~e** ***Leistung*** singing, vocal performance

Geˈsang·pro·be *f* audition

Geˈsangs|ein·la·ge *f* vocal number; **~kunst** *f* (art of) singing

Geˈsang(s)|leh·rer *m* singing teacher; **~stun·de** *f* singing lesson (*or* class)

Geˈsangs·tech·nik *f* singing technique

Geˈsang(s)|ˌun·ter·richt *m* singing lessons (*or* classes) *pl.*; **~ver·ein** *m* (*usu.* male) choir, *Am.* glee club; choral society

Ge·säß [gəˈzɛːs] *n* (-es; -e) buttocks *pl.*, seat, F behind; **~backe** *f* buttock; **~kno·chen** *m* ischium; **~mus·kel** *m* gluteal muscle; **~ta·sche** *f* back (*or* hip) pocket

geˈsät *adj.*: ***dünn*** ~ few and far between

ge·sät·tigt [gəˈzɛtɪçt] *adj.* full; ⚗ *and fig.* ☤ saturated

Ge·sau·fe [gəˈzaʊfə] F *n* (-s; *no pl.*) F boozing

geˈschaf·fen *p.p. of* ***schaffen¹***

geˈschafft F *adj.* F whacked, bushed; ***ich bin*** ~ *a.* F I've had it

Ge·schäft [gəˈʃɛft] *n* (-[e]s; -e) a) business; transaction, F deal, b) *no pl.* business, *stock exchange*: trading; trade, c) business, affair; work; trade, line, job; duty, d) business, firm, company; shop, *esp. Am.* store; ***gutgehendes*** ~ thriving business; ***dunkles*** ~ F racket; ~ ***in Wolle*** wool trading; **~e** ***machen mit*** *dat.* do business with *s.o.*, deal in *s.th.*; ***wie gehen die*** **~e?** how's business?; ***die*** **~e** ***gehen gut*** (***schlecht***) business is good (slack); ~ ***ist*** ~ business is business; (***groß***) ***ins*** ~ ***kommen*** make (a lot of) money (***mit*** *dat.* out of); ***sie versucht, aus allem ein*** ~ ***zu machen*** she tries to make money out of everything; ***s-n*** **~en** ***nachgehen*** go about one's business; ***er versteht sein*** ~ he knows what he's doing; ***das*** ~ ***mit der Angst*** exploiting (*or* playing on) people's fear and insecurity; F *fig.* ***sein*** ~ ***verrichten*** F do one's business; F ***kleines*** (***großes***) ~ F small (big) job

geˈschäf·te·hal·ber [-halbɐ] *adv.*: ~ ***unterwegs*** away on business; ~ ***mit j-m zu tun haben*** have business dealings with s.o.

Geˈschäf·te·ma·cher *m* (-s; -) profiteer, F wheeler-dealer

ge·schäf·tig [gəˈʃɛftɪç] *adj.* busy, active; **Geˈschäf·tig·keit** *f* (-; *no pl.*) activity; bustle, bustling

geˈschäft·lich I. *adj.* business ...; **~e** ***Angelegenheit*** business matter; **II.** *adv.* on business; ~ ***unterwegs*** away on business; ~ ***verhindert*** prevented by business; ~ ***zu tun haben mit*** *dat.* do business with *s.o.*; ~ ***in Köln zu tun haben*** a) have business (to do) in Cologne, b) be in Cologne on business; ~ ***geht es ihm gut*** (***schlecht***) his business is doing well (isn't doing too well)

Geˈschäfts|ab·schluß *m* (business) transaction (F deal); **~adres·se** *f* business address; **~an·teil** *m* share, business interest; ***maßgeblicher*** ~ control(l)ing interest; **~an·zei·ge** *f* business advertisement; **~auf·ga·be** *f* closing of a business; retirement from business; ***Räumungsverkauf wegen*** ~ closing-down sale; **~bank** *f* (-; -en) commercial bank; **~be·din·gun·gen** *pl.* terms of business; **~be·reich** *m* scope of business; ⚖ jurisdiction; *pol.* portfolio; ***Minister ohne*** ~ minister without portfolio; **~be·richt** *m* business report; ***jährlicher*** ~ annual (*or* market) report; **~be·trieb** *m* **1.** business (activity); **2.** business; **~be·zie·hun·gen** *pl.* business relations; **~brief** *m* business letter; **~bü·cher** *pl.* account books; **ℒer·fah·ren** *adj.* experienced in business; ~ ***sein*** *a.* have had business experience; **~er·fah·rung** *f* business experience; **~er·öff·nung** *f* **1.** opening of a shop (*or* store); **2.** starting-up of (*or* starting up) a business

ge'schäfts·fä·hig *adj.* legally competent (to contract); ***voll*** (***beschränkt***) ~ with full (restricted) legal capacity; **Ge'schäfts·fä·hig·keit** *f* (-; *no pl.*) legal (*or* contractual) capacity

Ge'schäfts|frau *f* businesswoman; **~freund** *m* business friend

ge'schäfts·füh·rend *adj.* managing, executive; *pol.* **~e *Regierung*** caretaker government; **Ge'schäfts·füh·rer** *m* ✝ manager; *sport etc.*: secretary; *pol.* party chairman; **Ge'schäfts·füh·rung** *f* (-; *no pl.*) management

Ge'schäfts|gang *m* (-[e]s; *no pl.*) **1.** (run of) business; business routine; **2.** errand; ***e-n*** ~ ***machen*** run an errand; **~ge·ba·ren** *n* business policy (*or* practi|ces [*Am. a.* -ses] *pl.*); ***anständiges*** ~ fair practi|ces (*Am. a.* -ses); ***unlauteres*** ~ unfair (trade) practi|ces (*Am. a.* -ses); **~ge·heim·nis** *n* trade secret; **~grund·la·ge** *f* basis of a (*or* the) transaction; **~haus** *n* a) firm, company, b) business premises *pl.*; office building; **~in·ha·ber** *m* proprietor; **~in·ter,es·se** *n* business interest; ***in j-s*** ~ in the interests of s.o.'s business; **~jahr** *n* business year; *pol.* financial (*or* fiscal) year; **~ju·bi,lä·um** *n* company anniversary; **~kar·te** *f* business card; **~ko·sten** *pl.* business expenses; ***auf*** ~ on expense account; **~krei·se** *pl.* business circles; **~la·ge** *f* business situation; **~le·ben** *n* business; ***ins*** ~ ***eintreten*** go into business; **~lei·ter** *m*, **~lei·tung** *f* → ***Geschäftsführer, Geschäftsführung***; **~leu·te** *f* businessmen, business men and women; **~mann** *m* (-[e]s; -leute) businessman

ge'schäfts·mä·ßig *adj.* businesslike; impersonal

Ge'schäfts|mo,ral *f* business ethics *pl.*; **~ord·nung** *f* **1.** *parl.* standing orders *pl.*; **2.** a) rules *pl.* (of procedure), b) agenda; **~pa,pie·re** *pl.* business papers; **~part·ner** *m* business partner; **~po·li,tik** *f* company (*or* corporate) policy; **~räu·me** *f* business premises; **~rei·se** *f* business trip; *pl. a.* business travel *sg.*; **~rei·sen·de** *m* business travel(l)er; travel(l)ing businessman; **~ri·si·ko** *n* business risk; **~rück·gang** *m* decline in business

ge'schäfts·schä·di·gend *adj.* ⚖ damaging to business (interests); **Ge'schäfts·schä·di·gung** *f* trade libel, injurious malpractice

Ge·schäfts|schluß *m* closing time; ***nach*** ~ *a.* after business (*or* office) hours; **~sinn** *m* (-[e]s; *no pl.*) (a) head for business; **~sitz** *m* place of business; registered office; **~spra·che** *f* commercial language, F commercialese; *pol.* official language; **~stel·le** *f* office; branch; **~stra·ße** *f* shopping street; **~stun·den** *pl.* business (*or* office) hours; **~tä·tig·keit** *f* business activity; **~teil·ha·ber** *m* partner; **~ton** *m*: (***im*** ~ in a) businesslike tone; **~trä·ger** *m pol.* chargé d'affaires; ✝ representative

ge'schäfts·tüch·tig *adj.* efficient; smart; ***er ist sehr*** ~ *a.* he's a good businessman; **Ge'schäfts·tüch·tig·keit** *f* business acumen; smartness

Ge'schäfts|,über·ga·be *f* handing over of a (*or* the) business (***an*** *acc.* to); **~,über·nah·me** *f* (business) takeover; **~,um·fang** *m* **1.** volume of business; **2.** scope of business

ge'schäfts·un·fä·hig *adj.* legally incapacitated (*or* incompetent); **Ge'schäfts·un·fä·hig·keit** *f* legal incapacity

Ge'schäfts|un·ko·sten *pl.* business expenses; overheads; **~,un·ter·la·gen** *pl.* business papers; **~ver·bin·dung** *f* business contacts *pl.*; ***in*** ~ ***stehen mit*** *dat.* do business with; ***in*** ~ ***treten mit*** *dat.* enter into business relations with; **~ver·kehr** *m* business (dealings *pl. or* transactions *pl.*); **~vier·tel** *n* business quarter, commercial district; shopping cent|re (*Am.* -er); **~voll·macht** *f* power of attorney; **~wa·gen** *m* company car; **~welt** *f* (-; *no pl.*) business world (*or* community); **~wert** *m* goodwill; **~zei·chen** *n* reference (*or* file) number; **~zeit** *f* → ***Geschäftsstunden***; **~zim·mer** *n* office; **~zweig** *m* line (of business)

ge·schah [gəˈʃaː] *pret. of* ***geschehen***

Ge·schä·ker [gəˈʃɛːkɐ] F *n* (-s; *no pl.*) flirting

ge'schätzt *adj.* **1.** estimated; **2.** *fig.* respected, *formal*: esteemed; valued *friend*; well-liked

ge·scheckt [gəˈʃɛkt] *adj.* piebald *horse etc.*, brindled *cow etc.*, tabby *cat*

ge·sche·hen [gəˈʃeːən] **I.** *v/i.* (geschah, geschehen, sn) a) happen, occur; take place, b) happen (***j-m*** to s.o.), c) be done; ~ ***lassen*** let *s.th.* happen, allow, turn a blind eye to; ***es geschieht ihm recht*** it serves him right; ***was geschieht, wenn*** what happens if; ***was soll damit*** ~? what am I *etc.* supposed to do with it?; ***es muß etwas*** ~ something must be done about it; ***es wird dir nichts*** ~ nothing will happen to you, you'll be all right (*Am.* alright), *w.s.* they won't do anything to you; ***es geschieht in d-m Interesse*** it's for your own good (*or* sake); ***er wußte nicht, wie ihm geschah*** he didn't know what was happening to him; ***es ist um sie*** ~ that's the end of her, F she's done for, she's had it; ***Dein Wille geschehe*** Thy will be done; ~ ***ist*** ~ it's no use crying over spilt milk; ***ℒes kann man nicht rückgängig machen*** you can't put the clock back; → ***gern***(***e***), ***Unrecht*** II; **II.** ℒ *n* (-s; *no pl.*) events *pl.*; ***in das*** ~ ***eingreifen*** intervene; ***das*** ~ ***auf der Straße faszinierte ihn*** he was fascinated by what was going on in the street

Ge·scheh·nis [gəˈʃeːnɪs] *n* (-ses; -se) event, incident; ***die*** **~*se der letzten Tage*** the events of the past few days, what has been happening in the past few days

ge·scheit [gəˈʃaɪt] *adj.* bright, clever; sensible; F decent *helping etc.*; ***sei doch*** ~! be sensible; ***du bist wohl nicht*** ~ you must be mad; ***ich werde nicht*** ~ ***daraus*** I can't make head or tail of it, I don't get it; ***das ist immer am*** **~*sten*** that's always the best policy; F ***nichts ℒes*** nothing (doing F); ***das ist doch nichts ℒes*** that's no good; ***er weiß nichts ℒes mit sich anzufangen*** he doesn't know what to do with himself; ***wie soll aus dir was ℒes werden?*** what 'is to become of you?; F ***etwas ℒes zu essen*** F a decent bite to eat, F a decent meal; F ***etwas ℒes zu trinken*** F a decent drink, F a good stiff drink; F ***hier gibt's nichts ℒes zu essen*** there's nothing worth eating here

ge'schei·telt *adj.*: ***das Haar*** ~ ***tragen*** have a parting, part one's hair

ge'schei·tert *adj.*: ***ein*** **~*er Versuch*** an unsuccessful (*or* a failed) attempt

Ge·schenk [gəˈʃɛŋk] *n* (-[e]s; -e) gift, present; ✝ free gift; ⚖ donation; ***j-m et. zum*** ~ ***machen*** give s.o. s.th. as a present; *fig.* ~ ***des Himmels*** godsend; **~abon·ne,ment** *n* gift subscription

Ge'schenk·ar,ti·kel *pl.* gifts; **~la·den** *m* gift shop

Ge'schenk|etui *n* presentation case; **~gut·schein** *m* gift voucher; **~idee** *f* gift idea, idea for a present; **~korb** *m* (gift) hamper; **~packung** *f* gift wrapping; presentation box; ***in*** ~ gift-wrapped; **~pa,ket** *n* **1.** present; box of presents; **2.** → ***Geschenksendung***; **~pa,pier** *n* (gift) wrapping paper; **~sen·dung** *f* gift parcel (*Am. a.* package)

ge'schenkt *p.p. and adj.*: ***das ist ja*** (***fast***) ~! F it's a snip (*or* giveaway, *Am. a.* steal); ***ich möcht's nicht einmal*** ~ ***haben*** I wouldn't take it if you paid me for it; F ~! forget it!; → ***Gaul***

ge·schert [gəˈʃeːɐt] F *dial. adj.* ignorant; **~*er Lackel*** ignorant oaf

Ge·schich·te [gəˈʃɪçtə] *f* (-; -n) **1.** story, tale; F ***immer die alte*** ~! it's the same old story every time; F ***erzähl mir keine*** **~*n!*** don't give me any of your nonsense; **2.** *no pl.* history; *w.s.* story; ***die*** ~ ***des X*** the X story, the story of X; ~ ***machen*** make history; ***in die*** ~ ***eingehen*** go down in history; ***das ist*** (***bereits***) ~ that's (already) part of history; **3.** F affair, business; ***e-e dumme*** ~ (such) a stupid thing; ***e-e schöne*** ~! a fine mess; ***die ganze*** ~ the whole business; ***da haben wir die*** ~! there you are; ***mach keine*** **~*n!*** a) don't make such a fuss, b) don't be a fool; ***das ist e-e böse*** ~ ***mit s-m Knie*** that's a nasty business he's got with his knee

Ge'schich·ten|buch *n* storybook; **~er·zäh·ler** *m* storyteller

ge'schicht·lich I. *adj.* historical; historic; ***von*** **~*er Bedeutung*** historically important, of historic(al) importance; **II.** *adv.* historically; **Ge'schicht·lich·keit** *f* (-; *no pl.*) historicity

Ge'schichts|at·las *m* historical atlas; **~auf·fas·sung** *f* view of history (*or* the past); **~be·wußt·sein** *n* sense of history (*or* the past), historical awareness (*or* consciousness); **~bild** *n* view of history; **~buch** *n* history book; **~deu·tung** *f* interpretation (*or* view) of history; **~dra·ma** *n* historical play (*or* drama); *pl.* historical plays (*or* drama *sg.*); **~epo·che** *f* period of history, historical period (*or* era); **~fäl·schung** *f* falsification of history; corruption of historical fact(s); **~for·scher** *m* historian; **~for·schung** *f* historical research; **~kennt·nis**(**se** *pl.*) *f* knowledge (*sg.*) of history; **~klit·te·rung** [-klɪtərʊŋ] *f* (-; *no pl.*) **1.** bias(s)ed historical account; **2.** → ***Geschichtsfälschung***; **~leh·rer** *m* history teacher

ge'schichts·los *adj.* without (a) history; ahistorical

Ge'schichts|phi·lo·so,phie *f* philosophy of history; **~quel·le** *f* historical source; **~ro,man** *m* historical novel; **~schrei·ber** *m* historian; **~schrei·bung** *f* historiography, *the* writing of history; **~stun·de** *f* history class (*or* lesson)

ge'schichts·träch·tig *adj. place etc.* steeped in history, (very) historical, historically important; historic *moment etc.*; **dies ist ein ~es Ereignis** *a.* this event will go down in history

Ge'schichts|,un·ter·richt *m* **1.** history class(es *pl.*) *or* lessons *pl.*; **2.** *the* teaching of history; **~ver·ständ·nis** *n* conception of history; **~werk** *n* historical work; **~wis·sen·schaft** *f* history; **~wis·sen·schaft·ler** *m* historian

Ge·schick[1] [gə'ʃɪk] *n* (-[e]s; -e) **1.** fate; **trauriges ~** sad fate (*or* lot); **schweres ~** cruel fate; **2.** *pl.* destiny *sg.*, fortunes

Ge'schick[2] *n* (-[e]s; *no pl.*) **1.** talent (**zu** *dat.* for); F knack; **er hat nicht das ~ dazu** F he hasn't got the knack, he hasn't got what it takes; *iro.* **ein (besonderes) ~ haben zu** *inf.* F have the knack of *ger.*, F have a special knack for *ger.*; **2.** → **Geschicklichkeit**

Ge'schick·lich·keit *f* (-; *no pl.*) skill; dexterity, deftness

Ge'schick·lich·keits|fah·ren *n mot.* skill tests *pl.*, *Am.* gymkhana; **~prü·fung** *f* test of skill; **~spiel** *n* game of skill; **~übung** *f* exercise in skill

ge'schickt I. *adj.* skil(l)ful (**in** *dat.* at); dext(e)rous, deft; *fig.* clever, quick; **er ist besonders ~ in** *dat.* F he has a knack for *ger.*; → **Zug** 12; **II.** *adv.* skil(l)fully *etc.*; **~ vorgehen** play one's cards well; → **Affäre**

Ge·schie·be [gə'ʃi:bə] *n* (-s; -) **1.** *no pl.* pushing, F shoving; pushing and shoving; **2.** *geol.* glacial drift

ge·schie·den [gə'ʃi:dən] **I.** *p.p. of* **scheiden**; **II.** *adj.* divorced; dissolved; **~er Mann, 2er, ~e Frau, 2e** divorcee; **die Zahl der 2en** the number of divorced people; *fig.* **wir sind ~e Leute** F we're through, I'm through with you (*or* him *etc.*)

ge·schie·nen [gə'ʃi:nən] *p.p. of* **scheinen**[1] *and* **scheinen**[2]

Ge·schimp·fe [gə'ʃɪmpfə] F *n* (-s; *no pl.*) ranting and raving; cursing and swearing

ge'schirmt *adj.* ⚡ shielded

Ge·schirr [gə'ʃɪr] *n* (-[e]s; -e) **1.** *no pl.* crockery, F crocks *pl.*; china; tea things *pl.*; kitchen things *pl.*, pots and pans *pl.*, ☤ kitchenware; **~ spülen** do (*or* wash) the dishes; **das ~ abräumen** clear the dishes away, clear the table; **das ~ einräumen** put the dishes away; **2.** harness; horse and carriage; **sich ins ~ legen** pull hard, *fig.* put one's back into it; **~schrank** *m* (china) cupboard, F cupboard where the plates are (kept); **~spü·ler** *m a.* ⚙ dishwasher; **~spül·korb** *m* dish drainer; **~spül·ma,schi·ne** *f* dishwasher; **2spül·ma,schi·nen·fest** *adj.* dishwasher-safe; **~spül·mit·tel** *n* washing-up liquid, detergent; **~tuch** *n* tea towel, drying-up cloth, *Am.* dish towel

ge·schis·sen [gə'ʃɪsən] *p.p. of* **scheißen**

ge'schla·fen *p.p. of* **schlafen**

ge'schla·gen I. *p.p. of* **schlagen**; **II.** *adj.*: **sich ~ geben** give in, admit defeat; **ein ~er Mann** a broken man; **zwei ~e Stunden (lang)** (for) two solid hours

ge'schlaucht F *adj.* F whacked, bushed, dead beat; **ich bin ~** *a.* F I've had it

Ge·schlecht [gə'ʃlɛçt] *n* (-[e]s; -er) **1.** *no pl.* sex; **das andere ~** the opposite sex; **das starke ~** the strong sex; **das schwache (schöne) ~** the weaker (fair) sex; **beiderlei ~s** of both sexes; **2.** *no pl.* species; **das menschliche ~** the human race, mankind; **3.** a) family; dynasty, b) descent, lineage; **4.** generation; **die kommenden ~er** generations to come; **5.** *no pl. ling.* gender; **welches ~ hat das Wort?** what gender is the word?; **6.** *no pl. lit.* sex

Ge·schlech·ter|rol·le [gə'ʃlɛçtɐ-] *f* sex (*or* gender) role; **~tren·nung** *f* segregation of the sexes

ge'schlecht·lich I. *adj.* sexual, sex ...; *biol. a.* generic; **II.** *adv.*: **mit j-m ~ verkehren** have (sexual) intercourse with s.o.; **Ge'schlecht·lich·keit** *f* (-; *no pl.*) sexuality

Ge'schlechts|akt *m* sex(ual) act; **der ~** *a.* coitus; **~be·stim·mung** *f* sex determination; **~chro·mo,som** *n* sex chromosome; **~drü·se** *f* gonad; **2ge·bun·den** *adj. biol.* sex-linked; **~hor,mon** *n* sex hormone; **2krank** *adj.* VD *patients etc.*; **~ sein** have venereal disease (*or* VD); **~krank·heit** *f* venereal disease, VD; **~le·ben** *n* sex life

ge'schlechts·los *adj.* sexless, *a. biol.* asexual; *ling.* neuter

Ge'schlechts|merk·mal *n* sex characteristic; **~or,gan** *n* sex(ual) organ, *pl. a.* genitals; **~part·ner** *m* (sexual) partner; **2reif** *adj.* sexually mature; **~rei·fe** *f* sexual maturity; **die ~ erlangen** reach sexual maturity; **2spe,zi·fisch** *adj.* sex-specific; **~teil** *n, m* genitals *pl.*; **~trieb** *m* sex(ual) drive; **~,um·wand·lung** *f*: **(e-e ~ durchmachen** have a) sex change (operation); **~,un·ter·schie·de** *pl.* differences between the sexes; **~ver·hält·nis** *n* sex ratio; **~ver·ir·rung** *f* sexual perversion; **~ver·kehr** *m* (sexual) intercourse, sex; **~wort** *n* (-[e]s; ⁼er) *ling.* article; **~zuge·hö·rig·keit** *f* sex; **Benachteiligung aufgrund der ~** sex discrimination

ge·schli·chen [gə'ʃlɪçən] *p.p. of* **schleichen**

ge·schlif·fen [gə'ʃlɪfən] **I.** *p.p. of* **schleifen**[1]; **II.** *fig. adj.* polished, refined

ge·schlos·sen [gə'ʃlɔsən] **I.** *p.p. of* **schließen**; **II.** *adj.* closed (*a. ling. vowel*, ⚡ *circuit*); self-contained *unit*, *whole*; cohesive *group etc.*; well-rounded, finished *performance etc.*; ⚔ *etc.* closed, serried *ranks*; uniform; united; **~e Gesellschaft (Vorstellung)** private party (performance); **~e Ortschaft** built-up area; **~e Wolkendecke** overcast skies; **e-e ~e Front bilden** form a united front; ⚖ **in ~er Sitzung** in camera; **III.** *adv.* a) all together, b) unanimously; **~ hinter j-m stehen** be solidly behind s.o.; **sie waren ~ dafür (dagegen)** they were unanimously in support of it (against it), they were unanimous in their support for it (opposition to it); **Ge'schlos·sen·heit** *f* (-; *no pl.*) a) unity, solidarity, b) unanimity

ge·schlun·gen [gə'ʃlʊŋən] *p.p. of* **schlingen**

Ge·schlür·fe [gə'ʃlʏrfə] *n* (-s; *no pl.*) (loud) slurping

Ge·schmack [gə'ʃmak] *m* (-[e]s; Geschmäcke [gə'ʃmɛkə], *hum.* Geschmäcker [gə'ʃmɛkɐ]) (*sep.* -k·k-) **1.** *no pl.* taste, flavo(u)r; **ich habe gar keinen ~ mehr** I've got no sense of taste, I can't taste anything any more; **ohne ~** → **geschmacklos**; **2.** *no pl. fig.* taste; **~ haben** have (good) taste; **keinen ~ haben** have no (sense of) taste; **e-n teuren ~ haben** have expensive tastes; **es ist nicht jedermanns ~** it's not everyone's taste; **mit ~** → **geschmackvoll**; **3.** taste, liking (**an** *dat.* for); **~ finden an** *dat.* (get *or* come to) like; **den ~ verlieren an** *dat.* lose one's taste for; **auf den ~ kommen** acquire a taste for it, get to like it, F get hooked; **j-n auf den ~ bringen** whet s.o.'s appetite (for s.th.); **wir werden dich schon auf den ~ bringen!** you'll get to like it soon enough; *usu. iro.* **ist es nach d-m ~?** is it to your liking (*or* taste)?; **(das ist) ein Mann nach m-m ~!** that's the kind of man I like, that's my kind of man; **jeder nach s-m ~** everyone to his own taste; **die Geschmäcker sind verschieden, über ~ läßt sich streiten** *a.* there's no accounting for tastes; **was hat sie für e-n musikalischen ~?** what are her musical tastes (*or* tastes in music)?; **es zeugt nicht gerade für s-n ~** it doesn't say much for his taste(s); **der ~ von heute** today's tastes (*or* fashions)

ge'schmack·lich *adv.*: **~ verschieden sein** taste different; **~ verfeinern** improve the taste of; *fig.* **~ unmöglich** absolutely tasteless

ge'schmack·los *adj.* tasteless (*a. fig.*); *fig. a.* in bad taste; tactless; **das war äußerst ~** that was in very bad taste; **Ge'schmack·lo·sig·keit** *f* (-; -en) **1.** *no pl.* tastelessness; *fig. a.* bad taste; tactlessness; offen|ce (*Am.* -se) against good taste; **2.** tasteless remark; **das war e-e ~** that was in bad taste

Ge'schmacks|fra·ge *f* → **Geschmackssache**; **~knos·pe** *f* taste bud; **~nerv** *m* gustatory nerve; **2neu,tral** *adj.* tasteless; **~or,gan** *n* organ of taste; **~pro·be** *f* **1.** tasting; **2.** sample; **~rich·tung** *f* taste; **~sa·che** *f* (a) matter of taste; **~sinn** *m* (-[e]s; *no pl.*) (sense of) taste; **~stö·rung** *f* impaired taste; **~ver·ir·rung** *f* insult to good taste; (definite) mistake; F **sie leidet an ~** she's never heard of the word taste; **~ver·stär·ker** *m* flavo(u)r enhancer; **~zu·satz** *m* flavo(u)r(ing); **mit ~** flavo(u)red

ge'schmack·voll I. *adj.* tasteful, in good taste; elegant, stylish; **das war nicht sehr ~ von ihm** that wasn't very tactful of him, that was in bad taste; **II.** *adv.*: **er kleidet sich ~** he's very well dressed, he has good dress sense

ge·schmei·dig [gə'ʃmaɪdɪç] *adj.* smooth (*a. fig.*); elastic (*a. fig.*), pliant; soft *leather*; lithe *body*; *fig.* adroit, F slick; **Ge'schmei·dig·keit** *f* (-; *no pl.*) smoothness; elasticity, pliancy; softness; litheness; *fig.* adroitness, F slickness

Ge·schmeiß [gə'ʃmaɪs] *n* (-es; *no pl.*) *a. fig. contp.* vermin

Ge·schmet·ter [gə'ʃmɛtɐ] *n* (-s; *no pl.*) flourish *of trumpets etc.*; *contp.* blaring

Ge'schmie·re *n* (-s; *no pl.*) a) smearing, b) scribble, c) daub, d) hotchpotch

ge·schmis·sen [gə'ʃmɪsən] *p.p. of* **schmeißen**

ge·schmol·zen [gə'ʃmɔltsən] *p.p. of* **schmelzen**

Ge·schmor·te [gə'ʃmo:ɐtə] *n* (-n; *no pl.*) stewed (*or* braised) meat

Ge·schmun·zel [gəˈʃmʊntsəl] *n* (-s; *no pl.*) smirk(ing)
Ge·schmu·se [gəˈʃmu:zə] *n* (-s; *no pl.*) (kissing and) cuddling; F smooching
Ge·schnar·che [gəˈʃnarçə] *n* (-s; *no pl.*) snoring
Ge·schnat·ter [gəˈʃnatɐ] *n* (-s; *no pl.*) quacking *of ducks*; cackling *of geese*; *fig.* chatter(ing)
ge·schnie·gelt [gəˈʃni:gəlt] *adj.* (*a.* ~ ***und gebügelt***) (*pred.* all) spruced up
ge·schnit·ten [gəˈʃnɪtən] *p.p. of* ***schneiden***
Geˈschnör·kel *n* (-s; *no pl.*) curlicues *pl.*; F fiddly (*or* fancy) bits *pl.*
Ge·schnüf·fel [gəˈʃnʏfəl] *n* (-s; *no pl.*) sniffling, sniffing; *fig.* snooping (around)
ge·scho·ben [gəˈʃo:bən] *p.p. of* ***schieben***
ge·schol·ten [gəˈʃɔltən] *p.p. of* ***schelten***
Ge·schöpf [gəˈʃœpf] *n* (-[e]s; -e) **1.** creature; F ***süßes*** (***armes***) ~ lovely (poor) creature *or* thing; **2.** *fig.* creation (*gen.* of)
ge·scho·ren [gəˈʃo:rən] *p.p. of* ***scheren***[1]
Ge·schoß[1] [gəˈʃɔs] *n* (-sses; -sse) stor(e)y, floor; ***im ersten*** ~ on the first (*Am.* second) floor; ***im oberen*** (***unteren***) ~ upstairs (downstairs)
Geˈschoß[2] *n* (-sses; -sse) missile; bullet; shell; **~bahn** *f* trajectory; **~ha·gel** *m* hail of bullets (*or* shells)
ge·schos·sen [gəˈʃɔsən] *p.p. of* ***schießen***
ge·schraubt [gəˈʃraʊpt] **I.** *adj.* ⚙ screwed, bolted; *fig.* stilted, affected, artificial; **II.** *adv.*: **~ *reden*** talk like a book; **Geˈschraubt·heit** *f* (-; *no pl.*) affectation, artificiality
Geˈschrei *n* (-[e]s; *no pl.*) shouting, screaming; shouts *pl.*, screams *pl.*; cheering; *fig.* howls *pl.* of protest, hue and cry; huge (F almighty) fuss; ***ein großes ~ machen*** raise a hue and cry, make a huge fuss (***um*** *acc.*, ***wegen*** *gen.* about)
Ge·schreib·sel [gəˈʃraɪpsəl] *n* (-s; *no pl.*) scrawl, scribble; *fig.* scribblings *pl.*
ge·schrie·ben [gəˈʃri:bən] *p.p. of* ***schreiben***
ge·schrie·en [gəˈʃri:ən] *p.p. of* ***schreien***
ge·schrit·ten [gəˈʃrɪtən] *p.p. of* ***schreiten***
ge·schun·den [gəˈʃʊndən] **I.** *p.p. of* ***schinden***; **II.** *adj.* maltreated
geˈschuppt *adj.* scaly; scalloped
Ge·schütz [gəˈʃʏts] *n* (-es; -e) gun; ***schweres*** ~ heavy gun, *coll.* heavy artillery; *fig.* ***schweres ~ auffahren*** bring in the big guns (***gegen*** *acc.* against); **~feu·er** *n* gunfire, shelling; **~füh·rer** *m* gunner
geˈschützt *adj.* protected; safe, secure; sheltered *from the wind etc.*; **~*e Tierart*** protected species; ***patentamtlich*** ~ patented; (***gesetzlich***) **~*es Warenzeichen*** registered trademark; → ***urheberrechtlich***
Ge·schwa·der [gəˈʃva:dɐ] *n* (-s; -) ⚓ squadron; ✈ group, wing; F *fig.* troop
Ge·schwa·fel [gəˈʃva:fəl] F *n* (-s; *no pl.*) drivel
Ge·schwätz [gəˈʃvɛts] *n* (-es; *no pl.*) talk, prattle; nonsense; gossip; ***leeres*** ~ hot air; **geˈschwät·zig** *adj.* talkative, garrulous; gossipy; ***er ist ein ~er Typ*** he talks an awful lot, he never stops talking; **Geˈschwät·zig·keit** *f* (-; *no pl.*) talkativeness; gossiping
geˈschwe·felt *adj.* sulphonated, *Am.* sulfonated
geˈschweift *adj.* curved; **~*e Klammern*** braces; ~ ***sein*** *comet etc.*: have a tail
geˈschwei·ge *cj.*: **~ *denn*** let alone, never mind, much less
ge·schwellt [gəˈʃvɛlt] *adj.*: ***von Stolz*** ~ puffed up (with pride)
ge·schwie·gen [gəˈʃvi:gən] *p.p. of* ***schweigen***
ge·schwind [gəˈʃvɪnt] **I.** *adj.* fast; **II.** *adv.* quickly; **~!** quick!
Ge·schwin·dig·keit [gəˈʃvɪndɪçkaɪt] *f* (-; -en) speed; pace; *phys.* velocity; rate; momentum; ***mit e-r ~ von*** *dat.* at a rate (*or* speed) of; ***mit größter*** ~ full speed, at top speed; F ***er macht es mit e-r ~!*** he does it so fast (*or* at such speed)
Geˈschwin·dig·keits|ab·fall *m* loss of speed; **~be·gren·zung** *f*, **~be·schrän·kung** *f* speed limit; **~kon͵trol·le** *f* speed check; **~mes·ser** *m mot.* speedometer; **~rausch** *m* thrill of speed; ***im*** ~ drunk with speed; **~re͵kord** *m* speed record; **~über͵schrei·tung** *f* speeding
Ge·schwirr [gəˈʃvɪr] *n* (-s; *no pl.*) whirring, buzz(ing)
Ge·schwi·ster [gəˈʃvɪstɐ] *pl.* brother(s) and sister(s); *esp. formal*: siblings; ***hat er noch ~?*** has he got any brothers or sisters?; **Geˈschwi·ster·chen** *n* little (*or* baby) brother *or* sister; **geˈschwi·ster·lich** *adj.* brotherly, sisterly
Geˈschwi·ster|lie·be *f* brotherly (*or* sisterly) love; **~paar** *n* brother and sister
ge·schwol·len [gəˈʃvɔlən] **I.** *p.p. of* ***schwellen***; **II.** *adj.* swollen; *fig.* pompous, inflated
ge·schwom·men [gəˈʃvɔmən] *p.p. of* ***schwimmen***
ge·schwo·ren [gəˈʃvo:rən] **I.** *p.p. of* ***schwören***; **II.** *adj.*: **~*er Gegner*** (*or* ***Feind***) sworn enemy; **Geˈschwo·re·ne** *m, f* (-n; -n) ⚖ **1.** juror, member of the jury; ***die ~n*** the jury (*sg.*); **2.** *obs.* lay judge
Geˈschwo·re·nen|bank *f*: (***auf der*** ~ in the) jury box; **~ge·richt** *n* jury court
Ge·schwulst [gəˈʃvʊlst] *f* (-; Geschwülste [gəˈʃvʏlstə]) ⚕ growth, tumo(u)r; lump; **⁀ar·tig** *adj.*: **~*e Gewebebildung*** tumescent growth
ge·schwun·den [gəˈʃvʊndən] *p.p. of* ***schwinden***
ge·schwun·gen [gəˈʃvʊŋən] **I.** *p.p. of* ***schwingen***; **II.** *adj.* curved, sweeping
Ge·schwür [gəˈʃvy:ɐ] *n* (-[e]s; -e [gəˈʃvy:rə]) ⚕ ulcer; sore; boil; **⁀ar·tig** *adj.* ulcerous
geˈseg·net *adj.* blessed (***mit*** *dat.* with); **~*e Mahlzeit!*** enjoy your meal; **~*es neues Jahr!*** Happy New Year!; ***im ~en Alter von*** at the ripe old age of
geˈse·hen *p.p. of* ***sehen***
Ge·selch·te [gəˈzɛlçtə] *dial. n* (-n; *no pl.*) smoked meat
Ge·sel·le [gəˈzɛlə] *m* (-n; -n) **1.** journeyman (*e.g.* ***Schneider⁀*** journeyman tailor); **2.** F lad; *esp. contp.* type
ge·sel·len [gəˈzɛlən] *v/refl.* (h) **1.** ***sich ~ zu*** *dat.* join *s.o. etc.*; ***zu uns gesellte sich e-e junge Dame*** we were joined by a young lady; → ***gleich*** 1; **2.** ***dazu gesellten sich noch andere Probleme*** in addition to that other problems cropped up
Geˈsel·len|brief *m* apprenticeship diploma; **~prü·fung** *f* (apprentices') final examination; **~stück** *n* diploma piece
ge·sel·lig [gəˈzɛlɪç] *adj.* **1.** sociable, *a. zo.* gregarious; **~*es Wesen*** social being; **2.** **~*es Beisammensein*** (little) get-together; **~*er Abend*** *a.* pleasant evening together; **Geˈsel·lig·keit** *f* (-; *no pl.*) sociability; socializing
Ge·sell·schaft [gəˈzɛlʃaft] *f* (-; -en) **1.** *no pl.* society; ***die feine*** ~ high society; ***e-e Dame der*** ~ a society lady; ***sich in guter ~ bewegen*** move in high circles; *iro.* ***du bewegst dich ja in guter ~!*** you don't mix with the hoi polloi, do you?; *iro.* ***benimm dich, wir sind hier in guter ~!*** (watch your manners -) we're not at home now; **2.** *no pl.* company; ***schlechte*** (***gute***) ~ bad (good) company; ***in schlechte ~ geraten*** get in with the wrong crowd; ***in j-s*** ~ in the company of s.o.; ***j-m ~ leisten*** keep s.o. company, ***bei*** *dat.*: join s.o. in *ger.*; ***komm, leiste mir ein bißchen*** ~ come and talk to me; ***hier hast du*** ~ here's someone to keep you company; ***wir kriegen*** ~ look who's coming; *fig. iro.* ***sich in guter ~ befinden*** be in good company; ***da bist du ja in guter ~!*** *a.* join the club; **3.** *no pl. fig. contp.* lot, bunch, crowd; ***ihr seid ja e-e langweilige ~!*** what a boring lot you are; **4.** social gathering; party; ***e-e ~ geben*** have (*or* give) a party; **5.** a) society, association, b) ✝ company, *Am. a.* corporation, c) partnership; *eccl.* ~ ***Jesu*** Society of Jesus; → ***Aktiengesellschaft, Handelsgesellschaft, Haftung*** 2
Ge·sell·schaf·ter [gəˈzɛlʃaftɐ] *m* (-s; -) **1.** ***er ist ein guter*** ~ he's good company; **2.** ✝ partner, associate; ***stiller*** ~ sleeping (*Am.* silent) partner; **~ver·samm·lung** *f* ✝ corporate (*or* general) meeting
geˈsell·schaft·lich **I.** *adj.* social; **~*e Entwicklung*** development of society; **~*es Gefüge*** social fabric, fabric of society; **II.** *adv.* socially; ~ ***gewandt*** (*or* ***sicher***) ***sein*** have plenty of savoir-faire, move easily in society; ***sich ~ unmöglich machen*** disgrace o.s. in public; ***so kann man sich ~ nicht benehmen*** you can't behave like that in society
Geˈsell·schafts|abend *m* (dinner) party; **~an·zug** *m* formal suit; ~ ***erbeten*** black tie; **⁀fä·hig** *adj.* socially acceptable; presentable, respectable; ***nicht*** ~ risqué, near the knuckle; ***in der Hose bist du nicht*** ~ you can't go out in those trousers; **⁀feind·lich** *adj.* **1.** ~ ***sein*** threaten (*or* be a threat to) society; **2.** antisocial; **~form** *f* social system; **~ka·pi͵tal** *n* ✝ corporate capital; joint stock, share capital; **~klas·se** *f* (social) class; **~kri͵tik** *f* social criticism; **~kri·ti·ker** *m* social critic; **⁀kri·tisch** *adj.* sociocritical; socially critical, critical of society; **~kun·de** *f* social studies *pl.*; **~leh·re** *f* sociology; **~ord·nung** *f* social order; **~po·li͵tik** *f* sociopolitics *pl.*; **⁀po͵li·tisch** *adj.* sociopolitical; **~raum** *m* party room; *hotel etc.*: lounge; **~rei·se** *f* group tour; **~ro͵man** *m* social novel; **~schicht** *f* (social) class; **~spiel** *n* party (*or* parlo[u]r) game; **~struk͵tur** *f* social structure; structure of society; **~stück** *n thea.* drawing-room comedy; *art*: genre painting; **~sy͵stem** *n* social system; **~tanz** *m* ballroom dance; **~ver·mö·gen** *n* company assets *pl.*; **~ver·trag** *m* **1.** *pol., phls.* social contract; **2.** ✝ articles *pl.* of association
geˈsengt *adj.* → ***Sau*** 2
Ge·senk [gəˈzɛŋk] *n* (-[e]s; -e) ⚙ die
ge·ses·sen [gəˈzɛsən] *p.p. of* ***sitzen***
Ge·setz [gəˈzɛts] *n* (-es; -e) law (*a. fig.*);

⚖, *parl. a.* act; *parl.* bill; *a. fig.* rule, principle; *coll.* ***das ~*** the law; ***gegen das ~*** against the law, illegal; ***nach dem ~*** under the law; ***im Namen des ~es*** in the name of the law; ***zum ~ werden*** become law; ***mit dem ~ in Konflikt geraten*** come up against the law, F get tangled up with the law; ***es steht im ~, daß*** the law says (that); F ***das steht nicht im ~*** there's no law about that; → ***aufheben*** 4, ***erlassen*** 3, ***Hüter; das ~ des Dschungels*** the law of the jungle, jungle law; ***das ~ der Serie*** the law of continuity; *fig.* ***das oberste ~ der Werbung ist*** the first rule of advertising is; ***sich et. zum obersten ~ machen*** make s.th. a cardinal rule; **~blatt** *n* law gazette; **~buch** *n* code (of law); statute book; **~ent·wurf** *m parl.* bill

Ge·set·zes|hü·ter [gəˈzɛtsəs-] *iro. m* guardian of the law; **&kon,form** *adj. and adv.* within the law; **~kraft** *f* (-; *no pl.*) legal force; ***~ erlangen*** become law; **~lücke** *f* gap (*or* loophole) in the law; **~miß,ach·tung** *f* defiance of the law; **~no,vel·le** *f* amendment; **~samm·lung** *f* statute book; **&treu** *adj.* law-abiding; **~über,tre·tung** *f* offen|ce (*Am* -se); violation of the law; **~vor·la·ge** *f* bill; **~werk** *n* body of law

ge'setz·ge·bend *adj.* legislative; ***~e Gewalt*** legislature; ***~e Körperschaft*** legislative (body); **Ge'setz·ge·ber** *m* (-s; -) legislator, lawmaker; **Ge'setz·ge·bung** *f* (-; *no pl.*) legislation; **Ge'setz·ge·bungs·werk** *n* body of law

ge'setz·lich I. *adj.* legal, statutory; lawful; legitimate *claim etc.*; legislative; ***~es Alter*** legal age; ***~es Rentenalter*** compulsory retirement age; → ***Feiertag;*** **II.** *adv.* legally *etc.*; ***~ bestimmt*** prescribed by law, statutory; ***~ geschützt*** patented, registered *trademark*; ***~ zulässig*** legal, lawful; ***~ verboten*** prohibited (by law); ***~ verpflichtet*** bound by law; **Ge'setz·lich·keit** *f* (-; *no pl.*) legality; legitimacy

ge'setz·los *adj.* lawless; anarchic(al); **Ge'setz·lo·sig·keit** *f* (-; *no pl.*) lawlessness; anarchy

ge'setz·mä·ßig *adj.* legal, lawful; legitimate *claim etc.*; *fig.* regular, following a set pattern; **Ge'setz·mä·ßig·keit** *f* (-; *no pl.*) legality; lawfulness; legitimacy; *phys.* conformity with a natural law; *fig.* (inherent) law(s *pl.*), regularity; (predetermined) pattern(s *pl.*)

Ge'setz·samm·lung *f* statute book

ge'setzt I. *adj.* staid; sober; dignified; mature; ***~es Alter*** mature age; *ein Herr* ***in ~em Alter*** of mature years; **II.** *cj.*: ***~ den Fall, daß*** suppose, supposing, let's assume; **Ge'setzt·heit** *f*: ***~ des Alters*** staidness of old age

ge'setz·wid·rig *adj.* illegal; **Ge'setz·wid·rig·keit** *f* (-; -en) unlawful (*or* illegal) act

Ge·seuf·ze [gəˈzɔʏftsə] *n* (-s; *no pl.*) sighing

ge'si·chert *adj.* secured (***vor*** *dat.*, ***gegen*** *acc.* against), safe (from), protected (from); ⚙, *a.* ✝ secured; *gun*: at safe; *fig.* secure *existence etc.*

Ge·sicht [gəˈzɪçt] *n* (-[e]s; -er) face (*a. fig.*); expression; *fig.* look; *lit.* character; ***~er machen*** (*or* ***schneiden***) make (*or* pull) faces; ***ein böses ~ machen*** scowl; ***er machte ein langes ~*** a) his face fell, b) he pulled a face; ***was machst du für ein ~?*** what are you pulling (such) a face for?; ***mach nicht so ein ~!*** stop pulling such a face, wipe that look off your face; ***mach nicht so ein dummes ~!*** don't look so stupid, wipe that stupid look off your face; ***das sieht man ihm am ~ an*** you can tell by the look on his face; ***es steht ihm im ~ geschrieben*** it's written all over his face; ***j-m*** (***gerade***) ***ins ~ sehen*** look s.o. (straight) in the eye; ***e-r Gefahr*** *etc.* ***ins ~ sehen*** face up to a danger *etc.*; ***den Tatsachen ins ~ sehen*** face the facts; ***ich kann ihm nicht mehr ins ~ sehen*** I can't look him in the face (*or* eye) any more; ***j-m ins ~ schlagen*** slap s.o. in the face; ***j-m et. ins ~ sagen*** say s.th. to s.o.'s face; ***j-m ins ~ lügen*** lie to s.o.'s face; ***das springt einem doch ins ~*** it stares you in the face, it's so obvious; ***ich hätte ihm ins ~ springen können*** I could have strangled him; ***zu ~ bekommen*** catch sight (*or* a glimpse) of, set eyes (up)on, see; *lit.* ***aus dem ~ verlieren*** lose sight of; ***er ist s-m Vater wie aus dem ~ geschnitten*** he's the spitting image (*or* spit and image) of his father, F he's a chip off the old block; ***das ~ wahren*** save (one's) face; ***das ~ verlieren*** lose face; ***sein wahres ~ zeigen*** show its true face, show one's true colo(u)rs; ***ein anderes ~ bekommen*** take on a new (*or* different) look *or* complexion; ***das gibt der Sache ein anderes ~*** that puts a new (*or* different) light *or* complexion on the matter

Ge'sichts|aus·druck *m* (facial) expression; **~creme** *f* face cream; **~far·be** *f* complexion; **~feld** *n opt.* range of vision; **~haar** *n* facial hair; **~hälf·te** *f* side of the face; **~haut** *f* (facial) skin; **~kon,trol·le** F *f* appearance (*or* face) check; ***so kommst du nie durch die ~*** they'll never let you in like that; **~kreis** *m* **1.** *fig.* horizon(s *pl.*); ***das liegt außerhalb ihres ~es*** it's beyond her horizon; **2.** view; ***in den ~ treten*** come into view; ***aus dem ~ verschwinden*** *a. fig.* disappear from view; *fig.* ***ich habe sie aus m-m ~ verloren*** I've lost touch with her, I've lost sight of her; **~läh·mung** *f* Bell's palsy

ge'sichts·los *adj.* faceless

Ge'sichts|mas·ke *f* mask; ⚕ (face) mask; ⚙ face guard; fencing mask; → ***Gesichtspackung;*** **~mas,sa·ge** *f* facial massage; **~mus·kel** *m* facial muscle; **~nerv** *m* facial nerve; **~ope·ra·ti,on** *f* plastic surgery; **~packung** *f* face pack, facial; **~par,tie** *f* area (of the face); **~pfle·ge** *f* skin (*or* face) care; **~pla·stik** *f* ⚕ plastic surgery; **~pu·der** *m* face powder; **~punkt** *m* point of view, angle; factor; ***unter dem ~*** *gen. a.* in terms of; ***von diesem ~ aus gesehen*** seen from this angle (*or* point of view); **~sei·fe** *f* facial (*or* face) soap; **~straf·fung** *f* facelift; **~ver·lust** *m* loss of face; ***e-n ~ erleiden*** lose face; **~was·ser** *n* face lotion; **~win·kel** *m opt.* visual angle; *fig.* angle; **~zü·ge** *pl.* features

Ge·sims [gəˈzɪms] *n* (-es; -e) △ mo(u)lding; cornice; *a. geol.* ledge

Ge·sin·del [gəˈzɪndəl] *n* (-s; *no pl.*) rabble, good-for-nothings *pl.*

ge'sinnt *adj. in cpds.* ...-minded, ...-oriented; *well*-disposed *etc.*; ***feindlich ~*** hostile; ***anders ~ sein*** have different views (***als*** from); ***fortschrittlich ~ sein*** be (a) progressive, be in favo(u)r of progress; ***sozialistisch ~ sein*** have socialist leanings (*or* views); ***wie ist sie politisch ~?*** where does she stand politically?, what are her political leanings?

Ge·sin·nung [gəˈzɪnʊŋ] *f* (-; -en) mentality; way of thinking; opinions *pl.*, views *pl.*; attitude; conviction, persuasion; character; ***edle ~*** noble-mindedness; ***von edler ~*** noble-minded; ***treue ~*** loyalty; ***ein Mann mit liberaler*** (***demokratischer***) ***~*** a liberal-minded (democratically minded) man; ***s-e wahre ~ zeigen*** show one's true colo(u)rs

Ge'sin·nungs·ge·nos·se *m* fellow-communist *etc.*; *iro.* kindred spirit; *contp.* crony; adherent, supporter

ge'sin·nungs·los *adj.* unprincipled, lacking in character; disloyal; **Ge'sin·nungs·lo·sig·keit** *f* (-; *no pl.*) lack of principles

Ge'sin·nungs|lump *m* timeserver, opportunist; **~lum·pe·rei** *f* opportunism, timeserving; **~schnüf·fe·lei** F *f* ideological spying (F snooping); McCarthyism; **~tä·ter** *m* politically *etc.* motivated offender; **&treu** *adj.* loyal; **~treue** *f* loyalty; **~wan·del** *m*, **~wech·sel** *m* change of heart; *esp. pol.* about-turn, volte-face

ge·sit·tet [gəˈzɪtət] *adj.* civilized; moral; well-mannered; polite, courteous

Ge·socks [gəˈzɔks] F *n* (-; *no pl.*) rabble, F shower

Ge·söff [gəˈzœf] F *n* (-[e]s; -e) F brew

ge·sof·fen [gəˈzɔfən] *p.p. of* ***saufen***

ge·so·gen [gəˈzoːgən] *p.p. of* ***saugen***

ge·son·dert [gəˈzɔndɐt] *adj.* separate

ge·son·nen [gəˈzɔnən] **I.** *p.p. of* ***sinnen;*** **II.** *adj.*: ***~ sein zu*** *inf.* be inclined to *inf.* (*or* towards *ger.*); ***er scheint nicht ~ zu*** *inf. a.* he doesn't seem willing *or* prepared to *inf.* (*or* keen on *ger.*)

Ge·sot·te·ne [gəˈzɔtənə] *dial. n* (-n; *no pl.*) boiled meat

ge'spal·ten I. *p.p. of* ***spalten;*** **II.** *adj.* split; *pol. a.* divided; ***~er Gaumen*** cleft palate; *psych.* ***~e Persönlichkeit*** split personality

Ge·spann [gəˈʃpan] *n* (-[e]s; -e) team; horse and cart; *fig.* team, pair, duo, tandem; *die beiden* ***bilden ein ideales*** (***merkwürdiges***) ***~*** make a perfect team (make strange bedfellows)

ge·spannt [gəˈʃpant] **I.** *adj.* **1.** taut *rope*; tense *muscle*; **2.** *fig.* a) strained *relations etc.*; tense *situation etc.*, b) curious; ***ich bin ~ auf*** *acc.* I can't wait to see (*or* find out *etc.*), ***das Konzert:*** I wonder what the concert's going to be like; ***ich bin ~, ob*** I wonder if (*or* whether); F ***ich bin ~ wie ein Regenschirm*** I (just) can't wait, I can hardly wait, the suspense is killing me, F I'm dying (*or* bursting) to find out *etc.*; ***et. mit ~er Aufmerksamkeit verfolgen*** follow s.th. closely (*or* with keen interest); ***sie steht mit ihm auf ~em Fuß*** she doesn't get on (very well) with him; **II.** *adv.* intently; ***~ zusehen*** watch closely, be riveted; ***er hörte ~ zu*** he listened intently, he was all ears; ***wir warten schon ganz ~*** we can't wait (to hear *etc.*); **Ge'spannt·heit** *f* (-; *no pl.*) a) expectation, excited anticipation, b) intentness, c) tension; ***man konnte die ~ im Saal spüren*** the hall was buzzing with expectation (*or* anticipation, excitement)

Ge·spenst [gəˈʃpɛnst] *n* (-[e]s; -er) ghost; *fig.* spect|re (*Am.* -er); F ***du siehst ja***

~er! you're seeing (*or* imagining) things; ***wie ein ~ aussehen*** look like a ghost; ***da gehen ~er um*** the place is haunted; *fig.* ***das ~ der Anarchie*** *etc.* ***an die Wand malen*** raise (*or* conjure up) the spect|re (*Am.* -er) of anarchy *etc.*

Ge·spen·ster·ge·schich·te [gəˈʃpɛnstɐ-] *f* ghost story

geˈspen·ster·haft *adj.* ghostly; *fig.* uncanny

Geˈspen·ster|schiff *n* phantom ship; **~stun·de** *f* witching hour

ge·spen·stisch [gəˈʃpɛnstɪʃ] *adj.* ghostly, eerie; F incredible

geˈsperrt I. *adj.* **1.** closed (***für*** *acc.* to); ✝ blocked; stopped *check etc.*; ***für den Verkehr ~*** closed to all traffic; **2.** *typ.* spaced; **II.** *adv.*: ***~ gedruckt*** spaced out

geˈspickt *adj.* **1.** *gastr.* larded; **2.** F *fig.* ***~ mit*** *dat.* bristling with *mistakes*, interlarded with *quotations etc.*; ***s-e Brieftasche war ~*** F his wallet (*or* he) was loaded

ge·spie·en [gəˈʃpiːən] *p.p. of* ***speien***

Ge·spie·le [gəˈʃpiːlə] *m* (-n; -n), **Ge·spie·lin** [gəˈʃpiːlɪn] *f* (-; -nen) *lit. and iro.* playmate

geˈspielt *adj.*: ***~e Gleichgültigkeit*** *etc.* studied indifference *etc.*

Ge·spinst [gəˈʃpɪnst] *n* (-[e]s; -e) spun yarn; *textil.* web, tissue; *zo.* cocoon; (*spider's*) web; *fig.* web *of lies etc.*

ge·spon·nen [gəˈʃpɔnən] **I.** *p.p. of* ***spinnen*; II.** F *adj.*: ***alles ~es Zeug*** he's *etc.* made it all up

Ge·spons [gəˈʃpɔns] *hum. m, n* (-es; -e) spouse

Ge·spött [gəˈʃpœt] *n* (-[e]s; *no pl.*) mockery, ridicule; ***sich zum ~ (der Leute) machen*** make a fool of o.s., make o.s. into a laughing stock; ***zum ~ der Leute werden*** become a laughing stock; **Ge·spöt·tel** [gəˈʃpœtəl] *n* (-s; *no pl.*) (constant) mocking *or* mockery

Ge·spräch [gəˈʃprɛːç] *n* (-[e]s; -e) conversation (***über*** *acc.* about, on); discussion; dialog(ue); *pol.* talks *pl.*; telephone conversation, call; ***ein ~ führen mit*** *dat.* have a conversation with; ***~e führen mit*** *dat.* talk to, *esp. pol.* have talks with; ***ins ~ kommen mit*** *dat.* get into conversation with, get talking to, *fig.* make contact with; ***es ist im ~*** it's being considered, it's under discussion (*or* consideration), it's a talking point; ***das ~ bringen auf*** *acc.* bring the conversation round to; ***mit j-m im ~ bleiben*** keep in contact with s.o., keep up contacts (*or* the contact) with s.o.

ge·sprä·chig [gəˈʃprɛːçɪç] *adj.* talkative; communicative; ***sie ist nicht sehr ~*** *a.* she doesn't say much; ***heute bist du ja nicht sehr ~*** *a.* you haven't got much to say for yourself today, have you?; **Geˈsprä·chig·keit** *f* (-; *no pl.*) talkativeness

geˈsprächs·be·reit *adj. esp. pol.* ready for talks; prepared (*or* willing) to have talks; ready (*or* prepared, willing) to negotiate; **Geˈsprächs·be·reit·schaft** *f* willingness to have talks; desire for talks (*or* negotiations)

Geˈsprächs|dau·er *f*: *teleph.* ***bei e-r ~ von fünf Minuten*** a five-minute call *will cost etc.*; **~ein·heit** *f teleph.* unit; **~fet·zen** *pl.* snatches of (a *or* the) conversation; **~form** *f*: ***in ~*** in the form of a conversation *or* dialog(ue); **~ge·gen·stand** *m* topic (*or* subject) of conversation; **~grund·la·ge** *f* basis for talks; **~kli·ma** *n pol.* atmosphere of the talks; **~lei·ter** *m radio, TV*: host; anchorman; **~lei·tung** *f*: ***die ~ hat ...*** hosting the discussion we have ...; **~part·ner** *m*: ***er ist ein guter ~*** you can have good conversations with him; ***mein ~ war ...*** I was talking to ...; ***sie braucht e-n ~*** she needs someone to talk to; ***unsere ~ heute abend sind ...*** with us here this evening (to talk about it) are ...; *pol.* ***sein ~*** his partner in the talks; ***er trifft sich mit s-m ~ X*** he'll be meeting X for talks; **~pau·se** *f* lull in the conversation; **~run·de** *f pol.* round of talks; **~stoff** *m* topic(s *pl.*) of conversation; ***genügend ~ haben*** have plenty to talk about; → ***ausgehen*** 3; **~the·ma** *n* topic (of conversation); topic of discussion; ***~ Nummer eins*** topic number one; ***es ist zur Zeit ~ Nummer eins*** everyone's talking about it; ***das ist für mich kein ~*** that's not something I'm even prepared to discuss; **~the·ra͵pie** *f* counsel(l)ing

geˈsprächs·wei·se *adv.* a) in conversation, b) in the course of (the) conversation

geˈspreizt *fig. adj.* affected; stilted; **Geˈspreizt·heit** *f* (-; *no pl.*) affectation

geˈspren·kelt *adj.* speckled; mottled

geˈspritzt *adj.* ... with soda; ***~er Whisky*** whisk(e)y soda

ge·spro·chen [gəˈʃprɔxən] *p.p. of* ***sprechen***

ge·spros·sen [gəˈʃprɔsən] *p.p. of* ***sprießen***

ge·sprun·gen [gəˈʃprʊŋən] **I.** *p.p. of* ***springen*; II.** *adj.* cracked; ***die Tasse ist ~*** *a.* the cup's got a crack

Ge·spür [gəˈʃpyːɐ] *n* (-s; *no pl.*) feeling (***für*** *acc.* for); sense (of); ***feines ~*** *a.* antenna, nose (***für*** *acc.* for); ***sie hat ein ~ dafür*** she picks that kind of thing up straightaway

ge·spurt [gəˈʃpuːɐt] *adj. skiing*: tracked, prepared *trail*

Ge·sta·de [gəˈʃtaːdə] *lit. n* (-s; -) shore, beach

geˈstaf·felt *adj.* graduated, sliding scale ...; ***~e Arbeitszeiten (Urlaubszeiten)*** staggered working hours (holidays); ***~er Zinssatz*** progressive (interest) rate

Ge·sta·gen [gɛstaˈgeːn] *n* (-s; -e) progestin

Ge·stalt [gəˈʃtalt] *f* (-; -en) **1.** figure, form; shape; *fig.* character; ***dunkle ~*** dark shape (*or* figure), *fig.* shady character; **2.** *no pl.* shape, form; ***(feste) ~ annehmen*** take shape, materialize, be shaping up; ***die ~ e-r Pyramide haben*** be shaped like a pyramid; ***e-r Sache ~ geben*** give s.th. shape; ***in ~ von*** *dat.* in the form (*or* shape) of; ***in s-r jetzigen ~*** in its present shape (*or* form); **3.** *no pl.* build, frame; ***von hagerer ~*** of lean build, lean-built; ***sie ist e-e zierliche ~*** she's gracefully built; **4.** personality, figure; character; **5.** *no pl. fig.* shape, form; guise; ***in der ~ des Teufels*** in the shape (*or* guise) of the devil, disguised as the devil; ***sich in s-r wahren ~ zeigen*** reveal one's true character; **6.** *psych.* gestalt

ge·stal·ten [gəˈʃtaltən] (h) **I.** *v/t.* a) form, shape; *sculpture etc.*: model; *a.* ⚙ design, b) create, produce, make, c) decorate; arrange; ***et. interessanter*** *etc.* ***~*** make s.th. more interesting *etc.*; ***et. abwechslungsreich ~*** lend s.th. variety, lend (some) variety to s.th.; ***et. dramatisch ~*** dramatize s.th., lend s.th. a dramatic element; ***et. ~ zu*** *dat.* make s.th. out of, turn s.th. into; **II.** *v/refl.*: ***sich ~*** take shape; develop; ***sich gut*** *etc.* ***~*** go (*or* turn out) well *etc.*; ***sich zu*** *e-m Erfolg etc.* ***~*** prove, turn out (to be), be *a success etc.*; **Ge·stal·ter** [gəˈʃtaltɐ] *m* (-s; -) designer; creator; **ge·stal·te·risch** [gəˈʃtaltərɪʃ] *adj.* design ...; artistic; creative

geˈstalt·los *adj.* shapeless, amorphous; **Geˈstalt·lo·sig·keit** *f* (-; *no pl.*) shapelessness

Geˈstalt·psy·cho·lo͵gie *f* gestalt psychology

Ge·stal·tung [gəˈʃtaltʊŋ] *f* (-; *no pl.*) **1.** creation, production; shaping, *a.* ⚙ designing; arrangement; **2.** shape; form; structure; features *pl.*; style, *a.* ⚙ design; **3.** development

Geˈstal·tungs|kraft *f* creative power; **~trieb** *m* creative impulse

Ge·stam·mel [gəˈʃtaməl] *n* (-s; *no pl.*) stuttering, stammering; *contp.* F gobbledygook; ***was war denn das für ein ~?*** what was all that about?

geˈstand *pret. of* ***gestehen***

ge·stan·den [gəˈʃtandən] **I.** *p.p. of* ***stehen*** *and* ***gestehen*; II.** *adj.*: ***ein ~er Mann, ein ~es Mannsbild*** a man who's made it (*or* got somewhere) in life; ***ein ~er Politiker*** a seasoned politician

ge·stän·dig [gəˈʃtɛndɪç] *adj.*: ***~ sein*** a) confess, own up, b) have confessed (*or* owned up), have made a confession

Ge·ständ·nis [gəˈʃtɛntnɪs] *n* (-ses; -se) *a.* ⚖ confession; admission; avowal; ***ein ~ ablegen*** make a confession, confess (***über*** *acc.* s.th.); ***j-m ein ~ abringen*** get s.o. to confess (*or* make a confession); ***ich muß dir ein ~ machen*** there's something I have to tell (*or* confess to) you

Ge·stank [gəˈʃtaŋk] *m* (-[e]s; *no pl.*) smell, stench, stink

ge·stat·ten [gəˈʃtatən] *v/t.* (h) allow, permit; grant; ***Rauchen (Fotografieren) nicht gestattet*** no smoking (no photographs); ***j-m et. ~*** allow s.o. to do s.th.; ***~ Sie, daß ich rauche?*** do you mind my smoking (*or* if I smoke)?; ***~ Sie mir zu*** *inf.* allow me to *inf.*; ***~ Sie?*** may I?; ***heute gestatte ich mir ...*** today I'm going to allow myself (*or* treat myself to) ...

Ge·ste [ˈgɛstə, ˈgeːstə] *f* (-; -n) gesture (*a. fig.*); ***mit lebhaften ~n*** gesticulating wildly; *fig.* ***~ der Versöhnung*** conciliatory gesture, F peace offering; ***als ~ der Höflichkeit*** as a matter of politeness

Ge·steck [gəˈʃtɛk] *n* (-[e]s; -e) flower arrangement

geˈsteckt *adv.*: F ***~ voll*** (F jam)packed, F chock-a-block

geˈste·hen (gestand, gestanden, h) **I.** *v/t.* admit, *a.* ⚖ confess; ***ich muß ~, daß*** I must confess (*or* admit) that; ***offen gestanden*** to be quite honest; **II.** *v/i.* confess, make a confession (*a.* ⚖), own up

Ge·ste·hungs·ko·sten [gəˈʃteːʊŋs-] *pl.* cost price *sg.*

Geˈstein *n* (-[e]s; -e) rock(s *pl.*); ⚒ rock, stone

Geˈsteins|art *f* type of rock; **~bil·dung** *f* rock formation; **~kun·de** *f* petrology, mineralogy; **~mas·se** *f* rocky mass; **~pro·be** *f* rock sample; **~schicht** *f* stratum

Ge·stell [gəˈʃtɛl] *n* (-[e]s; -e) a) rack; shelves *pl.*; stand; support; trestle; pedestal; legs *pl.*, b) frame; → ***Bettgestell, Fahrgestell***

geˈstellt *adj.* **1.** posed *photograph*; acted *scene*; *w.s.* artificial, unnatural; ***es ist ~*** they're (just) acting; **2.** ***gut (schlecht) ~ sein*** be well (badly) off; ***er ist nicht besonders gut ~*** he doesn't do too well (moneywise); ***auf sich selbst ~ sein*** have to fend for o.s., have to paddle one's own canoe

geˈstelzt I. *adj.* affected; stilted; **II.** *adv.*: ***~ reden*** *a.* talk like a book

ge·stern [ˈgɛstɐn] *adv.* yesterday; ***~ früh, ~ morgen*** yesterday morning; ***~ abend*** last night; ***~ vor e-r Woche*** yesterday week, a week ago yesterday; ***von ~*** yesterday's; *fig.* ***er ist nicht von ~*** he wasn't born yesterday, he's nobody's fool

geˈstie·felt *adj.* in boots; ***der ≈e Kater*** Puss-in-Boots; *fig.* ***~ und gespornt*** ready and waiting, *iro.* raring to go

ge·stie·gen [gəˈʃtiːgən] *p.p. of* ***steigen***

ge·stielt [gəˈʃtiːlt] *adj.* stemmed *vase etc.*; ♣ stalked

Ge·stik [ˈgɛstɪk, ˈgeːstɪk] *f* (-; *no pl.*) gestures *pl.*; sign (*or* body) language; ***e-e lebhafte ~ haben*** gesticulate a lot, use one's hands a lot; ***sich durch ~ verständigen*** communicate through sign language, signal to s.o. (*or* to one another)

ge·sti·ku·lie·ren [gɛstikuˈliːrən] **I.** *v/i.* (h) gesticulate, wave one's hands about (in the air); **II.** ≈ *n* (-s) gesticulation

Ge·stirn [gəˈʃtɪrn] *n* (-[e]s; -e) star(s *pl.*); constellation; **ge·stirnt** [gəˈʃtɪrnt] *adj.* starry

ge·sto·ben [gəˈʃtoːbən[*p.p. of* ***stieben***

Ge·stö·ber [gəˈʃtøːbɐ] *n* (-s; *no pl.*) (snow)drift, (snow) flurry

ge·sto·chen [gəˈʃtɔxən] **I.** *p.p. of* ***stechen***; **II.** *adj.* very neat (*or* clear) *handwriting*; **III.** *adv.*: ***~ scharf*** pin-sharp *photographs etc.*

ge·stoh·len [gəˈʃtoːlən] **I.** *p.p. of* ***stehlen***; **II.** *adj.* stolen; ***~e Ware*** stolen goods; F *fig.* ***der (das) kann mir ~ bleiben*** *sl.* to hell with him (it)

Ge·stöh·ne [gəˈʃtøːnə] *n* (-s; *no pl.*) moaning, moans *pl.*

geˈstopft I. *adj.* a) stuffed, b) darned *socks etc.*; **II.** *adv.*: F ***~ voll*** F jampacked, chock-a-block

ge·stor·ben [gəˈʃtɔrbən] *p.p. of* ***sterben***

ge·stört [gəˈʃtøːɐt] *adj.* disturbed; ***~er Schlaf*** *a.* broken sleep; *radio etc.* ***~er Empfang*** bad reception; ***~e Leitung*** faulty line; ***~e Ehe*** unstable marriage; ***~e Erziehung*** troubled upbringing; ***Kinder aus ~em Elternhaus*** (*or* ***Umfeld***) children from unstable homes (*or* backgrounds); ***~es Verhältnis*** ambivalent (*or* uneasy *or* shaky) relationship (***zu*** *dat.* with); ***sie haben ein ~es Verhältnis*** *a.* it's not a straightforward relationship; ***er hat ein ~es Verhältnis zu sich selbst*** he finds it hard to come to terms with himself; ***geistig ~*** mentally disturbed (*or* imbalanced)

ge·sto·ßen *p.p. of* ***stoßen***

Ge·stot·ter [gəˈʃtɔtɐ] *n* (-s; *no pl.*) stuttering

Ge·stram·pel [gəˈʃtrampəl] *n* (-s; *no pl.*) kicking (and struggling)

geˈstran·det *adj.* stranded

Ge·sträuch [gəˈʃtrɔyç] *n* (-[e]s; -e) bushes *pl.*, shrubbery

geˈstreckt *adj.* stretched; ***in ~em Galopp*** at full gallop

geˈstreift *adj.* striped, F strip(e)y; ***rotblau ~*** with blue and red stripes, blue-and-red striped *jumper etc.*

geˈstreßt F *adj.* under a lot of pressure (*or* stress); ***er ist zur Zeit ziemlich ~*** *a.* F he's got an awful lot on his plate at the moment

geˈstreut *adj.* scattered; ✝ diversified

geˈstri·chelt *adj.*: ***~e Linie*** broken (F dotted) line

ge·stri·chen [gəˈʃtrɪçən] **I.** *p.p. of* ***streichen***; **II.** *adj.* painted; → ***frisch*** II; *typ.* deleted; ♪ bowed; ***drei ~e Teelöffel*** three level teaspoons(ful); **III.** *adv.*: ***~ voll*** filled to the brim; F *fig.* ***ich hab' die Nase ~ voll*** F I'm fed up to the back teeth (with it)

geˈstrie·gelt *adj.* (*a.* ***~ und gebügelt***) (*pred.* all) spruced up

ge·strig [ˈgɛstrɪç] *adj.* yesterday's; ***am ~en Tage*** yesterday; ***am ~en Abend*** last night; ***unser ~es Schreiben*** our letter of yesterday; ***auf unser ~es Gespräch zurückkommend*** a) coming back to what we were saying yesterday, b) with reference to our conversation of yesterday; ***ewig ≈e*** (*pol.* political) diehards, F old fogeys

ge·strit·ten [gəˈʃtrɪtən] *p.p. of* ***streiten***

Ge·strüpp [gəˈʃtrʏp] *n* (-[e]s; -e) brushwood, scrub; underbrush; *fig.* jungle, maze

Ge·stühl [gəˈʃtyːl] *n* (-[e]s; -e) chairs *pl.*, seats *pl.*; *eccl.* pews *pl.*, stalls *pl.*

Ge·stüm·per [gəˈʃtʏmpɐ] *n* (-s; *no pl.*) a) bungling, b) F botch-up

ge·stun·ken [gəˈʃtʊŋkən] *p.p. of* ***stinken***

geˈstürzt *adj. pol.* overthrown; *a. ex-president etc.*

Ge·stüt [gəˈʃtyːt] *n* (-[e]s; -e) stud farm; **~buch** *n* studbook; **~hengst** *m* stallion; **~stu·te** *f* stud mare

geˈstylt *adj.* designer ...; styled

Ge·such [gəˈzuːx] *n* (-[e]s; -e) petition; application

geˈsucht *adj.* **1.** (much) sought-after; ***~ sein*** *a.* be in demand; ***sehr ~ sein*** be in great demand, be very much in demand; **2.** wanted; **3.** *fig.* studied; affected; labo(u)red

Ge·su·del [gəˈzuːdəl] *n* (-s; *no pl.*) scrawl

Ge·sum·me [gəˈzʊmə] *n* (-s; *no pl.*) hum, humming (noise)

Ge·sums [gəˈzʊms] F *n* (-es; *no pl.*) fuss (and bother)

ge·sund [gəˈzʊnt] *adj.* healthy (*a. fig.*); *pred. a.* (very) well; fit; *fig.* sound *views, instinct*, ✝ *firm etc.*; ***~e Nahrung*** good(, wholesome) food; *Ihre Leber etc.* ***ist ~*** *a.* is in (perfectly) good shape; ***~ und munter*** alive and kicking; ***Obst ist ~*** fruit is good for you; ***Schokolade ist für die Zähne nicht ~*** chocolate is bad for your teeth; ***wir machen dich schon wieder ~*** we'll get you back on your feet again; ***bleib (schön) ~!*** look after yourself; ***~er Menschenverstand*** (sound) common sense; ***ein ~es Urteil*** sound judg(e)ment; *fig.* ***das ist ganz ~ für ihn*** it'll do him good; *iro.* ***sonst bist du ~?*** apart from that you're fine, are you?; → ***gesundmachen, gesundstoßen***

geˈsund·be·ten *v/t.* (*sep.*, h) cure *s.o.* by faith healing; **Geˈsund·be·ter** [-beːtɐ] *m* (-s; -) faith healer; **Geˈsund·be·te·rei** [-beːtəˈraɪ] *f* (-; *no pl.*) faith healing

Geˈsund·brun·nen *fig. m* fountain of youth

ge·sun·den [gəˈzʊndən] *v/i.* (sn) recover (*a. fig.*), get well

Geˈsund·heit *f* (-; *no pl.*) health; healthiness; ***bei bester ~*** in the best of health; ***e-e eiserne ~ haben*** have an iron constitution; ***vor ~ strotzen*** be the picture of health; ***auf j-s ~ trinken*** drink to s.o.'s health; ***auf Ihre ~!*** your health!; ***~!*** bless you!, *Am. a.* gesundheit!

geˈsund·heit·lich I. *adj.* health ...; healthy; ***~er Zustand*** state of health; **II.** *adv.* healthwise; ***wie geht's ~?*** how are things healthwise?, how's your health?

Geˈsund·heits|amt *n* health cent|re (*Am.* -er); **~apo·stel** *m* health freak; **~arˌti·kel** *m* health product; **~atˌtest** *n* health certificate; **~be·am·te** *m* public health officer; **~be·hör·de** *f* public health authority; **≈be·wußt** *adj.* health-conscious; **~dienst** *m* public health service; **~er·zie·hung** *f* health education; **~faˌna·ti·ker** *m* health freak; **≈för·dernd** *adj.* healthy, good for one's health; **~für·sor·ge** *f* health care; **≈ge·fähr·dend** *adj.* noxious; ***~ sein*** *a.* be a health hazard; **~ge·fähr·dung** *f* health hazard; **~grün·de** *pl.*: ***aus ~n*** → ***gesundheitshalber***

geˈsund·heits·hal·ber [-halbɐ] *adv.* for health reasons, for reasons of health

Geˈsund·heits|in·duˌstrie *f* health (care) industry; **~miˌni·ster** *m* health minister, minister for health; *in GB*: Health Secretary, Secretary of State for Health; *in the USA*: Secretary of Health; **~mi·niˌste·ri·um** *n* health ministry (*or* department); *in GB*: Health Department, *a. in the USA*: Department of Health; **~pfle·ge** *f* health care; **~po·liˌtik** *f* health policy; **~reˌform** *f* health service reform(s *pl.*); **~ri·si·ko** *n* health hazard; **~scha·den** *m* health injury; *pl. a.* damage *sg.* to one's health; **≈schäd·lich** *adj.* bad for one's health; noxious *gas etc.*; ***~e Auswirkungen*** adverse health effects; **~schuh** *m* orthop(a)edic shoe; **~schutz** *m* health protection; **~vor·sor·ge** *f* health care; **~we·sen** *n* (-s; *no pl.*) public health system; **~zeug·nis** *n* health certificate; **~zu·stand** *m* (state of) health, physical condition

geˈsund|ma·chen *v/refl.* (*sep.*, h) → ***gesundstoßen***; **~pfle·gen** *v/t.* (*sep.*, h) nurse *s.o.* back to health

geˈsund·schrump·fen (*sep.*, h) ✝ **I.** *v/t.* pare (*or* whittle) down, shake up; **II.** *v/refl.*: ***sich ~*** be pared (*or* whittled) down, have a shake-up; **Geˈsund·schrump·fung** *f* (-; *no pl.*) shakeout, shake-up

geˈsund·sto·ßen F *v/refl.* (*irr.*, *sep.*, h, → ***stoßen***): ***sich ~*** F make a packet (***an*** *dat.* on, with); ***mit dem Geschäft hat er sich gesundgestoßen*** *a.* F he got rich in that racket

Ge·sun·dung [gəˈzʊndʊŋ] *f* (-; *no pl.*) recovery (*a. fig.*)

ge·sun·gen [gəˈzʊŋən] *p.p. of* ***singen***

ge·sun·ken [gəˈzʊŋkən] *p.p. of* ***sinken***

geˈtä·felt *adj.* panel(l)ed

ge·tan [gəˈtaːn] **I.** *p.p. of* ***tun***; **II.** *adj.*: ***gesagt, ~*** no sooner said than done; ***nach ~er Arbeit*** when the day's work is done, after work

geˈtaucht *adj.*: ***in Licht ~*** bathed in light; ***in Dunkelheit ~*** shrouded *or* enveloped in darkness

ge'teilt *adj.* divided (*a. pol.*); ✿ parted; ⚙, ✝ split; **~er Meinung sein** disagree; **da sind wir ~er Meinung** *a.* our opinions differ on that; **die Meinungen sind ~** opinions differ (*or* are divided); **~es Leid ist halbes Leid** a sorrow shared is a sorrow halved; **~e Freude ist doppelte Freude** a joy shared is a joy doubled
Ge'tier *n* (-[e]s; *no pl.*) animals *pl.*; creatures *pl.*
ge·ti·gert [gə'ti:gɐt] *adj.* striped
ge'tönt *adj.* tinted
Ge·tö·se [gə'tø:zə] *n* (-s; *no pl.*) din, F racket; crash; uproar; roaring
ge'tra·gen I. *p.p. of* **tragen; II.** *adj.* **1.** old *clothes*; **2.** *fig.* solemn; ♪ portato (*a. adv.*)
Ge·tram·pel [gə'trampəl] *n* (-s; *no pl.*) trampling about
Ge·tränk [gə'trɛŋk] *n* (-[e]s; -e) drink
Ge'trän·ke|au·to,mat *m* drinks machine; **~in·du,strie** *f* beverage industry; **~kar·te** *f* list of beverages; wine list; **~kell·ner** *m* wine waiter; **~steu·er** *f* beverage tax; *tax on alcoholic beverages consumed in public*
ge'tränkt *adj.*: **mit Alkohol** *etc.* **~** soaked in alcohol *etc.*
Ge·trat·sche [gə'tra:tʃə] *n* (-s; *no pl.*) gossip
ge'trau·en *v/refl.* (h) **1. sich ~** dare (**et. zu tun** [to] do s.th.); **2. das getraue ich mich** (**nicht**) I (don't) think I could do that
Ge·trei·de [gə'traɪdə] *n* (-s; -) grain, cereals *pl.*, *Brit. a.* corn; **~an·bau** *m* growing of cereals; **~art** *f* cereal, (type of) grain; **~bör·se** *f* grain (*Brit.* corn) exchange; **~ern·te** *f* grain harvest; **~ex,port** *m* export(ing) of grain(s); **~feld** *n* cornfield, *Am.* grainfield; **~händ·ler** *m* grain merchant; **~im,port** *m* import(ing) of grain(s); **~korn** *n* grain; **~land** *n* grain-growing country; **~lie·fe·run·gen** *pl.* grain supply *sg.* (*or* supplies) (**an** *acc.* to); **~mehl** *n* flour; meal; **~müh·le** *f* grain mill; **~pro,duk·te** *pl.* cereal products; **~si·lo** *m, n*, **~spei·cher** *m* granary; silo, *Am. a.* (grain) elevator; **~stär·ke** *f* cereal starch; **~vor·rat** *m* grain supply (*or* supplies *pl.*)
ge'trennt *adj. and adv.* separate(ly); **~ leben** be separated (**von** *dat.* from), live apart; **~ schlafen** have separate bedrooms; *Begriffe* **~ halten** distinguish between; *Wort* **~ schreiben** write as two words; **mit ~er Post** under separate cover; **~e Kasse machen** go Dutch, go halves on s.th., have separate accounts; *im Urlaub* **machen wir ~e Kasse** *a.* we each pay for ourselves; **wir zahlen ~** *in restaurant*: could we have separate bills?
Ge'trennt·schrei·bung *f*: **die ~ findet man häufiger** it's usually written as two (*or* three *etc.*) words
ge'tre·ten *p.p.of* **treten**
ge'treu *lit. adj.* faithful, loyal (*dat.* to); **~e Abschrift** true copy; **~e Übersetzung** faithful translation; **~ s-m Eid** *etc.* true to his oath *etc.*; **sich selbst ~ bleiben** remain true to o.s.; **Ge'treue** *m, f* (-n; -n) follower, loyal supporter; **ge'treulich** *lit. adj.* faithful (*a. fig.*), loyal
Ge·trie·be [gə'tri:bə] *n* (-s; -) **1.** ⚙ gear unit; *mot. etc.* transmission; gearbox; drive; clockwork; **2.** *fig.* machinery; → **Sand; ~...** *in cpds. mst* transmission ...; **~brem·se** *f* gear brake; **~ge·häu·se** *n*, **~ka·sten** *m* gearbox
ge·trie·ben [gə'tri:bən] **I.** *p.p. of* **treiben; II.** *adj.* embossed; **~e Arbeit** *a.* chased work
Ge'trie·be|rad *n* gear wheel; **~scha·den** *m* transmission trouble (*or* failure); **~wel·le** *f* shaft
ge'trimmt *adj.*: **~ für** *acc.* trained for, in form for; **auf gutes Benehmen** *etc.* **~** trained to behave well *etc.*; **auf alt ~** done up to look old; **(sie ist) auf jugendlich ~** F mutton dressed up as lamb
ge·trof·fen [gə'trɔfən] **I.** *p.p. of* **treffen; II.** *adj.* **1. auf dem Foto bist du gut ~** it's a good photo of you; **2. sich ~ fühlen** feel hurt
ge·tro·gen [gə'tro:gən] *p.p. of* **trügen**
ge·trost [gə'tro:st] *adv.* a) safely, b) easily, c) confidently; **das kannst du ~ tun** there's no reason why you shouldn't do it, *a.* go ahead (and do it), feel free (to do so); **du kannst ~ nach Hause gehen** just go home, it'll be all right (*Am.* alright); **ihr kannst du es ~ sagen** you needn't worry about telling her; **man kann ~ behaupten, daß** one can safely say that
ge'trun·ken *p.p. of* **trinken**
Get·to ['gɛto] *n* (-s; -s) *a. fig.* ghetto; *hist.* **das Warschauer (Prager) ~** the Warsaw (Prague) Ghetto
Ge·tue [gə'tu:ə] *n* (-s; *no pl.*) **1.** fuss (**um** *acc.* about, over); **was soll das ganze ~?** what's the big fuss (all about)?; **2.** silly behavio(u)r; **3.** acting
Ge·tüm·mel [gə'tʏməl] *n* (-s; *no pl.*) tumult, hurly-burly; **sich ins ~ stürzen** enter (*or* throw o.s. into) the fray
ge·tunt [gə'tju:nt] F *adj. mot.* F souped up
ge'tüp·felt, ge'tupft *adj.* spotted; *dress etc.* with dots, polka-dot *dress etc.*; **gelb ~** with yellow dots (*or* spots)
ge·übt [gə'ʔy:pt] *adj.* practi|sed (*Am.* -ced); skilled, experienced; trained (*a. eye*); **er ist (darin) ~** he's had plenty of practi|ce (*Am. a.* -se) (at it); **Ge'übt·heit** *f* (-; *no pl.*) practi|ce (*Am. a.* -se), experience
Ge·viert [gə'fi:ɐt] *n*: **... im ~** ... square
Ge·wächs [gə'vɛks] *n* (-es; -e) **1.** ✿ plant; **2.** produce; wine, vintage; **unser eigenes ~** our own produce; **ein edles ~** a choice wine; **3.** ⚕ growth
ge'wach·sen I. *p.p. of* **wachsen¹; II.** *adj.* **1.** grown; natural, undisturbed; *fig.* deep-rooted *traditions etc.*; **wie aus dem Boden ~ erscheinen** suddenly appear (as if) from nowhere; **2.** *fig.* **j-m ~ sein** be a match for s.o.; **e-r Sache ~ sein** be up to s.th.; **der Sache ~ sein** *a.* be equal to the task; **sich der Lage ~ zeigen** rise to the occasion
Ge'wächs·haus *n* greenhouse, hothouse; **~pflan·ze** *f* hothouse plant
ge·wagt [gə'va:kt] *adj.* a) risky, b) daring, c) risqué *dress, a. joke*; **~es Unternehmen** risky business (*or* venture); **Ge'wagt·heit** *f* (-; *no pl.*) a) riskiness, b) daring
ge'wählt I. *adj.* refined *speech*; select *company*; **II.** *adv.*: **sich ~ ausdrücken** talk well, choose one's words well, be very articulate; **Ge'wählt·heit** *f*: **~ des Ausdrucks** careful choice of words
ge'wahr *adj.*: **~ werden** *gen.* notice; discover; realize *a danger etc.*; catch sight of, see
Ge·währ [gə'vɛ:ɐ] *f* (-; *no pl.*) guarantee, ⚖, ✝ *a.* security; **diese Angaben erfolgen ohne ~** no responsibility is accepted for the correctness of this information; **~ bieten** (*or* **leisten**) **für** guarantee
ge·wäh·ren [gə'vɛ:rən] *v/t.* (h) grant; allow; give, offer; **j-n ~ lassen** a) let s.o. have his way, b) leave s.o. alone; **j-m Einlaß ~** let s.o. in, admit s.o.; **es gewährt e-n Einblick** it affords an insight (**in** *acc.* into)
ge'währ·lei·sten *v/t.* (h) guarantee; ensure; **Ge'währ·lei·stung** *f* (-; -en) guarantee, *a.* ✝ warranty
Ge·wahr·sam [gə'va:ɐza:m] *m* (-s; *no pl.*) care; safekeeping; custody, detention; **et. in ~ haben** have s.th. in safekeeping; **j-n in ~ halten** keep s.o. in custody; **in ~ nehmen** take charge of *s.th.*, take *s.o.* into custody; place *s.o.* under detention; **in sicherem ~** in safekeeping, in custody
Ge'währs·mann *m* (-[e]s; ⸚er, -leute) authority, source
Ge'währs·trä·ger *m* guarantor
Ge·wäh·rung [gə'vɛ:rʊŋ] *f* (-; *no pl.*) granting
Ge·walt [gə'valt] *f* (-; -en) **1.** power (**über** *acc.* over); authority; control (of, over); *pol.* **die drei ~en** the three powers; **2.** *no pl.* a) force, power, b) violence, force, c) strength, might, d) force, impact; **höhere ~** an act (*or* acts) of God, force majeure; **(die) nackte** *or* **rohe ~** brute force; **mit ~** by force, using force, forcibly; **mit nackter** (*or* **roher**) **~** by brute force, through sheer force; **mit ~ öffnen** force (*or* break) open, break down; **mit sanfter ~** (by) using gentle force; **mit aller ~** for all he's *etc.* worth; **sie will es mit aller ~ schaffen** she desperately wants to make it; **er hat es mit aller ~ abgestritten** he vehemently denied it; **sich in der ~ haben** have o.s. under control; **die ~ verlieren über** *acc.* lose control over (*a. mot.*), lose one's grip on; **er verlor die ~ über den Wagen** *a.* the car went out of control; **in s-e ~ bringen** gain control of, take command of, *w.s.* hijack; **j-n in s-r ~ haben** have s.o. under one's thumb (*or* in one's sway); **sich in der ~ haben** be in control of o.s.; → **antun** 1, **anwenden; ~akt** *m* act of violence; *fig.* tour de force; **~an·dro·hung** *f*: (**unter ~** under) threat of violence; **~an·wen·dung** *f* (use of) force; (use of) violence; **unter ~** by force, using force; **~aus·bruch** *m* eruption of violence; **~aus·übung** *f* use of force; **~de·mon·stra·ti,on** *f* violent demonstration
Ge'wal·ten|tei·lung *f*, **~tren·nung** *f pol.* separation of powers
ge'walt·frei *adj.* nonviolent *protest etc.*; peaceful; **Ge'walt·frei·heit** *f* (-; *no pl.*) absence of violence
Ge'walt|herr·schaft *f* despotism, tyranny; **~herr·scher** *m* despot
ge·wal·tig [gə'valtɪç] **I.** *adj.* **1.** powerful; vehement, violent; **~er Schlag** powerful blow; **die ⁓en** the people in power, **der Industrie** *etc.*: the big names in industry *etc.*; **2.** enormous, immense, stupendous; gigantic, huge, vast; F tremendous, terrific; **~er Irrtum** big(, big) mistake; **~e Leistung** tremendous feat (*or* achievement); **~e Lüge** great big lie; **~e Menge** huge (*or* vast) amount; **~er Unterschied** vast difference; **e-n ~en Hunger haben** be ravenous; **e-n ~en Eindruck hinterlassen** make a big (*or* deep) impression (**bei** *dat.* on); **II.** *adv.* enormously *etc.*; → **I;** → *a.* **irren** II

Ge'walt|kri·mi·na·li̦tät *f* violent crime(s *pl.*); **~kur** *f* ⚕ *etc.* drastic cure; crash diet; *fig.* drastic measures *pl.*; *fig.* ***das ist e-e ziemliche*** ~ that's a bit drastic; **~leistung** *f* tour de force

ge'walt·los *adj.* nonviolent; bloodless; **Ge'walt·lo·sig·keit** *f* (-; *no pl.*) absence of violence; nonviolence

Ge'walt|lö·sung *f* drastic solution; **~marsch** *m* forced march; **~maß·nah·me** *f* drastic (*or* violent) measure; **~mensch** *m* brutal person

ge'walt·sam I. *adj.* violent; drastic; forcible; ***e-s ~en Todes sterben*** die a violent death; ***~es Vorgehen*** use of force; **II.** *adv.* violently; by force; **Ge'walt·sam·keit** *f* (-; -en) **1.** *no pl.* violence; force; **2.** act of violence

Ge'walt|schuß *m soccer*: F rocket; **~streich** *m* coup de main; **~tat** *f* act of violence; → ***terroristisch***; **~tä·ter** *m* violent criminal; **2tä·tig** *adj.* violent; **~tä·tig·keit** *f* (-; -en) **1.** *no pl.* brutality, violence; **2.** act of violence

Ge'walt|ver·bre·chen *n* violent crime; **~ver·bre·cher** *m* violent criminal; **~ver·zicht** *m* non-aggression; renunciation of force

Ge'walt·ver·zichts|ab·kom·men *n* non--aggression pact; **~klau·sel** *f* non--aggression clause; **~ver·trag** *m pol.* non-aggression treaty

Ge·wand [gə'vant] *n* (-[e]s; Gewänder [gə'vɛndɐ]) garment; robe, gown; *eccl.* robe, vestment; *fig.* look; *fig.* ***im*** ~ *gen.* in the guise of; ***die Zeitschrift*** *etc.* ***erscheint in neuem*** ~ the magazine *etc.* has had a face-lift

ge·wandt [gə'vant] **I.** *p.p. of* ***wenden***; **II.** *adj.* a) quick, agile, nimble, b) skil(l)ful, clever (*both a. fig.*); efficient; smart; elegant, *a. contp.* smooth; fluent *speaker*; ~ ***sein in*** *dat. a.* be good at; ~ ***sein im Umgang mit*** have a way with; **Ge'wandt·heit** *f* (-; *no pl.*) a) agility, b) skill; efficiency; smartness; elegance; smoothness; fluency

ge·wann [gə'van] *pret. of* ***gewinnen***

ge'wapp·net *adj.* armed (***gegen*** *acc.* against), prepared (for)

ge·wär·tig [gə'vɛrtɪç] *adj.*: ~ ***sein*** *gen.* expect, reckon with; be prepared for

Ge·wäsch [gə'vɛʃ] F *n* (-[e]s; *no pl.*) F twaddle, hogwash

ge'wa·schen *p.p. of* ***waschen***

Ge·wäs·ser [gə'vɛsɐ] *n* (-s; -) body of water; *pl.* lakes and rivers; waters; **~kun·de** *f* hydrology; **~rei·ni·gung** *f* cleaning up of rivers and lakes; **~schutz** *m* water pollution control; **~ver·schmut·zung** *f*, **~ver·un·rei·ni·gung** *f* water pollution

Ge·we·be [gə've:bə] *n* (-s; -) **1.** a) fabric, textile, b) texture; **2.** *anat.* tissue; **3.** *fig.* web; **~flüs·sig·keit** *f* tissue (*or* lymph) fluid; **~kul̦tur** *f* tissue culture; **~pro·be** *f* tissue sample; **~schicht** *f* layer of tissue; **2scho·nend** *adj.* kind to fabrics; **~stoff·wech·sel** *m* tissue metabolism; **~ver·pflan·zung** *f* tissue transplant(s *pl.*); **~ver·träg·lich·keit** *f* tissue tolerance

Ge·wehr [gə've:ɐ] *n* (-[e]s; -e) gun; rifle; *pl.* (fire)arms; *fig.* ~ ***bei Fuß stehen*** be ready for battle; **~feu·er** *n* rifle fire; **~gra̦na·te** *f* rifle-launched grenade; **~kol·ben** *m* (rifle) butt; **~ku·gel** *f* (rifle) bullet; **~lauf** *m* barrel; **~mün·dung** *f* muzzle (of a gun *or* rifle); **~mu·ni·ti̦on** *f* rifle (*or* small-arms) ammunition; **~pa̦tro·ne** *f* cartridge; **~sal·ve** *f* volley of gunfire; **~schuß** *m* rifle shot

Ge·weih [gə'vaɪ] *n* (-[e]s; -e) antlers *pl.*

ge'weiht *adj.* **1.** consecrated; ordained *priest*; **2.** dedicated (*dat.* to), devoted (to); ***dem Tode*** ~ doomed to die; ***dem Untergang*** ~ doomed

Ge·wer·be [gə'vɛrbə] *n* (-s; -) trade (*a. fig.*), business; craft; branch of industry; ***ehrliches*** ~ honest trade; ***dunkles*** ~ shady business; *hum.* ***das älteste*** ~ ***der Welt*** the oldest profession in the world; **~auf·sichts·amt** *n* trade supervisory board; **~aus·stel·lung** *f* trade exhibition; **~be·trieb** *m* business enterprise; **~frei·heit** *f* (-; *no pl.*) freedom of trade; **~ge·biet** *n* industrial estate (*or* park); **~ge·setz** *n* trade law; **~ord·nung** *f* trade regulations *pl.*; **~schein** *m* trading licen|ce (*Am.* -se); **~schu·le** *f* trade school; **~steu·er** *f* trade tax; **~tä·tig·keit** *f* commercial activity

ge'wer·be·trei·bend *adj.* engaged in a trade, trading; industrial, manufacturing; **Ge'wer·be·trei·ben·de** *m* (-n; -n) businessman; manufacturer; craftsman, artisan

Ge'wer·be·zweig *m* trade, branch of industry; line (of business)

ge·werb·lich [gə'vɛrplɪç] **I.** *adj.* industrial, commercial, trade ...; business ...; ***~e Einfuhr*** industrial imports; ***~es Fahrzeug*** commercial vehicle; ***~e Räume*** business premises; ***~e Wirtschaft*** trade and industry; **II.** *adv.* commercially, on a commercial basis; ~ ***tätig sein*** carry on (*or* out) a trade; ~ ***genutzt*** (used) for commercial purposes; ~ ***genutzte Räume*** business premises

ge·werbs·mä·ßig [gə'vɛrpsmɛ:sɪç] **I.** *adj.* professional (*a.* ⚖); ***~e Unzucht*** prostitution; **II.** *adv.* professionally, on a commercial basis

ge'werbs·tä·tig *adj.* → ***gewerbetreibend***

Ge·werk·schaft [gə'vɛrkʃaft] *f* (-; -en) (trade) union, *Am.* labor union; **Ge'werk·schaf·ter** [-tɐ] *m* (-s; -), **Ge'werk·schaft·ler** [-lɐ] *m* (-s; -) trade unionist; (trade) union official; **ge'werk·schaft·lich I.** *adj.* (trade) union ...; **II.** *adv.*: (***sich***) ~ ***organisieren*** form a union; ~ (***nicht***) ***organisiert*** (not) unionized, (non-)union ...

Ge'werk·schafts|bei·trä·ge *pl.* union dues; **~be·we·gung** *f* trade unionism, trade union movement; **~boß** F *m* union leader; **~bund** *m* federation of trade unions; **2feind·lich** *adj.* anti-union ...; **~füh·rer** *m* union (*or* labo[u]r) leader; **~funk·tio̦när** *m* (trade) union official; **~mit·glied** *n* (trade) union member; **~spre·cher** *m* union spokesman; **~ver·band** *m* federation of trade unions; **~we·sen** *n* (-s; *no pl.*) trade unionism; **~zu·ge·hö·rig·keit** *f* union membership

ge·we·sen [gə've:zən] **I.** *p.p. of* ***sein***[1]; **II.** *adj.* former, one-time

ge·wi·chen [gə'vɪçən] *p.p. of* ***weichen***[2]

Ge·wicht [gə'vɪçt] *n* (-[e]s; -e) **1.** weight, load; ***fehlendes*** ~ short weight; ⚙ ***totes*** ~ dead weight; → ***spezifisch***; ***nach*** ~ by weight; **2.** *fig.* weight, importance, significance; ***e-r Sache großes*** (***wenig***) ~ ***beimessen*** attach great (little) importance to s.th.; ~ ***erhalten, an*** ~ ***gewinnen*** gain in importance (*or* significance); ***e-r Sache*** ~ ***geben*** (*or* ***verleihen***) lend weight to s.th.; ~ ***haben*** carry weight (***bei*** *dat.* with); ~ ***legen auf*** *acc.* set great store by, place great emphasis on; ***das*** ~ ***legen auf*** *acc.* put the emphasis on, emphasize, stress; ***die ~e haben sich verlagert*** the emphasis has (*or* the priorities have) shifted; ***ins*** ~ ***fallen*** count, matter (a lot); ***nicht ins*** ~ ***fallen*** make no difference; ***fällt das überhaupt ins*** ~? *a.* is it important?; ***an*** ~ ***verlieren*** lose in (*or* its) importance *or* significance

ge·wich·ten [gə'vɪçtən] *v/t.* (h) weight; *fig.* assess; *fig.* ***neu*** ~ reassess, have another look at

Ge'wicht·he·ben *n* (-s) weight-lifting; **Ge'wicht·he·ber** *m* (-s; -) weight-lifter

ge'wich·tig *adj.* weighty (*a. fig.*), heavy; *fig.* momentous *decision etc.*; influential; imposing; self-important; *fig.* ***e-e ~e Person*** (*or* ***Persönlichkeit***) a) an influential figure, b) *hum.* a person of some weight; ***ein ~es Wort mitzureden haben*** have a big say in the matter

Ge'wichts|ab·nah·me *f* loss of weight, weight loss; **~ana̦ly·se** *f* gravimetric analysis; **~an·ga·be** *f* ✝ declared weight; weight; **~ein·heit** *f* unit of weight; **~gren·ze** *f* weight limit; **~klas·se** *f sport*: weight (class); **~kon̦trol·le** *f* weight check

ge'wichts·los *adj.* weightless; **Ge'wichts·lo·sig·keit** *f* (-; *no pl.*) weightlessness

ge'wichts·mä·ßig *adj.* in (terms of) weight

Ge'wichts|satz *m* set of weights; **~trai·ning** *n* weight training; **~̦un·ter·schied** *m* difference in weight; **~ver·hält·nis** *n* weight ratio; **~ver·la·ge·rung** *f* shifting of weight; *fig.* shift of emphasis; **~ver·lust** *m* loss of weight; **~zu·nah·me** *f* increase in weight

Ge·wich·tung [gə'vɪçtʊŋ] *f* (-; -en) *statistics*: weighting; *fig.* assessment; prioritization, establishing priorities

ge·wieft [gə'vi:ft] F *adj.* smart, clever; shrewd; sly; experienced; streetwise, streetsmart

ge·wie·sen [gə'vi:zən] *p.p. of* ***weisen***

ge·willt [gə'vɪlt] *adj.* willing; prepared; determined

Ge·wim·mel [gə'vɪməl] *n* (-s; *no pl.*) **1.** swarming, bustle; **2.** swarm, teeming crowd, mass of people

Ge·wim·mer [gə'vɪmɐ] *n* (-s; *no pl.*) whimpering

Ge·win·de [gə'vɪndə] *n* (-s; -) **1.** garland; wreath; **2.** ⚙ thread; **3.** *zo.* spire; whorl; **~boh·rer** *m* tap; **~frä·sen** *n* thread milling; **~gang** *m* (turn of a) thread; **~schlei·fen** *n* thread grinding

Ge·winn [gə'vɪn] *m* (-[e]s; -e) **1.** winnings *pl.*; prize; **2.** ✝ profit (*a. fig.*); yield, returns *pl.*; proceeds *pl.*; earnings *pl.*; *fig.* gain; advantage, benefit; improvement, enhancement; *pol.* ***~e*** gains; ***reiner*** ~ net profit; ~ ***bringen*** yield a profit; ***am*** ~ ***beteiligt sein*** have a share in the profits; ~ ***erzielen*** net a profit; ***mit*** ~ ***verkaufen*** (***arbeiten***) sell (work) at a profit; *fig.* ~ ***ziehen aus*** *dat.* profit from; ***die Reise war ein*** ~ ***für mich*** I really profited from (*or* got a lot out of) the trip; **~ab·füh·rung** *f* transfer of profits; **~ab·schöp·fung** *f* skimming-off of excess profits; **~an·teil** *m* share in (the) profits; dividend; **~aus·schüt·tung** *f* dividend payout; **~aus·sich·ten** *pl.* profit prospects;

~be·schrän·kung *f* control of profits; **~be·tei·li·gung** *f* profit sharing; **2brin·gend I.** *adj.* profitable (*a. fig.*), lucrative; **II.** *adv.*: ***Geld ~ anlegen*** invest money profitably; **~chan·cen** *pl.* chances of winning; odds

ge·win·nen [gəˈvɪnən] (gewann, gewonnen, h) **I.** *v/t.* **1.** a) win, get *prize etc.*; gain *an advantage etc.*, b) get, obtain; earn, make; *fig.* gain *an insight, s.o.'s confidence etc.*; ***j-n für sich (et.) ~*** win s.o. over (to s.th.); ***j-n für s-e Pläne etc. ~*** win s.o.'s support for one's plans *etc.*; ***j-s Herz ~*** win s.o.'s heart; ***was ist damit gewonnen?*** what good will it do?; ***damit ist nichts gewonnen*** it won't do any good; ***wie gewonnen, so zerronnen*** easy come, easy go; → ***Oberhand, Spiel*** 1; **2.** a) ⚒ *etc.* win, obtain, extract, b) recover, reclaim (***aus*** *dat.* from *waste material etc.*), c) ⚗ extract, derive; **II.** *v/i.* **3.** win, be the winner(s); win the match *etc.*; ***~ gegen*** *acc.* beat; ***gegen ihn kannst du nicht ~*** *a.* he's unbeatable; ***knapp ~*** *sport*: scrape home; → ***spielend***; **4.** ***~ an*** *dat.* gain (in) *importance etc.*; ***an Boden ~*** gain ground; **5.** gain, improve; ***~ durch*** *acc.* profit by, benefit from; ***sie gewinnt bei näherer Bekanntschaft*** she's not so bad when you get to know her; ***durch den Bart gewinnt er*** the beard improves him, he definitely suits a beard; **geˈwin·nend** *fig. adj.* winning, engaging

Geˈwinn·ent·nah·me *f* withdrawal of profits

Ge·win·ner [gəˈvɪnɐ] *m* (-s; -), **Ge·win·ne·rin** [gəˈvɪnərɪn] *f* (-; -nen) winner

Geˈwinn|ge·mein·schaft *f* profit pool; **~li·ste** *f* list of winners; **~los** *n* winning ticket (*or* number), winner; **2orien,tiert** *adj.* profit-minded; **~quo·te** *f* ✝ profit margin; *lottery etc.*: prize; *football pools*: dividend; **2reich** *adj.* profitable; **~schwel·le** *f* breakeven point; **~span·ne** *f* profit (*or* trade) margin; **~sträh·ne** *f* lucky streak; **~stre·ben** *n* pursuit of gain (*or* profit)

Geˈwinn·sucht *f* (-; *no pl.*) profit-seeking; greed; **ge·winn·süch·tig** *adj.* profit-seeking, grasping, profiteering; ⚖ ***in ~er Absicht*** with the object of gain

geˈwinn·träch·tig *adj.* high-profit ..., high-yield ..., lucrative

Geˈwinnum·mer (*sep.* -nn·n-) *f* winning ticket (*or* number), winner

Geˈwinn-und-Ver·lust-Rech·nung *f* profit and loss account

Geˈwin·nung [gəˈvɪnʊŋ] *f* (-; *no pl.*) a) ⚒ production, extraction; output, b) (*land*) reclamation, c) ⚗ preparation, extraction

Geˈwinn|ver·tei·lung *f* distribution of profits; **~zahl** *f* winning number; **~zu·schlag** *m* profit markup

Ge·win·sel [gəˈvɪnzəl] *n* (-s; *no pl.*) whining

Ge·wirr [gəˈvɪr] *n* (-[e]s; *no pl.*) tangle, snarl; maze; jumble, confusion

ge·wiß [gəˈvɪs] **I.** *adj.* **1.** certain, positive, sure; ***eines ist ~*** there's one thing for sure; ***der Preis ist ihm ~*** he's certain to win; ***sich s-r Sache ~ sein*** be sure of one's facts; ***m-e Unterstützung ist ihm ~*** he can count on my support; ***man weiß nichts Gewisses*** nothing definite is known, nobody knows anything for sure; **2.** certain; ***ein gewisser Herr X*** a certain (*or* one) Mr X; ***ein gewisses Etwas*** a certain something; ***in gewissem Sinne*** in a sense (*or* way); ***in gewisser Hinsicht*** in a way, in some ways; ***in gewissen Fällen*** in certain (*or* some) cases; **II.** *adv.* certainly; no doubt; ***~ nicht*** definitely not; ***das weiß ich ganz ~*** I know that for sure; ***~!*** certainly; yes, indeed; ***aber ~!*** yes, of course

Geˈwis·sen *n* (-s; *no pl.*) conscience; ***ein reines*** (*or* ***gutes, ruhiges***) ***~*** a clear conscience; ***ein schlechtes ~*** a bad (*or* guilty) conscience; ***ein schlechtes ~ haben wegen*** *gen. a.* feel bad about *ger.*; ***soziales ~*** social conscience; ***ihn plagt sein ~*** he's got a bad conscience; ***sein ~ erleichtern*** ease one's conscience; ***j-m ins ~ reden*** have a serious talk with s.o.; ***j-n (et.) auf dem ~ haben*** have s.o. (s.th.) on one's conscience; ***das hast du auf dem ~*** you've got to answer for that; ***das mußt du mit d-m ~ ausmachen*** you'll have to settle that with your conscience; ***sich kein ~ machen zu*** *inf.* have no scruples about *ger.*; ***sie macht sich kein ~ daraus*** *a.* it doesn't bother (*or* worry) her in the slightest; ***das kannst du mit gutem ~ behaupten*** you can say that with a safe conscience; → ***Wissen***

geˈwis·sen·haft *adj.* conscientious; thorough; scrupulous; **Geˈwis·sen·haf·tig·keit** *f* (-; *no pl.*) conscientiousness; thoroughness; scrupulousness

geˈwis·sen·los *adj.* unscrupulous; irresponsible; unconscionable; **Geˈwis·sen·lo·sig·keit** *f* (-; *no pl.*) unscrupulousness; irresponsibility

Geˈwis·sens|angst *f* (terrible) qualms *pl.* (about s.th.); **~bis·se** *pl.* pangs (*or* pricks) of conscience; ***~ bekommen*** get a guilty conscience, start to feel guilty (***wegen*** *gen.* about); ***sich ~ machen*** have a guilty conscience, feel guilty (***wegen*** *gen.* about); ***er macht sich überhaupt keine ~ deswegen*** it doesn't bother (*or* worry) him in the slightest; **~ent·schei·dung** *f* moral decision; **~fra·ge** *f* matter of conscience; **~frei·heit** *f* freedom of conscience; **~grün·de** *pl.*: ***aus ~n*** for reasons of conscience; ***Wehrdienstverweigerer aus ~n*** conscientious objector; **~kon,flikt** *m* moral conflict; **~not** *f* moral dilemma; **~pflicht** *f* moral obligation (*or* duty); ***es ist e-e ~ zu*** *inf.* we *etc.* have a moral duty to *inf.*, we're *etc.* under a moral obligation to *inf.*; **~qua·len** *pl.* terribly bad conscience; **~sa·che** *f* matter of conscience; **~zwang** *m* a) moral constraint, b) religious despotism; **~zwei·fel** *pl.* moral doubts

ge·wis·ser·ma·ßen [gəˈvɪsɐˈmaːsən] *adv.* as it were; so to speak; in a way; to a certain extent

Geˈwiß·heit *f* (-; *no pl.*) certainty; assurance; ***mit ~*** for certain, with certainty; ***zur ~ werden*** become certain (*or* a certainty); ***~ erlangen über*** *acc.* become certain of (*or* about); ***sich ~ verschaffen über*** *acc.* make sure about (*or* of), find out for certain about; ***die ~ haben, daß*** know for sure (*or* certain) that; ***ich muß ~ haben*** I want to be sure (of *or* about it)

Ge·wit·ter [gəˈvɪtɐ] *n* (-s; -) (thunder-)storm; ***schweres ~*** heavy *or* severe (thunder)storm; ***wie ein reinigendes ~ wirken*** clear the air; **~flie·ge** *f* thunder fly; **~front** *f* stormy front; **~luft** *f*: ***es ist ~*** there's a storm in the air

ge·wit·tern [gəˈvɪtɐn] *v/impers.* (h): ***es gewittert*** there's a storm on its way

Geˈwit·ter|nei·gung *f* possibility of thunderstorms; **~re·gen** *m*, **~schau·er** *m* thundery shower; **~stö·run·gen** *pl. radio*: static *sg.*; **~sturm** *m* thunderstorm; **~wol·ke** *f* thundercloud

ge·witt·rig [gəˈvɪtrɪç] *adj.* thundery; ***es sieht ~ aus*** it looks as though we're in for a storm

Ge·wit·zel [gəˈvɪtsəl] *n* (-s; *no pl.*) joking, (silly) jokes *pl.*

ge·wit·zigt [gəˈvɪtsɪçt] *adj.*: ***~ sein*** have learnt from experience

ge·witzt [gəˈvɪtst] *adj.* smart, clever, shrewd

ge·wo·ben [gəˈvoːbən] *p.p. of* ***weben***

ge·wo·gen [gəˈvoːgən] **I.** *p.p. of* ***wägen*** *and* ***wiegen¹***; **II.** *adj. dat.* well-disposed to(wards); **Geˈwo·gen·heit** *f* (-; *no pl.*) goodwill (***gegenüber*** *dat.* towards); affection (for)

ge·wöh·nen [gəˈvøːnən] (h) **I.** *v/refl.*: ***sich ~ an*** *acc.* get used (*or* accustomed) to; ***sich daran ~ zu*** *inf.* get used to *ger.*, get into the habit of *ger.*; ***du wirst dich daran ~ müssen*** *a.* you'll have to learn to put up with it; ***man wird sich daran ~ müssen*** it'll take a bit of getting used to; **II.** *v/t.*: ***j-n an et. ~*** get s.o. used to s.th.; familiarize s.o. with s.th.; ***gewöhnt (sein)*** → ***gewohnt*** 2

Ge·wohn·heit [gəˈvoːnhaɪt] *f* (-; -en) habit; ***aus (alter) ~*** out of habit; ***aus lauter ~*** out of sheer habit, from force of habit; ***das macht die ~*** a) it's (a) habit, b) that's what habit can do (to you); ***aus der ~ kommen*** get out of practi|ce (*Am. a.* -se); ***die ~ haben zu*** *inf.* be in the habit of *ger.*, have a habit of *ger.*; ***j-m zur ~ werden*** become a habit with s.o.; ***in die ~ verfallen zu*** *inf.* get into the habit of *ger.*; ***sich et. zur ~ machen*** make s.th. (into) a habit; ***zur ~ werden*** become (*or* grow into) a habit; ***ich komme aus der ~ nicht heraus*** I can't break (*or* get out of) the habit, I can't stop doing it; ***wie es s-e ~ war*** as he was in the habit of doing, *formal and iro.*: as was his wont; → ***ablegen*** 3, ***Macht***

geˈwohn·heits·mä·ßig I. *adj.* habitual (*a.* ⚖); usual; **II.** *adv.* habitually, out of habit

Geˈwohn·heits|mensch *m* creature of habit; **~recht** *n* (-[e]s; *no pl.*) customary (*or* common) law; prescriptive right; *w.s.* established right; **~sa·che** *f* matter of habit; **~tä·ter** *m* habitual (*or* persistent) offender; **~tier** *n* creature (*or* slave) of habit; **~trin·ker** *m* habitual drinker; **~ver·bre·cher** *m* habitual criminal

ge·wöhn·lich [gəˈvøːnlɪç] **I.** *adj.* a) usual; normal; ordinary, everyday; conventional; plain; average; mediocre, b) common, vulgar; ***unter ~en Umständen*** under ordinary (*or* normal) circumstances; ***der ~e Sterbliche*** we ordinary mortals; ***im ~en Leben*** in everyday life; ***mein ~es Pech!*** my usual luck; ***~ aussehen, ein ~es Aussehen haben*** look (rather) common; **II.** *adv.* usually *etc.*; ***für ~*** as a rule, generally, normally; ***wie ~*** as usual

ge·wohnt [gəˈvoːnt] *adj.* **1.** usual; familiar; ***in ~er*** (*or* ***auf ~e***) ***Weise*** (in) the usual way; ***zu ~er Stunde*** at the usual time; → ***Gang*** 3; **2.** ***et. ~ sein*** be used (*or* accustomed) to s.th. (*or ger.*); ***~ sein zu*** *inf.* be used (*or* accustomed) to *ger.*, be in

the habit of *ger.*; ***ich bin ~, früh aufzustehen*** I'm used to getting up early
ge•wöhnt [gəˈvøːnt] *adj.*: ***an et. ~ sein*** be used (*or* accustomed) to s.th.; ***es*** (*or* ***daran***) ***~ sein zu*** *inf.* be used (*or* accustomed) to *ger.*; ***ich bin ja viel ~, aber ...*** I've seen a lot (of things) in my time, but ...
ge•wohn•ter•ma•ßen [gəˈvoːntɐˈmaːsən] *adv.* as usual
Ge•wöh•nung [gəˈvøːnʊŋ] *f* (-; *no pl.*) **1.** ~ ***an*** *acc.* getting used to; adaptation to; ***die ~ daran wird lange dauern*** it'll take a long time to get used to it; **2.** ⚕ ~ ***an*** *acc.* becoming habituated to; addiction to; ***Kokain führt zur ~*** cocaine is a habit-forming drug; **3.** acclimatization
Ge•wöl•be [gəˈvœlbə] *n* (-s; -) vault (*a. fig.*); vaults *pl.*; **~bo•gen** *m* arch (of a *or* the vault); **~pfei•ler** *m* pier (of a *or* the vault)
ge•wölbt [gəˈvœlpt] *adj.* △ vaulted, arched; domed *forehead etc.*; ⚙ convex, curved
Ge•wölk [gəˈvœlk] *n* (-[e]s; *no pl.*) clouds *pl.*
ge•wollt [gəˈvɔlt] **I.** *p.p. of* ***wollen***[1]; **II.** *adj.* deliberate; studied; artificial; **III.** *adv.* deliberately; ~ ***gelassen*** with studied calm; ~ ***ungezwungen*** with forced casualness; ***sich ~ naiv*** *etc.* ***geben*** act (*or* pretend to be) naive *etc.*
ge•won•nen [gəˈvɔnən] *p.p. of* ***gewinnen***
ge•wor•ben [gəˈvɔrbən] *p.p. of* ***werben***
ge•wor•fen [gəˈvɔrfən] *p.p. of* ***werfen***
ge•wrun•gen [gəˈvrʊŋən] *p.p. of* ***wringen***
Ge•wühl [gəˈvyːl] *n* (-[e]s; *no pl.*) a) turmoil, b) crowd, crush
ge•wun•den [gəˈvʊndən] **I.** *p.p. of* ***winden***; **II.** *adj.* winding, twisting; *fig.* roundabout, tortuous; **II.** *adv.*: ***sich ~ ausdrücken*** express o.s. in a roundabout way, beat about (*or* around) the bush
geˈwünscht *adj.* desired, wished-for; expected; hoped-for
geˈwür•felt *adj.* checked
Ge•würz [gəˈvʏrts] *n* (-es; -e) spice; seasoning; **~bord** *n* spice rack; **~es•sig** *m* aromatic vinegar; **~gur•ke** *f* gherkin, *Am.* pickle; **~han•del** *m* spice trade; **~kräu•ter** *pl.* (pot) herbs; **~mi•schung** *f* mixed spices *pl.*; **~nel•ke** *f* clove; **~reˌgal** *n*, **~stän•der** *m* spice rack
geˈwürzt *adj.* seasoned, spiced; *fig.* spiced, spicy
Geˈwürz•tra•mi•ner [-tramiːnɐ] *m* (-s; -) gewürztraminer
ge•wußt [gəˈvʊst] *p.p. of* ***wissen***
Gey•sir [ˈgaɪziːɐ] *m* (-s; -e [-ziːrə]) geyser
geˈzackt *adj.* jagged; *esp.* ♣, ⚙ serrated
geˈzahnt, geˈzähnt *adj.* toothed (*a.* ⚙); notched; *biol.*, ♣ dentate; perforated
Ge•zänk [gəˈtsɛŋk] *n* (-[e]s; *no pl.*) squabbling, bickering
Ge•zap•pel [gəˈtsapəl] *n* (-s; *no pl.*) fidgeting, wriggling (about)
geˈzeich•net *adj.* a) drawn, b) signed, c) *fig. face etc.*: marked (***von*** *dat.* by); ***schön ~es Fell*** beautifully patterned fur; *fig.* ***realistisch ~*** realistically portrayed *characters etc.*; ***fürs Leben ~*** scarred (*or* branded) for life; ***vom Tod ~*** bearing the stamp of death; ***sie ist von der Krankheit ~*** the illness has left its mark (on her)
Geˈzei•ten *pl.* tide *sg.*; **~..., *den ~ unterworfen*** tidal; **~enerˌgie** *f* tidal energy; **~kraft•werk** *n* tidal power plant; **~strom** *m*, **~strö•mung** *f* tidal current; **~wech•sel** *m* turn of the tide, changing tide
Ge•ze•ter [gəˈtseːtɐ] *n* (-s; *no pl.*) yelling; hue and cry
geˈzielt I. *adj.* well-aimed *shot*; *fig.* selective; specific *question etc.*; calculated *measure*; *advertising*: targeted *campaign etc.*; pointed *remark*; ***~er Versuch*** *contp.* deliberate attempt (***zu*** *inf.* to *inf.*); ***durch e-n ~en Einsatz der Polizei*** through a concerted effort on the part of the police; **II.** *adv.*: ***~ schießen*** shoot to kill; *fig.* ***~ fragen*** ask specifically, F ask *s.o.* straight; ***~ vorgehen*** take calculated measures (*or* steps); ***das müssen wir ganz ~ angehen*** we've got to plan our approach carefully
ge•zie•men [gəˈtsiːmən] (h) **I.** *v/i.*: ***j-m ~*** befit s.o.; **II.** *v/refl.*: ***es geziemt sich nicht*** it's not done, it's not (considered) good form, it's not considered proper; ***wie es sich geziemt*** as is proper (*or* fitting); **geˈzie•mend** *adj.* decent; due, proper *respect etc.*; respectful *distance*
ge•ziert [gəˈtsiːɐt] *adj.* affected; ***tu nicht so ~!*** stop putting it on; **Geˈziert•heit** *f* (-; *no pl.*) affectation
ge•zinkt [gəˈtsɪŋkt] *adj.* **1.** ⚙ dovetailed; **2.** marked; *fig.* ***mit ~en Karten spielen*** play with a stacked deck
Ge•zi•schel [gəˈtsɪʃəl] *n* (-s; *no pl.*) whispering; gossip; ***was soll das ~?*** what's all this (secret) whispering going on?
ge•zo•gen [gəˈtsoːgn] **I.** *p.p. of* ***ziehen***; **II.** *adj. a.* ⚙ drawn; rifled
geˈzuckert (*sep.* -k·k-) *adj.* **1.** sugared; **2.** *phot.* ***~e Leinwand*** glass-beaded screen
Ge•zwin•ker [gəˈtsvɪŋkɐ] *n* (-s; *no pl.*) winking
Ge•zwit•scher [gəˈtsvɪtʃɐ] *n* (-s; *no pl.*) chirping, twittering
ge•zwun•gen [gəˈtsvʊŋən] **I.** *p.p. of* ***zwingen***; **II.** *adj.* unnatural; affected; stiff; forced *smile etc.*; strained *conversation etc.*; ***~ sein*** (***sich ~ sehen***) ***zu*** *inf.* be (find o.s., feel) compelled *or* constrained to *inf.*; **II.** *adv.*: ***~ lachen*** give a forced laugh, force a laugh; **geˈzwun•ge•nerˈma•ßen** *adv.*: ***~ et. tun*** be forced to do s.th.; **Geˈzwun•gen•heit** *f* (-; *no pl.*) affectation; stiffness
Gha•na•er [ˈgaːnaɐ] *m* (-s; -), **Gha•nae•rin** [ˈgaːnaərɪn] *f* (-; -nen), **gha•na•isch** [ˈgaːnaɪʃ] *adj.* Ghanaian
Ghet•to *n* → ***Getto***
Gicht[1] [gɪçt] *f* (-; *no pl.*) ⚕ gout
Gicht[2] *f* (-; -en) *metall.* furnace top; furnace charge
ˈGicht•an•fall *m* attack of gout
gich•tig [ˈgɪçtɪç] *adj.* gout-ridden
ˈGicht•kno•ten *m* chalkstone
ˈgicht•krank *adj.*: ***~ sein*** suffer from (*or* have) gout; **ˈGicht•kran•ke** *m, f* (-n; -n) gout sufferer
Gie•bel [ˈgiːbəl] *m* (-s; -) gable; pediment; **~dach** *n* gable(d) roof; **~feld** *n* tympanum; **~fen•ster** *n* gable window; **~sei•te** *f* side, gable end, end wall
Gier [giːɐ] *f* (-; *no pl.*) greed (***nach*** *dat.* for); craving (for)
gie•ren[1] [ˈgiːrən] *v/i.* (h): ***~ nach*** *dat.* crave, lust for (*or* after)
ˈgie•ren[2] *v/i.* (h) ⚓, ✈ yaw
gie•rig [ˈgiːrɪç] **I.** *adj.* greedy (***nach*** *dat.*, ***auf*** *acc.* for); gluttonous; **II.** *adv.*: ***~ essen*** eat greedily; ***~ verschlingen*** bolt down, *a. fig.* devour; ***~ lesen*** read avidly; ***es ~ in sich aufnehmen*** F lap it up; ***~ ansehen*** look at *s.o. or s.th.* with lust in one's eyes (*or* with lustful eyes)
Gieß•bach [ˈgiːs-] *m* torrent
gie•ßen (goß, gegossen, h) **I.** *v/t.* **1.** a) pour, b) spill; **2.** ⚘ water; **3.** ⚙ cast; **II.** *v/impers.*: ***es gießt*** it's pouring; ***es gießt in Strömen*** (F ***wie aus Kübeln***) F it's coming down in buckets; **Gie•ßer** [ˈgiːsɐ] *m* (-s; -) ⚙ caster; founder; **Gie•ße•rei** [giːsəˈraɪ] *f* (-; -en) **1.** foundry; **2.** *no pl.* casting
ˈGieß•form *f* ⚙ mo(u)ld; die
ˈGieß•kan•ne *f* watering can; **ˈGieß•kan•nen•prinˌzip** *n* watering-can principle; ***Gelder*** *etc.* ***nach dem ~ verteilen*** *a.* try to give everyone a slice of the cake
Gift [gɪft] *n* (-[e]s; -e) poison (*a. fig.*); ⚗, *biol.* toxin; *fig.* venom; *fig.* ***das ist das reinste ~ für ihn*** that's sheer poison for him, that's the worst thing you could give him, ***für die Beziehung***: that could kill off relations; ***darauf kannst du ~ nehmen*** F you can bet your bottom dollar on that; ***er spuckte ~ und Galle*** F he was really fuming; F ***blondes ~*** F blonde bombshell; **~amˌpul•le** *f* poison phial; **~be•cher** *m* cup of poison; **~bee•re** *f* poisonberry; **~bla•se** *f zo.* poison sac; **~drü•se** *f* poison gland
gif•ten [ˈgɪftən] (h) **I.** *v/t.* rile, (really) get to *s.o.*; **II.** *v/i.*: ***~ über*** *acc.* say (really) nasty things about; **III.** *v/refl.*: ***sich ~*** get het up *or* mad (***über*** *acc.* about); ***gifte dich nicht darüber*** *a.* don't let it get to you
ˈGift|faß *n* toxic waste drum; **~fla•sche** *f* bottle of poison; **~gas** *n* poison gas; **~gas•graˌna•te** *f* gas-filled (*or* poison gas) artillery shell
ˈgift•grün *adj.* bright green
ˈgift•hal•tig *adj.* toxic
gif•tig [ˈgɪftɪç] **I.** *adj.* poisonous; ⚗ toxic; ⚕ virulent, contagious; *fig.* vicious, (really) nasty; vitriolic *remark, reply etc.*; **II.** *fig. adv.* viciously; ***j-n ~ ansehen*** look daggers at s.o.; **ˈGif•tig•keit** *f* (-; *no pl.*) poisonousness, toxicity; *fig.* viciousness
ˈGift|kör•per *m* toxic agent; **~krö•te** F *f sl.* narky bastard, *sl.* bitch; **~kü•che** F *fig. f* hotbed of gossip (and intrigue); **~kun•de** *f* toxicology; **~mi•scher** *m* **1.** poison brewer; **2.** F *fig.* F poison peddler; **3.** F *fig.* ***er ist ein richtiger ~*** he's always stirring up trouble; **~mord** *m* (murder by) poisoning; **~mör•der** *m* poisoner, assassin; **~müll** *m* toxic waste; **~müll•de•poˌnie** *f* toxic waste dump; **~nu•del** F *f* F (old) shrew, *sl.* bitch; **~pfeil** *m* poison arrow (*or* dart); **~pflan•ze** *f* poisonous plant; **~pilz** *m* poisonous mushroom; toadstool; **~schlan•ge** *f* poisonous snake; F *fig.* F (old) shrew; **~schrank** *m* poison cabinet; **~spin•ne** *f* poisonous spider; **~sta•chel** *m* poison sting; venomous spine
ˈGift•stoff *m* poison(ous substance); ⚕ toxin, toxic agent; pollutant; **~be•sei•ti•gung** *f* disposal of toxic substances (*or* wastes)
ˈGift|wir•kung *f* effect of the poison; **~zahn** *m zo.* poison fang; **~zenˌtra•le** *f* public laboratory; **~zwerg** F *m* F nasty little man
Gi•gant [giˈgant] *m* (-en; -en) giant, *fig. a.* heavyweight; ***~en der Politik*** political giants (*or* heavyweights); **gi•gan•tisch**

[gi'gantɪʃ] *adj.* huge, gigantic; tremendous *achievement etc.*; **~es Unternehmen** *a.* momentous undertaking; **Gi·gan·tis·mus** [gigan'tɪsmʊs] *m* (-; *no pl.*) gigantism; **Gi·gan·to·ma·nie** [giganto-ma'ni:] *f* (-; *no pl.*) megalomania

Gi·go·lo ['ʒi:golo] *m* (-s; -s) gigolo

Gigue [ʒi:k] *f* (-; -en ['ʒi:gən]) ♪ gigue; jig

Gil·de ['gɪldə] *f* (-; -n) guild; **~haus** *n* guildhall

Gim·pel ['gɪmpəl] *m* (-s; -) *zo.* bullfinch; F *fig.* F dimwit; **~fang** F *m* F con (job[s *pl.*]); **auf ~ ausgehen** F go out on the con game

ging [gɪŋ] *pret. of* **gehen**

Gin·ster ['gɪnstɐ] *m* (-s; -) ⚘ broom; gorse

Gin To·nic [dʒɪn 'tɔnɪk] *m* gin and tonic

Gip·fel ['gɪpfəl] *m* (-s; -) **1.** summit, (mountain) peak, mountain top; (*tree*)top; peak *of curve*; **2.** *fig.* peak, height; **auf dem ~** *gen.* at the peak (*or* height) of *one's power etc.*; **der ~ der Frechheit** the height of cheek; **das ist der ~ der Geschmacklosigkeit** *a.* for tastelessness that's hard to beat; **das ist ja der ~!** that really is the limit, *Brit. a.* F that takes the biscuit; **3.** *pol.* → **Gipfelkonferenz**; **~ab·kom·men** *n pol.* summit agreement; **~di·plo·ma̦tie** *f pol.* summitry; **~ge·spräch** *n pol.* summit talks *pl.*; **~kon·fe̦renz** *f pol.* summit (conference); **~lei·stung** *f* peak (performance); record

gip·feln ['gɪpfəln] *v/i.* (h) culminate (**in** *dat.* in); *riots etc.*: *a.* escalate (into); *career, speech etc.*: climax (in), culminate (in)

'Gip·fel|punkt *m* highest point; *fig.* high point, culmination; *fig.* **s-n ~ erreichen** *a.* reach one's zenith; **~stür·mer** *m* mountaineering fanatic; *fig.* high flier; **~teil·neh·mer** *m pol.* summiteer; **~tref·fen** *n pol.* summit (meeting)

Gips [gɪps] *m* (-es; *no pl.*) **1.** *min.* gypsum, calcium sulphate; **2.** plaster (of Paris); ⚕ **das Bein in ~ legen** put s.o.'s leg in plaster (*or* in a [plaster] cast); **~ab·druck** *m* plaster cast; **~bein** *n*: **ein ~ haben** have one's leg in plaster (*or* in a [plaster] cast); **~bin·de** *f* plaster bandage; **~bü·ste** *f* plaster bust; **~decke** *f* plaster ceiling

gip·sen ['gɪpsən] *v/t.* (h) plaster

'Gips|fi̦gur *f* plaster figure; **~kopf** F *fig. m* F blockhead; **~mar·mor** *m* imitation marble; **~mas·ke** *f* face mask; death mask; **~mehl** *n* powdered plaster; **~mör·tel** *m* gypsum mortar; **~ver·band** *m* ⚕ plaster cast; **e-m Bein e-n ~ anlegen** put a leg in plaster (*or* in a [plaster] cast)

Gi·raf·fe [gɪ'rafə] *f* (-; -n) giraffe

gi·rie·ren [ʒi'ri:rən] *v/t.* (h) ⚜ endorse, indorse (**auf** *acc.* on)

Gir·lan·de [gɪr'landə] *f* (-; -n) garland; paper chain

Gi·ro ['ʒi:ro] *n* (-s; -s) **1.** endorsement, indorsement; **2.** bank (*or* giro) transfer; **~ab̦tei·lung** *f* giro department; **~auf·trag** *m* credit transfer order; **~bank** *f* (-; -en) clearing bank; **~gut·ha·ben** *n* current account balance; **~kon·to** *n* current account; *esp.* ✉ giro account; **~kun·de** *m* current account customer (*or* holder); **~über̦wei·sung** *f* giro transfer; **~ver·kehr** *m* clearing; **~zen̦tra·le** *f* clearing house, central giro institution

gir·ren ['gɪrən] *v/i.* (h) coo (*a. fig.*)

Gis [gɪs] *n* (-; -) ♪ G sharp

Gi·tar·re [gɪ'tarə] *f* (-; -n) guitar; **Gi'tar·ren·spie·ler** *m*, **Gi·tar·rist** [gita'rɪst] *m* (-en; -en) guitar player, guitarist

Git·ter ['gɪtɐ] *n* (-s; -) grating (*a. phys.*); grille; *esp.* ⚘ trellis; (iron) bars *pl.*; (*iron*) gate; bars *pl. of a cot etc.*; grate; screen; fence; railing; *electron., geogr.* grid; *fig.* **hinter ~n** behind bars; **hinter ~ kommen** be locked up; **2ar·tig** *adj.* latticed; **~bett** *n* cot, *Am.* crib; **~draht** *m* wire netting; ⚡ grid wire; **~fen·ster** *n* lattice window; window with iron bars; **~netz** *n geogr.* grid; **~rost** *m* **1.** grating; **2.** grill; **~span·nung** *f* grid voltage; **~stab** *m* bar; **~tor** *n* iron gate; **~werk** *n* latticework; **~zaun** *m* palings *pl.*; lattice fence

Gla·cé|hand·schu·he [gla'se:-] *pl.* kid gloves; *fig.* **j-n mit ~n anfassen** handle s.o. with kid gloves; **~le·der** *n* glacé (*or* kid) leather

gla·cie·ren [gla'si:rən] *v/t.* (h) *gastr.* glaze

Gla·dia·tor [gla'di̯a:toːɐ] *m* (-s; -en [gladi̯a'to:rən]) gladiator

Gla·dio·le [gla'di̯o:lə] *f* (-; -n) ⚘ gladiola, gladiolus

Glanz [glants] *m* (-es; *no pl.*) shine, lust|re (*Am.* -er); brilliance, sparkle; radiance, glow; glitter; glare; shine, polish; *textil.* sheen; *fig.* splendo(u)r; glory; pomp; glitter, tinsel; *fig.* **äußerer ~** gloss; **in vollem ~** *a. iro.* in all one's glory; (**die Prüfung**) **mit ~** (**und Gloria**) **bestehen** pass (the exam) with flying colo(u)rs; F **mit ~ und Gloria** *untergehen etc.*: F in style; *iro.* **welcher ~ in m-r Hütte** what gives me the hono(u)r?

glän·zen ['glɛntsən] (h) **I.** *v/i.* shine; be shiny; glitter, sparkle, *stars*: *a.* twinkle; *fig.* beam (**vor** *dat.* with *joy etc.*); shine; **~ in** *dat.* be brilliant at; **~ wollen** like (*or* want) to impress, **mit s-m Wissen** *etc.*: like (*or* want) to show off one's knowledge *etc.*; → **Abwesenheit, Gold**; **II.** *v/t.* ⚙ polish; glaze; **'glän·zend I.** *adj.* shining, shiny, bright, gleaming; glittering, sparkling; *fig.* radiant; *phot.* glossy; *fig.* brilliant, excellent; **~e Idee** brilliant (*iro. a.* bright) idea; **in ~er Form** in top form; **~e Kritik** glowing (F rave) review; **~es Comeback** blistering comeback (**in** *acc.* to); **II.** *fig. adv.* brilliantly; extremely well; **die Prüfung ~ bestehen** pass (the exam) with flying colo(u)rs, do brilliantly (in the exam); **sie verstehen sich ~** they get on like a house on fire; **ihm geht's ~** he's doing very well (*or* just fine), *a.* F he's in the pink; **~ aussehen** look tremendous (F great); **sich ~ amüsieren** have a great time (of it), F have a whale of a time

'Glanz|fo·to *n* glossy print; **~idee** *f a. iro.* brilliant idea; **~lack** *m* brilliant varnish; **~le·der** *n* patent leather; **~lei·stung** *f* brilliant feat (*or* performance); **es war nicht gerade e-e ~** it wasn't exactly brilliant (*or* a brilliant performance *etc.*); **~licht** *n* (-[e]s; -er) highlight; *fig.* **e-r Sache ~er aufsetzen** add a few highlights to s.th.

'glanz·los *adj.* dull; *esp. eyes and fig. a.* lacklust|re (*Am.* -er); *fig.* inglorious

'Glanz|num·mer *f* highlight; pièce de résistance, F party piece; **~pa̦pier** *n* glazed paper; **~pa̦ra·de** *f sport*: brilliant save; **~par̦tie** *f* **1.** brilliant performance; **2.** → **Glanzrolle**; **~pe·rio·de** *f* → **Glanzzeit**; **~punkt** *m* highlight; climax; **~rol·le** *f thea.* star role; best role; **~sei·de** *f* glossy silk; **~stel·le** *f textil.* shiny patch; **~stück** *n* **1.** showpiece; **2.** → **Glanzleistung, Glanznummer**; **2voll** *adj.* glittering; **~zeit** *f* heyday; golden age

Glas¹ [gla:s] *n* (-es; Gläser ['glɛ:zɐ]) **1.** *no pl.* glass; **2.** a) glass, tumbler, b) jar, c) *opt.* lens; binoculars *pl.*; opera glasses *pl.*, d) mirror; *opt.* **Gläser** glasses; **hinter ~** behind glass, (*a.* **unter ~**) in a glass case; **zwei ~ Wein** two glasses of wine; **et. bei e-m ~ Wein besprechen** discuss s.th. over a glass of wine; F **er hat zu tief ins ~ geguckt** he's had a drop too many, F he's had one over the eight

Glas² *n* (-es; -en) ⚓ bell; **acht ~en** eight bells

'Glas|au·ge *n* glass eye; **~bal̦lon** *m* demijohn; ⚗ balloon (flask); **~blä·ser** *m* glass blower; **~blä·se·rei** [-blɛ:zəraɪ] *f* (-; -en) **1.** *no pl.* glass blowing; **2.** glassworks *pl.*, glass factory; glass blowing workshop

'Glas·bo·den·boot *n* glass-bottomed boat

Gläs·chen ['glɛ:sçən] *n*: **ein ~ zuviel** a drop too many; **sich ein ~ genehmigen** F have a wee drop

'Glas·dach *n* glass roof

Gla·ser ['gla:zɐ] *m* (-s; -) glazier; **Gla·se·rei** [gla:zə'raɪ] *f* (-; -en) **1.** glazier's workshop; **2.** *no pl.* glazing

'Gla·ser·kitt *m* (glazier's) putty

glä·sern ['glɛ:zɐn] *adj.* (made of) glass; *fig.* **~e Augen** glazed eyes; **~er Blick** glassy stare; **~er Klang** tinkling sound; **~e Stimme** brittle voice

'Glas·fa̦brik *f* → **Glashütte**

'Glas·fa·ser *f* fibreglass, *Am.* fiberglass; **~ka·bel** *n* fibre-optic (*Am.* fiber-optic) cable; **~op·tik** *f* fibre (*Am.* fiber) optics *pl.*

'Glas|fen·ster *n* glass window; **~fi·ber** *f* → **Glasfaser**; **~fla·sche** *f* glass bottle; **~flüg·ler** [-fly:glɐ] *m* (-s; -) *zo.* clearwing; **~ge·schirr** *n* glassware; **~har·fe** *f*, **~har̦mo·ni·ka** *f* glass harmonica; **2hart** F *adj.* (as) hard as rock; cracking *blow etc.*; **~haus** *n* greenhouse; **wer im ~ sitzt, soll nicht mit Steinen werfen** people in glass houses shouldn't throw stones; **~hüt·te** *f* glassworks *pl.*, glass factory

gla·sie·ren [gla'zi:rən] *v/t.* (h) glaze; enamel; *gastr.* frost, ice; candy *fruit*

gla·sig ['gla:zɪç] *adj.* glassy; glazed *eyes*; *gastr.* transparent *onions etc.*; waxy *potatoes*

'Glas|in·du̦strie *f* glass industry; **~kasten** *m* glass case; F *contp.* F glass box; **2klar** *adj.* crystal-clear (*a. fig.*); **~kolben** *m* **1.** ⚗ (glass) flask; **2.** ⚡ (glass) bulb; **~kör·per** *m anat.* vitreous body; **~ku·gel** *f* glass ball; **~ma·le̦rei** *f* a) painting on glass, b) stained glass (window[s *pl.*]); **~nu·deln** *pl.* glass noodles, vermicelli; **~pa̦last** F *contp. m* F glass box; **~pa̦pier** *n* glass paper; **~per·le** *f* (glass) bead; **~plat·te** *f* a) sheet of glass, b) glass top; **~röh·re** *f* glass tube, *pharm. a.* vial; **~sam·mel·con̦tai·ner** *m* bottle bank; **~scha·le** *f* glass bowl; **~schei·be** *f* pane (of glass); **~scher·be** *f* piece of (broken) glass; *pl.* broken glass *sg.*; **~schlei·fer** *m* glass grinder (*or* cutter); **~schnei·der** *m* glass cutter; glazier's diamond; **~schrank** *m* glass cabinet;

~schüs·sel *f* glass bowl; **~split·ter** *m* splinter of glass; **~tür** *f* glass door
Gla·sur [gla'zu:ɐ] *f* (-; -en [-'zu:rən]) ⚙ glaze; gloss; *gastr.* icing, *Am.* frosting
'Glas|ve,ran·da *f* glass veranda, *Am.* sun parlor; **~wa·ren** *pl.* glassware *sg.*; **~wat·te** *f* glass wool
'glas·wei·se *adv.* by the glass
'Glas|wol·le *f* glass wool; **~zie·gel** *m* glass tile; glass brick
glatt [glat] **I.** *adj.* a) smooth; soft *skin etc.*, b) straight *hair*; level, c) calm *sea*, d) polished, e) slippery, icy *road etc.*, f) clean *cut, fraction etc.*; even *number*, g) *fig.* smooth; glib; F downright *nonsense etc.*; ***~e Landung*** smooth landing; ***Vorsicht, hier ist es ~!*** mind you don't slip (*mot.* skid); *fig.* ***~e Absage*** flat refusal; ***(ein) ~er Beweis*** proof positive; ***e-e ~e Eins*** a straight A; ***e-e ~e Lüge*** a downright (*or* an absolute) lie; ***ein ~er Sieg*** a straight win; F ***es kostete mich ~e 1000 Dollar*** F it cost me a quick thousand (dollars); **II.** *adv.* a) smoothly, *fig. a.* without a hitch, b) completely; ***~ anliegen*** fit closely, ***an der Wand*** *etc.*: be flush with the wall *etc.*; ***~ durchschneiden*** cut clean through; *fig.* ***~ ablehnen (ableugnen)*** flatly refuse (deny); ***~ gewinnen*** win hands down; F ***et. ~ heraussagen*** say s.th. (straight) to s.o.'s face; F ***er kam ~ zu spät*** he had the nerve to turn up late; F ***~ vergessen haben*** have completely (F clean) forgotten; ***~ verlaufen*** go off smoothly (*or* without a hitch); F ***ich könnte ~ ...*** F I've a good mind (*or* half a mind) to *inf.*; **~bü·geln** *v/t.* (*sep.*, h) iron; *fig.* iron out
Glät·te ['glɛtə] *f* (-; *no pl.*) smoothness (*a. fig.*); slipperiness; polish
'Glatt·eis *n* ice; *mot. a.* black ice; ***es ist ~ (auf den Straßen)*** the roads are icy (*or* iced over); *fig.* ***j-n aufs ~ führen*** put s.o. in a tricky situation; ***er war aufs ~ geraten*** he was skating on thin ice; **~ge·fahr** *f* (*a.* ***auf den Straßen ~***) icy roads *pl.*, ice on the roads
glät·ten ['glɛtən] (h) **I.** *v/t.* smooth out; smooth (down); take out *creases etc.*; smooth away *wrinkles*; ⚙ smooth, give *s.th.* a smooth finish; polish (*a. fig.*), *metall. a.* burnish; plane; **II.** *v/refl.*: ***sich ~*** smooth (itself) out; *skin*: become smooth; *features*: relax; *sea*: calm down; *fig.* blow over; ***das Hemd wird sich von alleine ~*** *a.* the creases will come out (of the shirt) by themselves
glat·ter·dings ['glatɐdıŋs] *adv.* absolutely *impossible etc.*; flatly *refuse etc.*
'glatt|fei·len *v/t.* (*sep.*, h) file *s.th.* smooth; **~ge·hen** F *v/i.* (*irr.*, *sep.*, sn, → ***gehen***) go off smoothly (*or* without a hitch); ***es geht eben nicht immer alles glatt*** it can't be plain sailing all the time; **~haa·rig** *adj.* straight-haired; *zo.* smooth-haired
'Glatt·heit *f* (-; *no pl.*) → ***Glätte***
'glatt|ho·beln *v/t.* (*sep.*, h) plane *s.th.* smooth; **~ma·chen** *v/t.* (*sep.*, h) **1.** → ***glätten***; **2.** ✝ settle; **~ra·siert** [-ra,zi:ɐt] *adj.* clean-shaven; **~rüh·ren** *v/t.* (*sep.*, h) *gastr.* beat until smooth; **~schlei·fen** *v/t.* (*irr.*, *sep.*, h, → ***schleifen***) polish
'glatt·stel·len *v/t.* (*sep.*, h) ✝ settle, square, even up; **'Glatt·stel·lung** *f* (-; *no pl.*) settlement
'glatt·strei·chen *v/t.* (*irr.*, *sep.*, h, → ***streichen***) smooth out; smooth (down) *one's hair*
'glatt·weg F *adv.* just like that; point-blank; absolutely; ***~ ablehnen*** flatly refuse; ***er hat ~ behauptet*** he literally said
'glatt·zün·gig [-tsʏŋıç] *adj.* smooth-tongued
Glat·ze ['glatsə] *f* (-; -n) bald head, *hum.* bald pate; bald patch; **'Glatz·kopf** *m* **1.** bald head; **2.** bald man, F baldie, slap-head; **'glatz·köp·fig** [-kœpfıç] *adj.* bald(-headed)
Glau·be *m* (-ns; *no pl.*) a) belief (***an*** *acc.* in); faith, trust (in), b) creed; (religious) faith *or* belief, religion, c) conviction; ***~ an die Zukunft*** faith in the future; ***fester ~*** firm belief; ***in gutem ~n*** in good faith; ***im ~n, daß*** believing (that), under the impression that; ***~n schenken*** *dat.* believe; ***den ~n verlieren*** lose (one's) faith (***an*** *acc.* in); ***des (festen) ~ns sein, daß*** firmly believe (that); ***j-n in dem ~n lassen, daß*** let s.o. go on believing (that); ***laß sie doch in dem ~n*** let her believe it, don't spoil her illusion(s); ***ich möchte Sie nicht von Ihrem ~n abbringen(, daß)*** I wouldn't like to disillusion you (about ... *ger.*)
'glau·ben (h) **I.** *v/t.* believe; think; ***das glaube ich gern*** I can (well) believe that; F ***es ist nicht zu ~*** it's incredible (*or* unbelievable); ***das ist kaum zu ~*** it's hard to believe; ***er glaubt alles*** he'll believe anything; ***ob du es glaubst oder nicht*** believe it or not; ***und das soll ich ~?*** you don't expect me to believe that, do you?; ***ich glaube dir kein Wort*** I don't believe a word (you're telling me); ***das glaubst du ja wohl selber nicht*** F tell me another one; F ***wer's glaubt, wird selig*** F that's a good one; ***er glaubte sich unbeobachtet*** he didn't think anyone was looking; ***ich glaubte, er sei Arzt*** I thought he was a doctor; **II.** *v/i.* believe (***j-m*** s.o.; ***an*** *acc.* in); ***~ an*** *acc.* have faith in; ***ich glaube schon*** I think so; ***sie ~ fest daran*** they swear by it; ***du kannst mir ~*** take my word for it; F ***dran ~ müssen*** F come a cropper; F ***jetzt mußt du dran ~*** you can't get out of it now; F ***e-s Tages müssen wir alle dran ~*** F we've all got to go one of these days; **III.** 2 *m* (-s; *no pl.*) → ***Glaube***
'Glau·bens|ar,ti·kel *m* article of faith; **~be·kennt·nis** *n* **1.** creed; *fig.* ***sein politisches ~ ablegen*** lay down one's political creed; **2.** confession; **~be·we·gung** *f* religious movement; **~bru·der** *m* → ***Glaubensgenosse***; **~ei·fer** *m* religious zeal; **~fra·ge** *f* **1.** matter of faith; **2.** religious question; **~frei·heit** *f* (-; *no pl.*) religious freedom, freedom of religion; **~ge·mein·schaft** *f* religious community; **~ge·nos·se** *m* fellow Christian (*or* Moslem, Socialist *etc.*); **~krieg** *m* religious war; **~leh·re** *f* religious doctrine, dogma; dogmatics *pl.*; **~sa·che** *f* matter of faith; **~satz** *m* dogma; **~spal·tung** *f* schism; **2stark** *adj.* deeply religious; **~streit** *m* religious controversy; **~stren·ge** *f* (strict) orthodoxy; **~treue** *f* (religious) faith; **~ver·fol·gung** *f* religious persecution; **~wech·sel** *m* change of faith; **~zwang** *m* religious coercion, intolerance; **~zwei·fel** *m a. pl.* (religious) doubt
glaub·haft ['glaʊphaft] **I.** *adj.* plausible; ⚖ ***~ machen*** substantiate; ***j-m et. ~ machen*** convince (*or* persuade) s.o. of s.th.; → ***glaubwürdig***; **II.** *adv.*: ***~ nachweisen*** satisfactorily show; **'Glaub·haf·tig·keit** *f* (-; *no pl.*) credibility, plausibility
gläu·big ['glɔʏbıç] *adj.* **1.** religious; devout; **2.** trusting, *contp.* gullible; faithful, loyal
Gläu·bi·ge ['glɔʏbıgə] *m, f* (-n; -n) (true) believer; ***die ~n*** the faithful
Gläu·bi·ger ['glɔʏbıgɐ] *m* (-s; -) ✝ creditor; guarantor; mortgagee; **~aus·schuß** *m* creditor's committee; **~staat** *m* creditor country (*or* nation); **~ver·samm·lung** *f* meeting of creditors
'Gläu·big·keit *f* (-; *no pl.*) **1.** (unquestioning) faith; devoutness; **2.** trustfulness, *contp.* gullibility
glaub·lich ['glaʊplıç] *adj.*: ***kaum ~*** hard to believe
glaub·wür·dig ['glaʊp-] *adj.* plausible; reliable *source etc.*; trustworthy; ***~er Zeuge*** credible witness; ***aus ~er Quelle*** on good authority; **'Glaub·wür·dig·keit** *f* (-; *no pl.*) plausibility, credibility; reliability; trustworthiness; ***Mangel an ~*** credibility gap
'Glaub·wür·dig·keits|kri·se *f* credibility crisis; **~ver·lust** *m* loss of credibility
Glau·kom [glaʊ'ko:m] *n* (-s; -e) ⚕ glaucoma
gla·zi·al [gla'tsïa:l] *adj.* glacial
Gla·zi'al|land·schaft *f* glacial landscape; **~zeit** *f* ice age, glacial period
gleich [glaıç] **I.** *adj.* **1.** *pred.* a) *the* same; identical; equal (*a. rights, payment etc.*), b) constant, c) uniform; ***fast ~*** very similar; Ꭿ ***~e Winkel*** equal angles; ***in ~em Abstand voneinander*** equidistant from each other; ***x ist ~ y*** x equals y; ***12 minus 3 ist ~ 9*** 12 minus 3 is (*or* leaves) 9; ***in ~er Weise*** (in) the same way; ***zu ~en Teilen*** equally; ***zu ~er Zeit*** at the same time, simultaneously; ***es geht uns diesmal allen ~*** we're all in the same boat this time; ***das sieht ihm ~*** that's just like him; ***ins ~e bringen*** settle; ***~ und ~ gesellt sich gern*** birds of a feather (flock together); ***das ~e*** (*or* ***2es***) ***gilt für*** *acc.* the same applies to (F goes for); ***er ist nicht mehr der ~e*** he's not the Peter *etc.* I (*or* we) used to know, he's really changed, you wouldn't recognize him any more; ***es kommt aufs ~e hinaus*** it boils down to the same thing; ***2es mit 2em vergelten*** give *s.o.* tit for tat, F an eye for an eye; *hum.* ***alle Menschen sind ~, nur einige sind ~er als die anderen*** all people (*or* men) are equal, only some are more equal than others; → ***gleichbleiben***; **2.** es ist mir ~ it's all the same to me; ***ganz ~ wann*** *or* ***wo*** *etc.* whenever *or* wherever *etc.* (it is), no matter when *or* where *etc.* (it is); ***es ist ganz ~ wann*** *or* ***wo*** *etc.* it doesn't matter (*or* make any difference) when *or* where *etc.*; ***das soll dir doch ~ sein*** why should you care?; **II.** *adv.* **3.** alike, equally; ***~ alt (groß*** *etc.*) the same age (size *etc.*); **4.** right, straight, just, directly; immediately, straightaway; ***~ zu Beginn*** right at the outset; to start off with; ***~ daneben*** right beside (*or* next to) it; ***~ gegenüber*** just opposite; ***~ als*** as soon as; ***~ nach(dem)*** right (*or* straight) after; ***ich ging ~ hin*** I went straight there; ***es muß nicht ~ sein*** there's no hurry; ***~ (jetzt)*** right now, this minute; ***(ich komme) ~!*** (I'm) coming!, I'm on my way!; ***Kollege***

kommt ~ you'll be served right away; ***~!*** just a minute, F give us a chance; ***ich bin ~ wieder da*** I won't be long, I won't be a minute; ***bis ~!*** see you in a minute (*or* later); ***geh doch nicht ~ in die Luft*** there's no need to get angry; ***das haben wir ~*** it won't take a minute, we'll have that done (*or* fixed) in no time; ***das dachte ich mir doch ~*** I thought so (*or* as much); ***habe ich es nicht ~ gesagt?*** what did I say?; ***es ist ~ zehn (Uhr)*** it's nearly ten (o'clock); **5.** ***wie heißt er ~?*** what's (*or* what was) his name again?; ***was wollte ich ~ sagen?*** what was I going to say?; ***wo war es ~?*** where was it now?; ***das hört sich ~ ganz anders an!*** that's better, that's more like it; ***willst du ~ den Mund halten!*** will you shut up!; ***es muß nicht ~ ... heißen*** it doesn't mean to say (that), ***sein:*** it doesn't (necessarily) have to be; **III.** *prp.* (*dat.*): ***~ e-m König*** like a king

'gleich·al·trig [-altrıç] *adj.* (of) the same age

'gleich·ar·tig *adj.* of the same kind; similar; **'Gleich·ar·tig·keit** *f* (-; *no pl.*) homogeneity; similarity

gleich'auf *adv.*: ***~ liegen*** *sport*: be on level pegging

'gleich·be·deu·tend *adj.* **1.** synonymous (***mit*** *dat.* with); ***~e Wörter*** synonyms; **2.** equivalent (***mit*** *dat.* to); ***das ist ~ mit e-r Annahme (Absage)*** it means you've *etc.* been accepted (turned down, it amounts to a refusal)

'Gleich·be·hand·lung *f* equal treatment

'gleich·be·rech·tigt I. *adj.* equal; ***~ sein*** *a.* have equal rights; **II.** *adv.*: ***~ behandeln*** treat *people etc.* on an equal basis, treat *s.o.* as an equal; **'Gleich·be·rech·ti·gung** *f* (-; *no pl.*) equality; ***~ der Frau*** *etc.* equal rights *pl.* for women *etc.*

'gleich·blei·ben *v/i. and v/refl.* (***sich ~***) (*irr., sep.*, sn, → ***bleiben***) stay the same; ***er wird sich immer ~*** he'll never change; ***das bleibt sich gleich*** it doesn't make any difference, it comes (*or* boils) down to the same thing; **'gleich·blei·bend** *adj.* always the same; constant, invariable; steady (*a.* ✈ *and meteor.*)

'gleich·den·kend *adj.* like-minded

glei·chen ['glaıçən] *v/i.* (glich, geglichen, h) be (*or* look) like, resemble (***j-m*** s.o.); ***er gleicht s-r Mutter*** *a.* he takes after his mother; → ***Ei*** 1

glei·cher·ma·ßen ['glaıçɐ'maːsən] *adv.* **1.** equally; ***~ ... wie ...*** both ... and ..., at one and the same time ... and ...; **2.** → **'glei·cher'wei·se** *adv.* in the same way

'gleich·falls *adv.* likewise; ***danke, ~!*** thanks, and (to) you

'gleich·far·big *adj.* (of) the same colo(u)r

'gleich·för·mig [-fœrmıç] *adj.* uniform; steady, constant, unchanging; monotonous; **'Gleich·för·mig·keit** *f* (-; *no pl.*) uniformity; steadiness; monotony

'gleich|ge·ar·tet *adj.* of the same kind; similar; **~ge·rich·tet** *adj.* **1.** similar, parallel; **2.** ⚙ synchronous; ⚡ unidirectional; **~ge·schlecht·lich** *adj.* homosexual; *twins* (of) the same sex

'gleich·ge·sinnt *adj.* like-minded; ***~e Leute*** people with the same kind of interest (*or* outlook *etc.*); **'Gleich·ge·sinn·te** *m, f* (-n; -n) kindred spirit

'gleich|ge·stellt *adj.* on an equal footing (*dat.* with); on the same social level; **~ge·stimmt** *adj.* ♪ tuned to the same pitch; *fig.* in tune (with one another); ***~e Seelen*** kindred spirits

'Gleich·ge·wicht *n* (-[e]s; *no pl.*) *a. fig.* balance, equilibrium; ***~ der Kräfte*** balance of power (*phys.* of forces); ***ökologisches ~*** balance of nature, ecological balance; ***seelisches ~*** inner harmony; ***im ~*** balanced; ***aus dem ~ kommen, das ~ verlieren*** lose one's balance, *fig.* be thrown (off balance); ***aus dem ~ bringen*** unbalance *s.th.*, put *s.o.* off balance, *fig. a.* throw *s.o.* (off balance); ***das ~ (be)halten*** *or* ***wahren, sich im ~ halten*** keep one's balance, *fig.* stay on an even keel; ***das ~ halten*** *dat.* counterbalance *s.o. or s.th.*; ***sich das ~ halten*** *a. fig.* balance each other out; ***wieder ins ~ kommen*** steady o.s., *fig.* get back on an even keel; *fig.* ***et. wieder ins ~ bringen*** put s.th. back on an even keel; ***das ~ wiederherstellen*** redress the balance

'Gleich·ge·wichts|la·ge *f* balanced position; *fig.* balance; **~or,gan** *n anat.* organ of equilibrium; **~sinn** *m* (-[e]s; *no pl.*) sense of balance; **~stö·rung** *f* imbalance; ***sie leidet unter ~en*** her sense of balance is upset

'gleich·gül·tig I. *adj.* a) indifferent (***gegen*** *acc.* to); careless, casual, b) listless; apathetic (about), c) unfeeling, callous, d) unimportant, trivial; ***es ist mir (vollkommen) ~*** it's all the same to me, I don't care (a bit *or* F a damn), I couldn't really care less; ***Sport ist mir ~*** I'm not interested in sports, sports don't interest me; ***er ist mir ~*** he means nothing to me; ***ich bin dir wohl ~*** I don't suppose you care about me at all; ***es läßt ihn ~*** it leaves him cold; ***es ist völlig ~*** it doesn't make any difference (at all); ***(ganz) ~, was du tust*** whatever you do, no matter what you do; **II.** *adv.*: ***~ zusehen*** (just) stand there and do nothing, (just) stand and watch; ***sie reagierte ~*** she didn't seem to care (*or* be bothered); **'Gleich·gül·tig·keit** *f* (-; *no pl.*) indifference (***gegen*** *acc.* to[wards]); apathy, couldn't-care-less attitude

'Gleich·heit *f* (-; *no pl.*) a) equality, b) identity, identical nature; similarity, c) uniformity, d) conformity; homogeneity; equivalence; ***~ vor dem Gesetz*** equality before the law

'Gleich'heits|prin,zip *n* principle of equality; **~zei·chen** *n* equals sign

'Gleich·klang *m* unison; *ling.* consonance; *fig.* (***im ~*** in) harmony, unison

'gleich·kom·men *v/i.* (*irr., sep.*, sn, → ***kommen***) **1.** *dat.* come up to, compare with; ***an ... kommt ihr (so schnell) keiner gleich*** there's no-one to touch her (she's hard to beat) when it comes to ...; **2.** *dat.* amount to, *b.s. a.* be nothing short of

'Gleich·lauf *m* (-[e]s; *no pl.*) ⚙, ⚡, *TV* synchronism, synchronized operation; ⟁ *etc.* parallelism; **'gleich·lau·fend** *adj.* parallel (***mit*** *dat.* to, with); ⚙ synchronous, synchronized; **'Gleich·lauf·schwan·kun·gen** *pl.* wow and flutter *sg.*

'gleich·lau·tend *adj.* identical, *text*: with the same wording; *content*: to the same effect; *ling.* homonymic, homophonic; ***~es Wort*** a) homonym, b) homophone; ***~e Abschrift*** true copy

'gleich·ma·chen *v/t.* (*sep.*, h) make equal (*dat.* to); level (with *or* to); standardize, *b.s.* reduce to the same level, rob of its (*or* their) individuality; ***dem Erdboden ~*** raze to the ground; ***der Tod macht alle gleich*** death is the great level(l)er (*or* equalizer); **'Gleich·ma·cher** *m* (-s; -) level(l)er, egalitarian; **'Gleich·ma·che·rei** [-maxəraı] *f* (-; *no pl.*) level(l)ing, egalitarianism; **'gleich·ma·che·risch** [-maxərıʃ] *adj.* egalitarian

'Gleich·maß *n* (-es; *no pl.*) symmetry; harmony; regularity; → *a.* ***Gleichmäßigkeit, Gleichgewicht***; **'gleich·mä·ßig I.** *adj.* a) regular; steady, even; consistent, b) well-proportioned; symmetrical; (very) regular *features*; **II.** *adv. distribute etc.* evenly; ***~ gut*** consistently good; **'Gleich·mä·ßig·keit** *f* (-; *no pl.*) a) regularity; steadiness, evenness; consistency, b) symmetry

'Gleich·mut *m* (-[e]s; *no pl.*) equanimity; ***heiterer ~*** serenity; ***stoischer ~*** stoicism; **'gleich·müt·ig** [-myːtıç] *adj.* a) calm, composed; imperturbable, b) indifferent; **'Gleich·mü·tig·keit** *f* (-; *no pl.*) a) equanimity; calmness, composure; imperturbability; stoicism, b) indifference

'gleich·na·mig [-naːmıç] *adj.* of the same name; *phys.* like *poles etc.*; ⟁ *fractions* with a common denominator; ***~ machen*** bring *fractions* down to a common denominator

Gleich·nis ['glaıçnıs] *n* (-ses; -se) **1.** *a. bibl.* parable; **2.** *rhetoric*: simile; image; **'gleich·nis·haft** *adj.* allegorical; symbolic(ally *adv.*)

'gleich·ran·gig [-raŋıç] *adj.* a) ⚔ *etc.* of equal rank, b) on the same level, on a par, c) of equal importance

'gleich·rich·ten *v/t.* (*sep.*, h) ⚡ rectify; **'Gleich·rich·ter** *m* (-s; -) ⚡ rectifier; **'Gleich·rich·tung** *f* (-; *no pl.*) ⚡ rectification

'gleich·sam *adv.* as it were, so to speak; ***~ als wollte er sagen*** as if (*or* as though) he wanted to say

'gleich·schal·ten *v/t.* (*sep.*, h) **1.** ⚙ synchronize; **2.** *fig.* bring into line, *pol. a.* impose political (and economic *etc.*) conformity on; **'Gleich·schal·tung** *f* (-; *no pl.*) **1.** ⚙ synchronization; **2.** *fig.* enforced (political *etc.*) conformity, *pol. a.* gleichschaltung

'gleich·schenk·lig [-ʃɛŋklıç] *adj.*: ⟁ ***~es Dreieck*** isosceles triangle

'Gleich·schritt *m*: ***im ~*** (marching) in step, *fig.* in step (***mit*** *dat.* with); ***im ~, marsch!*** forward, march!

'gleich·se·hen *v/i.* (*irr., sep.*, h, → ***sehen***) **1.** resemble, look (*or* be) like (*dat. s.o., s.th.*); **2.** ***das sieht ihm gleich*** that's just like him

'gleich·sei·tig [-zaıtıç] *adj.* ⟁ equilateral

'gleich·set·zen *v/t.* (*sep.*, h) *a.* ⟁ equate (*dat. or* ***mit*** *dat.* with); identify, put on a level (with); **'Gleich·set·zung** *f* (-; *no pl.*) identification, equation

'Gleich·span·nung *f* ⚡ DC voltage

'Gleich·stand *m* (-[e]s; *no pl.*) *sport*: tie; *tennis*: deuce; **'gleich·ste·hen** *v/i.* (*irr., sep.*, h, → ***stehen***) be on a par *or* level (*dat.* with); ***sie stehen gleich*** *sport*: they're drawing, *in the table*: they're level on points

'gleich·stel·len *v/t.* (*sep.*, h) put in the same category (*dat.* as)

'Gleich·strom *m* ⚡ direct current (*abbr.* DC); *in cpds.* direct-current ..., DC ...

'gleich·tun *v/t.* (*irr.*, *sep.*, h, → **tun**): **es j-m ~** a) emulate s.o., b) match s.o.; **es j-m ~ wollen** vie with s.o.; **an ... tut's ihm keiner gleich** there's no match for him (*or* there's no-one to touch him) when it comes to ...
Glei·chung ['glaɪçʊŋ] *f* (-; -en) equation; *fig.* **die ~ ging nicht auf** it (*or* things) didn't work out
gleich'viel *adv.* all the same; **~, ob** *etc.* no matter if *etc.*; **~, wo** no matter where, wherever
'gleich·wer·tig [-veːɐtɪç] *adj.* equivalent (*dat.* to); equally good; *fig.* equal (*dat.* to), on a par (with)
gleich'wie *cj. u. adv.* (just) as
'gleich·wink·lig *adj.* with equal angles, 🕮 equiangular
gleich'wohl *obs. adv.* nevertheless, all the same; yet, however
'gleich·zei·tig I. *adj.* simultaneous; concurrent; **II.** *adv.* at the same time, simultaneously; **'Gleich·zei·tig·keit** *f* (-; *no pl.*) simultaneousness; concurrence
'gleich·zie·hen *v/i.* (*irr.*, *sep.*, h, → **ziehen**) *sport*: draw even (**mit** *dat.* with), catch up (with) (*both a. fig.*); equalize
Gleis [glaɪs] *n* (-es; -e) a) rails *pl.*, track, b) platform, c) *fig.* rut; **einfaches ~** single track; **aus dem ~ springen** jump the rails; *fig.* **das alte ~** the same old rut; **j-n aus dem ~ werfen** (*or* **bringen**) throw s.o. (completely); **wieder ins rechte ~ bringen** set (*or* put) to rights again; **auf ein falsches ~ geraten** get onto the wrong track; **auf ein totes ~ schieben** shelve *s.th.*, put *s.o.* on the shelf, put *s.o.* out to pasture; **~an·la·ge** *f* track system; **~an·schluß** *m* works siding; **~an·zei·ge** *f* platform indicator; **~ket·te** *f* track chain; **~ket·ten·schlep·per** *m* crawler tractor; **~kör·per** *m* track
glei·ßen ['glaɪsən] *v/i.* (h) gleam; glare; **'glei·ßend** *adj.*: **~e Sonne** glaring sun; **~e Hitze** searing heat; **~es Licht** glaring (*or* blinding) light, strong glare
Gleit|bahn ['glaɪt-] *f* slide, chute; ⚓ slipway; ✈ glide path; **~boot** *n* hydroplane
glei·ten ['glaɪtən] *v/i.* (glitt, geglitten, sn) glide (**über** *acc.* across); slide; slip; *mot.* skid; ⚓ glide, skim (across); pass, run *one's hand* (over); *smile*: pass (over *s.o.'s face*); **~ über** *acc. eyes*: scan; **et. ~ lassen** slide *or* slip s.th. (**in** *acc.* into); **es ist mir aus der Hand geglitten** it slipped out of my hand; **die Hand ~ lassen über** *acc.* run one's hand over; **'glei·tend** *adj.* gliding; *a.* ⚙ *and fig.* sliding; **~e Arbeitszeit** flexible working hours, flexitime
'Gleit|flä·che *f* sliding surface; **~flug** *m* glide; **~flug·zeug** *n* glider; **~klau·sel** *f* ⚕ escalator clause; **~kom·ma** *n* floating point; **~la·ger** *n* ⚙ slide bearing; **~laut** *m ling.* glide; **~schie·ne** *f* slide bar, guide; *typewriter*: carriage rail
'Gleit·schirm *m* paraglider; **~flie·gen** *n* paragliding; **~flie·ger** *m* paraglider
'Gleit·schritt *m dancing*: glissade; *skiing*: gliding step
'Gleit·schutz *m* **1.** anti-skid protection; **2.** → **~vor·rich·tung** *f* anti-skid device
'Gleit·se·geln *n* hang-gliding; **'Gleit·seg·ler** *m* hang-glider
'gleit·si·cher *adj.* non-skid
'Gleit|sitz *m* sliding seat; **~tag** *m* flexiday; **~wachs** *n* gliding wax; **~win·kel** *m* gliding angle; **~zeit** *f* (-; *no pl.*) flexible working hours *pl.*, flexitime
Glet·scher ['glɛtʃɐ] *m* (-s; -) glacier; **~bach** *m* glacial stream; **~bil·dung** *f* glacier formation; **~bo·den** *m* glacial soil; **~brand** *m* glacial sunburn; **~bril·le** *f*: (**e-e ~** a pair of) (high protection) snow goggles *pl.*, glacier goggles *pl.*; **~eis** *n* glacial ice; **~kun·de** *f* glaciology; **~müh·le** *f* moulin; **~spal·te** *f* crevasse; **~tal** *n* glacial valley; **~tor** *n* mouth of a (*or* the) glacier; **~wan·de·rung** *f* glacier tour; **~was·ser** *n* glacier water
Glib·ber ['glɪbɐ] *m* (-s; *no pl.*) slime; **glib·be·rig** ['glɪbərɪç] *adj.* slimy; slippery
glich [glɪç] *pret. of* **gleichen**
Glied [gliːt] *n* (-[e]s; -er ['gliːdɐ]) a) limb, b) joint, c) penis, (male) member, d) ⚙ *and fig.* link, e) *bibl.* generation, f) ⚔ rank, g) ⚖ *etc.* term; *ling.* → **Satzteil; künstliches ~** artificial limb; **an allen ~ern zittern** tremble like a leaf; **s-e ~er strekken** stretch (o.s.); **ich konnte kein ~ rühren** I couldn't move (*or* budge an inch); **der Schreck fuhr ihm in alle ~er** it gave him quite a turn; **der Schreck sitzt mir noch in den ~ern** I'm still recovering (*or* reeling) from the shock
Glie·der|arm·band ['gliːdɐ-] *n* adjustable bracelet; **~fü·ßer** [-fyːsɐ] *m* (-s; -) *zo.* arthropod; **~ket·te** *f* link chain; **2lahm** *adj.* worn out; **ich bin ~** I can hardly walk (*or* move); **~läh·mung** *f* paralysis
glie·dern ['gliːdɐn] (h) **I.** *v/t.* arrange, classify; structure; (sub)divide (**in** *acc.* into); ⚔ organize, deploy; **II.** *v/refl.*: **sich ~ in** *acc.* be made up of; be divided into
Glie·der|pup·pe ['gliːdɐ-] *f* jointed doll; puppet; lay figure; mannequin; **~rei·ßen** *n*, **~schmerz** *m* pains *pl.* in one's arms *or* legs (*or* arms and legs); **~tier** *n* articulate
Glie·de·rung ['gliːdərʊŋ] *f* (-; -en) arrangement, classification; plan; pattern; structure, organization (*a.* ⚔); division (**in** *acc.* into); *zo.*, ⚘ segmentation
'Glied|ma·ßen [-maːsən] *pl.* limbs; **~satz** *m ling.* subordinate clause; **~staat** *m* member state
glim·men ['glɪmən] **I.** *v/i.* (glimmte, *lit.* glomm, geglimmt, *lit.* geglommen, h) smo(u)lder (*a. fig.*); glow (*a. fig.*); glimmer, gleam; *fig.* flicker; **II. 2** *n* (-s) smo(u)ldering (*a. fig.*); faint glow; gleam, glimmer
Glim·mer ['glɪmɐ] *m* (-s; -) *min.* mica
glim·mern ['glɪmɐn] *v/i.* (h) glimmer
'Glimm|lam·pe *f* glow lamp; **~sten·gel** F *obs. m* F smoke stick
glimpf·lich ['glɪmpflɪç] **I.** *adj.* mild; **II.** *adv.*: **~ davonkommen** get off lightly; **es ist noch einmal ~ abgelaufen** we *etc.* were lucky; **j-n ~ behandeln** be lenient with s.o., not to be too hard on s.o.
glit·schen ['glɪtʃən] F *v/i.* (sn) slip; **glit·schig** ['glɪtʃɪç] *adj.* slippery; slimy
glit·zern ['glɪtsɐn] *v/i.* (h) glitter; glisten
glo·bal [glo'baːl] **I.** *adj.* a) worldwide, global, b) overall, c) exhaustive; general; **II.** *adv.* a) worldwide, globally, b) as a whole; **~ gesehen** a) seen on a global scale, b) seen from a broader perspective
Glo'bal|ab·kom·men *n* overall (*or* global) agreement; **~be·trag** *m* ⚕ overall amount; **~kür·zung** *f* across-the-board cut; **~steue·rung** *f* overall control; **~stra·te·gie** *f* global strategy; **~ver·ein·ba·rung** *f* → **Globalabkommen; ~ver·si·che·rung** *f* blanket insurance; **~ver·trag** *m* global contract
Glo·be·trot·ter ['gloːbətrɔtɐ] *m* (-s; -) globetrotter
Glo·bu·lin [globu'liːn] *n* (-s; -e) globulin
Glo·bus ['gloːbʊs] *m* (-[ses]; Globen ['gloːbən], F -se) globe; **sie ist um den ganzen ~ gereist** she's been all around the globe (*or* all over the world)
Glöck·chen ['glœkçən] *n* (-s; -) little bell
Glocke ['glɔkə] (*sep.* -k·k-) *f* (-; -n) bell; globe *of lamp*; (*cheese etc.*) cover; ⚘ bell (jar); gong; *fig.* blanket *of smog etc.*, thick layer; *fig.* **et. an die große ~ hängen** make a big thing about (*or* of) s.th.; **du solltest es nicht an die große ~ hängen** I would keep quiet about it if I were you; **er weiß, was die ~ geschlagen hat** he knows what to expect (*or* what he's in for)
'Glocken|blu·me (*sep.* -k·k-) *f* bluebell; **2för·mig** [-fœrmɪç] *adj.* bell-shaped; **~ge·läut** *n* **1.** ringing of bells; **2.** bells *pl.*; chime(s *pl.*), chiming; **~gie·ßer** *m* bell founder; **~gie·ße·rei** *f* bell foundry; **2hell** *adj. and adv.* (as) clear as a bell; **~hut** *m* cloche; **~klang** *m* peal of bells; **2rein** *adj. and adv.* → **glockenhell; ~rock** *m* flared skirt; **~schlag** *m* stroke of the clock; **mit dem** (*or* **auf den**) **~** on the dot; **~seil** *n* bell rope; **~spiel** *n* chime(s *pl.*); ♪ glockenspiel, carillon; **~turm** *m* bell tower, belfry; **~zei·chen** *n* bell signal; **~zug** *m* bell pull
Glöck·ner ['glœknɐ] *m* (-s; -) bell ringer; sexton; **der ~ von Notre-Dame** the hunchback of Notre Dame
glomm [glɔm] *lit. pret. of* **glimmen**
Glo·rie ['gloːrĭə] *f* (-; -n) glory; **'Glo·ri·en·schein** *m* halo; **glo·ri·fi·zie·ren** [glorifi'tsiːrən] *v/t.* (h) glorify; **Glo·rio·le** [glo'rĭoːlə] *f* (-; -n) halo; **glo·ri·os** [glo'rĭoːs] → **'glor·reich** *adj.* glorious; *iro.* **~e Idee** bright idea; **wer ist denn auf die ~e Idee gekommen?** whose bright idea was that?
Glos·sar [glɔ'saːɐ] *n* (-s; -e [-'saːrə]) glossary (of terms)
Glos·se ['glɔsə] *f* (-; -n) *ling.* gloss; commentary, marginal note; **Gegenstand zahlreicher ~n werden** become the subject of endless commentaries; *fig.* **s-e ~n machen über** *acc.* sneer (*or* scoff) at; **glos·sie·ren** [glɔ'siːrən] *v/t.* (h) gloss; write (*radio*: do) a commentary on; *fig.* make fun of
glot·tal [glɔ'taːl] *adj. ling.* glottal
Glot'tal *m* (-s; -e), **~laut** *m ling.* glottal (sound)
Glotz·au·ge ['glɔts-] *n* goggle eye; ⚕ exophthalmos; **'glotz·äu·gig** [-ɔʏgɪç] *adj.* goggle-eyed
Glot·ze ['glɔtsə] F *f* (-; -n), **'Glotz·ka·sten** F *m* F *the* box, *Am. a.* F (boob) tube
glot·zen ['glɔtsən] F *v/i.* (h) stare; gape, F gawk; **glotz nicht so blöd!** stop gawking like an idiot
Glück [glʏk] *n* (-[e]s; *no pl.*) (good) luck, stroke of (good) luck; happiness; **eheliches ~** domestic (*or* marital) bliss; **zum ~** fortunately; **~ haben** be lucky, be in luck; **kein ~ haben** be out of luck; **das ~ haben zu** *inf.* be lucky enough to *inf.*, have the good fortune to *inf.*; **da hast du ~ gehabt** you were lucky (there); **da kannst du von ~ sagen** you can count yourself lucky; **damit wirst du bei ihr**

kein ~ haben that won't get you anywhere with her, that won't cut any ice with her(, I'm afraid); **ein ~, daß** thank goodness (that); **ein ~, daß du da warst** *a.* it's lucky (*or* a good thing) you were there; **j-m ~ wünschen** wish s.o. luck; (**ich wünsch' dir**) **viel ~!** good luck!, F best of luck!; **es soll ~ bringen** it's supposed to bring you (good) luck; **sein ~ machen** make one's fortune; **sein ~ versuchen** try one's luck (**bei** *dat.* with), **mit** *dat. a.* F have a shot at *s.th.*; **auf gut ~** on the off-chance; **wir sind auf gut ~ nach Florenz gefahren** we went to Florence on the off-chance of finding a room (*or* finding some good weather *etc.*); **nochmal ~ gehabt!** F that was a close shave; **ich hatte ~ im Unglück** I was lucky things didn't turn out worse; **er** (**sie**) **hat viel ~ bei den Frauen** (**Männern**) he's (she's) a great success with the ladies ([the] men); **mancher hat mehr ~ als Verstand** Fortune favo(u)rs fools; **dein ~!** lucky for you; F **das hat mir gerade noch zu m-m ~ gefehlt** that's all I wanted (*or* needed)

'glück·brin·gend *adj.* lucky *charm etc.*

Glucke ['glʊkə] (*sep.* -k·k-) *f* (-; -n) mother hen (*a. fig.*), sitting hen; **'glucken** (*sep.* -k·k-) *v/i.* (h) cluck

glücken ['glʏkən] (*sep.* -k·k-) *v/i.* (sn) succeed, be successful, turn (*or* work) out well, F come off; **es glückte ihm zu** *inf.* he succeeded in *ger.*, he managed to *inf.*; **ihm glückt aber auch alles** some people have all the luck; **es wollte ihm nicht ~** he just couldn't manage it, *a.* he just couldn't get it right; **es ist ihm gut geglückt** he did a good job of it; **nichts wollte ~** everything went wrong

gluckern ['glʊkɐn] (*sep.* -k·k-) (h) **I.** *v/i.* gurgle; **II.** F *v/t.* F swill down

'Gluck·hen·ne *f* → **Glucke**

'glück·lich I. *adj.* a) happy, b) lucky, fortunate, c) *fig.* most appropriate, happy; good, fortunate *decision, choice etc.*; inspired; **der ~e Gewinner** *lottery etc.*: the lucky winner, (*a.* **der ~e Sieger**) the happy winner(s); *fig.* **ein ~er Wurf** a smart move; **nicht sehr ~** a bit unfortunate; **~ sein** be (*or* feel) happy; **du kannst dich ~ schätzen** (*or* **preisen**) you can count yourself lucky; *fig.* **e-e ~e Hand haben** have the right touch (**bei** *dat.* for, when it comes to); **du 2er!** F you lucky thing; **wer ist denn der** (**die**) **2e?** who's the lucky man (lady *or* girl), then?; **II.** *adv.* happily *etc.*; → **I,** b) well; successfully, c) *iro.* F finally; **~ ankommen** arrive safely; **~ enden** have a happy end(ing); F **jetzt hat er ~ auch noch ...** F to cap it all he's ...; F **jetzt ist er ~ weg** F thank goodness he's gone; **'glück·li·cher·wei·se** *adv.* fortunately, luckily

'Glück·sa·che *f* → **Glückssache**

'Glücks|bot·schaft *f* good news (*sg.*); **~brin·ger** [-brɪŋɐ] *m* (-s; -) lucky charm; mascot; **du bist ein ~!** you've brought me good luck

glück'se·lig *adj.* blissful, happy, *pred. a.* overjoyed; **Glück'se·lig·keit** *f* (-; *no pl.*) bliss(fulness), happiness; **ewige ~** eternal bliss

gluck·sen ['glʊksən] *v/i.* (h) a) *zo.* cluck, b) *water etc.*: gurgle, c) chortle (**vor** *dat.* with)

'Glücks|fall *m*: (**durch e-n ~** by a) stroke of luck; *a.* lucky coincidence; **es war ein reiner ~, daß ich ihm begegnete** it was pure luck that I ran (*or* should have run) into him; **~fee** *f a. fig.* fairy godmother, good fairy; **~ge·fühl** *n* feeling of happiness; blissful sensation; **~göt·tin** *f*: **die ~** (F Dame) Fortune, F Lady Luck; **~gü·ter** *pl. the* blessings (*or* good things) in life; **~kind** *n*: **sie ist ein ~** she was born under a lucky star; **~klee** *m* four-leaf (*or* four-leaved) clover; **~pfen·nig** *m* lucky penny; **~pil·le** F *f* mood drug; **~pilz** F *m* lucky devil; **ist das ein ~!** *a.* some people have all the luck; **~rad** *n* wheel of fortune; **~rit·ter** *obs. m* soldier of fortune; **~sa·che** *f* a matter of luck; **~!** luck!; **reine ~** pure luck; **~spiel** *n* game of chance; *coll.* gambling; *fig.* gamble; **~spie·ler** *m* gambler; **~stern** *m* lucky star; **~sträh·ne** *f* streak *or* run of (good) luck, lucky streak; **~tag** *m* lucky day; **das ist für mich ein ~!** this is my lucky day

'glück·strah·lend *adj.* radiant(ly happy), beaming all over one's face

'Glücks|tref·fer *m* fluke, lucky shot (*a. sport*); *fig.* stroke of luck; windfall; **~zahl** *f* lucky number

'glück·ver·hei·ßend *adj.* propitious

'Glück·wunsch *m* congratulations *pl.* (**zu** *dat.* on); good wishes *pl.*; **herzlichen ~!** congratulations!, *a.* F well done!; → **Geburtstag; ~kar·te** *f* greetings card; **~te·le|gramm** *n* greetings telegram

Glu·co·se [glu'ko:zə] *f* (-; *no pl.*) glucose

Glüh|bir·ne ['gly:-] *f* (light) bulb; **~draht** *m* ↯ filament

glü·hen ['gly:ən] (h) **I.** *v/i.* glow (*a. fig.*), *metal*: be red-hot; *fig. face*: burn; *fig.* **vor Zorn** *etc.* **~** burn with anger *etc.*; **II.** *v/t.* make *s.th.* red-hot; *metall.* anneal; **'glü·hend** *adj.* glowing (*a. fig.*); red-hot; live *coals*; burning (*a. fig.*); *fig.* fervent, ardent *fan etc.*; **~e Hitze** scorching heat; *fig.* **et. in ~en Farben schildern** paint s.th. in glowing colo(u)rs, paint a glowing picture of s.th.; → **Farbe, Kohle; 'glü·hend·heiß** *adj.* red-hot; *fig.* **ein ~er Tag** F a (real) scorcher

Glüh|fa·den ['gly:-] *m* ↯ filament; **~ker·ze** *f mot.* glow plug; **~lam·pe** *f* electric light bulb; **~wein** *m* mulled wine, glühwein; **~würm·chen** *n zo.* glow-worm

Glupsch·au·gen ['glʊpʃ-] F *pl.* F goggle eyes; **~ machen** goggle; **'glupsch·äu·gig** [-ɔʏgɪç] F *adj.* F goggle-eyed

Glut [glu:t] *f* (-; -en) a) embers *pl.*, b) (scorching *or* blazing) heat, c) glow; *fig.* fervo(u)r, fire

Glut·amat [gluta'ma:t] *n* (-[e]s; *no pl.*) glutamate

Glut·amin [gluta'mi:n] *n* (-[e]s; -e) glutamine; **~säu·re** *f* glutamic acid

'glut·äu·gig [-ɔʏgɪç] *lit. adj.* fiery-eyed; **mit ~em Blick** with blazing eyes, *lit.* with eyes ablaze

Glu·ten [glu'te:n] *n* (-s; *no pl.*) gluten; **2frei** *adj.* gluten-free

'glut·rot *adj.* fiery red; **~ werden** turn crimson

Gly·kol [gly'ko:l] *n* (-s; -e) (ethylene) glycol

Gly·ze·rin [glytse'ri:n] *n* (-s; *no pl.*) glycerine

Gna·de ['gna:də] *f* (-; *no pl.*) a) mercy, *eccl. a.* grace, b) favo(u)r; blessing; **ohne ~** merciless(ly); **um ~ bitten** beg for mercy; **e-e ~ gewähren** grant a favo(u)r; **~ vor Recht ergehen lassen** be lenient; *obs.* **j-m auf ~ oder Ungnade ausgeliefert sein** be at s.o.'s mercy; **~ finden vor** *dat.* find favo(u)r with; **Euer ~n** Your Grace; *iro.* **hättest du die ~ zu** *inf.* do you think you could lower yourself to *inf.* (*or ger.*); **sie hatte die ~ zu** *inf.* she (actually) condescended to *inf.* (*or ger.*); → **Gott;** F **ein Künstler von eigenen ~n** a self-styled artist

gna·den ['gna:dən] *v/i.*: **dann gnade dir Gott** God help you

'Gna·den|akt *m* act of mercy (*or* clemency); **~be·weis** *m*, **~be·zei·gung** *f* show of favo(u)r (*or* mercy, clemency); **~bild** *n eccl.* miraculous image of the Virgin Mary *etc.*; **~brot** *n*: **bei j-m das ~ essen** live on s.o.'s charity; **~er·laß** *m* amnesty; **~frist** *f* reprieve; † **e-e ~ von fünf Tagen** (**e-r Woche**) five days' (one week's) grace; **~ge·such** *n* plea for clemency

'gna·den·los *adj.* merciless, pitiless

'gna·den·reich *adj.* **1.** happy *time*; **2.** *R.C.* blessed, *Maria*: full of grace

'Gna·den|stoß *m* coup de grâce; **~tod** *m*: **der ~** (death by) euthanasia; **~weg** *m*: **auf dem ~** by special grace

gnä·dig ['gnɛ:dɪç] **I.** *adj. a. iro.* gracious (**gegen**[**über**] to); kind, benevolent; merciful; lenient, mild *sentence etc.*; *obs.* **~e Frau, ~es Fräulein,** *a. iro.* (**die**) **2ste** Madam, *Am.* Ma'am; *iro.* **wärst du wohl so ~ zu** *inf.* do you think you might just be able to *inf.* (*or* just lower yourself to *inf. or ger.*); **das war ja noch ~** we *etc.* got off lightly there, it could have been a lot worse; **Gott sei ihm ~!** God have mercy on him; **II.** *adv.* graciously *etc.*; **noch ~ davonkommen** get off lightly; **mach's ~** don't be too hard (on us *etc.*); **gnä·di·ger·wei·se** ['gnɛ:dɪgɐvaɪzə] *adv.*: *iro.* **~ et. tun** condescend to do(ing) s.th.

Gneis [gnaɪs] *m* (-es; -e) *min.* gneiss

Gnom [gno:m] *m* (-en; -en) gnome; F *contp. a.* dwarf; **'gno·men·haft** *adj.* gnomic

Gno·sti·ker ['gnɔstikɐ] *m* (-s; -), **gno·stisch** ['gnɔstɪʃ] *adj.* Gnostic

Gnu [gnu:] *n* (-s; -s) gnu

Go [go:] *n* (-; *no pl.*) go

Go·be·lin [gobə'lɛ̃:] *m* (-s; -s) tapestry, Gobelin

Gockel ['gɔkəl] (*sep.* -k·k-) *m* (-s; -), **~hahn** *m* cock, rooster

Gold [gɔlt] *n* (-[e]s; *no pl.*) gold (*a. fig.*); *fig.* **sie ist nicht mit ~ zu bezahlen** (*or* **aufzuwiegen**) she's priceless, she's worth her weight in gold; **er hat ein Herz aus ~, er ist treu wie ~** he's got a heart of gold; **~ in der Kehle haben** have a voice of gold; **~ gewinnen** win gold (*or* a gold medal); **zweimal ~ gewinnen** win two golds (*or* two gold medals); → *a.* **olympisch; es ist nicht alles ~, was glänzt** all that glitters is not gold

'Gold|ader *f* vein of gold; **~am·mer** *f zo.* yellowhammer; **~am·sel** *f zo.* golden oriole; **~an·lei·he** *f* † gold loan; **~auf·la·ge** *f* gold plating; **~bar·ren** *m* gold ingot; † *pl. usu.* bullion *sg.*; **~barsch** *m zo.* rosefish, ocean perch; † Norway haddock; **~be·stand** *m* gold reserves *pl.*; **2be·stickt** *adj.* embroidered with gold; **~blatt** *n* gold leaf; **~blätt·chen** *n* (piece of) gold leaf; **~blech** *n* gold foil; **2blond** *adj.* golden(-haired); **2braun** *adj.* golden-brown; **~bro|kat** *m* gold brocade; **~buch·sta·be** *m* gold letter; **mit ~n**

in gold lettering; **~deckung** *f* ✝ gold backing; **~de,vi·sen·wäh·rung** *f* gold exchange standard; **~du,blee** *n* gold plate; ***es ist ~ a.*** it's gold-plated; **Ձdurch,wirkt** *adj.* interwoven with gold
gol·den ['gɔldən] *adj.* (of) gold; *fig.* golden; *fig.* ***~e Hochzeit*** golden wedding; ***~er Mittelweg*** golden mean; ***~e Regel*** golden rule; ***Ձe Schallplatte*** gold disc; ***~er Schnitt*** golden section; ***~es Zeitalter*** golden age; ***die ~e Jugendzeit*** golden youth; ***die ~en Zwanziger*** the roaring (*or* golden) twenties; ***das Ձe Buch*** the visitors' book; ***sich ins Ձe Buch (der Stadt) eintragen*** sign the visitors' book; F ***sich e-e ~e Nase verdienen*** F make (*or* earn) a mint (***an*** *dat.* with); F ***sich den ~en Schuß setzen*** *sl.* OD oneself; → ***Brücke, Käfig***
'Gold|erz *n* gold ore; **~esel** F *m*: ***ich bin doch kein ~*** F I'm not made of money(, you know); **~fa·den** *m* gold thread; **~far·be** *f* gold colo(u)r; **Ձfar·ben, Ձfar·big** *adj.* gold-colo(u)red, golden; **~fa,san** *m* golden pheasant; **~fe·der** *f* gold nib; **~fink** *m zo.* goldfinch; **~fisch** *m* goldfish; **~fül·lung** *f* gold filling; **~ge·halt** *m* gold content; **Ձgelb** *adj.* yellow(y)-gold; *a.* golden *wine*; **~ge·wicht** *n* troy (weight); **~grä·ber** [-grɛːbɐ] *m* (-s; -) gold digger; **~gru·be** *f* goldmine; *fig. a.* F moneyspinner; **~grund** *m art*: gold (back)ground
'gold·hal·tig [-haltɪç] *adj.* auriferous, gold-bearing
'Gold·ham·ster *m* golden hamster
gol·dig ['gɔldɪç] *adj.* lovely, cute, sweet
'Gold|jun·ge F *m* F blue-eyed boy; **~kä·fer** *m* rose chafer; **~ket·te** *f* gold chain; **~kind** *n* (little) darling; **~klum·pen** *m* gold nugget; **~kurs** *m* price of gold; **~le,gie·rung** *f* gold alloy; **~markt** *m* gold market; **~me,dail·le** *f* gold medal
'Gold·me,dail·len|ge·win·ner *m*, **~in·ha·ber** *m* gold medal(l)ist
'Gold|mi·ne *f* goldmine; **~mün·ze** *f* gold coin; **~pa,pier** *n* gold foil; **Ձplat,tiert** *adj.* gold-plated; **~plom·be** *f* gold filling; **~rah·men** *m* gold (*or* gilt) frame; **~rand** *m* gilt edge; ***mit ~*** gilt-edged; **~rausch** *m* gold fever; *hist.* gold rush; **~re·gen** *m* ♀ laburnum
'gold'rich·tig F **I.** *adj.* exactly (*or* just) right; F spot on; **II.** *adv.* exactly (*or* just) right; ***~ handeln*** do just the right thing
'Gold|ring *m* gold ring; **~schatz** *m* treasure of gold; F *fig.* darling; **~schmied** *m* goldsmith; **~schnitt** *m* gilt edge; ***mit ~*** gilt-edged; **~stan·dard** *m* gold standard; **~staub** *m* gold dust; **~stück** *n* gold coin; F *fig.* gem; **~su·cher** *m* gold prospector; **~tres·se** *f* gold braid; **~uhr** *f* gold watch; **Ձum,ran·det** *adj.* gilt-edged, edged in gold; **~vor·kom·men** *n* gold deposits *pl.*; **~vor·rat** *m* gold reserves *pl.*; **~waa·ge** *f* gold balance (*or* scales *pl.*); *fig.* ***jedes Wort auf die ~ legen*** a) weigh every word, b) take everything to heart; **~wäh·rung** *f* gold standard; **~wa·ren** *pl.* gold articles, jewellery *sg.*, *esp. Am.* jewelry *sg.*; **~wä·scher** *m* gold washer; **~wert** *m* a) gold value, b) price of gold; **~zahn** *m* gold tooth
Golf[1] [gɔlf] *m* (-[e]s; -e) *geogr.* gulf
Golf[2] *n* (-s; *no pl.*) *sport*: golf; **~ball** *m* golf ball; **~klub** *m* golf club; **~müt·ze** *f* golfing (*or* golfer's) cap; **~platz** *m* golf course (*or* links *pl.*); **~schlä·ger** *m* golf club; **~spiel** *n* **1.** golf; **2.** game of golf; **~spie·ler** *m* golfer
'Golf·strom *m* (-[e]s; *no pl.*) Gulf Stream
Go·li·ath ['goːlĭat] *fig. m* (-s; -s) giant
Gon·del ['gɔndəl] *f* (-; -n) gondola, basket; **~bahn** *f* cable railway, gondola (ski) lift, F bubble lift
gon·deln ['gɔndəln] *v/i.* (sn): F ***~ durch*** *acc.* wander through (*or* around in), F cruise around in
Gon·do·lie·re [gɔndo'lĭeːrə] *m* (-; -ri) gondolier
Gong [gɔŋ] *m* (-s; -s) gong; *sport*: bell; **gon·gen** ['gɔŋən] (h) **I.** *v/i.* sound the gong; **II.** *v/impers.*: ***es gongt*** there's the gong; **'Gong·schlag** *m*: ***beim ~ ist es 6 Uhr*** at the first stroke it will be 6 a.m.
gön·nen ['gœnən] *v/t.* (h): ***j-m et. ~*** a) not to grudge s.o. s.th., b) allow s.o. s.th.; ***ich gönne es ihm (von Herzen), das sei ihm (auch wirklich) gegönnt*** I'm really glad for him, he deserves it, *iro.* (it) serves him right; ***ich gönne ihm das Vergnügen*** I don't grudge him the pleasure (at all); ***er gönnt sich keine Pause*** he never stops for a minute; ***ich gönn' mir jetzt e-e kleine Pause*** I'm going to allow myself (*or* have) a little break now; ***gönn dir doch mal e-n Urlaub*** you really should have a holiday (- for your own sake); ***gönn's ihm doch!*** a) (go on,) let him; don't be so hard (on him), b) don't be so grudging; ***sie gönnte ihm keinen Blick*** she didn't so much as look at him
Gön·ner ['gœnɐ] *m* (-s; -) patron; benefactor; **'gön·ner·haft** *adj.* patronizing; ***er tut so ~*** he's so patronizing, he has such a patronizing manner; **'Gön·ner·haf·tig·keit** *f* (-; *no pl.*) patronizing air; **'Gön·ner·mie·ne** *f*: (***mit ~*** with a) patronizing air; **'Gön·ner·schaft** *f* (-; *no pl.*) patronage
Go·nor·rhö [gonɔ'røː] *f* (-; -en) ⚕ gonorrh(o)ea
Good·will ['gʊd'wɪl] *m* (-s; *no pl.*) goodwill; good name (*or* reputation); **~be·such** *m* goodwill visit; **~rei·se** *f*, **~tour** *f* goodwill tour
gor [goːɐ] *pret. of* ***gären***
Gör [gøːɐ] F *n* (-s; -en ['gøːrən]) F kid; *contp.* little minx
gor·disch ['gɔrdɪʃ] *adj.*: ***den Ձen Knoten zerhauen*** cut the Gordian knot
Gö·re ['gøːrə] F *f* (-; -n) → ***Gör***
Go·ril·la [go'rɪla] *m* (-s; -s) gorilla (*a.* F *bodyguard*)
Go·sche ['gɔʃə] F *dial. f* (-; -n) F mush; ***halt die ~!*** F shut up!
goß [gɔs] *pret. of* ***gießen***
Gos·se ['gɔsə] *f* (-; -n) gutter (*a. fig.*); *fig.* ***in der ~ enden*** land (*or* end up) in the gutter; ***j-n aus der ~ ziehen*** drag s.o. out of the gutter; ***j-n durch die ~ ziehen*** drag s.o.'s name through the mud (*or* mire)
Go·te ['goːtə] *m* (-n; -n) Goth
Go·tik ['goːtɪk] *f* (-; *no pl.*) **1.** Gothic (style); **2.** Gothic period; **go·tisch** ['goːtɪʃ] **I.** *adj.* Gothic; *typ.* ***~e Schrift*** Gothic (type); **II.** Ձ *n* (-en) *ling.* Gothic
Gott [gɔt] *m* (-[e]s; Götter ['gœtɐ]) a) god, deity, b) *no pl.* God; ***~ der Herr*** the Lord God; ***~ der Allmächtige*** God (*or* the) Almighty; ***der liebe ~*** God; F ***ach du lieber ~!, großer ~!*** F oh God!, oh no!; ***ach ~*** well; ***~ bewahre!*** God forbid; ***~ sei Dank!*** thank goodness, fortunately; ***leider ~es*** unfortunately; ***um ~es willen!*** for heaven's sake!, (oh,) goodness!, oh no!; ***dann mach's in ~es Namen!*** do it then, if you must, then for God's sake do it; ***so wahr mir ~ helfe!*** so help me God; ***weiß ~, wo er steckt*** God (*or* heaven) knows where he is; ***das wissen die Götter*** God knows, *a.* don't ask me; ***es ist weiß ~ nicht einfach*** God knows it isn't easy; ***von ~es Gnaden*** by the grace of God; ***um ~es Lohn*** for nothing; ***den lieben ~ e-n guten Mann sein lassen*** live for the day; ***den lieben ~ spielen*** play God; ***wie ~ in Frankreich leben*** F live the life of Riley, live (*or* be) in clover; ***er kennt ~ und die Welt*** he knows the world and his brother; ***über ~ und die Welt reden*** talk about everything under the sun; ***dein Wort in ~es Ohr!*** let's hope so; ***ein Bild für die Götter*** a sight for sore eyes
'gott·ähn·lich *adj.* godlike
'gott·be·gna·det *adj.* gifted, inspired
'Gott·chen *int.*: (***ach***) ***~!*** goodness!
'Gott·er·bar·men *n*: ***zum ~*** pitiful(ly)
Göt·ter|bild ['gœtɐ-] *n* statue (*or* picture *etc.*) of a god, idol; **~bo·te** *m* messenger of the gods; ***der ~*** Mercury, Hermes; **~däm·me·rung** *f* twilight of the gods; **~ga·be** *f* gift of the gods; **~gat·te** F *hum. m* F lord and master
'gott·er·ge·ben *adj.* a) resigned to (one's) fate, b) pious
Göt·ter|ge·schlecht ['gœtɐ-] *n* (race of) gods *pl.*; **~glau·be** *m* belief in (the) gods; **Ձgleich** *adj.* godlike; like a god; **~le·ben** *n*: ***ein ~ führen*** F live the life of Riley, live (*or* be) in clover; **~lieb·ling** *m* favo(u)rite of the gods; **~mahl** *n* feast for the gods; **~sa·ge** *f* myth; **~sitz** *m myth.* seat (*or* home) of the gods; **~spei·se** *f* **1.** *myth.* ambrosia; **2.** *gastr.* jelly; **~trank** *m* nectar; **~welt** *f* **1.** realm of the gods; **2.** *the* gods *pl.*
Got·tes|acker ['gɔtəs-] *m* graveyard; **~an·be·te·rin** [-anbeːtərɪn] *f* (-; -nen) *zo.* praying mantis; **~be·weis** *m* proof of the existence of God; **~dienst** *m* (church) service
Got·tes·furcht ['gɔtəs-] *f* fear of God; piety; **'got·tes·fürch·tig** [-fʏrçtɪç] *adj.* God-fearing; pious
Got·tes|ga·be ['gɔtəs-] *f* gift of God; godsend; **~gei·ßel** *f* scourge of God; **~ge·lehr·te** *obs. m* (-n; -n) theologian; **~ge·richt** *n* → ***Gottesurteil***; **~ge·schenk** *n* gift of God (*or* of the gods); **~glau·be** *m* belief in God; **~haus** *n* house of God, church; **~lamm** *n* lamb of God; **~lä·ste·rer** *m* blasphemer; **Ձlä·ster·lich** *adj.* blasphemous; **~lä·ste·rung** *f* blasphemy; **~lohn** *m*: ***für*** (*or* ***um***) ***~*** for charity; **~mut·ter** *f* Mother of God; **~sohn** *m* Son of God; **~staat** *m* theocracy; **~ur·teil** *n* trial by ordeal; **~wort** *n* Word of God
'gott|ge·ge·ben *adj.* god-given; **~ge·weiht** *adj.* dedicated to God; consecrated; **~ge·wollt** *adj.* divinely-ordained; **~gleich** *adj.* godlike
'Gott·heit *f* (-; -en) deity, divinity; god, goddess
Göt·tin ['gœtɪn] *f* (-; -nen) goddess
'Gott·kö·nig *m* divine king (*or* monarch); **~tum** *n* (-s; *no pl.*) divine kingship (*or* monarchy)
gött·lich ['gœtlɪç] *adj.* divine, heavenly (*both a.* F *fig.*); godlike; ***das Ձe*** the di-

vine; **~e Ordnung** divine order; F *fig.* **ein ~er Anblick** a sight for sore eyes; **das war ein ~er Spaß** it was hilarious; **'Gött·lich·keit** *f* (-; *no pl.*) divinity; godliness

gott·lob [gɔt'lo:p] *int.* thank God (*or* goodness); **es war ~ nichts Ernstes** *a.* thankfully it wasn't anything serious

'gott·los *adj.* godless, ungodly (*a.* F *fig.*); sinful, wicked; **'Gott·lo·sig·keit** *f* (-; *no pl.*) ungodliness, irreligion; wickedness

Gott·sei·bei·uns [gɔtzaɪ'baɪ'ʔʊns] F *m* (-; *no pl.*) F Old Nick

'gotts·er·bärm·lich, 'gotts·jäm·mer·lich *adj.* pitiful

Gott'va·ter *m* God the father

'gott·ver·ges·sen *adj.* → **gottlos**

'gott·ver·las·sen F *adj.* godforsaken

'Gott·ver·trau·en *n* faith in God

Göt·ze ['gœtsə] *m* (-n; -n) idol (*a. fig.*)

'Göt·zen|bild *n* idol; **~dienst** *m* idolatry; **~ treiben** worship idols; *fig.* **~ treiben mit** *dat.* make an idol *or* idols (out) of

Götz·zi‚tat ['gœts-] *n*: **er antwortete mit dem ~** F he told him *etc.* where to go

Gou·ache ['gŭaʃ] *f* (-; -n) gouache

Gour·mand [gʊr'mã:] *m* (-s; -s) **1.** gourmand, gormandizer; **2.** → **Gour·met** [gʊr'me:] *m* (-s; -s) gourmet

Gou·ver·nan·te [guvɛr'nantə] *f* (-; -n) governess; **gou·ver'nan·ten·haft** *adj.* schoolmarmish

Gou·ver·neur [guvɛr'nø:ɐ] *m* (-s; -e [-'nø:rə]) governor

G-Punkt *m anat.* G-spot

Grab [gra:p] *n* (-[e]s; Gräber ['grɛ:bɐ]) grave; *lit.* tomb; sepulch|er (*Brit.* -re); **am ~** at the graveside; **zu ~e tragen** *a. fig.* bury; **j-m ins ~ folgen** follow s.o. to the grave; **er nahm sein Geheimnis mit ins ~** he took his secret with him into the grave, his secret died with him; **bis ins ~** unto (*or* till) death; **über das ~ hinaus** beyond the grave; **er ist verschwiegen wie ein ~** his lips are sealed; *fig.* **er bringt mich noch ins ~** he'll be the death of me yet; **mit einem Bein** (*or* **Fuß**) **im ~(e) stehen** have one foot in the grave; **sein eigenes ~ graben** (*or* **schaufeln**) be digging one's own grave; **sich im ~e umdrehen** turn in one's grave; **~bei·ga·be** *f* burial object

grab·beln ['grabəln] *v/i.* (h) grope (*or* rummage) around (**nach** *dat.* for)

'Grab·bel·tisch F *m* ♆ bargain counter

gra·ben ['gra:bən] (grub, gegraben, h) **I.** *v/i.* dig (**nach** *dat.* for); *zo.* burrow; **II.** *v/t.* a) dig; burrow; sink *a shaft*; ⚠ dig out, excavate *foundations*, b) carve (**in** *acc.* into); ⚙ engrave, cut; F *fig.* **die Hände in die Taschen ~** dig one's hands into one's pockets; **III.** *v/refl.*: **sich ~ in** *acc.* dig into; bury o.s. into; *fig.* **sich in j-s Gedächtnis ~** engrave itself on s.o.'s memory

'Gra·ben *m* (-s; Gräben ['grɛ:bən]) ditch, *esp.* ⚔ trench; ⚙ drain, culvert; moat; *geol.* rift valley, trench; **e-n ~ ziehen** dig a ditch; **in den ~ fahren** ditch, run *a car* into a ditch; **~bruch** *m geol.* rift valley; **~krieg** *m* trench war(fare)

Grä·ber|feld ['grɛ:bɐ-] *n* burial ground, necropolis; **~fund** *m* grave find

Gra·bes|dun·kel ['gra:bəs-] *n* sepulchral darkness; **es herrschte ~** it was as dark as the tomb; **~stil·le** *f* deathly silence; **es herrschte ~** there was (a) deathly silence; **~stim·me** *f* sepulchral voice

'Grab|ge·läut *n* (death) knell (*a. fig.*); **~ge·sang** *m* funeral song, dirge; **~ge·wöl·be** *n* burial vault, crypt; **~hü·gel** *m* burial mound; **~in·schrift** *f* inscription (on a *or* the gravestone); epitaph; **~kam·mer** *f* burial chamber; **~ka‚pel·le** *f* funeral chapel

'Grab·le·gung [-le:gʊŋ] *f* (-; -en) **1.** *no pl.* burial; **2.** *eccl., art*: **~** (**Christi**) *the* Entombment (of Christ)

'Grab|mal *n* tomb; monument; **~pfle·ge** *f* looking after (*or* care of) a grave *or* graves; **~plat·te** *f* ledger; marble slab; **~räu·ber** *m* grave robber; **~re·de** *f* funeral address (*eccl.* sermon); **~re·li‚ef** *n* tomb relief; **~schän·der** *m* **1.** desecrator of graves; **2.** grave robber; **~schän·dung** *f* **1.** desecration of graves; **2.** grave robbery; **~stät·te** *f*, **~stel·le** *f* a) burial place, b) grave, tomb; **~stein** *m* gravestone, tombstone; **~sti·chel** *m* ⚙ graving tool, chisel

Gra·bung ['gra:bʊŋ] *f* (-; -en) excavation

'Gra·bungs|fund *m* arch(a)eological find; **~stät·te** *f* arch(a)eological site

'Grab·ur·ne *f* (funeral) urn

Grad [gra:t] *m* (-[e]s; -e ['gra:də]) degree (*a.* ⩘, *phys., geogr., univ.*); extent; stage; ⚔ rank; **bei ... ~** at (a temperature of) ... degrees; **es sind ... ~** it's ... degrees, the temperature is ... degrees; **... ~ Wärme** (**Kälte**) ... degrees above (below) zero; **... ~** (**Fieber**) **haben** have a temperature of ...; **40 ~ nördlicher Breite** 40° (= forty degrees) north (latitude); **Verbrennungen zweiten ~es** second-degree burns; **Vetter ersten ~es** first cousin; **dritter ~** third degree; **bis zu e-m gewissen ~** up to a point, to some extent; **in hohem ~e** to a high degree, highly, largely, to a great extent; **in höchstem ~e** extremely, highly; **in geringem ~e** slightly; **in dem ~e, daß** to such a degree that; **~bo·gen** *m* graduated arc; **~ein·tei·lung** *f* graduation, scale

Gra·di·ent [gra'dĭɛnt] *m* (-en; -en) ⩘, *phys.* gradient

gra·die·ren [gra'di:rən] *v/t.* (h) graduate; **Gra'die·rung** *f* (-; -en) graduation

'Grad|mes·ser *m* yardstick, measure, indication (*gen.* of); **~netz** *n geogr.* grid; **~strich** *m* graduation (mark)

Gra·dua·le [gra'dŭa:lə] *n* (-s; -lien [-lĭən]) *R.C.* gradual

gra·du·ell [gra'dŭɛl] **I.** *adj.* gradual; *difference etc.* of degree; **II.** *adv.* gradually, by degrees; *different* in degree

gra·du·ie·ren [gradu'i:rən] (h) **I.** *v/t.* **1.** ⚙ graduate; **2.** *univ.* confer a degree on; **II.** *v/i. univ.* graduate; **Gra·du·ier·te** [gradu'i:ɐrtə] *m, f* (-n; -n) *univ.* graduate

'Grad‚un·ter·schied *m* difference in degree

'grad·wei·se *adv.* by degrees

Graf [gra:f] *m* (-en; -en) count, Count; *in GB*: earl

Gra·fen|ge·schlecht *n* lineage of counts (*in GB*: earls); **~kro·ne** *f* count's (*in GB*: earl's) coronet

Graf·fi·ti [gra'fi:ti] *pl.* graffiti

Gra·fik(...) → **Graphik(...)**

Grä·fin ['grɛ:fɪn] *f* (-; -nen) countess

gräf·lich ['grɛ:flɪç] *adj.* count's, countess's; *in GB*: earl's; of a count(ess), of an earl

'Graf·schaft *f* (-; -en) county

Gral [gra:l] *m* (-s; *no pl.*): **der Heilige ~** the (Holy) Grail

'Grals|burg *f* Castle of the Grail; **~hü·ter** *m* keeper of the Grail; *fig. a.* guardian; **~rit·ter** *m* Knight of the Grail; **~su·che** *f* quest for the (Holy) Grail

Gram [gra:m] *m* (-[e]s; *no pl.*) grief, sorrow; **vor ~ vergehen** pine away; **vor ~ sterben** die of grief, die of a broken heart

gram *pred. adj.*: **j-m ~ sein** bear s.o. a grudge; be angry with s.o.

grä·men ['grɛ:mən] (h) **I.** *v/refl.*: **sich ~** grieve (**über** *acc.* over), fret (about); **sich zu Tode ~** pine away, die of a broken heart; **II.** *lit. v/t.* trouble *s.o.* (deeply)

'gram|er·füllt *adj.* grief-stricken; *life* beset with grief; **~ge·beugt** *adj.* bowed down with grief; **~ge·furcht** *adj.* careworn

gräm·lich ['grɛ:mlɪç] *adj.* morose, surly

Gramm [gram] *n* gramme, *Am.* gram

Gram·ma·tik [gra'matɪk] *f* (-; -en) **1.** *no pl.* grammar; **2.** grammar (book); **gram·ma·ti·ka·lisch** [gramati'ka:lɪʃ] *adj.* grammatical; **Gram·ma·ti·ker** [gra'matikɐ] *m* (-s; -) grammarian

Gram'ma·tik|feh·ler *m* grammar (*or* grammatical) mistake; **~re·gel** *f* rule of grammar, grammatical rule

gram·ma·tisch [gra'matɪʃ] *adj.* grammatical, grammar ...

Gram·mo·phon [gramo'fo:n] (*TM*) *obs. n* (-s; -e) gramophone, *Am.* phonograph

Gra·nat [gra'na:t] *m* (-[e]s, -en; -e, -en) **1.** *min.* garnet; **2.** *zo.* shrimp, prawn; **~ap·fel** *m* pomegranate

Gra·na·te [gra'na:tə] *f* (-; -n) shell; grenade

Gra'nat|feu·er *n* ⚔ shellfire, shelling; **~split·ter** *m* piece of shrapnel; *pl.* shrapnel *sg.*; **~trich·ter** *m* shell crater

Grand [grã:] *m* (-s; -s) *skat*: grand

Gran·de ['grandə] *m* (-n; -n) grandee

Gran·dez·za [gran'dɛtsa] *f* (-; *no pl.*) grandeur

gran·di·os [gran'dĭo:s] *adj.* grand, magnificent; F *fig.* brilliant; **~er Auftritt** *a.* heroic performance; **~e Einbildung** grand delusion

Gra·nit [gra'ni:t] *m* (-s; -e) *min.* granite; *fig.* **bei ihm wirst du auf ~ beißen** you'll be banging your head against a brick wall with him, you won't get anywhere with him; **~fel·sen** *m* granite rock; **~ge·bir·ge** *n* granite mountains *pl.*; **~ge·stein** *n* granite (rock)

Gran·ne ['granə] *f* (-; -n) ⚘ awn, beard, 🕮 arista

gran·tig ['grantɪç] F *dial. adj.* grumpy, grouchy, crabby

Gra·nu·lat [granu'la:t] *n* (-[e]s; -e) granules *pl.*; **gra·nu·lie·ren** [granu'li:rən] *v/t. and v/i.* (h) granulate

Grape·fruit ['gre:pfru:t] *f* (-; -s) grapefruit; **~saft** *m* grapefruit juice

Graph [gra:f] *m* (-en; -en) ⩘, *phys., ling.* graph

Gra·phem [gra'fe:m] *n* (-s; -e) *ling.* grapheme

Gra·phik ['gra:fɪk] *f* (-; -en) **1.** *no pl.* a) graphic arts *pl.*; ♆ commercial art, b) layout, artwork, c) *computer*: graphics *pl*; **2.** *art*: print; **3.** graph, diagram; **~bild·schirm** *m* graphics screen; **~cur·sor** *m* graphics cursor; **~drucker** *m* graphics printer

Gra·phi·ker ['gra:fikɐ] *m* (-s; -), **Gra·phi·ke·rin** ['gra:fikərɪn] *f* (-; -nen) graphic designer, commercial artist

'gra·phik|fä·hig *adj*: **~ sein** *computer*: have graphics capabilities; **ꝰfä·hig·keit** *f* graphics capability

'Gra·phik|kar·te *f computer*: graphics card (*or* board); **~mo·dus** *m* graphics mode; **~ta,blett** *n* graphics (*or* digitizing) tablet; **~zei·chen** *n* graphic character; **~zei·chen·satz** *m* graphic character set

gra·phisch ['gra:fɪʃ] *adj*. graphic(ally *adv*.); **~e Darstellung → Graphik** 3; **~e Gestaltung → Graphik** 1 b

Gra·phit [gra'fi:t] *m* (-s; -e) *min*. graphite; **~stift** *m* lead (*or* graphite) pencil

Gra·pho·lo·ge [grafo'lo:gə] *m* (-n; -n) graphologist; **Gra·pho·lo·gie** [grafolo'gi:] *f* (-; *no pl*.) graphology; **Gra·pho·lo·gin** [grafo'lo:gɪn] *f* (-; -nen) graphologist; **gra·pho·lo·gisch** [grafo'lo:gɪʃ] *adj*. graphological

grap·schen ['grapʃən] F *v/t. and v/i*. (h) grab (**nach** *dat*. at)

Gras [gra:s] *n* (-es; Gräser ['grɛ:zɐ]) grass; *fig*. F **er hört das ~ wachsen** a) he reads too much into things, he overinterprets, *contp*. F he thinks he's got a hot line to Heaven, b) he's got an answer for everything; F **ins ~ beißen** F bite the dust; **über et. ~ wachsen lassen** let the dust settle (on s.th.); **darüber ist längst ~ gewachsen** that's dead and buried

'gras·be·wach·sen *adj*. grassy

'Gras·bü·schel *n* tuft of grass

gra·sen ['gra:zən] *v/i*. (h) graze

'Gras|flä·che *f* patch of grass; lawn; **~fleck** *m* grass stain; **ꝰfres·send** *adj. zo*. grass-eating; **~es Tier → ~fres·ser** *m* grass-eater; **~frosch** *m* grass frog; **~fut·ter** *n* grass fodder; **ꝰgrün** *adj*. bright green; **~halm** *m* blade of grass; **~hüp·fer** *m* grasshopper

gra·sig ['gra:zɪç] *adj*. grassy

'Gras|karp·fen *m* grass carp; **~land** *n* (-[e]s; *no pl*.) grassland; **~mücke** *f* warbler; **~nar·be** *f* turf, sod; **~pflan·ze** *f* grass plant; **~platz** *m tennis*: grass court; **~sa·men** *m* grass seed(s *pl*.)

gras·sie·ren [gra'si:rən] *v/i*. (h) rage; *esp. b.s*. be rife, be rampant; *bad habit etc*.: take hold; *rumo(u)r*: spread; **gras'sie·rend** *adj*. widespread; raging, rampant

gräß·lich ['grɛslɪç] **I.** *adj*. horrible, terrible, awful (*all a*. F *fig*.); hideous; **II.** *adv*.: F **~ faul** *etc*. F terribly (*or* incredibly) lazy *etc*.; **'Gräß·lich·keit** *f* (-; -en) terrible thing to do, atrocity

'Gras|step·pe *f* grassy plains *pl*.; **~strei·fen** *m* strip of grass

'gras|über,wach·sen, ~über,wu·chert *adj*. overgrown with grass

Grat [gra:t] *m* (-[e]s; -e) *geol*. (sharp) edge; ridge; ⚙ bur(r), flash, fin; ⚠ arris, groin

Grä·te ['grɛ:tə] *f* (-; -n) (fish)bone

'Grä·ten|mu·ster *n* herringbone pattern; **~schritt** *m skiing*: herringbone

Gra·ti·fi·ka·ti·on [gratifika'tsǐo:n] *f* (-; -en) gratuity; (*Christmas*) bonus

grä·tig ['grɛ:tɪç] *adj*. **1.** *fish* full of bones; **2.** F *fig*. F grumpy, crabby

gra·ti·nie·ren [grati'ni:rən] *v/t*. (h) *gastr*. gratiné, gratinate

gra·tis ['gra:tɪs] *adv*. free (of charge); for nothing; into the bargain

'Gra·tis|ak·tie *f* bonus share; **~bei·la·ge** *f* free supplement; **~ex·em,plar** *n* free copy; **~pro·be** *f* free sample

Grät·sche ['grɛ:tʃə] *f* (-; -n) **1.** straddle; **in die ~ gehen** do the splits; **2.** straddle vault; **'grät·schen** *v/t. and v/i*. (h) straddle; do the splits; **'Grätsch·sprung** *m* straddle vault

Gra·tu·lant [gratu'lant] *m* (-en; -en) well-wisher; **Gra·tu·la·ti·on** [gratula'tsǐo:n] *f* (-; -en) congratulations *pl*. (**zu** *dat*. on); **gra·tu·lie·ren** [gratu'li:rən] *v/i*. (h) congratulate (**j-m zu et.** s.o. on s.th.); **j-m zum Geburtstag ~** wish s.o. a happy birthday; **ich gratuliere!** congratulations; F *fig*. **da kannst du dir ~!** you can count yourself lucky, *iro*. you'll regret it

'Grat·wan·de·rung *f* ridge walk; *fig*. tightrope walk; *fig*. **sich auf e-r ~ befinden** be walking a tightrope

grau [graʊ] **I.** *adj*. gray, *Brit*. grey; *fig*. dark, gloomy; **~ werden** turn *or* go grey (*Am*. gray); **sie hat schon ~e Haare bekommen** she's going grey (*Am*. gray) already; **~er Star** cataract(s); F **die ~en Zellen** the little grey (*Am*. gray) cells, one's grey (*Am*. gray) matter; **~ in ~** dismal *weather*; *fig*. **er sieht** (*or* **malt**) **alles ~ in ~** he's so negative about everything; **~er Alltag** *the* daily grind; **ich laß mir darüber keine ~en Haare wachsen** I'm not going to lose any sleep over it; **~er Markt** grey (*Am*. gray) market; **~er Flugscheinmarkt** bucket shop system; **e-e ~e Maus** a mousy person; **in ~er Vorzeit** in the dim and distant past; **in ~er Zukunft** (*or* **Ferne**) in the (long) distant future; **das liegt noch in ~er Zukunft** (*or* **Ferne**) that's still a long way off; **das ist alles ~e Theorie** it's all theory; **→ Eminenz; II.** ꝰ *n* (-s; -) grey, *Am*. gray; **~blau** *adj*. greyish-blue, *Am*. grayish-blue

'Grau·brot *n* mixed-grain bread

grau·en¹ ['graʊən] (h) **I.** *v/i*. dawn, be dawning; **der Tag** (*or* **Morgen**) **graut** day is (*or* it's) dawning; **II.** ꝰ *n*: **beim ~ des Tages** at daybreak

'grau·en² **I.** *v/impers*. (h): **es graut mir** (*or* **mir graut**) **vor** *dat*. I shudder at the thought of, I dread, I'm dreading; **II.** ꝰ *n* (-s; -) dread, horror (**vor** *dat*. of); **~ empfinden vor** *dat*. be horrified of, shudder at the thought of; **j-m ~ einflößen** fill s.o. with horror; **vom ~ gepackt** seized (*or* filled) with horror; **ein Bild des ~s** (**bieten**) (be) a horrific sight *or* scene, (be) a scene of horror

'grau·en·er·re·gend, 'grau·en·haft, 'grau·en·voll *adj*. horrific, ghastly, gruesome; F *fig*. dreadful, terrible

'grau·haa·rig *adj*. grey-haired, *Am*. gray-haired

grau·len ['graʊlən] *v/refl*. (h): **sich ~** be scared (**vor** *dat*. of), dread (*s.th*.)

gräu·lich ['grɔʏlɪç] *adj*. greyish, *Am*. grayish

'grau·me,liert *adj*. **1.** greying, *Am*. graying *hair*; grizzled; **2.** *textil*. mottled grey (*Am*. gray)

Grau·pe ['graʊpə] *f* (-; -n) barley

Grau·pel ['graʊpəl] *f* (-; -n) *meteor*. (soft) hail, *Am*. sleet; **'grau·peln** *v/impers*. (h): **es graupelt** it's hailing (*Am*. sleeting); **'Grau·pel·schau·er** *m* hail, *Am*. sleet

Graus [graʊs] *m* (-es; *no pl*.) horror, dread; *obs. and iro*. **o ~!** (oh) horrors!; **es ist ein ~** it's horrible; **das** (**er**) **ist mir ein ~** I can't stand it (him); **es ist ein ~ mit ihm** he's impossible

grau·sam ['graʊza:m] **I.** *adj*. cruel (**gegen** *acc*. to); F terrible, awful; **II.** *adv*.: **~ zu Tode kommen** die a horrible death; **'Grau·sam·keit** *f* (-; -en) **1.** *no pl*. cruelty; **2.** atrocity

'Grau|schim·mel *m* grey (horse), *Am*. gray (horse); **~schlei·er** *m* greyness, *Am*. grayness; **e-n ~ haben** be grey (*Am*. gray)

'grau·schwarz *adj*. grey(ish)-black, *Am*. gray(ish)-black

grau·sen ['graʊzən] *v/impers*. (h): **es graust mir** (*or* **mir graust**) **vor** *dat*. I shudder at the thought of, I dread, I'm dreading, I'm terrified of

grau·sig ['graʊzɪç] *adj*. **→ grauenerregend**

'Grau|tier F *n* donkey; **~ton** *m* shade of grey (*Am*. gray); **~wal** *m* Californian grey (*Am*. gray) whale; **~zo·ne** *fig*. *f* grey (*Am*. gray) area, twilight zone

Gra·veur [gra'vø:ɐ] *m* (-s; -e [-'vø:rə]) engraver; **gra·vie·ren** [gra'vi:rən] *v/t*. (h) engrave

gra'vie·rend *adj*. serious, grave

Gra'vier·na·del *f* engraving needle

Gra·vie·rung [gra'vi:rʊŋ] *f* (-; -en) engraving

gra·vi·me·trisch [gravi'me:trɪʃ] *adj*. gravimetric(ally *adv*.)

Gra·vis ['gra:vɪs] *m* (-; -) *ling*. grave (accent)

Gra·vi·ta·ti·on [gravita'tsǐo:n] *f* (-; *no pl*.) *phys*. gravitation, gravity

Gra·vi·ta·ti'ons|feld *n* gravitational field; **~ge·setz** *n* law of gravity

gra·vi·tä·tisch [gravi'tɛ:tɪʃ] *adj*. (*and adv*.) *a. iro*. solemn(ly), grave(ly); **mit ~em Ernst** very solemnly

gra·vi·tie·ren [gravi'ti:rən] *v/i*. (h) gravitate (**zu** *dat*., **nach** *dat*. towards)

Gra·vur [gra'vu:ɐ] *f* (-; -en), **Gra·vü·re** [gra'vy:rə] *f* (-; -n) engraving

Gra·zie ['gra:tsǐə] *f* (-; -n) **1.** *no pl*. grace(fulness); **mit ~ → graziös** II; **2. die drei ~n** the three Graces

gra·zil [gra'tsi:l] *adj*. delicate(ly built); willowy; graceful

gra·zi·ös [gra'tsǐø:s] **I.** *adj*. graceful; **II.** *adv*. gracefully; *a. fig*. elegantly

Greif [graɪf] *m* (-[e]s; -e) *myth*. griffin

'Greif|arm *m zo*. tentacle; ⚙ grip(per) arm; **~bag·ger** *m* grab dredger

'greif·bar *adj*. **1.** (*a*. **in ~er Nähe**) handy, within easy reach; ✝ available, in stock; **2.** *fig*. tangible, concrete; obvious; **er ist nie ~** you just can't get hold of him; **~e Gestalt annehmen** assume a definite form; **in ~e Nähe rücken** a) get closer (and closer), b) become a distinct possibility; **e-e Lösung schien in ~er Nähe** a solution seemed close at hand

grei·fen ['graɪfən] (griff, gegriffen, h) **I.** *v/t*. **1.** take; grasp; grab (hold of); ♪ play, hold down, stop; F grab *s.o*.; *fig*. **das ist** (**völlig**) **aus der Luft gegriffen** he's *etc*. made it up; **die Zahl ist zu hoch gegriffen** that's a very high estimate; F **sich j-n ~** F nab s.o.; **II.** *v/i*. **2. ~ an** *acc*. touch; **sich an die Stirn ~** clutch one's brow (*or* forehead); **~ in** *acc*. reach into; **~ nach** *dat*. reach for, snatch at, clutch at; **~ zu** *dat*. reach for, *fig*. resort to; **zu den Waffen ~** take up arms, rise in arms; **zu e-m Buch** *etc*. **~** pick up a book *etc*.; **ein Buch, zu dem man immer wieder** (**gerne**) **greift** a book to which one will always return (with pleasure), a book one wouldn't like to miss; **es war zum ꝰ nah** (*fig*. you felt) you could almost touch it; *fig*. **mit beiden Händen ~ nach**

dat. jump at, F grab *the opportunity etc.*; ***zum Äußersten*** ~ go to extremes; ***um sich*** ~ spread, proliferate; ***um sich ~d*** rampant; → ***Feder, Flasche, Strohhalm***; **3.** *wheels etc*: grip; **4.** *fig.* (begin to) take effect, be effective; catch on

Grei·fer ['graɪfɐ] *m* (-s; -) gripping device; claw; grab

'**Greif|fuß** *m zo.* prehensile foot; **~klaue** *f*, **~kral·le** *f* claw; **~vo·gel** *m* bird of prey; **~zan·ge** *f*: **(e-e** ~ a pair of) tongs *pl.*; **~zir·kel** *m* outside cal(l)ipers *pl.*

grei·nen ['graɪnən] F *v/i.* (h) F grizzle; F whinge

Greis [graɪs] **I.** *m* (-es; -e ['graɪzə]) old man; **II.** ≗ *adj.* old; grey, *Am.* gray; *iro.* ***er schüttelte sein ~es Haupt*** he shook his wise old head

Grei·sen·al·ter ['graɪzən-] *n*: ***im*** ~ as an old man, at a ripe old age

'**grei·sen·haft** *adj.* senile (*a.* ⚕), *the face etc.* of an old man (*or* woman); '**Grei·sen·haf·tig·keit** *f* (-; *no pl.*) senility

Grei·sin ['graɪzɪn] *f* (-; -nen) old woman (*or* lady)

grell [grɛl] **I.** *adj.* garish, loud, very bright *colo(u)r*; shrill, piercing *sound*; dazzling, glaring, *a.* harsh *light*; *fig.* stark *contrast etc.*; **II.** *adv.*: ~ ***gegen et. abstechen*** form a sharp (*or* stark) contrast to s.th.; **~be·leuch·tet** *adj.* blindingly bright, glaring; **~bunt** *adj.* gaudy; **~gelb** *adj.* bright yellow; **~grün** *adj.* bright green; **~rot** *adj.* bright red

Gre·mi·um ['greːmɪʊm] *n* (-s; -ien) committee; body

Grenz|ab·fer·ti·gung ['grɛnts-] *f* customs clearance; **~auf·sicht** *f* border surveillance; **~bahn·hof** *m* border station; **~be·am·te** *m* border official; **~be·fe·sti·gun·gen** *pl.* frontier fortifications; **~be·la·stung** *f* ⚙ critical load; **~be·reich** *m* **1.** border area; **2.** intermediate zone; **3.** limits *pl.*; **~be·rei·ni·gung** *f*, **~be·rich·ti·gung** *f* frontier revision; **~be·völ·ke·rung** *f* border population; **~be·woh·ner** *m* border dweller; **~be·zirk** *m* border district

Gren·ze ['grɛntsə] *f* (-; -n) boundary, border, frontier; *fig.* limit(s *pl.*); *fig.* **~n** bounds (*gen.* of); ***s-e ~n kennen*** know one's limitations; ***keine ~n kennen*** know no bounds; ***der Applaus kannte keine ~n*** the applause just wouldn't stop; ***du kennst wohl keine ~n*** you just don't know when to stop; ***~n setzen*** (*or* ***stecken***) set limits (*dat.* to); ***e-e*** (***scharfe***) ~ ***ziehen*** draw a (sharp) line; ***in ~n bleiben, sich in ~n halten*** keep within (reasonable) limits, be tolerable; ***s-e Begeisterung hielt sich in ~n*** he wasn't overly enthusiastic; ***die ~n überschreiten*** go too far, overstep the mark; ***es ist an der*** ~ F it's pushing it (a bit); ***alles hat s-e ~n*** there's a limit to everything; ***dem sind nach oben keine ~n gesetzt*** there's no upper limit, F the sky's the limit; ***ohne ~n*** → ***grenzenlos***

gren·zen ['grɛntsən] *v/i.* (h): ~ ***an*** *acc.* border on (*a. fig.*), be right next to, adjoin, abut on; *fig.* verge on, come close to, be little short of

'**gren·zen·los I.** *adj.* a) boundless, unbounded, b) immeasurable; ***e-e ~e Frechheit*** the height of impudence; ***ins ≗e gehen*** be endless, be never-ending; **II.** *adv.* immeasurably; ~ ***glücklich*** deliriously happy; ~ ***dumm*** stupid beyond belief, F incredibly stupid; ***j-n ~ lieben*** love s.o. with all one's being

Gren·zer ['grɛntsɐ] *m* (-s; -) border guard

'**Grenz|er·trag** *m* ⚕ marginal returns *pl.*; **~fall** *m* borderline case; **~flä·che** *f* interface; **~for·ma·li·tä·ten** *pl.* border formalities; **~gän·ger** [-gɛŋɐ] *m* (-s; -) **1.** cross-border commuter; **2.** illegal border crosser; **3.** smuggler; **4.** *fig.* crossover artist; **~ge·biet** *n* border area; interdisciplinary subject; **~gra·ben** *m* boundary ditch; **~jä·ger** *m* border patrolman; **~kämp·fe** *pl.* border fighting *sg.*; **~kon,flikt** *m* border dispute; **~kon,trol·le** *f* border control; ***erleichterte ~n*** relaxation of border controls; **~ko·sten** *pl.* ⚕ marginal cost *sg.*; **~krieg** *m* border war(fare); **~land** *n* **1.** border area; **2.** bordering country; **~leh·re** *f* ⚙ limit ga(u)ge; **~li·nie** *f* border; *pol.* demarcation line; *sport*: line; **~maß** *n* ⚙ limiting size; **~mau·er** *f* boundary wall; **~nut·zen** *m* marginal utility; **~ort** *m* border town (*or* village); **~pfahl** *m* boundary post; **~po·li,zei** *f* border police; **~po·sten** *m* border guard; **~punkt** *m* limit; **~schutz** *m* **1.** frontier protection; **2.** *coll.* border guard; **~si·tua·tion** *f* borderline situation; **~sper·re** *f* **1.** closing of the border(s); **2.** (frontier) barrier; **~stadt** *f* border town; **~sta·ti,on** *f* frontier station; **~stein** *m* boundary stone; **~strei·fe** *f* border patrol; **~,über·gang** *m* **1.** border crossing point; **2.** (border) crossing; **≗über,schrei·tend** *adj.* cross-border ...; international; *problems etc.* of international significance; **~über,schrei·tung** *f*, **~,über·tritt** *m* border crossing; **~ver·kehr** *m*: (***kleiner*** ~ local) border traffic; **~ver·lauf** *m* border; **~ver·let·zung** *f* border violation; **~wa·che** *f*, **~wäch·ter** *m* border guard; **~wert** *m* limit, threshold value; **~win·kel** *m* critical angle; **~zoll** *m* customs duty; **~zo·ne** *f* border zone; **~zwi·schen·fall** *m* border incident; *pl. usu.* border clashes

Gret·chen·fra·ge ['grɛːtçən-] *f the* big question, F *the* sixty-four thousand dollar question

Greu·el ['grɔʏəl] *m* (-s; -) a) horror (***vor*** *dat.* of), b) atrocity, outrage; ***er*** (***es***) ***ist mir ein*** ~ I loathe him (it); ***es ist mir ein ~ zu*** *inf.* I loathe *ger.*, I loathe having to *inf.*; **~ge·schich·te** *f*, **~mär·chen** *n* horror story; **~pro·pa,gan·da** *f* horror stories *pl.*; **~sze·ne** *f* scene of horror; **~tat** *f* atrocity

greu·lich ['grɔʏlɪç] *adj.* → ***gräßlich***

Grie·ben ['griːbən] *pl.* greaves, crackling *sg.*; **~schmalz** *n* dripping (with greaves *or* crackling)

Grie·che ['griːçə] *m* (-n; -n) **1.** Greek; **2.** F Greek restaurant; ***zum ~n gehen*** F go to a Greek place; ***in der Nähe ist ein*** ~ there's a Greek place near here

Grie·chin ['griːçɪn] *f* (-; -nen) Greek

grie·chisch ['griːçɪʃ] **I.** *adj.* Greek; ⚠ *and art*: *a.* Grecian; **II.** ≗ *n* (-en) *ling.* Greek; **~-or·tho'dox** *adj.* Greek Orthodox; **~-rö·misch** *adj.* Gr(a)eco-Roman

Gries·gram ['griːsgraːm] *m* (-[e]s; -e) F (old) grouch; '**gries·grä·mig** [-grɛːmɪç] *adj.* F grumpy, grouchy, crabby; '**Gries·grä·mig·keit** *f* (- *no pl.*) grumpiness

Grieß [griːs] *m* (-es; *no pl.*) a) *gastr.* semolina, b) ⚙ grit, c) ⚕ gravel; **~brei** *m* semolina; **~kloß** *m*, **~klöß·chen** *n* semolina dumpling

griff [grɪf] *pret. of* ***greifen***

Griff *m* (-[e]s; -e) **1.** grasping (***nach*** *dat.* at), snatching (at), clutching (at); movement (of the hand); *wrestling*: hold; *gym.* grip; *mountaineering*: (hand)hold; ♪ stop; chord; ***mit sicherem*** ~ right away, *fig.* with a sure touch; ***mit einem*** ~ with one swift movement, *fig.* in no time; ***mit wenigen ~en*** with a few (deft) movements; *fig.* ***e-n guten ~ tun*** make a good choice, strike lucky (***mit*** *dat.* with); ***e-n schlechten ~ tun*** make a bad choice, pick the wrong man *etc.*; ***im ~ haben*** have got the hang of, have *s.th.* under control, have a good grip on; ***in den ~ bekommen*** (F ***kriegen***) get the hang of, get a grip on; ***kühner*** ~ bold stroke; ~ ***nach der Macht*** attempt to seize power; ***der ~ zur Flasche*** *etc.* (turning to) drink *etc.*; **2.** handle; → ***Türgriff***; **3.** *textil.* feel; **≗be·reit** *adj.* handy; **~brett** *n* ♪ fingerboard

Grif·fel ['grɪfəl] *m* (-s; -) **1.** slate pencil; *hist.* stylus; **2.** ⚘ pistil; **3.** F ***nimm' deine ~ weg*** F take your (dirty) paws (*or* mitts) off

grif·fig ['grɪfɪç] *adj.* **1.** ~ ***sein*** *tool etc.*: handle (*or* hold) well; *tires, road etc.*: have a good grip; *textil.* have a good feel; **2.** coarse-grained *flour*; **3.** *fig.* catchy *phrase etc.*; '**Grif·fig·keit** *f* (-; *no pl.*) *mot.* grip, traction

'**Griff|loch** *n* ♪ fingerhole; **~stück** *n* grip; **~übung** *f* ♪ fingering exercise

Grill [grɪl] *m* (-s; -s) grill, *Am.* barbecue; ***... vom Grill*** roast *chicken etc.*

Gril·le ['grɪlə] *f* (-; -n) *zo.* cricket; *fig.* silly idea; *fig.* ***~n fangen*** mope; ***~n im Kopf haben*** be full of silly ideas; ***j-m ~n in den Kopf setzen*** put ideas into s.o.'s head

gril·len ['grɪlən] (h) **I.** *v/t.* grill, *Am. a.* barbecue, broil; **II.** *v/i.* (have a) barbecue; **III.** F *v/refl.*: ***sich in der Sonne*** ~ F roast in the sun

'**gril·len·haft** *adj.* strange, eccentric; moody; F grumpy

'**Grill|fest** *n* barbecue; **~fleisch** *n* **1.** grilled meat; **2.** meat for grilling; **~koh·le** *f* charcoal; **~par·ty** *f* barbecue; **~platz** *m* barbecue site; **~rost** *m* grill, rack; **~spieß** *m* spit

Gri·mas·se [gri'masə] *f* (-; -n) grimace, face; ***~n schneiden*** pull faces

Grimm [grɪm] *m* (-[e]s; *no pl.*) wrath, fury; '**Grimm·darm** *m* colon; **grim·mig** ['grɪmɪç] *adj.* **1.** a) fierce; grim *laughter etc.*, b) in a bad mood; **2.** *fig.* severe *cold, pain etc.*

Grind [grɪnt] *m* ([e]s; -e [-də]) ⚕ scab, scurf; *vet.* mange; ⚘ scurf; **grin·dig** ['grɪndɪç] *adj.* scabby

grin·sen ['grɪnzən] **I.** *v/i.* (h) grin; smirk, sneer (***über*** *acc.* at); **II.** ≗ *n* (-s) grin; sneer; ***dir wird das ~ schon noch vergehen*** I'll *etc.* wipe that grin off your face(, don't you worry)

grip·pal [grɪ'paːl] *adj.*: ⚕ ***~er Infekt*** influenza

Grip·pe ['grɪpə] *f* (-; -n) influenza, flu; **~epi·de,mie** *f* flu epidemic; **~imp·fung** *f* flu vaccination; **~mit·tel** *n* flu remedy; ***kannst du mir irgendein ~ mitbringen?*** do you think you could get me something for this cold (*or* flu) of mine?; **~vi·rus** *m* flu virus; **~wel·le** *f* flu epidemic

Grips [grɪps] F *m* (-es; *no pl.*) F nous

grob [groːp] **I.** *adj.* a) coarse (*a. fig.*); rough (*a. voice, fig. work etc.*), b) raw, crude; unfinished, c) coarse-grained, d) uncouth; very rough, brutal; rude; bluff, blunt; crude; ⚖ gross; *fig.* **~e Entfernung** approximate distance; ⚖ **~e Fahrlässigkeit** gross negligence; **~er Fehler** grave mistake; **~e Lüge** downright (*or* flagrant) lie; **~e Skizze** rough sketch; ⚖ **~es Vergehen** grievous offen|ce (*Am.* -se); **in ~en Zügen** very roughly; **~ werden** be rude (**gegen** *acc.* to), get offensive (towards); **der gröbste Dreck** the worst of the dirt; **aus dem Gröbsten heraus sein** be out of the wood(s), have broken the back of it; → **Holz, Schnitzer** 2; **II.** *adv.* coarsely *etc.*; → **I; ~ gerechnet** roughly, at a rough estimate; **et. ~ schätzen** make a rough guess at s.th.; **~ geschätzt** at a rough guess; **et. ~ umreißen** give a rough outline of s.th.; **j-m ~ kommen** be rude to s.o., get offensive towards s.o.; ⚖ **~ fahrlässig** grossly negligent

'**Grob|ein·stel·lung** *f* ⚙ coarse adjustment; **2fa·se·rig** *adj.* coarse-fibred (*Am.* fibered); coarse-grain(ed); **~fei·le** *f* ⚙ rough file; **2ge·hackt** *adj.* coarsely chopped; **2ge·mah·len** *adj.* coarse-ground

'**Grob·heit** *f* (-; -en) **1.** *no pl.* coarseness; roughness; crudeness; *fig.* rudeness; **2. ~en** abuse; **j-m ~en an den Kopf werfen** be rude to s.o.

Gro·bi·an ['groːbi̯aːn] *m* (-s; -e) boor

'**grob|klot·zig** *adj.* clumsy, hamfisted; **~kno·chig** *adj.* big-boned; **~kör·nig** *adj.* coarse-grained; *phot.* grainy

gröb·lich ['grøːplıç] **I.** *adj.* gross; **II.** *adv.*: **j-n ~ beleidigen** grossly insult s.o.

'**grob·ma·schig** [-maʃıç] *adj.* wide-meshed

'**Grob·ra·ster** *m* coarse screen

'**grob·schläch·tig** [-ʃlɛçtıç] *adj.* uncouth

'**Grob·schnitt** *m* coarse cut *tobacco*

Grog [grɔk] *m* (-s; -s) hot grog

grog·gy ['grɔgi] F *adj.* shattered, F whacked, pooped

grö·len ['grøːlən] *v/i. and v/t.* (h) bellow; roar; **~de Menge** noisy crowd

Groll [grɔl] *m* (-s; *no pl.*) rancour, resentment; animosity; **e-n ~ gegen j-n hegen** bear a grudge against s.o.; **grol·len** ['grɔlən] *v/i.* (h) **1.** *thunder etc.*: rumble; **2. j-m ~** bear s.o. a grudge; **er grollt seit Tagen** it (*or* something) has been galling him for days; '**grol·lend** *adj.* angry

Grön·län·der ['grøːnlɛndɐ] *m* (-s; -), **Grön·län·de·rin** ['grøːnlɛndərın] *f* (-; -nen) Greenlander; **grön·län·disch** ['grøːnlɛndıʃ] *adj.* Greenland ..., from Greenland

Gros [groː] *n* (-; *no pl.*) *the* vast (*or* great) majority

Gro·schen ['grɔʃən] *m* (-s; -) **1.** *östr.* groschen; **2.** F ten-pfennig piece, ten pfennigs *pl.*; *fig.* **keinen ~ wert** not worth a penny (*or* cent); **sich ein paar ~ dazuverdienen** earn a bit of pocket money (on the side); **der ~ ist gefallen!** the penny has dropped; **~blatt** *n* F rag; **~ro͵man** *m* penny dreadful, *Am.* dime novel

'**gro·schen·wei·se** *adv.* bit by bit, a little bit at a time

groß [groːs] **I.** *adj.* a) big, large, huge, vast, b) tall, c) long, great *distance etc.*, d) grown-up, e) *fig.* great; major, important; big *mistake etc.*; great, intense *heat etc.*; severe *cold*; heavy *loss etc.*; **größer** quite big *etc.*; **~er Buchstabe** capital letter; **~e Ferien** summer holiday(s), long vacation; **ein ~es Gebäude** a big(, tall) building; **~e Mehrheit** great majority; **~e Schwester** big sister; **ein ~er Tag** a great day; **der größere Teil** most of it (*or* them); **zum ~en Teil** largely; ♪ **~e Terz** major third; **~er Unterschied** big (*or* great) difference; **e-e ~e Zahl von** *dat.* a large number of, a great many; **~e Zehe** big toe; **gleich ~** the same size; **so ~ wie ein Fußballfeld** the size of a football pitch; **~ werden** grow up; **zu ~ werden für** *acc.* outgrow *s.th.*; **wie ~ ist er?** how tall is he?; **er ist ... ~** he's ... (tall); *das Grundstück* **ist ... m² ~** is ... metres (*Am.* meters) square; **~en Hunger haben** be very hungry, be starving; F **ganz ~** F great; F **im Rechnen ist er ganz ~** he's really good (*or* he's brilliant) at arithmetic; **ich bin kein ~er Tänzer** *etc.* I'm not much of a dancer *etc.*; **unser Umsatz war dreimal so ~ wie der der Konkurrenz** our sales were three times those of our rivals; **Friedrich der 2e** Frederick the Great; **Karl der 2e** Charlemagne; → **Auge** 1, **Bär** 2, **Glocke; II.** *adv.*: **~ auftreten** act big; F **~ angeben** a) talk big, b) throw one's weight around (*or* about); **er sah mich ganz ~ an** he just stared at me; F **~ ausgehen** have a real night out; **~ schreiben** capitalize; **schreibt man das ~?** does that have a capital (letter)?; F **er kümmert sich nicht ~ darum** he doesn't really bother about it; F **was ist schon ~ dabei?** so what's the problem?; F **was gibt es da ~ zu sagen?** what can you say?; F **er ist ganz ~ angekommen** the audience *etc.* loved him; **~ und breit dastehen** *etc.* stand there *etc.* as large as life; → **herausbringen**

'**Groß|ab·neh·mer** *m* ✝ bulk buyer; **~ad·mi͵ral** *m* ⚓ Admiral of the Fleet; **~ak·ti͵on** *f* major (*or* large-scale) campaign *or* operation; **~ak·tio͵när** *m* major shareholder; **~alarm** *m* red (*or* major) alert; **2an·ge·legt** *adj.* large-scale, full-scale; **~an·griff** *m* ⚔ major offensive, all-out attack, ✈ air blitz; **~an·schaf·fung** *f* major purchase (*or* investment)

'**groß·ar·tig I.** *adj.* tremendous, great; excellent; brilliant; wonderful, magnificent; grand; *contp.* pompous; **du warst ~!** you were tremendous (*or* just great); **II** *adv.*: **~ tun** put on airs; **sie haben ~ gespielt** they played really well; **sich ~ amüsieren** have a great time

'**Groß|auf·nah·me** *f phot., film*: close-up (shot); **~auf·trag** *m* ✝ large-scale order

'**groß·äu·gig** [-ɔygıç] *adj.* big-eyed, wide-eyed

'**Groß|bank** *f* (-; -en) big bank; **~bau·er** *m* (-n; -n) (big) farmer; **~bau·stel·le** *f* major building site; **~be·trieb** *m* large concern (🖌 farm)

'**Groß·bild·ka·me·ra** *f* large-format camera

'**Groß|brand** *m* big fire; **~buch·sta·be** *m* capital (letter); *typ.* uppercase letter; **in ~n** *a.* uppercase, F in caps

'**groß·bür·ger·lich** *adj.* upper middle class; '**Groß·bür·ger·tum** *n* (-s; *no pl.*) upper middle class(es *pl.*)

'**groß·deutsch** *adj.* pan-German

'**Groß·druck·aus·ga·be** *f* large-print edition

Gro·ße[1] ['groːsə] *m, f* (n; -n) **1. die ~n der Welt** (**des Films**) the great people of this world (the big names in the film industry); **2.** *pl.* grown-ups; **3.** *our etc.* eldest, oldest

'**Gro·ße**[2] *n* (-n) **1. ~s** great things (*or* deeds) *pl.*; **es hat sich nichts ~s ereignet** nothing important happened; **2. im 2n** on a large scale, large-scale ...; ✝ *buy etc.* wholesale, (in) bulk; **im ~n wie im Kleinen** at all levels; → **ganz** II, **Ganze**

Grö·ße ['grøːsə] *f* (-; -n) **1.** a) size, b) height, c) spaciousness, vastness, d) *esp.* ⚕ quantity; order, e) *fig.* extent; significance, greatness; enormity *of an offense etc.*; *ast.* magnitude; **dieselbe ~ haben** be the same size (*or* height); **er hat ungefähr d-e ~** he's about your height; **welche ~ haben** (*or* **tragen**) **Sie?** what size do you take?; **in voller ~** full-size, *w.s.* (as) large as life; **von mittlerer ~** medium-sized, of medium height; **Stern erster ~** star of the first magnitude; **2.** *fig.* magnanimity, largesse, *Am.* largess; **3.** celebrity, important figure, authority, *esp. iro.* worthy; *thea., sport*: star; **politische ~** political heavyweight; **(un)bekannte ~** (un)known quantity; **e-e vergangene ~** a has-been

'**Groß|ein·kauf** *m* **1. e-n ~ machen** do a big shop; **2.** ✝ a) bulk buying, b) bulk purchase; **~ein·satz** *m* large-scale (*or* major) operation; **~ der Polizei** large police deployment; **~el·tern** *pl.* grandparents; **~en·kel** *m* great-grandson; *pl.* great-grandchildren; **~en·ke·lin** *f* great--granddaughter

'**Grö·ßen|klas·se** *f* size; **~ord·nung** *f* order (of magnitude) (*a. ast.*); *Unternehmen etc.* **von dieser ~** of that scale; **es liegt in der ~ von** it's somewhere in the order (*or* region) of

'**gro·ßen·teils** *adv.* largely, to a great extent

'**Grö·ßen·ver·hält·nis** *n* ratio; proportions *pl.*, dimensions *pl.*; scale; **das ~ stimmt nicht** it's out of proportion (*or* scale)

'**Grö·ßen·wahn** *m* megalomania; delusions *pl.* of grandeur; '**grö·ßen·wahn·sin·nig** *adj.*, '**Grö·ßen·wahn·sin·ni·ge** *m, f* (-n; -n) megalomaniac

'**Groß|er·zeu·ger** *m* large-scale producer (*or* manufacturer); **~fahn·dung** *f* dragnet operation; **~fa͵mi·lie** *f* extended family; **~feu·er** *n* big fire; **2flä·chig** [-flɛçıç] *adj.* extensive; wide; **~flug·ha·fen** *m* international (*or* major) airport; **~for͵mat** *n* large size; *phot. etc.* large format; **im ~** → **2for·ma·tig** [-fɔr͵maːtıç] *adj.* large-format; **~fürst** *m* grand duke; **~für·sten·tum** *n* grand duchy; **~für·stin** *f* grand duchess; **2füt·tern** F *v/t.* (*sep.*, h) bring up; **wir haben ihn großgefüttert** *a.* we fed and clothed him all those years; **~ga͵ra·ge** *f* **1.** big garage; (underground) car park; **2.** major service station; **2ge·druckt** *adj.* in large letters (*or* print); **2ge·wach·sen** *adj.* tall, big; **~grund·be·sitz** *m* large estate(s *pl.*); **~grund·be·sit·zer** *m* big landowner

'**Groß·han·del** *m* a) wholesale trade (*or* trading), b) wholesaler's, wholesale store; **im ~ (ver)kaufen** buy (sell) wholesale (*or* [in] bulk)

'**Groß·han·dels|ge·schäft** *n* **1.** wholesale business; **2.** wholesaler's, wholesale

store; **~preis** *m* wholesale price; **~ra‚batt** *m* bulk discount
'Groß·händ·ler *m* wholesaler
'Groß·hand·lung *f* wholesale firm (*or* business)
'groß·her·zig *adj.* magnanimous; **'Groß·her·zig·keit** *f* (-; *no pl.*) magnanimity
'Groß|her·zog *m* grand duke; **~her·zog·tum** *n* grand duchy
'Groß·hirn *n anat.* cerebrum; **~rin·de** *f* cerebral cortex
'Groß|in·du‚strie *f* big industry; **~in·du·stri·el·le** *m* (-n; -n) big industrialist, F tycoon; **~in·qui‚si·tor** *m* Grand Inquisitor, Inquisitor General
Gros·sist ['grɔsɪst] *m* (-en; -en) wholesaler
'groß·jäh·rig [-jɛːrɪç] *adj.* of age; ~ ***werden*** come of age; **'Groß·jäh·rig·keit** *f* (-; *no pl.*) majority
'groß·ka·li·brig [-ka‚liːbrɪç] *adj.* large-calib|re (*Am.* -er)
'Groß|kampf·tag *fig. m* tough (*or* hard) day; **~ka·pi‚tal** *n* high finance, big business; *coll.* big financiers *pl.*; **~ka·pi·ta‚list** *m* capitalist; **♀ka‚riert** *adj.* large-checked; **~kat·ze** *f* big cat; **~kli·ma** *n* macroclimate; **~kon‚zern** *m* big concern
'groß·kot·zig [-kɔtsɪç] F *adj.* full of o.s.; flashy; ***er ist so ~*** *a.* he's such a show-off
'Groß|kraft·werk *n* large(-scale) power station (*or* plant); **~kü·che** *f* large kitchen; *w.s.* canteen; **~kund·ge·bung** *f* mass rally
'Groß·macht *f* great power; superpower; **~po·li‚tik** *f* superpower politics *pl.*; **~stel·lung** *f* position of power
'Groß·ma·ma F *f* grandma, granny; Grandma, Granny
'Groß·manns·sucht *f*: ***er leidet unter ~*** he always has to act the big shot, he likes to play lord of the manor
'Groß·markt *m* **1.** wholesale market (*or* store); **2.** hypermarket
'groß·ma·schig [-maʃɪç] *adj.* wide-meshed
'Groß·mast *m* ⚓ mainmast
'Groß·maul F *n* (-[e]s; *no pl.*) F loudmouth; **'groß·mäu·lig** [-mɔʏlɪç] F *adj.* F loudmouthed
'Groß|mei·ster *m* grand master; **~mo‚gul** *m hist.* Grand (*or* Great) Mogul; **~muf·ti** *m* grand mufti
'Groß·mut *f* (-; *no pl*) magnanimity, largesse, *Am.* largess; **'groß·mü·tig** [-myːtɪç] *adj.* magnanimous
'Groß·mut·ter *f* grandmother
'groß·müt·ter·lich *adj.* one's grandmother's; *fig.* grandmotherly; **'groß·müt·ter·li·cher·seits** *adv.* on one's grandmother's side
'Groß|nef·fe *m* grand-nephew; **~nich·te** *f* grand-niece; **~of·fen‚si·ve** *f* major offensive; **~on·kel** *m* great-uncle; **~pak·kung** *f* large (*or* economy) pack; **~pa·pa** F *m* F grandpa; Grandpa
'Groß·raum *m*: ***der ~ München*** the Munich area, Munich and its surrounding areas; **~bü‚ro** *n* open-plan office; **~flug·zeug** *n* wide-bodied jet
'groß·räu·mig [-rɔʏmɪç] *adj.* spacious; *w.s.* extensive; ***ortskundige Fahrer werden gebeten, den Stau ~ zu umfahren*** motorists are advised to keep well away from the congested area
'Groß·raum·wa·gen *m* 🚃 open-plan carriage
'Groß|raz·zia *f* large-scale raid (F swoop); **~rei·ne·ma·chen** F *n* big clean-up, big cleaning-up session; spring-clean(ing session); *fig.* purge
'groß·schnäu·zig [-ʃnɔʏtsɪç] F *adj.* F loudmouthed
'groß·schrei·ben *fig. v/t.* (*irr., sep.*, h, → ***schreiben***): ***großgeschrieben werden*** rate very highly, be very much in demand; ***bei ihm wird Pünktlichkeit großgeschrieben*** *a.* he sets great store by punctuality; **'Groß·schrei·bung** *f* capitalization; ***er hat Probleme mit der Groß- und Kleinschreibung*** he has problems with capitalization
'Groß|se·gel *n* mainsail; **~sen·der** *m* high-power transmitter (*w.s.* broadcasting station)
'Groß·spre·cher *m* loudmouth; **'Groß·spre·che·rei** [-ʃprɛçəraɪ] *f* (-; *no pl.*) bragging; loudmouthed behavio(u)r; **'groß·spre·che·risch** [-ʃprɛçərɪʃ] *adj.* loudmouthed
'groß·spu·rig [-ʃpuːrɪç] *adj.* high and mighty; pompous
'Groß·stadt *f* big town (*or* city), city; metropolis; **'Groß·städ·ter** *m* (-s; -) city-dweller; *contp.* city-slicker; **'groß·städ·tisch** *adj.* urban, (big-)city ...
'Groß·stadt|lärm *m* big-city noise, noise (*or* hubbub) of the (big) city; **~le·ben** *n* (big-)city life, life in the city; **~luft** *f* city air; **~mensch** *m* big-city person (*or* man, woman); *contp.* city-slicker; ***ich bin ein ~*** *a.* I grew up in the city; **~men·ta·li‚tät** *f* big-city mentality; **~rum·mel** *m* bustling city life (*or* life of the city), hubbub of the city; **~ver·kehr** *m* (big-) city traffic; traffic in the cities
'Groß·tank·stel·le *f* (large) service station
'Groß·tan·te *f* great-aunt
'Groß·tat *f* great feat
'Groß·teil *m* (-[e]s; *no pl.*) *a* large part, *the* majority, *the* bulk (*gen.* of)
größ·ten·teils ['grøːstəntaɪls] *adv.* mainly, for the most part
Größt·maß ['grøːst-] *n* **1.** maximum (size); maximum limit; **2.** → ***Höchstmaß***
'größt'mög·lich *adj.* greatest possible; *the* utmost *effort, care etc.*
'Groß·tu·er [-tuːɐ] *m* (-s; -) show-off; **Groß·tue·rei** [-tuːə'raɪ] *f* (-; *no pl.*) showing off; **'groß·tue·risch** [-tuːərɪʃ] *adj.* boastful; **'groß·tun** (*irr., sep.*, h, → ***tun***) **I.** *v/i.* act big, show off; **II.** *v/refl.*: ***sich mit et. ~*** show s.th. off; brag about s.th.
'Groß|un·ter‚neh·men *n* big business; **~un·ter‚neh·mer** *m* big businessman
'Groß·va·ter *m* grandfather
'groß·vä·ter·lich *adj.* one's grandfather's; *fig.* grandfatherly; **'groß·vä·ter·li·cher·seits** *adv.* on one's grandfather's side
'Groß·va·ter|ses·sel *m* (big,) comfy armchair; **~uhr** *f* grandfather clock
'Groß|ver·an·stal·tung *f* big event; *esp. pol.* mass rally; **~ver·brau·cher** *m* bulk consumer; **~ver·die·ner** *m* big(-income) earner; **~ver·such** *m* large-scale test (*or* experiment); **~vieh** *n* cattle and horses *pl.*; **~wet·ter·la·ge** *f* general weather situation; *fig.* general situation
'Groß·wild·jagd *f* big-game hunt(ing)
'Groß·wür·den·trä·ger *m* high dignitary
'groß·zie·hen *v/t.* (*irr., sep.*, h, → ***ziehen***) bring up, raise
'groß·zü·gig *adj.* **1.** generous; **2.** liberal, broadminded; permissive; **3.** large-scale, generous; spacious; **'Groß·zü·gig·keit** *f* (-; *no pl.*) **1.** generosity; **2.** liberality, broadmindedness; **3.** bold conception (*or* design)
gro·tesk [gro'tɛsk] **I.** *adj.* grotesque; gross; absurd; **II.** ♀ *f* (-; *no pl.*) *typ.* grotesque; **Gro'tes·ke** *f* (-; -n) *literature*: grotesque; △, *art*: grotesque(rie); *fig.* farce; **Gro'tesk·schrift** *f typ.* grotesque
Grot·te ['grɔtə] *f* (-; -n) grotto
grub *pret. of* ***graben***
Grüb·chen ['gryːpçən] *n* (-s; -) dimple; ⚘, *zo.* fossule; ⚙ pit
Gru·be ['gruːbə] *f* (-; -n) pit; ⚒ *a.* mine, colliery; hollow; hole; *fig.* ***j-m e-e ~ graben*** set (up) a trap for s.o.; ***wer andern e-e ~ gräbt, fällt selbst hinein*** you've got to watch you don't fall into your own trap (*or* watch you're not hoist with your own petard)
Grü·be·lei [gryːbə'laɪ] *f* (-; -en) *a. pl.* brooding; **grü·beln** ['gryːbəln] **I.** *v/i.* (h) brood (***über*** *acc. or dat.* over, about); ~ ***über*** *acc. or dat. a.* mull over; **II.** ♀ *n* (-s): ***ins ~ kommen*** start brooding
'Gru·ben|ar·bei·ter *m* miner; **~brand** *m* pit fire; **~ex·plo·si‚on** *f* explosion in a (*or* the) mine; **~gas** *n* pit gas, firedamp; **~lam·pe** *f* miner's lamp; **~schacht** *m* mineshaft; **~un·glück** *n* mining accident (*or* disaster), pit disaster
Grüb·ler ['gryːblɐ] *m* (-s; -) broody person; reflective person; **grüb·le·risch** ['gryːblərɪʃ] *adj.* brooding, broody; introspective
Gruft [grʊft] *f* (-; Grüfte ['grʏftə]) tomb; crypt; *poet.* grave
Gruf·ti ['grʊfti] F *m* (-s; -s) F crumbly, wrinkly, oldster
grün [gryːn] **I.** *adj.* green (*a. pol. and fig.*); unripe; *fig.* (still) wet behind the ears; *pol.* ecology ...; ***Aal ~*** stewed eel; ***die Ampel ist ~*** the lights are green, it's green; ***~e Heringe*** fresh herrings; ***die ♀e Insel*** the Emerald Isle; ***~er Salat*** lettuce; *die Bananen etc.* ***sind noch zu ~*** aren't ripe yet; *fig.* ***~er Junge*** greenhorn; ***j-m ~es Licht geben*** give s.o. the go-ahead (F thumbs up); ***~e Lunge*** green lung; ~ ***vor Neid*** green with envy; ***~e Weihnachten*** snow-free Christmas; ***j-n ~ und blau schlagen*** (*or* ***dreschen***) beat s.o. black and blue; ***sich ~ und blau ärgern*** F be really mad; ***ich hab' mich ~ und blau geärgert*** I could have kicked myself; ***ich komme auf keinen ~en Zweig*** I'm just not getting anywhere; ***er wird nie auf e-n ~en Zweig kommen*** he'll never get anywhere in life; F ***sie ist mir nicht ~*** she doesn't like me; → ***Bohne, Minna, Star, Tisch, Welle***; **II.** ♀ *n* (-s; -) green; ***im ~en*** out in the open; ***Fahrt ins ~e*** drive into the countryside; ***die Ampel steht auf ~*** the lights are green; ***bei ~*** at green; ***geht bitte nur bei ~ über die Straße*** don't cross the road until the lights are green; F ***das ist dasselbe in ~*** it's six of one and half a dozen of the other
'Grün·an·la·ge *f* park; green; **~n** green spaces
'grün|blau *adj.* greenish-blue; **~blind** *adj.* green-blind
Grund [grʊnt] *m* (-[e]s; Gründe ['grʏndə]) **1.** *no pl.* a) ground; land, property, b) bottom, c) △ foundations *pl.*; plot, d) background; ⚙ priming (coat); ***~ und Boden*** land, property; ⚓ ***auf ~ geraten*** (*or* ***laufen***) run aground; *fig.* ***den ~ le-***

gen zu lay the foundations of; ***e-r Sache auf den ~ gehen*** get to the bottom of s.th.; ***im ~e s-s Herzens*** at (the bottom of his) heart; ***von ~ aus*** (*or* ***auf***) completely, ... through and through; ***im ~e*** (***genommen***) basically, really; ***j-n in ~ und Boden reden*** talk s.o. into the ground; ***in ~ und Boden verdammen*** condemn outright; ***ich habe mich in ~ und Boden geschämt*** I wished the earth would open up and swallow me; **2.** reason (**zu** *inf.* to *inf.*, for *ger.*); cause (**für** *acc.* of); argument; ***Gründe für und wider*** arguments for and against, *the* pros and cons; ***auf ~ von*** *dat.* on grounds of; ***aus gesundheitlichen*** (***familiären***) ***Gründen*** for health (family) reasons, for reasons of health; ***aus diesem ~*** that's (*or* that was) why; ***aus welchem ~?*** why?; ***aus dem einfachen ~, daß*** for the simple reason that; ***mit*** (***gutem***) ***~*** with good reason; ***ein ~ mehr zu*** *inf.* all the more reason to *inf.*; ***aus diesem oder jenem ~*** for one (*or* some) reason or another; ***ich habe m-e Gründe dafür*** I have my reasons; ***es hat schon s-e Gründe*** he knows *etc.* what he's *etc.* doing; ***nicht ohne ~*** not without reason; ***ohne jeden ~*** for no apparent reason; ***jeden*** (***keinen***) ***~ haben zu*** *inf.* have every (no) reason to *inf.*; ***es besteht*** (***kein***) ***~ zu der Annahme, daß*** we *etc.* have (no) reason to suppose that; ***Gründe anführen*** state one's case (**für** *acc.* for); ***kein ~ zur Besorgnis*** no need to get worried, there's no cause for concern; → ***zugrunde***

'Grund|ak·kord *m* ♪ basic chord; **~an·schau·ung** *f* basic outlook

'grund'an·stän·dig *adj.* really decent

'Grund|an·strich *m* first coat(ing); **~aus·bil·dung** *f* basic training; **~aus·stat·tung** *f* basic equipment; **~bau** *m* (-[e]s; -ten) foundations *pl.*; **~bau·stein** *m* **1.** *phys.* elementary particle; **2.** basic component; **~be·darf** *m* basic needs (*or* requirements) *pl.*; **~be·deu·tung** *f* primary (*or* basic) meaning; **~be·din·gung** *f* basic condition; **~be·dürf·nis** *n* basic requirement (*or* need); **~be·griff** *m* **1.** *pl.* basics; **2.** basic concept; **~be·sitz** *m* property, real estate; immovables *pl.*; **~be·sit·zer** *m* landowner; **~be·stand·teil** *m* basic component; **~be·trag** *m* basic sum; **~buch** *n* real estate register

'grund'ehr·lich *adj.* absolutely honest

'Grund|ei·gen·schaft *f* basic (*or* fundamental) characteristic; essential aspect (*or* quality); **~ei·gen·tum** *n* → ***Grundbesitz***; **~ei·gen·tü·mer** *m* → ***Grundbesitzer***; **~ein·heit** *f* absolute unit; **~ein·kom·men** *n* basic income; **~ein·stel·lung** *f* basic attitude (*or* outlook); **~eis** *n* **1.** ground ice; **2.** V ***ihm geht der Arsch mit ~*** *sl.* he's got the wind up, V he's scared shitless

grün·den ['grʏndən] (h) **I.** *v/t.* found, establish, set up; create; form; start (up); launch; **et. ~ auf** *dat.* base (*or* found) s.th. on; **II.** *v/refl.*: ***sich ~ auf*** *dat.* be based on

Grün·der ['grʏndɐ] *m* (-s; -) founder, ✝ *a.* promoter; originator, creator; **~ak·ti·en** *pl.*, **~an·tei·le** *pl.* founders' shares (*Am.* stock *sg.*)

'Grund|er·fah·rung *f* basic experience; **~er·for·der·nis** *n* basic requirement

'Grün·der·jah·re *pl. period of industrial expansion in Germany from 1871 on*

'Grün·der·va·ter *m* founding father

'Grund·er·werb *m* acquisition of land; **'Grund·er·werbs·steu·er** *f* land transfer tax

'Grün·der·zeit *f* → ***Gründerjahre***

'grund'falsch *adj.* absolutely (*or* completely) wrong; ***was du machst, ist ~*** *a.* you're doing the completely wrong thing, you couldn't do worse

'Grund|far·be *f* **1.** primary colo(u)r; **2.** first coat; **~feh·ler** *m* basic *or* fundamental mistake (*or* error); **~fe·sten** *fig. pl.* foundations; ***an den ~ des Staates*** *etc.* ***rütteln*** rock the foundations of the state *etc.*; **et. in den** (*or* **s-n**) ***~ erschüttern*** shake s.th. to its (very) foundations; **~flä·che** *f* (surface) area; **~form** *f* basic form; *ling.* infinitive; **~for·mel** *f* basic formula; **~fra·ge** *f* basic question; **~frei·hei·ten** *pl. pol.* (basic) civil rights, basic freedoms; **~ge·bühr** *f* basic charge, flat rate; **~ge·dan·ke** *m* basic (*or* fundamental) idea

'Grund·ge·halt[1] *m* basic content

'Grund·ge·halt[2] *n* basic salary

'grund·ge'scheit *adj.* very intelligent (*or* bright)

'Grund|ge·setz *n* basic law; *pol.* constitution; **~hal·tung** *f* basic attitude

'grund'häß·lich *adj.* really ugly, ugly as sin (F hell)

'Grund·idee *f* basic idea

grun·die·ren [grʊn'di:rən] *v/t.* (h) ground; ⚙ *usu.* prime; stain *wood etc.*; **Grun·dier·far·be** [grʊn'di:ɐ-] *f* primer; **Grun'die·rung** *f* (-; -en) **1.** primer; **2.** *no pl.* priming; **3.** filler

'Grund|irr·tum *m* fundamental error; **~ka·pi,tal** *n* ✝ capital stock; **~kennt·nis·se** *pl.* basic knowledge *sg.* (**in** *dat.* of), basics; **~ko·sten** *pl.* basic cost *sg.*; **~kurs** *m* basic (*or* beginners') course

'Grund·la·ge *f* basis; F base; *pl.* fundamentals, basics; ***die ~ bilden für*** *acc.* form the basis of, be (*or* constitute) the basis for; ***die ~n schaffen für*** *acc.* lay the foundations for; ***jeder ~ entbehren*** be completely unfounded; ***jeder gesetzlichen ~ entbehren*** have no legal basis *or* authority (whatsoever); F ***für heute abend wirst du e-e gute ~ brauchen*** F you'll have to line your stomach well (*or* you'll need a good lining) for tonight; **'Grund·la·gen·for·schung** *f* basic research

'grund·le·gend **I.** *adj.* basic, fundamental; essential; **II.** *adv.* fundamentally; ***~ verändern*** *a.* radically change, change the whole face of

gründ·lich ['grʏntlɪç] **I.** *adj.* thorough; careful; proper; ***e-e ~e Arbeit*** a good piece of work; ***~e Kenntnisse haben in*** *dat.* be well-grounded in; **II.** *adv.* thoroughly *etc.*; F *a.* properly; ***sich ~ vorbereiten*** prepare o.s. well; ***ich habe mich ~ vorbereitet*** I'm well-prepared; ***er hat s-e Sache ~ gemacht*** he's done a very thorough job, *iro.* he's made a thorough job of it; ***j-m ~ die Meinung sagen*** give s.o. a piece of one's mind; ***da hast du dich ~ getäuscht*** you're very much mistaken there; ***ich habe mich in ihr ~ getäuscht*** I completely misjudged her; ***er hat sich ~ blamiert*** he made a real (F right, proper) fool of himself; **'Gründ·lich·keit** *f* (-; *no pl.*) thoroughness; carefulness

'Grund·li·nie *f* ⩓ base; *sport*: base line; *pl. fig.* outline *sg.*

'Grund·li·ni·en|schlag *m* base-line shot; **~spiel** *n* base-line game

'Grund·lohn *m* basic wage(s *pl.*)

'grund·los **I.** *adj.* **1.** bottomless; **2.** muddy *paths etc.*; **3.** *fig.* unfounded; **II.** *adv.* for no reason (at all)

'Grund|mau·er *f* foundation wall; **~me,tall** *n* base metal; **~mo,dell** *n* standard model; **~nah·rungs·mit·tel** *n* staple, basic (*or* staple) food

Grün'don·ners·tag *m* Maundy Thursday

'Grund|ord·nung *f pol. etc.*: fundamental order; **~pfei·ler** *m* main support; *fig.* mainstay, bedrock; **~po·si·ti,on** *f* basic point of view; **~preis** *m* basic price; **~prin,zip** *n* basic principle; **~pro,blem** *n* basic (*or* fundamental) problem; **~re·chen·art** *f*, **~rech·nungs·art** *f* basic (arithmetical) operation; **~rech·te** *pl.* basic (*or* fundamental) rights; **~re·gel** *f* basic rule; *fig.* maxim; **~ren·te** *f* **1.** basic pension; **2.** ground rent; **~rich·tung** *f* general tendency; **~riß** *m* **1.** ⚠ ground plan; layout; **2.** *fig.* outline, sketch; outline(s *pl.*)

'Grund·satz *m* principle, *fig. a.* maxim; *esp. phls.* axiom; tenet; ***nach dem ~, daß*** on the principle that; ***es sich zum ~ machen*** make it a rule; ***er ist ein Mann mit Grundsätzen*** he's a man of principle, he's got his principles; **~de,bat·te** *f* debate on basic principles; *pol.* policy debate; **~ent·schei·dung** *f* fundamental (*or* basic) decision; ⚖ landmark decision; ***wir müssen e-e ~ treffen*** *a.* we've got to make a decision and stick by it; **~er·klä·rung** *f* policy statement; **~fra·ge** *f* basic issue; key question

'grund·sätz·lich [-zɛtslɪç] **I.** *adj.* fundamental, basic; ... on principle; **II.** *adv.* fundamentally; basically; on principle, as a matter of principle; always, invariably; *w.s.* absolutely

'Grund·satz|pro,gramm *n pol.* (basic) policy statement; party platform; **~re·de** *f pol.* keynote speech (*or* address); **~ur·teil** *n* leading decision

'Grund|schlag *m* ♪ beat; **~schrift** *f typ.* main type; **~schul·bil·dung** *f* primary education; **~schuld** *f* land charge; **~schu·le** *f* primary school, *Am.* elementary (*or* grade) school; **~schü·ler** *m* primary pupil, *Am. a.* elementary (*or* grade) school student

'grund·so'li·de *adj.* absolutely dependable, rock solid

'Grund·stein *m* foundation stone; *fig.* cornerstone; ***den ~ legen zu*** *dat.* lay the foundation stone of, *fig.* lay the foundations for; **~le·gung** [-le:gʊŋ] *f* (-; *no pl.*) laying of the foundation stone; cornerstone ceremony

'Grund|stel·lung *f dancing*: starting position; *gym.* normal position; *boxing*: on-guard position; ⚔ position of attention; **~steu·er** *f* land tax; **~stim·mung** *f* general mood; tenor *of talks etc.*; **~stock** *m* basis; core

'Grund·stoff *m phys.* element; ⚙ raw material; **~in·du,strie** *f* basic industry

'Grund|stoff·wech·sel *m physiol.* basal metabolism; **~stück** *n* piece (*or* plot) of land; property; (building) site

'Grund·stücks|mak·ler *m* estate agent, *Am.* realtor; **~markt** *m* property market;

~spe·ku͵lant *m* land jobber; **~spe·ku·la·ti͵on** *f* land speculation
'Grund|stu·di·um *n* foundation course; **~stu·fe** *f* **1.** elementary stage; **2.** junior school; **3.** *ling.* positive degree; **~sub͵stanz** *f* basic substance; **~ta͵rif** *m* base (*or* basic) rate; **~ten͵denz** *f* general tendency (*or* direction); **~text** *m* original text; **~ton** *m* **1.** ♪ tonic, root; **2.** bottom shade; **3.** *fig.* general mood; **~tu·gend** *f* cardinal virtue; **~übel** *n* basic problem; ***das ~ ist ...*** *a.* the root of all the other problems is ..., all the other problems go back to ...; **~über͵zeu·gung** *f* fundamental conviction; **~͵um·satz** *m* **1.** ✝ basic turnover; **2.** *physiol.* basal metabolic rate
Grün·dung ['grʏndʊŋ] *f* (-; -en) foundation; formation; establishment, setting-up, opening, starting (up)
'Grün·dün·ger *m* green manure
'Grün·dungs|fei·er *f* inaugural celebrations *pl.* (*or* ceremony); **~jahr** *n* year of foundation; **~ka·pi͵tal** *n* initial capital stock; **~mit·glied** *n* founder member; **~ur·kun·de** *f* corporate charter
'grund·ver'kehrt *adj.* totally wrong; ***es wäre ~ zu*** *inf.* it would be a big mistake to *inf.*
'Grund·ver·mö·gen *n* **1.** ✝ basic assets *pl.*; **2.** → ***Grundbesitz***
'grund·ver'schie·den *adj.* totally (*or* fundamentally) different; ***~ sein*** be totally different personalities, F be poles apart
'Grund|vor͵aus·set·zung *f* basic (*or* absolute) prerequisite; **~wachs** *n skiing*: base wax; **~wahr·heit** *f* fundamental (*or* basic) truth
'Grund·was·ser *n* (-s; *no pl.*) (under)ground water; **~spie·gel** *m*, **~stand** *m* water table
'Grund|wis·sen *n* basic knowledge (***in*** *dat.* of); **~wort** *n ling.* primary word, 🕮 etymon; **~wort·schatz** *m* basic vocabulary; **~zahl** *f* cardinal number; base radix; base; **~zug** *m* characteristic (feature), main feature; *pl.* fundamentals, outline *sg.*; ***in s-n Grundzügen*** in outline
Grü·ne[1] ['gry:nə] *m*, *f* (-n; -n) *pol.* Green; ***die ~n*** the Greens, the German ecology party
'Grü·ne[2] *n* (-n) → **grün** II
grü·nen ['gry:nən] (h) **I.** *v/i.* a) be green (*or* verdant), b) turn green; *lit. fig.* flourish, blossom; **II.** *v/impers.*: ***es grünt*** (***und blüht***) everything's beginning to flower (again)
'Grün|fäu·le *f* green rot; **~fink** *m* greenfinch; **~flä·che** *f* **1.** green, lawn; **2.** *pl.* green spaces, unspoilt countryside *sg.*; **~fut·ter** *n* green fodder; **2gelb** *adj.* greenish-yellow; **~gür·tel** *m* green belt; **~kern** *m* unripe spelt grain; **~kohl** *m* kale; **~land** *n* (-[e]s; *no pl.*) grassland
'grün·lich *adj.* greenish
'Grün·ling *m* (-s; -e) **1.** greenfinch; **2.** greenling; **3.** ♣ green agaric; **4.** F *fig.* greenhorn
'Grün|pflan·ze *f* non-flowering plant; **~schna·bel** *fig. m* greenhorn; **~span** *m* (-[e]s; *no pl.*) verdigris
'Grün·stich *m* (-[e]s; *no pl.*) *phot.* green cast; **'grün·sti·chig** [-ʃtɪçɪç] *adj.*: ***~ sein*** have a green cast
'Grün·strei·fen *m* centre (*Am.* median) strip

grun·zen ['grʊntsən] **I.** *v/i. and v/t.* (h) grunt; **II.** 2 *n* (-s) grunt(ing)
'Grün·zeug F *n* raw (green) vegetables *pl.*
Grup·pe ['grʊpə] *f* (-; -n) group (*a.* ✝ *and fig.*); cluster *of houses etc.*; clump *of trees*; team, crew *of workmen etc.*; *fig.* category; ⚔ section, *Am.* squad; ✈ *Brit.* wing, *Am.* group; ✝ concern
'Grup·pen|abend *m* group get-together (*or* meeting); **~ak͵kord** *m* ✝ group piece work (*or* rate); **~ar·beit** *f* teamwork, *ped. a.* group work, work in groups; **~auf·nah·me** *f* → ***Gruppenbild***; **2be·wußt** *adj.* group-conscious; **~be·wußt·sein** *n* group consciousness (*or* awareness); group (*or* collective) identity; **~bild** *n* group portrait (*or* photo, shot), photo of the (*or* a) group; **~bil·dung** *f* formation (*or* forming) of groups, grouping; **~dy͵na·mik** *f psych.* group dynamics *pl.*; **2dy͵na·misch** *adj.* group--dynamic; **~ego͵is·mus** *m* sectional self-interest; **~fo·to** *n* group photo (*or* shot), photo of the (*or* a) group; **~füh·rer** *m* group leader; ⚔ *Brit.* section leader, *Am.* squad leader; **~lei·ter** *m* group manager; **~pra·xis** *f* group (*or* joint) practice; **~rei·se** *f* **1.** group (*or* organized) tour; **2.** *pl.* group travel *sg.*; **~sex** *m* group sex; **~sie·ger** *m* group winner(s *pl.*); **~the·ra͵pie** *f* group therapy; **~͵un·ter·richt** *m* group instruction
'grup·pen·wei·se *adv.* in groups
'Grup·pen·zwang *m* (peer) group pressure
grup·pie·ren [grʊ'pi:rən] (h) **I.** *v/t.* group, arrange in groups; **II.** *v/refl.*: ***sich ~*** form a group (*or* groups), group (o.s.) (***um*** *acc.* round); assemble; *sport*: line up; **Grup'pie·rung** *f* (-; -en) **1.** forming of groups; **2.** grouping; **3.** group(s *pl.*); *pol. etc.* group(ing)
Grus [gru:s] *m* (-es [-zəs]; *no pl.*) slack; *geol.* debris
Gru·sel|film ['gru:zəl-] *m* horror film; monster movie; **~ge·schich·te** *f* horror story
gru·se·lig ['gru:zəlɪç] *adj.* creepy, F scary; spine-chilling *story etc.*
gru·seln ['gru:zəln] **I.** *v/t.*, *v/i.*, *v/impers.* (h): ***mich*** *or* ***mir gruselt*** (***es***) I'm scared, this is creepy, this is giving me the creeps; ***mich*** (***or mir***) ***gruselt vor diesem Haus*** this place gives me the creeps; **II.** 2 *n* (-s) *the* creeps *pl.*; ***dabei kann man das ~ lernen*** it's enough to give you the creeps
Gruß [gru:s] *m* (-es; Grüße ['gry:sə]) **1.** greeting, *formal*: salutation; *pl.* regards, love (***an*** *acc.* to); ***schöne Grüße aus*** *dat.* greetings from; (***sag*** *or* ***bestell ihm***) ***e-n schönen ~ von mir!*** give him my regards (*or* my love), *a.* say hello to him from me; ***herzliche Grüße*** Kind regards, Best wishes, (With) Love; ***mit freundlichem ~*** Yours sincerely; **2.** ⚔ salute; **~adres·se** *f*, **~bot·schaft** *f* message of greeting
grü·ßen ['gry:sən] (h) **I.** *v/t.* greet, say hello (*or* good morning *etc.*) to; ⚔ salute; *fig.* greet; ***grüß dich!*** hello!, F hi!; ***~ Sie ihn von mir!*** give him my regards (*or* my love), *a.* say hello to him from me; ***er läßt Sie ~*** he sends his regards; **II.** *v/i.* greet s.o., say hello (*or* good morning *etc.*); ⚔ salute; ***kannst du nicht ~?*** have you forgotten how to say hello?; ***er hat überhaupt nicht gegrüßt*** he didn't even say hello

'Gruß|for·mel *f* salutation (*a. in letter*); complimentary close, ending; ***welche ~n benutzt man in englischen Briefen?*** how do you address people and sign off in English letters?; **~kar·te** *f* greetings card
'gruß·los *adv.* without a word (of greeting *or* of goodbye), without (even) saying hello *or* goodbye
'Gruß|te·le͵gramm *n* greetings telegram; **~wort** *n* (-[e]s; -e) word(s *pl.*) of welcome, opening words *pl.*
Grüt·ze ['grʏtsə] *f* (-; *no pl.*) **1.** groats *pl.*, *Am.* grits *pl.*; porridge; ***rote ~*** *dessert of semi-liquid red fruit*; **2.** F brains *pl.*
Gschaftl·hu·ber ['kʃaftlhu:bɐ] *dial. m*: ***er ist ein richtiger ~*** he has to get himself involved in everything
G-Schlüs·sel *m* ♪ treble clef
gucken ['gʊkən] (*sep.* -k·k-) F (h) **I.** *v/i.* look; peep; stare; ***guck mal!*** look!; ***guck mal, der Wagen da!*** look at that car; ***nicht ~!*** no looking, no peeping; ***laß mich mal ~!*** let me (F let's) have a look; ***guck nicht so skeptisch*** don't look so sceptical (*Am.* skeptical); **II.** *v/t.*: ***Fernsehen ~*** watch (the) television (*or* TV, F telly); **Gucker** ['gʊkɐ] (*sep.* -k·k-) F *m* (-s; -) **1.** telescope; opera glasses *pl.*; **2.** *pl.* F peepers
'Guck·fen·ster *n* peephole
'Guck·ka·sten *m* peep show (box); **~büh·ne** *f* picture-frame stage, proscenium (stage)
'Guck·loch *n* peephole
Gue·ril·la [ge'rɪlja] *m* (-s; -s) guer(r)illa; **~ein·heit** *f* guer(r)illa unit; **~kämp·fer** *m* guer(r)illa (fighter); **~krieg** *m* guer(r)illa warfare (*or* war)
Guil·lo·ti·ne [gɪljo'ti:nə] *f* (-; -n), **guil·lo·ti·nie·ren** [gɪljoti'ni:rən] *v/t.* (h) guillotine
Gu·lasch ['gu:laʃ] *n* (-[e]s; -s, -e) goulash; **~ka͵no·ne** *f* ⚔ field kitchen; **~sup·pe** *f* goulash soup
Gül·le ['gʏlə] *f* (-; *no pl.*) liquid manure
Gul·ly ['gʊli] *m* (-s; -s) drain
gül·tig ['gʏltɪç] *adj.* valid (*a. fig.*); effective, in force; legal; good *coin etc.*; *ticket*: valid, good (***drei Tage*** for three days); (***für***) ***~ erklären, ~ machen*** declare valid; ***~ sein → gelten***; **'Gül·tig·keit** *f* (-; *no pl.*) validity (*a. fig.*); legal force, legality; currency; ***s-e ~ verlieren*** cease to be valid, *contract, passport etc.*: expire; ***~ haben → gelten***
'Gül·tig·keits|be·reich *m* range of validity, scope; **~dau·er** *f* (period of) validity; *usu.* term *of a contract etc.*; life *of a patent etc.*
Gum·mi ['gʊmi] **1.** *m*, *n* (-s; *no pl.*) rubber; **2.** *m*, *n* (-s; -s) gum; **3.** *m* (-s; -s) rubber, eraser; **4.** *n* (-s; -s) rubber (*or* elastic) band; elastic; **5.** F *m* (-s; -s) F rubber; **~ab·satz** *m* rubber heel; **2ar·tig** *adj.* rubbery; **~ball** *m* rubber ball; **~band** *n* (-[e]s; ¨er) elastic band; **~bär(chen** *n*) *m* gummi (*or* jelly) bear; **~baum** *m* gumtree; (India) rubber tree; **~be·griff** *m* elastic concept; **~bei·ne** F *pl.*: ***~ haben*** F have wobbly knees; ***ich habe plötzlich ~ bekommen*** F my knees went all wobbly, my knees turned to jelly; **~boot** *n* rubber dinghy; **~dich·tung** *f* rubber seal
gum·mie·ren [gʊ'mi:rən] *v/t.* (h) gum; ⚙ rubberize; **gum·miert** [gʊ'mi:ɐt] *adj.* gummed; ⚙ rubberized
'Gum·mi|ge·schoß *n* rubber bullet;

~ham·mer *m* rubber mallet; **~hand·schuh** *m* rubber glove; **~harz** *n* gum resin; **~hös·chen** *n*: (**ein** ~ a pair of) rubber pants *pl.*; **~klau·sel** F *f* elastic (*or* catch-all) clause; **~knüp·pel** *m* (rubber) truncheon; **~lin·se** *f phot.* zoom lens; **~lö·we** *fig. m* paper tiger; **~man·tel** *m* rubber coat; **~mat·te** *f* rubber mat; **~pa·ra͵graph** F *m* elastic (*or* catch-all) clause; **~pup·pe** *f* rubber doll; **~rei·fen** *m* (rubber) tyre (*Am.* tire); **~ring** *m* a) rubber band, b) sealing ring, c) rubber ring, quoit; **~schlauch** *m* rubber hose; inner tube; **~schu·he** *pl.* galoshes, rubber overshoes, *Am. a.* rubbers; **~schür·ze** *f* rubber apron; **~soh·le** *f* rubber sole; **~stem·pel** *m* rubber stamp; **~stie·fel** *m* wellington, rubber boot; **~stöp·sel** *m* rubber stopper; **~strumpf** *m* elastic stocking; **~tier** *n* rubber animal; **~͵un·ter·la·ge** *f* rubber sheet; **~zel·le** *f* padded cell; **~zug** *m* elastic

Gunst [gʊnst] *f* (-; *no pl.*) favo(u)r; goodwill; ***in j-s ~ stehen*** be in s.o.'s good graces (F good books); ***um j-s ~ werben*** court (*or* try to win) s.o.'s favo(u)r, woo s.o.; ***j-s ~ verlieren*** fall out of favo(u)r with s.o.; ***zu m-n ~en*** in my favo(u)r; ***Saldo zu Ihren ~en*** balance in your credit; ***die ~ des Augenblicks nutzen*** make hay while the sun shines; → ***zugunsten***; **~be·weis** *m*, **~be·zei·gung** *f* (-; -en) (mark of) favo(u)r

gün·stig ['gʏnstɪç] **I.** *adj.* favo(u)rable (***für*** *acc.* to); positive; opportune, good *time*; promising; good (*a. offer*); ***e-n ~en Augenblick abwarten*** wait for the right moment; ***j-n ~ stimmen*** put s.o. in (*or* get s.o. into) the right mood; ***bei ~em Wetter*** weather permitting; ***im ~sten Fall*** at best; ***sich im ~sten Licht zeigen*** show o.s. off to one's best advantage; † ***zu ~en Bedingungen*** on easy terms; **II.** *adv.* favo(u)rably; positively; ~ ***gesinnt*** well-disposed (*dat.* towards); ~ ***abschneiden*** come off well (***bei*** *dat.* in); ***sich ~ entwickeln für j-n*** work out well for s.o.; ***dort kann man ~ einkaufen*** they're quite cheap; **'gün·stig·sten·falls** *adv.* at best; at (the) most

Günst·ling ['gʏnstlɪŋ] *m* (-s; -e) favo(u)rite; *contp.* minion; **'Günst·lings·wirt·schaft** *f* favo(u)ritism

Gur·gel ['gʊrgəl] *f* (-; -n) throat; ***j-n bei der ~ packen*** grab s.o. by the throat; ***j-m an die ~ springen*** jump at s.o.'s throat; ***j-m die ~ zudrücken*** (*or* ***abdrücken***) *a. fig.* strangle s.o.; F *fig.* ***sein Geld durch die ~ jagen*** F guzzle all one's money away

gur·geln ['gʊrgəln] *v/i. and v/t.* (h) gargle; *water etc.*: gurgle

'Gur·gel·was·ser *n* gargle

Gur·ke ['gʊrkə] *f* (-; -n) **1.** cucumber; gherkin; ***saure ~n*** pickled cucumbers, *Am.* pickles; **2.** F conk, beak; ***e-n auf die ~ kriegen*** F get a bonk (*or* biff) on the nose; **'Gur·ken·sa͵lat** *m* cucumber salad

gur·ren ['gʊrən] *v/i.* (h) coo

Gurt [gʊrt] *m* (-[e]s; -e) belt; strap; waistband; *mot.*, ✈ seatbelt; harness *of parachute*; ⚠ flange

Gür·tel ['gʏrtəl] *m* (-s; -) belt (*a. fig.*); *geogr.* zone; *fig.* ***den ~ enger schnallen*** tighten one's belt; **~li·nie** *f* waistline; ***unter der ~*** *boxing and fig.*: below the belt; **~rei·fen** *m mot.* radial-ply tyre (*Am.* tire); **~ro·se** *f* ⚕ shingles (*sg.*); **~schlau·fe** *f* loop (of a *or* the belt); **~schnal·le** *f* belt buckle; **~tier** *n zo.* armadillo

gur·ten ['gʊrtən] (h) **I.** *v/t.* strap; ⚠ brace; **II.** *v/i. mot.* put one's seatbelt on, strap o.s. in

'Gurt|muf·fel F *m* seatbelt offender; ***ein ~ sein*** *a.* hate wearing seatbelts; **~straf·fer** [-ʃtrafɐ] *m* (-s; -) *mot.* seatbelt tensioner; **~zeug** *n* harness *of parachute*

Gu·ru ['guːru] *m* (-s; -s) *a. fig.* guru

Guß [gʊs] *m* (Gusses; Güsse ['gʏsə]) **1.** jet of water *etc.*; shower, downpour; **2.** a) ⚙ founding, casting (process), b) ⚙ castings *pl.*, c) *typ.* fount, *Am.* font; ***aus einem ~*** made in one casting; *fig.* ***es ist*** (***wie***) ***aus einem ~*** it's a completely rounded piece of work; **3.** *gastr.* glaze, icing; **~as͵phalt** *m* poured asphalt; **~be͵ton** *m* cast concrete; **~ei·sen** *n* cast iron; **2ei·sern** *adj.* cast-iron ... (*a. fig.*); **~form** *f* mo(u)ld

Gu·sto ['gʊsto] *m*: ***nach j-s ~ sein*** be to s.o.'s taste (*or* liking); ***et. nach s-m ~ machen*** do s.th. (just) as one likes (*or* fancies); ***e-n ~ haben auf*** *acc.* feel like *s.th.*; ***mit ~*** with (great) relish *or* gusto

gut [guːt] **I.** *adj.* good; ***mein ~er Anzug*** my good (*or* best) suit; ***aus ~er Familie stammen*** come from a good family; ***sie spricht ein ~es Englisch*** she speaks good English; ***ganz ~*** not bad; ***das ist ganz ~ so, auch ~*** that's all right (*Am.* alright); ***schon ~!*** a) it's all right (*Am.* alright), b) okay, okay, c) that'll do; ***sei so ~ und*** do me a favo(u)r and ..., will you?; ***es ist ganz ~, daß*** it's good that; (***es ist***) ***nur ~, daß*** a good thing (that); ***so ~ wie unmöglich*** virtually impossible; *der Prozeß ist* ***so ~ wie gewonnen*** as good as won; ***so ~ wie fertig*** virtually (*or* more or less) finished; ***so ~ wie kein*** practically (*or* virtually) no; ***so ~ wie nichts*** next to nothing; ***zu ~er Letzt*** finally; → ***zugute***; ***e-e ~e Stunde*** a good hour; ***er ist ein ~er Läufer*** he's a good runner, he's good at running; ***~ sein für*** (*or* ***gegen***) *acc.* be good for *a cold etc.*; ***wozu soll das ~ sein?*** what's that for (F in aid of)?; ***mir ist nicht ~*** I don't feel well; ***nicht mehr ~ sein*** *food*: have gone off (*or* bad), *milk*: have gone off (*or* sour), have turned sour; ***dafür ist er sich zu ~*** he thinks he's above that sort of thing, he thinks it would be beneath him (*or* his dignity); ***~ werden*** turn out all right (*Am.* alright) *or* well; ***es wird schon wieder ~*** it'll all work out in the end; ***~ finden*** like; ***er ist kein besonders ~er Tänzer*** *etc.* he's not much of a dancer *etc.*; *iro.* ***du bist ~!*** I like that!, you're joking, of course; → ***Ding*** 1, ***Glaube, Glück, Gute***[2]; **II.** *adv.* well; ***~ und gern*** at least, easily; ***~ riechen*** (***schmecken***) smell (taste) good; ***~ aussehen*** a) look good, b) be good-looking; look well; ***da kennt sie sich ~ aus*** a) she knows all about that, b) she really knows her way around there; ***~ so!*** good!, well done!; ***paß ~ auf!*** a) watch carefully (now), b) watch yourself; ***dort hatte er es ~*** he was doing all right (*Am.* alright) (for himself) there; ***du hast's ~!*** it's all right (*Am.* alright) for some, you don't know how lucky you are; ***ich kann ihn nicht ~ darum bitten*** I can't really ask him; ***er täte ~ daran zu gehen*** it would be a good idea if he went; ***du hast ~ reden*** (***lachen***) you can talk (laugh, well may you laugh); ***das fängt ja ~ an*** that's a great start; ***das kann ~ sein*** that's quite possible, that may well be; → ***genausogut, gutgehen, gutmachen, guttun, halten*** I, III, ***machen*** I

Gut *n* (-[e]s; Güter ['gyːtɐ]) **1.** property; *pl.* goods, products; 🚂 freight; † assets; ***Hab und ~*** → ***Habe***; (***un***)***bewegliche Güter*** (im)movables; ***nicht für alle Güter der Welt*** not for all the money in the world; ***das höchste ~*** the greatest good; **2.** estate, farm

'Gut·ach·ten *n* (-s; -) expert's opinion; certificate, testimonial; ***ärztliches ~*** medical certificate; **'Gut·ach·ter** [-axtɐ] *m* (-s; -) expert; surveyor; valuer; consultant

'gut|ar·tig *adj.* good-natured, *a.* ⚕ harmless; ⚕ benign *tumo(u)r etc.*; **~aus·se·hend** *adj.* good-looking, attractive; **~be·setzt** *adj. thea. etc.* well-cast; **~es Haus** full house; **~be·tucht** [-bətuːxt] F *adj.* F well-heeled; **~be·zahlt** *adj.* well-paid; **~bür·ger·lich** *adj.* middle-class; **~e Küche** home cooking, *a.* traditional fare; **~do͵tiert** *adj.* well-paid

'Gut·dün·ken *n*: ***nach*** (***eigenem***) ~ at one's own discretion, as one sees fit

Gu·te[1] ['guːtə] *m, f* (-n; -n) good man (woman); ***die ~n*** the good (*pl.*), *bibl.* the righteous (*pl.*); F the goodies

'Gu·te[2] *n* (-n): ***etwas ~s*** (***zu essen***) something nice to eat; ***~s und Böses*** good and evil; ***~s tun*** do good; ***das ~ daran ist*** the good thing about it is; ***die Sache hat auch ihr ~s*** there's a good side to it too; ***des ~n zuviel tun*** overdo it; ***das ist des ~n zuviel*** that's too much of a good thing; ***sich zum ~n wenden*** change for the better; ***~s verheißen*** augur well; ***ich ahne nichts ~s*** I have a strange feeling (something has gone wrong *or* is going to go wrong); ***alles ~!*** all the best; ***daraus wird nichts ~s*** nothing good will come of it; ***im 2n*** amicably, on friendly terms; ***wir sind im 2n auseinandergegangen*** *a.* we parted as friends

Gü·te ['gyːtə] *f* (-; *no pl.*) **1.** goodness, kindness; generosity; (God's) grace; ***in*** (***aller***) ~ amicably; ***haben Sie die ~ zu*** *inf.* would you be so kind as to *inf.*; ***durch die ~ des Herrn X*** through the kindness of Mr X; F (***ach, du***) ***meine ~!*** goodness me!, (my) goodness!; good God!; **2.** quality; grade, class; superior quality; (***von***) ***erster ~*** first-class, first-rate, top-quality ...; *iro. Idiot etc.* ***erster ~*** of the first order; **~grad** *m* quality, grade; **~klas·se** *f* class, grade; **~ 1** Grade A quality; prime ...; **~kon͵trol·le** *f* quality control

Gu·te'nacht|ge·schich·te *f* bedtime story; **~kuß** *m* goodnight kiss; ***j-m e-n ~ geben*** kiss s.o. goodnight

Gü·ter|ab·fer·ti·gung ['gyːtɐ-] *f* dispatch of goods; **~an·nah·me** *f* goods (*Am.* freight) office; **~bahn·hof** *m* goods (*Am.* freight) station; **~fern·ver·kehr** *m* long-haul transportation; **~ge·mein·schaft** *f* ⚖ community of property; joint property; ***in ~ leben*** have joint property, share one's property; **~hal·le** *f* warehouse

'gut·er·hal·ten *adj.* in good condition

Gü·ter|kraft·ver·kehr ['gyːtɐ-] *m* road haulage; **~markt** *m* commodity market;

~nah·ver·kehr *m* short-haul transportation; **~trans,port** *m* transport of goods; **~tren·nung** *f* ⚖ separation of property; ***in ~ leben*** have separate property; **~ver·kehr** *m* goods (*Am.* freight) traffic; **~ver·sand** *m* goods shipment; **~ver·tei·lung** *f* distribution of goods; **~wa·gen** *m* 🚂 goods wag(g)on, *Am.* freight car; **~zug** *m* goods (*Am.* freight) train

'Gü·te|sie·gel *n* seal of quality; **~stem·pel** *m* quality stamp; hallmark (*a. fig.*); **~zei·chen** *n* quality label; seal of approval; hallmark (*a. fig.*)

'gut|ge·ar·tet *adj.* good-natured; **~ge·baut** *adj.* a) well-made, b) well-built; **~ge·fe·dert** *adj.* well-sprung *mattress etc.*

'gut·ge·hen *v/i.* (*irr.*, *sep.*, sn, → ***gehen***) **1.** go well, turn out all right (*Am.* alright); ***das konnte nicht ~*** it was bound to go wrong; ***das kann ja nicht ~*** F there's no way it's going to work; ***wenn das nur gutgeht!*** well, let's just hope for the best; ***das ist noch einmal gutgegangen*** that was close (*or* a close thing), F talk about lucky; **2.** ***mir geht's gut*** a) I'm fine, b) I'm doing fine; ***es sich ~ lassen*** have a good time, enjoy o.s.; **'gut·ge·hend** *adj.* flourishing, thriving

'gut|ge·launt *adj.* in a good mood; **~ge·meint** *adj.* well-meant; **~ge·pflegt** *adj.* well-looked-after; **~ge·pol·stert** *adj.* well-padded; **~ge·sinnt** *adj.* well-meaning

'gut·gläu·big I. *adj.* gullible, credulous; *esp.* ⚖ acting (*or* done) in good faith, bona fide ...; **II.** *adv.* gullibly, credulously; ⚖ in good faith, bona fide; **'Gut·gläu·big·keit** *f* (-; *no pl.*) gullibility, credulity; ⚖ good faith

'Gut·ha·ben I. *n* (-s; -) balance; assets *pl.*; **II.** ♀ *v/t.* (*irr.*, *sep.*, h, → ***haben***) have *s.th.* in hand; ✝ have credit for; ***du hast bei mir noch ein Essen gut*** I still owe you a meal

'gut·hei·ßen *v/t.* (*irr.*, *sep.*, h, → ***heißen***) approve of, sanction

'gut·her·zig *adj.* kind(hearted); **'Gut·her·zig·keit** *f* (-; *no pl.*) kindheartedness

gü·tig ['gy:tɪç] **I.** *adj.* good, kind (***gegen*** *acc.* to); kindhearted; well-meaning; ***mit Ihrer ~en Erlaubnis*** with your kind permission; *iro.* ***zu ~*** too kind (of you); *iro.* ***würdest du so ~ sein zu*** *inf.* would you be so kind as to *inf.*; **II.** *adv.* kindly; ***wollen Sie mir ~st gestatten, daß ich ...*** *a. iro.* (will you) kindly allow me to *inf.*

güt·lich ['gy:tlɪç] **I.** *adj.* amicable; **II.** *adv.*: ***sich ~ einigen*** come to (*or* reach) a friendly agreement, ***über*** *acc.*: settle *s.th.* amicably; ***sich ~ tun*** have a good time, enjoy o.s., ***an*** *dat.*: eat (*or* drink) one's fill of; ***sie taten sich an s-n Zigarren ~*** they helped themselves to his cigars

'gut·ma·chen *v/t.* (*sep.*, h) **1.** make up for; **2.** make *10 dollars etc.*; make up *time etc.*

'gut·mü·tig [-my:tɪç] *adj.* good-natured; **'Gut·mü·tig·keit** *f* (-; *no pl.*) good-naturedness

'gut·nach·bar·lich *adj.* neighbo(u)rly; ***zwischen ihnen bestehen ~e Beziehungen*** they get on well (enough) with each other

'gut·sa·gen *v/i.* (*sep.*, h) vouch (***für*** *acc.* for)

'Guts·be·sit·zer *m* landowner

'Gut·schein *m* voucher; gift token

'gut·schrei·ben *v/t.* (*irr.*, *sep.*, h, → ***schreiben***) credit; ***j-m e-n Betrag ~*** credit a sum to s.o.; ***e-n Betrag e-m Konto ~*** credit an account with an amount, credit an amount to an account; **'Gut·schrift** *f* (-; -en) credit entry; credit slip

'Guts|haus *n* manor house; **~herr** *m* **1.** *hist.* lord of the manor; **2.** estate owner; owner of the estate; **~hof** *m* estate; farm

'gut·si·tu·iert [-zitu,i:ɐt] *adj.* well-off, well-to-do, moneyed

'gut·sit·zend *adj.*: ***ein ~er Anzug*** a suit that fits properly (*or* well)

'gut·tun *v/i.* (*irr.*, *sep.*, h, → ***tun***) *dat.* do *s.o. or s.th.* good; *dat. or* ***bei*** *dat.* ~ be good for; ***sehr ~*** do a lot of good; ***das tut gut!*** that's just what I need, that feels good, that's better, what a relief; ***das tut ihm gut!*** *a. iro.* he could do with that; ***j-m nicht ~*** *drug etc.*: disagree with s.o.; ***das tut d-m Magen nicht gut*** it's no good for your stomach, it won't do your stomach any good

gut·tu·ral [gʊtu'ra:l] *adj.* guttural

Gut·tu'ral *m* (-s; -e), **~laut** *m ling.* guttural (sound)

'gut·un·ter,rich·tet *adj.* well-informed

'gut·ver·die·nend *adj.*: ***er ist ein ~er Mann*** he earns a good (*or* decent) salary

'gut·ver·träg·lich *adj. drug etc.*: well-tolerated; *w.s.* kind to the stomach; gentle, gentle-action ...; hypoallergenic

'gut·wil·lig I. *adj.* willing; obliging; voluntary; **II.** *adv.* willingly *etc.*; of one's own accord (*or* free will)

Gym·na·si·al|bil·dung [gʏmna'zi̯a:l-] *f* grammar (*Am.* high) school education; **~leh·rer** *m* grammar (*Am.* high) school teacher

Gym·na·si·ast [gʏmna'zi̯ast] *m* (-en; -en), **Gym·na·sia·stin** [gʏmna'zi̯astɪn] *f* (-; -nen) grammar (school) pupil, *Am.* high school student

Gym·na·si·um [gʏm'na:zi̯ʊm] *n* (-s; -ien) grammar (*Am.* high) school

Gym·na·stik [gʏm'nastɪk] *f* (-; *no pl.*) exercises *pl.*; gymnastics *pl.*; ***~ machen*** a) do gymnastics, b) do (one's) exercises; ***die tägliche ~*** *a.* F one's daily dozen; **~leh·rer** *m* PE (= physical education) instructor

gym·na·stisch [gʏm'nastɪʃ] *adj.* gymnastic; ***~e Übungen*** physical exercises

Gy·nä·ko·lo·ge [gʏnɛko'lo:gə] *m* (-n; -n) gyn(a)ecologist, F gyny; **Gy·nä·ko·lo·gie** [gʏnɛkolo'gi:] *f* (-; *no pl.*) gyn(a)ecology; **Gy·nä·ko·lo·gin** [gʏnɛko'lo:gɪn] *f* (-; -nen) (woman) gyn(a)ecologist, F gyny; **gy·nä·ko·lo·gisch** [gʏnɛko'lo:gɪʃ] *adj.* gyn(a)ecological

H

H, h [haː] *n* (-; -) H, h; ♪ B
ha [ha, haː] *int.* **1.** ah!, aha!; **2.** ha!
hä [hɛː] *int.* **1.** eh?; **2.** heh(, heh)!
Haar [haːɐ] *n* (-[e]s; -e [ˈhaːrə]) hair (*a.* ⚘); ***sich die ~e schneiden lassen*** get a haircut; ***du mußt dir mal die ~e schneiden lassen*** it's time you had a haircut; ***j-n an den ~en ziehen*** pull s.o.'s hair; *fig.* ***sich die ~e (aus)raufen*** tear one's hair (out); ***ich könnte mir die ~e ausraufen*** I could kick myself; ***aufs ~*** to a T; ***sich aufs ~ gleichen*** look absolutely identical, be as alike as two peas in a pod; ***um ein ~ wäre ich überfahren worden*** I just missed being run over by the skin of my teeth; ***um ein ~ hätten wir uns verpaßt*** we very nearly missed each other; ***um ein ~ hätte er gewonnen*** *etc.* he came within a whisper of winning *etc.*; ***um kein ~ besser*** not a bit better; ***~e spalten*** split hairs; ***j-m kein ~ krümmen*** not to touch a hair on s.o.'s head; ***er ließ kein gutes ~ an ihm*** he picked (*or* pulled) him to pieces, he didn't have a good word to say about him; ***an e-m ~ hängen*** hang by a thread; ***sie hat ~e auf den Zähnen*** she's a tough one, *sl.* she's a bitch; ***sich in die ~e geraten*** get into each other's hair; ***sich in den ~en liegen*** be at each other, be at loggerheads; ***(immer) ein ~ in der Suppe finden*** (always) find s.th. to criticize (*or* quibble about); ***an den ~en herbeigezogen*** far-fetched; ***die ~e standen mir zu Berge, mir sträubten sich die ~e*** it made my hair stand on end; ***laß dir deshalb keine grauen ~e wachsen*** don't lose any sleep over it; ***schwer ~e lassen (müssen)*** a) suffer heavy losses, pay dearly, b) take a real beating, F cop it hard
ˈHaar|an·satz *m* hairline; **~aus·fall** *m* hair loss, 📖 alopecia; **~balg** *m* hair follicle; **~band** *n* (-[e]s; ⸚er) hairband; (hair) ribbon; **~bo·den** *m* scalp; **~breit** *fig. n* **1.** ***nicht ein ~ (weichen*** *or* ***nachgeben)*** not (to give *or* budge) an inch; **2.** → ***Haaresbreite***; **~bür·ste** *f* hairbrush; **~bü·schel** *n* tuft of hair
haa·ren [ˈhaːrən] *v/i. and v/refl.* ***(sich ~)*** (h) lose (*or* shed) one's hair; *fur etc.*: lose (*or* shed) hairs
ˈHaar|ent·fer·ner [-ɛntfɛrnɐ] *m* (-s; -) depilatory (cream); **~er·satz** *m* false hair; wigs and toupets *pl.*
Haa·res·brei·te [ˈhaːrəs-] *f*: ***um ~*** by a hair's breadth; ***nicht um ~*** not an inch; → ***Haar***
Haa·re·schnei·den [ˈhaːrə-] *n* (-s) haircut
ˈHaar|far·be *f* colo(u)r of hair; ***was hat er für e-e ~?*** what colo(u)r hair has he got?; **~fa·ser** *f* capillary fib|re (*Am.* -er); **~fe·der** *f* ⚙ hairspring
ˈhaar·fein *adj.* **1.** ***~er Riß*** *etc.* hairline crack *etc.*; **2.** *fig.* subtle
ˈHaar|fe·sti·ger [-fɛstɪgɐ] *m* (-s; -) setting lotion; **~filz** *m* fur felt; **~fol,li·kel** *m* hair follicle; **~ge·fäß** *n* capillary (vessel)
ˈhaar·ge·nau I. *adj.* exact, (very) precise; **II.** *adv.* exactly, (very) precisely; to a T; ***das stimmt ~*** that's exactly right, F (that's) spot on; ***et. ~ kennen*** know s.th. like the back of one's hand
haa·rig [ˈhaːrɪç] *adj.* hairy (*a.* F *fig.*), *formal*: hirsute, ⚘ pilous
ˈHaar|kamm *m* (hair)comb; **~klam·mer** *f* → ***Haarklemme***; **~kleid** *n* coat of hair
ˈhaar·klein F *adv. describe etc.* down to the last detail; *calculate etc.* down to the last cent
ˈHaar|klem·me *f* hair clip, *Am. a.* bobby pin; **~krank·heit** *f* hair disease; **~kranz** *m* fringe of hair; **~locke** *f* curl; lock
ˈhaar·los *adj.* hairless; bald
ˈHaar|mit·tel *n* hair restorer; **~mo·de** *f* **1.** hairstyle; **2.** hair fashion(s *pl.*)
ˈHaar·na·del *f* hairpin; **~kur·ve** *f* hairpin bend
ˈHaar|netz *n* hairnet; **~öl** *n* hair oil
ˈHaar·pfle·ge *f* hair care; **~mit·tel** *n*, **~pro,dukt** *n* hair-care product
ˈHaar·riß *m* hairline crack; craze
haarˈscharf I. *adj.* very clear; very precise; very fine *distinction*; **II.** *adv.*: ***der Wagen fuhr ~ an mir vorbei*** the car missed me by an inch; ***~ e-m Unfall entgehen*** just miss having an accident; ***das hat er ~ erkannt*** he spotted it right away; ***das hast du ~ beobachtet*** very clever of you to notice that; ***~ unterscheiden*** make a very fine distinction (between)
ˈHaar|schlei·fe *f* (hair) ribbon, bow; **~schmuck** *m* hair accessories *pl.*; ***sie trägt nie ~*** she never wears anything in her hair; **~schnei·den** *n* haircut; **~schnitt** *m* haircut; **~schopf** *m* shock of hair; **~schup·pen** *pl.* dandruff *sg.*; **~sieb** *n* hair sieve
ˈHaar·spal·ter [-ʃpaltɐ] *m*: ***ein ~ sein*** like to split hairs; **Haar·spal·te·rei** [-ʃpaltəˈraɪ] *f* (-; -en) *a. pl.* splitting hairs; ***das ist reine ~*** that's just splitting hairs; ***~ treiben*** split hairs; **ˈhaar·spal·te·risch** [-ʃpaltərɪʃ] *adj.* hair-splitting
ˈHaar|span·ge *f* (hair) slide, *Am.* barrette; **~spray** *n, m* hairspray; **~sträh·ne** *f* strand of hair
ˈhaar·sträu·bend *adj.* dreadful; incredible; outrageous; ***das ist ja ~*** it's enough to make your hair stand on end
ˈHaar|strich *m* hairstroke; **~stu·dio** *n* hair stylist's; hairdresser's; **~teil** *n* hairpiece; **~tracht** *f* hairstyle; **~trock·ner** *m* hair drier; **~ver·pflan·zung** *f* hair transplant; **~wa·schen** *n* **1.** shampoo, wash; **2.** washing one's hair; ***bei jedem ~*** every time you wash your hair; **~wasch·mit·tel** *n* shampoo; **~was·ser** *n* hair tonic; **~wuchs** *m* a) growth of (the) hair, b) hair; **~wuchs·mit·tel** *n* hair restorer; **~wur·zel** *f* root of a (*or* the) hair; *fig.* ***bis zu den ~n erröten*** blush to the roots of one's hair
Hab [haːp] *without art.*: ***all sein ~ und Gut*** everything (he owns *or* owned)
Ha·be [ˈhaːbə] *f* (-; *no pl.*) property, possessions *pl.*; personal effects *pl.*; ***bewegliche ~*** movables; ***unbewegliche ~*** immovables, real estate
ha·ben [ˈhaːbən] (hatte, gehabt, h) **I.** *v/t.* have (got); ***sie will es so ~*** that's the way she wants it; ***das werden wir gleich ~!*** no problem, we'll have that done (*or* fixed) in no time; ***ich hab's bald*** (I'm) nearly finished; ***hast du's bald?*** how much longer are you going to take?; ***et. hinter sich ~*** have been through s.th.; ***das hätten wir hinter uns*** well, that's that; ***das ~ wir noch vor uns*** that's still to come, we've still got that to come; ***unter sich ~*** be in charge of, command; F ***es im Hals ~*** have a sore throat; F ***ich hab's nicht mit ihr (mit Pizza)*** I don't like *or* get on with her (I don't go for pizzas); ***zu ~*** *goods*: available, *house*: up for sale; ***ist es noch zu ~?*** *a.* is it still going?; F ***sie ist noch zu ~*** F she's still up for grabs; F ***ich hab's!*** (I've) got it!; F ***da hast du's!*** there you are, I told you so; ***was hast du?*** what's up (*or* wrong)?; F ***und damit hat sich's!*** and that's final; F ***er hat's ja!*** he can afford it; ***er hat Geburtstag*** it's his birthday; ***wir ~ April*** it's April; ***welche Farbe ~ s-e Augen?*** what colo(u)r are his eyes?; F ***hat man den Dieb schon?*** have they caught the thief yet?; ***es hat viel für sich*** there's a lot to be said for it; ***ich habe an ihm e-n Freund*** I have a friend in him; ***e-n Italiener zum Chef ~*** have an Italian boss; ***er hat etwas Überspanntes an sich*** there's something eccentric about him; ***er hat das so an sich*** that's just the way he is; F ***es hat sich was damit*** it's not that easy; F ***hat sich was!*** some hope; F ***hat sie was mit ihm?*** is there something going on between them?; F ***die Sache hat es in sich*** it's not easy, F it's a tough one; ***er hat viel von s-m Vater*** he takes after his father; ***woher hast du das?*** a) where did you get that from?, b) where did you hear that?; ***was hast du gegen ihn?*** what have you got against him?; ***jetzt ~ wir's nicht mehr weit*** not far to go now; ***dafür bin ich nicht zu ~*** you can count me out, that's not (really) my thing; ***für ein Bier bin ich immer zu ~*** I'm always game for a beer; ***was habe***

ich davon? what do I get out of it?, F what for?; ***das hast du jetzt davon*** see?; ***das hast du davon, wenn*** that's what you get from *ger.*; → ***Anschein, Auge*** 1, ***gehabt, gern***; **II.** F *v/refl.*: ***hab dich nicht so*** don't make such a fuss, don't take on like that; ***der hat sich vielleicht mit s-n Platten*** what a fuss he makes about his records; ***und damit hat sich's!*** and that's that; **III.** *v/aux.* have; ***hast du ihn gesehen?*** have you seen him?; ***du hättest es mir sagen sollen*** you should have told me; ***er hätte es machen können*** he could have done it

'Ha·ben *n* (-s; *no pl.*) ✝ credit (side); ***Soll und ~*** credit and debit

Ha·be·nichts ['ha:bənıçts] *hum. m* (-[es]; -e) have-not (*pl.* have-nots)

'Ha·ben|sal·do *m* credit balance; **~sei·te** *f* credit side; **~zin·sen** *pl.* credit interest *sg.*, interest *sg.* on deposits

Hab·gier ['ha:p-] *f* greed, avarice; **'hab·gie·rig** *adj.* greedy, grasping

hab·haft ['ha:phaft] *adj.*: ***~ werden*** *gen.* get hold of, *a.* seize, catch *s.o.*

Ha·bicht ['ha:bıçt] *m* (-s; -e) hawk; **'Ha·bichts·na·se** *f* hooked nose

Ha·bi·li·ta·ti·on [habilita'tsĭo:n] *f* (-; -en) *univ.* habilitation; *postdoctoral qualification*; **Ha·bi·li·ta·ti'ons·schrift** *f postdoctoral thesis*; **ha·bi·li·tie·ren** [habili'ti:rən] *v/i. and v/refl.* (***sich ~***) (h) habilitate; *obtain one's postdoctoral qualification*

Ha·bi·tat [habi'ta:t] *n* (-s; -e) *zo.* habitat

ha·bi·tu·ell [habi'tŭɛl] **I.** *adj.* habitual; **II.** *adv.* habitually, as a habit

Ha·b·itus ['ha:bitʊs] *m* (-; *no pl.*) **1.** bearing, deportment; disposition; **2.** *zo.* habit

Hab·se·lig·kei·ten ['ha:p-] *pl.* belongings, F bits and pieces

Hab·sucht ['ha:p-] *f*, **'hab·süch·tig** *adj.* → ***Habgier, habgierig***

Ha·ché [ha'ʃe:, a'ʃe:] *n* (-s; -s) *gastr.* hash

Hach·se ['haksə] *f* (-; -n) *zo.* hock; *gastr.* knuckles *pl.*; F *pl.* F pins, ham hocks

Hack|beil ['hak-] *n* chopper; **~block** *m* chopping block; **~bra·ten** *m* meat loaf; **~brett** *n* **1.** chopping board; **2.** ♪ dulcimer

Hacke¹ ['hakə] (*sep.* -k·k-) *f* (-; -n) ⚒ hoe, pick, pickax, *Brit.* pickaxe

'Hacke² (*sep.* -k·k-) *f* (-; -n) *anat.* heel; ***j-m auf die ~n treten*** tread on s.o.'s heels; ***j-m dicht auf den ~n sein*** be hard (*or* hot) on s.o.'s heels; ***die ~n zusammenschlagen*** click one's heels; → ***ablaufen*** 6

hacken¹ ['hakən] (*sep.* -k·k-) *v/t. and v/i.* (h) hack, ⚒ *a.* hoe; chop *wood etc.*; pick, peck (***nach*** *dat.* at)

'hacken² (*sep.* -k·k-) *v/i.* (h) *computer*: hack

'Hacken·trick *m soccer*: backheeler

Hacke·pe·ter ['hakəpe:tɐ] (*sep.* -k·k-) *m* (-s; *no pl.*) *raw minced meat mixed with onions and spices*

Hacker ['hakɐ] (*sep.* -k·k-) *m* (-s; -) *computer*: hacker

Hack|fleisch ['hak-] *n* minced (*Am.* ground) meat, mincemeat; *Am. a.* hamburger; F *fig.* ***aus j-m ~ machen*** F make mincemeat of s.o.; **~mes·ser** *n* chopper; **~ord·nung** *f zo. and fig.* pecking order

Häck·sel ['hɛksəl] *m, n* (-s; *no pl.*) ⚒ chaff, chopped straw

Hack·steak ['hak-] *n* beefburger, hamburger

Ha·der ['ha:dɐ] *m* (-s; *no pl.*) quarrel(l)ing; discord; **ha·dern** ['ha:dɐn] *v/i.* (h) quarrel (***mit*** *dat.* with)

Ha·fen¹ ['ha:fən] *m* (-s; Häfen ['hɛ:fən]) harbo(u)r, port; dock(s *pl.*); *fig.* haven; *fig.* ***in den ~ der Ehe einlaufen*** be joined in holy matrimony

'Ha·fen² *dial. m* (-s; -) pot

'Ha·fen|an·la·gen *pl.* docks; **~ar·bei·ter** *m* docker, *Am.* longshoreman; **~becken** *n* harbo(u)r basin, (wet) dock; **~be·hör·de** *f* port authorities *pl.*; **~damm** *m* pier, jetty; **~ein·fahrt** *f* harbo(u)r entrance; **~ge·büh·ren** *pl.* harbo(u)r dues; **~ka·pi,tän** *m*, **~mei·ster** *m* harbo(u)r master; **~mo·le** *f* mole; **~po·li,zei** *f* harbo(u)r police; **~rund·fahrt** *f* (boat) trip around a (*or* the) harbo(u)r; **~schleu·se** *f* dock gate(s *pl.*); **~sper·re** *f* barrage; embargo; blockade; **~stadt** *f* (sea)port; **~vier·tel** *n* dock area, docklands *pl.*

Ha·fer ['ha:fɐ] *m* (-s; *no pl.*) oats *pl.*; *fig.* ***dich sticht wohl der ~*** *iro.* are you feeling all right (*Am.* alright)?; **~brei** *m* porridge, *Am.* (cooked) oatmeal; **~brot** *n* oatmeal bread; **~flocken** *pl.* porridge oats, *Am.* oatmeal *sg.*; **~grüt·ze** *f* groats *pl.*, grits *pl.*; **~kleie** *f* oat bran; **~mehl** *n* oatmeal; **~schleim** *m*, **~schleim·sup·pe** *f* gruel

Haff [haf] *n* (-[e]s; -e) lagoon

Haft [haft] *f* (-; *no pl.*) custody; detention; imprisonment; ***strenge ~*** close confinement; ***in ~*** under arrest, in custody; ***zu drei Jahren ~ verurteilt werden*** be sentenced to three years' imprisonment (*or* three years in prison), be given a three-year (prison) sentence; ***aus der ~ entlassen*** release (from custody); ***in ~ behalten*** detain, hold in custody; ***in ~ nehmen*** take into custody, place under detention; **~an·stalt** *f* prison; detention cent|re (*Am.* -er); **~aus·set·zung** *f* suspended prison sentence

'haft·bar *adj.* responsible, ⚖ liable (***für*** *acc.* for); ***~ sein (für)*** → ***haften*** 2; ***j-n ~ machen für*** make s.o. liable for, hold s.o. responsible for; **'Haft·bar·keit** *f* (-; *no pl.*) responsibility, liability

'Haft|be·din·gun·gen *pl.* prison conditions; **~be·fehl** *m* arrest warrant; ***e-n ~ gegen j-n erlassen*** issue a warrant for s.o.'s arrest; **~be·schwer·de** *f*: (***~ einlegen*** lodge *or* make an) appeal against (a) remand in custody; **~dau·er** *f* term of confinement

haf·ten ['haftən] *v/i.* (h) **1.** cling, stick (***an*** *dat.* to); *fig.* ***~ an*** *dat.* focus on, revolve around; ***im Gedächtnis ~*** stick (in one's mind); **2.** ⚖ be liable, be responsible, answer (*all* ***für*** *acc.* for); be held responsible (for); ***~ für*** *acc.* guarantee; **~blei·ben** *v/i.* (*irr.*, *sep.*, sn, → ***bleiben***) → ***haften*** 1; ***bei ihr bleibt nichts haften*** F it's in one ear and out (of) the other (with her)

'Haft|ent·las·se·ne *m, f* (-n; -n) released prisoner; **~ent·las·sung** *f* release (from prison *or* custody); **~ent·schä·di·gung** *f* compensation for wrongful imprisonment

'haft·fä·hig *adj.* **1.** adhesive; ***~ sein*** *a.* stick; **2.** ⚖ fit to undergo detention; **'Haft·fä·hig·keit** *f* (-; *no pl.*) **1.** adhesive power(s *pl.*); **2.** ⚖ fitness to undergo detention

Häft·ling ['hɛftlıŋ] *m* (-s; -e) prisoner; ***politischer ~*** *a.* political detainee

'Häft·lings|klei·dung *f* prison clothes *pl.*; **~re,vol·te** *f* prison(ers') revolt

'Haft·lo,kal *n* detention room; ⚔ guard room, *Am.* guardhouse

'Haft·pflicht *f* (-; *no pl.*) liability; **'haft·pflich·tig** *adj.* liable (***für*** *acc.* for); **'Haft·pflicht·ver·si·che·rung** *f* third party insurance

'Haft|psy,cho·se *f* prison psychosis; **~pul·ver** *n* denture fixative; **~rich·ter** *m* committing magistrate; **~scha·le** *f opt.* contact lens; **~schicht** *f* adhesive surface; **~sitz** *m* ⚙ tight fit; **~stra·fe** *f* prison sentence

'haft·un·fä·hig *adj.* ⚖ unfit to undergo detention; **'Haft·un·fä·hig·keit** *f* (-; *no pl.*) unfitness to undergo detention

Haf·tung ['haftʊŋ] *f* (-; -en) **1.** adhesion; ⚗ absorption; **2.** ⚖ liability; guarantee; ***beschränkte (persönliche) ~*** limited (personal) liability; ***Gesellschaft mit beschränkter ~*** private limited (liability) company

'Haf·tungs|be·schrän·kung *f* restriction of liability; **~ver·hält·nis·se** *pl.* contingent liabilities

'Haft·ur·laub *m* prisoner's leave

'Haft·ver·mö·gen *n* adhesive power(s *pl.*)

Ha·ge·but·te ['ha:gəbʊtə] *f* (-; -n) ⚘ rose hip; **'Ha·ge·but·ten·tee** *m* rose hip tea

Ha·ge·dorn ['ha:gədɔrn] *m* (-s; -e) ⚘ hawthorn

Ha·gel ['ha:gəl] *m* (-s; *no pl.*) hail; *fig. a.* shower; volley, torrent *of abuse etc.*; ***ein ~ von Protesten*** a volley of protest; **2dicht** *fig. adv.* thick and fast; **~korn** *n* hailstone

ha·geln ['ha:gəln] *v/i. and v/t.* (h) hail (*a. fig.*); *fig.* ***die Schläge hagelten auf ihn nieder*** the blows rained down on him; ***es hagelte Vorwürfe*** there was a volley of reproaches, ***auf ihn:*** he was showered with reproaches

'Ha·gel|scha·den *m* damage caused by hail; **~schau·er** *m* hailstorm; **~schlag** *m* **1.** (heavy) hail(storm); **2.** damage caused by hail; **~schlo·ße** [-ʃlo:sə] *f* (-; -n) hailstone; **~sturm** *m* hailstorm; **~ver·si·che·rung** *f* hail insurance; **~wet·ter** *n* hailstorm(s *pl.*)

ha·ger ['ha:gɐ] *adj.* lean, gaunt

Ha·gio·gra·phie [hagĭogra'fi:] *f* (-; -n) hagiography

ha·ha [ha'ha:] *int.* ha ha!

Hä·her ['hɛ:ɐ] *m* (-s; -) jay

Hahn [ha:n] *m* (-[e]s; Hähne ['hɛ:nə]) **1.** a) *zo.* cock, rooster, b) weathercock; ***junger ~*** cockerel; *fig.* ***~ im Korb*** cock of the walk; ***es kräht kein ~ danach*** F nobody cares two hoots about it; **2.** ⚙ tap, *Am. a.* faucet; spigot; ***den ~ aufdrehen (zudrehen)*** turn the tap on (off); *fig.* ***j-m den ~ zudrehen*** stop giving (*or* sending) s.o. money; ***e-m Institut*** *etc.* ***den ~ zudrehen*** axe (*Am.* ax) an institute's *etc.* funds; **3.** *rifle*: hammer

Hähn·chen ['hɛ:nçən] *n* (-s; -) chicken; ***ein halbes ~*** half a chicken

Hah·nen|fuß ['ha:nən-] *m* (-es; *no pl.*) ⚘ crowfoot; **~kamm** *m a.* ⚘ cockscomb; **~kampf** *m* cockfight; **~schrei** *m*: *fig.* ***mit dem ersten ~*** at the crack of dawn; **~sporn** *m* cockspur; **~tritt** *m* **1.** *biol.* cock tread; **2.** *textil.* dog's-tooth check

Hahn·rei ['ha:nraı] *obs. m* (-s; -e) cuckold; ***zum ~ machen*** cuckold

Hai [haı] *m* (-[e]s; -e), **'Hai·fisch** *m* shark;

'**Hai·fisch·flos·sen·sup·pe** *f* sharkfin soup

Hain [haın] *lit. m* (-[e]s; -e) grove

Hai·tia·ner [hai'tĭa:nɐ] *m* (-s; -), **Hai·tia·ne·rin** [hai'tĭa:nərın] *f* (-; -nen), **hai·tia·nisch** [hai'tĭa:nıʃ] *adj.* Haitian

Häk·chen ['hɛ:kçən] *n* (-s; -) **1.** small hook; **2.** tick, *Am.* check; **3.** *ling.* apostrophe

Hä·kel·ar·beit ['hɛ:kəl-] *f*, **Hä·ke·lei** [hɛ:kə'laı] *f* (-; -en) crochet work; **hä·keln** ['hɛ:kəln] *v/t. and v/i.* (h) crochet; '**Hä·kel·na·del** *f* crochet needle (*or* hook)

ha·ken ['ha:kən] (h) **I.** *v/t.* hook (***an*** *acc.* onto *or* into); ***sich ~ an*** *dat.* catch (*or* be caught) on *or* in; **II.** *v/i.* get (*or* be) stuck *or* jammed

'**Ha·ken** *m* (-s; -) **1.** hook; peg; ***e-n ~ schlagen*** *hare etc.*: double back; **2.** tick, *Am.* check; **3.** ***~ und Öse*** hook and eye; F *fig.* ***mit ~ und Ösen spielen*** *sport*: play dirty; **4.** *boxing*: ***linker*** (***rechter***) ***~*** left (right) hook; **5.** *fig.* ***die Sache muß doch e-n ~ haben*** there must be a catch to it (somewhere); ***der ~ daran ist*** the (only) problem *or* thing is; ***ohne ~*** no strings attached; ***da sitzt der ~*** that's where the problem is (*or* lies)

'**ha·ken·för·mig** [-fœrmıç] *adj.* hooked

'**Ha·ken|kreuz** *n* swastika; **~na·se** *f* hooked nose; **~wurm** *m* hookworm

Ha·la·li [hala'li:] *n* (-s; -[s]) death halloo, mort; ***das ~ blasen*** sound the mort

halb [halp] **I.** *adj.* half; ***e-e ~e Stunde*** half an hour; ***~ drei*** half past two; ***~ Deutschland*** half of Germany; ♪ ***~e Note*** minim, *Am.* half note; ♪ ***~e Pause*** minim (*Am.* half note) rest; ***auf ~er Höhe*** halfway (up); ***die ~e Summe*** half the amount; ***zum ~en Preis*** for half the price, (at) half-price; ***nichts 2es und nichts Ganzes*** neither fish nor fowl; ***keine ~en Sachen machen*** not to do anything by halves; ***die ~e Wahrheit*** a half-truth; ***mit ~em Herzen*** half-hearted(ly); ***j-m auf ~em Wege entgegenkommen*** meet s.o. halfway; ***sich auf ~em Wege einigen*** meet halfway; ***er hörte nur mit ~em Ohr zu*** he was only half listening, he was just listening with one ear; F ***es dauert e-e ~e Ewigkeit*** F it's taking an age and a half; **II.** *adv.* half; almost; virtually; ***~ soviel*** half as much; ***~ und ~*** half and half, partly, (*a.* ***~e-~e***) fifty-fifty; ***~e-~e machen mit j-m*** go halves with s.o.; ***es ist ~ so schlimm*** (*or* ***wild***) it's not as bad as all that (*or* as we *etc.* thought); ***~ herausfordernd, ~ abwehrend*** half in challenge, half in defen|ce (*Am.* -se); ***~ Mensch, ~ Tier*** half-human, half-beast; ***das ist ja ~ geschenkt*** that's a give-away; ***sich ~ totlachen*** F (nearly) kill o.s. laughing; ***damit war die Sache ~ gewonnen*** that was half the battle; ***ich wünsche ~, daß*** I half wish (that); ***ich dachte mir schon ~*** I half suspected, I had a feeling; ***es war mir nur ~ bewußt*** I was only half aware of it

'**Halb|ach·se** *f* ⩓ semiaxis; ⚙ half axle; **~af·fe** *m* lemur; **2amt·lich** *adj.* semi-official; ***~e Meldung*** unconfirmed report; **~är·mel** *m* half-sleeve; **~au·to,mat** *m* semi-automatic machine(ry *a. pl.*); **2au·to,ma·tisch** *adj.* semi-automatic; **~band** *m* (-[e]s; ⸚e) *typ.* half-binding; **2be·klei·det** *adj.* half-dressed; **2be·wußt** *adj.* semiconscious; **~bil·dung** *contp. f* superficial knowledge, semi-literacy; **2bit·ter** *adj.* plain *chocolate*; **2blind** *adj.* semi-blind, partially blind

'**Halb·blut** *n* (-[e]s; *no pl.*) a) half-caste, b) *zo.* half-breed; '**Halb·blü·ter** [-bly:tɐ] *m* (-s; -) *zo.* half-breed; '**halb·blü·tig** [-bly:tıç] *adj.* half-breed *horse*

'**Halb|bril·le** *f*: (***e-e ~*** a pair of) half-moon glasses *pl.*; **~bru·der** *m* half-brother; **~cou,sin** *m*, **~cou,si·ne** *f* second cousin; **2dun·kel** *adj.* dimly-lit *room etc.*; dusky; **~dun·kel** *n* semi-darkness, twilight; **2,durch·läs·sig** *adj.* semi-permeable, semi-porous; **2,durch·sich·tig** *adj.* translucent

Hal·be ['halbə] *f* (-; -n) pint (of beer)

'**Halb·edel·stein** *m* semi-precious stone

...hal·ben [-halbən], **...hal·ber** [-halbɐ] *in cpds.* a) on account of, due to, b) for the sake of, c) for; ***gesundheitshalber*** for reasons of health, for health reasons, on grounds of health

'**halb|er·fro·ren** *adj.* half-frozen, F frozen to death; **~er·ha·ben** *adj. and adv.* (in) half relief; **~er·stickt** *adj.* half-suffocated; choked *voice*; **~er·wach·sen** *adj.* almost grown-up; ***~e Kinder*** *a.* teenage children

'**Halb·er·zeug·nis** *n* semi-finished product

'**halb|fer·tig** *adj.* half-done, half-finished; ⚙ semi-finished; *fig.* half-baked; **~fest** *adj.* semi-solid; soft *ice*; **~fett** *adj.* **1.** medium-fat *cheese etc.*; **2.** *typ.* semi-bold

'**Halb|fi,na·le** *n* semi-final; **~flie·gen·ge·wicht(ler** *m*) *n* light flyweight; **2flüs·sig** *adj.* semi-liquid; **~for,mat** *n phot.* half-frame

'**halb·gar** *adj.* underdone, rare

'**halb·ge·bil·det** *adj.* half-educated, semi-literate; '**Halb·ge·bil·de·te** *m, f* (-n; -n) F half-wit; *pl. a.* bunch *sg.* of half-wits, uneducated lot *sg.*

'**Halb|ge·fro·re·ne** *n* (-n; *no pl.*) *gastr.* parfait, soft ice; **~ge·schoß** *n* ⩓ mezzanine; **~ge·schwi·ster** *pl.* half-brothers, half-sisters; half-brother(s) and -sister(s); ***er und sie sind ~*** he's her half-brother; she's his half-sister; **~gott** *m* demigod; F *fig.* ***~ in Weiß*** F white-coated wizard, miracle-worker (in white); **~göt·tin** *f* demigoddess

'**Halb·heit** *f* (-; -en) half measure; ***er mag keine ~en*** he doesn't like doing things by halves (*or* in half measures)

'**halb|her·zig** *adj.* half-hearted(ly *adv.*); **~hoch I.** *adj.* medium-high (*or* -sized); low *table etc.*; *sport*: hip-high *shot*; **II.** *adv.*: ***~ gefüllt*** half full, ***mit*** *dat.*: half-full with, half-filled with

'**Halb·idi,ot** *contp. m* F cretin

hal·bie·ren [hal'bi:rən] *v/t.* (h) halve, cut in half, divide in half (*or* in two), F split in half (*or* in two); *fig.* halve, cut by (*or* in) half; ⩓ bisect; **Hal'bie·rung** *f* (-; -en) halving; ✂, ⩓ bisection

Hal'bie·rungs|ebe·ne *f*, **~flä·che** *f* ⩓ bisecting plane; **~li·nie** *f* ⩓ bisecting line, bisector

'**Halb|in·sel** *f* peninsula; **~in·va,li·de** *m* semi-invalid; **~jahr** *n* half-year; (period of) six months *pl.*

'**Halb·jah·res...** *in cpds. usu.* half-yearly; six-month; **~be·richt** *m* ✝ semi-annual report; **~zeug·nis** *n* half-yearly report

'**halb·jäh·rig** [-jɛ:rıç] *adj.* a) six-month *stay etc.*, *a stay etc.* of six months, b) six-month-old *baby etc.*

'**halb·jähr·lich I.** *adj.* half-yearly, semi-annual(ly *adv.*); **II.** *adv.* every six months, twice a year

'**Halb·kon·so,nant** *m* semi-consonant

'**Halb·kreis** *m* semicircle; '**halb·kreis·för·mig** [-fœrmıç] **I.** *adj.* semicircular; **II.** *adv.* in a semicircle

'**Halb·ku·gel** *f* hemisphere; '**halb·ku·gel·för·mig** [-fœrmıç] *adj.* hemispherical

'**Halb·ku,si·ne** *f* second cousin

'**halb·lang** *adj.* medium-length ...; knee-length *skirt etc.*; *ling.* half-long *vowel*; F ***nu' mach mal ~!*** F hold on a minute!, *sl.* hang about!

'**halb·laut I.** *adj.* low, subdued; **II.** *adv.* in an undertone, in undertones

'**Halb·le·der** *n* half leather; ***in ~ gebunden*** half-leather ...; **~band** *m* (-[e]s; ⸚e) a) half-leather binding, b) half-leather volume

'**halb·leer** *adj.* half-empty

'**Halb·lei·nen I.** *n* half-linen (cloth); ***in ~ gebunden*** half-cloth; **II.** 2 *adj.* half-linen; **~band** *m* a) half-cloth binding, b) half-cloth volume

'**Halb·lei·ter** *m electron.* semiconductor; **~tech·nik** *f* semiconductor technology

'**halb·mast** *adv.*: (***auf ~*** at) half-mast (*a. fig. trousers*); ***auf ~ stehen*** be (flying) at half-mast; ***auf ~ hissen*** hoist to half-mast

'**Halb|mes·ser** *m* (-s; -) radius; **~me,tall** *n* semi-metal; **2mi·li,tä·risch** *adj.* paramilitary; **~mit·tel·ge·wicht(·ler** *m*) *n* light middleweight

'**halb·mo·nat·lich I.** *adj.* half-monthly; **II.** *adv.* half-monthly, fortnightly; '**Halb·mo·nats·schrift** *f* fortnightly publication (*or* periodical)

'**Halb·mond** *m* half-moon, crescent; '**halb·mond·för·mig** [-fœrmıç] *adj.* crescent-shaped

'**halb|nackt** *adj.* half-naked; **~of·fen** *adj.* half-open (*a. ling.*); **~of·fi·zi,ell** *adj.* semi-official

'**halb·part** [-part] *adv.*: ***~ machen*** go halves, F go fifty-fifty

'**Halb|pen·si,on** *f* half-board; **~profi** *m* semi-pro(fessional); **~pro,fil** *n* three-quarters profile; **2reif** *adj.* half-ripe; **~re·li,ef** *n* half relief; **2rund** *adj.* semicircular; **~rund** *n* (-[e]s; -e) semicircle; **~schat·ten** *m* half-shade; *ast., art and fig.*: penumbra; **~schlaf** *m* doze; ***ich hab's im ~ gehört*** I heard it just as I was dozing off (*or* beginning to wake up); **~schluß** *m* ♪ imperfect cadence; **~schuh** *m* (low) shoe; **~schwer·ge·wicht(·ler** *m*) *n sport*: light heavyweight; **~schwe·ster** *f* half-sister; **2sei·den** *adj.* half-silk; *fig. contp.* shady

'**halb·sei·tig** [-zaıtıç] **I.** *adj.* **1.** *typ.* half-page ...; **2.** ⚕ unilateral; ***~e Lähmung*** 🕮 hemiplegia; **II.** *adv.* on one side; ***~ gelähmt*** paralyzed on one side, 🕮 hemiplegic

'**Halb·star·ke** F *m* (-n; -n) F yob(bo)

'**Halb·stie·fel** *m* ankle boot

'**halb·stün·dig** [-ʃtʏndıç] *adj.* half-hour ...; '**halb·stünd·lich I.** *adj.* half-hourly; **II.** *adv.* every half-hour

'**Halb·ta·ges·kar·te** *f* half-day pass

'**halb·tä·gig** [-tɛ:gıç] **I.** *adj.* half a day's ..., half-day ...; **II.** *adv.* → ***halbtags***

'**halb·tags** *adv.* (for) half the day; ***~ arbeiten*** work half-days, have a part-time job; ***~ geöffnet*** open in the mornings (*or* afternoons)

'Halb·tags|ar·beit *f* part-time job (*or* employment); **~be·schäf·ti·gte** *m, f* (-n; -n), **~kraft** *f* part-time worker (*or* employee), part-timer
'Halb·ton *m* **1.** ♪ semitone, *Am.* half tone; **2.** *phot., typ.* half-tone
'halb·tot *adj.* half-dead
'Halb|to,ta·le *f film*: medium long shot; **~trau·er** *f* half mourning
'halb|trocken *adj. gastr.* medium dry; **~ver·daut** *adj.* half-digested (*a. fig.*); **~ver·fault** *adj.* rotting; **~ver·hun·gert** *adj.* starving
'Halb|vet·ter *m* second cousin; **~vo,kal** *m* semivowel
'halb|voll *adj.* half-full; **~wach** *adj.* half-awake, dozing
'Halb|wahr·heit *f* half-truth; **~wai·se** *f*: ***er ist ~*** he('s) lost his father (*or* mother)
'halb·wegs [-'ve:ks] *adv.* halfway; *fig.* fairly, reasonably; more or less; *fig.* ***ich möchte e-n ~ anständigen Wagen*** *a.* I don't want just any old car; ***kannst du dich nicht mal ~ normal benehmen?*** can't you try and act like a human being for a change?; ***wie geht's? - so ~*** how are things? - oh, all right (*Am.* alright)
'Halb·welt *f* (-; *no pl.*) demimonde; **~da·me** *f* demimondaine
'Halb·wel·ter·ge·wicht(·ler *m*) *n* light welterweight
'Halb·wert(s)·zeit *f phys.* half-life (period)
'halb·wild *adj.* half-wild; semi-barbarian *tribe etc.*
'Halb·wis·sen *n* superficial (*or* bitty) knowledge
'halb·wö·chent·lich *adj.* half-weekly, twice-weekly
'halb·wüch·sig [-vy:ksıç] *adj.* teenage ...; **'Halb·wüch·si·ge** [-vy:ksıgə] *m, f* (-n; -n) adolescent, teenager
'Halb·wü·ste *f* semi-desert
'Halb·zeit *f* **1.** *sport*: *first, second* half; half-time; ***nach der ~*** in the second half; ***zur ~ steht es 2:1*** the half-time score is 2-1, the score at half-time was 2-1; **2.** *phys.* half-life (period); **~er·geb·nis** *n sport*: half-time score; **~pau·se** *f sport*: half-time; **~stand** *m sport*: half-time score
Hal·de ['haldə] *f* (-; -n) slope, hillside; ⚒ slagheap; ***auf~ stehen*** *cars etc.*: be in the storage yard
half [half] *pret. of* ***helfen***
Hälf·te ['hɛlftə] *f* (-; -n) half; ***die ~ (davon)*** half of it; ***gib mir die ~*** give me half (of it); ***die ~ der Leute*** half the people; ***die ~ m-r Zeit*** half my (*or* the) time; ***um die ~ teurer sein*** cost half as much again; ***bis zur ~ zahlen*** pay half; ***(nur) die ~ zahlen*** pay (only) half-price; ***Kosten*** *etc.* ***zur ~ tragen*** pay (*or* bear) half the costs *etc.*; ***sich je zur ~ beteiligen*** go half-shares (***an*** *dat.* in); ***wir haben's bis zur ~ geschafft*** we're halfway there; ***zur ~*** half (of it *or* them); F ***m-e bessere ~*** F my better half
Half·ter ['halftɐ] **1.** *m, n* (-s; -) halter; **2.** *n* (-s; -), *f* (-; -n) holster; **'half·tern** *v/t.* (h) halter
Hall [hal] *m* (-[e]s; *no pl.*) sound; echo
Hal·le ['halə] *f* (-; -n) hall; entrance hall; *hotel*: foyer, lobby; ⚙ shop; gymnasium, gym; *tennis*: covered court; ✈ hangar; ***in der ~ (spielen*** *etc.*) *sport*: (play *etc.*) indoors
Hal·le·lu·ja [hale'lu:ja] **I.** *n* (-s; -s) hallelujah; **II.** ♀ *int.* hallelujah!
hal·len ['halən] *v/i.* (h) echo, resound (***von*** *dat.* with)
'Hal·len|bad *n* indoor (swimming) pool; **~fuß·ball** *m* five-a-side football; **~hand·ball** *m* (indoor) handball; **~mei·ster·schaft** *f* indoor championship(s *pl.*); **~re,kord** *m* indoor record; **~schwimm·bad** *n* indoor (swimming) pool; **~sport** *m* indoor sports *pl.* (*or* athletics); **~ten·nis** *n* indoor tennis; **~tur,nier** *n* indoor tournament (*or* meeting)
Hal·lig ['halıç] *f* (-; -en [-gən]) *small island off Schleswig-Holstein*
hal·li hal·lo [ha'li: ha'lo:] *int.* **1.** yoo hoo!; **2.** well, hello there!
hal'lo I. *int.* hello, F hi; **~(, Sie)!** excuse me; **II.** ♀ *n* (-s; -s) **1.** hello; **2.** *fig.* fuss, hullabaloo; ***es gab ein großes ~, als sie ankam*** everyone made a big fuss (*or* there was a great hullabaloo) when she arrived
Hal·lo·dri [ha'lo:dri] *dial. m* (-s; -[s]) F scallywag, *Am.* scalawag
Hal·lu·zi·na·ti·on [halutsina'tsĭo:n] *f* (-; -en) hallucination; **hal·lu·zi·na·to·risch** [halutsina'to:rıʃ] *adj.* hallucinatory; **hal·lu·zi·nie·ren** [halutsi'ni:rən] *v/i.* (h) hallucinate; **hal·lu·zi·no·gen** [halutsino'ge:n] **I.** *adj.* hallucinogenic; **II.** ♀ *n* (-s; -e) hallucinogen, hallucinogenic drug
Halm [halm] *m* (-[e]s; -e) ⚘ blade; stalk; straw
Hal·ma ['halma] *n* (-s; *no pl.*) halma
Ha·lo ['ha:lo] *m* (-[s]; -s, Halonen [ha'lo:nən]) *ast.*, ⚡ halo
Ha·lo·gen [halo'ge:n] **I.** *n* (-s; -e) halogen; **II.** ♀ *adj.* halogenous; **~lam·pe** *f* halogen lamp; **~schein·wer·fer** *m mot.* halogen headlight (*or* headlamp)
Hals [hals] *m* (-es; Hälse ['hɛlzə]) a) *anat.* neck, throat, b) ⚙ neck, collar, c) neck *of a bottle, violin etc.*; ♪ tail *of a note*; ***steifer ~*** stiff neck; ***j-m in den ~ schauen*** (have a) look at s.o.'s throat; F ***ich hab's im ~*** I've got a sore throat; ***sich den ~ brechen*** break one's neck; ***j-m um den ~ fallen*** fling one's arms around s.o.'s neck; ***bis an den ~*** up to one's neck (*fig. a.* eyes, ears); ***er hat es in den falschen ~ bekommen*** it went down (*fig.* he took it) the wrong way; ***aus vollem ~(e) schreien (lachen)*** scream at the top of one's voice (roar with laughter); *fig.* ***et. (j-n) auf dem ~ haben*** be lumbered with s.th. (s.o.); ***sich et. auf den ~ laden*** lumber o.s. with s.th., get o.s. lumbered with s.th.; ***j-m die Polizei*** *etc.* ***auf den ~ hetzen*** get the police *etc.* onto s.o.; ***j-m den ~ umdrehen*** wring s.o.'s neck; ***sich j-m an den ~ werfen*** throw o.s. at s.o.; ***sich et. (j-n) vom ~(e) schaffen*** get rid of s.th. (s.o.); ***~ über Kopf*** headlong; ***sich ~ über Kopf verlieben in*** *acc.* fall head over heels in love with; ***e-r Flasche den ~ brechen*** crack a bottle; ***das kann ihn den ~ kosten*** that could cost him his head; ***das Wort blieb mir im ~(e) stekken*** the word stuck in my throat; ***es hängt mir zum ~(e) heraus*** F I'm fed up to the back teeth with it, I'm sick (and tired) of it; ***er kann den ~ nicht vollkriegen (nicht voll genug kriegen)*** he can't get enough (of it); ***schaff es (ihn) mir vom ~e*** a) get it (him) out of here (*or* out of my sight), b) I don't want to have anything to do with it (him), F get it (him) off my back; ***bleib mir damit vom ~e!*** I don't want to know about it; → ***ausrenken, Herz***
'Hals·ab·schnei·der *m* (-s; -) shark; **'hals·ab·schnei·de·risch** [-apʃnaıdərıʃ] *adj.* extortionate; cutthroat ...
'Hals|aus·schnitt *m* neckline; ***tiefer ~*** low neck(line); **~band** *n* (-[e]s; ⸚er) **1.** necklace; **2.** (*dog*) collar
'hals·bre·che·risch [-brɛçərıʃ] *adj.* hair-raising; breakneck *speed etc.*
'Hals|ent·zün·dung *f* ⚕ sore throat; **~ket·te** *f* necklace; **~kra·gen** *m* collar (*a. zo.*); **~krau·se** *f* ruff; ⚕ neck brace; **~län·ge** *f*: ***um e-e ~*** by a neck; **~mus·kel** *m* neck muscle, muscle in one's neck; **~-'Na·sen-'Oh·ren-Spe·zia'list** *m* ear, nose and throat (*or* ENT) specialist, otolaryngologist; **~par,tie** *f* neck (area), throat (area); throat and neck *pl.*; **~schlag·ader** *f* carotid (artery); **~schmer·zen** *pl.* sore throat; ***~ haben*** have a sore throat
'hals·star·rig [-ʃtarıç] *adj.* stubborn; **'Hals·star·rig·keit** *f* (-; *no pl.*) stubbornness
Hals·tuch *n* neckerchief; scarf
'Hals- und 'Bein·bruch F *int.* F break a leg!
'Hals|weh *n* → ***Halsschmerzen***; **~wei·te** *f* collar size; ***was haben Sie für e-e ~?*** what size collar do you take?; **~wir·bel** *m anat.* cervical vertebra (*pl.* vertebrae)
Halt [halt] *m* (-[e]s; *no pl.*) **1.** hold, foothold; support (*a. fig.*); *fig.* (moral) stability; *Mensch* ***ohne ~*** a) weak, unstable, b) helpless, disoriented; ***j-m ein ~ sein*** be a (great) support to s.o.; ***an j-m ~ finden*** find support in s.o.; **2.** stop; *dat.* ***~ gebieten*** call a halt to, halt, stop; → ***haltmachen***
halt I. *int.* a) stop!, don't move!; wait!, b) that'll do, c) wait a minute; ***~! Keine Bewegung!*** freeze!; ***~, wer da?*** halt, who goes there?; **II.** F *adv.* just; you know; ***das ist ~ so*** that's the way it is; ***da kann man ~ nichts machen*** there's nothing you can do (about it); ***dann tu's ~*** do it then(, if you must)
'halt·bar *adj.* **1.** non-perishable *food*; long-life *milk etc.*; ***~ sein*** keep (for a long time); ***~ machen*** preserve; ***~ bis*** best before; **2.** hardwearing, durable; strong, solid; ⚙ *a.* wear-resistant; **3.** fast *colo(u)rs*; **4.** *fig.* lasting; tenable, valid *argument etc.*; ***sich als nicht ~ erweisen*** prove untenable; **5. *das war ein ~er Schuß*** *sport*: he could have saved that (one); **'Halt·bar·keit** *f* (-; *no pl.*) ✝ shelf life; durability; stability (*a.* ⚗); ⚙ *a.* resistance to wear; service life; fastnes *of colo(u)rs*; **'Halt·bar·keits·da·tum** *n* best-by (*or* best-before) date, *Am.* pull date
'Hal·te|bo·gen *m* ♪ tie; **~bucht** *f* lay-by, *Am.* rest stop; **~griff** *m* strap
hal·ten ['haltən] (hielt, gehalten, h) **I.** *v/t.* a) hold (*a.* ♪), maintain *price etc.*; hold (up), support; keep *clean, fresh etc.*, b) hold *meeting etc.*, *a.* celebrate *wedding, mass*; have, take *a meal etc.*, c) hold, contain, d) keep *contract, promise etc.*, e) *sport*: hold *ball, record, title etc.*, stop, save *shot*, hold onto *the ball*; stop *opponent etc.*, *boxing*: *b.s.* hold *s.o.*, f) (*usu.* ***sich et. ~***) keep *a car etc.*, take *a newspaper etc.*, g) ✝ (keep in) stock; ***j-n an der Hand ~*** hold s.o.'s hand; ***ans Licht ~***

hold to the light; ***den Kopf hoch*** ~ hold one's head up; ***frisch*** (***warm***) ~ keep fresh (warm); ***das Zimmer ist in Blau gehalten*** the colo(u)r scheme in the room is blue; ***was hältst du von ...?*** what do you think of ...?, how about ...?; ***was hältst du davon?*** what do you think (of it)?; ***viel ~ von*** *dat.* think highly (*or* the world) of; F ***er hält e-e ganze Menge von dir*** F he thinks you're great; ***ich halte nicht viel davon*** I don't think much of it, I'm not keen on it; ***er hält nichts vom Sparen*** he doesn't believe in saving; ***ich halte es mit m-m Lehrer, der immer sagte*** I go by (*or* I set great store by) what my teacher always used to say; ~ ***für*** *acc.* consider *s.o.* (to be), think *s.o.* is, (mis)take *s.o.* for; ***er hält ihn für den Besitzer*** *usu.* he thinks he's the owner; ***ich halte es für richtig, daß er absagt*** I think he's right to refuse, I think it's right that he should refuse; ***ich hielte es für gut, wenn wir gingen*** I think we should go, I think it would be a good idea if we went; ***für wie alt hältst du ihn?*** how old do you think he is?; ***wofür ~ Sie mich*** (***eigentlich***)***?*** who do you think I am?; ***das kannst du ~, wie du willst*** please yourself; ***wie hältst du es mit ...?*** what do you usually do about ...?; ***so haben wir es immer gehalten*** we've always done it that way; ***diese Theorie läßt sich nicht ~*** this theory is untenable; ***er ließ sich nicht ~, er war nicht zu ~*** there was no stopping him, you couldn't hold him back; → ***Daumen, Gang*** 4, ***laufend*** I; **II.** *v/i.* a) hold, b) stop, *mot. a.* draw up, pull up, c) last; *food etc.*: keep; *weather*: hold, d) *sport*: save; ***links*** (***rechts***) ~ keep left (right); ~ ***auf*** *acc.* pay attention to, set great store by, insist on; ***auf sich ~*** be very particular about one's appearance, look after one's health; ***jeder Handwerker, der*** (***etwas***) ***auf sich hält*** any self-respecting craftsman; ***wir ~ nicht auf Formen*** we don't stand on ceremony; ***zu j-m ~*** stand by (F stick to) s.o., side with s.o.; ***an sich ~*** control o.s.; ***ich mußte an mich ~, um nicht zu*** *inf.* I could hardly stop myself (from) *ger.*; **III.** *v/refl.*: ***sich ~*** a) last, *food etc.*: keep, *weather*: hold, b) hold out; ***sich ~ an*** *dat.* hold onto; *fig.* ***sich ~ an*** *acc.* keep to, stick to *rules etc.*, rely on *s.o.*, ⚖ hold *s.o.* liable; ***sich*** (***auf*** *e-m Posten*, ***in*** *e-r Firma etc.*) ~ last *in a job, firm*; ***sich ~ als*** maintain one's position as; ***sich warm*** (***fit*** *etc.*) ~ keep warm (fit *etc.*); ***sich in Form ~*** keep in form, keep fit; ***sich bei guter Gesundheit*** (***Laune***) ~ stay healthy (keep up one's good mood), manage to stay healthy (cheerful); ***sich bereit ~*** be ready, ⚔ be on standby; ***sich gut ~*** *food etc.*: keep well; ***sich gut*** (*or* ***wacker***) ~ hold one's own (***gegen*** *acc.* against), do well; ***sie hat sich gut gehalten*** she looks good for her age; ***sich links*** (***rechts***) ~ keep to the left (right); ***sich südlich ~*** keep on south, keep going in a southerly direction; ***sich nicht*** (*or* ***kaum***) ***mehr ~ können*** be beside o.s. with joy (anger *etc.*); ***sich*** (***vor Lachen***) ***nicht mehr ~ können*** F be rolling about, be creasing (*or* creased) up; **IV.** 𝔖 *n* (-s): ***da gab es kein ~ mehr*** there was no holding them *etc.* (back)

Hal·te|platz ['haltə-] *m* stopping place; **~punkt** *m* stop; *phys.* critical point; *shooting*: point of aim

Hal·ter ['haltɐ] *m* (-s; -) **1.** holder; handle; **2.** owner

Hal·te·rung ['haltərʊŋ] *f* (-; -en) fixture

'Hal·te|schild *n mot.* stop sign; **~seil** *n* safety rope; **~si͵gnal** *n* stop signal; **~stel·le** *f* stop

'Hal·te·ver·bot *n sign*: no stopping; **'Hal·te·ver·bots·schild** *n* "no-stopping" sign

'Hal·te·vor·rich·tung *f* ⚙ (clamping *or* holding) fixture

'halt·los *adj.* **1.** disoriented, (completely) insecure, completely adrift, floundering; **2.** untenable *theory etc.*; unfounded *suspicions etc.*; **'Halt·lo·sig·keit** *f* (-; *no pl.*) **1.** *s.o.'s* lack of orientation; **2.** lack of foundation, untenable nature (*gen.* of *a theory etc.*)

'halt·ma·chen *v/i.* (*sep.*, h) (make a) stop; *fig.* ***er macht vor nichts halt*** he'll stop at nothing

Hal·tung ['haltʊŋ] *f* (-; *no pl.*) **1.** posture; *a. sport*: position; pose; ***e-e gute ~ haben*** have good posture; **2.** outlook (***zu*** *dat.* on), approach (to); attitude (***gegenüber*** *dat.* towards); ***politische ~*** political outlook (*or* views *pl.*); ***e-e konservative*** *etc.* ~ ***einnehmen*** take a conservative *etc.* approach (*or* line); **3.** bearing, manner; ***ihre ganze ~*** *a.* the way she comes across; **4.** poise, composure; self-possession; ~ ***bewahren*** keep a stiff upper lip, retain one's composure, F keep one's cool; ***um ~ ringen*** try to keep one's composure (F one's cool); **5.** keeping *of a dog etc.*; **'Hal·tungs·feh·ler** *m* **1.** ⚕ bad posture; **2.** *sport*: style fault

Ha·lun·ke [ha'lʊŋkə] *m* (-n; -n) rogue; rascal

Hä·me ['hɛːmə] *f* (-; *no pl.*) malice; **hä·misch** ['hɛːmɪʃ] **I.** *adj.* malicious; ***~e Bemerkung*** snide remark; **II.** *adv.* maliciously; ~ ***grinsen*** sneer (***über*** *acc.* at)

Ham·mel ['haməl] *m* (-s; -) **1.** *zo.* wether; *gastr.* mutton; **2.** F *fig.* lout, boor; ***blöder ~*** (F blithering) idiot; **~bei·ne** *pl.*: F ***j-m die ~ langziehen*** F give s.o. a good going over; **~bra·ten** *m* a) joint of mutton, b) roast mutton; **~fleisch** *n* mutton; **~keu·le** *f* leg of mutton; **~ko·te͵lett** *n* mutton chop; **~ra͵gout** *n* mutton stew; **~ripp·chen** *n* mutton chop; **~sprung** *m parl.* (vote by) division

Ham·mer ['hamɐ] *m* (-s; Hämmer ['hɛmɐ] **1.** hammer (*a.* ♪, *sport and auction*); mallet; *parl. etc.* gavel; ~ ***und Sichel*** hammer and sickle; *fig.* ***unter den ~ kommen*** come under the hammer; **2.** F *sport*: F hammer; **3.** F boo-boo; ***das ist ein ~!*** a) F that's great, b) F that's incredible, that really takes the biscuit; ***du hast wohl e-n ~*** F you must be off your nut; **~hai** *m* hammerhead (shark); **~kla͵vier** *n* pianoforte, fortepiano

häm·mern ['hɛmɐn] (h) **I.** *v/i.* hammer (*a. fig.*); *heart*: pound; *fig.* ~ ***auf*** *acc.* hammer away at; **II.** *v/t.* hammer; forge; *fig.* ***j-m et. in den Kopf ~*** hammer s.th. into s.o.

'Ham·mer|schlag *m* hammer blow, blow of the hammer; **~wer·fen** *n sport*: hammer throwing; **~wer·fer** *m sport*: hammer thrower; **~zeh** *m* ⚕ hammer toe

Hä·mo·glo·bin [hɛmoglo'biːn] *n* (-s; *no pl.*) h(a)emoglobin

Hä·mo·phi·le [hɛmo'fiːlə] *m* (-n; -n) ⚕ h(a)emophiliac; **Hä·mo·phi·lie** [hɛmofi'liː] *f* (-; *no pl.*) h(a)emophilia

Hä·mor·rhoi·den [hɛmɔro'iːdən] *pl.* ⚕ h(a)emorrhoids, F piles

Ham·pel·mann ['hampəlman] *m* (-[e]s; ⸚er) jumping jack; F *fig.* F wimp; **ham·peln** ['hampəln] F *v/i.* (h) jump around; fidget

Ham·ster ['hamstɐ] *m* (-s; -) hamster; **~backen** F *pl.* fat (F pudgy) cheeks; **~käu·fe** *pl.* hoarding *sg.*; panic buying *sg.*; ~ ***machen*** hoard (food *etc.*), stock up (on food *etc.*)

ham·stern ['hamstɐn] *v/t. and v/i.* (h) hoard

'Ham·ster|prei·se *pl.* inflated prices; **~wa·re** *f* hoarded goods *pl.*

Hand [hant] *f* (-; Hände ['hɛndə]) hand; ***et. mit der ~ machen*** *etc.* do *etc.* s.th. by hand; ***mit der ~ gemacht*** handmade; ***von ~ gemalt*** handpainted; ***j-m die ~ geben*** (*or* ***schütteln***) shake hands with s.o.; ***j-n an die ~ nehmen*** take s.o.'s hand; ***Hände hoch!*** hands up!; *parl.* ***durch Heben der Hände*** by a show of hands; *fig.* ***j-s rechte ~*** s.o.'s right-hand man (*or* woman); ***öffentliche ~*** authorities, state; ***an ~ von*** *dat.* with help of, on the basis of, in the light of; ***aus bester ~*** on good authority; ***aus erster ~*** first-hand; ***ich hab's aus erster ~*** I got it straight from the horse's mouth; ***aus zweiter ~*** *buy etc. s.th.* second-hand, *fig. experience etc. s.th.* vicarious(ly); ***aus der ~ geben*** part with, give up; ***er gibt es nicht aus der ~*** *a.* he won't let go of it, he won't let anyone else have it (*or* take it from him); ***aus der ~ legen*** put aside; ***bei der ~, zur ~*** at hand, handy; ***sie hat immer e-e Antwort zur ~*** *a.* she's always got an answer pat, she's never at a loss for words; ***mit vollen Händen*** liberally, ***sein Geld ausgeben:*** throw one's money about; ***unter der ~*** through unofficial channels, *buy etc.* privately, under the counter, on the side; ***von langer ~*** long beforehand; ***zu Händen*** c/o (= care of), *adm.* att., Attention; ***zur rechten*** (***linken***) ~ on the right-hand (left-hand) side; ~ ***anlegen*** lend a hand, put one's shoulder to the wheel; ~ ***an sich legen*** commit suicide; ***letzte ~ legen an*** *acc.* add the finishing touches to; ***j-n an der ~ haben*** have contacts with s.o.; ~ ***in ~ gehen*** walk hand in hand, *fig.* go hand in hand, go together (***mit*** *dat.* with); ~ ***in ~ arbeiten*** work together, cooperate (closely); ~ ***und Fuß haben*** *plan etc.*: make sense, hold water; ***was er macht, hat ~ und Fuß*** he doesn't do things in half measures; ***alle*** (*or* ***beide***) ***Hände voll*** (***zu tun***) ***haben*** have one's hands full, have a lot on one's plate; ***e-e offene ~ haben*** be open-handed, be generous; ***e-e glückliche*** (*or* ***geschickte***) ~ ***haben*** have the right touch (***mit*** *dat.* for), ***mit*** *dat.*: *a.* know how to handle, have a way with; ***die Arbeit geht ihm flott von der ~*** he's a fast worker; ***er hat e-e leichte ~*** a) things come easily to him, b) he doesn't take his time over things, he doesn't take things seriously enough; ***et. in die Hände bekommen*** get hold (*or* control) of s.th.; ***et. in die Hände nehmen*** take charge of s.th.; ***die Sache in die Hände nehmen*** take the initiative; ***j-m aus der ~ fressen*** eat out of s.o.'s hand; *lit.* ***j-m die ~ reichen*** marry s.o.;

einander die ~ geben *events etc.*: follow hard on each other's heels, happen in close succession; ***die Ereignisse gaben einander die ~*** *a.* one thing led to another; ***die beiden können einander die ~ reichen*** (*or* ***geben***) they're two of a kind, *contp. a.* they're as bad as each other; ***j-m (et.) in die Hände spielen*** play (s.th.) into s.o.'s hands; ***j-m freie ~ lassen*** give s.o. a free hand; ***j-n auf Händen tragen*** wait on s.o. hand and foot; ***j-n in der ~ haben*** have s.o. in one's grip; ***j-m in die Hände fallen*** fall into s.o.'s hands; ***mit beiden Händen zugreifen*** jump at the chance; ***es ist mit den Händen zu greifen*** F it sticks out a mile (*or* like a sore thumb); ***mit leeren Händen weggehen*** go away (*or* be left) empty-handed; ***s-e ~ im Spiel haben*** have a hand in it; ***s-e ~ ins Feuer legen für*** *acc.* put one's hand into the fire for; ***sich mit Händen und Füßen wehren*** fight tooth and nail; ***von der ~ in den Mund leben*** live from hand to mouth; ***von der ~ weisen*** a) dismiss, b) deny; ***es ist nicht von der ~ zu weisen*** it can't be denied, there's no denying (*or* getting away from) it, ***daß:*** there's no denying (*or* getting away from) the fact that; ***es liegt in s-r ~*** it's up to him; ***es liegt klar auf der ~*** it's (so) obvious; ***e-e ~ wäscht die andere*** you scratch my back and I'll scratch yours; ***sie ist in festen Händen*** she's accounted for, F she's booked; ***sich (fest) in der ~ haben*** have everything under (firm) control, have a firm grip on o.s.; ***wir haben die Lage fest in der ~*** we've got everything under control; ***er ist zu schnell bei der ~ mit s-r Kritik*** he's always very quick to criticize; → ***drücken*** 1, ***gebunden*** 2, ***link*** 1

'Hand·ap·pa,rat *m* (set of) reference works *pl.*

'Hand·ar·beit *f* (-; -en) **1.** handicrafts *pl.*; needlework; *pl.* handiwork; **2.** handmade article; ***feine ~*** skilled handiwork; **3.** *no pl.* manual work; **'Hand·ar·bei·ter** *m* **1.** manual worker; **2.** craftsman; **'Hand·ar·beits,un·ter·richt** *m* needlework (classes *pl.*)

'Hand|auf·he·ben *n*: *parl.* ***durch ~ abstimmen*** vote by a show of hands; **~auf·le·gen** *n* (-s), **~auf·le·gung** *f* (-; -en) *eccl.* laying on of hands; **~ball** *m* (-[e]s; ⸚e) a) *no pl.* handball, b) handball; **~bal·len** *m anat.* ball of the thumb; **~beil** *n* hatchet; **~be·sen** *m* (hand)brush; **~be·trieb** *m* manual operation; hand control; ***mit ~*** manual *set etc.*, hand-operated; **~be·we·gung** *f* movement (*or* sweep) of the hand, gesture; ***j-n durch e-e ~ auffordern*** motion s.o. (***zu*** *inf.* to *inf.*); **~bib·lio,thek** *f* reference library; **~boh·rer** *m* ⚙ gimlet; **~bohr·ma,schi·ne** *f* hand drill

'hand·breit *adj.* *a* hand's breadth; ***~ offenstehen*** be ajar; **'Hand·breit** *f* (-; -) hand's breadth

'Hand|brem·se *f* hand brake, *Am.* emergency (*or* parking) brake; **~buch** *n* textbook; manual, handbook; **~creme** *f* handcream

Händ·chen ['hɛntçən] *n* (-s; -) (little) hand; ***~ halten*** hold hands; ***j-m ~ halten*** hold s.o.'s hand; **2hal·tend** *adv.* hand in hand, holding hands

Hän·de|druck ['hɛndə-] *m* (-[e]s; ⸚e) handshake; ***et. mit e-m ~ bekräftigen*** shake hands on s.th.; **~klat·schen** *n* clapping, applause

Han·del¹ ['handəl] *m* (-s; *no pl.*) a) trade, commerce, *esp. stock exchange*: trading (***mit*** *dat.* in), b) market, c) (business) transaction, deal; barter; ***~ und Gewerbe*** trade and industry; ***im ~*** on the market; ***im ~ sein*** *a.* be available; ***nicht mehr im ~*** off the market, no longer available; ***in den ~ bringen*** (***kommen***) put on (come onto) the market; ***~ treiben*** trade, ***mit*** *dat.*: deal in *s.th.*, do business with *s.o.*

'Han·del² *lit. m* (-s; Händel ['hɛndəl]) affair, business; ***mit j-m in ~ geraten*** a) start squabbling (*or* arguing) with s.o., b) get involved in a scuffle with s.o.

han·deln ['handəln] (h) **I.** *v/i.* **1.** act; take action; proceed; behave; **2.** ✝ trade (***mit*** *dat.* with *s.o.*, in *goods*), deal (in *goods*); bargain (***um*** *acc.* for *goods*, over *a price*), *contp.* haggle (over); ***mit sich ~ lassen*** be open to offers, *fig.* be prepared to discuss things, be open to persuasion; **3.** *fig.* ***~ von*** *dat.* be about, deal with; **II.** *v/t.*: ***an der Börse gehandelt werden*** be traded (*or* listed) on the stock exchange; **III.** *v/impers.*: ***es handelt sich um*** *acc.* it's a question (*or* matter) of, it concerns; ***es handelt sich um folgendes*** the thing (*or* situation *etc.*) is (this); ***es handelt sich darum, ob*** *etc.* the question is whether *etc.*; ***gerade darum handelt es sich ja*** that's (just) the point; ***wenn es sich darum handelt zu helfen*** *etc.* when it comes to helping *etc.*; ***worum handelt es sich?*** a) what's it about?, b) what's the problem?; **IV.** 2 *n* (-s) action

'Han·dels|ab·kom·men *n* trade agreement; **~at·ta,ché** *m* commercial attaché; **~bank** *f* (-; -en) commercial (*or* merchant) bank; **~be·richt** *m* trade (*or* market) report; **~be·schrän·kun·gen** *pl.* trade restrictions; **~be·trieb** *m* commercial enterprise, business; **~be·zeich·nung** *f* trade name; **~be·zie·hun·gen** *pl.* trade relations; **~bi,lanz** *f* balance of trade; **~blatt** *n* trade journal; **~bü·cher** *pl.* account books; **~de·fi·zit** *n* trade deficit; **~de·le·ga·ti,on** *f* trade delegation; **~ein·heit** *f stock exchange*: unit of trading

'han·dels·ei·nig, 'han·dels·eins *adj.*: ***~ werden*** come to (*or* reach) an agreement (***mit*** *dat.* with)

'Han·dels·em,bar·go *n* trade embargo

'han·dels·fä·hig *adj.* negotiable

'Han·dels|flag·ge *f* merchant flag; **~flot·te** *f* merchant fleet; **~frei·heit** *f* (-; *no pl.*) freedom of trade, *w.s.* free trade; **~geist** *m* (-[e]s; *no pl.*) commercialism; **~ge·richt** *n* commercial court; **~ge·sell·schaft** *f* (trading) company, *Am.* (business) corporation; **~ge·wer·be** *n* trade, business; **~ge·wicht** *n* avoirdupois; **~ha·fen** *m* commercial port; **~hoch·schu·le** *f* commercial college, *Am.* business school; **~kam·mer** *f* chamber of commerce; **~ka·pi,tal** *n* trading capital; **~ket·te** *f* chain (of stores); **~klas·se** *f* grade; **~kor·re·spon,dent** *m* commercial correspondent; **~kor·re·spon,denz** *f* commercial correspondence; **~kre,dit** *m* business loan; **~krieg** *m* trade war (-fare); **~luft·fahrt** *f* commercial aviation; **~macht** *f* trading nation; **~ma,ri·ne** *f* merchant navy; **~mar·ke** *f* trademark; **~me·tro,po·le** *f* commercial capital, cent|re (*Am.* -er) of commerce; **~mi,ni·ster** *m* minister (*Am.* secretary) of commerce; *in GB*: Secretary of State for Trade and Industry; *in the USA*: Secretary of Commerce; **~mi·ni,ste·ri·um** *n* department of commerce; *in GB*: Department of Trade and Industry; *in the USA*: Department of Commerce; **~mo·no,pol** *n* trade monopoly; **~na·me** *m* trade name; **~na·ti,on** *f* trading nation; **~nie·der·las·sung** *f* **1.** business establishment; **2.** ⚖ registered seat; **3.** branch; **~part·ner** *m* trading partner; **~platz** *m* trading cent|re (*Am* -er)

'Han·dels·po·li,tik *f* commercial policy; **'han·dels·po,li·tisch** *adj.* trade ...

'Han·dels·recht *n* (-[e]s; *no pl.*) commercial law; **'han·dels·recht·lich I.** *adj.* in accordance with (*or* relating to) commercial law; **II.** *adv.* under (*or* according to) commercial law

'Han·dels|re,gi·ster *n* commercial (*or* trade) register; ***ins ~ eintragen*** register *a firm*; **~rei·sen·de** *m* → ***Handlungsreisende***; **~schiff** *n* merchant ship, trading vessel; **~schiffahrt** (*sep.* -ff·f-) *f* merchant shipping; **~schu·le** *f* commercial (*or* business) school; **~span·ne** *f* profit margin, markup; **~sper·re** *f* embargo; **~stadt** *f* commercial cent|er (*Brit.* -re); **~stra·ße** *f* trade route; **~stütz·punkt** *m* trading base; **~teil** *m* financial pages *pl.* (*or* section); **~,über·schuß** *m* trade surplus

'han·dels·üb·lich *adj.* usual in the trade; commercial; ***~e Qualität*** commercial quality; ***~e Bezeichnung*** trade name; ***~e Verpackung*** standard packaging

'Han·dels|un·ter,neh·men *n* commercial enterprise; **~ver·bin·dung** *f* **1.** trade route; **2.** ***~en*** trade relations; **~ver·kehr** *m* trading; commerce; **~ver·trag** *m* trade agreement; **~ver·tre·ter** *m* travel(l)ing salesman; **~ver·tre·tung** *f* commercial agency; *pol.* trade mission; **~volk** *n* trading nation, nation of traders; **~wa·re** *f* commodity; *pl.* merchandise *sg.*; **~wech·sel** *m* trade bill; **~weg** *m* trade route; **~wert** *m* market value; **~zen·trum** *n* commercial cent|re (*Am.* -er); **~zweig** *m* line of business

'han·del·trei·bend *adj.* trading

hän·de·rin·gend ['hɛndə-] *adv.* a) imploringly, b) despairingly; ***j-n ~ anflehen*** implore s.o.

'Hän·de|schüt·teln *n* shaking of hands, handshake; **~trock·ner** *m* drier

'Hand|ex·em,plar *n* personal copy; **~fe·ger** *m* (hand)brush; **~fer·tig·keit** *f* manual skill, dexterity

'hand·fest *adj.* sturdy, strong; *fig.* tangible, concrete; hard *evidence etc.*; serious *threat etc.*; full-blown *scandal etc.*; ***~e Mahlzeit*** good, square meal; ***~e Lüge*** out and out lie

'Hand|feu·er·lö·scher *m* fire extinguisher; **~feu·er·waf·fe** *f* portable firearm; *pl.* small arms; **~flä·che** *f* palm (of one's hand); **2ge·ar·beitet** *adj.* handmade; **~ge·brauch** *m*: ***zum ~*** for everyday use; **2ge·fer·tigt** *adj.* handmade; **2ge·knüpft** *adj.* handwoven; **~geld** *n* **1.** ✝ earnest money; **2.** *sport*: signing-on fee; **~ge·lenk** *n* wrist; F *fig.* ***aus dem ~*** off the cuff, just like that; ***ich kann keine Rede so einfach aus dem ~ schütteln*** I can't come up with a speech just like that

'**hand|ge·macht** *adj.* handmade; **~ge·malt** *adj.* handpainted
'**hand·ge·mein** *adj.*: **~ *werden*** come to blows (***mit j-m*** with s.o.)
'**Hand|ge·men·ge** *n* brawl, scuffle; ***es kam zu e-m*** ~ scuffling (*or* scuffles) broke out; **2ge·näht** *adj.* hand-sewn; **~ge·päck** *n* hand luggage (*Am.* baggage), carry-on luggage (*Am.* baggage)
'**hand|ge·recht** *adj.* handy; practical; **~ge·schnitzt** *adj.* hand-carved; **~ge·schrie·ben** *adj.* handwritten; **~ge·stickt** *adj.* hand-embroidered; **~ge·strickt** *adj.* hand-knitted; F *fig.* home-made; **~ge·webt, ~ge·wirkt** *adj.* hand-woven
'**Hand·gra,na·te** *f* hand grenade
'**hand·greif·lich** [-graɪflɪç] **I.** *adj.* violent *clashes, dispute*; *fig.* palpable; evident, manifest; **~*e Lüge*** out and out (*or* blatant) lie; ~ ***werden*** a) turn (*or* get) violent, lash out, F get rough, come to blows, b) F start pawing; **II.** *adv.*: ***j-m et.*** ~ ***vor Augen führen*** show s.o. s.th. quite plainly
'**Hand·griff** *m* **1.** grip, handle; **2.** movement, manipulation; *pl.* mechanical jobs; ***mit e-m*** ~ with a flick of the wrist, in no time, just like that; ***er tut keinen*** ~ he doesn't lift a finger
'**hand·groß** *adj.* ... the size of a hand
'**Hand·ha·be** *f* grounds *pl.* (***um et. zu tun*** for doing s.th.); proof, evidence; ***gesetzliche*** ~ legal grounds; ***e-e gesetzliche*** ~ ***haben gegen*** *acc.* have a case against *s.o.*; ***keinerlei*** ~ ***gegen j-n haben*** F have nothing on s.o.; ***er hat keinerlei*** ~ he hasn't got a leg to stand on
'**hand·ha·ben** *v/t.* (handhabte, gehandhabt, h) **1.** use *tool etc.*, go about with; operate *machine etc.*; **2.** *fig.* handle, deal with; apply; ***das wurde immer so gehandhabt*** it's always been done like that; '**Hand·ha·bung** *f* (-; *no pl.*) **1.** use; operation; **2.** *fig.* handling
Han·di·kap ['hɛndikɛp] *n* (-s; -s) handicap; drawback
'**Hand|kan·te** *f* side of the hand; ***Schlag mit der*** ~ chop; **~kar·ren** *m* handcart; **~kof·fer** *m* small suitcase; **~kuß** *m*: ***j-m e-n*** ~ ***geben*** kiss s.o.'s hand; *fig.* ***er hat es mit*** ~ ***angenommen*** he was only too glad to have (*or* accept) it
'**Hand·lan·ger** [-laŋɐ] *m* (-s; -) odd-job man; *contp.* dogsbody; accomplice; *pol. etc.* henchman, F stooge; F ***den*** ~ ***machen*** F do the donkey (*or* dirty) work, ***für j-n***: act as s.o.'s servant; **~dien·ste** *pl.* donkey (*or* dirty) work *sg.*; ***j-m*** ~ ***leisten*** fetch and carry for s.o., do the dirty work (for s.o.)
Händ·ler ['hɛndlɐ] *m* (-s; -) trader, merchant; retailer, dealer; shopkeeper; ***wenden Sie sich an Ihren*** ~ ask at your local dealer's; **~preis** *m* trade price; **~ra,batt** *m* trade discount
'**Hand·le·se·kunst** *f* (- *no pl.*) palmistry; '**Hand·le·ser** *m* palmist
'**Hand·leuch·te** *f* (portable) lamp
'**hand·lich** *adj.* handy; convenient; practical; compact; *mot. etc.* easy to handle
Hand·lung ['handlʊŋ] *f* (-; -en) **1.** act, action; **2.** action, story *of novel etc.*, plot (*a. thea.*); ***Ort der*** ~ scene (of action); ***Ort der*** ~ ***ist ...*** the scene (*or* story *etc.*) is set in ..., the action (*or* story *etc.*) takes place in ...
'**Hand·lungs|ab·lauf** *m* sequence (*or* course) of events; *thea. etc.* plot; **2arm** *adj.*: ***ein*** **~*er Roman*** *etc.* a novel *etc.* without much action (*or* much of a plot); **~be·darf** *m*: ***es besteht kein (dringender)*** ~ there's no (urgent) call for action; **~be·voll·mäch·tig·te** *m, f* (-n; -n) (authorized) agent, proxy
'**hand·lungs·fä·hig** *adj.* ⚖ capable of acting; *w.s. pol.* working; functioning; '**Hand·lungs·fä·hig·keit** *f* (-; *no pl.*) ⚖ legal capacity; *w.s.* capacity to act
'**Hand·lungs|frei·heit** *f* (-; *no pl.*) freedom of action; ***j-m*** ~ ***geben*** *a.* give s.o. a free hand; **~ket·te** *f* chain of events; **2reich** *adj. novel etc.* full of action, action-packed; ***es ist e-e*** **~*e Geschichte*** *etc. a.* there's plenty of action in the story *etc.*; **~rei·sen·de** *m* travel(l)ing salesman; **~sche·ma** *n* plot; **~spiel·raum** *m* room for manoeuvre (*Am.* maneuver); **~strang** *m* strand (of the plot)
'**hand·lungs·un·fä·hig** *adj.* ⚖ incapable of acting; *w.s. pol.* immobilized; '**Hand·lungs·un·fä·hig·keit** *f* ⚖ legal incapacity; *w.s. pol.* immobilization
'**Hand·lungs|ver·lauf** *m* sequence (*or* course) of events; *thea. etc.* plot; **~voll·macht** *f* limited authority to act and sign; **~wei·se** *f* behavio(u)r, conduct; procedure; methods *pl.*
'**Hand|mi·kro,phon** *n* hand microphone; **~müh·le** *f* hand mill; **~pfle·ge** *f* hand care, care of the hands; manicure; **~pres·se** *f* hand press; **~pum·pe** *f* hand pump; **~pup·pe** *f* (hand) puppet
'**Hand·rei·chung** [-raɪçʊŋ] *f* (-; -en) *a. pl.* help; **~*en tun*** help out
'**Hand|rücken** *m* back of the (*or* one's) hand; **~sä·ge** *f* hand saw; **~satz** *m typ.* hand composition; **~schel·le** *f* handcuff; ***j-m*** **~*n anlegen*** handcuff s.o.; **~schlag** *m* handshake; ***durch*** ~ ***bekräftigen*** shake hands on; **~schrei·ben** *n* handwritten letter
'**Hand·schrift** *f* (-; -en) **1.** handwriting, hand; ***e-e gute*** ~ good (*or* nice) handwriting, a nice hand; *fig.* ***es trägt s-e*** ~ it carries his trademark; **2.** manuscript
'**Hand·schrif·ten|ab,tei·lung** *f* manuscript section (*or* department); **~deu·tung** *f* graphology; **~kun·de** *f* pal(a)eography; **~pro·be** *f* specimen of s.o.'s handwriting
'**hand·schrift·lich I.** *adj.* **1.** handwritten; **2.** manuscript ...; **II.** *adv.* in writing
'**Hand·schuh** *m* (-[e]s; -e) glove; mitten; *fig.* ***j-m den*** ~ ***hinwerfen*** throw down the gauntlet to s.o.; ***den*** ~ ***aufheben*** take up the gauntlet; **~fach** *n* glove compartment; **~num·mer** *f* glove size
'**Hand|set·zer** *m typ.* (hand) compositor; **2si,gniert** *adj.* autographed, signed (by the artist); **~skiz·ze** *f* rough sketch; **~spie·gel** *m* hand mirror; **~spiel** *n soccer*: hand ball, hands; **~stand** *m* (***e-n*** ~ ***machen*** do a) handstand; **~steue·rung** *f* ⚙ manual control; **~sticke·rei** *f* hand embroidery; **~streich** *m* surprise attack; *pol.* coup; ***im*** ~ ***nehmen*** take in a surprise attack; ***durch*** ~ ***stürzen*** overthrow by coup; ***durch*** ~ ***an die Macht kommen*** come to power in a coup; **~ta·sche** *f* handbag, *Am. a.* purse; **~tel·ler** *m anat.* palm (of one's hand)
'**Hand·tuch** *n* (-[e]s; ¨er) towel; ***das*** ~ ***werfen*** *boxing and fig.*: throw in the towel; **~au·to,mat** *m* towel dispenser; **~hal·ter** *m*, **~stän·der** *m* towel rack
'**Hand|um,dre·hen** *n*: ***im*** ~ in no time
'**hand·ver·le·sen** *adj.* handpicked (*a. fig.*)
'**Hand·voll** *f* (-; -) handful (*a. fig.*)
'**Hand|waf·fe** *f* → ***Handfeuerwaffe***; **~wa·gen** *m* handcart; **2warm** *adj.* lukewarm; **~wasch·becken** *n* hand basin; **~wä·sche** *f* hand wash(ing)
Hand·werk ['hantvɛrk] *n* (-s; -e) craft, trade; ***das*** ~ (*a. coll.*) the craft, the trade; ***ein*** ~ ***lernen*** learn a trade; ***sein*** ~ ***verstehen*** *a. fig.* know one's business (F stuff); *fig.* ***j-m das*** ~ ***legen*** throw a spanner (*Am.* monkey wrench) into the works, put a stop to s.o.('s game); ***j-m ins*** ~ ***pfuschen*** meddle in s.o. else's affairs; ***ich möchte Ihnen nicht ins*** ~ ***pfuschen*** I wouldn't like to tread on your toes; '**Hand·wer·ker** [-vɛrkɐ] *m* (-s; -) **1.** workman; ***morgen kommen die*** ~ *a.* we're having (the) workmen in tomorrow; **2.** craftsman; '**hand·werk·lich** *adj.* (handi)craft ...; **~*er Beruf*** skilled trade; **~*e Fähigkeiten*** craft skills
'**Hand·werks|ge·sel·le** *m* journeyman; **~kam·mer** *f* chamber of handicrafts; **~ka·sten** *m* tool box; **~mei·ster** *m* master craftsman; **~zeug** *n* tools *pl.*; *fig.* tools *pl.* of the trade, stock-in-trade
'**Hand·wör·ter·buch** *n* concise dictionary
'**Hand·wur·zel** *f anat.* wrist, 🕮 carpus; **~kno·chen** *m* wristbone, 🕮 carpal bone
'**Hand|zei·chen** *n* a) sign, b) *parl.* show of hands, c) cross *of an illiterate person*; **~zeich·nung** *f* sketch; **~zet·tel** *m* leaflet
ha·ne·bü·chen ['ha:nəby:çən] *adj.* incredible
Hanf [hanf] *m* (-[e]s; *no pl.*) hemp
Hänf·ling ['hɛnflɪŋ] *m* (-s; -e) *zo.* linnet
'**Hanf|öl** *n* hempseed oil; **~sa·men** *m* hempseed; **~seil** *n* hemp rope
Hang[1] [haŋ] *m* (-[e]s; Hänge ['hɛŋə]) **1.** slope (*a. skiing*); **2.** *gym.* hang
Hang[2] *m* (-[e]s; *no pl.*) (natural) inclination (***zu*** *dat.* to *stoutness etc.*, ***zu*** *inf.* to *do*); bent (***zu*** *dat.* for *language etc.*, ***zu*** *inf.* for *doing*); tendency (***zu*** *dat.* towards *s.th. or doing*, ***zu*** *inf.* to *do*); propensity (***zu*** *inf.* to *do*, ***zu*** *dat.* to *s.th.*, for *doing*), penchant (***zu*** *dat.* for *s.th.*); partiality (***zu*** *dat.* for *s.th.*), fondness (for, of *s.th.*); proneness (***zu*** *dat.* to *s.th.*)
Han·gar ['haŋga:ɐ] *m* (-s; -s) ✈ hangar
Hän·ge|arsch ['hɛŋə-] V *m* **1.** drooping buttocks *pl.*; **2.** F droopy drawers *pl.*; **~backen** *pl.* flabby cheeks; **~bahn** *f* suspension railway; **~bauch** *m* paunch, potbelly, flabby stomach; **~brücke** *f* suspension bridge; **~brust** *f*, **~bu·sen** *m* sagging breasts *pl.*; **~la·ger** *n* ⚙ hanging bearing; **~lam·pe** *f* hanging lamp
han·geln ['haŋəln] *v/i.* (h) work one's way along *s.th.* (with one's hands)
Hän·ge·mat·te ['hɛŋə-] *f* hammock
Han·gen ['haŋən] *n*: ***mit*** ~ ***und Bangen*** a) in anxious anticipation, b) barely; ***mit*** ~ ***und Bangen bestehen*** scrape through
hän·gen[1] ['hɛŋən] *v/i.* (hing, gehangen, h) a) hang (***an*** *dat.* on; ***von*** *dat.* from), be suspended (from), b) cling, stick (***an*** *dat.* to), ⚙ catch, be caught, c) ⚠ sag; slope, d) F *fig.* be stuck; ***es hängt schief (zu tief*** *etc.*) it's not straight (it's too low *etc.*); ***voller Früchte*** ~ be laden with fruit; ***voller Bilder*** ~ *wall*: be covered in paintings, *house*: be full of paintings; *fig.* ~ ***an*** *dat.* cling to *s.o. or s.th.*, be very attached (*or* devoted) to *s.o.*, depend on

s.th.; ***die ganze Arbeit hängt an mir*** a) I'm responsible for all the work, b) F I've been lumbered with all the work; F ***er hängt dauernd am Telefon*** he's on the phone all day, he's never off the phone; F ***er hängt dauernd vor dem Fernseher*** he can't take his eyes off the TV, F he's glued to the TV most of the time; → ***Faden, Lippe***; *fig.* ~ ***über*** *dat.* hang over; F *ped.* ***sie hängt in Latein*** she's not very good at Latin, Latin's her weak subject; ***woran hängt's?*** what's the problem?; ~ ***lassen*** → ***Flügel, Kopf*** 5; → ***hängenlassen***

'hän·gen² *v/t.* (h) a) hang (***an*** *acc.* [up] on *the wall*, from *the ceiling*), suspend (from); fix, fasten, attach (***an*** *acc.* to); hook on(to), b) hang *s.o.*; ***gehängt werden*** be hanged; *fig.* ***sich an j-n*** ~ cling to s.o., *sport*: drop in behind s.o.; ***sein Herz an et.*** ~ set one's heart on s.th.; → ***Glocke, Mantel, Nagel***

'Hän·gen *n*: F ***mit*** ~ ***und Würgen*** only just, ***et. schaffen***: only just manage (s.th.), ***die Prüfung bestehen***: scrape through (the exam)

'hän·gen·blei·ben *v/i.* (*irr.*, *sep.*, sn, → ***bleiben***) get (*or* be) caught (***an*** *dat.* on), catch (on, in); get (*or* be) stuck (***in*** *dat.* in); ⚙ jam, stick; be held up; *sport*: be stopped (***an*** *dat.* by); ~ ***in*** (***bei***) *dat.* end up in (at); ~ ***an*** *dat.* get stuck on *s.th.*; ***an mir bleibt alles hängen*** F I get lumbered with everything, I end up having to do everything; *fig.* ***im Gedächtnis*** ~ stick in one's mind; ***von dem Vortrag ist bei mir nicht viel hängengeblieben*** I can't remember much of (what was said in) the talk

'hän·gen·las·sen (*irr.*, *sep.*, h, → ***lassen***) **I.** *v/t.* **1.** leave *washing* on the line; leave (hanging); **2.** F *fig.* ***j-n*** ~ leave s.o. in the lurch; **II.** *v/refl.*: ***sich*** ~ let o.s. go

Hän·ge|oh·ren ['hɛŋə-] *pl.* drooping (*or* floppy) ears; **~par͵tie** *f chess*: adjourned game; **~pflan·ze** *f* hanging plant

Hän·ger ['hɛŋɐ] *m* (-s; -) loose dress (*or* coat), smock

Hän·ge|reck ['hɛŋə-] *n* trapeze; **~schloß** *n* padlock; **~schrank** *m* wall cupboard; **~wei·de** *f* weeping willow

'Hang·la·ge *f* hillside location

Häns·chen ['hɛnsçən] *n*: ***was*** ~ ***nicht lernt, lernt Hans nimmermehr*** you can't teach an old dog new tricks

Hans'dampf [hans-] F *m*: ***er ist ein richtiger*** ~ ***in allen Gassen*** he's a jack-of-all-trades, *w.s.* he's got his finger in every pie

Han·se ['hanzə] *f* (-; *no pl.*) *hist.* Hansa, Hanseatic League

han·sea·tisch [hanze'a:tɪʃ] *adj.* Hanseatic

Hän·se·lei [hɛnzə'laɪ] *f* (-; -en) teasing; **hän·seln** ['hɛnzəln] *v/t.* (h) tease

'Han·se·stadt *f* Hansa (*or* Hanseatic) city; ~ ***Hamburg*** the Hanseatic city of Hamburg

Hans'wurst *m* (-[e]s; -e) clown; *thea.* pantaloon; F fool, idiot, buffoon; ***den*** ~ ***machen für*** *acc.* do the donkey work for

Han·tel ['hantəl] *f* (-; -n) dumbbell

han·tie·ren [han'ti:rən] *v/i.* (h) bustle (*or* potter) around (*or* about); ~ ***mit*** *dat.* work with, handle, F wield; ~ ***an*** *dat.* work on, *contp.* fiddle with, mess around with

ha·pern ['ha:pɐn] F *v/impers.* (h): ***es hapert mit*** (*or* ***bei***) *dat.* there are problems with; ***es hapert an*** *dat.* ... the problem is ..., *a.* there isn't (*or* aren't) enough ...; ***woran hapert's?*** what's the problem?; ***bei uns hapert's am Geld*** the problem (with us) is money; ***im Englischen hapert's bei ihm*** English is his weak point

Häpp·chen ['hɛpçən] *n* (-s; -) titbit, *Am.* tidbit; small snack; gobbet, morsel

Hap·pen ['hapən] *m* (-s; -) bite (to eat); *fig.* catch; ***großer*** ~ hunk; ***e-n*** ~ ***essen*** have a bite to eat; *fig.* ***fetter*** ~ good catch (*or* haul)

Hap·pe·ning ['hɛpənɪŋ] *n* (-s; -s) (art) happening

hap·pig ['hapɪç] F *adj.* F steep *price etc.*; F stiff *problem etc.*; ***das ist ganz schön*** ~ *a.* F that's a bit much

hap·py ['hɛpi] F *adj.* (as) pleased as Punch, F over the moon, high

'Hap·py-End [-'ɛnt] *n* (-[s]; -s) happy end(ing)

Ha·ra·ki·ri [hara'ki:ri] *n* (-[s]; -s): (~ ***machen*** commit) hara-kiri

Här·chen ['hɛ:ɐçən] *n* (-s; -) little (*or* tiny) hair; *biol.* cilium

Hard·ware ['ha:dvɛ:ɐ] *f* (-; *no pl.*) *computer*: hardware

Ha·rem ['ha:rɛm] *m* (-s; -s) harem; **'Ha·rems·da·me** *f* member of a (*or* the) harem

hä·ren ['hɛ:rən] *adj.* (made of) hair; **~es *Gewand*** hairshirt

Hä·re·sie [hɛre'zi:] *f* (-; -n) heresy; **Hä·re·ti·ker** [hɛ're:tikɐ] *m* (-s; -) heretic; **hä·re·tisch** [hɛ're:tɪʃ] *adj.* heretical

Har·fe ['harfə] *f* (-; -n) harp; **Har·fe·nist** [harfə'nɪst] *m* (-en; -en), **Har·fe·ni·stin** [harfə'nɪstɪn] *f* (-; -nen), **'Har·fen·spie·ler** *m* harpist

Har·ke ['harkə] *f* (-; -n) rake; *fig.* ***j-m zeigen, was e-e*** ~ ***ist*** tell s.o. what's what; **'har·ken** *v/t.* (h) rake

Har·le·kin ['harleki:n] *m* (-s; -e) harlequin

Harm [harm] *m* (-[e]s; *no pl.*) grief, sorrow; injury

här·men ['hɛrmən] → ***grämen***

'harm·los I. *adj.* harmless; innocuous; *a.* (perfectly) safe *drug etc.*; easy *test etc.*; insignificant; innocent *expression etc.*; guileless; ***er ist ein*** **~*er Typ*** he's harmless, you needn't worry about him; ***der Film ist eher*** ~ it's a harmless sort of film; ***das ist ja noch*** ~! that's nothing; **II.** *adv.*: ~ ***verlaufen*** *illness etc.*: take its normal course; ***ganz*** ~ ***fragen*** ask in all innocence

Har·mo·nie [harmo'ni:] *f* (-; -n) harmony (*a. fig.*); **~leh·re** *f* harmony

har·mo·nie·ren [harmo'ni:rən] *v/i.* (h) **1.** ♪ harmonize (***mit*** *dat.* with); **2.** a) go (well) together, b) get on well (together), *a.* make a good couple

Har·mo·ni·ka [har'mo:nika] *f* (-; -s) ♪ accordion; concertina; mouthorgan, harmonica; ***er spielt*** ~ he plays the accordion *etc.*

har·mo·nisch [har'mo:nɪʃ] **I.** *adj.* a) ♪ harmonic (*a.* ⩘), *a. fig.* harmonious, b) *gastr.* well-balanced, harmonious *wine*; **~e *Schwingungen*** harmonics; **II.** *adv.*: (***vollkommen***) ~ ***zusammenleben*** *etc.* live *etc.* in (perfect) harmony; ~ ***ablaufen*** go (off) smoothly (*or* without a hitch)

har·mo·ni·sie·ren [harmoni'zi:rən] *v/t.* (h) harmonize

Har·mo·ni·um [har'mo:nĭʊm] *n* (-s; -ien) ♪ harmonium

Harn [harn] *m* (-[e]s; *no pl.*) urine, F water; ~ ***lassen*** pass water; **~ana͵ly·se** *f* urinalysis; **~bla·se** *f* bladder; **~drang** *m* urge to pass water; **~gang** *m* ureter; **~grieß** *m* gravel

Har·nisch ['harnɪʃ] *m* (-[e]s; -e) (suit of) armo(u)r; *fig.* ***j-n in*** ~ ***bringen*** infuriate s.o., raise s.o.'s hackles; ***in*** ~ ***geraten*** get (really) furious

'Harn|lei·ter *m* ureter; **~pro·be** *f* urine sample; **~röh·re** *f* urethra; **~säu·re** *f* uric acid; **~stein** *m* urinary calculus; **~stoff** *m* urea; **≈trei·bend** *adj.* (*a.* **~*es Mittel***) diuretic; **~un·ter͵su·chung** *f* urinalysis; **~we·ge** *pl.* urinary tract *sg.*; **~zwang** *m* strangury

Har·pu·ne [har'pu:nə] *f* (-; -n) harpoon; **har·pu·nie·ren** [harpu'ni:rən] *v/t.* (h) harpoon

har·ren ['harən] *v/i.* (h) wait (*gen. or* ***auf*** *acc.* for), hope (for), await (*s.th.*); ***der Dinge*** ~, ***die da kommen sollen*** wait and see what happens, await events

harsch [harʃ] *adj.* **1.** crusted *snow*; **2.** *fig.* harsh *manner, voice etc.*

Harsch *m* (-[e]s; *no pl.*), **~schnee** *m* crusted snow

hart [hart] **I.** *adj.* **1.** a) hard; firm, solid; stale *bread*; hard-boiled *egg*, b) *fig.* hard; tough; hardened; severe; harsh; **~e *Droge*** hard drug; F ***die*** **~*en Sachen*** F the hard stuff; **~*es Geld*** hard cash; **~e *Währung*** hard currency; **~*es Los*** hard lot; **~*er Schlag*** (***Verlust***) heavy blow (loss); **~*es Spiel*** *sport*: tough game; **~e *Strafe*** severe (*or* harsh) punishment; **~e *Tatsachen*** hard facts; **~*er Winter*** hard (*or* severe) winter; **~e *Worte*** harsh words; **~e *Zeiten*** hard times; ~ ***machen*** (*or* ***werden***) harden; ***j-n*** ~ ***machen*** F toughen s.o. up; ***er blieb*** ~ he was adamant, he wouldn't relent; ***durch e-e*** **~e *Schule gegangen sein*** have learnt it the hard way; ***e-n*** **~*en Stand haben*** have no easy time of it; ***mit*** (*or* ***zu***) ***j-m*** ~ ***sein*** be hard on s.o.; F ***das ist ganz schön*** ~ F it's tough (going); **II.** *adv.* **2.** hard; ~ ***arbeiten*** work hard; ***j-n*** ~ ***bestrafen*** punish s.o. hard (*or* severely); ***j-n*** ~ ***anfassen*** be firm (F tough) with s.o.; ***es kommt ihn*** ~ ***an*** it's hard on him, he's finding it hard; ***j-n*** ~ ***treffen*** hit s.o. hard; ~ ***aneinandergeraten*** come to blows, F go at each other hammer and tongs; ~ ***aufsetzen*** ✈ *etc.* land with a bump; ***es ging*** ~ ***auf*** ~ it was a pitched battle, *a.* both sides were driving a hard bargain; ***es kommt*** ~ ***auf*** ~ it's one problem after another; **3.** ~ ***an*** *dat.* hard by, close to; ~ ***vorbeistreifen an*** *dat.* graze; ~ ***am Wind segeln*** sail close to the wind

Här·te ['hɛrtə] *f* (-; -n) a) hardness, *metall. a.* temper; stability, b) *fig.* toughness; *sport*: tough play; severity; hardship; harshness, c) *phot.* contrast; ***soziale*** ~ social hardship; ⚖ ***unbillige*** ~ undue hardship; ***mit aller*** ~ a) extremely hard, fiercely, relentlessly, b) drastically; ***es traf sie in s-r ganzen*** ~ it hit her with all its force; **~aus·gleich** *m* hardship allowance; **~bad** *n* ⚙ hard-treating (*metall.* tempering) bath; **~fall** *m* a) case of hardship, b) hardship case; **~fonds** *m* hardship fund; **~grad** *m* degree of hardness; *metall.* temper; **~klau·sel** *f* ⚖ hardship clause; **~mit·tel** *n* hardening agent, hardener

här·ten ['hɛrtən] (h) **I.** *v/t.* harden; *metall.* temper; **II.** *v/i.* harden, grow hard

'**Här·te|ofen** *m* ⚙ hard-treating (*metall.* tempering) furnace; **~po·sten** *m* hardship post; **~ska·la** *f* scale of hardness
'**Hart·fa·ser·plat·te** *f* hardboard, *Am.* fiberboard
'**Hart·fut·ter** *n* grain fodder
'**hart|ge·fro·ren** *adj.* frozen; *pred. a.* frozen solid (*or* hard); **~ge·kocht** *adj.* hard-boiled
'**Hart·geld** *n* hard cash, coins *pl.*
'**hart|ge·lö·tet** *adj.* hard-soldered; **~ge·sot·ten** [-gəzɔtən] *fig. adj.* hard-boiled; hardened *criminal etc.*
'**Hart|glas** *n* hard(ened) glass; **~gum·mi** *n, m* hard rubber; ⚘ vulcanite
'**hart·her·zig** *adj.* hard-hearted, unfeeling, callous; '**Hart·her·zig·keit** *f* (- *no pl.*) hard-heartedness, callousness
'**Hart|holz** *n* hardwood; **~kä·se** *m* hard cheese; **♀lö·ten** *v/t.* (*only inf. and p.p.* hartgelötet, h) ⚙ hard-solder; **~me,tall** *n* hard metal; ⚙ cutting metal
hart·näckig ['hartnɛkɪç] *adj.* stubborn (*a.* ⚕); persistent, dogged *attempt etc.*; intractable *problem etc.*; '**Hart·näckig·keit** (*sep.* -k·k-) *f* (-; *no pl.*) stubbornness; persistence, doggedness; intractability
'**Hart·platz** *m tennis*: hard court
Här·tung ['hɛrtʊŋ] *f* (-; *no pl.*) hardening, *metall. a.* tempering; '**Här·tungs·mit·tel** *n* hardening agent
'**Hart·wei·zen** *m* durum wheat; **~grieß** *m* semolina
'**Hart·wurst** *f* dry sausage
Harz [harts] *n* (-es; -e) resin; *a.* ♪ rosin; *mot.* gum; **har·zig** ['hartsɪç] *adj.* resinous
'**Harz|lack** *m* resin varnish; **~säu·re** *f* resin acid
Ha·sar·deur [hazar'døːʁ] *m* (-s; -e [-'døːrə]) gambler (*a. fig.*); **ha·sar·die·ren** [hazar'diːrən] *v/i.* (h) gamble, take a risk (*or* risks); **Ha·sard·spiel** *n* game of chance; *fig.* gamble
Hasch [haʃ] F *n* (-s; *no pl.*) F hash, pot
Ha·schee [ha'ʃeː] *n* (-s; -s) hash
ha·schen[1] ['haʃən] (h) **I.** *v/t.* catch; ***sich ~*** play catch; **II.** *v/i.*: ***~ nach*** *dat.* grasp at, try to catch; *fig.* strive after; *fig.* ***nach Anerkennung*** (***Komplimenten***) ***~*** strive for recognition (fish for compliments)
'**ha·schen**[2] F *v/i.* (h) F smoke pot
Häs·chen ['hɛːsçən] *n* (-s; -) young hare, leveret; F bunny
Hä·scher ['hɛʃɐ] *contp. m* (-s; -) bloodhound
Ha·scherl ['haʃɐl] *dial. n* (-s; -n): ***armes ~*** poor little thing (*or* mite)
Ha·schisch ['haʃɪʃ] *n* (-[s]; *no pl.*) hashish, cannabis; **~zi·ga,ret·te** *f* joint
Ha·se ['haːzə] *m* (-n; -n) **1.** hare; ***junger ~*** leveret; ***männlicher ~*** buck (hare); *gastr.* ***falscher ~*** meat loaf; F *fig.* ***alter ~*** old hand; F ***sehen, wie der ~ läuft*** see how things develop; F ***da liegt der ~ im Pfeffer*** that's the real problem; F ***mein Name ist ~(, ich weiß von nichts!)*** F search me; **2.** *dial.* → ***Kaninchen***
Ha·sel|busch ['haːzəl-] *m* hazelnut (tree), hazel; **~maus** *f* dormouse
'**Ha·sel·nuß** *f* **1.** hazelnut; **2.** → ***Haselstrauch***; **♀braun** *adj.* hazel; **♀groß** *adj.* ... the size of a hazelnut
'**Ha·sel·strauch** *m* hazelnut (tree), hazel
'**Ha·sen|bra·ten** *m* roast hare; **~fuß** *fig. m* coward; **~jagd** *f* hare hunt(ing); **~klein** *n* (-s; *no pl.*), **~pfef·fer** *m gastr.* jugged hare, *Am.* hasenpfeffer; **♀rein** F *adj.*: ***nicht ganz ~*** F a bit fishy, not quite kosher; **~rücken** *m gastr.* saddle of hare; **~schar·te** *f* ⚕ hare lip
Hä·sin ['hɛːzɪn] *f* (-; -nen) female hare, doe
Has·pe ['haspə] *f* (-; -n) hasp
Has·pel ['haspəl] *f* (-; -n) reel; windlass, winch; ⚓ capstan; '**has·peln** (h) **I.** *v/t.* **1.** reel; **2.** splutter (out); **II.** *v/i.* splutter
Haß [has] *m* (Hasses; *no pl.*) hatred, hate (***auf*** *acc.*, ***gegen*** *acc.* for); animosity; loathing; enmity; ***aus ~*** out of hatred; ***e-n ~ haben auf*** *acc.* really hate; F ***e-n ~ kriegen*** see red, F go wild; **~brie·fe** *pl.* hatemail *sg.*
has·sen ['hasən] *v/t.* (h) hate; loathe, detest; → ***Pest***; '**has·sens·wert** *adj.* hateful, odious
'**haß·er·füllt I.** *adj.* full of hatred, seething with hatred; **II.** *adv.*: ***j-n ~ anblicken*** give s.o. a look of hatred, look daggers at s.o.
'**Haß|ge·füh·le** *pl.* feelings of hatred, ranco(u)r *sg.*; **~ge·sang** *m* litany of hate
häß·lich ['hɛslɪç] **I.** *adj.* ugly (*a. fig.*); hideous; unsightly; *fig.* nasty *weather, action etc.*; unpleasant; ***~er Anblick*** ugly sight, (real) eyesore; **II.** *adv.*: ***sich ~ benehmen*** be nasty, behave nastily; ***~ über j-n reden*** say nasty things about s.o.
'**Haß|lie·be** *f* love-hate relationship (***für j-n*** with s.o.); ***mit e-r Art ~ an j-m hängen*** have a (kind of) love-hate relationship with s.o.; **~ob,jekt** *n* object of hate; F ***bevorzugtes ~*** pet hate; **~ti,ra·de** *f* vitriolic attack
Hast [hast] *f* (-; *no pl.*) hurry(ing); *fig.* mad rush; ***ohne ~*** without hurrying (*or* rushing); ***sich ohne ~ fertigmachen*** *a.* take one's time getting ready; ***in großer ~*** in a great hurry, *lit.* in great haste; ***nur keine ~!*** no need to rush; **ha·sten** ['hastən] *v/i.* (sn) hurry; rush, race; **ha·stig** ['hastɪç] **I.** *adj.* a) hurried, rushed, b) rash, c) slapdash; **II.** *adv.* quickly, in a hurry; ***nicht so ~!*** just a minute!; (***noch***) ***~ et. aufschreiben*** jot s.th. down quickly
Hät·schel·kind ['hɛːtʃəl-] *n* pampered child, *a.* Mummy's boy (*or* girl); **hät·scheln** ['hɛːtʃəln] *v/t.* (h) a) pamper, mollycoddle, spoil, b) (kiss and) cuddle, pet; ***sie hätschelt das Kind*** (***den Hund***) ***dauernd*** *a.* she smothers that child (dog), she's all over that child (dog)
hat·schi [ha'tʃiː, 'hatʃi], **hat·zi** [ha'tsiː, 'hatsi] *int.* achoo!, atishoo!
hat·te ['hatə] *pret. of* ***haben***
Hatz [hats] *f* (-; -en) hunt, chase
Hau·be ['haʊbə] *f* (-; -n) **1.** bonnet; hood; *hist.* coif; ⚔ helmet; *eccl.* cornet; *fig.* ***unter die ~ bringen*** find a husband for, get *one's daughter etc.* married; ***unter die ~ kommen*** get married, be married off; **2.** *mot.* bonnet, *Am.* hood; ✈ cowling; **3.** ⚙ cover, cap, dome; dust cover; **4.** hair drier; **5.** *orn.* crest; hood; **6.** *zo.* second stomach, bonnet
'**Hau·ben|ler·che** *f* crested lark; **~mei·se** *f* crested tit(mouse); **~tau·cher** *m* (great) crested grebe
Hau·bit·ze [haʊ'bɪtsə] *f* (-; -n) ⚔ howitzer; F *fig.* ***voll wie e-e ~*** F drunk to the gills, plastered
Hauch [haʊx] *m* (-[e]s; *no pl.*) breath; breath (of wind), breeze; whiff; *ling.* aspiration; *fig.* trace, touch, tinge, hint; (thin) film; air; *fig.* ***ein ~ von Ironie*** a touch of irony; ***nicht der leiseste ~ von*** not a trace of
'**hauch·dünn** *adj.* wafer-thin (*a. fig.*); flimsy *fabric etc.*; sheer *stockings etc.*; eggshell *china etc.*; *fig.* very slim *majority, advantage etc.*; ***~er Sieg*** knife-edge victory; ***~ schneiden*** cut into very fine (*or* wafer-thin) slices
hau·chen ['haʊxən] (h) **I.** *v/i.* breathe; (***sich***) ***in die Hände ~*** blow on one's hands; **II.** *v/t.* breathe, whisper; *ling.* aspirate
'**hauch·fein** *adj.* wafer-thin; flimsy *fabric*; *fig.* very fine, subtle *distinction etc.*
'**Hauch·laut** *m ling.* aspirate
'**hauch·zart** *adj.* very delicate
Hau·de·gen ['haʊdeːgən] *m* (-s; -) (*a.* ***alter ~***) old trooper (*or* warhorse)
Haue[1] ['haʊə] *f* (-; -n) hoe
Haue[2] *dial. f*: ***~ kriegen*** get a smack (*or* spanking)
hau·en ['haʊən] (haute, hieb, gehauen) **I.** *v/t.* (h) **1.** a) hit, beat *s.o.*; smack *a child*, b) chop; chop down *trees*, c) hew, make *statue etc.* (***aus*** *dat.* from), d) ⚙ cut, make *hole etc.*, e) F throw, bang (down) *on the table etc.*; ***sich ~*** (have a) fight; ***haut ihn!*** F let him have it!; ***j-m et. auf den Kopf ~*** hit s.o. over the head with s.th.; ***e-n Nagel in die Wand ~*** bang a nail into the wall; F ***et.*** (***die Wohnung, j-n***) ***kurz und klein ~*** F smash s.th. to pieces (tear the place apart, make mincemeat of s.o.); **II.** *v/i.* **2.** (h) ***~ nach*** *dat.* lash out at; ***um sich ~*** hit out in all directions; ***nicht ~!*** don't hit me (*or* him *etc.*)!; ***j-m ins Gesicht ~*** hit (*or* slap) s.o. in the face; ***auf den Tisch ~*** bang (one's fist on) the table; **3.** (sn) ***mit dem Kopf an die Tür ~*** knock (*or* bang) one's head against the door; → ***Pauke***; **III.** *v/refl.* (h): ***sich ~*** knock o.s., hit o.s.; → ***Ohr***
Hau·er ['haʊɐ] *m* (-s; -) **1.** ⚒ face worker; **2.** *zo.* tusk; **3.** *östr.* vintner, wine grower
Haue·rei ['haʊə'raɪ] F *f* (-; -en) fight(ing), F scrap(ping)
Häuf·chen ['hɔʏfçən] F *n* (-s; -) **1.** (pile of) dog's *etc.* muck; **2.** ***wie ein ~ Unglück*** (*or* ***Elend***) the picture of misery
häu·feln ['hɔʏfəln] *v/t.* (h) heap up
Hau·fen ['haʊfən] *m* (-s; -) pile, heap; mass; stack *of wood*; *fig.* swarm, crowd; ***zu e-m ~ zusammenkehren*** sweep into a pile; F ***ein ~*** F piles (*gen.* of), masses (of); ***ein ~ Arbeit*** a pile (*or* piles) of work; ***ein ~ Geld*** F heaps (*or* stacks) of money; ***e-n ~*** (***Geld***) ***verdienen*** F rake it in, F make a pile; ***es hat e-n ~ Geld gekostet*** F it cost a packet; F ***in hellen ~*** in droves; *contp.* ***der große ~*** the rabble; F ***auf e-m ~ sitzen*** *etc.* sit *etc.* in a big group; F ***auf e-n ~ kommen*** *etc.* come *etc.* all at the same time; F ***j-n über den ~ rennen*** (***schießen***) F (nearly) knock s.o. flying (bump s.o. off); F ***über den ~ werfen*** a) mess up *plans etc.*, put paid to *s.th.*, F scupper, throw overboard, b) upset, explode *a theory etc.*
häu·fen ['hɔʏfən] (h) **I.** *v/t.* pile up, heap up; ***~ auf*** *acc.* pile (up) on, pile onto; → ***gehäuft*** I; **II.** *v/refl.*: ***sich ~*** a) pile up, accumulate, mount, b) *fig.* multiply, increase; spread; happen (*or* occur) more and more often, be on the increase; ***die Beschwerden ~ sich*** more and more complaints are being made (*or* are coming in); ***die Todesfälle ~ sich*** the number of deaths is going up (*or* is on the increase); ***die Hinweise ~ sich*** evidence is mounting; → ***gehäuft*** II
'**hau·fen·wei·se** *adv.* a) in piles, b) in

droves; ***wir kriegen ~ Beschwerden*** we get an endless stream of complaints; ***er hat ~ Platten*** F he's got masses (*or* piles) of records

'Hau·fen·wol·ke *f* cumulus (cloud); ***geschichtete ~*** stratocumulus

häu·fig ['hɔʏfɪç] **I.** *adj.* frequent; widespread; ***ein ~er Fehler*** a common mistake; ***~er werden*** (be on the) increase, be increasing; **II.** *adv.* frequently, (quite) often, F a lot; ***das ist ~ so*** that's often the case; **'Häu·fig·keit** *f* (-; *no pl.*) frequency; incidence *of accidents, crime etc.*

'Häu·fig·keits|kur·ve *f* frequency curve; **~ver·tei·lung** *f* frequency distribution

Häuf·lein ['hɔʏflaɪn] *n* (-s; -) → ***Häufchen***

Häu·fung ['hɔʏfʊŋ] *f* (-; *no pl.*) accumulation (*gen.* of); spread(ing) (of); increase (in, of), increased number (of)

Haupt [haʊpt] *n* (-[e]s; Häupter ['hɔʏptɐ]) head (*a. fig.*); *lit.* ***zu Häupten*** *gen.* at the head of; *fig.* ***an ~ und Gliedern reformieren*** reform root and branch

Haupt... *in cpds. usu.* main, chief, principal; **~ab·neh·mer** *m* † biggest buyer (*or* importer); **~ab·schnitt** *m* 🚂 *etc.* main stretch; **~ab·sicht** *f* main intention (*or* purpose); **~ab|tei·lungs·lei·ter** *m* (senior) head of department; **~ach·se** *f* main axis; *fig.* main thoroughfare; **~ader** *f* ⚒ master lode; **~ak·tio|när** *m* † principal shareholder (*Am.* stockholder); **~ak|zent** *m ling.* primary stress; *fig.* main emphasis; *fig.* ***der ~ liegt auf*** *dat.* the main emphasis is on; **~al|tar** *m* high altar

'haupt·amt·lich I. *adj.* full-time; **II.** *adv. a.* on a full-time basis

'Haupt|an·ge·klag·te *m, f* (-n; -n) principal defendant; **~an·griffs·ziel** *n* main (*or* chief) target; **~an·kla·ge·punkt** *m* main (*or* principal) charge; **~an·lie·gen** *n* main (*or* chief) concern; **~an·schluß** *m teleph.* main line; **~an·teil** *m* † principal share; *fig.* lion's share (***an*** *dat.* of); **~arbeit** *f* **1.** ***die ~*** most (*or* the main part) of the work; **2.** → ***Hauptaufgabe***; **~argu|ment** *n* main (*or* chief) argument; **~ar|ti·kel** *m* †, ⚖ main article; **~attrak·ti|on** *f* main (*or* chief) attraction, big draw; **~auf·ga·be** *f* main (*or* chief) task; **~au·gen·merk** *n*: ***sein ~ richten auf*** *acc.* focus (one's) attention on; **~aus·gang** *m* main exit; **~aus·sa·ge** *f* main statement (*or* point); **~aus·schuß** *m* central committee; **~bahn·hof** *m* main (*or* central) station; **~be·deu·tung** *f ling.* primary meaning; *fig.* main (*or* primary) significance; **~be·din·gung** *f* main (*or* principal) condition; **~be·la·stungszeu·ge** *m* chief witness for the prosecution

'Haupt·be·ruf *m* main job; **'haupt·beruf·lich I.** *adj.* full-time ...; **II.** *adv.* as one's main job; *work* full-time; ***~ ist er Lehrer*** his main job is teaching; ***was machen Sie ~?*** what's your main job?

'Haupt|be·schäf·ti·gung *f* main job; **~be·stand·teil** *m* main constituent (*esp.* ⚙ component); **~be·tei·lig·te** *m, f* (-n; -n) principal party (*or* person) concerned; chief protagonist; **~be·trieb** *m* **1.** main office(s *pl.*) *or* plant; **2.** peak period; **~be·weg·grund** *m* main reason; **~be·weis** *m* main proof (*or* evidence); **~dar·stel·ler** *m* leading actor, lead; **~da|tei** *f computer*: master file; **~deck** *n* ⚓ main deck; **~ei·gen·schaft** *f* chief characteristic; **~ein·fahrt** *f*, **~ein·gang** *m* main entrance; **~ein·kaufs·zeit** *f* peak shopping hours *pl.*; **~ein·nah·me·quelle** *f* chief (*or* main) source of income; **~ein·schalt·quo·te** *f* highest viewer (*or* listener) rating; **~er·be** *m* chief heir; **~er·bin** *f* chief heiress; **~er·for·der·nis** *n* chief requirement; **~er·zeug·nis** *n* main product; **~fach** *n* main subject, *Am.* major; ***was hast du als ~?*** what's your main subject (*Am.* major, what do you major in)?; **~fak·tor** *m* main factor; **~feh·ler** *m* chief mistake; main fault; **~feind** *m* chief enemy; **~feld·we·bel** *m* ⚔ staff sergeant, *Am.* sergeant major; **~fi|gur** *f* main (*or* central) figure; *thea. etc.* main character; hero, *f* heroine; protagonist; **~fi·li|ale** *f* main branch; **~film** *m* main feature; **~fra·ge** *f* main question (*or* issue); **~funk·ti|on** *f* main function (*or* purpose); **~gang** *m* **1.** *gastr.* main course; **2.** main corridor (*zo.* passage); **~ge·bäu·de** *n* main building; **~ge·danke** *m* main idea; **~ge·fahr** *f* main (*or* primary) danger; **~ge·frei·te** *m* ⚔ lance corporal, *Am.* private 1st class; **~gericht** *n gastr.* main course; **~ge·schäft** *n* **1.** head office; **2.** a) peak business hours *pl.*, b) → ***Haupteinkaufszeit***; **~geschäfts·stel·le** *f* → ***Hauptgeschäft*** 1; **~ge·schäfts·zeit** *f* → ***Hauptgeschäft*** 2; **~ge·sichts·punkt** *m* main (*or* major) consideration; **~ge·sprächs·the·ma** *n* main topic of conversation, conversation topic number one; **~ge·wicht** *fig. n* main emphasis; **~ge·winn** *m* first prize; † main profit; **~gläu·bi·ger** *m* principal creditor; **~grund** *m* main reason; **~hahn** *m* main tap (*Am.* faucet); **~hand·lung** *f thea. etc.* main plot; **~hin·der·nis** *n* main obstacle (*or* hurdle); **~in·halt** *m* essence; **~in·ter|es·se** *n* main interest; ***sein ~ gilt ...*** he's mainly (*or* primarily) interested in ...; **~in·ter|es·sen·ge·biet** *n* main area (*or* field) of interest; **~kasse** *f* main cash desk; *thea.* box office; **~ka·ta|log** *m* main catalog(ue); **~kläger** *m* principal plaintiff; **~last** *f* main burden; brunt (of it); ***die ~ zu tragen haben*** have to bear the brunt (of it); **~lei·den·schaft** *f* great(est) passion; **~leid·tra·gen·de** *m, f* (-n; -n) main victim; ***der ~*** *a.* the one to suffer most; ***die ~n*** those who suffer most; **~lei·tung** *f* mains *pl.*; **~lie·fe|rant** *m* main (*or* chief) supplier

Häupt·ling ['hɔʏptlɪŋ] *m* (-s; -e) headman; tribal chief; (Indian) chief; F boss

'Haupt|mahl·zeit *f* main meal (of the day); **~man·gel** *m* main fault (*or* weakness); **~mann** *m* (-[e]s; -leute) ⚔ captain; **~mas·se** *f* bulk, main body; **~me|nü** *n computer*: main menu; **~merk·mal** *n* main feature, chief characteristic; **~mieter** *m* main tenant; **~mo|tiv** *n* **1.** main motive (*or* motivation); **2.** *art*: central motif (*or* theme); **~nach·richt** *f* **1.** lead story; **2.** *pl.* main news (*sg.*); **~nah·rung** *f*, **~nah·rungs·mit·tel** *n* staple (food), *pl. a.* staple diet *sg.*; **~nen·ner** *m* 𝔄 *and fig.* common denominator; *fig.* ***um es auf e-n ~ zu bringen*** to bring it down to a common denominator; **~nie·der·lassung** *f* † head (*or* central) office, headquarters *pl.*; **~per|son** *f* → ***Hauptfigur***; ***er will immer die ~ sein*** he always wants to be number one (*or* the cent|re [*Am.* -er] of attention); **~por|tal** *n* main entrance (*gen.* of, to), main door(way) (of, into); **~post(·amt** *n*) *f* main (*Am.* general) post office; **~pro·be** *f thea.* dress rehearsal; ♪ general rehearsal; **~pro|blem** *n* main problem; **~punkt** *m* main point (*or* issue); **~quar|tier** *n* headquarters *pl.*; **~rech·ner** *m computer*: mainframe (computer); **~red·ner** *m* main speaker; **~re·gel** *f* principal (*or* most important) rule, rule number one; **~rei·se·zeit** *f* (peak) tourist season; **~rich·tung** *f* **1.** main (*or* general) direction; **2.** major (*or* main) trend; **~rol·le** *f* leading role, main part, lead; title role; ***die ~ spielen*** *thea.* play the lead(ing role) *or* main part, *fig.* a) be the central figure, be the chief protagonist, b) play the most important role, be the most important thing

'Haupt·sa·che *f* **1.** main (*or* most important) thing; ***das ist die ~*** *a.* that's what matters most; ***~ sie gewinnt*** the main thing is that she wins (*or* is for her to win); ***in der ~*** mainly, in the main, for the main part; **2.** ⚖ main issue; **'hauptsäch·lich I.** *adj.* main ..., most important, essential; **II.** *adv.* mainly, chiefly, essentially; above all; ***worauf es ~ ankommt, ist*** what matters most is, the most important thing is

'Haupt|sai|son *f* peak season; **~satz** *m* **1.** *ling.* main clause; **2.** *phys. etc.* first principle (*or* law); **~schal·ter** *m* **1.** ⚡ main (*or* master) switch; **2.** main desk (*or* counter); 🚂 *etc.* main booking office (*or* ticket desk, ticket counter); **~schiff** *n* △ nave; **~schlag·ader** *f anat.* aorta; **~schlüs·sel** *m* master key; **~schuld** *f* **1.** ***er trägt die ~ daran*** it's mainly his fault, he's mostly to blame (for it); **2.** † principal debt; **~schul·di·ge** *m, f* (-n; -n) major offender; **~schuld·ner** *m* principal debtor; **~schu·le** *f* secondary modern school; **~schwie·rig·keit** *f* main (*or* chief, major) difficulty; **~se·mi|nar** *n* (advanced) seminar; **~sen·de·zeit** *f TV* peak viewing hours *pl.*, prime time; **~si·che·rung** *f* ⚡ main fuse; **~sitz** *m* † head office, headquarters *pl.*; **~sor·ge** *f* main (*or* chief) concern, main worry; **~spei·cher** *m computer*: main memory; **~spei·se** *f* main course; **~stadt** *f* capital (city); **~stamm** *m* chief tribe; **~stär·ke** *f* strong point, main (*or* chief) strength; **~stoß·rich·tung** *f* ⚔ general thrust (of the attack); **~stra·ße** *f* main street; **~strecke** *f* main route; 🚂 main line; **~streit·punkt** *m* main issue (*or* point of contention); **~strom** *m* ⚡ main current; **~strö·mung** *f* main current (*or* trend); **~stüt·ze** *fig. f* mainstay; **~tä·ter** *m* ⚖ principal offender; **~tä·tig·keit** *f* main job; main duty (*or* function); **~teil** *m* main part; ***der ~*** most of it, the greater part; **~the·ma** *n* main subject; ♪ principal theme; **~ton** *m* main stress; ♪ keynote; **~tor** *n* main gate; **~tref·fer** *m* first prize, F jackpot; ***den ~ gewinnen*** hit the jackpot; **~trep·pe** *f* main (*or* grand) staircase; **~tri|bü·ne** *f* grandstand; **~trieb·fe·der** *f* mainspring (*a. fig.*); **~trieb·kraft** *fig. f* prime mover (*gen.* of), powerhouse (behind); **~trieb·werk** *n* main rocket engine; **~tu·gend** *f* cardinal virtue; **~|un·ter·schied** *m* main difference; **~ur·sa·che** *f* main cause; ***die ~ ist ...*** *a.* at the bottom of it all is ...; **~verant·wor·tung** *f* chief (*or* prime) responsibility; ***die ~ übernehmen*** take chief (*or* prime) responsibility (***für*** *acc.* for); **~ver·die·ner** *m* chief earner (F breadwinner)

'Haupt·ver·dienst¹ *m* main income

'Haupt·ver·dienst² *n* major (*or* greatest) achievement

'Haupt|ver·hand·lung *f* ⚖ trial, hearing; main proceedings *pl.*; **~ver·kehr** *m* **1.** rush-hour traffic; **2.** ***der ~*** most of the traffic

'Haupt·ver·kehrs|stra·ße *f* main road; main thoroughfare; **~zeit** *f* rush hour; peak traffic hours *pl.*

'Haupt|ver·samm·lung *f* ✝ general meeting; **~ver·tre·ter** *m* general agent; **~ver·wal·tung** *f* head office, headquarters *pl.*; **~vor·stand** *m* governing board; **~wacht·mei·ster** *m* police sergeant; ⚔ → ***Hauptfeldwebel***; **~wasch·gang** *m* main wash; **~werk** *n* **1.** major work; **2.** ⚙ main plant; **~wohn·sitz** *m* main (place of) residence; **~wort** *n* (-[e]s; ⸚er) *ling.* noun; **~zeu·ge** *m* chief witness; **~ziel** *n* main objective; **~zug** *m* **1.** 🚂 regular train; **2.** *fig.* main (*or* chief) characteristic; main (character) trait; ***et. in s-n Hauptzügen schildern*** outline s.th., give an (*or* a rough) outline of s.th.; **~zweck** *m* main (*or* chief, primary) purpose

hau ruck ['haʊ 'rʊk] *int.* heave-ho!

Haus [haʊs] *n* (-es [-zəs]; Häuser ['hɔʏzɐ]) **1.** house (*a. ast. and fig. tenants*); building, *a.* block (of flats); home, *fig. a.* family; dynasty; *parl.* House; hotel; restaurant; shop, store; ***im ~*** inside; ***zu ~e*** at home; ***zu ~e sein*** *a.* be in; ***wieder zu ~e sein*** be back home again; ***nach ~e*** home; ***j-n nach ~e bringen*** take (*or* see) s.o. home; ***er ist in X zu ~e*** his home is (in) X, he comes from X; ***bei uns zu ~e*** a) in my family, F at our place, b) where I come from; ***er ist außer ~e*** he's out, he's not in, he's gone out; ✝ ***außer ~ geben*** contract out; ***von ~ zu ~*** from door to door; ***ein ~ weiter*** a) next door, b) in the next block (of flats); ***zwei Häuser weiter*** a) next door but one, b) two blocks (further) down *or* up; ***~ an ~ wohnen*** live next door to each other, be next-door neighbo(u)rs, ***mit j-m:*** live next door to s.o.; ***tut, als ob ihr zu ~e wäret*** make yourselves at home; ***ein offenes ~ haben*** have an open door; ***das kommt mir nicht ins ~!*** I'm not having that in the (*or* my) house; ✝ ***frei ~*** carriage paid; *thea.* ***volles ~*** full house; ***immer volle Häuser haben*** always be sold out; ***das ~ tobte*** the audience went wild, *a.* they nearly brought the house down; ***das erste ~ am Platz(e)*** the best hotel (*or* restaurant, store) in town, the number one hotel *etc.* around here; ***~ und Hof*** house and home; *fig.* ***aus gutem ~e sein*** come from a good family; ***sein ~ bestellen*** (*or* ***beschicken***) put one's house in order; ***in e-r Sache zu ~e sein*** be well up in s.th.; ***auf ihn kann man Häuser bauen*** he's rock solid; ***es stehen Neuwahlen ins ~*** elections are coming up, there are elections ahead (*or* on the doorstep); ***ihm steht e-e Versetzung ins ~*** he's got a posting coming up, he's in for a posting; ***von ~ aus*** actually, originally; ***er ist von ~ aus Chirurg*** he's (actually) a qualified surgeon, he was originally a surgeon; **2.** *hum.* ***altes ~*** old chap; ***fideles ~*** cheerful type

'Haus|al,tar *m* family altar; **~an·ge·stell·te** *f* domestic (servant); maid; **~an,ten·ne** *f* roof aerial (*or* antenna); **~apo,the·ke** *f* medicine cabinet (*or* chest); **~ar·beit** *f* housework; *ped. a. pl.* homework; **~ar,rest** *m*: (***unter ~ stellen*** place under) house arrest; **~arzt** *m* family doctor, GP (= general practitioner); **~auf·ga·be** *f a. pl.* homework

'haus·backen (*sep.* -k·k-) *adj.* homemade; *fig.* homely *person*; plain, prosy, F boring *thing*

'Haus|ball *m* private ball, dinner and dance; **~bar** *f* cocktail cabinet; bar; **~bau** *m* (-[e]s; *no pl.*) house building; **~be·darf** *m* household requirements *pl.*; ***für den ~*** for the home, *w.s.* for (your *etc.* own) private use; **~be·set·zer** *m* squatter; **~be·set·zung** *f* squatting; **~be·sit·zer** *m* house owner; landlord; **~be·such** *m* ⚕ home visit; ***~e machen*** *a.* be on (*or* doing) one's rounds; **~be·woh·ner** *m* occupant; tenant; **~bib·lio,thek** *f* private library; **~boot** *n* houseboat; **~brand** *m* (-[e]s; *no pl.*) domestic fuel

Häus·chen ['hɔʏsçən] *n* (-s; -) a) small house; cottage; lodge, b) F loo, *Am.* F john; F *fig.* (***ganz***) ***aus dem ~ geraten*** F flip one's lid, throw a wobbly; F ***ganz aus dem ~ sein*** be all excited, F be over the moon, ***vor*** *dat.*: F be wild with *excitement etc.*

'Haus|da·me *f* housekeeper; **~de·tek,tiv** *m* store detective; **~dra·chen** F *m* battle-ax(e); **~durch,su·chung** *f* house search; **~ei·gen·tü·mer** *m* → ***Hausbesitzer***; **~ein·gang** *m* entrance (to a *or* the house), front door (*or* entrance)

hau·sen ['haʊzən] *v/i.* (h) **1.** live; **2.** *contp.* wreak havoc; ***sie haben dort wie die Vandalen gehaust*** *a.* F they wrecked the place

Häu·ser|block ['hɔʏzɐ-] *m* block (of houses); **~flucht** *f* row of houses; **~front** *f* **1.** housefront; **2.** row of houses; **~makler** *m* estate agent, *Am.* realtor; **~meer** *n* (-[e]s; *no pl.*) sea of houses; ***ein ~*** *a.* houses as far as the eye can see

'Haus·flur *m* hall(way)

'Haus·frau *f* housewife; *Am. a.* homemaker; *w.s.* lady of the house; **'Haus·frau·en·da·sein** *n* life of a housewife; ***das ~ satt haben*** be fed up of being (just) a housewife; **'haus·frau·lich** *adj.* housewifely; domestic; ***~e Pflichten*** duties of a housewife; ***ich habe keine ~en Fähigkeiten*** I'm (*or* I'd be) no good as a housewife

'Haus·freund *m* friend of the family; *iro.* boyfriend, F man

'Haus·frie·dens·bruch *m* ⚖ illegal entry of s.o.'s house

'Haus|ge·brauch *m*: ***für den ~*** for use in the home; F *fig.* for (one's own) pleasure; F *fig.* ***für den ~ reichen*** be enough to get by on, be good enough for one's own simple needs (*or* requirements); **~ge·hil·fin** [-gəhɪlfɪn] *f* (-; -nen) maid; **2ge·macht** *adj.* homemade (*a.* F *fig.*); **~ge·mein·schaft** *f* **1.** tenants *pl.*; **2.** community, household; ***wir haben e-e nette ~*** we have nice neighbo(u)rs, we all get on with each other (in our block of flats)

'Haus·halt *m* (-[e]s; -e) **1.** a) household, b) *no pl.* housekeeping; ***den ~ führen*** run the household, ***j-m:*** *a.* keep house for s.o.; ***im ~ helfen*** help (out) in (*or* around) the house; **2.** *pol.* budget;

'haus·hal·ten *v/i.* (*irr.*, *sep.*, h, → ***halten***) economize; ***~ mit*** *dat.* be economical with, economize on, *a. fig.* F go easy on *one's strength etc.*; *fig.* ***mit der Zeit*** (***s-r Energie***) ***~*** divide one's time (energies) up sensibly; **'Haus·häl·te·rin** [-hɛltərɪn] *f* (-; -nen) housekeeper; **'haus·häl·te·risch** [-hɛltərɪʃ] **I.** *adj.* economical; **II.** *adv.*: ***~ umgehen mit*** *dat.* → ***haushalten***

'Haus·halts|ar,ti·kel *m* household article; **~aus·schuß** *m parl.* budget(ary) committee; **~de,bat·te** *f* budget(ary) debate, debate on the budget; **~de·fi·zit** *n* budget deficit; **~ent·wurf** *m* budget proposals *pl.*; **~ex,per·te** *m* budget expert; **~füh·rung** *f* housekeeping; **~geld** *n* (-[e]s; *no pl.*) housekeeping money; **~ge·rät** *n* household appliance; **~ge·setz** *n* budget law; **~jahr** *n* fiscal (*or* financial) year; **~mit·glied** *n* member of a (*or* the) household; **~mit·tel** *pl.* budgetary means; appropriations; **~packung** *f* economy pack; **~plan** *m parl.* budget; **~pla·nung** *f* budgeting; **~po·li,tik** *f* budgetary policies *pl.*; **2po,li·tisch** *adj.* budgetary; **~,über·schuß** *m* budget surplus; **~vor·la·ge** *f* budget proposals *pl.*; **~vor·stand** *m* head of a (*or* the) household; **~wa·ren** *pl.* household articles

'Haus·hal·tung *f* (-; -en) **1.** *no pl.* housekeeping; **2.** household; **'Haus·hal·tungs·ko·sten** *pl.* household expenses

'Haus-'Haus-Ver·kehr *m* 🚂 door-to-door service

'Haus·herr *m* head of a (*or* the) household; host; **'Haus·her·rin** *f* lady of the house; hostess

'haus'hoch I. *adj.* very high, huge; *fig.* vast, enormous; ***haushohe Niederlage*** shattering (*or* crushing) defeat; ***haushoher Sieg*** walkover, *Am.* walkaway; **II.** *adv.*: ***~ gewinnen*** win hands down; ***~ schlagen*** trounce, *sport*: *a.* play *s.o.* into the ground; ***~ verlieren*** suffer a crushing defeat, F be thrashed; *dat.* ***~ überlegen sein*** be more than a match for *s.o.*, *a team etc.*, *a.* be head and shoulders above *s.o.*, be streets ahead of *s.o.*, outnumber by far; ***sie ist ihm ~ überlegen*** *a.* he's no match for her, he can't hold a candle to her

'Haus|huhn *n* domestic fowl; **~hund** *m* (domestic) dog

hau·sie·ren [haʊ'zi:rən] *v/i.* (h) hawk, *a. fig.* peddle (***mit et.*** s.th.); ***Betteln und 2 verboten!*** no hawkers; *fig.* ***~ mit*** *dat.* tell the whole world (about) *s.th.*; **Hau·sie·rer** [haʊ'zi:rɐ] *m* (-s; -) hawker, peddler; door-to-door salesman

'Haus|in·du,strie *f* cottage industry; **2in,tern** *adj.* internal, in-house ...; **~ju,rist** *m* company (*or* corporate) lawyer; **~ka,pel·le** *f* **1.** private chapel; **2.** resident band (*or* orchestra); **~kat·ze** *f* (domestic) cat; **~käu·fer** *m* home buyer; **~klin·gel** *f* (front) doorbell; **~kon,zert** *n* private (*or* house) concert; **~kor·rek,tur** *f typ.* house corrections *pl.*; **~leh·rer** *m* private tutor

häus·lich ['hɔʏslɪç] **I.** *adj.* a) domestic (*a. fig.*); household ..., family ..., b) domesticated; ***er ist ein ~er Typ*** *a.* he's quite happy to be at home (with the family) *or* around the house; **II.** *adv.*: ***sich ~ einrichten*** (*or* ***niederlassen***) make o.s. at home (***bei j-m*** in s.o.'s flat *etc.*), F camp down (at s.o.'s place); **'Häus·lich·keit** *f*

(-; *no pl.*) family life; domesticity; home
'**Haus·ma·cher·art** *f*: ***nach*** ~ traditional-style ...
'**Haus·mäd·chen** *n* maid
'**Haus·mann** *m* (-[e]s; ⸚er) house husband; '**Haus·manns·kost** *f* good plain cooking
'**Haus|mar·der** *m zo.* beech marten; ~**mar·ke** *f* own brand; house wine; F *w.s. one's* favo(u)rite brand; ~**mei·ster** *m* caretaker, *Am.* janitor; ~**mit·tel** *n* household (*or* home) remedy; ~**müll** *m* household waste; ~**mu,sik** *f* music-making in the home
'**Haus·mut·ter** *f* matron; '**Haus·müt·ter·chen** F *n* F homebody; '**haus·müt·ter·lich** *adj.* homely
'**Haus|num·mer** *f* house number, number of the house; ~**ord·nung** *f* rules *pl.* (for residents); *iro.* ***die*** ~ ***besagt, daß*** the rules in this house say that; ~**per·so,nal** *n* domestic staff (*or* servants *pl.*); ~**pfle·ge** *f* ⚕ home nursing; home care; ~**post** *f* internal (*or* in-house) mail; ~**putz** *m* spring-clean(ing); ~ ***machen*** give the house a spring-clean
'**Haus·rat** *m* (-s; *no pl.*) household effects *pl.*; ~**ver·si·che·rung** *f* household contents insurance
'**Haus|samm·lung** *f* door-to-door collection; ~**schlach·tung** *f* home slaughtering; ~**schlüs·sel** *m* (front) doorkey, key to the (front) door; ~**schuh** *m* slipper; ~**schwal·be** *f* (house) martin; ~**schwamm** *m* house fungus; ***Echter*** ~ dry rot; ~**schwein** *n* (domestic) pig
Hausse ['ho:s(ə)] *f* (-; -n) ✝ bull market; ***auf*** ~ ***spekulieren*** bull the market
'**Haus·se·gen** *m*: F ***der*** ~ ***hängt*** (***bei ihnen***) ***schief*** F they've been having a row
'**Hausse|markt** *m* ✝ bull(ish) market; ~**spe·ku·la·ti,on** *f* ✝ bull operation
Haus·sier [(h)o'sie:] *m* (-s; -s) ✝ bull operator
'**Haus·sprech·an·la·ge** *f* intercom; ***über die*** ~ on the intercom
'**Haus·stand** *m* household; ***e-n*** ~ ***gründen*** set up house
'**Haus·staub·mil·be** *f* dust mite
'**Haus·su·chung** [-zu:xʊŋ] *f* (-, -en) house search; '**Haus·su·chungs·be·fehl** *m* search warrant
'**Haus|te·le,fon** *n* intercom; ~**tier** *n* **1.** domestic animal; **2.** pet
'**Haus·tür** *f* front door; ~**schlüs·sel** *m* front doorkey
'**Haus|ty,rann** *m* household tyrant; ~**va·ter** *m* warden; ~**ver·bot** *n* order to stay away; ***er hat bei ihnen*** ~ he's been told to stay away, they're not letting him into the house (*or* building *etc.*); ~**ver·wal·ter** *m* **1.** property manager, *Am.* superintendent; **2.** caretaker, *Am.* janitor; ~**ver·wal·tung** *f* property management; ~**wand** *f* outside wall, (outer) wall of a (*or* the) house; ~**wirt** *m* landlord; ~**wir·tin** *f* landlady
'**Haus·wirt·schaft** *f* housekeeping; *ped.* domestic science; '**haus·wirt·schaft·lich** *adj.* domestic, household ...; '**Haus·wirt·schafts·leh·re** *f* domestic science, home economics *pl.*
'**Haus·zeit·schrift** *f* company *or* in-house magazine (F rag)
Haut [haʊt] *f* (-; Häute ['hɔʏtə]) **1.** *no pl.* skin (*a.* ✂ *etc.*); ***obere*** ~ epidermis; ***dünne*** ~ membrane (*a.* ⚘); ***bis auf die*** ~ ***durchnäßt*** soaked to the skin; ***auf bloßer*** ~ ***tragen*** wear next to one's skin; ***er trägt die Jacke auf der bloßen*** ~ *a.* he's got nothing on under his jacket; ***sich die*** ~ ***aufschürfen*** graze o.s., ***an den Knien*** *etc.*: skin (*or* graze) one's knees *etc.*; F *fig.* ***e-e ehrliche*** (***gute***) ~ an honest (a good) soul; F ***mit*** ~ ***und Haaren*** completely, F hook, line and sinker; F ***auf der faulen*** ~ ***liegen*** take it easy, have an easy time of it; F ***aus der*** ~ ***fahren*** F go through (*or* hit) the roof; F ***das ist ja zum Aus-der-Haut-Fahren*** F it's enough to drive you spare; F ***e-e dicke*** ~ ***haben*** have a thick skin, be thick-skinned; F ***mit heiler*** ~ ***davonkommen*** come out of it unscathed (*or* F in one piece); F ***s-e*** (***eigene***) ~ ***retten*** save one's skin (F *hum.* bacon); F ***sich s-r*** ~ ***wehren*** defend o.s. (with all one's might); F ***ihr ist nicht wohl in ihrer*** ~ she feels (rather) uncomfortable (*or* uneasy); F ***ich möchte nicht in s-r*** ~ ***stekken*** I wouldn't like to be in his shoes; F ***er ist nur noch*** ~ ***und Knochen*** he's just skin and bones; F ***es kann eben keiner aus s-r*** ~ a leopard can't change its spots; F ***das geht einem unter die*** ~ it gets under your skin; F ***s-e*** ~ ***zu Markte tragen*** a) risk one's neck, b) sell o.s., sell one's charms; → ***heil*** I; **2.** *zo. and* ✝ hide; ⚘ skin, peel; ⚙ film; ***e-m Tier die*** ~ ***abziehen*** skin an animal
'**Haut|ab·schür·fung** *f* abrasion, graze; ~**arzt** *m* dermatologist, skin specialist; ~**at·mung** *f* cutaneous respiration; ~**aus·schlag** *m* (skin) rash
Häut·chen ['hɔʏtçən] *n* (-s; -) thin coat(ing); film; *anat.*, ⚘ membrane
'**Haut|creme** *f* skin cream; ~**drü·se** *f* cutaneous gland
Haute Cou·ture [(h)o:tku'ty:ʁ] *f* (- -; *no pl.*) (*a.* ***die*** ~) haute couture
häu·ten ['hɔʏtən] (h) **I.** *v/t.* skin, flay; **II.** *v/refl.*: ***sich*** ~ shed one's skin, *snake etc.*: slough off; F peel
'**haut·eng** *adj.* skintight, body-hugging
'**Haut·ent·zün·dung** *f* inflammation of the skin; skin rash
Haute·vo·lee [(h)o:tvo'le:] *f* (-; *no pl.*) F upper crust; top knobs *pl.*
'**Haut·fal·te** *f* skin fold; wrinkle
'**Haut·far·be** *f* colo(u)r (of one's skin); complexion; '**haut·far·ben** [-farbən] *adj.* flesh-colo(u)red, *cosmetics*: skin-colo(u)red
'**Haut|farb·stoff** *m* (skin) pigment; ~**fet·zen** *m* piece of skin
'**Haut·flüg·ler** [-fly:glɐ] *m* (-s; -) *zo.* hymenopteron
'**haut·freund·lich** *adj.* kind to the skin
'**Haut·gift** *n* skin (*or* contact) poison, 🕮 vesicant
Haut·gout [o'gu:] *m* (-s; *no pl.*) **1.** *gastr.* high flavo(u)r; ~ ***haben*** be high; **2.** *fig.* shadiness; shady touch
'**Haut|jucken** *n* itching, irritation of the skin, 🕮 pruritus; ~**krank·heit** *f* skin disease; ~**krebs** *m* skin cancer
'**haut·nah I.** *adj. sport*: close, tight; *fig.* graphic, vivid; **II.** *adv. sport*: closely; *fig.* ***j-n*** ~ ***berühren*** affect s.o. directly, go straight to the core, get under s.o.'s skin; ***wir haben es*** ~ ***miterlebt*** it happened right in front of our eyes; ***durch das Fernsehen kann man das Weltgeschehen*** ~ ***miterleben*** television brings world events right into your living room
'**Haut|nerv** *m* cutaneous nerve; ~**öl** *n* skin oil
'**Haut·pfle·ge** *f* skin care; ~**mit·tel** *n* skin care product
'**Haut|pilz** *m* **1.** skin (*or* cutaneous) fungus; **2.** fungal infection; ~**pla·stik** *f* ⚕ dermoplasty; ~**rei·zung** *f* skin irritation; ~**rö·tung** *f* red (patch of) skin; ~**sal·be** *f* skin ointment; ~**sche·re** *f* cuticle scissors *pl.*; ~**trans·plan·ta·ti,on** *f* skin graft(ing); ~**typ** *m* skin type; ***was für e-n*** ~ ***hat sie?*** what type of skin has she got?; ***für jeden*** ~ for all skin types
Häu·tung ['hɔʏtʊŋ] *f* (-; -en) sloughing
'**Haut|un·rein·heit** *f* (skin) blemish; spot; ~***en*** *a.* spots and blackheads; ~**ver·let·zung** *f* superficial wound, (skin) lesion; ~**ver·pflan·zung** *f* skin graft(ing); ~**ver·träg·lich** *adj.* non-irritant, hypoallergenic; ~**wun·de** *f* → ***Hautverletzung***; ~**zip·fel** *m* skin tag
Ha·va·rie [hava'ri:] *f* (-; -n) damage, average; accident; ~**kom·mis,sar** *m* average adjuster, claims agent
H-Bom·be *f* H-bomb
he [he:] *int.* hey!, *sl.* oy!
Heb·am·me ['he:pˀamə] *f* (-; -n) midwife
He·be|arm ['he:bə-] *m*, ~**baum** *m* lever; ~**büh·ne** *f mot.* hydraulic lift; ~**kran** *m* hoist(ing crane)
He·bel ['he:bəl] *m* (-s; -) lever (*a. fig.*); handle; crank; *fig.* ***den*** ~ ***ansetzen*** get things moving; ***alle*** ~ ***in Bewegung setzen*** do everything in one's power, move heaven and earth, leave no stone unturned; ***am längeren*** ~ ***sitzen*** have more pull; ***an den*** ~***n der Macht sitzen*** be at the controls
'**He·bel|arm** *m* lever arm; ~**ge·setz** *n phys.* lever law; ~**griff** *m sport*: lever hold; ~**kraft** *f*, ~**mo,ment** *n* leverage; ~**stütz·punkt** *m* fulcrum; ~**waa·ge** *f* beam scale; ~**werk** *n* lever gear; ~**wir·kung** *f* leverage; ***e-e*** ~ ***haben*** have a levering effect
he·ben ['he:bən] (hob, gehoben, h) **I.** *v/t.* lift (*a. sport*); raise (*a. one's glass, one's voice, a treasure etc., fig. standards, quality etc.*); hoist; *mot.* jack up; *fig.* increase; improve; add to; ***j-s Moral*** (***Selbstbewußtsein***) ~ boost s.o.'s morale (self-confidence); F ***einen*** ~ F hoist one; **II.** *v/refl.*: ***sich*** ~ rise (*a. voice*), go up; *curtain, fog etc.*: lift; *fig.* improve; ***sich*** ~ ***und senken*** rise and fall; → ***Angel***², ***Himmel***; **III.** ♀ *n* (-s) weight lifting
He·ber ['he:bɐ] *m* (-s; -) *phys.* siphon; pipette; ⚙ *esp. in cpds.* ...-lifter, ...-raiser; *mot.* jack
He·be|satz ['he:bə-] *m* rate of assessment; ~**schiff** *n* salvage ship; ~**vor·rich·tung** *f* lifting gear, hoisting apparatus; elevating mechanism; hydraulic jack; ~**zeug** *n* lifting gear, hoist
He·brä·er [he'brɛ:ɐ] *m* (-s; -), **He·bräe·rin** [he'brɛ:ərɪn] *f* (-; -nen), **he·brä·isch** [he'brɛ:ɪʃ] *adj.*, **He'brä·isch** *n* (-en) *ling.* Hebrew
He·bung ['he:bʊŋ] *f* (-; -en) **1.** lifting, raising; *geol.* elevation, rise; **2.** *fig.* improvement; increase; **3.** *metrics*: stress; stressed syllable
He·chel ['hɛçəl] *f* (-; -n) hackle, flax comb; **He·che·lei** [hɛçə'laɪ] F *f* (-; -en) *a. pl.* (malicious) gossip; '**he·cheln** *v/i.* (h) **1.** *dog etc.*: pant; **2.** F gossip
Hecht [hɛçt] *m* (-[e]s; -e) **1.** pike; *fig.* F ***ein toller*** ~ F some guy; ***er ist der*** ~ ***im***

Karpfenteich he really stirs things up; **2.** F fug

hech·ten ['hɛçtən] *v/i.* (sn) *swimming*: do a racing dive; *gym.* do a long-fly; *soccer etc.*: dive (full-length)

'**Hecht|sprung** *m swimming*: racing dive; *gym.* long-fly; *soccer etc.*: (flying) dive; **~sup·pe** *f*: F ***hier zieht's wie ~*** F it's like a gale-force wind blowing in here

Heck [hɛk] *n* (-s; -s) ⚓ stern; *mot.* rear; ✈ tail; **~an·trieb** *m mot.* rear-wheel drive

Hecke ['hɛkə] (*sep.* -k·k-) *f* (-; -n) hedge; hedgerow

hecken ['hɛkən] (*sep.* -k·k-) *v/t. and v/i.* (h) hatch; breed

'**Hecken|ro·se** (*sep.* -k·k-) *f* dogrose; **~sche·re** *f*: (***e-e ~*** a pair of) hedge clippers *pl.*; **~schüt·ze** *m* ⚔ sniper; **~zaun** *m* hedge(s *pl.*), hedge fencing

'**Heck|fen·ster** *n mot.* rear window; **~flos·se** *f mot.* tailfin; **~klap·pe** *f mot.* tailgate

'**heck·la·stig** [-lastıç] *adj.* ✈ *and mot.* tail-heavy

'**Heck·licht** *n* ✈ *and mot.* tail-light

Heck·meck ['hɛkmɛk] F *m* (-s; *no pl.*) **1.** fuss; ***mach keinen ~*** stop making such a fuss; **2.** rubbish

'**Heck|mo·tor** *m mot.* rear engine; **~schei·be** *f mot.* rear windscreen; **~schei·ben·wi·scher** *m mot.* rear (windscreen) wiper; **~spoi·ler** *m mot.* back spoiler; **~tür** *f mot.* tailgate

he·da ['he:da] *int.* hey(, you there)!

He·de·rich ['he:dərıç] *m* (-s; *no pl.*) 🌿 wild radish; wild mustard

He·do·nis·mus [hedo'nısmʊs] *m* (-; *no pl.*) hedonism; **He·do·nist** [hedo'nıst] *m* (-en; -en) hedonist; **he·do·ni·stisch** [hedo'nıstıʃ] *adj.* hedonistic(ally *adv.*)

Heer [he:ɐ] *n* (-[e]s; -e ['he:rə]) army; *fig. a.* huge crowd

Hee·res|be·stän·de ['he:rəs-] *pl.* military stores; **~dienst** *m* (-es; *no pl.*) military service; **~füh·rung** *f* army command; ***Oberste ~*** *the* Supreme Command; **~lie·fe,rant** *m* army contractor (*or* supplier)

'**Heer|fahrt** *f* expedition; **~füh·rer** *m* **1.** military leader; **2.** commander (of the army); **~schar** *f* host; *bibl.* ***himmlische ~en*** heavenly hosts

He·fe ['he:fə] *f* (-; *no pl.*) a) (baker's) yeast, leaven, b) (brewer's) yeast, c) *fig.* dregs *pl.*; *fig.* ***die ~ des Volkes*** the scum of the earth; **~ex,trakt** *m* yeast extract; **~ge·bäck** *n* yeast pastries *pl.*; **~kloß** *m gastr.* yeast dumpling; F *fig.* ***er ist aufgegangen wie ein ~*** he's really put on weight, F he's like a balloon; **~ku·chen** *m* yeast cake; **~pilz** *m* yeast fungus; **~prä·pa,rat** *n pharm.* yeast preparation; **~teig** *m* yeast dough

he·fig ['he:fıç] *adj.* yeasty; *wine* full of dregs

Heft [hɛft] *n* (-[e]s; -e) **1.** *ped.* notebook; exercise book; **2.** magazine; number; copy; issue; **3.** *fig.* ***das ~ fest in der Hand haben*** have things firmly under control; ***das ~ aus der Hand geben*** hand over control (*or* the controls, the reins); ***j-m das ~ aus der Hand nehmen*** seize control from s.o.

Heft·chen ['hɛftçən] *n* (-s; -) book

hef·ten ['hɛftən] (h) **I.** *v/t.* a) fix, pin (***an*** *acc.* to), b) baste, tack, *a. typ.* stitch, sew (*all* ***an*** *acc.* to); → ***geheftet***; *fig.* ***s-e Augen*** (***s-n Blick***) ***~ auf*** *acc.* fix one's eyes (one's gaze) on; **II.** *fig. v/refl.*: ***sich ~ auf*** *acc. eyes*: a) fix (themselves) on, b) be glued to; ***sich an j-s Fersen ~*** stick hard on s.o.'s heels; **Hef·ter** ['hɛftɐ] *m* (-s; -) **1.** file; **2.** stapler

'**Heft|fa·den** *m*, **~garn** *n* tacking thread

hef·tig ['hɛftıç] **I.** *adj.* a) violent; vehement; fierce; passionate, b) hot-tempered; furious, c) intense, intensive; sharp, severe (*a. criticism*); bad, severe *cold etc.*; angry *words*; ***~er Regen*** heavy rain(fall) *or* showers; ***~es Kopfweh*** a severe (*or* splitting) headache; ***~e Kämpfe*** fierce fighting; ***~ werden*** lose one's temper; ***sei doch nicht gleich so ~*** calm down, no need to get upset; **II.** *adv.* violently *etc.*; → **I**; ***es stürmt ~*** there's a real storm going (*or* outside); ***der Wind bläst ~*** there's a strong wind blowing

'**Heft|klam·mer** *f* paper clip; staple; **~ma,schi·ne** *f* stitching machine, stitcher; stapler; **~pfla·ster** *n* (sticking) plaster; **~stich** *m* tack

'**heft·wei·se** *adv.* in fascicles

'**Heft·zwecke** *f* drawing pin, *Am.* thumbtack

He·ge ['he:gə] *f* (-; *no pl.*) care, preservation

He·ge·mo·nie [hegemo'ni:] *f* (-; -n) hegemony, supremacy

he·gen ['he:gən] *v/t.* (h) look after; protect; tend; *fig.* cultivate *the arts etc.*; cherish, entertain *hope etc.*; have *doubts, a suspicion etc.*; ***Haß*** (***e-n Groll***) ***gegen j-n ~*** harbo(u)r hatred (bear a grudge) against s.o.; ***~ und pflegen*** take great care of, look after *s.th.* well, attend to *s.o.'s* every need

Hehl [he:l] *n*: ***kein ~ machen aus*** make no secret of, make no bones about; ***kein ~ daraus machen, daß*** make no secret of the fact that, make no bones about the fact that (*or* about *ger.*)

Heh·ler ['he:lɐ] *m* (-s; -) ⚖ receiver of stolen goods, F fence; **Heh·le·rei** [he:lə'raı] *f* (-, *no pl.*) receiving (of) *or* accepting stolen goods

hehr [he:ɐ] *lit. adj.* sublime, noble; august

heia ['haıa]: ***~ machen*** go bye-byes; **Heia** *f*: ***in die ~ gehen*** go to beddy-byes, go bye-byes; '**Heia·bett** *n* bed, beddy-byes

Hei·de[1] ['haıdə] *m* (-n; -n) heathen; pagan; *bibl.* gentile

'**Hei·de**[2] *f* (-; *no pl.*) **1.** heath(land); **2.** → **~kraut** *n* (-[e]s; *no pl.*) heather

Hei·del·bee·re ['haıdəl-] *f* 🌿 bilberry, blueberry

'**Hei·de·moor** *n* moorland

Hei·den|angst ['haıdən-] F *f* (-; *no pl.*): ***e-e ~ haben*** be scared to death, F be scared stiff (***vor*** *dat.* of); **~ar·beit** F *f* (-; *no pl.*) *a* huge (*sl.* hell of a) job; ***das war e-e ~*** *a.* F that was a real sweat; **~geld** F *n* (-[e]s; *no pl.*): ***ein ~*** a fortune, F a packet, pots (*or* stacks) of money; **~lärm** F *m* F dreadful racket (*or* din); ***ihr macht ja e-n ~!*** *a.* you'll bring the roof down in a minute

hei·den·mä·ßig ['haıdən-] F *adv.*: ***~ viel Geld*** F pots (*or* stacks) of money; ***~ schreien*** F scream blue murder, scream one's head off

Hei·den|re,spekt ['haıdən-] F *m*: ***e-n ~ haben vor*** *dat.* have a healthy respect for, be scared to death of; ***sie haben e-n ~ vor ihm*** *a.* they wouldn't dare put a foot wrong when he's around; **~spaß** F *m* (-es; *no pl.*): ***e-n ~ haben*** F have a whale of a time (***an*** *dat.* with)

Hei·den·tum ['haıdən-] *n* (-s; *no pl.*) a) heathenism, paganism, b) heathendom, *the* pagans *pl.*

'**Hei·de·rös·chen** *n* briar-rose

Hei·din ['haıdın] *f* (-; -nen) → ***Heide***[1]; **heid·nisch** ['haıdnıʃ] *adj.* heathen; pagan; ***~e Bräuche*** pagan customs (*or* rites)

Heid·schnucke ['haıtʃnʊkə] *f* (-; -n) *zo.* (North German) moorland sheep

hei·kel ['haıkəl] *adj.* **1.** awkward *business etc.*, *a.* tricky *problem etc.*; ***heikles Thema*** delicate subject; **2.** fussy, hard to please; choosy; ***sie ist im Essen ~*** she's fussy about her food (*or* what she eats), she's a fussy eater

heil [haıl] *adj.* a) unhurt, unharmed, safe and sound; undamaged, intact, b) healed, cured; ***~e Welt*** intact (*or* ideal, *iro.* sugarcoated) world; ***et. ~ überstehen*** come through (s.th.) unscathed; *iro.* ***da bist du noch mal mit ~er Haut davongekommen*** you got off lightly this time; ***wieder ~ machen*** a) fix, mend, b) make *s.th.* better; ***wieder ~ sein*** be better; *die Vase etc.* ***ist ~ geblieben*** didn't break, is still intact (*or* in one piece)

Heil I. *n* (-[e]s; *no pl.*) welfare, well-being; *eccl.* salvation; ***sein ~ in der Flucht suchen*** take flight; ***sein ~ bei j-m*** (***mit et.***) ***versuchen*** try one's luck with s.o. (s.th.); **II.** *int. hist.* hail!

Hei·land ['haılant] *m* (-[e]s; *no pl.*) *eccl.* Savio(u)r

'**Heil|an·stalt** *f* sanatorium; (mental) home; **~an·zei·ge** *f* ⚕ indication; **~bad** *n* **1.** health resort, spa; **2.** therapeutic bath

'**heil·bar** *adj.* curable; ***nicht ~*** incurable; ***es ist nicht ~*** *a.* it can't be cured; '**Heil·bar·keit** *f* (-; *no pl.*) curability

'**heil·brin·gend** *adj.* salutary

'**Heil·brun·nen** *m* mineral spring

Heil·butt ['haılbʊt] *m* (-[e]s; -e) halibut

hei·len ['haılən] **I.** *v/t.* (h) cure *s.o.*; heal *wound*; *fig.* ***j-n ~ von*** *dat.* cure s.o. of; ***jetzt ist er für immer geheilt*** that seems to have cured him (good and proper *or* once and for all); **II.** *v/i.* (sn) heal; *wound*: *a.* heal up; '**hei·lend** *adj.* healing; curative

'**Heil|er·de** *f* healing earth; **~er·folg** *m* successful cure (*or* treatment), success; ***damit hat man gute ~e erzielt*** it has proved a successful cure; **~fa·sten** *n* **1.** fasting (cures *pl.*); **2.** fasting cure

'**heil'froh** F *adj.* really glad; relieved; ***ich war ~, als ich wegkam*** I was glad (*or* relieved) to get away

'**Heil|gym·nast** [-gym,nast] *m* (-en; -en) physiotherapist; **~gym,na·stik** *f* physiotherapy

hei·lig ['haılıç] *adj.* a) holy; sacred; hallowed, b) pious, devout, c) sacred, inviolable, sacrosanct, d) venerable; Saint (*abbr.* St); ***der ~e Antonius*** St Anthony; ***Ձer Abend*** Christmas Eve; ***das Ձe Römische Reich*** the Holy Roman Empire; ***der Ձe Geist*** (***Stuhl, Vater***) the Holy Spirit *or* Ghost (See, Father); ***das Ձe Grab*** the Holy Sepulchre; ***das Ձe Land*** the Holy Land; ***die Ձe Schrift*** the Bible, the Scriptures *pl.*; ***~e Pflicht*** sacred duty; ***ihm ist nichts ~*** nothing is sacred to him; ***schwören bei allem, was ~ ist*** swear by all that is holy; F ***~ tun*** act the saint; → ***Jungfrau, Kuh***

Hei·lig'abend *m* Christmas Eve

Hei·li·ge ['haılıgə] *m, f* (-n; -n) saint
hei·li·gen ['haılıgən] *v/t.* (h) hallow, sanctify; hold *s.th.* sacred; → ***Zweck***
'**Hei·li·gen|bild** *n* depiction (*or* picture, statue) of a saint; **~fiˌgur** *f* figure (*or* statue) of a saint; **~le·ben** *n* life of a saint; **~leˌgen·de** *f* life (*or* legend) of a saint; **~schein** *m* halo, gloriole; **~ver·eh·rung** *f* worship of saints
'**hei·lig·hal·ten** *v/t.* (*irr.*, *sep.*, h, → ***halten***) hold *s.th.* sacred; keep *s.th.* (holy), observe
'**Hei·lig·keit** *f* (-; *no pl.*) holiness, sanctity, sacredness; saintliness; ***Seine ~*** His Holiness
'**hei·lig·spre·chen** *v/t.* (*irr.*, *sep.*, h, → ***sprechen***) canonize; '**Hei·lig·spre·chung** *f* (-; -en) canonization
'**Hei·lig·tum** *n* (-s; -tümer [-ty:mɐ]) (holy) shrine; (sacred) relic; *fig.* something sacred; *hum.* sanctum
Hei·li·gung ['haılıgʊŋ] *f* (-; *no pl.*) hallowing, sanctification (*a. fig.*)
'**Heil·kli·ma** *n* healthy climate
'**Heil·kraft** *f* healing power(s *pl.*); '**heil·kräf·tig** *adj.* curative
'**Heil|kraut** *n* medicinal herb; **~kun·de** *f* medicine, therapeutics *pl.*
'**heil·los** F **I.** *adj.* dreadful, F unholy; ***dort herrscht ein ~es Durcheinander*** F the place is an absolute shambles, it's absolutely chaotic there; **II.** *adv.* hopelessly; ***~ verschuldet*** up to one's neck in debt
'**Heil·meˌtho·de** *f* (method of) treatment, therapy, cure
'**Heil·mit·tel** *n* remedy, cure (***gegen*** *acc.* for) (*a. fig.*); medicine; **~kun·de** *f*, **~leh·re** *f* pharmacology
'**Heil|pflan·ze** *f* medicinal plant (*or* herb); **~pfla·ster** *n* healing (*or* medicated) plaster; **~ˌprak·ti·ker** *m* non-medical practitioner; **~quel·le** *f* mineral spring; **~sal·be** *f* healing ointment
'**heil·sam** *fig. adj.* salutary; *iro.* ***das wäre sehr ~ für ihn*** that would do him good, he could do with (s.th. like) that; '**Heil·sam·keit** *fig. f* (-; *no pl.*) salutary nature (*or* effect)
'**Heils|arˌmee** *f* Salvation Army; **~bot·schaft** *f* gospel (*a. fig.*)
'**Heil|schlaf** *m* healing sleep; hypnotherapy; **~se·rum** *n* ⚕ antiserum
'**Heils|ge·schich·te** *f eccl.* history of salvation, Heilsgeschichte; **~leh·re** *f eccl.* doctrine of salvation
'**Heil|stät·te** *f* sanatorium, *Am.* sanitarium; **~trank** *m* medicinal potion; **~-und Pfle·ge·an·stalt** *f* **1.** sanatorium, *Am.* sanitarium; **2.** mental home (*or* institution)
Hei·lung ['haılʊŋ] *f* (-; *no pl.*) a) cure, b) curing, healing *of wounds*, c) recovery
'**Hei·lungs|aus·sich·ten** *pl.*, **~chan·cen** *pl.* chances of recovery; **~proˌzeß** *m* a) healing process, b) recovery; **~quo·te** *f* cure rate
'**Heil|ver·fah·ren** *n* (medical) treatment, therapy; **~was·ser** *n* healing water(s *pl.*); **~wir·kung** *f* therapeutic effect
heim [haım] *adv.* home
Heim *n* (-[e]s; -e) **1.** *no pl.* home; **2.** a) ⚕ *etc.* home, b) students' hostel, hall of residence, *Am.* dormitory, c) club (-house), d) recreation cent|re (*Am.* -er), e) hostel; **~abend** *m* social (evening); **~ar·beit** *f* (-; *no pl.*) homework, outwork; *w.s.* cottage industry; **~ar·bei·ter** *m* homeworker, outworker

Hei·mat ['haıma:t] *f* (-; *no pl.*) home; home country; home town; ⚘ habitat; ***zweite ~*** second home, F home from home; **~adres·se** *f*, **~an·schrift** *f* home address; **~dich·ter** *m* regional writer; **~dich·tung** *f* regional literature; **~er·de** *f* native soil; **~film** *m* (*sentimental*) *film with a regional background*; **~for·scher** *m* local historian; **~for·schung** *f* local heritage studies *pl.*; **~ha·fen** *m* home port; **~kun·de** *f ped.* local studies *pl.*; **~land** *n* (-[e]s; ⸗er) home country, homeland
'**hei·mat·lich** *adj.* home ...; like home, *Am.* hom(e)y; ***~er Boden*** *one's* native soil; ***~e Klänge*** familiar sounds; ***das sind ~e Klänge*** *a.* it sounds just like home
'**hei·mat·los** *adj.* homeless; outcast; uprooted
'**Hei·mat|muˌse·um** *n* local heritage museum; **~ort** *m* home town (*or* village); **~recht** *n* right of abode; **~roˌman** *m novel set in a regional background*; **~spra·che** *f* native language (*or* tongue), mother tongue; **~staat** *m* native country, country of origin; **~stadt** *f* home town; **~ver·band** *m* homeland association; *association of regional compatriots stemming from Germany's former eastern territories*; **2ver·bun·den** *adj.* tied to one's roots; **~ver·trie·be·ne** *m, f* (-n; -n) displaced person, expellee (*from one of Germany's former eastern territories*)
'**heim|be·ge·ben** *v/refl.* (*irr.*, *sep.*, h, → ***begeben***): ***sich ~*** make one's way home; **~be·glei·ten** *v/t.* (*sep.*, h), **~brin·gen** *v/t.* (*irr.*, *sep.*, h, → ***bringen***) see (*or* take) *s.o.* home
Heim·chen ['haımçən] *n* (-s; -) **1.** *zo.* (house) cricket; **2.** *contp.* ***ein ~ (am Herd)*** (just a) housewife, an ordinary housewife
hei·me·lig ['haıməlıç] *adj.* cosy, *Am.* cozy, hom(e)y
'**Heim·er·zie·hung** *f* upbringing in an institution, institution upbringing
'**heim·fah·ren** *v/i.* (*irr.*, *sep.*, sn, → ***fahren***) go home; go back; *mot.* (*a. v/t.* [h]) drive home (*or* back); '**Heim·fahrt** *f* ride (*or* journey) back *or* home, return journey (*or* trip); ***auf der ~*** *a.* on the (*or* our *etc.*) way back
'**Heim·fall** *m* (-[e]s; *no pl.*) ⚖ reversion, escheat; '**heim·fal·len** *v/i.* (*irr.*, *sep.*, sn, → ***fallen***) revert (***an*** *acc.* to)
'**heim|fin·den** *v/i.* (*irr.*, *sep.*, h, → ***finden***) find one's way home; **~füh·ren** *v/t.* (*sep.*, h) **1.** take *s.o.* home; **2.** *obs.* marry
'**Heim·gang** *m* (-[e]s; *no pl.*) death, decease; '**Heim·ge·gan·ge·ne** *m, f* (-n; -n) departed, deceased; '**heim·ge·hen** *v/i.* (*irr.*, *sep.*, sn, → ***gehen***) **1.** go home; **2.** *fig.* die, pass away
'**heim|ge·sucht** *p.p. and adj.* → ***heimsuchen***; **~ho·len** *v/t.* (*sep.*, h) fetch home; *fig.* ***heimgeholt werden*** be called to one's Maker
'**Heim·in·duˌstrie** *f* cottage industry
hei·misch ['haımıʃ] *adj.* home ...; ⚘ *etc.* native, indigenous; ***~e Gewässer*** home waters; ***~ sein in*** *dat.* be indigenous to, live in, *a. fig.* be at home in; ***~ werden*** acclimatize o.s. (***in*** *dat.* to); ***sich ~ fühlen*** feel at home; ***auch nach 5 Jahren fühlte er sich nicht ~*** *a.* even after 5 years he didn't feel he belonged (there)

(*or* he felt no sense of belonging)
Heim·kehr ['haımke:ɐ] *f* (-; *no pl.*) return, homecoming; '**heim·keh·ren** [-ke:rən] *v/i.* (*sep.*, sn) come (*or* return) home, come back; '**Heim·keh·rer** [-ke:rɐ] *m* (-s; -) homecomer; ⚔ *etc.* returnee
'**Heim|kind** *n* institution child; **~ki·no** *n* a) cine-projector, movie-projector, b) movie-night, c) F *the* box
'**heim·kom·men** *v/i.* (*irr.*, *sep.*, sn, → ***kommen***) → ***heimkehren***; '**Heim·kunft** *f* (-; *no pl.*) → ***Heimkehr***
'**Heim|lei·ter** *m* a) director (of a home), b) warden
'**heim·leuch·ten** F *fig. v/i.* (*sep.*, h): ***j-m ~*** F tell s.o. what's what, F tell s.o. where to go
heim·lich ['haımlıç] **I.** *adj.* secret, clandestine *meeting, agreement etc.*; surreptitious, furtive *glance etc.*; **II.** *adv.* secretly *etc.*; → ***I***; F on the quiet (*a.* ***~, still und leise***); inwardly; ***j-n ~ anblicken*** steal a (furtive) glance at s.o.; ***sich ~ entfernen*** sneak (*or* slip) away; '**Heim·lich·keit** *f* (-; -en) **1.** *no pl.* secrecy; **2.** ***~en*** secrets
'**Heim·lich·tu·er** [-tu:ɐ] *m* (-s; -), '**Heim·lich·tue·rin** [-tu:ərın] *f* (-; -nen) mystery-monger; **Heim·lich·tue·rei** [-tu:ə'raı] *f* (-; -en) secretiveness, mysteriousness; '**heim·lich·tun** *v/i.* (*irr.*, *sep.*, h, → ***tun***) be very secretive (***mit*** *dat.* about), make a mystery (out of)
'**heim|müs·sen** *v/i.* (*irr.*, *sep.*, h, → ***müssen***) have to go home; **~neh·men** *v/t.* (*irr.*, *sep.*, h, → ***nehmen***) take home
'**Heim|nie·der·la·ge** *f sport*: home defeat; **~or·gel** *f* electric organ
'**Heim·rei·se** *f* journey home, return trip (*or* journey); ***auf der ~*** *a.* on the (*or* our *etc.*) way home; ***die ~ antreten*** set off (for) home; '**heim·rei·sen** *v/i.* (*sep.*, sn) go (*or* drive, fly *etc.*) home
'**heim·schicken** *v/t.* (*sep.*, h) send home
'**Heim|sieg** *m sport*: home win; **~son·ne** *f* sun-ray (*or* UV) lamp; **~spiel** *n sport*: home game; **~stät·te** *f* home; homeland; ***nationale ~*** national home
'**heim·su·chen** *v/t.* (*sep.*, h) hit, strike, *bibl.* visit; ravage; haunt (*a. fig.*); descend on (*a. hum. visit s.o.*); ***heimgesucht von*** *dat.* struck *etc.* by; ***heimgesucht werden von*** *dat. a.* suffer *severe drought etc.*, come down with *a severe illness etc.*; ***von Dürre (Krieg) heimgesucht*** drought-stricken (war-torn); ***vom Streik heimgesucht*** strike-ridden; '**Heim·su·chung** [-zu:xʊŋ] *f* (-; -en) disaster; ***~ Gottes*** divine retribution; *eccl.* ***~ Mariä*** *the* Visitation
'**heim·tra·gen** *v/t.* (*irr.*, *sep.*, h, → ***tragen***) carry home; ***wie wollen wir das ~?*** how are we going to get it home?
'**Heim·trai·ner** *m* home exerciser
Heim·tücke ['haımtʏkə] (*sep.* -k·k-) *f* (-; *no pl.*) insidiousness; malice, maliciousness; treachery; '**heim·tückisch** (*sep.* -k·k-) *adj.* insidious (*a.* ⚕); malicious; treacherous (*a. fig. road etc.*)
'**Heim·vor·teil** *m a. fig.* home advantage
'**heim·wärts** [-vɛrts] *adv.* homeward(s), home; ***sie gingen gerade ~*** they were on their (*or* the) way home
'**Heim|weg** *m* (-[e]s; *no pl.*) way home; ***auf dem ~*** on the (*or* my *etc.*) way home; ***sich auf den ~ machen*** set off (for) home; **~weh** *n* (-s; *no pl.*) homesickness; ***~ haben*** be homesick; ***~ haben nach*** *dat. a.* pine for (*or* after), yearn for

'Heim·wer·ker [-vɛrkɐ] *m* (-s; -) do-it--yourselfer, DIYer, handyman

'heim·zah·len *v/t.* (*sep.*, h): ***j-m et.*** ~ get one's own back on s.o. for s.th.

Hein [haɪn] *m*: ***Freund*** ~ the Grim Reaper, Death

Hei·ni ['haɪni] F *contp. m* (-s; -s) idiot, F twerp; ***komischer*** ~ F queer customer

Hein·zel·männ·chen ['haɪntsəl-] *pl. the* little people, fairies

Hei·rat ['haɪra:t] *f* (-; -en) marriage; ***gute*** ~ good match; **'hei·ra·ten** (h) **I.** *v/i.* get married, marry; **II.** *v/t.* marry, get married to

'Hei·rats|ab·sich·ten *pl.* marriage plans; ***~ haben, sich mit ~ tragen*** be thinking of getting married, be planning to get married; **~al·ter** *n*: (***durchschnittliches*** ~ average) age at marriage; **~an,non·ce** *f* marriage ad; **~an·trag** *m* (marriage) proposal; ***j-m e-n ~ machen*** propose to s.o., F pop the question to s.o.; **~an·zei·ge** *f* **1.** marriage announcement; **2.** → ***Heiratsannonce***; **2~fä·hig** *adj.* marriageable; ***in ~em Alter*** of marriageable age; **~in·sti,tut** *n* marriage bureau; **~kan·di,dat** *m* **1.** groom-to-be; **2.** eligible young man; **~kan·di,da·tin** *f* **1.** bride-to-be; **2.** marriageable young woman; **2~lu·stig** *adj.* keen to get married; **~markt** *m* **1.** marriage ads *pl.*; **2.** marriage (*contp.* F cattle) market; **~muf·fel** F *m* confirmed bachelor; **~plä·ne** *pl.* → ***Heiratsabsichten***; **~schwin·del** *m* marriage fraud; **~schwind·ler** *m* marriage impostor; fortune hunter; **~ur·kun·de** *f* marriage certificate; **~ur·laub** *m* wedding leave; **~ver·mitt·ler** *m* marriage broker; **~ver·mitt·lung** *f* marriage brokerage (*or* bureau); **~zif·fer** *f* marriage rate

hei·ser ['haɪzɐ] *adj.* hoarse; husky; croaky; ***sich ~ reden (schreien)*** talk (shout) o.s. hoarse; **'Hei·ser·keit** *f* (-; *no pl.*) hoarseness; huskiness

heiß [haɪs] **I.** *adj.* hot; torrid, b) *fig.* fiery, passionate; vehement, fierce; fervent, c) *zo.* on heat; ***glühend*** ~ red-hot, scorching; ***~es Blut*** hot blood (*or* temper); ***~er Krieg*** shooting war; F ***~e Musik*** hot sounds (*or* rhythms); ***~er Sommer*** *fig.* long, hot (*or* turbulent) summer; ***~e Spur*** hot trail; ***~es Thema*** (highly) controversial issue; ***~er Tip*** hot tip; F ***~er Typ*** F hunk; ***~e Ware*** hot goods; ***~ machen*** heat (up); ***~e Tränen weinen*** weep bitterly; ***mir ist ~*** I'm hot; ***mir wird ~*** I'm getting hot; ***ihm wurde ~ und kalt (vor Angst)*** he went hot and cold (with fear); ***das Kind ist ganz ~*** the baby feels hot; ***sie haben sich die Köpfe ~ geredet*** they talked themselves silly, they talked till they were blue in the face, F they went at it hammer and tongs; ***was ich nicht weiß, macht mich nicht ~*** ignorance is bliss; ***es wird nichts so ~ gegessen, wie es gekocht wird*** things are never as bad as they look; F ***ganz ~ sein auf*** *acc.* F be wild about; *sl.* ***echt ~!*** *sl.* brill!; → ***Draht, Eisen, Hölle***; **II.** *fig. adv.* fervently, ardently; ***~ (und innig) lieben*** love *s.o.* madly, adore, F be wild about; ***et. ~ ersehnen*** long for s.th. (fervently); ***~ begehrt sein*** ✝ *etc.* be in great demand; ***die Stadt ist ~ umkämpft*** fierce battles are being fought over the town; F ***den haben sie wohl zu ~ gebadet*** F they must have dropped him on his head when he was a baby; → ***hergehen*** 2

'heiß·be·gehrt *adj.* coveted

'heiß·blü·tig [-bly:tɪç] *adj.* hot-blooded; passionate, fiery

hei·ßen (hieß, geheißen, h) **I.** *v/i.* a) be called, b) mean; ***ich heiße ...*** my name is ...; ***wie heißt du?*** what's your name?; ***wie heißt das?*** what's that called?; ***wie heißt das auf englisch?*** what's that (called) in English?; ***wie heißt ... auf englisch?*** *a.* what's the English (word *or* expression) for ...?; ***das heißt*** (*abbr.* ***d.h.***) that is (to say) (*abbr.* i.e.); ***das hieße*** (*or* ***würde*** ~) that would mean; ***das will (et)was ~*** that's saying something; ***das will nicht viel ~*** that doesn't mean much; ***was heißt das schon?*** so?, that doesn't mean a thing; ***es heißt, daß*** they say that, apparently; ***es heißt in dem Brief*** it says in the letter, the letter says; ***das soll nicht ~, daß*** that doesn't mean (to say) that; ***es soll nicht ~, daß*** I don't want it to be said that; ***damit es nicht (nachher) heißt, ...*** so that nobody can say ...; ***nun heißt es handeln*** *etc.* the situation calls for action *etc.*, it's time to act *etc.*; ***soll das ~, daß ...?, das heißt also, daß ...*** does that mean (that) ...?, do you mean to say (that) ...?; ***das heißt doch nicht etwa, daß ...?*** you don't mean to say (that) ...?; ***was soll das eigentlich ~?*** what's this all about?, F what's the big idea?; **II.** *lit. v/t.* call; ***j-n et. tun ~*** tell s.o. to do s.th.; ***das heiße ich e-e gute Nachricht*** that's what I call good news; → ***willkommen***

'heiß|er·sehnt *adj.* longed-for; *a.* long--awaited *letter etc.*; **~ge·liebt** *adj.* dearly (*or* passionately) loved; ***~e(r) ...*** dearly beloved ...

'Heiß·hun·ger *m* (sudden) craving (***auf*** *acc.*, ***nach*** *dat.* for); **'heiß·hung·rig** *adj.* ravenous, *esp. fig.* voracious

'heiß·lau·fen *v/i. and v/refl.* (***sich*** ~) (*irr.*, *sep.*, h, → ***laufen***) overheat; ***der Motor ist heißgelaufen*** the engine is overheated

'Heiß·luft *f* hot air; **~bal,lon** *m* hot-air balloon; **~be·hand·lung** *f* hot-air treatment; **~herd** *m* convection oven

'Heiß·sporn *fig. m* (-[e]s; -e) hothead

'heiß|um,kämpft *adj.* embattled; *fig.* much sought-after; **~um,strit·ten** *adj.* highly controversial; hotly debated *topic*

'Heiß·was·ser·be·rei·ter *m* water heater, *Brit. a.* geyser

hei·ter ['haɪtɐ] *adj.* a) *meteor.* bright, b) cheerful; amusing, funny; humorous *story etc.*; serene, c) F merry; ***~ bis wolkig*** fair to cloudy; ***~(er) werden*** brighten up; ***wie aus ~em Himmel*** completely out of the blue; *iro.* ***das ist ja ~!*** F that's just (*or* really) great; ***das kann ja ~ werden*** F looks like we're in for some fun and games; **'hei·ter-be'sinn·lich** *adj. film etc.*: serio-comic, amusing but thought-provoking; ***~er Film*** *a.* contemplative (*or* serious) comedy

'Hei·ter·keit *f* (-; *no pl.*) cheerfulness; amusement; mirth; ***zur allgemeinen ~*** to everybody's amusement; **'Hei·ter·keits·er·folg** *m*: ***damit hatte er e-n ~*** it gave everyone a good laugh

Heiz|an·la·ge ['haɪts-] *f* heating system; **~ap·pa,rat** *m* heater

heiz·bar ['haɪtsba:ɐ] *adj.* heatable; *room etc.* with heating; *mot.* ***~e Heckscheibe*** heated rear windscreen (*Am.* windshield)

Heiz|decke ['haɪts-] *f* electric blanket; **~draht** *m* heating wire; **~ele,ment** *n* heating element

hei·zen ['haɪtsən] (h) **I.** *v/t.* heat *room etc.*; fire *stove*; **II.** *v/i.* put (*or* have) the heating on; ***der Ofen heizt gut*** the stove heats well (*or* gives off plenty of heat); **III.** *v/refl.*: ***sich gut ~*** *room*: get warm quickly; **Hei·zer** ['haɪtsɐ] *m* (-s; -) boilerman; ⚓ *etc.* stoker, *Am.* fireman

Heiz|flä·che ['haɪts-] *f* heating surface; **~ge·blä·se** *n* fan heater; **~ge·rät** *n* heating appliance, heater; **~kes·sel** *m* boiler; **~kis·sen** *n* electric pad

Heiz·kör·per ['haɪts-] *m* heater; radiator; **~ver·klei·dung** *f* radiator cover

Heiz·ko·sten ['haɪts-] *pl.* heating costs; **~ab·rech·nung** *f* heating bill

Heiz|kraft·werk ['haɪts-] *n* thermal power station; **~lüf·ter** *m* fan heater; **~ma·te·ri,al** *n* fuel; **~ofen** *m* stove; (electric, oil *etc.*) heater; **~öl** *n* heating oil; **~pe·rio·de** *f* heating period; **~plat·te** *f* hotplate; **~schlan·ge** *f* heating coil; **~son·ne** *f* electric fire; **~strah·ler** *m* (heater-)reflector; **~strom** *m* heating current

Hei·zung ['haɪtsʊŋ] *f* (-; -en) (central) heating; radiator

'Hei·zungs|an·la·ge *f* heating system; **~bau·er** *m* (-s; -) heating engineer; **~kel·ler** *m* boiler room; **~mon,teur** *m* heating engineer; **~rohr** *n* heating pipe; **~tech·nik** *f* heating engineering

Heiz·wert ['haɪts-] *m phys.* thermal (*or* calorific) value

Hek·tar ['hɛkta:ɐ] *n* (-s; -[s]) hectare

Hek·tik ['hɛktɪk] *f* (-; *no pl.*) mad rush, frantic pace; commotion, hectic atmosphere *of a place*; *s.o.'s* nervousness; ***in der ~ habe ich m-e Tasche liegenlassen*** in the general rush I have left my purse behind; ***nur keine ~!*** (just) take your time, F take it easy; ***das machen wir ohne ~*** we'll take our time, we'll take it nice and easy; ***wozu die ~?*** what's the rush?; ***sie bringt viel ~ hinein*** she makes everybody nervous; ***das ist e-e ~ heute*** it's one of those days, it's all go; **Hek·ti·ker** ['hɛktikɐ] *m* (-s; -): ***er ist ein absoluter ~*** he's always rushing around like a madman; **hek·tisch** ['hɛktɪʃ] *adj.* hectic; frantic *activity*; excited, frenzied *atmosphere*; nervous *person*; ***~es Treiben*** hustle and bustle, frantic activity; ***ein paar ~e Stunden*** a few frantic hours

Hek·to·li·ter ['hɛkto-] *m*, *n* hectolit|re (*Am.* -er)

Held [hɛlt] *m* (-en; -en ['hɛldən]) hero; *thea.*, *literature etc.*: protagonist; *fig.* champion; *fig.* ***~ des Tages*** man of the moment; F ***er ist kein ~ in Mathematik*** F he's not the world's best mathematician; ***den ~en spielen*** *thea.* play the hero, *fig. iro.* act the hero('s part); *iro.* ***das ist vielleicht ein ~!*** some hero he is

Hel·den|dich·tung ['hɛldən-] *f* epic poetry; **~epos** *n* epic (poem)

hel·den·haft ['hɛldənhaft] *adj.* heroic(ally *adv.*)

Hel·den·mut ['hɛldən-] *m* bravery, heroism; **hel·den·mü·tig** [-my:tɪç] *adj.* heroic(ally *adv.*)

Hel·den|rol·le ['hɛldən-] *f thea.* part of a (*or* the) hero; **~sa·ge** *f* saga; **~stück** *n* → **~tat** *f* heroic deed; F ***nicht gerade e-e ~*** F nothing to write home about; **~te,nor** *m* heroic tenor, Heldentenor; **~tod** *m*

heroic death; ⚔ death in action; ***den ~ sterben*** die a hero's death, ⚔ be killed in action
Hel·den·tum ['hɛldəntu:m] *n* (-s; *no pl.*) heroism
Hel·den·ver·eh·rung ['hɛldən-] *f* hero worship
Hel·din ['hɛldɪn] *f* (-; -nen) heroine (*a. thea.*)
hel·disch ['hɛldɪʃ] *adj.* heroic(ally *adv.*)
hel·fen ['hɛlfən] *v/i.* (half, geholfen, h) a) help (***j-m*** s.o.; ***bei*** *dat.* with); lend *s.o.* a hand, b) help, be of use; ***j-m et. tun ~*** help s.o. (to) do s.th.; ***kann ich irgendwie ~?*** is there anything I can do?, can I (be of any) help?; ***im Haushalt ~*** help (out) with the housework; ***~ gegen*** *acc.* (*or* ***bei*** *dat.*) be good for *colds etc.*; ***j-m über die Straße ~*** help s.o. across the road; ***j-m aus dem*** (***in den***) ***Mantel ~*** help s.o. off (on) with his (*or* her) coat; ***j-m aus e-r Verlegenheit ~*** help s.o. out of a difficulty; ***j-m bei der Arbeit ~*** help s.o. with his (*or* her) work; ***da ist nicht zu ~*** there's nothing you can do (about it); ***das hilft mir wenig*** that's not much help; ***hat's was geholfen?*** was it any use (*or* good)?; ***es hat nichts geholfen*** it was no good, *a. pharm.* it didn't help, it didn't do any good; ***er weiß sich zu ~*** he can cope, he can look after himself; ***er weiß sich immer zu ~*** he's never at a loss as to what to do; ***er weiß sich nicht*** (***mehr***) ***zu ~*** he's at a loss as to what to do, he's at his wits' end; ***sie läßt sich von niemandem ~*** she won't accept anybody's help, she won't let anybody help her; ***es hilft nichts*** it's no use; ***da hilft kein Jammern*** it's no use complaining; ***da hilft nur eins*** there's only one thing for it; ***was hilft es, wenn*** what's the use of *ger.*; ***es hilft alles nichts, wir müssen gehen*** we've got to go whether we like it or not; ***ich kann mir nicht ~*** I can't help it; ***ich kann mir nicht ~, ich muß einfach lachen*** I can't help laughing (about it); ***ihm ist nicht*** (***mehr***) ***zu ~*** there's no hope for him, *iro. a.* he's hopeless, F he's a dead loss; *iro.* ***ihm werd' ich schon ~*** I'll show him; ***dir werd' ich ~!*** just you try; ***das half*** that worked, F that did the trick
Hel·fer ['hɛlfɐ] *m* (-s; -) helper; assistant; *fig.* help; ***ein ~ in der Not*** a friend in need; **'Hel·fers·hel·fer** *m* (-s; -) accomplice, F stooge
He·li·kop·ter [heli'kɔptɐ] *m* (-s; -) helicopter
He·lio·graph [helio'gra:f] *m* (-en; -en) heliograph
He·lio·skop [helio'sko:p] *n* (-s; -e) helioscope
He·lio·trop [helio'tro:p] *n* (-s; -e) heliotrope
he·lio·zen·trisch [helio'tsɛntrɪʃ] *adj.* heliocentric(ally *adv.*)
He·li·um ['he:lium] *n* (-s; *no pl.*) helium
hell [hɛl] **I.** *adj.* a) bright; shining, b) light *colo(u)r etc.*; fair *hair, complexion etc.*; light-colo(u)red *dress etc.*, c) clear *sound*; *ling.* bright *vowel*, d) *fig.* (F *a.* ***helle***) bright, clever; ***~es Bier*** lager; ***es wird ~*** a) it's getting light, b) it's brightening up (again); ***es ist schon ~*** it's light (already), the sun's up (already); *fig.* ***~er Neid*** pure envy; ***er ist ein ~er Kopf*** F he's a bright young spark; ***er hatte s-e ~e Freude daran*** he really enjoyed it; ***das ist ja ~er Wahnsinn*** that's (sheer) madness, F that's (absolutely) crazy; ***in ~er Verzweiflung*** out of sheer desperation; **II.** *adv. lamp etc.*: *shine* brightly, *moon etc.*: *shine* bright
'hell'auf *adv.*: ***sie waren ~ begeistert*** they thought it was tremendous, they were all for it
'hell·blau *adj.*, **'Hellblau** *n* light blue
'hell·blond *adj.* very fair
'Hell·dun·kel *n art*: chiaroscuro
hel·le ['hɛlə] F *adj.* bright, clever
'Hel·le[1] *f* (-; *no pl.*) (bright) light; brightness
'Hel·le[2] F *n* (-n; -n) lager
Hel·le·bar·de [hɛlə'bardə] *f* (-; -n) *hist.* halberd
Hel·le·ne [hɛ'le:nə] *m* (-n; -n) Hellene, (ancient) Greek; **Hel'le·nen·tum** *n* (-s; *no pl.*) Hellenism, Hellenic culture; **hel·le·ni·sie·ren** [hɛleni'zi:rən] *v/t.* (h) Hellenize; **Hel·le·nis·mus** [hɛle'nɪsmʊs] *m* (-; *no pl.*) Hellenism; **Hel·le·nist** [hɛle'nɪst] *m* (-en; -en) Hellenist, Greek scholar; **Hel·le·ni·stik** [hɛle'nɪstɪk] *f* (-; *no pl.*) ancient (*or* classical) Greek, Greek studies *pl.*; **hel·le·ni·stisch** [hɛle'nɪstɪʃ] *adj.* Hellenistic
Hel·ler ['hɛlɐ] *m* (-s; -): ***es ist keinen ~ wert*** it's not worth a cent; ***er besitzt keinen roten ~*** he hasn't got a penny to his name, *Am.* he doesn't have a red cent; ***auf ~ und Pfennig*** down to the last penny (*or* cent)
'helleuch·tend (*sep.* -ll·l-) *adj.* bright(ly shining)
'hell|far·big *adj.* light(-colo[u]red); **~gelb** *adj.* pale (*or* straw) yellow; **~grün** *adj.* light green; **~haa·rig** *adj.* fair-haired
'hell·häu·tig [-hɔytɪç] *adj.* light-skinned, fair-skinned
'hell·hö·rig [-hø:rɪç] *adj.* **1.** *fig.* sensitive (***für*** *acc.* to); alert (to); ***~ sein*** *a.* have keen senses; ***~ werden*** prick up one's ears; ***da wurde er ~*** that made him sit up straight (*or* prick up his ears); ***sie ist für solche Dinge sehr ~*** she picks that kind of thing up very quickly; **2.** wafer-thin *walls*; badly soundproofed *house etc.*; ***die Wand ist sehr ~*** *a.* you can hear (virtually) everything through that wall; ***das Haus ist sehr ~*** *a.* the house has got very thin walls, you can hear (virtually) everything in this house
hellicht ['hɛlɪçt] (*sep.* -ll·l-) *adj.*: ***am ~en Tage*** in broad daylight
Hel·lig·keit ['hɛlɪçkaɪt] *f* (-; *no pl.*) brightness (*a. TV*); *phys.* light intensity
'Hel·lig·keits|re·ge·lung *f*, **~reg·ler** *m TV* brightness control
Hel·ling ['hɛlɪŋ] *f* (-; -en) ⚓ slip(way); ✈ (assembly) cradle
'hell|klin·gend *adj.* clear-sounding; **~ro·sa** *adj.* pale pink; **~rot** *adj.* light red
'hell·sehen I. *v/i.* (*only inf.*) have second sight (*or* psychic powers), be clairvoyant, be psychic; **II.** 2 *n* (-s) clairvoyance; **'Hell·se·her** *m*, **'Hell·se·he·rin** *f*, **'hell·se·he·risch** *adj.* clairvoyant, psychic
'hell·sich·tig [-zɪçtɪç] *adj.* perceptive; shrewd; **'Hell·sich·tig·keit** *f* (-; *no pl.*) perceptiveness; shrewdness
'hell'wach *adj.* wide-awake (*a. fig.*)
Helm [hɛlm] *m* (-[e]s; -e) **1.** helmet; **2.** ⌂ cap, spire; **~dach** *n* helm roof
Hel·ve·tis·mus [hɛlve'tɪsmʊs] *m* (-; -men) *ling.* Helveticism
Hemd [hɛmt] *n* (-[e]s; -en) a) shirt, b) vest, *Am.* undershirt; *fig.* ***j-m sein letztes ~ geben*** give s.o. the shirt off one's back; ***er hat kein*** (***ganzes***) ***~ mehr auf dem Leib*** he hasn't got a shirt to his back; ***j-n bis aufs ~ ausziehen*** fleece s.o.; F ***mach dir nicht ins ~!*** F no need to wet yourself; **~blu·se** *f* shirt; **~brust** *f* shirt front; **~kleid** *n* shirtwaister
'Hemds·är·mel *m* shirt sleeve; ***in ~n*** in one's shirt sleeves; **'hemds·är·me·lig** [-ɛrməlɪç] *adj.* shirt-sleeved; F *fig.* casual, shirt-sleeve ...; **'Hemds·är·me·lig·keit** F *f* (-; *no pl.*) (over)casual manner
He·mi·sphä·re [hemi'sfɛ:rə] *f* (-; -n) hemisphere
hem·men ['hɛmən] *v/t.* (h) a) stop, b) impede, hamper; restrain; check *progress etc.*; hold back *development etc.*; *psych.* inhibit *s.o.*; ***sich gegenseitig ~*** hold each other back; → ***gehemmt***; **'hem·mend** *adj.* obstructive; hampering, impeding; *psych. etc.* inhibitory; **Hem·mer** ['hɛmɐ] *m* (-s; -) *biol., physiol. etc.* inhibitor; **Hemm·nis** ['hɛmnɪs] *n* (-ses; -se) obstacle
Hemm|schuh ['hɛm-] *m* brake shoe; *fig.* obstacle (***für*** *acc.* to), impediment (to); **~schwel·le** *f psych.* inhibition threshold; ***e-e ~ überwinden müssen*** have to overcome one's inhibitions
Hem·mung ['hɛmʊŋ] *f* (-; -en) **1.** inhibition; scruple; ***~en haben*** be inhibited; ***ohne ~en*** uninhibited(ly); ***nur keine ~en!*** don't be shy!; ***~en haben zu*** *inf.* have inhibitions (*or* scruples) about *ger.*, feel awkward about *ger.*; ***keine ~en haben zu*** *inf.* have no compunction (*or* inhibitions, scruples) about *ger.*; ***die haben überhaupt keine ~en*** F they don't give a damn; **2.** *no pl.* hampering; checking *etc.*; → ***hemmen***; **3.** jam, stoppage; **4.** ⚙ stop, catch; escapement *of watch*
'hem·mungs·los *adj.* unscrupulous; unrestrained; ***~ sein*** *a.* have no scruples, have no sense of shame; **'Hem·mungs·lo·sig·keit** *f* (-; *no pl.*) shamelessness; shameless behavio(u)r
Hendl ['hɛndl] *dial. n* (-s; -n) chicken
Hengst [hɛŋst] *m* (-[e]s; -e) stallion; F *fig.* stud; **~foh·len** *n*, **~fül·len** *n* colt
Hen·kel ['hɛŋkəl] *m* (-s; -) handle; **~krug** *m* jug
'hen·kel·los *adj.* without a handle
'Hen·kel·mann F *m* (-[e]s; ⸚er) **1.** F canteen; **2.** F ghetto-blaster
hen·ken ['hɛŋkən] *v/t.* (h) hang; **Hen·ker** ['hɛŋkɐ] *m* (-s; -) executioner; F ***scher dich zum ~!*** F go to hell!; F ***zum ~!*** F to hell with it!; F ***wer zum ~?*** F who the hell?
'Hen·kers|beil *n* executioner's axe; **~knecht** *m* executioner's assistant; *fig.* henchman; **~mahl·zeit** *f* condemned man's breakfast (*or* last meal); *fig.* final binge
Hen·na ['hɛna] *f* (-; *no pl.*), *n* (-s; *no pl.*) henna; **'hen·na·rot** *adj.* henna(-colo[u]red), hennaed
Hen·ne ['hɛnə] *f* (-; -n) hen
He·pa·ti·tis [hepa'ti:tɪs] *f* (-; -titiden [-ti'ti:dən]) ⚕ hepatitis
her [he:ɐ] *adv.* **1.** ***von*** *dat.* ***... ~*** from; ***er ist von weit ~ gekommen*** he's come a long way; ***von oben ~*** from above; ***von links ~*** from the left; → ***herhaben, hersein*** 2; **2.** ***j-n von früher ~ kennen*** know s.o. from before; **3.** ***~ damit!*** give it to me!,

hand it over!; **4. um mich ~** around me, round about me; **5.** *fig.* **von** *dat.* **... ~** from the point of view of; **vom Technischen ~** from a technical point of view, technically (speaking); **vom Inhalt ~** as far as the content goes, F contentwise

her·ab [hɛ'rap] *adv. in cpds. usu.* ... down; **von oben ~** from above, *fig.* from on high, condescendingly; **~blicken** *v/i.* (*sep.*, h) → **herabsehen; ~ge·setzt** *adj.* reduced, cut-rate *prices etc.*; reduced, cut-price *goods*; **zu ~en Preisen** at reduced prices, cut-rate ...; **~hän·gen** *v/i.* (*irr.*, *sep.*, h, → **hängen**) → **herunterhängen; ~kom·men** *v/i.* (*irr.*, *sep.*, sn, → **kommen**) → **herunterkommen**

her'ab·las·sen (*irr.*, *sep.*, h, → **lassen**) **I.** *v/t.* let down, lower; **II.** *fig. v/refl.*: **sich ~** lower o.s., **zu** *dat. or inf.*: deign (*or* condescend, stoop) to *talk to s.o. etc.*; **her'ab·las·send** *adj.* (*and adv.*) condescending(ly); **~e Art** condescending attitude (*or* approach); **Her'ab·las·sung** [-lasʊŋ] *f* (-; *no pl.*) condescension; **j-n mit ~ behandeln** patronize s.o., be (very) patronizing towards s.o.

her'ab|min·dern *v/t.* (*sep.*, h) a) reduce, diminish, b) belittle *s.o.'s achievement etc.*, c) minimize; **~se·hen** *v/i.* (*irr.*, *sep.*, h, → **sehen**): **~ auf** *acc. a. fig.* look down on

her'ab·set·zen *v/t.* (*sep.*, h) reduce, lower; ✝ reduce (in price); cut (back); *fig.* disparage *s.o.*, run *s.o.* down; belittle *s.o.'s achievement etc.*; → **herabgesetzt; her'ab·set·zend** *adj.* (*and adv.*) disparaging(ly); **Her'ab·set·zung** [-zetsʊŋ] *f* (-; *no pl.*) lowering, reduction (*a.* ✝); cut (**von** *dat.* in); *fig.* disparagement

her'ab|stei·gen *v/i.* (*irr.*, *sep.*, sn, → **steigen**) descend, walk (*or* climb, come) down; dismount *horse*; **~stür·zen** *v/i.* (*sep.*, sn) → **herunterstürzen; ~trop·fen** *v/i.* (*sep.*, sn) drip (onto the ground *or* floor *etc.*); **von e-m Baum ~** drip from a tree

her'ab·wür·di·gen *v/t.* (*sep.*, h) degrade (**sich** o.s.), lower (o.s.); **her'ab·wür·di·gend I.** *adj.* disparaging; **II.** *adv.* disparagingly; **~ behandeln** *a.* treat with disdain; **Her'ab·wür·di·gung** *f* (-; *no pl.*) degradation

He·ral·dik [he'raldɪk] *f* (-; *no pl.*) heraldry; **he·ral·disch** [he'raldɪʃ] *adj.* heraldic

her·an [hɛ'ran] *adv.* near, close; **~ an** *acc.* up (*or* close, next) to; **mehr links ~** more (*or* closer) to the left; **nur ~!** come closer!; **~ar·bei·ten** *v/refl.* (*sep.*, h): **sich ~ an** *acc.* work one's way forward to (*or* through towards, *fig.* towards); **~bil·den** (*sep.*, h) **I.** *v/t.* **1.** train (**zu** *dat.* to be); **II.** *v/refl.*: **sich ~ 2.** be in the making; **3.** train (**zu** *dat.* to be); **~brin·gen** *v/t.* (*irr.*, *sep.*, h, → **bringen**) bring (**an** *acc.* [up] to); *fig.* → **heranführen; ~drän·gen** *v/refl.* (*sep.*, h): **sich ~** push forward (**an** *acc.* towards); **~fah·ren** *v/i.* (*irr.*, *sep.*, sn, → **fahren**) drive up (**an** *acc.* to); **~füh·ren** *v/t.* (*sep.*, h) lead, take (**an** *acc.* to); bring (to); *fig.* **j-n (langsam) an et. ~** introduce s.o. to s.th. (gradually); **~ge·hen** *v/i.* (*irr.*, *sep.*, sn, → **gehen**): **~ an** *acc.* go up to; *fig.* approach, tackle; **geh nicht so nah heran** don't go too close; **~ho·len** *v/t.* (*sep.*, h) fetch, get; *phot.* zoom in on; **~kämp·fen** *v/refl.* (*sep.*, h): **sich ~** close in (**an** *acc.* on), pull up (to)

'her'an·kom·men *v/i.* (*irr.*, *sep.*, sn, → **kommen**) come up, approach; **~ an** *acc.* a) come up to, b) reach, get hold of, c) be able to get (through) to, be able to get at (*or* get hold of), d) *fig.* come up to, come near, approach; **die Sache** (*or* **es**) **an sich ~ lassen** wait and see; **er** (**es**) **kommt nicht an ... heran** *a.* he (it) can't touch ...; **er kommt an sie nicht heran** *a.* he can't hold a candle to her

her'an|las·sen *v/t.* (*irr.*, *sep.*, h, → **lassen**): **er läßt niemanden an sich** (**s-e Bücher**) **heran** he won't let anyone (come) near him (touch his books); **~ma·chen** F *v/refl.* (*sep.*, h): **sich ~ an** *acc.* set to work on *s.th.*, get going on *s.th.*; sidle up to *s.o.*, *fig.* approach *s.o.*, make up to *s.o.*, start working on *s.o.*

her'an·na·hen I. *v/i.* (*sep.*, sn) approach, draw near; **II.** ♀ *n* (-s) approach

her'an|pir·schen *v/refl.* (*sep.*, h): **sich ~ an** stalk (up on), stalk (*or* creep, sneak) up on *s.o.*; **~rei·chen** *v/i.* (*sep.*, h): **~ an** *acc.* reach, *water etc.*: *a.* come up to; *fig.* come up to, equal; come (very) close to; **sie reicht ihm bis an die Schulter heran** she comes up to his shoulders; *fig.* **sie reicht lange nicht an ihn heran** she can't touch him, she can't hold a candle to him; **der Film reicht lange nicht an s-n letzten heran** the film isn't nearly as good as his last one (*or* isn't a patch on his last one); **~rei·fen** *v/i.* (*sep.*, sn) ripen; *fig. plan etc.*: mature; *person*: grow up (**zu** *dat.* into); *fig.* **er reift zu e-m wahren Profi heran** he's fast becoming a real professional; **~rücken** (*sep.*) **I.** *v/t.* (h) move (*or* push) nearer; pull up *chair*; **II.** *v/i.* (sn) approach, draw near; **an j-n ~** move up (close) to s.o.; **~schlei·chen** *v/refl.* (*irr.*, *sep.*, h, → **schleichen**): **sich ~** sneak (*or* creep) up (**an** *acc.* to, on *s.o.*); **~stür·men** *v/i.* (*sep.*, sn) come rushing up (*or* along); **~ta·sten** *v/refl.* (*sep.*, h): **sich ~ an** *acc.* grope one's way towards, *fig.* feel one's way towards, cautiously approach *a problem etc.*; **~tra·gen** *v/t.* (*irr.*, *sep.*, h, → **tragen**) bring (over); *fig.* **et. an j-n ~** approach s.o. with s.th.; **~trau·en** *v/refl.* (*sep.*, h): **sich ~** dare to go near (*or* approach), **an** *acc.*: dare to go near (*or* up to *a dog etc.*); **sich nicht ~ an** *acc. a. fig.* be scared of; **ich trau' mich an die Maschine nicht heran** I wouldn't like to tinker with the machine, I daren't touch the machine; *fig.* **ich trau' mich an das Projekt nicht heran** I don't think I can handle the project; **er hat sich schon an schlimmere Probleme herangetraut** he's tackled (*or* had to deal with) worse problems than that; **~tre·ten** *v/i.* (*irr.*, *sep.*, sn, → **treten**) approach (**an j-n** s.o.) (*a. fig.*); **~ an** *acc.* go (*or* step) up to; *fig.* **es traten einige Probleme an ihn heran** he had to face up to (*or* he was confronted with) a number of problems

her'an·wach·sen *v/i.* (*irr.*, *sep.*, sn, → **wachsen**) grow up; **~ zu** *dat.* grow (up) into; **die ~de Jugend** the youth of today; **Her'an·wach·sen·de** *m, f* (-n; -n) adolescent; ⚖ young person

her'an|wa·gen *v/refl.* (*sep.*, h) → **herantrauen; ~win·ken** *v/t.* (*sep.*, h) wave *s.o.* over, motion *s.o.* to come nearer; hail *a taxi*; **~zie·hen** (*irr.*, *sep.*, → **ziehen**) **I.** *v/t.* (h) **1.** pull up; **2.** raise; train; **3.** *fig.* a) draw *s.o.*; call on *s.o.*, enlist *s.o.*(*'s services*), *a.* ⚔ mobilize, recruit (**zu** *dat.* for); consult, call in *expert, doctor etc.*, b) draw on, use *funds etc.*, c) cite, quote; **II.** *v/i.* (sn) approach, draw near; ⚔ *a.* advance; *clouds*: gather

her·auf [hɛ'raʊf] *adv.* up, upwards; up here; **den Berg ~** up the hill, uphill; **den Fluß ~** up the river, upstream; **die Treppe ~** up the stairs, upstairs; (**von**) **unten ~** from below; *in cpds. usu.* ... up; **~arbei·ten** *v/refl.* (*sep.*, h): **sich ~** *a. fig.* work one's way up; **~be·ge·ben** *v/refl.* (*irr.*, *sep.*, h, → **begeben**): **sich ~** go up(stairs); **~be·schwö·ren** *v/t.* (*irr.*, *sep.*, h, → **beschwören**) **1.** bring on, provoke; **wir wollen es nicht ~** let's not tempt fate; **2.** evoke, recall, conjure up; **~bit·ten** *v/t.* (*irr.*, *sep.*, h, → **bitten**) ask *s.o.* (to come) up; **~blicken** *v/i.* (*sep.*, h) look up (**zu** *dat.* at); **~brin·gen** *v/t.* (*irr.*, *sep.*, h, → **bringen**) bring up(stairs)

her'auf·däm·mern I. *v/i.* (*sep.*, sn) *day*: dawn; *morning*: break; **II.** ♀ *fig. n* (-s) dawning

her'auf|drin·gen *v/i.* (*irr.*, *sep.*, sn, → **dringen**) *scent etc.*: waft up; **der Lärm drang von unten herauf** the noise could be heard from below; **~kom·men** *v/i.* (*irr.*, *sep.*, sn, → **kommen**) come up(stairs); *thunderstorm*: come up; **die Straße ~** come up (*or* along) the street; **~schal·ten** *v/i.* (*sep.*, h) *mot.* shift into higher gear, shift up; **~se·hen** *v/i.* (*irr.*, *sep.*, h, → **sehen**) look up (**zu** *dat.* at); **~set·zen** *v/t.* (*sep.*, h) raise, put up; **~stei·gen** *v/i.* (*irr.*, *sep.*, sn, steigen) go (*or* climb) up; *fumes etc.*: rise; *thunderstorm*: come up, be brewing; **~zie·hen** (*irr.*, *sep.*, → **ziehen**) **I.** *v/t.* (h) pull up; **II.** *v/i.* (sn) *thunderstorm*: come up, be brewing

her·aus [hɛ'raʊs] *adv.* out; out of; **zum Fenster ~** out of the window, *Am. a.* out the window; **nach vorn ~ wohnen** live at the front; **von innen ~** from inside; **aus einem Gefühl der Verlassenheit** *etc.* **~** from (*or* out of) a sense of loneliness *etc.*; **~ mit ihm!** out with him; **~ damit!** (come on,) out with it; **~ mit der Sprache!** out with it!; **da ~** out there; **geht es da ~?** is that the way out?; **frei** (*or* **gerade, offen, rund**) **~** openly, bluntly, point-blank; → **heraushaben, heraussein;** *in cpds usu.* ... out; **~ar·bei·ten** (*sep.*, h) **I.** *v/t.* work out (*a. fig.*); carve out; *fig.* elaborate; **II.** *v/refl.*: **sich ~** work one's way out (**aus** *dat.* of), struggle out (of); *fig.* manage to get out (of); **~be·kom·men** *v/t.* (*irr.*, *sep.*, h, → **bekommen**) **1.** get out (**aus** *dat.* of); find out *secret etc.*; work out, solve *riddle etc.*; make (*or* figure) out *meaning etc.*; **2. sein Geld wieder ~** get one's money back; **etwas** (**Wechselgeld**) **~** get some change; **Sie bekommen zwei Mark heraus** you get two marks change; **~brin·gen** *v/t.* (*irr.*, *sep.*, h, → **bringen**) bring out, get out (**aus** *dat.* of); *fig.* bring out *product etc.*, *a.* publish *book etc.*; release *record*; *thea.* produce *play etc.*; **groß ~** give *s.o. or s.th.* a big buildup; **sie brachte kein Wort heraus** she couldn't say a word; **~bü·geln** *v/t.* (*sep.*, h) iron out; **~de·stil·lie·ren** *v/t.* (*sep.*, h) ⚗ top, remove through distillation; *fig.* distil (**aus** *dat.* from); **~drücken** *v/t.* (*sep.*, h) **1.** squeeze out (**aus** *dat.* of); **2.** stick out *one's chest*; **~fah·ren** (*irr.*, *sep.*, → **fahren**) **I.** *v/i.* (sn) come (*or* drive) out (**aus** *dat.* of); *fig.*

words: slip out; **II.** *v/t.* (h) drive out (**aus** *dat.* of); **~fal·len** *v/i.* (*irr., sep.,* sn, → ***fallen***) fall out; drop out; **~fil·tern** *v/t.* (*sep.,* h) filter out (*a. fig.*); **~fin·den** (*irr., sep.,* h, → ***finden***) **I.** *v/t.* find out; find; **II.** *v/i. and v/refl.* (**sich ~**) find one's way out (**aus** *dat.* of); *fig.* get out (of); **~fi·schen** *v/t.* (*sep.,* h) *a. fig.* fish out (**aus** *dat.* of); **~flie·gen** *v/i.* (*irr., sep.,* sn, → ***fliegen***) fly out (**aus** *dat.* of); **~flie·ßen** *v/i.* (*irr., sep.,* sn, → ***fließen***) flow out (**aus** *dat.* of)

Her'aus·for·de·rer [-fɔrdərɐ] *m* (-s; -) challenger; *pol.* rival candidate, opponent; **her'aus·for·dern** *v/t.* (*sep.,* h) challenge (**zu** *dat.* to); provoke (into *ger.*); ***das Unglück ~*** court disaster; ***das Schicksal ~*** tempt fate; ***zur Kritik ~*** invite criticism; ***das fordert direkt dazu heraus zu*** *inf.* that's an open invitation to (*doing*) *s.th.*; **her'aus·for·dernd I.** *adj.* a) challenging; defiant; provocative; arrogant, b) inviting; ***~er Blick*** F come-hither look; **II.** *adv.*: ***j-n ~ ansehen*** give s.o. a challenging look; **Her'aus·for·de·rung** *f* (-; -en) challenge (*a. fig. task etc.*); provocation

her'aus·füh·len *v/t.* (*sep.,* h) sense, feel; ***ich fühle es aus s-m Verhalten heraus*** I can sense from (*or* tell by) his behavio(u)r

Her'aus·ga·be *f* (-; *no pl.*) ⚖ surrender; delivery; publication; **her'aus·ge·ben** (*irr., sep.,* h, → ***geben***) **I.** *v/t.* a) hand over; give back, return, b) publish, edit *book*; issue *stamps etc.*; ***(j-m) zwei Mark ~*** give s.o. two marks change; **II.** *v/i.* give s.o. change; ***können Sie ~?*** can you change this?; ***~ auf*** *acc.* give change for; **Her'aus·ge·ber** *m* (-s; -) publisher; editor

her'aus|ge·hen *v/i.* (*irr., sep.,* sn, → ***gehen***) go out; *stain*: come out; *fig.* ***aus sich ~*** come out of one's shell; **~grei·fen** *v/t.* (*irr., sep.,* h, → ***greifen***) pick out; cite *example etc.*; ***sich ein Opfer*** *etc.* ***~*** single out a victim *etc.*; **~gucken** *v/i.* (*sep.,* h) **1.** look out (**aus** *dat.* of); **2.** peep out; **~ha·ben** *v/t.* (*irr., sep.,* h, → ***haben***) a) have got *s.th.* out, b) have found *s.th.* out; have solved (*or* got) *s.th.*; ***jetzt hat er es heraus*** he's got (the hang of) it now; **~hal·ten** (*irr., sep.,* h, → ***halten***) **I.** *v/t.*: ***j-n (et.) ~ aus*** *dat.* keep s.o. (s.th.) out of *s.th.*; **II.** *v/refl.*: ***sich ~*** keep out of it; ***sich ~ aus*** *dat.* keep out of *s.th.*; ***halt dich da heraus*** don't get involved; **~hän·gen** *v/t.* (*sep.,* h) *and v/i.* (*irr., sep.,* h, → ***hängen¹***) hang out; **~hau·en** *v/t.* (*irr., sep.,* h, → ***hauen***) **1.** a) knock out, b) carve out; **2.** *fig.* ***j-n (sich) ~*** get s.o. (o.s.) out (**aus** *dat.* of *a difficulty etc.*); **~he·ben** *v/t.* (*irr., sep.,* h, → ***heben***) **1.** lift (*or* take) out; **2.** *fig.* → ***hervorheben***; **~hel·fen** *v/i.* (*irr., sep.,* h, → ***helfen***): ***j-m ~*** help s.o. out (*a. fig.*) (**aus** *dat.* of); **~ho·len** *v/t.* (*sep.,* h) a) get out (*a. fig.*) (**aus** *dat.* of); bring (*or* fetch) out; *fig.* gain, F notch up *profit, win etc.*, b) *fig.* bring out *merit etc.*; *fig.* ***et. ~ aus*** *dat.* get s.th. out of; ***was (wieviel) hast du herausgeholt?*** what did you manage to achieve? (how much did you get out of it?); ***alles aus sich ~*** give everything one has got; → ***letzt*** II; **~hö·ren** *v/t.* (*sep.,* h) hear; *fig.* detect (**aus** *dat.* in); *fig.* ***es war deutlich herauszuhören*** it was obvious to anyone with ears, you couldn't overhear it; **~in·ter·pre·tie·ren** *v/t.* (*sep.,* h) deduce, derive (**aus** *dat.* from); **~keh·ren** *fig. v/t.* (*sep.,* h) a) act, play *the expert etc.*, b) show, display, parade *s.th.*

her'aus·kom·men *v/i.* (*irr., sep.,* sn, → ***kommen***) a) come out (**aus** *dat.* of); appear, emerge (from), b) get out (*a. fig.*) (**aus** *dat.* of), c) *fig.* come out, *book etc.*: *a.* be published, appear, *stamps etc.*: be issued; A be the result; ***groß ~*** be a great success; ***komisch*** *etc.* ***~*** sound funny *etc.*; F ***~ mit*** *dat.* come out with, admit; ***es kommt aufs gleiche*** (*or* ***auf dasselbe***) ***heraus*** it boils (*or* comes) down to the same thing; ***~ bei*** *dat.* come (out) of *s.th.*; ***es kommt nichts dabei heraus*** it's not worth it, it doesn't pay; ***dabei ist nichts Gutes herausgekommen*** nothing good has come (out) of it; ***was ist dabei herausgekommen?*** what was the outcome?, *a.* what was decided?; ***ist irgend etwas dabei herausgekommen?*** was it any good?, did you *etc.* achieve anything (F get anywhere)?; ***wir kamen aus dem Lachen (Staunen) nicht mehr heraus*** we just couldn't stop laughing (we couldn't believe our eyes)

her'aus|kön·nen *v/i.* (*irr., sep.,* h, → ***können***) be able to get out (**aus** *dat.* of); ***ich kann nicht heraus*** I can't get out, I'm stuck; **~krie·gen** F *v/t.* (*sep.,* h) → ***herausbekommen***; **~kri·stal·li·sie·ren** (*sep.,* h) **I.** *v/refl.*: ***sich ~*** crystallize (**zu** *dat.* into; **aus** *dat.* out of, *a. fig.* from); **II.** *v/t.* crystallize (**aus** *dat.* out of, from); *fig.* distil, extract (from); **~las·sen** *v/t.* (*irr., sep.,* h, → ***lassen***) **1.** let *s.o.* out (**aus** *dat.* of); **2.** *fig.* leave *s.o. or s.th.* out (**aus** *dat.* of); **~lau·fen** *v/i.* (*irr., sep.,* sn, → ***laufen***) run out; **~le·gen** *v/t.* (*sep.,* h) put out (*dat.* for); **~le·sen** *v/t.* (*irr., sep.,* h, → ***lesen***) **1.** pick out (**aus** *dat.* of); **2.** *fig.* gather (**aus** *dat.* from); read (into); **~locken** *v/t.* (*sep.,* h) lure out (**aus** *dat.* of); *fig.* ***et. aus j-m ~*** worm s.th. out of s.o.; ***j-n aus s-r Reserve ~*** draw s.o. out of his (*or* her) shell; **~lü·gen** *v/refl.* (*irr., sep.,* h, → ***lügen***): ***sich ~*** lie one's way out (**aus** *dat.* of); **~ma·chen** (*sep.,* h) **I.** *v/t.* take out; **II.** F *fig. v/refl.*: ***sich ~*** be coming along well, improve; be doing nicely *after one's illness etc.*; **~müs·sen** *v/i.* (*irr., sep.,* h, → ***müssen***) a) *tooth etc.*: have to come out, b) have to get out (**aus** *dat.* of *one's flat etc.*), c) have to go out(side), d) have to get up; ***das mußte noch heraus*** it had to be said, I *etc.* had to say it

her'aus·nehm·bar [-neːmbaːɐ] *adj.* removable; **her'aus·neh·men** *v/t.* (*irr., sep.,* h, → ***nehmen***) take out (**aus** *dat.* of); *w.s.* remove (from); ***sich den Blinddarm*** *etc.* ***~lassen*** have one's appendix *etc.* (taken) out; *mot.* ***den Gang ~*** go into neutral, put the gear in neutral; *fig.* ***sich et. ~*** arrogate s.th. (to o.s.); ***sich Freiheiten ~*** take liberties (***j-m gegenüber*** with s.o.); ***sich zuviel ~*** go too far, overstep the mark; ***nimm dir ja nicht zuviel heraus!*** watch you don't overdo it (*or* overstep the mark)

her'aus|plat·zen *v/i.* (*sep.,* sn) burst out (laughing); ***~ mit*** *dat.* blurt out *the truth etc.*; **~pres·sen** *v/t.* (*sep.,* h) press (*or* squeeze) out; **~put·zen** *v/t.* (*sep.,* h) spruce (**sich** o.s.) up; **~quet·schen** *v/t.* (*sep.,* h) squeeze out (*a. fig.*)

her'aus·ra·gen *v/i.* (*sep.,* h) jut out; *building etc.*: tower, rise (**aus** *dat.* above); *fig.* stand out; **her'aus·ra·gend** *fig. adj.* outstanding

her'aus|re·den *v/refl.* (*sep.,* h): ***sich ~*** talk one's way out of it, wriggle out of it, **aus** *dat.*: talk one's way out of, wriggle out of; **~rei·ßen** *v/t.* (*irr., sep.,* h, → ***reißen***) pull out; tear out *page etc.*; *fig.* tear *s.o.* (**aus** *dat.* from); get *s.o.* out (of); shake *s.o.* out (of); F save; F *fig.* ***diese Leistung hat ihn noch herausgerissen*** this performance saved him (from the worst); F ***das reißt alles (wieder) heraus*** that makes up for it; **~rücken** (*sep.*) **I.** *v/t.* (h) push (*or* move) out; F *fig.* → **II.** F *v/i.* (sn): ***~ mit*** *dat.* come out with; F fork out, cough up *money etc.*; ***mit der Sprache ~*** talk, come out with it; ***jetzt rück mal heraus (mit der Sprache)*** come on, out with it; **~ru·fen** *v/t.* (*irr., sep.,* h, → ***rufen***) call out; *thea.* call for, call before the curtain; **~rut·schen** *v/i.* (*sep.,* sn) slip out (*a. fig.*); *fig.* ***das ist mir so herausgerutscht*** it just slipped out; **~sa·gen** *v/t.* (*sep.,* h): ***et. (frei) ~*** say s.th. straight out; **~schaf·fen** *v/t.* (*sep.,* h) take (*or* move, carry) out; **~schä·len** *fig.* (*sep.,* h) **I.** *v/t.* **1.** sift out; **II.** *v/refl.* **2.** F ***sich aus s-n Sachen ~*** F peel one's clothes off; **3. *sich ~*** emerge; **~schau·en** *v/i.* (*sep.,* h) **1.** look out; **2.** *fig.* → ***herausspringen*** 2; **~schin·den** F *v/t.* (*irr., sep.,* h, → ***schinden***) → ***herausschlagen*** 2; **~schla·gen** (*irr., sep.,* → ***schlagen***) **I.** *v/t.* (h) **1.** knock out (**aus** *dat.* of); **2.** *fig.* get (**aus** *dat.* out of); ***Geld ~ aus*** *dat.* make money out of; ***möglichst viel ~*** get as much as one can (**aus** *dat.* out of); ***e-n Vorteil ~*** wangle an advantage (**aus** *dat.* out of); **II.** *v/i.* (sn) *flames*: leap out (**aus** *dat.* of); **~schleu·dern** *v/t.* (*sep.,* h) **1.** throw (*or* hurl, catapult) out (**aus** *dat.* of); ***aus e-m Auto herausgeschleudert werden*** be thrown (*or* hurled) out of a car; **2.** *fig.* burst out with *accusations etc.*; **~schlüp·fen** *v/i.* (*sep.,* sn) slip out; **~schmecken** *v/t.* (*sep.,* h) taste; ***et. ~ aus*** *dat.* taste s.th. in *the sauce etc.*; **~schmei·ßen** F *v/t.* (*irr., sep.,* h, → ***schmeißen***) throw out (**aus** *dat.* of); **~schnei·den** *v/t.* (*irr., sep.,* h, → ***schneiden***) cut out; **~schöp·fen** *v/t.* (*sep.,* h) ladle *soup* out (**aus** *dat.* of), scoop out *water*, bale out *boat*; **~schrau·ben** *v/t.* (*sep.,* h) unscrew (**aus** *dat.* from); **~schrei·ben** *v/t.* (*irr., sep.,* h, → ***schreiben***) copy (**aus** *dat.* from, out of); **~schüt·teln** *v/t.* (*sep.,* h) shake out (**aus** *dat.* of); **~schüt·ten** *v/t.* (*sep.,* h) pour out (**aus** *dat.* of); **~schwin·deln** *v/refl.* (*sep.,* h): ***sich ~*** wriggle (one's way) out of it, **aus** *dat.*: wriggle out of; **~se·hen** *v/i.* (*irr., sep.,* h, → ***sehen***) look out; **~sein** F *v/i.* (*irr., sep.,* sn, → ***sein***) be out; ***jetzt ist es heraus!*** *a.* now the secret's out, now the cat's been let out of the bag; ***es ist noch nicht heraus, ob*** it's still open as to whether; → ***fein*** II; **~sickern** *v/i.* (*sep.,* sn) seep (**aus** *dat.* out of); trickle (out of); **~sprin·gen** *v/i.* (*irr., sep.,* sn, → ***springen***) **1.** jump out (**aus** *dat.* of); **2.** F *fig.* ***was springt für mich dabei heraus?*** what's in it for me?; **~sprit·zen** *v/i.* (*sep.,* sn) squirt out; **~spru·deln** (*sep.*) **I.** *v/i.* (sn) bubble out; *fig. words*: come spluttering out; **II.** *fig. v/t.* (h) splutter out; **~ste·chen** *v/i.* (*irr., sep.,* h, → ***stechen***) *colo(u)r etc.*: stand out; **~ste·hen** *v/i.* (*irr.*, *sep.*, h, → ***stehen***) stand out; stick out; jut out

her'aus·stel·len (*sep.*, h) **I.** *v/t.* **1.** put out(side); **2.** *fig.* a) emphasize, underline, bring out (clearly), b) publicize, c) highlight, feature (*a. thea.*), bring out; set off, throw into (sharp) relief; ***et. klar und deutlich ~*** make s.th. quite clear; **II.** *v/refl.*: ***sich ~ als*** turn out (to be); ***es hat sich herausgestellt, daß*** it turned out (that), ***er ein Drogenschmuggler ist***: he turned out to be (*or* it turned out he was) a drug smuggler; ***es hat sich herausgestellt, daß er sehr kompetent ist*** *a.* he proved (to be) very competent; ***das hat sich erst später herausgestellt*** that only came out (*or* came to light) later

her'aus|strecken *v/t.* (*sep.*, h) stick *one's head* out (***aus*** *dat.* of); → ***Zunge***; **~strei·chen** (*irr.*, *sep.*, h, → ***streichen***) **I.** *v/t.* **1.** cross out (***aus*** *dat.* of), delete (from); **2.** *fig.* praise to the skies; **II.** *v/refl.*: ***sich ~*** blow one's own trumpet; **~strö·men** *v/i.* (*sep.*, sn) *a. fig.* pour out (***aus*** *dat.* of); **~stür·zen** *v/i.* (*sep.*, sn) a) fall out (***aus*** *dat.* of), b) rush (*or* storm) out (of), come rushing (*or* storming) out (of); **~su·chen** *v/t.* (*sep.*, h) choose, pick out; **~tra·gen** *v/t.* (*irr.*, *sep.*, h, → ***tragen***) carry out (***aus*** *dat.* of); **~tren·nen** *v/t.* (*sep.*, h) detach, remove (***aus*** *dat.* from); **~tre·ten** *v/i.* (*irr.*, *sep.*, sn, → ***treten***) step (*or* come) out (***aus*** *dat.* of); **~wach·sen** *v/i.* (*irr.*, *sep.*, sn, → ***wachsen***[1]): ***~ aus*** *dat.* grow out of, *a.* outgrow *one's clothes*; F ***das wächst mir zum Hals heraus*** I'm sick and tired of it; **~wa·gen** *v/refl.* (*sep.*, h): ***sich ~*** venture out(side); **~wa·schen** *v/t.* (*irr.*, *sep.*, h, → ***waschen***) wash out; **~wer·fen** *v/t.* (*irr.*, *sep.*, h, → ***werfen***) throw out (***aus*** *dat.* of); **~win·den** *fig.* *v/refl.* (*irr.*, *sep.*, h, → ***winden***): ***sich ~*** wriggle out of it, ***aus*** *dat.*: wriggle out of *s.th.*; **~win·ken** (*sep.*, h) **I.** *v/t.* flag down *a car etc.*; **II.** *v/i.*: ***aus dem Fenster*** *etc.* ***~*** wave from the window *etc.*; **~wirt·schaf·ten** *v/t.* (*sep.*, h) get (***aus*** *dat.* out of); ***e-n Gewinn ~*** make a profit (***aus*** *dat.* out of); **~wol·len** *v/i.* (*irr.*, *sep.*, h, → ***wollen***) want to get out; *fig.* ***er will nicht mit der Sprache heraus*** he won't open up, he's clammed up; **~zie·hen** *v/t.* (*irr.*, *sep.*, h, → ***ziehen***) pull out (***aus*** *dat.* of); extract (from) (*a.* ⚒, ⚕ *and fig.*); drag out (of); ⚔ withdraw (from), pull out (of); *fig.* cull (from)

herb [hɛrp] *adj.* a) sour, tart; *gastr.* dry; tangy *scent etc.*, b) *fig.* harsh, severe; bitter *disappointment*, *defeat etc.*; austere *beauty etc.*

Her·ba·ri·um [hɛr'baːrium] *n* (-s; -rien) herbarium

her·bei [hɛɐ'baɪ] *adv.* here; **~ei·len** *v/i.* (*sep.*, sn) come running (up); **~füh·ren** *v/t.* (*sep.*, h) a) cause, bring about; lead to, b) force; *esp.* ⚕ induce; **~ho·len** *v/t.* (*sep.*, h) fetch; call (*or* send) for *a doctor etc.*; **~kom·men** *v/i.* (*irr.*, *sep.*, sn, → ***kommen***) come along; **~lau·fen** *v/i.* (*irr.*, *sep.*, sn, → ***laufen***) come running (along); **~locken** *v/t.* (*sep.*, h) attract, lure; **~re·den** *v/t.* (*sep.*, h) provoke; ***wir wollen es nicht ~*** let's not tempt fate; **~ru·fen** *v/t.* (*irr.*, *sep.*, h, → ***rufen***) call over; call (*or* send) for *a doctor etc.*; **~schaf·fen** *v/t.* (*sep.*, h) fetch; provide, get; produce *evidence etc.*; **~schlep·pen** *v/t.* (*sep.*, h) drag along (*or* in); **~seh·nen** *v/t.* (*sep.*, h) long for; ***sie sehnt den Frühling (ihre Kinder) herbei*** *a.* she can't wait for spring (she wishes her children were there *or* with her); **~strö·men** *v/i.* (*sep.*, sn) flock to the scene; come in crowds; ***~ zu*** *dat.* flock to; ***die Menschen sind herbeigeströmt*** crowds of people came; **~stür·zen** *v/i.* (*sep.*, sn) rush up (to the scene); **~win·ken** *v/t.* (*sep.*, h) beckon *s.o.* to come; hail, flag down *taxi*; **~wün·schen** *v/t.* (*sep.*, h): (***sich***) ***et. ~*** long for s.th.; ***sich j-n ~*** wish s.o. were (*or* was) there; **~zau·bern** *v/t.* (*sep.*, h) conjure up; **~zie·hen** *v/t.* (*irr.*, *sep.*, h, → ***ziehen***) pull near; pull up *chair*; *fig.* → ***Haar***; **~zi·tie·ren** *v/t.* (*sep.*, h) send for *s.o.*, ask *s.o.* to come and see one

'her|be·kom·men *v/t.* (*irr.*, *sep.*, h, → ***bekommen***) get (hold of); **~be·mü·hen** (*sep.*, h) **I.** *v/t.*: ***j-n ~*** ask s.o. to come (there *or* here); **II.** *v/refl.*: ***sich ~*** take the trouble to come; ***Sie haben sich leider umsonst herbemüht*** I'm afraid you've come all this way for nothing; **~be·or·dern** *v/t.* (*sep.*, h) summon

Her·ber·ge ['hɛrbɛrgə] *f* (-; -n) a) inn, b) (youth *etc.*) hostel, c) shelter (*a. fig.*); **'Her·bergs·mut·ter** *f*, **'Her·bergs·va·ter** *m* warden

'her|be·stel·len *v/t.* (*sep.*, h) ask *s.o.* to come; send for *s.o.*; order *taxi etc.*; **~be·ten** *v/t.* (*sep.*, h) reel (*or* rattle) off

Herb·heit ['hɛrphaɪt] *f* (-; *no pl.*) a) sourness; *gastr.* dryness, dry quality, b) *fig.* severity; bitterness; austerity

'her·bit·ten *v/t.* (*irr.*, *sep.*, h, → ***bitten***) ask *s.o.* to come

Her·bi·zid [hɛrbi'tsiːt] *n* (-[e]s; -e [-də]) herbicide

'her·brin·gen *v/t.* (*irr.*, *sep.*, h, → ***bringen***) bring (along); → ***hergebracht***

Herbst [hɛrpst] *m* (-[e]s; -e) autumn, *Am. a.* fall; **~an·fang** *m* beginning of autumn (*Am. a.* fall); **~blu·me** *f* autumn flower; **~fär·bung** *f* autumn(al) colo(u)rs *pl.*; **~fe·ri·en** *pl.* autumn break *sg.*; **~kol·lek·ti·on** *f* autumn collection

'herbst·lich **I.** *adj.* autumn(al); **II.** *adv.*: ***~ kühles Wetter*** (***kühler Abend*** *etc.*) cool autumn weather (evening *etc.*)

'Herbst|mo·nat *m* autumn month; **~ro·se** *f* hollyhock; **~tag** *m* autumn day; **~wet·ter** *n* autumn weather; **~wind** *m* autumn(al) wind; **~zeit·lo·se** [-tsaɪtloːzə] *f* (-; -n) ⚘ meadow saffron, naked lady

Herd [heːɐt] *m* (-[e]s; -e ['heːɐdə]) **1.** stove, cooker; range; oven; *fig.* hearth, home; ***den ganzen Tag am ~ stehen*** stand in the kitchen all day long; *fig.* ***am häuslichen ~*** at home; ***eigener ~ ist Goldes wert*** there's no place like home; **2.** *fig.* cent|re (*Am.* -er); focus (*a.* ⚕); epicent|re (*Am.* -er)

Her·de ['heːɐdə] *f* (-; -n) **1.** herd; flock *of sheep*; *zo.* ***in der ~ leben*** live in herds; **2.** *fig.* herd, masses *pl.*; ***mit der ~ laufen*** (just) follow the herd; ***aus der ~ ausbrechen*** break away from the others, go one's own way

'Her·den|geist *m* (-[e]s; *no pl.*) herd mentality; **~in·stinkt** *m* herd instinct; **~mensch** *m* sheep; **~tier** *n* **1.** gregarious animal; **2.** *fig. contp.* sheep; **~trieb** *m* (-[e]s; *no pl.*) herd (*fig. a.* sheep) instinct; **~vieh** *fig. contp. n the* herd

'her·den·wei·se *adv.* in herds (*a. fig.*)

'Herd|in·fek·ti·on *f* ⚕ focal infection; **~plat·te** *f* hotplate

he·re·di·tär [heredi'tɛːɐ] *adj.* hereditary

her·ein [hɛ'raɪn] *adv.* in; ***von draußen ~*** from outside; ***~!*** come in!; ***hier ~!*** this way, please; **~be·kom·men** *v/t.* (*irr.*, *sep.*, h, → ***bekommen***) *a.* † get in; recover; **~bit·ten** *v/t.* (*irr.*, *sep.*, h, → ***bitten***) ask *s.o.* to come in; **~blicken** *v/i.* (*sep.*, h) look in(side); ***~ in*** *acc.* look into (*or* inside); **~bre·chen** *fig.* *v/i.* (*irr.*, *sep.*, sn, → ***brechen***) *night*: fall; *storm*: break; *winter*: set in; ***~ über*** *acc.* hit, strike, *misfortune etc.*: *a.* befall *s.o.*; **~brin·gen** *v/t.* (*irr.*, *sep.*, h, → ***bringen***) bring in, get in; **~drin·gen** *v/i.* (*irr.*, *sep.*, sn, → ***dringen***) → ***eindringen***; **~fal·len** *v/i.* (*irr.*, *sep.*, sn, → ***fallen***) **1.** *light etc.*: come in; **2.** *fig.* be taken in (***auf*** *acc.* by), (*a.* ***darauf ~***) F fall for it; ***~ auf*** *a. acc.* fall for; ***~ mit*** *dat.* make a mistake with *s.o. or s.th.*; **~füh·ren** *v/t.* (*sep.*, h) show in(to ***in*** *acc.*); **~ho·len** *v/t.* (*sep.*, h) fetch (*or* bring) in; † get (in) *orders*; *fig.* recoup *losses etc.*; make up for *lost time*; **~kom·men** *v/i.* (*irr.*, *sep.*, sn, → ***kommen***) come in(side); walk in; get in; † come in; ***~ in*** *acc.* come into (*or* inside); **~las·sen** *v/t.* (*irr.*, *sep.*, h, → ***lassen***) let in; **~le·gen** *v/t.* (*sep.*, h) F take *s.o.* for a ride, take *s.o.* in; **~locken** *v/t.* (*sep.*, h) lure in(side); **~neh·men** *v/t.* (*irr.*, *sep.*, h, → ***nehmen***) take in; **~plat·zen** *v/i.* (*sep.*, sn) burst in(to ***in*** *acc.*); **~reg·nen** *v/impers.* (*sep.*, h): ***es regnet herein*** it's raining in, the rain's coming in (*or* through the roof *etc.*); ***~ in*** *acc.* rain into; **~rei·chen** (*sep.*, h) **I.** *v/t.*: ***j-m et. ~*** hand s.th. in to s.o.; **II.** *v/i.*: ***~ in*** *acc.* reach as far as; **~rei·ßen** F *v/t.* (*irr.*, *sep.*, h, → ***reißen***), **~rei·ten** F *v/t.* (*irr.*, *sep.*, h, → ***reiten***) get (*or* land) *s.o.* in a (real) mess; ***j-n in et. ~*** land s.o. in s.th., drag s.o. into s.th.; **~ru·fen** *v/t.* (*irr.*, *sep.*, h, → ***rufen***) call in; **~schau·en** *v/i.* (*sep.*, h) look in; F look in, drop by (***bei*** *dat.* at); ***~ in*** *acc.* look into; ***zur Tür ~*** pop one's head around the door; **~schmug·geln** *v/t.* (*sep.*, h) smuggle in(to ***in*** *acc.*); **~schnei·en** (*sep.*) **I.** *v/impers.* (h): ***es schneit herein*** it's snowing in, the snow's coming in (*or* through the door *etc.*); ***~ in*** *acc.* snow into; **II.** F *fig.* *v/i.* (sn) F blow in, breeze in; **~se·hen** *v/i.* (*irr.*, *sep.*, h, → ***sehen***) → ***hereinschauen***; **~spa·zie·ren** *v/i.* (*sep.*, sn) stroll in, walk in; ***hereinspaziert kommen*** come waltzing (*or* strolling) in; ***hereinspaziert kam(en) ...*** in strolled ..., in walked ..., who should walk in but ...; ***hereinspaziert!*** come in!, come in!; **~strö·men** *v/i.* (*sep.*, sn) pour in (*a. fig.*); **~stür·men** *v/i.* (*sep.*, sn), **~stür·zen** *v/i.* (*sep.*, sn) rush in(to ***in*** *acc.*); **~tre·ten** *v/i.* (*irr.*, *sep.*, sn, → ***treten***) come in, walk in, enter; ***~ in*** *acc.* come into, enter; **~zie·hen** (*irr.*, *sep.*, → ***ziehen***) **I.** *v/t.* (h) pull in; *fig.* → ***hineinziehen***; ***~ in*** *acc.* pull into (*or* inside); **II.** *v/i.* (sn) → ***einziehen***

'her·fah·ren (*irr.*, *sep.*, → ***fahren***) **I.** *v/t.* (h) bring (*or* drive) here; bring by car; **II.** *v/i.* (sn) drive (here); come by car; ***~ hinter*** *dat.* drive behind; follow; ***~ vor*** *dat.* drive in front (*or* ahead) of; **'Her·fahrt** *f* (-; -en) journey (*or* trip) here; ***auf der ~*** on the (*or* my *etc.*) way here

'her|fal·len *v/i.* (*irr.*, *sep.*, sn, → ***fallen***): ~

über *acc.* pounce on, attack; F have a (real) go at *s.o.*; F go for, pitch into *one's food*; **~fin·den** *v/i.* (*irr.*, *sep.*, h, → **finden**) find one's way here; **~füh·ren** (*sep.*, h) **I.** *v/t.* bring here; **was führt Sie her?** what brings you here?; **II.** *v/i.*: **~ neben** *dat.* run *or* go along(side) s.th.

Her·gang ['he:ɐgaŋ] *m* (-[e]s; *no pl.*) sequence of events; circumstances *pl.*, details *pl.*; **den ~ schildern** describe exactly what happened

'her|ge·ben (*irr.*, *sep.*, h, → **geben**) **I.** *v/t.* a) give (*or* hand) back, b) give away; **gib her!** give it to me, hand it over; **gib mal her!** let me have a look; **ich gebe es nicht gerne her** I don't like to part with it; **s-n Namen ~ zu** *dat.* associate o.s. with; *fig.* **e-e Menge ~** F be pretty good, *w.s.* be well worth the effort; **es gibt nichts her** it's not much use, it's not worth it, *book, subject etc.*: there isn't much to it; **II.** *v/refl.*: **sich ~ zu** *dat.* get involved in *s.th.*, stoop to *s.th.*; **sich dazu ~ zu** *inf.* lower o.s. to *inf.*, stoop to *ger.*; **dazu gebe ich mich nicht her** *a.* I'm not going to have anything to do with that (*or* be a party to that)

'her·ge·bracht I. *p.p. of* **herbringen; II.** *adj.* usual, customary; traditional, old

'her|ge·hen *v/i.* (*irr.*, *sep.*, sn, → **gehen**) **1. ~ hinter** *dat.* follow, walk behind; **~ vor** *dat.* walk in front (*or* ahead) of; **2. es ging heiß her** things got pretty lively, they were having a great time *at the party etc.*; **hier geht es hoch her** there's plenty of action (*or* plenty going on) around here; **es ging lustig her** it was great fun; **3. über j-n ~** pull s.o. to pieces; **~ge·hö·ren** *v/i.* (*sep.*, h) → **hierhergehören**

'her·ge·lau·fen I. *p.p. of* **herlaufen; II.** *contp. adj.*: **jeder ~e Kerl** any (old) Tom, Dick or Harry; **du kannst doch nicht einfach diesen ~en Kerl heiraten** you can't just marry the first man who happens to come your way

'her|ha·ben *v/t.* (*irr.*, *sep.*, h, → **haben**): **wo hast du das her?** where did you get that (from)?; **~hal·ten** (*irr.*, *sep.*, h, → **halten**) **I.** *v/t.* hold out; **II.** *v/i.*: **~ müssen** F have to take the rap; **~ho·len** *v/t.* (*sep.*, h) fetch, get; **~ lassen** send for; *fig.* **weit hergeholt** far-fetched; **~hö·ren** *v/i.* (*sep.*, h) listen; **hört mal alle her!** listen, everyone

He·ring ['he:rɪŋ] *m* (-s; -e) **1.** *zo.* herring; F *fig.* F matchstick; **wie die ~e zusammengedrängt** packed like sardines; **2.** tent peg

'He·rings|fi·sche·rei *f* herring fishery; **~hai** *m* mackerel shark; **~milch** *f* herring milt; **~sa‚lat** *m* pickled herring salad

'her·ja·gen (*sep.*) **I.** *v/i.* (sn): **~ hinter** *dat.* chase after *s.o.*, try to chase up *s.th.*; **II.** *v/t.* (h): **vor sich ~** drive *an animal etc.* along in front of one

'her·kom·men I. *v/i.* (*irr.*, *sep.*, sn, → **kommen**) come (here); approach; **~ von** *dat. a. fig.* come from; **wo kommt er her?** where does he come from?; **II. ≈** *n* (-s) **1.** → **Herkunft; 2.** tradition; **'her·kömm·lich** [-kœmlɪç] *adj.* customary; traditional; conventional *weapons etc.*

Her·ku·les·ar·beit ['hɛrkulɛs-] *fig. f* Herculean task

her·ku·lisch [hɛr'ku:lɪʃ] *adj.* Herculean

Her·kunft ['he:ɐkʊnft] *f* (-; *no pl.*) origin; *a. s.o.'s* background; *ling. a.* derivation; **der ~ nach** by origin; **er ist chinesischer ~** he's of Chinese origin (*or* descent), he has a Chinese background; **es ist kanadischer ~** it comes from Canada

'Her·kunfts|be·zeich·nung *f* ✝ mark of origin; **~land** *n* ✝ country of origin; **~ort** *m* ✝ place of origin

'her|lau·fen *v/i.* (*irr.*, *sep.*, sn, → **laufen**) run (here); **~ hinter** *dat.* run (*or* chase) after; → **hergelaufen; ~lei·ern** *v/t.* (*sep.*, h) reel off

'her·lei·ten (*sep.*, h) **I.** *v/t.* derive (**von** *dat.* from); deduce (from), infer (from); **II.** *v/refl.*: **sich ~ von** *dat.* a) derive (*or* be derived) from; go back to, b) descend (*or* be descended) from; **'Her·lei·tung** *f* (-; -en) *ling.* derivation

'her|locken *v/t.* (*sep.*, h) lure (over here); **~ma·chen** (*sep.*, h) **I.** *v/refl.*: **sich ~ über** *acc.* tackle *book, work etc.*, F get stuck into; F go for, pitch into *one's food*; F have a (real) go at *s.o.*; **II.** *v/i.*: **etwas (viel) ~** be quite (very) impressive, *clothes etc.*: look good (great); **es macht nicht viel her** F it's not up to much, it's not much to look at

Her·ma·phro·dit [hɛrmafro'di:t] *m* (-en; -en) hermaphrodite; **her·ma·phro·di·tisch** [hɛrmafro'di:tɪʃ] *adj.* hermaphroditic(al)

Her·me·lin¹ [hɛrmə'li:n] *n* (-s; -e) *zo.* ermine, stoat

Her·me'lin² *m* (-s; -e) ermine

her·me·tisch [hɛr'me:tɪʃ] **I.** *adj.* hermetic, airtight; **II.** *adv.* hermetically; **~ verschlossen** (*or* **abgeriegelt**) hermetically sealed

'her·müs·sen *v/i.* (*irr.*, *sep.*, h, → **müssen**) have to come (here); **das Buch muß her!** we must get hold of (*or* get our hands on) that book

her·nach [hɛɐ'na:x] *dial. adv.* afterwards; later (on)

'her·neh·men *v/t.* (*irr.*, *sep.*, h, → **nehmen**) **1.** get (**von** *dat.* from), find; **2.** a) F put *s.o.* through the mill, b) F give *s.o.* a good going over; **den muß ich mir mal ~** I'll have to have words with him

Her·nie ['hɛrnĭə] *f* (-; -n) ⚕ hernia, rupture

her·oben [hɛ'ro:bən] *dial. adv.* up here

He·ro·en·kult [he'ro:ən-] *m* hero worship

He·ro·in [hero'i:n] *n* (-s; *no pl.*) heroin; **~ spritzen** shoot heroin

He·roi·ne [hero'i:nə] *f* (-; -n) *thea.* heroine

He·ro'in|op·fer *n* → **Herointote; ~sucht** *f* heroin addiction; **≈süch·tig** *adj.* addicted to heroin; **~süch·ti·ge** *m, f* (-n; -n) heroin addict; **~to·te** *m, f* (-n; -n) heroin victim; **die Zahl der ~n** *a.* the number of heroin deaths

he·ro·isch [he'ro:ɪʃ] *adj.* heroic(ally *adv.*); **He·ro·is·mus** [hero'ɪsmʊs] *m* (-; *no pl.*) heroism

He·rold ['he:rɔlt] *m* (-[e]s; -e [-də]) herald; *fig. a.* harbinger

He·ros ['he:rɔs] *m* (-; -roen [he'ro:ən]) hero

Her·pes ['hɛrpɛs] *m* (-; *no pl.*) ⚕ herpes

'her·plap·pern *v/t.* (*sep.*, h) rattle off

Herr [hɛr] *m* (-en; -en) **1.** man, gentleman; Mr *Miller etc.*; **die ~en N. und M.** Messrs N and M; **~ Doktor (Professor** *etc.*) doctor (professor *etc.*); **~ Präsident!** Mr Chairman, *parl. Brit.* Mr Speaker, *USA*: Mr President; **der ~ Präsident** the Chairman *etc.*; **meine (Damen und) ~en!** (ladies and) gentlemen!; **Sehr geehrter ~ N.** Dear Sir, Dear Mr N; **Ihr ~ Vater** your father; **~en** *sign*: Gentlemen, Men; **bei den ~en** *sport*: in the men's event (*or* finals *etc.*); **meine ~en!** would you believe it; **2.** master (*a. of dog*), lord; ruler; **mein ~ und Gebieter** my lord and master; **s-n ~n und Meister finden in** *dat.* meet one's match in *s.o.*; **aus aller ~en Länder** from the four corners of the earth; **sein eigener ~ sein** be one's own boss; **~ im eigenen Hause sein** be master (*or* have the say) in one's own house; **zwei ~en dienen** serve two masters; **~ der Lage sein** have everything under control; **~ über Leben und Tod sein** have power over life and death; **~ werden** *gen.* get *s.th.* under control, get on top of *problems etc.*; **s-r Gefühle ~ werden** get a grip of oneself; **den (großen) ~n spielen** play lord of the manor, F act the big shot; **wie der ~, so's Gescherr** like master, like man; **3.** *eccl.* Lord; **Gott, der ~** the Lord God; **der ~ Jesus** the Lord Jesus; **im Jahre des ~n** in the year of our Lord

'Herr·chen F *n* (-s; -) master; **komm zu ~!** come to Daddy!

'Her·rei·se *f* → **Herfahrt; 'her·rei·sen** *v/i.* (*sep.*, sn) come (*or* get) here

'Her·ren|abend *m* stag party; **~an·zug** *m* man's suit; **~ar‚ti·kel** *pl.* men's accessories; **~aus·stat·ter** *m* men's outfitter, *Am.* haberdasher; **~be·glei·tung** *f*: **in ~** accompanied by a man, in male company, with a man; **~be·klei·dung** *f* men's clothing, menswear; **~be·such** *m* male visitor(s *pl.*); **~dop·pel** *n tennis etc.*: men's doubles *pl.*; **~ein·zel** *n tennis*: men's singles *pl.*; **~fahr·rad** *n* men's bicycle; **~fri‚seur** *m* a) men's hairdresser, barber, b) men's hairdresser's, barber's, barber('s) shop; **~ge·sell·schaft** *f* **1.** stag party; **2.** → **Herrenbegleitung; ~grö·ße** *f* men's size; **~hemd** *n* man's shirt; **~hof** *m* manor; **~ho·se** *f*: **(e-e ~** a pair of) men's trousers (*Am.* pants) *pl.*; **~hut** *m* men's hat; **~klei·dung** *f*, **~kon·fek·ti‚on** *f* men's clothing, menswear; **~le·ben** *n* life of luxury; **ein ~ führen** live like a lord

her·ren·los ['hɛrənlo:s] *adj.* abandoned; stray *dog etc.*; **~e Güter** unclaimed property

Her·ren|ma·ga‚zin ['hɛrən-] *n* men's magazine; **~mann·schaft** *f* men's team; **~mo·de** *f* men's fashion(s *pl.*); **~ober·be·klei·dung** *f* menswear; **~ras·se** *f* master race; **~schirm** *m* men's umbrella; **~schnei·der** *m* men's tailor; **~sitz** *m* **1.** manor; **2. im ~ reiten** ride astride; **~toi‚let·te** *f* men's lavatory (*or* toilet, *Am.* restroom); *sign*: Gentlemen, Men; **~‚un·ter·wä·sche** *f* men's underwear; **~volk** *n* master race; **~welt** *f* (-; *no pl.*) *the* men *pl.*; **~witz** *m* dirty joke

'Herr·gott *m* (-[e]s; *no pl.*) God, *the* Lord (God); **'Herr·gotts·frü·he** *f*: **in aller ~** at the crack of dawn, at an (*or* some) unearthly hour

'her·rich·ten (*sep.*, h) **I.** *v/t.* a) get ready; tidy up, b) do up; **II.** *dial. v/refl.*: **sich ~** get ready, smarten o.s. up, get all spruced up

Her·rin ['hɛrɪn] *f* (-; -nen) **1.** mistress, lady; **2.** ruler

her·risch ['hɛrɪʃ] *adj.* domineering, imperious, dictatorial; commanding; arrogant, overbearing

herrlich ['hɛrlɪç] **I.** *adj.* wonderful, marvel(l)ous; *a.* beautiful, glorious *weather etc.*; splendid; **II.** *adv.* marvel(l)ously *etc.*; ~ ***und in Freuden leben*** live in clover; '**Herr·lich·keit** *f* (-; -en) **1.** *no pl.* magnificence; splendo(u)r; (great) beauty; ***die*** ~ ***Gottes*** the glory (*or* majesty) of God; F ***das war die ganze*** ~ that was it; **2.** *pl.* wonderful things, treasures

'**Herr·schaft** *f* (-; -en) **1.** *no pl.* rule; government, reign; power (*a. fig.*); supremacy; *fig.* control (***über*** *acc.* of); ***unter j-s*** ~ ***fallen*** (***kommen***) fall (come) under s.o.'s sway; *fig.* ***die*** ~ ***verlieren über*** *acc.* lose control of; **2.** ***meine*** ~***en!*** ladies and gentlemen; ***hohe*** ~***en*** dignitaries, F *iro.* F top nobs; F ~ (***noch mal***)***!*** damnation!; '**herr·schaft·lich** *adj.* a) manorial; territorial *rights*, b) grand

'**Herr·schafts|an·spruch** *m* claim to power (*or* the throne); ***e-n*** ~ ***geltend machen*** a) make a territorial claim (***auf*** *acc.* on), b) lay claim to the throne; ~**be·reich** *m* **1.** sphere of control; **2.** territory; ~**form** *f* form (*or* system) of rule; ~**in·stru**ˌ**ment** *n* instrument of power; ~**struk**ˌ**tur** *f* power structure; ~**sy**ˌ**stem** *n* system of rule (*or* government)

herr·schen ['hɛrʃən] *v/i.* (h) **1.** rule (***über*** *acc.* over); govern (***über e-n Staat*** *etc.* a state *etc.*); *monarch*: reign (over); *fig.* rule (*s.th.*, *s.o.*), be in control (of); **2.** a) be; prevail, b) *epidemic etc.*: be raging, be rife, c) be the fashion; *fig.* ~ ***über*** *acc. a.* control; ***es herrscht ...*** there is ...; ***bei uns herrscht ...*** we have ..., we're having ...; ***es herrschte e-e gute Stimmung*** a) everyone was in good spirits, b) the general mood was positive; '**herr·schend** *adj.* a) ruling, in power, b) prevailing (*a. opinion*), prevalent, current; present; *a.* latest *fashion*; ~***e Ansichten*** *a.* climate of opinion; ***die*** ~***en Gesellschaftsschichten*** the ruling (*or* governing) classes; ***nach der*** ~***en Meinung ...*** current opinion has it that ...; ***unter den*** ~***en Verhältnissen*** (*or* ***Umständen***) under the present circumstances, conditions being as they are

Herr·scher ['hɛrʃɐ] *m* (-s; -) ruler; monarch, sovereign; ~**blick** *m* imperious look; ~**ge·schlecht** *n* dynasty; ~**ge·walt** *f* (-; *no pl.*) sovereign power; ~**haus** *n* **1.** dynasty; **2.** ruling house

Herr·sche·rin ['hɛrʃərɪn] *f* (-; -nen) → ***Herrscher***

'**Herr·scher|kult** *m* ruler cult; ~**mie·ne** *f* commanding air; ~**paar** *n* ruler (*or* sovereign) and his *or* her consort; ~**stab** *m* scept|er (*Brit.* -re)

'**Herrsch·sucht** *f* (-; *no pl.*) lust (*or* thirst) for power; *fig.* domineering (*or* tyrannical) nature; '**herrsch·süch·tig** *adj.* power-mad; *fig.* domineering, tyrannical

'**her|rücken** (*sep.*) **I.** *v/i.* (sn) move up (*or* closer); **II.** *v/t.* (h) move closer; ~**ru·fen** *v/t.* (*irr.*, *sep.*, h, → ***rufen***) call (over); ~**rüh·ren** *v/i.* (*sep.*, h): ~ ***von*** *dat.* come (*or* stem, result, derive) from, be due to; ~**sa·gen** *v/t.* (*sep.*, h) recite *poem etc.*; say *prayer etc.*; *b.s.* reel off; ~**schaf·fen** *v/t.* (*sep.*, h) get here; get hold of; ~**schen·ken** *dial. v/t.* (*sep.*, h) give away; ~**schicken** *v/t.* (*sep.*, h) send here (*or* over); ~**schie·ben** *v/t.* (*irr.*, *sep.*, h, → ***schieben***) push over (here), push this way; ***vor sich*** ~ push (along), *fig.* keep putting off; ~**schlei·chen** *v/i.* (*irr.*, *sep.*, sn, → ***schleichen***) *and v/refl.* (***sich*** ~) (h) sneak over; ~**schlep·pen** *v/t.* (*sep.*, h) drag *or* lug over (here) (*or* all the way here); ~**se·hen** *v/i.* (*irr.*, *sep.*, h, → ***sehen***) look (here *or* this way); ~**sein** *v/i.* (*irr.*, *sep.*, sn, → ***sein***) **1.** ***es ist drei Tage her*** it was three days ago, it's three days now, ***daß:*** it's three days since, it was three days ago that; ***wie lange ist es schon her?*** how long ago was it?, how long has it been now?; **2.** ***wo ist er her?*** where is he from?, where does he come from?; **3.** F ~ ***hinter*** *dat.* be after *s.o. or s.th.*, be trying to get hold of; **4.** F ***mit ihm*** (***dem Roman***) ***ist es nicht weit her*** F he's (the novel's) no great shakes; ~**set·zen** (*sep.*, h) **I.** *v/t.* put (*or* place) here; **II.** *v/refl.*: ***sich zu j-m*** ~ sit (down) next to (*or* beside) s.o.; ***setz dich zu mir her!*** come and sit down next to (*or* beside) me; ~**stam·men** *v/i.* (*sep.*, h) **1.** ~ ***von*** *dat.* come from; **2.** → ***herrühren***

'**her·stell·bar** *adj.*: ***leicht*** (***schwer***) ~ easy (difficult) to make *or* produce; '**her·stel·len** (*sep.*, h) **I.** *v/t.* **1.** put here; **2.** a) produce, make, b) build, c) ⚗ prepare; **3.** a) restore, repair, b) restore to health; **4.** establish; **II.** *v/refl.*: ***sich*** ~ **5.** come and stand over here; ***stell dich her zu mir!*** come and stand over here (*or* next to me, beside me); **6.** come about, be established; **Her·stel·ler** ['he:ɐʃtɛlɐ] *m* (-s; -) **1.** manufacturer; **2.** *typ.* production man; '**Her·stel·lung** *f* (-; *no pl.*) a) production, b) establishment *of relationship etc.*, c) restoration, repair

'**Her·stel·lungs|be·trieb** *m* manufacturing *or* production firm (*or* plant); ~**ko·sten** *pl.* production cost(s); prime cost *sg.*; ~**land** *n* producer country; country of origin; ~**preis** *m* production price, cost of manufacture; ~**ver·fah·ren** *n* manufacturing process

'**her|stür·zen** *v/i.* (*sep.*, sn) rush here (*or* over); ~**tra·gen** *v/t.* (*irr.*, *sep.*, h, → ***tragen***) carry here; ~**trei·ben** *v/t.* (*irr.*, *sep.*, h, → ***treiben***)***: vor sich*** ~ drive along (in front of one); F ***was treibt dich her?*** what brings you here?

Hertz [hɛrts] *n* (-; -) *phys.* hertz, cycle per second

her·über [hɛ'ry:bɐ] *adv.* (over) here; ~ ***und hinüber*** to and fro; ~***... in cpds. usu.*** ... over, ... across; ~**bit·ten** *v/t.* (*irr.*, *sep.*, h, → ***bitten***) ask *s.o.* (to come) over; ~**blicken** *v/i.* (*sep.*, h) look (*or* glance) over; ~**brin·gen** *v/t.* (*irr.*, *sep.*, h, → ***bringen***) bring over (*or* round); ~ ***über*** *acc.* take *s.o.* across *the border etc.*; ~**drin·gen** *v/i.* (*irr.*, *sep.*, sn, → ***dringen***) find its (*or* their) way over; *sounds etc.*: carry over (***an*** *acc.* to); ~**ei·len** *v/i.* (*sep.*, sn) hurry (*or* rush) over; ~**flie·gen** *v/i.* (*irr.*, *sep.*, sn, → ***fliegen***) fly over; ~**ge·lan·gen** *v/i.* (*sep.*, sn) get over; ~**hel·fen** *v/i.* (*irr.*, *sep.*, h, → ***helfen***)***: j-m*** ~ help s.o. (to get) over; ~**ho·len** *v/t.* (*sep.*, h) (over); ~**klet·tern** *v/i.* (*sep.*, sn) climb over; ~**kom·men** *v/i.* (*irr.*, *sep.*, sn, → ***kommen***) come over (*or* round); ~ ***über*** *acc.* get across *a street etc.*; ~**las·sen** *v/t.* (*irr.*, *sep.*, h, → ***lassen***) let *s.o.* (come) over; ~**lau·fen** *v/i.* (*irr.*, *sep.*, sn, → ***laufen***) come running over; ~**rei·chen** (*sep.*, h) **I.** *v/t.* hand (over), pass (across); **II.** *v/i.* reach (across); ***das Kabel*** *etc.* ***reicht nicht herüber*** the cable won't reach (*or* isn't long enough); ~**ret·ten** *v/t.* (*sep.*, h) → ***hinüberretten***; ~**schwim·men** *v/i.* (*irr.*, *sep.*, sn, → ***schwimmen***) swim over; ~**sprin·gen** *v/i.* (*irr.*, *sep.*, sn, → ***springen***) jump over; ~**wech·seln** *v/i.* (*sep.*, sn) change sides; ***auf die linke Fahrbahn*** ~ switch to the left(-hand) lane; ~**we·hen** (*sep.*) **I.** *v/i.* (sn) *scent etc.*: waft over (*or* across); *leaves, paper etc.*: be blown over (*or* across); **II.** *v/t.* (h) blow over (*or* across)

her·um [hɛ'rʊm] *adv.* **1.** (a)round, about; ~ ***um*** *acc.* (a)round *the lake etc.*; round about, (all) around; ***hier*** ~***!*** this way!; ***gleich um die Ecke*** ~ just (a)round the corner; **2.** ***um*** *acc.* ***...*** ~ about; in the region of; ***er ist um die vierzig*** ~ he's about forty, he's fortyish; ***um zehn Uhr*** ~ (at) about ten o'clock; ***um Weihnachten*** ~ round about Christmas (time); ***hier*** ~ ***muß es sein*** it must be somewhere (a)round here; **3.** over; ***die Zeit ist*** ~ time's up; ~**al·bern** *v/i.* (*sep.*, h) fool around; ~**är·gern** *v/refl.* (*sep.*, h): ***sich*** ~ ***mit*** *dat.* (be having a constant) battle with; ~**bal·gen** *v/refl.* (*sep.*, h): ***sich*** ~ romp around; *fig.* ***sich*** ~ ***mit*** *dat.* wrangle with; ~**ba·steln** *v/i.* (*sep.*, h) tinker around; ~ ***an*** *dat.* tinker *or* fiddle (around) with; ~**brül·len** *v/i.* (*sep.*, h) shout one's head off, yell; ***was brüllt der so herum?*** what's he shouting (his head off) about?; ~**bum·meln** *v/i.* (*sep.*)**1.** (sn) stroll around; gad about (the place); ***in Indien*** ~ gad about India; **2.** (h) mess around; ~**deu·teln** (*sep.*, h) **I.** *v/i.*: ~ ***an*** *dat.* quibble (*or* split hairs) over; **II.** *v/t.*: ***daran ist nichts herumzudeuteln*** it's perfectly plain; ~**di·ri**ˌ**gie·ren** *v/t.* (*sep.*, h) boss around; ~**dok·tern** [-dɔktɐn] F *v/i.* (*sep.*, h): ~ ***an*** *dat.* tinker *or* fiddle (around) with, tinker around with *s.o.*, treat *s.o.* like a guinea pig; ~**dre·hen** *v/t. and v/refl.* (***sich*** ~) (*sep.*, h) turn (a)round, turn over; ~**drücken** F *v/refl.* (*sep.*, h) **1.** ***sich*** ~ hang (a)round (*in a place*); **2.** ***sich*** ~ ***um*** *acc.* try to get out of *s.th.*; ***sich um das wahre Problem*** ~ (try to) avoid the issue; ~**druck·sen** F *v/i.* (*sep.*, h) hum and haw; ~**ex·pe·ri·men**ˌ**tie·ren** *v/i.* (*sep.*, h) experiment (***mit*** *dat.* with); *contp.* experiment around (with); ~**fah·ren** *v/i.* (*irr.*, *sep.*, sn, → ***fahren***) drive (*or* ride, ⚓ sail) (a)round; ***um die Stadt*** ~ drive round the outskirts of the town; ***in der Stadt*** ~ drive around (the) town; ***um e-e Ecke*** ~ drive round (*or* turn) a corner; ~**fin·gern** *v/i.* (*sep.*, h): ~ ***an*** *dat.* fiddle around with, touch, finger; ~**flie·gen** *v/i.* (*irr.*, *sep.*, sn, → ***fliegen***) fly (a)round (***um et.*** s.th.); ~**fra·gen** *v/i.* (*sep.*, h) ask (a)round; ~**fuch·teln** *v/i.* (*sep.*, h) gesticulate; ~ ***mit*** *dat.* wave *s.th.* around, brandish, wield; ~**füh·ren** (*sep.*, h) **I.** *v/t.* **1.** show *s.o.* (a)round (*in a place*); → ***Nase***; **2.** ***e-n Graben*** *etc.* ~ ***um*** *acc.* run a ditch *etc.* (a)round; **II.** *v/i.*: ~ ***um*** *acc.* *road etc.*: go (*or* run) (a)round; F *fig.* ***da führt kein Weg*** (***drum***) ***herum*** there's no getting round it; ~**fuhr·wer·ken** F *v/i.* (*sep.*, h) bustle about; ~ ***mit*** *dat.* wield *s.th.* about; ~**fum·meln** F *v/i.* (*sep.*, h): ~ ***mit*** *dat.* fiddle (*or* mess) around with; ~**ge·hen** *v/i.* (*irr.*, *sep.*, sn, → ***gehen***) a) walk around, b) be passed (a)round, c) *ditch etc.*: run round, d) *time*: pass; ~ ***um*** *acc.* walk (*or* go) (a)round; ~ ***in*** *dat.* walk around *a place*; ***et.*** ~ ***lassen*** pass s.th. (a)round; *fig.* ***im Kopf*** ~ go round and round in one's head; **~gei·stern** F *v/i.* (*sep.*, sn) F flit around (**in** *dat. a place*); **in j-m** (*or* **j-s Kopf**) **~** *idea etc.*: dart about in s.o.'s head, haunt s.o.; **in den Köpfen ~** be on people's minds; **~gon·deln** F *v/i.* (*sep.*, sn) F coast (*or* swan) around (**in** *dat. a place*); **~hacken** F *v/i.* (*sep.*, h): **auf j-m ~** pick on s.o., go on at s.o.; **~hän·gen** F *v/i.* (*irr.*, *sep.*, h, → **hängen**¹) hang (a)round; **~ in** *dat.* hang around (in) *a place*; **~han,tie·ren** *v/i.* (*sep.*, h): **~ mit** *dat.* fiddle around with; **~het·zen** (*sep.*) **I.** *v/i.* (sn) run around (like mad); **II.** *v/t.* (h) chase *s.o.* (a)round, keep *s.o.* on the run; **~hor·chen** *v/i.* (*sep.*, h) keep one's ears open, ask around (**ob** to see whether, in case); **~hu·ren** *v/i.* (*sep.*, h) whore around; **~ir·ren** *v/i.* (*sep.*, sn) wander around *or* about (lost *or* like a lost soul), **in** *dat.*: wander around *a place*; **~kom·man,die·ren** *v/t.* (*sep.*, h) boss around (*or* about); **~kom·men** *v/i.* (*irr.*, *sep.*, sn, → **kommen**) **1.** (*a.* **~ um** *acc.*) come (a)round *the corner etc.*; F come round (*or* over); **2.** get around; *rumo(u)r*: spread; **3. ~ um** *acc.* get (a)round *s.th.* (*a. fig.*); *fig.* **du kommst um die Tatsachen** (**Prüfung**) **nicht herum** there's no getting away from the facts (around the exam); **~kreb·sen** F *v/i.* (*sep.*, h) struggle along; **~krie·gen** F *v/t.* (*sep.*, h) **1.** get (*or* talk, bring) *s.o.* round; **j-n dazu ~ zu** *inf.* get s.o. to *inf.*, get s.o. round to *ger.*, talk s.o. into *ger.*; **2.** pass; **wie kriegen wir den Abend** (**die Stunde**) **herum?** what are we going to do all evening (for the next hour)?; **~kri·ti,sie·ren** *v/i.* (*sep.*, h): **~ an** *dat.* keep finding fault with, pick (*or* keep picking) holes in; **~kur·ven** F *v/i.* (*sep.*, sn) F cruise around (**in** *dat. a place*); **~kut,schie·ren** F (*sep.*) **I.** *v/t.* (h) chauffeur (F cart) *s.o.* around (the place); **II.** *v/i.* (sn) F drive (*or* chauffeur people) around the place; **~lau·fen** *v/i.* (*irr.*, *sep.*, sn, → **laufen**) run (a)round; **~ um** *acc.* run (a)round *s.th.*; **~ mit** *dat.* sport *s.th.*; **~lie·gen** *v/i.* (*irr.*, *sep.*, h, → **liegen**) lie around; **~ um** *acc.* surround; **~lüm·meln** F *v/i.* (*sep.*, h) lounge around, F loll about; **~lun·gern** F *v/i.* (*sep.*, h) hang (a)round; **~ma·chen** F *v/i.* (*sep.*, h) **1. ~ an** *dat.* fiddle around with *s.th.*; **2. ~ an** *dat.* go on at *s.o.*, go on about *s.th.*; **3. mach nicht so lang herum** a) F stop dawdling, b) make up your mind; **~mä·keln** F *v/i.* (*sep.*, h) find fault (**an** *dat.* with), **an** *dat.*: *a.* pick holes in *s.th.*; **~meckern** F *v/i.* (*sep.*, h) moan (about everything), keep moaning, F whinge; **~murk·sen** F *v/i.* (*sep.*, h) mess around; **~nör·geln** F *v/i.* (*sep.*, h) find fault (**an** *dat.* with), **an** *dat.*: *a.* pick holes in *s.th.*; **~pfu·schen** *v/i.* (*sep.*, h): **~ an** *dat.* fiddle around with, tamper with; **~pla·gen** *v/refl.* (*sep.*, h): **sich ~ mit** *dat.* a) have a hard time with, b) have to mess around with; **~quä·len** *v/refl.* (*sep.*, h): **sich ~ mit** *dat.* a) be plagued by, go around with, try to fight off *a cold etc.*, b) → **herumplagen**; **~ra·sen** *v/i.* (*sep.*, sn) rush around (like a madman *or* an idiot); **~rät·seln** *v/i.* (*sep.*, h) rack one's brains (**an** *dat.* over); **~ an** *dat. a.* try to figure (*or* work) *s.th.* out; **~re·den** *v/i.* (*sep.*, h): **~ um** *acc.* talk round *s.th.*; **darum ~** beat around (*or* about) the bush, avoid the issue; **~rei·chen** *v/t.* (*sep.*, h) hand (*or* pass) round; **~rei·sen** *v/i.* (*sep.*, sn) travel around (**in e-m Land** *etc.* a country *etc.*); **~rei·ten** *v/i.* (*irr.*, *sep.*, sn, → **reiten**) ride around; *fig.* **~ auf** *dat.* harp (*or* go) on about *s.th.*; **~rut·schen** *v/i.* (*sep.*, sn) slide around; **~schar·wen·zeln** F *v/i.* (*sep.*, sn): **~ um** *acc.* F suck up to; **~schla·gen** *v/refl.* (*irr.*, *sep.*, h, → **schlagen**): **sich ~ mit** *dat.* scuffle with; *fig.* grapple with; **~schlep·pen** *v/t.* (*sep.*, h) drag around; **~schmei·ßen** F *v/t.* (*irr.*, *sep.*, h, → **schmeißen**) throw around; **~schnüf·feln** *v/i.* (*sep.*, h) snoop around (**in** *dat. a place*); **~schub·sen** F *v/t.* (*sep.*, h) push *s.o.* around; **~schwän·zeln** F *v/i.* (*sep.*, sn): **~ um** *acc.* F suck up to; **~schwir·ren** *v/i.* (*sep.*, sn) **1.** (*a.* **~ um** *acc.*) buzz around, fly around; **~ um** *acc. a.* circle; **2.** *fig.* mill around *or* about (**in** *dat.* in); flit around (the place); **~sit·zen** *v/i.* (*irr.*, *sep.*, h, → **sitzen**) sit around (doing nothing); **~spie·len** *v/i.* (*sep.*, h) play around (**mit** *dat.*, **an** *dat.* with); **~spio,nie·ren** *v/i.* (*sep.*, h) snoop around; **~spre·chen** *v/refl.* (*irr.*, *sep.*, h, → **sprechen**): **sich ~** get around; **es sprach sich herum** *a.* word got out; **~ste·hen** *v/i.* (*irr.*, *sep.*, h, → **stehen**) stand (a)round; **~stö·bern** *v/i.* (*sep.*, h) poke around; **~ in** *dat.* dig (*or* nose) around in; **~sto·chern** *v/i.* (*sep.*, h): **~ in** *dat.* poke around in; **im Essen ~** pick at one's food; **~stol,zie·ren** *v/i.* (*sep.*, sn) strut around (**in** *dat. a place*); **~sto·ßen** *v/t.* (*irr.*, *sep.*, h, → **stoßen**) *a. fig.* push *s.o.* around; **~strei·chen** *v/i.* (*irr.*, *sep.*, sn, → **streichen**), **~strei·fen** *v/i.* (*sep.*, sn) prowl (**in den Straßen** the streets), roam around (**in** *dat. a place*); **~strei·ten** *v/refl.* (*irr.*, *sep.*, h, → **streiten**): **sich ~** argue; **ich will mich mit dir nicht ~** *a.* I don't want to waste time arguing with you; **~streu·nen** *v/i.* (*sep.*, sn) *dog etc.*: roam around, wander around (the streets *etc.*); **~su·chen** *v/i.* (*sep.*, h) look (*or* hunt) around (**nach** *dat.* for); **~tan·zen** *v/i.* (*sep.*, sn) dance around (**um et.** s.th.); → **Nase**; **~tap·pen** F *v/i.* (*sep.*, sn), **~ta·sten** *v/i.* (*sep.*, h) grope (*or* feel) around (**nach** *dat.* for); **~te·le·fo,nie·ren** *v/i.* (*sep.*, h) ring up all over the place; **den ganzen Tag ~** spend the whole day on the phone (*or* ringing people up); **~to·ben** *v/i.* (*sep.*, h), **~tol·len** *v/i.* (*sep.*, sn) romp around; **~tra·gen** *v/t.* (*irr.*, *sep.*, h, → **tragen**) carry (a)round; *fig.* spread *news etc.*; *fig.* **mit sich ~** nurse *one's sorrows etc.*; **~tram·peln** *v/i.* (*sep.*, sn) trample around (**auf** *dat.* on), stamp around (on); *fig.* **~ auf** *dat.* trample on *s.o.'s feelings etc.*, treat *s.o.* like a doormat

her'um·trei·ben *v/refl.* (*irr.*, *sep.*, h, → **treiben**): **sich ~** roam around (**in** *dat. a place*); hang out (in); **wo hast du dich wieder herumgetrieben?** what have you been up to then?; **Her'um·trei·ber** *m* (-s; -) loafer; tramp

her'um|trö·deln *v/i.* (*sep.*, h) dawdle (**mit** *dat.* over); **~tur·nen** *v/i.* (*sep.*, h) scramble about; **~wäl·zen** (*sep.*, h) **I.** *v/t.* turn (*or* roll) over; **II.** *v/refl.*: **sich ~** turn (a)round; toss and turn; **~wan·dern** *v/i.* (*sep.*, sn) wander (a)round (**in** *dat. a place*); **~wer·fen** (*irr.*, *sep.*, h, → **werfen**) **I.** *v/t.* throw (*or* toss) around; pull round *the wheel*; **II.** *v/refl.*: **sich ~** toss and turn; **~wickeln** *v/t.* (*sep.*, h) wrap (*or* tie) (a)round; **~wir·beln** *v/t.* (*sep.*, h) *and v/i.* (sn) spin *or* whirl (*s.o.*) (a)round; **~wirt·schaf·ten** F *v/i.* (*sep.*, h) potter about; **~wüh·len** *v/i.* (*sep.*, h) rummage (**in** *dat.* [around] in); *fig.* dig around (in *s.o.'s past etc.*); **~wur·steln** F *v/i.* (*sep.*, h) mess around (**an** *dat.* with); **~zan·ken** *v/refl.* (*sep.*, h): **sich ~** argue, squabble; **~zei·gen** *v/t.* (*sep.*, h) show (a)round; **~zer·ren** (*sep.*, h) **I.** *v/t.* pull (F yank) round; drag (a)round; **II.** *v/i.*: **~ an** *dat.* tug at

her'um·zie·hen (*irr.*, *sep.*, → **ziehen**) **I.** *v/t.* (h) drag around; **II.** *v/i.* (sn) wander about; *fig.* **~ mit** *dat.* F hang around with *s.o.*; **her'umzie·hend** *adj.* nomadic *tribe*; ✝ itinerant; *thea.* strolling *player*

her'um·zi·geu·nern *v/i.* (*sep.*, sn) rove around

her·un·ten [hɛ'rʊntən] *dial. adv.* down here

her·un·ter [hɛ'rʊntɐ] *adv.* down; **da ~** down there; **hier ~** down here; **die Treppe ~** down the stairs, downstairs; **~ von dem Bett!** get off the bed!; **~be·kom·men** *v/t.* (*irr.*, *sep.*, h, → **bekommen**) a) get *s.th.* down, b) get *s.th.* off; **~be·ten** F *v/t.* (*sep.*, h) reel off, rattle off; **~blicken** *v/i.* (*sep.*, h) look down (**auf** *acc.* at); **~brin·gen** *v/t.* (*irr.*, *sep.*, h, → **bringen**) bring down (*a. fig. prices*, ⚕ *temperature etc.*); get down; *fig.* ruin; **~drücken** *v/t.* (*sep.*, h) press down; press *key*; *fig.* bring (*or* force) down *prices etc.*; **~fal·len** *v/i.* (*irr.*, *sep.*, sn, → **fallen**) fall (down); **~ von** *dat.* fall (*or* drop) off *s.th.*; **fall nicht herunter!** mind you don't fall; **~ge·hen** *v/i.* (*irr.*, *sep.*, sn, → **gehen**) **1.** go down; *temperature etc.*: *a.* drop (**bis auf** *acc.* to); *prices*: *a.* fall, drop; ✈ *a.* descend; **~ mit** *dat.* reduce, lower *prices*, *speed etc.*; **2.** go down (**zu** *dat.* to); **3. ~ von** *dat.* get off *s.th.*

her'un·ter·ge·kom·men **I.** *p.p. of* **herunterkommen**; **II.** *adj.* a) dowdy, down-at-heel, scruffy, b) dissolute, c) in bad shape, d) run-down, neglected *farm etc.*, dilapidated *building etc.*; **~ sein** *a.* be going to rack and ruin

her'un·ter|han·deln *v/t.* (*sep.*, h) beat *s.o.*, *price* down (**auf** *acc.* to); get *20 marks etc.* knocked off (**vom Preis** the price); **et. ~** (manage to) get s.th. cheaper; **et. um 20 Mark ~** get 20 marks knocked off s.th., get s.th. 20 marks cheaper; **~hän·gen** *v/i.* (*irr.*, *sep.*, h, → **hängen**¹) hang down; dangle (**von** *dat.* from); **~hel·fen** *v/i.* (*irr.*, *sep.*, h, → **helfen**): **j-m ~** help s.o. (to get) down; **~ho·len** *v/t.* (*sep.*, h) fetch (*or* get) down; ⚔ shoot down; **~klap·pen** *v/t.* (*sep.*, h) turn down; **~klet·tern** *v/i.* (*sep.*, sn) climb down (**von** *dat.* from); **~kom·men** (*irr.*, *sep.*, sn; → **kommen**) **I.** *v/i.* **1.** come down; get down (**von** *dat.* from); **~ von** *dat. a.* get off *s.th.*; **2.** *fig.* a) go downhill; *business*, *economy* go to rack and ruin, b) come down in the world, go to the dogs, sink low; → **heruntergekommen** II; **II.** *v/t.* come down *the street etc.*; **die Treppe ~** *a.* come downstairs; **~krie·gen** F *v/t.* (*sep.*, h) **1.** → **herunterbekommen**; **2. ich krieg's nicht herunter** I can't eat (*or* drink) it, I can't get it down; **~las·sen** *v/t.* (*irr.*, *sep.*, h, → **lassen**) let down, lower; drop; **~lau·fen** (*irr.*, *sep.*, sn, → **laufen**) **I.** *v/t.* walk (*or* run) down *the street etc.*; **II.** *v/i.* *water etc.*: run down (***an der Wand*** *etc.* the wall *etc.*); **~lei·ern** *v/t.* (*sep.*, h) rattle off, reel off; **~ma·chen** *v/t.* (*sep.*, h) **1.** lower; turn down *one's collar*; **2.** *fig.* run *s.o.* down, pull *s.o.* to pieces; **~neh·men** *v/t.* (*irr.*, *sep.*, h, → ***nehmen***) take down; ~ ***von*** *dat.* take down from, take off *the wall etc.*; ***die Füße vom Tisch*** ~ take one's feet off the table; **~pras·seln** *v/i.* (*sep.*, sn) *rain etc.*: pelt down; *coins, beads etc.*: scatter all over the floor; **~pur·zeln** *v/i.* (*sep.*, sn) fall (*or* tumble) down; **~put·zen** F *v/t.* (*sep.*, h): ***j-n*** ~ give s.o. a dressing down, lambast s.o., F blow s.o. up; **~rei·chen** (*sep.*, h) **I.** *v/i.* reach down (***bis*** to, as far as); **II.** *v/t.* hand (*or* pass) *s.th.* down; **~rei·ßen** *v/t.* (*irr.*, *sep.*, h, → ***reißen***) **1.** pull down; **2.** *fig.* → ***heruntermachen*** 2; **~rut·schen** *v/i.* (*sep.*, sn) slide (*or* slip) down; **~schal·ten** *v/i.* (*sep.*, h) *mot.* change (*Am.* shift) down; **~schicken** *v/t.* (*sep.*, h) send down; **~schla·gen** *v/t.* (*irr.*, *sep.*, h, → ***schlagen***) **1.** knock down; **2.** turn down *one's collar*; **~schlucken** *v/t.* (*sep.*, h) swallow (*a. fig.*); **~schmei·ßen** F *v/t.* (*irr.*, *sep.*, h, → ***schmeißen***) throw down; knock down; **~schüt·teln** *v/t.* (*sep.*, h) shake down (*or* off); **~se·hen** *v/i.* (*irr.*, *sep.*, h, → ***sehen***) look down (***auf*** *acc.* at, *fig.* on); **~sein** F *v/i.* (*irr.*, *sep.*, sn, → ***sein***) **1.** *a.* ⚕ be run-down; ***er ist mit den Nerven herunter*** his nerves are shot; **2.** ⚕ *temperature*: have gone down; **~spie·len** *v/t.* (*sep.*, h) **1.** ♪ rattle off, rush through; **2.** *fig.* play *s.th.* down; **~sprin·gen** *v/i.* (*irr.*, *sep.*, sn, → ***springen***) jump down; **~spü·len** *v/t.* (*sep.*, h) wash off (***von*** *dat. s.th.*), wash down (from); wash *s.th.* down the sink; F wash down *one's food*; **~stei·gen** *v/i. and v/t.* (*irr.*, *sep.*, sn, → ***steigen***) climb down; ***die Treppe*** ~ *a.* come down the stairs, come downstairs; **~sto·ßen** *v/t.* (*irr.*, *sep.*, h, → ***stoßen***) knock down; **~stür·zen** *v/i.* (*sep.*, sn) fall down, come crashing down; **~tra·gen** *v/t.* (*irr.*, *sep.*, h, → ***tragen***) carry *or* take down(stairs); **~trop·fen** *v/i.* (*sep.*, sn) drip (down); **~wer·fen** *v/t.* (*irr.*, *sep.*, h, → ***werfen***) throw down; **~wirt·schaf·ten** *v/t.* (*sep.*, h) mismanage, run down; **~zie·hen** *v/t.* (*irr.*, *sep.*, h, → ***ziehen***) pull down; *fig. contp.* drag *s.o.* down (***auf*** *acc.* to *a lower level etc.*); *fig.* ***j-n zu sich*** ~ drag s.o. down to one's own level

her·vor [hɛɐ'fo:ɐ] *adv.* out; ~ ***aus*** *dat.* out of; ***hinter*** *dat.* ***...*** ~ from behind ...; ***unter*** *dat.* ***...*** ~ from under ...; **~blicken** *v/i.* (*sep.*, h) peep out (***hinter*** *dat.*, ***unter*** *dat.* of), appear; ***hinter e-m Baum*** *etc.* ~ peep from behind a tree *etc.*; **~bre·chen** *v/i.* (*irr.*, *sep.*, sn, → ***brechen***) burst out (*or* through); ⚔ rush forward; **~brin·gen** *v/t.* (*irr.*, *sep.*, h, → ***bringen***) a) produce (*a. offspring*); create, b) cause, give rise to, c) utter; **~drin·gen** *v/i.* (*irr.*, *sep.*, sn, → ***dringen***) come out (***von*** *dat.* of); ~ ***aus*** *dat. sounds etc.*: come (*or* penetrate) from; **~ge·hen** *v/i.* (*irr.*, *sep.*, sn, → ***gehen***): ~ ***aus*** *dat.* a) come (*or* emerge) from, b) develop (*or* arise) from, c) result from; ***daraus geht hervor, daß*** it follows that, this shows that; ***aus dem Brief geht nicht hervor, ob*** the letter doesn't indicate whether; ***wie aus der Umfrage hervorgeht, ...*** the survey shows that ...; ***als Sieger*** ~ emerge victorious; **~gucken** F *v/i.* (*sep.*, h) peep out

her'vor·he·ben *fig.* (*irr.*, *sep.*, h, → ***heben***) **I.** *v/t.* emphasize, underline, stress; *typ.* set off, bring out; **II.** *v/refl.*: ***sich*** ~ stand out (***aus*** *dat.* against); **Her'vor·he·bung** *f* (-; *no pl.*) emphasis; ***unter*** (***besonderer***) ~ *gen.* with (special) emphasis on

her'vor|ho·len *v/t.* (*sep.*, h) produce; take (*or* pull) *s.th.* out (***aus*** *dat.* of); **~keh·ren** *fig. v/t.* (*sep.*, h) **1.** emphasize; **2.** act, play *the big boss etc.*; **~kom·men** *v/i.* (*irr.*, *sep.*, sn, → ***kommen***) come out (***hinter*** *dat.* from behind); appear, emerge (***aus*** *dat.* from); **~kra·men** F *v/t.* (*sep.*, h) F fish out, dig up; *fig.* F dredge up *memories etc.*; **~leuch·ten** *v/i.* (*sep.*, h) shine (*a. fig.*); **~locken** *v/t.* (*sep.*, h) lure out; **~quel·len** *v/i.* (*irr.*, *sep.*, sn, → ***quellen***) **1.** *liquid etc.*: well up (***aus*** *dat.* out of, from); gush out (of); ~ ***aus*** *dat. a.* well (*or* gush) from; **2.** *smoke etc.*: pour (***aus*** *dat.* from); **3.** *eyes etc.*: bulge, protrude

her'vor·ra·gen *v/i.* (*sep.*, h) **1.** jut (*or* stick) out (***aus*** *dat.* of); project (from); ~ ***aus*** *dat.* rise (*or* tower) above; **2.** *fig.* stand out (***durch*** *acc.* by); **her'vor·ra·gend** *fig.* **I.** *adj.* excellent, outstanding, first-rate; ***sie hat 2es geleistet*** she has achieved some outstanding things; **II.** *adv.* extremely well, outstandingly

her'vor|ru·fen *v/t.* (*irr.*, *sep.*, h, → ***rufen***) **1.** *fig.* cause, give rise to; provoke *anger, protest etc.*; create *impression*; ***bei j-m Gelächter*** (***e-e Reaktion*** *etc.*) ~ make s.o. laugh (react *etc.*); **2.** *thea.* call for; **~sprin·gen** *v/i.* (*irr.*, *sep.*, sn, → ***springen***) **1.** jump out (***aus*** *dat.* of); **2.** jut out; ***~der Felsen*** protruding rock; ***~des Kinn*** (***~de Nase***) prominent chin (nose); ***sie hat ein ~des Kinn*** *a.* her chin juts out; **3.** hervorstechen

her'vor·ste·chen *fig. v/i.* (*irr.*, *sep.*, h, → ***stechen***) stand out (***aus*** *dat.* against); be prominent; be conspicuous; **her'vor·ste·chend** *fig. adj.* prominent; striking; (pre)dominant

her'vor·ste·hen *v/i.* (*irr.*, *sep.*, h, → ***stehen***) jut (*or* stick) out; *eyes*: protrude, bulge; *ears*: stick out; ***~de Backenknochen*** high cheekbones; ***~de Zähne*** buck teeth

her'vor·tre·ten *v/i.* (*irr.*, *sep.*, sn, → ***treten***) **1.** come out (***aus*** *dat.* of; ***hinter*** *dat.* from behind); *a.* emerge (from *hiding place*); **2.** *fig.* a) *eyes*: bulge, protrude, b) stand out, c) emerge; make o.s. a name (***als*** as); ~ ***mit*** *dat.* come out with *a novel etc.*; **her'vor·tre·tend** *adj.* a) *fig.* striking, prominent, b) protruding *eyes*

her'vor|tun *v/refl.* (*irr.*, *sep.*, h, → ***tun***): ***sich*** ~ **1.** distinguish o.s.; **2.** show off; ***sich*** ~ ***mit*** *dat. a.* flaunt *s.th.*; **~wa·gen** *v/refl.* (*sep.*, h): ***sich*** ~ venture out, dare to appear; **~zau·bern** *v/t.* (*sep.*, h) conjure up (*a. fig.*); **~zie·hen** *v/t.* (*irr.*, *sep.*, h, → ***ziehen***) pull out (***aus*** *dat.* of), *a.* produce (out of, from)

'her·wa·gen *v/refl.* (*sep.*, h): ***sich*** ~ dare to come (*or* put in an appearance) here

'Her·weg *m*: ***auf dem*** ~ on the way here

Herz [hɛrts] *n* (-ens; -en) heart (*a. fig.*); soul; *card game*: heart(s *pl.*); *fig.* core, cent|re (*Am.* -er); ***er hat's am ~en*** he has heart trouble (*or* a heart condition); *fig.* ***aus tiefstem ~en*** from the bottom of one's heart; ***ein Mann nach m-m ~en*** a man after my own heart; ***von ~en*** sincerely; ***von ~en kommend*** sincere, heartfelt; ***von ganzem ~en*** with all one's heart; ***ich bedanke mich von ganzem ~en*** I'm deeply grateful (to you); ***et. auf ~ und Nieren prüfen*** put s.th. through its paces; ***es läßt die ~en höher schlagen*** a) it makes your heart swell, b) it gets you going; ***er läßt die ~en höher schlagen*** he makes the ladies swoon (*or* go weak in the knees); ***sein ~ schlug höher*** his heart leapt; ***mir schlug das ~ bis zum Hals*** my heart was in my mouth; ***mir fiel das ~ in die Hosentasche*** my heart sank; ***et. auf dem ~en haben*** have s.th. on one's mind; ***j-m et.*** (***besonders***) ***ans ~ legen*** a) urge s.o. to do s.th., b) entrust s.o. with the task of doing s.th.; ***j-m zu ~en gehen*** move s.o.; ***j-n in sein ~ schließen*** grow very fond of s.o., become very attached to s.o.; ***j-s ~ brechen*** (***gewinnen, stehlen***) break (win, steal) s.o.'s heart; ***sein ~ an et. hängen*** set one's heart on s.th.; ***sein ganzes ~ hängt daran*** it means the world to him; ***sein ~ auf der Zunge tragen*** wear one's heart on one's sleeve; ***sich ein ~ fassen*** pluck (F screw) up some courage; ***sich et. zu ~en nehmen*** take s.th. to heart; ***Hand aufs ~!*** cross my heart; ***es liegt mir am ~en*** it means a lot to me (***zu*** *inf.* to be able to *inf.*), ***zu*** *inf.*: *a.* I'm (very) anxious to *inf.*; ***mit ganzem ~en dabeisein*** *etc.* take part *etc.* heart and soul; ***er ist mit ganzem ~en bei der Arbeit*** his heart's in his work; ***es tut dem ~en wohl*** it does you good; ***ich kann es nicht übers ~ bringen*** I can't bring myself to do it, I haven't got the heart (to do it); ***mein ~ blutete*** my heart bled (***für ihn*** for him; ***bei dem Anblick*** at the sight); ***alles, was das ~ begehrt*** everything your heart desires, everything you could possibly wish for; ***ein ~ für Kinder*** (***Tiere*** *etc.*) ***haben*** have a place in one's heart for children (animals *etc.*); ***ein ~ u. eine Seele sein*** be inseparable; → ***ausschütten*** 2, ***Fleck, gebrochen, leicht*** 1, ***schwer*** I

'Herz|an·fall *m* heart attack; **~as** *n* ace of hearts; **~asth·ma** *n* cardiac asthma

'her·zau·bern *v/t.* (*sep.*, h) conjure up

'Herz·be·schwer·den *pl.* heart trouble *sg.*

'Herz·beu·tel *m anat.* pericardium; **~ent·zün·dung** *f* ⚕ pericarditis

'herz·be·we·gend *adj.* (deeply) moving, heart-rending

'Herz|blatt *n* **1.** *pl.* heart *sg. of lettuce etc.*; **2.** ⚘ grass-of-Parnassus; **3.** F sweetheart; **~blut** *fig. n one's* lifeblood; ***et. mit s-m ~ tun*** put one's entire heart into s.th.; **~bu·be** *m* jack of hearts

'Herz·chen *n* (-s; -) **1.** darling, sweetheart; **2.** *iro.* simple soul

'Herz|chir·urg *m* heart surgeon; **~chir·ur,gie** *f* heart (*or* cardiac) surgery; **~da·me** *f* queen of hearts

'her·zei·gen *v/t.* (*sep.*, h) show, let *s.o.* see *s.th.*; ***zeig mal her!*** *a.* let's have a look

her·zen ['hɛrtsən] *v/t.* (h) hug, cuddle

Her·zens|an·ge·le·gen·heit ['hɛrtsəns-] *f* **1.** matter of the heart; **2.** something close to one's heart; **~bre·cher** *m* lady-killer; **2froh** *adj.* overjoyed, very happy; **~grund** *m*: ***aus tiefstem ~*** from the bottom of one's heart; **2gut** *adj.* very kind(hearted); ***ein ~er Mensch*** *a.* a

good soul; **~gü·te** *f* kindheartedness; **~lust** *f*: ***nach ~*** to one's heart's content; **~wunsch** *m* great desire; *one's* dearest wish
'Herz·ent·zün·dung *f* ⚕ carditis
'herz|er·fri·schend *adj.* heart-warming, very refreshing; **~er·grei·fend** *adj.* deeply moving; **~er·quickend** *adj.* → ***herzerfrischend***; **~er·wär·mend** *adj.* heart-warming; **~er·wei·chend** *adj.* heart-rending
'Herz|er·wei·te·rung *f* dilatation of the heart; **~feh·ler** *m* heart defect; **~flat·tern** *n* **1.** F *fig.* palpitations *pl.*; ***dabei kriege ich ~*** *a.* F it makes my heart go pitter-patter; **2.** → **~flim·mern** *n* ⚕ heart flutter; ventricular fibrillation
'herz·för·mig [-fœrmɪç] *adj.* heart-shaped
'Herz|ge·gend *f* cardiac region; ***in der ~*** *a.* around the heart; **~ge·räusch** *n* cardiac murmur
'herz·haft I. *adj.* good, decent; substantial, robust *food etc.*; firm *handshake*; hearty *wine*; ***~er Kuß*** big kiss, F smack on the cheek (*or* lips); **II.** *adv.*: ***~ lachen*** have a good laugh; ***~ zulangen*** F dig in
'her·zie·hen (*irr., sep.,* → ***ziehen***) **I.** *v/t.* (h) **1.** pull (*or* draw) up; ***hinter sich ~*** pull along; **II.** *v/i.* (sn) **2.** ***~ hinter*** *dat.* follow; **3.** come to live here, move here (*or* to this place); **4.** F *fig.* ***~ über*** *acc.* run down, pull to pieces
her·zig ['hɛrtsɪç] *adj.* cute
'Herz|in,farkt *m* heart attack, coronary, 🕮 cardiac infarction; **~in·suf·fi·zi·enz** *f* heart failure, 🕮 cardiac insufficiency; **~ja·gen** *n* tachycardia; **~kam·mer** *f* ventricle; **~ka,the·ter** *m* cardiac catheter; **~klap·pe** *f* (heart) valve; **~klap·pen·feh·ler** *m* valvular defect; **~klop·fen** *n* **1.** ⚕ palpitations *pl.*; **2.** ***mit ~ ging ich hinein*** my heart was thumping when I went in; **~kol·laps** *m* heart failure; **~kö·nig** *m* king of hearts
'herz·krank *adj.*: ***~ sein*** suffer from a heart disease (*or* condition); **'Herz·kran·ke** *m, f* (-n; -n) heart (*or* cardiac) patient; **'Herz·krank·heit** *f* heart disease (*or* complaint)
'Herz·kranz·ge·fäß *n* coronary vessel
'Herz-'Kreis·lauf|-Er·kran·kung *f* cardiovascular disease (*or* complaint); **~-Sy,stem** *n* cardiovascular system
'Herz·lei·den *n* heart disease (*or* complaint)
'herz·lich I. *adj.* warm; heartfelt, sincere; affectionate; ***~e Grüße*** best regards, love; ***~en Dank*** many thanks (indeed), I'm much obliged; ***~en Glückwunsch!*** congratulations! (***zu*** *dat.* on); ***~es Beileid*** I'm so sorry (to hear about your father *etc.*); ***ich habe e-e ~e Bitte an dich*** I wonder if you could do me a big favo(u)r; **II.** *adv.* warmly *etc.*; ***~ gern*** gladly, with pleasure; ***~ schlecht*** pretty bad; ***~ wenig*** not very much at all, ***verdienen***: earn a pittance; ***~ lachen*** have a good laugh; ***~ empfangen werden*** be given a warm welcome; ***ich gratuliere ~!*** congratulations! (***zu*** *dat.* on); ***ich danke Ihnen ~*** many thanks indeed, I'm much obliged to you; **'Herz·lich·keit** *f* (-; *no pl.*) warmth; sincerity
'Herz·li·nie *f* **1.** cardioid; **2.** *palmistry*: heart line
'herz·los *adj.* heartless, unfeeling; **'Herz·lo·sig·keit** *f* (-; *no pl.*) heartlessness
'Herz-'Lun·gen-Ma,schi·ne *f* heart-lung machine
'Herz|mas,sa·ge *f* cardiac massage; **~mit·tel** *n* cardiac stimulant
'Herz·mus·kel *m* cardiac muscle; **~ent·zün·dung** *f* myocarditis; **~stö·rung** *f* myocardiac insufficiency (*or* lesion)
'Herz·neu,ro·se *f* cardiac neurosis
Her·zog ['hɛrtso:k] *m* (-s; Herzöge ['hɛrtsø:gə]) duke; **Her·zo·gin** ['hɛrtso:gɪn] *f* (-; -nen) duchess; **'her·zog·lich** *adj.* ducal; **'Her·zog·tum** *n* (-s; -tümer [-ty:mɐ]) duchy
'Herz|ope·ra·ti,on *f* heart surgery (*or* operation); **~pa·ti,ent** *m* heart (*or* cardiac) patient; **~pfla·ster** *n* nitrate (*or* angina) patch; **~rhyth·mus·stö·run·gen** *pl.* irregular heartbeat *sg.*, cardiac arrhythmia (*or* dysrhythmia) *sg.*; **~ri·si·ko·pa·ti,ent** *m* coronary-risk patient; **~scha·den** *m* heart (*or* cardiac) defect; **~schei·de·wand** *f* septum of the heart; **~schlag** *m* **1.** heartbeat; *w.s.* pulse; **2.** heart failure; **~schmer·zen** *pl.* pain(s) in the chest; **~schritt·ma·cher** *m* pacemaker; **~schwä·che** *f* (-; *no pl.*) cardiac insufficiency; syncope; **~spe·zia,list** *m* heart specialist, cardiologist; **2stär·kend** *adj.* cardiotonic; ***~es Mittel*** cardiac stimulant; **~still·stand** *m* cardiac arrest; **~stück** *fig. n* heart, core; **~tä·tig·keit** *f* cardiac activity; ***Aussetzen der ~*** cardiac arrest; **~tod** *m* cardiac (*or* heart-related) death; ***den ~ sterben*** die of heart failure; **~tö·ne** *pl.* cardiac sounds; **~trans·plan·ta·ti,on** *f* heart transplant
her'zu(...) → ***herbei(...)***, ***hinzu(...)***
'Herz- und 'Kreis·lauf-'Krank·heiten *pl.* cardiovascular diseases
'Herz|ver·fet·tung *f* fatty degeneration of the heart; **~ver·grö·ße·rung** *f* cardiac enlargement; **~ver·pflan·zung** *f* heart transplant; **~ver·sa·gen** *n* heart failure; **~vor·kam·mer** *f* atrium; **~wand** *f* cardiac wall
'herz·zer·rei·ßend *adj.* heart-rending
Hes·se ['hɛsə] *m* (-n; -n), **Hes·sin** ['hɛsɪn] *f* (-; -nen) Hessian; ***~ sein*** *a.* come from Hesse; **hes·sisch** ['hɛsɪʃ] *adj.* Hessian
he·te·ro ['he:tero] F **I.** *adj.* F straight; **II. 2** *m* (-s; -s) F het
he·te·ro·gen [hetero'ge:n] *adj.* heterogeneous; **He·te·ro·ge·ni·tät** [heterogeni'tɛ:t] *f* (-; *no pl.*) heterogeneity
he·te·ro·nym [hetero'ny:m] **I.** *adj.* heteronymous; **II. 2** *n* (-s; -e) heteronym
He·te·ro·se·xua·li'tät *f* heterosexuality; **he·te·ro·se·xu'ell** *adj.* heterosexual; **He·te·ro·se·xu'el·le** *m, f* (-n; -n) heterosexual
He·thi·ter [he'ti:tɐ] *m* (-s; -) Hittite
Hetz|ar,ti·kel [hɛts-] *m* inflammatory article; **~blatt** *n* smearsheet
Het·ze ['hɛtsə] *f* (-; *no pl.*) **1.** rush, *a.* F rat race; ***was soll die ~?*** what's the big rush?; **2.** smear campaign; agitation; ***~ gegen die Juden*** *etc.* Jew-baiting *etc.*; **3.** → ***Hetzjagd*** 1
het·zen ['hɛtsən] **I.** *v/t.* (h) **1.** rush; ***j-n ~*** *a.* breathe down s.o.'s neck; ***ich lasse mich nicht ~*** I won't be rushed; ***gehetzt werden*** (***von*** *dat.*) a) be put under pressure (by), b) be under pressure (from); **2.** hunt (with hounds), chase; **3.** ***~ auf*** *acc.* set *s.o., dog etc.* on(to); **4.** *fig.* chase, hunt; ***zu Tode ~*** hound to death, *w.s.* flog *s.th.* to death; **II.** *v/i.* **5.** (sn) *and v/refl.* (***sich ~***) (h) rush; ***du brauchst*** (***dich***) ***nicht zu ~*** there's no (great) rush; ***hetz nicht so!*** not so fast!; **6.** (h) *fig.* stir (things up); ***~ gegen*** *acc.* stir up hatred against; ***~ zu*** *dat.* agitate for *s.th.*; **Het·zer** ['hɛtsɐ] *m* (-s; -) agitator, rabble-rouser; **Het·ze·rei** [hɛtsə'raɪ] *f* (-; *no pl.*) → ***Hetze*** 1, 2; **het·ze·risch** ['hɛtsərɪʃ] *adj.* inflammatory; rabble-rousing
'Hetz|jagd *f* **1.** hunt(ing) (with hounds); **2.** *fig.* hunt, chase; **3.** *fig.* (mad) rush; **4.** → **~kam,pa·gne** *f* smear campaign; **~pa,ro·le** *f* demagogic slogan; **~re·de** *f* inflammatory (*or* rabble-rousing) speech; **~ti,ra·de** *f* inflammatory harangue
Heu [hɔʏ] *n* (-[e]s; *no pl.*) hay; *fig.* ***Geld wie ~ haben*** have money to burn; **~bo·den** *m* hayloft
Heu·che·lei [hɔʏçə'laɪ] *f* (-; *no pl.*) hypocrisy; dissimulation; insincerity; deceit; **heu·cheln** ['hɔʏçəln] (h) **I.** *v/i.* be hypocritical; be insincere; cant; (dis)simulate, dissemble; **II.** *v/t.* feign, affect, F fake; **Heuch·ler** ['hɔʏçlɐ] *m* (-s; -), **Heuch·le·rin** ['hɔʏçlərɪn] *f* (-; -nen) hypocrite; **heuch·le·risch** ['hɔçlərɪʃ] *adj.* hypocritical; deceitful, insincere; **'Heuch·ler·mie·ne** *f* hypocritical air
heu·er ['hɔʏɐ] *dial. adv.* this year
Heu·er [hɔʏɐ] *f* (-; -n) ⚓ pay; **'heu·ern** *v/t.* (h) ⚓ sign on; F *w.s.* (*a.* ***sich j-n ~***) hire *s.o.*
'Heu|ern·te *f* a) hay harvest, b) haymaking season; **~fie·ber** *n* hay fever; **~ga·bel** *f* pitchfork; **~hau·fen** *m* haystack
Heul·bo·je ['hɔʏl-] *f* whistling buoy
heu·len ['hɔʏlən] **I.** *v/i.* (h) cry, howl (*a. wind*); *owl*: hoot; *siren*: wail; *bomb etc.*: scream; ***er heulte vor Wut*** he wept with rage; **II. 2** *n* (-s) crying, howling *etc.*; → ***I; es ist zum ~*** it's enough to make you weep; *bibl.* ***~ und Zähneklappern*** weeping and gnashing of teeth; **Heu·ler** ['hɔʏlɐ] *m* (-s; -) **1.** F ***das ist ja der letzte ~!*** a) would you believe it, b) *sl.* it's (absolutely) brill; **2.** baby seal, seal pup; **Heu·le·rei** [hɔʏlə'raɪ] *f* (-; *no pl.*) crying, howling; ***hör auf mit der ~!*** stop howling!
Heul|su·se ['hɔʏl-] F *f* (-; -n) F crybaby; **~ton** *m* wailing sound; sound of a siren
Heu·pferd *n zo.* grasshopper; locust
heu·rig ['hɔʏrɪç] *dial. adj.* this year's (*or* season's), new; **Heu·ri·ge** ['hɔʏrɪgə] *m* (-n; -n) **1.** new wine; **2.** (Austrian) wine tavern (*selling new wine*)
'Heu|schnup·fen *m* hay fever; **~scho·ber** *m* haystack
Heu·schrecke ['hɔʏʃrɛkə] (*sep.* -k·k-) *f* (-; -n) grasshopper; locust; **'Heu·schrek·ken·pla·ge** *f* plague of locusts
heu·te ['hɔʏtə] **I.** *adv.* today; ***~ abend*** this evening, tonight; ***~ früh, ~ morgen*** this morning; ***~ nacht*** a) tonight, b) last night; ***~ in acht Tagen*** a week (from) today, today week; ***~ in einem Jahr*** a year from today; ***~ vor acht Tagen*** a week ago (today); ***von ~ an, ab ~*** from today, as of today; ***von ~ auf morgen*** overnight, from one day to the next; ***lieber ~ als morgen*** the sooner the better; (***noch***) ***bis ~*** to this day; ***er hat bis ~*** (***noch***) ***nicht bezahlt*** he hasn't paid to this day, I'm *etc.* still waiting for him to pay (up); ***... von ~*** ... of today, today's ..., *w.s.* present-day ...; (***die***) ***Ausgabe von ~*** today's issue; ***das Amerika von ~*** present-day America, America today; ***die Frau von ~*** today's women, the women of today; **II. 2** *n*: ***das ~*** the present

heu·tig ['hɔʏtɪç] *adj.* today's; present(-day...), of today, modern; ***der ~e Tag*** today; ***die ~e Zeitung*** today's paper; ***bis zum ~en Tag*** to this day; ***in der ~en Zeit*** → ***heutzutage***
heut·zu·ta·ge ['hɔʏttsuta:gə] *adv.* these days, nowadays, today
'**Heu·wa·gen** *m* haywag(g)on, haycart
He·xa·de·zi'mal|sy,stem [hɛksa-] *n* hexadecimal system; **~zahl** *f* hexadecimal number
He·xa·gon [hɛksa'go:n] *n* (-s; -e) Ⱥ hexagon; **he·xa·go·nal** [hɛksago'na:l] *adj.* hexagonal
He·xa·me·ter [hɛ'ksa:metɐ] *m* (-s; -) hexameter
He·xe ['hɛksə] *f* (-; -n) witch; *fig. contp.* old hag; '**he·xen** *v/i.* (h) practi|se (*Am.* -ce) witchcraft; ***ich kann doch nicht ~*** I can't perform miracles; → ***gehext***
He·xen|ein·mal,eins ['hɛksən-] *n* magic square; **~glau·be** *m* belief in witches; **~häus·chen** *n* gingerbread house; **~jagd** *fig. f* witch-hunt(ing); **~kes·sel** *m* **1.** witch's (*or* witches') cauldron; **2.** *fig.* chaos; *esp. pol.* inferno; *pol.* ***mitten im ~ sitzen*** be sitting on a powder keg; **~kü·che** *f* witches' kitchen; **~kunst** *f a. pl.* witchcraft; **~mei·ster** *m* wizard, sorcerer; **~pro,zeß** *m* witch('s) trial; **~sab·bat** *m* witches' sabbath; *fig.* inferno; **~schuß** *m* (-sses; *no pl.*) ⚕ lumbago; **~ver·bren·nung** *f* burning of witches (*or* of a witch); **~ver·fol·gung** *f* witch-hunt(ing)
He·xe·rei [hɛksə'raɪ] *f* (-; *no pl.*) witchcraft, sorcery; magic
Hex·zahl ['hɛks-] *f* hex number
Hick·hack ['hɪkhak] F *n* (-s; -s) wrangling, squabbling
hie [hi:] *adv.*: ***~ und da*** a) now and then, b) here and there
hieb [hi:p] *pret. of* ***hauen***
Hieb *m* (-[e]s; -e ['hi:bə]) **1.** a) blow, punch; lash *of the whip*; *fencing*: cut, b) ⚕ cut, gash, c) *fig.* dig (***auf*** *acc.* at); **~e** beating; ***j-m e-n ~ versetzen*** *a. fig.* deal s.o. a blow; *fig.* ***auf den ersten ~*** first time round; ***der ~ saß*** that hit home; F ***e-n*** (***leichten***) ***~ haben*** F be (slightly) cracked; **2.** felling *of trees*; **3.** ⚙ cut
'**hieb- und 'stich·fest** *adj.* watertight *arguments etc.*; cast-iron *evidence etc.*
hielt [hi:lt] *pret. of* ***halten***
hier [hi:ɐ] **I.** *adv.* **1.** here; in this place; ***~*** (***drüben***) over here; ***~ draußen*** (***drinnen***) out (in) here; ***~ oben*** (***unten***) up (down) here; ***~ entlang*** this way; ***~ hinein*** this way, in here; ***~!*** present!, here!; *teleph.* ***~*** (***spricht***) ***John B.*** (this is) John B speaking; ***ich bin auch nicht von ~*** I'm a stranger here myself; ***das Haus ~*** this house; ***~ und da*** a) now and then, b) here and there; ***~ und jetzt*** here and now; F ***es steht mir bis ~*** F I'm fed up to the back teeth with it; F ***nicht ganz ~*** F not all there; **2.** a) here, in this case, b) at this point; ***~ ist nichts mehr zu machen*** there's nothing more we can do; **II.** ≈ *n*: ***das ~ und Jetzt*** the here and now; ***im ~ und Jetzt*** here and now
hier·an ['hi:'ran] *adv.* at (*or* by, in, on, to) this; ***wenn ich ~ denke*** when I think of this; ***er wird sich ~ erinnern*** he'll remember this; ***~ kann ich es erkennen*** I can recognize it by that; ***~ wird sich entscheiden, ob*** this will decide whether; ***~ schließt sich ... an*** following this is (*or* are) ...
Hier·ar·chie [hĭerar'çi:] *f* (-; -n) hierarchy; **hier·ar·chisch** [hĭe'rarçɪʃ] *adj.* hierarchical
hie·ra·tisch [hĭe'ra:tɪʃ] *adj.* hieratic
hier·auf ['hi:'raʊf] *adv.* **1.** on this (*or* that), here; **2.** then, thereupon
hier·aus ['hi:'raʊs] *adv.* from (*or* out of) this; ***~ geht hervor, daß*** it follows (*or* would appear) from this that
'**hier·be·hal·ten** *v/t.* (*irr.*, *sep.*, h, → ***behalten***) keep here
'**hier'bei** *adv.* a) here, on this occasion, b) in this connection, c) in this case, d) during this, while doing so
'**hier·blei·ben** *v/i.* (*irr.*, *sep.*, sn, → ***bleiben***) stay here; ***hiergeblieben!*** don't you move!, you just stay put!
'**hier'durch** *adv.* **1.** through here, this way; **2.** this way; because of this; that's how
hier·ein ['hi:'raɪn] *adv.* in here
'**hier'für** *adv.* for this (*or* it)
'**hier'ge·gen** *adv.* against this (*or* it); in comparison
'**hier'her** *adv.* here; this way, over here; (***komm***) ***~!*** come here!; ***bis ~*** up to here, this far; ***bis ~ und nicht weiter*** this far and no (*or* not a step) further
'**hier·her'auf** *adv.* up here
'**hier·her|be·mü·hen** (*sep.*, h) **I.** *v/t.* trouble *s.o.* to come here; **II.** *v/refl.*: ***sich ~*** take the trouble to come here; **~brin·gen** *v/t.* (*irr.*, *sep.*, h, → ***bringen***) bring here; **~ge·hö·ren** *v/i.* (*sep.*, h) belong here; ***er gehört hierher*** *a.* this is where he belongs; *fig.* ***das gehört nicht hierher*** it's out of place, it's irrelevant; **~kom·men** *v/i.* (*irr.*, *sep.*, sn, → ***kommen***) come here; come this way; **~pas·sen** *v/i.* (*sep.*, h) fit, look right; *fig. a.* be appropriate; ***es paßt nicht hierher*** *a.* it looks out of place; **~tra·gen** *v/t.* (*irr.*, *sep.*, h, → ***tragen***) carry *s.o.*, *s.th.* here
'**hier·her'um** *adv.* **1.** this way round; **2.** somewhere (a)round here
'**hier·her·wa·gen** *v/refl.* (*sep.*, h): ***wie kannst du dich ~?*** how dare you come near this place?
'**hier'hin** *adv.* here, this way
'**hier·hin'aus** *adv.* out here
'**hier·hin'ein** *adv.* in here
hier·in ['hi:'rɪn] *adv.* **1.** in here, in it; **2.** here, in this
'**hier'mit** *adv.* **1.** with this; ***~ ist die Sache erledigt*** that settles that; ***~ bin ich einverstanden*** I'll agree to that, that's all right (*Am.* alright) by me; ***~ wird bescheinigt*** this is to certify; ***~ geht unsere Sendung zu Ende*** that brings us to the end of our program(me); ***~ möchte ich mich verabschieden*** and that's all from me (for today *etc.*); **2.** with these words, with this, saying this
'**hier'nach** *adv.* **1.** after this; **2.** according to this
Hie·ro·gly·phe [hĭero'gly:fə] *f* (-; -n) hieroglyph; **Hie·ro'gly·phen·schrift** *f* hieroglyphic writing (*or* script); **hie·ro·gly·phisch** [hĭero'gly:fɪʃ] *adj.* hieroglyphic
Hie·ro·kra·tie [hĭerokra'ti:] *f* (-; -n) hierocracy; **hie·ro·kra·tisch** [hĭero'kra:tɪʃ] *adj.* hierocratic(ally *adv.*)
'**hier·sein** *v/i.* (*irr.*, *sep.*, sn, → ***sein***) be here; ***wann sollte er ~?*** when was he supposed to come (*or* be here)?
hier·über ['hi:'ry:bɐ] *adv.* **1.** about this (*or* it), on this (*or* it), on this (*or* the) subject; **2.** in the process; **3.** over here; over this (*or* it)
hier·um ['hi:'rʊm] *adv.* **1.** (a)round here; **2.** about this (*or* it); ***~ geht es nicht*** that's not the point
hier·un·ter ['hi:'rʊntɐ] *adv.* **1.** (included) among them *or* these; **2.** *understand etc.* by that; ***~ verstehe ich*** *a.* by that I mean; **3.** under(neath) this (*or* it)
'**hier'von** *adv.* **1.** of *or* from this (*or* it, these, them); **2.** about it (*or* this)
'**hier'vor** *adv.* → ***davor***
'**hier'zu** *adv.* a) for this (purpose), b) concerning this, on this score, c) to this (*or* these)
hier·zu·lan·de ['hi:ɐtsu'landə] *adv.* in this country, in these parts, around here, (over) here
'**hier'zwi·schen** *adv.* between them (*or* these, the two); in between
hie·sig ['hi:zɪç] *adj.* local, ... (around) here; **Hie·si·ge** ['hi:zɪgə] *m*, *f* (-n; -n) local
hieß [hi:s] *pret. of* ***heißen***
hie·ven ['hi:fən, 'hi:vən] *v/t.* (h) ⚓ heave (*a. fig.*), hoist
Hi-Fi|-An·la·ge ['haɪfi, haɪ'fi:] *f* stereo (system), hi-fi (system); **~-Fan** *m* stereo fan, audiophile; **~-Ge·rät** *n* piece of hi-fi equipment; *pl.* hi-fi equipment *sg.*; **~-Turm** *m* rack system
Hil·fe ['hɪlfə] *f* (-; -n) a) help (*a. person*); aid, assistance; support; cooperation, b) *usu. pl. teaching etc.* aids; (***j-n***) ***um ~ bitten*** ask for help (ask s.o. to help one, ask for s.o.'s help); ***Erste ~*** (***leisten***) (give) first aid; ***~!*** help!; ***mit ~*** *gen.* (*or* ***von*** *dat.*) with *s.o.'s* help, by means of *s.th.*; ***ohne ~*** without any help, single-handed, (by) himself *etc.*; ***~ suchen*** seek help; ***et. zu ~ nehmen*** make use of s.th.; ***j-m ~ leisten*** help s.o.; ***j-m zu ~ kommen*** come to s.o.'s assistance (*or* aid); ***um ~ rufen*** call (*or* shout) for help; *iro.* ***du bist mir e-e schöne ~*** you're a great help(, I must say); **~ge·such** *n* request for help; **~lei·stung** *f* help, assistance, aid; **~ruf** *m*, **~schrei** *m* call (*or* cry) for help (*a. fig.*); **~stel·lung** *f gym.* support; ***j-m ~ leisten*** support s.o., give s.o. support, *fig. a.* back s.o. up
'**hil·fe·su·chend** *adj.* ... seeking help; beseeching *look etc.*; ≈**e** those seeking (*or* in need of) help
'**hilf·los I.** *adj. a. fig.* helpless (***gegenüber*** *dat.* in the face of); ***j-m*** (***e-r Sache***) ***gegenüber völlig ~ sein*** be at a complete loss as to what to do with (*or* about) s.o. (s.th.); **II.** *adv.*: ***j-m ~ ausgeliefert sein*** be at s.o.'s mercy; '**Hilf·lo·sig·keit** *f* (-; *no pl.*) helplessness
'**hilf·reich I.** *adj.* helpful; supportive; ***es wäre ~, wenn wir wüßten ...*** it would be helpful to know ..., it would help if we knew ...; **II.** *adv.*: ***j-m ~ zur Seite stehen*** help s.o. out, support s.o.
'**Hilfs...** *in cpds. often* auxiliary, emergency; temporary; relief; assistant, junior; **~ak·ti,on** *f* relief campaign; **~ar·bei·ter** *m* unskilled worker (*or* labo[u]rer); *pl.* unskilled labo(u)r *sg.*; **~as·si,stent** *m univ.* graduate lecturer
'**hilfs·be·dürf·tig** *adj.* a) in need of help, b) needy
'**hilfs·be·reit** *adj.* (very) helpful; cooperative; '**Hilfs·be·reit·schaft** *f* (-; *no pl.*) helpfulness; cooperativeness

'Hilfs|brem·se *f* auxiliary brake; **~dienst** *m* auxiliary service; emergency service; **~fonds** *m* relief fund; **~gel·der** *pl.* subsidies; **~ zahlen an** *acc.* subsidize; **~kas·se** *f* relief fund; **~ko·mi,tee** *n* action committee; **~kraft** *f* temporary worker; (*esp. secretary*) F temp; *univ.* assistant; **~li·nie** *f* ♪ leger line; ⚒ *etc.* auxiliary line; **~maß·nah·men** *pl.* aid *sg.*; emergency measures; **~me,nü** *n computer*: help menu; **~mit·tel** *n* aid (*a.* ⚙, *a. pl.*); *w.s.* remedy; measure; expedient; **(finanzielle ~** financial) aid; **~ pl. für den Unterricht** teaching aids; **~mo·tor** *m* auxiliary engine (⚡ motor); **~or·ga·ni·sa·ti,on** *f* relief organization, aid agency; **~pa,ket** *n* aid package; **~per·so,nal** *n* ancillary staff; **~po·li,zei** *f* auxiliary police; **~po·li,zist** *m* special constable; **~pre·di·ger** *m* curate; **~pro,gramm** *n* aid program(me); **~quel·le** *f* **1.** (natural) resource; **2.** ✝ financial resources *pl.*; **3.** *fig.* source; **~tä·tig·keit** *f* auxiliary work; **e-e ~ ausüben** help out; **~trup·pen** *pl.* ⚔ reinforcements; **~verb** *n* auxiliary verb; **~vor·rich·tung** *f* auxiliary device; **~werk** *n* welfare (*or* relief) organization; **~wis·sen·schaft** *f* auxiliary science; **~zeit·wort** *n* auxiliary verb

Him·bee·re ['hɪmbeːrə] *f* (-; -n) raspberry

Him·beer|eis ['hɪmbeːɐ-] *n* raspberry ice cream; **~geist** *m* (-[e]s; *no pl.*) raspberry brandy; **~saft** *m* raspberry juice; **~strauch** *m* raspberry bush

Him·mel ['hɪməl] *m* (-s; -) **1.** *no pl.* sky; *meteor. a.* skies *pl.*; *lit.* heavens *pl.*; heaven; **am ~** in the sky; **im ~** in heaven; **unter freiem ~** in the open air; **unter südlichem ~** under southern skies; *fig.* **der ~ auf Erden** heaven on earth; **den ~ auf Erden haben** live in paradise; **~ und Hölle in Bewegung setzen** move heaven and earth; **aus allen ~n fallen** be crushed; **in den ~ heben** praise to the skies; **im sieb(en)ten ~ sein** be on cloud nine, be walking on air, be in the seventh heaven; **ihm hängt der ~ voller Geigen** he thinks life's a bed of roses; **wie vom ~ fallen** appear from nowhere; **(wie) aus heiterem ~** (completely) out of the blue; **das schreit** (F **stinkt**) **zum ~** it's a scandal; **... fallen nicht vom ~** ... don't grow on trees; **es ist noch kein Meister vom ~ gefallen** everyone has to learn; **ein neuer Stern am musikalischen (literarischen) ~** a new star on the music (literary) scene; **Wolken am politischen ~** clouds on the political horizon; **du lieber ~!** my goodness!, good Heavens!; **um ~s willen!** for Heaven's (*or* God's) sake!; **weiß der ~** God knows; **2.** canopy

'him·mel'angst F *adj.*: **mir wurde ~** I was scared to death

'Him·mel|bett *n* four-poster (bed); **2blau** *adj.*, **~blau** *n* sky-blue, azure; **~'don·ner'wet·ter** F *int.* F damnation!

'Him·mel·fahrt *f* (-; *no pl.*) *eccl.* **1.** (*a.* **Christi ~**) the Ascension (of Christ); **Mariä ~** the Assumption (of the Blessed Virgin); **2.** → **Himmelfahrtstag**

'Him·mel·fahrts|kom,man·do *n* **1.** suicide mission; **2.** suicide squad; **~na·se** F *f* snub nose; **~tag** *m* Ascension Day

'him·mel'hoch I. *adj.* sky-high, soaring; **II.** *adv.* high in the sky; *fig.* **~ jauchzend, zu Tode betrübt** up one minute, down the next

'Him·mel·reich *n* (-[e]s; *no pl.*) (Kingdom of) Heaven

'him·mel·schrei·end *adj.* outrageous; blatant *nonsense etc.*

'Him·mels... *in cpds.* heavenly; celestial; **~er·schei·nung** *f* celestial phenomenon; **~ga·be** *f* gift from heaven; **~glo·bus** *m* celestial globe; **~kar·te** *f* star chart, map of the night sky; **~kör·per** *m* celestial body; **~ku·gel** *f* sphere; **~kun·de** *f* astronomy; **~lei·ter** *f* (-; *no pl.*) Jacob's ladder (*a.* ✿); **~pfor·te** *f* gates *pl.* of Heaven, F pearly gates *pl.*; **~re,kla·me** *f* skywriting, aerial advertising; **~rich·tung** *f* **1.** point of the compass, cardinal point; **2.** direction; **aus allen ~en** from everywhere, from all four corners of the earth; **in alle vier ~en deuten** point north, south, west and east; **in alle ~en zerstreut werden** be scattered to the four winds; **~schlüs·sel** *m* ✿ cowslip; **~schrei·ber** *m* skywriter; **~schrift** *f* skywriting; **in ~** skywritten; **~spi,on** F *m* spy satellite, F spy in the sky; **~tor** *n*, **~tür** *f* → **Himmelspforte; ~zelt** *n* firmament

'him·mel·wärts [-vɛrts] *adv.* heavenward(s)

'him·mel'weit *fig. adj.* (*and adv.*) vast(ly), enormous(ly); **~ voneinander entfernt** worlds apart

himm·lisch ['hɪmlɪʃ] *adj.* heavenly; divine; F (absolutely) wonderful, *a.* gorgeous *dress etc.*; **~er Vater** Our Father in Heaven; **~e Geduld** *the* patience of Job

hin [hɪn] **I.** *adv.* **1.** there; **auf** *acc.* (*or* **nach, zu** *dat.*) **... ~** towards, to; **bis ~ zu** *dat.* as far as, up to; *fig.* including (even); **über** *acc.* **... ~** over; **an** *dat.* **... ~** along; **~ und her** to and fro, back and forth; **~ und zurück** there and back; **zweimal Kiel ~ und zurück** two returns (*Am.* round-trip tickets) to Kiel; **bis ... ist noch (ist nicht mehr) lange ~** ... is still a long way off (... isn't far away now); **bis Weihnachten sind noch einige Wochen ~** we've still got a few weeks to go before Christmas, Christmas is still a few weeks off; **et. ~ und her überlegen** turn s.th. over in one's mind; **wir haben ~ und her überlegt** we to-ed and fro-ed; **~ und her gerissen sein** be torn (**zwischen** *dat.* between), F be absolutely delighted (**von** *dat.* with, by), be entranced *or* mesmerized (by); **ich bin ~ und her gerissen** *a.* I just can't decide; **Freundschaft ~ oder her** friendship or no; **ein paar Mark ~ oder her** give or take a couple of marks, **das macht nichts:** a few marks more or less aren't going to make any difference; **~ und wieder** now and then; **vor sich ~** *walk etc.* along, *mumble, cry etc.* to o.s.; **ich muß ~** I've got to go (there); **nichts wie ~!** what are we waiting for?; **wo ist er ~?** where has he gone?, where has he got to?; **wo willst du ~?** a) where are you going?, b) where do you want to go?; **2. auf** *acc.* **~** a) as a result of, following, b) in reply to, on, c) concerning; **auf die Gefahr ~ zu** *inf.* at the risk of *ger.*; **auf s-n Rat ~** on his advice; **auf** *acc.* **... ~ konzipiert** designed for ..., with ... in mind; **j-n auf Krebs ~ untersuchen** test s.o. for cancer; → **Verdacht; 3.** → **hinsein; II.** 2 *n*: **~ und Her** coming and going, to-ing and fro-ing; *fig.* ifs and buts; *fig.* **nach vielem ~ und Her** after much discussion (*or* talk[ing], bargaining), after many attempts, after much experimentation, after a lot of to-ing and fro-ing

hin·ab(...) [hɪ'nap] → **hinunter(...)**

'hin·ar·bei·ten (*sep.*, h) **I.** *v/i.*: **~ auf** *acc.* work towards; **darauf ~ zu** *inf.* work towards *ger.*, strive to *inf.*; **II.** *v/refl.*: **sich ~ zu** *dat.* work one's way towards

hin·auf [hɪ'naʊf] *adv.* up, upwards; up there; **bis ~ zu** *dat.* up to; **den Berg ~** up the hill; **die Treppe ~** up the stairs, upstairs; **hier ~** up here, this way; **dort ~** up there; **~ar·bei·ten** *v/refl.* (*sep.*, h): **sich ~** work one's way up (*a. fig.*); **~be·ge·ben** *v/refl.* (*irr.*, *sep.*, h, → **begeben**): **sich ~** go up(stairs); **~blicken** *v/i.* (*sep.*, h) look up (**zu** *dat.* at, *fig.* to); **~brin·gen** *v/t.* (*irr.*, *sep.*, h, → **bringen**) bring (*or* carry, take) up(stairs); **~fah·ren** (*irr.*, *sep.*, → **fahren**) **I.** *v/i.* (sn) drive up, go up; **II.** *v/t.* (h) take (*or* drive) up; **~füh·ren** (*sep.*, h) **I.** *v/t.* **1.** take *s.o.* up(stairs); **2.** *path etc.*: lead (*or* go) up *the mountain etc.*; **II.** *v/i.* go up (there); **~ge·hen** (*irr.*, *sep.*, sn, → **gehen**) **I.** *v/i.* **1.** go (*or* walk) up; go upstairs; **2.** go up (there); **3.** *fig. prices*: go up, rise; **II.** *v/t.* **4.** go up, walk up *a mountain etc.*; **5.** *path etc.*: go up *the mountain etc.*; **~klet·tern** (*sep.*, sn) **I.** *v/t.* climb (up); **II.** *v/i.* climb up; **~kom·men** *v/i.* (*irr.*, *sep.*, sn, → **kommen**) come up; make it; **~lau·fen** *v/i. and v/t.* (*irr.*, *sep.*, sn, → **laufen**) run up (*s.th.*); **~rei·chen** (*sep.*, h) **I.** *v/t.* pass *s.th.* up (**j-m** to s.o.); **II.** *v/i.* reach (**[bis] zu** [as far as, up] to), reach up (to); **~schicken** *v/t.* (*sep.*, h) send up; **~schrau·ben** F *v/t.* (*sep.*, h) push (*or* force) up *prices etc.*; step up, F up *production etc.*; **~se·hen** *v/i.* (*irr.*, *sep.*, h, → **sehen**) look up (**zu** *dat.* at); **~set·zen** *v/t.* (*sep.*, h) put up *prices etc.*; **~stei·gen** (*irr.*, *sep.*, sn, → **steigen**) **I.** *v/t.* climb (up); go up *the stairs etc.*; **II.** *v/i.* climb up; **~tra·gen** *v/t.* (*irr.*, *sep.*, h, → **tragen**) carry *or* take up(stairs); **~trei·ben** *v/t.* (*irr.*, *sep.*, h, → **treiben**) push (*or* force) up *prices etc.*; **~zie·hen** (*irr.*, *sep.*, → **ziehen**) **I.** *v/t.* (h) pull up; **II.** *v/i.* (sn) move up; **III.** *v/refl.* (h): **sich ~** pull o.s. up; **sich ~ bis zu** *dat.* stretch up to

hin·aus [hɪ'naʊs] *adv.* out, out there; outside; **~ aus** *dat.* out of; **hier ~** out here, this way; **nach hinten (vorn) ~** *live* at the back (front); **über** *acc.* **... ~** a) beyond, past, b) above, more than; **zum Fenster ~** out of the window, *Am. a.* out the window; **ein Zimmer zur Straße (zum Hof) ~** a room facing *or* overlooking the street (overlooking *or* looking into a courtyard); *fig.* **er weiß nicht wo ~** he doesn't know which way to turn; **auf Jahre ~** for years (to come); **über die nächste Woche ~** till (at least) the week after next; **~!** get out!; **~ mit ihm!** throw him out!; **~ damit** out with it; → **darüber** 4; **~be·för·dern** *v/t.* (*sep.*, h) *usu. iro.* F kick *s.o.* out; **~be·glei·ten** *v/t.* (*sep.*, h) see *or* show *s.o.* out (*or* to the door); **~beu·gen** *v/refl.* (*sep.*, h): **sich ~** lean out (**aus, zu** *dat.* of); **~blicken** *v/i.* (*sep.*, h) look out (**aus, zu** *dat.* of); **~brin·gen** *v/t.* (*irr.*, *sep.*, h, → **bringen**) bring *or* take out(side); see *s.o.* out; **~ekeln** F *v/t.* (*sep.*, h) F freeze out; **~fah·ren** *v/i.* (*irr.*, *sep.*, → **fahren**) drive out (*a. v/t.* [h]); ⚓ sail out, put to sea; **~fal·len** *v/i.* (*irr.*, *sep.*, sn, → **fallen**) fall out (**aus, zu** *dat.* of); **~fin·den** *v/i.* (*irr.*, *sep.*, h, → ***finden***) find one's way out; ***allein*** ~ find one's own way out; **~flie·gen** *v/i.* (*irr.*, *sep.*, sn, → ***fliegen***) **1.** fly out; **2.** F be kicked out; F get the sack; **~füh·ren** (*sep.*, h) **I.** *v/t.* take out; **II.** *v/i. path etc.*: lead out; ~ ***auf*** *acc. door etc.*: open onto, lead to; **~ge·hen** *v/i.* (*irr.*, *sep.*, sn, → ***gehen***) go (*or* walk) out, leave; ***das Zimmer geht auf den Park hinaus*** the room looks out onto the park; ~ ***über*** *acc.* go beyond, *fig. a.* surpass; ~ ***auf*** *acc.* aim at; **~ge·lei·ten** *v/t.* (*sep.*, h) see (*or* show) *s.o.* out; **~grei·fen** *fig. v/i.* (*irr.*, *sep.*, h, → ***greifen***)**:** ~ ***über*** *acc.* go beyond; **~ja·gen** *v/t.* (*sep.*, h) *a. fig.* chase out; *fig.* F kick *s.o.* out; **~ka·ta·pul͵tie·ren** *v/t.* (*sep.*, h) eject; F *fig.* F chuck (*or* kick) *s.o.* out; **~kom·men** *v/i.* (*irr.*, *sep.*, sn, → ***kommen***) come out; get out; *fig.* ~ ***über*** *acc.* get beyond, get further than, manage (*or* do) more than; **~kom·pli·men͵tie·ren** *iro. v/t.* (*sep.*, h) get rid of *s.o.*, see *s.o.* off the premises; **~las·sen** *v/t.* (*irr.*, *sep.*, h, → ***lassen***) let out; **~lau·fen** *v/i.* (*irr.*, *sep.*, sn, → ***laufen***) **1.** run (*or* rush) out; **2.** *fig.* ~ ***auf*** *acc.* come (*or* boil) down to, end up in; ***es läuft auf dasselbe hinaus*** it comes (*or* amounts) to the same thing; **~leh·nen** *v/refl.* (*sep.*, h): ***sich*** ~ lean out (***aus, zu*** *dat.* of); ***nicht ~!*** 🚃 do not lean out (of the window); **~müs·sen** *v/i.* (*irr.*, *sep.*, h, → ***müssen***) have to go out; ***ich muß mal eben hinaus an die frische Luft*** I must just go out for (*or* to get some) fresh air; **~po͵sau·nen** *v/t.* (*sep.*, h) broadcast *s.th.*; **~ra·gen** *v/i.* (*sep.*, h) jut out; ~ ***über*** *acc.* tower above (*a. fig.*); **~rei·chen** (*sep.*, h) **I.** *v/t.* reach (*or* hand) *s.th.* out; **II.** *v/i.*: ~ ***über*** *acc.* a) reach (*or* stretch) beyond, b) last more than; **~schaf·fen** *v/t.* (*sep.*, h) take (*or* get) out; **~schau·en** *v/i.* (*sep.*, h) look out (***aus, zu*** *dat.* of); **~schicken** *v/t.* (*sep.*, h) send out; **~schie·ben** *v/t.* (*irr.*, *sep.*, h, → ***schieben***) **1.** push out; **2.** *fig.* put off, postpone; delay; **~schie·ßen** *v/i.* (*irr.*, *sep.*, sn, → ***schießen***)**:** ~ ***über*** *acc.* overshoot (***das Ziel*** the mark); **~schlei·chen** *v/i.* (*irr.*, *sep.*, sn, → ***schleichen***) sneak out; **~schlep·pen** *v/t.* (*sep.*, h) drag *s.o. or s.th.* out (***aus, zu*** *dat.* of); **~schlüp·fen** *v/i.* slip out, sneak out (***aus*** *dat.* of)

hin'aus·schmei·ßen F *v/t.* (*irr.*, *sep.*, h, → ***schmeißen***) → ***hinauswerfen***; **Hin'aus·schmiß** F *m* → ***Hinauswurf***

hin'aus|se·hen *v/i.* (*irr.*, *sep.*, h, → ***sehen***) look out; **~sein** *v/i.* (*irr.*, *sep.*, sn, → ***sein***)**:** ~ ***über*** *acc.* be past *s.th.*; ***ich bin längst darüber hinaus zu*** *inf.* I'm long past *ger.*; ***über die Vierzig*** ~ be over forty; ***darüber ist er hinaus*** he's got over that; ***über das Alter ist sie hinaus*** she's grown out of it; **~set·zen** *v/refl.* (*sep.*, h): ***sich*** ~ (go and) sit outside *or* out in the open; **~steh·len** *v/refl.* (*irr.*, *sep.*, h, → ***stehlen***)**: *sich*** ~ steal (*or* sneak) out (***aus*** *dat.* of); **~stel·len** *v/t.* (*sep.*, h) put out(side); *sport*: send off; **~sto·ßen** *v/t.* (*irr.*, *sep.*, h, → ***stoßen***) push out (***aus*** *dat.* of); **~stür·zen** (*sep.*) **I.** *v/i.* (sn) rush out; **II.** *v/refl.* (h): ***sich*** (***zum Fenster***) ~ jump out *or* throw o.s. out (of the window); **~tor·keln** *v/i.* (*sep.*, sn) stagger out; **~tra·gen** *v/t.* (*irr.*, *sep.*, h, → ***tragen***) carry out; **~trei·ben** *v/t.* (*irr.*, *sep.*, h, → ***treiben***) drive out; chase away; ***es treibt mich hinaus*** I've got to get out of (*or* away from) here; **~trom͵pe·ten** *v/t.* (*sep.*, h) broadcast *s.th.*; **~wach·sen** *v/i.* (*irr.*, *sep.*, sn, → ***wachsen***)**:** ~ ***über*** *acc.* grow bigger than; *fig.* outgrow *s.th.*; surpass *s.o.*; ***der Baum ist über die Garage hinausgewachsen*** the tree's taller than the garage now; *fig.* ***über sich selbst*** ~ rise above o.s.; **~wa·gen** *v/refl.* (*sep.*, h): ***sich*** ~ venture out; **~wei·sen** (*irr.*, *sep.*, h, → ***weisen***) **I.** *v/t.* show *s.o.* the door, ask *s.o.* to leave; **II.** *fig. v/i.*: ~ ***über*** *acc.* point (*or* go, reach) beyond; **~wer·fen** *v/t.* (*irr.*, *sep.*, h, → ***werfen***) throw out (***aus*** *dat.* of); *a.* F give *s.o.* the sack, sack (*or* fire) *s.o.*; *fig.* ***sein Geld zum Fenster*** ~ squander one's money; **~wol·len** *v/i.* (*irr.*, *sep.*, h, → ***wollen***) **1.** want to get out (***aus*** *dat.* of); **2.** *fig.* ~ ***auf*** *acc.* drive at; ***worauf will er hinaus?*** *a.* what's he getting at?; ***hoch*** ~ aim high, be ambitious; ***höher ~ als*** have set one's sights further than

Hin'aus·wurf *m*: ***j-m mit dem ~ drohen*** threaten to throw (F kick) s.o. out

hin'aus|zie·hen (*irr.*, *sep.*, → ***ziehen***) **I.** *v/t.* (h) **1.** pull out; **2.** *fig.* draw (*or* drag) out; **3.** *fig.* ***es zog ihn hinaus*** (***in die Welt***) he felt he had to go out into the big wide world; **II.** *v/i.* (sn): ***aufs Land*** ~ move out into the country; **III.** *v/refl.* (h): ***sich*** ~ drag on; be delayed; **~zö·gern** (*sep.*, h) **I.** *v/t.* put off; drag (F spin) out; **II.** *v/refl.*: ***sich*** ~ be delayed; take longer than expected

'hin|be·ge·ben *v/refl.* (*irr.*, *sep.*, h, → ***begeben***)**: *sich*** ~ go there; ***sich ~ zu*** *dat.* go to, make one's way to; **~be·kom·men** *v/t.* (*irr.*, *sep.*, h, → ***bekommen***) → ***hinkriegen***; **~bemü·hen** (*sep.*, h) **I.** *v/t.* ask *s.o.* to go there; **II.** *v/refl.*: ***sich*** ~ take the trouble to go there; **~bie·gen** F *v/t.* (*irr.*, *sep.*, h, → ***biegen***) put straight (*or* right), straighten out; iron out; **~blät·tern** F *v/t.* (*sep.*, h) F shell out *money*

'Hin·blick *m*: ***im ~ auf*** *acc.* in view of; regarding; with the prospect of, with ... in mind (*or* view); **'hin·blicken** *v/i.* (*sep.*, h) look (***zu*** *dat.* at)

'hin|brin·gen *v/t.* (*irr.*, *sep.*, h, → ***bringen***) **1.** take there; ***wo darf ich Sie ~?*** where would you like to go?; **2.** spend, pass (away); ***s-e Zeit mit Schreiben*** ~ spend one's time writing; **3.** F manage; **~brü·ten** *v/i.* (*sep.*, h): ***vor sich*** ~ brood; **~däm·mern** *v/i.* (*sep.*, h): ***vor sich*** ~ doze; **~deich·seln** F *v/t.* (*sep.*, h) sort out; → ***hinbiegen, hindrehen, hinkriegen***; **~den·ken** *v/i.* (*irr.*, *sep.*, h, → ***denken***)**: *wo denkst du hin?*** say that again?, you've got to be joking

hin·der·lich ['hɪndɐlɪç] *adj.* obstructive (*dat.* to); troublesome; inconvenient (to); ***j-m ~ sein*** be in s.o.'s way

hin·dern ['hɪndɐn] *v/t.* (h) hinder; block, obstruct; ***j-n an et. ~, j-n*** (***daran***) ~ ***zu*** *inf.* stop (*or* prevent) s.o. from *ger.*

Hin·der·nis ['hɪndɐnɪs] *n* (-ses; -se) **1.** barrier; *sport*: hurdle; *riding*: fence; **2.** *fig.* obstacle (***für*** *acc.* to); difficulty; ***kein ~ für*** *acc.* no obstacle to; ***auf ~se stoßen*** run into difficulties; ***j-m ~se in den Weg legen*** throw obstacles into s.o.'s path; **~lauf** *m*, **~ren·nen** *n* steeplechase

Hin·de·rung ['hɪndərʊŋ] *f* (-; -en) obstruction; **'Hin·de·rungs·grund** *m* reason (*for not coming etc.*); argument (*for not coming etc.*); excuse; ***das ist für mich kein ~ a.*** that's not going to stop me; ***ich sehe darin keinen*** ~ I don't see why that should stop me *etc.*

'hin·deu·ten *v/i.* (*sep.*, h): ~ ***auf*** *acc.* point to (*or* at); *fig.* point to, indicate

Hin·di ['hɪndi] *n* (-s; *no pl.*) *ling.* Hindi

'hin|drän·gen (*sep.*, h) **I.** *v/t.*: ~ ***zu*** *dat.* push towards; *fig.* ***es drängt ihn zu ihr hin*** he feels drawn to(wards) her; **II.** *v/refl.*: ***sich ~ zu*** *dat.* push (one's way) towards *or* (through) to; **III.** *v/i.*: ~ ***zu*** (*or* ***nach***) *dat.* push (one's way) towards *or* (through to); *fig.* ~ ***auf*** *acc.* a) urge, press for *reform etc.*, b) move irresistibly towards; ~ ***zu*** *dat.* feel drawn to(wards) *s.th.*; **~dre·hen** F *v/t.* (*sep.*, h) **1.** sort out, manage, *b.s.* F wangle; **2. *et. so ~, daß*** twist s.th. so that, ***alle glauben ...***: twist s.th. to make everyone believe ...; ***er dreht alles so hin, wie's ihm gerade paßt*** he twists everything to suit his purposes

Hin·du ['hɪndu] *m* (-[s]; -[s]) Hindu; **Hin·du·is·mus** [hɪndu'ɪsmʊs] *m* (-; *no pl.*) Hinduism; **hin·dui·stisch** [hɪndu'ɪstɪʃ] *adj.* Hindu

hin'durch *adv.* **1.** through; across; ***durch et.*** ~ through s.th.; ***mitten*** ~ right *or* straight through (the middle); **2.** through(out), during; ***den ganzen Tag*** ~ all day (long); ***die ganze Nacht*** ~ all night (long), the whole night long; ***das ganze Jahr*** ~ all year round, the whole year; *in cpds.* → ***durch...***

'hin·dür·fen *v/i.* (*irr.*, *sep.*, h, → ***dürfen***) be allowed to go (there)

'hin·ei·len *v/i.* (*sep.*, sn) hurry there

hin·ein [hɪ'naɪn] *adv.* in; ~ ***in*** *acc.* into, in(side); ***da*** (***hier***) ~ in there (here); ***bis*** (*or* ***mitten***) ~ ***in*** *acc.* right into (the middle of); ***bis in den Mai*** (***die Nacht***) ~ well (*or* right) into May (the night); ***bis tief in die Nacht*** ~ till the (wee) small hours; ***nur ~!*** go on in; ~ ***mit dir!*** in you go!; **~ar·bei·ten** *v/refl.* (*sep.*, h): ***sich*** ~ work one's way in(to ***in*** *acc.*); *fig.* get in(to); **~bei·ßen** *v/i.* (*irr.*, *sep.*, h, → ***beißen***)**:** ~ ***in*** *acc.* bite into; take a bite of; **~be·kom·men** *v/t.* (*irr.*, *sep.*, h, → ***bekommen***) get *s.th.* in(to ***in*** *acc.*); **~brin·gen** *v/t.* (*irr.*, *sep.*, h, → ***bringen***) take *or* bring *or* get in(to ***in*** *acc.*); F ***ich bring' nichts mehr hinein*** I couldn't eat another thing; **~den·ken** *v/refl.* (*irr.*, *sep.*, h, → ***denken***)**: *sich ~ in*** *acc.* put o.s. in *s.o.'s* place (*or* position); imagine one is in; think back to; **~deu·ten** *v/t.* (*sep.*, h) → ***hineininterpretieren***; **~drän·gen** (*sep.*, h) **I.** *v/t.* squeeze *or* force *s.th.* in(to ***in*** *acc.*); force *or* push *s.o.* in(to), *a.* herd *people* in(to); **II.** *v/refl.*: ***sich*** ~ push one's way in(to ***in*** *acc.*); **~fal·len** *v/i.* (*irr.*, *sep.*, sn, → ***fallen***) **1.** fall in(to ***in*** *acc.*); **2.** → ***hereinfallen***; **~fin·den** (*irr.*, *sep.*, h, → ***finden***) **I.** *v/i.* (*a.* ***sich*** ~) find one's way in(to ***in*** *acc.*); **II.** *fig. v/refl.*: ***sich ~ in*** *acc.* get into; **~ge·heim·nis·sen** [-gəhaɪmnɪsən] *v/t.* (*sep.*, *p.p.* hineingeheimnißt, h): ***et. ~ in*** *acc.* try to read s.th. into *s.th.*, try to find a hidden meaning in *s.th.*; ***viel in et.*** ~ read all sorts of things into s.th., try to find all sorts of things in s.th.; **~ge·hen** *v/i.* (*irr.*, *sep.*, sn, → ***gehen***) go in(to ***in*** *acc.*); ***in den Kanister gehen ... hinein*** *a.* the container holds ...; ***in den Saal gehen ... hinein*** *a.* the hall seats ... *persons*; **~ge·ra·ten** *v/i.*

(*irr., sep.*, sn, → **geraten**): ~ **in** *acc.* get into; get (o.s.) involved in; *a.* get caught up in; **≈grät·schen** *n* (-s) *soccer*: sliding tackle; **~hal·ten** *v/t.* (*irr., sep.*, h, → **halten**) put *s.th.* in; ~ **in** *acc.* put in(to); **~hän·gen¹** (*sep.*, h) **I.** *v/t.* **1.** hang *s.th.* inside (*or* in there); ~ **in** *acc.* hang *s.th.* in *the wardrobe etc.*; **II.** F *v/refl.*: **2. sich** ~ → **hineinknien; 3. sich** ~ **in** *acc.* F stick one's nose into; **~hän·gen²** *v/i.* (*irr., sep.*, h, → **hängen¹**) hang (**in** *acc.* in the *water etc.*); **~hor·chen** *v/i.* (*sep.*, h) **1. in sich** ~ do some soul-searching; **2.** ~ **in** *acc.* try to grasp the meaning of; **~in·ter·pre,tie·ren** *v/t.* (*sep.*, h): **et.** ~ **in** *acc.* read s.th. into; **~knien** *fig. v/refl.* (*sep.*, h): **sich** ~ put one's back into it, **in** *acc.*: get down to s.th.; **~kom·men** *v/i.* (*irr., sep.*, sn, → **kommen**) come in; get in(to **in** *acc.*); **das kommt hier** (**dort**) **hinein** that goes in here (there); *fig.* **ins Reden** *etc.* ~ start talking *etc.*; **~krie·chen** *v/i.* (*irr., sep.*, sn, → **kriechen**) creep in(to **in** *acc.*); **~la·chen** *v/i.* (*sep.*, h): **in sich** ~ laugh (*or* chuckle) to o.s.; **~lan·gen** *v/i.* (*sep.*, h): ~ **in** *acc.* reach into; **nicht ~!** hands off!; **~las·sen** *v/t.* (*irr., sep.*, h, → **lassen**) let in; **~lau·fen** *v/i.* (*irr., sep.*, sn, → **laufen**) run inside (*or* in there); ~ **in** *acc.* run inside (*or* into); F *fig.* **in j-n** ~ run (*or* bump) into s.o.; **~le·gen** *v/t.* (*sep.*, h) **1.** put in(to **in** *acc.*) *or* inside; **2.** F *fig.* → **hereinlegen; ~le·sen** *v/t.* (*irr., sep.*, h, → **lesen**): **et.** ~ **in** *acc.* read s.th. into; **~leuch·ten** *v/i.* (*sep.*, h) **1.** shine in(to **in** *acc.*); **mit e-r Taschenlampe** *etc.* ~ **in** *acc.* shine a torch (*Am.* flashlight) *etc.* into; **2.** *fig.* ~ **in** *acc.* probe into, (try to) throw light on; **~ma·nö,vrie·ren** *v/t.* (*sep.*, h) manoeuvre (*Am.* maneuver) in(to **in** *acc.*) *or* inside; **~pas·sen** *v/i.* (*sep.*, h) fit in(to **in** *acc.*), *a.* go in(to); **es paßt nicht hinein** it won't fit (in) *or* go in; **~pfu·schen** *v/i.* (*sep.*, h) meddle (**in** *acc.* in, with), interfere (in, with); **~plat·zen** *v/i.* (*sep.*, sn) burst in(to **in** *acc.*); **~pres·sen** *v/t.* (*sep.*, h) press in(to **in** *acc.*); ~ **in** *acc.* force into *a pattern etc.*; **~pro·ji,zie·ren** *v/t.* (*sep.*, h): ~ **in** *acc.* project onto; **~pum·pen** *v/t.* (*sep.*, h) pump in(to **in** *acc.*) (*a.* F *fig.*); **~quet·schen** *v/t.* (*sep.*, h) squeeze in(to **in** *acc.*); **~re·den** *v/i.* (*sep.*, h): ~ **in** *acc.* interfere with, interrupt; **~rei·chen** (*sep.*, h) **I.** *v/t.* pass in; **II.** *v/i.* reach in(side); **~ren·nen** *v/i.* (*irr., sep.*, sn, → **rennen**) run in(to **in** *acc.*); *fig.* **in sein Verderben** ~ rush headlong into disaster; **~rie·chen** F *v/i.* (*irr., sep.*, h, → **riechen**): ~ **in** *acc.* take a look at *a firm etc.*, have a go at *a task etc.*; **~schei·nen** *v/i.* (*irr., sep.*, h, → **scheinen**) shine in(to **in** *acc.*); **~schlit·tern** F *v/i.* (*sep.*, sn): ~ **in** *acc.* drift into, get involved in; **~spie·len** *v/i.* (*sep.*, h) be involved, play a role (*or* part), figure (**in** *acc.* in); **~stecken** *v/t.* (*sep.*, h) put in(to **in** *acc.*); *fig.* **Geld** ~ **in** *acc.* put (✝ sink) money into; → **Nase; ~stei·gern** *v/refl.* (*sep.*, h): **sich** ~ **in** *acc.* a) work o.s. up into *a rage etc.*, b) get all worked upover *a problem etc.*, c) get completely wrapped up in *one's work etc.*, go completely overboard for *an idea etc.*, get completely involved (*or* caught up) in *a role etc.*; **~stop·fen** *v/t.* (*sep.*, h) **1.** stuff in(to **in** *acc.*) (*a.* F *fig.*); **2.** F **in sich** ~ F stuff o.s. with *chocolate etc.*, *sl.* feed one's face with *sweets etc.*; **~sto·ßen** *v/t.* (*irr., sep.*, h, → **stoßen**) **1.** push in(to **in** *acc.*); **2.** ♪ ~ **in** *acc.* blow into; **~stür·men** *v/i.* (*sep.*, sn) storm in(side); ~ **in** *acc.* storm into (*or* inside); **~stür·zen** (*sep.*) **I.** *v/i.* (sn) fall in(to **in** *acc.*); burst in(to *a room etc.*); **II.** *v/t.* (h) push *s.o.* in(to **in** *acc.*); *fig.* ~ **in** *acc.* plunge *s.o.* into *difficulties etc.*; **III.** *v/refl.*: **sich** ~ (h) jump in(to **in** *acc.*), plunge in(to); *fig.* throw o.s. into the fray; **sich in die Arbeit** ~ throw o.s. into one's work; **~tap·pen** *v/i.* (*sep.*, sn): ~ **in** *acc.* walk into (*a. fig. a trap etc.*); *fig.* get (o.s.) involved in, get caught up in *a difficult situation etc.*; **~tun** *v/t.* (*irr., sep.*, h, → **tun**) put in(to **in** *acc.*); *fig.* **e-n Blick** ~ **in** *acc.* take a look at; **~ver·set·zen** *v/refl.* (*sep.*, h) → **versetzen** II, **hineindenken; ~wach·sen** *v/i.* (*irr., sep.*, sn, → **wachsen**): ~ **in** *acc.* grow into; **~wa·gen** *v/refl.* (*sep.*, h): **sich** ~ venture in; **ich wagte mich nicht hinein** I didn't dare (to) go in; **~we·hen** *v/i.* (*sep.*, sn) blow in(to **in** *acc.*); *a.* waft in(to); **~wer·fen** *v/t.* (*irr., sep.*, h, → **werfen**) throw in(to **in** *acc.*); *fig.* **e-n Blick** ~ (**in** *acc.*) take *or* have a quick look (at), **in ein Buch** *etc.*: *a.* glance at a book *etc.*; **~wol·len** *v/i.* (*irr., sep.*, h, → **wollen¹**) want to go (*or* get) in; **das will mir nicht in den Kopf hinein** I just can't understand it; **~zie·hen** *v/t.* (*irr., sep.*, h, → **ziehen**) **1.** pull in(to **in** *acc.*); **2.** *fig.* **j-n** ~ **in** *acc.* drag s.o. into *s.th.*; **~zwän·gen** *v/t.* (*sep.*, h) squeeze (*or* force) in(to **in** *acc.*)

'hin·fah·ren (*irr., sep.*, → **fahren**) **I.** *v/t.* (h) **1.** drive (*or* take) *s.o. or s.th.* there; ~ **zu** *dat.* drive (*or* take) to; **II.** *v/i.* (sn) **2.** drive (*or* go) there; ~ **zu** *dat.* drive (*or* go) to; **3.** *fig.* **mit der Hand über et.** ~ run one's hand over s.th.; **'Hin·fahrt** *f* journey there; **auf der** ~ on the (*or* our *etc.*) way there

'hin·fal·len *v/i.* (*irr., sep.*, sn, → **fallen**) fall (down); fall over

hin·fäl·lig ['hɪnfɛlɪç] *adj.* **1.** frail; **2.** invalid; ~ **machen** invalidate; **damit wird die Sache** ~ that disposes of that (*or* the matter); **'Hin·fäl·lig·keit** *f* (-; *no pl.*) **1.** frailty; **2.** invalidity

'hin|fin·den *v/i.* (*irr., sep.*, h, → **finden**) find the way (*or* one's way there); **~fle·geln** F *v/refl.* (*sep.*, h): **sich** ~ F sprawl all over the place, **auf** *acc.*: sprawl all over

'Hin·flug *m* outward flight; **auf dem** ~ *a.* flying over, on the way there

'hin·füh·ren (*sep.*, h) **I.** *v/t.* take there; **II.** *v/i.* go there; ~ **zu** *dat.* lead (*or* go) to; *fig.* **wo soll das ~?** where will it all end?; **wo soll** (*or* **würde**) **das** ~, **wenn ...** where would we all be if ...

hing [hɪŋ] *pret. of* **hängen**

'Hin·ga·be *f* (-; *no pl.*) devotion (**an** *acc.* to); **mit** (*or* **voller**) ~ devotedly, passionately, with abandon

'hin·ge·ben (*irr., sep.*, h, → **geben**) **I.** *v/t.* give away; sacrifice; **sein Leben** ~ lay down one's life; **II.** *v/refl.*: **sich** ~ *dat.* devote (*or* dedicate) o.s. to; *b.s.* indulge in; cherish *hope, illusion etc.*; surrender to; **sie gab sich ihm hin** she gave herself to him; **sich s-m Schmerz** *etc.* ~ abandon o.s. to one's grief *etc.*; **'Hin·ge·bung** *f* (-; *no pl.*) → **Hingabe; 'hin·ge·bungs·voll** *adj.* (*and adv.*) devoted(ly)

hin'ge·gen *adv.* however, on the other hand

'hin·ge·gos·sen I. *p.p. of* **hingießen; II.** *adj.*: F **wie** ~ **auf der Couch liegen** F lie draped over the settee

'hin|ge·hen *v/i.* (*irr., sep.*, sn, → **gehen**) **1.** go (*road*: *a.* lead) there; **zu j-m** ~ a) go up to s.o., b) go to (see) s.o., go and see s.o.; **wo gehst du hin?** where are you going?; F **wo kann man hier ~?** what sort of places can you go to around here?; **2.** *time*: pass (by); **3.** *fig.* pass; **et.** ~ **lassen** let s.th. pass, overlook s.th.; **~ge·hö·ren** *v/i.* (*sep.*, h) belong; **wo gehört das hin?** where does that belong (*or* go)?; **~ge·lan·gen** *v/i.* (*sep.*, sn) get there; **~ge·ra·ten** F *v/i.* (*irr., sep.*, sn, → **geraten**) F land, end up; **wo ist sie ~?** *a.* what became of her?

'hin·ge·ris·sen I. *p.p. of* **hinreißen; II.** *adj.* fascinated; enthralled; **III.** *adv.*: ~ **lauschen** listen with rapt attention; ~ **der Musik lauschen** *a.* be transported (*or* carried away) by the music

'hin·ge·wor·fen I. *p.p. of* **hinwerfen; II.** *adj.* casual *remark etc.*

'hin·hal·ten *v/t.* (*irr., sep.*, h, → **halten**) **1.** hold out (*dat.* to); **2.** *fig.* put *s.o.* off; keep *s.o.* hanging; **'hin·hal·tend** *adj.* delaying *action etc.*

'Hin·hal·te|po·li,tik *f*, **~tak·tik** *f* delaying (*or* stalling) tactics *pl.*

'hin|hau·en F (*sep.*, h) **I.** *v/i.* **1.** hit; **2.** *fig.* work; work out (just) right; **II.** *v/t.* **3.** slam *or* bang down (**auf** *acc.* on); **4.** *fig.* F knock off; F reel off; **III.** *v/refl.*: **sich** ~ F hit the sack (*or* hay); **sich aufs Bett** ~ flop down on the bed; **~hocken** *v/refl.* (*sep.*, h): **sich** ~ squat (down); F **hock dich hin!** F plonk yourself down; **~hö·ren** *v/i.* (*sep.*, h) listen

hin·ken ['hɪŋkən] *v/i.* **1.** (sn) limp; **2.** (h) have a limp; *fig.* **der Vergleich hinkt** the metaphor doesn't work

'hin|knal·len F (*sep.*) **I.** *v/t.* (h) slam *or* bang down (**auf** *acc.* on); **II.** *v/i.* (sn) crash down (**auf** *acc.* onto); **~knien** *v/i.* (*sep.*, sn) *and v/refl.* (**sich ~**) (h) kneel down; **~kom·men** *v/i.* (*irr., sep.*, sn, → **kommen**) **1.** come (*or* get) there; **2.** → **hingeraten; 3.** *fig.* **wo kämen wir hin, wenn ...** where would we be if ...; **4.** F a) manage, get along (**mit** *dat.* with), b) make it; **5.** F go, belong; **6.** → **hinhauen** 2; **~krie·gen** F *v/t.* (*sep.*, h) **1.** do, manage; **das hast du gut hingekriegt** you've done a good job of it; **2.** (*a.* **wieder ~**) fix, *a.* put *s.o.* right, patch *s.o.* up; put right (*or* straight); **das werden wir wieder** ~ *a.* we'll have that fixed again, no problem; **~lan·gen** *v/i.* (*sep.*, h) **1.** reach out (**nach** *dat.* for); ~ **nach** *dat.* touch; **2.** F put one's shoulder to the wheel; **3.** F take what one can get; **er hat ganz schön hingelangt** he didn't exactly hold back

hin·läng·lich ['hɪnlɛŋlɪç] *adj.* (*and adv.*) sufficient(ly), adequate(ly); *adv.* ~ **bekannt sein** be sufficiently well-known

'hin|lau·fen *v/i.* (*irr., sep.*, sn, → **laufen**) **1.** run (there); **2.** walk (there); **~le·gen** (*sep.*, h) **I.** *v/t.* a) lay (*or* put) down, b) put to bed; **II.** *v/refl.*: **sich** ~ lie down; **~len·ken** *v/t.* (*sep*, h): ~ **auf** *acc.* direct *conversation etc.* to(wards), *a.* draw *attention* to; **~lüm·meln** *v/refl.* (*sep.*, h) → **hinflegeln; ~ma·chen** F (*sep.*, h) **I.** *v/t.* **1.** put (there); **2.** smash (up); **3.** F finish off, burn out; **II.** *v/i.* F do something; **III.** *v/refl.*: **sich** ~ F burn o.s. out; **~neh·men** *v/t.* (*irr., sep.*, h, → **nehmen**) a) accept, take, b) *fig.* take, put up with *s.th.*, take *s.th.* lying down; → ***selbstverständlich*** I

'hin·nei·gen (*sep.*, h) **I.** *fig. v/i.*: ~ ***zu*** *dat.* be inclined (*or* incline) towards; ***zu der Auffassung*** (*or* ***Überzeugung, Meinung***) ~, ***daß*** be inclined to believe that; ***ich neige zu der Meinung hin, daß*** *a.* I rather think that; **II.** *v/refl.*: ***sich*** ~ ***zu*** *dat.* a) lean (over) towards *s.o.*, b) *terrain etc.*: be inclined towards; **III.** *v/t.* ~ ***zu*** *dat.* bow (*or* incline) *one's head etc.* towards; **'Hin·nei·gung** *f* (-; *no pl.*) inclination, leanings *pl.* (***zu*** *dat.* towards)

'hin|op·fern *v/t.* (*sep.*, h) sacrifice; **~pas·sen** *v/i.* (*sep.*, h) fit (in); **~pflan·zen** *v/t.* (*sep.*, h) **1.** plant; **2.** F plonk (***sich*** o.s.) down; **~plap·pern** F *v/t.* (*sep.*, h): ***das hat er nur so hingeplappert*** he just said it without (really) thinking (about it); **~raf·fen** *v/t.* (*sep.*, h) snatch away

'hin·rei·chen (*sep.*, h) **I.** *v/t.* hand, give; **II.** *v/i.* be enough, do; ~ ***bis zu*** *dat.* reach to (*or* as far as); **'hin·rei·chend I.** *adj.* enough, sufficient; adequate; ample; **II.** *adv.* sufficiently, enough; adequately

'Hin·rei·se *f* trip there; outward journey; ***auf der*** ~ on the way there; **'hin·rei·sen** *v/i.* (*sep.*, sn) travel (*or* go) there

'hin·rei·ßen *v/t.* (*irr.*, *sep.*, h, → ***reißen***) *fig.* enthral(l); ***sich*** ~ ***lassen*** let o.s. be carried away (***von*** *dat.* by); ***sich*** (***dazu***) ~ ***lassen zu*** *inf.* let o.s. be carried away and *do s.th.*; ***das Stück riß zu Beifallsstürmen hin*** the play received rapturous applause; → ***hingerissen*** II; **'hin·rei·ßend I.** *adj.* fascinating; marvel(l)ous; **II.** *adv.*: ~ ***schön*** stunningly beautiful; ***sie hat*** ~ ***gespielt*** she played beautifully, it was a wonderful performance

'hin·rich·ten *v/t.* (*sep.*, h) execute, put to death; electrocute; hang; **'Hin·rich·tung** *f* (-; -en) execution

'Hin·rich·tungs|be·fehl *m* orders *pl.* for execution; **~kom,man·do** *n* execution squad

'Hin·run·de *f sport* **1.** first half of the season; **2.** *corresponding match in the first half of the season*

'hin|schaf·fen *v/t.* (*sep.*, h) take (*or* get) there; **~schau·en** *v/i.* (*sep.*, h) → ***hinsehen***; **~schicken** *v/t.* (*sep.*, h) send (there); **~schie·len** *v/i.* (*sep.*, h) sneak a glance (***nach*** *or* ***zu*** *dat.* at); ~ ***nach*** (*or* ***zu***) *dat. a.* squint at; **~schlach·ten** *v/t.* (*sep.*, h) slaughter; **~schlep·pen** (*sep.*, h) **I.** *v/t.* drag along; **II.** *v/refl.*: ***sich*** ~ drag o.s. along; *fig. time, negotiations, trial etc.*: drag (on); **~schmei·ßen** F *v/t.* (*irr.*, *sep.*, h, → ***schmeißen***) throw down; *fig.* F chuck in; **~schmie·ren** *v/t.* (*sep.*, h) a) scribble, scrawl, b) daub; **~schrei·ben** *v/t.* (*irr.*, *sep.*, h, → ***schreiben***) write down

'hin·se·hen I. *v/i.* (*irr.*, *sep.*, h, → ***sehen***) look; **II.** 2 *n* (-s): ***vom bloßen*** ~ ***wird mir übel*** it makes me feel sick just to look (at it)

'hin·sein F *v/i.* (*irr.*, *sep.*, sn, → ***sein***) a) be broken, be smashed, b) be gone (*or* lost), c) be ruined, F be done for, d) F be done in, be all in, e) be dead, F be dead and gone, f) F be gone; ***er*** (***es***) ***ist hin*** *a.* F he's (it's) had it

'hin·set·zen (*sep.*, h) **I.** *v/t.* put (down); **II.** *v/refl.*: ***sich*** ~ sit down

'Hin·sicht *f*: ***in dieser*** ~ on that score; ***in gewisser*** ~ in a way; ***in einer*** ~ in one sense; ***in mancher*** ~ in some ways; ***in jeder*** ~ in every respect; ***in keiner*** ~ in no respect (*or* way); ***in politischer*** ~ politically; ***in*** ~ ***auf*** *acc.* → **'hin·sicht·lich** *prp.* (*gen.*) concerning, regarding, with regard to; as to

'Hin·spiel *n sport* **1.** first leg; **2.** away leg (*or* tie)

'hin|spre·chen *v/t.* (*irr.*, *sep.*, h, → ***sprechen***): ***et.*** (***nur so***) ~ say s.th. without thinking; ***vor sich*** ~ talk to o.s.; **~stel·len** (*sep.*, h) **I.** *v/t.* put (down); *fig.* ~ ***als*** make out to be; **II.** *v/refl.*: ***sich*** ~ stand (up); ***sich*** ~ ***vor*** *acc.* stand in front of; *fig.* ***sich*** ~ ***als*** make o.s. out to be, pose as; **~steu·ern** *v/i.* (*sep.*, sn): ~ ***auf*** *acc.* steer towards, make (*or* head) for (*a. fig.*); *fig.* be aiming at; **~stre·ben** *v/i.* (*sep.*, h): ~ ***zu*** (*or* ***nach***) *dat.* make (*or* head) for; *fig.* strive for (*or* after); *phys. and fig.* gravitate towards; **~strecken** (*sep.*, h) **I.** *v/t.* **1.** stretch *or* hold out (*dat.* to); **II.** *v/refl.*: ***sich*** ~ **2.** lie down, stretch out; **3.** *fig.* stretch (out), extend (***über Meilen*** for miles); **~strö·men** *v/i.* (*sep.*, sn) throng there; **~stür·zen** *v/i.* (*sep.*, sn) fall; ~ ***zu*** (*or* ***nach***) *dat.* rush to

hint·an|set·zen [hɪnt'an-] *v/t.* (*sep.*, h) a) put last, b) neglect, c) disregard, ignore; **~ste·hen** *v/i.* (*irr.*, *sep.*, h, → ***stehen***) come last (*or* second); **~stel·len** *v/t.* (*sep.*, h) → ***hintansetzen***

hin·ten ['hɪntən] *adv.* at the back; at the end; ~ ***in*** *dat.* in (*or* at) the back of; ***nach*** ~ (to the) back; ***ein nach*** ~ ***gelegenes Zimmer*** a room at the back; ***nach*** ~ ***hinausgehen*** *room etc.*: be at (*or* face) the back; ***von*** ~ from behind; ~ ***anfügen*** add; ***sich*** ~ ***anstellen*** join (*or* go to the back of) the queue (*Am.* line); F *fig.* ~ ***und vorn***(***e***) left, right and cent|er (*Brit.* -re); F ***es stimmt*** ~ ***und vorn***(***e***) ***nicht*** a) *check etc.*: it's totally wrong, b) F it's a pack of lies; F ***ich weiß nicht mehr, wo*** ~ ***und vorn***(***e***) ***ist*** I don't know whether I'm coming or going; ***ziemlich weit*** ~ ***sein*** be a long way behind; F ***ich hab' doch*** ~ ***keine Augen*** I haven't got eyes in the back of my head; **~'an** *adv.* behind, at the back; **~her'um** *adv.* (a)round the back; *fig. learn etc.* through the grapevine; *get etc.* under the counter

hin·ter[1] ['hɪntɐ] *prp.* (*dat.*) a) behind, at the back of, b) after; ~ ***m-m Rücken*** behind my back; ~ ***dem Hügel hervor*** from behind the hill; ~ ***e-e Sache kommen*** a) find out about s.th., b) get the hang of s.th.; ~ ***e-r Sache stecken*** be at the bottom of (*or* behind) s.th.; ~ ***e-r Sache stehen*** be behind s.th., back s.th.; ***et.*** ~ ***sich bringen*** get s.th. over (and done) with; ***et.*** ~ ***sich haben*** a) have got s.th. out of the way (*or* over [and done] with), b) have been through s.th.; ***viel*** ~ ***sich haben*** have been through a lot; ***er hat gerade e-e Niereninfektion*** ~ ***sich*** he's just got over a kidney infection; ***das Schlimmste haben wir*** ~ ***uns*** we've got over the worst part (of it), we're out of the wood(s) now; ***j-n*** (***et.***) ~ ***sich lassen*** leave s.o. (s.th.) behind; ***sich*** ~ ***e-e Sache machen*** get down to s.th.; ~ ***e-e Sache kommen*** find s.th. out

'hin·ter[2] *adj.* rear, back; **~es Ende** far end; ***die*** **~en Bänke** the back benches; ***die*** **~en Räume** *etc. a.* the rooms *etc.* at the back (*or* rear); 🚃 ***die*** **~en Wagen** the rear coaches; ***die*** **2en** those (*or* the ones) at the back

'Hin·ter·achs·an·trieb *m* rear-axle drive; **'Hin·ter·ach·se** *f* rear axle

'Hin·ter|an·sicht *f* rear view; **~aus·gang** *m* rear (*or* back) exit; **~backe** *f* buttock

'Hin·ter·bänk·ler [-bɛŋklɐ] *m* (-s; -) *parl.* backbencher

'Hin·ter·bein *n* hind leg; ***sich auf die*** **~e** ***stellen*** stand on its hind legs, *fig.* put up a fight, not to take it (*or* things) lying down

Hin·ter·blie·be·ne [hɪntɐ'bli:bənə] *m, f* (-n; -n) dependant, dependent; ***die*** **~n** the bereaved (*pl.*); **Hin·ter'blie·be·nen·ren·te** *f* survivor's pension (*or* benefit[s *pl.*])

hin·ter'brin·gen *v/t.* (*irr.*, h, → ***bringen***): ***j-m et.*** ~ inform s.o. about s.th.

'Hin·ter·deck *n* ⚓ afterdeck

hin·ter·ein·an·der [hɪntɐ'aɪ'nandɐ] *adv.* one behind the other; one after the other, one by one, b) in a row, at a stretch; ***drei Tage*** ~ three days running (*or* in a row); ***an drei Tagen*** ~ on three consecutive days; ***et.*** ~ ***tun*** do s.th. in turns, take turns (to do s.th.); ***dicht*** ~ close together; **~ge·hen** *v/i.* (*irr.*, *sep.*, sn, → ***gehen***) walk in single file

'Hin·ter·ein·gang *m* back (*or* rear) entrance

'hin·ter·fot·zig [-fɔtsɪç] F *adj.* false, F two-faced; **'Hin·ter·fot·zig·keit** F *f* (-; -en) **1.** *no pl.* falseness, F two-facedness; **2.** dirty trick

hin·ter'fra·gen *v/t.* (h) question, scrutinize; try to get to the bottom of

'Hin·ter|fuß *m* hind foot (*or* paw); **~ge·bäu·de** *n* back building; **~ge·dan·ke** *m* *b.s.* ulterior motive; ***ohne*** **~n** *a.* quite innocently; ***mein*** ~ ***dabei war ...*** what was at the back of my mind was ...

hin·ter'ge·hen *v/t.* (*irr.*, h, → ***gehen***) deceive, *a.* be unfaithful to *wife etc.*, go (*or* do s.th.) behind s.o.'s back; ***er fühlt sich von s-m Bruder hintergangen*** he thinks his brother should have come to him about it (and not done it behind his back); **Hin·ter'ge·hung** *f* (-; *no pl.*) deception

Hin·ter'glas·ma·le,rei *f* glass painting

'Hin·ter·grund *m* background (*a. art and fig.*); *thea. and fig.* backdrop; *fig.* ***die Hintergründe*** the background (*gen.* of), what's behind *s.th.*; ***den*** ~ ***e-r Sache bilden*** form the background to s.th.; ***sich vor dem*** ~ ***e-s Krieges*** *etc.* ***abspielen*** take place against a backdrop of war *etc.*; ***in den*** ~ ***treten*** F take a back seat; ***sich im*** ~ ***halten*** keep out of the way, watch from the sidelines; ***j-n in den*** ~ ***drängen*** push s.o. into the background, force s.o. onto the sidelines; ***et. im*** ~ ***haben*** have s.th. up one's sleeve; **'hin·ter·grün·dig** [-grʏndɪç] *fig. adj.* enigmatic; subtle; profound; hidden

'Hin·ter·grund|mu,sik *f* background music; **~rau·schen** *n hi-fi etc.*: background noise

'Hin·ter·halt *m*: ***aus dem*** ~ ***überfallen*** waylay, ambush; ***im*** ~ ***liegen*** (*or* ***lauern***) lie in ambush; *fig.* ***et. im*** ~ ***haben*** have s.th. up one's sleeve; **'hin·ter·häl·tig** [-hɛltɪç] *adj.* underhanded, *a.* underhand *methods etc.*; insidious

'Hin·ter|hand *f* (-; *no pl.*) **1.** *zo.* hindquarters *pl.*; **2.** *card game*: (***in der*** ~ ***sein*** be the) youngest hand; *fig.* ***et. in der*** ~ ***ha-***

ben have s.th. up one's sleeve; **~haus** *n* **1.** back (part) of the house; **2.** house at the back

hin·ter'her *adv.* **1.** after, behind; **2.** afterwards; *fig.* when it's (*or* it was) too late; **~ge·hen** *v/i.* (*irr., sep.*, sn, → ***gehen***) follow; **~hin·ken** *fig. v/i.* (*sep.*, sn) lag behind; **~kom·men** *v/i.* (*irr., sep.*, sn, → ***kommen***) come on later; **~lau·fen** *v/i.* (*irr., sep.*, sn, → ***laufen***), **~ren·nen** *v/i.* (*irr., sep.*, sn, → ***rennen***) run behind; ***j-m ~*** run (*esp. fig.* chase) after s.o.; *fig.* ***e-r Sache ~*** chase after s.th.; **~schicken** *v/t.* (*sep.*, h): ***j-n j-m ~*** send s.o. after s.o.; **~sein** F *v/i.* (*irr., sep.*, sn, → ***sein***) **1.** ***j-m ~*** be after s.o., be on s.o.'s heels; **2.** ***~ mit*** *dat.* be behind with *one's work etc.*; **3.** ***~, daß*** see (to it) that, make sure that; ***~ bei*** *dat.* see (to it) that *s.th.* is done, keep an eye on *s.o.*, F make sure *s.o.* does his (*or* her) stuff; **~tra·gen** *v/t.* (*irr., sep.*, h, → ***tragen***): ***j-m et. ~*** run after s.o. with s.th.

'Hin·ter|hirn *n* hind brain; **~hof** *m* backyard; **~kopf** *m* back of the head; *fig.* ***et. im ~ haben*** have s.th. at the back of one's mind; **~land** *n* (-[e]s; *no pl.*) hinterland

hin·ter'las·sen I. *v/t.* (*irr., sep.*, h, → ***lassen***) leave (behind); *fig.* leave *impression etc.*; ⚖ leave behind, be survived by; ***j-m et. ~*** leave s.th. to s.o.; ***e-e Nachricht ~*** leave a message; **II.** *adj.* posthumous *works etc.*; **Hin·ter'las·sen·schaft** *f* (-; -en) estate; *fig.* bequest

'Hin·ter·lauf *m zo.* hind leg

hin·ter'le·gen *v/t.* (*sep.*, h) deposit (***bei*** *dat.* with); **Hin·ter'le·gung** *f*: ***gegen ~*** *gen.* on depositing *s.th.*, *a.* against payment of

'Hin·ter·leib *m zo.* hindquarters *pl.*; abdomen *of insects etc.*

'Hin·ter·list *f* (-; *no pl.*) cunning, deceit; underhandedness; **'hin·ter·li·stig** *adj.* cunning, deceitful; underhanded; *a.* underhand *methods*

'Hin·ter|mann *m* (-[e]s; ⸚er) person behind (me, him *etc.*); *fig.* wirepuller, *the* brains behind it; **~mann·schaft** *f sport*: defen|ce (*Am.* -se)

Hin·tern ['hɪntɐn] F *m* (-s; -) F backside, bottom, behind; ***du kriegst gleich ein paar auf den ~*** you'll get your bottom smacked; *fig.* ***ich hätte mich in den ~ beißen können*** I could have kicked myself; ***j-m in den ~ treten*** F give s.o. a kick up the backside; ***j-m in den ~ kriechen*** F suck up to s.o.

'Hin·ter·pfo·te *f zo.* hind paw

'Hin·ter·rad *n* back (*or* rear) wheel; **~ach·se** *f* rear axle; **~an·trieb** *m* rear-wheel drive; **~brem·se** *f* rear-wheel brake

'Hin·ter·rei·fen *m* back (*or* rear) tyre (*Am.* tire)

hin·ter·rücks ['hɪntɐrʏks] *adv.* from behind; *fig.* behind s.o.'s back

'Hin·ter·sei·te *f* back; reverse

'Hin·ter·sinn *m* (-[e]s; *no pl.*) deeper (*or* hidden) meaning; **'hin·ter·sin·nig** *adj.* *story, remark etc.* with a deeper (*or* hidden) meaning

'Hin·ter·sitz *m* back seat

hin·terst ['hɪntɐst] *adj.* (very) last; ***~e Reihe*** *a.* back row; ***der ~e Baum*** *etc. a.* the tree *etc.* right at the back; ***das ~e Ende*** the tail end; ***die 2en*** those (*or* the ones) (right) at the back

'Hin·ter|stüb·chen *n*: ***et. im ~ haben*** have s.th. at the back of one's mind; **~teil** *n* back (part); F backside, behind; **~tref·fen** *n*: ***im ~ sein*** a) be at a disadvantage, b) lag behind, ***mit*** *dat.*: have fallen behind with *one's work etc.*; ***ins ~ geraten*** (*or* ***kommen***) fall behind

hin·ter'trei·ben *v/t.* (*irr., sep.*, h, → ***treiben***) obstruct, thwart, prevent *s.th.* (from being carried out *or* taking place *etc.*); counteract; torpedo; **Hin·ter'trei·bung** *f* (-; *no pl.*) obstruction

'Hin·ter·trep·pe *f* back stairs *pl.*

'Hin·ter·trep·pen|po·li,tik *f* backstairs politics *pl.*; **~ro,man** *m* F penny dreadful, *Am.* F dime novel

Hin·ter·tup·fin·gen [-'tʊpfɪŋən] F *n* F: (***in ~*** at) the back of beyond

'Hin·ter·tür *f* back door; *fig. a.* loophole; *fig.* ***sich e-e ~ offenhalten*** leave o.s. a way out; ***durch die ~ wieder hereinkommen*** come back in through the back door

'Hin·ter·wäld·ler [-vɛltlɐ] *m* (-s; -) country bumpkin (*or* yokel), *Am. a.* hick

hin·ter'zie·hen *v/t.* (*irr., sep.*, h, → ***ziehen***) evade *tax*; **Hin·ter'zie·hung** *f* (-; -en) *tax* evasion

'Hin·ter·zim·mer *n* back room

'hin|tra·gen *v/t.* (*irr., sep.*, h, → ***tragen***) carry (*or* take) there; **~träu·men** *v/i.* (*sep.*, h): ***vor sich ~*** daydream; **~tre·ten** *v/i.* (*irr., sep.*, sn, → ***treten***) step, tread; ***vor j-n ~*** go up to s.o., *fig.* stand before s.o.; **~tun** *v/t.* (*irr., sep.*, h, → ***tun***) put (there); ***wo soll ich es ~?*** where shall I put it?; F *fig.* ***ich weiß nicht, wo ich ihn ~ soll*** I can't place him

hin·über [hɪ'nyːbɐ] *adv.* over (there); to the other side; ***über*** *acc.* ... ***~*** over, across; **~blen·den** *v/i.* (*sep.*, h) *film*: ***~ nach*** *dat.* cut to, switch over to; **~blik·ken** *v/i.* (*sep.*, h) look over *or* across (***zu*** *dat.* to); ***er blickte zu mir hinüber*** *a.* he looked my way; **~brin·gen** *v/t.* (*irr., sep.*, h, → ***bringen***) take over (*or* across); **~fah·ren** (*irr., sep.*, → ***fahren***) **I.** *v/t.* (h) drive (*or* run, take) *s.o., s.th.* over; **II.** *v/i.* (sn) go *or* drive over (***nach*** *dat.* to); ***über die Grenze ~*** cross the border; **~füh·ren** (*sep.*, h) **I.** *v/i. road etc.*: go across (***nach*** *dat.* to); ***es führt hinüber nach*** *a.* it takes you across to; **II.** *v/t.* take (*or* lead) *s.o.* across; **~ge·hen** *v/i.* (*irr., sep.*, sn, → ***gehen***) go over, walk across; *fig.* pass away; ***~ über*** *acc.* cross; **~ge·lei·ten** *v/t.* (*sep.*, h) walk *s.o.* across; **~hel·fen** *v/i.* (*irr., sep.*, h, → ***helfen***): ***j-m ~*** help s.o. across (*or* over); **~kom·men** *v/i.* (*irr., sep.*, sn, → ***kommen***) get over (*or* across); **~las·sen** *v/t.* (*irr., sep.*, h, → ***lassen***) let *s.o.* over (*or* across); **~müs·sen** *v/i.* (*irr., sep.*, h, → ***müssen***) have to go *or* get across (*or* over); **~rei·chen** (*sep.*, h) **I.** *v/t.* pass (*or* hand) over *or* across; **II.** *v/i.* reach (across); **~ret·ten** *v/t.* (*sep.*, h) save, salvage; ***et. ~ in*** *acc.* ensure the survival of s.th. into *the next century etc.*; ***j-n über die Grenze ~*** get s.o. over the border; **~schau·en** *v/i.* (*sep.*, h) → ***hinüberblicken***; **~schlum·mern** *v/i.* (*sep.*, sn) (***friedlich***) ***~*** pass away peacefully; **~schwim·men** *v/i.* (*irr., sep.*, sn, → ***schwimmen***) swim across *or* over (***zu*** *dat.* to); **~se·hen** *v/i.* (*irr., sep.*, h, → ***sehen***) → ***hinüberblicken***; **~sein** F *v/i.* (*irr., sep.*, sn, → ***sein***) a) be bad, be off, b) be broken, be smashed, c) F be done in, be all in, d) be dead, e) have passed (F conked) out; ***er ist hinüber*** *a.* F he's had it; **~spie·len** *fig. v/i.* (*sep.*, h): ***~ in*** *acc.* a) verge on, have a tinge of *blue etc.*, b) border on; **~sprin·gen** *v/i.* (*irr., sep.*, sn, → ***springen***) jump over (*or* across); F run over *or* across (***zu*** *dat.* to); **~tra·gen** *v/t.* (*irr., sep.*, h, → ***tragen***) carry over *or* across (***zu*** *dat.* to); **~wech·seln** *v/i.* (*sep.*, sn) cross over (***zu*** *dat.* to); *fig.* switch over (to), go over (to); **~wer·fen** *v/t.* (*irr., sep.*, h, → ***werfen***) throw over (*or* across); **~wol·len** *v/i.* (*irr., sep.*, h, → ***wollen***) want to go over (there); **~zie·hen** (*irr., sep.*, → ***ziehen***) **I.** *v/t.* (h) pull across (*or* over); **II.** *v/i.* (sn) move across (*or* over)

Hin·und'her|ge·re·de *n* talk; ***was soll das ganze ~?*** all this talk isn't going to get you *etc.* anywhere; **~über,le·gen** *n* indecision, humming and hawing

hin·un·ter [hɪ'nʊntɐ] *adv.* down; ***den Hügel ~*** down the hill; ***die Treppe ~*** down the stairs; ***da ~*** down there, down that way; **~blicken** *v/i.* (*sep.*, h) look *or* glance down (***auf*** *acc.* at); **~brin·gen** *v/t.* (*irr., sep.*, h, → ***bringen***) take down; **~fah·ren** *v/i.* (*irr., sep.*, sn, → ***fahren***) drive (*or* go) down; **~fal·len** *v/i.* (*irr., sep.*, sn, → ***fallen***) fall down; **~füh·ren** (*sep.*, h) **I.** *v/t.* take down; **II.** *v/i. stairs*: lead down, *path*: *a.* run down; **~ge·hen** *v/i.* (*irr., sep.*, sn, → ***gehen***) **1.** go (*or* walk) down; **2.** *stairs, path etc.*: go *or* lead down (***zu*** *dat.* to); **~hel·fen** *v/i.* (*irr., sep.*, h, → ***helfen***): ***j-m ~*** help s.o. down; **~las·sen** *v/t.* (*irr., sep.*, h, → ***lassen***) let down, lower; **~müs·sen** *v/i.* (*irr., sep.*, h, → ***müssen***) have to go down(stairs); **~rei·chen** (*sep.*, h) **I.** *v/t.* hand down; **II.** *v/i.*: ***~ (bis) auf*** *acc. or* ***zu*** *dat.* reach down to *the floor etc.*; **~schau·en** *v/i.* (*sep.*, h) → ***hinunterblicken***; **~schlin·gen** *v/t.* (*irr., sep.*, h, → ***schlingen***) bolt (*or* wolf) down; **~schlucken** *v/t.* (*sep.*, h) swallow (*a. fig.*); **~se·hen** *v/i.* (*irr., sep.*, h, → ***sehen***) → ***hinunterblicken***; **~sprin·gen** *v/i.* (*irr., sep.*, sn, → ***springen***) jump down; **~spü·len** *v/t.* (*sep.*, h) wash down; *fig.* ***s-n Kummer (mit Alkohol) ~*** drown one's sorrows in drink; **~stür·zen** (*sep.*) **I.** *v/i.* (sn) **1.** fall (*or* crash) down, crash to the floor (*or* ground); *fig.* plummet; ***~ von*** *dat.* fall off, fall out of; **2.** rush (*or* run) downstairs *or* down the stairs; **II.** *v/t.* **3.** (sn) ***die Treppe ~*** → **2**; ***den Berg ~*** fall down the mountainside; **4.** (h) F knock back *a glass of beer etc.*; gulp down *a cup of coffee etc.*; **~tra·gen** *v/i.* (*irr., sep.*, h, → ***tragen***) take *or* carry down(stairs); **~wer·fen** *v/t.* (*irr., sep.*, h, → ***werfen***) throw down; **~wol·len** *v/i.* (*irr., sep.*, h, → ***wollen***) want to go down(stairs); **~wür·gen** *v/t.* (*sep.*, h) choke (*or* force) down; **~zie·hen** (*irr., sep.*, → ***ziehen***) **I.** *v/t.* (h) pull down; **II.** *v/i.* (sn) move down

'hin·wa·gen *v/refl.* (*sep.*, h): ***sich ~ zu*** *dat.* dare to go to (*or* near), venture near

'Hin·weg *m*: ***auf dem ~*** on the way there

hin·weg [hɪn'vɛk] *adv.* **1.** away; **2.** ***~ über*** *acc.* over (*or* across) *s.th.*; **3.** *fig.* ***über Jahre ~*** for years (and years); ***über alle Unterschiede ~*** despite (*or* transcending) all differences; **~brin·gen** *v/t.* (*irr., sep.*, h, → ***bringen***): ***j-n über e-n Verlust*** *etc.* ***~*** help s.o. (to) get over a loss *etc.*; ***dies wird uns über die kritische Zeit*** ~ this will see us through the critical period; **~ge·hen** *v/i.* (*irr.*, *sep.*, sn, → ***gehen***): ~ ***über*** *acc.* pass over *s.th.*; laugh *s.th.* off; shrug *s.th.* off; skip; ignore; **~hel·fen** *v/i.* (*irr.*, *sep.*, h, → ***helfen***): ***j-m*** ~ ***über*** *acc.* help s.o. (to) get over *s.th.*, *fig.* tide s.o. over *the winter etc.*; **~kom·men** *v/i.* (*irr.*, *sep.*, sn, → ***kommen***): ~ ***über*** *acc.* get over; ***ich komme nicht darüber hinweg, daß*** I can't get over the fact that, *w.s.* I can't get it into my head that; **~raf·fen** *lit.* *v/t.* (*sep.*, h) snatch away; **~re·den** *v/i.* (*sep.*, h): ~ ***über*** *acc.* ignore, pretend *s.th.* doesn't exist; **~se·hen** *v/i.* (*irr.*, *sep.*, h, → ***sehen***): ~ ***über*** *acc.* see (*or* look) over; *fig.* overlook, turn a blind eye to; **~sein** F *v/i.* (*irr.*, *sep.*, sn, → ***sein***): ~ ***über*** *acc.* be past *s.th.*, have got over *s.th.*; **~set·zen** (*sep.*) **I.** *v/i.* (sn): ~ ***über*** *acc.* jump (over) *a fence etc.*; **II.** *fig.* *v/refl.* (h): ***sich*** ~ ***über*** *acc.* ignore, shrug *s.th.* off; ***sich rücksichtslos*** ~ ***über*** *acc.* ride roughshod over *s.th.*; **~täu·schen** (*sep.*, h) **I.** *v/t.*: ***j-n*** ~ ***über*** *acc.* mislead s.o. as to; **II.** *v/i.*: ~ ***über*** *acc.* obscure the fact *that*; **III.** *v/refl.*: ***sich*** ~ ***über*** *acc.* ignore, be blind to; ***sich nicht darüber*** ~, ***daß*** not to have any illusions about (*or* as to) the fact that; **~trö·sten** (*sep.*, h) **I.** *v/t.*: ***j-n*** ~ ***über*** *acc.* help s.o. get over *s.th.*; ***das tröstet mich nicht darüber hinweg*** that's no consolation to me, that doesn't make up for it; **II.** *v/refl.*: ***sich*** ~ ***über*** *acc.* (try to) get over *s.th.*

Hin·weis ['hınvaıs] *m* (-es; -e [-zə]) tip, *some* advice; clue, pointer; indication, evidence (*a. pl.*); reference; remark; ***anonymer*** ~ anonymous tip-off; ***mit*** (*or* ***unter***) ~ ***auf*** *acc.* referring to; **'hin·weisen** (*irr.*, *sep.*, h, → ***weisen***) **I.** *v/t.* **1.** ***j-n*** ~ ***auf*** *acc.* point *s.th.* out to s.o.; ***ich möchte Sie nochmals auf die Gefahren*** ~ I'd like to remind you once again of the dangers; **II.** *v/i.* **2.** ~ ***auf*** *acc.* point to; allude to; refer to; ***darauf*** ~, ***daß*** point out that, stress (*or* emphasize, underline) that; **3.** ~ ***auf*** *acc.* point to (*or* out); **'Hin·weis·schild** *n* sign

'hin|wen·den (*irr.*, *sep.*, h, → ***wenden***) **I.** *v/refl.* **1.** ***sich*** ~ ***zu*** *dat.* turn to(wards), turn round to; **2.** *fig.* ***sich*** ~ ***an*** *acc.* turn to, *a.* go to; ***ich wußte nicht, wo ich mich*** ~ ***sollte*** I didn't know which way to turn; **II.** *v/t.*: ***den Kopf*** ~ ***zu*** *dat.* turn (one's head) round to; ***die Augen*** ~ ***zu*** *dat.* turn to look at; **~wer·fen** (*irr.*, *sep.*, h, → ***werfen***) **I.** *v/t.* **1.** throw down; ***e-m Hund et.*** ~ throw a dog s.th., throw s.th. to a dog; **2.** *fig.* give up, F chuck in; → ***Kram***; **3.** *fig.* (casually) drop, throw in *remark etc.*; → ***hingeworfen*** II; **II.** *v/refl.*: ***sich*** ~ throw o.s. down (*or* onto the floor *or* ground); **~wir·ken** *v/i.* (*sep.*, h): ~ ***auf*** *acc.* work towards; ***darauf*** ~, ***daß j-d et. tut*** try and bring s.o. to do s.th.; ***darauf*** ~, ***daß sich die Lage verbessert*** work towards improving the situation; **~wol·len** *v/i.* (*irr.*, *sep.*, h, → ***wollen***) want to go (there); ***wo willst du hin?*** where are you going?

Hinz [hınts] *m*: ~ ***und Kunz*** [kʊnts] every (*or* any old) Tom, Dick and Harry

'hin|zäh·len *v/t.* (*sep.*, h) count out; **~zau·bern** F *v/t.* (*sep.*, h) conjure up; F whip up *a meal etc.*; **~zei·gen** *v/i.* (*sep.*, h) point there; ~ ***auf*** *acc.* point at

'hin·zie·hen (*irr.*, *sep.*, → ***ziehen***) **I.** *v/t.* (h) **1.** pull there; *fig.* ***sich hingezogen fühlen zu*** *dat.* be drawn to(wards); **2.** *fig.* draw (*or* drag) out *negotiations etc.*; **II.** *v/refl.*: ***sich*** ~ (h) **3.** drag on, ***bis zu*** *dat.*: *a.* go on until (*or* till); ***sich über Jahre*** ~ go on for years (and years); ***die Entscheidung wird sich noch*** ~ it will be some time (yet) before a decision is reached; **4.** stretch (***bis an*** *acc.* to, as far as); ***sich*** ~ ***an*** *dat.* stretch along *the coast etc.*; **III.** *v/i.* (sn) move; ***wo zieht ihr hin?*** where are you moving (to)?

'hin·zie·len *v/i.* (*sep.*, h): ~ ***auf*** *acc.* aim at; *remark etc.*: be directed at, be meant for

hin'zu|ad͵die·ren *v/t.* (*sep.*, h) add on; **~be·kom·men** *v/t.* (*irr.*, *sep.*, h, → ***bekommen***) get *s.th.* on top of it (*or* into the bargain); **~den·ken** *v/t.* (*irr.*, *sep.*, h, → ***denken***) (try to) imagine (there is *or* are), (try to) visualize; ***das übrige können Sie sich*** ~ I'm sure you can fill in (*or* imagine) the rest, I'll leave the rest to your imagination

hin'zu·fü·gen *v/t.* (*sep.*, h) add (*dat.* to); enclose; append; **Hin'zu·fü·gung** *f* (-; -en) addition; ***unter*** ~ ***von*** *dat.* (by) adding

hin'zu|ge·sel·len *v/refl.* (*sep.*, h): ***sich*** ~ join the group (*or* us, them *etc.*); **~kom·men** *v/i.* (*irr.*, *sep.*, sn, → ***kommen***) **1.** come along; **2.** join (**zu** *dat. s.o. or s.th.*); ***zur Mannschaft kamen noch zwei neue Spieler hinzu*** the team was joined by two new players; **3.** ***hinzu kommt noch, daß*** on top of this (is the fact that), and we mustn't forget that; ***es kommen noch die Heizkosten hinzu*** we've *etc.* got to add the heating costs (to that), and we *etc.* mustn't forget the heating costs, on top of that there are the heating costs; ***es kamen weitere Probleme hinzu*** more problems cropped up; **~neh·men** *v/t.* (*irr.*, *sep.*, h, → ***nehmen***) add (**zu** *dat.* to), *a.* include *s.o.* (in); **~set·zen** (*sep.*, h) **I.** *v/t.* add (**zu** *dat.* to); **II.** *v/refl.*: ***sich zu j-m*** ~ join s.o.; **~tre·ten** *v/i.* (*irr.*, *sep.*, sn, → ***treten***) → ***hinzukommen***; **~tun** F *v/t.* (*irr.*, *sep.*, h, → ***tun***) add (**zu** *dat.* to); **~zäh·len** *v/t.* (*sep.*, h) add (**zu** *dat.* to)

hin'zu·zie·hen *v/t.* (*irr.*, *sep.*, h, → ***ziehen***) **1.** call in *doctor, expert etc.*, consult *s.o. or s.th.*; **2.** include; **Hin'zu·zie·hung** *f*: ***unter*** ~ ***von*** *dat.* (*or gen.*) with the help of

Hi·obs|bo·te ['hi:ɔps-] *m* bearer of bad tidings; **~bot·schaft** *f* bad news (*sg.*)

Hip·pie ['hıpi] *m* (-s; -s) hippy

hip·po·kra·tisch [hıpo'kra:tıʃ] *adj.* ⚕ Hippocratic *oath etc.*

Hirn [hırn] *n* (-[e]s; -e) brain; *gastr. and fig.* brains *pl.*; *fig.* mind; **~an·hang·drü·se** *f* pituitary (gland); **~ar·beit** *f* brainwork; **~blu·tung** *f* cerebral (*or* brain) h(a)emorrhage; **~er·wei·chung** *f* softening of the brain; **~for·scher** *m* brain researcher; **~funk·ti͵on** *f* function(ing) of the brain

'hirn·ge·schä·digt *adj.* brain-damaged

'Hirn|ge·spinst *n* crazy idea; delusion; pipe dream; **~hälf·te** *f*: ***rechte*** (***linke***) ~ right (left) half of the brain

'Hirn·haut *f* cerebral membrane; **~ent·zün·dung** *f* meningitis

Hir·ni ['hırni] F *m* (-s; -s) F screwball

'Hirn·ka·sten F *m*: ***nichts im*** ~ ***haben*** F have (nothing but) sawdust between one's ears

'hirn·los F *adj.* F brainless; **~er** ***Mensch*** *a.* F moron, cretin; **'Hirn·lo·sig·keit** F *f* (-; -en) **1.** *no pl.* F brainlessness; **2.** F crazy thing to do

'Hirn|mas·se *f* cerebral matter; **~quet·schung** *f* contusion of the brain; **~rin·de** *f* cerebral cortex

'hirn·ris·sig F *adj.* F crazy, whacky

'Hirn|scha·den *m* brain damage; **~scha·le** *f* *anat.* cranium; **~schlag** *m* ⚕ stroke; **~schmalz** F *n* F grey (*Am.* gray) matter; **~schwund** *m* shrinking of the brain; **~sub͵stanz** *f* cerebral matter; ***graue*** ~ grey (*Am.* gray) matter; ***weiße*** ~ white matter; **~tod** *m* brain death; **~trau·ma** *n* brain (*or* cerebral) trauma; **~tu·mor** *m* brain tumo(u)r

'hirn·ver·brannt F *adj.* mad, F crazy, cracked

'Hirn|ver·let·zung *f* brain injury; **~zel·le** *f* brain cell

Hirsch [hırʃ] *m* (-[e]s; -e) **1.** stag; *w.s.* (red) deer; **2.** *gastr.* venison; **3.** F clod; **~brunft** *f* rutting season; **~ge·weih** *n* (stag's) antlers *pl.*; **~horn** *n* (-[e]s; *no pl.*) staghorn, buckhorn; **~jagd** *f* stag hunt(ing); **~kä·fer** *m* stag beetle; **~kalb** *n* fawn, calf; **~kuh** *f* hind

'Hirsch·le·der *n*, **'hirsch·le·dern** *adj.* buckskin (...)

Hir·se ['hırzə] *f* (-; -n) millet; **~brei** *m* millet gruel; **~korn** *n* **1.** millet (seed); **2.** ⚕ sty(e); **~mehl** *n* millet flour

Hirt [hırt] *m* (-en; -en) herdsman; shepherd (*a. fig.*); *eccl.* ***der Gute*** **~e** the Good Shepherd

Hir·ten|amt ['hırtən-] *n* *eccl.* pastorate; **~brief** *m* *eccl.* pastoral letter; **~dich·tung** *f* pastoral poetry; **~ge·dicht** *n* pastoral poem, eclogue; **~jun·ge** *m*, **~kna·be** *m* shepherd boy; **~le·ben** *n* pastoral life; **~lied** *n* pastoral song; **~mäd·chen** *n* (young) shepherdess; **~spiel** *n* pastoral play; **~stab** *m* shepherd's crook; *eccl.* crosier, crozier; **~tä·schel(kraut)** [-tɛʃəl-] *n* ⚘ shepherd's purse; **~volk** *n* pastoral tribe

His [hıs] *n* (-; -) ♪ B sharp

his·sen ['hısən] *v/t.* (h) hoist (up), raise *flag etc.*

Hi·sta·min [hısta'mi:n] *n* (-s; *no pl.*) histamine

Hi·sto·lo·gie [hıstolo'gi:] *f* (-; *no pl.*) ⚕ histology

Hi·stör·chen [hıs'tø:ɐçən] *n* (-s; -) anecdote, little story

Hi·sto·ri·en|ma·ler [hıs'to:rĭən-] *m* historical painter; **~ma·le͵rei** *f* historical painting

Hi·sto·ri·ker [hıs'to:rikɐ] *m* (-s; -) historian

Hi·sto·rio·graph [hıstorĭo'gra:f] *m* (-en; -en) historiographer; **Hi·sto·rio·gra·phie** [hıstorĭogra'fi:] *f* (-; *no pl.*) historiography

hi·sto·risch [hıs'to:rıʃ] **I.** *adj.* a) historical, b) historic; **~es** ***Verständnis*** sense (*or* understanding) of history; **II.** *adv.*: ~ ***bedeutend sein*** be historically significant, be of historical significance; **~-kri·tisch** *adj.* historicocritical

hi·sto·ri·sie·ren [hıstori'zi:rən] *v/t.* (h) historicize; **Hi·sto·ris·mus** [hısto'rısmʊs] *m* (-; *no pl.*) historicism; **hi·sto·ri·stisch** [hısto'rıstı] *adj.* historicist; **Hi·sto·ri·zis·mus** [hıstori'tsısmʊs] *m* → ***Historismus***

Hit [hɪt] *m* (-[s]; -s) hit

Hit·ler|gruß ['hɪtlɐ-] *m* (-es; *no pl.*) *hist.* Nazi salute; **~ju·gend** *f hist.* Hitler Youth; **~jun·ge** *m hist.* member of the Hitler Youth; **~zeit** *f* (-; *no pl.*) *hist.* Hitler era; ***in der ~ a.*** at the time of Hitler, in Hitler's time

'Hit|li·ste *f* hit parade, top twenty, top one hundred *etc.*; ***auf Platz 1 der ~ sein*** be number one in the hit parade *etc.*; **~pa,ra·de** *f* hit parade *etc.*; → ***Hitliste***

Hit·ze ['hɪtsə] *f* (-; *no pl.*) heat (*a. fig.*); ***das ist heute e-e ~!*** it's sweltering (*or* really hot) today; ***hier drinnen ist aber e-e ~!*** it's like an oven in here; ***bei dieser ~*** in this heat; *fig.* ***in ~ geraten*** get all worked up; ***in der ~ des Gefechtes*** in the heat of the moment; **~aus·schlag** *m* ⚕ heat rash

'hit·ze·be·stän·dig *adj.* heat-resistant, heat-proof; oven-proof *dishes etc.*; **'Hit·ze·be·stän·dig·keit** *f* heat-resistance

'Hit·ze|bläs·chen *pl.* heat blisters; **~ein·wir·kung** *f* effect of (the) heat

'hit·ze|emp·find·lich *adj.* heat-sensitive, sensitive to heat; **~fest** *adj.* → ***hitzebeständig***; **~frei** *adj.*: ***~ haben*** be off school because of the heat

'Hit·ze|grad *m* temperature; **~mau·er** *f* wall of heat; **~pe·rio·de** *f* hot spell; **~schild** *m space travel*: heat shield; **~schweif** *m* exhaust plume *of rocket*; **~wel·le** *f* **1.** heat wave; **2. ~n** ⚕ hot flushes

hit·zig ['hɪtsɪç] *adj.* a) quick-tempered; rash, b) violent; heated *debate etc.*; ***~ werden*** flare up; ***nicht so ~!*** don't get excited

'Hitz·kopf *m* hothead; **'hitz·köp·fig** [-kœpfɪç] *adj.* hotheaded

'Hitz·schlag *m* heatstroke

HIV-ne·ga·tiv [haːʔiː'faʊ-] *adj.* HIV-negative; **~-po·si·tiv** *adj.* HIV-positive; **~-Po·si·ti·ve** *m, f* (-n; -n) HIV-carrier

Hi·wi ['hiːvi] *m* (-s; -s) *univ.* assistant

hm [hm] *int.* **1.** um; **2.** mm; **3.** huh?

H-Milch ['haː-] *f* long-life milk

HNO-Arzt [haːʔɛn'oː-] *m* ear, nose and throat doctor, *esp. Am.* ENT specialist

hob [hoːp] *pret. of* ***heben***

Hob·by ['hɔbi] *n* (-s; -s) hobby; **~gärt·ner** *m* amateur gardener; **~kel·ler** *m* workshop (in the cellar); **~koch** *m* keen cook

Ho·bel ['hoːbəl] *m* (-s; -) ⚙ plane; *gastr.* slicer; **~bank** *f* (-; ¨e) carpenter's bench, workbench; **~ei·sen** *n* plane iron; **~ma,schi·ne** *f* planer, planing machine; **~mes·ser** *n* plane iron

ho·beln ['hoːbəln] *v/t.* (h) plane; *fig.* polish; → ***Span***

'Ho·bel·spä·ne *pl.* (wood) shavings; facings

hoch [hoːx] **I.** *adj.* → ***höher, höchst***; high; tall *person, tree, building etc.*; long *ladder etc.*; *fig.* high, big *income etc.*; heavy, severe *sentence etc.*; high, important *post etc.*; great *hono(u)r etc.*; ***3 Meter ~ sein*** be 3 met|res (*Am.* -ers) high (*or* deep); ♪ ***zu ~*** sharp; ***hoher Adel*** nobility, *Brit. a.* peerage; ***hohes Alter*** great (*or* advanced) age; ***ein hohes Alter erreichen*** *a.* live to be very old (*or* to a ripe old age); ***hohe Ehre*** great hono(u)r; ***hoher Gast*** distinguished guest, VIP; ***hohe Geburt*** high birth; ***hohes Gericht*** a) high court, b) Your Lordship (*Am.* Your Honor), Members of the Jury; ***das hohe Mittelalter*** the High Middle Ages; ***der hohe Norden*** the far north; ***hoher Offizier*** *etc.* high-ranking officer *etc.*; ***hohe Politik*** high politics; ***ein hohes Lied singen auf*** *acc.* sing the praises of; ***e-e hohe Meinung haben von*** *dat.* think very highly of; ***das ist mir zu ~*** that's above my head (*or* beyond me); ***s-e Rede war zu ~ für sie*** he was talking over their heads; → ***Ansehen*** II, ***höchst*** I, ***Kante, Roß***; **II.** *adv.* high(ly); *a.* extremely; ***drei Mann ~*** three of them; ***~ oben*** high up, a long way up, ***im Norden***: far up in the north; ***~ und heilig versprechen*** promise solemnly, swear; ***~ in den Achtzigern*** (F ***in die achtzig***) ***sein*** be well into one's eighties; ***~ spielen*** play (for) high (stakes) (*a. fig.*); ***~ verehren*** esteem highly; ***zu ~ singen*** (***spielen***) sing (play) sharp; ***zwei Treppen ~*** (***höher***) ***wohnen*** live on the second (*Am.* third) floor (live two floors up); ***zu ~ einschätzen*** overestimate, overrate; ***~ verschuldet*** heavily (*or* deep) in debt; ***das ist zu ~ gegriffen*** that's a bit high, that's an exaggeration; ***wenn es ~ kommt*** at (the) most; ***j-m et. ~ anrechnen*** respect s.o. for (doing) s.th.; ***er rechnet dir das ~ an*** *a.* F that really impressed him; ***Hände ~!*** hands up!; ***Kopf ~!*** chin up!; ***~ lebe ...!*** three cheers for ...!; ***~ lebe der König!*** long live the King!; → ***hergehen*** 2, ***höchst*** II; **III.** ⚟ *prp.*: **4 ~ 5** four to the fifth (power)

Hoch *n* (-s; -s) **1.** cheers *pl.* (***auf*** *acc.* for); ***ein~ für*** *acc.* three cheers for; **2.** *fig.* high, peak; **3.** *meteor.* high(-pressure area)

'hoch·ach·ten *v/t.* (*sep.*, h) greatly respect, hold in high esteem; **'Hoch·ach·tung** *f* (great) respect (***vor*** *dat.* for); admiration (for); ***bei aller ~ vor*** *dat.* with all respect to; ***mit vorzüglicher ~*** → **'hoch·ach·tungs·voll** *adv.* Yours sincerely, *esp. Am.* Yours truly

'Hoch·adel *m* higher nobility

'hoch|ak·tu,ell *adj.* highly topical; up-to-the-minute; very much in the news; **~al,pin** *adj.* alpine

'Hoch|al,tar *m* high altar; **~amt** *n* high mass

'hoch|an·ge·se·hen *adj.* highly regarded; very distinguished; **~an·stän·dig** *adj.* very decent

'Hoch·an,ten·ne *f* outdoor aerial (*or* antenna)

'hoch|ar·bei·ten *v/refl.* (*sep.*, h): ***sich ~*** work one's way up; **~auf·ge·schos·sen** *adj.* lanky; **~auf·lö·send** *adj. phot.* high-resolution; *TV* high-definition; **~es *Fernsehbild*** high-definition TV (screen), HDTV; **~auf·ra·gend** *adj.* towering

'Hoch|bahn *f* elevated railway (*Am.* railroad); **~ba,rock** *m, n* high baroque (period)

'Hoch·bau *m* (-[e]s; *no pl.*) building construction; → ***Hoch- und Tiefbau***; **~amt** *n* municipal building department; **~in·ge·ni,eur** *m*, **~tech·ni·ker** *m* structural engineer

'hoch|be·deut·sam *adj.* highly significant; **~be·frie·digt** *adj.* very (*or* extremely) satisfied; **~be·gabt** *adj.* very (*or* highly) gifted; **~be·glückt** *adj.* extremely (*or* blissfully) happy

'hoch·bei·nig [baɪnɪç] *adj.* long-legged

'hoch|be·rühmt *adj.* very famous; **~be·steu·ert** *adj.* heavily taxed; **~be·tagt** *adj.* (very) advanced in years; ***~ sterben*** die at a very old age, die a very old man (*or* woman)

'Hoch·be·trieb *m* (-[e]s; *no pl.*) **1.** ***es herrscht ~, wir*** *etc.* ***haben ~*** things are really busy, F it's all go; **2.** rush hour, peak hours *pl.*; **3.** peak season

'hoch|be·zahlt *adj.* highly paid; **~bin·den** *v/t.* (*irr.*, *sep.*, h, → ***binden***) tie up; **~blicken** *v/i.* (*sep.*, h) look up

'Hoch·blü·te *f* (-; *no pl.*) **1.** ✿ ***in ~ stehen*** be in full bloom; **2.** *fig.* golden age; heyday; ***die ~ des Mittelalters*** (***der italienischen Malerei*** *etc.*) the flowering of the Middle Ages (of Italian painting *etc.*); ***e-e*** (***s-e***) ***~ erleben*** experience a peak (have its heyday); ***e-e wirtschaftliche ~ erleben*** go through a period of economic power (*or* prosperity, expansion)

'hoch|brin·gen *v/t.* (*irr.*, *sep.*, h, → ***bringen***) bring up (*a.* ⚕ *vomit*); lift, get up; *fig.* ***e-e Firma*** (***e-n Kranken***) ***wieder ~*** get a company (a sick person) back on its (his *or* her) feet; ***j-n ~*** raise s.o.'s hackles, F get s.o.'s back up; **~bri,sant** *fig. adj.* highly charged, explosive

'Hoch·burg *fig. f* stronghold

'hoch·deutsch *adj.*, **'Hoch·deutsch** *n ling.* standard (*n.s.* High) German

'hoch·do,tiert *adj.* highly paid

'Hoch·druck *m* (-[e]s; *no pl.*) high pressure (*a. meteor.*); ⚕ high blood pressure; *fig.* ***mit ~*** *work etc.* flat out

'hoch·drücken *v/t.* (*sep.*, h) press *or* push up(wards)

'Hoch·druck|ge·biet *n meteor.* high, high-pressure area; **~keil** *m* wedge of high pressure; **~kern** *m* high-pressure cent|re (*Am.* -er) *or* core; **~zo·ne** *f* → ***Hochdruckgebiet***

'Hoch·ebe·ne *f* plateau

'hoch|ele,gant *adj.* very elegant; **~emp·find·lich** *adj.* highly sensitive; *phot.* high-speed ..., fast; F *fig.* hypersensitive, *a.* very touchy; **~ent·wickelt** *adj.* highly developed, sophisticated; very advanced *technology etc.*; **~er·freut** *adj.* delighted (***über*** *acc.* at); **~er·ho·ben** *adj.*: ***~en Hauptes*** with one's head (*or* nose) in the air; **~er·staunt** *adj.* (absolutely) amazed; **~ex·plo,siv** *adj.* highly explosive

'hoch·fah·ren (*irr.*, *sep.*, → ***fahren***) **I.** *v/i.* (sn) **1.** drive (*or* go) up; **2.** a) start, b) flare up; **II.** *v/t.* (h) **3.** a) take *s.o. or s.th.* up, b) drive *s.o. or s.th.* up (there); **'hoch·fah·rend** *adj.* overbearing, arrogant

'hoch·fein *adj.* a) ✝ first-class, top quality, b) *fig.* very refined

'Hoch·fi,nanz *f* high finance

'hoch·flie·gen *v/i.* (*irr.*, *sep.*, sn, → ***fliegen***) a) soar (up), b) blow up, explode; **'hoch·flie·gend** *fig. adj.* ambitious; high-flown *plans etc.*

'Hoch|flut *f* high tide; *fig.* flood, deluge; **~form** *f*: ***in ~*** in top form; **~for,mat** *n* upright format; ***Foto im ~*** upright photo

'hoch·fre,quent *adj.* high-frequency ...

'Hoch·fre,quenz *f* ⚡ high frequency; **~be·reich** *m* high-frequency range; **~tech·nik** *f* high-frequency engineering

'Hoch·ga,ra·ge *f* multi-stor(e)y car park

'hoch|ge·ach·tet *adj.* highly esteemed; **~ge·bil·det** *adj.* (very) erudite

'Hoch·ge·bir·ge *n* high mountain region(s *pl.*); **'Hoch·ge·birgs...** *in cpds.* high mountain, alpine

ˈ**hoch·ge·ehrt** *adj.* highly hono(u)red
ˈ**Hoch·ge·fühl** *n* (-[e]s; *no pl.*) feeling of elation; ***das ist ein*** ~ it's a wonderful feeling
ˈ**hoch|ge·hen** *v/i.* (*irr.*, *sep.*, sn, → ***gehen***) **1.** go up, *curtain*, *fig. prices etc.*: *a.* rise; **2.** F a) blow up, b) *fig.* flare up, F hit the roof; ~ ***lassen*** blow up *bomb etc.*, F *fig.* F bust *a gang etc.*; **~gei·stig** *adj.* (highly) intellectual, *iro.* highbrow; **~ge·le·gen** *adj.* high-up, high up in the mountains; **~ge·lehrt** *adj.* very learned, erudite
ˈ**Hoch·ge·nuß** *m* absolute delight, real treat
ˈ**hoch|ge·schätzt** *adj.* highly esteemed; **~ge·schlos·sen** *adj.* high-necked, with a high neckline; **~ge·schraubt** *fig. adj.* high, exaggerated; high-flown *ambitions etc.*
ˈ**Hoch·ge·schwin·dig·keits|strecke** *f* high-speed rail link; **~zug** *m* high-speed train
ˈ**hoch|ge·sinnt** *adj.* high-minded; **~ge·spannt** *adj.* ⚙ high-pressure ...; ⚡ high-voltage ...; *fig.* great, high *expectations etc.*; ambitious *plans etc.*; **~ge·steckt** *adj.* high-flown; ***~es Ziel*** *a. iro.* lofty mission; **~ge·stellt** *adj.* high-ranking *personality*; **~ge·stimmt** *adj.* elated; expectant; **~ge·sto·chen** F *adj.* F jumped-up; F high-falutin; highbrow; **~ge·wach·sen** *adj.* lanky; **~ge·züch·tet** *adj.* high-bred; ⚙ sophisticated; *mot. etc.* F souped up; **~gif·tig** *adj.* highly toxic
ˈ**Hoch·glanz** *m* high polish; ***et. auf ~ polieren*** give s.th. a high polish; *fig.* ***auf ~ bringen*** spruce up; **~ab·zug** *m phot.* glossy print; **~paˌpier** *n phot.* glossy paper; **~po·liˌtur** *f* mirror finish
ˈ**Hoch·go·tik** *f* High Gothic period; ***das ist ~*** that's High Gothic, that's from the High Gothic period
ˈ**hoch·gra·dig** [-graːdɪç] **I.** *adj.* extreme; intense; ⚕ highly concentrated; *fig.* utter *nonsense etc.*; **II.** *adv.* extremely, to a high degree
ˈ**hoch·gucken** *v/i.* (*sep.*, h) look up
ˈ**hoch·hackig** [-hakɪç] (*sep.* -k·k-) *adj.* high-heeled *shoes*
ˈ**hoch·hal·ten** *v/t.* (*irr.*, *sep.*, h, → ***halten***) hold up; *fig.* hono(u)r; cherish *memory etc.*; uphold, preserve *traditions etc.*
ˈ**Hoch·haus** *n* block of flats, high-rise, tower block
ˈ**hoch|he·ben** *v/t.* (*irr.*, *sep.*, h, → ***heben***) lift (up); *parl.* ***durch*** ♀ ***der Hände*** by show of hands; **~hei·lig** *adj.* (most) holy; **~herr·schaft·lich I.** *adj.* grand; **II.** *adv.*: ***dort geht es ~ zu*** they live in grand style; **~her·zig** *adj.* high-minded; magnanimous; **~in·du·stria·liˌsiert** *adj.* highly industrialized; **~in·tel·lek·tuˌell** *adj.* highly intellectual; **~in·tel·liˌgent** *adj.* very (*or* highly) intelligent; **~in·ter·esˌsant** *adj.* very (*or* most) interesting; **~ja·gen** *v/t.* (*sep.*, h) **1.** rouse; **2.** *mot.* rev up *the engine*; **~ju·beln** F *v/t.* (*sep.*, h) F crack up; **~käm·men** *v/t.* (*sep.*, h) comb (*or* sweep) *one's hair* up
ˈ**hoch·kant** [-kant] *adv.* on end; ~ ***stellen*** upend; F *fig.* ~ ***hinausfliegen*** F be turned out on one's ear, *a.* F get the boot; F ***j-n ~ hinauswerfen*** F kick s.o. out, F give s.o. the boot
ˈ**Hoch·ka·pi·taˌlis·mus** *m* heyday of capitalism
ˈ**hoch·ka·rä·tig** [-kaˌrɛːtɪç] *adj.* high-carat ...; *fig.* high-calib|re (*Am.* -er), top-flight ...
ˈ**hoch·kip·pen** *v/t.* (*sep.*, h) tilt up
ˈ**Hoch·kir·che** *f in GB*: High Church
ˈ**hoch|klapp·bar** *adj.* tip-up ...; folding *bed*; **~klap·pen** *v/t.* (*sep.*, h) turn up *collar*; fold up *bed*, *a.* tip up *seat*; **~klet·tern** *v/i.* (*sep.*, sn) climb up (*a. fig.*); ~ ***an*** *dat.* climb (up) *s.th.*; *fig.* ***langsam*** ~ *interest rate etc.*: creep up; **~kom·forˌta·bel** *adj.* luxury *flat etc.*; **~kom·men** *v/i.* (*irr.*, *sep.*, sn, → ***kommen***) a) come up, b) get up, get on one's feet, c) *fig.* get on (*or* ahead); get back on one's feet; F ***mir kam alles wieder hoch*** I brought everything up again, *fig.* it all came (flooding) back; ***wenn es hochkommt*** at (the) most, at best
ˈ**Hoch·kon·junkˌtur** *f* ✝ (economic) boom; ~ ***haben*** be going through (*or* be experiencing) an economic boom
ˈ**hoch|kon·zenˌtriert I.** *adj.* highly concentrated; **II.** *adv. read etc.* with great concentration, very concentratedly; **~krem·peln** *v/t.* (*sep.*, h) roll up; *fig.* ***die Ärmel*** ~ roll up one's sleeves, F get down to it; **~krie·gen** *v/t.* (*sep.*, h) **1.** get *s.o. or s.th.* up; **2.** V ***einen*** ~ *sl.* get (*or* have) a hard on; V ***er kriegt keinen hoch*** *sl.* he can't get it up; **~kul·tiˌviert** *adj.* highly civilized; highly cultivated (*or* cultured) *person*
ˈ**Hoch·kulˌtur** *f* advanced civilization
ˈ**hoch|kur·beln** *v/t.* (*sep.*, h) wind up; **~la·gern** *v/t.* (*sep.*, h) put *one's legs* up; prop *s.o.'s head* up
ˈ**Hoch·land** *n* uplands *pl.*; mountains *pl.*
ˈ**hoch·le·ben: *er lebe hoch!*** three cheers!; ***j-n ~ lassen*** give s.o. three cheers
ˈ**Hoch·lei·stung** *f* top performance; ⚙ *a.* high output
ˈ**Hoch·lei·stungs...** ⚙ *in cpds.* high-capacity, high-output, high-performance, high-power(ed); **~mo·tor** *m* high-performance engine; **~sport** *m* high-performance sport(s *pl.*); **~sport·ler** *m* top sportsman; top athlete
ˈ**Hoch·lei·tung** *f* ⚡ overhead wire
ˈ**hoch·löb·lich** [-løːplɪç] *adj. esp. iro.* most esteemed
ˈ**Hoch·mit·tel·al·ter** *n* High Middle Ages *pl.*
ˈ**hoch·moˌdern I.** *adj.* very modern, ultramodern; **II.** *adv.*: ***sich ~ kleiden*** wear the latest fashions; ***e-e ~ eingerichtete Küche*** a kitchen with all the latest mod cons
ˈ**Hoch·moor** *n* moor, sphagnum bog
ˈ**Hoch·mut** *m* (-s; *no pl.*) arrogance, pride; ~ ***kommt vor dem Fall*** pride goes before a fall; ˈ**hoch·mü·tig** [-myːtɪç] *adj.* haughty, arrogant
ˈ**hoch·nä·sig** [-nɛːzɪç] *adj.* F stuck-up, snooty, snotty-nosed; ˈ**Hoch·nä·sig·keit** *f* (-; *no pl.*) F snootiness
ˈ**Hoch·ne·bel** *m* low stratus; **~decke** *f* extended low stratus; **~fel·der** *pl.* patches of low stratus
ˈ**hoch·neh·men** *v/t.* (*irr.*, *sep.*, h, → ***nehmen***) **1.** pull *s.o.'s* leg; **2.** F bust
ˈ**hoch·not·pein·lich** *iro. adj.* severe; scrutinizing
ˈ**Hoch·ofen** *m* blast furnace
ˈ**hoch|or·ga·niˌsiert** *adj.* highly organized; **~päp·peln** *v/t.* (*sep.*, h) get *s.o.* back on his (*or* her) feet; *w.s.* feed *s.o.* up; nurse *a plant etc.* back to life
ˈ**Hoch|parˌterre** *n* raised ground floor; **~plaˌteau** *n* plateau
ˈ**hoch|poˌli·tisch** *adj.* highly political; **~pro·zen·tig** [-proˌtsɛntɪç] *adj.* high-proof *alcohol*; **~qua·li·fiˌziert** *adj.* highly qualified (*or* trained); **~ra·dio·akˌtiv** *adj.* highly radioactive (*or* contaminated); **~ra·gen** *v/i.* (*sep.*, h) tower *or* rise (up); **~ran·ken** *v/refl.* (*sep.*, h): ***sich*** ~ climb (up), ***an*** *dat.*: climb (*or* creep) up *s.th.*; **~rap·peln** *v/refl.* (*sep.*, h) → ***aufrappeln***
ˈ**hoch·rech·nen** (*sep.*, h) **I.** *v/t.* project; **II.** *v/i.* make a projection; ˈ**Hoch·rech·nung** *f* projection; *elections*: computer prediction; exit poll; ***die ersten ~en haben ergeben ...*** early indications point to ...
ˈ**hoch|recken** (*sep.*, h) **I.** *v/refl.*: ***sich*** ~ stretch up; **II.** *v/t.* stretch *one's arms etc.* up (into the air); **~rei·chen** *v/t.* (*sep.*, h) pass *s.th.* up
ˈ**Hoch|re·liˌef** *n* high relief; **~re·naisˌsance** *f* High Renaissance
ˈ**hoch|rot** *adj.* bright red, crimson; **~rut·schen** *v/i.* (*sep.*, sn) **1.** *dress etc.*: ride up; **2.** move up
ˈ**Hoch·saiˌson** *f*: (***in der*** ~ in the) peak season, (at the) height of the season
ˈ**hoch|schät·zen** *v/t.* (*sep.*, h) think (very) highly of; **~schau·keln** *v/t.* (*sep.*, h) play up; ***sich*** (***gegenseitig***) ~ get each other (all) worked up; **~schie·ben** *v/t.* (*irr.*, *sep.*, h, → ***schieben***) push up; **~schie·ßen** *v/i.* (*irr.*, *sep.*, sn, → ***schießen***) shoot up; **~schla·gen** (*irr.*, *sep.*, → ***schlagen***) **I.** *v/t.* (h) turn up *collar etc.*; **II.** *v/i.* (sn) *waves*: be high; *fig. feelings*: run high; **~schnel·len** *v/i.* (*sep.*, sn) jump up; *prices*: soar, F go sky-high, skyrocket; **~schrau·ben** *v/t.* (*sep.*, h) push (*or* force) up *prices*; raise *expectations etc.*; **~schrecken** *v/t.* (*sep.*, h) startle, frighten (away), disturb
ˈ**Hoch·schul·ab·solˌvent** *m* (university *or* college) graduate; ˈ**Hoch·schu·le** *f* university; college; ***technische*** ~ college of advanced technology, *Am.* institute of technology; ***pädagogische*** ~ college of education
ˈ**Hoch·schul|ge·setz** *n legislation governing higher education*; **~leh·rer** *m* (university *or* college) lecturer; **~reˌform** *f* higher education reforms *pl.*; **~rei·fe** *f* university entrance qualification(s *pl.*)
ˈ**hoch·schwan·ger** *adj.* highly pregnant; ~ ***sein*** *a.* be at an advanced stage of pregnancy
ˈ**Hoch·see** *f* (-; *no pl.*) high sea(s *pl.*), open sea; **~fi·scheˌrei** *f* deep-sea fishing; **~flot·te** *f* **1.** deep-sea fishing fleet; **2.** navy fleet; **~jacht** *f* ocean yacht
ˈ**Hoch·seil** *n* tightrope, high wire; **~akroˌbat** *m* tightrope artist; **~akt** *m* tightrope (*or* high-wire) act; *fig.* tightrope walk
ˈ**Hoch·si·cher·heits|ge·fäng·nis** *n* top-security prison; **~trakt** *m* security wing
ˈ**Hoch·sitz** *m* raised hide (*Am.* blind)
ˈ**Hoch·som·mer** *m* middle of summer; ˈ**hoch·som·mer·lich** *adj.* summery; ***~e Temperaturen*** temperatures in the (high) eighties
ˈ**Hoch·span·nung** *f* **1.** ⚡ high voltage; **2.** *fig.* great suspense; ***es herrscht*** ~ things are very tense
ˈ**Hoch·span·nungs|lei·tung** *f* ⚡ power line; **~mast** *m* ⚡ pylon

'hoch|spe·zia·li,siert *adj.* highly specialized; **~spie·len** *fig. v/t.* (*sep.*, h) play up, blow up; build up

'Hoch·spra·che *f*: ***die deutsche ~*** standard German; **'hoch·sprach·lich** *adj.* standard (German *etc.*) ...

'hoch·sprin·gen *v/i.* (*irr.*, *sep.*, sn, → ***springen***) jump up (in the air); **'Hoch·sprin·ger** *m* high-jumper; **'Hoch·sprung** *m* high jump

'hoch·spü·len *v/t.* (*sep.*, h) wash up (*fig.* bring) to the surface

höchst [hø:çst] **I.** *adj.* highest; *fig.* greatest, utmost; *fig.* ***~e Instanz*** highest authority; ***~er Punkt*** peak; ***~e Vollkommenheit*** peak of perfection; ***in den ~en Tönen loben*** praise to the skies; ***es ist ~e Zeit*** it's high time *you went to bed etc.*; ***von ~er Wichtigkeit*** extremely important; ***das ist das ~e der Gefühle*** it's the most wonderful feeling, it's an amazing experience; → ***äußerst, Höchste***; **II.** *adv.* (*a.* ***aufs ~e***) highly; greatly, extremely, most

'Höchst|al·ter *n* age limit; ***das ~ überschritten haben*** be over the age limit, be too old; **~an·ge·bot** *n* highest offer (*or* bid)

'hoch·stäm·mig *adj.* tall

Hoch·sta·pe·lei [ho:xʃta:pə'laı] *f* (-; -en) **1.** confidence trickery (*or* trick), swindling; **2.** *fig.* overstatement, exaggeration; boasting; ***geistige ~*** intellectual fraud; **'hoch·sta·peln** *v/i.* (h) **1.** swindle (s.o. *or* people); **2.** *fig.* exaggerate, overstate things (*or* the case *etc.*); boast; **'Hoch·stap·ler** [-ʃta:plɐ] *m* (-s; -) **1.** F con man; **2.** fake

'Höchst|be·la·stung *f* ⚙ peak stress (*a.* ↯ load); **~be·trag** *m* maximum (amount), limit; **~bie·ten·de** *m, f* (-n; -n) highest bidder

Höch·ste ['hø:çstə] *n*: ***das ~*** the (ut)most; ***das ist ja das ~!*** that's the limit

'hoch|ste·hend *adj.* turned-up *collar*; F sticking-out, ... standing up; *typ.* superior; *fig.* ***~e Persönlichkeit*** leading figure, distinguished personality, VIP; **~stei·gen** (*irr.*, *sep.*, sn, → ***steigen***) **I.** *v/i.* **1.** *fig. prices etc.*: go up; rise; **2.** climb up; **3.** *fig. anger etc.*: well up (***in j-m*** inside s.o.); **II.** *v/t.* climb (up) *stairs etc.*

'höchst|'ei·gen *hum. adj.*: ***in ~er Person*** in person; ***der Präsident in ~er Person*** *a.* the president himself(, no less); **~'ei·gen·hän·dig** *hum. adj.* personally

'hoch|stel·len *v/t.* (*sep.*, h) **1.** put *s.th.* up; **2.** stand *s.th.* upright (*or* on end); **3.** turn up *heating etc.*; **~stem·men** (*sep.*, h) **I.** *v/t.* lift (*or* heave) up; **II.** *v/refl.*: ***sich ~*** push o.s. up

höch·stens ['hø:çstəns] *adv.* at (the) most, at the outside; only; ***er ist ~ zwanzig*** he can't be more than twenty; ***es ist ~ neun Uhr*** it can't be later than nine o'clock; ***ich trinke ~ mal ein Bier*** very occasionally I might have a beer; ***das gibt es ~ noch in*** *dat.* ... the only place you might find it is (in) ...; ***das gibt es ~ im Fachhandel*** you might find it at a specialist's; ***~, wenn*** unless; ***~ ein Wunder würde ...*** only (*or* nothing short of) a miracle would ..., it would take a miracle to ...

'Höchst|fall *m*: ***im ~*** → ***höchstens***; **~form** *f*: ***in ~*** in top form; **~ge·bot** *n* highest offer; **~ge·schwin·dig·keit** *f* maximum (*or* top) speed; *mot.* ***zulässige ~*** speed limit; **~ge·wicht** *n* maximum weight; **~ge·winn** *m* maximum win(nings *pl.*); **~gren·ze** *f* limit, ceiling; ***e-e ~ festsetzen für*** *acc.* put a ceiling on

'hoch·sti·li,sie·ren *v/t.* (*sep.*, h) build up; ***~ zu*** *dat.* turn *s.o. or s.th.* into, make *s.o. or s.th.* out to be

'Hoch·stim·mung *f* (-; *no pl.*) high spirits *pl.*; ***in ~ sein*** *a.* be excited

'Höchst|last *f* maximum load; **~leistung** *f* top performance, ⚙ *a.* maximum output; *sport*: record (performance); *science etc.*: great achievement; **~lohn** *m* maximum wage(s *pl.*) *or* salary; **~maß** *n*: ***ein ~*** a maximum (***an*** *dat.* of); a great deal (of *patience etc.*); **~men·ge** *f* maximum (amount); **~mög·lich** *adj.* highest possible; **~no·te** *f sport*: top score, top marks *pl.*; **~per,sön·lich** **I.** *adj.* strictly personal; **II.** *adv.* himself (*f* herself), in person, personally; **~preis** *m* top (*or* maximum) price, price ceiling

'Hoch·stra·ße *f* **1.** mountain road; **2.** elevated highway

'hoch|stre·bend *adj.* soaring; *fig.* ambitious; **~strecken** *v/t.* (*sep.*, h) stretch up (into the air)

'höchst·rich·ter·lich *adj.*: ***~e Entscheidung*** decision by the supreme court

'Höchst|satz *m* maximum rate; **~stand** *m* highest level, all-time high; high-water mark; **~stra·fe** *f* maximum penalty (*or* sentence); **~sum·me** *f* maximum sum (*or* amount); **~tem·pe·ra,tu·ren** *pl.* maximum temperatures

'höchst·wahr'schein·lich *adv.* very probably (*or* likely), in all probability

'Höchst|wert *m* maximum value; **~zahl** *f* maximum (figure)

'höchst·zu·läs·sig *adj.* maximum (permitted)

'Hoch·tal *n* high-lying valley

'hoch·tech·ni,siert *adj.* sophisticated; high-tech ...; **'Hoch·tech·no·lo,gie** *f* high tech(nology)

'Hoch·tem·pe·ra,tur·re,ak·tor *m* high-temperature reactor

'hoch·tö·nend *adj.* high-sounding, grandiloquent

'Hoch·tö·ner [-tø:nɐ] *m* (-s; -) *hi-fi*: tweeter

'Hoch·tou·ren *pl.*: ***auf ~ sein*** a) be running at full power (*mot.* speed), F *fig.* be working flat out, *party etc.*: be in full swing, *esp. project etc.*: be going full steam ahead, b) *sl.* be freaking out; F ***j-n auf ~ bringen*** F make s.o. wild; **'hoch·tou·rig** [-tu:rıç] *adv.*: ***~ fahren*** run at high revs

'hoch|tra·bend *adj.* pompous, high-falutin, high-sounding; **~trei·ben** *v/t.* (*irr.*, *sep.*, h, → ***treiben***) force up

'Hoch- und 'Tief·bau *m* structural and civil engineering

'hoch|ver·dient *adj.* meritorious, *man etc.* of great merit; well-deserved, well-earned *victory etc.*; **~ver·ehrt** *adj.* a) esteemed, greatly respected, b) *address*: dear

'Hoch|ver·rat *m* high treason; **~ver·rä·ter** *m* traitor

'hoch·ver·zins·lich *adj.* yielding high interest, high-interest-bearing

'Hoch·wald *m* timber forest

'Hoch·was·ser *n* (-s; *no pl.*) a) high water (*or* tide), b) flood(s *pl.*); ***~ haben*** (*or* ***führen***) be swollen; F *fig.* ***er hat ~*** F his trousers are at half-mast; **~ho·sen** F *pl.*: ***er trägt immer ~*** F he always wears his trousers at half-mast; **~ka·ta,stro·phe** *f* flood disaster; **~scha·den** *m* flood damage; **~stand** *m* high-water level

'hoch·wer·fen *v/t.* (*irr.*, *sep.*, h, → ***werfen***) throw up (in the air)

'hoch·wer·tig [-ve:ɐtıç] *adj.* high-grade ..., high-quality ...; ***~e Nahrungsmittel*** highly nutritive food

'hoch·wich·tig *adj.* highly important

'Hoch·wild *n larger game animals, esp. deer, elk, fallow deer*

'hoch|will·kom·men *adj.* most welcome; **~win·den** (*irr.*, *sep.*, h, → ***winden***) **I.** *v/t.* hoist up; **II.** *v/refl.*: ***sich (am Berg, den Berg) ~*** *road etc.*: wind its way up (the mountain); **~wirk·sam** *adj.* highly effective; **~wuch·ten** *v/t.* (*sep.*, h) heave up; lever up

'Hoch·wür·den: ***Eure*** (*or* ***Euer***) ***~!*** Reverend (Father); ***Seine ~*** the Most Reverend ...

'Hoch·zahl *f* 𝔄 exponent

Hoch·zeit[1] ['hɔxtsaıt] *f* (-; -en) wedding; ***~ feiern*** a) get married, b) have a wedding; ***wann feiert ihr denn ~?*** *a. iro.* when's the wedding (*or* big) day then?; *fig.* ***man kann nicht auf zwei ~en tanzen*** a) you can't be in more than one place at the same time, b) you can't have your cake and eat it

Hoch·zeit[2] ['ho:x-] *f* golden age

Hoch·zeits|fei·er ['hɔxtsaıts-] *f*, **~fest** *n* wedding (reception); **~flug** *m zo.* nuptial flight; **~fo·to** *n* wedding photo; **~gast** *m* wedding guest; **~ge·schenk** *n* wedding present; **~kleid** *n* wedding dress; **~kuchen** *m* wedding cake; **~nacht** *f* wedding night; **~paar** *n* bride and groom, F happy couple; **~rei·se** *f* honeymoon; ***auf ~ sein*** be on one's honeymoon, F be honeymooning; **~strauß** *m* bridal bouquet; **~tag** *m* a) wedding day, b) (wedding) anniversary; **~tor·te** *f* wedding cake

'hoch·zie·hen (*irr.*, *sep.*, → ***ziehen***) **I.** *v/t.* (h) a) pull up; hitch up *trousers*; draw up *legs*; raise *eyebrows*, b) build, erect *wall etc.*, c) ✈ pull up; ***die Nase ~*** sniff; **II.** *v/refl.*: ***sich ~*** (h) pull o.s. up (***an*** *dat.* by); *fig.* ***sich ~ an*** *dat.* a) get a thrill out of, b) make a fuss about; **III.** *v/i.* (sn) *thunderstorm*: come up

'Hoch·zins·po·li,tik *f* policy of high interest rates

'hoch·zi·vi·li,siert *adj.* highly civilized

'hoch·züch·ten *v/t.* (*sep.*, h) breed selectively; *fig.* F soup up *engine*; nurture *feelings*

Hocke ['hɔkə] (*sep.* -k·k-) *f* (-; -n) *gym. etc.* crouch, squatting position; ***in die ~ gehen*** crouch down, squat (down)

hocken ['hɔkən] (*sep.* -k·k-) (h) **I.** *v/i.* squat, crouch; F sit; sit around; ***~ über*** *dat.* be poring over; **II.** *v/refl.*: ***sich ~*** squat down; F plonk o.s. down; **~bleiben** F *v/i.* (*irr.*, *sep.*, sn, → ***bleiben***) *ped.* have to repeat a year

Hocker ['hɔkɐ] (*sep.* -k·k-) *m* (-s; -) stool

Höcker ['hœkɐ] (*sep.* -k·k-) *m* (-s; -) hump (*a. zo.*); bump

höcke·rig ['hœkərıç] (*sep.* -k·k-) *adj.* bumpy

Hockey ['hɔki] (*sep.* -k·k-) *n* (-s; *no pl.*) hockey; **~schlä·ger** *m* hockey stick; **~spie·ler** *m* hockey player

'Hock·stel·lung *f* squatting position

Ho·den ['ho:dən] *m* (-s; -) *anat.* testicle; **~sack** *m* scrotum

Ho·do·me·ter [hodo'meːtɐ] *m* (-s; -) (h)odometer

Hof [hoːf] *m* (-[e]s; Höfe ['høːfə]) **1.** yard; courtyard; backyard; *ped.* playground; **2.** court; ***bei*** (*or* ***am***) ***~e*** at court; *fig.* ***j-m den ~ machen*** court s.o.; **3.** farm; **4.** *ast.* halo (*a. opt. and* ⚕), corona; *anat.* areola; **~da·me** *f* lady-in-waiting; **~dich·ter** *m in GB*: Poet Laureate; **2fä·hig** *adj.* socially acceptable; *n.s.* presentable

Hof·fart ['hɔfart] *f* (-; *no pl.*) haughtiness, pride

hof·fen ['hɔfən] **I.** *v/t. and v/i.* (h) hope (***auf*** *acc.* for); **~ *auf*** *acc. a.* set (*or* pin) one's hopes on; **~ *wir das Beste*** let's hope for the best; ***ich hoffe es*** (***sehr***) I (sincerely *or* certainly) hope so; ***das will ich doch ~!*** he'd better; ***ich hoffe nicht*** I hope not; ***verzweifelt ~*** hope against hope; **II. 2** *n* (-s) hoping, hope

hof·fent·lich ['hɔfəntlɪç] *adv.* hopefully, I hope ...; I hope so, let's hope so; **~ *nicht*** I hope not, let's hope not

Hoff·nung ['hɔfnʊŋ] *f* (-; -en) hope (***auf*** *acc.* for, of); expectation; prospect; ***in der ~ zu*** *inf.* in the hope of *ger.*, hoping to *inf.*; ***die ~ verlieren*** lose hope; ***die ~ aufgeben*** give up (*or* abandon) hope; ***man darf die ~ nie aufgeben*** *a.* never say die; ***j-m ~(en) machen, in j-m ~(en) erwecken*** raise s.o.'s hopes; ***sich ~en machen*** be hopeful, be hoping; ***j-m ~ machen, daß*** lead s.o. to believe (*or* expect) that; ***j-m ~en auf et. machen*** hold out the prospect of s.th. to s.o.; ***mach dir keine allzu großen ~en*** don't be too hopeful, don't expect too much; ***ich habe keine große ~, daß*** I don't hold out much hope that (*or of ger.*); ***s-e ~en setzen auf*** *acc.* pin one's hopes on, place one's hopes in, bank on; ***es besteht noch ~*** there's still hope, there's hope yet; ***ist*** (*or* ***besteht***) ***noch ~?*** is there any hope (left)?; ***er*** (***es***) ***ist unsere letzte ~*** he's (it's) our last hope; ***er ist unsere große ~*** we're pinning all our hopes on him, he's our great hope

'**hoff·nungs·los** *adj.* hopeless (*a.* F *fig.*); desperate; F ***ein ~er Fall*** a hopeless case; '**Hoff·nungs·lo·sig·keit** *f* (-; *no pl.*) hopelessness; despair

'**Hoff·nungs|schim·mer** *m* glimmer of hope; **~trä·ger** *m* F *the* great white hope; **2voll** *adj.* hopeful; promising

'**hof·hal·ten** *v/i.* (*irr.*, *sep.*, h, → ***halten***) hold court

ho·fie·ren [ho'fiːrən] *v/t.* (h): ***j-n ~*** court s.o.'s favo(u)r

hö·fisch ['høːfɪʃ] *adj.* courtly

'**Hof|ka,pel·le** *f* **1.** court chapel; chapel royal; **2.** ♪ court orchestra; **~le·ben** *n* life at court; **~leu·te** *pl.* courtiers

höf·lich ['høːflɪç] **I.** *adj.* polite, courteous (***zu*** *dat.* to[wards]); **~, *aber bestimmt*** polite but firm; **II.** *adv.* politely *etc.*; ***wir bitten Sie ~ zu*** *inf.* may we ask you to *inf.* (*or* request that you ...); **~, *aber bestimmt*** politely but firmly; '**Höf·lich·keit** *f* (-; -en) **1.** *no pl.* politeness, courtesy; *iro.* ***darüber schweigt des Sängers ~*** a) we won't say any more about that, b) that will have to remain a mystery; **2.** compliment

'**Höf·lich·keits|be·such** *m* courtesy call; **~be·zei·gung** *f* mark of respect; **~flos·kel** *f*, **~for·mel** *f* polite phrase; *letter*: complimentary close

'**Hof·lie·fe,rant** *m* purveyor to the court (*in GB*: to His *or* Her Majesty)

Höf·ling ['høːflɪŋ] *m* (-s; -e) courtier

'**Hof|ma·ler** *m* court painter; **~narr** *m* court jester; **~pre·di·ger** *m* court chaplain; **~rat** *m in GB*: Privy Councillor; *Austrian* Hofrat; **~staat** *m* (-s; *no pl.*) royal (*or* princely) household (*or* retinue); **~ze·re·mo·ni,ell** *n* court etiquette

HO-Ge·schäft [ha'oː-] *n hist. DDR*: state-owned store; *pl. coll.* state-owned store chain *sg.*

ho·he(r, -s) ['hoːhə, 'hoːhɐ, 'hoːhəs] *adj.* → ***hoch***

Hö·he ['høːhə] *f* (-; -n) a) height; *ast.*, *geogr.*, ✈ altitude, b) hill, elevation, c) summit, top, *fig.* height, peak, d) *no pl. fig.* level; extent; importance, magnitude, e) ♪ pitch; *phys.* intensity, f) *fig.* size, amount *of payment etc.*; severity *of a sentence etc.*; ***in e-r ~ von*** *dat.* ... at a height (✈ an altitude) of ...; ***e-e Summe in ~ von*** *dat.* ... a sum (to the amount, F to the tune) of ...; ***ein Zuwachs in ~ von*** *dat.* ... an increase at the rate of ...; ***e-e Strafe bis zu e-r ~ von*** *dat.* ... a maximum of ...; ***auf der ~ von*** *dat.* on the same latitude as *London*, ⚓ off *Dover*; ***auf gleicher ~ mit*** *dat.* on a level with; ***aus der ~*** from above; ***in die ~*** up, upwards; ***in die ~ gehen*** go up, increase; ***in die ~ treiben*** force up; ***trotz der ~ s-s Alters*** despite his (advanced *or* great) age *or* advanced years; *fig.* ***die ~n und Tiefen des Lebens*** the ups and downs of life; ***auf der ~ s-s Ruhms*** *etc.* at the height (*or* peak) of his fame *etc.*; ***auf der ~ sein*** a) be in good form, b) be up to date; ***sich nicht ganz auf der ~ fühlen*** not to feel quite up to the mark; ***e-e gewaltige ~ erreichen*** reach great heights; F ***in die ~ gehen*** F hit the roof; F ***das ist ja wohl die ~!*** F that really is the limit!

Ho·heit ['hoːhaɪt] *f* (-; -en) **1.** *no pl. pol.* sovereignty; **2.** His *etc.* Highness; Your Highness; ***Seine*** (***Ihre***) ***Königliche ~*** His (Her) Royal Highness; **3.** *no pl. fig.* a) *s.o.'s* dignity, b) grandeur, majesty; '**ho·heit·lich** *adj.* sovereign

'**Ho·heits|akt** *m pol.* sovereign act; **~be·reich** *m* **1.** jurisdiction (*of the state etc.*); **2.** → **~ge·biet** *n* (sovereign) territory; ***deutsches ~*** German territory; **~ge·walt** *f* sovereignty; **~ge·wäs·ser** *pl.* territorial waters; **~recht** *n* sovereign right; **2voll** *adj.* majestic(ally *adv.*); imperious; **~zei·chen** *n* national emblem

'**Ho·he·lied** *n* (-[e]s; *no pl.*) **1.** *bibl.* Song of Solomon, Song of Songs; **2.** *fig.* hymn (*gen.* in praise of)

'**Hö·hen|angst** ['høːən-] *f* (-; *no pl.*) fear of heights; **~flos·se** *f* ✈ stabilizer; **~flug** *m* high-altitude flight; *fig.* ***geistiger ~*** flight of fancy; ***der ~ des Dollars*** the soaring dollar; **~ka,bi·ne** *f* pressurized cabin; **~kar·te** *f* relief map; **~kli·ma** *n* mountain climate; **~krank·heit** *f* altitude sickness; **~kur·ort** *m* high-altitude health resort; **~la·ge** *f* altitude; ***in den ~n*** at higher altitudes; **~leit·werk** *n* ✈ horizontal tail; **~luft** *f* (-; *no pl.*) mountain air; **~mes·ser** *m* altimeter; **~mes·sung** *f* measurement of altitude; **~rausch** *m* high-altitude euphoria; **~reg·ler** *m radio etc.*: treble control; **~re,kord** *m* altitude record; **~ru·der** *n* ✈ elevator; **~schrei·ber** *m* altigraph; **~son·ne** *f* (-; -n) **1.** *no pl.* mountain sun; **2.** sun-ray lamp; **~strah·lung** *f* cosmic radiation; **~,un·ter·schied** *m* difference in altitude; **~ver·lust** *m* ✈ loss of altitude; **2ver·stell·bar** *adj.* height-adjustable; **~wind** *m* upper wind; **~zug** *m* ridge

'**Ho·he·prie·ster** *m* high priest

'**Hö·he·punkt** *m* climax (*a. sexually*); *fig. a.* highlight *of a party etc.*; height *of* (*one's*) *power*; critical stage; high-water mark *of s.o.'s career etc.*; ***auf dem ~*** *gen.* at the height of; ***s-n ~ erreichen*** culminate (***in*** *dat.* in), climax (in), ✝ *etc.* peak, reach its (*or* their) peak

hö·her ['høːɐ] **I.** *adj.* higher; **~*e Bildung*** higher education; **~*es Dienstalter*** seniority; **~*e Instanz*** ⚖ higher court, *adm.* higher authority; **~*e Mathematik*** higher mathematics (*sg.*); → ***Gewalt, Schule;*** **II.** *adv.* higher, more highly; higher up; ***immer ~*** higher and higher; **~ *bewerten*** rate higher (*or* more highly); **~be·steu·ert** *adj.* more heavily taxed; **~be·zahlt** *adj.* better (*or* more highly) paid

Hö·he·re ['høːərə] *fig. n* (-n; *no pl.*): ***das ~*** higher things

hö·her|ent·wickelt ['høːɐ-] *adj.* more highly developed; **~ge·le·gen** *adj.* higher, *pred. a.* situated higher (*or* further) up; **~ge·stellt** *adj.* higher(-ranking); **~lie·gend** *adj.* → ***höhergelegen;*** **~qua·li·fi,ziert** *adj.* more highly qualified; **~schrau·ben** F *v/t.* (*sep.*, h) push up *prices etc.*; step up *demands etc.*; **~ste·hend** *adj.* higher(-ranking); *biol.* more highly developed; **~stu·fen** *v/t.* (*sep.*, h) upgrade

Hö·her·ver·si·che·rung ['høːɐ-] *f* increased insurance

hohl [hoːl] *adj.* hollow (*a. tooth*); sunken *a. eyes, cheeks*; empty *nut*; cupped *hand*; *opt.* concave; *fig.* hollow, empty; ***e-e ~e Hand machen*** cup one's hand; ***et. in der ~en Hand halten*** hold s.th. cupped in one's hand (*or* in the hollow of one's hand); F *fig.* ***e-n ~en Kopf haben*** F have nothing but sawdust in one's head; F ***das ist was für den ~en Zahn*** that's not enough to keep a sparrow alive

'**hohl·äu·gig** [-ɔʏɡɪç] *adj.* hollow-eyed

'**Hohl·block(stein)** *m* hollow block

'**hohl·brü·stig** [-brʏstɪç] *adj.* pigeon-chested

Höh·le ['høːlə] *f* (-; -n) a) cave, grotto, b) hollow, c) *zo.* den, lair (*both a. fig.*), burrow, d) *anat.* cavity; (*eye*) socket, e) F *contp.* F hole, hovel; *fig.* ***sich in die ~ des Löwen wagen*** venture into the lion's den; F *fig.* ***sich in s-e ~ verkriechen*** retreat into one's den

'**Hohl·ei·sen** *n* gouge; spoon chisel

'**Höh·len|be·woh·ner** *m* caveman, cave-dweller, troglodyte; **~for·scher** *m* cave explorer, spel(a)eologist; potholer; **~for·schung** *f* spel(a)eology; **~fund** *m* cave find; **~kun·de** *f* spel(a)eology; **~ma·le,rei** *f* cave painting; **~mensch** *m* caveman; **~zeich·nung** *f* cave drawing

'**hohl|er·ha·ben** *adj. phys.* concavo-convex; **~ge·schlif·fen** *adj.* concave; **2glas** *n* hollow glass(ware)

'**Hohl·heit** *f* (-; *no pl.*) hollowness; *fig. a.* emptiness

'**hohl·klin·gend** *adj.* hollow-sounding

'**Hohl·kopf** F *m contp.* F numskull; '**hohl·köp·fig** [-kœpfɪç] *adj.* empty-headed

'**Hohl|kör·per** *m* hollow body; **~kreuz** *n* ⚕ hollow back; **~ku·gel** *f* hollow sphere;

~maß *n* measure of capacity; dry measure; **~mei·ßel** *m* gouge; **~na·del** *f* ⚕ cannula; **~raum** *m* hollow (space), *a. anat.*, ⚕, *metall.* cavity; **~raum·ver·sie·ge·lung** *f mot.* vacuum sealing; **~saum** *m* hemstitch
'hohl·schlei·fen *v/t.* (h) grind *s.th.* hollow; **'Hohl·schliff** *m* hollow grinding
'Hohl|spie·gel *m* concave mirror; **~tier** *n* zoophyte, *pl.* coelenterata
Höh·lung ['hø:lʊŋ] *f* (-; -en) hollow, *a. anat.* cavity
'hohl·wan·gig [-vaŋɪç] *adj.* hollow-cheeked
'Hohl|weg *m* hollow; ravine, gorge; narrow pass; **~zie·gel** *m* hollow brick; hollow tile
Hohn [ho:n] *m* (-[e]s; *no pl.*) scorn, disdain; mockery, derision, scoffing, sneering; sarcasm; ***der reinste ~*** sheer mockery; ***zum ~(e)*** *gen.* in defiance of; ***ein ~ sein auf*** *acc.* make a mockery of *s.th.*; ***nur ~ und Spott ernten*** be(come) a laughing stock
höh·nen ['hø:nən] *v/i.* (h) sneer, mock, scoff (*all **über** acc.* at)
'Hohn·ge·läch·ter *n* derisive laughter
höh·nisch ['hø:nɪʃ] *adj.* disdainful; sneering, mocking, derisive; gloating; ***~es Lächeln*** sneer
'hohn·lä·cheln I. *v/i.* (h) sneer (***über*** *acc.* at); **II. 2** *n* (-s) sneer; **'hohn·lä·chelnd I.** *adj.* sneering; **II.** *adv. a.* with a sneer
'hohn·la·chen I. *v/i.* (h) laugh derisively (***über*** *acc.* at *s.o.*, about *s.th.*); **II. 2** *n* (-s) derisive laughter
'hohn·spre·chen *v/i.* (*irr.*, *sep.*, h, → ***sprechen***) make a mockery (*dat.* of)
Ho·kus·po·kus [ho:kʊs'po:kʊs] *m* (-; *no pl.*) **1.** abracadabra; **2.** mumbo-jumbo; **3.** eyewash; **4.** nonsense
hoi [hɔʏ] *int.* hey!
hold [hɔlt] **I.** *adj.* **1.** *poet.* lovely, sweet, fair; **2.** ***j-m*** (***e-r Sache***) ***~ sein*** be well-disposed towards s.o. (s.th.); ***das Glück war ihm ~*** fortune smiled upon him, he was in luck; **II.** *adv.*: ***~ lächeln*** *etc.* smile *etc.* sweetly
Hol'ding·ge·sell·schaft ['ho:ldɪŋ-] *f* † holding company
ho·len ['ho:lən] *v/t.* (h) (go and) get, fetch; go for; call for, pick up; *fig.* (*a.* ***sich ~***) get, win, take *first prize etc.*; ***~ lassen*** send for, call *s.o.*; ***j-n ans Telefon ~*** get s.o. (to come) to the phone; ***j-n aus dem Bett ~*** get s.o. out of bed, wake s.o. up; ***sich et. ~*** get (F *fig.* catch) s.th.; ***sich bei j-m Rat ~*** ask s.o.'s advice; F ***hier ist nichts zu ~*** there's nothing going here; → ***Atem, Luft***
Ho·lis·mus [ho'lɪsmʊs] *m* (-; *no pl.*) holism; **ho·li·stisch** [ho'lɪstɪʃ] *adj.* holistic(ally *adv.*)
Hol·län·der ['hɔlɛndɐ] *m* (-s; -) **1.** Dutchman; ***die ~*** the Dutch; **2.** Dutch cheese; **Hol·län·de·rin** ['hɔlɛndərɪn] *f* (-; -nen) Dutchwoman; **hol·län·disch** ['hɔlɛndɪʃ] *adj.*, **'Hol·län·disch** *n* (-en) *ling.* Dutch
Hol·land·rad ['hɔlant-] *n* (heavy-duty) town bike
Höl·le ['hœlə] *f* (-; *no pl.*) hell; ***in der ~*** in hell; ***in die ~ kommen*** go to (*or* end up in) hell; *fig.* ***die ~ auf Erden*** hell on earth; ***j-m die ~ heiß machen*** a) put the fear of death into s.o., b) give s.o. a hard time, make things unpleasant for s.o.; ***j-m die ~ heiß machen, daß er et. tut*** keep on at s.o. to do s.th., put s.o. under pressure to do s.th.; ***j-m das Leben zur ~ machen*** make life hell for s.o.; ***die ~ war los*** it was sheer pandemonium; F ***zur ~ damit!*** F to hell with it
'Höl·len|angst F *f*: ***e-e ~ haben*** F be scared stiff; **~fahrt** *f eccl.* Christ's Descent into Hell; **~feu·er** *n* hellfire; **~gestank** F *m* diabolical smell; **~hit·ze** F *f*: ***es war e-e ~*** the heat was unbearable, *sl.* it was hot as hell; **~lärm** F *m* F terrible racket, almighty din; **~qua·len** F *pl.*: ***~ ausstehen*** go through hell; **~tem·po** F *n*: ***in e-m ~*** at breakneck speed
höl·lisch ['hœlɪʃ] **I.** *adj.* devilish; F *fig.* dreadful, F hellish; ***e-e ~e Arbeit*** a hellish job; **II.** F *fig. adv.*: ***~ schwer*** F hellishly difficult; ***es tut ~ weh*** *sl.* it hurts like hell; ***du mußt ~ aufpassen*** you've really got to watch out
Hol·ly·wood·schau·kel ['hɔliwʊd-] *f* swing seat
Ho·lo·caust ['ho:lokaʊst] *m* (-[s]; -s): (***atomarer ~*** nuclear) holocaust
Ho·lo·gramm [holo'gram] *n* (-s; -e) hologram; **Ho·lo·gra·phie** [hologra'fi:] *f* (-; -n) holography; **ho·lo·gra·phisch** [holo'gra:fɪʃ] *adj.* holographic(ally *adv.*)
hol·pe·rig ['hɔlpərɪç] → ***holprig***; **hol·pern** ['hɔlpɐn] *v/i.* (sn) bump (along); *fig.* stumble (along); *verse etc.*: be clumsy; **Hol·per·schwel·le** ['hɔlpɐ-] *f mot.* sleeping policeman; **holp·rig** ['hɔlprɪç] **I.** *adj.* rough; *a.* bumpy *path etc.*; *fig.* clumsy *verse etc.*; ***sie spricht ein ~es Englisch*** her English is very shaky; **II.** *adv.* a) haltingly, b) clumsily; ***et. ~ vorlesen*** (*or* ***vortragen***) stumble through s.th.
hol·ter·die·pol·ter [hɔltɐdi'pɔltɐ] *adv.* helter-skelter
Ho·lun·der [ho'lʊndɐ] *m* (-s; *no pl.*) elder; **~bee·re** *f* elderberry; **~strauch** *m* elder
Holz [hɔlts] *n* (-es; Hölzer ['hœltsɐ]) a) wood, b) timber; ***aus ~*** made of wood, wooden; F ***ich bin doch nicht aus ~*** I've got feelings too, you know; *fig.* ***sie sind*** (***er ist***) ***aus demselben ~ geschnitzt*** they're two of a kind (he's a chip off the old block); ***aus anderem ~ geschnitzt sein*** be made of different stuff; ***aus grobem ~ geschnitzt*** rough and insensitive; F *fig.* ***~ sägen*** F saw wood; F ***wie ein Stück ~ dastehen*** F stand there (*or* around) like a lemon; F ***~ vor der Hütte haben*** F be well-stacked; **~ap·fel** *m* crab apple; **~ar·beit** *f* **1.** woodwork; **2.** piece of woodwork; wood carving, wooden figure; **~art** *f* (kind of) wood; **~asche** *f* wood ashes *pl.*; **~au·ge** *n*: F ***~, sei wachsam!*** F keep your eyes peeled; **~bal·ken** *m* wooden beam; **~bank** *f* (-; ⸚e) wooden bench; **~ba·racke** *f* wooden hut; **~bau** *m* (-[e]s; -ten) **1.** wooden structure; **2.** *no pl.* → **~bau·wei·se** *f* timber construction; **~bein** *n* wooden leg; **~bir·ne** *f* wild pear; **~blä·ser** *m* ♪ woodwind player; ***die ~*** the woodwind (*pl.*); **~blas·in·stru·ment** *n* woodwind (instrument); **~block** *m* **1.** block of wood; **2.** ♪ woodblock; **~bock** *m* **1.** *zo.* (wood) tick; **2.** ⚙ sawhorse, *Am. a.* sawbuck; **~bo·den** *m* wooden floor; **~boh·rer** *m* wood drill; gimlet; **~brett** *n* wooden board (*or* plank); **~decke** *f* wooden ceiling; **~druck** *m* (-[e]s; -e) **1.** *no pl.* woodblock printing; **2.** woodblock print
hol·zen ['hɔltsən] F *v/i.* (h) *soccer*: kick everything above the grass
höl·zern ['hœltsɐn] *adj.* wooden (*a. fig. movement, style etc.*); *fig.* awkward
'Holz·fäl·ler [-fɛlɐ] *m* (-s; -) woodcutter, *esp. Am.* lumberjack
'Holz·fa·ser *f* wood fib|re (*Am.* -er); grain; **~plat·te** *f* wood fibreboard (*Am.* fiberboard)
'Holz|fäu·le *f* dry rot; **~fi·gur** *f* wood carving, wooden figure; **~floß** *n* (wooden) raft; **2frei** *adj.* wood-free *paper*; **~fuß·bo·den** *m* wooden floor; **~ge·rüst** *n* wooden scaffolding; **2ge·tä·felt** *adj.* wood-panel(l)ed, wainscot(t)ed; **~ge·wächs** *n* woody plant; **~hacken** *n* wood chopping, chopping wood; **~hacker** *m* **1.** woodchopper; **2.** *soccer*: butcher
'holz·hal·tig [-haltɪç] *adj.* ligneous; woody *paper*
'Holz·ham·mer *m* mallet; F *in cpds.* sledge-hammer *method, diplomacy etc.*
'Holz|han·del *m* wood (*or* timber) trade; **~haus** *n* wooden house; **~hüt·te** *f* wooden hut
hol·zig ['hɔltsɪç] *adj.* woody; *gastr.* stringy
'Holz|in·du·strie *f* wood (*or* timber) industry; **~ki·ste** *f* wooden box (*or* crate); **~klotz** *m* **1.** block of wood; **2.** → **~klötz·chen** *n* wooden brick
'Holz·koh·le *f* charcoal; **'Holz·koh·len·grill** *m* charcoal grill
'Holz|kon·struk·ti·on *f* **1.** wood (*or* timber) construction; **2.** wooden structure; **~kopf** F *m* F blockhead; **~la·ger** *n* timber yard; **~leim** *m* wood glue; **~lei·ste** *f* strip (*or* thin piece) of wood; **~löf·fel** *m* wooden spoon; **~ma·se·rung** *f* wood grain, grain of the wood; **~na·gel** *m* wooden nail (*or* peg); **~ofen** *m* wood-burning stove; **~pan·tof·feln** *pl.* clogs; **~pa·pier** *n* wood(-pulp) paper; **~pla·stik** *f* wooden figure (*or* statue); **~plat·te** *f* wooden board; **~pup·pe** *f* wooden doll; **~rah·men** *m* wooden frame; **~schäd·ling** *m* wood pest; **~scha·le** *f* wooden bowl; **~scheit** *n* piece of wood; **~schliff** *m* (mechanical) wood pulp; **~schnitt** *m* woodcut; **~schnit·zer** *m* wood carver; **~schnit·ze·rei** *f* wood carving; **~schrau·be** *f* wood screw; **~schuh** *m* clog; **~schup·pen** *m* **1.** wooden shed; **2.** woodshed; **~schutz·mit·tel** *n* wood preserver; **~schwamm** *m* dry rot; **~sor·te** *f* (kind of) wood; **~spä·ne** *pl.* wood shavings; **~span·plat·te** *f* (wood) chipboard; **~spi·ri·tus** *m* wood alcohol; **~split·ter** *m* splinter (of wood); **~sta·pel** *m* pile of wood; **~stich** *m* wood engraving; **~stift** *m* wooden peg; **~stock** *m* woodblock; **~tä·fe·lung** *f* wood panel(l)ing, wainscot(t)ing; **~teer** *m* wood tar; **~tel·ler** *m* wooden plate; **~trep·pe** *f* wooden staircase; **~tür** *f* wooden door; **2ver·ar·bei·tend** *adj.*: ***~e Industrie*** wood-processing industry; **~ver·ar·bei·tung** *f* **1.** woodworking; **2.** → **~ver·ede·lung** *f* wood processing; **~ver·klei·dung** *f* wood panel(l)ing, wainscot(t)ing; **~ver·scha·lung** *f* timber facing, boarding; **~ver·schlag** *m* wooden partition; **~wa·re** *f* wooden article(s *pl.*); **~weg** *m*: *fig.* ***auf dem ~ sein*** a) be barking up the wrong tree, b) be very much mistaken; **~wirt·schaft** *f* wood (*or* timber) industry; **~wol·le** *f* excelsior; **~wurm** *m* woodworm; **~zaun** *m* wooden fence; hoarding; **~zell·stoff** *m* wood cellulose
Hom·burg ['hɔmbʊrk] *m* (-s; -s) Homburg (hat)

ho·me·risch [ho'me:rɪʃ] *adj.* Homeric; **~es Gelächter** Homeric laughter
Ho·mi·le·tik [homi'le:tɪk] *f* (-; *no pl.*) homiletics *pl.*
Ho·mi·ni·de [homi'ni:də] *m* (-n; -n) *biol.* hominid
Ho·mo ['ho:mo] F *m* (-s; -s) F gay, *contp.* queer
'ho·mo... *in cpds.* homo
Ho·mo·ero·tik [-e'ro:tɪk] *f* (-; *no pl.*) homoeroticism; **ho·mo·ero·tisch** [-e'ro:tɪʃ] *adj.* homoerotic
ho·mo·gen [homo'ge:n] *adj.* homogeneous; **ho·mo·ge·ni·sie·ren** [homogeni'zi:rən] *v/t.* (h) homogenize; **Ho·mo·ge·ni·tät** [homogeni'tɛ:t] *f* (-; *no pl.*) homogeneity
Ho·mo·graph ['ho:mogra:f] *n* (-s; -e) homograph
Ho·mo·nym [homo'ny:m] *n* (-s; -e) *ling.* homonym
Ho·möo·path [homøo'pa:t] *m* (-en; -en) ⚕ hom(o)eopath; **Ho·möo·pa·thie** [homøopa'ti:] *f* (-; *no pl.*) hom(o)eopathy; **ho·möo·pa·thisch** [homøo'pa:tɪʃ] *adj.* hom(o)eopathic(ally *adv.*)
Ho·mo·phon [homo'fo:n] *n* (-s; -e) *ling.* homophone
Ho·mo·se·xua·li'tät *f* homosexuality; **ho·mo·se·xu'ell** *adj.* homosexual; **Ho·mo·se·xu'el·le** *m,f* (-n; -n) homosexual
Ho·nig ['ho:nɪç] *m* (-s; *no pl.*) honey; F *fig.* ***j-m ~ um den Bart schmieren*** F butter s.o. up; **~bie·ne** *f* honey bee; **2far·ben, 2gelb** *adj.* honey-colo(u)red; **~klee** *m* sweet clover; **~ku·chen** *m* honey cake; **~me,lo·ne** *f* sugar (*or* honeydew) melon; **~schlecken** *fig. n*: ***das ist kein ~*** it's no bed of roses; **~schleu·der** *f* honey extractor; **2süß** *adj.* honey-sweet, (*a. adv.*) as sweet as honey; **~wa·be** *f* honeycomb; **~wein** *m* mead
Ho·no·rar [hono'ra:ɐ] *n* (-s; -e [-'ra:rə]) fee; royalties *pl.*; **2frei** *adj.* free of charge; **~kon·sul** *m* honorary consul; **~pro,fes·sor** *m* honorary professor
Ho·no·ra·tio·ren [honora'tsio:rən] *pl.* local dignitaries
ho·no·rie·ren [hono'ri:rən] *v/t.* (h) pay for; pay, remunerate *s.o.* (**für** *acc.* for); ✝ hono(u)r; *fig.* acknowledge, reward; *fig.* ***es wird überhaupt nicht honoriert*** you get no credit (*or* thanks) for it; **Ho·no·rie·rung** [hono'ri:rʊŋ] *f* (-; -en) remuneration, payment; *fig.* acknowledg(e)ment, reward
Hop·fen ['hɔpfən] *m* (-s; *no pl.*) ♣ hop; ✓ *coll.* hops *pl.*; F *fig.* ***an ihm ist ~ und Malz verloren*** F he's a dead loss; **~anbau** *m* hop growing; **~bau·er** *m* hop farmer; **~bier** *n* hopped beer; **~ern·te** *f* hop picking; hop-picking time (*or* season); **~klee** *m* hop clover; **~stan·ge** *f* **1.** hop pole; **2.** F beanpole
hopp [hɔp] *int.* jump!; quick!; ***nun mal ~!*** F get a move on!, chop, chop!; **~, *raus aus dem Bett!*** come on, up you get!
hop·peln ['hɔpəln] *v/i.* (sn) hop; *vehicle etc.*: jolt (along), bump along
hopp·hopp [hɔp'hɔp] **I.** *int.* chop, chop!; **II.** *adv.*: ***bei ihr muß alles ~ gehen*** she wants everything done in double-quick time
hopp·la ['hɔpla] *int.* (wh)oops(-a-daisy)!; F **~, *jetzt komm' ich!*** F look out, here I come!; **hopp·la'hopp** F *adv.* slapdash; chop-chop; ***so ~ geht das nicht*** you can't rush these things, it takes time
hops [hɔps] F *adj.*: ***~ sein* → *hinsein***
hop·sa ['hɔpsa], **hop·sas·sa** ['hɔpsasa] *int.* (wh)oops(-a-daisy)!
hop·sen ['hɔpsən] F *v/i.* (sn) hop, skip, hop and skip; **Hop·ser** ['hɔpsɐ] F *m* (-s; -) hop; ***e-n ~ machen*** give a little hop; **Hop·se·rei** [hɔpsə'raɪ] F *f* (-; -en) jumping around
'hops|ge·hen F *v/i.* (*irr.*, *sep.*, sn, → ***gehen***) a) F snuff it, pop one's clogs, b) get lost; *money etc.*: F go down the drain, c) F get nabbed; **~neh·men** F *v/t.* (*irr.*, *sep.*, h, → ***nehmen***) F nab *a thief etc.*
Hör·ap·pa,rat ['hø:ɐ-] *m* hearing aid
hör·bar ['hø:ɐba:ɐ] *adj.* audible; ***sich ~ machen*** make o.s. heard; **'Hör·bar·keit** *f* (-; *no pl.*) audibility
hör·be·hin·dert ['hø:ɐ-] *adj.* partially deaf; **'Hör·be·hin·de·rung** *f* impaired hearing; partial deafness
Hör|be·reich ['hø:ɐ-] *m* auditory range; *radio*: broadcasting range; **~bib·lio,thek** *f* audio library; **~bild** *n* radio feature; **~buch** *n* talking book
hor·chen ['hɔrçən] *v/i.* (h) listen (***auf*** *acc.* to); eavesdrop
Hor·de[1] ['hɔrdə] *f* (-; -n) **1.** *contp.* horde, mob; **2.** (wandering) tribe
'Hor·de[2] *f* (-; -n) rack
'hor·den·wei·se *adv.* in hordes
hö·ren ['hø:rən] **I.** *v/t. and v/i.* (h) a) hear, b) overhear, c) listen; ***hör mal!*** listen; ***Radio ~*** listen to the radio; ***~ an*** *dat.* be able to tell by; ***~ auf*** *acc.* listen to; ***auf den Namen ... ~*** answer to the name of ...; ***gut ~*** have good ears (*or* hearing); ***schwer*** (*or* ***schlecht***) ***~*** be slightly deaf, be hard of hearing; ***ich hör' dich so schlecht*** I can't hear you very well; ***du hörst wohl schlecht?*** are you (going) deaf?; ***bei Professor B. Geschichte ~*** go to Professor B's history lectures; ***~ von*** *dat.* hear of (*or* about); ***ich hab's von ihr gehört*** I heard it from her, she told me; ***ich habe von ihm gehört*** a) I've heard of him, b) I've heard from him; ***ich habe schon viel von ihm gehört*** I've heard a lot about him; ***ich habe gehört, daß*** they say (that); ***ich will davon nichts ~*** I don't want to hear about it; ***das ist das erste, was ich höre*** that's the first I've heard of it; ***soviel ich gehört habe*** as far as I've heard; ***nach allem, was ich höre*** from what I've heard; ***was muß ich da ~?*** what's this you're telling me?; F ***ich glaube, ich höre nicht recht*** did I hear (you) right?, F say that again; ***er hat nichts von sich ~ lassen*** he hasn't written (*or* phoned), we *etc.* haven't heard from him at all; ***man hörte nie mehr etwas von ihm*** he was never heard of again; ***laßt mal von euch ~*** keep in touch; ***ich lasse von mir ~*** I'll let you know; ***Sie werden noch von mir ~!*** you haven't heard the last of this!; ***das läßt sich ~*** that doesn't sound too bad at all; ***er hört sich gerne reden*** he likes the sound of his own voice; ***man höre und staune*** would you believe it; ***wer nicht ~ will, muß fühlen*** that's what you get for not listening; **II.** 2 *n* (-s): ***beim ~ des Vortrags*** while listening to the lecture; ***ihm verging ~ und Sehen*** (***dabei***) F he almost passed out; ***..., daß dir ~ und Sehen vergeht*** ... that you'll wish you were never born
'Hö·ren·sa·gen *n*: ***vom ~*** by hearsay
Hö·rer ['hø:rɐ] *m* (-s; -) **1.** (*a. radio*) listener; *univ.* student; ***liebe Hörerinnen und ~!*** a) hello everybody, hello to our listeners everywhere, b) dear listeners; **2.** *teleph.* receiver; ***den ~ abheben*** pick up (*or* answer) the phone; ***den ~ auflegen*** put the phone down; **~brief** *m* letter (from a listener); *pl.* listeners' letters
Hö·re·rin ['hø:rərɪn] *f* (-; -nen) → ***Hörer***; **'Hö·rer·kreis** *m*, **'Hö·rer·schaft** *f* (-; *no pl.*) listeners *pl.*, audience
'Hö·rer·wunsch *m* request (from a listener); *pl.* (listeners') requests
Hör|fä·hig·keit ['hø:ɐ-] *f* (-; *no pl.*) hearing ability; **~feh·ler** *m* **1.** misunderstanding; **2.** ⚕ hearing defect; impaired hearing; **~fre,quenz** *f* audio frequency; **~funk** *m* sound broadcasting, radio; **~ge·rät** *n* hearing (*or* deaf) aid; **2ge·schä·digt** *adj.* hard of hearing, partially deaf; **~hil·fe** *f* → ***Hörgerät***
hö·rig ['hø:rɪç] *adj.* (*a. sexually*) dependent (*dat.* on); ***j-m ~ sein*** be in bondage to s.o.; **'Hö·rig·keit** *f* (-; *no pl.*) (total) dependence (***gegenüber*** *dat.* on), *a. hist.* bondage (to)
Ho·ri·zont [hori'tsɔnt] *m* (-[e]s; -e) horizon (*a. geol. and fig.*); ***am ~*** on the horizon; ***die Sonne sank unter den ~*** the sun sank (*or* disappeared) behind the horizon; *fig.* ***enger*** (*or* ***beschränkter***) ***~*** narrow horizons; ***großer*** (*or* ***weiter***) ***~*** broad view (*or* horizon); ***s-n ~ erweitern*** broaden one's horizons; ***das erweitert den ~*** it broadens your horizons (*or* the mind); ***das geht über m-n ~*** that's beyond me
ho·ri·zon·tal [horitsɔn'ta:l] *adj.* horizontal; F ***das ~e Gewerbe*** F the oldest profession in the world; **Ho·ri·zon·ta·le** [horitsɔn'ta:lə] *f* (-; -n) horizontal; F ***sich in die ~ begeben*** F *iro.* (go and) recline
Ho·ri·zon'tal|kon,zern *m* ✝ horizontal group; **~la·ge** *f* horizontal position
Hor·mon [hɔr'mo:n] *n* (-s; -e) hormone; **hor·mo·nal** [hɔrmo'na:l] *adj.* hormonal
Hor'mon|be·hand·lung *f* hormonal treatment; course of hormone tablets (*or* injections); **~drü·se** *f* hormone gland
hor·mo·nell [hɔrmo'nɛl] **I.** *adj.* hormonal; hormone ...; **II.** *adv. treat etc.* with hormones
Hor'mon|haus·halt *m* hormone balance; **~man·gel** *m* lack of hormones; **~prä·pa,rat** *n* hormone preparation; **~spie·gel** *m* hormone level; **~sprit·ze** *f* hormone injection, F shot of hormones
Hör·mu·schel ['hø:ɐ-] *f teleph.* earpiece
Horn [hɔrn] *n* (-[e]s; Hörner ['hœrnɐ]) **1.** *zo.* horn (*a. material*); feeler; *fig.* ***die Hörner einziehen*** pull in one's horns; ***j-m Hörner aufsetzen*** cuckold s.o.; ***sich die Hörner abstoßen*** sow one's wild oats; → ***Stier*** 1; **2.** ♪ (French) horn; ⚔ bugle; ***ins ~ stoßen*** blow one's horn; *fig.* ***ins gleiche ~ stoßen*** play the same tune, be of one mind (in the matter), ***mit j-m***: chime in with s.o., go along with s.o. (wholeheartedly); **3.** *mot.* horn
Hörn·ber·ger Schie·ßen ['hɔrnbɛrgɐ] *n*: ***ausgehen wie das ~*** be a complete flop
'Horn|blen·de *f min.* hornblende; **~bril·le** *f*: (***e-e ~*** a pair of) horn-rimmed glasses *pl. or* spectacles *pl.*
Hörn·chen ['hœrnçən] *n* **1.** *gastr.* croissant; **2.** *zo.* squirrel
hör·nern ['hœrnɐn] *adj.* horn ..., made of horn

Hör·nerv ['hø:ɐ-] *m* auditory nerve
'**Horn·haut** *f* **1.** callus(es *pl.*); **2.** *anat.* cornea; **~ent·zün·dung** *f* inflammation of the cornea, keratitis; **~trü·bung** *f* nebula; **~ver·let·zung** *f* injured cornea
hor·nig ['hɔrnɪç] *adj.* horny *skin etc.*
Hor·nis·se [hɔr'nɪsə] *f* (-; -n) hornet; **Hor'nis·sen·nest** *n* hornets' nest
Hor·nist [hɔr'nɪst] *m* (-en; -en) (French) horn player
'**Horn·och·se** F *m* idiot, F clod
Hör·or,gan ['hø:ɐ-] *n* organ of hearing
Ho·ro·skop [horo'sko:p] *n* (-[e]s; -e) horoscope
Hör|pro·be ['hø:ɐ-] *f* audition; test recording; **~prü·fung** *f* ⚕ hearing test
hor·rend [hɔ'rɛnt] *adj.* shocking, ridiculous *price etc.*; ***e-e ~e Dummheit*** sheer lunacy
Hör·rohr ['hø:ɐ-] *n* **1.** ear trumpet; **2.** ⚕ stethoscope
Hor·ror ['hɔro:ɐ] *m* (-s; *no pl.*) **1.** ***e-n ~ haben vor*** *dat.* F have a thing about, be terrified of *s.o. or s.th.*; ***ich habe e-n ~ vor Spinnen*** *etc. a.* I can't stand spiders *etc.*; **2.** ***es ist der reinste ~*** it's excruciating, F it's sheer hell; **~film** *m* horror film (*or* movie); **~ge·schich·te** *f* horror story; **~sze·ne** *f* scene of horror; *film*: horror (*or* horrific) scene; **~vi·deo** *n* video nasty
Hör|saal ['hø:ɐ-] *m* lecture hall, auditorium; **~scha·den** *m* hearing defect (*or* impairment); impaired hearing; **~schär·fe** *f* hearing acuity; **~schwel·le** *f* auditory threshold; **~spiel** *n* radio play
Horst [hɔrst] *m* (-[e]s; -e) **1.** nest; eyrie; **2.** thicket; **3.** ✈ air base
Hör·sturz ['hø:ɐ-] *m* acute hearing loss; sudden deafness
Hort [hɔrt] *m* (-[e]s; -e) **1.** *poet.* a) treasure, b) safe retreat, refuge; **2.** after-school care cent|re (*Am.* -er)
hor·ten ['hɔrtən] *v/t.* (h) hoard; stockpile
Hor·ten·sie [hɔr'tɛnzĭə] *f* (-; -n) ♣ hydrangea
Hör·test ['hø:ɐ-] *m* hearing test; ***e-n ~ machen lassen*** have one's ears tested
Hor·tung ['hɔrtʊŋ] *f* (-; *no pl.*) hoarding; stockpiling
Hör|ver·mö·gen ['hø:ɐ-] *n* (-s; *no pl.*) hearing; **~wei·te** *f*: ***außer*** (***in***) ~ out of (within) earshot
Hös·chen ['hø:sçən] *n* (-s; -) **1.** (***ein ~*** a pair of) panties *pl.*; **2.** (ein ~ a pair of) short trousers *pl.*
Ho·se ['ho:zə] *f* (-; -n): (***e-e ~*** a pair of) trousers (*Am.* pants) *pl.*; ***kurze ~*(*n*)** (pair of) shorts *pl.*; ***in die ~ machen*** a) wet o.s. (*a.* F *fig.*), b) fill (*or* make a mess in) one's pants; F ***die ~n*** (***gestrichen***) ***voll haben*** F be in a blue funk; F ***j-m die ~n strammziehen*** give s.o. a good hiding; F ***die ~n anhaben*** wear the trousers (*Am.* pants); F ***es ist in die ~n gegangen*** a) F it was a flop (*or* washout), b) it didn't work out, F it was a bit of a disaster, c) *joke etc.*: nobody got it, it didn't come over; *sl.* ***tote ~ sein*** a) F be a washout, b) F be a dump
'**Ho·sen|an·zug** *m* trouser (*Am.* pants) suit; **~auf·schlag** *m* turn-up, *Am.* cuff; **~bein** *n* trouser leg; **~bo·den** *m* seat of the *or* one's trousers (*esp. Am.* pants); F *fig.* ***sich auf den ~ setzen*** a) sit down (F and shut up), b) F knuckle under; F ***j-m den ~ versohlen*** F tan s.o.'s hide; **~bü·gel** *m* trouser (*Am.* pants) hanger; **~bund** *m*, **~gurt** *m* waistband; **~latz** *m* flies *pl.*, fly; **~matz** F *m* F little guy; **~rock** *m*: (***ein ~*** a pair of) culottes *pl.*; **~schei·ßer** F *m* F scaredy-pants, scaredy-cat; **~schlitz** *m* flies *pl.*, fly; **~ta·sche** *f* trouser pocket; F *fig.* ***et. wie s-e ~ kennen*** know s.th. like the back of one's hand; **~trä·ger** *m*: (***ein ~*** a pair of) braces (*Am.* suspenders) *pl.*
Hos·pi·tant [hɔspi'tant] *m* (-en; -en) auditor; **hos·pi·tie·ren** [hɔspi'ti:rən] *v/i.* (h) sit in (***bei*** *dat.* on)
Hos·piz [hɔs'pi:ts] *n* (-es; -e) **1.** hospice; **2.** Christian-run hotel
Ho·stess ['hɔstɛs] *f* (-; -en), '**Ho·steß** *f* (-; -ssen) hostess (*a. euphem.*); ✈ air hostess
Ho·stie ['hɔstĭə] *f* (-; -n) *eccl.* host
Ho·tel [ho'tɛl] *n* (-s; -s) hotel; ***~ garni*** bed and breakfast hotel; ***in welchem ~ seid ihr?*** which hotel are you (staying) at?; **~an·ge·stell·te** *m, f* (-n; -n) hotel employee; **~bar** *f* hotel bar; **~be·sit·zer** *m* hotel owner; **~bett** *n* **1.** hotel bed; **2.** ***hier gibt es wenig ~en*** hotel accommodation here is limited; **~di,rek·tor** *m* hotel manager; **~fach** *n* (-[e]s; *no pl.*) hotel business; **~fach·schu·le** *f* school for hotel management; **~füh·rer** *m* hotel guide; **~gast** *m* hotel guest; **~ge·wer·be** *n* hotel trade (*or* industry); **~hal·le** *f* foyer, (hotel) lobby
Ho·te·lier [hote'lĭe:] *m* (-s; -s) hotelier
Ho'tel|ket·te *f* hotel chain; **~koch** *m* hotel chef; **~kü·che** *f* hotel kitchen; **~nach·weis** *m* **1.** hotel information service; **2.** list of hotels; **~pen·si,on** *f* residential hotel, boarding house; **~per·so,nal** *n* hotel staff; **~por·tier** *m* (hotel) doorman; **~- und 'Gast·stät·ten·ge·wer·be** *n* catering trade; **~ver·zeich·nis** *n* list of hotels; **~zim·mer** *n* hotel room
hott [hɔt] *int.* gee!; → ***hü***
hu [hu:] *int.* a) ugh!, b) whew!, c) brrr!, d) boo!
hü [hy:] *int.* gee up!; wo hi!; *fig.* ***~ oder hott!*** make up your mind; ***einmal sagt er ~, einmal hott*** first he says one thing and then he says something completely different
Hub [hu:p] *m* (-[e]s; Hübe ['hy:bə]) ⚙, *mot.* stroke; lift; **~brü·cke** *f* lift bridge
hü·ben ['hy:bən] *adv.* on this side; ***~ und*** (*or* ***wie***) ***drüben*** on either side
'**Hub|kraft** *f*, **~lei·stung** *f* lifting capacity; *mot.* output per unit of displacement; **~raum** *m* cubic capacity; → ***Hubvolumen***
hübsch [hʏpʃ] **I.** *adj.* **1.** pretty; nice-looking *boy*; good-looking, handsome *man*; **2.** *w.s.* nice; **3.** F nice; ***e-e ~e Summe*** F a tidy sum; ***ein ~es Stück Weg*** quite a way; *iro.* ***~e Aussichten*** nice prospects; *iro.* ***e-e ~e Angelegenheit!*** a fine state of affairs; **II.** *adv.* **4.** nicely; **5.** F pretty; **6.** F ***das wirst du ~ sein lassen*** you'll do nothing of the sort; ***sei ~ artig!*** be a good boy (*or* girl); ***immer ~ der Reihe nach!*** one after the other, please
'**Hub·schrau·ber** [-ʃraʊbɐ] *m* (-s; -) helicopter; **~lan·de·platz** *m* heliport; **~pi,lot** *m* helicopter pilot
'**Hub|stap·ler** [-ʃta:plɐ] *m* (-s; -) forklift truck; **~vo,lu·men** *n* piston displacement; **~weg** *m* piston travel
huch [hu:x] *int.* ooh!
Hucke ['hʊkə] (*sep.* -k·k-) F *f*: ***j-m die ~ voll hauen*** give s.o. a good hiding; ***sich die ~ voll saufen*** F get plastered; ***j-m die ~ voll lügen*** F tell s.o. a pack of lies; ***sich die ~ voll lachen*** F kill o.s. (laughing)
hucke·pack ['hʊkəpak] *adv.* piggyback; '**Hucke·pack·ver·kehr** *m* piggyback transport (*or* traffic), piggybacking
Hu·de·lei [hu:də'laɪ] F *f* (-; -en) **1.** *no pl.* sloppiness; **2.** sloppy work; **hu·de·lig** ['hu:dəlɪç] F *adj.* sloppy; **hu·deln** ['hu:dəln] F *v/i.* (h) be sloppy; do a sloppy job; **Hud·ler** ['hu:dlɐ] F *m* (-s; -) sloppy person (*or* worker)
Huf [hu:f] *m* (-[e]s; -e) hoof
'**Huf·ei·sen** *n* horseshoe; **~bo·gen** *m* ⚠ horseshoe arch
'**huf·ei·sen·för·mig** [-fœrmɪç] *adj.* horseshoe ..., horseshoe-shaped
Huf·lat·tich ['hu:flatɪç] *m* (-s; *no pl.*) ♣ coltsfoot
'**Huf|na·gel** *m* horseshoe nail; **~schlag** *m* **1.** hoofbeat; **2.** (horse's) kick; **~schmied** *m* blacksmith; **~spur** *f* hoof mark
Hüft|bein ['hʏft-] *n* hip-bone, 📖 ilium; **~beu·ge** *f* groin
Hüf·te ['hʏftə] *f* (-; -n) *anat.* hip; *zo.* haunch; ***sich in den ~n wiegen*** sway one's hips; ***mit den ~n wackeln*** wiggle one's hips; ***die Arme in die ~n stemmen*** put one's hands on one's hips; ***die Arme*** (***or mit den Armen***) ***in den ~n*** *a.* (with) arms akimbo; ***bis an die ~ reichend → hüfthoch***
Hüft|ge·lenk ['hʏft-] *n* hip joint; **~hal·ter** *m* (-s; -) suspender belt; **2hoch** *adj.* waist-high; waist-deep
'**Huf·tier** *n* hoofed animal
Hüft|kno·chen ['hʏft-] *m* hip-bone; **~lei·den** *n* hip complaint; **~wei·te** *f* hip measurement
Hü·gel ['hy:gəl] *m* (-s; -) hill; hillock; **~grab** *n* burial mound; *in GB*: barrow, *in Scotland*: cairn; *in Europe*: tumulus; *in the USA*: mound
hü·ge·lig ['hy:gəlɪç] *adj.* hilly
'**Hü·gel|ket·te** *f* range of hills; **~land·schaft** *f* hill(y) country
Hu·ge·not·te [hugə'nɔtə] *m* (-n; -n), **Hu·ge·not·tin** [hugə'nɔtɪn] *f* (-; -nen), **hu·ge·not·tisch** [hugə'nɔtɪʃ] *adj.* Huguenot
Huhn [hu:n] *n* (-[e]s; Hühner ['hy:nɐ]) chicken; hen; *fig.* ***verrücktes ~*** F (real) nutcase; F ***mit den Hühnern zu Bett gehen*** (***aufstehen***) go to bed early (get up at the crack of dawn); F ***da lachen ja die Hühner!*** don't make me laugh
Hühn·chen ['hy:nçən] *n* (-s; -) chicken; *gastr.* roast chicken; *fig.* ***mit j-m ein ~ zu rupfen haben*** have a bone to pick with s.o.
Hüh·ner|au·ge ['hy:nɐ-] *n* corn; F *fig.* ***j-m auf die ~n treten*** a) tread on s.o.'s toes (*or* corns), b) (*a.* ***j-m auf die ~n steigen***) give s.o. a subtle reminder; **~au·gen·pfla·ster** *n* corn plaster; **~brü·he** *f* chicken broth; **~brust** *f* chicken breast; ⚕ pigeon chest; F *fig.* ***e-e ~ haben*** F be pigeon-chested
Hüh·ner·ei ['hy:nɐ-] *n* hen's egg; **2groß** *adj.* the size of an (*or* a chicken's) egg
Hüh·ner|farm ['hy:nɐ-] *f* poultry (*or* chicken) farm; **~fleisch** *n* chicken (meat); **~fri·kas,see** *n* chicken fricassee; **~fut·ter** *n* chicken feed; **~ha·bicht** *m* goshawk; **~haus** *n* henhouse; **~hof** *m* **1.** chicken run; **2.** → ***Hühnerfarm***; **~jagd** *f* partridge shoot(ing); **~le·ber** *f* chicken liver (*gastr.* livers *pl.*); **~lei·ter** *f* chicken

ladder; **~pa͵ste·te** *f* chicken pie; **~pest** *f* fowl pest; **~schlag** *m*, **~stall** *m* chicken coop; **~stan·ge** *f* perch, (chicken) roost; **~sup·pe** *f* chicken soup; **~vö·gel** *pl.* gallinaceous birds; **~zucht** *f* **1.** chicken farming; **2.** chicken farm; **3.** chickens *pl.*, hens *pl.*

hui [hoi] *int.* a) ooh!, b) wow!; ***außen ~, innen pfui*** it's all right (*Am.* alright) until you take the wrappings off

Huld [hʊlt] *f* (-; *no pl.*) *a. iro.* grace, favo(u)r; benevolence; ***in j-s ~ stehen*** be in s.o.'s good graces; ***j-m s-e ~ schenken*** bestow one's favo(u)r on s.o.; **hul·di·gen** ['hʊldɪgən] *v/i.* (h) (*dat.*) pay tribute (*or* homage) to *s.o.*; *fig.* subscribe to *a way of thinking*; *b.s.* indulge in; hold *a belief etc.*; follow, worship *a fashion etc.*; **'Hul·di·gung** *f* (-; -en) tribute (***an*** *acc.* to); applause; **'huld·reich, 'huld·voll** *adj. a. iro.* gracious

Hül·le ['hʏlə] *f* (-; -n) a) cover; (record) sleeve; jacket; case; *phys.* shell, b) *fig.* veil; *fig.* ***sterbliche*** (*or* ***irdische***) ~ mortal remains; ***... in ~ und Fülle*** ... galore, plenty of; ***die ~ des Schweigens über et. breiten*** draw a veil of silence over s.th.; F *hum.* ***s-e ~n abstreifen*** F peel off; **'hül·len** *v/t.* (h): ~ ***in*** *acc.* wrap (up) in *s.th.*; *fig.* ***in Flammen gehüllt*** enveloped in flames; ***in Dunkel*** (***Nebel***) ***gehüllt*** shrouded in darkness (mist); ***in Wolken gehüllt*** covered in clouds; ***sich in Schweigen ~*** remain silent (***über*** *acc.* about); ***er hüllt sich in Schweigen*** *a.* his lips are sealed; **'Hül·len·elek·tron** *n phys.* orbital electron; **'hül·len·los** *adj.* naked; F *hum.* stark naked, F starkers; ***er stand ~ da*** *a.* F he stood there without a stitch on

Hül·se ['hʏlzə] *f* (-; -n) ✿ husk; shell; pod; capsule; ⚙ case, sleeve; tube; cap *of fountain pen*; **'Hül·sen·frucht** *f* legume; *pl.* pulses

hu·man [hu'ma:n] *adj.* human, humane; F decent

Hu'man|bio͵lo·ge *m* human biologist; **~bio·lo͵gie** *f* human biology; **~ge͵ne·tik** *f* human genetics *pl.*; **~ge͵ne·ti·ker** *m* human geneticist

hu·ma·ni·sie·ren [humani'zi:rən] *v/t.* (h) make more human

Hu·ma·nis·mus [huma'nɪsmʊs] *m* (-; *no pl.*) humanism; **Hu·ma·nist** [huma'nɪst] *m* (-en; -en) humanist; classicist; **hu·ma·ni·stisch** [huma'nɪstɪʃ] *adj.* humanist; ***~e Bildung*** classical education; ***~es Gymnasium*** grammar school (*emphasizing the study of the classics*)

hu·ma·ni·tär [humani'tɛ:ɐ] *adj.* humanitarian

Hu·ma·ni·tät [humani'tɛ:t] *f* (-; *no pl.*) humanitarianism; **Hu·ma·ni'täts·du·se·lei** [-du:zə͵laɪ] *f* (-; *no pl.*) sentimental humanitarianism

Hu'man|me·di͵zin *f* human medicine; **~me·di͵zi·ner** *m* doctor (of medicine); **~ver·such** *m* human experiment; **~wis·sen·schaf·ten** *pl.* human sciences (*or* studies)

Hum·bug ['hʊmbʊk] *m* (-s; *no pl.*) nonsense; humbug

Hum·mel ['hʊməl] *f* (-; -n) bumblebee

Hum·mer ['hʊmɐ-] *m* (-s; -) lobster; **~cock·tail** *m* lobster cocktail; **~fleisch** *n* lobster (meat); **~ga·bel** *f* lobster fork; **~ge·richt** *n* lobster dish; **~krab·ben** *pl.* king prawns; **~sche·re** *f* lobster claw

Hu·mor [hu'mo:ɐ] *m* (-s; *no pl.*) humo(u)r; sense of humo(u)r; ***er hat keinen ~*** he has no sense of humo(u)r, *a.* he can't take a joke; ***et. mit ~ ertragen*** take s.th. in good humo(u)r; *iro.* ***du hast*** (***vielleicht***) ***~!*** you've got a nerve; ***das kann einem wirklich den ~ verderben*** F it can really get to you

Hu·mo·res·ke [humo'rɛskə] *f* (-; -n) humorous sketch (*or* story); ♪ humoresque

hu·mo·rig [hu'mo:rɪç] *adj.* humorous

Hu·mo·rist [humo'rɪst] *m* (-en; -en) a) humorous writer, b) comedian; **hu·mo·ri·stisch** [humo'rɪstɪʃ] *adj.* humorous

hu'mor·los *adj.* humo(u)rless, unfunny; ***~ sein*** have no sense of humo(u)r; ***sei doch nicht so ~!*** don't take everything so seriously; can't you take a joke?; **Hu'mor·lo·sig·keit** *f* (-; *no pl.*) lack of humo(u)r; ***an ~ leiden*** have no sense of humo(u)r

hu'mor·voll *adj.* humorous, funny

hum·peln ['hʊmpəln] *v/i.* (sn) hobble; (have a) limp

Hum·pen ['hʊmpən] *m* (-s; -) tankard

Hu·mus ['hu:mʊs] *m* (-; *no pl.*) humus; **~bo·den** *m* humus soil; **~er·de** *f* humus; **~schicht** *f* humus layer

Hund [hʊnt] *m* (-[e]s; -e ['hʊndə]) **1.** dog; *hunt. a.* hound; ***junger ~*** puppy; → ***bissig*** 1; **2.** F *fig.* (***gemeiner***) ~ *sl.* (rotten) swine; ***armer*** (***schlauer, fauler***) ~ F poor (sly, lazy) devil; ***blöder ~!*** idiot!, F cretin!; ***so ein blöder ~!*** what a stupid bastard; ***auf den ~ bringen*** ruin; (***ganz***) ***auf dem ~ sein*** be in a real mess, *a.* be a wreck; ***mit den Nerven auf dem ~ sein*** be a nervous wreck; ***vor die ~e gehen*** go to the dogs; ***wie ~ und Katze leben*** fight like cat and dog; ***da liegt der ~ begraben*** that's why; ***er ist bekannt wie ein bunter ~*** everybody knows him; ***er ist mit allen ~en gehetzt*** he knows all the tricks of the trade; ***das ist ein dicker ~*** F that's a bit thick; ***damit kann man keinen ~ hinter dem Ofen hervorlocken*** who's interested in that?; ***~e, die*** (***viel***) ***bellen, beißen nicht*** barking dogs seldom bite

Hun·de|au·gen ['hʊndə-] *pl.*: *fig.* ***treue ~*** big faithful eyes; ***j-n mit traurigen ~ ansehen*** give s.o. a hangdog look; **~aus·stel·lung** *f* dog show; **~be·sit·zer** *m* dog owner; **~biß** *m* dog bite; **~blick** *m* → ***Hundeaugen***; **~dreck** F *m* F dog's muck; **~dres͵sur** *f* dog training; **≈elend** F *adj.*: ***sich ~ fühlen*** feel rotten (F lousy); **~fän·ger** *m* dog-catcher; **~fraß** F *m* F muck; ***das ist ja ein ~*** it's not fit for a dog; **~fut·ter** *n* dogfood; **~ge·bell** *n* (sound of) barking dogs (*or* a dog barking), barking; **~haa·re** *pl.* dog's hair *sg.* (*or* hairs); **~hals·band** *n* dog collar; **~hal·ter** *m* dog owner; **~hüt·te** *f* (dog) kennel, *Am.* doghouse; **~käl·te** F *f*: ***es ist e-e ~*** it's absolutely freezing; **~kot** *m* dog('s) dirt, F dog's muck; **~krank·heit** *f* dog's disease; **~ku·chen** *m* dog biscuit; **~le·ben** *n*: F ***ein ~ führen*** lead a dog's life; **~lei·ne** *f* lead, leash; **~lieb·ha·ber** *m* dog-lover; **~lohn** F *m* pittance; ***für e-n ~*** *a.* F for peanuts; **~mar·ke** *f* dog tag (*a.* F ⚔ *etc.*); **~meu·te** *f* pack of dogs; **≈mü·de** F *adj.* F dog-tired, *sl.* zonked; **~narr** *m* F dog freak; ***er ist ein ~*** he's crazy about dogs; **~pfle·ge** *f* dog care; **~ras·se** *f* breed (of dog); **~ren·nen** *n* dog (*or* greyhound) racing

hun·dert ['hʊndɐt] *adj.* a (*Am.* one) hundred

'Hun·dert¹ *n* (-s; -[e]) hundred; ***fünf vom ~*** (*abbr.* ***v.H.***) five per cent (*or* percent); ***~e von Menschen*** hundreds of people; ***zu ~en*** by the (*or* in their) hundreds; ***in die ~e gehen*** *costs etc.*: run into the hundreds

'Hun·dert² *f* (-; -en) hundred

hun·dert'acht·zig: F ***auf ~ sein*** F be hitting the roof, *sl.* be freaking out

Hun·der·ter ['hʊndɐtɐ] *m* (-s; -) ℞ *the* hundred; hundred; three-digit number; F hundred-mark *etc.* note (*Am.* bill)

hun·der·ter·lei ['hʊndɐtɐ'laɪ] *adj.* hundreds of different *things etc.*

'hun·dert·fach **I.** *adj.* a hundredfold; ***die ~e Summe*** a hundred times the sum; ***in ~er Vergrößerung*** enlarged (*or* magnified) a hundred times; **II.** *adv.* a hundred times; **'Hun·dert·fa·che** *n* (-n; *no pl.*): ***das ~*** a hundred times that (*or* as much)

hun·dert'fünf·zig·pro͵zen·tig F *adj.* ultra ...; ***so ein ≈er*** one of those fanatics

Hun·dert'jahr·fei·er *f* centenary, *Am.* centennial

'hun·dert·jäh·rig [-jɛ:rɪç] *adj.* *a* hundred-year-old ..., *pred.* a hundred years old; a hundred years of *fighting, experience etc.*; ***~es Jubiläum*** centenary, *Am.* centennial; *hist.* ***der ≈e Krieg*** the Hundred Years' War; **'Hun·dert·jäh·ri·ge** [-jɛ:rɪgə] *m, f* (-n; -n) centenarian

'hun·dert·mal *adv.* a hundred times

Hun·dert'mark·schein *m* hundred-mark note (*Am.* bill)

Hun·dert'me·ter·lauf *m the* 100 (= hundred) met|res (*Am.* -ers)

'hun·dert·pro·zen·tig [-pro'tsɛntɪç] **I.** *adj.* a hundred per cent (*or* percent); pure *alcohol*; *fig. a.* one hundred per cent ..., out-and-out ...; ***~e Tochtergesellschaft*** wholly-owned subsidiary; **II.** *fig. adv.* a (*or* one) hundred per cent *or* percent; absolutely; ***das weiß ich ~*** *a.* I know that for sure; ***ich stimme ~ mit Ihnen überein*** I couldn't agree with you more

'Hun·dert·satz *m* percentage

'Hun·dert·schaft *f* (-; -en) contingent of a hundred police *etc.*, hundred-strong police *etc.* contingent; ***mehrere ~en*** several hundred police *etc.*

hun·dertst ['hʊndɐtst] *adj.* hundredth; *fig.* ***wir kamen vom ≈en ins Tausendste*** one thing led to another; we just got talking and couldn't stop; ***das geht vom ≈en ins Tausendste*** it just goes on forever, there's no end to it; **Hun·dert·stel** ['hʊndɐtstəl] *n* (-s; -) hundredth

'hun·dert'tau·send *adj.* a (*or* one) hundred thousand; ***≈e von Exemplaren*** hundreds of thousands of copies

'hun·dert·wei·se *adv.* by the hundred, in (their) hundreds

Hun·de|sa͵lon ['hʊndə-] *m* dog (F pooch) parlo(u)r; **~schei·ße** *sl.* *f* F dog's muck, V dog shit; **~schlit·ten** *m* dog sleigh (*or* sled); **~schnau·ze** *f* dog's nose; F ***kalt wie e-e ~*** (as) cold as a fish; **~sohn** *contp. m sl.* bastard, *esp. Am. sl.* son of a bitch; **~steu·er** *f* dog licen|ce (*Am.* -se) fee; **~typ** *m* kind of dog; **~wet·ter** F *n* nasty weather; **~zucht** *f* dog breeding; kennel (of dogs); **~züch·ter** *m* dog breeder; **~zwin·ger** *m* (dog) kennel(s *pl.*)

Hün·din ['hʏndɪn] *f* (-; -nen) bitch

hün·disch ['hʏndɪʃ] *fig. contp.* **I.** *adj.* servile; ***~e Ergebenheit*** abject devotion;

II. *adv.*: ~ ***ergeben*** abjectly (*or* utterly) devoted (*dat.* to)

hunds·ge·mein ['hʊnts-] F **I.** *adj.* really mean, nasty *remark, lie etc.*; ~***er Kerl*** *a. sl.* bastard; ***er*** (***sie***) ***kann*** ~ ***werden*** *sl.* he (she) can be a real bastard (bitch); **II.** *adv.* a) nastily, b) F damn, *sl.* bloody *cold etc.*; ***es tut*** ~ ***weh*** *sl.* it hurts like hell; **'Hunds·ge·mein·heit** F *f* (-; -en) **1.** *no pl.* nastiness; **2.** F dirty trick

'hunds·mi·se͵ra·bel F *adj.* F lousy

'Hunds|ro·se *f* dogrose; ~**stern** *m* Sirius, Dog Star; ~**ta·ge** *pl.* dog days

Hü·ne ['hyːnə] *m* giant; ***er ist ein*** ~ *a.* he's gigantic (*or* huge); **'Hü·nen·grab** *n* megalithic grave, dolmen; **'hü·nen·haft** *adj.* giant, gigantic

Hun·ger ['hʊŋɐ] *m* (-s; *no pl.*) a) hunger; appetite, b) famine, c) *fig.* hunger, thirst (***nach*** *dat.* for); ~ ***haben*** (***bekommen***) be (get) hungry (***auf*** *acc.* for); ***ich habe*** ~ ***auf*** *acc.* ... *a.* I feel like ..., F I (could just) fancy ...; ~ ***leiden*** starve; ***vor*** ~ ***sterben*** die of starvation, starve to death; F *fig.* ***ich sterbe vor*** ~ F I'm famished, I'm ravenous; ~ ***ist der beste Koch*** hunger is the best sauce; ~**blocka·de** *f* hunger blockade; ~**da·sein** *n* miserable existence; ***ein*** ~ ***fristen*** eke out a living; ~**ge·fühl** *n* hungry feeling; ***starkes*** ~ hunger pangs, gnawing hunger; ~**jahr** *n* year of famine; *pl.* lean years; ~**künst·ler** *m* professional faster; ~**kur** *f* starvation diet; ~**le·ben** *n* life of want

'Hun·ger·lei·der [-laɪdɐ] F *m* (-s; -) pauper

'Hun·ger·lohn *m* pittance

hun·gern ['hʊŋɐn] (h) **I.** *v/i.* go hungry, starve; fast; *fig.* ~ ***nach*** *dat.* hunger (*or* long) for; **II.** *v/refl.*: ***sich zu Tode*** ~ starve o.s. to death; **'hun·gernd** *adj.* hungry, starving

Hun·gers·not ['hʊŋɐs-] *f* famine; ***es herrscht*** ~ ***in*** *dat.* ... there is a (*or* widespread) famine in ...

'Hun·ger|streik *m* hunger strike; ***in den*** ~ ***treten*** go on hunger strike; ~**tod** *m* (death from) starvation; ***den*** ~ ***sterben*** die of starvation, starve to death; ~**tuch** *n*: ***am*** ~ ***nagen*** be on the breadline

hung·rig ['hʊŋrɪç] *adj.* hungry; starving, famished; *fig.* hungry (*a. look etc.*), starved (***nach*** *dat.* for)

Hun·ne ['hʊnə] *m* (-n; -n) Hun; **'Hun·nen·kö·nig** *m* king of the Huns

Hu·pe ['huːpə] *f* (-; -n) *mot.* horn; ***auf die*** ~ ***drücken*** sound (F toot, beep) one's horn; **'hu·pen** *v/i.* (h) hoot, honk; sound (F toot, beep) one's horn; **Hu·pe·rei** [huːpə'raɪ] *f* (-; *no pl.*) honking, tooting

hup·fen ['hʊpfən] *v/i.* (sn) → ***hüpfen***; F ***das ist gehupft wie gesprungen*** F it's six of one and half a dozen of the other

hüp·fen ['hʏpfən] *v/i.* (sn) hop; jump (***vor Freude*** for joy); *fig.* ***sein Herz hüpfte ihm vor Freude*** his heart leapt for joy; **Hüp·fer** ['hʏpfɐ] *m* (-s; -) hop, (little) jump; ***e-n*** ~ ***machen*** give a hop (*or* little jump)

'Hup|kon͵zert F *n* barrage of honking, F car-horn (⚓ foghorn) opera; ~**si͵gnal** *n* hoot; ***j-m ein*** ~ ***geben*** hoot (*or* toot one's horn) at s.o.; ~**ton** *m* sound of a horn; ***ein anhaltender*** ~ prolonged tooting; ~**ver·bot** *n* no horn signals; ~**zei·chen** *n* → ***Hupsignal***

Hür·de ['hʏrdə] *f* (-; -n) **1.** *sport*: hurdle (*a. fig.*); ***e-e*** ~ ***nehmen*** take (*or* clear) a hurdle; **2.** fold, pen

'Hür·den|lauf *m* hurdles *pl.*; ~**läu·fer** *m* hurdler

Hu·re ['huːrə] *f* (-; -n) whore; **'hu·ren** *v/i.* (h) whore around

'Hu·ren|bock *contp. m* lecher; ~**sohn** *contp. m sl.* son of a bitch; ~**vier·tel** F *n* red-light district

Hu·re·rei [huːrə'raɪ] *f* (-; *no pl.*) whoring

hur·ra [hʊ'raː] *int.* hooray!; **Hur'ra** *n* (-s; -s) hooray, cheer

Hur'ra·pa·tri͵ot *m* jingoist, flag-waver; **hur'ra·pa·trio·tisch** *adj.* jingoistic; **Hur'ra·pa·trio͵tis·mus** *m* jingoism

Hur'ra·ruf *m* cheer(s *pl.*), hooray(ing)

Hur·ri·kan ['hʊrikaːn] *m* (-s; -e) hurricane

hur·tig ['hʊrtɪç] *adj.* swift, quick; nimble

Hu·sar [hu'zaːɐ] *m* (-en; -en) hussar

husch [hʊʃ] *int.* a) shoo!, b) quick!; ~ ***ins Bett!*** off to bed with you!; **hu·schen** ['hʊʃən] *v/i.* (sn) dart, flit, F whizz, *Am.* whiz; whoosh

hü·steln ['hyːstəln] **I.** *v/i.* (h) a) give a little cough, b) have a slight cough; **II.** ♀ *n* (-s) slight cough(ing)

hu·sten ['huːstən] (h) **I.** *v/i.* cough; ***stark*** ~ have a bad cough; F *fig.* ***ich huste drauf*** F I couldn't give a damn (about it); **II.** *v/t.* cough (*or* bring) up; ***Blut*** ~ spit blood; F *fig.* ***sich die Gedärme*** (*or* ***die Seele***) ***aus dem Leib*** ~ cough one's heart out, *sl.* cough one's guts up; F ***ich werde dir was*** ~ F you'll be lucky, you know what you can do

'Hu·sten *m* (-s; *no pl.*) cough; ***e-n*** (***schlimmen*** *or* ***bösen***) ~ ***haben*** have a (bad *or* nasty) cough; ~**an·fall** *m* coughing fit; ~**bon͵bon** *m, n* cough sweet (*or* drop); ~**mit·tel** *n* cough medicine; ~**reiz** *m* tickle in one's throat; ~**saft** *m*, ~**si·rup** *m* cough mixture; ♀**stil·lend** *adv.*: ~ ***wirken*** relieve coughs; ~**tee** *m* bronchial tea; ~**trop·fen** *pl.* cough drops

Hu·ster ['huːstɐ] F *m* (-s; -) cough

Hut¹ [huːt] *m* (-[e]s; Hüte ['hyːtə]) hat; ♀ cap; *fig.* ***vor j-m den*** ~ ***ziehen*** take one's hat off to s.o.; ~ ***ab!*** I take my hat off; F ***unter einen*** ~ ***bringen*** reconcile *different opinions etc.*, *a.* get *people* to agree (*or* cooperate *etc.*), coordinate, sort out, fit in; F ***s-n*** ~ ***nehmen müssen*** have to go; F ***mit Politik*** *etc.* ***habe ich nichts am*** ~ politics *etc.* isn't my cup of tea, I'm not very politically-minded *etc.*, I don't know the first thing about politics *etc.*; F ***ein alter*** ~ F old hat; F ***ihm ging der*** ~ ***hoch*** F he blew his top (*sl.* stack); F ***eins auf den*** ~ ***kriegen*** F get a rap across the knuckles; F ***das kannst du dir an den*** ~ ***stecken!*** *sl.* you can stick that

Hut² *f* (-; *no pl.*) **1.** care, keeping; protection; **2.** ***auf der*** ~ ***sein*** be on one's guard (***vor*** *dat.* against), look (*or* watch) out (for), be on the lookout (for), be careful (***nicht zu*** *inf.* not to *inf.*); ***nicht auf der*** ~ ***sein*** be off one's guard

'Hut|ab·la·ge *f* hat rack; ~**ab͵tei·lung** *f* hat (*or* millinery) department; ~**band** *n* (-[e]s; ⸚er) hatband

hü·ten ['hyːtən] (h) **I.** *v/t.* guard, protect (***vor*** *dat.* from); watch (over); tend *cattle etc.*; look after *children*; *fig.* keep, guard *secret etc.*; **II.** *v/refl.*: ***sich*** ~ → ***Hut²*** 2; ***sich*** ~ ***zu*** *inf.* be careful not to *inf.*, take care not to *inf.*; ***sich*** ~ ***vor*** *dat.* watch out for; ***hüte dich vor ihm*** *a.* be careful of him; F ***ich werd' mich*** ~***!*** I'll make sure I don't, F I'll be blowed if I do, F not likely!; ***er soll sich*** ~***(, das zu tun)*** he'd better not (try); **Hü·ter** ['hyːtɐ] *lit. m* (-s; -) custodian; *hum.* ***der*** ~ ***des Gesetzes*** the arm of the law

'Hut|ge·schäft *n* hat shop; *a.* milliner's (shop); ~**grö·ße** *f* hat size; ***welche*** ~ ***haben Sie?*** what size hat do you take?; ~**krem·pe** *f* brim (of a *or* the hat); ~**la·den** *m* → ***Hutgeschäft***; ~**ma·cher** *m* (-s; -) hat maker; *a.* milliner; ~**na·del** *f* hatpin; ~**schach·tel** *f* hatbox; ~**schnur** *f* hat string; F *fig.* ***das geht mir über die*** ~ F that's a bit much; ~**stän·der** *m* hatstand

Hüt·te ['hʏtə] *f* (-; -n) **1.** a) hut; hovel, shack, b) alpine hut; refuge; hunting lodge; **2.** *metall.* steelworks *pl.*; smelting works *pl.*; glassworks *pl.*

'Hüt·ten|ar·bei·ter *m* (iron-and-)steelworker; ~**be·trieb** *m* metal plant (*or* factory); ~**fest** *n bibl.* Feast of Tabernacles; ~**in·du͵strie** *f* iron and steel industry; ~**in·ge·ni͵eur** *m* metallurgical engineer; ~**kä·se** *m* cottage cheese; ~**kun·de** *f* metallurgy; ~**schu·he** *pl.* slipper socks; ~**we·sen** *n* (-s; *no pl.*) metallurgy

hut·ze·lig ['hʊtsəlɪç] *adj.* shrivel(l)ed, withered; wizened *old woman etc.*

Hyä·ne ['hÿɛːnə] *f* (-; -n) *zo.* hyena

Hya·zinth [hÿa'tsɪnt] *m* (-[e]s; -e) *min.* hyacinth

Hya·zin·the [hÿa'tsɪntə] *f* (-; -n) ♀ hyacinth

hy·brid [hy'briːt] *adj.*, **Hy·bri·de** [hy'briːdə] *f* (-; -n) hybrid

Hy·bris ['hyːbrɪs] *f* (-; *no pl.*) hubris

Hy·dra ['hyːdra] *f* (-; Hydren [-drən]) hydra

Hy·drant [hy'drant] *m* (-en; -en) fire hydrant

Hy·drat [hy'draːt] *n* (-[e]s; -e) hydrate

Hy·drau·lik [hy'draʊlɪk] *f* (-; *no pl.*) *phys.* hydraulics *pl.*; **hy·drau·lisch** [hy'draʊlɪʃ] *adj.* hydraulic(ally *adv.*); ~***es Getriebe*** hydrodynamic drive

Hy·dro... [hydro-] *in cpds.* hydro...

Hy·dro·dy'na·mik *f phys.* hydrodynamics *pl.*

hy·dro·elek·trisch [-e'lɛktrɪʃ] *adj.* hydroelectric

Hy·dro·gra·phie [hydrogra'fiː] *f* (-; *no pl.*) hydrography

Hy·dro·kul͵tur ['hyːdro-] *f* (-; -en) hydroponics *pl.*

Hy·dro·lo·gie [hydrolo'giː] *f* (-; *no pl.*) hydrology

Hy·dro·ly·se [hydro'lyːzə] *f* (-; -n) hydrolysis; **hy·dro·ly·tisch** [hydro'lyːtɪʃ] *adj.* hydrolytic

Hy·dro·me·ter [hydro'meːtɐ] *n* (-s; -) hydrometer

Hy·dro·pho'bie *f* (-; *no pl.*) ⚕ hydrophobia

Hy·dro'sphä·re *f* (-; *no pl.*) hydrosphere, hydrospace

Hy·dro'sta·tik *f* (-; *no pl.*) hydrostatics *pl.*; **hy·dro'sta·tisch** *adj.* hydrostatic(ally *adv.*)

Hy·dro'tech·nik *f* (-; *no pl.*) hydraulic engineering

Hy·dro·the·ra'pie *f* (-; -n) ⚕ hydrotherapy

Hy·gie·ne [hy'gǐeːnə] *f* (-; *no pl.*) hygiene; ***mangelnde*** ~ lack of hygiene, unhygienic conditions; ~**ar͵ti·kel** *pl.* toiletries; ~**vor·schrif·ten** *pl.* rules of hygiene

hy·gie·nisch [hy'gǐeːnɪʃ] *adj.* hygienic(ally *adv.*)

Hy·gro·me·ter [hygro'meːtɐ] *n* (-s; -) hygrometer

Hy·gro·skop [hygro'skoːp] *n* (-s; -e) hygroscope

Hy·men ['hyːmən] *n* (-s; -) *anat.* hymen

Hym·ne ['hʏmnə] *f* (-; -n) hymn (***an*** *acc.* to); *a.* ode (to); national anthem

'Hym·nen|dich·ter *m* hymn composer (*or* writer); **~me·lo͵die** *f* melody of a (*or* the) hymn; **~samm·lung** *f* book of hymns

hym·nisch ['hʏmnɪʃ] *adj.* hymnic; *fig.* eulogistic, panegyrical

Hy·per·bel [hy'pɛrbəl] *f* (-; -n) ⍝ hyperbola; *ling.* hyperbole; **hy·per·bo·lisch** [hypɐ'boːlɪʃ] *adj.* hyperbolic(al)

hy·per|ge'nau [hypɐ-] *adj.* overexact, extremely meticulous; **~kor'rekt** *adj.*: ***~er Mensch*** stickler for etiquette (*or* form); **~mo'dern** *adj.* ultramodern, hypermodern; **~sen'si·bel** *adj.* hypersensitive, highly strung

Hy·per·to·nie [hypɐto'niː] *f* (-; *no pl.*) ⚕ hypertension; hypertonia; **Hy·per·to·ni·ker** [hypɐ'toːnikɐ] *m* (-s; -) hypertension sufferer

hy·per·troph [hypɐ'troːf] *adj.* ⚕ hypertrophied; *fig.* exaggerated; **Hy·per·tro·phie** [hypɐtro'fiː] *f* (-; *no pl.*) ⚕ hypertrophy; **hy·per·tro·phiert** [hypɐtro'fiːɐt] *adj.* hypertrophied (*a. fig.*)

Hyp·no·se [hʏp'noːzə] *f* (-; *no pl.*) hypnosis; ***in ~ versetzen*** hypnotize, put under hypnosis; ***unter ~*** in a state of hypnosis, in a hypnotic state; ***aus der ~ erwachen*** come out of one's hypnosis, F wake up again; **Hyp·no·the·ra'pie** [hʏpno-] *f* (-; -n) hypnotherapy; **hyp·no·tisch** [hʏp'noːtɪʃ] *adj.* hypnotic(ally *adv.*); **Hyp·no·ti·seur** [hʏpnoti'zøːɐ] *m* (-s; -e [-'zøːrə]) hypnotist; **hyp·no·ti·sie·ren** [hʏpnoti'ziːrən] *v/t.* (h) hypnotize; *fig.* mesmerize; **hyp·no·ti·siert** [hʏpnoti'ziːɐt] *adj.* hypnotized; *fig.* (*a.* ***wie ~***) mesmerized (***von*** *dat.* by); **Hyp·no·tis·mus** [hʏpno'tɪsmʊs] *m* (-; *no pl.*) hypnotism

Hy·po·chon·der [hypo'xɔndɐ] *m* (-s; -) hypochondriac; **Hy·po·chon·drie** [hypoxɔn'driː] *f* (-; *no pl.*) hypochondria; **hy·po·chon·drisch** [hypo'xɔndrɪʃ] *adj.* hypochondriac

Hy·po·phy·se [hypo'fyːzə] *f* (-; -n) *anat.* pituitary (gland)

Hy·po·sta·se [hypo'staːzə] *f* (-; -n) *ling.*, *phls.* hypostasis

Hy·po·te·nu·se [hypote'nuːzə] *f* (-; -n) hypotenuse

Hy·po·thek [hypo'teːk] *f* (-; -en) mortgage; *fig.* burden; ***e-e ~ aufnehmen*** take out a mortgage (***auf*** *acc.* on); ***mit e-r ~ belasten*** mortgage; **hy·po·the·ka·risch** [hypote'kaːrɪʃ] **I.** *adj.* mortgage ...; **II.** *adv.*: ***~ belasten*** mortgage; ***~ belastet*** mortgaged; ***~ belastbar*** mortgageable; ***~ gesichert*** secured by a mortgage

Hy·po'the·ken|bank *f* (-; -en) mortgage bank; **~brief** *m* mortgage (deed); **~dar·le·hen** *n* mortgage loan; **≈frei** *adj.* unencumbered; **~gläu·bi·ger** *m* mortgagee; **~pfand·brief** *m* mortgage bond; **~schuld** *f* mortgage debt; **~schuld·ner** *m* mortgagor; **~zin·sen** *pl.* mortgage interest *sg.*

Hy·po·the·se [hypo'teːzə] *f* (-; -n) hypothesis, supposition; **hy·po·the·tisch** [hypo'teːtɪʃ] *adj.* hypothetical

Hy·po·to·nie [hypoto'niː] *f* (-; *no pl.*) ⚕ hypotension; hypotonia; **Hy·po·to·ni·ker** [hypo'toːnikɐ] *m* (-s; -) hypotension sufferer

Hy·ste·rie [hʏste'riː] *f* (-; -n) hysteria; **Hy·ste·ri·ker** [hʏs'teːrikɐ] *m* (-s; -), **Hy·ste·ri·ke·rin** [hʏs'teːrikərɪn] *f* (-; -nen) hysterical person; **hy·ste·risch** [hʏs'teːrɪʃ] *adj.* hysterical; ***e-n ~en Anfall bekommen*** ⚕ have a hysterical fit, F *fig.* (*a.* ***~ werden***) go hysterical, go into hysterics; F ***werd' nicht gleich ~!*** F keep your hair on

I

I, i [iː] **I.** *n* (-; -) I, i; → ***Tüpfelchen*; II.** *int.* ***i!*** ugh!; F ***i wo!*** oh no, F get away
ibe·risch [iˈbeːrɪʃ] *adj.* Iberian; ***die 2e Halbinsel*** the Iberian Peninsula
Ibis [ˈiːbɪs] *m* (-ses; -se) ibis
IC [iˈtseː] *m* intercity (train); ***mit dem ~ fahren*** travel (*or* go) by intercity, go intercity
ich [ɪç] **I.** *pers. pron.* I; ***~ bin's!*** it's me; ***wer, ~?*** who, me?; ***~ nicht*** not me; ***wer will es? - ~!*** who wants it? - me!, I do!; ***immer ~!*** why (always) me?; ***~ selbst würde es nicht machen*** personally, I wouldn't do it; if you ask me, I wouldn't do it; ***~ Idiot!*** how stupid can you get, what an idiot I am; ***du und ~, wir machen uns e-n schönen Abend*** you and me, we're going to have a nice evening together; ***hier bin ~!*** here I am!, *a. iro.*: hi everybody, it's me!; **II. 2** *n* (-[s]; -[s]) self; *psych., phls.* ego; ***mein zweites*** (***or anderes***) ***~*** a) my other self, b) my alter ego; ***sein besseres ~*** his better self; ***das liebe ~*** one's own sweet self
ˈich·be·zo·gen *adj.* egocentric, self-centred (*Am.* self-centered); **ˈIch·be·zo·gen·heit** *f* (-; *no pl.*) self-centredness (*Am.* self-centeredness)
ˈIch-Er·zäh·ler *m* first-person narrator; **ˈIch-Er·zäh·lung** *f* first-person narrative
ˈIch-Form *f*: ***Roman in der ~*** novel written in the first person (singular)
ˈIch-Ge·fühl *n* consciousness (*or* perception) of the self
ˈIch-Mensch *m* self-centred (*Am.* self-centered) person; ***ein ~ sein*** *a.* be totally self-centred (*Am.* self-centered)
Ich·thyo·lo·gie [ɪçtÿoloˈgiː] *f* (-; *no pl.*) ichthyology
Ich·thyo·sau·rus [ɪçtÿoˈzaʊrʊs] *m* (-; -rier [-rïɐ]) ichthyosaurus
IC|-Netz *n* 🚆 intercity network; **~Zug** *m* intercity (train)
Id [iːt] *n* (-[s]; Ide [ˈiːdə]) *psych.* id
ide·al [ideˈaːl] **I.** *adj.* **1.** ideal, perfect; *a.* model *husband etc.*; **2.** *phls.* ideal; conceptual; **3.** idealistic; **II. 2** *n* (-s; -e) ideal; F *a.* dream
Ideˈal|bild *n* ideal; **~fall** *m* ideal case; ***im ~*** ideally; **~fiˌgur** *f the* perfect figure; **~gewicht** *n* optimum weight
idea·li·sie·ren [idealiˈziːrən] *v/t.* (h) idealize; **Idea·liˈsie·rung** *f* (-; -en) idealization
Idea·lis·mus [ideaˈlɪsmʊs] *m* (-; *no pl.*) idealism; **Idea·list** [ideaˈlɪst] *m* (-en; -en) idealist; **idea·li·stisch** [ideaˈlɪstɪʃ] *adj.* idealistic(ally *adv.*)
Ideˈal|lö·sung *f* ideal solution; **~typ** *m*: ***der ~ des Lehrers*** a) the ideal teacher, b) a model teacher; **~vor·stel·lung** *f* ideal; idealistic view; **~zu·stand** *m* ideal (state of affairs)

Idee [iˈdeː] *f* (-; -n) **1.** idea; thought; concept; ***gute ~*** good idea; ***ich habe keine ~*** (I've) no idea; ***ich kam auf die ~ zu*** *inf.* it occurred to me to *inf.* (*or* that I could ...), I (suddenly) had the idea to *inf.*; ***wie kamst du auf die ~?*** what made you think of it?, what made you decide that?; ***wie kamst du auf die ~ zu*** *inf.*? what made you think of *ger.* (*or* decide to *inf.*)?; ***das ist die ~!*** that's it, that's the answer; ***ein Mann mit ~n*** a man of ideas; ***allein die ~!*** even just to think of it; F ***ich hab' so 'ne ~, daß*** I have an idea (*or* a feeling) that; → ***fix*** 1; **2.** F ***eine ~*** just a (F a wee) bit *darker etc.*
ide·ell [ideˈɛl] *adj.* **1.** non-material(istic), idealistic; *a.* spiritual *values*; moral, ethical; ***~er Wert*** sentimental value; **2.** ***der ~e Gehalt e-s Buches*** *etc.* the ideas in (*or* behind) a book *etc.*; **3.** *phls. and* ⚒ ideal
ide·en·arm [iˈdeːən-] *adj.* lacking in ideas; unimaginative; **Ide·en·ar·mut** *f* lack of ideas (*or* imagination)
Ide·en|as·so·zia·tiˌon [iˈdeːən-] *f* association of ideas; **~aus·tausch** *m* exchange of ideas; **~dra·ma** *n* drama of ideas; **~ge·schich·te** *f* history of ideas; **~leh- re** *f phls.* ideology; ***Platos ~*** Plato's theory of ideas
ide·en·los [iˈdeːən-] *adj.* → ***ideenarm***; **Ide·en·lo·sig·keit** *f* (-; *no pl.*) → ***Ideenarmut***
ide·en·reich [iˈdeːən-] *adj.* full of ideas, very (*or* highly) imaginative; *a.* inventive *person*; **Ide·en·reich·tum** *m* (-s; *no pl.*) *m* wealth of ideas; inventiveness
Ide·en·welt [iˈdeːən-] *f* (world of) ideas *pl.*
iden·ti·fi·zier·bar [idɛntifiˈtsiːɐbaːɐ] *adj.* identifiable; **iden·ti·fi·zie·ren** [idɛntifiˈtsiːrən] (h) **I.** *v/t.* identify (***mit*** *dat.* with); **II.** *v/refl.*: ***sich ~ mit*** *dat.* identify with, relate to; **Iden·ti·fiˈzie·rung** *f* (-; -en) identification
iden·tisch [iˈdɛntɪʃ] *adj.* identical (***mit*** *dat.* with)
Iden·ti·tät [idɛntiˈtɛːt] *f* (-; *no pl.*) identity
Iden·tiˈtäts|kri·se *f* crisis of identity; **~nach·weis** *m* proof of (one's) identity; **~ver·lust** *m* loss of identity
Ideo·gramm [ideoˈgram] *n* (-s; -e) *ling.* ideogram
Ideo·lo·ge [ideoˈloːgə] *m* (-n; -n) ideologist; *contp.* ideologue; **Ideo·lo·gie** [ideoloˈgiː] *f* (-; -n) ideology; **ideo·lo·gisch** [ideoˈloːgɪʃ] *adj.* ideological; **ideo·lo·gi·sie·ren** [ideologiˈziːrən] *v/t.* (h) ideologize
Idio·blast [idïoˈblast] *m* (-en; -en) *biol.* idioblast
Idio·la·trie [idïolaˈtriː] *f* (-; *no pl.*) idiolatry
Idio·lekt [idïoˈlɛkt] *m* (-[e]s; -e) idiolect

Idi·om [iˈdïoːm] *n* (-s; -e) idiom; language; **Idio·ma·tik** [idïoˈmaːtɪk] *f* (-; *no pl.*) idioms (and phrases) *pl.*; phraseology; **idio·ma·tisch** [idïoˈmaːtɪʃ] *adj.* idiomatic(ally *adv.*); ***~e Wendung*** idiom, idiomatic phrase (*or* expression)
Idi·ot [iˈdïoːt] *m* (-en; -en) idiot
Idio·ten·ar·beit [iˈdïoːtən-] F *f* mindless work (*or* job), F donkeywork
idio·ten·haft [iˈdïoːtənhaft] *adj.* idiotic, ridiculous
Idio·ten·hü·gel [iˈdïoːtən-] F *m skiing*: nursery slope, F dope slope
idio·ten·si·cher [iˈdïoːtən-] F *adj.* foolproof
Idio·tie [iˈdïoˈtiː] F *f* (-; -n): ***e-e ~*** (sheer) lunacy
idio·tisch [iˈdïoːtɪʃ] *adj.* idiotic, ridiculous
Idol [iˈdoːl] *n* (-s; -e) idol; *a. s.o.'s* hero *or* heroine; ***ein ~ der sechziger Jahre*** *a.* an icon of the sixties; **Ido·la·trie** [idolaˈtriː] *f* (-; *no pl.*) idolatry
Idyll [iˈdʏl] *n* (-s; -e) idyll; **Idyl·le** [iˈdʏlə] *f* (-; -n) idyll, *art*: *a.* pastoral scene; pastoral poem; **idyl·lisch** [iˈdʏlɪʃ] *adj.* idyllic
Igel [ˈiːgəl] *m* (-s; -) hedgehog
igit·ti·gitt [iˈgɪtigɪt] *int.* ugh!, F yuk!
Ig·lu [ˈiːglu] *m, n* (-s; -s) igloo
igno·rant [ɪgnoˈrant] *adj.* ignorant; **Ignoˈrant** *m* (-en; -en) ignorant person; **Ignoˈran·ten·tum** *n* (-s; *no pl.*) ignorance; **Igno·ranz** [ɪgnoˈrants] *f* (-; *no pl.*) ignorance; **igno·rie·ren** [ɪgnoˈriːrən] *v/t.* (h) ignore, take no notice of; *a.* cut *s.o.* dead
ihm [iːm] *pers. pron.* (*dat. of er and es*) **1.** (to) him; (to) it; for him; ***ich hab's ~ gesagt*** (***gegeben***) I told him (I gave it to him, I gave him it); ***wie geht's ~?*** how is he?; **2.** *after prp.*: him, *i.e.* ***von ~*** from him; ***ein Freund von ~*** a friend of his, one of his friends
ihn [iːn] *pers. pron.* (*acc. of er and es*) him, it
ih·nen [ˈiːnən] *pers. pron.* (*dat. pl. of er, sie, es*) **1.** (to) them; ***ich hab's ~ gesagt*** (***gegeben***) I told them (I gave it to them, I gave them it); ***wie geht's ~?*** how are they?; **2.** *after prp.*: them; ***bei ~*** with them; at their place; **3. 2** (*dat. of Sie*) (to) you
ihr [iːɐ] **I.** *pers. pron.* **1.** (*dat. of sie sg.*) (to) her, (to) it; for her; ***ich hab's ~ gesagt*** (***gegeben***) I told her (I gave it to her, I gave her it); ***wie geht's ~?*** how is she?; **2.** (*nom. pl. of du, in letter 2*) you; **II.** *poss. pron.* (*see a. sein² I*) **3.** *adj. sg.* her, its; *pl.* their; ***einer ~er Verwandten*** one of her (*pl.* their) relatives, a relative of hers (*pl.* theirs); **4.** *su.* **der** (**die, das**) **~(ig)e** hers, *pl.* theirs, *address*: **der** (**die, das**) **2(ig)e** yours
ˈih·rer·seits *adv.* as far as she's (*pl.*

they're) concerned, *address*: ♀ as far as you're concerned
ih·res'glei·chen ['i:rəs-] *pron.* her (*pl.* their) equals *pl.*, *contp.* the likes of her (*pl.* them), her (*pl.* their) sort, *address*: ♀ your equals *pl.*, *contp.* the likes of you, your sort
ih·ret|hal·ben ['i:rət'halbən] *obs. adv.* → **~'we·gen** *adv.* **1.** because of her (*pl.* them), on her (*pl.* their) account, *address*: ♀ because of you, on your account; **2.** because of her (*pl.* them), for her (*pl.* their) sake, *address*: ♀ because of you, for your sake; **3.** on her (*pl.* their) behalf, *address*: ♀ on your behalf; **~'wil·len** *adv.*: **um** ~ a) for her (*pl.* their) sake, b) on her (*pl.* their) behalf; *address*: **um** ♀ a) for your sake, b) on your behalf
ih·ri·ge ['i:rɪgə] → ***ihr*** 4
Iko·ne [i'ko:nə] *f* (-; -n) icon; **Iko·nen·ma·le,rei** *f* **1.** icon painting, painting of icons; **2.** → ***Ikone***
Iko·no·gra·phie [ikonogra'fi:] *f* (-; *no pl.*) iconography
Iko·no·klas·mus [ikono'klasmʊs] *m* (-; -men) iconoclasm; **Iko·no·klast** [ikono'klast] *m* (-en; -en) iconoclast; **iko·no·kla·stisch** [ikono'klastɪʃ] *adj.* iconoclastic
Iko·no·sta·se [ikono'sta:zə] *f* (-; -n) iconostasis
Ilias ['i:lĭas] *f* (-; *no pl.*) Iliad
il·le·gal ['ɪlega:l] *adj.* illegal; **Il·le·ga·li·tät** ['ɪlegalitɛ:t] *f* (-; *no pl.*) **1.** illegality; **2.** illegal status; **3.** illegal act
il·le·gi·tim ['ɪlegiti:m] *adj.* illegitimate; **Il·le·gi·ti·mi·tät** ['ɪlegitimitɛ:t] *f* (-; *no pl.*) illegitimacy
Il·lu·mi·na·ti·on [ɪlumina'tsĭo:n] *f* (-; -en) **1.** illumination; **2.** illuminations *pl.*, lights *pl.*; **il·lu·mi·nie·ren** [ɪlumi'ni:rən] *v/t.* (h) illuminate
Il·lu·si·on [ɪlu'zĭo:n] *f* (-; -en) illusion; *psych. a.* delusion; ***das ist e-e reine*** ~ that's an illusion, that's pure illusion; ***sich ~en machen*** delude o.s., fool o.s., ***über*** *acc.*: *a.* be under an illusion about; ***darüber mache ich mir keine ~en*** I have no illusions about that; ***mach dir keine ~en!*** don't fool (F kid) yourself!; ***laß ihm doch s-e ~en*** let him dream
il·lu·sio·när [ɪluzĭo'nɛ:ʀ] *adj.* illusory
Il·lu·sio·nis·mus [ɪluzĭo'nɪsmʊs] *m* (-; *no pl.*) *art, phls. etc.* illusionism; **Il·lu·sio·nist** [ɪluzĭo'nɪst] *m* (-en; -en) illusionist
il·lu·si'ons·los *adj.* **1.** free from illusions; realistic, sober *assessment etc.*; ~ ***sein*** *a.* have no illusions; **2.** disillusioned
il·lu·so·risch [ɪlu'zo:rɪʃ] *adj.* illusory; ***das ist doch ~!*** that's an illusion, you're fooling yourself
il·lu·ster [ɪ'lʊstʀ] *adj.* distinguished
Il·lu·stra·ti·on [ɪlʊstra'tsĭo:n] *f* (-; -en) illustration, picture; ***zur*** ~ to illustrate (what I mean); **il·lu·stra·tiv** [ɪlʊstra'ti:f] *adj.* illustrative; **Il·lu·stra·tor** [ɪlʊs'tra:to:ʀ] *m* (-s; -en [-tra'to:rən]) illustrator; **il·lu·strie·ren** [ɪlʊs'tri:rən] *v/t.* (h) illustrate, *fig. a.* demonstrate; **il·lu·striert** [ɪlʊs'tri:ʀt] *adj.* illustrated; ***ist es ~?*** *a.* has it got illustrations (*or* pictures)?
Il·lu'strier·te *f* (-n; -n) (glossy) magazine, F glossy
im [ɪm] (= ***in dem***) → ***in***
Image ['ɪmɪtʃ] *n* ([s]; -s ['ɪmɪdʒɪs]) image; **~pfle·ge** *f* image cultivation (*or* building)
ima·gi·när [imagi'nɛ:ʀ] *adj.* imaginary
Ima·go [i'ma:go] *f* (-; -gines [-gine:s]) *psych. and zo.* imago
Imam [i'ma:m] *m* (-s; -s, -e) imam
Im·biß ['ɪmbɪs] *m* (-sses; -sse) **1.** snack, F bite to eat; **2.** → ***Imbißstand, Imbißstube;*** **~stand** *m* snack booth; *a.* hot-dog stand (*or* stall); **~stu·be** *f* snack bar
Imi·ta·ti·on [imita'tsĭo:n] *f* (-; -en) a) imitation, copy, b) fake; **Imi·ta·tor** [imi'ta:to:ʀ] *m* (-; -en [-ta'to:rən]) imitator; impersonator; **imi·tie·ren** [imi'ti:rən] *v/t.* (h) **1.** imitate; impersonate *s.o.*; **2.** copy
Im·ker ['ɪmkʀ] *m* (-s; -) bee-keeper, *formal*: apiarist; **Im·ke·rei** [ɪmkə'raɪ] *f* (-; -en) **1.** *no pl.* bee-keeping; **2.** apiary
im·ma·nent [ɪma'nɛnt] *adj.* inherent (*dat.* in); *phls.* immanent; **Im·ma·nenz** [ɪma'nɛnts] *f* (-; *no pl.*) immanence
im·ma·te·ri·ell ['ɪmaterĭɛl] *adj.* immaterial
Im·ma·tri·ku·la·tion [ɪmatrikula'tsĭo:n] *f* (-; -en) *univ.* enrol(l)ment; **im·ma·tri·ku·lie·ren** [ɪmatriku'li:rən] *v/t. and v/refl.* (***sich*** ~) (h) *univ.* enrol(l), register (***an*** *dat.* at)
im·mens [ɪ'mɛns] *adj.* tremendous, vast
im·mer ['ɪmʀ] *adv.* **1.** always; every time; constantly, all the time; ~ ***noch, noch*** ~ still; ***es ist ~ noch nicht da*** it still hasn't arrived; ***er ist ~ noch dein Chef*** he 'is your boss after all; ~ ***wenn*** every time, whenever; ***für*** ~ *leave etc.* for good; ~ ***wieder*** over and over again, time and again; ***et. ~ wieder tun*** do s.th. over and over again, keep (on) doing s.th.; ***es ist ~ wieder dasselbe*** it's the same (thing) every time; ~ ***weiter reden*** keep (on) talking, F go on and on; ~ ***und ewig*** for evermore; F ~ ***zu!*** don't stop!; F ~ ***mit der Ruhe!*** F (take it) easy now; **2.** *with comp.*: ~ ***besser*** better and better; ~ ***schlimmer*** worse and worse; ~ ***größer werdend*** ever-increasing; **3.** F at a time; ~ ***den dritten Tag*** every third day; ~ ***zu zweit*** in twos; **4.** *generalizing*: ***wann auch*** ~ whenever; ***was auch*** ~ whatever; ***wer auch*** ~ whoever; ***wie auch*** ~ however, ***du es machen willst*** *etc.*: whichever way you choose *etc.*; ***wo auch*** ~ wherever; ***wann*** (***wo*** *etc.*) ***auch ~ ich ...*** *a.* it doesn't matter when (where *etc.*) I ..., no matter when (where *etc.*) I ...
'im·mer·fort *obs. adv.* continually, all the time
'im·mer·grün *adj.*, **'Im·mer·grün** *n* (-s; *no pl.*) ♀ evergreen
'im·mer'hin *adv.* a) still, though, b) after all; at least; **~!** a) not bad, considering, b) well, that's something at least; ***das ist ~ etwas*** well, it's better than nothing, I suppose; ***es war ~ das zweitbeste Ergebnis*** it 'was the second-best score; ***er ist ~ dein Chef*** he 'is your boss after all; don't forget he's your boss
'im·mer'wäh·rend *adj.* perpetual; eternal
'im·mer'zu *adv.* all the time; ***et. ~ tun*** *a.* keep (on) doing s.th.
Im·mi·grant [ɪmi'grant] *m* (-en; -en) immigrant; **Im·mi·gra·ti·on** [ɪmigra'tsĭo:n] *f* (-; -en) immigration; **Im·mi·gra·ti·'ons·be·stim·mun·gen** *pl.* immigration laws; **im·mi·grie·ren** [ɪmi'gri:rən] *v/i.* (sn) immigrate
Im·mis·si·on [ɪmɪ'sĭo:n] *f* (-; -en) (harmful effects *pl.* of) noise *or* pollutants *pl. etc.*
Im·mo·bi·li·en [ɪmo'bi:lĭən] *pl.* real estate *sg.*, property *sg.*; **~ma,gnat** *m* property giant; **~mak·ler** *m* estate agent, *Am.* realtor; **~markt** *m* property market
im·mo·bi·li·sie·ren [ɪmobili'zi:rən] *v/t.* (h) immobilize
Im·mor·tel·le [ɪmɔr'tɛlə] *f* (-; -n) ♀ everlasting (flower), immortelle
im·mun [ɪ'mu:n] *adj. a. fig.* immune (***gegen*** *acc.* to, *pol. etc.* from); **~*machen*** → ***immunisieren***
Im'mun·bio·lo,gie *f* immunobiology
Im'mun·de·fi·zi,enz *f* immunodeficiency
im·mu·ni·sie·ren [ɪmuni'zi:rən] *v/t.* (h) make immune (***gegen*** *acc.* against, to); immunize (against)
Im·mu·ni·tät [ɪmuni'tɛ:t] *f* (-; *no pl.*) immunity (***gegen*** *acc.* to, against, *pol. etc.* from); *a.* (parliamentary) privilege
Im'mun·kör·per *m* antibody
Im·mu·no·lo·ge [ɪmuno'lo:gə] *m* (-n; -n) immunologist; **Im·mu·no·lo·gie** [ɪmunolo'gi:] *f* (-; *no pl.*) immunology
Im'mun|re·ak·ti,on *f* immunological reaction, immunoreaction; **~schwä·che** *f* immunodeficiency; **~sy,stem** *n* immune system; **~the·ra,pie** *f* immunotherapy
Im·pe·danz [ɪmpe'dants] *f* (-; -en) ⚡ impedance
Im·pe·ra·tiv ['ɪmperati:f] *m* (-s; -e [-və]) *ling.* imperative (mood); *phls.* ***kategorischer*** ~ categorical imperative; **im·pe·ra·ti·visch** [ɪmpera'ti:vɪʃ] *adj.* imperative
Im·per·fekt ['ɪmpɛrfɛkt] *n* (-s; -e) *ling.* imperfect (tense)
Im·pe·ria·lis·mus [ɪmperĭa'lɪsmʊs] *m* (-; *no pl.*) imperialism; **Im·pe·ria·list** [ɪmperĭa'lɪst] *m* (-en; -en) imperialist; **im·pe·ria·li·stisch** [ɪmperĭa'lɪstɪʃ] *adj.* imperialist(ic)
Im·pe·ri·um [ɪm'pe:rĭʊm] *n* (-s; -rien [-rĭən]) empire (*a. fig.*)
im·per·ti·nent [ɪmpɛrti'nɛnt] *adj.* impertinent, insolent; **Im·per·ti·nenz** [ɪmpɛrti'nɛnts] *f* (-; -en) **1.** *no pl.* impertinence; **2.** impertinence, impertinent remark (*or* thing to do)
Impf|ak·ti,on [ɪmpf-] *f* vaccination program(me); **~an·stalt** *f* vaccination clinic *or* centre (*Am.* center)
imp·fen ['ɪmpfən] *v/t.* (h) vaccinate, inoculate; *fig.* → ***einimpfen*** 1; ***sich ~ lassen*** be vaccinated, get a vaccination
Impf|nar·be ['ɪmpf-] *f* vaccination scar; **~paß** *m* vaccination card; **~pi,sto·le** *f* vaccination gun; **~schein** *m* vaccination certificate; **~stoff** *m* vaccine, serum
Imp·fung ['ɪmpfʊŋ] *f* (-; -en) vaccination, inoculation
'Impf·zwang *m* (-[e]s; *no pl.*) compulsory vaccination
Im·plan·tat [ɪmplan'ta:t] *n* (-[e]s; -e) ⚕ implant; **Im·plan·ta·ti·on** [ɪmplanta'tsĭo:n] *f* (-; -en) implantation; **im·plan·tie·ren** [ɪmplan'ti:rən] *v/t.* (h) implant
Im·pli·ka·ti·on [ɪmplika'tsĭo:n] *f* (-; -en) implication; **im·pli·zie·ren** [ɪmpli'tsi:rən] *v/t.* (h) imply; ***es impliziert(, daß)*** *a.* it would indicate *or* suggest (that)
im·pli·zit [ɪmpli'tsi:t] *adj.* implicit
im·pli·zi·te [ɪm'pli:tsite] *adv.* implicitly
im·plo·die·ren [ɪmplo'di:rən] *v/i.* (sn) implode; **Im·plo·si·on** [ɪmplo'zĭo:n] *f* (-; -en) implosion
Im·pon·de·ra·bi·li·en [ɪmpɔndera'bi:lĭən] *pl.* imponderables
im·po·nie·ren [ɪmpo'ni:rən] *v/i.* (h) (*dat.*) impress *s.o.*; command *s.o.'s* respect; **im-**

po'nie·rend *adj.* impressive; ***~es Auftreten*** commanding presence; **Im·po·nier·ge·ha·be** [ımpo'ni:ɐ-] *n* (-s; *no pl.*) **1.** showing off, posturing, exhibitionism; attempt to impress; ***der mit s-m ~!*** he's just trying to impress (people); **2.** *zo.* display behavio(u)r

Im·port [ım'pɔrt] *m* (-[e]s; -e) ✝ **1.** *no pl.* import(ing); **2.** *a. pl.* imports *pl.*; **~ab·ga·be** *f* import duty; **~ar,ti·kel** *m* import, imported article (*pl. a.* goods); **~be·schrän·kung** *f* import restriction

Im·por·teur [ımpɔr'tø:ɐ] *m* (-s; -e [-'tø:rə]) importer

Im'port|fir·ma *f* importer, importing company; **~ge·schäft** *n* **1.** import trade; **2.** → ***Importfirma***

im·por·tie·ren [ımpɔr'ti:rən] *v/t.* (h) import

Im'port|kon·tin,gent *n* import quota; **~stopp** *m* ban on imports; **~wa·re** *f* imported goods *pl.*; **~zoll** *m* import duty

im·po·sant [ımpo'zant] *adj.* impressive; imposing; striking

im·po·tent ['ımpotɛnt] *adj.* impotent; **Im·po·tenz** ['ımpotɛnts] *f* (-; *no pl.*) impotence

im·prä·gnie·ren [ımprɛ'gni:rən] *v/t.* (h) impregnate; *esp. textil.* waterproof; **Im·prä·gnier·mit·tel** [ımprɛ'gni:ɐ-] *n* impregnating agent; **Im·prä'gnie·rung** *f* (-; -en) impregnation; waterproofing

'im·prak·ti,ka·bel *adj.* impracticable

Im·pre·sa·rio [ımpre'za:rĭo] *m* (-s; -s) impresario, agent

Im·pres·sio·nen [ımprɛ'sĭo:nən] *pl.* impressions

Im·pres·sio·nis·mus [ımprɛsĭo'nısmʊs] *m* (-; *no pl.*) Impressionism; **Im·pres·sio·nist** [ımprɛsĭo'nıst] *m* (-en; -en) Impressionist; **im·pres·sio·ni·stisch** [ımprɛsĭo'nıstıʃ] *adj.* impressionist(ic); *art:* Impressionist

Im·pres·sum [ım'prɛsʊm] *n* (-s; -ssen) *typ.* imprint; *newspaper: a.* masthead

Im·pri·ma·tur [ımpri'ma:tʊr] *n* (-s; *no pl.*) *typ.* imprimatur; ***das ~ erteilen für*** *acc.* pass *s.th.* for press; ***~!*** ready for press

Im·prom·ptu [ɛ̃prõ'ty:] *n* (-s; -s) ♪ impromptu

Im·pro·vi·sa·ti·on [ımproviza'tsĭo:n] *f* (-; -en) improvisation; **Im·pro·vi·sa·tor** [ımprovi'za:to:ɐ] *m* (-s; -en [-za'to:rən]) improviser; **im·pro·vi·sie·ren** [ımprovi'zi:rən] *v/t. and v/i.* (h) improvise (*a. fig.*); ♪ *etc. a.* ad-lib, extemporize; **im·pro·vi·siert** [ımprovi'zi:ɐt] *adj.* improvised; *a.* off-the-cuff *speech etc.*; improvised, F instant ..., *pred.* thrown together

Im·puls [ım'pʊls] *m* (-es; -e [-zə]) **1.** impulse; *a.* idea; *a. pl.* inspiration (*sg.*); ***e-r Sache neue ~e geben*** give a fresh impetus to s.th.; **2.** impulse; ***aus e-m ~ heraus, e-m plötzlichen ~ folgend*** on an (*or* a sudden) impulse; **3.** *electron.* pulse

im·pul·siv [ımpʊl'zi:f] **I.** *adj.* impulsive; spur-of-the-moment *decision etc.*; **II.** *adv.*: ***~ handeln*** act on impulse (*or* on the spur of the moment); **Im·pul·si·vi·tät** [ımpʊlzivi'tɛ:t] *f* (-; *no pl.*) impulsiveness

Im'puls·kauf *m* impulse purchase; *pl. a.* impulse buying *sg.*

im·stan·de [ım'ʃtandə] *pred. adj.*: ***~ sein zu*** *inf.* (***zu*** *dat.*) be capable of *ger.* (of *s.th.*), be in a position to *inf.* (to do *s.th.*); ***nicht ~ zu*** *inf.* unable to *inf.*, incapable of *ger.*; ***er ist nicht ~ aufzustehen*** *a.* he just can't get up; ***sie ist durchaus ~, das zu tun*** she's perfectly capable of doing it, there's nothing to stop her doing it; *iro.* ***dazu ist er glatt ~*** I wouldn't put it past him; ***er ist ~ und ...*** he's quite capable of *ger.*; ***er ist zu allem ~*** he'll stop at nothing

in [ın] **I.** *prp.* **1.** a) in, at, b) within, c) into, in; ***im Haus*** in(side) the house, indoors; ***im ersten Stock*** on the first (*Am.* second) floor; ***~ der*** (***die***) ***Kirche*** (***Schule***) at (to) church (school); ***im*** (***ins***) ***Theater*** at (to) the theat|re (*Am. a.* -er); ***~ England*** in England; ***waren Sie schon ~ England?*** have you ever been to England?; **2.** a) in, b) during, c) within; ***~ drei Tagen*** in three days; ***~ diesem*** (***im letzten, nächsten***) ***Jahr*** this (last, next) year; ***heute ~ acht Tagen*** a week from today; ***im Jahr 1990*** in (the year) 1990; ***im*** (***Monat***) ***Februar*** in (the month of) February; ***im Frühling*** (***Herbst***) in (the) spring (autumn, *Am.* fall); ***~ der Nacht*** at night, during the night; ***~ letzter Zeit*** lately; **3.** ***~ größter Eile*** in a great rush; ***im Kreis*** in a circle; **4.** ***im Alter von ...*** at the age of ...; ***~ Behandlung sein*** be having treatment; ***~ Vorbereitung*** being prepared, F in the pipeline; ***~ e-m Klub*** *etc.* ***sein*** be in a club *etc.*, belong to a club *etc.*; ***~ Biologie ist er schwach*** he's not very good at biology; **II.** F *adj.*: ***~ sein*** F be in, be the fashion

in·ad·äquat ['ınʔadɛkva:t] *adj.* a) inappropriate, b) unsatisfactory, inadequate

in·ak·tiv ['ınʔakti:f] *adj.* inactive; ⚗ *a.* inert; non-active *member etc.*; **in·ak·ti·vie·ren** [ınʔakti'vi:rən] *v/t.* (h) inactivate

in·ak·zep·ta·bel ['ınʔaktsɛpta:bəl] *adj.* unacceptable

In·an·griff·nah·me [ın'ʔangrıfna:mə] *f* (-; *no pl.*) launching *of a project etc.*; tackling *of a task etc.*; ***seit ~ des Projekts*** since the project was launched (*or* started); ***seit ~ der Arbeit*** since the job *or* work was started (*or* taken up)

In·an·spruch·nah·me [ın'ʔanʃprʊxna:mə] *f* (-; *no pl.*) a) (laying) claim (*gen.* to), b) use (of), utilization (of), c) resort (to), d) demands *pl.* (on); claims *pl.* on *s.o.'s* time; strain (on); ✝ ***~ von Kredit*** availment of credit

In·au·gen·schein·nah·me [ın'ʔaʊgənʃaınna:mə] *f* (-; -n) inspection

'In·be·griff *m* (-[e]s; *no pl.*) epitome (*gen.* of); ***der ~ von Qualität*** *etc.* a byword for quality *etc.*

'in·be·grif·fen **I.** *pred. adj.* included; ***Mahlzeiten ~*** meals included, including meals; **II.** *prp.* including, inclusive of

In·be·sitz·nah·me [ınbə'zıtsna:mə] *f* (-; *no pl.*) appropriation, seizure; occupation

In·be·trieb·nah·me [ınbə'tri:pna:mə] *f* (-; -n), **In·be'trieb·set·zung** *f* (-; -en) opening; ⚙ starting up, switching on; ***vor ~*** *gen.* before starting (*or* switching on) ...

In·brunst ['ınbrʊnst] *f* (-; *no pl.*) ardo(u)r, fervo(u)r; **in·brün·stig** ['ınbrʏnstıç] **I.** *adj.* ardent, fervent; **II.** *adv.*: ***~ hoffen, daß*** *a.* hope and pray that

in·de·kli·na·bel [ındekli'na:bəl] *adj.* indeclinable

in·de·li·kat ['ındelika:t] *adj.* indelicate; tactless

in·dem [ın'de:m] *cj.* **1.** as, while; ***~ er mich ansah, sagte er*** looking at me he said; ***~ er dies sagte, verließ er das Zimmer*** saying this (*or* with these words) he left the room; **2.** by (*ger.*); ***er gewann, ~ er mogelte*** he won by cheating

In·der ['ındɐ] *m* (-s; -) **1.** Indian; **2.** F Indian restaurant; ***zum ~ gehen*** F go to an Indian; ***in der Nähe ist ein ~*** there's an Indian place near here; **In·de·rin** ['ındərın] *f* (-; -nen) Indian

in·des [ın'dɛs], **in·des·sen** [ın'dɛsən] *adv.* a) meanwhile, in the meantime, b) nevertheless, still; **II.** *cj.* whereas

In·dex ['ındɛks] *m* (-es; -e) index; 𝔄 *a.* exponent; *eccl.* ***Bücher auf den ~ setzen*** put books on the Index; **~lohn** *m* ✝ index-linked wages *pl.*; **~preis** *m* index-linked price; **~wäh·rung** *f* ✝ index-based currency; **~zahl** *f*, **~zif·fer** *f* index (number)

In·dia·ner [ın'dĭa:nɐ] *m* (-s; -), **In·dia·ne·rin** [ın'dĭa:nərın] *f* (-; -nen) (American) Indian

In'dia·ner|häupt·ling *m* Indian chief; **~re·ser,vat** *n*, **~re·ser·va·ti,on** *f* Indian reservation; **~spra·che** *f* American Indian language; **~stamm** *m* Indian tribe; **~zelt** *n* wigwam

in·dia·nisch [ın'dĭa:nıʃ] *adj.* (American) Indian

in·dif·fe·rent ['ındıfərɛnt] *adj.* indifferent (***gegenüber*** *dat.* to); *phys.*, ⚗ *a.* neutral; inert *gas*; **In·dif·fe·renz** ['ındıfərɛnts] *f* (-; *no pl.*) indifference (***gegenüber*** *dat.* to)

in·di·gniert [ındi'gni:ɐt] *adj.* indignant (***über*** *acc.* at)

In·di·go ['ındigo] *m* (-s; -s) indigo; **~blau** *n* ⚗ indigo

In·di·ka·ti·on [ındika'tsĭo:n] *f* (-; -en) ⚕ indication; **In·di·ka·ti'ons·mo,dell** *n* grounds *pl.* for legal abortion

In·di·ka·tiv ['ındikati:f] *m* (-s; -e [-və]) *ling.* indicative (mood)

In·di·ka·tor [ındi'ka:to:ɐ] *m* (-s; -en [-ka'to:rən]) indicator; **~en** *a.* indications

In·dio ['ındĭo] *m* (-s; -s) South American Indian

in·di·rekt ['ındirɛkt] **I.** *adj.* indirect; oblique; (***die***) ***~e Rede*** indirect (*or* reported) speech; **II.** *adv.* indirectly; obliquely; *express o.s. etc. a.* in a roundabout way

in·disch ['ındıʃ] *adj.* Indian

in·dis·kret ['ındıskre:t] *adj.* indiscreet; tactless; **In·dis·kre·ti·on** [ındıskre'tsĭo:n] *f* (-; -en) indiscretion; tactless remark (*or* thing to do)

in·dis·ku·ta·bel ['ındıskuta:bəl] *adj.* a) not worth considering; *theory etc.*: out of court; out of the question, b) appalling, impossible *performance etc.*

in·dis·po·niert ['ındısponi:ɐt] *adj.* indisposed

In·di·vi·du·al·be·reich [ındivi'dŭa:l-] *m* personal sphere

in·di·vi·dua·li·sie·ren [ındividŭali'zi:rən] *v/t.* (h) individualize

In·di·vi·dua·lis·mus [ındividŭa'lısmʊs] *m* (-; *no pl.*) individualism; **In·di·vi·dua·list** [ındividŭa'lıst] *m* (-en; -en) individualist; **in·di·vi·dua·li·stisch** [ındividŭa'lıstıʃ] *adj.* individualist(ic)

In·di·vi·dua·li·tät [ındividŭali'tɛ:t] *f* (-; *no pl.*) individuality

In·di·vi·du·al|psy·cho·lo,gie [ındivi'dŭa:l-] *f* individual psychology; **~recht** *n* right(s *pl.*) of an (*or* the) individual

in·di·vi·du·ell [ındivi'dŭɛl] **I.** *adj.* a) individual; personal, b) original; ***die ~e Note*** the personal touch; **II.** *adv.*: ***~ gestal-***

ten do (*or* arrange *etc.*) according to one's own tastes *etc.*, individualize, personalize; ***das ist ~ verschieden*** that varies from person to person; ***man kann es sich ~ aussuchen*** (***zusammenstellen***) you can choose whatever you like *or* whatever suits you best (you can arrange it whichever way you like *or* as it suits you best)

In·di·vi·du·um [ɪndi'viːduʊm] *n* (-s; -en) individual (*a. fig.*)

In·diz [ɪn'diːts] *n* (-es; Indizien [ɪn'diːtsĭən]) **1.** indication, sign; **2.** ⚖ *pl.* circumstantial evidence *sg.*

In·di·zi·en|be·weis [ɪn'diːtsĭən-] *m* ⚖ *a. pl.* circumstantial evidence; **~ket·te** *f* chain of evidence; **~pro͵zeß** *m trial based on circumstantial evidence*

in·di·zie·ren [ɪndi'tsiːrən] *v/t.* (h) **1.** indicate; **2.** index; *eccl.* put on the Index; **in·di·ziert** [ɪndi'tsiːɐt] *adj.* ⚕ *and fig.* indicated

in·do·eu·ro'pä·isch ['ɪndo-] *adj.* Indo-European

in·do·ger'ma·nisch ['ɪndo-] *adj.* Indo-European; **In·do·ger·ma'ni·stik** *f* Indo-European studies *pl.*

In·dok·tri·na·ti·on [ɪndɔktrina'tsĭoːn] *f* (-; -en) indoctrination; **in·dok·tri·nie·ren** [ɪndɔktri'niːrən] *v/t.* (h) indoctrinate; **In·dok·tri'nie·rung** *f* (-; -en) indoctrination

in·do·lent [ɪndo'lɛnt] *adj.* indolent, idle; **In·do·lenz** [ɪndo'lɛnts] *f* (-; *no pl.*) indolence

In·do·lo·ge [ɪndo'loːgə] *m* (-n; -n) Indologist; **In·do·lo·gie** [ɪndolo'giː] *f* (-; *no pl.*) Indology

In·do·ne·si·er [ɪndo'neːzĭɐ] *m* (-s; -), **In·do·ne·sie·rin** [ɪndo'neːzĭərɪn] *f* (-; -nen), **in·do·ne·sisch** [ɪndo'neːzɪʃ] *adj.* Indonesian

In·dos·sa·ment [ɪndɔsa'mɛnt] *n* (-[e]s; -e) ☤ endorsement; **In·dos·sant** [ɪndɔ'sant] *m* (-en; -en) endorser; **In·dos·sat** [ɪndɔ'saːt] *m* (-en; -en) endorsee; **in·dos·sie·ren** [ɪndɔ'siːrən] *v/t.* (h) endorse

In·duk·ti·on [ɪndʊk'tsĭoːn] *f* (-; -en) *phls. and* ⚡ induction

In·duk·ti'ons|be·weis *m phls.* inductive proof; **~mo·tor** *m* induction motor; **~spu·le** *f* induction coil; **~strom** *m* induced current

in·duk·tiv [ɪndʊk'tiːf] *adj.* inductive; **In·duk·ti·vi·tät** [ɪndʊktivi'tɛːt] *f* (-; -en) inductivity, inductance

in·du·stria·li·sie·ren [ɪndʊstriali'ziːrən] *v/t.* (h) industrialize; **In·du·stria·li'sie·rung** *f* (-; *no pl.*) industrialization; **In·du·stria·lis·mus** [ɪndʊstria'lɪsmʊs] *m* (-; *no pl.*) industrialism

In·du·strie [ɪndʊs'triː] *f* (-; -n) (branch of) industry; ***in der ~*** (***tätig***) ***sein*** be (employed) in industry; **~ab·fäl·le** *pl.* industrial waste *sg.*; **~ab·ga·se** *pl.* industrial emissions (*or* waste gases); **~ab·wäs·ser** *pl.* industrial sewage (*or* effluent) *sg.*; **~an·la·ge** *f* industrial plant; **~ar·bei·ter** *m* industrial worker; **~ar·chäo·lo͵gie** *f* industrial arch(a)eology; **~be·ra·ter** *m* industrial consultant; **~be·trieb** *m* industrial concern (*or* plant); **~boß** F *m* captain of industry; **~er·zeug·nis** *n* industrial product; **~ge·biet** *n* **1.** industrial area; **2.** → **~ge·län·de** *n* industrial estate (*or* park); **~ge·sell·schaft** *f* industrial society; **~ge·werk·schaft** *f* industrial (*or* industry-wide) union; ***~ Metall*** Metal Workers' Union; **~gi͵gant** *m* industrial giant; **~kauf·mann** *m white-collar worker in an industrial company*; **~kom͵plex** *m* industrial complex; **~kon͵zern** *m* industrial concern; **~land** *n* (-[e]s; ¨er) industrial (*or* developed) nation; **~land·schaft** *f* industrial landscape; **~lärm** *m* industrial noise

in·du·stri·ell [ɪndʊstri'ɛl] *adj.* industrial; **In·du·stri'el·le** *m, f* (-n; -n) industrialist

In·du'strie|macht *f* industrial power; **~ma͵gnat** *m* industrial magnate, captain of industry, tycoon; **~mes·se** *f* industrial fair; **~müll** *m* industrial waste; **~na·ti͵on** *f* industrialized nation; ***die ~en*** *a.* the developed world; **~norm** *f* industrial standard; ***Deutsche ~*** German Standard Specification; **~park** *m* industrial park; **~po·ten·ti͵al** *n* industrial potential (*or* capacity); **~pro͵dukt** *n* industrial product; **~ro·bo·ter** *m* industrial robot; **2schwach** *adj.* under-industrialized; **~spi͵on** *m* industrial spy; **~spio͵na·ge** *f* industrial espionage; **~staat** *m* industrial nation; **~stadt** *f* industrial town (*or* city); **~tech·nik** *f* industrial engineering; **~- und 'Han·dels·kam·mer** *f* Chamber of Industry and Commerce; **~ver·band** *m* confederation of industries; **~vier·tel** *n* industrial area (*or* part of town); **~werk** *n* industrial plant; **~wer·te** *pl.* industrials; **~wirt·schaft** *f* industry; **~zeit·al·ter** *n* industrial age; **~zen·trum** *n* industrial cent|re (*Am.* -er); **~zweig** *m* (branch of) industry

in·du·zie·ren [ɪndu'tsiːrən] *v/t.* (h) induce (*a. phys.*)

in·ef·fi·zi·ent ['ɪnˀɛfitsĭɛnt] *adj.* **1.** ineffective; **2.** uneconomical; inefficient *method etc.*

in·ein·an·der [ɪnˀaɪ'nandɐ] *adv.* in(to) one another; *a.* in(to) each other; *in cpds. a.* inter...; ***~ verliebt*** in love (with each other); **~flech·ten** *v/t.* (*irr.*, *sep.*, h, → ***flechten***) intertwine; **~flie·ßen** *v/i.* (*irr.*, *sep.*, sn, → ***fließen***) merge (into one another); *colo(u)rs*: *a.* run; **~fü·gen** *v/t.* (*sep*, h) fit together, fit *things* into each other, join; **~ge·schach·telt** *adj.* fitted into each other; a. nested *boxes etc.*; closely interlocking *buildings etc.*; encapsulated *sentences*; **~grei·fen** *v/i.* (*irr.*, *sep.*, h, → ***greifen***) interlock; *fig. facts etc.*: be interconnected; **~grei·fend** *adj.* interlocking; *fig.* interconnected; **~pas·sen** *v/i. and v/t.* (*sep.*, h) fit together (*or* into each other); **~schach·teln** *v/t.* (*sep.*, h) fit *things* into each other; **~schie·ben** *v/t. and v/refl.* (***sich ~***) (*irr.*, *sep.*, h, → ***schieben***) telescope; **~stecken** *v/t.* (*sep.*, h) fit *things* together; **~wach·sen** *v/i.* (*irr.*, *sep.*, sn, → ***wachsen***) grow together

in·ex·akt ['ɪnˀɛksakt] *adj.* inaccurate

in·fam [ɪn'faːm] *adj.* disgraceful, shameless; F *fig.* awful; ***~e Lüge*** *a.* disgusting lie

In·fan·te·rie ['ɪnfantəriː] *f* (-; *no pl.*) infantry; **In·fan·te·rist** ['ɪnfantərɪst] *m* (-en; -en) infantryman

in·fan·til [ɪnfan'tiːl] *adj.* childish, infantile, puerile; **In·fan·ti·li·tät** [ɪnfantili'tɛːt] *f* (-; *no pl.*) childishness; childish (*or* infantile, puerile) behavio(u)r

In·farkt [ɪn'farkt] *m* (-[e]s; -e) ⚕ **1.** infarct; **2.** heart attack, coronary, 🕮 cardiac infarction; **2ge·fähr·det** *adj.* coronary-risk *patient etc.*; **~per͵sön·lich·keit** *f* coronary-risk type

In·fekt [ɪn'fɛkt] *m* (-[e]s; -e), **In·fek·ti·on** [ɪnfɛk'tsĭoːn] *f* (-; -en) ⚕ infection

In·fek·ti'ons|ab͵tei·lung *f* isolation ward; **~er·re·ger** *m* pathogen; **~ge·fahr** *f* risk of infection; **~herd** *m* focus of infection; **~krank·heit** *f* infectious disease; **~trä·ger** *m* (infection) carrier; **~weg** *m* path of infection

in·fek·ti·ös [ɪnfɛk'tsĭøːs] *adj.* infectious, contagious

in·fer·na·lisch [ɪnfɛr'naːlɪʃ] *adj.* **1.** infernal; fiendish *laughter*; **2.** dreadful *smell etc.*; ***~er Krach*** terrible din

In·fer·no [ɪn'fɛrno] *n* (-s; -s) inferno (*a. fig.*)

In·fil·tra·ti·on [ɪnfɪltra'tsĭoːn] *f* (-; -en) infiltration (*a. fig.*); **in·fil·trie·ren** [ɪnfɪl'triːrən] *v/t. and v/i.* (h) infiltrate (*a. fig.*)

in·fi·nit ['ɪnfiniːt] *adj. ling.* non-finite

In·fi·ni·te·si·mal·rech·nung [infinitezi'maːl-] *f* infinitesimal calculus

In·fi·ni·tiv ['ɪnfinitiːf] *m* (-s; -e [-və]) infinitive; **~satz** *m* infinitive clause

In·fix [ɪn'fɪks] *n* (-es; -e) *ling.* infix

in·fi·zie·ren [ɪnfi'tsiːrən] (h) **I.** *v/t.* infect; ***j-n*** (***mit et.***) ***~*** *a.* pass s.th. on to s.o.; **II.** *v/refl.*: ***sich ~*** get an infection; ***bei*** *dat.* infect o.s. doing *s.th.*; **In·fi'zie·rung** *f* (-; -en) infection

in fla·gran·ti [ɪn fla'granti] *adv.*: ***~ ertappt werden*** be caught in the act (*or* red-handed)

In·fla·ti·on [ɪnfla'tsĭoːn] *f* (-; -en) inflation; **in·fla·tio·när** [ɪnflatsĭo'nɛːɐ], **in·fla·tio·ni·stisch** [ɪnflatsĭo'nɪstɪʃ] *adj.* inflationary

In·fla·ti'ons|aus·gleich *m* inflationary adjustment; **~be·kämp·fung** *f* fight against inflation; **~er·schei·nung** *f* symptom of inflation; **~ge·fahr** *f* risk of inflation; **2hem·mend** *adj.* anti-inflationary; **~po·li͵tik** *f* inflationary policies *pl.*; **~ra·te** *f* rate of inflation, inflation rate; **~rück·gang** *m* easing-off of inflation, drop in the inflation rate; **2si·cher** *adj.* inflation-proof; **2trei·bend** *adj.* inflationary; **~zeit** *f* time of inflation; inflationary period

in·fle·xi·bel ['ɪnflɛksiːbəl] *adj.* inflexible; *ling.* invariable

In·fo ['ɪnfo] F *n* **1.** (-s; -s) F *a. pl.* info, *Brit. sl.* gen; **2.** F info sheet

in'fol·ge *prp.* (*gen*) as a result of

in·fol·ge'des·sen *adv.* as a result (of this), consequently

In·for·mant [ɪnfɔr'mant] *m* (-en; -en) source; *a. pol. etc.* informant; *b.s.* informer

In·for·ma·tik [ɪnfɔr'maːtɪk] *f* (-; *no pl.*) information (*or* computer) science, *Brit.* informatics *pl.*; **In·for·ma·ti·ker** [ɪnfɔr'maːtikɐ] *m* (-s; -) information (*or* computer) scientist

In·for·ma·ti·on [ɪnfɔrma'tsĭoːn] *f* (-; -en) **1.** *a. pl.* information (***über*** *acc.* on, about); ***zu Ihrer ~*** for your information; **2.** information (*or* inquiry) desk

In·for·ma·ti'ons|aus·tausch *m* exchange of information; **~be·such** *m* fact-finding mission; **~blatt** *n* information sheet; news sheet; **~bü͵ro** *n* inquiry office; **~dienst** *m* information service; **~fluß** *m* (-sses; *no pl.*) flow of information; **~flut** *f* information explosion; **~frei·heit** *f* (-; *no pl.*) freedom of information; **~ge·halt** *m* informational content; **~ge·sell·schaft**

f informed society; **~ge·spräch** *n* exchange of information; **2hung·rig** *adj.* starved for information; **~lücke** *f* information gap; **~ma·te·ri,al** *n* information; information leaflets *pl.*; **~netz** *n* information network; **~po·li,tik** *f* information policy; **~quel·le** *f* source (of information); **~recht** *n* right to be informed; **~rei·se** *f* fact-finding tour (*or* mission); **~sen·dung** *f* informational program(me); **~stand** *m* **1.** ***nach dem neuesten ~*** according to the latest information (available); **2.** information stand (*or* desk); **~tech·nik** *f*, **~tech·no·lo,gie** *f* information technology; **~wert** *m* informational value; **~wis·sen·schaft** *f* information science; **~wis·sen·schaft·ler** *m* information scientist; **~zeit·al·ter** *n* information age; **~zen·trum** *n* information cent|re (*Am.* -er)

in·for·ma·tiv [ɪnfɔrma'ti:f] *adj.* informative, instructive

in·for·ma·to·risch [ɪnfɔrma'to:rɪʃ] *adj.* informational

in·for·mell ['ɪnfɔrmɛl] *adj.* informal

in·for·mie·ren [ɪnfɔr'mi:rən] (h) **I.** *v/t.* **1.** let *s.o.* know (***über*** *acc.* about), tell *s.o.* (about), *adm. a.* notify *s.o.* (of); ***falsch ~*** misinform; **2.** inform (***über*** *acc.* about, of); **3.** instruct; *esp.* ⚔ brief; **II.** *v/refl.*: ***sich ~*** find out, inform o.s., keep informed (*all* ***über*** *acc.* about); ***sich ~ über*** *acc. a.* read up on; **in·for·miert** [ɪnfɔr'mi:ɐt] *adj.* informed; *a.* in the picture; ***~e Kreise*** well-informed circles; ***er ist gut ~*** he knows a lot (***über*** *acc.* about), ***über*** *acc.*: *a.* he's well up on; ***ich bin darüber ~*** I've been told (*or* I know) about it; **In·for'miert·heit** *f* (-; *no pl.*) (extent of) knowledge; ***ich war erstaunt über ihre ~*** I was amazed at how much they knew (*or* how well-informed they were)

'In·fo·stand *m* information stand

In'fra·ge·stel·lung *f* (-; *no pl.*) questioning, calling in question; jeopardizing

in·fra·rot ['ɪnfra-] *adj.*, **'In·fra·rot** *n* infrared

'In·fra·rot|be·strah·lung *f* infrared heat treatment; **~film** *m* infrared film; **~fo·to·gra,fie** *f* infrared photography; **~ka·me·ra** *f* infrared camera; **~lam·pe** *f* infrared lamp

'In·fra·schall *m* infrasound

'In·fra·struk,tur *f* infrastructure

In·fu·si·on [ɪnfu'zi̯o:n] *f* (-; -en) infusion, F *the* drip

In·fu·si'ons·tier·chen *pl.*, **In·fu·so·ri·en** [ɪnfu'zo:ri̯ən] *pl.* infusoria

In'gang·set·zung *f* (-; *no pl.*) starting (up)

In·ge·nieur [ɪnʒe'ni̯ø:ɐ] *m* (-s; -e [-'ni̯ø:rə] engineer; **~bü,ro** *n* consulting engineers *pl.*; engineering office; **~schu·le** *f* school of engineering

In·gre·di·en·zen [ɪngre'di̯ɛntsən] *pl.* **1.** *gastr.* ingredients; **2.** *pharm. etc.* constituents, components, constituent parts

Ing·wer ['ɪŋvɐ] *m* (-s; *no pl.*) ginger; **~stäb·chen** *n* ginger stick

In·ha·ber ['ɪnha:bɐ] *m* (-s; -) owner, proprietor; ⚖, ✝ *and sport*: holder, ✝ *a.* bearer; **~ak·tie** *f* bearer share (*Am.* stock)

In·ha·be·rin ['ɪnha:bərɪn] *f* (-; -nen) → ***Inhaber***

'In·ha·ber|scheck *m* cheque (*Am.* check) to bearer; **~schuld·ver·schrei·bung** *f* bearer bond; **~zer·ti·fi,kat** *n* bearer certificate

in·haf·tie·ren [ɪnhaf'ti:rən] *v/t.* (h) arrest, take *s.o.* into custody; **In·haf'tie·rung** *f* (-; -en) imprisonment

In·ha·la·ti·on [ɪnhala'tsi̯o:n] *f* (-; -en) inhalation; **In·ha·la·ti'ons·ap·pa,rat** *m* inhaler; **in·ha·lie·ren** [ɪnha'li:rən] *v/t. and v/i.* (h) inhale

In·halt ['ɪnhalt] *m* (-[e]s; -e) **1.** contents *pl.*; **2.** ⩓ capacity; volume; area; **3.** *fig.* content; plot, contents *pl. of a novel etc.*; subject matter; essence, substance; ***den ~ e-s Romans erzählen*** summarize the contents of a novel, give a summary of what happens in a novel; **4.** *fig.* meaning; ***ein Leben ohne ~*** a meaningless life; **'in·halt·lich I.** *adj.* textual; ***~e Zusammenfassung*** summary of the plot (*or* contents); ***~e Analyse*** analysis of the content (*or* plot); **II.** *adv.* in content; as far as the content (*or* plot) is concerned; ***~ ist der Film gut*** the film has a good storyline

'in·halt·los *adj.* → ***inhaltslos***

'in·halt·reich *adj.* → ***inhaltsreich***

'In·halts|an·ga·be *f* **1.** summary, synopsis; ***e-e ~ machen von*** *dat.* summarize; **2.** → ***Inhaltsverzeichnis***; **2arm** *adj.* lacking in substance, shallow; thin on plot; **~er·klä·rung** *f* ✉ description of contents; **2gleich** *adj.* ⩓ equal

'in·halts·leer, 'in·halts·los *adj. a. fig.* empty, meaningless; *book etc.* lacking in substance, shallow

'in·halts|reich *adj. book etc.* rich in content, F meaty; weighty, momentous; full, rich *life*; **~schwer** *adj.* fraught with meaning; momentous

'In·halts|,über·sicht *f* **1.** summary, synopsis; abstract; **2.** → **~ver·zeich·nis** *n* list (*or* table) of contents; *computer*: directory

in·hä·rent [ɪnhɛ'rɛnt] *adj.* inherent (*dat.* in); **In·hä·renz** [ɪnhɛ'rɛnts] *f* (-; *no pl.*) inherence

in·hu·man ['ɪnhuma:n] *adj.* inhuman; **In·hu·ma·ni·tät** ['ɪnhumanitɛ:t] *f* (-; -en) **1.** *no pl.* inhumanity; **2.** inhuman act, act of inhumanity (*or* cruelty)

In·itia·le [ini'tsi̯a:lə] *f* (-; -n) initial

In·iti·al·zün·dung [ini'tsi̯a:l-] *f* **1.** booster; **2.** *fig.* initial (*or* original) idea; ***die ~ kam von ihr*** it was her idea that sparked it all off

In·itia·ti·ve [initsi̯a'ti:və] *f* (-; -n) **1.** initiative; ***die ~ ergreifen*** take the initiative; ***auf s-e ~ hin*** on his initiative; ***aus eigener ~*** on one's own initiative, of one's own accord; **2.** action group; **In·itia·tiv·grup·pe** [initsi̯a'ti:f-] *f* action group; **In·itia·tor** [ini'tsi̯a:to:ɐ] *m* (-s; -en [initsi̯a'to:rən] initiator; ***er war der ~*** *a.* he was behind it all, he got the whole thing going; **in·iti·ie·ren** [initsi'i:rən] *v/t.* (h) initiate, start *s.th.* off

In·jek·ti·on [ɪnjɛk'tsi̯o:n] *f* (-; -en) injection

In·jek·ti'ons|na·del *f* hypodermic needle; **~sprit·ze** *f* hypodermic syringe

in·ji·zie·ren [ɪnji'tsi:rən] *v/t.* (h) inject

In·ka ['ɪŋka] *m* (-[s]; -[s]) *hist.* Inca; **~kul,tur** *f*: ***die ~*** Inca civilization; **~reich** *n* Inca Empire

In·kar·na·ti·on [ɪnkarna'tsi̯o:n] *f* (-; -en) *eccl.* incarnation; *fig. a.* embodiment

In·kas·so [ɪn'kaso] *n* (-s; -s, -si) ✝ collection; ***zum ~*** for collection; **2be·voll·mäch·tigt** *adj.* authorized to collect; **~bü,ro** *n* collection agency; **~voll·macht** *f* authority to collect; **~wech·sel** *m* bill for collection

In·klu·si·on [ɪnklu'zi̯o:n] *f* (-; -en) ⩓, ⚕, *min.* inclusion

In·klu·siv·an·ge·bot [ɪnklu'zi:f-] *n* all-in package

in·klu·si·ve [ɪnklu'zi:və] **I.** *prp.* (*gen.*) including, inclusive of; ***✝ ~ Verpackung*** packing included; **II.** *adv.*: ***bis zum 3. Mai ~*** up to and including May 3rd; ***Montag bis ~ Freitag*** Monday to Friday, *Am.* Monday through Friday

In·klu·siv·preis [ɪnklu'zi:f-] *m* inclusive (*or* all-in) price

in·kog·ni·to [ɪn'kɔgnito] **I.** *adv. travel etc.* incognito; **II.** 2 *n* (-s; -s) disguise; ***sein ~ wahren*** (manage to) hide one's true identity; ***sein ~ lüften*** reveal one's true identity, drop one's mask

in·kom·pa·ti·bel [ɪnkɔmpa'ti:bəl] *adj.* incompatible; **In·kom·pa·ti·bi·li·tät** ['ɪnkɔmpatibilitɛ:t] *f* (-; *no pl.*) incompatibility

in·kom·pe·tent ['ɪnkɔmpetɛnt] *adj.* incompetent; **In·kom·pe·tenz** ['ɪnkɔmpetɛnts] *f* (-; *no pl.*) incompetence

in·kon·gru·ent ['ɪnkɔngruɛnt] *adj.* ⩓ incongruent; *fig.* incongruous; **In·kon·gru·enz** ['ɪnkɔngruɛnts] *f* (-; *no pl.*) incongruity

in·kon·se·quent ['ɪnkɔnzekvɛnt] *adj.* **1.** inconsistent *behavio(u)r etc.*; **2.** illogical, not logical; **In·kon·se·quenz** ['ɪnkɔnzekvɛnts] *f* (-; -en) **1.** inconsistency; **2.** illogicality, lack of logic

in·kor·rekt ['ɪnkɔrɛkt] *adj.* incorrect; inaccurate; inappropriate, improper *behavio(u)r, clothes etc.*

In'kraft|set·zung *f* (-; *no pl.*) ⚖ introduction, enactment; **~tre·ten** *n*: ***bei ~ des Gesetzes*** *etc.* when the law *etc.* comes into effect (*or* is introduced); ***Tag des ~s*** effective date

in·kri·mi·nie·ren [ɪnkrimi'ni:rən] *v/t.* (h) incriminate

In·ku·ba·ti·ons·zeit [ɪnkuba'tsi̯o:ns-] *f* incubation (⚕ *a.* latency) period

In·ku·ba·tor [ɪnku'ba:to:ɐ] *m* (-s; -en [-ba'to:rən]) incubator

In·ku·bus ['ɪnkubʊs] *m* (-; -ben [ɪn'ku:bən]) incubus

In·ku·na·bel [ɪnku'na:bəl] *f* (-; -n) incunabulum (*pl.* incunabula), cradle book, incunable; early printed book

In·land ['ɪnlant] *n* (-[e]s; *no pl.*) home; ***im In- und Ausland*** at home and abroad; ***im ~ hergestellt*** domestic *product etc.*; ***für das ~ bestimmt*** for home consumption

'In·land... *usu.* home; internal; domestic; **~eis** *n* ice sheet; **~flug** *m* domestic (*or* internal) flight

in·län·disch ['ɪnlɛndɪʃ] *adj.* home ..., domestic ...; internal *traffic*

'In·lands|ab·satz *m* ✝ domestic sales *pl.*; **~ab,tei·lung** *f* domestic (sales) department; **~auf·trag** *m* domestic order; **~brief** *m* inland (*Am.* domestic) letter; **~han·del** *m* domestic trade; **~markt** *m* home (*or* domestic) market; **~por·to** *n* inland (*Am.* domestic) postage; **~post** *f* inland (*Am.* domestic) mail; **~pres·se** *f* domestic press; **~ta,rif** *m* inland (*Am.* domestic) rate; **~te·le,gramm** *n* inland (*Am.* domestic) telegram; **~wech·sel** *m* inland (*Am.* domestic) bill of exchange

In·lay ['ınleı] *n* (-s; -s) ⚕ inlay
In·lett ['ınlɛt] *n* (-[e]s; -e) ticking
in me·di·as res [ın 'meːdĭaːs reːs]: ~ **gehen** get straight to the point, *formal*: plunge in medias res
in'mit·ten I. *prp.* (*gen.*) in the middle (*lit.* midst) of; **II.** *adv.*: ~ **von** *dat.* among(st), surrounded by
in na·tu·ra [ın na'tuːra] *adv.* in real life; *a.* in the flesh
in·ne|ha·ben ['ınə-] *v/t.* (*irr.*, *sep.*, h, → **haben**) hold *office*, *record etc.*; **~hal·ten** *v/i.* (*irr.*, *sep.*, h, → **halten**) stop, pause
in·nen ['ınən] *adv.* (on the) inside; ~ **und außen** inside and out(side); **nach** ~ **tragen** *etc.* carry *etc.* inside; **nach** ~ (**zu**) inwards; **die Tür geht nach** ~ **auf** the door opens inwards (*or* into the hall *etc.*); **nach** ~ **gekehrt** inside-out, *fur lining etc.*: on the inside, facing inwards, *fig.* introspective, introverted *person*; **von** ~ from (the) inside; **hast du das Haus von** ~ **gesehen?** have you been inside the house?; **hast du ein Filmstudio** (**Fernsehgerät**) **schon einmal von** ~ **gesehen?** *a.* have you ever seen a film studio (TV set) from the inside?, F have you ever seen the insides of a film studio (TV set)?
'**In·nen|ab·mes·sun·gen** *pl.* inside measurements (*or* dimensions); **~an·sicht** *f* interior view; **~an,ten·ne** *f* indoor aerial (*or* antenna); **~ar·bei·ten** *pl.* ⚠ indoor work *sg.*; **~ar·chi,tekt** *m* interior designer; **~ar·chi·tek,tur** *f* interior design; **~auf·nah·me** *f phot.* indoor (*film*: studio) shot; **~aus·schuß** *m* committee on internal affairs; **~aus·stat·tung** *f* décor; *mot.* interior fittings *pl.*; ✈ inside furnishings *pl.*; **~bahn** *f sport*: inside lane; **~be·leuch·tung** *f* interior lighting; **~dienst** *m* office work; **im** ~ **tätig sein** work in the office (F at base); **~,durch·mes·ser** *m* inside diameter; **~ein·rich·tung** *f* → **Innenausstattung**; **~flä·che** *f* **1.** inside surface; **2.** *anat.* palm; **~fut·ter** *n* inside lining, liner; **~hof** *m* (inner) courtyard; **~kan·te** *f* inside (*or* inner) edge; **~la·ge** *f skiing*: inward lean; **~le·ben** *n* **1.** inner life; *iro.* **erzähl mir etwas aus d-m** (**reichen**) ~ tell me what's been going on in that mind of yours; **2.** *fig.* internal *or* inner mechanism (*or* workings *pl.*), F insides *pl.* *of a watch etc.*; **~lei·tun·gen** *pl.* internal wiring *sg.*; **~leuch·te** *f mot.* courtesy light; **~mi,ni·ster** *m* minister of the interior; *in GB*: Home Secretary; *in the USA*: Secretary of the Interior; **~mi·ni,ste·ri·um** *n* interior ministry; *in GB*: Home Office; *in the USA*: Department of the Interior; **~ohr** *n* inner ear; **~po·li,tik** *f* domestic policy (*or* policies *pl.*); **ᴥpo,li·tisch I.** *adj.* domestic (political), internal, home *affairs*; **~e Auseinandersetzung** dispute over domestic policy; **II.** *adv.* on the domestic front; ~ **gesehen** as far as domestic policy is (*or* home affairs are) concerned; **~raum** *m* **1.** interior; **2.** cent|re (*Am.* -er), central part (*or* area) *of a city etc.*; **~sei·te** *f* inside; **~ski** *m* inside ski; **~spie·gel** *m mot.* inside mirror; **~stadt** *f* town (*or* city) cent|re (*Am.* -er), *Am. a.* downtown; **in der** ~ **leben** *Am.* live downtown; **~ta·sche** *f* inside pocket; **~tem·pe·ra,tur** *f* inside (*or* indoor) temperature; **~tür** *f* inside door; **~ver·klei·dung** *f* inside (*or* interior) lining; **~wand** *f* inside wall; **~,wi·der·stand** *m* ⚡ internal resistance; **~win·kel** *m* ⩘ internal angle
in·ner ['ınɐ] *adj.* inside; *pol.* internal, domestic; *fig.* inner; mental; ⚕ internal *bleeding*, *medicine etc.*; *fig.* **das ~e Auge** one's mind's eye; **ohne ~en Halt** very insecure; **~er Konflikt** inner conflict; **e-n ~en Konflikt haben** be torn; **~er Monolog** interior monolog(ue); **~e Ordnung** internal order; **~e Unruhe** agitation; **~e Uhr** body clock, 🕮 circadian rhythms; **~e Ruhe** peace of mind; **~e Stimme** inner voice, voice inside (*or* within) one; **~er Wert** intrinsic value; **~er Widerspruch** contradiction in itself, *w.s.* inconsistency; **~be·trieb·lich** *adj.* ✝ internal; in-company *training etc.*; **~deutsch** *adj.* **1.** German, domestic, internal; **2.** *hist.* German-German, inter-German; **~e Grenze** inner-German border
In·ne·re[1] ['ınərə] *n* (-n; *no pl.*) interior (*a. geogr.*), inside; heart, core, cent|re (*Am.* -er); *fig.* *s.o.'s* inner being, mind, heart, soul; **im ~n** inside, *geogr.* in the interior, *pol.* on the home front; *fig.* at heart, secretly; **Minister des ~n** → **Innenminister**; *fig.* **tief im ~n** deep down (inside); **ich würde gern wissen, was in s-m ~n so vor sich geht** I'd like to know what's going on inside him (*or* what's going through his mind *or* head)
'**In·ne·re**[2] F *f* (-n; *no pl.*) ⚕ **1.** internal medicine; **2. in der ~n arbeiten** (**liegen**) F be in medical
In·ne·rei·en [ınə'raıən] *pl.* **1.** *gastr.* innards; giblets; guts; **2.** F *fig.* F insides, innards, entrails
in·ner·halb ['ınɐhalp] **I.** *prp.* (*gen.*) a) inside, within (*a. fig.*), b) within, in; during; ~ **e-r Woche** within a week; **II.** *adv.*: ~ **von** *dat.* within; *a.* within a period of
in·ner·lich ['ınɐlıç] **I.** *adj.* **1.** ⚕ internal; **2.** *fig.* inner; introspective; emotional; **II.** *adv.* **3.** ⚕ internally; *pharm.* ~ (**anzuwenden**) for internal use (only); **4.** *fig.* *moved etc.* inwardly; (deep down) inside; secretly; ~ **lachen** laugh to o.s.; '**In·ner·lich·keit** *f* (-; *no pl.*) sensitivity; depth; introspection
'**in·ner|par·la·men,ta·risch** *adj.* intra-parliamentary; **~par,tei·lich** *adj. pol.* inner-party ...., internal; **~e Kämpfe** (party) infighting; **~po,li·tisch** *adj.* → **innenpolitisch**
in·nerst ['ınɐst] *adj.* innermost; *fig. a.* inmost; **die ~en Gedanken** (**Wünsche**) one's most secret thoughts (desires)
'**in·ner|staat·lich** *adj.* internal; **~städ·tisch** *adj.* urban, inner-city ...
In·ner·ste ['ınɐstə] *n* (-n; *no pl.*) the innermost part; heart, core; **im ~n des Waldes** in the heart of the forest; *fig.* **bis ins** ~ to the heart (*or* core); **in s-m ~n, im ~n s-r Seele** deep down (inside), in his heart of hearts
'**in·ne|sein** *v/i.* (*only inf. and p.p.* innegewesen, sn): **e-r Sache** ~ be aware of s.th.; **~wer·den** *v/i.* (*only inf. and p.p.* innegeworden, sn): **e-r Sache** ~ become aware of s.th.; **~woh·nen** *v/i.* (*sep.*, h): **e-r Sache** ~ be inherent in s.th.; **~woh·nend** *adj.* inherent (*dat.* in), innate (in)
in·nig ['ınıç] **I.** *adj.* tender, affectionate; ardent, fervent; heartfelt, sincere; close *friendship etc.*; **II.** *adv.* tenderly *etc.*; → **heiß** II; '**In·nig·keit** *f* (-; *no pl.*) tenderness; ardo(u)r; sincerity; closeness; **in·nig·lich** ['ınıklıç] *adv.* → **innig** II; **in·nigst** ['ınıçst] *adj.*: **mein ~er Wunsch** my greatest desire
In·no·va·ti·on [ınova'tsĭoːn] *f* (-; -en) innovation
in·no·va·ti'ons|feind·lich *adj.* hostile to (any form of) innovation, unwilling to adapt (to the times); **~freu·dig** *adj.* innovative
in·no·va·tiv [ınova'tiːf] *adj.* innovative; **in·no·va·to·risch** [ınova'toːrıʃ] *adj.* innovational; **in·no·vie·ren** [ıno'viːrən] *v/t. and v/i.* (h) innovate
in nu·ce [ın 'nuːtsə] *adv.* in nuce, in a nutshell, in short, in a word
In·nung ['ınʊŋ] *f* (-; -en) (trade) guild; F *fig.* **die ganze** ~ **blamieren** F let the side down; '**In·nungs·ver·band** *m* association of trade guilds
in·of·fi·zi·ell ['ınˀɔfitsĭɛl] *adj.* unofficial; off-the-record *statement*; informal *talks etc.*
in·ope·ra·bel ['ınˀoperaːbəl] *adj.* ⚕ inoperable; **es ist** ~ *a.* it can't be operated on
in pet·to [ın 'pɛto] *adv.*: **et.** ~ **haben** have s.th. up one's sleeve
in punc·to [ın 'pʊŋkto] *prp.* (*gen.*) when it comes to, where (*or* as far as) ... is (*or* are) concerned, in matters of, as regards
In·qui·si·ti·on [ınkvizi'tsĭoːn] *f* (-; -en) **1.** *no pl. hist.* Inquisition; **2.** *fig.* inquisition; **In·qui·si·ti'ons·ge·richt** *n* Court of Inquisition; **In·qui·si·tor** [ınkvi'ziːtoːɐ] *m* (-s; -en [-kvizi'toːrən] inquisitor
ins [ıns] (= **in das**) → **in**
In·sas·se ['ınzasə] *m* (-n; -n) *mot.* passenger; (*prison*) inmate; '**In·sas·sen·ver·si·che·rung** *f mot.* passenger insurance (cover); **In·sas·sin** ['ınzasın] *f* (-; -nen) → **Insasse**
ins·be·son·de·re [ınsbə'zɔndərə] *adv.* particularly, (e)specially, in particular
'**In·schrift** *f* (-; -en) inscription; *a.* epigraph
In·sekt [ın'zɛkt] *n* (-[e]s; -en) insect, *esp. Am.* bug
In·sek·ten|be·kämp·fung [ın'zɛktən-] *f* insect (*or* pest) control; **~be·kämp·fungs·mit·tel** *n* insecticide; **~for·scher** *m* entomologist; **~fraß** *m* insect damage; **ᴥfres·send** *adj.* insectivorous; **~fres·ser** *m* insectivore, insect-eater; **~gift** *n* **1.** *zo.* insect poison; **2.** insecticide; **~kun·de** *f*, **~leh·re** *f* entomology; **~pla·ge** *f* plague of insects; **~spray** *m*, *n* insect spray; **~staat** *m* insect state; **~stich** *m* insect bite; **~ver·til·gungs·mit·tel** *n* insecticide
In·sek·ti·zid [ınzɛkti'tsiːt] *n* (-[e]s; -e [-də]) insecticide
In·sel ['ınzəl] *f* (-; -n) island (*a. fig.*); *poet.* isle; **die** ~ **Wight** the Isle of Wight; **die Britischen ~n** the British Isles
'**In·sel·be·woh·ner** *m* islander
In·sel·chen ['ınzəlçən] *n* (-s; -) islet
'**In·sel|grup·pe** *f* group of islands, archipelago; **~ket·te** *f* string of islands; **~la·ge** *f* island position; **~meer** *n* archipelago; **~pa·ra,dies** *n* island (*or* tropical) paradise; **~re·pu,blik** *f* island republic; **~staat** *m* island state; **~volk** *n* (nation of) islanders *pl.*; **~welt** *f* (group of) islands *pl.*
In·se·rat [ınze'raːt] *n* (-[e]s; -e) advertisement, ad, *Brit. a.* advert; **ein** ~ **aufgeben** → **inserieren** II; **In·se·rent** [ınze'rɛnt] *m* (-en; -en) advertiser; **in·se·rie·ren** [ınze'riːrən] (h) **I.** *v/t.* advertise; **II.** *v/i.* advertise, place an ad *or* advertisement (in the *or* a paper)

ins·ge·heim [ɪnsgə'haɪm] *adv.* secretly; behind s.o.'s back
ins·ge·mein [ɪnsgə'maɪn] *obs. adv.* generally; on the whole
ins·ge·samt [ɪnsgə'zamt] *adv.* a) altogether, in all, b) as a whole; ***er erhielt ~ 500 Briefe*** he received a total of 500 letters; ***s-e Schulden betragen ~ ...*** his debts total ...
In·si·der ['ɪnsaɪdɐ] *m* (-s; -) insider; **~ge·schäf·te** *pl.* insider trading *sg.*, insider dealings (*or* dealing *sg.*)
In·si·gni·en [ɪn'zɪgnĭən] *pl.* insignia
in·si·stie·ren [ɪnzɪs'tiːrən] *v/i.* (h) insist (***auf*** *dat.* on); ***darauf ~, daß*** insist that; ***er insistierte darauf, daß ich komme*** *a.* he insisted on my coming
in·so·fern [ɪn'zoːfɛrn] **I.** *adv.* as far as that goes (*or* is concerned), from that point of view; **II.** *cj.*: ~ (***als***) in so far as, insofar as, inasmuch as, in that; if; ***er hat ~ recht, als*** he's right in so far as *etc.*
in·sol·vent ['ɪnzɔlvɛnt] *adj.* ✝ insolvent; **In·sol·venz** ['ɪnzɔlvɛnts] *f* (-; -en) insolvency
in'so·weit *adv. and cj.* → ***insofern***
in spe [ɪn 'speː] *adj.* ...-to-be, future ...; ***ein Arzt ~*** *a.* a doctor in the making
In·spek·teur [ɪnspɛk'tøːɐ] *m* (-s; -e [-'tøːrə]) inspector; ⚔ Chief of Staff
In·spek·ti·on [ɪnspɛk'tsĭoːn] *f* (-; -en) **1.** inspection; **2.** *mot.* service; ***zur ~ bringen*** put *the car* in for a service; **3.** inspectorate; **In·spek·ti'ons·gang** *m* inspection round
In·spek·tor [ɪn'spɛktoːɐ] *m* (-s; -en [ɪnspɛk'toːrən]) inspector
In·spi·ra·ti·on [ɪnspira'tsĭoːn] *f* (-; -en) inspiration; **in·spi·rie·ren** [ɪnspi'riːrən] *v/t.* (h) inspire; ***j-n zu e-m Gedicht*** (***e-m Gemälde*** *etc.*) ~ inspire s.o. to write a poem (paint a picture *etc.*); ***j-n zu e-r Idee ~*** give s.o. an idea; ***sich ~ lassen von*** *dat.* draw inspiration from; F ***laß dich mal ~!*** see if you can come up with something; F ***ich muß mich mal ~ lassen*** I'll have to go away and think about it; **in·spi·riert** [ɪnspi'riːɐt] *adj.* inspired
In·spi·zi·ent [ɪnspi'tsĭɛnt] *m* (-en; -en) *thea.* stage manager
in·spi·zie·ren [ɪnspi'tsiːrən] *v/t.* (h) inspect; examine
in·sta·bil ['ɪnstabiːl] *adj.* unstable; ⚙ *a.* not stable; **In·sta·bi·li·tät** ['ɪnstabilitɛːt] *f* (-; *no pl.*) instability
In·stal·la·teur [ɪnstala'tøːɐ] *m* (-s; -e [-'tøːrə]) plumber; gas fitter; ⚡ electrician; **In·stal·la·ti·on** [ɪnstala'tsĭoːn] *f* (-; -en) **1.** installation; **2.** installation; plumbing; **in·stal·lie·ren** [ɪnsta'liːrən] (h) **I.** *v/t.* put in, fit, instal(l); **II.** *v/refl.*: ***sich ~*** instal(l) o.s.
in·stand [ɪn'ʃtant] *adv.*: ~ ***halten*** keep in good condition (*or* repair); maintain, service; ~ ***setzen*** repair, renovate, recondition; ***j-n ~ setzen zu*** *inf.* enable s.o. to *inf.*, put s.o. in a position to *inf.*
in'stand·be·set·zen *v/t.* (h) occupy and refurbish; **In'stand·be·set·zung** *f* (-; -en) squatter-renovation
In'stand·hal·tung *f* (-; *no pl.*) upkeep, maintenance; ⚙, *mot.* servicing; **In'stand·hal·tungs·ko·sten** *pl.* maintenance costs
in·stän·dig ['ɪnʃtɛndɪç] **I.** *adj.* urgent; **II.** *adv.*: ***j-n ~ bitten*** implore *s.o.*; **'In·stän·dig·keit** *f* (-; *no pl.*) urgency
In'stand·set·zung *f* (-; *no pl.*) repair; renovation; **In'stand·set·zungs·ar·beit** *f* repair work, repairs *pl.* (***an*** *dat.* on)
In·stanz [ɪn'stants] *f* (-; -en) authority; ⚖ instance; ***höhere ~en*** higher authorities (⚖ courts); ⚖ ***in erster ~*** at first instance; ***Gericht erster ~*** court of first instance, *a.* trial court; ***in letzter ~*** without further appeal, ***entscheiden:*** make the final decision, *fig.* have the final say, ultimately decide; **In·stan·zen·weg** [ɪn'stantsən-] *m* ⚖ (successive) stages *pl.* of appeal; ***auf dem ~*** through the prescribed channels
In·stinkt [ɪn'stɪŋkt] *m* (-[e]s; -e) instinct; *w.s. a.* feeling; ***aus ~*** instinctively; ***s-m ~ folgen*** follow one's instincts (F one's nose); ***mein ~ sagt mir*** my instinct tells me, I have an instinctive feeling; ***e-n ~ haben für*** *acc.* have an instinctive feel for, F have a nose for; ***an die niederen ~e des Menschen appellieren*** appeal to the baser human instincts; **in'stinkt·haft** *adj.* instinctive; **In'stinkt·hand·lung** *f* instinctive act (*or* reaction); **in·stink·tiv** [ɪnstɪŋk'tiːf] **I.** *adj.* instinctive, intuitive; *a.* visceral *reaction etc.*; instinctive, innate *fear etc.*; ***~e Begabung*** natural talent; **II.** *adv.* instinctively, intuitively; **in'stinkt·los** *adj.* lacking in instinct; *w.s.* tactless, insensitive; **in'stinkt·mä·ßig** **I.** *adj.* instinctive; **II.** *adv.* instinctively, on (an) instinct; **in'stinkt·si·cher** **I.** *adj.*: ~ ***sein*** have a good (*or* an unerring) instinct, F have a good nose; **II.** *adv.*: ~ ***handeln*** rely on one's instincts; ***er hat wieder einmal ~ gehandelt*** his instinct proved him right again
In·sti·tut [ɪnsti'tuːt] *n* (-[e]s; -e) institute; **In·sti·tu·ti·on** [ɪnstitu'tsĭoːn] *f* (-; -en) institution (*a. fig.*); **in·sti·tu·tio·na·li·sie·ren** [ɪnstitutsĭonali'ziːrən] *v/t.* (h) institutionalize; **in·sti·tu·tio·nell** [ɪnstitutsĭo'nɛl] *adj.* institutional(ly *adv.*)
in·stru·ie·ren [ɪnstru'iːrən] *v/t.* (h) give *s.o.* instructions (***über*** *acc.* on); *a.* ⚔ brief (on); inform (about); **In·struk·ti·on** [ɪnstrʊk'tsĭoːn] *f* (-; -en) instruction; *a.* directions *pl.*; **in·struk·tiv** [ɪnstrʊk'tiːf] *adj.* instructive
In·stru·ment [ɪnstru'mɛnt] *n* (-[e]s; -e) instrument; ⚙ *a.* tool, implement
in·stru·men·tal [ɪnstrumɛn'taːl] *adj.* instrumental
In·stru·men'tal|auf·nah·me *f* instrumental version; **~be·glei·tung** *f* instrumental accompaniment; **~mu·sik** *f* instrumental music; **~stück** *n* instrumental (piece)
In·stru·men·ta·ri·um [ɪnstrumɛn'taːrĭʊm] *n* (-s; -rien) *a. fig.* instruments *pl.*
In·stru·men·ten|bau [ɪnstru'mɛntən-] *m* (-[e]s; *no pl.*) instrument making; **~bau·er** *m* (-s; -) instrument maker; **~be·leuch·tung** *f mot.* dashboard lighting; **~brett** *n* instrument panel; *mot. a.* dashboard; ✈ *a.* control panel; **~flug** *m* instrument flying (*or* flight)
in·stru·men·tie·ren [ɪnstrumɛn'tiːrən] *v/t.* (h) ♪ arrange (for instruments); **In·stru·men'tie·rung** *f* (-; -en) arrangement (for instruments), instrumentation
In·sub·or·di·na·ti·on ['ɪnzʊpˀɔrdinatsĭoːn] *f* (-; -en) insubordination
In·suf·fi·zi·enz ['ɪnzʊfitsĭɛnts] *f* (-; -en) *esp.* ⚕ insufficiency
In·su·la·ner [ɪnzu'laːnɐ] *m* (-s; -), **In·su·la·ne·rin** [ɪnzu'laːnərɪn] *f* (-; -nen) islander
In·su·lin [ɪnzu'liːn] *n* (-s; *no pl.*) insulin; **~man·gel** *m* insulin deficiency; **~schock** *m* insulin (*or* hypoglyc[a]emic) shock; **~sprit·ze** *f* insulin injection (F jab)
in·sze·nie·ren [ɪnstse'niːrən] *v/t.* (h) *thea.* (put on) stage, produce (*a. film*), mount; direct *a film*; *fig.* stage *a revolt, strike etc.*, *a.* F kick up *a row*; conduct, orchestrate *a campaign etc.*; **In·sze'nie·rung** *f* (-; -en) production; **~: *X*** produced by X
in·takt [ɪn'takt] *adj.* intact (*a. fig.*); ⚕ *a.* in good shape; *mot.*, ⚙ *a.* in good working order; ***das Dach ist ~ geblieben*** the roof is still intact (*or* in one piece)
In·tar·si·en [ɪn'tarzĭən] *pl.* inlaid work *sg.*, marquetry *sg.*
in·te·ger [ɪn'teːgɐ] *adj. man* of integrity
in·te·gral [ɪnte'graːl] *adj.* 𝔸 integral
In·te'gral|bau·wei·se *f* integral construction; **~glei·chung** *f* integral equation; **~rech·nung** *f* integral calculus; **~zei·chen** *n* integral sign
In·te·gra·ti·on [ɪntegra'tsĭoːn] *f* (-; -en) integration; **In·te·gra·ti'ons·pro,zeß** *m* process of integration
in·te·grie·ren [ɪnte'griːrən] (h) **I.** *v/t.* 𝔸 *and fig.* integrate (***in*** *acc.* into); **II.** *v/refl.*: ***sich ~*** integrate (o.s.), become integrated (***in*** *acc.* into); **in·te·griert** [ɪnte'griːɐt] *adj.* integrated; ***~er Schaltkreis*** integrated circuit, IC
In·te·gri·tät [ɪntegri'tɛːt] *f* (-; *no pl.*) integrity (*a. pol.*)
In·tel·lekt [ɪntɛ'lɛkt] *m* (-[e]s; *no pl.*) intellect; **in·tel·lek·tu·ell** [ɪntɛlɛk'tŭɛl] *adj.* intellectual, F highbrow; cerebral; **In·tel·lek·tu·el·le** [ɪntɛlɛk'tŭɛlə] *m, f* (-n; -n) intellectual, F highbrow
in·tel·li·gent [ɪntɛli'gɛnt] *adj.* intelligent, bright
In·tel·li·genz [ɪntɛli'gɛnts] *f* (-; *no pl.*) **1.** intelligence; **2.** intelligentsia; **~be·stie** F *f* F brain(box); ***das ist e-e ~*** F he's (*or* she's) a real brain; **~grad** *m* level of intelligence; **~lei·stung** *f* feat of (human) intelligence
In·tel·li·genz·ler [ɪntɛlɪ'gɛntslɐ] F *m* (-s; -) F egghead
In·tel·li'genz|quo·ti,ent *m* intelligence quotient, IQ; **~test** *m* intelligence test
In·ten·dant [ɪntɛn'dant] *m* (-en; -en) *thea. etc.* director; **In·ten·danz** [ɪntɛn'dants] *f* (-; -en) **1.** directorship; ***die ~ von ... übernehmen*** take over as director of ...; **2.** director's office(s *pl.*)
in·ten·die·ren [ɪntɛn'diːrən] *v/t.* (h) intend; aim at, plan
In·ten·si·tät [ɪntɛnzi'tɛːt] *f* (-; *no pl.*) intensity; **in·ten·siv** [ɪntɛn'ziːf] **I.** *adj.* intensive, thorough; intense *pain, interest etc.*; **II.** *adv.* intensively; intensely; ***sich ~ bemühen*** try very hard, make a great (*or* tremendous) effort; ***sich ~ auf e-e Prüfung vorbereiten*** study hard for an exam, F grind (*Brit.* swot) away; ~ ***nachdenken*** think hard; ***j-n ~ ansehen*** give s.o. a long, hard look; **in·ten·si·vie·ren** [ɪntɛnzi'viːrən] *v/t.* (h) intensify; a. step up *one's efforts etc.*; **In·ten·si'vie·rung** *f* (-; *no pl.*) intensification; *a.* stepping up *of efforts*
In·ten'siv|in·ter·view *n* (in-)depth interview; **~kurs** *m* crash course; **~sta·ti,on** *f* ⚕ intensive care unit
In·ten·ti·on [ɪntɛn'tsĭoːn] *f* (-; -en) intention

In·ter·ak·ti·on [ɪntɐʔak'tsĭoːn] *f* (-; -en) interaction
In·ter·ci·ty(-Zug) [ɪntɐ'sɪti-] *m* inter-city (train)
In·ter·dikt [ɪntɐ'dɪkt] *n* (-[e]s; -e) *eccl.* interdict
in·ter·dis·zi·pli·när [ɪntɐdɪstsipli'nɛːɐ] *adj.* interdisciplinary
in·ter·es·sant [ɪntərɛ'sant] **I.** *adj.* interesting; attractive *deal etc.*; ***das* ≗*e daran*** the interesting thing about it; ***er will sich bei ihr bloß ~ machen*** he's just trying to impress her; ***das ist überhaupt nicht ~*** that's totally irrelevant; **II.** *adv.*: ***er kann ~ erzählen*** he's a good story-teller; **in·ter·es·san·ter·wei·se** [ɪntərɛ'santɐ'vaɪzə] *adv.* interestingly, it's interesting that ...
In·ter·es·se [ɪntə'rɛsə] *n* (-s; -n) interest (***an*** *dat.*, ***für*** *acc.* in); ***das ~ verlieren*** lose interest; ***~ zeigen*** show an (*or* some) interest (***für*** *acc.* in); ***~ haben an*** *dat.* (*or* ***für*** *acc.*) be interested in; ***es ist für mich nicht von ~*** it's of no interest to me; ***sein besonderes ~ gilt*** *dat.* **...** he's particularly interested in ..., his special area of interest is ...; ***in j-s ~ sein*** be in s.o.'s interest; ***ich tat es in d-m ~*** I did it for your sake; ***im öffentlichen ~*** in the public interest; ***es besteht kein ~ an*** *dat.* nobody's interested in, there's no demand for; **in·ter'es·se·hal·ber** [-halbɐ] *adv.* out of interest, as a matter of interest
in·ter'es·se·los *adj.* uninterested, indifferent; **In·ter'es·se·lo·sig·keit** *f* (-; *no pl.*) indifference, apathy
In·ter·es·sen|aus·gleich [ɪntə'rɛsən-] *m* balancing of interests; **~ge·biet** *n* field (*or* area) of interest; **~ge·gen·satz** *m* conflict of interests; **~ge·mein·schaft** *f* **1.** interest group; ✝ pooling agreement; combine, pool; syndicate; **2.** common interest(s *pl.*); **~kol·li·si͵on** *f* clash of interests; **~kon͵flikt** *m* conflict of interests; **~la·ge** *f*: ***die ~ erforderte es, daß*** it was in their *etc.* interests to *inf.*; **~schwer·punkt** *m* focus of interest; **~sphä·re** *f* sphere of influence
In·ter·es·sent [ɪntərɛ'sɛnt] *m* (-en; -en) **1.** ✝ prospective buyer; ***wir haben schon drei ~en*** *a.* there are already three people interested, three people have rung up *etc.* already; **2.** interested person; ***~en sollen sich melden*** *etc.* anyone (*or* those) interested please apply *etc.*; **3.** applicant; **4.** interested party; **In·ter·es·sen·ten·kreis** [ɪntərɛ'sɛntən-] *m* group of interested people, those *pl.* interested; ✝ prospective buyers *pl.*, market
In·ter·es·sen|ver·band [ɪntə'rɛsən-] *m* pressure group, lobby; **~ver·tre·ter** *m* representative, spokesman, spokesperson; **~wahr·neh·mung** *f* (-; *no pl.*) safeguarding of interests
in·ter·es·sie·ren [ɪntərɛ'siːrən] (h) **I.** *v/refl.* **1. *sich ~ für*** *acc.* be interested in; ***sich gar nicht ~ für*** *acc. a.* take no interest in; ***er interessiert sich für nichts*** he's not interested in anything; **II.** *v/t.* **2. *das Buch*** *etc.* ***interessiert mich nicht*** I'm not interested in the book *etc.*, the book *etc.* doesn't interest me; ***das interessiert mich überhaupt nicht*** I'm not in the least bit interested, I couldn't care less; ***es wird dich ~ zu erfahren*** you'll be interested to know; **3. *j-n für et. ~*** interest s.o. in s.th., get s.o. interested in s.th.; **III.** *v/i.* ***das interessiert nicht*** that's of no interest, that's irrelevant; **in·ter·es·siert** [ɪntərɛ'siːɐt] **I.** *adj.* interested (***an*** *dat.* in); ***politisch*** *etc.* **~** interested in politics *etc.*, politically *etc.* aware; ***musikalisch* ≗*e*** *the* musically minded, music lovers; ***sehr daran ~ sein, daß es klappt*** *etc.* be keen to see it work out *etc.*; **II.** *adv.*: ***~ zuhören*** (***zuschauen***) listen (watch) intently
In·ter·fe·renz [ɪntɐfe'rɛnts] *f* (-; -en) *phys. and ling.* interference; **~er·schei·nung** *f* interference phenomenon
In·ter·fe·ron [ɪntɐfe'roːn] *n* (-s; -e) *biol.*, ⚕ interferon
In·te·rieur [ɛ̃te'rĭøːɐ] *n* (-s; -s) interior
In·te·rim ['ɪnterɪm] *n* (-s; -s) **1.** temporary arrangement, interim solution; **2.** interim; **in·te·ri·mi·stisch** [ɪnteri'mɪstɪʃ] *adj.* interim ...
'In·te·rims|ab·kom·men *n* temporary agreement; **~lö·sung** *f* interim (*or* stop-gap) solution; **~re͵gie·rung** *f* caretaker (*or* interim, transitional) government
In·ter·jek·ti·on [ɪntɐjɛk'tsĭoːn] *f* (-; -en) interjection
in·ter·kon·fes·sio·nell [ɪntɐkɔnfɛsĭo'nɛl] *adj.* interdenominational
in·ter·kon·ti·nen·tal [ɪntɐkɔntinɛn'taːl] *adj.* intercontinental
In·ter·kon·ti·nen'tal|flug *m* intercontinental flight; **~ra͵ke·te** *f* intercontinental ballistic missile
in·ter·li·ne·ar [ɪntɐline'aːɐ] *adj.*, ≗... *in cpds.* interlinear
In·ter·mez·zo [ɪntɐ'mɛtso] *n* (-s; -zi [-tsi]) ♪ intermezzo, interlude (*a. fig.*)
in·tern [ɪn'tɛrn] **I.** *adj.* internal; ***das ist e-e ~e Sache*** *a.* that's something that concerns us (*or* them *etc.*); **II.** *adv.* internally; among ourselves (*or* themselves *etc.*); (*a.* ***~ gesehen***) seen from the inside, on the inside
in·ter·na·li·sie·ren [ɪntɛrnali'ziːrən] *v/t.* (h) internalize; **In·ter·na·li'sie·rung** *f* (-; *no pl.*) internalization
In·ter·nat [ɪntɐ'naːt] *n* (-[e]s; -e) boarding school
in·ter·na·tio·nal [ɪntɐnatsĭo'naːl] **I.** *adj.* international; **II.** *adv.*: ***~ bekannt*** internationally known, world-renowned
In·ter·na·tio·na·le [ɪntɐnatsĭo'naːlə] *f* (-; -n) International(e)
in·ter·na·tio·na·li·sie·ren [ɪntɐnatsĭonali'ziːrən] *v/t.* (h) internationalize; **In·ter·na·tio·na·li'sie·rung** *f* (-; *no pl.*) internationalization
In·ter·na·tio·na·lis·mus [ɪntɐnatsĭona'lɪsmʊs] *m* (-; *no pl.*) internationalism
In·ter·na·tio·na·li·tät [ɪntɐnatsĭonali'tɛːt] *f* (-; *no pl.*) international character; mix of nationalities, international mix
In·ter'nats|schu·le *f* boarding school; **~schü·ler** *m* boarder
In·ter·ne [ɪn'tɛrnə] *m, f* (-n; -n) boarder
in·ter·nie·ren [ɪntɐ'niːrən] *v/t.* (h) intern; ⚕ isolate; **In·ter·nier·te** [ɪntɐ'niːɐtə] *m, f* (-n; -n) internee; **In·ter'nie·rung** *f* (-; -en) internment; **In·ter'nie·rungs·la·ger** *n* detention camp
In·ter·nist [ɪntɐ'nɪst] *m* (-en; -en) ⚕ internist; **in·ter·ni·stisch** [ɪntɐ'nɪstɪʃ] *adj.* internal(-medical)
in·ter·par·la·men·ta·risch [ɪntɐparlamɛn'taːrɪʃ] *adj.* interparliamentary
In·ter·pel·lant [ɪntɐpɛ'lant] *m* (-en; -en) *parl.* questioner; **In·ter·pel·la·ti·on** [ɪntɐpɛla'tsĭoːn] *f* (-; -en) (parliamentary) question; **in·ter·pel·lie·ren** [ɪntɐpɛ'liːrən] *v/i.* (h) ask (*or* put) a question (in parliament)
in·ter·pla·ne·ta·risch [ɪntɐplane'taːrɪʃ] *adj.* interplanetary
In·ter·po·la·ti·on [ɪntɐpola'tsĭoːn] *f* (-; -en) interpolation; **in·ter·po·lie·ren** [ɪntɐpo'liːrən] *v/t. and v/i.* (h) interpolate
In·ter·pret [ɪntɐ'preːt] *m* (-en; -en) **1.** interpreter; exponent; **2.** ♪ performer; singer; ***er ist ein bekannter Schubert-~*** he's famous for his Schubert interpretations (*or* performances); **In·ter·pre·ta·ti·on** [ɪntɐpreta'tsĭoːn] *f* (-; -en) interpretation; ♪ *etc.*: *a.* rendering; **in·ter·pre·tie·ren** [ɪntɐpre'tiːrən] *v/t.* (h) interpret (*a.* ♪); *a.* understand; ⚖ construe; ***et. ~ als*** interpret s.th. as, take s.th. as *an insult etc.*
In·ter·punk·ti·on [ɪntɐpʊŋk'tsĭoːn] *f* (-; *no pl.*) punctuation
In·ter·punk·ti'ons|feh·ler *m* punctuation mistake; **~zei·chen** *n* punctuation mark
in·ter·ro·ga·tiv ['ɪntɐrogatiːf] *adj. ling.* interrogative
'In·ter·ro·ga·tiv|pro͵no·men *n ling.* interrogative pronoun; **~satz** *m ling.* interrogative clause
In·ter·vall [ɪntɐ'val] *n* (-s; -e) interval (*a.* ♪); ***in regelmäßigen ~en wiederkehren*** occur at regular intervals; **~trai·ning** *n sport*: interval training
in·ter·ve·nie·ren [ɪntɐve'niːrən] *v/i.* (h) intervene; **In·ter·ven·ti·on** [ɪntɐvɛn'tsĭoːn] *f* (-; -en) intervention
In·ter·ven·ti'ons|krieg *m* war of intervention; **~recht** *n* right to intervene, right of intervention
In·ter·view ['ɪntɐvjuː] *n* (-s; -s) interview; **in·ter·view·en** [ɪntɐ'vjuːən] *v/t.* (h) interview; **In·ter·view·er** [ɪntɐ'vjuːɐ] *m* (-s; -) interviewer
In·thro·ni·sa·ti·on [ɪntroniza'tsĭoːn] *f* (-; -en) enthronement
in·tim [ɪn'tiːm] *adj.* a) intimate (*a. fig. knowledge etc.*); *a.* cosy, *Am.* cozy *room etc.*; close *friendship*; F chummy, b) intimate, sexual; ***im ~en Kreis*** with close friends (and relatives); ***ich bin mit ihnen nicht so ~*** I don't know them that well; ***~er Kenner → Intimkenner; mit j-m ~ sein*** F sleep with s.o.; ***miteinander ~ sein*** sleep together (*or* with each other)
In'tim|be·reich *m* **1.** genitals *pl.*; **2.** → ***Intimsphäre***; **~feind** *m* personal enemy number one; **~hy͵gie·ne** *f* → ***Intimpflege***
In·ti·mi·tät [ɪntimi'tɛːt] *f* (-; -en) **1.** *no pl.* familiarity; closeness *of friendship*; intimacy *of a room etc.*; **2.** *pl.* liberties
In'tim|ken·ner *m* expert (*gen.* on), connoisseur (of); ***er ist ein ~ von*** *dat. a.* he has an intimate knowledge of; **~kon͵takt** *m* sexual contact; **~le·ben** *n* sex (*or* love) life; **~pfle·ge** *f* intimate (*or* feminine) hygiene; **~sphä·re** *f* private sphere, privacy; ***in j-s ~ eindringen*** invade (*or* encroach on) s.o.'s privacy; **~spray** *m, n* vaginal (*or* feminine) spray
In·ti·mus ['ɪntimʊs] F *m* (-; -mi) F best buddy
In'tim·ver·kehr *m* intercourse
in·to·le·rant ['ɪntolerant] *adj.* intolerant (***gegen[über]*** towards *s.o.*, *a.* of *s.th.*); **In·to·le·ranz** ['ɪntolerants] *f* (-; *no pl.*) intolerance (***gegen[über]*** towards *s.o.*, *a.* of *s.th.*)

In·to·na·ti·on [ɪntona'tsĭo:n] *f* (-; -en) ♪, *ling.* intonation; **in·to·nie·ren** [ɪnto'ni:rən] *v/t.* (h) intonate

in·tra·mus·ku·lär [ɪntramʊsku'lɛ:ɐ] *adj.* ⚕ intramuscular

in·tran·si·tiv ['ɪntranziti:f] *adj. ling.* intransitive

In·tra·ute·rin·pes,sar [ɪntraʔute'ri:n-] *n* intrauterine device, IUD

in·tra·ve·nös [ɪntrave'nø:s] *adj.* ⚕ intravenous

in·tri·gant [ɪntri'gant] *adj.* scheming; **In·tri'gant** *m* (-en; -en), **In·tri·gan·tin** [ɪntri'gantɪn] *f* (-; -nen) schemer; **In·tri·ge** [ɪn'tri:gə] *f* (-; -n) intrigue, scheme; **~n spinnen** plot and scheme; **In'tri·gen·spiel** *n*, **In'tri·gen·wirt·schaft** *f* plotting and scheming; *a.* infighting; **in·tri·gie·ren** [ɪntri'gi:rən] *v/i.* (h) (plot and) scheme

In·tro·ver·si·on [ɪntrovɛr'zĭo:n] *f* (-; -en) introversion; **in·tro·ver·tiert** [ɪntrovɛr'ti:ɐt] *adj.* introverted; **~er Mensch** introvert; **In·tro·ver'tiert·heit** *f* (-; *no pl.*) introversion

in·tui·tiv [ɪntui'ti:f] *adj.* intuitive; **In·tui·ti·on** [ɪntui'tsĭo:n] *f* (-; -en) **1.** intuition; **2.** (sudden) intuition; (flash of) inspiration

in·tus ['ɪntʊs] F *adv.*: **~ haben** F have put away *food*, F have downed *drink*, *a.* F have knocked back *alcoholic drink*; **jetzt, wo ich drei Tassen Kaffee ~ habe** *a.* with three cups of coffee inside me; *fig.* **jetzt hab' ich's ~** F it's finally sunk in, I've got it now

In·va·li·de [ɪnva'li:də] *m* (-n; -n) invalid

In·va'li·den|ren·te *f* disability pension; **~ver·si·che·rung** *f* disability insurance

In·va·li·di·tät [ɪnvalidi'tɛ:t] *f* (-; *no pl.*) disablement, disability

in·va·ria·bel ['ɪnvarĭa:bəl] *adj.* invariable

In·va·si·on [ɪnva'zĭo:n] *f* (-; -en) invasion (*a. fig.*); **In·va·si'ons·krieg** *m* war of invasion; **In·va·so·ren** [ɪnva'zo:rən] *pl.* invaders, invading forces

In·ven·tar [ɪnvɛn'ta:ɐ] *n* (-s; -e [-rə]) inventory; stock; **~ aufnehmen → inventarisieren; festes ~** fixture(s), office furniture and equipment; F *fig.* **zum ~ gehören** F be one of the fixtures; **in·ven·ta·ri·sie·ren** [ɪnvɛntari'zi:rən] (h) **I.** *v/i.* take inventory (*or* stock); **II.** *v/t.* take an inventory of

In·ven'tar|li·ste *f*, **~ver·zeich·nis** *n* inventory

In·ven·tur [ɪnvɛn'tu:ɐ] *f* (-; -en [-rən]) ✝ inventory, stocktaking; **~ machen** take inventory (*or* stock); **~aus·ver·kauf** *m* stocktaking sale

In·ver·si·on [ɪnvɛr'zĭo:n] *f* (-; -en) inversion; **In·ver·si'ons·la·ge** *f meteor.* temperature inversion

in·ve·stie·ren [ɪnvɛs'ti:rən] (h) **I.** *v/t.* invest (**in** *acc.* in); *fig.* put *time, effort etc.* (into), invest (in); **Geld ~ in** *a.* F sink money into; **II.** *v/i.* invest; **In·ve'stie·rung** *f* (-; -en) investment; **In·ve·sti·ti·on** [ɪnvɛsti'tsĭo:n] *f* (-; -en) ✝ investment; capital expenditure

In·ve·sti·ti'ons... *in cpds. usu.* investment *loan, bank etc.*; **~ab·ga·be** *f* investment tax; **~an·reiz** *m* investment incentive; **~bei·hil·fe** *f* investment grant; **~gü·ter** *pl.* capital goods; **~pro,gramm** *n* investment program(me); **~tä·tig·keit** *f* investment activity; **~zu·la·ge** *f* capital investment bonus

In·ve·sti·tur [ɪnvɛsti'tu:ɐ] *f* (-; -en) investiture; **~streit** *m hist.*: **der ~** the investiture controversy

In·vest·ment|an·teil [ɪn'vɛstmənt-] *m* investment share; **~fonds** *m* unit trust; **~ge·sell·schaft** *f* investment company

in·wen·dig ['ɪnvɛndɪç] *adv.* **→ auswendig**

in·wie·fern [ɪnvi'fɛrn] *cj.* in what way, how

in·wie·weit [ɪnvi'vaɪt] *cj.* to what extent

In'zah·lung·nah·me [-na:mə] *f* (-; *no pl.*) part exchange, trade-in

In·zest ['ɪntsɛst] *m* (-[e]s; -e) incest; **in·ze·stu·ös** [ɪntsɛs'tŭø:s] *adj.* incestuous

'In·zucht *f* (-; *no pl.*) intermarriage, *a. zo.* inbreeding

in'zwi·schen *adv.* **1.** in the meantime, meanwhile; *a.* before (*or* till, until) then; by then; **ich mache ~ das Mittagessen** (meanwhile) I'll be getting on with the lunch; **2.** now; already; **ich habe ~ an die 600 Münzen** I've managed to collect about 600 coins so far

Ion [ĭo:n] *n* (-s; Ionen ['ĭo:nən]) *phys.* ion; **'Io·nen·aus·tau·scher** *m* ion(ic) exchanger; **Io·ni·sa·tor** [ĭoni'za:to:ɐ] *m* (-s; -en [-za'to:rən]) ionizer; **io·ni·sie·ren** [ĭoni'zi:rən] *v/t.* (h) ionize; **Io·ni'sie·rung** *f* (-; -en) ionization; **Io·no·sphä·re** [ĭono'sfɛ:rə] *f* (-; -n) ionosphere

Io·ta ['ĭota] *n* **→ Jota**

I-Punkt *m* dot over the i; *fig.* **bis auf den ~** down to the last detail

Ira·ker [i'ra:kɐ] *m* (-s; -) Iraqi; **Ira·ke·rin** [i'ra:kərɪn] *f* (-; -nen) Iraqi (woman); **ira·kisch** [i'ra:kɪʃ] *adj.* Iraqi

Ira·ner [i'ra:nɐ] *m* (-s; -) Iranian; **Ira·ne·rin** [i'ra:nərɪn] *f* (-; -nen) Iranian (woman); **ira·nisch** [i'ra:nɪʃ] *adj.* Iranian

ir·den ['ɪrdən] *adj.* earthenware

ir·disch ['ɪrdɪʃ] *adj.* earthly; temporal; worldly; mortal; **→ Hülle; 'Ir·di·sche** *n* (-n): **den Weg alles ~n gehen** go the way of all flesh

Ire ['i:rə] *m* (-n; -n) Irishman; **die ~n** the Irish (*pl.*)

ir·gend ['ɪrgənt] *adv.* **1. wenn es ~ geht** if (it's) at all possible, if I *etc.* possibly can; **wann (wo) es ~ geht** whenever (wherever) it might be possible; **wer nur ~ geeignet ist** anyone who is even remotely qualified; **so rasch wie ~ möglich** as soon as at all possible; **2. ~ etwas** something, anything; **nicht ~ etwas!** not just anything; **~ jemand** somebody, someone, anybody, anyone; **er ist ja (schließlich) nicht ~ jemand** (I mean,) he isn't just anybody (F any old Joe Bloggs); **~ so ein Politiker** one of those politicians, some politician or other

'ir·gend'ein *indef. pron.*: **~e Tasse** a cup; some cup or other; **nimm ~e Tasse** take any cup, it doesn't matter what (sort of) cup; **~ anderer** someone else, anyone else; **besteht ~e Hoffnung?** is there any hope at all?; **'ir·gend'ei·ne(r, -s)** *indef. pron.* **1.** somebody, someone; anybody, anyone; **2.** something, anything

'ir·gend|ein'mal *adv.* **→ irgendwann; ~'eins** *indef. pron.* **→ irgendeine(r, -s); ~'wann** *adv.* sometime (or other), any time, whenever you like *etc.*, whenever it suits you *etc.*; **~'was** *indef. pron.* something, anything; **nicht ~!** not just anything; **~'wel·che** *indef. pron.* any; **ohne ~ Kosten** without any expense (at all); **~'wer** *indef. pron.* somebody, someone, anybody, anyone; **er ist ja (schließlich) nicht ~** (I mean,) he isn't just anybody (F any old Joe Bloggs); **~'wie** *adv.* somehow (or other); any old how; **~'wo** *adv.* somewhere (or other), anywhere; **~ anders** somewhere else, anywhere else; **~wo'her** *adv.* from somewhere (or other), from anywhere; **~wo'hin** *adv.* somewhere (or other), anywhere

Irin ['i:rɪn] *f* (-; -nen) Irishwoman; **sie ist ~** she's Irish

Iris ['i:rɪs] *f* (-; -) *anat.*, ⚘ iris

irisch ['i:rɪʃ] **I.** *adj.* Irish; **die ♀e Republik** the Irish Republic, Eire; **II.** ♀ *n* (-en) *ling.* Irish

iri·sie·rend [iri'zi:rənt] *adj.* iridescent

Ir·län·der ['ɪrlɛndɐ] *m* (-s; -) **→ Ire; Ir·län·de·rin** ['ɪrlɛndərɪn] *f* (-; -nen) **→ Irin**

Iro·ke·se [iro'ke:zə] *m* (-n; -n) Iroquois (Indian); **Iro'ke·sen·schnitt** *m* Mohican (haircut)

Iro·nie [iro'ni:] *f* (-; *no pl.*) irony (**des Schicksals** of fate); **Iro·ni·ker** [i'ro:nikɐ] *m* (-s; -) ironist; **iro·nisch** [i'ro:nɪʃ] *adj.* ironic(ally *adv.*); **das ♀e daran war** the irony of it was, the ironic thing about it was; **iro·ni·sie·ren** [ironi'zi:rən] *v/t.* (h) treat with irony

ir·ra·tio·nal ['ɪratsĭona:l] *adj.* irrational; **Ir·ra·tio·na·lis·mus** [ɪratsĭona'lɪsmʊs] *m* (-; *no pl.*) irrationalism; **Ir·ra·tio·nali·tät** ['ɪratsĭonalitɛ:t] (-; *no pl.*) *f* irrationality, irrational nature (*gen.* of)

ir·re ['ɪrə] **I.** *adj.* **1.** mad, F crazy *person, laughter etc.*; wild, crazed *look*; **~s Lächeln** crazy grin, wild sneer; **~s Zeug reden** rave; F **wie ~ schuften** *etc.* F work *etc.* like mad (*or* like a madman, *sl.* like crazy); **in e-m ~n Tempo fahren** drive like a maniac; **2.** ⚕ mad, insane, demented; **3.** F incredible; **ein ~r Typ** *a.* F an amazing guy; **es ist ~** *a.* F it's unreal; **4.** (totally) confused; **→ *a.* irremachen; 5. ~ werden an** *dat.* begin to have one's doubts about; **II.** *adv.* **6.** F incredibly; *work etc.* F like mad (*sl.* crazy, hell)

'Ir·re[1] *f*: **j-n in die ~ führen** lead s.o. astray; **in die ~ gehen** go astray

'Ir·re[2] *m, f* (-n; -n) madman (*f* madwoman); F *fig.* F lunatic; F **wie ein ~r** F like an idiot (*or* a maniac)

ir·re·al ['ɪrea:l] *adj.* **1.** unreal: **2.** unrealistic

'ir·re·füh·ren *v/t.* (*sep.*, h) mislead; deceive; **sich ~ lassen** be deceived (**von** *dat.* by); **'ir·re·füh·rend** *adj.* misleading; **'Ir·re·füh·rung** *f* (-; *no pl.*) deception; F pulling the wool

'ir·re·ge·hen *v/i.* (*irr.*, *sep.*, sn, **→ gehen**) **1.** be mistaken; **gehe ich irre in der Annahme, daß ...?** am I wrong in assuming that ...?; **2.** *lit.* go astray

'ir·re·ge·lei·tet *adj.* misguided

ir·re·gu·lär ['ɪregulɛ:ɐ] *adj.* irregular

'ir·re·lei·ten *v/t.* (*sep.*, h) misguide, lead astray

ir·re·le·vant ['ɪrelevant] *adj.* irrelevant (**für** *acc.* to); **Ir·re·le·vanz** ['ɪrelevants] *f* (-; -en) irrelevance

'ir·re·ma·chen *v/t.* (*sep.*, h) **1.** totally confuse, F throw; **2. j-n ~ an** *dat.* have s.o. wondering about

ir·ren[1] ['ɪrən] (h) **I.** *v/i.* be wrong, be mistaken; **II.** *v/refl.*: **sich ~** be wrong, be mistaken; **sich ~ in** *dat.* be wrong about *s.o. or s.th.*, *n.s.* get *date etc.* wrong, go to the wrong *door etc.*, *teleph.* get (*or* dial) the wrong number; **sich um tausend Mark ~** be out by a thousand marks, be a thousand marks out; ***ich kann mich (auch)*** ~ I may be wrong; ***wenn ich mich nicht irre*** if I'm not mistaken, I think I'm right in saying (that); ***da irrst du dich aber gewaltig*** you couldn't be more wrong, that's where you make your big mistake; *wenn sie glaubt, daß ich das mache etc.*, ***dann irrt sie sich gewaltig*** she's got another think coming; **III.** ♀ *n*: ~ ***ist menschlich*** we all make mistakes, *lit. and iro.* 'tis human to err

'ir·ren² *v/i.* (sn) wander, roam

'Ir·ren|an·stalt *f* mental asylum; **~haus** *n*: F *fig.* ***hier geht's zu wie im*** ~ F it's like a madhouse (here), it's (sheer) bedlam; ***er ist reif fürs*** ~ F he ought to be certified

ir·re·pa·ra·bel ['ɪrepara:bəl] *adj.* irreparable

'ir·re·re·den *v/i.* (*sep.*, h) rave

ir·re·ver·si·bel ['ɪrevɛrzi:bəl] *adj.* irreversible

'Irr|fahrt *f* wild-goose chase, odyssey; **~flug** *m* odyssey (in the air); **~gar·ten** *m* maze, labyrinth; **~glau·be(n)** *m* misconception, delusion; heresy

ir·rig ['ɪrɪç] *adj.* wrong, mistaken, erroneous; ***~e Ansicht*** *a.* misconception; **ir·ri·ger'wei·se** ['ɪrɪgɐ-] *adv.* wrongly, erroneously

ir·ri·tier·bar [ɪri'ti:ɐba:ɐ] *adj.*: ***leicht*** ~ a) easily annoyed, b) easily put off (F thrown), c) easily distracted; **ir·ri·tie·ren** [ɪri'ti:rən] *v/t.* (h) a) irritate, get on *s.o.'s* nerves, annoy, b) distract, c) put *s.o.* off (***bei*** *dat. s.th.*), F throw; ***sich ~ lassen*** be put off, F be thrown (***durch*** *acc.* by)

'Irr|läu·fer *m* **1.** stray (*or* misdirected) letter *etc.*; **2.** rogue satellite; **~leh·re** *f* false doctrine, heresy; **~licht** *n* (-[e]s; -er) will-o'-the-wisp (*a. fig.*)

Irr·sinn ['ɪrzɪn] *m* (-s; *no pl.*) madness (*a. fig.*); **irr·sin·nig** ['ɪrzɪnɪç] **I.** *adj.* insane, mad; F *fig.* F crazy, mad; F incredible; **II.** F *adv.* F incredibly; **Irr·sin·ni·ge** ['ɪrzɪnɪgə] *m, f* (-n; -n) → ***Irre²***

Irr·tum ['ɪrtu:m] *m* (-s; Irrtümer ['ɪrty:mɐ]) mistake; misunderstanding; ***im ~ sein, sich im ~ befinden*** be mistaken, be wrong, be in the wrong (***über*** *acc.* about); ~ ***vorbehalten*** errors (and omissions) excepted; **irr·tüm·lich** ['ɪrty:mlɪç] **I.** *adj.* wrong; **II.** *adv.* wrongly; ***ich war ~ der Meinung*** I was wrong in thinking; **irr·tüm·li·cher'wei·se** ['ɪrty:mlɪçɐ-] *adv.* by mistake, mistakenly

'Irr·weg *m fig.*: ***auf e-n ~ geraten sein*** be on the wrong track completely; ***j-n auf e-n ~ führen*** lead s.o. astray

Irr·wisch ['ɪrvɪʃ] *m* (-[e]s; -e) **1.** will-o'-the-wisp; **2.** jack-in-the-box; ***er ist ein richtiger ~*** *a.* he's up and down like a yo-yo, he can't sit still for one minute

'irr·wit·zig *adj.* ridiculous, absurd, F crazy, hare-brained

Is·chi·as ['ɪʃi̯as] *m, n* (-; *no pl.*) ⚕ sciatica; **~nerv** *m* sciatic nerve

Is·lam [ɪs'la:m] *m* (-[s]; *no pl.*) Islam; **is·la·misch** [ɪs'la:mɪʃ] *adj.* Islamic; **is·la·mi·sie·ren** [ɪslami'zi:rən] *v/t.* (h) convert to Islam, Islamize, *Brit. a.* Islamise; **Is·la·mi'sie·rung** *f* (-; *no pl.*) Islamization, *Brit. a.* Islamisation

Is·län·der ['i:slɛndɐ] *m* (-s; -), **Is·län·de·rin** ['i:slɛndərɪn] *f* (-; -nen) Icelander; **is·län·disch** ['i:slɛndɪʃ] *adj.* Icelandic

Is·mus ['ɪsmʊs] F *iro. m* (-; Ismen ['ɪsmən]) F ism

Iso·ba·re [izo'ba:rə] *f* (-; -n) isobar

Iso·glos·se [izo'glɔsə] *f* (-; -n) isogloss

Iso·gon [izo'go:n] *n* (-s; -e) Ᾰ isogon

Iso·la·ti·on [izola'tsi̯o:n] *f* (-; -en) **1.** *pol.* isolation; **2.** ⚡, ⚙ insulation

Iso·la·tio·nis·mus [izolatsi̯o'nɪsmʊs] *m* (-; *no pl.*) *pol.* isolationism; **Iso·la·tio·nist** [izolatsi̯o'nɪst] *m* (-en; -en) isolationist; **iso·la·tio·ni·stisch** [izolatsi̯o'nɪstɪʃ] *adj.* isolationist

Iso·la·ti'ons·haft *f* solitary confinement

Iso·la·tor [izo'la:to:ɐ] *m* (-s; -en [-la'to:rən]) insulator

Iso·lier·band [izo'li:ɐ-] *n* (-[e]s; ⸚er) insulating tape

iso·lie·ren [izo'li:rən] (h) **I.** *v/t.* ⚕ isolate (*a. pol.*); ⚡, ⚙ insulate; **II.** *fig. v/refl.*: ***sich*** ~ isolate o.s., cut o.s. off; **III.** *v/i.*: ***gut*** ~ insulate well, be a good insulator

Iso·lier|haft [izo'li:ɐ-] *f* solitary confinement; **~kan·ne** *f* thermos jug (*TM*); **~lack** *m* insulating varnish (*or* paint); **~mas·se** *f* insulating compound; **~ma·te·ri·al** *n* insulating material; **~schicht** *f* insulating layer; **~schutz** *m* (thermal) insulation; **~sta·ti·on** *f* ⚕ isolation ward

iso·liert [izo'li:ɐt] **I.** *adj.* isolated (*a.* ⚕, *pol.*), cut off; *patient, prisoner* in isolation; ***~e Fälle*** isolated cases; **II.** *adv.*: ~ ***betrachten*** view *s.th.* in isolation; ***man darf es nicht ~ betrachten*** *a.* you've got to see it in context; **Iso'liert·heit** *f* (-; *no pl.*) isolation

Iso·lie·rung [izo'li:rʊŋ] *f* (-; -en) **1.** isolation; **2.** ⚡, ⚙ insulation

Iso·lier·wir·kung [izo'li:ɐ-] *f* insulating action

iso·me·trisch [izo'me:trɪʃ] *adj.* isometric; ***~e Übungen*** isometric exercises

iso·morph [izo'mɔrf] *adj.* isomorph

Iso·top [izo'to:p] *n* (-s; -e) isotope

iso·trop [izo'tro:p] *adj.* isotropic

Is·rae·li [ɪsra'e:li] *m* (-[s]; -[s]), **is·rae·lisch** [ɪsra'e:lɪʃ] *adj.* Israeli

Is·rae·lit [ɪsrae'li:t] *m* (-en; -en), **Is·rae·li·tin** [ɪsrae'li:tɪn] *f* (-; -nen), **is·rae·li·tisch** [ɪsrae'li:tɪʃ] *adj.* Israelite

Ist-Be·stand ['ɪst-] *m* ✝ actual stock

Isth·mus ['ɪstmʊs] *m* (-; -men [-mən]) *geogr.* isthmus

'Ist|-Lei·stung *f* ✝ actual output; **~-Stär·ke** *f* ⚔ effective (*or* actual) strength; **~-Wert** *m* actual (*or* true) value

Ita·ker ['i:takɐ] *contp. m* (-s; -) F dago, wop, Eyetie

Ita·lie·ner [ita'li̯e:nɐ] *m* (-s; -) **1.** Italian; **2.** F Italian place; ***laß uns zum ~ gehen*** F let's go to an Italian; ***um die Ecke ist ein*** ~ F there's an Italian (place) round the corner; **Ita·lie·ne·rin** [ita'li̯e:nərɪn] *f* (-; -nen) Italian (woman); **ita·lie·nisch** [ita'li̯e:nɪʃ] **I.** *adj.* Italian; ***die ~e Schweiz*** Italian-speaking Switzerland; **II.** ♀ *n* (-en) *ling.* Italian

Ita·lo-We·stern ['i:talo-] F *m* F spaghetti western

I-Trä·ger *m* I-beam

I-Tüp·fel·chen *n* → ***I-Punkt***

J

J, j [jɔt] *n* (-; -) J, j

ja [jaː] **I.** *adv.* **1.** yes; F yeah, yep; *parl.* aye, *Am.* yea; *wedding*: I do; um, er, well; **~?** really?, F oh yeah?, *teleph.* hello?; **wenn ~** if so; **~ sagen** say yes, *a.* agree (**zu** *dat.* to); *wird er kommen?* - **ich glaube ~** I think so; **aber ~!** a) yes, of course, b) yes, yes, *iro.* yes, dear; **2. er ist ~ mein Freund** I mean, he's a friend (after all); **dazu ist es ~ da** that's what it's (there) for (after all); **es ist ~ nicht so schlimm** it's not that bad; **du kennst ihn ~** you know what he's like; **3. ~, wissen Sie** well, you know; **4. da bist du ~!** there you are!; **da haben wir's ~!** there we are, isn't that (just) what I said?; **ich sagte es dir ~** didn't I tell you?; **das ist ~ unglaublich** that's really incredible; **5. sag's ihm ~ nicht** don't you tell (*or* go telling) him; **laß sie ~ in Ruhe** just (*or* you'd better) leave her alone; **bring es ~ mit** make sure you bring it; **6. ~, weißt du denn nicht, daß** do you mean to say you didn't know (that); **~, so e-e Überraschung!** well, this really is a surprise; **7. ich würde es ~ gern tun, aber** I'd really like to do it, but; **8. du weißt ~ gar nicht ...** you have no idea; **das sag ich ~** that's what I mean; **9. er genießt die Filme, ~ verschlingt sie** he really enjoys the films, or rather devours them (*or* or devours them is more like it); **10. du kommst doch später, ~?** you 'are coming later on, aren't you?; **gibst du's mir, ~?** will you give it to me (, please)?, are you going to give it to me then?; **II. Ձ** *n* (-[s]; -[s]) yes; *parl.* aye, *Am.* yea; **mit ~ oder Nein antworten** answer yes or no; **mit ~ (be)antworten** say yes (to); **er (es) bleibt bei s-m ~** he's said yes and he means it

Jacht [jaxt] *f* (-; -en) yacht; **~klub** *m* yacht club

Jacke ['jakə] (*sep.* -k·k-) *f* (-; -n) a) jacket, *Am. a.* coat, b) cardigan; F **das ist ~ wie Hose** it's much of a muchness, it's (a case of) six of one and half a dozen of the other; F **j-m die ~ voll hauen** give s.o. a good hiding; **'Jacken·kleid** *n* two-piece dress

Jacket·kro·ne ['dʒekɪt-] (*sep.* -k·k-) *f* jacket crown

Jackett [ʒa'kɛt] (*sep.* -k·k-) *n* (-s; -s) jacket, *Am. a.* coat

Ja·de ['jaːdə] *m* (-s; *no pl.*), *f* (-; *no pl.*) *min.* jade; **Ձgrün** *adj.* jade(-colo[u]red)

Jagd [jaːkt] *f* (-; *no pl.*) **1.** a) hunt(ing), shoot(ing), b) hunting (*or* shooting) party; **auf (die) ~ gehen** go hunting; **auf der ~ sein** be hunting; **ein Tiger** *etc.* **bei der ~** a tiger *etc.* hunting for prey; **2.** *fig.* chase, pursuit; **die ~ auf** *acc.* the hunt for *terrorists etc.*; **~ machen auf** *acc.* chase (after), hunt for, try to track down; **3.** *fig.* pursuit (**nach** *dat.* of), chasing (after *money etc.*); **e-e wilde ~** a mad scramble *or* rush (**nach** *dat.* for); **die ~ hat begonnen** the race (*or* chase) is on; **~aufseher** *m* gamekeeper

'jagd·bar *adj.* fit for hunting; **~es Wild** fair game

'Jagd|beu·te *f* bag; **~bom·ber** *m* ✈ fighter bomber; **~fie·ber** *n* hunting fever; **~flie·ger** *m* ✈ fighter pilot; **~flin·te** *f* shotgun; **~flug·zeug** *n* fighter (jet, plane, aircraft); interceptor (aircraft); **~fre·vel** *m* poaching; **~ge·biet** *n* hunting ground; **~ge·sell·schaft** *f* hunting party; **~ge·setz** *n* game law; **~ge·wehr** *n* shotgun; **~grün·de** *pl.* hunting grounds; **in die ewigen ~ eingehen** go to the happy hunting grounds; **~haus** *n* (hunting) lodge; **~horn** *n* hunting horn, bugle; **~hund** *m* a) hound, b) short-haired pointer; **~hüt·te** *f* (hunting) lodge; **~lei·den·schaft** *f* passion for hunting; **~mes·ser** *n* hunting knife; **~pacht** *f* (tenancy of a) shoot; **~recht** *n* **1.** hunting rights *pl.*; **2.** game law; **~ren·nen** *n* steeplechase; **~re,vier** *n* hunting ground; **~ruf** *m* hunting call; **~schein** *m* shooting licen|ce (*Am.*-se); F *fig.* **er hat e-n ~** F he needs certifying; **~schloß** *n*, **~schlöß·chen** *n* hunting lodge; **~staf·fel** *f* ✈ fighter squadron; **~stück** *n art*: hunting scene; **~stuhl** *m* shooting stick; **~sze·ne** *f* → **Jagdstück; ~ta·sche** *f* game bag; **~tro,phäe** *f* hunting trophy; **~waf·fe** *f* hunting weapon; **~wild** *n* game, game animal(s *pl.*); **~zeit** *f* hunting (*or* shooting) season

ja·gen ['jaːgən] (h) **I.** *v/t.* **1.** a) hunt, b) drive; chase; hound, c) shoot; **2.** *fig.* chase (after); hunt for; **j-n aus dem Bett** *etc.* **~** chase s.o. out of bed *etc.*; **in die Luft ~** blow up, F blow *s.th.* sky-high; F **j-m e-e Nadel in den Arm ~** stick a (F whopping great) needle into s.o.'s arm; F **j-m ein Messer in den Leib ~** run a knife into s.o.; F **j-m (sich) e-e Kugel durch den Kopf ~** put a bullet through s.o.'s (one's) head, *sl.* blow s.o.'s (one's) brains out; **den Ball ins Netz ~** *soccer*: slam (*or* drive) the ball home; **ein Ereignis jagt(e) das andere** things are really happening *or* starting to happen (things were happening really fast); F **damit kannst du mich ~!** F I wouldn't touch it with a bargepole; → **Gurgel; II.** *v/i.* **3.** go hunting, go shooting, hunt; *fig.* **~ nach** *dat.* chase after; **4.** (sn) *fig.* race, tear; *wind etc.*: sweep; *clouds*: scud *across the sky*; **III. Ձ** *n* (-s) hunt(ing), shooting

Jä·ger ['jɛːgɐ] *m* (-s; -) **1.** huntsman; ranger; gamekeeper; *ethnology*: hunter; **2.** ⚔ rifleman; **3.** fighter (jet, plane, aircraft); **ein ~ vom Typ F117** an F117 fighter jet (*or* plane); **Jä·ge·rei** [jɛːgə'raɪ] *f* (- *no pl.*) hunting

'Jä·ger|la,tein *n* cock-and-bull story (*or* stories *pl.*); **~mei·ster** *m* professional huntsman; **~schnit·zel** *n gastr.* escalope alla cacciatora

Ja·gu·ar ['jaːgŭaːɐ] *m* (-s; -e ['jaːgŭaːrə]) *zo.* jaguar

jäh [jɛː] **I.** *adj.* **1.** a) sudden, abrupt, b) impetuous; rash; **~er Aufbruch** abrupt departure; **~es Erwachen** *a. fig.* rude awakening; **~er Schmerz** sudden sharp pain; **~er Tod** sudden death; **~e Wendung** sudden (*or* unexpected) turn *for the worse etc.*; **2.** steep; **~er Abhang** sheer drop, precipice; **II.** *adv.* **3.** a) all of a sudden; abruptly, b) headlong; **4.** precipitously; **~ abfallend** precipitous; **dort fällt die Straße nach rechts ~ ab** at that point the road drops away to the right (*or* there's a sheer drop to the right)

Jahr [jaːɐ] *n* (-[e]s; -e ['jaːrə]) year; **ein halbes ~** six months; **anderthalb ~e** a year and a half, eighteen months; **dreiviertel ~** nine months; **im ~ 1996** in (the year) 1996; **bis zum 31. Dezember d. J.** (= **dieses Jahres**) until December 31st of this year; **Anfang der achtziger ~e** in the early eighties; **alle ~e** every year; **auf ~e hinaus** for years to come; **im Lauf der ~ e** through (*or* over) the years; **in die ~e kommen** be getting on (a bit); **in diesem (im nächsten) ~** this (next) year; **mit den ~en** with (the) years; **mit (*or* im Alter von) 20 ~en** at the age of twenty; **nach ~en** after (many) years; **nach ~ und Tag** after a very long time, (many) years later; **seit ~ und Tag** for a long time, for many years; **heute vor einem ~** a year ago today; **von ~ zu ~** from year to year, *w.s.* as the years go by; **~ für ~** year after year; **in den besten ~en sein** be in the prime of life; → **Buckel** 2

jahr'aus *adv.*: **~, jahrein** year in, year out

'Jahr·buch *n* yearbook; almanac

Jähr·chen ['jɛːɐçən] F *n* (-s; -) year; **ein paar ~ noch** another year or two, another couple of years

jah·re·lang ['jaːrəlaŋ] **I.** *adj.* longstanding; **~e Erfahrung** years of experience; **ein ~er Kampf** *a.* years of struggle (*or* struggling); **e-e ~e Freundschaft** *a.* a friendship that goes back a long time; **II.** *adv.* for years (and years), for years on end

jäh·ren ['jɛːrən] *v/refl.* (h): **1995 jährt sich die Erfindung des ... zum 200. Mal** 1995 will see the 200th anniversary (*or* the bicentennial) of the invention of ...; **heute (morgen) jährt sich sein To-**

destag it's a year today since he died, it's a year ago today that he died (it'll be a year ago tomorrow that he died)

Jah·res... ['ja:rəs-] *in cpds. usu.* annual, yearly; **~abon·ne,ment** *n* annual subscription; *thea. etc.* yearly season ticket; **~ab·rech·nung** *f*, **~ab·schluß** *m* annual (statement of) accounts *pl.*; **~an·fang** *m*: (***zu*** at the) beginning of the year; **~aus·gleich** *m* annual tax adjustment; **~be·ginn** *m*: (***zu*** at the) beginning of the year; **~bei·trag** *m* annual subscription (*or* contribution); **~be·richt** *m* annual report; **~best·lei·stung** *f* best performance of the year (so far); **~best·zeit** *f* best time of the year (so far); **~bi,lanz** *f* annual balance (sheet); **~ein·kom·men** *n* yearly income; **~en·de** *n* end of the year; **~etat** *m* annual budget; **~fehl·be·trag** *m* annual deficit, net loss for the year; **~frist** *f*: ***binnen ~*** within a year; ***nach ~*** after one year; **~ge·halt** *n* annual salary; **~hälf·te** *f*: ***erste*** (***zweite***) ~ first (second) half of the year; **~haupt·ver·samm·lung** *f* annual general meeting, AGM; **~haus·halt** *m* annual budget; **~hoch** *n* annual high; **~kar·te** *f* yearly season ticket; **~mit·te** *f* middle of the year; ***... zur ~*** mid-year ...; **~mit·tel** *n* yearly average; **~ring** *m* ⚘ annual ring; **~rück·blick** *m* review of (*or a* look back at) the year's events; **~schluß** *m* end of the year; ***... zum ~ ...*** at the end of the year, year-end ...; **~tag** *m* anniversary; **~tem·pe·ra,tur** *f*: ***mittlere ~*** annual mean temperature; **~tief** *n* annual low; **~,über·schuß** *m* net earnings *pl.*; **~,um·satz** *m* annual turnover; **~ur·laub** *m* annual holiday (allowance), *Am.* annual vacation (allowance); **~ver·dienst** *m* annual income (*or* earnings *pl.*); **~ver·samm·lung** *f* annual meeting; **~ver·trag** *m* one-year contract; **~wa·gen** *m* employee('s) car; **~wech·sel** *m*, **~wen·de** *f* turn of the year; New Year; **~wirt·schafts·be·richt** *m* annual economic report; **~zahl** *f* date, year; ***ich kann mir keine ~en merken*** I'm hopeless at dates

'Jah·res·zeit *f* season, time of the year; ***zu jeder ~*** (in) any season, in all seasons; **'jah·res·zeit·lich I.** *adj.* seasonal; **II.** *adv.* seasonally; ***~ bedingt*** seasonal

'Jahr·gang *m* (-[e]s; ⸚e) age group, 📖 cohort; *ped.* year; *gastr.* vintage (*a. fig.*), year; *magazine etc.*: volume, year; ***der ~ 1968*** those born in 1968, *gastr.* the 1968 vintage; *gastr.* ***wie ist der ~ 1983?*** what's the 1983 (vintage) like?; ***wir sind derselbe ~*** we're the same age, we were born in the same year; ***was ist er für ein ~?*** what year was he born (in)?; ***ich bin ~ 62*** I was born in (19)62

Jahr'hun·dert *n* (-s; -e) century

jahr'hun·der·te|alt *adj.* centuries-old; ancient; **~lang I.** *adj.* centuries of ...; **II.** *adv.* for centuries, for hundreds of years

Jahr'hun·dert|er·eig·nis *n* **1.** event (*or* happening) of the century; **2.** once-in-a--lifetime event; **~fei·er** *f* centenary, centennial; **~hälf·te** *f*: ***erste*** (***zweite***) ~ first (second) half of the century; **~mit·te** *f*: (***um die ~*** around the) middle of the century; **~wein** *m* vintage of the century; rare vintage; **~wen·de** *f*: (***um die ~*** around the) turn of the century

jähr·lich ['jɛ:ɐlɪç] **I.** *adj.* yearly, annual; **II.** *adv.* every year, yearly, once a year; *1,000 dollars* a year, per annum

Jähr·ling ['jɛ:ɐlɪŋ] *m* (-s; -e) *zo.* yearling

'Jahr·markt *m* fair; *fig.* ***~ der Eitelkeiten*** vanity fair; **'Jahr·markt·schrei·er** *m* fairground barker; **'Jahr·markts·trei·ben** *n* fairground (hustle and) bustle

Jahr|mil·li'ar·den *pl.*: ***vor ~*** thousands of millions of years ago, billions of years ago; ***seit ~*** for thousands of millions of years, for billions of years; **~mil·lio·nen** [-mɪ'lĭo:nən] *pl.*: ***vor ~*** millions of years ago; ***seit ~*** for millions of years

Jahr'tau·send *n* (-s; -e) millennium; **~fei·er** *f* millenary; **~wen·de** *f* turn of the millennium

Jahr'zehnt *n* (-s; -e) decade, ten years *pl.*; **jahr'zehn·te·lang I.** *adj.* decades of ...; **II.** *adv.* for decades

Jäh·zorn ['jɛ:tsɔrn] *m* (-[e]s; *no pl.*) **1.** violent temper; **2.** sudden (outburst of) rage

'jäh·zor·nig I. *adj.* hot-tempered; ***er ist ein ~er Mensch*** *a.* he's got a violent temper, he tends to flare up; **II.** *adv.* angrily, in a temper

Ja·kob ['ja:kɔp] *m*: F ***nicht gerade der wahre ~*** not quite what I *etc.* want

Ja·ko·bi·ner [jako'bi:nɐ] *m* (-s; -) **1.** *hist. pol.* Jacobin; **2.** *eccl.* Dominican (friar), Jacobin

'Ja·kobs|lei·ter *f* ⚓ *and bibl.* (***die ~***) Jacob's ladder; **~mu·schel** *f* scallop shell

Ja·lou·sie [ʒalu'zi:] *f* (-; -n) (Venetian) blind(s *pl.*)

Ja·mai·ka·ner [jamaɪ'ka:nɐ] *m* (-s; -), **Ja·mai·ka·ne·rin** [jamaɪ'ka:nərɪn] *f* (-; -nen), **ja·mai·ka·nisch** [jamaɪ'ka:nɪʃ] *adj.* Jamaican

Jam·be ['jambə] *f* (-; -n), **Jam·bus** ['jambʊs] *m* (-; Jamben) iamb(us)

Jam·mer ['jamɐ] *m* (-s; *no pl.*) a) misery, b) despair, c) lamentation; ***es ist ein ~*** it's such a shame; ***der ~ ist, daß*** the trouble is that; ***es ist immer derselbe ~*** it's the same old story every time; **~bild** *n* pitiful sight, *a.* picture of misery; **~ge·schrei** *n* wailing; **~ge·stalt** *f* miserable wretch (*a. fig. contp.*); **~lap·pen** F *m* F spineless jellyfish

jäm·mer·lich ['jɛmɐlɪç] **I.** *adj.* miserable, wretched, pitiful (*all a. fig. contp.*); deplorable; heart-rending; ***~ aussehen*** look wretched; ***ihm war ~ zumute*** he felt utterly miserable; **II.** *adv.*: ***~ weinen*** weep bitterly, cry one's eyes out; ~ (***schlecht***) ***singen*** *etc.* sing *etc.* miserably; ***~ frieren*** be dreadfully cold, be freezing, freeze; ***~ vernachlässigt werden*** be woefully neglected

jam·mern ['jamɐn] (h) **I.** *v/i.* **1.** moan, wail; whimper; ***~ nach*** *dat.* cry for; **2.** moan, F bellyache; **II.** *v/t.*: ***es jammert mich zu sehen*** it breaks my heart to see; ***er jammert mich*** I feel sorry for him; **III.** ♀ *n* (-s) moaning, wailing

jam·mer'scha·de *adj.*: ***es ist ~*** it's such a shame (***um*** *acc.* about), F it's too bad (about)

'Jam·mer·tal *lit. n* (-[e]s; *no pl.*) *lit.* vale of tears

Jan·ker ['jaŋkɐ] *m* (-s; -) Janker jacket

Jän·ner ['jɛnɐ] *Austrian m* (-s; -) January

Ja·nu·ar ['janŭa:ɐ] *m* (-s; -e) January; ***im ~*** in January

ja·nus·köp·fig ['ja:nʊskœpfɪç] *adj.* two-sided, Janus-faced

Ja·pa·ner [ja'pa:nɐ] *m* (-s; -) Japanese; **Ja·pa·ne·rin** [ja'pa:nərɪn] *f* (-; -nen) Japanese (woman); **ja·pa·nisch** [ja'pa:nɪʃ] *adj.*, **Ja'pa·nisch** *n* (-en) *ling.* Japanese

Ja·pa·no·lo·ge [japano'lo:gə] *m* (-n; -n) Japanologist; **Ja·pa·no·lo·gie** [japanolo'gi:] *f* (-; *no pl.*) Japanese studies *pl.*, Japanology

Ja·pan·sei·de ['ja:pan-] *f* Japanese silk

Japs [japs] F *contp. m* (-en; -e[n]) F Nip, slit-eye

jap·sen ['japsən] *v/i.* (h) gasp (***nach Luft*** for breath), pant

Jar·gon [ʒar'gõ:] *m* (-s; -s) jargon; slang

Ja·sa·ger ['ja:za:gɐ] *m* (-s; -) yes-man

Jas·min [jas'mi:n] *m* (-s; -e) jasmin(e); **~öl** *n* jasmine oil; **~tee** *m* jasmine tea

Jas·pis ['jaspɪs] *m* (-[ses]; -se) *min.* jasper

'Ja·stim·me *f parl.* aye, *Am.* yea

jä·ten ['jɛ:tən] (h) **I.** *v/t.* weed (out); ***Unkraut ~*** pull out (the) weeds; **II.** *v/i.* weed (the garden), pull out (the) weeds

Jau·che ['jaʊxə] *f* (-; *no pl.*) liquid manure; F *fig.* swill; **~gru·be** *f* manure pit

jau·chen ['jaʊxən] *v/t. and v/i.* (h) manure, dung

jauch·zen ['jaʊxtsən] **I.** *v/i.* (h) cheer; shout for joy, whoop with joy; **II.** ♀ *n* (-s) cheers *pl.*; *lit.* jubilation; **'jauch·zend** *adj.* cheering; exultant, jubilant; **Jauch·zer** ['jaʊxtsɐ] *m* (-s; -) (loud) whoop, shout of joy; ***e-n ~ ausstoßen*** give a loud whoop, whoop with joy

jau·len ['jaʊlən] *v/i.* (h) howl; *guitar*: *a.* whine, scream

Jau·se ['jaʊzə] *Austrian f* (-; -n) snack; ***e-e ~ machen*** have a snack (*or* bite to eat)

Ja·va·mensch ['ja:va-] *m*: ***der ~*** Pithecanthropus, Java Man

Ja·va·ner [ja'va:nɐ] *m* (-s; -), **Ja·va·ne·rin** [ja'va:nərɪn] *f* (-; -nen), **ja·va·nisch** [ja'va:nɪʃ] *adj.* Javanese

ja·wohl [ja'vo:l] *adv.* yes; will do; ⚔ *etc.*, *a. iro.* yes, Sir!, yessir!

'Ja·wort *n*: ***sie gab ihm das ~*** she said yes

Jazz [dʒɛs] *m* (-; *no pl.*) jazz; **~band** *f* jazz band; **~fe·sti·val** *n* jazz festival; **~ka,pel·le** *f* jazz band; **~mu,sik** *f* jazz (music); **~mu·si·ker** *m* jazz musician; **~sän·ger** *m* jazz singer

je[1] [je:] *int.*: ***ach ~!*** oh no!, oh dear!

je[2] [je:] *adv. and cj.* **1.** → **eh** 2; **2.** ever; ***ohne ihn ~ gesehen zu haben*** without ever having seen him; ***hast du ~ so etwas gehört?*** did you ever hear (of) such a thing?; **3.** ***~ sechs*** six each; ***sie kosten ~ einen Dollar*** they cost a dollar each; ***er gab den Jungen ~ einen Apfel*** he gave each of the boys an apple, he gave the boys an apple each; ***für ~ zehn Wörter*** for every ten words; ***in Schachteln mit ~ zehn Stück*** in boxes of ten; ***~ zwei und zwei*** in twos; **4.** ***~ nach*** *dat.* according to; ***~ nachdem*** *as adv.*: it (all) depends, *as cj.*: according to, depending on *what he says etc.*; **5.** *with comp.*: ***~ ... desto ...*** the ... the ...; ***~ länger, ~ lieber*** the longer the better

Jeans [dʒi:nz] *pl., a. f*: (***e-e ~*** a pair of) jeans; **~an·zug** *m* denim suit; **♀far·ben** *adj.* denim(-colo[u]red); **~jacke** *f* denim jacket; **~stoff** *m* denim

jeck [jɛk] *dial. adj.* mad, F crazy; ***bist du ~?*** *a.* have you gone mad?

je·de ['je:də], **je·der** ['je:dɐ], **je·des** ['je:dəs] *indef. pron.* **1.** *adj.* a) every; each, b) each and every, c) any, d) either, e) all; ***jeder einzelne ...*** every single ...; ***jeder zweite ...*** every other ...; ***ohne jeden Zweifel*** without (any) doubt; (***zu***) ***jeder Zeit*** any time; ***sie kann jeden Moment***

dasein she could be here any minute; ***um jeden Preis*** whatever the cost (*or* price); ***bei jedem Wetter*** in any weather; ***fern jeder Zivilisation*** far away from civilization; → ***Fall*** 2; **2.** *su.* a) everyone, every single one (*or* person), b) anyone, c) every (*or* each) one, d) any (of them); ***jeder von ihnen*** all (*or* each) of them; ***alles und jedes*** everything (under the sun); ***jeder hat seine Fehler*** we all have our faults; ***da kann jeder machen, was er will*** you can do what(ever) you like there

je·den·falls ['je:dən'fals] *adv.* **1.** anyway, in any case, at any rate; **2.** at any rate, at all events; **3.** be that as it may; **4.** at least, at any rate; ***ich bin es ~ nicht*** a) it's not me, anyway, b) I for one am not *surprised etc.*

je·der·lei ['je:dɐ'laɪ] *adj.* all sorts (*or* kinds) of ...

'je·der·mann *indef. pron.* everyone, everybody; anyone, anybody; ***nicht ~s Sache*** not everybody's cup of tea; *thea.* ***Jedermann*** Everyman

'je·der'zeit *adv.* **1.** any time, always; **2.** any minute (*or* day) (now); ***er rechnet ~ mit s-r Entlassung*** he's waiting to be given notice any day now

'je·des'mal *adv.* every time; always; ***~ wenn*** every time, whenever

je·doch [je'dɔx] *adv.* however, still; ... though

jed·we·de ['je:t've:də], **jed·we·der** ['je:t've:dɐ], **jed·we·des** ['je:t've:dəs] *indef. pron.* every single; all; ***ohne jedweden ...*** without a trace of, bar all, devoid of (all); ***ihm fehlt jedweder Sinn für Humor*** *etc.* he hasn't got the slightest sense of humo(u)r *etc.*

jeg·li·che ['je:klɪçə], **jeg·li·cher** ['je:klɪçɐ], **jeg·li·ches** ['je:klɪçəs] *indef. pron.* → ***jedwede, jedweder, jedwedes***

je·her ['je:he:ɐ] *adv.*: ***von ~*** always; all along; from time immemorial, ever since I *etc.* can remember

jein [jaɪn] *adv.* yes and no

Je·län·ger·je·lie·ber [je'lɛŋɐje'li:bɐ] *n* (-s; -) ⚘ honeysuckle

je·mals ['je:ma:ls] *adv.* ever

je·mand ['je:mant] *indef. pron.* somebody, someone; anybody, anyone; ***es kommt ~*** somebody's coming; ***ist ~ da?*** is there anybody here (*or* home)?; ***~ anders*** somebody (*or* anybody) else; ***sonst noch ~?*** anyone else (*iro.* while I'm at it)?; → ***irgend*** 2; ***ein gewisser ♀*** a certain somebody

Je·me·nit [jeme'ni:t] *m* (-en; -en), **Je·me·ni·tin** [jeme'ni:tɪn] *f* (-; -nen), **je·me·ni·tisch** [jeme'ni:tɪʃ] *adj.* Yemenite, Yemeni

je·ner ['je:nɐ], **je·ne** ['je:nə], **je·nes** ['je:nəs] *dem. pron.* **1.** *adj.* that, *pl.* those; ***seit jenem Tag*** from that day on; **2.** *su.* that one, *pl.* those; the former; → ***dieser, diese, dieses*** 2

jen·sei·tig ['je:nzaɪtɪç] *adj.* **1.** on the other side; ***am ~en Ufer*** on the opposite bank; **2.** *fig.* otherworldly

jen·seits ['je:nzaɪts] **I.** *prp.* (*gen.*) on the other side of, across, beyond; **II.** *adv.* on the other side; ***~ von*** beyond; F ***~ von Gut und Böse*** F past it; **III.** ♀ *n* (-; *no pl.*) *the* hereafter; F ***j-n ins ~ befördern*** F send s.o. up the river

Je·re·mia [jere'mi:a] *m* (-[s]; *no pl.*) *bibl.* Jeremiah; ***das Buch ~*** (the Book of) Jeremiah; ***die Klagelieder ~s*** the Lamentations of Jeremiah; **Je·re·mia·de** [jere'mia:də] *f* (-; -n) jeremiad, lamentation

Jer·sey ['dʒø:ɐzi] *m* (-[s]; -s) jersey

Jes·ses ['jɛsəs] *int.* (*a.* ***~ Maria!***) good Lord!

Je·suit [je'zŭi:t] *m* (-en; -en) Jesuit

Je·sui·ten|dra·ma [je'zŭi:tən-] *n* (-s; *no pl.*) Jesuit play; *coll.* Jesuit plays *pl.* (*or* drama); **~or·den** *m* Jesuit Order, Order of Jesuits; Jesuits *pl.*; **~schu·le** *f* Jesuit school

je·sui·tisch [je'zŭi:tɪʃ] *adj.* Jesuit ..., Jesuitic(al); *contp.* jesuitical

Je·sus ['je:zʊs] *m* (-; *no pl.*) Jesus; ***~ Christus*** Jesus Christ; ***der Herr ~*** the Lord Jesus; **~kind** *n* (-[e]s; *no pl.*): ***das ~*** the infant (*or* child) Jesus, (the) baby Jesus; **~lat·schen** F *pl.* F Jesus sandals; (leather) thongs

Jet [dʒɛt] *m* (-[s]; -s) ✈ jet

Je·ton [ʒə'tõ:] *m* (-s; -s) chip

Jet-set ['dʒɛtsɛt] *m* (-s; *no pl.*) jet set

jet·ten ['dʒɛtən] *v/i.* (sn): ***~ nach*** *dat.* jet off to

jet·zig ['jɛtsɪç] *adj.* present; current; existing; prevailing; ***in der ~en Zeit*** these days, nowadays

jetzt [jɛtst] **I.** *adv.* **1.** now; these days, nowadays; ***erst ~*** only now; ***gleich ~*** right now; ***noch ~*** even now, to this day; ***ich habe ~ keine Zeit*** I haven't got (any) time right now; **2.** ***~ erhob er sich*** then he got up; **3.** *after prp.*: ***bis ~*** so far, *negative*: *a.* as yet; ***von ~ an*** from now on; **4.** ***wo hab' ich's ~ hingetan?*** where did I put it now?; ***was hast du denn ~?*** what's wrong now (*or* this time)?; **II.** ♀ *n* (-; *no pl.*) → ***Hier***

'Jetzt·zeit *f* (-; *no pl.*) present (time)

je·wei·lig ['je:'vaɪlɪç] **I.** *adj.* respective; particular; relevant; prevailing; ***der ~e Präsident*** the president in office; ***der ~e Abteilungsleiter*** the head of department in each case; ***den ~en Umständen nach*** according to the circumstances (at the time); **II.** *adv.* → **je·weils** ['je:'vaɪls] *adv.* **1.** *two etc.* at a time; **2.** always; a time; ***sie kommt ~ am Montag*** she comes every Monday (*or* on Mondays); ***er gibt ~ zwei Stunden Geschichte*** he does two hours of history a time; **3.** each; ***Übungen mit ~ 20 Fragen*** exercises with twenty questions each; **4.** in each case; ***die ~ erforderlichen Maßnahmen*** the relevant (*or* appropriate) measures

jid·disch ['jɪdɪʃ] *adj.*, ♀ *n* (-n) *ling.* Yiddish

Jiu-Jit·su ['dʒi:u'dʒɪtsu] *n* (-[s]; *no pl.*) j(i)ujitsu

Job [dʒɔp] *m* (-s; -s) job; **job·ben** ['dʒɔbən] *v/i.* (h) job around; *student*: work during the vac; F work, have a job

Joch [jɔx] *n* (-[e]s; -e) **1.** yoke (*a.* ⚡ *and fig.*); *fig.* ***unter das ~ bringen*** bring under one's yoke (*or* sway); **2.** *geol.* saddleback; **3.** △ bay; → **~bal·ken** *m* crossbeam, girder; **~bein** *n anat.* cheekbone

Jockei → **Jockey** ['dʒɔke, 'dʒɔki] (*sep.* -k·k-) *m* (-s; -s) jockey

Jod [jo:t] *n* (-[e]s; *no pl.*) ⚗ iodine

jo·deln ['jo:dəln] *v/i. and v/t.* (h) yodel

'jod·hal·tig [-haltɪç] *adj.*: ***~ sein*** contain iodine

jo·die·ren [jo'di:rən] *v/t.* (h) ⚗ iodinate; ⚕ *and phot.* iodize

Jod·ler ['jo:dlɐ] *m* (-s; -) **1.** yodel(l)er; **2.** yodel

'Jod|lö·sung *f* iodine solution; **~prä·pa,rat** *n* iodine preparation; **~sal·be** *f* iodine ointment; **~salz** *n* iodized salt; **~sil·ber** *n* silver iodide; **~tink,tur** *f* iodine tincture, tincture of iodine

Jo·ga ['jo:ga] *m, n* (-[s]; *no pl.*) yoga; **~übung** *f* yoga exercise

jog·gen ['dʒɔgən] *v/i.* (h, sn) jog, go jogging; **Jog·ger** ['dʒɔgɐ] *m* (-s; -), **Jog·ge·rin** ['dʒɔgərɪn] *f* (-; -nen) jogger

Jog·ging ['dʒɔgɪŋ] *n* (-s; *no pl.*) jogging; **~an·zug** *m* tracksuit; **~ho·se** *f* tracksuit trousers (*or* bottoms) *pl.*; **~schu·he** *pl.* running shoes

Jog·hurt ['jo:gʊrt] *m, n* (-[s]; -s) yog(h)urt

Jo·gi ['jo:gɪ] *m* (-s; -s) yogi

Jo·han·nes [jo'hanəs] *m bibl.* John; ***~ der Täufer*** John the Baptist; → ***Offenbarung*** 2; **~evan,ge·li·um** *n*: ***das ~*** (the Gospel of) St John, St John's Gospel

Jo·han·nis·bee·re [jo'hanɪs-] *f*: ***rote ~*** redcurrant; ***schwarze ~*** blackcurrant

Jo'han·nis|brot *n* carob; **~feu·er** *n* Midsummer Eve bonfire; **~kä·fer** *m* glow-worm; **~kraut** *n* ⚘ St John's wort; **~nacht** *f* Midsummer Eve (*or* Night), Eve of St John; **~trieb** *m* **1.** ⚘ lammas shoot; **2.** F *fig.* late love

Jo·han·ni·ter·or·den [johaˈni:tɐ-] *m* Order of (the Knights of) St John of Jerusalem

joh·len ['jo:lən] **I.** *v/i.* (h) bawl, yell; **II.** ♀ *n* (-s) bawling, yelling

Jo·ker ['jo:kɐ, 'dʒo:kɐ] *m* (-s; -) joker; *fig.* trump card

Jol·le ['jɔlə] *f* (-; -n) dinghy

Jon·gleur [ʒõ'glø:ɐ, ʒɔŋ'lø:ɐ] *m* (-s; -e [-rə]) juggler; **jon·glie·ren** [ʒõ'gli:rən, ʒɔŋ'li:rən] *v/t. and v/i.* (h) juggle (***mit*** *dat.* [with] *s.th.*) (*a. fig.*)

Jop·pe ['jɔpə] *f* (-; -n) jacket

Jor·dan ['jɔrdan] *m* (-s; *no pl.*) (River) Jordan; *fig.* ***über den ~ gehen*** go to meet one's Maker, pass on

Jor·da·ni·er [jɔr'da:nǐɐ] *m* (-s; -), **Jor·da·nie·rin** [jɔr'da:nǐərɪn] *f* (-; -nen), **jor·da·nisch** [jɔr'da:nɪʃ] *adj.* Jordanian

Jo·ta ['jo:ta] *n*: *fig.* ***kein ~*** not one jot (or tittle); ***kein ~ nachgeben*** not to budge (*or* give) an inch

Joule [dʒu:l] *n* (-[s]; -) *phys.* joule

Jour·nal [ʒʊr'na:l] *n* (-s; -e) journal, magazine; **Jour·na·lis·mus** [ʒʊrna'lɪsmʊs] *m* (-; *no pl.*) journalism; **Jour·na·list** [ʒʊrna'lɪst] *m* (-en; -en) journalist

Jour·na'li·sten|deutsch *n*, **~stil** *m* journalese

Jour·na·li·stik [ʒʊrna'lɪstɪk] *f* (-; *no pl.*) journalism; **Jour·na·li·stin** [ʒʊrna'lɪstɪn] *f* (-; -nen) journalist; **jour·na·li·stisch** [ʒʊrna'lɪstɪʃ] *adj.* journalistic(ally *adv.*)

jo·vi·al [jo'vĭa:l] *adj.* genial, affable

Jo·via·li·tät [jovĭali'tɛ:t] *f* (-; *no pl.*) geniality; affability

Ju·bel ['ju:bəl] *m* (-s; *no pl.*) cheering, cheers *pl.*; rejoicing; ***es herrschte allgemeiner ~*** there was great rejoicing; ***es herrschte ~, Trubel, Heiterkeit*** there was much merrymaking; **~fei·er** *f*, **~fest** *n* anniversary (celebration[s *pl.*]); **~geschrei** *n* cheering; **~greis** F *m* sprightly old fellow; **~jahr** *n* jubilee year; F ***alle ~e einmal*** F once in a blue moon

ju·beln ['ju:bəln] *v/i.* (h) cheer, shout for joy; rejoice; ***zu früh ~*** rejoice too soon; F *fig.* ***j-m et. unter die Weste ~*** fob s.th. off on s.o., F land s.o. with s.th.

Ju·bi·lar [jubi'la:ɐ] *m* (-s; -e), **Ju·bi·la·rin** [jubi'la:rɪn] *f* (-; -nen) *person celebrating an anniversary*; F birthday boy *or* girl

Ju·bi·lä·um [jubiˈlɛːʊm] *n* (-s; -en) anniversary

Ju·biˈlä·ums|aus·ga·be *f* anniversary edition; **~fei·er** *f* anniversary celebration(s *pl.*)

ju·bi·lie·ren [jubiˈliːrən] *v/i.* (h) **1.** rejoice (**über** *acc.* over), *a.* gloat (over); **2.** *bird*: trill, carol

juch·he [jʊxˈheː] *int.* whoopee!

Juch·ten [ˈjʊxtən] *n* Russia leather; (*scent*) Russian leather; **~le·der** *n* Russia leather

juch·zen [ˈjʊxtsən] *v/i.* (h) → ***jauchzen***; **Juch·zer** [ˈjʊxtsɐ] *m* (-s; -) → ***Jauchzer***

juckeln [ˈjʊkəln] (*sep.* -k·k-) F *v/i.* (sn) **1.** fidget (F twitch) around; ***hör doch auf mit dem ≈ a.*** F have you got ants in your pants?; **2.** *mot.* chug along

jucken [ˈjʊkən] (*sep.* -k·k-) (h) **I.** *v/t. and v/i.* itch; ***mich juckt's*** I'm itching; ***es juckt mich am Arm*** my arm's itching; ***der Pullover juckt*** the pullover's scratchy; *fig.* ***es juckt(e) mich zu*** *inf.* I'd love to *inf.* (I was tempted to *inf.*); ***dir juckt wohl das Fell*** what's got into you all of a sudden?; ***das juckt mich nicht*** why should I care?; ***es scheint ihn nicht zu ~*** it doesn't seem to bother him (in the slightest); ***wen juckt's?*** who cares?; ***das juckt niemanden*** nobody could care less (F give a damn); **II.** F *v/refl.*: ***sich ~*** scratch o.s.; **III.** ≈ *n* (-s) itch(ing)

Juck|pul·ver [ˈjʊk-] *n* itching powder; **~reiz** *m* itch(ing), itchiness

Ju·dai·ka [juˈdaːika] *pl.* Judaica

Ju·da·is·mus [judaˈɪsmʊs] *m* (-; *no pl.*) Judaism; **Ju·dai·stik** [judaˈɪstɪk] *f* (-; *no pl.*) Jewish (*or* Judaic) studies *pl.*

Ju·das [ˈjuːdas] *m* (-; -se) **1.** *no pl. bibl.* Judas; **2.** *fig.* Judas, traitor; **~baum** *m* ⚘ Judas tree; **~brief** *m*: *bibl.* ***der ~*** (the Epistle of) Jude; **~kuß** *m* Judas kiss; ***der ~*** *art*: the Betrayal; **~lohn** *m* traitor's reward, (*one's*) thirty pieces of silver

Ju·de [ˈjuːdə] *m* (-n; -n) Jew

ˈJu·den·stern *m* Star of David

ˈJu·den·tum *n* (-s; *no pl.*) **1.** ***das ~*** Judaism; **2.** *the* Jews *pl.*, *the* Jewish people, *modern etc.* Jewry

ˈJu·den|ver·fol·gung *f* persecution of the Jews; **~vier·tel** *n* Jewish quarter

Ju·di·ka·ti·ve [judikaˈtiːvə] *f* (-; -n) judiciary

Jü·din [ˈjyːdɪn] *f* (-; -nen) Jew, Jewess

jü·disch [ˈjyːdɪʃ] *adj.* Jewish

Ju·do [ˈjuːdo] *n* (-[s]; *no pl.*) judo; **~an·zug** *m* judo outfit; **~griff** *m* judo hold; **~ho·se** *f* judo pyjamas (*Am.* pajamas) *pl.*; **~jacke** *f* judo jacket

Ju·do·ka [juˈdoːka] *m* (-[s]; -[s]) judoka

ˈJu·do·wurf *m* judo throw

Ju·gend [ˈjuːgənt] *f* (-; *no pl.*) **1.** youth; childhood; ***in m-r ~*** when I was young; ***von ~ auf*** since I was (*or* you were *etc.*) young *or* a child; **2.** youth(fulness); **3.** *coll.* ***die ~*** young people, the younger generation, *a.* the youth of today, today's youth; ***die deutsche ~*** the young Germans (of today); **4.** → ***Jugendmannschaft***; **~al·ter** *n*: (***im ~*** in) adolescence; **~amt** *n* youth welfare office; **~ar·beits·lo·sig·keit** *f* youth unemployment; **~arˌrest** *m* ⚖ *short-term detention for young offenders*; **~ban·de** *f* gang of youths; **~be·we·gung** *f* youth movement; **~bild(nis)** *n*: ***ein ~ von X*** a portrait of X as a young man (*or* woman); **~buch** *n* book for young people (*or* adolescents); **~bü·cheˌrei** *f* junior library, library for young people; **~elf** *f sport*: youth team; **~er·in·ne·run·gen** *pl.* memories of one's youth; **~fo·to** *n*: ***ein ~ von X*** a photo of X as a young man (*or* woman), a photo of X when he (*or* she) was young; **≈frei** *adj. film*: suitable for all ages, U-certificate, *Am.* G-rated; ***nicht ~*** for adults only; **~freund** *m* friend from one's youth; ***er ist ein ~ von mir*** we've been friends ever since we were young; **~fri·sche** *f* youthfulness; **≈ge·fähr·dend** *adj.* harmful (to young people); **~ge·fäng·nis** *n* → ***Jugendstrafanstalt***; **~ge·richt** *n* juvenile court; **~grup·pe** *f* youth group; **~haft** *f* youth custody; **~heim** *n* youth cent|re (*Am.* -er); **~her·ber·ge** *f* youth hostel

ˈJu·gend·her·bergs|mut·ter *f*, **~va·ter** *m* youth hostel warden; **~ver·band** *m* Youth Hostel Association

ˈJu·gend|hil·fe *f* youth welfare (services *pl.*); **~jah·re** *pl.*: ***die ~*** one's youth; ***in m-n ~n*** in my youth, when I was young, when I was a young lad (*or* girl); **~kam·mer** *f* ⚖ juvenile division; **~klas·se** *f sport*: youth class; **~kri·mi·na·liˌtät** juvenile delinquency; **~la·ger** *n* youth camp

ˈju·gend·lich *adj.* youthful (*a. look, clothes etc.*); young; ⚖ *a.* juvenile; ***~er Leichtsinn*** youthful abandon (*or* innocence); ***~er Täter*** youth offender; ***~ aussehen*** look young; ***~ wirken*** *a.* come across as quite young; ***sich ~ geben*** act young

ˈJu·gend·li·che *m, f* (-n; -n) young person, *m a.* youth, ⚖ *a.* juvenile

ˈJu·gend·lich·keit *f* (-; *no pl.*) youthfulness

ˈJu·gend|lie·be *f* **1.** *my etc.* old flame; **2.** puppy love; **~li·te·raˌtur** *f* books *pl.* for young people, young adult literature; **~mann·schaft** *f* youth team; **~mei·ster** *m* youth champion; **~mei·ster·schaft** *f* youth championships *pl.*; **~or·ga·ni·sa·tiˌon** *f* youth organization; **~pfle·ge** *f* youth welfare; **~pfle·ger** *m* youth welfare worker; **~recht** *n* juvenile law (*or* legislation); **~rich·ter** *m* juvenile court judge

ˈJu·gend·schutz *m legal protection for children and young persons*; **~ge·setz** *n in GB*: Children and Young Persons Act

ˈJu·gend|spra·che *f* teenage slang; **~stil** *m* Jugendstil, *a.* art nouveau; **~straf·an·stalt** *f* youth custody unit, remand centre, *Am.* reform school; **~streich** *m* youthful escapade (*or* exploit); **~sün·de** *f* sin (*or* transgression) of one's youth; → **~tor·heit** *f* youthful escapade (*or* exploit), folly of one's youth; **~traum** *m* childhood dream; ambition of one's youth; ***es ist ein ~ von mir (gewesen)*** *a.* it's something I've always dreamt of (doing); **~ver·bot** *n*: ***der Film hat ~*** the film is for adults only; **~werk** *n* early work; **~zeit** *f* → ***Jugend*** 1; **~zeit·schrift** *f* teenage magazine; **~zen·trum** *n* youth cent|re (*Am.* -er)

Ju·go·sla·we [jugoˈslaːvə] *hist. m* (-n; -n) **1.** Yugoslav; **2.** F Yugoslavian place; **Ju·go·sla·win** [jugoˈslaːvɪn] *hist. f* (-; -nen) Yugoslav; **ju·go·sla·wisch** [jugoˈslaːvɪʃ] *hist. adj.* Yugoslav

Ju·li [ˈjuːli] *m* (-[s]; -s) July; ***im ~*** in July

Jum·bo [ˈjʊmbo] *m* (-s; -s), **~-Jet** *m* jumbo (jet)

jung [jʊŋ] *adj.* young; youthful; ***~es Unternehmen*** new company; ***~er Wein*** new wine; ***~es Glück*** new-found happiness; ***von ~ auf*** from childhood; ***~ und alt*** young and old; ***~ heiraten (sterben*** *etc.*) marry (die *etc.*) young *or* at an early age; ***die ≈en*** the young ones, the young(er) generation; ***die ≈en und die Alten*** young and old; → ***jünger, jüngst*** I, ***Gemüse, Hund*** I

ˈJung|brun·nen *m* fountain of youth; **~de·moˌkrat** *m* Young Democrat

Jun·ge[1] [ˈjʊŋə] *m* (-n; -n) a) boy; F lad, b) *card game*: F jack; ***dummer ~*** silly little boy; ***armer ~*** poor lad; F ***~, ~!*** F boy oh boy; → ***schwer*** I

ˈJun·ge[2] *n* (-n; -n) *zo.* F baby; puppy; kitten; cub; calf; ***~ werfen (or bekommen)*** have young (*or* a litter), have puppies (*or* kittens), *cow etc.*: calve, *deer*: fawn

ˈJun·gen·ge·sicht *n* boy's face; boyish face

ˈjun·gen·haft *adj.* boyish

ˈJun·gen·haf·tig·keit *f* (-; *no pl.*) boyishness

ˈJun·gen|klas·se *f* boys' class; **~schu·le** *f* boys' school; **~streich** *m* schoolboy prank

jün·ger [ˈjʏŋɐ] *adj.* a) younger; *w.s.* youngish, b) more recent, later; ***der ≈e (d. J.)*** the Younger; ***~en Datums*** more recent; ***sie sieht ~ aus als sie ist*** she looks younger than her age, she doesn't look her age

ˈJün·ger *m* (-s; -) disciple; *fig. a.* follower; **ˈJün·ger·schaft** *f* (-; *no pl.*) (body of) followers *pl. or* disciples *pl.*

Jung·fer [ˈjʊŋfɐ] *f* (-; -n): ***alte ~*** old maid

ˈJung·fern|fahrt *f* maiden (*or* inaugural) voyage; **~flug** *m* maiden (*or* inaugural) flight; **~häut·chen** *n anat.* hymen; **~öl** *n* virgin oil; **~re·de** *f* maiden speech; **~zeu·gung** *f biol.* parthenogenesis

ˈJung·frau *f* **1.** virgin; ***sie ist noch ~*** she's still a virgin; ***die ~ Maria*** the Virgin Mary; ***die Heilige ~*** the Blessed Virgin; ***Eiserne ~*** Iron Maiden; ***die ~ von Orleans*** the Maid of Orleans, Joan of Arc; F ***er ist dazu gekommen wie die ~ zum Kind*** it just (F sort of) fell into his lap; **2.** *ast.* Virgo; ***(e-e) ~ sein*** be (a) Virgo; **ˈJung·frau·en·ge·burt** *f bibl.* Virgin Birth

ˈjung·fräu·lich [-frɔʏlɪç] *adj.* chaste; virginal; *fig.* virgin ...; **ˈJung·fräu·lich·keit** *f* (-; *no pl.*) virginity; chasteness

ˈJung·ge·sel·le *m* bachelor, single man; ***eingefleischter (alter) ~*** confirmed (old) bachelor; ***er ist noch ~*** he's still a bachelor, he's still single

ˈJung·ge·sel·len|bu·de F *f* F bachelor pad; **~da·sein** *n* life of a bachelor, bachelor life; **~haus·halt** *m* bachelor household; **~le·ben** *n* → ***Junggesellendasein***

ˈJung·ge·sel·len·tum *n* (-s; *no pl.*) bachelorhood

ˈJung·ge·sel·len|wirt·schaft *f* bachelor household; **~zeit** *f* bachelor years (*or* days) *pl.*

Jung·ge·sel·lin [ˈjʊŋgəzɛlɪn] *f* (-; -nen) single girl (*or* woman), unmarried woman; *adm.* spinster

Jüng·ling [ˈjʏŋlɪŋ] *m* (-s; -e) youth; *contp.* stripling; **ˈJüng·lings·al·ter** *n*: (***im ~*** in one's) youth, (in) adolescence

ˈjüng·lings·haft *adj.* youthful, ... of youth

ˈ**Jung|pflan·ze** *f* seedling, young plant; **~so·zia͵list** *m* Young Socialist

jüngst [jʏŋst] **I.** *adj.* a) youngest, b) latest; **2er Tag** Day of Judg(e)ment; ***Vorgänge der ~en Vergangenheit*** recent events; ***sein ~es Werk*** his latest work; F ***sie ist auch nicht mehr die 2e*** she's not getting any younger, F she's no spring chicken any more; ***unser 2er, unsere 2e*** our youngest (one *or* child); ***in ~er Zeit*** → **II.** *adv.* recently; the other day

ˈ**Jung|stein·zeit** *f* Neolithic Age; **~tier** *n* young animal; *hunt.* young deer (*or* doe); **~tür·ke** *m pol.* Young Turk; **~un·ter·͵neh·mer** *m* young entrepreneur (*or* businessman); **2ver·hei·ra·tet, 2ver·mählt** *adj.* newly-wed; **~vieh** *n* young stock; **~wäh·ler** *m* young voter

Ju·ni [ˈjuːni] *m* (-[s]; -s) June; ***im ~*** in June

ju·ni·or [ˈjuːnĭoːɐ] **I.** *adj.* **1.** junior; ***X ~*** X junior, young X; **II. 2** *m* (-s; -en [juˈnĭoːrən]) **2.** *sport and* F junior; **3.** ✝ owner's son; → ˈ**Ju·ni·or·chef** ✝ *m* junior partner

Ju·nio·ren... [juˈnĭoːrən-] *in cpds. sport*: junior *class etc.*

Jun·ker [ˈjʊŋkɐ] *m* (-s; -) **1.** (young) nobleman; (country) squire; **2.** *hist.* Junker; ˈ**Jun·ker·tum** *n* (-s; *no pl.*) **1.** squir(e)archy; **2.** *hist.* Junkerdom

Junk·tim [ˈjʊŋktɪm] *n* (-s; -s) *pol.* nexus

Ju·no [ˈjuːno] *m* (-s; *no pl.*) June; ***im ~*** in June

Jun·ta [ˈxʊnta] *f* (-; Junten [ˈxʊntən]) *pol.* junta

Ju·ra[1] [ˈjuːra] law

ˈ**Ju·ra**[2] *m* (-s; *no pl.*) *geol.* Jurassic (period); **~for·ma·ti͵on** *f* Jurassic system

ˈ**Ju·ra|stu͵dent** *m* law student; **~stu·di·um** *n* law studies *pl.*; study of law; law degree

ˈ**Ju·ra·zeit** *f geol.* Jurassic period

Ju·ris·pru·denz [jurɪspruˈdɛnts] *f* (-; *no pl.*) jurisprudence

Ju·rist [juˈrɪst] *m* (-en; -en) lawyer; *univ.* law student

Ju·ri·sten|deutsch [juˈrɪstən-] *n*, **~spra·che** *f* legalese

Ju·ri·stin [juˈrɪstɪn] *f* (-; -nen) → ***Jurist***

ju·ri·stisch [juˈrɪstɪʃ] *adj.* legal; ***~e Fakultät*** faculty of law, law school; ***~e Laufbahn*** career in law, legal career; ***~e Person*** legal entity

Ju·ry [ʒyˈriː] *f* (-; -s) **1.** jury, (panel of) judges *pl.*; *exhibition*: selection committee; **2.** ⚖ jury; **Juˈry·mit·glied** *n* **1.** panel(l)ist; **2.** ⚖ member of the jury

Jus [jʊs] law

Ju·so [ˈjuːzo] *m* (-s; -s) young member of the SPD

just [jʊst] *obs. adv. a. hum.* just; ***~ als*** just as; ***~ in dem Moment*** at that very moment, just then; ***~ er*** him of all people

ju·stier·bar [jʊsˈtiːɐbaːɐ] *adj.* adjustable

ju·stie·ren [jʊsˈtiːrən] *v/t.* (h) adjust, set; true up *gun etc.*; ⚙ calibrate; *typ.* justify; **Juˈstie·rung** *f* (-; -en) adjustment; calibration

Ju·sti·tia [jʊsˈtiːtsĭa] *f* (-; *no pl.*) Justice; goddess of justice

Ju·sti·ti·ar [jʊstiˈtsĭaːɐ] *m* (-s; -e [-rə]) legal adviser

Ju·stiz [jʊsˈtiːts] *f* (-; *no pl.*) justice; *the* law; **~be·amte** *m* judicial officer; **~be·hör·de** *f* legal authority; **~ge·bäu·de** *n* law courts *pl.*; **~ge·walt** *f* judiciary (power); **~irr·tum** *m* error of justice; **~mi͵ni·ster** *m* justice minister; *in GB*: Lord Chancellor; *in the USA*: Attorney General; **~mi·ni͵ste·ri·um** *n* ministry of justice; *in the USA*: Department of Justice; **~mord** *m* judicial murder; **~pa͵last** *m* (central) law courts *pl.*; **~ver·wal·tung** *f* **1.** administration of justice; **2.** legal administrative body; **~voll͵zugs·an·stalt** *f* prison; **~we·sen** *n* (-s; *no pl.*) judicial system, judiciary

Ju·te [ˈjuːtə] *f* (-; *no pl.*) jute

Jü·te [ˈjyːtə] *m* (-n; -n) Jute

ˈ**Ju·te|fa·ser** *f* jute fibre (*Am.* fiber); **~lei·nen** *n*, **~lein·wand** *f* burlap; **~pflan·ze** *f* jute plant; **~ta·sche** *f* jute bag

Ju·wel [juˈveːl] *n* (-s; -en) **1.** jewel; *pl.* jewellery, *esp. Am.* jewelry; precious stones; **2.** (*pl.* -e) *fig.* jewel, gem

Juˈwe·len|händ·ler *m* jewel(l)er; **~schmuck** *m* jewellery, *esp. Am.* jewelry

Ju·we·lier [juveˈliːɐ] *m* (-s; -e [-rə]) jewel(l)er; **~ge·schäft** *n* jewel(l)er's shop

Jux [jʊks] F *m* (-es; *no pl.*) (practical) joke; ***aus ~*** for fun, for a laugh, F for (*or* as) a lark; ***er macht nur ~*** F he's just kidding; ***sich e-n ~ machen*** have a lark; ***sich e-n ~ daraus machen zu*** *inf.* have a bit of fun *ger.*

jwd [jɔtveːˈdeː] F *hum. adv.*: ***~ wohnen*** F live at the back of beyond, live out in the sticks (*Am. a.* boondocks)

K

K, k [kaː] *n* (-; -) K, k
Ka·ba·rett [kabaˈrɛt] *n* (-s; -s) (political) revue; **Ka·ba·ret·tist** [kabarɛˈtɪst] *m* (-en; -en), **Ka·ba·ret·ti·stin** [kabarɛˈtɪstɪn] *f* (-; -nen) revue artist; (political) satirist; **ka·ba·ret·ti·stisch** [kabarɛˈtɪstɪʃ] *adj.* cabaret ...
Ka·bäus·chen [kaˈbɔʏsçən] F *n* (-s; -) a) (gatekeeper's) cabin, b) cubbyhole, c) commentary box, d) booth
Kab·ba·la [ˈkabala] *f* (-; *no pl.*) cabbala, kabbala; **Kab·ba·li·stik** [kabaˈlɪstɪk] *f* (-; *no pl.*) cabbalism; **kab·ba·li·stisch** [kabaˈlɪstɪʃ] *adj.* cabbalistic
kab·be·lig [ˈkabəlɪç] *adj.*: **~e See** choppy water (*or* seas)
Ka·bel [ˈkaːbəl] *n* (-s; -) ⚡, ⚙ cable; **~ader** *f* cable core; **~an·schluß** *m* cable connection; **~baum** *m* ⚡ cable harness; **~brand** *m*: ***das Feuer entstand durch ~*** the fire was caused by an electrical fault; **~fern·se·hen** *n* cable TV; **~fern·seh·zen,tra·le** *f* cablehead
Ka·bel·jau [ˈkaːbəljaʊ] *m* (-s; -e, -s) cod
ˈKa·bel|klem·me *f* cable terminal; **~man·tel** *m* cable sheath; **~netz** *n* cable network; **~rund·funk** *m* cable broadcasting; **~schnur** *f* flex; **~trom·mel** *f* cable drum; **~tu·ner** *m* cable decoder (*or* tuner); **~ver·bin·dung** *f* cable link
Ka·bi·ne [kaˈbiːnə] *f* (-; -n) cabin; ⚓ stateroom (*a. Am.* ✈); cubicle; *sport*: dressing room; car *of a cable railway*; telephone booth; booth *of a language laboratory*
Kaˈbi·nen|bahn *f* cable railway; **~per·so,nal** *n* cabin staff; **~pre·digt** F *f* F *sport*: half-time roasting
Ka·bi·nett [kabiˈnɛt] *n* (-s; -e) **1.** *pol.* cabinet; **2.** *gastr.* Kabinett wine
Ka·biˈnetts|be·schluß *m* cabinet decision; **~bil·dung** *f* formation of a cabinet; **~ju,stiz** *f* **1.** *hist.* star-chamber justice; **2.** *fig.* arbitrary government; **~kri·se** *f* cabinet crisis; **~li·ste** *f* list of cabinet members; **~mit·glied** *n* cabinet member; **~sit·zung** *f* cabinet meeting; **~tisch** *m*: ***auf den ~ kommen*** be put before the cabinet
Ka·biˈnett·stück *n* **1.** *art*: showpiece; **2.** *fig.* masterstroke; flash of genius, *sport*: *a.* F beautiful little trick
Ka·biˈnetts|,um·bil·dung *f* cabinet reshuffle; **~vor·la·ge** *f* cabinet bill
Ka·biˈnett·wein *m* Kabinett wine
Ka·brio [ˈkaːbrio] *n* (-s; -s) → **Ka·brio·lett** [kabrioˈlɛt] *n* (-s; -s) convertible
Ka·buff [kaˈbʊf] F *n* (-s; -s) cubbyhole
Ka·chel [ˈkaxəl] *f* (-; -n), **ˈka·cheln** *v/t.* (h) tile
ˈKa·chel|ofen *m* tiled stove; **~wand** *f* tiled wall
Kacke [ˈkakə] (*sep.* -k·k-) V *f* (-; *no pl.*) V shit; ***die ~ ist am Dampfen*** V the shit's really flying now; **ˈkacken** (*sep.* -k·k-) V *v/i.* (h) V shit
Ka·da·ver [kaˈdaːvɐ] *m* (-s; -) carcass (*a. fig.*); corpse; **~ge·hor·sam** *m* slavish obedience; **~ver·wer·tung** *f* animal waste processing
Ka·denz [kaˈdɛnts] *f* (-; -en) ♪ cadence
Ka·der [ˈkaːdɐ] *m* (-s; -) ⚔, *pol. etc.* cadre; *sport*: pool *of players etc.*; **~schmie·de** *f* cadre training unit; *w.s.* elite training cent|re (*Am.* -er)
Ka·dett [kaˈdɛt] *m* (-en; -en) cadet
Ka·det·ten·an·stalt [kaˈdɛtən-] *f* cadet school
Ka·di [ˈkaːdi] *m*: F ***j-n vor den ~ schleppen*** have s.o. up (***wegen*** *gen.* for); ***zum ~ laufen*** go to court
Kad·mi·um [ˈkatmiʊm] *n* (-s; *no pl.*) ⚗ cadmium; **~gelb** *n*, **~sul,fid** *n* cadmium sulphide (*or* yellow)
ka·du·zie·ren [kaduˈtsiːrən] *v/t.* (h) ⚖ cancel; ***kaduzierte Aktie*** forfeited share
Kä·fer [ˈkɛːfɐ] *m* (-s; -) beetle (*a.* F *VW*)
Kaff [kaf] F *n* (-s; -e) F hole, dump
Kaf·fee [ˈkafe, kaˈfeː] *m* (-s; -s) coffee; ***~ kochen*** make (some *or* the) coffee; ***e-e Tasse ~*** a cup of coffee; ***~ mit*** (***ohne***) ***Milch*** white (black) coffee; F ***das ist kalter ~*** F that's old hat
ˈKaf·fee|an·bau *m* coffee growing; **~au·to,mat** *m* coffee machine; **~boh·ne** *f* coffee bean; **⁓braun** *adj.* coffee-colo(u)red; **~-Er·satz** *m* coffee substitute, ersatz coffee; **~fahrt** *f* *type of magical mystery tour involving sales promotion*; **~fil·ter** *m* **1.** coffee filter; **2.** filter, paper cone; **~ge·schirr** *n* a) coffee things *pl.*, b) coffee service
Kafˈfee·haus *n* café, coffee house; **~li·te,rat** *m* coffee-house writer; *pl.* coffee-house literati; **~phi·lo,soph** *m* coffee-house philosopher
ˈKaf·fee|kan·ne *f* coffee pot; **~klatsch** F *m* coffee party, *Am.* F coffee klatch; **~löf·fel** *m* teaspoon; **~ma,schi·ne** *f* coffee machine (*or* maker); **~müh·le** *f* coffee grinder; **~pau·se** *f* coffee break; **~plan,ta·ge** *f* coffee plantation; **~sah·ne** *f* (coffee) cream; **~satz** *m* coffee grounds *pl.*; **~ser,vice** *n* coffee service; **~tan·te** F *f* F coffee freak (*or* addict); **~tas·se** *f* coffee cup; **~trin·ker** *m*: ***ich bin*** (***kein***) ***~*** I (don't) drink coffee; **~was·ser** *n*: ***das ~ aufsetzen*** put the kettle on for some coffee; **~wei·ßer** *m* (-s; -) coffee whitener (*Am.* creamer)
Kaf·fer [ˈkafɐ] F *m* (-s; -) (F blithering) idiot
Kä·fig [ˈkɛːfɪç] *m* (-s; -e) cage (*a.* ⚡, ⚙); *fig.* ***im goldenen ~ sitzen*** be a bird in a gilded cage; **~hal·tung** *f* (-; *no pl.*) caging of animals
kaf·ka·esk [kafkaˈɛsk] *adj.* Kafkaesque
Kaf·tan [ˈkaftan] *m* (-s; -e) caftan
kahl [kaːl] *adj.* bald, shorn; *fig.* bare *rocks, walls etc.*; bare, leafless *trees*; barren, bleak *landscape*; plain *room etc.*; empty *walls etc.*; ***~ werden*** go bald
ˈKahl·fraß *m* complete defoliation
ˈkahl·fres·sen *v/t.* (*irr.*, *sep.*, h, → ***fressen***) strip (of its *or* their leaves)
ˈkahl·ge·scho·ren *adj.* shaven
ˈKahl·kopf *m* a) bald head, b) F baldy, slap-head; **ˈkahl·köp·fig** [-kœpfɪç] *adj.* bald(-headed); **ˈKahl·köp·fig·keit** *f* (-; *no pl.*) baldness
ˈkahl·ra,sie·ren *v/t.* (*sep.*, h) shave
ˈKahl·schlag *m* (-[e]s; ⁓e) **1.** *no pl.* complete deforestation; *w.s.* eradication; *fig.* wiping the slate clean; **2.** clearing, deforested area; **~sa,nie·rung** *f* wholesale redevelopment
ˈKahl·wei·den *n* overgrazing
Kahn [kaːn] *m* (-[e]s; Kähne [ˈkɛːnə]) **1.** (rowing *or* fishing) boat; barge; F tub; **2.** F *fig.* ***in den ~ gehen*** F turn in; **3.** F *pl.* F beetle-crushers; **~fahrt** *f* boat trip
Kai [kaɪ] *m* (-s; -s) quay(side), wharf; **~an·la·ge** *f* wharf, wharves *pl.*; **~ar·bei·ter** *m* docker
Kai·man [ˈkaɪman] *m* (-s; -e) *zo.* cayman
ˈKai·mau·er *f* quayside
Kains·mal [ˈkaɪnsmaːl] *n* (-[e]s; -e) mark of Cain
Kai·ser [ˈkaɪzɐ] *m* (-s; -) emperor; ***der deutsche ~*** the German Emperor, (*1871-1918*) *a.* the Kaiser; *fig.* ***sich um des ~s Bart streiten*** squabble over little things; ***gebt dem ~, was des ~s ist*** render unto Caesar the things that are Caesar's; **~ad·ler** *m zo.* imperial eagle; **~haus** *n* imperial dynasty
Kai·se·rin [ˈkaɪzərɪn] *f* (-; -nen) empress
ˈKai·ser·kro·ne *f* **1.** imperial crown; **2.** ⚘ crown imperial
ˈkai·ser·lich *adj.* imperial
ˈKai·ser|reich *n* empire; **~schmar·ren** *Austrian m shredded pancake with sugar and raisins*; **~schnitt** *m* ⚕ C(a)esarean (section); ***durch ~ zur Welt kommen*** be born by C(a)esarean
ˈKai·ser·tum *n* (-s; *no pl.*) **1.** imperial rule; **2.** imperial status
ˈKai·ser|wet·ter *n* glorious weather; ***das ist ja ein ~ heute*** what a glorious day; **~wür·de** *f* imperial status; ***die ~ erlangen*** become emperor
Ka·jak [ˈkaːjak] *m*, *n* (-s; -s) kayak
Ka·jü·te [kaˈjyːtə] *f* (-; -n) ⚓ cabin
Ka·ka·du [ˈkakadu] *m* (-s; -s) cockatoo
Ka·kao [kaˈkaʊ] *m* (-s; *no pl.*) **1.** cocoa; F ***durch den ~ ziehen*** make fun of, F kid, pull to pieces; **2.** → **~baum** *m* ⚘ cocoa tree, cacao tree; **~boh·ne** *f* cocoa bean; **~pul·ver** *n* cocoa (powder)
Ka·ker·lak [ˈkaːkɐlak] *m* (-s, -en; -en) cockroach, *Am.* roach

Ka·ko·pho·nie [kakofo'niː] *f* (-; -n) cacophony

Kak·tee [kak'teː] *f* (-; -n [-'teːən]), **Kaktus** ['kaktʊs] *m* (-; -teen [-'teːən]) ♣ cactus; *pl.* cacti, cactuses

Ka·la·mi·tät [kalami'tɛːt] *f* (-; -en) difficulty

Ka·lan·der [ka'landɐ] *m* (-s; -) calender, roller; **ka'lan·dern** *v/t.* (h) calender, roll

Ka·lau·er ['kaːlaʊɐ] *m* (-s; -) low pun; corny joke; **'ka·lau·ern** *v/i.* (h) pun; tell corny jokes

Kalb [kalp] *n* (-[e]s; Kälber ['kɛlbɐ]) calf; *gastr.* veal; *fig.* ***der Tanz um das goldene*** ~ the pursuit of mammon; F ***dummes*** ~ F silly goose; **kal·ben** ['kalbən] *v/i.* (h) calve

kal·bern ['kalbɐn], **käl·bern** ['kɛlbɐn] F *v/i.* (h) fool around; ***hör auf zu*** ~ F stop acting the goat

'Kalb|fell *n* calfskin; **~fleisch** *n* veal

'Kalbs|bra·ten *m* a) joint of veal, b) roast veal; **~bries** *n* sweetbread; **~brust** *f* breast of veal; **~fi,let** *n* fillet of veal; **~fri·kas,see** *n* veal fricassee; **~ha·xe** *f* knuckle of veal; **~keu·le** *f* leg of veal; **~kopf** *m* **1.** calf's head; **2.** F *fig.* F stupid oaf (*or* twit); **~ko·te,lett** *n* veal cutlet (*or* chop); **~le·ber** *f* calf's liver

'Kalbs·le·der *n* calf (leather); ***in ~ gebunden*** calfbound; **'kalbs·le·dern** *adj.* calfskin

'Kalbs·schnit·zel *n* veal cutlet

Kal·dau·nen [kal'daʊnən] *pl. gastr.* tripe *sg.*

Ka·le·bas·se [kale'basə] *f* (-; -n) **1.** calabash; **2.** ♣ (bottle) gourd

Ka·lei·do·skop [kalaɪdo'skoːp] *n* (-s; -e) kaleidoscope; **ka·lei·do·sko·pisch** [kalaɪdo'skoːpɪʃ] *adj.* kaleidoscopic

ka·len·da·risch [kalɛn'daːrɪʃ] *adj.* calendrical, calendar ...; according to the calendar

Ka·len·der [ka'lɛndɐ] *m* (-s; -) calendar (*a. w.s.*); ***et. rot im ~ anstreichen*** mark s.th. down as a red-letter day, *iro.* put s.th. on the record; **~blatt** *n* page of a (*or* the) calendar; **~jahr** *n* calendar year

Kal·fak·ter [kal'faktɐ] *m* (-s; -), **Kal·fak·tor** [kal'faktoːɐ] *m* (-s; -en [-'toːrən]) a) handyman, odd-job man, b) trusty

kal·fa·tern [kal'faːtɐn] *v/t.* (h) ⚓ caulk

Ka·li ['kaːli] *n* (-s; *no pl.*) potash (*a.* ✓); (***kohlensaures***) ~ potassium carbonate; ***salpetersaures*** ~ potassium nitrate

Ka·li·ber [ka'liːbɐ] *n* (-s; -) calib|re (*Am.* -er) (*a. fig.*), bore; ⚙ ga(u)ge; *fig. a.* type, sort; *fig.* ***kleineren*** (***größeren***) **~s** a) small-scale (large-scale), b) low-calibre (high-calibre)

'Ka·li·berg·werk *n* potassium mine

ka·li·brie·ren [kali'briːrən] *v/t.* ⚙ calibrate, ga(u)ge

'Ka·li·dün·ger *m* potash fertilizer

Ka·lif [ka'liːf] *m* (-en; -en) *hist.* caliph

Ka·li·fat [kali'faːt] *n* (-[e]s; -e) *hist.* caliphate

Ka·li·for·ni·er [kali'fɔrnĭɐ] *m* (-s; -), **Ka·li·for·nie·rin** [kali'fɔrnĭərɪn] *f* (-; -nen), **ka·li·for·nisch** [kali'fɔrnɪʃ] *adj.* Californian

Ka·li·ko ['kaliko] *m* (-s; -s) calico; *typ.* cloth (binding)

'Ka·li|lau·ge *f* potash lye; **~sal,pe·ter** *m* potassium nitrate, saltpet|re (*Am.* -er); **~salz** *n* potassium salt

Ka·li·um ['kaːlĭʊm] *n* (-s; *no pl.*) potassium; **~chlo,rat** *n* potassium chlorate

Kalk [kalk] *m* (-[e]s; *no pl.*) a) ⚒ lime, b) *geol.* limestone, chalk, c) ⚕ calcium; ***gelöschter*** ~ slaked lime; F *fig.* ***bei ihm rieselt schon der*** ~ F he's past it; **~ab·la·ge·rung** *f* **1.** *geol.* lime deposit; **2.** ⚕ a) calcification, b) calcium deposit; **ⵔarm** *adj.* deficient in lime (⚕ calcium); **~bo·den** *m* chalky soil; **~bren·ne,rei** *f* limekiln; **~dün·ger** *m* lime (fertilizer)

kal·ken ['kalkən] *v/t.* (h) **1.** ✓ lime; **2.** whitewash

'Kalk|ge·bir·ge *n* limestone mountains *pl.*; **~gru·be** *f* limepit

'kalk·hal·tig [-haltɪç] *adj.* hard *water*; chalky *soil*

'Kalk·hüt·te *f* limekiln

kal·kig ['kalkɪç] *adj.* **1.** → ***kalkhaltig***; **2.** *fig.* chalky *complexion etc.*

'Kalk|man·gel *m* ⚕ calcium deficiency; **~ofen** *m* limekiln; **~stein** *m* limestone; **~stick·stoff** *m* calcium cyanamide

Kal·kül [kal'kyːl] *n* (-s; -e) calculation; (***mit***) ***ins ~ ziehen*** take into consideration (*or* account)

Kal·ku·la·ti·on [kalkula'tsĭoːn] *f* (-; -en) calculation; estimate; **Kal·ku·la·ti'ons·feh·ler** *m* miscalculation; **Kal·ku·la·tor** [kalku'laːtoːɐ] *m* (-s; -en [-la'toːrən]) cost accountant

kal·ku·lier·bar [kalku'liːɐbaːr] *adj.* calculable; ✝ **~e *Risiken*** insurable risks

kal·ku·lie·ren [kalku'liːrən] *v/t. and v/i.* (h) calculate; **kal·ku·liert** [kalku'liːɐt] *fig. adj.* studied *nonchalance etc.*

Kal·li·gra·phie [kaligra'fiː] *f* (-; *no pl.*) calligraphy

Kal·me ['kalmə] *f* (-; -n) *meteor.* calm

'Kal·men·gür·tel *m* calm belt; ***äquatorialer ~*** *the* doldrums

Ka·lo·rie [kalo'riː] *f* (-; -n) calorie

ka·lo'ri·en|arm *adj.* low-calorie, low in calories; **ⵔbe·darf** *m* calorie requirement; **~be·wußt** *adj.* calorie-conscious; **ⵔbom·be** *f* fattener; **~re·du,ziert** *adj.* low-calorie; **~reich** *adj.* high-calorie, high in calories

Ka·lo'ri·en|ta,bel·le *f* calorie chart; **~wert** *m* calorific value; **~zu·fuhr** *f* calorie intake

Ka·lo·ri·me·ter [kalori'meːtɐ] *n* (-s; -) calorimeter

kalt [kalt] **I.** *adj.* **1.** cold; *meteor. a.* chilly; ***mir ist*** ~ I'm cold; ***mir wird*** ~ I'm getting cold; ~ ***werden*** get cold, cool down; **2.** *psych.* frigid; **3.** *fig.* cold; cool *reception, look etc.*; **~!** cold; ***j-m die ~e Schulter zeigen*** give s.o. the cold shoulder; ***j-n ~ erwischen*** F catch s.o. with his pants down; → ***Dusche, Fuß*** 1, ***Küche***; **II.** *adv.* coldly; ~ ***stellen*** put in a cool place, put in the fridge; ***wir zahlen ~ 1200 Mark*** we pay 1200 marks without heating; → ***Rücken***

'kalt·blei·ben *fig. v/i.* (*irr., sep.,* sn, → ***bleiben***) keep cool

'Kalt·blut *n* draught (*Am.* draft) horse

'Kalt·blü·ter [-blyːtɐ] *m* (-s; -) cold-blooded animal

'kalt·blü·tig [-blyːtɪç] **I.** *adj. zo. and fig.* cold-blooded; *fig.* cool; **II.** *fig. adv. kill etc.* in cold blood; *react etc.* calmly

'Kalt·blü·tig·keit *f* (-; *no pl.*) cold-bloodedness; calmness, sangfroid

Käl·te ['kɛltə] *f* (-; *no pl.*) **1.** cold; ***drei Grad*** ~ three degrees below zero; ***draußen in der*** ~ (out) in the cold; ***vor ~ zittern*** shiver with cold; **2.** *psych.* frigidity; **3.** *fig.* coldness; **~an·la·ge** *f* refrigerating plant; **~be·hand·lung** *f* ⚕ cryotherapy; **ⵔbe·stän·dig** *adj.* cold-resistant; **~chir·ur,gie** *f* cryosurgery; **~ein·bruch** *m* cold snap, sudden cold spell; **ⵔemp·find·lich** *adj.* sensitive to (the) cold; **~ge·fühl** *n* cold feeling; **~grad** *m* temperature (below zero); **~hoch** *n* cold-weather high; **~ma,schi·ne** *f* refrigerating machine; **~mit·tel** *n* refrigerant; **~pe·rio·de** *f* cold spell; **~sturz** *m* cold snap, sudden drop in temperature; **~tech·nik** *f* refrigeration engineering; **~the·ra,pie** *f* ⚕ cryotherapy; **~tod** *m* (death through) hypothermia; ***den ~ sterben*** die of hypothermia (*or* exposure), freeze to death; **~wel·le** *f* cold spell

'Kalt·front *f* cold front

'kalt|ge·preßt *adj.* cold-pressed *oil*; **~her·zig** *adj.* cold-hearted, unfeeling; **~lä·chelnd** F *fig. adv.* without turning a hair; **~las·sen** *v/t.* (*irr., sep.,* h, → ***lassen***): ***das läßt mich kalt*** that leaves me cold

'Kalt·luft *f* (-; *no pl.*) *meteor.* cold air; **~ein·bruch** *m* cold snap; **~mas·se** *f* cold air mass; **~schnei·se** *f* fresh air corridor

'kalt·ma·chen F *v/t.* (*sep.,* h) F bump off

'Kalt|mie·te *f* basic rent (without heating); **~scha·le** *f gastr.* iced fruit soup

'kalt·schmie·den *v/t.* (*sep.,* h) cold-hammer

'kalt·schnäu·zig [-ʃnɔʏtsɪç] F *adj.* callous; cheeky

'Kalt·start *m a. fig.* cold start

'kalt·stel·len F *fig. v/t.* (*sep.,* h) neutralize

'Kalt·ver·pfle·gung *f* cold dishes *pl.*

'kalt·wal·zen *v/t.* (*sep.,* h) cold-roll

'Kalt·was·ser|be·hand·lung *f* cold-water treatment, hydrotherapy; **~kur** *f* cold-water therapy (*or* cure)

'Kalt·wel·le *f* cold wave

Kal·va·ri·en·berg [kal'vaːrĭən-] *m*: ***der*** ~ Calvary

Kal·vi·nis·mus [kalvi'nɪsmʊs] *m* (-; *no pl.*) Calvinism; **Kal·vi·nist** [kalvi'nɪst] *m* (-en; -en), **Kal·vi·ni·stin** [kalvi'nɪstɪn] *f* (-; -nen) Calvinist; **kal·vi·ni·stisch** [kalvi'nɪstɪʃ] *adj.* Calvinist(ic)

kal·zi·nie·ren [kaltsi'niːrən] *v/t.* (h) calcine

Kal·zi·um ['kaltsĭʊm] *n* (-s; *no pl.*) calcium; **~chlo,rid** *n* calcium chloride; **~kar·bo,nat** *n* calcium carbonate; **~man·gel** *m* ⚕ calcium deficiency; ***unter ~ leiden*** have a calcium deficiency, be low on calcium; **~spie·gel** *m* calcium level

kam [kaːm] *pret. of* ***kommen***

Ka·ma·ril·la [kama'rɪla] *f* (-; -len) camarilla

Kam·bo·dscha·ner [kambo'dʒaːnɐ] *m* (-s; -), **Kam·bo·dscha·ne·rin** [kambo'dʒaːnərɪn] *f* (-; -nen), **kam·bo·dscha·nisch** [kambo'dʒaːnɪʃ] *adj.* Cambodian

Ka·mee [ka'meː] *f* (-; -n) cameo

Ka·mel [ka'meːl] *n* (-s; -e) camel; F *fig.* idiot; ***eher geht ein ~ durchs Nadelöhr*** it's easier for a camel to go through the eye of a needle; **~garn** *n* mohair

Ka'mel·haar *n* (-[e]s; *no pl.*), **~...** *in cpds.* camelhair; **ka'mel·haar·far·ben** [-farbən] *adj.* camel(-colo[u]red)

Ka·me·lie [ka'meːlĭə] *f* (-; -n) ♣ camellia

Ka·mel·len [ka'mɛlən] *pl.*: F ***olle*** ~ F old hat, F old chestnuts; ***das sind doch olle ~*** *a.* they're as old as the hills

Ka'mel·trei·ber *m* camel driver

Ka·me·ra ['kaməra] *f* (-; -s) camera; **~aus·rü·stung** *f* photographic equipment

Ka·me·rad [kamə'ra:t] *m* (-en; -en [-'ra:dən]) companion, F mate; → ***Schulkamerad, Spielkamerad***; **Ka·me'rad·schaft** *f* (-; *no pl.*) comradeship; loyalty; **ka·me'rad·schaft·lich** **I.** *adj.* friendly; ***rein ~*** purely platonic; ***unser Verhältnis ist rein ~*** *a.* we're just good friends; ***das war nicht sehr ~ von dir*** that wasn't very nice of you, a fine friend 'you are; **II.** *adv.* as a friend; **Ka·me'rad·schafts·geist** *m* (-[e]s; *no pl.*) esprit de corps

'Ka·me·ra|ein·stel·lung *f* **1.** camera position (*or* angle); *film*: *a. long etc.* shot; **2.** camera setting; **~füh·rung** *f film*: camera work, photography; **~mann** *m* (-[e]s; ⁼er, -leute) cameraman; **≈scheu** *adj.* camera-shy; **~schwenk** *m* pan; *vertical*: tilt; **~ta·sche** *f* camera case (*or* holdall); **~team** *n* camera team (*or* crew); **~wa·gen** *m* dolly

Ka·me·ru·ner ['kaməru:nɐ] *m* (-s; -), **Ka·me·ru·ne·rin** ['kaməru:nərɪn] *f* (-; -nen), **ka·me·ru·nisch** ['kaməru:nɪʃ] *adj.* Cameroonian

Ka·mi·ka·ze|flie·ger [kami'ka:tsə-] *m hist.* kamikaze pilot; **~un·ter,neh·men** *fig. n* suicide mission, kamikaze operation

Ka·mil·le [ka'mɪlə] *f* (-; -n) ✿ camomile

Ka'mil·len·tee *m* camomile tea

Ka·min [ka'mi:n] *m* (-s; -e) a) fireplace, b) chimney (*a. geol.*); ***am ~ sitzen*** sit in front of the fire; *fig.* ***et. in den ~ schreiben*** write s.th. off; ***das kannst du dir in den ~ schreiben*** *a.* you can wave goodbye to that (*or* forget that); **~feu·er** *n* (open) fire; ***am ~*** by the fireside; **~keh·rer** [-ke:rɐ] *dial. m* (-s; -) chimney sweep; **~sims** *m* mantelpiece

Kamm [kam] *m* (-[e]s; Kämme ['kɛmə]) comb; *geol.* ridge; crest *of wave*; *orn.* comb, crest; ⚙ cog; → ***Kammstück***; *fig.* ***man kann nicht alle(s) über e-n ~ scheren*** you can't just lump them all (everything) together; ***ihm schwoll der ~*** it went to his head

käm·men ['kɛmən] *v/t.* (h) comb; ***sich ~*** comb one's hair

Kam·mer ['kamɐ] *f* (-; -n) **1.** small room; cubbyhole; **2.** *pol.* chamber; ⚖ division; **3.** *anat.* ventricle, chamber; **4.** ✿ valve; **~chor** *m* chamber choir; **~die·ner** *m* valet

Käm·me·rer ['kɛmərɐ] *m* (-s; -) treasurer

'Kam·mer|frau *f*, **~fräu·lein** *n hist.* lady-in-waiting; **~ge·richt** *n* Court of Appeal (in Berlin); **~jä·ger** *m* pest controller; **~kon,zert** *n* a) chamber concert, b) chamber concerto

Käm·mer·lein ['kɛmɐlaɪn] *n*: F ***im stillen ~*** in private

'Kam·mer|mu,sik *f* chamber music; **~or,che·ster** *n* chamber orchestra; **~sän·ger** *m title conferred on singer of outstanding merit*; **~spiel** *n* **1.** society play; **2.** *pl.* studio theat|re (*Am. a.* -er); **~ton(hö·he** *f*) *m* concert pitch; **~zo·fe** *f* lady's maid

'Kamm|garn *n* worsted; **~ge·bir·ge** *n* ridged mountains *pl.*; **~la·gen** *pl.*: ***in den ~*** on the peaks; **~stück** *n gastr.* neck

'Kammu·schel (*sep.* -mm·m-) *f* scallop

Kam·pa·gne [kam'panjə] *f* (-; -n) campaign; ***e-e ~ starten*** launch a campaign

Kampf [kampf] *m* (-[e]s; Kämpfe ['kɛmpfə]) fight, battle (*both a. fig.*); *fig.* struggle (*all* ***um*** *acc.* for; ***gegen*** *acc.* against); conflict (*a. pol.*); feud; rivalry; *psych.* inner conflict; *sport*: contest; match; *boxing*: fight; ***~ ums Dasein*** fight for survival; ***~ dem Hunger*** *etc.* war on hunger *etc.*; ***~ auf Leben und Tod*** life-and-death struggle; ***j-m den ~ ansagen*** challenge s.o.; **~ab·stim·mung** *f* crucial vote; *trade union*: strike ballot; **~an·sa·ge** *f* challenge (***an*** *acc.* to); **~an·zug** *m* ⚔ battle dress; **~aus·bil·dung** *f* combat training; **~aus·rü·stung** *f* riot gear; **~bahn** *f sport*: stadium; **~be·fehl** *m* ⚔ order to attack; **≈be·reit** *fig. adj.* ready to do battle, ready for the fray; **≈be·tont** *adj. sport*: tough, hard; **~bund** *m* (-[e]s; ⁼e) pressure (*or* action) group; **~ein·heit** *f* ⚔ combat unit; **~ein·satz** *m* operational mission; ***zum ~ kommen*** be sent into action, see action

kämp·fen ['kɛmpfən] (h) **I.** *v/i.* fight (***für*** *acc.*, ***um*** *acc.* for) (*a. fig.*); struggle (***mit*** *dat.* with; ***gegen*** *acc.* against) (*a. fig.*), wrestle (***mit*** *dat.* with); ***~ gegen*** *acc.* fight (against); *fig.* ***~ mit*** *dat. a.* fight (against), contend (*or* grapple) with, be up against, (have to) face *difficulties etc.*; ***mit dem Schlaf ~*** struggle to keep awake; ***mit den Tränen ~*** fight back one's tears; **II.** *v/t.*: ***e-n schweren Kampf ~*** *a. fig.* fight a hard battle; **III.** *v/refl.*: ***sich ~ durch*** *acc. a. fig.* fight (*or* battle) one's way through *s.th.*; *fig.* ***sich nach oben ~*** fight one's way to the top; **IV.** ≈ *n* (-s) → ***Kampf***

Kamp·fer ['kampfɐ] *m* (-s; *no pl.*) camphor

Kämp·fer ['kɛmpfɐ] *m* (-s; -) **1.** ⚔ combatant; **2.** *fig.* champion (***für*** *acc.* of), fighter (for); **3.** *sport* a) contestant, b) wrestler, c) *boxing*: fighter

'kampf|er·fah·ren, ~er·probt *adj.* battle-hardened; *fig.* seasoned, *a. sport*: veteran ...

kämp·fe·risch ['kɛmpfərɪʃ] *adj.* combative; belligerent, aggressive; *pol. etc.* militant; *sport*: physically strong; ***~e Maßnahmen*** combative measures

'Kämp·fer·na,tur *f* (-; -en) fighter

'kampf·fä·hig *adj.* ⚔ fit for action, *a. sport*: fighting fit

'Kampf|fahr·zeug *n* combat vehicle; **~flie·ger** *m* combat (*hist.* bomber) pilot; **~flug·zeug** *n* fighter aircraft; *hist.* bomber; **~gas** *n* war gas; **~ge·biet** *n* conflict area; **~ge·fähr·te** *m* comrade-in-arms; **~geist** *m* (-[e]s; *no pl.*) fighting spirit; ***~ zeigen*** put up a good fight; **~ge·mein·schaft** *f* activist group; **~ge·richt** *n sport*: *the* judges *pl.*; **~ge·sche·hen** *n* fighting, action; ***Ort des ~s*** scene of the fighting; **~ge·tüm·mel** *n* fighting; ***sich ins ~ stürzen*** throw o.s. into the fray; **~ge·wicht** *n sport*: fighting weight; ***sein ~ ist 60 kg*** he has weighed in at 60 kilos; **~hahn** *m* **1.** fighting cock; **2.** F *fig.* F pugnacious so-and-so; ***er ist ein richtiger ~*** *a.* he's always looking for a fight; ***guck dir die zwei Kampfhähne an*** look at those two fighting like cat and dog; **~hand·lung** *f* ⚔ *a. pl.* action, fighting; **~hub·schrau·ber** *m* (helicopter) gunship; **~kraft** *f* (-; *no pl.*) (fighting) strength; **~lied** *n* **1.** battle song; **2.** revolutionary song

'kampf·los *adj. and adv.* without a fight; ***~er Sieg*** walkover, *Am.* walkaway; ***~ e-e Runde weiterkommen*** reach the next round by default

'Kampf·lust *f* (-; *no pl.*) aggressiveness, pugnacity; **'kampf·lu·stig** *adj.* belligerent

'Kampf|maß·nah·me *f* ⚔ *a. pl.* military (*pol.* militant) action; **~mo,ral** *f* morale (of the soldiers *or* troops); **≈mü·de** *adj.* battle-weary; **~pau·se** *f* lull in the fighting; **~platz** *m* battleground; *sport*: arena; *fig.* scene of the action; **~preis** *m* ✝ cut-rate price; **~rich·ter** *m* judge; referee, *tennis, swimming*: umpire; **~schrift** *f* pamphlet, political broadside; **~sport** *m* combative sports *pl.*; (*judo, karate etc.*) martial arts *pl.*; **≈stark** *adj.* ⚔ *and sport*: strong; **~stoff** *m*: ***chemischer (biologischer) ~*** chemical (biological) weapon; **~stra·te,gie** *f* tactics *pl.*; **~tag** *m*: ***am dritten*** *etc.* ***~*** on the third *etc.* day of action; **~trup·pe** *f* combat troops *pl.*; **≈un·fä·hig** *adj.* out of action; ***~ machen*** *a. sport*: put out of action; **~ver·band** *m* ⚔ combat unit; **~wei·se** *f* tactics *pl.*, strategy; **~ziel** *n* objective; **~zo·ne** *f* ⚔ fighting zone

kam·pie·ren [kam'pi:rən] *v/i.* (h) camp; F *fig.* ***bei j-m ~*** sleep (F crash out) on s.o.'s floor (*or* sofa)

Ka·na·di·er[1] [ka'na:dĭɐ] *m* (-s; -), **Ka·na·die·rin** [ka'na:dĭərɪn] *f* (-; -nen), **ka·na·disch** [ka'na:dɪʃ] *adj.* Canadian

Ka'na·di·er[2] *m* (-s; -) Canadian (canoe); ***~-Einer (~-Zweier)*** Canadian single (double)

Ka·nail·le [ka'naljə] *contp.* *f* (-; -n) **1.** mob, rabble; **2.** *sl.* swine

Ka·na·ke [ka'na:kə] *m* (-n; -n) **1.** Kanaka; **2.** *contp. sl.* bloody foreigner, wog

Ka·nal [ka'na:l] *m* (-s; Kanäle [ka'nɛ:lə]) canal; *geogr.* channel (*a. fig.*); ⚙ drain; *anat.* duct; *radio, TV*: channel; ***der ~*** the (English) Channel; *fig.* ***diplomatische Kanäle*** diplomatic channels; ***roter (grüner) ~*** ✈ red (green) channel; F ***den ~ voll haben*** a) F be fed up to the back teeth, b) F be full to the gills; **~ar·bei·ter** *m* **1.** sewage worker; **2.** F *fig. pol.* F backroom boy; **~deckel** *m* manhole cover; **~ge·büh·ren** *pl.* canal dues

Ka·na·li·sa·ti·on [kanaliza'tsĭo:n] *f* (-; -en) **1.** sewage system; **2.** canalization *of a river*; **Ka·na·li·sa·ti'ons·netz** *n* sewage system; network of sewers

ka·na·li·sie·ren [kanali'zi:rən] *v/t.* (h) **1.** provide *city etc.* with sewers; **2.** canalize *river*; **3.** *fig.* channel

Ka'nal|schleu·se *f* canal lock; **~schwim·mer** *m* (cross-)Channel swimmer; **~sy,stem** *n* a) irrigation system, b) drainage system; **~tun·nel** *m* Channel tunnel, F Chunnel; **~wäh·ler** *m TV* channel selector

Ka·na·pee ['kanape] *n* (-s; -s) **1.** *gastr.* canapé; **2.** sofa

ka·na·ri·en·gelb [ka'na:rĭən-] *adj.* canary yellow; **Ka'na·ri·en·vo·gel** *m* canary

Kan·da·re [kan'da:rə] *f* (-; -n) bit; *fig.* ***j-n an die ~ nehmen*** keep a tighter rein on s.o., bring s.o. to heel (*or* into line)

Kan·de·la·ber [kandə'la:bɐ] *m* (-s; -) candelabra

Kan·di·dat [kandi'da:t] *m* (-en; -en) candidate (*a. fig.*), contender; *pol.* ***vorgeschlagener ~*** nominee; **Kan·di'da·ten·li·ste** *f* list of candidates; *pol. Am.* party ticket

Kan·di·da·tur [kandida'tu:ɐ] *f* (-; -en [-rən]) candidature; **kan·di·die·ren** [kandi'di:rən] *v/i.* (h) stand *or* run for election (*or* an office *etc.*); ***für das Amt des Präsidenten (Bürgermeisters)*** ~ run for the presidency (the office of mayor); ***erneut*** ~ run for re-election, stand (for election) again
kan·die·ren [kan'di:rən] *v/t.* (h) crystallize; **kan·diert** [kan'di:ɐt] *adj.* candied, glacé
Kan·dis ['kandɪs] *m* (-; *no pl.*), **~zucker** *m* sugar (*or* rock) candy
Ka·neel [ka'ne:l] *m* (-s; -e) cinnamon
Kän·gu·ruh ['kɛŋguru] *n* (-s; -s) kangaroo
Ka·nin·chen [ka'ni:nçən] *n* (-s; -) rabbit; **~bau** *m* (-[e]s; -e) burrow; **~fell** *n* rabbit skin; **~stall** *m* rabbit hutch; **~züch·ter** *m* rabbit breeder
Ka·ni·ster [ka'nɪstɐ] *m* (-s; -) canister, can
'**Kann·be·stim·mung** *f* ⚖ discretionary clause
Känn·chen ['kɛnçən] *n* (-s; -) jug; ***ein ~ Kaffee*** a pot of coffee
Kan·ne ['kanə] *f* (-; -n) jug; (*coffee etc.*) pot; (*oil etc.*) can; (*milk*) churn
kan·ne·liert [kanə'li:ɐt] *adj.* fluted; **Kan·ne'lie·rung** *f* (-; -en) fluting
'**kan·nen·wei·se** *adv.* **1.** in cans; **2.** ***~ Kaffee trinken*** F drink pots of coffee, drink coffee by the gallon
Kan·ni·ba·le [kani'ba:lə] *m* (-n; -n) cannibal; *fig.* savage; **kan·ni·ba·lisch** [kani'ba:lɪʃ] **I.** *adj.* cannibal ...; *fig.* brutal, savage; **II.** *adv.*: F *fig.* ***sich ~ wohl fühlen*** feel terrific (*or* on top of the world); **Kan·ni·ba·lis·mus** [kaniba'lɪsmʊs] *m* (-; *no pl.*) cannibalism
kann·te ['kantə] *pret. of* ***kennen***
'**Kann·vor·schrift** *f* ⚖ discretionary clause
Ka·non ['ka:nɔn] *m* (-s; -s) **1.** canon, code; **2.** *bibl.*, *eccl.*, ⚖, *a.* 🎨 canon; **3.** ♪ canon, round
Ka·no·na·de [kano'na:də] *f* (-; -n) cannonade; *fig.* volley, salvo *of abuse*
Ka·no·ne [ka'no:nə] *f* (-; -n) **1.** gun; cannon; *sl.* iron, *Am. sl.* rod; → ***Spatz***; **2.** F *fig.* wizard, *esp. sport*: ace; **3.** F *fig.* ***unter aller ~*** F lousy, *sl.* the pits
Ka'no·nen·auf·schlag *m tennis*: powerful serve
Ka'no·nen·boot *n* gunboat; **~di·plo·ma·ˌtie** *f* gunboat diplomacy
Ka'no·nen|fut·ter *fig. n* cannon fodder; **~ku·gel** *f* cannonball; **~ofen** *m* cylindrical stove; **~rohr** *n* gun barrel; **~schlag** *m* cannon cracker; **~schuß** *m* cannon shot; ***man hörte die Kanonenschüsse*** you could hear the guns being fired
Ka·no·nier [kano'ni:ɐ] *m* (-s; -e [-'ni:rə]) gunner
ka·no·nisch [ka'no:nɪʃ] *adj.* canonical; *eccl.* ***~es Recht*** canon law
ka·no·ni·sie·ren [kanoni'zi:rən] *v/t.* (h) canonize
Ka·nos·sa [ka'nɔsa] *n*: *fig.* ***nach ~ gehen*** pocket one's pride; **~gang** *m*: ***es war für ihn ein ~*** he had to pocket his pride
Kä·no·zoi·kum [kɛno'tso:ikʊm] *n* (-s; *no pl.*) *geol.* Cenozoic (era)
Kan·ta·te [kan'ta:tə] *f* (-; -n) ♪ cantata
Kan·te ['kantə] *f* (-; -n) edge; *textil.* selvage; F *fig.* ***etwas auf die hohe ~ legen*** put something aside for a rainy day; ***etwas auf der hohen ~ haben*** have something tucked away (somewhere)
Kan·ten ['kantən] *m* (-s; -) crust *of bread*
'**kan·ten** (h) **I.** *v/t.* tilt; carve *ski*; ✝ ***nicht ~!*** this side up; **II.** *v/i. skiing*: carve
'**Kan·ten·ball** *m table tennis*: (table-)edge deflection
Kan·ter ['kantɐ] *m* (-s; -) canter; **~sieg** *m sport*: runaway victory, walkover, *Am.* walkaway
Kant·ha·ken ['kant-] *m*: F *fig.* ***j-n beim ~ kriegen*** F give s.o. a good going-over
kan·tig ['kantɪç] *adj.* **1.** squared; angular *face*; square *chin*; **2.** *fig.* difficult, awkward
Kan·ti·ne [kan'ti:nə] *f* (-; -n) canteen
Kan'ti·nen|es·sen *n* canteen meal(s *pl.*); **~fraß** F *contp. m* F canteen slop
Kan·ton [kan'to:n] *m* (-s; -e) canton
Kan·to·nist [kanto'nɪst] *m* (-en; -en): F *fig.* ***unsicherer ~*** F fly-by-night
Kan·tor ['kanto:ɐ] *m* (-s; -en [kan'to:rən]) choirmaster
Ka·nu ['ka:nu] *n* (-s; -s) canoe; **~sport** *m* canoeing
Ka·nü·le [ka'ny:lə] *f* (-; -n) ⚕ can(n)ula, (drain) tube
Ka·nu·te [ka'nu:tə] *m* (-n; -n) canoeist
Kan·zel ['kantsəl] *f* (-; -n) **1.** pulpit; ***auf der ~*** in the pulpit; **2.** ✈ cockpit; **~re·de** *f* sermon
kan·ze·ro·gen [kantsero'ge:n] *adj.* carcinogenic
Kanz·lei [kants'laɪ] *f* (-; -en) office; **~deutsch** *n* officialese
Kanz·ler ['kantslɐ] *m* (-s; -) *pol.* chancellor; *univ.* vice-chancellor; *hist.* ***der Eiserne ~*** (*Bismarck*) the Iron Chancellor; **~amt** *n* **1.** chancellorship; **2.** chancellor's office, chancellery; **~amts·miˌni·ster** *m* chancellery minister; **~kan·diˌdat** *m* candidate for the chancellorship
Kao·lin [kao'li:n] *n* (-s; -e) *min.* kaolin
Kap [kap] *n* (-s; -s) *geogr.* cape
Ka·paun [ka'paʊn] *m* (-s; -e) capon
Ka·pa·zi·tät [kapatsi'tɛ:t] *f* (-; -en) *phys.*, ⚙, ⚡ *and fig.* capacity; *fig.* (leading) authority (***auf dem Gebiet*** *gen.* on, in the field of)
Ka·pa·zi'täts|ab·bau *m* cutback(s *pl.*) in capacity; **~aus·la·stung** *f*, **~aus·nut·zung** *f* capacity utilization; **~er·wei·te·rung** *f* increase in capacity
Ka·pee [ka'pe:]: F ***schwer von ~*** F a bit dense (*or* slow on the uptake)
Ka·pel·le [ka'pɛlə] *f* (-; -n) **1.** *eccl.* chapel; **2.** ♪ band; orchestra
Ka'pell·mei·ster *m* **1.** director of music; **2.** conductor; **3.** chorusmaster, choral director; **4.** ⚔ bandmaster
Ka·per[1] ['ka:pɐ] *f* (-; -n) ⚘ caper
'**Ka·per**[2] ⚓ *m* (-s; -) privateer
ka·pern ['ka:pɐn] *v/t.* (h) ⚓ capture, seize; F *fig.* F nab
'**Ka·per·schiff** *n* → ***Kaper***[2]
ka·pie·ren [ka'pi:rən] (h) F **I.** *v/t.* F get, twig; ***ich kapier' das nicht!*** I (just) don't get it; **II.** *v/i.* catch on, F twig; get the message; ***kapiert?*** got it?, *threateningly*: do you read me?
ka·pil·lar [kapɪ'la:ɐ] *adj.* capillary
Ka·pil·la·re [kapɪ'la:rə] *f* (-; -n) ⚕, *phys.* capillary (tube)
Ka·pil'lar|ge·fäß *n anat.* capillary (tube); **~netz** *n* capillary network
Ka·pi·tal [kapi'ta:l] **I.** *n* (-s; -e, -ien [-lĭən]) **1.** capital; funds *pl.*; capital stock; ***flüssiges ~*** available funds; **2.** *fig.* asset; ***~ schlagen aus*** *dat.* capitalize on *s.th.*, cash in on *s.th.*; **II.** ♀ *adj.* **3.** ***ein ~er Fehler*** an absolute (*or* a colossal) blunder; **4.** royal *stag etc.*; **~ab·fin·dung** *f* lump-sum compensation; **~ab·fluß** *m*, **~ab·wan·de·rung** *f* capital outflow
Ka·pi'tal·an·la·ge *f* (capital) investment; **~ge·sell·schaft** *f* investment trust
Ka·pi'tal|an·le·ger *m* investor; **~an·teil** *m* capital share; **~auf·stockung** *f* capital increase; **~auf·wand** *m* capital expenditure; **~aus·fuhr** *f* capital exports *pl.*; **~be·darf** *m* capital requirements *pl.*; **~be·schaf·fung** *f* raising of funds; **~be·sitz** *m* capital holdings *pl.*; **~be·tei·li·gung** *f* **1.** participation; **2.** stake; ***er hält e-e ~ von 27%*** he has a 27% stake (***an*** *dat.* in); **~biˌlanz** *f* balance of capital transactions; **~bil·dung** *f* accumulation of capital
Ka·pi·täl·chen [kapi'tɛ:lçən] *n* (-s; -) *typ.* small capital (F cap)
Ka·pi'tal|ein·la·ge *f* capital contribution; **~er·hö·hung** *f* capital increase
Ka·pi'tal·er·trag *m* capital yield; **~(s)steu·er** *f* capital gains tax
Ka·pi'tal|flucht *f* flight of capital; **~ge·ber** *m* sponsor; **~ge·sell·schaft** *f* corporation
Ka·pi'tal·ge·winn *m* capital gains *pl.*; **~steu·er** *f* capital gains tax
Ka·pi'tal|gü·ter *pl.* capital goods; **~hil·fe** *f* financial aid
'**ka·pi'tal·in·tenˌsiv** *adj.* capital-intensive
ka·pi·ta·li·sie·ren [kapitali'zi:rən] *v/t.* (h) capitalize; **Ka·pi·ta·li'sie·rung** *f* (-; -en) capitalization
Ka·pi·ta·lis·mus [kapita'lɪsmʊs] *m* (-; *no pl.*) capitalism; **Ka·pi·ta·list** [kapita'lɪst] *m* (-en; -en) capitalist; **ka·pi·ta·li·stisch** [kapita'lɪstɪʃ] *adj.* capitalist(ic)
Ka·pi'tal|knapp·heit *f* shortage of capital; **~kon·to** *n* capital account; **~kraft** *f* (-; *no pl.*) financial strength; **♀kräf·tig** *adj.* well-funded, (financially) powerful; **~man·gel** *m* lack of capital; **~markt** *m* capital (*or* money) market; **~mehr·heit** *f* majority shareholding, controlling interest; **~rück·la·ge** *f* capital reserve(s *pl.*); **~sprit·ze** *f* cash injection, (fiscal) shot in the arm; **~ver·bre·chen** *n* capital crime (*or* offen|ce, *Am.* -se); **~ver·bre·cher** *m* dangerous criminal; **~ver·kehr** *m* turnover of capital; **~ver·mö·gen** *n* capital assets *pl.*; **~wert** *m* capital value; **~zins** *m* interest on capital; **~zu·fluß** *m* influx of capital
Ka·pi·tän [kapi'tɛ:n] *m* (-s; -e) **1.** ⚓, ✈ captain; skipper; **2.** *sport*: captain, F skipper
Ka·pi'täns·paˌtent *n* master's certificate
Ka·pi·tel [ka'pɪtəl] *n* (-s; -) **1.** chapter (*a. eccl.*); **2.** *fig.* chapter; story; ***das ist ein ~ für sich*** that's another story
Ka·pi·tell [kapi'tɛl] *n* (-s; -e) ⚠ capital
Ka·pi·tu·la·ti·on [kapitula'tsĭo:n] *f* (-; -en) capitulation, surrender
ka·pi·tu·lie·ren [kapitu'li:rən] *v/i.* (h) capitulate, surrender; *fig.* give in (*or* up)
Ka·plan [ka'pla:n] *m* (-s; Kapläne [ka'plɛ:nə]) chaplain
Kap·pe ['kapə] *f* (-; -n) a) cap, b) top, c) (toe)cap; *fig.* ***et. auf s-e ~ nehmen*** take (the) responsibility for s.th., ***müssen***: *a.* have to carry the can for s.th.
kap·pen ['kapən] *v/t.* (h) cut *rope*; lop, top *tree*; *zo.* capon; *fig.* cut off
Kap·pes ['kapəs] *dial. m* (-s; *no pl.*) rubbish, F rot, *Am.* F garbage
Käp·pi ['kɛpi] *n* (-s; -s) cap; ⚔ forage (*Am.* garrison) cap

'**Kapp·naht** *f* French seam

Ka·prio·le [kapri'oːlə] *f* (-; -n) **1.** caper; **2.** prank; **3.** *riding*: capriole

ka·pri·zie·ren [kapri'tsiːrən] *v/refl.* (h): ***sich ~ auf*** *acc.* insist on (*ger.*)

ka·pri·zi·ös [kapri'tsǐøːs] *adj.* capricious

Kap·sel ['kapsəl] *f* (-; -n) a) *anat.*, ✿, *pharm.* capsule, *space travel*: *a.* module, b) case, c) cap, d) detonator; **~ent·zün·dung** *f* ⚕ capsulitis

'**kap·sel·för·mig** [-fœrmɪç] *adj.* capsule-shaped

kap·seln ['kapsəln] *v/t.* (h) ⚙ encase, enclose; *phys.* jacket

Kap·si·kum ['kapsikʊm] *n* (-s; *no pl.*) capsicum

ka·putt [ka'pʊt] F *adj.* **1.** broken; *a.* not working; ***die Birne ist ~*** the light bulb's gone; *fig.* ***was ist denn jetzt schon wieder ~?*** what's up now?; **2.** *fig.* F bust; broken *marriage*; **3.** ⚕ *etc.* bad *heart etc.*, F no good (any more); *a.* ruined *liver*; **4.** shattered; ***~er Typ*** (human) wreck; ***ich bin nervlich ~*** my nerves are shot; ***er ist seelisch ~*** he's emotionally drained, he's a broken man; **~ar·bei·ten** F *v/refl.* (*sep.*, h): ***sich ~*** work o.s. to death; **~är·gern** F *v/refl.* (*sep.*, h): ***ich hab' mich kaputtgeärgert*** F I was really mad, F I could have kicked myself; **~drücken** F *v/t.* (*sep.*, h): ***j-n vor Liebe ~*** F squeeze s.o. to death; **~fah·ren** F *v/t.* (*irr.*, *sep.*, h, → ***fahren***) smash up, wreck *a car*; **~ge·hen** F *v/i.* (*irr.*, *sep.*, sn, → ***gehen***) a) get broken, break, b) *fig. firm etc.*: F go bust; *marriage*, *friendship*: break up, c) go to pieces, crack up; **~la·chen** F *v/refl.*: ***sich ~*** (*sep.*, h) F kill o.s. laughing; **~ma·chen** (*sep.*, h) F **I.** *v/t.* break; smash; **II.** *v/refl.*: ***sich ~*** kill o.s. *doing s.th.*; **~schla·gen** F *v/t.* (*irr.*, *sep.*, h, → ***schlagen***) smash

Ka·pu·ze [ka'puːtsə] *f* (-; -n) hood; cowl

Ka'pu·zen·man·tel *m* hooded coat

Ka·pu·zi·ner [kapu'tsiːnɐ] *m* (-s; -) Capuchin (monk); **~kres·se** *f* ✿ nasturtium; **~mönch** *m* Capuchin monk; **~or·den** *m* Capuchin Order

Kar [kaːɐ] *n* (-[e]s; -e ['kaːrə]) *geol.* cirque

Ka·ra·bi·ner [kara'biːnɐ] *m* (-s; -) **1.** carbine; **2.** → **~ha·ken** *m* karabiner, snaplink

Ka·ra·bi·nie·re [karabi'nǐeːrə] *m* (-[s]; -ri) carabiniere

Ka·ra·cho [ka'raxo] *n*: F ***mit ~*** F like a bomb

Ka·raf·fe [ka'rafə] *f* (-; -n) carafe, decanter

Ka·ram·bo·la·ge [karambo'laːʒə] *f* (-; -n) **1.** *billiards*: cannon, *Am.* carom; **2.** F collision, crash; **ka·ram·bo·lie·ren** [karambo'liːrən] *v/i.* (h) cannon, *Am.* carom

Ka·ra·mel [kara'mɛl] *m* (-s; *no pl.*) caramel; **Ka·ra'mel·bon͵bon** *m, n,* **Ka·ra·mel·le** [kara'mɛlə] *f* (-; -n) caramel (sweet)

ka·ra·me·li·sie·ren [karameli'ziːrən] *v/t.* (h) caramelize

Ka·rat [ka'raːt] *n* (-[e]s; -e) carat

Ka·ra·te [ka'raːtə] *n* (-[s]; *no pl.*) karate

Ka·ra·te·ka [kara'teːka] *m* (-[s]; -[s]) karateka

Ka'ra·te|kämp·fer *m* karate expert; **~kurs** *m* karate course; ***e-n ~ machen*** take karate lessons; **~schlag** *m* karate chop

...ka·rä·ter [-ka͵rɛːtɐ] *m* (-s; -) *in cpds.* ***Zweikaräter*** two-carat diamond (*or* sapphire *etc.*); **...ka·rä·tig** [-ka͵rɛːtɪç] *adj. in cpds.* ***achtzehnkarätiges Gold*** 18-carat gold

Ka·ra·wa·ne [kara'vaːnə] *f* (-; -n) caravan

Ka·ra'wa·nen·stra·ße *f* caravan route

Ka·ra·wan·se·rei [karavanzə'raɪ] *f* (-; -en) caravanserai

Kar·bid [kar'biːt] *n* (-[e]s; *no pl.*) carbide; **~lam·pe** *f* carbide lamp

Kar·bol [kar'boːl] *n* (-s; *no pl.*), **~säu·re** *f* carbolic acid; **~sei·fe** *f* carbolic soap

Kar·bon [kar'boːn] *n* (-s; *no pl.*) *geol.* Carboniferous (period)

Kar·bo·nat [karbo'naːt] *n* (-[e]s; -e) ⚗ carbonate

kar·bo·ni·sie·ren [karboni'ziːrən] *v/t.* (h) carbonize

Kar·bun·kel [kar'bʊŋkəl] *m* (-s; -) ⚕ carbuncle

Kar·da·mom [karda'moːm] *m, n* (-s; -e[n]) cardamom

Kar·dan|an·trieb [kar'daːn-] *m* ⚙ Cardan drive; **~ge·lenk** *n* universal joint

kar·da·nisch [kar'daːnɪʃ] *adj.* Cardan(ic)

Kar'dan|tun·nel *m* transmission tunnel; **~wel·le** *f* drive (*or* propeller) shaft

Kar·dia·kum [kar'diːakʊm] *n* (-s; -ka) ⚕ cardiac stimulant

kar·di·al [kar'dǐaːl] *adj.* ⚕ cardiac

Kar·di·nal [kardi'naːl] *m* (-s; Kardinäle [kardi'nɛːlə]) cardinal (*a. zo.*)

Kar·di'nal|feh·ler *m* cardinal error; **~fra·ge** *f* essential question

Kar·di'nals·hut *m* red (cardinal's) hat

Kar·di'nal|tu·gend *f* cardinal virtue; **~zahl** *f* cardinal number

Kar·dio·gramm [kardǐo'gram] *n* (-s; -e) ⚕ cardiogram

Kar·dio·lo·ge [kardǐo'loːgə] *m* (-n; -n) heart specialist, cardiologist; **Kar·dio·lo·gie** [kardǐolo'giː] *f* (-; *no pl.*) cardiology

Ka·renz·zeit [ka'rɛnts-] *f* a) *insurance*: waiting period, b) ✝ period of restriction, c) ⚕ period of rest

Kar·fi·ol [kar'fǐoːl] *Austrian m* (-s; *no pl.*) cauliflower

Kar'frei·tag [kaːɐ-] *m*: (***am ~*** on) Good Friday

Kar·fun·kel [kar'fʊŋkəl] *m* (-s; -) *min. and* ⚕ carbuncle

karg [kark] *adj.* meag|re (*Am.* -er), paltry; frugal *life etc.*; barren *soil etc.*; bare *room etc.*; ***~ sein mit*** *dat.* → **kar·gen** ['kargən] *v/i.* (h): ***~ mit*** *dat.* be sparing of; ***nicht ~ mit*** *dat.* lavish; '**Karg·heit** *f* (-; *no pl.*) meagreness, *Am.* meagerness; paltriness; frugality; barrenness; bareness

kärg·lich ['kɛrklɪç] *adj.* → ***karg***; ***die ~en Reste*** the paltry remains

Kar·go ['kargo] *m* (-s; -s) cargo

Ka·ri·be [ka'riːbə] *m* (-n; -n) Caribbean, Carib; **ka·ri·bisch** [ka'riːbɪʃ] *adj.* Caribbean; ***der ~e Raum*** the Caribbean (basin)

ka·riert [ka'riːɐt] *adj.* **1.** checked; squared *paper*; **2.** F ***~es Zeug reden*** F talk rot

Ka·ri·es ['kaːrǐɛs] *f* (-; *no pl.*) ⚕ tooth decay, caries

Ka·ri·ka·tur [karika'tuːɐ] *f* (-; -en) caricature (*a. fig.*); cartoon; **Ka·ri·ka·tu·rist** [karikatu'rɪst] *m* (-en; -en) caricaturist; cartoonist; **ka·ri·ka·tu·ri·stisch** [karikatu'rɪstɪʃ] *adj.*: ***~e Darstellung*** cartoon, caricature; **ka·ri·kie·ren** [kari'kiːrən] *v/t.* (h) caricature

ka·ri·ös [ka'rǐøːs] *adj.* ⚕ decayed, F bad, rotten

ka·ri·ta·tiv [karita'tiːf] *adj.* charitable; ***es dient ~en Zwecken*** it's for a good cause, it's for charity

Kar·kas·se [kar'kasə] *f* (-; -n) **1.** *gastr.* bones *pl.*, (chicken) carcass; **2.** ⚙ casing

Kar·ma ['karma] *n* (-s; *no pl.*) karma

Kar·me·li·ter [karme'liːtɐ] *m* (-s; -) Carmelite (monk); **Kar·me·li·te·rin** [karme'liːtərɪn] *f* (-; -nen) Carmelite (nun)

kar·me·sin(rot) [karme'ziːn-] *adj.* crimson

Kar·min [kar'miːn] *n* (-s; *no pl.*), **kar'min·rot** *adj.* crimson

Kar·ne·ol [karne'oːl] *m* (-s; -e) *min.* carnelian

Kar·ne·val ['karnəval] *m* (-s; -s, -e) carnival; **kar·ne·va·li·stisch** [karnəva'lɪstɪʃ] *adj.* carnival ...; '**Kar·ne·vals(͵um)zug** *m* carnival procession

Kar·nickel [kar'nɪkəl] (*sep.* -k·k-) *n* (-s; -) **1.** rabbit; **2.** F *fig.* stupid idiot

kar·ni·vor [karni'voːɐ] *adj. zo. and* ✿ carnivorous; **Kar·ni·vo·re** [karni'voːrə] **I.** *m* (-n; -n) *zo.* carnivore; **II.** *f* (-; -n) ✿ carnivorous plant, carnivore

Kärnt·ner ['kɛrntnɐ] *m* (-s; -), **Kärnt·ne·rin** ['kɛrntnərɪn] *f* (-; -nen), **kärnt·ne·risch** ['kɛrntnərɪʃ] *adj.* Carinthian

Ka·ro ['kaːro] *n* **1.** *textil.* check, square; **2.** *card game*: a) diamonds *pl.*, b) diamond; '**Ka·ro...** *in cpds.* → ***Herz...***

Ka·ro·lin·ger ['kaːrolɪŋɐ] *m* (-s; -), **ka·ro·lin·gisch** ['kaːrolɪŋɪʃ] *adj. hist.* Carolingian

'**Ka·ro·mu·ster** *n* check(ed) pattern

Ka·ros·se [ka'rɔsə] *f* (-; -n) state coach

Ka·ros·se·rie [karɔsə'riː] *f* (-; -n) (car) body, coachwork; **~bau·er** *m* (-s; -) panel-beater

Ka·ro·tin [karo'tiːn] *n* (-s; *no pl.*) carotin

Ka·rot·te [ka'rɔtə] *f* (-; -n) carrot

Karp·fen ['karpfən] *m* (-s; -) carp; **~teich** *m* carp pond; → ***Hecht*** 1

Kar·re ['karə] *f* (-; -n) → ***Karren***

Kar·ree [ka'reː] *n* (-s; -s) square; block; ***ums ~ gehen*** go for a walk round the block

Kar·ren ['karən] *m* (-s; -) cart; F ***alter ~*** F old banger; ***ein ~ voll Äpfel*** a cartload of apples; *fig.* ***den ~ in den Dreck fahren*** mess things up; ***den ~ aus dem Dreck ziehen*** straighten things out; ***den ~ (einfach) laufen lassen*** let things go; ***j-n vor s-n ~ spannen*** F rope s.o. in; ***ich laß mich nicht vor s-n ~ spannen*** I'm not going to be his dogsbody

'**kar·ren** *v/t.* (h) *a.* F *fig.* cart

Kar·rie·re [ka'rǐeːrə] *f* (-; -n) **1.** career; ***~ machen*** get ahead (*or* to the top); **2.** *riding*: full gallop; **2be·wußt** *adj.* career-minded; **~di·plo͵mat** *m* career diplomat; **~frau** *f* career girl (*or* woman); **~kof·fer** *m* VIP briefcase; **~ma·cher** *m*, **~typ** *m* careerist

Kar·rie·rist [karǐe'rɪst] *m* (-en; -en) careerist

Karst [karst] *m* (-[e]s; -e) *geol.* karst; **~land·schaft** *f* karstland, karst country; *a.* rocky desert

Kar·täu·ser [kar'tɔʏzɐ] *m* (-s; -) Carthusian (monk); **Kar·täu·se·rin** [kar'tɔʏzərɪn] *f* (-; -nen) Carthusian (nun)

Kar·te ['kartə] *f* (-; -n) a) card, b) *geogr.* map; ⚓ chart, c) ticket, d) *gastr.* menu; wine list; *sport*: ***gelbe (rote) ~*** yellow (red) card; ***~n spielen*** play cards; ***gute (schlechte) ~n haben*** have a good (bad) hand; ***~n geben*** deal; ***j-m die ~n legen*** tell s.o.'s fortune (from the cards);

fig. ***alles auf e-e ~ setzen*** put all one's eggs in one basket; ***auf die falsche ~ setzen*** bet on the wrong horse; ***mit offenen ~n spielen*** put one's cards on the table; ***mit verdeckten ~n spielen*** play one's cards close to one's chest

Kar•tei [kar'taɪ] *f* (-; -en) card index; ~ ***führen über*** *acc.* keep a file on; **~kar•te** *f* index card; **~ka•sten** *m* card-index box; **~zet•tel** *m* index slip (*or* card)

Kar•tell [kar'tɛl] *n* (-s; -e) ✝, *pol.* cartel; **~ab•spra•che** *f* cartel agreement; **~amt** *n* Federal Cartel Office; **~ge•setz** *n* antitrust law; **~recht** *n* antitrust law; **~ver•bot** *n* ban on cartels; **~we•sen** *n* (-s; *no pl.*) cartel system

'Kar•ten|blatt *n*: ***gutes*** (***schlechtes***) ~ good (bad) hand; **~haus** *n* **1.** house of cards; *fig.* ***wie ein ~ einstürzen*** fold up like a house of cards; **2.** ⚓ chart house; **~kunst•stück** *n* card trick; **~le•gen** *n* reading the cards; **~le•ger** [-le:gɐ] *m* (-s; -), **~le•ge•rin** [-le:gərɪn] *f* (-; -nen) fortune-teller; **~netz** *n* map grid; **~spiel** *n* **1.** card game, game of cards; **2.** pack of cards; **~spie•ler** *m* card player; **~te•le|fon** *n* cardphone; **~tisch** *m* **1.** card table; **2.** map table; **~ver•kauf** *m* **1.** sale of tickets; **2.** box office; **~vor•ver•kauf** *m* **1.** advance booking; **2.** box office; **~zei•chen** *n* sign *or* symbol (on a map); **~zeich•ner** *m* cartographer

kar•te•sisch [kar'te:zɪʃ] *adj.* Cartesian

kar•tie•ren [kar'ti:rən] *v/t.* (h) map; ⚓ chart

Kar•tof•fel [kar'tɔfəl] *f* (-; -n) potato; F *fig.* (***sich***) ***die ~n von unten ansehen*** F be pushing up the daisies; ***j-n wie e-e heiße ~ fallen lassen*** F drop s.o. like a hot potato; **~brei** *m* mashed potatoes *pl.*; ~ ***mit ...*** *a.* F ... and mash; **~chips** *pl.* potato crisps (*Am.* chips); **~ern•te** *f* a) potato harvest, b) potato crop; **~fäu•le** *f* potato rot; **~feld** *n* potato field; **~gra|tin** *n* gratinée potatoes *pl.*; **~kä•fer** *m* Colorado beetle; **~kloß** *m*, **~knö•del** *m* potato dumpling; **~puf•fer** *m* potato fritter; **~pü|ree** *n* mashed potatoes *pl.*; **~sa|lat** *m* potato salad; **~scha•len** *pl.* potato peels; **~schä•ler** *m* potato peeler; **~stamp•fer** *m* potato masher; **~sup•pe** *f* potato soup

Kar•to•graph [karto'gra:f] *m* (-en; -en) cartographer; **Kar•to•gra•phie** [kartogra'fi:] *f* (-; *no pl.*) cartography; **kar•to•gra•phisch** [karto'gra:fɪʃ] *adj.* cartographic(ally *adv.*)

Kar•ton [kar'tɔŋ, kar'tõ:] *m* (-s; -s) **1.** cardboard, pasteboard; **2.** cardboard box; **3.** cartoon; **Kar•to•na•gen** [karto'na:ʒən] *pl.* (cardboard) packaging materials

kar•to•niert [karto'ni:ɐt] *adj.* hardcover

Kar•to•thek [karto'te:k] *f* (-; -en) card index

Kar•tu•sche [kar'tʊʃə] *f* (-; -n) **1.** ⚠ cartouche; **2.** ⚔ cartridge

Ka•rus•sell [karʊ'sɛl] *n* (-s; -s, -e) roundabout, merry-go-round, *Am.* car(r)ousel; *fig.* merry-go-round; F *fig.* ***mit j-m ~ fahren*** haul s.o. over the coals

Kar•wo•che ['ka:ɐ-] *f* (*a.* ***die*** ~) Holy Week

Kar•zer ['kartsɐ] *m* (-s; -) **1.** *hist.* detention room; **2.** detention

kar•zi•no•gen [kartsino'ge:n] **I.** *adj.* carcinogenic; **II.** ♀ *n* (-s; -e) carcinogen

Kar•zi•nom [kartsi'no:m] *n* (-s; -e) carcinoma

Ka•schem•me [ka'ʃɛmə] *contp.* *f* (-; -n) F (low) dive

ka•schie•ren [ka'ʃi:rən] *v/t.* (h) **1.** hide, cover up; **2.** laminate *paper*; *thea.* mo(u)ld

Kasch•mir ['kaʃmi:ɐ] *m* (-s; -e [-rə]) cashmere; **~zie•ge** *f* Kashmir goat

Kä•se ['kɛ:zə] *m* (-s; -) **1.** cheese; **2.** *no pl.* F *fig.* F rubbish, *Am.* F garbage; stupid business; **~auf•lauf** *m* cheese soufflé; **~auf•schnitt** *m* assorted cheese slices *pl.*; cheese platter; **~blatt** F *n* F (local) rag; **~brot** *n* (open) cheese sandwich; **~ecke** *f* cheese triangle; **~fon|due** *n* cheese fondu; **~fü•ße** F *pl.* smelly (F cheesy) feet; **~ge•bäck** *n* cheese savo(u)ries *pl.*; **~glocke** *f* cheese cover

Ka•se•in [kaze'i:n] *n* (-s; *no pl.*) ⚗ casein

'Kä•se•ku•chen *m* cheesecake

Ka•se•mat•te [kazə'matə] *f* (-; -n) *hist.* casemate

'Kä•se|mes•ser *n* cheese knife; **~plat•te** *f* cheese platter; **~rin•de** *f* cheese rind

Ka•ser•ne [ka'zɛrnə] *f* (-; -n) barracks *pl.*

Ka'ser•nen•ar|rest *m*: ~ ***haben*** be confined to barracks

Ka'ser•nen•hof *m* parade ground; **~drill** *m* parade-ground drill, F square-bashing; **~ton** *m* parade-ground voice (*or* manner)

ka•ser•nie•ren [kazɛr'ni:rən] *v/t.* (h) barrack

'Kä•se|schmie•re *f* ⚕ vernix caseosa; **~stan•ge** *f* cheese straw; **~tor•te** *f* cheesecake; ♀**'weiß** F *adj.* (as) white as a sheet; **~wür•fel** *pl.* diced cheese *sg.*

kä•sig ['kɛ:zɪç] *adj.* **1.** cheesy; **2.** F pale

Ka•si•no [ka'zi:no] *n* (-s; -s) **1.** ⚔ officers' mess; **2.** cafeteria; **3.** casino

Kas•ka•de [kas'ka:də] *f* (-; -n) cascade (*a.* *phys.*, ⚡); **Kas'ka•den•schal•tung** *f* ⚡ cascade connection

Kas•ka•deur [kaska'dø:ɐ] *m* (-s; -e [-rə]) (circus) acrobat

Kas•ko•ver•si•che•rung *f* **1.** *mot.* *insurance against damage to one's own vehicle*; **2.** ⚓ hull insurance

Kas•per ['kaspɐ] *m* (-s; -) **1.** → ***Kasperle***; **2.** F *fig.* clown; **Kas•perl** ['kaspɐl] *m* (-s; -[n]), **Kas•per•le** ['kaspɐlə] *n, m* (-s; -) Punch

'Kas•per•le•thea•ter *n* Punch and Judy show

kas•pern ['kaspɐn] F *v/i.* (h) fool around

Kas•sa|ge•schäft ['kasa-] *n* ✝ spot transaction; **~kurs** *m* spot price

Kas•sa•ti•on [kasa'tsĭo:n] *f* (-; -en) ⚖ annulment; **Kas•sa•ti'ons•hof** *m* court of cassation (*or* appeal)

'Kas•sa•zah•lung *f* ✝ cash payment

Kas•se ['kasə] *f* (-; -n) **1.** a) till, cash register, b) cash desk; checkout (counter); **2.** cashier's office; *bank*: counter; *thea. etc.* box office; *sport*: ticket window; *card game etc.*: pool; ***j-n zur ~ bitten*** present s.o. with the bill; **3.** → ***Krankenkasse***; **4.** takings *pl.*, receipts *pl.*; **5.** cash; F ***gut*** (***knapp***) ***bei ~ sein*** F be flush (a bit hard up); ~ ***machen*** a) ✝ cash up, b) F check one's accounts, c) F be raking it in; → ***getrennt***

Kas•se•ler ['kasəlɐ] *n* (-s; *no pl.*) *gastr.* smoked pork

'Kas•sen|an•wei•sung *f* order for payment; **~arzt** *m* panel doctor; **~be•richt** *m* cash report; **~be•stand** *m* cash balance; **~bi|lanz** *f* cash balance; **~bon** *m* receipt; **~bril•le** *f*: (***e-e*** ~ a pair of) national health glasses *pl.* (*Brit.*); **~buch** *n* cashbook; **~de•fi•zit** *n* cash shortfall; **~ein•gän•ge** *pl.* cash receipts, takings; **~er•folg** *m* box-office hit; **~ma|gnet** *m* crowd-puller, draw; box-office hit; **~ob•li•ga•ti|on** *f* medium-term bond; **~pa•ti|ent** *m* health plan patient, non-private patient; *in GB*: NHS patient; *in the USA*: Medicaid patient; ***er nimmt keine ~en*** *a.* he only takes private patients; **~prü•fung** *f* cash audit; **~schal•ter** *m* counter; **~schla•ger** *m* **1.** → ***Kassenerfolg***; **2.** money-spinner; **~stun•den** *pl.* business hours; **~sturz** *m*: F ~ ***machen*** count one's cash; ♀**träch•tig** *adj.* lucrative, money-spinning ...; **~wart** *m* treasurer; **~zet•tel** *m* receipt; **~zwang** *m* compulsory medical insurance

Kas•se•rol•le [kasə'rɔlə] *f* (-; -n) casserole

Kas•set•te [ka'sɛtə] *f* (-; -n) a) cashbox, b) (*jewelry*) case, box, c) slipcase; box set, d) *phot.* cassette, cartridge, e) ⚠ coffer, f) cassette (tape)

Kas'set•ten|deck *n* cassette deck; **~dek•ke** *f* ⚠ coffered ceiling; **~re|cor•der** *m*, **~spie•ler** *m* cassette recorder (*or* player)

Kas•si•ber [ka'si:bɐ] *sl.* *m* (-s; -) *sl.* stiff

kas•sie•ren [ka'si:rən] (h) **I.** *v/t.* **1.** collect; **2.** F a) charge; take, b) make; **3.** F *fig.* pocket; take *a blow etc.*; **4.** F nab; **5.** ⚖ quash *sentence*; **II.** *v/i.* take (*or* collect) the money; ***dürfte ich jetzt ~?*** do you mind if I give you the bill now?; F ***ganz schön ~*** F be raking it in; F *iro.* ***und er kassiert*** F and he pockets it all; **Kas•sie•rer** [ka'si:rɐ] *m* (-s; -), **Kas•sie•re•rin** [ka'si:rərɪn] *f* (-; -nen) cashier; teller

Ka•sta•gnet•te [kastan'jɛtə] *f* (-; -n) castanet

Ka•sta•nie [kas'ta:nĭə] *f* (-; -n) (horse) chestnut; ***eßbare*** ~ (sweet) chestnut

Ka'sta•ni•en|baum *m* chestnut (tree); ♀**braun** *adj.* chestnut (brown)

Käst•chen ['kɛstçən] *n* (-s; -) small box; *newspaper, form etc.*: box; *paper*: square

Ka•ste ['kastə] *f* (-; -n) caste

ka•stei•en [kas'taɪən] *v/refl.* (h): ***sich*** ~ a) chastise o.s., b) deny o.s.; **Ka'stei•ung** *f* (-; -en) self-chastisement

Ka•stell [kas'tɛl] *n* (-s; -e) fortress, citadel; **Ka•stel•lan** [kastɛ'la:n] *m* (-s; -e) castle warden

Ka•sten ['kastən] *m* (-s; Kästen ['kɛstən]) **1.** a) box; case; (*beer etc.*) crate, b) letterbox, c) *gym.* box, d) showcase, e) *dial.* → ***Schrank***; F ***im ~ sein*** *film*: F be in the can; **2.** F *fig.* a) F crate, b) F box, c) F jug, clink; **3.** F ***er hat was auf dem ~*** he's not daft; ***er hat nicht viel auf dem ~*** F he's a bit thick; **~brot** *n* square (*or* tin) loaf; **~dra•chen** *m* box kite; **~form** *f* loaf tin

'ka•sten•för•mig [-fœrmɪç] *adj.* box-shaped

'Ka•sten|geist *m* (-[e]s; *no pl.*) caste spirit; **~we•sen** *n* (-s; *no pl.*) caste system

Ka•strat [kas'tra:t] *m* (-en; -en) eunuch; ♪ castrato; **Ka•stra•ti•on** [kastra'tsĭo:n] *f* (-; -en) castration; *zo. a.* gelding

Ka•stra•ti'ons|angst *f* fear of castration; **~kom|plex** *m psych.* castration complex

ka•strie•ren [kas'tri:rən] *v/t.* (h) castrate; *zo. a.* geld, spay

Ka•sui•stik [ka'zŭɪstɪk[*f* (-; *no pl.*) casuistry; **ka•sui•stisch** [ka'zŭɪstɪʃ] *adj.* casuistic(ally *adv.*)

Ka•sus ['ka:zʊs] *m* (-; - ['kazu:s]) *ling.* case; **~en•dung** *f* case ending

Ka•ta•falk [kata'falk] *m* (-s; -e) catafalque

Ka·ta·kom·be [kata'kɔmbə] *f* (-; -n) catacomb
Ka·ta·la·ne [kata'la:nə] *m* (-n; -n), **Ka·ta·la·nin** [kata'la:nɪn] *f* (-; -nen), **ka·ta·la·nisch** [kata'la:nɪʃ] *adj.*, **Ka·ta'la·nisch** *n* (-en) *ling.* Catalan
Ka·ta·log [kata'lo:k] *m* (-[e]s; -e [-'lo:gə]) catalog(ue); *fig.* package; *fig.* ***ein ganzer ~ von Fragen*** a long list of questions; **~preis** *m* list price; **~wert** *m* catalog(ue) price
Ka·ta·ly·sa·tor [kataly'za:to:ɐ] *m* (-s; -en [-za'to:rən]) catalyst (*a. fig.*); *mot. a.* catalytic converter; **Ka·ta·ly'sa·tor·au·to** *n* catalyst (*or* catalyser) car, F cat car
ka·ta·ly·sie·ren [kataly'zi:rən] *v/t.* (h) catalyse; **ka·ta·ly·tisch** [kata'ly:tɪʃ] *adj. a. fig.* catalytic
Ka·ta·ma·ran [katama'ra:n] *m* (-s; -e) catamaran
ka·ta·pul·tie·ren [katapʊl'ti:rən] (h) **I.** *v/t.* catapult; *fig. a.* propel (***in*** *acc.*, ***auf*** *acc.* [in]to); *fig.* ***~ in*** *acc.* launch into *a career etc.*; **II.** *fig. v/refl.*: ***sich an die Spitze ~*** shoot to the top
Ka·ta·pult|sitz [kata'pʊlt-] *m* ejector seat; **~start** *m* catapult takeoff
Ka·ta·rakt [kata'rakt] *m* (-[e]s; -e) cataract
Ka·tarrh [ka'tar] *m* (-s; -e) catarrh
Ka·ta·ster [ka'tastɐ] *m*, *n* (-s; -) land register; **~amt** *n* land registry
ka·ta·stro·phal [katastro'fa:l] *adj. a. fig.* disastrous
Ka·ta·stro·phe [katas'tro:fə] *f* (-; -n) disaster (*a. fig.*), catastrophe; cataclysm
Ka·ta'stro·phen|alarm *m* red alert; **~dienst** *m* emergency relief organization; **~ein·satz** *m* emergency help (*or* operation); **~fall** *m* emergency; ***im ~*** in an emergency, in the event of a disaster; **~ge·biet** *n* disaster area; **~hil·fe** *f* disaster relief; **~me·di'zin** *f* disaster medicine; **~schutz** *m* disaster control; **~stim·mung** *f* doomsday atmosphere
Kat-Au·to ['kat-] F *n* F cat car
Ka·te ['ka:tə] *f* (-; -n) cottage
Ka·te·che·se [katɛ'çe:zə] *f* (-; -n) catechesis; **Ka·te·chet** [katɛ'çe:t] *m* (-en; -en) catechist; **Ka·te·chis·mus** [katɛ'çɪsmʊs] *m* (-; -men) catechism
Ka·te·go·rie [katego'ri:] *f* (-; -n) category
ka·te·go·risch [kate'go:rɪʃ] *adj.* categorical
ka·te·go·ri·sie·ren [kategori'zi:rən] *v/t.* (h) categorize; **Ka·te·go·ri'sie·rung** *f* (-; -en) categorization
Ka·ter[1] ['ka:tɐ] *m* (-s; -) tom(cat); ***der Gestiefelte ~*** Puss in Boots
'**Ka·ter**[2] F *m* (-s; -) hangover, *fig. a. the* morning after; **~früh·stück** F *n* hangover cure; **~stim·mung** F *f* morning-after feeling
Ka·thar·sis ['ka:tarzɪs, ka'tarzɪs] *f* (-; *no pl.*) catharsis; **ka·thar·tisch** [ka'tartɪʃ] *adj.* cathartic(ally *adv.*)
Ka·the·der [ka'te:dɐ] *n*, *m* (-s; -) (teacher's *or* lecturer's) desk; **~weis·heit** *f* academic (*or* bookish) knowledge
Ka·the·dra·le [kate'dra:lə] *f* (-; -n) cathedral
Ka·the·ter [ka'te:tɐ] *m* (-s; -) ⚕ catheter
Ka·tho·de [ka'to:də] *f* (-; -n) ⚡ cathode
Ka'tho·den|röh·re *f* cathode ray tube; **~strah·len** *pl.* cathode rays
Ka·tho·le [ka'to:lə] F *m* (-n; -n) F papist
Ka·tho·lik [kato'li:k] *m* (-en; -en), **Ka·tho·li·kin** [kato'li:kɪn] *f* (-, -nen), **ka·tho·lisch** [ka'to:lɪʃ] *adj.* (Roman) Catholic
Ka·tho·li·zis·mus [katoli'tsɪsmʊs] *m* (-; *no pl.*) Catholicism
Kat·tun [ka'tu:n] *m* (-s; -e) calico, *w.s.* cotton; dungaree
Katz [kats] *f*: *fig.* ***~ und Maus spielen mit*** *dat.* play cat and mouse with; ***(alles) für die ~!*** I don't know why I bothered
'**katz|bal·gen** F *v/refl.* (h): ***sich ~*** **1.** F scrap, tussle; **2.** squabble; **~buckeln** *v/i.* (h) bow and scrape (***vor*** *dat.* before)
Kätz·chen ['kɛtsçən] *n* (-s; -) **1.** *zo.* kitten; **2.** ⚘ catkin
Kat·ze ['katsə] *f* (-; -n) **1.** cat; *fig.* ***falsch wie e-e ~*** as false as they come; ***die ~ aus dem Sack lassen*** let the cat out of the bag, give the show away; ***wie die ~ um den heißen Brei gehen*** beat about (*or* around) the bush; ***die ~ im Sack kaufen*** buy a pig in a poke; ***zäh wie e-e ~ sein*** have as many lives as a cat; ***die ~ läßt das Mausen nicht*** a leopard can't change his spots; ***wenn die ~ aus dem Haus ist, tanzen die Mäuse auf dem Tisch*** when the cat's away the mice will play; → ***Katz***; **2.** ⚙ → ***Laufkatze***
'**kat·zen·ar·tig** *adj.* catlike, feline
'**Kat·zen|au·ge** *n* **1.** cat's eye (*a. fig. and min.*); **2.** ⚙ reflector, cat's eye; **~buckel** *m*: ***e-n ~ machen*** arch one's back; **~dreck** *m* cat's droppings *pl.*; F *fig.* ***ein ~*** nothing, F chickenfeed; **~fell** *n* catskin; **2freund·lich** *adj.* sugary; **~ge·schrei** *n* yowling cats *pl.*
'**kat·zen·haft** *adj.* catlike, feline
'**Kat·zen|hai** *m* dogfish; **~jam·mer** *m* hangover (*a. fig.*); the blues *pl.*; **~kopf** *m* cobble(stone); **~mu'sik** *f* caterwauling; **~mut·ter** *f* mother cat; **~pföt·chen** *n* **1.** *zo.* cat's paw; **2.** ⚘ cat's foot; **~sprung** *fig. m a* stone's throw; **~streu** *f* cat litter; **~tisch** *m*: F ***am ~ essen müssen*** have to eat at the little table; **~wä·sche** F *f* F a lick and a promise; ***~ machen*** give o.s. a lick and a promise, (just) splash o.s.; ***hast du wieder mal ~ gemacht?*** you've hardly got yourself wet; **~zun·ge** *f gastr.* langue de chat
Kau·ap·pa'rat ['kaʊ-] *m anat.* masticatory organs *pl.* (*or* apparatus)
Kau·der·welsch ['kaʊdɐvɛlʃ] *n* (-[s]; *no pl.*) gibberish; jargon; **kau·der·wel·schen** ['kaʊdɐvɛlʃən] *v/i.* (h) talk gibberish
kau·en ['kaʊən] *v/t. and v/i.* (h) chew; ***an den Nägeln ~*** bite one's nails; *fig.* ***~ an*** *dat.* chew *s.th.* over
kau·ern ['kaʊɐn] *v/i. and v/refl.* (***sich ~***) (h) crouch *or* squat (down)
Kauf [kaʊf] *m* (-[e]s; Käufe ['kɔʏfə]) a) purchase, F buy, b) purchasing, buying; ***günstiger ~*** bargain, F good buy; ***zum ~ anbieten*** offer for sale; *fig.* ***mit in ~ nehmen*** accept; **~an·reiz** *m* incentive to buy; **~auf·trag** *m* buying order; **~be·din·gun·gen** *pl.* conditions of sale; **~boom** F *m* high-street boom
kau·fen ['kaʊfən] (h) **I.** *v/t.* **1.** buy; F *fig.* ***dafür kann ich mir nichts ~*** F a fat lot of use that is; → ***teuer*** I; **2.** bribe, buy; **3.** F ***den werde ich mir ~*** F I'll tell him what's what; **II.** *v/i.* shop; ***~ bei*** *dat.* go to
Käu·fer ['kɔʏfɐ] *m* (-s; -) buyer; customer; **~for·schung** *f* buyer research; **~ge·wohn·hei·ten** *pl.* buying habits; **~grup·pe** *f* group of buyers
Käu·fe·rin ['kɔʏfərɪn] *f* (-; -nen) → ***Käufer***
'**Käu·fer|markt** *m* buyer's market; **~schicht** *f* group of buyers
'**Kauf|frau** *f* businesswoman; **~ge·le·gen·heit** *f* opportunity (to buy); **~ge·wohn·hei·ten** *pl.* buying habits; **~hal·le** *f* small department store
'**Kauf·haus** *n* department store; **~de·tek'tiv** *m* store detective; **~ket·te** *f*, **~kon'zern** *m* (department) stores group
'**Kauf|in·ter'es·se** *n* (buyer) demand; **~in·ter·es'sent** *m* prospective buyer
'**Kauf·kraft** *f* (-; *no pl.*) buying (*or* purchasing) power; spending power
'**kauf·kräf·tig** *adj.* well-funded; strong *currency*
'**Kauf·kraft·schwund** *m* dwindling purchasing power
'**Kau·flä·che** *f* masticatory surface
'**Kauf·la·den** *m* shop, *esp. Am.* store
'**Kauf·leu·te** *pl.* → ***Kaufmann***
käuf·lich ['kɔʏflɪç] **I.** *adj.* for sale; *fig.* open to bribery; **~e *Liebe*** venal love; **II.** *adv.*: ***~ erwerben*** purchase; '**Käuf·lich·keit** *f* (-; *no pl.*) corruptibility
'**Kauf·lust** *f* (-; *no pl.*) urge to spend; spending; ☨ demand for consumer goods; '**kauf·lu·stig** *adj.*: ***~e Touristen*** tourists with plenty of money to spend, *n.s.* dollar-happy (*or* pound-happy) tourists
'**Kauf·mann** *m* (-[e]s; -leute) a) businessman; trader, b) shopkeeper, *Am.* storekeeper; '**kauf·män·nisch** [-mɛnɪʃ] **I.** *adj.* commercial; business *qualities etc.*; ***~er Angestellter*** clerk; ***~er Betrieb*** business enterprise; ***~es Personal*** office staff; **II.** *adv.*: ***~ ausgebildet sein*** have had business training
'**Kauf·manns·la·den** *m* (toy) shop
'**Kauf|ob'jekt** *n* article, object; **~or·gie** F *f* F splurge; **~preis** *m* purchase price; **~rausch** *m*: ***sie ist im ~*** she can't stop buying things, F she's having a big splurge; **~un·lust** *f* lack of spending; ☨ lack of demand for consumer goods; **~ver·hal·ten** *n* buying patterns *pl.*; **~ver·trag** *m* contract for sale; **~wert** *m* purchase value; **~wut** *f* buying craze; **~zwang** *m*: ***kein ~*** no obligation
Kau·gum·mi ['kaʊ-] *m* chewing gum
Kau·ka·si·er [kaʊ'ka:ziɐ] *m* (-s; -), **Kau·ka·sie·rin** [kaʊ'ka:ziərɪn] *f* (-; -nen), **kau·ka·sisch** [kaʊ'ka:zɪʃ] *adj.* Caucasian
Kaul·quap·pe ['kaʊl-] *f* tadpole
kaum [kaʊm] *adv.* hardly; only just, barely; with great difficulty; ***~ je*** hardly ever; ***~ hatte er ...*** (*or* ***~ daß er ... hatte***)***, als*** he had hardly ... when, no sooner had he ... than; ***(wohl) ~!*** hardly, I doubt it very much; ***es ist ~ zu sehen*** you can hardly see it
'**Kau·mus·kel** *m* masticatory muscle
kau·sal [kaʊ'za:l] *adj.* causal
Kau'sal|be·griff *m* causal concept; **~be·zie·hung** *f* causal connection; **~ge·setz** *n* law of causality, law of cause and effect
Kau·sa·li·tät [kaʊzali'tɛ:t] *f* (-; -en) causality; **Kau·sa·li'täts·prin'zip** *n* principle of causality
Kau'sal|satz *m ling.* causal clause; **~zu'sam·men·hang** *m* causal connection
kau·stisch ['kaʊstɪʃ] *adj.* ⚗ *and fig.* caustic(ally *adv.*)
'**Kau·ta·bak** *m* chewing tobacco
Kau·ti·on [kaʊ'tsĭo:n] *f* (-; -en) ☨ security; ⚖ *usu.* bail; deposit; ***gegen ~ entlassen*** release on bail; ***gegen ~ freigelassen***

werden be granted bail; ***j-n durch ~ freibekommen*** bail s.o. out
Kau·ti'ons·sum·me *f* (amount of) security *or* bail
Kau·tschuk ['kaʊtʃʊk] *m* (-s; *no pl.*) (India) rubber; **~baum** *m* rubber tree; **~milch** *f* latex; **~pa·ra͵graph** F *m* elastic clause
'Kau·werk·zeu·ge *pl.* masticatory organs
Kauz [kaʊts] *m* (-es; Käuze ['kɔʏtsə]) **1.** *zo.* tawny owl; **2.** F *fig.* ***komischer ~*** F strange customer, *sl.* weirdo; **Käuz·chen** ['kɔʏtsçən] *n* (-s; -) → ***Kauz*** 1; **kau·zig** ['kaʊtsɪç] *adj.* strange, odd
Ka·va·lier [kava'li:ɐ] *m* (-s; -e [-rə]) gentleman; ***ein ~ der alten Schule*** a (*or* the) perfect gentleman; **ka·va'lier·mä·ßig** *adj.* gentlemanly, F chivalrous
Ka·va'liers·de͵likt F *n* peccadillo, harmless crime; ***es gilt als ~*** *a.* it's considered a (national) sport
Ka·va'lier(s)·start *m* racing start
Ka·val·ka·de [kaval'ka:də] *f* (-; -n) cavalcade
Ka·val·le·rie ['kavaləri:] *f* (-; -n) cavalry
Ka·val·le·rist ['kavalərɪst] *m* (-en; -en) cavalryman
Ka·vi·ar ['ka:vi̯ar] *m* (-s; *no pl.*) caviar(e); ***~ fürs Volk*** caviar(e) to the general
Ka·vi·tät [kavi'tɛ:t] *f* (-; -en) ⚕ cavity
Ke·bab [ke'ba:p] *m* (-[s]; *no pl.*) kebab
keck [kɛk] *adj.* cheeky, saucy (*a. fig. hat etc.*); bold (as brass)
Ke·fir ['ke:fɪr] *m* (-s; *no pl.*) kefir
Ke·gel ['ke:gəl] *m* (-s; -) **1.** skittle, pin; **2.** *esp.* 𝔄 *and* ⚙ cone; taper; → ***Kind***; **~abend** *m* bowling evening; ***Dienstag ist ~*** Tuesday's bowling night; **~bahn** *f* bowling alley; **~bru·der** F *m* **1.** F bowling mate; **2.** F bowling freak
'ke·gel·för·mig [-fœrmɪç] *adj.* conical
'Ke·gel|ge·trie·be *n* ⚙ bevel gear; **~klub** *m* bowling club; **~ku·gel** *f* bowling ball
ke·geln ['ke:gəln] **I.** *v/i.* (h) bowl; go bowling; **II.** 2 *n* (-s) bowling
'Ke·gel|pro·jek·ti͵on *f* conical projection; **~rad** *n* bevel gear; **~rad·an·trieb** *m* bevel drive; **~schnitt** *m* 𝔄 conic section; **~spiel** *n*, **~sport** *m* bowling; **~stumpf** *m* 𝔄 truncated cone; **~ven͵til** *n* cone valve
Keg·ler ['ke:glɐ] *m* (-s; -), **Keg·le·rin** ['ke:glərɪn] *f* (-; -nen) bowler
Kehl·deckel ['ke:l-] *m anat.* epiglottis
Keh·le ['ke:lə] *f* (-; -n) **1.** *anat.* throat; windpipe; ***aus voller ~*** at the top of one's voice; ***j-m das Messer an die ~ setzen*** put a knife to s.o.'s throat, *fig.* point a gun at s.o.'s head; *fig.* ***er hat es in die falsche ~ bekommen*** F he got the wrong end of the stick; ***ihm geht's an die ~*** he's in for it now; F ***(immer) e-e trockene ~ haben*** F be a bit of a tippler; ***sich die ~ anfeuchten*** F wet one's whistle; F ***et. durch die ~ jagen*** F sluice s.th. down the hatch; → ***zusammenschnüren***; **2.** △ chamfer, *a.* ⚙ flute
Kehl·kopf ['ke:l-] *m* larynx; **~ent·zün·dung** *f* laryngitis; **~krebs** *m* cancer of the larynx; **~mi·kro͵phon** *n* throat microphone; **~schnitt** *m* laryngotomy; **~spie·gel** *m* laryngoscope; **~spie·ge·lung** *f* laryngoscopy
Kehl|laut ['ke:l-] *m ling.* guttural (sound); **~lei·ste** *f* △ mo(u)lding
Kehr·aus ['ke:ɐ̯ʔaʊs] *m* (-; *no pl.*) last dance; *fig.* (grand) finale
Keh·re ['ke:rə] *f* (-; -n) a) (sharp) bend, b) turning space, loop (*a.* 🚗), c) *gym.* rear vault, back dismount, d) ✈, *skiing*: turn
keh·ren¹ ['ke:rən] *dial. v/i. and v/t.* (h) sweep (up); *fig.* ***er soll mal vor der eigenen Tür ~*** he should put his own house in order (first)
'keh·ren² (h) **I.** *v/t.* **1.** turn; ***j-m den Rücken ~*** *a. fig.* turn one's back on s.o.; *fig.* ***in sich gekehrt*** withdrawn; **II.** *v/refl.* **2.** ***sich ~ gegen*** *acc.* turn against; ***sich zum Besten ~*** turn out all right (*Am.* alright) in the end; **3.** ***sich nicht ~ an*** *dat.* pay no attention to; **III.** *v/i.*: ⚔ ***kehrt!*** about turn!
Keh·richt ['ke:rɪçt] *m, n* (-s; *no pl.*) dirt; F *fig.* ***das geht dich e-n feuchten ~ an*** F that's none of your (bloody) business; **~ei·mer** *m* rubbish bin, *Am.* trashcan; **~hau·fen** *m* (pile of) dirt; **~schau·fel** *f* dustpan
Kehr|ma͵schi·ne ['ke:ɐ-] *f* **1.** road sweeper; **2.** carpet sweeper; **~reim** *m* refrain; **~sei·te** *f* other side, reverse; F backside; F ***j-m s-e ~ zuwenden*** turn one's back on s.o.; *fig.* ***die ~ der Medaille*** the other side of the coin; ***die ~ des Lebens*** the seamy side of life
kehrt·ma·chen ['ke:ɐt-] *v/i.* (*sep.*, h) turn back; turn on one's heels, do an about-turn (*fig. a.* about-face)
'Kehrt·wen·dung *f*: ***(e-e ~ machen*** do a[n]) about-turn, U-turn, *fig. a.* about-face
Kehr·wert ['ke:ɐ-] *m* reciprocal
kei·fen ['kaɪfən] *v/i.* (h) nag
Keil [kaɪl] *m* (-[e]s; -e) a) wedge (*a. meteor.*); chock, b) gusset, c) ⚔ spearhead; *fig.* ***e-n ~ treiben zwischen*** drive a wedge between; **~ab·satz** *m* wedge heel
Kei·le ['kaɪlə] *f*: ***~ kriegen*** get a hiding
kei·len ['kaɪlən] (h) **I.** *v/t.* **1.** wedge; **2.** F rope *s.o.* in (***für*** *acc.* for); **II.** F *v/refl.*: ***sich ~*** fight, scuffle, F tussle
Kei·ler ['kaɪlɐ] *m* (-s; -) *zo.* wild boar
Kei·le·rei [kaɪlə'raɪ] *f* (-; -en) fight, scuffle, F tussle, scrap
'Keil|flos·se *f* ✈ vertical tail fin; **~form** *f* ✈ V-formation
'keil·för·mig [-fœrmɪç] *adj.* wedge-shaped; cuneiform *letters, script etc.*
'Keil|ho·se *f*: ***(e-e ~*** a pair of) stretch trousers *pl.* (*Am.* pants *pl.*); **~kis·sen** *n* (wedge-shaped) bolster; **~rie·men** *m* ⚙ V-belt; **~schrift** *f* cuneiform (script)
Keim [kaɪm] *m* (-[e]s; -e) ⚕ germ; ⚘ shoot; sprout; embryo; *fig.* seed(s *pl.*); ***~e treiben*** germinate; *fig.* ***im ~ ersticken*** nip in the bud, scotch *rumo(u)r etc.*; **~blatt** *n* ⚘ cotyledon; *biol.* germ layer; **~bo·den** *m biol.* substratum
'Keim·drü·se *f* gonad; **'Keim·drü·sen·hor͵mon** *n* sex hormone
kei·men ['kaɪmən] *v/i.* (h) germinate; sprout; bud; *fig.* grow; stir
'keim·fä·hig *adj.* germinable, viable
'keim·frei *adj.* sterile; ***~ machen*** sterilize
Keim·ling ['kaɪmlɪŋ] *m* (-s; -e) seedling
'Keim|plas·ma *n* germ plasm; **2tö·tend** *adj.* antiseptic; **~trä·ger** *m* ⚕ (germ) carrier; **~zel·le** *f* germ cell, gamete; *fig.* nucleus
kein [kaɪn] *indef. pron.* **1.** *adj.* **~(e)** no, not any; ***er hat ~ Auto*** he hasn't got a car; ***sie hat ~e Freunde*** she hasn't got any friends; ***~ anderer als*** none other than; ***sie ist ~ Ungeheuer*** she's not a (*or* no) monster; **2.** *su.* **~er, ~e, ~(e)s** a) none, not any, b) no-one, nobody; *hast du welche gesehen?* - **nein, ~e** no, I didn't see any; **~er (~e, ~s) *von beiden*** neither (of them); ***~er von uns*** neither (*or* none) of us; F ***uns kann ~er*** F there are no flies on us, you can't catch us out (as easily as that)
kei·ner·lei ['kaɪnɐ'laɪ] *adj.* no ... at all; ***~ Schmerzen*** *a.* no pain whatsoever; ***auf ~ Weise*** in no way
kei·nes·falls ['kaɪnəs'fals] *adv.* under no circumstances, on no account; (in) no way; certainly not, F no way
kei·nes·wegs ['kaɪnəs've:ks] *adv.* not at all; anything but
'kein·mal *adv.* not once, never
Keks [ke:ks] *m* (-es; -e) biscuit, *Am.* cookie; F *fig.* ***j-m auf den ~ gehen*** F get on s.o.'s wick
Kelch [kɛlç] *m* (-[e]s; -e) cup, goblet; *eccl.* chalice, communion cup; ⚘ calyx; ***der ~ ist noch einmal an uns vorübergegangen*** we've been spared, F that was close; **~blatt** *n* sepal
'kelch·för·mig [-fœrmɪç] *adj.* cup-shaped; ⚘ calyciform
'Kelch·glas *adj.* (crystal *or* glass) goblet
Kel·le ['kɛlə] *f* (-; -n) *gastr.* ladle; △ trowel; 🚗 *etc.* signal(l)ing disc
Kel·ler ['kɛlɐ] *m* (-s; -) cellar; basement; *fig.* ***in den ~ fallen*** hit rock bottom; **~as·sel** *f zo.* woodlouse; **~bar** *f* cellar bar
Kel·le·rei [kɛlə'raɪ] *f* (-; -en) wine cellars *pl.*
'Kel·ler|fal·te *f* box pleat; **~ge·schoß** *n* basement; **~ge·wöl·be** *n* (underground) vault, cellar; **~kind** F *n* **1.** deprived child; **2.** *fig.* **~er** *sport*: bottom-of-the-table team(s); **~lo͵kal** *n* cellar restaurant (*or* bar); **~mei·ster** *m* cellarer; **~tem·pe·ra͵tur** *f* cellar temperature; **~trep·pe** *f* cellar steps (*or* stairs) *pl.*; **~wech·sel** *m* ☤ dummy bill; **~woh·nung** *f* basement (flat)
Kell·ner ['kɛlnɐ] *m* (-s; -) waiter; **Kell·ne·rin** ['kɛlnərɪn] *f* (-; -nen) waitress; **kell·nern** ['kɛlnɐn] F *v/i.* (h) work (*or* job around) as a waiter (*or* waitress)
Kel·te ['kɛltə] *m* (-n; -n) Celt
Kel·ter ['kɛltɐ] *f* (-; -n) wine press; **Kel·te·rei** [kɛltə'raɪ] *f* (-; -en) press house; **kel·tern** ['kɛltɐn] *v/t.* (h) press
Kel·tin ['kɛltɪn] *f* (-; -nen) Celt; **kel·tisch** ['kɛltɪʃ] *adj.* Celtic
Ken·do ['kɛndo] *n* (-[s]; *no pl.*) kendo
Ke·nia·ner [ke'ni̯a:nɐ] *m* (-s; -), **Ke·nia·ne·rin** [ke'ni̯a:nərɪn] *f* (-; -nen), **ke·nia·nisch** [ke'ni̯a:nɪʃ] *adj.* Kenyan
Kenn|buch·sta·be ['kɛn-] *m* code letter; **~da·ten** *pl.* data
ken·nen *v/t.* (kannte, gekannt, h) a) know, b) recognize (**an** *dat.* by); ***das ~ wir!*** we know all about that!; ***wir ~ uns schon*** we 'have met; ***du kennst mich schlecht*** you don't know me (at all) yet; ***kennst du mich noch?*** remember me?; ***er kannte sich nicht mehr vor Wut*** he was beside himself with anger; ***kennst du den (Witz) vom ...*** did you hear the one about ...?; ***die ~ keine Rücksicht*** they're absolutely ruthless
'ken·nen·ler·nen *v/t.* (*sep.*, h) get to know, meet; ***als ich ihn kennenlernte*** when I first met him; ***näher ~*** get to know *s.o. or s.th.* better; F ***der soll mich noch ~!*** F he hasn't seen anything yet
Ken·ner ['kɛnɐ] *m* (-s; -) connoisseur; ex-

pert (*gen.* on), authority (on); **~blick** *m*: (**mit ~** with an *or* one's) expert eye
'ken·ner·haft, ken·ne·risch ['kɛnərɪʃ] *adj.* discerning
'Ken·ner·mie·ne *f*: **mit ~** with the air of a connoisseur
'Ken·ner·schaft *f* (-; *no pl.*) expertise
'Kenn|far·be *f* identifying colo(u)r; **~kar·te** *f* identity card; **~li·nie** *f* 𝔄, *phys.* characteristic curve; **~mar·ke** *f* identity tag
kennt·lich ['kɛntlɪç] *adj.* recognizable; distinguishable; discernible; marked; **~ machen** mark, label; **sich ~ machen** make o.s. known
Kennt·nis ['kɛntnɪs] *f* (-; -se) **1.** knowledge (*gen. or* **von** *dat.* of); **~ haben von** *dat.* know (about), be aware of; **j-n von et. in ~ setzen** inform s.o. of s.th., bring s.th. to s.o.'s attention; **~ nehmen von** *dat.* take note of; **es ist uns zur ~ gelangt, daß** we have learned (*or* been informed) that; **das entzieht sich m-r ~** I don't know anything about it; **2.** *pl.* knowledge (*gen. or* **in** *dat.* of); experience (in, of); understanding (of); **gute ~se haben in** *dat.* be well grounded in
'Kennt·nis·nah·me [-naːmə] *f*: **zu Ihrer ~** for your attention; **mit der Bitte um ~** please take note
'kennt·nis|reich *adj.* knowledgeable, well-informed; **2stand** *m* (-[e]s; *no pl.*) state of knowledge (*or* information)
Ken·nung ['kɛnʊŋ] *f* (-; -en) identification; ⚓, ✈ route marking
Kenn|wort ['kɛn-] *n* (-[e]s; ⸚er) password, *a.* ✝ *etc.* code word; box number; **Zuschriften unter dem ~ X** mark your letters (*or* envelopes) X; **~zahl** *f* **1.** *teleph.* (area) code, *Am.* prefix; **2.** → **Kennziffer**
Kenn·zei·chen ['kɛn-] *n* (-s; -) (distinguishing) feature, characteristic; badge, emblem; brand; *mot.* registration (*Am.* license) number; aircraft marking; **besondere ~** *passport*: distinguishing marks; **ein sicheres ~, daß** a sure sign that
'kenn·zeich·nen *v/t.* (h) **1.** mark, identify, label; signpost *path etc.*; brand *animals*; **2.** reflect; **j-n ~ als** show s.o. to be; **3.** describe, *a.* portray *s.o.*; **'kenn·zeich·nend** *adj.* characteristic, typical (**für** *acc.* of); distinguishing
Kenn·zif·fer ['kɛn-] *f* code number; 𝔄 characteristic, index (*of logarithm*); *statistics*: index (number); *newspaper etc.*: box number
ken·tern ['kɛntɐn] *v/i.* (sn) capsize
Ke·ra·mik [ke'raːmɪk] *f* (-; -en) **1.** *no pl.* ceramics *pl.*, pottery; **2.** (piece of) pottery; **ke·ra·misch** [ke'raːmɪʃ] *adj.* ceramic
Ker·be ['kɛrbə] *f* (-; -n) notch, groove; *fig.* **in dieselbe ~ hauen** do (*or* say) exactly the same thing
Ker·bel ['kɛrbəl] *m* (-s; *no pl.*) ♣ chervil
ker·ben ['kɛrbən] *v/t.* (h) notch; knurl
Kerb·holz ['kɛrp-] *n*: *fig.* **etwas auf dem ~ haben** have done s.th. wrong; **einiges auf dem ~ haben** have quite a record
'Kerb·tier ['kɛrp-] *n* insect
Ker·ker ['kɛrkɐ] *m* (-s; -) *hist.* jail, *Brit. a.* gaol, prison; dungeon; ⚖ → **~haft** *f* imprisonment; **~mei·ster** *m hist.* jailer, *Brit. a.* gaoler
Kerl [kɛrl] F *m* (-s; -e) F bloke, guy; **armer ~** F poor devil; **ein ganzer ~** a real man; **ein anständiger ~** F a decent sort; **sie ist ein feiner ~** F she's a good sort; **blöder ~** idiot
Kern [kɛrn] *m* (-[e]s; -e) **1.** pip, seed; stone; kernel; **2.** ⚙, ⚡, *phys.* core; 📖 nucleus; **3.** *fig.* core, essence; nucleus; (*town etc.*) cent|re (*Am.* -er), heart; **der ~ der Sache** the heart (*or* core) of the matter; **bis zum ~ e-r Sache vordringen** get to the core of s.th.; **harter ~** hard core; **im ~ verdorben** rotten to the core; **sie hat e-n guten ~** she's good at heart; **~brenn·stoff** *m* nuclear fuel; **~che,mie** *f* nuclear chemistry
'Kern·ener,gie *f* nuclear energy; **~pro,gramm** *n* nuclear energy program(me); **~ri·si·ko** *n* nuclear (energy) risk
'Kern|ex·plo·si,on *f* nuclear explosion; **~fach** *n ped.* core subject; **~fa,mi·lie** *f* nuclear family; **~for·schung** *f* nuclear research; **~for·schungs·an·la·ge** *f* nuclear research plant; **~fra·ge** *f* hard-core issue; **~fu·si,on** *f* nuclear fusion; **~ge·dan·ke** *m* central idea; **~ge·häu·se** *n* ♣ core
'kern·ge·sund *adj.* (as) fit as a fiddle
ker·nig ['kɛrnɪç] *adj.* **1.** *fruit* full of pips; **2.** *fig.* pithy; robust, vigorous; earthy; **3.** sturdy *wine*; **4.** full *leather*
'Kern·kraft *f* (-; *no pl.*) nuclear power (*or* energy); **~geg·ner** *m* antinuclear protester (*or* campaigner); **~werk** *n* nuclear power plant
'Kern·la·dung *f* nuclear charge; **'Kern·la·dungs·zahl** *f* atomic number
'kern·los *adj.* ♣ seedless
'Kern|mo,dell *n* nuclear model; **~obst** *n* pomaceous fruit, pome(s *pl.*); **~phy,sik** *f* nuclear physics; **~phy·si·ker** *m* nuclear physicist; **~punkt** *m* essential (*or* central) point; **~re·ak·ti,on** *f* nuclear reaction; **~re,ak·tor** *m* nuclear reactor; **~schat·ten** *m* deepest shadow; *ast.* umbra; **~schmel·ze** *f* core meltdown; **~sei·fe** *f* curd soap; **~spal·tung** *f* nuclear fission; **~spei·cher** *m computer*: core memory; **~spin·to·mo·gra,phie** *f* ⚕ magnetic resonance; **~spruch** *m* pithy saying; **~stück** *n* main item; pièce de résistance; **~tech·nik** *f* nuclear technology
'Kern·waf·fe *f* nuclear weapon
'kern·waf·fen·frei *adj.*: **~e Zone** nuclear-free zone
'Kern·waf·fen·ver·such *m* nuclear test
'Kern|zeit *f* core time; **~zo·ne** *f* cent|re (*Am.* -er); *geol.* nucleus
Ke·ro·sin [kero'ziːn] *n* (-s; *no pl.*) kerosene
Ker·ze ['kɛrtsə] *f* (-; -n) **1.** candle (*a.* ⚡ *and phys.*); *mot.* spark(ing) plug; **2.** *gym.* shoulder stand; **e-e ~ fabrizieren** (*or* **produzieren**) *soccer*: sky one's clearance
ker·zen·ge·ra·de ['kɛrtsən-] *adj. and adv.* (as) straight as an arrow; (as) straight as a ramrod; bolt upright
'Ker·zen|hal·ter *m* candleholder; **~leuch·ter** *m* candelabrum, candlestick; sconce; **~licht** *n*: (**bei ~** by) candlelight; **Essen bei ~** a candlelight dinner; **~stecker** *m mot.* spark-plug cap
Ke·scher ['kɛʃɐ] *m* (-s; -) net; landing net
keß [kɛs] F *adj.* pert, saucy
Kes·sel ['kɛsəl] *m* (-s; -) **1.** kettle; ca(u)ldron; boiler; **2.** *geol.* hollow; basin; **3.** ⚔ pocket; **~haus** *n* boiler house (*or* room); **~pau·ke** *f* kettledrum; **~schlacht** *f* battle of encirclement, cauldron battle; **~stein** *m* (-[e]s; *no pl.*) fur, scale; **den ~ entfernen von** *dat.* descale; **~trei·ben** *n hunt.* battue; *fig. pol.* witch-hunt (**gegen** *acc.* against)
Ketch·up ['kɛtʃap] *m, n* (-s; -s) (tomato) ketchup, tomato sauce
Ke·ton [ke'toːn] *n* (-s; -e) ⚗ ketone
Ketsch [kɛtʃ] *f* (-; -en) ⚓ ketch
Ket·te ['kɛtə] *f* (-; -n) **1.** a) chain (*a.* ⚗, ✝), b) necklace, chain, bracelet, c) *fig. usu. pl.* chains, fetters; **an die ~ legen** put *a dog* on the chain, *fig.* put *s.o.* on a short leash, *sport*: mark *s.o.* out of the game; **2.** *mot.* track; **3.** *textil.* warp; **~ und Schuß** warp and woof; **4.** *geogr.* chain, range *of mountains*; chain, string *of lakes*; **5.** *fig.* chain, series *of events etc.*; **6.** cordon; **e-e ~ bilden** form a cordon (*or* line), *a. demonstrators*: form a human chain
ket·ten ['kɛtən] *v/t.* (h) chain (**an** *acc.* to) (*a. fig.*)
'Ket·ten|an·trieb *m* ⚙ chain drive; **~arm·band** *n* chain bracelet; **~brief** *m* chain letter; **~bruch** *m* 𝔄 continued fraction; **~brücke** *f* suspension bridge; **~fahr·zeug** *n mot.* tracked vehicle; **~för·de·rer** *m* ⚙ chain conveyor
'ket·ten·för·mig [-fœrmɪç] *adj.* aliphatic
'Ket·ten|ge·bir·ge *n* mountain range; **~ge·lenk** *n* chain (*mot.* track) link; **~ge·schäft** *n* chain store; **~glied** *n* chain link; **~hund** *m* watchdog; **~ka·rus,sell** *n* chairoplane; **~la·den** *m* chain store; **~pan·zer** *m hist.* coat of mail; **~rad** *n* ⚙ sprocket wheel; **~rau·chen** *n* chain smoking; **~rau·cher** *m* chain smoker; **~re·ak·ti,on** *f phys. and fig.* chain reaction; **~re·stau,rant** *n* chain restaurant; **~sä·ge** *f* chain saw; **~schluß** *m phls.* chain syllogism, sorites; **~schutz** *m* ⚙ chain guard; **~stich** *m* chain stitch; **~ver·trag** *m* chain contract
Kett·fa·den ['kɛt-] *m* warp
Ket·zer ['kɛtsɐ] *m* (-s; -) heretic; **Ket·ze·rei** [kɛtsə'raɪ] *f* (-; -en) heresy; **'Ket·zer·ge·richt** *n hist.* (court of) inquisition; **Ket·ze·rin** ['kɛtsərɪn] *f* (-; -nen) heretic; **ket·ze·risch** ['kɛtsərɪʃ] *adj.* heretical
keu·chen ['kɔʏçən] *v/i.* (h) pant, wheeze; gasp; *train etc.*: puff
Keuch·hu·sten ['kɔʏç-] *m* ⚕ whooping cough
Keu·le ['kɔʏlə] *f* (-; -n) **1.** club, cudgel, *hist.* mace; *pharm.* pestle; **2.** *zo.* haunch; *gastr.* leg, haunch, drumstick; **3. chemische ~** chemical mace
'Keu·len|schlag *m* cudgel blow; *fig.* **es traf ihn wie ein ~** it came as a tremendous blow to him; **~schwin·gen** *n sport*: (Indian) club swinging
keusch [kɔʏʃ] *adj.* chaste; virginal; **'Keusch·heit** *f* (-; *no pl.*) chastity
'Keusch·heits|ge·lüb·de *n* vow of chastity; **~gür·tel** *m* chastity belt
Kfz [kaːʔɛf'tsɛt] *n* (-; -[s]) → **Kraftfahrzeug**; **~-Kenn·zei·chen** *n* car registration (*Am.* license) number; **~-Me,cha·ni·ker** *m*, **~-Schlos·ser** *m* (car) mechanic; **~-Steu·er** *f* road (*Am.* automobile) tax; **~-Werk·statt** *f* garage; **~-Zu·las·sungs·stel·le** *f* vehicle registration cent|re (*Am.* -er)
Kha·ki ['kaːki] *m, n* (-[s]; *no pl.*) khaki
Khmer¹ [kmeːɐ] *m* (-; -) Khmer; **die ~** the Khmer (people); **die Roten ~** the Khmer Rouge
Khmer² *n* (-; *no pl.*) *ling.* Khmer
khmer *adj.* Khmer
Kib·buz [kɪ'buːts] *m* (-; -) (**in e-m ~** in *or* on a) kibbutz
Ki·cher·erb·se ['kɪçɐ-] *f* chickpea

ki·chern ['kɪçɐn] **I.** *v/i.* (h) giggle; snigger; **II.** ♀ *n* (-s) giggling; sniggering
Kick [kɪk] F *m* (-[s]; -s) **1.** kick; **2.** game; **kicken** ['kɪkən] (*sep.* -k·k-) (h) F **I.** *v/t.* kick; **II.** *v/i.* play football; **Kicker** ['kɪkɐ] (*sep.* -k·k-) F *m* (-s; -) (football) player
'**Kick·star·ter** *m mot.* kickstarter
kid·nap·pen ['kɪtnɛpən] *v/t.* (h) kidnap
Kid·nap·per ['kɪtnɛpɐ] *m* (-s; -), **Kid·nap·pe·rin** ['kɪtnɛpərɪn] *f* (-; -nen) kidnapper
Kie·bitz ['ki:bɪts] *m* (-es; -e) **1.** *zo.* peewit, lapwing; **2.** F kibitzer; **kie·bit·zen** ['ki:bɪtsən] F *v/i.* (h) F sneak a look; *card game etc.*: F kibitz
Kie·fer¹ ['ki:fɐ] *m* (-s; -) jaw(bone); *zo.* mandible
'**Kie·fer**² *f* (-; -n) ♣ pine (tree); pine(wood)
'**Kie·fer|bruch** *m* fractured jaw; **~chir·ur,gie** *f* oral surgery; **~höh·le** *f* (maxillary) sinus; **~höh·len·ent·zün·dung** *f* (maxillary) sinusitis; **~klem·me** *f* lockjaw; **~kno·chen** *m* jawbone
'**Kie·fern|holz** *n* pine(wood); **~na·del** *f* pine needle; **~öl** *n* pine oil; **~wald** *m* pinewood; **~zap·fen** *m* pine cone
'**Kie·fer|or·tho,pä·de** *m* orthodontist; **~or·tho·pä,die** *f* orthodontics *pl.*
kie·ken ['ki:kən] F *dial. v/i.* (h) → ***guk·ken***; **Kie·ker** ['ki:kɐ] *m*: F ***j-n auf dem ~ haben*** a) have one's eye on s.o., b) F have it in for s.o.
Kiel [ki:l] *m* (-[e]s; -e) **1.** ⚓, ✈ keel; ***auf ~ legen*** lay down *a ship*; **2.** quill; **~flos·se** *f* ✈ tail fin; **~li·nie** *f* **1.** line ahead; **2.** ⚓ keel line; ♀'**oben** *adj.* bottom up; **~raum** *m* bilge; **~was·ser** *n* wake; ***im ~ fahren*** *a. fig.* follow in the wake (*gen.* of)
Kie·me ['ki:mə] *f* (-; -n) *zo.* gill
'**Kie·men|at·mung** *f* gill breathing; **~deckel** *m* gill cover; **~spal·te** *f* gill slit
Kien [ki:n] *m* (-[e]s; *no pl.*) resinous (pine)wood; **~ap·fel** *m* pine cone; **~span** *m* pine(wood) chip; **~zap·fen** *m* pine cone
Kie·pe ['ki:pə] *f* (-; -n) pannier
Kies [ki:s] *m* (-es; *no pl.*) **1.** gravel; grit; ***grober ~*** shingle; **2.** *min.* pyrite; **3.** F lolly; **~be,ton** *m* gravel concrete; **~bo·den** *m* gravelly soil
Kie·sel ['ki:zəl] *m* (-s; -) pebble; **~al·ge** *f* diatom; **~er·de** *f* silica; ♀**sau·er** *adj.* siliceous; **~säu·re** *f* silicic acid; **~stein** *m* pebble
'**Kies·gru·be** *f* gravel pit
kie·sig ['ki:zɪç] *adj.* gravelly
'**Kies|strand** *m* shingle beach; **~weg** *m* gravel path
Kiez [ki:ts] *m* (-es; -e) **1.** area, quarter; **2.** *sl.* red-light district
kif·fen ['kɪfən] *sl. v/i.* (h) F smoke pot
ki·ke·ri·ki [kikəri'ki:] *int.*, ♀ *n* (-s; -s) cock-a-doodle-doo
kil·le·kil·le ['kɪlə'kɪlə] F *int.* tickle-tickle
kil·len ['kɪlən] F *v/t.* (h) F bump off
Kil·ler ['kɪlɐ] F *m* (-s; -) F hit man, killer, hatchet man; **~kom,man·do** F *n* F hit squad; **~sa·tel,lit** F *m* (hunter-)killer satellite
Ki·lo ['ki:lo] *n* (-s; -[s]) kilogram(me)
Ki·lo|'byte [kilo-] *n* kilobyte; **~'gramm** *n* kilogram(me); **~'hertz** *n* kilocycle (per second), kilohertz; **~ka·lo'rie** *f* kilocalorie
Ki·lo'me·ter [kilo-] *m* (-s; -) kilomet|re (*Am.* -er); ***60 ~ (in der Stunde) fahren*** do 60 kilomet|res (*Am.* -ers); **~fres·ser** F *m* (-s; -) F speed merchant; **~geld** *n* mileage allowance; ♀**lang I.** *adj.* stretching for miles, miles (and miles) of ...; **II.** *adv.* for miles (and miles); **~pau,scha·le** *f* flat mileage rate; **~stand** *m mot.* mileage (reading); **~stein** *m* milestone; ♀**weit** *adj.* → ***kilometerlang***; **~zahl** *f mot.* mileage; **~zäh·ler** *m* mileometer, mileage indicator
Ki·lo|'ohm [kilo-] *n* kilohm, *a* thousand ohms *pl.*; **~pond** [-'pɔnt] *n* kilogram(me) weight; **~'ton·ne** *f* kiloton
Ki·lo·volt [kilo'vɔlt] *n* kilovolt; **Ki·lo·volt·am·pere** [kilovɔlt'ʔam'pɛ:ɐ] *n* kilovolt-ampere
Ki·lo·watt [kilo'vat] *n* kilowatt; **~stun·de** *f* kilowatt hour
Kilt [kɪlt] *m* (-[e]s; -s) kilt
Kim·ber ['kɪmbɐ] *m* (-s; -n) *hist.* Cimbrian; ***die ~n*** the Cimbri; **kim·brisch** ['kɪmbrɪʃ] *adj.* Cimbrian
Kimm [kɪm] *f* (-; *no pl.*) ⚓ **1.** visual horizon; **2.** bilge
Kim·me ['kɪmə] *f* (-; -n) notch
Ki·mo·no ['ki:mono] *m* (-s; -s) kimono
Kind [kɪnt] *n* (-[e]s; -er ['kɪndɐ]) child; baby; *fig.* product; ***sie ist kein ~ mehr*** she's not a little kid any more; ***ein großes ~*** a big baby; ***ein ~ bekommen*** (*or* ***erwarten***) be pregnant, be expecting a baby; ***von ~ auf*** (ever) since I was (*or* you were *etc.*) a child; ***das ist nichts für kleine ~er*** you're too young for that; ***~er, ~er!*** my goodness!; ***eure ~er und Kindeskinder*** your children and children's children; ***das weiß doch jedes ~!*** any child knows that; ***(ein) gebranntes ~ scheut das Feuer*** once bitten, twice shy; F *fig.* ***wie sag ich's m-m ~e?*** a) how shall I put it now?, b) how am I going to put it to him (*or* her)?; F ***wir werden das ~ schon schaukeln*** we'll work it out (somehow); ***das ~ mit dem Bade ausschütten*** throw the baby out with the bathwater; ***ein Berliner ~*** a Berliner born and bred; ***sich lieb ~ machen bei j-m*** try to get into s.o.'s good books; ***sie sind mit ~ und Kegel losgezogen*** the whole clan went off; ***das ~ beim rechten Namen nennen*** call a spade a spade; ***~er, hört mal!*** listen (to this), folks
'**Kind·bett** *n* (-[e]s; *no pl.*) childbed; ***im ~ liegen*** be lying in; ***im ~ sterben*** die in childbed; **~fie·ber** *n* childbed (*or* puerperal) fever
'**Kind·chen** *n* (-s; -) small child; *iro.* ***aber ~!*** my dear child!
Kin·der|ar·beit ['kɪndɐ-] *f* (-; *no pl.*) child employment *or* labo(u)r; **~arzt** *m*, **~ärz·tin** *f* p(a)ediatrician; **~bett** *n* cot, *Am.* crib; **~buch** *n* children's book; **~chor** *m* children's choir; **~dorf** *n* children's village; → ***SOS-Kinderdorf***; **~er·mä·ßi·gung** *f* reduction for children, children's rate; **~er·zie·hung** *f* bringing up children; **~fahr·rad** *n* children's bicycle; ♀**feind·lich** *adj.*: ***~ sein*** hate children; **~fern·se·hen** *n* children's TV (program[me]s *pl.*); **~fest** *n* children's party; **~film** *m* children's film; **~frau** *f* child minder; **~frei·be·trag** *m* child allowance; **~freund** *m*: ***ein ~ sein*** be very fond of children; ♀**freund·lich** *adj.* very fond of children; *surroundings etc.* suitable for children; ***ein ~es Hotel*** *etc.* a hotel *etc.* that welcomes children; **~funk** *m* children's TV (*or* radio); **~gar·ten** *m* kindergarten; **~gärt·ne·rin** *f* kindergarten teacher; **~geld** *n* child benefit, *Brit. a.* children's allowance; **~ge·sicht** *n* child's face; *w.s.* babyface; **~got·tes·dienst** *m* children's service; **~heil·kun·de** *f* p(a)ediatrics *pl.*; **~heim** *n* children's home; **~hort** *m* after-school care cent|re (*Am.* -er); **~ka·rus,sell** *n* roundabout, merry-go-round, *Am.* car(r)ousel; **~klei·dung** *f* children's wear; **~kli·nik** *f* children's hospital; **~krank·heit** *f* ⚕ children's illness; *fig.* **~en** teething troubles; **~krebs** *m* childhood cancer; **~krie·gen** *n*: F ***es ist zum ~*** it's enough to drive you up the wall; **~krip·pe** *f* crèche, day nursery; **~la·den** *m* **1.** children's shop; **2.** (antiauthoritarian) playgroup; **~läh·mung** *f* ⚕ polio, 📖 poliomyelitis
'**kin·der|'leicht** *adj.* really (F dead) easy; ***es ist ~*** *a.* it's a pushover (F cinch); **~lieb** *adj.* very fond of children
'**Kin·der·lied** *n* children's song; *n.s.* nursery rhyme
kin·der·los ['kɪndɐlo:s] *adj.* childless
'**Kin·der·lo·sig·keit** *f* (-; *no pl.*) childlessness; inability to have children
Kin·der|mäd·chen ['kɪndɐ-] *n* nanny; **~mo·de** *f* children's fashions *pl.*; children's wear; **~mord** *m* child murder; ⚖ infanticide; *bibl.* ***der ~ zu Bethlehem*** the massacre of the innocents; **~mör·der** *m* child murderer; **~mund** *fig. m* (-[e]s; *no pl.*) things *pl.* children say; ***~ tut Wahrheit kund*** out of the mouths of babes and sucklings; **~nah·rung** *f* baby food; **~narr** *m*: ***ein ~ sein*** F be crazy about children, go potty over children; **~pfle·ge·rin** *f* children's nurse; **~po,po** F *m*: ***glatt wie ein ~*** (as) smooth as a baby's bottom; **~psy·cho,lo·ge** *m* child psychologist; **~pu·der** *m* baby powder; ♀**reich** *adj.*: ***~e Familie*** large family; **~reim** *m* nursery rhyme; **~schreck** *m* (-[e]s; *no pl.*) bogeyman; **~schu·he** *pl.* children's shoes; *fig.* *das Unternehmen* ***steckt noch in den ~n*** is still in its infancy; ***er steckt politisch*** *etc.* ***noch in den ~n*** he's still in his political *etc.* nappies; **~schutz·bund** *m* child welfare association; **~schwe·ster** *f* children's nurse; **~sen·dung** *f* children's program(me); ♀**si·cher** *adj.* childproof; **~si·che·rung** *f* child lock; **~sitz** *m* child seat; **~spiel** *n* **1.** children's game; **2.** *fig.* pushover; ***das ist für ihn ein ~*** *a.* that's child's play for him; **~spiel·platz** *m* children's playground; **~spiel·zeug** *n* (children's) toys *pl.*; **~spra·che** *f* a) children's language, b) baby talk; **~star** *m* child star; **~sta·ti,on** *f* children's ward, p(a)ediatric ward; **~sterb·lich·keit** *f* child (*or* infant) mortality; **~stu·be** *fig. f* upbringing; ***er hat keine (e-e gute) ~*** he's got no manners (he's been brought up well); **~stun·de** *f TV* children's program(me); **~ta·ges·stät·te** *f* day nursery, day care cent|re (*Am.* -er); **~tel·ler** *m* children's portion; **~wa·gen** *m* pram, *Am.* baby carriage; **~zim·mer** *n* children's room; playroom; **~zu·schuß** *m* child benefit
Kin·des|al·ter ['kɪndəs-] *n* childhood; infancy; **~aus·set·zung** *f* abandoning of a child (*or* of children); **~bei·ne** *pl.*: ***von ~n an*** from childhood; **~ent·füh·rung** *f* child kidnapping; **~kind** *n* → ***Kind***; **~miß,hand·lung** *f* child abuse; **~mord** *m* infanticide; **~mör·der** *m* child murderer; **~mut·ter** *f* child's mother; **~tö·tung** *f* infanticide; **~va·ter** *m* child's father

'Kind·frau *f* **1.** nymphet; **2.** ***sie ist e-e*** ~ she's like a young girl

'kind|ge·mäß I. *adj.* suitable for children (*or* a child); **II.** *adv.*: ***et.*** ~ ***ausdrücken*** express s.th. in children's terms; **~ge·recht** *adj.* suitable for children (*or* a child)

'Kind·heit *f* (-; -en) childhood; infancy; ***von*** ~ ***an*** from childhood

'Kind·heits|er·in·ne·rung *f* childhood memory; **~er·leb·nis** *n* childhood experience

kin·disch ['kındıʃ] *adj.* childish

'kind·lich *adj.* childish; childlike; innocent; naive

'Kinds|kopf *m*: F ***er ist ein richtiger*** ~ he's just like a little boy; **~la·ge** *f* ⚕ presentation; **~tau·fe** *f* christening, baptism; **~tod** *m*: ***plötzlicher*** ~ cot death, 🕮 sudden infant death syndrome, F Sids

Ki·ne·ma·thek [kinema'teːk] *f* (-; -en) film library

Ki·ne·ma·to·gra·phie [kinematogra'fiː] *f* (-; *no pl.*) cinematography

ki·ne·ma·to·gra·phisch [kinemato'graːfıʃ] *adj.* cinematographic(ally *adv.*)

Ki·ne·tik [ki'neːtık] *f* (-; *no pl.*) *phys.* kinetics *pl.*; **ki·ne·tisch** [ki'neːtıʃ] *adj.* kinetic(ally *adv.*)

King [kıŋ] F *m* (-s; -s) F top dog

Kin·ker·litz·chen ['kıŋkɐlıtsçən] F *pl.* **1.** odds and ends; **2.** F monkey business *sg.*

Kinn [kın] *n* (-[e]s; -e) chin; **~backe** *f*, **~backen** *m* jaw; **~bart** *m* goatee; **~ha·ken** *m* left (*or* right) hook; **~la·de** *f* jaw; ***er ließ die*** ~ ***fallen*** his jaw dropped; **~rie·men** *m* chinstrap; **~stüt·ze** *f* ♪ *etc.* chin rest

Ki·no ['kiːno] *n* (-s; -s) **1.** cinema, *Am.* movie theater; ***ins*** ~ ***gehen*** go to the cinema (*Am.* movies), go and see a film (*Am.* movie); **2.** *no pl.* cinema, *esp. Am. the* movies *pl.*; *w.s. the* screen; **~be·su·cher** *m* cinemagoer, *Am.* moviegoer; **~film** *m* (cinema) film; **~hit** *m* film hit; **~pro'gramm** *n* cinema program(me); **~pub·li·kum** *n* cinema audience(s *pl.*); **~re'kla·me** *f* **1.** cinema (*or* screen) advertising; **2.** film publicity

Kin·topp ['kiːntɔp] F *m* (-s; *no pl.*) *the* movies *pl.*

Ki·osk ['kiːɔsk, kĭɔsk] *m* (-[e]s; -e) kiosk; *a.* newsstand

kipp·bar ['kıp-] *adj.* tiltable, hinged

'Kipp|be·we·gung *f* tipping movement; **~büh·ne** *f* tilting stage

Kip·pe ['kıpə] *f* (-; -n) **1.** F cigarette butt (*or* end), F fag end; **2.** ***er*** (***die Firma***) ***steht auf der*** ~ it's touch and go with him (the company's on the verge of bankruptcy); **3.** (*rubbish*) dump

kip·pe·lig ['kıpəlıç] F *adj.* wobbly

kip·peln ['kıpəln] F *v/i.* (h) **1.** *chair etc.*: be wobbly; **2.** go back on one's chair

kip·pen ['kıpən] **I.** *v/i.* (sn) tip over; *boat*: capsize; → ***Latsche²***; **II.** *v/t.* (h) a) tip up; tilt *window*, b) tip, pour *water etc.* (***aus*** *dat.* out of); ***nicht*** ~***!*** (please) do not tilt; F ***einen*** ~ F have a quick one

Kip·per ['kıpɐ] *m* (-s; -) **1.** ⚙ dumper; **2.** → ***Kippwagen***

'Kipp|fen·ster *n* tilting window; **~he·bel** *m* tilting lever; **~schal·ter** *m* toggle switch; **~schal·tung** *f* ⚡ trigger circuit; **&si·cher** *adj.* stable; **~vor·rich·tung** *f* tipping device; **~wa·gen** *m mot.* tipper lorry, *a. Am.* dump truck

Kir·che ['kırçə] *f* (-; -n) **1.** ⛪ church; *fig.* ***wir wollen die*** ~ ***im Dorf lassen*** let's not get carried away; **2.** *no pl.* (church) service; ***in der*** ~ at church; ***in die*** (*or* ***zur***) ~ ***gehen*** go to church

Kir·chen|äl·te·ste ['kırçən-] *m* (-n; -n) elder; **~amt** *n* church office; **~bank** *f* (-; ⸚e) pew; **~bann** *m* excommunication; **~be·such** *m* **1.** church attendance; **2.** → ***Kirchgang***; **~be·su·cher** *m* churchgoer; **~buch** *n* parish register; **~chor** *m* (church) choir; **~die·ner** *m* sexton; **&feind·lich** *adj.* anticlerical; **~fen·ster** *n* church window; **~füh·rer** *m* church leader; **~funk** *m* religious broadcasting; **~fürst** *m* church dignitary; **~ge·mein·de** *f* a) parish, b) congregation; **~ge·schich·te** *f* church history; **~ge·stühl** *n* pews *pl.*; **~glocke** *f* church bell; **~jahr** *n* ecclesiastical year; **~ka'len·der** *m* ecclesiastical calendar; **~kampf** *m* struggle between church and state; **~kon'zert** *n* church concert; **~la'tein** *n* Church Latin; **~leh·re** *f* church doctrine; **~lied** *n* hymn; **~mann** *m* (-[e]s; ⸚er) churchman; **~maus** *f*: *fig.* ***arm wie e-e*** ~ (as) poor as a church mouse; **~mu'sik** *f* sacred (*or* church) music; **~po·li'tik** *f* church policy; **~raub** *m* theft from a church (*or* churches); ***er wurde wegen*** **~*s*** ***verurteilt*** he was sentenced for stealing from a church; **~recht** *n* canon law; **&recht·lich** *adj.* canonical; **~schän·dung** *f* sacrilege; **~schiff** *n* nave; **~spal·tung** *f* schism; **~staat** *m* **1.** *hist.* Papal States *pl.*; **2.** *the* Vatican City; **~steu·er** *f* church tax; **~tag** *m* church congress; **~ton·art** *f* church mode; **~va·ter** *m hist.* church father; ***die Kirchenväter*** the Early Fathers (of the Church); **~vor·stand** *m* parish council

'Kirch·gang *m*: ***der*** ~ ***am Sonntag war Familientradition*** (***Pflicht***) going to church on Sundays was a family tradition (we had to go to church on Sundays)

'Kirch·gän·ger [-gɛŋɐ] *m* (-s; -) churchgoer

'Kirch·hof *m* churchyard

'Kirch·hofs|frie·den *fig. m* uneasy peace; **~ru·he** *f* **1.** peace of the graveyard; *fig.* ***es herrschte e-e*** ~ it was silent as the grave; **2.** → ***Kirchhofsfrieden***

'kirch·lich I. *adj.* church *wedding etc.*; ecclesiastical; clerical; religious, devout; **II.** *adv.*: ***sich*** ~ ***trauen lassen*** have a church wedding

'Kirch·turm *m* (church) steeple, spire; church tower; **~po·li'tik** *f* parish-pump politics *pl.*; **~spit·ze** *f* (top of a) church spire; **~uhr** *f* church clock

Kirch·weih ['kırçvai] *f* (-; -en) (parish) fair

'Kirch·wei·he *f* consecration of a church

Kir·mes ['kırmɛs] *f* (-; -sen) fair

kir·re ['kırə] F *adj.* (*a.* ~ ***machen***) tame

Kirsch [kırʃ] *m* (-[e]s; -) kirsch; **~baum** *m* a) cherry tree, b) cherrywood; **~blü·te** *f* cherry blossom

Kir·sche ['kırʃə] *f* (-; -n) cherry; ***saure*** ~ sour cherry, morello; *fig.* ***mit ihm ist nicht gut*** **~*n*** ***essen*** F he's a tough customer

Kirsch|kern ['kırʃ-] *m* cherry stone; **~li'kör** *m* cherry brandy; **&rot** *adj.*, **~rot** *n* cherry(-red), cerise; **~saft** *m* cherry juice; **~tor·te** *f* cherry gateau; **~was·ser** *n* kirsch

Kis·sen ['kısən] *n* (-s; -) cushion; pillow; **~be·zug** *m*, **~hül·le** *f* cushion cover; pillowcase, pillowslip; **~schlacht** *f* pillow fight

Ki·ste ['kıstə] *f* (-; -n) **1.** box; chest; ✝ case; crate; **2.** F *mot.*, ✈ F crate; ***alte*** ~ F old banger; **3.** F business, job; ***faule*** ~ fishy business; **'ki·sten·wei·se** *adv.* in crates; by the crate

Kitsch [kıtʃ] *m* (-es; *no pl.*) kitsch; trash, junk; **kit·schig** ['kıtʃıç] *adj.* kitschy; trashy; **'Kitsch·ro'man** *m* trashy novel

Kitt [kıt] *m* (-[e]s; *no pl.*) putty; (sealing) cement; filling compound

Kitt·chen ['kıtçən] F *n* (-s; -) F clink, jug, *Am.* F slammer; ***im*** ~ ***sitzen*** be in clink (*or* jug), *Am.* be in the slammer

Kit·tel ['kıtəl] *m* (-s; -) overall, *Am.* workcoat, (white) coat; smock; **~schür·ze** *f* overall

kit·ten ['kıtən] *v/t.* (h) cement; putty; *w.s.* glue together; F *fig.* patch up

Kitz [kıts] *n* (-es; -e), **Kit·ze** ['kıtsə] *f* (-; -n) kid; fawn

Kit·zel ['kıtsəl] *m* (-s; -) tickle, tickling; *fig.* thrill, F kick; F itch (***nach*** *dat.* for)

kit·zeln ['kıtsəln] *v/t. and v/i.* (h) tickle (*a. fig.*); ***mich kitzelt's am Fuß*** (***im Hals***) my foot's tickling (I've got a tickle in my throat); *fig.* ***es kitzelte ihn zu*** *inf.* he was itching to *inf.*

Kitz·ler ['kıtslɐ] *m* (-s; -) *anat.* clitoris

kitz·lig ['kıtslıç] *adj.* ticklish (*a. fig.*)

Ki·wi¹ ['kiːvi] *m* (-s; -s) *zo.* kiwi

'Ki·wi² *f* (-; -s) kiwifruit

Kla·bau·ter·mann [kla'bautɐman] *m* (-[e]s; ⸚er) hobgoblin

Klacks [klaks] F *m* (-es; -e) F blob; *gastr.* (small) dollop; *fig.* ***das ist doch nur ein*** ~ that's nothing

Klad·de ['kladə] *f* (-; -n) **1.** (rough) notebook; (scribbling) pad; ✝ waste book; **2.** rough draft

klad·de·ra·datsch [kladəra'datʃ] F **I.** *int.* bang!; **II.** & *m* (-[e]s; -e) crash (*a.* ✝); *fig.* mess; scandal, F to-do

klaf·fen ['klafən] *v/i.* (h) *abyss, wound, dress etc.*: gape

kläf·fen ['klɛfən] *v/i.* (h) yap, yelp; F *fig.* F whinge; **Kläf·fer** ['klɛfɐ] *m* (-s; -) yelper, F noisy little critter; F *fig.* F whinger

klag·bar ['klaːkbaːɐ] *adj.* ⚖ actionable; suable *claim*

Kla·ge ['klaːgə] *f* (-; -n) **1.** complaint; lament; **2.** complaint; (***keinen***) ***Grund zur*** ~ ***haben*** have (no) cause for complaint; **3.** ⚖ suit, action; ~ ***erheben gegen*** *acc.* file a suit against, sue (***wegen*** *gen.* for); **~ab·wei·sung** *f* ⚖ dismissal of action; **~er·he·bung** *f* ⚖ filing of an action; **~ge·schrei** *n* wailing; **~grund** *m* ⚖ cause of action; **~laut** *m* moan; **~lied** *n* dirge; *fig.* lamentation; *fig.* ***ein*** ~ ***anstimmen*** set up a wail; → ***Jeremia***; **~mau·er** *f*: ***die*** ~ the Wailing Wall

kla·gen ['klaːgən] (h) **I.** *v/i.* **1.** complain (***über*** *acc.* about, of; ***bei*** *dat.* to); wail, lament; ~ ***über*** *acc.* complain of; **2.** ⚖ bring an action (***gegen*** *acc.* against; ***auf*** *acc.*, ***wegen*** *gen.* for), go to court (***auf*** *acc.*, ***wegen*** *gen.* about), sue (for); **II.** *v/t.*: ***j-m sein Leid*** ~ pour one's heart out to s.o.; **'kla·gend** *adj.*: ⚖ ***der*** **~*e*** ***Teil*** the plaintiff(s *pl.*)

Klä·ger ['klɛːgɐ] *m* (-s; -), **Klä·ge·rin** ['klɛːgərın] *f* (-; -nen) ⚖ plaintiff; complainant; petitioner

'Kla'ge|schrift *f* ⚖ statement of claim; **~weg** *m* ⚖ litigation; ***auf dem*** ~ by

taking legal action; **~weib** *n* professional mourner
kläg·lich ['klɛːklɪç] **I.** *adj.* pitiful *look etc.*; *a.* miserable, wretched *existence, situation etc.*; **II.** *adv.*: **~ versagen** fail miserably; **~ weinen** cry pitifully, F howl; **der Gewinn ist ~ ausgefallen** we *etc.* made a pittance
klag·los ['klaːkloːs] *adv.* without complaining
Kla·mauk [kla'maʊk] F *m* (-s; *no pl.*) **1.** a) F row, racket, b) F to-do; **2.** *thea.* slapstick
klamm [klam] *adj.* clammy; numb
Klamm *f* (-; -en) *geol.* gorge
Klam·mer ['klamɐ] *f* a) clip, staple, b) peg, c) ⚕ clip; brace, d) ⚙ clamp, e) *typ.* bracket, *a. Am.* parenthesis; **eckige ~** square bracket, *Am.* bracket; **~ auf (zu)** open (close) brackets (*Am.* parentheses); **~af·fe** *m zo.* spider monkey; *fig.* **er ist ein ~** he's like a leech; **~beu·tel** *m* peg bag; F *fig.* **mit dem ~ gepudert sein** F be off one's head; **~griff** *m* (tight) grip
klam·mern ['klamɐn] (h) **I.** *v/t.* clip, attach (**an** *acc.* to); **II.** *v/refl.*: **sich ~ an** *acc. a. fig.* cling to; **III.** *v/i. boxing*: clinch
'klamm'heim·lich F *adv.* F on the quiet
Kla·mot·te [kla'mɔtə] F *f* (-; -n) **1.** *pl.* F things, *sl.* gear, clobber; **2.** *pl.* F things, stuff; **3.** F oldie; **Kla'mot·ten·ki·ste** *f*: F *fig.* **das hast du wohl aus der ~** F where did you dig that up?
Klam·pe ['klampə] *f* (-; -n) ⚓ cleat; chock
Klamp·fe ['klampfə] F *f* (-; -n) guitar
klang [klaŋ] *pret. of* **klingen**
Klang [klaŋ] *m* (-[e]s; Klänge ['klɛŋə]) a) sound, clinking *of glasses etc.*, tinkling, chinking *of coins etc.*, clanking *of metal*, b) tone, c) timbre, d) resonance, e) *fig.* ring; ♪ **Klänge** strains, sounds; **zu den Klängen von** *dat.* to the sound (*or* strains) of; *fig.* **sein Name hat e-n guten ~** he's got a good reputation; **~bild** *n* sound; **~ef,fekt** *m* (sound) effect; **~farbe** *f* timbre; **~fi,gu·ren** *pl.* sound figures; **~fül·le** *f* sonority; **~kör·per** *m* orchestra; **~leh·re** *f* acoustics *pl.*
'klang·lich *adj.* tonal, tone ...; sound ...
'klang·los *adj.* toneless; → **sang- und ~**
'Klang|reg·ler *m* tone control; **≈rein** *adj.*: **~ sein** have a pure sound (*or* tone); **~spek·trum** *n* range of sound(s); **≈voll** *adj.* sonorous; melodious; *fig.* illustrious; **~wel·le** *f* sound wave; **~,wie·der·ga·be** *f* sound reproduction
Klapp|bett ['klap-] *n* folding bed; **~brücke** *f* bascule bridge; **~deckel** *m* hinged lid
Klap·pe ['klapə] *f* (-;-n) a) flap, leaf *of table*, b) lid; ⚙ shutter, c) *mot.* tailboard, drop side, d) ⚙ flap valve; ♪ key, e) *film*: clapper board(s *pl.*), f) ⚕, *zo.* valve, g) F mouth, *sl.* trap; **die ~ fällt am ...** *film*: shooting starts on (the) ...; **nach der letzten ~** *film*: when shooting finishes (*or* finished); F **bei mir ist die ~ runtergegangen** I don't want to hear any more about it; F **~ zu, Affe tot!** (thank goodness) that's the end of that; F **halt die ~!** F shut up; F **(immer) die ~ aufreißen, e-e große ~ haben** have a big mouth; F **in die ~ gehen** F hit the sack (*esp. Am.* hay)
klap·pen ['klapən] (h) **I.** *v/t.* **1.** fold; **der Sitz läßt sich nach hinten ~** the seat folds back; **II.** *v/i.* **2.** *door etc.*: click; **3.** F work; go off well; **es klappt nicht** it won't work; **wenn alles klappt** if all goes well; **(es) wird schon ~!** it'll work out all right (*Am.* alright)
'Klap·pen|feh·ler *m* ⚕ valvular defect; **~text** *m* blurb
Klap·per ['klapɐ] *f* (-; -n) rattle; ♪, *R.C.* clapper; **≈dürr** F *adj.*: **~ sein** F be a bag of bones; **~ge·stell** F *n* **1.** F bag of bones; **2.** → **Klapperkasten**
klap·pe·rig ['klapərɪç] *adj.* → **klapprig**
'Klap·per|ka·sten F *m*, **~ki·ste** F *f mot.* F old banger, boneshaker; ✈ F crate
klap·pern ['klapɐn] **I.** *v/i.* (h) (*a.* **mit et. ~**) rattle; clatter (*a. zo.*); *heels*: clip-clop; *knitting needles*: click; **er klapperte (vor Kälte) mit den Zähnen** his teeth were chattering (with cold); **II. ≈** *n* (-s) rattling, rattle, clatter(ing); **~ gehört zum Handwerk** puff is part of the trade
'Klap·per|schlan·ge *f zo.* rattlesnake; **~storch** *m* stork; **er glaubt noch an den ~** he doesn't know about the birds and the bees yet, *iro.* he still thinks the earth is flat
Klapp|hut ['klap-] *m* crush hat, opera hat; **~mes·ser** *n* jack-knife; **~rad** *n* folding bicycle
klapp·rig ['klaprɪç] *adj.* shaky, F doddery; rickety *chair etc.*
Klapp|sitz ['klap-] *m* jump (*or* folding) seat; **~stuhl** *m* folding chair; **~tisch** *m* folding table; drop-leaf table; ✈ *etc.* foldaway table; **~ven,til** *n* flap valve; **~ver·deck** *n mot.* folding hood (*Am.* top)
Klaps [klaps] *m* (-es; -e) **1.** smack; **2.** F **e-n ~ haben** F have a screw loose; **~müh·le** F *f* F funny farm, nut-house, *Am. a.* F booby hatch
klar [klaːɐ] **I.** *adj.* **1.** clear (*a. gastr., a. fig. sky, voice etc.*); colo(u)rless, white *schnapps*; **~er Blick** open, honest look; **2.** clear; plain; **bei ~em Bewußtsein sein** be fully conscious, know (exactly) what's going on; **~er Augenblick** lucid moment; **er hat e-n ~en Blick** he knows what he's doing; **e-n ~en Kopf behalten** keep a clear head, keep one's wits about one; **sie ist ein ~er Kopf** F she's got her head screwed on the right way; **3.** a) clear(-cut), definite *decision etc.*, b) clear, straight; **~e Verhältnisse schaffen** get things straight; **zwischen ihnen ist alles ~** they've settled everything; **4.** *sport etc.*: clear *victory etc.*; **5. es ist ~, daß** it's obvious that; **es ist mir ~, daß, ich bin mir darüber ~, daß** I realize that; **es ist mir nur zu ~, daß** I'm only too well aware that; **ich bin mir noch nicht ~ (darüber), was ich tun soll** I'm not quite sure what to do; **ist das ~?** is that clear?, have you got that straight?; F **(na) ~!** of course, oh yes; **sich über e-e Sache im ~en sein** realize s.th., be aware of s.th.; → **Kloßbrühe; 6.** ⚓, ✈ clear, ready; **~ zum Gefecht** ready for action, clear the decks; **II.** *adv.* clearly; **~ und deutlich** quite clearly; **~ zutage treten** be obvious; **er brachte es ~ zum Ausdruck, daß** he made it quite clear that
Klär|an·la·ge ['klɛːɐ-] *f* sewage (*or* water treatment) plant; **~becken** *n* clearing tank
'klar|blickend *adj.* clear-sighted; **~denkend** *adj.* clear-thinking
Kla·re ['klaːrə] F *m* (-n; -n) schnapps
klä·ren ['klɛːrən] (h) **I.** *v/t.* **1.** purify; **2.** clear up, clarify *a matter etc.*; **II.** *v/i.* **3.** *sport*: clear; **III.** *v/refl.*: **sich ~ 4.** *sky etc.*: clear (up); **5.** *question*: be settled; *problem*: be solved
'klar·ge·hen F *v/i.* (*irr., sep.*, sn, → **gehen**): **(es) geht klar!** F it's okay
Klär·gru·be ['klɛːɐ-] *f* cesspit
'Klar·heit *f* (-; *no pl.*) a) brightness, b) transparency; *fig.* clarity, lucidity; **~ gewinnen, sich ~ verschaffen** get things straight (**über** *acc.* concerning)
kla·rie·ren [kla'riːrən] *v/t.* (h) ⚓ clear; **Kla'rie·rung** *f* (-; -en) clearance
Kla·ri·net·te [klari'nɛtə] *f* (-; -n) clarinet
Kla·ri·net·tist [klarinɛ'tɪst] *m* (-en; -en) clarinettist
'klar|kom·men F *v/i.* (*irr., sep.*, sn, → **kommen**) manage (**mit** *dat. s.th.*); **~ (mit** *dat.*) understand; **mit j-m ~** get along with s.o.; **~krie·gen** F *v/t.* (*sep.*, h) F sort *it* out; **~le·gen** *v/t.* (*sep.*, h): **j-m et. ~** explain s.th. to s.o.; **~ma·chen** *v/t.* (*sep.*, h) **1. j-m et. ~** make s.th. clear to s.o., explain s.th. to s.o.; **sich et. ~** get s.th. straight in one's (own) mind; **2.** ⚓ *etc.* (*a. v/i.*) clear, get ready (**zu** *dat.* for)
Klär|mit·tel ['klɛːɐ-] *n* clarifier; **~schlamm** *m* (sewage) sludge
'Klar·schrift·le·ser *m computer*: (optical) character reader
'klar·se·hen F *v/i.* (*irr., sep.*, h, → **sehen**) see the light
'Klar·sicht|fo·lie *f* cling film, *Am.* plastic wrap; **~hül·le** *f* plastic cover (*or* wallet); **~packung** *f* transparent pack
'Klar|spü·ler *m*, **~spül·mit·tel** *n* (liquid) rinse
'klar·stel·len *v/t.* (*sep.*, h): **et. ~** get s.th. straight
'Klar·text *m* text in clear; *fig.* **im ~** in plain English; **mit j-m ~ reden** level with s.o., F talk turkey with s.o.
Klä·rung [klɛːrʊŋ] *f* (-; -en) purification; *fig.* clarification
'klar·wer·den *v/i.* (*irr., sep.*, sn, → **werden**) become clear (**j-m** to s.o.); **es wurde mir klar** I realized, it dawned on me; **sich ~ über** *acc.* realize *s.th.*; **sich ~** make up one's mind (**über** *acc.* about)
Klas·se ['klasə] **I.** *f* (-; -n) **1.** *ped.* a) class, *Am. a.* grade; *Brit. in cpds.* form (*e.g.* **zweite ~** second form), b) classroom; **2.** class; ✝ grade, quality; *soccer*: division, league; (*salary, tax etc.*) bracket; **Fahrkarte erster ~** first-class ticket; **erster ~ reisen** travel first-class; **er ist e-e ~ für sich** he's in a class of his own; **II.** F *int. attr., pred.*: **≈(!), (ganz große) ~(!)** F great, fantastic; **~frau** F *f*: **das ist e-e ~** F she's a real smasher
Klas·se·ment [klasə'mɑ̃ː] *n* (-s; -s) *sport*: rankings *pl.*
'Klas·sen|äl·te·ste *m, f* (-n; -n) oldest (pupil) in the class; **~ar·beit** *f* (class) test; **~be·ste** *m, f* (-n; -n): **~(r) sein** be top of the class; **≈be·wußt** *adj.* class-conscious; **~be·wußt·sein** *n* class consciousness; **~buch** *n* register; **~,durch·schnitt** *m* class average; **~feind** *m* class enemy; **~ge·sell·schaft** *f* class society; **~haß** *m* class hatred; **~herr·schaft** *f* class rule; **~ju,stiz** *f* class justice; **~ka·me,rad** *m* classmate; **~kampf** *m* class struggle; **~leh·rer** *m*, **~lei·ter** *m* form teacher (*or* master)
'klas·sen·los *adj.* classless
'Klas·sen|schran·ken *pl.* class barriers; **~spre·cher** *m* form captain, *esp. Am.*

class president; **~tref·fen** *n* class reunion; **~,un·ter·schie·de** *pl.* class differences; **~ziel** *n*: ***das ~ erreichen*** complete the school year successfully, *fig.* make the grade; **~zim·mer** *n* classroom
klas·sie·ren [kla'si:rən] *v/t.* (h) classify
Klas·si·fi·ka·ti·on [klasifika'tsĭo:n] *f* (-; -en) classification; **klas·si·fi·zie·ren** [klasifi'tsi:rən] *v/t.* (h) classify; **Klas·si·fi'zie·rung** *f* (-; -en) classification
Klas·sik ['klasık] *f* (-; *no pl.*) **1.** classical period (*or* age); ***die antike ~*** classical antiquity; ***die deutsche ~*** the classical period of German literature; ♪ ***die Wiener ~*** the Vienna classical period (of music); **2.** classical music
Klas·si·ker ['klasikɐ] *m* (-s; -) **1.** classical author; ***die antiken ~*** the classical authors of antiquity; **2.** *fig.* a) great artist (*or* author *etc.*), b) classic
klas·sisch ['klasıʃ] *adj.* **1.** classical (*a.* ♪); ***~es Werk*** classic; **2.** *fig.* classic (*a. mistake, example etc.*); **3.** classical
Klas·si·zis·mus [klasi'tsısmʊs] *m* (-; *no pl.*) classicism; **Klas·si·zist** [klasi'tsıst] *m* (-en; -en) classicist; **klas·si·zi·stisch** [klasi'tsıstıʃ] *adj.* classicistic
klatsch [klatʃ] *int.* bang!; splat!; splash!
Klatsch *m* (-[e]s; -e) **1.** splat; splash; thud; **2.** *no pl.* gossip; **~ba·se** F *f* (old) gossip; **~blatt** F *n* F gossip sheet
Klat·sche ['klatʃə] *f* (-; -n) **1.** fly swat(ter); **2.** F sneak; **3.** F crib
klat·schen ['klatʃən] (h) **I.** *v/i.* **1.** smack; *rain etc.*: splash; *flag etc.*: flap; **2.** clap; **3.** F *fig.* gossip (***über*** *acc.* about); **II.** *v/t.* **4.** swat *a fly*; **5.** F bang (***auf*** *acc.* on); **6.** ***Beifall ~*** applaud
'**Klatsch·ge·schich·te** *f* piece of gossip
'**klatsch·haft** *adj.* gossipy
'**Klatsch|ko,lum·ne** *f* gossip column; **~ko·lum,nist** *m* gossip columnist; **~maul** F *n* F old gossip; **~mohn** *m* corn poppy; **ℒnaß** *adj.* drenched, soaking (wet), soaked (to the skin); **~spal·te** *f* gossip column; **~tan·te** F *f*, **~weib** F *n* F old gossip
klau·ben ['klaʊbən] *dial. v/t.* (h) a) collect, b) sort out; *fig.* ***Worte ~*** split hairs
Klaue ['klaʊə] *f* (-; -n) **1.** *zo.* claw, talon; paw (*a. fig. contp. hand*); foot; *fig.* ***in j-s ~n geraten*** fall into s.o.'s clutches; ***die ~n des Todes*** the jaws of death; **2.** F scrawl; ***was ist denn das für e-e ~?*** what a dreadful scrawl, it looks as if a spider's been all over this
klau·en ['klaʊən] (h) F **I.** *v/t.* steal, F pinch, snitch, swipe; **II.** *v/i.* steal (things)
'**Klau·en|fuß** *m* claw foot; **~seu·che** *f vet.* foot-and-mouth disease
Klau·se ['klaʊzə] *f* (-; -n) retreat; cell; F den; *geogr.* defile
Klau·sel ['klaʊzəl] *f* (-; -n) ⚖ clause; proviso; stipulation
Klaus·ner ['klaʊsnɐ] *m* (-s; -) hermit, recluse
Klau·stro·pho·bie [klaʊstrofo'bi:] *f* (-; *no pl.*) claustrophobia
Klau·sur [klaʊ'zu:ɐ] *f* (-; -en [-rən]) **1.** *univ.* test, exam; **2.** *eccl.* enclosure; F ***in ~ gehen*** F retreat (from the world); **~ta·gung** *f* closed conference; ***dreitägige ~*** three-day retreat
Kla·via·tur [klavĭa'tu:ɐ] *f* (-; -en) keyboard, keys *pl.*; *organ*: manual
Kla·vi·chord [klavi'kɔrt] *n* (-[e]s; -e [-də]) clavichord
Kla·vier [kla'vi:ɐ] *n* (-s; -e [-'vi:rə]) piano; ***~ spielen*** (***können***) play the piano; **~abend** *m* piano recital; **~aus·zug** *m* piano score; **~bau·er** *m* (-s; -) piano maker; **~be·ar·bei·tung** *f* piano arrangement; **~be·glei·tung** *f* piano accompaniment; **~duo** *n* piano duet; **~hocker** *m* piano stool; **~kon,zert** *n* a) piano concert (*or* recital), b) piano concerto; **~leh·rer** *m* piano teacher; **~mu,sik** *f* piano music; **~quar,tett** *n* piano quartet; **~quin,tett** *n* piano quintet; **~sai·te** *f* piano string; **~schu·le** *f* piano tutor; **~so,na·te** *f* piano sonata; **~spiel** *n* piano playing; **~spie·ler** *m* pianist; **~stim·mer** [-ʃtımɐ] *m* (-s; -) piano tuner; **~stück** *n* piano piece, piece for piano; **~stuhl** *m* piano stool; **~stun·den** *pl.* piano lessons; **~ta·ste** *f* piano key; **~trio** *n* piano trio; **~,un·ter·richt** *m* piano lessons *pl.*; **~ver·leih** *m* piano rental (shop)
Kle·be|band ['kle:bə-] *n* adhesive (*or* sticky) tape; **~bin·dung** *f typ.* perfect binding; **~fo·lie** *f* adhesive foil; **~mit·tel** *n* adhesive
kle·ben ['kle:bən] (h) **I.** *v/i.* **1.** a) stick (***an*** *dat.* to), b) be sticky; *fig.* (***am ganzen Körper***) **~** be hot and sticky; ***m-e Haare ~ vor Schweiß*** my hair's (all) sticky with sweat; ***m-e Schuhe ~ vor Dreck*** my shoes are plastered with mud; *fig.* ***an j-m ~*** cling to s.o. (like a leech), *sport*: mark s.o. very closely; ***an s-m Posten ~*** cling to one's job; ***am Buchstaben ~*** stick to the letter (of the law); ***an j-s Stoßstange ~*** tailgate s.o.('s car), hang on s.o.'s tail; **2.** F *obs.* pay stamps; **II.** *v/t.* glue, stick; splice *film*; F ***j-m e-e ~*** F give s.o. a wallop, land s.o. one; **~blei·ben** *v/i.* (*irr., sep.*, sn, → ***bleiben***) **1.** get stuck (*a. fig.*); stay stuck; *fig.* ***an Einzelheiten ~*** get stuck on details; ***das wird an ihm ~*** he won't be allowed to forget that for a long time to come; **2.** → ***sitzenbleiben***
'**kle·bend** *adj.* adhesive
Kle·be·pfla·ster ['kle:bə-] *n* sticking plaster
Kle·ber ['kle:bɐ] *m* (-s; -) **1.** F glue; **2.** ♀ gluten
Kle·be|stift ['kle:bə-] *m* glue stick; **~strei·fen** *m* **1.** sticky (*or* adhesive) tape; **2.** adhesive strip *on envelope etc.*; **~ver·band** *m* adhesive dressing; **~zet·tel** *m* adhesive label
Kleb·fe·stig·keit ['kle:p-] *f* (-; *no pl.*) adhesive strength, sticking power
kle·brig ['kle:brıç] *adj.* sticky; viscous
Kleb|stel·le ['kle:p-] *f* joint; *film*: splice; **~stoff** *m* glue; paste
Klecker·frit·ze ['klɛkɐfrıtsə] (*sep.* -k·k-) F *m* (-n; -n) F mucky pup
kleckern ['klɛkɐn] (*sep.* -k·k-) F **I.** *v/i.* **1.** (h) make a mess; **2.** (sn) *paint*: drip; **3.** (sn) *fig.* trickle along; **4.** → ***klotzen***; **II.** *v/t.* (h) spill *soup etc.* (***auf*** *acc.* on), drip *ice-cream etc.* (on)
klecker·wei·se ['klɛkɐ-] (*sep.* -k·k-) *adv.* in bits and pieces, *arrive etc.* in dribs and drabs
Klecks [klɛks] *m* (-es; -e) **1.** mark, blotch; **2.** blob; **kleck·sen** ['klɛksən] (h) **I.** *v/i.* make a mess, spill something; *fountain pen*: blot; **II.** *v/t.* splash
Klee [kle:] *m* (-s; *no pl.*) clover; F ***über den grünen ~ loben*** praise to the skies
'**Klee·blatt** *n* **1.** cloverleaf; shamrock (*national emblem of Ireland*); ***vierblättriges ~*** four-leaf(ed) clover; **2.** *fig.* threesome, trio; **3.** cloverleaf junction; **~bo·gen** *m* ⚠ trefoil arch
Kleid [klaıt] *n* (-[e]s; -er ['klaıdɐ]) dress; *pl. coll.* clothes; ***~er machen Leute*** fine feathers make fine birds; **klei·den** ['klaıdən] (h) **I.** *v/t.* dress; ***j-n*** (***gut***) **~** suit s.o.; *fig.* ***in Worte ~*** put into words; **II.** *v/refl.*: ***sich ~*** dress; ***sich modern*** *etc.* **~** wear fashionable *etc.* clothes
Klei·der|ab·la·ge ['klaıdɐ-] *f* coat rack (*or* stand); cloakroom, *Am.* checkroom; **~bad** *n* dry clean(ing); **~bü·gel** *m* (coat) hanger; **~bür·ste** *f* clothes brush; **~ha·ken** *m* coat hook; *pl. coll.* coat rack *sg.*; **~ord·nung** *f* dress regulations *pl.*; **~sack** *m* garment bag; **~schrank** *m* wardrobe; F *fig.* F gorilla, great hulk; **~stän·der** *m* coat stand; ✝ clothes rack
'**kleid·sam** *adj.* flattering
Klei·dung ['klaıdʊŋ] *f* (-; *no pl.*) clothes *pl.*; F *usu. iro.* garb; *lit.* attire; ***warme ~*** warm clothing (*or* clothes); ***komische ~*** strange garb; ***in voller ~*** fully clothed
'**Klei·dungs·stück** *n* piece (*or* article) of clothing; *pl. a.* clothing *sg.*
Kleie ['klaıə] *f* (-; *no pl.*) bran
klein [klaın] **I.** *adj.* a) small, *a.* short; *esp. attr.* little *toe, finger etc.*; tiny, b) *fig.* small *letter etc.*, little, minor *mistake etc.*; short *rest etc.*; brief *interruption etc.*, c) ♪ minor *third etc.*; ***mein ~er Bruder*** my little (*or* younger) brother; ***ein häßlicher ~er Mann*** an ugly little man; ***~er Bauer*** (***Geschäftsmann***) small farmer (businessman); ***es ist ein ~er Anfang*** it's a start; ***als ich noch ~ war*** when I was a little boy (*or* girl); ***er ist doch noch ~*** he's only a (little) child, *to a child*: he's much smaller than you, remember; ***von ~ auf*** from an early age, since childhood, since I was *etc.* a child; ***s-e ~en Launen*** (***Intrigen***) his little moods (intrigues); ***der ~e Mann*** the man in the street; ***~e Leute*** ordinary people; ***da wurde er ganz ~*** that shut him up; ***könnt ihr euch ~ machen?*** can you squeeze up a bit?; ***im ~en*** on a small scale, *n.s.* in miniature; ***bis ins ~ste*** down to the last detail; ***~e Augen haben*** look tired; ***aus ~en Verhältnissen stammen*** come from a humble background; ***und er hat daran kein ~es Verdienst*** and it's no small thanks to him; F ***es ~ haben*** have the right change; **~, *aber fein*** the best things come in small packages; F ***~, aber oho!*** F a mighty midget, a pocket dynamo; → ***Übel***; **II.** *adv.* small; **~ *anfangen*** start off small; **~ *denken*** be small-minded; **~ *schreiben*** write with a small letter
'**Klein|ak·tie** *f* midget share (*Am.* stock); **~ak·tio,när** *m* small shareholder; **~an·zei·gen** *pl.* small (*or* classified) ads; **~ar·beit** *f* finicky work; ***in mühevoller ~*** painstakingly
klein·asia·tisch [-a'zĭa:tıʃ] *adj.* of (*or* from) Asia Minor
'**Klein·bau·er** *m* (-n; -n) small farmer
'**klein·be·kom·men** *v/t.* (*irr., sep.*, h, → ***bekommen***) → ***kleinkriegen***
'**Klein|be·trieb** *m* small business; ***landwirtschaftlicher ~*** smallholding; **~bild·ka·me·ra** *f* 35 mm (= thirty-five millimet|re, *Am.* -er) camera; **~buch·sta·be** *m* small (*typ.* lowercase) letter
'**Klein·bür·ger** *m*, '**klein·bür·ger·lich** *adj.* petty (*or* petit) bourgeois; '**Klein·bür·ger·tum** *n* petty bourgeoisie
'**Klein|bus** *m* minibus, *Am.* passenger van; **~dar·stel·ler** *m* bit player, small part actor

'klein·dre·hen F *v/t.* (*sep.*, h) turn down
Klei·ne'leu·te·mi·li,eu *n* kitchen-sink environment (*or* setting); ***der Film spielt im ~*** it's a kitchen-sink film
Klei·ne ['klaɪnə] *m, f* (-n; -n): ***der*** (***die***) ~ the little boy (girl); F ***m-e ~*** my girl; ***die ~n*** the little ones; ***hallo, ~(r)!*** hello my little girl (lad)!
'Klein|er·zeu·ger *m* small(-scale) producer; **~fa,mi·lie** *f* nuclear family; **~for,mat** *n*: ***... im ~*** small-format ...; **~gärt·ner** *m* allotment gardener; **~ge·bäck** *n* (fancy) biscuits *pl.*, *Am.* cookies *pl.*
'klein|ge·druckt *adj. and adv.* in small print; ***das 2e*** the small print; **~ge·hackt** *adj.* (finely) chopped
'Klein·geld *n* (small) change; ***das nötige ~*** the wherewithal
'klein|ge·mu·stert *adj.* with a small pattern, small-patterned; **~ge·wach·sen** *adj.* small, short
'Klein·ge·wer·be *n* small trade; *coll.* small-scale industries *pl.*
'klein·gläu·big *adj.* of little faith
'klein·hacken *v/t.* (*sep.*, h) chop (up)
'Klein·han·del *m* retail trade
'Klein·han·dels·preis *m* retail price
'Klein·händ·ler *m* retailer
'Klein·heit *f* (-; *no pl.*) smallness
'Klein·hirn *n anat.* cerebellum
'Klein·holz *n* firewood; F *fig.* ***~ machen aus*** *dat.* smash *s.th.* to pieces, F make mincemeat of *s.o.*
Klei·nig·keit ['klaɪnɪçkaɪt] *f* (-; -en) a) little thing; minor detail, b) *a* little something, c) bite; ***das ist e-e ~*** that's nothing; ***es kostet die ~ von zwei Millionen Dollar*** it costs a mere two million dollars; ***e-e ~ zu lang*** a little bit on the long side; ***e-e ~ essen*** have a bite to eat; ***ich habe noch ein paar ~en zu erledigen*** I've still got a few (little) things to see to; ***mußt du bei jeder ~ heulen?*** do you have to cry about every little thing?
'Klei·nig·keits·krä·mer *m* pedant
'Klein·ka,li·ber·ge·wehr *n* small-bore rifle
'klein|ka·li·brig [-ka,li:brɪç] *adj.* small-bore ...; **~ka,riert** *fig. adj.* small-minded
'Klein·kind *n* toddler, small child; *formal*: infant
Klein·kleckers·dorf [-'klɛkɐs-] F *without art.*: ***in ~*** F out in the sticks, at the back of beyond, *Am. a.* in hicksville
'Klein|kli·ma *n* microclimate; **~kram** *m* trivia *pl.*; **~kre,dit** *m* personal loan; **~krieg** *m* guer(r)illa war(fare)
'klein·krie·gen F *v/t.* (*sep.*, h) a) get through *one's money etc.*, b) cut *s.o.* down to size; ***ich lasse mich nicht ~*** I'm not going to let them *etc.* get to me; ***nicht kleinzukriegen sein*** be indestructible, keep bouncing back
'Klein|kunst *f* (-; *no pl.*) minor arts *pl.*; **~kunst·büh·ne** *f* cabaret; **~künst·ler** *m* minor artist
'klein·laut I. *adj.* subdued; ***da wurde er ganz ~*** that shut him up; **II.** *adv.* meekly
'Klein·le·be·we·sen *n* microorganism
'klein·lich *adj.* a) petty, b) pedantic, fussy, c) stingy
'klein·ma·chen *v/t.* (*sep.*, h) a) chop *wood*, b) change *a banknote*, c) get through *one's money etc.*
'Klein·mö·bel *pl.* small pieces of furniture
'Klein·mut *m* (-[e]s; *no pl.*) faint-heartedness; despondency; **'klein·mü·tig** [-my:tɪç] *adj.* faint-hearted; despondent
Klein·od ['klaɪnʔo:t] *n* (-[e]s; -e [-ʔo:də]) *a. fig.* jewel, gem
'klein·schnei·den *v/t.* (*irr.*, *sep.*, h, → ***schneiden***) cut up (into small pieces)
'klein·schrei·ben *v/t.* (*irr.*, *sep.*, h, → ***schreiben***): ***Höflichkeit*** *etc.* ***wird bei ihr kleingeschrieben*** politeness *etc.* is not one of her priorities; **'Klein·schrei,bung** *f* → ***Großschreibung***
'Klein·spa·rer *m* small saver
'Klein·staat *m* small state
Klein·staa·te·rei [-sta:tə'raɪ] *f* (-; *no pl.*) particularism
'Klein·stadt *f* small town; **'Klein·städ·ter** *m* small-towner; **'klein·städ·tisch** *adj.* small-town ..., provincial
'klein·stamp·fen *v/t.* (*sep.*, h) crush
Kleinst·be·trieb ['klaɪnst-] *m* small business, F hole in the wall
'klein·stel·len *v/t.* (*sep.*, h) turn down *the gas etc.*, put on low
'Kleinst|for,mat *n*: ***Radio*** *etc.* ***im ~*** miniature (*or* minute) radio *etc.*; **~kind** *n* baby
'kleinst·mög·lich *adj.* smallest possible
'Klein|tier *n* small (farm) animal; **~trans,por·ter** *m* (pickup) van, *Am.* pickup (truck); **~ver·die·ner** *m* low earner; *pl. coll.* low income bracket *sg.*; **~vieh** *n* small livestock; *fig.* ***~ macht auch Mist*** every little thing (*or* penny *etc.*) counts; **~wa·gen** *m* runabout; **~wild** *n* small game
'Klein·wuchs *m* stunted growth, 🕮 hyposomia; **'klein·wüch·sig** [-vy:ksɪç] *adj.* small
Klei·ster ['klaɪstɐ] *m* (-s; -) paste; F *fig.* F goo; **'klei·stern** *v/t.* (h) paste; F *fig.* ***j-m e-e ~*** F paste s.o. one, give s.o. a clip round the ears
Kle·men·ti·ne [klemɛn'ti:nə] *f* (-; -n) clementine
Klem·me ['klɛmə] *f* (-; -n) **1.** clamp; ⚡ terminal; **2.** F *fig.* ***in der ~ sein*** (*or* ***sitzen***) F be in a fix (*or* tight spot)
klem·men ['klɛmən] (h) **I.** *v/t.* **1.** a) squeeze; wedge, jam (***hinter*** *acc.* behind), b) stick, tuck *under one's arm etc.*; ***sich den Finger ~*** jam one's finger; **2.** F swipe; **II.** *v/i.* be stuck, be jammed; **III.** F *fig. v/refl.*: ***sich ~ hinter*** *acc.* F get cracking on *s.th.*; ***sich hinter die Arbeit ~*** put one's shoulder to the wheel, F get stuck in; ***sich hinter j-n ~*** get to work on s.o.
Klemm|lam·pe ['klɛm-] *f* clamp-on lamp; **~zan·ge** *f* ⚕ blunt forceps
Klemp·ner ['klɛmpnɐ] *m* (-s;-) plumber; **Klemp·ne·rei** [klɛmpnə'raɪ] *f* (-; -en) **1.** *no pl.* plumbing; **2.** plumbing shop
Klep·per ['klɛpɐ] *m* (-s; -) (old) nag
klep·to·man [klɛpto'ma:n] *adj.*, **Klep·to·ma·ne** [klɛpto'ma:nə] *m* (-n; -n), **Klep·to·ma·nin** [klɛpto'ma:nɪn] *f* (-; -nen) kleptomaniac, F klepto; **Klep·to·ma·nie** [klɛptoma'ni:] *f* (-; *no pl.*) kleptomania; **klep·to·ma·nisch** [klɛpto'ma:nɪʃ] *adj.* kleptomaniac, F klepto
kle·ri·kal [kleri'ka:l] *adj.*, **Kle·ri·ka·le** [kleri'ka:lə] *m* (-n; -n) clerical
Kle·ri·ka·lis·mus [klerika'lɪsmʊs] *m* (-; *no pl.*) clericalism; **Kle·ri·ker** ['kle:rikɐ] *m* (-s; -) clergyman, cleric; **Kle·rus** ['kle:rʊs] *m* (-; *no pl.*) clergy
Klet·te ['klɛtə] *f* (-; -n) burr; *fig.* ***sich wie e-e ~ an j-n hängen*** cling to s.o. like a leech; **'Klet·ten·wur·zel** *f* burr root
Klet·te·rei [klɛtə'raɪ] *f* (-; -en) climbing
Klet·te·rer ['klɛtərɐ] *m* (-s; -) climber
Klet·ter|ge·rüst ['klɛtɐ-] *n* climbing frame; **~ma·xe** [-maksə] *m*: ***er ist ein richtiger ~*** he climbs all over the place
klet·tern ['klɛtɐn] **I.** *v/i.* (sn) climb (*a.* ✿ *and fig.*); ***~ auf*** *acc.* climb (up) *a tree, mountain etc.*; clamber (*or* scramble) up; **II.** 2 *n* (-s) climbing
Klet·ter|par,tie ['klɛtɐ-] *f* climbing tour; **~pflan·ze** *f* climbing plant; **~schu·he** *pl.* (rock-)climbing shoes; **~seil** *n* climbing rope; **~stan·ge** *f* climbing pole; **~tour** *f* climbing tour
Klett·ver·schluß ['klɛt-] *m* velcro fastening (*TM*)
klick [klɪk] *int.*, **Klick** *m* (-s; -s) click
klicken ['klɪkən] (*sep.* -k·k-) **I.** *v/i.* (h) click; ***erst ~, dann starten!*** clunk, click, every trip; **II.** 2 *n* (-s) click; clicking
Kli·ent [kli'ɛnt] *m* (-en; -en) client
Kli·en·tel [kliɛn'te:l] *f* (-; -en) clientele
Kli·en·tin [kli'ɛntɪn] *f* (-; -nen) → ***Klient***
Kliff [klɪf] *n* (-[e]s; -e) cliff
Kli·ma ['kli:ma] *n* (-s; -s, -te [kli'ma:tə]) climate; *fig. a.* atmosphere; **~än·de·rung** *f* change in climate; **~an·la·ge** *f* air conditioning; **~be·hand·lung** *f* climatotherapy; **~for·scher** *m* climatologist; **~for·schung** *f* climatology; **~gür·tel** *m* climatic zone; **~kam·mer** *f* climatic chamber; **~ka·ta,stro·phe** *f* climatic upheavals *pl.*
kli·mak·te·risch [klimak'te:rɪʃ] *adj.* ⚕ climacteric, menopausal; **Kli·mak·te·ri·um** [klimak'te:rĭʊm] *n* (-s; *no pl.*) menopause, change of life
'Kli·ma·tech·nik *f* air-conditioning technology
kli·ma·tisch [kli'ma:tɪʃ] *adj.* climatic(ally *adv.*); **kli·ma·ti·sie·ren** [klimati'zi:rən] *v/t.* (h) air-condition; **kli·ma·ti·siert** [klimati'zi:ɐt] *adj.* air-conditioned; ***der Raum ist ~*** the room has air conditioning
Kli·ma·to·lo·gie [klimatolo'gi:] *f* (-; *no pl.*) climatology
'Kli·ma·wech·sel *m* change in climate (*a. fig.*)
Kli·max ['kli:maks] *f* (-; *no pl.*) climax
'Kli·ma·zo·ne *f* climatic zone
Klim·bim [klɪm'bɪm] F *m* (-s; *no pl.*) a) fuss, F to-do, b) rubbish; ***der ganze ~*** F the whole caboodle
klim·men ['klɪmən] *v/i.* (klomm, geklommen, sn) climb
Klimm·zug ['klɪm-] *m*: (***e-n ~ machen*** do a) chinup; F *fig.* ***geistige Klimmzüge machen*** go into mental contortions
Klim·per·ka·sten ['klɪmpɐ-] F *m* F honky-tonk, *sl.* joanna
klim·pern ['klɪmpɐn] *v/i.* (h) jingle (*a. ~ mit dat.*); tinkle (away) *on the piano*; strum *on the guitar*, strum away *at the guitar*
Klin·ge ['klɪŋə] *f* (-; -n) blade; *fig.* ***mit j-m die ~n kreuzen*** cross swords with s.o.; ***j-n über die ~ springen lassen*** a) get rid of s.o., b) ruin s.o., F squeeze s.o. out
Klin·gel ['klɪŋəl] *f* (-; -n) bell; **~beu·tel** *m* collection bag
klin·ge·ling [klɪŋə'lɪŋ] *int.* dingaling!, ding, ding!
'Klin·gel·knopf *m* bell (push)
klin·geln ['klɪŋəln] (h) **I.** *v/i.* ring; ***es hat geklingelt*** a) there's somebody at the door, b) *ped. etc.* the bell's gone, c) F *fig.* F the penny's dropped; **II.** *v/t.*: ***j-n aus dem Schlaf ~*** get s.o. out of bed; **III.** 2 *n* (-s) ring; ringing; *w.s.* bell

'Klin·gel|zei·chen *n* ring; **~zug** *m* bell pull
klin·gen ['klɪŋən] *v/i.* (klang, geklungen, h) sound (*a. fig.*); *bell etc.*: (*a.* **~ lassen**) ring; *glasses*: clink; ***es klingt bis zu uns herüber*** you can hear it all the way over here; ***die Gläser ~ lassen*** clink glasses; ***mir ~ die Ohren*** my ears are ringing; ***es klingt verrückt*** it sounds crazy; ***das klingt nach schlechtem Gewissen*** it sounds as if she's *etc.* got a guilty conscience; ***das klingt schon besser*** that's more like it; **'klin·gend** *adj.* ringing, resounding *voice etc.*; ***schön ~e Worte*** nice-sounding words; → ***Münze***
Kli·nik ['kli:nɪk] *f* (-; -en) clinic, hospital
Kli·ni·ker ['kli:nikɐ] *m* (-s; -) **1.** clinician; **2.** houseman, *Am.* intern; **Kli·ni·kum** ['kli:nikʊm] *n* (-s; -ken) **1.** *no pl.* pre-registration (period), F pre-reg year; *Am.* internship; **2.** clinic; **kli·nisch** ['kli:nɪʃ] **I.** *adj.* clinical; **II.** *adv.*: **~ *tot*** clinically dead
Klin·ke ['klɪŋkə] *f* (-; -n) (door-)handle; ⚙ pawl, catch; F *fig.* ***die Bewerber gaben sich die ~ in die Hand*** there was an endless queue of applicants
'Klin·ken·put·zer F *m* (-s; -) hawker; door-to-door salesman
Klin·ker ['klɪŋkɐ] *m* (-s; -) clinker; **~stein** *m* clinker (brick)
Kli·no·mo·bil [klinomo'bi:l] *n* (-s; -e) mobile clinic
Kli·no·stat [klino'sta:t] *m* (-[e]s, -en; -en) *biol.* clinostat
klipp [klɪp] **I.** *int.*: **~, *klapp*** click-clack, *horse*: clip-clop; **II.** *adv.*: **~ *und klar*** in no uncertain terms; point-blank, straight out
Klipp [klɪp] *m* (-s; -s) **1.** clip; **2.** earclip
Klip·pe ['klɪpə] *f* (-; -n) cliff; rock; *fig.* obstacle; *fig.* ***alle ~n umschiffen*** clear all the hurdles, get round all the tricky bits, steer clear of any difficult topics *etc.*
'Klip·pen·kü·ste *f* rocky coast(line)
'klip·pen·reich *adj.* rocky
Klip·per ['klɪpɐ] *m* (-s; -) clipper
'Klipp·fisch *m* dried cod
klir·ren ['klɪrən] *v/i.* (h) *chains etc.*: jangle, *keys etc.*: *a.* jingle; *windowpanes etc.*: rattle; *swords etc.*: clash; **'klir·rend** *adj.*: *fig.* ***~e Kälte*** icy (*or* arctic) cold, biting frost, F brass monkey weather; ***heute ist e-e ~e Kälte*** *a.* it's bitter(ly) cold today
Klirr·fak·tor ['klɪr-] *m* harmonic distortion
Kli·schee [kli'ʃe:] *n* (-s; -s) **1.** stereotype, cliché; **2.** *typ.* (printing) block; **~fi͜gur** *f* stereotype
kli'schee·haft *adj.* stereotyped; ***es ist so ~*** *a.* it's such a cliché
Kli·stier [klɪs'ti:ɐ] *n* (-s; -e) enema
kli·stie·ren [klɪs'ti:rən] *v/t.* (h) give *s.o.* an enema
Kli'stier·sprit·ze *f* enema syringe
kli·to·ral [klito'ra:l] *adj.* clitoral
Kli·to·ris ['kli:torɪs] *f* (-; -) clitoris
klitsch·naß ['klɪtʃ-] *adj.* → ***klatschnaß***
klit·schig ['klɪtʃɪç] *adj.* soggy, doughy
klit·tern ['klɪtɐn] *v/t.* (h) throw *s.th.* together; ***Tatsachen ~*** lump all the facts together
klit·ze'klein [klɪtsə-] F *adj.* tiny (little ...), F teeny weeny; *Am.* F itty bitty
Klo [klo:] F *n* (-s; -s) F loo, *Am.* F john; ***aufs*** (***im, auf dem***) **~** to (in) the loo (*Am.* john); ***ich muß*** (***dringend***) ***aufs ~*** I've got to go (I'm dying to go) to the loo (*Am.* john)
Kloa·ke [klo'a:kə] *f* (-; -n) **1.** sewer; **2.** *zo.* cloaca
'Klo·becken F *n* toilet bowl
klo·big ['klo:bɪç] *adj.* **1.** bulky; chunky; heavy; ***~e Schuhe*** *a.* F clodhoppers; **2.** *fig.* clumsy; rough, uncouth
'Klo|bril·le F *f* toilet (F loo) seat; **~bür·ste** F *f* toilet (F loo) brush; **~deckel** F *m* toilet lid; **~fen·ster** F *n* toilet (F loo) window; **~frau** F *f* toilet (F loo) attendant
klomm [klɔm] *pret. of* ***klimmen***
⚕**klo·nen** ['klo:nən] *v/i.* (h) clone
klö·nen ['klø:nən] F *dial. v/i.* (h) F (have a) natter
'Klo·pa͜pier F *n* F loo paper (*or* roll)
klop·fen ['klɔpfən] (h) **I.** *v/i.* knock (*a. mot.*); tap (***an*** *acc.*, ***auf*** *acc.* at, on); *heart*: beat, thump (***vor*** *dat.* with); ***es klopft*** there's somebody (knocking) at the door; ***j-m auf die Schulter ~*** give s.o. a pat on the back; **II.** *v/t.* beat *carpet etc.*; break *stones*; ***e-n Nagel in die Wand ~*** knock a nail into the wall; **III.** ♀ *n* (-s) knock(ing); tap(ping); *mot.* knocking
Klop·fer ['klɔpfɐ] *m* (-s; -) **1.** doorknocker; **2.** carpet beater; **3.** *gastr.* mallet; **4.** *teleph.* sounder
klopf·fest ['klɔpf-] *adj. mot.* antiknock ...; **'Klopf·fe·stig·keit** *f* (-; *no pl.*) *mot.* antiknock rating
Klopf|sau·ger ['klɔpf-] *m* vacuum cleaner (with beating action); **~spra·che** *f* tapping code; **~zei·chen** *n* tap, knock
Klöp·pel ['klœpəl] *m* (-s; -) **1.** tongue *of bell*; **2.** (lace) bobbin; **'klöp·peln** *v/i.* (h) make lace; **'Klöp·pel·spit·zen** *pl.* bone lace *sg.*; **Klöpp·le·rin** ['klœplərɪn] *f* (-; -nen) lacemaker
Klops [klɔps] *dial. m* (-es; -e) meatball
Klo·sett [klo'zɛt] *n* (-[e]s; -e, -s) toilet, F loo, *Am.* F john; **~becken** *n* toilet bowl; **~bril·le** *f* toilet seat; **~bür·ste** *f* toilet brush; **~deckel** *m* toilet lid; **~fen·ster** *n* toilet window; **~frau** *f* toilet (*or* lavatory) attendant; **~pa͜pier** *n* toilet paper; **~sitz** *m* toilet seat
Klo'settür (*sep.* -tt·t-) *f* toilet door
Kloß [klo:s] *m* (-es; Klöße ['klø:sə]) **1.** clump, clod (of earth); **2.** *gastr.* dumpling, meatball; *fig.* ***e-n ~ im Hals haben*** have a lump in one's throat; **~brü·he** *f*: F ***klar wie ~*** (as) clear as daylight
Klo·ster ['klo:stɐ] *n* (-s; Klöster ['klø:stɐ]) monastery; convent; ***ins ~ gehen*** go into a monastery (*or* convent), *a.* take the veil; *iro.* ***da kann ich ja gleich ins ~ gehen*** I may as well join a monastery (*or* convent); **~an·la·ge** *f* monastery (*or* convent) complex *or* grounds *pl.*; **~bru·der** *m* monk; **~gar·ten** *m* monastery (*or* convent) gardens *pl.*; **~ge·mein·schaft** *f* monastic community, community of monks (*or* nuns); **~kir·che** *f* monastery (*or* convent) church
klö·ster·lich ['klø:stɐlɪç] *adj.* monastic; *fig. a.* secluded
'Klo·ster|re·gel *f* monastic rule; **~schu·le** *f* monastic (*or* convent) school
'Klo·tür F *f* toilet (F loo) door
Klotz [klɔts] *m* (-es; Klötze ['klœtsə]) block of wood; stump; *fig.* lout; *fig.* **~ *am Bein*** handicap, millstone round *s.o.'s* neck
klot·zen ['klɔtsən] F *v/i.* (h) **1.** F go the whole hog; **~, *nicht kleckern!*** think big!, we don't want any half measures; **2.** F slog away, put in some hard graft
klot·zig ['klɔtsɪç] **I.** *adj.* unwieldy; **II.** *adv.*: F **~ *viel Geld*** F stacks of money
Klub [klʊb] *m* (-s; -s) club; **~haus** *n* clubhouse; **~jacke** *f* blazer; **~mit·glied** *n* (club) member; **~ses·sel** *m* armchair
Kluft[1] [klʊft] *f* (-; Klüfte ['klʏftə]) gap, crevice, fissure; chasm, abyss; *fig.* gulf; rift
Kluft[2] F *f* (-; -en) F gear, get-up
klug [klu:k] *adj.* clever, intelligent; smart; wise; sensible; bright; ***es wäre das klügste zu*** *inf.* the best idea would be to *inf.*; **klu·ger·wei·se** ['klu:gɐ'vaɪzə] *adv.* sensibly; **~ *schwieg er*** *a.* he had the good sense not to say anything
'Klug·heit *f* (-; *no pl.*) cleverness, intelligence; wisdom; good sense; smartness
'klug·re·den *v/i.* (*sep.*, h) F play the wise guy; always know the answer; ***hör doch auf klugzureden*** stop acting clever
'klug·schei·ßen V *v/i.* (*only inf.*) *sl.* shoot one's mouth off; **'Klug·schei·ßer** V *m* (-s; -) V smart arse
'klug·schnacken *dial. v/i.* → ***klugreden***
Klum·pen ['klʊmpən] *m* (-s; -) a) lump; (*blood*) clot, b) nugget, c) F heap, d) huddle; **~ *Erde*** clod of earth
Klump·fuß ['klʊmp-] *m* clubfoot
klum·pig ['klʊmpɪç] *adj.* lumpy
Klün·gel ['klʏŋəl] *m* (-s; -) clique, crowd; ***er und sein ~*** F him and his cronies; **Klün·ge·lei** [klʏŋə'laɪ] *f* (-; -en) **1.** F cronyism; **2.** *dial.* dawdling; **klün·geln** ['klʏŋəln] *v/i.* (h) **1.** band together; **2.** *dial.* dawdle
Klu·nia·zen·ser [klunĭa'tsɛnzɐ] *m* (-s; -) Cluniac (monk); **klu·nia·zen·sisch** [klunĭa'tsɛnzɪʃ] *adj.* Cluniac
Klun·kern ['klʊŋkɐn] F *pl.* F rocks, *a.* F ice *sg.*
Klü·se ['kly:zə] *f* (-; -n) ⚓ hawse
Klü·ver ['kly:vɐ] *m* (-s; -) ⚓ jib; **~baum** *m* jib boom
Kly·stron ['klʏstrɔn] *n* (-s; -e [klʏs'tro:nə]) klystron
Knab·be·rei·en [knabə'raɪən] *pl.* nibbles
knab·bern ['knabɐn] *v/i. and v/t.* (h) nibble (***an*** *dat.* at); *fig.* ***daran wird er noch lang zu ~ haben*** he'll be chewing on that for a while to come
Kna·be ['kna:bə] *m* (-n; -n) boy; F ***alter ~*** F old chap
'Kna·ben|al·ter *n* boyhood; ***im ~*** as a boy; **~chor** *m* boys' choir
'kna·ben·haft *adj.* boyish
'Kna·ben·stim·me *f* ♪ treble
Knäcke·brot ['knɛkə-] (*sep.* -k·k-) *n* crispbread
knacken ['knakən] (*sep.* -k·k-) (h) **I.** *v/i.* crack; *branch etc.*: snap; *fire, radio*: crackle; *metal*: click; **II.** *v/t.* crack (open) *nut, safe etc.*; break into *a car etc.*; break open *lock etc.*; crack *secret code etc.*; *fig.* ***j-m e-e harte Nuß zu ~ geben*** give s.o. s.th. to chew on
Knacker ['knakɐ] (*sep.* -k·k-) F ⚕⚕ *m* (-s; -) **1.** ***alter ~*** F old fogey; **2.** → ***Knackwurst***
knack·frisch ['knak-] *adj.* (nice and) crisp, crunchy
Knacki ['knaki] (*sep.* -k·k-) F *m* (-s; -s) F con, jailbird
knackig ['knakɪç] (*sep.* -k·k-) F *adj. gastr.* crisp, crunchy; *fig.* F ripe; taut, firm *body*
Knack·laut ['knak-] *m ling.* glottal stop
Knack·punkt ['knak-] F *m* sticking point
Knacks [knaks] *m* (-es; -e) crack; F *fig.* ***er hat e-n ~ weg*** a) his health has taken a bad knock, b) something's snapped; ***ihre Ehe*** (*or* ***Freundschaft*** *etc.*) ***hat e-n***

~ there's a rift between them; ***e-n leichten ~ haben*** F be slightly cracked

Knack·wurst ['knak-] *f* frankfurter, *Am. a.* F frank

Knall [knal] *m* (-[e]s; -e) bang; thud; loud bang, (*the* sound of an) explosion; shot; pop *of a cork*; ✈ (sonic) boom; F *fig.* row, flare-up; *fig.* (***auf***) ***~ und Fall*** just like that, without a word of warning; F ***du hast wohl 'nen ~*** F you must be off your nut; **~bon͵bon** *m, n* cracker; **♀'bunt** *adj.* brightly colo(u)red, *contp.* gaudy, garish; **~ef͵fekt** *fig. m* sensation

knal·len ['knalən] **I.** *v/i.* **1.** (h) bang; ***mit der Peitsche ~*** crack one's whip; ***plötzlich knallte es*** suddenly there was a loud bang (*or* shot); **2.** (sn) ***ins Schloß ~*** *door*: bang shut; F ***~ gegen*** *acc.* crash into; F ***sonst knallt's!*** F or else (you'll cop it)!; **II.** *v/t.* (h) a) fire, shoot, b) fling; slam, bang; ***den Ball ins Tor ~*** slam the ball home; F ***er knallte ihm eine*** F he gave him a wallop

Knal·ler ['knalɐ] *m* (-s; -) **1.** → ***Knallkörper***; **2.** F gun

'Knall|erb·se *f* (toy) torpedo; **~frosch** *m* jumping jack

'knall|'hart F *adj.* (as) hard as rock (*or* nails); brutal; tough; ***~er Bursche*** F tough guy; ***der Film*** *etc.* ***ist ~*** the film *etc.* doesn't pull any punches; **~'heiß** F *adj.* scorching

knal·lig ['knalıç] F *adj.* loud *colo(u)r*

'Knall|kopf F *m* F blockhead; **~kör·per** *m* banger; **♀'rot** *adj.* bright red; **~tü·te** F *f* F twerp

'knall'voll F *adj.* **1.** F chock-a-block; **2.** F paralytic, *sl.* pissed out of one's mind

knapp [knap] **I.** *adj.* a) tight *dress etc.*; *fig.* concise, terse; brief, b) meag|re (*Am.* -er); limited, *a.* scarce, tight *funds*; ~ (***bei Kasse***) short (of cash), F hard up; ***~e fünf Jahre*** just under (*or* not quite) five years; ***~e Mehrheit*** slim majority; ***~ sein*** *food etc.*: be in short supply, be scarce; ***~ werden*** run short; ***mit ~er Not*** only just; ***er ist mit ~er Not entkommen*** F it was a close shave; **II.** *adv.* only just; narrowly; ***et. ~ bemessen*** measure s.th. too short, *contp.* be stingy with s.th.; ***das ist ~ bemessen*** (***berechnet***) that's a bit on the short (low) side; ***m-e Zeit ist ~ bemessen*** I'm pushed for time; ***er starb ~ 65jährig*** he died shortly after his 65th birthday; F ***und nicht zu ~!*** F and how!

'knapp·hal·ten *v/t.* (*irr., sep.,* h, → ***halten***) **1.** ***j-n ~*** keep s.o. short (***mit*** *dat.* on); **2.** ⚕ keep in short supply

'Knapp·heit *f* (-; *no pl.*) shortage; *fig.* conciseness

'Knapp·schaft *f* (-; -en) ⚒ body of miners; **'Knapp·schafts·kas·se** *f* miners' social security fund

knap·sen ['knapsən] F *v/i.* (h) be stingy; ***~ mit*** *dat. a.* F be tight with

Knar·re ['knarə] *f* (-; -n) **1.** rattle; **2.** F gun

knar·ren ['knarən] *v/i.* (h) creak; ***~de Stimme*** grating (*or* rasping) voice

Knast [knast] F *m* (-[e]s; *no pl.*) jail, F clink, *Am.* F slammer; ***im ~ sitzen*** F be in clink (*or* the slammer); **~bru·der** F *m* F jailbird

Kna·ster ['knastɐ] F *m* (-s; -) cheap(, smelly) tobacco

Knatsch [kna:tʃ] F *m* (-es; *no pl.*) row; ***es gab ~*** we *etc.* had a row; **'knat·schen** F *v/i.* (h) F grizzle; **knat·schig** ['kna:tʃıç] F *adj.* F grumpy

knat·tern ['knatɐn] *v/i.* (h) *mot.* put-put; *machine gun*: rat-a-tat-tat; *flag*: flap

Knäu·el ['knɔʏəl] *m, n* (-s; -) ball *of wool etc.*; *fig.* tangle; *a.* cluster *of people*

Knauf [knaʊf] *m* (-[e]s; Knäufe ['knɔʏfə]) knob; pommel; △ capital

Knau·ser ['knaʊzɐ] F *m* (-s; -) F skinflint; **knau·se·rig** ['knaʊzərıç] *adj.* stingy, mean; ***~ mit*** *dat. a.* F tight with; **knau·sern** ['knaʊzɐn] *v/i.* (h) be stingy, be mean; ***~ mit*** *dat. a.* F be tight with

Knaus-Ogi·no-Me͵tho·de ['knaʊsˀo'gi:-no-] *f* rhythm method

knaut·schen ['knaʊtʃən] F *v/t. and v/i.* (h) crumple up, crease

Knautsch|lack(le·der *n*) ['knaʊtʃ-] *m* wet-look leather; **~zo·ne** *f mot.* crumple zone

Kne·bel ['kne:bəl] *m* (-s; -) a) gag, b) ⚙ lever, c) toggle; **'Kne·bel·bart** *m* handlebar moustache; **kne·beln** ['kne:bəln] *v/t.* (h) gag; **'Kne·bel·ver·band** *m* tourniquet

Knecht [knɛçt] *m* (-[e]s; -e) farmhand; stableboy; servant; slave (*a. fig.*); serf

knech·ten ['knɛçtən] *v/t.* (h) enslave; tyrannize, oppress; subjugate

'Knecht·schaft *f* (-; *no pl.*) slavery, bondage

knei·fen ['knaıfən] (kniff, gekniffen, h) **I.** *v/t.* **1.** pinch; **II.** *v/i.* **2.** *clothes etc.*: pinch; **3.** F shirk (***vor*** *dat. s.th.*), F chicken out (of *s.th.*); ***hier wird nicht gekniffen!*** no shirking now; **Knei·fer** ['knaıfɐ] *m* (-s; -) **1.** pince-nez; **2.** F shirker; **Kneif·zan·ge** ['knaıf-] *f*: (***e-e*** ~ a pair of) pincers *pl.*

Knei·pe ['knaıpə] *f* (-; -n) pub, *Am.* bar; **'Knei·pen·wirt** *m*, **Knei·pier** [knaı'pie:] F *m* (-s; -s) pub-owner, *Am.* barkeeper

kneip·pen ['knaıpən] *v/i.* (h) take a Kneipp cure; **Kneipp·kur** ['knaıp-] *f* Kneipp cure

Kne·te ['kne:tə] *f* (-; *no pl.*) **1.** plasticine; **2.** F dough; **'kne·ten** *v/t.* (h) knead; mo(u)ld; **Knet·mas͵sa·ge** ['kne:t-] *f* pummel(l)ing massage; **'Knet·mas·se** *f* plasticine

Knick [knık] *m* (-[e]s; -e) a) crease, b) dog-ear, c) kink; buckle, d) angle (*a.* △); sharp bend; *in a diagram*: blip; *fig.* setback (***in*** *dat.* to, in *s.o.'s career etc.*); dent; **knicken** ['knıkən] (*sep.* -k·k-) **I.** *v/i.* (sn) bend; break, snap; *knees, metal*: buckle, give way; **II.** *v/t.* (h) bend; crease; break, snap; *fig.* dent *s.o.'s pride etc., a.* crush *s.o.*; → ***geknickt***

Knicker ['knıkɐ] F *m* (-s; -) F skinflint

Knicker·bocker ['knıkɐbɔkɐ] (*sep.* -k·k-) *pl.* plus fours

knicke·rig ['knıkərıç] (*sep.* -k·k-) F *adj.* stingy, mean

'Knick|fe·stig·keit *f* (-; *no pl.*) ⚙ buckling strength; **~flü·gel** *m* ✈ cranked (*or* gull) wing; **~fuß** *m* ⚕ skew foot

Knicks [knıks] *m* (-es; -e) curts(e)y; ***e-n ~ machen*** → **knick·sen** ['knıksən] *v/i.* (h) curts(e)y (***vor*** *dat.* to)

Knie [kni:] *n* (-s; - ['kni:(ə)]) a) *anat.* knee, b) bend, c) ⚙ elbow, knee; ***j-n auf den ~n bitten*** beg s.o. on bended knee; ***auf die ~ fallen*** fall to one's knees; ***in die ~ gehen*** bend one's knees, crouch on one's knees, *fig.* go to the wall; *fig.* ***j-n auf die ~ zwingen*** force s.o. to his (*or* her) knees; F ***j-n übers ~ legen*** give s.o. a good hiding; ***et. übers ~ brechen*** rush s.th.; F ***ich wurde ganz weich in den ~n*** F my legs turned to jelly; **~beu·ge** *f* **1.** *gym.* knee-bend; **2.** *eccl.* genuflection; **~bund·ho·se** *f*: (***e-e*** ~ a pair of) knee breeches *pl.*; **~fall** *m*: ***e-n ~ vor j-m machen*** *a. fig.* go down on one's knees before s.o.; **♀frei** *adj.*: ***~er Rock*** skirt that goes above the knee; ***ich trage meistens ~e Röcke*** I usually wear my skirts above the knee; **~ge·lenk** *n* knee joint; **♀hoch** *adj.* up to one's knees, knee-high; *snow, water*: knee-deep; **~keh·le** *f* hollow of the knee; ***in der ~*** *a.* at the back of one's knee

'knie·lang *adj.* knee-length

knien [kni:n] *v/i.* (h) a) kneel, be on one's knees, b) kneel down, go down on one's knees

'Knie|re͵flex *m* knee jerk; **~rohr** *n* elbow pipe; **~schei·be** *f* kneecap; **~scho·ner** *m*, **~schüt·zer** [-ʃʏtsɐ] *m* (-s; -) knee pad; **~strumpf** *m* (knee-length) sock; **~stück** *n* ⚙ bend, elbow; **♀tief I.** *adj.* knee-deep; **II.** *adv.* up to one's knees; **~wel·le** *f gym.* knee circle

kniff [knıf] *pret. of* ***kneifen***

Kniff *m* (-[e]s; -e) **1.** pinch; **2.** crease; dent; **3.** *fig.* trick

kniff·lig ['knıflıç] F *adj.* tricky

Knig·ge ['knıgə] *m*: ***er hat s-n ~ nie gelesen*** he doesn't know his etiquette

Knilch [knılç] F *m* (-[e]s; -e) F creep

knip·sen ['knıpsən] (h) **I.** *v/i.* **1.** take photos; ***hast du schon geknipst?*** have you taken it already?; **2.** ***mit den Fingern ~*** snap one's fingers; **II.** *v/t.* **3.** take a picture (*or* shot) of; ***hast du's geknipst?*** have you got it?; **4.** punch *ticket*

Knirps [knırps] *m* (-es; -e) little lad; *contp.* F squirt

knir·schen ['knırʃən] *v/i.* (h) crunch; ***mit den Zähnen ~*** grind one's teeth

kni·stern ['knıstɐn] **I.** *v/i.* (h) rustle; *fire*: crackle; *fig.* ***es knisterte vor Spannung*** the atmosphere was electric; **II.** ♀ *n* (-s) rustling; crackling

Knit·tel·vers ['knıtəl-] *m* doggerel

Knit·ter ['knıtɐ] *m* (-s; -) crease; **'knit·ter·frei** *adj.* non-crease; **'Knit·ter·look** *m* crumple look; **'knit·tern** *v/t. and v/i.* (h) crease

Kno·bel·be·cher ['kno:bəl-] *m* **1.** dice cup; **2.** F *pl.* jackboots

kno·beln ['kno:bəln] *v/i.* (h) throw dice; toss (***um*** *acc.* for); *fig.* ***~ an*** *dat.* puzzle over

Knob·lauch ['kno:plaʊx] *m* (-[e]s; *no pl.*) garlic; **~kap·sel** *f* garlic pill; **~pres·se** *f* garlic press; **~pul·ver** *n* garlic powder; **~salz** *n* garlic salt; **~ze·he** *f* clove of garlic

Knö·chel ['knœçəl] *m* (-s; -) **1.** ankle; **2.** knuckle; **♀lang** *adj.* ankle-length *dress*; **♀tief I.** *adj.* ankle-deep; **II.** *adv.* up to one's ankles

Kno·chen ['knɔxən] *m* (-s; -) bone; *fig.* ***mir tun sämtliche ~ weh*** every bone in my body is aching; ***naß bis auf die ~*** soaked to the skin; ***es ist ihm in die ~ gefahren*** it really got to him; ***es sitzt mir noch in den ~*** I still haven't got over it (completely); ***sich bis auf die ~ blamieren*** make an absolute fool of o.s.; F ***fauler ~*** F lazybones; F ***harter ~*** F tough job; **~ar·beit** F *f* (-; *no pl.*) F hard graft; **~bau** *m* (-[e]s; *no pl.*) bone structure; **♀bil·dend** *adj.* bone-building; **~bil·dung** *f* bone formation; **~bruch** *m* fracture; **~ent·zün·dung** *f* inflammation of the bones; 📖 ostitis; **~er·wei·chung** *f* softening of the bones; 📖 osteomalacia;

~ge·rüst *n* skeleton; **~ge·we·be** *n* bone tissue; **2'hart** *adj.* (as) hard as rock; *fig. sport*: tough
'Kno·chen·haut *f* (-; *no pl.*) periosteum; **~ent·zün·dung** *f* periostitis
'Kno·chen·krebs *m* bone cancer
'Kno·chen·mark *n* bone marrow; **~ent·zün·dung** *f* osteomyelitis; **~krebs** *m* bone-marrow cancer
'Kno·chen|mehl *n* bonemeal; **~müh·le** F *f* **1.** F sweatshop; **2.** F boneshaker; **~naht** *f* bone suture; **~sä·ge** *f* butcher's (*or* bone) saw; **~schin·ken** *m* ham on the bone; **~schwund** *m* atrophy of the bone(s); **~split·ter** *m* bone fragment, piece of bone; **2'trocken** F *adj.* bone-dry; **~tu·mor** *m* bone tumo(u)r; **~ver·let·zung** *f* bone injury
knö·chern ['knœçɐn] *adj.* **1.** bony; **2.** made of bone, bone ...
kno·chig ['knɔxɪç] *adj.* skinny; bony
Knö·del ['knœ:dəl] *m* (-s; -) dumpling
Knöll·chen ['knœlçən] F *n* (-s; -) parking ticket
Knol·le ['knɔlə] *f* (-; -n) ♀ tuber; bulb; node
Knol·len ['knɔlən] *m* (-s; -) **1.** lump; **2.** F (parking) ticket; **~blät·ter·pilz** *m* amanita; **~na·se** *f* bulbous nose; **~sel·le·rie** *m* celeriac; **~wur·zel** *f* tuberous root
knol·lig ['knɔlɪç] *adj.* knotty; lumpy; ♀ bulbous
Knopf [knɔpf] *m* (-[e]s; Knöpfe ['knœpfə]) **1.** button (*a.* ⚡); (*door etc.*) knob; ***auf den ~ drücken*** press the button; **2.** F chap, *Am.* guy; **~au·gen** *pl.* big brown eyes; **~druck** *m*: ***auf ~*** at the touch of a button, *fig. a.* at the flick of a switch
knöp·fen ['knœpfən] *v/t.* (h) button (up); ***falsch geknöpft*** buttoned up the wrong way
'Knopf·loch *n* buttonhole; F *fig.* ***aus allen Knopflöchern platzen*** be bursting at the seams; ***ihm scheint die Neugier (Eitelkeit) aus allen Knopflöchern*** he's just bursting with curiosity (he just oozes vanity); *iro.* ***mit e-r Träne im ~*** with a tear in my *etc.* eye
Knor·pel ['knɔrpəl] *m* (-s; -) cartilage; *gastr.* gristle; **knor·pe·lig** ['knɔrpəlɪç] *adj.* gristly
Knor·ren ['knɔrən] *m* (-s; -) knot
knor·rig ['knɔrɪç] *adj.* knotty, gnarled; *fig.* gruff
Knos·pe ['knɔspə] *f* (-; -n) ♀ bud; *fig.* tender bud; ***~n treiben*** → **'knos·pen** *v/i.* (h) bud, *w.s.* sprout; *fig.* bud
Knöt·chen ['knø:tçən] *n* (-s; -) ⚕ nodule
kno·ten ['kno:tən] *v/t. and v/i.* (h) knot, make knots (in *a rope etc.*)
'Kno·ten *m* (-s; -) knot (*a.* ⚓); *a.* bun; ♀ joint, *a. phys., ast.* node; ⚕ lump; *fig.* plot *of drama etc.*; ***e-n ~ ins Taschentuch machen*** tie a knot in one's handkerchief; *thea.* ***der ~ schürzt (löst) sich*** the plot thickens (unravels); → ***gordisch***; **~punkt** *m* (*road etc.*) junction; 🚂, *opt., phys.* nodal point; *fig.* cent|re (*Am.* -er); hub; **~schrift** *f* quipu; **~stock** *m* gnarled (walking) stick
Knö·te·rich ['knø:tərɪç] *m* (-s; -e) ♀ knotgrass
kno·tig ['kno:tɪç] *adj.* knotty; ⚕ nodular
Know-how [noʊ'haʊ] *n* (-[s]; *no pl.*) know-how, expertise, expert knowledge, F savvy; ***geschäftliches (technisches** etc.) **~** a.* business (technical *etc.*) skills
Knülch [knʏlç] F *m* (-[e]s; -e) F creep
knül·le ['knʏlə] F *adj.* F tight
knül·len ['knʏlən] (h) **I.** *v/i.* crumple; crease; **II.** *v/t.* crease; screw up *paper*
Knül·ler ['knʏlɐ] F *m* (-s; -) sensation; scoop; F *thea., film etc.* blockbuster; (*record*) F smash hit
knüp·fen ['knʏpfən] (h) **I.** *v/t.* a) tie *knot*, make *net*; knot *carpet*, b) attach, fasten (***an*** *acc.* to); *fig.* ***ein Bündnis (e-e Freundschaft) ~*** form an alliance (a friendship); ***~ an*** *acc.* pin *one's hopes* on, attach *conditions* to; **II.** *v/refl.*: ***sich ~ an*** *acc.* a) be tied up with, *conditions*: be attached to, b) arise from; ***daran ~ sich für mich glückliche Erinnerungen*** it holds happy memories for me
Knüp·pel ['knʏpəl] *m* (-s; -) (heavy) stick, club; truncheon; ✈ control stick, F joystick; *fig.* ***j-m e-n ~ zwischen die Beine werfen*** put a spoke in s.o.'s wheels
'knüp·pel'dick F *adj. and adv.*: ***es kommt immer gleich ~*** it never rains but it pours; ***dann kam's ~*** then it came thick and fast (*or* with a vengeance), then things really started happening, then it was just one thing after another; ***ich hab's ~ (satt)*** F I'm fed up to the back teeth; ***er hat's ~ hinter den Ohren*** F he knows all the tricks of the trade
'knüp·pel'dicke'voll (*sep.* -k·k-) F *adj.* F chock-a-block, jampacked
knüp·peln ['knʏpəln] *v/t.* (h) beat (with a stick *etc.*)
'Knüp·pel·schal·tung *f mot.* floor shift
'knüp·pel'voll F *adj.* F chock-a-block, jampacked
knur·ren ['knʊrən] *v/i.* (h) growl; *fig.* grunt, grumble (***über*** *acc.* at); *empty stomach*: rumble
Knurr·hahn [knʊr-] *m zo.* gurnard
knur·rig ['knʊrɪç] F *adj.* F grumpy
Knus·per·häus·chen ['knʊspɐ-] *n* gingerbread house
knus·pe·rig, knusp·rig ['knʊsp(ə)rɪç] *adj.* crunchy; crisp
Knu·te ['knu:tə] *f*: ***unter j-s ~*** under s.o.'s thumb; **'knu·ten** *v/t.* (h) oppress
knut·schen ['knu:tʃən] F *v/i.* (h) F snog; **Knutsch·fleck** ['knu:tʃ-] F *m* F lovebite, *Am.* F hickey
K.o. [ka:'ʔo:] *m* (-; -) knockout, k.o.; **k.o. I.** *adj.* **1.** knocked out, k.o.; **2.** F whacked, bushed; **II.** *adv.*: ***j-n ~ schlagen*** knock s.o. out, k.o. s.o.
koa·gu·lie·ren [koʔagu'li:rən] *v/i.* (sn) *and v/t.* (h) coagulate
Koa·la [ko'a:la] *m* (-s; -s), **~bär** *m* koala (bear)
koa·lie·ren [koʔa'li:rən] *v/i.* (h) form a coalition; **Koa·li·ti·on** [koʔali'tsĭo:n] *f* (-; -en) coalition; ***große ~*** grand coalition
Koa·li·ti'ons|par,tei *f* coalition party; **~part·ner** *m* coalition partner; **~recht** *n* right of association; **~re,gie·rung** *f* coalition government; **~zwang** *m* obligatory compliance with a coalition agreement
Ko·au·tor ['ko:ʔaʊto:ɐ] *m* co-author
ko·axi·al [koʔa'ksĭa:l] *adj.* coaxial
Ko·axi'al·ka·bel *n* coaxial cable
Ko·balt ['ko:balt] *n* (-[e]s; *no pl.*) cobalt; **~blau** *n* cobalt blue; **~bom·be** *f* cobalt bomb
Ko·ben ['ko:bən] *m* (-s; -) (pig)sty
Ko·bold ['ko:bɔlt] *m* (-[e]s; -e ['ko:bɔldə]) (hob)goblin; F *fig.* F imp
Ko·bra ['ko:bra] *f* (-; -s) cobra
Koch [kɔx] *m* (-[e]s; Köche ['kœçə]) cook; chef; ***viele Köche verderben den Brei*** too many cooks spoil the broth; **~an·lei·tung** *f* cooking instructions *pl.*; **~ap·fel** *m* cooking apple; **~beu·tel** *m*: ***Reis** etc. **im ~*** boil-in-the-bag rice *etc.*; **~buch** *n* cookery book, cookbook; **~ecke** *f* kitchenette
kö·cheln ['kœçəln] *v/i.* (h) simmer
Kö·chel·ver·zeich·nis ['kœçəl-] *n* ♪ Köchel catalog(ue); ***~ 421*** (*abbr.* ***KV 421***) Köchel (number) 421 (*abbr.* K421)
ko·chen ['kɔxən] (h) **I.** *v/i.* a) cook, do the cooking, b) be cooking, be boiling; *fig.* be seething with rage; ***sie kocht gut*** she's a good cook; **II.** *v/t.* cook; boil *water, egg etc.*; make *tea, coffee etc.*; ***das Essen ~*** make (*or* cook) the dinner; → ***gekocht***; **III. 2** *n* (-s) cooking, cookery; ***zum ~ bringen*** bring to the boil, *fig.* make *s.o.'s* blood boil; ***et. am ~ haben*** have s.th. on the boil (*a.* F *fig.*)
'ko·chend'heiß *adj.* boiling hot, scalding
Ko·cher ['kɔxɐ] *m* (-s; -) cooker, boiler
Kö·cher ['kœçɐ] *m* (-s; -) quiver; *phot.* lens case
'koch|fer·tig *adj.* (ready) prepared; oven-ready; boil-in-the-bag ...; **~fest** *adj.* boil-wash ...
'Koch|fett *n* cooking fat; **~ge·le·gen·heit** *f* cooking facilities *pl.*; **~ge·schirr** *n* cooking (*or* kitchen) utensils *pl. or* things *pl.*; ⚔ mess kit; **~herd** *m* cooker, stove
Kö·chin ['kœçɪn] *f* (-; -nen) cook
'Koch|kä·se *m* cooking cheese; **~kunst** *f* cookery, (art of) cooking; **~kurs** *m* cookery course; **~löf·fel** *m* wooden spoon; **~ni·sche** *f* kitchenette; **~plat·te** *f* hot plate; **~re,zept** *n* recipe
'Koch·salz *n* table salt; **~lö·sung** *f* salt solution
'Koch|schin·ken *m* boiled ham; **~topf** *m* saucepan; **~wä·sche** *f* boil wash; **~was·ser** *n* cooking water
Ko·da ['ko:da] *f* (-; -s) ♪ coda; *fig. a.* tailpiece
Kode [ko:t] *m* (-s; -s) code
Ko·de·in [kode'i:n] *n* (-s; *no pl.*) codeine
Kö·der ['kø:dɐ] *m* (-s;-) bait (*a. fig.*); *fig.* ***auf den ~ anbeißen*** fall for (*or* swallow) the bait; **'kö·dern** *v/t.* (h) bait; *fig.* lure, entice
Ko·dex ['ko:dɛks] *m* (-[es]; -e, -dizes ['ko:ditse:s]) codex, manuscript; ⚖ code; *fig.* code *of hono(u)r etc.*
ko·die·ren [ko'di:rən] *v/t.* (h) (en)code; **Ko'die·rung** *f* (-; -en) (en)coding
ko·di·fi·zie·ren [kodifi'tsi:rən] *v/t.* (h) codify
Ko·edu·ka·ti·on ['ko:ʔedukatsĭo:n] *f* (-; *no pl.*) coeducation
Ko·ef·fi·zi·ent [koʔɛfi'tsĭɛnt] *m* (-en; -en) coefficient
Ko·exi·stenz ['ko:ʔɛksɪstɛnts] *f* (-; *no pl.*) *esp. pol.* coexistence; **ko·exi·stie·ren** ['ko:ʔɛksɪsti:rən] *v/i.* (h) coexist
Kof·fe·in [kɔfe'i:n] *n* (-s; *no pl.*) caffeine
kof·fe'in·frei *adj.* decaffeinated; ***~er Kaffee*** *a.* F decaf
Kof·fer ['kɔfɐ] *m* (-s; -) suitcase; case; ***s-e ~ packen*** pack (one's bags), *fig.* pack one's bags (and leave); *fig.* ***aus dem ~ leben*** live out of a suitcase; ***noch e-n ~ in Berlin haben*** still have half a foot in Berlin; **~an·hän·ger** *m* address tag; **~ge·rät** *n* portable (set); **~kleid** *n* travel(l)ing dress; **~ku·li** *m* trolley; **~ra·dio** *n* transistor radio; **~raum** *m* boot, *Am.* trunk

Kog·ge ['kɔgə] *f* (-; -n) *hist.* ⚓ cog

Ko·gnak ['kɔnjak] *m* (-s; -s) brandy, cognac; **~schwen·ker** *m* brandy balloon

ko·gni·tiv [kɔgni'ti:f] *adj.* cognitive

Ko·ha·bi·ta·ti·on [kohabita'tsi̯o:n] *f* (-; -en) cohabitation

Ko·hä·renz [kohɛ'rɛnts] *f* (-; *no pl.*) coherence

Ko·hä·si·on [kohɛ'zi̯o:n] *f* (-; *no pl.*) cohesion; **Ko·hä·si'ons·kraft** *f* cohesive force

Kohl [ko:l] *m* (-[e]s; *no pl.*) cabbage; F *fig.* rubbish, F rot, *Am.* F garbage; *fig.* ***s-n ~ anbauen*** cultivate one's garden; F ***alten ~ aufwärmen*** dig up old stories; ***das ist doch alter ~*** F that's old hat; **~dampf** F *m*: ***~ haben*** F be starving

Koh·le ['ko:lə] *f* (-; -n) **1.** *no pl.* a) coal, b) ⚗, ⚡ carbon, c) charcoal, d) F cash, readies *pl.*; **2.** coal; *fig.* ***glühende ~n auf j-s Haupt sammeln*** heap coals of fire on s.o.'s head; ***(wie) auf (glühenden) ~n sitzen*** be on tenterhooks; **~kraft·werk** *n* coal(-fired) power station

'Koh·len|berg·bau *m* coal-mining (industry); **~berg·werk** *n* coalmine, colliery; **~bren·ner** *m* charcoal burner; **~di·oxyd** *n* carbon dioxide; **~ei·mer** *m* coal scuttle; **~feue·rung** *f* coal firing; **~flöz** *n* coal seam; **~för·de·rung** *f* a) extraction of coal, b) coal output; **~gas** *n* coal gas; **~gru·be** *f* coal pit; **~hal·de** *f* coal dump; **~händ·ler** *m* coal merchant; **~hei·zung** *f* coal heating; **~hy͵drat** *n* carbohydrate; **~la·ger** *n* **1.** ✝ coal depot; **2.** *geol.* coal bed; **~mei·ler** *m* charcoal pile; **~(mon)oxyd** *n* carbon monoxide; **~mon·oxyd·ver·gif·tung** *f* carbon monoxide poisoning; **~pott** F *m* the Ruhr coal basin

'koh·len·sau·er *adj.* carbonic; ***kohlensaures Salz*** carbonate; ***kohlensaures Kali*** potassium carbonate

'Koh·len·säu·re *f* carbonic acid; ***ohne ~*** still, flat, *Am.* non-carbonated *drink*; ***mit ~*** → **'koh·len·säu·re·hal·tig** [-haltɪç] *adj.* fizzy, sparkling, *Am.* carbonated

'Koh·len|schacht *m* coal pit; **~schau·fel** *f* coal shovel; **~schicht** *f* coal bed; **~staub** *m* coal dust; **~stoff** *m* ⚗ carbon

'Koh·len·was·ser·stoff *m*, **~gas** *n* hydrocarbon; **~ver·bin·dung** *f* carbohydrate compound

'Koh·len·ze·che *f* coalmine

'Koh·le|ofen *m* coal stove; **~pa͵pier** *n* carbon paper; **~prä·pa͵rat** *n* ⚕ medicinal charcoal

Köh·ler ['kø:lɐ] *m* (-s; -) **1.** charcoal burner; **2.** *zo.* coalfish

'Koh·le|stift *m* **1.** piece of charcoal; **2.** ⚡ carbon rod; **~ta͵blet·te** *f* charcoal tablet; **~ver·ede·lung** *f* coal conversion; **~vor·kom·men** *n* coal deposit(s *pl.*); **~zeich·nung** *f* charcoal drawing

'Kohl·kopf *m* (head of) cabbage

'Kohl·mei·se *f* great tit

'kohl'ra·ben'schwarz *adj.* jet-black *hair etc.*; pitch-black *night etc.*

Kohl·ra·bi [ko:l'ra:bi] *m* (-[s]; -[s]) kohlrabi

'Kohl|rou͵la·den *pl. gastr.* stuffed cabbage leaves; **~rü·be** *f* swede, *Am. a.* rutabaga; **~weiß·ling** [-vaɪslɪŋ] *m* (-s; -e) cabbage white butterfly

Ko·hor·te [ko'hɔrtə] *f* (-; -n) cohort

koi·tie·ren [koi'ti:rən] *v/i.* (h) have sexual intercourse, copulate; **Koi·tus** ['ko:itʊs] *m* (-; - [-tu:s]) coitus, sexual intercourse

Ko·je ['ko:jə] *f* (-; -n) ⚓ bunk, berth

Ko·jo·te [ko'jo:tə] *m* (-n; -n) coyote

Ko·ka·in [koka'i:n] *n* (-s; *no pl.*) cocain(e); **~süch·ti·ge** *m, f* (-n; -n) cocain(e) addict

ko·kett [ko'kɛt] *adj.* coquettish, F flirty

ko·ket·tie·ren [kokɛ'ti:rən] *v/i.* (h) *a. fig.* flirt (***mit*** *dat.* with)

Kok·ken ['kɔkən] *pl.* cocci

Ko·ko·lo·res [koko'lo:rɛs] F *m* (-; *no pl.*) rubbish, F rot, *Am.* F garbage

Ko·kon [ko'kõ:] *m* (-s; -s) cocoon

Ko·kos|baum ['ko:kɔs-] *m* coconut tree (*or* palm); **~fett** *n* coconut fat; **~flocken** *pl.* desiccated coconut *sg.*; **~ma͵kro·ne** *f* macaroon; **~mat·te** *f* coconut mat(ting); **~milch** *f* coconut milk; **~nuß** *f* coconut; **~öl** *n* coconut oil; **~pal·me** *f* coconut palm (*or* tree); **~ras·peln** *pl.* desiccated coconut *sg.*

Koks [ko:ks] *m* (-es; *no pl.*) **1.** coke; **2.** *sl.* coke; **kok·sen** ['ko:ksən] *sl. v/i.* (h) *sl.* take (*or* sniff) coke; **'Koks·feue·rung** *f* coke firing

Ko·la·nuß ['ko:la-] *f* cola nut

Kol·ben ['kɔlbən] *m* (-s; -) a) *mot.* piston, b) (*rifle*) butt, c) ⚗ flask; ⚡ bulb, d) ✿ spike; (*corn*)cob, e) F conk; **~an·trieb** *m* piston drive; **~fres·ser** F *m*: ***ich hatte e-n ~*** the engine seized (up); **~hub** *m* piston stroke; **~mo·tor** *m* piston engine; **~stan·ge** *f* piston rod; **~ver·dich·ter** *m* reciprocating compressor

Kol·cho·se [kɔl'ço:zə] *f* (-; -n) kolkhoz, collective farm

Ko·li·bak͵te·ri·en ['ko:li-] *pl.* coli

Ko·li·bri ['ko:libri] *m* (-s; -s) humming bird

Ko·lik ['ko:lɪk] *f* (-; -en) colic

Kolk·ra·be ['kɔlk-] *m* (common) raven

kol·la·bie·ren [kɔla'bi:rən] *v/i.* (sn) ⚕ collapse

Kol·la·bo·ra·teur [kɔlabora'tø:ɐ] *m* (-s; -e [-rə]) *pol.* collaborator; **kol·la·bo·rie·ren** [kɔlabo'ri:rən] *v/i.* (h) collaborate

Kol·la·gen [kɔla'ge:n] *n* (-s; -e) collagen

Kol·laps ['kɔlaps] *m* (-es; -e): (*a.* ***e-n ~ erleiden***) collapse

kol·la·te·ral [kɔlate'ra:l] *adj.* collateral

Kol·leg [kɔ'le:k] *n* (-s; -s) **1.** *ped.* sixth-form college; **2.** *R.C.* theological college

Kol·le·ge [kɔ'le:gə] *m* (-n; -n) **1.** colleague; **2.** fellow student (*or* cyclist *etc.*); **3.** F mate

Kol'le·gen|kreis *m*: ***im ~*** among colleagues; ***im ~ behauptet man*** *etc.* colleagues maintain *etc.*; **~ra͵batt** *m* trade discount

kol·le·gi·al [kɔle'gi̯a:l] *adj.* friendly; helpful; loyal; ***das war nicht sehr ~ von dir*** that wasn't very nice of you; **Kol·le·gia·li·tät** [kɔlegi̯ali'tɛ:t] *f* (-; *no pl.*) helpfulness; loyalty (to one's colleagues)

Kol·le·gin [kɔ'le:gɪn] *f* (-; -nen) → ***Kollege***

Kol·le·gi·um [kɔ'le:gi̯ʊm] *n* (-s; Kollegien [kɔ'le:gi̯ən]) a) committee, b) teaching staff

Kol'leg|map·pe *f* document case; **~stu·fe** *f ped.* sixth-form college, *Am.* junior college

Kol·lek·te [kɔ'lɛktə] *f* (-; -n) collection

Kol·lek·ti·on [kɔlɛk'tsi̯o:n] *f* (-; -en) ✝ collection, range

kol·lek·tiv [kɔlɛk'ti:f] *adj.* collective

Kol·lek'tiv|be·dürf·nis *n* collective need; **~be·wußt·sein** *n* collective consciousness

Kol·lek·ti·vis·mus [kɔlɛkti'vɪsmʊs] *m* (-; *no pl.*) collectivism

Kol·lek'tiv|schuld *f* collective guilt; **~ver·si·che·rung** *f* group insurance; **~ver·trag** *m* collective agreement (*pol.* treaty); **~wirt·schaft** *f* collective economy

Kol·lek·tor [kɔ'lɛkto:ɐ] *m* (-s; -en [kɔlɛk'to:rən]) **1.** ⚡ commutator; **2.** collector; **3.** → ***Sonnenkollektor***

Kol·ler ['kɔlɐ] F *fig. m* (-s; -) tantrum; ***e-n ~ kriegen*** F flip one's lid

kol·lern¹ ['kɔlɐn] *v/i.* (sn) roll

'kol·lern² *v/i.* (h) *turkey*: gobble; *fig. stomach*: rumble

kol·li·die·ren [kɔli'di:rən] *v/i.* **1.** (sn) collide; **2.** (h) *fig.* clash

Kol·lier [kɔ'lje:] *n* a) necklace, b) necklet

Kol·li·si·on [kɔli'zi̯o:n] *f* (-; -en) collision; *fig.* clash, *a.* ⚖ conflict; **Kol·li·si'ons·kurs** *m*: ***auf ~ sein*** *a. fig.* be on a collision course

Kol·lo·ka·ti·on [kɔloka'tsi̯o:n] *f* (-; -en) collocation

Kol·lo·qui·um [kɔ'lo:kvi̯ʊm] *n* (-s; -quien [-kvi̯ən]) colloquium

Kol·lu·si·on [kɔlu'zi̯o:n] *f* (-; -en) ⚖ collusion

Köl·nisch·was·ser ['kœlnɪʃ-] *n* eau de Cologne

Ko·lon ['ko:lɔn] *n* (-s; -s, Kola ['ko:la]) *ling., anat.* colon

Ko·lo·ni·al... [kolo'ni̯a:l-] *in cpds.* colonial; **~her·ren** *pl.* colonial masters; **~herr·schaft** *f* colonial rule

Ko·lo·nia·lis·mus [koloni̯a'lɪsmʊs] *m* (-; *no pl.*) colonialism

Ko·lo·ni'al|krieg *m* colonial war; **~macht** *f* colonial power; **~stil** *m* colonial style; **~zeit** *f* colonial age; ***in der ~*** *a.* in colonial times, in the colonial days

Ko·lo·nie [kolo'ni:] *f* (-; -n [-ən]) colony (*a. biol.*); **Ko·lo·ni·sa·ti·on** [koloniza'tsi̯o:n] *f* (-; *no pl.*) colonization; **Ko·lo·ni·sa·tor** [koloni'za:to:ɐ] *m* (-s; -en [-za'to:rən]) colonizer; **ko·lo·ni·sie·ren** [koloni'zi:rən] *v/t.* (h) colonize; **Ko·lo·nist** [kolo'nɪst] *m* (-en; -en) colonist, settler

Ko·lon·na·de [kolɔ'na:də] *f* (-; -n) colonnade

Ko·lon·ne [ko'lɔnə] *f* (-; -n) column; *mot.* convoy; crew *of workers etc.*; *pol.* ***Fünfte ~*** Fifth Column; ***~ fahren*** drive in line

Ko'lon·nen|sprin·ger F *m mot.* F queue-jumper; **~ver·kehr** *m* single-line traffic

Ko·lo·pho·ni·um [kolo'fo:ni̯ʊm] *n* (-s; *no pl.*) rosin, 📖 colophony

Ko·lo·ra·tur [kolora'tu:ɐ] *f* (-; -en [-rən]) ♪ coloratura; **~sän·ge·rin** *f* coloratura; **~so͵pran** *m* coloratura soprano

ko·lo·rie·ren [kolo'ri:rən] *v/t.* (h) colo(u)r; colo(u)rize *film*; **Ko·lo'rie·rung** *f* (-; -en) colo(u)ring; *film*: colo(u)rization

Ko·lo·ri·me·ter [kolori'me:tɐ] *n* (-s; -) colorimeter; **Ko·lo·ri·me·trie** [kolorime'tri:] *f* (-; *no pl.*) colorimetry

Ko·lo·ris·mus [kolo'rɪsmʊs] *m* (-; *no pl.*) *art*: colo(u)rism

Ko·lo·rit [kolo'ri:t] *n* (-[e]s; -e) colo(u)r, colo(u)ring; *fig.* local colo(u)r, atmosphere

Ko·loß [ko'lɔs] *m* (-sses; -sse) colossus; *fig. a.* giant; **ko·los·sal** [kolɔ'sa:l] *adj.* gigantic; *fig.* mammoth *task etc.*

Ko·los'sal|film *m* screen epic, (Hollywood) spectacular; **~ge·mäl·de** *n* monumental painting; **~schin·ken** F *m* **1.** → ***Kolossalfilm***; **2.** → ***Kolossalgemälde***; **~sta·tue** *f* giant statue

Ko·lo·strum [koˈlɔstrʊm] *n* (-s; *no pl.*) colostrum, first milk

Kol·por·ta·ge [kɔlpɔrˈtaːʒə] *f* (-; -n) **1.** a) sensationalism, b) trash; **2.** rumo(u)r-mongering; **~li·te·ra͵tur** *f* trashy literature; **~ro͵man** *m* trashy novel

Kol·por·teur [kɔlpɔrˈtøːɐ] *m* (-s; -e [-rə]) rumo(u)r-monger; **kol·por·tie·ren** [kɔlpɔrˈtiːrən] *v/t.* (h) spread

Ko·lum·bia·ner [kolʊmˈbi̯aːnɐ] *m* (-s; -), **Ko·lum·bia·ne·rin** [kolʊmˈbi̯aːnərɪn] *f* (-; -nen), **ko·lum·bia·nisch** [kolʊmˈbi̯aːnɪʃ] *adj.* Colombian

Ko·lum·ne [koˈlʊmnə] *f* (-; -n) *typ.* column; **Koˈlum·nen·ti·tel** *m* running title (*or* headline); **Ko·lum·nist** [kolʊmˈnɪst] *m* (-en; -en) columnist

Ko·ma [ˈkoːma] *n* (-s; -s, Komata [-ta]) ⚕ coma; ***im ~ liegen*** be in a coma

Kom·bi [ˈkɔmbi] F *m* (-s; -s) → ***Kombiwagen***

Kom·bi·nat [kɔmbiˈnaːt] *n* (-[e]s; -e) *hist. DDR* collective combine

Kom·bi·na·ti·on [kɔmbinaˈtsi̯oːn] *f* (-; -en) **1.** a) combination (*a. chess*, ⚗, ⚙ *etc.*, *a. of a lock*), b) matching jacket and trousers (*or* skirt *etc.*) *pl.*; overalls *pl.*; ***Alpine*** (***Nordische***) *~ skiing*: Alpine (Nordic) combination; ***e-e tolle ~ soccer etc.***: a lovely move; **2.** deduction; conjecture

Kom·bi·na·tiˈons|ga·be *f* (-; *no pl.*) power(s *pl.*) of deduction; **~lauf** *m skiing*: combined event; **~mö·bel** *pl.* **1.** add-on furniture *sg.*; **2.** all-purpose furniture *sg.*; **~prä·pa͵rat** *n* compound preparation *sg.*; **~schloß** *n* combination lock; **~spiel** *n* teamwork; **~zan·ge** *f* → ***Kombizange***

kom·bi·nie·ren [kɔmbiˈniːrən] (h) **I.** *v/t.* combine (***mit*** *dat.* with); ***das läßt sich gut miteinander ~*** a) *clothes etc.*: they go together very well, b) *appointments etc.*: we *etc.* could combine that very nicely; **II.** *v/i.* deduce

ˈKom·bi|wa·gen *m* estate car, *Am.* station wagon; **~zan·ge** *f*: (***e-e ~*** a pair of) combination pliers *pl.*

Kom·bü·se [kɔmˈbyːzə] *f* (-; -n) galley

Ko·met [koˈmeːt] *m* (-en; -en) comet; **koˈme·ten·haft** *adj.*: ***~er Aufstieg*** meteoric rise; **Koˈme·ten·schweif** *m* tail of a (*or* the) comet

Kom·fort [kɔmˈfoːɐ] *m* (-s; *no pl.*) conveniences *pl.*; luxury; ***mit allem ~ apartment etc.*** with all the conveniences, *appliances etc.* with all the extras; **kom·for·ta·bel** [kɔmfɔrˈtaːbəl] *adj.* comfortable *life*; well-appointed *apartment etc.*, *a.* good *hotel etc.*; plush *car etc.*; **Komˈfort·woh·nung** *f* luxury apartment

Ko·mik [ˈkoːmɪk] *f* (-; *no pl.*) humo(u)r; *the* funny side (***an*** *dat.* of); ***voller ~*** very funny

Ko·mi·ker [ˈkoːmikɐ] *m* (-s; -) comedian, comic (*both a. fig.*); comic actor; *fig. contp.* idiot; **Ko·mi·ke·rin** [ˈkoːmikərɪn] *f* (-; -nen) comedienne; comic actress

ˈKo·mi·ker·paar *n* comedy duo

ko·misch [ˈkoːmɪʃ] *adj.* funny (*a. fig.*); *thea.* comic *opera etc.*; F ***~er Vogel*** F funny guy; ***das ꝯe daran*** the funny thing about it; ***mir ist so ~*** I feel really funny; **ko·mi·scher·wei·se** [ˈkoːmɪʃɐˈvaɪzə] *adv.* funnily enough

Ko·mi·tee [komiˈteː] *n* (-s; -s) committee; body

Kom·ma [ˈkɔma] *n* (-s; -s, -ta [-ta]) comma; decimal point; ***sechs ~ vier*** six point four; ***null ~ fünf*** (nought) point five; ***hier fehlt ein ~*** there's a comma (*or* decimal point) missing here (*or* somewhere); **~ba͵zil·lus** *m* comma bacillus; **~feh·ler** *m* comma mistake

Kom·man·dant [kɔmanˈdant] *m* (-en; -en) commander, commanding officer (*abbr.* CO); commandant; **Kom·man·dan·tur** [kɔmandanˈtuːɐ] *f* (-; -en [-rən]) **1.** commander's office; **2.** garrison headquarters *pl.*; **Kom·man·deur** [kɔmanˈdøːɐ] *m* (-s; -e [-rə]) commander

kom·man·die·ren [kɔmanˈdiːrən] *v/t. and v/i.* (h) a) command, be in command (of), b) command, order; give the orders; F (*only v/t.*) boss *s.o.* about; ***~ zu*** *dat.* detach to, detail to (*or* for)

Kom·man·dit·ge·sell·schaft [kɔmanˈdiːt-] *f* limited partnership

Kom·man·di·tist [kɔmandiˈtɪst] *m* (-en; -en) limited partner

Kom·man·do [kɔˈmando] *n* (-s; -s) a) command, order, b) command, headquarters *pl.*, c) detachment; commando (unit); ***das ~ führen*** be in command; ***auf ~*** on command; ***wie auf ~*** as if by command, as if he *etc.* had rehearsed it; ***ich kann nicht auf ~ lachen*** *etc.* I can't just turn it on; ***~ zurück!*** hold it!; **~brücke** *f* ⚓ bridge; **~ge·walt** *f* power of command; **~kap·sel** *f space travel*: command module; **~spra·che** *f computer*: command language; **~stel·le** *f* command post; **~ton** *m*: (***im ~*** in a *or* one's) sergeant-major's voice; **~trupp** *m* command unit; **~trup·pe** *f* Commandos *pl.*, *Am.* Rangers *pl.*

ˈKom·ma·zei·chen *n* comma

kom·men [ˈkɔmən] **I.** *v/i.* (kam, gekommen, sn) **1.** a) come, arrive; get (***bis*** to), b) come, happen; ***komm schon!*** come on!, hurry up!; ***ich komme schon!*** I'm coming; ***er wird bald ~*** he won't be long; ***es kommt ein Gewitter*** there's a storm coming up; ***der Morgen kommt*** it's nearly morning, it's starting to get light; ***spät ~*** come (*or* be) late; ***angelaufen*** *etc.* ~ come running *etc.* along (*or* up); ***j-n ~ lassen*** send for s.o.; ***er soll nur ~!*** (just) let him come; ***et. ~ lassen*** send for (*or* order) s.th.; ***et. ~ sehen*** see s.th. coming; ***wie weit bist du gekommen?*** how far did you get?; ***es ist so weit gekommen, daß*** things have got to the stage where; F ***es wird noch so weit ~, daß er rausgeschmissen wird*** he'll be thrown out one of these days; ***wenn Sie mir so ~*** if you talk to me like that; ***komm mir ja nicht so frech!*** I don't want any of your cheek; F ***na, komm schon!*** come on(, now)!; ***komme, was da wolle*** come what may; ***es wird noch ganz anders ~*** there's worse to come (yet); ***das mußte ja so ~*** it had to (*or* was bound to) happen; ***wie kommt das?*** how come?; ***wie*** (***or woher***) ***kommt es, daß*** how is it that, how come; ***das kommt daher, daß*** it's because; ***es kam mir*** (***der Gedanke***), ***daß*** it occurred to me that; ***es kommt mir e-e Idee*** I've got an idea, I know what we can do; ***wer zuerst kommt, mahlt zuerst*** first come, first served; *iro.* ***mir ~ die Tränen*** don't make me weep; **2.** *with prp.*: ***~ an*** *acc.* a) come (*or* get) to, arrive at, b) go (*or* fall) to *s.o.*; ***an j-s Stelle ~*** take s.o.'s place; ***~ auf*** *acc.* a) think of, hit upon *the idea*, b) think of, remember, c) come to, total; ***auf die Rechnung ~*** go (*or* be put) on the bill; ***das kommt auf Seite 12*** that comes (*or* is) on page 12; ***auf et. zu sprechen ~*** get onto the subject of; ***wie kommst du darauf?*** what makes you say that?, what gives you that idea?; ***darauf wäre ich nie gekommen*** it would never have occurred to me; ***ich komme nicht darauf!*** I just can't think of it; ***darauf komme ich gleich*** I'll be coming to that; ***auf 1000 Einwohner kommt ein Arzt*** there's a (*or* one) doctor for every 1000 inhabitants; ***ich lasse nichts auf ihn ~*** I won't have anything said against him; ***~ durch*** *acc.* pass (*or* come) through; ***hinter e-e Sache ~*** find s.th. out; ***~ in*** *acc.* come (*or* go) into, enter; ***das Buch kommt ins oberste Regal*** (***ins Arbeitszimmer***) the book goes on the top shelf (into the study); ***komm mir nur nicht mit diesen Ausreden*** spare me your excuses; ***damit kannst du mir nicht ~*** you don't expect me to believe that, do you?; ***komm mir nicht dauernd mit der Geschichte*** I wish you wouldn't keep going on (*or* I wish you'd shut up) about that business; ***er kommt einfach mit diesen Ideen*** he just trots out these ideas; ***~ nach*** *dat.* a) come (*or* get) to, b) come after; ***wie komme ich nach ...?*** how do I get to ...?; ***~ über*** *acc.* a) come via *Berlin*, b) get over *a fence etc.*, c) *fig. feeling etc.*: come over *s.o.*; *curse etc.*: come upon *s.o.*; ***um et. ~*** be done out of s.th.; ***ums Leben ~*** die, be killed; ***~ unter*** *acc.* go under *the heading etc.*; ***das kommt davon!*** see?, what did I tell you?; ***~ vor*** *dat.* come (*or* go) before; ***vors Gericht ~*** come up before the court; ***zu et. ~*** a) come (*or* get) to s.th., b) come by s.th., get hold of s.th., come into *a fortune*; ***zu der Ansicht ~, daß*** come to the conclusion that, decide that; ***zur Sprache ~*** come up (for discussion); (***wieder***) ***zu sich ~*** come to (*or* round); ***wie kamst du bloß dazu***(***, das zu tun***)***?*** what on earth made you do that?; ***es kam zum Streit*** they (*or* we *etc.*) ended up arguing; ***es kam zu Kämpfen zwischen ...*** fighting broke out between ...; ***ich komme einfach nicht zum Lesen*** I just don't get the time to read anything; ***ich komme aber erst morgen dazu*** I won't get round to it (*or* manage it) before tomorrow; ***wie ~ Sie dazu?*** how dare you?; → ***Kraft*** 1, ***Sache***; **II.** ꝯ *n* (-s) arrival; ***ein ständiges ~ und Gehen*** a constant coming and going; ***es ist ein ständiges ~ und Gehen*** people are in and out all day, there's a constant stream of traffic (*or* of people going in and out); *fig.* ***im ~ sein*** be on the ascendancy; ***kurze Röcke sind wieder im ~*** short hemlines are coming in again; ***dieser Dirigent ist im ~*** he's an up-and-coming (young) conductor; **ˈkom·mend** *adj.* coming, *a.* future; forthcoming; ***im ~en Jahr*** next year; ***in*** (***den***) ***~en Jahren*** in (the) years to come; ***die ~e Generation*** the rising (*or* up-and-coming) generation; ***~e Geschlechter*** future generations; ***~er Mann*** F up-and-comer

kom·men·su·ra·bel [kɔmɛnzuˈraːbəl] *adj.* commensurable

Kom·men·tar [kɔmɛnˈtaːɐ] *m* (-s; -e [-rə]) commentary; comment; *newspaper*: opinion column; ***e-n ~ geben zu*** *dat.*

comment on *s.th.*; ***er muß ständig s-n ~ abgeben*** he always has to have his say; ***kein ~!*** no comment; **kom·men'tar·los** *adv.* without comment

Kom·men·ta·tor [kɔmɛn'ta:to:ʁ] *m* (-s; -en [-ta'to:rən]) commentator; **Kom·men·ta'to·ren·box** *f sport etc.* commentary box

kom·men·tie·ren [kɔmɛn'ti:rən] *v/t.* (h) comment on; give (*or* write) a commentary on; annotate *texts*

Kom·merz [kɔ'mɛrts] *m* (-es; *no pl.*) commerce; ***reiner ~*** pure commercialism; ***nur auf ~ aussein*** be out for profit

kom·mer·zia·li·sie·ren [kɔmɛrtsĭali-'zi:rən] *v/t.* (h) commercialize; **Kom·mer·zia·li'sie·rung** *f* (-; *no pl.*) commercialization

kom·mer·zi·ell [kɔmɛr'tsĭɛl] *adj.* commercial

Kom·mi·li·to·ne [kɔmili'to:nə] *m* (-n; -n), **Kom·mi·li·to·nin** [kɔmili'to:nın] *f* (-; -nen) fellow student; ***m-e Kommilitonen*** the other students

Kom·mis·sar [kɔmı'sa:ʁ] *m* (-s; -e [-rə]) **1.** commissioner; *hist. in Russia*: commissar; **2.** (police) superintendent; (detective) superintendent; **Kom·mis·sa·ri·at** [kɔmısa'rĭa:t] *n* (-[e]s; -e) a) commissionership, b) commissioner's *etc.* office, c) *Austrian* police station; **kom·mis·sa·risch** [kɔmı'sa:rıʃ] *adj.* provisional, temporary

Kom·mis·si·on [kɔmı'sĭo:n] *f* (-; -en) ✝ commission; ***in ~ geben*** commission; **Kom·mis·sio·när** [kɔmısĭo'nɛ:ʁ] *m* (-s; -e [-rə]) ✝ commission agent

Kom·mis·si'ons|ba·sis *f*: ***auf ~*** on commission; **~ge·bühr** *f* commission; **~ge·schäft** *n* commission business; **~la·ger** *n* consignment stock; **~ver·kauf** *m* sale on commission; **~wa·re** *f* consigned goods *pl.*

kom·mis·si'ons·wei·se *adv.* on commission

Kom·mit·tent [kɔmı'tɛnt] *m* (-en; -en) ✝ consigner

Kom·mo·de [kɔ'mo:də] *f* (-; -n) chest of drawers, *Am.* bureau

Kom·mo·do·re [kɔmo'do:rə] *m* (-s; -n, -s) commodore

kom·mu·nal [kɔmu'na:l] *adj.* municipal, communal, local

'Kom·mu'nal|ab·ga·ben *pl.* (*local*) rates, *Am.* local taxes; *in GB*: council tax *sg.*; **~an·lei·he** *f* municipal loan; **~bank** *f* (-; -en) municipal bank; **~be·am·te** *m* municipal civil servant; **~po·li,tik** *f* local politics *pl.*; **~steu·er** *f* → ***Kommunalabgaben***; **~ver·wal·tung** *f* local government; **~wah·len** *pl.* local elections

Kom·mu·nar·de [kɔmu'nardə] *m* (-n; -n) **1.** *hist.* Communard; **2.** ***~ sein*** live in a commune

Kom·mu·ne [kɔ'mu:nə] *f* (-; -n) **1.** community; **2.** commune

Kom·mu·ni·kant [kɔmuni'kant] *m* (-en; -en) *R.C.* communicant

Kom·mu·ni·ka·ti·on [kɔmunika'tsĭo:n] *f* (-; -en) communication; **kom·mu·ni·ka·ti'ons·fä·hig** *adj.* able to communicate; **Kom·mu·ni·ka·ti'ons·fä·hig·keit** *f* (-; *no pl.*) ability to communicate

'Kom·mu·ni·ka·ti'ons|fluß *m* flow of communication, intercommunication; ***gestörter ~*** communications breakdown; **~for·schung** *f* communications research; **~lücke** *f* communications gap; **~mit·tel** *n* means (*sg.*) of communication; (*radio, TV etc.*) media; **~sa·tel,lit** *m* communications satellite; **~schwie·rig·kei·ten** *pl.*: ***es gab ~*** we *etc.* had difficulty communicating, we *etc.* had difficulty getting across; **~wis·sen·schaft** *f* communication(s) science; **~zen·trum** *n* meeting place; community cent|re (*Am.* -er)

kom·mu·ni·ka·tiv [kɔmunika'ti:f] *adj.* communicative

Kom·mu·ni·on [kɔmu'nĭo:n] *f* (-; -en) *R.C.* (Holy) Communion

Kom·mu·ni·qué [kɔmyni'ke:, kɔmuni-'ke:] *n* (-s; -s) communiqué

Kom·mu·nis·mus [kɔmu'nısmʊs] *m* (-; *no pl.*) communism; **Kom·mu·nist** [kɔmu'nıst] *m* (-en; -en), **Kom·mu·ni·stin** [kɔmu'nıstın] *f* (-; -nen) communist; Communist; **kom·mu·ni·stisch** [kɔmu-'nıstıʃ] *adj.* communist

kom·mu·ni·zie·ren [kɔmuni'tsi:rən] *v/i.* (h) communicate; ***~de Röhren*** communicating tubes

Ko·mö·di·ant [komø'dĭant] *m* (-en; -en) **1.** actor; ***er ist ein echter ~*** he's a full-blooded actor; **2.** *fig. contp.* play-actor; hypocrite; **Ko·mö·di·an·tin** [komø-'dĭantın] *f* (-; -nen) actress; → ***Komödiant*** 2; **ko·mö·di·an·tisch** [komø'dĭantıʃ] *adj.* acting ...; **Ko·mö·die** [ko-'mø:dĭə] *f* (-; -n) comedy; *fig.* farce; play-acting; **ko'mö·di·en·haft** *adj.* theatrical, histrionic; **Ko'mö·di·en·schrei·ber** *m* comedy writer, comic playwright

Kom·pa·gnon [kɔmpan'jõ:] *m* (-s; -s) partner

kom·pakt [kɔm'pakt] *adj.* compact

Kom'pakt·an·la·ge *f* music cent|re (*Am.* -er)

Kom'pakt·heit *f* (-; *no pl.*) compactness

Kom'pakt|ka·me·ra *f* compact camera; **~ski** *m* compact ski; **~wa·gen** *m* compact car

Kom·pa·nie [kɔmpa'ni:] *f* (-; -n) ⚔ company; **~chef** *m*, **~füh·rer** *m* company commander

kom·pa·ra·bel [kɔmpa'ra:bəl] *adj.* comparable

Kom·pa·ra·tist [kɔmpara'tıst] *m* (-en; -en) comparatist; **Kom·pa·ra·ti·stik** [kɔmpara'tıstık] *f* (-; *no pl.*) comparative literature (*or* studies *pl.*)

Kom·pa·ra·tiv ['kɔmparati:f] *m* (-s; -e [-və]), ♀ *adj. ling.* comparative

Kom·par·se [kɔm'parzə] *m* (-n; -n), **Kom·par·sin** [kɔm'parzın] *f* (-; -nen) bit player, *film*: *a.* extra

Kom·paß ['kɔmpas] *m* (-sses; -sse) compass; **~na·del** *f* compass needle

kom·pa·ti·bel [kɔmpa'ti:bəl] *adj.* compatible; **Kom·pa·ti·bi·li·tät** [kɔmpatibili-'tɛ:t] *f* (-; *no pl.*) compatibility

Kom·pen·di·um [kɔm'pɛndĭʊm] *n* (-s; -ien) compendium

Kom·pen·sa·ti·on [kɔmpɛnza'tsĭo:n] *f* (-; -en) *a.* ⚡, ⚖, *psych.* compensation; **Kom·pen·sa·ti'ons·ge·schäft** *n* barter transaction; **Kom·pen·sa·tor** [kɔmpɛn'za:to:ʁ] *m* (-s; -en [-za'to:rən]) ⚡ compensator, potentiometer; **kom·pen·sa·to·risch** [kɔmpɛnza'to:rıʃ] *adj.* compensatory; **kom·pen·sie·ren** [kɔmpɛn'zi:rən] *v/t.* (h) compensate for (*a. psych.*); ⚡, ⚒ compensate

kom·pe·tent [kɔmpe'tɛnt] *adj.* competent; responsible; qualified

Kom·pe·tenz [kɔmpe'tɛnts] *f* (-; -en) competence; responsibility; ***in die ~*** *gen.* ***fallen*** be the responsibility of; ***s-e ~en überschreiten*** exceed one's authority; **~be·reich** *m* area (*or* sphere) of authority; **~kon,flikt** *m*, **~streit** *m* conflict of powers; demarcation (*or* jurisdictional) dispute

Kom·pi·la·ti·on [kɔmpila'tsĭo:n] *f* (-; -en) compilation; **Kom·pi·la·tor** [kɔmpi'la:to:ʁ] *m* (-s; -en [-la'to:rən]) compiler; **kom·pi·lie·ren** [kɔmpi'li:rən] *v/t.* (h) compile

kom·ple·men·tär [kɔmplemɛn'tɛ:ʁ] **I.** *adj.* complementary; **II.** ♀ *m* (-s; -e [-rə]) ✝ general partner; **Kom·ple·men'tär·far·be** *f* complementary colo(u)r

kom·ple·men·tie·ren [kɔmplemɛn'ti:-rən] *v/t.* (h) complement

Kom·plet[1] [kõ'ple:, kɔm'ple:] *n* (-s; -s) matching dress and coat (*or* jacket)

Kom·plet[2] [kɔm'ple:t] *f* (-; -e) *eccl.* compline

kom·plett [kɔm'plɛt] *adj.* complete; F *contp. a.* utter *nonsense etc.*; **kom·plet·tie·ren** [kɔmplɛ'ti:rən] *v/t.* (h) complete

Kom·plex [kɔm'plɛks] **I.** *m* (-es; -e) complex (*a. psych.*, ⚒, ⚗ *etc.*); ***voller ~e*** complex-ridden, full of complexes; **II.** ♀ *adj.* complex; **kom'plex·be·la·den** *adj. psych.* full of complexes; **Kom·ple·xi·tät** [kɔmplɛksi'tɛ:t] *f* (-; *no pl.*) complexity

Kom·pli·ka·ti·on [kɔmplika'tsĭo:n] *f* (-; -en) complication; **kom·pli·ka·ti'ons·los I.** *adj.* straightforward, uncomplicated; **II.** *adv. go etc.* without a hitch

Kom·pli·ment [kɔmpli'mɛnt] *n* (-[e]s; -e) compliment; ***(mein) ~!*** congratulations!; ***j-m ~e machen*** pay s.o. compliments

kom·pli·men·tie·ren [kɔmplimɛn'ti:rən] *v/t.* (h) escort; *euphem.* ***j-n zur Tür ~*** usher s.o. out

Kom·pli·ze [kɔm'pli:tsə] *m* (-n; -n) accomplice

kom·pli·zie·ren [kɔmpli'tsi:rən] *v/t.* (h) complicate; ***das kompliziert die Sache*** that complicates matters; **kom·pli·ziert** [kɔmpli'tsi:ʁt] *adj.* complicated; complex *character etc.*; intricate; ⚕ ***~er Bruch*** compound fracture; **Kom·pli'ziert·heit** *f* (-; *no pl.*) complexity

Kom·plott [kɔm'plɔt] *n* (-[e]s; -e) plot, conspiracy; ***ein ~ schmieden*** plot, conspire (***gegen*** *acc.* against), hatch a plot

Kom·po·nen·te [kɔmpo'nɛntə] *f* (-; -n) component; *fig. a.* element

kom·po·nie·ren [kɔmpo'ni:rən] *v/t. and v/i.* (h) compose (*a. fig.*); write *a song etc.*

Kom·po·nist [kɔmpo'nıst] *m* (-en; -en) composer; **Kom·po·si·ti·on** [kɔmpozi'tsĭo:n] *f* (-; -en) composition (*a. fig.*); *typ.* page make-up, layout; **Kom·po·si·ti'ons·leh·re** *f* (theory of) composition; **kom·po·si·to·risch** [kɔmpozi'to:rıʃ] *adj.* compositional; ***sein ~es Werk*** his musical works

Kom·po·si·tum [kɔm'po:zitʊm] *n* (-s; -ta) *ling.* compound

Kom·post [kɔm'pɔst] *m* (-[e]s; -e) compost; **~hau·fen** *m* compost heap

kom·po·stie·ren [kɔmpɔs'ti:rən] *v/t.* (h) a) compost, b) put compost on, add compost to; **Kom·po'stie·rung** *f* (-; *no pl.*) composting

Kom·pott [kɔm'pɔt] *n* (-[e]s; -e) stewed fruit; **~scha·le** *f*, **~schüs·sel** *f* dessert bowl

Kom·pres·se [kɔm'prɛsə] *f* (-; -n) compress

Kom·pres·si·on [kɔmprɛ'sĭo:n] *f* (-; -en) ⚙ compression; **Kom·pres·si'ons·ver·band** *m* ⚕ pressure bandage
Kom·pres·sor [kɔm'prɛso:ɐ] *m* (-s; -en [kɔmprɛ'so:rən]) ⚙ compressor; *mot.* supercharger
kom·pri·mie·ren [kɔmpri'mi:rən] *v/t.* (h) compress; condense (*a. fig.*); **kom·pri·miert** [kɔmpri'mi:ɐt] **I.** *adj.* condensed; concise; **II.** *adv.*: ***et.*** ~ ***ausdrücken*** put s.th. concisely
Kom·pro·miß [kɔmpro'mɪs] *m* (-sses; -sse) compromise; tradeoff; ***e-n*** ~ ***schließen*** (make a) compromise (***über*** *acc.* on); **≗be·reit** *adj.* willing to compromise; **~for·mel** *f* compromise (solution)
Kom·pro·miß·ler [kɔmpro'mɪslɐ] *m* (-s; -) compromiser; **kom·pro·miß·le·risch** [kɔmpro'mɪslərɪʃ] *adj.* too ready to make concessions; ***~e Haltung*** *esp. pol.* softly-softly approach
kom·pro'miß·los *adj.* uncompromising; *pol. a.* hard-line ...; relentless
Kom·pro'miß|lö·sung *f* compromise solution; **~vor·schlag** *m* compromise proposal
kom·pro·mit·tie·ren [kɔmpromɪ'ti:rən] *v/t.* (h) compromise (***sich*** o.s.)
Kom·teß [kɔm'tɛs] *f* (-; -ssen), **Kom·tes·se** [kɔm'tɛsə] *f* (-; -n) countess
Kom·tur [kɔm'tu:ɐ] *m* (-s; -e [-rə]) commander (of an order)
Kon·den·sat [kɔndɛn'za:t] *n* (-[e]s; -e) condensate; **Kon·den·sa·ti·on** [kɔndɛnza'tsĭo:n] *f* (-; -en) condensation
Kon·den·sa·tor [kɔndɛn'za:to:ɐ] *m* (-s; -en [-za'to:rən]) ⚡ capacitor, *esp.* ⚙, ⚗ condenser; **~mi·kro,phon** *n* condenser microphone
kon·den·sie·ren [kɔndɛn'zi:rən] *v/t.* (h, sn) condense; **Kon·den'sie·rung** *f* (-; *no pl.*) condensation
Kon·dens|milch [kɔn'dɛns-] *f* evaporated (*or* condensed) milk; **~strei·fen** *m* ✈ condensation (*or* vapo[u]r) trail; **~was·ser** *n* condensation
Kon·di·ti·on [kɔndi'tsĭo:n] *f* (-; -en) **1.** *no pl.* condition; ***e-e gute*** (***keine***) ~ ***haben*** be very fit (have no stamina); **2.** *usu. pl.* ⚚ condition; ***zu günstigen ~en*** on favo(u)rable terms
Kon·di·tio·nal [kɔnditsĭo'na:l] *m* (-s; -e), ≗ *adj. ling.* conditional; **~satz** *m* conditional clause
kon·di·tio·nell [kɔnditsĭo'nɛl] *adv.* stamina-wise; ~ ***am Ende*** on one's last legs; ~ ***ganz oben*** in top form
kon·di·tio·nie·ren [kɔnditsĭo'ni:rən] *v/t.* (h) condition
Kon·di·ti'ons|man·gel *m* → ***Konditionsschwäche;*** **≗schwach** *adj.*: ~ ***sein*** have no stamina, be very unfit; **~schwä·che** *f* lack of stamina; ***an*** ~ ***leiden*** be very unfit; **≗stark** *adj.* very fit; **~trai·ning** *n* fitness training
Kon·di·tor [kɔn'di:to:ɐ] *m* (-s; -en [kɔndi'to:rən]) pastry cook; **Kon·di·to·rei** [kɔndito'raɪ] *f* (-; -en) cake shop; café
Kon·do·lenz|be·such [kɔndo'lɛnts-] *m* visit of condolence; **~brief** *m* letter of condolence; **~buch** *n*: ***sich ins*** ~ ***eintragen*** sign the condolences book; **~schrei·ben** *n* letter of condolence
kon·do·lie·ren [kɔndo'li:rən] *v/i.* (h): ***j-m*** ~ express one's condolences to s.o. (***zu*** *dat.* on)
Kon·dom [kɔn'do:m] *n* (-s; -e) condom
Kon·do·mi·ni·um [kɔndo'mi:nĭʊm] *n* (-s; -ien) condominium
Kon·dor ['kɔndo:ɐ] *m* (-s; -e [-rə]) condor
Kon·fekt [kɔn'fɛkt] *n* (-[e]s; *no pl.*) chocolates *pl.*
Kon·fek·ti·on [kɔnfɛk'tsĭo:n] *f* (-; *no pl.*) (manufacture of) ready-to-wear clothing
kon·fek·tio·nie·ren [kɔnfɛktsĭo'ni:rən] *v/t.* (h) mass-produce; **kon·fek·tio·niert** [kɔnfɛktsĭo'ni:ɐt] *adj.* mass-produced, off-the-peg *clothes*
Kon·fek·ti'ons|an·zug *m* ready-made (*or* off-the-peg) suit; **~ge·schäft** *n* clothes shop; **~grö·ße** *f* size; **~n** clothes sizes
Kon·fe·renz [kɔnfe'rɛnts] *f* (-; -en) conference; **~dol·met·scher** *m* conference interpreter; **~raum** *m*, **~saal** *m* conference room; **~schal·tung** *f* conference circuit; **~sen·dung** *f* hookup; **~teil·neh·mer** *m* conference member; **~tisch** *m* conference table; ***am*** ~ *a. fig.* at the round table
kon·fe·rie·ren [kɔnfe'ri:rən] *v/i.* (h) **1.** confer (***über*** *acc.* on); **2.** (*a. v/t.*) *thea.* compère
Kon·fes·si·on [kɔnfɛ'sĭo:n] *f* (-; -en) religion, (religious) denomination; ***welcher*** ~ ***gehören Sie an?*** what (religious) denomination (*or* religion) are you?
kon·fes·sio·nell [kɔnfɛsĭo'nɛl] *adj.* denominational
kon·fes·si'ons·los *adj.* non-denominational
Kon·fes·si'ons·schu·le *f* denominational school
Kon·fet·ti [kɔn'fɛti] *n* (-[s]; *no pl.*) confetti; **~pa,ra·de** *f* ticker-tape parade
Kon·fi·gu·ra·ti·on [kɔnfigura'tsĭo:n] *f* (-; -en) configuration
Kon·fir·mand [kɔnfɪr'mant] *m* (-en; -en [-dən]), **Kon·fir·man·din** [kɔnfɪr'mandɪn] *f* (-; -nen) confirmand; **Kon·fir·man·den,un·ter·richt** [kɔnfɪr'mandən-] *m* confirmation classes *pl.*; **Kon·fir·ma·ti·on** [kɔnfɪrma'tsĭo:n] *f* (-; -en) *eccl.* confirmation; **kon·fir·mie·ren** [kɔnfɪr'mi:rən] *v/t.* (h) confirm
kon·fis·zie·ren [kɔnfɪs'tsi:rən] *v/t.* (h) confiscate, seize; **Kon·fis'zie·rung** *f* (-; -en) confiscation
Kon·fi·tü·re [kɔnfi'ty:rə] *f* (-; -n) jam
Kon·flikt [kɔn'flɪkt] *m* (-[e]s; -e): (***bewaffneter, innerer*** ~ armed, inner) conflict; ***in*** ~ ***geraten*** come into conflict (***mit*** *dat.* with), ***mit*** *dat.*: *a.* clash with; → ***Gesetz;*** **~be·wäl·ti·gung** *f* conflict management; **~for·schung** *f* conflict studies *pl.*; **≗frei** *adj.* peaceful; **≗freu·dig** *adj.* belligerent; **~herd** *m* cent|re (*Am.* -er) of conflict; trouble spot; **≗reich** *adj.* conflict-ridden; **≗scheu** *adj.*: ***er ist*** ~ he hates any sort of confrontation; **~si·tua·ti,on** *f* conflict situation; **~stoff** *m* seeds *pl.* of conflict; **≗träch·tig** *adj.* (potentially) explosive; ***die Situation ist*** ~ *a.* the least thing could spark off a conflict
Kon·fö·de·ra·ti·on [kɔnfødera'tsĭo:n] *f* (-; -en) confederation, confederacy; **kon·fö·de·rie·ren** [kɔnføde'ri:rən] *v/i. and v/refl.* (***sich*** ~) (h) form a confederation (***mit*** *dat.* with); **Kon·fö·de·rier·te** [kɔnføde'ri:ɐtə] *m* (-n; -n) confederate
kon·form [kɔn'fɔrm] *adj.* conforming (***mit*** *dat. or dat.* to), in conformity (with); ~ ***gehen*** be in agreement, concur (***mit*** *dat.* with); ***unsere Meinungen sind da*** (***nicht***) ~ we see it the same way (we don't see eye to eye on it); **Kon·for·mis·mus** [kɔnfɔr'mɪsmʊs] *m* (-; *no pl.*) conformism; **Kon·for·mist** [kɔnfɔr'mɪst] *m* (-en; -en), **kon·for·mi·stisch** [kɔnfɔr'mɪstɪʃ] *adj.* conformist
Kon·fron·ta·ti·on [kɔnfrɔnta'tsĭo:n] *f* (-; -en) confrontation; face-off; **Kon·fron·ta·ti'ons·kurs** *m* collision course; ***sich auf e-m*** ~ ***befinden*** be on a collision course; **kon·fron·tie·ren** [kɔnfrɔn'ti:rən] *v/t.* (h) confront (***mit*** *dat.* with)
kon·fus [kɔn'fu:s] *adj.* confused, muddled; ***~es Zeug reden*** rave; **Kon·fu·si·on** [kɔnfu'zĭo:n] *f* (-; -en) confusion, muddle
kon·ge·ni·al [kɔnge'nĭa:l] *adj.* ideal *partner etc.*; very sensitive *translation etc.*; perfectly matched; ***~er Geist*** kindred spirit, (spiritual) soulmate
Kon·glo·me·rat [kɔnglome'ra:t] *n* (-[e]s; -e) ⚚, *geol.* conglomerate; *fig.* conglomeration
Kon·greß [kɔn'grɛs, kɔŋ'grɛs] *m* (-sses; -sse) congress; conference; *Am.* convention (*a. pol.*); *Am. pol.* ***der*** ~ Congress; **~hal·le** *f* convention hall; **~teil·neh·mer** *m* conference member
kon·gru·ent [kɔngru'ɛnt, kɔŋ-] *adj.* 𝔄 congruent, perfectly equal; **Kon·gru·enz** [kɔngru'ɛnts, kɔŋ-] *f* (-; *no pl.*) congruence, congruency
K.-o.-Nie·der·la·ge [ka:'ʔo:-] *f* knockout
Ko·ni·fe·re [koni'fe:rə] *f* (-; -n) conifer
Kö·nig ['kø:nɪç] *m* (-s; -e ['kø:nɪgə]) king; *eccl.* ***die Heiligen Drei ~e*** the Three Wise Men (from the East), the Magi; ***j-n zum*** ~ ***machen*** make s.o. king
Kö·ni·gin ['kø:nɪgɪn] *f* (-; -nen) queen; **~mut·ter** *f* queen mother; **~pa,ste·te** *f* *gastr.* chicken vol-au-vent
kö·nig·lich ['kø:nɪklɪç] **I.** *adj.* royal; regal; princely *gift etc.*; sumptuous *meal etc.*; **II.** *adv.*: ***j-n*** ~ ***bewirten*** entertain s.o. lavishly; ***sich*** ~ ***amüsieren*** have a marvel(l)ous time
Kö·nig·reich ['kø:nɪk-] *n* kingdom (*a. eccl.*), *lit.* realm
'Kö·nigs|ad·ler *m* golden eagle; **~bau·er** *m chess*: king's pawn; **≗blau** *adj.* royal blue; **~haus** *n* royal dynasty; **~hof** *m* royal court; **~ker·ze** *f* ⚘ mullein; **~kro·ne** *f* royal crown; **~ma·cher** *m* kingmaker; **~paar** *n* royal couple; **~schloß** *n* royal castle; **~ti·ger** *m zo.* Bengal tiger; **≗treu** *adj.* loyal (to the king), loyalist, royalist; **~was·ser** *n* ⚗ aqua regia, nitrohydrochloric acid
'Kö·nig·tum *n* (-s; -tümer [-ty:mɐ]) monarchy
ko·nisch ['ko:nɪʃ] *adj.* conical; tapering, tapered
Kon·ju·ga·ti·on [kɔnjuga'tsĭo:n] *f* (-; -en) conjugation; **kon·ju·gie·ren** [kɔnju'gi:rən] *v/t.* (h) conjugate (*a.* 𝔄, ⚕, ⚡)
Kon·junk·ti·on [kɔnjʊŋk'tsĭo:n] *f* (-; -en) *ling.* conjunction; **Kon·junk·tio·nal·satz** [kɔnjʊŋktsĭo'na:l-] *m* conjunctive clause
Kon·junk·tiv ['kɔnjʊŋkti:f] *m* (-s; -e [-və]) *ling.* subjunctive
Kon·junk·tur [kɔnjʊŋk'tu:ɐ] *f* (-; -en [-rən]) ⚚ economic situation; business activity; trade cycle; boom; *fig.* ~ ***haben*** *goods etc.*: be in great demand, *clothes etc.*: be in fashion, F be in; ***dieses Modell hat im Moment*** ~ *a.* everyone's buying this model right now; **≗ab·hän·gig** *adj.* cyclical; **~ab·schwä·chung** *f* downward trend, downturn, downswing; **~auf·schwung** *m* upward trend,

upturn, upswing, (business) revival; **~aus·sich·ten** *pl.* economic outlook *sg.*; **~ba·ro·me·ter** *n* business barometer; **2be·dingt** *adj.* cyclical; **~be·le·bung** *f* business revival; **~be·we·gung** *f* cyclical movement

kon·junk·tu·rell [kɔnjʊŋktu'rɛl] *adj.* cyclical; economic, business *trend etc.*

Kon·junk'tur|ent·wick·lung *f* economic trend; **~for·schung** *f* business research; **~kri·se** *f* economic depression; **~la·ge** *f* economic situation; **~pha·se** *f* trade cycle; **~po·li·tik** *f* trade cycle policy; **2po·li·tisch** *adj.* economic(ally *adv.*); **~pro·gno·se** *f* economic (*or* business) forecast; **~pro·gramm** *n* program(me) of economic measures, stimulus program(me); **~rit·ter** *m* opportunist; **~rück·gang** *m* → ***Konjunkturabschwächung***; **~rück·schlag** *m* (economic) slump; **~schwan·kun·gen** *pl.* cyclical (*or* business) fluctuations; **~sprit·ze** F *f* F shot in the arm; **~ver·lauf** *m* business cycle; economic trend; **~zy·klus** *m* business (*or* trade) cycle

kon·kav [kɔn'ka:f, kɔŋ-] *adj.* concave; sculptured *keys*; **2lin·se** *f* concave lens

Kon·kla·ve [kɔn'kla:və, kɔŋ-] *n* (-s; -n) *R.C.* conclave

Kon·kor·danz [kɔnkɔr'dants, kɔŋ-] *f* (-; -en) concordance

kon·kret [kɔn'kre:t, kɔŋ-] **I.** *adj.* concrete; tangible; specific; actual; ***~e Poesie*** concrete poetry; **II.** *adv.*: ***was willst du ~ damit sagen?*** what do you actually mean by that?; **kon·kre·ti·sie·ren** [kɔnkreti'zi:rən, kɔŋ-] (h) **I.** *v/t.* put in concrete terms; **II.** *v/refl.*: ***sich ~*** take shape, materialize; *idea etc.*: gel

Kon·ku·bi·nat [kɔnkubi'na:t, kɔŋ-] *n* (-[e]s; -e) concubinage; **Kon·ku·bi·ne** [kɔnku'bi:nə, kɔŋ-] *f* (-; -n) concubine

Kon·kur·rent [kɔnkʊ'rɛnt, kɔŋ-] *m* (-en; -en) competitor, rival; *pl. a.* competition *sg.*

Kon·kur·renz [kɔnkʊ'rɛnts, kɔŋ-] *f* (-; -en) **1.** *no pl.* competition, rivalry; ***j-m ~ machen*** compete with s.o.; ***außer ~ stehen*** be unrival(l)ed; **2.** *no pl.* competitor(s *pl.*), rival(s *pl.*), *coll.* competition; **3.** *sport*: event, competition, contest; ***außer ~*** as a non-official competitor; **4.** ⚖ concurrence; **~an·ge·bot** *n* rival offer; **~blatt** *n* rival newspaper; **~den·ken** *n* competitive mentality; **~druck** *m* (-[e]s; *no pl.*) competitive pressure; **~er·zeug·nis** *n* rival product; **2fä·hig** *adj.* competitive, able to compete; **~fä·hig·keit** *f* (-; *no pl.*) competitiveness; **~fir·ma** *f*, **~ge·schäft** *n* rival firm; **~kampf** *m* competition; rivalry; **~klau·sel** *f* restraint clause

kon·kur'renz·los *adj.* unrival(l)ed, unbeatable; unmatched *prices*

Kon·kur'renz|neid *m* professional jealousy; **~pro·dukt** *n* rival product; **~ver·bot** *n* (agreement on) restraint of trade; **~wa·ren** *pl.* competing goods

kon·kur·rie·ren [kɔnkʊ'ri:rən, kɔŋ-] *v/i.* (h) compete (***mit*** *dat.* with; ***um*** *acc.* for); **kon·kur'rie·rend** *adj.* competing, rival

Kon·kurs [kɔn'kʊrs, kɔŋ-] *m* (-es; -e) ✝ bankruptcy; ***~ anmelden*** file for bankruptcy; ***in ~ gehen*** (*or* ***geraten***), ***~ machen*** go bankrupt; **~an·trag** *m* petition in bankruptcy; **~de·likt** *n* bankruptcy offen|ce (*Am.* -se); **~er·klä·rung** *f* declaration of insolvency; **~ge·richt** *n* bankruptcy court; **~gläu·bi·ger** *m* bankrupt's creditor; **~mas·se** *f* bankrupt's estate, assets *pl.*; **~ver·fah·ren** *n*: ***das ~ eröffnen*** open bankruptcy proceedings; **~ver·wal·ter** *m* receiver, liquidator; trustee (in bankruptcy)

kön·nen I. *v/aux.* (konnte, hat können) **1.** be able to *inf.*, be capable of *ger.*; be in a position to *inf.*; ***er hätte es tun ~*** he could have done it; ***sie kann mit ihm machen, was sie will*** she's got him twisted round her little finger; ***du kannst machen, was du willst*** it's like banging your head on a brick wall; ***ich kann das nicht mehr hören*** I can't stand it any more; ***er tut, was er kann*** he does his best; ***man kann nie wissen*** you never know; ***das war ein Reinfall, kann ich dir sagen*** what a disaster; **2.** be allowed to *inf.*; ***er kann gehen*** he can go; ***Sie ~ es mir glauben*** take my word for it; F ***kannst du machen!*** go ahead; I don't mind; **3.** ***das kann*** (***schon***) ***sein*** it's possible, that may be true; ***das kann nicht sein*** (that's) impossible; ***wer kann es gewesen sein?*** who could it have been?; ***ich kann mich auch täuschen*** I may be wrong, of course; ***du könntest recht haben*** you may (well) be right; ***es kann*** (***könnte***) ***etwas länger dauern*** it could (*or* might) take a while; **II.** *v/t. and v/i.* (konnte, gekonnt, h) **4.** ***er kann schwimmen*** he can (*or* knows how to) swim; ***ich kann es*** (***nicht***) I can('t) do it; ***er kann es*** (***gut***) he can do it (well); ***er kann Spanisch*** he knows (*or* speaks) Spanish; ***sie kann gut Englisch*** she speaks good English; ***er kann gar nichts*** he's useless; ***man kann alles, wenn man will*** you can do anything if you put your mind to it; ***ich kann nicht mehr*** a) F I've had it, b) I couldn't eat another thing, c) I can't take any more; F ***wir konnten nicht mehr*** F we were rolling about; F ***er kann's mit ihm*** he gets on all right (*Am.* alright) with him; F ***du kannst mich mal*** F you know what you can do; **5.** ***ich kann nichts dafür*** I can't help it; ***er kann nichts dafür, daß er ...*** he can't help *ger.*

'Kön·nen *n* (-s) ability, skill(s *pl.*); ***sportliches ~*** athletic prowess

Kön·ner ['kœnɐ] *m* (-s; -) expert, F ace

Kon·nex [kɔ'nɛks] *m* (-es; -e) **1.** connection; **2.** contact

Kon·nos·se·ment [kɔnɔsə'mɛnt] *n* (-[e]s; -e) ✝ bill of lading

Kon·no·ta·ti·on [kɔnota'tsĭo:n] *f* (-; -en) connotation

konn·te ['kɔntə] *pret. of* ***können***

Kon·rek·tor ['kɔnrɛkto:ɐ] *m* (-s; -en [-'to:rən]) deputy headmaster; **Kon·rek·to·rin** [kɔnrɛk'to:rɪn] *f* (-; -nen) deputy headmistress

kon·se·ku·tiv [kɔnzeku'ti:f] *adj.* consecutive; **2dol·met·scher** *m* consecutive interpreter; **2satz** *m* consecutive clause

Kon·sens [kɔn'zɛns] *m* (-es; -e) **1.** consensus; **2.** consent

kon·se·quent [kɔnze'kvɛnt] *adj.* a) logical, b) consistent, c) uncompromising, d) firm, persistent, e) resolute, f) thorough; ***~ bleiben*** remain firm, F stick to one's guns; **kon·se·quen·ter'wei·se** [kɔnze'kvɛntɐ-] *adv.* logically; to be consistent

Kon·se·quenz [kɔnze'kvɛnts] *f* (-; -en) **1.** *no pl.* persistence; determination; ***mit eiserner ~*** doggedly; **2.** consequence; ***bis zur äußersten ~*** a) to the bitter end, b) regardless of the consequences; ***die ~en tragen*** bear the consequences; ***die ~en ziehen*** take the necessary steps; ***er zog die ~ und trat zurück*** he had no alternative but to resign; ***die*** (***logische***) ***~ aus et. ziehen*** draw the logical conclusion from s.th.

Kon·ser·va·tis·mus [kɔnzɛrva'tɪsmʊs] *m* (-; *no pl.*) conservatism

kon·ser·va·tiv [kɔnzɛrva'ti:f] *adj. a. w.s.* conservative; *pol. etc.* Conservative, *in GB*: *a.* Tory; **Kon·ser·va·ti·ve** [kɔnzɛrva'ti:və] *m, f* (-n; -n) conservative; *pol.* Conservative, *in GB*: *a.* Tory

Kon·ser·va·tor [kɔnzɛr'va:to:ɐ] *m* (-s; -en [-va'to:rən]) curator

Kon·ser·va·to·ri·um [kɔnzɛrva'to:rĭʊm] *n* (-s; -ien) music academy, conservatory; conservatoire

Kon·ser·ve [kɔn'zɛrvə] *f* (-; -n) **1.** tin, can; *pl.* tinned (*or* canned) foods; **2.** ⚕ unit of (stored) blood; **3.** F ***Musik aus der ~*** F canned music

Kon'ser·ven|büch·se *f*, **~do·se** *f* tin, can; **~fa·brik** *f* canning factory, *esp. Am.* cannery

kon·ser·vie·ren [kɔnzɛr'vi:rən] (h) **I.** *v/t.* preserve (*a. fig.*), conserve; tin, can; *fig.* uphold *traditions etc.*; **II.** *v/refl.*: ***sich ~*** preserve (itself), F *fig.* F preserve o.s.; ***du hast dich gut konserviert*** *a.* you've kept yourself in good shape; **Kon·ser'vie·rung** *f* (-; *no pl.*) preservation; conservation

Kon·ser'vie·rungs|maß·nah·men *pl.* conservation measures; **~mit·tel** *n* preservative; **~stoff** *m* preservative

Kon·si·gnant [kɔnzɪ'gnant] *m* (-en; -en) ✝ consigner; **Kon·si·gna·ti·ons·wa·re** [kɔnzɪgna'tsĭo:ns-] *f* consigned goods *pl.*

Kon·si·li·um [kɔn'zi:lĭʊm] *n* (-s; -ien) consultation

Kon·si·stenz [kɔnzɪs'tɛnts] *f* (-; -en) consistency

Kon·so·le [kɔn'zo:lə] *f* (-; -n) ⚠, ⚙ console, bracket, support

kon·so·li·die·ren [kɔnzoli'di:rən] (h) **I.** *v/t.* consolidate; **II.** *v/refl.*: ***sich ~*** be consolidated, consolidate; **Kon·so·li'die·rung** *f* (-; *no pl.*) consolidation

Kon·so·nant [kɔnzo'nant] *m* (-en; -en) *ling.* consonant; **Kon·so·nanz** [kɔnzo'nants] *f* (-; -en) ♪ consonance, concord

Kon·sor·te [kɔn'zɔrtə] *m* (-n; -n) **1.** F *contp.* ***Lehmann u. ~n*** F Lehmann and co., Lehmann and his lot; ***gib dich ja nicht mit solchen ~n ab*** I should keep away from that crowd; **2.** ✝ consortium (*or* syndicate) member

Kon·sor·ti·al|bank [kɔnzɔr'tsĭa:l-] *f* (-; -en) consortium bank; **~ge·schäft** *n* syndicate transaction

Kon·sor·ti·um [kɔn'zɔrtsĭʊm] *n* (-s; -ien) syndicate, group

Kon·spi·ra·ti·on [kɔnspira'tsĭo:n] *f* (-; -en) conspiracy; **kon·spi·ra·tiv** [kɔnspira'ti:f] *adj.* conspiratorial; ***~e Wohnung*** safe flat (*or* house), terrorist hideout

kon·stant [kɔn'stant] **I.** *adj.* steady, *sport*: *a.* consistent *performance etc.*; fixed *costs, income etc.*; *phys.* constant; ***~e Größe*** constant; ***~ halten*** maintain; **II.** *adv.* consistently; **Kon·stan·te** [kɔn'stantə] *f* (-; -n) ⚗, *phys.* constant; *fig.* constant factor

kon·sta·tie·ren [kɔnsta'ti:rən] *v/t.* (h) a) note, b) state, c) ascertain

Kon·stel·la·ti·on [kɔnstɛla'tsĭo:n] *f* (-; -en) *ast.*, ⚕ *and fig.* constellation
kon·ster·niert [kɔnstɛr'ni:ɐt] *adj.* completely taken aback, flabbergasted
Kon·sti·pa·ti·on [kɔnstipa'tsĭo:n] *f* (-; -en) constipation
Kon·sti·tu·en·te [kɔnsti'tŭɛntə] *f* (-; -n) *ling.* constituent
kon·sti·tu·ie·ren [kɔnstitu'i:rən] (h) **I.** *v/t.* constitute; establish; **II.** *v/refl.*: ***sich*** ~ *parl.* assemble, convene; become established
Kon·sti·tu·ti·on [kɔnstitu'tsĭo:n] *f* (-; -en) *pol.*, ⚕ constitution; **kon·sti·tu·tio·nell** [kɔnstitutsĭo'nɛl] *adj.* constitutional
kon·stru·ie·ren [kɔnstru'i:rən] *v/t.* (h) construct (*a.* ⚠ *and fig.*); *ling.* construe; ⚙ create; fabricate; **kon·stru·iert** [kɔnstru'i:ɐt] *adj. fig.* contrived
Kon·strukt [kɔn'strʊkt] *n* (-[e]s; -e) working model; creation
Kon·struk·teur [kɔnstrʊk'tø:ɐ] *m* (-s; -e [-rə]) designing engineer
Kon·struk·ti·on [kɔnstrʊk'tsĭo:n] *f* (-; -en) construction (*a. ling.*); ⚙ design
Kon·struk·ti'ons|bü,ro *n* drawing office; **~feh·ler** *m* constructional flaw; faulty design; **~merk·mal** *n* constructional feature; **2tech·nisch** *adj.* constructional; **~teil** *n* structural component, element; **~zeich·ner** *m* draughtsman, *Am.* draftsman; designer
kon·struk·tiv [kɔnstrʊk'ti:f] *adj.* **1.** constructive; **2.** ⚙ constructional, design ...
Kon·sul ['kɔnzu:l] *m* (-s; -n) consul
Kon·su·lar... [kɔnzu'la:ɐ-] *in cpds.*, **kon·su·la·risch** [kɔnzu'la:rɪʃ] *adj.* consular
Kon·su·lat [kɔnzu'la:t] *n* (-[e]s; -e), **Kon·su'lats·ge·bäu·de** *n* consulate
Kon·su'lats·ge·büh·ren *pl.* consular fees
Kon·sul·ta·ti·on [kɔnzʊlta'tsĭo:n] *f* (-; -en) consultation
kon·sul·ta·tiv [kɔnzʊlta'ti:f] *adj.* consultative; **2pakt** *m pol.* consultative pact
kon·sul·tie·ren [kɔnzʊl'ti:rən] *v/t.* (h) consult; *a.* see *a doctor etc.*
Kon·sum [kɔn'zu:m] *m* (-s; *no pl.*) consumption (*a. fig.*); intake *of alcohol*; **~ar,ti·kel** *m* consumer article (*pl.* goods); **~den·ken** *n* consumer mentality; consumerism
Kon·su·ment [kɔnzʊ'mɛnt] *m* (-en; -en) consumer; **Kon·su'men·ten·nach·fra·ge** *f* consumer demand
Kon'sum|for·schung *f* consumer research; **~ge·nos·sen·schaft** *f* consumers' cooperative; **~ge·sell·schaft** *f* consumer society; **~gü·ter** *pl.* consumer goods; **~herr·schaft** *f* consumerism
kon·su·mie·ren [kɔnzu'mi:rən] *v/t.* (h) consume (*a. fig.*)
Kon'sum|kli·ma *n* buyer demand; ***das ~ ist gut*** (***schlecht***) buyer demand is up (down); **~müll** *m* consumer waste; **~ter·ror** *m* → ***Konsumzwang***; **~ver·wei·ge·rer** [-fɛɐvaɪgərɐ] *m* (-s; -) anti-consumerist; **~zwang** *m* hard sell, aggressive marketing
Kon·takt [kɔn'takt] *m* (-[e]s; -e) contact (*a.* ⚡); ***enger ~*** close contact(s); ***mit j-m ~ aufnehmen*** get in touch with s.o.; ***mit j-m in ~ stehen*** be in contact (*or* touch) with s.o.; *pol.* ***die ~e abbrechen*** break ties (***mit*** *dat.* with); **~ab·zug** *m phot.* contact print; **~an·zei·ge** *f* personal (ad); **~n** personal column; **2arm** *adj.*: ***er ist ~*** a) he's not a mixer, b) he hasn't got many friends; **~auf·nah·me** *f*: ***bei der ersten ~*** when I *etc.* first took up contact (*or* got in touch with him *etc.*); **~bild·schirm** *m computer*: touch screen; **~bü,ro** *n pol.* liaison mission
Kon·tak·ter [kɔn'taktɐ] *m* (-s; -) contact man
Kon'takt|flä·che *f* contact area; **2freu·dig** *adj.* sociable, gregarious; **~ge·sprä·che** *pl.* initial talks; **~gift** *n* contact poison
kon·tak·tie·ren [kɔntak'ti:rən] *v/t.* (h) contact
Kon'takt|lin·se *f* contact lens; **~man·gel** *m*: ***sie leidet unter ~*** she hasn't got many friends; **~mann** *m* contact; **~per,son** *f esp.* ⚕ contact; **~pfle·ge** *f* human relations *pl.*; **~schal·ter** *m* ⚡ contact switch; **2scheu** *adj.* shy; ***er ist ~*** *a.* he shies away from social contact; **~schwie·rig·kei·ten** *pl.*: ***~ haben*** be shy, be introverted, find it hard to make friends; **~sper·re** *f* ⚖ incommunicado confinement; **~stel·le** *f* contact point; **~stu·di·um** *n* refresher course
Kon·ta·mi·na·ti·on [kɔntamina'tsĭo:n] *f* (-; -en) contamination; **kon·ta·mi·nie·ren** [kɔntami'ni:rən] *v/t.* (h) contaminate
Kon·tem·pla·ti·on [kɔntɛmpla'tsĭo:n] *f* (-; -en) contemplation; *religious etc.* meditation
Kon·ter ['kɔntɐ] F *m* (-s; -) → ***Konterschlag***
'Kon·ter·ad·mi,ral *m* rear admiral
Kon·ter·fei ['kɔntɐfaɪ] *n* (-s; -s, -e) *hum.* portrait
kon·ter·ka·rie·ren [kɔntɐka'ri:rən] *v/t.* (h) go against; thwart
kon·tern ['kɔntɐn] *v/t. and v/i.* (h) *boxing and fig.* counter; *soccer*: counterattack; *fig.* ***er versteht es immer wieder zu ~*** he's never at a loss for a reply; ***gut gekontert!*** touché!
'Kon·ter|re·vo·lu·ti,on *f* counter-revolution; **~schlag** *m* counterblow; *fig. a.* counterattack
Kon·text ['kɔntɛkst] *m* (-[e]s; -e): (***im ~*** in) context; ***aus dem ~ gerissen*** (taken) out of context
Kon·ti·nent ['kɔntinɛnt] *m* (-[e]s; -e) continent; ***der*** (***europäische***) ~ the Continent; **kon·ti·nen·tal** [kɔntinɛn'ta:l] *adj.* continental
kon·ti·nen'tal·eu·ro,pä·isch *adj.* Continental
'Kon·ti·nen'tal|kli·ma *n* continental climate; **~sockel** *m* continental shelf; **~ver·schie·bung** *f* continental drift
Kon·tin·gent [kɔntɪŋ'gɛnt] *n* (-[e]s; -e) *esp.* ⚔ contingent; ✝ *a.* quota
kon·tin·gen·tie·ren [kɔntɪŋgɛn'ti:rən] *v/t.* (h) fix (*or* impose) a quota on, subject to quota; ration *goods*; ***kontingentierte Einfuhren*** quota imports; **Kon·tin·gen'tie·rung** *f* (-; -en) quota fixing; output limitation
kon·ti·nu·ier·lich [kɔntinu'i:ɐlɪç] **I.** *adj.* continuous; steady; **II.** *adv.* continuously; steadily; *work etc. a.* solidly, without interruption; **Kon·ti·nui·tät** [kɔntinui'tɛ:t] *f* (-; *no pl.*) continuity
Kon·ti·nu·um [kɔn'ti:nuʊm] *n* (-s; -nua [-nŭa]) continuum
Kon·to ['kɔnto] *n* (-s; -s, Konten ['kɔntən]) (bank) account; ***auf ~ von*** *dat.* chargeable to the account of; ***die Getränke gehen auf mein ~*** the drinks are on me; *fig.* ***das geht auf sein ~*** that's his doing; **~aus·zug** *m* bank statement; **~er·öff·nung** *f* opening of an account; **~füh·rungs·ge·bühr** *f* service charge; **~in·ha·ber** *m* account holder
Kon·to·kor·rent [kɔntokɔ'rɛnt] *n* (-s; -e) current account; **~num·mer** *f* account number
Kon·tor [kɔn'to:ɐ] *n* (-s; -e [-rə]) branch (office); *fig.* ***das war ein Schlag ins ~*** it came like a bombshell; **Kon·to·rist** [kɔnto'rɪst] *m* (-en; -en), **Kon·to·ri·stin** [kɔnto'rɪstɪn] *f* (-; -nen) clerk
'Kon·to·stand *m* balance (of account); ***wie ist der ~?*** how does the account stand?
kon·tra ['kɔntra] *prp.*, *adv.* against; *esp.* ⚖ *and fig.* versus (*abbr.* vs.); ***er ist immer ~*** he always has to take the opposite line, he's a contrarian
'Kon·tra *n*: ***~ geben*** *card game*: double; *fig.* ***j-m ~ geben*** hit back at s.o.; → ***Pro;*** **~alt** *m* ♪ contralto; **~baß** *m* ♪ double bass
Kon·tra·dik·ti·on [kɔntradɪk'tsĭo:n] *f* (-; -en) contradiction
Kon·tra·hent [kɔntra'hɛnt] *m* (-en; -en) ⚖ contracting party; *sport etc.*: opponent; **kon·tra·hie·ren** [kɔntra'hi:rən] *v/t. and v/i.* (h) contract
Kon·tra·in·di·ka·ti'on *f* ⚕ contraindication
Kon·trakt [kɔn'trakt] *m* (-[e]s; -e) contract, agreement; ***e-n ~*** (***ab***)***schließen*** make (*or* conclude) a contract
Kon·trak·ti·on [kɔntrak'tsĭo:n] *f* (-; -en) contraction
'Kon·tra·punkt *m* ♪ counterpoint
kon·tra·punk·tie·rend [kɔntrapʊŋk'ti:rənt] *adj.*, **kon·tra·punk·tisch** [kɔntra'pʊŋktɪʃ] *adj.* contrapuntal
kon·trär [kɔn'trɛ:ɐ] *adj.* opposing, antithetical; (completely) opposite *characters etc.*; contrary *aims etc.*
Kon·trast [kɔn'trast] *m* (-[e]s; -e) contrast; ***e-n ~ bilden zu → kontrastieren;*** **2arm** *adj. phot.* low-contrast ...; **~brei** *m* ⚕ barium meal; **~far·be** *f* contrasting colo(u)r; **~fi,gur** *f* foil
kon·tra·stie·ren [kɔntras'ti:rən] *v/i.* (h): ***~ mit*** *dat.* contrast with, form a contrast to
Kon'trast|mit·tel *n* ⚕ contrast medium; **~reg·ler** *m* contrast control
kon'trast·reich *adj.* varied, colo(u)rful; *phot. etc.* high-contrast ..., contrasty
Kon·tri·bu·ti·on [kɔntribu'tsĭo:n] *f* (-; -en) contribution
Kon·troll·ab·schnitt [kɔn'trɔl-] *m* counterfoil, stub; **Kon'trollam·pe** (*sep.* -ll·l-) *f* pilot light; warning light
Kon'troll|aus·schuß *m pol.* supervisory committee; **~be·am·te** *m* inspector
Kon·trol·le [kɔn'trɔlə] *f* (-; -n) a) supervision; check(ing), ⚙, *gastr. etc.* inspection; control, b) checkpoint, c) passport control; customs *sg.*; ***unter ärztlicher ~*** under medical supervision; ***unter ~ bringen*** (***haben, halten***) get (have, keep) under control; ***die Inflation*** *etc.* ***unter ~ halten*** *a.* F keep the lid on inflation *etc.*; ***die ~ verlieren über*** *acc.* lose control of; ***er verlor die ~ über s-e Leute*** his men got out of hand; ***er verliert leicht die ~ über sich*** he's quick to lose his temper, he tends to flare up (very quickly)
Kon·trol·leur [kɔntrɔ'lø:ɐ] *m* (-s; -e [-rə]) inspector
Kon'troll|funk·ti,on *f* controlling function; **~gang** *m* round; *police*: beat; **~ge-**

rät *n* monitor; **~grup·pe** *f esp.* ✈ control group
kon·trol·lier·bar [kɔntrɔ'li:ɐba:ɐ] *adj.* checkable; controllable; ***schwer ~*** difficult to check (*or* to keep a check on)
kon·trol·lie·ren [kɔntrɔ'li:rən] *v/t.* (h) **1.** supervise; check, *a.* check up on *s.o.*; ***hör auf, mich dauernd zu ~!*** I wish you'd stop checking up on me all the time!; **2.** check, ⚙, *gastr. etc.* inspect; **3.** control
Kon'trolli·ste (*sep.* -ll·l-) *f* checklist
Kon·troll|kar·te *f* time card; **~maß·nah·men** *pl.* control(ling) measures; **~num·mer** *f* code number; **~or,gan** *n pol.* controlling body; **~punkt** *m* checkpoint; **~schirm** *m* monitor; **~stel·le** *f* checkpoint; **~stem·pel** *m* inspection stamp; **~turm** *m* control tower; **~uhr** *f* time clock; **~ver·such** *m* control test; **~zet·tel** *m* check slip
kon·tro·vers [kɔntro'vɛrs] *adj.* controversial; ***~e Frage*** *a.* contentious issue
Kon·tro·ver·se [kɔntro'vɛrzə] *f* (-; -n) controversy, dispute
Kon·tur [kɔn'tu:ɐ] *f* (-; -en [-rən]) **1.** *pl.* contours, outline; **2.** *fig.* ***an ~ gewinnen*** (begin to) take shape, *pol. etc.* (begin to) make a name for o.s., begin to make one's mark; **kon·tu·ren·los** [kɔn'tu:rənlo:s] *adj.* shapeless, flat
Kon'tu·ren|schär·fe *f phot.* definition; **~stift** *m* liner
Ko·nus ['ko:nʊs] *m* (-; -se) cone; ⚙ *a.* taper
Kon·va·les·zent [kɔnvalɛs'tsɛnt] *m* (-en; -en) convalescent; **Kon·va·les·zenz** [kɔnvalɛs'tsɛnts] *f* (-; *no pl.*) convalescence
Kon·vek·tor [kɔn'vɛkto:ɐ] *m* (-s; -en [kɔnvɛk'to:rən]) convector, convection heater
Kon·vent [kɔn'vɛnt] *m* (-[e]s; -e) **1.** convention; **2.** monastery; convent
Kon·ven·ti·on [kɔnvɛn'tsĭo:n] *f* (-; -en) convention; *a. pl.* (social) convention
Kon·ven·tio·nal·stra·fe [kɔnvɛntsĭo'na:l-] *f* contract penalty
kon·ven·tio·nell [kɔnvɛntsĭo'nɛl] *adj.* conventional
kon·ver·gent [kɔnvɛr'gɛnt] *adj.* convergent; **Kon·ver·genz** [kɔnvɛr'gɛnts] *f* (-; -en) convergence; **kon·ver·gie·ren** [kɔnvɛr'gi:rən] *v/i.* (h) converge
Kon·ver·sa·ti·on [kɔnvɛrza'tsĭo:n] *f* (-; -en) conversation
Kon·ver·sa·ti'ons|le·xi·kon *n* encyclop(a)edia; **~stück** *n thea.* comedy of manners
Kon·ver·ter [kɔn'vɛrtɐ] *m* (-s; -) converter
kon·ver·ti·bel [kɔnvɛr'ti:bəl] *adj.*, **kon·ver·tier·bar** [kɔnvɛr'ti:ɐba:ɐ] *adj.* convertible; **kon·ver·tie·ren** [kɔnvɛr'ti:rən] **I.** *v/t.* (h) convert (**zu** *dat.* to); **II.** *v/i.* (h, sn) convert; ***zum Protestantismus ~*** convert to Protestantism, become a Protestant, turn Protestant; **Kon·ver·tit** [kɔnvɛr'ti:t] *m* (-en; -en) convert
kon·vex [kɔn'vɛks] *adj.* convex
Kon'vex·lin·se *f* convex lens
Kon·voi ['kɔnvɔʏ] *m* (-s; -s) convoy
Kon·vul·si·on [kɔnvʊl'zĭo:n] *f* (-; -en) convulsion; **kon·vul·siv** [kɔnvʊl'zi:f] *adj.* convulsive
kon·ze·die·ren [kɔntse'di:rən] *v/t.* (h) concede (***j-m*** to s.o.)
Kon·zen·trat [kɔntsɛn'tra:t] *n* (-[e]s; -e) concentrate; *fig.* résumé
Kon·zen·tra·ti·on [kɔntsɛntra'tsĭo:n] *f* (-; -en) concentration
Kon·zen·tra·ti'ons|fä·hig·keit *f* (-; *no pl.*) powers *pl.* of concentration; **~la·ger** *n* concentration camp; **~man·gel** *m*: ***unter ~ leiden*** have difficulty concentrating; **~schwä·che** *f* lack of concentration
kon·zen·trie·ren [kɔntsɛn'tri:rən] *v/t. and v/refl.* (**sich ~**) (h) concentrate (**auf** *acc.* upon); *a.* focus *one's attention* (on)
kon·zen·triert [kɔntsɛn'tri:ɐt] *adj.* concentrated; **Kon·zen'triert·heit** *f* (-; *no pl.*) concentration
kon·zen·trisch [kɔn'tsɛntrɪʃ] *adj.* concentric(ally *adv.*)
Kon·zept [kɔn'tsɛpt] *n* (-[e]s; -e) a) (rough) draft, notes *pl.*, b) plan(s *pl.*); ***aus dem ~ kommen*** lose the thread; ***j-n aus dem ~ bringen*** put s.o. off; ***das paßt ihm nicht ins ~*** a) it doesn't fit in with his plans, b) he doesn't like it
Kon·zep·ti·on [kɔntsɛp'tsĭo:n] *f* (-; -en) **1.** concept; plan; **2.** ✈ conception
kon·zep·tio·nell [kɔntsɛptsĭo'nɛl] *adj.* conceptual
kon·zep·ti'ons·los *adj.*: ***~ sein*** have no concept
Kon'zept·pa,pier *n* notepaper
Kon·zern [kɔn'tsɛrn] *m* (-[e]s; -e) ✝ group
Kon·zert [kɔn'tsɛrt] *n* (-[e]s; -e) a) concert; recital, b) concerto; ***ins ~ gehen*** go to a concert; **~agen,tur** *f* concert agency
kon·zer·tant [kɔntsɛr'tant] *adj.*: ***~e Aufführung*** concert performance
Kon'zert|be·su·cher *m* concertgoer; ***die ~ waren begeistert*** the audience was delighted; **~flü·gel** *m* classical grand; **~gi,tar·re** *f* classical guitar; **~hal·le** *f* concert hall, auditorium
kon·zer·tie·ren [kɔntsɛr'ti:rən] *v/i.* (h) give a concert (*or* concerts)
kon·zer·tiert [kɔntsɛr'ti:ɐt] *adj.*: ***~e Aktion*** concerted action
Kon'zert|mei·ster *m* leader (of the *or* an orchestra), *esp. Am.* concertmaster; **~pia,nist** *m* concert pianist; **~pro,gramm** *n* **1.** (concert) program(me); **2.** program(me) of concerts; **~pu·bli·kum** *n* concert audience; **~rei·he** *f* series of concerts; **~rei·se** *f* concert tour; **~saal** *m* concert hall; **~sai,son** *f* concert season; **~sän·ger** *m* concert singer; **~tour,nee** *f* concert tour; ***auf ~*** on (a concert) tour; **~ver·an·stal·ter** *m* (concert) promoter; **~ver·an·stal·tung** *f* concert
Kon·zes·si·on [kɔntsɛ'sĭo:n] *f* (-; -en) **1.** licence, *Am.* license, franchise; ⚒ *etc.* concession; **2.** concession (**an** *acc.* to); ***~en machen*** make concessions (*dat. or* **an** *acc.* to); **kon·zes·sio·nie·ren** [kɔntsɛsĭo'ni:rən] *v/t.* (h) grant a licen|ce (*Am.* -se) to
kon·zes·si'ons·be·reit *adj.* willing to make concessions, conciliatory
Kon·zes·si'ons·in·ha·ber *m* concessionaire
kon·zes·siv [kɔntsɛ'si:f] *adj.* concessive
Kon·zes'siv·satz *m* concessive clause
Kon·zil [kɔn'tsi:l] *n* (-s; -e, -lien [-lĭən]) *eccl.* council
kon·zi·li·ant [kɔntsi'lĭant] *adj.* conciliatory
kon·zi·pie·ren [kɔntsi'pi:rən] *v/t.* (h) plan; ⚙ design; prepare a draft for; ***konzipiert für*** designed for
Ko·ope·ra·ti·on [ko?opera'tsĭo:n] *f* (-; -en) cooperation; **Ko·ope·ra·ti'ons·ver·trag** *m* cooperative agreement; **ko·ope·ra·tiv** [ko?opera'ti:f] *adj.* cooperative; **Ko·ope·ra·ti·ve** [ko?opera'ti:və] *f* (-; -n) cooperative; **ko·ope·rie·ren** [ko?ope'ri:rən] *v/i.* (h) cooperate
ko·op·tie·ren [ko?ɔp'ti:rən] *v/t.* (h) coopt
Ko·or·di·na·te [ko?ɔrdi'na:tə] *f* (-; -n) coordinate; **Ko·or·di'na·ten·sy,stem** *n* system of coordinates
Ko·or·di·na·ti·on [ko?ɔrdina'tsĭo:n] *f* (-; -en) coordination; **Ko·or·di·na·tor** [ko?ɔrdi'na:to:ɐ] *m* (-s; -en [-na'to:rən]) coordinator; **ko·or·di·nie·ren** [ko?ɔrdi'ni:rən] *v/t.* (h) coordinate; **Ko·or·di'nie·rung** *f* (-; -en) coordination
Kö·per ['kø:pɐ] *m* (-s; -) twill; **~bin·dung** *f* twill weave
Ko·pe·ke [ko'pe:kə] *f* (-; -n) kopeck
Kopf [kɔpf] *m* (-[e]s; Köpfe ['kœpfə]) **1.** a) head (*a.* ⚙), b) letterhead; top *of page etc.*, c) (*pipe*) bowl; ***~ an ~*** closely packed, *horse racing etc.*: neck and neck; ***es steht auf dem ~*** it's upside down; ***von ~ bis Fuß*** from head to foot, from top to toe; **2.** *fig.* a) head, mind, b) memory; ***aus dem ~*** *recite etc.* from memory, by heart; ***et. im ~ ausrechnen*** work s.th. out in one's head; **3.** *fig.* a) (great) thinker, b) head, leader, c) mastermind, driving force; ***der ~ sein von*** *dat.* mastermind *s.th.*; **4.** person, head; ***pro ~*** a head, per person, each; **5.** ***s-n eigenen ~ haben*** have a mind of one's own; ***s-n ~ retten*** save one's skin; ***mir steht der ~ nicht danach*** I don't really feel like it; ***den ~ hängen lassen*** hang one's head; ***den ~ in den Sand stecken*** hide one's head in the sand; ***den ~ oben behalten*** F keep one's pecker up; ***~ hoch!*** F chin up!; ***den ~ (nicht) verlieren*** lose one's head (keep one's cool); ***e-n roten ~ bekommen*** go red, blush; ***er ist nicht auf den ~ gefallen*** he's no fool; ***ich weiß nicht, wo mir der ~ steht*** I don't know whether I'm coming or going; ***j-m den ~ verdrehen*** turn s.o.'s head; ***~ und Kragen riskieren*** risk one's neck; ***j-m den ~ zurechtrücken*** straighten s.o. out; F ***sein ganzes Geld auf den ~ hauen*** F blow all one's money; ***et. auf den ~ stellen*** turn s.th. upside down; F ***die Bude auf den ~ stellen*** a) turn the place upside down, b) F have a wild fling; ***Tatsachen auf den ~ stellen*** twist things (*or* the facts); ***ich habe andere Dinge im ~*** I've got other things on my mind (*or* to think about); ***den ~ voll haben*** have a lot (*or* too much) on one's mind; ***er hat nur Fußball im ~*** all he ever thinks about is football; ***das kannst du dir aus dem ~ schlagen*** you can forget (about) that; ***das will mir nicht aus dem ~*** I can't get it out of my mind; ***sich et. durch den ~ gehen lassen*** think s.th. over; ***er hat es sich in den ~ gesetzt, es zu tun*** he's determined to do it, F he's dead set on doing it; ***j-m in den ~*** (*or* ***zu ~[e]***) ***steigen*** go to s.o.'s head; ***immer mit dem ~ durch die Wand wollen*** be pigheaded; ***bis über den ~ in Schulden stecken*** be up to one's neck (F eyeballs) in debt; ***j-m über den ~ wachsen*** a) outgrow s.o., b) *work etc.*: get too much for s.o.; ***über s-n ~ hinweg*** over his head; ***j-n vor den ~ stoßen*** F put s.o.'s nose out of joint; ***j-m Beleidigungen an den ~ werfen*** hurl insults at s.o.; ***wie vor den ~ geschlagen*** speechless; ***Köpfe werden rollen*** heads will roll; ***er ist nicht ganz richtig im ~*** F he's got a screw loose somewhere;

da faßt man sich doch an den ~ it really makes you wonder; ***und wenn du dich auf den ~ stellst*** you can do what you like, *a.* you can talk until you're blue in the face

'Kopf-an-'Kopf-Ren·nen *n* neck-and--neck (*or* close) race

'Kopf|ar·beit *f* brainwork; **~ar·bei·ter** *m* brainworker; **~bahn·hof** *m* terminus; **~ball** *m sport*: header; **~be·deckung** (*sep.* -k·k-) *f* headgear; ***mit ~*** with something on one's head; ***ohne ~*** bareheaded

Köpf·chen ['kœpfçən] *n* (-s; -) little head; F ***~, ~!*** F it's brains you need

köp·fen ['kœpfən] (h) **I.** *v/t.* **1.** behead, cut (*or* chop) off *s.o.'s* head; ⚘ top; **2.** head *ball*; **II.** *v/i. soccer*: head

'Kopf|en·de *n* head; 🚗 front; **~form** *f*: ***runde*** *etc.* **~** round(-shaped) *etc.* head; **~geld** *n* reward; *w.s.* blood money; **~grip·pe** *f* head cold; **~haar** *n* hair (on one's head)

'kopf·hän·ge·risch [-hɛŋərɪʃ] *adj.* down (in the dumps)

'Kopf|haut *f* scalp; **~hö·rer** *m*: (***ein ~*** a pair of) headphones *pl.*; **~jä·ger** *m* headhunter (*a. fig.*); **~jucken** *n an* itchy scalp

'Kopf·kis·sen *n* pillow; **~be·zug** *m* pillowcase, pillowslip

'Kopf|la·ge *f* ⚕ head presentation; **~län·ge** *f*: ***um e-e ~*** by a head

'kopf·la·stig [-lastɪç] *adj.* top-heavy; ✈ nose-heavy

'Kopf|laus *f* head louse; **~lei·ste** *f typ.* headpiece

'kopf·los *adj.* headless; *fig.* panic-stricken; **~e *Flucht*** stampede; **'Kopf·lo·sig·keit** *fig. f* (-; *no pl.*) panic; rashness

'Kopf|mas͵sa·ge *f* scalp massage; **~mensch** *m* cerebral person; **~nicken** *n* nod(ding); **~nuß** F *f* **1.** F biff on the head; **2.** brainteaser; **~rech·nen** *n* mental arithmetic; **~sa͵lat** *m* lettuce; **≈scheu** *adj.* timid; ***j-n ~ machen*** intimidate s.o.

'Kopf·schmer·zen *pl.* headache *sg.*; ***~ haben*** have a headache; F *fig.* ***j-m ~ bereiten*** give s.o. a headache; ***was mir am meisten ~ bereitet*** my biggest headache

'Kopf·schmerz·ta͵blet·te *f* headache pill (*or* tablet)

'Kopf·schuß *m* shot in the head

'Kopf·schüt·teln *n* shaking (*or* shake) of the head; ***allgemeines ~*** general disapproval; **'kopf·schüt·telnd** *adv.* shaking one's head; *refuse etc.* with a shake of the head

'Kopf|schutz *m* protective headgear; helmet; **~sprung** *m*: ***e-n ~ machen*** dive (headfirst)

'Kopf·stand *m* headstand; ✈ nose-over; ***e-n ~ machen*** → **'kopf·ste·hen** *v/i.* (*irr., sep.,* h, → ***stehen***) stand on one's head; ✈ nose over; be upside down; F *fig.* go mad (***wegen*** *gen.* over)

'Kopf|stein·pfla·ster *n* cobblestones *pl.*; **~steu·er** *f hist.* poll tax; **~stim·me** *f* head voice; *w.s.* falsetto; **~stoß** *m boxing*: butt; *soccer*: header; **~stüt·ze** *f* headrest; *mot. a.* head restraint; **~teil** *m, n* headboard; **~tuch** *n* (head)scarf

kopf'über *adv.* headfirst (*a. fig.*)

'Kopf|ver·let·zung *f* head injury; **~wä·sche** *f* hairwash; F *fig.* dressing down; **~weh** F *n* → ***Kopfschmerzen***; **~wun·de** *f* head wound; **~zahl** *f* number of persons; **~zer·bre·chen** *n*: ***es hat uns viel ~ bereitet*** we really had to rack our brains (over it), it gave us quite a headache; ***mach dir kein ~ darüber*** don't lose any sleep over it

Ko·pie [ko'piː] *f* (-; -n) copy (*a. fig.*); duplicate; *art*: reproduction, replica

Ko·pier|an·stalt [ko'piːɐ-] *f* print lab; **~dienst** *m* copy shop (*or* service), photocopying service

ko·pie·ren [ko'piːrən] *v/t.* (h) copy; imitate; *phot.* print; **Ko·pie·rer** [ko'piːrɐ] *m* (-s; -) photocopier

Ko·pier|ge·rät [ko'piːɐ-] *n* photocopier; **~pa͵pier** *n* photocopying paper; **~stift** *m* indelible pencil

Ko·pi·lot ['koːpiloːt] *m* (-en; -en) copilot

Ko·pist [ko'pɪst] *m* (-en; -en) copyist; copier, imitator

Kop·pel¹ ['kɔpəl] *f* (-; -n) **1.** paddock; enclosure; **2.** leash; **3.** pack *of dogs etc.*

Kop·pel² *n* (-s; -) ⚔ belt

kop·peln ['kɔpəln] *v/t.* (h) **1.** link up (*a. spaceships*); *mot. etc.* couple; **2.** tie (*or* leash) *animals* together; **3.** *fig.* couple *s.th.* (***mit*** *dat.* with)

Kopp·ler ['kɔplɐ] *m* (-s; -) *radio*: coupler

Kopp·lung ['kɔplʊŋ] *f* (-; -en) coupling

'Kopp·lungs... *in cpds.* ⚡ coupling; **~ge·schäft** *n* tie-in sale; **~ma͵nö·ver** *n space travel*: docking

Ko·pro·duk·ti·on ['koː-] *f* coproduction, joint production; **'Ko·pro·du·zent** *m* coproducer

Kop·te ['kɔptə] *m* (-n; -n) Copt; **kop·tisch** ['kɔptɪʃ] *adj.* Coptic

Ko·pu·la·ti·on [kopula'tsǐoːn] *f* (-; -en) **1.** copulation; **2.** ⚘ whip graft(ing)

ko·pu·lie·ren [kopu'liːrən] (h) **I.** *v/t.* ⚘ splice-graft; **II.** *v/i.* copulate

Ko·ral·le [ko'ralə] *f* (-; -n) coral

Ko'ral·len|in·sel *f* coral island; **~ket·te** *f* coral necklace; **~riff** *n* coral reef

Ko·ran [ko'raːn] *m* (-s; *no pl.*) Koran; **~schu·le** *f* Koranic school; **~schü·ler** *m* student of the Koran

Korb [kɔrp] *m* (-[e]s; Körbe ['kœrbə]) a) basket (*a. sport*), b) hive, c) ⚙ cage; F *fig.* ***j-m e-n ~ geben*** turn s.o. down, F give s.o. the brush-off; ***e-n ~ bekommen*** be turned down, F be given the brush-off; **~ball** *m* (-[e]s; *no pl.*) *sport*: netball

'Korb·blüt·ler [-blyːtlɐ] *m* (-s; -) ⚘ composite

Körb·chen ['kœrpçən] *n* (-s; -) **1.** (*dog's etc.*) basket; *fig.* ***ab ins ~!*** off to bed with you; **2.** cup *of bra*

kör·be·wei·se ['kœrbəvaɪzə] *adv.*: ***~ pflücken*** *etc.* pick *etc.* basketfuls of

'Korb|fla·sche *f* demijohn; **~ge·flecht** *n* wickerwork; **~ma·cher** *m* basket maker; **~mö·bel** *pl.* wicker furniture *sg.*; **~ses·sel** *m*, **~stuhl** *m* wicker chair; **~wa·gen** *m* bassinet, wicker pram; **~wa·ren** *pl.* wickerwork *sg.*; **~wei·de** *f* osier, basket willow

Kord [kɔrt] *m* (-[e]s; -e [-də]) corduroy

Kor·del ['kɔrdəl] *f* (-; -n) cord

'Kord|ho·se *f*: (***e-e ~*** a pair of) cords *pl.* *or* cord(uroy) trousers *pl.*; **~jacke** *f* cord(uroy) jacket

Kor·don [kɔr'dõː] *m* (-s; -s) cordon; ***e-n ~ ziehen*** form a cordon (***um*** *acc.* around), ***um*** *acc.*: *a.* cordon off

Ko·rea·ner [kore'aːnɐ] *m* (-s; -), **Ko·rea·ne·rin** [kore'aːnərɪn] *f* (-; -nen), **ko·rea·nisch** [kore'aːnɪʃ] *adj.*, **Ko·rea·nisch** *n* (-en) *ling.* Korean

Ko·ri·an·der [ko'riandɐ] *m* (-s; *no pl.*) coriander

Ko·rin·the [ko'rɪntə] *f* (-; -n) currant; **Ko'rin·then·kacker** F *m* pedant, F nit-picker

Kork [kɔrk] *m* (-[e]s; -e) ⚘ cork; **~ei·che** *f* cork oak

Kor·ken ['kɔrkən] *m* (-s; -) cork

'Kor·ken·zie·her *m* corkscrew; **~locken** *pl.* corkscrew curls

'Kork·ge·schmack *m*: ***e-n ~ haben*** *wine etc.*: be corked

'Kork·mund·stück *n* cork tip; ***mit ~*** cork--tipped

Kor·mo·ran [kɔrmo'raːn] *m* (-s; -e) cormorant

Korn¹ [kɔrn] *n* (-[e]s; Körner ['kœrnɐ]) **1.** grain; seed; **2.** *no pl.* grain; rye; wheat; **3.** *no pl. phot. etc.* grain; *fig.* ***aufs ~ nehmen*** attack, take aim at

Korn² F *m* (-s; *no pl.*) schnapps

'Korn·blu·me *f* cornflower

'korn·blu·men·blau *adj.* cornflower (blue)

Körn·chen ['kœrnçən] *n* (-s; -) small grain; *fig.* ***~ Wahrheit*** grain (*or* modicum) of truth

kör·nen ['kœrnən] (h) **I.** *v/i. salt, sugar etc.*: granulate; **II.** *v/t. metall.* granulate, grain

Kör·ner|fres·ser ['kœrnɐ-] F *contp. m* F muesli freak; **~frucht** *f* cereal; **~fut·ter** *n* grain feed

Kor·nett [kɔr'nɛt] *n* (-[e]s; -s, -e) ♪ cornet

'Korn·feld *n* cornfield, *Am.* grainfield

kör·nig ['kœrnɪç] *adj.* grainy; *rice etc.*: al dente; *in cpds.* ...-grained

'Korn·kam·mer *f* granary (*a. fig.*)

'Korn·ra·de [-raːdə] *f* (-; -n) ⚘ corn cockle

'Korn·spei·cher *m* granary

Kör·nung ['kœrnʊŋ] *f* (-; -en) grain

Ko·ro·na [ko'roːna] *f* (-; -nen) **1.** *ast.*, ⚡ corona; **2.** F crowd, bunch

Ko·ro·nar|er·kran·kung [koro'naːɐ-] *f* coronary disease; **~ge·fäß** *n* coronary vessel; **~in·suf·fi·zi͵enz** *f* coronary failure; **~throm͵bo·se** *f* cardiac infarction, coronary (thrombosis)

Kör·per ['kœrpɐ] *m* (-s; -) body (*a. phys., gastr. of wine*); *phys.*, 𝔄 solid; ***am ganzen ~ zittern*** tremble from head to foot (*or* all over); **~bau** *m* (-[e]s; *no pl.*) build, physique; **~be·herr·schung** *f* body control; **≈be·hin·dert** *adj.* (physically) disabled, handicapped; **~be·hin·der·te** *m, f* (-n; -n) handicapped person; *pl. the* handicapped, handicapped people; **~be·hin·de·rung** *f* (physical) disability *or* handicap; **~be·we·gung** *f* (body) movement; **~en** *gym.* motions

Kör·per·chen ['kœrpɐçən] *n* (-s; -) *biol.* corpuscle

kör·per·ei·gen ['kœrpɐ-] *adj.* endogenic; ***die ~en Abwehrkräfte*** *etc.* the body's own (*or* in-built) defen|ces (*Am.* -ses) *etc.*

Kör·per|fül·le ['kœrpɐ-] *f* corpulence; **~funk·ti͵on** *f* bodily function; **≈ge·recht** *adj.* contoured *seat etc.*; **~ge·ruch** *m* body odo(u)r, b.o., BO; **~ge·wicht** *n* (body) weight; **~grö·ße** *f* height; **~haa·re** *pl.* bodily hair *sg.*; **~hälf·te** *f*: ***die rechte*** (***linke***) **~** the right (left) half (*or* side) of the body; ***die obere*** (***untere***) **~** the upper (lower) part (*or* half) of the body; **~hal·tung** *f*: (***e-e gute, schlechte ~*** good, bad) posture; **~kon͵takt** *m* physical (*or* bodily) contact; *sport*: body (*or* bodily) contact; **~kraft** *f* physical strength

kör·per·lich ['kœrpɐlɪç] *adj.* physical; carnal; corporeal; material; A solid; **~e** ***Arbeit*** physical (*or* manual) labo(u)r *or* work; **~e** ***Betätigung*** physical exercise; **~e** ***Genüsse*** physical (*or* carnal) pleasures *or* delights, pursuits of the flesh; **~e** ***Züchtigung*** corporal punishment
kör·per·los ['kœrpɐloːs] *adj.* disembodied; *sport*: without bodily contact
Kör·per|ma·ße ['kœrpɐ-] *pl.* (body) measurements; **~öff·nung** *f* orifice; **~pfle·ge** *f* personal hygiene; **~pu·der** *m* talcum powder; **2reich** *adj.* full-bodied *wine*; **~säf·te** *pl.* body juices
Kör·per·schaft ['kœrpɐʃaft] *f* (-; -en) corporation, body; ***gesetzgebende ~*** legislative (body); **'kör·per·schaft·lich** *adj.* corporate; **'Kör·per·schafts·steu·er** *f* corporation tax
Kör·per|schwä·che ['kœrpɐ-] *f* physical weakness; **~spra·che** *f* body language, *formal*: non-verbal communication; **~spray** *m, n* deodorant (spray); **~teil** *m* part of the body; **~tem·pe·ra,tur** *f* body temperature; **~ver·let·zung** *f* (physical) injury; ⚖ (***schwere ~*** grievous) bodily harm; **~wär·me** *f* body heat
Kor·po·ral [kɔrpo'raːl] *m* (-s;-e) corporal
Kor·po·ra·ti·on [kɔrpora'tsĭoːn] *f* (-; -en) corporation; *univ.* fraternity; **kor·po·ra·tiv** [kɔrpora'tiːf] *adj.* corporate
Korps [koːɐ] *n* (-; - [koːɐs]) corps
kor·pu·lent [kɔrpu'lɛnt] *adj.* corpulent, stout; **Kor·pu·lenz** [kɔrpu'lɛnts] *f* (-; *no pl.*) corpulence
Kor·pus¹ ['kɔrpʊs] F *m* (-; -se) body
'Kor·pus² *n* (-; Korpora ['kɔrpora]) **1.** corpus; **2.** *no pl.* ♪ resonance box
Kor·re·fe·rat ['kɔreferaːt] *n* (-[e]s; -e) follow-up paper; **Kor·re·fe·rent** ['kɔreferɛnt] *m* (-en; -en) **1.** follow-up speaker; **2.** coexaminer
kor·rekt [kɔ'rɛkt] **I.** *adj.* correct; proper; fair; honest, above board; **~es** ***Benehmen*** (social) etiquette, the right behavio(u)r; ***j-m ~es Benehmen beibringen*** teach s.o. to behave in public; ***er ist sehr ~*** he knows the rules of etiquette; ***er ist ~ wie ein Beamter*** he's a stickler for the rules; **II.** *adv.*: ***sich ~ verhalten*** do the right thing; **kor·rek·ter'wei·se** [kɔ'rɛktɐ-] *adv.* by rights, as a matter of courtesy; F so as not to offend anyone; **Kor'rekt·heit** *f* (-; *no pl.*) correctness
Kor·rek·tiv [kɔrɛk'tiːf] *n* (-s; -e [-və]) corrective
Kor·rek·tor [kɔ'rɛktoːɐ] *m* (-s; -en [kɔrɛk'toːrən]) *typ.* proofreader
Kor·rek·tur [kɔrɛk'tuːɐ] *f* (-; -en [-rən]) correction; **~** ***lesen*** proofread, read (the) proofs, do (the) proofreading; **~ab·zug** *m* (galley) proof; **~band** *n* (-[e]s; ⸚er) correction tape; **~bo·gen** *m* page proof; **~fah·ne** *f* galley (proof); **~ta·ste** *f* correction key; **~zei·chen** *n* proofreader's mark, correction mark
Kor·re·lat [kɔre'laːt] *n* (-[e]s; -e) correlative; **Kor·re·la·ti·on** [kɔrela'tsĭoːn] *f* (-; -en) correlation; **kor·re·lie·ren** [kɔre'liːrən] *v/i.* (h) (*a.* ***miteinander ~***) correlate
kor·re·pe·tie·ren [kɔrepe'tiːrən] *v/i.* (h) ♪, *thea.* coach; **~** ***mit*** *dat.* coach; **Kor·re·pe·ti·tor** [kɔrepe'tiːtoːɐ] *m* (-s; -en [-ti'toːrən]) repetiteur
Kor·re·spon·dent [kɔrɛspɔn'dɛnt] *m* (-en; -en) correspondent; **Kor·re·spon·'den·ten·be·richt** *m* correspondent's report; **Kor·re·spon·denz** [kɔrɛspɔn'dɛnts] *f* (-; -en) correspondence
kor·re·spon·die·ren [kɔrɛspɔn'diːrən] *v/i.* (h) **1.** correspond (***mit*** *dat.* with), write (to); **2.** *fig.* correspond (***mit*** *dat.* to)
Kor·ri·dor ['kɔridoːɐ] *m* (-s; -e [-rə]) hall; corridor
kor·ri·gie·ren [kɔri'giːrən] *v/t.* (h) correct; adjust; *typ.* read *the proofs*
kor·ro·die·ren [kɔro'diːrən] *v/t.* and *v/i.* (h) corrode; **Kor·ro·si·on** [kɔro'zĭoːn] *f* (-; *no pl.*) corrosion
kor·ro·si'ons·fest *adj.* non-corroding
Kor·ro·si'ons|mit·tel *n* corrosive; **~schutz** *m* corrosion protection; **2ver·hü·tend** *adj.* anti-corrosive
kor·rum·pie·ren [kɔrʊm'piːrən] *v/t.* (h) corrupt; **kor·rupt** [kɔ'rʊpt] *adj.* corrupt; **Kor·rup·ti·on** [kɔrʊp'tsĭoːn] *f* (-; -en) corruption; bribery; **Kor·rup·ti'ons·af,fä·re** *f* corruption scandal
Kor·sa·ge [kɔr'zaːʒə] *f* (-; -n) corsage
Kor·sar [kɔr'zaːɐ] *m* (-en; -en [-rən]) corsair
Kor·se ['kɔrzə] *m* (-n; -n) Corsican
Kor·sett [kɔr'zɛt] *n* (-s; -s, -e) corset (*a.* ⚕)
Kor·sin ['kɔrzɪn] *f* (-; -nen), **kor·sisch** ['kɔrzɪʃ] *adj.* Corsican
Kor·so ['kɔrzo] *m* (-s; -s) **1.** parade, procession; **2.** corso, boulevard
Kor·tex ['kɔrtɛks] *m* (-[es]; -e) cortex
Kor·ti·ko·id [kɔrtiko'iːt] *n* (-[e]s; -e [-'iːdə]) corticosteroid, corticoid
Kor·ti·sol [kɔrti'zoːl] *n* (-s; *no pl.*) hydrocortisone, cortisol
Kor·ti·son [kɔrti'zoːn] *n* (-s; *no pl.*) cortisone
Kor·vet·te [kɔr'vɛtə] *f* (-; -n) ⚓ corvette
Ko·ry·phäe [kory'fɛːə] *f* (-; -n) luminary (*gen.* of); great authority (***auf*** *e-m Gebiet*: on), F big name (in)
Ko·sak [kɔ'zak] *m* (-en; -en) Cossack
ko·scher ['koːʃɐ] *adj.* kosher (*a. fig.*)
K.-o.-Schlag [kaː'ʔoː-] *m* knockout blow, F finisher
Ko·se·form ['koːzə-] *f* affectionate form
ko·sen ['koːzən] *v/i.* and *v/t.* (h) caress; (***miteinander***) **~** kiss and cuddle
Ko·se|na·me ['koːzə-] *m* pet name; **~wort** *n* (-[e]s; ⸚er) term of affection
Ko·si·nus ['koːzɪnʊs] *m* (-; -[se]) A cosine
Kos·me·tik [kɔs'meːtɪk] *f* (-; *no pl.*) **1.** beauty treatment; **2.** *fig.* cosmetics *pl.*; ***geschickte ~*** skil(l)ful patching-up; **Kos·me·ti·ka** [kɔs'meːtika] *pl.* cosmetics, makeup *sg.*; **Kos·me·ti·ke·rin** [kɔs'meːtikərɪn] *f* (-; -nen) beautician
Kos'me·tik|in·du,strie *f* cosmetics industry; **~kof·fer** *m* vanity case; **~sa,lon** *m* beauty parlo(u)r (*or* salon, *Am. a.* shop); **~ta·sche** *f* makeup bag
kos·me·tisch [kɔs'meːtɪʃ] *adj.* cosmetic(ally *adv.*); *fig. a.* just for show (*or* effect)
kos·misch ['kɔsmɪʃ] *adj.* cosmic(ally *adv.*)
Kos·mo·go·nie [kɔsmogo'niː] *f* (-; -n) cosmogony
Kos·mo·lo·gie [kɔsmolo'giː] *f* (-; -n) cosmology
Kos·mo·naut [kɔsmo'naʊt] *m* (-en; -en) cosmonaut
Kos·mo·po·lit [kɔsmopo'liːt] *m* (-en; -en), **kos·mo·po'li·tisch** *adj.* cosmopolitan
Kos·mos ['kɔsmɔs] *m* (-; *no pl.*) universe
Kost [kɔst] *f* (-; *no pl.*) food; *lit. and fig.* fare; board; ***magere ~*** low-fat diet, *fig.* meag|re (*Am.* -er) offerings; ***leichte ~*** light food(s), *fig.* light fare, light reading; *fig.* ***das Buch ist schwere ~*** this book is heavy-going; → ***Logis***
kost·bar ['kɔstbaːɐ] *adj.* precious, valuable (*a. fig.*); expensive; **'Kost·bar·keit** *f* (-; -en) **1.** precious object, treasure; **2.** *no pl.*) (great) value
ko·sten¹ ['kɔstən] *v/t.* (h) taste, try (*a. fig.*); *fig.* enjoy; *b.s.* get a taste of
'ko·sten² *v/t.* (h) cost (***j-n*** s.o.); *fig. a.* take *time etc.*; ***was kostet es?*** how much is it?; ***es kostete ihn sein Leben*** (*or* ***den Kopf***) it cost him his life, he paid for it with his life; ***er ließ es sich viel ~*** he spent a lot of money on it; ***koste es, was es wolle*** whatever it costs
Ko·sten ['kɔstən] *pl.* a) cost(s *pl.*) *sg.*; expenses, b) fees, charges, ⚖ costs; ***auf anderer Leute*** (***eigene***) **~** *a. fig.* at other people's (one's own) expense; ***auf ~ der Allgemeinheit*** at the public expense; ***ohne ~*** at no cost (***für*** *acc.* to); ***die ~ tragen*** bear (*or* pay) the costs; ***keine ~ scheuen*** spare no expense; ***sie scheuen die ~*** they're not prepared to spend the money (*or* pay that kind of money); ***auf s-e ~ kommen*** cover one's expenses, *fig.* get one's money's worth; *fig.* ***das geht auf ~ der Gesundheit*** it'll take its toll on your health; **~an·schlag** *m* estimate; quotation; **~an·stieg** *m* increase in costs; **~auf·wand** *m* expenditure; ***mit e-m ~ von*** *dat.* at a cost of; **~be·rech·nung** *f* costing; **~be·tei·li·gung** *f* cost sharing; **2be·wußt** *adj.* cost-conscious; **~dämp·fung** *f* curbing (of) costs; **2deckend I.** *adj.* cost-covering; **II.** *adv.*: **~** ***arbeiten*** break even; **~deckung** *f* breaking even; **~druck** *m* (-[e]s; *no pl.*) ⚕ rising costs *pl.*; **2ef·fi·zi,ent** *adj.* cost-effective; **~ent·schei·dung** *f* ⚖ order for costs; **~er·spar·nis** *f* (cost) saving; **~er·stat·tung** *f* refund (of expenses); **~ex·plo·si,on** *f* runaway costs *pl.*; **~fak·tor** *m* cost factor; **~fra·ge** *f* question of cost; **2frei** *adj.* free (of cost); **2gün·stig I.** *adj.* (very) reasonable, cheap; **II.** *adv.* at (*or* for) a reasonable price, cheaply; **~la,wi·ne** *f* spiral(l)ing (*or* escalating) costs *pl.*
'Ko·sten-'Lei·stungs-Ver·hält·nis *n* cost-(*or* price-)performance ratio
'ko·sten·los *adj. and adv.* free (of charge), *get s.th. etc.* for nothing
'Ko·sten-'Nut·zen|-Ana,ly·se *f* cost-benefit analysis; **~-Ver·hält·nis** *n* cost-benefit ratio
'ko·sten·pflich·tig [-pflɪçtɪç] **I.** *adj.* liable to pay the costs; **II.** *adv. tow off etc.* at the owner's expense; ⚖ ***e-e Klage ~ abweisen*** dismiss an action with costs
'Ko·sten|pla·nung *f* expense budgeting; **~preis** *m* ⚕ cost price; ***unter dem ~*** below cost, at a loss; **~punkt** F *m* **1.** → ***Kostenfrage*; 2. *~?*** how much?; ***~ 7000 Mark*** cost 7000 marks; **~rech·nung** *f* cost accounting; **2sen·kend** *adj.* cost-cutting; **~sen·kung** *f a. pl.* reduction in costs; **2spa·rend** *adj.* cost-saving; **~stei·ge·rung** *f* increase in costs; **~ver·tei·lung** *f* cost distribution; **~vor·an·schlag** *m* estimate; quotation; **~vor·schuß** *m* advance on costs
Kost·gän·ger ['kɔstgɛŋɐ] *m* (-s; -) boarder, lodger
'Kost·geld *n* board, F keep
köst·lich ['kœstlɪç] **I.** *adj.* a) delicious; exquisite; delightful, wonderful, b) highly amusing; **II.** *adv.*: ***sich ~ amüsieren*** enjoy o.s. immensely, F have a great time;

'Köst·lich·keit *f* (-; -en) *gastr. etc.* titbit, *Am.* tidbit

'Kost·pro·be *f* sample; *fig. a.* taste

kost·spie·lig ['kɔstʃpi:lɪç] *adj.* expensive; sumptuous

Ko·stüm [kɔs'ty:m] *n* (-s; -e) **1.** costume, *a.* fancy dress; *hist. a.* dress (*a. pl.*); **2.** suit; **~ball** *m* fancy-dress ball; **~bild·ner** [-bɪldnɐ] *m* (-s; -) costume designer; **~fest** *n* fancy-dress ball

ko·stü·mie·ren [kɔsty'mi:rən] *v/refl.* (h): ***sich ~*** dress up

Ko'stüm|pro·be *f thea.* dress rehearsal; **~ver·leih** *m* costume rental

'Kost·ver·äch·ter *m*: F ***er ist kein ~*** he's a bit of a bon vivant

K.-o.-Sy,stem [ka:'ʔo:-] *n* knockout system

Kot [ko:t] *m* (-[e]s; *no pl.*) excrement, f(a)eces *pl.*; *a.* F (*dog's etc.*) muck; *fig.* ***in den ~ ziehen*** drag through the mud

Ko·tan·gens ['ko:taŋgɛns] *m* (-; -) ⩓ cotangent

Ko·tau [ko'taʊ] *m* (-s; -s) kowtow; ***vor j-m e-n ~ machen*** kowtow to s.o.

Ko·te·lett [kotə'lɛt, kɔ'tlɛt] *n* (-s; -s) chop, cutlet; **Ko·te'let·ten** *pl.* sideburns

Kö·ter ['kø:tɐ] *contp. m* (-s; -) cur

'Kot·flü·gel *m mot.* mudguard, *Am.* fender

ko·tig ['ko:tɪç] *adj.* mucky

Kotz·brocken ['kɔts-] V *m sl.* nasty piece of work

Kot·ze ['kɔtsə] V *f* (-; *no pl.*) *sl.* puke

kotz'elend ['kɔts-] V *adj.*: ***sich ~ fühlen*** F feel like death warmed up

kot·zen ['kɔtsən] V *v/i.* (h) *sl.* puke, spew, throw up; ***es ist doch zum ≗*** it's absolutely sickening

kotz|'lang·wei·lig ['kɔts-] V *adj. sl.* boring as hell; **~'übel** V *adj.*: ***mir ist ~*** *sl.* I think I'm going to puke (*or* throw up)

Krab·be ['krabə] *f* (-; -n) *zo.* crab; shrimp, prawn

Krab·bel·al·ter ['krabəl-] *n*: (***im ~*** at the) crawling stage; **krab·beln** ['krabəln] **I.** *v/i.* (sn) crawl; **II.** F *v/t.* (h) tickle; scratch

'Krab·ben·cock·tail *m* prawn cocktail

Krach [krax] **I.** *m* (-[e]s; Kräche ['krɛçə]) **1.** *no pl.* a) noise, F racket, b) crash; ***~ machen*** make a noise (F racket); **2.** F a) F row, b) ✝ crash; F ***~ bekommen mit*** *dat.* get into trouble with; ***bei denen gibt's ständig ~*** F they're always having rows; **II.** ≗ *int.* crash!, bang!

kra·chen ['kraxən] *v/i.* **1.** (h) crash (*a. thunder*); *fire, radio*: crackle; **2.** (sn) a) *door etc.*: bang, slam, b) burst, explode; *ice*: crack, c) ✝ crash; ***~ gegen*** (*or* ***in***) *acc.* crash into; ***auf dieser Straße kracht es dauernd*** there's one accident after another on that road; F ***du tust, was ich dir sage, sonst kracht's*** F you'll do as I tell you, or else; F ***daß es nur so krachte*** F like crazy

'krach·le·dern *adj.* rough and ready; blunt and outspoken; ***~er Typ*** *a.* robust personality; **'Krach·le·der·ne** [-le:dɐnə] *dial. f* (-n; -n) lederhosen *pl.*

kräch·zen ['krɛçtsən] *v/i.* (h) *crow*: caw; *parrot*: squawk; F *fig.* F croak; ***~de Stimme*** croaking voice

Krack·ver·fah·ren ['krak-, 'krɛk-] *n* ⚗ cracking (process)

Kraft [kraft] *f* (-; Kräfte ['krɛftə]) **1.** strength (*a. fig.*); force (*a. phys. and pol.*); power (*a.* ⚙, ⚡ *and pol.*); energy (*a. phys.*); F punch; *phys.* ***~ u. Masse*** force and mass; ***heilende ~*** healing power; ***überirdische Kräfte*** supernatural forces; *pol.* ***dritte ~*** third force; ***treibende ~*** driving force, *fig. a.* powerhouse; ***rohe ~*** brute force; ***am Ende s-r Kräfte*** at the end of his tether; ***bei Kräften*** on one's feet; ***aus eigener ~*** under one's own steam; ***mit aller ~*** with all one's might; ***mit frischen Kräften*** with renewed strength (*or* vigo[u]r); ***mit letzter ~*** with one's last ounce of strength; ***volle ~ voraus*** full speed ahead; ***nach besten Kräften*** to the best of one's ability; ***das geht über m-e Kräfte*** that's more than I can handle; ***Kräfte sammeln*** gather strength; ***wieder zu Kräften kommen*** get back on one's feet; ***~ verleihen*** give strength (*dat.* to), *fig.* lend force (to *an argument etc.*); → ***Spiel*** 1, ***vereint***; **2.** ***in ~ sein*** be in force, be effective; ***in ~ setzen*** put into force, enforce; ***in ~ treten*** come into effect (*or* force), become effective; ***außer ~ setzen*** annul, repeal *law*, cancel *contract etc.*, *a.* overrule; suspend; ***außer ~ treten*** expire; **3.** employee, *pl. a.* personnel (*pl.*)

kraft *prp.* (*gen.*) by virtue of; on the strength of

'Kraft|akt *m* strong-man act; *fig.* great feat, tour de force; **~an·stren·gung** *f* effort, exertion; **~an·trieb** *m* power drive; ***mit ~*** power-driven; **~auf·wand** *m* energy involved; effort; **~aus·druck** *m* expletive, swearword; **~brü·he** *f* beef tea

Kräf·te|aus·gleich ['krɛftə-] *m pol. etc.* balance of power; **~drei·eck** *n* triangle of forces; **≗mä·ßig** *adv.* physically; ***~ geht's mir gut*** I feel quite strong (*or* fit); **~mes·sen** *n* trial of strength; **~pa·ral·le·lo,gramm** *n* parallelogram of forces; **~spiel** *n* interplay of forces; **~ver·fall** *m* loss of strength; **~ver·hält·nis** *n* relative strength

'Kraft·fah·rer *m* driver, motorist

'Kraft·fahr·zeug *n* motor vehicle; **~bau** *m* (-[e]s; *no pl.*) **1.** car (*or* automobile) manufacturing; **2.** → ***Kraftfahrzeugindustrie***; **~brief** *m* vehicle registration document; **~hal·ter** *m* (registered) car owner; **~in·du,strie** *f* car (*or* automobile) industry; **~me,cha·ni·ker** *m* (car) mechanic; **~schein** *m* vehicle registration document; **~steu·er** *f* road (*Am.* automobile) tax; **~steu·er·mar·ke** *f* tax sticker

'Kraft|feld *n phys.* field (of force); **~fut·ter** *n* concentrate(d feed)

kräf·tig ['krɛftɪç] **I.** *adj.* a) strong (*a. meteor.*); powerful *engine etc.*, b) heavy, powerful *blow etc.*, c) big; bouncing *baby*; healthy, d) nourishing, robust *a. wine*, F decent *meal etc.*, e) bright, strong *colo(u)r etc.*, f) firm *handshake*; ***e-n ~en Durst haben*** be really thirsty; ***~er Schluck*** F good (old) swig; **II.** *adv.*: ***~ schütteln*** give *s.th.* a good shake, *pharm. etc.* shake well; ***j-m ~ die Hand schütteln*** give s.o. a firm handshake; ***~ zuschlagen*** a) hit out, b) *fig.* tuck in, F get stuck in

kräf·ti·gen ['krɛftɪgən] *v/t.* (h) a) strengthen (*a. fig.*); harden, steel, b) refresh, revive; **'kräf·ti·gend** *adj.* refreshing; invigorating, *a.* bracing *air*; ***~es Mittel*** tonic; ***das wirkt ~*** that'll give you strength

Kräf·ti·gung ['krɛftɪgʊŋ] *f* (-; *no pl.*) strengthening; recovery; **'Kräf·ti·gungs·mit·tel** *n* ⚕ tonic

'Kraft|lei·stung *f* feat of strength; *fig.* great feat, tour de force; **~li·ni·en** *pl. phys.* lines of force

'kraft·los *adj.* weak (*a. fig.*); limp

'Kraft·lo·sig·keit *f* (-; *no pl.*) lack of energy; ***sie klagt über ~*** she complains that she has no energy

'Kraft·ma,schi·ne *f* engine

'Kraft·mei·er [-maiɐ] F *m* (-s; -) muscle man; **Kraft·meie·rei** [-maiə'rai]) F *f* (-; *no pl.*) swaggering

'Kraft|mensch *m* F strong guy; **~pro·be** *f* trial of strength; **~protz** *m* F gorilla, bruiser; **~quel·le** *f* source of power (*fig.* strength); **~rad** *n* motorcycle; **~re,ser·ve(n** *pl.*) *f* (energy) reserves *pl.*; **~sport** *m* strength events *pl.*; **~sprü·che** *pl.* big words

'Kraft·stoff *m* fuel; **~an·zei·ger** *m* fuel ga(u)ge; **~-Luft-Ge·misch** *n* fuel-air mixture; **≗spa·rend** *adj.* fuel-efficient; **~ver·brauch** *m* fuel consumption

'Kraft|strom *m* power current; **≗strot·zend** *adj.* bursting with energy; **~stück** *n* strong-man act; **~über,tra·gung** *f* power transmission; **~ver·schwen·dung** *f* waste of energy

'kraft·voll *adj.* strong, powerful (*a. fig.*)

'Kraft|wa·gen *m* motor vehicle; **~werk** *n* ⚡ power station; **~wort** *n* (-[e]; ⸗er) swear word

Kra·gen ['kra:gən] *m* (-s; -) collar (*a.* ⚙); *fig.* ***j-n beim ~ nehmen*** collar s.o.; ***jetzt geht's ihm an den ~*** he's had it now; ***j-m den ~ umdrehen*** wring s.o.'s neck; ***da platzte mir der ~*** that was the last straw; **~knopf** *m* collar stud; **~stäb·chen** *n* collar stiffener; **~wei·te** *f* collar size; F *fig.* ***das ist nicht m-e ~*** F it's not my cup of tea

Krag·stein ['kra:k-] *m* ⩓ console, corbel stone

Krä·he ['krɛ:ə] *f* (-; -n) crow; rook

krä·hen ['krɛ:ən] *v/i.* (h) crow; *fig. baby*: coo

'Krä·hen|fü·ße *pl.* **1.** crow's feet; **2.** scrawl *sg.*; **~nest** *n* crow's nest (*a.* ⚓)

Kräh·win·kel ['krɛ:-] *n* (-s; *no pl.*) (sleepy) backwater, *Am.* F hick town

Kra·ke ['kra:kə] *m* (-n; -n) *zo.* octopus; *myth.* kraken

Kra·keel [kra'ke:l] F *m* (-s; *no pl.*) F row; F racket; **kra'kee·len** *v/i.* (h) make (*or* have) a row; **Kra·kee·ler** [kra'ke:lɐ] *m* (-s; -) brawler

kra·ke·lig ['kra:kəlɪç] *adj.*: ***~e Schrift*** spidery handwriting; **kra·keln** ['kra:kəln] *v/t. and v/i.* (h) scrawl

Kral [kra:l] *m* (-s; -e) kraal

Kral·le ['kralə] *f* (-; -n) claw (*a. fig. and* F *fingernail*); *fig.* ***die ~n zeigen*** bare one's teeth; ***j-n fest in den ~n haben*** have s.o. in one's clutches; **'kral·len** (h) **I.** *v/refl.*: ***sich ~ an*** *acc.* cling to, clutch (at); *zo.* dig its claws into; ***sich ~ in*** *acc.* dig one's feet (*or* nails *etc.*) into; **II.** *v/t.*: ***die Finger*** (*or* ***Nägel***) ***~ in*** *acc.* dig one's nails into; F *fig.* ***sich j-n ~*** collar s.o.

Kram [kra:m] F *m* (-s; *no pl.*) **1.** rubbish; **2.** business; ***der ganze ~*** F the whole caboodle; ***den ganzen ~ hinschmeißen*** F chuck the whole thing; ***das paßt mir überhaupt nicht in den ~*** F that's the last thing I could do with; ***soll er s-n ~ alleine machen*** let him get on with it(, then)

kra·men ['kra:mən] *v/i.* (h) rummage (***in*** *dat.*, ***unter*** *dat.* in; ***nach*** *dat.* for); *fig.* ***in***

s-n Erinnerungen ~ take a trip down memory lane, revel in memories
Krä·mer·geist ['krɛːmɐ-] *m* (-[e]s; *no pl.*) **1.** petty-mindedness; **2.** petty-minded person
'Kram·la·den *contp. m* junk shop
Kram·pe ['krampə] *f* (-; -n) ⚙ staple
Krampf [krampf] *m* (-[e]s; Krämpfe ['krɛmpfə]) **1.** ⚕ cramp; spasm, convulsions *pl.*; fit; ***epileptische Krämpfe*** an epileptic fit; F *fig.* ***Krämpfe kriegen*** F have a fit; **2.** F ***so ein*** ~ F what a bind; ***das Konzert*** *etc.* ***war der reinste*** ~ F the concert *etc.* was diabolical
'Krampf·ader *f* ⚕ varicose vein
'krampf·ar·tig *adj.* spasmodic, convulsive
kramp·fen ['krampfən] (h) **I.** *v/refl.*: ***sich*** ~ cramp up; **II.** *v/t.* clench (***um*** *acc.* around)
'krampf·haft *adj.* convulsive; *fig.* forced *smile etc.*; desperate *efforts etc.*
'Krampf·hu·sten *m* convulsive cough
'krampf|lö·send, ~stil·lend I. *adj.* antispasmodic; **II.** *adv.*: *pharm.* ***... wirkt*** ~ a) eases cramps, b) will ease the cramps
Kran [kraːn] *m* (-[e]s; Kräne ['krɛːnə]) crane; **~arm** *m* jib; **~brücke** *f* gantry (bridge); **~füh·rer** *m* crane driver
Kra·nich ['kraːnɪç] *m* (-s; -e) *zo.* crane
krank [kraŋk] *adj.* sick (*a. mentally*); *pred. a.* ill, not well; diseased *organ, a.* ♘; bad *tooth etc.*; *fig.* sick *mind etc.*; ⚘ *a.* ailing; ~ ***werden*** fall ill (*or* sick); ***sich*** ~ ***melden*** ring in sick; ***j-n*** ~ ***schreiben*** give s.o. a sick note; ~ ***spielen*** malinger, pretend to be sick; ***j-n*** ~ ***machen*** make s.o. ill, *fig.* get s.o. down; ***er macht mich*** ~ F he's driving me round the bend; *fig.* ~ ***vor Sorge*** sick with worry; **Kran·ke** ['kraŋkə] *m, f* (-n; -n) sick person; patient; ***die*** ~***n*** the sick (*pl.*)
krän·keln ['krɛŋkəln] *v/i.* (h): ***sie kränkelt seit einiger Zeit*** (***schon immer***) she hasn't been in the best of health lately (she's never been the healthiest of people)
kran·ken ['kraŋkən] *fig. v/i.* (h): ~ ***an*** *dat.* suffer from
krän·ken ['krɛŋkən] *v/t.* (h) offend, hurt *s.o.'s* feelings; ***das kränkt*** that hurts; ***es kränkt mich, daß*** it upsets me that
'Kran·ken|an·stalt *f* hospital; **~bah·re** *f* stretcher; **~be·richt** *m* medical report; bulletin; **~be·such** *m* visit (to the hospital); *doctor's* visit, *pl.* rounds; **~bett** *n* sickbed; ***am*** ~ at the bedside; ***Unterricht am*** ~ bedside teaching; ***ans*** ~ ***gefesselt*** bedridden; **~blatt** *n* doctor's notes *pl.*, medical record; **~geld** *n* sickness benefit; **~ge·schich·te** *f* medical history; **~gymˌnast** *m* physiotherapist; **~gymˌna·stik** *f* physiotherapy
'Kran·ken·haus *n* hospital; ***im*** ~ ***liegen*** be in hospital; ***ins*** ~ ***gebracht werden*** be taken to hospital; **~auf·ent·halt** *m* stay in hospital; **~be·hand·lung** *f* hospital treatment; **~bett** *n* hospital bed; **~kosten** *pl.* hospital fees
'kran·ken·haus·reif *adj.*: ***j-n*** ~ ***schlagen*** F hospitalize s.o., F *fig.* beat s.o. to pulp
'Kran·ken·haus·ta·ge·geld *n* (hospital) daily benefit; **~ver·si·che·rung** *f* (hospital) daily benefits insurance
'Kran·ken|kas·se *f* health insurance scheme; **~kost** *f* light foods *pl.*; *w.s.* convalescent diet; **~la·ger** *n* → ***Krankenbett***; **~pfle·ge** *f* nursing; **~pfle·ger** *m* auxiliary, orderly; male nurse; **~pfle·ge·rin** *f* nurse; **~saal** *m* ward; **~schein** *m* health insurance certificate; **~schwe·ster** *f* nurse; **~tra·ge** *f* stretcher; **~trä·ger** *m* stretcher bearer; ambulance man; **~transˌport** *m* ambulance service(s *pl.*); **~ur·laub** *m* sick leave
'kran·ken·ver·si·chern (*only inf. and p.p.* krankenversichert, h) **I.** *v/t.* take out medical insurance for; **II.** *v/refl.*: ***sich*** ~ take out medical (*or* health) insurance; **'kran·ken·ver·si·chert** *adj.* medically insured; ***sind Sie*** ~***?*** do you have medical (*or* health) insurance?
'Kran·ken·ver·si·che·rung *f* health insurance
'Kran·ken|wa·gen *m* ambulance; **~wär·ter** *m* (medical) orderly; **~zim·mer** *n* sickroom, patient's room, sick bay
'krank·fei·ern F *v/i.* (*sep.*, h) malinger, go sick, F skive, take a sicky
'krank·haft *adj.* **1.** pathological; **2.** abnormal, obsessive
'Krank·heit *f* (-; -en) illness, sickness; disease (*a.* ♘ *and fig.*); complaint; ***psychische*** ~ *usu.* psychological disorder
'Krank·heits|be·richt *m* medical report (*or* bulletin); **~bild** *n* syndrome; **≗er·re·gend** *adj.* pathogenic; **~er·re·ger** *m* germ, 🕮 pathogen; **~er·schei·nung** *f* symptom; **~fall** *m* case (of illness)
'krank·heits·hal·ber [-halbɐ] *adv.* owing to illness
'Krank·heits|herd *m* focus of a (*or* the) disease; **~keim** *m* germ; **~leh·re** *f* pathology; **~trä·ger** *m* carrier; **~überˌtra·gung** *f* transmission of a (*or* the) disease; **~ver·lauf** *m* course of an (*or* the) illness; **~zei·chen** *n* symptom
'krank·la·chen F *v/refl.* (*sep.*, h): ***sich*** ~ F kill o.s. (laughing)
kränk·lich ['krɛŋklɪç] *adj.* frail; **'Kränk·lich·keit** *f* (-; *no pl.*) sickliness, infirmity
'krank·ma·chen F *v/i.* (*sep.*, h) → ***krankfeiern***
'Krank|mel·dung *f* notification of sickness; **~schrei·bung** *f* sick note
Krän·kung ['krɛŋkʊŋ] *f* (-; -en) insult
'Kran·wa·gen *m* **1.** crane truck; **2.** breakdown lorry, *Am.* tow truck
Kranz [krants] *m* (-es; Kränze ['krɛntsə]) garland; wreath; △ cornice; ⚙ rim; face; *gastr. and fig.* ring; *fig.* circle
Kränz·chen ['krɛntsçən] *fig. n* (-s; -) F hen party
krän·zen ['krɛntsən] *v/t.* (h) crown (with a wreath, garland *etc.*)
'Kranz|ge·fäß *n anat.* coronary artery; **~ge·sims** *n* cornice; **~nie·der·le·gung** *f* (ceremonial) laying of a wreath; wreath-laying ceremony; **~spen·de** *f* wreath, flowers *pl.*; ***es wird gebeten, von*** ~***n abzusehen*** no flowers please
Krap·fen ['krapfən] *m* (-s; -) doughnut
kraß [kras] *adj.* crass (*a. example*); *a.* stark *contrast etc.*; blatant *lie etc.*; gross *exaggeration etc.*; ***dazwischen ist ein krasser Unterschied*** *a.* there's a world of difference (between them); ***krasser Außenseiter*** rank outsider
Kra·ter ['kraːtɐ] *m* (-s; -) crater; **~landschaft** *f* crater landscape; **~see** *m* crater lake
Kratz·bür·ste ['krats-] *f* wire brush; F *fig.* ***sie ist e-e richtige*** ~ she's vicious
'kratz·bür·stig [-bʏrstɪç] F *fig. adj.* vicious
Krät·ze ['krɛtsə] *f* (-; *no pl.*): ***die*** ~ scabies
krat·zen ['kratsən] (h) **I.** *v/t.* a) scratch, b) scrape; ***sich die Nase*** ~ scratch one's nose; F *fig.* ***das kratzt mich nicht*** that doesn't worry me; **II.** *v/i.* a) scratch, b) scrape, c) *smoke etc.*: get to one's throat; ***mir kratzt der Hals*** I've got a tickle in my throat; F ***auf der Geige*** ~ F saw away at the violin; **III.** *v/refl.*: ***sich*** ~ scratch o.s.; ***sich am Ohr*** *etc.* ~ scratch one's ear *etc.*; **IV** ≗ *n* (-s) a) scratching (noise), b) tickle (in one's throat)
Krat·zer ['kratsɐ] *m* (-s; -) **1.** scratch; **2.** scraper
kratz·fest ['krats-] *adj.* non-scratch, scratchproof
'Kratz·fuß F *m*: ***e-n*** ~ ***machen*** bow and scrape
krat·zig ['kratsɪç] *adj.* scratchy
Kratz·putz ['krats-] *m* **1.** scratchwork; **2.** *art:* sgraffito
Kraul [kraʊl] *n* (-s; *no pl.*) *swimming*: crawl; **krau·len¹** ['kraʊlən] *v/i.* (sn) do the crawl
'krau·len² *v/t.* (h): ***e-n Hund*** *etc.* ~ ruffle a dog's *etc.* fur (*or* neck); ***j-m das Haar*** ~ run one's fingers through s.o.'s hair; ***sich den Kopf*** ~ scratch one's head
'Kraul·stil *m swimming*: crawl
kraus [kraʊs] *adj.* very curly, frizzy, F fuzzy *hair*; crinkly *dress etc.*; *fig.* muddled, confused *ideas etc.*; ***die Stirn*** ~ ***ziehen*** knit one's brow
Krau·se ['kraʊzə] *f* (-; -n) ruffle; ruff
Kräu·sel·krepp ['krɔʏzəl-] *m* crepe
kräu·seln ['krɔʏzəln] (h) **I.** *v/t.* frizz; crimp *one's hair*; gather *material*; screw up *one's nose*; ***die Stirn*** ~ frown; **II.** *v/refl.*: ***sich*** ~ *water*: ripple; *smoke*: curl up; *hair*: curl
krau·sen ['kraʊzən] *v/t.* (h) → ***kräuseln***
Kraus|haar ['kraʊs-] *n* very curly (*or* frizzy) hair; **~kopf** *m* curlyhead
Kraut [kraʊt] *n* (-[e]s; Kräuter ['krɔʏtɐ]) **1.** *no pl.* a) leaves *pl.*, top(s *pl.*), b) cabbage; ***ins*** ~ ***schießen*** run to leaf, *fig.* run riot; *fig.* ***das macht das*** ~ ***auch nicht fett*** that's not going to make any difference; ***wie*** ~ ***und Rüben*** (***durcheinander***) a complete muddle (*or* mess); **2.** *gastr.*, ⚘ herb; ***dagegen ist kein*** ~ ***gewachsen*** there's no cure for that yet; **3.** F weed
Kräu·ter|buch ['krɔʏtɐ-] *n* herbal (book); **~but·ter** *f* herb-flavo(u)red butter; **~es·sig** *m* aromatic vinegar; **~gar·ten** *m* herb garden; **~kä·se** *m* herb-flavo(u)red cheese; **~liˌkör** *m* herb-flavo(u)red liqueur; **~tee** *m* herb(al) tea
'Kraut·saˌlat *m* coleslaw
Kra·wall [kra'val] F *m* (-s; -e) **1.** *pl.* riot(s), rioting; **2.** *no pl.* F row; → *a.* ***Krach*** (***machen***); **~ma·cher** F *m* rioter
Kra·wat·te [kra'vatə] *f* (-; -n) tie
Kra'wat·ten|muf·fel F *m*: ***er ist ein*** ~ a) he hates wearing a tie, b) he always wears the same tie; **~na·del** *f* tiepin; **~zwang** *m* (-[e]s; *no pl.*) collar and tie compulsory
Kra·xe ['kraksə] *dial. f* (-; -n) pannier
kra·xeln ['kraksəln] *dial. v/i.* (sn) **1.** climb, go climbing; **2.** scramble (***auf*** *acc.* up)
Krea·ti·on [krea'tsi̯oːn] *f* (-; -en) creation, design
krea·tiv [krea'tiːf] *adj.* creative
Krea·ti·vi·tät *f* (-; *no pl.*) creativity
Krea'tiv·ur·laub *m* activity holiday
Krea·tur [krea'tuːɐ] *f* (-; -en [-rən]) creature; *fig. contp. a.* minion
Krebs [kreːps] *m* (-es; -e) **1.** *zo.* crustacean; *gastr.* crayfish; crab; ***e-n*** ~ ***fangen***

rowing: catch a crab; **2.** ⚕ cancer; **3.** *ast.* Cancer; **(ein)** ~ ***sein*** be (a) Cancer, be a Cancerian; **~angst** *f* fear of cancer; **~be·hand·lung** *f* treatment of cancer
'krebs·be·kämp·fend *adj.*: ***~e Mittel*** anti-cancer drugs; **'Krebs·be·kämp·fung** *f the* fight against cancer
kreb·sen ['kre:psən] F *v/i.* (sn) F crawl
'krebs·er·re·gend *adj.* cancer-causing, carcinogenic; **'Krebs·er·re·ger** *m* carcinogen
'Krebs|for·schung *f* cancer research; **~früh·er·ken·nung** *f* early cancer diagnosis; **~gang** *m* (-[e]s; *no pl.*) retrogression; ***im ~ gehen*** be going downhill; **~ge·schwulst** *f*, **~ge·schwür** *n* carcinoma; **~kli·nik** *f* cancer clinic; **⁀krank** *adj.*: ***er ist ~*** he's got cancer; ***~e Kinder*** children with (*or* suffering from) cancer; **~kran·ke** *m, f* (-n; -n) cancer patient; **~krank·heit** *f*, **~lei·den** *n* cancer(ous disease); **⁀rot** *adj.* (as) red as a lobster; **~spe·zia,list** *m* cancer specialist; **~sta·ti,on** *f* cancer ward; **~sup·pe** *f* crayfish soup; **~tier** *n* crustacean; **~ver·dacht** *m*: ***es besteht ~*** (there are fears) it may be cancer, F suspected cancer; **~vor·sor·ge** *f* cancer prevention; F → **~vor·sor·ge·un·ter,su·chung** *f* cancer screening (test), *pl. coll.* cancer screening *sg.*; **~zel·le** *f* cancer(ous) cell
kre·den·zen [kre'dɛntsən] *v/t.* (h): ***j-m et. ~*** offer s.o. s.th.
Kre·dit [kre'di:t] *m* (-[e]s; -e) ✝ credit; loan; *fig.* standing; ***auf ~*** on credit, F on tick; ***e-n ~ aufnehmen*** take out a loan; ***j-m e-n ~ gewähren*** grant s.o. a loan; *fig.* ***du hast bei mir keinen ~ mehr*** F I'm through with you; **~ab·bau** *m* loan repayment; **~ab,tei·lung** *f* loan department; **~an·stalt** *f* credit bank; **~an·trag** *m* loan application; **~auf·nah·me** *f* borrowing; **~auf·trag** *m* credit order; **~aus·zah·lung** *f* loan payout; **~bank** *f* (-; -en) credit bank; **~be·darf** *m* borrowing requirement(s *pl.*); **~be·din·gun·gen** *pl.* credit terms; **~be·schrän·kun·gen** *pl.* lending restrictions; **~brief** *m* letter of credit; **~er·öff·nung** *f* opening of a credit (***bei*** *dat.* with)
kre'dit·fä·hig *adj.* sound, solvent; **Kre'dit·fä·hig·keit** *f* (-; *no pl.*) borrowing power; credit standing (*Am.* rating)
Kre'dit|ge·ber *m* lender; **~ge·schäft** *n* **1.** credit transaction; **2.** lending business; **~hai** F *m* F loan shark
kre·di·tie·ren [kredi'ti:rən] *v/t.* (h): ✝ ***j-m et. ~*** credit s.o.('s account) with s.th.; **Kre·di'tie·rung** *f* (-; -en) crediting; credit advice; credit note
Kre'dit|in·sti,tut *n* credit institute (*or* bank); **~kar·te** *f* credit card; **~kauf** *m* credit sale; **~knapp·heit** *f* credit crunch; **~lauf·zeit** *f* credit period; **~li·mit** *n* overdraft limit; **~li·nie** *f* credit line; **~markt** *m* credit market; **~neh·mer** [-ne:mɐ] *m* (-s; -) borrower; **~po·li,tik** *f* lending policy; **~po·sten** *m* credit item; **~rück·zah·lung** *f* repayment of a loan; **~schöp·fung** *f* credit formation; **~schrau·be** *f* F credit screw
Kre·dit·sei·te ['kre:dɪt-] *f* credit side
Kre'dit|sper·re *f* credit freeze; **~sprit·ze** *f* credit injection; **~sy,stem** *n* credit system; instal(l)ment plan; **~ver·ein·ba·rung** *f* credit agreement; **~ver·kehr** *m* credit transactions *pl.*; **~wirt·schaft** *f* paper economy

kre'dit·wür·dig *adj.* creditworthy; *fig.* credible; **Kre'dit·wür·dig·keit** *f* (-; *no pl.*) creditworthiness, credit rating (*or* standing); *fig.* credibility
Kre'dit·zins *m* lending rate
Kre·do → ***Credo***
Krei·de ['kraɪdə] *f* (-; -n) **1.** *no pl.* chalk; *fig.* ***tief in der ~ sitzen*** be up to one's ears (F eyeballs) in debt, ***bei j-m:*** owe s.o. a lot of money; **2.** → ***Kreidestift***; **⁀'bleich** *adj.* (as) white as a ghost (*or* sheet); **~fel·sen** *m* chalk cliff
'krei·de·hal·tig [-haltɪç] *adj.* chalky, 🕮 cretaceous
'Krei·de|stift *m* (piece of) chalk; **~strich** *m* chalk line; **⁀'weiß** *adj.* → ***kreidebleich***; **~zeich·nung** *f* chalk drawing; **~zeit** *f* (-; *no pl.*) Cretaceous period
krei·dig ['kraɪdɪç] *adj.* chalky; *geol. a.* cretaceous
kre·ie·ren [kre'i:rən] *v/t.* (h) create; design
Kreis [kraɪs] *m* (-es; -e ['kraɪzə]) *a.* 𝔄 *and fig.* circle; ring; *ast.* orbit; ⚡ circuit; *biol.* cycle; *adm.* district; *fig.* sphere; ***im ~*** in a circle; ***mir dreht sich alles im ~*** my head's spinning; ***e-n ~ schließen um*** *acc.* form a circle around; ***sich im ~ drehen*** revolve, rotate, spin round (in circles), *fig. discussion etc.*: go round in circles; ***~e ziehen*** *bird etc.*: circle; ***immer weitere ~e ziehen*** *rumo(u)r*: spread further and further (afield), *affair etc.*: have far-reaching implications; ***in weiten ~en*** widely; ***in den besten ~en verkehren*** move in the best circles; ***der ~ schließt sich*** we've come full circle
'Kreis|ab·schnitt *m* 𝔄 segment (of a circle); **~amt** *n* district administration; **~aus·schnitt** *m* 𝔄 sector (of a circle); **~bahn** *f ast.* orbit; 𝔄 circular path; **~be·hör·de** *f* district authority; **~be·we·gung** *f* rotation, circular motion; **~bo·gen** *m* 𝔄 arc of a circle
krei·schen ['kraɪʃən] *v/i. and v/t.* (h) screech (*a. fig. brakes etc.*); squeal *with pleasure etc.*; **'krei·schend** *adj.* shrill
'Kreis|dia,gramm *n* circular (*or* pie) chart; **~,durch·mes·ser** *m* diameter
Krei·sel ['kraɪzəl] *m* (-s; -) (spinning) top; ⚙ gyroscope; ⚓, ✈ gyro stabilizer; **~be·we·gung** *f* gyration; **~kom·paß** *m* gyrocompass
krei·seln ['kraɪzəln] *v/i.* **1.** (h) play with a top; **2.** (sn) spin (around)
'Krei·sel·pum·pe *f* centrifugal pump
krei·sen ['kraɪzən] **I.** *v/i.* (sn) circle (***um*** *acc.* around); revolve, rotate, spin; ⚕, ✝ circulate; ***~ lassen*** pass round; ***~ um*** *acc. thoughts etc.*: revolve around; **II.** *v/t.* (h) *gym.* ***die Arme ~*** swing one's arms around; **III.** ⁀ *n* (-s) rotation; *ast.* revolution
'Kreis·flä·che *f* 𝔄 area of a circle
'kreis·för·mig [-fœrmɪç] **I.** *adj.* circular; **II.** *adv.*: ***~ angeordnet*** arranged in a circle
'Kreis|in·halt *m* → ***Kreisfläche***; **~ke·gel** *m* circular cone; **~kol·ben·mo·tor** *m* rotary-piston engine
'Kreis·lauf *m biol. and fig.* cycle; ⚕, ✝ circulation; **~kol·laps** *m* circulatory failure (*or* breakdown, collapse); ***ich hatte e-n ~*** F I fainted (*or* passed out, collapsed); **~mit·tel** *n* circulatory preparation; **~stö·run·gen** *pl.* bad circulation *sg.*, problems *pl.* with one's circulation; **~ver·sa·gen** *n* circulatory failure (*or* breakdown, collapse)

'kreis·rund *adj.* circular
'Kreis·sä·ge *f* circular saw
Kreiß·saal ['kraɪs-] *m* delivery room
'Kreis|stadt *f* district (*Brit.* county) town; **~,um·fang** *m* 𝔄 circumference (of a circle); **~ver·kehr** *m* roundabout traffic; ***im ~*** on a roundabout
Krem *f* → ***Creme***
Kre·ma·to·ri·um [krema'to:rĭʊm] *n* (-s; -rien) crematorium, *Am.* crematory
Krem·pe ['krɛmpə] *f* (-; -n) brim
Krem·pel ['krɛmpəl] F *m* (-s; *no pl.*) → ***Kram***
krem·peln ['krɛmpəln] *v/t.* (h): ***die Ärmel etc. nach oben ~*** roll up one's sleeves *etc.*
Kren [kre:n] *dial. m* (-[e]s; *no pl.*) horseradish
Kreo·le [kre'o:lə] *m* (-n; -n), **Kreo·lin** [kre'o:lɪn] *f* (-; -nen), **kreo·lisch** [kre'o:lɪʃ] *adj.* Creole
kre·pie·ren [kre'pi:rən] *v/i.* (sn) **1.** *animal*: die, perish; F *person*: die a wretched death; **2.** *bomb etc.*: burst, explode
Krepp [krɛp] *m* (-s; -s) crepe
'Kreppa,pier (*sep.* -pp·p-) *n* crepe paper
'Krepp|sei·de *f* crepe de Chine; **~soh·le** *f* crepe sole
Kres·se ['krɛsə] *f* (-; -n) cress
Kre·ter ['kre:tɐ] *m* (-s; -) Cretan
Kre·thi und Ple·thi ['kre:ti ʊnt 'ple:ti] *pl.* every Tom, Dick and Harry
Kre·tin [kre'tɛ̃:] *m* (-s; -s) cretin; *contp. a.* moron
kre·tisch ['kre:tɪʃ] *adj.* Cretan
kreuz [krɔʏts] *adv.*: ***~ und quer*** *liegen etc.*: all over the place; ***~ und quer durch die Stadt*** all over town
Kreuz *n* (-es; -e) a) cross (*a. fig.*); *eccl.* crucifix, b) *anat.* lower back, small of the back, 🕮 sacrum, c) intersection, d) *card game*: club(s *pl.*), e) ♪ sharp, f) *typ.* dagger; ***über ~*** crosswise; ***das ~ schlagen*** make the sign of the cross, *a.* cross o.s. (*a. fig.*); ***das Eiserne ~*** the Iron Cross; *ast.* ***~ des Südens*** Southern Cross; F ***ich hab's wieder im ~*** F my back's playing me up again; *fig.* ***sein ~ auf sich nehmen (tragen)*** take up (bear) one's cross; ***zu ~e kriechen*** eat humble pie, *Am. a.* eat crow; ***er ist mit ihm über(s) ~*** they've fallen out (with each other); ***es ist ein ~ mit ihm*** it's one thing after another with him; F ***j-n aufs ~ legen*** F take s.o. for a ride; F ***j-m et. aus dem ~ leiern*** F scrounge s.th. off s.o.; ***ich hab' drei ~e gemacht*** I was glad to see (*or* hear) the last of that; **~ab·nah·me** *f* descent from the cross; **~al,tar** *m* lay altar; **~band** *n* (-[e]s; ⸚er) **1.** *anat.* crucial ligament; **2.** ✉ wrapper; **~bein** *n anat.* sacrum
'Kreuz·blüt·ler [-bly:tlɐ] *m* (-s; -) ⚘ crucifer
'kreuz'brav F *adj.* very virtuous
kreu·zen ['krɔʏtsən] **I.** *v/t.* (h) **1.** cross, intersect *line, road etc.*; ***die Beine ~*** cross one's legs; ***die Arme ~*** fold one's arms; **2.** *biol.* cross(breed), interbreed; **3.** ***sich ~*** cross; *fig. interests etc.*: clash; *eyes* meet; **II.** *v/i.* (sn) ⚓, ✈ cruise
Kreu·zer ['krɔʏtsɐ] *m* (-s; -) a) ⚔ cruiser, b) (cabin) cruiser
Kreu·zes·tod ['krɔʏtsəs-] *m* (death by) crucifixion; ***den ~ sterben*** die on the cross
'Kreuz|fah·rer *m hist.* crusader; **~fahrt** *f* cruise; **~feu·er** *n* crossfire (*a. fig.*); *fig.*

ins ~ geraten come under fire, F come in for a shelling; ***im ~ der Kritik stehen*** be under fire; **2fi,del** F *adj.* F very chirpy (*Am.* chipper)

'kreuz·för·mig [-fœrmɪç] *adj.* cross-shaped, cruciform

'Kreuz|gang *m* ⚠ cloisters *pl.*; **~ge·lenk** *n* ⚙ universal joint; **~ge·wöl·be** *n* ⚠ cross (*or* groined) vault

kreu·zi·gen ['krɔʏtsɪgən] *v/t.* (h) crucify (*a. fig.*), *eccl. a.* nail to the cross; **'Kreu·zi·gung** *f* (-; -en) crucifixion

'kreuz·lahm F *adj.*: ***jetzt bin ich aber ~*** a) F I'm shattered, b) my back!

'Kreuz|ot·ter *f zo.* adder; **~pro·be** *f* ⚕ cross-matching; ***die ~ machen*** cross-match; **~reim** *m* alternate rhyme; **~rip·pen·ge·wöl·be** *n* ⚠ ribbed vault

'Kreuz·rit·ter *m* **1.** crusader; **2.** Teutonic Knight; **~or·den** *m* Teutonic Order of Knights

'Kreuz|schiff *n* ⚠ transept; **~schlitz·schrau·be** *f* cross-recessed screw; **~schmer·zen** *pl.* backache *sg.*; **~schna·bel** *m zo.* crossbill; **~spin·ne** *f* cross (*or* garden) spider; **~stich** *m* cross-stitch

Kreu·zung ['krɔʏtsʊŋ] *f* (-; -en) **1.** crossroads *pl.*, *esp. Am.* intersection; **2.** *biol.* a) cross-breeding, b) cross(-breed)

'kreu·zungs·frei *adj.* non-intersecting

'Kreu·zungs·punkt *m* point of intersection

'Kreuz|ver·hör *n* ⚖ cross-examination; *w.s.* interrogation, F grilling; ***ins ~ nehmen*** cross-examine, *w.s.* F give *s.o.* a grilling; **~ver·weis** *m* cross-reference; **~weg** *m* **1.** crossroads *pl.* (*a. fig.*); **2.** *eccl.* stations *pl.* of the Cross; **~weh** *n* backache; **2wei·se** *adv.* crosswise, across; *sl.* ***du kannst mich mal ~*** *sl.* you know what you can do; **~wort·rät·sel** *n* crossword (puzzle); **~zei·chen** *n eccl.* sign of the cross; **~zug** *m* crusade (*a. fig.*)

Kre·vet·te [kre'vɛtə] *f* (-; -n) shrimp (*Am. a. pl.*); **Kre'vet·ten·cock·tail** *m* shrimp cocktail

krib·be·lig ['krɪbəlɪç] *adj.* nervous, F jittery; *pred.* on edge; ***das macht mich ganz ~*** *a.* F it gives me the heebie-jeebies

krib·beln ['krɪbəln] **I.** *v/i.* (h) **1.** tickle; itch; ***mir kribbelt's in den Fingern*** I've got pins and needles in my fingers, *fig.* I'm itching to do it *etc.*; **2.** ***es kribbelt von Ameisen*** *etc.* the place is crawling with ants *etc.*; **II.** 2 *n* (-s) tingling, pins and needles *pl.*

Kricket ['krɪkət] (*sep.* -k·k-) *n* (-s; *no pl.*) cricket; **~spie·ler** *m* cricket player

krie·chen ['kriːçən] *v/i.* (kroch, gekrochen, sn) a) crawl (*a. fig.*); creep (*a. mot.*), b) *zo.* crawl, slither; ***~de Pflanze*** creeper; *fig.* ***vor j-m ~*** F toady (*or* suck up) to s.o.; **Krie·cher** ['kriːçɐ] *m* (-s; -) F toady; **krie·che·risch** ['kriːçərɪʃ] *adj.* bootlicking ...; ***ich kann s-e ~e Art nicht ausstehen*** F I can't stand the way he sucks up to people

Kriech|pflan'ze ['kriːç-] *f* creeper; **~spur** *f* **1.** *mot.* slow lane; **2.** *zo.* trail; **~strom** *m* ⚡ (surface) leakage current; **~tem·po** *n*: ***sich im ~ fortbewegen*** crawl along; **~tier** *n* reptile

Krieg [kriːk] *m* (-[e]s; -e ['kriːgə]) war (*a. fig.*); warfare; feud (*a. fig.*); ***kalter ~*** cold war; ***totaler ~*** total warfare; ***im ~*** at war (***mit*** *dat.* with); ***vom ~ verwüstet*** war-torn; ***~ führen gegen*** *acc.* a) make war on, b) be at war with; ***e-m Land den ~ erklären*** declare war on a country; *fig.* ***j-m*** (***e-r Sache***) ***den ~ ansagen*** declare war on s.o. (s.th.)

krie·gen ['kriːgən] F *v/t.* (h) get; *a.* catch *a disease, a criminal, a train etc.*; *a.* come down with *the flu etc.*, have *a coronary etc.*; ***j-n dazu ~, et. zu tun*** get s.o. to do s.th.; ***das werden wir schon ~!*** we'll sort that out, don't you worry; ***ich krie·ge es nicht über mich zu*** *inf.* I can't bring myself to *inf.*; ***er kriegt was von mir zu hören!*** I'll have something to say to him; ***gleich kriegst du was!*** just watch your step

Krie·ger ['kriːgɐ] *m* (-s; -) warrior; soldier; *hum.* ***alter ~*** old campaigner; *pol.* ***kalter ~*** cold warrior; **~denk·mal** *n* war memorial

krie·ge·risch ['kriːgərɪʃ] *adj.* warlike, *a. fig.* belligerent; military, armed *conflict etc.*; ***~e Auseinandersetzung(en)*** armed conflict

'Krie·ger·wit·we *f* war widow

'krieg·füh·rend *adj.* warring *nations etc.*; **'Krieg·füh·rung** *f* strategy; ***biologische*** *etc.* **~** biological *etc.* warfare

'Kriegs|an·lei·he *f* war loan; **~aus·bruch** *m* outbreak of (the) war; ***bei ~*** when the war broke out; **~aus·zeich·nung** *f* war decoration; **~beil** *n*: *fig.* ***das ~ begraben*** bury the hatchet; **~be·ma·lung** *f* war paint; F *fig.* ***in voller ~*** F with her war paint on; **~be·richt·er·stat·ter** *m* war correspondent; **2be·schä·digt** *adj.* war-disabled; **~be·schä·dig·te** *m* (-n; -n) disabled veteran; **~beu·te** *f* spoils *pl.* of war; **~braut** *f* war bride

'Kriegs·dienst *m* military service; **~ver·wei·ge·rer** [-fɛɐvaɪgərɐ] *m* (-s; -) conscientious objector

'Kriegs|dro·hung *f* threat of war; **~en·de** *n* end of the war; ***bei*** (***nach, vor***) **~** *a.* when (after, before) the war ended; **~ent·schä·di·gung** *f* reparations *pl.*; **~er·klä·rung** *f* declaration of war; **~er·leb·nis** *n* wartime experience; **~fall** *m*: ***im ~*** in the event of (a) war; **~film** *m* war film; **~flot·te** *f* navy; **~frei·wil·li·ge** *m* (-n; -n) war volunteer; **~fuß** *m*: ***auf ~ stehen mit*** *dat.* be at loggerheads with *s.o.*, be having a hard time (*or* a real struggle) with *s.th.*; **~ge·biet** *n* war zone; **~ge·fahr** *f* threat of war; **~ge·fan·ge·ne** *m* prisoner of war (*abbr.* POW); **~ge·fan·gen·schaft** *f* captivity; ***in ~ geraten*** be put into a prisoner-of-war camp; ***aus der ~ heimkehren*** return from a prisoner-of-war camp; **~geg·ner** *m* **1.** wartime enemy; **2.** pacifist; **~ge·ne·ra·ti,on** *f* war generation; **~ge·richt** *n* court martial; ***vor ein ~ gestellt werden*** be tried by court martial; **~ge·schrei** *n* battle cry; **~ge·setz** *n* martial law

'Kriegs·ge·winn·ler [-gəvɪnlɐ] *m* (-s; -) war profiteer

'Kriegs|gott *m* god of war; **~göt·tin** *f* goddess of war; **~grä·ber·für·sor·ge** *f* War Graves Commission; **~greu·el** *pl.* war atrocities; **~ha·fen** *m* naval port; **~held** *m* war hero; *hist.* great warrior; **~herr** *m*: ***oberster ~*** commander-in-chief, supreme commander; *w.s.* warlord; **~het·ze** *f* warmongering; **~het·zer** *m* warmonger; **~hin·ter,blie·be·ne** *pl.* war widows and orphans, surviving dependants; **~in·du,strie** *f* war industry; **~in·va,li·de** *m* disabled veteran; **~jahr** *n* year of (the) war; **~ka·me,rad** *m* wartime comrade; ***wir sind ~en*** *a.* we fought together in the war; **~ma·schi·ne,rie** *f* machinery of war; **~ma·te·ri,al** *n* matériel; **2mü·de** *adj.* war-weary

'Kriegs·op·fer *n* war victim; **~ren·te** *f* war pension

'Kriegs|pfad *m*: ***auf dem ~ sein*** be on the warpath; **~po·ten·ti,al** *n* military resources *pl.*; **~pro·pa,gan·da** *f* war propaganda; **~rat** *m*: *fig.* **~ *halten*** have a conference (*or* pow-wow); **~recht** *n* (-[e]s; *no pl.*) ⚖ law of war; ⚔ martial law; **~ro,man** *m* war novel; **~scha·den** *m* war damage; **~schau·platz** *m* theat|re (*Am. a.* -er) of war; **~schiff** *n* warship; *hist.* man-of-war; **~schuld** *f* war guilt; **~schul·den** *pl.* war debts; **~spiel·zeug** *n* toy weapons *pl.*; **~stär·ke** *f* wartime strength; **~ta·ge·buch** *n* war diary; **~tanz** *m* war dance; **~teil·neh·mer** *m* a) combatant, b) (war) veteran, c) warring nation; **~to·te** *pl.* war dead (*pl.*); ***30000 ~*** *a.* 30,000 killed in action; **~trei·ber** *m* warmonger; **~ver·bre·chen** *n* war crime

'Kriegs·ver·bre·cher *m* war criminal; **~pro,zeß** *m* war crimes trial

'Kriegs|ver·bün·de·te *m* (-n; -n) wartime ally; **~ver·let·zung** *f* war injury; **~ver·sehr·te** *m* (-n; -n) disabled veteran; **~waf·fe** *f* weapon of war; **~wai·se** *f* war orphan; **~wirt·schaft** *f* wartime economy; **~zeit** *f* wartime; ***in ~en*** in times of war; **~zu·stand** *m* (-[e]s; *no pl.*) (state of) war; ***im ~*** at war

Kri·mi ['kriːmi, 'krɪmi] F *m* **1.** crime thriller; detective novel; **2.** *film*: crime thriller; *TV* crime series; **3.** F *fig.* F nailbiter

Kri·mi·nal·be·am·te [krimi'naːl-] *m*, **Kri·mi·na·le** [krimi'naːlə] F *m* (-n; -n) detective

Kri·mi'nal|film *m* crime thriller; **~ge·schich·te** *f* **1.** history of crime; **2.** → ***Krimi*** 1; **~in,spek·tor** *m* detective inspector

kri·mi·na·li·sie·ren [kriminali'ziːrən] *v/t.* (h) criminalize

Kri·mi·na·list [krimina'lɪst] *m* (-en; -en) detective; criminologist; **Kri·mi·na·li·stik** [krimina'lɪstɪk] *f* (-; *no pl.*) criminology; **kri·mi·na·li·stisch** [krimina'lɪstɪʃ] *adj.* criminal

Kri·mi·na·li·tät [kriminali'tɛːt] *f* (-; *no pl.*) crime

Kri·mi'nal|kom·mis,sar *m* detective superintendent; **~ko,mö·die** *f* comedy thriller; **~po·li,zei** *f* criminal investigation department (*abbr.* CID), F plain-clothes police *pl.*; **~psy·cho·lo,gie** *f* psychology of crime, criminal psychology; **~ro,man** *m* crime thriller, detective novel; *pl. coll.* crime (*or* detective) fiction *sg.*; **~so·zio·lo,gie** *f* criminology, sociology of crime; **~sta,ti·stik** *f* crime statistics *pl.*; *n.s.* crime figures *pl.*; **~stück** *n thea.* detective play, crime thriller; **~tech·nik** *f* forensic science; **2tech·nisch** *adj.* forensic

kri·mi·nell [krimi'nɛl] *adj.*, **Kri·mi·nel·le** [krimi'nɛlə] *m, f* (-n; -n) criminal

Kri·mi·no·lo·ge [krimino'loːgə] *m* (-n; -n) criminologist; **Kri·mi·no·lo·gie** [kriminolo'giː] *f* (-; *no pl.*) criminology; **kri·mi·no·lo·gisch** [krimino'loːgɪʃ] *adj.* criminological

Krim·mer ['krɪmɐ] *m* (-s; -) lambskin, astrakhan

Krims·krams ['krɪmskrams] F *m* (-[e]s; *no pl.*) odds and ends *pl.*; (piece of) junk

Krin·gel ['krɪŋəl] *m* (-s; -) ring (*a. gastr.*); squiggle; **'krin·geln** *v/refl.* (h): ***sich ~*** curl (up); F ***sich (vor Lachen) ~*** F crease up (laughing)
Kri·no·li·ne [krino'li:nə] *f* (-; -n) crinoline
Kri·po ['kri:po, 'krɪpo] F *f* (-; *no pl.*) → ***Kriminalpolizei***
Krip·pe ['krɪpə] *f* (-; -n) **1.** a) *a. bibl.* manger, b) (*Christmas*) crib; *fig.* ***an der ~ sitzen*** be in clover; **2.** crèche, day nursery
'Krip·pen|fi,gur *f* nativity figure; **~spiel** *n* nativity play
Kri·se ['kri:zə] *f* (-; -n) crisis
kri·seln ['kri:zəln] F *v/impers.* (h): ***es kriselt*** there's something in the air, there's trouble brewing; ***in der Partei (in ihrer Ehe) kriselt es*** the party's (they're) going through a bit of a sticky patch, *iro.* all is not well in the party (their marriage)
'kri·sen·an·fäl·lig *adj.* unstable, crisis-prone
'Kri·sen|be·schwö·rer *m* alarmist; **~be·wäl·ti·gung** *f* crisis management; **~fest** *adj.* stable; **~ge·biet** *n* trouble spot; **~ge·schüt·telt** *adj.* crisis-ridden; **~herd** *m* trouble spot; **~ma·nage·ment** *n* crisis management; **~plan** *m* contingency plan; **~si·tua·ti,on** *f* crisis (situation); **~sit·zung** *f* crisis meeting; **~stab** *m* crisis management group, F crisis squad; **~stim·mung** *f* apprehensive climate; **~zeit** *f* time of crisis
Kri·stall[1] [krɪs'tal] *m* (-s; -e) crystal
Kri'stall[2] *n* (-s; *no pl.*) crystal
Kri'stall·bil·dung *f* crystallization
kri·stal·len [krɪs'talən] *adj.* crystal; *fig.* crystal clear *water etc.*
Kri'stalleuch·ter (*sep.* -ll·l-) *m* crystal chandelier
Kri'stall|git·ter *n* ⚒ crystal lattice; **~glas** *n* (-[e]s; ¨er) **1.** *no pl.* crystal; **2.** crystal glass
Kri·stal·li·sa·ti·on [krɪstaliza'tšo:n] *f* (-; -en) crystallization; **kri·stal·li·sie·ren** [krɪstali'zi:rən] *v/t., v/i. and v/refl.* (***sich ~***) (h) crystallize (*a. fig.*); **Kri·stal·li'sie·rung** *f* (-; -en) crystallization
kri'stall·klar *adj.* crystal clear
Kri'stall|ku·gel *f* crystal ball; **~nacht** *f hist.* kristallnacht, Night of the Broken Glass; **~wa·ren** *pl.* crystal(ware) *sg.*; **~zucker** *m* (refined) sugar crystals *pl.*
Kri·te·ri·um [kri'te:rĭum] *n* (-s; -ien) criterion
Kri·tik [kri'ti:k] *f* (-; -en) **1.** *no pl.* criticizing; criticism (***über*** *acc.*, ***an*** *dat.* of), censure; F ***unter aller ~*** beneath contempt; ***~ üben (an*** *dat.*) → ***kritisieren***; **2.** review, write-up; ***gute ~en haben*** have a good press; ***was sagt die ~?*** what do the critics say?; → ***glänzend*** I; **3.** critique (***über*** *acc.* of)
Kri·ti·ka·ster [kriti'kastɐ] *contp. m* (-s; -) faultfinder; hack critic
Kri·ti·ker ['kri:tikɐ] *m* (-s; -), **Kri·ti·ke·rin** ['kri:tikərɪn] *f* (-; -nen) a) critic, b) reviewer
Kri'tik·fä·hig·keit *f* (-; *no pl.*) critical faculties *pl.*; powers *pl.* of discernment
kri'tik·los *adj.* uncritical
Kri'tik·lo·sig·keit *f* (-; *no pl.*) uncriticalness; lack of discrimination
kri·tisch ['kri:tɪʃ] *adj.* **1.** critical (***gegenüber*** *dat.* of); discriminating, discerning; **2.** critical (*a. phys.*, ⚙); **~er *Augenblick*** critical moment
kri·ti·sie·ren [kriti'zi:rən] *v/t.* (h) a) criticize, b) review; ***er hat an allem etwas zu ~*** he's always got something to criticize
Krit·te·lei [krɪtə'laɪ] *f* (-; -en) F nitpicking; **krit·teln** ['krɪtəln] *v/i.* (h) find fault (***an*** *dat.* with)
Krit·ze·lei [krɪtsə'laɪ] *f* (-; -en) **1.** *no pl.* scribbling; **2.** scribble; **krit·zeln** ['krɪtsəln] *v/i.* (h) a) scribble, b) doodle
Kroa·te [kro'a:tə] *m* (-n; -n), **Kroa·tin** [kro'a:tɪn] *f* (-; -nen), **kroa·tisch** [kro'a:tɪʃ] *adj.* Croatian
kroch [krɔx] *pret. of* ***kriechen***
Krocket ['krɔkət] (*sep.* -k·k-) *n* (-s; *no pl.*) croquet
Kro·kant [kro'kant] *m* (-[e]s; *no pl.*) cracknel
Kro·ket·ten [kro'kɛtən] *pl. gastr.* croquettes
Kro·ko ['kro:ko] F *n* (-[s]; -s) crocodile, F croc
Kro·ko·dil [kroko'di:l] *n* (-s; -e) crocodile; **~le·der** *n* crocodile (skin)
Kro·ko'dils·trä·nen F *fig. pl.* crocodile tears; ***ein paar ~ weinen*** squeeze a tear
Kro·kus ['kro:kʊs] *m* (-; -se) ⚘ crocus
Kro·ne ['kro:nə] *f* (-; -n) **1.** crown; coronet; ***die päpstliche ~*** the papal tiara; **2.** *fig.* climax; crowning glory; ***die ~ der Schöpfung*** the pride of creation; ***e-r Sache die ~ aufsetzen mit*** *dat.* crown s.th. with; ***das setzt allem die ~ auf*** that beats everything; F ***das ist ihm in die ~ gestiegen*** it's gone to his head; F ***was ist ihm in die ~ gefahren?*** what's up with him?; F ***(ganz schön) e-n in der ~ haben*** have had one too many; ***dir wird kein Stein (***or* ***Zacken) aus der ~ fallen, wenn*** it won't kill you to *inf.*; ***brich dir keinen Stein (***or* ***Zacken) aus der ~!*** don't put yourself out!; **3.** ⚘ a) corolla, b) (*tree*) top; **4.** ⚕ crown; **5.** ⚙ top *of a dam*; △ coping; **6.** winder *of a watch*
krö·nen ['krø:nən] *v/t.* (h) **1.** crown; ***j-n zum König ~*** crown s.o. king; **2.** *fig.* crown, cap; round *s.th.* off; → ***gekrönt***
'Kro·nen|kor·ken *m* crown cork; **~mut·ter** *f* castle nut; **~ver·schluß** *m* crown cap
Kron|er·be ['kro:n-] *m* heir to the throne (*or* crown); **~gut** *n* crown estate; **~ju,we·len** *pl.* crown jewels; **~ko·lo,nie** *f* crown colony; **~land** *n* crown estate; **~leuch·ter** *m* chandelier; F ***mir geht ein ~ auf*** F I've seen the light; **~prinz** *m* crown prince; *in GB*: Prince of Wales; **~prin,zes·sin** *f* crown princess; *in GB*: Princess Royal
Krö·nung ['krø:nʊŋ] *f* (-; -en) **1.** coronation; **2.** *fig.* climax, high point; crowning moment (*or* event); ***zur ~ des Ganzen*** to crown (*or* top) it all
'Krö·nungs|eid *m* coronation oath; **~fei·er** *f* coronation (ceremony)
Kron·zeu·ge ['kro:n-] *m* chief witness; state witness, accomplice witness; ***als ~ auftreten*** *in GB*: turn Queen's (*or* King's) evidence
Kropf [krɔpf] *m* (-[e]s; Kröpfe ['krœpfə]) ⚕ goitre, *Am.* goiter; *zo.* crop; F ***überflüssig wie ein ~*** F as useful as a hole in the head
kröp·fen ['krœpfən] *v/t.* (h) stuff
Kropp·zeug ['krɔp-] F *n* (-s; *no pl.*) **1.** F dregs *pl.*, scum, peasants *pl.*; **2.** F junk
kroß [krɔs] *adj.* crisp
Krö·sus ['krø:zʊs] *fig. m*: ***ich bin doch kein ~!*** I'm not made of money, you know
Krö·te ['krø:tə] *f* (-; -n) toad; *fig.* ***giftige ~*** *sl.* nasty bit of stuff, F nasty customer; F ***freche ~*** little rascal; F ***m-e letzten ~n*** my last few pennies (*or* cents)
Krücke ['krʏkə] (*sep.* -k·k-) *f* (-; -n) **1.** a) crutch, b) handle; ***an ~n gehen*** walk on crutches; **2.** F *fig.* F dead loss, washout; **3.** *fig.* support; shoulder to lean on
Krück·stock ['krʏk-] *m* walking stick
Krug [kru:k] *m* (-[e]s; Krüge ['kry:gə]) **1.** jug; (*beer*) mug, stein, tankard; ***der ~ geht so lange zum Brunnen, bis er bricht*** a) you *etc.* won't get away with that forever, b) there's a limit to everything, you do that one more time; **2.** *dial* inn
Krüm·chen ['kry:mçən] *fig. n* (-s; -) tiny bit; ***er zeigte kein ~ Interesse*** he wasn't the least bit interested
Kru·me ['kru:mə] *f* (-; -n) **1.** crumb; **2.** ✓ topsoil
Krü·mel ['kry:məl] *m* (-s; -) crumb
krü·me·lig ['kry:məlɪç] *adj.* crumbly; full of crumbs; **'krü·meln** *v/i.* (h) be crumbly; ***bitte nicht ~!*** no crumbs on the floor, please
krumm [krʊm] *adj. and adv.* **1.** crooked (*a. nose*); bent; winding; twisted; ***e-e ~e Haltung*** bad posture, a stoop; ***~ gehen*** stoop; ***~ biegen*** bend; *fig.* ***alt und ~*** bowed down with age; **2.** F *fig.* ***~e Finger machen*** F walk off with s.th.; ***~e Sachen machen*** F get up to no good, get onto the wrong side of the law; ***es auf die ~e Tour machen (versuchen)*** F (try to) pull a fast one; **'krumm·bei·nig** [-baɪnɪç] *adj.* bandy- (*or* bow-)legged
krüm·men ['krʏmən] (h) **I.** *v/t.* bend; *cat etc.*: arch *its back*; → ***Finger, Haar***; **II.** *v/refl.*: ***sich ~*** *road*: curve, be very windy, *river*: bend, wind its way, meander; *wood*: warp; *worm*: wriggle; *fig.* ***sich ~ vor*** *dat.* be doubled up (*or* convulsed) with *pain, laughter etc.*, squirm with *embarrassment*
Krüm·mer ['krʏmɐ] *m* (-s; -) ⚙ elbow, bend
Krumm·horn ['krʊm-] *n* ♪ crumhorn
'krumm·le·gen F *v/refl.* (*sep.*, h): ***sich ~*** F scrimp and save, have to count every penny
'krumm·li·nig [-li:nɪç] *adj.* 𝒜 curvilinear
'krumm·neh·men F *v/t.* (*irr.*, *sep.*, h, → ***nehmen***): ***(j-m) et. ~*** take offen|ce (*Am.* -se) at s.th.
'Krumm|sä·bel *m* scimitar; **~stab** *m* crook; *eccl.* crosier, crozier
Krüm·mung ['krʏmʊŋ] *f* (-; -en) bend; 𝒜, ⚕, *phys.* curvature; twist
Krupp [krʊp] *m* (-s; *no pl.*) ⚕ croup
Krup·pe ['krʊpə] *f* (-; -n) *zo.* croup
Krüp·pel ['krʏpəl] *m* (-s; -) cripple; F *fig. contp.* F cretin; ***zum ~ machen*** cripple, maim; ***zum ~ werden*** be crippled; **krüp·pe·lig** ['krʏpəlɪç] *adj.* deformed, crippled
'Krupp·hu·sten *m* barking cough
Kru·ste ['krʊstə] *f* (-; -n) *a.* ⚕, *geol.* crust
'Kru·sten·tier *n* crustacean
Kru·zi·fix ['kru:tsifɪks] *n* (-es; -e) crucifix
Kryo·chir·ur'gie [kryo-] *f* cryosurgery
Kryp·ta ['krʏpta] *f* (-; -ten) crypt
Kryp·ton ['krʏptɔn] *n* (-s; *no pl.*) krypton
Ku·ba·ner [ku'ba:nɐ] *m* (-s; -), **Ku·ba·ne·rin** [ku'ba:nərɪn] *f* (-; -nen), **ku·ba·nisch** [ku'ba:nɪʃ] *adj.* Cuban
Kü·bel ['ky:bəl] *m* (-s; -) bucket; tub; ***es gießt wie aus ~n*** it's coming down in buckets; **~wa·gen** *m* jeep (*TM*)

'kü·bel·wei·se *adv.* by the bucket(load)

ku·bie·ren [ku'bi:rən] *v/t.* (h) Ꭿ cube

Ku·bik|in·halt [ku'bi:k-] *m* cubic content; **~maß** *n* cubic measure; **~me·ter** *m, n* cubic metre (*Am.* meter); **~wur·zel** *f* Ꭿ cube root; **~zahl** *f* Ꭿ cube number

ku·bisch ['ku:bɪʃ] *adj.* cubic

Ku·bis·mus [ku'bɪsmʊs] *m* (-; *no pl.*) cubism; **Ku·bist** [ku'bɪst] *m* (-en; -en) cubist; **ku·bi·stisch** [ku'bɪstɪʃ] *adj.* cubist

Ku·bus ['ku:bʊs] *m* (-; Kuben ['ku:bən]) Ꭿ cube

Kü·che ['kʏçə] *f* (-; -n) a) kitchen; ⚓, ✈ galley, b) cooking, cuisine; ***kalte*** ~ cold dishes; ***warme*** ~ hot meals; ***französische*** ~ French cuisine; → ***gutbürgerlich, Teufel***

Ku·chen ['ku:çən] *m* (-s; -) cake

'Kü·chen|ab·fäl·le *pl.* kitchen waste *sg.*, kitchen scraps; **~be·nüt·zung** *f*: ***mit*** ~ use of kitchen

'Ku·chen·blech *n* baking tin (*or* tray)

'Kü·chen|chef *m* chef; **~dienst** *m*: ***du hast heute*** ~ it's your turn to do the washing-up (*or* cooking)

'kü·chen·fer·tig *adj.* pre-cooked

'Ku·chen|form *f* cake tin; **~ga·bel** *f* pastry (*or* cake) fork

'Kü·chen|ge·rät *n* kitchen appliance; **~herd** *m* (electric *or* gas) cooker; **~hil·fe** *f* kitchen help; **~la,tein** *n* dog Latin; **~mei·ster** *m* chef; **~mes·ser** *n* kitchen knife; **~per·so,nal** *n* kitchen staff *sg.*; **~scha·be** *f* cockroach, *Am.* roach

'Ku·chen·schlacht F *f* cake orgy

'Kü·chen·schrank *m* kitchen cupboard

'Ku·chen|teig *m* cake mixture; **~tel·ler** *m* dessert plate

'Kü·chen|uhr *f* kitchen clock; **~waa·ge** *f*: (***e-e*** ~ a pair of) kitchen scales *pl.*; **~wecker** *m* timer; **~zei·le** *f* kitchen units *pl.*

Kuckuck ['kʊkʊk] (*sep.* -k·k-) *m* (-s; -e) a) *zo.* cuckoo, b) F ⚖ bailiff's seal; F ***zum ~!*** damn it!; ***wo*** (***wie*** *etc.*) ***zum ~ ...?*** where (how *etc.*) the devil ...?

'Kuckucks|ei *n* cuckoo's egg; **~uhr** *f* cuckoo clock

Kud·del·mud·del ['kʊdəlmʊdəl] F *m, n* (-s; *no pl.*) muddle; jumble, mess

Ku·fe ['ku:fə] *f* (-; -n) runner; ✈ skid

Kü·fer ['ky:fɐ] *m* (-s; -) cooper; cellarman

Ku·gel ['ku:gəl] *f* (-; -n) Ꭿ sphere; *sport etc.*: ball, shot; *anat.* head; ⚔ bullet; (*Christmas*) bauble; ***die ~ stoßen*** *sport*: put the shot; ***die Erde ist e-e ~*** the earth is a sphere; F ***e-e ruhige ~ schieben*** have a cushy job (F number); **~ab·schnitt** *m* Ꭿ spherical segment; **~bak,te·ri·en** *pl.* cocci; **~blitz** *m* ball lightning; **~fang** *m* butt; **Ձfest** *adj.* bulletproof; **~fisch** *m* puffer, globefish

'ku·gel·för·mig [-fœrmɪç], **ku·ge·lig** ['ku:gəlɪç] *adj.* spherical

'Ku·gel|ge·lenk *n anat.*, ⚙ ball-and-socket joint; **~ha·gel** *m* hail of bullets

'Ku·gel·kopf *m* golf ball; **~ma,schi·ne** *f* golf-ball typewriter

'Ku·gel·la·ger *n* ⚙ ball bearing

ku·geln ['ku:gəln] **I.** *v/t.* (h) *and v/i.* (sn) roll; **II.** *v/refl.* (h): ***sich ~*** roll about (*a.* F ***vor Lachen***); **III.** Ձ *n*: F ***es war zum ~*** F it was a scream

'Ku·gel|re·gen *m* hail of bullets; **Ձrund** *adj.* a) perfectly round, b) F like a balloon; **~schrei·ber** *m* ballpoint (pen), *Brit. a.* biro (*TM*); F pen; **~seg,ment** *n* Ꭿ spherical segment; **Ձsi·cher** *adj.* bulletproof; ***~e Weste*** bulletproof vest

'Ku·gel·sto·ßen *n sport*: shot-put(ting); **'Ku·gel·sto·ßer** [-ʃto:sɐ] *m* (-s; -), **'Ku·gel·sto·ße·rin** [-ʃto:sərɪn] *f* (-; -nen) shot-putter

Kuh [ku:] *f* (-; Kühe ['ky:ə]) cow; *fig.* ***heilige*** ~ sacred cow; ***melkende*** ~ mealticket; *sl.* ***blöde*** ~ *sl.* silly old cow; **~au·gen** F *pl.* F goggle eyes; **~dorf** F *n* backwater, *Am.* F hick town; **~fla·den** *m* cowpat; **~glocke** *f* cow bell; **~han·del** F *fig. m esp. pol.* horse trading; **~haut** *f* cowhide; *fig.* ***das geht auf keine*** ~ F it's just incredible; **~hirt** *m* cowherd

kühl [ky:l] **I.** *adj.* cool (*a. fig.*); *meteor. a.* chilly; ***~es Bier*** cold beer; ***~ werden*** cool (down); ***e-n ~en Kopf bewahren*** keep one's cool; ***mir ist*** ~ I feel a bit chilly; ***~ stellen*** chill *wine etc.*, let *s.th.* cool down; **II.** *adv.* coolly; ***~ aufbewahren*** (***or lagern***)***!*** keep in a cool place

'Kühl|ag·gre,gat *n* cooling aggregate; **~an·la·ge** *f* cold-storage plant; *mot. etc.* cooling system; **~box** *f* ice box

Küh·le ['ky:lə] *f* (-; *no pl.*) coolness (*a. fig.*); cool *of the night etc.*

küh·len ['ky:lən] *v/t.* (h) a) cool, b) refresh, c) *gastr.* refrigerate; chill *wine etc.*

Küh·ler ['ky:lɐ] *m* (-s; -) **1.** cooler; **2.** *mot.* a) radiator, b) bonnet, *Am.* hood; **~fi,gur** *f* radiator emblem (*or* mascot); **~grill** *m* radiator grille; **~hau·be** *f* bonnet, *Am.* hood

'Kühl|fach *n* freezing compartment; **~flüs·sig·keit** *f* coolant; **~haus** *n* cold store; **~ket·te** *f* cold chain; **~la·ge·rung** *f* cold storage; **~luft** *f* cooling air; **~mit·tel** *n* coolant; **~raum** *m* cold room (*or* store); **~rip·pen** *pl.* cooling ribs; **~schiff** *n* refrigerator ship; **~schlan·ge** *f* cooling coil; **~schrank** *m* fridge, refrigerator; **~stoff** *m* coolant; **~sy,stem** *n* cooling system; **~ta·sche** *f* ice box; **~tru·he** *f* (deep) freeze, (chest) freezer; **~turm** *m* cooling tower

Küh·lung ['ky:lʊŋ] *f* (-; -en) **1.** *no pl.* a) cooling, ⚙ *a.* refrigeration, b) coolness; **2.** cooling system

'Kühl|wa·gen *m* 🚃 refrigerator van (*Am.* car); *mot.* refrigerator lorry (*esp. Am.* truck); **~was·ser** *n* coolant

'Kuh|milch *f* cow's milk; **~mist** *m* cow dung

kühn [ky:n] *adj.* a) bold (*a. fig.*); daring, b) audacious; ***j-s ~ste Träume übertreffen*** go beyond s.o.'s wildest dreams; **'Kühn·heit** *f* (-; *no pl.*) a) boldness; daring, b) audacity

'Kuh|pocken *pl.* cowpox *sg.*; **~stall** *m* cowshed; **Ձwarm** *adj.* still warm (from the cow); **~wei·de** *f* cow pasture

Kü·ken ['ky:kən] *n* (-s; -) **1.** chick; **2.** F *fig.* F young thing; **3.** ⚙ plug

ku·lant [ku'lant] *adj.* ✝ accommodating; fair; **Ku·lanz** [ku'lants] *f* (-; *no pl.*) goodwill; fairness; *die Reparatur* ***geht auf*** ~ will be carried out at the firm's expense

Ku·li¹ ['ku:li] *m* (-s; -s) coolie; *fig.* slave

'Ku·li² F *m* (-s; -s) → ***Kugelschreiber***

ku·li·na·risch [kuli'na:rɪʃ] *adj.* culinary; ***~e Genüsse*** culinary delights

Ku·lis·se [ku'lɪsə] *f* (-; -n) **1.** *thea.* set; flat; backdrop; *pl.* wings; *fig.* background (*a.* ♪); setting; façade, front; ***hinter die*** (***den***) ***~n*** backstage, *esp. fig.* behind the scenes; ***e-n Blick hinter die ~n werfen*** take a look behind the scenes (***auf*** *acc.* at), ***auf*** *acc.*: *a.* take a backstage look at; **2.** ✝ unofficial market

Ku'lis·sen·schie·ber *m* scene-shifter

Kul·ler·au·gen ['kʊlɐ-] F *pl.* big wide eyes; ***~ machen*** goggle

kul·lern ['kʊlɐn] *v/i.* **1.** (sn) roll; **2.** (h) ***mit den Augen ~*** roll one's eyes

Kul·mi·na·ti·on [kʊlmina'tsi̯o:n] *f* (-; -en) culmination; **Kul·mi·na·ti'ons·punkt** *m ast.* culmination point, *fig. a.* apex; **kul·mi·nie·ren** [kʊlmi'ni:rən] *v/i.* (h) *a. fig.* culminate (***in*** *dat.* in)

Kult [kʊlt] *m* (-[e]s; -e) cult; ***e-n ~ treiben mit*** *dat.* make a cult out of, idolize; **~fi,gur** *f* cult figure; **~film** *m* cult film; **~hand·lung** *f* rite

kul·tisch ['kʊltɪʃ] *adj.* ritual

kul·ti·vier·bar [kʊlti'vi:ɐba:ɐ] *adj.* arable; **kul·ti·vie·ren** [kʊlti'vi:rən] *v/t.* (h) cultivate; **kul·ti·viert** [kʊlti'vi:ɐt] *adj.* cultivated *atmosphere etc.*; *a.* cultured *person*; civilized *people, country etc.*; **Kul·ti'vie·rung** *f* (-; *no pl.*) cultivation

'Kult|stät·te *f* place of worship; **~tanz** *m* ritual dance

Kul·tur [kʊl'tu:ɐ] *f* (-; -en) **1.** *no pl.* culture; civilization; ***die antike*** (***abendländische***) ~ ancient (western) civilization; ***die römische*** (***griechische***) ~ Roman (ancient Greek) civilization, the civilization of Rome (ancient Greece); **2.** *no pl.* culture; ***er hat*** ~ he's got education; F ***etwas für die ~ tun*** F (try and) educate oneself; ***~ des Essens*** (***Wohnens***) cultivated eating habits (living); **3.** *no pl.* ⸙ cultivation; **4.** *biol.*, ⚘ culture; **~ab·kom·men** *n* cultural agreement; **~ar·beit** *f* (-; *no pl.*) cultural activities *pl.*; **~at·ta,ché** *m* cultural attaché; **~aus·tausch** *m* cultural exchange; **~ba,nau·se** *contp. m* philistine; **Ձbe·flis·sen** *adj.* (very) culturally-minded; **~be·trieb** F *m* (-[e]s; *no pl.*) cultural scene; **~beu·tel** *m* toilet bag; **~bo·den** *m* **1.** cultivated soil; **2.** ***uralter*** ~ site of an ancient culture; **3.** *biol.* culture medium; **~denk·mal** *n* cultural monument; work of art; *pl. a.* cultural heritage *sg.*; ***die Kulturdenkmäler Ägyptens*** *a.* the Egyptian antiquities, *a.* the ancient Egyptian monuments

kul·tu·rell [kʊltu'rɛl] *adj.* cultural

Kul'tur·er·be *n* cultural heritage

Kul'tur·feind *m* philistine, cultural Bolshevik; **kul'tur·feind·lich** *adj.* philistine

Kul'tur·füh·rer *m* cultural guide

Kul'tur·ge·schich·te *f* **1.** history of civilization (*a. book*); **2.** cultural history *of Denmark etc.*; **3.** history of culture; **kul'tur·ge·schicht·lich** *adj.* cultural-historical

Kul'tur|gü·ter *pl.* cultural assets; **~ho·heit** *f* (-; *no pl.*) cultural and educational autonomy; **~kreis** *m* society; **~land·schaft** *f* man-made landscape; **~le·ben** *n* cultural life

kul'tur·los *adj.* uncultured

Kul'tur|ma·ga,zin *n* arts journal; **~me·tro,po·le** *f* cultural capital; **~papst** *m* cultural guru; **~pes·si,mis·mus** *m* pessimistic view of civilization; **~pflan·ze** *f* cultivated plant

Kul'tur·po·li,tik *f* cultural and educational policy; **kul'tur·po,li·tisch** *adj.* politico-cultural

Kul'tur|pro,gramm *n* program(me) of cultural events; **~raum** *m* area of culture; ***im südostasiatischen ~*** in the Southeast Asian cultural area; **~re·dak,teur** *m* arts (features) editor; **~re·fe,rent** *m* head of cultural affairs;

~re·vo·lu·ti͵on *f* cultural revolution; **~schan·de** *f* **1.** disgrace to (civilized) society; **2.** F eyesore; **~schock** *m* culture shock; **~spe͵zi·fisch** *adj.* culture-specific; **~staat** *m* civilized nation; **~sze·ne** *f* cultural scene; **~volk** *n* civilized race (*or* people); **~zen·trum** *n* **1.** cultural cent|re (*Am.* -er); **2.** arts cent|re (*Am.* -er)

Kul·tus|mi͵ni·ster ['kʊltʊs-] *m* minister (*Am.* secretary) of education and cultural affairs; **~mi·ni͵ste·ri·um** *n* ministry of education and cultural affairs

'Kult·wa·gen *m* cult car

Küm·mel ['kʏməl] *m* (-s; -) **1.** caraway (seed); ⚘ (***echter*** ~) cumin; **2.** kümmel

Kum·mer ['kʊmɐ] *m* (-s; *no pl.*) worry, worries *pl.*, problems *pl.*; ~ ***haben*** have problems; ***j-m*** ~ ***machen*** (*or* ***bereiten***) cause s.o. a lot of worry; ***du machst mir*** ~ I'm worried about you; ***s-n*** ~ ***herunterspülen*** drown one's sorrows; ***das ist mein geringster*** ~ that's the least of my worries; **~bund** *m* (-[e]s; -e) cummerbund; **~fal·ten** *pl.* worry lines

'Kum·mer·ka·sten F *m* complaints box; **~tan·te** F *f* F agony aunt

küm·mer·lich ['kʏmɐlɪç] **I.** *adj.* a) miserable; measly, paltry *wages etc.*, b) stunted; **II.** *adv.*: ***sich*** ~ ***durchschlagen*** just manage to get by

Küm·mer·ling ['kʏmɐlɪŋ] *m* (-s; -e) weakling; stunted plant (*or* specimen); F pathetic little specimen

küm·mern ['kʏmɐn] (h) **I.** *v/refl.*: ***sich*** ~ ***um*** *acc.* **1.** look after, take care of, *a.* see to *s.th.*; ***ich muß mich um alles*** ~ I have to see to everything; ***du mußt dich um Karten*** ~ you'll have to see about getting tickets; **2.** worry about; ***ich kümmere mich nicht um solche Sachen*** I don't have (the) time to worry about that sort of thing; → ***Dreck***; **3.** pay attention to; ***sich nicht*** ~ ***um*** *acc.* a) not to bother about, ignore, b) neglect; **4.** *contp.* poke one's nose into; ***kümmere dich um d-e eigenen Angelegenheiten*** just mind your own business; **II.** *v/t.*: ***was kümmert's mich?*** it's not my problem (F pigeon)

'Kum·mer·speck F *m*: ~ ***ansetzen*** put on weight with worry

'kum·mer·voll *adj.* sorrowful

Kum·pan [kʊm'pa:n] F *m* (-s; -e) **1.** F mate; **2.** partner; **Kum·pa·nei** [kʊmpa'naɪ] F *f* (-; -en) **1.** crowd, F lot; **2.** *no pl.* camaraderie

Kum·pel ['kʊmpəl] *m* (-s; -) **1.** ⚒ miner; **2.** F mate, *Am.* F buddy; **'kum·pel·haft** *adj.* F pally

Ku·mu·la·ti·on [kumula'tsio:n] *f* (-; -en) accumulation; **ku·mu·la·tiv** [kumula'ti:f] *adj.* cumulative; **ku·mu·lie·ren** [kumu'li:rən] *v/t. and v/i.* (h) accumulate

Ku·mu·lus ['ku:mulʊs] *m* (-; -li], **~wol·ke** *f* cumulus (cloud)

künd·bar ['kʏntba:ɐ] *adj.* terminable; *job, lease etc.* subject to notice; callable *capital*; redeemable *loan*; ***wir sind jederzeit*** ~ we can be given notice at any time

Kun·de¹ ['kʊndə] *m* (-n; -n) **1.** customer; client; patron; ***fester*** ~ regular customer; ***„Nur für ~n"*** For Patrons Only; ***der*** ~ ***ist König*** the customer is always right; **2.** F *fig.* F customer; ***merkwürdiger*** (***übler***) ~ queer (nasty) customer

'Kun·de² *f* (-; *no pl.*) knowledge; ~ ***geben von*** *dat.* bear witness to; ***frohe*** ~ good news (*sg.*), *lit.* glad tidings

kün·den ['kʏndən] *lit.* (h) **I.** *v/t.* announce (*dat.* to), tell (*s.o.*) of; **II.** *v/i.*: ~ ***von*** *dat.* tell of; bear witness to

'Kun·den|be·ra·tung *f* customer advisory service (*or* office); **~be·such** *m* (customer) call; **~dienst** *m* (-[e]s; *no pl.*) **1.** after-sales service; **2.** (customer) service; ***das gehört zum*** ~ it's (all) part of the service; **3.** a) service department, b) technician(s *pl.*); ***morgen kommt der*** ~ ***wegen m-s Kühlschranks*** they're sending someone (*or* someone's coming) to have a look at my fridge tomorrow; **~fang** *m* (-[e]s; *no pl.*) touting; **~kar͵tei** *f* customer file; **~kre͵dit** *m* consumer credit; **~kreis** *m* customers *pl.*, clients *pl.*, clientele; **~stamm** *m* regular customers *pl.*; **~werbung** *f* canvassing (of customers)

kund·ge·ben ['kʊnt-] *v/t.* (*irr.*, *sep.*, h, → ***geben***) make known (*dat.* to), announce (to); declare; **'Kund·ge·bung** [-ge:bʊŋ] *f* (-; -en) *pol.* rally; demonstration

kun·dig ['kʊndɪç] *adj.* (well-)informed; expert (*gen.* in); skil(l)ful

kün·di·gen ['kʏndɪgən] (h) **I.** *v/i.* hand (*or* give) in one's notice (***bei*** *dat.* to; ***zu*** *dat.* for); ***j-m*** ~ a) give s.o. notice (F the sack), b) give s.o. (his *etc.*) notice; **II.** *v/t.* cancel, *formal*: terminate *contract etc.*; call in *loan etc.*; ***er hat uns die Wohnung gekündigt*** he's told us we have to leave the flat (*Am.* apartment); ***wir haben die Wohnung gekündigt*** (we've given notice that) we're moving out of the flat (*Am.* apartment); **'Kün·di·gung** *f* (-; -en) a) notice, b) dismissal, c) calling in *of a loan etc.*; ***s-e*** ~ ***erhalten*** be given notice (F the sack); ***mit monatlicher*** ~ at (*or* subject to) a month's notice

'Kün·di·gungs|frist *f* period of notice; ***mit halbjähriger*** ~ at six months' notice; **~grund** *m* grounds *pl.* for giving notice; **~recht** *n* right to give notice; **~schrei·ben** *n* a) written notice, b) letter of dismissal; **~schutz** *m* protection against unlawful dismissal (*or* unwarranted eviction); **~ter͵min** *m* (last) date for giving notice

Kun·din ['kʊndɪn] *f* (-; -nen) (female) customer *etc.*; → ***Kunde¹***

Kund·schaft ['kʊntʃaft] *f* (-; *no pl.*) ✝ a) customers *pl.*, clients *pl.*; clientele; F customer, b) patronage

Kund·schaf·ter ['kʊntʃaftɐ] *m* (-s; -) scout, spy

kund·tun ['kʊnt-] *v/t.* (*irr.*, *sep.*, h, → ***tun***) → ***kundgeben***

künf·tig ['kʏnftɪç] **I.** *adj.* future; (up-and-)coming *generations etc.*, ... to come; ***in ~en Zeiten*** in times to come; ***in e-m*** (***im***) ***~en Leben*** in a future life (in the next life); **II.** *adv.* in future, from now on

Kun·ge·lei [kʊŋə'laɪ] *f* (-; -en) wheeling and dealing; **kun·geln** ['kʊŋəln] *v/i.* (h) fiddle (things)

Kunst [kʊnst] *f* (-; Künste ['kʏnstə]) art; *a.* skill; *fig.* trick; ***die schönen*** (***freien***) ***Künste*** the fine (liberal) arts; ***die griechische*** ~ Greek art; ***die bildende*** ~ the graphic arts; ***die*** ~ ***zu schreiben*** (***der Liebe***) the art of writing (of love); ***alle Künste der Überredung*** all the tricks of persuasion; ***jetzt bin ich mit m-r*** ~ ***am Ende*** I give up, I've tried everything; ***nach allen Regeln der*** ~ F good and proper; ***das ist keine*** ~***!*** F that's no great shakes, F big deal; F ***was macht die*** ~***?*** F how's things?; → ***brotlos***; **~aka·de͵mie** *f* academy of arts, art college; **~au·ge** *n* artificial (*or* glass) eye; **~auk·ti͵on** *f* art auction; **~aus·stel·lung** *f* art exhibition; **~ba͵nau·se** *contp.* *m* philistine; ***er ist ein*** ~ *a.* he doesn't know the first thing about art; **~bei·la·ge** *f* art supplement; **~be·we·gung** *f* art movement; **~blatt** *n* **1.** art print; **2.** art journal; **~blu·me** *f* artificial flower; **~buch** *n* art book; **~darm** *m* (artificial) sausage skin; **~denk·mal** *n* art monument; great work of art; **~dieb** *m* art thief

'Kunst·druck *m* (-[e]s; -e) **1.** art reproduction; **2.** *no pl.* art printing; **~pa͵pier** *n* art paper

'Kunst|dün·ger *m* artificial fertilizer; **~eis** *n* artificial ice

Kün·ste·lei [kʏnstə'laɪ] *f* (-; *no pl.*) artificiality; affectation; **kün·steln** ['kʏnstəln] *v/t.* → ***gekünstelt***

'Kunst|er·zie·her *m* art teacher; **~er·zie·hung** *f* art education; **~ex͵per·te** *m* art connoisseur; **~fäl·schung** *f* art forgery, fake; **~fa·ser** *f* man-made fibre (*Am.* fiber); **~feh·ler** *m* ⚕ professional (*or* medical) blunder; *pl. a.* medical malpractice *sg.*

'kunst·fer·tig *adj.* skilled; skil(l)ful, expert; **'Kunst·fer·tig·keit** *f* (artistic *or* technical) skill; craftsmanship

'Kunst|flie·ger *m* stunt pilot; **~flug** *m* aerobatics *pl.*; **~form** *f* art form; **~freund** *m* art lover; **~füh·rer** *m* art guide; **~ga·le͵rie** *f* art gallery; **~gat·tung** *f* art form, genre; **~ge·gen·stand** *m* art object, objet d'art; **~ge·nuß** *m* **1.** enjoyment of art; **2.** (a)esthetic treat

'kunst·ge·recht *adj.* expert, professional

'Kunst·ge·schich·te *f* history of art, art history; **'Kunst·ge·schicht·ler** [-gəʃɪçtlɐ] *m* (-s; -) art historian; **'kunst·ge·schicht·lich** *adj.* art-historical

'Kunst|ge·wer·be *n* arts and crafts *pl.*; applied art(s *pl.*); **~glied** *n* artificial limb; **~griff** *m* (clever) trick; ***ein*** ~ *a.* sleight of hand; **~hal·le** *f* art gallery; **~han·del** *m* art trade; **~händ·ler** *m* art dealer; **~hand·lung** *f* art dealer('s); **~hand·werk** *n* → ***Kunstgewerbe***; **~hand·wer·ker** *m* artist-craftsman; **~harz** *n* synthetic resin; **~herz** *n* artificial heart

'Kunst·hi͵sto·ri·ker *m* art historian; **'kunst·hi͵sto·risch** *adj.* art-historical

'Kunst|hoch·schu·le *f* art academy (*or* college); **~ho·nig** *m* artificial honey; **~ka͵len·der** *m* art calendar; **~ken·ner** *m* (art) connoisseur

'Kunst·kopf *m radio*: dummy head; **~auf·nah·me** *f* binaural recording

'Kunst|kri͵tik *f* a) art criticism, b) art critics *pl.*; **~kri·ti·ker** *m* art critic; **~le·der** *n* imitation leather

Künst·ler ['kʏnstlɐ] *m* (-s; -), **Künst·le·rin** ['kʏnstlərɪn] *f* (-; -nen) artist; ♪, *thea.* performer; (*circus etc.*) artiste; *fig.* genius; **künst·le·risch** ['kʏnstlərɪʃ] **I.** *adj.* artistic; ***~e Form*** art form; ***~er Leiter*** art director; ***~e Ader*** artistic vein; **II.** *adv.* artistically; ***ein*** ~ ***wertvoller Film*** a film of artistic merit

'Künst·ler|ko·lo͵nie *f* artists' colony; **~le·ben** *n the* life of an artist; **~na·me** *m* a) stage name, b) pseudonym, pen name, nom de plume; **~pech** F *n* bad luck

'Künst·ler·tum *n* (-s; *no pl.*) artistry; *coll. the* artistic world

'Künst·ler|vier·tel *n* artists' quarter; **~werk·statt** *f* studio

künst·lich ['kʏnstlɪç] **I.** *adj.* artificial (*a. respiration, insemination, flower, light etc., a. fig. smile etc.*); *a.* false *teeth*; imitation *leather etc.*; fake; synthetic; man-made; *fig. esp. attr.* forced *smile etc.*; **~e Niere** kidney machine; **II.** *adv.* artificially; **~ in die Länge ziehen** (deliberately) stretch out; F **sich ~ aufregen** F make a big thing out of it; **'Künst·lich·keit** *f* (-; *no pl.*) artificiality

'Kunst·licht *n* artificial light; **~film** *m* indoor film

'Kunst|lieb·ha·ber *m* art lover; **~lied** *n* lied

'kunst·los *adj.* simple, unsophisticated

'Kunst|ma·ler *m* painter, artist; **~ob͵jekt** *n* art object, objet d'art; **~pau·se** *f* pause for effect; *iro.* awkward pause; **e-e ~ machen** pause for effect; **~preis** *m* art award (*or* prize); **~ra·sen** *m* astroturf (*TM*); **~raub** *m* art theft; **~räu·ber** *m* art thief

'kunst·reich *adj.* (very) artistic; elaborate, ornate

'Kunst|rich·tung *f* style (of painting *etc.*); art movement, art school; **~samm·ler** *m* art collector; **~samm·lung** *f* art collection; **~schät·ze** *pl.* art treasures; **~schmied** *m* ornamental iron-worker, artist blacksmith; **~schu·le** *f* art school; **~sei·de** *f* rayon; **~spra·che** *f* artificial language; **~sprin·gen** *n* (springboard) diving; **~sprin·ger** *m* (springboard) diver

'Kunst·stoff *m* plastic; **aus ~** (made of) plastic; **~bahn** *f* artificial track; **2be·schich·tet** *adj.* plastic-coated; **~in·du͵strie** *f* plastics industry; **~ra·sen** *m* artificial turf

'Kunst|stop·fen *n* invisible mending; **~stück** *n* **1. das ist schon ein ~** that takes some doing; **das ist kein ~** (there's) nothing to it; *iro.* **wie er wohl dieses ~ fertiggebracht hat** how on earth did he manage that?; F *iro.* **~!** F big deal; **2.** (*conjuring etc.*) trick; **~stu͵dent** *m* art student; **~sze·ne** *f* art scene; **~tisch·ler** *m* cabinet-maker; **~tur·nen** *n* gymnastics *pl.*; **~tur·ner** *m* gymnast; **~ver·ein** *m* arts society; **~ver·stand** *m*, **~ver·ständ·nis** *n* **1.** knowledge of art; **2.** (a)esthetic sense

'kunst·voll *adj.* very artistic; elaborate, ornate; skil(l)ful

'Kunst|werk *n* work of art; **~wis·sen·schaft** *f* (theory of) art; **~wort** *n* (-[e]s; ⸚er) coinage; **~zeit·schrift** *f* art journal (*or* magazine)

kun·ter·bunt ['kʊntɐbʊnt] **I.** *adj.* **1.** colo(u)rful; multicolo(u)red; **2.** *fig.* untidy; **ein ~es Durcheinander** a (real) mess; **3.** *fig.* chequered, very varied; **~e Mischung** mixed bag; **es gab ein ~es Programm** there were all sorts of things going on (*or* being shown *etc.*); **II.** *adv.*: **alles ~ durcheinanderwerfen** throw everything into a heap, *fig.* lump everything together; **hier geht's ja ~ zu!** what on earth's going on here?

Kup·fer ['kʊpfɐ] *n* (-s; *no pl.*) copper; **~berg·werk** *n* copper mine; **~blech** *n* sheet copper; **~dach** *n* copper roof; **~draht** *m* copper wire; **~druck** *m* (-[e]s; -e) copperplate engraving, print

'kup·fer·far·ben *adj.* copper-colo(u)red

'kup·fer·hal·tig [-haltɪç] *adj.* containing copper

'Kup·fer|kes·sel *m* copper kettle; **~mün·ze** *f* copper coin

kup·fern ['kʊpfɐn] *adj.* (made of) copper

'kup·fer·rot *adj.* copper-colo(u)red

'Kup·fer|schmied *m* coppersmith; **~ste·cher** *m* (-s; -) copperplate engraver; **~stich** *m* copperplate engraving; **~sul͵fat** *n* copper sulphate (*Am.* sulfate); **~ver·gif·tung** *f* copper poisoning

ku·pie·ren [ku'piːrən] *v/t.* (h) dock, crop

Ku·pon [ku'põː] *m* (-s; -s) → **Coupon**

Kup·pe ['kʊpə] *f* (-; -n) **1.** hilltop; **2.** fingertip; **3.** ⚙ head

Kup·pel ['kʊpəl] *f* (-; -n) dome, cupola; **~bau** *m* domed building; **~dach** *n* domed roof

'kup·pel·för·mig [-fœrmɪç] *adj.* dome-shaped

Kup·pe·lei [kʊpə'laɪ] *f* (-; *no pl.*) ⚖ procuration

kup·peln ['kʊpəln] (h) **I.** *v/t.* → **koppeln**; **II.** *v/i. mot.* operate the clutch, (let in the) clutch, declutch

Kupp·ler ['kʊplɐ] *m* (-s; -) ⚖ procurer, pimp; **Kupp·le·rin** ['kʊplərɪn] *f* (-; -nen) ⚖ procuress

Kupp·lung ['kʊplʊŋ] *f* (-; -en) ⚙ coupling (*a.* 🚂, ⚡); *mot.* clutch; **die ~ schleifen lassen** let the clutch slip

'Kupp·lungs|au·to͵mat *m* automatic clutch; **~be·lag** *m* clutch lining; **~pe͵dal** *n* clutch pedal; **~schei·be** *f* clutch disc

Kur [kuːɐ] *f* (-; -en ['kuːrən]) (course of) treatment; cure; **e-e ~ machen, zur ~ gehen** go for a cure

Kür [kyːɐ] *f* (-; -en ['kyːrən]) *sport*: voluntary exercise; → *a.* **Kürlauf**

Ku·rat [ku'raːt] *m* (-en; -en) curate

Ku·ra·tor [ku'raːtoːɐ] *m* (-s; -en [kura'toːrən]) ⚖ trustee; *museum, univ.*: curator

Ku·ra·to·ri·um [kura'toːrĭʊm] *n* (-s; -ien) board of trustees

'Kur·bad *n* spa (town)

Kur·bel ['kʊrbəl] *f* (-; -n) winder; ⚙ crank; **~dach** *n* (winding) sunroof; **~ge·häu·se** *n* crankcase; **~ge·trie·be** *n* crank mechanism

kur·beln ['kʊrbəln] (h) **I.** *v/t.* wind (*or* crank) up *etc.*; **II.** *v/i.* wind; *mot.* crank the engine; F **ich mußte (mit dem Lenkrad) ganz schön ~** it was hard work steering

'Kur·bel|stan·ge *f* connecting rod; **~wel·le** *f* crankshaft

Kür·bis ['kʏrbɪs] *m* (-ses; -se) **1.** ♀ pumpkin; **2.** F nut; **~fla·sche** *f* gourd; **~kern** *m* pumpkin seed

Kur·de ['kʊrdə] *m* (-n; -n), **Kur·din** ['kʊrdɪn] *f* (-; -nen) Kurd; **kur·disch** ['kʊrdɪʃ] *adj.* Kurdish

ku·ren ['kuːrən] F *v/i.* (h) take (*or* be on) a cure

kü·ren ['kyːrən] *v/t.* (h) choose

Kü·ret·ta·ge [kyrɛ'taːʒə] *f* (-; -n) ⚕ curettage; **Kü·ret·te** [ky'rɛtə] *f* (-; -n) curette

'Kur·fürst *m* (prince) elector; **'Kur·für·sten·tum** *n* electorate; **'Kur·für·stin** *f* electress; **'kur·fürst·lich** *adj.* electoral

'Kur|gast *m* patient (at a health resort); **~haus** *n* casino (of a health resort); **~ho͵tel** *n* health-resort hotel, spa hotel

Ku·rie ['kuːrĭə] *f* (-; -n) *R.C.* curia; *the* papal Court

Ku·rier [ku'riːɐ] *m* (-s; -e [-rə]) courier, messenger; dispatch rider; **~dienst** *m* courier service

ku·rie·ren [ku'riːrən] *v/t.* (h) *a. fig.* cure (**von** *dat.* of); *fig.* **davon bin ich kuriert** I've had my taste (*or* share) of that

ku·ri·os [ku'rĭoːs] *adj.* strange, funny

Ku·rio·si·tät [kurĭozi'tɛːt] *f* (-; -en) **1.** *no pl.* oddness; **2.** → **Kuriosum**; **3.** curio, curiosity; **Ku·rio·sum** [ku'rĭoːzʊm] *n* (-s; -sa) oddity, odd thing (*or* fact); curiosity

'Kur·kli·nik *f* sanatorium; *a.* health farm

Kur·ku·ma ['kʊrkuma] *f* (-; -men) curcuma; **~pa͵pier** *n* ⚗ turmeric paper

Kur·laub ['kuːɐlaʊp] *m* (-[e]s; -e [-bə]) holiday-cum-cure

'Kür·lauf *m* free skating

'Kur|ort *m* health resort, spa (town); **~packung** *f* conditioner; **~park** *m* health-resort gardens *pl.*, spa gardens *pl.*

'Kur·pfu·scher *m* charlatan, F quack

Kur·pfu·sche'rei *f* charlatanism

Kurs [kʊrs] *m* (-es; -e) **1.** ✝ price; quotation; exchange rate; **zum ~ von** *dat.* at the rate of; **hoch im ~ stehen** be at a premium, *fig.* rate highly (**bei** *dat.* with); **in ~ setzen** circulate; **2.** a) ⚓, ✈ course; *radar*: track; route, b) *fig. pol.* course, line, policy; **~ halten** stay on course; **vom ~ abweichen** go off course; **~ nehmen auf** *acc.* head for (*a. fig.*); *fig.* **e-n neuen ~ einschlagen** take a new line; **3.** → **Kursus**

'Kur·saal *m* kursaal, casino

'Kurs|ab·schlag *m* markdown; **~ab·schwä·chung** *f* easing off of (market) prices; **~ab·wei·chung** *f* ⚓ *etc.* deviation (from the route); **~än·de·rung** *f* change of course; *fig. a.* policy change; **~an·stieg** *m* rise in (market) prices; **~auf·schlag** *m* markup; **~blatt** *n* stock market report; **~buch** *n* 🚂 (railway) timetable

Kürsch·ner ['kʏrʃnɐ] *m* (-s; -) furrier; **Kürsch·ne·rei** [kʏrʃnə'raɪ] *f* (-; -en) **1.** *no pl.* furrier's trade; **2.** furrier's (work)shop

'Kurs|ein·bruch *m* sudden fall in prices; **~ein·bu·ße** *f* price decline; **~ent·wick·lung** *f* trends *pl.* in prices; **~er·ho·lung** *f* rally in prices; **~fest·set·zung** *f* fixing of the exchange rate (*or* price); **~ge·winn** *m* price gain

kur·sie·ren [kʊr'ziːrən] *v/i.* (h) circulate; *rumo(u)r*: go round

'Kurs·in·dex *m* share prices index

kur·siv [kʊr'ziːf] *adj.* italic; (*a. adv.*) in italics; **Kur·si·ve** [kʊr'ziːvə] *f* → **Kur'siv·schrift** *f* italics *pl.*; **in ~ setzen** italicize

'Kurs|kor·rek͵tur *f* correction of course; *fig.* shift in policy; **~lei·ter** *m* instructor, teacher; **~mak·ler** *m* official (*or* inside) broker; **~no͵tie·rung** *f* (price *or* market) quotation

kur·so·risch [kʊr'zoːrɪʃ] *adj.* cursory

'Kurs|rück·gang *m* decline in prices; **~schwan·kun·gen** *pl.* price fluctuations; **~stei·ge·rung** *f* price increase; **~sturz** *m* sharp fall in prices; **~stüt·zung** *f* price pegging; **~sy͵stem** *n ped.* streaming; **~teil·neh·mer** *m* course participant; **~trei·be·rei** [-traɪbəraɪ] *f* (-; -en) share pushing

Kur·sus ['kʊrzʊs] *m* (-; Kurse ['kʊrzə]) course; class

'Kurs|ver·lust *m* exchange loss; **~wa·gen** *m* 🚂 through coach; **~wech·sel** *m* change of course (*fig. a.* policy); **~wert** *m* market value; **~zet·tel** *m* stock exchange list

'Kur·ta·xe *f* health resort tax

Kur·ti·sa·ne [kʊrtiˈzaːnə] *f* (-; -n) courtesan

ˈKür|tur·nen *n* free exercises *pl.*; **~übung** *f* free exercise

Kur·ve [ˈkʊrvə] *f* (-; -n) curve (*a.* 𝔄); bend; F *hum.* **~n** F curves; **e-e ~ schneiden** cut a corner; **zu schnell in die ~ gehen** take a (*or* the) corner too fast; ✈ **in die ~ gehen** bank; F *fig.* **die ~ kratzen** F make a quick getaway; F **ich hab' die ~ nicht gekriegt** I didn't quite make it; **ˈkur·ven** *v/i.* (sn) drive round; ✈ circle; **um die Ecke ~** F zoom around the corner; F **durch die Gegend ~** cruise (F bomb) around

ˈkur·ven·för·mig [-fœrmɪç] *adj.* curved

ˈKur·ven|la·ge *f mot.* holding on bends; **e-e gute ~ haben** hold well on bends; **~li·neˌal** *n* curve; **2reich** *adj.* winding, twisting, full of bends; F *hum.* F curvaceous; **~schar** *f* 𝔄 family of curves; **~schrei·ber** *m* plotter; **2si·cher** *adj.*: **der Wagen ist ~** the car holds well on bends, the car corners well; **~star** *m* sex star, F blonde (*or* brunette) bombshell; **~ver·hal·ten** *n mot.* → **Kurvenlage**; **~vor·ga·be** *f sport*: stagger

kur·vig [ˈkʊrvɪç] *adj.* winding, twisting

kurz [kʊrts] **I.** *adj.* **1.** short; **~ und dick** dumpy; **~e Hose** shorts (*pl.*); **mit ~en Ärmeln** short-sleeved; **sie trägt ~es Haar** she's got short hair; **sich die Haare ~ schneiden lassen** have one's hair cut short; **hinten und an den Seiten ~** short back and sides; **die Hose ist ihm zu ~ geworden** he's grown out of those trousers; **die Röcke werden dieses Jahr ~ getragen** hemlines are high this year; **kürzer machen** shorten; F **~ und klein schlagen** smash to pieces; **alles ~ und klein schlagen** F wreck the place; *fig.* **den kürzeren ziehen** come off worst, lose out, F get the rough end of the stick, get the thin end of the wedge; **2.** short, brief *report, outline etc.*; *fig.* short, curt (**gegen** *acc.* with *s.o.*); **~e Darstellung** (*or* **Zusammenfassung**) (brief) summary; **~es Gedächtnis** short memory; **~er Blick** quick glance; **in ~en Worten** in a few words; → **Prozeß** 2; **seit ~em geht es ihm besser** he's been feeling better lately; **vor ~em** recently, not long ago; **die Tage werden kürzer** the days are getting shorter; **II.** *adv.* **3. er sprang zu ~** he jumped too short, he didn't jump far enough; **~ vor Lissabon** just before (we *etc.* got to) Lisbon; **es liegt ~ hinter der Post** it's a little way up (*or* just up) from the post office; *fig.* **zu ~ kommen** come off worst; **sieh zu, daß du nicht zu ~ kommst** make sure you get your fair share of the deal; **das Problem ist viel zu ~ gekommen** the problem didn't get the attention it deserved; F **er ist mit dem Verstand zu ~ gekommen** F he was at the back of the queue when brains were being handed out; → **kurzhalten, kurztreten**; **4.** briefly; for a while; for a moment; **könntest du ~ herüberkommen?** could you come over for a minute?; **~ darauf** shortly after (this); **~ zuvor** shortly before (this); **über ~ oder lang** sooner or later; **~ (gesagt), um es ~ zu sagen** (*or* **zu machen**) to cut a long story short; **~ (und bündig)** briefly, curtly, bluntly, point-blank, *refuse etc.* flatly; **~ angebunden** short, curt (**gegen** *acc.* with *s.o.*); **~ gesagt** very briefly, in a word, in short; **j-m ~ schreiben** drop s.o. a line; **~ nicken** give a brief (*or* quick) nod; **laß mich mal ~ überlegen** let me have a quick think; **ich will ihn nur ~ anrufen** I just want to give him a quick call; **fasse dich ~!** try to make it short; **er wird ~ Will genannt** he's called Will for short; → **abfertigen** 2

ˈKurz·ar·beit *f* (-; *no pl.*) short-time work; **ˈkurz·ar·bei·ten** *v/i.* (*sep.*, h) work (*or* be on) short time; **ˈKurz·ar·bei·ter** *m* short-time worker; **~ sein** *a.* be on short time

ˈkurz·är·me·lig [-ɛrməlɪç] *adj.* short-sleeved

ˈkurz·at·mig [-aːtmɪç] *adj.* short of breath, short-winded

ˈKurz·aus·ga·be *f* abridged edition

ˈkurz·bei·nig [-baɪnɪç] *adj.* short-legged

ˈKurz|be·richt *m* brief report; summary; **~bio·graˌphie** *f* profile

Kür·ze [ˈkʏrtsə] *f* (-; -n) shortness; *a.* brevity *of a report etc.*; conciseness; **in ~** shortly, soon; **in aller ~** very briefly; **in der ~ liegt die Würze** brevity is the soul of wit

Kür·zel [ˈkʏrtsəl] *n* (-s; -) **1.** abbreviation (**für** *acc.* of); contraction (of); **2.** shorthand symbol; *fig.* **das ist ein ~ für** *acc.* ... that's shorthand for ...

kür·zen [ˈkʏrtsən] *v/t.* (h) shorten (**um** *acc.* by); abridge *book etc.*; reduce (*a.* 𝔄), cut; **drastisch ~** F slash

kur·zer·hand [ˈkʊrtsɐˈhant] *adv.* unceremoniously, F just like that; *a.* there and then; **~ leugnen** flatly deny; **et. ~ ablehnen** reject s.th. out of hand

kür·zer·tre·ten [ˈkʏrtsɐ-] *v/i.* (*irr.*, *sep.*, h, → **treten**) a) tighten one's belt, b) slow down, take things a bit slower; **~ mit** *dat.* go easy on

ˈKurz|fas·sung *f* abridged version; **~film** *m* short; **~form** *f* short(ened) form; **~for·mel** *f*: **et. auf e-e ~ bringen** put s.th. in a nutshell

ˈkurz·fri·stig [-frɪstɪç] **I.** *adj.* a) short-term ..., b) sudden; immediate; **II.** *adv.* a) at short notice; at the last minute, b) quickly

ˈkurz|ge·bra·ten *adj.* quick-fried; **~gefaßt** *adj.* brief

ˈKurz·ge·schich·te *f* short story

ˈkurz|ge·schnit·ten *adj.* short; **~ge·scho·ren** *adj.* very short, close-cropped

ˈKurz·haar·dackel *m* short-haired dachshund

ˈkurz·haa·rig *adj.* short-haired

ˈkurz·hal·ten F *v/t.* (*irr.*, *sep.*, h, → **halten**) keep *s.o.* on a tight rein (*or* short leash); **j-n mit Geld** *etc.* **~** keep s.o. in short supply, stint s.o. of money *etc.*

ˈKurz·kom·menˌtar *m* brief commentary (*or* analysis)

ˈkurz·le·big [-leːbɪç] *adj.* short-lived (*a. fig. and phys.*), ✿, *zo.* ephemeral; ✝ perishable *goods*; **es war ziemlich ~** *a.* it didn't last very long

ˈKurz·lehr·gang *m* crash course

kürz·lich [ˈkʏrtslɪç] *adv.* recently, the other day; **erst ~** just the other day

ˈKurz|mel·dung *f* news flash; **~en** → **~nach·rich·ten** *pl.* news *sg.* in brief, summary *sg.* of the news, news briefing *sg.*; **~par·ker** [-parkɐ] *m* (-s; -) short-term parker; **~park·zo·ne** *f* limited parking zone; **~paß** *m sport*: short pass; **~re·feˌrat** *n* short paper (*or* talk); **ein ~ halten über** *acc.* give a short talk on; **~ruf·num·mer** *f teleph.* code number

ˈKurz·schä·del *m* shorthead; **ˈkurz·schä·de·lig** [-ʃɛːdəlɪç] *adj.* shortheaded

ˈkurz·schlie·ßen *v/t.* (*irr.*, *sep.*, h, → **schließen**) ⚡ short-circuit

ˈKurz·schluß *m* ⚡ short circuit, F short; *fig.* moment of madness; **~hand·lung** *f* panic reaction

ˈKurz·schrift *f* shorthand, stenography

ˈkurz·sich·tig [-zɪçtɪç] *adj.* shortsighted (*a. fig.*), ⚕ myopic; **ˈKurz·sich·tig·keit** *f* (-; *no pl.*) shortsightedness (*a. fig.*), ⚕ myopia

ˈKurz|ski *m* short ski; **~start** *m* ✈ short takeoff; **~star·ter** *m* short takeoff aircraft; **~strecke** *f* short haul

ˈKurz·strecken|be·trieb *m* short-haul traffic; **~flug** *m* short-haul flight; **~flug·zeug** *n* short-haul aircraft; commuter plane; **~läu·fer** *m* sprinter; **~raˌke·te** *f* short-range missile; **~waf·fe** *f* short-range weapon

ˈkurz·tre·ten F *v/i.* (*irr.*, *sep.*, h, → **treten**) **1.** cut down (expenses), **mit** *dat.*: go easy on *the sugar etc.*; **2.** take things easy

kurzˈum *adv.* in a word, to cut a long story short

Kür·zung [ˈkʏrtsʊŋ] *f* (-; -en) abridg(e)ment; cut, cutback (*gen.* in *wages etc.*); 𝔄 reduction; **~en vornehmen in** *dat.* cut, shorten *a film etc.*, cut down on *the staff etc.*

ˈKür·zungs·po·liˌtik *f* policy of retrenchment (*or* low spending)

ˈKurz|ur·laub *m* short trip, short-break holiday; **~wahl** *f teleph.* abbreviated dial(l)ing

ˈKurz·wa·ren *pl.* haberdashery *sg.*, *Am.* dry goods, notions; **~ge·schäft** *n* haberdashery, *Am.* dry goods store

ˈkurz·wei·lig [-vaɪlɪç] *adj.* entertaining

ˈKurz·wel·le *f* short wave

ˈKurz·wel·len|be·reich *m* short-wave range; **~emp·fän·ger** *m* short-wave receiver; **~sen·der** *m* short-wave radio station (*or* transmitter); **~the·raˌpie** *f* ⚕ short-wave therapy

ˈKurz·wort *n* (-[e]s; ⸚er) contraction, abbreviation; acronym

ˈKurz·zeit·ge·dächt·nis *n* short-term memory

ˈkurz·zei·tig *adj.* short; short-lived

ˈKurz·zeit·wecker *m* timer

ku·sche·lig [ˈkʊʃəlɪç] *adj.* soft and cuddly; cosy, *Am.* cozy; **ku·scheln** [ˈkʊʃəln] (h) **I.** *v/refl.*: **sich ~ an** *acc.* snuggle (*or* cuddle) up to *s.o.*, snuggle against *s.th.*; **II.** *v/t.*: **s-n Kopf ~ an** (**in**) *acc.* nestle one's head against (bury one's head into); **III.** *v/i.* cuddle

Ku·schel|tier [ˈkʊʃəl-] *n* soft (*or* cuddly) toy; **2weich** *adj.* soft and cuddly

ku·schen [ˈkʊʃən] *v/i.* (h) *dog.*: lie down; *fig.* knuckle under (**vor** *dat.* to)

Ku·si·ne [kuˈziːnə] *f* (-; -n) cousin

Kus·kus [ˈkʊskʊs] *m* (-; -) *gastr.* couscous

Kuß [kʊs] *m* (Kusses; Küsse [ˈkʏsə]) kiss; **Gruß u. ~** love and kisses

Küß·chen [ˈkʏsçən] *n* (-s; -) (little) kiss; peck on the cheek; F **~!** F give us a kiss

ˈkuß·echt *adj.* kiss-proof

küs·sen [ˈkʏsən] *v/t.* (h) kiss; **sie küßten sich** they kissed (each other); **j-n zum Abschied ~** kiss s.o. goodbye; **j-n auf den Mund ~** kiss s.o.'s lips, kiss s.o. on the lips

ˈKuß·hand *f*: **j-m e-e ~ zuwerfen** blow s.o. a kiss; *fig.* **mit ~** gladly, with pleas-

ure; ***ich würde es mit ~ nehmen*** *a.* I'd be only too glad to take it
Kü·ste ['kʏstə] *f* (-; -n) coast, shore
'**Kü·sten|be·woh·ner** *m* coastal inhabitant; **~damp·fer** *m* coaster; **~ebe·ne** *f* coastal plain; **~fi·sche,rei** *f* inshore fishing; **~ge·biet** *n* coastal area; **~ge·wäs·ser** *pl.* coastal waters; **~han·del** *m* coastal trade (*or* trading); **&nah** *adj.* coastal, offshore ..., near the coast; **~schiffahrt** (*sep.* -ff·f-) *f* coastal shipping; **~schutz** *m* coastal protection (*or* preservation); **~staat** *m* littoral state; **~stadt** *f* coastal town; **~stra·ße** *f* coastal road (*or* route); road along the coast; **~strei·fen** *m*, **~strich** *m* coastal strip; beach; **~ver·schmut·zung** *f* coastal pollution; **~ver·tei·di·gung** *f* coastal defen|ce (*Am.* -se); **~wa·che** *f* coastguard (station); **~wach·schiff** *n* coastal patrol vessel
Kü·ster ['kʏstɐ] *m* (-s; -) sexton, sacristan
Ku·sto·de [kʊs'to:də] *m* (-n; -n), **Ku·stos** ['kʊstɔs] *m* (-; Kustoden) curator, keeper
Kutsch·bock ['kʊtʃ-] *m* coach box
Kut·sche ['kʊtʃə] *f* (-; -n) coach; F *mot.* ***alte ~*** F old banger
Kut·scher ['kʊtʃɐ] *m* (-s; -) coachman
kut·schie·ren [kʊt'ʃi:rən] **I.** *v/i.* (sn) drive (*or* ride) in a coach; drive (a coach); F *mot.* drive; **II.** *v/t.* (h) drive; F ***ich habe keine Lust, sie durch die Gegend zu ~*** why should I act as her chauffeur?
Kut·te ['kʊtə] *f* (-; -n) (monk's) habit
Kut·teln ['kʊtəln] *pl.* tripe *sg.*
Kut·ter ['kʊtɐ] *m* (-s; -) ⚓ cutter
Ku·vert [ku've:ɐ] *n* (-s; -s) **1.** envelope; **2.** *gastr.* cover
Ku·ver·tü·re [kuvɛr'ty:rə] *f* (-; -n) *gastr.* (chocolate) coating
Ku·wai·ter [ku'vaɪtɐ] *m* (-s; -), **Ku·wai·te·rin** [ku'vaɪtərɪn] *f* (-; -nen), **ku·wai·tisch** [ku'vaɪtɪʃ] *adj.* Kuwaiti
Ky·ber·ne·tik [kybɛr'ne:tɪk] *f* (-; *no pl.*) cybernetics *pl.*; **ky·ber·ne·tisch** [kybɛr'ne:tɪʃ] *adj.* cybernetic(ally *adv.*)
Ky·rie(elei·son) ['ky:rïe(ʔe'laɪzɔn)] *n* (-s; -s) *eccl.* Kyrie (eleison)
ky·ril·lisch [ky'rɪlɪʃ] *adj.* Cyrillic
KZ [ka:'tsɛt] *n* (-s; -s) concentration camp; **KZ-Häft·ling** *m*, **KZler** [ka:'tsɛtlɐ] F *m* (-s; -) concentration camp internee (*or* inmate); **KZ-Me,tho·den** *pl.* concentration camp methods

L

L, l [ɛl] *n* (-; -) L, l

Lab [laːp] *n* (-[e]s; -e [ˈlaːbə]) *biol., zo.* rennet, rennin

lab·be·rig [ˈlabərɪç] F *adj.* **1.** a) tasteless, insipid, b) runny *blancmange etc.*, watery *soup etc.*; soggy *salad, bread etc.*; ***das schmeckt total*** ~ it tastes like nothing; ***dieses ~e Zeug kann ich nicht essen*** F I can't eat this mush; **2.** sloppy, shapeless *clothes, a.* baggy *trousers*; slack *elastic band etc.*; **3.** *fig.* limp *handshake etc.*; **4.** ***mir ist ganz*** ~ I feel a bit queasy

La·bel [ˈleːbəl] *n* (-s; -) label

la·ben [ˈlaːbən] (h) **I.** *v/refl.*: ***sich*** ~ refresh o.s., revive o.s. (***an*** *dat.* with); *fig.* ***sich*** ~ ***an*** *dat.* relish, gloat over; **II.** *v/t.* refresh, revive; **ˈla·bend** *adj.* refreshing

la·bern [ˈlaːbɐn] F *v/i.* (h) F blather

la·bi·al [laˈbi̯aːl] *adj.* labial; **La·biˈal** *m* (-s; -e), **La·biˈal·laut** *m ling.* labial

la·bil [laˈbiːl] *adj.* unstable; weak, easily influenced, very impressionable; susceptible; bad *circulation*; ***~e Gesundheit*** weak constitution; **La·bi·li·tät** [labiliˈtɛːt] *f* (-; *no pl.*) instability; weakness; susceptibility

la·bio·den·tal [labi̯odɛnˈtaːl] *adj.* labiodental; **La·bio·denˈtal** *m* (-s; -e), **La·bio·denˈtal·laut** *m ling.* labiodental

la·bio·ve·lar [labi̯oveˈlaːɐ] *adj.* labiovelar; **La·bio·veˈlar** *m* (-s; -e [-rə]), **La·bio·veˈlar·laut** *m ling.* labiovelar

ˈLab|kraut *n* ♣ bedstraw; **~ma·gen** *m zo.* fourth stomach; 📖 abomasum

La·bor [laˈboːɐ] *n* (-s; -s, -e [-rə]) laboratory, F lab; **La·bo·rant** [laboˈrant] *m* (-en; -en), **La·bo·ran·tin** [laboˈrantɪn] *f* (-; -nen) laboratory assistant; **La·bo·ra·to·ri·um** [laboraˈtoːri̯ʊm] *n* (-s; -ien) laboratory

Laˈborbeˌfunˌde *pl.* test results; **laˈbor·ge·prüft** *adj.* lab-tested

la·bo·rie·ren [laboˈriːrən] F *v/i.* (h): ~ ***an*** *dat.* be suffering from *a gastritis etc.*, be trying to shake off *the flu etc.*

Laˈbor|platz *m* lab place; **~tech·ni·ker** *m* laboratory technician; **~un·terˌsu·chung** *f* laboratory test; **~ver·such** *m* laboratory experiment

Lab·sal [ˈlaːpzaːl] *n* (-[e]s; -e), *f* (-; -e) refreshment; *fig.* a) treat, feast, b) comfort; ***es war ein*** ~ it was very refreshing, *fig.* a) it was a great comfort, b) it was a treat

La·by·rinth [labyˈrɪnt] *n* (-[e]s; -e) labyrinth (*a. anat.*); maze (*a. fig.*); *fig.* warren

la·by·rin·thisch [labyˈrɪntɪʃ] *adj.* labyrinthine

Lach·an·fall [ˈlax-] *m* laughing fit, fit of laughter; ***e-n ~ kriegen*** go into fits (of laughter), burst out laughing

La·che[1] [ˈlaxə] F *f* (-; *no pl.*) laugh; ***dreckige*** ~ dirty laugh

La·che[2] [ˈlaxə, ˈlaːxə] *f* (-; -n) pool; puddle

lä·cheln [ˈlɛçəln] **I.** *v/i.* (h) smile (***über*** *acc.* at); grin (at); ***höhnisch*** ~ sneer; ***immer nur ~!*** keep smiling!; ***über das ganze Gesicht*** ~ be all smiles, be grinning from ear to ear; *fig. lit.* ***ihm lächelte das Glück*** fortune smiled (up)on him; **II.** ≈ *n* (-s; *no pl.*) smile; grin; ***höhnisches*** ~ sneer

la·chen [ˈlaxən] **I.** *v/i. and v/t.* (h) laugh (***über*** *acc.* at); smile; ***laut*** ~ laugh out loud; ***leise vor sich hin*** ~ chuckle (to o.s.); F ***sich e-n Ast*** ~ F nearly die laughing, kill o.s. (laughing), crease up (with laughter); ***du hast gut*** ~ you can laugh; ***daß ich nicht lache!, da kann ich nur ~!*** don't make me laugh; ***lach*** (***du***) ***nur!*** just you wait and see; ***es wäre doch gelacht, wenn*** it would be ridiculous if *we couldn't do it*; ***da gibt's nichts zu*** ~ it's not funny, *formal*: this is no laughing matter; ***was gibt's da zu ~?*** what's so funny about that?; ***bei ihm hat sie nichts zu*** ~ he really gives her a hard time; ***er hat nicht viel zu*** ~ life's no bed of roses for him; ***du wirst ~, aber*** you won't believe this, but; ***wer zuletzt lacht, lacht am besten*** he who laughs last, laughs loudest; ***lach doch mal!*** come on, give us a smile; *fig.* ***die Sonne lacht*** the sun is smiling; *lit.* ***ihm lachte das Glück*** fortune smiled (up)on him; → ***Fäustchen***; **II.** ≈ *n* (-s; *no pl.*) laugh(ing), laughter; ***j-n zum ~ bringen*** make s.o. laugh; ***ich konnte ihn nicht zum ~ bringen*** I couldn't get him to laugh; ***in lautes ~ ausbrechen*** burst out laughing; ***sich biegen*** (***or ausschütten, kugeln***) ***vor*** ~ F kill o.s. (laughing), split one's sides (laughing); ***das ist nicht zum*** ~ it's no joke; ***das ist ja zum*** ~ that's ridiculous; ***ich werde dir das ~ schon abgewöhnen*** I'll wipe that smile off your face; ***ihm wird das ~ schon noch vergehen*** he'll be laughing on the other side of his face before he knows it; ~ ***ist gesund*** laughter is the best medicine; → ***verbeißen, zumute***; **ˈla·chend** *adj.* laughing; *fig.* smiling *sun*; ***die ~en Erben*** the laughing heirs; ***der ~e Dritte*** the real winner; **La·cher** [ˈlaxɐ] *m* (-s; -) **1.** ***er hatte die ~ auf seiner Seite*** he had the laugh on his side; **2.** laugh

ˈLach·er·folg *m*: ***es war ein großer*** ~ F it was a scream; ***~e ernten*** have everybody laughing

lä·cher·lich [ˈlɛçɐlɪç] **I.** *adj.* a) ridiculous; laughable, absurd, b) ridiculous, F piddling; ~ ***machen*** ridicule; ***sich ~ machen*** make a fool of o.s.; ***~e Kleinigkeit*** trivial matter, *pl. a.* trivia; ***das ≈e daran*** the ridiculous thing about it; ***ins ≈e ziehen*** make fun of, ridicule; **II.** *adv.*: ***~ wenig*** *etc.* ridiculously little *etc.*, a ridiculously small amount *etc.*; **ˈLä·cher·lich·keit** *f* (-; -en) **1.** *no pl.* ridiculousness; ***der ~ preisgeben*** make *s.o. or s.th.* look ridiculous; **2.** trivial matter, F piddling affair, *pl. a.* trivia

ˈLach|fal·ten *pl.* laughter lines; **~gas** *n* laughing gas

ˈlach·haft *adj.* ridiculous, laughable

ˈLach|ka·biˌnett *n* crazy house; **~krampf** *m* laughing fit; ***e-n ~ bekommen*** (F ***kriegen***) start laughing uncontrollably, have a laughing fit; ***ich bekam e-n ~ a.*** I couldn't stop laughing; F *iro.* ***ich krieg' e-n ~*** F you're kidding; **~mö·we** *f* laughing gull; **~mus·kel** *m* laughing muscle; **~reiz** *m* (sudden) urge to laugh, *the* giggles *pl.*; ***ein ~ überfiel ihn*** he suddenly got the giggles

Lachs [laks] *m* (-es; -e) salmon

ˈLach·sal·ve *f* peals *pl.* of laughter

ˈLachs|er·satz *m* (thinly sliced) rock salmon; **~fang** *m* salmon fishing; **≈far·ben, ≈far·big** *adj.* salmon(-colo[u]red), salmon pink; **~foˌrel·le** *f* salmon trout; **≈ro·sa** *adj.* salmon pink, salmon-colo(u)red; **~schin·ken** *m smoked, rolled, lean ham*

Lack [lak] *m* (-[e]s; -e) **1.** lacquer, varnish; enamel; **2.** *mot.* paintwork, *Am.* paint job; **3.** *fig.* veneer; ***fertig ist der ~!*** F hey presto!; and Bob's your uncle!; ***der ~ ist ab*** the novelty has worn off, the initial glamo(u)r has gone; **~af·fe** F *m* fop; **~ar·bei·ten** *pl.* lacquerwork *sg.*

Lackel [ˈlakəl] (*sep.* -k·k-) F *m* F peasant; F clumsy oaf

lackie·ren [laˈkiːrən] (*sep.* -k·k-) *v/t.* (h) varnish; *mot.* paint; F *fig.* take *s.o.* in; ***sich die Fingernägel*** ~ put some nail varnish on, paint one's nails; ***der Lakkierte sein*** → ***gelackmeiert***

Lackie·rer [laˈkiːrɐ] (*sep.* -k·k-) *m* (-s; -) varnisher; *mot.* body painter

Lackie·rung [laˈkiːrʊŋ] (*sep.* -k·k-) *f* (-; -en) varnish; enamel; *mot.* paintwork, *Am.* paint job

Lack|krat·zer *m* → ***Lackschaden***; **~le·der** *n* patent leather; **~ma·leˌrei** *f* lacquer painting; **~man·tel** *m* patent leather coat

lack·mei·ern [ˈlakmaiɐn] F *v/t.* → ***gelackmeiert***

Lack·mus [ˈlakmʊs] *m, n* (-; *no pl.*) ⚗ litmus; **~paˌpier** *n* litmus paper

ˈLack|scha·den *m mot.* scratch (on the paintwork [*Am.* paint job]); **~schu·he** *pl.* patent leather shoes; **~stie·fel** *pl.* patent leather boots

La·de [ˈlaːdə] *obs. f* (-; -n) chest; drawer

ˈLa·de|baum *m* derrick; **~brü·cke** *f* loading bridge; **~büh·ne** *f* loading platform; **~fä·hig·keit** *f* loading capacity; ⚓ tonnage; ⚡ storage capacity; **~flä·che** *f*

loading space; **~ge·rät** *n* ⚡ battery charger; **~ge·wicht** *n* maximum load; **~hem·mung** *f* jam, stoppage; **~ haben** *gun etc.*: be jamming, F *fig.* have a mental block, *n.s.* not to be able to get a word out; **~ka·pa·zi·tät** *f* → **Ladefähigkeit; ~klap·pe** *f mot.* tailboard, tailgate; **~kran** *m* loading crane; **~li·nie** *f* ⚓ load line; **~li·ste** *f* cargo list; **~lu·ke** *f* hatch(way)

la·den¹ ['la:dən] *v/t.* (lud, geladen, h) load; ⚡ charge; *mot.* supercharge, boost; *computer*: boot (up); *fig.* **auf sich ~** saddle o.s. with, incur *s.o.'s hatred etc.*; F *fig.* **schwer geladen haben** F have had one over the eight, be tight; → **geladen**

'la·den² *v/t.* (lud, geladen, h) invite; ⚖ **vor Gericht ~** summon before a court, subpoena

'La·den *m* (-s; Läden ['lɛ:dən]) **1.** shop, *esp. Am.* store; **2.** F *fig.* business; **den ~ hinschmeißen** F chuck the whole thing; **den ~ schmeißen** a) F run the show, b) F swing it; **den ~ dichtmachen** F shut up shop, *a.* F fold up; **der ~ läuft** F everything's hunky-dory; **wie ich den ~ (so) kenne** if you ask me; **3.** shutter(s *pl.*); **~be·sit·zer** *m* shop owner, proprietor; **~de·tek·tiv** *m* store detective; **~dieb** *m* shoplifter; **~dieb·stahl** *m* shoplifting; **~ein·bruch** *m* shopbreaking; **~ein·rich·tung** *f* shop (*Am. a.* store) fittings *pl.*; **~fen·ster** *n* shop window; **~front** *f* shop (*Am. a.* store) front; **~hü·ter** F *m* F shelf-warmer; ✝ *pl.* soiled goods; **~in·ha·ber** *m* → **Ladenbesitzer; ~kas·se** *f* till; **~ket·te** *f* chain (of stores); **~pas·sa·ge** *f* shopping mall; **~preis** *m* retail price; publisher's price; **~schild** *n* (shop) sign, facia, fascia

'La·den·schluß *m* closing time; **nach ~** after hours; **~ge·setz** *n* shop closing laws *pl.*; *in GB*: shops act

'La·den|stra·ße *f* shopping street; **~tisch** *m* counter; *fig.* **unter dem ~** under the counter; **~ver·kauf** *m* retail (sale)

La·der ['la:dɐ] *m* (-s; -) ⚙ loader, charger; *mot.* supercharger, booster; ⚡ battery charger

'La·de|ram·pe *f* loading ramp; **~raum** *m* loading (*or* cargo) bay; a) ⚓ (ship's) hold, b) ⚓ tonnage; ✈ stowage compartment; **~schein** *m* ⚓ bill of lading; **~strom** *m* ⚡ charging current; **~zo·ne** *f* loading area (*or* bay)

lä·die·ren [lɛ'di:rən] *v/t.* (h) a) damage, b) injure; **lä·diert** [lɛ'di:ɐt] *adj.* **1.** a) damaged, battered, b) injured; **leicht ~** the worse for wear; **er sah ziemlich ~ aus** he looked as if he'd taken a bit of a beating (*or* had a rough time); **2.** *fig.* battered *reputation etc.*; injured *pride*

La·dung¹ ['la:dʊŋ] *f* (-; -en) **1.** ✝ load, freight, ⚓, ✈ cargo; shipment; truckload; **2.** ⚔ (explosive) charge; ⚡, *phys.* charge; **3.** F **e-e ~ Sand** *etc.*: F a pile (*or* load) of, a fistful of; *fig.* **e-e geballte ~ von Vorwürfen** a volley of criticism

'La·dung² *f* (-; -en) ⚖ summons, subpoena

La·dy ['le:di] *f* (-; -s) real lady

La·fet·te [la'fɛtə] *f* (-; -n) (gun) carriage, mount

Laf·fe ['lafə] F *m* (-n; -n) fop

lag [la:k] *pret. of* **liegen**

La·ge ['la:gə] *f* (-; -n) **1.** a) position, b) site, location; *mot.* → **Straßenlage; ein Haus in schöner ~** a beautifully situated house; **in höheren ~n** higher up; **2.** *fig.* a) situation; circumstances *pl.*, *usu. b.s.* state of affairs, b) condition, state; **rechtliche ~** legal position; **wirtschaftliche (finanzielle) ~** economic (financial) situation; **in allen ~n** in any situation; **nach ~ der Dinge** as matters stand; **die ~ der Dinge erfordert es, daß er zurücktritt** the situation calls for his resignation; **(nicht) in der ~ sein zu** *inf.* be (un)able to *inf.*, (not to) be in a position to *inf.*; **j-n in die ~ versetzen zu** *inf.* enable s.o. to *inf.*, make it possible for s.o. to *inf.*; **in der glücklichen ~ sein zu** *inf.* be in the fortunate position *or* be fortunate enough to (be able to) *inf.*; **ich bin nicht in der ~ zu** *inf.* I'm in no position to *inf.*; **in derselben ~ sein** *a.* be in the same boat; **versetzen Sie sich in m-e ~** put yourself in my place (*or* position); **wenn ich in d-r ~ wäre** if I were you, (if I were) in your position *or* place; **in e-r unangenehmen** (*or* **unglücklichen**) **~ sein** be in an awkward position (*or* situation); **Herr der ~ sein (bleiben)** be (remain) in control of the situation (*or* of things); → **peilen** I; **3.** layer, *geol. a.* stratum; tier; ⚙ ply; coat *of paint etc.*; **4.** ♪ register; position *of chords*; **die höheren ~n** the upper registers; **5.** volley; **6. e-e ~ Bier ausgeben** buy (*or* stand) a round of beer; **~be·richt** *m* progress report; **~be·spre·chung** *f* briefing

'La·gen·staf·fel *f swimming*: medley relay

'La·ge·plan *m* layout plan

La·ger ['la:gɐ] *n* (-s; -) **1.** ✝ a) warehouse, storeroom, b) stock, stores *pl.*; ⚔ depot; **auf ~ haben** have in stock, *fig.* have up one's sleeve; **das haben wir nicht auf ~** we haven't got it in stock, it's out of stock; **ab ~** ex warehouse; *fig.* **et. für j-n auf ~ haben** have s.th. in store for s.o.; **2.** ⚔ a) camp, b) cache; **3.** *fig.* camp; **im feindlichen ~** in the enemy camp; **ins andere ~ überwechseln** change sides; **4.** ⚙ a) support, b) bearing; **5.** *geol.* layer, deposit; **6.** *obs.* bed; **~ap·fel** *m* winter apple; **~ar·bei·ter** *m* warehouse employee; storekeeper, storeman; **~be·stand** *m* stock (on hand); **den ~ aufnehmen** take stock, do the stocktaking (*or* inventory); **~be·stands·auf·nah·me** *f* stocktaking, inventory; **~bier** *n* lager; **~buch** *n* stock book, stores ledger

'la·ger·fä·hig *adj.* storable

'La·ger·fä·hig·keit *f* (-; *no pl.*) shelf life; **große (geringe) ~** long (short) shelf life

'La·ger·feu·er *n* camp fire; **~ro·man·tik** *f* campfire romanticism

'La·ger|ge·büh·ren *pl.* storage charges, storage *sg.*; **~hal·le** *f* warehouse; **~hal·tung** *f* stockkeeping; **~haus** *n* warehouse

La·ge·rist [la:gə'rɪst] *m* (-en; -en) stockkeeper, storekeeper, storeman

'La·ger|kol·ler F *m* camp psychosis; **~ko·sten** *pl.* storage charges, storage *sg.*; **~le·ben** *n* camp life; **~li·ste** *f* stock list

la·gern ['la:gɐn] (h) **I.** *v/t.* **1.** store; keep; → **kühl** II; **2.** season *wood etc.*; **3.** *esp.* ⚕ rest (up) *one's leg etc.*; **4.** put, lay; **5.** ⚙ mount; support; position; → **gelagert; II.** *v/i.* **6.** camp; **~ auf** *dat.* camp down on; **7.** ✝ be stored; **8.** mature; **9.** ⚙ rest; **III.** *v/refl.*: **sich ~** settle (down)

'La·ger|obst *n* storing fruit; **~platz** *m* **1.** place to spend the night; **2.** ✝ storage place; **~psy·cho·se** *f* camp psychosis; **~raum** *m* storeroom; **~schup·pen** *m* storage shed; **~seu·che** *f* camp epidemic; **~stät·te** *f geol.* deposit

La·ge·rung ['la:gərʊŋ] *f* (-; *no pl.*) **1.** ✝ storage; **2.** seasoning; **3.** ⚙ mounting; *mot.* suspension; **4.** *geol.* stratification

'La·ger|ver·wal·ter *m* storekeeper, stockkeeper; **~ver·zeich·nis** *n* stock list; **~vor·rat** *m* stock, supply

La·gu·ne [la'gu:nə] *f* (-; -n) lagoon

lahm [la:m] *adj.* **1.** lame; ⚕ paralyzed; crippled; **~ sein** *a.* (have a) limp; **2.** F limp; stiff; **3.** F *fig.* a) slow, sluggish, b) dull; tame *film, joke etc.*, c) lame, poor *excuse etc.*; **~e Ente** sluggard, *mot.* crawler; **~er Verein** F hopeless lot

'Lahm·arsch *sl. m* F drip; **diese Lahmärsche!** F what a bunch of drips, what a hopeless lot; **komm, du ~!** *sl.* come on, get off that butt of yours!; **'lahm·ar·schig** [-arʃɪç] *sl. adj.* slow; hopeless

lah·men ['la:mən] *v/i.* (h) *zo.* be lame (**auf** *dat.* in)

läh·men ['lɛ:mən] *v/t.* (h) paralyze (*a. fig.*); → **lahmlegen, gelähmt; 'läh·mend** *adj.* paralyzing (*a. fig. fear etc.*)

'lahm·le·gen *fig. v/t.* (*sep.*, h) paralyze, cripple; bring to a standstill (*or* halt, stop); ⚙ knock out *machine etc.*; **'Lahm·le·gung** *fig. f* (-; *no pl.*) paralyzing, crippling

Läh·mung ['lɛ:mʊŋ] *f* (-; -en) ⚕ paralysis; *fig.* paralyzing; **einseitige (doppelseitige) ~** paralysis on *or* down one side (both sides) of one's body, 📖 hemiplegia (paraplegia); **'Läh·mungs·er·schei·nung** *f* symptom of paralysis

Laib [laɪp] *m* (-[e]s; -e ['laɪbə]) loaf

Laich [laɪç] *m* (-[e]s; -e) spawn; **'lai·chen** *v/i.* (h) spawn; **'Laich·platz** *m a. pl.* spawning ground; **'Laich·zeit** *f* spawning season

Laie ['laɪə] *m* (-n; -n) *eccl.* layman (*a. fig.*); laywoman; *fig.* **da bin ich absoluter ~** I don't know the first thing about it; F **da staunt der ~ (und der Fachmann wundert sich)** that's unbelievable, F that's too much

'Lai·en|bru·der *m* lay brother; **~büh·ne** *f* amateur theat|re (*Am. a.* -er)

'lai·en·haft I. *adj.* amateurish, unprofessional, dilettante; **II.** *adv.*: **~ ausgedrückt** (to put it) in layman's terms

'Lai·en|in·ve·sti·tur *f* lay investiture; **~pre·di·ger** *m*, **~prie·ster** *m* lay preacher; **~rich·ter** *m* lay judge; **~spiel** *n thea.* amateur play; **~spra·che** *f* layman's language; **~thea·ter** *n* amateur theat|re (*Am. a.* -er) (group); **~theo·lo·ge** *m* lay theologian

'Lai·en·tum *n* (-s; *no pl.*) **1.** *coll.* laity; **2.** laymanship

'Lai·en·ver·stand *m* layman's way of thinking; **das sagt mir schon mein ~** even I as a layman realize (*or* know) that

La·kai [la'kaɪ] *m* (-en; -en) **1.** *hist.* lackey, footman; **2.** *contp.* minion, flunkey; **la'kai·en·haft** *adj.* servile, cringing

La·ke ['la:kə] *f* (-; -n) brine, pickle

La·ken ['la:kən] *n* (-s; -) sheet

la·ko·nisch [la'ko:nɪʃ] *adj.* laconic(ally *adv.*)

La·krit·ze [la'krɪtsə] *f* (-; -n) liquorice; **La'krit·zen·stan·ge** *f* liquorice stick, stick of liquorice

Lak·ta·ti·on [lakta'tsio:n] *f* (-; -en) lactation

Lak·to·se [lak'to:zə] *f* (-; -n) lactose

la·la ['la'la] F *adj. and adv.*: **so ~** F so-so

lal·len ['lalən] *v/i. and v/t.* (h) *baby*: babble; *drunk*: blabber

La·ma¹ ['la:ma] *n* (-s; -s) *zo.* llama

'**La·ma²** *m* (-[s]; -s) *buddhism*: lama; **La·ma·is·mus** [lama'ɪsmʊs] *m* (-; *no pl.*) lamaism; **la·mai·stisch** [lama'ɪstɪʃ] *adj.* Lamaist(ic); '**La·ma·klo·ster** *n* lamasery

La·mäng [la'mɛŋ] F *f*: ***aus der*** **~** F off the top of one's head, just like that

'**La·ma·wol·le** *f* llama (wool)

La·mé [la'me:] *m* (-[s]; -s) lamé

La·mel·le [la'mɛlə] *f* (-; -n) ⚙ lamella; ⚡ (commutator) segment; *mot.* rib; *phot.* blade, leaf; slat, blade *of a blind*; ⚘ gill; **la'mel·len·för·mig** [-fœrmɪç] *adj.* lamellar

La'mel·len|kupp·lung *f* multiple-disc clutch; **~ver·schluß** *m phot.* iris diaphragm, bladed shutter

la·men·tie·ren [lamɛn'ti:rən] *v/i.* (h) complain, moan; **La·men·to** [la'mɛnto] *n* (-s; -s, -ti) **1.** (howl of) complaint; ***ein großes ~ anstimmen*** set up a howl of complaint (***über*** *acc.* about), F kick up a big fuss (about); **2.** ♪ lament

La·met·ta [la'mɛta] *n* (-s; *no pl.*) **1.** tinsel; **2.** F *fig.* F fruit salad

la·mi·nie·ren [lami'ni:rən] *v/t.* (h) ⚙ laminate

Lamm [lam] *n* (-[e]s; Lämmer ['lɛmɐ]) lamb (*a. fig.*); ***das ~ Gottes*** the Lamb of God; **~bra·ten** *m* roast lamb

lam·men ['lamən] *v/i.* (h) lamb

Läm·mer|gei·er ['lɛmɐ-] *m* lammergeyer, bearded vulture; **~wol·ken** *pl.* fleecy (*or* cotton-wool) clouds

'**Lamm·fell** *n* lambskin; **~haus·schu·he** *pl.* lambskin slippers; **~jacke** *f* lambskin (*or* sheepskin) jacket; **~man·tel** *m* lambskin (*or* sheepskin) coat

'**Lamm|fleisch** *n* lamb; **≗fromm** *adj.* (as) meek as a lamb; **~ko·te,lett** *n* lamb chop

Lämm·lein ['lɛmlaɪn] *n* (-s; -) little lamb

'**Lamms·ge·duld** *f the* patience of Job (*or* of a saint)

'**Lamm·wol·le** *f* lambswool

Lämp·chen ['lɛmpçən] *n* (-s; -) (small) lamp; **Lam·pe** ['lampə] *f* (-; -n) **1.** lamp; *w.s.* light; **2.** bulb

'**Lam·pen|fas·sung** *f* bulb socket; **~fie·ber** *n* stage fright; *a.* first-night nerves *pl.*; **~licht** *n* (-[e]s; *no pl.*) lamplight; **~schein** *m* lamplight, light of the lamp; **~schirm** *m* lampshade

Lam·pi·on [lam'piõ:, 'lampiɔŋ] *m, n* (-s; -s) Chinese lantern

lan·cie·ren [lã:'si:rən] *v/t.* (h) **1.** launch; build *s.o.* up; **~ *in*** *acc.* launch *s.th. or s.o.* into *the charts etc.*; **2.** † float *a loan etc.*; **Lan'cie·rung** *f* (-; -en) launch(ing); † flotation

Land [lant] *n* (-[e]s; Länder ['lɛndɐ]) **1.** *no pl.* land, † *a.* property, ⚒ *a.* soil; ***10 Hektar ~*** 10 hectares of land; **~ *in Sicht*** land ahead; ***an ~*** ashore; ***an ~ gehen*** go ashore, disembark; ***an ~ ziehen*** land, pull ashore, F *fig.* F land o.s., hook o.s. *a nice job etc.*; **~ *sehen*** see land; F *fig.* (***wieder***) **~ *sehen*** see the light at the end of the tunnel; ***ich sehe noch kein ~*** there's no end in sight yet; ***kein ~ mehr sehen*** be completely at sea, be floundering; → ***unter¹***; **2.** *no pl.* country(side); ***auf dem ~*** in the country; ***aufs ~ fahren*** go (*or* drive) out into the country(side); ***aufs ~ ziehen*** move to the country(side); ***hügeliges ~*** hill(y) country; *fig.* ***ins ~ gehen*** *time*: pass, elapse, go by; **3.** *geogr.* country; *pol. a.* nation, state; *lit.* land; → ***gelobt, heilig; andere Länder, andere Sitten*** when in Rome, do as the Romans do; **~ *und Leute kennenlernen*** get to know the country (and its people); ***aus aller Herren Länder*** from all four corners of the earth; F *fig.* ***wieder im ~e sein*** be back again, be back in circulation; F ***bist du wieder mal im ~e?*** F returned from your wanderings, have you?, *iro.* well hello there, stranger!; **4.** territory, land; country; *fig.* **~ *der Träume*** *etc.* land of dreams *etc.*; **5.** *pol. within Germany*: (federal) state, Land (*pl.* Laender, Länder); *in Austria*: province, Land (*pl.* Laender, Länder); ***das ~ Bayern*** the state of Bavaria; ***das ~ Kärnten*** the province of Carinthia; **~adel** *m* (landed) gentry; **~ar·beit** *f* farming; **~ar·bei·ter** *m* farm worker; **~arzt** *m* country doctor

land'auf *adv.*: **~, *landab*** up and down the country

'**Land·auf·ent·halt** *m* stay in the country

land'aus *adv.*: **~, *landein*** all over the place, *wander etc.* from country to country

'**Land|be·sitz** *m* landed property, ⚖ real estate; **~be·sit·zer** *m* landowner; **~be·stel·lung** *f* tillage; **~be·völ·ke·rung** *f* rural population; **~be·woh·ner** *m* country dweller; *pl. a.* countryfolk *sg.*; **~be·zirk** *m* rural district; **~brot** *n* farm bread; **~brücke** *f geol.* land bridge; **~but·ter** *f* farm butter

Lan·de|an·flug ['landə-] *m* landing approach (***auf*** *acc.* to); **~bahn** *f* runway, airstrip, landing strip; **~brücke** *f* ⚓ landing stage, pier, jetty; **~deck** *n* ⚓, ⚔ landing (*or* flight) deck; **~er·laub·nis** *f* ✈ landing clearance, permission to land; ***die ~ erhalten*** be given permission to land

'**Land·ei·er** *pl.* farm eggs

land'ein·wärts *adv.* (further) inland

Lan·de|klap·pe ['landə-] *f* ✈ landing flap; **~kopf** *m* ⚔ beachhead; **~licht** *n* *airport*: approach light; *airplane*: landing light; **~ma,nö·ver** *n* ✈ landing approach

lan·den ['landən] **I.** *v/i.* (sn) ✈ land, touch down; *space capsule*: land, splash down; ⚓ dock; *passengers*: disembark, go ashore; *fig.* land *on the floor etc.*; F arrive; F land (up), end up, wind up; ***auf dem dritten Platz ~*** *sport*: come in third; F ***bei ihm kannst du*** (***damit***) ***nicht ~*** you won't get (that won't get you) anywhere with him; **II.** *v/t.* (h) disembark *troops etc.*; *fig.* land *a blow*; **III.** ≗ *n* (-s; *no pl.*) landing; ***beim ~*** as we (*or* the plane *etc.*) landed

'**Land·en·ge** *f* isthmus

Lan·de|pi·ste ['landə-] *f* landing strip; **~platz** *m* ✈ airstrip; ⚓ pier, wharf, quay; **~recht** *n* landing rights *pl.*

Län·de·rei·en [lɛndə'raɪən] *pl.* property *sg.*, land *sg.*

Län·der|kampf ['lɛndɐ-] *m sport*: international competition; *soccer etc.*: international match; **~kenn·zahl** *f teleph.* country code; **~kun·de** *f* (-; *no pl.*) geography; **~na·me** *m* name of a country; *pl.* names of countries, geographical names; **~spiel** *n* international match

Lan·des·bank ['landəs-] *f* (-; -en) regional bank

Lan·de·schlei·fe ['landə-] *f* circuit; **~n *ziehen*** be in a holding pattern, circle above an airport; ***wir mußten eine Stunde lang ~n ziehen*** *a.* we were stacked for an hour

Lan·des|ebe·ne ['landəs-] *f*: ***auf ~*** on a regional level; **≗ei·gen** *adj.* state-owned; **~er·zeug·nis** *n* domestic product; *pl. a.* home produce *sg.*; **~far·ben** *pl.* national colo(u)rs; **~flag·ge** *f* national flag; **~fürst** *m* → ***Landesherr***; **~ge·biet** *n* national territory; **~gren·ze** *f* frontier, border; **~haupt·mann** *Austrian m* head of a (*or* the) provincial government; **~haupt·stadt** *f* a) capital, b) (state) capital, c) *in Austria*: (provincial) capital; **~herr** *m* sovereign; **~ho·heit** *f* (-; *no pl.*) sovereignty; **~in·ne·re** *n* interior; **~kir·che** *f* a) national church, b) regional church; **~kun·de** *f* (-; *no pl.*) background studies *pl.*; **~li·ste** *f pol.* state ticket; **~po·li,tik** *f* regional politics *pl.*; **~pro,dukt** *n* → ***Landeserzeugnis***; **~re,gie·rung** *f* a) (central) government, b) *in Germany*: (state) government, c) *in Austria*: (provincial) government; **~sit·te** *f* national (*or* local) custom; **~spra·che** *f* (national) language, language of a country; official language

Lan·de·steg ['landə-] *m* landing stage

Lan·des|thea·ter ['landəs-] *n* regional theat|re (*Am. a.* -er); **~tracht** *f* national (*or* local) costume

Lan·de|strecke ['landə-] *f* landing run; **~strei·fen** *m* landing strip

lan·des·üb·lich ['landəs-] *adj.* customary

Lan·des|va·ter ['landəs-] *iro. m* patron; sovereign; **~ver·mes·sung** *f* ordnance survey; **~ver·rat** *m* treason; **~ver·rä·ter** *m* traitor; **~ver·tei·di·gung** *f* national defen|ce (*Am.* -se); **~wäh·rung** *f* national (*or* local) currency

lan·des·weit ['landəs-] *adj.* nationwide

Lan·de|trupp ['landə-] *m* ⚔ landing party; **~ver·bot** *n*: ***e-r Maschine ~ erteilen*** refuse an aircraft permission to land; ***wegen starken Nebels herrschte am Flughafen ~*** the airport was closed due to heavy fog; **~zeit** *f* ✈ landing time; *space capsule*: splashdown

'**Land·flucht** *f* (-; *no pl.*) rural exodus, drift to the cities

'**land·fremd** *adj.* foreign

'**Land·frie·de** *m hist.* King's peace; '**Land·frie·dens·bruch** *m* breach of the peace

'**Land|ge·mein·de** *f* rural community; **~ge·richt** *n* district court

'**land·ge·stützt** *adj.*: **~e *Rakete*** land-based missile

'**Land|ge·win·nung** *f* land reclamation; **~gut** *n* estate; **~haus** *n* country house, villa, cottage; **~kar·te** *f* map; **~kreis** *m* district

'**land·läu·fig** **I.** *adj.* current, common, generally accepted; popular; ***im ~en Sinn*** in the conventional sense (of the word); ***der ~en Meinung nach*** according to popular opinion (*or* belief), conventional wisdom has it that; ***entgegen ~er Meinung*** contrary to popular opinion (*or* belief); **II.** *adv.* commonly, in popular usage

'**Land·le·ben** *n* (-s; *no pl.*) country life, life in the country

Länd·ler ['lɛntlɐ] *m* (-s; -) ländler, country waltz
'**Land·leu·te** *pl.* countryfolk (*pl.*)
länd·lich ['lɛntlɪç] *adj.* rural, country ...; rustic; *contp.* F countrified; '**Länd·lich·keit** *f* (-; *no pl.*) rural nature (*or* character); rural (*or* country) atmosphere
'**länd·lich-'sitt·lich** *hum. adj.* untouched by civilization
'**Land|luft** *f* country air; **~macht** *f* land power; **~mar·ke** *f* landmark; **~ma,schi·nen** *pl.* agricultural machinery *sg.*, farming equipment *sg.*; **~mas·se** *f geogr.* landmass; **~mi·ne** *f* ⚔ landmine
'**Land·nah·me** [-na:mə] *f* (-; *no pl.*) (conquest and) settlement
'**Land|pfar·rer** *m* country parson; **~pla·ge** *f* **1.** serious plague, scourge; **2.** F *iro.* F nuisance, pest; **~po·me,ran·ze** *hum. f* F country miss
'**Land·rat** *m* district administrator
'**Land·rats·amt** *n* district administration
'**Land|rat·te** F *f* F landlubber; **~re·gen** *m* continuous rainfall (*or* showers *pl.*); **~rei·se** *f* (overland) journey; **~rücken** *m geol.* ridge of land
'**Land·schaft** *f* (-; -en) **1.** scenery; landscape (*a. geol.*); countryside; *fig. political etc.* scene, landscape; F *fig.* ***das paßt nicht in die ~*** it doesn't fit into the picture; ***was stehst du in der ~ herum?*** what are you waiting (F hanging around) for?; **2.** *art*: landscape; '**land·schaft·lich I.** *adj.* **1.** scenic *attractions etc.*; ***~e Unterschiede*** differences in the landscape (*or* countryside); **2.** regional; **II.** *adv.* **3.** ***e-e ~ sehr schöne Gegend*** a beautiful area (*or* part of the country), a beauty spot; ***dort ist es ~ sehr schön*** *a.* the countryside around there is beautiful; ***~ schöne Strecke*** scenic route (*or* road); **4.** ***ein ~ gefärbter Akzent*** a slight regional accent; ***das ist ~ verschieden*** that varies from region to region
'**Land·schafts|ar·chi,tekt** *m* landscape architect; **~ar·chi·tek,tur** *f* landscape architecture, landscaping; **~bild** *n* landscape (painting); **~gärt·ner** *m* landscape gardener; **~ma·ler** *m* landscape painter (*or* artist); **~ma·le,rei** *f* landscape painting; **~pfle·ge** *f*, **~schutz** *m* conservation of the countryside; **~schutz·ge·biet** *n* nature reserve, conservation area
'**Land|schild·krö·te** *f* (land) tortoise; **~schul·heim** *n school's field cent|re (Am. -er) in the country*; **~sitz** *m* country house (*or* estate)
'**Lands·knecht** *m hist.* lansquenet; mercenary; F ***fluchen wie ein ~*** swear like a trooper
'**Lands·mann** *m* (-[e]s; -leute) (fellow) countryman, compatriot; ***was sind Sie für ein ~?*** where (*or* which part of the world) do you come from?; '**Lands·män·nin** [-mɛnɪn] *f* (-; -nen) (fellow) countrywoman, compatriot; '**Lands·mann·schaft** *f* homeland association; *association of regional compatriots stemming from Germany's former eastern territories*
'**Land|spit·ze** *f* point, promontory, headland; **~stadt** *f* country town; **~stra·ße** *f* country road; ***wir sind über die ~ gefahren*** *a.* we took the road (*or* route) through the country(side)
'**Land·strei·cher** *m* (-s; -) tramp
Land·strei·che·rei [lantʃtraɪçə'raɪ] *f* (-; *no pl.*) ⚖ vagrancy
'**Land|strei·fen** *m* strip (of land); **~streit·kräf·te** *pl.* land (*or* ground) forces; **~strich** *m* region, district
'**Land·tag** *m* (-[e]s; *no pl.*) *pol.* Landtag, state parliament; '**Land·tags·wah·len** *pl.* state elections
'**Land|tier** *n* terrestrial animal; **~trans·,port** *m* overland transport; **~trup·pen** *pl.* ⚔ land (*or* ground) forces
'**land·um,schlos·sen** *adj.* landlocked
Lan·dung ['landʊŋ] *f* (-; -en) landing; ⚓ disembarkation; ⚔ assault; *w.s.* arrival; ✈ ***zur ~ ansetzen*** come in to land; ***zur ~ zwingen*** force down
'**Lan·dungs|boot** *n* landing craft; **~brücke** *f*, **~steg** *m* gangway; **~trupp** *m* ⚔ landing party; **~trup·pen** *pl.* ⚔ landing force *sg.*
'**Land|ur·laub** *m* ⚓ shore leave; **~ver·mes·ser** *m* (land) surveyor; **~ver·mes·sung** *f* ordnance survey; **~vo·gel** *m* land bird; **~volk** *n* rural population
'**land·wärts** [-vɛrts] *adv.* landward(s)
'**Land|weg** *m* **1.** country road (*or* lane); **2.** overland route; ***auf dem ~*** by land, overland; **~wein** *m* vin ordinaire
'**Land·wirt** *m* (-[e]s; -e) farmer; '**Land·wirt·schaft** *f* (-; -en) **1.** *no pl.* agriculture, farming; **2.** farm; '**land·wirt·schaft·lich** *adj.* agricultural; ***~er Betrieb*** farm; ***~e Maschinen*** agricultural machinery *sg.*, farm equipment *sg.*; ***~e Hochschule*** agricultural college
'**Land·wirt·schafts...** *in cpds.* agricultural; **~hoch·schu·le** *f* agricultural college; **~mi,ni·ster** *m* minister of agriculture, farm minister; **~mi·ni,ste·ri·um** *n* ministry (*or* department) of agriculture
'**Land·zun·ge** *f* promontory
lang [laŋ] **I.** *adj. and adv.* **1.** a) long, b) tall; ***zehn Meter ~ und vier Meter breit*** ten metres (*Am.* meters) by four; ***sie sind gleich ~*** they're the same length; ***das Haar ~ tragen*** have long hair; ***e-n ~en Hals machen*** crane one's neck, *Am.* rubberneck; *fig.* ***sich des ~en und breiten*** (*or* ***~ und breit***) ***über et. auslassen*** expatiate on s.th.; → ***Bank***[1] 1, ***Gesicht***; **2.** long, (for) a long time; ***~e Jahre*** for years; ***seit ~em*** for a long time; ***vor nicht allzu ~er Zeit*** not so long ago; ***in nicht zu ~er Zeit*** before long; ***nicht ~e darauf*** not long after(wards); ***mir wird die Zeit ~*** the days are beginning to drag; ***er braucht immer ~e*** it always takes him a while, *contp.* he's so slow; ***~ werden*** *days*: get longer; ***drei Jahre ~*** for three years; ***die ganze Woche ~*** all week long, the whole week; ***~ anhaltend*** long, continuous; ***~ entbehrt*** (*or* ***vermißt***) sorely missed; ***das ist schon ~e her*** that was a long time ago; ***es ist schon ~e her, daß*** it's been a long time since, it's ages since; ***wie ~e lernen Sie schon Englisch?*** how long have you been learning English?; ***~e nicht*** not nearly ..., F not by a long chalk, nowhere near ...; (***noch***) ***~e nicht fertig*** (***gut genug*** *etc.*) not nearly ready (good enough *etc.*); *ist er fertig?* - ***noch ~e nicht*** F not by a long chalk, *iro.* you must be joking; ***so ~e wie*** as long as; ***so ~e bis*** till, until; ***da kannst du ~e warten*** F you can wait till the cows come home; ***du brauchst nicht ~e zu fragen*** you don't need to ask; ***er fragte nicht erst ~e*** he didn't stop to ask; ***das ist noch ~e kein Grund, um zu*** *inf.* that's no reason for *ger.*; ***deswegen brauchst du dir noch ~e nichts einzubilden*** don't imagine that's anything special; → ***dauern, kurz*** 4, ***länger, längst, Leitung*** 2, ***Lulatsch***; **II.** *dial. prp.* (*acc.*) along; ***die Straße ~*** along (*or* down) the street
'**lang·är·me·lig** [-ɛrməlɪç] *adj.* long-sleeved
'**lang·at·mig** [-a:tmɪç] *adj.* long-winded; wordy *text etc.*; '**Lang·at·mig·keit** *f* (-; *no pl.*) long-windedness
'**lang·bei·nig** [-baɪnɪç] *adj.* long-legged, F leggy
lan·ge ['laŋə] *adv.* → ***lang*** 2
Län·ge ['lɛŋə] *f* (-; -n) **1.** length (*a. time*); height; *geogr., ast.*, ⛵ longitude; *ling. and metrics*: long; ***20 Meter in der ~, mit e-r ~ von 20 Metern*** 20 metres (*Am.* meters) long (*or* in length); ***der ~ nach*** lengthwise, ***hinfallen***: fall flat on one's face, go sprawling; ***in s-r vollen ~ senden*** broadcast in full; *fig.* ***in die ~ ziehen*** draw (*or* drag) out, spin out *a tale*; ***sich in die ~ ziehen*** drag (on); F ***auf die ~*** in the long run; **2.** *sport*: length; ***mit einer ~ gewinnen*** win by a length; **3.** *fig.* longueur
'**län·ge·lang** *adv.*: ***~ hinfallen*** go sprawling (*or* flying)
lan·gen ['laŋən] (h) **I.** *v/i.* **1.** be enough (***für*** *acc.* for); ***das langt uns für die nächsten Tage*** *a.* that'll last us for the next few days; ***damit lange ich e-e Woche*** that'll last me a week; ***langt das?*** is that enough?, will that do?; F ***mir langt's*** I've had enough; F ***jetzt langt's mir aber!*** I've had enough of this (business), F that's it; **2.** ***~ nach*** *dat.* reach for, grab at; ***~ in*** *acc.* reach into; **3.** ***~ bis an*** *or* ***auf*** *acc.* reach to (*or* as far as); **II.** *v/t.*: ***j-m et. ~*** hand s.o. s.th.; F *fig.* ***j-m e-e ~*** F land s.o. one
län·gen ['lɛŋən] *v/t.* (h) **1.** ⚙ lengthen, elongate; **2.** *gastr.* thin down, stretch
Län·gen|ein·heit ['lɛŋən-] *f* unit of length; **~grad** *m* degree of longitude; **~kreis** *m* meridian; **~maß** *n* measure of length
län·ger ['lɛŋɐ] *adj. and adv.* **1.** (*comp. of lang*) longer; ***ich kann es nicht ~ ertragen*** I can't stand (*or* take) it any longer; ***je ~, je lieber*** the longer, the better; ***~ machen*** make *s.th.* longer, lengthen, *a.* let down *skirt etc.*; **2.** fairly long; (*a.* ***~e Zeit***) (for) quite a while, (for [quite]) some time; ***über ~e Zeiträume*** for (*or* over) prolonged periods (of time)
'**län·ger·fri·stig** [-frɪstɪç] **I.** *adj.* long(er)-term, for the long(er) term; **II.** *adv. plan etc.* for the long(er) term, for the future; *invest etc.* on a long(er)-term basis; ***~ gesehen*** seen in the long term
Lan·ger·hans-In·seln ['laŋɐhans] *pl. anat.* islets of Langerhans
'**lang|er·hofft** *adj.* long-hoped-for; **~er·sehnt** *adj.* long-awaited; **~er·war·tet** *adj.* long-awaited
'**Lan·ge·wei·le** *f* (-; *no pl.*) boredom; ***aus*** (*or* ***vor***) ***~*** out of (sheer) boredom; ***~ haben*** be (*or* feel) bored, suffer from boredom; ***sich die ~ vertreiben*** while away the time
'**Lang·fin·ger** F *m* thief; pickpocket; '**lang·fing·rig** [-fɪŋrɪç] *adj.* long-fingered; F *fig.* light-fingered
'**lang·fri·stig** [-frɪstɪç] **I.** *adj.* long-term; ✝ ***~e Anleihe*** long-term bond; ***~er Wechsel*** long(-dated) bill; **II.** *adv.*: (***~ gese-***

hen seen) in the long term; ~ ***investieren*** *etc.* invest *etc.* long term
'lang·ge·hegt [-gəhe:kt] *adj.* long-cherished (*or* -nourished, -nurtured) *hope etc.*
'lang·ge·hen F *fig. v/i.* (*irr.*, *sep.*, sn, → ***gehen***): ***wissen, wo's langgeht*** know what's what; ***j-m zeigen, wo's langgeht*** show s.o. what's what, tell s.o. a few home truths
'lang·ge·streckt *adj.* long, extended; *geogr. a.* extensive *mountain ridge etc.*
'Lang·haar·dackel *m* long-haired dachshund
'lang·haa·rig *adj.* long-haired
'Lang·haar·kat·ze *f* long-haired cat
'lang·hal·sig [-halzıç] *adj.* long-necked
'lang·jäh·rig [-jɛ:rıç] *adj.* longstanding; ***~e Freiheitsstrafe*** long prison sentence; ***~e Erfahrung*** (many) years of experience
'Lang·korn·reis *m* long-grain rice
'Lang·lauf *m* (-[e]s; *no pl.*) cross-country skiing; **'lang·lau·fen** *v/i.* (*only inf.*) do (*or* go) cross-country skiing; **'Lang·läu·fer** *m* cross-country skier
'Lang·lauf|schu·he *pl.* cross-country skiing boots; **~ski** *m* cross-country ski; **~strecke** *f* cross-country trail (*or* circuit)
'lang·le·big [-le:bıç] *adj.* long-lived (*a.* ⚙ *and fig.*); ✝ durable; *fig.* lasting; ***es war e-e ~e Angelegenheit*** it lasted (*or* was around) for a long time; **'Lang·le·big·keit** *f* (-; *no pl.*) longevity; ✝ durability
'lang·le·gen F *v/refl.* (*sep.*, h): ***sich ~*** have a lie-down, stretch out on the bed (*or* couch *etc.*)
läng·lich ['lɛŋlıç] *adj.* long; oblong; **~rund** *adj.* oval
'Lang·mut *f* (-; *no pl.*) patience, forbearance; **'lang·mü·tig** [-my:tıç] **I.** *adj.* patient, longsuffering; **II.** *adv.* patiently; **'Lang·mü·tig·keit** *f* → ***Langmut***
'lang·na·sig [-na:zıç] *adj.* long-nosed
Lan·go·bar·de [laŋo'bardə] *m* (-n; -n) *hist.* Langobard, Longobard; **lan·go·bar·disch** [laŋo'bardıʃ] *adj.* Langobardic, Longobardic, Lombard
'Lang·ohr F *n* a) Mister Hare, b) bunny rabbit, c) Neddy
längs [lɛŋs] **I.** *prp.* (*gen.*) along(side); **II.** *adv.* longwise
'Längs·ach·se *f* longitudinal axis
lang·sam ['laŋza:m] **I.** *adj.* slow; sluggish; heavy, plodding; *fig.* slow (on the uptake); ***~er werden*** slow down, slacken; **II.** *adv.* slowly *etc.*; gradually; ~, ***aber sicher*** slowly but surely, ***nähern wir uns dem Ziel:*** we're getting there (slowly but surely); ***immer ~!*** not so fast, F easy does it; *mot.* ***~ fahren!*** slow down; ***es wird ~ Zeit, daß er anruft*** it's time he called up; ***es wird ~ Zeit, daß du gehst*** you'd better be thinking about going; ***es wird mir ~ zuviel*** it's getting too much for me, it's beginning to get on top of me; **'Lang·sam·keit** *f* (-; *no pl.*) slowness; sluggishness; slackness
'lang·sam·tre·ten *v/i.* (*irr.*, *sep.*, h, → ***treten***) slow down, take things easy
'Längs|auf·riß *m* longitudinal view; **~bal·ken** *m* longitudinal beam, stringer
'Lang·schä·del *m* longhead
'lang·schä·de·lig *adj.* longheaded
'Lang|schiff *n* nave; **~schlä·fer** *m* late riser, F sleepyhead
'längs|ge·rich·tet *adj.* longitudinal; **~ge·streift** *adj.*: ***~es Kleid*** dress with vertical stripes

'Lang·spiel·plat·te *f* LP, long-playing record
'Längs|rich·tung *f* longitudinal direction; ***in der ~*** lengthways, lengthwise; **~schnitt** *m* longitudinal section; sectional elevation
'längs·seits [-zaıts] *adv. and prp.* (*gen.*) alongside *the ship etc.*
längst [lɛŋst] *adv.* long ago, long since; ***ich weiß es ~*** I've known that for a long time; ***das solltest du ~ wissen*** you really ought to know that; ***er sollte ~ dasein*** he should have been here long ago; ***das ist ~ vorbei*** (***vergessen***) that's long past (forgotten); ***als ich ankam, war er ~ weg*** when I arrived he had long since left; ***am ~en*** longest; → ***fällig***; ***~ nicht*** not nearly ..., F not by a long chalk, nowhere near ...; ***das ist ~ nicht so gut*** that's not nearly (F nowhere near) as good; ***er ist ~ nicht fertig*** he hasn't nearly finished yet, F he's nowhere near finished yet, he's still got a long way to go;
läng·stens ['lɛŋstəns] *adv.* a) at the latest, b) at (the) most
'lang·stie·lig [-ʃti:lıç] *adj.* long-handled *tool etc.*; long-stemmed *glass, rose etc.*
'Lang·strecke *f* long distance
'Lang·strecken|flug *m* long-haul flight; **~flug·zeug** *n* long-haul aircraft; **~kom,fort** *m mot.* long-distance comfort; **~lauf** *m* (long-)distance run *or* race; **~läu·fer** *m* (long-)distance runner; **~ra,ke·te** *f* long-range missile; **~waf·fe** *f* long-range weapon
Lan·gu·ste [laŋ'gʊstə] *f* (-; -n) rock lobster
lang·wei·len ['laŋvaılən] (h) **I.** *v/t.* bore (***zu Tode*** to death, to tears, stiff); **II.** *v/refl.*: ***sich ~*** be (*or* feel) bored; ***sich zu Tode ~*** be bored to death (*or* to tears, stiff, F out of one's tiny little mind);
Lang·weiler ['laŋvaılɐ] F *m* (-s; -) **1.** F bore; **2.** F slowcoach, *Am.* slowpoke;
lang·wei·lig ['laŋvaılıç] *adj.* boring, tedious; humdrum *life*; ***e-e ~e Sache*** *a.* F a drag; F ***~er Betrieb*** F slow show; F ***~er Verein*** F dull (*or* boring) lot; ***es war so was von ~*** it was an absolute (F a crushing) bore; **'Lang·wei·lig·keit** *f* (-; *no pl.*) boringness, boredom; tediousness, tedium
'Lang·wel·le *f radio*: long wave
'Lang·wel·len|be·reich *m* long-wave band; **~sen·der** *m* long-wave radio station (*or* transmitter)
lang·wie·rig ['laŋvi:rıç] *adj.* long-drawn-out; lengthy, prolonged, protracted; tedious; ***es war e-e ~e Sache*** *a.* it dragged on for a long time
'Lang·zeit|ar·beits·lo·se *m, f* (-n; -n) long-term unemployed; *pl.* the long-term unemployed (*pl.*); **~-EK'G** *n* long-term ECG (*Am.* EKG); **~ge·dächt·nis** *n* long-term memory; **~pro,gno·se** *f* long-term prediction (*or* forecast); **~pro,gramm** *n* long-term program(me); **~stu·die** *f*, **~un·ter,su·chung** *f* long-term study; **~ver·such** *m* long-term trial; **~wir·kung** *f* long-term effect(s *pl.*)
La·no·lin [lano'li:n] *n* (-s; *no pl.*) lanolin
Lan·ze ['lantsə] *f* (-; -n) lance; spear; *fig.* ***für j-n*** (***et.***) ***e-e ~ brechen*** go to battle (*or* take up the cudgels) for s.o. (s.th.)
'Lan·zen|spit·ze *f* lancehead; spearhead; **~ste·chen** *n hist.* joust(ing)
Lan·zet·te [lan'tsɛtə] *f* (-; -n) ⚕ lancet
Lan'zett·fisch·chen *n* lancelet

lan·zett·för·mig [lan'tsɛtfœrmıç] *adj.* lance-shaped
Lao·te [la'o:tə] *m* (-n; -n), **Lao·tin** [la'o:tın] *f* (-; -nen) Laotian; ***Laote sein*** *a.* come from Laos; **lao·tisch** [la'o:tıʃ] *adj.* Laotian, from Laos
la·pi·dar [lapi'da:ɐ] *adj.* terse, succinct
La·pis·la·zu·li [lapıs'la:tsuli] *m* (-; -) lapis lazuli
Lap·pa·lie [la'pa:lĭə] *f* (-; -n) little (*or* minor) thing, trivial matter, trifle
Lap·pe ['lapə] *m* (-n; -n) Lapp
Lap·pen ['lapən] *m* (-s; -) **1.** a) cloth, b) flannel, *Am.* washcloth, c) F *fig.* rag, d) *sl.* smacker; F *fig.* ***j-m durch die ~ gehen*** a) give s.o. the slip, b) slip right through s.o.'s fingers; **2.** *anat.*, ♣ lobe; **3.** ⚕ flap
läp·pern ['lɛpɐn] (h) **I.** *v/t. and v/i.* sip; **II.** F *v/refl.*: ***sich ~*** add up; ***es läppert sich*** it all adds up
lap·pig ['lapıç] *adj.* **1.** limp; flabby *skin*; **2.** *anat.*, ♣ lobed
Lap·pin ['lapın] *f* (-; -nen) Lapp (woman)
läp·pisch ['lɛpıʃ] *adj.* silly; ridiculous; ***wegen ~er zehn Mark regt er sich auf*** F he makes a fuss about a measly ten marks
Lapp·län·der ['laplɛndɐ] *m* (-s; -), **Lapp·län·de·rin** ['laplɛndərın] *f* (-; -nen) Laplander; **lapp·län·disch** ['laplɛndıʃ] *adj.* Lapp, from Lapland
Lap·sus ['lapsʊs] *m* (-; - ['lapsu:s]): (***e-n ~ begehen*** make a) slip
Lär·che ['lɛrçə] *f* (-; -n) larch
La·ri·fa·ri [lari'fa:ri] *n* (-s; *no pl.*) nonsense, rubbish
Lärm [lɛrm] *m* (-s; *no pl.*) noise; racket, din; ***macht nicht so e-n ~*** *a.* keep the noise down; ***bei dem ~ kann ich nicht schlafen*** I can't sleep with that noise (going on); ***~ am Arbeitsplatz*** workplace noise; *fig.* ***großen ~ um e-e Sache machen*** make a big fuss about s.th.; ***viel ~ um nichts*** much ado about nothing, (it's) just a lot of noise, **machen:** make a big thing out of nothing; ***~ schlagen*** make a noise; **~be·kämp·fung** *f* noise abatement (*or* control); **~be·lä·sti·gung** *f* noise pollution; **2emp·find·lich** *adj.* sensitive to noise; ***sie ist sehr ~*** *a.* she's got very sensitive ears
lär·men ['lɛrmən] *v/i.* (h) make a (lot of) noise; *radio, music etc.*: blare (away); **'lär·mend** *adj.* noisy
lar·moy·ant [larmŏa'jant] *adj.* maudlin, F soppy; lachrymose, F whing(e)ing
'Lärm|pe·gel *m* noise (emission) level; **~schlep·pe** *f* ✈ noise footprint
'Lärm·schutz *m* noise protection; **~wall** *m* noise barrier
'Lärm|taub·heit *f* noise deafness; **~tep·pich** *m* sonic boom carpet; **~wand** *f* noise barrier; **~zo·ne** *f* noise field
Lar·ve ['larvə] *f* (-; -n) **1.** *zo.* larva; **2.** mask; **3.** *fig.* face
La·ryn·gi·tis [larʏn'gi:tıs] *f* (-; -gitiden [-gi'ti:dən]) ⚕ laryngitis
La·ryn·go·lo·ge [larʏŋgo'lo:gə] *m* (-n; -n) laryngologist
las [la:s] *pret. of* ***lesen***[1] *and* ***lesen***[2]
La·sa·gne [la'zanjə] *f* (-; -n) lasagna
lasch [laʃ] *adj.* limp *handshake etc.*; slack, lax; *gastr.* tasteless, insipid; ***~er Typ*** F wimp
La·sche ['laʃə] *f* (-; -n) strap; tongue *of shoe*; loop; flap *of an envelope etc.*
La·ser ['le:zɐ] *m* (-s; -) *phys.* laser; **~ab·ta-**

stung *f* laser scanning; **~chir·ur,gie** *f* laser surgery; **~drucker** *m* laser (beam) printer; **~kopf** *m* laser head; **~strahl** *m* laser beam; **~tech·nik** *f* laser technology
la·sie·ren [la'zi:rən] *v/t.* (h) glaze; **La'sie·rung** *f* (-; -en) **1.** *no pl.* glazing; **2.** glaze
Lä·si·on [lɛ'zĭo:n] *f* (-; -en) ⚕ lesion, injury
las·sen (ließ, lassen *with inf.*, h) **I.** *v/t.* **1.** let; ***j-n gehen*** (***schlafen*** *etc.*) ~ let s.o. go (sleep *etc.*); ***er hat es fallen*** ~ he dropped it; ***sehen*** ~ show; ***laß mich mal sehen!*** let me see (*or* have a look); ***laß ihn nur kommen!*** just let him come; ***laß mich nur machen!*** (just) leave it to me; ***er läßt sich nichts sagen*** he won't listen (to anyone); ***er ließ ihn ins Haus*** he let him in(to the house); ***Wasser in die Wanne*** ~ run ([the] water into) the bath; *sl.* ***einen*** (***fahren***) ~ *sl.* let off; → ***bieten, schmecken*** II, ***sehen*** II, ***stören*** I, ***träumen*** II; **2.** ***j-n et. tun*** ~ get s.o. to do s.th., make s.o. do s.th.; ***er ließ ihn versetzen*** he had him transferred; ***er ließ sich e-n Anzug machen*** he had a suit made (for himself); ***sich et. schicken*** ~ have s.th. sent; ***sich e-n Zahn ziehen*** ~ have a tooth (taken) out; ***er ließ den Arzt*** (***die Polizei***) ***kommen*** he sent for *or* called the doctor (he called the police); ***er ließ mich warten*** he kept me waiting; ***ich habe mir sagen*** ~ I've heard (*or* been told); ~ ***Sie mich wissen*** let me know; ***ich lass' mich so nicht anreden*** I won't be spoken to like that, I won't have anyone speak to me like that; F ***ich lass' mich doch nicht verarschen*** *a.* who do they *etc.* take me for (*or* think I am)?; → ***laufen*** 1, 5, 7; **3.** ***laß(t) uns gehen!*** let's go; ***laßt*** (*or* ***lasset***) ***uns beten*** let us pray; **4.** ***laß es*** (***sein***) leave it, don't bother; ***laß das!*** don't!, stop it!; ~ ***wir das*** enough of that; ***laß das Weinen*** stop crying; ***laß den Lärm*** stop that noise; ***ich kann's nicht*** ~ I can't help it; ***er kann das Streiten nicht*** ~ he 'will (*or* 'must) argue; ***er kann's einfach nicht*** ~ he 'will keep on doing it; **5.** (*p.p.* gelassen, h) leave; ***alles so ~, wie es ist*** leave things as they are; ***die Tür offen*** ~ leave the door open; ***et.*** (***j-n***) ***hinter sich*** ~ leave s.th. (s.o.) behind; F ***das kann man so ~!*** (mm,) not bad; → ***brennen*** II, ***Ruhe***; **6.** (*p.p.* gelassen, h) leave; ***wo soll ich mein Gepäck ~?*** where shall I leave (*or* put) my luggage?; ***wo habe ich*** (***bloß***) ***m-n Schirm gelassen?*** where did I put (*or* what's happened to) my umbrella?; **7.** (*p.p.* gelassen, h) ***j-m et.*** ~ leave s.o. s.th.; ***ich lasse Ihnen das Bild für 400 Dollar*** you can have the picture for 400; ***j-m fünf Minuten*** ~ give s.o. five minutes; ***das muß man ihm*** ~ you've got to hand it to him; → ***Sorge, Vortritt, Wille, Zeit***; **8.** (*p.p.* gelassen, h) *poet.* leave *one's country, wife etc.*; ***sein Leben*** ~ lose one's life, be killed, die, ***für et.***: die (*or* lay down one's life) for s.th.; **II.** *v/refl.*: ***das läßt sich*** (***schon***) ***machen*** (*or* ***einrichten***) I'm sure we could manage that; ***es läßt sich nicht beweisen*** it can't be proved; ***das Wort läßt sich nicht übersetzen*** this word is untranslatable; ***es läßt sich nicht leugnen, daß*** there's no denying that; ***es läßt sich vielfach verwenden*** it can be put to a number of uses; ***es läßt sich gut mischen*** (***drehen***) it mixes well (turns easily); F ***der Wein läßt sich trinken*** this wine's not bad at all; → ***einfallen*** 1, ***hören*** I, ***sehen*** II; **III.** *v/i.* (*p.p.* gelassen, h): ~ ***von*** *dat.* a) leave *s.o.*, b) give up *s.th.*; **IV.** ♀ *n* (-s; *no pl.*) → ***tun*** IV
läs·sig ['lɛsɪç] **I.** *adj.* casual (*a. clothes*); nonchalant; F ***er ist total*** ~ F he's so laid-back; **II.** *adv.* easily, F no problem; ~ ***gekleidet*** dressed very casually, in casual dress; ***wir haben's ~ geschafft*** F we did it no problem, *sl.* it was a cinch; **'Läs·sig·keit** *f* (-, *no pl.*) casualness; nonchalance, offhandedness; ***die ~, mit der er es macht*** *a.* the offhanded way (in which) he does it
läß·lich ['lɛslɪç] *adj.*: *eccl.* ***~e Sünde*** venial (*or* pardonable) sin
Las·so ['laso] *m, n* (-s; -s) lasso, *Am. a.* lariat
Last [last] *f* (-; -en) load (*a.* ⚓, ✈); weight; tonnage; *fig.* burden; ⚖ ***die ~ der Beweise*** the weight of evidence; ***steuerliche*** ~ tax burden; ***soziale ~en*** welfare costs; ***zu ~en*** *gen.* ✝ payable by, to the debit of *s.o.'s* account, *fig.* at the expense of; ***der Betrag geht zu ~en*** *gen.* the amount is payable by (*or* will be debited to *s.o.'s* account); ***wir buchen es zu Ihren ~en*** we will debit (*or* charge) it to your account; ***j-m zur ~ fallen*** (***werden***) be(come) a burden to s.o., bother s.o.; ***ich will Ihnen nicht zur ~ fallen*** I don't want to be a nuisance; ***sich selbst e-e*** *or* ***zur ~ sein*** (***werden***) be(come) a burden to o.s.; ***j-m et. zur ~ legen*** charge s.o. with s.th.
'Last·au·to *n* → ***Lastkraftwagen***
la·sten ['lastən] *v/i.* (h) **1.** ~ ***auf*** *dat.* weigh down (*a. fig.*); *fig.* ***die Verantwortung lastet auf ihr*** the (burden of) responsibility rests on her (shoulders), she bears the (burden of) responsibility; **2.** ***auf dem Grundstück lastet e-e Hypothek*** the property is encumbered by a mortgage
'La·sten|auf·zug *m* goods lift, *Am.* freight elevator; **~aus·gleich** *m* ✝ equalization of (war) burdens
'la·stend *fig. adj.* oppressive *heat etc.*
'la·sten·frei *adj.* ✝ unencumbered
'La·sten·ver·tei·lung *fig. f* burden-sharing
La·ster[1] ['lastɐ] F *m* (-s; -) lorry, *esp. Am.* truck
'La·ster[2] *n* (-s; -) **1.** vice; **2.** F ***langes*** ~ F beanpole
Lä·ste·rei [lɛstə'raɪ] *f* (-; -en) negative remarks *pl.* (***über*** *acc.* about); ***hör auf mit der*** ~ stop making such negative remarks, ***über d-n Nachbarn***: *a.* stop running your neighbo(u)r down; **Lä·ste·rer** ['lɛstərɐ] *m* (-s; -) **1.** *eccl.* blasphemer; **2.** → ***Lästermaul*** 2
'la·ster·haft *adj.* dissolute; profligate; corrupt; **'La·ster·haf·tig·keit** *f* (-; *no pl.*) dissoluteness; profligacy; corruptness, corruption
'La·ster|höh·le *f* den of iniquity; **~le·ben** *n* life of sin
lä·ster·lich ['lɛstɐlɪç] *adj.* blasphemous
Lä·ster·maul ['lɛstɐ-] F *n* **1.** vicious (*or* wagging) tongue; **2.** ***er ist ein*** ~ he's got a vicious tongue, he's always saying nasty things about people, *esp. Am.* he's always bad-mouthing people; **lä·stern** ['lɛstɐn] F *v/i.* (h) criticize (***über*** *acc. s.o., s.th.*); gossip, spread gossip (about); ***über j-n*** ~ *a.* F go on about s.o., talk about s.o. behind his (*or* her) back, say nasty things about s.o., *esp. Am.* bad-mouth s.o.; *sl.* bitch about s.o.; **Lä·ste·rung** ['lɛstərʊŋ] *f* (-; -en) blasphemy; **'Lä·ster·zun·ge** *f* vicious (*or* wagging) tongue
'Last|esel *m* (pack) mule; *fig.* workhorse; **~fah·rer** *m* → ***Lastwagenfahrer***
lä·stig ['lɛstɪç] *adj.* annoying; troublesome; tiresome; (***j-m***) ~ ***sein*** be a nuisance; ***ein ~er Mensch*** a pest; ***er ist einfach*** ~ *a.* he just gets in the way; ***es wird mir langsam*** ~ it's getting to be a nuisance, it's beginning to get on my nerves; ***~e Aufgabe*** tiresome (*or* irksome) task; ***ist dir die Musik ~?*** does the music bother you (*or* get on your nerves)?; ***ich will euch nicht ~ fallen*** I don't want to be a nuisance
'Last|kahn *m* barge; **~kraft·wa·gen** *m* lorry, *esp. Am.* truck; **~pferd** *n* pack horse; **~schiff** *n* freighter
'Last·schrift *f* ✝ a) debit note, b) direct debit; **~ver·fah·ren** *n* direct debiting
'Last·tier *n* beast of burden
'Last·wa·gen *m* lorry, *esp. Am.* truck; **~an·hän·ger** *m* truck trailer; **~fah·rer** *m* lorry (*or* truck) driver, F trucker
'Last|,wi·der·stand *m* ⚡ load resistance; **~zug** *m mot.* truck trailer, *Am. a.* F rig
La·sur [la'zu:ɐ] *f* (-; -en [-rən]) glaze; **~farbe** *f* transparent colo(u)r; **~lack** *m* clear (*or* transparent) varnish
las·ziv [las'tsi:f] *adj.* lascivious
Las·zi·vi·tät [lastsivi'tɛ:t] *f* (-; *no pl.*) lasciviousness
La·tein [la'taɪn] *n* (-s; *no pl.*) Latin; *fig.* ***mit s-m ~ am Ende sein*** be at a loss as to what to do (next); ***ich bin mit m-m ~ am Ende*** *a.* I give up
La'tein·ame·ri,ka·ner *m*, **la'tein·ame·ri,ka·nisch** *adj.* Latin American
la·tei·nisch [la'taɪnɪʃ] *adj.* Latin; ***auf*** ~ in Latin; ***die ~e Schrift*** the Latin alphabet
la·tent [la'tɛnt] *adj.* latent; **La·tenz** [la'tɛnts] *f* (-; *no pl.*) latency; **La'tenz·zeit** *f* latency period
La·te·rit [late'ri:t] *m* (-s; -e) *geol.* laterite
La·ter·ne [la'tɛrnə] *f* (-; -n) lantern; streetlamp; F *fig.* ***solche Leute kannst du mit der ~ suchen*** there aren't many of that sort around
La'ter·nen|ga,ra·ge F *f* F kerbside garage; **~par·ker** F *m* F kerbside parker; **~pfahl** *m* lamppost; **~,um·zug** *m* lantern procession
La·tex ['la:tɛks] *m* (-; Latizes ['la:titse:s]) latex
La·ti·num [la'ti:nʊm] *n* (-s; *no pl.*) *ped.* Latin proficiency certificate
La·tri·ne [la'tri:nə] *f* (-; -n) latrine
La'tri·nen|ge·rücht F *n*, **~pa,ro·le** F *f* latrine rumo(u)r
Lat·sche[1] ['latʃə] *f* (-; -n) ♣ dwarf pine
Lat·sche[2] ['la:tʃə] *f* (-; -n), **'Lat·schen** *m* (-s; -) a) (old) slipper, b) scruffy old shoe; F *fig.* ***aus den Latschen kippen*** F keel over; ***ich bin fast aus den Latschen gekippt*** F I nearly fell over backwards
lat·schen ['la:tʃən] F **I.** *v/i.* (sn) traipse (*or* slouch) along; ***latsch nicht so!*** walk properly!; **II.** *v/t.* (h): ***j-m eine*** ~ F land s.o. one; **lat·schig** ['la:tʃɪç] F *adj.* **1.** slouching, shuffling *gait etc.*; **2.** slack; slow
Lat·te ['latə] *f* (-; -n) slat; *sport:* (cross)bar; ***~!*** it's hit the bar; F *fig.* ***lange*** ~ F beanpole; F ***e-e*** (***lange***) ~ ***von Fragen*** *etc.* F

a whole string of questions *etc.*; F ***nicht alle auf der ~ haben*** F have a screw loose (somewhere); F ***j-n auf der ~ haben*** F have it in for s.o.

'Lat·ten|ki·ste *f* crate; **~rost** *m* a) duckboards *pl.*, b) ⚙ grid, c) slatted (bed)-frame; **~schuß** *m*, **~tref·fer** *m soccer*: shot against the bar; **~zaun** *m* picket fence, paling

Lat·tich ['latɪç] *m* (-s; -e) 🌱 lettuce

Latz [lats] *m* (-es; Lätze [lɛtsə]) a) bib, b) pinafore, c) flap, fly; F ***j-m eine vor den ~ knallen*** F give s.o. a punch (*or* thump)

Lätz·chen ['lɛtsçən] *n* (-s; -) bib

'Latz·ho·se *f*: (***e-e ~*** a pair of) dungarees *pl.*

lau [laʊ] *adj.* lukewarm (*a. fig.*); *meteor.* mild

Laub [laʊp] *n* (-[e]s; *no pl.*) foliage; leaves *pl.*; ***in ~ stehen*** be in leaf; **~baum** *m* deciduous tree

Lau·be ['laʊbə] *f* (-; -n) **1.** arbo(u)r, bower; summer house; F ***fertig ist die ~!*** F and Bob's your uncle!; **2.** △ porch; portico; arcade

'Lau·ben|gang *m* **1.** pergola; **2.** △ arcade, loggia, covered way; **~ko·lo,nie** *f* allotment area

'Laub|fär·bung *f* colo(u)r(s *pl.*) of the leaves (*or* foliage); **~frosch** *m* tree frog; **~grün** *n* leaf green; **~holz** *n* a) hardwood, b) deciduous tree

'Laub·hüt·ten·fest *n* Feast of Tabernacles

'Laub·sä·ge *f* fretsaw; **~ar·beit** *f* fretwork

'Laub·sän·ger *m zo.* wood warbler

'laub·tra·gend *adj.* leafy, leafed

'Laub|wald *m* deciduous forest; *pl. a.* deciduous woodland *sg.*; **~werk** *n* (-[e]s; *no pl.*) foliage; △ *a.* leafwork

Lauch [laʊx] *m* (-[e]s; *no pl.*) 🌱 leek

Lau·da·tio [laʊ'da:tsɪo] *f* (-; -nes [laʊda-'tsɪo:ne:s]) eulogy

Lau·des ['laʊde:s] *pl. eccl.* lauds

Lau·er ['laʊɐ] *f*: ***auf der ~ sein nach*** *dat.* be on the lookout for; ***auf der ~ liegen*** be lying in wait; **'lau·ern** *v/i.* (h) lie in wait (***auf*** *acc.* for); *danger*: lurk; ***auf e-e Gelegenheit*** *etc.* **~** be on the lookout (*or* watch out) for an opportunity *etc.*; **'lau·ernd** *adj.* lurking *danger etc.*; shifty *look*

Lauf [laʊf] *m* (-[e]s; Läufe ['lɔʏfə]) **1.** a) *no pl.* run(ning), b) race; heat, run; ***100-Meter-~*** hundred-metre (*Am.* -meter) sprint; ***in vollem ~*** F (at) full tilt; **2.** *no pl.* movement, motion; flow; ⚙ action, running, operation; **3.** *no pl. fig.* course; ***s-n ~ nehmen*** take its course; ***freien ~ lassen*** *dat.* let *s.th.* take its course, allow free (*or* full) rein to *s.th.*, let *one's emotions, imagination* run wild; ***der ~ der Ereignisse*** the course of events; ***der ~ der Geschichte*** the tide of history; ***das ist der ~ der Dinge*** that's the way things are, that's life; ***den Dingen ihren ~ lassen*** let things take their course; ***den ~ der Dinge aufhalten*** stop the course of events, *w.s.* hold up history; ***im ~e*** *gen.* in the course of *our conversation etc.*; ***im ~e der nächsten Woche*** *a.* some time next week; ***im ~e der Jahre*** over the years; ***im ~e der Zeit*** in time, as time went on; **4.** *no pl.* ***am oberen*** (***unteren***) ***~ des Indus*** along the upper (lower) reaches of the Indus; **5.** ♪ run; roulade; **6.** barrel; ***mit zwei Läufen*** double-barrel(l)ed; ***vor den ~ bekommen*** *hunt. and fig.*: get *an animal etc.* in one's sights; **7.** *zo.* leg, foot; **~ach·se** *f* ⚙ running axle; **~bahn** *f* career; ***gehobene ~*** profession; ***e-e ~ einschlagen*** choose (*or* take up) a career; **~bur·sche** *m* errand boy (*a. fig. contp.*), *Am. a.* F gofer; *usu. fig. contp.* ***für j-n den ~n machen*** (*or* ***spielen***) run errands for s.o., fetch and carry for s.o.; **~dis·zi,plin** *f sport*: running event

lau·fen ['laʊfən] (lief, gelaufen) **I.** *v/i.* (sn) **1.** run, rush, race; ***gelaufen kommen*** come running along; ***lauf!*** run!, quick!; ***ein Pferd ~ lassen*** run a horse; ***ein Schiff auf ein Riff*** *etc.* ***~ lassen*** run a ship onto a reef *etc.*; → *a.* **7**; → ***Arm, Grund*** 1, ***Strand***; **2.** walk, go (on foot); ***viel ~*** do a lot of walking; ***gern ~*** like walking; **3.** ⚙, *mot. etc.* run; go, work; **4.** ***~ um*** *acc.* revolve (*or* move) round *the sun etc.*; **5.** *line, road etc.*: run (***durch*** *acc.* through); *liquid, a. sweat, blood etc.*: run, *tears*: *a.* stream (***über j-s Gesicht*** down s.o.'s face); ***Wasser ~ lassen in*** *acc.* run water into *s.th.*; → ***Rücken***; **6.** run, stretch (***von*** *dat.* ***... bis an*** *acc. or* ***zu*** *dat.* from ... to); **7.** *fig.* be under way; *film*: run, be on, be showing; *contract etc.*: be valid; ***~ bis*** *acc.* (***über ... Jahre***) *a.* run until (for ... years); ***der Antrag läuft*** the application is being considered; ***das Abonnement läuft noch drei Monate*** the subscription runs (*or* is valid) for another three months; ***das Stück lief drei Monate*** the play ran for three months (*or* had a three-month run); ***die Dinge ~ lassen*** let things ride; ***die Sache ist gelaufen*** a) it's all over (*or* settled), b) everything's all right (*Am.* alright), c) there's nothing you *etc.* can do about it now; F ***wie läuft es so?*** how are things?, how are you getting on?; F ***da läuft nichts!*** F nothing doing!; F ***das ist ein Ding, das nicht läuft*** it's just not on, you can forget it; → ***Name*** *etc.*; **8.** *nose, eyes etc.*: run; *sore*: weep; *candle*: drip; *container*: leak; *butter, chocolate, ice cream etc.*: melt; *cheese*: be runny; **II.** *v/t.* **9.** (sn) run, do; ***das Auto läuft 160 Stundenkilometer*** the car does 100 miles an hour; **10.** (h) ***sich ein Loch in den Socken ~*** wear a hole into one's sock; ***sich Blasen*** (***an den Füßen***) ***~*** get blisters (on one's feet) from walking; → ***Gefahr, Sturm, wund***; **III.** *v/refl.* (h): ***sich müde ~*** wear o.s. out running; ***sich warm ~*** warm up, *sport*: *a.* do a warm-up run; ⚙ ***sich heiß ~*** overheat; **IV.** *v/impers.* (h): ***es läuft sich schlecht hier*** it's hard to walk (*or* run *etc.*) along here, F it's hard going along here; ***es läuft sich gut*** (***schlecht***) ***in diesen Schuhen*** these shoes are very (un)comfortable to walk in; **V.** ♀ *n* (-s; *no pl.*) a) running, b) walking

'lau·fend I. *adj.* **1.** *engine etc.*: running; ***bei ~em Motor*** with the engine running (*or* on); **2.** *fig.* a) current; continuous; regular, b) ongoing, c) ✝ running, in circulation; *patent*: pending; ***~en Monats*** of this month; ***~e Berichterstattung*** running commentary; ***~e Kosten*** overheads; ***~e Nummer*** (serial) number; ***~e Nummern*** consecutive numbers; ***~e Rechnung*** current account; ***~e Wartung*** (***Prüfung***) routine maintenance (check); ***auf dem ~en sein*** be up to date (***über*** *acc.* on), be in the picture (about); ***j-n*** (***sich***) ***auf dem ~en halten*** keep s.o. informed *or* posted (keep up with things); ***et. aufs ~e bringen*** bring s.th. up to date, update s.th.; **II.** *adv.* a) continuously, b) increasingly; ***~ besser werden*** get better and better (all the time); ***~ zunehmen*** (***abnehmen***) put on (lose) more and more weight; ***wir haben ~ zu tun*** there's (always) plenty of work to do, there's no shortage of work

'lau·fen·las·sen *v/t.* (*irr., sep.*, h, → ***lassen***): ***j-n ~*** a) let s.o. go, b) let s.o. off; ***ein Tier ~*** let an animal go, set an animal free

Läu·fer ['lɔʏfɐ] *m* (-s; -) **1.** *sport*: runner; **2.** *chess*: bishop; **3.** a) rug, b) runner, c) stair carpet; **4.** ⚡ rotor

Lau·fe·rei [laʊfə'raɪ] *f* (-; -en) running around; *w.s.* ***j-m ~en bereiten*** cause s.o. a lot of bother (*or* trouble)

Läu·fe·rin [lɔʏfərɪn] *f* (-; -nen) *sport*: runner

'Lauf|feu·er *n* brush fire; *fig.* ***sich wie ein ~ verbreiten*** spread like wildfire; **~flä·che** *f* tread *of tire*; running surface *of ski*; **~ge·räusch** *n* running noise; **~ge·schirr** *n* walking harness; **~ge·schwin·dig·keit** *f* ⚙ running speed; **~ge·wicht** *n* sliding weight; **~git·ter** *n* playpen

läu·fig ['lɔʏfɪç] *adj.*: ***~e Hündin*** bitch on heat

'Lauf|jun·ge *m* → ***Laufbursche***; **~kat·ze** *f* ⚙ crab; **~kran** *m* travel(l)ing crane; **~kund·schaft** *f* casual customers *pl.*; passing trade

'Lauf·ma·sche *f* ladder, run

'lauf·ma·schen·si·cher *adj.* ladder-proof, runproof

'Lauf|num·mer *f* serial (*or* consecutive) number; **~paß** *iro. m*: ***j-m den ~ geben*** give s.o. his (*or* her) marching orders, *Am.* give s.o. the pink slip, F give s.o. the boot, F ditch (*or* drop, jilt) s.o.; ***den ~ bekommen*** F get the boot, *boyfriend etc.*: *a.* F be ditched (*or* dropped, jilted); **~plan·ke** *f* gangplank; **~rad** *n* running wheel; *mot.* impeller; *turbine*: runner; **~rich·tung** *f* direction (of movement); **~rie·men** *m* drive belt; **~rol·le** *f* ⚙ roller; **~rost** *m* duckboards *pl.*; **~schie·ne** *f* guide rail, track; **~schrift** *f* moving screen; **~schritt** *m* run, jog; ⚔ double; ***im ~ ins Büro eilen*** (***die Straße überqueren***) run to the office (across the street); **~schu·he** *pl.* **1.** walking shoes; **2.** *sport*: trainers; **~soh·le** *f* outer sole, outsole; **~sport** *m* running; **~stall** *m* playpen; **~steg** *m* catwalk; **~stil** *m sport*: running style; **~stuhl** *m* (baby) walker; **~trai·ning** *n* running; **~vo·gel** *m* running bird; **~werk** *n* ⚙ drive; *computer*: *a.* disk drive; mechanism; 🚂 *etc.* running gear; F *fig.* F pins *pl.*; **~wett·be·werb** *m* race; **~zeit** *f* **1.** term, life *of contract etc.*; repayment period *of loan etc.*; **2.** *film etc.*: run; length, running time; **3.** ⚙ hours *pl.* of operation; (service) life; **~zet·tel** *m* memo; control slip *on files*

Lau·ge ['laʊgə] *f* (-; -n) lye; brine; suds *pl.*; **'lau·gen** *v/t.* (h) lye; **'lau·gen·ar·tig** *adj.* alkaline

'Lau·gen|bad *n* alkaline bath; **~bre·zel** *f* salt pretzel; **~salz** *n* alkaline salt

Lau·heit ['laʊhaɪt] *f* (-; *no pl.*) *esp. fig.* lukewarmness; *meteor.* mildness

Lau·ne ['laʊnə] *f* (-; -n) **1.** mood; ***guter*** (***schlechter***) ***~*** in a good (bad) mood; ***bester ~*** in a very good (F a great) mood, on top of the world; ***~n haben*** be moody, be subject to moods; ***er hat*** (***so***) ***s-e***

~n he has his little moods; ***j-n bei ~ halten*** keep s.o. in a good (*or* in the) mood, keep s.o. happy, humo(u)r s.o.; ***du hast mir die ~ gründlich verdorben*** you've really spoilt my day; → ***Lust***; **2.** whim; ***aus e-r ~ heraus*** on a whim; ***aus e-r ~ heraus haben wir den Wagen gekauft*** *a.* we just decided on the spur of the moment to buy the car; ***es war nur so e-e ~ von mir*** it was just one of my (little) whims; ***~n des Schicksals*** *etc.* vagaries of fortune *etc.*; ***~ der Natur*** freak of nature

'lau·nen·haft *adj.* moody, subject to moods; **'Lau·nen·haf·tig·keit** *f* (-; *no pl.*) moodiness

lau·nig ['laʊnɪç] *adj.* humorous; witty

lau·nisch ['laʊnɪʃ] *adj.* **1.** moody; **2.** fickle, capricious; **3.** *meteor.* changeable

Laus [laʊs] *f* (-; Läuse ['lɔʏzə]) louse (*pl.* lice); *fig.* ***dem ist wohl e-e ~ über die Leber gelaufen*** I wonder what's eating (*or* biting) him

'Laus·bub *dial. m* (-en; -en) rascal

'laus·bu·ben·haft *adj.* impish

'Laus·bu·ben·streich *m* schoolboy (*or* silly) prank

'laus·bü·bisch [-byːbɪʃ] *adj.* mischievous

Lausch|ak·ti,on *f*, **~an·griff** ['laʊʃ-] *m* bugging operation, *a. pl.* electronic eavesdropping

lau·schen ['laʊʃən] *v/i.* (h) listen (*dat. or* ***auf*** *acc.* to); strain one's ears (for); eavesdrop (on), listen (in on)

Lausch·ge·rät ['laʊʃ-] *n* intercept set

lau·schig ['laʊʃɪç] *adj.*: ***~es Plätzchen*** (***~er Winkel***) nice quiet spot (corner)

Lau·se·jun·ge ['laʊzə-] F *m* rascal, (little) devil; **'lau·se'kalt** F *adj.* (absolutely) freezing; **'Lau·se·kerl** F *m* real devil

lau·sen ['laʊzən] *v/t. and v/refl.* (h): ***j-n*** (***sich***) ~ pick s.o.'s (one's) lice, delouse s.o. (o.s.); → ***Affe***

Lau·se·pack ['laʊzə-] F *n* bunch of good-for-nothings

lau·sig ['laʊzɪç] F **I.** *adj.* dreadful, F lousy; ***wegen ~er 10 Mark!*** F for the sake of 10 measly marks; **II.** *adv.*: ***~ viel Geld*** F pots of money, ***haben:*** *a.* F be rolling in it; ***~ kalt*** (absolutely) freezing

laut[1] [laʊt] **I.** *adj.* loud *voice, music etc., a. fig. colo(u)r*; noisy *street, machine etc.*; ***~er Schrei*** loud scream; ***~es Geräusch*** loud noise; ***~e Nachbarn*** noisy neighbo(u)rs; ***~ werden*** a) raise one's voice, start , b) *fig. request etc.*: be expressed, *protests*: be heard, *secret etc.*: get out; *fig.* ***es wurden Gerüchte ~, daß*** it was rumo(u)red that; ***laß das ja nicht ~ werden*** keep that to yourself; **II.** *adv.* loud(ly); noisily; *talk etc.* in a loud voice, loud; ***~ und deutlich*** loud and clear, openly; ***~ lesen*** read aloud; ***~ denken*** (*or* ***überlegen***) think aloud; ***~er, bitte!*** speak up, please; ***er schrie, so ~ er konnte*** he screamed at the top of his voice; *fig.* ***das kannst du ~ sagen*** you can say that again

laut[2] *prp.* (*gen. or dat.*) according to; ⚜ as per; ***~ Befehl*** as ordered, *gen.*: by order of; ***~ Vorschrift*** (*or* ***Verordnung***) as prescribed (*gen.* by)

Laut *m* (-[e]s; -e) sound (*a. ling.*); ***keinen ~ von sich geben*** not to say a word (*or* utter a sound); ***er gab keinen ~ mehr von sich*** *a.* F there wasn't another peep from him; ***~ geben*** a) *dog*: give tongue, b) F say something, speak up (*or* out), react, say what one wants; **~ar,chiv** *n* sound archives *pl.*; **~bil·dung** *f* articulation

Lau·te ['laʊtə] *f* (-; -n) ♪ lute

lau·ten ['laʊtən] *v/i.* (h) *text*: read, run, *line etc.*: go; *answer, request, opinion etc.*: be; sound; ***wie lautet der Brief*** (***die Antwort***)? what does the letter say (what's the answer)?; ***der Paß lautet auf m-n Namen*** the passport is in my name; ***das Urteil lautet auf ein Jahr Gefängnis*** the sentence is one year's imprisonment

läu·ten ['lɔʏtən] (h) **I.** *v/i.* ring; toll; tinkle; ***nach j-m ~*** ring for s.o.; *fig.* ***ich habe etwas davon ~ hören*** I heard something (*or* noises) to that effect; **II.** *v/t.* ring; **III.** *v/impers.*: ***es läutet*** a) there's somebody at the door, b) *ped. etc.* the bell's ringing; **IV.** ♀ *n* (-s; *no pl.*) ringing

Lau·te·nist [laʊtə'nɪst] *m* (-en; -en), **'Lau·ten·spie·ler** *m* lute player, lutenist

lau·ter ['laʊtɐ] **I.** *adj.* **1.** pure *gold etc.*; clear, transparent *liquid*; flawless *gem etc.*; genuine; **2.** *fig.* sincere, genuine; ***die ~e Wahrheit*** the plain truth; **II.** *adv.* nothing but; ***~ Unsinn*** a lot of nonsense; ***aus ~ Bosheit*** out of sheer spite; ***aus ~ Dankbarkeit ließ er ihn laufen*** he was so grateful (that) he let him off; ***vor ~ Aufregung habe ich s-n Namen vergessen*** in (*or* with all) the excitement I forgot his name; ***das sind ~ Lügen*** it's all lies; **'Lau·ter·keit** *fig. f* (-; *no pl.*) sincerity, integrity

läu·tern ['lɔʏtɐn] *v/t.* (h) purify; *fig.* ***die Erfahrung hat ihn geläutert*** it was a salutary experience for him; **Läu·te·rung** ['lɔʏtərʊŋ] *f*)(-; -en) purification; *fig.* purging; **'Läu·te·rungs·pro,zeß** *m* purification process; *fig.* cleansing process (*or* experience)

'Laut·ge·setz *n* sound (*or* phonetic) law, law of sound (*or* phonetics)

'laut·gesetz·lich **I.** *adj.* phonetic; **II.** *adv.* phonetically; according to the law(s) of sound (*or* phonetics)

laut·hals ['laʊthals] *adv.*: ***~ lachen*** (***schreien***) roar with laughter (scream at the top of one's voice)

'Laut·heit *f* (-; *no pl.*) loudness

'Laut·leh·re *f* phonetics *pl.*; phonology

'laut·lich *adj.* phonetic(ally *adv.*)

'laut·los **I.** *adj.* silent (*a. fig.*); noiseless, soundless; ***~e Stille*** complete (*or* absolute) silence; **II.** *adv.* silently; noiselessly, without a sound; ***er brach ~ zusammen*** he just collapsed without a murmur; **'Laut·lo·sig·keit** *f* (-; *no pl.*) silence; noiselessness, soundlessness

'Laut·ma·le·rei *f* onomatopoeia; **'laut·ma·le·risch** *adj.* onomatopoeic

'Laut·schrift *f* **1.** phonetic transcription; **2.** phonetic alphabet; ***die internationale ~*** the international phonetic alphabet, IPA

'Laut·spre·cher *m* loudspeaker; **~an·la·ge** *f*: ***öffentliche ~*** public address system, PA (system); **~box** *f* loudspeaker; loudspeaker cabinet; **~wa·gen** *m* loudspeaker van (*or* car)

'laut·stark **I.** *adj.* loud, strident, vehement *demands, protest etc.*, vociferous; ***~e Minderheit*** vocal minority; **II.** *adv.* loudly; *talk etc. a.* in a loud voice, so that everyone can (*or* could) hear; ***~ schimpfen*** shout (at s.o.); ***~ protestieren*** protest loudly (*or* vehemently); ***~ zustimmen*** express loud approval; ***~ argumentieren*** argue heatedly

'Laut·stär·ke *f* volume; **~re·ge·lung** *f* volume control; **~reg·ler** *m* volume control

'Laut|sym,bol *n ling.* phonetic symbol (*or* character); **~sy,stem** *n* phonetic (*or* phonological) system

'Laut|ver·schie·bung *f* sound shift; **~ver·schie·bungs·ge·setz** *n* sound (shift) law; **~wan·del** *m* phonetic change; **~zei·chen** *n* → ***Lautsymbol***

'lau·warm *adj.* → ***lau***

La·va ['laːva] *f* (-; *no pl.*) lava; **~ge·stein** *n* lava rock; **~strom** *m* stream of (molten) lava

La·ven·del [la'vɛndəl] *m* (-s; *no pl.*) ⚘ lavender; **♀blau** *adj.* lavender (blue)

la·vie·ren[1] [la'viːrən] *v/i.* (h) manoeuvre, *Am.* maneuver; ***~ zwischen*** *dat.* tack between

la'vie·ren[2] *v/t.* (h) *art*: wash (over)

La·wi·ne [la'viːnə] *f* (-; -n) avalanche; *fig.* torrent, inundation *of letters, questions etc.*; **la'wi·nen·ar·tig** *adj. and adv.* avalanche-like; ***~ anwachsen*** (*or* ***anschwellen***) snowball

La'wi·nen|ge·fahr *f* danger of avalanches; **♀ge·fähr·det** *adj.*: ***~es Gebiet*** avalanche-prone (F avalanchy) area, area exposed to avalanches; **~hund** *m* avalanche search dog; **~op·fer** *n* avalanche victim; **~un·glück** *n* avalanche disaster; **~war·nung** *f* avalanche warning

lax [laks] *adj.* lax, loose; **'Lax·heit** *f* (-; *no pl.*) laxness, laxity

Lay·out ['leːʔaʊt] *n* (-s; -s) layout

lay·ou·ten [leː'ʔaʊtən] *v/i.* (h) **1.** do a (*or* the) layout; **2.** do layouting

Lay·ou·ter ['leːʔaʊtɐ] *m* (-s; -) layout man; **Lay·ou·te·rin** ['leːʔaʊtərɪn] *f* (-; -nen) layout girl (*or* woman)

La·za·rett [latsa'rɛt] *n* (-s; -e) (military) hospital; **~flug·zeug** *n* air ambulance; **~schiff** *n* hospital ship; **~zug** *m* hospital train

lea·sen ['liːzən] *v/t.* (h) lease; **Lea·sing** ['liːzɪŋ] *n* (-s; *no pl.*) leasing

Le·be·da·me ['leːbə-] *f* demi-mondaine

Le·be·hoch [leːbə'hoːx] *n* (-s; -s) cheer(s *pl.*), three cheers *pl.*; ***ein ~ ausbringen*** give three cheers

Le·be·mann ['leːbə-] *m* (-[e]s; ⸚er) man about town

Le·ben ['leːbən] *n* (-s; -) a) life; existence; being, b) life(-time), c) (way of) life, *a. contp.* lifestyle, d) vitality; liveliness, animation, e) bustling activity, (hustle and) bustle, f) life, biography; ***das ~ in Australien*** life in Australia; ***auf dem Mond ist kein ~*** there's no life on the moon; ***so ist das ~*** (***nun einmal***) that's life, such is life, F that's the way the cooky crumbles; ***das einfache ~*** the simple life; ***am ~ sein*** be alive; ***am ~ bleiben*** stay alive, survive; ***mit dem ~ davonkommen*** survive, escape; ***am ~ erhalten*** keep alive; ***das ~ vor*** (***hinter***) ***sich haben*** have one's whole life ahead of one (have done with life); ***er hängt am ~*** he really enjoys life, *patient*: he's not ready to die yet; ***~ in e-e Sache bringen*** put some life into s.th.; ***das Stück hat kein ~*** there's no life in the play; F ***~ in die Bude bringen*** liven (F hot) things up; ***et. für sein ~ gern tun*** love doing s.th.; ***er spielt für sein ~ gern Golf*** *a.* he's a passionate golfer; ***ich würde für mein ~ gern*** I'd give anything to *inf.*, I'd love to *inf.*; ***nie im ~!*** never, F not on your life; ***ins ~ rufen*** call into being, start (up); ***ins ~ treten*** step into the big, wide world; ***j-m das ~ schenken*** spare s.o.'s life; ***das ~ genießen*** enjoy life; ***mein ganzes ~ (lang)*** all my life; ***das ~ ist schon schwer*** it's a hard life; ***wie das ~ so spielt*** life is full of surprises; ***sich das ~ nehmen*** commit suicide, take one's (own) life; ***ums ~ kommen*** be killed; → ***lassen*** 8; ***es geht um ~ und Tod*** it's a matter of life and death; ***nicht ums ~*** not for anything (in the world); ***das Stück ist aus dem ~ gegriffen*** the play is a slice of life; ***ein Stück nach dem ~*** a play taken from real life, a slice of life; ***voll(er) ~*** full of life (F beans); ***~ zeigen*** show signs of life; → ***abschließen*** 4, ***erwecken*** 2, ***froh, nackt, passieren*** II

'le·ben (h) **I.** *v/i.* live; be alive; *fig. memory etc.*: live on; ***man lebt nur einmal*** you only have one life to live; ***die Statue lebt*** the statue is very (*or* so) lifelike; ***das Stück lebt nicht*** there's no life in the play; ***~ nach*** *dat.* live by *principle etc.*; ***~ von*** *dat.* live on (*or* off) *s.th.*, live from (*or* off), make a living with (*or* by *ger.*); ***vegetarisch ~*** be a vegetarian; ***makrobiotisch ~*** live on macrobiotic food(s); ***(un)gesund ~*** a) lead a healthy (an unhealthy) life, b) live in (un)healthy conditions; ***sie ~ ganz gut*** they don't do too badly (for themselves); ***~ und ~ lassen*** live and let live; ***er wird nicht mehr lange ~*** he hasn't got much longer to live; his days are numbered; *iro.* ***wir ~ nicht mehr im 19. Jahrhundert*** this isn't the 19th century(, you know); ***wie lange ~ Sie schon hier?*** how long have you been living here?; ***so wahr ich lebe!*** I swear it; *iro.* ***lebst du noch?*** well, hello stranger; F *wie geht's?* - ***man lebt (so eben)*** surviving; ***es lebe ...!*** three cheers for ...!; ***es lebe der König (die Königin)!*** long live the King (Queen)!; *obs.* ***~ Sie wohl*** *obs.* farewell; → ***Tag;*** **II.** *v/t.*: ***ein angenehmes (bequemes*** *etc.*) ***Leben ~*** lead a pleasant (comfortable *etc.*) life, have a pleasant (an easy *etc.*) lifestyle; ***sein Leben noch einmal ~*** live one's life (over) again; **III.** *v/impers.*: ***es lebt sich ganz angenehm (bequem*** *etc.*) life's quite pleasant (comfortable *etc.*) enough; ***hier lebt es sich gut*** it's not a bad life here, life's not bad over (*or* around) here; **'le·bend** *adj.* living (*a. language*); *biol.* live; ***~es Inventar*** livestock; ***~er Schild*** human shield; ***~e Ziele*** live targets; ***kein ~es Wesen*** not a living soul; ***der größte ~e Künstler*** the greatest artist alive; ***ein noch ~er Zeuge*** a surviving witness; **Le·ben·de** ['le:bəndə] *m, f* (-n; -n) living person; ***die (noch) ~n*** the survivors; ***die ~n und die Toten*** the living and the dead; ***er nimmt's von den ~n*** he'd rob the dead

'le·bend·ge·bä·rend *adj. zo.* viviparous

'Le·bend|ge·burt *f* ⚕ live birth; **~ge·wicht** *n* live weight

le·ben·dig [le'bɛndɪç] *adj.* living, *pred.* alive; *fig.* lively, vivid *description etc.*; alert *mind*; lively *imagination*; cheerful *colo(u)rs*; living *faith etc.*; ***bei ~em Leibe (or ~en Leibes) verbrennen*** be burnt alive; ***wieder ~ machen (werden)*** bring (come) back to life; ***sehr ~ wirken*** be very lifelike; *fig.* ***~ werden*** come to life, liven up; ***~ bleiben*** *memory etc.*: be kept alive, survive; ***~es Museum*** working museum; **Le'ben·dig·keit** *f* (-; *no pl.*) → ***Lebhaftigkeit***

'Le·bens|abend *m* old age; retirement; *lit. the* eve of (one's) life; **~ab·schnitt** *m* stage of (one's) life, period in one's life; **~ader** *fig. f* lifeline; **~al·ter** *n* age; phase; ***ein hohes ~ erreichen*** live to a ripe old age; **~angst** *f* angst, existential fear (*or* anxiety); **~an·schau·ung** *f* approach to life; philosophy (of life); **~art** *f* way of life, lifestyle; ***feine ~*** savoir-vivre; ***er hat keine ~*** he has no style; **~auf·fas·sung** *f* view (*or* philosophy) of life; **~auf·ga·be** *f one's* purpose in life; ***es sich zur ~ machen zu*** *inf.* dedicate one's life to *ger.*; **~äu·ße·rung** *f* sign of life; **~baum** *m* tree of life; **~be·din·gun·gen** *pl.* living conditions; **2be·dro·hend** *adj.* life-threatening; **~be·dro·hung** *f* threat to (one's) life; **~be·dürf·nis·se** *pl.* necessities of life; **2be·ja·hend** *adj.* life-affirming, positive(-minded); **~be·ja·hung** *f* positive approach to life; **2be·rech·tigt** *adj.*: ***~ sein*** have the right to live (*or* exist); **~be·rech·ti·gung** *f* right to live (*or* exist); **~be·reich** *m* area of life; **~be·schrei·bung** *f* life, biography; **~bund** *m* lifelong union; **~chan·cen** *pl.* chances of survival; **~dau·er** *f* lifespan; *fig.*, ⚙ *etc.* life; **~drang** *m* urge (*or* will) to live, vital instinct

'le·bens·echt *adj.* true to life, lifelike

'Le·bens|eli,xier *n* elixir of life; **~en·de** *n* end of one's life; ***bis an sein ~*** till the end of one's days; **~er·fah·rung** *f* experience of life

'le·bens·er·hal·tend *adj.* life-saving; ***~e Maßnahmen*** measures to prolong life

'Le·bens|er·war·tung *f* (-; *no pl.*) life expectancy; **~fa·den** *m*: ***j-m den ~ abschneiden*** cut the thread of s.o.'s life

'le·bens·fä·hig *adj. a. fig.* capable of surviving, viable; **'Le·bens·fä·hig·keit** *f* (-; *no pl.*) viability; *fig. a.* ability to survive

'le·bens·feind·lich *adj.* hostile to life

'Le·bens|form *f* **1.** way of life; **2.** *biol.* life form, form of life; **~fra·ge** *f* vital issue

'le·bens·fremd *adj.* out of touch (with reality); remote from reality; unrealistic

'Le·bens|freu·de *f* joie de vivre; animal spirits *pl.*; **~frist** *f* lease of life

'le·bens·froh *adj.* full of the joys of life, full of joie de vivre

'Le·bens|füh·rung *f* life(style), *formal*: conduct of one's life; **~fun·ke** *m* vital spark, spark of life; **~funk·ti,on** *f* vital function

'Le·bens·ge·fahr *f* (-; *no pl.*): ***~!*** danger!; ***in ~ schweben*** be in a critical condition; ***außer ~ sein*** be out of danger, ⚕ be in a stable condition, be off the critical list; ***sie hat ihn unter ~ gerettet*** she risked her life to save him; **'le·bens·ge·fähr·lich I.** *adj.* extremely dangerous; ⚕ very serious, life-threatening; **II.** *adv.*: ***~ verletzt*** very seriously hurt

'Le·bens|ge·fähr·te *m*, **~ge·fähr·tin** *f* partner, (lifetime) companion, F lifemate; ⚖ common law husband (*f* wife); **~ge·fühl** *n* **1.** experience (*or* enjoyment) of life; ***es war ein völlig neues ~*** it was a completely new experience for me *etc.*; **2.** attitude towards life; **~gei·ster** *pl.*: ***j-s ~ wecken*** put some life (back) into s.o., F get s.o. going (again); ***nach dem Kaffee erwachten m-e ~ wieder*** after the coffee I felt revived (F I could feel the old adrenalin going again); **~ge·mein·schaft** *f* **1.** partnership; **2.** *biol.* symbiosis; **~ge·nuß** *m* enjoyment of life; **~ge·schich·te** *f* story of s.o.'s life; **~ge·wohn·hei·ten** *pl.* **1.** way *sg.* of life, (day to day) habits; **2.** *a people's* way *sg.* of life, customs; **~gier** *f* lust for life; **~glück** *n* happiness

'le·bens·groß *adj.* life-size(d)

'Le·bens·grö·ße *f*: ***in ~*** in its actual size; ***in doppelter ~*** twice its actual size; ***Gemälde in ~*** full-length painting (*or* portrait); F *fig.* ***in voller ~*** in the flesh

'Le·bens·hälf·te *f*: ***in der ersten (zweiten) ~*** during (*or* in) the first (second) half of one's life

'Le·bens·hal·tung *f* standard of living

'Le·bens·hal·tungs|in·dex *m* cost of living index; **~ko·sten** *pl.* cost *sg.* of living

'Le·bens·hun·ger *m* hunger (*or* thirst) for life; **'le·bens·hung·rig** *adj.* hungry (*or* thirsting) for life

'Le·bens|in·halt *m* purpose in life; ***sie hat keinen ~*** *a.* she's got nothing to live for; ***sich et. zum ~ machen*** make s.th. the focal point of one's life, dedicate one's life to s.th.; ***s-e Tiere sind sein einziger ~*** his animals are the only thing he lives for (*or* are his only purpose in life), he only lives for his animals, his whole life revolves around his animals; **~jahr** *n*: ***im 50. ~*** at the age of 50; → ***vollendet;*** **~kampf** *m* struggle (*or* fight) for survival; **2klug** *adj.* worldly-wise; **~klug·heit** *f* worldly wisdom; **~kraft** *f* vitality (*a.* ⚕); **~kri·se** *f* (personal *or* existential) crisis; **~kunst** *f* art of living (*or* survival); **~künst·ler** *m* survivor; **~la·ge** *f* situation (in life)

'le·bens·lang *adj.* lifelong ..., lifetime ...

'le·bens·läng·lich I. *adj.* lifelong ..., lifetime ...; ***~e Freiheitsstrafe*** life sentence (*or* imprisonment); **II.** *adv.* all one's life; ⚖ for life; **'Le·bens·läng·li·che** *m* (-n; -n) prisoner serving a life sentence, F lifer

'Le·bens|lauf *m* **1.** curriculum vitae, CV, *Am.* résumé, *one's* biodata *pl.*; **2.** life (story); **~li·nie** *f* life line; **~lü·ge** *f* grand delusion; **~lust** *f* (-; *no pl.*) joys *pl.* of living, joie de vivre, zest for life; **2lu·stig** *adj.* full of joie de vivre (*or* the joys of living); ***er ist sehr ~*** *a.* he's somebody who really enjoys life; **~ma,xi·me** *f* maxim (of life); principle by which *s.o.* lives; **~mit·te** *f* middle (*or* mid-point) of (one's) life, halfway stage of (one's) life

'Le·bens·mit·tel *pl.* food *sg.*, foodstuffs; **~ab,tei·lung** *f* food hall; **~be·strah·lung** *f* food irradiation; **~che,mie** *f* food chemistry; **~che·mi·ker** *m* food chemist (*or* analyst); **~ge·schäft** *n* food store, grocery (shop); **~ge·setz** *n* (pure) food law; **~händ·ler** *m* grocer; **~in·du,strie** *f* food industry; **~kar·te** *f* (food) ration card; **~knapp·heit** *f* food shortage(s *pl.*); **~kon,trol·le** *f* food quality control; **~pa,ket** *n* food parcel (*Am.* package); **~ver·gif·tung** *f* food poisoning; **~ver·sor·gung** *f* food supplies *pl.*

'Le·bens·mo·nat *m*: ***in den ersten ~en*** in (*or* during) the first few months of life

'le·bens·mü·de *adj.* tired of life; *w.s.* world-weary; ***~ sein*** *a.* have lost the will to live (*or* go on living); F ***du bist wohl ~!*** are you trying to kill yourself?

'Le·bens·mü·dig·keit *f* tiredness of life; *w.s.* world-weariness
'Le·bens·mut *m* courage to face life; *w.s.* will to live; ***er hatte keinen ~ mehr*** *a.* he had lost all interest in life
'le·bens·nah I. *adj. representation etc.* true to life; *a. w.s.* realistic; **II.** *adv.* realistically; **'Le·bens·nä·he** *f* realism
'Le·bens·nerv *fig. m* nerve centre (*Am.* center)
'le·bens·not·wen·dig *adj.* vital, essential; **'Le·bens·not·wen·dig·keit** *f* essential (for life), vital necessity
'le·ben·spen·dend *adj.* life-giving
'le·ben·sprü·hend *adj.* brimming over with life
'Le·bens|qua·li̦tät *f* (-; *no pl.*) quality of life; **~raum** *m* **1.** living space; *pol.* lebensraum; **2.** *biol.* habitat; **~re·gel** *f* rule of life, maxim (of life); **2ret·tend** *adj.* lifesaving; **~ret·ter** *m* lifesaver; ***mein ~*** *a.* the man who saved my life
'Le·bens·ret·tungs|maß·nah·men *pl.* lifesaving measures; **~me̦dail·le** *f* lifesaving medal
'Le·bens|rhyth·mus *m* rhythm (*or* pace) of life; **~span·ne** *f* lifespan; **~stan·dard** *m* standard of living, living standard; **~stel·lung** *f* permanent post, lifetime job; **~stil** *m* lifestyle; **~traum** *m* lifetime dream, dream of one's life; ***mein ~*** *a.* my life's dream; **~trieb** *m* vital instinct; libido
'le·bens·tüch·tig *adj.* fit for life, able to cope with life; ***sehr ~ sein*** *a.* cope very well with life; **'Le·bens·tüch·tig·keit** *f* ability to survive (*or* cope with life)
'Le·benșüber·druß *m* world-weariness; tiredness of life; **'le·benșüber·drüs·sig** *adj.* world-weary; tired of life
'Le·benșum·stän·de *pl.* circumstances of (*or* surrounding) s.o.'s life
'le·bens·un·fä·hig *adj.* non-viable; *a. fig.* unfit for life; **'Le·bens·un·fä·hig·keit** *f* non-viability; *a. fig.* inability to survive
'Le·benșun·ter·halt *m* (-[e]s; *no pl.*) livelihood, living; (***sich***) ***s-n ~ verdienen*** earn (*or* make) a living
'le·bens·un·tüch·tig *adj.* unfit for life, unable to cope with life; **'Le·bens·un·tüch·tig·keit** *f* inability to cope with life
'Le·bens|ver·hält·nis·se *pl.* **1.** living conditions; **2.** → ***Lebensumstände***; **~ver·län·ge·rung** *f* **1.** ⚕ prolongation of life; **2.** increased longevity
'le·bens·ver·nei·nend *adj.* negative (towards life); ***~ sein*** *a.* negate life
'Le·bens·ver·nei·nung *f* (-; *no pl.*) negation of life; negative attitude towards life
'Le·bens|ver·si·che·rung *f* life insurance; **2wahr** *adj.* true to life; realistic; **~wan·del** *m* life(style); **~weg** *m* (path through) life; **~wei·se** *f* way of life; habits *pl.*; ***sitzende ~*** sedentary life
'le·bens·wei·se *adj.* worldly-wise
'Le·bens·weis·heit *f* (-; -en) **1.** *no pl.* worldly wisdom; **2.** maxim, aphorism
'Le·bens·werk *n* life's work
'le·bens·wert *adj. a life* worth living; ***das Leben ~ machen*** a) make life more worthwhile, b) increase the quality of life
'le·bens·wich·tig *adj.* essential; ⚕ *and fig.* vital; ***~e Güter*** essentials; ⚕ ***~e Organe*** vital organs
'Le·bens|wil·le *m* will to live; **~zei·chen** *n* sign of life; *a.* news (*sg.*); ***kein ~ von sich geben*** *a. fig.* show no sign of life; *fig.* ***wir haben kein ~ von ihr bekommen*** *a.* F we haven't heard a peep from her; **~zeit** *f* life(time); ***auf ~*** for life; ***Mitglied auf ~*** life member; **~ziel** *n*, **~zweck** *m* aim in life
'le·ben·zer·stö·rend *adj.* life-destroying
Le·ber ['le:bɐ] *f* (-; -n) *anat. and gastr.* liver; *fig.* ***frei*** (*or* ***frisch***) ***von der ~ weg reden*** speak one's mind, not to mince one's words; ***sich et. von der ~ reden*** get s.th. off one's chest; → ***Laus***; **~blüm·chen** *n* ♣ liverwort; **~fleck** *m* mole; **~kä·se** *m gastr. type of meat loaf made of ham and pork or veal, sometimes including liver*; **~knö·del·sup·pe** *f gastr.* liver dumpling soup
'le·ber·krank *adj.*: ***~ sein*** have (*or* suffer from) a liver complaint; **'Le·ber·krank·heit** *f*, **'Le·ber·lei·den** *n* liver complaint (*or* disease)
'Le·ber|pa̦ste·te *f* liver pâté; **~punk·ti̦on** *f* liver puncture; **~scha·den** *m* damaged liver; **~schrump·fung** *f* → ***Leberzirrhose***; **~tran** *m* cod-liver oil; **~ver·fet·tung** *f* fatty degeneration of the liver; **~wer·te** *pl.* liver count *sg.*; **~wurst** *f* liver sausage, *Am.* liverwurst; → ***beleidigt***; **~zir̦rho·se** *f* cirrhosis of the liver
Le·be·we·sen ['le:bə-] *n* (-s; -) living being (*or* organism); ***menschliches ~*** human being
Le·be'wohl *lit. n* (-s; -s, -e) *lit.* farewell; ***j-m ~ sagen*** bid s.o. farewell
leb·haft ['le:phaft] **I.** *adj.* lively (*a. fig.*), buoyant (*a.* ✝); *fig.* vivid *description etc.*; animated, heated *discussion etc.*; enthusiastic *applause etc.*; bright, vivid *colo(u)rs*; busy *street*; vibrant *city*; heavy *traffic*; ***~e Nachfrage*** brisk demand; ***~er Handel*** brisk (*or* buoyant) trading; ***~e Börse*** buoyant trading on the stock market; ***es herrschte ~es Treiben*** there was a lot of activity (*or* a lot going on); ***~en Anteil nehmen*** show a lively interest (***an*** *dat.* in); **II.** *adv.* animatedly *etc.*; ***~ bedauern*** sincerely regret; ***~ begrüßen*** give a warm welcome to; ***~ darstellen*** vividly portray, paint a vivid portrait of; ***sich ~ erinnern an*** *acc.* remember (quite) vividly; ***sich ~ unterhalten*** have a lively (*or* an animated) conversation; ***das kann ich mir ~ vorstellen*** I can just imagine; **'Leb·haf·tig·keit** *f* (-; *no pl.*) liveliness; vividness; animation; buoyancy; briskness
Leb·ku·chen ['le:p-] *m* gingerbread
leb·los ['le:plo:s] *adj.* lifeless; inanimate *matter etc.*; *fig.* dull; expressionless *eyes*; dead; ***die Gegend*** *etc.* ***ist ~*** *a.* there's no life in the place *etc.*; ***~ liegenbleiben*** lie there motionless; **'Leb·lo·sig·keit** *f* (-; *no pl.*) lifelessness; inanimateness *of matter*; *fig.* lack of expression; lack of life (*gen.* in)
Leb·tag ['le:pta:k] *m*: ***mein ~*** all (*negated*: never in) my life
'Leb·zeit ['le:ptsaɪt] *f*: ***zu s-n ~en*** a) in his time, b) when he was still alive
lech·zen ['lɛçtsən] *v/i.* (h): ***~ nach*** *dat.* thirst after, F be dying for; **'lech·zend** *adj.* thirsty (***nach*** *dat.* for), thirsting (after); ***mit ~er Zunge*** with one's (*or* its) tongue hanging out
leck [lɛk] *adj.* leaking, leaky; ***~e Stelle*** leak; **Leck** *n* (-[e]s; -e, -s) leak; ⚓ ***ein ~ bekommen*** spring a leak; **lecken**[1] ['lɛkən] (*sep.* -k·k-) *v/i.* (h) leak, be leaking
'lecken[2] *v/t. and v/i.* (h) lick (*a.* ***~ an*** *dat.*); *fig.* ***sich die Finger ~ nach*** *dat.* F drool after; V ***leck mich doch!*** V piss off!; → ***Arsch, Blut*** 1, ***geleckt***
lecker ['lɛkɐ] (*sep.* -k·k-) *adj.* tasty, delicious; F *fig.* F yummy *girl etc.*
'Lecker|bis·sen *m* tasty titbit (*Am.* tidbit), delicacy; *fig.* (real) treat, something to savo(u)r; **~maul** *n*, **~mäul·chen** *n*: ***ein ~ sein*** have a sweet tooth
Le·der ['le:dɐ] *n* (-s; -) leather (*a.* F *football*); chamois; ***aus ~*** (made of) leather; *fig.* ***vom ~ ziehen*** let fly, F let rip (***gegen*** *acc.* against); → ***zäh*** I; **~ar·beit** *f a. pl.* leatherwork; leather article (*pl. a.* goods)
'le·der·ar·tig *adj.* leathery
'Le·der|ball *m* leather ball; **~band** (-[e]s; ⸚e) *m* leatherbound book (*or* volume); **~couch** *f* leather sofa; **~ein·band** *m* leather binding
'le·der·far·ben *adj.* buff(-colo[u]red)
'Le·der|fett *n* dubbin; **~gar·ni̦tur** *f* leather suite; **~gür·tel** *m* leather belt; **~hand·schuh** *m* leather glove; **~haut** *f anat.* corium; sclera; **~ho·se** *f*: (***e-e ~*** a pair of) leather trousers *pl. or* lederhosen *pl.*; **~imi·ta·ti̦on** *f* imitation leather; **~jacke** *f* leather jacket; **~kof·fer** *m* leather suitcase; **~kom·bi·na·ti̦on** *f* leather two-piece; **~look** *m* leather-look; **~man·tel** *m* leather coat; **~mon̦tur** F *f*: ***Motorradfahrer in ~*** F motorcyclist in (his *or* her) leather gear
le·dern[1] ['le:dɐn] *adj.* **1.** leather ..., made of leather; *gastr.* leathery; **2.** F *fig.* dull
'le·dern[2] *v/t.* (h) go over *s.th.* with a chamois
'Le·der|rie·men *m* leather strap (*or* belt); **~ses·sel** *m* leather armchair; **~wa·ren** *pl.* leather goods
le·dig ['le:dɪç] *adj.* **1.** single, unmarried *a. mother*; **2.** ***e-r Sache ~ sein*** be rid of s.th.
le·dig·lich ['le:dɪklɪç] *adv.* merely, only; ***ich habe ~ gesagt*** *a.* all I said was
Lee [le:] *f* (-; *no pl.*) ⚓ lee; ***nach ~*** leeward
leer [le:ɐ] **I.** *adj.* empty; vacant; blank *sheet of paper*; unfurnished *room etc.*; *fig.* blank *stare*; expressionless *look etc.*; unfounded; empty, idle *promise*, *threat etc.*; ***~es Gerede*** hot air, empty talk; ♆ ***~e Menge*** null set; ***die Batterie ist ~*** the battery has run out (*mot.* is dead); ***mit ~en Händen*** empty-handed; ***sein Glas ~ trinken*** empty one's glass; ***s-n Teller ~ essen*** empty (*or* clean) one's plate; *e-n Laden etc.* ***~ kaufen*** buy out, empty the shelves of; *den Tank* ***~ fahren*** run down; ***~ stehen*** be empty, be unoccupied; *e-e Zeile* ***~ lassen*** leave out; → ***ausgehen*** 8, ***Stroh***; **II.** *adv.*: ⚙ ***~ laufen*** idle, be idling
'Leer|kașset·te *f* blank tape (*or* cassette); **~darm** *m anat.* jejunum; **~dișket·te** *f* blank disk(ette)
Lee·re[1] ['le:rə] *n* (-n; *no pl.*) empty space; ***ins ~ starren*** stare into space; ***ins ~ greifen*** clutch at thin air
'Lee're[2] *f* (-; *no pl.*) vacuum; ***innere ~*** inner void; → ***gähnend***; **~ge·fühl** *n* feeling of emptiness
lee·ren ['le:rən] (h) **I.** *v/t.* empty; pour out; clear out, clear, evacuate; **II.** *v/refl.*: ***sich ~*** empty, *street*: grow empty
'Leer|for·mel *f* empty formula; *w.s.* empty phrase; **2ge·fegt** *adj.* empty *shelves etc.*, *a.* deserted *streets*; **~ge·wicht** *n* dead weight; tare (weight); **~gut** *n* ✝ empties *pl.*; ***~ bitte zurück*** please return empty container (*or* bottles *etc.*)

'Leer·lauf *m* (-[e]s; *no pl.*) ⚙ idling, idle motion; *mot.* neutral (gear); *fig.* a) unproductive phase, running on the spot, b) slack (*or* idle) period(s *pl.*), *sport etc.*: boring patch(es *pl.*); ~ ***haben*** a) be running on the spot, b) be having (*or* going through) a slack (*or* an idle) period, have nothing to do; ~... *in cpds.* idle, idling; **'leer·lau·fen** *v/i.* (*irr.*, *sep.*, sn, → ***laufen***) run dry; ~ ***lassen*** drain
'Leer·packung *f* ⚕ dummy
'leer·pum·pen *v/t.* (*sep.*, h) pump out
'leer·ste·hend *adj.* empty, unoccupied
'Leer|stel·le *f* blank (space); **~takt** *m mot.* idle stroke; **~ta·ste** *f* space bar (*computer*: *a.* key)
Lee·rung ['le:rʊŋ] *f* (-; -en) emptying; ✉ collection
'Leer|zei·chen *n computer*: blank (character), space (character); **~zei·le** *f* space, empty line; ***zwei ~n lassen*** leave two lines free (*or* two empty lines); **~zim·mer** *n* unfurnished room
'Lee·sei·te *f* lee(ward)
lee·wärts ['le:vɛrts] *adv.* leeward
Lef·zen ['lɛftsən] *pl. zo.* chaps
le·gal [le'ga:l] *adj.* legal; ***auf ~em Weg erwerben*** obtain by legal means
le·ga·li·sie·ren [legali'zi:rən] *v/t.* (h) legalize; **Le·ga·li'sie·rung** *f* (-; *no pl.*) legalization
le·ga·li·stisch [lega'lɪstɪʃ] *adj.* legalistic
Le·ga·li·tät [legali'tɛ:t] *f* (-; *no pl.*) legality
Leg·asthe·nie [legaste'ni:] *f* (-; *no pl.*) dyslexia; **Leg·asthe·ni·ker** [legas'te:nikɐ] *m* (-s; -), **leg·asthe·nisch** [legas'te:nɪʃ] *adj.* dyslexic
Le·gat[1] [le'ga:t] *m* (-en; -en) *R.C.* legate
Le'gat[2] *n* (-[e]s; -e) ⚖ legacy
Le·ga·ti·on [lega'tsĭo:n] *f* (-; - en) **1.** *R.C.* legation; **2.** *pol.* legation, mission
Le·ga·ti'ons·rat *m pol.* legation council(l)or
Le·ge|bat·te͵rie ['le:gə-] *f zo.* laying battery; **~hen·ne** *f* layer
le·gen ['le:gən] (h) **I.** *v/t.* **1.** lay; put; lay down; lay flat; put down *carpet etc.*; lay *cable etc.*; plant *a bomb*, lay *mines*; *wrestling*: pin to the floor; *soccer etc.*: floor; ***e-e Tischdecke auf den Tisch*** ~ spread (*or* put) a tablecloth on the table; ***ein Tuch um die Schultern*** ~ wrap a shawl round one's shoulders; ***Eier*** ~ lay eggs; ***sich die Haare ~ lassen*** have a set; ***den Kopf ~ an*** *acc.* rest one's head against; ***Feuer ~ an*** *acc.* set fire to; → ***beiseite, Hand, Handwerk***; **II.** *v/refl.* **2.** ***sich*** ~ lie down; ***sich schlafen*** ~ go to bed; ***sich ~ auf*** *acc.* lie on *s.th.*, *dust etc.*: settle on; *fig.* ***sich aufs Gemüt*** ~ get one down, be depressing; **3.** *fig.* ***sich*** ~ *storm, wind, noise, a. excitement, enthusiasm etc.*: die down; *scandal etc.*: blow over; *tension*: ease off; *pain*: ease, go away; **4.** *fig.* ***sich ~ auf*** *acc.* take up, specialize in *a subject etc.*; **III.** *v/i. zo.* lay (eggs)
le·gen·där [legɛn'dɛ:ɐ] *adj.* legendary (*a. fig.*); *fig.* ***~e Gestalt*** (*or* ***Sache***) legend
Le·gen·de [le'gɛndə] *f* (-; -n) **1.** legend (*a. fig.*); ***wie die ~ berichtet*** as legend has it; *fig.* ***er war schon zu Lebzeiten e-e*** ~ he was a legend in his own lifetime; **2.** *geogr. etc.*: legend; key; **Le'gen·den·bil·dung** *f* myth-making; **le'gen·den·haft** *adj.* legendary; **le'gen·den·um͵wo·ben** *adj.* shrouded in legend; fabled
le·ger [le'ʒe:ɐ] *adj.* casual; informal; relaxed, F laid-back

le·gie·ren [le'gi:rən] *v/t.* (h) **1.** *metall.* alloy; **2.** *gastr.* thicken; **le·giert** [le'gi:ɐt] *adj.* **1.** *metall.* alloy ..., alloyed; **2.** *gastr.* thickened; ***~e Suppe*** (***Sauce***) cream soup (sauce); **Le'gie·rung** *f* (-; -en) alloy
Le·gi·on [le'gĭo:n] *f* (-;-en) legion; *fig.* ***~en von*** *dat.* myriads of; ***ihre Zahl war*** ~ their number was legion; **Le·gio·när** [legĭo'nɛ:ɐ] *m* (-s; -e [-rə]) legionnaire; **Le·gio'närs·krank·heit** *f* ⚕ legionnaire's disease
Le·gis·la·ti·ve [legɪsla'ti:və] *f* (-; -n) *pol.* legislative; legislative assembly (*or* body)
Le·gis·la·tur [legɪsla'tu:ɐ] *f* (-; -en) legislation; **~pe·rio·de** *f* **1.** session; ***die erste*** (***zweite***) ***Hälfte der*** ~ the first (second) half of parliament; **2.** term of office
le·gi·tim [legi'ti:m] *adj.* legitimate; *fig. a.* (perfectly) justified
Le·gi·ti·ma·ti·on [legitima'tsĭo:n] *f* (-; -en) legitimation; proof of identity, credentials *pl.*; authority; **le·gi·ti·mie·ren** [legiti'mi:rən] (h) **I.** *v/t.* legitimize; authorize; justify; **II.** *v/refl.*: ***sich*** ~ prove one's identity; show one's credentials; **Le·gi·ti'mie·rung** *f* (-; *no pl.*) legitimizing; justification
Le·gi·ti·mi·tät [legitimi'tɛ:t] *f* (-; *no pl.*) legitimacy
Le·gu·an [le'gŭa:n] *m* (-s; -e) *zo.* iguana
Le·hen ['le:ən] *n* (-s; -) *hist.* fief; ***j-m Land zu ~ geben*** enfeoff s.o.
Lehm [le:m] *m* (-[e]s; *no pl.*) loam; clay; mud; **~bo·den** *m* loamy soil
'lehm·far·ben *adj.* loam-colo(u)red
'lehm·gelb *adj.* loam(y)
'Lehm·gru·be *f* loam pit
'lehm·hal·tig [-haltɪç] *adj.*: ***~er Boden*** soil containing loam
'Lehm·hüt·te *f* mud hut
leh·mig ['le:mɪç] *adj.* loamy
'Lehm·klum·pen *m* lump of clay
'Lehm·zie·gel *m* clay brick; adobe; **~hüt·te** *f* clay-brick (*or* adobe) hut
Lehn|be·deu·tung ['le:n-] *f ling.* semantic loan; **~bil·dung** *f* loan formation
Leh·ne ['le:nə] *f* (-; -n) back; arm(-rest); **'leh·nen I.** *v/i. and v/refl.* (***sich*** ~) (h) lean (***an*** *acc.* against; ***auf*** *acc.* on); ***sich aus dem Fenster*** ~ lean out of (*Am. a.* out) the window; **II.** *v/t.* lean, rest, prop (***gegen*** *acc.* against)
Lehns·dienst ['le:ns-] *m* feudal service
Lehn·ses·sel ['le:n-] *m* easy chair
Lehns|gut ['le:ns-] *n* manor; **~herr** *m* feudal lord; **~mann** *m* (-[e]s; ⸚er, -leute) vassal, liege man; **~recht** *n* feudal law; right of investiture
Lehn·stuhl ['le:n-] *m* easy chair
Lehns·we·sen ['le:ns-] *n* (-s; *no pl.*) feudal system
'Lehn|über͵set·zung *f* loan translation; **~über͵tra·gung** *f* loan transference; **~wort** *n* (-[e]s; ⸚er) loanword
Lehr·amt ['le:ɐ-] *n* teaching profession (*or* post)
Lehr·amts|an·wär·ter ['le:ɐ-] *m*, **~kan·di͵dat** *m* trainee teacher
Lehr|an·stalt ['le:ɐ-] *f* educational establishment; school, college; **~auf·trag** *m* teaching assignment; *univ.* part-time lectureship
lehr·bar ['le:ɐba:ɐ] *adj.* teachable
Lehr|be·auf·trag·te ['le:ɐ-] *m*, *f* (-n; -n) *univ.* part-time lecturer; **~be·ruf** *m* teaching profession; **~brief** *m* certificate (of apprenticeship); **~buch** *n* textbook
Leh·re[1] ['le:rə] *f* (-; -n) **1.** lesson; ***das war mir e-e*** ~ that was a lesson (for me); ***laß dir das e-e ~ sein*** let that be a lesson to you; ***e-e ~ ziehen aus*** *dat.* draw a lesson from, take a warning from; *w.s.* learn from; **2.** (piece of) advice; **3.** teaching, doctrine; tenets *pl.*; system; science; theory; **4.** moral *of a story etc.*; **5.** apprenticeship; ***bei j-m in die ~ gehen*** be an apprentice to s.o.; F *fig.* ***bei dem kannst du noch in die ~ gehen*** he can teach you a thing or two; ***e-e harte ~ durchmachen*** (***müssen***) (have to) pass through a tough school
'Leh·re[2] *f* (-; -n) ⚙ ga(u)ge
leh·ren ['le:rən] *v/t. and v/i.* (h) teach; ***j-n et.*** ~ teach s.o. (how to do) s.th.; ***j-n lesen*** ~ teach s.o. to read; ***die Erfahrung lehrt, daß*** experience teaches us (*or* shows [us], tells us) that; ***die Zeit wird es*** ~ time will tell
Leh·rer ['le:rɐ] *m* (-s; -) teacher; (*driving, skiing etc.*) instructor; (*private*) tutor; ***ist er noch ~?*** does he still teach?, is he still in teaching?; **~aus·bil·dung** *f* teacher training; **~be·ruf** *m* teaching profession; **~fort·bil·dung** *f* in-service training (for teachers)
'leh·rer·haft *adj.* schoolmasterly; F schoolmarmish
'Leh·rer·hand·rei·chun·gen *pl.* teachers' notes
Leh·re·rin ['le:rərɪn] *f* (-; -nen) → ***Lehrer***
'Leh·rer|kol͵le·gi·um *n* teaching staff, *Am. a.* faculty; **~kon·fe͵renz** *f* staff meeting; **~man·gel** *m* shortage of teachers
'Leh·rer·schaft *f* (-; *no pl.*) teachers *pl.*; teaching staff, *Am. a.* faculty
'Leh·rer|schwem·me *f* glut (*or* surplus) of teachers; **~zim·mer** *n* staff room, *Am. a.* teachers' room
Lehr|fach ['le:ɐ-] *n* (-[e]s; ⸚er) **1.** subject; **2.** *no pl.* teaching profession; **~film** *m* educational film; **~gang** *m* course; **~ge·bäu·de** *n* system of theories; **~ge·gen·stand** *m* subject of instruction; **~geld** *fig. n*: (***teures*** *or* ***schwer***) ***~ bezahlen*** (***müssen***) (have to) pay (dearly) for s.th., *n.s.* (have to) learn the hard way
lehr·haft ['le:ɐhaft] *adj.* instructive; *contp.* F know-(it-)all
Lehr|jahr ['le:ɐ-] *n* year of one's apprenticeship; ***die ~e*** one's (period of) apprenticeship; *fig.* ***harte ~e*** a tough school; ***~e sind keine Herrenjahre*** we've all got to start small; **~jun·ge** *m* apprentice; **~kör·per** *m* teaching staff, *Am. a.* faculty; **~kraft** *f* (qualified) teacher
Lehr·ling ['le:ɐlɪŋ] *m* (-s; -e) apprentice, trainee
Lehr|mäd·chen ['le:ɐ-] *n* (female) apprentice; **~ma·te·ri͵al** *n* teaching material; **~mei·nung** *f* school of thought; **~mei·ster** *m* **1.** master; **2.** *fig.* teacher, mentor; **~me͵tho·de** *f* teaching method; **~mit·tel** *pl.* teaching aids; **~per·so͵nal** *n* teaching staff; **~plan** *m* syllabus; curriculum; **~plan·ent·rüm·pe·lung** *f* curricular streamlining; **~pro·be** *f* demonstration lesson; **&reich** *adj.* instructive, informative; ***das war für mich sehr*** ~ I found it very instructive (*or* informative), I learnt a lot from it; **~saal** *m* lecture hall; **~satz** *m* doctrine, tenet; *phls. a.* dogma; ⩚ theorem, proposition; **~schwimm·becken** *n* beginners' pool; **~stel·le** *f* apprenticeship; **~stoff** *m* material

Lehr·stuhl ['le:ɐ-] *m* chair (***für*** *acc.* of); **~in·ha·ber** *m*: ***er ist ~ an der Universität X*** he has (*or* holds) a chair at the University of X (*or* at X University)

Lehr|tä·tig·keit ['le:ɐ-] *f* a) teaching, b) teaching post (*or* job); ***e-e ~ ausüben*** teach; **~ver·an·stal·tung** *f* lecture; seminar; ***die ~en in diesem Semester*** this semester's courses (and lectures); **~werk** *n* (school) textbook; **~werk·statt** *f* training workshop; **~zeit** *f* apprenticeship; *fig.* ***harte ~*** hard school; **~zeug·nis** *n* apprentice's diploma

Leib [laɪp] *m* (-[e]s; Leiber ['laɪbɐ]) a) body, b) abdomen, c) trunk, d) womb; ***~ und Seele*** body and soul; ***ein ~ und eine Seele werden*** become one flesh; ***mit ~ und Seele*** heart and soul; ***der ~ des Herrn*** the body of Christ; ***e-e Gefahr für ~ und Leben*** a risk to life and limb; ***am ganzen ~e zittern*** tremble from head to toe; ***er hat kein Hemd auf dem ~e*** he hasn't got a penny to his name; ***et. am eigenen ~e erfahren*** experience s.th. oneself (*or* first-hand); ***am eigenen ~e erfahren, was Armut heißt*** learn from experience (*or* the hard way) what it means to be poor; ***ich hab's am eigenen ~e erfahren*** (***or gespürt***) *a.* I know only too well; ***j-m*** (***hart***) ***auf den ~ rücken*** start breathing down s.o.'s neck; *dat.* ***zu ~e rücken*** (*or* ***gehen***) tackle *s.o. or s.th.*; ***die Rolle ist ihm auf den ~ geschrieben*** he was made for the part; ***sich j-n vom ~e halten*** keep s.o. at arm's length; ***sich et. vom ~e halten*** steer clear of s.th.; ***halt ihn mir bloß vom ~e*** just don't let him come near me; ***bleib mir damit vom ~e*** I don't want to hear about it; → ***Ehre, lebendig, Lunge***; **~arzt** *m* private physician; **~bin·de** *f* **1.** waistband, sash; **2.** ⚕ truss

'leib·ei·gen *adj. hist.* in bondage

'Leib·ei·ge·ne *m* (-n; -n) *hist.* serf

'Leib·ei·gen·schaft *f* (-; *no pl.*) *hist.* serfdom

lei·ben ['laɪbən] *only in*: ***das ist Michael, wie er leibt und lebt*** a) that's Michael to a T, he's the spitting image (*or* spit and image) of Michael, b) that's Michael all over

Lei·bes|er·zie·hung ['laɪbəs-] *f* physical education; **~frucht** *f* f(o)etus; *poet.* fruit of the womb; **~kräf·te** *pl.*: ***aus ~n*** with all one's might, *lit.* with might and main, *scream etc.* at the top of one's voice; **~übun·gen** *pl.* exercises *pl.*; gymnastics *pl.*; **~ˌum·fang** *m* waist(line); corpulence; **~vi·si·ta·tiˌon** *f* body search; ***j-n e-r ~ unterziehen*** search s.o.

'Leib|gar·de *f* bodyguard; **~ge·richt** *n* favo(u)rite food; ***Spaghetti sind mein ~*** *a.* I could live off spaghetti; **~ge·tränk** *n* favo(u)rite drink

leib·haf·tig [laɪp'haftɪç] **I.** *adj.* real(-life), F real live; ***ein ~es Gespenst*** *a.* F a ghost, would you believe; ***der ~e Teufel*** the devil incarnate; ***sie war die ~e Faulheit*** she was laziness in person (*or* the epitome of laziness); ***er sah aus wie mein ~er Bruder*** he was the spitting image (*or* spit and image) of my brother; ***wie der ~e Tod aussehen*** look like death warmed up, look like a corpse; **II.** *adv.*: ***da stand er ~ vor mir*** there he was in the flesh; ***ich seh' ihn noch ~ vor mir*** (***stehen***) I can see him now, I can still see him in my mind's eye; **Leib·haf·ti·ge** [laɪp'haftɪgə] *m* (-n; *no pl.*): ***der ~*** the devil, Satan

leib·lich ['laɪplɪç] *adj.* a) bodily (*a. adv.*), physical, b) worldly, c) natural *heir, parents etc.*; ***~er Bruder*** blood brother; ***~e Mutter*** natural (*or* biological) mother; ***ihr ~er Sohn*** her own son; ***~e Genüsse*** physical comforts; ***die ~e Hülle*** *gen.* the mortal remains of; ***~es Wohl***(***ergehen***) physical well-being, *w.s.* creature comforts; *iro.* ***wir werden schon für dein ~es Wohl sorgen*** we'll make sure you don't go hungry; **'Leib·lich·keit** *f* (-; *no pl.*) physical nature, corporeality

'Leib|ren·te *f* life annuity; **~schmer·zen** *pl.* stomache-ache *sg.*

'Leib-'See·le-Proˌblem *n* body-mind problem; **'leib'see·lisch** *adj.* body-mind ...; ⚕ *etc.* psychosomatic

'Leib-und-'Ma·gen-Ge·richt *n* → ***Leibgericht***

'Leib|wa·che *f* bodyguard(s *pl.*); team of bodyguards; **~wäch·ter** *m* bodyguard; **~wä·sche** *f* underwear

Lei·che ['laɪçə] *f* (-; -n) corpse, (dead) body; *zo.* carcass, cadaver; ***die Opfer konnten nur noch als ~n geborgen werden*** all help for the victims came too late; *fig.* ***sie sieht aus wie e-e wandelnde*** (*or* ***lebende***) ***~*** she looks like death warmed up (*or* like a corpse); ***er geht über ~n*** he'll stop at nothing; ***nur über m-e ~!*** over my dead body!

'Lei·chen|be·fund *m* post-mortem findings *pl.*; **~be·gäng·nis** [-bəgɛŋnɪs] *n* (-ses; -se) funeral, burial; funeral service, *formal*: obsequies *pl.*; **~be·schau** *f* inquest; **~be·schau·er** *m* coroner; **~be·stat·ter** *m* undertaker, *Am.* mortician, *formal*: funeral director; **~bit·ter·mie·ne** *f* doleful expression

'lei·chen'blaß *adj.* deathly pale, (as) white as a sheet (*or* ghost); **'Lei·chen·bläs·se** *f* deathly pallor

'Lei·chen|fei·er *f* funeral reception; **~fled·de·rei** [-flɛdəraɪ] *f* (-; -en) body-stripping; **~fled·de·rer** [-flɛdərɐ] *m* (-s; -) body-stripper; **~frau** *f* layer-out; **~ge·ruch** *m* smell of (decaying) corpses *or* a (decaying) corpse; **~gift** *n* ptomaine

'lei·chen·haft *adj.* corpse-like, cadaverous; ***~e Blässe*** deathly pallor

'Lei·chen|hal·le *f*, **~haus** *n* mortuary; **~hemd** *n* shroud; **~öff·nung** *f* postmortem (examination), autopsy; **~raub** *m* **1.** body-snatching; **2.** → ***Leichenfledderei***; **~räu·ber** *m* **1.** body-snatcher; **2.** → ***Leichenfledderer***; **~re·de** *f* funeral oration; *fig.* ***e-e ~ halten*** have a post-mortem; ***es hat keinen Sinn, ~n zu halten*** it's no use crying over spilt milk; **~red·ner** *m* funeral orator; person holding the funeral oration; **~re·ste** *pl.* remains of a (*or* the) body *or* of (the) bodies; **~sack** *m* body bag; **~schän·der** *m* necrophiliac; **~schän·dung** *f* necrophilia; **~schau** *f* ⚖ (coroner's) inquest, post-mortem (examination); **~schau·haus** *n* morgue; **~schmaus** *m* funeral reception (*or* party), wake; *sl.* cold-meat party; **~star·re** *f* rigor mortis; **~tuch** *n* shroud (*a. fig.*), winding sheet; **~ver·bren·nung** *f* cremation; **~wa·gen** *m* hearse; **~zug** *m* funeral procession

Leich·nam ['laɪçna:m] *m* (-s; -e) corpse, body; ***der ~ Christi*** the body of Christ

leicht [laɪçt] **I.** *adj.* **1.** light (*a. food, wine, clothing, reading, music etc.*); mild *cigar*; ⚙ light(weight); ***~en Fußes*** lightfootedly, nimbly, *fig.* with a spring in one's gait; ***~en Herzens*** a) happily, relieved, b) readily; ***jetzt ist mir ~er*** (***ums Herz***)***!*** what a relief!; ***er hat e-n ~en Schlaf*** he's a light sleeper; F ***danach war ich um hundert Mark ~er*** I came away a hundred marks lighter; → ***Kost***; **2.** gentle *breeze, touch etc.*; **3.** slight (*a. cold*); *a.* mild *concussion, inflammation*; minor *injury, mistake etc.*; little *mistake etc.*; *mot.* surface *scratch*; ***~er Regen*** (***Schnee***) light rainfall (snowfall); ⚕ ***ein ~er Fall*** a) nothing serious, b) (a) straightforward case; ***er hat e-e ~e Bronchitis*** he has a mild case of (F a touch of) bronchitis; ***ein ~es Vergehen*** a petty crime; ***e-e ~e Strafe*** a mild punishment, ⚖ a mild sentence; **4.** easy; ***~er Sieg*** walkover, *Am.* walkaway; ***nichts ~er als das!*** no problem (at all); ***mit ihm hat sie's nicht ~*** she has a rough time with him; ***er nimmt es auf die ~e Schulter*** he's taking it very lightly; → ***leichtmachen***; **5.** ***ein ~es Mädchen*** F a bit of a tart; **II.** *adv.* **6.** slightly; ***~ berühren*** touch gently (*or* carefully), brush against; ***das ist ~ übertrieben*** that's a slight (*or* a bit of an) exaggeration; **7.** easily; ***es geht ganz ~*** it's (very) easy; ***~er gesagt als getan, das ist ~ gesagt*** easier said than done; ***du hast ~ reden*** it's all right (*Am.* alright) for you, 'you can talk; ***sie ist ~ gekränkt*** she's easily offended; ***er erkältet sich ~*** he catches cold very easily, he's always catching cold; ***so etwas passiert ~*** that (sort of thing) can happen very easily (*or* before you know it); ***das wird so ~ nicht wieder passieren*** it's not likely to happen again; ***das wird mir so ~ nicht wieder passieren*** I'll make sure that doesn't happen again in a hurry; ***das wird er so ~ nicht vergessen*** I bet he won't forget that in a hurry; ***es ist ~ möglich*** that could well be, that's quite possible; ***du kannst dir ~ denken ...*** you can well imagine ...; ***die hat's*** (***nicht gerade***) ***~*** she has (doesn't exactly have) an easy time of it; ***er könnte ~ sein Bruder sein*** he could easily be his brother; ***es ist ihm ein ~es zu*** *inf.* it's no problem (F no big deal) for him to *inf.*

'Leicht·athˌlet *m* athlete; **'Leicht·athˌle·tik** *f* track-and-field sports *pl.*, athletics *pl.*; **'leicht·athˌle·tisch** *adj.* athletic, track-and-field

'Leicht·bau *m* (-[e]s; *no pl.*) lightweight construction; **~stoff** *m* lightweight construction material; **~wei·se** *f* lightweight construction

'leicht|be·deckt *adj.*: ***~er Himmel*** slightly overcast skies, slight cloud cover; **~be·klei·det** *adj.* lightly dressed; scantily dressed (*iro.* clad)

'Leicht·benˌzin *n* benzine

'leicht·be·schwingt *adj.* lilting *melody*, lighthearted

'Leicht·beˌton *m* lightweight concrete

'leicht|be·waff·net *adj.* lightly armed; **~be·weg·lich** *adj.* easily transportable; ⚙ easily adjustable

'leicht·blü·tig [-bly:tɪç] *adj.* lighthearted; **'Leicht·blü·tig·keit** *f* (-; *no pl.*) lightheartedness

'leicht·ent·zünd·lich *adj.* highly inflammable (*esp. Am. and* ⚙ flammable)

Leich·ter ['laɪçtɐ] *m* (-s; -) ⚓ lighter

'leicht·fal·len *v/i.* (*irr.*, *sep.*, sn, → ***fallen***) be easy (***j-m*** for s.o.); ***es fällt ihm nicht leicht*** it isn't easy for him (***zu*** *inf.* to *inf.*), he doesn't find it easy (*ger. or* to *inf.*); ***so etwas fällt ihm leicht*** he finds that sort of thing easy, that sort of thing comes easily (F easy) to him, he has no difficulty with that sort of thing

'leicht·fer·tig I. *adj.* careless, thoughtless; irresponsible; frivolous; facile; ***~es Gerede*** loose talk; **II.** *adv.*: ***et. ~ abtun*** shrug s.th. off; ***et. ~ aufs Spiel setzen*** gamble with s.th.; **'Leicht·fer·tig·keit** *f* (-; *no pl.*) carelessness *etc.*; → ***leichtfertig*** I

'Leicht·flug·zeug *n* light aircraft

'leicht·fü·ßig [-fy:sıç] *adj.* nimble, *lit.* fleet-footed

'leicht·gän·gig *adj.* ⚙ smooth

'leicht·ge·schürzt *hum. adj.* scantily clad

'Leicht·ge·wicht *n* (-[e]s; *no pl.*) *sport*: lightweight (*a.* F *fig.*); **'Leicht·ge·wicht·ler** [-gəvıçtlɐ] *m* (-s; -) lightweight

'leicht·gläu·big *adj.* gullible, credulous; **'Leicht·gläu·big·keit** *f* (-; *no pl.*) gullibility, credulity

'Leicht·heit *f* (-; *no pl.*) lightness

'leicht·her·zig *adj.* lighthearted; *a. contp.* carefree; **'Leicht·her·zig·keit** *f* (-; *no pl.*) lightheartedness; *contp.* carefree attitude (*or* outlook on life *etc.*); nonchalance

'leicht'hin *adv.* casually, F just like that

Leich·tig·keit ['laıçtıçkaıt] *f* (-; *no pl.*) **1.** easiness, ease; ***mit*** (***größter***) ***~*** with (the greatest of) ease, effortlessly; ***es ist für ihn e-e ~*** it's no problem (F big deal, great shakes) for him, it's the easiest thing in the world for him; **2.** lightness

'Leicht·in·du͵strie *f* light industry

'leicht·le·big [-le:bıç] *adj.* easygoing; happy-go-lucky; **'Leicht·le·big·keit** *f* (-; *no pl.*) easygoing (*or* happy-go-lucky) attitude *or* nature

'leicht·lös·lich *adj.* easily soluble

'leicht·ma·chen *v/t.* (*sep.*, h): ***j-m et. ~*** make s.th. easy for s.o.; ***es sich ~*** take the easy way out; ***du machst es dir zu leicht*** you're taking things too lightly, it's not as easy as that

'Leicht·ma͵tro·se *m* ordinary seaman

'Leicht·me͵tall *n* light metal; **~bau** *m* (-[e]s; -ten) light-metal construction; **~in·du͵strie** *f* light metals industry

'leicht·neh·men *v/t.* (*irr.*, *sep.*, h, → ***nehmen***) take *s.th.* lightly; ***er nimmt es zu leicht*** he doesn't take it seriously enough; ***das Leben ~*** take life as it comes; F ***nimm's leicht!*** don't worry about it

'Leicht·sinn *m* (-[e]s; *no pl.*) carelessness; ***sträflicher ~*** criminal negligence; ***jugendlicher ~*** youthful abandon; ***purer ~*** sheer recklessness; **'leicht·sin·nig I.** *adj.* careless; **II.** *adv.*: ***~ umgehen mit*** *dat.* be careless with; **'leicht·sin·ni·ger·'wei·se** *adv.* carelessly; rashly, unthinkingly; **'Leicht·sinns·feh·ler** *m* careless mistake

'leicht·tun *v/i. and v/refl.* (*irr.*, *sep.*, h, → ***tun***): ***sich ~ mit e-r Sache*** have no difficulties with s.th., have no difficulty doing s.th., find it easy to do s.th.; ***mit so etwas tut er sich leicht*** *a.* that sort of thing comes easily (F easy) to him

'leicht|ver·dau·lich *adj.* easily digestible, *a. fig.* light; **~ver·derb·lich** *adj.* perishable; ***~e Waren*** perishables; **~ver·dient** *adj.*: ***~es Geld*** easy money

'leicht·ver·letzt *adj.* slightly hurt (*or* injured); **'Leicht·ver·letz·te** *m, f* (-n; -n) minor casualty; slightly injured person

'leicht·ver·ständ·lich *adj.* easy to understand (*or* follow); (very) straightforward; ***~e Lektüre*** easy reading; ***in ~er Form*** in comprehensible (*or* accessible) form

'leicht·ver·wun·det *adj.* slightly wounded; **'Leicht·ver·wun·de·te** *m* (-n; -n) minor casualty

leid [laıt] *adj.* **1.** (***es***) ***tut mir ~*** (I'm) sorry; ***das tut mir aber ~*** I'm sorry to hear that; ***es tut mir leid, aber ...*** I'm afraid ..., much as I'd like to, ...; ***es tut mir ~ um ihn*** I feel sorry for him; ***es tut mir um die Kinder*** (***Möbel***) ***~*** it's the children I feel sorry for (it's the furniture I'm worried about); ***es wird dir ~ tun*** you'll be sorry, you'll regret it; **2.** ***ich bin es ~*** I've had enough of it, I'm sick and tired of it; ***ich habe es so ~*** *a.* I can't take it any more

Leid [laıt] *n* (-[e]s; *no pl.*) a) suffering, b) sorrow, grief, c) harm; ***j-m ein ~ zufügen*** harm s.o., lay hands on s.o.; ***j-m tiefes ~ zufügen*** cause s.o. great suffering; ***es wird ihm kein ~ geschehen*** he won't come to any harm; ***j-m sein ~ klagen*** pour one's heart out to s.o.; *lit.* ***~ tragen*** mourn (***um*** *acc.* for); → ***geteilt***

Lei·de·form ['laıdə-] *f ling.* passive (voice)

lei·den ['laıdən] (litt, gelitten, h) **I.** *v/i.* suffer (***an*** *dat.*, ***unter*** *dat.* from); be in (considerable) pain; *fig.* smart (***unter*** *dat.* from); ***er leidet an e-r Leberkrankheit*** (***Herzkrankheit*** *etc.*) he's got a liver (heart *etc.*) condition; ***s-e Gesundheit litt darunter*** it took its toll on his health; ***der Motor hat stark gelitten*** the engine has been severely affected; ***die Bäume haben am meisten gelitten*** the trees have suffered most (*or* have come off worst); **II.** *v/t.* suffer *hunger*, *want etc.*; *w.s.* put up with; stand, endure; ***gut ~ können*** like, *a.* have a soft spot for *s.o.*; ***ich kann ihn*** (***es***) ***nicht ~*** I can't stand him (it); ***ich hab' ihn*** (***es***) ***nie ~ können*** I've never liked him (it); ***er war dort nur gelitten*** he was tolerated there; **III.** ♀ *n* (-s; -) suffering(s *pl.*); illness, ailment; *in cpds.* condition (*e.g.* ***Leberleiden*** liver condition); ***es ist das alte ~*** it's the same old complaint; ***das ~ Christi*** the Passion; F *fig.* ***aussehen wie das ~ Christi*** F look like death warmed up; **'lei·dend I.** *adj.* suffering; ailing; *fig.* woeful *look etc.*; ***~ aussehen*** look ill; **II.** *adv.*: *fig.* ***j-n ~ ansehen*** give s.o. a woeful look

'Lei·den·schaft *f* (-; -en) passion; (powerful) emotion; ardo(u)r; zeal, fervo(u)r; ***mit ~*** *tun etc.*: passionately, with a passion; ***Angeln ist s-e ~*** he's a passionate angler; ***Musik ist s-e ~*** music is his passion, *a.* he's a passionate musician; ***ein Gärtner aus ~*** a dedicated gardener

'lei·den·schaft·lich I. *adj.* passionate; very emotional; hotheaded; *fig.* impassioned *appeal, speech etc.*; ardent *desire, request etc.*; enthusiastic; violent; ***er ist ein ~er Skifahrer*** he loves (*or* adores) skiing; **II.** *adv. love, hate etc.* passionately; ***et. ~ gern tun*** love (*or* adore) doing s.th.; ***~ gern ins Kino gehen*** love (going to) the cinema (*Am.* movies); ***ich esse ~ gern Schokolade*** I love chocolate, F I'm a chocolate addict (*or* a chocoholic);

'Lei·den·schaft·lich·keit *f* (-; *no pl.*) passion(ateness); ardo(u)r; enthusiasm; vehemence

'lei·den·schafts·los *adj.* unemotional, cool; impassive; **'Lei·den·schafts·lo·sig·keit** *f* (-; *no pl.*) lack of emotion; coolness; impassiveness

'Lei·dens|ge·nos·se *m* fellow sufferer; companion in distress; **~ge·schich·te** *f* **1.** sad story (*or* history); *iro.* tale of woe; **2.** *eccl. the* Passion; **~mie·ne** *f* woeful look (*or* expression); **~weg** *m* **1.** long ordeal; **2.** *eccl.* way of the Cross; **~werk·zeu·ge** *pl. eccl.* instruments of the Passion; **~zeit** *f* time of suffering

lei·der ['laıdɐ] *adv.* unfortunately; ***~ müssen wir jetzt gehen*** *a.* I'm afraid we have to go now; ***~ ja!*** I'm afraid so; ***~ nicht!*** I'm afraid not; ***~*** (***Gottes***)***!*** unfortunately(, yes)

'leid·er·füllt *adj.* grief-stricken

'leid·ge·beugt *adj.* bowed down with grief

'leid·ge·prüft *adj.* sorely tried; ***das ist e-e ~e Familie*** that family has been through a lot

lei·dig ['laıdıç] *adj.* annoying; tiresome; wretched; ***das ~e Geld*** filthy lucre; ***es ist e-e ~e Geschichte*** it's an unpleasant affair; ***immer diese ~en Kopfschmerzen*** these wretched headaches

leid·lich ['laıtlıç] **I.** *adj.* bearable; passable; ***sein Englisch ist ~*** his English isn't too bad; **II.** *adv.* passably, tolerably, reasonably *clean etc.*; (*a.* ***~ gut***) not too bad(ly), reasonably good (well); ***er spielt ~ gut Violine*** *a.* he's a passable violin-player; *wie geht's?* - ***~*** fair to middling, F so-so

'Leid·tra·gen·de *m, f* (-n; -n): ***der ~*** the one who suffers; ***die ~n*** the ones who suffer; ***er ist immer der ~*** *a.* he's always the one to suffer

'leid·voll *adj.* sorrowful *expression*; ***ein ~es Leben*** a life of sorrow

'Leid·we·sen *n*: ***zu m-m*** (***großen***) ***~*** much to my regret; ***zum ~*** *gen.* to the chagrin of

Lei·er ['laıɐ] *f* (-; -n) **1.** barrel organ; *fig.* ***immer die alte*** (*or* ***dieselbe***) ***~*** (it's) the same old story every time, F can't he *etc.* change the record?; **2.** *ast.* Lyra; **3.** ⚙ crank; **'Lei·er·ka·sten** *m* barrel organ; **'Lei·er(ka·sten)mann** *m* (-[e]s; ¨er) organ grinder; **'lei·ern** F (h) **I.** *v/t.* **1.** ***nach oben ~*** crank up; ***nach unten ~*** lower; **2.** *fig.* rattle off, drone out; **II.** *v/i.* **3.** *wheel*: be wobbly; **4.** *fig.* drone (on), rattle on

Leih|amt ['laı-] *n* pawnshop; **~ar·bei·ter** *m* loan worker, seconded employee; **~ar·beits·ver·hält·nis** *n* secondment; **~bi·blio͵thek** *f*, **~bü·che͵rei** *f* lending library

lei·hen ['laıən] *v/t.* (lieh, geliehen, h) **1.** lend (out); lend, loan *money*; loan *painting etc.* (*dat.* to *a museum etc.*); ***j-m et. ~*** lend (*Am. a.* loan) s.o. s.th. (*or* s.th. to s.o.), lend s.th. (out) to s.o.; ***kannst du mir dein Auto ~?*** could you lend me your car?; *fig.* ***j-m sein Ohr ~*** lend s.o. one's ear; **2.** borrow; ***sich et. von j-m ~*** borrow (*or* hire, *Am.* rent) s.th. from s.o.; ***es ist*** (***nur***) ***geliehen*** it's not mine, I (only) borrowed it, *painting etc.*: it's on loan

Leih|frist ['laı-] *f* lending period; **~ga·be** *f* object (*or* painting *etc.*) *on loan*; ***es ist e-e ~ von*** *dat.* it's on loan from; **~ge-**

bühr *f* rental (*or* lending) fee; **~ge·schäft** *n* lending business; **~haus** *n* pawnshop; **~mut·ter** *f* surrogate mother; **~mut·ter·schaft** *f* surrogate motherhood, surrogacy; **~schein** *m* **1.** pawn ticket; **2.** *library*: borrowing slip; **~ski·er** *pl.* rental (*or* hired) skis; **~stim·me** *f*: ***wir haben keine ~n zu vergeben*** we can't afford to sacrifice any votes; **~wa·gen** *m* hire (*Am.* rented) car

'leih·wei·se *adv.* on loan; on hire; ***j-m et. ~ überlassen*** lend (*Am. a.* loan) s.o. s.th.; ***könnten Sie es mir ~ geben?*** *a.* could I borrow it (for a while)?

Leim [laɪm] *m* (-[e]s; -e) glue; F ***aus dem ~ gehen*** a) *a. fig.* fall apart, come apart at the seams, b) F *fig.* balloon; F ***auf den ~ führen*** take *s.o.* for a ride; F ***j-m auf den ~ gehen*** (*or* ***kriechen***) fall for s.o.'s line, be taken in by s.o.; **lei·men** ['laɪmən] *v/t.* (h) glue (together); F *fig.* ***geleimt werden*** be taken in (*or* for a ride), F be had

'Leim·far·be *f* distemper

lei·mig ['laɪmɪç] *adj.* gluey

'Leim|ru·te *f* lime twig; **~sie·der** [-ziːdɐ] F *m* (-s; -) F slowcoach, *Am.* F slowpoke

Lein [laɪn] *m* (-[e]s; -e) flax

Lei·ne ['laɪnə] *f* (-; -n) a) (thin) rope; clothes line, b) lead, leash; *fig.* ***j-n an der (kurzen) ~ haben*** *or* ***halten*** keep s.o. on a short lead, keep a tight rein on s.o.; *sl.* ***zieh ~!*** *sl.* push off!

lei·nen ['laɪnən] *adj.* linen

'Lei·nen *n* (-s; *no pl.*) linen; ***in ~ gebunden*** clothbound; **~band** *m* (-[e]s; ⸚e) clothbound book; **~bettuch** (*sep.* -tt·t-) *n* (linen) sheet; **~ein·band** *m* cloth binding; **~sack** *m* burlap bag; **~schu·he** *pl.* canvas shoes; **~zeug** *n* linen; **~zwang** *m* mandatory leashing of dogs; ***dort herrscht ~*** dogs have to be kept on a lead (*or* leash) there

'Lein·öl *n* linseed oil

'Lein·sa·men *m* linseed; **~brot** *n* bread with linseed; **~öl** *n* linseed oil

'Lein·tuch *n* linen; (linen) sheet

'Lein·wand *f* **1.** canvas; ***auf ~ malen*** paint on canvas; **2.** *film*: screen; ***die Helden der ~*** the heroes of the silver screen; ***auf die ~ bannen*** preserve on celluloid; **~grö·ße** *f* screen celebrity; **~held** *m* screen hero

lei·se ['laɪzə] **I.** *adj.* faint *noise*; soft *voice, music etc.*; quiet *person*; *fig.* faint *hope etc.*; slight *suspicion etc.*; ***mit ~r Stimme*** in a low voice; ***seid bitte ~!*** quiet, please; not so loud, please; F *iro.* can you turn the volume down, please; **~r *stellen*** turn down; ***wir müssen ~ sein*** we'll have to keep the noise (*or* our voices) down; ***ich habe nicht die ~ste Ahnung*** I haven't the faintest idea; **II.** *adv. sing, knock etc.* softly; *a. speak etc.* in a low voice; quietly; gently; ***sprich ~(r)*** not so loud, keep your voice down (a bit); ***~ vor sich hin murmeln*** mumble away to oneself; ***~ (auf)treten*** tread softly, *fig.* sing small

'Lei·se·tre·ter [-treːtɐ] *m* (-s; -) pussyfooter; **'Lei·se·tre·te·rei** [-treːtəraɪ] *f* (-; *no pl.*) pussyfooting

Lei·ste ['laɪstə] *f* (-; -n) **1.** border; strip of wood; skirting board; ⚙ (guide) rail; *typ.* edge; *textil.* selvage; **2.** *anat.* groin

lei·sten ['laɪstən] *v/t.* (h) **1.** do; manage; achieve, accomplish; ***du hast aber nicht sehr viel geleistet*** you haven't come up with much; ***ich habe schon einiges geleistet*** I haven't been idle; ***was leistet der Wagen?*** what does (*or* can) the car do?; ***gute Arbeit ~*** do a good job; ***da mußt du schon was ~*** you've got to show what you can do; ***er hat Großes geleistet*** he has some remarkable achievements to his name, it was a great performance; → ***Dienst*** 2, ***Eid, Folge***; **2.** ***ich kann mir das nicht ~*** I can't afford that (*fig.* to do that); ***ich kann es mir nicht ~ zu*** *inf. a. fig.* I can't afford to *inf.*; ***leiste dir doch mal etwas*** give yourself a treat; ***heute leiste ich mir e-n Kognak*** I'm going to treat myself to (*iro.* splash out on) a brandy today; *fig.* ***was hast du dir da wieder geleistet?*** what have you been up to this time?; ***du leistest dir ja Dinge!*** you certainly get up to things(, don't you)?

Lei·sten ['laɪstən] *m* (-s; -) shoe tree; last; *fig.* ***alles über e-n ~ schlagen*** tar everything with the same brush

'Lei·sten|bruch *m* ⚕ hernia; **~ge·gend** *f* groin; **~zer·rung** *f* groin injury; ***e-e ~ haben*** *a.* have pulled a groin muscle

Lei·stung ['laɪstʊŋ] *f* (-; -en) **1.** achievement; (great) feat; *a. sport etc.* performance; work; results *pl.*; ***e-e hervorragende ~!*** an excellent job; ***schwache ~!*** poor show; ***nach ~ bezahlt werden*** be paid by results; ***unter (über) der üblichen ~*** below (above) standard; **2.** ⚙, ✝ performance; power; capacity (*a.* ⚕); output; **3.** ⚡ power, wattage, output, input; **4.** a) service(s *pl.* rendered), b) payment, *insurance etc.*: benefit, c) contribution

'Lei·stungs|ab·fall *m ped.* deterioration in *a pupil's* work; ✝, *sport*: drop in performance; ⚕ loss of energy; ⚙ drop in efficiency (*or* output); ⚡ power drop; **~an·ga·be** *f* ⚙ power rating; **~an·spruch** *m* entitlement to benefits; **~an·stieg** *m ped. etc.* improvement in *s.o.'s* work (*sport*: performance); ⚙ increase in efficiency (*or* output)

'lei·stungs·be·rech·tigt *adj. insurance etc.*: entitled to benefits; **'Lei·stungs·be·rech·ti·gung** *f* entitlement to (receive) benefits

'lei·stungs·be·zo·gen *adj.* performance-oriented

'Lei·stungs|bi̦lanz *f* balance of payments; **~den·ken** *n* performance orientation, competitive thinking; **~druck** *m* (-[e]s; *no pl.*) pressure to perform; *ped.* pressure (to get higher marks *or* grades); **~ein·heit** *f phys.* unit of power; **~emp·fän·ger** *m* beneficiary

'lei·stungs·fä·hig *adj.* efficient (*a.* ⚙, ✝); fit; *ped. etc.* capable; ✝ solvent; **'Lei·stungs·fä·hig·keit** *f* (-; *no pl.*) efficiency; ⚙ *a.* performance, output; fitness; *ped. etc.* ability

'Lei·stungs·fak·tor *m* ⚙ power factor

'lei·stungs·ge·recht *adj.*: ***~e Bezahlung*** adequate pay

'Lei·stungs|ge·sell·schaft *f* achievement- (*or* performance-)oriented society, achieving society; **~gren·ze** *f* limit(s *pl.*) (of performance *etc.*); ✝ maximum output; ***s-e ~*** his limits; **~grup·pe** *f* ability group; **~knick** *m* sudden drop in performance; **~kurs** *m ped.* special subject; ***ich bin im ~ Geschichte*** I'm taking history as a special subject; **~kur·ve** *f* performance chart; **~lohn** *m* incentive pay; **~mensch** *m* (high) achiever; **~nach·weis** *m* certificate; **~ni̦veau** *n* standard (of performance); *ped. a.* achievement level

'lei·stungs·ori·en̦tiert *adj.* achievement-oriented

'Lei·stungs·pflicht *f* ✝ liability

'lei·stungs·pflich·tig [-pflɪçtɪç] *adj.* liable to pay

'Lei·stungs|prä·mie *f* incentive bonus; **~prin̦zip** *n* achievement principle; **~prü·fung** *f* performance (*ped.* achievement) test; **~rück·gang** *m* → ***Leistungsabfall***

'lei·stungs·schwach *adj.* ⚙ low-performance ...; *ped. etc.* weak; ***~er Schüler*** *a.* underachiever

'Lei·stungs|soll *n* target; **~sport** *m* serious sport(s *pl.*); **~sport·ler** *m* **1.** serious runner (*or* athlete *etc.*); **2.** → ***Spitzensportler***; **~stand** *m* performance level

'lei̦·stungs·stark *adj.* ⚙, ✝ *etc.* powerful; *ped. etc.* (more) capable; *sport*: strong *team*; ***~er Schüler*** *a.* high achiever

'lei·stungs·stei·gernd *adj.* performance-enhancing; **'Lei·stungs·stei·ge·rung** *f* increase in efficiency *etc.*; ⚙ *a.* increased output

'Lei·stungs|test *m* → ***Leistungsprüfung***; **~ver·mö·gen** *n* → ***Leistungsfähigkeit***; **~zen·trum** *n* (exclusive) training centre (*Am.* center); **~zwang** *m* → ***Leistungsdruck***

Leit·ar̦ti·kel ['laɪt-] *m* leader, leading article (*Am.* editorial); **'Leit·ar·tik·ler** [-artiːklɐ] F *m* (-s; -) leader (*Am.* editorial) writer

'Leit·bild *n* (role) model

lei·ten ['laɪtən] (h) **I.** *v/t.* **1.** lead; steer; direct; *fig.* guide; ***sich von s-n Gefühlen ~ lassen*** be guided (*or* governed) by one's emotions; **2.** head; *pol.* govern; run, be in charge of *a department etc.*; supervise; chair *a meeting etc.*; ***wer leitet die Delegation?*** who is head of (*or* heading) the delegation?; **3.** ♪ conduct; ***e-e Kapelle ~*** be leader of a (*or* the) band, be (the) bandleader; **4.** *sport*: referee; **5.** *phys., physiol. etc.* conduct; **6.** ⚙ pipe *gas, oil etc.*; **7.** pass *letter etc.* on(to ***an*** *acc.*), direct (to); **II.** *v/i.*: *phys. etc.* ***gut (schlecht) ~*** be a good (bad) conductor; **'lei·tend** *adj.* **1.** leading; ***~e Stellung*** managerial post; ***~er Angestellter*** managerial employee, *esp. Am.* executive, *pl.* senior staff *sg.*; ***~er Ingenieur*** chief engineer; **2.** *phys.* conductive; ***nicht ~*** non-conductive

Lei·ter[1] ['laɪtɐ] *m* (-s; -) **1.** ✝ manager, director; head of department; head; chairman; ♪ conductor; leader; ***technischer ~*** technical director; ***~ sein von*** *dat. a.* be in charge of; **2.** *phys.*, ⚡ conductor

'Lei·ter[2] *f* (-; -n) ladder (*a. fig.*); (e-e ~ a pair of) steps *pl.*; **~wa·gen** *m* (hand)cart

Leit·fa·den ['laɪt-] *m* **1.** main thread *or* theme (running through s.th.); **2.** guide (*gen.* to *zoology etc.*)

leit·fä·hig ['laɪt-] *adj. phys.* conductive; **'Leit·fä·hig·keit** *f* (-; *no pl.*) conductivity

Leit|feu·er ['laɪt-] *n* beacon; **~fi̦gur** *f* model (to follow), F bellwether; **~foșsil** *n geol.* index fossil; **~ge·dan·ke** *m* central theme; guiding principle; **~ham·mel** *m* bellwether; F *fig.* leader of the pack; *fig.* ***manche Leute brauchen immer e-n ~*** some people always have to play follow-the-leader; **~idee** *f* central theme; **~ke·gel** *m mot.* traffic cone;

~li•nie *f* **1.** guideline; **2.** *mot.* dotted line; **~mo,tiv** *n* ♪ *and fig.* leitmotif; **~plan•ke** *f mot.* crash barrier, *Am.* guard rail; **~satz** *m* guiding principle; **~spruch** *m* motto; **~stel•le** *f* central office; *subway etc.*: control cent|re (*Am.* -er); **~stern** *m* lode star; *fig. a.* guiding star; **~stu•die** *f* pilot study; **~the•ma** *n* main (*or* keynote) theme; leitmotif; key issue; **~tier** *n* leader; **~ton** *m* ♪ leading note

Lei•tung ['laɪtʊŋ] *f* (-; -en) **1.** *no pl.* management; administration; direction, control, supervision; organization; chairmanship; management committee; **...** ***wurde ausgeführt unter der ~ von X*** ... was carried out under the direction of X; ♪ ***das Sinfonieorchester unter der ~ von X*** the symphoy orchestra conducted by X; ***die ~ haben*** be in charge (**von** *dat.* of), ♪ be the conductor (of), **von** *dat.*: *a.* be conducting; ***unter der ~ stehen von*** *dat.* (*or gen.*) be directed (*or* headed, supervised, ♪ conducted) by; **2.** ⚡ lead; wire; circuit; ⚙ pipes *pl.*, pipeline; main(s *pl.*); duct; *teleph.* ***in der ~ bleiben*** hold the line; ***die ~ ist besetzt*** the line is engaged (*or* busy); ***da ist jemand in der ~*** the lines seem to be crossed; F *fig.* ***e-e lange ~ haben*** be slow on the uptake; F ***du stehst wohl auf der ~*** F not quite with it today, are we?

'Lei•tungs|draht *m* lead wire; **~mast** *m* (electricity) pylon; **~netz** *n* supply network; mains system; **~rohr** *n* water pipe; gas pipe; **~was•ser** *n* tap water; **~,wi•der•stand** *m* ⚡ line resistance

Leit|ver•mö•gen ['laɪt-] *n* (-s; *no pl.*) *phys.* conductivity; **~wäh•rung** *f* key currency; **~werk** *n* ✈ tail (unit); **~wert** *m* ⚡ conductance; **~wort** *n* (-[e]s; -e) motto; **~zahl** *f phot.* guide number; **~zins** *m* key interest rate, central bank discount rate

Lek•ti•on [lɛk'tsĭo:n] *f* (-; -en) chapter, unit; *fig.* lesson; *fig.* ***j-m e-e ~ erteilen*** teach s.o. a lesson

Lek•tor ['lɛkto:ɐ] *m* (-s; -en [lɛk'to:rən]) **1.** *univ.* language assistant, F lektor; **2.** editor; **Lek•to•rat** [lɛkto'ra:t] *n* (-[e]s; -e) **1.** *univ.* language teaching (*or* assistant's) post, F lektorship; **2.** (editorial) department

Lek•tü•re [lɛk'ty:rə] *f* (-; -n) reading (matter), something to read; books *pl.*; ***leichte*** (***schwere*** *etc.*) **~** light (heavy *etc.*) reading; ***bei der ~ des Buchs entdeckte ich ...*** when I read (*or* while I was reading) the book I discovered ...; ***... ist keine geeignete ~ für*** ... isn't suitable (reading) for; ***das ist keine ~ für dich*** that's not the right (kind of) book for you, that's not the sort of book you want to be reading; ***was können Sie mir als ~ empfehlen?*** what can you recommend me to read?; ***sich et. als ~ mitnehmen*** take s.th. to read

Lem•ming ['lɛmɪŋ] *m* (-s; -e) *zo.* lemming

Le•mu•re [le'mu:rə] *m* (-n; -n) *zo.* lemur

Len•de ['lɛndə] *f* (-; -n) **1.** *anat.* lumbar region, lower back; **2.** *gastr.* loin; **3.** *lit. pl.* loins

'Len•den|bra•ten *m* roast loin, sirloin; **~ge•gend** *f anat.* lumbar region; **~schurz** *m* loincloth; **~steak** *n* sirloin steak; **~stück** *n* (piece of) tenderloin; **~wir•bel** *m anat.* lumbar vertebra (*pl.* vertebrae)

Le•ni•nis•mus [leni'nɪsmʊs] *m* (-; *no pl.*) Leninism; **Le•ni•nist** [leni'nɪst] *m* (-en; -en), **le•ni•ni•stisch** [leni'nɪstɪʃ] *adj.* Leninist

Lenk•ach•se ['lɛŋk-] *f* steering axle

lenk•bar ['lɛŋkba:ɐ] *adj.* ⚙ manoeuvrable, *Am.* maneuverable; *fig.* tractable; ***leicht ~*** manageable; **'Lenk•bar•keit** *f* ⚙ manoeuvrability, *Am.* maneuverability; *fig.* manageability

len•ken ['lɛŋkən] *v/t.* (h) *mot.* steer; ✈ pilot, be at the controls of; turn (**nach** *dat.* towards, to); drive; *fig.* guide; *pol.* govern; ✝ control; ***die Aufmerksamkeit ~ auf*** *acc.* draw attention to, **sich**: *a.* attract attention; ***s-n Blick ~ auf*** *acc.* turn one's gaze to(wards); ***das Gespräch ~ auf*** *acc.* steer the conversation round to; ***s-e Schritte ~ nach*** *dat.* turn one's steps to(wards); → ***gelenkt, Verdacht***

Len•ker ['lɛŋkɐ] *m* (-s; -) **1.** a) steering wheel, b) handlebars *pl.*; **2.** *lit.* ruler, *lit.* helmsman

Lenk•flug•kör•per ['lɛŋk-] *m* guided missile

Lenk•rad ['lɛŋk-] *n* steering wheel; **~schal•tung** *f* steering-column change (*Am.* gearshift); **~schloß** *n* steering(-column) lock

lenk•sam ['lɛŋkza:m] *adj.* manageable, tractable; **'Lenk•sam•keit** *f* (-; *no pl.*) manageability, tractability

Lenk|säu•le ['lɛŋk-] *f mot.* steering column; **~stan•ge** *f* handlebars *pl.*

Len•kung ['lɛŋkʊŋ] *f* (-; -en) **1.** a) *mot.* steering system, b) *no pl.* steering; **2.** *no pl.* guidance (*a. fig.*); *pol.* government; ✝ control; **'Len•kungs•aus•schuß** *m* steering committee

Lenz [lɛnts] *poet. m* (-es; -e) **1.** *no pl.* spring; **2.** *fig.* prime (of life); ***er zählte zwanzig ~e*** he was twenty years of age; ***er zählte gerade zwanzig ~e*** he had just turned twenty; **3.** *fig.* ***sich e-n schönen*** (*or* ***faulen***) **~ *machen*** take things easy, have an easy time of it

len•zen ['lɛntsən] ⚓ (h) **I.** *v/t.* pump out; **II.** *v/i.* scud

Leo•pard [leo'part] *m* (-en; -en [-dən]) *zo.* leopard

Leo•par•den|fell [leo'pardən-] *n* leopardskin; **~man•tel** *m* leopardskin coat

Le•pra ['le:pra] *f* (-; *no pl.*) ⚕ leprosy; **~ko•lo,nie** *f* lepers' colony; **≈krank** *adj.*: **~ *sein*** have (*or* be suffering from) leprosy; **~kran•ke** *m, f* (-n; -n) leper

lep•to•som [lɛpto'zo:m] *adj.*, **Lep•to•so•me** [lɛpto'zo:mə] *m, f* (-n; -n) leptosome

Ler•che ['lɛrçə] *f* (-; -n) *zo.* lark

Lern•be•gier•de ['lɛrn-] *f* thirst for knowledge; **'lern•be•gie•rig** *adj.* eager to learn; ***ein ~er Schüler*** a (very) keen pupil

lern•be•hin•dert ['lɛrn-] *adj.* learning-disabled; educationally subnormal; **'Lern•be•hin•der•te** *m, f* (-n; -n) learning-disabled (*or* educationally subnormal) child; **'Lern•be•hin•de•rung** *f* learning handicap

Lern•ei•fer ['lɛrn-] *m* eagerness to learn; *ped. a.* keenness; **'lern•eif•rig** *adj.* eager to learn; *a.* keen *pupil*

ler•nen ['lɛrnən] (h) **I.** *v/t.* learn; pick up; ***lesen ~*** learn (how) to read; ***j-n schätzen ~*** come to appreciate s.o.; ***j-n lieben ~*** grow (*or* learn) to love s.o.; ***du wirst es nie ~*** you'll never learn; ***das will gelernt sein!*** it's not as easy as it looks; **II.** *v/i.* learn; study; *ped.* do (one's) homework; revise, do one's revision *for an exam*; be a trainee; ***fleißig ~*** work (*or* study) hard; ***schnell*** (***leicht***) **~** be a fast (good) learner; ***langsam*** (***schwer***) **~** be a slow (poor) learner; → ***gelernt***; **III.** *v/refl.*: ***das lernt sich leicht*** (***schwer***) that's easy (hard) to learn *od.* remember; ***das lernt sich schnell*** you'll learn that (*or* pick that up) in no time; **IV.** ≈ *n* (-s; *no pl.*) learning, studying; ***er tut sich mit dem ~ schwer*** he's not a good (*or* he's a poor) learner; ***j-m beim ~ helfen*** help s.o. with his (*or* her) homework *or* studies

lern•fä•hig ['lɛrn-] *adj.* educable; capable of learning; **'Lern•fä•hig•keit** *f* (-; *no pl.*) educability; learning ability (*or* capacity)

Lern•mit•tel ['lɛrn-] *n* learning aid; **~frei•heit** *f* (-; *no pl.*) free learning aids *pl.*

Lern|pro,zeß ['lɛrn-] *m* learning process; **~psy•cho•lo,gie** *f* psychology of learning; **~schwe•ster** *f* trainee nurse; **~schwie•rig•kei•ten** *pl.* difficulties (with) learning; **~spiel** *n* educational game; **~stoff** *m* learning matter; **~ver•mö•gen** *n* (-s; *no pl.*) learning ability; **~ziel** *n* (learning) objective *or* target

Les•art ['le:s-] *f* (-; -en) reading, version; ***verschiedene ~en*** variants, variant readings

les•bar ['le:sba:ɐ] *adj.* readable; legible *hand*; **'Les•bar•keit** *f* (-; *no pl.*) readability; legibility

Les•be ['lɛsbə] F *f* (-; -n) lesbian, *sl.* dike; **'Les•ben•treff** F *m* F lesbian hangout

Les•bie•rin ['lɛsbĭərɪn] *f* (-; -nen), **les•bisch** ['lɛsbɪʃ] *adj.* lesbian

Le•se ['le:zə] *f* (-; -n) vintage; harvest

Le•se•abend ['le:zə-] *m* (evening) reading session; (evening) play reading *or* poetry reading

le•se•blind ['le:zə-] *adj.* alexic; **'Le•se•blind•heit** *f* alexia

Le•se|bril•le ['le:zə-] *f*: (***e-e ~*** a pair of) reading glasses *pl.*; **~buch** *n* reading book, reader; **~dra•ma** *n* closet drama; **~ecke** *f* reading corner; **~ge•rät** *n computer*: scanner; **~ge•wohn•hei•ten** *pl.* reading habits *pl.*; **~hun•ger** *m* appetite for books; **≈hung•rig** *adj.* starved for books; **~kopf** *m computer*: reading head; **~kreis** *m* reading circle; **~lam•pe** *f* reading lamp

le•sen[1] ['le:zən] (las, gelesen, h) **I.** *v/t.* read (*a. computer*); make out; ***falsch ~*** misread; *univ.* ***Geschichte*** *etc.* **~** teach history *etc.*; **II.** *v/i.* read; *univ.* **~ *über*** *acc.* teach, lecture on; ***viel ~*** read a lot, do a lot of reading; **III.** *v/refl.*: ***sich gut ~*** a) be very readable, be a good read, b) be very legible, *print*: read well; ***sich schlecht ~*** be hard to read, F be tough going; ***es liest sich wie ein Roman*** (***Krimi***) it's like reading a novel (it makes for exciting reading); ***in diesem Licht liest es sich schlecht*** this light isn't good for reading (in); **IV.** ≈ *n* (-s; *no pl.*) reading

'le•sen[2] *v/t.* (las, gelesen, h) gather; pick, harvest *grapes*

'le•sens•wert *adj.* worth reading

Le•se|pro•be ['le:zə-] *f* **1.** *thea.* first rehearsal; **2.** sample; **~pu•bli•kum** *n* readership, readers *pl.*; **~pult** *n* lectern; bookstand

Le•ser ['le:zɐ] *m* (-s; -) reader

Le•se•rat•te ['le:zə-] F *f* bookworm

'Le•ser|brief *m* letter (to the editor); **~e**

letters to the editor, *a.* letters page; **~echo** *n* reader(s') response
Le·se·rin ['le:zərɪn] *f* (-; -nen) reader
'**Le·ser·kreis** *m* (circle of) readers *pl.*; ***e-n weiten ~ haben*** be widely read
le·ser·lich ['le:zɐlɪç] **I.** *adj.* legible, readable; ***fein ~*** nice and neat; **II.** *adv.* legibly
Le·ser·lich·keit *f* (-; *no pl.*) legibility
'**Le·ser·schaft** *f* (-; *no pl.*) readership, readers *pl.*
'**Le·ser|schicht** *f* type of reader; readership (range); ***breite ~*** broad readership (*or* spectrum of readers); **~schwund** *m* declining circulation, drop in circulation; **~stamm** *m* regular readers *pl.*; **~stim·me** *f* reader's opinion; *pl.* readers' opinions; **~,um·fra·ge** *f* survey among (our *etc.*) readers; **~zu·schrift** *f* letter (to the editor)
Le·se|saal ['le:zə-] *m* reading room; **~stoff** *m* reading (matter), something to read; **~stück** *n* closet drama; **~übung** *f* reading exercise; **~wut** *f* reading mania; **~zei·chen** *n* bookmark; **~zir·kel** *m* magazine circle
Le·sung ['le:zʊŋ] *f* (-; -en) **1.** *parl.* reading; ***in zweiter ~*** on second reading; ***zur dritten ~ kommen*** come up for the third reading; **2.** reading, recital; ***e-e ~ halten*** give a reading; **3.** *eccl.* lesson, reading
le·tal [le'ta:l] *adj.* lethal; **Le'tal·do·sis** *f* lethal dose
Le·thar·gie [letar'gi:] *f* (-; *no pl.*) ⚕ lethargy (*a. fig.*); **le·thar·gisch** [le'targɪʃ] *adj.* lethargic
Let·te ['lɛtə] *m* (-n; -n) Latvian
Let·ten ['lɛtən] *m* (-s; -) clay
Let·ter ['lɛtɐ] *f* (-; -n) letter; character
Let·tin ['lɛtɪn] *f* (-; -nen) Latvian (woman); **let·tisch** ['lɛtɪʃ] *adj.*, '**Let·tisch** *n* (-en; *no pl.*) *ling.* Latvian, Lettish
Letzt [lɛtst] *f*: ***zu guter ~*** a) finally, in the end, b) last but not least
letzt *adj.* a) last; final, b) latest; ***als ~er Ausweg*** as a last resort; ***die ~en Nachrichten*** the latest news (*sg.*), ***vom Tage:*** the late-night news (*sg.*); ***... vom ~en Monat*** last month's ...; ***(am) ~en Sonntag*** last Sunday; ***im ~en Sommer*** last summer; ***in den ~en Jahren*** in recent years; ***in ~er Zeit*** lately; ***die ~en Stunden*** the closing hours; ***im ~en Augenblick*** just in time, at the last minute; ***Änderungen im ~en Augenblick*** last-minute changes; ***an ~er Stelle liegen*** be last; ***bis auf den ~en Platz gefüllt*** filled to capacity; ***m-e ~en Ersparnisse*** the last of my savings; ***~en Endes*** in the end, when all is said and done, ultimately; → ***Ehre, Loch, Ölung***
Letz·te ['lɛtstə]: ***der, die, das ~*** the last (one); ***das ~*** *a.* the last thing, the most (I can do *etc.*); ***der ~ des Monats*** the last day of the month; ***als ℒr et. tun*** be the last to do s.th.; ***als ℒr ins Ziel kommen*** come in last; ***es geht ums ~*** it's a case of do or die, everything's at stake; ***sein ~s hergeben, das ~ aus sich herausholen*** make an all-out (*or* a supreme) effort; F ***das ist ja wohl das ~!*** F that really takes the biscuit; F ***er ist doch der ~*** *sl.* he really is the pits; ***bis ins ℒ*** down to the last detail; ***bis zum ℒn*** to the utmost, as far as is (humanly) possible; ***bis zum ~n gehen*** a) go all the way, F go the whole hog, b) stop at nothing
letz·te·mal ['lɛtstəma:l] *adv.*: ***das ~*** the last time
'**letzt'end·lich** *adv.* in the end
letz·tens ['lɛtstəns] *adv.* **1.** lastly, finally; **2.** the other day, recently
letz·te·re ['lɛtstərə] *adj.*: ***~(r), ~s, der, die, das ~*** the latter
'**letzt·ge·nannt** *adj.* last-named
'**letzt'hin** *adv.* **1.** recently; **2.** in the end
'**letzt·jäh·rig** [-jɛ:rɪç] *adj.* last year's
'**letzt·lich** *adv.* **1.** in the end; in the final analysis; **2.** → ***letztens*** 2
'**letzt·ma·lig** [-ma:lɪç] *adj.* last; final; '**letzt·mals** [-ma:ls] *adv.* for the last time
'**letzt·mög·lich** *adj.* last possible ..., last ... possible
'**letzt·wil·lig** ⚖ **I.** *adj.* testamentary, by will; ***~e Verfügung*** last will and testament; **II.** *adv.*: ***~ verfügen*** state in one's last will and testament (***daß*** that)
Leucht|an·zei·ge ['lɔʏçt-] *f* LED display; **~bo·je** *f* light buoy; **~bom·be** *f* ✈ flare; **~buch·sta·ben** *pl.* neon letters; **~di·ode** *f* light-emitting diode, LED; **~di·oden·an·zei·ge** *f* LED display
Leuch·te ['lɔʏçtə] *f* (-; -n) light, lamp; *fig.* ***e-e (keine) große ~*** a leading light (not exactly a shining *or* leading light); ***er ist e-e (keine) ~ in Physik*** *a.* he's a brilliant physicist (he's not exactly the most brilliant physicist)
leuch·ten ['lɔʏçtən] *v/i.* (h) shine; glow; *candle, fire:* burn; *fig.* beam (***vor*** *dat.* with); *eyes:* glow, light up; ***j-m ~*** light the way for s.o.; ***mit e-r Kerze (e-m Scheinwerfer*** *etc.*) ***~*** shine a candle (a spotlight *etc.*); ***die Lampe leuchtet nur schwach*** the lamp doesn't give off much light; ***unter das Bett ~*** shine a light (*or* torch) under the bed; '**leuch·tend** *adj.* vivid, brilliant *colo(u)rs*; *a.* glowing *red, organge*; *fig.* ***~e Augen*** gleaming (*or* sparkling) eyes; ***~es Beispiel*** (*or* ***Vorbild***) shining example; ***et. in ~en Farben schildern*** paint a glowing picture of s.th.
Leuch·ter ['lɔʏçtɐ] *m* (-s; -) candlestick; chandelier; candelabra
Leucht|fa·den ['lɔʏçt-] *m* ⚡ filament; **~far·be** *f* luminescent paint; **~feu·er** *n* flare; beacon; **~fisch** *m* lantern fish; **~kä·fer** *m* glow-worm; **~kom·paß** *m* luminous(-dial) compass; **~kör·per** *m* (source of) light; **~kraft** *f* (-; *no pl.*) brightness, luminosity; brilliance; **~ku·gel** *f* flare; **~mel·der** *m* indicator light; **~pa,tro·ne** *f* flare cartridge; **~pi,sto·le** *f* flare pistol; **~quarz** *m* luminous quartz; **~ra,ke·te** *f* flare; **~re,kla·me** *f* neon lights (*or* signs) *pl.*; **~röh·re** *f* fluorescent lamp (*or* tube); **~schirm** *m* fluorescent screen (*a.* ⚕); **~schrift** *f* illuminated letters *pl.*; **~si,gnal** *n* flare signal; **~ska·la** *f* luminous dial
Leucht·spur ['lɔʏçt-] *f* tracer path; **~ge·schoß** *n* tracer (bullet); **~mu·ni·ti,on** *f* tracer ammunition
Leucht|stär·ke ['lɔʏçt-] *f* candlepower; **~stift** *m* light pen; **~stoff** *m* illuminant; **~stoff·röh·re** *f* fluorescent lamp (*or* tube); **~turm** *m* lighthouse; **~turm·wär·ter** *m* lighthouse man; **~uhr** *f* luminous clock (*or* watch); **~zei·ger** *m* luminous hand; **~zif·fer·blatt** *n* luminous dial; **~zif·fern** *pl.* luminous figures
leug·nen ['lɔʏgnən] (h) **I.** *v/t.* deny; ***~, et. getan zu haben*** deny having done s.th.; ***es ist nicht zu ~(, daß)*** it can't be denied (that), it's undeniable (that), there's no denying it (there's no denying the fact that); **II.** *v/i.* deny everything; **III.** ℒ *n* (-s; *no pl.*) denying; denial; ***da half kein ~*** all his (*or* her *etc.*) denials were useless
Leu·kä·mie [lɔʏkɛ'mi:] *f* (-; -n) ⚕ leuk(a)emia; **leu·kä·misch** [lɔʏ'kɛ:mɪʃ] *adj.* leuk(a)emic
Leu·kom [lɔʏ'ko:m] *n* (-s; -e) ⚕ leucoma
Leu·ko·plast [lɔʏko'plast] (*TM*) *n* (-[e]s; -e) sticking plaster
Leu·ko·zyt [lɔʏko'tsy:t] *m* (-en; -en) leucocyte; **Leu·ko'zy·ten·zäh·lung** *f* white cell count
Leu·mund ['lɔʏmʊnt] *m* (-[e]s; *no pl.*) reputation, name; ***ihr ~ ist gut (schlecht)*** she's got a good (bad) reputation *or* name; ***ein böser ~ behauptet ...*** there's some nasty gossip going round (to the effect) that ...; '**Leu·munds·zeug·nis** *n* character reference
Leu·te ['lɔʏtə] *pl.* **1.** people, persons, individuals; ***die ~*** people; F ***m-e ~*** my people, F my folks; ***die ~ sagen*** people (*or* they) say; ***was werden die ~ sagen?*** what will people say?; ***es gibt manche ~, die ...*** some people ..., there are certain individuals who ...; ***unter die ~ bringen*** a) make *s.th.* public, F tell the world about *s.th.*, b) F spend, F get rid of *one's money*; ***unter die ~ gehen*** (*or* ***kommen***) mix with people, socialize; ***vor allen ~n*** in front of everyone (*or* everybody); F ***hört mal zu, ~!*** listen, everyone (*or* everybody)!; ***aber, liebe ~!*** oh come on, now; → ***geschieden***; **2.** staff *sg.*; workers; *sport etc.*: men (and women); **~schin·der** *m* slave-driver
Leut·nant ['lɔʏtnant] *m* (-s; -s) second lieutenant (*Am. a.* ✈); ✈ *Brit.* pilot officer; ***~ zur See*** *Brit.* acting sub-lieutenant, *Am.* ensign
leut·se·lig ['lɔʏtze:lɪç] *adj.* affable; '**Leut·se·lig·keit** *f* (-; *no pl.*) affability
Le·van·te [le'vantə] *obs. f* (-; *no pl.*) Levant; **Le·van·ti·ner** [levan'ti:nɐ] *m* (-s; -.) Levantine; ***~ sein*** *a.* come from the Levant; **le·van·ti·nisch** [levan'ti:nɪʃ] *adj.* Levantine
Le·vi·ten [le'vi:tən] *pl.*: ***j-m die ~ lesen*** read s.o. the riot act
Lev·ko·je [lɛf'ko:jə] *f* (-; -n) ⚘ gillyflower
Le·xem [lɛ'kse:m] *n* (-s; -e) *ling.* lexeme
Le·xik ['lɛksɪk] *f* (-; *no pl.*) *ling.* lexis
le·xi·ka·lisch [lɛksi'ka:lɪʃ] *adj.* lexical
Le·xi·ko·graph [lɛksiko'gra:f] *m* (-en; -en) lexicographer; **Le·xi·ko·gra·phie** [lɛksikogra'fi:] *f* (-; *no pl.*) lexicography; **le·xi·ko·gra·phisch** [lɛksiko'gra:fɪʃ] *adj.* lexicographic(al); **Le·xi·ko·lo·ge** [lɛksiko'lo:gə] *m* (-n; -n) lexicologist; **Le·xi·ko·lo·gie** [lɛksikolo'gi:] *f* (-; *no pl.*) lexicology
Le·xi·kon ['lɛksikɔn] *n* (-s; -ka) **1.** encyclop(a)edia; → ***wandelnd***; **2.** dictionary
Le·zi·thin [letsi'ti:n] *n* (-s; -e) lecithin
Li·ai·son [lĭɛ'zõ:] *f* (-; -s) liaison (*a. ling.*); affair
Lia·ne ['lĭa:nə] *f* (-; -n) liana
Li·ba·ne·se [liba'ne:zə] *m* (-n; -n), **Li·ba·ne·sin** [liba'ne:zɪn] *f* (-; -nen), **li·ba·ne·sisch** [liba'ne:zɪʃ] *adj.* Lebanese
Li·bel·le [li'bɛlə] *f* (-; -n) **1.** dragonfly; **2.** ⚙ bubble
li·be·ral [libe'ra:l] *adj.* open-minded, liberal; tolerant; *pol.* Liberal; **Li·be'ra·le** *m, f* (-n; -n) *pol.* Liberal
li·be·ra·li·sie·ren [liberali'zi:rən] *v/t.* (h) liberalize; **Li·be·ra·li'sie·rung** *f* (-; *no pl.*) liberalization

Li·be·ra·lis·mus [libera'lɪsmʊs] *m* (-; *no pl.*) liberalism; *pol.* Liberalism
Li·be·ra·li·tät [liberali'tɛ:t] *f* (-; *no pl.*) liberality
Li·be·ria·ner [libe'rĭa:nɐ] *m* (-s; -), **Li·be·ria·ne·rin** [libe'rĭa:nərɪn] *f* (-; -nen) Liberian; **li·be·ria·nisch** [libe'rĭa:nɪʃ] *adj.* Liberian; ***unter ~er Flagge*** under a Liberian flag
Li·be·ro ['li:bero] *m* (-s; -s) sweeper, libero
li·bi·di·nös [libidi'nø:s] *adj.* libidinous
Li·bi·do [li'bi:do] *f* (-; *no pl.*) libido
Li·bret·tist [librɛ'tɪst] *m* (-en; -en) librettist; **Li·bret·to** [li'brɛto] *n* (-s; -s) libretto
Li·by·er ['li:bÿɐ] *m* (-s; -), **Li·bye·rin** ['li:bÿərɪn] *f* (-; -nen), **li·bysch** ['li:bʏʃ] *adj.* Libyan
Licht [lɪçt] *n* (-[e]s; -er) a) *no pl.* light; daylight; brightness, b) lighting; lamp; (*traffic*) light, c) *no pl.* F electricity; ***offenes ~*** *an* open flame; ***~ machen*** turn on the lights; ***gegen das ~ halten*** hold up to the light; ***j-m im ~ stehen*** stand in the (*or* s.o.'s) light; ***j-m aus dem ~ gehen*** get out of the (*or* s.o.'s) light; *fig.* ***ans ~ bringen*** (***kommen***) bring (come) to light; ***das ~ der Welt erblicken*** see the light of day; ***im ~e*** *gen.* in the light (*esp. Am.* in light) of *these facts etc.*; ***~ bringen in*** *acc.*, ***ein ~ werfen auf*** *acc.* shed (*or* throw) light on; ***ein schlechtes ~ werfen auf*** *acc.* throw a bad light on, reflect badly on, (*a.* ***in e-m schlechten ~ zeigen***) show in a bad light; ***ein neues ~ werfen auf*** *acc.* put a new complexion on; ***et. ins rechte ~ rücken*** a) put (*or* show) s.th. in a favo(u)rable light, b) put (*or* show) s.th. in its true light; ***et. in e-m (un)günstigen ~ erscheinen lassen*** make s.th. appear in a favo(u)rable (an unfavo[u]rable) light; ***in ein schiefes*** (*or* ***falsches***) ***~ geraten*** be put in the wrong light; ***et. in ein schiefes*** (*or* ***falsches***) ***~ rücken, ein schiefes ~ auf et. werfen*** put a wrong complexion on s.th., show s.th. in the wrong light; ***bei ~e besehen*** a) on closer inspection, b) (seen) in the cold light of day; ***das ~ scheuen*** have something to hide; ***j-n hinters ~ führen*** pull the wool over s.o.'s eyes, lead s.o. up the garden path; ***sich im wahren ~e zeigen*** show one's true colo(u)rs; ***in X gehen die ~er aus*** things are beginning to look pretty grim in X; ***es ging mir ein ~ auf*** the truth began to dawn on me; F ***j-m ein ~ aufsetzen*** (*or* ***aufstecken***) put s.o. in the picture; F ***er ist kein großes ~*** he's no shining light; *bibl. and hum.* ***es werde ~*** let there be light; → ***grün*** I
licht *adj.* **1.** bright; ***bei ~em Tage*** in broad daylight; ***~er Augenblick*** (*or* ***Moment***) lucid moment; **2.** thin, sparse; bald; ***~(er) werden*** thin (out); **3.** ⚙ ***~e Breite*** (***Höhe***) clear breadth (height); ***~e Weite*** inside (*or* clearance) width
'**Licht|ag·gre,gat** *n* lighting set; **~an·la·ge** *f* lighting system; **℘arm** *adj.* badly lit, dingy; **~bad** *n* ⚕ light bath; **~be·hand·lung** *f* ⚕ phototherapy
'**licht·be·stän·dig** *adj.* light-resistant; *textil.* non-fading
'**Licht·bild** *n* **1.** photo(graph); **2.** *obs.* transparency, slide; '**Licht·bil·der·vor·trag** *m* slide talk (*or* show)
'**licht·blau** *adj.* light blue
'**Licht·blick** *m* something to look forward to (*or* to brighten up one's life); bright spot on the horizon; ***der einzige ~ in m-m Leben*** the only bright spot in my life
'**Licht·bo·gen** *m* ⚡ arc; **~schwei·ßung** *f* ⚙ arc welding
'**licht·bre·chend** *adj. opt.* refractive; '**Licht·bre·chung** *f* refraction (of light)
'**Licht·bün·del** *n* light beam, pencil of rays
'**licht·dicht** *adj.* lightproof
'**licht·durch,flu·tet** *adj.* flooded with light, bathed in light
'**licht,durch·läs·sig** *adj.* translucent; transparent; '**Licht,durch·läs·sig·keit** *f* translucency; transparency
'**licht·echt** *adj.* lightproof; *textil.* non--fading
'**Licht|ef,fekt** *m* lighting effect; **~ein·fall** *m* **1.** incidence of light; **2.** light leakage; **~ein·wir·kung** *f* action of light
'**licht·emp·find·lich** *adj.* sensitive to light; *phys.* photosensitive; *phot.* sensitized *paper*; self-adjusting *sunglasses*; ***~ machen*** sensitize; '**Licht·emp·find·lich·keit** *f* (light-)sensitivity; *phot.* speed
lich·ten¹ ['lɪçtən] (h) **I.** *v/t.* **1.** clear; **2.** thin out; **II.** *v/refl.*: ***sich ~*** **3.** thin out (*a. fig.*); **4.** clear up
'**lich·ten²** *v/t.* (h): ⚓ ***den Anker ~*** weigh anchor
Lich·ter|baum ['lɪçtɐ-] *m* Christmas tree; **~fest** *n* Hanukkah, Festival of Lights
'**licht·er·füllt** *adj. lit.* suffused with light
Lich·ter·glanz ['lɪçtɐ-] *m* bright lights *pl.*
lich·ter·loh ['lɪçtɐ'lo:] *adv.*: ***~ brennen*** be ablaze
Lich·ter·meer ['lɪçtɐ-] *n* sea of lights
'**Licht|fil·ter** *m, n* filter; **~ge·schwin·dig·keit** *f* (-; *no pl.*) speed of light; **~grif·fel** *m* light pen; **℘grün** *adj.* light green; **~hof** *m* **1.** ⛬ atrium; **2.** *phot.* halo; **~hu·pe** *f mot.* flasher; ***die ~ betätigen*** flash one's lights; **~jahr** *n* light year; **~ke·gel** *m* beam (of light); **~kreis** *m* circle of light; **~kup·pel** *f* light dome, domed roof light; **~leh·re** *f* (-; *no pl.*) *phys.* optics *pl.*
'**licht·los** *adj.* (completely) dark; devoid of sunlight
'**Licht·ma,schi·ne** *f mot.* dynamo, *Am.* generator; alternator
'**Licht·meß** [-mɛs] *f*: *R.C.* (***Mariä***) ~ Candlemas
'**Licht|mes·ser** *m* light meter; **~mes·sung** *f* photometry; **~or·gel** *f* lighting console; **~pau·se** *f* photocopy; blueprint; **~punkt** *m* point of light; *fig.* bright spot; **~quel·le** *f* source of light; **~re,flex** *m* light reflection, reflection of light; **~re,gie** *f thea.* lighting control; ***~ hatte ...*** F on lights we had ...; **~schacht** *m* light well; **~schal·ter** *m* light switch; **~schein** *m* (beam of) light; **℘scheu** *adj.* **1.** *fig.* ***~er Mensch*** shady character; ***~es Gesindel*** shady characters (F bunch); **2.** sensitive to light; ***~e Tiere*** *etc.* animals *etc.* that avoid (*or* shun) the light; **~schim·mer** *m* glimmer of light; **~schleu·se** *f* light trap; **℘schluckend** *adj.* light-absorbing; **~schran·ke** *f* light barrier; F magic eye
'**Licht·schutz** *m* protection against the light (*or* sun); **~fak·tor** *m* sun protection factor
'**licht·schwach** *adj.* dim, faint
'**Licht|sei·te** *fig. f* bright side; **~si,gnal** *n* light signal; *mot.* flashing lights *pl.*; ***ein ~ geben*** flash one's lights; **~spalt** *m* crack of light; **~spek·trum** *n* light spectrum; **~spiel·haus** *obs. n* cinema, *Am.* movie theater; **℘stark** *adj.* powerful; *phot. a.* fast, high-speed *lens*; **~stär·ke** *f* brightness; *phot.* F-number, speed; **~strahl** *m* ray (*or* beam) of light; **~the·ra,pie** *f* ⚕ phototherapy
'**licht,un·durch·läs·sig** *adj.* opaque; '**Licht,un·durch·läs·sig·keit** *f* opacity, opaqueness
'**licht·un·emp·find·lich** *adj.* insensitive to light; '**Licht·un·emp·find·lich·keit** *f* insensitivity to light
Lich·tung ['lɪçtʊŋ] *f* (-; -en) clearing
'**Licht|ver·hält·nis·se** *pl.* lighting conditions, lighting *sg.*; **~zel·le** *f* photovoltaic cell
Lid [li:t] *n* (-[e]s; -er ['li:dɐ]) eyelid; **~schat·ten** *m* eye shadow; **~spalt** *m anat.* palpebral fissure
lieb [li:p] **I.** *adj.* kind, good; nice; sweet; dear; ***ein ~er Kerl*** a nice guy; ***ein ~es Ding*** a darling; ***~er Herr N.*** *in a letter*: Dear Mr N; ***der ~e Gott*** God; ***~er Gott*** dear God; ***du ~er Himmel!*** goodness me!; F ***mein ~er Mann*** (*or* ***Schwan***)***!*** F I tell you!; ***den ~en langen Tag*** the whole day long; ***~ sein zu*** *dat.* be nice to; ***warst du auch ~?*** have you been a good boy (*or* girl)?; ***es wäre mir ~, wenn*** I'd appreciate it if; ***sei ~!*** be good!; ***sei so ~ und ...*** do me a favo(u)r and ...(, will you?); ***sei so ~*** do you mind?; ***das ist ~ von dir*** that's very sweet of you; ***mehr, als ihm ~ ist*** more than he really wanted; ***alles, was ihr ~ war*** all that was dear to her; ***wenn dir dein Leben ~ ist*** if you value your life; ***j-m etwas ℘s tun*** (*or* ***erweisen***) be very kind to s.o.; → ***lieber, liebst, Not***; **II.** *adv.* lovingly, fondly; kindly; nicely; tenderly; gently; ***j-n ~ behandeln*** be nice to s.o.; ***er hat es so ~ hergerichtet*** *etc.* he took such a lot of care over it
lieb·äu·geln ['li:pʔɔʏgəln] *v/i.* (h): ***mit e-r Sache ~*** have one's eyes on s.th.; ***mit dem Gedanken*** (*or* ***der Idee***) ***~ zu*** *inf.* toy with the idea of *ger.*
Lieb·chen ['li:pçən] *obs. n* (-s; -s) sweetheart
Lie·be¹ ['li:bə] *f* **1.** *no pl.* a) love (**zu** *dat.* for *s.o., fig.* of *s.th.*); liking (for), b) sex; ***aus ~*** for love; ***aus ~ zu*** *dat.* for the love of; ***bei aller ~*** a) much as I'd like to, b) listen, my dear, F listen, mate; ***mit ~ gemacht*** *etc.* made (*or* done) *etc.* with tender loving care; ***die ~ geht durch den Magen*** the way to a man's heart is through his stomach; → ***blind*** 1; **2.** F sweetheart; idol; ***m-e große ~*** my idol, F my big crush, *fig.* my great passion; ***e-e alte ~*** F an old flame; **3.** *no pl.* favo(u)r; ***tu mir die ~*** will you do it for me?; ***tu mir die ~ und ...*** be a dear and ...; do me a favo(u)r and ..., will you?
'**Lie·be²** *m, f* (-n; -n) dear (person); ***mein ~r!*** my dear man; ***meine ~!*** my dear (girl); ***meine ~n!*** my dears; ***~s*** love
'**lie·be·be·dürf·tig** *adj.*: ***~ sein*** need (*or* crave) love and affection
'**lie·be·leer** *adj.* loveless
Lie·be·lei [li:bə'laɪ] *f* (-; -en) little affair
lie·ben ['li:bən] (h) **I.** *v/t.* a) love; (really) like, b) make love to; ***er liebt es zu*** *inf.* he loves *ger.* (*or* to *inf.*); ***er liebt es nicht zu*** *inf.* he doesn't like *ger.* (*or* to *inf.*); ***er liebt es nicht, wenn man zu spät kommt*** he doesn't like people to arrive late, he doesn't appreciate people arriv-

ing late, he doesn't like it when people arrive late; ***sich*** ~ a) love each other (*or* one another), be in love (with each other), b) make love; → ***lernen*** I; **II.** *v/i.* a) love, b) make love; **'lie·bend I.** *adj.* loving; **II.** *adv.*: ~ ***gern*** gladly; ***ich würde*** ~ ***gern*** I'd love to; ***er spielt*** ~ ***gern Schach*** he loves (to play) chess; ***ich esse*** ~ ***gern Kartoffeln*** I (just) love potatoes

Lie·ben·de ['li:bəndə] *m, f* (-n; -n) lover

'lie·bens·wert *adj.* lovely *person*; *fig.* endearing *quality etc.*; ***ein*** ~***er Mensch*** *a.* such a nice person

'lie·bens·wür·dig *adj.* (very) kind; charming; ***wären Sie so*** ~ ***zu*** *inf.* would you be so kind as to *inf.* (*or* kind enough to *inf.*); **'lie·bens·wür·di·ger'wei·se** *adv.* (very) kindly; ***er hat es mir*** ~ ***geliehen*** *a.* he was kind enough to lend it to me; **'Lie·bens·wür·dig·keit** *f* (-; *no pl.*) kindness; charm, charming nature; ***hätten Sie die*** ~ ***zu*** → ***liebenswürdig***

lie·ber ['li:bɐ] **I.** *adj.* (*comp. of lieb I*); **II.** *adv.*: ~ ***haben,*** ~ ***mögen*** like *s.th. or s.o.* better, prefer; ***ich möchte*** ~ ***nicht*** I'd rather not; ***ich bleibe*** ~ ***zu Hause*** I'd rather stay at home; ***du solltest*** ~ ***gehen*** you'd (= you had) better go, it would be better if you left; ***das hättest du*** ~ ***nicht machen sollen*** you shouldn't (really) have done that; ***laß es*** ~ better leave it; ***machen wir es*** ~ ***gleich*** let's do it now, I think we should do it now; ***was wäre dir*** ~***?*** what would you prefer?; ***mir wäre*** ~***, wenn ...*** I'd prefer it if ..., I'd prefer us *etc.* to *inf.*; ***mir wäre nichts*** ~ ***als das*** there's nothing I'd rather do (*or* have *etc.*), that for me would be perfect

'Lie·bes|aben·teu·er *n* amorous adventure (*or* escapade); ~**af,fä·re** *f* love affair; ~**akt** *m* sexual act; ~**be·dürf·nis** *n* need (*or* craving) for love and affection; ~**be·zie·hung** *f* love relationship; *n.s.* sexual relationship; ~**brief** *m* love letter; ~**dich·tung** *f* love poetry; ~**dienst** *m* favo(u)r; ***j-m e-n*** ~ ***erweisen*** do s.o. a good turn; ~**ent·zug** *m* withdrawal of love (and affection); ***j-n mit*** ~ ***bestrafen*** punish s.o. by withdrawing one's love (and affection) from him (*or* her); ~**er·klä·rung** *f* declaration of love; ***(j-m) e-e*** ~ ***machen*** declare one's love (to s.o.); ~**er·leb·nis** *n* love affair; ~**film** *m* (filmed) love story; ~**freu·den** *pl.* pleasures of love; ~**ge·dicht** *n* love poem; ~**ge·schich·te** *f* love story; ~**glück** *n* a) joy(s *pl.*) of love, b) happy love affair; ~**gott** *m* god of love; Cupid, Eros; ~**göt·tin** *f* goddess of love; Venus, Aphrodite; ~**hei·rat** *f* love match; ⁀**krank** *adj.* lovesick; ~**kum·mer** *m*: ~ ***haben*** have man (*or* woman) problems; be lovesick; ~**kunst** *f* art of love; ~**le·ben** *n* love life; ~**lied** *n* love song; ~**mü·he** *f*: ***das ist vergebliche*** ~ that's a waste of time (and effort); ~**nacht** *f* night of love; ~**nest** *n* love nest; ~**ob,jekt** *n* object of love; ~**paar** *n*, ~**pär·chen** *n* couple; (two) lovers *pl.*; ~**ro,man** *m* love story; romance; ~**schwur** *m* lover's oath; ~**spiel** *n* loveplay; *zo.* mating ritual; ~**sze·ne** *f* love scene; ⁀**toll** *adj.* love-crazed; *lit.* love-stricken; ~**tö·ter** [-tø:tɐ] F *pl.* F bloomers; ~**tra,gö·die** *f* tragedy of love; ~**trank** *m* love potion; ⁀**trunken** *adj.* besotted; ~**ver·hält·nis** *n* relationship; ~**ver·lust** *m* deprivation of love; ~**vö·gel** *pl. zo.* lovebirds; ~**werben** *n* wooing, courtship; ~**zau·ber** *m* spell of love; ~**zei·chen** *n* token of love

'lie·be·voll I. *adj.* loving; very kind; **II.** *adv.* lovingly; ~ ***zubereitet*** prepared with loving care; ***er wird*** ~ ***umsorgt*** he's well looked after; ***j-n*** ~ ***ansehen*** give s.o. a tender look (*or* a look of affection)

'lieb·ge·win·nen *v/t.* (*irr., sep.*, h, → ***gewinnen***) grow fond of, come to like

'lieb·ge·wor·den *adj.* cherished; ***ein mir*** ~***es Fleckchen*** a place I have come to cherish (*or* have grown very fond of)

'lieb·ha·ben *v/t.* (*irr., sep.*, h, → ***haben***) like; love

Lieb·ha·ber ['li:pha:bɐ] *m* (-s; -) **1.** lover; admirer; *thea. obs.* ***erster*** ~ leading (gentle)man; *thea.* ***jugendlicher*** ~ juvenile lead; ***er ist ein guter (schlechter)*** ~ he's (not very) good in bed; **2.** ~ ***der Kunst*** *etc.* art *etc.* lover (F fan); **3.** connoisseur; ~**aus·ga·be** *f* de luxe (*or* collector's) edition

Lieb·ha·be·rei [li:pha:bə'raɪ] *f* (-; -en) hobby; ***aus*** ~ as a hobby, for pleasure

'Lieb·ha·ber|preis *m* collector's price; ~**stück** *n* collector's item; ~**wert** *m* collector's value

lieb'ko·sen *v/t.* (h) caress; kiss and cuddle; **Lieb·ko·sung** [li:p'ko:zʊŋ] *f* (-; -en) caress

'lieb·lich I. *adj.* lovely, sweet; *fig.* lovely, charming, delightful *scenery etc.*; suave, pleasant *wine*; **II.** *adv.*: ~ ***duften (klingen*** *etc.*) have a lovely smell (sound *etc.*), smell (sound *etc.*) lovely; **'Lieb·lich·keit** *f* (-; *no pl.*) loveliness; sweetness; charm; pleasantness

Lieb·ling ['li:plɪŋ] *m* (-s; -e) darling; (my) love; favo(u)rite; ***der*** ~ ***der Damen*** the ladies' darling; ***er war ein*** ~ ***der Götter*** he was beloved of the gods

'Lieb·lings|kind *n* favo(u)rite child; *fig.* baby; ~**schü·ler** *m* teacher's pet; ***er ist ihr*** ~ he's the teacher's pet; ~**the·ma** *n* pet (*or* favo[u]rite) subject; ***er ist wieder bei s-m*** ~ he's on his hobby-horse again, he's onto his favo(u)rite (*or* pet) subject again, F he's away again

'lieb·los I. *adj.* unkind; cold; uncaring; **II.** *adv.*: ***sie geht sehr*** ~ ***mit ihm um*** she doesn't treat him very well

'Lieb·lo·sig·keit *f* (-; *no pl.*) unkindness; coldness; lack of love; couldn't-care-less attitude

'Lieb·reiz *m* (-es; *no pl.*) charm, attractiveness

Lieb·schaft ['li:pʃaft] *f* (-; -en) affair

liebst [li:pst] **I.** *adj.* (*sup. of lieb I*); ***m-e*** ~***e Pflanze*** *etc.* my favo(u)rite plant *etc.*; **II.** *adv.*: ***am*** ~***en schwimme ich*** I like swimming best; ***am*** ~***en würde ich bleiben*** (F ***ihm eine runterhauen***) I'd really like to stay (I'd love to just hit him)

Lieb·ste ['li:pstə] *m, f* (-n; -n) (*a.* ***meine*** ~, ***mein*** ~***r***) darling, (my) love

Lieb·stöckel ['li:pʃtœkəl] (*sep.* -k·k-) *m, n* (-s; -) ✿ lovage

Lied [li:t] *n* (-[e]s; -er ['li:dɐ]) song; tune; lied; poem; ballad; *fig.* ***es ist immer das alte*** ~ it's the same old story every time; ***er kann dir ein*** ~ ***davon singen*** he can tell you a thing or two about that; ***das Ende vom*** ~ the upshot (of the whole affair); ***und das war das Ende vom*** ~ and that was that

Lie·der|abend ['li:dɐ-] *m* lieder recital; ~**buch** *n* songbook

lie·der·lich ['li:dɐlɪç] *adj.* **1.** untidy; sloppy, slovenly (*both a. fig. work etc.*); **2.** dissolute; **'Lie·der·lich·keit** *f* (-; *no pl.*) **1.** untidiness; sloppiness, slovenliness; **2.** dissipation, dissolution

Lie·der|ma·cher ['li:dɐ-] *m* (-s; -) singer-songwriter; ~**sän·ger** *m* lieder singer; ~**zy·klus** *m* song cycle

'Lied·text *m* lyrics *pl. or* words *pl.* (of a *or* the song)

lief [li:f] *pret. of* ***laufen***

Lie·fe·rant [li:fə'rant] *m* (-en; -en) supplier; **Lie·fe'ran·ten·ein·gang** *m* tradesman's (*or* goods) entrance

Lie·fer·auf·trag ['li:fɐ-] *m* order

lie·fer·bar ['li:fɐba:ɐ] *adj.* available, in stock; ***nicht*** ~ not available, out of stock; ***sofort*** ~***e Waren*** spot goods

Lie·fer|be·din·gun·gen ['li:fɐ-] *pl.* terms of delivery; ⁀**be·reit** *adj.* ready for delivery; ~**eng·paß** *m* supply shortage; ~**firma** *f* supplier(s *pl.*); ~**frist** *f* delivery deadline; ~**ko·sten** *pl.* delivery charges; ~**land** *n* supplier country; ~**men·ge** *f* quantity delivered (*or* ordered); ~**mono,pol** *n*: ***das*** ~ ***haben für*** *acc.* have a monopoly on the supply of

lie·fern ['li:fɐn] *v/t. and v/i.* (h) deliver (*dat. or* ***an*** *acc.* to); supply (***j-m et.*** s.o. with s.th.); produce; yield; *fig.* supply, provide, furnish, come up with *evidence etc.*; ***es lieferte uns genug Gesprächsstoff*** it gave us plenty to talk about; ***er lieferte e-n harten Kampf (ein gutes Spiel)*** he put up a good fight (he played well); → ***geliefert***

Lie·fer|ort ['li:fɐ-] *m* place of delivery; ~**po·sten** *m* supply item, lot; ~**preis** *m* contract price; ~**schein** *m* delivery note; ~**sper·re** *f* halt of deliveries; ~**tag** *m* delivery date; ~**ter,min** *m* **1.** delivery deadline; **2.** delivery date

Lie·fe·rung ['li:fərʊŋ] *f* (-; -en) a) delivery, *Am. a.* shipment; supply, b) consignment, shipment; instal(l)ment (*a. of book*)

'Lie·fe·rungs... → ***Liefer...***

Lie·fer|ver·trag ['li:fɐ-] *m* supply contract; ~**wa·gen** *m* delivery van, *Am.* panel truck, pickup (truck); ~**zeit** *f* delivery period; ***die*** ~ ***einhalten*** deliver on time

Lie·ge ['li:gə] *f* (-; -n) a) couch, b) sunbed, c) campbed; ~**deck** *n* ⚓ lounge deck; ~**kur** *f* ⚕ rest cure

lie·gen ['li:gən] **I.** *v/i.* (lag, gelegen, h) lie, be lying; ⚕ be in bed, *w.s.* be laid up; *fig.* lie, be (situated *or* located); ⚓ lie; ~ ***müssen*** *patient*: have to stay in bed, have to lie flat; ***er hat drei Wochen gelegen*** he was in bed (*or* was laid up) for three weeks; ***der Boden lag voller Zeitungen*** the floor was strewn with newspapers; ***es lag viel Schnee*** there was a lot of snow (on the ground); ***liegt mein Haar richtig?*** is my hair all right (*Am.* alright)?; ***da liegt der Fehler*** that's where the trouble lies; ***wie die Sache jetzt liegt*** as matters (now) stand, as things are at the moment; ***das liegt mir nicht*** it's not my thing; ***er liegt mir überhaupt nicht*** a) he's not my type of person, b) he's not my type; ***nichts liegt mir ferner*** nothing could be further from my mind; *with prp.*: ~ ***an*** *dat.* a) be near, be on; be next to, b) *fig.* be because of; ***an der Spitze*** *etc.* ~ be in front *etc.*; ***es liegt an dir*** it's your fault, ***et. zu tun:***

it's up to you to do s.th.; ***an mir soll's nicht*** ~ a) I'll certainly do my best, b) I won't stand in the way; ***an mir soll's nicht*** ~, ***wenn die Sache schiefgeht*** it won't be my fault (*or* through any fault of mine) when things go wrong; ***es liegt daran, daß*** it's because; ***es liegt mir daran zu*** *inf.* I'm keen to *inf.*; ***es liegt mir sehr viel daran*** it means a lot to me; ***es liegt mir nichts daran*** it doesn't mean much to me, ***zu gewinnen***: it doesn't make any difference to me whether I win or not; ~ ***auf*** *dat.* lie on, *stress*: be on; → ***Hand, Seele***; *mot.* ***der Wagen liegt gut*** (***auf der Straße***) the car holds (the road) well; ***es liegt Nebel auf den Feldern*** there's fog over the fields; ***der Gewinn liegt bei fünf Millionen*** the profit amounts to five million; ***die Temperaturen*** ~ ***bei 30 Grad*** temperatures are around 30 degrees; ***die Entscheidung liegt bei dir*** it's your decision, it's up to you; *fig.* ***es liegt hinter uns*** it's behind us; *fig.* ~ ***in*** *dat. advantage etc.*: lie in; ***in ihrer Stimme lag leise Ironie*** there was a hint of irony in her voice; ***die Schwierigkeit liegt darin, daß*** the problem is that; ~ ***nach*** *dat.* face *the street etc.*, look out on, overlook *the park etc.*; → ***Blut*** 1, ***Magen***; **II.** ≈ *n* (-s; *no pl.*) lying; lying position; ***im*** ~ lying down; ***das*** ~ ***bekommt ihm nicht*** he can't take all this lying down

'lie·gen·blei·ben *v/i.* (*irr.*, *sep.*, sn, → ***bleiben***) **1.** not to get up; (just) lie there; stay in bed; *boxing*: stay down; **2.** be left (***auf*** *dat.* on); *snow*: settle; be left (behind); *a. fig.* be forgotten; *fig. task etc.*: be left unfinished; *fig.* ***das kann*** ~ that can wait; **3.** ☤ be left unsold, F be left on the shelf; **4.** *mot.* break down; ***wir sind unterwegs liegengeblieben*** we had a breakdown on the way

'lie·gend *adj.* **1.** resting; *art*: reclining; ***auf dem Rücken*** ~ lying on one's back; **2.** *fig.* situated

'lie·gen·ge·blie·ben I. *p.p. of* ***liegenbleiben***; **II.** *adj. books etc.* left behind; forgotten; *mot.* stranded, abandoned

'lie·gen·las·sen *v/t.* (*irr.*, *sep*, h, → ***lassen***) **1.** leave behind, forget; **2.** leave alone; ***laß es liegen!*** don't touch it!; **3.** leave (unfinished); ***die Arbeit*** ~ stop work, leave everything lying, F down tools; **4.** leave *s.th.* lying around; → ***links*** I

'Lie·gen·schaf·ten *pl.* real estate *sg.*

'Lie·ge|sitz *m* reclining seat, recliner; **~stuhl** *m* deckchair; **~stütz** *m* press-up, *a. Am.* push-up; **~ter,ras·se** *f* sun terrace; **~wa·gen** *m* 🚃 couchette car; **~wie·se** *f* lawn

lieh [liː] *pret. of* ***leihen***

Lies·chen ['liːsçən] *n* (-s; -) **1.** F ~ ***Müller*** the (average) woman in the street, F Mrs Average; **2.** ⚘ → ***fleißig*** I

ließ [liːs] *pret. of* ***lassen***

Lift¹ [lɪft] *m* (-[e]s; -e) lift, *Am.* elevator; (ski) lift

Lift² *m*, *n* (-s; -s) ⚕ facelift

lif·ten¹ ['lɪftən] *v/t.* (h): ***sich*** ~ ***lassen*** have a facelift

'lif·ten² *v/i.* (sn) take the ski lift

'Lift·kar·te *f skiing*: lift ticket

Li·ga ['liːga] *f* (-; Ligen) league (*a. sport*); **~spiel** *n* league match (*or* game)

Li·ga·tur [liga'tuːɐ] *f* (-; -en [-rən]) *anat.*, *typ.* ligature; ♪ tie

Li·gnit [lɪ'gniːt] *m* (-s; -e) lignite

Li·gu·ster [li'gʊstɐ] *m* (-s; -) ⚘ (common) privet; **~hecke** *f* privet hedge

li·ie·ren [li'iːrən] *v/refl.* (h): ***sich*** ~ get together, ☤ *etc.* join forces (***mit*** *dat.* with); **li·iert** [li'iːɐt] *adj.*: (***fest***) ~ attached; ***mit j-m*** ~ ***sein*** be going out with s.o.

Li·kör [li'køːɐ] *m* (-s; -e [-rə]) liqueur

Li·la ['liːla] *n* (-s; -), **'li·la·far·ben** *adj.* purple; lilac

Li·lie ['liːlĭə] *f* (-; -n) ⚘ lily; *heraldry*: *a.* fleur-de-lis; ***gelbe*** ~ gold lily; ***weiße*** ~ white (*or* Madonna) lily; ***blaue*** ~ iris

Li·li·pu·ta·ner [lilipu'taːnɐ] *m* (-s; -), **Li·li·pu·ta·ne·rin** [lilipu'taːnərɪn] *f* (-; -nen) midget

Li·met·te [li'mɛtə] *f* (-; -n) lime

Li·mit ['lɪmɪt] *n* (-s; -s) limit; ☤ *a.* ceiling; *auction*: reserve (price); **li·mi·tie·ren** [limi'tiːrən] *v/t.* (h) limit; ☤ *a.* put a ceiling on; **li·mi·tiert** [limi'tiːɐt] *adj.* limited; ***nicht*** ~ unlimited, open-ended

Li·mo ['lɪmo] F *f* (-; -[s]), **Li·mo·na·de** [limo'naːdə] *f* (-; -n) fizzy drink, *Am.* soda pop; lemonade; orangeade

Li·mo·ne [li'moːnə] *f* (-; -n) lime

Li·mou·si·ne [limu'ziːnə] *f mot.* saloon, *Am.* sedan

lind [lɪnt] *adj.* gentle, mild

Lin·de ['lɪndə] *f* (-; -n) a) lime, linden, b) limewood; **'Lin·den·baum** *m* lime tree; **'Lin·den·blü·ten·tee** *m* lime blossom tea; **'Lin·den·holz** *n* limewood

lin·dern ['lɪndɐn] *v/t.* (h) alleviate, ease *pain etc.*; bring down *temperature*; relieve *poverty etc.*; mitigate *sentence etc.*; **Lin·de·rung** ['lɪndərʊŋ] *f* (-; *no pl.*) alleviation; easing; relief; mitigation; ***j-m*** ~ ***verschaffen*** bring relief to s.o.

Lind·wurm ['lɪnt-] *m* dragon

Li·ne·al [line'aːl] *n* (-s; -e) ruler

li·ne·ar [line'aːɐ] *adj.* linear; ☤ across-the-board

Li·ne'ar|be·schleu·ni·ger *m phys.* linear accelerator; **~schrift** *f* linear script; **~zeich·nung** *f* line drawing

Lin·gu·ist [lɪŋ'gŭɪst] *m* (-en; -en) linguist; **Lin·gui·stik** [lɪŋ'gŭɪstɪk] *f* (-; *no pl.*) linguistics *pl.*; **lin·gui·stisch** [lɪŋ'gŭɪstɪʃ] *adj.* linguistic(ally *adv.*)

Li·nie ['liːnĭə] *f* (-; -n) **1.** line (*a.* ⚔, *sport etc.*); *fig.* ***in erster*** ~ first of all, in the first place; ***in vorderster*** ~ ***stehen*** be in the front line; ***auf der ganzen*** ~ (right) down the line; **2.** route; ***die*** ~ ***20*** bus number 20, the number 20 (bus); ***auf der*** ~ ***Köln-Hamburg*** on the Cologne-Hamburg line (✈ route); **3.** airline; **4.** *fig.* a) trend, b) *pol.* course; party line, c) editorial policy; ***e-e klare*** ~ ***haben*** be clear-cut, (*a.* ***e-e klare*** ~ ***einhalten***) be consistent; ***e-e mittlere*** ~ ***einschlagen*** (*or* ***verfolgen***) follow a middle course; **5.** figure, waistline; ***ich muß auf m-e*** (***schlanke***) ~ ***achten*** *a.* I've got to watch what I eat; **6.** line; ***in direkter*** ~ ***abstammen von*** *dat.* be a direct descendant of

'Li·ni·en|blatt *n* (sheet of) lined paper; **~bus** *m* public service bus; **~dienst** *m* scheduled services *pl.*; ✈ *a.* regular flights *pl.*; **~flug** *m* scheduled flight; **~flug·zeug** *n* → ***Linienmaschine***; **~füh·rung** *f* flow of the lines; **~ma,schi·ne** *f* scheduled aircraft (*or* plane); **~netz** *n* (rail *etc.*) network; **~pa,pier** *n* ruled (*or* lined) paper; **~rich·ter** *m sport*: linesman; **~schiff** *n* liner; **~sy,stem** *n* ♪ staff, stave

'li·ni·en·treu *adj. pol.* loyal; ~ ***sein*** *a.* toe the line; **'Li·ni·en·treue** *f* loyalty to the party line; **'Li·ni·en·treue** *m* party liner

'Li·ni·en·ver·kehr *m* scheduled services *pl.*; ✈ scheduled air traffic

li·nie·ren [li'niːrən] *v/t.* (h) rule, line

li·niert [li'niːɐt] *adj.* ruled, lined

link [lɪŋk] *adj.* **1.** left; ~***e Seite*** left-hand side, left; *fig.* ***zwei*** ~***e Hände haben*** have two left hands; ***das mache ich mit der*** ~***en Hand*** (F ***mit*** ~***s***) I can do that no problem (*or* with my hands tied); ***er ist wohl mit dem*** ~***en Fuß*** (*or* ***Bein***) ***zuerst aufgestanden*** he must have got out of the wrong side of the bed this morning; **2.** *pol.* left-wing, leftist; left *wing*; **3.** F dirty, mean, nasty; underhand(ed); two-faced; ~***e Tour*** underhand(ed) (*or* dirty, mean) trick; (*a.* ~***e Touren***) underhand(ed) (*or* fishy) dealings *pl.*; ***j-m auf die*** ~***e Tour kommen*** F try and play s.o. for a sucker, F do the dirty on s.o.; ***komm mir ja nicht auf die*** ~***e Tour!*** *a.* F just don't try it on me(, mate); ~***er Hund***, V ~***e Sau*** *sl.* two-faced swine (V bastard); ~***er Vogel*** V scheming bastard

Lin·ke¹ ['lɪŋkə] *f* (-n; *no pl.*) left hand; *boxing*: left; *pol. the* left, left wing; ***zur*** ~***n*** to (*or* on) the left; ***zu s-r*** ~***n*** to (*or* on) his left; **'Lin·ke²** *m*, *f* (-n; -n) *pol.* leftist, left-winger; F leftie

lin·ken ['lɪŋkən] F *v/t.* (h) F do the dirty on *s.o.*

lin·ker·hand ['lɪŋkɐ-] *adv.* on the left

lin·kisch ['lɪŋkɪʃ] *adj.* clumsy, gauche; awkward

links [lɪŋks] **I.** *adv.* a) on the left(-hand side), b) (to the) left, c) inside out; ~ ***von*** *dat.* to the left of; ~ ***von ihm*** on (*or* to) his left; ~ ***oben*** (***unten***) on the top (bottom) left; ***drittes Regal*** ~ third shelf on the left; ~ ***abbiegen*** turn left; ***sich*** ~ ***halten***, ~ ***fahren*** (*or* ***gehen***) keep to the left; *pol.* ~ ***stehen*** be on the left, be a left-winger; *fig.* ~ ***liegenlassen*** completely ignore, give *s.o.* the cold shoulder; ***ich weiß nicht mehr, was*** ~ ***und was rechts ist*** I'm totally confused, I don't know which way to turn; **II.** *prp.* (*gen.*) on (*or* to) the left of; ~ ***der Spree*** on the left bank of the Spree; *pol.* ~ ***der Mitte*** left of cent|re (*Am.* -er); **III.** F *adj.* left-handed

'Links|ab·bie·gen *n*: ~ ***verboten*** no left turn(s); **~ab·bie·ger** [-apbiːgɐ] *m* (-s; -) car *etc.* turning left, *pl.* traffic *sg.* turning left; **~ab·bie·ge·spur** *f* left-hand turn(-off) lane; **~au·ßen** *m soccer*: outside left, left wing; *fig. pol.* extreme left-winger; **≈bün·dig** *adj. typ.* flush left; **~drall** *m* left-hand twist; *fig. pol.* leftist tendencies *pl.*; **~dre·hung** *f* anticlockwise rotation

'Links·ex·tre,mist *m* left-wing extremist; **'links·ex·tre,mi·stisch** *adj.* (of the) extreme left

'Links·füß·ler [-fyːslɐ] *m* (-s; -) left-footed player

'links·ge·rich·tet *adj. pol.* left-wing

'Links·ha·ken *m boxing*: left hook

'Links·hän·der [-hɛndɐ] *m* (-s; -) left-hander; ***er ist*** ~ he's left-handed; **'links·hän·dig** [-hɛndɪç] *adj.* left-handed; left hand *blow etc.*

'links·her,um *adv.* anticlockwise; (to the) left

'Links|in·tel·lek·tu,el·le *m*, *f* (-n; -n) left-wing intellectual; **~ka·tho·li,zis·mus** *m* left-wing Catholicism; **~kurs** *m* leftist

policy (*or* tendencies *pl.*); **~kur·ve** *f* left turn (✈ bank); left-hand bend
'links·la·stig [-lastɪç] *adj.*: **~ *sein*** lean to the left, *fig.* lean towards the left, have leftist tendencies (*or* leanings)
'Links·len·ker *m mot.* left-hand drive
'links·ori·en,tiert *adj.* leftist; **'Links·ori·en,tie·rung** *f* leftist tendencies *pl.*
'Links·par,tei *f* left-wing party
'links·ra·di,kal *adj.*, **'Links·ra·di,ka·le** *m, f* (-n; -n) left-wing extremist
'Links|ruck *m*, **~rutsch** *m*, **~schwen·kung** *f pol.* swing to the left
'links·sei·tig [-zaɪtɪç] **I.** *adj.* left; on the left(-hand) side; **II.** *adv.* → ***gelähmt***
'Links|steue·rung *f mot.* left-hand drive; **~ver·kehr** *m*: *mot.* ***in Großbritannien ist*** **~** in Britain they drive on the left(-hand side); **~wen·dung** *f pol.* shift to the left
Li·no·le·um [li'no:leʊm] *n* (-s; *no pl.*) linoleum, lino
Li·nol|säu·re [li'no:l-] *f* linoleic acid; **~schnitt** *m* linocut
Lin·se ['lɪnzə] *f* (-; -n) **1.** ♣ lentil; **2.** *anat. and opt.* lens; F ***j-n vor die*** **~** ***kriegen*** F get s.o. into one's (camera) sights
lin·sen ['lɪnzən] F *v/i.* (h) peep, F peek
'lin·sen·för·mig [-fœrmɪç] *adj.* lenticular
'Lin·sen|ge·richt *n* lentil dish; *fig.* ***et. für ein*** **~** ***hergeben*** sell s.th. for a song; **~sup·pe** *f* lentil soup; **~trü·bung** *f* ⚕ cataract
Li·pom [li'po:m] *n* (-s; -e) ⚕ lipoma, skin tag
Lip·pe ['lɪpə] *f* (-; -n) *anat.* lip; ♣ labellum; ***von den*** **~n** ***lesen*** lip-read; *fig.* ***sich auf die*** **~n** ***beißen*** bite one's tongue; ***an j-s*** **~n** ***hängen*** hang on s.o.'s every word; ***das bringe ich nicht*** (***nur schwer***) ***über die*** **~n** I can't (I can hardly) bring myself to say it; ***das soll nicht über m-e*** **~n** ***kommen*** I won't breathe a word, my lips are sealed; F ***e-e große*** (*or* ***freche***) **~** ***riskieren*** F shoot one's mouth off
'Lip·pen·be·kennt·nis *n* lip service; ***ein*** **~** ***ablegen*** pay lip service
'Lip·pen·blüt·ler [-bly:tlɐ] *m* (-s; -) ♣ labiate
'lip·pen·för·mig [-fœrmɪç] *adj.* ♣ *etc.* labiate
'Lip·pen|laut *m ling.* labial; **~stift** *m* lipstick
'lip·pen·syn,chron *adj.*, **'lip·pen·syn·chro·ni·sie·ren** *v/t. and v/i.* (h), **'Lip·pen·syn·chro·ni·sa·ti,on** *f film*: F lip-sync
li·quid [li'kvi:t] *adj.* ⚚ liquid *funds*; solvent *customer*; **Li·qui·da·ti·on** [likvida'tsi̯o:n] *f* (-; -en) ⚚ liquidation, *esp. Brit.* winding-up; *stock exchange*: settlement; ***in*** **~** ***treten*** go into liquidation; **Li·qui·da·tor** [likvi'da:to:ɐ] *m* (-s; -en [-da'to:rən]) liquidator; **li·qui·die·ren** [likvi'di:rən] *v/t.* (h) ⚚ liquidate (*a. fig. s.o.*), wind up; **Li·qui'die·rung** *f* (-; -en) liquidation (*a. fig.*); **Li·qui·di·tät** [likvidi'tɛ:t] *f* liquidity; solvency
lis·peln ['lɪspəln] (h) **I.** *v/i.* (have a) lisp; **II.** *v/t.* lisp; whisper
List [lɪst] *f* (-; -en) cunning; ruse, trick, ploy; ***zu e-r*** **~** ***greifen*** a) use (*or* employ, resort to) a trick, b) use a bit of cunning; ***er steckt voller*** **~** he's a sly old fox; ***mit*** **~** ***und Tücke*** with a great deal of cunning
Li·ste ['lɪstə] *f* (-; -n) list; *adm.* register; ⚖, ⚕ panel; → ***Wahlliste; schwarze*** **~** black list; ***auf die schwarze*** **~** ***setzen*** blacklist
'Li·sten|platz *m pol.* place; **~** ***vier haben*** be in fourth place; **~preis** *m* ⚚ list price
'li·sten·reich *adj.* full of cunning
li·stig ['lɪstɪç] *adj.* cunning, crafty, wily; sly *look etc.*
Li·ta·nei [lita'naɪ] *f* (-; -en) *eccl. and fig.* litany; *fig.* ***die ganze*** **~** *a.* F the whole spiel; ***immer dieselbe*** **~** the same old story every time
Li·tau·er [li:'taʊɐ] *m* (-s; -), **Li·taue·rin** ['li:taʊərɪn] *f* (-; -nen), **li·tau·isch** ['li:taʊɪʃ] *adj.* Lithuanian
Li·ter ['li:tɐ] *m, n* (-s; -) litre, *Am.* liter
li·te·rar·ge·schicht·lich [lɪtə'ra:ɐ-] *adj.* literary historical
Li·te'rar·hi,sto·ri·ker *m* literary historian; **li·te'rar·hi,sto·risch** *adj.* literary historical
li·te·ra·risch [lɪtə'ra:rɪʃ] **I.** *adj.* literary; **II.** *adv.*: **~** ***gebildet*** literate, well-read; **~** ***tätig sein*** be a writer, write
Li·te·rat [lɪtə'ra:t] *m* (-en; -en) **1.** man of letters, belletrist; writer, literary figure; *pl.* literati, literary establishment *sg.*; **2.** *contp.* scribe
Li·te'ra·ten|ca,fé *n* literary café; **~krei·se** *pl.*: ***in*** **~n** in (*or* among) literary circles
Li·te·ra·tur [lɪtəra'tu:ɐ] *f* (-; -en) literature; **~agent** *m* literary agent; **~an·ga·be** *f* bibliographical reference; *pl.* bibliography *sg.*; **~bei·la·ge** *f* literary supplement; **~be·trieb** *m* (-[e]s; *no pl.*) literary scene (*contp.* mill); **~gat·tung** *f* literary genre; **~ge·schich·te** *f* history of literature, literary history; **~,hin·wei·se** *pl.* recommendations for (F tips on) further reading; *heading*: further reading *sg.*; **~hi,sto·ri·ker** *m* literary historian; **~kri,tik** *f* literary criticism; **~kri·ti·ker** *m* literary critic; **~le·xi·kon** *n* dictionary (*or* encyclop[a]edia) of literature; **~nach·weis** *m* bibliography; **~papst** F *m* literary guru; **~preis** *m* literary award; **~spra·che** *f* written language; **~ver·zeich·nis** *n* bibliography; **~wis·sen·schaft** *f* literature, literary studies *pl.*; **~wis·sen·schaft·ler** *m* literary scholar; ***er ist*** **~** ***an der Universität Wien*** he teaches literature at Vienna university; **~zeit·schrift** *f* literary journal
'Li·ter·fla·sche *f* litre (*Am.* liter) bottle
'li·ter·wei·se *adv.* by the litre (*Am.* liter); F *fig.* ***sie saufen das Zeug*** **~** F they knock the stuff back by the bottle
Lit·faß·säu·le ['lɪtfas-] *f* advertising column
Li·tho·gra·phie [litogra'fi:] *f* (-; -n) **1.** *no pl.* lithography; **2.** lithograph
Li·tho·trip·ter [lito'trɪptɐ] *m* (-s; -) ⚕ lithotripter
Lit·schi ['lɪtʃi] *f* (-; -s) lychee
litt [lɪt] *pret. of* ***leiden***
Li·tur·gie [litʊr'gi:] *f* (-; -n) *eccl.* liturgy
li·tur·gisch [li'tʊrgɪʃ] *adj.* liturgical
Lit·ze ['lɪtsə] *f* (-; -n) cord, braid; ⚡ flex
live [laɪf] *adj. and adv.* live
'Live|-Auf·nah·me *f* live recording; **~-Auf·tritt** *m* live performance; **~-Auf·zeich·nung** *f* → ***Live-Aufnahme***; **~-Be·richt** *m* **1.** *sport etc.*: live commentary; **2.** → ***Live-Reportage***; **~-Be·richt·er·stat·tung** *f* **1.** *sport*: live commentary; **2.** live (*or* on-the-spot) reporting; **~-Re·por,ta·ge** *f* on-the-spot report; **~-Sen·dung** *f* live broadcast; **~-Über,tra·gung** *f* live transmission
Liv·län·der ['li:flɛndɐ] *m* (-s; -), **Liv·län·de·rin** ['li:flɛndərɪn] *f* (-; -nen), **liv·län·disch** ['li:flɛndɪʃ] *adj.* Livonian
Li·vree [li'vre:] *f* (-; -n) livery; **li·vriert** [li'vri:ɐt] *adj.* liveried
Li·zenz [li'tsɛnts] *f* (-; -en) licen|ce (*Am.* -se); ***j-m die*** **~** ***erteilen zu*** *inf.* give s.o. a licen|ce (*Am.* -se) to *inf.*, licen|se (*Am. a.* -ce) s.o. to *inf.*; ***in*** **~** under licen|ce (*Am.* -se); **~bau** *m* (-[e]s; *no pl.*) licen|sed (*Am. a.* -ced) manufacture; **~ge·bühr** *f* licen|ce (*Am.* -se) fee, royalty; **~in·ha·ber** *m* licensee; **~spie·ler** *m sport*: professional, F pro; **~ver·trag** *m* licen|ce (*Am.* -se) agreement
Lkw ['ɛlkave:] *m* (-[s]; -s) lorry, *esp. Am.* truck; **~-Fah·rer** *m* lorry (*esp. Am.* truck) driver, *esp. Am. a.* F trucker
Lob[1] [lo:p] *n* (-[e]s; *no pl.*) praise; approval; ***j-m ein*** **~** ***aussprechen*** praise s.o. (for s.th.); ***großes*** **~** ***ernten*** earn a great deal of praise; ***des*** **~es** ***voll sein*** be full of praise (***über*** *acc.* for), ***über j-n***: *a.* sing s.o.'s praises; ***über alles*** **~** ***erhaben*** beyond praise; ***zu s-m*** **~e** to his credit
Lob[2] [lɔp] *m* (-[s]; -s) *tennis*: lob
lob·be·gie·rig ['lo:p-] *adj.* eager for praise; **~** ***sein*** *a.* always be looking for (*or* seeking) praise
lob·ben ['lɔbən] *v/i. and v/t.* (h) *tennis*: lob
Lob·by ['lɔbi] *f* (-; -s) lobby; **Lob·by·is·mus** [lɔbi'ɪsmʊs] *m* (-; *no pl.*) lobbyism, lobbying; **Lob·by·ist** [lɔbi'ɪst] *m* (-en; -en) lobbyist
lo·ben ['lo:bən] *v/t.* (h) praise; speak very highly of; extol; ***da lobe ich mir ...*** give me ... any time; → ***Abend***; **'lo·bend I.** *adj.*: **~es** ***Wort*** word of praise; **~e** ***Erwähnung*** positive (*or* hono[u]rable) mention; **II.** *adv.*: **~** ***erwähnen*** give *s.o. or s.th.* a positive (*or* an hono[u]rable) mention; **~** ***sprechen über*** *acc.* be full of praise for
'lo·bens·wert *adj.* commendable, laudable
Lo·bes·hym·ne ['lo:bəs-] *f* hymn (*or* song) of praise; *fig.* ***in*** **~n** ***ausbrechen über*** *acc.* praise *s.o. or s.th.* to the skies
Lob·ge·sang ['lo:p-] *m* song of praise; *fig.* → ***Loblied***
Lob·hu·de·lei [lo:phu:də'laɪ] *f* (-; -en) *a. pl.* adulation, sycophancy; **lob·hu·deln** ['lo:phu:dəln] *v/t. and v/i.* (h) heap praise on *s.o.*, adulate; **Lob·hud·ler** ['lo:phu:dlɐ] *m* (-s; -) sycophant
löb·lich ['lø:plɪç] *adj.* commendable, creditable, laudable; *iro.* brilliant
Lob|lied ['lo:p-] *n* hymn (*or* song) of praise; *fig.* ***ein*** **~** ***auf j-n singen*** sing s.o.'s praises, praise s.o. to the skies; **~re·de** *f* eulogy
Loch [lɔx] *n* (-[e]s; Löcher ['lœçɐ]) hole (*a. fig. contp.*); opening; gap; *billiards*: pocket; F *fig.* F clink, jug, *Am.* F slammer; V cunt, hole; *fig.* ***auf dem letzten*** **~** ***pfeifen*** be on one's last legs; F ***j-m Löcher*** (*or* ***ein*** **~**) ***in den Bauch fragen*** (***reden***) bombard s.o. with questions (go on and on at s.o.); F ***Löcher in die Luft starren*** (*or* ***in die Wand stieren***) stare into space; ***j-m ein großes*** **~** ***in den Geldbeutel reißen*** burn a big hole in s.o.'s pocket; ***ein*** **~** ***mit dem anderen zustopfen*** rob Peter to pay Paul; F ***er säuft wie ein*** **~** F he drinks like a fish
'Loch·ei·sen *n* ⚙ punch
lo·chen ['lɔxən] *v/t.* (h) punch; **Lo·cher** ['lɔxɐ] *m* (-s; -) punch; **lö·che·rig** ['lœçərɪç] *adj.* **1.** full of holes (*a. fig.*); F holey; **2.** ⚕ perforated; pitted; **lö·chern**

['lœçɐn] F *v/t.* (h) go on at *s.o.*, pester *s.o.*; ***sie löchert mich seit Tagen, wann wir wegfahren*** she's been pestering me (*or* going on at me) for days about when we're going away
'Loch|kar·te *f* punchcard; **~sä·ge** *f* keyhole saw; **~strei·fen** *m* ticker tape
Lo·chung ['lɔxʊŋ] *f* (-; -en) a) punching, b) perforation
'Loch|ver·stär·ker *m* paper reinforcement; **~zan·ge** *f*: (**e-e ~** a pair of) punch pliers *pl.*; ⚒ punch; **~zie·gel** *m* air brick
Lock·ar,ti·kel ['lɔk-] *m* ✝ loss leader
Locke ['lɔkə] (*sep.* -k·k-)] *f* (-; -n) curl, lock; (***blonde***) ***schwarze ~n haben*** have curly blond (black) hair; ***das Haar in ~n legen*** put curlers in (one's hair)
locken¹ ['lɔkən] (*sep.* -k·k-) *v/t. and v/refl.* (***sich ~***) (h) curl; → ***gelockt***
'locken² (*sep.* -k·k-) *v/t.* (h) **1.** lure, call *animal*; bait *fish*; **2.** *fig.* lure; tempt; **~ *in*** *acc.* (***aus*** *dat.*) lure into (out of); ***es lockt mich*** I feel tempted; ***das lockt mich sehr*** (***gar nicht***) *a.* I really like the idea (it doesn't interest me at all, F it doesn't grab me); ***mich würde Portugal ~*** I quite fancy Portugal; ***j-m das Geld aus der Tasche ~*** entice s.o. into spending his (*or* her) money, cheat s.o. out of his (*or* her) money; **'lockend** *fig. adj.* attractive, enticing
'Locken|kopf (*sep.* -k·k-) *m* a) curly hair, b) curly head, c) curlyhead; **~stab** *m* curling tongs *pl.*; **~wick·ler** *m* curler
locker ['lɔkɐ] (*sep.* -k·k-) **I.** *adj.* loose; slack; *gastr.* light; *fig.* relaxed; easygoing, F cool *person*; lax *morals*; (very) casual *relationship*; ***e-e ~e Hand haben*** be quick to lash out; → ***Mundwerk; ~ machen*** (***werden***) → (***sich***) ***lockern***; **II.** *adv.* loosely; F *fig.* easily, F *do s.th.* no problem; ***et. ~ handhaben*** deal with s.th. very casually; ***es geht sehr ~ zu*** it's all very relaxed; ***bei ihm sitzt das Geld ziemlich ~*** he doesn't think twice when it comes to spending money; ***bei ihm sitzt das Geld nicht ~*** he has to go easy on his money, he has to count his pennies; ***das mußt du etwas ~er sehen*** you mustn't see it so narrowly; F ***das schafft er ~*** F he'll manage it no problem
'locker·las·sen (*sep.* -k·k-) *v/i.* (*irr.*, *sep.*, h, → ***lassen***): ***nicht ~*** keep at it, keep going; ***nicht ~!*** don't give up!, no slacking now!; ***er ließ nicht locker, bis*** he wouldn't give up until
'locker·ma·chen (*sep.* -k·k-) F *v/t.* (*sep.*, h) F fork out, cough up; ***bei j-m 20 Mark ~*** F get s.o. to fork out 20 marks
lockern ['lɔkɐn] (*sep.* -k·k-) (h) **I.** *v/t.* loosen; slacken *rope etc.*; *a.* relax (*one's grip etc.*, *a. fig. discipline etc.*); loosen up *one's muscles*; **II.** *v/refl.*: ***sich ~*** loosen, come loose; *rope etc.*: slacken; *sport*: loosen (*or* limber) up; *fig.* relax; *fig.* ***die Sitten haben sich gelockert*** morals have become lax (*or* slack); **Locke·rung** ['lɔkərʊŋ] (*sep.* -k·k-) *f* (-; *no pl.*) loosening; relaxation; slackening; *sport*: limbering-up; **'Locke·rungs·übung** *f* loosening-up (*or* limbering-up) exercise
lockig ['lɔkɪç] (*sep.* -k·k-) *adj.* curly
'Lock|mit·tel *n* bait; **~ruf** *m zo.* mating call; **~spit·zel** *m* stool pigeon; *pol.* agent provocateur
Lockung ['lɔkʊŋ] (*sep.* -k·k-) *f* (-; -en) *a. pl.* lure; temptation
'Lock·vo·gel *m a. fig.* decoy; **~an·ge·bot** *n* ✝ loss leader; **~wer·bung** *f* bait advertising
Lod·del ['lɔdəl] F *m* (-s; -) F pimp
Lo·den ['lo:dən] *m* (-s; *no pl.*) loden; **~man·tel** *m* loden coat
lo·dern ['lo:dɐn] *v/i.* (h) blaze; *torch*: burn, shine; *fig.* glow; burn; **'lo·dernd** *adj.*: ***~e Flammen*** burning flames; *fig.* ***~e Begeisterung*** *etc.* burning (*or* glowing) enthusiasm *etc.*
Löf·fel ['lœfəl] *m* (-s; -) spoon; ⚙ scoop; F *fig. pl.* ears, *sl.* lugholes; F *fig.* ***den ~ weglegen*** F kick the bucket, pop one's clogs; F ***er hat die Weisheit nicht mit ~n gefressen*** F he must have been at the back of the queue when they were handing brains out; ***mit e-m goldenen*** (*or* ***silbernen***) ***~ im Mund geboren sein*** have been born with a silver spoon in one's mouth; F ***schreib dir das hinter die ~*** F and don't you forget it; F ***j-n über den ~ barbieren*** F play s.o. for a sucker, take s.o. for a ride; **~bis,kuit** *m*, *n* sponge finger
löf·feln ['lœfəln] *v/t.* (h) spoon; ladle; spoon *s.th.* up
'Löf·fel·stiel *m* spoon handle
'löf·fel·wei·se *adv.* in spoonfuls, by the spoonful
log [lo:k] *pret. of* ***lügen***
Log·arith·men·ta·fel [loga'rɪtmən-] *f* log(arithmic) tables *pl.*
log·arith·mie·ren [logarɪt'mi:rən] (h) **I.** *v/t.* take the logarithm of; **II.** *v/i.* take the logarithm
log·arith·misch [loga'rɪtmɪʃ] *adj.* logarithmic
Log·arith·mus [loga'rɪtmʊs] *m* (-; -men) logarithm
Log·buch ['lɔkbu:x] *n* log(book)
Lo·ge ['lo:ʒə] *f* (-; -n) **1.** *thea.* box; **2.** (*freemason's*) lodge
'Lo·gen|bru·der *m* fellow mason; **~meister** *m* master of a (*or* the) lodge; **~platz** *m thea.* box seat
Log·gia ['lɔdʒa] *f* (-; Loggien ['lɔdʒĭən]) ⚠ loggia; recessed balcony
lo·gie·ren [lo'ʒi:rən] *v/i.* (h) stay (***bei*** *dat.* with; ***in*** *dat.* at); **Lo·gier·be·such** [lo-'ʒi:ɐ-] *m* (overnight) guest(s *pl.*)
Lo·gik ['lo:gɪk] *f* (-; *no pl.*) logic; **Lo·gi·ker** ['lo:gikɐ] *m* (-s; -) logician
Lo·gis [lo'ʒi:] *n* (-; - [lo'ʒi:s]) lodgings *pl.*; ***Kost und ~*** board and lodgings
lo·gisch ['lo:gɪʃ] *adj.* logical; ***es ist doch völlig ~*** it stands to reason(, doesn't it?); ***ist doch ~!*** it's logical, isn't it (*hum.* innit)?, of course!, F you bet!; **lo·gi·scher·wei·se** ['lo:gɪʃɐ-] *adv.* logically; obviously; ***~ muß er ...*** *a.* it's obvious (*or* only logical) that he has to ...
Lo·gi·stik ['lo'gɪstɪk] *f* (- *no pl.*) *phls. and* ⚔ logistics *pl.*; **lo·gi·stisch** [lo'gɪstɪʃ] *adj.* logistic(ally *adv.*)
lo·go ['lo:go] *sl. int. sl.* sure thing!, F you bet!
Lo·go ['lo:go] *m*, *n* (-s; -s) ✝ logo
Lo·go·pä·de [logo'pɛ:də] *m* (-n; -n), **Lo·go·pä·din** [logo'pɛ:dɪn] *f* (-; -nen) speech therapist; **Lo·go·the·ra'pie** [logo-] *f* speech therapy, logotherapy
Lo·he ['lo:ə] *f* (-; -n) tan
Lohn [lo:n] *m* (-[e]s; Löhne ['lø:nə]) a) wage(s *pl.*), pay; payment, b) reward; ***zum ~*** as a reward (***für*** *acc.* for), *fig. a.* in return (for); ***bei j-m in ~ stehen*** be in s.o.'s pay (*or* service); ***j-n um ~ und Brot bringen*** deprive s.o. of his (*or* her) livelihood, take the bread out of s.o.'s mouth; *iro.* ***er hat s-n*** (***gerechten***) ***~ bekommen*** he got his just deserts; **~ab·bau** *m* wage cuts *pl.*
'lohn·ab·hän·gig *adj.* wage-earning ..., wage-dependent; **'Lohn·ab·hän·gi·ge** *m*, *f* (-n; -n) wage earner
'Lohn|ab·kom·men *n* wage agreement; **~ab·rech·nung** *f* **1.** pay slip; **2.** payroll accounting; **~ab·zug** *m* wage (*or* salary) deduction; **~an·glei·chung** *f* wage adjustment; **~an·stieg** *m* rise in wages; **~ar·beit** *f* paid labo(u)r; **~auf·trag** *m* farming-out contract; ***e-n ~ vergeben*** farm out work to a subcontractor; **~aus·fall** *m* loss of earnings; **~aus·gleich** *m*: ***bei vollem ~*** without cuts in payment; **~aus·zah·lung** *f* payment of wages; **~be·schrän·kung** *f* wage restraint; **~buch·hal·ter** *m* payroll clerk; **~buch·hal·tung** *f* **1.** payroll accounting; **2.** payroll department; **~dif·fe,renz** *f* wages gap, wage differential; **~dik,tat** *n* imposed pay settlement; **~drift** *f* wage drift; **~emp·fän·ger** *m* wage earner; ***Lohn- und Gehaltsempfänger*** salaried and wage-earning employees
loh·nen ['lo:nən] (h) **I.** *v/refl.* **1. *sich ~*** be worthwhile, be worth one's while, pay; ***es lohnt sich*** it's worth it, ***zu*** *inf.*: it's worth *ger.*, it pays to *inf.*; ***es lohnt sich nicht*** a) it's not worth it, b) it's no use; ***der Film lohnt sich*** it's a good film, the film's worth seeing, you should go and see the film; ***ein Versuch lohnt sich*** it's worth a try; ***die Mühe lohnt sich*** it's worth (making) the effort *or* (taking) the trouble; **II.** *v/t.* **2. *j-m et. ~*** repay (*or* reward) s.o. for s.th.; **3. *es lohnt die Mühe*** it's worth the effort
löh·nen ['lø:nən] F *v/i.* (h) F cough up, pick up the tab
'loh·nend *adj.* worthwhile; rewarding; worth seeing *etc.*
'Lohn|er·hö·hung *f* wage increase, pay rise (*Am.* raise); **~for·de·rung** *f* wage claim; **~fort·zah·lung** *f* continued pay (in case of sickness); **~front** *f*: (***an der ~*** on the) wages front; **~ge·fäl·le** *n* wage differential, wages gap; **~grup·pe** *f* wage bracket; **~in·dex** *m* wage index; **ℒin·ten,siv** *adj.* wage-intensive; **~kampf** *m* wage dispute; **~ko·sten** *pl.* labo(u)r costs; **~kür·zung** *f* pay cut; **~nach·zah·lung** *f a. pl.* back pay; **~pau·se** *f* temporary wage freeze; **~po·li,tik** *f* wages policy; **~-'Preis-Spi,ra·le** *f* wages-price spiral; **~run·de** *f* round of wage talks, wage round; **~sen·kung** *f* cut in wages, wages cut; **~ska·la** *f* wage scale; **~staf·fe·lung** *f* graduated salary
'Lohn·steu·er *f* income tax; **~jah·res·aus·gleich** *m* annual adjustment of income tax; ***s-n ~ machen*** do one's tax return; **~kar·te** *f* tax card
'Lohn|stopp *m* wage freeze, pegging of wages; **~strei·fen** *m* pay slip; **~tü·te** *f* wage packet; **~ver·ein·ba·rung** *f* wage (*or* pay) agreement; **~ver·hand·lun·gen** *pl.* wage negotiations (*or* talks), wage round *sg.*; **~vor·sprung** *m* wage differential; **~zet·tel** *m* pay slip
Loi·pe ['lɔʏpə] *f* (-; -n) *skiing*: (cross-country) trail *or* circuit
Lok [lɔk] *f* (-; -s) engine
lo·kal [lo'ka:l] *adj.* local
Lo·kal [lo'ka:l] n (-s; -e) restaurant; pub, bar, F *hum.* watering hole; ***ich kenne ein gutes ~*** *a.* F I know a good place

Lo'kal|an·äs·the,sie *f* (-; -n) ⚕ local an(a)esthetic; **~an·zei·ger** *m* free paper, local freesheet (*or* advertiser); **~be·richt** *m* local report; **~blatt** *n* local paper; **~der·by** *n* local derby
Lo·ka·le [lo'ka:lə] *n* (-n; *no pl.*) *newspaper*: local news (*sg.*)
lo·ka·li·sie·ren [lokali'zi:rən] *v/t.* (h) **1.** locate; pinpoint; **2.** localize
Lo·ka·li·tät [lokali'tɛ:t] *f* (-; -en) place, locality
Lo'kal|ko·lo,rit *n* local colo(u)r; **~ma·ta,dor** *m* local hero; **~nach·rich·ten** *pl.* local news *sg.*; **~pa·trio·tis·mus** *m* local (*or* regional) patriotism; **~pres·se** *f* local (*or* regional) press; **~re·dak,teur** *m* local (*or* regional) news editor; **~re·dak·ti,on** *f* local newsroom; **~run·de** *f*: **e-e ~ ausgeben** (F **schmeißen**) buy drinks for everyone (in the house); **~sei·te** *f* local news page (*or* section); **~teil** *m* local news pages *pl.* (*or* section); **~ter,min** *m* ⚖ visit to the scene of the crime; **~ver·bot** *n*: **~ (erteilt) bekommen** be barred from (entering) the place; **er hat (hier) ~** he's been barred from the place; **~ver·hält·nis·se** *pl.* local conditions; **~zei·tung** *f* local paper
Lo·ka·tiv ['lo:kati:f] *m* (-s; -e [-və]) *ling.* locative
'Lok·füh·rer *m* → **Lokomotivführer**
Lo·ko|ge·schäft ['lo:ko-] *n* ✝ spot transaction; **~han·del** *m* spot trading
Lo·ko·mo·ti·ve [lokomo'ti:və] *f* (-; -n) engine; **Lo·ko·mo'tiv·füh·rer** *m* engine driver, *Am.* engineer
Lo·ko·preis ['lo:ko-] *m* ✝ spot price
Lo·kus ['lo:kʊs] F *m* (-; -se) F loo, *Am.* F john; **er ist auf dem ~** he's in (*or* he's gone to) the loo (*Am.* john)
Lom·bard|kre,dit ['lɔmbart-] *m* ✝ collateral loan; **~satz** *m* Lombard rate
Loo·ping ['lu:pɪŋ] *m* (-s; -s) loop; **e-n ~ drehen** do a loop
Lor·beer ['lɔrbe:ɐ] *m* (-s; -en [-be:rən]) **1.** ♣ laurel; **2.** *no pl. gastr.* bay leaf (*or* leaves *pl.*); **3.** → **Lorbeerkranz; 4.** *fig. pl.* laurels; **sich auf s-n ~en ausruhen** rest on one's laurels; **die ersten ~en ernten** win one's first laurels; **damit wird sie keine ~en ernten** that won't win her any laurels; **~baum** *m* laurel (tree), bay (tree); **~blatt** *n* bay leaf; **~kranz** *m* laurel wreath (*a. fig.*); **~zweig** *m* sprig of laurel
Lo·re ['lo:rə] *f* (-; -n) tipper lorry, *a. Am.* dump truck
Lor·gnet·te [lɔrn'jɛtə] *f* (-; -n) lorgnette
Los [lo:s] *n* (-es; -e ['lo:zə]) **1.** (lottery) ticket; **das große ~ ziehen** win first prize, *fig.* hit the jackpot; **2. durchs ~ entscheiden** decide by drawing lots (*or* by lot); *fig.* **ihm fiel das ~ zu zu** *inf.* it fell to his lot to *inf.*; **das ~ fiel auf mich** *iro.* I was the lucky one; **3.** fate; **ein schweres ~** a hard lot; **es war mein ~ zu** *inf.* it was my lot (*or* fate, destiny) to *inf.*; **4.** ✝ lot
los [lo:s] **I.** *pred. adj. and adv.* **1.** → **lose** 1; **2.** a) off, b) loose, off the leash (*or* lead); **der Knopf ist ~** the button is (*or* has come) off; **3.** F **ich bin's immer noch nicht ~** a) I haven't got rid of it yet, b) *fig.* I still haven't got over it; **den wären wir endlich ~** thank goodness he's gone; **den Auftrag bist du ~** you can say goodbye to that job; **4.** F **was ist (mit ihm) ~?** what's wrong (with him)?; **was ist denn schon wieder ~?** what's the matter this time (*or* now)?; **da ist etwas ~** a) there's something going on, b) there's something wrong, c) something has happened; **da war (schwer) was ~** a) the sparks were flying, b) things were really happening; **da ist immer was ~** there's always something going on there; **hier ist nichts ~** F nothing doing around here; **wo ist hier was ~?** where can you go around here?; **mit ihm ist nicht viel ~** he isn't up to much; **heute ist mit ihr nichts ~** you can forget her (for) today; → **losgehen, Teufel; 5.** F **er ist schon ~** he's gone (*or* left) already; **willst du schon ~?** are you going already?; **II.** *int.*: **~!** a) go on!, *sport*: go!, b) let's go!, come on!; **jetzt aber ~!** okay, let's go!, F go for it!; **~ar·bei·ten** *v/i.* (*sep.*, h) start working; work away (**auf** *acc.* at); **auf et. ~** start work(ing) on s.th.; **~bal·lern** F *v/i.* (*sep.*, h) F start banging away
lös·bar ['lø:sba:ɐ] *adj. a. fig.* soluble; ⚗ *etc. a.* solvable; **'Lös·bar·keit** *f* (-; *no pl.*) solubility
'los|bei·ßen (*irr.*, *sep*, h, → **beißen**) **I.** *v/t.* bite off (*or* through); **II.** *v/refl.*: **sich ~** bite o.s. free; **~be·kom·men** *v/t.* (*irr.*, *sep.*, h, → **bekommen**) get off (*or* out); **~bel·len** *v/i.* (*sep.*, h) start barking; **~bin·den** *v/t.* (*irr.*, *sep.*, h, → **binden**) untie; free; take *a dog* off the lead; set *an animal* free; **~brau·sen** F *v/i.* (*sep.*, sn) F zoom off; **~bre·chen** (*irr.*, *sep.*, → **brechen**) **I.** *v/t.* (h) break off; **II.** *fig. v/i.* (sn) *storm*: break; *laughter etc.*: break out; **~brül·len** *v/i.* (*sep.*, h) start shouting (*or* screaming)
Lösch|an·la·ge ['lœʃ-] *f* fire-fighting equipment; **~ar·bei·ten** *pl.* fire-fighting operations (*or* operation *sg.*); **die ~ dauern noch an** firemen are still fighting (*or* trying to put out) the blaze
lösch·bar ['lœʃba:ɐ] *adj.* **1.** erasable *tape etc.*; **2. schwer ~** not easy to put out
Lösch|blatt ['lœʃ-] *n* (piece of) blotting paper; **~ei·mer** *m* fire bucket
lö·schen ['lœʃən] *v/t.* (h) **1.** put out *fire*; *a.* blow out *candle*; **2.** douse *coals*; **3.** put out, switch off *the light etc.*; **4. den Durst ~** quench one's thirst; **5.** take out *word etc.*, *computer*: erase, delete; cross out *entry etc.*, strike (*or* cross) *name etc.* off (the list); erase, wipe everything off *a tape*, tape over; *fig.* wipe *memory*, *trace etc.* out (**aus** *dat.* of), erase (from); **aus dem Gedächtnis ~** wipe out of (*or* erase from) one's memory *or* mind; **6.** ✝ cancel; clear, pay off *mortgage etc.*; close *account*; **7.** ⚓ unload; **Lö·scher** ['lœʃɐ] *m* (-s; -) **1.** fire extinguisher; **2.** blotter
Lösch|ge·rät ['lœʃ-] *n* fire-extinguisher; *coll.* fire-fighting equipment; **~kalk** *m* quicklime; **~kom,man·do** *n* fire-fighting squad; **~kopf** *m* erasing head; **~mann·schaft** *f* fire-fighting team, fire brigade; **~pa,pier** *n* blotting paper; **~schaum** *m* extinguishing foam; **~ta·ste** *f tape recorder etc.*: erase (*or* record) button; *computer*: delete key; *typewriter*: erase key; *radio, CD-player etc.*: clear button; **~trupp** *m* fire-fighting team (*or* squad)
Lö·schung ['lœʃʊŋ] *f* (-; -en) **1.** deletion; ✝ cancellation, *a.* discharge *of a mortgage etc.*; striking off the register *of a firm*; **2.** ⚓ unloading
Lösch|wa·gen ['lœʃ-] *m* fire engine; **~zug** *m* fire brigade
'los|don·nern *v/i.* (*sep.*) **1.** (h) a) start thundering, b) *fig.* explode; **2.** (sn) *mot.* roar off; **~dre·hen** *v/t.* (*sep.*, h) twist off; *a.* loosen *a screw*; **~drücken** *v/i.* (*sep.*, h) pull the trigger
lo·se ['lo:zə] **I.** *adj.* **1.** loose (*a.* ✝ *goods etc.*); slack; movable; **~ Blätter** loose leaves; **~ Teile** separate parts; **2.** *fig.* loose *contact etc.*; **in ~r Folge** sporadically, at (varying) intervals; **3.** *fig.* loose; malicious; *hum.* naughty, mischievous; F **~s Maul** (*or* **Mundwerk**) loose (*or* nasty, malicious) tongue; **~ Reden führen** indulge in loose talk; **~ Sitten** loose morals; **II.** *adv.* loosely; **die Haare ~ tragen** wear one's hair down
Lo·se'blatt·aus·ga·be *f* loose-leaf edition
Lö·se·geld ['lø:zə-] *n* ransom (money)
'los·ei·sen F (*sep.*, h) **I.** *v/t.* get *s.o. or s.th.* away (**von** *dat.* from), get *s.o. or s.th.* out (of); **et. von j-m ~** get s.th. from (*or* out of) s.o.; **II.** *v/refl.*: **sich ~** get away (**von** *dat.* from), get out (of)
Lö·se·mit·tel ['lø:zə-] *n* solvent
lo·sen ['lo:zən] *v/i.* (h) draw lots (**um** *acc.* for); toss (for); **beim ♀ gewinnen (verlieren)** win (lose) the toss
lö·sen ['lø:zən] (h) **I.** *v/t.* **1.** untie, undo; **2.** loosen; release (*brake, one's grip, a. fig. tension etc.*); ⚕ loosen (up) *cough*; *fig.* **j-m die Zunge ~** loosen s.o.'s tongue; → **gelöst; 3.** remove; separate (from s.th.); **4.** dissolve; **5.** disentangle, *a. fig.* unravel; **6.** *fig.* solve *riddle, task etc.*; answer *question etc.*; resolve, settle *conflict etc.*; **7.** *fig.* break off *one's engagement, a relationship etc.*; dissolve *a marriage*; **8.** cancel *contract etc.*; **9.** buy *a ticket*; **II.** *v/refl.*: **sich ~ 10.** *knot etc.*: come undone; **11.** come loose; ⚕ *cough*, *fig. tongue*: loosen up; *tension*: ease; **12.** come off (*a.* **sich ~ von** *dat.*); **13.** *fig.* **sich ~ von** *dat.* leave; break away from; free o.s. of; **14.** dissolve; **15.** *problem etc.*: be solved, **von alleine**: solve (*or* resolve) itself; *conflict*: be settled
'los·fah·ren *v/i.* (*irr.*, *sep.*, sn, → **fahren**) leave (*a.* 🚗), drive off; **~ auf** *acc.* make *or* head (straight) for, *fig.* fly at *s.o.*
'los·ge·hen *v/i.* (*irr.*, *sep.*, sn, → **gehen**) **1.** go, leave; **ich geh' jetzt los** *a.* I'm off now; **~ auf** *acc.* go up to, go for (*a. fig.*); **aufeinander ~** go for each other('s throats); **2.** F start; **jetzt geht's los!** here we go!, this is it (now)!; **jetzt geht's schon wieder los** here we go again; **es kann ~** we're (*or* I'm *etc.*) ready; **wann geht es endlich los?** a) when is it going to start?, b) when are we going?; **3.** *gun etc.*: go off; explode; **die Pistole ist nicht losgegangen** the gun didn't fire; *fig.* **nach hinten ~** backfire (on one)
'los·ge·las·sen I. *p.p. of* **loslassen; II.** *adj.*: **wie ~** like mad (F crazy)
'los·ge·löst I. *adj. a. fig.* detached (**von** *dat.* from); separate, isolated (from); **II.** *adv.*: *fig.* **~ betrachten (behandeln)** view (treat) separately *or* in isolation
'los|ha·ben F *v/t.* (*irr.*, *sep.*, h, → **haben**): **er hat was los** he's not bad at all, he's got what it takes, he knows a thing or two, F he's on the ball; **er hat in Physik viel (nichts) los** he knows a thing or two about physics (he's not up to much *or* F he's not much cop when it comes to physics); **~ha·ken** *v/t.* (*sep.*, h) unhook; **~het·zen** *v/i.* (*sep.*, sn) rush off (like mad); **~heu·len** F *v/i.* (*sep.*, h) start (*or*

burst out) crying, *baby*: *a.* start screaming; **~kau·fen** *v/t. and v/refl.* (*sep.*, h) → ***freikaufen***; **~ket·ten** *v/t.* (*sep.*, h) take *a dog etc.* off the chain; **~kom·men** *v/i.* (*irr.*, *sep.*, sn, → ***kommen***) get away; *fig.* ~ ***von*** *dat.* tear o.s. away from *s.o. or s.th.*, get off *drugs etc.*; ***ich komme nicht los davon*** a) I can't stop doing it, I can't kick the habit, b) I can't get it out of my mind; **~krie·gen** F *v/t.* (*sep.*, h) a) get *s.th.* off, b) get rid of *s.th.*, shake *s.th.* off; **~la·chen** *v/i.* (*sep.*, h) burst out laughing; **~las·sen** *v/t.* (*irr.*, *sep.*, h, → ***lassen***) **1.** let go; ***laß mich los!*** let go!; ***nicht ~!*** hold tight!, hang on!; ***der Gedanke*** *etc.* ***läßt mich nicht los*** I can't get it out of my mind; **2.** ~ ***auf*** *acc.* set *the dog* on *s.o.*, let *s.o.* loose on *s.o.*; F ***j-n auf die Menschheit*** ~ unleash s.o. on an unsuspecting world; **3.** let fly with *a letter etc.*; crack *a joke*; **4.** V ***einen*** ~ V let off; **~lau·fen** *v/i.* (*irr.*, *sep.*, sn, → ***laufen***) start running (***auf*** *acc.* towards); run off; ~ ***auf*** *acc.* run towards; **~le·gen** F *v/i.* (*sep.*, h) **1.** F get cracking; **2.** ***dann legte er los*** then it all came out, then he really got going; ***leg los!*** F fire away!; ~ ***gegen*** → ***losziehen***

lös·lich ['løːslıç] *adj.* ⚗ soluble; ***leicht*** ~ readily soluble; **'Lös·lich·keit** *f* (-; *no pl.*) solubility

'los|lö·sen (*sep.*, h) **I.** *v/t.* remove, detach; **II.** *v/refl.*: ***sich*** ~ come off, *a.* peel off; *fig.* free o.s. (***von*** *dat.* of), cut o.s. loose (from), break away (from); → ***losgelöst***; **~ma·chen** (*sep.*, h) **I.** *v/t.* take off; take away; untie, undo; take *dog etc.* off the chain (*or* lead); ⚓ unmoor; **II.** *v/refl.*: ***sich*** ~ get free, free o.s. (***von*** *dat.* from), *fig.* get away (from), break away (from *s.o.*); **III.** F *v/i.*: ***mach jetzt endlich los!*** F get a move on!; **~mar,schie·ren** *v/i.* (*sep.*, sn) march off, *fig.* go off; ~ ***auf*** *acc.* march towards, *fig.* make (*or* head) for

'Los·num·mer *f* (ticket) number

'los|plat·zen F *v/i.* (*sep.*, sn) **1.** burst out laughing; **2.** ~ ***mit*** *dat.* blurt *s.th.* out; **~ra·sen** *v/i.* (*sep.*, sn) zoom (*mot. a.* roar) off; **~rei·ßen** (*irr.*, *sep.*, h, → ***reißen***) **I.** *v/t.* tear (*or* rip) off; **II.** *v/refl.*: ***sich*** ~ break loose; free o.s.; *fig.* tear o.s. away (***von*** from); **~ren·nen** *v/i.* (*irr.*, *sep.*, sn, → ***rennen***) → ***loslaufen***

Löß [lœs] *m* (Lösses; Lösse) *geol.* loess

'los·sa·gen *v/refl.* (*sep.*, h): ***sich*** ~ ***von*** *dat.* renounce, disown; **'Los·sa·gung** [-zaːgʊŋ] *f* (-; -en) renunciation (***von*** *dat.* of), break (with)

'los|sau·sen F *v/i.* (*sep.*, sn) F zoom off; **~schicken** *v/t.* (*sep.*, h) send; send off *letter*; **~schie·ßen** F *v/i.* (*irr.*, *sep.*, → ***schießen***) **1.** (h) shoot, start shooting (***auf*** *acc.* at); F ***schieß los!*** F fire away!; **2.** (sn) F zoom off; **~schla·gen** (*irr.*, *sep.*, h, → ***schlagen***) **I.** *v/t.* ✝ sell off; *auction*: knock down; **II.** *v/i.* ⚔ strike; ~ ***auf*** *acc.* start hitting *s.o.*, let fly at *s.o.*; **~schnal·len** (*sep.*, h) **I.** *v/t.* unstrap; **II.** *v/refl.*: ***sich*** ~ unstrap o.s., ✈ *etc.* undo one's seatbelt; **~schrau·ben** *v/t.* (*sep.*, h) unscrew

'los·spre·chen *v/t.* (*irr.*, *sep.*, h, → ***sprechen***): ~ ***von*** *dat.* release from, *eccl.* absolve from; **'Los·spre·chung** [-ʃprɛçʊŋ] *f* (-; -en) *eccl.* absolution

'los|sprin·gen *v/i.* (*irr.*, *sep.*, sn, → ***springen***) jump (off); F rush (*or* run) off; ~ ***auf*** *acc.* leap at; **~steu·ern** *v/i.*: ~ ***auf*** *acc.* make for, *fig.* have set one's sights on, be working towards *an examination etc.*; be heading for *disaster*; **~stür·men, ~stür·zen** *v/i.* (*sep.*, sn) tear off; ~ ***auf*** *acc.* fly at; **~tren·nen** *v/t.* (*sep.*, h) → ***abtrennen***

Lo·sung¹ ['loːzʊŋ] *f* (-; -en) watchword; password

'Lo·sung² *f* (-; -en) *hunt.* droppings *pl.*

Lö·sung ['løːzʊŋ] *f* (-; -en) **1.** solution; answer (*gen.* to); ***zur*** ~ *gen.* to (help) resolve *the difficulty etc.*; ***zur*** ~ ***des Problems beitragen*** help solve the problem; **2.** ⚗ solution; **3.** separation

'Lö·sungs·mit·tel *n* solvent; thinner; **~,miß·brauch** *m* solvent abuse

'Lö·sungs|vor·schlag *m* suggested solution, suggestion; answer; **~wort** *n* (-[e]s; ⸚er) answer

'Los·ver·fah·ren *n* decision by lot; ***et. im*** ~ ***entscheiden*** decide s.th. by lot (*or* by drawing lots)

'los|wer·den *v/t.* (*irr.*, *sep.*, sn, → ***werden***) a) get rid of, b) lose, c) spend; F ***ich bin dabei viel Geld losgeworden*** F it put me back a pretty penny; ***ich werde den Gedanken*** (***das Gefühl***) ***nicht los, daß*** I can't help thinking (feeling) that; **~zie·hen** F *v/i.* (*irr.*, *sep.*, sn, → ***ziehen***) set off; *fig.* ~ ***gegen*** *acc.* lash out at, F have a real go at

Lot [loːt] *n* (-[e]s; -e) plumbline; ⚓ sounding line; ⩘ perpendicular; ⚙ solder; ***aus dem*** ~ out of plumb; ***im*** ~ perpendicular, *fig.* all right, *Am.* alright; *fig.* ***aus dem*** ~ ***geraten*** come unstuck, be thrown (off balance); ***wieder ins*** ~ ***bringen*** straighten out; ***wieder ins*** ~ ***kommen*** straighten itself out, get o.s. sorted out, get back on one's feet again; **lo·ten** ['loːtən] *v/t.* (h) plumb; ⚓ sound

lö·ten ['løːtən] *v/t.* (h) solder

Loth·rin·ger ['loːtrıŋɐ] *m* (-s; -) **1.** *hist.* Lotharingian; **2.** inhabitant of Lorraine; ~ ***sein*** *a.* be (*or* come) from Lorraine

loth·rin·gisch ['loːtrıŋıʃ] *adj.* Lotharingian (*a. hist.*); from Lorraine

Lo·ti·on [lo'tsĭoːn] *f* (-; -en) lotion

Löt|kol·ben ['løːt-] *m* soldering iron; **~lam·pe** *f* blowlamp, blowtorch; **~me,tall** *n* solder

Lo·tos ['loːtɔs] *m* (-; -), **~blu·me** *f* lotus; **~säu·le** *f* lotus column; **~sitz** *m yoga etc.*: lotus position

Löt·pi,sto·le ['løːt-] *f* soldering gun

lot·recht ['loːtrɛçt] *adj.* perpendicular

Lot·se ['loːtsə] *m* (-n; -n) ⚓ pilot; *mot.* guide; → ***Fluglotse, Schülerlotse***

'lot·sen *v/t.* (h) guide; ⚓ pilot; *fig.* steer *s.o.*; ***j-n ins Kino*** *etc.* ~ drag s.o. (off) to the movies *etc.*; ***j-n*** ~ ***durch*** *acc.* see s.o. through *a difficulty*, *an exam etc.*

'Lot·sen|boot *n* pilot vessel; **~dienst** *m mot.* driver-guide service

Löt|spit·ze ['løːt-] *f* (soldering) bit; **~sta·ti,on** *f* soldering station; **~stel·le** *f* (soldered) joint

Lot·te·rie [lɔtə'riː] *f* (-; -n) lottery; **~ge·winn** *m* **1.** win in the lottery; **2.** lottery prize; **~los** *n* lottery ticket; **~spiel** *n* lottery; *fig.* gamble

Lot·ter·le·ben ['lɔtɐ-] *n* dissolute life(style)

Lot·to ['lɔto] *n* (-s; *no pl.*) **1.** lottery, lotto; **2.** bingo; **~an·nah·me·stel·le** *f* (local) lottery counter *or* kiosk; **~ge·winn** *m* **1.** win in the lottery; **2.** lottery winnings *pl.*; **~schein** *m* lottery coupon; **~spie·ler** *m* lottery player (*or* participant); **~zah·len** *pl.* (winning) lottery numbers

Lo·tus ['loːtʊs] *m* → ***Lotos***

Löt·zinn ['løːt-] *n* solder

Lö·we ['løvə] *m* (-n; -n) **1.** *zo.* lion; **2.** *ast.* Leo; (***ein***) ~ ***sein*** be (a) Leo

'Lö·wen|an·teil *m* lion's share; ***sich den*** ~ ***sichern*** make sure one gets the lion's share; **~bän·di·ger** *m* lion tamer; **~gru·be** *f* lion's den; **~jagd** *f* lion hunt(ing); **~jun·ge** *n* lion cub; **~kä·fig** *m* lion's cage; **~mäh·ne** *f* lion's mane; *fig.* sweeping mane; **~maul** *n* ⚘ snapdragon; **~mut** *m* boldness (*or* courage) of a lion; **~mut·ter** *f* mother lion; **~zahn** *m* ⚘ dandelion

Lö·win ['løːvın] *f* (-; -nen) *zo.* lioness

loy·al [lŏa'jaːl] *adj.* loyal; **Loya·li·tät** [lŏajali'tɛːt] *f* (-; *no pl.*) loyalty

LP [ɛl'peː] *f* (-; -s) LP; **~-Samm·lung** *f* collection of LPs, LP collection

LSD [ɛlɛs'deː] *n* (-[s]; *no pl.*) LSD; **~-süch·tig** *adj.* addicted to LSD; **~-Süch·ti·ge** *m, f* (-n; -n) LSD addict

Luchs [lʊks] *m* (-es; -e) *zo.* lynx; *fig.* ***Augen wie ein*** ~ eyes like a hawk; ***aufpassen wie ein*** ~ watch like a hawk; **~au·gen** F *pl.*: (~ ***haben*** have) eyes like a hawk

luch·sen ['lʊksən] F *v/i.* (h) peep, F squint, peer; *a. fig.* ~ ***auf*** *acc.* have an eye on; *fig.* ***auf s-n Vorteil*** ~ be out for one's own advantage; ***auf jede Gelegenheit*** ~ be ready to grab every opportunity that comes along

Lü·cke ['lʏkə] (*sep.* -k·k-) *f* (-; -n) gap (*a. fig.*); (empty) space; *fig.* void; ⚖ loophole; ✝ need; ***e-e*** ~ ***ausfüllen*** (*or* ***schließen***) fill a gap, *fig. a.* supply a need, *person*: *a.* step into the breach; ***e-e*** ~ ***reißen*** make a gap, (*a.* ***e-e*** ~ ***hinterlassen***) leave a gap (*or* void)

'Lücken·bü·ßer (*sep.* -k·k-) *m* (-s; -) stopgap; fill-in

'lücken·haft (*sep.* -k·k-) *adj.* full of gaps; *fig. a.* incomplete; fragmentary; *chain of evidence etc.* full of holes; *law* full of loopholes; **~es Gebiß** F gappy teeth

'lücken·los (*sep.* -k·k-) *adj.* complete; unbroken; watertight *alibi*; **~er Lebenslauf** complete CV; ***e-e*** **~e Beweisführung** (*or* ***Beweiskette***) a watertight case, an unbroken chain of evidence

'Lücken|sprin·ger (*sep.* -k·k-) *m mot.* lane-hopper; **~text** *m* completion exercise

lud [luːt] *pret. of* ***laden***

Lu·der ['luːdɐ] *n* (-s; -) wretched woman, F hussy; ***freches*** ~ F cheeky cow (*or* F brat); ***armes*** ~ poor thing; **~le·ben** *n* dissipated life(style)

Lu·es ['luːɛs] *f* (-; *no pl.*) ⚕ lues, syphilis; **lue·tisch** ['lŭeːtıʃ] *adj.* luetic, syphilitic

Luft [lʊft] *f* (-; Lüfte ['lʏftə]) **1.** *no pl.* a) air; atmosphere, b) breath, c) ⚕ wind, d) *fig.* room; room to move *or* manoeuvre (*Am.* maneuver), leeway, e) ⚙ clearance, f) *fig.* breathing space; F ***frische*** ~ ***schnappen, an die*** ~ ***gehen*** get some fresh air; ***er kommt zu wenig an die*** ~ he doesn't get out into the fresh air enough; ***den ganzen Tag an der frischen*** ~ ***sein*** be out in the open all day; ~ ***holen*** take a (*or* draw) breath, pause for breath; ***tief*** ~ ***holen*** take a deep breath, *fig.* swallow hard; *fig.* ***da mußte ich erstmal tief*** ~ ***holen*** I had to swallow hard; ***keine*** ~ ***haben*** be out of breath; ***ich bekam*** (***beinahe***) ***keine*** ~ ***mehr*** I couldn't breathe properly, I felt I was going to suffocate (I could hardly breathe); F ***nach ~ schnappen*** gasp for breath; ***wieder ~ bekommen*** get one's breath back (*a. fig.*); *fig.* ***mir blieb die ~ weg*** it took my breath away, F I just stood gaping; F *fig.* ***halt mal die ~ an!*** F give us a break; put a sock in it, will you; ***die ~ herauslassen aus*** let the air out of, *a.* let down *tire*, F *fig.* uncork; ***in der ~ schwebend*** *etc.* floating *etc.* in mid-air; ***es liegt ein Gewitter*** (***etwas***) ***in der ~*** there's a storm (something, *a. fig.*) in the air; ***vor Freude in die ~ springen*** jump for joy; ***in die ~ fliegen*** blow up, explode; F ***in die ~ jagen*** blow up; ***et. an die ~ hängen*** hang s.th. out (in the air); F *fig.* ***j-n an die ~ setzen*** throw s.o. out; ***j-n wie ~ behandeln*** act as if s.o. wasn't there; ***sie ist für mich ~*** she doesn't exist as far as I'm concerned; F ***in die ~ gehen*** F hit the roof; ***leicht in die ~ gehen*** be quick to lose one's temper; ***von der ~*** (F ***von ~ und Liebe***) ***leben*** live on air; ***s-r Wut*** *etc.* ***~ machen*** let out one's anger *etc.*; ***sich*** (*or* ***s-n Gefühlen***) ***~ machen*** let it all out; ***sich ~ machen*** get out; ***jetzt hab' ich endlich wieder ~*** I can breathe again at last; ***ich muß mir ~ schaffen*** I've got to get some of this work *etc.* out of the way; ***sobald ich etwas ~ habe*** as soon as I've got a breathing space (*or* a moment to spare); ***wir haben genügend ~*** there's plenty of time; F ***die ~ ist raus*** they're *etc.* finished; ***sich in ~ auflösen*** disappear into thin air, *plans etc.*: go up in smoke; ***das hängt*** (*or* ***schwebt***) ***alles*** (***noch***) ***in der ~*** it's all up in the air; ***die ~ ist rein*** the coast is clear; → ***ausgehen*** 3, ***dick, greifen*** I, ***Loch***; **2.** *lit.* air; ***sich in die Lüfte schwingen*** soar into the air

'Luft·ab·wehr *f* air defen|ce (*Am.* -se); *in cpds.* anti-aircraft

'Luft|ab·zug *m* ⚙ air exhaust; **~akro,bat** *m* trapeze artist; **~akro,ba·tik** *f* high-wire act(s *pl.*); ✈ stunt flying; **~alarm** *m* air alert; **~an·griff** *m* air attack (*or* strike); **~an·sicht** *f* aerial view; **~auf·klä·rung** *f* aerial reconnaissance; **~auf·nah·me** *f* aerial photograph (*or* shot, view); **~bal,lon** *m* balloon; **~be·feuch·ter** [-bəfɔʏçtɐ] *m* (-s; -) humidifier; **~be·we·gung** *f* flow of air; ***schwache ~*** light breeze(s)

'Luft·bild *n* aerial photograph (*or* shot, view); **~ar·chäo·lo,gie** *f* aerial arch(a)eology; **~ver·mes·sung** *f* aerial survey

'Luft|bläs·chen *n*, **~bla·se** *f* air bubble; **~-'Bo·den-Ra,ke·te** *f* air-to-surface missile; **~brem·se** *f* ⚙ air brake; **~brücke** *f* ✈ airlift

Lüft·chen ['lʏftçən] *n* (-s; -) breeze, breath of air (*or* wind); ***es weht kein ~*** there's not a breath of wind (in the air)

'Luft·de·to·na·ti,on *f* airburst

'luft·dicht I. *adj.* airtight; **II.** *adv.*: ***~ verschließen*** seal hermetically, airseal; ***~ verschlossen*** airtight, hermetically sealed; ***~ verpackt*** vacuum-packed

'Luft·dich·te *f phys.* atmospheric density

'Luft·druck *m* (-[e]s; *no pl.*) *meteor.* atmospheric pressure; ⚔ blast; ⚙ air pressure; **~mes·ser** *m* barometer

'luft,durch·läs·sig *adj.* pervious to air; *textil.* cellular, breathing ...; **'Luft,durch·läs·sig·keit** *f* air permeability; *textil.* breathing ability

'Luft|dü·se *f* air nozzle, air jet; **~em·bo,lie** *f* ⚕ air embolism

lüf·ten ['lʏftən] *v/t.* (h) **1.** air; *mot.* bleed *brakes etc.*; ***hier muß mal gelüftet werden*** this place needs airing; **2.** lift; raise *one's hat etc.*; **3.** *fig.* reveal, F take the wraps off *a secret etc.*; ***sein Inkognito ~*** drop one's mask; ***das Geheimnis ist gelüftet*** F the wraps are off

Lüf·ter ['lʏftɐ] *m* (-s; -) ⚙ fan, ventilator

'Luft·fahrt *f* (-; *no pl.*) **1.** aviation, flying; **2.** aeronautics *pl.*; **~be·hör·de** *f*: ***zivile ~*** civil aeronautics board; **~elek,tro·nik** *f* avionics *pl.*; **~ge·sell·schaft** *f* airline (company); **~in·du,strie** *f* aviation industry; **~mi·ni,ste·ri·um** *n* ministry of aviation; **~recht** *n* aviation law(s *pl.*)

'Luft|fahr·zeug *n* aircraft; **~fe·de·rung** *f* ⚙ air cushioning (*mot.* suspension); **~feuch·tig·keit** *f* humidity; **~feuch·tig·keits·mes·ser** *m* hygrometer; **~fil·ter** *m, n* air filter; **~flot·te** *f* air fleet

'luft·för·mig [-fœrmɪç] *adj. phys.* aeriform

'Luft·fracht *f* air cargo; (***per ~*** by) airfreight; ***per ~ schicken*** *a.* airfreight; **~brief** *m* air waybill

'Luft|ge·fecht *n* aerial battle; **~geist** *m* aerial spirit; **2ge·kühlt** *adj.* air-cooled; **~ge·schwin·dig·keit** *f* air speed; **2ge·stützt** *adj.*: ***~e Rakete*** air-launched missile; **2ge·trock·net** *adj.* air-dried; **~ge·wehr** *n* airgun; **~hauch** *m* breath of air; **~hei·zung** *f* hot-air heating; **~herr·schaft** *f* air supremacy, control of the air; **~ho·heit** *f* (-; *no pl.*) air sovereignty; **~hül·le** *f* atmosphere

'Luft·hun·ger *m* hunger for (fresh) air; **'luft·hung·rig** *adj.* hungry for (fresh) air

luf·tig ['lʊftɪç] **I.** *adj.* airy; breezy *spot etc.*; light, cool *clothing etc.*; **II.** *adv.*: ***~ gekleidet sein*** be wearing light clothes

Luf·ti·kus ['lʊftikʊs] F *m* (-[ses, -se) happy-go-lucky sort; ***er ist ein ~*** *a.* F he's easy come, easy go

'Luft·kampf *m* air (*or* aerial) combat; dogfight

'Luft·kis·sen *n* air cushion (*a.* ⚙); **~fahr·zeug** *n* hovercraft

'Luft|klap·pe *f* ⚙ *etc.* air flap, *mot.* choke; **~kor·ri·dor** *m* air corridor

'luft·krank *adj.* airsick; **'Luft·krank·heit** *f* airsickness

'Luft|krieg *m* aerial warfare (*or* war); **~küh·lung** *f* air cooling; **~kur·ort** *m* (climatic) health resort; **~lan·de·trup·pen** *pl.* airborne troops, paratroops

'luft·leer *adj.* (completely) airless; ***~ sein*** *a.* be a vacuum; ***~er Raum*** vacuum

'Luft|li·nie *f*: ***500 km ~*** 500 km as the crow flies; **~loch** *n* air hole, vent; ✈ air pocket; **~-'Luft-Ra,ke·te** *f* air-to-air missile; **~macht** *f* air power; **~man·gel** *m* (-s; *no pl.*) lack of air; **~ma·sche** *f* chain stitch; **~mas·se** *f meteor.* air mass; **~ma,trat·ze** *f* air mattress, *Brit. a.* lilo (*TM*); **~mi·ne** *f* aerial mine; **~not** *f*: ***Flugzeug in ~*** aircraft in distress; **~of·fen,si·ve** *f* air offensive; **~pa,ra·de** *f* flypast; **~pas·sa,gier** *m* air(line) passenger; **~per·spek,ti·ve** *f* **1.** aerial perspective; **2.** *art*: degradation; **~pi,rat** *m* hijacker, *esp. Am.* skyjacker; **~pi·ra·te,rie** *f* hijacking (of aircraft), *esp. Am.* skyjacking; **~pi,sto·le** *f* air pistol; **~pol·ster** *n* air cushion

'Luft·post *f* airmail; ***mit*** (*or* ***per***) ***~*** (by) airmail; **~brief** *m* airmail letter; **~leicht·brief** *m* aerogram(me); **~pa,ket** *n* airmail parcel (*Am.* package); **~pa,pier** *n* airmail paper

'Luft·pum·pe *f* air (*or* pneumatic) pump; bicycle pump

'Luft·raum *m* airspace; **~über,wa·chung** *f* air traffic control

'Luft·rei·fen *m* pneumatic tyre (*Am.* tire)

'Luft·rein·hal·tung *f* air pollution control; **'Luft·rein·hal·tungs·ge·setz** *n* air cleanliness (*or* clean air) law (*pl.* legislation *sg.*)

'Luft|rein·heit *f* purity of the air; air cleanliness; **~rei·ni·ger** *m* air filter; deodorizer; **~re,kla·me** *f* aerial advertisement (*or* advertising); skywriting; **~ret·tungs·dienst** *m* air rescue service; **~röh·re** *f anat.* windpipe

'Luft·röh·ren·schnitt *m* tracheotomy

'Luft|sack *m* ✈ windsock; *mot.* air bag; *zo.* air sac; **~sau·er·stoff** *m* atmospheric oxygen; **~schacht** *m* ventilation (*or* air) shaft; **~schad·stoff** *m* air pollutant; **~schicht** *f* air layer; layer of the atmosphere, stratum

'Luft·schiff *n* airship; **'Luft·schiffahrt** (*sep.* -ff·f-) *f* aerial navigation

'Luft|schlacht *f* air battle; **~schlan·ge** *f* streamer; **~schlauch** *m* inner tube; **~schleu·se** *f* air lock; **~schloß** *n* pie in the sky, pipe dream; ***Luftschlösser bauen*** build castles in the air; **~schnei·se** *f* air lane

'Luft·schutz *m* civil air defen|ce (*Am.* -se); **~bun·ker** *m*, **~kel·ler** *m*, **~raum** *m* air-raid shelter

'Luft|si·che·rung *f* air traffic control; **~sog** *m* air suction; vacuum; **~spe·di,teur** *m* air carrier; **~sperr·ge·biet** *n* restricted airspace; **~spie·ge·lung** *f* mirage; **~sprung** *m*: (***vor Freude***) ***e-n ~ machen*** jump in the air (jump for joy); **~stick·stoff** *m* atmospheric nitrogen; **~stoß** *m* gust of wind (*or* air)

'Luft·strahl *m* air jet; **~trieb·werk** *n* jet engine

'Luft|strecke *f* air route; **~streit·kräf·te** *pl.* air force *sg.*; air combat forces; **~strom** *m* **1.** flow of air; **2.** → **~strö·mung** *f* current of air; *meteor.* airstream; **~stütz·punkt** *m* air base; **~tan·ken** *n* in-flight refuel(l)ing; **~ta·xi** *n* air taxi; **~tem·pe·ra,tur** *f* air temperature; **~trans,port** *m* air transport(ation *Am.*)

'luft·trock·nen *v/t.* (h) air-dry

'luft·tüch·tig *adj.* ✈ airworthy; **'Luft·tüch·tig·keit** *f* airworthiness

'Luft|über,le·gen·heit *f* air superiority; **~über,wa·chung** *f* air surveillance

'Luft- und 'Raum·fahrt·in·du,strie *f* aerospace industry

Lüf·tung ['lʏftʊŋ] *f* (-; -en) **1.** *no pl.* airing, ventilation; **2.** → ***Lüftungsanlage***

'Lüf·tungs|an·la·ge *f* ventilation (system); **~rohr** *n* vent pipe; **~schacht** *m* ventilation (*or* air) shaft

'Luft|ven,til *n* air valve; **~ver·än·de·rung** *f* change of air; **~ver·dich·ter** *m* (air) compressor; **~ver·kehr** *m* air traffic; **~ver·kehrs·ge·sell·schaft** *f* airline (company); **~ver·mes·sung** *f* aerial survey; **~ver·pe·stung** *f*, **~ver·schmut·zung** *f* air pollution; ***~ durch Abgase*** exhaust pollution; **~ver·tei·di·gung** *f* air defen|ce (*Am.* -se); **~ver·un·rei·ni·gung** *f* → ***Luftverpestung***; **~waf·fe** *f* air force; **~war·nung** *f* air(-raid) warning; **~wech·sel** *m* change of air; **~weg** *m* **1.** ✈ air route; *pl. a.* airways; ***auf dem ~*** by air; **2.** *pl. anat.* respiratory tract *sg.*; **~ˌwi·der·stand** *m* air resistance; ✈ *a.* drag; **~wir·bel** *m* air eddy; **~wur·zel** *f bot.* aerial root; **~zie·gel** *m* air brick; **~zu·fuhr** *f* air supply; **~zug** *m* draught, *Am.* draft

Lug [lu:k] *m*: ~ ***und Trug*** lies and deception; ***es war alles ~ und Trug*** *a.* it was all lies (F a pack of lies)

Lü·ge ['ly:gə] *f* (-; -n) lie; ***alles ~*** all lies; ***j-n (et.) ~n strafen*** give the lie to s.o. (s.th.); ***j-n bei e-r ~ ertappen*** catch s.o. out, catch s.o. lying; ***~n haben kurze Beine*** your lies will always catch up with you in the end

lu·gen ['lu:gən] *v/i.* (h) peer; ***~ nach*** *dat.* look out for, *fig.* have an eye on

lü·gen ['ly:gən] (log, gelogen, h) **I.** *v/i.* lie, tell a lie (*or* lies); ***er lügt*** he's lying, he's a liar; ***ich müßte ~, wenn*** I'd be lying (*or* telling a lie) if; ***wer einmal lügt(, dem glaubt man nicht, und wenn er auch die Wahrheit spricht)*** once a liar always a liar; → ***Balken*** 1, ***gedruckt***; **II.** *v/t.*: ***das ist gelogen!*** that's a lie; ***alles gelogen!*** (it's) all lies, F it's a pack of lies; **III.** ~ *n* (-s; *no pl.*) lying

'Lü·gen|deˌtek·tor *m* lie detector, polygraph; **~ge·schich·te** *f* fairy story; **~gespinst** *n* web of lies

'lü·gen·haft *adj.* untrue, false, fabricated

'Lü·gen|kamˌpa·gne *f* campaign of lies; **~mär·chen** *n* fairy story; **~pro·paˌganda** *f* propaganda lie(s *pl.*)

Lüg·ner ['ly:gnɐ] *m* (-s; -), **Lüg·ne·rin** ['ly:gnərɪn] *f* (-; -nen) liar; **lüg·ne·risch** ['ly:gnərɪʃ] *adj.* untrue

Lu·ke ['lu:kə] *f* (-; -n) skylight; hatch

lu·kra·tiv [lukra'ti:f] *adj.* lucrative

lu·kul·lisch [lu'kʊlɪʃ] *adj. gastr.* exquisite; sumptuous; ***~e Leckerbissen*** gastronomic delights

Lu·latsch ['lu:latʃ] F *m* (-[e]s; -e): ***langer ~*** F beanpole

lul·len ['lʊlən] *v/t.* (h): ***in den Schlaf ~*** lull to sleep

Lu·men ['lu:mən] *n* (-s; -, Lumina ['lu:mina]) *phys. and biol.* lumen

Lu·mi·nes·zenz [luminɛs'tsɛnts] *f* (-; -en) *phys.* luminescence

Lüm·mel ['lʏməl] *m* (-s; -) lout; **Lüm·me·lei** [lʏmə'laɪ] *f* (-; -en) **1.** loutishness; **2.** *no pl.* lounging around (all day), lolling about; **'lüm·mel·haft** *adj.* loutish; **'Lüm·mel·haf·tig·keit** *f* (-; *no pl.*) loutishness; **'lüm·meln** *v/i. and v/refl.* (***sich*** ~) (h) loll about; ***auf dem Sofa ~*** lie sprawled across the sofa

Lump [lʊmp] *m* (-en; -en) rogue, F louse

Lum·pen ['lʊmpən] *m* (-s; -) **1.** *pl.* rags (*a. fig. clothes*); **2.** *dial.* rag

lum·pen ['lʊmpən] F (h) **I.** *v/i.* F live it up, go (*or* be) out on the tiles; **II.** *v/t.*: ***sich nicht ~ lassen*** do things (*or* it) in style, be generous; ***wir wollen uns nicht ~ lassen*** we don't want it to be said that we're stingy

'Lum·pen|ban·de F *f* F bunch of no-gooders; **~hund** F *m*, **~kerl** F *m* good-for-nothing, F louse; **~pack** F *n* → ***Lumpenbande***; **~pro·le·ta·riˌat** *n* lumpenproletariat; **~samm·ler** *m* **1.** rag-and-bone man; **2.** F *fig.* last bus (*or* underground *etc.*)

Lum·pe·rei [lʊmpə'raɪ] *f* (-; -en) mean (*or* dirty) trick

lum·pig ['lʊmpɪç] **I.** *adj.* **1.** shabby (*a. fig. behavio[u]r etc.*); **2.** F ***wegen ~er zehn Mark*** because of a measly ten marks; **II.** *adv.*: ***~ gekleidet*** *etc.* shabbily dressed *etc.*; ***~ verpackt*** sloppily packed

lu·nar [lu'na:ɐ] *adj.* lunar

Lunch [lanʃ] *m* (-[e]s; -[e]s, -e) lunch

'lun·chen *v/i.* (h) (have) lunch

'Lunch·paˌket *n* packed (*Am.* box) lunch

Lun·ge ['lʊŋə] *f* (-; -n) *anat.* lungs *pl.*; lung; ***auf ~ rauchen*** inhale; ⚕ ***eiserne ~*** iron lung; ***er hat es auf der ~*** he's got lung trouble (*or* trouble with his lungs); F *fig.* ***sich die ~ aus dem Leib schreien*** F scream one's head off

'Lun·gen|abˌtei·lung *f* respiratory (*or* pulmonary) ward *or* section; **~bläs·chen** *n* (pulmonary) alveolus (*pl.* alveoli); **~em·boˌlie** *f* embolism of the lung, pulmonary embolism; **~em·phyˌsem** *n* pulmonary emphysema; **~ent·zün·dung** *f* pneumonia; **~fisch** *m* lungfish; **~flü·gel** *m* (lobe of the) lung; ***rechter (linker) ~*** right (left) lung; **~ge·we·be** *n* lung tissue; **~heil·an·stalt** *f* sanatorium (*Am.* sanitarium) for lung patients

'lun·gen·krank *adj.*: ***~ sein*** have a lung disease; **'Lun·gen·kran·ke** *m, f* (-n; -n) lung patient; **'Lun·gen·krank·heit** *f* lung disease (*or* complaint)

'Lun·gen|kraut *n* ♀ lungwort; **~krebs** *m* ⚕ lung cancer; **~spit·ze** *f* apex of the lung; **~tu·ber·kuˌlo·se** *f* tuberculosis (of the lung); **~zug** *m*: ***e-n ~ (or Lungenzüge) machen*** inhale

lun·gern ['lʊŋɐn] *v/i.* (h) hang around

Lun·te ['lʊntə] *f* (-; -n) **1.** fuse; *fig.* F ***~ riechen*** a) sense danger, b) smell a rat; **2.** *hunt.* brush

Lu·pe ['lu:pə] *f* (-; -n) magnifying glass; *fig.* ***unter die ~ nehmen*** have a good look at, scrutinize; ***die kann (or muß) man mit der ~ suchen*** there aren't many of them around, they're not easy to get hold of; **'lu·pen·rein** *adj.* flawless *diamond etc.*; *fig.* perfect; *fig.* ***es ist ~*** *a.* you can't fault it; ***nicht ganz ~*** F not quite kosher

lüp·fen ['lʏpfən] *v/t.* (h) lift; raise *one's hat*

Lu·pi·ne [lu'pi:nə] *f* (-; -n) ♀ lupin

Lurch [lʊrç] *m* (-[e]s; -e) *zo.* amphibian

Lust [lʊst] *f* (-; Lüste ['lʏstə]) **1.** *no pl.* desire; craving (***auf*** *acc.* for); ***ich habe (keine) ~ zu*** *inf.* I (don't) feel like *ger.*; ***ich hätte (große) ~ zu*** *inf.* I wouldn't mind *ger.* (I'd love to *inf.*); ***ich hätte ~ auf ein Bier*** I wouldn't mind a beer; ***ich habe keine ~ mehr (zu arbeiten)*** I've had enough (I don't feel like doing any more work); ***ich habe keine ~*** I don't feel like it, I'm not in the mood; ***ich hätte gute ~ zu*** *inf.* I've a good mind (*or* half a mind) to *inf.*; ***alle ~ an et. verlieren*** lose all interest in s.th.; ***et. aus (purer) ~ tun*** do s.th. for the (sheer) fun of it; ***sie haben mir ~ gemacht*** they've whet my appetite, F they've got me at it; ***dabei kann einem die ~ vergehen*** it can really put you off; ***mir ist die ~ vergangen*** I don't feel like it any more, that's put me off (now); ***s-e ~ an et. haben*** F get a kick out of s.th.; ***(je) nach ~ und Laune*** as the mood takes you, just as you fancy; ***dort kannst du nach ~ und Laune schwimmen (malen)*** you can go swimming there whenever you feel like it *or* as often as you like (you can paint [whenever and] whatever you like there); ***er kann schlafen, solange er ~ hat*** he can sleep as long as he likes; ***es ist e-e wahre ~, ihr zuzusehen*** it's a pleasure to watch her; ***das ist für mich die höchste ~*** that for me is the ultimate; ***mit ~ und Liebe*** heart and soul; **2.** pleasure; *an* appetite (***auf*** *acc.* for); sexual appetite, *contp.* lust; sensual (*or* sexual) pleasure

Lust·bar·kei·ten ['lʊstba:ɐkaɪtən] *obs. pl.* festivities; merrymaking (*sg.*)

'lust·be·tont *adj.* hedonistic(ally *adv.*); pleasure-seeking

'Lust·emp·fin·dung *f* pleasurable sensation

Lü·ster ['lʏstɐ] *m* (-s; -) **1.** chandelier; **2.** lustre, *Am.* luster; **~klem·me** *f* strip connector

lü·stern ['lʏstɐn] **I.** *adj.* a) greedy (***nach*** *dat.* for), b) lewd, lecherous; **II.** *adv.*: ***~ schauen nach*** *dat.* F lech after

'Lü·stern·heit *f* (-; *no pl.*) a) greed, b) lecherousness

'Lust|gar·ten *m* pleasure grounds *pl.*; **~ge·fühl** *n* **1.** pleasurable sensation; ***das ist ein ~!*** what a (wonderful) sensation; **2.** (feeling of) sexual pleasure; *one's* enjoyment of sex; **~ge·winn** *m* (experience of) pleasure; ***nach ~ streben*** try to gain as much pleasure as possible; **~greis** F *m* F old lecher, dirty old man; **~haus** *n* summer house (*or* mansion)

lu·stig ['lʊstɪç] **I.** *adj.* funny; amusing; merry; ***es war sehr ~*** it was great fun; ***ein ~er Abend (Film*** *etc.*) a fun evening (film *etc.*); ***er ist ein ~er Typ*** he's good fun; ***das kann ja ~ werden!*** *iro.* F looks like we're in for some fun and games; ***du bist ~!*** *iro.* F you're a right one, F don't make me laugh; ***sich ~ machen über*** *acc.* laugh at, make fun of; **II.** *adv.* a) funnily; amusingly; merrily, b) blithely; ***er spielte ~ weiter*** he carried on playing as if nothing had happened; ***hier geht's ja ~ zu!*** they *etc.* seem to be having a good time, *iro.* we 'are having a good time, aren't we?; ***~ drauflos singen (hämmern*** *etc.*) sing (hammer *etc.*) away; **'Lu·stig·keit** *f* (-; *no pl.*) a) fun atmosphere, b) funny personality, *s.o's* sense of humo(u)r, c) funny side (of it)

Lüst·ling ['lʏstlɪŋ] *m* (-s; -e) lecher

'lust·los I. *adj.* **1.** listless; uninterested; ***er ist völlig ~*** he's not interested in (*or* he can't be bothered with) anything; **2.** ✝ inactive, dull, sluggish; **II.** *adv.* without any (*or* much) enthusiasm; listlessly; *w.s.* half-heartedly; **'Lust·lo·sig·keit** *f* (-; *no pl.*) listlessness; lack of interest (*or* enthusiasm); ✝ dullness, slackness

'Lust|molch F *m* lecher; *iro.* F sex-fiend; **~mord** *m* sex murder; **~mör·der** *m* sex killer; **~obˌjekt** *n* sex object, object of sexual desire (*or* lust); **~prinˌzip** *n psych.* pleasure principle; **~schloß** *n* summer residence; **~spiel** *n* comedy

'lust·voll I. *adj.* joyful; *sigh etc.* of pleasure; voluptuous; **II.** *adv.*: ***~ verspeisen*** *etc.* consume *etc.* with relish

'lust·wan·deln *v/i.* (sn) *hum.* stroll

Lu·the·ra·ner [lutə'ra:nɐ] *m* (-s; -), **Lu·the·ra·ne·rin** [lutə'ra:nərɪn] *f* (-; -nen), **lu·the·ra·nisch** [lutə'ra:nɪʃ] *adj.* Lutheran

lut·schen ['lʊtʃən] *v/i. and v/t.* (h) (*a.* ***~ an*** *dat.*) suck; ***am Daumen ~*** suck one's thumb; ***er ist dauernd am ~, dauernd lutscht er etwas*** he's always got something in his mouth

Lut·scher ['lʊtʃɐ] *m* (-s; -) lollipop, F lolly

Luv [lu:f] *f* (-; *no pl.*), **lu·ven** ['lu:vən] *v/i.* (h), '**Luv·sei·te** *f* ⚓ luff
Lux [lʊks] *n* (-; -) *phys.* lux
Lu·xem·bur·ger ['lʊksəmbʊrgɐ] *m* (-s; -), **Lu·xem·bur·ge·rin** ['lʊksəmbʊrgərɪn] *f* (-; -nen) Luxemb(o)urger; **lu·xem·bur·gisch** ['lʊksəmbʊrgɪʃ] *adj.* Luxemb(o)urgian, from Luxemb(o)urg
lu·xu·ri·ös [lʊksu'rĭø:s] **I.** *adj.* luxurious; luxury *apartment, car etc*; **~es Leben** life of luxury; **II.** *adv.*: ~ **ausgestattet** luxuriously furnished, *car, kitchen etc.* with luxury fittings
Lu·xus ['lʊksʊs] *m* (-; *no pl.*) luxury; **im ~ leben** live in luxury, live a life of luxury; **das ist reiner ~** that's sheer extravagance; **sich den ~ erlauben zu** *inf.* allow o.s. the luxury of *ger.*; **den ~ kann ich mir nicht erlauben** I can't afford that kind of luxury (*w.s.* the luxury of *ger.*); **~apart·ment** *n* luxury flat (*Am.* apartment); **~arˌti·kel** *m* luxury article; *pl. a.* luxury goods; **~aus·füh·rung** *f* de luxe model; **~aus·ga·be** *f* de luxe edition; **~bus** *m* luxury coach; **~damp·fer** *m* luxury liner; **~hoˌtel** *n* five-star (*or* luxury) hotel; **~jacht** *f* luxury yacht; **~kaˌbi·ne** *f* de luxe cabin; **~klas·se** *f*: **... der ~** luxury ...; **~li·mouˌsi·ne** *f* luxury sedan; **~re·stauˌrant** *n* top-class (*or* three-star) restaurant; **~steu·er** *f* luxury tax; **~vil·la** *f* luxury mansion; **~wa·gen** *m* luxury car; **~wa·re** *f* → **Luxusartikel**
Lu·zer·ne [lu'tsɛrnə] *f* (-; -n) ⚘ lucerne
Lymph·drü·se ['lʏmf-] *f* lymph(atic) gland; '**Lymph·drü·sen·schwel·lun·gen** *pl.* swollen lymph glands
Lym·phe ['lʏmfə] *f* (-; -n) lymph; vaccine
Lymph·ge·fäß ['lʏmf-] *n* lymph vessel
Lymph·kno·ten ['lʏmf-] *m* lymph node; **~ent·zün·dung** *f* adenitis
Lymph·syˌstem ['lʏmf-] *n* lymphatic system
lyn·chen ['lʏnçən] *v/t.* (h) lynch; F *hum.* **nächstes Mal werde ich dich ~!** I'll strangle you if you do that again
Lynch|juˌstiz ['lʏnç-] *f* mob law; **~mord** *m* lynching
Ly·ra ['ly:ra] *f* (-; Lyren) ♪ lyre; *ast.* Lyra
Ly·rik ['ly:rɪk] *f* (- *no pl.*) **1.** poetry; **2.** lyricism
Ly·ri·ker ['ly:rikɐ] *m* (-s; -), **Ly·ri·ke·rin** ['ly:rikərɪn] *f* (-; -nen) (lyric) poet
ly·risch ['ly:rɪʃ] *adj.* lyrical

M

M, m [ɛm] *n* (-; -) M, m

Mä·an·der [mɛ'andɐ] *m* (-s; -) *geol.* meander; **mä·an·drisch** [mɛ'andrɪʃ] *adj.* meandering

Maat [maːt] *m* (-[e]s; -[n]) ⚓ (ship's) mate

Mach [max] *n* (-[s]; -) *phys.* Mach

Mach·art ['max-] *f* make, style, design

mach·bar ['maxbaːɐ] *adj.* feasible, F doable; ***es müßte ~ sein*** it ought to be doable; **'Mach·bar·keit** *f* (-; *no pl.*) feasibility

Ma·che ['maxə] F *f* (-; *no pl.*) **1.** show; ***das ist alles nur ~*** it's all show, it's just an act; **2.** ***in der ~ sein*** be in the pipeline; ***et. in der ~ haben*** have s.th. in the pipeline, F be hatching s.th. out; ***et. (j-n) in die ~ nehmen*** take s.th. in hand (give s.o. a good going-over); **3.** F mo(u)ld

ma·chen ['maxən] (h) **I.** *v/t.* **1.** do; make; prepare; ***was machst du?*** a) what are you doing?, b) what do you do?; ***ein Foto ~*** take a photograph; ***das Zimmer ~*** do (*or* tidy up) the room; ***Hausaufgaben ~*** do one's homework; ***e-e Prüfung ~*** take (*or* pass) an exam; ***e-n Spaziergang ~*** go for a walk; ***e-n Fehler ~*** make a mistake; ***e-n Kurs ~*** do (*or* take) a course; ***e-e (un)angenehme Erfahrung ~*** have a pleasant (an unpleasant) experience; ***j-n zum General ~*** make s.o. a general; ***den Schiedsrichter ~*** be (*or* act as) umpire (*or* referee); F ***der Wagen macht 160 km/h*** the car does 100 mph; ***4 mal 5 macht 20*** four times five is twenty, four fives are twenty; ***was macht das?*** how much is that?, F what's the damage?; ***das macht drei Mark*** that's (*or* that'll be) three marks; ***j-n traurig (glücklich*** *etc.*) ~ make s.o. sad (happy *etc.*); ***das macht das Wetter*** it's the weather; ***so was macht man nicht*** that isn't done, you just don't do that; ***was macht das schon?*** does it really matter?, what difference does it make?, F so what?; ***das macht nichts*** never mind, it doesn't matter; ***es macht mir nichts (aus)*** I don't mind; ***da kann man nichts ~*** it's (just) one of those things; ***sie macht sich nichts (or nicht viel) aus Geld*** she doesn't care much about money, money doesn't mean much to her, F she's not really bothered about money; ***er macht sich nicht viel aus Kuchen (Alkohol*** *etc.*) he doesn't care (much) for cake (alcohol *etc.*), he's not particularly keen on cake (alcohol *etc.*); ***mach dir nichts draus!*** don't worry about it; ***das macht Durst*** it makes you thirsty; ***was macht die Familie?*** how's the family (getting on)?; ***mach's gut!*** a) see you, b) all the best; ***das läßt sich schon ~*** that can be arranged, that's no problem; F *iro.* ***mit mir könnt ihr's ja ~!*** the things I put up with; F ***er wird's nicht mehr lange ~*** he's on his last legs; → ***Ferien, Hoffnung, Krach, Licht;*** **II.** *v/refl.* **2.** ***sich (gut) ~*** be coming along (well *or* fine), be getting on fine; ***sich gut ~*** a) look good (***bei j-m*** on s.o.), b) make a good impression; ***sich schlecht ~*** a) not to look good, b) make a bad impression; ***er macht sich gut als ...*** he makes a good ...; ***wie macht sich der Kleine?*** how's the little one coming along (*or* getting on)?; ***die Vase macht sich sehr gut in der Ecke*** the vase looks very nice in the corner; **3.** ***sich ~ an*** *acc.* get down to (doing) *s.th.*; → ***Weg;*** **III.** *v/i.:* ***macht, daß ihr bald zurück seid!*** make sure you get back soon!; ***mach, daß du wegkommst!*** get out of here!; ***mach schon!*** hurry up!, F get a move on!; ***laß ihn nur ~*** a) let him if he wants to, let him have his way, just let him do it (*or* get on with it), b) leave it to him; ✝ ***~ in*** *dat.* deal in, sell; F ***in Politik ~*** be in politics; F ***er macht in Schriftstellerei*** he's some sort of writer; F ***~ auf*** *acc.* act (*or* play) *s.th.*, pretend to be *s.th.*; ***auf Künstler ~*** act (*or* play) the artist, F do one's artist act; ***auf unschuldig (doof) ~*** act *or* play the innocent (the fool), pretend to be innocent (stupid); → ***gemacht***

'Ma·chen·schaf·ten *pl.* wheelings and dealings, machinations, intrigues; ***heimliche (or dunkle) ~*** underhand dealings, dark machinations

Ma·cher ['maxɐ] *m* (-s; -) man of action, doer

Ma·che·te [ma'xeːtə] *f* (-; -n) machete

Ma·chia·vel·lis·mus [makĭavɛ'lɪsmʊs] *m* (-; *no pl.*) Machiavellianism; **ma·chia·vel·li·stisch** [makĭavɛ'lɪstɪʃ] *adj.* Machiavellian

Ma·cho ['matʃo] *m* (-s; -s) macho

Macht [maxt] *f* (-; Mächte ['mɛçtə]) **1.** *no pl.* power, strength, *esp. lit.* might; ***mit aller ~*** with all one's might, *lit.* with might and main; **2.** *no pl.* power, authority; ***es steht nicht in m-r ~*** it's not within my power; ***wenn es in m-r ~ stünde(, es zu tun)*** if I had it within my power (to do so); ***~ der Gewohnheit*** force of habit; **3.** *pol.* power; force; ***die ~ ergreifen*** seize power; ***an die ~ kommen, zur ~ gelangen*** come (in)to power; ***an der ~ sein*** be in power; **4.** *fig.* power, force; ***die ~ des Schicksals*** the force of destiny; ***die Mächte der Finsternis*** the powers of darkness; **~ab·lö·sung** *f* transfer of power; **~an·häu·fung** *f* accumulation (*or* concentration) of power; **~an·spruch** *m* claim to power; **~aus·übung** *f* exercise of power; **~be·reich** *m* sphere of influence

'macht·be·ses·sen *adj.* power-crazed; **Macht·be·ses·se·ne** *m, f* (-n; -n) power maniac; **'Macht·be·ses·sen·heit** *f* power mania, obsession with power

'Macht|block *m* power bloc; **~ent·fal·tung** *f* development (*or* expansion) of power, growth in power; ***Ära der ~*** period of political growth (*or* expansion); **~er·grei·fung** *f* **1.** seizure of power; **2.** *hist.* Hitler's seizure of power in 1933; **~fra·ge** *f* question of who is (the) more powerful, question of superior strength; **~ge·fü·ge** *n* power structure

'Macht·gier *f* lust for power; **'macht·gie·rig** *adj.* power-hungry

'Macht·ha·ber [-haːbɐ] *m* (-s; -) ruler; *contp.* dictator; *iro.* ***die ~*** the powers that be

'Macht·hun·ger *f* lust for power; **'macht·hung·rig** *adj.* power-hungry

mäch·tig ['mɛçtɪç] **I.** *adj.* a) powerful (*a. voice, blow etc.*), *lit.* mighty, b) massive, huge, enormous; ***e-r Sprache ~ sein*** be able to speak (*or* have a good command of) a language; ***der Sprache ~ sein*** be able to speak; *iro.* ***sind Sie der Sprache nicht ~?*** have you lost your tongue?; ***s-r selbst (s-r Sinne) nicht mehr ~ sein*** have lost control of oneself (one's senses); **II.** F *adv.* tremendously, F incredibly, *Am.* F mighty *proud etc.*; ***~ groß*** (really) huge, massive; ***~ schreien*** scream at the top of one's voice (F like mad); ***sich ~ anstrengen*** push (*or* write *etc.*) for all one is worth (F like mad); **Mäch·ti·ge** ['mɛçtɪgə] *m* (n; -n) powerful figure; ***die ~n dieser Erde*** the rulers of (*or* the people who rule) this world

'Macht|in·stru,ment *n* instrument of power; **~kampf** *m* power struggle, struggle for power

'macht·los *adj.* powerless, helpless; F ***da ist man ~*** there's nothing you can do (about it); **'Macht·lo·sig·keit** *f* (-; *no pl.*) powerlessness, helplessness

'Macht|mensch *m* power-seeker; **~,miß·brauch** *m* abuse of power; **~mit·tel** *n* instrument of power; means (*sg.*) of enforcing power; **~mo·no,pol** *n* monopoly of power; **~or,gan** *n* organ of power

'Macht·po·li,tik *f* power politics *pl.*; **'Macht·po,li·ti·ker** *m* power politician; **'macht·po,li·tisch** *adj.* power-political

'Macht|po·si·ti,on *f* position of power; **~pro·be** *f* test of strength, F showdown, face-off; **~stel·lung** *f* position of power; **~stre·ben** *n* striving for power; **~struk,tur** *f* power structure; **~,über·nah·me** *f* assumption of power; **~va·ku·um** *n* power vacuum; **~ver·hält·nis·se** *pl.* balance *sg.* (*or* hierarchy *sg.*) of power, F pecking order *sg.*; **~ver·tei·lung** *f* distribution of power

'macht·voll *adj.* powerful (*a. fig.*)

'Macht|voll,kom·men·heit *f* absolute power; ***aus eigener ~*** on one's own authority, at one's own discretion; **~wech·sel** *m* changeover of power; **~wil·le** *m* will to power; **~wort** *n*: ***ein ~ sprechen*** F put one's foot down; **~zen,tra·le** *f*, **~zen·trum** *n* cent|re (*Am.* -er) of power, powerhouse
Mach·werk ['maxvɛrk] *n* (-[e]s; -e) (*a.* ***elendes ~***) miserable effort (*or* piece of work), F lousy (*or* botched-up) job
Macke [makə] (*sep.* -k·k-) F *f* (-; -n) **1.** fault, defect; **2.** ***e-e ~ haben*** F have a screw loose
Macker ['makɐ] (*sep.* -k·k-) *sl. m* (-s; -) **1.** F bloke, guy; F punter; *sl.* fella, bloke; **2.** ***den großen ~ spielen*** throw one's weight around, act as if one owns the place
Ma·da·gas·se [mada'gasə] *m* (-n; -n), **Ma·da·gas·sin** [mada'gasın] *f* (-; -nen), **ma·da·gas·sisch** [mada'gasıʃ] *adj.* Madagascan
Ma·dam [ma'dam] F *hum. f* (-; -s, -en) **1.** F madam, *the* mistress; **2.** F *the* missus; **3.** F old dame
Mäd·chen ['mɛːtçən] *n* (-s; -) girl; maid; *fig.* ***~ für alles*** (general) dogsbody; **~al·ter** *n*: (***schon***) ***im ~*** as a girl
'mäd·chen·haft *adj.* girlish; **'Mäd·chen·haf·tig·keit** *f* (-; *no pl.*) girlishness
'Mäd·chen|han·del *m* white slave trade; **~händ·ler** *m* white slave trader; **~na·me** *m* a) girl's name, b) maiden name
Ma·de ['maːdə] *f* (-; -n) maggot; ***wie die ~ im Speck leben*** be (*or* live) in clover
Ma·dei·ra [ma'deːra] *m* (-s; -s) Madeira
Mä·del ['mɛːdəl] *n* (-s; -) girl, lass
ma·dig ['maːdıç] *adj.* full of maggots, F maggoty; F *fig.* ***~ machen*** run down, F knock; (***j-m***) ***et. ~ machen*** spoil s.th. (for s.o.), take the fun out of s.th. (for s.o.); ***mach mir doch nicht alles ~*** I wish you wouldn't keep spoiling things for me
Ma·don·na [ma'dɔna] *f* (-; -nen) Madonna; **Ma'don·nen·bild** *n* (picture of the) Madonna; **ma'don·nen·haft** *adj.* Madonna-like; **Ma'don·nen·kult** *m* worship of the Virgin Mary, *contp.* Mariolatry
Ma·dri·gal [madri'gaːl] *n* (-s; -e) madrigal
Ma·fia ['mafĭa] *f* (-; -s) Mafia; *fig.* mafia; **~boß** *m* Mafia boss; head of the Mafia; **~me,tho·den** *pl.* Mafia(-type) methods
Ma·fio·so [ma'fĭoːzo] *m* (-[s]; -si) member of the Mafia, Mafioso
Ma·ga·zin [maga'tsiːn] *n* (-s; -e) **1.** warehouse; depot; storeroom; *library*: stacks *pl.*; **2.** ⚙ magazine (*a. of a gun*); hopper; **3.** *phot.* magazine, tray; **4.** magazine; *TV*, *radio*: magazine program(me)
Magd [maːkt] *lit. f* (-; Mägde ['mɛːkdə]) *lit.* maiden; farmgirl; *obs.* maid(servant)
Ma·gen ['maːgən] *m* (-s; Mägen ['mɛːgən]) stomach; ***mit leerem ~, auf nüchternen ~*** on an empty stomach; ***ich habe noch nichts im ~*** I haven't eaten a thing; ***ich habe mir den ~ verdorben*** (F ***verkorkst***) I've got an upset stomach; ***es liegt mir schwer im ~*** I'm having trouble digesting it, *fig.* it's really bothering me (F getting to me); ***dabei drehte es ihr den ~ um*** it turned her stomach, she felt sick; ***j-m auf den ~ schlagen*** ⚕ settle on s.o.'s stomach, *fig.* get to s.o., (begin to) give s.o. ulcers; → ***knurren, Liebe***; **~be·schwer·den** *pl.* stomach trouble *sg.*; **~bit·ter** *m* (-s; -) bitters *pl.*; **~blu·tung** *f* ⚕ stomach bleeding
'Ma·gen-'Darm-Ka,tarrh *m* ⚕ gastroenteritis
'Ma·gen|drücken *n* stomach pains *pl.*; **~er·wei·te·rung** *f* dilation of the stomach; **~ge·schwür** *n* ⚕ stomach (*or* peptic) ulcer; **~gru·be** *f* pit of one's stomach; **~knur·ren** *n* rumbling stomach; ***ich habe ~*** my stomach's rumbling; **~krämp·fe** *pl.* stomach cramps; **⁲krank** *adj.*: ***~ sein*** suffer from a stomach complaint; **~krank·heit** *f* stomach disease (*or* complaint); **~krebs** *m* stomach cancer; **~lei·den** *n* stomach complaint (*or* trouble); **~ope·ra·ti,on** *f* stomach operation; **~rei·zung** *f* gastric irritation; **~saft** *m* gastric juices *pl.*; **~säu·re** *f* gastric (*or* stomach) acid
'Ma·gen·schleim·haut *f* stomach lining; **~ent·zün·dung** *f* gastritis
'Ma·gen|schmer·zen *pl.* stomach-ache *sg.*; **~son·de** *f* stomach probe; **~spie·gel** *m* gastroscope; **~spie·ge·lung** *f* gastroscopy; **~ver·stim·mung** *f* indigestion, upset stomach; **~wand** *f* wall of the stomach
ma·ger ['maːgɐ] *adj.* **1.** thin, F skinny; **2.** *gastr.* lean *meat*; low-fat *cheese etc.*; **3.** *fig.* meag|re (*Am.* -er), poor; lean *harvest*; ***~e Jahre*** lean years; ***~es Lob*** scant praise; **4.** ***~e Schrift*** light-face(d) type
'Ma·ger|jo·ghurt *m* low-fat yoghurt; **~kä·se** *m* low-fat cheese; **~milch** *f* skimmed milk; **~mo·tor** *m* lean-burn engine; **~quark** *m* low-fat curd cheese
'Ma·ger·sucht *f* (-; *no pl.*) ⚕ anorexia (nervosa)
Mag·gi·kraut ['magi-] *n* ⚘ lovage
Ma·gie [ma'giː] *f* (-; *no pl.*): (***schwarze, weiße ~***) black, white) magic; **Ma·gier** ['maːgĭɐ] *m* (-s; -) magician; conjuror; **ma·gisch** ['maːgıʃ] **I.** *adj.* magic; magical *atmosphere*, *attraction etc.*; ***~e Künste*** magic arts; **II.** *adv.* magically; by magic; ***j-n ~ anziehen*** have a magical attraction for s.o.
Ma·gi·ster [ma'gıstɐ] *m* (-s; -) *univ.* Master's degree; ***~ Artium*** Master of Arts (*abbr.* MA); ***den ~ machen*** do a (*or* one's) MA *or* Master's degree; **~ar·beit** *f* MA (*or* Master's) thesis; **~prü·fung** *f* MA (*or* Master's) exam
Ma·gi·strat [magıs'traːt] *m* (-[e]s; -e) municipal authorities *pl.*, town council
Mag·ma ['magma] *n* (-s; Magmen [-mən]) magma
Ma·gnat [ma'gnaːt] *m* (-en; -en) magnate, tycoon
Ma·gne·sia [ma'gneːzĭa] *f* (-; *no pl.*) magnesia
Ma·gne·si·um [ma'gneːzĭʊm] *n* (-s; *no pl.*) ⚗ magnesium
Ma·gnet [ma'gneːt] *m* (-en; -en) magnet (*a. fig.*), lodestone; **~band** *n* (-[e]s; ⸚er) magnetic tape; **~feld** *n* magnetic field
ma·gne·tisch [ma'gneːtıʃ] *adj.* magnetic(ally *adv.*) (*a. fig.*)
Ma·gne·ti·seur [magneti'zøːɐ] *m* mesmerist
ma·gne·ti·sie·ren [magneti'ziːrən] *v/t.* (h) magnetize; *a. fig.* mesmerize; **Ma·gne·ti'sie·rung** *f* (-; -en) magnetization
Ma·gne·tis·mus [magne'tısmʊs] *m* (-; *no pl.*) magnetism (*a. fig.*); mesmerism
Ma'gnet|ka·me·ra *f* (electro)magnetic camera; **~kar·te** *f computer*: magnetic card; **~kern** *m* magnet core; **~kom·paß** *m* magnetic compass; **~kopf** *m* magnetic head; **~na·del** *f* magnetic (*or* compass) needle; **~plat·te** *f* magnetic disk; **~pol** *m* magnetic pole; **~schal·ter** *m mot.* solenoid switch; **~schwe·be·bahn** *f* magnetic levitation train, maglev; **~strei·fen** *m* magnetic strip; **~wir·kung** *f* magnetic effect (*or* attraction); **~zün·dung** *f* magneto ignition
Ma·gno·lie [ma'gnoːlĭə] *f* (-; -n) ⚘ magnolia
Ma·ha·go·ni [maha'goːni] *n* (-s; *no pl.*) mahogany; **~baum** *m* mahogany (tree); **~holz** *n* mahogany
Ma·ha·rad·scha [maha'raːdʒa] *m* (-s; -s) maharaja(h); **Ma·ha·ra·ni** [maha'raːni] *f* (-; -s) maharanee
Mahd [maːt] *dial. f* (-; Maden ['maːdən]) **1.** mowing; hay harvest; **2.** cut grass
Mäh·dre·scher ['mɛːdrɛʃɐ] *m* (-s; -) combine (harvester)
mä·hen ['mɛːən] (h) **I.** *v/t.* mow *the lawn*; cut *the grass*, *a.* reap *the corn etc.*; **II.** *v/i.* mow (the lawn *or* grass); reap (the corn *etc.*); **Mä·her** ['mɛːɐ] *m* (-s; -) **1.** mower; reaper; **2.** → ***Mähmaschine***
Mahl [maːl] *n* (-[e]s; -e, Mähler ['mɛːlɐ]) meal; banquet
mah·len ['maːlən] (mahlte, gemahlen, h) **I.** *v/t.* **1.** mill; grind; → ***gemahlen***; **II.** *v/i.* **2.** grind; *fig.* ***wer zuerst kommt, mahlt zuerst*** first come first served; **3.** *wheels*: spin
'Mahl·zeit *f* (-; -en) meal; ***~!*** afternoon!; F ***prost ~!*** F that's (just) great!, goodnight!
Mäh·ma,schi·ne ['mɛː-] *f* mower; reaper
Mahn|be·scheid ['maːn-] *m* ⚖ default summons; **~brief** *m* reminder
Mäh·ne ['mɛːnə] *f* (-; -n) mane; *fig.* (*iro.* sweeping) mane
mah·nen ['maːnən] (h) **I.** *v/t.* a) urge, exhort, admonish, b) remind (***an*** *acc.* of) (*a. debtor etc.*); ✝ send *s.o.* a reminder; ***j-n zur Vorsicht*** *etc.* ***~*** urge s.o. to be careful *etc.*; (***j-n***) ***zum Aufbruch ~*** remind s.o. that it's time to leave; **II.** *v/i.*: ***zur Vorsicht*** (***Geduld*** *etc.*) ***~*** urge caution (patience *etc.*); **'mah·nend I.** *adj.* admonishing, warning; ***~es Wort*** word of admonishment (*or* warning); **II.** *adv.* in admonishment, in (*or* as a) warning; ***~ den Finger heben*** raise a warning finger; ***~ die Stimme erheben*** raise one's voice in warning
'Mahn|ge·bühr *f* fine; **~mal** *n* memorial; **~pre·digt** *f* exhortatory sermon; **~ruf** *m* exhortation; **~schrei·ben** *n* reminder
Mah·nung ['maːnʊŋ] *f* (-; -en) warning; ✝ reminder, *library*: *a.* overdue notification
'Mahn|ver·fah·ren *n* ⚖ collection proceedings *pl.*; **~wa·che** *f* vigil; **~wort** *n* (-[e]s; -e) word of admonishment (*or* exhortation, warning)
Mäh·re ['mɛːrə] *f* (-; -n) (old) nag, jade
mäh·risch ['mɛːrıʃ] *adj.* Moravian
Mai [maı] *m* (-s; -e) May; ***im ~*** in May; ***der Erste ~*** May Day; **~baum** *m* maypole; **~fei·er** *f* May Day celebrations *pl.*; **~fei·er·tag** *m* May Day, *Brit. a.* May Bank Holiday; **~glöck·chen** *n* ⚘ lily of the valley; **~kä·fer** *m* cockchafer, maybug; **~kund·ge·bung** *f* May Day rally
Mais [maıs] *m* (-es ['maızəs]; *no pl.*) maize, *Am.* corn; **~brot** *n* cornbread
Mai·sche ['maıʃə] *f* (-; -n), **'mai·schen** *v/t.* (h) mash
'mais·far·ben *adj.* corn-colo(u)red

'**Mais|feld** *n* field of maize, *Am.* cornfield; **~flocken** *pl.* cornflakes; **2gelb** *adj.* corn-colo(u)red; **~kol·ben** *m* (corn)cob; *gastr.* corn on the cob; **~mehl** *n* Indian meal, *Am.* cornmeal
Mai·so·nette·woh·nung [mɛzo'nɛt-] *f* maisonette, *esp. Am.* duplex apartment
'**Mais·stär·ke** *f* cornflour, *Am.* cornstarch
Ma·je·stät [majɛs'tɛːt] *f* (-; -en) majesty (*a. fig.*); ***Seine*** (***Eure***) ~ His (Your) Majesty; **ma·je·stä·tisch** [majɛs'tɛːtɪʃ] *adj.* majestic(ally *adv.*); **Ma·je'stäts·be·lei·di·gung** *f esp. iro.* lèse-majesté
Ma·jo·li·ka [ma'joːlika] *f* (-; -ken, -s) majolica
Ma·jor [ma'joːɐ] *m* (-s; -e [-rə]) major
Ma·jo·ran [majo'raːn] *m* (-s; -e) marjoram
ma·jo·ri·sie·ren [majori'ziːrən] *v/t.* (h) outvote
Ma·jo·ri·tät [majori'tɛːt] *f* (-; -en) majority
Ma·jo·ri'täts|be·schluß *m* majority vote; **~prin͵zip** *n* principle of majority rule
Ma·jus·kel [ma'jʊskəl] *f* (-; -n) capital (letter)
ma·ka·ber [ma'kaːbɐ] *adj.* macabre, grim; F horrible
Ma·kel ['maːkəl] *m* (-s; -) **1.** flaw, defect, imperfection, fault; **2.** *fig.* flaw, blemish, taint; **3.** (***e-n*** ~ ***tragen*** bear a) stigma
Mä·ke·lei [mɛːkə'laɪ] *f* (-; -en) fault-finding (***an*** *dat.* with), carping (at); **mä·ke·lig** ['mɛːkəlɪç] *adj.* fussy, finicky
'**ma·kel·los** *adj.* flawless, immaculate, perfect; *fig. a.* impeccable; *fig.* ~***e Vergangenheit*** blameless past; '**Ma·kel·lo·sig·keit** *f* (-; *no pl.*) flawlessness, immaculateness; impeccableness
mä·keln ['mɛːkəln] *v/i.* (h) find fault (***an*** *dat.* with); ~ ***an*** *dat. a.* criticize, F pick holes in
Make-up [meːk'ʔap] *n* (-s; -s) makeup; **~-'Un·ter·la·ge** *f* makeup base
Mak·ka·ro·ni [maka'roːni] *pl.* macaroni *sg.*
Mak·ler ['maːklɐ] *m* (-s; -) ✝ broker; stockbroker; estate agent, *Am.* realtor; → ***ehrlich*** I
Mäk·ler ['mɛːklɐ] *m* (-s; -) fault-finder, carper, *formal:* caviller
'**Mak·ler|fir·ma** *f* (firm of) brokers *pl.*, brokerage company (*or* concern); **~ge·bühr** *f* broker's commission; **~ge·schäft** *n* broker's business
Ma·ko ['mako] *f* (-; -s) maco, Egyptian cotton
Ma·kra·mee [makra'meː] *n* (-[s]; -s) macramé
Ma·kre·le [ma'kreːlə] *f* (-; -n) mackerel
Ma·kro ['maːkro] *n* (-s; -s) **1.** *computer:* macro; **2.** *phot.* macro (lens); **~auf·nah·me** *f* macro shot
Ma·kro·bio·tik [makro'bĭoːtɪk] *f* (-; *no pl.*) macrobiotics *pl.*; **ma·kro·bio·tisch** [makro'bĭoːtɪʃ] *adj.* macrobiotic
Ma·kro·fo·to·gra͵fie ['maːkro-] *f* macrophotography
Ma·kro'kos·mos [makro-] *m* macrocosm
Ma·kro·ne [ma'kroːnə] *f* (-; -n) macaroon
Ma·kro-Ob·jek'tiv ['maːkro-] *n* macro lens
Ma·kro·öko·no'mie [makro-] *f* macroeconomics *pl.*
Ma·kro·struk͵tur ['maːkro-] *f* macrostructure
Ma·ku·la·tur [makula'tuːɐ] *f* (-; -en) waste paper; *w.s.* useless stuff; F *fig.* F rubbish, *esp. Am.* F garbage, trash; F *fig.* ~ ***reden*** *a.* F talk (a lot of) rot
mal [maːl] *adv.* **1.** ⩓ times, multiplied by; ***vier*** ~ ***zehn*** (***ist***) *a.* four tens (are); ***das Zimmer ist sechs*** ~ ***vier Meter*** the room is six metres (*Am.* meters) by four; ***sechs*** ~ ***vier*** six by four; **2.** ***guck*** ~ look; here, have a look at this; ***komm*** ~ ***her*** come here a minute(, will you?); **3.** ***er macht es*** ~ ***so,*** ~ ***so*** he does it differently every time; *iro.* ~ ***dies,*** ~ ***jenes*** it's something different every time
Mal[1] [maːl] *n* (-[e]s; -e) time; ***dieses eine*** ~ this once; ***ein paar*** ~ a few (F a couple of) times; ***ein anderes*** ~ some other time; ***das nächste*** ~ next time; ***beim ersten*** ~ the first time, *manage etc.* (the) first time round; ***beim letzten*** ~, ***letztes*** ~ the last time; ***ein letztes*** ~ one last time; ***das nächste*** ~ next time (round); ***zum ersten*** ~ for the first time; ***ein ums andere*** ~ time after time; ***das eine oder andere*** ~ now and then, now and again; ***zum wiederholten*** ~ repeatedly; ***zu wiederholten*** ~***en*** repeatedly, time and again; ***von*** ~ ***zu*** ~ every time, all the time; ***ein einziges*** ~ just once; ***kein einziges*** ~ not once; ***für dieses*** ~ for now, for the time being; ***mit einem*** ~(***e***) all of a sudden
Mal[2] [maːl] *n* (-[e]s; -e) **1.** mark (*a.* ⚕), sign; ⚕ birthmark; *fig.* stigma; **2.** monument, memorial; **3.** *sport:* start; base, home
Ma·la·chit [mala'xiːt] *m* (-s; -e) *min.* malachite
Ma·laie [ma'laɪə] *m* (-n; -n), **Ma·lai·in** [ma'laɪɪn] *f* (-; -nen) **1.** Malay(an); **2.** Malaysian; **ma·lai·isch** [ma'laɪɪʃ] *adj.*, **Ma'lai·isch** *n* (-en) *ling.* Malay(an)
Ma·la·ria [ma'laːrĭa] *f* (-; *no pl.*) malaria; **~an·fall** *m* attack of malaria; **~er·re·ger** *m* malaria parasite; **~ge·biet** *n*, **~ge·gend** *f* malaria(l) (*or* malaria-infested) territory; **~imp·fung** *f* malaria vaccination (*or* inoculation); **2krank** *adj.*: ~ ***sein*** be suffering from (*or* have) malaria; **~kran·ke** *m, f* (-n; -n) malaria patient (*or* victim); **~mücke** *f* malaria mosquito, 🕮 anopheles; **~pro·phy͵la·xe** *f* malaria prophylaxis; course of malaria tablets
Ma·lay·si·er [ma'laɪzĭɐ] *m* (-s; -), **Ma·lay·sie·rin** [ma'laɪzĭərɪn] *f* (-; -nen), **ma·lay·sisch** [ma'laɪzɪʃ] *adj.* Malaysian
'**Mal·buch** *n* colo(u)ring book
ma·len ['maːlən] (h) **I.** *v/t.* paint (*a. fingernails etc.*); draw; *fig.* portray, paint, depict; ***sich*** ~ ***lassen*** sit for a portrait; ***wie gemalt*** like a painting; *fig.* ***et. rosig*** (***schwarz***) ~ paint a rosy (black) picture of s.th.; **II.** *v/i.* paint; draw; **III.** *fig. v/refl.*: ***sich*** ~ be reflected, be mirrored; show (***auf j-s Gesicht*** in s.o.'s face)
Ma·ler ['maːlɐ] *m* (-s; -) painter, artist; **~ar·bei·ten** *pl.* painting *sg.* (jobs)
Ma·le·rei [maːlə'raɪ] *f* (-; -en) painting
Ma·le·rin ['maːlərɪn] *f* (-; -nen) painter, artist
ma·le·risch ['maːlərɪʃ] **I.** *adj.* **1.** ~***e Tätigkeit*** work as a painter, artistic work; ~***es Talent*** artistic talent, gift for painting; **2.** picturesque; **II.** *adv.*: ~ ***gesehen*** from an artistic point of view, as a painting
'**Ma·ler|lein·wand** *f* artist's canvas; **~mei·ster** *m* master painter
'**Mal·grund** *m* grounding; primer
Mal·heur [ma'løːɐ] *n* (-s; -e [-rə]): (***kleines*** ~ slight) mishap, (little) accident
ma·li·zi·ös [mali'tsĭøːs] *adj.* spiteful, malicious; ~***e Bemerkung*** *a.* snide remark
'**Mal|ka·sten** *m* paintbox; **~kunst** *f* art of painting
'**mal·neh·men** *v/t.* (*irr., sep.*, h, → ***nehmen***) ⩓ multiply
Ma·lo·che [ma'lɔxə] *sl. f* (-; *no pl.*) F (hard) graft, grind; **ma·lo·chen** [ma'lɔxən] *sl. v/i.* (h) F slog away; **Ma·lo·cher** [ma'lɔxɐ] *sl. m* (-s; -) workhorse
'**Mal|stift** *m* crayon; **~tech·nik** *f* painting technique
Mal·te·ser [mal'teːzɐ] *m* (-s; -), **Mal·te·se·rin** [mal'teːzərɪn] *f* (-; -nen) Maltese
Mal'te·ser|kreuz *n* Maltese cross; **~or·den** *m* order of the Knights of Malta; **~rit·ter** *m* Knight of Malta, Hospitaller
mal·te·sisch [mal'teːzɪʃ] *adj.* Maltese
Mal·to·se [mal'toːzə] *f* (-; *no pl.*) maltose
mal·trä·tie·ren [maltrɛ'tiːrən] *v/t.* (h) ill-treat, mistreat, maltreat; treat (*or* handle) *s.th.* roughly
Mal·ve ['malvə] *f* (-; -n) ⚘ mallow
'**mal·ven·far·big** *adj.* mauve
Malz [malts] *n* (-es; *no pl.*) malt; **~bier** *n* (low-alcohol) malt beer; **~bon͵bon** *n* malt(-flavo[u]red) sweet (*Am.* candy)
'**Mal·zei·chen** *n* ⩓ multiplication sign
mäl·zen ['mɛltsən] *v/i.* (h) malt; **Mäl·zer** ['mɛltsɐ] *m* (-s; -) maltster; **Mäl·ze·rei** [mɛltsə'raɪ] *f* (-; -en) malthouse
'**Malz|ex͵trakt** *m* malt extract; **~kaf͵fee** *m* malt coffee, ersatz coffee, coffee substitute (*made from malt*); **~zucker** *m* malt sugar, maltose
Ma·ma ['mama] *f* (-; -s) mummy, mum, *Am.* mommy, mom
Mam·mo·gramm [mamo'gram] *n* (-s; -e) ⚕ mammogram; **Mam·mo·gra·phie** [mamogra'fiː] *f* (-; -n) ⚕ mammography
Mam·mon ['mamɔn] *m* (-s; *no pl.*) mammon; ***schnöder*** ~ filthy lucre
Mam·mut ['mamuːt] *n* (-s; -s, -e) *zo.* mammoth; **~...** *in cpds. usu.* mammoth, giant; **~bau** *m* (-[e]s; -ten) megastructure; **~baum** *m* sequoia; **~film** *m* (screen) epic, (screen, *n.s.* Hollywood) spectacular; **~kon͵zern** *m* giant (*or* mammoth) company; **~kon͵zert** *n* giant concert; **~pro͵zeß** *m* marathon trial; **~sit·zung** *f* marathon (F jumbo) session *or* meeting; **~un·ter͵neh·men** *n* giant (*or* mammoth) enterprise
mamp·fen ['mampfən] F *v/i.* (h) munch, F chomp
man [man] *indef. pron.* **1.** one, you, we; ~ ***weiß nie,*** ~ ***kann nie wissen*** there's no telling (*or* knowing); ***wenn*** ~ ***ihn so hört*** to hear him talk, the way he talks *you'd think ...*; ~ ***trägt wieder Röcke*** *etc.* skirts *etc.* are in again (*or* are back in fashion); ~ ***darf ja wohl noch fragen*** there's no harm in asking, is there?; **2.** they, people; ~ ***hat mir gesagt*** I've been told; ~ ***sagt*** they say, people say; ~ ***holte ihn*** he was fetched; **3.** ~ ***nehme*** take; ~ ***wende sich an*** *acc.* apply to; ~ ***lasse sich nicht täuschen*** don't be deceived
Mä·na·de [mɛ'naːdə] *f* (-; -n) *myth. and fig.* maenad
Ma·nage·ment ['mænɪdʒmənt] *n* (-s; -s) **1.** management; *fig.* executive floor; ***ins*** ~ ***aufsteigen*** *a.* reach the boardroom; **2.** running *of foreign affairs etc.*; **~be·ra·tung** *f* management consulting
ma·na·gen ['mɛnɛdʒən] F *v/t.* (h) **1.** manage, F wangle; **2.** run *a campaign etc.*; **3.**

sport etc.: be (the) manager of, be *s.o.'s* manager; **Ma·na·ger** ['mɛnɛdʒɐ] *m* (-s; -) manager; **Ma·na·ge·rin** ['mɛnɛdʒərɪn] *f* (-; -nen) manager(ess)
'**Ma·na·ger|krank·heit** *f* executive stress; **~typ** *m* management (*or* executive) type
manch [manç] *adj. and indef. pron.* many a; **~ eine(r)** many (people), *lit.* many a one; ***in ~em hat er recht*** he's right about some things; ***so ~er*** a number of people; ***so ~es*** a fair bit; a thing or two; a few things; ***ich habe ~es zu berichten (kritisieren)*** I've got a few things to report (criticize, I've got a fair number of criticisms to make); **man·che** ['mançə] *pl.* some (people); quite a few (people)
man·cher·lei ['mançɐ'laɪ] *adj.* a) many, a good deal of, quite a few, b) various; all sorts (*or* kinds) of, c) *su.* a number of (*or* quite a few, various) things, all sorts (*or* kinds) of things
'**manch·mal** *adv.* sometimes, occasionally
Man·dant [man'dant] *m* (-en; -en), **Man·dan·tin** [man'dantɪn] *f* (-; -nen) ⚖ client
Man·da·ri·ne [manda'riːnə] *f* (-; -n) tangerine, mandarin
Man·dat [man'daːt] *n* (-[e]s; -e) ⚖, *pol., parl.* mandate; ⚖ *a.* brief; *parl.* ***sein ~ niederlegen*** resign (*or* vacate) one's seat
Man'dats|ge·biet *n* mandate; **~macht** *f* mandatory power; **~trä·ger** *m* (political) representative
Man·del ['mandəl] *f* (-; -n) **1.** ♣ almond; **2.** *anat.* tonsil; '**man·del·äu·gig** [-ɔʏgɪç] *adj.* almond-eyed
'**Man·del|baum** *m* almond (tree); **~ent·zün·dung** *f* tonsillitis
'**man·del·för·mig** [-fœrmɪç] *adj.* almond-shaped
'**Man·del|kern** *m* almond (kernel); **~kleie** *f* almond meal; **~öl** *n* almond oil; **~ope·ra·ti·on** *f* tonsillectomy; ***sich e-r ~ unterziehen*** have one's tonsils taken out, have a tonsillectomy; **~split·ter** *pl.* chopped almonds
Man·do·li·ne [mando'liːnə] *f* (-; -n) ♪ mandolin
Man·dra·go·ra [man'draːgora] *f* (-; -ren [mandra'goːrən]) ♣ mandrake
man·dschu·risch [man'dʒuːrɪʃ] *adj.* Manchurian
Ma·ne·ge [ma'neːʒə] *f* (-; -n) (circus) ring
Man·gan [maŋ'gaːn] *n* (-s; *no pl.*) manganese; **~knol·len** *pl.* manganese nodules
man'gan·sau·er *adj.* manganic; ***mangansaures Salz*** manganate
Man·gel¹ ['maŋəl] *f* (-; -n) ⚙ mangle; F *fig.* ***j-n durch die ~ drehen, j-n in die ~ nehmen*** F put s.o. through the mill, F give s.o. a grilling
'**Man·gel²** *m* (-s; Mängel ['mɛŋəl]) a) defect, fault, flaw, b) shortcoming, imperfection, weakness, c) lack, shortage, *lit.* dearth (***all an*** *dat.* of); *a.* ⚕ deficiency (***an*** *dat.* in); ***aus ~ an*** *dat.* for lack (*or* want) of; ***~ leiden*** suffer hardship (*or* privation); ***keinen ~ leiden*** *a.* want for nothing; ***Mängel aufweisen*** be flawed, have (its) faults (*or* shortcomings, imperfections); ***e-n ~ beseitigen*** remedy a fault (*or* defect)
Män·gel·an·zei·ge ['mɛŋəl-] *f* notice of defect(s)
'**Man·gel·be·ruf** *m* understaffed profession
Män·gel·be·sei·ti·gung ['mɛŋəl-] *f* correction of faults
'**Man·gel·er·schei·nung** *f* ⚕ deficiency symptom
'**man·gel·frei** *adj.* faultless, free of faults (*or* defects); '**Man·gel·frei·heit** *f* (-; *no pl.*) flawlessness
'**man·gel·haft** *adj.* faulty, defective *goods etc.*; *fig.* poor *quality, memory etc.*; unsatisfactory *performance, grades etc.*; imperfect, insufficient, inadequate *knowledge etc.*; '**Man·gel·haf·tig·keit** *f* (-; *no pl.*) faultiness, defectiveness, poor quality; imperfection, insufficiency
Män·gel·haf·tung ['mɛŋəl-] *f* liability for defects
'**Man·gel·krank·heit** *f* deficiency disease
Män·gel·li·ste ['mɛŋəl-] *f* list of faults (*w.s.* complaints)
man·geln¹ ['maŋəln] *v/t.* (h) mangle
'**man·geln²** *v/impers.* (h): ***es mangelt an*** *dat.* there's a lack (*or* shortage) of; ***es mangelt mir an Geld*** *etc.* I'm short of (*or* I need) money *etc.*; ***es mangelt ihm an Mut*** he lacks (*or* is lacking in) courage; ***es mangelt ihr an nichts*** she's got everything she needs, *lit.* she wants for nothing; ***~des Selbstvertrauen*** lack of self-confidence; ***wegen ~der Nachfrage*** due to lack of demand
Män·gel·rü·ge ['mɛŋəl-] *f* ✝ notice of defects, complaint
man·gels ['maŋəls] *prp.* (*gen.*) for lack (*or* want) of; *esp.* ⚖ in default of; ***~ Beweisen*** in the absence of evidence; ***~ Masse*** ⚖ for lack of assets, F for lack of money
'**Man·gel·wa·re** *f* scarce commodity; ***~ sein*** *a.* F *fig.* be scarce, be in short supply, be hard to come by, *w.s.* be rare
Man·go ['maŋgo] *f* (-; -s) mango
Man·gold ['maŋgɔlt] *m* (-[e]s; *no pl.*) ♣ mangold
Man·gro·ve [maŋ'groːvə] *f* (-; -n) mangrove; **Man'gro·ven·sumpf** *m* mangrove swamp
Ma·ni·chä·er [manɪ'çɛːɐ] *m* (-s; -) Manich(a)ean; **ma·ni·chä·isch** [manɪ'çɛːɪʃ] *adj.* Manich(a)ean; **Ma·ni·chä·is·mus** [manɪçɛ'ɪsmʊs] *m* (-; *no pl.*) Manich(a)eanism
Ma·nie [ma'niː] *f* (-; -n) mania; obsession; ***zur ~ werden*** become a mania *or* an obsession (***bei*** *dat.* with)
Ma·nier [ma'niːɐ] *f* (-; -en [-rən]) **1.** manner, way (of doing s.th.); *art*: style; ***in englischer ~*** in the English style; ***in Rembrandtscher ~*** in the style of Rembrandt; → ***altbewährt*; 2.** *usu. pl.* manner(s *pl.*); ***gute (schlechte) ~en haben*** be well-mannered (bad-mannered); ***keine ~en haben*** have no manners
ma·nie·riert [mani'riːɐt] *adj.* affected, mannered; stilted; **Ma·nie'riert·heit** *f* (-; -en) mannerism; mannered behavio(u)r, affectation
Ma·nie·ris·mus [mani'rɪsmʊs] *m* (-; -men) mannerism; **Ma·nie·rist** [mani'rɪst] *m* (-en; -en) mannerist; **ma·nie·ri·stisch** [mani'rɪstɪʃ] *adj.* mannerist(ic)
ma·nier·lich [ma'niːɐlɪç] **I.** *adj.* well-behaved, well-mannered; *w.s.* decent, acceptable *price etc.*; **II.** *adv.* properly, decently; ***sich ~ benehmen*** behave o.s., behave well (*or* properly)
ma·ni·fest [mani'fɛst] *adj.* manifest
Ma·ni'fest *n* (-[e]s; -e) manifesto
Ma·ni·fe·sta·ti·on [manifɛsta'tsi̯oːn] *f* (-; -en) manifestation; **ma·ni·fe·stie·ren** [manifɛs'tiːrən] (h) **I.** *v/refl.*: ***sich ~*** manifest itself, become manifest; come to the fore; **II.** *v/t.* manifest, show, display
Ma·ni·kü·re [mani'kyːrə] *f* (-; -n) **1.** manicure; **2.** manicurist; **ma·ni·kü·ren** [mani'kyːrən] *v/t. and v/i.* (h) manicure
Ma·ni·la·hanf [ma'niːla-] *m* Manila hemp
Ma·ni·pu·la·ti·on [manipula'tsi̯oːn] *f* (-; -en) manipulation; **Ma·ni·pu·la·tor** [manipu'laːtoːɐ] *m* (-s; -en [-la'toːrən]) manipulator, fixer; **ma·ni·pu·lier·bar** [manipu'liːɐbaːɐ] *adj.* manipulable; ***sind sie ~?*** *a.* can they be manipulated?; **Ma·ni·pu'lier·bar·keit** *f* (-; *no pl.*) manipulability; **ma·ni·pu·lie·ren** [manipu'liːrən] *v/t.* (h) manipulate (*a. pol.*), influence; fiddle with *engine etc.*; rig *elections etc.*; massage *figures, report etc.*
ma·nisch ['maːnɪʃ] *adj.* manic(ally *adv.*); ***~depressiv*** manic-depressive; ***~depressiv sein*** be a manic-depressive
Man·ko ['maŋko] *n* (-s; -s) **1.** ✝ deficiency, shortage; deficit, shortfall; **2.** *fig.* (***entscheidendes ~*** major) shortcoming, drawback
Mann [man] *m* (-[e]s; Männer ['mɛnɐ]) a) man (*pl.* men), b) husband; ***der ~ auf der Straße*** the man in the street, the ordinary man; ***~ für ~*** one after the other; ***ein Gespräch von ~ zu ~*** a man-to-man talk; ***wie ein ~*** as one; ***bis auf den letzten ~*** to a man; ***et. wie ein ~ ertragen*** *etc.* bear *etc.* s.th. like a man; ***alle ~ hoch*** the whole lot of us (*or* them); ***alle ~ mitmachen!*** come on, everyone!; ***wir waren drei ~ hoch*** there were three of us; ***wir brauchen drei ~*** we need three men (*or* people); ***~s genug sein für etwas*** be man enough for (*or* to do) s.th.; ***an den ~ bringen*** a) place *goods etc.*, b) find a husband for, F marry off, c) F find an audience for *one's jokes*, get *one's opinions etc.* across; ***s-n ~ stehen*** hold one's own, stand one's ground, do a fine job; ***s-n ~ gefunden haben*** have found one's match; ***der vierte ~*** *card game*: the fourth player; ⚓ ***alle ~ an Deck!*** all hands on deck; ***da sind wir an den rechten ~ gekommen*** he's the (right) man for us; ***ein ~ von Welt*** a man with savoir-faire; ***ein ~, ein Wort*** a promise is a promise; ***ein ~ von Wort*** a man of his word; ***10 Mark pro ~*** 10 marks each (*or* per head); ***~ Gottes!*** for God's sake!; F ***~!*** F wow!, F hey!; → ***selbst*** I, ***stark*** I, ***tot***
Man·na ['mana] *n* (-[s]; *no pl.*), *f* (-; *no pl.*) *bibl. and fig.* manna (from heaven)
Männ·chen ['mɛnçən] *n* (-s; -) **1.** little man, manikin; **2.** *zo.* a) male, b) cock; **3.** ***~ machen*** a) *animal*: stand on its hind legs, *dog*: *a.* sit up and beg, b) F ⚔ snap to attention, c) F grovel, bow and scrape; **4.** F ***~ malen*** doodle
'**Mann·deckung** *f* man-to-man marking
Man·ne·quin ['manəkɛ̃] *n* (-s; -s) model
Män·ner ['mɛnɐ] *pl.* men; *in cpds.* men's; *WC*: Men, Gentlemen; **~be·kannt·schaft** *f* male (*or* man) friend, boyfriend; **~be·ruf** *m* male(-oriented *or* -dominated) profession; **~chor** *m* ♪ male(-voice) *or* all-male choir; **~fang** F *m*: ***auf ~ ausgehen (aussein)*** F go (be) manhunting
'**män·ner·feind·lich** *adj.* anti-male, *pred. a.* anti-men; ***sie ist ~*** *a.* she doesn't like men, she hates men, she's bias(s)ed against men (*or* the male sex); '**Män·ner·feind·lich·keit** *f* hostility towards men, anti-male attitude
'**Män·ner|ge·sell·schaft** *f* male(-dominated) society; **~haß** *m* hatred towards

men; 2mor·dend *hum. adj.* man-eating; ~sa·che *f* a man's job (*or* business); **das ist ~!** *a.* leave that to the men!; ~sta·ti͵on *f* men's ward; ~stim·me *f* man's (♪ male) voice; ~͵über·schuß *m* surfeit of men; ~welt *f* (-; *no pl.*) **1.** *a* man's world; **2.** men *pl.*, *the* male population; ~wirt·schaft F *f* **1.** (all-)male setup; **2.** male household; **typische ~!** you can tell it's a man (*or* men) running the place; ~witz *m* male joke

Man·nes|al·ter ['manəs-] *n* manhood; **im besten ~** in one's prime; ~jah·re *pl.* years (*or* period *sg.*) of manhood; ~kraft *f* (-; ⸚e) a) masculine strength, b) *no pl.* virility

'mann·haft *adj.* manly, brave, valiant; resolute; **'Mann·haf·tig·keit** *f* (-; *no pl.*) manliness

man·nig·fach ['manıçfax] *adj.* various, diverse, manifold

man·nig·fal·tig ['manıçfaltıç] *adj.* varied, multifarious, manifold; **'Man·nig·fal·tig·keit** *f* (-; *no pl.*) diversity

Männ·lein ['mɛnlaın] *n* (-s; -) little man; F **~ und Weiblein** men and women, boys and girls; F **na ~!** F well (*or* hello), sonny

männ·lich ['mɛnlıç] *adj. biol.*, ⚘, ⚙ male; masculine (*a. ling.*); manly; **~e Entsprechung** male equivalent; **'Männ·lich·keit** *f* (-; *no pl.*) masculinity; manliness, virility; **'Männ·lich·keits·wahn** *m* machismo

'Manns·bild F *n* man; **ein stattliches ~** a fine figure of a man

'Mann·schaft *f* (-; -en) **1.** *sport*: team; side; F squad; **2.** crew; **3.** *fig.* team (*a. pol.*), F squad; group (of people); **vor versammelter ~** in front of everyone (*or* the whole department *etc.*); **4.** ⚔ **~en** enlisted men, other ranks

'Mann·schafts|auf·stel·lung *f sport*: (team) line-up; ~füh·rer *m* (team) captain, F skipper; ~geist *m* (-[e]s; *no pl.*) team spirit; ~kampf *m* team event; ~ka·pi͵tän *m* (team) captain, F skipper; ~spiel *n* team game; ~sport *m* team sport; ~wa·gen *m* personnel carrier; police van; ~wer·tung *f sport*: team classification; ~wett·be·werb *m sport*: team event

'manns·hoch *adj. and adv.* head-high

'manns·toll *adj.* oversexed, nymphomaniac; **'Manns·toll·heit** *f* (-; *no pl.*) nymphomania

'Mann·weib *n* **1.** *biol.* gynander; **2.** *contp.* F butch

Ma·no·me·ter [mano'me:tɐ] **I.** *n* (-s; -) ⚙ pressure ga(u)ge; **II.** F *int.* F wow!

Ma·nö·ver [ma'nø:vɐ] *n* (-s; -) **1.** manoeuvre, *Am.* maneuver; *fig.* **ein geschicktes ~** a clever move; **2.** ⚔ manoeuvres *pl.*, *Am.* maneuvers *pl.*, exercise; ~ge·län·de *n* exercise area; ~kri͵tik *fig. f* postmortem(s *pl.*); **~ halten** have (*or* hold) a postmortem

ma·nö·vrier·bar [manø'vri:ɐba:ɐ] *adj.* → **manövrierfähig**; **Ma·nö'vrier·bar·keit** *f* → **Manövrierfähigkeit**

ma·nö·vrie·ren [manø'vri:rən] *v/i.* (h) manoeuvre, *Am.* maneuver (*a. fig.*)

ma·nö'vrier·fä·hig *adj.* manoeuvrable, *Am.* maneuverable; **Ma·nö'vrier·fä·hig·keit** *f* manoeuvrability, *Am.* maneuverability; **ma·nö'vrier·un·fä·hig** *adj.* disabled

Man·sar·de [man'zardə] *f* (-; -n) attic

Man'sar·den|dach *n* mansard roof; ~fen·ster *n* dormer window; ~woh·nung *f* attic flat (*or* apartment); ~zim·mer *n* attic room, room in the attic

Mansch [manʃ] F *m* (-[e]s; *no pl.*) F mush; mud, slush; **'man·schen** F (h) **I.** *v/t.* mash (up); **II.** *v/i.* mess about

Man·schet·te [man'ʃɛtə] *f* (-; -n) cuff; ⚙ sleeve, collar; frill *of flowerpot etc.*; F *fig.* **~n haben vor** *dat.* F be scared stiff of; F **~n bekommen** F get the wind up, F get cold feet; **Man'schet·ten·knopf** *m* cufflink

Man·tel ['mantəl] *m* (-s; Mäntel ['mɛntəl]) **1.** coat; cloak (*a. fig.*); *fig.* mantle; **im ~** in a (*or* one's) coat, wearing a coat; **ohne ~** without a coat (on); **gib mir d-n ~** a) let me take your coat, b) let me help you on with your coat; *fig.* **~ der Nächstenliebe** (*or* **Barmherzigkeit**) cloak of charity; **den ~ nach dem Wind hängen** swim with the tide, trim one's sails to the wind; → **Verschwiegenheit**; **2.** ⚙ jacket; casing

Män·tel·chen ['mɛntəlçən] *n* (-s; -): *fig.* **e-r Sache ein ~ umhängen** gloss over s.th., cover s.th. up; **sich ein frommes ~ umhängen** play the saint

'Man·tel|ge·setz *n* skeleton law; ~kleid *n* coat dress; ~pa·vi·an *m* sacred (*or* grey, *Am.* gray) baboon; ~ta͵rif(ver·trag) *m* collective agreement on working conditions

'Man·tel-und-'De·gen|-Film *m* cloak-and-dagger film; ~-Stück *n* cloak-and-dagger piece

Ma·nu·al [ma'nŭa:l] *n* (-s; -e) **1.** ♪ manual, keyboard; **2.** (reference *or* user) manual

ma·nu·ell [ma'nŭɛl] **I.** *adj.* manual; **II.** *adv.*: **~ begabt sein** be skilled with one's hands

Ma·nu·fak·tur [manufak'tu:ɐ] *f* (-; -en) **1.** factory; **2.** manufacture, manufacturing; ~wa·ren *pl.* piece goods; *n.s.* textiles, *Am.* yard goods

Ma·nu·skript [manu'skrıpt] *n* (-[e]s; -e) manuscript; *film etc.*: script; **ohne ~ sprechen** speak without a script (*or* notes); **sie sprach ohne ~** *a.* she didn't have any notes

Mäpp·chen ['mɛpçən] *n* (-s; -) (pencil) case

Map·pe ['mapə] *f* (-; -n) a) briefcase, b) schoolbag, c) folder, file; portfolio

Mär [mɛ:ɐ] *f* (-; Mären ['mɛ:rən]) **1.** F *hum.* (tall) story; **2.** *obs.* fairytale; F **nur e-e fromme ~** just an old fairytale

Ma·ra·bu ['ma:rabu] *m* (-s; -s) *zo.* marabou

Ma·ras·chi·no(li͵kör) [maras'ki:no-] *m* maraschino

Ma·ra·thon ['ma:ratɔn] *m* (-s; -s) *a. fig.* marathon; ~lauf *m* marathon (race); ~läu·fer *m* marathon runner; ~rad·ren·nen *n* cycling marathon, F bikeathon; ~schwim·men *n* swimming marathon, F swimathon; ~sit·zung *f* marathon (F jumbo) session *or* meeting; ~strecke *f* **1.** marathon route; **2.** marathon distance; ~tanz *m* dance marathon, F danceathon

Mär·chen ['mɛ:ɐçən] *n* (-s; -) fairytale; *fig.* (tall) story, yarn; F **erzähl doch keine ~!** F pull the other leg; ~buch *n* book of fairytales; ~dich·ter *m* fairytale writer (*or* author); ~er·zäh·ler *m* teller of fairytales; F *fig.* storyteller; ~fi͵gur *f*, ~ge·stalt *f* fairytale character, figure from a fairytale

'mär·chen·haft *adj. a. fig.* magical, fairytale ...; *fig.* fantastic; **~e Möglichkeiten** (**Aussichten**) utopian possibilities (prospects)

'Mär·chen|land *n* fairyland, land of fairytales; ~oper *f* fairytale opera; ~prinz *m* Prince Charming (*a. fig.*); ~samm·lung *f* **1.** collection of fairytales; **2.** → **Märchenbuch**; ~stun·de *f* story time; ~welt *f* **1.** → **Märchenland**; **2.** *fig.* fairytale world

Mar·der ['mardɐ] *m* (-s; -) marten; ~fell *n* marten skin; ~pelz *m* marten fur

Mar·ga·ri·ne [marga'ri:nə] *f* (-; *no pl.*) margarine

Mar·ge ['marʒə] *f* (-; -n) margin

Mar·ge·ri·te [margə'ri:tə] *f* (-;-n) ⚘ oxeye daisy

Mar·gi·na·lie [margi'na:lĭə] *f* (-;-n) marginal note

Ma·ri·en|bild [ma'ri:ən-] *n* Madonna; ~kä·fer *m* ladybird, *Am. a.* ladybug; ~kult *m*, ~ver·eh·rung *f* worship of the Virgin Mary, *contp.* Mariolatry

Ma·ri·hua·na [mari'hŭa:na] *n* (-s; *no pl.*) marijuana, *sl.* pot

Ma·ril·le [ma'rılə] *Austrian f* (-; -n) apricot

Ma·rim·ba [ma'rımba] *f* (-; -s) ♪ marimba

Ma·ri·na·de [mari'na:də] *f* (-; -n) marinade

Ma·ri·ne [ma'ri:nə] *f* (-; -n) merchant navy; ⚔ navy; **ma'ri·ne·blau** *adj.*, **Ma'ri·ne·blau** *n* navy (blue)

Ma'ri·ne|flie·ger *m* naval pilot; ~in·fan·te·rie *f* marines *pl.*; ~in·fan·te·rist *m* marine; ~of·fi͵zier *m* naval officer; ~sol͵dat *m* marine, member of the marines; ~streit·kräf·te *pl.* naval forces; navy *sg.*; ~stütz·punkt *m* naval base; ~trup·pen *pl.* marines

ma·ri·nie·ren [mari'ni:rən] *v/t.* (h) marinate

Ma·rio·net·te [marĭo'nɛtə] *f* (-; -n) *a. fig.* marionette, puppet; **ma·rio'net·ten·haft** *adj.* puppet-like, *a. adv.* like a puppet

Ma·rio'net·ten|re͵gie·rung *f* puppet government; ~spiel *n* puppet show; ~spie·ler *m* puppet player; ~thea·ter *n* puppet theat|re (*Am. a.* -er)

ma·ri·tim [mari'ti:m] *adj.* maritime

Mark¹ [mark] *n* (-s; *no pl.*) marrow; ⚘ pulp; pith; *fig. a.* core; *fig.* **j-m durch ~ und Bein** (*or* **Knochen**) **gehen** set s.o.'s teeth on edge; **j-n bis ins ~ treffen** cut s.o. to the quick; **faul** (*or* **verderbt**) **bis ins ~** rotten to the core; **j-m das ~ aus den Knochen saugen** bleed s.o. white

Mark² *f* (-; -en) *hist.* march; **die ~ Brandenburg** the Brandenburg Marches

Mark³ *f* (-; -) mark; **Deutsche ~** German mark, deutschmark; **zehn ~** ten marks; F **jede ~ umdrehen** (**müssen** have to) count every penny; → **müde** I

mar·kant [mar'kant] *adj.* striking (*a. fig.*); prominent *figure etc.*; *fig.* clear-cut; distinctive; pithy; full of character; **~er Wein** wine with a distinctive flavo(u)r (*or* character)

'mark·durch͵drin·gend *adj.* bloodcurdling *scream etc.*

Mar·ke ['markə] *f* (-; -n) **1.** make, type, *esp. mot. a.* marque; brand, sort; **2.** *surv.* mark; **3.** *sport*: record; **4.** F odd character; **du bist mir e-e ~!** you're a fine one!; **5.** → **Briefmarke, Dienstmarke**

'Mar·ken|al·bum *n* stamp album; ~ar͵ti·kel *m* brand-name article; ~be·wußt-

sein *n* brand awareness; **~but·ter** *f* best quality butter; **~er·zeug·nis** *n*, **~fa·bri̦kat** *n* brand-name article (*or* product); **~ge·rät** *n* brand-name model (*or* appliance *etc.*); **~heft·chen** *n* stamp book; **~na·me** *m* trade (*or* brand) name; **~samm·ler** *m* stamp collector; **~samm·lung** *f* stamp collection; **~schutz** *m* trademark protection; **~treue** *f* brand loyalty; **~wa·re** *f* brand-name article (*pl. a.* goods); **~zei·chen** *n a. fig.* trademark

Mar·ker ['markɐ] *m* (-s; -) **1.** *ling. and genetics*: marker; **2.** marker pen

'mark·er·schüt·ternd *adj.* bloodcurdling

Mar·ke·ten·der [markə'tɛndɐ] *m* (-s; -), **Mar·ke·ten·de·rin** [markə'tɛndərɪn] *f* (-; -nen) *hist.* sutler

Mar·ke·ting ['markətɪŋ] *n* (-[s]; *no pl.*) ✝ marketing

'Mark·graf *m* margrave; **'Mark·grä·fin** *f* margravine; **'Mark·graf·schaft** *f* margrav(i)ate

mar·kie·ren [mar'ki:rən] (h) **I.** *v/t.* **1.** mark; **2.** accentuate, underline; **3.** act, play, pretend to be; feign *illness etc.*; ***e-e Kolik*** *~ a.* put on (*or* pretend to be having) a colic; ***den starken Mann*** *~* (try to) act tough; ***den Dummen*** *~* play the fool; **4.** *sport*: a) mark *a player*, b) score *a goal etc.*; **II.** *v/i.* **5.** pretend, act, pose; ***sie markiert nur*** she's putting it on

Mar·kier·stein [mar'ki:ɐ-] *m* marker

mar·kiert [mar'ki:ɐt] *adj.* **1.** marked; **2.** put-on; ***es ist*** *~ a.* it's all an act

Mar'kie·rung *f* (-; -en) a) marking, b) mark

Mar'kie·rungs|fähn·chen *n sport*: (course) marker; **~li·nie** *f* (marked) line; **~punkt** *m* mark

mar·kig ['markɪç] *fig. adj.* powerful (*a. wine*); *a.* pithy *words etc.*

Mar·ki·se [mar'ki:zə] *f* (-; -n) sun blind; awning

'Mark|klöß·chen *n* marrow dumpling; **~kno·chen** *m* marrowbone

'Mark·stein *m* boundary stone; *fig.* landmark, milestone

'Mark·stück *n* (one-)mark piece

Markt [markt] *m* (-[e]s; Märkte ['mɛrktə]) a) market; trading cent|re (*Am.* -er), b) marketplace, market square, c) fair, d) trade, business; ***freier*** (***inländischer, schwarzer***) *~* free (home, black) market; ***auf dem*** *~* at the market, in the marketplace, ✝ in (*or* on) the market; ***auf den*** *~* ***bringen*** (put on the) market; ***auf den*** *~* ***kommen*** come on(to) the market; → ***gemeinsam***; **~ab·spra·che** *f* marketing agreement; **~ana̦ly·se** *f* market analysis; **~an·teil** *m* share of the market

'markt·be·herr·schend *adj.* dominant; *~* ***sein*** *a.* control the market; ***~e Stellung*** dominant market role; **'Markt·be·herr·schung** *f* control of the market, market control

'Markt|be·ob·ach·ter *m* market observer (*or* analyst); **~be·richt** *m* market report; **~bu·de** *f* market stall; **~chan·cen** *pl.* sales opportunities; **~ent·wick·lung** *f* market trend; **⁀fä·hig** *adj.* marketable, sal(e)able; **~flecken** *m* (small) market town

'Markt·for·scher *m* market researcher; **'Markt·for·schung** *f* market research; **'Markt·for·schungs·in·sti̦tut** *n* marketing research institute

'Markt|frau *f* market woman (*or* vendor); **~füh·rer** *m* market leader

'markt|gän·gig *adj.* marketable, sal(e)able; current *price*; **~ge·recht** *adj.* in line with market requirements

'Markt|hal·le *f* covered market; **~la·ge** *f* market conditions *pl.*; **~lücke** *f* opening, gap in the market; **~ord·nung** *f* market regulations *pl.*; **~platz** *m* market place (*or* square); **~preis** *m* market *or* going price (*or* rate)

'Markt·schrei·er *m* (fairground) barker; **'markt·schreie·risch** [-ʃraɪərɪʃ] *fig. adj.* ostentatious, loud

'Markt|schwan·kun·gen *pl.* market fluctuations; **~stu·die** *f* market analysis; **~tag** *m* market day; **~̦über·sicht** *f* market survey; **~über̦sät·ti·gung** *f* market saturation; **⁀üb·lich** *adj.*: ***~er Zins*** market interest rate; **~weib** *contp. n* fishwife; **~wert** *m* (current) market value, commercial value

'Markt·wirt·schaft *f* market economy; ***freie*** *~ a.* free enterprise; ***soziale*** *~* social market economy; **'markt·wirt·schaft·lich** *adj.* free-enterprise ...

Mar·kus·evan·ge·li·um ['markʊs-] *n*: ***das*** *~* (the Gospel of) St Mark, St Mark's Gospel

Mar·me·la·de [marmə'la:də] *f* (-; -n) jam; marmalade

Mar·me'la·den|brot *n* jam sandwich, *Brit. a.* F jam butty; **~glas** *n* jam jar

Mar·mor ['marmo:ɐ] *m* (-s; -e [-rə]) marble; **~bild** *n* marble statue

mar·mo·rie·ren [marmo'ri:rən] *v/t.* (h) marble; **Mar·mo'rie·rung** *f* (-; -en) marbling; marbled pattern

'Mar·mor·ku·chen *m* marble cake

mar·morn ['marmɔrn] *adj.* marble ... (*a. fig.*), made of marble

'Mar·mor|plat·te *f* marble slab; marble top; **~säu·le** *f* marble column; **~sta·tue** *f* marble statue; **~ta·fel** *f* marble plaque; **~trep·pe** *f* marble staircase (*or* steps *pl.*)

ma·ro·de [ma'ro:də] F *adj.* **1.** ailing *economy etc.*; degenerate, rotten to the core; ***die Wirtschaft ist*** *~ a.* F the economy is on its last legs; **2.** F washed out, whacked

Ma·rok·ka·ner [marɔ'ka:nɐ] *m* (-s; -), **Ma·rok·ka·ne·rin** [marɔ'ka:nərɪn] *f* (-; -nen), **ma·rok·ka·nisch** [marɔ'ka:nɪʃ] *adj.* Moroccan

Ma·rok·ko·le·der [ma'rɔko-] *n* Morocco (leather)

Ma·ro·ne [ma'ro:nə] *f* (-; -n) **1.** ⚘ (sweet) chestnut; **2.** ⚘ → **Ma'ro·nen·röhr·ling** [-rø:ɐlɪŋ] *m* (-s; -e) cep

Ma·rot·te [ma'rɔtə] *f* (-; -n) (strange) quirk; fad

Mar·quis [mar'ki:] *m* (-; - [-ki:s]) marquis, marquess; **Mar·qui·se** [mar'ki:zə] *f* (-; -n) marchioness, marquise

Mars [mars] *m* (-; *no pl.*) *ast. and myth.* Mars; **~be·woh·ner** *m* Martian

marsch [marʃ] *int.*: ⚔ ***vorwärts, ~!*** forward march!; ***~!*** hurry up!, F get a move on!, chop, chop!; *~* ***ins Bett!*** off to bed with you!; *~* ***an die Arbeit!*** F let's get cracking(, then)!

Marsch[1] *m* (-es; Märsche ['mɛrʃə]) a) ⚔ march (*a.* ♪), b) ⚔ marching; *w.s.* walk; trek; ***sich in*** *~* ***setzen*** march (*or* move) off, *fig. a.* set out (*or* off); *fig.* ***in*** *~* ***setzen*** get *s.o. or s.th.* moving; F *fig.* ***j-m den*** *~* ***blasen*** F haul s.o. over the coals

Marsch[2] *f* (-; -en) marsh

Mar·schall ['marʃal] *m* (-s; Marschälle ['marʃɛlə]) marshal; **~stab** *m* (field) marshal's baton

'Marsch·be·fehl *m* marching orders *pl.*

'marsch·be·reit *adj.* ready to march

'Marsch·bo·den *m* marshy ground

'Marsch·flug·kör·per *m* cruise missile

'Marsch·ge·päck *n* field kit

mar·schie·ren [mar'ʃi:rən] *v/i.* (sn) **1.** ⚔ march (*a.* *~* ***lassen***); **2.** walk, trek; stride, march (***nach*** *dat.*, ***zu*** *dat.* off to); **3.** F *fig.* ***die Sache marschiert*** F things are moving along nicely

'Marsch|ko̦lon·ne *f* route column; **~kom·paß** *m* prismatic compass

'Marsch·land *n* marsh(es *pl.*)

'Marsch|lied *n* marching song; **~mu̦sik** *f* military marches *pl.*; **~ord·nung** *f* march formation; **~rou·te** *f* ⚔ route; *fig.* line of approach, tactics *pl.*; **~ver·pfle·gung** *f* ⚔ marching (*or* travel) rations *pl.*; *fig.* provisions *pl.* (for the road)

'Mars·son·de *f* Mars probe

Mar·stall ['marʃtal] *m* (-[e]s; Marställe ['marʃtɛlə]) (royal) stables *pl.*

Mar·ter ['martɐ] *f* (-; -n) torture; *fig. a.* ordeal, torment; **'mar·tern** *v/t.* (h) torture; *fig. a.* torment

'Mar'ter|pfahl *m* stake; ***am*** *~* ***sterben*** die at the stake; **~tod** *m* death by torture; *a* martyr's death; **~werk·zeug** *n* instrument(s *pl.*) of torture

mar·tia·lisch [mar'tsĭa:lɪʃ] *adj.* martial

Mar·tins|fest ['marti:ns-] *n* Martinmas; **~horn** *n* (police, ambulance *or* fire-engine) siren; **~tag** *m* Martinmas

Mär·ty·rer ['mɛrtyrɐ] *m* (-s; -), **Mär·ty·re·rin** ['mɛrtyrərɪn] *f* (-; -nen) martyr; ***j-n*** (***sich***) ***zum Märtyrer machen*** *a. iro.* make a martyr of s.o. (o.s.); *iro.* ***er macht sich gern zum Märtyrer*** *a.* he likes to act the martyr; **'Mär·ty·rer·tod** *m a* martyr's death; ***den*** *~* ***sterben*** die a martyr's death, die a martyr

'Mär·ty·rer·tum *n* (-s; *no pl.*) martyrdom

Mar·ty·ri·um [mar'ty:rĭʊm] *n* (-s; -rien) martyrdom; *fig.* ***ein*** (***einziges***) *~* torture, torment, an ordeal, hell on earth

Mar·xis·mus [mar'ksɪsmʊs] *m* (-; *no pl.*) Marxism; **Mar·xist** [mar'ksɪst] *m* (-en; -en), **Mar·xi·stin** [mar'ksɪstɪn] *f* (-; -nen), **mar·xi·stisch** [mar'ksɪstɪʃ] *adj.* Marxist

März [mɛrts] *m* (-[es]; -e) March; ***im*** *~* in March

Mar·zi·pan [martsi'pa:n] *n* (-s; -e) marzipan

Ma·sche ['maʃə] *f* (-; -n) **1.** a) stitch, b) mesh, c) ladder, run; *fig.* ***durch die ~n des Gesetzes schlüpfen*** find a loophole in the law; ***j-m durch die ~n gehen*** slip through s.o.'s hands (*or* fingers, net), give s.o. the slip; **2.** F a) trick, ploy, b) fad, craze; ***es mit der sanften*** *~* ***versuchen*** F try a bit of soft soap (***bei j-m*** with s.o.); ***komm mir nicht mit der ~!*** don't try that one on me, don't try it on with me; ***das ist die ~!*** that's brilliant; ***auf die*** *~* ***ist er reingefallen*** F he fell for the line; ***die*** *~* ***raushaben*** have got the hang of it

'Ma·schen·draht *m* wire netting

Ma·schi·ne [ma'ʃi:nə] *f* (-; -n) a) machine, b) engine, c) plane, d) F bike; ***er fliegt mit der nächsten*** *~* he's taking the next plane (*or* flight); → ***Nähmaschine, Schreibmaschine*** *etc.*

ma'schi·ne·ge·schrie·ben I. *p.p. of* ***maschineschreiben***; **II.** *adj.* → ***maschinengeschrieben***

ma·schi·nell [maʃi'nɛl] **I.** *adj.* machine ...; **II.** *adv.* by machine, machine-...; *~* ***bearbeiten*** machine; *~* ***hergestellt*** machine-made

Ma'schi·nen|an·la·ge *f* plant, machinery; **~an·trieb** *m* machine drive; **mit ~** machine-driven

Ma'schi·nen·bau *m* (-[e]s; *no pl.*) mechanical engineering; **Ma'schi·nen·bau·er** *m* (-s; -), **Ma'schi·nen·bau·in·ge,nieur** *m* mechanical engineer

Ma'schi·nen|fa,brik *f* engineering works *pl.*; **~garn** *n* machine twist; **2ge·schrie·ben** *adj.* typewritten, typed; **2ge·strickt** *adj.* machine-knitted; **~ge·wehr** *n* machine gun; **~hal·le** *f*, **~haus** *n* engine room; **2les·bar** *adj.* machine-readable; **~mei·ster** *m* machine minder; *thea.* stage machinist; *typ.* pressman; **~öl** *n* machine (*or* lubricating) oil; **~park** *m coll.* machinery; **~pi,sto·le** *f* submachine gun; **~raum** *m* engine room; **~scha·den** *m* mechanical breakdown; *mot.*, ✈ engine trouble; **~schlos·ser** *m* engine (*or* machine) fitter

ma'schi·nen·schrei·ben I. *v/i.* → ***maschineschreiben***; **II. 2** *n* (-s; *no pl.*) typewriting, typing; typing ability, typewriting skills *pl.*; **Ma'schi·nen·schrift** *f* typescript; ***in ~*** typewritten; **ma'schi·nen·schrift·lich I.** *adj.* typewritten; **II.** *adv.* in typewritten form, in typescript

Ma'schi·nen·zeit·al·ter *n* machine age

Ma·schi·ne·rie [maʃinə'riː] *f* (-; -n) machinery (*a. fig.*)

ma'schi·ne·schrei·ben *v/i.* (schrieb Maschine, maschinegeschrieben, h) type; ***gut*** (***schlecht***) **~** be a good (bad, F hopeless) typist, be good (not very good, F hopeless) at typing

Ma·schi·nist [maʃi'nɪst] *m* (-en; -en) machine operator; 🚂 engine driver, *Am.* engineer

Ma·ser ['maːzɐ] *f* (-; -n) vein; ***feine ~n*** fine grain; **ma·se·rig** ['maːzərɪç] *adj.* veined, streaked; **'ma·sern** *v/t.* (h) grain

Ma·sern ['maːzɐn] *pl.* ⚕ measles *sg.*

Ma·se·rung ['maːzərʊŋ] *f* (-; -en) grain; veins *pl.*

Mas·ke ['maskə] *f* (-; -n) mask (*a.* ⚕, *phot.*, *computer*, *sport and fig.*); *thea.* makeup; *fig.* guise; *thea.* ***in ~*** (fully) made up; *fig.* ***ihr Gesicht wurde zur ~*** her face turned to stone; ***in der ~*** *gen.* under the guise of; ***die ~ fallen lassen*** show one's true face, drop one's mask; ***j-m die ~ vom Gesicht reißen*** unmask s.o.; F *hum.* ***s-e ~ aufsetzen*** F put one's face (*or* war paint) on

'Mas·ken|ball *m* fancy-dress ball; **~bild·ner** *m* makeup artist

'mas·ken·haft *adj.* mask-like; expressionless

'Mas·ken|spiel *n thea.* masque; **~zug** *m* masked procession

Mas·ke·ra·de [maskə'raːdə] *f* (-; -n) **1.** costume; **2.** masquerade, masked ball; **3.** *fig.* masquerade; ***~ sein*** *a.* be a preten|ce (*Am.* -se)

mas·kie·ren [mas'kiːrən] (h) **I.** *v/t.* a) dress up, b) disguise, conceal; **II.** *v/refl.*: ***sich ~*** a) dress up, b) disguise o.s.; put on a mask; **Mas'kie·rung** *f* (-; -en) **1.** dressing up; **2.** disguise; mask

Mas·kott·chen [mas'kɔtçən] *n* (-s; -) mascot

mas·ku·lin [masku'liːn] *adj.*, **Mas·ku·li·num** ['maskuliːnʊm] *n ling.* masculine

Ma·so·chis·mus [mazɔ'xɪsmʊs] *m* (-; *no pl.*) masochism; **Ma·so·chist** [mazɔ'xɪst] *m* (-en; -en) masochist; **ma·so·chi·stisch** [mazɔ'xɪstɪʃ] *adj.* masochistic(ally *adv.*)

maß [maːs] *pret. of* ***messen***

Maß¹ [maːs] *n* (-es; -e) **1.** measure, unit of measurement; *fig.* ***das ~ ist voll*** enough is enough, I've had just about all I can take; ***um das ~ vollzumachen*** to cap it all; ***das ~ aller Dinge*** *lit.* the measure of all things; ***das ~ überschreiten*** overstep (*or* overshoot) the mark; → ***zweierlei***; **2.** extent, degree; ***ein gewisses ~*** (***an*** *dat.*) a certain degree of, some; ***ein gerüttelt ~*** (***an*** *dat.*) a fair bit of; ***ein hohes ~*** (***an*** *dat.*) a high degree (*or* measure) of; ***in hohem ~e*** to a great (*or* high) degree, highly; ***in höchstem ~e*** to an extremely high degree, extremely; ***in gleichem ~e*** to the same extent; ***in zunehmendem ~e*** increasingly, to an increasing extent; ***in dem ~e, daß*** to such an extent that; ***in dem ~e, wie sich die Lage verschlechtert, steigt die Zahl der Flüchtlinge*** as the situation worsens, the number of refugees rises accordingly; ***in besonderem ~e*** especially; ***in geringem ~e*** to a minimal extent, minimally; ***in beschränktem ~e*** to a limited extent (*or* degree); ***in reichem ~e*** in plenty; ***Obst war in reichem ~e vorhanden*** there was an abundance of fruit, there was fruit in plenty; ***et. auf ein vernünftiges ~ reduzieren*** bring s.th. down to an acceptable level; ***über alle ~en*** exceedingly, ... beyond all measure; **3.** moderation; ***weder ~ noch Ziel kennen, ohne ~ und Ziel sein*** know no bounds; ***in ~en trinken*** *etc.* drink *etc.* in moderation (*or* moderately); **4.** *pl. s.o.'s* measurements; *a.* dimensions *of a room etc.*; ***sich ~ nehmen lassen*** have one's measurements taken; ***j-m ~ nehmen*** take s.o.'s measurements; ***et. nach ~ anfertigen lassen*** have s.th. custom-built (*or* custom-made)

Maß² *f* (-; -) litre (*Am.* liter) of beer

Mas·sa·ge [ma'saːʒə] *f* (-; -n) massage; **~pra·xis** *f* physiotherapy practice; **~sa,lon** *m a. euphem.* massage parlo(u)r; **~stab** *m* vibrator

Mas·sa·ker [ma'saːkɐ] *n* (-s; -) massacre, bloodbath; ***ein ~ anrichten*** carry out a massacre (*or* bloodbath)

mas·sa·krie·ren [masa'kriːrən] *v/t.* (h) massacre, slaughter; F *fig.* ***den massakrier' ich, wenn ich ihn sehe*** F I'm going to tear him apart when I see him

'Maß|an·fer·ti·gung *f* made-to-measure (*or* tailor-made, custom-made) item (*or* shirt, shoes *etc.*); specially-made (*or* custom-made, custom-built) table (*or* bookcase *etc.*); **~an·zug** *m* tailor-made (*or* custom-made) suit; **~ar·beit** *fig. f* precision work (*or* job)

Mas·se ['masə] *f* (-; -n) **1.** mass (*a. phys.*); **2.** F masses (*or* loads, heaps, piles) *pl.* of; ***in ~n*** in masses; ***... in ~n*** masses (*or* loads, heaps, piles) of ...; ***die ~ bringt's*** it's quantity that counts; **3.** bulk, majority; **4.** crowd; ***die breite ~*** the masses; **5.** ⚡ earth, *Am.* ground; ***et. an ~ legen*** earth (*Am.* ground) s.th.; **6.** mixture, compound; **7.** → ***Erbmasse, Konkursmasse***; → ***mangels***

'Maß·ein·heit *f* measure, unit of measurement

'Mas·se·ka·bel *n* earth (*Am.* ground) cable

Mas·sel ['masəl] F *m* (-s; *no pl.*) (good) luck; (***e-n***) **~** ***haben*** be lucky; ***da hast du aber*** (***e-n***) ***~ gehabt*** *a.* F talk about lucky

'Mas·sen|ab·fer·ti·gung *f usu. contp.* mass processing; **~ab·füt·te·rung** *f contp.* feeding of the masses (F of the five thousand); **~ab·satz** *m* bulk selling; **~an·drang** *m* **1.** rush (of people *or* visitors *etc.*); **2.** huge crowd, crowds *pl.* of people; **~ar·beits·lo·sig·keit** *f* mass unemployment; **~ar,ti·kel** *m* ✝ mass-produced article; **~auf·ge·bot** *n* large (*or* huge) force (***an*** *dat.* of); ⚔ levy en masse; ***~ an Polizisten*** *a.* large police presence; **~auf·la·ge** *f newspaper*: mass circulation; *book*: large circulation

'Mas·sen·be·darf *m* mass demand; **'Mas·sen·be·darfs·gü·ter** *pl.* mass market commodities

'Mas·sen|be·för·de·rung *f* mass transportation; **~be·we·gung** *f* mass movement; **~blatt** *n* mass-circulation paper; **~de·mon·stra·ti,on** *f* mass demonstration; **~ent·las·sun·gen** *pl.* mass dismissals (*or* redundancies); **~er·zeu·gung** *f*, **~fa·bri·ka·ti,on** *f*, **~fer·ti·gung** *f* → ***Massenproduktion***; **~flucht** *f* mass exodus; stampede; **~ge·sell·schaft** *f* mass society; **~grab** *n* mass grave

'Mas·sen·gü·ter *pl.* bulk goods; **~trans,port** *m* bulk haulage

'mas·sen·haft I. *adj.*: ***~es Auftreten von ...*** ... in masses, vast numbers of ...; ***es gab ~e Entlassungen*** there were an enormous number of dismissals; **II.** *adv.* ... in masses; ***et. ~ haben*** F have masses (*or* heaps, piles) of s.th.; ***es gibt ~ ...*** there are masses of ...; ***~ töten*** kill *cows etc.* in their hundreds (*or* thousands); ***es entstanden ~ neue Siedlungen*** vast numbers of settlements arose

'Mas·sen|,hin·rich·tun·gen *pl.* mass executions; **~hy·ste,rie** *f* mass hysteria; **~ka·ram·bo,la·ge** *f mot.* pileup, multiple crash; ***~ auf der Autobahn*** motorway pileup; **~kund·ge·bung** *f* mass demonstration, rally; **~me·di·um** *n* mass media (*a. pl.*); **~mord** *m* mass murder; **~mör·der** *m* mass murderer; **~par,tei** *f* party of the masses; **~pro·duk·ti,on** *f* mass production; **~psy·cho·lo,gie** *f* crowd psychology; **~psy,cho·se** *f* mass hysteria; **~quar,tier** *n a. pl.* mass accommodation; **~schlä·ge,rei** *f* big punch-up, riot; **~sport** *m* popular (*or* mass-participant) sport; **~ster·ben** *n* widespread deaths *pl.* (*zo.* dying-off, *fig.* closures *pl. of theatres etc.*); **~sze·ne** *f film etc.*: crowd scene; **~tier·hal·tung** *f* large-scale animal husbandry; **~tou,ris·mus** *m* mass tourism; **~ver·an·stal·tung** *f* popular event; ***musikalische ~*** mammoth concert; **~ver·haf·tun·gen** *pl.* mass arrests; **~ver·kehrs·mit·tel** *n* means (*sg.*) of mass transportation; **~ver·nich·tung** *f* mass extermination

'Mas·sen·ver·nich·tungs|la·ger *n* extermination camp; **~mit·tel** *pl.* weapons of mass destruction

'Mas·sen|ver·samm·lung *f* mass meeting; **~wahn** *m* mass hysteria; **~wa·re** *f* mass-produced goods (*or* articles) *pl.*

'mas·sen·wei·se *adj. and adv.* → ***massenhaft***

'mas·sen·wirk·sam *adj.*: ***~ sein*** have mass appeal

'Mas·sen|wir·kung *f* mass appeal;

~zu,sam·men·stoß *m* → ***Massenkarambolage***
Mas·seur [ma'søːʀ] *m* (-s; -e [-rə]), **Mas·seu·rin** [ma'søːrɪn] *f* (-; -nen) masseur; **Mas·seu·se** [ma'søːzə] *f* (-; -n) *euphem.* masseuse
'Maß·ga·be *f*: ***nach ~*** *gen.* according to, in accordance with; ***mit der ~, daß*** provided that; **'maß·ge·bend** *adj.* important; definitive, authoritative, *a.* standard *work etc.*; influential *personality etc.*; ***die ~en Personen auf diesem Gebiet*** the leading authorities in this field; ***das ist nicht ~*** that is no criterion
'maß·geb·lich [-geːplɪç] **I.** *adj.* a) decisive, b) relevant, competent; ✝ ***~e Beteiligung*** controlling interest; **II.** *adv.*: ***~ beteiligt sein*** play a decisive role (***an*** *dat.* in); ***es wird ~ davon abhängen, ob*** it will largely depend on whether
'maß·ge·recht *adj.* **1.** true to size; **2.** true to scale; ***~es Modell*** (accurate) scale model
'maß·ge·schnei·dert *adj.* made-to-measure, tailor-made (*a. fig.*), custom-made
'maß·hal·ten I. *v/i.* (*irr., sep.*, h, → ***halten***) be moderate; ***im Essen*** (***Trinken*** *etc.*) ~ be a moderate eater (drinker *etc.*), eat (drink *etc.*) in moderation; **II.** ♀ *n* (-s; *no pl.*) moderation, restraint; temperance
mas·sie·ren¹ [ma'siːrən] *v/t.* (h) massage
mas'sie·ren² *v/t. and v/refl.* (***sich ~***) (h) mass, concentrate; **Mas'sie·rung** *f* (-; -en) ⚔ massing *of troops*, buildup *of weapons*
mas·sig ['masɪç] **I.** *adj.* massive; bulky; **II.** F *adv.* F masses (*or* heaps) of
mä·ßig ['mɛːsɪç] **I.** *adj.* a) moderate, b) temperate, c) F (fair to) middling, d) mediocre, (rather) poor; **II.** *adv.*: ***~ trinken*** *etc.* drink *etc.* moderately (*or* in moderation); **mä·ßi·gen** ['mɛːsɪgən] (h) **I.** *v/t.* moderate *demands, opinion etc.*; curb *one's anger, hatred etc.*; tone down *criticism etc.*; ***das Tempo ~*** slow down, reduce (one's) speed; **II.** *v/refl.*: ***sich ~*** restrain (*or* control) o.s.; ***sich beim Essen*** *etc.* ~ cut down on food *etc.*; *iro.* ***könntest du dich etwas ~?*** could you exercise a bit of self-control (*or* restraint)?; → ***gemäßigt***
'Mas·sig·keit *f* (-; *no pl.*) massiveness; bulkiness
Mä·ßig·keit ['mɛːsɪçkaɪt] *f* (-; *no pl.*) **1.** moderation; **2.** mediocrity
Mä·ßi·gung ['mɛːsɪgʊŋ] *f* (-; *no pl.*) moderation, restraint
mas·siv [ma'siːf] *adj.* **1.** solid *wood etc.*; **2.** solidly built; massive, heavy; **3.** *fig.* heavy, massive *resistance, attack etc.*; severe, vehement *criticism etc.*; grave *insults, threats etc.*; excessive *demands etc.*; F ***~ werden*** F cut up rough; ***es kam zu e-m ~en Einsatz der Polizei*** the police arrived in force
Mas'siv *n* (-s; -e [-və]) *geol.* massif; **~bau** *m* (-[e]s; -ten) **1.** massive structure; **2.** *no pl.* → **~bau·wei·se** *f* massive construction
Mas·si·vi·tät [masivi'tɛːt] *f* (-; *no pl.*) **1.** solidity, solid nature; **2.** *fig.* massiveness; severity; vehemence; gravity
'Maß|klei·dung *f*, **~kon·fek·ti,on** *f* made-to-measure (*or* tailor-made, custom-made) clothes *pl.*
'Maß·krug *m* litre (*Am.* liter) beer mug; stein
'maß·los I. *adj.* **1.** immoderate; intemperate; boundless, unrestrained *emotions etc.*; **2.** excessive; F ***das ist ja e-e ~e Frechheit!*** F what an absolute cheek!; **II.** *adv.* **3.** a) immoderately, b) excessively, to excess, c) without restraint; **4.** extremely, terribly; ***~ empört*** (***erregt***) boiling *or* seething with indignation (rage); ***~ übertrieben*** grossly exaggerated; ***~ enttäuscht*** deeply disappointed; ***sich ~ ärgern*** be (*or* get) really annoyed; ***ich habe mich ~ geärgert*** *a.* F I could have kicked myself
'Maß·lo·sig·keit *f* (-; *no pl.*) **1.** immoderateness, lack of moderation; intemperance; lack of restraint; boundlessness; **2.** excessiveness
Maß·nah·me ['maːsnaːmə] *f* (-; -n) measure, step; ***~n ergreifen*** *or* ***treffen gegen*** *acc.* take measures (*or* steps, action) against; **'Maß·nah·men·ka·ta,log** *m* package of measures
'Maß·re·gel *f* rule, guideline; ***strenge ~n treffen*** establish strict guidelines
'maß·re·geln *v/t.* (h) reprimand, take to task (***wegen*** *gen.* for, about); punish, discipline; *sport*: penalize; **'Maß·re·ge·lung** *f* (-; -en) reprimand; disciplinary action; *sport*: penalty
'Maß·schnei·der *m* bespoke (*Am.* custom) tailor
'Maß·stab *m* **1.** standard; yardstick, criterion, benchmark; ***e-n ~ setzen*** set a (*or* the) standard; ***e-n strengen ~ anlegen*** apply a strict standard (***an*** *acc.* to); ***j-n*** (***et.***) ***als ~ nehmen*** take s.o. (s.th.) as an example, model o.s. on s.o. (s.th.); ***das ist*** (***für mich***) ***kein ~*** that's no criterion (as far as I'm concerned); **2.** *geogr. etc.* scale; ***im ~ 1:5*** on a scale of 1:5; ***in großem*** (***kleinem***) ***~*** large-(small-)scale; ***in verkleinertem*** (***vergrößertem***) ***~ zeichnen*** draw to (*or* on) a reduced (an enlarged) scale; **'maß·stab·ge·recht, 'maß·stab·ge·treu I.** *adj.* (true) to scale; **II.** *adv.*: ***~ vergrößern*** (***verkleinern***) scale up (down)
'maß·voll I. *adj.* moderate, restrained; reasonable; **II.** *adv.* moderately, with (*or* in) moderation
Mast¹ [mast] *m* (-[e]s; -e[n]) ⚓ mast; pole; ⚡ pylon
Mast² *f* (-; *no pl.*) **1.** fattening; **2.** (fattening) feed
'Mast·baum *m* → ***Mast¹***
'Mast·darm *m anat.* rectum
Mast·ek·to·mie [mastɛkto'miː] *f* (-; -n) ⚕ mastectomy
mä·sten ['mɛstən] (h) **I.** *v/t.* fatten; **II.** *v/refl.*: ***sich ~*** gorge o.s., F stuff o.s.
'Mast|en·te *f* **1.** fattened duck; **2.** fattening (*or* feeder) duck; **~fut·ter** *n* (fattening) feed
'Mast·korb *m* ⚓ crow's nest
'Mast|och·se *m* **1.** fattened ox; **2.** fattening (*or* feeder) ox; **~rind** *n* beef cow; **~schwein** *n* **1.** fattened pig, porker; **2.** fattening (*or* feeder) pig
'Mast·spit·ze *f* masthead
Mä·stung ['mɛstʊŋ] *f* (-; *no pl.*) fattening (process)
Ma·stur·ba·ti·on [masturba'tsi̯oːn] *f* (-; -en) masturbation; **ma·stur·bie·ren** [mastʊr'biːrən] *v/i. and v/t.* (h) masturbate
'Mast·ver·stär·ker *m radio, TV*: masthead amplifier
'Mast·vieh *n* fat stock
Ma·ta·dor [mata'doːʀ] *m* (-s; -e [-rə]) **1.** matador; **2.** *fig.* hero, star
Match [mɛtʃ] *n* (-[e]s; -s, -e) match, game; **~ball** *m tennis*: match point; **~beu·tel** *m*, **~sack** *m* duffle (*or* duffel) bag
Ma·te·ri·al [mate'ri̯aːl] *n* (-s; -alien [-li̯ən]) material; *coll.* materials *pl.*; ⚔ materiel; **~auf·wand** *m* cost of materials; **~aus·ga·be** *f* **1.** stores *pl.*; **2.** issue of stores; **~be·darf** *m* material requirements *pl.*; **~be·schaf·fung** *f* obtaining (*or* getting hold of) materials; *w.s.* availability of materials; **~er·mü·dung** *f* material fatigue; **~feh·ler** *m* material fault
ma·te·ria·li·sie·ren [materi̯ali'ziːrən] *v/t.* (h) materialize
Ma·te·ria·lis·mus [materi̯a'lɪsmʊs] *m* (-; *no pl.*) materialism; **Ma·te·ria·list** [materi̯a'lɪst] *m* (-en; -en) materialist; **ma·te·ria·li·stisch** [materi̯a'lɪstɪʃ] *adj.* materialist(ic); ***~es Weltbild*** materialistic outlook
Ma·te·ri'al|knapp·heit *f* shortage (*or* scarcity) of materials; ***es herrscht ~*** materials are in short supply; **~ko·sten** *pl.* cost *sg.* of materials, material costs; **~krieg** *m* war of materiel; **~la·ger** *n* stores *pl.*; **~prü·fung** *f* material test(ing); **~samm·lung** *f* gathering of material (*or* information); **~scha·den** *m* material defect; **~wert** *m* material value
Ma·te·rie [ma'teːri̯ə] *f* (-; -n) **1.** *no pl. phys., phls.* matter; **2.** subject (matter); ***die ~ beherrschen*** F know one's stuff; **ma·te·ri·ell** [mate'ri̯ɛl] **I.** *adj.* material; *esp. contp.* materialistic; **II.** *adv.*: ***~ eingestellt*** materially-minded
Ma·the ['matə] F *f* (-; *no pl.*) maths *pl.*, *Am.* math; **Ma·the·ma·tik** [matema'tiːk] *f* (-; *no pl.*) mathematics *pl.*, maths *pl.*, *Am.* math; **Ma·the·ma·ti·ker** [mate'maːtikʀ] *m* (-s; -) mathematician; **ma·the·ma·tisch** [mate'maːtɪʃ] *adj.* mathematical
Ma·ti·nee [mati'neː] *f* (-; -n) *thea.* morning performance, matinee (performance)
Mat·jes·he·ring ['matjəs-] *m* soused herring
Ma·trat·ze [ma'tratsə] *f* (-; -n) mattress
Mä·tres·se [mɛ'trɛsə] *f* (-; -n) mistress
ma·tri·ar·cha·lisch [matriar'çaːlɪʃ] *adj.* matriarchal; **Ma·tri·ar·chat** [matriar'çaːt] *n* (-[e]s; -e) matriarchy
Ma·tri·kel [ma'triːkəl] *f* (-; -n) register
Ma·trix ['maːtrɪks] *f* (-; Matrizes [ma'triːtseːs] *and* Matrizen [ma'triːtsən]) *biol., ling.,* ⚡ matrix; **~drucker** *m typ.* matrix printer
Ma·tri·ze [ma'triːtsə] *f* (-; -n) **1.** ⚙, *typ.* matrix; **2.** stencil; ***et. auf ~ schreiben*** stencil s.th.
Ma·tro·ne [ma'troːnə] *f* (-; -n) matron; **ma'tro·nen·haft** *adj.* matronly
Ma·tro·se [ma'troːzə] *m* (-n; -n) sailor, seaman; ⚔ ordinary sailor, *Am.* seaman recruit
Ma'tro·sen|an·zug *m* sailor suit; **~lied** *n* (sea) shanty
Matsch [matʃ] *m* (-es; -e) **1.** F mush; **2.** mud; slush; **mat·schig** ['matʃɪç] *adj.* **1.** *gastr.* mushy; **2.** muddy; slushy; **'Matsch·wet·ter** *n* mucky weather
matt [mat] **I.** *adj.* **1.** dull; matt *paper, paint etc.*; frosted *glass*; pearl, opal *bulb*; dim *light*; **2.** exhausted, worn out; feeble, weak (*a. fig.*); *fig.* faint *voice, smile etc.*; ***~ vor Hunger*** faint (*or* weak) with hunger; **3.** *fig.* dull; colo(u)rless, insipid; feeble, lame *joke, excuse etc.*; **4.** ✝ dull, slack; **5.**

chess: checkmate; ***j-n ~ setzen*** checkmate s.o.; **II.** ♀ *n* (-s; -s) *chess*: checkmate
Mat·te¹ ['matə] *f* (-; -n) mat; ***j-n auf die ~ legen*** *sport*: floor s.o.
'Mat·te² *f* (-; -n) (alpine) meadow
'Matt|glanz *m* matt finish; **~glas** *n* ground (*or* frosted) glass; **~gold** *n* dead gold
Mat·thäi [ma'tɛːi]: F ***bei ihm ist ~ am letzten*** a) F he's done for, b) F he's (stony) broke
Mat·thä·us·evan·ge·li·um [ma'tɛːʊs-] *n*: ***das ~*** (the Gospel of) St Matthew, St Matthew's Gospel
'Matt·heit *f* (-; *no pl.*) **1.** dullness; dimness; **2.** lack of energy, tiredness; exhaustion
mat·tie·ren [ma'tiːrən] *v/t.* (h) matt; frost *glass*; **Mat'tie·rung** *f* (-; *no pl.*) **1.** matting; frosting; **2.** matt finish; frosting
Mat·tig·keit ['matɪçkaɪt] *f* (-; *no pl.*) lack of energy, tiredness; exhaustion
'Matt·schei·be *f* **1.** F tube, *esp. Brit.* F telly, box; ***vor der ~ sitzen*** *a.* be glued to the tube *etc.*; **2.** *phot.* focus(s)ing screen; **3.** F *fig.* ***ich hab' ~*** F I'm not twigging, I've got a mental block
'matt·schlei·fen *v/t.* (*irr.*, *sep.*, h, → ***schleifen***) dull-grind; frost *glass*
'matt·schwarz *adj.*, **'Matt·schwarz** *n* matt black
'matt·ver·gol·det *adj.* dead-gilt
'matt·weiß *adj.*, **'Matt·weiß** *n* matt white
Ma·tu·ra [ma'tuːra] *Austrian f* (-; *no pl.*) → ***Abitur***
Ma·tu·tin [matu'tiːn] *f* (-; -e[n]) *eccl.* matins *pl.*
Matz [mats] F *m* (-es; -e, Mätze ['mɛtsə]): ***kleiner ~*** little lad (*or* man)
Mätz·chen ['mɛtsçən] F *pl.* **1.** nonsense *sg.*; ***~ machen*** fool (*or* mess) around; ***mach bloß keine ~!*** don't do anything stupid; **2.** tricks; ***mach keine ~!*** none of your tricks!
Mat·ze ['matsə] *f* (-; -n), **Mat·zen** ['matsən] *m* (-s; -) matzo
mau [maʊ] F *adj. and adv.* bad(ly); ***mir ist ~*** I feel funny (*or* queasy); ***die Wirtschaft ist ~*** the economy is in a bad way
Mau·er ['maʊɐ] *f* (-; -n) wall (*a. fig. and sport*); *hist.* ***die (Berliner) ~*** the (Berlin) Wall; **~bau** *m hist.* building of the Berlin Wall; **~blüm·chen** F *fig. n* wallflower
mau·ern ['maʊɐn] *v/i.* (h) **1.** build a wall *etc.*; **2.** *sport*: play defensively; *card game*: hold back; **3.** *fig.* stonewall, stall
'Mau·er|schwal·be *f* swift; **~schwamm** *m* dry rot; **~seg·ler** *m* swift; **~stein** *m* brick; **~vor·sprung** *m* wall projection; **~werk** *n* masonry; brickwork; **~zie·gel** *m* brick
Maul [maʊl] *n* (-[e]s; Mäuler ['mɔʏlɐ]) **1.** *zo.* mouth; jaws *pl.*; muzzle, snout; **2.** *sl.* trap, gob; ***ein großes ~ haben*** have a big mouth, be a big-mouth; ***ein böses (loses) ~ haben*** have a wicked (loose) tongue; ***das ~ (zu weit) aufreißen*** F shoot one's mouth off; ***das ~ halten*** keep one's mouth shut; ***halt's ~!*** F shut up!; ***sich das ~ zerreißen*** gossip (***über*** *acc.* about); ***darüber werden sie sich die Mäuler zerreißen*** that'll give them something to gossip about, that'll have plenty of tongues wagging; ***j-m das ~ stopfen*** F shut s.o. up; ***er hat sechs Mäuler zu stopfen*** he's got six hungry mouths to feed; ***j-m ums ~ gehen*** F soft-soap s.o.; ***dem Volk aufs ~ schauen*** listen to what people really say (*or* think)
'Maul·af·fen F *pl.*: ***~ feilhalten*** stand around gaping
'Maul·beer·baum *m* mulberry tree; **'Maul·bee·re** *f* mulberry
mau·len ['maʊlən] F *v/i.* (h) moan, F gripe
'Maul·esel *m* mule
'maul·faul F *adj.* too lazy to talk; uncommunicative; ***~e Person*** F clam
'Maul|held F *m* F big-mouth; ***er ist ein ~*** *a.* it's all talk with him; **~korb** *m* muzzle; ***e-m Hund*** (*fig.* ***j-m***) ***e-n ~ anlegen*** muzzle a dog (s.o.); **~sper·re** *f* lock-jaw; **~tier** *n* mule; **~trom·mel** *f* ♪ Jew's harp
'Maul-und-'Klau·en·seu·che *f* foot-and-mouth disease
Maul·wurf ['maʊlvʊrf] *m* (-[e]s; -würfe [-vʏrfə]) mole; **'Maul·wurfs·hü·gel** *m* molehill
maun·zen ['maʊntsən] *v/i.* (h) miaow
Mau·re ['maʊrə] *m* (-n; -n) Moor
Mau·rer ['maʊrɐ] *m* (-s; -) bricklayer, F brickie; **~ar·beit** *f* bricklaying; **~ge·sel·le** *m* journeyman bricklayer; **~hand·werk** *n* bricklaying; **~kel·le** *f* trowel; **~mei·ster** *m* master bricklayer
mau·risch ['maʊrɪʃ] *adj.* Moorish
Maus [maʊs] *f* (-; Mäuse ['mɔʏzə]) **1.** *a. computer*: mouse (*pl.* mice); *hum.* ***weiße ~*** traffic policeman; ***weiße Mäuse sehen*** see pink elephants; F ***graue ~*** nondescript person; F ***da beißt die ~ keinen Faden ab*** there's no way round it, that's the way things are; → ***Katz, Katze***; **2.** F *fig. pl.* F lolly, *sl.* brass, bread
mau·scheln ['maʊʃəln] *v/i.* (h) **1.** fiddle; cheat; **2.** mumble
Mäus·chen ['mɔʏsçən] *n* (-s; -) **1.** *dim. of Maus*: F ***da möchte ich ~ sein*** I'd like to be a fly on the wall; **2.** F love, pet, *Am.* honey, F hon; **'mäus·chen'still** *adj.* (as) quiet as a mouse; ***es war ~*** you couldn't hear a sound
Mäu·se·bus·sard ['mɔʏzə-] *m* (common) buzzard
Mau·se·fal·le ['maʊzə-] *f* mousetrap; *fig.* death-trap
Mäu·se|fang ['mɔʏzə-] *m* mousehunting; ***auf ~ sein*** be mousehunting, be running after mice; **~fraß** *m* damage (done) by mice; **~gift** *n* mouse poison
Mau·se·loch ['maʊzə-] *n* mousehole; *fig.* ***am liebsten hätte ich mich in ein ~ verkrochen*** I just wished the ground would open up and swallow me
Mäu·se·mel·ken ['mɔʏzə-] *n*: F ***es ist ja zum ~!*** F it's enough to drive you spare
mau·sen ['maʊzən] F *v/t.* (h) F pinch
Mau·ser ['maʊzɐ] *f* (-; *no pl.*) mo(u)lt, mo(u)lting period; ***in der ~ (sein*** be) mo(u)lting; **'mau·sern** (h) **I.** *v/i.* mo(u)lt; **II.** *v/refl.*: ***sich ~*** mo(u)lt; *fig.* shape up nicely; *fig.* ***sich ~ zu*** *dat.* turn out (*or* into), *esp. young girl*: blossom (out) into
mau·se'tot ['maʊzə-] F *adj.* F stone dead; (as) dead as a doornail
'maus·grau *adj.* mouse-colo(u)red
mau·sig ['maʊzɪç] F *adj.*: ***sich ~ machen*** F get fresh (*esp. Brit.* cheeky)
Mau·so·le·um [maʊzo'leːʊm] *n* (-s; -leen [-leːən]) mausoleum
Maut [maʊt] *f* (-; -en), **~ge·bühr** *f* toll
'maut·pflich·tig [-pflɪçtɪç] *adj.* toll *road etc.*
'Maut|stel·le *f* toll booth (*or* gate); **~stra·ße** *f* turnpike (road), toll road
ma·xi·mal [maksi'maːl] **I.** *adj.* maximum; **II.** *adv.* maximally, at (the) most; *reach, amount to etc.* a maximum of
Ma·xi'mal... *in cpds. usu.* maximum; **~be·trag** *m* maximum (amount); **~ge·schwin·dig·keit** *f* maximum (*or* top) speed; ***zulässige ~*** maximum allowed speed; **~stra·fe** *f* maximum penalty (*or* sentence)
Ma·xi·me [ma'ksiːmə] *f* (-; -n) maxim
ma·xi·mie·ren [maksi'miːrən] *v/t.* (h) maximize; **Ma·xi'mie·rung** *f* (-; *no pl.*) maximization; **Ma·xi·mum** ['maksimʊm] *n* (-s; -ma) maximum
Ma·xi-'Sin·gle ['maksi-] *f* maxi single
Ma·yon·nai·se [majɔ'nɛːzə] *f* (-; -n) mayonnaise, *Am. a.* F mayo
Mä·zen [mɛ'tseːn] *m* (-s; -e) patron
Mä·ze·na·ten·tum [mɛtse'naːtəntuːm] *n* (-s; *no pl.*) patronage
Me·cha·nik [me'çaːnɪk] *f* (-; -en) *phys.* mechanics *pl.*; ⚙ mechanism
Me·cha·ni·ker [me'çaːnikɐ] *m* (-s; -) mechanic
me·cha·nisch [me'çaːnɪʃ] **I.** *adj.* mechanical (*a. fig.*); *fig.* ***~es Auswendiglernen*** rote learning; **II.** *adv.* mechanically; *fig.* ***~ herunterleiern*** reel (*or* rattle) off (like an automaton)
me·cha·ni·sie·ren [meçani'ziːrən] *v/t.* (h) mechanize; **Me·cha·ni'sie·rung** *f* (-; -en) mechanization
Me·cha·nis·mus [meça'nɪsmʊs] *m* (-; -men) mechanism (*a. fig. and psych.*, *phls.*); *fig. pl. a.* workings
me·cha·ni·stisch [meça'nɪstɪʃ] *adj.* mechanistic(ally *adv.*)
Mecke·rei [mɛkə'raɪ] (*sep.* -k·k-) *f* (-; -en) grumbling, F grousing, griping
Mecke·rer ['mɛkərɐ] (*sep.* -k·k-) *m* (-s; -) grumbler
Mecker·ka·sten ['mɛkɐ-] (*sep.* -k·k-) *m* suggestion box
meckern ['mɛkɐn] (*sep.* -k·k-) *v/i.* (h) **1.** *goat*: bleat; **2.** *fig.* grumble, grouse, F gripe, bellyache
Mecki|fri,sur ['mɛki-] (*sep.* -k·k-) F *f*, **~schnitt** F *m* crew cut
Me·dail·le [me'daljə] *f* (-; -n) medal; → ***Kehrseite***; **Me'dail·len·ge·win·ner** *m* *sport*: medal(l)ist
me'dail·len·träch·tig *adj.*: ***~ sein*** be a medal hopeful (*or* certainty)
Me·dail·lon [medal'jõː] *n* (-s; -s) medallion (*a. art and gastr.*); locket
Me·diä·vist [medĭɛ'vɪst] *m* (-en; -en) medi(a)evalist, medi(a)eval scholar
Me·diä·vi·stik [medĭɛ'vɪstɪk] *f* (-; *no pl.*) medi(a)eval studies *pl.*
Me·di·en ['meːdĭən] *pl.* media; **~for·schung** *f* media research (*or* studies *pl.*); **~fürst** *m* media magnate; **~land·schaft** *f* media landscape; **~po·li,tik** *f* media politics *pl.*; **♀po,li·tisch** *adj.* media-political; **~rum·mel** *m*, **~spek,ta·kel** *n* media circus; **~ver·bund** *m* **1.** multimedia system; **2.** ***Unterricht im ~*** multimedia teaching; **~zen·trum** *n* multimedia information cent|re (*Am.* -er)
Me·di·ka·ment [medika'mɛnt] *n* (-[e]s; -e) drug, medicine, medicament; tablet, pill; *pl. a.* medication *sg.*; **Me·di·ka'men·ten,miß·brauch** *m* drug abuse
me·di·ka·men·tös [medikamɛn'tøːs] **I.** *adj.* medicinal; ***~e Behandlung*** medication, *a.* course of tablets (*or* drugs); **II.** *adv.*: ***~ behandeln*** treat with drugs (*or* tablets)
Me·di·ka·ti·on [medika'tsĭoːn] *f* (-; -en) medication

Me·dio·thek [medĭo'te:k] *f* (-; -en) media resource centre (*Am.* center)
Me·di·ta·ti·on [medita'tsĭo:n] *f* (-; -en) meditation; **Me·di·ta·ti'ons·übung** *f* meditation exercise; **me·di·ta·tiv** [medita'ti:f] **I.** *adj.* meditative; **II.** *adv.*: **~ *veranlagt sein*** be a meditative type
me·di·ter·ran [meditɛ'ra:n] *adj.* Mediterranean; ***~er Typ*** *a.* Latin (*or* Southern) type
me·di·tie·ren [medi'ti:rən] *v/i.* (h) meditate (***über*** *acc.* on)
Me·di·um ['me:dĭʊm] *n* (-s; Medien ['me:dĭən]) medium; (*mass*) media; → ***Medien***
Me·di·zin [medi'tsi:n] *f* (-; -en) **1.** *no pl.* medicine; ***Doktor der ~*** doctor of medicine (*abbr.* MD); **2.** → ***Medikament***
Me·di·zi·nal|as·si͵stent [meditsi'na:l-] *m* houseman, *Am.* intern; **~rat** *m* senior medical officer
Me·di'zin·ball *m* medicine ball
Me·di·zi·ner [medi'tsi:nɐ] *m* (-s; -) **1.** medical student, F medic; **2.** doctor, physician, F medic
Me·di'zin·ge·schich·te *f* history of medicine
me·di·zi·nisch [medi'tsi:nɪʃ] *adj.* a) medical, b) medicinal; **me·di'zi·nisch-'tech·ni·sche As·si͵sten·tin** *f* medical laboratory assistant
Me·di'zin|mann *m* (-[e]s; ⸚er) witchdoctor; medicine man; **~schränk·chen** *n* medicine cabinet; **~stu͵dent** *m* medical student, F medic; **~stu·di·um** *n* medical studies *pl.*; degree in medicine
Meer [me:ɐ] *n* (-[e]s; -e ['me:rə]) sea (*a. fig.*), ocean; ***das offene ~*** the high seas; ***am ~*** by the sea, *a. holiday* at the seaside; ***auf dem ~*** (out) at sea; ***auf dem offenen ~*** on the high seas; ***über dem ~*** above sea level; **~bu·sen** *m* gulf; **~en·ge** *f* strait(s *pl.*)
Mee·res|arm ['me:rəs-] *m* arm of the sea, inlet; **~berg·bau** *m* deep-sea mining; **~bio·lo͵gie** *f* marine biology; **~blick** *m* seaview; ***Zimmer mit ~*** room with (a) seaview; **~bo·den** *m* → ***Meeresgrund***; **~for·schung** *f* marine research, oceanography; **~früch·te** *pl.* seafood *sg.*; **~grund** *m* seafloor, bottom of the sea; **~kun·de** *f* oceanography; **~luft** *f* **1.** sea air; **2.** *meteor.* Atlantic wind(s *pl.*); **~ober·flä·che** *f* surface of the sea; **~schild·krö·te** *f* turtle; **~spie·gel** *m*: (***über dem ~*** above) sea level; **~strei·fen** *m* belt of sea; **~strö·mung** *f* ocean current; **~tie·fe** *f* depth (of the sea); **~ver·schmut·zung** *f* marine pollution
'Meer|gott *m* sea god; **≈grün** *adj.* sea-green; **~jung·frau** *f* mermaid; **~kat·ze** *zo. f* long-tailed monkey; **~ret·tich** *m* horseradish; **~salz** *n* sea salt
'Meer·schaum *m* (-[e]s; *no pl.*) meerschaum; **~pfei·fe** *f* meerschaum pipe
'Meer|schwein·chen *n* guinea pig; **~un·ge·heu·er** *n* sea monster, *lit.* monster of (*or* from) the deep; **~was·ser** *n* seawater
Mee·ting ['mi:tɪŋ] *n* (-s; -s) meeting; *sport: a.* meet
Me·ga'byte [mega-] *n* megabyte
Me·ga'hertz [mega-] *n* megahertz, megacycle
Me·ga·lith [mega'li:t] *m* (-s, -en; -e[n]) megalith; **~kul͵tur** *f* megalithic culture
me·ga·lo·man [megalo'ma:n] *adj.* megalomaniac; **Me·ga·lo·ma·nie** [megaloma'ni:] *f* (-; -n) megalomania
Me·ga·phon [mega'fo:n] *n* (-s; -e) megaphone
Me·gä·re [me'gɛ:rə] *f* (-; -n) **1.** *myth.* Megaera; **2.** *fig.* termagant, virago
Me·ga'ton·ne [mega-] *f* megaton
Me·ga'volt [mega-] *n* ⚡ megavolt
Me·ga'watt [mega-] *n* ⚡ megawatt
Mehl [me:l] *n* (-[e]s; -e) flour, meal; dust, powder; **meh·lig** ['me:lɪç] *adj.* mealy
'Mehl|kloß *m*, **~knö·del** *m* dumpling; **~sack** *m* a) flour bag, b) sack of flour; F ***wie ein ~*** like a sack of potatoes; **~schwit·ze** *f* roux; **~spei·se** *f* **1.** batter pudding; **2.** *Austrian* sweet, pudding, dessert; **~tau** *m* mildew, blight; **~wurm** *m* mealworm
mehr [me:ɐ] **I.** *indef. pron.* more; ***~ als genug*** more than enough; ***~ als 20 Leute*** more than (*or* over) 20 people; ***und dergleichen ~*** and the like; ***je ~ ..., desto besser*** the more ..., the better; **II.** *adj.* more; ***~ und ~*** (*or* ***immer ~***) ***Tiere*** more and more animals; **III.** *adv.* more; ***~ oder weniger*** more or less; ***der Hahn tropft immer ~*** the tap is dripping more and more; ***je ~ er sich isoliert, desto ~ leidet er*** the more he isolates himself, the more he suffers; ***um so ~*** all the more; ***nicht ~*** no longer, not any longer (*or* more); ***nie ~*** never again; ***ich habe keins*** (*or* ***keine*** *pl.*) ***~*** I haven't got any more; ***ich habe nichts ~*** I've got nothing left; ***was will er ~?*** what more does he want?; ***kein Wort ~*** not another word; ***das ist ein Grund ~ um zu*** *inf.* that's one more (*or* another) reason to *inf.*; ***ich kann nicht ~*** a) I couldn't eat another thing, b) F I've had it, c) F I can't take it any more; ***er ist ~ ein praktischer Mensch*** he's more of a practical man; → ***schmecken*** II; **IV.** **≈** *n*: ***ein ~ an Zeit*** (***Erfahrung*** *etc.*) more *or* extra time (experience *etc.*)
'Mehr·ar·beit *f* extra work; overtime
'mehr·ato·mig [-ato:mɪç] *adj.* polyatomic
'Mehr|auf·wand *m* extra *or* additional time (*or* cost *etc.*); **~aus·ga·ben** *pl.* additional *or* extra expenditure *sg.* (*or* expenses)
'mehr·bän·dig [-bɛndɪç] *adj.* multivolume ..., in several volumes
'Mehr|be·darf *m* extra (*or* increased) demand; **~be·la·stung** *f* additional (*or* extra) load (*fig.* burden); **~be·trag** *m* surplus; extra charge
'mehr·deu·tig [-dɔʏtɪç] *adj.* ambiguous; **'Mehr·deu·tig·keit** *f* (-; *no pl.*) ambiguity
'mehr·di·men·sio͵nal *adj.* multidimensional; **'Mehr·di·men·sio·na·li͵tät** *f* (-; *no pl.*) multidimensionality, multidimensional nature (*gen.* of)
'Mehr·ehe *f* polygamous marriage
'Mehr·ein·nah·men *pl.* surplus *sg.*, surplus earnings
meh·ren ['me:rən] (h) **I.** *v/t.* increase, augment, add to; **II.** *v/refl.*: ***sich ~*** increase, grow; be on the increase; ***die Fälle*** (***Gründe*** *etc.*) ***~ sich*** there are an increasing number of cases (reasons *etc.*); ***die Anzeichen ~ sich, daß*** there is mounting evidence that
meh·re·re ['me:rərə] **I.** *adj.* several; **II.** *indef. pron.* several; **~s** several (*or* a number of) things
meh·rer·lei ['me:rɐ'laɪ] **I.** *adj.* several *or* various (kinds of); **II.** *indef. pron.* several (*or* various) things
'Mehr|er·lös *m* additional revenue; **~er·trag** *m* additional (*or* surplus) yield
'mehr·fach **I.** *adj.* repeated; ***~e Verletzungen*** multiple injuries; ***in ~er Hinsicht*** in several respects; ***~er deutscher Meister*** several times German champion; ***ein ~er Millionär*** a multimillionaire, a millionaire several times over; **II.** *adv.* several times; repeatedly; ***~ vorbestraft sein*** have had several previous convictions; → ***ungesättigt***
'Mehr·fach... *in cpds. usu.* multiple
'mehr·fach·be·hin·dert *adj.* multiple-handicap ...; ***~ sein*** have more than one handicap, have several handicaps
'Mehr·fach|be·lich·tung *f phot.* multiple exposure; **~be·steue·rung** *f* multiple taxation
'Mehr·fa·che [-faxə] *n* (-n; *no pl.*): ***das ~*** *gen.*, ***ein ~s*** *gen.* several times the ...; ***das ~, ein ~s*** several times as much, several times over; ***ein ~s der Summe*** several times the amount
'Mehr·fach|spreng·kopf *m* multiple warhead; **~stecker** *m* multiple plug; **~ta͵lent** *n* multitalented person, man (*or* woman) of many talents
'Mehr·fa͵mi·li·en·haus *n house divided into flats*; apartment house; *adm.* multiple dwelling (unit)
'Mehr·far·ben·druck *m* (-[e]s; -e) **1.** multicolo(u)r print; **2.** *no pl.* multicolo(u)r printing; **'mehr·far·big** *adj.* multicolo(u)r ..., multicolo(u)red
'Mehr|ge·bot *n auction etc.*: higher bid; **~ge·päck** *n* excess luggage (*or* baggage)
'mehr·ge·schos·sig [-gəʃɔsɪç] *adj.* multistor(e)y ..., multistoried
'Mehr|ge·wicht *n* excess weight; **~ge·winn** *m* additional (*or* surplus) profits *pl.*
'mehr·glei·sig [-glaɪzɪç] *adj.* multitrack ..., multitracked
'mehr·glied·rig [-gli:drɪç] *adj.* **1.** ⚙ multisectional; **2.** ⩚ polynomial
Mehr·heit ['me:ɐhaɪt] *f* (-; -en) majority; mainstream; *parl.* ***mit absoluter*** (***einfacher, knapper, großer***) ***~*** by an absolute (a simple, narrow, large) majority; ***mit zehn Stimmen ~*** by a majority of ten; ***... wurde mit ~ beschlossen*** ... was carried by a majority of votes; ***die ~ auf sich vereinigen*** be supported by the majority of votes; → ***schweigend*** I
'mehr·heit·lich **I.** *adj.* majority *decision etc.*; **II.** *adv.* by a majority (of votes); ***~ getroffener Beschluß*** majority decision
'Mehr·heits|ak·tio͵när *m* majority shareholder; **~be·schluß** *m* majority decision; **~be·tei·li·gung** *f* ✝ majority holding; **~ent·schei·dung** *f* majority decision; **≈fä·hig** *adj.* capable of obtaining a majority; **~prin͵zip** *n* principle of majority rule; **~ver·hält·nis** *n* distribution of power; **~wahl·recht** *n*, **~wahl·sy͵stem** *n* majority vote system, F first past the post system
'mehr·jäh·rig [-jɛ:rɪç] *adj.* of (*or* lasting, stretching over) several years; several years' ..., several years of ...
'mehr·köp·fig [-kœpfɪç] *adj.*: ***~e Familie*** (***Delegation*** *etc.*) family (delegation *etc.*) consisting of several members
'Mehr|ko·sten *pl.* additional *or* extra cost *sg.* (*or* costs, expenses); extra charge *sg.*; **~lei·stung** *f* increased performance
'mehr·ma·lig [-ma:lɪç] *adj.* repeated; ***nach ~er Warnung*** (***~em Versuch*** *etc.*)

after several warnings (attempts *etc.*); **'mehr·mals** [-ma:ls] *adv.* several times
'mehr·mo·to·rig [-mo,to:rıç] *adj.* multi--engine ..., multi-engined
'Mehr·par,tei·en·sy,stem *n* multiparty system
'Mehr·per,so·nen·haus·halt *m* multi-person household
'Mehr·pha·sen·strom *m* ⚡ multiphase current; **'mehr·pha·sig** [-fa:zıç] *adj.* multiphase ...
'mehr·po·lig [-po:lıç] *adj.* multipole ...
'Mehr·preis *m* extra charge
'mehr·schich·tig [-ʃıçtıç] *adj. a. fig.* multilayered
'mehr·sei·tig [-zaıtıç] *adj.* **1.** polygonal; **2.** *pol.* multilateral *treaty etc.*
'mehr·sil·big [-zılbıç] *adj.* polysyllabic; ***ein ~es Wort*** *a.* a word consisting of several syllables
'mehr·spal·tig [-ʃpaltıç] *adj.* multicolumn ...; in several columns
'mehr·spra·chig [-ʃpra:xıç] **I.** *adj.* multilingual, polyglot; **II.** *adv.*: ***~ aufwachsen*** grow up speaking several languages
'mehr·spu·rig [-ʃpu:rıç] *adj.* **1.** multitrack *recording etc.*; **2.** *mot.* multilane ...
'Mehr·stär·ken·glas *n* varifocal lens
'mehr·stel·lig [-ʃtɛlıç] *adj.* multidigit
'mehr·stim·mig [-ʃtımıç] **I.** *adj.* for several voices, polyphonic; ***~er Gesang*** part singing; ***~es Lied*** part song; **II.** *adv.*: ***~ singen*** (***spielen***) sing (play) in harmony, harmonize; ***et. ~ setzen*** set s.th. for several parts, harmonize s.th.; **'Mehr·stim·mig·keit** *f* (-; *no pl.*) ♪ polyphony
'mehr·stöckig [-ʃtœkıç] (*sep.* -k·k-) *adj.* multistor(e)y ..., multistoried
'Mehr·stu·fen·ra,ke·te *f* multistage rocket
'mehr·stün·dig [-ʃtʏndıç] *adj.* of (*or* lasting) several hours; several hours' ..., several hours of ...
'mehr·tä·gig [-tɛ:gıç] *adj.* of (*or* lasting) several days; several days' ..., several days of ...
'mehr·tei·lig [-taılıç] *adj.* **1.** *apparatus etc.*: consisting of several parts; **2.** *film etc.* in several parts
Meh·rung ['me:rʊŋ] *f* (-; *no pl.*) increase, augmentation
'Mehr·ver·brauch *m* increased consumption
'Mehr·weg·fla·sche *f* returnable (*or* deposit) bottle
'Mehr·wert *m* ✝ increase in value; appreciation; *according to Marx*: surplus value; **~steu·er** *f* VAT, value-added tax, *esp. Am.* sales tax
'Mehr·zahl *f* (-; *no pl.*) **1.** majority; ***die ~ der Befragten*** the majority of those interviewed; **2.** *ling.* plural
'mehr·zei·lig [-tsaılıç] *adj.* (consisting) of several lines; ***e-e ~e Notiz*** *a.* a note several lines long
'mehr·zel·lig [-tsɛlıç] *adj.* multicellular, polycellular
'Mehr·zweck... *in cpds.* utility, multipurpose; **~fahr·zeug** *n* utility vehicle
mei·den ['maıdən] *v/t.* (mied, gemieden, h) avoid, steer clear of, shun *s.o.*
Mei·le ['maılə] *f* (-; -n) mile; **'Mei·len·stein** *m* milestone; *fig. a.* landmark; **'mei·len·weit I.** *adj.* miles and miles of; **II.** *adv.* for miles (and miles); ***~ entfernt von*** *a. fig.* miles (away) from; ***~ voneinander entfernt sein*** be miles (*fig. a.* worlds) apart

Mei·ler ['maılɐ] *m* (-s; -) **1.** charcoal pile; **2.** pile, nuclear reactor
mein [maın] **I.** *poss. pron.* **1.** *adj.* my; ***e-r ~er Wagen*** one of my cars; ***e-r ~er Freunde*** (***Kollegen***) a friend (colleague) of mine, one of my friends (colleagues); ***~e Damen und Herren*** ladies and gentlemen; **2.** *su.* mine; ***~er, ~e, ~(e)s, der*** (***die, das***) ***~(ig)e*** mine; ***ich habe das ~(ig)e getan*** I've done my share (F bit), I've done my best (*or* all I can); **II.** *pers. pron.* (*gen. of ich*) of me; ***gedenke ~(er)*** remember me
Mein·eid ['maın?aıt] *m* (-[e]s; -e) perjury; ***e-n ~ schwören*** swear a false oath
mein·ei·dig ['maın?aıdıç] *adj.* perjured; ***~ werden*** perjure o.s., ⚖ commit perjury
mei·nen ['maınən] (h) **I.** *v/t.* **1.** think, believe; ***was ~ Sie dazu?*** what do you think (*or* say)?; ***ich meine überhaupt nichts*** it's all the same to me; ***~ Sie*** (***wirklich***)***?*** do you (really) think so?; ***das will ich ~!*** I should (jolly well) hope so; **2.** mean; ***wie ~ Sie das?*** how do you mean?, what do you mean by that?; ***~ Sie das ernst?*** do you really mean it (*or* that)?; ***so war es nicht gemeint*** she *etc.* didn't mean it (like that); ***sie meint es gut*** she means well; ***es war gut gemeint*** it was well-meant; ***sie meint es gut mit dir*** she's only thinking of (*or* doing it for) your own good; ***er hat es nicht böse gemeint*** he meant no harm; **3.** mean; refer to, speak of; ***meinst du ihn?*** do you mean him?; ***er meinte mich*** he meant me, he was referring to me; **4.** say; ***was ~ Sie?*** what did you say?, I beg your pardon?; **II.** *v/i.*: ***wenn du meinst*** if you say so; ***wie Sie ~*** as you wish; ***ich meine ja nur*** it was just a thought
mei·ner ['maınɐ] → **mein** 2, II
mei·ner·seits ['maınɐzaıts] *adv.* for my part, as far as I'm (*or* I was) concerned; ***ich ~*** I for one; ***ganz ~*** the pleasure is (*or* has been) mine
mei·nes·glei·chen ['maınəs'glaıçən] *pron.* people like me; *iro.* my sort, the likes of me
mei·net·hal·ben ['maınət'halbən] *obs. adv.* → **'mei·net'we·gen** *adv.* **1.** a) because of me, on my account, b) because of me, for my sake; **2.** I don't mind, it's all right (*Am.* alright) by (*or* with) me, please yourself; ***~ kann er gehen*** he can go as far as I'm concerned, I don't mind if he goes; **3.** let's say, shall we say; **'mei·net'wil·len** *adv.*: (***um***) ***~*** for my sake; on my behalf
mei·ni·ge ['maınıgə] → ***mein*** 2
Mei·nung ['maınʊŋ] *f* (-; -en) opinion (***über*** *acc.* of, about, on); ***meiner ~ nach*** in my opinion; ***der ~ sein, daß*** think (believe, be of the opinion) that; ***ich bin auch der ~, daß*** I agree that, I also think (*or* believe) that; ***e-e ~ äußern*** express (*or* put forward) an opinion; ***derselben*** (***anderer***) ***~ sein*** agree (disagree); ***ganz meine(r) ~!*** I quite agree; ***s-e ~ ändern*** change one's views (*or* opinion), change one's mind; ***sich e-e ~ bilden*** form an opinion (***über*** *acc.* on, about); ***e-e hohe*** (***schlechte***) ***~ von j-m*** *or* ***et. haben*** have a high (low) opinion of s.o. *or* s.th.; ***ich habe keine ~ dazu*** I don't really have any thoughts on the matter; ***die allgemeine ~ geht dahin, daß*** opinion has it that, the conventional wisdom is that; ***j-m*** (***gehörig***) ***die ~ sagen*** give s.o. a piece of one's mind; → ***öffentlich*** I, ***vorgefaßt***
'Mei·nungs|än·de·rung *f* change of opinion; **~äu·ße·rung** *f* expression of one's opinion; ***freie ~*** freedom of expression; **~aus·tausch** *m* exchange of views (***über*** *acc.* on); **~be·fra·gung** *f* opinion poll
'mei·nungs·bil·dend I. *adj.* opinion--forming; **II.** *adv.*: ***~ wirken*** help to shape public opinion; **'Mei·nungs·bild·ner** *m* opinion-maker (*or* -former); **'Mei·nungs·bil·dung** *f* forming of an opinion; opinion-forming, shaping of public opinion
'Mei·nungs·for·scher *m* (opinion) pollster, poll-taker; **'Mei·nungs·for·schung** *f* (-; *no pl.*) opinion research; **'Mei·nungs·for·schungs·in·sti,tut** *n* polling institute
'Mei·nungs|frei·heit *f* (-; *no pl.*) freedom of speech; **~füh·rer** *m* opinion leader
'mei·nungs·los *adj.* devoid of (all) opinion; ***~ sein*** *a.* have no opinion(s); ***~e Masse*** unthinking masses
'Mei·nungs|ma·che F *f* manipulation of public opinion; **~ma·cher** *m* opinion--maker; **~streit** *m* controversy, dispute; conflict of views (*or* opinions); **~,um·fra·ge** *f* (public) opinion poll; **~,um·schwung** *m* shift in (*or* swing of) opinion; **~ver·schie·den·heit** *f* difference of opinion, disagreement
Mei·se ['maızə] *f* (-; -n) *zo.* tit(mouse); F ***du hast wohl 'ne ~?*** F you must be nuts
Mei·ßel ['maısəl] *m* (-s; -) chisel
'mei·ßeln *v/t. and v/i.* (h) chisel; carve
meist [maıst] **I.** *adj.* **1.** most of, (the) most; ***die ~en Leute*** most people; ***die ~e Zeit*** most of the time; ***er hat das ~e Geld*** he's got (the) most money; **II.** *indef. pron.* **2.** ***das ~e*** (the) most, most of it; ***wer das ~e schreibt*** whoever writes (the) most; ***das ~e*** (***davon***) ***habe ich mir gemerkt*** I can remember most of it; **3.** ***die ~en*** (the) most, most (of them); ***sie ist ruhiger als die ~en*** she's quieter than most; ***die ~en*** (***davon***) ***kenne ich*** I know most of them; ***wer die ~en hat, gewinnt*** whoever has the most, wins; **III.** *adv.* **4.** ***am ~en*** (*superlative of* **viel**) (the) most, (*superlative of* **sehr**) most (of all), the most, *w.s.* best (of all); ***er hat am ~en*** he's got (the) most; ***sie spricht am ~en*** she talks (the) most; ***das hat mich am ~en geärgert*** that annoyed me (the) most (*or* most of all); ***am ~en verkauft*** best-selling; **5.** → ***meistens, meistenteils***
'meist·be·gün·stigt *adj.* most-favo(u)red; ***~es Land*** most-favo(u)red nation, MFN; **'Meist·be·gün·sti·gung** *f* most-favo(u)red nation treatment
'Meist·be·gün·sti·gungs·klau·sel *f* most-favo(u)red nation clause
'meist·bie·tend I. *adj.*: ***~er Interessent*** highest bidder; **II.** *adv.*: ***~ verkaufen*** sell to the highest bidder; **'Meist·bie·ten·de** *m, f* (-n; -n) highest bidder
'meist·dis·ku,tiert *adj.*: ***~es Thema*** most popular topic of discussion, topic number one
mei·stens ['maıstəns] *adv.* a) usually, b) most of the time, c) → **mei·sten·teils** ['maıstəntaıls] *adv.* mostly, for the most part
Mei·ster ['maıstɐ] *m* (-s; -) **1.** master (craftsman); master baker *etc.*; ***s-n ~***

machen take one's master craftsman's diploma; **2.** master (*a. fig., iro.*); ***alter ~*** ♪, *art etc.*: past master; ***ein ~ im Lügen*** a master at (*or* in the art of) lying; ***Übung macht den ~*** practi|ce (*Am. a.* -se) makes perfect; *fig.* ***s-n ~ finden*** find (*or* meet) one's match; → ***Himmel*; 3.** *sport etc.*: champion(s *pl.*); **4.** foreman; **5.** *sl.* guv, chief, *Am.* Mac; **~brief** *m* master craftsman's diploma; **~de·tek,tiv** *m* master detective

'mei·ster·haft I. *adj.* masterly; **II.** *adv.* in masterly fashion, brilliantly; ***es ~ verstehen zu mogeln*** be an expert at cheating, be an expert cheat; **'Mei·ster·haf·tig·keit** *f* (-; *no pl.*) masterliness

'Mei·ster·hand *f* master's touch; ***ein Werk von ~*** the work of a master

Mei·ste·rin ['maɪstərɪn] *f* (-; -nen) qualified dressmaker (*or* interior decorator *etc.*); master crafts(wo)man

'Mei·ster|klas·se *f* master class; **~lei·stung** *f* superb feat (*or* performance); ***technische ~*** engineering feat; ***musikalische*** (***künstlerische***) **~** superb feat of musicianship (artistry)

mei·stern ['maɪstɐn] *v/t.* (h) master; control; overcome *difficulties etc.*; ***sein Leben ~*** cope with life

'Mei·ster·prü·fung *f examination for the master craftsman's diploma*

'Mei·ster·schaft *f* (-; -en) **1.** *no pl.* mastery; ***es*** (***bis***) ***zur ~ bringen in*** become a master in, *formal*: attain mastery in; **2.** *sport*: championship; title; ***e-e ~ gewinnen*** win a championship, gain a title; **'Mei·ster·schafts·spiel** *n* championship game (*soccer etc.*: *a.* match)

'Mei·ster|schü·ler *m* ♪, *art etc.*: master-class pupil (*or* student); ***ein ~ von X*** *w.s.* one of X's best pupils (*or* students); **~sin·ger** [-zɪŋɐ] *m* (-s; -) *hist.* meistersinger; **~spi,on** *m* master spy; **~stück** *n* **1.** a) masterpiece, b) masterstroke; **2.** *work submitted for the master craftsman's diploma*; **~ti·tel** *m* **1.** *sport*: championship title; **2.** master craftsman's title

Mei·ste·rung ['maɪstərʊŋ] *f* (-; *no pl.*) mastery

'Mei·ster|werk *n* masterpiece; **~wür·de** *f* → ***Meistertitel*** 2

'Meist·ge·bot *n* highest bid

'meist|ge·braucht *adj.* most widely (*or* frequently) used; **~ge·fragt** *adj.* most popular, most sought-after; ... most in demand; **~ge·kauft** *adj.* best-selling; **~ge·le·sen** *adj.* most widely read; **~ge·nannt** *adj.* most frequently cited; **~ver·kauft** *adj.* best-selling

Mek·ka ['mɛka] *fig. n* (-s; -s) mecca (*gen.* of; ***für*** *acc.* for, of)

Me·lan·cho·lie [melaŋko'liː] *f* (-; *no pl.*) melancholy; **Me·lan·cho·li·ker** [melaŋ'koːlikɐ] *m* (-s; -) melancholic; **me·lan·cho·lisch** [melaŋ'koːlɪʃ] *adj.* melancholy

Mel·de|amt ['mɛldə-] *n* → ***Einwohnermeldeamt***; **~frist** *f* registration period (*or* deadline)

mel·den ['mɛldən] (h) **I.** *v/t.* **1.** report; **2.** announce; ***würden Sie mich bei ihm ~?*** would you tell him I'm here?; ***wen darf ich ~?*** who shall I say is here?; **3.** *adm. etc.*: notify the authorities *etc.* of, *a.* register *a birth etc.*; report *an accident, a crime etc.* (***der Polizei*** *etc.* to the police *etc.*); ***j-m et. ~*** notify s.o. of s.th.; F ***nichts zu ~ haben*** have no say (in the matter); F ***du hast hier nichts zu ~!*** *iro.* we don't need any help from you(, thank you very much); **II.** *v/refl.*: ***sich ~* 4.** report (***bei*** *dat.* to; ***zur Arbeit*** for work); **5.** register with the police; **6.** answer (the [tele]phone); ***es meldet sich keiner*** nobody's answering; **7.** volunteer (for s.th.); **8.** make itself felt; **9.** *ped.* put one's hand up; **10.** sign up (***zu*** *dat.* for *an examination etc.*); **11. *sich auf ein Inserat ~*** answer an ad (*or* advertisement); **12. *er wird sich schon ~*** a) he'll be in touch, b) he'll shout (*or* make himself heard); **13.** *wenn du mich brauchst,* ***melde dich*** let me know, just shout; → ***anmelden, krank***

Mel·de·pflicht ['mɛldə-] *f* obligatory registration; ⚕ duty of notification

'mel·de·pflich·tig [-pflɪçtɪç] *adj.* subject to registration; ⚕ notifiable

Mel·de|schluß ['mɛldə-] *m* closing date (for entries); **~stel·le** *f* registration office

Mel·dung ['mɛldʊŋ] *f* (-; -en) **1.** announcement; **2.** (*press*) report; news (*sg.*); announcement; ***letzte ~en des Tages*** final news headlines (for today); **3.** report; ***~ machen*** report (***bei*** *dat.* to); **4.** *adm.* registration; **5.** *sport*: entry

me·liert [me'liːɐt] *adj.* mixed; mottled; → ***graumeliert***

Me·lis·se [me'lɪsə] *f* (-; -n) balm

Me'lis·sen·geist *m* (-[e]s; *no pl.*) Carmelite spirit

mel·ken ['mɛlkən] *v/t. and v/i.* (melkte, *obs.* molk, gemolken, h) milk (*a. fig.*); ***~de Kuh → Melkkuh***

Mel·ker ['mɛlkɐ] *m* (-s; -), **Mel·ke·rin** ['mɛlkərɪn] *f* (-; -nen) milker

Melk|kü·bel ['mɛlk-] *m* milk(ing) pail; **~kuh** *f* dairy cow; *fig.* milch cow; **~ma,schi·ne** *f* milking machine

Me·lo·die [melo'diː] *f* (-; -n) melody; tune

Me·lo·dik [me'loːdɪk] *f* (-; *no pl.*) **1.** melody, melodic pattern; **2.** theory of melody

me·lo·di·ös [melo'dĭøːs] *adj.* melodious

me·lo·disch [me'loːdɪʃ] *adj.* melodic(ally *adv.*)

Me·lo'dra·ma [melo-] *n* melodrama (*a.* F *fig.*); **me·lo·dra'ma·tisch** *adj.* melodramatic(ally *adv.*)

Me·lo·ne [me'loːnə] *f* (-; -n) **1.** ⚘ melon; **2.** F bowler (hat), *Am.* derby

Mem·bra·ne [mɛm'braːnə] *f* (-; -n) *anat. and phys.* membrane; *a.* ⚙ diaphragm

Me·men·to [me'mɛnto] *n* (-s; -s) warning, admonition

Mem·me ['mɛmə] *f* (-; -n) coward, F cissy; **'mem·men·haft** *adj.* cowardly

Me·mo ['meːmo] F *n* (-s; -s) memo

Me·moi·ren [me'mŏaːrən] *pl.* memoirs

Me·mo·ran·dum [memo'randʊm] *n* (-s; -den, -da) memorandum, memo

me·mo·rie·ren [memo'riːrən] *v/t.* (h) memorize, learn *s.th.* by heart

Me·na·ge [me'naːʒə] *f* (-;-n) **1.** *gastr.* cruet stand; **2.** *Austrian* ⚔ rations *pl.*

Me·ne·te·kel [mene'teːkəl] *n*: ***das ~ ist an der Wand*** the writing is on the wall

Men·ge ['mɛŋə] *f* (-; -n) **1.** quantity; amount; **2.** a lot (of), F lots (of); ***e-e ~ Autos*** a lot (F lots) of cars; ***e-e ~ zu essen*** a lot (F lots) to eat; ***... in ~n*** any amount of ...; ***... in großen ~n*** large quantities (*or* vast amounts) of ...; a large number (*or* crowds) of ...; F ***jede ~ Geld, Geld in rauhen ~n*** F piles (*or* stacks, heaps) of money; **3.** crowd; *fig.* ***mit der ~ laufen*** follow the crowd; **4.** ⅍ set

'men·gen (h) **I.** *v/t.* mix; ***et. ~ in*** *acc.* mix s.th. with (*or* into) *s.th.*; **II.** *v/refl.*: ***sich ~ unter*** *acc.* mingle (*or* mix) with *the crowd etc.*

'Men·gen|an·ga·be *f* (indication of) quantity; **~leh·re** *f* ⅍ set theory

'men·gen·mä·ßig I. *adj.* quantitative; **II.** *adv.* quantitatively, in terms of quantity

'Men·gen·ra,batt *m* bulk (*or* quantity) discount

Me·nis·kus [me'nɪskʊs] *m* (-; -en) meniscus; ***am ~ operiert werden*** have a cartilage operation; **~ope·ra·ti,on** *f* cartilage operation

Men·ni·ge ['mɛnɪgə] *f* (-; *no pl.*) minium, red lead

Me·no·pau·se [meno'paʊzə] *f* (-; -n) menopause

Men·sa ['mɛnza] *f* (-; Mensen) *univ.* refectory, canteen, *Am. a.* commons *pl.*

Mensch [mɛnʃ] **I.** *m* (-en; -en) **1.** *no pl.* human being; ***der ~*** man; ***ich bin auch nur ein ~*** I'm only human; ***e-e Seele von ~ sein*** have a heart of gold; ***als ~*** *ist er in Ordnung etc.*: as a person (*or* human being), from a personal point of view; ***mit j-m von ~ zu ~ reden*** have a heart-to-heart (talk) with s.o.; F ***sich anstellen wie der erste ~*** F act like one was born yesterday; **2. *der ~*** man, mankind; **3.** person, man, woman; (***die***) ***~en*** people; ***gern unter ~en sein*** enjoy (human) company; ***kein ~*** nobody, not a soul; F ***~ Meier!*** → **II.** F *int.* a) goodness!, F wow!, b) for goodness' (*sl.* Christ's) sake!

Mensch är·ge·re dich nicht *n* (-[s]; *no pl.*) ludo

men·scheln ['mɛnʃəln] F *v/i.* (h): ***es menschelt sehr*** a) there are lots of people around, b) *iro.* humans will be humans

Men·schen|af·fe ['mɛnʃən-] *m* ape, anthropoid; **≗ähn·lich** *adj.* manlike, anthropoid, hominoid; **~al·ter** *n* generation; lifetime; **~an·samm·lung** *f* crowd (of people), cluster of people; **~bild** *n* image of man (***des Mittelalters*** *etc.* in the Middle Ages *etc.*); **~feind** *m* misanthropist; **≗feind·lich** *adj.* **1.** misanthropic(ally *adv.*); **2.** *living conditions etc.* hostile to man; inhuman; **~feind·lich·keit** *f* (-; *no pl.*) **1.** misanthropy; **2.** hostility; inhumanity *of living conditions etc.*; **~fleisch** *n* human flesh; **≗fres·send** *adj.* cannibal ...; *zo.* man-eating ...; **~fres·ser** *m* (-s; -) cannibal; *zo.* man-eater; **~freund** *m* philanthropist; **≗freund·lich** *adj.* **1.** philanthropic(ally *adv.*); **2.** humane, hospitable *environment etc.*; **~freund·lich·keit** *f* (-; *no pl.*) **1.** philanthrophy; **2.** hospitable (*or* humane) nature (*gen.* of *the environment etc.*); **~füh·rung** *f* (-; *no pl.*) leadership; ***er versteht einiges von ~*** he's a good leader, he has good leadership qualities; **~ge·den·ken** *n*: ***seit ~*** within living memory; from (*or* since) time immemorial; **~ge·schlecht** *n*: ***das ~*** the human race, mankind; **~ge·stalt** *f*: ***in ~*** in human form; ***ein Teufel in ~*** a devil incarnate; **~hand** *f*: ***von ~ geschaffen*** made (*or* created) by human beings (*lit.* by the hand of man); ***es liegt nicht in ~*** it is beyond the control of man; **~han·del** *m* slave (*or* body) trade; **~haß** *m* misanthrophy; hatred of people (*or* mankind); **~has·ser** [-hasɐ] *m* (-s; -) misanthropist; hater of men (*or* of the human race); **~ken·ner** *m* good judge of character (*or* human nature); **~kennt·nis** *f* knowledge of (*or* insight into) human nature; **~ket·te** *f* human chain; **~le·ben** *n* **1.** (human) life; ~ ***sind nicht zu beklagen*** there were no fatalities; **2.** lifetime; *w.s.* life; **2leer** *adj.* deserted; ***es war*** ~ *a.* there was nobody (*or* there wasn't a soul) in sight *or* to be seen; **~lie·be** *f* human kindness, charity; **~los** *n the* human lot; **~men·ge** *f* crowd (of people); **2mög·lich** *adj.* humanly possible; ***das ~e*** everything humanly possible; **~op·fer** *n* **1.** *pl.* ⚔ human sacrifice *sg.*, *a. accident*: deaths, fatalities, casualties; ***es gab zahlreiche*** ~ *a.* many lives were lost; ***zahlreiche ~ fordern*** take a huge toll on human life; **2.** human sacrifice; **~pflicht** *f one's* duty as a human being; **~ras·se** *f* race (of people); **~raub** *m* kidnapping, abduction

Men·schen·rech·te ['mɛnʃən-] *pl.* human rights; **'Men·schen·recht·ler** [-rɛçtlɐ] *m* (-s; -) human rights activist

Men·schen·rechts|ab·kom·men ['mɛnʃən-] *n* agreement on human rights; **~ka·ta͵log** *m* catalog(ue) of human rights; **~kom·mis·si͵on** *f* human rights commission; ***Europäische*** ~ European Commission for Human Rights; **~kon·ven·ti͵on** *f* Human Rights Convention; **~ver·let·zung** *f* human rights abuse, violation of human rights

men·schen·scheu ['mɛnʃən-] **I.** *adj.* shy; unsociable; **II.** **2** *f* (-; *no pl.*) shyness; unsociableness

Men·schen|schin·der ['mɛnʃən-] *m* slavedriver; **~schin·de͵rei** *f* slavedriving; **~schlag** *m* (-[e]s; *no pl.*) breed of people; **~see·le** *f* human soul; ***keine*** ~ not a living soul

Men·schens·kind ['mɛnʃəns-] *int.* a) goodness!, good heavens!, b) for goodness' sake!

Men·schen|sohn ['mɛnʃən-] *m eccl.* Son of Man; **~stim·me** *f* human voice; **~strom** *m* stream (*or* flood) of people; **~typ** *m* **1.** type (*or* sort) of person; **2.** 📖 anthropological type; **~ty·pus** *m* → ***Menschentyp*** 2; **2un·mög·lich** *adj.* humanly impossible; **2un·wür·dig** *adj.* degrading, inhumane *treatment etc.*; *conditions etc.* unfit for human beings; **~ver·äch·ter** *m* misanthropist, *lit.* despiser of men; **~ver·ach·tung** *f* contempt for human beings (*or* humankind); **~ver·stand** *m* human intellect; ***gesunder*** ~ common sense; ***das sagt einem schon der gesunde*** ~ common sense will tell you that; **~werk** *n the* work of man; **~wür·de** *f* (*a.* ***die*** ~) human dignity; **2wür·dig** **I.** *adj.* humane *treatment etc.*; *conditions etc.* fit for human beings; *behavio(u)r etc.* befitting a human being; **II.** *adv.*: ***j-n ~ behandeln*** treat s.o. like a human being

'Mensch·heit *f* (-; *no pl.*): ***die*** ~ mankind, humankind, humanity, the human race, man

'Mensch·heits|ge·schich·te *f* history of man(kind) *or* of the human race; **~ide͵al** *n* human ideal, *pl. a.* ideals of man

'mensch·lich **I.** *adj.* human; humane; F tolerable; ***die ~e Natur*** human nature; ***nach ~em Ermessen*** as far as one can possibly judge; ***es ist nur ~, daß*** (*or* ***wenn***) it's only human that (*or* for *s.o. to inf.*); F ***ganz ~ aussehen*** F look halfway civilized; → ***Irren, Rühren***; **II.** *adv.*: ***j-n ~ behandeln*** treat s.o. like a human being, treat s.o. humanely; ***et. ~ betrachten*** look at s.th. from a human point of view; ***rein ~ gesehen*** from a purely human point of view; ***sich ~ benehmen*** behave like a human being; **'Mensch·lich·keit** *f* (-; *no pl.*) **1.** human nature; **2.** humaneness, humanity; ***Verbrechen gegen die*** ~ crime against humanity

'Mensch·wer·dung *f* (-; *no pl.*) **1.** *eccl.* incarnation (***Christi*** of Christ); **2.** *biol.* anthropogenesis

Men·strua·ti·on [mɛnstrua'tsi̯o:n] *f* (-; -en) (*a.* ***die*** ~) menstruation

Men·strua·ti'ons|be·schwer·den *pl.* **1.** period pains; **2.** PMT, premenstrual tension (*or* syndrome) *sg.*; **~zy·klus** *m* menstrual cycle

men·stru·ie·ren [mɛnstru'i:rən] *v/i.* (h) menstruate

Men·sur [mɛn'zu:ɐ] *f* (-; -en [-rən]) **1.** *fencing*: distance; **2.** (student's) duel; **3.** fencing slash; **4.** ♪ scale; *wind instruments*: bore; *string instruments*: stop

men·tal [mɛn'ta:l] *adj.* mental; **Men·ta·li·tät** [mɛntali'tɛ:t] *f* (-; -en) mentality; way of thinking; **men·ta·li'täts·mä·ßig** *adj.* in (their *etc.*) mentality, in their *etc.* way of thinking

Men·thol [mɛn'to:l] *n* (-s; *no pl.*) menthol; **~zi·ga͵ret·te** *f* menthol(ated) cigarette

Men·tor ['mɛnto:ɐ] *m* (-s; -en [mɛn'to:rən]) mentor; *univ.* adviser, tutor

Me·nü [mə'ny:] *n* (-s; -s) **1.** set meal, set lunch; **2.** *computer*: menu

Me·nu·ett [me'nŭɛt] *n* (-s; -e, -s) ♪ minuet

Mer·gel ['mɛrgəl] *m* (-s; -) *geol.* mar

Me·ri·di·an [meri'dĭa:n] *m* (-s; -s, -e) *ast.* meridian; **~kreis** *m* meridian circle

me·ri·dio·nal [meridĭo'na:l] *adj.* meridional

Me·rin·ge [me'rɪŋə] *f* (-; -n) meringue

Me·ri·no [me'ri:no] *m* (-s; -s) merino; **~schaf** *n* Merino sheep; **~wol·le** *f* Merino wool

Me·ri·ten [me'ri:tən] *pl.* merits; ***ein Mann mit zahlreichen*** ~ a man of great merit (*or* of many merits, with many merits to his name); ***sich große ~ erwerben um*** *acc.* render great services to

mer·kan·til [mɛrkan'ti:l] *adj.* mercantile; **Mer·kan·ti·lis·mus** [mɛrkanti'lɪsmʊs] *m* (-; *no pl.*) mercantilism; **Mer·kan·ti·list** [mɛrkanti'lɪst] *m* (-en; -en) mercantilist; **mer·kan·ti·li·stisch** [mɛrkanti'lɪstɪʃ] *adj.* mercantilist(ic)

merk·bar ['mɛrkba:ɐ] *adj.* → ***merklich***

Merk·blatt ['mɛrk-] *n* leaflet; *a.* instructions *pl.*

mer·ken ['mɛrkən] *v/t.* (h) a) notice, b) feel, sense, c) realize, see; be aware of, know; ***merkt man es?*** can you tell?, does it show?; ***man merkte es an s-r Stimme*** you could tell by his voice; ***ich habe nichts gemerkt*** I didn't notice a thing (*or* anything), nothing struck me; ***er hat etwas gemerkt*** he smelled a rat; ***~ lassen*** show, F let on; *iro.* ***du merkst*** (***aber***) ***auch alles*** you don't miss a thing, do you?; ***sich et. ~*** remember s.th., make a mental note of s.th.; ***~ Sie sich das!*** (and) don't you forget it!; ***das werde ich mir ~!*** I shan't forget that (in a hurry); ***ihn wird man sich ~ müssen*** he's a man to watch

Merk|fä·hig·keit ['mɛrk-] *f* (powers *pl.* of) memory; **~heft** *n* notebook; *ped. a.* rough book; **~hil·fe** *f* mnemonic (aid)

merk·lich ['mɛrklɪç] **I.** *adj.* a) noticeable; distinct, marked, visible, b) considerable, appreciable; **II.** *adv.* noticeably; markedly; visibly; → ***I; es ist ~ kühler geworden*** it's gone really cold

Merk·mal ['mɛrkma:l] *n* (-[e]s; -e) characteristic feature; symptom; sign; ***unterscheidendes*** ~ distinctive mark (*or* feature); ***besondere ~e*** distinguishing marks (*or* features)

Merk|satz ['mɛrk-] *m* **1.** mnemonic (phrase); **2.** maxim; **~spruch** *m* **1.** mnemonic (verse); **2.** maxim

merk·wür·dig ['mɛrk-] *adj.* strange, odd, curious, peculiar; **'merk·wür·di·ger·wei·se** *adv.* strangely (*or* oddly) enough; **'Merk·wür·dig·keit** *f* (-; -en) **1.** strangeness, oddness, curiousness, peculiarity; **2.** (strange) quirk

Merk·zei·chen ['mɛrk-] *n* mark(er)

mer·ze·ri·sie·ren [mɛrtsəri'zi:rən] *v/t.* (h) *textil.* mercerize

me·schug·ge [me'ʃʊgə] F *adj.* F crazy, off one's head, nuts

Mes·ka·lin [mɛska'li:n] *n* (-s; *no pl.*) *pharm.* mescaline

Mes·ner ['mɛsnɐ] *m* (-s; -) sexton

Me·so·li·thi·kum [mezo'li:tikʊm] *n* (-s; *no pl.*) Mesolithic (period); **me·so·li·thisch** [mezo'li:tɪʃ] *adj.* Mesolithic

Me·so·zoi·kum [mezo'tso:ikʊm] *n* (-s; *no pl.*) Mesozoic (period); **me·so·zo·isch** [mezo'tso:ɪʃ] *adj.* Mesozoic

Meß·band ['mɛs-] *n* (-[e]s; ¨er) tape measure

meß·bar ['mɛsba:ɐ] *adj.* measurable; ***es ist nicht*** ~ *a.* it can't be measured (*or* ga[u]ged); **'Meß·bar·keit** *f* (-; *no pl.*) measurability

Meß|be·cher ['mɛs-] *m* measuring cup (*or* jug); **~be·reich** *m* (measuring) range; **~bild·ver·fah·ren** *n* photogrammetry; **~da·ten** *pl.* measuring data

Meß·die·ner ['mɛs-] *m R.C.* server

Mes·se[1] ['mɛsə] *f* (-; -n) *R.C.* mass; (***die***) ***~ lesen*** say Mass

'Mes·se[2] *f* (-; -n) ⚔ mess

'Mes·se[3] *f* (-; -n) (trade) fair; **~amt** *n* fair office; **~aus·weis** *m* fair pass; **~be·su·cher** *m* visitor to a (*or* the) fair; **~ge·län·de** *n* exhibition site (*or* centre, *Am.* center); **~hal·le** *f* exhibition hall; **~ho͵stess** *f* hostess (at a fair); **~lei·tung** *f* fair management

mes·sen ['mɛsən] (maß, gemessen, h) **I.** *v/t.* measure; ⚙ *a.* ga(u)ge; *fig.* size up; ***die Zeit*** ~ do the timing, ***bei*** *dat.* time; ***s-e Kräfte mit j-m*** ~ pit one's strength against s.o.; → ***Fieber***; **II.** *fig. v/refl.*: ***sich mit j-m*** ~ match o.s. against s.o., pit one's wits against s.o., *sport*: compete against s.o.; ***sich nicht ~ können mit*** *dat.* be no match for *s.o.*, not to bear comparison with *s.th.*; **III.** *v/i.* measure, be ... long (*or* high, wide *etc.*); be ... (tall); → ***gemessen***

'Mes·se·neu·heit *f* newcomer to the market

Mes·ser ['mɛsɐ] *n* (-s; -) **1.** knife; *fig.* ***Kampf bis aufs*** ~ fight to the death (*or* finish); ***auf*** (***des***) ***~s Schneide stehen*** be hanging in the balance, be on a knife edge, be on the razor's edge; ***es steht auf ~s Schneide, ob ...*** it's touch and go whether ...; *fig.* ***j-n ans ~ liefern*** F put s.o.'s head on the block, F blow the whistle on s.o.; ***ins offene ~ rennen*** F take it on the chin; → ***Kehle*** 1; **2.** ⚙ knife, blade; **3.** ⚕ scalpel, knife; ***unters ~ kommen*** come under the (surgeon's) knife; **~griff** *m* knife handle; **~haar·schnitt** *m* razor cut; **~held** *m* knifer; **~klin·ge** *f* knife blade; **~rücken** *m* back of a (*or* the) knife; **2scharf I.** *adj.* razor-sharp; *fig. a.* keen, acute; *fig.* ***~er Verstand*** razor-sharp mind; ***e-n ~en Verstand haben*** *a.* be razor-sharp; **II.** *adv.*: *iro.* ***das war ~ geschlossen!*** that was good thinking; **~schmied** *m* cutler; **~schnitt** *m* **1.** knife cut (*or* wound); **2.** razor cut; **~spit·ze** *f* knife point; ***e-e ~ Salz*** a pinch of salt

'Mes·ser·ste·cher [-ʃtɛçɐ] *m* (-s; -) knifer; **'Mes·ser·ste·che·rei** [-ʃtɛçəraɪ] *f* (-; -en) knife fight; stabbing; **'Mes·ser·stich** *m* a) stab, b) stab wound

'Mes·se|schla·ger *m* highlight of the exhibition (*or* trade fair); **~stadt** *f* exhibition centre (*Am.* center); *town famous for its fairs and exhibitions*; **~stand** *m* exhibition stand; **~teil·neh·mer** *m* exhibitor; **~ver·an·stal·ter** *m* fair organizer; **~zen·trum** *n* exhibition centre (*Am.* center)

Meß|ge·rät ['mɛs-] *n* measuring instrument; ga(u)ge; meter; **~glas** *n* measuring jug

mes·sia·nisch [mɛ'sia:nɪʃ] *adj.* messianic; **Mes·si·as** [mɛ'si:as] *m* (-; *no pl.*): ***der ~*** the Messiah

Mes·sing ['mɛsɪŋ] *n* (-s; *no pl.*) brass; **~blech** *n* sheet brass; **~draht** *m* brass wire; **~schild** *n* brass (name)plate

Meß·in·stru,ment ['mɛs-] *n* → ***Meßgerät***

Meß·kelch ['mɛs-] *m R.C.* (Communion) chalice

Meß·lat·te ['mɛs-] *f* surveyor's pole

Meß·op·fer ['mɛs-] *n R.C.* Sacrifice of the Mass

Meß|schnur ['mɛs-] *f* measuring cord; **~stab** *m* **1.** *mot.* dipstick; **2.** → ***Meßlatte***; **~tech·nik** *f* metrology; **~uhr** *f* meter, dial ga(u)ge

Mes·sung ['mɛsʊŋ] *f* (-; -en) measurement; reading; ***e-e ~ vornehmen*** take a measurement (*or* reading)

Meß|ver·fah·ren ['mɛs-] *n* measuring method; **~war·te** *f* survey (control) station

Meß·wein ['mɛs-] *m R.C.* altar (*or* sacramental) wine

Meß|wert ['mɛs-] *m* measurement, reading; **~zahl** *f*, **~zif·fer** *f* measurement; *statistics*: index (number)

Me·sti·ze [mɛs'ti:tsə] *m* (-n; -n), **Me·sti·zin** [mɛs'ti:tsɪn] *f* (-; -nen) mestizo

Met [me:t] *m* (-[e]s; *no pl.*) mead

me·ta·bo·lisch [meta'bo:lɪʃ] *adj.* metabolic; **Me·ta·bo·lis·mus** [metabo'lɪsmʊs] *m* (-; *no pl.*) metabolism

Me·tall [me'tal] *n* (-s; -e) metal; **~ar·bei·ter** *m* metalworker; **~be·ar·bei·tung** *f* metalworking; **~be·schlä·ge** *pl.* metal fittings (*or* mountings); **~bör·se** *f* metal exchange

me·tal·len [me'talən] *adj.* metal; metallic (*a. fig.*)

Me·tal·ler [me'talɐ] *m* (-s; -) metalworker

Me'tall|er·mü·dung *f* metal fatigue; **~geld** *n* metallic currency; coins *pl.*

me'tall·hal·tig *adj.* metalliferous

me·tal·lic [me'talɪk] *adj.* metallic; ***~grün*** *etc.* metallic green *etc.*

Me'tal·lic-Lackie·rung *f* metallic finish

Me'tall·in·du,strie *f* metal (and engineering) industry

me·tal·lisch [me'talɪʃ] *adj.* metallic

Me'tall|kun·de *f* metallurgy; **~oxyd** *n* metallic oxide; **~,über·zug** *m* metal coating

Me·tall·ur·gie [metalʊr'gi:] *f* (-; *no pl.*) metallurgy; **me·tall·ur·gisch** [meta'lʊrgɪʃ] *adj.* metallurgic(al)

me'tall·ver·ar·bei·tend metal-processing *industry etc.*; **Me'tall·ver·ar·bei·tung** *f* metal processing

Me'tall·wa·ren *pl.* metal goods, hardware *sg.*

Me·ta·mor·pho·se [metamɔr'fo:zə] *f* (-; -n) metamorphosis; *fig. a.* transformation; *fig.* ***e-e ~ durchmachen*** undergo a metamorphosis (*or* transformation, complete change)

Me·ta·pher [me'tafɐ] *f* (-; -n) metaphor

Me·ta·pho·rik [meta'fo:rɪk] *f* (-; *no pl.*) (use of) imagery; **me·ta·pho·risch** [meta'fo:rɪʃ] *adj.* metaphorical

Me·ta·phy'sik [meta-] *f* metaphysics *pl.*; **Me·ta'phy·si·ker** *m* metaphysician; **me·ta'phy·sisch** *adj.* metaphysical

Me·ta·spra·che ['me:ta-] *f* metalanguage; **'me·ta·sprach·lich** *adj.* metalinguistic

Me·ta·sta·se [meta'sta:zə] *f* (-; -n) ⚕ secondary, 📖 metastasis

Me·te·or [mete'o:ɐ] *m* (-s; -e [-rə]) meteor; **me·te'or·haft** *fig. adj.* meteoric; ***~er Aufstieg*** meteoric rise; **Me·teo·rit** [meteo'ri:t] *m* (-s, -en; -e[n]) meteorite; **Me·teo'ri·ten·kra·ter** *m* meteor(ite) crater

Me·teo·ro·lo·ge [meteoro'lo:gə] *m* (-n; -n) meteorologist; weatherman

Me·teo·ro·lo·gie [meteorolo'gi:] *f* meteorology

Me·teo·ro·lo·gin [meteoro'lo:gɪn] *f* (-; -nen) meteorologist; weatherlady

me·teo·ro·lo·gisch [meteoro'lo:gɪʃ] *adj.* meteorological

Me·te'or·stein *m* meteorite

Me·ter ['me:tɐ] *n*, *m* (-s; -) metre (*Am.* meter); yard

'me·ter|dick *adj.* a metre (*Am.* meter) in diameter (*or* thick), a yard in diameter (*or* thick); metre-thick ..., *Am.* meter-thick ..., yard-thick ...; **~hoch** *adj.* metre-high ..., *Am.* meter-high ..., yard-high ...; waist-deep *snow*, three-foot deep ..., *pred.* three feet deep; **~lang** *adj.* metre-long ..., *Am.* meter-long ..., yard-long ...; *fig.* very long, F great long ...

'Me·ter|maß *n* tape measure; measuring rod, rule; **~wa·re** *f* yard goods *pl.*

'me·ter·wei·se *adv.* by the metre (*Am.* meter)

Me·than [me'ta:n] *n* (-s; *no pl.*), **~gas** *n* methane

Me·tha·nol [meta'no:l] *n* (-s; *no pl.*) methanol

Me·tho·de [me'to:də] *f* (-; -n) **1.** method; ***et. mit ~ machen*** do s.th. methodically; ***es hat ~*** there's method in (*or* behind) it; ***er hat ~*** he's very methodical, he's a man of method; **2.** *pl.* ways, behavio(u)r *sg.*

Me·tho·dik [me'to:dɪk] *f* (-; -en) **1.** methodology; **2.** method; **me·tho·disch** [me'to:dɪʃ] *adj.* methodical

Me·tho·dist [meto'dɪst] *m* (-en; -en), **me·tho·di·stisch** [meto'dɪstɪʃ] *adj.* Methodist

Me·tho·do·lo·gie [metodolo'gi:] *f* (-; -n) methodology; **me·tho·do·lo·gisch** [metodo'lo:gɪʃ] *adj.* methodological

Me·thu·sa·lem [me'tu:zalɛm] *m* (-[s]; -s) *bibl.* Methuselah; *fig.* ***so alt wie ~*** as old as Methuselah (*or* as the hills)

Me·thyl·al·ko·hol [me'ty:l-] *m* methyl alcohol

Me·tier [me'tie:] *n* (-s; -s) profession, job; trade; *fig.* ***das ist nicht mein ~*** that's not my line

Me·trik ['me:trɪk] *f* (-; *no pl.*) **1.** metrics *pl.* (*a.* ♪), prosody; **2.** metre (*Am.* meter)

me·trisch ['me:trɪʃ] *adj.* ⚙ metric; ♪ *etc.* metrical

Me·tro·nom [metro'no:m] *n* (-s; -e) ♪ metronome

Me·tro·po·le [metro'po:lə] *f* (-; -n) metropolis

Me·tro·po·lit [metropo'li:t] *m* (-en; -en) *eccl.* metropolitan

Me·trum ['me:trʊm] *n* (-s; Metren ['me:trən]) metre, *Am.* meter

Met·te ['mɛtə] *f* (-; -n) *eccl.* → ***Frühmette, Nachtmette***

Mett·wurst ['mɛt-] *f* smoked sausage spread

Met·ze·lei [mɛtsə'laɪ] *f* (-; -en) slaughter, massacre; **met·zeln** ['mɛtsəln] *v/t.* (h) butcher, slaughter

Metz·ger ['mɛtsgɐ] *m* (-s; -) butcher; ***zum ~ gehen*** go to the butcher's; **Metz·ge·rei** [mɛtsgə'raɪ] *f* (-; -en) butcher's (shop); **'Metz·ger·gang** *fig. m*: ***(e-n ~ tun*** go on a) wild goose chase

Meu·chel|mord ['mɔʏçəl-] *m* treacherous killing; **~mör·der** *m* murderer, assassin

meuch·le·risch ['mɔʏçlərɪʃ] *adj.* treacherous

meuch·lings ['mɔʏçlɪŋs] *adv.*: ***j-n ~ umbringen*** murder s.o. treacherously, commit a treacherous murder against s.o.

Meu·te ['mɔʏtə] *f* (-; -n) **1.** pack (of hounds); **2.** *fig.* mob; F gang

Meu·te·rei [mɔʏtə'raɪ] *f* (-; -en) mutiny

Meu·te·rer ['mɔʏtərɐ] *m* (-s; -) mutineer

meu·tern ['mɔʏtɐn] *v/i.* (h) mutiny; F *fig.* rebel

Me·xi·ka·ner [mɛksi'ka:nɐ] *m* (-s; -), **Me·xi·ka·ne·rin** [mɛksi'ka:nərɪn] *f* (-; -nen), **me·xi·ka·nisch** [mɛksi'ka:nɪʃ] *adj.* Mexican

Mez·zo·so·pran ['mɛtsozopra:n] *m* (-s; *no pl.*) mezzo-soprano

MG|-Sal·ve [ɛm'ge:-] *f* burst of machine-gun fire; **~-Schüt·ze** *m* (machine-)gunner

mi·au [mi'aʊ] *int.* miaow!; **mi·au·en** [mi'aʊən] *v/i.* (h) miaow

mich [mɪç] **I.** *pers. pron.* (*acc. of ich*) me; **II.** *refl. pron.* myself; *after prp.* me; ***hinter ~*** behind me; *often untranslated*: ***ich setzte ~*** I sat down

mick·rig ['mɪkrɪç] F *adj.* a) measly, pathetic, F lousy, b) puny, sickly

Mid·life-cri·sis ['mɪdlaɪf'kraɪsɪs] *f* (- *no pl.*) midlife crisis, male menopause

mied [mi:t] *pret. of* ***meiden***

Mie·der ['mi:dɐ] *n* (-s; -) bodice; **~hös·chen** *n* panty girdle; **~wa·ren** *pl.* foundation garments

Mief [mi:f] F *m* (-[e]s; *no pl.*) fug; F stink; *fig.* stuffy atmosphere; ***~ der Provinz*** provincial atmosphere; **'mie·fen** F *v/i.* (h) F pong, stink; ***das mieft aber!*** what a pong (*or* stink); **mie·fig** ['mi:fɪç] F *adj.* stuffy, F frowsty

Mie·ne ['mi:nə] *f* (-; -n) expression; face; ***überlegene*** (***unschuldsvolle***) ***~*** superior (innocent) expression *or* air; ***e-e ernste ~ aufsetzen*** look serious; ***gute ~ zum bösen Spiel machen*** put on a brave face (*or* front), F grin and bear it; ***~***

machen, et. zu tun make as if to do s.th.; ***ohne e-e ~ zu verziehen*** without batting an eyelid, without flinching; **'Mie·nen·spiel** *n* facial expressions *pl.* (*or* play)

mies [mi:s] F *adj.* F lousy, rotten; ***~er Laune sein*** F be in a foul mood; → ***miesmachen***; **Mie·se·pe·ter** ['mi:zəpe:tɐ] F *m* (-s; -) F (old) grouch, sourpuss; **'mies·ma·chen** F *v/t.* (*sep*, h): ***j-n (et.) ~*** run *or* put s.o. (s.th.) down; ***er muß alles ~*** he's always running (*or* putting) things down; ***er muß alle Leute ~*** he's always running (*or* putting) people down, he hasn't got a good word to say about anyone; **'Mies·ma·cher** F *m* moaner, F whinger; fault-finder; killjoy

Mies·mu·schel ['mi:s-] *f zo.* mussel

Miet|aus·fall ['mi:t-] *m* loss of rent; **~au·to** *n* hire(d) car, *Am.* rented (*or* rental) car; **~bei·hil·fe** *f* rent allowance; **~dau·er** *f* (period of) tenancy

Mie·te¹ ['mi:tə] *f* (-; -n) rent; ***in*** (*or* ***zur***) ***~ wohnen*** live in a rented flat (*Am.* apartment) *or* house, live in lodgings, rent a room; F *fig.* ***das ist ja schon die halbe ~*** that's half the battle

'Mie·te² *f* (-; -n) ⚒ pit; stack

Miet·ein·nah·men ['mi:t-] *pl.* rental income *sg.*

mie·ten ['mi:tən] *v/t.* (h) rent; *a.* hire *a car etc.*; **Mie·ter** ['mi:tɐ] *m* (-; -) tenant; lodger, *Am.* roomer

Miet·er·hö·hung ['mi:t-] *f* rent increase

Mie·te·rin ['mi:tərɪn] *f* (-; -nen) → ***Mieter***

'Mie·ter·schutz *m* protection of tenants' rights; **~bund** *m* tenants' rights association; **~ge·setz** *n Brit.* Rent Act

'Mie·ter·ver·band *m* tenants' association

miet·frei ['mi:t-] *adj. and adv.* rent-free; ***sie wohnt dort ~ a.*** she doesn't have to pay any rent; **'Miet·frei·heit** *f* (-; *no pl.*) rent exemption

Miet|kau·ti͵on ['mi:t-] *f* deposit; **~ob͵jekt** *n* rental property; **~par͵tei** *f* tenant; **~preis** *m* rent; rental (fee, *Am.* rate), *Brit. a.* hire charge; **~preis·bin·dung** *f* rent control; **~recht** *n* (-[e]s; *no pl.*) laws *pl.* governing tenancy; **~rück·stän·de** *pl.* rent arrears

Miets|haus ['mi:ts-] *n* block of flats, *Am.* apartment house; **~ka͵ser·ne** *f* tenement block

Miet|spie·gel ['mi:t-] *m* rental table; **~ver·hält·nis** *n* tenancy; **~ver·län·ge·rung** *f* extension of one's (*or* the) lease; **~ver·trag** *m* lease; hire (*Am.* rental) contract; **~vor͵aus·zah·lung** *f* advance rent; **~wa·gen** *m* hire(d) car, *Am.* rented (*or* rental) car; **~wa·gen·ver·leih** *m* car rental (service); **~wert** *m* rental value; **~woh·nung** *f* (rented) flat, *Am.* apartment; **~wu·cher** *m* rack renting; **~zah·lung** *f* payment of rent; **~zins** *m* rental (fee); **~zu·schuß** *m* rent allowance

Mie·ze ['mi:tsə] F *f* (-; -n) **1.** F pussy(cat); **2.** *fig.* F bird, *Am.* F chick

Mi·grä·ne [mi'grɛ:nə] *f* (-; -n) migraine; **~an·fall** *m* migraine (attack)

Mi·kro ['mi:kro] F *n* (-s; -s) F mike; → ***Mikrophon***

Mi·kro·be [mi'kro:bə] *f* (-; -n) microbe

Mi·kro|bio·lo'gie [mikro-] *f* microbiology; **~che'mie** *f* microchemistry

Mi·kro·chip ['mi:kro-] *m* microchip

Mi·kro·chir·ur'gie [mikro-] *f* ⚕ microsurgery

Mi·kro·com͵pu·ter ['mi:kro-] *m* microcomputer

Mi·kro·elek'tro·nik [mikro-] *f* microelectronics *pl.*

Mi·kro·fiche ['mi:krofi:ʃ] *m, n* (-s; -s) microfiche

Mi·kro·film ['mi:kro-] *m* microfilm

Mi·kro|'kos·mos [mikro-] *m* microcosm; **~or·ga'nis·mus** *m* microorganism

Mi·kro·phon [mikro'fo:n] *n* (-s; -e) microphone; **~buch·se** *f* microphone jack

Mi·kro·phy'sik [mikro-] *f* microphysics *pl.*

Mi·kro·pro͵zes·sor ['mi:kro-] *m* microprocessor

Mi·kro·skop [mikro'sko:p] *n* (-s; -e) microscope; **mi·kro·sko·pisch** [mikro'sko:pɪʃ] **I.** *adj.* microscopic (*a. fig.*); **II.** *adv.* microscopically; ***~ untersuchen*** examine under the microscope

Mi·kro|struk͵tur ['mi:kro-] *f* microstructure; **~ver·fil·mung** *f* microfilming; **~wel·le** *f* microwave (*a.* F oven)

Mi·kro·wel·len|be·hand·lung ['mi:kro-] *f* microwave treatment; **~herd** *m* microwave oven

Mil·be ['mɪlbə] *f* (-; -n) mite

Milch [mɪlç] *f* (-; *no pl.*) **1.** milk; **2.** ♃ milk, juice; **3.** *zo.* (soft) roe; **~bar** *f* milk bar; **~brei** *m* milk pudding; **~drü·se** *f* mammary gland; **~ei·weiß** *n* lactoprotein; **~fett** *n* milk fat; **~fla·sche** *f* milk bottle

'milch·frei *adj.* non-milk ...

'Milch|ge·schäft *n* dairy, creamery; **~ge·sicht** *contp. n* babyface; **~glas** *n* ⚙ frosted glass; **~händ·ler** *m* dairyman

mil·chig ['mɪlçɪç] *adj.* milky

'Milch|kaf͵fee *m* milky coffee; **~känn·chen** *n* milk jug; **~kan·ne** *f* milk churn; milk can; **~kuh** *f* dairy cow; **~lei·stung** *f* milk yield; **~mäd·chen·rech·nung** F *f* simple-minded reasoning; **~mann** F *m* milkman; **~mix·ge·tränk** *n* milkshake

Milch·ner ['mɪlçnɐ] *m* (-s; -) *zo.* milter

'Milch|pro͵duk·te *pl.* milk (*or* dairy) products; **~pul·ver** *n* powdered milk; **~reis** *m* rice pudding; **~säu·re** *f* lactic acid; **~schorf** *m* ⚕ milk crust; **~stra·ße** *f ast.* Milky Way; **~stra·ßen·sy͵stem** *n* galaxy; **~trin·ker** *m* milk drinker; **~vieh** *n* dairy cattle *pl.*; **~wirt·schaft** *f* dairy farming; **~zahn** *m* milk tooth; **~zen·tri·fu·ge** *f* (cream) separator; **~zucker** *m* milk sugar, lactose

mild [mɪlt] → **mil·de** ['mɪldə] **I.** *adj.* mild (*a. gastr., meteor.*); *gastr.* smooth *wine etc.*; *fig.* lenient *sentence etc.*; gentle *or* wan *smile*; soft *colo(u)rs etc.*; ***e-e ~ Gabe*** alms, something for charity; **II.** *adv.*: ***~ gesagt*** to put it mildly; ***et. ~ beurteilen*** take a lenient view of s.th.; *iro.* ***da kann ich nur ~ lächeln*** don't make me laugh

'Mil·de *f* (-; *no pl.*) mildness; gentleness; leniency; ***~ walten lassen*** be lenient, show some leniency

mil·dern ['mɪldɐn] (h) **I.** *v/t.* soothe, ease, alleviate *pain*; moderate; mitigate *sentence*; qualify *statement etc.*; reduce, soften *effect etc.*; ⚖ ***~de Umstände*** extenuating (*or* mitigating) circumstances; **II.** *v/refl.*: ***sich ~*** *pain*: ease; *emotions*: cool off; **Mil·de·rung** ['mɪldərʊŋ] *f* (-; *no pl.*) alleviation *of pain*; mitigation *of sentence*; qualification *of statement*; moderation; **'Mil·de·rungs·grund** *m* ⚖ extenuating cause

'mild·tä·tig *adj.* charitable; **'Mild·tä·tig·keit** *f* (-; *no pl.*) charity

Mi·lieu [mi'liø:] *n* (-s; -s) environment (*a. biol.*); surroundings *pl.*; background

mi'lieu|be·dingt *adj.* due to environmental factors (*or* social background); ***es ist ~ a.*** it goes back to the environment he *etc.* grew up in; **~ge·schä·digt** *adj.* maladjusted

Mi'lieu|scha·den *m* environmental disturbance; **~schil·de·rung** *f* background description; **~theo͵rie** *f* environmentalism

mi·li·tant [mili'tant] *adj.* militant; **Mi·li·tanz** [mili'tants] *f* (-; *no pl.*) militancy

Mi·li·tär [mili'tɛ:ɐ] *n* (-s; *no pl.*) **1.** armed forces *pl.*, military; army; ***beim ~ sein*** be in the army; **2.** military personnel, soldiers *pl.*; **~ab·kom·men** *n* military agreement (*or* pact); **~aka·de͵mie** *f* military academy; **~arzt** *m* medical officer; **~at·ta͵ché** *m* military attaché; **~be·ra·ter** *m* military adviser; **~bünd·nis** *n* military alliance; **~dienst** *m* military service; **~dik·ta͵tur** *f* military dictatorship; **~flug·zeug** *n* military aircraft; **~ge·fäng·nis** *n* military prison; **~ge·richt** *n* military court; court martial; **~ho·heit** *f* (-; *no pl.*) military authority; ***unter ~ a.*** under military command

mi·li·tä·risch [mili'tɛ:rɪʃ] *adj.* military; martial

mi·li·ta·ri·sie·ren [militari'zi:rən] *v/t.* (h) militarize; **Mi·li·ta·ri'sie·rung** *f* (-; *no pl.*) militarization

Mi·li·ta·ris·mus [milita'rɪsmʊs] *m* (-; *no pl.*) militarism; **Mi·li·ta·rist** [milita'rɪst] *m* (-en; -en) militarist; **mi·li·ta·ri·stisch** [milita'rɪstɪʃ] *adj.* militaristic

Mi·li'tär|jun·ta *f* military junta; **~ka͵pel·le** *f* military band; **~macht** *f* military power; **~marsch** *m* ♪ military march; **~mu͵sik** *f* military marches *pl.* (*or* music); **~po·li͵zei** *f* military police; **~putsch** *m* military putsch; **~re͵gie·rung** *f* military government; **~re͵gime** *n* military regime; **~spra·che** *f* military (*or* forces) slang; **~spre·cher** *m*: (***~ des Weißen Hauses*** White House) military spokesman; **~straf·an·stalt** *f* detention (*Am.* disciplinary) barracks *pl.*; **~stütz·punkt** *m* military base; **~wis·sen·schaft** *f* military science

Mi·li·ta·ry ['mɪlɪtərɪ] *f* (-; -s) three-day event; **~rei·ter** *m* three-day eventer

Mi·li'tär·zeit *f* military service; ***während m-r ~*** when I was in the Army (*or* Navy *etc.*)

Mi·liz [mi'li:ts] *f* (-; -en) militia; **~sol͵dat** *m* militiaman

Mil·le ['mɪlə] F *n* (-; -) F grand, K, thou, thou'; **25 ~** 25 grand, 25K, 25 thou (*or* thou')

Mil·len·ni·um [mɪ'lɛnĭʊm] *n* (-s; -en) millennium

Mil·li·ar·där [mɪlĭar'dɛ:ɐ] *m* (-s; -e [-rə]), **Mil·li·ar·dä·rin** [mɪlĭar'dɛ:rɪn] *f* (-; -nen) multimillionaire; **Mil·li·ar·de** [mɪ'lĭardə] *f* (-; -n) billion, *Brit. obs. a.* thousand million; ***in die ~n gehen*** run into billions (of dollars *etc.*)

Mil·li'ar·den|be·trag *m* billions (*Brit. obs. a.* thousands of millions) of pounds *etc.*; ***es sind Milliardenbeträge*** it runs into billions (*Brit. obs. a.* thousands of millions); **~hö·he** *f*: ***Kredit in ~*** billion-dollar *etc.* loan; **~loch** *n*: ***das ~ im Haushalt*** the billion-dollar *etc.* deficit

mil·li·ardst [mɪ'lĭardst] *adj.* billionth, *Brit. obs. a.* thousand millionth

Mil·li·ard·stel [mɪˈlĭardstəl] *n* (-s; -) billionth (part), *Brit. obs. a.* thousand millionth (part)
Mil·li·bar [ˈmɪlibaːɐ] *n* (-s; -s) *meteor.* millibar
Mil·li·me·ter [ˈmɪlimeːtɐ] *n*, *m* millimet|re (*Am.* -er); **~ar·beit** F *f* (-; *no pl.*) *a* precision job; **~pa,pier** *n* graph paper
Mil·li·on [mɪˈlĭoːn] *f* (-; -en) million; ***fünf ~en Dollar*** five million dollars; ***in die ~en gehen*** run into millions (of dollars *etc.*)
Mil·lio·när [mɪlĭoˈnɛːɐ] *m* (-s; -e [-rə]), **Mil·lio·nä·rin** [mɪlĭoˈnɛːrɪn] *f* (-; -nen) millionaire, *f a.* millionairess
Mil·lio·nen|auf·la·ge [mɪˈlĭoːnən-] *f* circulation of over a million (*or* of several millions); ***das Buch hat inzwischen e-e ~ erreicht*** the book has sold over a million copies; **~be·trag** *m* millions of pounds *etc.*; **~ding** F *n* million-dollar *etc.* deal
mil·lio·nen·fach [mɪˈlĭoːnənfax] **I.** *adj.* millionfold; **II.** *adv.* a million times (over)
Mil·lio·nen|ge·schäft [mɪˈlĭoːnən-] *n* multimillion-dollar (*or* -pound *etc.*) business (*or* deal); **~ge·win·ne** *pl.* profits running into millions; **~hö·he** *f*: ***Kredit in ~*** (multi)million-dollar *etc.* loan; ***die Explosion verursachte e-n Schaden in ~*** the explosion caused damage running into millions of marks *etc.*; **~scha·den** *m* damage running into millions of marks *etc.*; **&schwer** F *adj.* worth millions; **~stadt** *f* city of over a million inhabitants
mil·li·onst [mɪˈlĭoːnst] *adj.* millionth
Mil·li·on·stel [mɪˈlĭoːnstəl] *n* (-s; -) millionth (part)
Milz [mɪlts] *f* (-; -en) *anat.* spleen; **~brand** *m vet.* anthrax
Mi·me [ˈmiːmə] *m* (-n; -n) *thea.* actor
ˈmi·men *v/t.* (h) act, play (*both a. fig.*); ***den Kranken (Überraschung** etc.**)*** ~ pretend to be sick (surprised *etc.*), feign sickness (surprise *etc.*)
Mi·mik [ˈmiːmɪk] *f* (-; *no pl.*) facial play
Mi·mi·kry [ˈmɪmikri] *f* (-; *no pl.*) *biol.* mimicry
mi·misch [ˈmiːmɪʃ] *adj.* mimic
Mi·mo·se [miˈmoːzə] *f* (-; -n) **1.** ♀ mimosa; **2.** *fig.* sensitive creature; **miˈmo·sen·haft** *fig. adj.* (over)sensitive
Mi·na·rett [minaˈrɛt] *n* (-s; -e) minaret
min·der [ˈmɪndɐ] **I.** *adv.* less; ***nicht ~*** no less; **II.** *adj.* less(er); smaller; minor; inferior; ***Waren ~er Güte*** inferior (*or* low-quality) goods
ˈMin·der|aus·ga·ben *pl.* reduced expenditure *sg.*; **~be·darf** *m* reduced demand, drop in demand
ˈmin·der|be·deu·tend *adj.* less important (*or* significant); **~be·gabt** *adj.* less gifted; **~be·mit·telt** *adj.* less well-off, needy; ***geistig ~*** mentally less gifted, F not very bright, a bit slow
ˈMin·der|be·trag *m* deficit; **~be·wer·tung** *f* undervaluation; **~ein·nah·me** *f* shortfall in receipts; **~er·trag** *m* reduced yield (✝ profit); **~ge·wicht** *n* short weight
ˈMin·der·heit *f* (-; -en) minority
ˈMin·der·hei·ten|fra·ge *f* minorities question; **~recht** *n* rights *pl.* of minorities; **~schutz** *m* protection of minorities
ˈMin·der·heits·re,gie·rung *f* minority(-party) government
ˈmin·der·jäh·rig [-jɛːrɪç] *adj.* under age; **ˈMin·der·jäh·ri·ge** [-jɛːrɪgə] *m*, *f* (-n; -n) minor; **ˈMin·der·jäh·rig·keit** *f* (-; *no pl.*) minority
min·dern [ˈmɪndɐn] (h) **I.** *v/t.* diminish, lessen, decrease; reduce, lower; depreciate; **II.** *v/refl.*: ***sich ~*** diminish, decrease; *enthusiasm etc.*: *a.* abate; **Min·de·rung** [ˈmɪndərʊŋ] *f* (-; *no pl.*) decrease, reduction; depreciation
ˈMin·der·wert *m* reduced value
ˈmin·der·wer·tig [-veːɐtɪç] *adj.* inferior, of inferior quality, ✝ *a.* low-grade ...; **ˈMin·der·wer·tig·keit** *f* (-; *no pl.*) inferiority; ✝ inferior quality
ˈMin·der·wer·tig·keits|ge·fühl *n* feeling of inferiority, sense of being inferior; → **~kom,plex** *m* inferiority complex
ˈMin·der·zahl *f* (-; *no pl.*): ***(in der ~ sein*** be in the) minority
min·dest [ˈmɪndəst] *adj.* least; slightest; minimum ...; ***nicht im ~en*** not in the least, not at all; ***nicht die ~e Chance*** not the slightest chance; ***ich habe nicht die ~e Ahnung*** I haven't the slightest idea, ***davon:*** I don't know the first thing about it; ***zum ~en*** at least; ***das ~e*** the very minimum (*or* least); ***das wäre das ~e gewesen*** that's the (very) least one could have expected; ***das ~e wäre, daß du mich angerufen hättest*** you could have at least rung me up
ˈMin·dest|al·ter *n* minimum age; **~an·for·de·run·gen** *pl.* minimum requirements; **~be·trag** *m* minimum amount
min·de·stens [ˈmɪndəstəns] *adv.* at least
ˈMin·dest·for·de·rung *f* minimum (wage) demand
ˈMin·dest·ge·halt[1] *n* minimum wage
ˈMin·dest·ge·halt[2] *m* minimum content; ***~ an Alkohol*** minimum alcohol content
ˈMin·dest·halt·bar·keits·da·tum *n* best-before (*or* best-by) date, *Am.* pull date
ˈMin·dest|lohn *m* minimum wage; **~maß** *n* minimum; ***auf ein ~ herabsetzen*** reduce to a minimum; **~preis** *m* minimum price; **~stra·fe** *f* minimum penalty; **~ta,rif** *m* minimum wage; **~,um·tausch** *m* minimum currency exchange; **~ver·brauch** *m* minimum consumption; **~wert** *m* minimum value; **~wort·schatz** *m* minimum vocabulary; ***ein ~ von ...*** *a.* a minimum (number) of ... words; **~zahl** *f* minimum (number)
Mi·ne [ˈmiːnə] *f* (-; -n) **1.** ⚒, ⚔, ⚓ mine; ***~n legen*** lay mines; ***auf e-e ~ laufen*** hit a mine; **2.** a) lead, b) cartridge, refill
ˈMi·nen|ar·bei·ter *m* ⚒ mineworker, miner; **~feld** *n* ⚔ minefield; **~le·ger** [-leːgɐ] *m* (-s; -) ⚔ ⚓ mine layer; **~räum·boot** *n* minesweeper; **~sper·re** *f* ⚓ mine barrier; ⚔ mine roadblock; **~such·boot** *n* mine hunter, minesweeper
ˈmi·nen·ver·seucht *adj.* mine-infested
Mi·ne·ral [mineˈraːl] *n* (-s; Mineralien [-lĭən]) mineral; **~bad** *n* a) mineral bath, b) spa; **~brun·nen** *m* mineral spring; **~dün·ger** *m* mineral fertilizer
mi·ne·ra·lisch [mineˈraːlɪʃ] *adj.* mineral
Mi·neˈral·kun·de *f* mineralogy
Mi·ne·ra·lo·ge [mineraˈloːgə] *m* (-n; -n) mineralogist; **Mi·ne·ra·lo·gie** [mineraloˈgiː] *f* (-; *no pl.*) mineralogy; **mi·ne·ra·lo·gisch** [mineraˈloːgɪʃ] *adj.* mineralogical
Mi·neˈral·öl *n* mineral oil; **~er·zeug·nis** *n* petroleum product; **~ge·sell·schaft** *f* oil company; **~in·du,strie** *f* oil industry; **~kon,zern** *m* oil company; **~steu·er** *f* tax on oil
Mi·neˈral|quel·le *f* mineral spring; **~salz** *n* mineral salt; **~vor·kom·men** *n* mineral deposit(s *pl.*); **~was·ser** *n* mineral water
Mi·nia·tur [minĭaˈtuːɐ] *f* (-; -en) miniature; *in manuscripts*: *a.* illumination; **~aus·ga·be** *f* miniature edition
mi·nia·tu·ri·sie·ren [minĭaturiˈziːrən] *v/t.* (h) miniaturize
Mi·niaˈtur|ma·ler *m* miniaturist; **~ma·le,rei** *f* miniature painting
Mi·ni|bar [ˈmɪni-] *f* minibar; **~car** [-kaːɐ] *m* (-s; -s) minicab; **~for,mat** *n* mini-format, tiny format; ***... in ~*** mini-format ...
ˈMi·ni·golf *n* crazy golf; **~platz** *m* crazy golf course
mi·ni·mal [miniˈmaːl] *adj.* minimal, minimum ...; *fig.* insignificant
Mi·niˈmal|be·trag *m* minimum (amount); **~for·de·rung** *f* minimum demand
Mi·ni·ma·list [minimaˈlɪst] *m* (-en; -en) minimalist
Mi·niˈmal·pro,gramm *n* (basic) policy plan
Mi·ni·mum [ˈmiːnimʊm] *n* (-s; -ma) minimum; ***et. auf ein ~ beschränken*** keep s.th. to a minimum
Mi·ni|pil·le [ˈmɪni-] *f* minipill; **~rock** *m* miniskirt; **~slip** *m*: ***(ein ~*** a pair of) bikini briefs *pl.*
Mi·ni·ster [miˈnɪstɐ] *m* (-s; -) minister (*gen.* of, for), *in GB*: Secretary of State (for), *in the USA*: Secretary (of); **~amt** *n* ministerial office; portfolio; **~an·kla·ge** *f* impeachment of a minister; **~bank** *f* (-; ¨e) government front bench; **~ebe·ne** *f*: ***auf ~*** at cabinet level; ***Gespräche auf ~*** *a.* ministerial-level talks
Mi·ni·ste·ri·al|be·am·te [minɪsteˈrĭaːl-] *m* ministry official; **~bü·ro·kra'tie** *f* departmental red tape (*or* bureaucracy); **~di,rek·tor** *m* under-secretary (of state), *Am.* assistant secretary of state; **~er·laß** *m* ministerial decree; **~rat** *m* principal; **~zu·la·ge** *f* ministerial salary benefits *pl.*
mi·ni·ste·ri·ell [minɪsteˈrĭɛl] *adj.* ministerial
Mi·ni·ste·rin [miˈnɪstərɪn] *f* (-; -nen) → ***Minister***
Mi·ni·ste·ri·um [minɪsˈteːrĭʊm] *n* (-s; -rien) ministry, (government) department
Mi·niˈste·ri·ums·spre·cher *m* ministerial spokesman, spokesman for the ministry
Miˈni·ster|kon·fe,renz *f* ministerial conference; **~po·sten** *m* ministerial post; **~prä·si,dent** *m* prime minister, premier; **~rat** *m* cabinet; *EC etc.*: Council of Ministers
Mi·ni·strant [minɪsˈtrant] *m* (-en; -en) *eccl.* server
Min·na [ˈmɪna] F *f* (-; -s): ***grüne ~*** F Black Maria, *Am.* paddy wagon; ***j-n zur ~ machen*** F give s.o. a roasting, bawl (*Am.* chew) s.o. out
Min·ne [ˈmɪnə] *f* (-; *no pl.*) (*a.* ***hohe ~***) courtly love; **~sang** *m* (-s; *no pl.*) minnesang; **~sän·ger** *m* minnesinger
Mi·no·ri·tät [minoriˈtɛːt] *f* (-; -en) minority; **Mi·no·riˈtä·ten·fra·ge** *f* question of minorities
mi·nus [ˈmiːnʊs] **I.** *prp.* (*gen.*) minus; **II.** *adv.*: ***~ 10 Grad*** 10 (degrees) below zero
ˈMi·nus *n* (-; *no pl.*) deficit; overdraft; *fig.* disadvantage, drawback; ***~ machen***

make a loss; ***im ~ sein*** be in the red; **~be·trag** *m* deficit

Mi·nus·kel [mi'nʊskəl] *f* (-; -n) small (*or* lowercase) letter, minuscule

'Mi·nus|pol *m* ⚡ negative pole (*or* element); **~punkt** *m* **1.** penalty point; *sport*: point against; **2.** *fig.* disadvantage, drawback, minus factor; **~re,kord** *m* record (*or* all-time) low; **~sei·te** *f* ✝ *and fig.*: (***auf der ~*** on the) debit side; **~stun·de** *f* minus hour; **~zei·chen** *n* minus sign

Mi·nu·te [mi'nu:tə] *f* (-; -n) minute (*a. ast.*, ⩘); ***auf die ~*** on the dot; ***es klappte auf die ~*** it was perfectly timed, the timing was perfect; ***in letzter ~*** at the last minute; ***bis zur letzten ~*** right up to the last minute; ***~ auf ~ verging*** the minutes passed by; ***auf die ~ kommt es nicht an*** a) it doesn't have to be timed down to the minute, b) you *etc.* don't have to be absolutely punctual (*or* be there on the minute); → ***ruhig*** I; **mi'nu·ten·lang I.** *adj.* lasting several minutes; several minutes of ...; **II.** *adv.* for (several) minutes; **Mi'nu·ten·zei·ger** *m* minute hand

mi·nu·ti·ös, mi·nu·zi·ös [minu'tsi̯ø:s] *adj.* minutely detailed; scrupulously precise; meticulous

Min·ze ['mɪntsə] *f* (-; -n) ⚘ mint

mir [mi:ɐ] *pers. pron.* (*dat. of ich*) (to) me; (*a.* ***~ selbst***) myself; ***er gab es ~*** he gave it to me, he gave me it; ***~ ist kalt*** I feel cold; ***ein Freund von ~*** a friend of mine; ***du bist ~ ein schöner Freund*** a fine friend you are; ***laß ~ m-e Ruhe*** leave me alone; ***von ~ aus*** → ***meinetwegen***; ***wie du ~, so ich dir*** an eye for an eye; ***ich putzte ~ die Zähne*** I brushed my teeth; → ***nichts***

Mi·ra·bel·le [mira'bɛlə] *f* (-; -n) yellow plum

Mis·an·throp [mizan'tro:p] *m* (-en; -en) misanthropist; **mis·an·thro·pisch** [mizan'tro:pɪʃ] *adj.* misanthropic(ally *adv.*)

misch·bar ['mɪʃba:ɐ] *adj.* mixable; ***gut ~ sein*** mix well

Misch|bat·te,rie ['mɪʃ-] *f* mixer tap; **~be·cher** *m* shaker; **~brot** *n* mixed-grain bread; **~ehe** *f* mixed marriage

mi·schen ['mɪʃən] (h) **I.** *v/t.* **1.** mix; blend *tobacco, coffee etc.*; ***et. ~ in*** *acc.* mix s.th. into *s.th.*, add s.th. to *s.th.*; ***Gift ~*** concoct (*or* mix) a poison; **2.** *card game*: shuffle; **3.** *radio, TV* mix; **II.** *v/refl.* **4.** ***sich*** (***gut*** *etc.*) **~** mix (well *etc.*); **5.** ***sich ~ unter*** *acc.* mix (*or* mingle) with; ***sich ~ in*** *acc.* interfere (*or* meddle) in; butt in on; ***sich in ein Gespräch ~*** join in the conversation; **III.** *v/i. card game*: shuffle; → ***gemischt***

Mi·scher ['mɪʃɐ] *m* (-s; -) mixer (*a. TV*)

Misch|far·be ['mɪʃ-] *f* compound colo(u)r; **2far·big** *adj.* of mixed (*or* various) colo(u)rs; **~form** *f* **1.** *ling.* hybrid (form); **2.** mixture; ***e-e ~ zwischen ... und ...*** *a.* a fusion of ... and ...; **~fut·ter** *n* mixed feed; **~ge·we·be** *n* mixed fabric, F mixture; **~haut** *f* combination skin; **~kon,zern** *m* conglomerate; **~kost** *f* mixed diet; **~kul,tur** *f* **1.** mixed(-race) culture; **2.** ⚒ mixed cultivation

Misch·ling ['mɪʃlɪŋ] *m* (-s; -e) hybrid (*a.* ⚘), crossbreed; half-caste, *esp. contp.* half-breed

Misch·masch ['mɪʃmaʃ] F *m* (-[e]s; -e) hotchpotch; *contp. a.* jumble

Misch·ma,schi·ne ['mɪʃ-] *f* (cement) mixer

Misch·po·che [mɪʃ'po:xə], **Misch·po·ke** [mɪʃ'po:kə] F *contp. f* (-; *no pl.*) **1.** F clan; **2.** F rabble, shower

Misch|pult ['mɪʃ-] *n radio, TV* mixer, mixing console; **~ras·se** *f* mixed race; *zo.* mixed breed, crossbreed; **~trom·mel** *f* ⚙ mixing drum

Mi·schung ['mɪʃʊŋ] *f* (-; -en) mixture (*a. fig.*); blend *of tobacco etc.*; assortment *of biscuits etc.*; ***e-e ~ aus*** *dat.* a mixture of; **'Mi·schungs·ver·hält·nis** *n* mixing ratio

Misch|wald ['mɪʃ-] *m* mixed forest; **~wort** *n* hybrid (word)

mi·se·ra·bel [mizə'ra:bəl] *adj.* terrible, dreadful, F lousy; F rotten; ***miserable Leistung*** *a.* pathetic performance

Mi·se·re [mi'ze:rə] *f* (-; -n) plight; *pol.*, ✝ *a.* malaise

Mis·pel ['mɪspəl] *f* (-; -n) ⚘ medlar (tree)

miß'ach·ten [mɪs-] *v/t.* (h) ignore; neglect; disdain, despise; **Miß'ach·tung** *f* (-; *no pl.*) disregard (*gen.* of); neglect (of); disdain (for); ⚖ ***~ des Gerichts*** contempt of court

Miß·be·ha·gen ['mɪs-] *n* (-s; *no pl.*) feeling of unease, uncomfortable feeling; misgivings *pl.*; displeasure, discontent

Miß·bil·dung ['mɪs-] *f* (-; -en) deformity

miß'bil·li·gen [mɪs-] *v/t.* (h) disapprove (of); **'Miß·bil·li·gung** *f* (-; *no pl.*) disapproval; **'Miß·bil·li·gungs·an·trag** *m* motion of disapproval

Miß·brauch ['mɪs-] *m* (-[e]s; ⸚e) abuse; misuse, improper use; ***der ~ von Medikamenten*** drug abuse; ***~ e-s Amtes*** abuse of office; ***unter ~ von*** *dat.* by abusing (*or* misusing); ***~ treiben mit*** *dat.* abuse, misuse, put *s.th.* to improper use; **miß'brau·chen** *v/t.* (h) abuse (*a. sexually*); misuse; **'miß·bräuch·lich** [-brɔʏçlɪç] *adj.*: ***~e Verwendung*** improper use, misuse

miß'deu·ten [mɪs-] *v/t.* (h) misinterpret, misconstrue; **'Miß·deu·tung** *f* (-; -en) misinterpretation

mis·sen ['mɪsən] *v/t.*: ***nicht ~ können*** *or* ***mögen*** not to be able to do without *s.o. or s.th.*; ***das möchte ich nicht ~*** I wouldn't like to do (*or* be *or* have done) without it, I wouldn't like to miss out (*or* have missed out) on it

Miß|er·folg ['mɪs-] *m* failure; flop; **~ern·te** *f* bad harvest, crop failure

Mis·se·tat ['mɪsə-] *f* misdeed; **'Mis·se·tä·ter** *m* malefactor, miscreant; *a.* ⚖ offender

miß'fal·len ['mɪs-] *v/i.* (mißfiel, mißfallen, h): ***er*** (***es***) ***mißfällt ihr*** she doesn't like him (it); **'Miß·fal·len** *n* (-s; *no pl.*) displeasure, disapproval; ***j-s ~ erregen*** cause s.o. displeasure, incur s.o.'s displeasure (*or* disapproval); **'Miß·fal·lens·äu·ße·rung** *f* expression of disapproval

miß·ge·bil·det ['mɪs-] *adj.* deformed, misshapen

Miß·ge·burt ['mɪs-] *f* **1.** deformed child (*or* animal); freak; **2.** *fig.* failure, flop; **3.** F *contp.* F obnoxious creature, *sl.* scab

miß·ge·launt ['mɪs-] *adj.* bad-tempered ...; ***~ sein*** be in a bad mood

Miß·ge·schick ['mɪs-] *n* bad luck, misfortune; mishap

Miß·ge·stalt ['mɪs-] *f* misshapen figure; **'miß·ge·stal·tet** *adj.* misshapen, deformed

miß·ge·stimmt ['mɪs-] *adj.* → ***mißgelaunt***

miß'glücken [mɪs-] *v/i.* (sn) fail, be a failure, be unsuccessful, not to come off; ***der Plan ist ihm mißglückt*** his plan failed, the plan turned out a failure *or* didn't work out (for him), his plan didn't come off; ***der Kuchen ist mir mißglückt*** the cake didn't turn out; **miß'glückt** *adj.* unsuccessful *attempt etc.*; ***es war ein*** (***völlig***) ***~er Plan*** the plan didn't come off (was a complete failure *or* a disaster)

miß'gön·nen [mɪs-] *v/t.* (h): ***j-m et. ~*** (be)grudge s.o. s.th.

Miß·griff ['mɪs-] *m* mistake; wrong move; bad choice; ***e-n ~ tun*** make a mistake (*or* wrong move, bad choice); ***damit hat er e-n absoluten ~ getan*** that was a bad (*or* fatal) mistake

Miß·gunst ['mɪs-] *f* (-; *no pl.*) envy, jealousy; ill will, malevolence; **'miß·gün·stig** *adj.* envious, jealous; malevolent

miß'han·deln [mɪs-] *v/t.* (h) ill-treat, maltreat; **miß'han·delt** *adj.*: ***~es Kind*** (***~e Frau***) battered child (wife); **Miß'hand·lung** *f* ill-treatment, maltreatment; ⚖ assault and battery

Miß·hel·lig·kei·ten ['mɪshɛlɪçkaɪtən] *pl.* **1.** differences (of opinion), disagreement *sg.*; **2.** trouble *sg.*

Mis·si·on [mɪ'si̯o:n] *f* (-; -en) mission; delegation; **Mis·sio·nar** [mɪsi̯o'na:ɐ] *m* (-s; -e [-rə]) missionary; **mis·sio·na·risch** [mɪsi̯o'na:rɪʃ] **I.** *adj.* missionary; *fig.* ***mit ~em Eifer*** with a missionary zeal; **II.** *adv.*: ***~ tätig sein*** do missionary work; proselytize; **mis·sio·nie·ren** [mɪsi̯o'ni:rən] (h) **I.** *v/i.* do missionary work; proselytize; **II.** *v/t.* do missionary work in *a country*, take (*or* preach) the Gospel *etc.* to; proselytize, *w.s.* convert *people*

Mis·si'ons|chef *m* head of a (*or* the) mission; **~sta·ti,on** *f* mission; missionary outpost

Miß|klang ['mɪs-] *m* discordant note, *a. pl.* dissonance, discord; *fig. a.* note of discord; **~kre,dit** *m* discredit, disrepute; ***in ~ bringen*** bring discredit upon, bring dishono(u)r to; ***in ~ geraten*** fall into disrepute, get (o.s. *or* itself) a bad name

miß·lang [mɪs'laŋ] *pret. of* ***mißlingen***

miß·lich ['mɪslɪç] *adj.* disagreeable, awkward; difficult; unfortunate; ***~e Lage*** awkward (*or* unpleasant) situation, predicament; **'Miß·lich·keit** *f* (-; -en) **1.** *no pl.* disagreeable nature *of a situation etc.*; awkwardness; **2.** awkward (*or* unpleasant) situation, predicament; *pl.* unpleasant things (*or* aspects), F little problems

miß·lie·big ['mɪsli:bɪç] *adj.* unpopular; **'Miß·lie·big·keit** *f* (-; *no pl.*) unpopularity

miß·lin·gen [mɪs'lɪŋən] *v/i.* (mißlang, mißlungen, sn) fail, be unsuccessful, turn out (to be) a failure; ***es mißlang ihm*** he was unsuccessful (with it), he didn't manage it, ***zu*** *inf.*: he failed (in his attempt) to *inf.*, he was unsuccessful in *ger.*; **miß·lun·gen** [mɪs'lʊŋən] **I.** *p.p. of* ***mißlingen***; **II.** *adj.* unsuccessful *attempt etc.*; ***~er Staatsstreich*** abortive coup

Miß·mut ['mɪs-] *m* (-[e]s; *no pl.*) disgruntlement; **'miß·mu·tig** *adj.* bad-tempered ..., *pred.* in a bad mood; disgruntled

miß'ra·ten[1] [mɪs-] *v/i.* (mißriet, mißraten, sn) fail; turn out a failure, go wrong; ***es ist mir ~*** I've made a mess of it; ***der Kuchen ist mir ~*** the cake hasn't turned out

miß'ra·ten² I. *p.p. of* **mißraten¹**; II. *adj.* wayward *child*

Miß·stand ['mɪs-] *m* (-[e]s; ⸚e) *a. pl.* deplorable state of affairs; abuse; *pl.* mismanagement; **soziale Mißstände** social injustices; **Mißstände abschaffen** remedy abuses *etc.*; **es herrschen Mißstände in** *dat.* **...** *a.* things are not as they should be in ...

Miß·stim·mung ['mɪs-] *f* (-; -en) bad (*or* ill) feeling, note of discord; (note of) disagreement

Miß·ton ['mɪs-] *m* discordant (*or* grating) note; *fig.* sour note, note of discord; **'miß·tö·nend** *adj.* discordant; grating

miß'trau·en [mɪs-] *v/i.* (h) distrust, mistrust; have no confidence in; **ich mißtraue der Sache** I have my doubts (*or* suspicions) about it; **'Miß·trau·en** *n* (-s; *no pl.*) distrust, mistrust (**gegen** *acc.* of); suspicion (of); doubt(s *pl.*) (concerning); **voller ~ sein** be very distrustful (*or* suspicious, doubtful)

'Miß·trau·ens|an·trag ['mɪs-] *m* motion of no-confidence; **e-n ~ stellen** propose a vote of no-confidence; **~vo·tum** *n* vote of no-confidence

miß·trau·isch ['mɪstraʊɪʃ] *adj.* distrustful; suspicious, wary; sceptical, *Am.* skeptical

Miß·ver·gnü·gen ['mɪs-] *n* (-s; *no pl.*) annoyance, displeasure (**über** *acc.* at); discontent(ment) (at, about); **'miß·vergnügt** *adj.* disgruntled (**über** *acc.* at, about), not (exactly) pleased (about), upset (at, about); discontented (at, about); sullen, F grumpy; **etwas ~ sein über** *acc. a.* not to be too happy about

Miß·ver·hält·nis ['mɪs-] *n* imbalance, disproportion; discrepancy, disparity; **in e-m ~ stehen** be out of proportion (**zu** *dat.* to)

miß·ver·ständ·lich ['mɪs-] *adj.* misleading, unclear; ambiguous; **'Miß·verständ·lich·keit** *f* (-; *no pl.*) misleading nature *of a statement*; **'Miß·ver·ständnis** *n* (-ses; -se) misunderstanding; disagreement

'miß·ver·ste·hen *v/t.* (mißverstand, mißverstanden, h) misunderstand; misinterpret, misconstrue, *a.* mistake *s.o.'s intentions etc.*; **du hast mich mißverstanden** *a.* you've got me wrong

Miß·wahl ['mɪs-] *f* beauty contest

Miß·wirt·schaft ['mɪs-] *f* (-; *no pl.*) mismanagement, bad management

Mist [mɪst] *m* (-[e]s; *no pl.*) **1.** dung; droppings *pl.*; manure; F *fig.* **das ist nicht auf m-m ~ gewachsen** I had nothing to do with it; **2.** F rubbish, F junk; **3.** F rubbish, rot, F trash, garbage; **~ machen** (*or* **bauen**) a) F (make a) boob, b) make a mess of it, F botch it (up), cock it up; **mach keinen ~!** don't do anything stupid; **~ verzapfen** F talk rot; (**so ein**) **~!** F damn (it)!

Mi·stel ['mɪstəl] *f* (-; -n) ♀ mistletoe; **~zweig** *m* sprig of mistletoe

mi·sten ['mɪstən] *v/t.* (h) **1.** manure; **2.** muck out

'Mist|fink F *m sl.* dirty slob; **~ga·bel** *f* pitchfork; **~hau·fen** *m* manure heap; **~kä·fer** *m zo.* dung beetle; **~kerl** F *contp. m sl.* swine, bastard; **~stück** F *contp. n*, **~vieh** F *contp. n sl.* bastard, *sl.* bitch; **~wet·ter** F *n* rotten weather, F bloody awful weather; **~zeug** F *n* → **Mist** 2, 3

mit [mɪt] I. *prp.* (*dat.*) **1.** with; **ein Mann ~ Hund** a man with a dog; **Tee ~ Rum** tea with rum; **Zimmer ~ Frühstück** bed and breakfast; **ein Korb ~ Obst** a basket of fruit; **2.** with; **~ der Bahn** (**Post** *etc.*) by train (post *etc.*); **~ Bleistift** (**Kugelschreiber**) **schreiben** write in pencil (with a ballpoint, in pen); **~ Gewalt** by force; **~ Bargeld** (**Scheck, Kreditkarte**) **bezahlen** pay in cash (by cheque [*Am.* check], by credit card); **~ dem nächsten Bus fahren** (**ankommen**) take (arrive on) the next bus; **3.** with; **~ Absicht** intentionally; **~ lauter Stimme** in a loud voice; **~ Verlust** at a loss; **~ einem Mal** all of a sudden, suddenly; **~ einem Wort** in a word; **~ 8 zu 11 Stimmen beschließen** carry by 8 votes to 11; **~ e-r Mehrheit von** by a majority of; **4. was ist ~ ihm?** what's the matter with him?; **wie steht es ~ Ihrer Arbeit?** how's your work getting on?; **wie steht's ~ dir?** how about you?; **wie wär's ~ ...?** how about ...?; **~ mir nicht!** don't (*or* they *etc.* needn't) try it on with me; **5. ~ 20 Jahren** at (the age of) twenty; **~ dem 3. Mai** as of May 3rd; → **Zeit**; II. *adv.* also, too; **~ dabeisein** be there too; **er war ~ der beste** he was one of the (very) best; → **dazugehören**

'Mit·an·ge·klag·te *m, f* (-n; -n) codefendant

'Mit·ar·beit *f* (-; *no pl.*) cooperation, collaboration; assistance (**bei** *dat.* in); *w.s.* work; **ihre langjährige ~ bei** *dat.* **...** her many years of work(ing) with (*or* for) ...; **'mit·ar·bei·ten** *v/i.* (*sep.*, h) cooperate, collaborate; help out; **~ an** *dat.* work on *s.th.* (too), contribute to; *ped.* participate in, join in; **'Mit·ar·bei·ter** *m* a) employee, b) contributor (*gen. or* **bei** *dat.* to *a newspaper etc.*); **freier ~** freelance, collaborator; **er war ~ an dem Projekt** he worked on (*or* was involved in) the project; **wie viele ~ hat die Firma?** how many people work for the company?; **'Mit·ar·bei·ter·stab** *m* staff, F team; **sie gehört zu s-m engsten ~** she's one of his closest collaborators

'Mit·au·tor *m* co-author

'Mit·be·grün·der *m* co-founder

'mit·be·kom·men *v/t.* (*irr., sep*, h, → **bekommen**) **1.** a) get (*or* be given) *s.th.* (to take with one (*or* for the road), b) get *s.th.* as a dowry; **2.** F catch; hear; realize; F get

'mit·be·nut·zen *v/t.* (*sep*, h) share (with s.o.); **ich darf es ~** I'm allowed to use it (too); **'Mit·be·nut·zer** *m* co-user; **'Mit·be·nut·zung** *f* joint (*or* shared) use

'Mit·be·sit·zer *m* co-owner, joint owner

'mit·be·stim·men (*sep.*, h) I. *v/t.* a) decide *s.th.* along with (the) others, b) have an influence on, influence; II. *v/i.*: (**bei e-r Sache**) **~** have a say (in the matter)

'Mit·be·stim·mung *f* (-; *no pl.*), **'Mit·be·stim·mungs·recht** *n* co-determination; worker participation

'Mit·be·wer·ber *m* competitor

'Mit·be·woh·ner *m* fellow occupant

'mit·brin·gen *v/t.* (*irr., sep.*, h, → **bringen**) bring (*or* take) along (with one); *fig.* have, be endowed with; **j-m etwas ~** take something along for s.o., take s.o. a (little) present; **hast du mir was mitgebracht?** have you got (*or* brought) anything for me?; **Mit·bring·sel** ['mɪtbrɪŋzəl] *n* (-s; -) little present, F pressie; souvenir, memento

'Mit·bür·ger *m* fellow citizen

'mit·den·ken *v/i.* (*irr., sep.*, h, → **denken**) **1.** show some initiative, think (things through); **2. denk mal mit!** help me (*or* us) think; **ich muß immer für andere ~** I have to do all the thinking; **er denkt nie mit** he lets others do all the thinking, he leaves the thinking to others; **3.** follow s.o.'s train of thought

'mit·dür·fen *v/i.* (*irr., sep.*, h, → **dürfen**) be allowed to go *or* come (with s.o.); **darf ich mit?** can I come *or* go (too)?

'Mit·ei·gen·tü·mer *m* joint owner, co-owner

mit·ein'an·der I. *adj.* with each other; together; **alle ~** everyone; **~ verheiratet** married; **~ verwandt** related; **sie sind ~ bekannt** they know each other; **sie sind ~ zerstritten** they've fallen out; II. **2** *n* (-s; *no pl.*) coexistence; getting along together

'mit·emp·fin·den (*irr., sep.*, h, → **empfinden**) I. *v/t.* share *s.o.'s troubles etc.*; II. *v/i.*: **mit j-m ~** feel for s.o., sympathize (with s.o.)

'Mit·er·be *m*, **'Mit·er·bin** *f* co-heir(ess *f*), joint heir(ess *f*)

'mit·er·le·ben *v/t.* (*sep.*, h) see (with one's own eyes); **ich hab's miterlebt** *a.* I was there, I saw it happen, I was around at the time; **sie hat den Krieg noch miterlebt** she was still alive during the war; **das wird er nicht mehr ~** he won't live (*or* be around) to see that (day); **ich mußte ~, wie er an Krebs starb** I had to watch him die of cancer

'mit·es·sen (*irr., sep.*, h, → **essen**) I. *v/i.* eat with us *etc.*; II *v/t.*: **kann man die Schale** *etc.* **~?** can you eat the peel *etc.* (too)?

'Mit·es·ser *m* (-s; -) ⚕ blackhead

'mit·fah·ren *v/i.* (*irr., sep.*, sn, → **fahren**) drive (*or* go, ride) with s.o.; **j-n ~ lassen** give s.o. a lift (*Am.* ride); **darf ich ~?** can you give me a lift (*Am.* ride)?

'Mit·fahr|ge·le·gen·heit *f* lift, *Am.* ride; **biete ~ nach Köln** lift (*Am.* ride) offered to Cologne; **~zen,tra·le** *f* car pool(ing) service

'mit·flie·gen *v/i.* (*irr., sep.*, sn, → **fliegen**) fly with s.o.; **fliegt er mit?** *a.* is he flying too?; **mit derselben Maschine ~** be on the same flight

'mit·freu·en *v/refl.* (*sep.*, h): **sich ~** be (very) pleased for s.o.; **wir haben uns alle mitgefreut** *a.* we were all thrilled (at the news)

'mit·füh·len *v/t. and v/i.* (*sep.*, h) → **mitempfinden**; **'mit·füh·lend** *adj.* sympathetic, compassionate; understanding

'mit·füh·ren *v/t.* (*sep.*, h) **1.** have *s.th.* with (*or* on) one; **2.** *river etc.*: carry (along) with it

'mit·ge·ben *v/t.* (*irr., sep.*, h, → **geben**): **j-m et. ~** give s.o. s.th. (to take with him *or* her), *fig.* give s.o. s.th. (along the way); **j-m j-n ~** send s.o. along with s.o.

'mit·ge·fan·gen *adj.*: **~, mitgehangen** in for a penny(, in for a pound)

'Mit·ge·fan·ge·ne *m, f* (-n; -n) fellow prisoner; **die ~n** the other prisoners

'Mit·ge·fühl *n* (-[e]s; *no pl.*) sympathy; **j-m sein ~ ausdrücken** offer one's sympathies (*formal*: condolences) to s.o.; **du hast mein ~** *esp. iro.* I sympathize, you have my (deepest) sympathy

'mit·ge·hen *v/i.* (*irr., sep.*, sn, → **gehen**) **1.** go (*or* come) along (**mit j-m** with s.o.);

ich geh' noch ein Stückchen mit I'll come along part of the way with you, I'll walk you part of the way; F ***et. ~ lassen*** F walk off with s.th.; **2.** *fig. audience etc.*: respond, play along; ***~ mit*** *dat. a.* go along with; ***begeistert ~*** respond wholeheartedly
ˈmit·ge·nom·men I. *p.p. of* ***mitnehmen***; **II.** *adj.* the worse for wear; battered; exhausted, strained
Mit·gift [ˈmɪtgɪft] *f* (-; -en) dowry; **~jä·ger** *m* fortune-hunter
Mit·glied [ˈmɪtgliːt] *n* (-[e]s; -er [-dɐ]) member; ***ordentliches (förderndes, zahlendes) ~*** full (supporting, subscribing) member; ***~ sein von*** *dat.* be a member of, belong to; sit on *a committee*
Mit·glie·der|ver·samm·lung [ˈmɪtgliː-dɐ-] *f* general meeting; **~zahl** *f* membership
ˈMit·glieds·bei·trag *m* (membership) fees (*Am.* dues *pl.*)
ˈMit·glied·schaft *f* (-; *no pl.*) membership
ˈMit·glieds·kar·te *f* membership card
ˈMit·glied(s)|land *n* member country (*or* nation); **~staat** *m* member state
ˈmit·ha·ben *v/t.* (*irr.*, *sep.*, h, → ***haben***): ***et. ~*** have (brought) s.th. with one, have s.th. on (*or* with) one
ˈmit·haf·ten *v/i.* (*sep.*, h) be jointly liable
ˈMit·häft·ling *m* fellow prisoner
ˈmit·hal·ten *v/i.* (*irr.*, *sep.*, h, → ***halten***) keep up, keep pace; ***~ mit*** *dat. a.* keep abreast of; ***wacker ~*** hold one's own
ˈmit·hel·fen *v/i.* (*irr.*, *sep.*, h) → ***helfen***
ˈMit·her·aus·ge·ber *m* co-editor
ˈMit·hil·fe *f* help, assistance, cooperation
mitˈhin *adv.* consequently, therefore, thus
ˈmit·hö·ren (*sep.*, h) **I.** *v/t.* **1.** listen in on, listen to; eavesdrop on; overhear; ***ich hab's zufällig mitgehört*** I happened to hear it, I couldn't help overhearing it; ***man hört von oben alles mit*** you can hear everything that goes on upstairs; **2.** monitor, listen in on; intercept *radio messages etc.*; **3.** *radio*: listen to, hear; **II.** *v/i.* **4.** listen in; eavesdrop; **5.** tap the wire
ˈMit·in·ha·ber *m* joint owner (*or* proprietor); ☨ partner
ˈmit·kämp·fen *v/i.* (*sep.*, h) join in the struggle; ***mit j-m ~*** fight on s.o.'s side; **ˈMit·kämp·fer** *m* ⚔ fellow combatant, *lit.* comrade-in-arms; *fig. a.* fellow (*or* militant) supporter (***für*** *acc.*, ***in Sachen*** *gen.* of)
ˈMit·klä·ger *m* co-plaintiff
ˈmit·klin·gen *v/i.* (*irr.*, *sep.*, h, → ***klingen***) → ***mitschwingen***
ˈmit·kom·men *v/i.* (*irr.*, *sep.*, sn, → ***kommen***) **1.** come (along); ***kommst du mit?*** are you coming (too)?; **2.** keep up, keep pace; **3.** *fig.* be able to follow; ***da komme ich (einfach) nicht mit*** it's above my head, I must be too stupid for that kind of thing; **4.** *ped.* ***gut ~*** do (*or* get along) well; ***nicht ~*** do badly, lag behind
ˈmit·kön·nen *v/i.* (*irr.*, *sep.*, h, → ***können***) **1.** be able to come *or* go (too); **2.** *fig.* → ***mitkommen*** 3
ˈmit·krie·gen F *v/t.* (*sep.*, h) → ***mitbekommen***
ˈmit·las·sen *v/t.* (*irr.*, *sep.*, h, → ***lassen***) let *s.o.* go *or* come along (too)
ˈmit·lau·fen *v/i.* (*irr.*, *sep.*, sn, → ***laufen***) **1.** run (*or* go) along too; ***~ mit*** *dat.* run (along) with; **2.** *sport*: run (in the race); **3.** F *fig.* get done on the side (*or* in between); **ˈMit·läu·fer** *contp. m* hanger-on; *pol.* fellow travel(l)er
ˈMit·laut *m* consonant
ˈMit·leid *n* (-[e]s; *no pl.*) pity, compassion; sympathy; ***aus ~ für*** *acc.* out of pity for; ***mit j-m ~ haben*** have (*or* take) pity on s.o., pity s.o., feel sorry for s.o.
ˈMit·lei·den·schaft *f*: ***in ~ ziehen*** (begin to) affect; spread to; take its toll on ... (as well)
ˈmit·leid·er·re·gend *adj.* pitiful, pitiable, *lit.* piteous; **mit·lei·dig** [ˈmɪtlaɪdɪç] *adj.* compassionate, sympathetic; ***ein ~es Lächeln*** a contemptuous smile
ˈmit·leid(s)·los *adj.* unfeeling, pitiless; ***~ sein*** have no pity
ˈmit·leid(s)·voll *adj.* full of pity, compassionate
ˈmit·le·sen *v/t.* (*irr.*, *sep.*, h, → ***lesen***) read *s.th.* too (*or* with s.o.); ***et. ~*** read s.th. along with s.o.
ˈmit·ma·chen (*sep.*, h) **I.** *v/i.* **1.** join in, take part (***bei*** *dat.* in); F play along, go along with it; ***da mach' ich nicht mit*** a) you can count me out on that, b) I'm not going to go along with that; **2.** cooperate; *fig.* ***wenn das Wetter mitmacht*** weather permitting; ***m-e Beine machen nicht mehr mit*** my legs are giving up (on me); ***der Motor macht nicht mehr mit*** the engine has packed up; **II.** *v/t.* **3.** a) take part in, join in, b) be at; **4.** follow, go with *the fashions*; **5.** live through; go through, suffer; ***sie hat einiges mitgemacht*** *a.* she's got a few tales to tell; F ***da machst du was mit!*** it's a hard life
ˈMit·men·schen *pl.*: ***die ~*** one's fellow human beings; people; *iro.* ***die lieben ~!*** people!; **ˈmit·mensch·lich** *adj.*: ***~e Beziehungen*** human relations; ***~e Kontakte*** social (*or* human) contact
ˈmit·mi·schen F *v/i.* (*sep.*, h) F be in on it (*or* s.th.); ***er muß immer ~*** he's always got to be in on everything
ˈmit·müs·sen *v/i.* *irr.*, *sep.*, h, → ***müssen***) have to go *or* come (too)
Mit·nah·me·preis [ˈmɪtnaːmə-] *m* cash and carry price
ˈmit·neh·men *v/t.* (*irr.*, *sep.*, h, → ***nehmen***) **1.** take along (*or* with one); take away; ***darf ich eins ~?*** can I take one?; ***j-n (im Auto) ~*** give s.o. a lift (*Am.* ride); ***zum ℒ*** please take one; *Pizza etc.* ***zum ℒ*** takeaway ..., *Am.* carryout ..., ... to go; **2.** F *fig.* F take *s.th.* along (as well); *iro.* ***wolltest du die Tür noch ~?*** are you going to leave the door here?; **3.** F walk off with; **4.** exhaust, wear out, take it out of one; ***das hat ihn ziemlich*** (F ***schwer***) ***mitgenommen*** it hit him hard, it's really taken it out of him; → ***mitgenommen*** II; **5.** F do *s.th.* on the side; take *sights etc.* in (on the way), F do; make the most of; ***jede Gelegenheit ~*** F grab every opportunity; ***alles ~, was man kann*** make the most of life
mit·nich·ten [mɪtˈnɪçtən] *adv.* certainly not
Mi·tra [ˈmiːtra] *f* (-; Mitren) mitre, *Am.* miter
ˈmit·rau·chen (*sep.*, h) **I.** *v/i.* **1.** breathe in the (cigarette) smoke; **II.** *v/t.* **2.** breathe in; **3.** ***rauchst du eine mit?*** will you have a cigarette with me?; **III.** ℒ *n* (-s; *no pl.*) passive smoking; **ˈMit·rau·cher** *m* passive smoker; ***wir armen ~*** we poor people who have to breathe in all the smoke
ˈmit·rech·nen *v/t.* (*sep.*, h) include, count (as well), count in; ***... nicht mitgerechnet*** not counting ...
ˈmit·re·den (*sep.*, h) **I.** *v/i.* a) join in (the conversation), b) have a say; ***da kann ich nicht ~*** I don't know anything about that; **II.** *v/t.*: ***etwas*** (*or* ***ein Wörtchen***) ***mitzureden haben*** have a say (***bei*** *dat.* in)
ˈmit·rei·sen *v/i.* (*sep.*, sn) travel (*or* go, come) with s.o.; ***er reist mit*** *a.* he's going (*or* coming) too; **ˈMit·rei·sen·de** *m, f* (-n; -n) fellow passenger (*or* travel[l]er); tour member (*or* participant)
ˈmit·rei·ßen *v/t.* (*irr.*, *sep.*, h, → ***reißen***) drag (*or* carry, sweep) along; *fig.* carry *or* sweep along (*or* away); **ˈmit·rei·ßend** *fig. adj.* rousing *speech, music etc.*; infectious *rhythm etc.*; exciting *play etc.*
mitˈsamt *prp.* (*dat.*) together (*or* along) with
ˈmit·schicken *v/t.* (*sep.*, h) send (along); enclose
ˈmit·schlei·fen *v/t.* (*sep.*, h) (*a.* F *fig. s.o.*) drag along (with one)
ˈmit·schlep·pen *v/t.* (*sep.*, h) F cart along (with one), F hump along; F *fig.* drag *s.o.* along (with one); F *fig.* ***er hat die Kinder alle mitgeschleppt*** *a.* F he had all the kids in tow
ˈmit·schnei·den *v/t.* (*irr.*, *sep.*, h, → ***schneiden***) record; **ˈMit·schnitt** *m* recording
ˈmit·schrei·ben (*irr.*, *sep.*, h, → ***schreiben***) **I.** *v/t.* **1.** write (*or* take) down, make notes on; **2.** take part in, F do *an exam*; **II.** *v/i.* make notes
ˈMit·schuld *f* (-; *no pl.*) share of the blame, *esp.* ⚖ partial responsibility; ***ihn trifft e-e ~*** he is partly to blame (***an*** *dat.* for), he is partly responsible (for), he has a share in the blame (for)
ˈmit·schul·dig *adj.*: ***~ sein*** be partly responsible (***an*** *dat.* for), be partly to blame (for); **ˈMit·schul·di·ge** *m, f* (-n; -n) accomplice (***an*** *dat.* in)
ˈMit·schü·ler *m* schoolmate; classmate
ˈmit·schwin·gen *v/i.* (*irr.*, *sep.*, h, → ***schwingen***) resonate; *fig.* ***darin schwingt ... mit*** it has overtones of ...
ˈmit·sin·gen *v/i.* (*irr.*, *sep.*, h, → ***singen***) join in the singing, sing along; ***in e-m Konzert ~*** sing in a concert
ˈmit·sol·len F *v/i.* (*sep.*, h) be supposed to go *or* come (too)
ˈmit·spie·len *v/i.* (*sep.*, h) **1.** join in, play with s.o.; *sport*: play (***bei*** *dat.* for), be on the team; *thea.* appear, have a part (in); **2.** *fig.* play along; **3.** play a role *or* part (***bei*** *dat.* in); **4.** ***j-m übel*** (*or* ***böse***) ***~*** be really hard (F tough) on s.o., give s.o. a really hard time; **ˈMit·spie·ler** *m* player; *thea.* member of the (supporting) cast
ˈMit·spra·che·recht *n* right to a say (***bei*** *dat.* in); ***wir haben kein ~*** we have no say (whatsoever); ***er hat hier kein ~*** he has no say in things (*or* in the matter); **ˈmit·spre·chen** (*irr.*, *sep.*, h, → ***sprechen***) **I.** *v/t.* **1.** say *s.th.* together with s.o.; ***alle sprachen den Eid mit*** they all said the oath together; **II.** *v/i.* **2.** → ***mitreden***; **3.** → ***mitspielen*** 3
ˈMit·strei·ter *m* fellow combatant *or* supporter (***für*** *acc.*, ***in Sachen*** *gen.* of), *lit.* comrade-in-arms
ˈMitt·acht·zi·ger *m* man in his mid-eighties; ***ein ~ sein*** *a.* be in one's mid-eighties
Mit·tag [ˈmɪtaːk] *m* (-s; -e [-taːgə]) midday,

noon(time); lunchtime; ***heute*** ≗ at noon (*or* midday) today; ***zu ~ essen*** have lunch; ***et. zu ~ essen*** have s.th. for lunch, have some lunch; F ***~ machen*** have one's lunchbreak; ***wir haben über ~ geschlossen*** we close for lunch, we're closed at lunchtime; **~es·sen** *n* lunch; ***was gibt's zum ~?*** what's for lunch?

mit·täg·lich ['mɪtɛːklɪç] *adj.* midday, noonday *a. heat etc.*; lunchtime *break etc.*; **mit·tags** ['mɪtaːks] *adv.* at midday (*or* noon); at lunchtime; ***von (bis, gegen) ~*** from (until, around) noon

'**Mit·tags|hit·ze** *f* midday heat; **~mü·dig·keit** *f* afternoon low point; **~pau·se** *f* lunchbreak; lunchhour; **~ru·he** *f* **1.** afternoon quiet hour; **2.** → ***Mittagsschlaf***; **3.** ***von 12-14h ~*** closed for lunch 12-2 p.m.; **~schlaf** *m*, **~schläf·chen** *n* afternoon nap, siesta; **~son·ne** *f* midday sun; **~stun·de** *f* noon, midday; **~tem·pe·ra͵tu·ren** *pl.* midday temperatures (*or* highs); **~tisch** *m* dinner table; ***den ~ decken*** lay the table for lunch; ***am ~ sitzen*** be having lunch; **~zeit** *f* (-; *no pl.*) lunchtime; ***in*** (*or* ***während***) ***der ~*** at lunchtime

'**Mit·tä·ter** *m* ⚖ accomplice; accessory (to the crime); '**Mit·tä·ter·schaft** *f* complicity

'**Mitt·drei·ßi·ger** *m* man in his mid-thirties; ***ein ~ sein*** *a.* be in one's mid-thirties

Mit·te ['mɪtə] *f* (-; *no pl.*) middle; centre (*Am.* center); *fig.* ***die goldene ~*** the golden mean, a (*or* the) happy medium; *pol.* ***die ~*** the centre (*Am.* center); ***e-e Politik der ~*** a policy of moderation; ***in unserer ~*** with us, in our midst; *lit.* ***er wurde aus unserer ~ gerissen*** *lit.* he was taken from our midst; ***in der ~ zwischen*** half-way between; ***~ Juli*** in the middle of July, (in) mid-July; ***~ des Jahres*** halfway through the year; ***~ der Woche*** midweek, in the middle of the week; ***~ nächster Woche*** in the middle of next week; ***in der ~ des 18. Jahrhunderts*** in the mid-18th century; ***~ Dreißig*** in one's mid-thirties; ***wir nahmen ihn in die ~*** we took him between us, we sat down on either side of him, F we sandwiched him; F ***ab durch die ~!*** off you go!

'**mit·teil·bar** *adj.* communicable

'**mit·tei·len** (*sep.*, h) **I.** *v/t.* **1.** ***j-m et. ~*** inform s.o. of s.th., tell s.o. s.th., *adm.* notify s.o. of s.th., ✝ advise s.o. of s.th.; ***hiermit teilen wir Ihnen mit, daß ...*** this is to inform you that (*or* of) ...; **2.** impart *knowledge etc.* (*dat.* to), convey *a. mood etc.*; **3.** *phys.* impart (*dat.* to); **II.** *v/refl.* **4.** ***sich j-m ~*** confide in s.o., open up to s.o.; **5.** ***sich ~*** *dat. mood etc.*: spread to, (begin to) infect; **6.** *phys.* ***sich ~*** impart itself (*dat.* to)

'**mit·tei·lens·wert** *adj.* worth telling; ***~e Nachricht*** interesting piece of news

mit·teil·sam ['mɪtaɪlzaːm] *adj.* communicative, forthcoming, open; talkative; '**Mit·teil·sam·keit** *f* (-; *no pl.*) communicativeness, openness; talkativeness

'**Mit·tei·lung** *f* (-; -en) *adm.* communication; notification; announcement; (*press*) report; ***~ machen*** → ***mitteilen*** 1

'**Mit·tei·lungs|be·dürf·nis** *n*, **~drang** *m* need *or* urge to communicate (*or* talk [to s.o.])

Mit·tel ['mɪtəl] *n* (-s; -) **1.** means (*sg.*) (***[um] zu*** *inf.* of *ger.*); method (for *ger.*), way (of *ger.*); expedient; *fig.* tool, device; weapon; ***als letztes ~, wenn alle ~ versagen*** as a last resort; ***ihm ist jedes ~ recht*** he'll stop (F stick) at nothing, he'll go to any length(s); ***~ und Wege finden*** find ways and means (***[um] zu*** *inf.* to *inf.*); ***über die ~ verfügen*** (***um***) ***zu*** *inf.* be in a position to *inf.*; ***kein ~ unversucht lassen*** try every possible means (*or* avenue), leave no stone unturned; ***et. mit allen ~n tun*** go to great lengths (*or* do one's utmost) to do s.th.; ***ich hab's mit allen ~n versucht*** I tried everything (possible); → ***Zweck***; **2.** a) ⚕ cure, remedy (***gegen*** *acc.* for); medicine; tablets *pl.*; ointment, b) (*cleaning*) agent; (*household*) cleaner; ***ein ~ gegen Kopfschmerzen*** *etc.* something for a headache *etc.*; ***ein starkes ~*** a) strong medicine (*or* tablets), b) a powerful agent; **3.** *pl.* resources (*a. fig.*); means, funds; ***aus öffentlichen ~n*** from the public purse; ***m-e ~ erlauben es nicht*** it's beyond my means; **4.** average; mean

'**mit·tel** **I.** *adj.* → ***mittler***; **II.** F *adv.* (fair to) middling, so-so

'**Mit·tel·ach·se** *f* central axis

'**Mit·tel·al·ter** *n* (-s; *no pl.*) **1.** Middle Ages *pl.*; ***im ~*** *a.* in medi(a)eval times; ***dunkles ~*** (*the*) Dark Ages; *fig.* ***dort herrscht dunkles ~*** they're going through a dark age; ***das sind Zustände wie im ~!*** it's like (going back to) the Dark Ages; **2.** F middle age; '**mit·tel·al·ter·lich** *adj.* medi(a)eval (*a. fig.*); *fig.* ***~e Zustände*** *a.* conditions going back to the Middle (*or* Dark) Ages

'**Mit·tel·ame·ri͵ka·ner** *m*, '**mit·tel·ame·ri͵ka·nisch** *adj.* Central American

'**Mit·tel·arm·leh·ne** *f mot.* central arm rest

'**mit·tel·bar** *adj.* indirect

'**Mit·tel|bau** *m* (-[e]s; -ten) **1.** ⚠ central part (of a building); **2.** *no pl.* ✝ middle range, middle-range positions *pl.*; *univ.* non-professorial staff; **~be·trieb** *m* medium-size(d) business

'**Mit·tel·chen** F *n* (-s; -) cure; *w.s.* (little) trick

'**mit·tel·deutsch** *adj.* **1.** *geogr.* Central German; **2.** *ling.* Central (*or* Middle) German

'**Mit·tel·ding** *n* (-[e]s; *no pl.*) cross, something in between; ***ein ~ zwischen ... und ...*** a cross between ... and ...

'**Mit·tel·eu·ro͵pä·er** *m* Central European; '**mit·tel·eu·ro͵pä·isch** *adj.* Central European; ***~e Zeit*** (***MEZ***) Central European Time

'**mit·tel·fein** *adj.* ✝ medium-grade (*or* -fine, -size)

'**Mit·tel·feld** *n* centrefield, *Am.* centerfield; *soccer*: midfield; **~spie·ler** *m* midfield player

'**Mit·tel·fin·ger** *m* middle finger

'**mit·tel·fri·stig** [-frɪstɪç] **I.** *adj.* ✝ medium-term *loan etc.*; ***~e Anleihe*** medium-term bond; ***~es Ziel*** medium-range (*or* intermediate) target; ***~e Prognose*** (***Planung***) medium-range forecast (planning); **II.** *adv.*: (***~ gesehen*** seen) in the medium term; ***~ planen*** plan for the medium term

'**Mit·tel·fuß** *m anat.* metatarsus; **~kno·chen** *m* metatarsal

'**Mit·tel·gang** *m* (cent|re, *Am.* -er) aisle

'**Mit·tel·ge·bir·ge** *n* highlands *pl.*; low mountain range

'**Mit·tel·gewicht** *n* (-[e]s; *no pl.*), '**Mit·tel·ge·wicht·ler** [-gəvɪçtlɐ] *m* (-s; -) *boxing*: middleweight

'**Mit·tel·glied** *n* middle (*or* connecting) joint

'**mit·tel·groß** *adj.* middle-sized, medium-sized; '**Mit·tel·grö·ße** *f* medium size

'**Mit·tel·grund** *m art*: middle ground

'**Mit·tel·hand** *f anat.* metacarpus; **~kno·chen** *m* metacarpal

'**Mit·tel·hirn** *n anat.* midbrain, 🕮 mesencephalon

'**mit·tel·hoch·deutsch** *adj.*, '**Mit·tel·hoch·deutsch** *n* (-en; *no pl.*) *ling.* Middle High German

'**Mit·te-'Links|-'Bünd·nis** *n* centre-left (*Am.* center-left) coalition; **~-Re͵gie·rung** *f* centre-left (*Am.* center-left) government

'**Mit·tel·klas·se** *f* (-; *no pl.*) **1.** ✝ medium price range; ***e-e Anlage*** *etc.* ***der ~*** a medium-range (*or* mid-price) hi-fi system *etc.*; **2.** middle classes *pl.*; **~ho͵tel** *n* mid-price hotel; **~wa·gen** *m* middle-of-the-market car

'**Mit·tel·la·ge** *f* **1.** central position, mid-position; **2.** ♪ middle voice

'**mit·tel·län·disch** [-lɛndɪʃ] *adj.* Mediterranean

'**Mit·tel·la͵tein** *n*, '**mit·tel·la͵tei·nisch** *adj. ling.* Medi(a)eval Latin

'**Mit·tel|lauf** *m* middle course *of a river*; **~li·nie** *f* halfway line, *a. sport*: cent|re (*Am.* -er) line; *tennis*: cent|re (*Am.* -er) service line; 𝔄 median line

'**mit·tel·los** *adj.* penniless, destitute, impoverished, *formal*: impecunious

'**Mit·tel·lo·sig·keit** *f* (-; *no pl.*) impoverishment, destitution

'**Mit·tel·maß** *n* average; *an* average performance; *contp.* mediocrity; ***gutes ~*** above average; ***ein vernünftiges*** (*or* ***gesundes***) ***~*** a (*or* the) happy medium; '**mit·tel·mä·ßig** *adj.* mediocre; average; F middling; '**Mit·tel·mä·ßig·keit** *f* mediocrity; mediocre standards *pl.* (*gen.* of)

'**Mit·tel·meer...** *in cpds.* Mediterranean; **~raum** *m* Mediterranean area; ***im ~*** *a.* around the Mediterranean

'**Mit·tel·ohr** *n anat.* middle ear; **~ent·zün·dung** *f* inflammation of the (*or* infection in one's) middle ear

'**Mit·tel·pfo·sten** *m* mullion

'**mit·tel·präch·tig** F **I.** *adj.* **1.** middling; **2.** quite a ...; **II.** F *adv.*: *wie geht's?* - ***~*** so-so, (fair to) middling

'**Mit·tel·punkt** *m* centre (*Am.* center); *a.* heart *of a town etc.*; *fig.* cent|re (*Am.* -er) of interest (*or* attraction); focus, hub; *fig.* ***sie will immer im ~ stehen*** she always wants to be the focus of attention; ***et. in den ~ e-r Rede*** *etc.* ***stellen*** focus on s.th. in a speech *etc.*, make s.th. the focal point of a speech *etc.*; ***in den ~ rücken*** move into cent|er (*Brit.* -re) stage

mit·tels ['mɪtəls] *prp.* (*gen.*) by (means of), through, with (the help of)

'**Mit·tel|schei·tel** *m* middle (*or* cent|re [*Am.* -er]) parting; ***e-n ~ tragen*** have a middle parting, part one's hair in the middle; **~schicht** *f* (-; *no pl.*) middle classes *pl.*; **~schiff** *n* ⚠ nave; **~schu·le** *f* → ***Realschule***

'**Mit·tels|mann** *m* (-[e]s; ⸚er), **~per͵son** *f* mediator, go-between, *a.* ✝ middleman

'**Mit·tel·stadt** *f* middle-sized town

'**Mit·tel·stand** *m* (-[e]s; *no pl.*) middle classes *pl.*; '**mit·tel·stän·disch** [-ʃtɛndɪʃ] *adj.* **1.** bourgeois; **2.** ***~e Betriebe*** small and medium-size(d) businesses; **'Mit·tel·ständ·ler** [-ʃtɛntlɐ] *m* (-s; -) member of the middle classes

'Mit·tel·stands... *in cpds.* middle-class; **~bür·ger** *m* middle-class citizen, member of the middle classes

'Mit·tel|sta·ti,on *f* halfway station, mid-station; **~stein·zeit** *f* Mesolithic period; **~stel·lung** *f* intermediate position; ***e-e ~ einnehmen zwischen*** be halfway between, *fig. a.* be a cross between

'Mit·tel·strecken|flug *m* medium-haul flight; **~flug·zeug** *n* medium-haul aircraft; **~läu·fer** *m* middle-distance runner; **~ra,ke·te** *f* medium-range missile

'Mit·tel|strei·fen *m* central reservation, *Am.* median strip; **~stück** *n* middle part; *gastr.* middle, F middle bit; **~stu·fe** *f* **1.** intermediate stage; **2.** *ped.* middle school, *Am.* junior high; **~stür·mer** *obs. m sport*: centre (*Am.* center) forward; **~teil** *m, n* → ***Mittelstück***; **~weg** *fig. m* middle course; ***der goldene ~*** the golden mean; ***e-n ~ einschlagen*** steer a middle course; **~wel·le** *f radio*: medium wave

'Mit·tel·wel·len|be·reich *m* medium-wave band; **~sen·der** *m* medium-wave radio station (*or* transmitter)

'Mit·tel|wert *m* average, mean (value); **~wort** *n* (-[e]s; ⸚er) *ling.* participle; ***~ der Vergangenheit*** past participle

mit·ten ['mɪtən] *adv.*: ***~ in*** (***an, auf, unter***) *dat.* in the middle of, right in (against, on, under), in the thick of; ***~ unter uns*** in our (very) midst; ***~ aus*** *dat.* right out of; ***~ hinein in*** *acc.* right into *s.th.*; ***~ entzwei*** right in two, clean through; ***~ im Winter*** in the middle (*lit.* depth) of winter; ***~ in der Nacht*** in the middle of the night; ***~ am Tag*** in broad daylight; ***er stand ~ im Leben*** a) he was living life to the full, b) he had firmly established himself in life; ***~ ins Herz*** right into the heart; ***~ im Satz*** in mid-sentence (*or* mid-speech); ***~ in der Luft*** in mid-air; ***~ auf dem Meer*** in mid-ocean

mit·ten|'drin F *adv.* right in the middle (of it); **~'durch** *adv.* right *or* straight through (*or* across); *break, cut etc. a.* clean through

Mit·ter·nacht ['mɪtɐ-] *f* (-; *no pl.*) midnight; **'mit·ter·nacht·blau** *adj.*, **'Mit·ter·nacht·blau** *n* midnight blue

'mit·ter·nächt·lich *adj.* midnight ...

'mit·ter·nachts *adv.* at (*or* around) midnight

'Mit·ter·nachts|mes·se *f* midnight mass; **~son·ne** *f* midnight sun

'Mitt·fünf·zi·ger *m* man in his mid-fifties; ***ein ~ sein*** *a.* be in one's mid-fifties

mit·tig ['mɪtɪç] *adj.* ⚙ concentric, *pred. a.* O.C., on centre (*Am.* center)

mitt·ler ['mɪtlɐ] *adj.* a) middle, central, b) average, medium; 𝔄, *phys.*, ⚙ mean; middling; ***von ~em Alter*** middle-aged; ***~er Beamter*** lower-grade civil servant; ***~es Einkommen*** middle income; ***von ~er Größe*** medium-sized; ***~e Leistungen*** average performance; ***~es Management*** middle management; ***~er Osten*** Middle East; ***~e Qualität*** medium quality; → ***Reife***

'Mitt·ler *m* (-s; -) mediator; **~funk·ti,on** *f*, **~rol·le** *f* role as (a) mediator

'mitt·ler'wei·le *adv.* meanwhile, (in the) meantime; since

'Mitt·neun·zi·ger *m* man in his mid-nineties; ***ein ~ sein*** *a.* be in one's mid-nineties

'mit·tra·gen (*irr., sep.*, h, → ***tragen***) **I.** *v/t.* **1.** help (to) carry; **2.** *fig.* share, bear (*or* carry) one's share of; **II.** *v/i.* help carrying, help with (the) carrying

'mit·trin·ken *v/t. and v/i.* (*irr., sep.*, h, → ***trinken***): ***trinkst du*** (***einen***) ***mit uns mit?*** are you going to have a drink with us (*or* join us for a drink)?

'mitt·schiffs *adv.* ⚓ amidships

'Mitt·sech·zi·ger *m* man in his mid-sixties; ***ein ~ sein*** *a.* be in one's mid-sixties

'Mitt·sieb·zi·ger *m* man in his mid-seventies; ***ein ~ sein*** *a.* be in one's mid-seventies

'Mitt·som·mer *m* midsummer; **~nacht** *f* midsummer night

'Mitt·vier·zi·ger *m* man in his mid-forties; ***ein ~ sein*** *a.* be in one's mid-forties

Mitt·woch ['mɪtvɔx] *m* (-s; -e) Wednesday; (***am***) ~ on Wednesday; **'mitt·wochs** *adv.* on Wednesdays

'Mitt·zwan·zi·ger *m* young man in his mid-twenties; ***ein ~ sein*** *a.* be in one's mid-twenties

mit'un·ter *adv.* now and then, sometimes, occasionally

'mit·un·ter,zeich·nen *v/t.* (*sep.*, h) co-sign; countersign; **'Mit·un·ter,zeich·ner** *m* cosignatory

'mit·ver·ant·wort·lich *adj.* jointly responsible; **'Mit·ver·ant·wort·lich·keit** *f* share of the responsibility; **'Mit·ver·ant·wor·tung** *f* joint responsibility

'mit·ver·die·nen *v/i.* (*sep.*, h) be earning as well; **'Mit·ver·die·ner** *m* second (*or* extra) earner

'Mit·ver·fas·ser *m* co-author

'Mit·ver·schul·den I. *n* (-s; *no pl.*) ⚖ contributory negligence; **II.** ♀ *v/t.* (*sep.*, h) be partly responsible for

'Mit·ver·schwo·re·ne *m, f* (-n; -n) fellow conspirator

'mit·ver·si·chern *v/t.* (*sep.*, h) include in the insurance; **'Mit·ver·si·cher·te** *m, f* (-n; -n) jointly insured party; **'Mit·ver·si·che·rung** *f* coinsurance; joint insurance

'mit·ver·ur·sa·chen *v/t.* (*sep.*, h) be partly responsible for; ***von et. mitverursacht sein*** be partly caused by s.th.

'Mit·welt *f* (-; *no pl.*) a) society in which one lives, b) *one's* contemporaries *pl.*; F ***er präsentierte sich der staunenden ~ als ...*** to everyone's astonishment he appeared as ...

'mit·wir·ken *v/i.* (*sep.*, h) **1.** a) help (***bei*** *dat.* in), b) take part (in); play one's (*or* its) part (in), ***bei*** *dat.*: *a.* play (*or* have) a part in; **2.** *thea.* take part (***bei*** *dat.* in), appear (in); ♪ perform, play, sing (in); **'Mit·wir·ken·de** *m, f* (-n; -n) participant; performer, *thea. a.* actor (*f* actress), player; ***die ~n*** the cast; **'Mit·wir·kung** *f* (-; *no pl.*) participation; cooperation, assistance; ***unter ~ von ...*** assisted by ..., *thea.* starring (*or* featuring) ...

'Mit·wis·sen *n* knowledge; connivance; ***ohne mein ~*** without my knowledge, unbeknown(st) to me; **'Mit·wis·ser** [-vɪsɐ] *m* (-s; -) someone who is in on the secret; confidant; ⚖ accessory; ***es sind zu viele ~*** too many people know about it; **'Mit·wis·ser·schaft** *f* (-; *no pl.*) connivance

'mit·wol·len *v/i.* (*sep.*, h) want to go *or* come (too)

'mit·zäh·len (*sep.*, h) **I.** *v/i.* **1.** help (s.o.) count; count as well; ***ich hab' nicht mitgezählt*** I wasn't counting; **2.** *fig.* count, be important; ***das zählt nicht mit*** that doesn't count, that's not important; **II.** *v/t.* **3.** count (in), include; **4.** include; take into account

'mit·zie·hen (*irr., sep.*, → ***ziehen***) **I.** *v/i.* **1.** (h) help (to) pull, help pulling; **2.** (sn) travel (*or* go) too; ***mit j-m ~*** travel (*or* go) along with s.o.; **3.** (h) follow suit; F play along; ***~ mit*** *dat. a.* go along with; **II.** *v/t.* (h) **4.** help (to) pull; **5.** pull *s.th. or s.o.* along with (*or* behind) one

Mix·be·cher ['mɪks-] *m* (cocktail) shaker

mi·xen ['mɪksən] *v/t.* (h) mix; **Mi·xer** ['mɪksɐ] *m* (-s; -) **1.** bartender; **2.** *TV etc.* mixer; **3.** blender, liquidizer

Mix|ge·rät ['mɪks-] *n* mixer; **~ge·tränk** *n* mixed drink; cocktail

Mix·tur [mɪks'tuːɐ] *f* (-; -en [-rən]) mixture

Mne·mo'tech·nik [mnemo-] *f* mnemonics *pl.*; **mne·mo'tech·nisch** *adj.* mnemonic(ally *adv.*); ***~e Hilfe*** mnemonic (aid)

Mob [mɔp] *m* (-s; *no pl.*) mob

Mö·bel ['møːbəl] *n* (-s; -) piece of furniture; *pl.* furniture *sg.*; **~ge·schäft** *n* furniture shop (*esp. Am.* store); **~händ·ler** *m* furniture dealer; **~packer** *m* removal man; **~po·li,tur** *f* furniture polish; **~schrei·ner** *m* cabinet-maker; **~spe·di,teur** *m* removal man; *pl.* → **~spe·di·ti,on** *f* removal firm; **~stoff** *m* furniture fabric; **~stück** *n* → ***Möbel***; **~tisch·ler** *m* cabinet-maker; **~wa·gen** *m* furniture (*or* removal) van, *obs.* pantechnicon, *Am.* furniture truck

mo·bil [mo'biːl] *adj.* a) mobile, b) *fig.* flexible; active; sprightly; ⚔ ***~e Streitmacht*** mobile force; *a. fig.* ***~ machen*** mobilize

Mo·bi·le ['moːbilə] *n* (-s; -s) mobile

Mo·bi·li·ar [mobi'li̯aːɐ] *n* (-s; *no pl.*) furniture, furnishings *pl.*

Mo·bi·li·en [mo'biːli̯ən] *pl.* movables, movable property *sg.*

mo·bi·li·sie·ren [mobili'ziːrən] *v/t. and v/i.* (h) ⚔ *and fig.* mobilize; ⚕ realize (*v/i.* assets *or* property); **Mo·bi·li'sie·rung** *f* (-; *no pl.*) mobilization; ⚕ realization

Mo·bi·li·tät [mobili'tɛːt] *f* (-; *no pl.*) mobility; *fig.* agility

Mo'bil·ma·chung *f* (-; -en) ⚔ *and fig.* mobilization

Mo'bil·te·le,fon *n* mobile phone

mö·blie·ren [mø'bliːrən] *v/t.* (h) furnish; ***neu ~*** refurnish; **mö·bliert** [møː'bliːɐt] *adj.* furnished; ***~es Zimmer*** furnished room, *Brit. a.* bedsit(ter)

moch·te ['mɔxtə] *pret. of* ***mögen***

möch·te(n) ['mœçtə(n)] *etc.* → ***mögen***

Möch·te·gern... ['mœçtəgɛrn-] *in cpds.* would-be *writer etc.*

mo·dal [mo'daːl] *adj.* modal; **Mo·da·li·tät** [modali'tɛːt] *f* (-; -en) modality; *pl.* details; (precise) terms *of contract etc.*

Mo'dal·verb *n* modal (verb)

Mo·de ['moːdə] *f* (-; -n) fashion; ***die neueste ~*** the latest fashion; ***in ~*** in fashion; ***~ sein*** be in fashion, F be in; (***die***) ***große ~ sein*** be all the rage; ***in*** (***aus der***) ***~ kommen*** come into (go *or* fall out of) fashion; ***in ~ bleiben*** continue (to be) in fashion; ***mit der ~ gehen*** follow (*or* keep up with) the (latest) fashions; *fig.* ***es ist*** (***nicht***) ***~ zu*** *inf.* it's (not) the fashion to *inf.*, it's (not) considered fashionable to *inf.*; **~ar,ti·kel** *m* fashionable article; *n.s.* novelty; **~aus·druck** *m* vogue expression (*or* word), F in word; *pl. a. the* latest jargon *sg.*; **~be·ruf** *m* fashionable (F in) career; **Ձbe·wußt** *adj.* fashion-conscious, F trendy; **~bran·che** *f* fashion trade (*or* industry), F rag trade; **~dro·ge** *f* recreational drug; F in drug; **~far·be** *f this* season's colo(u)r, F in colo(u)r; **~fo·toˌgraf** *m* fashion photographer; **~ge·schäft** *n* fashion shop; **~haus** *n* **1.** fashion house; **2.** → ***Modegeschäft***; **~jourˌnal** *n* fashion magazine; **~krank·heit** *f* fashionable complaint, F the thing to have

Mo·dell [mo'dɛl] *n* (-s; -e) **1.** a) model, b) mock-up; **2.** *paint. etc.* model; ~ ***stehen*** work as a model; ***j-m* ~ *stehen*** sit (*or* pose) for s.o.; ***für ein Bild* ~ *stehen*** model for a painting; **3.** model, design; **4.** draft; **5.** *euphem.* call girl; **~bau** *m* (-[e]s; *no pl.*) model construction; making models; **~bau·ka·sten** *m* construction kit; **~ei·sen·bahn** *f* model railway (*Am.* railroad); **~fall** *m* **1.** model case; **2.** classic case (*or* example), case in point; **~flug·zeug** *n* model aeroplane (*Am.* airplane)

mo·del·lie·ren [modɛ'li:rən] *v/t.* (h) model; mo(u)ld

Mo·del'lier|mas·se *f*, **~ton** *m* model(l)ing clay

Mo'dell|kleid *n* model (dress); **~schrei·ner** *m*, **~tisch·ler** *m* pattern maker; **~ver·such** *m* **1.** pilot experiment (*or* scheme); **2.** *phys. etc.* experiment on (*or* with) a model; **~zeich·nung** *f art*: drawing (*or* sketch) of a model

mo·deln ['mo:dəln] *v/t.* (h) model, mo(u)ld, form; change

Mo·dem ['mo:dɛm] *n*, *m* (-s; -s) *computer*: modem

'Mo·den·schau *f* fashion show

'Mo·de|püpp·chen F *n*, **~pup·pe** F *f* dolly bird

Mo·der ['mo:dɐ] *m* (-s; *no pl.*) mo(u)ld; decay, putrefaction

Mo·de·ra·ti·on [modera'tsĭo:n] *f* (-; -en) *TV* presentation, *Am.* moderation; ***die* ~ *hat ...*** the presenter (*Am.* moderator) is ...; **Mo·de·ra·tor** [mode'ra:to:ɐ] *m* (-s; -en [-ra'to:rən]) *TV* presenter, host, *Am.* moderator, anchorman; **Mo·de·ra·to·rin** [modera'to:rın] *f* (-; -nen) *TV* presenter, host, *Am.* moderator, anchorwoman

'Mo·der·ge·ruch *m* mo(u)ldy (*or* musty) smell; smell of decay (*or* putrefaction)

mo·de·rie·ren [mode'ri:rən] *v/t.* (h) *TV* present, *Am.* anchor, moderate

mo·de·rig ['mo:dərıç] *adj.* mo(u)ldy; musty *smell*; decaying, putrid

mo·dern¹ ['mo:dɐn] *v/i.* (h, sn) mo(u)lder, rot (away)

mo·dern² [mo'dɛrn] *adj.* modern; progressive; *contp.* newfangled; up-to-date ..., *pred.* up to date; fashionable

Mo·der·ne [mo'dɛrnə] *f* (-; *no pl.*) **1.** modern age; **2.** ***Kunst*** *etc.* ***der* ~** modern(ist) art *etc.*

mo·der·ni·sie·ren [modɛrni'zi:rən] *v/t.* (h) modernize; *a.* F give *a company etc.* a facelift; update, bring *s.th.* up to date; **Mo·der·ni'sie·rung** *f* (-; -en) modernization; F facelift; updating

Mo·der·nis·mus [modɛr'nısmʊs] *m* (-; *no pl.*) modernism; **mo·der·ni·stisch** [modɛr'nıstıʃ] *adj.* modernistic(ally *adv.*)

Mo·der·ni·tät [modɛrni'tɛ:t] *f* (-; *no pl.*) modernity

'Mo·de|sa·che *f*: ***das ist*** (***reine***) ~ it's (just) the fashion; **~saˌlon** *m* fashion house; **~schmuck** *m* costume jewellery (*esp. Am.* jewelry); **~schöp·fer** *m* creator and designer; couturier; **~schrift·stel·ler** *m* fashionable writer (*or* author), F in author; **~tanz** *m* latest (F in) dance; dancing craze; **~tor·heit** *f* fad; **~welt** *f* (-; *no pl.*) world of fashion; **~wort** *n* (-[e]s; ⸚er) vogue expression, F in word; **~zeich·ner** *m* fashion designer; **~zeit·schrift** *f* fashion magazine

Mo·di·fi·ka·ti·on [modifika'tsĭo:n] *f* (-; -en) modification; qualification; **mo·di·fi·zie·ren** [modifi'tsi:rən] *v/t.* (h) modify; qualify *term etc.*; **Mo·di·fi'zie·rung** *f* (-; -en) modification; qualification

mo·disch ['mo:dıʃ] *adj.* fashionable, stylish; fashion ..., F in ...

Mo·dul¹ [mo'du:l] *n* (-s; -e) ⚡, *computer*: module

Mo·dul² ['mo:dʊl] *m* (-s; -n) *phys.*, ⚙ module

Mo·du·la·ti·on [modula'tsĭo:n] *f* (-; -en) modulation; **mo·du·lie·ren** [modu'li:rən] *v/t.* (h) modulate

Mo·dus ['mo:dʊs] *m* (-; Modi ['mo:di]) **1.** way, method; approach; **2.** ♪ mode; **3.** *ling.* mood

Mo·fa ['mo:fa] *n* (-s; -s) moped

Mo·ge·lei [mo:gə'laı] F *f* (-; -en) cheating

mo·geln ['mo:gəln] F (h) **I.** *v/i.* cheat; **II.** *v/refl.*: ***sich ins Konzert* ~** wangle one's way into the concert

Mo·gel·packung ['mo:gəl-] *f* **1.** cheat package; *pl. coll.* deceptive packaging *sg.*; **2.** F *fig.* cosmetic change; F *fig.* ***das ist wieder e-e ihrer ~en*** F they're trying to sell us short again

mö·gen ['mø:gən] (mochte, gemocht, h) **I.** *v/i.* **1.** want; ***ich mag nicht*** I don't want to, I don't feel like it; ***ich möchte schon, aber*** I'd like to, but; **II.** *v/t.* **2.** want; ***was möchtest du denn?*** what is it you want?; **3.** like, be fond of; ***nicht* ~** not to like, not to be keen on, dislike; ***lieber* ~** like better, prefer; **III.** *v/aux.* (mochte, hat mögen): ***ich möchte ihn sehen*** I want (*or* I'd like) to see him; ***möchtest du mitkommen?*** do you want (*or* would you like) to come?; ***ich möchte wissen*** a) I'd like to know, b) I wonder; ***ich möchte lieber ins Kino gehen*** I'd rather go to the cinema; ***das möchte ich doch einmal sehen!*** I'd like to see that; ***er mag nicht nach Hause gehen*** he doesn't want to go home; *ich gehe jetzt spazieren* (*essen etc.*) - ***möchtest du auch?*** do you want to come too?; ***mag er sagen, was er will*** he can say what he wants; ***das mag*** (***wohl***) ***sein*** that may be (so); ***mag sein, daß*** perhaps, maybe; ***was ich auch tun mag*** whatever I do, no matter what I do; ***wo er auch sein mag*** wherever he may be; ***wie dem auch sein mag*** be that as it may; ***was mag er dazu sagen?*** I wonder what he'll say to that; ***was mag das bedeuten?*** what can it mean?, I wonder what it could mean?; ***sie mochte 30 Jahre alt sein*** she would have been (*or* she looked) about 30; ***man möchte meinen ...*** you might think ...; ***man möchte verrückt werden!*** F it's enough to drive you up the wall

Mog·ler ['mo:glɐ] F *m* (-s; -) cheat

mög·lich ['mø:klıç] *adj.* possible (***j-m*** for s.o.); practicable, feasible; potential *reaction etc.*; ***alle ~en*** all sorts of; ***alles ~e*** all sorts of things *etc.*; ***alles Ձe tun*** do everything possible; ***sein ~stes tun*** do one's best (*or* utmost), do everything in one's power; ***im Bereich des Ձen*** within the realm (*or* bounds) of possibility; ***es*** (***j-m***) ***~ machen zu*** *inf.* make it possible (for s.o.) to *inf.*; ***nicht ~!*** I don't believe it!, F no kidding!; ***das ist*** (***gut***) ~ that's (quite) possible; ***das ist eher* ~** that's more likely; ***es ist ~, daß er kommt*** he may come; ***es ist mir nicht ~ zu*** *inf.* I can't (possibly) ..., there's no way I can ...; ***es war mir nicht ~*** I wasn't able to do it, I didn't manage (to do) it; ***wenn es mir*** (***irgendwie***) ***~ ist*** if I can (possibly) manage it; ***wenn irgend ~*** if at all possible; *a. iro.* ***wäre es ~, daß du mir hilfst?*** do you think you might possibly be able to help me?; ***man sollte es nicht für ~ halten*** would you credit it; ***so bald*** *etc.* ***wie ~*** as soon *etc.* as possible; **mög·li·chen·falls** ['mø:klıçənfals] *adv.* **1.** if possible; **2.** → **mög·li·cher'wei·se** ['mø:klıçɐ-] *adv.* possibly, it is possible that; perhaps; ***~ ist er schon da*** he may already be there; **'Mög·lich·keit** *f* (-; -en) possibility; opportunity; chance; *pl.* potentialities; ***nach ~*** as far as possible; if possible; ***es besteht die ~*** there is a (*or* that) possibility, ***daß:*** there is a (*or* the) possibility that, it's possible that; ***es besteht die ~, daß sie uns verläßt*** *a.* there's a chance (*or* possibility) of her leaving us, it's possible that she might leave us; ***ich sehe keine ~ zu*** *inf.* I don't see any chance of *ger.*; ***ist das die ~!*** would you credit it; **mög·lichst** ['mø:klıçst] *adv.*: ***~ bald*** *etc.* as soon *etc.* as possible; ***~ klein*** as small as possible, *attr. the* smallest possible ..., *a* minimum of *losses etc.*; ***~ wenig*** as little (...) as possible; ***ein ~ billiges Zimmer*** a very cheap room, a room at the cheap end, the cheapest possible room; ***ich brauche e-n ~ schnellen Wagen*** I need the fastest car available (*or* you've got)

Mo·gul ['mo:gʊl] *m* (-s; -n) *hist.* Mogul

Mo·hair [mo'hɛ:ɐ] *m* (-s; -e [-rə]) mohair

Mo·ham·me·da·ner [mohame'da:nɐ] *m* (-s; -), **Mo·ham·me·da·ne·rin** [mohame'da:nərın] *f* (-; -nen), **mo·ham·me·da·nisch** [mohame'da:nıʃ] *adj.* Moslem, Muslim

Mo·hi·ka·ner [mohi'ka:nɐ] *m* (-s; -) Mohican; *fig.* ***der letzte* ~** the last of the Mohicans

Mohn [mo:n] *m* (-s; *no pl.*) ⚘ poppy; poppy seed; **~blu·me** *f* poppy; **~bröt·chen** *n roll sprinkled with poppy seed*; **~ku·chen** *m* poppy-seed cake; **~saft** *m* poppy juice; *w.s.* opium

Mohr [mo:ɐ] *obs.* *m* (-en; -en ['mo:rən]) *obs.* Moor; *fig.* ***der ~ hat s-e Schuldigkeit getan, der ~ kann gehen*** now that I'm (*or* he's *etc.*) not needed any more, I (*or* he *etc.*) can just go

Möh·re ['mø:rə] *f* (-; -n) carrot

Moh·ren·kopf ['mo:rən-] *m gastr.* **1.** *spherical, chocolate-coated cream cake*; **2.** → ***Negerkuß***

'Möh·ren·saft *m* carrot juice

'Moh·ren·wä·sche *f* whitewash attempt

Mohr·rü·be ['mo:ɐ-] *f* carrot

Moi·ré [mŏa're:] *m*, *n* (-s; -s) moiré

mo·kant [mo'kant] *adj.* mocking, sneering, sardonic(ally *adv.*)

Mo·kas·sin [moka'si:n] *m* (-s; -s) **1.** slip-on; **2.** moccasin

mo·kie·ren [mo'ki:rən] *v/refl.* (h): ***sich ~ über** acc.* make fun of, sneer at
Mok·ka ['mɔka] *m* (-s; -s) mocha (coffee); **~tas·se** *f* demitasse
Molch [mɔlç] *m* (-[e]s; -e) *zo.* newt
Mo·le ['mo:lə] *f* (-; -n) mole, jetty
Mo·le·kül [mole'ky:l] *n* (-s; -e) molecule
mo·le·ku·lar [moleku'la:ɐ] *adj.*, **Mo·le·ku'lar...** *in cpds.* molecular *biology etc.*
molk [mɔlk] *obs. pret. of* ***melken***
Mol·ke ['mɔlkə] *f* (-; *no pl.*) whey
Mol·ke·rei [mɔlkə'raɪ] *f* (-; -en) dairy; **~but·ter** *f* standard (quality) butter; **~ge·nos·sen·schaft** *f* dairy cooperative; **~pro͵dukt** *n* dairy product
Moll [mɔl] *n* (-; *no pl.*) ♪ minor (key); ***a-~*** A minor; **~ak͵kord** *m* minor chord
mol·lig ['mɔlɪç] F **I.** *adj.* **1.** plump, F dumpy; **2.** cosy, *Am.* cozy; snug (*a. pullover etc.*); **II.** *adv.*: ***~ warm*** warm and cosy (*Am.* cozy)
'Moll|ton·art *f* minor key; **~ton·lei·ter** *f* minor scale
Mol·lus·ke [mɔ'lʊskə] *f* (-; -n) *zo.* mollusc, *Am.* mollusk
Mo·loch ['mo:lɔx] *fig. m* (-s; -e) Moloch
Mo·lo·tow·cock·tail ['mo:lotɔf-] *m* Molotov cocktail, petrol (*Am.* gasoline) bomb
Mo·lyb·dän [molʏp'dɛ:n] *n* (-s; *no pl.*) ⚗ molybdenium
Mo·ment¹ [mo'mɛnt] *m* (-[e]s; -e) moment; instant; ***~!*** just a minute; ***~ mal!*** wait a minute!, F hang on (a minute)!; ***im ~*** at the moment, right now; ***im ~ nicht*** not at the moment, not just now; ***im ersten ~*** for a moment, at first; ***im letzten ~*** at the last minute, just in time; ***jeden ~*** any minute *or* moment (now)
Mo'ment² *n* (-[e]s; -e) motive; factor; ⚙ momentum; ***das auslösende ~ für et. sein*** trigger s.th. off
mo·men·tan [momɛn'ta:n] **I.** *adj.* **1.** momentary, passing; **2.** present; ***die ~e Situation*** *a.* the situation at present (*or* right now); **II.** *adv.* at the moment; for the time being
Mo'ment·auf·nah·me *f phot.* snapshot (*a. fig.*); candid shot
Mo·na·de [mo'na:də] *f* (-; -n) monad; **Mo'na·den·leh·re** *f* theory of monads; **Mo·na·do·lo·gie** [monadolo'gi:] *f* (-; *no pl.*) monadology
Mon·arch [mo'narç] *m* (-en; -en) monarch, sovereign; **Mon·ar·chie** [monar'çi:] *f* (-; -n) monarchy; **Mon·ar·chin** [mo'narçɪn] *f* (-; -nen) → ***Monarch***; **mon·ar·chisch** [mo'narçɪʃ] *adj.* monarchic(al); **Mon·ar·chist** [monar'çɪst] *m* (-en; -en) monarchist; **mon·ar·chi·stisch** [monar'çɪstɪʃ] *adj.* monarchist
mo·na·stisch [mo'nastɪʃ] *adj.* monastic; ***das ~e Leben*** *a.* the life of a monk
Mo·nat ['mo:nat] *m* (-s; -e) month; ***der ~ Januar*** the month of January; ***im ~ verdienen*** *etc.*: a (*or* per) month, monthly; ***im dritten ~ sein*** be three months pregnant, be in the third month
'mo·na·te·lang **I.** *adj.* months (and months) of; **II.** *adv.* for months (on end)
'mo·nat·lich **I.** *adj.* monthly; **II.** *adv.* monthly, a month
'Mo·nats|an·fang *m* beginning of the month; **~ein·kom·men** *n* monthly income; **~en·de** *n* end of the month; **~er·ste** *m*: (***am ~n*** on the) first of the month; **~frist** *f* term (*or* period) of one month; ***binnen ~*** within a month; **~ge·halt** *n* monthly salary (*or* pay); ***ein ~*** a (*or* one) month's pay *or* salary; **~kar·te** *f* monthly (season) ticket; **~lohn** *m* monthly wage(s *pl.*); **~mie·te** *f* monthly rent; ***eine ~*** a (*or* one) month's rent; **~mit·te** *f* middle of the month; **~na·me** *m* name of a (*or* the) month; ***die ~n*** the names of the months; **~ra·te** *f* monthly instal(l)ment; **~schrift** *f* monthly (journal, periodical, publication); **~tem·pe·ra͵tur** *f*: ***durchschnittliche ~*** average monthly temperature
'mo·nats·wei·se *adv.* monthly
Mönch [mœnç] *m* (-s; -e) monk; friar; **mön·chisch** ['mœnçɪʃ] *adj.* monastic; ***ein ~es Leben führen*** live the life of a monk
'Mönchs|klo·ster *n* monastery; **~kut·te** *f* monk's habit; **~or·den** *m* monastic order
'Mönch(s)·tum *n* (-s; *no pl.*) monkhood; monastic life, life of a monk
'Mönchs·zel·le *f* monk's cell
Mond [mo:nt] *m* (-[e]s; -e ['mo:ndə]) moon; satellite; F *fig.* ***hinter dem ~ leben*** F be way behind the times; ***du lebst wohl hinter dem ~!*** where have you been all your life?; ***ich könnte ihn auf den ~ schießen!*** F I could wring his neck; ***d-e Uhr geht nach dem ~*** *sl.* your watch is up the creek; ***in den ~ schreiben*** write off; ***in den ~ gucken*** be left (*or* come away) empty-handed, be left out
mon·dän [mɔn'dɛ:n] *adj.* fashionable, chic; ***~e Frau*** society woman
'Mond|auf·gang *m* moonrise; **~bahn** *f* lunar (*or* moon's) orbit; **⁀be·schie·nen** *poet. adj.* moonlit, *pred. a.* bathed in moonlight; **~fäh·re** *f* lunar module; **~fin·ster·nis** *f* eclipse of the moon, lunar eclipse; **~flug** *m* flight to the moon; **~ge·bir·ge** *n* lunar mountain range; **~ge·sicht** F *n* moonface; **~ge·stein** *n* lunar rock(s *pl.*), rocks *pl.* from the moon; **~glo·bus** *m* lunar (*or* moon) globe; **⁀hell** *adj.* moonlit *night*; ***es war ~*** the moon was shining brightly; **~jahr** *n* lunar year; **~kalb** F *n* simpleton, F dumbo; **~kar·te** *f* map of the moon, moon chart; **~kra·ter** *m* lunar crater, crater on the moon; **~lan·de·fäh·re** *f* lunar module; **~land·schaft** *f* lunar landscape, moonscape; **~lan·dung** *f* moon landing, landing on the moon; **~licht** *n* (-[e]s; *no pl.*) moonlight
'mond·los *adj.* moonless *night*
'Mond|nacht *f* moonlit night; **~pha·se** *f* phase of the moon; **~pha·sen·uhr** *f* moon-phase watch; **~ra͵ke·te** *f* lunar rocket; **~schat·ten** *m* shadow of the moon
'Mond·schein *m* (-s; *no pl.*) moonlight; F *fig.* ***du kannst mir im ~ begegnen!*** F you can take a running jump; **~ta͵rif** *m teleph.* cheap rate
'Mond|si·chel *f* crescent (of the moon); **~son·de** *f* lunar probe; **~staub** *m* lunar dust; **~stein** *m* moonstone
'mond·süch·tig *adj.* somnambulist ..., somnambulistic; *w.s.* moonstruck; ***~ sein*** *usu.* sleepwalk, walk in one's sleep; **'Mond·süch·ti·ge** *m, f* (-n; -n) sleepwalker, somnambulist
'Mond|um͵krei·sung *f* lunar orbit; **~͵un·ter·gang** *m* moonset; ***e-n ~ beobachten*** watch the moon go down; **~vier·tel** *n*: ***erstes*** (***letztes***) ***~*** first (last *or* third) quarter (of the moon)
Mo·ne·gas·se [mone'gasə] *m* (-n; -n), **Mo·ne·gas·sin** [mone'gasɪn] *f* (-; -nen) Monacan; ***Monegasse sein*** *a.* come from Monaco; **mo·ne·gas·sisch** [mone'gasɪʃ] *adj.* Monacan, Monegasque
mo·ne·tär [mone'tɛ:ɐ] *adj.* monetary
Mo·ne·ten [mo'ne:tən] F *pl.* F lolly *sg.*, *sl.* brass *sg.*, bread *sg.*
Mon·go·le [mɔŋ'go:lə] *m* (-n; -n), **Mon·go·lin** [mɔŋ'go:lɪn] *f* (-; -nen) Mongolian; **mon·go·lisch** [mɔŋ'go:lɪʃ] *adj.* Mongol, Mongolian
Mon·go·lis·mus [mɔŋgo'lɪsmʊs] *m* (-; *no pl.*) ⚕ mongolism, Down's syndrome; **mon·go·lo·id** [mɔŋgolo'i:t] *adj.* mongoloid
mo·nie·ren [mo'ni:rən] *v/t.* (h) complain about, criticize (***daß*** the fact that); query *check etc.*; make a complaint about *s.th.*
Mo·ni·tor ['mo:nito:ɐ] *m* (-s; -e [-rə]) *TV*, ⚕ *etc.* monitor
mo·no ['mo:no] *adj.* mono
'Mo·no·auf·nah·me *f* mono recording
mo·no·chrom [mono'kro:m] *adj.* monochrome
'Mo·no·emp·fän·ger *m* mono receiver
mo·no·gam [mono'ga:m] *adj.* monogamous; ***~er Mann*** *a.* F one-woman man; **Mo·no·ga·mie** [monoga'mi:] *f* (-; *no pl.*) monogamy
Mo·no·gramm [mono'gram] *n* (-s; -e) monogram; ***... mit ~*** monogrammed ...
Mo·no·gra·phie [monogra'fi:] *f* (-; -n) monograph
Mon·okel [mo'nɔkəl] *n* (-s; -) monocle
'Mo·no·kul͵tur *f* ⚘ monoculture
Mo·no·lith [mono'li:t] *m* (-s, -en; -[e]n) monolith; **mo·no·li·thisch** [mono'li:tɪʃ] *adj.* monolithic
Mo·no·log [mono'lo:k] *m* (-s; -e [-gə]) monolog(ue); *thea.* soliloquy; **mo·no·lo·gi·sie·ren** [monologi'zi:rən] *v/i.* (h) soliloquize, hold monolog(ue)s
mo·no·man [mono'ma:n] *adj.* monomaniac, monomaniacal; **Mo·no·ma·nie** [monoma'ni:] *f* (-; -n) monomania; **mo·no·ma·nisch** [mono'ma:nɪʃ] *adj.* → ***monoman***
Mo·no·phthong [mono'ftɔŋ] *m* (-s; -e) *ling.* monophthong
Mo·no·pol [mono'po:l] *n* (-s; -e) monopoly (***auf*** *acc.* of); **mo·no·po·li·sie·ren** [monopoli'zi:rən] *v/t.* (h) monopolize; **mo·no·po·li·stisch** [monopo'lɪstɪʃ] **I.** *adj.* monopolistic; **II.** *adv.*: ***~ beherrschter Markt*** captive market
Mo·no'pol|par͵tei *f* dominant party; **~pres·se** *f* monopoly press; **~stel·lung** *f* monopoly; ***e-e ~ innehaben*** hold (*or* have) a monopoly (***für*** *acc.* on)
'Mo·no·sen·dung *f* mono broadcast
Mo·no·the·is·mus [monote'ɪsmʊs] *m* (-; *no pl.*) monotheism; **Mo·no·the·ist** [monote'ɪst] *m* (-en; -en) monotheist; **mo·no·thei·stisch** [monote'ɪstɪʃ] *adj.* monotheistic
mo·no·ton [mono'to:n] *adj.* monotonous; **Mo·no·to·nie** [monoto'ni:] *f* (-; *no pl.*) monotony
'Mo·no͵wie·der·ga·be *f* mono reproduction (*or* sound)
Mon·oxyd ['mo:nɔksy:t] *n* (-s; -e) monoxide
Mon·ster ['mɔnstɐ] *n* (-s; -) monster
'Mon·ster... *in cpds. usu.* mammoth; **~film** *m* **1.** monster film; **2.** mammoth production
Mon·stranz [mɔn'strants] *f* (-; -en) monstrance

mon·strös [mɔn'strøːs] *adj.* monstrous
Mon·stro·si·tät [mɔnstrozi'tɛːt] *f* (-; -en) monstrosity
Mon·strum ['mɔnstrʊm] *n* (-s; Monstren ['mɔnstrən]) monster
Mon·sun [mɔn'zuːn] *m* (-s; -e) monsoon; **~re·gen** *m* monsoon rain(s *pl.*); **~wald** *m* monsoon forest; **~zeit** *f* monsoon (period)
Mon·tag ['moːntaːk] *m* (-s; -e [-taːgə]) Monday; (***am***) ~ on Mondays
Mon·ta·ge [mɔn'taːʒə] *f* (-; -n) ⚙ mounting, fitting; erection; installation; assembly; *phot., film etc.*: montage; ***auf*** **~ *sein*** be away on a construction job; **~an·lei·tung** *f* assembly instructions *pl.*; **~hal·le** *f* assembly shop; **~werk** *n* assembly plant
mon·tags ['moːntaːks] *adv.* on Mondays
'Mon·tags|au·to *n*, **~pro·duk·ti͵on** *f* Monday model; **~stim·mung** *f* Monday(-morning) blues
Mon·tan·in·du͵strie [mɔn'taːn-] *f* coal, iron and steel industries *pl.*
Mon·teur [mɔn'tøːɐ] *m* (-s; -e [-rə]) ⚙ fitter; *mot.*, ✈ mechanic; ⚡ electrician; **~an·zug** *m* overalls *pl.*
mon·tie·ren [mɔn'tiːrən] *v/t.* (h) ⚙ mount, fit; set up; assemble; instal(l)
Mon·tur [mɔn'tuːɐ] *f* (-; -en [-rən]) **1.** F gear, F get-up; ***in voller*** ~ fully clothed; **2.** *obs.* uniform
Mo·nu·ment [monu'mɛnt] *n* (-[e]s; -e) monument (***für*** *acc.* to); **mo·nu·men·tal** [monumɛn'taːl] *adj.* monumental
Mo·nu·men'tal... *in cpds. usu.* monumental; mammoth; epic; **~bau** *m* (-[e]s; -ten) monumental structure; **~film** *m*, **~schin·ken** F *m* (screen) epic, (Hollywood) spectacular; **~werk** *n* monumental (*or* epic) work
Moor [moːɐ] *n* (-[e]s; -e ['moːrə]) moor, fen; bog; **~bad** *n* mudbath; **~bo·den** *m* marshy ground; **~huhn** *n* grouse
moo·rig ['moːrɪç] *adj.* marshy, boggy
'Moor|land *n* moorland, marshland; **~land·schaft** *f* moorland(s *pl.*), marshland, marshy landscape; **~lei·che** *f* bog body; **~packung** *f* ⚕ mudpack
Moos [moːs] *n* (-es; -e ['moːzə]) **1.** ♀ moss; **2.** moor; bog; **3.** *sl.* brass; **≈be·deckt** *adj.* moss-covered; **≈grün** *adj.* moss-green; **~rös·chen** [-røːsçən] *n* (-s; -) moss rose
Mop [mɔp] *m* (-s; -s) mop
Mo·ped ['moːpɛt] *n* (-s; -s) moped, motorbike
Mops [mɔps] *m* (-es; Möpse ['mœpsə]) pug(dog)
mop·sen ['mɔpsən] F (h) **I.** *v/t.* F pinch, snitch; **II.** *v/refl.*: ***sich*** ~ be peeved
Mo·ral [mo'raːl] *f* (-; *no pl.*) **1.** morals *pl.*, moral standards *pl.*; ***doppelte*** ~ double standards; ~ ***predigen*** moralize; **2.** morality, ethics *pl.*; **3.** moral; ***die*** ~ ***der Geschichte*** the moral of the tale; **4.** morale; ***die*** ~ ***der Mannschaft*** (***Truppen***) ***ist gut*** morale in the team (among the troops) is high; **~apo·stel** *m* moralizer; **~be·griff** *m* concept of morality; moral (*or* ethical) standards *pl.*
Mo·ra·lin [mora'liːn] F *n* (-s; *no pl.*) priggishness; **mo·ra'lin·sau·er** F *adj.* priggish
mo·ra·lisch [mo'raːlɪʃ] *adj.* moral; F ***e-n ≈en haben*** a) be feeling down, F have the blues, b) have pangs of remorse (*or* conscience); ***er hat e-n ≈en*** *a.* his conscience is pricking him; **mo·ra·li·sie·ren** [morali'ziːrən] *v/i.* (h) moralize, *contp. a.* preach; **Mo·ra·list** [mora'lɪst] *m* (-en; -en) moralist; **Mo·ra·li·tät** [morali'tɛːt] *f* (-; *no pl.*) morality
Mo'ral|ko·dex *m* code of ethics; ethical standards *pl.*; **~pre·di·ger** *m* moralizer; **~pre·digt** *f iro.* sermon, lecture; ***j-m e-e*** ~ ***halten*** give s.o. a lecture, preach at s.o.; **~*en halten*** preach; **~theo·lo͵gie** *f* moral theology
Mo·rä·ne [mo'rɛːnə] *f* (-; -n) moraine
Mo·rast [mo'rast] *m* (-[e]s; -e) morass; *fig. a.* mire; *fig.* ***im*** ~ ***waten*** wallow in the mire
Mo·ra·to·ri·um [mora'toːrĭʊm] *n* (-s; -ien) moratorium
mor·bid [mɔr'biːt] *adj.* **1.** decadent; degenerate, moribund; **2.** sickly, deathly *pallor etc.*; **Mor·bi·di·tät** [mɔrbidi'tɛːt] *f* (-; *no pl.*) **1.** decadence; degeneracy; **2.** sickly nature, sickliness
Mor·chel ['mɔrçəl] *f* (-; -n) ♀ morel (mushroom)
Mord [mɔrt] *m* (-[e]s; -e ['mɔrdə]) murder (***an*** *dat.* of); ⚖ first-degree murder; ***e-n*** ~ ***begehen*** commit (a) murder; F *fig.* ***das gibt*** ~ ***und Totschlag*** F all hell will be let loose; ***es ist der reinste*** ~ it's (sheer) murder; **~an·kla·ge** *f*: ***unter*** ~ ***stehen*** be charged with murder; ***j-n unter*** ~ ***stellen*** charge s.o. with murder; **~an·schlag** *m* attempted murder (***auf*** *acc.* of), brutal attack (on), assassination attempt (against, on); ***e-n*** ~ ***verüben*** carry out a brutal attack *or* assassination attempt (***auf*** *acc.* on), ***auf j-n***: *a.* make an attempt on s.o.'s life; **~de·zer͵nat** *n* murder (*or* homicide) squad; **~dro·hung** *f* death threat; ~ ***gegen j-n*** *a.* threat on s.o.'s life
mor·den ['mɔrdən] (h) **I.** *v/i.* commit murder, kill; **II.** *v/t.* murder; kill; **III.** **≈** *n* (-s; *no pl.*) murder(ing), killing, slaughter(ing)
Mör·der ['mœrdɐ] *m* (-s; -) murderer, killer; assassin; **~ban·de** *f* gang of murderers; **~bie·ne** *f* killer bee; **~hand** *f*: ***durch*** ~ ***sterben*** die at the hands of a murderer
Mör·de·rin ['mœrdərɪn] *f* (-; -nen) murderer, *a.* murderess; killer; assassin
mör·de·risch ['mœrdərɪʃ] **I.** *adj.* murderous; *fig. a.* deadly; *fig.* breakneck *speed etc.*; cutthroat *competition, prices etc.*; **II.** *fig. adv.* dreadfully, F incredibly; ~ ***heiß*** *a. sl.* hot as hell; ~ ***schreien*** *sl.* scream blue murder; ~ ***fluchen*** *sl.* swear like hell
'Mord·gier *f* lust for murder (*or* to kill); **'mord·gie·rig** *adj.* bloodthirsty
'Mord|in·stru͵ment *n* murder weapon; **~kom͵man·do** *n* death squad; **~kom·mis·si͵on** *f* murder (*or* homicide) squad; **~pro͵zeß** *m* murder trial
Mords... [mɔrts-] F *in cpds.* great, F terrific, fantastic; dreadful; **~angst** F *f*: ***e-e*** ~ ***haben*** F be in a flat panic (***vor*** *dat.* about), be scared stiff (of); **~ding** F *n* (-[e]s; -er) F whopper, humdinger; **~durst** F *m*: ***e-n*** ~ ***haben*** be dying of thirst, *sl.* be thirsty as hell; **~glück** F *n* fantastic stroke of luck; **~hit·ze** F *f* scorching heat; ***es ist e-e*** ~ ***heute!*** F it's a real scorcher today; **~hun·ger** F *m*: ***e-n*** ~ ***haben*** be famished, be dying for something to eat (*or*. of hunger); **~kerl** F *m* F great guy; **~krach** F *m*, **~lärm** F *m* F dreadful row (*or* racket)
'mords·mä·ßig F **I.** *adj.* F terrific; **II.** *adv.* F like crazy (*sl.* hell); ***ich habe mich*** ~ ***gefreut*** I was thrilled to bits, F I was over the moon
'Mords|schreck F *m sl. one* hell of a fright; ***e-n*** ~ ***bekommen*** *a.* be frightened out of one's skin; **~skan͵dal** F *m* full-blown scandal; **~spaß** F *m*: ***e-n*** ~ ***haben*** have a great time; ***e-n*** ~ ***machen*** be great fun; **~spek͵ta·kel** F *m* **1.** F hullabaloo, incredible racket; ruckus; ***e-n*** ~ ***machen*** kick up an incredible racket; **2.** F great (big) rumpus (*or* row), ruckus; ***e-n*** ~ ***machen*** kick up a great big row (*or* rumpus); **3.** F hullabaloo, great palaver, hue and cry; **~wut** F *f*: ***e-e*** ~ (***im Bauch***) ***haben*** be seething, be ready to explode
'Mord|tat *f* murder(ous deed); **~ver·dacht** *m* suspicion of murder; ***unter*** ~ ***stehen*** be suspected of murder; **~ver·such** *m* attempted murder; **~waf·fe** *f* murder weapon
Mo·res ['moːreːs] *pl.*: ***j-n*** ~ ***lehren*** teach s.o. what's what
Mor·gen[1] ['mɔrgən] *m* (-s; -) morning; *fig. a.* dawn(ing); ***am*** ~ in the morning, (in the) mornings; (***guten***) ~***!*** (good) morning!; ***es wird*** ~ it's getting light
'Mor'gen[2] *obs. m* (-s; -) *unit of measurement comprising between 2,500 and 3,400 square metres* (*Am. meters*)
'mor·gen *adv.* tomorrow; ~ ***früh*** (***abend***) tomorrow morning (evening *or* night); ***heute*** ~ this morning; ~ ***in acht Tagen*** a week (from) tomorrow, tomorrow week; ~ ***vor acht Tagen*** a week ago tomorrow; ~ ***um diese Zeit*** (by) this time tomorrow; ~ ***ist auch noch ein Tag*** tomorrow's another day
'Mor·gen|an·dacht *f* morning service; **~aus·ga·be** *f* morning edition; **~däm·me·rung** *f* dawn, daybreak
mor·gend·lich ['mɔrgəntlɪç] *adj.* (early) morning ...
'Mor·gen|fri·sche *f* fresh morning air; **~grau·en** *n*: ***beim*** (*or* ***im***) ~ at dawn, at daybreak, *get up etc. a.* F at the crack of dawn; **~gym͵na·stik** *f* morning exercises *pl.*, F *one's* daily dozen
'Mor·gen·land *lit. n* (-[e]s; *no pl.*) Orient, East; **'mor·gen·län·disch** [-lɛndɪʃ] *adj.* Eastern, from the East, Oriental; **~*e Märchen*** tales from the East
'Mor·gen|luft *f* morning air; *fig.* ~ ***wittern*** see an opportunity coming up (*or* up ahead); **~muf·fel** F *m*: ***er ist ein*** ~ he's not a morning person; **~post** *f* morning post (*Am.* mail); **~rock** *m* dressing gown; **~rot** *n*, **~rö·te** *f* (red) dawn, sunrise
'mor·gens *adv.* in the morning; (in the) mornings, every morning; ***um vier Uhr*** ~ at four (o'clock) in the morning; ~ ***als erstes*** first thing in the morning; ***von*** ~ ***bis abends*** from morning till night, all day long, *lit.* from dawn to dusk
'Mor·gen|son·ne *f* (early) morning sun; **~spa͵zier·gang** *m* (early) morning walk; **~stern** *m* morning star; **~stun·de** *f*: ***in den*** **~*n*** in the morning(s); ***die frühen*** **~*n*** the early morning hours; ***bis in die frühen*** **~*n*** into the small *or* wee (*or* small wee) hours; ***Morgenstund hat Gold im Mund*** the early bird catches the worm; **~zei·tung** *f* morning paper; **~zug** *m* morning train
mor·gig ['mɔrgɪç] *adj.* tomorrow's; ***der*** **~*e Tag*** tomorrow

Mo·ri·tat ['mo:rita:t] *f* (-; -en) street ballad (*relating a usually horrific event*)

Mor·mo·ne [mɔr'mo:nə] *m* (-n; -n), **mor·mo·nisch** [mɔr'mo:nɪʃ] *adj.* Mormon

Mor·phem [mɔr'fe:m] *n* (-s; -e) *ling.* morpheme

Mor·phin [mɔr'fi:n] *n* (-s; *no pl.*) morphine; **Mor·phi·nis·mus** [mɔrfi'nɪsmʊs] *m* (-; *no pl.*) morphine addiction; **Mor·phi·nist** [mɔrfi'nɪst] *m* (-en; -en) morphine addict

Mor·phi·um ['mɔrfiʊm] *n* (-s; *no pl.*) morphine; **∼sprit·ze** *f* morphine injection

'Mor·phi·um·sucht *f* morphine addiction; **'mor·phi·um·süch·tig** *adj.* addicted to morphine; **'Mor·phi·um·süch·ti·ge** *m, f* (-n; -n) morphine addict

Mor·pho·lo·gie [mɔrfolo'gi:] *f* (-; *no pl.*) morphology; **mor·pho·lo·gisch** [mɔrfo'lo:gɪʃ] *adj.* morphological

morsch [mɔrʃ] *adj.* rotting, rotten; brittle; **∼ *werden*** (start to) rot; *fig.* ***alt und*** **∼** old and decrepit, ***sein***: *a.* F be slowly falling apart; **'Morsch·heit** *f* (-; *no pl.*) rottenness; brittleness

Mor·se·al·pha,bet ['mɔrzə-] *n*: ***das*** **∼** Morse code; **mor·sen** ['mɔrzən] *v/t. and v/i.* (h) morse

Mör·ser ['mœrzɐ] *m* (-s; -) mortar (*a.* ⚔)

'Mor·se·zei·chen *n* Morse signal

Mor·ta·del·la [mɔrta'dɛla] *f* (-; -s) mortadella, baloney

Mor·ta·li·tät [mɔrtali'tɛ:t] *f* (-; *no pl.*) mortality (rate)

Mör·tel ['mœrtəl] *m* (-s; -) mortar; **∼kel·le** *f* trowel; **∼trog** *m* hod

Mo·sa·ik [moza'i:k] *n* (-s; -e[n]) *a. fig.* mosaic; **∼ar·beit** *f* **1.** mosaic (*or* tesse[l]lated) work; **2.** mosaic

mo·sa'ik·ar·tig *adj.* tessel(l)ated, mosaic-like

Mo·sa'ik|fuß·bo·den *m* mosaic (*or* tessel[l]ated) floor; **∼stein(chen** *n*) *m* **1.** mosaic piece (*or* stone); tessera; **2.** piece of (*or* from a) mosaic; **3.** *fig.* piece of a *or* the (jigsaw) puzzle

mo·sa·isch [mo'za:ɪʃ] *adj.* Mosaic; ***das*** **∼*e Gesetz*** Mosaic law

Mo·schee [mɔ'ʃe:] *f* (-; -n) mosque

Mo·schus ['mɔʃʊs] *m* (-, *no pl.*) musk; **∼ge·ruch** *m* musky odo(u)r; **∼och·se** *m* musk ox; **∼rat·te** *f* muskrat

Mo·se(s) ['mo:zə(s)]: ***das 1.*** (***2.***, ***3.***, ***4.***, ***5.***) ***Buch*** **∼** (the Book of) Genesis (Exodus, Leviticus, Numbers, Deuteronomy); ***die 5 Bücher Mosis*** the Pentateuch

Mö·se ['mø:zə] V *f* (-; -n) V cunt, *sl.* fanny, pussy

mo·sern ['mo:zɐn] F *v/i.* (h) grumble, F gripe, grizzle

Mos·ki·to [mɔs'ki:to] *m* (-s; -s) mosquito; **∼netz** *n* mosquito net; **∼stich** *m* mosquito bite

Mos·lem ['mɔslɛm] *m* (-s; -s), **mos·le·misch** [mɔs'le:mɪʃ] *adj.* Moslem, Muslim

Most [mɔst] *m* (-[e]s; -e) **1.** fruit juice; (freshly-pressed) grape juice, must; apple (*or* pear) juice; **2.** fruit wine; *n.s.* cider, perry; **∼ap·fel** *m* cider apple; **∼bir·ne** *f* perry pear

mo·sten ['mɔstən] *v/i.* (h) make fruit juice *etc.*; → ***Most***

Mo·tel ['mo:təl, mo'tɛl] *n* (-s; -s) motel

Mo·tet·te [mo'tɛtə] *f* (-; -n) ♪ motet

Mo·tiv [mo'ti:f] *n* (-[e]s; -e [-və]) **1.** motive (***zu*** *dat.* for); ***aus welchem*** **∼ *heraus hat er es getan?*** what made him (want to) do it?; **2.** *art*, ♪ *etc.*: motif; *film etc.*: *a.* theme; *phot.* subject; **Mo·ti·va·ti·on** [motiva'tsi̯o:n] *f* (-; -en) motivation; incentive; **Mo'tiv·for·schung** *f* motivation research; **mo·ti·vie·ren** [moti'vi:rən] *v/t.* (h) **1.** motivate; be behind *an action etc.*; ***was hat dich dazu motiviert?*** what made you (want to) do it?; ***ich konnte ihn nicht dazu*** **∼** I couldn't persuade (*or* get) him to do it; **2.** explain; **mo·ti·viert** [moti'vi:ɐt] *adj.* motivated; ***sehr*** **∼** highly motivated; ***sie sind nicht gerade*** **∼** *a.* they're not exactly keen (F raring to go); **Mo·ti'viert·heit** *f* (-; *no pl.*) (degree of) motivation; **Mo·ti'vie·rung** *f* (-; -en) motivation

Mo·tor ['mo:to:ɐ, mo'to:ɐ] *m* (-s; -en [mo'to:rən]) engine, *esp.* ⚡ motor (*a. fig.*)

'Mo·tor... *in cpds.* engine, *esp.* ⚡ motor; **∼block** *m* engine block; **∼boot** *n* motorboat; **∼brem·se** *f* engine brake

Mo·to·ren|lärm [mo'to:rən-] *m* noise (*or* roar) of engines; **∼öl** *n* engine oil

'Mo·tor|ge·räusch *n* engine noise; **∼hau·be** *f* bonnet, *Am.* hood; ✈ (engine) cowl

Mo·to·rik [mo'to:rɪk] *f* (-; *no pl.*) *physiol.* motor activity; **mo·to·risch** [mo'to:rɪʃ] *adj.* motor *nerve etc.*

mo·to·ri·sie·ren [motori'zi:rən] (h) **I.** *v/t.* motorize, *esp.* ⚔ mechanize; **II.** *v/refl.*: ***sich*** **∼** become motorized, buy (o.s.) a car (*or* motorbike); **mo·to·ri·siert** [motori'zi:ɐt] *adj.* motorized, mobile; ***sind Sie*** **∼*?*** *a.* a) have you got a car?, b) did you come by car?; **Mo·to·ri'sie·rung** *f* (-; *no pl.*) motorization, *esp.* ⚔ mechanization

'Mo·tor|jacht *f* motor yacht; **∼kol·ben** *m* engine piston; **∼lei·stung** *f* engine performance (*or* power); **∼öl** *n* engine oil; **∼pum·pe** *f* power pump

'Mo·tor·rad *n* motorbike, motorcycle; **∼ *fahren*** ride a motorbike (*or* motorcycle); **∼fah·rer** *m* motorcyclist; **∼helm** *m* motorbike helmet; **∼ren·nen** *n* **1.** motorbike race; **2.** motorbike (*or* motorcycle) racing

'Mo·tor|raum *m* engine compartment; **∼rol·ler** *m* (motor) scooter; **∼sä·ge** *f* power saw; **∼scha·den** *m* engine trouble; **∼schlit·ten** *m* snowmobile; **∼sport** *m* motor sport; **∼wech·sel** *m* engine replacement

Mot·te ['mɔtə] *f* (-; -n) moth; ***von*** **∼*n zerfressen*** moth-eaten; F ***ach, du kriegst die*** **∼*n!*** F that's all I (*or* we) needed!

'mot·ten·fest *adj.* mothproof

'Mot·ten|fraß *m* moth damage; **∼ki·ste** *f*: ***e-e Geschichte*** *etc.* ***aus der*** **∼** (***holen*** dig up) an old (*or* ancient) story *etc.*; ***das gehört in die*** **∼** that should be dead and buried; **∼ku·gel** *f* mothball; **∼pul·ver** *n* moth powder

'mot·ten·zer·fres·sen *adj.* moth-eaten

Mot·to ['mɔto] *n* (-s; -s) motto; ***nach dem*** **∼*(, daß) ...*** according to the principle that ...; ***unter dem*** **∼ *... stehen*** have as a motto ...

mot·zen ['mɔtsən] F *v/i.* (h) moan, F gripe, beef

mous·sie·ren [mʊ'si:rən] *v/i.* (h) sparkle, fizz; be fizzy; **mous'sie·rend** *adj.* sparkling *wine*; fizzy *lemonade etc.*

Mö·we ['mø:və] *f* (-; -n) (sea)gull

Mo·zart·ku·gel ['mo:tsart-] *f rum truffle with marzipan*

Mucke ['mʊkə] (*sep.* -k·k-) F *f* (-; -n) whim; *fig.* ***die Sache hat ihre*** **∼*n*** it's got its snags; ***er hat so s-e*** **∼*n*** he has his little moods; ***der Motor hat s-e*** **∼*n*** the engine's rather temperamental; ***j-m s-e*** **∼*n austreiben*** straighten s.o. out

Mücke ['mʏkə] (*sep.* -k·k-) *f* (-; -n) mosquito, midge; *fig.* ***aus e-r*** **∼ *e-n Elefanten machen*** make a mountain out of a molehill

Mucke·fuck ['mʊkəfʊk] (*sep.* -k·k-) F *m* (-s; *no pl.*) coffee substitute, F kiddies' coffee

mucken ['mʊkən] (*sep.* -k·k-) F *v/i.* (h) grumble; ***ohne zu*** **∼** F without a peep

'Mücken|schwarm *m* swarm of mosquitoes; **∼spray** *m, n* mosquito spray (*or* repellant); **∼stich** *m* mosquito bite

Mucks [mʊks] *m* (-es; -e): ***keinen*** **∼ *tun*** a) be as quiet as a mouse, b) not to budge (*or* stir); ***sie haben keinen*** **∼ *getan*** *a.* we *etc.* didn't hear a peep from them; **muck·sen** ['mʊksən] *v/i. and v/refl.* (***sich*** **∼**) (h) stir, move, budge

'mucks'mäus·chen'still F *adj.* → ***mäuschenstill***

mü·de ['my:də] **I.** *adj.* tired; **∼*s Lächeln*** weary smile; ***keine*** **∼ *Mark*** not a penny (*or* cent, F tinker's cuss); ***e-r Sache*** **∼ *werden*** grow weary (*or* tired) of s.th., get fed up with s.th.; ***ich bin es jetzt*** **∼** I've had enough (of it); ***nicht*** **∼ *werden zu*** *inf.* never tire of *ger.*; **II.** *adv.* wearily, tiredly; **∼ *lächeln*** smile wearily, give a weary smile; **∼ *abwinken*** give a weary gesture of refusal; **Mü·dig·keit** ['my:dɪçkaɪt] *f* (-; *no pl.*) tiredness; fatigue, exhaustion

Muff [mʊf] *m* (-[e]s; -e) muff

Muf·fe ['mʊfə] *f* (-; -n) ⚙ sleeve, socket; coupling box

Muf·fel ['mʊfəl] F *m* (-s; -) **1.** F sourpuss, *sl.* misery-guts; **2.** stick-in-the-mud; → ***Krawattenmuffel, Partymuffel***

muf·feln ['mʊfəln] F *v/i.* (h) **1.** smell musty, smell mo(u)ldy; **2.** F have the grumps; F be in a huff

'Muf·fen·sau·sen F *n*: **∼ *kriegen*** F get the wind up; **∼ *haben*** F have the wind up, be in a flat panic

muf·fig ['mʊfɪç] *adj.* **1.** musty, stuffy *air*; musty-smelling *cellar etc.*; **2.** *fig. contp.* stuffy; **3.** F grumpy; **'Muf·fig·keit** *f* (-; *no pl.*) **1.** mustiness; **2.** *fig. contp.* stuffiness; **3.** F grumpiness

muh [mu:] *int.* moo!; **∼ *machen*** go moo

Mü·he ['my:ə] *f* (-; -n) trouble; effort; ***mit Müh(e) und Not*** with great difficulty, just about; (***nicht***) ***die*** **∼ *wert*** (not) worth the effort; ***sich*** **∼ *geben*** (***mit*** *dat.*) take great trouble *or* pains (over *s.th.*); ***sich große*** **∼ *geben*** (***or machen***) ***zu*** *inf.* go to great trouble (*or* pains) to *inf.*; ***sich die*** **∼ *machen zu*** *inf.* go to the trouble of *ger.*; ***er machte sich nicht einmal die*** **∼ *zu*** *inf.* he couldn't even be bothered to *inf.*; ***keine*** **∼ *scheuen*** spare no effort *or* pains (***zu*** *inf.* in *ger.*); ***machen Sie sich keine*** **∼*!*** don't go to any trouble; ***s-e*** (***liebe***) **∼ *haben zu*** *inf.* have a hard time *ger.*

'mü·he·los I. *adj.* effortless, easy; **II.** *adv.* easily, with ease; effortlessly; ***sie hat es*** **∼ *geschafft*** *a.* it didn't take much effort on her part; **'Mü·he·lo·sig·keit** *f* (-; *no pl.*) effortlessness, lack of effort, (great) ease, facility

mu·hen ['mu:ən] *v/i.* (h) moo, low

mü·hen ['my:ən] *v/refl.* (h): ***sich*** **∼** make an effort, try hard, take pains (***zu*** *inf.* to *inf.*)

'mü·he·voll *adj.* difficult, hard; laborious

Mühl·bach ['my:l-] *m* mill stream

Müh·le ['my:lə] *f* (-; -n) **1.** mill; **2.** *fig.* treadmill; ***in die ~ der Justiz (Bürokratie) geraten*** get caught up in the machinery *or* labyrinth of the law (in the bureaucratic machine); F ***j-n durch die ~ drehen*** F put s.o. through the mill; → ***Wasser*; 3.** nine men's morris

Mühl|rad ['my:l-] *n* mill wheel; **~stein** *m* millstone

Müh·sal ['my:za:l] *f* (-; *no pl.*) drudgery, toil (and trouble); hardship; strain

müh·sam ['my:za:m] **I.** *adj.* difficult; strenuous; tiring; labo(u)red *conversation etc.*; **II.** *adv.* with difficulty, after a lot of effort; ***sich ~ erheben*** struggle to one's feet; ***~ nährt sich das Eichhörnchen*** it's uphill all the way

'Müh·samkeit *f* (-; *no pl.*) effort, strain (*gen.* of, involved in)

müh·se·lig ['my:ze:lɪç] **I.** *adj.* laborious; arduous, hard *life etc.*; ***~es Unterfangen*** uphill task; **II.** *adv.* a) laboriously, b) painstakingly

Mu·ko·vis·zi·do·se [mukovɪstsi'do:zə] *f* (-; *no pl.*) ⚕ cystic fibrosis

Mu·lat·te [mu'latə] *m* (-n; -n), **Mu·lat·tin** [mu'latɪn] *f* (-; -nen) mulatto

Mul·de ['mʊldə] *f* (-; -n) hollow; *geol. a.* depression; *skiing*: bowl

Mu·li ['mu:li] *dial. n* (-s; -s) mule

Mull [mʊl] *m* (-s; *no pl.*) gauze, lint

Müll [mʏl] *m* (-s; *no pl.*) rubbish, garbage, trash (*all a.* F *fig.*); *formal*: refuse; (*a. industrial, special, toxic*) waste; ***radioaktiver ~*** radioactive waste; ***et. in den ~ werfen*** throw s.th. in(to) the dustbin (*Am.* trashcan *or* garbage can); **~ab·fuhr** *f* **1.** refuse (*or* garbage) disposal; **2.** dustmen *pl.*, *Am.* garbage men (*or* collectors *pl.*), *Brit.* dustmen *pl.*; **~ab·la·de·platz** *m* → ***Mülldeponie*; ~auf·be·rei·tung** *f* waste disposal

Mülla͵wi·ne (*sep.* -ll·l-) *f* mountain of rubbish (*Am.* garbage)

'Müll|berg *m* **1.** pile of rubbish (*Am.* garbage); *w.s.* mountain of rubbish (*Am.* garbage); **2.** artificial hill; **~be·sei·ti·gung** *f* waste disposal (*or* management); **~beu·tel** *m* dustbin liner, *Am.* garbage bag

'Mull·bin·de *f* gauze bandage

'Müll|con͵tai·ner *m* rubbish (*or* refuse) skip; **~de·po͵nie** *f* rubbish tip (*or* dump), *Am.* (garbage) dump; dumping (*or* waste disposal) site, landfill (site); **~ei·mer** *m* rubbish bin, *Am.* garbage can

Mül·ler ['mʏlɐ] *m* (-s; -), **Mül·le·rin** ['mʏlərɪn] *f* (-; -nen) miller

'Müll|fah·rer *m* dustman, *Am.* garbage man (*or* collector); **~gru·be** *f* refuse pit; **~hal·de** *f* → ***Mülldeponie***; *iro.* ***fließende ~*** (public) sewer; **~hau·fen** *m* rubbish (*Am.* garbage) heap; *fig.* scrapheap; *fig.* ***auf dem ~ landen*** end up on the scrapheap; **~mann** *m* → ***Müllfahrer*; ~platz** *m* rubbish tip (*or* dump), *Am.* (garbage) dump; **~sack** *m* **1.** dustbin liner, *Am.* garbage bag; **2.** sack of rubbish (*Am.* garbage); **~schlucker** *m* rubbish (*Am.* garbage) chute, waste disposal unit; **~ton·ne** *f* dustbin, *Am.* trashcan, garbage can; **~tren·nung** *f* waste separation, separation of waste; **~ver·bren·nungs·an·la·ge** *f* incinerator, (waste) incineration plant; **~ver·wer·tung** *f* recycling; **~wa·gen** *m* dustbin lorry, dustcart, *Am.* garbage truck; **~zer·klei·ne·rung** *f* waste maceration (*or* compaction)

mul·mig ['mʊlmɪç] F *adj.* **1.** threatening; ***es sieht ziemlich ~ aus*** things aren't looking too good; **2. *mir ist ganz ~ zumute*** a) I feel weak in the knees, b) I feel a bit queasy, c) I've got a funny feeling in the pit of my stomach

Mul·ti ['mʊlti] F *m* (-s; -s) multinational (concern)

mul·ti·la·te·ral [mʊltilate'ra:l] *adj.* multilateral

mul·ti·me·di·al [mʊltime'dĭa:l] *adj.* multimedia ...

Mul·ti'me·dia·ver·an·stal·tung *f* multimedia show (*or* event)

Mul·ti'me·di·en·zen·trum *n* multimedia centre (*Am.* center)

Mul·ti·mil·lio'när [mʊlti-] *m* multimillionaire

mul·ti·na·tio'nal [mʊlti-] *adj.* multinational

Mul·ti·pli·ka·ti·on [mʊltiplika'tsĭo:n] *f* (-; -en) multiplication; **Mul·ti·pli·ka·tor** [mʊltipli'ka:to:ɐ] *m* (-s; -en [-ka'to:rən]) multiplier; **mul·ti·pli·zie·ren** [mʊltipli'tsi:rən] *v/t.* (h) multiply (***mit*** *dat.* by)

Mu·mie ['mu:mĭə] *f* (-; -n) mummy

'mu·mi·en·haft *adj.* mummy-like

Mu·mi·fi·ka·ti·on [mumifika'tsĭo:n] *f* (-; -en) mummification

mu·mi·fi·zie·ren [mumifi'tsi:rən] *v/t.* (h) mummify; **Mu·mi·fi'zie·rung** *f* (-; -en) mummification

Mumm [mʊm] F *m* (-s; *no pl.*) **1.** gumption, F guts *pl.*, *sl.* bottle; **2.** drive, verve, F get-up-and-go, oomph

Mum·mel·greis ['mʊməl-] *m* old dodderer

mum·meln ['mʊməln] *v/t.* (h) **1.** mumble *s.th.* (into one's beard); **2.** wrap *s.o.* up (***in*** *acc.* into)

müm·meln ['mʏməln] F *v/t.* (h) nibble (away) at; chew away at, chew on

Mum·men·schanz ['mʊmənʃants] *m* (-es; *no pl.*) masquerade

Mum·pitz ['mʊmpɪts] F *m* (-es; *no pl.*) F rubbish, poppycock; F garbage

Mumps [mʊmps] *m* (-es; *no pl.*) ⚕ mumps (*sg.*)

Mund [mʊnt] *m* (-[e]s; Münder ['mʏndɐ]) mouth; ***den ~ aufmachen*** open one's mouth, *fig.* speak up; ***machen Sie bitte den ~ auf*** open wide(, please); ***mit vollem ~ sprechen*** talk with one's mouth full; ***aus dem ~ riechen*** have bad breath; ***den ~ halten*** keep one's mouth shut; ***halt den ~!*** shut up!; *fig.* ***kriegst du den ~ nicht auf?*** have you lost your tongue?; ***sie hat den ~ nicht aufgekriegt*** she didn't say a word; ***den ~ voll nehmen*** talk big, F shoot one's mouth off; ***et. ständig im ~e führen*** never stop talking about s.th.; ***j-m et. in den ~ legen*** put words into s.o.'s mouth; ***j-m das Wort aus dem ~ nehmen*** take the words right out of s.o.'s mouth; ***j-m das Wort im ~ umdrehen*** twist s.o.'s words; ***j-m über den ~ fahren*** cut s.o. short; ***es ist in aller ~e*** everyone's talking about it, it's the talk of the town; ***nicht auf den ~ gefallen sein*** F have the gift of the gab; ***sich den ~ verbrennen*** put one's foot in it; ***so ein Wort würde er nie in den ~ nehmen*** he would never use such a word; ***und das aus s-m ~(e)*** fancy him saying that (*or* such a thing); ***von ~ zu ~ gehen*** be passed on from one person to the next, F do the rounds; → ***Blatt*** 1, ***stopfen*** 3, ***wässerig***

'Mund·art *f* dialect; **~dich·tung** *f* dialect literature (*n.s.* poetry); **~for·scher** *m* dialectologist; **~for·schung** *f* dialectology, dialect research

'mund·art·lich *adj.* dialect ..., dialectal

'Mund·du·sche *f* dental water jet, mouth rinse

Mün·del ['mʏndəl] *n* (-s; -) ward

'mün·del·si·cher *adj.* ✝ gilt-edged; ***~e Papiere*** gilt-edged securities, gilts

mun·den ['mʊndən] *v/i.* (h) taste good, be delicious; ***es mundet mir*** it's delicious; ***sich et. ~ lassen*** savo(u)r s.th., relish s.th.

mün·den ['mʏndən] *v/i.* (h, sn): ***~ in*** *acc.* lead to (*a. fig.*); *river*: flow (*or* empty) into; *road*: lead into

'mund·faul *adj.* too lazy to open one's mouth

'Mund|fäu·le *f* ⚕ stomatitis; **~flo·ra** *f* (bacterial) flora of the mouth

'mund·ge·recht *adj.* bite-sized; *fig.* ***j-m et. ~ machen*** make s.th. palatable for s.o.

'Mund|ge·ruch *m* (*a.* ***übler ~***) bad breath, halitosis; **~har͵mo·ni·ka** *f* mouthorgan, harmonica; **~höh·le** *f* oral cavity; **~hy͵gie·ne** *f* oral hygiene

mün·dig ['mʏndɪç] *adj.* ⚖ of age; *fig.* responsible, mature; ***~er Bürger*** responsible citizen; ***~ werden*** come of age; ***j-n (für) ~ erklären*** declare s.o. of age; **Mün·di·ge** ['mʏndɪgə] *m, f* (-n; -n) major; **'Mün·dig·keit** *f* (-; *no pl.*) ⚖ (age of) majority; *fig.* maturity

'mün·dig·spre·chen *v/t.* (*irr.*, *sep.*, h, → ***sprechen***) declare *s.o.* of age

münd·lich ['mʏntlɪç] **I.** *adj.* verbal *statement*; oral *examination*; ***~e Überlieferung*** oral tradition; ***~er Vertrag*** verbal agreement; **II.** *adv.* orally, verbally; ***et. ~ weitergeben*** pass s.th. on by word of mouth; ***alles Weitere ~*** I'll tell you the rest when I see you

'Mund|par͵tie *f* area around the mouth; mouth and lips *pl.*; **~pfle·ge** *f* oral hygiene; **~pro·pa͵gan·da** *f*: (***durch*** by) word-of-mouth recommendation; **~raub** *m* petty larceny; **~schleim·haut** *f* mucous membrane of the mouth; **~schutz** *m* ⚕ mask; *boxing*: gumshield

M-und-S-Reifen [ɛmʊnt'ˀɛs-] *m* snow tyre (*Am.* tire)

'Mund·stück *n* **1.** ♪ mouthpiece; **2.** tip

'mund·tot *adj.*: ***~ machen*** silence, F shut *s.o.* up; *pol.* gag, muzzle

Mün·dung ['mʏndʊŋ] *f* (-; -en) **1.** *geogr.* mouth, estuary; **2.** *anat. and* ⚙ mouth; **3.** muzzle *of a gun*

'Mund|voll *m* (-; -) mouthful, gobbet; gulp; **~vor·rat** *m* provisions *pl.*; **~was·ser** *n* mouth wash, gargle; **~werk** F *n* (-[e]s; *no pl.*) mouth; ***ein loses (or lockeres) ~ haben*** have a loose tongue; ***ein gutes ~ haben*** F have the gift of the gab; **~win·kel** *m* corner of one's mouth; ***die ~ verziehen*** grimace

'Mund-zu-'Mund-Be'at·mung *f* ⚕ mouth-to-mouth resuscitation, F kiss of life

Mun·go ['mʊŋgo] *m* (-s; -s) *zo.* mungo

Mu·ni·ti·on [muni'tsĭo:n] *f* (-;-en) ammunition (*a. fig.*); ***s-e ~ verschießen*** use up one's ammunition, *fig.* shoot one's bolt; *fig.* ***j-m ~ liefern*** provide s.o. with (plenty of) ammunition

Mu·ni·ti'ons|faˌbrik *f* munitions factory; *in GB*: *a.* Royal Ordnance factory; **~la·ger** *n* ammunition depot (*or* dump)
Mun·ke·lei [mʊŋkə'laɪ] *f* (-; -en) talk, gossip, whisperings *pl.*; **mun·keln** ['mʊŋkəln] (h) **I.** *v/i.* talk; **II.** *v/t.* say, whisper; ***man munkelt, daß*** people are saying (that)
Mün·ster ['mʏnstɐ] *n* (-s; -) minster; cathedral
mun·ter ['mʊntɐ] **I.** *adj.* awake; up (and about); *fig.* lively; cheerful, F chirpy, *Am.* F chipper; ***~ werden*** wake up, perk up; ***j-n ~ machen*** perk s.o. up, get s.o. going; ***Kaffee macht ~*** coffee gets you going; → ***gesund***; **II.** *fig. adv.* blithely; **'Mun·ter·keit** *f* (-; *no pl.*) liveliness; cheerfulness, high spirits *pl.*; **'Mun·ter·ma·cher** *m* (-s; -) stimulant; pep pill
'Münz|an·stalt *f* mint; **~au·toˌmat** *m* slot machine
Mün·ze ['mʏntsə] *f* (-; -n) **1.** coin; *fig.* ***klingende ~*** hard cash; ***et. für bare ~ nehmen*** take s.th. at face value; ***j-m et. mit gleicher ~ heimzahlen*** pay s.o. back in his (*or* her) own coin; **2.** mint
Münz|ein·heit ['mʏnts-] *f* monetary unit; **~ein·wurf** *m* coin slot
mün·zen ['mʏntsən] *v/t. and v/i.* (h) coin, mint; *fig.* ***auf j-n gemünzt sein*** be meant for s.o.
Münz|fern·rohr ['mʏnts-] *n* coin(-operated) telescope; **~fern·se·hen** *n* pay TV; **~fern·spre·cher** *m* pay phone; **~ge·wicht** *n* (standard) weight of a coin (*or* coins); **~samm·ler** *m* coin collector, *formal*: numismatist; **~samm·lung** *f* coin collection; **~stät·te** *f* mint; **~tank(au·toˌmat)** *m* coin-operated (petrol, *Am.* gas) pump; **~te·leˌfon** *n* pay phone; **~wä·scheˌrei** *f* laund(e)rette, laundromat; **~wechs·ler** *m* change machine; **~zäh·ler** *m* slot meter
Mu·rä·ne [mu'rɛːnə] *f* (-; -n) *zo.* moray
mür·be ['mʏrbə] *adj.* **1.** mellow, very ripe *fruit*; tender, well-cooked *meat*; crumbly *pastry*; rotten *wood*; **2.** *fig.* worn-out, *pred.* worn out; ***ich bin ~ a.*** my resistance has gone; ***j-n ~ machen*** wear s.o. down; ***j-n ~ kriegen*** break s.o.'s resistance
'Mür·be·teig *m* short(-crust) pastry
Murks [mʊrks] F *m* (-es; *no pl.*) F botch-up; ***~ machen*** → **'murk·sen** F *v/i.* (h) F mess around; make a mess of things
Mur·mel ['mʊrməl] *f* (-; -n) marble
mur·meln ['mʊrməln] **I.** *v/i. and v/t.* (h) murmur, mutter; **II.** ♀ *n* (-s; *no pl.*) murmur
'Mur·mel·tier *n* marmot, *Am. a.* woodchuck; *fig.* ***schlafen wie ein ~*** sleep like a log (*or* top)
mur·ren ['mʊrən] *v/i.* (h) grumble (***über*** *acc.* about)
mür·risch ['mʏrɪʃ] *adj.* sullen, F grumpy
Mus [muːs] *n* (-es; -e) mush; puree; (plum) jam; F *fig.* ***zu ~ schlagen*** F beat to a pulp, make mincemeat out of
Mu·schel ['mʊʃəl] *f* (-; -n) **1.** *zo.* mussel; shell; **2.** *teleph.* a) earpiece, b) mouthpiece; **~bank** *f* (-, ⁼e) mussel (*or* shell) bank
'mu·schel·för·mig [-fœrmɪç] *adj.* shell-shaped
'Mu·schel|kalk *m* muschelkalk; **~scha·le** *f* shell; **~tier** *n* mollusc, *Am.* mollusk
Mu·schi ['mʊʃi] *sl. f* (-; -s) *sl.* pussy
Mu·se ['muːzə] *f* (-; -n) Muse; *fig.* ***die leichte ~*** light entertainment; ***von der ~ geküßt werden*** be inspired by the muses
mu·se·al [muze'aːl] *adj.* museum ...; *fig.* antiquated; ***~en Wert haben*** be a museum piece
'Mu·sen·sohn *hum. m* poet
Mu·se·um [mu'zeːʊm] *n* (-s; -en) museum
Mu'se·ums|füh·rer *m* **1.** museum guide; **2.** guide to a (*or* the) museum; **♀reif** *adj.*: ***~ sein*** belong in a museum; **~stück** *n* museum piece; **~wär·ter** *m* museum attendant; **~wert** *m*: ***~ haben*** be a museum piece, *contp.* belong in a museum
Mu·si·cal ['mjuːzikəl] *n* (-s; -s) musical
Mu·sik [mu'ziːk] *f* (-; *no pl.*) **1.** music; ***~ machen*** play music; ***et. in ~ setzen*** set s.th. to music; ***die ~ schreiben zu*** *dat.* write the music (*film etc.*: *a.* score) for *or* to *s.th.*; *fig.* ***~ im Blut haben*** be a born musician; ***das ist ~ in m-n Ohren*** that's music to my ears; **2.** band; **~aka·deˌmie** *f* academy of music, musical academy
Mu·si·ka·li·en [muzi'kaːliən] *pl.* **1.** (printed) music *sg.*; **2.** musical instruments and accessories; **~hand·lung** *f* music shop
mu·si·ka·lisch [muzi'kaːlɪʃ] *adj.* musical; ***~es Talent*** musical talent, gift for music; *ling.* ***~er Akzent*** pitch accent
Mu·si·ka·li·tät [muzikali'tɛːt] *f* (-; *no pl.*) musicality
Mu·si·kant [muzi'kant] *m* (-en; -en) musician; **Mu·si'kan·ten·kno·chen** F *m* F funny bone
mu'sik·be·gei·stert *adj.* very keen on music; ***~ sein*** *a.* love music; **Mu'sik·be·gei·ste·rung** *f* love of music
Mu'sik|be·glei·tung *f* (musical) accompaniment; **~be·rie·se·lung** *f* piped music, Muzak (*TM*); **~bi·blioˌthek** *f* music library; **~box** *f* juke box; **~kasˌset·te** *f* music cassette; **~dra·ma** *n* music drama
Mu·si·ker ['muːzikɐ] *m* (-s; -), **Mu·si·ke·rin** ['muːzikərɪn] *f* (-; -nen) musician
Mu'sik|er·zie·hung *f* musical education (*or* training); **~fest·spie·le** *pl.* music festival *sg.*; festspiele; **~freund** *m* music lover; **~ge·schäft** *n* **1.** music shop; **2.** music business; **~ge·schich·te** *f* history of music; **~hoch·schu·le** *f* conservatory; **~in·struˌment** *n* musical instrument; **~kaˌpel·le** *f* band; **~konˌser·ve** F *f a. pl. coll.* F canned music; **~kri·ti·ker** *m* music critic; **~leh·rer** *m* music teacher
Mu·si·ko·lo·ge [muziko'loːgə] *m* (-n; -n) musicologist; **Mu·si·ko·lo·gie** [muzikolo'giː] *f* (-; *no pl.*) musicology
Mu'sik|pa·vil·lon *m* bandstand, music pavilion; **~saal** *m* music room; **~schu·le** *f* music school; **~stück** *n* piece of music; **~stuˌdent** *m* music student, student of music; **~stun·de** *f* music lesson; **~ˌun·ter·richt** *m* music lesson(s *pl.*)
Mu·si·kus ['muːzikʊs] F *m* (-; -se) musician, F music-man
Mu'sik|ver·lag *m* music publishers *pl.*; **~vi·deo** *n* music video; **~werk** *n* composition, musical work, piece of music; **~wis·sen·schaft** *f* musicology
mu·sisch ['muːzɪʃ] **I.** *adj.* artistic; ***~e Fächer*** fine arts (subjects); **II.** *adv.*: ***~ veranlagt sein*** have an artistic bent
mu·si·zie·ren [muzi'tsiːrən] *v/i.* (h) play music, play (the piano *etc.*); ***am Wochenende ~ wir gerne*** we like to get together to play music at the weekends
Mu·si·zier·wei·se [muzi'tsiːɐ-] *f* style of playing
Mus·kat [mʊs'kaːt] *m* (-[e]s; -e) nutmeg; **~blü·te** *f* mace
Mus·ka·tel·ler [mʊska'tɛlɐ] *m* (-s; -) muscatel (wine); **~trau·be** *f* muscat (*or* muskat) grape; **~wein** *m* muscatel wine
Mus'kat·nuß *f* nutmeg
Mus·kel ['mʊskəl] *m* (-s; -n) muscle; ***s-e ~n spielen lassen*** flex one's muscles; **~ka·ter** *m* sore (*or* stiff) muscles *pl.*; **~kraft** *f* muscle power, F muscle, beef; **~krampf** *m* cramp, ⚕ muscle spasm; ***an Muskelkrämpfen leiden*** suffer from cramp, get cramp(s); **~paˌket** F *n*, **~protz** F *m* F muscleman, muscles (*sg.*); **~riß** *m* torn muscle; **~schwund** *m* ⚕ muscular atrophy (*or* dystrophy); **~spiel** *n a. fig.* flexing of muscles; **~trai·ning** *n* muscle exercises *pl.*; **~zer·rung** *f* pulled muscle; ***sich e-e ~ zuziehen*** pull a muscle
Mus·ke·te [mʊs'keːtə] *f* (-; -n) musket
Mus·ke·tier [mʊske'tiːɐ] *m* (-s; -e [-rə]) musketeer
mus·ku·lär [mʊsku'lɛːɐ] *adj.* muscular
Mus·ku·la·tur [mʊskula'tuːɐ] *f* (-; -en) muscular system, muscles *pl.*
mus·ku·lös [mʊsku'løːs] *adj.* muscular
Müs·li ['myːsli] *n* (-s; -s) muesli; **~rie·gel** *m* cereal bar
Muß [mʊs] *n*: ***es ist ein ~*** it's a (*or* an absolute) must; **~be·stim·mung** *f* ⚖ mandatory provision
Mu·ße ['muːsə] *f* (-; *no pl.*) leisure; leisure time; ***mit ~*** at (one's) leisure; ***dazu habe ich nicht die ~*** I don't have the time (or the peace of mind) for that kind of thing
'Muß·ehe F *f* involuntary marriage
Mus·se·lin [mʊsə'liːn] *m* (-s; -e) muslin
müs·sen ['mʏsən] **I.** *v/aux.* (mußte, hat müssen) have (got) to; must; ***ich muß*** a) I have to, I've got to, b) I must; ***ich muß unbedingt*** I really must; ***ich mußte*** I had to; ***ich werde ~*** I'll have to; ***ich müßte (eigentlich)*** I ought to; ***er muß nicht hingehen*** a) he doesn't have to go, b) he needn't go; ***er mußte nicht gehen*** he didn't have to go; ***er hätte nicht gehen ~*** he needn't have gone; ***du mußt doch nicht gleich die Wut kriegen*** there's no need to get angry; ***du mußt dich nicht von ihm ärgern lassen*** don't let him annoy you (like that); ***er muß verrückt sein*** he must be mad; ***er muß es gewesen sein*** it must have been him; ***ich muß es vergessen haben*** I must have forgotten; ***es müßte sofort gemacht werden*** it ought to be done straightaway; ***man müßte mehr Zeit haben*** I wish we had more time, we could do with more time (for that sort of thing); ***sie ~ bald kommen*** they're bound to be here soon; ***der Zug müßte längst hier sein*** the train should have arrived long ago; ***ich mußte (einfach) lachen*** I couldn't help laughing, I just had to laugh; ***er hätte hier sein ~*** he ought to (*or* should) have been here; *so wie es aussieht*, ***muß es bald regnen*** it looks as if we're in for some rain; ***er muß immer alles wissen*** he's always got to know about everything; ***was sein muß, muß sein*** that's just the way it is, that's life; ***muß das sein?*** a) is that really necessary?, b) do you have to?; ***wenn es (unbedingt) sein muß*** if there's no other way, if you *etc.* (absolutely) must; ***das mußte ja passieren*** that was bound to (*or* just had to) happen; *iro.* ***das mußte natürlich jetzt passieren*** it 'would have to happen right now, trust it

to happen right now; ***das muß man gesehen haben*** a) you've got to have seen it, b) you've got to see it to believe it; **II.** *v/i.* (mußte, gemußt, h) have to, be forced to; must; ***ich muß!*** I've got no choice; ***ich muß nach Hause*** a) I have to go home, b) I must go home; ***er muß zur Schule*** he has to go to school; F ***ich muß mal*** F I must go to the loo (*Am.* bathroom); I need the toilet

'Mu·ße·stun·de *f* leisure hour; ***in e-r ~*** in a moment of leisure

'Muß·hei·rat F *f* F shotgun wedding

mü·ßig ['my:sɪç] **I.** *adj.* idle; useless, futile; ***es ist ~ zu*** *inf.* it's no use *ger.*, it's useless *ger.*; **II.** *adv.*: ***~ dabeistehen*** stand idly by (and watch)

'Mü·ßig·gang *m* (-[e]s; *no pl.*) idleness; ***~ ist aller Laster Anfang*** the devil finds work for idle hands

'Mü·ßig·gän·ger [-gɛŋɐ] *m* (-s; -) idler

'mü·ßig·gän·ge·risch [-gɛŋərɪʃ] *adj.* idle

'mü·ßig·ge·hen *v/i.* (*irr.*, *sep.*, sn, → ***gehen***) idle about; idle away one's life

muß·te ['mʊstə] *pret. of* ***müssen***

'Muß·vor·schrift *f* mandatory provision

Mu·stang ['mʊstaŋ] *m* (-s; -s) mustang

Mu·ster ['mʊstɐ] *n* (-s; -) **1.** pattern; ***nach e-m ~ arbeiten*** work from a pattern; **2.** sample, specimen; ✝ ***~ ohne Wert*** sample; **3.** pattern, design; **4.** *fig.* model; example; ***sie ist ein ~ von e-r Lehrerin*** *etc.* she's a model teacher *etc.*; ***ein ~ an Tugend*** a paragon of virtue; ***nach dem ~ von*** *dat.* following the example of; ***j-n als ~ hinstellen*** hold s.o. up as a paragon; **~bei·spiel** *n* classic example (***für*** *acc.* of), case in point; **~be·trieb** *m* model plant; **~bild** *n* → ***Muster*** 4; **~brief** *m* specimen letter; **~buch** *n* ✝ pattern book; samples folder; **~ehe** *f* perfect (*or* ideal, model) marriage; **~ex·em͜plar** *n* **1.** sample, specimen; **2.** *typ.* specimen copy; **3.** *esp. iro.* perfect example; **~fall** *m* model case; *w.s.* perfect (*or* classic) example; **~gat·te** *m* model (*or* ideal) husband

'mu·ster·gül·tig *adj. and adv.* → ***musterhaft***; **'Mu·ster·gül·tig·keit** *f* (-; *no pl.*) → ***Musterhaftigkeit***

'mu·ster·haft I. *adj.* exemplary, model ...; **II.** *adv.*: ***sich ~ benehmen*** behave impeccably, be on one's best behavio(u)r; **'Mu·ster·haf·tig·keit** *f* (-; *no pl.*) exemplariness, model nature (*gen.* of)

'Mu·ster|haus *n* showhouse; **~kna·be** *m* *esp. iro.* paragon, *contp.* prig, F goody-goody; **~kof·fer** *m* sample case; **~kol·lek·ti͜on** *f* ✝ sample collection; **~lei·stung** *f a. iro.* brilliant achievement

mu·stern ['mʊstɐn] *v/t.* (h) **1.** study, scrutinize; look *s.o.* up and down; ⚔ inspect, review *troops*; **2.** ⚔ muster; **3.** *textil.* pattern; → ***gemustert***

'Mu·ster|pro͜zeß *m* ⚖ test case; **~schü·ler** *m* model pupil (*Am.* student); F swot, *Am.* grind

Mu·ste·rung ['mʊstərʊŋ] *f* (-; -en) **1.** inspection, scrutiny; ⚔ review *of troops*; **2.** ⚔ mustering

Mut [mu:t] *m* (-[e]s; *no pl.*) **1.** courage, bravery; pluck, F guts *pl.*; daring; ***~ fassen*** take heart, pluck up courage; ***j-m ~ machen*** boost s.o.'s courage, (*a.* ***j-m ~ zusprechen***) give s.o. a few words of encouragement; ***j-m den ~ nehmen*** dishearten s.o.; ***den ~ verlieren*** (*or* ***sinken lassen***) lose heart; ***es gehört schon ~ dazu*** it takes a bit of courage; ***mir fehlt einfach der ~*** (***dazu***) I just haven't got the courage (for it); ***nur ~!*** chin up!, F keep your pecker up!; → ***antrinken***; **2.** ***guten ~es sein*** be optimistic; → ***zumute***

Mu·ta·gen [muta'ge:n] *n* (-s; -e) *biol.* mutagen; **Mu·tant** [mu'tant] *m* (-en; -en) *biol.* mutant; **Mu·ta·ti·on** [muta'tsi̯o:n] *f* (-; -en) *biol.* mutation

Müt·chen ['my:tçən] *n*: ***sein ~ kühlen*** let off steam, ***an j-m:*** take it out on s.o.

mu·tie·ren [mu'ti:rən] *v/i.* (h) **1.** *biol.* mutate; **2.** ***er mutiert*** (***gerade***) his voice is breaking

mu·tig ['mu:tɪç] *adj.* brave, courageous, F gutsy; bold; daring

'mut·los *adj.* disheartened; despondent; **'Mut·lo·sig·keit** *f* (-; *no pl.*) despondency; despair

mut·ma·ßen ['mu:tma:sən] *v/i.* (h) guess, conjecture; **mut·maß·lich** ['mu:tma:slɪç] *adj.* probable; suspected, presumed; ***~er Mörder*** *a.* murder suspect; ***~er Terrorist*** *a.* terrorist suspect

'Mut·ma·ßung *f* (-; -en) *a. pl.* speculation; suspicion; ***~en anstellen*** speculate (***über*** *acc.* about, on)

'Mut·pro·be *f* test of courage

Mutt·chen ['mʊtçən] *n* (-s; -) **1.** Mummy, *Am.* Mommy; *iro.* Mummy dear, *Am.* Mommy dear; **2.** little old lady, F old biddy

Mut·ter ['mʊtɐ] *f* (-; Mütter ['mʏtɐ]) **1.** mother; ***werdende ~*** expectant mother; ***sie wird ~*** she's expecting (*or* going to have) a baby; ***~ von zwei Kindern sein*** be a (*or* the) mother of two children, be a mother of two; F ***wie bei ~(n)*** just like home; F ***es schmeckt wie bei ~(n)*** it tastes like Mum's (*Am.* Mom's) cooking; *fig.* ***~ Erde*** mother earth; **2.** ⚙ nut

Müt·ter·be·ra·tungs·stel·le ['mʏtɐ-] *f* child welfare centre, *Am.* maternity center

'Mut·ter|bild *n psych.* mother image; **~bin·dung** *f psych.* attachment (*or* ties *pl.*) to one's mother; **~bo·den** *m* ⛏ topsoil; **~brust** *f* mother's breast

Müt·ter·chen ['mʏtɐçən] *n* (-s; -) **1.** mother (dear); **2.** ***altes ~*** little old lady, F old biddy

'Mut·ter|er·de *f* topsoil; **~er·satz** *m* substitute mother; **~freu·den** *pl.*: ***~ entgegensehen*** be expecting a baby; **~ge·sell·schaft** *f* ✝ parent company; **~ge·stein** *n* bedrock; **~ge·win·de** *n* ⚙ female thread; **~glück** *n* joy(s *pl.*) of motherhood

Mut·ter'got·tes *f* (Virgin) Mary; Madonna

Müt·ter·heim ['mʏtɐ-] *n* maternity home

'Mut·ter|herz *n* motherly feelings *pl.*; **~in͜stinkt** *m* maternal (*or* motherly) instinct(s *pl.*); **~kir·che** *f eccl.* mother church; **~kom͜plex** *m psych.* mother fixation; **~korn** *n* ♣ ergot; **~ku·chen** *m* ⚕ placenta; **~land** *n* (-[e]s; ⸚er) mother country; **~leib** *m* womb

müt·ter·lich ['mʏtɐ-] **I.** *adj.* motherly; maternal; **II.** *adv.* like a mother; ***j-n ~ umsorgen*** (*or* ***umhegen***) *a.* mother s.o.; **'müt·ter·li·cher·seits** *adv.* on one's mother's side; maternal *uncle etc.*; **'Müt·ter·lich·keit** *f* (-; *no pl.*) motherliness

'Mut·ter·lie·be *f* motherly love

'mut·ter·los *adj.* motherless; (*a. adv.*) without a mother

'Mut·ter|mal *n* birthmark; **~milch** *f* mother's milk; ***mit ~ genährt*** breast-fed; *fig.* ***et. mit der ~ einsaugen*** learn s.th. from the cradle; **~mord** *m* matricide; **~mör·der** *m* matricide; **~mund** *m anat.* uterine orifice, 🕮 os uteri

'Mut·tern·schlüs·sel *m* ⚙ spanner, *Am.* wrench

'Mut·ter|pflich·ten *pl. one's* duties as a mother; **~recht** *n* matriarchy; **~schaf** *n* ewe

'Mut·ter·schaft *f* (-; *no pl.*) motherhood

'Mut·ter·schafts|geld *n* maternity benefit; **~ur·laub** *m* maternity leave

'Mut·ter·schutz *m legal protection for expectant mothers*

'mut·ter'see·len·al'lein *adj.* all alone, all on one's own, F on one's tod

'Mut·ter·söhn·chen *n* mummy's (*Am.* mommy's) boy *or* darling; sissy, cissy

'Mut·ter·spra·che *f* mother tongue, native language; **'Mut·ter·sprach·ler** [-ʃpra:xlɐ] *m* (-s; -) native speaker

'Mut·ter·stel·le *f*: ***~ vertreten bei j-m*** be like a (*or* a second) mother to s.o.

Müt·ter·sterb·lich·keit ['mʏtɐ-] *f* maternal mortality

'Mut·ter|tag *m* Mother's Day; **~tier** *n zo.* dam; **~witz** *m* nous; natural wit

Mut·ti ['mʊti] *f* mum(my), *Am.* mom(my); Mum(my), *Am.* Mom(my)

'Mut·wil·le *m* (-n; *no pl.*) wil(l)fulness

'mut·wil·lig I. *adj.* wil(l)ful; wanton *destruction etc.*; **II.** *adv.* wil(l)fully, wantonly; ***~ zerstören*** *a.* vandalize

'Mut·wil·lig·keit *f* (-; *no pl.*) wil(l)fulness; wantonness, wanton nature (*gen.* of)

Müt·ze ['mʏtsə] *f* (-; -n) cap; wool(l)y hat; **'Müt·zen·schirm** *m* peak

My·ko·lo·gie [mykolo'gi:] *f* (-; *no pl.*) mycology

Myo·kar·di·tis [myokar'di:tɪs] *f* (-; -ditiden [-di'ti:dən]) ⚕ myocarditis

My·om [my'o:m] *n* (-s; -e) ⚕ myoma

Myo·pie [myo'pi:] *f* (-; *no pl.*) ⚕ myopia; **myo·pisch** [my'o:pɪʃ] *adj.* myopic

My·ria·de [my'ri̯a:də] *f* (-; -n) myriad

Myr·rhe ['mʏrə] *f* (-; -n) myrrh

Myr·te ['mʏrtə] *f* (-; -n) myrtle

my·ste·ri·ös [mʏste'ri̯ø:s] *adj.* mysterious

My·ste·ri·um [mʏs'te:ri̯ʊm] *n* (-; -en) mystery; *formal*: arcanum (*pl.* arcana)

My·sti·fi·ka·ti·on [mʏstifika'tsi̯o:n] *f* (-; -en) mystification; **my·sti·fi·zie·ren** [mʏstifi'tsi:rən] *v/t.* (h) make a mystery of

My·stik ['mʏstɪk] *f* (-; *no pl.*) mysticism

My·sti·ker ['mʏstikɐ] *m* (-s; -) mystic

my·stisch ['mʏstɪʃ] *adj.* **1.** mystic *symbol etc.*; mystical; **2.** mysterious

My·sti·zis·mus [mʏsti'tsɪsmʊs] *m* (-; *no pl.*) mysticism

My·the ['my:tə] *f* (-; -n) myth; **my·thisch** ['my:tɪʃ] *adj.* mythical

My·tho·lo·ge [myto'lo:gə] *m* (-n; -n) mythologist; **My·tho·lo·gie** [mytolo'gi:] *f* (-; -n) mythology; **my·tho·lo·gisch** [myto'lo:gɪʃ] *adj.* mythological; **my·tho·lo·gi·sie·ren** [mytologi'zi:rən] *v/t.* (h) mythologize

My·thos ['my:tɔs] *m* (-; Mythen ['my:tən]) **1.** myth; **2.** *a. fig.* legend; ***zu Lebzeiten zum ~ werden*** become a legend in one's own lifetime, become a living legend

N

N, n [ɛn] *n* (-; -) N, n

na [na] *int.* a) well!, b) hey!; ~, ~! come on (now), *sl.* oy!; ~ ***also!***, ~ ***bitte!*** see?, there you are, what did I tell you?; ~ ***ja*** well(, what can one say?), well(, you know); ~, ***ich weiß nicht*** (well,) I'm not so sure; ~, ***gut!***, ~ ***schön!*** all right, *Am.* alright; ~ ***gut*** fair enough; ~, ***so was!*** fancy that, F what do you know; ~ ***und?*** so (what)?; ~ ***warte!*** just you wait!; ~ ***endlich!*** about time too; ~, ***du?*** *to a child*: well(, what have you got to say for yourself)?; ~, ***wie geht's?*** how are things, then?; ~, ***denn mal los!*** let's get going, then!; ~ ***und ob!*** F you bet

Na·be ['na:bə] *f* (-; -n) hub

Na·bel ['na:bəl] *m* (-s; -) navel; *fig.* ~ ***der Welt*** cent|re (*Am.* -er) of the universe; **~bruch** *m* ⚕ umbilical hernia; **~schau** F *f* F navel gazing; ~ ***betreiben*** do some navel gazing, be all bound (*or* wrapped) up with o.s.; **~schnur** *f*, **~strang** *m* umbilical cord

'Na·ben·kap·pe *f* hub cap

nach [na:x] **I.** *prp.* (*dat.*) **1.** to, towards; for, bound for; ~ ***rechts*** to the right; ~ ***unten*** down, downstairs; ~ ***oben*** up, upstairs; ~ ***England reisen*** go to England; ~ ***England abreisen*** leave for England; ***der Zug*** ~ ***London*** the train to London; ***das Schiff fährt*** ~ ***Australien*** the ship is bound for (*or* is going to) Australia; ~ ***Hause*** home; ***das Zimmer geht*** ~ ***hinten*** (***vorn***) ***hinaus*** the room faces the back (front); ***der Balkon geht*** ~ ***Süden*** the balcony faces south; ***Balkon*** ~ ***Süden*** south-facing balcony; ***wir fahren*** ~ ***Norden*** we're travel(l)ing north (*or* northwards); ***die Blume richtet sich*** ~ ***der Sonne*** the flower turns towards the sun; ~ ***dem Arzt schicken*** send for the doctor; **2.** after; ***fünf*** (***Minuten***) ~ ***eins*** five (minutes) past (*Am. a.* after) one; ~ ***zehn Minuten*** ten minutes later; ~ ***einer Stunde*** in an hour('s time); ~ ***Ankunft*** (***Erhalt***) on arrival (receipt) (*gen.* of); **3.** after; ***einer*** ~ ***dem anderen*** one by one, one after the other; ***der Reihe*** ~ in turn; ***der Reihe*** ~! take it in turns!, one after the other!; *fig.* ~ ***ihm kommt lange keiner*** he's in a class of his own, he's streets ahead of the rest; **4.** according to; ~ ***dem, was er sagte*** *a.* going by what he said; ~ ***Ansicht*** *gen.* in (*or* according to) the opinion of; ~ ***Gewicht verkaufen*** sell by weight; ~ ***Bedarf*** as required; ***s-e Uhr stellen*** ~ *dat.* set one's watch by *the radio etc.*; ***wenn es*** ~ ***mir ginge*** if I had my way; ***dem Namen*** ~ by name; ***s-m Namen*** (***Akzent*** *etc.*) ~ judging *or* going by his name (accent *etc.*); ~ ***Musik tanzen*** *etc.* dance *etc.* to music; ~ ***Noten*** from music; ***es ist nicht*** ~ ***s-m Geschmack*** it's not to his taste; ***schmecken*** (***riechen***) ~ *dat.* taste (smell) of; ~ ***s-r Weise*** in his usual way; ~ ***bestem Wissen*** to the best of one's knowledge; ~ ***Stunden*** (***Dollar*** *etc.*) ***gerechnet*** in (terms of) hours (dollars *etc.*); → ***Ermessen, Meinung***; **5.** ~ ***j-m fragen*** ask for s.o.; ***die Suche*** ~ ***dem Glück*** *etc.* the pursuit of (*or* search for) happiness *etc.*; **II.** *adv.* after; ***mir*** ~! follow me!; ~ ***und*** ~ gradually, bit by bit; ~ ***wie vor*** still, as ever

nach·äf·fen ['na:xʔɛfən] *v/t.* (*sep.*, h) ape, mimic, take off; parrot; **Nach·äf·fe·rei** [na:xʔɛfə'raɪ] *f* (-; -en) aping, mimicking; parroting

nach·ah·men ['na:xʔa:mən] *v/t.* (*sep.*, h) **1.** imitate, copy; (try to) emulate; **2.** → ***nachäffen***; **'nach·ah·mens·wert** *adj.* exemplary; **~es** ***Beispiel*** example worth following (*or* trying to follow); **Nach·ah·mer** ['na:xʔa:mɐ] *m* (-s; -) imitator; ~ ***finden*** be imitated (*or* copied, emulated); **Nach·ah·mung** ['na:xʔa:mʊŋ] *f* (-; -en) **1.** imitation; ***zur*** ~ ***empfohlen!*** it's an example worth following; **2.** imitation, copy; **'Nach·ah·mungs·trieb** *m* imitative instinct

'nach·ar·bei·ten (*sep.*, h) **I.** *v/t.* **1.** make up (for) *lost time etc.*; **2.** copy; **3.** ⚙ a) finish, b) touch up; **II.** *v/i.* make up for lost time, catch up (on one's working hours); work late

'nach·ar·ten *v/i.* (*sep.*, sn): ***j-m*** ~ take after s.o.

Nach·bar ['naxba:ɐ] *m* (-n, -s; -n) neighbo(u)r (*a. fig.*); next-door neighbo(u)r; *ped. etc.*: person (*or* boy *etc.*) sitting next to one; → ***spitz*** 4; **~dorf** *n* neighbo(u)ring village; **~gar·ten** *m* neighbo(u)rs' (*or* neighbo[u]r's, neighbo[u]ring) garden, garden next door; **~haus** *n* house next door; ***im*** ~ next door

Nach·ba·rin ['naxba:rɪn] *f* (-; -nen) → ***Nachbar***

'Nach·bar|in·sel *f* neighbo(u)ring island; *pl. a.* islands round about; **~land** *n* (-[e]s; ¨er) neighbo(u)ring country

'nach·bar·lich I. *adj.* **1.** neighbo(u)rly; **2.** next-door *garden etc.*, *pred. the garden etc.* next door; **II.** *adv.*: ~ ***verkehren mit*** *dat.* be on (good) neighbo(u)rly terms with

'Nach·bar·ort *m* nearby village (*or* town, place)

'Nach·bar·schaft *f* (-; *no pl.*) a) neighbo(u)rhood, b) neighbo(u)rs *pl.*, c) vicinity; **'Nach·bar·schafts·hil·fe** *f* **1.** neighbo(u)rly help; **2.** community aid

'Nach·bars|fa,mi·lie *f* family next door; **~frau** *f* lady next door; **~kind** *n* boy (*or* girl) next door, *pl.* children next door; **~leu·te** *pl.* neighbo(u)rs, people next door

'Nach·bar|staat *m* neighbo(u)ring state; **~tisch** *m*: (***am*** ~ at the) next table; **~volk** *n* neighbo(u)ring people (*sg.*) *or* nation; **~wis·sen·schaft** *f* related discipline; **~zim·mer** *n* next room, room next door

'Nach·bau *m* (-[e]s; -ten) copy, reproduction; ⚙ ~ ***unter Lizenz*** construction under licen|ce (*Am.* -se); **'nach·bau·en** *v/t.* (*sep.*, h) copy, reproduce

'Nach·be·ben *n* (-s; -) aftershock

'nach·be·han·deln *v/t.* (*sep.*, h) **1.** ⚕ give *s.o. or s.th.* follow-up treatment, give *s.o.* aftercare; **2.** ⚙ *etc.* a) finish, b) touch up; **'Nach·be·hand·lung** *f* (-; -en) **1.** ⚕ follow-up treatment; aftercare; **2.** ⚙ *etc.* a) finishing work, b) touching-up

'nach·be·kom·men *v/t.* (*irr.*, *sep.*, h, → ***bekommen***) **1.** get another helping (*or* more helpings) of; **2.** get *s.th.* (later on), get hold of *spare parts etc.*

'nach·be·rei·ten *v/t.* (*sep.*, h) *ped.* go over

'nach·bes·sern *v/t.* (*sep.*, h) touch up, do some touching-up on; *w.s.* repair, do up; **'Nach·bes·se·rung** *f* (-; -en) finishing touches *pl.*; *w.s.* repairs *pl.*

'nach·be·stel·len ⚕⚗ *v/t.* (*sep.*, h) order some more of; ☤ place a repeat order for; **'Nach·be·stel·lung** *f* (-; -en) repeat order (*gen.* for)

'nach·be·ten F *v/t.* (*sep.*, h) parrot; **'Nach·be·ter** *m* (-s; -) parrot

'nach·be·zah·len (*sep.*, h) **I.** *v/t.* pay for *s.th.* afterwards (*or* later); pay the rest; **II.** *v/i.* pay afterwards (*or* later)

'nach·bil·den *v/t.* (*sep.*, h) copy, reproduce; replicate; **'Nach·bil·dung** *f* (-; -en) copy, reproduction; replica

'nach·blicken *v/i.* (*sep.*, h): ***j-m*** ~ gaze after s.o., watch s.o. go *etc.*

'Nach·blü·te *f* (-; *no pl.*) *a. fig.* second flowering

'nach·blu·ten *v/i.* (*sep.*, h) start bleeding again; **'Nach·blu·tung** *f* (-; -en) ⚕ *a. pl.* secondary bleeding

'nach·boh·ren F *fig. v/i.* (*sep.*, h) probe, dig deeper; ***bei j-m wegen e-r Sache*** ~ *a.* F pump s.o. for s.th.; ***da muß ich mal*** ~ I'll have to do a bit of probing

'nach·brin·gen *v/t.* (*irr.*, *sep.*, h, → ***bringen***) bring (*or* take) *s.th.* later

'nach·christ·lich *adj.*: ***im ersten*** **~en** ***Jahrhundert*** in the first century AD

'nach·da,tie·ren *v/t.* (*sep.*, h) antedate

nach'dem *cj.* **1.** after, when; ~ ***sie das gesagt hatte*** after she had said that, (after) having said that, after saying that; **2.** since, as, seeing as; ~ ***er es nicht wollte*** since (*or* as, seeing as) he didn't want it; **3.** ***je*** ~! it all depends; ***je*** ~, ***was er sagt*** depending on what he says

'nach·den·ken I. *v/i.* (*irr.*, *sep.*, h, → ***denken***) think (***über*** *acc.* about); ***ich werde darüber*** ~ I'll think about it, I'll think it over; ***denk mal nach*** think (hard); ***darüber ~, wie*** (***warum*** *etc.*) think about *or* consider how (why *etc.*); **II.** ≈ *n* (-s; *no pl.*) thinking; reflection; ***Zeit zum ~ brauchen*** need time to think (it over); ***in ~ versunken*** lost in thought; ***nach einigem ~*** after thinking about it, after giving it some thought; **'nach·denk·lich** [-dɛŋklɪç] *adj.* (*a. adv.* ~ ***gestimmt***) pensive, thoughtful; lost in thought; ***~es Gesicht*** thoughtful expression; ***du machst aber ein ~es Gesicht*** what are you looking so thoughtful about?; ***j-n ~ machen*** set s.o. thinking, have s.o. wondering; ***er wurde ~*** it had him thinking (*or* wondering); **'Nach·denk·lich·keit** *f* (-; *no pl.*) pensiveness; *w.s.* reservations *pl.*, doubts *pl.*

'nach·dich·ten *v/t.* (*sep.*, h) (freely) adapt; **'Nach·dich·tung** *f* (-; -en) (free) adaptation, free rendering

'nach·drän·gen *v/i.* (*sep.*, h) *crowd etc.*: push from behind; *fig.* build up

'nach·dre·hen *v/t.* (*sep.*, h) *film*: reshoot

'Nach·druck¹ *m* (-[e]s; *no pl.*) stress, emphasis; ~ ***legen auf*** *acc.*, ~ ***verleihen*** *dat.* stress, emphasize; ***mit ~ hinweisen auf*** *acc.* make a point of stressing *s.th.*; ***et. mit ~ verfolgen*** strenuously (*or* vigorously) pursue s.th.; ***mit ~ eintreten für*** *acc.* press for *s.th.*

'Nach·druck² *m* (-[e]s; -e) *typ.* reprint; ~ ***verboten*** all rights reserved

'nach·drucken *v/t.* (*sep.*, h) reprint

nach·drück·lich ['na:xdrʏklɪç] **I.** *adj.* emphatic; insistent; firm; explicit; ***~e Warnung*** (***Bitte***) urgent warning (plea); **II.** *adv.* emphatically; ***et. ~ empfehlen*** strongly recommend s.th.; ***j-n ~ warnen*** give s.o. an urgent warning; ***~ dementieren*** strenuously deny; ***et. ~ verlangen*** insist on s.th.; ***er riet ~ davon ab*** he strongly advised against it; ***ich habe dir doch ~ gesagt, daß ...*** didn't I make it quite clear to you that ...?; **'Nach·drück·lich·keit** *f* (-; *no pl.*) emphasis; insistence; firmness; explicitness; urgency

'nach·dun·keln *v/i.* (*sep.*, sn) darken, get darker

'Nach·durst *m* (alcohol-induced) dehydration

'nach·ei·fern *v/i.* (*sep.*, h): ***j-m ~*** (strive to) emulate s.o., try to follow in s.o.'s footsteps

'nach·ei·len *v/i.* (*sep.*, sn): ***j-m ~*** hurry (*or* run) after s.o.

nach·ein'an·der *adv.* one after the other; in succession; ***drei Tage ~*** three days running (*or* in a row); ***kurz ~*** in quick succession, at short intervals

'nach·emp·fin·den *v/t.* (*irr.*, *sep.*, h, → ***empfinden***) **1.** understand *s.o.'s feelings etc.*; imagine what *s.th.* is like; ***ich kann es dir ~*** I can understand exactly how you feel, I can really sympathize with you; **2.** ***et. ~*** *dat.* model (*or* base) s.th. on; ***e-r Sache nachempfunden sein*** *a.* be an adaptation of s.th.

'nach·emp·fun·den I. *p.p. of* ***nachempfinden***; **II.** *adj.* shared *emotions etc.*; vicarious *pleasure*, *experience etc.*

Na·chen ['naxən] *poet. m* (-s; -) boat; barge, *poet.* bark, barque

'nach·er·le·ben *v/t.* (*sep.*, h) relive

'Nach·ern·te *f* (-; -n) **1.** second harvest; **2.** a) gleaning, b) gleanings *pl.*

'nach·er·zäh·len *v/t.* (*sep.*, h) retell; *ped.* give a summary of; tell the story of *a film etc.*; **'Nach·er·zäh·lung** *f* (-; -en) summary; retelling of a story (in one's own words); recall test

Nach·fah·re ['na:xfa:rə] *m* (-n; -n) descendant

'nach·fah·ren *v/i.* (*irr.*, *sep.*, sn, → ***fahren***) follow on; ***j-m ~*** follow s.o., drive after s.o.

'nach·fär·ben *v/t.* (*sep.*, h) re-dye

'nach·fas·sen (*sep.*, h) **I.** *v/i.* **1.** go into it; ***bei j-m ~*** remind s.o. (***wegen*** *gen.* about); ***da muß ich mal ~*** *a.* I'll have to (ring up and) ask what's going on; **2.** have (*or* take) another helping; ***zum dritten Mal ~*** have one's third helping; **II.** *v/t.* have (*or* take) another helping of, help o.s. to some more

Nach·faß·wer·bung ['na:xfas-] *f* follow-up publicity

'nach·fei·ern *v/t.* (*sep.*, h) celebrate *s.th.* later; ***et. ~*** *a.* catch up with the celebrations later

'Nach·fol·ge *f* (-; *no pl.*) succession; ***die ~ antreten*** succeed to the throne (*or* title *etc.*); ***j-s ~ antreten*** succeed s.o.; ***ein Favorit für die ~ von X*** a favo(u)rite for the successor of X; ***~kan·di,dat*** *m* successor candidate; ***~kon·fe,renz*** *f* follow-up conference

'nach·fol·gen *v/i.* (*sep.*, sn) follow on; ***j-m ~*** follow s.o.; ***e-r Sache ~*** follow (on from) s.th.; ***j-m im Amt ~*** succeed s.o. in office; **'nach·fol·gend** *adj.* subsequent; following; ensuing, resulting; ***~er Verkehr*** traffic coming from behind; ***~er Präsident*** *etc.* incoming president *etc.*; ***die ~en Generationen*** later (*or* future, coming) generations; ***im ~en*** below

'Nach·fol·ge·or·ga·ni·sa·ti,on *f* successor organization

'Nach·fol·ger [-fɔlgɐ] *m* (-s; -) successor

'Nach·fol·ge·re·ge·lung *f* regulations *pl.* governing the succession

'Nach·fol·ge·rin [-fɔlgərɪn] *f* (-; -nen) → ***Nachfolger***

'Nach·fol·ger·staat *m hist.* successor state

'nach·for·dern *v/t.* (*sep.*, h) demand *s.th.* in addition; put in a claim for an extra *thousand marks etc.*; **'Nach·for·de·rung** *f* (-; -en) additional demand (*or* charge)

'nach·for·schen *v/i.* (*sep.*, h) investigate, inquire (*or* look) into the matter; make inquiries (*or* enquiries)

'Nach·for·schung *f* (-; -en) investigation, inquiry, enquiry; ***~en anstellen*** → ***nachforschen***

'Nach·fra·ge *f* (-; *no pl.*) **1.** inquiry, enquiry; ***danke der ~!*** kind of you to ask; **2.** ☤ demand (***nach*** *dat.* for); ***starke*** (***geringe***) ~ great (little) demand; → ***Angebot***; **'nach·fra·gen** *v/i.* (*sep.*, h): ***bei j-m ~*** ask s.o. (***wegen*** *gen.* about); ***bei e-m Amt*** *etc.* ~ ask at an office *etc.* (***wegen*** *gen.* about), inquire at (about)

'Nach·frist *f* extension

'nach·füh·len *v/t.* (*sep.*, h) understand; ***das kann ich dir ~*** I know exactly how you (must) feel

'nach·fül·len *v/t.* (*sep.*, h) a) refill, b) top up; ***j-m das Glas ~*** fill (*or* top) up s.o.'s glass

'Nach·füll·pack *m* (-s; -e) refill (pack)

'nach·gä·ren *v/i.* (*sep.*, h) ferment again; **'Nach·gä·rung** *f* (-; -en) secondary fermentation

'nach·ge·ben (*irr.*, *sep.*, h, → ***geben***) **I.** *v/i.* **1.** give in (*dat.* to), yield (to), relent; ***zu schnell ~*** give in too easily; ***j-m zuviel ~*** be too soft with s.o.; **2.** *material*: give; *wall etc.*: give way, collapse; **3.** ☤ *rates, prices*: drop; **II.** *v/i. and v/t.*: ***j-m*** (***et.***) ~ give s.o. another helping (of s.th.); ***j-m Kartoffeln*** *etc.* ~ *a.* give s.o. some more potatoes *etc.*; ***sich*** (***et.***) ***~ lassen*** have another helping (of s.th.); **III.** *fig. v/t.*: ***einander nichts ~*** be equals, be just as good (*or* bad *etc.*) as each other; ***j-m nichts ~*** be just as good as s.o.

'nach·ge·bo·ren *adj.* **1.** posthumous; **2.** younger; late-born

'Nach|ge·bühr *f* excess postage, (postal) surcharge; ***~ge·burt*** *f* ⚕ afterbirth, placenta

'nach·ge·hen *v/i.* (*irr.*, *sep.*, sn, → ***gehen***) **1.** ***j-m ~*** follow (*or* go after) s.o.; **2.** pursue *a profession, one's pleasure etc.*; see to *one's business*; indulge in *one's hobbies etc.*; **3.** *fig.* ***j-m ~*** a) linger in s.o.'s mind, haunt s.o., b) prey on s.o.'s mind, weigh heavily on s.o.'s conscience; ***die Sache geht ihm nach*** he's haunted by it; ***mir geht es ziemlich nach*** *a.* I can't get it out of my mind, I can't stop thinking about it; **4.** look into, follow *s.th.* up, investigate; **5.** *watch*: be slow; ***jeden Tag zwei Minuten ~*** lose two minutes a day

'nach|ge·las·sen I. *p.p. of* ***nachlassen***; **II.** *adj.* posthumous *works*; ***~ge·macht*** *adj.* a) counterfeit, b) imitation ...; ***~ge·ord·net*** *adj.* subordinate

'nach·ge'ra·de *adv.* **1.** virtually; almost; absolutely; really; **2.** by now; **3.** slowly, gradually

'nach·ge·ra·ten *v/i.* (*irr.*, *sep.*, sn, → ***geraten***): ***j-m ~*** take after s.o.

'Nach·ge·schmack *m* aftertaste (*a. fig.*); *fig.* ***es hinterläßt e-n*** (***unangenehmen***) ~ *a.* it leaves a bad taste in your mouth

'nach·ge·stellt I. *p.p. of* ***nachstellen***; **II.** *adj. ling.* postpositive; ***~e Position*** postposition

'nach·ge·wie·se·ner·ma·ßen [-gəvi:zənɐ'ma:sən] *adv.* as has been proved (*or* shown); ***er ist ~ ...*** he has been proved to be ...

'nach·gie·big [-gi:bɪç] *adj.* **1.** soft; pliable, flexible; **2.** *fig.* compliant; soft

'Nach·gie·big·keit *f* (-; *no pl.*) **1.** flexibility, pliability; **2.** *fig.* compliance

'nach·gie·ßen *v/t.* (*irr.*, *sep.*, h, → ***gießen***) pour (out) some more; add some more; ***darf ich dir noch etwas Kaffee ~?*** can I pour you some more coffee?, can I top you up again?

'nach·glü·hen I. *v/i.* (*sep.*, h) continue to glow; **II.** ≈ *n* (-s; *no pl.*) afterglow

'nach|grü·beln *v/i.* brood (***über*** *acc.* over); ***~gucken*** *v/i.* (*sep.*, h) → ***nachsehen*** I; ***~ha·ken*** F *v/i.* (*sep.*, h) broach the subject again; go into it; do a bit of probing; ***bei j-m ~*** press s.o. (***in*** *dat.* on *a matter etc.*)

'Nach·hall *m* reverberation; *fig.* echo; **'nach·hal·len** *v/i.* (*sep.*, h) reverberate; *fig.* echo

'nach·hal·tig [-haltɪç] **I.** *adj.* lasting; ***~er Geschmack*** lingering aftertaste, *wine*: long finish; **II.** *adv.* for a long time; strongly, deeply; ***~ wirken*** have a lasting (*or* long-term) effect, *w.s. a.* make itself felt for a long time (to come); ***j-n ~ beeindrucken*** a) leave a lasting impression on s.o., b) deeply impress s.o.; ***~ beeinflussen*** have a lasting effect on

'nach·hän·gen *v/i.* (*irr.*, *sep.*, h, → ***hän-***

gen²) **1.** dwell on *a problem etc.*; hang onto *one's memories, thoughts etc.*; **2.** lag behind (***in*** *dat.* in *a subject etc.*)

Nach'hau·se·weg *m*: (***auf dem ~*** on the) way home

'nach·hel·fen *v/i.* (*irr., sep.*, h, → ***helfen***) **1.** help (out); ***j-m ~ in*** *dat.* help s.o. (out) with *s.th., a.* coach s.o. in *s.th.*, give s.o. private lessons in *s.th.*; F ***bei j-m ~*** a) help s.o. along, b) push s.o. (along); F *iro.* ***j-m*** (*or* ***j-s Gedächtnis***) ***ein wenig ~*** jog s.o.'s memory; **2.** help things along, use a trick or two; ***e-r Sache ~*** help s.th. along; ***den Dingen etwas ~*** steer things in the right direction; ***dem Zufall*** (***Glück***) ***~*** help fate (fortune) along the way, give fate (fortune) a helping hand

nach'her *adv.* afterwards; later (on); ***bis ~!*** see you later!; ***paß auf, sonst passiert ~ was!*** watch out, otherwise there's going to be an accident (*or* there'll be an accident before you know it)

'Nach·hil·fe *f* → ***Nachhilfeunterricht***; **~leh·rer** *m* coach, private tutor; **~schü·ler** *m* private pupil; **~stun·de** *f* private lesson; **~ˌun·ter·richt** *m* private lessons *pl.*, coaching

'nach·hin·ein *adv.*: ***im ~*** afterwards; in retrospect, with hindsight; after the event

'Nach·hol·be·darf *m* (-[e]s; *no pl.*) ✝ *etc.* (unsatisfied) demand (***an*** *dat.* for); *fig.* (unsatisfied) need (for); ***großen ~ haben*** have a lot of catching up to do, have to make up for lost time; **'nach·ho·len** *v/t.* (*sep.*, h) **1.** fetch later; **2.** make up for *lost time etc.*; catch up on *one's sleep etc.*; **'Nach·hol·spiel** *n sport*: rescheduled match (*or* game)

Nach·hut ['na:xhu:t] *f* (-; -en) rearguard; ***die ~ bilden*** *a. fig.* bring up the rear

'nach·imp·fen *v/t.* (*sep.*, h) give *s.o.* a booster; **'Nach·imp·fung** *f* booster, reinoculation

'nach|ja·gen (*sep.*) **I.** *v/i.* (sn) chase (after); run after; *fig.* chase after *money etc.*; **II.** *v/t.* (h) send after *s.o.*; **~jam·mern** *v/i.* (*sep.*, h): ***e-r Sache ~*** mourn the loss of s.th., mourn after s.th.

'Nach·klang *m* **1.** echo (in one's ear); **2.** *fig.* a) reminiscence, b) (after)effect; ***unangenehmer ~*** unpleasant repercussions; **'nach·klin·gen** *v/i.* (*irr., sep.*, h, → ***klingen***) echo, *a. fig.* linger, ring in one's ears; *fig.* ***lange ~*** leave a deep impression (***in j-m*** on s.o.), linger on (in s.o.['s mind])

Nach·kom·me ['na:xkɔmə] *m* (-n; -n) descendant; ***ohne ~n sterben*** *formal*: die without issue

'nach·kom·men *v/i.* (*irr., sep.*, sn, → ***kommen***) **1.** follow (on) later; **2.** follow; **3.** keep up (*dat.* with); **4.** comply (*dat.* with *an order, a request etc.*); fulfil(l), carry out *duty, promise etc.*

'Nach·kom·men·schaft *f* (-; *no pl.*) descendants *pl.*

Nach·kömm·ling ['na:xkœmlɪŋ] *m* (-s; -e) **1.** → ***Nachkomme***; **2.** late arrival, *hum.* afterthought

'nach·kon·trolˌlie·ren *v/t.* (*sep.*, h) check *s.th.* again (*or* to make sure); ***et. ~*** *a.* do a double check

'Nach·kriegs|ge·ne·ra·tiˌon *f* postwar generation; **~li·te·raˌtur** *f* postwar literature; **~wir·ren** *pl.* postwar turmoil *sg.*; **~zeit** *f* postwar era (*or* years *pl.*)

'nach·la·den *v/t. and v/i.* (*irr., sep.*, h, → ***laden***) reload; ⚡ recharge

Nach·laß ['na:xlas] *m* (-sses; Nachlässe [-lɛsə]) **1.** estate; ***literarischer ~*** unpublished works; **2.** discount (***auf*** *acc.* on), reduction (on)

'nach·las·sen (*irr., sep.*, h, → ***lassen***) **I.** *v/t.* **1.** slacken; **2.** ***etwas*** (***10 Dollar***) ***vom Preis ~*** give a discount (of 10 dollars); **II.** *v/i.* a) decrease, diminish, weaken, *interest etc.* flag, *pace*: slacken, *rain, storm*: let up, *wind, fig. performance, production etc.*: drop, *pain*: ease, *effect*: wear off, *temperature*: go down, b) deteriorate, *one's health, eyes etc.*: begin to fail; *person*: slack; ***nicht ~!*** no slacking!; ***mein Gedächtnis*** (***Hirn***) ***läßt allmählich nach*** my memory (brain) is (slowly) going

'Nach·laß|ge·richt *n* probate court; **~gläu·bi·ger** *m* creditor of the estate

'nach·läs·sig *adj.* a) careless, negligent, b) slovenly, sloppy, c) indifferent; **'Nach·läs·sig·keit** *f* (-; *no pl.*) a) negligence, carelessness, b) slovenliness

'Nach·laß|steu·er *f* estate tax; **~ver·wal·ter** *m* executor

'nach·lau·fen *v/i.* (*irr., sep*, sn, → ***laufen***) run after (*dat. s.o. or s.th.*); chase (*or* run, be) after *a girl etc.*; *fig.* chase after

'nach·le·ben **I.** *v/i.* (*sep.*, h) live up to, emulate; **II.** ♀ *n* (-s; *no pl.*) afterlife

'nach·le·gen (*sep.*, h) **I.** *v/t.* put some more *coal etc.* on; **II.** *v/i.* put some more coal (*or* wood *etc.*) on (the fire)

'Nach·le·se *f* (-; *no pl.*) **1.** ✔ a) gleaning, b) gleanings *pl.*; **2.** *fig.* selection (of highlights), selection of previously unpublished works; **'nach·le·sen** *v/t.* (*irr., sep.*, h, → ***lesen***) **1.** ✔ glean; **2.** read (through), read up on, check, look up

'nach·leuch·ten **I.** *v/i.* (*sep.*, h) continue to glow; **II.** ♀ *n* (-s; *no pl.*) afterglow; *phys.* luminescence

'nach·lie·fern *v/t.* (*sep.*, h) send on (later), supply; **'Nach·lie·fe·rung** *f* later (*or* additional) delivery

'nach|lö·sen *v/t.* (*and v/i.*) (*sep.*, h) buy (a ticket) on the train *etc.* (*or* at the other end); **~ma·chen** *v/t.* (*sep.*, h) **1.** a) copy (***j-m et.*** s.th. s.o. does); imitate, mimic, F take off, b) forge; ***das soll mir erst mal einer ~!*** I'd like to see anyone do better; ***so schnell macht ihm das keiner nach*** he's hard to beat (when it comes to that); **2.** do (later); ***~ müssen*** still have to do; **~ma·len** *v/t.* (*sep.*, h) copy

nach·ma·lig ['na:xma:lɪç] *adj.* later, subsequent; **nach·mals** ['na:xma:ls] *adv.* later, subsequently

'nach·mes·sen *v/t.* (*irr., sep.*, h, → ***messen***) measure (again), check (the measurements of)

'Nach·mie·ter *m* new tenant; next tenant; ***sein ~*** the person who took over his flat (*Am.* apartment); ***ich muß e-n ~ suchen*** I've got to find someone to take over the flat (*Am.* apartment)

'Nach·mit·tag *m* afternoon; ***am ~*** in the afternoon; ***am späten ~*** (in the) late afternoon; **'nach·mit·tag** *adv.*: ***heute ~*** this afternoon; **'nach·mit·täg·lich** *adj.* afternoon ...; **'nach·mit·tags** *adv.* in the afternoon(s), afternoons; ***~ geschlossen*** open mornings only

'Nach·mit·tags·vor·stel·lung *f* matinee

Nach·nah·me ['na:xna:mə] *f* (-; *no pl.*) cash (*Am.* collect) on delivery (*abbr.* COD); ***gegen*** (*or* ***per***) ***~*** COD, to be paid for on delivery; ***per ~ schicken*** send COD; **~ge·bühr** *f* COD charge; **~sen·dung** *f* COD delivery (✝ *a.* consignment)

'Nach·na·me *m* surname, last name

'nach|neh·men *v/t.* (*irr., sep.*, h, → ***nehmen***): ***sich et. ~*** have (*or* take) another helping of, have (*or* take) some more ...; ***nimm dir noch etwas nach!*** have some more; **~plap·pern** (*sep.*, h) **I.** *v/t.* parrot, repeat; **II.** *v/i.* parrot

'Nach·por·to *n* excess postage

'nach·prä·gen *v/t.* (*sep.*, h) a) copy, b) forge, counterfeit

'nach·prüf·bar *adj.* verifiable; **'Nach·prüf·bar·keit** *f* (-, *no pl.*) verifiability; **'nach·prü·fen** *v/t.* (*sep.*, h) **1.** check; investigate; **2.** *ped. etc.* a) re-examine, b) examine at a later date; **'Nach·prü·fung** *f* **1.** check(ing); inspection; **2.** *ped. etc.* a) re-examination, b) examination at a later date

'nach·rech·nen *v/t. and v/i.* (*sep.*, h) check; ***ich muß erst ~*** let me think (*or* try and work it out)

'Nach·re·de *f*: ***üble ~*** malicious gossip, ⚖ defamation (of character), slander

'nach·re·den *v/t.* (*sep.*, h) **1.** repeat; *contp.* parrot, echo; **2.** ***j-m et. ~*** say s.th. about s.o.

'Nach·red·ner *m* follow-up (*or* next) speaker

'nach|rei·chen *v/t.* (*sep.*, h) **1.** hand *s.th.* in (*or* send *s.th.* on) later; **2.** serve some more ...; ***j-m et. ~*** *a.* give s.o. another helping of s.th.; **~rei·fen** *v/i.* (*sep.*, sn) carry on ripening; **~rei·sen** *v/i.* (*sep.*, sn) follow on (later), come on later; ***j-m ~*** join s.o. later; **~ren·nen** *v/i.* (*irr., sep.*, sn, → ***rennen***) → ***nachlaufen***

Nach·richt ['na:xrɪçt] *f* (-; -en): (***e-e ~*** a piece of) news (*sg.*); message; *pl. radio, TV*: news (*sg.*); ***in den ~en*** in (*TV* on) the news; ***~en hören*** (***sehen***) listen to (watch) the news; ***die ~ vom Erdbeben*** *etc.* (the) news of the earthquake *etc.*; ***e-e gute*** (***schlechte***) ***~*** good (bad) news; ***~ bekommen von*** *dat.* hear from; ***die ~ bekommen, daß*** be informed that, receive news of *s.o. or s.th. ger.*; ***j-m ~ geben*** let s.o. know (***über*** *acc.* about), inform s.o. (of); ***e-e ~ hinterlassen*** leave a message

'Nach·rich·ten|agenˌtur *f* news (*or* press) agency, wire service; **~aus·tausch** *m* news exchange; **~bei·trag** *m* news item; **~büˌro** *n* → ***Nachrichtenagentur***; **~dienst** *m* **1.** intelligence service; **2.** *TV etc.* news service; **~in·duˌstrie** *f* communications industry; **~ma·gaˌzin** *n* news magazine; **~netz** *n* communications network; **~quel·le** *f* news (*or* information) source; **~re·dak·tiˌon** *f* newsroom; **~sa·telˌlit** *m* communications satellite; **~sen·dung** *f* news broadcast (*or* program[me]), *Am.* newscast; **~sper·re** *f* news blackout; ***e-e ~ verhängen*** impose a ban on all news; **~spre·cher** *m* newsreader, news presenter, *Am.* newscaster; **~stu·dio** *n* news studio; **~tech·nik** *f* communications engineering; **~überˌmitt·lung** *f* news transmission; **~we·sen** *n* (-s; *no pl.*) communications *pl.*; **~zenˌtra·le** *f* news centre (*Am.* center)

'nach·rücken *v/i.* (*sep.*, sn) **1.** move up (*a. fig.*); **2.** ⚔ follow on; **3.** *parl.* ***für j-n ~*** take over s.o.'s seat in parliament

Nach·rücker ['na:xrʏkɐ] (*sep.* -k·k-) *m*

(-s; -) *parl.* successor (to a *or* the parliamentary seat)
'Nach·ruf *m* obituary (**auf** *acc.* on)
'nach·ru·fen (*irr.*, *sep.*, h, → **rufen**) **I.** *v/i.*: **j-m ~** call (*or* shout) after s.o.; **II.** *v/t.*: **j-m et. ~** call (*or* shout) s.th. after s.o.
'Nach·ruhm *m* posthumous fame
'nach·rüh·men *v/t.* (*sep.*, h): **ihm wird nachgerühmt, daß er ein guter Vermittler sei** he's said to be (*or* credited with being, known as) a good mediator
'nach·rü·sten (*sep.*, h) **I.** *v/i.* ⚔ stock up on arms, (try to) close the armaments gap; **II.** *v/t.* ⚙ *etc.* retrofit, *w.s.* extend, expand; upgrade *computer etc.*
'nach·sa·gen *v/t.* (*sep.*, h) **1.** repeat; *contp.* parrot, echo; **2. j-m et. ~** claim s.th. of s.o.; **j-m Schlechtes ~** speak badly (*formal*: ill) of s.o., cast a slur on s.o.; **j-m nur Gutes ~** not to have a bad word to say about s.o.; **man kann ihm nichts Schlechtes (Gutes) ~** there's nothing bad to be said about him (there's not a good word to be said for him); **man sagt ihm nach, daß** he's said to *inf.*; **ihr wird Unehrlichkeit** *etc.* **nachgesagt** she's said to be dishonest *etc.*; **das lasse ich mir nicht ~!** I won't have that said of me; **ich lasse mir nichts ~** I won't have anyone speak badly of me
'Nach·sai,son *f* low (*or* off-peak) season
'nach·sal·zen *v/i.* *and* *v/t.* (*sep.*, h) add some more salt (to)
'Nach·satz *m* **1.** additional (*or* added) remark; postscript; **et. in e-m ~ erwähnen** mention s.th. in addition; **2.** *ling.* final clause
'nach|schau·en *v/i.* (*sep.*, h) → **nachsehen; ~schen·ken** *v/t.* *and* *v/i.* (*sep.*, h) pour some more (wine *etc.*) out; **darf ich dir (etwas Wein) ~?** can I pour you some more wine?, can I top you up again?; **~schicken** *v/t.* (*sep.*, h) → **nachsenden**
'Nach·schlag *m* second helping
'nach·schla·gen (*irr.*, *sep.*, h, → **schlagen**) **I.** *v/t.* **1.** look up; **II.** *v/i.* **2.** look s.th. (*or* it) up; **~ in** *dat.* *a.* check (it) in; **3. j-m ~** take after s.o.; **'Nach·schla·ge·werk** *n* reference book (*or* work)
'nach|schlei·chen *v/i.* (*irr.*, *sep.*, sn, → **schleichen**): **j-m ~** creep after s.o.; shadow s.o.; **~schlei·fen¹** *v/t.* (*irr.*, *sep.*, h, → **schleifen¹**) ⚙ regrind; **~schlei·fen²** *v/t.* (*sep.*, h) trail (along) behind one; drag *or* lug (behind one); drag; **~schlep·pen** *v/t.* (*sep.*, h) drag *or* lug (behind one)
'Nach·schlüs·sel *m* a) duplicate key, b) skeleton key
'nach|schmecken *v/i.* (*sep.*, h) have (*or* leave) an aftertaste; **~schmei·ßen** F *v/t.* (*irr.*, *sep.*, h, → **schmeißen**) **1. j-m et. ~** throw s.th. after s.o.; **2.** *fig.* **sie werden einem nachgeschmissen** F they're ten a penny (*or* dirt cheap); **das ist ja nachgeschmissen** that's dirt cheap, that's (next to) nothing; **~schmin·ken** *v/t.* (*sep.*, h): **j-n ~** freshen up s.o.'s makeup; **~schrei·ben** *v/t.* (*irr.*, *sep.*, h, → **schreiben**) a) take down, b) copy, c) *ped.* do later; **e-e Arbeit zwei Wochen später ~** do (*or* sit) a test two weeks later
'Nach·schrift *f* postscript (*abbr.* PS, P.S.)
'Nach·schub *m* (-s; *no pl.*) **1.** ⚔ a) supplies *pl.*, b) reinforcements *pl.*; **2.** *fig.* supply (**an** *dat.* of), supplies *pl.* (of); **für ~ sorgen** keep the supplies coming (in), make sure there's enough work to go round
'Nach·schuß *m* **1.** *sport*: follow-up shot; **2.** → **~zah·lung** *f* additional payment
'nach·schwat·zen F *v/t.* (*sep.*, h) parrot
'nach·se·hen (*irr.*, *sep.*, h, → **sehen**) **I.** *v/i.* **1.** go and see, (go and) have a look, go and check (*or* make sure); **da hätte ich ja als erstes nachgesehen** that would have been the first place to look, surely; **2. j-m ~** gaze after s.o., follow s.o. with one's gaze, watch s.o. go; **e-m Auto** *etc.* **~** follow a car *etc.* with one's gaze, watch a car *etc.* leave; **3.** → **nachschlagen** II; **II.** *v/t.* **4.** examine, inspect; check; *ped.* correct; **5. j-m s-e Fehler** *etc.* **~** overlook (*or* turn a blind eye to) s.o.'s mistakes *etc.*; **III. ♀** *n*: **das ~ haben** lose out, go away empty-handed
'Nach·sen·de·an·schrift *f* forwarding address; **'nach·sen·den** *v/t.* (*irr.*, *sep.*, h, → **senden**) **1.** send on, forward; **bitte ~!** please forward; **2.** send on (later)
'nach·set·zen *v/i.* (*sep.*, h): **j-m ~** go (*or* run) after s.o., chase (after) s.o., be after s.o., be at s.o.'s heels
'Nach·sicht *f* (-; *no pl.*) forbearance; patience, tolerance; leniency; **~ üben** be lenient; **mit ~ behandeln** show (some) leniency towards, make allowances for, not to be too hard on; **da kenn' ich keine ~** I have no sympathy for that sort of thing; **'nach·sich·tig** [-zıçtıç] *adj.* indulgent (**gegenüber** *dat.* towards, with), *formal*: forbearing; patient (with), tolerant (towards); **'nach·sichts·voll** *adj.* → **nachsichtig**
'Nach·sil·be *f* *ling.* suffix
'nach·sin·nen *v/i.* (*irr.*, *sep.*, h, → **sinnen**) reflect (**über** *acc.* on), muse (over, on), ponder (over, on)
'nach·sit·zen *v/i.* (*irr.*, *sep.*, h, → **sitzen**) *ped.* be kept in, have detention; **j-n ~ lassen** give s.o. detention
'Nach|som·mer *m* late (*or* Indian) summer; **~sor·ge** *f* (-; *no pl.*) ⚕ aftercare
Nach·spann ['na:xʃpan] *m* (-[e]s; -e) *film*: credits *pl.*
'Nach·spei·se *f* → **Nachtisch**
'Nach·spiel *n* **1.** *thea.* epilog(ue); ♪ postlude; **2.** *fig.* sequel; **es hatte ein ~** there was a sequel (to it); **es wird noch ein ~ geben** the matter won't rest at that, there are bound to be consequences; **3.** afterplay; **'nach·spie·len** (*sep.*, h) **I.** *v/t.* ♪ play; **j-m et. ~** play s.th. after s.o., play s.th. like s.o., *n.s.* copy s.th. from s.o.; **II.** *v/i.* *sport*: play time; **~ lassen** add time on for injuries
'nach·spio,nie·ren *v/i.* (*sep.*, h) spy (*dat.* on)
'nach·spre·chen (*irr.*, *sep.*, h, → **sprechen**) **I.** *v/t.* repeat (**j-m et.** what s.o. has just said); **II.** *v/i.*: **sprechen Sie mir nach** repeat after me
'Nach·sprech·übung *f* repetition drill
'nach|spü·len (*sep.*, h) **I.** *v/t.* **1.** rinse; **II.** *v/i.* **2.** rinse; run water down the sink *etc.*; **3.** F wash everything (*or* it) down (**mit** *dat.* with); **~spü·ren** *v/i.* (*sep.*, h) **1. j-m ~** follow (*or* shadow) s.o.; spy on s.o.; **2.** *fig.* look into, investigate; try to get to the bottom of *a secret etc.*
nächst [nɛ:çst] **I.** *adj.* a) next, b) nearest; **~en Sonntag** next Sunday, Sunday next; **am ~en Tag** the next (*or* following) day; **aus ~er Entfernung** at close range; **bei ~er Gelegenheit** as soon as I get (*or* he gets *etc.*) a chance, at the next best opportunity; **im ~en Augenblick** the next minute; **in den ~en Tagen** in the next few days; **in ~er Zeit** (some time) soon; **~es Mal** next time; **die ~en Verwandten** s.o.'s nearest relatives; **II.** *su.* **der, die, das ~e** the next one (*or* person, thing *etc.*); **was kommt als ~es?** what's next (on the agenda)?; **der ~e, bitte!** next, please!; **du bist als ~er dran** it's your turn next, you're next; → **Nächste; III.** *adv.*: **am ~en** nearest; **fürs ~e** for the time being; **j-m am ~en stehen** be nearest to s.o.('s heart); **e-r Sache am ~en kommen** come closest to s.th.; **IV.** *prp.* (*dat.*) next to, close to; *fig.* after; **~ der Musik ist ihm die Lyrik am wichtigsten** after (*or* apart from) music, poetry is the most important thing for him
'nach·star·ren *v/i.* (*sep.*, h): **j-m (e-r Sache) ~** stare after s.o. (s.th.); **er starrte ihr einfach nach** *a.* he couldn't take his eyes off her
'nächst'best *adj.* next best; F any old; **ins ~e Restaurant** *etc.* **gehen** *a.* go into the first restaurant *etc.* one happens to find (*or* come across); **bei der ~en Gelegenheit** at the next best opportunity, as soon as I *etc.* get a chance; **'Nächst'be·ste** *m, f, n* (-n; -n) *the* next best person (*or* thing, hotel *etc.*), *the* first hotel *etc.* one happens to find (*or* come across)
Näch·ste ['nɛ:çstə] *m, f* (-n; -n) fellow human being; *bibl.* neighbo(u)r; **jeder ist sich selbst der ~** charity begins at home; *bibl.* **du sollst deinen ~n lieben wie dich selbst** thou shalt love thy neighbo(u)r as thyself
'nach·ste·hen *v/i.* (*irr.*, *sep.*, h, → **stehen**): **keinem ~** be second to none; **sie steht ihm in nichts nach** she can take him on any time; **'nach·ste·hend** *adj.* following; **siehe ~e Beschreibung** see description below
'nach·stei·gen *v/i.* (*irr.*, *sep.*, sn, → **steigen**) **1. j-m ~** climb (up) after s.o.; **2.** F be (*or* run) after *a girl etc.*
'nach·stel·len (*sep.*, h) **I.** *v/t.* **1.** ⚙ (re)adjust, reset; put back *watch*; **2.** *ling.* place after (s.th.); **II.** *v/i.*: **j-m ~** be after s.o., chase s.o., hunt *an animal*; **'Nach·stel·lung** *f* (-; -en) **1.** ⚙ (re)adjustment; **2.** *ling.* postposition; **3.** *usu. pl.* a) persecution, b) advances *pl.*
'näch·ste·mal *adv.*: **das ~, beim** (*or* **zum**) **nächstenmal** (the) next time
'Näch·sten·lie·be *f* charity
näch·stens ['nɛ:çstəns] *adv.* soon, before long; F **~ heiratet er sie noch!** he'll be marrying her next (*or* before we know it)
'nächst|fol·gend *adj.* following, next; **~ge·le·gen** *adj.* nearest
'Nächst·grö·ße·re *m, f, n* (-n; -n) *the* next size up
'nächst'hö·her *adj.* next *position etc.* up
'nächst·jäh·rig [-jɛ:rıç] *adj.* next year's
'nächst|lie·gend *adj.* nearest; *fig.* **das ♀e** the (most) obvious thing (to do *etc.*), the next thing (to do *etc.*); **~'mög·lich** *adj.* next possible, *a.* earliest possible; **zum ~en Termin** at the earliest possible date, as soon as possible
'nach|stre·ben *v/i.* (*sep.*, h) *dat.* strive after, aspire to; emulate *s.o.*; **~strö·men** *v/i.* (*sep.*, sn) **1.** *water, gas etc.*: come gushing (out) after; **2.** *fig.* *people etc.*: follow in their hundreds (*or* thousands); **~stür·zen** F *v/i.* (*sep.*, sn) *dat.* rush after

s.o.; **~su·chen** *v/i.* (*sep.*, h) **1.** have a (good) look, look and see; **2. *um et.* ~** apply for s.th.
'Nach·syn·chro·ni·sa·ti,on *f* post-dubbing, F post-sync; **'nach·syn·chro·ni·,sie·ren** *v/t.* (*sep.*, h) post-dub, F post-sync *film etc.*
nacht [naxt] *adv.*: ***heute* ~** a) last night, b) tonight; ***gestern* ~** last night; ***Freitag* ~** Friday night
Nacht *f* (-; Nächte ['nɛçtə]) night; ***bei* ~** at night; ***bei ~ und Nebel, im Schutze der ~*** under cover of darkness, *w.s.* clandestinely; ***bis in die ~ arbeiten*** work till late in the night; ***bis tief in die ~*** until (*or* right into) the small hours (of the night); ***in finsterer ~*** at the dead of night; ***gute ~!*** *a. iro.* goodnight!; ***die ganze ~ (hindurch)*** all night (long); ***über ~*** overnight (*a. fig.*); ***die ~ zum Tage machen*** turn night into day; ***es wird ~*** it's getting dark; ***häßlich wie die ~*** ugly as sin; → ***mitten, Ohr, schwarz*** I
'nacht·ak,tiv *adj. zo.* nocturnal
'nach·tan·ken (*sep.*, h) **I.** *v/i.* fill up (the tank), get some more petrol (*Am.* gas); **II.** *v/t.*: ***10 Liter* ~** put in another 10 litres (*Am.* liters), put another 10 litres (*Am.* liters) in the tank
'Nacht|ar·beit *f* night work, night shift(s *pl.*); **~asyl** *n* night shelter; **~aus·ga·be** *f* late edition; **~be·leuch·tung** *f* dimmed lights *pl.* (*or* lighting)
'nacht·blau *adj.* midnight blue
'nacht·blind *adj.* night blind; **'Nacht·blind·heit** *f* night blindness
'Nacht·dienst *m* night duty (*or* shift); **~ *haben*** a) *pharmacy etc.*: be open all night, b) be on night duty (*or* shift)
'Nacht·ef,fekt·auf·nah·me *f film*: day for night shot
Nach·teil ['na:xtaıl] *m* (-s; -e) disadvantage (***an*** *dat.* of); drawback, shortcoming; *sport and fig.*: handicap; ***die Sache hat nur einen ~*** there's just one disadvantage in it; ***im ~ sein*** be at a disadvantage (***j-m gegenüber*** compared with s.o.); ***ich bin ihr gegenüber im ~*** *a.* she's got an advantage over me; ***von ~ sein*** be disadvantageous, be a disadvantage; ***zum ~ von*** *dat.* to the detriment of; ***sich zu s-m ~ verändern*** change for the worse; ***j-m zum ~ gereichen*** be to s.o.'s disadvantage (*or* detriment); ***e-r Sache zum ~ gereichen*** be to the detriment of s.th.; ***dadurch entstehen uns nur ~e*** it will only bring us disadvantages; ***es soll nicht dein ~ sein*** it won't be to your disadvantage, you only stand to gain by it; **'nach·tei·lig** [-taılıç] **I.** *adj.* disadvantageous; detrimental; ***~e Folgen*** negative consequences; **II.** *adv.*: ***~ beeinflussen, sich ~ auswirken auf*** *acc.* have a detrimental (*or* an adverse) effect on
'Nacht·ein·satz *m* ⚔ night mission, night(-time) operation
näch·te·lang ['nɛçtəlaŋ] **I.** *adj.*: ***~e Gespräche*** *etc.* night after night of discussion(s) *etc.*; **II.** *adv.* for nights on end, night after night
'Nacht·eu·le F *fig. f* night owl
'Nacht·fahr·ver·bot *n* ban on nighttime driving; ***Lastwagen haben ~*** *a.* lorries (*or* trucks) aren't allowed on the roads at night
'Nacht·fal·ter *m* moth
'Nacht·flug *m* night flight; *pl. a.* night flying *sg.*; **~ver·bot** *n* ban on nighttime flying
'Nacht·frost *m* night(time) frost; *meteor.* ***strenger* ~** severe overnight frost; **~ge·fahr** *f* possible nighttime frost
'Nacht|ge·bet *n* evening (*or* bedtime) prayer; **~ge·spenst** *n* ghost; F ***aussehen wie ein ~*** look like a ghost; **~hemd** *n* nightdress, F nightie; nightshirt; **~him·mel** *m* night sky, sky at night
Nach·ti·gall ['naxtıgal] *f* (-; -en) nightingale; F ***~, ick hör' dir trapsen*** F I get the picture (now), *n.s.* so that's what he's *etc.* after(, is it?)
näch·ti·gen ['nɛçtıgən] *v/i.* (h) spend the night
'Nach·tisch *m* (-[e]s; *no pl.*) dessert, sweet, F afters (*sg.*), pudding
'Nacht|klub *m* night club; **~la·ger** *n* place to sleep, place for the night; bed; **~le·ben** *n* night life; *a. s.o.'s* nighttime activities *pl.*
nächt·lich ['nɛçtlıç] *adj.* nightly, nocturnal; ***~e Ausgangssperre*** dusk-to-dawn (*or* nighttime) curfew; ***~e Ruhestörung*** nighttime disturbance(s); ***~es Treiben*** a) *s.o.'s* night life, *s.o.'s* nighttime (*iro.* nocturnal) activities *pl.*, b) bustling night life
'Nacht|lo,kal *n* night club, *Am. a.* night-spot; **~luft** *f* night air; **~mensch** *m* night owl; **~met·te** *f* nocturn
'nach·tö·nen¹ *v/i.* (*sep.*, h) echo, linger
'nach·tö·nen² *v/t.* (*sep.*, h) retint
'Nacht|por·tier *m* night porter; **~pro·,gramm** *n radio etc.*: nighttime program(me)s *pl.*; **~quar,tier** *n* place for the night
Nach·trag ['na:xtra:k] *m* (-[e]s; Nachträge ['na:xtrɛ:gə]) supplement, addendum (*pl.* addenda); additional comment; postscript; appendix; ***ich hätte noch e-n ~ zu dem, was X sagte*** may I add something to what X said
'nach·tra·gen *v/t.* (*irr.*, *sep.*, h, → ***tragen***) **1. *j-m et.* ~** carry s.th. behind s.o.; go after s.o. with s.th.; **2.** *fig.* ***j-m et.* ~** hold s.th. against s.o., bear s.o. a grudge for s.th.; ***j-m ~, daß*** hold against s.o. the fact that, bear s.o. a grudge for *ger.*; **3.** add (later); **'nach·tra·gend** *adj.* unforgiving, resentful
nach·träg·lich ['na:xtrɛ:klıç] **I.** *adj.* additional, supplementary; later; belated; **II.** *adv.* afterwards; later; ***~ herzliche Glückwünsche*** belated best wishes
'Nach·trags... *in cpds.* additional, supplementary; **~haus·halt** *m* supplementary budget
'nach·trau·ern *v/i.* (*sep.*, h) mourn (*dat. s.o. or s.th.*); ***ihm wird keiner ~*** they *etc.* won't be sorry to see him go, F they'll *etc.* be glad to see the back of him; ***dem trauere ich nicht nach*** *a.* F good riddance to bad rubbish(, is all I can say)
'Nacht·ru·he *f* **1.** sleep; ***j-n in s-r ~ stören*** disturb s.o.'s sleep; **2.** nighttime peace; ***die ~ einhalten*** keep the peace at night
nachts [naxts] *adv.* at night, during the night, in the night; ***um ein Uhr ~*** (at) one o'clock at night (*or* in the morning)
'Nacht·schat·ten·ge·wächs *n* ⚘ solanum; *pl.* Solanaceae
'Nacht·schicht *f* night shift; ***~ haben*** be on night shift
'nacht·schla·fend *adj.*: ***zu ~er Zeit*** in the middle of the night
'Nacht|schränk·chen *n* bedside locker, *Am.* nightstand; **~schwär·mer** F *m* night owl; **~schwe·ster** *f* night nurse; **~sei·te** *f ast.* nightside, *a. fig.* dark side; **~spei·cher·ofen** *m* (night) storage heater; **~strom** *m* (-[e]s; *no pl.*) off-peak electricity
'nachts·über *adv.* during (*or* in) the night
'Nacht|ta,rif *m* off-peak (*or* cheap) rates *pl.*; **~tisch** *m* bedside locker, *Am.* nightstand; **~topf** *m* chamber pot, F jerry; **~tre,sor** *m* night safe
'Nacht-und-'Ne·bel-Ak·ti,on *f* (dawn) swoop *or* raid, nighttime raid
'Nacht|vor·stel·lung *f* late-night show (*or* performance); **~wa·che** *f* night watch; **~wäch·ter** *m* night watchman; F *contp.* F twit, dope
'nacht·wan·deln *v/i.* (h, sn) → ***schlafwandeln*; nacht·wand·le·risch** ['naxtvandlərıʃ] *adj.* somnambulistic
'Nacht|zeit *f* night(time); ***zur ~*** at night; **~zeug** *n* overnight things *pl.*, F toothbrush and pyjamas (*Am.* pajamas) *pl. or* nightie; **~zug** *m* (over)night train; **~zu·schlag** *m* nighttime bonus
'nach·un·ter,su·chen *v/t.* (*sep.*, h): ***j-n* ~** give s.o. a further checkup, do a further checkup on s.o.; **'Nach·un·ter,su·chung** *f* (-; -en) follow-up check, further checkup
'nach·voll,zieh·bar *adj.* understandable; ***es ist mir nicht ~*** I can't understand it, it's beyond me; **'nach·voll,zie·hen** *v/t.* (*irr.*, *sep.*, h, → ***vollziehen***) re-enact (in one's mind); understand, fathom; ***ich kann das nicht ~*** *a.* it's beyond me
'nach·wach·sen *v/i.* (*irr.*, *sep.*, sn, → ***wachsen***) grow again; **'nach·wach·send** *adj.*: ***die ~e Generation*** the up-and-coming (*or* rising, *Am.* upcoming) generation
'Nach|wahl *f parl.* by-election; **~we·hen** *pl.* afterpains; *fig.* painful consequences (*or* aftermath *sg.*)
'nach·wei·nen *v/i.* (*sep.*, h) cry over the loss of; ***keine Träne ~ → nachtrauern***
Nach·weis ['na:xvaıs] *m* (-es; -e) proof (***für*** *acc.* of), evidence (of *s.th.*, for *a theory etc.*); certificate; ***der wissenschaftliche ~ für et.*** scientific proof (*or* evidence) of s.th.; ***den ~ führen*** (*or* ***erbringen***), ***daß*** prove that, furnish proof of *s.th.*, provide evidence of *s.th.*
'nach·weis·bar *adj.* verifiable; ⚗ detectable; evident
'nach·wei·sen *v/t.* (*irr.*, *sep.*, h, → ***weisen***) prove, show; ***j-m et.* ~** prove that s.o. has done s.th.; ***j-m s-e (Un)Schuld ~*** prove s.o.'s guilt (innocence), prove s.o. to be guilty (innocent); ***j-m e-n Irrtum ~*** a) show that s.o. has made a mistake, b) point out a mistake to s.o.; ***sie konnten ihm nichts ~*** they couldn't prove anything (against him) *or* prove that he had done anything wrong
nach·weis·lich ['na:xvaıslıç] **I.** *adj.* demonstrable; **II.** *adv.* demonstrably; ***sie war ~ da*** it has been proved (*or* there is evidence) that she was there
'Nach·welt *f* (-; *no pl.*): ***die* ~** posterity, future (*or* later) generations; ***für die ~ festhalten*** record (*or* preserve) for posterity
'nach|wer·fen *v/t.* (*irr.*, *sep.*, h, → ***werfen***) **1. *j-m et.* ~** throw s.th. after s.o.; **2.** *fig.* → ***nachschmeißen*; 3.** *teleph.* ***noch e-e Münze ~*** put in another coin; **~win·ken** *v/i.* (*sep.*, h): ***j-m* ~** wave after s.o.
'nach·wir·ken *v/i.* (*sep.*, h) **1. *die Tabletten*** *etc.* ***wirken lange nach*** it'll take a

while before the effects of the tablets *etc.* wear off; **2.** *fig.* ***lange*** ~ leave a deep impression (on s.o.), have a lasting effect (on s.o.); **'Nach·wir·kung** *f* (-; -en) aftereffect(s *pl.*); consequences *pl.*, aftermath *of war etc.*

'Nach·wort *n* (-[e]s; -e) epilog(ue)

Nach·wuchs ['na:xvu:ks] *m* (-es; *no pl.*) **1.** *the* young (*or* up-and-coming, *Am.* upcoming) generation; new blood; ⚔ recruits; ⚕ junior staff, trainees *pl.*; ***ärztlicher*** (***wissenschaftlicher***) ~ *the* new generation (F breed) of doctors (academics), young doctors (academics); **2.** a) offspring, b) new arrival, addition to the family; ***sie bekommen*** ~ they're going to have a baby, there's a baby on the way; **~au·tor** *m* up-and-coming (*or* upcoming) writer, promising young writer; **~be·darf** *m* need for recruits (*or* young teachers *etc.*); **~kraft** *f* junior worker (*or* employee); **~man·gel** *m* **1.** shortage of recruits; **2.** dearth of young talent; **~schau·spie·ler** *m* up-and-coming (*Am.* upcoming) (young) actor; **~sorgen** *pl.*: ~ ***haben*** have difficulty (in) finding recruits (*or* young talent); **~ta͵lent** *n* promising young talent

'nach|wür·zen *v/i. and v/t.* (*sep.*, h) season to taste; ***ihr müßt*** (***es***) ***vielleicht*** ~ it might need some more salt and pepper *etc.*; **~zah·len** *v/t. and v/i.* (*sep.*, h) pay extra (*or* later); **~zäh·len** *v/t.* (*sep.*, h) check; count

'Nach·zah·lung *f* (-; -en) additional (*or* extra) payment

'nach·zeich·nen *v/t.* (*sep.*, h) copy; trace

'nach·zie·hen (*irr.*, *sep.*, → ***ziehen***) **I.** *v/t.* (h) **1.** drag (*or* pull) behind one; drag *one's leg etc.*; *fig.* ***nach sich ziehen*** bring with it (*or* in its wake); **2.** trace; pencil *eyebrows*; **3.** tighten up *screw etc.*; **II.** *v/i.* (sn) **4.** follow; **5.** *chess*: make the next move; **5.** (h) F *fig.* follow suit

Nach·züg·ler ['na:xtsy:klɐ] *m* (-s; -) **1.** straggler; latecomer; **2.** *hum.* late arrival, *hum.* afterthought

'Nach·zugs·ak·ti·en *pl.* ⚕ deferred shares (*or* stock *sg.*)

'Nach·zün·dung *f* ⚙, *mot.* retarded ignition

Nacke·dei ['nakədaɪ] (*sep.* -k·k-) F *m* (-s; -s) F nudie

Nacken [nakən] (*sep.* -k·k-) *m* (-s; -) nape (*or* back) of the neck, neck; ***den Kopf in den*** ~ ***werfen*** throw back one's head; ***den Hut in den*** ~ ***schieben*** tilt one's hat back; *fig.* ***halt den*** ~ ***steif!*** chin up!, *Brit. a.* F keep your pecker up!; ***j-n im*** ~ ***haben*** have s.o. after one (*or* hard on one's heels), have s.o. breathing down one's neck; ***ihm sitzt die Angst*** (***das Grauen***) ***im*** ~ he's scared (terrified) out of his wits *or* mind; ***mir sitzt die Prüfung*** (***der Termin***) ***im*** ~ I'm under terrible exam (deadline) pressure; → ***Faust, Schalk***; **~haar** *n* neck hair, hair on the back of one's neck; **~rol·le** *f* bolster; **~schlag** *fig. m* blow, knock; setback; ***e-n*** ~ ***erhalten*** (*or* ***hinnehmen***) take a knock, suffer a setback; **~stüt·ze** *f* headrest, *mot. etc. a.* head (*or* neck) support; **~wir·bel** *m* cervical vertebra (*pl.* vertebrae)

nackt [nakt] *adj.* naked (*a. fig.*), *a. art*: nude; bare *arms, legs etc.*, *a. fig. wall, tree etc.*; ~ ***sein*** *a.* be in the nude, have nothing on, F be in the raw; ***mit*** **~*en*** ***Füßen*** barefoot; ***mit*** **~*em*** ***Oberkörper*** stripped to the waist; ***sich*** ~ ***ausziehen*** strip (naked); ~ ***baden*** swim in the nude (F the raw), *Am.* F skinnydip; ***j-n*** ~ ***malen*** paint s.o. (in the) nude; *fig.* ***die*** **~*e*** ***Armut*** naked poverty; *fig.* ***mit dem*** **~*en*** ***Auge*** with the (*or* one's) naked eye; *fig.* ***auf dem*** **~*en*** ***Boden*** on the bare ground; *fig.* ***mit dem*** **~*en*** ***Leben davonkommen*** escape with one's bare life; *fig.* **~*e*** ***Tatsachen*** (cold,) hard facts; *fig.* ***die*** **~*e*** ***Wahrheit*** the plain truth; → ***Gewalt***

'Nackt·ba·den *n* nude bathing, *Am.* F skinnydipping; **'Nackt·ba·de·strand** *m* nudist beach

'Nackt·fo·to *n* nude photograph

'Nackt·fo·to·gra͵fie *f* nude photography

'Nackt·frosch F *m* F nudie

'Nackt'heit *f* (-; *no pl.*) nakedness, nudity

'Nackt|ma·ga͵zin *n* nude (F girlie) magazine; **~schnecke** *f* slug

Na·del ['na:dəl] *f* (-; -n) a) needle (*a.* ⚘, ⚙, ⚕ *etc.*), b) pin; brooch, c) stylus; *fig.* ***e-e*** ~ ***im Heuhaufen*** a needle in a haystack; (***wie***) ***auf*** **~*n*** ***sitzen*** be on tenterhooks; F ***an der*** ~ ***hängen*** F be on the needle, *sl.* be a junkie; F ***sie kommt von der*** ~ ***nicht los*** F she can't kick the (drugs) habit; **~ab·wei·chung** *f* magnetic deviation; **~baum** *m* conifer, coniferous tree; **~drucker** *m computer*: dot matrix printer; **~höl·zer** *pl.* conifers; **~kis·sen** *n* pin-cushion; **~kopf** *m* pinhead; **~la·ger** *n mot.* needle bearing

na·deln ['na:dəln] *v/i.* (h) lose (*or* shed) its needles

'Na·del|öhr *n* **1.** eye of a (*or* the) needle; **2.** *fig.* bottleneck; → ***Kamel***; **~stich** *m* **1.** pinprick (*a. fig.*); **2.** stitch

'Na·del·strei·fen·an·zug *m* pinstripe suit

'Na·del·wald *m* coniferous forest (*pl. a.* woodland *sg.*)

Na·dir [na'di:ɐ] *m* (-s; *no pl.*) *ast.* nadir

Na·gel ['na:gəl] *m* (-s; Nägel ['nɛ:gəl]) **1.** ⚙ nail; tack; *fig.* ***ein*** ~ ***zu j-s Sarg*** a nail in s.o.'s coffin; ***et. an den*** ~ ***hängen*** give s.th. up, F chuck s.th. in; ***den*** ~ ***auf den Kopf treffen*** hit the nail on the head; ***Nägel mit Köpfen machen*** do a proper job of it (*or* things), not to do things by halves; **2.** nail; ***an den Nägeln kauen*** bite (*or* chew) one's nails; ***schwarze Nägel*** black (finger)nails; *fig.* ***es brennt mir unter den Nägeln*** I'm itching to get it out of the way; ***mir brennt die Zeit auf den Nägeln*** I haven't got a minute to spare; F ***er hat nicht das Schwarze unter dem*** ~ he hasn't got a penny to his name; ***er gönnt ihm nicht das Schwarze unter dem*** ~ he begrudges him the air he breathes; F ***sich et. unter den*** ~ ***reißen*** F swipe (*or* pinch) s.th., walk off with s.th., make sure one gets (hold of) s.th.

'Na·gel·bett *n* nail bed; **~ent·zün·dung** *f* 🕮 onychitis

'Na·gel|boh·rer *m* gimlet; **~bür·ste** *f* nail brush; **~fei·le** *f* nail file; **~haut** *f* cuticle

'Nä·gel·kau·en *n* nailbiting

'Na·gel·lack *m* nail varnish (*Am.* polish); **~ent·fer·ner** *m* nail varnish (*Am.* polish) remover

na·geln ['na:gəln] (h) **I.** *v/t.* nail (***an*** *acc.*, ***auf*** *acc.* to); nail together; **II.** *v/i. engine*: knock

'na·gel'neu *adj.* brand-new

'Na·gel|pfle·ge *f* nail care; manicure; **~pro·be** *fig. f* **1.** litmus test; ***die*** ~ ***machen*** do a litmus test (***mit*** *dat.* on); **2.** touchstone (***für*** *acc.* of); **~sche·re** *f*: (***e-e*** ~ a pair of) nail scissors *pl.*; **~schuh** *m* hobnail boot; **~zan·ge** *f* **1.** (***e-e*** ~ a pair of) nail clippers *pl.*; **2.** ⚙ (***e-e*** ~ a pair of) pincers *pl.*

na·gen ['na:gən] *v/t. and v/i.* (h) gnaw, nibble (***an*** *dat.* at); ~ ***an*** *dat. a. geol.* eat into, corrode, *fig.* gnaw at; ***an e-m Knochen*** ~ gnaw at a bone; ***an der Unterlippe*** ~ bite one's (lower) lip; *fig.* ***an j-s Gesundheit*** ~ undermine s.o.'s health; → ***Hungertuch***; **'na·gend** *adj.* gnawing *hunger*; *fig.* nagging *pain, doubt etc.*

Na·ger ['na:gɐ] *m* (-s; -), **'Na·ge·tier** *n zo.* rodent

nah [na:] → ***nahe***; ***von*** ~ ***und fern*** from far and near (*or* wide)

'Nah|an·griff *m* ⚔ close-range attack; **~auf·nah·me** *f phot.* close-up (shot); **~be·reich** *m* **1.** neighbo(u)rhood, vicinity; surroundings *pl.*; suburbs *pl.*, suburban area(s *pl.*); *w.s.* area, region; ***der*** ~ ***von München*** the Munich area; ***im*** ~ *a.* nearby *shops etc.*, local *trains etc.*; **2.** *phot.* close-up range; ***im*** ~ at close range; **~bril·le** *f*: (***e-e*** ~ a pair of) reading glasses *pl.*

na·he ['na:ə] **I.** *adj.* **1.** *pred.* near, close; *attr.* nearby ...; ***von*** **~*m*** from close up; **~*r*** ***Osten*** Middle (*or* Near) East; **2.** forthcoming, imminent; **3.** *fig.* close *relative, friend etc.*; ***sich sehr*** ~ ***sein*** be very close; **II.** *adv.* **4.** near, close; nearby; ~ ***an*** *dat.* (*or* ***bei*** *dat.*) near (to), close to; ***komm mir nicht zu*** **~*!*** a) (just) keep your distance, b) don't get too close to me; **5.** *fig.* ~ ***verwandt*** closely related; ***j-m zu*** ~ ***treten*** offend s.o., tread on s.o.'s toes; ***ich war*** ~ ***daran zu kündigen*** I very nearly handed in my notice, I was about to hand in my notice, I was (very) tempted to hand in my notice; → ***näher, nächst, nahekommen, naheliegen***; **III.** *prp.* (*dat.*) near, close to (*a. fig.*); ***den Tränen*** ~ on the verge of tears, ready to burst into tears; ***der Verzweiflung*** ~ on the verge of despair, getting desperate; ***dem Tode*** ~ on the point of death, approaching death, close to death

Nä·he ['nɛ:ə] *f* (-; *no pl.*) a) nearness, proximity, b) vicinity, neighbo(u)rhood; ***in der*** ~ nearby; ***in der*** ~ ***von*** (*or* *gen.*) near (to), quite close to; ***der Park in der*** ~ the nearby park, the park nearby; ***bei uns in der*** ~ near (to) where we live, not far from where we live; ***in der*** ~ ***der Stadt*** near the town; ***hier in der*** ~ somewhere around here; ***in der*** ~ ***bleiben*** stay around; ***in s-r*** ~ near (to) where he lives, near (to) him; ***ich möchte in s-r*** ~ ***sein*** I'd like to be with (*or* close to) him, I'd like to have him around me; ***aus der*** ~ close up, at close range; ***aus der*** ~ ***betrachten*** (***betrachtet***) take a close(r) look at (seen at close range, on closer view); ***menschliche*** ~ human contact; → ***greifbar***

'na·he'bei *adv.* nearby, close by

'na·he|brin·gen *fig. v/t.* (*irr.*, *sep.*, h, → ***bringen***) **1.** ***j-m et.*** ~ make s.th. accessible to s.o., help s.o. to appreciate (*or* understand) s.th.; **2.** ***Menschen einander*** ~ bring people (close) together, create a bond between people; **3.** ***j-n der Verzweiflung*** (***dem Ruin***) ~ drive s.o. to the verge of despair (the brink of ruin); **~ge·hen** *fig. v/i.* (*irr.*, *sep.*, sn, → ***gehen***) *dat.* deeply affect *s.o.*, have a deep effect on *s.o.*; **~ge·le·gen** *adj.* nearby; ***der ~e Wald*** the nearby woods, the woods nearby; **~kom·men** *fig. v/i.* (*irr.*, *sep.*, sn, → ***kommen***) **1.** ***j-m ~*** get to know s.o.; ***einander*** (***sehr***) **~** get to know each other (grow close, develop a close relationship); **2.** *dat.* come close to, approach; ***es kommt der Wahrheit ziemlich nahe*** it's (*or* it comes) pretty close to the truth; **~le·gen** *fig. v/t.* (*sep.*, h) suggest (***j-m et.*** s.th. to s.o.); ***j-m ~, et. zu tun*** urge s.o. to do s.th.; ***es legt den Verdacht nahe, daß*** it would seem to suggest that

na·he·lie·gen *fig. v/i.* (*irr.*, *sep.*, h, → ***liegen***) be obvious, stand to reason; ***die Vermutung liegt nahe, daß*** it would appear that; **'na·he·lie·gend** *adj.* obvious

'Nah·emp·fang *m radio etc.*: short-distance reception

na·hen ['na:ən] **I.** *v/i.* (sn) approach; draw near; *fig. a.* be on its way; **II.** *v/refl.* (h): ***sich ~*** be approaching, be imminent; ***sich j-m ~*** approach s.o.

nä·hen ['nɛ:ən] (h) **I.** *v/t.* sew; stitch; ⚕ stitch (up); **~ *an*** (*or* ***auf***) *acc.* sew onto; ⚕ ***es muß genäht werden*** *a.* it'll have to have stitches; *fig.* ***doppelt genäht hält besser*** a) better safe than sorry, just to make sure, b) two heads are better than one; **II.** *v/i.* sew; do needlework

'na·hend *adj.* approaching; imminent, impending *danger etc.*

nä·her ['nɛ:ɐ] **I.** *adj.* closer, nearer; shorter *way etc.*; more detailed (*or* precise), in greater detail; → ***Nähere; die ~e Umgebung*** the immediate vicinity; ***bei ~er Betrachtung*** on closer inspection, *fig.* on further consideration; **II.** *adv.* closer, nearer; **~ *treten*** come closer; ***treten Sie ~!*** a) come in!, this way, please!, b) come closer; (***immer***) **~ *rücken*** get closer (and closer); ***Weihnachten*** *etc.* ***rückt immer ~*** *a.* Christmas *etc.* is just around the corner; **~ *betrachten*** have a closer look at, look at *s.th.* more closely; ***sich ~ befassen mit*** *dat.* go into *a matter*; ***et. ~ beschreiben*** be more precise (about s.th.); go into more detail (about s.th.); ***j-n ~ kennen*** know s.o. quite (*or* fairly) well; ***kennen Sie ihn ~?*** how well do you know him?; **~brin·gen** *fig. v/t.* (*irr.*, *sep.*, h, → ***bringen***): ***j-m et. ~*** make s.th. (more) accessible to s.o., help s.o. to appreciate (*or* understand) s.th. better

Nä·he·re ['nɛ:ərə] *n* (-n; *no pl.*) (further) details *pl.*

Nä·he·rei [nɛ:ə'raɪ] *f* (-; -en) **1.** *no pl.* sewing; **2.** needlework

'Nah·er·ho·lungs·ge·biet *n* greenbelt recreation area

Nä·he·rin ['nɛ:ərɪn] *f* (-; -nen) seamstress

'nä·her·kom·men *fig. v/i.* (*irr.*, *sep.*, sn, → ***kommen***) **1.** ***j-m ~*** get closer to s.o.; ***einander*** (*or* ***sich***) **~** get closer; **2.** ***jetzt kommen wir der Sache näher!*** now we're getting there; ***das kommt der Wahrheit*** (*or* ***den Tatsachen***) ***schon näher*** that's more like the truth

'nä·her·lie·gen *fig. v/i.* (*irr.*, *sep.*, h, → ***liegen***) be more likely (*or* obvious); be better, be more reasonable (*or* sensible); ***es liegt näher zu*** *inf.* it would be better to *inf.*, the more obvious thing would be to *inf.*; **'nä·her·lie·gend** *adj.* more obvious *etc.*; → ***näherliegen; das Näherliegende*** the (more) obvious thing (to do)

nä·hern ['nɛ:ɐn] (h) **I.** *v/t.* bring near(er) (*dat.* to); **II.** *v/refl.*: ***sich ~*** approach (*dat. s.o. or s.th.*); go (*or* come) up (*dat.* to); ***sich*** *e-r Frau* **~** try to approach; ***sich dem Ende ~*** draw to a close

nä·he·rungs·wei·se ['nɛ:ərʊŋs-] *adv.* approximately

'Nä·he·rungs·wert *m* approximate value

'na·he·ste·hen *fig. v/i.* (*irr.*, *sep.*, h, → ***stehen***) **1.** ***j-m ~*** be close to s.o.; ***sich*** (*or* ***einander***) **~** be very close; **2.** ***dem Liberalismus*** *etc.* **~** have liberal *etc.* sympathies; **'na·he·ste·hend** *adj.* **1.** close (*dat.* to); ***einander ~*** close; **2.** ***e-e den Konservativen ~e Zeitschrift*** a conservatively orien(ta)ted magazine, a magazine with conservative leanings

'na·he'zu *adv.* virtually, almost; **~ *unmöglich*** virtually (*or* well-nigh) impossible; **~ *10 Tage*** almost (F going on for) 10 days

'Näh|fa·den *m*, **~garn** *n* (sewing) cotton *or* thread

'Nah·kampf *m* ⚔ close combat, hand-to-hand fight(ing); ✈ dogfight(ing); *boxing, fencing*: infighting; **~mit·tel** *pl.* close-range weapons

'Näh|käst·chen *n* sewing box; *fig.* ***aus dem ~ plaudern*** tell tales out of school, give away secrets; **~korb** *m* work basket

nahm [na:m] *pret. of* ***nehmen***

'Näh|ma'schi·ne *f* sewing machine; **~na·del** *f* (sewing) needle

Nah'ost... *in cpds.*, **nah'öst·lich** *adj.* Middle Eastern, Near Eastern

Nähr|bo·den ['nɛ:ɐ-] *m biol.*, ⚕ culture medium; *fig.* breeding ground (***für*** *acc.* of, for); **~creme** *f* nutrient cream

näh·ren ['nɛ:rən] (h) **I.** *v/t.* **1.** feed; **2.** *fig.* nurture *hope etc.*, fuel *hatred, suspicion etc.*; **II.** *v/i.* be nourishing

Nähr·flüs·sig·keit ['nɛ:ɐ-] *f* nutrient fluid

nahr·haft ['na:ɐhaft] *adj.* **1.** nutritious, nourishing; **~e *Mahlzeit*** *a.* substantial (F good square) meal; **2.** F *fig.* lucrative

Nähr|lö·sung ['nɛ:ɐ-] *f* ⚕ nutrient solution; **~mit·tel** *pl.* cereal products; **~prä·pa'rat** *n* nutrient (preparation), patent food; **~salz** *n* nutrient salt; **~stoff** *m* nutrient

Nah·rung ['na:rʊŋ] *f* (-; *no pl.*) **1.** food; ***flüssige ~*** liquids; **~ *zu sich nehmen*** eat, take food; → ***verweigern; 2.*** *fig.* ***geistige ~*** food for the mind; **~ *geben*** *dat.* fuel; (***neue***) **~ *erhalten*** be fuel(l)ed, receive fresh impetus

'Nah·rungs|auf·nah·me *f* eating, food intake; 🕮 ingestion; → ***verweigern***; **~grund·la·ge** *f* basic food; **~ket·te** *f* food chain; **~man·gel** *m* food shortage; lack of food

'Nah·rungs·mit·tel *pl.* food *sg.*, foodstuffs; **~che'mie** *f* food chemistry; **~che·mi·ker** *m* food chemist; **~in·du'strie** *f* food industry; **~kon·zen'trat** *n* food concentrate; **~ver·gif·tung** *f* food poisoning

'Nah·rungs|quel·le *f* source of food; **~su·che** *f* search for food; ***auf ~ gehen*** go in search of food, go (out) hunting for food, search for food; **~ver·wei·ge·rung** *f* refusal to eat; *w.s.* hunger strike; **~zu·fuhr** *f* food intake; 🕮 ingestion

Nähr·wert ['nɛ:ɐ-] *m* nutritional value; ***e-n hohen ~ haben*** be highly nutritious; F *fig.* (***praktischer***) **~** practical value; ***das hat keinen ~*** that's a waste of time, that's useless

'Nah·schnell·ver·kehrs·zug *m* fast local train

'Näh·sei·de *f* sewing silk

Naht [na:t] *f* (-; Nähte ['nɛ:tə]) seam; ⚙ *a.* joint, *a.* weld; *anat.*, ⚘ suture; ⚕ suture, stitches *pl.*; ***aus den*** (*or* ***allen, sämtlichen***) ***Nähten platzen*** *a. fig.* be bursting at the seams

'naht·los I. *adj.* seamless; *fig.* **~er *Übergang*** smooth transition; **~e *Bräune*** all-over tan; **II.** *adv.*: **~ *ineinander übergehen*** run on smoothly from one another, merge into one another

'Naht·stel·le *f* **1.** ⚙ joint, weld; ⚕ suture; **2.** *fig.* interface

'Nah·ver·kehr *m* local traffic; 🚂 suburban services *pl.*; **'Nah·ver·kehrs·zug** *m* commuter (*or* local) train

Näh·zeug ['nɛ:-] *n* sewing kit

'Nah·ziel *n* immediate *or* short-term target (*or* objective)

na·iv [na'i:f] *adj.* naive (*a. art*); **~er *Maler*** *etc.* naive painter *etc.*; **Nai·ve** [na'i:və] *f* (-n; -n) *thea. the* Ingénue; **Nai·vi·tät** [naivi'tɛ:t] *f* (-; *no pl.*) naivety; **Na'iv·ling** *contp. m* (-s; -e) simpleton

Na·me ['na:mə] *m* (-ns; -n) a) name, b) name, reputation; ***mit ~n ...*** by the name of ..., called ...; ***den ~n ... tragen*** go by the name of ..., be called ..., be known as ...; **~*n nennen*** mention names; ***s-n ~n nennen*** give one's name; ***j-n nach s-m ~n fragen*** ask s.o. his (*or* her) name, ask s.o.'s name; (***nur***) ***dem ~n nach*** in name only; ***dem ~n nach kennen*** know *s.o. or s.th.* by name; ***das Kind*** (*or* ***die Dinge***) ***beim rechten ~n nennen*** call a spade a spade; F ***damit das Kind e-n ~n hat*** just to give it a name; ***sich e-n ~n machen*** make a name for o.s.; ***die Rechnung*** *etc.* ***geht auf m-n ~n*** the check *etc.* is on me; ***es läuft unter s-m ~n*** it's in his name; ***im ~ von*** *dat.* in the name of, on behalf of; F ***in Gottes ~n!*** F for heaven's sake!; → ***Hase, Schall***

'Na·men|ge·bung [-ge:bʊŋ] *f* (-; -en) naming; **~ge·dächt·nis** *n* memory for names; **~kun·de** *f* onomastics *pl.*; **~li·ste** *f* list of names

'na·men·los I. *adj.* **1.** anonymous, unnamed; ⚚ **~er *Artikel*** (**~e *Marke***) no-name product (brand); **2.** *fig.* indescribable; **II.** *fig. adv.* utterly, unspeakably

na·mens ['na:məns] **I.** *adv.* named, by the name of, called; **II.** *prp.* (*gen.*) in the name of, on behalf of

'Na·mens|ak·tie *f* registered share; **~än·de·rung** *f* change of name; **~pa'pier** *n* registered security; **~recht** *n* right to a name; **~schild** *n* nameplate; badge, name-tag; **~tag** *m* name day; **~ver·zeich·nis** *n* list of names; **~vet·ter** *m* namesake; **~zug** *m* signature

na·ment·lich ['na:məntlɪç] **I.** *adj.* **1.** **~e *Aufführung*** naming; *parl.* **~e *Abstimmung*** roll-call vote; **II.** *adv.* **2.** by name; → ***erwähnen; 3.*** especially, particularly, above all

'Na·men·ver·zeich·nis *n* list of names

nam·haft ['na:mhaft] *adj.* **1.** noted; renowned, famous; **2.** considerable, substantial; **3.** **~ *machen*** name, identify

näm·lich ['nɛ:mlɪç] **I.** *adv.* namely, that is (to say), ... to be precise (*or* exact); ***er war ~ krank*** he was ill, you see; **II.** *adj.*

the (very) same; ***der ~e Busfahrer*** the (very) same bus driver
nann·te ['nantə] *pret. of* ***nennen***
na·nu [na'nu:] F *int.*: ***~, wo ist denn m-e Tasche?*** F wait a minute, what have I done with my bag?; ***~, was haben wir denn da?*** F (well, well,) what's this we've got here then?; ***~, da hat ja einer aufgeräumt!*** well, well, (it looks as if) somebody's been tidying up; ***~, was ist denn hier los?*** F hey, what's all this about?
Na·palm ['na:palm] *n* (-s; *no pl.*) napalm; **~bom·be** *f* napalm bomb
Napf [napf] *m* (-[e]s; Näpfe ['nɛpfə]) bowl; dish; **~ku·chen** *m* (tall) ring cake
Naph·tha·lin [nafta'li:n] *n* (-s; *no pl.*) naphthalene
Nap·pa ['napa] *n* (-[s]; -s), **~le·der** *n* nappa (leather)
Nar·be ['narbə] *f* (-; -n) **1.** scar; ***es wird ohne ~ verheilen*** it won't leave a scar; *fig.* ***~n hinterlassen*** leave a scar (*or* its scar[s]); **2.** ⚘ stigma; **3.** ⚒ topsoil
'**nar·ben** *v/t.* (h) grain *leather*
'**Nar·ben|bil·dung** *f* scarring; **~ge·sicht** *n* scarred face; ***ein ~ haben*** *a.* have scars all over one's face
'**nar·ben·los** *adj.* unscarred, without a scar
'**Nar·ben·sei·te** *f* grain side *of leather*
nar·big ['narbɪç] *adj.* scarred
Nar·de ['nardə] *f* (-; -n) ⚘ nard
Nar·ko·lep·sie [narkolɛ'psi:] *f* (-; -n) narcolepsy
Nar·ko·se [nar'ko:zə] *f* (-; -n) an(a)esthetic; ***in ~*** under anaesthetic (*Am.* anesthesia); ***e-e ~ bekommen*** be given an an(a)esthetic; ***aus der ~ aufwachen*** come round (*or* to); **~fach·arzt** *m* anaesthetist, *Am.* anesthesiologist; **~ge·wehr** *n* tranquil(l)izer gun
Nar·ko·ti·kum [nar'ko:tikʊm] *n* (-s; -ka) an(a)esthetic, narcotic; **nar·ko·tisch** [nar'ko:tɪʃ] *adj.* an(a)esthetic, narcotic; **nar·ko·ti·sie·ren** [narkoti'zi:rən] *v/t.* (h) an(a)esthetize
Narr [nar] *m* (-en; -en) fool; *hist.* jester; *fig.* ***e-n ~en gefressen haben an*** *dat.* F be wild (*or* crazy) about; ***zum ~en halten*** → **nar·ren** ['narən] *v/t.* (h) make a fool of *s.o.*; fool
'**Nar·ren|frei·heit** *f* (-; *no pl.*) fool's licen|ce (*Am.* -se); ***bei ihr hat er ~*** she lets him do what he likes; **~haus** *n* madhouse; **~kap·pe** *f* fool's cap; **~ko,stüm** *n* jester's outfit; **2si·cher** *adj.* foolproof; **~streich** *m* silly prank
Nar·re·tei [narə'taɪ] *f* (-; -en), '**Narr·heit** *f* (-; -en) *a. pl.* tomfoolery; folly
När·rin ['nɛrɪn] *f* (-; -nen) fool
när·risch ['nɛrɪʃ] *adj.* **1.** mad, F crazy (***auf*** *acc.* about); **2.** ***~es Treiben*** carnival atmosphere; ***es herrscht ~es Treiben*** the carnival mood (*or* atmosphere) has taken over
Nar·zis·se [nar'tsɪsə] *f* (-; -n) ⚘ narcissus; ***gelbe ~*** daffodil
Nar·ziß·mus [nar'tsɪsmʊs] *m* (-; *no pl.*) narcissism; **Nar·zißt** [nar'tsɪst] *m* (-en; -en) narcissist; **nar·ziß·tisch** [nar'tsɪstɪʃ] *adj.* narcissistic
na·sal [na'za:l] *adj.* nasal
na·sa·lie·ren [naza'li:rən] *v/t.* (h) nasalize
Na'sal·laut *m* nasal (sound)
na·schen ['naʃən] *v/i. and v/t.* (h) nibble (between meals); eat (s.th. *or* things) on the sly; ***gern ~*** like to nibble (things), have a sweet tooth; ***wer hat von den Pralinen genascht?*** who's been at the chocolates?; **Na·scher** ['naʃɐ] *m* (-s; -) nibbler; **Na·sche·rei** [naʃə'raɪ] *f* (-; -en) **1.** nibbling; eating on the sly; **2.** sweets (and chocolates) *pl.*, *Am.* candy
nasch·haft ['naʃhaft] *adj.*: ***~ sein*** love to nibble things, have a sweet tooth
'**Nasch·kat·ze** *f*: ***sie ist e-e richtige ~*** she's always nibbling things (*or* eating sweet things)
Na·se ['na:zə] *f* (-; -n) **1.** nose (*a.* ✈ *etc. and physiol.*); *zo. a.* snout; ***e-e gute ~ haben*** have a keen sense of smell, *fig.* have good instincts, ***für et.***: *fig.* have a nose for s.th.; ***auf die ~ fallen*** *a.* F *fig.* fall flat on one's face; F ***eins auf die ~ kriegen*** get a punch on the nose, *fig.* F get a rap over the knuckles, F get it in the neck; F ***j-m eins auf die ~ geben*** give s.o. a punch on the nose, *fig.* F give s.o. a rap over the knuckles; F *fig.* ***pro ~ 10 Dollar*** 10 dollars each (*or* a head); F ***j-m et. auf die ~ binden*** tell s.o. all about s.th.; F ***j-n an der ~ herumführen*** lead s.o. up the garden path; F ***j-m auf der ~ herumtanzen*** play s.o. up, do what one likes with s.o.; ***j-m e-e lange ~ machen*** thumb one's nose at s.o., F cock a snook at s.o.; F *fig.* ***auf der ~ liegen*** be laid up; F ***s-e ~ in alles (hinein)stecken*** poke one's nose into everything; ***er muß immer die ~ vorn haben*** he's always got to be one step ahead; F ***j-n mit der ~ auf et. stoßen*** shove s.th. under s.o.'s nose; F ***es j-m unter die ~ reiben*** F rub s.o.'s nose in it, rub it in; F ***es j-m dauernd unter die ~ reiben*** keep rubbing it in; F ***die ~ voll haben*** be fed up (to the back teeth) (***von*** *dat.* with); F ***j-m et. aus der ~ ziehen*** worm (*or* winkle) s.th. out of s.o.; F ***immer der ~ nach!*** just follow your nose; F ***es liegt direkt vor d-r ~*** it's right under (*or* in front of) your nose; F ***der Zug fuhr uns vor der ~ weg*** we missed the train by seconds; F ***j-m die Tür vor der ~ zumachen*** shut the door in s.o.'s face; F ***j-m et. vor der ~ wegschnappen*** snatch s.th. from right under s.o.'s nose, *fig. a.* beat s.o. to s.th.; ***er sieht nicht weiter als s-e ~ (reicht)*** he can't see beyond the end of his nose; ***man kann es ihm an der ~ ansehen*** it's written all over his face; ***faß dich an d-e eigene ~!*** you can talk!; **2.** F drip
'**na·se·lang** F *adv.*: ***alle ~*** a) every few minutes, *w.s.* over and over again, b) every other step; ***er ruft alle ~ an*** *a.* he's forever ringing up
nä·seln ['nɛ:zəln] *v/i.* (h) speak through one's nose (*or* with a twang)
'**Na·sen|af·fe** *m* proboscis monkey; **~bein** *n* nosebone, nasal bone; **~blu·ten** *n* nosebleed(s *pl.*); **~boh·ren** *n* poking one's nose; **~flü·gel** *m* nostril; ***weite ~*** flared nostrils; **~gang** *m* nasal passage; **~haar** *n* nasal hair, F hairs *pl.* in one's nose; **~höh·le** *f* nasal cavity; **~kor·rek,tur** *f* rhinoplasty, F nose job
'**na·sen·lang** F *adv.* → ***naselang***
'**Na·sen|län·ge** *f*: *fig.* ***um e-e ~*** by an inch; ***j-n um e-e ~ schlagen*** *a.* F beat s.o. by a whisker, pip s.o. at the post; **~loch** *n* nostril; **~pla·stik** *f* → ***Nasenkorrektur***; **~ring** *m* nose ring; **~rücken** *m* bridge of the nose; **~schei·de·wand** *f* nasal septum; **~schleim·haut** *f* mucous membrane of the nose; **~schmuck** *m* nose jewellery (*esp. Am.* jewelry); **~son·de** *f* nasal probe; **~spit·ze** *f* tip of the nose; F ***man sieht's ihm an der ~ an*** you can tell (by the look on his face); **~spray** *m, n* nose (*or* nasal) spray
'**Na·sen·stü·ber** [-ʃty:bɐ] *m* (-s; -) **1.** F biff on the nose; **2.** F *fig.* F rap over the knuckles, wigging
'**Na·sen|trop·fen** *pl. pharm.* nose drops; **~wur·zel** *f* base of the nose
'**na·se·rümp·fend** *adj. and adv.* disapproving(ly *adv.*); reluctant(ly *adv.*); disdainful(ly *adv.*)
'**na·se·weis** [-vaɪs] *adj.* F smart-alecky, know-(it-)all; F saucy, brassy; '**Na·se·weis** *m* (-es; -e) **1.** F saucy (*or* cheeky) little brat; **2.** F smart aleck, know-(it-)all, wise guy, *Am.* F smarty pants
Nas·horn ['na:shɔrn] *n* (-[e]s; Nashörner ['na:shœrnɐ]) rhinoceros, F rhino
naß [nas] **I.** *adj.* wet; ***triefend ~*** dripping wet, soaking, drenched, wet through; ***~ machen*** wet; ***sich ~ machen*** wet o.s., wet his (*or* her) pants; ***~ werden*** get wet; F *fig.* ***j-n ~ machen*** *sport*: F give s.o. a thrashing; **II.** *adv.*: ***sich ~ rasieren*** wet-shave
Naß *lit. n* (Nasses; *no pl.*) **1.** water; F ***ins kühle ~ springen*** take a plunge; **2.** ***edles ~*** precious liquid (*or* drop)
Nas·sau·er ['nasaʊɐ] F *m* (-s; -) sponger, F scrounger; '**nas·sau·ern** (h) **I.** *v/i.* sponge (***bei*** *dat.* on *s.o.*), F scrounge (off *s.o.*); **II.** *v/t.* scrounge *s.th.* (***von j-m*** off s.o.)
Näs·se ['nɛsə] *f* (-; *no pl.*) wet(ness); damp(ness), moisture; ☂ humidity; ***vor ~ schützen!*** keep dry (*or* in a dry place); **~ge·fahr** *f mot.* slippery roads *pl.*
näs·sen ['nɛsən] (h) **I.** *v/t.* wet; moisten; **II.** *v/i.* ⚕ weep
'**Naß·fäu·le** *f* wet rot
'**naß|forsch** F *adj.* very forward, F cocky; **~ge·schwitzt** *adj.* soaked in sweat, dripping with sweat; **~kalt** *adj.* cold and damp; ***~es Wetter*** cold, damp weather
'**Naß|ra,sie·rer** *m* wet shaver; ***er ist ~*** *a.* he likes a wet shave; **~ra,sur** *f* wet shave; **~zel·le** *f* (prefabricated) bathroom unit
Na·ti·on [na'tsĭo:n] *f* (-; -en) nation
na·tio·nal [natsĭo'na:l] *adj.* national; ***~e Gesinnung*** nationalism; ***~e Minderheit*** ethnic minority
Na·tio'nal|be·wußt·sein *n* (feeling of) national identity; **~cha,rak·ter** *m* national character; **~elf** *f* national team (*or* side); ***Deutschlands ~*** the German team; **~far·ben** *pl.* national colo(u)rs; **~fei·er·tag** *m* national (public) holiday; **~flag·ge** *f* national flag; **~ge·fühl** *n* national consciousness; patriotism; **~ge·richt** *n gastr.* national dish; **~hei·lig·tum** *n* national shrine; **~held** *m* national hero; **~hym·ne** *f* national anthem
na·tio·na·li·sie·ren [natsĭonali'zi:rən] *v/t.* (h) **1.** nationalize; **2.** naturalize
Na·tio·na·lis·mus [natsĭona'lɪsmʊs] *m* (-; *no pl.*) nationalism; **Na·tio·na·list** [natsĭona'lɪst] *m* (-en; -en) nationalist; **na·tio·na·li·stisch** [natsĭona'lɪstɪʃ] *adj.* nationalist ..., nationalistic(ally *adv.*)
Na·tio·na·li·tät [natsĭonali'tɛ:t] *f* (-; -en) **1.** nationality; ***sie ist griechischer ~*** she's of Greek nationality, she's Greek; **2.** ethnic minority
Na·tio·na·li'tä·ten|fra·ge *f* problem of ethnic minorities, ethnic issue (*or* problem); **~kon,flikt** *m* ethnic conflict

Na·tio'nal|mann·schaft *f sport*: national team (*or* side); ***die englische*** ~ the English team; ***er spielt in der spanischen*** ~ he plays for Spain; **~öko·no,mie** *f* economics *pl.*; **~park** *m* national park
Na·tio'nal·so·zia,lis·mus *m* National Socialism; **Na·tio'nal·so·zia,list** *m* National Socialist; **na·tio'nal·so·zia,li·stisch** *adj.* National Socialist
Na·tio'nal|spie·ler *m sport*: international (player); **~sport** *m* national sport; **~spra·che** *f* national language
Na·tio'nal·staat *m* nation state
na·tio'nal·staat·lich *adj.* nation-state ...
Na·tio'nal|stolz *m* national pride; **~trai·ner** *m*: ***Deutschlands*** ~ ***X*** German manager X; ***Englands*** ~ ***X*** England('s) manager X; **~ver·samm·lung** *f* National Assembly
Na·to ['na:to] *f* (-; *no pl.*): ***die*** ~ NATO, Nato; **~län·der** *pl.* NATO (*or* Nato) countries *or* members; **~mit·glied(s·staat** *m*) *n* member of NATO (*or* Nato), NATO (*or* Nato) member
Na·tri·um ['na:triʊm] *n* (-s; *no pl.*) ⚗ sodium; **~chlo,rid** *n* sodium chloride
Na·tron ['na:trɔn] *n* (-s; *no pl.*) ⚗ sodium; ***kohlensaures*** ~ sodium carbonate; **~lau·ge** *f* sodium hydroxide, caustic soda
Nat·ter ['natɐ] *f* (-; -n) *zo.* adder, viper; *fig.* ***e-e*** ~ ***am Busen nähren*** nurse a viper in one's bosom
'Nat·tern·brut *fig. f*, **'Nat·tern·ge·zücht** [-gətsʏçt] *fig. n* (-[e]s; *no pl.*) vipers' brood
Na·tur [na'tu:ɐ] *f* (-; -en [-rən]) **1.** *no pl.* (*a.* ***die*** ~) nature; natural surroundings *pl.*, countryside; natural environment; *hum.* mother nature; ***in der freien*** ~ out in the open, *animals* in their natural habitat; ***er liebt die*** ~ he's a real nature lover, *w.s.* he loves to be out in the open; **2.** *no pl.* ***es ist*** ~ it's natural; ***Eiche*** ~ natural oak; **3.** temperament, disposition; character; ***von*** ~ ***(aus)*** by nature; ***e-e gesunde*** ~ ***haben*** have a strong constitution; ***es liegt (nicht) in ihrer*** ~ it's (not) in her nature; ***j-m zur zweiten*** ~ ***werden*** become second nature to s.o.; ***es geht ihm wider die*** ~ it's not in (*or* it's against) his nature (***zu*** *inf.* to *inf.*); ***die menschliche*** ~ human nature; ***gegen die*** ~ unnatural; **4.** *no pl. fig.* nature; ***Themen allgemeiner*** ~ topics of a general nature; ***die Sache ist ernster*** ~ it's a serious matter; ***es liegt in der*** ~ ***der Sache*** it's in the nature of it (*or* of things)
na·tu·ra [na'tu:ra]: ***in*** ~ *payment* in kind; ***in*** ~ *see etc. s.o. or s.th.* in real life, *a. see etc. s.o.* in the flesh
Na·tu·ral|ab·ga·ben [natu'ra:l-] *pl.* contributions (*or* payment *sg.*) in kind; **~be·zü·ge** *pl.* remuneration *sg.* in kind
Na·tu·ra·li·en [natu'ra:liən] *pl.* **1.** natural produce *sg.*; ***in*** ~ ***bezahlen*** *etc.* pay *etc.* in kind; **2.** natural history objects (*or* specimens)
na·tu·ra·li·sie·ren [naturali'zi:rən] *v/t.* (h) naturalize; **Na·tu·ra·li'sie·rung** *f* (-; -en) naturalization
Na·tu·ra·lis·mus [natura'lɪsmʊs] *m* (-; *no pl.*) naturalism; **Na·tu·ra·list** [natura'lɪst] *m* (-en; -en) naturalist; **na·tu·ra·li·stisch** [natura'lɪstɪʃ] *adj.* naturalist(ic)
Na·tu·ral|lei·stung [natu'ra:l-] *f* payment in kind; **~lohn** *m* wages *pl.* in kind; **~wert** *m* value in kind; **~wirt·schaft** *f* barter economy

Na'tur·apo·stel F *m* F nature freak
na'tur·be·las·sen *adj.* natural, in its (*or* their) natural state; untreated; unspoilt, left in its natural (*or* original) state; **~e** ***Nahrungsmittel*** untreated (*or* conservation) food
Na'tur|be·ob·ach·tung *f* nature study; observation of one's natural surroundings; wildlife observation; **~be·schrei·bung** *f* description of nature; **~bur·sche** *m* nature boy; **~denk·mal** *n* natural monument
na·ture [na'ty:r] *adj. gastr.* plain, au naturel; unbreaded *cutlet etc.*
Na·tu·rell [natu'rɛl] *n* (-s; -e) temperament, disposition
Na'tur|er·eig·nis *n*, **~er·schei·nung** *f* natural phenomenon
na'tur·far·ben *adj.* natural-colo(u)red
Na'tur|fa·ser *f* natural fibre (*Am.* fiber); **~film** *m* nature film; **~for·scher** *m* naturalist; **~for·schung** *f* (natural) science; **~freund** *m* nature lover
na'tur·ge·ge·ben *adj.* natural, decreed by nature; a gift of nature
na'tur·ge·mäß I. *adj.* natural; organic; **II.** *adv.* naturally; by definition; ***es ist*** ~ ***e-e gefährliche Sache*** *a.* it's in the nature of it that it's dangerous, it's bound to be dangerous
Na'tur·ge·schich·te *f* natural history; **na'tur·ge·schicht·lich** *adj.* natural history ...
Na'tur|ge·setz *n* law of nature; **2ge·treu** *adj.* true to nature; realistic(ally *adv.*); **~ge·wal·ten** *pl.* elements; **~gott·heit** *f* god of nature, natural deity; **~haus·halt** *m* balance of nature, ecological balance; **~heil·kun·de** *f* (-; *no pl.*) naturopathy; **~heil·ver·fah·ren** *n* naturopathic treatment; *pl. a.* naturopathy *sg.*
na'tur·iden·tisch *adj.* nature-identical
Na'tur|ka·ta,stro·phe *f* natural disaster; **~kind** *n* child of nature; **~kos,me·tik** *f* natural makeup; **~kost** *f* health food(s *pl.*); **~kost·la·den** *m* health food shop (*or* store); **~kraft** *f* natural force
na'tur·kraus *adj.* naturally frizzy; **Na'tur·krau·se** *f* naturally frizzy hair, F natural frizz
Na'tur|kun·de *f* (-; *no pl.*) (study of) natural history; *ped.* nature study; **~land·schaft** *f* (*a.* ***e-e*** ~) unspoilt (*or* untouched, natural) countryside; **~lehr·pfad** *m* nature trail
na·tür·lich [na'ty:ɐlɪç] **I.** *adj.* natural (*a. fig.*); normal; **~e** ***Größe*** actual (*or* full) size; ***die*** **~ste** ***Sache der Welt*** the most natural thing in the world; ***das ist doch*** ~ it's only natural; ***e-s*** **~en** ***Todes sterben*** die a natural death; ***das geht nicht mit*** **~en** ***Dingen zu*** F there's something fishy about it; **II.** *adv.* naturally; *a. int.* of course; ***aber*** **~!** but of course!; ***sich*** ~ ***verhalten*** act natural(ly); ***ich könnte*** ~ ***...*** of course I could ..., I could always ...
Na'tür·lich·keit *f* (-; *no pl.*) naturalness
Na'tur|mensch *m* child of nature, *iro.* nature boy; **2nah I.** *adj.* close to nature; *fig.* realistic, lifelike; **II.** *adv.*: ~ ***leben*** live in close touch with nature; **~park** *m* nature reserve; **~per·le** *f* natural pearl; **~pro,duk·te** *pl.* natural products (*or* produce *sg.*); **~recht** *n* natural law
na'tur·rein *adj.* pure, unadulterated
Na'tur|schät·ze *pl.* natural resources; **~schau·spiel** *n* spectacle of nature; ***ein*** ~ *a.* one of nature's spectacles; **~schön·heit** *f* beauty spot, area of natural beauty; **~schutz** *m* nature conservation; **~schüt·zer** *m* conservationist; **~schutz·ge·biet** *n* nature reserve, conservation area; **~schwär·me,rei** *f* nature worship; **~sei·de** *f* natural silk; **~stoff** *m* natural substance; **~ta,lent** *n* natural
na'tur·trüb *adj.* naturally cloudy *juice etc.*
na'tur·ver·bun·den *adj.* close to (*or* in touch with) nature; nature-loving ...; ~ ***sein*** a) live in close touch with nature, b) be a nature lover; **Na'tur·ver·bun·den·heit** *f* (-; *no pl.*) close relationship to nature; love of nature
Na'tur·volk *n* primitive people
Na'tur·wis·sen·schaft *f* (natural) science; **Na'tur·wis·sen·schaft·ler** *m* scientist; **na'tur·wis·sen·schaft·lich** *adj.* scientific; **~es** ***Fach*** science subject
Na'tur|wun·der *n* a) natural wonder, b) *fig.* prodigy; **~zu·stand** *m* (-[e]s; *no pl.*) natural state
Nau·tik ['naʊtɪk] *f* (-; *no pl.*) navigation, nautical science; **nau·tisch** ['naʊtɪʃ] *adj.* nautical
Na·vi·ga·ti·on [naviga'tsio:n] *f* (-; *no pl.*) navigation
Na·vi·ga·ti'ons|feh·ler *m* navigational error; **~ge·rät** *n* navigation system; **~kar·te** *f* navigation chart; **~raum** *m* chart room
Na·vi·ga·tor [navi'ga:to:ɐ] *m* (-s; -en [-ga'to:rən]) navigator; **na·vi·ga·to·risch** [naviga'to:rɪʃ] *adj.* navigational; **na·vi·gie·ren** [navi'gi:rən] *v/i.* (h) navigate
Na·zi ['na:tsi] *contp. m* (-s; -s) Nazi; **~herr·schaft** *f* (*a.* ***die*** ~) Nazi rule; **~re,gime** *n* Nazi regime
Na·zis·mus [na'tsɪsmʊs] *contp. m* (-; *no pl.*) Nazism; **na·zi·stisch** [na'tsɪstɪʃ] *contp. adj.* Nazi ...
'Na·zi|ver·bre·chen *n* Nazi crime (*or* atrocity); **~ver·gan·gen·heit** *f* Nazi past; **~zeit** *f* Nazi era, (period of) Nazi rule; ***in der*** ~ *a.* at the time of the Nazis (*or* of Nazi rule)
ne [ne:] F *adv.* → ***nicht*** 1
Ne·an·der·ta·ler [ne'andɐta:lɐ] *m* (-s; -) (*a.* ***der*** ~) Neanderthal man
Ne·bel ['ne:bəl] *m* (-s; -) fog; mist (*a. fig.*); haze; ⚔ smoke; *ast.* nebula; *fig.* veil, cloud; ***bei (dichtem)*** ~ in (thick) fog; F *fig.* ***fällt aus wegen*** **~!** it's off(, I'm afraid); **~bank** *f* (-; ¨e) fog bank; **~bil·dung** *f* (formation *or* buildup of) fog; **~decke** *f* fog cover; blanket of fog; **~feld** *n* fog bank; patch of fog; **~fet·zen** *pl.* fog patches, patchy fog *sg.*; **2feucht** *adj. road etc.* wet with fog; dank *weather*; **~fleck** *m ast.* nebula; **~glocke** *f* blanket of fog; **~gra,na·te** *f* smoke grenade
'ne·bel·haft *fig. adj.* hazy, dim, nebulous; fuzzy
'Ne·bel·horn *n* foghorn
ne·be·lig ['ne:bəlɪç] *adj.* → ***neblig***
'Ne·bel|kam·mer *f phys.* cloud chamber; **~lam·pe** *f*, **~leuch·te** *f*, **~schein·wer·fer** *m mot.* fog lamp; **~schlei·er** *m* veil of mist (*or* fog), haze; **~schluß·leuch·te** *f mot.* rear fog lamp; **~schwa·den** *pl.* patchy fog *sg.*, fog patches; **~wand** *f* fog bank; ⚔ smoke screen; **~wet·ter** *n* foggy weather
ne·ben ['ne:bən] *prp.* (*dat.*) **1.** next to, beside; by; **2.** *fig.* compared with (*or* to); **3.** apart (*esp. Am.* aside) from, besides; in addition to; ~ ***anderen Dingen*** amongst other things

'Ne·ben|ab·re·de *f* collateral agreement; **~ab·sicht** *f* secondary objective; ulterior motive; **~ak,zent** *m* secondary stress; **~al,tar** *m* side altar

'Ne·ben·amt *n* subsidiary office; *teleph.* branch exchange; **'ne·ben·amt·lich I.** *adj.* part-time *job etc.*; **II.** *adv.* part-time, on the side

ne·ben'an *adv.*: (***im Haus*** ~) next door; (***im Zimmer*** ~) *a.* in the next room; ***bei uns*** ~ next-door to us

'Ne·ben|an·schluß *m teleph.* extension; **~ar·beit** *f* **1.** job on the side, sideline; **2. ~en** less important (*or* secondary) jobs; **~arm** *m geogr.* branch; **~aus·ga·ben** *pl.* extras; † incidental expenses; **~aus·gang** *m* side exit; **~be·deu·tung** *f ling.* connotation

ne·ben'bei *adv.* **1.** in passing; ~ ***bemerkt*** incidentally, by the way, apropos of nothing; ***das nur ~ bemerkt*** that's just by the way; **2.** on the side; **3.** ... as well, ... besides

'Ne·ben·be·mer·kung *f* aside

'Ne·ben·be·ruf *m* sideline, job on the side; **'ne·ben·be·ruf·lich I.** *adj.*: ***~e Arbeit*** sideline, job on the side; **II.** *adv.* as a sideline, on the side

'Ne·ben|be·schäf·ti·gung *f* → ***Nebenarbeit, Nebenberuf***; **~be·trieb** *m* branch; subsidiary plant

'Ne·ben·buh·ler [-bu:lɐ] *m* (-s; -), **'Ne·ben·buh·le·rin** [-bu:lərɪn] *f* (-; -nen) rival

'Ne·ben|dar·stel·ler *m thea. etc.* supporting actor; *pl.* supporting cast *sg.*; **~din·ge** *pl.* trivialities; **~ef,fekt** *m* side effect

'ne·ben·ein'an·der I. *adv.* a) next to each other; *a. fig.* side by side, b) at the same time, simultaneously; concurrently; ~ ***bestehen*** coexist; **II.** ≈ *n* (-s; *no pl.*): *pol.* (***friedliches*** ~ peaceful) coexistence; **~le·gen** *v/t.* (*sep.*, h) place *or* lay next to each other (*or* side by side); **~lie·gen** *v/i.* (*irr.*, *sep.*, h, → ***liegen***) lie next to each other (*or* side by side); **~sit·zen** *v/i.* (*irr.*, *sep.*, h, → ***sitzen***) sit next to each other (*or* side by side); **~stel·len** *v/t.* (*sep.*, h) **1.** put *or* place next to each other (*or* side by side); **2.** *fig.* compare

'Ne·ben|ein·gang *m* side entrance; **~ein·kom·men** *n* extra income (on the side); **~ein·künf·te** *pl.* additional earnings; **~ein·nah·men** *pl.* extra income *sg.*; **~er·schei·nung** *f* side effect; ⚕ secondary symptom; **~er·werb** *m* extra income; job on the side; ***im*** ~ as a sideline

'Ne·ben·er·werbs|land·wirt *m* part-time farmer; **~land·wirt·schaft** *f* part-time farming

'Ne·ben|fach *n* **1.** *ped.* subsidiary (*or* secondary) subject, F subsid, *Am.* minor (subject); **2.** side compartment; **~fi,gur** *f* minor character; **~fluß** *m* tributary; **~form** *f* variant; **~fra·ge** *f* side issue; **~frau** *f* concubine; **~gas·se** *f* side street; **~ge·bäu·de** *n* building next door, next(-door) building; outbuilding, annex(e); **~ge·büh·ren** *pl.* extra charges; **~ge·dan·ke** *m* **1.** secondary consideration; ***es war nur ein ~*** *a.* it was just a thought that occurred to me; **2.** ulterior motive; **~ge·räusch** *n* **1.** *a. pl.* (background) noise; *radio*: *a.* interference; **2.** ⚕ secondary murmur; **~ge·richt** *n gastr.* side dish; **~gleis** *n* siding, *Am.* sidetrack; *fig.* ***aufs ~ schieben*** sideline, *Am.* sidetrack; **~hand·lung** *f* subplot; **~haus** *n* house (*or* building) next door, next house (*or* building)

ne·ben'her *adv.* **1.** alongside, by my *etc.* side; **2.** at the same time; **3.** *earn etc.* on the side; **~fah·ren** *v/i.* (*irr.*, *sep.*, sn, → ***fahren***) drive *or* ride along beside s.o. *or* s.th., drive (*or* ride) alongside; **~lau·fen** *v/i.* (*irr.*, *sep.*, sn, → ***laufen***) run along beside s.o. *or* s.th.

ne·ben'hin *adv. remark etc.* in passing, casually

'Ne·ben|ho·den *m* epididymis (*pl.* epididymides); **~höh·le** *f anat.* sinus; **~höh·len·ent·zün·dung** *f* sinusitis; **~kla·ge** *f* ⚖ incidental action; **~klä·ger** *m* co-plaintiff; **~ko·sten** *pl.* extra costs (*or* expenses), extras; **~li·nie** *f* **1.** collateral line; **2.** 🚂 branch line; **~mann** *m* (-[e]s; ⸚er, -leute) person (sitting *etc.*) next to one; **~nie·re** *f* adrenal gland

'Ne·ben·nie·ren|hor,mon *n* adrenaline; **~rin·de** *f* adrenal cortex

'ne·ben·ord·nen *v/t.* (*sep.*, h) coordinate; **'Ne·ben·ord·nung** *f* coordination

'Ne·ben|per,son *f thea.* minor character; **~pro,dukt** *n* by-product (*gen.* of); spin-off (from); **~raum** *m* **1.** a) side room, b) storeroom; **2.** room next door, next room; **~rech·te** *pl.* subsidiary rights; **~rol·le** *f thea. etc.* minor part (*fig.* role); ***kleine*** ~ bit part; **~sa·che** *f* minor consideration; ***das ist*** ~ that's not so important

'ne·ben·säch·lich *adj.* unimportant, *pred. a.* not important; irrelevant

'Ne·ben·säch·lich·keit *f* (-; -en) irrelevant matter, irrelevancy; triviality

'Ne·ben|sai,son *f* low (*or* off-peak) season; **~satz** *m ling.* subordinate clause; **~schild·drü·se** *f* parathyroid (gland); **~schluß** *m* ⚡ *etc.* parallel connection

'ne·ben·ste·hend *adj. and adv.* in the margin; ~ (***abgebildet***) opposite

'Ne·ben|stel·le *f* **1.** branch; **2.** *teleph.* extension; **~stra·ße** *f* side street; byroad; **~strecke** *f* 🚂 branch line; **~tä·tig·keit** *f* job on the side, sideline; **~tisch** *m*: (***am*** ~ at the) next table; **~ti·tel** *m* subtitle; **~ton** *m* **1.** *ling.* secondary stress; **2.** *pl.* ♪ secondary notes; **~tür** *f* side door; **~ver·an·stal·tung** *f* a) side show, b) fringe event; **~ver·dienst** *m* extra earnings *pl.* (*or* income); **~weg** *m* side road; **~win·kel** *m* 𝔸 adjacent angle; **~wir·kung** *f* side effect; *fig. pl.* fallout *sg.*; **~zim·mer** *n* **1.** next (*or* adjoining) room, room next door; **2.** side room, room at the back *of a restaurant etc.*; **~zweck** *m* secondary aim (*or* objective)

neb·lig ['ne:blɪç] *adj.* foggy, misty; **~-trüb** misty and dull (*or* overcast)

nebst [ne:pst] *obs. prp.* (*dat.*) together (*or* along) with; including

ne·bu·los [nebu'lo:s], **ne·bu·lös** [nebu'lø:s] *fig. adj.* nebulous, hazy

Ne·ces·saire [nesɛ'sɛ:ɐ] *n* (-s; -s) **1.** toilet bag; **2.** manicure set

necken ['nɛkən] (*sep.* -k·k) *v/t.* (h) tease

neckisch ['nɛkɪʃ] (*sep.* -k·k) *adj.* playful, teasing *a. remark etc.*; coquettish

nee [ne:] F *adv.* no, F na, *Am.* F *a.* nope

Nef·fe ['nɛfə] *m* (-n; -n) nephew

Ne·ga·ti·on [nega'tsi̯o:n] *f* (-; -en) negation

ne·ga·tiv ['ne:gati:f] **I.** *adj.* negative (*a. phys.*, 𝔸, ⚕, ⚡, *phot.*); ***~e Auswirkungen haben*** have an adverse effect (***auf*** *acc.* on); ***das ≈e daran*** the negative side of it (*or* thing about it); ***das ist nichts ≈es*** there's nothing wrong with it; ***er erzählt nur ≈es über sie*** he hasn't got a positive (*or* good) word to say about her; **II.** *adv.* negatively; ***et. ~ beurteilen*** see s.th. negatively, take a negative view of s.th.; ***alles nur ~ sehen*** *a.* always look on the negative side (of things); ***sich ~ über et. äußern*** be rather negative about s.th.

'Ne·ga·tiv *n* (-s; -e [-ti:və]) *phot.* negative

'Ne·ga·tiv|bei·spiel *n* negative example; **~bi,lanz** *f* debit balance; **~druck** *m* **1.** reverse printing; **2.** reverse print; **~film** *m* negative film; **~held** *m* antihero; **~image** *n* negative image; **~wer·bung** *f* negative advertising

Ne·ger ['ne:gɐ] *m* (-s; -) **1.** black; negro; **2.** F *TV* F idiot board; **Ne·ge·rin** ['ne:gərɪn] *f* (-; -nen) black (woman); negro woman, negress

'Ne·ger·kuß *m small, cream-filled chocolate cake*

ne·gie·ren [ne'gi:rən] *v/t.* (h) deny; negate; **Ne'gie·rung** *f* (-;-en) denial; negation

Ne·gli·gé [negli'ʒe:] *n* (-s; -s) negligee

ne·gro·id [negro'i:t] *adj.* negroid

neh·men ['ne:mən] *v/t.* (nahm, genommen, h) a) take; receive, b) ⚔ take, capture, c) take, clear *obstacle etc.*; *mot.* take, negotiate *bend etc.*, d) help o.s. to, e) use; take *bus etc.*, f) take *s.th., s.o.*, *a.* get (hold of) *a lawyer etc.*, *a.* charge *price etc.*, g) *fig.* deprive of *hope*, *rights etc.*; ***j-m die Angst*** *etc.* ~ take away s.o.'s fear *etc.*; ***et. an sich*** ~ take s.th.; ***zu sich*** ~ a) have *a cup of tea etc.*, b) take *s.o.* in; ***man nehme*** *recipe*: take; ***auf sich*** ~ undertake, take upon o.s., assume *office, burden etc.*, accept, take *responsibility etc.*; ***die Folgen auf sich*** ~ bear the consequences; ~ ***wir den Fall, daß*** let's assume that, suppose that; ***das lasse ich mir nicht*** ~ a) I won't be done out of that, b) nobody's going to talk me out of that; ***er läßt es sich nicht ~ zu*** *inf.* he insists on *ger.*; ***woher ~ und nicht stehlen?*** where (on earth) am I supposed to get hold of that (*or* them *etc.*)?; ***j-n zu ~ wissen*** know how to handle s.o.; ***er versteht es, die Kunden richtig zu ~*** he has a way with customers; ***wie man's nimmt*** it depends; ***er ist hart im ≈*** he can take a lot (of punishment); → ***geben*** 17

Neh·rung *f* (-; -en) spit

Neid [naɪt] *m* (-[e]s; *no pl.*) envy (***auf*** *acc.* of *s.o.*, at *s.th.*); jealousy; ***aus (purem)*** ~ out of (sheer) envy; ***grün vor ~*** green with envy; ***vor ~ vergehen*** (*or* ***erblassen***, F ***platzen***) be eaten up with envy; ***das muß ihm der ~ lassen*** you have to hand it to him; ***das ist nur der ~ der Besitzlosen*** he's *etc.* just jealous because he *etc.* hasn't got one; → ***blaß***; **nei·den** ['naɪdən] *v/t.* (h): ***j-m et.*** ~ envy s.o. s.th.; **Nei·der** ['naɪdɐ] *m* (-s; -) envious person; ***viele ~ haben*** be the envy of many; **'neid·er·füllt I.** *adj.* filled with envy, envious; **II.** *adv.* (filled) with envy, enviously; **'Neid·ham·mel** F *m* envious (*or* jealous) person; **nei·disch** ['naɪdɪʃ] *adj.* envious, jealous (***auf*** *acc.* of); **'neid·los** *adj. and adv.* without envy, ungrudging(ly)

Nei·ge ['naɪgə] *f* (-; *no pl.*) **1.** decline; ***zur ~ gehen*** decline, wane, *supplies*: run low, *a.* ✝ run short, *day*, *life etc.*: be drawing to an end; **2.** dregs *pl.*; ***den Kelch bis zur ~ leeren*** drain the cup to the last drop (*or* to the dregs); *fig.* ***et. bis zur ~ auskosten*** savo(u)r s.th. to the last (*or* the full); ***bis zur bitteren ~*** to the bitter end

nei·gen ['naɪgən] (h) **I.** *v/t.* bend, *formal*: incline; bow (down); tilt, tip; **II.** *v/refl.*: ***sich ~*** a) bend, lean; *plane*: slant; *ground*: slope, b) bow; *fig.* ***sich (dem Ende zu) ~*** be drawing to a close (*or* an end); **III.** *fig. v/i.*: ***~ zu*** *dat.* tend to *inf.*, have a tendency to *inf.* (*or* towards *ger. or s.th.*), be susceptible to *s.th.*, be prone to *s.th.* (*or inf.*, *ger.*); ***zu Unfällen ~*** be accident-prone; ***zum Kommunismus*** *etc.* ***~*** have communist *etc.* leanings; ***er neigt zu Übertreibungen*** he tends to exaggerate; ***ich neige zu der Ansicht, daß*** I'm inclined to think (that), I rather think (that); → ***geneigt***

Nei·gung ['naɪgʊŋ] *f* (-; -en) **1.** *no pl.* a) inclination, b) slope, incline; gradient; ✈ dip; **2.** *fig.* a) inclination (***zu*** *dat.* to, towards), propensity (to, for); liking, penchant, predilection (for); ✝, *pol.* tendency, trend (towards); disposition (for), *esp. b.s.* proclivity (for), b) affection (***zu*** *dat.* for), love (of); ***e-e ~ zur Kunst (Philosophie*** *etc.*) ***haben*** have an artistic (a philosophical *etc.*) bent; ***ein Mensch mit künstlerischen (philosophischen*** *etc.*) ***~en*** *a.* an artistically (philosophically *etc.*) inclined person; ***s-n ~en nachgeben*** (*or* ***leben***) follow one's inclinations; ***wenig ~ zeigen zu*** *inf.* show little inclination to *inf.*; ***er zeigt wenig ~ dazu*** he shows little talent in that direction

'Nei·gungs·win·kel *m* angle of inclination (*or* tilt)

nein [naɪn] *adv.* no; ***~ und abermals ~!*** for the last time, no!; ***aber ~!*** a) of course not, b) no!; ***geht er? - ~*** is he going? - no, he isn't; ***haben Sie gerufen? - ~!*** did you call? - no, I didn't; ***~, ist das schön!*** oh, how beautiful that is!

Nein *n* (-[s]; *no pl.*) no; refusal; ***ein klares ~*** a straight no; ***mit e-m ~ antworten*** say no, *a.* refuse; **'Nein·sa·ger** [-za:gɐ] *m* (-s; -) obstructionist; **'Nein·stim·me** *f parl.* no (*pl.* noes), *Am.* nay

Ne·kro·log [nekro'lo:k] *m* (-[e]s; -e [-gə]) obituary

Ne·kro·man·tie [nekroman'ti:] *f* (-; *no pl.*) necromancy

Ne·kro·phi·lie [nekrofi'li:] *f* (-; *no pl.*) necrophilia

Ne·kro·po·le [nekro'po:lə] *f* (-; -n) necropolis

Ne·kro·se [ne'kro:zə] *f* (-; -n) necrosis

Nek·tar ['nɛkta:ɐ] *m* (-s; -e [-rə]) **1.** ⚘ *and myth.* nectar; **2.** fruit juice (*containing crushed fruit*)

Nek·ta·ri·ne [nɛkta'ri:nə] *f* (-; -n) nectarine

Nel·ke ['nɛlkə] *f* (-; -n) **1.** ⚘ carnation; **2.** *gastr.* clove; **'Nel·ken·pfef·fer** *m* allspice, pimento

Nenn... [nɛn-] *in cpds.* nominal; ⚙ *usu.* rated

nenn·bar ['nɛnba:ɐ] *adj.* a) nameable, b) worth mentioning; appreciable *sum etc.*

'Nenn·be·trag *m* nominal amount (*or* sum)

nen·nen ['nɛnən] (nannte, genannt, h) **I.** *v/t.* a) name, call, *formal*: designate; dub, b) mention; quote, c) reveal, give away; nominate *candidate*; ***kannst du mir den höchsten Berg der Welt ~?*** can you name (*or* what's) the highest mountain in the world?; ***das nenne ich e-e Überraschung!*** well, that really is a surprise!; ***das nenne ich ein gelungenes Buch*** that's what I call a well-written book; ***das nennst du e-n guten Wein?*** is that what you call a good wine?; ***~ wir mal ...*** let's take ...(, for example); **II.** *v/refl.*: ***sich ~*** be called; *sport*: enter (***für*** *acc.* for); ***wie nennt sich ...?*** what's ... called?; *iro.* ***und das nennt sich Lehrer*** and he calls himself a teacher; ***und das nennt sich Kultur*** and that's supposed to be culture, and that goes by the name of culture, and they call it culture; → ***genannt***; **'nen·nens·wert** *adj.* worth mentioning; appreciable *sum etc.*; ***kein ~er Musiker*** *etc.* no musician *etc.* to speak of; ***keine ~e Leistung*** F nothing to write home about

Nen·ner ['nɛnɐ] *m* (-s; -) ✈ denominator; ***auf e-n gemeinsamen ~ bringen*** *a. fig.* bring down to a common denominator; *fig.* ***e-n gemeinsamen ~ finden für*** *acc.* find some common ground on which to base *a project etc.*

'Nenn·lei·stung *f* ⚙ rated power (*or* output)

Nen·nung ['nɛnʊŋ] *f* (-; -en) naming; mention; *sport*: entry; *pol. etc.* nomination; ***bei der ~ ihres Namens*** when her name was mentioned (*or* called out)

'Nenn·wert *m* nominal (*or* face) value; ✝ ***zum (über, unter) ~*** at (above, below) par

neo... [neo-], **Neo...** *in cpds.* neo(-)..., Neo(-)...

Neo·fa'schis·mus *m* neo-fascism, neo-Fascism; **Neo·fa'schist** *m*, **neo·fa'schi·stisch** *adj.* neo-fascist, neo-Fascist

Neo·klas·si'zis·mus *m* neoclassicism

Neo·klas·si'zist *m* neoclassicist

neo·klas·si'zi·stisch *adj.* neoclassical

Neo·li·thi·kum [neo'li:tikʊm] *n* (-s; *no pl.*) Neolithic period; **neo'li·thisch** [neo'li:tɪʃ] *adj.* Neolithic

Neo·lo·gis·mus [neolo'gɪsmʊs] *m* (-; -men) neologism

Ne·on ['ne:ɔn] *n* (-s; *no pl*) neon

Neo·na·zi ['ne:o-] *conpt.* *m* neo-Nazi; **Neo·na'zis·mus** [neo-] *contp.* *m* neo-Nazism; **neo·na'zis·tisch** [neo-] *conpt. adj.* neo-Nazi

'Ne·on|lam·pe *f*, **~leuch·te** *f* neon light (*or* lamp); **~licht** *n* neon light; **~re,kla·me** *f* neon sign; **~röh·re** *f* neon tube; *pl. a.* strip lighting *sg.*

Ne·pa·le·se [nepa'le:zə] *m* (-n; -n), **Ne·pa·le·sin** [nepa'le:zɪn] *f* (-; -nen) Nepalese, Nepali; **ne·pa·le·sisch** [nepa'le:zɪʃ] *adj.* Nepali, Nepalese, Nepal ...

Nepp [nɛp] F *m* daylight robbery, F *a* rip-off; ***es ist der reinste ~*** it's a real rip-off; **~bu·de** F *f* → ***Nepplokal***

nep·pen ['nɛpən] F *v/t.* (h) F fleece, rip *s.o.* off; **Nep·per** ['nɛpɐ] F *m* (-s; -) F rip-off artist

'Nepp|lo,kal F *n* F clip joint, rip-off place; **~preis** F *m* F rip-off price

Nerv [nɛrf] *m* (-s; -en) *anat.* nerve; ⚘ *a.* vein; ***j-m auf die ~en fallen*** (*or* ***gehen***), ***j-m den ~ töten*** (*or* ***rauben***) F get on s.o.'s nerves; ***die ~en behalten*** keep calm (F one's cool); ***die ~en verlieren*** lose one's nerve (*or* head), F snap, lose one's temper (F one's cool); ***er ist mit den ~en (völlig) fertig*** his nerves are (absolutely) shot, he's a(n absolute) nervous wreck, F his nerves have been worn to a frazzle; ***es kostet ~en*** it's nerve-racking, it takes it out on your nervous system; ***er hat ~en wie Drahtseile*** his nerves must be made of steel; F ***den ~ haben zu*** *inf.* have the nerve to *inf.*; F ***der hat vielleicht ~en!*** F he's got a nerve (*or* cheek); F ***d-e ~en möcht' ich haben!*** I'd like to have some of your nerves; F ***dazu braucht's ganz schöne ~en!*** it takes a fair bit of nerve (to do that); **'ner·ven** F *v/t.* (h): ***j-n ~*** get on s.o.'s nerves; ***der nervt mich vielleicht!*** F he doesn't half get on my nerves (*or* wick); → ***genervt***

'Ner·ven|an·span·nung *f* nervous tension; **~arzt** *m* neurologist; **Ⓢauf·rei·bend** *adj.* nerve-racking; **~bahn** *f* nerve tract; **~be·la·stung** *f* nervous strain; **Ⓢbe·ru·hi·gend** *adj.*: ***~ sein*** (*or* ***wirken***) calm the nerves; **~bün·del** *n* **1.** F *fig.* F bag (*or* bundle) of nerves; **2.** *anat.* nerve fascicle; **~ent·zün·dung** *f* neuritis; **~fa·ser** *f* nerve fibre (*Am.* fiber); **~gas** *n* nerve gas; **~gift** *n* nerve poison, neurotoxin; **~kit·zel** *m* (*contp.* cheap) thrill(s *pl.*); **~kli·nik** *f* psychiatric clinic; **~ko,stüm** F *n* nerves *pl.*; ***schwaches ~*** weak nerves; **Ⓢkrank** *adj.* neuropathic; neurotic; mentally ill; **~krank·heit** *f* nervous disease; **~krieg** *m* war of nerves; **~kri·se** *f* mental crisis; **~läh·mung** *f* neuroparalysis; **~lei·den** *n* nervous disease; **~pro·be** *f* ordeal; **~reiz** *m* nervous impulse; **~sa·che** *f*: (***es ist reine ~*** it's all) a question of nerves; **~sä·ge** F *f* F pain in the neck; ***sie ist e-e solche ~*** *a.* she really gets on your nerves, F she drives you up the wall; **~schmerz** *m a. pl.* neuralgia; **~schock** *m* nervous shock; **Ⓢschwach** *adj.*: ***~ sein*** have weak (*or* bad) nerves; **~schwä·che** *f* weak nerves *pl.*, ⚕ neurasthenia; **Ⓢstär·kend** *adj.*: ***~es Mittel*** tonic; **~strang** *m* (peripheral) nerve; **~sy,stem** *n* nervous system; **~zen·trum** *n* nerve centre (*Am.* center); (*a. fig.*); **Ⓢzer·rüt·tend** *adj.* nerve-shattering; **~zer·rüt·tung** *f* shattered nerves *pl.*; **~zu,sam·men·bruch** *m*: (***e-n ~ erleiden*** have a) nervous breakdown

ner·vig ['nɛrfɪç] *adj.* **1.** sinewy; **2.** F *fig.* nerve-racking *business etc.*

'nerv·lich I. *adj.* nervous; ***~e Belastung*** nervous strain, strain on the nerves; ***sein ~er Zustand*** (the state of) his nerves; **II.** *adv.*: ***~ bedingt*** nervous; ***es ist ~ bedingt*** *a.* it's my *etc.* nerves; ***sie ist ~ (völlig) am Ende*** (F ***kaputt***) her nerves are (absolutely) shot, she's a(n absolute) nervous wreck, F her nerves have been worn to a frazzle; ***er ist ~ zerrüttet*** his nerves are shattered; ***j-n ~ belasten*** be a strain on s.o.'s nerves; ***j-n ~ fertigmachen*** ruin s.o.'s nerves, F wear s.o's nerves to a frazzle, *w.s.* F drive s.o. up the wall

ner·vös [nɛr'vø:s] *adj.* **1.** tense; fidgety, F twitchy; edgy, F uptight; on edge, nervous; ***e-n ~en Eindruck machen*** seem nervous (*or* on edge); ***mach mich nicht ~!*** don't make me nervous, *w.s.* stop getting on my nerves; **2.** ⚕, *biol.* nervous

Ner·vo·si·tät [nɛrvozi'tɛ:t] *f* (-; *no pl.*) tenseness; edginess; nervousness

'nerv·tö·tend *adj.* soul-destroying, mind-

less *job etc.*; nerve-racking *noise etc.*; ***er ist einfach ~*** F he's such a pain in the neck, he drives you round the bend
Nerz [nɛrts] *m* (-es; -e) **1.** *zo.* mink; **2.** mink (coat, stole *etc.*); **~man·tel** *m* mink (coat); **~sto·la** *f* mink stole
Nes·sel ['nɛsəl] *f* (-; -n) ☘ nettle; *fig.* ***sich in die ~n setzen*** F put one's foot in it; **~aus·schlag** *m*, **~fie·ber** *n*, **~sucht** *f* (-; *no pl.*) nettle rash, hives (*sg.*)
Nest [nɛst] *n* (-[e]s; -er) a) nest, *fig. a.* home, b) F one-horse town, F dump, hole, c) F bed; F ***ins ~ gehen*** F turn in, hit the sack (*esp. Am.* hay); ***sein eigenes ~ beschmutzen*** foul one's own nest; ***das ~ leer finden*** find the bird has flown; ***da hat er sich aber ins gemachte*** (*or* ***warme***) ***~ gesetzt*** he's done nicely for himself there, he's got everything laid on; **~bau** *m* (-[e]s; *no pl.*) nest-building; **~be·schmut·zer** *fig. m*: ***er ist ein richtiger ~*** he's always running his own family (*or* company *etc.*) down
ne·steln ['nɛstəln] *v/i.* (h): ***~ an*** *dat.* fumble (around) with
'**Nest|häk·chen** *fig. n* pet of the family; **~hocker** *m* **1.** *fig.* stay-at-home; **2.** *zo.* nidiculus
Ne·stor ['nɛsto:ɐ] *m* (-s; -en [nɛs'to:rən]) doyen
'**Nest·wär·me** *fig. f* warmth and security (of the home)
nett [nɛt] *adj.* a) *a. iro.* nice (***von j-m*** of s.o.); kind, b) sweet, pretty, cute; ***~, daß du kommst*** (it's) nice of you to come; ***sei so ~ und bring mir ein Bier*** do me a favo(u)r and get me a beer, will you?; **net·ter·wei·se** ['nɛtɐ'vaɪzə] *adv.* very kindly; ***könnten Sie mir ~ ...?*** do you think you could possibly ... (for me)?
Net·tig·keit ['nɛtɪçkaɪt] *f* (-; -en) **1.** *no pl.* ***die ~ haben zu*** *inf.* be kind enough to *inf.*; **2.** ***j-m ein paar ~en (ins Ohr) sagen*** say a few nice words to s.o.
net·to ['nɛto] *adv.* ✝ net, clear
'**Net·to|ein·kom·men** *n* net income; **~ein·nah·men** *pl.*, **~er·trag** *m* net proceeds (*pl.*); **~ge·halt** *n* net salary; ***mein ~ ist ...*** *a.* I net ..., I take home ...; **~ge·wicht** *n* net weight; **~ge·winn** *m* clear profit; **~kre,dit·be·darf** *m* net borrowing requirement; **~lohn** *m* take-home pay; **~preis** *m* net price; **~,um·satz** *m* net turnover (*or* sales *pl.*)
Netz [nɛts] *n* (-es; -e) net (*a.* ⚔ *and fig.*); netting, mesh; (*baggage*) rack; 🚂, *teleph. etc.* network; ⚡ mains *pl.*; ***soziales ~*** safety net (of social benefits); ***ins ~ befördern*** *soccer*: put *the ball* into the net; ***ins ~ schlagen*** *tennis*: send *the ball* into the net; ***ans ~ gehen*** a) *tennis*: go up to the net, b) *power plant etc.*: go on line (*or* stream); *fig.* ***j-m ins ~ gehen*** walk into s.o.'s trap; ***s-e ~e auswerfen*** cast one's nets; ***sich im eigenen ~ verfangen*** get caught in one's own trap; ***sich im ~ s-r Lügen verstricken*** get caught up in a web of lies
'**Netz·an·schluß** *m* ⚡ mains connection
'**netz·ar·tig** *adj.* net-shaped, *formal*: reticular
'**Netz|auf·schlag** *m* let; **~au·gen** *pl.* compound eyes; **~aus·fall** *m* ⚡ power failure; **~ball** *m tennis*: net (ball)
net·zen ['nɛtsən] *v/t.* (h) wet, moisten
'**Netz·feh·ler** *m volleyball*: net (contact)
'**Netz·flüg·ler** [-fly:glɐ] *m* (-s; -) neuropteran (*pl.* neuroptera)
'**netz·för·mig** [-fœrmɪç] *adj.* → ***netzartig***
'**Netz|ge·rät** *n* ⚡ mains appliance; **~ge·wöl·be** *n* △ net vault
'**Netz·haut** *f anat.* retina; **~ab·lö·sung** *f* detached retina; **~ent·zün·dung** *f* retinitis
'**Netz|hemd** *n* string vest; **~kar·te** *f* 🚂 *etc.* runaround ticket; **~ma·gen** *m zo.* reticulum; **~rol·ler** *m tennis*: net cord; **~span·nung** *f* ⚡ mains voltage; **~spiel** *n tennis*: playing at the net; **~strümp·fe** *pl.* fishnet stockings; **~teil** *n* power supply; mains adapter; **~werk** *n* network
neu [nɔʏ] **I.** *adj.* a) new; novel, b) recent, c) modern, d) rising, e) renewed, f) clean *shirt etc.*; ***ganz ~*** brand-new; ***~er Anfang*** fresh start; ***~e Hoffnung*** renewed hope; ***~e Schwierigkeiten*** more (*or* renewed) difficulties; ***~ere Literatur*** modern literature; ***~ere Sprachen*** modern languages; ***~eren Datums*** recent; ***in ~erer Zeit*** in recent times, of late; ***~este Nachrichten*** latest news (*sg.*); ***die ~este Mode*** the latest fashion(s); ***ein ~es Leben beginnen*** make a fresh start (in life); ***das ist mir ~!*** that's new(s) to me; ***das ist mir nicht ~*** that's nothing new to me; ***noch wie ~*** as good as new; ***seit ~estem*** of late, since very recently, ***kann man ...:*** the latest thing is you can ...; **II.** *su.* ***aufs ~e, von ~em*** afresh, anew; ***von ~em anfangen*** start anew (*or* afresh); **III.** *adv.*: ***~ anfangen*** start anew (*or* afresh); ***~ beleben*** revive; ***~ schreiben*** rewrite; ***~ entdeckt*** newly(-)discovered; ***sich ~ einkleiden*** get a new set of clothes; ***sich ~ eindecken*** get in fresh supplies
'**Neu·an·kömm·ling** *m* newcomer
'**Neu·an·schaf·fung** *f* **1.** recent purchase, new acquisition; *pl. library*: recent acquisitions; ***letzte ~*** latest acquisition; ***es ist e-e ~*** *a. we etc.* only recently bought it; ***schon wieder e-e ~!*** something new again!; **2.** ***die ~ von Möbeln*** *etc.* buying new furniture *etc.*
'**neu·ar·tig** *adj.* new, *a* new type of; '**Neu·ar·tig·keit** *f* (-; *no pl.*) newness, novelty, novel aspect (*gen.* of)
'**Neu|auf·la·ge** *f* **1.** new edition; reprint; **2.** reissue *of a record*; **3.** F *fig.* repeat (performance); **~aus·ga·be** *f* → ***Neuauflage*** 1
'**Neu·bau** *m* (-[e]s; -ten) **1.** new building; **2.** *no pl.* reconstruction; **~sied·lung** *f* modern estate; **~woh·nung** *f* modern flat (*Am.* apartment)
'**neu·be·ar·bei·tet** *adj.* new(ly revised); '**Neu·be·ar·bei·tung** *f* **1.** new (*or* revised) version; revised edition; *thea. etc.* adaptation; **2.** revision
'**Neu|be·ginn** *m* fresh start, new beginning; ***es ist ein ~*** *a.* it's the start of something new; **~be·le·bung** *f* revival; **~be·set·zung** *f thea.* recasting; new cast; **~be·wer·tung** *f* reappraisal, reassessment, revaluation; **~bil·dung** *f* **1.** *physiol.* regeneration; **2.** *fig.* new formation, reorganization; **3.** *ling.* neologism; **~druck** *m* reprint
Neue[1] *m, f* (-n; -n) new man (woman); newcomer
Neue[2] *n* (-n; *no pl.*): ***das ~ daran*** what's new about it; ***das ~ste*** the latest thing *in fashion etc.*; ***weißt du schon das ~ste?*** have you heard the latest (news) *or* the news?; ***nichts ~s*** nothing new; ***das ist mir nichts ~s, das ist nichts ~s für mich*** that's nothing new to me; ***was gibt es ~s?*** what's new?
'**Neu|ein·spie·lung** *f* new recording; **~ent·deckung** *f* (new) discovery; **~ent·wick·lung** *f* (new) development
neu·er·dings ['nɔʏɐ'dɪŋs] *adv.* recently, as of late; ***~ gibt es ...*** a) there have (*or* has) recently been ..., b) the latest thing is there are (*or* is) ...; ***~ trinkt er wieder*** he's recently started drinking again, the latest (thing) is he's started drinking again
Neue·rer ['nɔʏərɐ] *m* (-s; -) innovator
neu·er·lich ['nɔʏɐlɪç] **I.** *adj.* recent; new, *a.* repeated; further; ***ein ~er Versuch*** *etc. a.* another attempt *etc.*; **II.** *adv.* recently, of late, for a while now
'**Neu·er·öff·nung** *f* (re)opening
'**Neu·er·schei·nung** *f* new *or* recent book (*or* publication); new (*or* recent) release
Neue·rung ['nɔʏərʊŋ] *f* (-; -en) innovation; change; reform
'**neue·rungs·feind·lich** *adj.* hostile *or* opposed to (any form of) innovation (*or* reform)
'**Neue·rungs·geist** *m* (-[e]s; *no pl.*) spirit of innovation
'**Neue·rungs·sucht** *f* (-; *no pl.*) mania for innovation (*or* reform); '**neue·rungs·süch·tig** *adj.* bent on innovation (*or* reform); ***~ sein*** *a.* be a fanatical innovator (*or* reformist)
'**Neu·er·wer·bung** *f* new acquisition; *pl. library etc.*: recent acquisitions
'**Neu·fas·sung** *f* revised version
Neu·fund·län·der [nɔʏ'fʊntlɛndɐ] *m* (-s; -) **1.** Newfoundlander; **2.** Newfoundland (dog)
'**neu|ge·backen** F *adj.* → ***frischgebacken***; **~ge·bo·ren** *adj.* new-born (*a. fig.*); ***sich wie ~ fühlen*** feel a different person, *a.* feel as good as new
'**Neu·ge·stal·tung** *f* **1.** a) redesigning, reshaping, b) reorganization; restructuring; **2.** new design (*or* structure)
'**Neu·gier** *f*, '**Neu·gier·de** [-gi:ɐdə] *f* (-; *no pl.*) curiosity, inquisitiveness; ***aus*** (***reiner***) ***~*** out of (sheer) curiosity
'**neu·gie·rig** *adj.* curious (***auf*** *acc.* about); inquisitive, F nosy; ***j-n ~ machen*** arouse s.o.'s curiosity; ***bin ich aber ~ auf den neuen Wagen!*** I can't wait to see the new car; ***ich bin ~, ob*** I wonder whether (*or* if); ***ich bin ~ darauf, was*** (***wie*** *etc.*) *a.* I'll be interested to know what (how *etc.*); ***du bist aber ~!*** F you're a real nosy-parker
'**Neu·glie·de·rung** *f* reorganization, restructuring
'**Neu·go·tik** *f* Gothic Revival, neo-Gothic style (*or* architecture); '**neu·go·tisch** *adj.* neo-Gothic
'**neu·grie·chisch** *adj.*, '**Neu·grie·chisch** *n ling.* modern Greek
'**Neu|grün·dung** *f* **1.** new establishment; **2.** re-establishment; **3.** ***~ e-s Vereins*** *etc.* (recent) establishment of a new association *etc.*; **~grup,pie·rung** *f* regrouping, *esp. pol.* reshuffling
'**neu·he·brä·isch** *adj.*, '**Neu·he·brä·isch** *n* (-en) *ling.* modern Hebrew
'**Neu·heit** *f* (-; -en) **1.** *no pl.* novelty; ***der Reiz der ~*** the novelty value; ***den Reiz der ~ verlieren*** lose its novelty (***für*** *acc.* for), begin to pall (on); ***es hat den Reiz der ~ verloren*** *a.* the novelty has worn (*or* begun to wear) off; **2.** new development (*or* idea *etc.*); ***~en auf dem Mode-***

markt (***Automarkt***) the latest fashions (car models)
'neu·hoch·deutsch *adj.*, **'Neu·hoch·deutsch** *n* (-en) *ling.* New High German
Neu·ig·keit ['nɔʏıçkaıt] *f* (-; -en) (***e-e*** ~ a piece of) news (*sg.*)
'Neu·in·sze,nie·rung *f thea.* new production
'Neu·jahr *n* (-s; *no pl.*) New Year('s Day); ***Pros(i)t*** ~! Happy New Year!
'Neu·jahrs|abend *m* New Year's Eve; **~an·spra·che** *f* New Year speech; **~bot·schaft** *f* New Year message; **~emp·fang** *m* New Year reception; **~grü·ße** *pl.* New Year greetings, greetings for the new year; **~tag** *m* New Year's day; **~wün·sche** *pl.* (best) wishes for the new year
'Neu·land *n* (-[e]s; *no pl.*) virgin soil; *fig.* new territory (*or* ground); ~ ***erschließen*** *a. fig.* break new ground; *fig.* ~ ***betreten*** (***erobern***) enter unknown (conquer new) territory; **~ge·win·nung** *f* land reclamation
'neu·lich *adv.* the other day, recently; not so long ago; ~ ***abends*** the other evening
Neu·ling ['nɔʏlıŋ] *m* (-s; -e) novice, beginner, tyro; *contp.* greenhorn
'neu·mo·disch *adj.* fashionable; *contp.* newfangled
'Neu·mond *m* (-[e]s; *no pl.*) new moon
neun [nɔʏn] *adj.* nine; ***alle ~e!*** strike!
Neun *f* (-; -en) **1.** ♠ nine; **2.** *bus etc.* (number) nine; **~au·ge** *n zo.* lamprey
'neun·bän·dig [-bɛndıç] *adj.* nine-volume ..., in nine volumes
'Neun·eck *n* nonagon
'neun·fach *adj.* ninefold; ***die ~e Menge*** nine times the amount
'neun'hun·dert *adj.* nine hundred
'neun·jäh·rig [-jɛːrıç] *adj.* **1.** nine-year-old ...; **2.** nine-year ...; ***ein ~es ...*** *a.* nine years of ...; **'Neun·jäh·ri·ge** [-jɛːrıgə] *m, f* (-n; -n) nine-year-old
'neun·köp·fig [-kœpfıç] *adj. family etc.* of nine; ***~e Delegation*** *etc. a.* nine-member (*or* nine-man) delegation *etc.*
'neun·mal *adv.* nine times
'neun·mal·klug *iro. adj.* F smart-alecky; **'Neun·mal·klu·ge** *m, f* (-n; -n) F know-(it-)all, smart aleck, *Am.* F smarty pants; ***das ist so ein ~r*** *a.* he thinks he knows it all
'neun·stel·lig [-ʃtɛlıç] *adj.* nine-digit *figure etc.*
'neun·stöckig [-ʃtœkıç] (*sep.* -k·k-) *adj.* nine-stor(e)y *building etc.*
'neun·stün·dig [-ʃtʏndıç] *adj.* nine-hour(-long) ...
neunt [nɔʏnt] **I.** *adj.* ninth; ***~es Kapitel*** chapter nine; ***am ~en April*** on the ninth of April, on April the ninth; ***9. April*** 9th April, April 9(th); **II.** *adv.*: ***wir waren zu*** ~ there were nine of us; ***wir gingen zu ~ hin*** nine of us went there
'neun·tä·gig [-tɛːgıç] *adj.* **1.** nine-day(-long) ...; **2.** nine-day-old ...
'neun'tau·send *adj.* nine thousand
Neun·te ['nɔʏntə] *m, f* (-n; -n) (the) ninth; ***er war ~r*** he was (*or* came) ninth; ***Papst Johannes IX.*** Pope John IX (= Pope John the Ninth); ***heute ist der*** ~ it's the ninth today
'neun·tei·lig [-taılıç] *adj.* nine-part ..., in nine parts
Neun·tel ['nɔʏntəl] *n* (-s; -) ninth
neun·tens ['nɔʏntəns] *adv.* ninth(ly), nine, in ninth place
'neun·wö·chig [-vœçıç] *adj.* **1.** nine-week ...; **2.** nine-week-old ...
'neun·zehn *adj.* nineteen; **'neun·zehnt** *adj.* nineteenth; **'Neun·zehn·tel** *n* (-s; -) nineteenth (part)
neun·zig ['nɔʏntsıç] *adj.* ninety; ***in den ~er Jahren*** in the nineties; ***er ist in den*** ***Ⱡern*** he's in his nineties; **Neun·zi·ger** ['nɔʏntsıgɐ] *m* (-s; -), **Neun·zi·ge·rin** ['nɔʏntsıgərın] *f* (-; -nen) man (woman) in his (her) nineties, *formal*: nonagenarian; F ninetysomething; **'neun·zig·jäh·rig** [-jɛːrıç] *adj.* ninety-year-old *man etc.*; ninety-year(-long) *period etc.*
neun·zigst ['nɔʏntsıçst] *adj.* ninetieth; ***sie hat heute ihren Ⱡen*** she's ninety today, it's her ninetieth birthday today
'Neu·ord·nung *f* reform
'Neu·ori·en,tie·rung *f* reorientation
'Neu·phi·lo,lo·ge *m* student (*or* teacher) of modern languages; **'Neu·phi·lo·lo,gie** *f* modern languages *pl.*
'Neu·prä·gung *f* recent coinage, neologism
Neur·al·gie [nɔʏral'giː] *f* (-; -n) ⚕ neuralgia; **neur·al·gisch** [nɔʏ'ralgıʃ] *adj.* neuralgic; *fig.* ***~er Punkt*** *s.o.'s* sore spot (*or* point), touchy subject; critical spot; *pol.* trouble spot; ***das ist sein ~er Punkt*** it's his sore spot (*or* point), it's a sore spot (*or* sore point, touchy subject) with him
Neur·asthe·nie [nɔʏraste'niː] *f* (-; -n) ⚕ neurasthenia; **Neur·asthe·ni·ker** [nɔʏras'teːnikɐ] *m*, **neur·asthe·nisch** [nɔʏras'teːnıʃ] *adj.* neurasthenic
'Neu·re·ge·lung *f* revision; reorganization
'Neu·rei·che *m, f* (-n; -n) nouveau riche; ***die ~n*** the nouveaux riches
Neu·ro·chir'urg [nɔʏro-] *m* neurosurgeon; **Neu·ro·chir·ur'gie** *f* neurosurgery
Neu·ro·lo·ge [nɔʏro'loːgə] *m* (-n; -n) neurologist; **Neu·ro·lo·gie** [nɔʏrolo'giː] *f* (-; *no pl.*) **1.** neurology; **2.** neurological wing (*or* section); **neu·ro·lo·gisch** [nɔʏro'loːgıʃ] *adj.* neurological
Neu·ro·se [nɔʏ'roːzə] *f* (-; -n) neurosis
Neu·ro·ti·ker [nɔʏ'roːtikɐ] *m* (-s; -) *a. fig.* neurotic; *fig.* ***er ist ein*** ~ he's neurotic
neu·ro·tisch [nɔʏ'roːtıʃ] *adj.* neurotic(ally *adv.*)
'Neu·schnee *m* fresh snowfall
'Neu·schöp·fung *f* **1.** new creation; **2.** *ling.* neologism
Neu·see·län·der [nɔʏ'zeːlɛndɐ] *m* (-s; -), **Neu·see·län·de·rin** [nɔʏ'zeːlɛndərın] *f* (-; -nen) New Zealander; **neu·see·län·disch** [nɔʏ'zeːlɛndıʃ] *adj.* New Zealand ..., from New Zealand
Neu·sprach·ler ['nɔʏʃpraːxlɐ] *m* (-s; -) → ***Neuphilologe***; **'neu·sprach·lich** *adj.* modern language *teaching etc.*; ***~es Gymnasium*** *grammar school with special emphasis on modern languages*
'Neu·struk·tu,rie·rung *f* restructuring
'neu·te·sta,ment·lich *adj.* New Testament *theology etc.*
neu·tral [nɔʏ'traːl] **I.** *adj.* **1.** neutral (*a.* ⚗, ⚡); ***geschmacklich ~ sein*** have a neutral taste; **2.** *ling.* neuter; **II.** *adv.*: ***sich ~ verhalten*** remain neutral; **Neu'tra·le** *m, f* (-n; -n) *pol.* neutral
neu·tra·li·sie·ren [nɔʏtrali'ziːrən] *v/t.* (h) neutralize; **Neu·tra·li'sie·rung** *f* (-; -en) neutralization
Neu·tra·li·tät [nɔʏtrali'tɛːt] *f* (-; *no pl.*) neutrality
Neu·tra·li'täts|ab·kom·men *n* neutrality pact; **~er·klä·rung** *f* declaration of neutrality; **~po·li,tik** *f* policy of neutrality; **~ver·let·zung** *f* violation of neutrality
Neu·tro·nen|bom·be [nɔʏ'troːnən-] *f* neutron bomb; **~waf·fe** *f* neutron weapon; **~zahl** *f* neutron count
Neu·trum ['nɔʏtrʊm] *n* (-s; -tren) **1.** *ling.* neuter noun; **2.** *fig.* sexless person; ***er ist ein*** ~ *a.* he's completely sexless
'Neu·ver·fil·mung *f* remake
'Neu·ver·hand·lung *f* renegotiation
'neu·ver·mählt *adj.* newly married (*or* wed), newly-wed ...; ***die Neuvermählten*** the newly-weds
'Neu|ver·schul·dung *f* new indebtedness; new borrowings *pl.*; **~ver·tei·lung** *f* redistribution; **~wahl** *f* election; ***die ~ des Vorsitzenden*** the election of a new chairman (*or* chairperson); *pol.* ***~en*** elections
'Neu·wert *m* value as new; **'neu·wer·tig** *adj.* as (good as) new; **'Neu·wert·ver·si·che·rung** *f* new for old insurance
'Neu·wort *n* (-[e]s; ⸚er) new word, neologism
'Neu·zeit *f* (-; *no pl.*) modern age; ***Geschichte*** *etc.* ***der*** ~ modern history *etc.*; **'neu·zeit·lich** *adj.* modern
'Neu|züch·tung *f* ⚘ new variety; *zo.* new breed; **~zu·gang** *m* new acquisition; new member; *univ.*, ⚕ *etc.* new admission, *pl. a.* new intake *sg.* of students *etc.*, incoming students *etc.*; **~zu·las·sun·gen** *pl.* new cars registered
New·tonsch ['njuːtənʃ] *adj.* Newtonian; ***das ~e Gravitationsgesetz*** Newton's law of gravity
Ni·be·lun·gen·treue ['niːbəlʊŋən-] *f* undying (*or* absolute) loyalty
nicht [nıçt] *adv.* **1.** not; ***er trinkt*** ~ he doesn't drink; ***ich ging*** ~ I didn't go; ~ ***füttern!*** (please) do not feed; ***willst du oder ~?*** do you want to or not?; ***ich*** ~ not me; ***der Apparat wollte ~ funktionieren*** the machine wouldn't work; ***gar*** ~ not at all; ***das wollte ich doch gar*** ~ that's not what I wanted (at all), but I didn't want that; ~ ***doch!*** don't!, stop it!; ~ ***einmal*** not even; ***nur das ~!*** anything but that!; ~ ***daß ich wüßte*** not that I know of; ~ ***daß es mich überrascht hätte*** not that I was surprised; ***ich glaube*** ~ I don't think so, ***daß***: I don't think (that); ***ich kenne ihn auch*** ~ I don't know him either; *sie sah es* ~, ***und ich auch*** ~ and nor (*or* neither) did I; *du kennst ihn ~?* - ***ich auch*** ~ nor do I; ***er ist krank, ~ wahr?*** he's ill, isn't he?; ***du tust es, ~ wahr?*** you 'will do it, won't you?; ***du kennst ihn, ~ wahr?*** you know him, don't you?; ***dann eben*** ~ don't, then, *a. iro.* nobody's forcing you; ***was du sagst!*** you don't say!; ***wie oft hab' ich ~ behauptet ...*** how many times have I said ..., haven't I said a hundred times ...; **2.** *with comp.*: no; ~ ***besser*** no better; ~ ***mehr*** no longer, not ... any more; **3.** *often a.* in... (*e.g.* ~ ***ratsam*** inadvisable); non-... (*e.g.* ~ ***abtrennbar*** non-detachable); un... (*e.g.* ~ ***gefärbt*** uncolo[u]red)
'Nicht·ach·tung *f* disregard (*gen.* of); ***j-n mit ~ strafen*** send s.o. to Coventry
'nicht·ade·lig *adj.* common
'Nicht·ade·li·ge *m, f* (-n; -n) commoner
'nicht·amt·lich *adj.* unofficial, nonofficial
'Nicht|an·er·ken·nung *f pol.* nonrecog-

nition; **~an·griffs·pakt** *m* nonaggression pact; **~be·ach·tung** *f*, **~be·fol·gung** *f* disregard (*gen.* of), failure to comply (with), noncompliance (with)
'nicht·be·rufs·tä·tig *adj.* nonemployed; **'Nicht·be·rufs·tä·ti·ge** *m,f* (-n; -n) nonemployed person
'Nicht|be·ste·hen *n* **1.** nonexistence; **2.** failure; ***das ~ der Prüfung*** failure of (*or* in) the exam(ination), failing (to pass) the exam(ination); **~be·zah·lung** *f* nonpayment
'Nicht·christ *m*, **'nicht·christ·lich** *adj.* non-Christian
Nich·te ['nɪçtə] *f* (-; -n) niece
'nicht·ehe·lich *adj.* illegitimate *child*
'Nicht|ein·hal·tung *f* noncompliance (*gen.* with); **~ein·lö·sung** *f*: ***bei ~*** if not cashed; **~ein·mi·schung** *f* nonintervention; **~er·fül·lung** *f* nonfulfil(l)ment, default; **~er·schei·nen** *n* nonappearance, failure to attend; ⚖ *a.* default
'nicht·exi,stent *adj.* nonexistent
'Nicht|fach·mann *m* non-expert, layman; *n.s.* non-professional; **~ge·brauch** *m*: ***bei ~*** when not in use; **~ge·fal·len** *n*: ***bei ~*** if not satisfied; ***bei ~ Geld zurück*** satisfaction or money back
nich·tig ['nɪçtɪç] *adj.* **1.** trivial; vain; **2.** ⚖ invalid; ***null und ~*** null and void; ***für ~ erklären*** declare null and void
'Nich·tig·keit *f* (-; -en) **1.** triviality; **2.** *no pl.* vanity; **3.** *no pl.* ⚖ nullity
'Nich·tig·keits|er·klä·rung *f* annulment, nullification; **~kla·ge** *f* nullity action
'Nicht·in·an·spruch·nah·me *f*: ***bei ~*** if not claimed
'nicht·kom·mu,ni·stisch *adj.* non-Communist
'nicht·krieg·füh·rend *adj.* nonbelligerent
'nicht·lei·tend *adj.* ⚡ nonconducting; **'Nicht·lei·ter** *m* nonconductor
'Nicht·me,tall *n* nonmetal
'Nicht·mit·glied *n* nonmember; **~staat** *m* nonmember (*or* nonaligned) state
'Nicht·nu·kle,ar·staat *m* nonnuclear state
'nicht·öf·fent·lich *adj.* private; ⚖ ***~e Sitzung*** session in camera
'nicht·or·ga·ni,siert *adj.* nonunionized; ***~e Arbeitnehmer*** nonunion(ized) workers
'Nicht·rau·cher *m* nonsmoker; ***ich bin ~*** I don't smoke; **~ab,teil** *n* nonsmoking compartment, F nonsmoker; **~lo,kal** *n* nonsmoking restaurant (*or* bar *etc.*); **~zo·ne** *f* nonsmoking area
'nicht·ro·stend *adj.* rustproof; stainless
nichts [nɪçts] *indef. pron.* nothing; ***~ Neues*** nothing new; ***ich höre*** (***sehe*** *etc.*) ***~*** I can't hear (see *etc.*) a thing; ***~ als Ärger*** *etc.* nothing but trouble *etc.*; ***~ anderes als*** nothing but; ***~ ist schöner als*** there's nothing nicer than (*ger. or to inf.*); ***es geht ~ über*** there's nothing like; ***~ dergleichen*** no such thing, nothing of the kind; ***gar ~*** nothing at all; ***fast gar ~*** hardly anything; ***für ~ und wieder ~*** all for nothing; ***mir ~, dir ~*** just like that, *leave etc. a.* without so much as a word (of goodbye, of explanation *etc.*); ***soviel wie ~*** next to nothing; ***~ weiter, weiter ~*** nothing else, *a.* nothing further *to discuss etc.*; ***weiter ~?*** is that all?; ***daraus ist ~ geworden*** nothing came of it; ***daraus wird ~*** a) nothing will come of it, b) we'll have to forget about that(, I'm afraid); ***das geht dich ~ an*** it's none of your business; ***aus ~ wird ~*** you can't make something out of nothing; ***wie ~*** F like nobody's business; ***das ist ~ für mich*** F that's not my thing; ***~ zu danken!*** not at all; don't mention it; ***es macht ~!*** it doesn't matter, never mind; ***~ zu machen!*** a) F nothing doing, b) it can't be helped; ***er wird es zu ~ bringen*** he'll never get anywhere (in life); ***sich in ~ auflösen*** *project etc.*: go up in smoke, vanish into thin air; ***ich komme zu ~*** I never get time for anything, I never get round to doing anything; F ***~ wie weg!*** run!, F let's move!; F ***~ wie raus!*** let's get out of here quick!; F ***~ wie hin!*** what are we waiting for?
Nichts *n* (-; *no pl.*) **1.** nothing(ness); void; ***aus dem ~*** from nowhere; ***et. aus dem ~ schaffen*** create s.th. out of nothing; ***vor dem ~ stehen*** be left with nothing, have to start from scratch; **2.** ***ein ~*** nothing; ***sich um ein ~ streiten*** fight over nothing (*or* a triviality); **3.** *contp. a* nobody; ***ein ~ sein*** *a.* be totally insignificant
'nichts·ah·nend I. *adj.* unsuspecting; **II.** *adv.* unsuspectingly, not suspecting a thing
'Nicht·schwim·mer *m* nonswimmer; **~becken** *n* beginners' pool
nichts·de·sto'trotz, nichts·de·sto'we·ni·ger *adv.* nevertheless, nonetheless
'Nicht·sein *n* nonexistence
'Nicht·seß·haf·te *m, f* (-n; -n) person of no fixed abode, vagrant
'Nichts·kön·ner *m* incompetent (person), F washout, dead loss; ***er ist ein ~*** *a.* he's not capable of anything, he's useless
Nichts·nutz ['nɪçtsnʊts] *m* (-es; -e) good-for-nothing; **'nichts·nut·zig** [-nʊtsɪç] *adj.* useless; **'Nichts·nut·zig·keit** *f* (-; *no pl.*) uselessness
'nichts·sa·gend *adj.* empty, meaningless *words etc.*; *a.* trite *remark etc.*; vague *answer etc.*; vacuous *report etc.*; vacant, blank *expression etc.*; colo(u)rless, dull; insipid; nondescript *face, person etc.*
'nicht·staat·lich *adj.* nongovernmental; private
Nichts·tu·er ['nɪçtstuːɐ] *m* (-s; -) idler, loafer, F layabout; **'nichts·tue·risch** [-tuːərɪʃ] *adj.* idle; **'Nichts·tun** *n* (-s; *no pl.*) idleness; ***seine Zeit*** *etc.* ***mit ~ verbringen*** idle away one's time *etc.*
Nichts·wis·ser ['nɪçtsvɪsɐ] *m* (-s; -) ignoramus
'nichts·wür·dig *adj.* base; contemptible; **'Nichts·wür·dig·keit** *f* (-; *no pl.*) baseness; contemptible nature (*gen.* of), contemptibility
'Nicht|tän·zer *m* nondancer; ***er ist ~*** he doesn't dance; **~teil·nah·me** *f* nonparticipation; **~trin·ker** *m* teetotal(l)er; ***ich bin ~*** I don't drink, I'm a teetotal(l)er; **~vor·han·den·sein** *n* absence; **~wis·sen** *n* ignorance; **~zah·lung** *f* nonpayment (***von*** *dat.* of), default (on); ***bei ~*** in default of payment; **~zu·tref·fen·de** *n*: ***~s streichen!*** delete where inapplicable
Nickel ['nɪkəl] (*sep.* -k·k-) *n* (-s; *no pl.*) ⚗ nickel; **~bril·le** *f*: (***e-e ~*** a pair of) steel-rimmed glasses *pl.*, F granny glasses *pl.*
nicken ['nɪkən] (*sep.* -k·k-) **I.** *v/i.* (h) **1.** (*a.* ***mit dem Kopf ~***) nod (one's head); give a nod; ***zustimmend ~*** nod in agreement; ***beifällig ~*** nod approvingly, nod (one's) approval; **2.** F doze, F be having forty winks; **II.** 𝔖 *n* (-s; *no pl.*) nod(ding)
Nicker·chen ['nɪkɐçən] (*sep.* -k·k-) F *n* (-s; -): ***ein ~ machen*** take a nap, F have forty winks, get (*or* have) a bit of shut-eye
Nicki ['nɪki] *m* (-[s]; -s) velour top
nie [niː] *adv.* never; ***fast ~*** hardly ever; ***~ wieder*** never again; ***noch ~*** never (before); ***man soll ~ „~" sagen*** never say never; ***~ und nimmer!*** never in a lifetime!, never in my *etc.* life!
nie·der ['niːdɐ] **I.** *adj.* low; inferior *rank etc.*; lower *office etc.*; *contp.* common, low, base, mean; *biol. etc.* lower, primitive *orders, instincts, life forms etc.*, early *stage of evolution*; ***der ~e Adel*** the gentry; ***von ~er Geburt*** of low(ly) birth, low-born; **II.** *adv.* low; down; ***auf und ~*** up and down; ***~ mit den Verrätern!*** down with the traitors!; **~beu·gen** *v/t.* (*sep.*, h) **1.** *a. v/refl.* (***sich ~***) bend down; **2.** *fig.* weigh down; **~bren·nen** (*irr.*, *sep.*, → ***brennen***) **I.** *v/i.* (sn) burn down (*or* to the ground), be burnt down (*or* to the ground); **II.** *v/t.* (h) burn *s.th.* down (*or* to the ground); **~brül·len** *v/t.* (*sep.*, h) shout *s.o.* down; **~bü·geln** F *v/t.* (*sep.*, h) **1.** F make mincemeat of *s.o.*; **2.** *sport*: F thrash, slaughter, clobber
'nie·der·deutsch *adj.*, **'Nie·der·deutsch** *n* (-en) *ling.* Low German
'Nie·der·druck *m* low pressure
'nie·der·drücken *v/t.* (*sep.*, h) **1.** press down; depress *key etc.*; **2.** *fig.* depress, weigh on *s.o.'s* mind
Nie·de·re ['niːdərə] *n* (-n; *no pl.*): ***das ~*** the baser instincts
'nie·der·fal·len *v/i.* (*irr.*, *sep.*, sn, → ***fallen***) fall down; ***auf die Knie ~*** fall down on one's knees, fall to one's knees
'Nie·der·fre,quenz *f* ⚡ low frequency; audio frequency; **'Nie·der·fre,quenz...** *in cpds.* low-frequency ...
'Nie·der·gang *m* (-s; *no pl.*) decline; *pol. etc. a.* decline and fall, *w.s.* collapse
'nie·der·ge·drückt *fig. adj.* dejected; ***~ sein*** be feeling (very) dejected
'nie·der·ge·hen *v/i.* (*irr.*, *sep.*, sn, → ***gehen***) **1.** *avalanche etc.*: come down; *rain etc.*: fall; *storm*: break; *curtain etc.*: come down, drop; ✈ descend, touch down; **2.** *fig.* rain down (***auf*** *acc.* on *s.o.*)
'nie·der·ge·schla·gen I. *p.p. of* ***niederschlagen***; **II.** *fig. adj.* depressed, dejected, F down in the dumps; **'Nie·der·ge·schla·gen·heit** *f* (-; *no pl.*) dejection, despondency; F *the* blues *pl.*
'nie·der|ha·geln *v/i.* (*sep.*, h) hail down (***auf*** *acc.* on); *fig.* rain down (on); **~hal·ten** *v/t.* (*irr.*, *sep.*, h, → ***halten***) hold (*or* keep) down; *fig.* suppress, oppress; **~ho·len** *v/t.* (*sep.*, h) lower *flag, sail*; **~kämp·fen** *v/t.* (*sep.*, h) *a. fig.* fight down, overcome; **~kau·ern** *v/refl.* (*sep.*, h): ***sich ~*** crouch (down); **~knal·len** F *v/t.* (*sep.*, h) F put a bullet through *s.o.*; **~kni·en** *v/i.* (*sep.*, sn) kneel down; **~knüp·peln** *v/t.* (*sep.*, h) club *s.o.* down
'nie·der·kom·men *v/i.* (*irr.*, *sep.*, sn, → ***kommen***) give birth (to a child); *formal, lit.*: ***~ mit*** *dat.* be delivered of
Nie·der·kunft ['niːdɐkʊnft] *f* (-; -künfte [-kʏnftə]) delivery, birth
'Nie·der·la·ge *f* (-; -n) ⚔ *and fig.* defeat; *esp. sport*: *a.* F drubbing, thrashing; ***e-e ~ erleiden*** (*or* ***erleben***, F ***einstecken***) be defeated, *formal*: suffer defeat (***gegen*** *acc.* at the hands of); ***j-m e-e ~ beibringen*** (*or* ***zufügen***) inflict a defeat on s.o., defeat s.o.; ***e-e 0:1-~*** a 1-0 (= one-nil) defeat

Nie·der·län·der ['ni:dɐlɛndɐ] *m* (-s; -) Dutchman; ~ ***sein*** be a Dutchman, come from Holland (*or* the Netherlands); '**Nie·der·län·de·rin** [-lɛndərɪn] *f* (-; -nen) Dutchwoman; → *a.* ***Niederländer***; '**nie·der·län·disch** [-lɛndɪʃ] *adj.*, '**Nie·der·län·disch** *n* (-en) *ling.* Dutch

'**nie·der·las·sen** (*irr.*, *sep.*, h, → ***lassen***) **I.** *v/t.* **1.** let down, lower; **II.** *v/refl.*: ***sich*** ~ **2.** sit down, take a seat; *bird*: settle, alight; **3.** take up residence, settle; **4.** ***sich*** ~ ***als*** set o.s. up as *a lawyer etc.*

'**Nie·der·las·sung** *f* (-; -en) **1.** establishment (*gen.* of); **2.** ✝ place of business; branch office; branch *of a bank*

'**Nie·der·las·sungs|frei·heit** *f* (-; *no pl.*) freedom of establishment; **~recht** *n* (-[e]s; *no pl.*) right of establishment

'**nie·der·le·gen** (*sep.*, h) **I.** *v/t.* lay (*or* put) down; *fig.* resign from *office etc.*; give up *business etc.*; ***die Waffen*** ~ lay down one's weapons; ***die Arbeit*** ~ (go on) strike, down tools, walk out; ***et. schriftlich*** ~ set s.th. down, put s.th. down in writing; **II.** *v/refl.*: ***sich*** ~ lie down; *a.* go to bed; '**Nie·der·le·gung** *f* (-; -en) resignation (*gen.* from *office*); abdication (from *the throne*)

'**nie·der|ma·chen** F *v/t.* (*sep.*, h) **1.** → ***niedermetzeln***; **2.** F give *s.o.* a roasting, bawl *s.o.* out; **~mä·hen** *fig. v/t.* (*sep.*, h) mow down

'**nie·der·met·zeln** *v/t.* (*sep.*, h) massacre, slaughter; '**Nie·der·met·ze·lung** *f* (-; -en) massacre, slaughter(ing)

'**nie·der|pras·seln** *v/i.* (*sep.*, sn) **1.** pelt (*or* lash) down; **2.** *fig.* rain down (***auf*** *acc.* on); **~reg·nen** *v/i.* (*sep.*, h) rain down; **~rei·ßen** *v/t.* (*irr.*, *sep.*, h, → ***reißen***) tear down (*a. fig. barriers etc.*); pull down, demolish *building etc.*; **~rin·gen** *fig. v/t.* (*irr.*, *sep.*, h, → ***ringen***) overpower

'**nie·der·rhei·nisch** *adj.* from the Lower Rhine

'**Nie·der·sach·se** *m*, '**Nie·der·säch·sin** *f* man (woman) from Lower Saxony; ~ ***sein*** *usu.* come (*or* be) from Lower Saxony; '**nie·der·säch·sisch** *adj.* from Lower Saxony

'**nie·der·schie·ßen** (*irr.*, *sep.*, → ***schießen***) **I.** *v/t.* (h) shoot (*or* gun) down; **II.** *v/i.* (sn) shoot (*or* swoop) down

'**Nie·der·schlag** *m* (-[e]s; ⸚e) **1.** *meteor.* rain(fall), *formal*: precipitation; ***radioaktiver*** ~ nuclear fallout; **2.** ⚗ precipitate; deposit, sediment; **3.** *boxing*: knockdown, knockout; **4.** *fig.* ***s-n*** ~ ***finden in*** *dat.* find expression in, show (itself) in, manifest itself in; be reflected in

'**nie·der·schla·gen** (*irr.*, *sep.*, h, → ***schlagen***) **I.** *v/t.* **1.** knock *s.o.* down; *boxing*: *a.* floor *s.o.*, knock *s.o.* out; **2.** cast down *one's eyes*; **3.** *fig.* suppress; put down, crush, quell *revolt etc.*; **4.** ⚖ quash; **II.** *v/refl.* **5.** ***sich*** ~ ⚗ precipitate, deposit; **6.** *fig.* ***sich*** ~ ***in*** *dat.* → ***Niederschlag*** 4

'**nie·der·schlags·arm** *adj.*: ~***es Gebiet*** *etc.* low-precipitation area *etc.*

'**nie·der·schlags·frei** *adj.* dry

'**Nie·der·schlags·men·ge** *f* rainfall, precipitation

'**nie·der·schlags·reich** *adj.*: ~***es Gebiet*** *etc.* high-precipitation area *etc.*

'**Nie·der·schla·gung** *f* (-; -en) **1.** suppression, quelling *of a revolt etc.*; **2.** ⚖ quashing

'**nie·der·schmet·tern** *v/t.* (*sep.*, h) **1.** floor *s.o.*; dash *s.th.* to the ground; **2.** *fig.* crush, shatter; '**nie·der·schmet·ternd** *adj.* shattering, crushing

'**nie·der|schrei·ben** *v/t.* (*irr.*, *sep.*, h, → ***schreiben***) write (*or* set) down, record; **~schrei·en** *v/t.* (*irr.*, *sep.*, h, → ***schreien***) shout *s.o.* down

'**Nie·der·schrift** *f* (-; -en) **1.** writing (*or* setting) down (*gen.* of), recording (of); **2.** notes *pl.*; minutes *pl.*

'**nie·der|set·zen** (*sep.*, h) **I.** *v/t.* put (*or* set) down; **II.** *v/refl.*: ***sich*** ~ sit down; **~sin·ken** *v/i.* (*irr.*, *sep.*, sn, → ***sinken***) sink (down); collapse

'**Nie·der·span·nung** *f* ⚡ low voltage

'**nie·der|ste·chen** *v/t.* (*irr.*, *sep.*, h, → ***stechen***) stab (to death); **~stei·gen** *v/i.* *and v/t.* (*irr.*, *sep.*, sn, → ***steigen***) descend; **~stel·len** *v/t.* (*sep.*, h) put (*or* set) down; **~stim·men** *v/t.* (*sep.*, h) vote down; **~sto·ßen** (*irr.*, *sep.*, → ***stoßen***) **I.** *v/t.* (h) knock *s.o.* down; **II.** *v/i.* (sn): ~ ***auf*** *acc.* swoop down on; **~strecken** *v/t.* (*sep.*, h) floor *s.o.*, knock *s.o.* down; **~stür·zen** *v/i.* (*sep.*, sn) **1.** fall down, *horse*: *a.* stumble; *rocks etc.*: come (crashing) down; **2.** *a. v/refl.* (***sich*** ~) swoop down (***auf*** *acc.* on)

nie·der·tou·rig ['ni:dɐtu:rɪç] *adv.*: ~ ***fahren*** run at low revs

Nie·der·tracht ['ni:dɐtraxt] *f* (-; *no pl.*) **1.** baseness, meanness; **2.** mean (*or* base) deed, F dirty trick; '**nie·der·träch·tig** [-trɛçtɪç] *adj.* base, mean, low; sordid; ***das war aber*** ~***!*** what a base (*or* mean) thing to do; '**Nie·der·träch·tig·keit** *f* (-; -en) **1.** *no pl.* baseness, meanness; **2.** mean (*or* base) deed, F dirty trick

'**nie·der|tram·peln** *v/t.* (*sep.*, h) trample down (*lit.* underfoot); trample on *s.o.*; ***niedergetrampelt werden*** be (*or* get) trampled on, be trampled to death; **~tre·ten** *v/t.* (*irr.*, *sep.*, h, → ***treten***) tread down; tread on, crush *flowers etc.*

Nie·de·rung ['ni:dərʊŋ] *f* (-; -en) **1.** *geogr.* depression; *pl.* low-lying areas; **2.** *fig.* ***die*** ~***en des Lebens*** the seamy side of life; ***die*** ~***en der Gesellschaft*** the dregs of society

'**Nie·der·wald** *m* copse

'**nie·der·wal·zen** *v/t.* (*sep.*, h) **1.** flatten, mow down; **2.** *fig.* steamroller

'**nie·der·wärts** [-vɛrts] *adv.* downward(s)

'**nie·der·wer·fen** (*irr.*, *sep.*, h, → ***werfen***) **I.** *v/t.* **1.** throw (*or* fling) down *or* to the ground; *fig.* ***niedergeworfen werden*** be laid low *with flu etc.*; **2.** *fig.* put down, crush, quell *revolt etc.*; **II.** *v/refl.*: ***sich vor j-m*** ~ throw o.s. at s.o.'s feet

'**Nie·der·wer·fung** *f* (-; -en) quelling

'**Nie·der·wild** *n* small game

'**nie·der·zwin·gen** *v/t.* (*irr.*, *sep.*, h, → ***zwingen***) overpower, overcome; *a.* bring *s.o.* to his (*or* her) knees

nied·lich ['ni:tlɪç] *adj.* sweet, cute

Nied·na·gel ['ni:t-] *m* hangnail

nied·rig ['ni:drɪç] *adj.* low (*a. adv.*); *a.* inferior *quality etc.*; *fig.* low(ly), humble *rank etc.*; *fig.* low, mean, base; ~ ***halten*** keep down; ***zu*** ~ ***angeben*** understate; *mot.* ~***er Gang*** low gear; *fig.* ~***e Instinkte*** base(r) instincts

'**Nied·rig·hal·tung** *f*: ~ ***von Preisen*** *etc.* keeping down prices *etc.*

'**Nied·rig·keit** *f* (-; *no pl.*) lowness; ✝ low level; *fig.* humbleness *of rank etc.*; *fig.* baseness *of character etc.*

'**Nied·rig·lohn** *m* low income; **~grup·pe** *f* low-wage bracket; **~land** *n* low-wage (*or* cheap labo[u]r) country

'**Nied·rig·was·ser** *n* low tide (*or* water)

nie·mals ['ni:ma:ls] *adv.* never; ~***!*** *a.* F not on your life (*Brit. a.* nelly)!

nie·mand ['ni:mant] **I.** *indef. pron.* nobody, no-one; not ... anybody; ~ ***anders*** nobody else; ~ ***anders als*** none other than; **II.** ♀ *contp. m* (-s; *no pl.*) a nobody

'**Nie·mands·land** *n* (-[e]s; *no pl.*) ⚔ *and fig.* no-man's-land

Nie·re ['ni:rə] *f* (-; -n) kidney; → ***künstlich***; F *fig.* ***j-m an die*** ~***n gehen*** F get to s.o., F take it out of s.o.; → ***Herz***

'**Nie·ren·becken** *n anat.* renal pelvis; **~ent·zün·dung** *f* ⚕ pyelitis

'**Nie·ren·ent·zün·dung** *f* kidney infection, 🕮 nephritis

'**nie·ren·för·mig** [-fœrmɪç] *adj.* kidney-shaped

'**Nie·ren|ko·lik** *f* renal colic; ♀**krank** *adj.*: ~ ***sein*** have kidney trouble (*or* a kidney disease); **~krank·heit** *f*, **~lei·den** *n* kidney disease (*or* trouble); **~scha·le** *f* kidney dish; **~spen·der** *m* kidney donor

'**Nie·ren·stein** *m* kidney stone; **~zer·trüm·me·rer** *m* lithotripter

'**Nie·ren|ta·sche** *f* belt bag, F bum bag; **~tisch** *m* kidney-shaped table; **~trans·plan·ta·ti·on** *f*, **~ver·pflan·zung** *f* kidney transplant; **~ver·sa·gen** *n* kidney failure; **~wär·mer** *m* body belt

nie·seln ['ni:zəln] *v/i.* (h), '**Nie·sel·re·gen** *m* drizzle

nie·sen ['ni:zən] *v/i.* (h) sneeze

Nies|pul·ver ['ni:s-] *n* sneezing powder; **~reiz** *m* urge to sneeze; ***e-n*** ~ ***haben*** keep wanting to sneeze

Nieß·brauch ['ni:s-] *m* (-[e]s; *no pl.*) usufruct; '**Nieß·brau·cher** [-braʊxɐ] *m* (-s; -), '**Nieß·nut·zer** *m* usufructuary

Nies·wurz ['ni:svʊrts] *f* (-; -en) ❀ hellebore

Niet [ni:t] *m*, *n* (-[e]s; -e) → ***Niete***[1]

Nie·te[1] ['ni:tə] *f* (-; -n) ⚙ rivet; stud

'**Nie·te**[2] *f* (-; -n) **1.** blank; ***e-e*** ~ ***ziehen*** *a. fig.* draw a blank; **2.** *fig.* a) F flop, washout, b) F washout, dead loss

nie·ten ['ni:tən] *v/t.* (h) rivet

'**Nie·ten|gür·tel** *m* studded belt; **~ho·se** *f* jeans (with studs)

'**Niet|ham·mer** *m* riveting hammer; **~kopf** *m* rivet head

'**niet- und** '**na·gel·fest** F *adj.*: ***alles, was nicht*** ~ ***war*** everything that wasn't nailed down

Ni·ge·ria·ner [nige'ria:nɐ] *m* (-s; -), **Ni·ge·ria·ne·rin** [nige'ria:nərɪn] *f* (-; -nen), **ni·ge·ria·nisch** [nige'ria:nɪʃ] *adj.* Nigerian

Ni·hi·lis·mus [nihi'lɪsmʊs] *m* (-; *no pl.*) nihilism; **Ni·hi·list** [nihi'lɪst] *m* (-en; -en) nihilist; **ni·hi·li·stisch** [nihi'lɪstɪʃ] *adj.* nihilistic

Ni·ko·laus(tag) ['nɪkolaʊs-] *m* St Nicholas' Day

Ni·ko·tin [niko'ti:n] *n* (-s; *no pl.*) nicotine; **ni·ko'tin·arm** *adj.* low in nicotine; low-nicotine ...; **ni·ko'tin·frei** *adj.* nicotine-free; **Ni·ko'tin·ge·halt** *m* nicotine content; **ni·ko'tin·hal·tig** [-haltɪç] *adj.*: ~ ***sein*** contain nicotine; **Ni·ko'tin·säu·re** *f* niacin; **ni·ko'tin·süch·tig** *adj.* addicted to nicotine; **Ni·ko'tin·süch·ti·ge** *m*, *f* (-n; -n) nicotine addict; **Ni·ko'tin·ver·gif·tung** *f* nicotine poisoning

Nil·pferd ['ni:l-] *n* hippopotamus, F hippo

Nim·bus ['nɪmbʊs] *m* (-; -se) **1.** nimbus, halo; **2.** *no pl. fig.* aura; ***der ~ des Mystischen*** *etc.* an aura of mysticism *etc.*; ***von e-m geheimnisvollen ~ umgeben*** surrounded by a (certain) mystique

nim·mer ['nɪmɐ] F *dial. adv.* never; → ***nie***

'nim·mer'mü·de *adj.* untiring, indefatigable

'nim·mer·satt *adj.* insatiable; **'Nim·mer·satt** *m* (-s; -e) insatiable person; ***er ist ein ~ a.*** he just can't get enough

Nim·mer'wie·der·se·hen *n*: ***auf ~*** for good

Nip·pel ['nɪpəl] *m* (-s; -) ⚙ fitting; nipple

nip·pen ['nɪpən] *v/i. and v/t.* (h) sip (***an*** *dat.* at)

Nip·pes ['nɪpəs] *pl.*, **Nipp·sa·chen** ['nɪp-] *pl.* knick-knacks, *esp. contp.* bric-a-brac *sg.*

nir·gend(s) ['nɪrgənt(s)], **'nir·gend'wo, 'nir·gend·wo'hin** *adv.* nowhere, not ... anywhere

Nir·wa·na [nɪr'va:na] *n* (-[s]; *no pl.*) nirvana, Nirvana; ***ins ~ eingehen*** enter into nirvana (*or* Nirvana); *fig. iro.* go to meet one's Maker

Ni·sche ['ni:ʃə] *f* (-; -n) niche (*a. fig.*); recess

Nis·se ['nɪsə] *f* (-; -n) *zo.* nit

'Nis·sen·hüt·te *f* Nissen (*Am.* Quonset) hut

ni·sten ['nɪstən] *v/i.* (h) (build a) nest

Nist|ka·sten ['nɪst-] *m* nesting box; **~platz** *m* nesting place

Ni·trat [ni'tra:t] *n* (-s; -e) ⚗ nitrate; **~ge·halt** *m* nitrate level(s *pl.*)

ni·trie·ren [ni'tri:rən] *v/t.* (h) **1.** ⚗ nitrate; **2.** → **ni·trier·här·ten** [ni'tri:ɐ-] *v/t.* (h) *metall.* nitride

Ni'trier·stahl *m* nitriding steel

Ni·trit [ni'tri:t] *n* (-s; -e) ⚗ nitrite

Ni·tro·gly·ze'rin [nitro-] *n* nitroglycerine

Ni·tro·lack ['ni:tro-] *m* nitrocellulose paint

Ni·veau [ni'vo:] *n* (-s; -s) **1.** (*a. price etc.*) level; **2.** level, standard *of education etc.*; ***unter dem ~*** not up to standard (F scratch); ***~ haben*** a) have class (*or* style), b) (*a.* ***ein hohes ~ haben***) be of a high standard, be on a high level; ***kein ~ haben*** have no culture, be (totally) uncultured; ***der Film*** *etc.* ***hat kein ~*** it's a very ordinary (*or* mediocre) film *etc.*; ***jemand von d-m ~*** someone of your calibre (*Am.* caliber); ***es ist unter s-m ~*** it's not his level, it's beneath him (*iro. a.* his dignity)

ni'veau·los *fig. adj.* mediocre; uncultured; **Ni'veau·lo·sig·keit** *f* (-; *no pl.*) mediocrity; *s.o.'s* lack of culture (*or* style)

Ni'veau|ˌun·ter·schied *m* difference in level (*fig. a.* standard); **~ver·lust** *fig. m* drop in standard

ni'veau·voll *adj.* a) of a high standard, b) cultivated, cultured, *w.s.* sophisticated

ni·vel·lie·ren [nivɛ'li:rən] *v/t.* (h) level

Ni·vel·lier|ge·rät [nivɛ'li:ɐ-] *n*, **~in·stru·ˌment** *n* (telescope) level; **~lat·te** *f* level(l)ing rod

Ni·vel·lie·rung [nivɛ'li:rʊŋ] *f* (-; -en) level(l)ing

Ni·xe ['nɪksə] *f* (-; -n) water nymph

no·bel ['no:bəl] *adj.* **1.** noble, high-minded; **2.** generous; **3.** F classy, posh

'No·bel|ge·gend *f* F posh area (*or* part of town); **~her·ber·ge** F *f*, **~hoˌtel** *n* high-class (F posh) hotel; **~kaˌros·se** F *f*, **~li·mouˌsi·ne** *f* F big flash(y) car

No·bel·preis [no'bɛl-] *m* Nobel Prize; **~trä·ger** *m* Nobel Prize winner, Nobel laureate

'No·bel·re·stauˌrant *n* top-class (F classy, posh) restaurant

No·bles·se [no'blɛsə] *obs. f* high-mindedness, noble-mindedness

noch [nɔx] **I.** *adv.* **1.** still; ***immer ~, ~ immer*** still; ***~ nicht*** not yet; ***~ ist es nicht zu spät*** it's not too late yet; ***~ nie*** never (before); ***~ besser*** (***mehr***) even better (more); ***~ am selben Tag*** that (very) same day; ***~ gestern*** only yesterday; ***heute ~*** to this day; ***~ jetzt*** even now; ***~ im 11. Jahrhundert*** as late as the 11th century, ***benutzte man sie:*** *a.* they were still in use in the 11th century; ***er hat nur ~ 10 Dollar*** he's only got 10 dollars left; ***~ lange nicht*** F not by a long chalk; ***wir sind ~ lange nicht fertig*** *etc.* we're not nearly (*or* nowhere near) ready *etc.*; ***wie heißt sie ~?*** what's (*or* what was) her name again?; ***was hattest du ~ gesagt?*** what was it you said (again)?; ***auch das ~!*** that's all I *etc.* needed; F ***er hat Geld ~ und ~*** (*or* ***nöcher***) F he's got piles (*or* stacks) of money; ***sie redet ~ und ~*** she never stops talking; ***da haben wir ja ~ Glück gehabt*** we were lucky there; → ***fehlen*** 3, ***gerade*** II, ***schön*** I; **2.** more; ***~ dazu*** on top of that; ***dazu kommt ~, daß er trinkt*** not only that - he drinks too; and then he drinks on top of it (all); ***~ einer*** one more, another one; ***~ ein Stück*** another (*or* one more) piece; ***~ ein Bier*** the same again; another beer, please; ***~ (ein)mal*** once more, one more time, again, F let's try that (one) again; → ***gutgehen*** 1; ***~ einmal so viel*** as much again; ***und ~ etwas*** and another thing; ***~ etwas?*** anything else?; ***was wollen Sie ~?*** what more do you want?; ***wer kommt ~?*** who else is coming?; ***~ schlauer als du*** even smarter than you; ***es klingt nur ~ verdächtiger*** it sounds even (*or* all the) more suspicious; ***~ fünf Minuten*** five minutes to go, five more minutes, another five minutes; **3.** ***sei es ~ so klein*** no matter how small it is, however small it may be; **II.** *cj.* → ***weder***

noch·ma·lig ['nɔxma:lɪç] *adj.* renewed, second; ***~e Untersuchung*** re-examination; **'noch·mals** [-ma:ls] *adv.* once more (*or* again), again; *a.* re... (*e.g.* ***~ untersuchen*** reinvestigate)

Nocken ['nɔkən] (*sep.* -k·k-) *m* (-s; -) ⚙ cam; **~wel·le** *f* camshaft

no·lens-vo·lens ['no:lɛns'vo:lɛns] *adv.* like it or not, *formal:* willy-nilly

No·ma·de [no'ma:də] *m* (-n; -n) nomad

No'ma·den|le·ben *n* nomadic life, life of a nomad (*or* nomads); **~stamm** *m* nomadic tribe

No'ma·den·tum *n* (-s; *no pl.*) nomadism

No'ma·den|volk *n* nomadic tribe (*or* people); **~zelt** *n* nomad('s) tent

no·ma·disch [no'ma:dɪʃ] *adj.* nomadic

No·men ['no:mən] *n* (-s; -, Nomina ['no:mina]) *ling.* noun

No·men·kla·tur [no:mɛnkla'tu:ɐ] *f* (-; -en [-'tu:rən]) nomenclature

no·mi·nal [nomi'na:l] *adj.* nominal

No·mi'nal·ein·kom·men *n* nominal income

No·mi·na·lis·mus [nomina'lɪsmʊs] *m* (-; *no pl.*) *phls.* nominalism; **No·mi·na·list** [nomina'lɪst] *m* (-en; -en) *phls.* nominalist

No·mi'nal|ver·zin·sung *f* nominal interest rate; **~wert** *m* nominal (*or* face) value

No·mi·na·tiv ['no:minati:f] *m* (-s; -e [-və]) *ling.* nominative (case)

no·mi·nell [nomi'nɛl] *adj.* nominal

no·mi·nie·ren [nomi'ni:rən] *v/t.* (h) nominate; **No·mi'nie·rung** *f* (-; -en) nomination

Non·cha·lance [nõʃa'lã:s] *f* (-; *no pl.*) nonchalance; **non·cha·lant** [nõʃa'lã:] *adj.* nonchalant

No·ne ['no:nə] *f* (-; -n) **1.** ♪ ninth; **2.** *eccl.* nones *pl.*

Non·kon·for'mis·mus [nɔn-] *m* (-; *no pl.*) nonconformism; **Non·kon·for'mist** *m* (-en; -en), **non·kon·for'mi·stisch** *adj.* nonconformist

Non·ne ['nɔnə] *f* (-; -n) nun

'Non·nen|hau·be *f* coif; **~klo·ster** *n* convent; *lit.* nunnery; **~or·den** *m* order of nuns

Non·plus·ul·tra [nɔnplʊs'ʔʊltra] *n*: ***das ~*** the ultimate (***was ... angeht*** in ...)

Non·sens·dich·tung ['nɔnzɛns-] *f* nonsense verse (*or* poem); *pl.* nonsense poetry (*or* verse) *sg.*

Non·stop|flug [nɔn'ʃtɔp-] *m* nonstop flight; **~ki·no** *n* continuous performance cinema

Nord [nɔrt] *without art.* north; ***von*** (*or* ***aus***) ***~*** from the north; ***Duisburg ~*** the north of Duisburg; ***Eingang ~*** the north entrance

'Nord·afri'ka·ner *m*, **'nord·afri'ka·nisch** *adj.* North African

'Nord·ame·ri'ka·ner *m*, **'nord·ame·ri'ka·nisch** *adj.* North American

'Nord·at'lan·tik·pakt *m pol.* North Atlantic Treaty

'nord·deutsch *adj.* North German; ***im ~en Raum*** in the north of Germany, in Northern Germany; **'Nord·deut·sche** *m, f* (-n; -n) North German

Nor·den ['nɔrdən] *m* (-s; *no pl.*) north; North; ***nach ~*** north(wards), northbound *traffic etc.*; ***von ~*** from the north; ***der kalte ~*** the cold north; ***im kalten ~*** up in the cold north; → ***hoch***

'nord·eng·lisch *adj.* northern (*or* Northern) English

'Nord·eu·ro'pä·er *m*, **'nord·eu·ro'pä·isch** *adj.* North (*or* Northern) European

'Nord|halb·ku·gel *f* northern hemisphere; **~hang** *m* northern (*or* north-facing) slope

'Nord'ire *m*, **'Nord'irin** *f* man (woman) from Northern Ireland; ***~ sein*** *usu.* come (*or* be) from Northern Ireland

nor·disch ['nɔrdɪʃ] *adj.* northern; Nordic

Nor·di·stik [nɔr'dɪstɪk] *f* (-; *no pl.*) Scandinavian studies *pl.*

'Nord·ko·rea·ner *m*, **'nord·ko·rea·nisch** *adj.* North Korean

'Nord·kü·ste *f* north coast; ***an der ~*** on the north coast

Nord·län·der ['nɔrtlɛndɐ] *m* (-s; -) Northerner; Nordic type; **'nord·län·disch** [-lɛndɪʃ] *adj.* northern, *a.* Nordic *type etc.*

nörd·lich ['nœrtlɪç] **I.** *adj.* northern, north ...; northerly *wind etc.*; ***in ~er Richtung*** north(wards); northbound *traffic etc.*; **II.** *adv.* (to the) north (***von*** *dat.* of)

'nörd·lichst *adj.* northernmost

'Nord·licht *n* (-[e]s; -er) **1.** northern lights *pl.*, aurora borealis; **2.** F Northerner

Nord'ost *without art.*, **Nord'osten** *m* (*abbr.* **NO**) northeast (*abbr.* NE)

nord'öst·lich **I.** *adj.* northeast(ern);

northeasterly *wind etc.*; **II.** *adv.* (to the) northeast

'Nord·pol *m* (-[e]s; *no pl.*) North Pole

'Nord·po·lar|ge·biet *n* Arctic; **~kreis** *m* Arctic Circle

'Nord·pol·ex·pe·di·ti,on *f* expedition to the North Pole

'Nord|sei·te *f* north (*or* northern) side; **~staa·ten** *pl.* the northern states *of the USA*; **~stern** *m* (-[e]s; *no pl.*) pole star, North Star

'Nord-'Süd|-Dia,log *m pol.* North-South Dialog(ue); **~-Ge·fäl·le** *n* north-south divide

'Nord'süd·rich·tung *f*: ***in ~ verlaufen*** run from north to south

'Nord·wand *f* north face *of a mountain*

'nord·wärts [-vɛrts] *adv.* north(wards)

Nord'west *without art.*, **Nord'we·sten** *m* (*abbr.* ***NW***) northwest (*abbr.* NW)

nord'west·lich I. *adj.* northwest(ern); northwesterly *wind etc.*; **II.** *adv.* (to the) northwest

'Nord·wind *m* north wind

Nör·ge·lei [nœrgə'laɪ] *f* (-; -en) grumbling, moaning; niggling, F grizzling; **nör·geln** ['nœrgəln] *v/i.* (h) grumble, moan; *child*: niggle, F grizzle; **Nörg·ler** ['nœrglɐ] *m* (-s; -) grumbler, moaner

Norm [nɔrm] *f* (-; -en) **1.** norm, standard; rule; ***als ~ gelten*** be (considered) the norm; ***sich an die ~en halten*** stick to the norm; **2.** ⚙ *etc.* standard specification; ***technische ~en*** technical standards (*or* specifications); **3.** ☤ norm, (production) quota

nor·mal [nɔr'ma:l] *adj.* normal; conventional; ordinary; ⚙ *etc.* standard ...; ***das ist doch ganz ~*** that's perfectly normal (*or* natural); ***das ist doch nicht mehr ~*** that's not normal; ***es ist ~, daß es heiß wird*** it's normal for it to get hot; ***jeder ~e Mensch*** any normal person, anyone in his right mind; ***du bist wohl nicht mehr ~!*** have you gone out of your mind?

Nor'mal|ben,zin *n* regular petrol (*Am.* gas); **~bür·ger** *m the* average citizen, *the* man in the street

nor·ma·ler·wei·se [nɔr'ma:lɐ'vaɪzə] *adv.* normally; under normal circumstances

Nor'mal|fall *m* normal case; ***im ~*** normally; **~ge·wicht** *n* standard (*or* average) weight; **~grö·ße** *f* normal (*or* standard) size

nor·ma·li·sie·ren [nɔrmali'zi:rən] (h) **I.** *v/t.* normalize; regulate; **II.** *v/refl.*: ***sich ~*** return to normal; regulate itself

Nor·ma·li'sie·rung *f* (-; *no pl.*) normalization

Nor·ma·li·tät [nɔrmali'tɛ:t] *f* (-; *no pl.*) normality

Nor'mal|maß *n* **1.** standard measurement; **2.** *fig.* standard, norm; ***auf ein ~ bringen*** (***zurückführen***) bring (back) down to normal; **~null** *n* (-[e]s; *no pl.*) sea level; **~spur** *f* 🚂 standard ga(u)ge; **~ton** *m* ♪ standard pitch; **~ver·brauch** *m* average (*or* standard) consumption; **~ver·brau·cher** *m* average consumer; → ***Otto***; **~wert** *m* standard value; **~zeit** *f* (-; *no pl.*) standard time; **~zu·stand** *m* normal conditions *pl.*; F *iro.* ***das ist der ~*** that's the way things are (around here); ***das ist kein ~*** things aren't usually like that

Nor·man·ne [nɔr'manə] *m* (-n; -n), **Nor·man·nin** [nɔr'manɪn] *f* (-; -nen), **nor·man·nisch** [nɔr'manɪʃ] *adj.* Norman

nor·ma·tiv [nɔrma'ti:f] *adj.* normative

'Norm·blatt *n* standard specifications list

nor·men ['nɔrmən] *v/t.* (h) standardize

'Norm·er·fül·lung *f* fulfil(l)ment of quotas

'norm·ge·recht *adj.* complying with standards

nor·mie·ren [nɔr'mi:rən] *v/t.* (h) standardize

Nor'mie·rung *f* (-; -en), **Nor·mung** ['nɔrmʊŋ] *f* (-; -en) standardization

Nor·we·ger ['nɔrve:gɐ] *m* (-s; -), **Nor·we·ge·rin** ['nɔrve:gərɪn] *f* (-; -nen), **nor·we·gisch** ['nɔrve:gɪʃ] *adj.*, **'Nor·we·gisch** *n* (-en) *ling.* Norwegian

Nost·al·gie [nɔstal'gi:] *f* (-, *no pl.*) nostalgia; **~wel·le** *f* wave of nostalgia

Nost·al·gi·ker [nɔs'talgɪkɐ] *m* (-s; -) nostalgic; **nost·al·gisch** [nɔs'talgɪʃ] *adj.* nostalgic(ally *adv.*)

Not [no:t] *f* (-; Nöte ['nø:tə]) a) want, need, poverty, b) plight, misery, c) difficulty, trouble; distress; danger, d) *pl.* difficulties, problems; ***wirtschaftliche ~*** economic plight; ***zur ~*** if necessary, if need be, at a pinch, if the worst comes to the worst; ***wenn ~ am Mann ist*** if need be, if the worst comes to the worst; ***~ leiden*** suffer want (*or* privation); ***in ~ sein*** be in trouble; ***in tausend Nöten sein*** be in real trouble (*or* a real mess); ***in ~ geraten*** run into difficulties; ***in der Stunde der ~*** at the hour of need; ***für Zeiten der ~*** for a rainy day; ***s-e liebe ~ haben*** have a hard time (of it), ***mit*** *dat.*: have a hard time with; ***es täte dir ♀ zu*** *inf.* you would do well to *inf.*; what you really need is to *inf.*; ***aus der ~ e-e Tugend machen*** make a virtue of necessity; ***~ macht erfinderisch*** necessity is the mother of invention; ***in der ~ frißt der Teufel Fliegen*** any port in a storm, beggars can't be choosers; ***~ kennt kein Gebot*** necessity knows no law; → ***Mühe, knapp*** I

no·ta·be·ne [nota'be:nə] *obs. adv.* **1.** mind you; **2.** by the way

'Not·an·ker *m a. fig.* sheet anchor

No·tar [no'ta:ɐ] *m* (-s; -e [no'ta:rə]) notary

No·ta·ri·at [nota'rĭa:t] *n* (-[e]s; -e) notary's office

no·ta·ri·ell [nota'rĭɛl] **I.** *adj.* notarial, attested by (a) notary; **II.** *adv.* by (a) notary; ***~ beglaubigt*** attested by (a) notary

'Not·arzt *m* a) emergency doctor, b) doctor on call; **~wa·gen** *m* emergency ambulance

No·ta·ti·on [nota'tsĭo:n] *f* (-; -en) (system of) notation

'Not·auf·nah·me *f* **1.** ⚕ a) emergency admission, b) casualty (department); **2.** provisional accommodation *of refugees etc.*; **~la·ger** *n* (refugee) transit camp, reception centre (*Am.* center)

'Not|aus·ga·be *f* skeleton edition *of a newspaper*; **~aus·gang** *m* emergency exit; fire exit (*or* door); **~aus·stieg** *m* escape hatch; **~be·helf** *m* stopgap; **~be·leuch·tung** *f* emergency lighting; **~brem·se** *f* emergency brake; 🚂 *Brit.* communication cord; ***die ~ ziehen*** apply the emergency brake(s), pull the communication cord, *fig.* call a halt before it's too late, *sport*: commit a professional foul; **~dienst** *m* standby duty; ***~ haben*** be on standby, *doctor*: *a.* be on call; *pharmacy*: be open all night

Not·durft ['no:tdʊrft] *f*: ***s-e ~ verrichten*** relieve o.s.

'not·dürf·tig I. *adj.* **1.** scanty, meagre (*Am.* meager); **2.** makeshift; emergency ...; provisional, stopgap ...; **II.** *adv.* **3.** scantily *furnished etc.*; **4.** a) as a makeshift (*or* stopgap), b) somehow or other, c) just about; ***et. ~ reparieren*** patch s.th. up (temporarily); ***sich ~ durchschlagen*** just about (manage to) scrape through

No·te ['no:tə] *f* (-; -n) **1.** *ped.* mark, *Am.* grade; **2.** ♪ note; *pl. coll.* music; ***ganze ~*** semibreve, *Am.* whole note; ***halbe ~*** minim, *Am.* half note; ***nach ~n singen*** sing from music; ***er kennt*** (*or* ***kann***) ***keine ~n*** he can't read music; **3.** *pol.* memorandum; **4.** *no pl.* touch, note; ***e-e besondere*** (***persönliche***) ***~ verleihen*** add a special (personal) touch (*dat.* to); ***das ist s-e persönliche ~*** a) that's his particular way of doing things, b) that's his (personal) trademark

No·ten|aus·tausch ['no:tən-] *m pol.* exchange of notes; **~bank** *f* (-; -en) central bank; **~blatt** *n* (sheet of) music; **~,durch·schnitt** *m* average mark (*Am.* grade)

No·ten·ge·bung ['no:təngeːbʊŋ] *f* (-; *no pl.*) → ***Benotung***

No·ten|heft ['no:tən-] *n* music book; **~li·ni·en** *pl.* ♪ lines; **~pa,pier** *n* manuscript paper; **~pult** *n* music stand; **~schlüs·sel** *m* ♪ clef; **~schrift** *f* musical notation; **~stän·der** *m* music stand; **~sy,stem** *n* **1.** *ped.* marking (*or* grading) system; **2.** ♪ system of notation; **~wert** *m* ♪ (time) value (of a *or* the note)

'Not·fall *m* emergency; ***im*** (***äußersten***) ***~*** in an emergency, if the worst comes to the worst; ***für den ~*** just in case; **~aus·weis** *m* emergency ID

'not·falls *adv.* if need be, if necessary; at a pinch

'not·ge·drun·gen I. *adj.* (en)forced, involuntary; **II.** *adv.* of necessity; ***~ mußte er ...*** he had no choice but to ..., he was forced to ...

'Not|geld *n* emergency money; **~ge·mein·schaft** *f* **1.** emergency action group; **2.** companions *pl.* in distress; ***wir bilden sozusagen e-e ~*** *a.* we're all in the same boat; **~gro·schen** *m* nest egg; (***sich***) ***e-n ~ beiseite legen*** save up (*or* put some money aside) for a rainy day; **~hel·fer** *m* helper in (time of) need

no·tie·ren [no'ti:rən] (h) **I.** *v/t.* make a note of, take down, jot down; ☤ quote (***zu*** *dat.* at); *sport*: book; ♪ notate; **II.** *v/i.* ☤ be quoted (***mit*** *dat.* at); ***... notierte um vier Punkte weniger*** ... was four points down

No'tie·rung *f* (-; -en) **1.** ♪ notation; **2.** ☤ quotation

nö·tig ['nø:tɪç] *adj.* necessary; ***wenn ~*** if necessary, if need be; ***et.*** (***dringend***) ***~ haben*** (badly) need s.th., need s.th. (badly), be in (dire) need of s.th.; ***es ist nicht*** (***unbedingt***) ***~, daß du kommst*** there's no (real) need for you to come, you don't (really) need to (*or* have to) come; ***es ist wohl nicht ~, daß ich euch sage*** I don't suppose there's any need for me to tell you (*or* there's any need for you to be told); ***das war doch wirklich nicht ~*** did you *etc.* have to (do that)?; ***das wäre aber wirklich nicht ~ gewesen*** you really shouldn't have; ***er hielt***

es nicht mal für ~ zu *inf.* he didn't even think (*or* consider) it necessary to *inf.*; *iro.* ***das habe ich nicht ~*** a) I can do very well without that(, thank you), b) I don't have to stand for that; ***hast du das ~?*** do you really have to (do that)?; *iro.* ***du hast es*** (***gerade***) ***~!*** you of all people; ***mit dem ~en Respekt*** with due respect

Nö·ti·ge ['nøːtɪgə] *n* (-n; *no pl.*): ***das ~*** (***tun*** do) whatever is necessary; ***ich werde das ~ tun*** *w.s.* I'll see to it; ***das ~ veranlassen*** make the necessary arrangements; ***das Nötigste*** the essentials; ***nehmt nur das Nötigste mit*** take only what you absolutely need (*or* what you need most)

nö·ti·gen ['nøːtɪgən] *v/t.* (h) a) urge, press, b) force, compel; ***lassen Sie sich nicht ~!*** help yourself!; ***er läßt sich nicht lange ~*** he doesn't need much coaxing (*or* encouragement); ***sich genötigt sehen zu*** *inf.* feel compelled to *inf.*

'nö·ti·gen·falls *adv.* if need be, if necessary

'Nö·ti·gung *f* (-; *no pl.*) constraint, coercion; ⚖ duress

No·tiz [no'tiːts] *f* (-; -en) **1.** note; ***sich ~en machen*** make (*or* take) notes (***über*** *acc.* on); **2.** (*press*) item; **3.** → ***Notierung*** 2; **4.** ***~ nehmen von*** *dat.* take note of; ***keine ~ nehmen von*** ignore, take no notice of; **~block** *m* notepad, *esp. Am.* memo pad; **~buch** *n* notebook

'Not|jah·re *pl.* lean years; **~la·ge** *f* predicament; plight; *w.s.* awkward (*or* difficult) situation; ***wirtschaftliche ~*** economic plight; **~la·ger** *n* makeshift bed, F shakedown

'not·lan·den *v/i.* (sn) make a forced landing, force-land; **'Not·lan·dung** *f* forced (*or* emergency) landing

'not·lei·dend *adj.* needy; **'Not·lei·den·de** *m, f* (-n; -n) needy person; ***die ~n*** the needy (*pl.*)

'Not|lei·ne *f* emergency cord; **~lö·sung** *f* stopgap (solution *or* measure); provisional (*or* temporary) solution; expedient; **~lü·ge** *f* white lie; **~maß·nah·me** *f* emergency (*or* stopgap) measure, expedient; **~na·gel** F *m* stopgap; fill-in; **~ope·ra·ti,on** *f* emergency operation; *a. pl. coll.* emergency surgery; **~op·fer** *n* emergency tax

no·to·risch [no'toːrɪʃ] *adj.* compulsive, habitual, addictive; *a.* notorious *liar, gambler etc.*; ***~er Optimist*** incorrigible optimist

'Not·pro·vi,ant *m* emergency rations *pl.*

'Not·ruf *m* **1.** *teleph.* emergency call; **2.** → **~num·mer** *f* emergency number; **~säu·le** *f* emergency telephone

'Not|rut·sche *f* ✈ emergency chute; **~schlach·tung** *f* forced slaughter; **~si·,gnal** *n* distress signal; **~si·tua·ti,on** *f* emergency (situation); **~sitz** *m* jump seat

'Not·stand *m* **1.** → ***Notlage;*** **2.** *pol.* state of emergency; ***den ~ ausrufen*** declare a state of emergency

'Not·stands|ge·biet *n* **1.** depressed area; **2.** disaster area; **~ge·set·ze** *pl. pol.* emergency legislation *sg.*, emergency powers act *sg.*

'Not·strom·ag·gre,gat *n* emergency generator

'Not·tau·fe *f* baptism in extremis

'not·tau·fen *v/t.* (h) baptize *a child* in extremis

'Not|te·sta,ment *n* emergency will; **~,un·ter·kunft** *f* provisional accommodation (*a. pl.*); emergency shelter *for the homeless*; **~ver·band** *m* ⚕ emergency dressing; **~ver·kauf** *m* distress sale; **~ver·ord·nung** *f pol.* emergency decree; **~was·se·rung** *f* crash-landing (in the sea)

Not·wehr ['noːtveːɐ] *f* (-; *no pl.*): (***aus*** *or* ***in ~*** in) self-defen|ce (*Am.* -se); **~hand·lung** *f* act of self-defen|ce (*Am.* -se); ***es war e-e ~*** he *etc.* acted in self-defen|ce (*Am.* -se)

not·wen·dig ['noːtvɛndɪç] **I.** *adj.* necessary; urgent; essential; indispensable; inevitable; ***unbedingt ~*** absolutely vital; **II.** *adv.* urgently; ***~ brauchen*** *a.* need badly, badly need; **not·wen·di·gen·falls** ['noːtvɛndɪgən'fals] *adv.* if necessary, if need be; **not·wen·di·ger·wei·se** ['noːtvɛndɪgɐ'vaɪzə] *adv.* necessarily, of necessity; inevitably; **'Not·wen·dig·keit** *f* (-; -en) **1.** necessity; requirement; ***e-e absolute ~*** a must; **2.** *no pl.* urgency

'Not·zei·ten *pl.* times (*or* time *sg.*) of need

'Not·zucht *f* (-; *no pl.*) rape; ***~ begehen an*** *dat.* commit rape on; **'not·züch·ti·gen** *v/t.* (h) rape, commit rape on

Nou·gat ['nuːgat] *m, n* (-s; *no pl.*) *sweet paste made from cocoa, sugar and crushed nuts*

No·vel·le [no'vɛlə] *f* (-; -n) **1.** novella; **2.** *parl.* amendment

no·vel·lie·ren [novɛ'liːrən] *v/t.* (h) *parl.* amend; **No·vel'lie·rung** *f* (-; -en) amendment

No·vel·list [novɛ'lɪst] *m* (-en; -en) novella writer

No·vem·ber [no'vɛmbɐ] *m* (-s; -) November; ***im ~*** in November

No·vi·tät [novi'tɛːt] *f* (-; -en) novelty, something new; ☤ new article, F newcomer to the market; ***e-e ~ auf dem Buchmarkt*** (***Plattenmarkt***) a (brand-)new publication (release); ***e-e ~ auf dem Modemarkt*** the latest fashion (F thing)

No·vi·ze [no'viːtsə] *m* (-n; -n), **No·vi·zin** [no'viːtsɪn] *f* (-; -nen) *eccl. and fig.* novice

No·vum ['noːvʊm] *n* (-s; *no pl.*) novelty, something new

NS... [ɛn'ʔɛs] *in cpds. contp.* Nazi; **~-Dik·ta,tur** *f* Nazi dictatorship; **~-Re,gime** *n* Nazi regime; **~-Ver·bre·chen** *n* Nazi crime (*or* atrocity); **~-Ver·bre·cher** *m* Nazi war criminal; **~-Zeit** *f* Nazi era, (period of) Nazi rule

nu [nuː] F *int.* → ***nun***

Nu *m*: ***im ~*** in no time, in a flash, before you knew it

Nu·an·ce ['nỹãːsə] *f* (-; -n) nuance, shade (*a. fig.*); *fig.* trace, tinge; ***um e-e ~ zu süß*** *etc.* a shade too sweet *etc.*; ***die*** (***keine***) ***~n unterscheiden können*** recognize (be unable to distinguish) the subtleties *or* subtle differences; **nu'an·cen·reich** *adj.* rich in nuance, finely nuanced, full of nuances; **Nu'an·cen·reich·tum** *m* (-s; *no pl.*) wealth of nuances; **nu·an·cie·ren** [nỹãː'siːrən] *v/t.* (h) nuance; **nu·an·ciert** [nỹãː'siːɐt] *adj.* subtle; finely (*or* subtly) distinguished; subtly graded *colo(u)rs etc.*; **Nu·an'ciert·heit** *f* (-; *no pl.*) subtlety; subtle distinctions *pl.*; subtle gradations *pl. of colo(u)rs etc.*

nüch·tern ['nʏçtɐn] **I.** *adj.* **1.** sober; ***wieder ~ werden*** sober up; ***vollkommen ~*** F stone cold sober; **2.** ***auf ~en Magen*** on an empty stomach; ***ich war ~*** I hadn't eaten anything; ⚕ ***kommen Sie bitte ~*** please don't eat or drink anything before you come; **3.** functional, austere *building etc.*; sober *clothes*; cold, bare *wall*; **4.** sober *assessment etc.*; *w.s.* rational, down-to-earth; plain, bare *facts etc.*; **II.** *adv. fig.* soberly; *w.s.* matter-of-factly; **~denkend** realistic, sober(-minded); ***~ betrachtet*** seen in a sober light

'Nüch·tern·heit *f* (-; *no pl.*) sobriety; austerity; coldness *etc.*; → ***nüchtern***

Nuckel ['nʊkəl] (*sep.* -k·k-) *m* (-s; -) **1.** teat, *Am.* nipple; **2.** dummy, *Am.* pacifier; **'nuckeln** *v/i.* (h): ***~ an*** *dat.* suck (at)

Nuckel·pin·ne ['nʊkəlpɪnə] (*sep.* -k·k-) F *f* (-; -n) F phut-phut car

Nu·del ['nuːdəl] *f* (-; -n) noodle; *pl.* pasta *sg.*, pastas; F *fig.* ***ulkige ~*** F funny character; **~ge·richt** *n* pasta dish; **~holz** *n* rolling pin

nu·deln ['nuːdəln] *v/t.* (h) stuff, fatten; F ***wie genudelt sein*** F be (absolutely) stuffed

'Nu·del|sa,lat *m* noodle salad; **~sup·pe** *f* noodle soup

Nu·dis·mus [nu'dɪsmʊs] *m* (-; *no pl.*) nudism; **Nu·dist** [nu'dɪst] *m* (-en; -en), **Nu·di·stin** [nu'dɪstɪn] *f* (-; -nen) nudist

nu·kle·ar [nukle'aːɐ] *adj.*, **Nu·kle'ar...** *in cpds.* nuclear

Nu·kle'ar|macht *f pol.* nuclear power; **~me·di,zin** *f* nuclear medicine; **~park** *m* nuclear park; **~stütz·punkt** *m* nuclear base; **~un·fall** *m* nuclear accident; **~waf·fe** *f* nuclear weapon

Nu·kle·in·säu·re [nukle'iːn-] *f* nucleic acid

null [nʊl] *adj.* **1.** nought (*a.* ⩘), *Am. and* 🕮 zero, *after decimal point*: O (*a. teleph.*), *Am. a.* zero; *sport*: nil, *Am.* zero; *tennis*: love; ***~ Grad*** zero degrees; ***~ Fehler*** no (*Am.* zero) mistakes; ***zwei zu ~*** two-nil, *Am.* two-zero; ***um ~ Uhr zehn*** at ten past (*Am.* after) midnight, *formal*: at zero hours ten; **2.** → ***nichtig***

Null *f* (-; -en) **1.** nought, *teleph.* O, *Am.* zero (*a. teleph.*); ***das Thermometer steht auf*** (***über, unter***) ***~*** the thermometer is at (above, below) zero; ***wieviel ~en hat ...?*** how many noughts (*Am.* zeros) are there in ... (*or* has ... got)?; *fig.* ***die Stunde ~*** (the) zero hour; ***in der Stunde ~*** at (the) zero hour; F ***gleich ~*** nil; F ***in ~ Komma nix*** in next to no time; ***bei ~ anfangen*** start from scratch; **2.** *contp.* nobody, F dead loss, complete washout

null·acht'fünf·zehn F *adj.*, **Null·acht·'fünf·zehn...** *in cpds.* run-of-the-mill, nondescript

'Null·di,ät *f* no-calorie (*or* starvation) diet

'Nullei·ter (*sep.* -ll·l-) *m* ⚡ earth (wire), *Am.* ground (wire)

'Null|men·ge *f* ⩘ null set; **~me·ri·di,an** *m* prime (*or* zero) meridian

'Null-'Null F *n* (-; -[s]) F loo, *Am.* F john; *on sign*: WC

'Null·num·mer *f* pilot issue *of a paper etc.*

'Nullö·sung (*sep.* -ll·l-) *f pol.* zero option

'Null|punkt *m* zero; *a.* freezing point; *fig.* rock bottom; ***den ~ erreichen*** drop to zero (*or* freezing point), *fig.* (*a.* ***auf dem ~ ankommen***) reach rock bottom; **~ta·,rif** *m* free admission; free fares; ***zum ~*** free; **~wachs·tum** *n* ☤ zero growth

nu·me·rie·ren [nume'riːrən] *v/t.* (h) number; **Nu·me'rie·rung** *f* (-; -en) numbering

nu·me·risch [nu'meːrɪʃ] *adj.* numerical
Nu·me·rus clau·sus ['nuːmerʊs 'klaʊzʊs] *m univ.* limited (*or* restricted) admission
Nu·mis·ma·tik [numɪs'maːtɪk] *f* (-; *no pl.*) numismatics *pl.*; **Nu·mis·ma·ti·ker** [numɪs'maːtikɐ] *m* (-s; -) numismatist; **nu·mis·ma·tisch** [numɪs'maːtɪʃ] *adj.* numismatic
Num·mer ['nʊmɐ] *f* (-; -n) a) number (*abbr.* No., *pl.* Nos.), b) number, issue *of a paper etc.*, c) ✝ size, d) *thea. etc.* number, routine, (*circus etc.*) act, e) *fig.* cipher; ***sie erreichen ihn unter der ~ ...*** you can ring (*or* call) him on ...; ***laufende ~*** serial number; F *fig.* ***komische ~*** funny character, F weirdo; ***er ist die ~ eins*** he's number one; ***auf ~ Sicher gehen*** play it safe
'**Num·mern|kon·to** *n* numbered (bank) account; **~schei·be** *f teleph.* dial; **~schild** *n mot.* number (*Am.* license) plate; **~ska·la** *f* graduated scale
nun [nuːn] **I.** *adv.* a) now, b) well; ***von ~ an*** a) from now on, *formal*: henceforth, b) from that time (onwards); ***~ denn!*** come on, then; ***~ ja*** well(, you see); ***~ gut!*** all right, *Am.* alright; ***~?*** well?, well, how are things?; ***was ~?*** what now (*or* next)?; ***was sagst du ~?*** what do you say to that (then)?; F ***~ sag bloß ...*** don't say ..., you don't mean to say ...; ***~ erst sah er ...*** only then did he see ...; ***wenn er ~ ...?*** what if he ...?; ***da es ~ einmal so ist*** since (*or* being as) that's the way it is; ***er mag ~ kommen oder nicht*** whether he comes or not; **II.** *obs. cj.*: ***~ (da)*** now that, since
'**nun'mehr** *adv.* now; from now on; ***es läuft ~ zwei Jahre lang*** it's been going on for two years now
Nun·ti·us ['nʊntsi̯ʊs] *m* (-; -ien) nuncio
nur [nuːɐ] **I.** *adv.* a) only; nothing but; just, b) except, c) simply; ***~ einmal*** just once; ***~ sie*** only she, she alone *knew etc.*; ***~ sie wußte*** *etc. a.* she was the only one to know *etc.*; ***~ weil*** just because; ***nicht ~, sondern auch*** not only, but also; ***wenn er ~ käme*** if only he would come; ***~, daß*** except (that), apart from the fact that; ***es ist ~, daß ...*** it's just that ...; ***in ~ zwei Jahren*** in just two (short) years, within two (short) years; ***~ aus Bosheit*** *etc.* out of sheer spite *etc.*; ***ohne auch ~ zu lächeln*** without so much as a smile; ***~ zu!*** go on!, F what are you waiting for?; ***na, warte ~!*** you just wait!; ***verkaufe es ~ ja nicht*** don't sell it whatever you do, just don't sell it; ***wie kam er ~ hierher?*** how on earth did he get here?; ***was will er damit ~ sagen?*** I wonder what he means (*or* is driving at)?; ***das weißt du ~ zu gut*** you know very (*or* perfectly) well; ***warum ist er ~ gegangen?*** what on earth made him go?, why (on earth) did he go?; ***was habe ich ~ getan?*** what (on earth) have I done?; ***wer kann es ~ gewesen sein?*** who (on earth) *or* whoever can it have been?; ***wie hat er es ~ geschafft?*** how (on earth) did he manage that?; ***wo kann sie ~ sein?*** where (on earth) can she be?; ***was hat sie ~?*** I wonder what's up (*or* wrong) with her; ***soviel ich ~ kann*** as much as I possibly can; ***so bald wie ~ möglich*** as soon as you *etc.* possibly can; ***es muß so schnell wie ~ möglich fertig werden*** it's got to be finished in the quickest possible time; *warum hast du ihn gehauen?* - F ***~ so*** I don't know; because I felt like it; F ***~ so*** *usu.* F like mad; ***der Wind hat ~ so gepfiffen*** the wind was howling like mad; ***es hat ~ so gescheppert*** F there was an almighty crash; **II.** *cj.*: ***~ habe ich vergessen ...*** only I forgot ...
nu·scheln ['nʊʃəln] *v/i. and v/t.* (h) mumble; ***(et.) in den Bart ~*** mumble *or* mutter (s.th.) into one's beard
Nuß [nʊs] *f* (-; Nüsse ['nʏsə]) nut; *fig.* ***harte ~*** hard nut to crack, F tough one; F ***du dumme ~!*** F you twit!; F ***j-m e-e auf die ~ geben*** F bop s.o. on the head, F give s.o. a biff on the nose; **~baum** *m* **1.** walnut (tree); **2.** walnut; **2braun** *adj.* hazel(-colo[u]red); **~knacker** *m* (-s; -) nutcracker; **~scha·le** *f* nutshell; **~scho·ko·|la·de** *f* chocolate with nuts, nut chocolate
Nü·ster ['nʏstɐ, 'nyːstɐ] *f* (-; -n) nostril
Nut [nuːt] *f* (-; -en) ⚙ groove; ***~ und Feder*** tongue and groove, *metall.* slot and key
Nut·te ['nʊtə] F *f* (-; -n) *sl.* tart, *Am. sl.* hooker; '**nut·ten·haft, nut·tig** ['nʊtɪç] F *adj. sl.* tarty
nutz [nʊts] *adj.* → **nütze**
Nutz *m*: ***zu j-s ~ und Frommen*** to s.o.'s benefit; **~an·wen·dung** *f* practical use (*or* benefit)
nutz·bar ['nʊtsbaːɐ] *adj.* usable; useful; productive; ***~ machen*** utilize, ✝ *a.* exploit; harness; take advantage of; ***den Boden ~ machen*** cultivate the land; '**Nutz·bar·keit** *f* (-; *no pl.*) usability; usefulness; '**Nutz·bar·ma·chung** *f* (-; *no pl.*) utilization; ✝ *a.* exploitation
'**nutz·brin·gend I.** *adj.* profitable; **II.** *adv.*: ***~ anwenden*** turn to good account
nüt·ze ['nʏtsə] *adj.*: ***zu nichts ~ sein*** be (completely) useless, F be a dead loss; ***es war wenigstens zu etwas ~*** at least it served some purpose; ***zu was soll das ~ sein?*** what's that supposed to achieve?
'**Nutz·ef|fekt** *m* ✝ *etc.* efficiency; *w.s.* (practical) use *or* value; ***der ~ ist null*** it has (*or* is of) no practical value (*or* use) whatsoever
Nut·zen ['nʊtsən] *m* (-s; *no pl.*) a) use, b) profit, gain, c) advantage, *a.* ⚖ benefit; ***praktischer ~*** practical use (*or* value); ***von ~*** useful, helpful; ***zum ~ von*** *dat.* for the benefit of; ***~ bringen*** yield a profit; ***~ ziehen aus*** *dat.* profit (*or* benefit) from, capitalize on; ***davon habe ich wenig ~*** it's not much use to me
'**nut·zen, nüt·zen** ['nʏtsən] (h) **I.** *v/i.* a) be of use, be useful (***zu et.*** for s.th.; ***j-m*** to s.o.), b) be of advantage *or* benefit (to s.o.); ***j-m ~*** *a.* benefit s.o.; ***das nützt (mir) nichts*** that's no use *or* good (to me); ***nützt (dir) das in irgendeiner Weise?*** is that any use (to you)?; ***das nützt wenig*** that doesn't help much, that's not much help; ***was nützt es, daß ...?*** what's the use (*or* good) of (*s.o. or s.th.*) *ger.?*; ***Heulen nützt nichts, es nützt nichts zu heulen*** it's no use crying; **II.** *v/t.* a) use, make use of; put to good use, b) take advantage of, seize *the opportunity*
'**Nut·zen-'Ko·sten-Ana|ly·se** *f* cost-benefit analysis
'**Nutz|fahr·zeug** *n* utility (*or* commercial) vehicle; **~flä·che** *f* usable area (✝ floor space); ⚒ agricultural acreage; **~gar·ten** *m* kitchen garden; **~holz** *n* timber, *Am.* lumber; **~last** *f* payload; **~lei·stung** *f* effective output (*or* power)
nütz·lich ['nʏtslɪç] *adj.* useful; helpful; handy; ***sich ~ machen*** make o.s. useful; ***er (es) könnte dir ~ sein*** he (it) might be of some use to you; ***sich als ~ erweisen*** prove (to be) very useful; '**Nütz·lich·keit** *f* (-; *no pl.*) usefulness
'**Nütz·lich·keits...** *in cpds. usu.* utilitarian; **~den·ken** *n* utilitarianism, utilitarian thinking; **~prin|zip** *n* utility principle; **~stand·punkt** *m* utilitarian point of view
Nütz·ling ['nʏtslɪŋ] *m* (-s; -e) *zo.* beneficial animal
'**nutz·los** *adj.* useless; futile, *pred. a.* no use; ***es ist ~ zu*** *inf.* it's useless (*or* pointless, no use) *ger.*; '**Nutz·lo·sig·keit** *f* (-; *no pl.*) uselessness; futility
Nutz·nie·ßer ['nʊtsniːsɐ] *m* (-s; -) beneficiary; ***die ~ des neuen Gesetzes*** those who (will) reap the benefits of the new law; **Nutz·nie·ßung** ['nʊtsniːsʊŋ] *f* (-; *no pl.*) ⚖ usufruct
'**Nutz|pflan·ze** *f* useful plant; **~tier** *n* domestic (*or* working) animal
Nut·zungs|dau·er ['nʊtsʊŋs-] *f* ✝ useful life; **~grad** *m* level of utilization; **~recht** *n* right of use
Ny·lon ['naɪlɔn] (*TM*) *n* (-s; *no pl.*) nylon; **~strümp·fe** *pl.* nylon stockings, nylons
Nym·phe ['nʏmfə] *f* (-; -n) nymph
nym·pho·man [nʏmfo'maːn] *adj.* nymphomaniac, F nympho
Nym·pho·ma·nie [nʏmfoma'niː] *f* (-; *no pl.*) nymphomania
Nym·pho·ma·nin [nʏmfo'maːnɪn] *f* (-; -nen) nymphomaniac, F nympho

O

O, o [oː] *n* (-; -) O, o; → ***A***
o *int.* oh!; ~ ***ja!*** oh yes!, yes, indeed!; ~ ***nein!*** oh no!, goodness, no!
Oa·se [oˈaːzə] *f* (-; -n) oasis; *fig. a.* haven
ob¹ [ɔp] *cj.* whether, if; ***als*** ~ as if, as though; ***nicht als*** ~ not that; ~ ***... oder nicht*** whether ... or not; (***na***) ***und*** ~***!*** F you bet!; (***ich frage mich,***) ~ ***er wohl kommt?*** I wonder if he'll come; ***so tun, als*** ~ ***...*** pretend to *inf.* (*or* that ...)
ob² *obs. prp.* (*gen.*) on account of
Ob·acht [ˈoːbaxt] *dial. f* (-; *no pl.*) attention; ~***!*** look (*or* watch) out!, careful!; ~ ***geben*** (***auf*** *acc.*) a) pay attention (to), b) be careful (with), c) look (*or* watch) out (for)
Ob·dach [ˈɔpdax] *n* (-[e]s; *no pl.*) shelter
ˈob·dach·los *adj.* homeless; ***Tausende wurden*** ~ thousands were left homeless
ˈOb·dach·lo·se *m, f* (-n; -n) homeless person; ***die*** ~***n*** the homeless (*pl.*); ***Asyl für*** ~ → **ˈOb·dach·lo·sen·asyl** *n*, **ˈOb·dach·lo·sen·heim** *n* shelter for the homeless
ˈOb·dach·lo·sig·keit *f* (-; *no pl.*) homelessness
Ob·duk·ti·on [ɔpdʊkˈtsi̯oːn] *f* (-; -en) ⚕, ⚖ postmortem, autopsy
Ob·duk·tiˈons|be·fund *m* postmortem findings *pl.*, autopsy result; ~**be·richt** *m* postmortem (*or* autopsy) report
ob·du·zie·ren [ɔpduˈtsiːrən] *v/t.* (h) carry out a postmortem (*or* an autopsy) on
ˈO-Bei·ne F *pl.* bandy (*or* bow) legs
O-bei·nig [ˈoːbaɪnɪç] *adj.* bandy-legged, bow-legged
Obe·lisk [obeˈlɪsk] *m* (-en; -en) obelisk
oben [ˈoːbən] *adv.* at the top; on (the) top; upstairs; ~***!*** this side up!; ***siehe*** ~ see above; ~ ***links*** on the top left, in the top left-hand corner; ~ ***am Tisch*** at the head of the table; ***da*** ~ up there; ***hier*** ~ up here; ***nach*** ~ up(wards), upstairs; ***von*** ~ from above, from upstairs; (***mit dem***) ***Gesicht*** (***Bauch*** *etc.*) ***nach*** ~ face (belly *etc.*) up; *fig.* ***von*** ~ ***herab*** condescendingly; ***von*** ~ ***bis unten*** a) from top to bottom, b) from top to toe, from head to foot; ***sich*** ~ ***halten*** stay on top; ***jetzt ist er ganz*** ~ he's made it to the top now; F ***die da*** ~ F the powers that be; ***mir steht es bis hier*** ~ F I'm fed up to the back teeth (with it); ***er kommt von da*** ~ F he's from up north; ~ ***ohne*** topless
ˈoben'an *adv.* at the top; ~**ste·hen** *v/i.* (*irr.*, *sep.*, h, → ***stehen***) be at the top; be in first place
ˈoben|ˈauf *adv.* on (the) top; F *fig.* (***ganz***) ~ ***sein*** a) be on top, b) be on a high, c) F be in the pink; ~**ˈdrauf** *adv.* on top; ~**ˈdrein** *adv.* on top of everything, to top it all; ~**er·wähnt,** ~**ge·nannt** *adj.* above(-mentioned), ... mentioned above; ~**herˈum** *adv.* around the top (*or* chest); ~**ˈhin** *adv.* superficially, perfunctorily; ~ ***bemerken*** remark casually (*or* in passing)
ˈOben-ˈoh·ne|-Ba·de·an·zug *m* topless swimsuit; ~**-Be·die·nung** *f* topless waitress; ~**-Loˌkal** *n* topless bar
ˈoben·ste·hend *adj.* above(-mentioned), ... above
ober [ˈoːbɐ] *adj.* upper; higher; → ***oberst, zehntausend***
Ober [ˈoːbɐ] *m* (-s; -) **1.** waiter; (***Herr***) ~***!*** waiter; **2.** *card game*: queen
ˈOber·arm *m* upper arm; ~**kno·chen** *m* humerus
ˈOber|arzt *m* assistant medical director; ~**auf·sicht** *f*: ***die*** ~ ***haben*** (*or* ***führen***) have overall control (***über*** *acc.* over), be in charge (of); ~**bau** *m* (-[e]s; -bauten) superstructure; ~**bauch** *m* upper abdomen
ˈOber·be·fehl *m* supreme command (***über*** *acc.* of); ***den*** ~ ***haben*** (*or* ***führen***) be commander-in-chief (***über*** *acc.* of); **ˈOber·be·fehls·ha·ber** *m* supreme commander, commander-in-chief, F supremo
ˈOber|be·griff *m* **1.** generic term; **2.** heading; ~**be·klei·dung** *f* outer garments *pl.*; ~**bett** *n* quilt; ~**be·wußt·sein** *n psych.* consciousness, conscious self; ~**bon·ze** F *m* F big boss, big shot; ***die*** ~***n*** *a.* the top brass; ~**bun·des·an·walt** *m* chief public prosecutor; ~**bür·ger·mei·ster** *m* mayor, *in GB*: Lord Mayor; ~**deck** *n* ⚓ upper deck
ˈober·deutsch *adj.*, **ˈOber·deutsch** *n* (-en) *ling.* Upper (*or* Southern) German
ˈober·faul F *adj.* very strange (indeed)
ˈOber·feld·we·bel *m* ⚔ staff sergeant; ✈ flight (*Am.* master) sergeant
ˈOber·flä·che *f* surface; ***an*** (***unter***) ***der*** ~ *a. fig.* on (below) the surface; (***wieder***) ***an die*** ~ ***steigen*** (re)surface
ˈOber·flä·chen|be·hand·lung *f* surface treatment; ~**span·nung** *f phys.* surface tension; ~**strukˌtur** *f a. ling.* surface structure
ober·fläch·lich [ˈoːbɐflɛçlɪç] **I.** *adj.* superficial; shallow; perfunctory, cursory; ~***e Bekanntschaft*** casual (*or* nodding) acquaintance; ***es ist bei ihm sehr*** ~ *a.* it doesn't go very deep with him; **II.** *adv.* superficially, perfunctorily, cursorily; ~ ***betrachtet*** on the surface; ***ich kenne sie nur*** ~ I don't know her very well
ˈOber·fläch·lich·keit *f* (-; -en) superficiality; shallowness
ˈOber·för·ster *m* head forester
ober·gä·rig [ˈoːbɐgɛːrɪç] *adj.* top-fermented
ˈOber|ge·frei·te *m* ⚔ lance corporal, *Am.* private 1st class; ✈ leading aircraftman, *Am.* airman 3rd class; ~**ge·schoß** *n* upper floor (*or* stor[e]y); ~**ge·walt** *f*: (***die*** ~ ***ausüben*** have) supreme power; ~**gren·ze** *f* upper limit; ✝, *statistics etc.*: *a.* ceiling
ober·halb [ˈoːbɐhalp] *prp.* (*gen.*) above
ˈOber|hand *f*: *fig.* ***die*** ~ ***haben*** have the upper hand; ***die*** ~ ***gewinnen*** get (*or* gain) the upper hand (***über*** *acc.* over), ***über j-n:*** *a.* get the better of s.o., F get the jump on s.o.; ~**haupt** *n* head; ~ ***der Familie*** *a.* pater familias; ~**haus** *n* (-es; *no pl.*) *parl.* Upper House, *in GB*: *a.* House of Lords; ~**haut** *f* epidermis; ~**hemd** *n* shirt; ~**herr·schaft** *f* (-; *no pl.*) supremacy; ~**hit·ze** *f* top heat; (***nur***) ***mit*** ~ ***backen*** bake in the top oven; ~**ho·heit** *f* (-; *no pl.*) supremacy; sovereignty
Obe·rin [ˈoːbərɪn] *f* (-; -nen) **1.** *R.C.* Mother Superior; **2.** ⚕ head nursing officer, *Am.* head nurse
ˈOber·inˌspek·tor *m* chief inspector
ˈober·ir·disch *adj.* surface ..., *pred. and adv.* above ground; ⚡ ~***e Leitung*** overhead line
ˈOber|kan·te *f* upper (*or* top) edge; ~**kell·ner** *m* head waiter; ~**kell·ne·rin** *f* head waitress; ~**kie·fer** *m* upper jaw; ~**klas·se** *f* **1.** *ped.* top form, *Am.* senior class; **2.** upper class(es *pl.*); ~**kom·manˌdie·ren·de** *m* (-n; -n) → ***Oberbefehlshaber;*** ~**komˌman·do** *n* → ***Oberbefehl;*** ~**kör·per** *m* upper part of the body; chest; ~**land** *n* (-[e]s; *no pl.*) uplands *pl.*; ***Berner*** ~ Bernese Oberland; ~**lan·des·ge·richt** *n* higher regional court
ober·la·stig [ˈoːbɐlastɪç] *adj.* top-heavy
ˈOber·lauf *m* upper course *of river*
ˈOber·le·der *n* uppers *pl.*
ˈober·leh·rer·haft *adj.* schoolmasterly, schoolmarmish
ˈOber·lei·tung *f* **1.** (senior) management, direction, control; **2.** ⚡ overhead contact line; **ˈOber·lei·tungs·bus** *m* trolley bus
ˈOber·leut·nant *m* ⚔ (*Am.* first) lieutenant; ✈ flying officer, *Am.* first lieutenant
ˈOber·licht *n* **1.** (*pl.* -er) skylight; fanlight; **2.** *no pl.* light (falling in) from above; *phot.* top light(ing)
ˈOber·lip·pe *f* upper lip
ˈOber·lip·pen·bart *m* moustache
ˈOber·motz [-mɔts] F *m* (-es; -e) F top dog
ˈOber|prie·ster *m* hight priest; ~**pri·ma** *obs. f ped.* top form, *in the USA*: senior grade, *in GB*: Upper Sixth; ~**rabˌbi·ner** *m* chief rabbi
ˈober·rhei·nisch *adj.* from the Upper Rhine
Obers [ˈoːbɐs] *Austrian n* (-; *no pl.*) cream
ˈOber·schen·kel *m* thigh; ~**hals** *m* head of the femur; ~**kno·chen** *m* femur, thigh bone
ˈOber·schicht *f* upper class(es *pl.*)

'Ober·schle·si·er *m* Upper Silesian; ~ ***sein*** come from Upper Silesia
'ober·schle·sisch *adj.* Upper Silesian, from Upper Silesia
'Ober|schu·le *f* secondary school, *Am.* high school; **~schwe·ster** *f* senior nursing officer, *Am.* head nurse; **~sei·te** *f* top (*or* upper) surface; **~se·mi,nar** *n* postgraduate seminar
oberst ['o:bɐst] *adj.* uppermost, topmost, highest; top ...; *fig.* chief ..., principal, highest; ***~e Aufsichtsbehörde*** supervisory authority; ***Oberstes Gericht*** High (*Am.* Supreme) Court; *fig.* ***das Oberste zuunterst kehren*** turn everything upside down
Oberst *m* (-en, -s; -en, -e) ⚔ colonel
'Ober|staats·an·walt *m* senior public prosecutor; **~stabs·feld·we·bel** *m* ⚔ warrant officer 1st class (*abbr.* WOI), *Am.* warrant officer; ✈ warrant officer, *Am.* chief master sergeant; **~stim·me** *f* treble
'Oberst·leut·nant *m* ⚔ lieutenant colonel; ✈ *Brit.* wing commander
'Ober|stoff *m* outer fabric; **~stüb·chen** F *fig. n*: ***er ist nicht ganz richtig im ~*** F he's got a screw loose somewhere; **~stu·di·en·di,rek·tor** *m* headmaster, *Am.* principal; **~stu·di·en·rat** *m* senior teacher; **~stu·fe** *f ped.* higher grade, senior class(es *pl.*); **~teil** *n* upper part, top; **~ton** *m* ♪ harmonic, overtone; **~ver·wal·tungs·ge·richt** *n* higher administrative court; **~was·ser** *n lock*: upper water; *mill*: overshot water; *fig.* ~ ***haben*** have the upper hand, be riding high; ~ ***bekommen*** get the upper hand; **~wei·te** *f* bust (measurement)
ob·gleich [ɔp'glaɪç] *cj.* (al)though
Ob·hut ['ɔphu:t] *f* (-; *no pl.*) care; protection; ⚖ custody; ***j-n in s-e ~ nehmen*** take charge of s.o., F take s.o. under one's wing
obig ['o:bɪç] *adj.* above(-mentioned)
Ob·jekt [ɔp'jɛkt] *n* (-[e]s; -e) **1.** object (*a. ling., phls.*); **2.** ⚚ property; **3.** *phot.* subject
ob·jek·tiv [ɔpjɛk'ti:f] *adj.* objective; impartial, *formal*: dispassionate, *a.* unbias(s)ed *judgement etc.*; actual
Ob·jek'tiv *n* (-[e]s; -e [-və]) objective; *phot.* lens; **~deckel** *m phot.* lens cap; **~fas·sung** *f phot.* lens mount
ob·jek·ti·vie·ren [ɔpjɛkti'vi:rən] *v/t.* (h) objectivize; **Ob·jek·ti'vie·rung** *f* (-; -en) objectivization
Ob·jek·ti·vis·mus [ɔpjɛkti'vɪsmʊs] *m* (-; *no pl.*) *phls.* objectivism; **Ob·jek·ti·vist** [ɔpjɛkti'vɪst] *m* (-en; -en) objectivist; **ob·jek·ti·vi·stisch** [ɔpjɛkti'vɪstɪʃ] *adj.* objectivistic(ally *adv.*)
Ob'jekt|satz *m ling.* object clause; **~trä·ger** *m* slide
Ob·la·te [o'bla:tə] *f* (-; -n) wafer
ob·lie·gen ['ɔp-] *v/i.* (oblag, oblegen, h): ***j-m ~*** be incumbent on s.o.; **'Ob·lie·gen·heit** *f* (-; -en) obligation, duty
ob·li·gat [obli'ga:t] *adj.* **1.** obligatory; *iro. a.* inevitable; **2.** ♪ obligato; ***mit ~er Violine*** with violin obligato
Ob·li·ga·ti·on [obliga'tsĭo:n] *f* (-; -en) ⚚ bond, debenture (bond)
ob·li·ga·to·risch [obliga'to:rɪʃ] *adj.* obligatory (*a. iro.*), compulsory
Ob·li·go ['o:bligo] *n* (-s; -s) ⚚ liability
Ob·mann ['ɔp-] *m* (-[e]s; ⸚er, -leute) chairman; shop steward, spokesman

Oboe [o'bo:ə] *f* (-; -n) ♪ oboe; **Obo·ist** [obo'ɪst] *m* (-en; -en) oboist, oboe-player
Obo·lus ['o:bolʊs] *m* (-; -se): ***s-n ~ entrichten*** pay one's mite
Ob·rig·keit ['o:brɪçkaɪt] *obs. f* (-; -en) *the* authorities *pl.*, *iro. the* powers *pl.* that be (*or* on high); government; ***weltliche und kirchliche ~*** temporal and spiritual authorities
'Ob·rig·keits|den·ken *n* blind faith in authority; **~staat** *m* authoritarian state
ob'schon *cj.* (al)though
Ob·ser·vanz [ɔpzɛr'vants] *f* (-; -en) **1.** observance; **2.** leanings *pl.*; kind, type; ***ein ... strengster ~*** a ... of the strictest kind, a hardline *socialist etc.*
Ob·ser·va·to·ri·um [ɔpzɛrva'to:rĭʊm] *n* (-s; -ien) *ast.* observatory
ob·ser·vie·ren [ɔpzɛr'vi:rən] *v/t.* (h) keep *s.o.* under surveillance
ob·skur [ɔps'ku:ɐ] *adj.* obscure; dubious
Ob·sku·ran·tis·mus [ɔpskuran'tɪsmʊs] *m* (-; *no pl.*) obscurantism
Ob·sku·ran·tist [ɔpskuran'tɪst] *m* (-en; -en) obscurantist
Ob·sku·ri·tät [ɔpskuri'tɛ:t] *f* (-; *no pl.*) obscurity; dubiousness, dubious nature (*gen.* of)
Obst [o:pst] *n* (-[e]s; *no pl.*) fruit; **~bau** *m* (-[e]s; *no pl.*) fruit growing; **~bau·er** *m* (-s; -n) fruit grower (*or* farmer); **~baum** *m* fruit tree; **~brannt·wein** *m* fruit schnapps; **~ern·te** *f* fruit harvest; fruit crop; fruit harvest(ing season); **~gar·ten** *m* (fruit) orchard; **~händ·ler** *m* fruiterer, fruit seller
ob·sti·nat [ɔpsti'na:t] *adj.* obstinate
'Obst·ku·chen *m* fruit flan (*Am.* pie)
Obst·ler ['o:pstlɐ] *m* (-s; -) fruit schnapps
'Obst·mes·ser *n* fruit knife
Ob·struk·ti·on [ɔpstrʊk'tsĭo:n] *f* (-; -en) *parl.* obstruction; **Ob·struk·ti'ons·po·li,tik** *f* obstructionism, filibustering
'Obst|saft *m* fruit juice; **~sa,lat** *m* fruit salad; **~tag** *m* fruit-only day; ***ich habe m-n ~*** I'm only eating fruit today; **~tor·te** *f* fruit flan (*Am.* pie); **~wein** *m* fruit wine
ob·szön [ɔp'tsø:n] *adj.* obscene; *fig.* disgusting; **Ob·szö·ni·tät** [ɔptsøni'tɛ:t] *f* (-; -en) obscenity
Obus ['o:bʊs] *m* (-ses; -se) trolley bus
ob'wohl *cj.* (al)though
Och·se ['ɔksə] *m* (-n; -n) ox (*pl.* oxen); bullock; F *fig.* oaf, dope; ***dastehen wie der ~ vorm Berg*** (*or* ***Scheunentor***) be at a complete loss (as to what to do); *fig.* ***den ~en hinter den Pflug spannen*** put the cart before the horse
och·sen ['ɔksən] (h) F **I.** *v/i.* F cram, swot; **II.** *v/t.* F swot up (on), bone (*or* mug) up on
'Och·sen|au·ge *n* **1.** bull's-eye (window); **2.** ✿ ox-eye (daisy); **3.** *dial. gastr.* fried egg (sunny side up *Am.*); **~fleisch** *n* beef; **~frosch** *m* bullfrog; **~ge·spann** *n* team of oxen; **~kar·ren** *m* bullock cart
'Och·sen·schwanz·sup·pe *f* oxtail soup
'Och·sen·tour F *f* **1.** F hard graft; **2.** F slow (uphill) grind; slow, hard road to the top
Ocker ['ɔkɐ] (*sep.* -k·k-) *m*, *n* (-s; *no pl.*) ochre (*Am.* ocher); **'ocker·far·ben, 'ocker·gelb** *adj.* (yellow) ochre (*Am.* ocher)
Ode ['o:də] *f* (-; -n) ode (***an*** *acc.* to)
öde ['ø:də] *adj.* **1.** deserted, desolate; **2.** dull, tedious; **3.** bleak, dreary; **4.** barren;

Öde *f* (-; *no pl.*) **1.** waste(land); **2.** *fig.* dreariness; tedium
Ödem [ø'de:m] *n* (-s; -e) ⚕ (o)edema
oder ['o:dɐ] *cj.* or; → ***entweder***; ~ (***aber***) otherwise, (or) else, *threateningly*: or else!; ~ ***auch*** or rather; ~ ***so*** or something like that, or something along those lines; ***du bleibst doch, ~?*** you 'are staying, aren't you?; ***gehen wir ins Bett, ~?*** let's go to bed, shall we?
ödi·pal [ødi'pa:l] *adj. psych.* oedipal
Ödi·pus·kom,plex ['ø:dipʊs-] *m psych.* Oedipus complex
Odi·um ['o:dĭʊm] *n* (-s; *no pl.*) odium
Öd·land ['ø:t-] *n* wasteland
Odys·see [odʏ'se:] *fig. f* (-; -n) odyssey
Oeu·vre ['ø:vrə] *n* (-; -s) works *pl.*, life's work; ***das Beethovensche ~*** Beethoven's works
Ofen ['o:fən] *m* (-s; Öfen ['ø:fən]) stove; oven; ⚙ kiln; furnace; *mot. sl.* ***heißer ~*** F hot rod; *fig.* ***hinterm ~ hocken*** be a stay-at-home; F ***jetzt ist der ~ aus!*** F that's it, it's 'curtains (for us *etc.*); → ***Hund*** 2; **~bank** *f* (-; ⸚e) bench by the stove
'ofen|fer·tig *adj. gastr.* oven-ready; **~frisch** *adj.* oven-fresh, hot from the oven; **~ge·trock·net** *adj.* ⚙ kiln-dried
'Ofen|hei·zung *f* stove heating; **~klap·pe** *f* damper; **~plat·te** *f* hot plate; **~rohr** *n* stovepipe; **~röh·re** *f* oven; **~schirm** *m* fire screen; **~set·zer** *m* stove fitter; **~trock·nung** *f* ⚙ kiln-drying; **~tür** *f* oven door
off [ɔf] *adj. TV etc.* out of vision (*abbr.* OOV), off(-screen); **Off** *n* (-; *no pl.*): ***im ~*** → ***off***; ***aus dem ~ sprechen*** *etc.* speak *etc.* off-screen
of·fen ['ɔfən] **I.** *adj.* a) open; loose *hair*; vacant *post*, b) open, sincere, candid; frank; open(-minded); ~ ***für*** *acc.* open to; ***~e Abstimmung*** open vote; ***~e Anspielung*** broad allusion (***auf*** *acc.* to); ***~er Blick*** open (*or* honest) face; ***~er Brief*** open letter; ***ein ~es Geheimnis*** an open (*or* everybody's) secret; ***~es Gelände*** (wide) open country; ***~es Hemd*** open-necked shirt; ***~e Rechnung*** outstanding account; ***mit ~en Haaren*** with one's hair (hanging) loose; ***auf ~er See*** on the open sea; ***auf ~er Straße*** in the middle of the street; ***auf ~er Strecke*** on the open road, 🚆 between stations; ***bei ~em Fenster*** with the window open; ~ ***und ehrlich*** open and above-board; ***mit ~em Mund dastehen*** stand gaping; ***es ist noch alles ~*** nothing has been decided yet, it's all still up in the air; ***ich will ganz ~ mit dir sein*** I'll be quite frank with you; **II.** *adv.* openly *etc.*; ~ ***zugeben*** *a.* admit (quite) frankly; ~ ***reden*** talk openly (*or* freely); ~ ***s-e Meinung sagen*** speak one's mind (quite openly), ***j-m***: be quite (*or* perfectly) open *or* frank with s.o.; ~ ***gestanden*** frankly speaking, quite frankly; ~ ***zur Schau stellen*** make no secret of, make a public exhibition of; → ***offenlassen*** *etc.*
'of·fen·bar I. *adj.* obvious, evident; clear; blatant *lie etc.*; apparent; **II.** *adv.* evidently, it seems ..., it would seem ...
of·fen·ba·ren [ɔfən'ba:rən] (h) **I.** *v/t.* reveal, disclose, unveil *secret etc.*; show, manifest (*all dat.* to); **II.** *v/refl.*: ***sich ~*** reveal o.s., open one's heart to *s.o.*
Of·fen'ba·rung *f* (-; -en) **1.** revelation,

eye-opener; **2.** *bibl.* **die ~ (Johannis)** Revelation, the Book of Revelations

Of·fen'ba·rungs·eid *m* **1.** ⚖ oath of manifestation (*or* disclosure); ***den ~ leisten*** swear an oath of manifestation (*or* disclosure); **2.** *fig. political etc.* bankruptcy

'of·fen|blei·ben *v/i.* (*irr., sep.*, sn, → ***bleiben***) **1.** stay open; **2.** *fig.* remain (*or* be left) open *or* unanswered; **~hal·ten** *v/t.* (*irr., sep.*, h, → ***halten***) **1.** hold open *door etc.*; keep open *store etc., a. one's eyes*; **2.** *fig.* keep (*or* leave) open, reserve

'Of·fen·heit *f* (-; *no pl.*) openness, frankness; honesty

'of·fen·her·zig *adj.* open, frank, outspoken; sincere, candid; F *fig.* F (rather) revealing *dress etc.*; **'Of·fen·her·zig·keit** *f* (-; *no pl.*) openness, frankness; sincerity

'of·fen·kun·dig *adj.* obvious, evident, clear, manifest; patent, blatant *lie*; ***es war ein ~er Irrtum*** *etc.* it was obviously (*or* clearly) a mistake *etc.*

'of·fen·las·sen *v/t.* (*irr., sep.*, h, → ***lassen***) *a. fig.* leave open; *fig.* ***die Möglichkeit ~*** not to discount the possibility (*gen.* of *s.th.*)

'of·fen·le·gen *fig. v/t.* (*sep.*, h) disclose

'of·fen·sicht·lich I. *adj.* obvious; visible, clear, plain; **II.** *adv.* obviously; **'Of·fen·sicht·lich·keit** *f* (-; *no pl.*) obviousness

of·fen·siv [ɔfɛn'ziːf] *adj.* offensive

Of·fen·si·ve [ɔfɛn'ziːvə] *f* (-; -n) offensive; ***die ~ ergreifen*** take the offensive

Of·fen'siv|krieg *m* offensive war(fare); **~spiel** *n sport*: offensive play (*or* game); **~spie·ler** *m* attacker; **~waf·fe** *f* offensive weapon

'of·fen·ste·hen *v/i.* (*irr., sep.*, h, → ***stehen***) **1.** be (*door: a.* stand) open; **2.** *fig. account etc.*: be outstanding, remain unsettled; **3.** *fig.* be open to *s.o.*; ***es steht ihm offen zu*** *inf.* he's free to *inf.*

'of·fen·ste·hend *adj.* **1.** open *door etc.*; ***mit ~em Mund*** open-mouthed; **2.** *fig.* outstanding, unsettled *account etc.*

öf·fent·lich ['œfəntlıç] **I.** *adj.* public; ***~e Anleihen*** government securities; ***~er Aufruhr*** civil disturbance; ***~e Bekanntmachung*** public announcement; ***~e Betriebe*** public utilities; ***~er Dienst*** public sector; ***Angestellter des ~en Dienstes*** public(-sector) employee; ***~e Hand*** *the* authorities; ***die ~e Meinung*** public opinion; ***~es Recht*** public law; ***in ~er Sitzung*** in open session; ***~e Versteigerung*** sale by public auction; **II.** *adv.* publicly, in public; ⚖ in open session; ***~ bekanntmachen*** make public, publicize; ***et. ~ machen*** bring s.th. to the public's attention

'Öf·fent·lich·keit *f* (-; *no pl.*) a) (general) public, b) public opinion, c) public nature (*gen.* of), publicity; ***die breite ~*** the public (*or* people) at large; ***in aller ~*** in public, quite openly; ***an die ~ treten*** appear before the public, ***mit*** *dat.*: bring *s.th.* before the public, come out with *s.th.*; ***zum ersten Mal an die ~ treten*** make one's first public appearance; ***an die ~ bringen*** bring before the public, bring (out) into the open; ***der ~ übergeben*** a) inaugurate, b) bring out, publish; ***an die ~ dringen*** leak out; → ***Ausschluß***

'Öf·fent·lich·keits|ar·beit *f* (-; *no pl.*) public relations *pl.*; *police etc.*: community relations *pl.*; **~scheu** *adj.* publicity-shy; ***er ist ~*** *a.* he doesn't like (any kind of) publicity

'öf·fent·lich-'recht·lich *adj.* under public law

of·fe·rie·ren [ɔfe'riːrən] *v/t.* (h) offer

Of·fer·te [ɔ'fɛrtə] *f* (-; -n) ☤ offer, tender, bid

Of·fi·zi·al·ver·tei·di·ger [ɔfi'tsĭaːl-] *m* ⚖ assigned counsel

of·fi·zi·ell [ɔfi'tsĭɛl] **I.** *adj.* official; formal; accepted *text etc.*; ***von ~er Seite ist bekanntgegeben worden*** it has been officially announced; **II.** *adv.* officially; ***~ bekanntgeben, daß*** make an official statement (to the effect) that

Of·fi·zier [ɔfi'tsiːɐ] *m* (-s; -e [-rə]) (commissioned) officer; ***hoher ~*** high-ranking officer

Of·fi'ziers|an·wär·ter *m* officer cadet; **~ka͵si·no** *n* officers' mess; **~lauf·bahn** *f* career as an officer, officer's career; **~rang** *m* rank of an officer, officer's rank; **~schu·le** *f* officer candidate school (*abbr.* OCS)

of·fi·zi·ös [ɔfi'tsĭøːs] *adj.* semi-official

'Off-Kom·men͵tar *m TV etc.* voice-over

öff·nen ['œfnən] *v/t. and v/i.* (h) (*a. v/refl.*: ***sich ~***) open; ***niemand öffnete*** nobody answered (*or* came to) the door; ***vor dem ~ schütteln*** shake before use; **Öff·ner** ['œfnɐ] *m* (-s; -) opener; **Öff·nung** ['œfnʊŋ] *f* (-; -en) opening (*a. fig.* ***nach*** *dat.* to *the East etc.*); hole; gap; *anat.* orifice; ⚙ vent; mouth (*gen.* of *a cave etc.*), entrance (to)

'Öff·nungs·zei·ten *pl.* opening (☤ business, banking) hours

Off·set·druck ['ɔfsɛt-] *m* offset (printing)

'Off|-Spre·cher *m TV etc.* voice-over; **~-Stim·me** *f* voice off

oft [ɔft] *adv.* often, frequently; ***schon ~*** *a.* many times, *lit.* many a time; ***ziemlich ~*** quite often, quite a lot; ***das ist mir schon so ~ passiert*** *a.* I don't know how many times that's happened to me

öf·ter ['œftɐ] *adv.* **1.** more often; ***je ~ ich ihn sehe, desto mehr ...*** the more I see of him, the more ...; **2.** (*a.* ***des ~en***, F ***~s***) repeatedly; quite often, quite a lot

oft·ma·lig ['ɔftmaːlıç] *adj.* frequent; repeated; **oft·mals** ['ɔftmaːls] *adv.* often, frequently, many times; repeatedly

oh [oː] *int.* oh!; → ***o***

Oheim ['oːhaım] *obs. m* (-[e]s; -e) uncle

Ohm [oːm] *n phys.* ohm; **ohmsch** [oːmʃ] *adj.* ohmic; ***das Ohmsche Gesetz*** Ohm's law; **'Ohm·zahl** *f* ohmage

oh·ne ['oːnə] **I.** *prp.* (*acc.*) without, F minus; not counting, excluding; ***~ Zweifel*** undoubtedly; ***~ seine Schuld*** through no fault of his (own); ***~ mein Wissen*** without my knowledge, unknown (*or* unbeknown[st]) to me; ***~ mich!*** (you can) count me out!, not me!; ***~ weiteres*** just like that, without any (great) effort, F no problem; ***das machen wir ~ weiteres*** we'll manage that easily enough (F no problem); ***das kannst du ~ weiteres akzeptieren*** you needn't worry (*or* hesitate) about accepting that; ***das geht nicht so ~ weiteres*** that's not so easy; F ***das ist gar nicht so ~*** a) F it's not bad, you know, b) there's more to it than meets the eye, it's harder *etc.* than you think; → ***oben***; **II.** *cj.*: ***~ daß***, ***~ zu*** *inf.* without *ger.*; ***~ auch nur zu lächeln*** without so much as a smile; ***~ daß ich ihn gesehen hatte*** without (my) having seen him

oh·ne'dem, oh·ne'dies *obs. adv.* → ***ohnehin***

oh·ne'glei·chen *adj.* unequal(l)ed, unparalleled, *formal*: peerless; *contp.* unheard-of; ***e-e Frechheit ~*** the height of impudence

oh·ne'hin *adv.* anyhow, anyway

Ohn·macht ['oːnmaxt] *f* (-; -en) **1.** ⚕ faint(ing fit); ***in ~ fallen*** (*or* ***sinken***) faint, pass out; *fig.* ***ich bin fast in ~ gefallen*** I nearly fainted (*or* keeled over); **2.** *no pl.* (sheer) helplessness, powerlessness, impotence (***gegenüber*** *dat.* in the face of)

ohn·mäch·tig ['oːnmɛçtıç] *adj.* **1.** ⚕ unconscious; ***~ werden*** faint, pass out; ***er ist ~*** he's fainted (*or* passed out); **2.** (utterly) helpless, powerless (***gegenüber*** *dat.* in the face of)

'Ohn·machts·an·fall *m* fainting fit

Ohr [oːɐ] *n* (-[e]s; Ohren ['oːrən]) ear (*a. fig.*); ***ich habe es noch im ~*** I can still hear it, it's still ringing in my ears; *fig.* ***die ~en aufmachen*** listen carefully; ***die ~en spitzen, lange ~en bekommen*** prick up one's ears; ***ganz ~ sein*** be all ears; ***ein ~ haben für*** *acc.* have an ear for; ***ein feines ~ haben für*** *acc.* have a good ear for; ***ein offenes ~ für j-n haben*** be prepared to listen to s.o.; ***ein offenes ~ finden*** find s.o. who will listen (to one); ***j-m in den ~en liegen*** pester s.o.; F ***j-m eins hinter die ~n hauen*** F give s.o. a clip round the ears; F ***j-n übers ~ hauen*** F rip s.o. off; F ***sich die Nacht um die ~en schlagen*** not to get a wink of sleep all night; F ***sich aufs ~ legen*** F get some shuteye; F ***schreib dir das hinter die ~en!*** and don't you forget it!; F ***bis über die*** (*or* ***beide***) ***~en in Arbeit*** (***Schulden*** *etc.*) ***stecken*** be up to one's ears (*or* eyeballs) in work (debt *etc.*); F ***bis über die*** (*or* ***beide***) ***~en verliebt*** head over heels in love; F ***viel um die ~en haben*** have an awful lot on one's plate; ***mir klingen die ~en*** my ears are burning; F ***halt die ~en steif!*** chin up!, *Brit. a.* F keep your pecker up!; ***mir kam zu ~en, daß*** I happened to hear that; ***was kommt mir da zu ~en?*** what's this I hear?; ***ich traute m-n ~en nicht*** I couldn't believe my ears; ***es ist nichts für fremde ~en*** it's not for public consumption; ***er hört nur mit halbem ~ hin*** he's only half listening; F ***wasch dir mal die ~en!*** when was the last time you washed your ears out?; ***zum einen ~ hinein, zum andern hinaus*** in one ear, out the other; → ***faustdick*** I, ***taub*** 1, ***trocken*** I

Öhr [øːɐ] *n* (-[e]s; -e ['øːrə]) eye

'oh·ren·be·täu·bend *adj.* deafening, earsplitting

'Oh·ren|klap·pe *f* earflap; **~sau·sen** *n* buzzing (*or* ringing) in one's ear(s); **~schmalz** *n* ear wax; **~schmaus** *m* (-es; *no pl.*) treat for the ears; **~schmer·zen** *pl.* earache *sg.*; **~schüt·zer** *pl.* earmuffs; **~ses·sel** *m* wing chair; **~spe·zia͵list** *m* ear specialist; **~spie·gel** *m* ⚕ auriscope; **~zeu·ge** *m* earwitness

Ohr·fei·ge ['oːɐfaıgə] *f* (-; -n) box (F clip) round the ears; **ohr·fei·gen** ['oːɐfaıgən] *v/t.* (h): ***j-n ~*** box s.o.'s ears; F ***ich könnte mich ~!*** I could kick myself

'Ohr·fei·gen·ge·sicht F *n* dull, brutish face

'**Ohr|hö·rer** *m* earphone; **~ge·hän·ge** *n* pendant (F drop) earrings *pl.*; **~klipp** *m* (ear-)clip; **~läpp·chen** [-lɛpçən] *n* (-s; -) earlobe; **~mu·schel** *f* (outer) ear

Oh·ro·pax [o:ro'paks] (*TM*) *n* (-; *no pl.*) ear plugs *pl.*

'**Ohr|ring** *m* earring; **~spei·chel·drü·se** *f* parotid gland; **~stecker** *m* stud; **~wurm** *m* **1.** *zo.* earwig; **2.** F *fig.* catchy tune

okay [o'ke:] **I.** *int.* OK, okay, F okey-doke(y); **II.** ≈ *n* (-[s]; -s) OK, okay; ***sein ~ geben*** give one's *or* the OK (*or* okay), give the go-ahead

ok·kult [ɔ'kʊlt] *adj.* occult; **Ok·kul·te** [ɔ'kʊltə] *n* (-n; *no pl.*): ***das ~*** the occult; **Ok·kul·tis·mus** [ɔkʊl'tɪsmʊs] *m* (-; *no pl.*) occultism; **ok·kul·ti·stisch** [ɔkʊl'tɪstɪʃ] *adj.* occult ...

Ok·ku·pa·ti·on [ɔkupa'tsi̯o:n] *f* (-; -en) occupation; **ok·ku·pie·ren** [ɔku'pi:rən] *v/t.* (h) occupy

Öko|bau·er ['ø:ko-] *m* (-n; -n) organic farmer; **~be·we·gung** *f* ecological movement; **~la·den** *m* health-food shop

Öko·lo·ge [øko'lo:gə] *m* (-n; -n) ecologist; **Öko·lo·gie** [økolo'gi:] *f* (-; *no pl.*) ecology; **öko·lo·gisch** [øko'lo:gɪʃ] *adj.* ecological; → ***Gleichgewicht***

Öko·nom [øko'no:m] *m* (-en; -en) **1.** economist; economics student; **2.** farmer; **Öko·no·mie** [økono'mi:] *f* (-; -n) **1.** economy; **2.** *no pl.* economics *pl.*; **öko·no·misch** [øko'no:mɪʃ] *adj.* **1.** economic; **2.** economical

Öko·sy͵stem ['ø:ko-] *n* ecosystem

Öko·top [øko'to:p] *n* (-s; -e) ecotope

Ok·ta·eder [ɔkta'ʔe:dɐ] *m* (-s; -) octahedron

Ok·tan [ɔk'ta:n] *n* (-s; -e) octane; **~zahl** *f mot.* octane number (*or* rating)

Ok·tav [ɔk'ta:f] *n* (-s; *no pl.*) **1.** ♪ octave; **2.** *typ.* octavo; **Ok·ta·ve** [ɔk'ta:və] *f* (-; -n) ♪ octave

Ok·tett [ɔk'tɛt] *n* (-[e]s; -e) ♪ octet

Ok·to·ber [ɔk'to:bɐ] *m* (-s; -) October; ***im ~*** in October

Oku·lar [oku'la:ɐ] *n* (-s; -e [-rə]) *opt.* eyepiece

oku·lie·ren [oku'li:rən] *v/t.* (h) ✓ graft

Öku·me·ne [øku'me:nə] *f* (-; *no pl.*) *eccl.* ecumenicalism; **öku·me·nisch** [øku'me:nɪʃ] *adj.* ecumenical

Ok·zi·dent ['ɔktsidɛnt] *m* (-s; *no pl.*) Occident, West; **ok·zi·den·tal** [ɔktsidɛn'ta:l] *adj.* occidental, western

Öl [ø:l] *n* (-[e]s; -e) oil; ***auf ~ stoßen*** strike oil; ***in ~ malen*** paint in oils; *fig.* ***~ ins Feuer gießen*** add fuel to the fire (*or* flames); ***~ auf die Wogen gießen*** pour oil on troubled waters; **~bad** *n* ⚙ oil bath; **~baum** *m* ⚘ olive (tree); **~berg** *m* (-[e]s; *no pl.*) *bibl.* Mount of Olives; **~bild** *n* oil painting; **~boh·rung** *f* oil drilling

Ol·die ['o:ldi] F *m* (-s; -s) **1.** F oldie; **2.** F old-timer

'**Öl·druck** *m* **1.** *art*: oleograph; **2.** ⚙ oil pressure; **~an·zei·ger** *m* oil-pressure ga(u)ge

Old·ti·mer ['o:ltaɪmɐ] *m* (-s; -) **1.** *mot.* vintage (*before 1905*: veteran) car; **2.** F old-timer

Ole·an·der [ole'andɐ] *m* (-s; -) ⚘ oleander

'**Öl·em͵bar·go** *n* oil embargo

ölen ['ø:lən] *v/t.* (h) oil, ⚙ *a.* lubricate; anoint; ***wie geölt*** like clockwork; → ***Blitz***

'**Öl|far·be** *f* oil (paint); **~feld** *n* oilfield; **~feue·rung** *f* oil firing; **~för·der·land** *n* oil-producing country; **~för·de·rung** *f* oil production; **~ge·mäl·de** *n* oil painting; **~ge·win·nung** *f* oil production; **~göt·ze** F *m*: ***wie ein ~*** like a stuffed dummy

'**öl·hal·tig** [-haltɪç] *adj.* **1.** oily; ***~ sein*** *a.* contain oil; **2.** ⚘ oleaginous

'**Öl|han·del** *m* oil trade; **~haut** *f textil.* oilskin; **~hei·zung** *f* oil heating

ölig ['ø:lɪç] *adj.* oily (*a. fig.*); rich *wine*; *fig.* ***~e Stimme*** soapy voice

Oli·garch [oli'garç] *m* (-en; -en) oligarch; **Oli·gar·chie** [oligar'çi:] *f* (-; *no pl.*) oligarchy; **oli·gar·chisch** [oli'garçɪʃ] *adj.* oligarchic

Olim ['o:lɪm] *without art.*: ***seit ~s Zeiten*** from (*or* since) the year dot

'**Öl·in·du͵strie** *f* oil (*or* petroleum) industry

oliv [o'li:f] *adj.* olive

Oli·ve [o'li:və] *f* (-; -n) ⚘ olive

Oli·ven|baum *m* olive (tree); **~gar·ten** *m*, **~hain** *m* olive grove; **~öl** *n* olive oil

oliv·far·ben *adj.* olive(-colo[u]red)

oliv·grün *adj.* olive(-green)

'**Öl|jacke** *f* oilskin; **~ka͵ni·ster** *m* oil canister; **~känn·chen** *n*, **~kan·ne** *f* oil can; **~ka·ta͵stro·phe** *f* oil spill; **~kon͵zern** *m* oil company; **~kri·se** *f* oil crisis; **~lam·pe** *f* oil lamp

Ol·le ['ɔlə] F *m*, *f* (-n; -n): ***der ~*** F the (*sl.* me) old man; ***die ~*** F the (*sl.* me) old woman, *a.* F the missus

'**Öl|lei·tung** *f* oil pipeline; **~ma·le͵rei** *f* oil painting; **~meß·stab** *m* dipstick; **~mul·ti** *m* multinational oil corporation; **~ofen** *m* oil stove; **~pa͵pier** *n* oil paper; **~pest** *f* oil pollution; **~quel·le** *f* oil well; **~raf·fi·ne͵rie** *f* oil refinery; **~rück·stän·de** *pl.* oil residues; **~sar͵di·nen** *pl.* (tinned, *Am.* canned) sardines; *w.s.* tin *or* can *sg.* of sardines; **~scheich** *m* oil sheik(h); **~schwem·me** *f* oil glut

'**Öl·stand** *m mot.* oil level; **~an·zei·ger** *m* oil ga(u)ge

'**Öl|tank** *m* oil tank; **~tan·ker** *m* oil tanker; **~tep·pich** *m* oil slick

Ölung ['ø:lʊŋ] *f*: *eccl.* ***die Letzte ~*** the last rites

'**Öl|vor·kom·men** *n* oil field(s *pl.*); oil resources *pl.*; **~wan·ne** *f mot.* sump; **~wech·sel** *m mot.* oil change; **~wirt·schaft** *f* oil industry

Olym·pia·aus·wahl [o'lʏmpi̯a-] *f* Olympic team

Olym·pia·de [olʏm'pi̯a:də] *f* (-; -n) **1.** Olympic Games *pl.*, Olympics *pl.*; **2.** olympiad

Olym·pia|dorf [o'lʏmpi̯a-] *n* Olympic village; **~ge·län·de** *n* Olympic complex (*or* park); **~mann·schaft** *f* Olympic team; **~sie·ger** *m* Olympic champion; **~sta·di·on** *n* Olympic stadium; **~teil·neh·mer** *m* Olympic athlete (*or* competitor)

Olym·pio·ni·ke [olʏmpi̯o'ni:kə] *m* (-n; -n) a) Olympic athlete, b) Olympic champion

olym·pisch [o'lʏmpɪʃ] *adj.* *sport*: Olympic; ***≈e Spiele*** → ***Olympiade*** 1; ***~es Gold (Silber) ge·winnen***: win a gold (silver) medal at the Olympics; ***der ~e Gedanke*** the Olympic ideal

'**Öl|zen͵tral·hei·zung** *f* oil-fired central heating; **~zeug** *n* oilskin, oils *pl.*; **~zu·fuhr** *f* oil feed; **~zweig** *m* ⚘ olive branch

Oma ['o:ma] F *f* (-; -s) grandma, granny; Grandma, Granny

Om·buds·mann ['ɔmbʊtsman] *m* (-[e]s; ⸚er, -leute) **1.** *parl.* ombudsman; **2.** representative, spokesman

Ome·lett [ɔm(ə)'lɛt] *n* (-[e]s; -e), **Ome·lette** [ɔm(ə)'lɛt] *f* (-; -n) omelette

Omen ['o:mən] *n* (-s; -) omen; ***das ist ein gutes (schlechtes) ~*** *a.* that augurs well (badly)

Omi ['o:mi] F *f* (-; -s) grandma, granny; Grandma, Granny

omi·nös [omi'nø:s] *adj.* ominous

Om·ni·bus ['ɔmnibʊs] *m* (-ses; -se) bus, coach; **~...** *in cpds.* → ***Bus...***

Ona·nie [ona'ni:] *f* (-; *no pl.*) masturbation; **ona·nie·ren** [ona'ni:rən] *v/i.* (h) masturbate

On·dit [õ'di:] *n* (-[s]; -s): ***e-m ~ zufolge ...*** rumo(u)r has it that ...

on·du·lie·ren [ɔndu'li:rən] *v/t.* (h) crimp

On·kel ['ɔŋkəl] *m* (-s; -) a) uncle, b) (nice) man; ***der ~ Doktor*** the (nice) doctor; F *fig.* ***der dicke (or große) ~*** one's big toe; ***über den großen ~ gehen*** (F ***latschen***) be pigeon-toed; '**on·kel·haft** *adj.* avuncular

On-Stim·me ['ɔn-] *f TV etc.* voice on

On·to·lo·gie [ɔntolo'gi:] *f* (-; *no pl.*) ontology; **on·to·lo·gisch** [ɔnto'lo:gɪʃ] *adj.* ontological

Onyx ['o:nʏks] *m* (-[es]; -e) onyx

OP [o'pe:] *m* (-s; -s) → ***Operationssaal***

Opa ['o:pa] F *m* (-s; -s) grandpa, grandad; Grandpa, Grandad

Opal [o'pa:l] *m* (-s; -e) *min.* opal

opa·li·sie·rend [opali'zi:rənt] *adj.* opalescent

Op-art ['ɔpʔa:ɐt] *f* (-; *no pl.*) op art

OPEC-Land ['o:pɛk-] *n* OPEC country (*or* nation)

Open-end-Dis·kus·si͵on ['oʊpn 'ɛnd-] *f* open-ended discussion

Oper ['o:pɐ] *f* (-; -n) (*a.* ***die ~***) opera; opera (house); ***komische ~*** comic opera; ***in die ~ gehen*** go to the opera

ope·ra·bel [opə'ra:bəl] *adj.* ⚕ operable

Ope·ra·teur [opəra'tø:ɐ] *m* (-s; -e [-rə]) ⚕ surgeon

Ope·ra·ti·on [opəra'tsi̯o:n] *f* (-; -en) **1.** ⚕ operation; ***e-e ~*** *a.* surgery (*a. pl. coll.*); F *fig.* ***~ gelungen, Patient tot*** it was a perfectly organized disaster (F cock-up); **2.** ⚔ operation

ope·ra·ti'ons·fä·hig *adj.* operable

Ope·ra·ti'ons|fol·gen *pl.* postoperative complications; ***an den ~ sterben*** die after the operation; **~ko·sten** *pl.* cost *sg.* of an (*or* the) operation; **~mas·ke** *f* surgeon's mask; **~nar·be** *f* scar from an (*or* the) operation, 📖 postoperative scar; **~saal** *m* ⚕ operating theatre (*Am.* room); **~schwe·ster** *f* theatre nurse, *Am.* operating room nurse; **~team** *n* surgical team; **~tisch** *m* operating table

ope·ra·tiv [opəra'ti:f] **I.** *adj.* **1.** ⚕ operative, surgical; ***ein ~er Eingriff*** surgery; **2.** ⚔ operational, strategic; **II.** *adv.*: ***et. ~ entfernen*** remove s.th. surgically (*or* by surgery)

Ope·ra·tor [opə'ra:to:ɐ] *m* (-s; -en [-ra'to:rən]) *computer*: operator

Ope·ret·te [opə'rɛtə] *f* (-; -n) operetta; **ope'ret·ten·haft** *contp. adj.* operatic(ally *adv.*)

ope·rie·ren [opə'ri:rən] (h) **I.** *v/t.* **1.** ⚕ ***j-n ~*** operate on s.o.; ***am Magen operiert werden*** have a stomach operation; ***sich ~ lassen*** have an operation; **II.** *v/i.* **2.** ⚔ operate; **3.** *fig.* proceed; ***vorsichtig ~***

proceed with caution, handle matters carefully

'**Opern|arie** *f* operatic aria; **~ball** *m* opera ball; **~fan** *m* opera buff; **~film** *m* filmed opera, film of an opera; **~freund** *m* opera fan, opera-goer; **~glas** *n*: (**ein ~** a pair of) opera glasses *pl.*

'**opern•haft** *adj.* operatic(ally *adv.*) (*a. fig. contp.*)

'**Opern|haus** *n* opera (house); **~kom-po,nist** *m* operatic composer; **~mu,sik** *f* operatic music; **~sän•ger** *m* opera singer; **~stadt** *f* centre (*Am.* center) for opera; **~text** *m* libretto

Op•fer ['ɔpfɐ] *n* (-s; -) **1.** a) sacrifice (*a. fig.*); offering, b) victim; ***ein ~ bringen*** make a sacrifice; *fig.* ***~ bringen*** make sacrifices (*dat.* for); ***viele ~ an Zeit*** (***Geld*** *etc.*) ***bringen*** invest a great deal of time (money *etc.*) (***für*** *acc.* into); ***keine ~ scheuen*** spare no sacrifice; ***unter großen ~n*** at great cost; **2.** victim (*a. fig.*), casualty; ***zahlreiche ~ fordern*** take a heavy toll on human life, cause heavy casualties, claim many victims; *fig. dat.* ***zum ~ fallen*** fall victim to *s.o. or s.th.*; **~al,tar** *m* sacrificial altar

'**op•fer•be•reit,** '**op•fer•freu•dig** *adj.* **1.** willing to make sacrifices; **2.** self-sacrificing; '**Op•fer•be•reit•schaft** *f*, '**Op•fer•freu•dig•keit** *f* willingness to make sacrifices

'**Op•fer|ga•be** *f* sacrificial offering; **~gang** *fig. m* self-sacrifice; **~geist** *m* (-[e]s; *no pl.*) spirit of self-sacrifice; **~lamm** *n* sacrificial lamb; *fig.* innocent victim

op•fern ['ɔpfɐn] (h) **I.** *v/t.* sacrifice; immolate *animal*; ***sein Leben ~*** give (*or* lay down) one's life; **II.** *v/i.* (make a) sacrifice; **III.** *v/refl.*: ***sich ~*** sacrifice o.s. (***für*** *acc. or dat.* for)

'**Op•fer|prie•ster** *m* sacrificial priest; **~stät•te** *f* sacrificial site; **~stock** *m* offertory box; **~tier** *n* sacrificial animal; **~tod** *m* self-sacrifice; ***den ~ sterben*** a) be sacrificed (***für*** *acc.* for), b) lay down one's life (for)

Op•fe•rung ['ɔpfərʊŋ] *f* (-; -en) sacrificing, sacrifice; immolation

Oph•thal•mo•lo•gie [ɔftalmolo'gi:] *f* (-; *no pl.*) ophthalmology; **oph•thal•mo•lo•gisch** [ɔftalmo'lo:gɪʃ] *adj.* ophthalmological

Opi ['o:pi] F *m* (-s; -s) grandpa, grandad; Grandpa, Grandad

Opi•at [o'pĭa:t] *n* (-[e]s; -e) opiate

Opi•um ['o:pĭʊm] *n* (-s; *no pl.*) opium; *fig.* ***~ fürs Volk*** opium for the masses (*or* people); **~an•bau** *m* **1.** opium growing; **2.** opium plantation(s *pl.*); **~höh•le** *f* opium den

'**Opi•um•sucht** *f* opium addiction

'**opi•um•süch•tig** *adj.* addicted to opium; '**Opi•um•süch•ti•ge** *m, f* (-n; -n) opium addict

Op•po•nent [ɔpo'nɛnt] *m* (-en; -en) opponent; **op•po•nie•ren** [ɔpo'ni:rən] *v/i.* (h) oppose; resist (***gegen*** *acc. s.th.*)

op•por•tun [ɔpɔr'tu:n] *adj.* opportune; ***nicht ~*** inopportune; ***das wäre im Augenblick nicht ~*** it's an inopportune time (*or* it's not the right moment) for it; **Op•por•tu•nis•mus** [ɔpɔrtu'nɪsmʊs] *m* (-; *no pl.*) opportunism; **Op•por•tu•nist** [ɔpɔrtu'nɪst] *m* (-en; -en) opportunist, timeserver; **op•por•tu•ni•stisch** [ɔpɔrtu'nɪstɪʃ] *adj.* opportunist, opportunistic(ally *adv.*)

Op•po•si•ti•on [ɔpozi'tsĭo:n] *f* (-; -en) opposition (*a. pol.*); **op•po•si•tio•nell** [ɔpozitsĭo'nɛl] *adj.* oppositional

Op•po•si•ti'ons|füh•rer *m* opposition leader, leader of the opposition; **~geist** *m* (-[e]s; *no pl.*) spirit of opposition; **~par,tei** *f* opposition (party)

Op•tik ['ɔptɪk] *f* (-; *no pl.*) **1.** *phys.* optics *pl.*; **2.** *phot.* optics *pl.*; lens; **3.** ✝ optical industry, optical instruments *pl.*; **4.** *fig.* point of view; ***das ist e-e Frage der ~*** that depends on how you look at it; **5.** F *fig.* visual effect, image; ***das ist nur für die ~*** that's just for show; ***das macht sich gut für die ~*** it makes a good impression; ***die ~ aufbessern*** improve the image (*gen.* of)

Op•ti•ker ['ɔptikɐ] *m* (-s; -) optician

op•ti•mal [ɔpti'ma:l] *adj.* best (possible), optimum, *a.* optimal; *a. pred.* ideal

op•ti•mie•ren [ɔpti'mi:rən] *v/t.* (h) optimize

Op•ti•mis•mus [ɔpti'mɪsmʊs] *m* (-; *no pl.*) optimism; ***vorsichtiger ~*** guarded optimism; **Op•ti•mist** [ɔpti'mɪst] *m* (-en; -en), **Op•ti•mi•stin** [ɔpti'mɪstɪn] *f* (-; -nen) optimist; **op•ti•mis•tisch** [ɔpti'mɪstɪʃ] *adj.* optimistic(ally *adv.*); ***~e Stimmung*** *a.* F upbeat mood; ✝ ***~e Börse*** bullish market

Op•ti•mum ['ɔptimʊm] *n* (-s; Optima [-ma]) optimum

Op•ti•on [ɔp'tsĭo:n] *f* (-; -en) option; ✝ *a.* (right of) first refusal

Op•ti'ons|an•lei•he *f* optional bond; **~han•del** *m* options trading

op•tisch ['ɔptɪʃ] *adj.* optic(al); visual; ***aus ~en Gründen*** for visual effect; ***~e Täuschung*** optical illusion

Op•to•elek'tro•nik [ɔpto-] *f* optoelectronics *pl.*; **op•to•elek'tro•nisch** *adj.* optoelectronic(ally *adv.*)

Op•to•me•trie [ɔptome'tri:] *f* (-; *no pl.*) optometry

opu•lent [opu'lɛnt] *adj.* opulent, sumptuous; **Opu•lenz** [opu'lɛnts] *f* (-; *no pl.*) opulence, sumptuousness

Opus ['o:pʊs, 'ɔpʊs] *n* (-; Opera ['o:pəra]) work; ♪ opus

Ora•kel [o'ra:kəl] *n* (-s; -) oracle; **ora•kel•haft** *adj.* oracular; **Ora•kel•spruch** *m* oracle

oral [o'ra:l] *adj.* oral; **Oral•ver•kehr** *m* oral intercourse

Oran•ge [o'rã:ʒə] *f* (-; -n) orange

oran•ge(far•ben) *adj.* orange

Oran•gea•de [orã'ʒa:də] *f* (-; -n) orangeade

Oran•gen|haut *f* ⚕ orange skin; **~marme,la•de** *f* (orange) marmalade; **~saft** *m* orange juice; **~scha•le** *f* orange peel; *gastr. a. the* zest of an orange; **~schei•be** *f* slice of orange, orange slice

Oran•ge•rie [orãʒə'ri:] *f* (-; -n) orangery

Orang-Utan ['o:raŋ'ʔu:tan] *m* (-s; -s) orang-utan(g)

Ora•to•ri•um [ora'to:rĭʊm] *n* (-s; -rien) ♪ oratorio

Or•che•ster [ɔr'kɛstɐ] *n* (-s; -) **1.** orchestra; *a. jazz etc.* band; **2.** → ***Orchestergraben***; **~be•glei•tung** *f* orchestral accompaniment; **~fas•sung** *f* orchestra (*or* orchestral) version; **~gra•ben** *m* orchestra pit; **~mu•si•ker** *m* orchestra musician; **~sitz** *m thea.* stall, *Am.* orchestra (seat); **~stück** *n* orchestra piece, piece for orchestra; **~wart** *m* orchestra attendant

or•che•stral [ɔrkɛs'tra:l] *adj.* orchestral

or•che•strie•ren [ɔrkɛs'tri:rən] *v/t.* (h) orchestrate; **Or•che'strie•rung** *f* (-; -en) orchestration

Or•chi•dee [ɔrçi'de:ə] *f* (-; -n) orchid

Or•chi'de•en•fach *n univ.* remote (*or* luxury) subject

Or•den ['ɔrdən] *m* (-s; -) **1.** *eccl. etc.* order; **2.** decoration, medal

'**Or•dens|bru•der** *m* monk; **~geist•li•che** *m* monk in holy orders; **~geist•lich•keit** *f* regular clergy; **~prie•ster** *m* monk in holy orders; **~rit•ter** *m* knight of an order; **~schwe•ster** *f eccl.* sister, nun; **~tracht** *f* habit (of a religious order); **~ver•lei•hung** *f* conferral of an order

or•dent•lich ['ɔrdəntlɪç] **I.** *adj.* **1.** tidy, neat, orderly; **2.** orderly *life etc.*; **3.** respectable; **4.** regular *job, contract etc.*; **5.** decent *food etc.*; ***e-e ~e Leistung*** a good job (*or* piece of work); ***in ~em Zustand*** in good order; **6.** ***~er Professor*** (full) professor; **7.** F proper, decent; ***e-e ~e Tracht Prügel*** a sound thrashing; → ***Gericht²***; **II.** *adv.* **8.** tidily, neatly; ***die Flaschen waren ~ aufgereiht*** the bottles stood in a neat row; **9.** (***ganz***) ~ quite (*or* fairly) well; ***er hat es ganz ~ gemacht*** he did quite a good job of it; **10.** F really; ***es hat ~ geschneit*** F there's a fair bit of snow on the ground; F ***ich hab's ihm ~ gegeben!*** I really let him have it

Or•der ['ɔrdɐ] *f* (-; -n) order; ✝ ***an eigene ~*** to my own order; '**or•dern** *v/t.* (h) order

Or•di•nal•zahl [ɔrdi'na:l-] *f* ordinal (number)

or•di•när [ɔrdi'nɛ:ɐ] *adj.* **1.** vulgar; dirty *joke etc.*; **2.** common *person, appearance etc.*; **3.** cheap, F cheapo

Or•di•na•ri•at [ɔrdina'rĭa:t] *n* (-[e]s; -e) *univ.* chair; **Or•di•na•ri•us** [ɔrdi'na:rĭʊs] *m* (-; -rien) (full) professor

Or•di•na•te [ɔrdi'na:tə] *f* (-; -n) 𝔄 ordinate; **Or•di'na•ten•ach•se** *f* axis of ordinates

Or•di•na•ti•on [ɔrdina'tsĭo:n] *f* (-; -en) **1.** *eccl.* ordination; **2.** ⚕ prescription

or•di•nie•ren [ɔrdi'ni:rən] *v/t.* (h) **1.** *eccl.* ordain; **2.** ⚕ prescribe

ord•nen ['ɔrdnən] (h) **I.** *v/t.* sort out, arrange; file *records etc.*; settle *one's affairs etc.*; put *one's life etc.* in order; ***s-e Kleider ~*** tidy o.s. up; ***alphabetisch ~*** arrange alphabetically (*or* in alphabetical order); ***nach Klassen ~*** classify; → ***geordnet***; **II.** *v/refl.*: ***sich ~ zu*** *dat.* form into; **Ord•ner** ['ɔrdnɐ] *m* (-s; -) **1.** steward; **2.** file

Ord•nung ['ɔrdnʊŋ] *f* (-; *no pl.*) **1.** ordering, putting in order *etc.*; → ***ordnen***; **2.** order; ***die öffentliche ~*** law and order; ***die göttliche ~*** the divine order; ***~ halten*** keep things in order; ***für ~ sorgen*** maintain order; ***~ schaffen*** sort things out, tidy up; ***in ~ bringen*** a) fix, b) settle, F fix, sort out *a problem etc.*; ***in ~ sein*** be all right (*Am.* alright); F ***er ist in ~*** he's all right (*Am.* alright), F he's okay; (***das ist***) ***in ~!, geht in ~!*** (that's) all right (*Am.* alright), F (that's) okay; ***es ist alles in bester ~*** everything's just fine; ***er ist nicht in ~*** he's not well; ***der Motor*** *etc.* ***ist nicht in ~*** there's something wrong with the engine *etc.*; *parl.* ***zur ~ rufen*** call to order; ***das finde ich nicht in ~*** I don't think that's right; **3.** rules *pl.*, regulations *pl.*; **4.** routine; **5.** order; ***... erster ~*** ... of the first order, first-class ..., first-rate ...; ***Stern erster*** ~ star of the first magnitude

'**Ord·nungs|amt** *n* (municipal) public affairs office; **~fim·mel** F *m* obsession with tidiness (*or* orderliness); ***e-n ~ haben*** *a.* be obsessively tidy

'**ord·nungs·ge·mäß I.** *adj.* proper, according to the rules; **II.** *adv.* duly

'**ord·nungs·hal·ber** [-halbɐ] *adv.* as a matter of form

'**Ord·nungs·hü·ter** *m iro. the* law, representative of the law

'**Ord·nungs·lie·be** *f* tidiness, (strong sense of) orderliness; '**ord·nungs·lie·bend** *adj.* orderly, tidy

'**Ord·nungs·macht** *f* law enforcement agency; peacekeeper

'**ord·nungs·mä·ßig** *adj. and adv.* → ***ordnungsgemäß***

'**Ord·nungs|prin‚zip** *n* system; **~ruf** *m parl.* call to order; **~sinn** *m* (-[e]s; *no pl.*) sense of order; **~stra·fe** *f* fine

'**ord·nungs·wid·rig** *adj.* against the regulations; '**Ord·nungs·wid·rig·keit** *f* breach of the law

'**Ord·nungs·zahl** *f* ordinal (number); ⚗ atomic number

Or·don·nanz [ɔrdɔ'nants] *f* (-; -en) ⚔ orderly

Ore·ga·no [o're:ga:no] *m* (-s; *no pl.*) ⚘ oregano

Or·gan [ɔr'ga:n] *n* (-s; -e) **1.** *anat.* organ; *fig.* ***kein*** (***ein***) ***~ haben für*** *acc.* have no (a) feeling for; **2.** F voice; ***die hat aber ein lautes ~!*** F she's got a voice like a foghorn; **3.** *fig.* organ; **4.** authority; *pol.* ***ausführendes*** ~ executive body; **~bank** *f* (-; -en) organ bank; **~emp·fän·ger** *m* organ recipient; **~han·del** *m* sale of (transplant) organs

Or·ga·ni·sa·ti·on [ɔrganiza'tsĭo:n] *f* (-; -en) organization; **Or·ga·ni·sa·ti'ons·ta‚lent** *n* organizational talent

Or·ga·ni·sa·tor [ɔrgani'za:to:ɐ] *m* (-s; -en [-za'to:rən]) organizer; **or·ga·ni·sa·to·risch** [ɔrganiza'to:rɪʃ] *adj.* organizational, organizing ...

or·ga·nisch [ɔr'ga:nɪʃ] *adj. a. fig.* organic(ally *adv.*)

or·ga·ni·sie·ren [ɔrgani'zi:rən] (h) **I.** *v/t.* a) organize, arrange; mount *an exhibition etc.*, b) F rustle up; ***das organisierte Verbrechen*** organized crime; **II.** *v/refl.*: ***sich ~*** get together; → ***gewerkschaftlich***

Or·ga·nis·mus [ɔrga'nɪsmʊs] *m* (-; -men) organism

Or·ga·nist [ɔrga'nɪst] *m* (-en; -en) organist

Or'gan|kon‚ser·ve *f* ⚕ stored organ; **~spen·de** *f* donation of an organ; **~spen·der** *m* organ donor; **~trans·plan·ta·ti‚on** *f*, **~ver·pflan·zung** *f* organ transplant

Or·gas·mus [ɔr'gasmʊs] *m* (-; -men) orgasm, climax; **or·ga·stisch** [ɔr'gastɪʃ] *adj.* orgasmic

Or·gel ['ɔrgəl] *f* (-; -n) ♪ organ; **~bau·er** *m* (-s; -) organ builder; **~kon‚zert** *n* **1.** organ recital; **2.** ♪ organ concerto

or·geln ['ɔrgəln] *v/i.* (h) **1.** grind a barrel organ; **2.** *fig.* roar

'**Or·gel|pfei·fe** *f* organ pipe; ***wie die ~n*** in order of size; **~punkt** *m* organ point; **~re‚gi·ster** *n* organ stop, register

Or·gie ['ɔrgĭə] *f* (-; -n) orgy; ***~n feiern*** have orgies; **or·gia·stisch** [ɔr'gĭastɪʃ] *adj.* orgiastic(ally *adv.*)

Ori·ent ['o:rĭɛnt] *m* (-s; *no pl.*) Orient, East; ***der Vordere ~*** the Near East, *pol. usu.* the Middle East; *hist.* the Levant

Ori·en·ta·le [orĭɛn'ta:lə] *m* (-n; -n), **Ori·en·ta·lin** [orĭɛn'ta:lɪn] *f* (-; -nen) Oriental; **ori·en·ta·lisch** [orĭɛn'ta:lɪʃ] *adj.* Oriental; (Far *or* Middle) Eastern

Ori·en·ta·li·stik [orĭɛnta'lɪstɪk] *f* (-; *no pl.*) Oriental studies *pl.*; Middle Eastern studies *pl.*

ori·en·tie·ren [orĭɛn'ti:rən] (h) **I.** *v/t.* **1.** inform (***über*** *acc.* about), put *s.o.* in the picture (about), fill *s.o.* in (on); **2.** orientate, *Am. a.* orient (***nach*** *dat.* according to); **II.** *v/refl.*: ***sich ~*** **3.** orient(ate) o.s. (***an*** *dat.* by), find one's bearings; ***sich nicht mehr ~ können*** have lost one's bearings; **4.** inform o.s. (***über*** *acc.* about, on); → ***orientiert***; **5.** ***sich ~ an*** *dat.* orient(ate) o.s. by, model o.s. on

ori·en·tiert [orĭɛn'ti:ɐt] *adj. in cpds.* ...-oriented (*i.e.* ***gewinnorientiert*** profit-oriented, ***verbraucherorientiert*** consumer-oriented); *pol.* (***nach***) ***links*** (***rechts***) ~ oriented towards the left (right); ***gut ~*** well-informed, in the picture; ***schlecht ~*** badly informed, uninformed

Ori·en·tie·rung [orĭɛn'ti:rʊŋ] *f* (-; *no pl.*) orientation (***nach*** *dat.*, ***auf*** *acc.* towards) (*a. fig.*); ***zu Ihrer ~*** for your guidance; ***die ~ verlieren*** *a. fig.* lose one's bearings

Ori·en'tie·rungs|da·ten *pl.* ✝ guideline data; **~hil·fe** *f* a) *a. pl.* guidance, b) guide, c) landmark; reference point; **~lauf** *m* orienteering (race)

ori·en'tie·rungs·los *adj.* disoriented; *fig.* ***~ sein*** *a.* be drifting

Ori·en'tie·rungs|punkt *m* landmark; reference point; **~sinn** *m* (-[e]s; *no pl.*) sense of direction; **~stu·fe** *f ped. two-year assessment stage after which pupils are allocated to appropriate secondary schools*; **~ver·mö·gen** *n* → ***Orientierungssinn***

Ori'ent·tep·pich *m* oriental carpet

Ori·ga·no [o'ri:gano] *m* (-s; *no pl.*) ⚘ oregano

Ori·gi·nal [origi'na:l] *n* (-[e]s; -e) **1.** original; (*document etc.*) *a.* original copy; (*tape etc.*) master (copy); **2.** F (*person*) F real character; **ori·gi'nal I.** *adj.* original; **II.** *adv.* genuine *Dresden china etc.*

Ori·gi'nal|ab·fül·lung *f label*: estate-bottled; **~aus·ga·be** *f* first edition; **~fas·sung** *f* original version

ori·gi'nal·ge·treu *adj.*: ***~e Nachbildung*** faithful copy

Ori·gi'nal·grö·ße *f* actual (*or* original) size; ***... in ~*** full-size ...

Ori·gi·na·li·tät [originali'tɛ:t] *f* (-; *no pl.*) originality

Ori·gi'nal|packung *f* original packaging; ***in ~*** factory-packed; **~text** *m* original (text); **~ton** *m* original sound; *film*: live sound(track); ***Aufnahmen im ~*** original sound recordings; ***~ X*** the original sound of X; **~über‚tra·gung** *f TV etc.* live broadcast

ori·gi·när [origi'nɛ:ɐ] *adj.* original

ori·gi·nell [origi'nɛl] *adj.* a) original, b) funny; witty; F ***~er Typ*** F real character

Or·kan [ɔr'ka:n] *m* (-s; -e) hurricane

or'kan·ar·tig *adj.* violent *storm*; *fig.* thunderous *applause etc.*; ***~e Winde*** gale-force winds

Or'kan·stär·ke *f* gale force

Or·na·ment [ɔrna'mɛnt] *n* (-[e]s; -e) ornament, decoration; ***mit ~en*** decorated, ornamented; **or·na·men·tal** [ɔrnamɛn'ta:l] *adj.* ornamental; **Or·na·men·tik** [ɔrna'mɛntɪk] *f* (-; *no pl.*) **1.** ornamentation; **2.** decorative art

Or·nat [ɔr'na:t] *m*, *n* (-[e]s; -e) robes *pl.*, vestments *pl.*; F ***in vollem ~*** in full array

Or·ni·tho·lo·ge [ɔrnito'lo:gə] *m* (-n; -n) ornithologist; **Or·ni·tho·lo·gie** [ɔrnitolo'gi:] *f* (-; *no pl.*) ornithology; **or·ni·tho·lo·gisch** [ɔrnito'lo:gɪʃ] *adj.* ornithological

Ort[1] [ɔrt] *m* (-[e]s; -e) **1.** place; ***~ der Handlung*** (***des Grauens***) scene of the action (of horror); ***an ~ und Stelle*** on the spot, *fig. a.* there and then; ***an ~ und Stelle gelangen*** get there, reach one's destination; ***es steht nicht an s-m ~*** it's not where it should be (*or* usually is); ***vor ~*** a) on the spot, b) on the job, c) locally; ***Besichtigung vor ~*** on-site visit; *fig.* ***dies ist nicht der ~ für*** *acc.* ***...*** this is not the time or place for ...; ***höheren ~(e)s*** at a higher level; → ***Platz***; **2.** place, *a.* village, *a.* town; ***von ~ zu ~*** from place to place

Ort[2] *n* (-[e]s; Örter ['œrtɐ]) ⚒ coalface; ***vor ~*** at the face

Ört·chen ['œrtçən] F *n* (-s; -) (*a.* ***stilles ~***) F loo, *Am.* F john

or·ten ['ɔrtən] *v/t.* (h) ⚓, ✈ locate

Or·tho·don·tie [ɔrtodɔn'ti:] *f* (-; *no pl.*) orthodontics *pl.*

or·tho·dox [ɔrto'dɔks] *adj.* orthodox

Or·tho·do·xie [ɔrtodɔ'ksi:] *f* (-; *no pl.*) orthodoxy

Or·tho·gra·phie [ɔrtogra'fi:] *f* (-; -n) orthography, spelling

or·tho·gra·phisch [ɔrto'gra:fɪʃ] **I.** *adj.* spelling ...; orthographic(al); **II.** *adv.*: ***~ falsch*** (***richtig***) wrongly (correctly) spelt

Or·tho·pä·de [ɔrto'pɛ:də] *m* (-n; -n) orthop(a)edist; **Or·tho·pä·die** [ɔrtopɛ'di:] *f* (-; *no pl.*) orthop(a)edics *pl.*; **or·tho·pä·disch** [ɔrto'pɛ:dɪʃ] *adj.* orthop(a)edic(ally *adv.*)

ört·lich ['œrtlɪç] *adj.* local; → ***Betäubung***; '**Ört·lich·keit** *f* (-; -en) locality, place; ***die ~en kennenlernen*** familiarize o.s. with the place

'**Orts·an·ga·be** *f* address, name of place

'**orts·an·säs·sig** *adj.* local; '**Orts·an·säs·sige** *m*, *f* (-n; -n) local resident

'**Orts|be·schaf·fen·heit** *f* topography; **~be·stim·mung** *f* location

'**orts·be·weg·lich** *adj.* ⚙ *etc.* mobile

'**Ort·schaft** *f* (-;-en) place, locality; village; ***geschlossene ~*** built-up area

'**Orts·emp·fang** *m* local reception

'**orts|fest** *adj.* ⚙ *etc.* stationary; **~fremd** *adj.* non-local, outside ...; ***er ist hier ~*** he's a stranger here; **~ge·bun·den** *adj.* stationary; resources-bound *industries etc.*; tied to one's place of work (*or* residence)

'**Orts|ge·spräch** *n teleph.* local call; **~grup·pe** *f* local branch; **~kennt·nis** *f*: ***~(se) besitzen*** know one's way around; **~kran·ken·kas·se** *f*: ***Allgemeine ~*** *general health insurance scheme*

'**orts·kun·dig** *adj.*: ***~ sein*** know one's way around

'**Orts|na·me** *m* place name; **~netz** *n teleph.* local exchange network; **~po·li‚zei** *f* local police; **~schild** *n* town sign; **~sen·der** *m* local transmitter; **~sinn** *m* (-[e]s; *no pl.*) sense of direction; **~ta‚rif** *m*: *teleph.* (***zum ~*** at) local rates *pl.*

'**orts|üb·lich** *adj.* local; ***das ist ~*** it's a

local custom; **~un·ge·bun·den** *adj.* mobile, *w.s.* flexible
'Orts|ver·än·de·rung *f* → ***Ortswechsel***; **~ver·ein** *m* local association; **~ver·kehr** *m* local traffic (*a. teleph.*); **~wech·sel** *m* **1.** change of location; **2.** *fig.* change of scenery; **~zeit** *f* local time; **~zu·schlag** *m* weighting (allowance)
Or·tung ['ɔrtʊŋ] *f* (-; -en) location, locating; **'Or·tungs·ge·rät** *n* position-finder
Öse ['ø:zə] *f* (-; -n) eye; eyelet *of a shoe*
Os·kar ['ɔskar] *m*: F ***er ist frech wie ~*** F he's a cheeky devil
os·ma·nisch [ɔs'ma:nɪʃ] *adj.* Ottoman; ***das 2e Reich*** the Ottoman Empire
Os·mo·se [ɔs'mo'zə] *f* (-; -n) osmosis
Ost [ɔst] *without art.* east; ***von*** (*or* ***aus***) ~ from the east; ***München*** ~ the east of Munich; ***Eingang*** ~ the east entrance; *fig.* ***aus ~ und West*** from all four corners of the earth; **~agent** *m* **1.** *hist.* East-Bloc agent (*or* spy); **2.** *n.s.* Russian (*or* KGB) spy; **~asia·ti·ka** [-azĭa:tika] *pl.* East Asian art *sg.* (*or* antiquities)
'Ost·block *m hist.* Eastern Bloc; **~staat** *m hist.* East(ern)-Bloc state
'ost·deutsch *adj.* East German; ***im ~en Teil*** in the eastern part of Germany, in Eastern Germany; **'Ost·deut·sche** *m, f* **1.** Eastern German; ***~(r) sein*** *a.* be from Eastern Germany; **2.** *hist. DDR*: East German
Osten ['ɔstən] *m* (-s; *no pl.*) east; East; ***nach*** ~ east(wards); eastbound *traffic etc.*; ***von*** ~ from the east; ***der*** ~ the East End (*Am.* Side); → ***fern*** I, ***mittler, nah*** 1
osten·ta·tiv [ɔstɛnta'ti:f] *adj.* unmistakable, pointed; demonstrative
Osteo·pa·thie [ɔsteopa'ti:] *f* (-; -n) ⚕ osteopathy
Osteo·po·ro·se [ɔsteopo'ro:zə] *f* (-; -n) ⚕ osteoporosis, brittle-bone disease
Oster·ei ['o:stɐ-] *n* Easter egg
'Oster·ei·er·su·che *f* Easter egg hunt; ***auf ~ sein*** be hunting for Easter eggs
'Oster|fei·er·tag *m*: ***am ersten*** (***zweiten***) ~ on Easter Sunday (Monday); ***über die ~e*** over the Easter weekend; **~fest** *n* Easter; **~glocke** *f* ⚘ narcissus; **~ha·se** *m* Easter bunny; **~lamm** *n* paschal lamb
öster·lich ['ø:stɐlɪç] *adj.* Easter ...; ***es sieht sehr ~ aus*** it loooks (very much) like Easter
'Oster·marsch *m* Easter march (*or* rally)
Oster'mon·tag *m* Easter Monday
Ostern ['o:stɐn] *n*: (***an*** *or* ***zu*** ~ at) Easter; ***frohe*** (*or* ***fröhliche***) ***~!*** Happy Easter
Öster·rei·cher ['ø:stəraɪçɐ] *m*(-s; -), **Öster·rei·che·rin** ['ø:stəraɪçərɪn] *f* (-; -nen), **öster·rei·chisch** ['ø:stəraɪçɪʃ] *adj.* Austrian
Oster'sonn·tag *m* Easter Sunday
'Oster·ver·kehr *m* Easter traffic
'Ost·eu·ro,pä·er *m*, **'ost·eu·ro,pä·isch** *adj.* East (*or* Eastern) European
'Ost·go·te *m* Ostrogoth; **'ost·go·tisch** *adj.* Ostrogothic; ***das ~e Reich*** the Ostrogothic Empire
Osti·na·to [ɔsti'na:to] *m, n* (-s; -s, -ti) ♪ ostinato
'Ost|kir·che *f* Eastern Orthodox Church; **~kü·ste** *f* east coast; ***an der ~*** on the east coast
öst·lich ['œstlɪç] **I.** *adj.* eastern, east ...; easterly *wind*; ***in ~er Richtung*** east(wards), eastbound *traffic etc.*; **II.** *adv.* (to the) east (*gen. or* ***von*** *dat.* of); **'öst·lichst** *adj.* easternmost
'Ost|mark *f hist.* East German mark; **~po·li,tik** *f* ostpolitik
'ost·preu·ßisch *adj.* East Prussian
Östro·gen [œstro'ge:n] *n* (-s; -e) (o)estrogen; **~spie·gel** *m* (o)estrogen level
'Ost·sei·te *f* east(ern) side
'ost·wärts *adj.* east(wards)
'Ost-'West|-Be·zie·hun·gen *pl.* East-West relations; **~-Dia,log** *m pol.* East-West dialog(ue)
Ost'west·rich·tung *f*: ***in ~ verlaufen*** run from east to west
'Ost·wind *m* east wind
'Ost·zo·ne *obs. f* Eastern (*or* Soviet-occupied) zone
Os·zil·la·tor [ɔstsɪ'la:to:ɐ] *m* (-s; -en [-la-'to:rən]) oscillator; **os·zil·lie·ren** [ɔstsɪ-'li:rən] *v/i.* (h) oscillate
Os·zil·lo·graph [ɔstsɪlo'gra:f] *m* (-en; -en) oscillograph
Os·zil·lo·skop [ɔstsɪlo'sko:p] *n* (-s; -e) oscilloscope, F scope
'O-Ton F *m* original sound; → *a.* ***Originalton***
Ot·ter¹ ['ɔtɐ] *f* (-; -n) viper, adder
'Ot·ter² *m* (-s; -) otter
Ot·to ['ɔto] *m*: F ***den flotten ~ haben*** F have the runs
'Ot·to·mo·tor *m* internal combustion engine, petrol (*Am.* gas) engine
'Ot·to Nor'mal·ver·brau·cher F *m* F Mr Average, Joe Blow, *Brit. a.* Joe Bloggs, the man on the Clapham omnibus, your high-street punter
out [aʊt] *adv.*: ***~ sein*** be out; ***das ist ~*** *a.* F that's died a death
Ou·ver·tü·re [uver'ty:rə] *f* (-; -n) ♪ overture (*a. fig.*)
oval [o'va:l] *adj.*, **Oval** *n* (-[e]s; -e) oval
Ova·ti·on [ova'tsĭo:n] *f* (-; -en) ovation; ***j-m ~en bereiten*** give s.o. an ovation
Over·all ['o:vəra:l] *m* (-s; -s) jump suit; boiler suit, overalls *pl.*, *Am.* overall
Over·head|fo·lie ['o:vəhɛd-] *f* overhead transparency; **~pro,jek·tor** *m* overhead projector
Over·kill ['o:vəkɪl] *n, m* (-s; *no pl.*) overkill (*a. fig.*)
Ovu·la·ti·on [ovula'tsĭo:n] *f* (-; -en) ovulation; **Ovu·la·ti'ons·hem·mer** *m* (-s; -) ovulation inhibitor
Oxyd [ɔ'ksy:t] *n* (-s; -e [-də]) ⚗ oxide
Oxy·da·ti·on [ɔksyda'tsĭo:n] *f* (-; -en) oxidation; **oxy·die·ren** [ɔksy'di:rən] *v/i.* (h *or* sn) oxidize; **Oxy'die·rung** *f* (-; -en) oxidization
Oze·an ['o:tsea:n] *m* (-s; -e) ocean; ***der Atlantische ~*** the Atlantic; ***der Große*** (*or* ***Stille***) ~ the Pacific; **~damp·fer** *m* ocean liner
ozea·nisch [otse'a:nɪʃ] *adj.* oceanic
Ozea·no·gra·phie [otseanogra'fi:] *f* (-; *no pl.*) oceanography
'Oze·an·über,que·rung *f* ocean crossing
Oze·lot ['o:tselɔt] *m* (-s; -e, -s) *zo.* ocelot
Ozon [o'tso:n] *m, n* (-s; *no pl.*) ozone
ozon·freund·lich *adj.* ozone-friendly
ozon·hal·tig [-haltɪç] *adj.* ozoniferous
Ozon·loch *n* ozone hole, hole in the ozone layer; ***das ~*** *a.* ozone depletion
ozon·reich *adj.* high (*or* rich) in ozone
Ozon·schicht *f* ozone layer
Ozon·wer·te *pl.* ozone levels

P

P, p [peː] *n* (-; -) P, p

paar [paːɐ] *indef. pron.*: ***ein ~*** a few, some, F a couple of; ***ein ~ hundert*** a few hundred; ***vor ein ~ Tagen*** the other day; ***alle ~ Minuten*** every few minutes; ***die ~ Mark wirst du wohl noch ausgeben können*** surely you can spare a couple of marks; → ***Zeile***

Paar [paːɐ] *n* (-[e]s) **1.** *pl.* ***Paar*** pair (*a. iro.*); ***ein (zwei) ~ Socken*** a pair (two pairs) of socks; ***ein ~ Frankfurter*** two frankfurters; **2.** *pl.* ***Paare*** ['paːrə] couple; ***sich zu ~en aufstellen*** line up in twos; ***sie treten immer als ~ auf*** you never see one without the other; → ***ungleich*** I; **~bil·dung** *f phys.* pair production

paa·ren ['paːrən] (h) **I.** *v/refl.*: ***sich ~*** **1.** *zo.* mate; **2.** *fig.* combine, be combined; ***bei ihr paart sich Schnelligkeit mit Genauigkeit*** she's fast and very accurate at the same time, she combines speed with accuracy; **II.** *v/t.* **3.** *zo.* pair, mate; **4.** *fig.* combine, couple (***mit*** *dat.* with); **5.** *sport*: draw against each other

'Paar·hu·fer [-huːfɐ] *m* (-s; -) cloven-hoofed animal

paa·rig ['paːrɪç] *adj.* in pairs, paired

'Paar|lauf *m sport*: pair skating; **~läu·fer** *m* pair skater

'paar·mal *adv.*: ***ein ~*** a few times, F a couple of times

'Paar·reim *m* rhyming couplets *pl.*; ***das ist ein ~*** it's rhyming couplets

Paa·rung ['paːrʊŋ] *f* (-; -en) **1.** *zo.* mating; **2.** *sport*: match, tie; **3.** *fig.* combination

'Paa·rungs|trieb *m zo.* mating urge; **~ver·hal·ten** *n* mating behavio(u)r; **~zeit** *f* mating season

'paar·wei·se *adv.* in pairs, in twos; ***~ anordnen*** arrange in pairs

Pacht [paxt] *f* (-; -en) **1.** *no pl.* lease; ***et. in ~ haben*** have s.th. on lease(hold); ***et. in ~ nehmen*** take s.th. on lease; **2.** rent; **~dau·er** *f* duration of a (*or* the) lease

pach·ten ['paxtən] *v/t.* (h) (take on) lease; ***er tut so, als hätte er die Weisheit gepachtet*** he acts as if he was the only person in the world with any brains

Päch·ter ['pɛçtɐ] *m* (-s; -) leaseholder, tenant

'pacht·frei *adj.* rent-free

'Pacht|geld *n* rent; **~grund·stück** *n* leasehold (property); **~gut** *n* (leasehold) estate, holding; **~hof** *m* (leasehold) farm; **~ver·län·ge·rung** *f* renewal (*or* extension) of a (*or* the) lease; **~ver·trag** *m* lease; **~zeit** *f* term of lease; **~zins** *m* rent

Pack[1] [pak] *m* (-s; -e) pile; bundle; ***ein ~ Spielkarten*** a pack of cards

Pack[2] *contp. n* (-s; *no pl.*) rabble

Päck·chen ['pɛkçən] *n* (-s; -) parcel, small packet, *Am.* package; ***ein ~ Zigaretten*** a pack(et) of cigarettes; *fig.* ***wir haben alle unser ~ zu tragen*** we all have our little crosses to bear

'Pack·eis *n* pack ice

Packen ['pakən] (*sep.* -k·k-) *m* (-s; -) pile; bundle; ***ein großer ~*** *gen. a.* F a great wodge of

packen ['pakən] (*sep.* -k·k-) (h) **I.** *v/t.* **1.** pack *a suitcase, one's things etc.*; wrap up *package etc.*; *fig.* ***j-n ins Bett ~*** pack s.o. off to bed; **2.** grab (hold of); **3.** *fig.* grip; ***von Furcht*** *etc.* ***gepackt*** gripped (*or* seized) with fear *etc.*; ***mich packt die Wut, wenn ich höre, daß ...*** I get so angry when I hear that ..., it makes me so mad to hear that ...; ***mich hat der Film gepackt*** I was totally gripped by the film; F ***ihn hat's gepackt*** a) F he's been laid low, b) F he's smitten; **4.** F *fig.* manage; ***es ~*** F make it, do it, manage, cope; F ***wir haben es gerade noch gepackt*** we just made it (in time); **II.** F *v/refl.*: ***sich ~*** F clear off, beat it; **III.** *v/i.* pack; ***ich muß noch ~*** I still have to pack (my case), I've still got my packing to do

'packend (*sep.* -k·k-) *fig.* **I.** *adj.* gripping, exciting, riveting; ***~er Bericht*** gripping account; **II.** *adv.*: ***es ist ~ erzählt*** it's (*or* it makes for) exciting reading

Packer ['pakɐ] (*sep.* -k·k-) *m* (-s; -) packer; **Packe·rei** [pakə'raɪ] (*sep.* -k·k-) *f* (-; -en) packing department (*or* office); **Packe·rin** ['pakərɪn] (*sep.* -k·k-) *f* (-; -nen) packer

'Pack|esel *m* (pack) mule; *fig.* packhorse; **~lei·nen** *n* sacking; **~ma·te·ri̦al** *n* packing material; **~pa̦pier** *n* (brown) wrapping paper; **~pferd** *n* packhorse; **~raum** *m* packing room; **~sat·tel** *m* pack saddle; **~schnee** *m* hard-packed snow; **~ta·sche** *f* pannier; **~tier** *n* pack animal

Packung ['pakʊŋ] (*sep.* -k·k-) *f* (-; -en) **1.** packet; ***e-e ~ Tee*** a packet of tea; ***e-e ~ Zigaretten*** a pack(et) of cigarettes; ***große ~*** large pack; **2.** package, wrapping; **3.** ⚕, *cosmetics*: pack; **4.** *sport*: beating; ***e-e ~ bekommen*** F get thrashed (*or* slaughtered); **'Packungs·bei·la·ge** *f* package insert, F blurb

'Pack|wa·gen *m* luggage van, *Am.* baggage car; **~zet·tel** *m* packing slip

Päd·ago·ge [pɛda'goːgə] *m* (-n; -n) education(al)ist, educator; **Päd·ago·gik** [pɛda'goːgɪk] *f* (-; *no pl.*) education(al theory), pedagogics *pl.*; **Päd·ago·gin** [pɛda'goːgɪn] *f* (-; -nen) → ***Pädagoge***; **päd·ago·gisch** [pɛda'goːgɪʃ] **I.** *adj.* educational, pedagogical; ***&e Hochschule*** college of education, *Am.* teachers' college; ***~er Wert*** educational value; ***er hat keinerlei ~e Fähigkeiten*** he doesn't know the first thing about teaching; **II.** *adv.*: ***das ist ~ falsch*** that's not the way to teach children

Pad·del ['padəl] *n* (-s; -) paddle

'Pad·del·boot *n* canoe

'pad·deln *v/i.* (sn) paddle

Päd·erast [pɛdə'rast] *m* (-en; -en) pederast; **Päd·era·stie** [pɛdəras'tiː] *f* (-; *no pl.*) pederasty

Päd·ia·trie [pɛdia'triː] *f* (-; *no pl.*) ⚕ pediatrics *pl.*

paff [paf] *int.* bang!

paf·fen ['pafən] *v/i. and v/t.* (h) puff away (***s-e Pfeife*** *etc.* at one's pipe *etc.*)

Pa·ge ['paːʒə] *m* (-n; -n) page

'Pa·gen·kopf *m* pageboy (hair)style

pa·gi·nie·ren [pagi'niːrən] *v/t.* (h) paginate; **Pa·gi'nie·rung** *f* (-; -en) pagination, page numbering

Pa·go·de [pa'goːdə] *f* (-; -n) pagoda

Pail·let·te [paɪ'jɛtə] *f* (-; -n) sequin

pail'let·ten·be·setzt *adj.* sequined

Pa·ket [pa'keːt] *n* (-[e]s; -e) **1.** parcel, *Am.* package (*a. pol.*); bundle; **2.** large pack; **3.** ☿ parcel (of shares); **~an·nah·me** *f* parcels counter; **~bom·be** *f* parcel bomb; **~kar·te** *f* (parcel) mailing form; **~post** *f* parcel post; **~schal·ter** *m* parcels counter; **~sen·dung** *f* parcel, *Am.* package; **~zu·stel·lung** *f* parcel delivery

Pa·ki·sta·ni [pakɪs'taːni] *m* (-[s]; -[s]), **pa·ki·sta·nisch** [pakɪs'taːnɪʃ] *adj.* Pakistani

Pakt [pakt] *m* (-[e]s; -e) pact; ***e-n ~ schließen*** → **pak·tie·ren** [pak'tiːrən] *v/i.* (h) make a deal (***mit*** *dat.* with)

Pa·lais [pa'lɛː] *n* (-; - [pa'lɛːs]) palace

Pa·läo·li·thi·kum [palɛo'liːtikʊm] *n* (-s; *no pl.*) paleolithic age; **pa·läo·li·thisch** [palɛo'liːtɪʃ] *adj.* paleolithic

Pa·läo·lo·ge [palɛo'loːgə] *m* (-n; -n) paleologist; **Pa·läo·lo·gie** [palɛolo'giː] *f* (-; *no pl.*) paleology; **pa·läo·lo·gisch** [palɛo'loːgɪʃ] *adj.* paleological

Pa·lä·on·to·lo·ge [palɛɔnto'loːgə] *m* (-n; -n) paleontologist; **Pa·lä·on·to·lo·gie** [palɛɔntolo'giː] *f* (-; *no pl.*) paleontology; **pa·lä·on·to·lo·gisch** [palɛɔnto'loːgɪʃ] *adj.* paleontological

Pa·last [pa'last] *m* (-[e]s; Paläste [pa'lɛstə]) palace; **~an·la·ge** *f* palace complex

pa'last·ar·tig *adj.* palatial

Pa·lä·sti·nen·ser [palɛsti'nɛnzɐ] *m* (-s; -), **Pa·lä·sti·nen·se·rin** [palɛsti'nɛnzərɪn] *f* (-; -nen) Palestinian

Pa·lä·sti'nen·ser·la·ger *n* Palestinian refugee camp

pa·lä·sti·nen·sisch [palɛsti'nɛnzɪʃ] *adj.* Palestinian

Pa'last|re̦vol·te *fig. f* palace coup; **~wa·che** *f* palace guard

pa·la·tal [pala'taːl] *adj.* ⚕, *ling.*, **Pa·la'tal·laut** *m ling.* palatal

Pa·la·ver [pa'laːvɐ] F *contp. n* (-s; -) palaver; fuss; **pa'la·vern** F *contp. v/i.* (h) F yak; ***~ über*** *acc.* yak (on) about

Pa·le·tot ['paləto] *m* (-s; -s) overcoat

Pa·let·te [pa'lɛtə] *f* (-; -n) **1.** *art*: palette; **2.** *fig.* (***breite ~*** wide) range; ***bunte ~*** mixed bag; ***die ganze ~*** the whole panoply; **3.** ⚙ pallet
pa·let·ti [pa'lɛti]: F (***es ist***) ***alles ~*** F everything's hunky dory
Pa·limp·sest [palɪmp'sɛst] *m*, *n* (-[e]s; -e) palimpsest
Pa·lin·drom [palɪn'dro:m] *n* (-s; -e) palindrome
Pa·li·sa·de [pali'za:də] *f* (-; -n) palisade; **Pa·li'sa·den·zaun** *m* stockade
Pa·li·san·der [pali'zandɐ] *m* (-s; *no pl.*), **~holz** *n* rosewood
Pal·me ['palmə] *f* (-; -n) palm; F *fig.* ***j-n auf die ~ bringen*** F get s.o.'s goat; F ***auf die ~ gehen*** F lose (*sl.* blow) one's cool; F ***von der ~ herunterkommen*** F cool down
'**Pal·men|hain** *m* palm grove; **~her·zen** *pl. gastr.* heart *sg.* of palm; **~strand** *m* palm(-lined) beach
'**Palm|kätz·chen** *n* catkin; **~öl** *n* palm oil
Palm'sonn·tag *m* Palm Sunday
'**Palm·we·del** *m* palm frond
Pam·pa ['pampa] *f* (-; -s) pampas *pl.*; **~(s)·gras** *n* pampas grass
Pam·pe ['pampə] *contp. f* (-; -n) stodge
Pam·pel·mu·se [pampəl'mu:zə] *f* (-; -n) grapefruit
Pam·phlet [pam'fle:t] *n* (-[e]s; -e) (political) pamphlet
pam·pig ['pampɪç] F *adj.* **1.** F stroppy, F bolshy; ***werd nicht ~!*** don't you get stroppy (*or* bolshy) with me; **2.** *contp.* stodgy
pan..., Pan... [pan-] *in cpds.* pan(-)...
Pa·na·de [pa'na:də] *f* (-; -n) *gastr.* batter
Pa·na·ma·er ['panamaɐ] *m* (-s; -), **Pa·na·mae·rin** ['panamaərɪn] *f* (-; -nen) Panamanian
'**Pa·na·ma·hut** *m* panama (hat)
pa·na·ma·isch [pana'ma:ɪʃ] *adj.* Panamanian
pan·ame·ri'ka·nisch *adj.* Pan-American; **Pan·ame·ri·ka'nis·mus** *m* Pan-Americanism
Pan·da ['panda] *m* (-s; -), **~bär** *m* panda
Pan·do·ra [pan'do:ra] *f*: *fig.* ***die Büchse der ~*** Pandora's box
Pa·neel [pa'ne:l] *n* (-s; -e) panel, wainscot
pan·eu·ro'pä·isch *adj.* Pan-European
Pan·flö·te ['pa:n-] *f* panpipes *pl.*
päng [pɛŋ] *int.* bang!, pow!
pa·nie·ren [pa'ni:rən] *v/t.* (h) bread
Pa·nier·mehl [pa'ni:ɐ-] *n* breadcrumbs *pl.*
Pa·nik ['pa:nɪk] *f* (-; -en) a) panic; scare, b) stampede; ***in ~ geraten*** panic, start panicking; ***er hat uns in ~ versetzt*** he had us panicking; ***keine ~!*** don't panic
'**pa·nik·ar·tig I.** *adj.* panic ...; **II.** *adv.* in (a) panic
'**Pa·nik|ma·che** *f* (-; *no pl.*) scaremongering, panicmongering, scare tactics *pl.*; ***das ist reine ~*** that's just scare tactics, he's *etc.* just trying to scare people; **~ma·cher** *m* alarmist; **~stim·mung** *f*: ***in ~ geraten*** start panicking
pa·nisch ['pa:nɪʃ] *adj.* panic ...; ***~e Angst*** (feeling of) sheer terror, (mortal) terror; ***~e Angst haben*** be terrified (out of one's wits), be frightened out of one's mind; ***ich habe e-e ~e Angst davor, daß mir der Computer abstürzt*** I live in terror of my computer crashing
Pan·kre·as ['pankreas] *n* (-; Pankreaten [pankre'a:tən]) *anat.* pancreas

Pan·ne ['panə] *f* (-; -n) breakdown; puncture, blowout, flat tyre (*Am.* tire), F flat; *fig.* mishap; hitch; *fig.* ***e-e kleine ~*** a) a little accident, b) a slight hitch
'**Pan·nen|dienst** *m* breakdown service; **~kof·fer** *m* breakdown kit; **~kurs** *m* car maintenance course
'**pan·nen·si·cher** *adj.* failsafe
Pan·op·ti·kum [pa'nɔptikʊm] *n* (-s; -en) waxworks *pl.*
Pan·ora·ma [pano'ra:ma] *n* (-s; -en) panorama; **~bild** *n phot.* panoramic view; **~bus** *m* sightseeing bus (*or* coach); **~fen·ster** *n* panoramic (*or* observation, picture) window; **~re·stau,rant** *n* panoramic (*or* revolving) restaurant; **~schei·be** *f mot.* panoramic windscreen (*Am.* windshield); **~schwenk** *m film*: pan(ning) shot
pan·schen ['panʃən] (h) **I.** *v/t.* water down *wine*; adulterate; → ***gepanscht***; **II.** *v/i.* splash about
Pan·sen ['panzən] *m* (-s; -) **1.** *zo.* rumen; **2.** F *fig.* belly; ***sich den ~ vollschlagen*** F stuff o.s.
Pan·the·is·mus [pante'ɪsmʊs] *m* (-; *no pl.*) pantheism; **Pan·the·ist** [pante'ɪst] *m* (-en; -en) pantheist; **pan·thei·stisch** [pante'ɪstɪʃ] *adj.* pantheist(ic)
Pan·ther ['pantɐ] *m* (-s; -) panther
Pan·ti·ne [pan'ti:nə] *f* (-; -n) clog; F *fig.* ***aus den ~n kippen*** a) F keel over, b) F fall over backwards
Pan·tof·fel [pan'tɔfəl] *m* (-s; -n) slipper; F *fig.* ***er steht unter dem ~*** he's a henpecked husband; ***sie hat ihn unter dem ~, sie schwingt den ~*** she wears the trousers (*Am.* pants); **~blu·me** *f* slipperwort; **~held** F *m* henpecked husband; **~ki·no** F *n* F box, tube
Pan·to·let·te [panto'lɛtə] *f* (-; -n) open-back shoe
Pan·to·mi·me[1] [panto'mi:mə] *f* (-; -n) mime, dumb show
Pan·to'mi·me[2] *m* (-n; -n) mime (artist)
pan·to·mi·misch [panto'mi:mɪʃ] *adj.* pantomime ...
pant·schen ['pantʃən] *v/t. and v/i.* (h) → ***panschen***
Pan·zer ['pantsɐ] *m* (-s; -) **1.** ⚔ a) tank, b) armo(u)r plating; **2.** *hist.* (suit of) armo(u)r; coat of mail; **3.** *fig.* wall *of silence etc.*; **4.** *zo.* shell, armo(u)r
'**Pan·zer·ab·wehr** *f* antitank defen|ce (*Am.* -se); **~hub·schrau·ber** *m* antitank helicopter; **~ka,no·ne** *f* antitank gun; **~ra,ke·te** *f* antitank missile (*or* rocket)
'**Pan·zer|di·vi·si,on** *f* armo(u)red division; **~faust** *f* bazooka, antitank rocket launcher; **~glas** *n* bulletproof glass; **~gra·ben** *m* antitank ditch; **~gre·na·dier** [-grenadi:ɐ] *m* (-s; -e [-di:rə]) armo(u)red infantry rifleman; **~hemd** *n hist.* coat of mail; **~jä·ger** *m* antitank gunner; **~ka,no·ne** *f* tank gun; **~ket·te** *f* tank track; **~kreu·zer** *m* ⚓ armo(u)red cruiser
pan·zern ['pantsɐn] (h) **I.** *v/t. a.* ⚙ armo(u)r-plate; → ***gepanzert***; **II.** *fig.* *v/refl.*: ***sich ~*** shield o.s., arm o.s.
'**Pan·zer|re·gi,ment** *n* armo(u)red regiment; **~schiff** *n* armo(u)r-plated vessel; **~schrank** *m* safe; **~späh·wa·gen** *m* armo(u)red scout car; **~trup·pen** *pl.* armo(u)red troops, tank corps *sg.*
Pan·ze·rung ['pantsərʊŋ] *f* (-; -en) **1.** armo(u)ring; **2.** armo(u)r
'**Pan·zer·wa·gen** *m* tank

Pa·pa [pa'pa:, 'papa] F *m* (-s; -s) dad(dy), *Am. a.* pa; Dad(dy), *Am. a.* Pa
Pa·pa·gal·lo [papa'galo] *m* (-[s]; -s, -li) beach romeo
Pa·pa·gei [papa'gaɪ] *m* (-en; -en) parrot (*a. fig.*); **pa·pa'gei·en·haft** *adj.* parrot-like
Pa·pa'gei·en|krank·heit *f* ⚕ psittacosis; **~vo·gel** *m* (type of) parrot; ***es ist ein ~ a.*** it belongs to the parrot family
Pa·pier [pa'pi:ɐ] *n* (-[e]s; -e [-rə]) paper; *pl.* papers, documents; (identity) papers; † securities; ***zu ~ bringen*** write down, commit to paper; ***das steht nur auf dem ~*** it's a pure formality; ***die Ehe besteht nur auf dem ~*** it's a marriage on paper only; ***s-e ~e bekommen*** get one's cards (*Am.* pink slip); ***~ ist geduldig*** the rubbish that ends up on paper; ***auf dem ~ sieht es leicht aus*** it looks easy on paper; **~ab·fäl·le** *pl.* waste paper *sg.*; **~block** *m* notepad; **~blu·me** *f* paper flower; **~brei** *m* pulp; **~deutsch** *n* officialese, bureaucratese
pa'pier·dünn *adj.* wafer-thin
pa·pie·ren [pa'pi:rən] *adj.* paper ..., made of paper; *fig.* prosy *style*
Pa'pier|fa,brik *f* paper mill; **~fei·le** *f* emery board; **~fet·zen** *m* scrap of paper; **~flie·ger** *m* paper (aero)plane; **~for,mat** *n* size of paper, paper size; ***welches ~ brauchst du?*** what size paper do you need?; **~geld** *n* (-[e]s; *no pl.*) paper money; notes *pl.*, *Am.* bills *pl.*; **~ge·schäft** *n* stationer's (shop); **~ge·wicht** *n* weight of paper; **~hand·tuch** *n* paper towel; **~korb** *m* wastepaper (*Am.* waste) basket; **~kram** F *m* paperwork; **~krieg** F *contp. m* red tape; ***e-n ~ führen mit*** *dat.* be involved in an endless stream of correspondence with; **~rand** *m* margin; **~sche·re** *f*: (***e-e ~*** a pair of) paper scissors *pl.*; **~schlan·ge** *f* streamer; **~schnit·zel** *pl.* paper cuttings; **~ser·vi,et·te** *f* paper napkin; **~stau** *m* jam; **~ta·schen·tuch** *n* paper tissue (F hankie); **~ti·ger** *m* paper tiger; **~tü·te** *f* paper bag
pa'pier·ver·ar·bei·tend *adj.* paper-processing; **Pa'pier·ver·ar·bei·tung** *f* paper processing
Pa'pier·vor·schub *m* paper feed
Pa'pier·wa·ren *pl.* stationery *sg.*; **~hand·lung** *f* stationer's (shop)
papp [pap] F *int.*: ***ich kann nicht mehr ~ sagen*** I couldn't eat another thing
Papp [pap] *m* (-s; *no pl.*) **1.** pap, *contp. a.* F goo; **2.** paste; **3.** → ***Pappschnee***
'**Papp|band** *m* (-[e]s; ⸚e) hard paperback; **~be·cher** *m* paper cup; **~deckel** *m* (piece of) cardboard; (piece of) pasteboard
Pap·pe ['papə] *f* (-; -n) cardboard; F *fig.* ***das ist nicht von ~*** it's not to be sniffed at; F ***er ist nicht von ~*** he's a force to be reckoned with
Pap·pel ['papəl] *f* (-; -n) poplar
päp·peln ['pɛpəln] F *v/t.* (h) feed up; *fig.* coddle, pamper; *fig.* ***j-s Eitelkeit ~*** feed (*or* pander to) s.o.'s vanity
pap·pen ['papən] (h) **I.** *v/t.* paste, stick; **II.** *v/i. snow etc.*: stick
'**Pap·pen·deckel** *m* → ***Pappdeckel***
Pap·pen·hei·mer ['papənhaɪmɐ] *pl.*: F ***ich kenne meine ~*** I know who I'm dealing with
'**Pap·pen·stiel** F *m*: ***für e-n ~*** for a song; ***das ist kein ~*** F it's no chickenfeed; ***es***

ist keinen ~ wert F it's not worth a bean (*or* a tinker's cuss)
pap·per·la·papp [papɐla'pap] *int.* rubbish!
pap·pig ['papɪç] *adj.* **1.** sticky; **2.** stodgy
'Papp|ka·me,rad *m* (cardboard) dummy, effigy; **~kar,ton** *m* cardboard box, carton
Papp·ma·ché [papma'ʃe:] *n* (-s; -s) papier mâché; *fig. in cpds.* cardboard ...
'Papp|na·se *f* false nose; **~schach·tel** *f* cardboard box; **~schnee** *m* wet (*or* sticky, heavy) snow; **~tel·ler** *m* paper plate
Pa·pri·ka ['paprika] *m* (-s; -[s]) **1.** paprika; **2.** → **~scho·te** *f* pepper
Papst [pa:pst] *m* (-es; Päpste ['pɛ:pstə]) pope; **~kro·ne** *f* (papal) tiara
päpst·lich ['pɛ:pstlɪç] *adj.* papal; *formal*: pontifical; ***2er Stuhl*** Holy See; ***~er als der Papst sein*** be more Catholic than the Pope
'Papst·mes·se *f* papal mass
'Papst·tum *n* (-[e]s; *no pl.*) papacy
'Papst·wahl *f* papal elections *pl.*, election of a new pope
Pa·py·rus [pa'py:rʊs] *m* (-; -ri) papyrus; **~hand·schrift** *f* papyrus manuscript; **~rol·le** *f* papyrus scroll; **~stau·de** *f* papyrus plant
Pa·ra·bel [pa'ra:bəl] *f* (-; -n) **1.** parable; **2.** ⩓ parabola
Pa·ra·bol·an,ten·ne [para'bo:l-] *f* satellite dish, dish aerial (*or* antenna)
pa·ra·bo·lisch [para'bo:lɪʃ] *adj.* parabolic
Pa·ra'bol·spie·gel *m* parabolic reflector
Pa·ra·de [pa'ra:də] *f* (-; -n) **1.** ⚔ parade, review; march-past; ***die ~ abnehmen*** take the salute; **2.** *fencing, boxing*: parry; *riding*: halt; *soccer etc.*: (***glänzende ~*** brilliant) save; *fig.* ***j-m in die ~ fahren*** a) cut s.o. short, b) throw a spanner (*Am.* monkey wrench) in(to) the works; **~bei·spiel** *n* classic example; **~marsch** *m* **1.** march-past; **2.** → ***Paradeschritt***; **3.** ♪ military march; **~pferd** *n* showhorse; *fig.* showpiece; **~rol·le** *f*: ***das ist s-e ~*** that's his party piece; ***das ist für sie e-e ~*** she was made (*or* cut out) for the part; ***das war e-e ihrer ~n*** it was one of her classic (*or* best, most famous, most successful) roles (*or* parts); **~schritt** *m* drill step; goose-step; ***im ~*** in drill step; goose-stepping; **~stück** *fig. n* showpiece; **~uni,form** *f* dress uniform
pa·ra·die·ren [para'di:rən] *v/i.* (h) parade; *fig.* **~ *mit*** *dat.* show off (with) *s.th.*
Pa·ra·dies [para'di:s] *n* (-es; -e [-zə]) paradise; *bibl.* Garden of Eden; ***ein ~ für Urlauber*** a holidaymaker's paradise; ***das verlorene ~*** paradise lost; ***das ~ auf Erden*** heaven on earth; ***ich fühle mich wie im ~*** (I feel as if) I'm walking on air; ***das ist das wahre ~*** it's absolute paradise; **pa·ra·die·sisch** [para'di:zɪʃ] **I.** *adj.* heavenly; *lit.* paradisiacal; **II.** *adv.*: ***hier ist es ~ schön*** it's like paradise (here)
Pa·ra'dies·vo·gel *m* bird of paradise
Pa·ra·dig·ma [para'dɪgma] *n* (-s; -men) paradigm
pa·ra·dox [para'dɔks] **I.** *adj.* paradoxical; ***das 2e daran*** the paradoxical side of it; **II.** 2 *n* (-es; -e) → **Pa·ra·do·xon** [pa'ra:dɔksɔn] *n* (-s; -xa [-sa]) paradox
Pa·raf·fin [para'fi:n] *n* (-s; -e) paraffin, *Am.* kerosene
Pa·ra·graph [para'gra:f] *m* (-en; -en) ⚖ section, article; paragraph

Pa·ra'gra·phen|dickicht *n* (jungle of) red tape; **~hengst** F *m* F legal eagle; **~rei·ter** *m* stickler for the rules
Pa·ra·guay·er ['pa:ragvaɪɐ] *m* (-s; -), **Pa·ra·guay·erin** ['pa:ragvaɪərɪn] *f* (-; -nen), **pa·ra·guay·isch** ['pa:ragvaɪɪʃ] *adj.* Paraguayan
Par·al·la·xe [para'laksə] *f* (-; -n) *phys.* parallax
par·al·lel [para'le:l] **I.** *adj.* parallel (***mit*** *dat.* to, with); **II.** *adv.* parallel; ***~ laufen zu*** *dat.* run parallel to
Par·al'lel·drucker *m* parallel printer
Par·al·le·le [para'le:lə] *f* (-; -n) parallel (line); *fig.* parallel; *fig.* ***e-e ~ ziehen zu*** *dat.* draw a parallel to
Par·al'lel|fall *m* parallel case; **~klas·se** *f* parallel class
Par·al·le·lo·gramm [paralelo'gram] *n* (-s; -e) parallelogram
Par·al'lel|schal·tung *f* ⚡ parallel connection; **~schwung** *m skiing*: parallel turn; **~stra·ße** *f* road (*or* street) running parallel; ***es ist e-e ~ zur X-Straße*** it runs parallel to X Street; ***die nächste ~*** the road parallel to this one
Pa·ra·ly·se [para'ly:zə] *f* (-; -n) paralysis
pa·ra·ly·sie·ren [paraly'zi:rən] *v/t.* (h) paralyze
Pa·ra·ly·ti·ker [para'ly:tikɐ] *m* (-s; -), **pa·ra·ly·tisch** [para'ly:tɪʃ] *adj.* paralytic
Pa·ra·me·ter [pa'ra:metɐ] *m* (-s; -) parameter
pa·ra·mi·li,tä·risch ['pa:ra-] *adj.* paramilitary
Pa·ra·noia [para'nɔya] *f* (-; *no pl.*) *psych.* paranoia; **pa·ra·no·id** [parano'i:t] *adj.* paranoid; **Pa·ra·noi·ker** [para'no:ikɐ] *m* (-s; -), **pa·ra·no·isch** [para'no:ɪʃ] *adj.* paranoiac
Pa·ra·nuß ['pa:ra-] *f* Brazil nut
pa·ra·phie·ren [para'fi:rən] *v/t.* (h) initial
Pa·ra·phra·se [para'fra:zə] *f* (-; -n), **pa·ra·phra·sie·ren** [parafra'zi:rən] *v/t.* (h) paraphrase
Pa·ra·psy·cho,lo·ge ['pa:ra-] *m* (-n; -n) parapsychologist; **'Pa·ra·psy·cho·lo,gie** *f* (-; *no pl.*) parapsychology
Pa·ra·sit [para'zi:t] *m* (-en; -en) parasite (*a. fig.*)
pa·ra·si·tär [parazi'tɛ:ɐ] *adj.* parasitic(al)
Pa·ra'si·ten·da·sein *n* parasitic existence, parasitism; ***er führt ein ~*** he just lives off other people
pa·ra·si·tisch [para'zi:tɪʃ] *adj.* parasitic(al)
pa·rat [pa'ra:t] *adj.* ready; ***immer ein Blatt Papier ~ haben*** always have a piece of paper at hand (*or* at the ready); ***immer e-n Witz ~ haben*** always have a joke up one's sleeve; ***er hat immer e-e Antwort (Ausrede) ~*** he's never at a loss for an answer (excuse)
Pa·ra·ta·xe [para'taksə] *f* (-; -n) *ling.* parataxis
Pär·chen ['pɛ:ɐçən] *n* (-s; -) **1.** couple; ***ein ideales ~*** the ideal couple; ***so ein nettes ~*** what (*or* such) a nice couple; **2.** *zo.* pair
Par·cours [par'ku:ɐ] *m* (-; - [-s]) *sport*: course
Par·don [par'dõ:] **I.** *m, n* (-s; *no pl.*): ***kein(en) ~ kennen*** be (absolutely) ruthless; **II.** *int.* (I'm) sorry, *Am.* excuse me
Par·en·the·se [parɛn'te:zə] *f* (-; -n) parenthesis; ***in ~ setzen*** put in parenthesis (*or* parentheses); **par·en·the·tisch** [parɛn'te:tɪʃ] **I.** *adj.* parenthetical; **II.** *adv.* in parenthesis

Par·force|jagd [par'fɔrs-] *f* coursing; course, hunt; ***auf ~ gehen*** go coursing; **~ritt** *m* **1.** forced ride; **2.** *fig.* feat
Par·füm [par'fy:m] *n* (-s; -s, -e) perfume; scent; **~duft** *m* smell of perfume; scent
Par·fü·me·rie [parfymə'ri:] *f* (-; -n) perfume shop (*Am.* store); **~ab,tei·lung** *f* perfume department
Par'füm·fla·sche *f* perfume bottle
par·fü·mie·ren [parfy'mi:rən] (h) **I.** *v/t.* perfume, scent; **II.** *v/refl.*: ***sich ~*** put (some) perfume on; **par·fü·miert** [parfy'mi:ɐt] *adj.* scented
Par'füm|wol·ke *f* cloud of perfume; **~zer·stäu·ber** *m* atomizer
pa·ri ['pa:ri] *adv.* ✝ par; ***auf*** (*or* ***al***) ~ at par; ***über (unter) ~*** above (below) par
Pa·ria ['pa:rĭa] *m* (-s; -s) pariah
pa·rie·ren [pa'ri:rən] (h) **I.** *v/t. fencing etc.*: parry (*a. fig. question etc.*); pull up *horse*; save *ball*; **II.** *v/i. fencing*: parry; *fig.* knuckle under
Pa·ri·kurs ['pa:ri-] *m* ✝ parity price
Pa·ri·ser [pa'ri:zɐ] **I.** *m* (-s; -) **1.** Parisian; **2.** F rubber; **II.** *adj.* Parisian, (of) Paris
Pa·ri·tät [pari'tɛ:t] *f* (-; -en) parity (*a.* ✝); **pa·ri·tä·tisch** [pari'tɛ:tɪʃ] *adj.* equal, on equal terms; parity ...
Park [park] *m* (-[e]s; -s) **1.** park; **2.** *mot.* fleet (of cars)
Par·ka ['parka] *m* (-s; -s) parka
'Park·an·la·ge *f* park
'Park|aus·weis *m* parking ID; **~bahn** *f space travel*: parking orbit
'Park·bank *f* (-; ⁻̈e) park bench
'Park|bucht *f* parking bay; lay-by; **~deck** *n* parking level
par·ken ['parkən] (h) **I.** *v/t.* park; **II.** *v/i.* park; *car*: be parked; ***2 verboten!*** no parking
Par·kett [par'kɛt] *n* (-[e]s; -e) **1.** a) parquet (floor), b) dance floor; *fig.* ***ein Tänzchen aufs ~ legen*** trip the light fantastic; ***sich auf dem ~ bewegen können*** be perfectly at ease in society, have plenty of savoir-faire; **2.** *no pl. thea.* stalls *pl.*, *Am.* orchestra; **~(fuß)bo·den** *m* parquet floor
'Park|ge·bühr *f* parking fee; **~(hoch)·haus** *n* multi-storey car park
Par·kin·son·sche Krank·heit ['parkɪnzɔnʃə]: ***die ~*** Parkinson's disease
'Park|kral·le *f* wheel clamp; **~leuch·te** *f*, **~licht** *n* parking light; **~lücke** *f* parking space; **~mög·lich·keit** *f* place to park; *pl.* room to park; parking provision; ***es gibt keine ~(en)*** there's nowhere (*or* no place) to park; **~pla,ket·te** *f* parking sticker; **~platz** *m* **1.** → ***Parklücke***; **2.** car park, *Am.* parking lot; **~pro,blem** *n* parking problem; **~schei·be** *f* parking disc; **~stu·di·um** *n* stopgap studies *pl.*; **~sün·der** *m* parking offender; **~uhr** *f* parking meter; **~ver·bot** *n*: ***hier ist ~*** there's no parking here; **~ver·bots·schild** *n* no-parking sign; **~ver·ge·hen** *n* parking offen|ce (*Am.* -se); **~wäch·ter** *m* car park (*Am.* parking lot) attendant
Par·la·ment [parla'mɛnt] *n* (-[e]s; -e) parliament
Par·la·men·ta·ri·er [parlamɛn'ta:rĭɐ] *m* (-s; -), **Par·la·men·ta·rie·rin** [parlamɛn'ta:rĭərɪn] *f* (-; -nen) member of parliament; parliamentarian
par·la·men·ta·risch [parlamɛn'ta:rɪʃ] *adj.* parliamentary
Par·la·men·ta·rismus [parlamɛnta'rɪsmʊs] *m* (-; *no pl.*) parliamentarianism

Par·la'ments|ab·ge·ord·ne·te *m, f* (-n; -n) member of parliament; parliamentarian; **~auf·lö·sung** *f* dissolving (*or* dissolution) of parliament; **~aus·schuß** *m* parliamentary committee; **~de‚bat·te** *f* parliamentary debate; **~fe·ri·en** *pl.* (parliamentary) recess *sg.*; ***in die ~ gehen*** rise for the recess; **~ge·bäu·de** *n* parliament (building); *in London*: Houses *pl.* of Parliament; **~mehr·heit** *f* parliamentary majority, majority in parliament; **~mit·glied** *n* member of parliament; *in GB*: *a.* MP; **~prä·si‚dent** *m* (parliamentary) president; *in GB*: Speaker; **~sit·zung** *f* sitting of parliament; **~wah·len** *pl.* parliamentary elections; *in GB*: general election *sg.*

Par·me·san [parme'za:n] *m* (-[s]; *no pl.*), **~kä·se** *m* Parmesan (cheese)

Pa·ro·die [paro'di:] *f* (-; -n) parody (***auf*** *acc.* on), F send-up (of); **pa·ro·die·ren** [paro'di:rən] *v/t.* (h) parody, F do a take-off (*or* send-up) of; **Pa·ro·dist** [paro'dɪst] *m* (-en; -en) parodist; **pa·ro·di·stisch** [paro'dɪstɪʃ] *adj.* parodistic

Par·odon·to·se [parodɔn'to:zə] *f* (-; -n) pyorrh(o)ea

Pa·ro·le [pa'ro:lə] *f* (-; -n) ⚔ password; *fig.* watchword, *pol. a.* slogan

Pa·ro·li [pa'ro:li] *n*: ***j-m*** (*or* ***e-r Sache***) ***~ bieten*** stand up to s.o. (*or* s.th.), give as good as one gets

Part [part] *m* (-s; -s) *thea.*, ♪ part; share

Par·tei [par'taɪ] *f* (-; -en) party (*a. pol.*, ⚖); *sport*: side; ✝ tenant(s *pl.*), household; ***hier wohnen vier ~en*** there are four parties occupying this house (*or* building); ***gegnerische ~*** ⚖ opponent(s *pl.*), *sport*: *a.* opposite side, opposing team; ***~ nehmen für j-n*** side with s.o.; ***gegen j-n ~ ergreifen*** take sides against s.o.; ***über den ~en stehen*** remain impartial; ***~ sein*** be bias(s)ed, be prejudiced; **~ab·zei·chen** *n* party badge; **~ap·pa‚rat** *m* party machine; **~aus·schluß** *m* expulsion from a party; **~aus·tritt** *m* party defection; **~ba·sis** *f* rank and file, grassroots (members) *pl.*; **~bon·ze** *m* party bigwig; **~buch** *n* party card; **~chef** *m* party leader; **~chi‚ne·sisch** F *n* F party lingo; **~dis·zi‚plin** *f* party discipline; ***sich der ~ beugen*** toe the party line

Par'tei·en|fi·nan‚zie·rung *f* funding of political parties; **~land·schaft** *f* party scene, political constellation; **~staat** *m* party state

Par'tei|freund *m* fellow member (of the party); **~füh·rer** *m* party leader; **~funk·tio‚när** *m* party official

Par'tei·gän·ger [-gɛŋɐ] *m* (-s; -) party liner

Par'tei|ge·nos·se *m*, **~ge·nos·sin** *f* party member; **~ideo‚lo·ge** *m* party ideologist (*or* theorist)

par'tei·in‚tern **I.** *adj.* (inner-)party ..., within the party; ***~e Querelen*** party in-fighting; **II.** *adv.* within the party

par·tei·isch [par'taɪɪʃ] *adj.* bias(s)ed, prejudiced (***für*** *acc.* in favo[u]r of; ***gegen*** *acc.* against)

Par'tei·kas·se *f* party funds *pl.*

par'tei·lich *adj.* party ...

Par'tei·li·nie *f* party line

par'tei·los *adj.* independent, non-party ...; **Par'tei·lo·se** *m, f* (-n; -n) independent

Par'tei·mit·glied *n* party member

Par'tei·nah·me [-na:mə] *f* (-; *no pl.*) siding (***für*** *acc.* with); ***sich e-r ~ enthalten*** not to take sides, sit on the fence

Par'tei|or‚gan *n* party organ; **~po·li‚tik** *f* party politics *pl.*; party policy (*or* policies *pl.*); **~po‚li·ti·ker** *m* party politician; **~po‚li·tisch** *adj.* party political; **~pres·se** *f* party press; **~pro‚gramm** *n* (party) manifesto *or* platform; **~schä·di·gend** *adj.* detrimental to the party (interests); **~schu·le** *f* party cadre training institution; **~spen·de** *f* party (political) donation; **~spen·den·af‚fä·re** *f* party funding scandal; **~spit·ze** *f* party leadership (*or* leaders *pl.*); **~tag** *m* party conference (*Am.* convention); **~‚über·grei·fend** *adj.* cross-party ...; **~ver·samm·lung** *f* party meeting (*or* rally); **~volk** *n* (-[e]s; *no pl.*) (party) rank and file; **~vor·sit·zen·de** *m, f* (-n; -n) party leader; **~vor·stand** *m* party executive; **~zei·tung** *f* party newspaper; **~zen‚tra·le** *f* party headquarters *pl.*; **~zu·ge·hö·rig·keit** *f* party affiliation; party membership

Par·terre [par'tɛr(ə)] **I.** *n* (-s; -s) ground (*Am.* first) floor; *thea.* rear stalls *pl.*, *Am.* parquet; **II.** ~ *adv.* on the ground (*Am.* first) floor; *thea.* in the stalls (*Am.* parquet); **~woh·nung** *f* ground-floor flat, *Am.* first-floor apartment

Par·ti·al... [par'tsĭa:l-] *in cpds usu.* partial

Par·tie [par'ti:] *f* (-; -n) **1.** part; ⚘ *a.* area, region; **2.** *sport etc.*: game; **3.** *thea.*, ♪ part; **4.** ✝ consignment, batch; **5.** ***e-e gute ~*** a good match; ***e-e gute ~ machen*** marry well; **6.** ***mit von der ~ sein*** be in on it; ***ich bin mit von der ~!*** you can count me in

par·ti·ell [par'tsĭɛl] *adj.* partial

Par·ti·kel¹ [par'ti:kəl] *n* (-s; -) particle

Par'ti·kel² *f* (-; -n) *ling.* particle

Par·ti·ku·la·ris·mus [partikula'rɪsmʊs] *m* (-; *no pl.*) particularism; **par·ti·ku·la·ri·stisch** [partikula'rɪstɪʃ] *adj.* particularist(ic)

Par·ti·san [parti'za:n] *m* (-s, -en; -en) partisan, guer(r)illa; **Par·ti'sa·nen·krieg** *m* partisan warfare

Par·ti·tur [parti'tu:ɐ] *f* (-; -en) ♪ score

Par·ti·zip [parti'tsi:p] *n* (-s; Partizipien [parti'tsi:pĭən]) *ling.* participle; ***~ Präsens*** (***Perfekt***) present (past) participle

Par·ti·zi·pi·al|kon·struk·ti‚on [partitsi'pĭa:l-] *f ling.* participial construction; **~satz** *m ling.* participial clause

par·ti·zi·pie·ren [partitsi'pi:rən] *v/i.* (h) participate (***an*** *dat.* in)

Part·ner ['partnɐ] *m* (-s; -) a) partner, b) boyfriend; ***als j-s ~ spielen*** *sport*: play as partner of s.o., *film etc.*: play opposite s.o.; **~be·zie·hung** *f* relationship (between two people)

Part·ne·rin ['partnərɪn] *f* (-; -nen) a) partner, b) girlfriend; → ***Partner***

'Part·ner|look [-lʊk] *m* (-s; *no pl.*) matching clothes *pl.*; ***im ~*** wearing matching clothes; **~pro‚ble·me** *pl.* problems with one's partner

'Part·ner·schaft *f* (-; -en) partnership

'part·ner·schaft·lich *adj.* fair; *relationship etc.* based on partnership; ***~es Verhalten*** cooperation; ***auf ~er Basis*** on a joint basis, on a basis of (mutual trust and) cooperation; ***sie führen e-e ~e Ehe*** their marriage is more of a partnership

'Part·ner|stadt *f* twin town; ***Frankfurt hat Birmingham als ~*** Frankfurt is twinned with Birmingham; **~su·che** *f* finding a (*or* the right) partner, F finding a mate; ***auf ~ sein*** be looking for a partner (*or* for someone, F for a mate); **~tausch** *m* wife (*or* partner) swapping; **~ver·mitt·lung** *f* dating agency; marriage bureau; **~wahl** *f* choice of partner; ***bei der ~*** when choosing a partner (F mate); **~wech·sel** *m* change of partners; changing partners; ***bei häufigem ~*** with (*or* in the case of) frequently changing partners

par·tout [par'tu:] F *adv.*: ***sie wollte es ~ nicht machen*** she absolutely refused to do it; ***es wollte ~ nicht klappen*** it just wouldn't work

Par·ty ['pa:ɐti] *f* (-; -s; Parties) party; **~kel·ler** *m* (basement) party room; **~lö·we** F *m* F party lion; **~muf·fel** F *m* F party pooper; **~raum** *m* party room; **~ser·vice** *m* party (*or* catering) service

Par·zel·le [par'tsɛlə] *f* (-; -n) plot (of land), allotment, *esp. Am.* lot; **par·zel·lie·ren** [partsɛ'li:rən] *v/t.* (h) divide into lots, *Am. a.* plot; **Par·zel'lie·rung** *f* (-; -en) division of land

Pas·cal [pas'kal] *n* (s; -) *phys.* pascal

Pa·scha ['paʃa] *m* (-s; -s) pasha; *fig.* ***sich wie ein ~ bedienen lassen*** let o.s. be waited on hand and foot

Paß [pas] *m* (Passes; Pässe ['pɛsə]) **1.** passport; **2.** *geogr.* pass; **3.** *sport*: pass; ***langer ~*** long ball; **4.** amble

pas·sa·bel [pa'sa:bəl] **I.** *adj.* passable, tolerable; ***ganz ~*** *a.* all right, *Am.* alright; not too bad; **II.** *adv.* passably, reasonably well; ***er hat es ganz ~ gemacht*** *a.* he didn't do too bad a job of it

Pas·sa·ge [pa'sa:ʒə] *f* (-; -n) **1.** passage(way); shopping arcade; **2.** ♪, *text*: passage; *film*: sequence; **3.** ⚓ crossing, passage; **4.** passage

Pas·sa·gier [pasa'ʒi:ɐ] *m* (-s; -e [-rə]) passenger; ***blinder ~*** stowaway; **~damp·fer** *m* passenger steamer, liner; **~flug·zeug** *n* passenger plane; **~gut** *n* luggage, *Am.* baggage; **~li·ste** *f* list of passengers

Pas·sah ['pasa] *n* (-s; *no pl.*) Passover; **~fest** *n* Passover; **~mahl** *n* Passover meal

'Paß·amt *n* passport office

Pas·sant [pa'sant] *m* (-en; -en), **Pas·san·tin** [pa'santɪn] *f* (-; -nen) passerby (*pl.* passersby), *pl. a.* people passing by; pedestrian; ***ein paar Passanten befragen*** interview a few people in the street

Pas·sat [pa'sa:t] *m* (-[e]s; -e), **~wind** *m* trade wind

'Paß|be·stim·mun·gen *pl.* passport regulations; **~bild** *n* passport photo(graph)

pas·sé [pa'se:] *adj.* passé(e), F out; ***das ist endgültig*** (***längst***) ***~*** F that's died a death (F that went out with the ark)

pas·sen ['pasən] (h) **I.** *v/i.* **1.** fit (***j-m*** s.o.; ***auf*** *acc. s.th.*); ***es paßt genau*** it fits perfectly, it's a perfect fit; **2.** ***~ zu*** *dat.* suit s.o., go with *s.th.*, match *s.th.*; ***die Hose paßt gut zu dir*** the trousers suit you; ***die Krawatte paßt nicht zur Jacke*** the tie doesn't go with the jacket; *fig.* ***das paßt zu ihm*** that's just like him, that's him all over; ***das paßt überhaupt nicht zu ihm*** that's not like him at all; **3.** *fig.* fit; ***sie ~ gut zueinander*** they suit each other; ***er paßt nicht in diese Kreise*** he doesn't fit (*or* he's out of place) in these circles; ***die Bemerkung paßt hier nicht*** that remark is out of place here; **4.** suit (*dat. s.o.*

or s.th.), be suitable *or* convenient (for *s.o. or s.th.*); ***morgen paßt es ihm nicht*** tomorrow doesn't suit him (*or* is inconvenient for him); ***das paßt mir gut*** that suits me fine; ***nur wenn es ihnen*** (F ***in den Kram***) ***paßt*** only when they feel like it; F ***das paßt mir überhaupt nicht in den Kram*** it doesn't suit me at all, that's the last thing I want; ***mein neues Zimmer paßt mir*** (***überhaupt***) ***nicht*** I don't like (I'm not at all happy with) my new room; ***das könnte dir so ~!*** you'd like that, wouldn't you?; **5.** *card game*: pass; ***ich passe!*** pass; *fig.* ***da muß ich ~*** F you've got me there; ***da mußte er ~*** F he couldn't answer that one, that had him stumped; **6.** *sport*: pass; **II.** *v/t.* ⚙ fit (***in*** *acc.* into); **'pas·send** *adj.* suitable; *a.* convenient *date etc.* (***für*** *acc.* to, for); apt, fitting *remark etc.*; right *word*; matching *blouse etc.*; ***~ zu*** *dat.* to go with, to match *the trousers etc.*; ***der ~e Augenblick*** the right moment; ***ich halte es nicht für ~, daß er ...*** I don't think it would be right (*or* proper) for him to *inf.*; ***hast du's ~?*** have you got the right change?

Passe·par·tout [paspar'tu:] *n* (-s; -s) mount

'Paß|fäl·schung *f* passport forgery; **~form** *f* fit; ***e-e gute ~ haben*** be a good fit; **~fo·to** *n* passport photo(graph); **~gang** *m* amble; ***im ~ gehen*** amble; **~ge·bühr** *f* passport fee

pas·sier·bar [pa'si:ɐba:ɐ] *adj.* passable

pas·sie·ren [pa'si:rən] **I.** *v/t.* (h) **1.** pass (by, through *etc.*) *a place etc.*; cross *bridge*, *river*; **2.** *sport*, ⚓ clear; **3.** *gastr.* strain, pass through a sieve; **II.** *v/i.* (sn) happen; ***j-m ~*** happen to s.o.; ***was ist passiert?*** what's wrong?, what('s) happened?; ***das kann jedem mal ~*** that can happen to the best of us; ***das kann auch nur dir ~*** it's just like you, isn't it?; ***das passiert mir zum erstenmal*** (***im Leben***) that's the first time (ever) anything like that has happened to me; ***mir ist nichts passiert*** I'm all right (*Am.* alright); ***ist was passiert?*** is everything all right (*Am.* alright)?; ***mir ist gerade was Merkwürdiges passiert*** I just had a strange experience; F ***jetzt ist es passiert!*** that's done it (now); ***... sonst passiert was!*** ... or else!; ***was passiert mit diesem Zeug?*** what's to be done with this stuff?, where's this stuff supposed to go?

Pas·sier·schein [pa'si:ɐ-] *m* pass, permit

Pas·si·on [pa'sĭo:n] *f* (-; -en) **1.** passion; ***Schach ist s-e ~*** he's a passionate chess player; **2.** *eccl.*, ♪, *art*: Passion

pas·sio·niert [pasĭo'ni:ɐt] *adj.* (very) keen, enthusiastic, fanatical; ***er ist ein ~er Gärtner*** *a.* he's very keen on (*or* he loves) gardening

Pas·si'ons|spiel *n* passion (*or* Passion) play; **~wo·che** *f* Holy Week

pas·siv ['pasi:f] **I.** *adj.* passive (*a. ling.*, *sport*, ⚔, ⚡, ☤); ***~er Widerstand*** passive resistance; ***~es Wahlrecht*** eligibility; ***~er Teilhaber*** sleeping partner; ***~e Handelsbilanz*** adverse balance of trade; **II.** *adv.*: ***sich ~ verhalten*** remain passive, *esp. pol.* maintain a passive stance; ***man kann nicht einfach ~ zusehen*** you can't just sit back and watch (it all happen)

'Pas·siv *n* (-s; *no pl.*) *ling.* passive (voice)

Pas·si·va [pa'si:va] *pl.* ☤ liabilities

pas·si·visch [pa'si:vɪʃ] *adj. ling.* passive

Pas·si·vi·tät [pasivi'tɛ:t] *f* (-; *no pl.*) passiveness, passivity (*a. sport*); inaction; apathy; inertia

'Pas·siv|po·sten *m* ☤ debit item; **~rau·chen** *n* passive smoking; **~rau·cher** *m* passive smoker; **~satz** *m ling.* passive clause

'Paß|kon,trol·le *f* passport control; **~le·se·ge·rät** *n* passport scanner; **~stel·le** *f* passport office; **~stra·ße** *f* mountain pass

Pas·sus ['pasʊs] *m* (-; - ['pasu:s]) passage

'Paß|ver·län·ge·rung *f* extension (*or* renewal) of a *or* one's passport; **~zwang** *m* passport(s) required

Pa·ste ['pastə] *f* (-; -n) *a. gastr.* paste

Pa·stell [pas'tɛl] *n* (-s; -e) pastel; ***in ~ gemalt*** painted in pastel colo(u)rs; **~bild** *n* pastel drawing; **~far·be** *f* **1.** pastel; **2.** pastel colo(u)r (*or* shade); **~ma·le,rei** *f* pastel (drawing)

Pa·ste·te [pas'te:tə] *f* (-; -n) pie, pâté

pa·steu·ri·sie·ren [pastøri'zi:rən] *v/t.* (h) pasteurize; ***pasteurisierte Milch*** pasteurized milk

Pa·stil·le [pas'tɪlə] *f* (-; -n) lozenge, pastille

Pa·stor ['pasto:ɐ] *m* (-s; -en [pas'to:rən]), **Pa·sto·rin** [pas'to:rɪn] *f* (-; -nen) pastor, minister, vicar; **pa·sto·ral** [pasto'ra:l] *adj.* pastoral; ***in ~em Ton*** solemnly

Pa·te ['pa:tə] *m* (-n; -n) **1.** godfather, *pl.* godparents; ***bei j-m ~ stehen*** be s.o.'s godfather (*f* godmother); *fig.* ***~ stehen bei*** *dat.* be the inspiration for *a poem etc.*, be behind *an idea etc.*, *chance*: play an important part in; ***dabei hat die Überlegung ~ gestanden, daß*** the idea behind it was that; **2.** → ***Patenkind***

'Pa·ten|kind *n* godchild; **~on·kel** *m* godfather

'Pa·ten·schaft *f* (-; -en) **1.** godparenthood; **2.** sponsorship; ***e-e ~ übernehmen für*** *acc.* sponsor *a child etc.*

'Pa·ten·sohn *m* godson

pa·tent [pa'tɛnt] F *adj.* clever, brilliant; ***~er Kerl*** F great guy, F good sort; ***sie ist e-e ~e Frau*** F she's all right (*Am.* alright), she's great

Pa'tent *n* (-[e]s; -e) **1.** patent (***auf*** *acc.* for); ***ein ~ anmelden*** (***erteilen***) apply for (issue) a patent; ***~ angemeldet*** patent pending; **2.** ⚔ commission; ***sein ~ erwerben*** get one's commission; **~amt** *n* patent office; **~an·mel·dung** *f* (patent) application

'Pa·ten·tan·te *f* godmother

Pa'tent|an·walt *m* patent agent (*Am.* attorney); **~dau·er** *f* life of a patent; **~er·tei·lung** *f* issue of a patent; **𝔏fä·hig** *adj.* patentable; **~ge·setz** *n* patent law

pa·ten·tier·bar [patɛn'ti:ɐba:ɐ] *adj.* patentable; **pa·ten·tie·ren** [patɛn'ti:rən] *v/t.* (h) patent; (***sich***) ***et. ~ lassen*** take out a patent for s.th.

Pa'tent|in·ha·ber *m* patentee; **~lö·sung** *fig. f* magic formula, nostrum; ***dafür gibt es keine ~*** there's no ready-made solution for that

'Pa·ten·toch·ter *f* goddaughter

Pa'tent·recht *n* a) patent law, b) patent right(s *pl.*); **pa'tent·recht·lich** *adj. and adv.* under patent law; ***~ geschützt*** patented, protected (by patent)

Pa'tent|re,zept *n* → ***Patentlösung***; **~schutz** *m* patent protection; **~ver·let·zung** *f* patent infringement

Pa·ter ['pa:tɐ] *m* (-s; Patres ['patre:s]) *eccl.* father

Pa·ter·na·lis·mus [patɛrna'lɪsmʊs] *m* (-; *no pl.*) paternalism; **pa·ter·na·li·stisch** [patɛrna'lɪstɪʃ] *adj.* paternalistic

Pa·ter·no·ster¹ [patɐ'nɔstɐ] *n* (-s; -) *eccl. the* Lord's Prayer, paternoster

Pa·ter'no·ster² *m* (-s; -) paternoster

pa·the·tisch [pa'te:tɪʃ] *adj.* lofty, emotional; *contp.* dramatic

pa·tho·gen [pato'ge:n] *adj.* pathogenic

Pa·tho·lo·ge [pato'lo:gə] *m* (-n; -n) pathologist; **Pa·tho·lo·gie** [patolo'gi:] *f* (-; *no pl.*) **1.** pathology; **2.** pathology department; **pa·tho·lo·gisch** [pato'lo:gɪʃ] *adj.* pathological (*a. fig.*)

Pa·thos ['pa:tɔs] *n* (-; *no pl.*) emotionalism; ***falsches ~*** bathos

Pa·ti·ence [pa'sĭã:s] *f* (-; -n) (game of) patience, *Am.* (game of) solitaire; ***e-e ~ legen*** play (a game of) patience (*Am.* solitaire)

Pa·ti·ent [pa'tsĭɛnt] *m* (-en; -en) patient

Pa·ti'en·ten|kar,tei *f* patients' file; **~über,wa·chung** *f* monitoring of patients

Pa·ti·en·tin [pa'tsĭɛntɪn] *f* (-; -nen) patient

Pa·tin ['pa:tɪn] *f* (-; -nen) godmother

Pa·ti·na ['pa:tina] *f* (-; *no pl.*) patina (*a. fig.*); ***~ ansetzen*** develop a patina, *fig. contp.* wear thin; **pa·ti·nie·ren** [pati'ni:rən] *v/t.* (h) patinate

Pat·na·reis ['patna-] *m* Patna rice

Pa·tri·arch [patri'arç] *m* (-en; -en) patriarch (*a. fig.*); **pa·tri·ar·cha·lisch** [patriar'ça:lɪʃ] *adj.* patriarchal; **Pa·tri·ar·chat** [patriar'ça:t] *n* (-[e]s; -e) patriarchy, patriarchal society

Pa·tri·ot [patri'o:t] *m* (-en; -en) patriot

pa·trio·tisch [patri'o:tɪʃ] *adj.* patriotic(ally *adv.*)

Pa·trio·tis·mus [patrio'tɪsmʊs] *m* (-; *no pl.*) patriotism

Pa·tri·zi·er [pa'tri:tsĭɐ] *m* (-s; -), **pa·tri·zisch** [pa'tri:tsɪʃ] *adj.* patrician

Pa·tron [pa'tro:n] *m* (-s; -e) patron; *eccl.* patron saint; F *contp.* ***übler ~*** nasty customer; **Pa·tro·nat** [patro'na:t] *n* (-s; -e) patronage

Pa·tro·ne [pa'tro:nə] *f* (-; -n) cartridge; *phot. a.* cassette

Pa'tro·nen|fül·ler *m*, **~füll·hal·ter** *m* cartridge pen; **~gurt** *m*, **~gür·tel** *m* cartridge belt; **~hül·se** *f* cartridge case; **~ta·sche** *f* ammunition pouch

Pa·tro·nin [pa'tro:nɪn] *f* (-; -nen) patroness; *eccl.* patron saint

Pa·trouil·le [pa'trʊljə] *f* (-; -n) patrol

Pa'trouil·len·boot *n* patrol boat

pa·trouil·lie·ren [patrʊl'ji:rən] *v/i.* (h, sn) patrol; *fig.* ***auf und ab ~*** pace up and down

patsch [patʃ] *int.* splat!; smack!

Pat·sche ['patʃə] F *f* (-; -n): (***ganz schön***) ***in der ~ sitzen*** F be in a real mess; ***j-m aus der ~ helfen*** get s.o. out of a tight spot, F bale s.o. out

pat·schen ['patʃən] *v/i.* (h) splash; smack; (***mit den Händen***) ***ins Wasser ~*** splash (the water about); (***in die Hände***) ***~*** clap (one's hands)

'Patsch|hand *f*, **~händ·chen** *n* (little) hand *or* F mitt

'patsch'naß *adj.* soaked to the skin, soaking (wet), drenched

Patt [pat] *n* (-s; -s), **patt** *adj. chess and fig. pol.* stalemate; *fig. a.* deadlock

'Patt·si·tua·ti,on *f* deadlock, stalemate

pat·zen ['patsən] F *v/i.* (h) F fluff (it), make a boob; **Pat·zer** ['patsɐ] F *m* (-s; -) F (real) boob

pat·zig ['patsɪç] F *adj.* F snotty; ***sei nicht so*** ~ F don't you get fresh with me

Pau·ke ['paʊkə] *f* (-; -n) kettledrum, *pl. a.* timpani; ~ ***spielen*** play the kettledrums (*or* timpani); F *fig.* ***mit*** ~***n und Trompeten durchfallen*** fail miserably, F make a real mess of it; F ***auf die*** ~ ***hauen*** a) F have a real binge, b) F blow one's horn

pau·ken ['paʊkən] (h) **I.** *v/i.* **1.** ♪ play the timpani (*or* [kettle]drums); **2.** F *ped.* F cram, swot; **II.** *v/t.* F swot (*or* bone) up on

'**Pau·ken|höh·le** *f anat.* tympanum; ~**schlag** *m* drumbeat; *fig.* ***mit e-m*** ~ ***beginnen*** (***enden***) get off to a dramatic start (come to a dramatic end *or* finish); ~**schlä·ger** *m* timpanist, drummer; ~**schle·gel** *m* timpani (*or* kettledrum) stick

Pau·ker ['paʊkɐ] *m* (-s; -) **1.** ♪ timpanist, drummer; **2.** F *ped.* F crammer

Pau·ke·rei [paʊkə'raɪ] F *f* (-; *no pl.*) *ped.* F cramming, swotting

Pauk·stu·dio ['paʊk-] F *n* F crammer

Paus·backen ['paʊs-] *pl.* chubby cheeks; '**paus·backig** ['paʊsbakɪç] (*sep.* -k·k-), '**paus·bäckig** [-bɛkɪç] (*sep.* -k·k-) *adj.* chubby(-cheeked); ***sie hat ein*** ~***es Gesicht*** she's got chubby cheeks

pau·schal [paʊ'ʃa:l] **I.** *adj.* **1.** lump *sum*; all-in *price etc.*, (all-)inclusive; ~***e Erhöhung*** across-the-board increase; **2.** *fig.* general; sweeping *statement*; **II.** *adv.* **3.** ~ ***vergüten*** pay a lump sum (*or* flat rate) for; ~ ***festsetzen*** set a flat rate for; ***j-m et.*** ~ ***berechnen*** charge s.o. a flat rate for s.th.; ***es kostet*** ~ ***3000 Mark*** it's 3,000 marks all in (*or* [all-]inclusive); **4.** *fig.* ***et.*** ~ ***verurteilen*** condemn s.th. wholesale; ***ich möchte es nicht*** ~ ***beurteilen*** I wouldn't like to draw any general conclusions (*or* make any general statements on the matter)

Pau'schal·an·ge·bot *n* package deal

Pau·scha·le [paʊ'ʃa:lə] *f* (-; -n) lump sum; *hotel etc.*: all-inclusive price; → ***Pauschalgebühr***

Pau'schal|ge·bühr *f* flat rate; ~**ho·no·ˌrar** *n* flat-rate fee

pau·scha·li·sie·ren [paʊʃali'zi:rən] (h) **I.** *v/i.* generalize; F lump everything together, tar everything with the same brush; **II.** *v/t.*: ***man kann es nicht*** ~ you can't generalize (*or* make generalizations) like that

Pau'schal|rei·se *f* package tour; ~**sum·me** *f* lump sum; ~**ur·laub** *m* package holiday; ~**ur·teil** *fig. n* sweeping statement, (broad) generalization; ~**wert** *m* overall value

Pausch·be·trag ['paʊʃ-] *m* lump sum

Pau·se[1] ['paʊzə] *f* (-; -n) break; pause; *ped.* break, *Am.* recess; *thea.*, *sport*: interval, *Am. a. film*: intermission; ♪ rest; ***kleine*** ~ short (*or* quick, little) break; ***e-e*** ~ ***machen*** (*or* ***einlegen***) a) take (*or* have) a break, b) pause for a moment; ***sie gönnt sich keine*** ~ she never lets up

'**Pau·se**[2] *f* (-; -n) **1.** tracing; **2.** copy; blueprint; **pau·sen** ['paʊzən] *v/t.* (h) **1.** trace; **2.** copy

'**Pau·sen|brot** *n* breaktime snack; ~**fül·ler** *m* filler

'**pau·sen·los** *adj.* uninterrupted, incessant, nonstop ...; unrelenting

'**Pau·sen|pfiff** *m sport*: half-time whistle; ~**stand** *m sport*: half-time score; ~**ta·ste** *f* pause button; ~**zei·chen** *n* **1.** ♪ rest; **2.** *radio*: interval (*or* station identification) signal

pau·sie·ren [paʊ'zi:rən] *v/i.* (h) take a break; ~ ***müssen*** *sport*: be out of action

'**Paus·pa|pier** *n* tracing paper

Pa·vi·an ['pa:vĭa:n] *m* (-s; -e) baboon

Pa·vil·lon ['pavɪljɔŋ, 'pavɪljõ] *m* (-s; -s) pavilion

pa·zi·fisch [pa'tsi:fɪʃ] *adj.* Pacific; ***der*** ≈***e Ozean*** the Pacific

Pa·zi·fis·mus [patsi'fɪsmʊs] *m* (-; *no pl.*) pacifism; **Pa·zi·fist** [patsi'fɪst] *m* (-en; -en), **pa·zi·fi·stisch** [patsi'fɪstɪʃ] *adj.* pacifist

PC [pe:'tse:] *m* (-s; -s) PC (= personal computer); ~**-Be·nut·zer** *m* PC user

Pech [pɛç] *n* (-s; *no pl.*) **1.** bad luck; ~ ***haben*** be unlucky (***bei*** *dat.*, ***mit*** *dat.* with); ***großes*** ~ ***haben*** be really unlucky; ~ ***gehabt!*** bad (F tough) luck; ***so ein*** ~***!*** F that's too bad, just my luck; ***er wird wirklich vom*** ~ ***verfolgt*** his bad luck never lets up, he seems to have been born unlucky; ***wie kann man nur so ein*** ~ ***haben!*** how can anyone be so unlucky?; ***sie hat*** ~ ***mit den Männern*** she has no luck with men, somehow she always seems to choose the wrong man; ***er hatte das*** ~***, beide Mitarbeiter zu verlieren*** he was unlucky enough (*or* he had the bad luck) to lose both colleagues; **2.** pitch; F *fig.* ***wie*** ~ ***und Schwefel zusammenhalten*** be (as) thick as thieves

'**pech'schwarz** *adj.* jet-black *hair*; pitch-dark *night*

'**Pech|stein** *m* pitchstone; ~**sträh·ne** *f* run (*or* streak) of bad luck; ***e-e*** ~ ***haben*** be down on one's luck, be going through an unlucky patch; ~**vo·gel** *m* unlucky person; ***er ist ein richtiger*** ~ some people are just born unlucky

Pe·dal [pe'da:l] *n* (-s; -e) **1.** pedal (*a.* ♪); ***in die*** ~***e treten*** pedal hard (*or* away), pedal for all one is worth; ***tret mal aufs*** ~***!*** step on it!; **2.** F *pl.* F trotters

Pe·dant [pe'dant] *m* (-en; -en) pedant, stickler; **Pe·dan·te·rie** [pedantə'ri:] *f* (-; -n) pedantry; **pe·dan·tisch** [pe'dantɪʃ] *adj.* pedantic(ally *adv.*)

Ped·dig·rohr ['pɛdɪç-] *n* (-[e]s; *no pl.*) rattan

Pe·dell [pe'dɛl] *m* (-s; -e) *univ.* porter; *ped.* janitor, caretaker

Pe·di·kü·re [pedi'ky:rə] *f* (-; -n) **1.** *no pl.* pedicure; **2.** pedicurist; **pe·di·kü·ren** [pedi'ky:rən] *v/t.* (h) pedicure; ***sich*** ~ ***lassen*** have a pedicure

Pee·ling ['pi:lɪŋ] *n* (-s; -s) facial (*or* body) scrub

Peep-Show ['pi:pʃo:] *f* (-; -s) peep show

Pe·gel ['pegəl] *m* (-s; -) ⚙ a) *a. fig.* level, b) water ga(u)ge; ~**an·zei·ge** *f* level meter; ~**reg·ler** *m* level control; ~**stand** *m* water level

Peil·an·la·ge ['paɪl-] *f* direction finder

pei·len ['paɪlən] (h) **I.** *v/t.*: ***ein Schiff*** *etc.* ~ take a ship's *etc.* bearings; F *fig.* ***die Lage*** ~ see how the land lies, *pol.* test the water; **II.** *v/i.* take one's bearings

Peil|funk ['paɪl-] *m* radio direction finding; ~**ge·rät** *n* direction finder; ~**sen·der** *m* radio beacon

Pei·lung ['paɪlʊŋ] *f* (-; -en) location; *radio*, ✈ direction finding; bearing(s *pl.*)

Pein [paɪn] *f* (-; *no pl.*) suffering; torment; ***seelische*** ~ mental anguish; **pei·ni·gen** ['paɪnɪgən] *v/t.* (h) torment, torture; harass, pester; **Pei·ni·ger** ['paɪnɪgɐ] *m* (-s; -), **Pei·ni·ge·rin** ['paɪnɪgərɪn] *f* (-; -nen) tormentor; **Pei·ni·gung** ['paɪnɪgʊŋ] *f* (-; -en) torment, torture

pein·lich ['paɪnlɪç] **I.** *adj.* **1.** embarrassing, *a.* awkward *situation*; F painful; ***es war mir sehr*** ~***(, daß ich es vergessen hatte)*** I was (*or* felt) really embarrassed (at *or* about having forgotten it); ***j-n in e-e*** ~***e Lage bringen*** put s.o. in an awkward situation; **2.** meticulous, painstaking; **II.** *adv.* **3.** ***j-n*** ~ ***berühren*** embarrass s.o.; **4.** ~ ***sauber*** scrupulously clean; ~ ***genau*** very exact (***bei*** *dat.* about); ***bei e-r Sache*** ~ ***genau sein*** *a.* take s.th. very seriously; ~***st vermeiden zu*** *inf.* take great care to avoid *ger.*

'**Pein·lich·keit** *f* (-; -en) **1.** *no pl.* embarrassment; **2.** embarrassing remark (*or* situation *etc.*)

Peit·sche ['paɪtʃə] *f* (-; -n) whip; '**peit·schen** *v/t. and v/i.* (h) whip, *a. fig. rain etc.*: lash (***gegen*** *acc.* against); *fig.* ~***der Wind*** (***Regen***) lashing winds (rain); ***von Ehrgeiz gepeitscht*** spurred on by ambition

'**Peit·schen|hieb** *m* lash (of the whip); ~**knall** *m* crack of the whip; ~**schlag·ver·let·zung** *f* whiplash (injury)

pe·jo·ra·tiv [pejora'ti:f] *adj.* pejorative

Pe·ki·ne·se [peki'ne:zə] *m* (-n; -n) *zo.* Pekin(g)ese

Pe·king·mensch ['pe:kɪŋ-] *m*: ***der*** ~ Peking man

Pek·tin [pɛk'ti:n] *n* (-s; -e) pectin

pek·to·ral [pɛkto'ra:l] *adj.* pectoral

pe·ku·ni·är [peku'nĭɛ:ɐ] *adj.* financial

Pe·le·ri·ne [pelə'ri:nə] *f* (-; -n) cape

Pe·li·kan ['pe:lika:n] *m* (-s; -e) pelican

Pel·le ['pɛlə] *f* (-; -n) peel, (*a. sausage etc.*) skin; F *fig.* ***j-m auf die*** ~ ***rücken*** crowd s.o.; ***j-m mit e-r Sache auf der*** ~ ***liegen*** keep pestering s.o. with s.th.; ***rück mir nicht so auf die*** ~ F get off my back, will you; ***j-m mit e-m Messer auf die*** ~ ***rücken*** go for s.o. with a knife; '**pel·len** (h) **I.** *v/t.* peel (*a. egg*), skin; **II.** *v/refl.*: ***sich*** ~ *skin, back etc.*: peel

'**Pell·kar|tof·feln** *pl.* jacket potatoes, potatoes boiled in their skins

Pelz [pɛlts] *m* (-es; -e) a) fur, b) skin, hide, c) fur (coat); F *fig.* ***j-m auf den*** ~ ***rücken*** crowd s.o.; ~**be·satz** *m* fur trimming; ≈**be·setzt** *adj.* fur-trimmed; ~**fut·ter** *n* fur lining; ≈**ge·füt·tert** *adj.* fur-lined; ~**han·del** *m* fur trade; ~**händ·ler** *m* furrier

pel·zig ['pɛltsɪç] *adj.* furry; ⚕ furred *tongue*; ♆ stringy *radish etc.*

'**Pelz|jacke** *f* fur jacket; ~**kra·gen** *m* fur collar; ~**man·tel** *m* fur coat; ~**müt·ze** *f* fur hat; ~**stie·fel** *m* fur boot; ~**tie·re** *pl.* fur-bearing animals, *coll.* furs; ~**werk** *n* (-[e]s; *no pl.*) furs *pl.*

Pen·dant [pã'dã:] *n* (-s; -s) matching piece; *fig.* complement; counterpart (*a. person*); ***dies ist das*** ~ ***dazu*** *a.* this is the other piece (*or* painting *etc.*) that goes with it

Pen·del ['pɛndəl] *n* (-s; -) pendulum (*a. fig.*); *fig.* ***das*** ~ ***schlug zurück*** the pendulum swung back; ~**bus** *m* shuttle bus; ~**di·plo·ma|tie** *f* shuttle diplomacy; ~**flug·zeug** *n* shuttle aircraft (*or* plane)

pen·deln ['pɛndəln] *v/i.* (h) **1.** swing, 📖 oscillate; ***mit den Beinen*** ~ dangle one's legs; (***mit dem Oberkörper***) ~ *boxing*: weave; **2.** 🚂 *etc.* shuttle; *person*: commute; ***zwischen X und Y*** ~ shuttle back and forth between X and Y, commute from X to Y

'**Pen·del|tür** *f* swing door; ~**uhr** *f* pendulum clock; ~**ver·kehr** *m* **1.** shuttle service; **2.** → ***Pendlerverkehr***; ~**zug** *m* **1.** shuttle train; **2.** → ***Pendlerzug***

Pend·ler ['pɛndlɐ] *m* (-s; -) commuter; ~**ver·kehr** *m* commuter traffic; ~**zug** *m* commuter train

pe·ne·trant [pene'trant] *adj.* **1.** penetrating, pungent *smell etc.*; **2.** F insistent, F pushy *person*; ***sie ist furchtbar*** ~ *a.* she's a real nuisance (*or* pest); **Pe·ne·tranz** [pene'trants] *f* (-; *no pl.*) **1.** pungency; **2.** F pushiness

Pe·ne·tra·ti·on [penetra'tsĭo:n] *f* (-; -en) penetration; **pe·ne·trie·ren** [pene'tri:rən] *v/t.* (h) penetrate

peng [pɛŋ] *int.* bang!

pe·ni·bel [pe'ni:bəl] *adj.* meticulous; *contp.* fussy, pernickety (*all* ***in*** *dat.* about); ***e-e penible Arbeit*** pernickety (*or* fiddly) work

Pe·nis ['pe:nɪs] *m* (-; -se) penis; ~**neid** *m* *psych.* penis envy

Pe·ni·zil·lin [penitsɪ'li:n] *n* (-s; *no pl.*) penicillin

Pen·nä·ler [pɛ'nɛ:lɐ] F *m* (-s; -) schoolboy

Penn·bru·der ['pɛn-] F *m* → ***Penner*** 1

Pen·ne ['pɛnə] F *f* (-; -n) school

pen·nen ['pɛnən] F *v/i.* (h) F kip, have a kip; **Pen·ner** ['pɛnɐ] F *m* (-s; -) **1.** tramp, down-and-out, F dosser, *Am.* hobo, bum; *pl. a.* street people; **2.** F sleepyhead; F dope; ***er ist ein richtiger*** ~ he spends most of his time asleep

Pen·si·on [pã'zĭo:n, paŋ-, pɛn-] *f* (-; -en) **1.** (old-age) pension; **2.** ***in*** ~ ***gehen*** retire; ***in*** ~ ***sein*** be retired, live in retirement; **3.** boarding house, pension

Pen·sio·när [pãzĭo'nɛ:ɐ, paŋ-, pɛn-] *m* (-s; -e [-rə]), **Pen·sio·nä·rin** [pãzĭo'nɛ:rɪn, paŋ-, pɛn-] *f* (-; -nen) pensioner

Pen·sio·nat [pãzĭo'na:t, paŋ-, pɛn-] *n* (-s; -e) boarding school

pen·sio·nie·ren [pãzĭo'ni:rən, paŋ-, pɛn-] *v/t.* (h) pension off; ***sich*** ~ ***lassen*** retire, go into retirement, take early retirement; **pen·sio·niert** [pãzĭo'ni:ɐt, paŋ-, pɛn-] *adj.* retired; **Pen·sio'nie·rung** *f* (-; -en) retirement; **Pen·sio'nie·rungs·tod** *m* retirement-induced death

Pen·sio·nist [pãzĭo'nɪst, paŋ-, pɛn-] *m* (-en; -en), **Pen·sio·ni·stin** [pãzĭo'nɪstɪn, paŋ-, pɛn-] *f* (-; -nen) pensioner

Pen·si'ons|al·ter *n* retirement age; ***im*** ~ ***sein*** have reached retirement age; ~**an·spruch** *m* pension claim; ≈**be·rech·tigt** *adj.* eligible for a pension; ~**kas·se** *f* pension fund; ≈**reif** *adj.* due for retirement

Pen·sum ['pɛnzʊm] *n* (-s; Pensen [-zən]) (work) quota; ***sein tägliches*** ~ ***schaffen*** F do one's daily stint

Pep [pɛp] F *m* (-; *no pl.*) F zip

Pe·pe·ro·ni [pepe'ro:ni] *f* (-; -[s]) chil(l)i

Pep·sin [pɛ'psi:n] *n* (-s; -e) pepsin

Pep·tid [pɛp'ti:t] *n* (-[e]s; -e [-'ti:də]) peptide

per [pɛr] *prp.* (*acc.*) per, by; ~ ***Adresse*** care of (*abbr.* c/o); ~ ***Bahn*** by train, by rail; ~ ***Luftpost*** airmail; ~ ***pedes*** on foot, F on shanks's pony, under one's own steam; → ***du*** I

per·fekt [pɛr'fɛkt] **I.** *adj.* perfect; *pred. contract etc.*: settled, F in the bag; ***e-e Sache*** ~ ***machen*** settle, F clinch *a deal*; ~ ***im Kochen*** an expert cook; ***e-e*** ~***e Gastgeberin*** the perfect hostess; ***ein*** ~***es Verbrechen*** the perfect crime; ***der*** ~***e Wagen*** the ultimate car; ***in Spanisch ist er fast*** ~ his Spanish is near-perfect, he speaks almost perfect Spanish; **II.** *adv.*: ***er spricht*** (*or* ***kann***) ~ ***Englisch*** his (spoken) English is perfect, he speaks perfect English

Per·fekt ['pɛrfɛkt] *n* (-s; -e) *ling.* perfect (tense)

Per·fek·ti·on [pɛrfɛk'tsĭo:n] *f* (-; *no pl.*) perfection; ***mit*** ~ to perfection; ***et. bis zur*** ~ ***treiben*** do (*or* practi|se, *Am.* -ce *etc.*) s.th. to the point of perfection

per·fek·tio·nie·ren [pɛrfɛktsĭo'ni:rən] *v/t.* (h) perfect

Per·fek·tio·nis·mus [pɛrfɛktsĭo'nɪsmʊs] *m* (-; *no pl.*) perfectionism

Per·fek·tio·nist [pɛrfɛktsĭo'nɪst] *m* (-en; -en), **per·fek·tio·ni·stisch** [pɛrfɛktsĭo'nɪstɪʃ] *adj.* perfectionist

per·fid [pɛr'fi:t] *adj.* insidious; *lit.* perfidious

Per·fo·ra·ti·on [pɛrfora'tsĭo:n] *f* (-; -en) perforation; *film etc.*: sprocket holes *pl.*

Per·fo·ra·ti'ons·li·nie *f*: ***an der*** ~ ***abreißen*** tear along the perforation

per·fo·rie·ren [pɛrfo'ri:rən] *v/t.* (h) perforate; **Per·fo'rie·rung** *f* (-; -en) perforation

Per·ga·ment [pɛrga'mɛnt] *n* (-[e]s; -e) parchment; vellum; ~**hand·schrift** *f* parchment (manuscript); vellum manuscript; ~**pa,pier** *n* greaseproof paper

Per·go·la ['pɛrgola] *f* (-; -len) bower, arbo(u)r

Pe·ri·ode [pe'rĭo:də] *f* (-; -n) **1.** period; ⚡ cycle; **2.** ⚕ period; ***m-e*** ~ ***ist ausgeblieben*** I've missed my period

Pe·ri'oden·sy,stem *n* ⚗ periodic system

Pe·ri·odi·kum [pe'rĭo:dikʊm] *n* (-s; -ka) periodical

pe·ri·odisch [pe'rĭo:dɪʃ] **I.** *adj.* periodic(al); 𝔄 ~***er Dezimalbruch*** recurring decimal; **II.** *adv.*: ~ ***auftretend*** periodically recurring

pe·ri·odi·sie·ren [perĭodi'zi:rən] *v/t.* (h) divide (up) into periods; **Pe·ri·odi'sie·rung** *f* (-; -en) division into periods

Pe·ri·pa·te·ti·ker [peripa'te:tikɐ] *m* (-s; -), **pe·ri·pa·te·tisch** [peripa'te:tɪʃ] *adj.* peripatetic

pe·ri·pher [peri'fe:ɐ] *adj.* peripheral

Pe·ri·phe·rie [perife'ri:] *f* (-; -n) **1.** periphery; *a.* outskirts *pl. of a town etc.*; **2.** *computer*: peripherals *pl.*; ~**ge·rät** *n* *computer*: peripheral; *pl.* peripheral equipment *sg.*

Pe·ri·skop [peri'sko:p] *n* (-s; -e) periscope

Pe·ri·stal·tik [peri'staltɪk] *f* (-; *no pl.*) peristalsis

Pe·ri·to·ne·um [perito'ne:ʊm] *n* (-s; -neen) *anat.* peritoneum

Per·kus·si·on [pɛrkʊ'sĭo:n] *f* (-; -en) *a.* ⚕ percussion

per·ku·tan [pɛrku'ta:n] *adj.* percutaneous

Per·le ['pɛrlə] *f* (-; -n) pearl; bead (*a. fig. of perspiration etc.*); *fig.* gem; *fig.* ~***n vor die Säue*** (***werfen*** cast) pearls before swine

'**per·len** *v/i.* **1.** (h) *drink*: bubble, sparkle; **2.** (sn) ~ ***von*** *dat.* drip from; **3.** (h) ***der Schweiß perlte ihr auf der Stirn*** her forehead was beaded with sweat; ***der Tau perlte auf den Blättern*** the leaves were beaded with dew

'**Per·len|au·ster** *f* pearl oyster; ~**fi·scher** *m* pearl fisher (*or* diver); ~**ket·te** *f* pearl necklace; ~**schnur** *f* string of pearls; ~**sticke,rei** *f* beadwork; ~**tau·cher** *m* pearl diver (*or* fisher); ~**zucht** *f* pearl cultivation

'**perl·grau** *adj.* pearl grey (*Am.* gray)

'**Perl|huhn** *n* guinea fowl; ~**lein·wand** *f* beaded screen; ~**mu·schel** *f* pearl oyster

Perl·mutt ['pɛrlmʊt] *n* (s; *no pl.*), '**Perl·mut·ter** *f* (-; *no pl.*) mother-of-pearl

'**Perl|schrift** *f* pearl; ~**wein** *m* sparkling wine; ≈**weiß** *adj.* pearly white; ~**zwie·bel** *f* pearl onion

per·ma·nent [pɛrma'nɛnt] *adj.* permanent; **Per·ma'nent·ma,gnet** *m* permanent magnet; **Per·ma·nenz** [pɛrma'nɛnts] *f* (-; *no pl.*) permanence

Per·man·ga·nat [pɛrmaŋga'na:t] *n* (-s; -e) permanganate

Per·mu·ta·ti·on [pɛrmuta'tsĭo:n] *f* (-; -en) permutation (*a.* 𝔄)

per·plex [pɛr'plɛks] *adj.* amazed; bewildered, nonplussed

Per·sen·ning [pɛr'zɛnɪŋ] *f* (-; -e[n], -s) tarpaulin

Per·ser ['pɛrzɐ] *m* (-s; -) **1.** Persian; **2.** → ***Perserteppich***; **Per·se·rin** ['pɛrzərɪn] *f* (-; -nen) Persian

'**Per·ser·tep·pich** *m* Persian carpet

Per·sia·ner [pɛr'zĭa:nɐ] *m* (-s; -) Persian lamb (coat)

Per·si·fla·ge [pɛrzi'fla:ʒə] *f* (-; -n) satire (***auf*** *acc.* on), pastiche (on), F send-up (of); **per·si·flie·ren** [pɛrzi'fli:rən] *v/t.* (h) satirize, burlesque, F send up

Per·sil·schein [pɛr'zi:l-] F *m* **1.** *hist.* denazification certificate; **2.** *fig.* clean bill of health

per·sisch ['pɛrzɪʃ] *adj.*, ≈ *n* (-en; *no pl.*) *ling.* Persian

Per·son [pɛr'zo:n] *f* (-; -en) person; individual; *thea.* character; *pl.* people; *ling.* ***erste*** ~ first person; *10 Mark* ***pro*** ~ each, a head; ***wir sind vier*** ~***en*** there are four of us; ***e-e aus zehn*** ~***en bestehende Gruppe*** a group of ten; ***für sechs*** ~***en*** *recipe*: serves six; ***keine einzige*** ~ not one person, not a single person; ***ich für m-e*** ~ I for my part; as for me, I ...; ***in*** (***eigener***) ~ in person, himself (*f* herself); ***Angaben zur*** ~ personal data; ***sich in der*** ~ ***irren*** mistake s.o. for s.o. else; ***man muß die*** ~ ***von der Sache trennen*** you've got to keep personal factors out of it; ***so e-e freche*** ~! F cheeky old so-and-so; ***er ist die Geduld in*** ~ he's the epitome of patience

Per·so·nal [pɛrzo'na:l] *n* (-s; *no pl.*) staff, employees *pl.*, personnel; servants *pl.*; ~**ab·bau** *m* cut(s *pl.*) *or* cutback(s *pl.*) in staff, staff reduction(s *pl.*), manpower cuts *pl.*; ~**ab,tei·lung** *f* personnel department; ~**ak·te** *f* personal file; ~**an·ga·ben** *pl.* particulars; ~**an·ge·le·gen·hei·ten** *pl.* personnel matters; ~**auf·wand** *m* personnel costs *pl.*; ~**aus·weis** *m* identity card; ~**be·darf** *m* manpower requirement(s *pl.*); ~**be·schaf·fung** *f* (personnel) recruitment; ~**bü,ro** *n* personnel department; ~**chef** *m* personnel manager

Per·so'nal·com,pu·ter *m* personal computer

Per·so·na·li·en [pɛrzo'na:lĭən] *pl.* particulars; ***j-s*** ~ ***aufnehmen*** take down s.o.'s particulars

per·so'nal·in·ten,siv *adj.* labo(u)r-intensive
Per·so'nal|ko·sten *pl.* payroll (*or* personnel) costs; **~man·gel** *m* manpower shortage, shortage of staff; ***an ~ leiden*** be understaffed; **~po·li,tik** *f* manpower policy; **~pro,no·men** *n ling.* personal pronoun; **~uni,on** *f* **1.** *pol.* personal union; **2.** ***zwei Ämter in ~ ausüben*** hold two offices; ***er ist ... und ... in ~*** he is both ... and ..., he holds the office of ... and ... (concurrently); **~wech·sel** *m* change in staff; staff turnover; **~we·sen** *n* (-s; *no pl.*) personnel
Per·sön·chen [pɛr'zøːnçən] *n* (-s; -): ***ein reizendes*** *etc.* **~** a charming *etc.* little creature
per·so·nell [pɛrzo'nɛl] *adj.* personnel ...
Per'so·nen|auf·zug *m* lift, *Am.* elevator; **~be·för·de·rung** *f* passenger transport; **~be·schrei·bung** *f* personal description; **~damp·fer** *m* passenger steamer; **~fahn·dung** *f* manhunt; **~fäh·re** *f* passenger ferry; **2ge·bun·den** *adj.* non-transferable; **~ge·dächt·nis** *n* memory for (people and) faces; **~kenn·zif·fer** *f* identity number, personal code; **~kraft·wa·gen** *m* (*abbr.* ***Pkw***) (motor)car, *Am. a.* auto(mobile); **~kreis** *m* circle; **~kult** *m* personality cult; **~re,gi·ster** *n* index of names; **~scha·den** *m* personal injury; **~schutz** *m* personal protection; **~über·,prü·fung** *f* identity check; **~ver·kehr** *m* passenger traffic; **~waa·ge** *f*: (***e-e ~*** a pair of) scales *pl.*; *a.* (a pair of) bathroom scales *pl.*; **~wa·gen** *m* **1.** 🚗 passenger coach (*Am.* car); **2.** → ***Personenkraftwagen***; **~zug** *m* **1.** passenger train; **2.** local train
Per·so·ni·fi·ka·ti·on [pɛrzonifika'tsi̯oːn] *f* (-; -en) personification
per·so·ni·fi·zie·ren [pɛrzonifi'tsiːrən] *v/t.* (h) personify
per·sön·lich [pɛr'zøːnlɪç] **I.** *adj.* personal; private, confidential; ***darf ich Ihnen e-e ~e Frage stellen?*** can (*or* may) I ask you something personal?; **~ *werden*** get personal; ***Persönliches*** *newspaper*: personals; **II.** *adv.* personally, in person; himself (*f* herself); **~ *haften*** be personally liable; ***et. ~ nehmen*** take s.th. personally; ***das ist nicht ~ gemeint*** (please) don't take it personally; ***das ist für dich ~*** it's personal, it's for you and you alone
Per'sön·lich·keit *f* (-; -en) **1.** *no pl.* personality; → ***gespalten***; **2.** personality; ***öffentliche ~*** public figure; ***der Kleine ist schon e-e ~*** he's a real little personality
Per'sön·lich·keits|ent·fal·tung *f* personality development; **~kult** *m* personality cult; **~spal·tung** *f* split personality; **~struk,tur** *f* personality structure
Per·spek·ti·ve [pɛrspɛk'tiːvə] *f* (-; -n) **1.** perspective; ***hier stimmt die ~ nicht*** he's *etc.* got the perspective wrong; **2.** *fig.* perspective, point of view, angle; *fig.* ***enge ~*** narrow view (*or* perspective); ***et. aus der richtigen ~ sehen*** see s.th. in perspective, get the right angle on s.th.; ***et. aus e-r anderen ~ betrachten*** look at s.th. from a different angle; **3.** prospect(s *pl.*)
per·spek·ti·visch [pɛrspɛk'tiːvɪʃ] **I.** *adj.* perspective ...; *pred. drawing etc.* in perspective; **II.** *adv.*: ***es stimmt ~*** (***nicht***) the perspective is right (wrong)
Pe·rua·ner [pe'rŭaːnɐ] *m* (-s; -), **Pe·rua·ne·rin** [pe'rŭaːnərɪn] *f* (-; -nen), **pe·rua·nisch** [pe'rŭaːnɪʃ] *adj.* Peruvian
Pe·rücke [pe'rʏkə] (*sep.* -k·k-) *f* (-; -n) wig
per·vers [pɛr'vɛrs] *adj.* perverse (*a. fig.*), F kinky; **~es *Hirn*** twisted mind; **~er *Mensch*** pervert; **Per·ver·si·on** [pɛrvɛr'zi̯oːn] *f* (-; -en) perversion; **Per·ver·si·tät** [pɛrvɛrzi'tɛːt] *f* (-; -en) perverseness, perversity; **per·ver·tie·ren** [pɛrvɛr'tiːrən] *v/t.* (h) pervert
Pes·sar [pɛ'saːɐ] *n* (-s; -e [-rə]) pessary; diaphragm, cap
Pes·si·mis·mus [pɛsi'mɪsmʊs] *m* (-; *no pl.*) pessimism; **Pes·si·mist** [pɛsi'mɪst] *m* (-en; -en) pessimist; **pes·si·mi·stisch** [pɛsi'mɪstɪʃ] *adj.* pessimistic(ally *adv.*)
Pest [pɛst] *f* (-; *no pl.*) plague; ***ich hasse es wie die ~*** I can't stand it; ***er haßt ihn wie die ~*** *a.* F he hates his guts; ***wie die ~ meiden*** avoid like the plague; F ***das stinkt ja wie die ~*** F it stinks something awful, what a stench; **~beu·le** *f* (plague) boil; **~epi·de,mie** *f* plague epidemic; **~ge·stank** *m* stench; **~hauch** *fig. m* miasma
Pe·sti·zid [pɛsti'tsiːt] *n* (-s; -e [-'tsiːdə]) pesticide
'pest·krank *adj*: **~ *sein*** have (caught) the plague
Pe·ter·si·lie [peːtɐ'ziːli̯ə] *f* (-; -n) parsley; F *fig.* ***das hat ihm gründlich die ~ verhagelt*** that really messed things up for him, that really threw a spanner (*Am.* monkey wrench) in(to) the works (for him); **Pe·ter'si·li·en·kar,tof·feln** *pl.* parsley potatoes
Pe·ti·ti·on [peti'tsi̯oːn] *f* (-; -en) petition
Pe·ti·ti'ons|aus·schuß *m* committee on petitions; **~recht** *n* right to petition
Pe·tro·che'mie [petro-] *f* petrochemistry
pe·tro'che·misch *adj.* petrochemical
Pe·tro·dol·lar ['peːtro-] *m* petrodollar
Pe·tro·le·um [pe'troːleʊm] *n* (-s; *no pl.*) paraffin, *Am.* kerosene; **~ko·cher** *m* paraffin (*Am.* kerosene) stove; **~lam·pe** *f* paraffin (*Am.* kerosene) lamp
Pe·trus ['peːtrʊs] *m* (-; *no pl.*) *bibl.* Peter; St Peter
pet·to ['pɛto]: ***et. in ~ haben*** have s.th. up one's sleeve
Pe·tu·nie [pe'tuːni̯ə] *f* (-; -n) ⚘ petunia
Pet·ze ['pɛtsə] F *f* (-; -n) → ***Petzer***
'pet·zen F *v/i.* (h) tell on s.o., F sneak (on s.o.); tell tales; ***petz doch nicht!*** stop telling tales
Pet·zer ['pɛtsɐ] F *m* (-s; -) F telltale, sneak
peu à peu [pøa'pø] *adv.* gradually, bit by bit
Pfad [pfaːt] *m* (-[e]s; Pfade ['pfaːdə]) path (*a. fig.*); *fig.* ***auf dem ~ der Tugend wandeln*** keep to the straight and narrow; ***vom ~ der Tugend abweichen*** come off the straight and narrow
'Pfad·fin·der *m* (-s; -) boy scout
'Pfad·fin·de·rin *f* (-; -nen) girl (guide), *Am.* girl scout
Pfaf·fe ['pfafə] *contp. m* (-n; -n) cleric, F *hum.* sky pilot, holy Joe
Pfahl [pfaːl] *m* (-[e]s; Pfähle ['pfɛːlə]) stake; post; pile; *fig.* ***j-m ein ~ im Fleisch sein*** be a thorn in s.o.'s side (*or* flesh); **~bau** *m* (-[e]s; -ten) lake dwelling
pfäh·len ['pfɛːlən] *v/t.* (h) **1.** prop up, support; stake; **2.** *hist.* impale
'Pfahl|rost *m* pile grating; **~werk** *n* paling; ⚔ palisade
Pfalz [pfalts] *f* (-; -en) *hist.* palatinate; *geogr.* ***die ~*** the (Rhineland) Palatinate
Pfäl·zer ['pfɛltsɐ] *m* (-s; -), **Pfäl·ze·rin** ['pfɛltsərɪn] *f* (-; -nen) Palatine; ***Pfälzer sein*** *usu.* come from the Palatinate
'Pfalz·graf *m hist.* Count Palatine
pfäl·zisch ['pfɛltsɪʃ] *adj.* Palatine, from the Palatinate
Pfand [pfant] *n* (-[e]s; Pfänder ['pfɛndɐ]) **1.** ✝ pledge; security; ***als ~ für*** *acc.* as a pledge for; ***als ~ geben*** pledge, pawn; ***sein Wort als ~ geben*** pledge one's word; **2.** deposit; **~ *für et. zahlen*** pay a deposit on s.th.; **3.** *games*: forfeit
pfänd·bar ['pfɛntbaːɐ] *adj.* ⚖ attachable, distrainable
'Pfand·brief *m* ✝ debenture bond
pfän·den ['pfɛndən] *v/t.* (h) ⚖ seize *s.th.*, distrain upon
Pfän·der·spiel ['pfɛndɐ-] *n* (game of) forfeits *pl.*; ***ein ~ machen*** play forfeits
'Pfand|fla·sche *f* deposit (*or* returnable) bottle; ***keine ~*** no deposit no return; **~geld** *n* deposit
'Pfand·lei·he [-laɪə] *f* (-; -n) pawnshop; **'Pfand·lei·her** [-laɪɐ] *m* (-s; -) pawnbroker
'Pfand|recht *n* lien; **~schein** *m* pawn ticket
Pfän·dung ['pfɛndʊŋ] *f* (-; -en) ⚖ seizure (*gen.* of); distraint (upon)
'Pfän·dungs·be·fehl *m* ⚖ warrant of distress
Pfan·ne ['pfanə] *f* (-; -n) **1.** *gastr.* (frying) pan; F ***ich werd' mir ein paar Eier in die ~ hauen*** F I'm going to fry up a couple of eggs; F *fig.* ***j-n in die ~ hauen*** F give s.o. a (real) roasting, haul s.o. over the coals; **2.** pantile; **3.** *anat.* socket; **4.** F *fig.* ***et. auf der ~ haben*** have s.th. up one's sleeve
'Pfan·nen|ge·richt *n* fried dish; **~stiel** *m* (frying-pan) handle
Pfann·ku·chen ['pfan-] *m* pancake, *Am. a.* flapjack; ***Berliner ~*** doughnut
Pfarr|amt ['pfar-] *n* rectory, vicarage; **~be·zirk** *m* parish
Pfar·rei [pfa'raɪ] *f* (-; -en) → ***Pfarramt***
Pfar·rer ['pfarɐ] *m* (-s; -) *R.C.* (parish) priest; *Anglican Church*: vicar, *nonconformist or Am.* minister
Pfarr|ge·mein·de ['pfar-] *f* parish; **~ge·mein·de·rat** *m* parish council; **~haus** *n* parsonage; rectory, vicarage; **~kir·che** *f* parish church
Pfau [pfaʊ] *m* (-[e]s, -en; -e) peacock; ***wie ein ~ einherstolzieren*** strut about like a peacock
Pfau·en|au·ge ['pfaʊən-] *n* **1.** peacock butterfly; **2.** eye, 🕮 ocellus *of a peacock feather*; **~fe·der** *f* peacock feather; **~hen·ne** *f* peahen
Pfef·fer ['pfɛfɐ] *m* (-s; *no pl.*) pepper; ***geh hin, wo der ~ wächst!*** F get lost, jump in the lake; F **~ *im Hintern haben*** F have plenty of oomph; F ***dem muß man ~ geben*** (V **~ *in den Arsch blasen***) F he needs a real kick in the pants (*or* up the backside); → ***Hase***; **~gur·ke** *f* gherkin
pfef·fe·rig ['pfɛfərɪç] *adj.* → ***pfeffrig***
'Pfef·fer|korn *n* peppercorn; **~ku·chen** *m* gingerbread
'Pfef·fer·minz·bon,bon *m, n* peppermint
'Pfef·fer·min·ze *f* (-; *no pl.*) ⚘ mint
'Pfef·fer·minz|li,kör *m* crème de menthe; **~tee** *m* mint tea
'Pfef·fer·müh·le *f* pepper mill
pfef·fern ['pfɛfɐn] *v/t.* (h) **1.** pepper; *fig.* spice; **2.** F fling, F chuck; F ***j-m e-e ~*** F

give s.o. a clout (round the ears); → ***gepfeffert***
'Pfef·fer|steak *n* pepper steak, steak au poivre; **~streu·er** *m* pepper caster
pfeff·rig ['pfɛfrɪç] *adj.* peppery
Pfei·fe ['pfaɪfə] *f* (-; -n) **1.** whistle; ♪ pipe; ⚔ fife; (organ) pipe; *fig.* ***nach j-s ~ tanzen*** dance to s.o.'s tune; **2.** pipe; **3.** F dead loss
'pfei·fen ['pfaɪfən] (pfiff, gepfiffen, h) **I.** *v/i.* whistle (*a. fig. wind, bullet etc.*); blow the whistle; *thea.* hiss, boo; *sport*: (be) referee; ***vor sich hin ~*** whistle to o.s.; ***~des Geräusch*** whistling (sound); ***~der Atem*** wheezing; F *fig.* ***ich pfeif' drauf!*** F I don't give a damn; ***ich pfeif' aufs Geld*** F I don't give a damn (*or* two hoots) about the money; ***ich pfeif' auf die Meinung der Leute*** F I don't give a damn what people think; **II.** *v/t.* a) whistle *a tune etc.*, b) referee *a football match etc.*, c) give, award *a free kick etc.*; F *fig.* ***ich werd' dir was ~!*** F you know what you can do; ***dem werd' ich was ~!*** F he can take a running jump
'Pfei·fen|be·steck *n* pipe knife; **~kopf** *m* pipe bowl; **~rauch** *m* pipe smoke; **~rau·cher** *m* pipe smoker; ***er ist ~ a.*** he smokes a pipe; **~rei·ni·ger** *m* pipe cleaner; **~stän·der** *m* pipe rack; **~stiel** *m* pipe stem; **~stop·fer** *m* tobacco tamper; **~ta·bak** *m* pipe tobacco
Pfei·fer ['pfaɪfɐ] *m* (-s; -) whistler; ♪ piper
'Pfeif|kon,zert F *n* whistling and booing; **~ton** *m* **1.** whistling sound; *esp. radio etc.*: high-pitched whine; **2.** whistle
Pfeil [pfaɪl] *m* (-[e]s; -e) a) arrow, b) dart; *fig.* ***wie ein ~*** like a shot; ***alle s-e ~e verschossen haben*** have played all one's trumps
Pfei·ler ['pfaɪlɐ] *m* (-s; -) pillar (*a. fig.*); pier; **~brücke** *f* pier bridge
'Pfeil·flü·gel *m* ✈ swept-back wing
'pfeil·ge·ra·de I. *adj.* (as) straight as an arrow; **II.** *adv.* straight; *sit* erect; ***er kam ~ auf uns zu*** he made a beeline for us
'Pfeil|gift *n* arrow poison; **~kraut** *n* ⚘ arrowhead; **~rich·tung** *f*: ***in ~*** in the direction of the arrow; **2schnell** *adj. and adv.* (as) quick as lightning; ***~ fuhr er weg*** he was off like a shot; **~spit·ze** *f* arrowhead; **~ta·ste** *f computer*: arrow key; **~wurf·spiel** *n* darts *pl.*
Pfen·nig ['pfɛnɪç] *m* (-s; -e ['pfɛnɪgə]) pfennig; *fig.* ***er hat keinen ~*** he hasn't (got) a penny to his name; ***jeden ~ umdrehen (müssen)*** (have to) count every penny; ***s-n letzten ~ für et. ausgeben*** just manage to scrape together enough to buy s.th.; ***das ist keinen ~ wert*** it's not worth a bean; ***ich würde keinen ~ für ihn geben*** I wouldn't bet a penny on his chances; ***er hat keinen ~ Mut (Anstand*** *etc.*) he hasn't got an ounce of courage (decency *etc.*); ***wer den ~ nicht ehrt, ist des Talers nicht wert*** look after the pennies and the pounds will look after themselves; **~ab·satz** *m* stiletto heel; **~ar,ti·kel** *m* cheap article; **~be·trä·ge** *pl.*: ***das sind doch bloß ~*** F that's chickenfeed
'Pfen·nig·fuch·ser [-fʊksɐ] F *m* (-s; -) F penny-pincher, skinflint
'Pfen·nig·kraut *n* ⚘ moneywort
Pferch [pfɛrç] *m* (-[e]s; -e) fold, pen
pfer·chen ['pfɛrçən] *v/t.* (h) pen; *fig. a.* cram
Pferd [pfeːɐrt] *n* (-[e]s; -e [-də]) a) *zo.* horse, b) *chess*: knight, c) *gym.* (vaulting) horse; ***aufs ~ steigen*** mount a horse; ***vom ~ steigen*** dismount; ***zu ~e*** on horseback, mounted *police etc.*; *fig.* ***aufs falsche (richtige) ~ setzen*** back the wrong (right) horse; ***das ~ beim Schwanz aufzäumen*** put the cart before the horse; ***er arbeitet wie ein ~*** he works like a Trojan; ***keine zehn ~e bringen mich dahin*** wild horses couldn't drag me there; ***mit ihr kann man ~e stehlen*** she's a good sport; ***er ist unser bestes ~ im Stall*** he's our best man; ***mit ihm gehen leicht die ~e durch*** he tends to fly off the handle; F ***immer langsam mit den jungen ~en!*** F hold your horses!; F ***ich glaub', mich tritt ein ~*** F well blow me
Pfer·de|äp·fel ['pfeːɐdə-] F *pl.* horse droppings; **~decke** *f* horse blanket; **~dieb** *m* horse thief; **~dün·ger** *m* horse manure; **~fleisch** *n* horsemeat; **~fuhr·werk** *n* horse and cart; **~fuß** *m fig.* a) cloven hoof, b) drawback, snag; ***die Sache hat e-n ~*** there's a snag (to it); **~fut·ter** *n* (horse's) feed; **~ge·biß** F *n* F horsy teeth *pl.*; ***er lächelte mit s-m ~*** F he gave a horsy grin; **~ge·sicht** F *n* F horsy face; **~haar** *n* horsehair; **~han·del** *m* horse trade; **~händ·ler** *m* horse dealer (*Am.* trader); **~knecht** *m* groom; **~kop·pel** *f* paddock; **~kuß** F *m sport*: thigh knock; **~kut·sche** *f* horse-drawn carriage; **~län·ge** *f* length; ***um zwei ~n gewinnen*** win by two lengths; **~lieb·ha·ber** *m* horse lover; **~narr** *m* F horse freak; **~na,tur** *f*: ***e-e ~ haben (or sein)*** have an iron constitution; **~pfle·ger** *m* groom; **~renn·bahn** *f* racecourse, racetrack; **~ren·nen** *n* a) horseracing, b) horserace; **~schlach·ter** *m* horse butcher; **~schlach·te,rei** *f* horse butcher's; **~schlit·ten** *m* horse-drawn sleigh; **~schwanz** *m* **1.** *zo.* horse's tail; **2.** ponytail; **~sport** *m* equestrian sports *pl.*; **~stall** *m* stable; **~stär·ke** *f* ⚙ horsepower (*abbr.* HP); **~trans,por·ter** *m* horsebox; **~wa·gen** *m* horse-drawn carriage; **~wet·te** *f* horseracing bet; **~zucht** *f* horse breeding; **~züch·ter** *m* horse breeder
pfiff [pfɪf] *pret. of* ***pfeifen***
Pfiff *m* (-[e]s; -e) **1.** whistle; *pl. thea. etc.*: whistling *sg.*; **2.** F ***der Mantel hat ~*** that coat's got style; F ***es hat keinen ~*** it's boring; F ***der Sache den richtigen ~ geben*** give it that extra something; F ***das ist ein Ding mit ~*** there's a trick to it
Pfif·fer·ling ['pfɪfɐlɪŋ] *m* (-s; -e) ⚘ chanterelle; F *fig.* ***keinen ~ wert*** F not worth a bean (*or* a tinker's cuss); F ***er schert sich keinen ~ drum*** F he doesn't care two hoots about it
pfif·fig ['pfɪfɪç] *adj.* smart; **Pfif·fi·kus** ['pfɪfikʊs] F *m* (-; -se) F crafty devil
Pfing·sten ['pfɪŋstən] *n* (-; -) Whitsun; *eccl. a.* Pentecost
Pfingst·fe·ri·en ['pfɪŋst-] *pl.* Whitsun holidays (*or* holiday *sg.*), Whitsun break *sg.*
Pfingst'mon·tag *m* Whit Monday
'Pfingst|och·se *m*: F ***geputzt wie ein ~*** dressed up to the nines; **~ro·se** *f* ⚘ peony
Pfingst'sonn·tag *m* Whit Sunday; *eccl. a.* Pentecost
Pfir·sich ['pfɪrzɪç] *m* (-s; -e) peach; **~baum** *m* peach tree; **~haut** *f* peach (*or* peaches and cream) complexion; **~kern** *m* peach stone
Pflan·ze ['pflantsə] *f* (-; -n) **1.** plant; **2.** F character; ***komische ~*** odd character (*or* sort)
'pflan·zen (h) **I.** *v/t.* plant (*a. fig.*); ***in Töpfe ~*** pot; → ***anpflanzen, aufpflanzen, einpflanzen***; **II.** F *v/refl.*: ***sich ~*** F plonk o.s. (down) (***auf*** *acc.* on)
'Pflan·zen|ei·weiß *n* vegetable albumin (*or* protein); **~ex,trakt** *m* vegetable extract; **~farb·stoff** *m* vegetable dye; **~fett** *n* vegetable fat; **2fres·send** *adj.* herbivorous; **~fres·ser** *m* herbivore; **~gift** *n* **1.** vegetable poison; **2.** herbicide; **~kost** *f* vegetable diet; **~kun·de** *f* botany; **~öl** *n* vegetable oil; **2reich** *adj.* rich in plant life; **~reich** *n* (-[e]s; *no pl.*) flora, vegetable kingdom; **~saft** *m* sap; **~schutz·mit·tel** *n* pesticide; **~welt** *f* (-; *no pl.*) **1.** → ***Pflanzenreich***; **2.** flora, plant life
Pflan·zer ['pflantsɐ] *m* (-s; -) planter
pflanz·lich ['pflantslɪç] *adj.* vegetable ...
Pflänz·ling ['pflɛntslɪŋ] *m* (-s; -e) seedling
Pflan·zung ['pflantsʊŋ] *f* (-; -en) **1.** planting; **2.** plantation
Pfla·ster ['pflastɐ] *n* (-s; -) **1.** ⚕ plaster; **2.** road (surface); *fig.* ***teures ~*** expensive strip (*or* place); ***heißes ~*** dangerous place; **~ma·ler** *m* pavement (*Am.* sidewalk) artist; **~ma·le,rei** *f* **1.** pavement (*Am.* sidewalk) art; **2.** pavement (*Am.* sidewalk) drawing
pfla·stern ['pflastɐn] *v/t.* (h) surface *road*; pave *sidewalks*
'Pfla·ster·stein *m* paving stone
Pflau·me ['pflaʊmə] *f* (-; -n) **1.** a) plum, b) prune; **2.** F twit
'Pflau·men|baum *m* plum tree; **2groß** *adj.* plum-sized; **~kern** *m* plum stone; **~ku·chen** *m* plum flan (*Am.* pie); **~mus** *n* plum jam (*Am.* jelly); **~schnaps** *m* plum brandy; **2weich** *adj.* **1.** ***~es Ei*** soft-boiled egg; **2.** F ***er ist ~*** F he's a real softie
Pfle·ge [pfleːgə] *f* (-; *no pl.*) care; *a.* grooming; ⚕ nursing care; ⚒ tending; *fig.* cultivation; ⚙ maintenance; service; *computer*: keeping up, updating; ***viel ~ brauchen*** need a lot of care (*or* attention); ***ein Kind in ~ nehmen*** take a child into one's care; ***ein Kind (bei j-m) in ~ geben*** put a child into (s.o.'s) care, farm a child out (to s.o.); **2be·dürf·tig** *adj.* in need of care; **~dienst** *m* **1.** ⚙ servicing, service; **2.** ⚕ nursing service; **~el·tern** *pl.* foster parents; **~fall** *m* invalid; **~fa,mi·lie** *f* foster family; **~heim** *n* nursing home; **~kind** *n* foster child; **~ko·sten** *pl.* nursing fees; **2leicht** *adj.* easy-care; *fig. person* easy to get along with; **~mit·tel** *n* shoe-care (*or* skin-care *etc.*) product; **~mut·ter** *f* foster mother
pfle·gen ['pfleːgən] (h) **I.** *v/t.* **1.** look after; *a.* nurse *child, invalid etc.*; ⚒ tend; *fig.* cultivate *friendship etc.*; ***sein Äußeres ~*** groom o.s., take care of one's appearance; **2.** ***zu tun ~*** be in the habit of doing; ***sie pflegte zu sagen*** she used to say, she would say; ***solche Versuche ~ fehlzuschlagen*** such attempts usually fail (*or* tend to fail); **II.** *v/refl.*: ***sich ~*** a) look after o.s., b) take care of one's appearance
'Pfle·ge·per·so,nal *n* nursing staff
Pfle·ger ['pfleːgɐ] *m* (-s; -), **Pfle·ge·rin** ['pfleːgərɪn] *f* (-; -nen) **1.** → ***Krankenpfleger(in)***; **2.** ⚖ curator, guardian
'Pfle·ge|satz *m* hospital allowance; **~sohn** *m* foster son; **~toch·ter** *f* foster daughter; **~va·ter** *m* foster father

pfleg·lich ['pfle:klıç] **I.** *adj.* careful; **II.** *adv.*: ~ ***behandeln*** take good care of

Pfleg·schaft ['pfle:kʃaft] *f* (-; -en) guardianship; trusteeship

Pflicht [pflıçt] *f* (-; -en) duty; *sport*: compulsory exercise(s *pl.*); ***die ehelichen ~en*** one's marital duties, one's duties as a husband (*or* wife); ***s-e ~ tun*** do one's duty; ***et. aus ~ tun*** do s.th. out of a sense of duty (*or* moral obligation); ***es sich zur ~ machen zu*** *inf.* make it one's duty to *inf.*; ***die ~ ruft*** duty calls; ***j-n in die ~ nehmen*** take s.o. up on his (*or* her) promise; **~bei·trag** *m* compulsory contribution; **~be·such** *m* courtesy call

'pflicht·be·wußt *adj.* conscientious; **'Pflicht·be·wußt·sein** *n* sense of duty

'Pflicht·ei·fer *m* devotion to duty, zeal; **'pflicht·eif·rig** *adj.* zealous

'Pflich·ten|kol·li·si͵on *f* **1.** conflicting duties *pl.*; **2.** conflict of loyalties; **~kreis** *m* range of tasks

'Pflicht|er·fül·lung *f* discharge of duties; **~ex·em͵plar** *n* deposit copy; **~fach** *n ped.* compulsory subject; **~ge·fühl** *n* (-[e]s; *no pl.*) sense of duty; **&ge·mäß** **I.** *adj.* due, dutiful; **II.** *adv.* duly, dutifully; **~lauf** *m figure skating etc.*: compulsory figures *pl.*; **~lei·stun·gen** *pl.* standard insurance benefits; **~lek͵tü·re** *f* required reading (*a. hum.*), set book(s *pl.*); *hum.* ***es ist ~*** *a.* you must read it, it's a must; **~mensch** *m* very zealous person; ***er ist ein ~*** *a.* he takes his duties very seriously; **~mit·glied·schaft** *f* compulsory membership; **&schul·dig** *adv.* dutifully; **~teil** *m, n* ⚖ legal portion (*or* share), *Am.* statutory share; **~übung** *f sport*: compulsory (*or* set) exercise; *fig.* ***et. als (reine) ~ tun*** do s.th. (purely) out of a sense of duty; **~͵un·ter·richt** *m* compulsory class(es *pl.*); **&ver·ges·sen** *adj.* neglectful, irresponsible; **~ver·let·zung** *f* breach of duty; **~ver·säum·nis** *n a.* ⚖ neglect *or* dereliction (of duty); **~ver·si·che·rung** *f* compulsory insurance; **~ver·tei·di·ger** *m* ⚖ assigned counsel; **~vor·le·sung** *f* compulsory lecture

'pflicht·wid·rig **I.** *adj.* disloyal, contrary to (one's) duty; **II.** *adv.*: ***sich ~ verhalten*** go against one's duty; **'Pflicht·wid·rig·keit** *f* breach of duty

Pflock [pflɔk] *m* (-[e]s; Pflöcke ['pflœkə]) peg; post, stake

pflücken ['pflʏkən] (*sep.* -k·k-) *v/t.* (h) pick; **Pflücker** ['pflʏkɐ] (*sep.* -k·k-) *m* (-s; -), **Pflücke·rin** ['pflʏkərın] (*sep.* -k·k-) *f* (-; -nen) picker; **pflück·reif** ['pflʏk-] *adj.* ready for picking

Pflug [pflu:k] *m* (-[e]s; Pflüge ['pfly:gə]) plough, *Am.* plow; **~bo·gen** *m skiing*: plough, *Am.* plow

pflü·gen ['pfly:gən] *v/t. and v/i.* (h) plough, *Am.* plow

Pflü·ger ['pfly:gɐ] *m* (-s; -) ploughman, *Am.* plowman

'Pflug·schar *f* (-; -en) ploughshare, *Am.* plowshare

Pfort·ader ['pfɔrt-] *f anat.* portal vein

Pfor·te ['pfɔrtə] *f* (-; -n) gate, door; *fig.* gateway; ***s-e ~n öffnen*** open its gates; *fig.* ***die ~n des Himmels (der Hölle)*** the gates of heaven (of hell)

Pfört·ner ['pfœrtnɐ] *m* (-s; -) gatekeeper; porter, *Am. a.* doorman; **~haus** *n* gatekeeper's lodge, gatehouse; **~lo·ge** *f* reception; gatekeeper's cabin, F gate; ***in*** (*or* ***an***) ***der ~*** at the gate

Pfo·sten ['pfɔstən] *m* (-s; -) post, pole; *sport*: (goal)post; **~schuß** *m* shot against the post; **~!** it's hit the post

Pfo·te ['pfo:tə] *f* (-; -n) **1.** *zo.* paw; **2.** F *hum.* F mitt, paw; ***~n weg!*** hands off!, F get your dirty mitts (*or* paws) off!; ***er hat s-e ~n überall drin*** F he's into everything, *contp.* F he has to be in on everything; **3.** F scrawl

Pfropf [pfrɔpf] *m* (-[e]s; -e) plug (*a.* ⚕); ⚕ (blood)clot

pfrop·fen ['pfrɔpfən] *v/t.* (h) **1.** plug, stop(per); stopper, cork *a bottle*; **2.** ⚘ graft; **3.** cram (***in*** *acc.* into); → ***gepfropft***

'Pfrop·fen *m* (-s; -) stopper; cork

Pfrün·de ['pfrʏndə] *f* (-; -n) *eccl.* prebend; benefice; *fig.* sinecure

Pfuhl [pfu:l] *m* (-[e]s; -e) murky pool; *fig.* slough

pfui [pfui] *int.* ugh!; *to a child or dog*: no!; *sport etc.*: boo!; → ***Teufel***

'Pfui·ruf *m* boo; *pl. a.* booing *sg.*

Pfund [pfʊnt] *n* (-[e]s; -e [-də]) **1.** pound (*abbr.* lb, *pl.* lbs); ***vier ~ Butter*** four pounds of butter; ***ein halbes ~ Bohnen*** half a pound of beans; **2.** ✝ pound; ~ ***Sterling*** pound sterling (*abbr.* £)

pfun·dig ['pfʊndıç] F *adj.* F great

'Pfund·no·te *f* pound note

'Pfunds|idee F *f* brilliant idea; **~kerl** F *m* F great guy

'pfund·wei·se *adv.* by the pound

'Pfund·zei·chen *n* pound sign (*abbr.* £)

Pfusch·ar·beit ['pfʊʃ-] *f* → ***Pfuscherei***

pfu·schen ['pfʊʃən] F *v/i. and v/t.* (h) bungle; **Pfu·scher** ['pfʊʃɐ] F *m* (-s; -) bungler; amateur; F cowboy; F quack

Pfu·sche·rei [pfʊʃə'raı] F *f* (-; -en) a) bungling, b) bad job, F botch-up

Pfüt·ze ['pfʏtsə] *f* (-; -n) puddle

Pha·lanx ['fa:laŋks] *f* (-; Phalangen [fa-'laŋən]) phalanx, *fig. a.* battery

phal·lisch ['falıʃ] *adj.* phallic

Phal·lus ['falʊs] *m* (-; Phalli) phallus; **~sym͵bol** *n* phallic symbol

Phä·no·men [fɛno'me:n] *n* (-s; -e) phenomenon (*a. fig.*); *fig. a.* real phenomenon; *a.* mystery; **phä·no·me·nal** [fɛno-me'na:l] *adj.* phenomenal (*a. fig.*)

Phä·no·me·no·lo·gie [fɛnomenolo'gi:] *f* (-; *no pl.*) phenomenology

Phä·no·typ [fɛno'ty:p] *m* (-en; -en) phenotype

Phan·ta·sie [fanta'zi:] *f* (-; -n [-zi:ən]) **1.** *no pl.* imagination; ***blühende ~*** vivid imagination; ***schmutzige ~*** dirty (F one-track) mind; ***~ haben*** have imagination; ***das ist reine ~*** it's all in the mind, you're *etc.* imagining things; → ***durchgehen*** 3, ***Lauf*** 3, ***Reich***; **2.** fantasy; ⚕ hallucination; ***sich in ~n flüchten*** escape into a fantasy world (*or* world of fantasies); **&arm** *adj.* unimaginative, lacking in imagination; **~ge·bil·de** *n* figment of the imagination; **~ge·stalt** *f* imaginary character; **~land·schaft** *f* imaginary (*or* fantastic) landscape

phan·ta·sie·los *adj.* unimaginative; boring; unresourceful; ***sei doch nicht so ~!*** have some imagination; **Phan·ta'sie·lo·sig·keit** *f* (-; *no pl.*) lack of imagination; unresourcefulness

Phan·ta'sie·preis *m* exorbitant (F wild) price

phan·ta·sie·ren *v/i.* (h) (day)dream, fantasize; ♪ improvise; ⚕ hallucinate, be delirious; F rave (***von*** *dat.* about); ***sie phantasiert davon, Astronautin zu werden*** she has this fantasy about becoming an astronaut

phan·ta'sie·voll *adj.* imaginative; creative

Phan·ta'sie|vor·stel·lung *f* fantasy; **~welt** *f* world of fantasy, fantasy world

Phan·tast [fan'tast] *m* (-en; -en) dreamer; **Phan·ta·ste·rei** [fantastə'raı] *f* (-; -en) **1.** (pure) fantasy; ***das ist ~*** *a.* it's his *etc.* imagination run wild; **2.** *pl.* F crazy ideas; **phan·ta·stisch** [fan'tastıʃ] *adj.* fantastic (*a.* F); bizarre; incredible; F terrific

Phan·tom [fan'to:m] *n* (-s; -e) phantom; **~bild** *n* identikit (*TM*) (*or* photofit) picture; **~glied** *n* phantom limb; **~schmer·zen** *pl.* phantom pain *sg.*

Pha·rao ['fa:rao] *m* (-s; Pharaonen [fara-'o:nən]) *hist.* Pharaoh

Pha·rao·nen|grab [fara'o:nən-] *n* Pharaoh's (*or* Pharaonic) tomb; **~reich** *n* **1.** Pharaonic kingdom (*or* reign); **2. *das ~*** *coll.* Ancient Egypt

Pha·ri·sä·er [fari'zɛ:ɐ] *m* (-s; -) **1.** *hist.* Pharisee; **2.** *fig.* self-righteous person; hypocrite; bigot; ***er ist ein richtiger ~*** *a.* he's so holier-than-thou

pha·ri'sä·er·haft *adj.* self-righteous, holier-than-thou; hypocritical; bigoted

Pha·ri'sä·er·tum *n* (-s; *no pl.*) self-righteousness, holier-than-thou attitude; hypocrisy; bigotry

Phar·ma·in·du͵strie ['farma-] *f* pharmaceutical(s) industry

Phar·ma·ko·lo·ge [farmako'lo:gə] *m* (-n; -n) pharmacologist; **Phar·ma·ko·lo·gie** [farmakolo'gi:] *f* (-; *no pl.*) pharmacology; **phar·ma·ko·lo·gisch** [farmako-'lo:gıʃ] *adj.* pharmacological

Phar·ma|kon͵zern ['farma-] *m* pharmaceutical company; **~re·fe͵rent** *m* medical rep(resentative); **~un·ter͵neh·men** *n* pharmaceuticals (*or* drug) company

Phar·ma·zeut [farma'tsɔʏt] *m* (-en; -en) pharmacist; **Phar·ma·zeu·tik** [farma-'tsɔʏtık] *f* (-; *no pl.*) pharmaceutics *pl.*; **phar·ma·zeu·tisch** [farma'tsɔʏtıʃ] *adj.* pharmaceutical

Phar·ma·zie [farma'tsi:] *f* (-; *no pl.*) pharmaceutics *pl.*

Pha·se ['fa:zə] *f* (-; -n) phase (*a. ast.*, ⚡); stage (*a.* ⚕); ***in dieser ~*** during this phase (*or* stage), at this stage; ***sich in e-r kritischen ~ befinden*** be going through a critical phase (*or* stage); ***in die entscheidende*** (F ***heiße***) ***~ treten*** enter the (*or* its, their) critical phase *or* stage

'Pha·sen|dia͵gramm *n* phase diagram; **&gleich** *adj.* in phase; **~mes·ser** *m* phase meter; **~ver·schie·bung** *f* phase displacement; **&ver·scho·ben** *adj.* out of phase; **~wand·ler** *m* phase adapter

Phe·nol [fe'no:l] *n* (-s; *no pl.*) phenol

Phe·ro·mon [fero'mo:n] *n* (-s; -e) *biol.* pheromone

Phil·an·throp [filan'tro:p] *m* (-en; -en) philanthropist; **Phil·an·thro·pie** [filan-tro'pi:] *f* (-; *no pl.*) philanthropy; **phil·an·thro·pisch** [filan'tro:pıʃ] *adj.* philanthropic(al)

Phil·ate·lie [filate'li:] *f* (-; *no pl.*) philately; **Phil·ate·list** [filate'lıst] *m* (-en; -en) philatelist

Phil·har·mo·nie [fılharmo'ni:] *f* **1.** philharmonic orchestra; **2.** philharmonic concert hall; **Phil·har·mo·ni·ker** [fıl-har'mo:nikɐ] *pl.*: ***die Berliner*** *etc.* ~ the Berlin *etc.* Philharmonic (Orchestra)

Phi·lip·pi·ka [fi'lıpika] *fig. f* (-; -ken) philippic, tirade

Phi·lip·pi·ner [fɪlɪ'piːnɐ] *m* (-s; -), **Phi·lip·pi·ne·rin** [fɪlɪ'piːnərɪn] *f* (-; -nen) Filipino; **phi·lip·pi·nisch** [fɪlɪ'piːnɪʃ] *adj.* Philippine, Filipino
Phi·li·ster [fi'lɪstɐ] *fig. m* (-s; -), **phi'li·ster·haft** *adj.* Philistine, philistine
Phi·lo·lo·ge [filo'loːgə] *m* (-n; -n), **Phi·lo·lo·gin** [filo'loːgɪn] *f* (-; -nen) language and literature teacher (*or* expert, F man, woman), *Am.* philologist; **Phi·lo·lo·gie** [filolo'giː] *f* (-; *no pl.*) (study of) language and literature, *Am.* philology; **phi·lo·lo·gisch** [filo'loːgɪʃ] *adj.* language and literature ..., *Am.* philological
Phi·lo·soph [filo'zoːf] *m* (-en; -en) philosopher; **Phi·lo·so·phie** [filozo'fiː] *f* (-; -n [-'fiːən]) philosophy; **phi·lo·so·phie·ren** [filozo'fiːrən] *v/i.* (h) philosophize (***über*** *acc.* on); **phi·lo·so·phisch** [filo'zoːfɪʃ] *adj.* philosophical; ***vom ~en Standpunkt*** from a philosophical point of view, looking at it philosophically; ***er ist ein ~er Mensch*** he has a philosophical mind (*or* bent), he's a bit of a philosopher
Phio·le ['fioːlə] *f* (-; -n) phial, vial
Phleg·ma ['flɛgma] *n* (-s; *no pl.*) lethargy, apathy; **Phleg·ma·ti·ker** [flɛg'maːtikɐ] *m* (-s; -) apathetic type; **phleg·ma·tisch** [flɛg'maːtɪʃ] *adj.* lethargic, apathetic
Pho·bie [fo'biː] *f* (-; -n) phobia
Pho·bi·ker ['foːbikɐ] *m* (-s; -), **pho·bisch** ['foːbɪʃ] *adj.* phobic
Phon [foːn] *n* (-s; -) *phys.* phon
Pho·nem [fo'neːm] *n* (-s; -e) phoneme
Pho·ne·tik [fo'neːtɪk] *f* (-; *no pl.*) phonetics *pl.*; **Pho·ne·ti·ker** [fo'neːtikɐ] *m* (-s; -) phonetician; **pho·ne·tisch** [fo'neːtɪʃ] **I.** *adj.* phonetic; ***~e Schrift*** phonetic transcription; **II.** *adv.* phonetically; ***~ darstellen*** transcribe
Phö·nix ['føːnɪks] *m*: ***wie ein ~ aus der Asche steigen*** rise (like a phoenix) from the ashes
Phö·ni·zi·er [fø'niːtsǐɐ] *m* (-s; -), **Phö·ni·zie·rin** [fø'niːtsǐərɪn] *f* (-; -nen), **phö·ni·zisch** [fø'niːtsiʃ] *adj.* Phoenician
Pho·no|ein·gang ['foːno-] *m* phono input; **~ein·gangs·buch·se** *f* phono input jack; **~ka·bel** *n* phono cable (*or* cord)
Pho·no·lo·ge [fono'loːgə] *m* (-n; -n) phonologist; **Pho·no·lo·gie** [fonolo'giː] *f* (-; *no pl.*) phonology
Pho·no·me·trie [fonome'triː] *f* (-; *no pl.*) phonometry
Pho·no·ty·pi·stin [fonoty'pɪstɪn] *f* (-; -nen) audiotypist
Phos·phat [fɔs'faːt] *n* (-[e]s; -e) ⚗ phosphate; **≈frei** *adj.* phosphate-free
phos'phat·hal·tig [-haltɪç] *adj.* containing phosphates; ***~ sein*** contain phosphates
Phos·phor ['fɔsfoːɐ] *m* (-s; *no pl.*) ⚗ phosphorus; **~bom·be** *f* incendiary bomb
Phos·pho·res·zenz [fɔsforɛs'tsɛnts] *f* (-; *no pl.*) phosphorescence
phos·pho·res·zie·ren [fɔsforɛs'tsiːrən] *v/i.* (h) phosphoresce; **~d** phosphorescent
'phos·phor·hal·tig [-haltɪç] *adj.* phosphoric
'Phos·phor|säu·re *f* phosphoric acid; **~ver·gif·tung** *f* phosphorus poisoning
Pho·to(...) → *a.* ***Foto(...)***
Pho·to|bio·lo'gie [foto-] *f* photobiology; **~che'mie** *f* photochemistry
Pho·to·di̦ode ['foːto-] *f* photodiode
pho·to·e'lek·trisch [foto-] *adj.* photoelectric, photovoltaic
Pho·to·ele̦ment ['foːto-] *n* photovoltaic cell
Pho·to·me·trie [fotome'triː] *f* (-; *no pl.*) photometry
Pho·ton ['foːtɔn, fo'toːn] *n* (-s; -en) *phys.* photon
Pho·to·syn'the·se [foto-] *f* photosynthesis
Pho·to·zel·le ['foːto-] *f* photoelectric cell, electric eye
Phra·se ['fraːzə] *f* (-; -n) phrase (*a.* ♪); cliché, platitude; *esp. pol.* catchphrase; ***leere ~n*** empty talk, F claptrap; ***~n dreschen*** talk in platitudes, F beat the air
'Phra·sen|dre·scher *m* phrasemonger; **~dre·sche̦rei** *f* phrasemongering, F hot air
'phra·sen·haft *adj.* empty, meaningless
Phra·seo·lo·gie [frazeolo'giː] *f* (-;-n) phraseology; **phra·seo·lo·gisch** [frazeo'loːgɪʃ] *adj.* phraseological
phra·sie·ren [fra'ziːrən] *v/t.* (h) ♪ phrase
pH-Wert [pe'haː-] *m phys.* pH factor
Phy·lo·ge·ne·se [fyloge'neːzə] *f* (-; -n) *biol.* phylogenesis; **phy·lo·ge·ne·tisch** [fyloge'neːtɪʃ] *adj.* phylogenetic
Phy·sik [fy'ziːk] *f* (-; *no pl.*) physics *pl.*
phy·si·ka·lisch [fyzi'kaːlɪʃ] *adj.* **1.** physical; **2.** physics ...; ***~es Gesetz*** law of physics; ***~es Institut*** institute (*or* department) of physics; **3.** physical; ***~e Therapie*** *a.* physiotherapy
Phy·si·ker ['fyːzikɐ] *m* (-s; -), **Phy·si·ke·rin** ['fyːzikərɪn] *f* (-; -nen) physicist
Phy·si·kum ['fyːzikʊm] *n* (-s; -ka) ⚕ preliminary medical examination
Phy·sio·gno·mie [fyzǐogno'miː] *f* (-; -n) physiognomy; **phy·sio·gno·misch** [fyzǐo'gnoːmɪʃ] *adj.* physiognomical
Phy·sio·lo·ge [fyzǐo'loːgə] *m* (-n; -n) physiologist; **Phy·sio·lo·gie** [fyzǐolo'giː] *f* (-; *no pl.*) physiology; **phy·sio·lo·gisch** [fyzǐo'loːgɪʃ] *adj.* physiological
Phy·sio·the·ra'peut [fyzǐo-] *m* physiotherapist, F physio; **Phy·sio·the·ra'pie** *f* physiotherapy
Phy·sis ['fyːzɪs] *f* (-; *no pl.*) physical constitution
phy·sisch ['fyːzɪʃ] *adj.* physical
Pi [piː] *n* (-[s]; *no pl.*) ⅌ pi
Pia·ni·no [pǐa'niːno] *n* (-s; -s) miniature upright
Pia·nist [pǐa'nɪst] *m* (-en; -en), **Pia·ni·stin** [pǐa'nɪstɪn] *f* (-; -nen) pianist
Pia·no ['pǐaːno] *n* (-s; -s) ♪ piano
Pi·ca·dor [pika'doːɐ] *m* (-s; -es [-'doːrɛs]) picador
pi·cheln ['pɪçəln] (h) F **I.** *v/i.* tipple, F booze; ***er hat anständig gepichelt*** F he was knocking them back; **II.** *v/t.*: ***einen ~*** F wet one's whistle; ***ein paar Flaschen ~*** F knock back a few bottles
Picke ['pɪkə] (*sep.* -k·k-) *f* (-; -n) pick(axe), *Am.* pick(ax)
Pickel[1] ['pɪkəl] (*sep.* -k·k-) *m* (-s; -) ⚕ spot, pimple
'Pickel[2] (*sep.* -k·k-) *m* (-s; -) ⚙ pick(axe), *Am.* pick(ax); ice pick
'Pickel·ge·sicht (*sep.* -k·k-) *n* **1.** spotty face; **2.** spotty person; pimply youth; *pl. a.* spotty (*or* pimply) teenagers, F *the* acne brigade *sg.*
'Pickel·hau·be (*sep.* -k·k-) *f* spiked helmet
picke·lig ['pɪkəlɪç] (*sep.* -k·k-) *adj.* spotty, pimply
picken ['pɪkən] (*sep.* -k·k-) *v/t. and v/i.* (h) peck; ***et. ~ aus*** *dat.* pick s.th. out of *s.th.*
Pick·nick ['pɪknɪk] *n* (-s; -s) picnic; ***ein ~ machen*** have (*or* go for) a picnic
pick·nicken ['pɪknɪkən] (*sep.* -k·k-) *v/i.* (h) (have a) picnic
'Pick·nick·korb *m* picnic basket (*or* hamper)
pi·co·bel·lo [piko'bɛlo] F **I.** *adj.* perfect, F spot on; **II.** *adv.*: ***~ sauber*** *etc.* absolutely spotless *etc.*; ***~ gekleidet*** immaculately dressed; ***er hat die Wohnung ~ aufgeräumt*** he got the flat into shipshape order; ***das Zimmer war ~ aufgeräumt*** *a.* there wasn't a thing out of place (in the room)
Pi·co·wel·len·herd ['piko-] *m* picowave oven
piek|fein ['piːk'faɪn] F **I.** *adj.* (very) smart, F posh, F swish; **II.** *adv.*: ***sich ~ anziehen*** F put on one's Sunday best, *sl.* put some smart gear on; **~'sau·ber** F *adj.* spotless, F squeaky clean
piep [piːp] *int.*: ***er sagte nicht mal ~*** F there wasn't a peep from him; ***er konnte nicht mehr ~ sagen*** it left him speechless, he just sat (*or* stood) there gaping
Piep F *m* → ***Pieps***
pie·pe ['piːpə], **piep·egal** ['piːpˀeˈgaːl] F *adj.*: ***das ist mir ~*** F I don't care two hoots, F I don't give a damn (*or* a tinker's cuss)
pie·pen ['piːpən] *v/i.* (h) cheep, chirp; *mouse*: squeak; F ***bei dir piept's wohl*** F you must be off your rocker; ***es (er) war zum ≈*** F it (he) was a scream
'Pie·pen F *pl. sl.* brass *sg.*, bread *sg.*
'Piep·matz [-mats] F *m* (-es; -mätze [-mɛtsə]) F dickybird, birdie
Pieps [piːps] F *m* (-es; -e) **1.** peep, cheep; ***er machte keinen ~*** F there was not a peep to be heard from him; ***ich will keinen ~ mehr hören!*** F I don't want to hear another peep out of you; **2.** ***du hast wohl einen ~*** F you must be off your rocker; **piep·sen** ['piːpsən] *v/i.* (h) **1.** → ***piepen***; **2.** ⚙ bleep; **Piep·ser** ['piːpsɐ] F *m* (-s; -) **1.** → ***Pieps*** 1; **2.** F ⚙ bleeper; **piep·sig** ['piːpsɪç] *adj.* squeaky *voice*
'Pieps·stim·me *f* squeaky voice
Pier [piːɐ] *m* (-s; -s, -e [-rə]) ⚓ pier
pie·sacken ['piːzakən] F *v/t.* (h) torment; pester
pie·seln ['piːzəln] F *dial. v/i.* (h) F have a pee; ***~ gehen*** F go for a pee
Pie·tät [pǐe'tɛːt] *f* (-; *no pl.*) reverence, piety; **pie'tät·los** *adj.* irreverent; **pie'tät·voll** *adj.* reverent
Pie·tis·mus [pǐe'tɪsmʊs] *m* (-; *no pl.*) **1.** *hist.* Pietism; **2.** pietism; **Pie·tist** [pǐe'tɪst] *m* (-en; -en) **1.** *hist.* Pietist; **2.** pietist; **pie·ti·stisch** [pǐe'tɪstɪʃ] *adj.* **1.** *hist.* Pietist; **2.** pietistic(al)
pie·zo·elek·trisch [pǐetsoˀe'lɛktrɪʃ] *adj.* piezoelectric; **Pie·zo·elek·tri·zi'tät** *f* piezoelectricity
Pig·ment [pɪ'gmɛnt] *n* (-[e]s; -e) pigment; **~feh·ler** *m* pigmentation defect; **~fleck** *m* pigmentation mark, F brown spot; → ***Altersfleck***
pig·men·tie·ren [pɪgmɛn'tiːrən] *v/t.* (*a.* ***sich ~***) (h) pigment; **Pig·men'tie·rung** *f* (-; -en) pigmentation
Pik[1] [piːk] *m*: ***e-n ~ auf j-n haben*** F have a grudge against s.o.
Pik[2] *n* (-s; -) spade(s *pl.*); *in cpds.* → ***Herz...***
pi·kant [pi'kant] *adj.* **1.** *gastr.* piquant (*a.*

wine), spicy; **2.** *fig.* off-colo(u)r, risqué *joke etc.*; **~es Thema** delicate subject; **3.** *fig.* attractive *face*; **Pi·kan·te·rie** [pikantəˈriː] *f* (-; -n) **1.** piquancy; ***darin liegt e-e gewisse ~*** it has a certain piquancy; **2.** risqué remark (*or* story *etc.*)
pi·ka·resk [pikaˈrɛsk] *adj.* picaresque
Pi·ke [ˈpiːkə] *f*: *fig.* ***et. von der ~ auf lernen*** learn s.th. from scratch, start at the bottom
pi·kiert [piˈkiːɐt] *adj.* put out, piqued, F miffed
Pik·ko·lo[1] [ˈpɪkolo] *m* (-s; -s) **1.** champagne miniature; **2.** trainee waiter
ˈ**Pik·ko·lo**[2] *n* (-s; -s), **~flö·te** *f* piccolo
Pik·to·gramm [pɪktoˈgram] *n* (-s; -e) pictograph; symbol
Pi·la·tus [piˈlaːtʊs] *m* → ***Pontius***
Pil·ger [ˈpɪlgɐ] *m* (-s; -) pilgrim; ˈ**Pil·ger·fahrt** *f* pilgrimage; **Pil·ge·rin** [ˈpɪlgərɪn] *f* (-; -nen) pilgrim; ˈ**pil·gern** *v/i.* (sn) go on a pilgrimage; F**~ *nach*** *dat.* trail off to
Pil·le [ˈpɪlə] *f* (-; -n) pill, tablet; ***die ~ nehmen*** take (*or* be on, go on) the pill; ***~ danach*** morning-after pill; *fig.* ***e-e bittere ~*** a bitter pill (to swallow); ***(j-m) die ~ versüßen*** sugar the pill (for s.o.); F ***da helfen keine ~n*** F it's hopeless; F ***bei ihm helfen keine ~n*** F he's a dead loss
ˈ**Pil·len|knick** *m* drop in the birthrate (*due to the introduction of the pill*), F baby bust; **2mü·de** F *adj.* tired of the pill, pill-weary; **~pau·se** *f*: ***e-e ~ einlegen*** go off (*or* stop taking) the pill for a while; **~schlucker** F *m* F pill popper
Pi·lot [piˈloːt] *m* (-en; -en) pilot; **~aus·ga·be** *f* pilot edition
Piˈlo·ten·schein *m* pilot's licen|ce (*Am.* -se)
Piˈlot·film *m* pilot film
Pi·lo·tin [piˈloːtɪn] *f* (-; -nen) pilot
Piˈlot|proˌjekt *n* pilot project (*or* scheme); **~sen·dung** *f* pilot broadcast; **~stu·die** *f* pilot study; **~ton** *m* pilot signal (*or* tone)
Pils [pɪls] *n* (-; -) Pils(e)ner (beer)
Pilz [pɪlts] *m* (-es; -e) mushroom; 𝕄, *a.* ⚘ fungus; → ***Fußpilz, Giftpilz, Hautpilz, Pilzkrankheit***; *fig.* ***wie ~e aus dem Boden schießen*** shoot up like mushrooms, mushroom; **~ge·richt** *n* mushroom dish; **~krank·heit** *f* fungus infection, 𝕄 mycosis; **~ver·gif·tung** *f* mushroom (*or* toadstool) poisoning
Pi·ment [piˈmɛnt] *m, n* (-[e]s; -e) *gastr.* allspice, pimento
Pim·mel [ˈpɪməl] *sl. m* (-s; -) *sl.* willy
Pimpf [pɪmpf] F *m* (-[e]s; -e) F squirt
pin·ge·lig [ˈpɪŋəlɪç] F *adj.* fussy, F nitpicking ...
Ping·pong [ˈpɪŋpɔŋ] *n* (-s; *no pl.*) ping-pong
Pin·gu·in [ˈpɪŋguiːn] *m* (-s; -e) penguin
Pi·nie [ˈpiːnĭə] *f* (-; -n) (stone) pine
ˈ**Pi·ni·en·kern** *m* pine nut
pink [pɪŋk] *adj.*, **Pink** *n* (-s; -s) shocking pink
Pin·ke [ˈpɪŋkə] F *obs. f* (-; *no pl.*) F cash, *sl.* bread, brass
Pin·kel [ˈpɪŋkəl] F *m* (-s; -): ***feiner ~*** F toff, poser
pin·keln [ˈpɪŋkəln] F *v/i.* (h) F (have a) piddle *or* pee; ***~ gehen*** F go for a pee, *a. sl.* take a leak; ˈ**Pin·kel·pau·se** F *f* F loo stop, stop for a pee; ***machen wir mal ~*** F time for a pee
pin·nen [ˈpɪnən] F *v/t.* (h) pin, F stick (***an*** *acc.*, ***auf*** *acc.* on[to])
Pinn·wand [ˈpɪn-] *f* pinboard
Pin·scher [ˈpɪnʃɐ] *m* (-s; -) **1.** *zo.* pinscher; **2.** F *contp.* pipsqueak
Pin·sel [ˈpɪnzəl] *m* (-s; -) **1.** (paint)brush; **2.** F *contp.* F twit; ***eingebildeter ~*** F arrogant ponce; **~füh·rung** *f* brushwork
pin·seln [ˈpɪnzəln] *v/i. and v/t.* (h) paint (*a.* ⚕)
ˈ**Pin·sel|stiel** *m* (paint)brush handle; **~strich** *m* brushstroke
Pin·zet·te [pɪnˈtsɛtə] *f* (-; -n): (***e-e ~*** a pair of) tweezers *pl.*
Pio·nier [pĭoˈniːɐ] *m* (-s; -e [-rə]) **1.** pioneer; **2.** ⚔ engineer; **~ar·beit** *f* pioneering work; **~geist** *m* (-[e]s; *no pl.*) pioneering spirit; **~lei·stung** *f* pioneering feat; **~trup·pe** *f* ⚔ engineers *pl.*
Pi·pa·po [pipaˈpoː] F *n*: ***und das ganze ~*** and all the rest (of it), and all that nonsense; ***Auto*** *etc.* ***mit allem ~*** car *etc.* with all the extras (*or* trimmings)
Pipe·line [ˈpaɪplaɪn] *f* (-; -s) pipeline
Pi·pet·te [piˈpɛtə] *f* (-; -n) pipette
Pi·pi [piˈpiː] F *n* (-s; *no pl.*) F wee-wee(s *pl.*); ***~ machen*** F do a wee-wee
Pi·rat [piˈraːt] *m* (-en; -en) pirate
Piˈra·ten|aus·ga·be *f* pirate edition; **~flag·ge** *f* Jolly Roger; **~sen·der** *m* pirate radio station; *pl. coll. a.* pirate radio *sg.*
Pi·ra·te·rie [piratəˈriː] *f* (-; -n) piracy
Pi·rou·et·te [piˈrŭɛtə] *f* (-; -n), **pi·rou·et·tie·ren** [pirŭɛˈtiːrən] *v/i.* (h) pirouette
Pirsch [pɪrʃ] *f* (-; *no pl.*) deerstalking, *Am.* still hunt; ***auf die ~ gehen*** → **pir·schen** [ˈpɪrʃən] *v/i.* (h) **1.** go deerstalking, stalk (the deer); **2.** (*a.* ***sich ~***) creep (***an*** *acc.* up to); ˈ**Pirsch·jagd** *f* → ***Pirsch***
Pis·se [ˈpɪsə] V *f* (-; *no pl.*), ˈ**pis·sen** V *v/i.* (h) V piss; **Pis·soir** [pɪˈsŏaːɐ] *n* (-s; -s, -e [-rə]) (men's) urinal
Pi·sta·zie [pɪsˈtaːtsĭə] *f* (-; -n) pistachio; **Piˈsta·zi·en·kern** *m* (shelled) pistachio
Pi·ste [ˈpɪstə] *f* (-; -n) a) (racing) track, b) piste, ski run, c) ✈ runway
ˈ**Pi·sten|row·dy** F *m*, **~sau** F *f* ski hooligan, terror of the slopes; **~wa·che** *f* ski patrol
Pi·sto·le [pɪsˈtoːlə] *f* (-; -n) pistol, gun; *fig.* ***j-m die ~ auf die Brust setzen*** hold a gun to s.o.'s head; ***wie aus der ~ geschossen*** like a shot
Piˈsto·len|held F *m* F gunslinger; **~schuß** *m* pistol shot; **~ta·sche** *f* holster
pit·to·resk [pɪtoˈrɛsk] *adj.* picturesque
Piz·za [ˈpɪtsa] *f* (-; -s, Pizzen [ˈpɪtsən]) pizza
Piz·ze·ria [pɪtseˈriːa] *f* (-; -s, -rien) pizza house (F place), pizzeria
Pla·ce·bo [plaˈtseːbo] *n* (-s; -s) placebo; **~efˌfekt** *m* placebo effect
pla·cie·ren [plaˈtsiːrən] *v/t. and v/refl. etc.* (h) → ***plazieren*** *etc.*
placken [ˈplakən] (*sep.* -k·k-) *v/refl.* (h) → ***plagen*** II; **Placke·rei** [plakəˈraɪ] (*sep.* -k·k-) *f* (-; -en) drudgery, F grind
plä·die·ren [plɛˈdiːrən] *v/i.* (h) plead (***auf*** *acc.*, ***für*** *acc.* for) (*a.* ⚖)
Plä·doy·er [plɛdŏaˈjeː] *n* (-s; -s) plea; ⚖ (final) speech; ***ein ~ halten für*** *acc.* make a speech for
Pla·fond [plaˈfõː] *m* (-s; -s) **1.** *Austrian* ceiling; **2.** ✝ ceiling, upper limit
Pla·ge [ˈplaːgə] *f* (-; -n) (real) nuisance; F (real) grind; *bibl.* plague; F ***man hat schon s-e ~ mit dir!*** you don't make life any easier; ***es macht das Leben zur ~*** it makes life unbearable (*or* a misery); ***es ist ihr zur ~ geworden*** it's become a real problem for her; **~geist** *m* F pest
pla·gen [ˈplaːgən] (h) **I.** *v/t.* torment, F plague; pester; worry, bother, dog; ***was plagt dich?*** what's eating at you?; → ***geplagt***; **II.** *v/refl.*: ***sich ~*** slave away (***mit*** *dat.* at *a job etc.*); go to great lengths; ***er plagt sich mit s-n Zähnen*** (***mit ständigem Kopfweh***) his teeth are giving him a lot of trouble (his constant headaches are getting him down); ***sie plagt sich mit ihren Schülern*** her pupils give her a hard time
Pla·gi·at [plaˈgĭaːt] *n* (-[e]s; -e) plagiarism; ***ein ~ begehen*** plagiarize; **Pla·gia·tor** [plaˈgĭaːtoːɐ] *m* (-s; -en [plagĭaˈtoːrən]) plagiarist; **pla·gi·ie·ren** [plagiˈiːrən] *v/t. and v/i.* (h) plagiarize
Pla·kat [plaˈkaːt] *n* (-[e]s; -e) poster; placard; **~far·be** *f* poster colo(u)r
pla·ka·tie·ren [plakaˈtiːrən] *v/t.* (h) placard
pla·ka·tiv [plakaˈtiːf] *adj.* striking; *contp.* ostentatious, sensational; simplistic
Plaˈkat|kle·ber *m* poster sticker; **~kunst** *f* poster art; **~ma·ler** *m* poster artist (*or* designer); **~säu·le** *f* advertising pillar; **~trä·ger** *m* sandwich man; **~wand** *f* hoarding, *Am. esp.* billboard; **~wer·bung** *f* poster advertising
Pla·ket·te [plaˈkɛtə] *f* (-; -n) badge; sticker
plan [plaːn] **I.** *adj.* level; **II.** *adv.*: ***~ liegen*** lie flat (***auf*** *dat.* on, against)
Plan[1] *m* (-[e]s; Pläne [ˈplɛːnə]) **1.** plan; intention; ***Pläne schmieden*** make plans, *b.s.* plot, scheme; ***voller Pläne stecken*** have all sorts of plans (*or* ideas); ***ich habe noch keine konkreten Pläne*** I haven't made any definite plans yet; **2.** plan; draft, design; diagram; **3.** (*city etc.*) map, (*layout etc.*) plan; **4.** schedule, plan
Plan[2] *m*: ***auf den ~ treten*** turn up, come onto the scene; ***auf den ~ rufen*** call into action
Pla·ne [ˈplaːnə] *f* (-; -n) tarpaulin; awning
pla·nen [ˈplaːnən] (h) **I.** *v/t.* **1.** plan; design; **2.** plan; ***ich habe nichts geplant*** I've got nothing planned; **II.** *v/i.* plan; plan ahead; budget; **Pla·ner** [ˈplaːnɐ] *m* (-s; -), **Pla·ne·rin** [ˈplaːnərɪn] *f* (-; -nen) planner; ✝ policy maker; **pla·ne·risch** [ˈplaːnərɪʃ] *adj.* planning ...
Pla·net [plaˈneːt] *m* (-en; -en) planet
pla·ne·ta·risch [planeˈtaːrɪʃ] *adj.* planetary
Pla·ne·ta·ri·um [planeˈtaːrĭʊm] *n* (-s; -en) planetarium
Plaˈne·ten|bahn *f* orbit; **~syˌstem** *n* planetary system
pla·nie·ren [plaˈniːrən] *v/t.* (h) level, grade
Pla·nier·rau·pe [plaˈniːɐ-] *f* bulldozer
Pla·ni·me·trie [planimeˈtriː] *f* (-; *no pl.*) plane geometry; **pla·ni·me·trisch** [planiˈmeːtrɪʃ] *adj.* planimetric(al)
Plan·ke [ˈplaŋkə] *f* (-; -n) plank, board
Plän·ke·lei [plɛŋkəˈlaɪ] *f* (-; -en) , **plän·keln** [ˈplɛŋkəln] *v/i.* (h) banter
ˈ**plan·konˌkav** *adj.* plano-concave
ˈ**plan·konˌvex** *adj.* plano-convex
ˈ**Plan·ko·sten** *pl.* target cost *sg.*
Plank·ton [ˈplaŋktɔn] *n* (-s; *no pl.*) plankton
ˈ**plan·los I.** *adj.* aimless, haphazard; **II.** *adv.* aimlessly, haphazardly
ˈ**Plan·lo·sig·keit** *f* (-; *no pl.*) haphazardness, haphazard nature (*gen.* of)
ˈ**plan·mä·ßig I.** *adj.* a) planned, b) ✈ *etc.* scheduled, c) systematic; **II.** *adv.* a) as

planned; *work etc.* according to plan (*or* schedule), b) *arrive etc.* on schedule, c) systematically

'Plan·qua͵drat *n* grid square

Plansch·becken ['planʃ-] *n* paddling pool

plan·schen ['planʃən] *v/i.* (h) splash (around); **Plan·sche·rei** [planʃə'raɪ] *f* (-; *no pl.*) splashing; ***hör auf mit der ~!*** stop splashing around

'Plan|soll *n* → ***Planziel***; **~spiel** *n* experimental game(s *pl.*); **~stel·le** *f* (authorized *or* established) post

Plan·ta·ge [plan'taːʒə] *f* (-; -n) plantation

Plan'ta·gen|ar·bei·ter *m* plantation worker; **~be·sit·zer** *m* planter, owner of a (*or* the) plantation

Pla·nung ['plaːnʊŋ] *f* (-; -en) **1.** planning; timing, scheduling; **2.** → ***Plan***[1] 2

'Pla·nungs|ab͵tei·lung *f* planning department; **~aus·schuß** *m* planning committee; **~sta·di·um** *n* planning stage; **~zeit·raum** *m* planning period

'plan·voll *adj.* systematic(ally *adv.*), methodical

'Plan·wa·gen *m* covered wagon

'Plan|wirt·schaft *f* planned economy; **~ziel** *n* target; **~zif·fer** *f* target (figure)

Plap·per·maul ['plapɐ-] *n* chatterbox; ***er ist ein richtiges ~*** *a.* he never stops talking

plap·pern ['plapɐn] **I.** *v/i.* (h) babble (on); **II.** ♀ *n* (-s; *no pl.*) babble

plär·ren ['plɛrən] F *v/i. and v/t.* (h) bawl; *radio etc.*: blare

Plas·ma ['plasma] *n* (-s; Plasmen [-mən]) plasma; **~bild·schirm** *m* plasma display (*or* screen); **~bren·ner** *m* plasma torch; **~phy͵sik** *f* plasma physics *pl.*; **~phy·si·ker** *m* plasma physicist; **~zel·le** *f* plasma cell

Pla·stik[1] ['plastɪk] *f* (-; -en) **1.** *art*: sculpture; **2.** *no pl.* plasticity; **3.** ⚕ plastic surgery

'Pla·stik[2] *n* (-s; *no pl.*) plastic; **~be·steck** *n* plastic cutlery; **~beu·tel** *m* plastic (*or* polythene) bag; **~bom·be** *f* plastic bomb; **~fo·lie** *f* polythene sheet; **~geld** *n* (-[e]s; *no pl.*) plastic money; **~ge·schoß** *n* plastic bullet; **~spreng·stoff** *m* plastic explosive(s *pl.*); **~tü·te** *f* plastic bag

pla·stisch ['plastɪʃ] *adj.* **1.** *art*: sculptural, plastic *arts*; **2.** three-dimensional; **3.** graphic, vivid *description etc.*; **4.** ***~e Chirurgie*** plastic surgery

Pla·ta·ne [pla'taːnə] *f* (-; -n) plane (tree)

Pla·teau [pla'toː] *n* (-s; -s) plateau; **~soh·le** *f* platform sole

Pla·tin ['plaːtiːn] *n* (-s; *no pl.*) platinum

'pla·tin·blond *adj.* platinum blonde

Pla·ti·ne [pla'tiːnə] *f* (-; -n) ⚡ (circuit) board

Pla·ti·tü·de [plati'tyːdə] *f* (-; -n) platitude; ***~n reden*** talk in platitudes

pla·to·nisch [pla'toːnɪʃ] *adj.* Platonic; platonic *love etc.*

platsch [platʃ] *int.* splosh!

plat·schen [platʃən] *v/i.* (h, sn) splash

plät·schern ['plɛtʃɐn] *v/i.* **1.** (sn) *rain*: patter (***gegen*** *acc.* against); *waves*: lap (against); **2.** (h) *fountain*: splash; *brook etc*: murmur, babble; *children*: splash about; **3.** (sn) F *fig. conversation etc.*: meander along

platt [plat] *adj.* **1.** flat; level, even; ***~ klopfen*** (***drücken*** *etc.*) flatten; F *mot.* ***e-n Platten haben*** have a flat tyre (*Am.* tire), F have a flat; **2.** *fig.* trite, uninspired; **3.** downright, F rotten *lie etc.*; **4.** F flabbergasted, F floored; ***ich war einfach ~*** you could have knocked me down with a feather; ***da bin ich aber ~!*** F well blow me!

Platt *n ling.* → ***Plattdeutsch***

Plätt·brett ['plɛt-] *n* ironing board

Plätt·chen ['plɛtçən] *n* (-s; -) small plate; *a. anat.* lamina; ⚙, ♀ lamella; ⚕ platelet

'platt·deutsch *adj.*, **'Platt·deutsch** *n* (-en; *no pl.*) *ling.* Low German

Plat·te ['platə] *f* (-; -n) **1.** dish; *gastr.* ***kalte ~*** cold cuts; **2.** sheet *of glass, metal etc.*; (*wooden*) board; (*stone*) slab; tile; **3.** tabletop, leaf; **4.** hotplate; **5.** *geol.* ledge; **6.** record; F *fig.* ***die ~ kenn' ich schon*** I've heard that one before; F ***leg mal 'ne neue ~ auf*** F can you put the other side on for a change?; F ***der hat ganz schön was auf der ~*** F he's on the ball, he's really with it; **7.** *computer*: fixed disk; **8.** F bald pate, bald patch; ***e-e ~ haben*** be (going) bald

Plätt·ei·sen ['plɛt-] *n* iron

plät·ten ['plɛtən] *v/t.* (h) iron, press

'Plat·ten|ar͵chiv *n* record library; **~auf·nah·me** *f* recording; **~bar** *f* record listening counter; **~co·ver** *n* record sleeve; **~fir·ma** *f* record company; **~ge·schäft** *n* record shop; **~hül·le** *f* record sleeve; **~in·du͵strie** *f* record industry; **~lauf·werk** *n computer*: disk drive; **~rei·ni·ger** *m* record cleaner; **~samm·lung** *f* record collection; **~spie·ler** *m* record player, turntable; **~stän·der** *m* LP rack; **~sta·pel** *m computer*: disk pack; **~tek͵to·nik** *f geol.* plate tectonics *pl.*; **~tel·ler** *m* turntable; **~wechs·ler** *m* record changer

'Platt·fisch *m* flatfish

'Platt·form *f* platform (*a. fig. pol.*)

'Platt·fuß *m* flat foot; F *mot.* flat tyre (*Am.* tire), F flat; **'platt·fü·ßig** [-fyːsɪç] *adj.* flat-footed

'Platt·heit *f* (-; -en) **1.** *no pl.* flatness; *fig.* triteness; **2.** trite remark, platitude

'platt·na·sig [-naːzɪç] *adj.* flat-nosed

Platz [plats] *m* (-es; Plätze ['plɛtsə]) **1.** room, space; ***~ machen*** make room (***für*** *acc.* for), *a. fig.* make way (for); ***~ da!*** move along, please!; ***~ sparen*** save space; ***es ist kein ~ mehr*** there's no room left; ***es ist noch viel ~*** there's plenty of room (left); ***dafür finden wir noch ~*** we'll fit (*or* squeeze) that in somehow; ***der Wagen bietet fünf Personen ~*** the car has room for five (*or* seats five); ***der Saal bietet 300 Personen ~*** the hall seats 300; ***das Stadion hat ~ für 30000*** the stadium holds 30,000; ***das hat in s-m Leben keinen ~*** there's no room for that in his life; **2.** *a.* ✈ *etc.* seat, place; ***~ nehmen*** sit down; ***nehmen Sie doch ~!*** have a seat, (do) sit down; ***~!*** *to dog*: down!, sit!; ***j-m s-n ~ anbieten*** offer s.o. one's seat, give up one's seat for s.o.; ***ist der ~ frei?*** is this seat taken?; ***bis auf den letzten ~ gefüllt*** filled to capacity; ***er hat s-n festen ~*** he always likes to sit in the same place; **3.** place; spot; ***der Schlüssel hängt nicht an s-m ~*** the key isn't where it should be; ***die Ordner sind alle an ihrem ~*** the files are all in their proper place; ***auf die Plätze, fertig, los!*** on your marks, get set, go!; ***er wich nicht vom ~*** he didn't budge (*or* move from the spot); ***dein ~ ist bei d-r Firma*** your place is with your company, your company is where you belong; ***ein ~ an der Sonne*** *a. fig.* a place in the sun; ***fehl am ~(e) sein*** be out of place, *a.* be a square peg in a round hole; *remark etc.*: be uncalled for; ***hier ist Vorsicht am ~*** we've got to be careful here, this calls for great care; **4.** space; ***hier ist noch ein ~ (frei) für den Koffer*** here's a (an empty) space for the case; **5.** place; ***das beste Restaurant am ~e*** the best restaurant around here (*or* in [the] town); **6.** (*building, camping etc.*) site; **7.** open space; square; Circus; **8.** *sport*: field, pitch; (*tennis*) court; (*golf*) course; ***j-n vom ~ stellen*** send s.o. off; ***auf eigenem (gegnerischem) ~ spielen*** play at home (away [from home]); *fig.* ***vom ~ fegen*** play into the ground; **9.** *univ.* place (to study); ***hast du schon e-n ~ gefunden?*** have you been accepted anywhere?, have you got a place?; **10.** position; *sport*: place; ***den dritten ~ belegen*** come third; ***j-n auf den zweiten ~ verweisen*** beat s.o. into second place; ***s-e Gegner auf die Plätze verweisen*** leave one's opponents trailing; **~angst** *f* (-; *no pl.*) claustrophobia; ⚕ agoraphobia; **~an·wei·ser** [-anvaɪzɐ] *m* (-s; -) usher; **~an·wei·se·rin** [-anvaɪzərɪn] *f* (-; -nen) usherette; **~be·darf** *m* space required

Plätz·chen[1] ['plɛtsçən] *n* (-s; -) **1.** (little) place, spot; **2.** ***ist hier noch ein ~ frei?*** a) is there any room left for me?, b) is there a free seat anywhere?; **3.** *fig.* ***sich ein ~ erobern*** carve out a niche for o.s.

'Plätz·chen[2] *n gastr.* biscuit, *Am.* cookie

'Platz·deck·chen *n* place mat

Plat·ze ['platsə] F *f*: ***da kriegt man ja die ~*** a) F it can drive you spare, b) F what a scream

plat·zen ['platsən] *v/i.* (sn) **1.** burst (*a. seam, tire*); *seam etc.*: split; crack, ⚕ rupture; ***ihm ist e-e Ader geplatzt*** he burst a blood vessel; F *fig.* ***ins Zimmer ~*** burst into the room; ***~ vor*** *dat.* be bursting with *curiosity, impatience etc.*; ***vor Lachen ~*** split one's sides; F ***mir platzt die Blase!*** F I'm dying to go to the loo; → ***Kragen, Naht***; **2.** F *fig.* fall through; *engagement*: be broken off; *drugs cartel etc.*: be smashed; *draft*: bounce; ***~ lassen*** upset, thwart, put an end to *s.o.'s plans etc.*, explode *theory etc.*, break up *friendship etc.*, smash *gang etc.*, bounce *draft*

'Platz|er·spar·nis *f* space saving; ***aus Gründen der ~*** for reasons of space; **~grün·de** *pl.*: ***aus ~n*** for reasons of space; ***wir sind aus ~n umgezogen*** we moved because we needed more space; **~hirsch** F *fig. m* F top dog; **~kar·te** *f* 🚂 reservation (ticket); **~kon͵zert** *n* promenade concert; **~man·gel** *m* lack of space; ***aus ~*** for (*or* due to) lack of space, because there isn't (*or* wasn't) enough room; **~mie·te** *f* **1.** rental charge, rent; *tennis*: fee; **2.** *thea.* subscription; **~ord·ner** *m sport*: steward; **~pa͵tro·ne** *f* blank cartridge; **~re·gen** *m* cloudburst, downpour; **~re·ser͵vie·rung** *f* reservation; ♀**spa·rend** *adj.* space-saving; **~sper·re** *f sport*: *ban on playing on one's home ground*; **~ver·weis** *m sport*: sending-off; ***X erhielt e-n ~*** X was sent off; ***es gab im ganzen vier ~e*** four players were sent off altogether; **~vor·teil** *m sport*: home advantage

'Platz·wart [-vart] *m* (-[e]s; -e) *sport*: groundsman

'**Platz·wech·sel** *m* **1.** change of places (*sport*: ends); **2.** ✝ local bill
'**Platz·wun·de** *f* cut, ⚕ laceration
Plau·de·rei [plaʊdəˈraɪ] *f* (-; -en) chat
Plau·de·rer [ˈplaʊdərɐ] *m* (-s; -) conversationalist; *contp.* gossip; ***er ist ein netter*** ~ it's nice listening to him talk
plau·dern [ˈplaʊdɐn] *v/i.* (h) (have a) chat; *fig.* ***aus der Schule*** ~ F blab
Plau·der\|stünd·chen *n*, ~**stun·de** *f* (pleasant) chat; ~**ton** *m* chatty tone, (light) conversational tone; ***im ~ schreiben*** write in a chatty style
Plausch [plaʊʃ] *dial. m* (-[e]s; -e) chat, F natter; **plau·schen** [ˈplaʊʃən] *v/i.* (h) chat, F (have a) natter
plau·si·bel [plaʊˈziːbəl] *adj.* plausible; ***j-m et. ~ machen*** make s.th. clear to s.o.; ***es klingt*** ~ it sounds plausible (enough)
Play [pleɪ] *n*: ***auf ~ drücken*** press play (*or* the play button)
Play·back [ˈpleɪbɛk] *n* (-s; *no pl.*) **1.** *TV etc.*: miming, singing to playback; ***es ist ~*** *a.* he's *etc.* (just) miming, it's a recording; **2.** double-tracking, multiple-tracking
'**Play·ta·ste** *f* play button
Pla·zen·ta [plaˈtsɛnta] *f* (-; -s, -ten) *anat.*, ⚘ placenta
Pla·zet [ˈplaːtsɛt] *n* (-s; -s) approval; ***e-r Sache sein ~ geben*** give one's approval for (*or* blessing to) s.th.
pla·zie·ren [plaˈtsiːrən] (h) **I.** *v/t.* place (*a. sport*); **II.** *v/refl.*: ***sich*** ~ position o.s.; *sport*: be placed (***als Dritter*** *etc.* third *etc.*); **pla·ziert** [plaˈtsiːɐt] *adj. sport*: well-placed *shot etc.*; **Pla'zie·rung** *f* (-; -en) *sport*: placing; place
Ple·be·jer [pleˈbeːjɐ] *contp. m* (-s; -) plebeian, F pleb; **ple'be·jer·haft I.** *adj.* → ***plebejisch***; **II.** *adv.*: ***sich ~ benehmen*** F behave (*or* act) like a pleb
ple·be·jisch [pleˈbːjɪʃ] *adj.* plebeian, F plebby
Ple·bis·zit [plebɪsˈtsiːt] *n* (-[e]s; -e) plebiscite
Plebs [plɛps] F *m* (-es; *no pl.*) F plebs *pl.*
Plei·sto·zän [plaɪstoˈtsɛːn] *n* (-s; *no pl.*), **plei·sto'zän** *adj.* Pleistocene
plei·te [ˈplaɪtə] F *adj.* F broke; ***total*** ~ F stone broke
Plei·te [ˈplaɪtə] F *f* (-; -n) **1.** ✝ bankruptcy; ***~ machen*** go bankrupt, F go bust; **2.** *fig.* failure, F flop; ~**gei·er** F *m*: ***über vielen Firmen schwebt der*** ~ many firms are on the verge of bankruptcy (F about to go bust); ***der ~ schwebt über uns*** (*or* ***ihnen***) *a.* the wolves are at the door
Plek·tron [ˈplɛktrɔn] *n* (-s; -tren, -tra), **Plek·trum** [ˈplɛktrʊm] *n* (-s; -tren, -tra) plectrum
plem·plem [plɛmˈplɛm] F *adj.* F nuts
Ple·nar\|de·bat·te [pleˈnaːɐ-] *f* debate of the full house; ~**saal** *m* plenary assembly hall; ~**sit·zung** *f* plenary session; ~**ver·samm·lung** *f* plenary assembly
Ple·num [ˈpleːnʊm] *n* (-s; Plenen [ˈpleːnən]) *parl.* plenary assembly; ⚖ full court
Pleo·nas·mus [pleoˈnasmʊs] *m* (-; -men) pleonasm; **pleo·na·stisch** [pleoˈnastɪʃ] *adj.* pleonastic(ally *adv.*)
Pleu·el·stan·ge [ˈplɔʏəl-] *f* ⚙ connecting rod
Pleu·ri·tis [plɔʏˈriːtɪs] *f* (-; -ritiden [-riˈtiːdən]) ⚕ pleurisy
Ple·xi·glas [ˈplɛksi-] (*TM*) *n* (-es; *no pl.*) Perspex (*TM*)

Ple·xus [ˈplɛksʊs] *m* (-; - [ˈplɛksuːs]) *anat.* plexus
Plis·see [plɪˈseː] *n* (-s; -s) pleats *pl.*; ~**rock** *m* pleated skirt
plis·sie·ren [plɪˈsiːrən] *v/t.* (h) pleat; **plis·siert** [plɪˈsiːɐt] *adj.* pleated
PLO [peːɛlˈʔoː] *f* (-; *no pl.*) PLO (= Palestine Liberation Organization); ~**-Füh·rer** *m* PLO leader
Plom·be [ˈplɔmbə] *f* (-; -n) **1.** ⚙ (lead) seal; **2.** ⚕ filling; **plom·bie·ren** [plɔmˈbiːrən] *v/t.* (h) **1.** ⚙ seal, lead; **2.** ⚕ fill *tooth*
Plot·ter [ˈplɔtɐ] *m* (-s; -) *computer*: plotter
plötz·lich [ˈplœtslɪç] **I.** *adj.* sudden; → ***Kindstod***; **II.** *adv.* suddenly; all of a sudden; ***~ war er verschwunden*** *a.* before you knew it he had disappeared; ***~ war alles anders*** from one minute (*or* day) to the next everything had changed; ***das kommt mir alles zu*** ~ it's all happening too fast (for my liking); F ***aber ein bißchen ~!*** F and make it snappy!
'**Plötz·lich·keit** *f* (-; *no pl.*) suddenness
Plu·der·ho·sen [ˈpluːdɐ-] *pl.* harem pants, Turkish trousers; F *hum.* baggy breeches
plump [plʊmp] *adj.* **1.** ungainly; clumsy, awkward; **2.** *fig.* a) awkward, heavy-handed, b) crude, (very) direct, blunt; blatant, gross *lie etc.*; ***das war e-e ~e Ausrede*** that was obviously just an excuse; → ***plump-vertraulich***
'**Plump·heit** *f* (-; *no pl.*) ungainliness, clumsiness *etc.*; → ***plump***
Plumps [plʊmps] F **I.** *m* (-es; -e) thud; plop; **II.** ♀ *int.* bang!; plop!; '**plump·sen** F *v/i.* (sn) fall; *a.* plop *into the water*
'**Plumps·klo** F *n* earth closet, F outdoor loo; *esp.* ⚔ latrine
'**plump-ver'trau·lich I.** *adj.* pally, chummy; **II.** *adv.* in a pally way, as if we *etc.* were the best of pals
Plun·der [ˈplʊndɐ] *m* (-s; *no pl.*) rubbish, F junk
Plün·de·rei [plʏndəˈraɪ] *f* (-; -en) looting (and pillaging), plundering; **Plün·de·rer** [ˈplʏndərɐ] *m* (-s; -) looter, plunderer; **plün·dern** [ˈplʏndɐn] *v/t. and v/i.* (h) loot, plunder, pillage; F raid *s.o.'s fridge, account etc.*; strip (bare) *Christmas tree etc.*; scavenge *book etc.*; **Plün·de·rung** [ˈplʏndərʊŋ] *f* (-; -en) looting, plundering, pillaging
Plu·ral [ˈpluːraːl] *m* (-s; -e) *ling.* plural (number); ~**bil·dung** *f* formation of the plural; ~**en·dung** *f* plural ending; ~**form** *f* plural form
Plu·ra·lis·mus [pluraˈlɪsmʊs] *m* (-; *no pl.*) pluralism; **plu·ra·li·stisch** [pluraˈlɪstɪʃ] *adj.* pluralistic(ally *adv.*)
Plu·ra·li·tät [pluraliˈtɛːt] *f* (-; *no pl.*) plurality
plus [plʊs] *prp.* plus; ***~/minus einen Tag*** give or take a day; ***~/minus Null abschneiden*** break even
Plus [plʊs] *n* (-; *no pl.*) **1.** plus; profit; ***ein ~ von 10 Stunden*** 10 hours plus (*or* in hand); **2.** asset, advantage
Plüsch [plʏʃ, plyːʃ] *m* (-[e]s; *no pl.*) plush; ~**au·gen** F *pl.* dreamy eyes; ~**tier** *n* soft (*or* cuddly) toy
'**Plus\|pol** *m* ⚡ positive (*or* plus) pole, anode; ~**punkt** *m* credit point, F *hum.* brownie point; *fig.* advantage, plus (point)
Plus·quam·per·fekt [ˈplʊskvampɛrfɛkt] *n* (-[e]s; -e) *ling.* pluperfect (tense), past perfect

'**Plus·sei·te** *f* ✝ *and fig.*: (***auf der*** ~ on the) credit side
plu·stern [ˈpluːstɐn] *v/t. and v/refl.* (h) → ***aufplustern***
'**Plus·zei·chen** *n* plus (sign)
Plu·to·krat [plutoˈkraːt] *m* (-en; -en) plutocrat; **Plu·to·kra·tie** [plutokraˈtiː] *f* (-; *no pl.*) plutocracy; **plu·to·kra·tisch** [plutoˈkraːtɪʃ] *adj.* plutocratic
Plu·to·ni·um [pluˈtoːnĭʊm] *n* (-s; *no pl.*) ⚛ plutonium; ~**bom·be** *f* plutonium bomb
Pneu·ma·tik [pnɔʏˈmaːtɪk] *f* (-; *no pl.*) *phys.* pneumatics *pl.*; **pneu·ma·tisch** [pnɔʏˈmaːtɪʃ] *adj.* pneumatic(ally *adv.*)
Po [poː] F *m* (-s; -s) → ***Popo***
Pö·bel [ˈpøːbəl] *m* (-s; *no pl.*) *the* masses *pl.*, *the* hoi polloi; mob, rabble
Pö·be·lei [pøːbəˈlaɪ] *f* (-; -en) **1.** *a. pl.* vulgar behavio(u)r; **2.** vulgar remark
'**pö·bel·haft** *adj.* vulgar, uncouth
'**Pö·bel·herr·schaft** *f* (-; *no pl.*) mob rule
po·chen [ˈpɔxən] *v/i.* (h) knock, tap; *pulse*: throb; *heart*: beat, thump; *fig.* ~ ***auf*** *acc.* insist on; make a big thing out of
po·chie·ren [pɔˈʃiːrən] *v/t.* (h) *gastr.* poach
Pocke [ˈpɔkə] (*sep.* -k·k-) *f* (-; -n) ⚕ pock; *pl.* smallpox *sg.*
'**Pocken\|imp·fung** (*sep.* -k·k-) *f* smallpox vaccination; ~**nar·be** *f* pockmark
pockig [ˈpɔkɪç] (*sep.* -k·k-) *adj.* pockmarked
Po·dest [poˈdɛst] *n* (-[e]s; -e) **1.** platform; *fig.* ***j-n auf ein ~ erheben*** put s.o. on a pedestal; ***j-n von s-m ~ stoßen*** knock s.o. off his (*or* her) pedestal; **2.** half-landing
Po·di·um [ˈpoːdĭʊm] *n* (-s; Podien) platform, rostrum
'**Po·di·ums·dis·kus·si̦on** *f* panel (*or* round-table) discussion
Poe·sie [poeˈziː] *f* (-; *no pl.*) poetry (*a. fig.*); ~**al·bum** *n* autograph book
Po·et [poˈeːt] *m* (-en; -en) poet; **Poe·ta lau·rea·tus** [poˈeːta laʊreˈaːtʊs] *m* (- -; -tae -ti [-tɛ -ti]) poet laureate; **Poe·tik** [poˈeːtɪk] *f* (-; *no pl.*) poetics *pl.*, poetic theory; **poe·tisch** [poˈeːtɪʃ] *adj.* poetic(al), lyrical; ***~e Ader*** poetic vein
Po·grom [poˈgroːm] *n* (-s; -e) pogrom
Poin·te [ˈpõɛ̃ːtə] *f* (-; -n) point *of a funny story etc.*; punch line ; '**poin·ten·reich** *adj.* very witty; **poin·tiert** [põɛ̃ˈtiːɐt] *adj.* pointed
Poin·til·lis·mus [põɛ̃tiˈjɪsmʊs] *m* (-; *no pl.*) *painting*: pointillism; **Poin·til·list** [põɛ̃tiˈjɪst] *m* (-en; -en) pointillist
Po·kal [poˈkaːl] *m* (-s; -e) cup (*a. sport*), goblet; ***~ der Landesmeister*** European (Champions') Cup; ***~ der Pokalsieger*** European Cup Winners' Cup; ~**end·spiel** *n* cup final; ~**run·de** *f* round (of the cup); ~**sie·ger** *m* cup winner; ~**spiel** *n* cup tie (*or* match); ~**ver·tei·di·ger** *m* cup holder(s *pl.*)
Pö·kel [ˈpøːkəl] *m* (-s; -s) brine, pickle
'**Pö·kel·fleisch** *n* cured meat
'**pö·keln** *v/t.* (h) pickle
Po·ker [ˈpoːkɐ] *n*, *m* (-s; *no pl.*) poker; ~**ge·sicht** *n* poker face; ***X mit s-m ~*** *a.* po-faced X
po·kern [ˈpoːkɐn] *v/i.* (h) play poker; *fig.* gamble (***um*** *acc.* over); *fig.* ***sehr hoch*** ~ gamble with high stakes
'**Po·ker\|spiel** *n* **1.** poker; **2.** game of poker; ~**spie·ler** *m* poker player
Pol [poːl] *m* (-s; -e) pole, ⚡ *a.* terminal; *fig.* ***der ruhende*** ~ the stabilizing element

po·lar [po'laːɐ] *adj.* polar (*a.* ⚡, ⚗); *meteor. a.* arctic; *fig.* ***in ~em Gegensatz zu*** *dat.* diametrically opposed to
Po'lar|ach·se *f* polar axis; **~eis** *n* polar (*or* arctic) ice; **~ex·pe·di·ti̩on** *f* polar (*or* [Ant]Arctic) expedition, expedition to the Arctic (*or* Antarctic); **~for·scher** *m* (Ant)Arctic explorer; **~front** *f meteor.* polar front; **~fuchs** *m* Arctic fox; **~ge·biet** *n* polar region(s *pl.*); **~hund** *m* husky
Po·la·ri·sa·ti·on [polariza'tsĭoːn] *f* (-; -en) ⚗, *phys.* polarization (*a. fig.*); **Po·la·ri·sa·ti'ons·fil·ter** *m, n* polarization filter
po·la·ri·sie·ren [polari'ziːrən] (h) **I.** *v/t.* polarize; **II.** *v/refl.*: ***sich ~*** become (more and more) polarized
Po·la·ri·tät [polari'tɛːt] *f* (-; *no pl.*) polarity (*a. fig.*)
Po'lar|kap·pe *f* polar (ice)cap; **~kreis** *m*: ***nördlicher (südlicher) ~*** Arctic (Antarctic) Circle; **~licht** *n*: ***nördliches (südliches) ~*** northern (southern) lights *pl.*, 📖 aurora borealis (australis); **~luft** *f* polar current; **~meer** *n*: ***nördliches (südliches) ~*** Arctic (Antarctic) Ocean; **~nacht** *f* polar night; **~re·gi̩on** *f* polar region; **~rou·te** *f* polar route; ***über die ~ fliegen*** take the polar route, fly over the North Pole; **~sta·ti̩on** *f* polar research station; **~stern** *m* Pole Star; **~tief** *n meteor.* polar low; **~zo·ne** *f* frigid zone
Po·le ['poːlə] *m* (-n; -n) Pole
Po·le·mik [po'leːmɪk] *f* (-; -en) **1.** *no pl.* polemics *pl.*; **2.** controversy, dispute; **3.** polemic (***gegen*** *acc.* against), attack (on, against)
po·le·misch [po'leːmɪʃ] *adj.* polemic(al)
po·le·mi·sie·ren [polemi'ziːrən] *v/i.* (h) polemicize (***gegen*** *acc.* against)
po·len ['poːlən] *v/t.* (h) ⚡ polarize
Po·len·te [po'lɛntə] F *obs. f* (-; *no pl.*) F *the* cops *pl.*, *sl. the* fuzz *pl.*
'Pol·fil·ter *m, n phot.* polarization filter
Po·li·ce [po'liːsə] *f* (-; -n) (insurance) policy
Po·lier [po'liːɐ] *m* (-s; -e [-rə]) foreman
po·lie·ren [po'liːrən] *v/t.* (h) polish (*a. fig.*)
Po'lier|mit·tel *n* polish; **~tuch** *n* softcloth
Po·li·kli·nik ['poːli-] *f* outpatients' clinic
Po·lin ['poːlɪn] *f* (-; -nen) Pole, Polish woman
Po·lio ['poːlĭo] *f* (-; *no pl.*) ⚕ polio; **~imp·fung** *f* polio vaccination
Po·lio·mye·li·tis [polĭomy̆e'liːtɪs] *f* (-; *no pl.*) ⚕ poliomyelitis
Po·lit·bü̩ro [po'lɪt-] *n* Politburo
Po·li·tes·se [poli'tɛsə] *f* (-; -n) F (woman) traffic warden, *Am.* meter maid
Po·li·tik [poli'tiːk] *f* (-; *no pl.*) politics *pl.*; policy (***in bezug auf*** *acc.*, ***im Hinblick auf*** *acc.* on; ***gegenüber*** *dat.* towards); tactics *pl.*; ***die internationale ~*** international politics (*or* relations); ***~ der Härte*** hard-line policy (*or* politics); ***in die ~ gehen*** go into politics; ***über ~ sprechen*** talk politics; → ***machen*** III; **Po·li·ti·ker** [po'liːtikɐ] *m* (-s; -), **Po·li·ti·ke·rin** [po'liːtikərɪn] *f* (-; -nen) politician; statesman (*f* stateswoman); **Po·li·ti·kum** [po'liːtikʊm] *n* (-s; *no pl.*) political issue
Po·li'tik|wis·sen·schaft *f* political science; **~wis·sen·schaft·ler** *m* political scientist
po·li·tisch [po'liːtɪʃ] **I.** *adj.* political; *fig.* judicious, politic; **II.** *adv.* politically; ***~ tätig*** involved in politics, politically active; ***~ interessiert*** politically aware; ***~ Verfolgte*** victim of political persecution; ***wie ist er ~ eingestellt?*** where does he stand politically?; **Po'li·ti·sche** *m, f* (-n; -n) political prisoner
po·li·ti·sie·ren [politi'ziːrən] (h) **I.** *v/i.* talk politics; **II.** *v/t.* politicize; make *s.o.* politically aware
Po·li·to·lo·ge [polito'loːgə] *m* (-n; -n) political scientist; **Po·li·to·lo·gie** [polito-lo'giː] *f* (-; *no pl.*) political science; **po·li·to·lo·gisch** [polito'loːgɪʃ] *adj.* political; *research etc.* in (the field of) political science
Po·lit|pro·mi̩nenz [po'lɪt-] *f* political top brass, top brass politicians *pl.*; **~re̩vue** *f* political revue; **~ter·ror** *m* political terror; **~thril·ler** *m* political thriller
Po·li·tur [poli'tuːɐ] *f* (-; -en) **1.** polish; **2.** polish, finish
Po·li·zei [poli'tsaɪ] *f* (-; *no pl.*) police; police force; ***bei der ~ sein*** a) be in the police force, b) be at the police station; F ***es mit der ~ zu tun kriegen*** get into trouble with the police; **~ak·ti̩on** *f* police operation; **~ap·pa̩rat** *m* police force; **~ar̩rest** *m* police custody; **~auf·ge·bot** *n* police detachment; ***starkes ~*** *a.* large police presence; ***es gab ein starkes ~*** *a.* the police were out in force; **~au·to** *n* police car; **~be·am·te** *m* policeman, police officer, law enforcement officer; **~be·am·tin** *f* policewoman, police officer, law enforcement officer; **≈be·kannt** *adj.* known to the police; **~boot** *n* police launch; **~chef** *m* police chief; **~dienst·stel·le** *f* police station; **~ein·satz** *m* police action (*or* intervention); ***unter starkem ~*** with (*or* by) a large-scale intervention of the police; **~es·kor·te** *f* police motorcade; **~funk** *m* police radio; **~ge·walt** *f*: ***die Menge wurde mit ~ auseinandergetrieben*** the police dispersed the crowds by force; **~griff** *m* arm-lock; **~hund** *m* police dog; **~knüp·pel** *m* truncheon; **~kom·mis̩sar** *m* (police) inspector; **~kon̩trol·le** *f* police check; **~la̩bor** *n* forensic laboratory
po·li'zei·lich I. *adj.* (of *or* by the) police; ***unter ~er Überwachung*** under police surveillance; **II.** *adv.*: ***sich ~ anmelden (abmelden)*** register with the authorities (inform the authorities that one is moving); ***~ verboten*** prohibited by law; ***er wird ~ gesucht*** the police are looking for (F are after) him; ***... wird ~ bestraft*** ... is punishable by law
Po·li'zei|prä·si̩dent *m* chief of police; *in GB*: chief constable, police commissioner; **~prä̩si·di·um** *n* police headquarters *pl.*; **~re̩vier** *n* **1.** (police) district, *Am.* (police) precinct; **2.** police station; **~schutz** *m* police protection; **~spit·zel** *m* (police) informer, *sl.* stool pigeon; **~staat** *m* police state; **~strei·fe** *f* police patrol (*or* squad); police patrolman; **~stun·de** *f* closing time; ***um Mitternacht ist ~*** all restaurants and bars have to close at midnight; **~trup·pen** *pl.* security forces; **~uni̩form** *f* police uniform; **~wa·che** *f* police station
Po·li·zist [poli'tsɪst] *m* (-en; -en) policeman, (police) constable; **Po·li·zi·stin** [poli'tsɪstɪn] *f* (-; -nen) policewoman, ([woman] police) constable
Pol·ka ['pɔlka] *f* (-; -s) polka
'Pol·kap·pe *f* polar cap
Pol·len ['pɔlən] *m* (-s; -) ⚘ pollen; **~ana̩ly·se** *f* pollen analysis; **~be·richt** *m* (latest) pollen count; **~korn** *n* pollen grain; **~krank·heit** *f* pollinosis; **~sack** *m* pollen sac; **~vor̩her·sa·ge** *f* → ***Pollenbericht***
Pol·ler ['pɔlɐ] *m* (-s; -) ⚓ bollard
pol·nisch ['pɔlnɪʃ] *adj.*, **'Pol·nisch** *n* (-en; *no pl.*) *ling.* Polish
Po·lo ['poːlo] *n* (-s; *no pl.*) polo; **~hemd** *n* polo shirt; **~schlä·ger** *m* mallet; **~spie·ler** *m* polo player
'Pol·stär·ke *f* ⚡ pole strength
Pol·ster ['pɔlstɐ] *n* (-s; -) a) upholstery, b) padding, c) *fig.* reserves *pl.*; → ***Auftragspolster, Fettpolster***
Pol·ste·rer ['pɔlstərɐ] *m* (-s; -) upholsterer
'Pol·ster|gar·ni̩tur *f* living room (*or* three-piece) suite; **~mö·bel** *pl.* **1.** upholstery *sg.*; **2.** → ***Polstergarnitur***
pol·stern ['pɔlstɐn] *v/t.* (h) a) upholster, b) pad *jacket etc.*; → ***gepolstert***
'Pol·ster|ses·sel *m* armchair, easy chair; **~stuhl** *m* upholstered chair; **~tür** *f* padded door
Pol·ste·rung ['pɔlstərʊŋ] *f* (-; -en) upholstery
Pol·ter|abend ['pɔltɐ-] *m* eve-of-the-wedding party; **~geist** *m* poltergeist
pol·tern ['pɔltɐn] *v/i.* **1.** (h) make a racket; **2.** (sn) a) crash, b) rumble (along); **3.** (h) F rant and rave
'Pol·wan·de·rung *f* polar wandering
Po·ly·amid [polyˀa'miːt] *n* (-[e]s; -e [-də]) ⚗ polyamide
Po·ly·an·drie [polyˀan'driː] *f* (-; *no pl.*) polyandry
Po·ly·ar·thri·tis [polyˀar'triːtɪs] *f* (-; -tiden [-tri'tiːden]) ⚕ rheumatoid arthritis
Po·ly·äthy·len [polyˀɛty'leːn] *n* (-s; *-no pl.*) ⚗ polyethylene
po·ly·chrom [poly'kroːm] *adj.* polychrome
Po·ly·eder [poly'ˀeːdɐ] *n* (-s; -) ⚗ polyhedron
Po·ly·ester [poly'ˀɛstɐ] *m* (-s; -) ⚗ polyester
po·ly·gam [poly'gaːm] *adj.* polygamous
Po·ly·ga·mie [polyga'miː] *f* (-; *no pl.*) polygamy
po·ly·glott [poly'glɔt] *adj.*, **Po·ly·glot·te** [poly'glɔtə] *m, f* (-n; -n) polyglot
Po·ly·mer [poly'meːɐ] *n* (-s; -e [-rə]) ⚗ polymer
po·ly·morph [poly'mɔrf] *adj.* polymorphous, polymorphic
Po·ly·ne·si·er [poly'neːzĭɐ] *m* (-s; -), **Po·ly·ne·sie·rin** [poly'neːzĭərɪn] *f* (-; -nen), **po·ly·ne·sisch** [poly'neːzɪʃ] *adj.*, **Po·ly'ne·sisch** *n* (-en; *no pl.*) *ling.* Polynesian
Po·lyp [po'lyːp] *m* (-en; -en) **1.** *zo.* polyp; *obs.* octopus; **2.** *pl.* ⚕ adenoids; **3.** F cop(per), *pl.* cops, *sl. the* fuzz (*pl.*)
po·ly·phon [poly'foːn] *adj.* polyphonic; **Po·ly·pho·nie** [polyfo'niː] *f* (-; *no pl.*) polyphony
po·ly·sem [poly'zeːm] *adj. ling.* polysemous; **Po·ly·se·mie** [polyze'miː] *f* (-; *no pl.*) polysemy
Po·ly·the·is·mus [polyte'ɪsmʊs] *m* (-; *no pl.*) polytheism; **po·ly·thei·stisch** [polyte'ɪstɪʃ] *adj.* polytheistic
po·ly·va·lent [polyva'lɛnt] *adj.* polyvalent
Po·ma·de [po'maːdə] *f* (-; -n) pomade
po·ma·dig [po'maːdɪç] *adj.* **1.** *hair*: slicked back (*or* down); **2.** *fig.* smarmy; slow, sluggish

Po·me·ran·ze [pomə'rantsə] *f* (-; -n) bitter orange

Pom·mer ['pɔmɐ] *m* (-n; -n) Pomeranian; ~ ***sein*** be (a) Pomeranian, come from Pomerania; **pom·mersch** ['pɔmɐʃ] *adj.* Pomeranian

Pommes ['pɔməs] F *pl.* chips, *Am.* fries; ***einmal*** ~, ***bitte*** bag of chips, please; *Am.* fries, please; **Pommes frites** [pɔm'frɪt] *pl.* chips, *Am.* (French) fries, French fried potatoes

Pomp [pɔmp] *m* (-[e]s; *no pl.*) pomp

pom·pös [pɔm'pø:s] *adj.* pretentious; bombastic *speech etc.*; extravagant *reception etc.*

Pon·ti·fex ['pɔntifɛks] *hist. m* (-; Pontifizes [pɔn'ti:fitse:s]) pontiff; ~ ***maximus*** Pontifex maximus

Pon·ti·fi·kal·amt [pɔntifi'ka:l-] *n* Pontifical mass; **Pon·ti·fi·kat** [pɔntifi'ka:t] *n* (-[e]s; -e) papacy, pontificate

Pon·ti·us ['pɔntsi̯ʊs] *m*: ***von*** ~ ***zu Pilatus laufen*** run (*or* chase) from pillar to post

Pon·ton [põ'tõ:, pɔn'tõ:] *m* (-s; -s) pontoon; ~**brücke** *f* pontoon bridge

Po·ny¹ ['pɔni] *n* (-s; -s) pony

'Po·ny² *m* (-s; -s) fringe, *Am.* bangs *pl.*; ~**fri,sur** *f*: ***e-e*** ~ ***tragen*** have a fringe, *Am.* have bangs

Pop [pɔp] *m* (-s; *no pl.*) **1.** pop art; **2.** pop (music)

Po·panz ['po:pants] *m* (-es; -e) **1.** bogeyman; **2.** puppet

Pop-art ['pɔpʔa:ɐt] *f* (-; *no pl.*) pop art

Po·pe ['po:pə] *m* (-n; -n) **1.** (Greek *or* Russian Orthodox) priest; **2.** *contp.* cleric, F holy Joe

Po·pel ['po:pəl] F *m* (-s; -) F bog(e)y, V bit of snot; **po·pe·lig** ['po:pəlɪç] F *adj.* a) F miserable, b) F stingy

Po·pe·lin [popə'li:n] *m* (-s; -e) poplin

po·peln ['po:pəln] F *v/i.* (h) pick one's nose

'Pop|fe·sti·val *n* pop festival; ~**grup·pe** *f* pop group; ~**kon,zert** *n* pop concert; ~**mu,sik** *f* pop music

Po·po [po'po:] F *m* (-s; -s) F bottom, backside; F bot(ty); ~**schei·tel** F *m* middle parting

Pop·per ['pɔpɐ] *m* (-s; -), **pop·pig** ['pɔpɪç] *adj.* mod

'Pop|star *m* pop star; ~**sze·ne** *f* pop scene; ***was tut sich in der*** ~? *a.* what's going on in the world of pop?

po·pu·lär [popu'lɛ:ɐ] *adj.* popular

po·pu·la·ri·sie·ren [populari'zi:rən] *v/t.* (h) popularize

Po·pu·la·ri·tät [populari'tɛ:t] *f* (-; *no pl.*) popularity

po·pu'lär·wis·sen·schaft·lich *adj.* popular(ized), popular-science ...

Po·pu·la·ti·on [popula'tsi̯o:n] *f* (-; -en) population; **Po·pu·la·ti'ons·dich·te** *f* population density

Po·pu·lis·mus [popu'lɪsmʊs] *m* (-; *no pl.*) populism; **po·pu·li·stisch** [popu'lɪstɪʃ] *adj.* populist

Po·re ['po:rə] *f* (-; -n) pore; ***mir brach der Schweiß aus allen*** ~***n*** I broke out into a cold sweat; **po·rig** ['po:rɪç] *adj.* porous

Por·no ['pɔrno] F *m* (-s; -s) F porn; ~**film** *m* sex (*or* porn) film, blue movie

Por·no·gra·phie [pɔrnogra'fi:] *f* (-; *no pl.*) pornography; **por·no·gra·phisch** [pɔrno'gra:fɪʃ] *adj.* pornographic(ally *adv.*)

'Por·no|heft *n* porn magazine; ~**ki·no** *n* blue movie theat|re (*Am. a.* -er); ~**la·den** *m* sex (*od.* porn) shop

po·rös [po'rø:s] *adj.* porous; **Po·ro·si·tät** [porozi'tɛ:t] *f* (-; *no pl.*) porosity

Por·phyr ['pɔrfy:ɐ] *m* (-s; -e [pɔr'fy:rə]) porphyry

Por·ree ['pɔre] *m* (-s; -s) ♣ leek; *gastr.* leeks *pl.*

Por·tal [pɔr'ta:l] *n* (-s; -e) main entrance, portal

Porte·feuille [pɔrt(ə)'fø:j] *n* (-s; -s) *pol.* portfolio; ***Minister ohne*** ~ minister without portfolio

Porte·mon·naie [pɔrtmɔ'ne:] *n* (-s; -s) purse, *Am.* change purse; F *fig.* ***ein dikkes*** ~ ***haben*** F have wads of money

Por·tier [pɔr'tje:] *m* (-s; -s) porter, doorman

Por·ti·on [pɔr'tsi̯o:n] *f* (-; -en) **1.** helping, serving; pot *of coffee, tea*; ***e-e*** ~ ***Kaffee*** a pot of coffee; **2.** F *fig.* good deal (F dose) *of courage etc.*; ***in kleinen*** ~***en*** in small doses; **3.** F *fig.* ***halbe*** ~ F shrimp, titch

Por·tio·nie·rer [pɔrtsi̯o'ni:rɐ] *m* (-s; -) scoop

Por·to ['pɔrto] *n* (-s; -s) postage (***für*** *acc.* on, for); 2**frei** *adj.* postage paid; ~**kasse** *f* petty cash; F *fig.* ***das zahlen die doch aus der*** ~ F that's chickenfeed for them

Por·trät [pɔr'trɛ:] *n* (-s; -s) portrait; ~**aufnah·me** *f* portrait (photograph); ~**bü·ste** *f* portrait bust; ~**fo·to** *n* portrait (photograph); ~**fo·to,graf** *m* portrait photographer

por·trä·tie·ren [pɔrtrɛ'ti:rən] *v/t.* (h) paint a portrait of; *fig.* portray

Por·trä·tist [pɔrtrɛ'tɪst] *m* (-en; -en) portrait painter

Por'trät|ma·ler *m* portrait painter; ~**ma·le,rei** *f* portraiture; ~**stu·die** *f* portrait study

Por·tu·gie·se [pɔrtu'gi:zə] *m* (-n; -n), **Por·tu·gie·sin** [pɔrtu'gi:zɪn] *f* (-; -nen), **por·tu·gie·sisch** [pɔrtu'gi:zɪʃ] *adj.*, **Portu'gie·sisch** *n* (-en; *no pl.*) *ling.* Portuguese

Port·wein ['pɔrt-] *m* port

Por·zel·lan [pɔrtsɛ'la:n] *n* (-s; -e) porcelain, china; *fig.* ~ ***zerschlagen*** cause a lot of (unnecessary) trouble; ~**er·de** *f* china clay, kaolin; ~**fi,gur** *f* porcelain figure (*or* figurine); ~**ge·schirr** *n* china; ~**la·den** *m* china (*or* porcelain) shop; → ***Elefant***; ~**ma·le,rei** *f* painting on porcelain; ~**wa·re** *f* china(ware), porcelain

Po·sau·ne [po'zaʊnə] *f* (-; -n) trombone; *fig.* trumpet; **po'sau·nen** (h) **I.** *v/i.* play the trombone; **II.** *fig. contp. v/t.* trumpet; **Po'sau·nen·blä·ser** *m*, **Po·saunist** [pozaʊ'nɪst] *m* (-en; -en) trombonist

Po·se ['po:zə] *f* (-; -n) pose; ***e-e*** ~ ***einnehmen*** take up a pose; *fig.* pose (***als*** as); ***sich in*** ~ ***werfen*** put on one's best pose; ***er gefiel sich wieder einmal in der*** ~ ***des Beleidigten*** he put on his offended act again; ***es ist alles nur*** ~ it's all part of an (*or* the, his *etc.*) act; **Po·seur** [po'zø:ɐ] *m* (-s; -e [-rə]) poser; **po·sieren** [po'zi:rən] *v/i.* (h) pose

Po·si·ti·on [pozi'tsi̯o:n] *f* (-; -en) **1.** position; standing, status; ***gesellschaftliche*** ~ social standing, position in society; **2.** *sport*: place, position; ***in dritter*** ~ ***liegen*** be in third place (*or* position); **3.** position, post; **4.** position; ⚔ ***in*** ~ ***gehen*** take up one's position; ~ ***einnehmen!*** *film*: places, please!; *fig.* ~ ***beziehen*** take a stand; ***e-e*** ~ ***vertreten*** maintain a standpoint (*or* point of view); **5.** ✝ item

po·si·tio·nie·ren [pozitsi̯o'ni:rən] *v/t.* (h) position

Po·si·ti'ons|an·zei·ger *m* position indicator; ~**leuch·te** *f mot.* side lamp; ~**lichter** *pl.* ✈, ⚓ navigation lights

po·si·tiv ['po:ziti:f] **I.** *adj.* a) positive (*a. phys.*, ⚕, ⚗, ⚡, *phot.*); affirmative, b) concrete; ***das ist ja sehr*** ~ that's excellent; ~***e Kritiken bekommen*** get a good press (*or* good write-ups); ***das*** 2***e daran*** the good (*or* positive) thing about it, the positive side of it; ***er hat nur*** 2***es über dich erzählt*** he only had positive things to say about you; **II.** *adv.* positively; ***sich*** ~ ***auswirken auf*** *acc.* have a positive effect on *s.th.*; ***er hat sich*** ~ ***darüber geäußert*** he was quite positive about it, he was in favo(u)r of it; ***e-m Projekt*** *etc.* ~ ***gegenüberstehen*** support (*or* be in favo[u]r of) a project *etc.*; ***weißt du das auch*** ~? do you know that for certain (*or* for sure)?; ***ich weiß es ganz*** ~ it's a hundred per cent certain

Po·si·tiv¹ ['po:ziti:f] *n* (-s; -e [-və]) *phot.* positive

'Po·si·tiv² *m* (-s; -e [-və]) *ling.* positive

Po·si·ti·vis·mus [poziti'vɪsmʊs] *m* (-; *no pl.*) *phls.* positivism; **Po·si·ti·vist** [poziti'vɪst] *m* (-en; -en) positivist; **po·si·ti·vistisch** [poziti'vɪstɪʃ] *adj.* positivist(ic)

Po·si·tron ['po:zitro:n] *n* (-s; -e) *phys.* positron

Po·si·tur [pozi'tu:ɐ] *f* (-; -en [-rən]) pose; ***sich in*** ~ ***setzen*** strike a pose

Pos·se ['pɔsə] *f* (-; -n) *thea.* farce (*a. fig.*), burlesque

Pos·sen ['pɔsən] *m* (-s; -) **1.** *pl.* antics; ~ ***reißen*** act the clown; **2. *j-m e-n*** ~ ***spielen*** play a trick on s.o.

'pos·sen·haft *adj.* farcical

pos·ses·siv ['pɔsɛsi:f] *adj. ling.* possessive

'Pos·ses·siv *n* (-s; -e [-və]) possessive (form); ~**pro,no·men** *n* possessive pronoun

Pos·ses·si·vum [pɔsɛ'si:vʊm] *n* (-s; -va) → ***Possessiv***

pos·sier·lich [pɔ'si:ɐlɪç] *adj.* droll, comical

Post [pɔst] *f* (-, *no pl.*) a) post, *esp. Am.* mail, b) postal service, c) post office; ***elektronische*** ~ electronic mail; ***mit der*** ~ by post, by mail; ***mit getrennter*** ~ under separate cover; ***zur*** ~ ***geben, mit der*** ~ ***schicken*** post, mail; ***ist*** ~ ***für mich da?*** are there any letters for me?; ***ich lese gerade m-e*** ~ I'm just reading (*or* going through) my mail; ***ich warte auf die*** ~ I'm waiting for the postman (*Am.* mailman), I'm waiting for the mail (to come); ***bei der*** ~ ***arbeiten*** work for the post office; → ***ab*** 4; ~**ab·la·ge** *f* correspondence file

po·sta·lisch [pɔs'ta:lɪʃ] *adj.* postal; ***auf*** ~***em Weg*** by post, by mail

Po·sta·ment [pɔsta'mɛnt] *n* (-[e]s; -e) pedestal, base

'Post|amt *n* post office; ~**an·ge·stell·te** *m, f* (-n; -n) post office (*Am.* postal) employee; ~**an·schrift** *f* postal (*Am.* mailing) address; ~**an·wei·sung** *f* money (*or* postal) order; ~**aus·gang** *m* outgoing mail; ~**au·to** *n* mail van; ~**bar·scheck** *m* postal cheque (*Am.* check); ~**be·am·te** *m*, ~**be·am·tin** *f* post office (*Am.* postal) clerk; ~**be·zirk** *m* postal district; ~**bo·te** *m* postman, *Am.* mailman, F postie; ~**bo·tin** [-bo:tɪn] *f* (-; -nen) postwoman, F postie; ~**bus** *m* post office bus; ~**dienst**

m postal service; **~ein·gang** *m* incoming mail

Po·sten ['pɔstən] *m* (-s; -) **1.** sentry, guard; **~ *stehen*** (*or* ***schieben***) be on guard duty; *fig.* ***auf dem ~ sein*** a) be on the alert, b) be in good form (F nick); ***wieder auf dem ~ sein*** be back on one's feet (again), be fighting fit again; ***nicht recht auf dem ~ sein*** be a bit under the weather; → ***verloren*; 2.** post, position; **3.** ✝ a) lot, batch, b) item; entry; **~jä·ger** *m* careerist, F go-getter; **~ket·te** *f* cordon

Po·ster ['po:stɐ] *n, m* (-s; -) poster

'Post·fach *n* post office box, PO box

'post|fer·tig *adj.* ready for posting (*or* mailing); **~frisch** *adj.* mint *stamp*, in mint condition

'Post|ge·bühr *f a. pl.* postage; *pl. a.* postal rates (*or* charges); **~ge·heim·nis** *n* postal secrecy; **~ge·werk·schaft** *f* postal workers' union

'Post·gi·ro *n* postal giro transfer; **~amt** *n* Girobank, *Am.* postal giro (*or* check) office; **~kon·to** *n* (post office) giro account, *Am.* postal check account

post·gla·zi·al [pɔstgla'tsi̯a:l] *adj. geol.* postglacial

'Post·horn *n hist.* post horn

post·hum [pɔst'hu:m] *adj.* posthumous

po·stie·ren [pɔs'ti:rən] (h) **I.** *v/t.* position, place; ⚔ *a.* post; **II.** *v/refl.*: ***sich ~*** position o.s.

Po·stil·le [pɔs'tɪlə] *f* (-; -n) **1.** devotional book; **2.** *contp.* sheet

Po·stil·li·on [pɔstɪl'jo:n] *m* (-s; -e) *hist.* stagecoach driver

'Post·kar·te *f* (picture) postcard

'Post·kar·ten|grö·ße *f*: ***in ~*** postcard-size(d); **~gruß** *m* postcard (greetings *pl.*)

'Post|ka·sten *m* letterbox, postbox, *Am.* mailbox; **~kut·sche** *f hist.* stagecoach

'post·la·gernd *adv.* poste restante, *Am.* (in care of) general delivery

'Post·leit·zahl *f* postcode, *Am.* zip code

Post·ler ['pɔstlɐ] F *m* (-s; -) post office worker

'Post|map·pe *f* correspondence folder (*or* file); **~mi,ni·ster** *m* postmaster general

Post·mo'der·ne *f* (-; *no pl.*): ***die ~*** Postmodernism

post·nu·me·ran·do [pɔstnume'rando] *adv.*: **~ *bezahlen*** pay on receipt, settle at the end of the month

post·ope·ra'tiv *adj.* ⚕ post-operative

'Post|sack *m* mailbag; **~schal·ter** *m* post office counter

'Post·scheck *m* (post office) giro cheque, *Am.* postal check; **~amt** *obs. n* → ***Postgiroamt*; ~kon·to** *obs. n* → ***Postgirokonto***

'Post|schließ·fach *n* → ***Postfach*; ~sen·dung** *f* postal consignment; **~spar·buch** *n* post office (*Am.* postal) savings book; **~spar·kas·se** *f* post office (*Am.* postal) savings bank

Post·skript [pɔst'skrɪpt] *n* (-[e]s; -e) postscript

'Post|stel·le *f* mail room; **~stem·pel** *m* postmark; ***„Datum des ~s"*** date as per postmark; **~über,wei·sung** *f* postal (*or* giro) transfer

Po·stu·lat [pɔstu'la:t] *n* (-[e]s; -e) **1.** imperative; **2.** *phls.* postulate, thesis; **po·stu·lie·ren** [pɔstu'li:rən] *v/t.* (h) postulate

po·stum [pɔs'tu:m] *adj.* posthumous

'Post|ver·ein *m* postal union; **~wa·gen** *m* 🚂 mail van, *Am.* postal car; **~weg** *m*: ***auf dem ~*** by post, by mail

'post·wen·dend *adv.* by return (of post), by return mail; F *fig.* right away

'Post|wert·zei·chen *n* (postage) stamp; **~we·sen** *n* (-s; *no pl.*) postal system; **~wurf·sen·dung** *f* bulk mail consignment; *pl. a.* bulk mail *sg.*; **~zen,sur** *f* postal censorship; **~zug** *m* mail train; **~zu·stel·lung** *f* postal delivery

Pot [pɔt] F *n* (-s; *no pl.*) F pot, grass

po·tent [po'tɛnt] *adj.* **1.** *physiol.* virile; **2.** powerful; influential; **3.** solvent

Po·ten·tat [potɛn'ta:t] *m* (-en; -en) potentate

Po·ten·ti·al [potɛn'tsi̯a:l] *n* (-s; -e) **1.** potential; **2.** capacity; **3.** pool (***an*** *dat.* of)

po·ten·ti·ell [potɛn'tsi̯ɛl] *adj.* potential

Po·ten·tio·me·ter [potɛntsi̯o'me:tɐ] *n* (-s; -) ⚡ potentiometer

Po·tenz [po'tɛnts] *f* (-; -en) **1.** 𝔄 power; ***zweite ~*** square; ***dritte ~*** cube; ***acht in die zweite*** (***dritte***) **~ *erheben*** square (cube) eight; ***acht in die vierte*** (***fünfte*** *etc.*) **~ *erheben*** raise eight to the power of four (five *etc.*); **2.** *physiol.* virility; **3.** *fig.* ability; **~angst** *f* impotence-related anxiety

po·ten·zie·ren [potɛn'tsi:rən] *v/t.* (h) **1.** 𝔄 raise to a higher power; **2.** *fig.* (*a. v/refl.*: ***sich ~***) multiply, intensify

po'tenz·stei·gernd *adj.* potency *pills etc.*; **Po'tenz·stö·rung** *f* virility problem, temporary impotence

Pot·pour·ri ['pɔtpʊri] *n* (-s; -s) ♪ potpourri (*a. fig.*), medley

Pott [pɔt] *m* (-[e]s; Pötte ['pœtə]) **1.** *dial.* pot; **2.** *sport*: cup; **3.** F jerry; potty; **4.** F ***wir müssen mit diesem Projekt*** (***Vertrag***) ***zu ~e kommen*** we've got to get this project wound up (we've got to get this contract in the bag); F ***ich komm' damit nicht zu ~e*** I'm not getting anywhere with it; **5.** ⚓ F tub

Pott·asche ['pɔtʔaʃə] *f* (-; *no pl.*) potash

Pott·wal ['pɔtva:l] *m* sperm whale

Pou·lar·de [pu'lardə] *f* (-; -n) poulard

Power ['paʊɐ] F *f* (-; *no pl.*) power; **~ *haben*** be powerful

PR [pe:'ʔɛr] PR, public relations *pl.*

Prä·am·bel [prɛ'ambəl] *f* preamble (***zu*** *dat.* to)

P'R-Ab,tei·lung *f* PR (*or* public relations) department

Pracht [praxt] *f* (-; *no pl.*) splendo(u)r; richness *of colo(u)rs*; ***kalte ~*** cold splendo(u)r; ***die ~ bei Hofe*** courtly splendo(u)r; F ***es ist e-e ~*** F it's brilliant; F ***es ist e-e ~, wie er Klavier spielt*** it's a treat to hear him play the piano; **~aus·ga·be** *f* de luxe edition; **~bau** *m* (-[e]s; -ten) stately building; **~ent·fal·tung** *f* display of splendo(u)r; **~ex·em,plar** *n* (very) fine specimen, F beauty, humdinger; F cracker

präch·tig ['prɛçtɪç] **I.** *adj.* splendid, magnificent; stately *mansions etc.*; glorious *weather*; F great *guy etc.*; F brilliant, great *idea etc.*; **II.** F *adv.*: ***sich ~ unterhalten*** F have a great conversation; ***sich ~ verstehen*** F get on like a house on fire; ***das hast du ~ gemacht!*** good work (F show)

'Pracht|kerl F *m* F humdinger, cracker; F bouncing baby; **~stra·ße** *f* (splendid) boulevard; **~stück** *n* (very) fine specimen, F beauty

'pracht·voll *adj.* splendid; glorious *weather*; wonderful

Prä·de·sti·na·ti·on [prɛdɛstina'tsi̯o:n] *f* (-; *no pl.*) predestination

prä·de·sti·nie·ren [prɛdɛsti'ni:rən] *v/t.* (h) predestine; ***prädestiniert zu*** *dat. or* ***für*** *acc.* predestined for, cut out for; ***zum Lehrer*** *etc.* ***prädestiniert*** predestined to become a teacher *etc.*, cut out to be a teacher *etc.* (*or* for teaching *etc.*), a born teacher *etc.*; ***er ist für diese Rolle prädestiniert*** he's made (*or* cut out) for the part

Prä·di·kat [prɛdi'ka:t] *n* (-[e]s; -e) **1.** *ling.* predicate; **2.** title; **3.** rating; mark, grade; ***der Film erhielt das ~ „wertvoll"*** the film was highly commended; ***Qualitätswein mit ~*** → ***Prädikatswein***

Prä·di·ka·ten·lo·gik [prɛdi'ka:tən-] *f* predicate logic

Prä·di'kats·wein *m* quality-tested wine (with special attributes)

prä·dis·po·niert [prɛdɪspo'ni:ɐt] *adj.*: **~ *für*** *acc.* predisposed towards

Prä·fekt [prɛ'fɛkt] *m* (-en; -en) *a. hist.* prefect; **Prä·fek·tur** [prɛfɛk'tu:ɐ] *f* (-; -en [-rən]) prefecture

Prä·fe·renz [prɛfe'rɛnts] *f* (-; -en) preference; **~li·ste** *f* a) list of preferences, b) short list

Prä·fix [prɛ'fɪks, 'prɛ:fɪks] *n* (-es; -e) *ling.* prefix

Prä·ge·druck ['prɛ:gə-] *m* relief print (*or* printing); embossing; tooling

prä·gen ['prɛ:gən] *v/t.* (h) stamp; mint *coins*; emboss *leather, metal etc.*; *fig.* coin *word etc.*; form, mo(u)ld *s.o.('s personality)*; set the tone of, determine *s.th.*; ***geprägt sein von*** *dat.* be marked (*or* characterized) by; **~*der Einfluß*** formative influence; ***den Charakter ~*** form (*or* mo[u]ld) one's personality; ***diese Jahre haben sie geprägt*** they were formative years for her; ***Wälder und Seen ~ die Landschaft*** woods and lakes lend the landscape its character (*or* are the main features of this landscape); ***er ist von s-r Umwelt geprägt*** he's a product of his environment

Prä·ge·stem·pel ['prɛ:gə-] *m* minting die; *typ.* stamping die

prä·gla·zi·al [prɛgla'tsi̯a:l] *adj. geol.* preglacial

Prag·ma·tik [prag'ma:tɪk] *f* (-; *no pl.*) pragmatism; **Prag·ma·ti·ker** [prag'ma:tikɐ] *m* (-s; -) pragmatist; **prag·ma·tisch** [prag'ma:tɪʃ] *adj.* pragmatic(ally *adv.*)

prä·gnant [prɛ'gnant] *adj.* concise, to the point; pithy *style*; **~*es Beispiel*** perfect (*or* telling) example; **Prä·gnanz** [prɛ'gnants] *f* (-; *no pl.*) conciseness, concision; pithiness *of style*

Prä·gung ['prɛ:gʊŋ] *f* (-; -en) **1.** stamping, minting; embossing; *fig.* coinage *of word etc.*; **2.** *fig.* stamp, character; ***Demokratie englischer ~*** English-style democracy

Prä·hi·sto·rie [prɛhɪs'to:ri̯ə] *f* (-; *no pl.*) prehistory; **Prä·hi'sto·ri·ker** *m* prehistorian; **prä·hi'sto·risch** *adj.* prehistoric

prah·len ['pra:lən] *v/i.* (h) boast, brag (***mit*** *dat.* about); show off (***mit*** *dat.* [with] *s.th.*); **Prah·ler** ['pra:lɐ] *m* (-s; -) boaster, braggart; **Prah·le·rei** [pra:lə'raɪ] *f* (-; *no pl.*) boasting, bragging; **prah·le·risch** ['pra:lərɪʃ] *adj.* a) boastful, b) showy; **'Prahl·hans** *m* (-es; -hänse [-hɛnzə]) a) braggart, b) F show-off

prä·ju·di·zie·ren [prɛjudi'tsi:rən] *v/t.* (h) prejudge

prä·ko·lum·bisch [prɛkoˈlʊmbɪʃ] *adj.* pre-Columbian

Prak·tik [ˈpraktɪk] *f* (-; -en) practice, *Am. a.* practise, *pl. a.* methods; ***unsaubere ~en*** underhanded methods; **prak·ti·ka·bel** [praktiˈkaːbəl] *adj.* practicable, feasible; ***nicht ~*** impracticable, not feasible; **Prak·ti·kant** [praktiˈkant] *m* (-en; -en), **Prak·ti·kan·tin** [praktiˈkantɪn] *f* (-; -nen) trainee; **Prak·ti·ker** [ˈpraktikɐ] *m* (-s; -) **1.** practical person; **2.** practician (of the trade); ***ein alter ~*** an old hand; **3.** ⚕ GP; **Prak·ti·kum** [ˈpraktikʊm] *n* (-s; -ka) practical training (period), traineeship; (industrial) placement, *pl. a.* industrial training *sg.*; **Prak·ti·kus** [ˈpraktikʊs] F *m* (-; -se) practical man, handyman

PR-Ak·tiˌon [peːˈʔɛr-] *f* PR (*or* public relations) campaign

prak·tisch [ˈpraktɪʃ] **I.** *adj.* a) practical, b) handy (*a.* ⚙ *etc.*), c) actual; ***~er Arzt*** general practitioner, GP; ***~e Ausbildung*** practical (*or* on-the-job, hands-on) training; ***~es Beispiel*** concrete example; ⚙ ***~er Versuch*** field test; ***im ~en Leben*** in real life; ***keinen ~en Wert haben*** be of no practical value; **II.** *adv.* a) practically; virtually, more or less, b) in practice, in practise; ***~ nie*** very rarely; ***~ nichts*** virtually (*or* next to) nothing

prak·ti·zie·ren [praktiˈtsiːrən] (h) **I.** *v/t.* carry out, put into practise (*Am. a.* practice); apply *method etc.*; *eccl.* practise (*Am. a.* practice); **II.** *v/i.* practise (*Am. a.* practice); ***als Arzt*** (***Anwalt***) ~ practise (*Am. a.* practice) medicine (law), be a practi|sing (*Am. a.* -cing) doctor (lawyer, *Am.* attorney); ***~der Katholik*** practi|sing (*Am. a.* -cing) Catholic

Prä·lat [prɛˈlaːt] *m* (-en; -en) *eccl.* prelate

Pra·li·ne [praˈliːnə] *f* (-; -n), **Pra·li·né** [praliˈneː] *n* (-s; -s) chocolate; *pl. a.* box *sg.* of chocolates

Praˈli·nen·schach·tel *f* chocolate box

prall [pral] *adj.* **1.** hard *ball, balloon etc.*; full *sails*; firm *fruit*; bulging *pockets etc.*; taut *muscles*; firm *thighs, breast*; chubby *cheeks etc.*; **2.** blazing *sun*

pral·len [ˈpralən] *v/i.* (sn) **1.** ***~ auf*** (*or* ***gegen***) *acc.* bang (*or* crash) into; bump (*or* run) into *s.o.*; *ball*: hit; *waves etc.*: crash against; ***mit dem Kopf gegen et. ~*** hit one's head on (*or* against) s.th.; **2.** *sun*: beat down (***auf*** *acc.* on)

ˈPrall·sack *m mot.* airbag

ˈprallˈvoll F *adj.* full to bursting; F chock-a-block, jampacked

Prä·lu·di·um [prɛˈluːdiʊm] *n* (-s; -dien) prelude

prä·men·stru·ell [prɛmɛnstruˈɛl] *adj.* premenstrual; ***~e Beschwerden*** premenstrual tension, PMT

Prä·mie [ˈprɛːmiə] *f* (-; -n) award, prize; ✝ premium; bonus (*a. sport*)

ˈPrä·mi·en·an·lei·he *f* premium bond

ˈprä·mi·en|be·gün·stigt *adj.* bonus-linked; ***~es Sparen*** → ***Prämiensparen***; **~frei** *adj.* paid-up *policy etc.*

ˈPrä·mi·en·spa·ren *n* bonus savings scheme

prä·mie·ren [prɛˈmiːrən], **prä·mi·ie·ren** [prɛmiˈiːrən] *v/t.* (h) award a prize to; ***präm(i)iert werden*** receive (*or* get) an award *or* a prize

PräˈmieÂ·rung *f* (-; -en), **Prä·miˈie·rung** *f* (-; -en) **1.** awarding of a prize; ***die ~ der Gruppe mit e-m Grammy*** the awarding of a Grammy to the group; **2.** presentation (*or* award, prize-giving) ceremony; **3.** award, prize

Prä·mis·se [prɛˈmɪsə] *f* (-; -n) premise; ***von falschen ~n ausgehen*** start out on the wrong premise

prä·na·tal [prɛnaˈtaːl] *adj.* prenatal

pran·gen [ˈpraŋən] *v/i.* (h) **1.** ***~ an*** *or* ***auf*** *dat. picture, name etc.*: be emblazoned on (*or* across); ***sein Gesicht prangte an allen Reklamewänden*** his face stared out from all the hoardings; **2.** *lit.* be resplendent (***mit*** *dat.* with); shine; *diamonds etc.*: sparkle, glitter; ***~ mit*** *dat. etc.*: be studded with *stars*; ***das Dorf prangte im Festschmuck*** (***in der Abendsonne***) the village was resplendent with festive decorations (was aglow in the evening sun); ***an den Bäumen prangten rote Blüten*** the trees were ablaze with red blossoms; **3.** ***~ mit*** *dat.* parade *s.th.*

Pran·ger [ˈpraŋɐ] *m* (-s; -) stocks *pl.*; *fig.* ***an den ~ stellen*** pillory; ***am ~ stehen*** be in the pillory

Pran·ke [ˈpraŋkə] *f* (-; -n) **1.** *zo.* paw; **2.** F *fig.* F (huge) paw

prä·nu·me·ran·do [prɛnumeˈrando] *adv.* in advance

Prä·pa·rat [prɛpaˈraːt] *n* (-[e]s; -e) **1.** *pharm. etc.* preparation, compound; **2.** slide preparation, *esp. anat.* specimen

prä·pa·rie·ren [prɛpaˈriːrən] *v/t.* (h) **1.** (*a.* ***sich ~***) prepare (***auf*** *acc.* for); **2.** dissect; **3.** preserve

Prä·po·si·ti·on [prɛpoziˈtsi̯oːn] *f* (-; -en) *ling.* preposition; **prä·po·si·tio·nal** [prɛpozitsi̯oˈnaːl] *adj.* prepositional

Prä·raf·fae·lit [prɛrafaeˈliːt] *m* (-en; -en) *art*: Pre-Raphaelite

Prä·rie [prɛˈriː] *f* (-; -n) prairie; **~hund** *m* prairie dog; **~wolf** *m* coyote

Prä·sens [ˈprɛːzɛns] *n* (-; *no pl.*) *ling.* present (tense)

prä·sent [prɛˈzɛnt] *adj.* a) present, b) fully alert, F with it; ***hast du's noch ~?*** can you remember?, is it still there?; ***das Ganze ist mir noch ~*** it's all still fresh in my mind; ***es ist mir momentan nicht ~*** it escapes me (*or* I can't think of it) right now

Präˈsent *n* (-[e]s; -e) present, gift

prä·sen·ta·bel [prɛzɛnˈtaːbəl] *adj.* presentable; **Prä·sen·ta·ti·on** [prɛzɛntaˈtsi̯oːn] *f* (-; -en) presentation; **Prä·sen·ta·tor** [prɛzɛnˈtaːtoːɐ] *m* (-s; -en [-taˈtoːrən]) *TV* presenter; **prä·sen·tie·ren** [prɛzɛnˈtiːrən] (h) **I.** *v/t.* present; ***stolz ~*** sport *a beard, car etc.*; *fig.* ***j-m die Rechnung ~*** make s.o. pay for (it); **II.** *v/refl.*: ***sich ~*** present o.s. (*dat.* to)

Prä·senˈtier·tel·ler [prɛzɛnˈtiːɐ-] *m*: F ***auf dem ~ sitzen*** F be on show (for all to see)

Präˈsent·korb *m* (food) hamper

Prä·senz [prɛˈzɛnts] *f* (-; *no pl.*) presence; **~bi·blioˌthek** *f* reference library; **~li·ste** *f* attendance list; *ped.* (attendance) register; **~stär·ke** *f* ⚔ effective strength

Prä·ser·va·tiv [prɛzɛrvaˈtiːf] *n* (-s; -e [-və]) condom

Prä·si·dent [prɛziˈdɛnt] *m* (-en; -en) president; chairman; *parl.* speaker; ⚖ presiding judge; **Prä·siˈden·ten·wahl** *f* presidential election

Prä·siˈdent·schaft *f* (-; *no pl.*) presidency; **Prä·siˈdent·schafts·kan·diˌdat** *m* presidential candidate

Prä·si·di·al|ge·walt [prɛziˈdi̯aːl-] *f* presidential power(s *pl.*); **~syˌstem** *n* presidential democracy

prä·si·die·ren [prɛziˈdiːrən] *v/i.* (h) preside (***über*** *acc.* over); **Prä·si·di·um** [prɛˈziːdiʊm] *n* (-s; -dien) **1.** presidency, chair(manship); **2.** → ***Polizeipräsidium***

pras·seln [ˈprasəln] *v/i.* (h) *rain, hail*: patter (***auf*** *acc.* on, against *the window*), beat down (on), beat (against *the window*); *blows etc., a. fig. questions etc.*: rain down (on); *fire*: crackle; ***~der Beifall*** thunderous applause

pras·sen [ˈprasən] *v/i.* (h) F live it up; ***mit dem Geld ~*** throw one's money about; ***mit den Vorräten ~*** squander one's reserves; **Pras·se·rei** [prasəˈraɪ] *f* (-; *no pl.*) carousing; lavish lifestyle; high life

Prä·ten·dent [prɛtɛnˈdɛnt] *m* (-en; -en) claimant (***auf*** *acc.* to); pretender (to *the throne*)

prä·ten·ti·ös [prɛtɛnˈtsi̯øːs] *adj.* pretentious

Prä·te·ri·tum [prɛˈteːritʊm] *n* (-s; -ta) *ling.* preterite, past tense

prä·ven·tiv [prɛvɛnˈtiːf] *adj.*, **≗...** *in cpds.* preventive, ⚕ *a.* prophylactic

Prä·venˈtiv|krieg *m* preventive war; **~maß·nah·me** *f* preventive measure; **~me·diˌzin** *f* preventive medicine; **~schlag** *m* ⚔ preemptive strike

Pra·xis [ˈpraksɪs] *f* (-; Praxen [ˈpraksən]) **1.** *no pl.* a) practice, *Am. a.* practise; usage, b) experience; ***in der ~*** in practice (*Am. a.* practise), in reality; ***in die ~ umsetzen*** put into practice (*Am. a.* practise), put *plan etc.* into effect; ***nicht in die ~ umsetzbar*** impracticable; ***mir fehlt die ~*** I haven't got the experience, I need more experience; ***ein Beispiel aus der ~*** a concrete (*or* real-life) example, *a.* a case I have experienced myself; **2.** ⚖, ⚕ *etc.* practice; consulting room, ⚕ *a.* surgery, *Am.* doctor's office

ˈpra·xis|be·zo·gen *adj.* practically orient(at)ed; **~fern** *adj.* theoretical, academic; **~fremd** *adj.* theoretical, academic *studies etc.*; ***~ sein*** have (had) no practical experience, have no idea of the practical demands of the job; **~ge·recht** *adj.* practical; **~nah** *adj.* practical(ly orient[at]ed); realistic; **~ori·enˌtiert** *adj.* practically orient(at)ed

ˈPra·xis·schock *m* reality shock

Prä·ze·denz·fall [prɛtseˈdɛnts-] *m* precedent; ⚖ *a.* test case; ***e-n ~ schaffen*** establish a precedent

prä·zi·se [prɛˈtsiːzə] *adj.* precise, exact; **prä·zi·sie·ren** [prɛtsiˈziːrən] *v/t.* (h) specify; ***können Sie es ~?*** can you specify what you mean?, can you be more precise?; **Prä·zi·si·on** [prɛtsiˈzi̯oːn] *f* (-; *no pl.*) precision, accuracy

Prä·zi·siˈons|ar·beit *f* ⚙ *and fig.* precision work; **~in·struˌment** *n* precision instrument; **~uhr** *f* precision watch (*or* clock); **~waa·ge** *f* precision scale(s *pl.*)

pre·di·gen [ˈpreːdɪgən] *v/i. and v/t.* (h) preach (*dat.* to, *fig.* at); *fig.* ***j-m Toleranz*** *etc.* ~ preach at s.o. about tolerance, preach tolerance to s.o.; ***j-m Vernunft ~*** try to make s.o. see reason (*or* sense)

Pre·di·ger [ˈpreːdɪgɐ] *m* (-s; -), **Pre·di·ge·rin** [ˈpreːdɪgərɪn] *f* (-; -nen) preacher

Pre·digt [ˈpreːdɪçt] *f* (-; -en) sermon (*a.* F *fig.*); ***e-e ~ halten*** give (*or* hold) a sermon (***über*** *acc.* on); *fig.* ***j-m e-e ~ halten*** give s.o. a lecture (***über*** *acc.* on)

Preis [praɪs] *m* (-es; -e [ˈpraɪzə]) **1.** price;

charge; rate; ***j-m e-n guten ~ machen*** make s.o. a good offer; ***unter ~ verkaufen*** undersell; ***weit unter ~ verkaufen*** sell (at) cut-price; ***zum halben ~ verkaufen*** sell (at) half-price; ***hoch im ~ stehen*** fetch high prices; ***~e vergleichen*** shop around; ***es kommt nicht auf den ~ an*** it's not a question of money; *fig.* ***es hat alles s-n ~*** there's a price to pay for everything; ***um keinen ~*** not for anything in the world; ***ich muß es um jeden ~ schaffen*** I've got to make it, come what may (*or* whatever happens); → ***drücken*** 4, ***stolz*** 2; **2.** prize (*a. fig.*); *film etc.*: *a.* award; ***der erste ~*** first prize; ***den zweiten ~ bekommen*** get second prize, come second; ***~ der Nationen*** *riding*: Prix des Nations; **3.** reward; ***e-n ~ auf j-s Kopf aussetzen*** put a price on s.o.'s head; **4.** *no pl.* praise; **~ab·spra·che** *f* price agreement; **~än·de·rung** *f* change in price; ***~en vorbehalten*** subject to change; **~an·ga·be** *f* quotation (of prices); **~an·ge·bot** *n* offer; ✝ quotation; **~an·stieg** *m* rise in prices; **~auf·schlag** *m* markup; **~aus·schrei·ben** *n* competition; **⁀be·wußt** *adj.* price-conscious; *adv.* ***~ einkaufen*** shop around; **~bin·dung** *f* retail price maintenance (*abbr.* RPM); **~bre·cher** *m* price cutter; **~dif·fe˛renz** *f* difference in price(s); **~dis·zi˛plin** *f* price restraint; **~druck** *m* (-[e]s; *no pl.*) pricing pressure; **~ein·bruch** *m* → ***Preissturz***

Prei·sel·bee·re ['praɪzəl-] *f* ⚘ cranberry

'Preis·emp·feh·lung *f* recommended price; ***unverbindliche ~*** recommended retail price

prei·sen ['praɪzən] *v/t.* (pries, gepriesen, h) praise, extol; ***~ als*** *a.* hail as; → ***glücklich*** I

'Preis|ent·wick·lung *f* price trend; **~er·hö·hung** *f* price increase; **~er·mä·ßi·gung** *f* price reduction; **~fra·ge** *f* **1.** prize question; sixty-four-thousand-dollar question; **2.** ***es ist e-e ~*** it's a question of price

'Preis·ga·be *f* (-; *no pl.*) **1.** revelation, unveiling *of secret etc.*; **2.** surrender *of territory etc.*; sellout

'preis·ge·ben *v/t.* (*irr.*, *sep.*, h, → ***geben***) give away, reveal *name, secret etc.* (*dat.* to); surrender, give up *territory, one's freedom etc.*; sacrifice *one's hono(u)r etc.*; ***sich der Kritik (dem Spott*** *etc.*) ***~*** expose o.s. (*or* lay o.s. open) to criticism (ridicule *etc.*); ***j-n dem Elend ~*** abandon s.o. to poverty; ***et. dem Verfall ~*** let s.th. go to rack and ruin; ***(hilflos) preisgegeben*** *dat.* at the mercy of; → ***Gelächter***

'preis·ge·bun·den *adj.* price-controlled

'Preis·ge·fü·ge *n* price structure

'preis·ge·krönt *adj.* prizewinning, *a.* award-winning *film etc.*

'Preis|ge·richt *n* jury; **~gren·ze** *f* price limit; ***obere ~*** *a.* ceiling; ***untere ~*** bottom price; **⁀gün·stig I.** *adj.* → ***preiswert***; **II.** *adv.*: ***er kauft immer sehr ~ ein*** he always shops around for bargains (*or* manages to find bargains); **~in·dex** *m* price index; **~kampf** *m* price war; **~ka·te·go˛rie** *f*, **~klas·se** *f* price range; ***in der oberen (unteren, mittleren) ~*** in the top (bottom, medium) price range *or* bracket; ***ein Auto der mittleren ~*** *a.* a medium-priced car; **~kon˛trol·le** *f* price control; **~krieg** *m* price war; **~la·ge** *f* price range; ***in mittlerer ~*** medium-priced; ***in der gleichen ~*** F around the same price; **~-'Lei·stungs-Ver·hält·nis** *n* price-performance ratio; F value for money

'preis·lich I. *adj.* price *differences etc.*; **II.** *adv.*: ***es ist ~ günstig*** it's a good price

'Preis|li·ste *f* price list; **~-'Lohn-Spi˛ra·le** *f* prices and wages spiral; **~nach·laß** *m* discount, markdown; **~ni˛veau** *n* price level; **~no˛tie·rung** *f* quotation; **~po·li˛tik** *f* prices policy; **~rät·sel** *n* competition; **~recht** *n* pricing laws *pl.*, price legislation; **~rich·ter** *m* judge; **~rück·gang** *m* fall (*or* drop) in prices; **~schild** *n* price tag; **~schla·ger** F *m* bargain offer; **~schwan·kun·gen** *pl.* price fluctuations; **~sen·kung** *f* price cut; **~ska·la** *f* price range; **~spi˛ra·le** *f* price spiral, spiral of rising prices; **~stei·ge·rung** *f* rise in prices; *pl. a.* rising prices; **~stopp** *m* price freeze; **~sturz** *m* steep fall in prices; **~trä·ger** *m* prizewinner

Preis·trei·be·rei [-traɪbə'raɪ] *f* (-; *no pl.*) profiteering

'Preis|über˛wa·chung *f* price control; **~über˛wa·chungs·stel·le** *f* price control board; **~˛un·ter·schied** *m* difference in price(s); **~ver·ein·ba·rung** *f* price agreement; **~ver·fall** *m* dramatic drop in prices; **~ver·gleich** *m* **1.** comparing prices; **2.** price comparison; **~ver·lei·hung** *f* presentation (of prizes); **~vor·teil** *m* saving; **⁀wert** *adj.* very reasonable; ***~ sein*** *a.* be good value (for money); **~zu·schlag** *m* surcharge

pre·kär [pre'kɛːɐ] *adj.* awkward, tricky *situation, question etc.*; really difficult; ***~er Friede*** uneasy peace; ***~e Lage*** *pol. a.* parlous state

Prell·bock ['prɛl-] *m* 🚂 *and fig.* buffer

prel·len ['prɛlən] *v/t.* (h) **1.** cheat swindle, F con (***um*** *acc.* out of); F ***die Zeche ~*** leave without paying, F do a bunk; **2.** ⚕ bruise

'Prell·schuß *m* ricochet

Prel·lung ['prɛlʊŋ] *f* (-; -en) ⚕ bruise; contusion; ***er hat e-e schlimme ~ abgekriegt*** he bruised himself badly, he got a bad bruise

Pre·mier [prə'mi̯eː] *m* (-s; -s) prime minister, premier

Pre·mie·re [prə'mi̯eːrə] *f* (-; -n) first (*or* opening) night, première; ***das Stück hat heute ~*** the play is having its première today, it's the première of the play today

Pre'mie·ren|abend *m* first night, night of the première; **~fie·ber** *n* first-night nerves *pl.*; **~ki·no** *n* first-run cinema; **~pu·bli·kum** *n* audience on the first night

Pre'mier·mi˛ni·ster *m* prime minister, premier

Pres·by·te·ria·ner [prɛsbyte'ri̯aːnɐ] *m* (-s; -), **pres·by·te·ria·nisch** [prɛsbyte'ri̯aːnɪʃ] *adj.* Presbyterian; **Pres·by·te·ria·nis·mus** [prɛsbyteri̯a'nɪsmʊs] *m* (-; *no pl.*) Presbyterianism

pre·schen ['prɛʃən] F *v/i.* (sn) F whiz(z), zoom; *horse*: gallop

pres·sant [prɛ'sant] *dial. adj.* urgent; ***es ~ haben*** be in a hurry

Pres·se[1] ['prɛsə] *f* (-; -n) ⚙, *typ.* press; squeezer

'Pres·se[2] *f* (-; *no pl.*) press; ***die ausländische ~*** the foreign press, foreign newspapers and magazines; ***er ist von der ~*** he's from the press; ***es stand in der ~*** it was in the papers; ***sie wurde von der ~ überallhin verfolgt*** the press were at her heels wherever she went; ***er hatte e-e gute (schlechte) ~*** he got *or* had a good (bad) press; **~agen˛tur** *f* press agency; **~amt** *n* press office; **~ar˛chiv** *n* press archives *pl.*; **~at·ta˛ché** *m* press attaché; **~aus·schnitt** *m* press (*or* news) clipping; **~aus·weis** *m* press card; **~be·richt** *m* press report; **~bü˛ro** *n* press agency; **~chef** *m* press officer; **~dienst** *m* news service; **~emp·fang** *m* press reception; **~er·klä·rung** *f* press release; **~fo·to˛graf** *m* press photographer; **~frei·heit** *f* (-; *no pl.*) freedom of the press; **~ge·setz** *n* press law; **~ge·spräch** *n* press interview; **~in·for·ma·ti˛on** *f* → ***Pressemeldung***; **~jar˛gon** *m* journalese; **~ka˛bi·ne** *f sport*: press box; **~kam˛pa·gne** *f* press campaign; **~kom·men˛tar** *m* press commentary; **~kon·fe˛renz** *f* press conference; **~kor·re·spon˛dent** *m* newspaper correspondent; **~mann** F *m* (-[e]s; -leute) F newspaper man, pressman; **~map·pe** *f* press kit; **~mel·dung** *f* press report; ***e-r ~ zufolge*** according to a press report

pres·sen ['prɛsən] *v/t.* (h) **1.** press *paper, flowers etc.*; bale *straw*; mo(u)ld *plastics*; make *wine*; **2.** press *grapes etc.*; squeeze *lemon etc.*; ***den Saft aus e-r Zitrone ~*** squeeze (the juice out of) a lemon; *fig.* ***et. aus j-m ~*** squeeze (*or* force) s.th. out of s.o.; **3.** ***~ in*** *acc.* force (*or* squeeze, F stuff) into; ***~ gegen*** *acc.* press against; ***an sich ~*** hold tightly, *a.* hug *s.o.* hard (*or* tightly); ***sich an die Wand ~*** press o.s. against the wall; ***sich flach an den Boden ~*** lie absolutely flat on the ground; ***j-m die Hand auf den Mund ~*** clasp one's hand over s.o.'s mouth; ***Luft ~ durch*** *acc.* force air through *s.th.*; *fig.* ***j-n zu et. ~*** force s.o. to do s.th.; ***et. in ein System ~*** force s.th. into a system; → ***gepreßt***

'Pres·se|or˛gan *n* (press) organ; **~recht** *n* press law; **~re·fe˛rent** *m* press officer; **~schau** *f* press review; **~spre·cher** *m* press spokesman; **~stel·le** *f* public relations department; **~stim·men** *pl.* press (*or* newspaper) comments; ***die ~ sind sich einig*** the newspapers agree; **~tri˛bü·ne** *f* press stand (*parl.* gallery); **~ver·laut·ba·rung** *f* press release; **~ver·tre·ter** *m* reporter, F pressman; **~zar** *m* press baron, newspaper tycoon; **~zen˛sur** *f* press censorship; **~zen·trum** *n* press centre (*Am.* center)

Preß|form ['prɛs-] *f* ⚙ compression mo(u)ld; **~glas** *n* pressed glass; **~he·fe** *f* press yeast; **~holz** *n* laminated wood

pres·sie·ren [prɛ'siːrən] *dial. v/i.* (h) be urgent; ***es pressiert mir*** I'm in a hurry; ***es pressiert nicht*** there's no hurry; ***es pressiert allmählich*** we're running out of time

Pres·si·on [prɛ'si̯oːn] *f* (-; -en) pressure; ***(e-r Fülle von) ~en ausgesetzt sein*** be under pressure (from all sides)

Preß·luft ['prɛs-] *f* compressed air; **~boh·rer** *m* pneumatic drill; **~ham·mer** *m* pneumatic hammer

Preß·sack ['prɛs-] *m gastr.* brawn, *Am.* headcheese

Preß·span ['prɛs-] *m* pressboard

Pres·sung ['prɛsʊŋ] *f* (-; -en) pressing

Preß·we·hen ['prɛs-] *pl.* bearing-down pains

Pre·sti·ge [prɛs'tiːʒə] *n* (-s; *no pl.*) prestige; status; ***an ~ verlieren (gewinnen)*** lose face (gain in prestige); ***hohes ~ genießen*** enjoy considerable prestige; ***sein ~ wahren*** save one's face; **~ar,ti·kel** *m* prestige item; **~den·ken** *n* status mentality; **~fra·ge** *f* matter of prestige; **~ge·winn** *m* gain in prestige; **2träch·tig** *adj.* prestigious, prestige ...; **~ver·lust** *m* loss of prestige (*or* face)

Preu·ße ['prɔʏsə] *m* (-n; -n) *hist.* Prussian; F *fig.* ***so schnell schießen die ~n nicht*** F hold your horses; **Preu·ßin** ['prɔʏsɪn] *f* (-; -nen) *hist.* Prussian; **preu·ßisch** ['prɔʏsɪʃ] *adj. a. fig.* Prussian

pre·zi·ös [pre'tsïø:s] *adj.* stilted, affected

prickeln ['prɪkəln] (*sep.* -k·k-) **I.** *v/i.* (h) **1.** *skin etc.*: tingle; **2.** *champagne etc.*: sparkle; ***auf der Zunge ~*** tickle one's tongue; **II.** 2 *n* (-s; *no pl.*) **3.** tingling (sensation), pins and needles *pl.*; **4.** *gastr.* prickle; **5.** *fig.* thrill; **'prickelnd** *fig. adj.* exciting, thrilling; titillating; *fig.* ***es ist ein ~es Gefühl*** it gives you goosepimples, it sends a tingle (*or* shiver) down your spine

Priel [pri:l] *m* (-[e]s; -e) tideway

Priem [pri:m] *m* (-[e]s; -e) quid, plug

prie·men ['pri:mən] *v/i.* (h) chew tobacco

pries [pri:s] *pret. of* ***preisen***

Prie·ster ['pri:stɐ] *m* (-s; -) priest; **~amt** *n* priesthood, ministry

Prie·ste·rin ['pri:stərɪn] *f* (-; -nen) priestess; **'prie·ster·lich** *adj.* priestly

'Prie·ster·schaft *f* (-; -en) priesthood

'Prie·ster·se·mi,nar *n* (Roman Catholic) seminary

'Prie·ster·tum *n* (-s; *no pl.*) priesthood

'Prie·ster·wei·he *f* ordination; ***die ~ empfangen*** take (holy) orders

Prim [pri:m] *f* (-; -en) **1.** ♪ prime; ***reine ~*** perfect unison; **2.** *eccl.* prime (song); **3.** *fencing*: prime

pri·ma ['pri:ma] F **I.** *adj.* F super, great; **II.** *adv.*: ***das hast du ~ gemacht*** well done, you've done a great job; ***wir haben uns ~ amüsiert*** we had a great time

'Pri·ma *f* (-; Primen) *ped.* **1.** *obs. last two years of grammar school*; *Brit.* sixth form; **2.** *Austrian* first year (of grammar school)

Pri·ma·bal·le'ri·na *f* prima ballerina

Pri·ma·don·na [prima'dɔna] *f* (-; -nen) prima donna (*a. fig.*)

Pri·ma-fa·cie-Be·weis [pri:ma'fa:tsïə] *m* prima facie evidence

Pri·ma·ner [pri'ma:nɐ] *m* (-s; -), **Pri·ma·ne·rin** [pri'ma:nərɪn] *f* (-; -nen) **1.** *obs. pupil in the* (*second to*) *last year of grammar school*; *Brit.* sixth former; **2.** *Austrian* first year (grammar school) pupil

pri·mär [pri'mɛ:ɐ] **I.** *adj.* primary; *a.* main *question, problem etc.*; **II.** *adv.* primarily; ***es geht uns ~ darum, daß die Firma überlebt*** what concerns us primarily (*or* our main concern) is that the company should survive

Pri'mär|ener,gie *f* primary energy; **~farbe** *f* primary colo(u)r; **~ge·stein** *n* primary rocks *pl.*; **~li·te·ra,tur** *f* primary literature; **~quel·le** *f* primary source; **~span·nung** *f* ⚡ primary voltage; **~ton** *m* simple (*or* primary) tone

Pri·mas ['pri:mas] *m* (-s; *no pl.*) *eccl.* primate

Pri·mat [pri'ma:t] *m, n* (-[e]s; -e) primacy (***über*** *acc.* over)

Pri·ma·ten [pri'ma:tən] *pl. zo.* primates

pri·ma vi·sta ['pri:ma 'vɪsta] *adv.* ♪ at sight

Pri·mel ['pri:məl] *f* (-; -n) primrose; F *fig.* ***eingehen wie e-e ~*** F wilt away, *lit.* wither on the vine, *sport*: F get a good drubbing

pri·mi·tiv [primi'ti:f] *adj.* primitive (*a. art*), crude *method, tool etc.*; ***die ~sten Kenntnisse*** the absolute basics; ***gegen die ~sten Regeln des Anstands verstoßen*** have absolutely no sense of decency

Pri·mi·ti·vis·mus [primiti'vɪsmʊs] *m* (-; *no pl.*) primitivism

Pri·mi·ti·vi·tät [primitivi'tɛ:t] *f* (-; *no pl.*) primitiveness; crudeness

Pri·mi'tiv·ling *contp. m* (-s; -e) F peasant

'Prim·zahl *f* ⅍ prime number

Print·me·di·en ['prɪnt-] *pl.* print media

Prinz [prɪnts] *m* (-en; -en) prince

Prin·zes·sin [prɪn'tsɛsɪn] *f* (-; -nen) princess

'Prinz·ge·mahl *m* prince consort

Prin·zip [prɪn'tsi:p] *n* (-[e]s; -pien [-pïən]) **1.** principle; ***aus ~*** on principle; ***im ~*** basically, in principle; ***ein Mann mit ~ien*** a man of principle; ***sein ~ ist zu*** *inf.* it's his principle to *inf.*; ***sie hat es sich zum ~ gemacht zu*** *inf.* she makes a point of *ger.*; ***mir geht's ums ~*** it's the principle of the matter (*or* thing); **2.** principle, law; ***es funktioniert nach dem ~*** *gen.* it works on the principle of

prin·zi·pi·ell [prɪntsi'pïɛl] **I.** *adj.* fundamental; ***ich habe keine ~en Einwände*** I have no real objections; **II.** *adv.* a) basically, in principle, b) on principle

Prin'zi·pi·en|fra·ge *f* question of principle; **~rei·ter** F *m* stickler for principles; **~rei·te,rei** *f* (-; *no pl.*) moralizing, harping on about principles; **~streit** *m* fight (*or* battle) over principles *or* fundamental issues

Pri·or ['pri:o:ɐ] *m* (-s; Prioren [pri'o:rən]) prior; **Prio·rin** [pri'o:rɪn] *f* (-; -nen) prioress

Prio·ri·tät [priori'tɛ:t] *f* (-; -en) priority (***über, vor*** *dat.* over) (*a.* ✝ *and patent law*); ***~en setzen*** establish priorities, take first things first, ***bei*** *dat.*: give priority to, prioritize; **Prio·ri'tä·ten·li·ste** *f* list of priorities

Pri·se ['pri:zə] *f* (-; -n) **1.** ***e-e ~ Salz (Tabak*** *etc.*) a pinch of salt (snuff *etc.*); **2.** ⚓ prize

Pris·ma ['prɪsma] *n* (-s; -men) prism; **pris·ma·tisch** [prɪs'ma:tɪʃ] *adj.* prismatic(ally *adv.*); **Pris·men·su·cher** ['prɪsmən-] *m phot.* prismatic viewfinder

Prit·sche ['prɪtʃə] *f* (-; -n) **1.** wooden bed; **2.** *mot.* platform; **'Prit·schen·wa·gen** *m* pickup (truck)

pri·vat [pri'va:t] **I.** *adj.* a) private, b) confidential, c) personal, d) privately owned; ***das ist m-e ~e Meinung*** that's my personal opinion; **II.** *adv.* privately, in private; ***haben Sie ~ mit ihr zu tun?*** do you have any private contact with her?

Pri'vat|ab·kom·men *n* private agreement; **~adres·se** *f* private (*or* home) address; **~an·ge·le·gen·heit** *f* private matter; ***das ist m-e ~*** that's my affair; **~au·di·enz** *f* private audience; **~aus·ga·ben** *pl.* personal expenses; **~au·to** *n* private car; **~bank** *f* (-; -en) private bank; **~be·sitz** *m* private property; ***in ~*** privately owned; ***in ~ gelangen*** pass into private hands; ***das Gemälde*** *etc.* ***stammt aus ~*** the painting *etc.* is from a private collection; **~bett** *n* ⚕ pay bed; **~brief** *m* personal letter; **~de·tek,tiv** *m* private detective (*or* investigator); **~do,zent** *m* (unsalaried) lecturer, *Am.* associate professor; **~ei·gen·tum** *n* → ***Privatbesitz***; **~fern·se·hen** *n* **1.** private (*or* commercial) television *or* TV; **2.** private (*or* commercial) TV station; **~ge·brauch** *m* private (*or* personal) use; ***die sind für d-n ~*** *a.* they're for your own (personal) use; **~ge·spräch** *n* private conversation; *teleph.* private call; **~grund·stück** *n*: ***ein ~*** private property; **~hand** *f*: ***aus ~*** from a private collection; ***in ~*** privately owned

Pri·va·tier [priva'tïe:] *m* (-s; -s) person of independent means; ***er ist ~*** he lives on a private income

pri·va·tim [pri'va:tɪm] *adv.* a) privately, in private, b) confidentially

Pri'vat|in·du,strie *f* private industry; **~ini·tia,ti·ve** *f* **1.** initiative; ***~ zeigen*** show some initiative; **2.** ✝ private venture

pri·va·ti·sie·ren [privati'zi:rən] *v/i.* (h) live on a (*or* one's) private income

Pri·va·ti'sie·rung *f* (-; -en) privatization (*gen.* of)

Pri'vat|kli·nik *f* private clinic (*or* nursing home, hospital); **~kor·re·spon,denz** *f* private (*or* personal) correspondence; **~krieg** *m* private feud; **~le·ben** *n* (-s; *no pl.*) private life; ***sich ins ~ zurückziehen*** retire from public life; ***ich habe kaum noch ein ~*** I hardly have any time for myself; **~leh·rer** *m* private tutor; **~mit·tel** *pl.* private means; **~num·mer** *f* private (*or* home) number; **~pa·ti,ent** *m* private patient; **~per,son** *f* **1.** private individual; ***als ~*** *a.* in private; **2. *es gehört e-r ~*** it's privately owned; **~pra·xis** *f* private practice (*Am. a.* practise); **~quar,tier** *n a. pl.* private accommodation; **~recht** *n* (-[e]s; *no pl.*) private (*or* civil) law; **2recht·lich** *adj.* under private law, private(-law) ...; **~sa·che** *f* private matter; **~samm·lung** *f* private collection; **~schu·le** *f* private school; **~se·kre,tär** *m* private secretary; **~sphä·re** *f* private sphere; privacy; **~sta·ti,on** *f* ⚕ private (patients') ward; **~stra·ße** *f* private road; **~stun·den** *pl.* private lessons (*or* tuition *sg.*); **~un·ter,neh·men** *n* private firm; **~,un·ter·richt** *m* → ***Privatstunden***; **~ver·brauch** *m* private (*or* personal) consumption; **~ver·gnü·gen** *n*: ***das mache ich nicht als ~*** I'm not doing it for my own pleasure; ***was Sie hier machen, ist Ihr ~*** what you do here is your (own) business; **~ver·mö·gen** *n* personal assets *pl.* (*or* fortune); **~weg** *m* private road (*or* footpath); **~wirt·schaft** *f* private enterprise; **~woh·nung** *f* private flat (*Am.* apartment) *or* home; **~zwecke** *pl.*: ***für ~*** for private use

Pri·vi·leg [privi'le:k] *n* (-s; Privilegien [privi'le:gïən]) privilege; ***ein ~ der Reichen*** a rich man's prerogative

pri·vi·le·gie·ren [privile'gi:rən] *v/t.* (h) grant *s.o.* a privilege; **pri·vi·le·giert** [privile'gi:ɐt] *adj.* (very) privileged

PR-Ma·na·ger [pe:'ʔɛr-] *m* PR (*or* public relations) manager

pro [pro:] *prp.* (*acc.*) per; ***~ Jahr*** per annum, a year; ***~ Kopf*** per head; ***Einkommen ~ Kopf*** per capita income; ***~ Stück*** each, a piece; ***~ Stunde*** an (*or* per) hour; ***fünf Mark ~ Person*** five marks each (*or* a head, per person); **Pro** *n*: ***~ und Kontra*** *the* pros and cons *pl.*

Pro·band [pro'bant] *m* (-en; -en [-dən]) **1.** ⚕ *etc.* test person; **2.** ⚖ probationer
pro·bat [pro'ba:t] *adj.* tried and tested
Pro·be ['pro:bə] *f* (-; -n) a) test, trial; trial run, practice (*Am. a.* practise) run, b) check, c) *thea.*, ♪ *etc.* rehearsal, choir practice (*Am. a.* practise); audition, d) sample; *iro.* taste; ***zur ~*** on a trial basis, F just to try it out; ***e-e ~ machen*** do a test, ⚙, *mot.* do a trial run; ***auf die ~ stellen*** (put to the) test; ***die ~ bestehen*** stand (*or* pass) the test; ***e-e ~ s-s Könnens*** (***Mutes*** *etc.*) ***ablegen*** give a sample (*iro.* taste) of his skill(s) (courage *etc.*), prove his skill(s) (courage *etc.*); *thea.* ***~n*** (***ab***)***halten*** have rehearsals, rehearse; ***ich muß zur ~*** I've got to go to rehearsals (*or* choir practi|ce, *Am. a.* -se); ⚙ ***~n nehmen*** take samples; ⚘ ***die ~ machen*** check; ***j-n auf ~ einstellen*** employ s.o. on a trial basis (*or* on probation); → ***Exempel***; **~ab·schuß** *m* test firing; **~ab·zug** *m typ., phot.* proof; **~alarm** *m* practice (*or* practise) alarm; **~ar·beit** *f* **1.** trial work; **2.** specimen (piece); **~auf·nah·me** *f* a) *film*: screen test, b) test recording; **~boh·rung** *f* trial drill; **~ehe** *f* trial marriage; **~ent·nah·me** *f* **1.** sampling; **2.** sample; ***e-e ~ machen*** take a sample; **~ex·em,plar** *n* specimen copy, sample (copy)
'pro·be·fah·ren (*irr., sep.*, → ***fahren***) **I.** *v/t.* (h) give *a car etc.* a trial run, test-drive; **II.** *v/i.* (sn) go for a trial run; **'Pro·be·fahrt** *f* test (*or* trial) run
'Pro·be·lauf *m* test run
pro·ben ['pro:bən] *v/t. and v/i.* (h) rehearse; practise, *Am.* practice
'Pro·be|num·mer *f* sample copy; **~sei·te** *f* specimen page; **~sen·dung** *f* sample sent on approval; **~stück** *n* sample
'pro·be·wei·se *adv.* on a trial basis, *employed etc.* on probation
'Pro·be·zeit *f* probationary (*or* trial) period; ***in der ~ sein*** be on probation
pro·bie·ren [pro'bi:rən] (h) **I.** *v/t.* **1.** try; try out; ***probier es noch mal*** try again, have another go; ***et.*** (***zu tun***) ***~*** try (to do) s.th.; ***es ~ mit*** *dat.* try *s.th., s.o. or ger.*, have a try at *s.th. or ger.*; F ***es bei j-m ~*** F try it on with s.o.; **2.** try, taste; ***probier mal, ob*** (***dir***) ***das schmeckt*** see if that tastes all right (*Am.* alright) (see if you like it); **II.** *v/i.* **3.** try; ***probier doch mal*** try, try it (out), have a go; ***⁰ geht über Studieren*** the proof of the pudding is in the eating; **4.** try, taste; ***kann ich mal ~?*** can I have a taste?
Pro·blem [pro'ble:m] *n* (-s; -e) problem (*a.* ⚘, *phls. etc.*); ***kein ~!*** no problem; ***vor e-m ~ stehen*** be faced with a problem; ***es ist nicht ohne ~e*** it's not without its (little) problems; *sie ist zu ungeduldig* - ***das ist ihr ~*** *a.* that's her trouble; ***er muß immer ein ~ daraus machen*** he always has to make a problem out of it (F a thing of it); **Pro·ble·ma·tik** [proble'ma:tɪk] *f* (-; *no pl.*) problem(s *pl.*); ***die ~ der Arbeitslosigkeit*** the problems of (*or* surrounding) unemployment; ***die ~ dieser Beziehung*** the problematic nature of this relationship; **pro·ble·ma·tisch** [proble'ma:tɪʃ] *adj.* problematic(al); questionable; **pro·ble·ma·ti·sie·ren** [problemati'zi:rən] *v/t.* (h) make a problem out of *s.th.*; ***man kann alles ~*** you can 'make problems
Pro'blem|fall *m* problem (case); **~haa·re** *pl.* problem hair *sg.*; **~haut** *f* problem skin; **~kind** *n* problem child; **~kom,plex** *m* complex of problems; **~kreis** *m* range (*or* complex) of problems
pro'blem·los I. *adj.* (completely) unproblematic(al), problem-free; **II.** *adv.*: ***~ ablaufen*** go off without a hitch
pro'blem·reich *adj.* (highly) problematic(al)
Pro'blem|stel·lung *f* **1.** presentation of a problem; **2.** problem; **~stück** *n thea.* problem (*or* issue, thesis) play
Pro·dukt [pro'dʊkt] *n* (-[e]s; -e) product (*a.* ⚘); *pl.* produce *sg.*
Pro'duk·ten·bör·se *f* commodity exchange
Pro'dukt·haf·tung *f* product liability
Pro·duk·ti·on [prodʊk'tsi̯o:n] *f* (-; -en) production; output; ***die ~ aufnehmen*** go into production
Pro·duk·ti'ons|ab·fall *m* drop in production; **~ab·lauf** *m* production run; **~an·la·ge** *f* production plant; **~aus·fall** *m* loss of production; **~brei·te** *f* horizontal range of production; **~ge·nos·sen·schaft** *f* **1.** producers' cooperative; **2.** ***landwirtschaftliche ~*** *hist. DDR* collective farm; **~gü·ter** *pl.* producer goods; **~ka·pa·zi,tät** *f* production (*or* productive) capacity; **~ko·sten** *pl.* production costs; **~lei·stung** *f* output capacity; **~lei·ter** *m* production manager; **~mit·tel** *pl.* means of production; **⁰reif** *adj.* ready for production; **~rück·gang** *m* fall in production; **~stät·te** *f* production plant; **~stei·ge·rung** *f* increase in production; increased productivity; **~tech·nik** *f* production technology; **~tie·fe** *f* vertical range of production; **~ver·fah·ren** *n* production process; **~wei·se** *f* production method; **~ziel** *n* production target; **~zweig** *m* line of production
pro·duk·tiv [prodʊk'ti:f] *adj.* productive; ***äußerst ~*** *a.* prolific; **Pro·duk·ti·vi·tät** [prodʊktivi'tɛ:t] *f* (-; *no pl.*) productivity
Pro·du·zent [produ'tsɛnt] *m* (-en; -en) producer (*a. film etc.*), manufacturer, maker; **Pro·du'zen·ten·haf·tung** *f* product (*or* manufacturer's) liability
pro·du·zie·ren [produ'tsi:rən] (h) **I.** *v/t.* produce; make; **II.** *v/refl.*: ***sich ~*** *contp.* show off, make an exhibition of o.s.
Prof [prɔf] F *m* (-s; -s) F prof
pro·fan [pro'fa:n] *adj.* **1.** profane, secular; **2.** ordinary, everyday ...
Pro'fan|ar·chi·tek,tur *f* civic architecture; **~bau** *m* (-[e]s; -ten) secular building
pro·fa·nie·ren [profa'ni:rən] *v/t.* (h) profane
Pro·fes·sio·na·lis·mus [profɛsi̯ona'lɪsmʊs] *m* (-; *no pl.*) professionalism
pro·fes·sio·nell [profɛsi̯o'nɛl] *adj.* professional; **Pro·fes·sio·nel·le** [profɛsi̯o'nɛlə] F *f* (-n; -n) F pro
Pro·fes·sor [pro'fɛso:ɐ] *m* (-s; -en [profɛ'so:rən]), **Pro·fes·so·rin** [profɛ'so:rɪn] *f* (-; -nen) professor; ***sie ist Professorin für Erdkunde*** she's a geography professor, she's Professor of Geography
pro·fes·so·ral [profɛso'ra:l] *adj.*, **pro·fes'so·ren·haft** *adj.* professorial
Pro·fes'so·ren·schaft *f* (-; *no pl.*) professorate
Pro·fes·sur [profɛ'su:ɐ] *f* (-; -en [-rən]) professorship, chair (***für*** *acc.* of)
Pro·fi ['pro:fi] F *m* (-s; -s) F pro; ***da waren ~s am Werk*** it looks like a professional job; **~bo·xen** *n* professional boxing; **~bo·xer** *m* professional boxer; **~fuß·ball** *m* professional football (*or* soccer); **~fuß·bal·ler** *m* professional footballer (*or* soccer player)
'pro·fi·haft *adj.* (very) professional
Pro·fil [pro'fi:l] *n* (-s; -e) **1.** profile; ⚙ *a.* section; (*tire*) tread; ***im ~*** in profile; **2.** *fig.* profile; personality; ***kein ~ haben*** a) have no personality, b) have no identity (*or* profile); ***die Partei*** *etc.* ***hat ein starkes ~*** it's a high-profile party *etc.*
Pro'fil·an·sicht *f* profile
pro·fi·lie·ren [profi'li:rən] (h) **I.** *v/t.* ⚙ profile, shape; *w.s.* streamline; *fig.* give *s.th.* a clear profile; **II.** *v/refl.*: ***sich ~*** *politician etc.*: distinguish o.s., make one's mark; **pro·fi·liert** [profi'li:ɐt] *fig. adj.* clearly defined, clear-cut; distinguished *personality*; ***er ist ein ~er Politiker*** he's made his mark as a politician
Pro'fil|neu,ro·se F *f* image neurosis; ***er hat e-e ~, er leidet an e-r ~*** he's obsessed with his image, he's always got to be in the limelight; **~rei·fen** *m* nonskid tyre (*Am.* tire); **~soh·le** *f* grip sole
Pro·fit [pro'fi:t] *m* (-[e]s; -e) profit
pro·fi·ta·bel [profi'ta:bəl] *adj.* profitable, lucrative
Pro'fit|den·ken *n* money-grubbing mentality; **⁰gie·rig** *adj.* profit-seeking, money-grubbing
pro·fi·tie·ren [profi'ti:rən] *v/i.* (h) profit; ***er kann dabei nur ~*** he only stands to gain
Pro'fit|jä·ger *m* profiteer; **~stre·ben** *n* profit-mongering
pro for·ma [pro: 'fɔrma] *adv.* as a matter of form
Pro'for·ma·rech·nung *f* ✝ pro forma invoice
pro·fund [pro'fʊnt] *adj.* profound
Pro·ge·ste·ron [progɛstə'ro:n] *n* (-s; *no pl.*) progesterone
Pro·gno·se [pro'gno:zə] *f* (-; -n) prediction; ✝, *meteor.* forecast; *esp.* ⚕ prognosis; ***ich möchte keine ~n stellen*** I wouldn't like to make any predictions (*or* forecasts); ***alle ihre ~n trafen ein*** everything happened as she had predicted (*or* foretold); **pro·gno·sti·zie·ren** [prognɔsti'tsi:rən] *v/t.* (h) forecast
Pro·gramm [pro'gram] *n* (-s; -e) programme, *Am.* program (*a. computer*); schedule; *pol.* (political) program(me), platform; ⚙ cycle *of a dishwasher etc.*; *TV* channel; ***im ersten ~*** on (channel) one; ***volles ~*** full schedule; ***mein ~ fürs Wochenende*** my weekend schedule; F ***was steht heute auf dem ~?*** F what's on the agenda today?; F ***das steht nicht auf unserem ~*** that's not on our list; F ***das paßt mir überhaupt nicht ins ~*** that doesn't suit me at all; **~ab·lauf·plan** *m computer*: flow chart; **~än·de·rung** *f* change of program(me)
pro·gram·ma·tisch [progra'ma:tɪʃ] *adj.* programmatic(ally *adv.*); ***~e Rede*** keynote speech (*or* address)
Pro'gramm|feh·ler *m computer*: program error; **⁰ge·mäß** *adj. and adv.* according to program(me), as scheduled; **~ge·stal·tung** *f* program(me) planning; **⁰ge·steu·ert** *adj.* computer-controlled; **~heft** *n* program(me); **~,hin·weis** *m TV* ***~e für heute abend*** details about tonight's program(me)s (*or* viewing); ***hier noch ein ~*** a word about a program(me) coming up shortly

pro·gram·mier·bar [progra'mi:ɐba:ɐ] *adj.* program(m)able

pro·gram·mie·ren [progra'mi:rən] *v/t.* (h) program(me)

Pro·gram·mie·rer [progra'mi:rɐ] *m* (-s; -), **Pro·gram·mie·re·rin** [progra'mi:rə-rɪn] *f* (-; -nen) program(m)er

Pro·gram·mier|feh·ler [progra'mi:ɐ-] *m* program(m)ing error; **~ge·rät** *n* program(m)er; **~spra·che** *f* program(m)ing language

pro·gram·miert [progra'mi:ɐt] *adj.* program(m)ed; *fig.* ***auf Erfolg ~ sein*** be program(m)ed for success; **Pro·gram-'mie·rung** *f* (-; -en) program(m)ing

Pro'gramm|ki·no *n* repertory cinema; **~platz** *m TV* program(me) slot; **~punkt** *m* item; *pol.* plank; **~steue·rung** *f* program(me) control; **~ta·ste** *f TV* channel selector button; *dishwasher etc.*: cycle setting button

Pro'grammu͵sik (*sep.* -mm·m-) *f* program(me) music

Pro'gramm|vor·schau *f* preview; *film*: trailer; **~wahl** *f TV* channel selection; *dishwasher etc.*: cycle selection; **~zeit-schrift** *f* program(me) guide, TV guide

Pro·gres·si·on [progrɛ'si̯o:n] *f* (-; -en) progression; **pro·gres·siv** [progrɛ'si:f] *adj.*, **Pro·gres·si·ve** [progrɛ'si:və] *m, f* (-n; -n) progressive

Pro·hi·bi·ti·on [prohibi'tsi̯o:n] *f* (-; -en) prohibition

Pro·jekt [pro'jɛkt] *n* (-[e]s; -e) project; **~grup·pe** *f* task force

pro·jek·tie·ren [projɛk'ti:rən] *v/t.* (h) project, plan; ***projektierte Zahl*** target figure

Pro·jek·til [projɛk'ti:l] *n* (-s; -e) projectile

Pro·jek·ti·on [projɛk'tsi̯o:n] *f* (-; -en) projection (*a.* ⚒, *psych.*)

Pro'jekt·lei·ter *m* project manager

Pro·jek·tor [pro'jɛkto:ɐ] *m* (-s; -en [-'to:-rən]) projector

Pro'jekt·stu·die *f* feasibility study

pro·ji·zie·ren [proji'tsi:rən] *v/t.* (h) project (***auf*** *acc.* onto) (*a. psych.*)

Pro·kla·ma·ti·on [proklama'tsi̯o:n] *f* (-; -en) proclamation; **pro·kla·mie·ren** [prokla'mi:rən] *v/t.* (h) proclaim

Pro-'Kopf|-Ein·kom·men *n* per capita income; **~-Ver·brauch** *m* per capita consumption

Pro·ku·ra [pro'ku:ra] *f* (-; -ren) ♆ power of attorney; **Pro·ku·rist** [proku'rɪst] *m* (-en; -en) authorized signatory

Pro·let [pro'le:t] *contp. m* (-en; -en) F pleb, prole; **Pro·le·ta·ri·at** [proleta'ri̯a:t] *n* (-s; *no pl.*) proletariat; **Pro·le·ta·ri·er** [prole'ta:ri̯ɐ] *m* (-s; -), **pro·le·ta·risch** [prole'ta:rɪʃ] *adj.* proletarian

pro'le·ten·haft *contp. adj.* plebeian, F plebby

Pro·log [pro'lo:k] *m* (-[e]s; -e [-gə]) prolog(ue)

pro·lon·gie·ren [prolɔŋ'gi:rən] *v/t.* (h) ♆ extend, renew

Pro·me·na·de [promə'na:də] *f* (-; -n) promenade

Pro·me'na·den|deck *n* ⚓ promenade deck; **~mi·schung** F *f* mongrel

pro·me·nie·ren [promə'ni:rən] *v/i.* (h, sn) promenade

Pro·mil·le [pro'mɪlə] *n* (-[s]; -) per thousand (*or* mil); F ~ (***Blutalkohol***) blood alcohol; **~gren·ze** *f* (blood) alcohol limit; **~sün·der** *m* drink driver

pro·mi·nent [promi'nɛnt] *adj.* prominent; ***~e Persönlichkeit*** well-known personality; **Pro·mi'nen·te** *m, f* (-n; -n) public figure, VIP; *esp. film etc.*: well-known personality, celebrity, F celeb

Pro·mi'nen·ten|mann·schaft *f* celebrity team; **~spiel** *n* celebrity match

Pro·mi·nenz [promi'nɛnts] *f* (-; *no pl.*) **1.** VIPs *pl.*, big names *pl.*, F top nobs *pl.*, F bigwigs *pl.*; ***die ganze ~*** *a.* all the important people; **2.** renown

Pro·mis·kui·tät [promɪskui'tɛ:t] *f* (-; *no pl.*) promiscuity

Pro·mo·ti·on [promo'tsi̯o:n] *f* (-; -en) *univ.* doctorate, PhD; **pro·mo·vie·ren** [promo'vi:rən] (h) **I.** *v/i.* do a *or* one's doctorate (*or* PhD); ***hat er promoviert?*** has he done a *or* his doctorate (*or* PhD)?, has he got a PhD?; **II.** *v/t.*: ***j-n ~*** award s.o. a doctorate (*or* PhD)

prompt [prɔmpt] **I.** *adj.* prompt, quick; **II.** *adv.* F *iro.* of course, needless to say; ***ich bin ~ drauf reingefallen*** of course I fell for it straightaway; ***als wir in Miami landeten, fing es ~ an zu regnen*** of course it had to start raining the minute we landed in Miami

Pro·no·men [pro'no:mən] *n* (-s; -, Pronomina [pro'no:mina]) *ling.* pronoun

pro·no·mi·nal [pronomi'na:l] *adj.*, **Pro·no·mi'nal...** *in cpds.* pronominal, pronoun ...

pro·non·ciert [pronõ'si:ɐt] **I.** *adj.* pronounced; firm, staunch; clear(-cut); ***~e Aussprache*** clear enunciation; **II.** *adv.*: ***sich ~ für (gegen) e-e Sache aussprechen*** take a firm stand in support of (against) s.th.; ***~ für e-e Sache eintreten*** give s.th. one's wholehearted support

Pro·pa·gan·da [propa'ganda] *f* (-; *no pl.*) propaganda; ***~ machen für*** *acc.* make propaganda for *s.th.*, F beat the big drum for *s.th.*; **~ap·pa͵rat** *m* propaganda machine; **~chef** *m* propaganda chief; **~feld-zug** *m* propaganda campaign; ♆ publicity (*or* advertising) campaign; **~film** *m* propaganda film; **~flut** *f* flood of propaganda; **~in·stru͵ment** *n* instrument of propaganda, propaganda medium; **~krieg** *m* propaganda war(fare); **~lü·ge** *f* propagandist lie; **~ma͵nö·ver** *n* propaganda move; **~ma·te·ri͵al** *n* propaganda material; **~rum·mel** F *m* F ballyhoo; ***e-n ~ machen um*** *acc.* make a great ballyhoo about; **~schrift** *f* propaganda leaflet; **~sen·der** *m* propaganda station; **~sen·dung** *f* propaganda broadcast; **~trom·mel** *f*: ***die ~ rühren für*** *acc.* drum up some support for, F beat the big drum for

Pro·pa·gan·dist [propagan'dɪst] *m* (-en; -en), **pro·pa·gan·di·stisch** [propagan-'dɪstɪʃ] *adj.* propagandist

pro·pa·gie·ren [propa'gi:rən] *v/t.* (h) propagate *idea etc.*; ♆ promote, F push

Pro·pan [pro'pa:n] (-s; *no pl.*), **~gas** *n* ⚗ propane

Pro·pel·ler [pro'pɛlɐ] *m* (-s; -) propeller, F prop; **~an·trieb** *m*: ***Maschine mit ~*** → ***Propellermaschine***; **~blatt** *n*, **~flü·gel** *m* propeller blade; **~ma͵schi·ne** *f* propeller aircraft, F prop plane

pro·per ['prɔpɐ] F *adj.* neat, clean and tidy

Pro·phet [pro'fe:t] *m* (-en; -en) prophet; ***falscher ~*** false prophet; ***ich bin doch kein ~*** I can't read the stars; ***der ~ gilt nichts in s-m eigenen Lande*** a prophet is not without hono(u)r save in his own country; **Pro'phe·ten·ga·be** *f* prophetic powers *pl.*, powers *pl.* (*or* gift) of prophecy; ***man braucht keine ~, um das zu sehen*** you don't have to be a prophet to see that; **pro·phe·tisch** [pro'fe:tɪʃ] *adj.* prophetic(ally *adv.*); ***~e Gabe*** → ***Prophetengabe***

pro·phe·zei·en [profe'tsaɪən] *v/t.* (h) prophesy; predict, forecast; ***j-m Reichtum ~*** prophesy that s.o. will become rich; F ***das hab' ich dir doch prophezeit*** I told you so, didn't I?

Pro·phe'zei·ung *f* (-; -en) prophecy; prediction, forecast

pro·phy·lak·tisch [profy'laktɪʃ] *adj.* prophylactic, preventive; **Pro·phy·la·xe** [profy'laksə] *f* (-; -n) prophylaxis; ***zur ~ gegen*** *acc.* as a precaution against

Pro·por·ti·on [propɔr'tsi̯o:n] *f* (-; -en) proportion; ***besorgniserregende ~en annehmen*** take on alarming proportions

pro·por·tio·nal [propɔrtsi̯o'na:l] *adj.* proportional; ***umgekehrt ~*** inversely proportional (***zu*** *dat.* to); **Pro·por·tio'nal-schrift** *f* proportional spacing

pro·por·tio·niert [propɔrtsi̯o'ni:ɐt] *adj.*: (***gut ~*** well-)proportioned

Pro·porz [pro'pɔrts] *m* (-es; -e) proportional representation

prop·pen'voll ['prɔpən-] F *adj.* F jam-packed, chock-a-block

Propst [pro:pst] *m* (-[e]s; Pröpste ['prø:p-stə] *eccl.* provost

Pro·sa ['pro:za] *f* (-; *no pl.*) prose; **~dich-tung** *f* **1.** prosework, work of prose; *coll.* prose writing; **2.** prose poem; *coll.* prose poetry; **~er·zäh·lung** *f* prose narrative; **~ge·dicht** *n* prose poem; *pl. a.* prose poetry *sg.*

Pro·sai·ker [pro'za:ikɐ] *fig. m* (-s; -) matter-of-fact (sort of) person

pro·sa·isch [pro'za:ɪʃ] *adj.* prosaic(ally *adv.*); *fig.* down-to-earth, matter-of-fact; mundane

Pro·sa·ist [proza'ɪst] *m* (-en; -en) prose writer

'Pro·sa|text *m* prose text; *pl. a.* prose writings; **~über͵set·zung** *f* prose translation

Pro·se·lyt [proze'ly:t] *m* (-en; -en) proselyte; **Pro·se'ly·ten·ma·cher** *m* proselytizer

Pro·se·mi·nar ['pro:zemina:ɐ] *n* (-s; -e [-rə]) *univ.* (introductory) seminar

pro·sit ['pro:zɪt] *int.* your health!, F cheers!; ***~ Neujahr!*** happy New Year!; **'Pro·sit** *n* (-s; -s) toast; ***ein ~ ausbringen auf*** *acc.* toast *s.o.*

Pro·spekt [pro'spɛkt] *m* (-[e]s; -e) **1.** brochure, leaflet; **2.** prospect

prost [pro:st] *int.* cheers!; → ***Mahlzeit***

Pro·sta·ta ['prɔstata] *f* (-; *no pl.*) *anat.* prostate (gland); **~krebs** *m* cancer of the prostate; **~ver·grö·ße·rung** *f* enlargement of the prostate (gland); enlarged prostate

pro·sti·tu·ie·ren [prostitu'i:rən] *v/refl.* (h): ***sich ~*** prostitute o.s.; **Pro·sti·tu·ier-te** [prostitu'i:ɐtə] *f* (-n; -n) prostitute; **Pro·sti·tu·ti·on** [prostitu'tsi̯o:n] *f* (-; *no pl.*) prostitution

Pro·sze·ni·um [pro'tse:ni̯ʊm] *n* (-s; -nien) *thea.* proscenium

Pro·ta·go·nist [protago'nɪst] *m* (-en; -en) protagonist; *fig. a.* champion (*gen.* of)

Pro·te·gé [prote'ʒe:] *m* (-s; -s) protégé(e *f*); **pro·te·gie·ren** [prote'ʒi:rən] *v/t.* (h) sponsor, promote

Pro·te·in [prote'iːn] *n* (-s; -e) protein **pro·te'in·reich** *adj.* high (*or* rich) in protein, high-protein ...

Pro·tek·ti·on [protɛk'tsĭoːn] *f* (-; *no pl.*) patronage, sponsorship; **Pro·tek·tio·nis·mus** [protɛktsĭo'nɪsmʊs] *m* protectionism; **pro·tek·tio·ni·stisch** [protɛktsĭo'nɪstɪʃ] *adj.* protectionist; **Pro·tek·ti'ons·wirt·schaft** *f* favo(u)ritism

Pro·tek·tor [pro'tɛktoːɐ] *m* (-s; -en [protɛk'toːrən]) protector; patron

Pro·tek·to·rat [protɛkto'raːt] *n* (-s; -e) protectorate; patronage; ***unter dem ~*** (*gen. or* ***von*** *dat.*) under the auspices of

Pro·test [pro'tɛst] *m* (-[e]s; -e) protest; ***öffentlicher ~*** *a.* public outcry; ***aus ~ gegen*** *acc.* in (*or* as a) protest against, in protest at; ***gegen et. ~ erheben*** protest against s.th., make a protest against s.th.; ***aus ~ weggehen*** leave in protest; ***aus ~ den Saal verlassen*** walk out (in protest); ⚚ ***e-n Wechsel zu ~ gehen lassen*** protest a bill; **~ak·ti͵on** *f* (public) protest; protest campaign

Pro·te·stant [protɛs'tant] *m* (-en; -en), **Pro·te·stan·tin** [protɛs'tantɪn] *f* (-; -nen), **pro·te·stan·tisch** [protɛs'tantɪʃ] *adj.* Protestant; **Pro·te·stan·tis·mus** [protɛstan'tɪsmʊs] *m* (-; *no pl.*) Protestantism

Pro'test|be·we·gung *f* protest movement; **~ge·schrei** *n* howls *pl.* of protest; **~hal·tung** *f* rebellious attitude

pro·te·stie·ren [protɛs'tiːrən] *v/i.* (h) protest (***gegen*** *acc.* [against] *s.th.*); ***er protestiert dagegen, daß*** he's protesting against the fact that

Pro'test|kund·ge·bung *f* protest rally, demonstration; **~lied** *n* protest song; **~marsch** *m* protest march; **~no·te** *f pol.* protest note; **~sän·ger** *m* protest singer; **~schrei·ben** *n* written protest; letter of protest; **~sturm** *m* storm of protest, public outcry; **~wäh·ler** *m* protest voter; **~wel·le** *f* wave of protest

Pro·the·se [pro'teːzə] *f* (-; -n) **1.** artificial limb (*or* arm, leg); **2.** dentures *pl.*; **Pro'the·sen·trä·ger** *m* **1.** person with an artificial limb; **2.** denture-wearer

Pro·to·koll [proto'kɔl] *n* (-s; -e) **1.** minutes *pl.*; **(*das*) *~ führen*** take (down) the minutes; ***ins ~ aufnehmen*** take down (in the minutes); ⚖ ***et. zu ~ geben*** give evidence of s.th., state s.th. in evidence; ***et. zu ~ nehmen*** take s.th. down in evidence, put s.th. on record; **2.** (***diplomatisches ~***) protocol; **3.** *dial.* ticket; **4.** *computer*: log; **pro·to·kol·la·risch** [protokɔ'laːrɪʃ] **I.** *adj.* **1.** recorded; ⚖ ***~e Aussage*** statement given in evidence; **2.** *pol.* ***~e Bestimmungen*** rules of protocol; **II.** *adv.*: ***~ festhalten*** take down (in the minutes), ⚖ take down as evidence

Pro·to'koll·füh·rer *m* minute-taker; ⚖ clerk of the court; ***wer ist ~?*** who's taking the minutes?

pro·to·kol·lie·ren [protokɔ'liːrən] (h) **I.** *v/t.* take down (in the minutes); take the minutes of (*or* at) *a meeting etc.*; ⚖ take down (on record); record *a hearing etc.*; **II.** *v/i.* take the minutes; ⚖ take the record

Pro·to·zo·on [proto'tsoːɔn] *n* (-s; -zoen) protozoon

Protz [prɔts] F *m* (-es; -e) F show-off; **prot·zen** ['prɔtsən] F *v/i.* (h) show off (***mit*** *dat.* [with] *s.th.*); ***er protzt gern mit s-m Geld*** he likes to flash his money around; **Prot·ze·rei** [prɔtsə'raɪ] F *f* (-; *no pl.*) showing off; **prot·zig** ['prɔtsɪç] F **I.** *adj.* ostentatious; F showy, swanky; F flash(y) *car*; **II.** *adv.* ostentatiously; ***er gab dem Kellner ~ e-n Fünfzigmarkschein*** *a.* he made a (big) show of giving the waiter a fifty-mark note (*Am.* bill)

Pro·ve·ni·enz [prove'nĭɛnts] *f* (-; -en) origin, provenance; ***Waren italienischer ~*** goods of Italian origin; ***unbekannter ~*** of unknown origin

Pro·vi·ant [pro'vĭant] *m* (-s; -e) provisions *pl.*, food; ⚔ rations *pl.*, food supply, supplies *pl.*

Pro·vinz [pro'vɪnts] *f* (-; -en) **1.** province (*a. fig.*); **2.** *no pl. the* provinces *pl.*; ***aus der ~ stammen*** come from the provinces (*or* country); *contp.* ***das ist ja hier tiefste ~*** what a backwater this is; ***sie leben in der hintersten ~*** F they live at the back of beyond; **~blatt** *n* backwoods newspaper, F local rag; **~haupt·stadt** *f* provincial centre (*Am.* center)

Pro·vin·zia·lis·mus [provɪntsĭa'lɪsmʊs] *m* (-; *no pl.*) provincialism

pro·vin·zi·ell [provɪn'tsĭɛl] *adj.* provincial

Pro·vinz·ler [pro'vɪntslɐ] *m* (-s; -) provincial, F country yokel; **pro·vinz·le·risch** [pro'vɪntslərɪʃ] *adj.* provincial

Pro'vinz|nest F *n* backwater, F hick town, one-horse town; **~stadt** *f* provincial town

Pro·vi·si·on [provi'zĭoːn] *f* (-; -en) ⚚ commission; ***auf ~*** on commission

Pro·vi·si'ons·ba·sis *f*: ***auf ~*** on commission, on a commission basis

pro·vi·so·risch [provi'zoːrɪʃ] **I.** *adj.* provisional, temporary; makeshift ...; ***~e Lösung*** stopgap solution; ***~e Regierung*** caretaker (*or* provisional) government; **II.** *adv.*: ***et. ~ reparieren*** do a makeshift job on s.th., patch s.th. up for the time being; **Pro·vi·so·ri·um** [provi'zoːrĭʊm] *n* (-s; -rien) provisional (*or* temporary) arrangement, stopgap

pro·vo·kant [provo'kant] *adj.* provocative; **Pro·vo·ka·teur** [provoka'tøːɐ] *m* (-s; -e [-rə]) troublemaker, agent provocateur; **Pro·vo·ka·ti·on** [provoka'tsĭoːn] *f* (-; -en) provocation; **pro·vo·ka·tiv** [provoka'tiːf] *adj.*, **pro·vo·ka·to·risch** [provoka'toːrɪʃ] *adj.* provocative

pro·vo·zie·ren [provo'tsiːrən] (h) **I.** *v/t.* a) provoke, b) torment *animals*; **~d** provocative; **II.** *v/i.* provoke; ***er will nur ~*** he's just trying to provoke (*or* be provocative)

Pro·ze·de·re [pro'tseːdərə] *n* (-; -) procedure

Pro·ze·dur [protse'duːɐ] *f* (-; -en [-rən]) procedure, process; F ***das war vielleicht e-e ~!*** what an ordeal (that was)

Pro·zent [pro'tsɛnt] *n* per cent, percent; ***~e*** percentage, a discount; ***zu fünf ~*** at five per cent (*or* percent); ***wieviel ~ Zinsen kriegt man? - fünf*** what's the interest rate? - five per cent (*or* percent); ***hast du ~e bekommen?*** did you get (*or* did they give you) a discount?; ***ich kann Ihnen zehn ~ geben*** I can knock off ten per cent (*or* percent)

pro·zen·tig [pro'tsɛntɪç] *adj.*: ***...~ in cpds.*** ... per cent (*or* percent)

Pro'zent|punkt *m* per cent, percent; ***sie haben sich bei der Wahl um fünf ~e verbessert*** they've gained another (*or* an extra) five per cent (*or* percent) of the vote; **~rech·nung** *f* percentages *pl.*; **~satz** *m* percentage

pro·zen·tu·al [protsɛn'tŭaːl] *adj.* proportional; ***~er Anteil*** percentage

Pro·zeß [pro'tsɛs] *m* (-sses; -sse) **1.** process; → ***Entwicklungsprozeß, Lernprozeß***; **2.** ⚖ lawsuit; trial; ***e-n ~ gewinnen*** (***verlieren***) win (lose) one's case; ***gegen j-n e-n ~ anstrengen*** bring an action against s.o., sue s.o.; ***in e-n ~ mit j-m verwickelt sein*** be involved in a lawsuit with s.o.; ***j-m den ~ machen*** take s.o. to court; *fig.* ***mit j-m (et.) kurzen ~ machen*** make short work of s.o. (s.th.)

pro'zeß|fä·hig *adj.* capable of suing or being sued; **~freu·dig** *adj.* litigious

Pro'zeß·geg·ner *m* opposing party

pro·zes·sie·ren [protsɛ'siːrən] *v/i.* (h) go to court; ***gegen j-n ~*** bring an action against s.o., take s.o. to court

Pro·zes·si·on [protsɛ'sĭoːn] *f* (-; -en) procession

Pro'zeß·ko·sten *pl.* legal costs; **~hil·fe** *f* legal aid

Pro·zes·sor [pro'tsɛsoːɐ] *m* (-s; -en [protsɛ'soːrən]) *computer*: processor

Pro'zeß|recht *n* adjective (*or* procedural) law; **~steue·rung** *f computer*: process control; **≈un·fä·hig** *adj.* ⚖ incapable of suing or being sued; **~voll·macht** *f* power of attorney

prü·de ['pryːdə] *adj.* prudish; ***ich bin (ja) nicht ~*** I'm no prude; ***tu doch nicht so ~*** don't be such a prude; **Prü·de·rie** [pryːdə'riː] *f* (-; *no pl.*) prudishness, prudery

Prüf·au·to͵mat ['pryːf-] *m* (automatic) testing equipment

prü·fen ['pryːfən] (h) **I.** *v/t.* a) *ped.* examine, test, give *s.o.* an exam (*or* test), b) check, test, c) try (out), (put to the) test; ⚙ inspect; *metall.* assay, d) examine, study; investigate, look into *a complaint, an incident etc.*; consider, have a close look at *a proposal etc.*; ⚚ audit; ⚖ review; (***auf Richtigkeit***) ~ verify, check; *der Antrag* ***wird geprüft*** is under consideration; ***j-s Russischkenntnisse ~*** test s.o.'s knowledge of Russian, give s.o. a Russian test; ***damit wird logisches Denken geprüft*** it's a test of logic; ***et. auf s-e Echtheit hin ~*** check to see whether s.th. is genuine (*or* authentic); ***j-n auf sein Reaktionsvermögen hin ~*** test s.o.'s reactions; ***er ist vom Leben schwer geprüft*** he hasn't been spared much in life; **II.** *v/i.* examine; ***er prüft sehr streng*** he's a tough examiner; ***es wird schriftlich und mündlich geprüft*** there will be a written and an oral test (*or* exam); **III.** *v/refl.*: ***sich ~*** do some soul-searching; **'prü·fend** *adj.*: ***~er Blick*** searching look; **Prü·fer** ['pryːfɐ] *m* (-s; -) *ped.* examiner; ⚙ *etc.* tester; inspector; *metall.* assayer; ⚚ auditor

'Prüf·ge·rät *n* testing apparatus

Prüf·ling ['pryːflɪŋ] *m* (-s; -e) **1.** *ped.* candidate; **2.** ⚙ (test) specimen

'Prüf|mu·ster *n* specimen; **~spit·ze** *f* ⚡ probe; **~stand** *m* ⚙ test bench, *mot. a.* test block; *fig.* ***auf dem ~ stehen*** be under close scrutiny, be on trial; ***es steht auf dem ~*** *a.* it's being put to the test, it's being tried and tested; **~stein** *fig. m* touchstone (***für*** *acc.* of); **~stück** *n* specimen

Prü·fung ['pryːfʊŋ] *f* (-; -en) **1.** *ped.* (***mündliche*** oral, ***schriftliche*** written) examination, exam; test (*a. fig.*); →

ablegen 5, ***abnehmen*** 4, ***bestehen*** 1; **2.** examination, investigation; scrutiny; verification, check(ing); ⚙ inspection; ☿ audit; ⚖ review; **3.** a) ⚙ trial, test, b) *fig.* trial, ordeal, c) *sport*: event

'Prü·fungs|an·for·de·run·gen *pl.* examination requirements; **~angst** *f* exam nerves *pl.*; **~ar·beit** *f*, **~auf·ga·be** *f* exam(ination) paper; **~aus·schuß** *m* board of examiners, examining board; review board; **~er·geb·nis** *n* examination results *pl.*; ⚙ test result; **~fach** *n* exam subject; **~fahrt** *f mot.* **1.** test drive; **2.** driving test; **~fra·ge** *f* (exam) question; **~kan·di͵dat** *m* (exam) candidate; **~kom·mis·si͵on** *f* → ***Prüfungsausschuß***; **~no·te** *f* exam mark; ***was hast du für e-e ~ bekommen?*** what mark (*Am.* grade) did you get in the exam?; **~ord·nung** *f* exam(ination) regulations *pl.*; **~ter͵min** *m* **1.** exam(ination) date; **2.** ⚖ meeting of creditors; **~ver·fah·ren** *n* **1.** *ped.* exam(ination) procedure; **2.** test (*or* testing) method; **~zeug·nis** *n* certificate, diploma

Prü·gel ['pry:gəl] *m* (-s; -) **1.** cudgel; **2.** *fig. pl.* (*a.* ***Tracht ~***) (good) hiding *sg.*

Prü·ge·lei [pry:gə'laɪ] *f* (-; -en) brawl, F scrap, free-for-all

'Prü·gel·kna·be *m* scapegoat, F fall guy

'prü·geln *v/t.* beat; ***sich ~*** (have a) fight; ***sich ~ um*** *acc.* fight over

'Prü·gel·stra·fe *f* corporal punishment

Prunk [prʊŋk] *m* (-[e]s; *no pl.*) splendo(u)r, magnificence; pageantry; pomp; **~bett** *n* bed of state

prun·ken ['prʊŋkən] *v/i.* (h) be resplendent; ***~ mit*** *dat.* flaunt, boast about

'Prunk·ge·mach *n* state apartment

'prunk·lie·bend *adj.*: ***der ~e König Ludwig XIV.*** Louis XIV with his love of pomp (and splendo[u]r)

'prunk·los *adj.* plain, unostentatious

'Prunk·stück *n* showpiece

'prunk·süch·tig *adj.* ostentatious

'prunk·voll *adj.* splendid, magnificent

pru·sten ['pru:stən] *v/i.* (h) a) snort, b) pant, gasp for air; ***vor Lachen ~*** snort with laughter; ***er kam ~d angelaufen*** he came panting along

PS¹ [pe:'ʔɛs] *n* (-; -) PS

PS² [pe:'ʔɛs] *n* (-; -) *mot.* horsepower (*abbr.* HP)

Psalm [psalm] *m* (-s; -en) psalm

Psal·mist [psal'mɪst] *m* (-en; -en) psalmist

Psal·ter ['psaltɐ] *m* (-s; -) psalter; *bibl.* ***der ~*** (the Book of) Psalms

Pseu·do..., pseu·do... ['psɔʏdo-] *in cpds.* pseudo..., mock ...

'Pseu·do·krupp *m* ⚕ mild croup

Pseu·do·nym [psɔʏdo'ny:m] *n* (-s; -e) pseudonym; pen name, nom de plume

'Pseu·do·wis·sen·schaft *f* pseudoscience; **'pseu·do·wis·sen·schaft·lich** *adj.* pseudoscientific

PS-stark [pe:'ʔɛs-] *adj.* high-horsepower, high-HP

pst [pst] *int.* **1.** ssh!; **2.** pst!

Psy·che ['psy:çə] *f* (-; -n) psyche; psychological makeup; mental state; state of mind; soul; (human) ego

Psy·chia·ter [psy'çĭa:tɐ] *m* (-s; -) psychiatrist; **Psy·chia·trie** [psyçĭa'tri:] *f* (-; -n) **1.** *no pl.* psychiatry; **2.** psychiatric ward; **psy·chia·trisch** [psy'çĭa:trɪʃ] *adj.* psychiatric

psy·chisch ['psy:çɪʃ] **I.** *adj.* psychological; mental; emotional; ***~e Belastung*** mental strain; ***~e Krankheit*** mental disease; **II.** *adv.*: ***~ bedingt*** psychological, F all in the mind; ***~ belastet*** under mental strain; ***~ krank*** mentally disturbed

Psy·cho·ana'ly·se [psyço-] *f* psychoanalysis; ***sich e-r ~ unterziehen*** have (*or* go for) psychoanalysis; **Psy·cho·ana'ly·ti·ker** *m* psychoanalyst, F analyst; *sl.* shrink; **psy·cho·ana'ly·tisch I.** *adj.* psychoanalytic(al); **II.** *adv.*: ***~ behandeln*** psychoanalyze

Psy·cho'dra·ma [psyço-] *n thea. and psych.* psychodrama

psy·cho·gen [psyço'ge:n] *adj.* psychogenic(ally *adv.*)

Psy·cho·gramm [psyço'gram] *n* (-s; -e) (personality) profile

Psy·cho·kri·mi ['psy:ço-] *m* psychological thriller

Psy·cho·lo·ge [psyço'lo:gə] *m* (-n; -n) psychologist; **Psy·cho·lo·gie** [psyçolo'gi:] *f* (-; *no pl.*) **1.** psychology; **2.** psychological insight; **psy·cho·lo·gisch** [psyço'lo:gɪʃ] **I.** *adj.* psychological; **II.** *adv.* psychologically, from a psychological point of view; ***~ hast du richtig gehandelt*** you did the right thing psychologically; **psy·cho·lo·gi·sie·ren** [psyçologi'zi:rən] *v/t.* (h) psychologize

Psy·cho·path [psyço'pa:t] *m* (-en; -en) psychopath; **psy·cho·pa·thisch** [psyço'pa:tɪʃ] *adj.* psychopathic

Psy·cho'phar·ma·ka [psyço-] *pl.* psychiatric (*or* mind) drugs

Psy·cho·se [psy'ço:zə] *f* (-; -n) psychosis (*a. fig.*)

psy·cho·so'ma·tisch [psyço-] *adj.* psychosomatic(ally *adv.*)

Psy·cho·ter·ror ['psy:ço-] *m* psychological blackmail

Psy·cho·the·ra'peut [psyço-] *m* psychotherapist; **psy·cho·the·ra'peu·tisch** *adj.* psychotherapeutic; ***~e Behandlung*** psychotherapy; **Psy·cho·the·ra'pie** *f* psychotherapy

Psy·cho·thril·ler ['psy:ço-] *m* psychological thriller

Psy·cho·ti·ker [psy'ço:tikɐ] *m* (-s; -) psychotic; **psy·cho·tisch** [psy'ço:tɪʃ] *adj.* psychotic(ally *adv.*)

pu·ber·tär [pubɛr'tɛ:ɐ] *adj.* adolescent; ***~e Probleme*** problems of adolescence; ***~er Junge*** boy in puberty; ***es ist nur e-e ~e Erscheinung*** it's all part of puberty

Pu·ber·tät [pubɐr'tɛ:t] *f* (-; *no pl.*) puberty, adolescence; ***in die ~ kommen*** reach (the age of) puberty; **Pu·ber'täts·jah·re** *pl.* (time of) puberty *sg.*

pu·ber·tie·ren [pubɛr'ti:rən] *v/i.* (h) be going through puberty

Pu·bli·ci·ty [pa'blɪsiti] *f* (-; *no pl.*) publicity; exposure

pu·blik [pu'bli:k] *adj.* public; ***~ machen*** publicize; ***die Sache ist längst ~*** everybody knows about it

Pu·bli·ka·ti·on [publika'tsĭo:n] *f* (-; -en) publication

Pu·bli·ka·ti'ons|rech·te *pl.* publication rights, rights of publication; **~ver·bot** *n* ban on publication; ***e-n Autor mit ~ belegen*** ban an author from publishing his works

Pu·bli·kum ['pu:blikʊm] *n* (-s; *no pl.*) **1.** *the* public; **2.** a) audience, *radio*: *a.* listeners *pl.*, b) *sport*: spectators *pl.*, crowd, c) readers *pl.*; ***er ist beim ~ gut angekommen*** the audience loved him; **3.** clientele; ***gemischtes ~*** a mixed crowd

'Pu·bli·kums|er·folg *m* great success, hit; **~ge·schmack** *m* popular taste; **~lieb·ling** *m* favo(u)rite; **~ma͵gnet** *m* crowd-puller; **~ver·kehr** *m* **1.** ***~ haben*** be open (to the public); ***keinen ~ haben*** be closed (for business); ***~ von 9 bis 12*** opening hours 9 to 12; **2.** ***~ haben*** deal directly with the public (*or* with customers); ***heute ist aber viel ~*** there's a lot of coming and going today

'pu·bli·kums·wirk·sam *adj.* popular; ***~ sein*** *a.* have public appeal, appeal to the public

pu·bli·zie·ren [publi'tsi:rən] *v/t.* (h) publish; **Pu·bli·zist** [publi'tsɪst] *m* (-en; -en) journalist; **Pu·bli·zi·stik** [publi'tsɪstɪk] *f* (-; *no pl.*) journalism; **pu·bli·zi·stisch** [publi'tsɪstɪʃ] *adj.* journalistic

Pu·bli·zi·tät [publitsi'tɛ:t] *f* (-; *no pl.*) publicity

Puck [pʊk] *m* (-s; -s) *ice hockey*: puck

Pud·ding ['pʊdɪŋ] *m* (-s; -e, -s) a) blancmange, b) pudding; F *fig.* ***das sind doch keine Muskeln, das ist nur ~*** that's not muscle, that's just flab; **~pul·ver** *n* pudding mixture

Pu·del ['pu:dəl] *m* (-s; -) poodle; F ***wie ein begossener ~ dastehen*** look (quite) crestfallen; *fig.* ***das also ist des ~s Kern*** so that's what it's all about; **~müt·ze** *f* woolly hat

'pu·del|'nackt F *adj.* stark naked, F starkers; ***er war ~*** *a.* F he didn't have a stitch on; **~'naß** F *adj.* soaking wet, drenched, soaked to the skin; **~'wohl** F *adj.*: ***sich ~ fühlen*** F feel great, feel on top of the world

Pu·der ['pu:dɐ] *m* (-s; -) powder; **~do·se** *f* powder compact

pu·dern ['pu:dɐn] *v/t.* (h) powder (***sich*** one's face)

'Pu·der|qua·ste *f* powder puff; **~zucker** *m* icing (*Am.* confectioner's) sugar

puff [pʊf] *int.* bang!

Puff¹ [pʊf] F *m* (-s; -s) brothel

Puff² *m* (-[e]s; Püffe ['pʏfə]) **1.** thump; poke, F dig (in the ribs); nudge; *fig.* ***er kann schon e-n ~ vertragen*** he can take a knock; **2.** bang, pop

Puff³ *m* (-[e]s; -s) linen basket

'Puff·är·mel *m* puffed sleeve

puf·fen ['pʊfən] (h) **I.** *v/t.* thump, jostle; poke *s.o.* in the ribs, nudge; **II.** *v/i.* 🚂 puff

Puf·fer ['pʊfɐ] *m* (-s; -) **1.** 🚂, *computer and fig.*: buffer; **2.** → ***Kartoffelpuffer***; **~bat·te͵rie** *f* buffer battery

puf·fern ['pʊfɐn] *v/t.* (h) buffer

'Puf·fer|staat *m* buffer state; **~vor·rä·te** *pl.* buffer stock *sg.*; **~zo·ne** *f* buffer zone

'Puff·mais *m* popcorn

'Puff·mut·ter F *f* madam

'Puff·reis *m* puffed rice

puh [pu:] *int.* **1.** phew!; **2.** poo!

pu·len ['pu:lən] *dial.* *v/i.* (h): ***~ an*** *dat.* pick at; ***~ in*** *dat.* poke around in; ***in der Nase ~*** *a.* pick one's nose

Pulk [pʊlk] *m* (-[e]s; -s, -e) crowd, *a. sport*: bunch; *mot.* group, convoy; ✈ group

Pul·le ['pʊlə] F *f* (-; -n) bottle; *fig.* ***volle ~ fahren*** F drive flat out; ***die Anlage volle ~ aufdrehen*** F turn the stereo up full blast; ***volle ~ schreien*** scream at the top of one's voice; ***volle ~ spielen*** play for what one is worth

pul·len ['pʊlən] *v/t. and v/i.* (h) row

pul·lern ['pʊlɐn] *dial.* *v/i.* (h) F piddle

Pul·li ['pʊli] F *m* (-s; -s), **Pull·over**

[pʊ'loːvɐ] *m* (-s; -) sweater, pullover, *Brit. a.* jumper
Pull·un·der [pʊ'lʊndɐ] *m* (-s; -) tank top
Puls [pʊls] *m* (-es; *no pl.*) pulse; ***hoher (niedriger)*** ~ high (low) pulse rate; ***j-m den ~ fühlen*** feel s.o.'s pulse, *fig.* sound s.o. out; **~ader** *f* artery
Pul·sar [pʊl'zaːɐ] *m* (-s; -e [-rə]) *astr.* pulsar
'**Puls·fre,quenz** *f* pulse rate
pul·sie·ren [pʊl'ziːrən] *v/i.* (h) pulsate (*a. fig.*); *pain*: throb; *fig.* ~ ***mit*** *dat.* throb (*or* pulsate, vibrate) with; *fig.* **~d** pulsating, vibrant
'**Puls|schlag** *m* pulse (beat); pulse rate; *fig.* vibrancy; *fig.* ~ ***der Großstadt*** *a.* pulsating city life; **~zahl** *f* pulse rate
Pult [pʊlt] *n* (-[e]s; -e) a) desk, b) lectern
Pul·ver ['pʊlvɐ] *n* (-s; -) a) powder, b) (gun)powder, c) F *fig.* F cash, *sl.* brass, bread; *fig.* ***er hat das ~ nicht erfunden*** F he's not exactly an Einstein; ***sein ~ verschossen haben*** have shot one's bolt; ***es (er) ist keinen Schuß ~ wert*** it's not worth a bean (he's useless); **~faß** *n* powder keg (*a. fig.*); *fig.* ***auf e-m ~ sitzen*** be sitting on top of a volcano
'**pul·ver·för·mig** [-fœrmɪç] *adj.* powdered ..., in powder form
pul·ve·ri·sie·ren [pʊlveri'ziːrən] *v/t.* (h) pulverize
'**Pul·ver|kaf,fee** *m* instant coffee; **~schnee** *m* powder snow
pulv·rig ['pʊlvrɪç] *adj.* powdery
Pu·ma ['puːma] *m* (-s; -s) *zo.* puma
Pum·mel ['pʊməl] F *m* F roly-poly
pum·me·lig ['pʊməlɪç] F *adj.* F dumpy, chubby
Pump [pʊmp] F *m*: ***auf ~ kaufen*** F buy on tick
Pum·pe ['pʊmpə] *f* (-; -n) **1.** pump; **2.** F ticker; '**pum·pen** *v/t. and v/i.* (h) **1.** pump (***in*** *acc.* into); **2.** F lend, *esp. Am.* loan; ***sich et.*** ~ borrow s.th. (***bei j-m*** from *or* F off s.o.); ***kannst du mir ein bißchen Geld ~?*** F can you lend me a bit of cash?; **3.** F do press-ups, *a. Am.* do push-ups
Pum·per·nickel ['pʊmpɐnɪkəl] (*sep.* -k·k-) *m* (-s; *no pl.*) pumpernickel
'**Pump·ho·se** *f* baggy trousers *pl.*
Pumps [pœmps] *m* (-; -) court shoe
'**Pump·spray** *m, n* pump-action spray; atomizer
Pun·ker ['paŋkɐ] *m* (-s; -) punk; **~haar·schnitt** *m* punk hairstyle
Punk·rock ['paŋk-] *m* punk rock
Punkt ['pʊŋkt] *m* (-[e]s; -e) a) dot, spot, b) *ling.* full stop, *Am.* period, c) ♪ point, d) point, place, spot, e) item, point; subject, topic; position, f) *sport etc.*: point; ***e-n ~ machen (or setzen)*** put a full stop (*Am.* period); ***~e und Striche*** dots and dashes; ***ein kleiner ~ am Horizont*** a tiny dot (*or* a speck) on the horizon; *fig.* ***dunkler ~*** dark chapter, skeleton in the cupboard (*Am.* closet); ***der springende ~*** the point; ***wunder ~*** sore point; ***e-n schwachen ~ treffen*** find a weak spot; ***~ für ~*** point by point; ***~ zehn Uhr*** ten o'clock sharp; ***bis zu e-m gewissen ~*** up to a point; ***in vielen ~en*** in many respects; ***in diesem ~ sind wir uns einig*** we agree on that point; ***e-n ~ hinter et. setzen*** bring s.th. to an end, settle s.th. (once and for all); ***ohne ~ und Komma reden*** talk nineteen to the dozen; ***nach ~en siegen (verlieren)*** *sport*: win (lose) on points; F ***nun mach mal e-n ~!*** F give it a break; → ***neuralgisch, strittig, tot***
punk·ten ['pʊŋktən] *v/i.* (h) *sport* a) collect (*or* pick up) points, b) award points
'**punkt·gleich** *adj.* level (on points); '**Punkt·gleich·heit** *f*: ***bei ~ entscheidet die Tordifferenz*** if teams are level on points, goal difference decides
punk·tie·ren [pʊŋk'tiːrən] *v/t.* (h) **1.** *a.* ♪ dot; ***punktierte Linie*** dotted line; **2.** ⚕ puncture; **Punk'tie·rung** *f* (-; -en) **1.** dotting; **2.** → **Punk·ti·on** [pʊŋk'tsi̯oːn] *f* (-; -en) ⚕ puncture
'**Punkt·lan·dung** *f* precision landing
pünkt·lich ['pʏŋktlɪç] **I.** *adj.* punctual; **II.** *adv.* punctually, on time; ***~ um 10 Uhr*** at ten o'clock sharp; '**Pünkt·lich·keit** *f* (-; *no pl.*) punctuality
'**Punkt|nie·der·la·ge** *f* defeat on points; **~rich·ter** *m sport*: judge; **~sieg** *m* win on points; **~sie·ger** *m* winner on points; **~strah·ler** *m* spot(light); **~sy,stem** *n* points system
punk·tu·ell [pʊŋk'tu̯ɛl] **I.** *adj.* selective; **II.** *adv.* selectively; point by point; ***~ Wirkung zeigen*** have its effect in places (*or* here and there)
'**Punk·tum:** ***und damit ~!*** and that's that
'**Punkt|wer·tung** *f* **1.** points system; **2.** → **~zahl** *f* score
Punsch [pʊnʃ] *m* (-es; -e) punch
Punz·ar·beit ['pʊnts-] *f* embossing
Pup [puːp] F *m* (-[e]s; -e) F guff, V fart; **pu·pen** ['puːpən] F *v/i.* (h) F let off
Pu·pil·le [pu'pɪlə] *f* (-; -n) pupil
Pu'pil·len|er·wei·te·rung *f* **1.** dilation of the pupil(s); **2.** enlarged pupil(s); **~ver·en·gung** *f* **1.** contraction of the pupil(s); **2.** contracted pupil(s)
Püpp·chen ['pʏpçən] *n* (-s; -) litte doll
Pup·pe ['pʊpə] *f* (-; -n) a) doll (*a.* F *fig. girl*), b) *a. fig.* puppet, marionette, c) dummy, mannequin, d) *zo.* pupa, chrysalis; cocoon; F *fig.* ***bis in die ~n schlafen*** sleep till all hours; F ***bis in die ~n feiern*** celebrate into the small hours; F ***alle ~n tanzen lassen*** F live it up, have a fling
'**Pup·pen|ge·sicht** *n* doll's face; **~haus** *n* doll's house; **~kli·nik** *f* doll's hospital; **~spiel** *n* puppet show; **~stu·be** *f* doll's house; **~thea·ter** *n* **1.** puppet theat|re (*Am. a.* -er); **2.** → ***Puppenspiel***; **~wa·gen** *m* doll's pram, *Am.* doll carriage
Pups [puːps] F *m* (-es; -e) → ***Pup***
pup·sen ['puːpsən] F *v/i.* → ***pupen***
Pup·ser ['puːpsɐ] F *m* (-s; -) → ***Pup***
pur [puːɐ] *adj.* pure; sheer; ***~er Unsinn*** pure nonsense; ***es war ~er Zufall*** it was sheer (*or* pure) coincidence; ***aus ~er Neugier (Bosheit)*** from sheer curiosity (out of sheer malice); ***Whisky ~*** neat (*Am.* straight) whisk(e)y; ***s-n Whisky ~ trinken*** drink one's whisk(e)y neat (*Am.* straight)
Pü·ree [py'reː] *n* (-s; -s) puree, mash
pü·rie·ren [py'riːrən] *v/t.* (h) *gastr.* mash, puree
pu·ri·fi·zie·ren [purifi'tsiːrən] *v/t.* (h) purify; **Pu·ri·fi'zie·rung** *f* (-; -en) purification
Pu·ris·mus [pu'rɪsmʊs] *m* (-; *no pl.*) purism; **Pu·rist** [pu'rɪst] *m* (-en; -en) purist; **pu·ri·stisch** [pu'rɪstɪʃ] *adj.* purist(ic)
Pu·ri·ta·ner [puri'taːnɐ] *m* (-s; -), **Pu·ri·ta·ne·rin** [puri'taːnərɪn] *f* (-; -nen) **1.** Puritan; **2.** *fig.* puritan; **pu·ri·ta·nisch** [puri'taːnɪʃ] *adj.* **1.** Puritan; **2.** *fig.* puritanical; **Pu·ri·ta·nis·mus** [purita'nɪsmʊs] *m* (-; *no pl.*) *hist.* Puritanism
Pur·pur ['pʊrpʊr] *m* (-s; *no pl.*), '**pur·purn** *adj.*, '**pur·pur·rot** *adj.* crimson
Pur·zel·baum ['pʊrtsəl-] *m* forward roll, somersault; ***e-n ~ schlagen*** do a forward roll (*or* somersault)
pur·zeln ['pʊrtsəln] *v/i.* (sn) *a. fig.* fall, tumble; ***aus dem Bett ~*** *a.* roll out of bed
pu·shen ['pʊʃən] *v/t.* (h) push *drugs*
Pu·sher ['pʊʃɐ] *m* (-s; -) (drugs) pusher
Pus·sel·ar·beit ['pʊsəl-] F *f* F fiddly *or* finicky work (*or* job); **Pus·se·lei** [pʊsə'laɪ] F *f* (-; -en) **1.** *no pl.* F fiddling (*or* tinkering) around; **2.** → ***Pusselarbeit***; **pus·se·lig** ['pʊsəlɪç] F *adj.* fussy *person*; F fiddly, finicky *job etc.*; **pus·seln** ['pʊsəln] F *v/i.* (h) F potter around; F tinker (*or* fiddle) around (***an*** *dat.* with)
Pu·ste ['puːstə] F *f* (-; *no pl.*) breath; ***ich hab' keine ~ mehr*** F I'm puffed; → ***ausgehen*** 3; **~blu·me** F *f* dandelion; **~ku·chen** F *int.* F no way; F no such luck
Pu·stel ['pʊstəl] *f* (-; -n) pimple; ⚕ pustule
pu·sten ['puːstən] F *v/i.* (h) blow; *mot.* ***er mußte ~*** he was breathalyzed (*or* breath-tested); ***ins ♎ kommen*** start puffing and panting
Pu·te ['puːtə] *f* (-; -n) turkey (hen); F *fig.* ***dumme ~*** F silly goose, stupid woman
'**Pu·ten|bra·ten** *m* roast turkey; **~fleisch** *n* turkey
Pu·ter ['puːtɐ] *m* (-s; -) turkey (cock)
'**pu·ter·rot** *adj.* (as) red as a lobster, scarlet
Putsch [pʊtʃ] *m* (-es; -e) *pol.* putsch, coup; **put·schen** ['pʊtʃən] *v/i.* (h) stage a coup; **Put·schist** [pʊt'ʃɪst] *m* (-en; -en) insurgent; '**Putsch·ver·such** *m* attempted coup, coup attempt
Put·te ['pʊtə] *f* (-; -n) *art*: putto
put·ten ['pʊtən] *v/i. and v/t.* (h) putt
Putz [pʊts] *m* (-es; *no pl.*) ⚠ plaster; ⚡ ***unter ~ (verlegt)*** concealed; F *fig.* ***auf den ~ hauen*** a) F have a fling, b) F kick up a row, c) show off
put·zen ['pʊtsən] (h) **I.** *v/t.* a) clean, b) polish (*Am.* shine) *shoes*, c) decorate; ***sich die Nase ~*** blow (*or* wipe) one's nose; ***sich die Zähne ~*** brush one's teeth; **II.** *v/i.* clean; do the cleaning; ***~ gehen*** work as a cleaner; **III.** *v/refl.*: ***sich ~*** *bird*: preen itself (*or* its feathers); *cat etc.*: wash itself
'**Putz|fim·mel** F *m* cleaning mania; **~frau** *f* cleaner, cleaning lady; **~hil·fe** *f* (part-time) cleaner
put·zig ['pʊtsɪç] F *adj.* comical, funny, droll
'**Putz|ko,lon·ne** *f* cleaning crew (*or* squad); **~lap·pen** *m* cloth; **~mit·tel** *n* a) cleaning agent, b) polish
'**putz'mun·ter** F *adj.* a) wide-awake, b) F perky, *Am.* F chipper
'**Putz|teu·fel** F *m* cleaning maniac; **~zeug** F *n* F cleaning things *pl.*
puz·zeln ['pazəln] *v/i.* (h) do a jigsaw puzzle; ***er puzzelt gerne*** he likes doing jigsaw puzzles; **Puz·zle·spiel** ['pazəl-] *n* (-s; -s) jigsaw puzzle
Pyg·mäe [pʏ'gmɛːə] *m* (-n; -n) pygmy
Py·ja·ma [py'dʒaːma] *m* (-s; -s): ***(ein) ~*** a pair of) pyjamas (*Am.* pajamas) *pl.*
Py·lon [py'loːn] *m* (-en; -en) ⚙ pylon
Py·ra·mi·de [pyra'miːdə] *f* (-; -n) pyramid

(*a.* A *and fig.*); **py·ra'mi·den·för·mig** [-fœrmıç] *adj.* pyramid-shaped, in the shape of a pyramid; pyramidal
Py·ro·ma·ne [pyro'maːnə] *m* (-n; -n) pyromaniac
Py·ro'tech·nik [pyro-] *f* pyrotechnics *pl.*
Pyr·rhus·sieg ['pyrʊs-] *m* Pyrrhic victory
py·tha·go·re·isch [pytago'reːıʃ] *adj.* Pythagorean; *~er Lehrsatz* Pythagoras' theorem
Py·thon ['pyːtɔn] *m* (-s; -s), **~schlan·ge** *f* python

Q

Q, q [kuː] *n* (-; -) Q, q

Quacke·lei [kvakəˈlaɪ] (*sep.* -k·k-) *dial. f* (-; *no pl.*) **1.** jabber(ing); **2.** grumbling, whing(e)ing; **3.** whining, grizzling; **quackeln** [ˈkvakəln] (*sep.* -k·k-) *dial. v/i.* (h) **1.** jabber (away); **2.** grumble, whinge; **3.** *child*: whine, grizzle

Quack·sal·ber [ˈkvakzalbɐ] *m* (-s; -) quack, charlatan; **Quack·sal·be·rei** [kvakzalbəˈraɪ] *f* (-; -en) quackery; **quack·sal·be·risch** [ˈkvakzalbərɪʃ] *adj.* quack *methods etc.*; **quack·sal·bern** [ˈkvakzalbɐn] *v/i.* (h) play the quack; ***er quacksalbert nur*** he's just a quack

Qua·der [ˈkvaːdɐ] *m* (-s; -) **1.** △ ashlar; **2.** ∧ rectangular parallelepiped; **~stein** *m* ashlar

Qua·drant [kvaˈdrant] *m* (-en; -en) quadrant

Qua·drat [kvaˈdraːt] *n* (-[e]s; -e) square; ***zwei Meter im ~*** two square metres (*Am.* meters), two metres (*Am.* meters) square; ***ins ~ erheben*** square; ***fünf zum ~*** five squared; **qua·dra·tisch** [kvaˈdraːtɪʃ] *adj.* square; ∧ quadratic

Quaˈdrat|ki·lo,me·ter *m* square kilometre (*Am.* kilometer); **~lat·schen** F *pl.* **1.** F boats, clodhoppers; **2.** F big trotters; **~me·ter** *m* square metre (*Am.* meter); **~me·ter·preis** *m* price per square metre (*Am.* meter); **~schä·del** F *m* **1.** square head, F block; **2.** ***er ist ein ~*** he's so pigheaded

Qua·dra·tur [kvadraˈtuːɐ] *f* (-; -en [-rən]) quadrature; *fig.* ***et. ist die ~ des Kreises*** it's like trying to square the circle

Quaˈdrat|wur·zel *f* square root; ***die ~ ziehen aus*** *dat.* get the square root of; **~zahl** *f* square number; **~zen·ti·me·ter** *m* square centimet|re (*Am.* -er)

qua·drie·ren [kvaˈdriːrən] *v/t.* (h) ∧ square

Qua·dro·pho·nie [kvadrofoˈniː] *f* (-; *no pl.*) quadraphonics *pl.*; **qua·dro·phon** [kvadroˈfoːn] *adj.* quadraphonic

qua·ken [ˈkvaːkən] *v/i.* (h) *frog*: croak; *duck*: quack; *baby*: whine, grizzle; *person*: squawk, whinge; *radio etc.*: squawk

quä·ken [ˈkvɛːkən] *v/i. and v/t.* (h) squawk

Quä·ker [ˈkvɛːkɐ] *m* (-s; -), **Quä·ke·rin** [ˈkvɛːkərɪn] *f* (-; -nen) Quaker; ***die Quäker*** *coll.* the Quakers, the Society of Friends

Qual [kvaːl] *f* (-; -en) *a. pl.* torture, agony; (mental) anguish; ***es ist e-e ~*** it's torture, it's agony, it's unbearable; ***unter ~en*** a) in great (*or* terrible) pain, b) with great difficulty; ***zur ~ werden*** become (*or* get) unbearable; ***ihr Leben war e-e ~*** life was unbearable for her; ***j-m das Leben zur ~ machen*** make s.o.'s life a misery; ***sein Rheuma hat ihm große ~en bereitet*** he went through agony with his rheumatism; ***die ~ der Ungewißheit*** the agony of not knowing; ***die ~en des Gewissens machen ihm zu schaffen*** he's tormented by a (*or* his) bad conscience; ***wir haben die ~ der Wahl*** we're spoilt for choice, we just can't decide; ***es ist e-e ~, ihn singen zu hören*** it's painful listening to him sing; ***ein Tier von s-n ~en erlösen*** put an animal out of its misery

quä·len [ˈkvɛːlən] (h) **I.** *v/t. a. fig.* torment, torture; *fig.* harass; pester, plague (***mit*** *dat.* with *requests, questions etc.*); ***j-n zu Tode ~*** torture s.o. to death; ***Hunger quälte ihn*** he was tormented by hunger; ***von Schmerzen gequält*** racked with (*or* tormented by) pain; ***mich quält dieser Schnupfen schon lange*** this cold has been tormenting me for a long time; ***dieser Gedanke quält mich seit einiger Zeit*** the thought has been tormenting (*or* haunting) me for some time; ***Zweifel quälten ihn*** he was torn by doubt; ***quäl ihn nicht so!*** stop tormenting him; F ***das Klavier ~*** F torture the piano; → ***gequält***; **II.** *v/refl.*: ***sich ~*** a) torment o.s. (***mit*** with *a thought etc.*), b) ✱ suffer, c) struggle; ***sich ~ mit*** *dat. a.* have a hard time with *s.th.*; ***sich durch den Schnee*** (***Regen***) ***~*** battle one's way through the snow (rain); ***sich durch ein Buch ~*** grapple with a book; ***sich ans Ziel ~*** *sport*: struggle to the finish; ***sich aufs Dach ~*** struggle (to get) onto the roof; ***sich umsonst ~*** labo(u)r in vain; ***sich zu Tode ~*** worry o.s. to death; **ˈquä·lend** *adj.* excruciating *pain*; agonizing *thought*; unbearable *heat, thirst etc.*; **Quä·le·rei** [kvɛːləˈraɪ] *f* (-; -en) a) torment(ing), torture, b) pestering, c) drudgery; ***Schreiben ist für mich e-e ~*** I can't stand writing

Quäl·geist [ˈkvɛːl-] *m* F pest

Qua·li·fi·ka·ti·on [kvalifikaˈtsi̯oːn] *f* (-; -en) qualification(s *pl.*); ability

Qua·li·fi·ka·tiˈons·run·de *f sport*: qualifying round

qua·li·fi·zie·ren [kvalifiˈtsiːrən] (h) **I.** *v/t.* **1.** qualify (***zu*** *dat.* for; ***als*** as); **2.** classify, qualify; **3.** qualify *remark etc.*; **II.** *v/refl.* **4.** ***sich ~ für*** *acc.* get one's (*or* the right) qualifications for; ***sich als Krankenschwester ~*** qualify as (*or* to become) a nurse; **5.** ***sich ~*** *sport*: qualify

qua·li·fi·ziert [kvalifiˈtsiːɐt] **I.** *adj.* a) qualified; highly trained *expert etc.*, b) qualified *statement etc.*; serious *discussion etc.*; *pol.* ***~e Mehrheit*** qualified majority; **II.** *adv.*: ***sich ~ zu et. äußern*** make a qualified statement on s.th.

Qua·li·tät [kvaliˈtɛːt] *f* (-; -en) quality; ✝ *a.* grade; ***erster ~*** first-rate; ***schlechte ~*** poor quality (*or* workmanship); ***er hat auch s-e ~en*** he's got his good points

qua·li·ta·tiv [kvalitaˈtiːf] **I.** *adj.* qualitative; **II.** *adv.* qualitatively, in quality, from the point of view of quality

Qua·liˈtäts|ar·beit *f* high-quality workmanship; ***das ist ~*** *a.* they've *etc.* done an excellent job on that; **~be·wußt I.** *adj.* quality-conscious; **II.** *adv.*: ***~ einkaufen*** shop for quality; **~er·zeug·nis** *n* (high-)quality product; **~kon,trol·le** *f* quality control; **~merk·mal** *n* mark of quality; **~min·dernd** *adv.*: ***sich ~ auswirken*** have a devaluing effect (***auf*** *acc.* on); **~min·de·rung** *f* reduction in quality; **~norm** *f* quality standard; **~si·che·rung** *f* quality assurance; **~stei·ge·rung** *f* quality improvement; **~,un·ter·schied** *m* difference in quality; **~wa·re** *f* quality goods *pl.*; **~wein** *m* quality-tested wine

Qual·le [ˈkvalə] *f* (-; -n) jellyfish

Qualm [kvalm] *m* (-s; *no pl.*) (thick) smoke; F *fig.* ***viel ~ machen*** make a big fuss; F ***bei ihnen herrscht ~ in der Bude*** they're having a row; **qual·men** [ˈkvalmən] (h) **I.** *v/i.* smoke; F *a.* F puff away (at a cigarette *etc.*); **II.** *v/t.* F puff away at; **Qual·me·rei** [kvalməˈraɪ] *f* (-; *no pl.*) smoking; **qual·mig** [ˈkvalmɪç] *adj.* smoky, *a.* smoke-filled *room etc.*

ˈqual·voll *adj.* excruciating, agonizing *pain etc.*; ***es war ~*** *a.* it was torture

Quant [kvant] *m* (-s; -en) *phys.* quantum

quan·teln [ˈkvantəln] *v/t.* (h) *phys.* quantize

Quan·ten [ˈkvantən] F *pl.* **1.** F boats, clodhoppers; **2.** F big trotters

Quan·ten|me,cha·nik [ˈkvantən-] *f phys.* quantum mechanics *pl.*; **~phy,sik** *f* quantum physics *pl.*; **~sprung** *m phys.* quantum leap (*or* jump); **~theo,rie** *f* quantum theory

quan·ti·fi·zier·bar [kvantifiˈtsiːɐbaːɐ] *adj.* quantifiable; **quan·ti·fi·zie·ren** [kvantifiˈtsiːrən] *v/t.* (h) quantify; **Quan·ti·fiˈzie·rung** *f* (-; -en) quantification

Quan·ti·tät [kvantiˈtɛːt] *f* (-; -en) quantity

quan·ti·ta·tiv [kvantitaˈtiːf] *adj.* quantitative; *adv. a.* in quantity

Quan·tum [ˈkvantʊm] *n* (-s; Quanten [ˈkvantən]) quantity; amount; share, quota; F ***das tägliche ~ Alkohol*** *etc.* one's daily ration of alcohol *etc.*; F ***ich hab' mein ~ schon gehabt*** F I've had my lot for today

Quap·pe [ˈkvapə] *f* (-; -n) *zo.* **1.** tadpole; **2.** burbot

Qua·ran·tä·ne [karanˈtɛːnə] *f* (-; -n) quarantine; ***unter ~ stellen*** put in quarantine; **~be·stim·mun·gen** *pl.* quarantine regulations; **~sta·ti,on** *f* quarantine ward

Quark[1] [kvark] *m* (-s; *no pl.*) **1.** skimmed

milk, cream cheese, quark; **2.** F → ***Quatsch***
Quark² [kwɔːk] *n* (-s; -s) *phys.* quark
quar·ren ['kvarən] *dial. v/i.* (h) *child*: grizzle, whine, *woman*: whinge
Quart¹ [kvart] *n* (-s; -e) **1.** quart; **2.** *no pl. typ.* quarto
Quart² *f* (-; -en) **1.** ♪ fourth; **2.** *fencing*: quart
Quar·ta ['kvarta] *f* (-; -en) *ped.* **1.** *obs.* third year (of grammar school); **2.** *Austrian* fourth year (of grammar school)
Quar·tal [kvar'taːl] *n* (-s; -e) quarter (year), quarterly period
Quar'tals... *in cpds.* quarterly; **~en·de** *n* end of a (*or* the) quarter; ***sechs Wochen vor ~ kündigen*** give notice six weeks before the end of the quarter; **~säu·fer** F *m* F dipso
quar'tal(s)·wei·se *adj. and adv.* quarterly
Quar·tär [kvar'tɛːɐ] *n* (-s; *no pl.*) *geol.* Quaternary
'Quart·band *m* (-[e]s; ¨e) quarto volume
Quar·te ['kvartə] *f* (-; -n) ♪ fourth
Quar·tett [kvar'tɛt] *n* (-[e]s; -e) **1.** ♪ quartet; **2.** happy families *pl.*; **3.** *fig.* foursome
'Quart·for,mat *n* quarto (format)
Quar·tier [kvar'tiːr] *n* (-s; -e [-rə]) **1.** accommodation; ***ein ~ für die Nacht*** accommodation (*or* a room, a bed) for the night; ***j-m ~ geben*** put s.o. up; **2.** ⚔ quarters *pl.*; ***~ beziehen*** take up quarters; ***bei j-m in ~ liegen*** be billeted on s.o.; **~su·che** *f*: ***auf ~ sein*** be looking for accommodation
Quarz [kvarts] *m* (-es; -e) quartz; ⚡ *a.* crystal; **2ge·steu·ert** *adj.* quartz(-controlled); **~glas** *n* quartz glass
Quar·zit [kvar'tsiːt] *m* (-s; -e) quartzite
'Quarz|kri,stall *m* quartz crystal; **~lam·pe** *f* quartz lamp; **~staub·lun·ge** *f* silicosis; **~uhr** *f* quartz clock (*or* [wrist]-watch); **~wecker** *m* quartz (alarm) clock
Qua·sar [kva'zaːɐ] *m* (-s; -e [-rə]) *ast.* quasar
qua·si ['kvaːzi] *adv.* more or less; as it were; **'Qua·si...** *in cpds.* quasi-...
Quas·sel·bu·de ['kvasəl-] F *f* talking shop
Quas·se·lei [kvasə'laɪ] F *f* (-; *no pl.*) **1.** F yakking, jabbering; **2.** F drivel, rubbish
Quas·sel|frit·ze ['kvasəlfrɪtsə] F *m* (-n; -n), **~kopf** F *m* F gasbag
quas·seln ['kvasəln] F *v/i.* (h) F yak (away), gas
Quas·sel·strip·pe ['kvasəlʃtrɪpə] F *f* **1.** F gasbag; **2.** F blower; ***an der ~ hängen*** be on the blower
Quast [kvast] *m* (-[e]s; -e) **1.** (wide) brush; **2.** → **Qua·ste** ['kvastə] *f* (-; -n) **1.** tassel; **2.** powder *etc.* puff
Quatsch [kvatʃ] F *m* (-[e]s; *no pl.*) F rubbish, *sl.* rot, F garbage, trash; ***~ machen*** a) fool around, get up to nonsense, b) do something stupid; ***so ein ~*** what a lot (*sl.* load) of rubbish; ***laß den ~!*** stop it!, *sl.* cut it out!; ***red keinen ~!*** a) don't talk rubbish *etc.*, stop talking rubbish *etc.*, b) F you're kidding; **quat·schen** ['kvatʃən] F *v/i.* (h) **1.** a) F blether, talk rubbish, b) F natter, *contp.* blather; gossip; **2.** *soil, shoes*: squelch; **'Quatsch·kopf** F *m* F driveller, windbag
Quecke ['kvɛkə] (*sep.* -k·k) *f* (-; -n) ♀ crouch (*or* quack) grass
Queck·sil·ber ['kvɛkzɪlbɐ] *n* (-s; *no pl.*) mercury, quicksilver; *fig.* ***er ist das reinste ~*** he's a real live wire; **~ba·ro,me·ter** *n* mercury barometer; **~ge·halt** *m* mercury level
'queck·sil·ber·hal·tig [-haltɪç] *adj.*: ***~ sein*** contain mercury; ***~e Fischprodukte*** fish products containing mercury
'queck·sil·bern *adj.* **1.** mercury; **2.** → ***quecksilbrig***
'Queck·sil·ber|säu·le *f* mercury (column); ***die ~ ist auf 30 Grad geklettert*** the mercury has risen to 30 degrees; **~ver·gif·tung** *f* mercury poisoning
queck·silb·rig ['kvɛkzɪlbrɪç] *fig. adj.* very lively, live-wire *personality*
Quell [kvɛl] *lit. m* (-s; *no pl.*) → ***Quelle***; **~code** *m computer*: source code
Quel·le ['kvɛlə] *f* (-; -n) **1.** spring; **2.** source *of river etc.*; **3.** *fig.* source; ***aus sicherer ~*** on good authority; ***aus erster ~*** firsthand; ***du sitzt doch an der ~*** you're in the right place (for that), you're right at the source; *lit.* ***die ~ des Lebens*** (***Wissens***) the fountain of life (the fountain[head] of knowledge); ***du mußt die ~n angeben*** you've got to quote your sources
'quel·len (quoll, gequollen) **I.** *v/i.* (sn) **1.** *a. fig.* pour, *blood*: *a.* gush (***aus*** *dat.* out of, from); ***aus dem Boden ~*** well up from under the ground; ***über den Rand ~*** well (*or* rise) over the edge; **2.** ***die Augen quollen ihr fast aus dem Kopf*** her eyes were popping out of her head; **3.** swell; **II.** *v/t.* (h) soak
'Quel·len|an·ga·be *f* reference; **~n** *coll.* list of sources, bibliography; **~for·schung** *f* basic research; **~ma·te·ri,al** *n* source material; **~nach·weis** *m* **1.** reference; **2.** list of sources, bibliography; **~steu·er** *f* withholding tax; **~stu·di·um** *n* basic research; **~ver·zeich·nis** *n* list of sources, bibliography
'Quell|fluß *m* headstream; **~ge·biet** *n geogr.* headwaters *pl.*; **~pro,gramm** *n computer*: source program; **~was·ser** *n* spring water
Quen·ge·lei [kvɛŋə'laɪ] F *f* (-; *no pl.*) whining, niggling; whing(e)ing; **quen·ge·lig** ['kvɛŋəlɪç] F *adj.* whining, niggly; whing(e)ing; **quen·geln** ['kvɛŋəln] F *v/i.* (h) whine, niggle; whinge
Quent·chen ['kvɛntçən] *n* (-s; -) tiny bit (of); ***ein ~ Salz*** *a.* a pinch of salt; *fig.* ***ein ~ Glück*** a little bit of luck; ***ein ~ Furcht*** (***Ehre***) a trace of fear (hono[u]r); ***ein ~ Vernunft*** a modicum of sense; ***ein ~ Mut*** (***Wahrheit***) a grain (*or* an ounce) of courage (truth); ***da ist kein ~ Wahrheit dran*** there isn't an ounce of truth to it
quer [kveːɐ] *adv.* a) crossways, crosswise; diagonally, b) at right angles; ***~ über*** (straight) across; ***~ über die Straße gehen*** cross the road; ***~ durch*** *acc.* (straight) through; ***~ gegenüber*** diagonally opposite; ***~ durch die Stadt laufen*** walk all over town; ***er lag ~ auf dem Bett*** he was lying across the bed; ***~ übereinanderlegen*** put crossways; ***~ durch die Parteien*** right across the parties; → ***kreuz*** II
'Quer|ach·se *f* transverse (axis); **~bal·ken** *m* crossbeam; lintel
quer'beet F *adv.* **1.** a) all over the place, b) across country; ***~ über die Felder laufen*** run across the fields in any old direction; ***j-n ~ durch die Stadt führen*** take s.o. all over town; **2.** at random, indiscriminately; ***~ auswählen*** pick *things* out at random; ***~ alle Probleme erörtern*** go through the whole gamut of problems; ***sie hat ~ gefragt*** she covered the whole range (with her questions)
'Quer·den·ker *m* unconventional thinker; ***~ sein*** *a.* have an unconventional way of thinking
Que·re ['kveːrə] *f* (-; *no pl.*) **1.** width; ***der ~ nach*** widthwise; ***et. der ~ nach messen*** measure s.th.'s width; **2.** *fig.* ***j-m in die ~ kommen*** get in s.o.'s (*or* the) way; ***ihm muß et. in die ~ gekommen sein*** a) something must have cropped up, b) something must be eating him
Que·re·len [kve'reːlən] *pl.* quarrel(l)ing *sg.*, squabbling *sg.*, bickering *sg.*; ***mit ~ enden*** end in a quarrel
que·ren ['kveːrən] *v/t.* (h) cross
'Quer·fal·te *f* cross pleat
quer·feld'ein *adv.* across country
Quer·feld'ein|lauf *m sport*: cross-country run(ning); **~ren·nen** *n* cyclo-cross
'Quer|flö·te *f* ♪ (transverse) flute; **~for,mat** *n* horizontal format; ***Foto im ~*** landscape-size photo
'quer·ge·streift *adj.* horizontally striped
'Quer·haus *n* ⛪ transept
'quer·kom·men F *v/i.* (*irr., sep.*, sn, → ***kommen***): ***j-m ~*** get in s.o.'s way
'Quer|kopf F *m* F awkward customer; ***er ist ein ~*** *a.* he likes being awkward, he likes to go against the grain; **~la·ge** *f* ⚕ transverse presentation; **~lat·te** *f sport*: crossbar
'quer·le·gen F *v/refl.* (*sep.*, h): ***sich ~*** be awkward
'Quer|lei·ste *f* ⚙ cross-rib; **2lie·gend** *adj. mot.* transverse-mounted *engine*; **~li·nie** *f* diagonal line; **~mo·tor** *m* transverse-mounted engine; **~paß** *m soccer*: cross pass; **~pfei·fe** *f* fife; **~ru·der** *n* ✈ aileron
'quer·schie·ßen F *v/i.* (*irr., sep.*, h, → ***schießen***) F put a spanner (*Am.* monkey wrench) in(to) the works
'Quer|schiff *n* ⛪ transept; **~schlä·ger** *m* **1.** ricochet; **2.** F → ***Quertreiber***
'Quer·schnitt *m* cross-section (*a. fig.* ***durch*** *acc.* of); *a.* sectional view; *fig.* highlights *pl.* (***durch*** *acc.* of *an opera etc.*)
'quer·schnitts|ge·lähmt *adj.* ⚕ paraplegic; paralyzed from the waist (*or* neck) down; **2läh·mung** *f* ⚕ paraplegia
'Quer|stra·ße *f* intersecting road; ***zweite ~ rechts*** second turning on the right; **~strei·fen** *m* horizontal stripe; **~strich** *m* horizontal line; **~sum·me** *f* sum of the digits; **~tal** *n* transverse valley
'Quer·trei·ber *m* obstructionist
Quer·trei·be·rei [-traɪbə'raɪ] *f* (-; *no pl.*) obstructionism
Que·ru·lant [kveru'lant] *m* (-en; -en) troublemaker, *Am.* grouch; **Que·ru'lan·ten·tum** *n* (-s; *no pl.*) querulousness
'Quer|ver·bin·dung *f* cross connection; link, connection; **~ver·weis** *m* cross-reference; **~wand** *f* partition
quet·schen ['kvɛtʃən] (h) **I.** *v/t.* squeeze; crush, squash; ⚕ bruise; ***sich den Finger ~*** get one's finger squashed, ***in der Tür***: get one's finger caught in the door; ***et. in e-n Koffer ~*** squeeze (F cram) s.th. into a suitcase; ***Saft aus e-r Zitrone ~*** squeeze a lemon; ***die Nase an die Scheibe ~*** press one's nose against the window; ***zu Tode gequetscht werden*** be crushed to death; **II.** *v/refl.*: ***sich ~*** ⚕

bruise o.s.; ***sich ~ in** acc.* squeeze (o.s.) into *a car etc.*; ***sich durch die Menge ~*** squeeze (*or* force) one's way through the crowd
'Quetsch|fal·te *f* box pleat; **~kom,mo·de** F *f* F squeeze-box
Quet·schung ['kvɛtʃʊŋ] *f* (-; -en), **'Quetsch·wun·de** *f* bruise, ⚕ contusion
Queue [kø:] *n, m* (-s; -s) (billiard) cue
Quiche [kɪʃ] *f* (-; -s) *gastr.* quiche
quick·le'ben·dig ['kvɪk-] *adj.* (very) lively *child*; sprightly *old lady etc.*
quie·ken ['kvi:kən], **quiek·sen** ['kvi:ksən] *v/i.* (h) squeak; squeal
quiet·schen ['kvi:tʃən] *v/i.* (h) squeak; squeal; screech; ***sie quietschte vor Vergnügen*** she squealed with delight
Quiet·scher ['kvi:tʃɐ] *m* (-s; -) squeak; squeal
'quietsch|fi'del F *adj.*, **~ver'gnügt** F *adj.* (very) chirpy, *Am.* F chipper
Quint [kvɪnt] *f* (-; -en) **1.** ♪ fifth; **2.** *fencing*: quinte
Quin·ta ['kvɪnta] *f* (-; -en) *ped.* **1.** *obs.* second year (of grammar school); **2.** *Austrian* fourth year (of grammar school)
Quin·te ['kvɪntə] *f* (-; -n) ♪ fifth
Quint·es·senz ['kvɪntɛsɛnts] *f* (-; -en) essence; ***die ~ war*** *a.* what it boiled (*or* came) down to was
Quin·tett [kvɪn'tɛt] *n* (-[e]s; -e) quintet
Quirl [kvɪrl] *m* (-[e]s; -e) **1.** beater; **2.** *fig.* live wire; **quir·len** ['kvɪrlən] (h) **I.** *v/t.* whisk, beat; **II.** *v/i.* whirl; **quir·lig** ['kvɪrlɪç] F *adj.* very lively *child*; bubbly *person*; mercurial *player*, *temperament etc.*; ***~es Treiben*** hustle and bustle
Quis·ling ['kvɪslɪŋ] *m* (-s; -e) *pol.* quisling, collaborator
quitt [kvɪt] *pred. adj.*: ***~ sein (werden) mit j-m*** be (get) quits (*or* even) with s.o. (*a. fig.*); ***jetzt sind wir ~*** now we're quits; ***ich bin doch mit dir ~, oder?*** I've squared up with you, haven't I?, we're quits now, aren't we?
Quit·te ['kvɪtə] *f* (-; -n) quince
'Quit·ten·baum *m* quince (tree)
'quit·te(n)·gelb *adj.* quince-yellow; *fig.* ***~ aussehen*** F look (a bit) green about the gills
quit·tie·ren [kvɪ'ti:rən] (h) **I.** *v/t.* **1.** give (*or* sign) a receipt for; ***den Empfang der Ware ~*** a) sign that one has received the goods, b) acknowledge receipt of the goods; *fig.* ***et. mit e-m Lächeln*** *etc.* ***~*** answer (*or* meet) s.th. with a smile *etc.*; ***es wurde mit Beifall quittiert*** it was met with applause; **2.** ***den Dienst ~*** resign; **II.** *v/i.* sign
Quit·tung ['kvɪtʊŋ] *f* (-; -en) receipt; ***e-e ~ ausstellen über*** *acc.* make a receipt out for; ***gegen ~*** on receipt; *fig.* ***das ist die ~ für d-n Leichtsinn*** that's what you get for (*or* that's what comes of) being so careless; ***das ist die ~*** that's what you end up with
'Quit·tungs·block *m* receipt book
Qui·vive [ki'vi:f] F *n*: ***auf dem ~ sein*** F be on the ball; ***bei dem mußt du auf dem ~ sein*** you've got to be on the ball (*or* you've got to watch things) with him; ***der ist auf dem ~!*** you can't fool him!
Quiz [kvɪs] *n* (-; *no pl.*) quiz; **~ma·ster** [-ma:stɐ] *m* (-s; -) quiz-show (*or* game-show) host, quizmaster, question master; **~sen·dung** *f* quiz show; gameshow
quoll [kvɔl] *pret. of* ***quellen***
Quo·rum ['kvo:rʊm] *n* (-s; *no pl.*) quorum
Quo·te ['kvo:tə] *f* (-; -n) proportion, ratio; rate; share; **'Quo·ten·re·ge·lung** *f* quota regulations *pl.*
Quo·ti·ent [kvo'tsĭɛnt] *m* (-en; -en) 𝔄 quotient
quo·tie·ren [kvo'ti:rən] *v/t.* (h) **1.** *stock exchange*: quote; **2.** fix quotas for; **Quo'tie·rung** *f* (-; -en) **1.** quotation; **2.** fixing of quotas

R

R, r [ɛr] *n* (-; -) R, r
Ra·batt [ra'bat] *m* (-[e]s; -e) ✝ discount (**auf** *acc.* on); **mit 10% ~** at a discount of 10 per cent (*or* percent)
Ra·bat·te [ra'batə] *f* (-; -n) ⚘ border
Ra'batt·mar·ke *f* trading stamp
Ra·batz [ra'bats] F *m* (-es; *no pl.*) F row, racket; **~ machen** F kick up a fuss, raise hell
Ra·bau·ke [ra'baʊkə] F *m* (-n; -n) hooligan
Rab·bi ['rabi] *m* (-[s]; -s), **Rab·bi·ner** [ra'biːnɐ] *m* (-s; -) rabbi; **rab·bi·nisch** [ra'biːnɪʃ] *adj.* rabbinical
Ra·be ['raːbə] *m* (-n; -n) raven; *fig.* **er stiehlt wie ein ~** he steals anything he can get his hands on
'Ra·ben|el·tern *pl.* uncaring parents; **~mut·ter** *f* uncaring mother
'ra·ben'schwarz *adj.* jet-black, raven *hair*; pitch-black *night*; **du bist ja ~!** you're black as coal!; *fig.* **~er Tag** black day
ra·bi·at [ra'bĭaːt] *adj.* rough, brutal; ruthless; drastic (*a. fig. measures etc.*); *fig.* radical *views etc.*; **ein ~er Kerl** a dangerous sort; **~ werden** go wild; get violent
Ra·che ['raxə] *f* (-; *no pl.*) revenge, *lit.* vengeance; retribution, retaliation; **Tag der ~** day of reckoning; **~ nehmen** take revenge (**an** *dat.* on); **aus ~** in (*or* out of) revenge; **auf ~ sinnen** plot revenge; **s-e ~ stillen** (*or* **befriedigen**) satisfy one's desire (*or* thirst) for revenge; **~ ist süß** revenge is sweet; F **~ ist Blutwurst!** just you wait!; **das ist die ~ des kleinen Mannes** it's the only way he can get his own back (*or* get back at the system); **~akt** *m* act of revenge; **~en·gel** *m* avenging angel; **~feld·zug** *m* retaliation campaign; **~ge·fühl** *n* desire for revenge; vindictive feeling
Ra·chen ['raxən] *m* (-s; -) *anat.* throat, 🕮 pharynx; *zo.* mouth, jaws *pl.*; *fig.* abyss; *lit.* **der ~ des Todes** the jaws of death; **j-m Geld in den ~ werfen** throw (even more) money at s.o.; **j-m den ~ stopfen** give s.o. s.th. to keep him (*or* her) quiet; **er kann den ~ nicht voll kriegen** he just can't get enough
rä·chen ['rɛçən] (h) **I.** *v/t.* avenge; *a.* take revenge for *s.th.*; **II.** *v/refl.*: **sich ~** get one's revenge, F get one's own back (**an j-m** on s.o.); **sich wegen et. an j-m ~** revenge o.s. (*or* take revenge) on s.o. for s.th.; **es wird sich bitter ~, daß** we'll *etc.* have to pay dearly for *ger.*; **s-e Eßgewohnheiten rächten sich** his eating habits took their toll; **die Vernachlässigung der Umwelt wird sich an unseren Kindern ~** our children will have to pay (the penalty) for our neglect of the environment
'Ra·chen|ab·strich *m* throat swab; **~höh·le** *f* pharynx, pharyngeal cavity; **~ka,tarrh** *m* pharyngitis; **~laut** *m ling.* pharyngeal; **~man·del** *f* adenoids *pl.*, 🕮 pharyngeal tonsil; **~put·zer** F *m* F rotgut, gutrot
Ra·che·plä·ne *pl.*: **~ schmieden** plot revenge
Rä·cher ['rɛçɐ] *m* (-s; -) avenger
'Ra·che·schwur *m* oath of revenge; **e-n ~ tun** swear vengeance
Rach·gier *f*, **'Rach·sucht** *f* thirst for revenge; vindictiveness; **'rach·gie·rig, 'rach·süch·tig** *adj.* revengeful, vindictive
Ra·chi·tis [ra'xiːtɪs] *f* (-; *no pl.*) ⚕ rickets *pl.*
Racker ['rakɐ] (*sep.* -k·k-) F *m* (-s; -) F little rascal
rackern ['rakɐn] (*sep.* -k·k-) F *v/i.* (h) slave (F slog) away; **ich mußte schwer ~** *a.* F it was a hard slog
Rad [raːt] *n* (-[e]s; Räder ['rɛːdɐ]) a) wheel (*a. fig.*), b) bicycle, F bike; **auf Rädern** on wheels; **mit dem ~ fahren** go by bicycle (*or* bike); → *a.* **radfahren; (ein) ~ schlagen** a) *peacock*: spread its tail, b) *gym.* turn (*or* do) a cartwheel; **unter die Räder kommen** be run over, *fig.* go to the dogs; *fig.* **das fünfte ~ am Wagen sein** be the odd man out, play gooseberry; *fig. lit.* **das ~ der Zeit (der Geschichte) anhalten wollen** try to stop the march of time (the course of history); *hist.* **aufs ~ geflochten werden** be broken on the wheel; **~ach·se** *f* ⚙ axle; **~an·trieb** *m* wheel drive
Ra·dar [ra'daːɐ, 'raːdaːɐ] *m, n* (-s; *no pl.*) radar; **~an·la·ge** *f* radar (unit); **~an,ten·ne** *f* radar aerial (*or* antenna); **~bild·schirm** *m* radar screen; **~echo** *n* radar echo; **~fal·le** *f* speed trap; **⁀ge·lenkt** *adj.* radar-guided; **~ge·rät** *n* radar (set); **~kon,trol·le** *f* radar speed check; **~pi,sto·le** *f* radar gun; **~schirm** *m* radar screen; **⁀si·cher** *adj.* radarproof; **~sta·ti,on** *f* radar station; **~über,wa·chung** *f* radar monitoring; **~ver·fol·gung** *f* radar tracking
Ra·dau [ra'daʊ] F *m* (-s; *no pl.*) F row, racket; **~ machen** a) make a racket, b) F kick up a fuss (*or* row); **~bru·der** F *m* hooligan, (F lager) lout
'Rad·auf·hän·gung *f* suspension
Ra'dau·ma·cher F *m* → **Radaubruder**
Räd·chen ['rɛːtçən] *n* (-s; -) **1.** small (*or* little) wheel; *fig.* **ein ~ im Getriebe sein** be a cog in the wheel (*or* machine); **2.** F (little) bike
'Rad·damp·fer *m* paddle steamer
ra·de·bre·chen ['raːdebreçən] *v/t.* (h): **Englisch** *etc.* **~** speak broken English *etc.*
ra·deln ['raːdəln] *dial.* F **I.** *v/i.* (sn) cycle, F bike; **II.** ⁀ *n* (-s; *no pl.*) cycling
Rä·dels·füh·rer ['rɛːdəls-] *m* ringleader
Rä·der|fahr·zeug ['rɛːdɐ-] *n* wheeled vehicle; **~ge·trie·be** *n* gearbox
rä·dern ['rɛːdɐn] *v/t.* (h) *hist.* break on the wheel; → **gerädert**
Rä·der·werk ['rɛːdɐ-] *n* a) mechanism, b) clockwork, c) gearing, d) *fig.* machinery; **ins ~ der Justiz geraten** get caught in the meshes of the law
rad·fah·ren ['raːt-] *v/i.* (fährt Rad, fuhr Rad, ist radgefahren) **1.** cycle, ride a bicycle (F bike), F bike; **2.** F *fig.* F suck up to people; **'Rad·fah·rer** *m* **1.** cyclist; **2.** F *fig.* F toady, bootlicker
'Rad·fahr·weg *m* → **Radweg**
Ra·di ['raːdi] *dial. m* (-s; -) mooli; (white) radish
ra·di·al [ra'dĭaːl] **I.** *adj.* radial; **II.** *adv.*: **~ angelegt** radially arranged, arranged in the shape of a star
Ra·di'al|bohr·ma,schi·ne *f* radial drill; **~ge·schwin·dig·keit** *f ast.* radial velocity; **~rei·fen** *m* radial (tyre, *Am.* tire)
Ra·dia·tor [ra'dĭaːtoːɐ] *m* (-s; -en [radĭa'toːrən]) radiator
ra·die·ren [ra'diːrən] *v/t. and v/i.* (h) **1.** rub out, erase; **2.** *art*: etch
Ra·dier|gum·mi [ra'diːɐ-] *m* rubber, eraser; **~kunst** *f* etching; **~mes·ser** *n* erasing knife; **~na·del** *f* etching needle
Ra·die·rung [ra'diːrʊŋ] *f* (-; -en) etching
Ra·dies·chen [ra'diːsçən] *n* (-s; -) radish; F **sich die ~ von unten ansehen** F be pushing up the daisies
ra·di·kal [radi'kaːl] **I.** *adj.* radical (*a. pol.*); drastic, sweeping *changes etc.*; extreme *measures etc.*; **der ~e linke (rechte) Flügel der Partei** the extreme left (right) wing of the party; **in s-r Haltung sehr ~ sein** have very radical views; **er ist mit s-n Schülern sehr ~** he's very hard on his pupils; **II.** *adv.*: **~ vorgehen gegen** *acc.* take drastic action (*or* radical steps) against; **~ mit der Vergangenheit brechen** make a clean (*or* radical) break with the past
Ra·di'kal *n* (-s; -e) **1.** ⚗ radical; **2.** 𝔄 root
Ra·di'ka·le *m, f* (-n; -n) *pol.* radical, extremist; **Ra·di'ka·len·er·laß** *m ban on the employment of teachers and civil servants with radical political views*
Ra·di·ka·lins·ki [radika'lɪnski] *contp. m* (-s; -s) (political) firebrand *or* extremist; *a.* F lefty
ra·di·ka·li·sie·ren [radikali'ziːrən] (h) **I.** *v/t.* radicalize; **II.** *v/refl.*: **sich ~** become more and more radical (*or* extreme)
Ra·di·ka·lis·mus [radika'lɪsmʊs] *m* (-; *no pl.*) radicalism; **Ra·di·ka·list** [radika'lɪst] *m* (-en; -en) radical, extremist
Ra·di'kal·kur *f* ⚕ drastic cure; *fig.* drastic measures *pl.*

Ra·dio ['ra:dĭo] *n* (-s; -s) a) radio, *Brit. a. obs.* wireless, b) radio, broadcasting; **~ *hören*** listen to the radio; ***im ~*** on the radio; ***im ~ übertragen*** broadcast (on the radio)
ra·dio·ak'tiv *adj.* radioactive; ***~e Abfälle, ~er Müll*** radioactive waste; ***~er Niederschlag*** (radioactive) fallout; ***~e Strahlung*** (atomic) radiation; ***~e Verseuchung*** radioactive contamination; ***~e Wolke*** radioactive cloud (*or* plume); ***~er Zerfall*** radioactive decay; ***~ machen*** (radio)activate; **Ra·dio·ak·ti·vi'tät** *f* (-; *no pl.*) radioactivity
'Ra·dio|an,ten·ne *f* radio aerial (*or* antenna); **~ap·pa,rat** *m* → ***Radiogerät***
Ra·dio|astro·no'mie *f* radio astronomy; **~che'mie** *f* radiochemistry
'Ra·dio|,durch·sa·ge *f* special announcement (on the radio); **~emp·fang** *m* radio reception; **~ge·rät** *n* radio (set); *Brit. a. obs.* wireless (set); **~hö·rer** *m* (radio) listener; *pl. a.* audience *sg.*
Ra·dio·kar'bon·me,tho·de *f* radio carbon dating
Ra·dio·la·ri·en [radĭo'la:rĭən] *pl. zo.* radiolaria; **~schlamm** *m* radiolarian ooze
Ra·dio·lo·ge [radĭo'lo:gə] *m* (-n; -n) radiologist; **Ra·dio·lo·gie** [radĭolo'gi:] *f* (-; *no pl.*) radiology; **ra·dio·lo·gisch** [radĭo'lo:gɪʃ] *adj.* radiological
Ra·dio·me·trie [radĭome'tri:] *f* (-; *no pl.*) radiometry
'Ra·dio|nach·rich·ten *pl.* radio news *sg.*, news *sg.* on the radio; **~quel·le** *f ast.* radio source; **~re,cor·der** *m* radio-cassette recorder; **~sen·der** *m* **1.** radio station; **2.** radio transmitter; **~sen·dung** *f* (radio) program(me), (radio) broadcast; **~sta·ti,on** *f* radio (*or* broadcasting) station; **~te·le,skop** *n* radio telescope; **~über,tra·gung** *f* (radio) broadcast; **~wecker** *m* clock radio; **~wer·bung** *f* a) radio advertising, b) radio advertisements (F ads) *pl.*, advertisements (F ads) *pl.* on the radio
Ra·di·um ['ra:dĭʊm] *n* (-s; *no pl.*) radium; **~be·hand·lung** *f*, **~the·ra,pie** *f* radium treatment
Ra·di·us ['ra:dĭʊs] *m* (-; Radien ['ra:dĭən]) ∡ *and fig.* radius
'Rad|kap·pe *f* hub cap; **~ka·sten** *m* wheel housing; **~kral·le** *f* wheel clamp; **~kranz** *m* (wheel) rim; **~kreuz** *n* wheel wrench
Rad·ler ['ra:dlɐ] F *m* (-s; -), **Rad·le·rin** ['ra:dlərɪn] F *f* (-; -nen) cyclist
'Rad·ler·maß *dial. f* large shandy
'Rad|mut·ter *f* wheel nut; **~na·be** *f* (wheel) hub
Ra·don ['ra:dɔn] *n* (-s; *no pl.*) ⚗ radon
'Rad|renn·bahn *f* cycling track; **~rennen** *n* cycle race; **~renn·fah·rer** *m* racing cyclist; **2schla·gen** *v/i.* (schlägt Rad, schlug Rad, hat radgeschlagen) *gym.* turn (*or* do) a cartwheel; **~sport** *m* cycling; **~stand** *m mot.* wheel base; **~tour** *f*, **~wan·de·rung** *f* bicycle tour; **~weg** *m* cycle track, bicycle path, cycleway
raf·fen ['rafən] *v/t.* (h) **1.** snatch, grab; **2.** amass *money*; **3.** gather up *one's dress etc*; gather *material, curtain etc.*; **4.** concentrate, condense *report, text etc.*; **5.** F get *s.th.*
Raff·gier ['raf-] *f* greed, *formal*: rapacity; **'raff·gie·rig** *adj.* greedy, grasping, *formal*: rapacious

Raf·fi·na·de [rafi'na:də] *f* (-; -n) refined sugar
Raf·fi·ne·ment [rafinə'mã:] *n* (-s; *no pl.*) a) finesse, b) refinement
Raf·fi·ne·rie [rafinə'ri:] *f* (-; -n) refinery
Raf·fi·nes·se [rafi'nɛsə] *f* (-; -n) a) shrewdness, finesse, b) refinement; ***er versuchte es mit allen ~n*** he tried all the tricks of the trade; ⚙ ***mit allen ~n*** with all the trimmings
raf·fi·nie·ren [rafi'ni:rən] *v/t.* (h) refine; **raf·fi·niert** [rafi'ni:ɐt] *adj.* **1.** refined; **2.** *fig.* a) clever, ingenious; shrewd, crafty, b) sophisticated *taste etc.*; **~!** very clever
Ra·ge ['ra:ʒə] *f* (-; *no pl.*) rage, fury; ***in ~ kommen*** get furious, F go wild; ***j-n in ~ bringen*** make s.o. furious (F wild)
ra·gen ['ra:gən] *v/i.* (h) tower, loom (***über*** *acc.* above); rise (***aus*** *dat.* from), project (from, out of)
Ra·glan|är·mel ['ragla(:)n-] *pl.* raglan sleeves; **~man·tel** *m* raglan (coat); **~pull·over** *m* raglan sweater
Ra·gout [ra'gu:] *n* (-s; -s) ragout
Rah [ra:] *f* (-; -en), **Ra·he** ['ra:ə] *f* (-; -n) ⚓ yard
Rahm [ra:m] *m* (-[e]s; *no pl.*) cream; ***den ~ abschöpfen*** skim off the cream, cream off the top of the milk, *fig.* skim (*or* cream) off the best, F take the pick of the bunch
rah·men ['ra:mən] *v/t.* (h) frame *picture etc.*
'Rah·men *m* (-s; -) **1.** a) frame (*a.* ⚙, *mot.*), b) edge, border; **2.** *no pl. fig.* a) framework, structure; scope *of a law etc.*, b) limits *pl.*, c) setting; ***im ~ gen.*** within the scope of; ***im ~ des Möglichen*** within the realms of possibility; ***im ~ der geltenden Gesetze*** within the framework of existing legislation; ***im ~ e-s kurzen Artikels*** within the limitations of a short article; ***e-n zeitlichen ~ setzen*** fix a time limit; ***den ~ e-r Sache sprengen*** go beyond the scope of s.th.; ***im ~ der Ausstellung finden ... statt*** the exhibition will include ...; ***im ~ bleiben*** a) stick to what's relevant, b) keep within bounds; ***aus dem ~ fallen*** a) be unusual, be out of the ordinary, b) step out of line, c) be out of place, *a.* be a square peg in a round hole; ***die Rede fiel ganz aus dem ~ des Üblichen*** it wasn't the sort of speech you hear every day; ***in engem (größerem) ~*** on a small (large) scale; ***e-e Feier in bescheidenem ~*** a modest little celebration (*or* affair); ***den richtigen ~ abgeben für*** *acc.* provide an appropriate setting for; ***e-r Sache den richtigen ~ geben*** do s.th. in style; ***der große ~ ist festgelegt*** the general outline (*or* framework) has been fixed
'Rah·men|ab·kom·men *n* outline agreement; **~an,ten·ne** *f* frame *or* loop aerial (*or* antenna); **~be·din·gun·gen** *pl.* **1.** general set-up *sg.*; **2.** general conditions *of a contract etc.*; **~er·zäh·lung** *f* frame story; **~ge·setz** *n* skeleton law; **~kampf** *m boxing*: supporting bout; **~pro,gramm** *n* supporting program(me); fringe events *pl.*; **~richt·li·ni·en** *pl.* overall policy *sg.*, general framework *sg.* (for regulations); **~ver·trag** *m* outline agreement
'Rahm|kä·se *m* cream cheese; **~so·ße** *f* cream sauce
'Rah·se·gel *n* ⚓ square sail
Rain [raɪn] *m* (-[e]s; -e) ba(u)lk

rä·keln ['rɛ:kəln] → ***rekeln***
Ra·ke·te [ra'ke:tə] *f* (-; -n) rocket; ✕ *a.* missile; ***e-e ~ abfeuern*** launch a rocket (✕ missile); ***mehrstufige ~*** multistage rocket (✕ missile); *fig.* ***wie e-e ~*** like a shot
Ra'ke·ten·ab·schuß|ba·sis *f* rocket launching site; **~ram·pe** *f* (rocket) launching pad
Ra'ke·ten|ab·wehr *f* antiballistic missile defen|ce (*Am.* -se); **~an·trieb** *m* rocket propulsion; ***mit ~*** rocket-propelled; **~artil·le,rie** *f* rocket (*or* missile) artillery; **~auf·schlag** F *m tennis*: explosive (*or* thundering) serve; **2be·stückt** *adj.* missile-carrying; **~ge·schoß** *n* missile; **~kopf** *m*, **~spit·ze** *f* rocket (✕ missile) head; **~start** *m* lift-off, takeoff; **~start·platz** *m* rocket (✕ missile) launching site; **~stu·fe** *f* (rocket) stage; **~stütz·punkt** *m* missile base; **~treib·stoff** *m* rocket fuel; **~trieb·werk** *n* rocket engine; **~wer·fer** *m* rocket launcher; **~zeit·al·ter** *n* missile age, age of the missile
Ral·lye ['rɛli] *f* (-; -s), *n* (-s; -s) *mot.* (motor) rally; **~fah·rer** *m* rally driver; **~-Strei·fen** *m* go-faster stripe
RAM [ram] *n* (-[s]; -[s]) *computer*: RAM, random access memory
Ramm|bär ['ram-] *m* ⚙ ram; **~bock** *m hist.* battering ram
ramm·dö·sig ['ramdø:zɪç] F *adj.* F woozy
Ram·me ['ramə] *f* (-; -n) ⚙ ram(mer); pile-driver
ram·meln ['raməln] *v/i.* (h) **1.** *zo.* mate; **2.** jostle, F shove; **3.** F ***an der Tür ~*** rattle at the door; **4.** V screw
ram·men ['ramən] *v/t.* (h) **1.** *mot.*, ⚓ ram; **2.** ***~ in*** *acc.* ram (*or* drive) *pile etc.* into, drive (*or* plunge) *a knife etc.* into
Ramm·klotz ['ram-] *m* ⚙ ram
Ramm·ler ['ramlɐ] *m* (-s; -) *zo.* buck
Ram·pe ['rampə] *f* (-; -n) ramp; *thea.* apron (stage)
'Ram·pen·licht *n* footlights *pl.*; *fig.* ***im ~ stehen*** be in the limelight; ***im ~ der Öffentlichkeit stehen*** *a.* be in the public eye
ram·po·nie·ren [rampo'ni:rən] F *v/t.* (h) F knock *s.th.* about; spoil, F mess up *one's hairdo etc.*; **ram·po·niert** [rampo'ni:ɐt] F *adj.* **1.** battered (old) *armchair etc.*; run-down *house etc.*; ***~ aussehen*** be (*or* look) the worse for wear; ***der Tisch ist ziemlich ~*** *a.* the table's seen better days; **2.** *fig.* dented *self-confidence etc.*; tarnished *reputation, image etc.*
Ramsch [ramʃ] *contp. m* (-es; *no pl.*) junk; **~la·den** *m* junk shop; **~ver·kauf** *m* jumble sale; **~wa·re** *f* cheap stuff
'RAM-Spei·cher *m* RAM, random access memory
ran [ran] F *int.*: ***~ an die Arbeit (an den Speck)!*** F let's get on with it then!; *in cpds.* → ***heran...***; → ***rangehen, ranhalten, ranlassen, rannehmen***
Rand [rant] *m* (-[e]s; Ränder ['rɛndɐ]) edge; rim *of plate etc.*; brim *of hat*; margin; ***Ränder unter den Augen*** (dark) rings (*or* circles) under one's eyes; ***bis zum ~ gefüllt*** *glass etc.* filled to the top (*or* brim); ***et. an den ~ schreiben*** write s.th. in the margin; ***am ~e des Waldes*** on the edge of the woods; ***am ~e der Stadt*** on the outskirts (of the town); *fig.* ***am ~e des Ruins (der Verzweiflung*** *etc.*) on the verge (*or* brink) of ruin (despair *etc.*); ***am ~e der Gesellschaft*** on

the fringe(s) of society; ***am ~e der Legalität*** just inside the law; ***an den ~ (des Geschehens** etc.) **geraten*** be marginalized; ***am ~e des Grabes stehen*** have one foot in the grave; ***am ~e erwähnen*** mention in passing; ***am ~e behandeln*** deal with *a problem etc.* in passing; ***es interessiert mich nur am ~e*** it's only of marginal interest to me; ***er hat es nur am ~e miterlebt*** he wasn't directly involved (*or* affected by it); ***außer ~ und Band sein*** be going wild, be beside o.s. (***vor*** *dat.* with *delight etc.*), ***geraten:*** go wild (with joy); ***zu ~e kommen mit*** *dat.* a) ***j-m:*** get on with s.o., b) ***e-r Sache:*** cope with s.th., get to grips with s.th.; F ***halt den ~!*** shut up!

Ran·da·le [ran'da:lə] F *f*: ***~ machen*** go on the rampage; **ran·da·lie·ren** [randa'li:rən] *v/i.* (h) riot, go on the rampage; **Ran·da·lie·rer** [randa'li:rɐ] *m* (-s; -) rioter; hooligan, F lager lout

'Rand|be·mer·kung *f* **1.** marginal note; **2.** passing remark (*or* comment); **~be·völ·ke·rung** *f* fringe population; **~er·schei·nung** *f* secondary (*or* peripheral) phenomenon; spin-off (*gen.* from); **~fi͵gur** *f* fringe figure; secondary (*or* peripheral) character *in a novel etc.*; **~ge·biet** *n* border region *of a state*; outskirts *pl. of a town*; *fig.* peripheral (*or* fringe) area; fringe subject; ***in den ~en*** *gen.* on the fringes of (*a. fig.*); ***~ der Physik*** subsidiary area of physics; **~grup·pe** *f* fringe group; ***radikale ~n*** *the* lunatic fringe

'rand·los *adj.* rimless *glasses*; *photograph* without borders

'Rand|pro͵blem *n* side issue; **~schär·fe** *f opt.* contour sharpness; **~sied·lung** *f* suburban estate; **~staat** *m* border state; **~stein** *m* kerbstone, *Am.* curbstone; **~stel·ler** [-ʃtɛlɐ] *m* (-s; -) margin stop; **~stel·lung** *f*: ***e-e ~ einnehmen*** be on the fringes (of society); **~strei·fen** *m* **1.** verge *of a road*; (hard) shoulder *of a motorway etc.*; **2.** margin; **~tief** *n meteor.* surrounding ridge of low pressure

'rand'voll *adj.* full to the brim, brimful

'Rand·zo·ne *f* peripheral area; ***in den ~n*** *gen. a.* on the edges of

rang [raŋ] *pret. of* ***ringen***

Rang [raŋ] *m* (-[e]s; Ränge ['rɛŋə]) **1.** a) rank, b) ⚔ rank, *Am.* grade, rating (*a.* ⚓); ***e-n hohen (den ersten, den gleichen) ~ einnehmen*** rank high (first, equally); **2.** *no pl. fig.* standing, status, quality; ***ersten ~es*** first-class, first-rate; ***ein gesellschaftliches Ereignis von hohem ~*** a top-notch social occasion; ***j-m den ~ ablaufen*** outdo s.o., outstrip s.o.; ***j-m den ~ streitig machen*** challenge s.o.; ***ein Mann von (ohne) ~ und Namen*** a distinguished personality (a nobody); ***alles, was ~ und Namen hat*** all the big names (F top nobs); **3.** *thea.* ***erster ~*** dress circle, *Am.* balcony; ***zweiter ~*** upper circle, *Am.* amphitheat|re (*or* -er); ***dritter ~*** gallery; **4.** ***die Ränge*** *sport*: the terraces; ***vor leeren Rängen spielen*** play to an empty stadium; **5.** *lottery etc.*: (dividend) class

'Rang|ab·zei·chen *n* badge of rank; *pl.* insignia; **~äl·te·ste** *m* (-n; -n) senior; ⚔ senior officer

'ran·ge·hen F *v/i.* (*irr.*, *sep.*, sn, → ***gehen***): ***~ an*** *acc.* tackle *s.th.*; ***der geht aber ran!*** a) F he's really laying into him *etc.*, b) F he's a fast worker

Ran·ge·lei [raŋə'laı] F *f* (-; -en) wrangling (***um*** *acc.* over); **ran·geln** ['raŋəln] F *v/i.* (h) scuffle; *fig.* ***~ um*** *acc.* wrangle about *s.th.*, jockey for *a position etc.*

'Rang·fol·ge *f* order of precedence (*or* priority); ranking

'rang·hoch *adj.* top- (*or* high-)ranking, senior; ***ranghoher Offizier (Vertreter)*** high-ranking officer (senior representative); **'rang·höchst** *adj.* highest-ranking, most senior

Ran·gier·bahn·hof [raŋ'ʒi:ɐ-] *m* 🚂 shunting yard, *Am.* switchyard; **ran·gie·ren** [raŋ'ʒi:rən] (h) **I.** *v/t.* 🚂 shunt, *Am.* switch; *mot. etc.* manoeuvre, *Am.* maneuver; **II.** *fig. v/i.*: ***~ vor*** *dat.* rank above; ***an erster Stelle ~*** rank highest; **Ran·gie·rer** [raŋ'ʒi:rɐ] *m* (-s; -) 🚂 shunter, *Am.* switchman; **Ran'gier·gleis** *n* siding, *Am.* switching track

'Rang|li·ste *f* a) *sport etc.*: ranking list, b) ⚔ Army (Navy, Air Force) List; **~ord·nung** *f* order of precedence (*or* priority); ranking; *biol. and fig.* pecking order; **~stu·fe** *f* a) rank, b) priority; **~͵un·ter·schied** *m* difference in rank

'ran·hal·ten F *v/refl.* (*irr.*, *sep.*, h, → ***halten***): ***sich ~*** a) F get a move on, b) F get cracking, get on with it, c) F keep at it, d) F dig in

rank [raŋk] *adj.* lithe, lissom *body*; slender *a. tree*; ***~ und schlank*** lithe and lissom

Ran·ke ['raŋkə] *f* (-; -n) ⚘ tendril

Rän·ke ['rɛŋkə] *obs. pl.* intrigues; ***~ schmieden*** plot and scheme

ran·ken ['raŋkən] *v/refl.* (h): ***sich ~ um*** *acc.* curl (a)round; *fig.* ***um die Familie ~ sich viele Geschichten*** a lot of stories have grown up around the family

'Ran·ken·ge·wächs *n* creeper

'ran|klot·zen F *v/i.* (*sep.*, h) F get cracking, get stuck in; F go at it hammer and tongs; **~krie·gen** F *v/t.* (*sep.*, h): ***j-n ~*** a) F make s.o. knuckle under, F put s.o. through the mill; F make s.o. pull his (*or* her) weight, b) F get s.o. (to answer for s.th.), c) F con s.o., take s.o. for a ride; **~las·sen** F *v/t.* (*irr.*, *sep.*, h, → ***lassen***): ***j-n ~ an*** *acc.* let s.o. get at *s.th.*; ***sie läßt niemanden an sich ran*** she won't let anyone (come) near her; ***laß mich mal ran!*** let me have a go; ***sie sollten die Jüngeren ~*** they should give the young ones a chance; **~ma·chen** F *v/refl.* (*sep.*, h): ***sich an j-n ~*** make a pass at s.o.; **~neh·men** F *v/t.* (*irr.*, *sep.*, h, → ***nehmen***): ***j-n ~*** a) put s.o. through his (*or* her) paces, b) F let s.o. have it

rann [ran] *pret. of* ***rinnen***

rann·te ['rantə] *pret. of* ***rennen***

Ran·zen ['rantsən] *m* (-s; -) **1.** satchel; **2.** → ***Wanst***

ran·zig ['rantsıç] *adj.* rancid

ra·pi·de [ra'pi:də] **I.** *adj.* rapid; ***~r Anstieg*** rapid rise, surge (*gen.* in); **II.** *adv.*: ***~ ansteigen*** surge; ***~ sinken*** plummet; ***mit der Wirtschaft geht es ~ bergab*** the economy is going downhill fast

Ra·pier [ra'pi:ɐ] *n* (-s; -e [-rə]) rapier

Rap·pe ['rapə] *m* (-n; -n) black horse; *fig.* ***auf Schusters ~n reiten*** go on shanks's pony, F hoof it

Rap·pel ['rapəl] F *m* (-s; *no pl.*) craze; ***e-n ~ haben*** F be off one's nut; ***e-n ~ kriegen*** F go mad

rap·peln ['rapəln] (h) F **I.** *v/i.* rattle; *fig.* ***bei ihm rappelt's wohl!*** F he must be off his nut; **II.** *v/refl.*: ***sich aus dem Bett ~*** heave o.s. out of bed; ***sich in die Höhe ~*** struggle up, *fig.* struggle back onto one's feet

'rap·pel'voll F *adj.* F jampacked, chock-a-block

Rap·pen ['rapən] *m* (-s; -) *Switzerland*: centime

Rap·port [ra'pɔrt] *m* (-[e]s; -s) **1.** report; ***sich zum ~ melden bei*** report to; **2.** *psych.* rapport

Raps [raps] *m* (-es; *no pl.*) ⚘ rape; rapeseed; **~öl** *n* rapeseed oil

Ra·pun·zel [ra'puntsəl] *f* (-; -n) ⚘ *a. pl.* lamb's lettuce

rar [ra:ɐ] *adj.* rare, scarce; ***sich ~ machen*** make o.s. scarce

Ra·ri·tät [rari'tɛ:t] *f* (-; -en) rarity

Ra·ri'tä·ten|ka·bi͵nett *n* curiosity cabinet; **~samm·lung** *f* collection of curios

ra·sant [ra'zant] *adj.* **1.** fast *car etc.*; *fig.* rapid *development etc.*; ***in e-m ~en Tempo*** at breakneck speed; **2.** F smashing; **3.** racy; **Ra·sanz** [ra'zants] *f* (-; *no pl.*) **1.** terrific (*or* breakneck) speed *of a development etc.*; **2.** F verve *of a show etc.*

rasch [raʃ] **I.** *adj.* quick; swift *action etc.*; fast *pace etc.*; **II.** *adv.* quickly *etc.*; ***~ machen*** be quick (***mit*** *dat.* about *s.th.*); ***~!*** hurry up!, quick!, F make it snappy!

ra·scheln ['raʃəln] **I.** *v/i.* (h) rustle; **II.** ♀ *n* (-s; *no pl.*) rustling, rustle

ra·sen ['ra:zən] *v/i.* (sn) **1.** F race (along), tear (along), speed (along); ***~ gegen*** *acc.* run into, *car*: *a.* crash into; **2.** *fig.* rave; *storm, sea*: rage; ***vor Zorn ~*** *a.* be wild with rage; ***vor Schmerz ~*** be delirious with pain; ***vor Begeisterung ~*** be wild with enthusiasm

Ra·sen ['ra:zən] *m* (-s; -) lawn

'ra·send I. *adj.* **1.** raving; ***~er Durst*** raging thirst; ***~er Hunger*** ravenous hunger; ***e-n ~en Hunger haben*** be ravenous; ***~e Schmerzen*** searing (*or* raging) pain; ***~e Kopfschmerzen haben*** have a splitting (*or* raging) headache; ***~e Wut*** violent rage; ***~er Applaus*** thunderous applause; ***~ werden*** go mad; ***er macht mich noch ~*** F he's driving me spare; **2.** breakneck ..., terrific *speed*; **II.** F *adv.*: ***~ verliebt*** madly in love, besotted; ***er spielt ~ gern Backgammon*** he loves backgammon, he's mad (F wild) about backgammon

'Ra·sen|hei·zung *f* under-soil heating; **~mä·her** *m* lawnmower; **~platz** *m tennis*: grass court; **~spren·ger** *m* sprinkler

Ra·ser ['ra:zɐ] F *m* (-s; -) *mot.* F speeder, speedster, speed freak, hot rodder

Ra·se·rei [ra:zə'raı] *f* (-; *no pl.*) **1.** a) rage, fury, b) frenzy, madness; ***j-n zur ~ treiben*** F drive s.o. round the bend; **2.** F *mot.* (reckless) speeding

Ra·sier|ap·pa͵rat [ra'zi:ɐ-] *m* razor; ***elektrischer ~*** *a.* electric shaver; **~creme** *f* shaving cream

ra·sie·ren [ra'zi:rən] *v/t.* (h) **1.** (*a.* ***sich ~***) shave; **2.** *fig.* raze to the ground; **3.** F *fig.* ***j-n ~*** F pull a fast one on s.o.

Ra·sier|klin·ge [ra'zi:ɐ-] *f* razor blade; **~mes·ser** *n* (straight) razor; **~pin·sel** *m* shaving brush; **~schaum** *m* shaving foam; **~sei·fe** *f* shaving soap; **~was·ser** *n* pre-shave lotion; aftershave (lotion); **~zeug** F *n* shaving things *pl.* (*or* kit)

Rä·son [rɛ'zõ:] *f*: ***j-n zur ~ bringen*** talk some sense into s.o., bring s.o. round; ***zur ~ kommen*** see reason

rä·so·nie·ren [rɛzoˈniːrən] *v/i.* (h) **1.** *dial.* moan; **2.** hold forth (**über** *acc.* on)
Ras·pel¹ [ˈraspəl] *f* (-; -n) **1.** ⚙ rasp; **2.** *gastr.* grater; **Ras·pel²** *m* (-s; -n) *usu. pl. gastr.* flake; **ˈras·peln** *v/t.* (h) **1.** ⚙ rasp; **2.** *gastr.* grate; → ***Süßholz***
raß [ras] *dial. adj.* strong *spirits etc.*, sharp *cheese etc.*; hot *spices*; *fig.* biting *wind*; crude *joke etc.*
Ras·se [ˈrasə] *f* (-; -n) race (*a. fig.*); *zo. a.* breed; *fig. a.* class; F *fig.* ***seltsame*** ~ strange breed; *contp.* ***sie sind e-e*** ~ ***für sich*** F they're an odd (*or* a strange) lot; **~hund** *m* pedigree (*or* pure-bred) dog
Ras·sel [ˈrasəl] *f* (-; -n) rattle; **~ban·de** F *f* F noisy lot; bunch of rascals
ras·seln [ˈrasəln] *v/i.* (h) rattle; *alarm clock*: shrill; ~ ***mit*** *dat.* rattle *s.th.*, *a.* jangle *keys*; **~*des Geräusch*** rattling (sound); F ***gegen e-e Mauer*** ~ crash against (*or* into) a wall; F ***durch e-e Prüfung*** ~ F flunk an exam
ˈRas·sen|dis·kri·miˌnie·rung *f* racial discrimination; **~faˌna·ti·ker** *m* racialist; **~fra·ge** *f* racial problem; **~haß** *m* racial hatred; **~het·ze** *f* racial aggression; **~ideoˌlo·ge** *m* racial theorist (*or* ideologist); **~ideo·loˌgie** *f* racial theory (*or* ideology); **~in·te·gra·tiˌon** *f* racial integration; **~kampf** *m*, **~konˌflikt** *m* racial conflict; **~kraˌwal·le** *pl.* race riots; **~kreu·zung** *f zo.* a) crossbreeding, b) crossbreed; **~kun·de** *f* racial anthropology; **~mi·schung** *f* a) *zo.* crossbreeding, b) interbreeding; **~po·liˌtik** *f* racial policy; **~schran·ke** *f* colo(u)r bar; **~tren·nung** *f* (racial) segregation; **~un·ru·hen** *pl.* race riots, racial unrest *sg.*; **~vor·ur·teil** *n* racial prejudice; **~wahn** *m* racial fanaticism
ˈRas·se|pferd *n* thoroughbred (horse); **~weib** F *n* F smasher
ras·sig [ˈrasɪç] *adj.* **1.** *zo.* thoroughbred; **2.** fiery; hot-blooded *woman etc.*; **3.** racy *wine etc.*
ras·sisch [ˈrasɪʃ] *adj.* racial
Ras·sis·mus [raˈsɪsmʊs] *m* (-; *no pl.*) racism; **Ras·sist** [raˈsɪst] *m* (-en; -en) racist; **ras·si·stisch** [raˈsɪstɪʃ] *adj.* racist
Rast [rast] *f* (-; *no pl.*) rest; break; ~ ***machen*** make a stop; have a rest
ra·sten [ˈrastən] *v/i.* (h) (take a) rest
Ra·ster¹ [ˈrastɐ] *m* (-s; -) **1.** *phot.*, *typ.* screen; **2.** *fig.* pattern, scheme; ***das fällt aus dem*** ~ ***heraus*** it doesn't fit into any pattern (*or* scheme)
ˈRa·ster² *n* (-s; -) *TV*, *computer*: raster; **~ein·heit** *f* raster unit; **~fahn·dung** *f* computer search
ra·stern [ˈrastɐn] *v/t.* (h) **1.** *phot.* print in halftone; **2.** *TV* scan
ˈrast·los I. *adj.* a) indefatigable, b) restless; **II.** *adv.*: ~ ***tätig sein*** work nonstop, F be on the go all the time
ˈRast|platz *m* place for a rest; *motorway*: lay-by, *Am.* rest stop; **~stät·te** *f* **1.** motorway restaurant; **2.** (motorway) service area; *sign*: Services *pl.*
Ra·sur [raˈzuːɐ] *f* (-; -en [-rən]) **1.** shave; **2.** erasure
Rat¹ [raːt] *m* (-[e]s; *no pl.*) a) advice; recommendation, b) suggestion, c) way out; ***ein*** ~ a piece of advice, some advice; ***ein guter*** ~ (some) good *or* sound advice; ***auf s-n*** ~ ***hin*** on his advice; ***j-n um*** ~ ***fragen*** ask s.o. for advice, ask s.o.'s advice; ~ ***suchen*** seek advice (**bei** *dat.* from); ***j-s*** ~ ***befolgen*** take (*or* follow) s.o.'s advice; ***nicht auf j-s*** ~ ***hören*** ignore s.o.'s advice; ***mit sich zu ~e gehen*** think things over; ***j-n zu ~e ziehen*** consult s.o., seek s.o.'s advice; ~ ***schaffen*** find ways and means; ~ ***wissen*** know what to do; ***keinen*** ~ ***mehr wissen*** be at a loss as to what to do; ***da ist guter*** ~ ***teuer*** it's hard to say what to do; ***j-m mit*** ~ ***und Tat beistehen*** give s.o. one's advice and support; → ***Zeit***
Rat² *m* (-[e]s; Räte [ˈrɛːtə]) **1.** council, board; ~ ***der EU*** Council of Ministers; **2.** council(l)or
Ra·te [ˈraːtə] *f* (-; -n) **1.** ✝ instal(l)ment; ***auf ~n kaufen*** buy in instal(l)ments (*Brit. a.* on hire purchase); **2.** rate
ra·ten¹ [ˈraːtən] *v/t. and v/i.* (riet, geraten, h) advise (**zu** *dat. s.th.*); ***zu et.*** ~ *a.* recommend s.th.; ***j-m*** ~, ***et. zu tun*** advise s.o. to do s.th.; ***er riet*** (***mir***) ***zur Vorsicht*** he advised me to be careful, he advised caution; ***ich rate dir zu diesem Modell*** I would advise you to take (*or* I think you should take) this model; ***das möchte ich dir geraten haben*** just as well (for your sake), F you'd damn well better (not); → ***geraten²***
ˈra·ten² *v/t. and v/i.* (riet, geraten, h) guess; ~ ***Sie mal!*** (have a) guess; ***gut geraten!*** good guess!; ***falsch geraten!*** wrong!; ***dreimal darfst du*** ~ I'll give you three guesses; ***du darfst noch mal*** ~ have another guess; ***das rätst du nie*** you'll never guess; ***das ist alles nur geraten*** it's all guesswork
ˈRa·ten|kauf *m* hire purchase, *Am.* installment plan; **~kreˌdit** *m* instal(l)ment credit; **&wei·se** *adv.* by instal(l)ments; **~zah·lung** *f* payment by instal(l)ments; ***auf*** ~ ***kaufen*** buy in instal(l)ments (*Brit. a.* on hire purchase)
Ra·te·spiel [ˈraːtə-] *n* guessing game
ˈRat·ge·ber *m* **1.** adviser, counsel(l)or; **2.** guide (**über** *acc.* to), self-help book (on), F how-to book (on); ~ ***für Arbeitslose*** *etc. a.* tips for the unemployed *etc.*
ˈRat·haus *n* town (*Am.* city) hall
Ra·ti·fi·ka·ti·on [ratifikaˈtsi̯oːn] *f* (-; -en) ratification
Ra·ti·fi·ka·tiˈons|klau·sel *f* ratification clause; **~ur·kun·de** *f* ratification document; **~ver·fah·ren** *n* ratification proceedings *pl.*
ra·ti·fi·zie·ren [ratifiˈtsiːrən] *v/t.* (h) ratify; **Ra·ti·fiˈzie·rung** *f* (-; -en) ratification; **Ra·ti·fiˈzie·rungs...** *in cpds.* → ***Ratifikations...***
Ra·tio [ˈraːtsi̯o] *f* (-; *no pl.*): ***die*** ~ reason
Ra·ti·on [raˈtsi̯oːn] *f* (-; -en) a) ration, b) allowance, share; ***eiserne*** ~ emergency (*or* iron) rations
ra·tio·nal [ratsi̯oˈnaːl] *adj.* rational (*a.* 𝔄)
ra·tio·na·li·sie·ren [ratsi̯onaliˈziːrən] *v/t.* (h) ✝ rationalize, streamline
Ra·tio·na·liˈsie·rung *f* (-; -en) rationalization; **Ra·tio·na·liˈsie·rungs·maß·nah·me** *f* efficiency measure
Ra·tio·na·lis·mus [ratsi̯onaˈlɪsmʊs] *m* (-; *no pl.*) rationalism; **Ra·tio·na·list** [ratsi̯onaˈlɪst] *m* (-en; -en) rationalist
ra·tio·na·li·stisch [ratsi̯onaˈlɪstɪʃ] *adj.* rationalist(ic)
ra·tio·nell [ratsi̯oˈnɛl] *adj.* rational, reasonable; efficient
ra·tio·nie·ren [ratsi̯oˈniːrən] *v/t.* (h) ration; **Ra·tioˈnie·rung** *f* (-; -en) rationing
ˈrat·los *adj.* helpless, at a loss
ˈRat·lo·sig·keit *f* (-; *no pl.*) helplessness
ˈrat·sam *adj.* advisable; wise; ***ich halte es nicht für*** ~ I don't think it's (*or* it would be) advisable *or* a good idea
ˈRat·sam·keit *f* (-; *no pl.*) advisability
Rat·sche [ˈraːtʃə] *f* (-; -n) rattle
rat·schen [ˈraːtʃən] F *v/i.* (h) a) F have a natter, b) gossip
ˈRat·schlag *m* (piece of) advice
Rät·sel [ˈrɛːtsəl] *n* (-s; -) riddle, puzzle (*a. fig.*); mystery; ***j-m*** ~ ***aufgeben*** ask s.o. riddles, *fig.* puzzle s.o., baffle s.o.; *fig.* ***in ~n sprechen*** speak in riddles; ***er ist mir ein*** ~ I can't make him out; ***es ist mir ein*** ~, ***ich stehe vor e-m*** ~ it's a complete mystery to me, F it beats me; ***vor e-m*** ~ ***stehen*** be baffled; ***das ist des ~s Lösung!*** that's the answer; **~ecke** *f* puzzle corner (*or* section); **~fra·ge** *f* puzzling question
ˈrät·sel·haft *adj.* puzzling; mysterious; ***es ist mir völlig*** ~ it's a complete mystery to me
ˈRät·sel·heft *n* puzzle book
rät·seln [ˈrɛːtsəln] *v/i.* (h) puzzle (**über** *acc.* over), speculate
ˈRät·sel·ra·ten *n* guessing games *pl.*; *fig.* speculation (**um** *acc.* about, over, on)
ˈRats|herr *m* (town) council(l)or, alderman; **~kel·ler** *m* rat(h)skeller; *city hall cellar-restaurant*; **~sit·zung** *f* council meeting
ˈrat·su·chend *adj.*: ***~e Personen, &e*** those (*or* anyone) seeking advice
ˈRats·ver·samm·lung *f* **1.** council, assembly; **2.** → ***Ratssitzung***
Rat·tan [ˈratan] *n* (-s; *no pl.*) rattan; **~mö·bel** *pl.* rattan (*or* cane) furniture
Rat·te [ˈratə] *f* (-; -n) rat
ˈRat·ten|fän·ger *m* ratcatcher; *fig. contp.* pied piper; **~gift** *n* rat poison; **~nest** *n* rat's nest; *fig.* lair, den of thieves *etc.*; **~schwanz** *m* **1.** *zo.* rat's tail; **2.** F pigtail; **3.** *fig.* ***ein*** (***ganzer***) ~ ***von*** *dat.* a whole string of; ***es zog e-n*** ~ ***von Problemen nach sich*** it brought a whole string of problems with it
rat·tern [ˈratɐn] *v/i.* (h), & *n* (-s; *no pl.*) rattle, clatter; *machine gun*: crackle; *engine etc.*: roar
rat·ze'kahl [ˈratsə-] F *adv.*: ***alles*** ~ ***auffressen*** F polish off the lot; ***e-n Baum*** ~ ***abfressen*** strip a tree clean (*or* bare)
Raub [raʊp] *m* (-es [ˈraʊbəs]; *no pl.*) **1.** robbery (*a.* ⚖); **2.** booty, loot; ***auf*** ~ ***ausgehen*** a) *zo.* hunt its prey, b) *thief*: go out on the prowl; *fig.* ***ein*** ~ ***der Flammen werden*** be destroyed by fire, be engulfed in flames; **~auf·nah·me** *f* pirate recording; **~aus·ga·be** *f* pirate edition; **~bau** *m* (-[e]s; *no pl.*) overexploitation (**an** *dat.* of), uncontrolled exploitation (of); ~ ***an der Landschaft*** despoliation of the countryside; ***mit s-r Gesundheit*** ~ ***treiben*** ruin one's health; **~druck** *m* (-[e]s; -e) pirate edition
rau·ben [ˈraʊbən] (h) **I.** *v/i.* rob, commit robbery; **II.** *v/t.* rob, steal; kidnap; ***j-m den Atem*** ~ take s.o.'s breath away; ***j-m den Schlaf*** *etc.* ~ rob *od.* deprive s.o. of his (*or* her) sleep *etc.*; ***es raubt mir zuviel Zeit*** it takes away too much of my time
Räu·ber [ˈrɔʏbɐ] *m* (-s; -) robber; highwayman; ~ ***und Gendarm spielen*** play cops and robbers; **~ban·de** *f* band of robbers; **~ge·schich·te** *f* story about robbers; F *fig.* F cock-and-bull story; **~höh·le** *f* den of robbers (*or* thieves); F

hier sieht's aus wie in e-r ~ F this place is an absolute mess, it's like a pigsty in here

räu·be·risch ['rɔʏbərɪʃ] *adj.* a) *zo.* predatory, b) thieving *person*; marauding *tribes etc.*; ***~e Erpressung*** extortion by means of force

räu·bern ['rɔʏbɐn] F *fig. v/i.* (h): ***im Kühlschrank*** *etc.* **~** F raid the fridge *etc.*

Räu·ber|pi,sto·le ['rɔʏbɐ-] *fig. f* F cock-and-bull story; **~zi,vil** F *n* F old togs; ***komm ruhig in ~*** come as you are

'Raub·fisch *m* predatory fish

'Raub·gier *f* rapacity; **'raub·gie·rig** *adj.* rapacious

'Raub|kat·ze *f* big cat; member of the cat family; **~ko,pie** *f* pirate copy; **~krieg** *m* **1.** marauding war(fare); **2.** war of annexation; **~mord** *m* murder and robbery; **~mör·der** *m* murderer and robber; **~plat·te** *f*, **~pres·sung** *f* F bootleg (record); **~rit·ter** *m hist.* robber baron; **~tier** *n* predator, (predatory) wild animal; **~,über·fall** *m*: (***bewaffneter ~*** armed) robbery, holdup; mugging; **~vo·gel** *m* bird of prey; **~zug** *m* predatory attack

Rauch [raʊx] *m* (-[e]s; *no pl.*) smoke; fumes *pl.*; ***in ~ aufgehen*** go up in smoke (*a. fig.*); *fig.* ***kein ~ ohne Flamme*** there's no smoke without fire; **~ab·zug** *m* flue; **~bier** *n* smoked beer; **~bom·be** *f* smoke bomb

rau·chen ['raʊxən] **I.** *v/i. and v/t.* (h) a) smoke, b) fume; ***er raucht stark*** he's a heavy smoker, he smokes a lot; ***er raucht wenig*** he doesn't smoke very much; F *fig.* ***wir arbeiteten, daß es nur so rauchte*** F we were going at it hammer and tongs; ***mir rauchte der Kopf*** my head started spinning; F ***..., sonst raucht es!*** F ... or you'll be in for it!; **II.** **2** *n* (-s; *no pl.*) smoking; ***~ verboten!*** no smoking

Rau·cher ['raʊxɐ] *m* (-s; -) **1.** smoker; **2.** smoking compartment, F smoker

Räu·cher·aal ['rɔʏçɐ-] *m* smoked eel

'Rau·cher|ab,teil *n* → ***Raucher*** 2; **~bein** *n* ⚕ smoker's leg, 📖 claudication

Räu·cher|ge·fäß ['rɔʏçɐ-] *n* censer; **~he·ring** *m* smoked herring, kipper

'Rau·cher·hu·sten *m* smoker's cough

Rau·che·rin ['raʊxərɪn] *f* (-; -nen) smoker

Räu·cher·ker·ze ['rɔʏçɐ-] *f* aromatic candle

'Rau·cher·krebs *m* smoker's (*or* smoking-related) cancer

Räu·cher·lachs ['rɔʏçɐ-] *m* smoked salmon

räu·chern ['rɔʏçɐn] (h) **I.** *v/t.* **1.** *gastr.* smoke, cure; **2.** fumigate; **II.** *v/i.* burn incense

Räu·cher|schin·ken ['rɔʏçɐ-] *m* smoked ham; **~stäb·chen** *n* joss stick

'Rauch|fah·ne *f* smoke trail; **~fang** *m* chimney hood

'rauch|far·ben *adj.* smoke-colo(u)red; **~frei** *adj.*: ***~e Zone*** no-smoking area (*or* part) *of a restaurant etc.*

'Rauch|gas *n* flue gas; **~ge·schmack** *m* taste of smoke; **2ge·schwärzt** *adj.* black with smoke; **~glas** *n* smoked glass

rau·chig ['raʊxɪç] *adj.* smoky (*a. voice*)

'Rauch|krin·gel *m* smoke ring; **~mel·der** *m* smoke detector; **~pilz** *m* mushroom cloud; **~quarz** *m* smoky quartz, cairngorm; **~säu·le** *f* pillar of smoke; **~schwa·den** *pl.* billows of smoke; **~schwal·be** *f* (barn) swallow; **~si,gnal** *n* smoke signal; **~to,pas** *m* smoky topaz; **~ver·bot** *n* ban on smoking; ***hier herrscht ~*** there's no smoking allowed here; **~ver·gif·tung** *f* smoke poisoning

'Rauch·wa·ren¹ *pl.* tobacco products

'Rauch·wa·ren² *pl.* furs

'Rauch|werk *n* (-[e]s; *no pl.*) → ***Rauchwaren²***; **~wol·ke** *f* cloud of smoke; **~zei·chen** *n* smoke signal

Räu·de ['rɔʏdə] *f vet.* mange

räu·dig ['rɔʏdɪç] *adj.* mangy

rauf [raʊf] F *adv.*, **rauf...** *in cpds.* **1.** → ***herauf(...)***; **2.** → ***hinauf(...)***

Rauf·bold ['raʊfbɔlt] *m* (-[e]s; -e [-də]) ruffian; **rau·fen** ['raʊfən] (h) **I.** *v/t.* pull (out); → ***Haar***; **II.** *v/i. and v/refl.*: (***sich ~***) scuffle, brawl, tussle; **Rau·fe·rei** [raʊfə'raɪ] *f* (-; -en) fight, brawl, scuffle; **'rauf·lu·stig** *adj.* pugnacious; ***~ sein*** *a.* love to tussle

rauh [raʊ] *adj.* a) rough (*a. skin, weather, tone etc.*), *a.* coarse *fur etc.*, b) raw *wind etc.*; biting, bitter *cold*; severe *winter*; harsh *climate*, c) desolate *region, country etc.*, d) sore *throat*; hoarse, harsh, grating, husky *voice*, e) tough, rough *life*, f) harsh; coarse; ***~e Behandlung*** rough treatment; ***~e Wirklichkeit*** harsh reality; ***der ~e Norden*** the cold north; F ***in ~en Mengen ...*** galore, F heaps of ...; ***~ aber herzlich*** bluff

'Rauh·bein *n* rough diamond

'rauh·bei·nig [-baɪnɪç] *adj.* bluff

'Rau·heit *f* (-; *no pl.*) roughness; severity; harshness; coarseness *etc.*; → ***rauh***

rau·hen ['raʊən] *v/t.* (h) rough(en); *textil.* tease, nap

'Rauh·fa·ser·ta,pe·te *f* woodchip paper

'Rauh·haar·dackel *m* wire-haired dachshund; **'rauh·haa·rig** *adj.* wire-haired

'Rauh·reif *m* white frost, hoarfrost

Raum [raʊm] *m* (-[e]s; Räume ['rɔʏmə]) a) room, b) *no pl.* area, c) space, expanse, c) *no pl. phys., phls.* space (*a. ast.*); volume, d) *no pl. fig.* scope, room; ***viel ~ beanspruchen*** take up a lot of space; ***auf engstem ~ leben*** live in cramped surroundings; ***freier ~*** *sport*: open space; ***Spiel in den freien ~*** opening up the game; ***im ~ München*** in the Munich area; ***es nahm in der Diskussion e-n breiten ~ ein*** it occupied a large part of the discussion; ***die grenzenlosen Räume des Weltalls*** the limitless expanses of the universe; ***~ geben*** *or* ***gewähren*** *dat.* give way to *an idea etc.*, entertain *hopes*, grant *a request etc.*; ***das Problem steht im ~*** the problem demands an answer; ***e-e Frage im ~ stehenlassen*** leave a question unanswered; ***ich möchte die Frage einfach in den ~ stellen*** I'd just like to throw up the question for us to be thinking about it

'Raum|aku·stik *f* acoustics *pl.* (of a *or* the room); **~an·zug** *m* space suit; **~aus·stat·ter** *m* interior decorator; **~aus·stat·tung** *f* interior decorating, interior (of a room); **~be·darf** *m* required space, space required

Räum·boot ['rɔʏm-] *n* minesweeper

'Raum·deckung *f sport*: zone marking

räu·men ['rɔʏmən] (h) **I.** *v/t.* **1.** clear away, remove; ***et. in den Schrank ~*** put s.th. away in the cupboard; ***aus dem Weg ~*** clear (*or* get) *s.th.* out of the way, *fig.* get rid of, *a.* solve *a problem etc.*; **2.** move out of, *formal*: vacate *house etc.*; check out of *a hotel room*; clear *scene of the accident, hall etc.*; clear out *drawers etc.*; evacuate, ⚔ *a.* leave *an area etc.*; ⚔ leave, retreat from *a position*; ✝ clear, sell off *stocks*; ***j-m den Platz ~*** give s.o. one's seat, *fig.* make way for s.o.; ⚖ ***den Saal ~ lassen*** have the court cleared; **II.** *v/i.* clear up

'Raum|fäh·re *f* space shuttle; **~fah·rer** *m* astronaut, spaceman

'Raum·fahrt *f* (-; *no pl.*) **1.** space travel; **2.** astronautics *pl.*; **~be·hör·de** *f* space agency; **~in·du,strie** *f* space industry; **~me·di,zin** *f* space medicine; **~pro,gramm** *n* space program(me); **~pro,jekt** *n* space project; **~tech·nik** *f* space technology; **~tech·ni·ker** *m* space engineer; **~zen·trum** *n* space centre (*Am.* center)

'Raum|fahr·zeug *n* spacecraft, spaceship; **~flug** *m* space flight; **~for·schung** *f* (aero)space research; **~ge·stal·ter** *m* interior decorator; **~ge·stal·tung** *f* interior decorating; **2grei·fend** *adj.*: ***~e Schritte*** long strides; **~in·halt** *m* volume, capacity; **~kap·sel** *f* space capsule; **~klang** *m* stereophonic sound; **~la,bor** *n* → ***Raumstation***

räum·lich ['rɔʏmlɪç] **I.** *adj.* spatial, space ...; three-dimensional; ***~e Wirkung*** depth, three-dimensionality; **II.** *adv.*: ***~ sehr beengt*** cramped (for space); ***~ gefällt mir die Wohnung*** I like the layout of the flat (*Am.* apartment)

'Räum·lich·keit *f* (-; -en) **1.** room; *pl. a.* premises; **2.** *no pl.* depth, three-dimensionality

'Raum|man·gel *m* lack of space (*or* room); restricted space; **~maß** *n* solid measure; **~not** *f* lack of space; cramped living conditions *pl.*; **~ord·nungs·plan** *m pol.* development plan; **~pfle·ge·rin** *f* cleaning lady; **~schiff** *n* spaceship; **~son·de** *f* space probe; **2spa·rend** *adj.* space-saving; **~sta·ti,on** *f* space station (*or* platform), skylab; **~tei·ler** *m* partition; **~tem·pe·ra,tur** *f* room temperature; **~ton** *m* stereophonic sound; **~trans,por·ter** *m* space shuttle

Räu·mung ['rɔʏmʊŋ] *f* (-; -en) **1.** removal; **2.** clearing, *esp.* ✝ clearance; **3.** a) vacating, b) eviction; ***die ~ der Wohnung muß bis ... erfolgen*** the flat must be vacated by ...; **4.** *a.* ⚔ evacuation

'Räu·mungs|ar·bei·ten *pl.* clear-up operation(s); **~be·fehl** *m* eviction order; **~kla·ge** *f* action for possession (*Am.* eviction); **~ver·kauf** *m* clearance sale

rau·nen ['raʊnən] *v/i. and v/t.* (h) whisper, murmur (*both a. fig.*)

Rau·pe ['raʊpə] *f* (-; -n) **1.** *zo.* caterpillar; grub; **2.** ⚙ a) caterpillar (*TM*), b) → ***Raupenkette***

'Rau·pen|fahr·zeug *n* tracked vehicle; **~ket·te** *f* track chain

raus [raʊs] F *adv.*, **raus...** *in cpds.* **1.** → ***heraus(...)***; **2.** → ***hinaus(...)***; ***~!*** (get) out!, *sl.* scram!; ***~ mit euch!*** (come on,) out you go *into the garden etc.*, (come on,) out you get; ***~ mit der Sprache!*** F (come on,) spit it out!

Rausch [raʊʃ] *m* (-es; Räusche ['rɔʏʃə]) **1.** intoxication, drunkenness; F high; ***sich e-n ~ antrinken*** get drunk; ***e-n ~ haben*** be drunk; ***s-n ~ ausschlafen*** sleep it off; ***im ~*** under the influence of alcohol; **2.** *no pl. fig.* a) delirious state, frenzy, b) rapture, exhilaration; ***im ~ des Glücks sein***

be deliriously happy; ***im ~ der Geschwindigkeit*** intoxicated (*or* drunk) with speed; ***im ~ der Begeisterung*** carried away by one's enthusiasm, in a fit of enthusiasm; ***im ~ des Erfolgs*** carried away by success; ***im ~ der Leidenschaft*** seized with (a burning) passion

'rausch·arm *adj.* low-noise

rau·schen ['raʊʃən] *v/i.* **1.** (h) *water*: rush; *brook*: murmur; *surf, storm*: roar; *leaves, silk etc.*: rustle; *applause*: ring, thunder; ***es rauscht im Radio*** there's (a lot of) interference (*or* static) on the radio; **2.** (sn) sweep, sail; **'rau·schend** *adj.* rustling *etc.*; → ***rauschen; ~er Beifall*** rapturous applause; ***~es Fest*** lavish party (*or* celebration)

'Rausch|fak·tor *m* noise ratio; **~fil·ter** *n* noise suppressor

'Rausch·gift *n* narcotic, drug; *coll.* narcotics *pl.*, drugs *pl.*; **~be·kämp·fung** *f* fight against drugs; **~de·zer,nat** *n* narcotics (*or* drugs) squad; **~han·del** *m* drug trafficking; **~händ·ler** *m* drug dealer; **~ma·fia** *f* drugs mafia; **~sucht** *f* drug addiction; **♀süch·tig** *adj.* addicted to drugs; **~süch·ti·ge** *m, f* drug addict

'Rausch|gold *n* gold foil; **~sper·re** *f hi-fi etc.*: noise gate; **~un·ter,drückungs·sy,stem** *n* noise reduction system

'raus·feu·ern F *v/t.* (*sep.*, h) fire, F give *s.o.* the sack (*or* boot)

'raus·flie·gen F *v/i.* (*irr.*, *sep.*, sn, → ***fliegen***) F be kicked (*or* booted, chucked, turfed) out; F get the sack (*or* boot)

'raus·hal·ten (*irr.*, *sep.*, h, → ***halten***) F **I.** *v/refl.*: ***sich ~*** keep out of it, ***aus e-r Sache***: keep out of s.th.; ***halt dich da raus!*** don't get involved, I'd keep out of it if I were you; **II.** *v/t.* keep *s.o. or s.th.* out of it; ***~ aus e-r Sache*** keep *s.o. or s.th.* out of s.th.

'raus·krie·gen F *v/t.* (*sep.*, h) → ***herausbekommen*** 1

räus·pern ['rɔʏspɐn] *v/refl.* (h): ***sich ~*** clear one's throat

'raus·rei·ßen F *v/t.* → ***herausreißen***

'raus·schmei·ßen F *v/t.* (*irr.*, *sep.*, h, → ***schmeißen***) throw out, F chuck out, *a.* F kick *s.o.* out (*all* ***aus*** *dat.* of); *a.* fire, F give *s.o.* the boot; **Raus·schmei·ßer** ['raʊsʃmaɪsɐ] F *m* (-s; -) F bouncer

Raus·schmiß ['raʊsʃmɪs] F *m* (-sses; -sse) sacking, F *the* boot

Rau·te ['raʊtə] *f* (-; -n) **1.** ♀ rue; **2.** ⩓ rhomb(us); **3.** *her.* lozenge; **4.** *cards*: diamond; **'rau·ten·för·mig** [-fœrmɪç] *adj.* diamond-shaped

Ra·vio·li [ra'vĭo:li] *pl.* ravioli

Raz·zia ['ratsĭa] *f* (-; Razzien ['ratsĭən]) (police) raid, police roundup, F swoop; ***e-e ~ machen*** make a raid (***auf*** *acc.* on), ***auf*** *acc.*: *a.* raid, F swoop on

Rea·genz|glas [rea'gɛnts-] *n* test tube; **~pa,pier** *n* test paper

rea·gie·ren [rea'gi:rən] *v/i.* (h) react (***auf*** *acc.* to, ⚗ on), respond (to *a.* ⚕ *a treatment etc.*); ***nicht ~ auf*** *acc.* ignore; ***sofort ~*** respond immediately; ***sie reagierten überhaupt nicht*** *a.* there was no reaction (from them); ***ich bin gespannt, wie er darauf ~ wird*** I wonder what he'll say (*or* how he'll take it)

Re·ak·ti·on [reak'tsĭo:n] *f* (-; -en) **1.** reaction (***auf*** *acc.* to, ⚗ on); ⚕ *a.* response (to), reflex; ***s-e erste ~ war Wut*** his initial reaction was to get angry, at first he was angry; **2.** *pol.* reactionary forces *pl.*

re·ak·tio·när [reaktsĭo'nɛ:ɐ] *adj.*, ♀ *m* (-s; -e [-rə]) reactionary

Re·ak·ti'ons|fä·hig·keit *f* (-; *no pl.*) reactions *pl.*; ***es schränkt die ~ ein*** it slows down your reactions; **♀schnell** *adj.*: ***~ sein*** have fast reactions; **~ver·mö·gen** *n* (-s; *no pl.*) → ***Reaktionsfähigkeit***; **~zeit** *f* reaction (*or* response) time

re·ak·ti·vie·ren [reakti'vi:rən] *v/t.* (h) reactivate

Re·ak·tor [re'akto:ɐ] *m* (-s; -en [reak'to:rən]) reactor; **~block** *m* reactor block; **~ge·bäu·de** *n* reactor housing (*or* dome); **~gift** *n toxic substance emanating from a nuclear reactor*; **~kern** *m* reactor core; **~si·cher·heit** *f* reactor safety; **~un·fall** *m* reactor accident; **~un·glück** *n* reactor disaster

re·al [re'a:l] *adj.* **1.** real (*a.* ✝); concrete; **2.** realistic

Re'al·ein·kom·men *n* real income

Rea·li·en [re'a:lĭən] *pl.* **1.** facts, realities; **2.** expert knowledge *sg.*

rea·li·sier·bar [reali'zi:ɐba:ɐ] *adj.* realizable; ***der Plan ist nicht ~*** the plan can't be put into practice (*or* practise)

rea·li·sie·ren [reali'zi:rən] (h) **I.** *v/t.* realize; ✝ *a.* convert into money; **II.** *v/refl.*: ***sich ~*** materialize, be realized

Rea·li'sie·rung *f* (-; *no pl.*) realization

Rea·lis·mus [rea'lɪsmʊs] *m* (-; *no pl.*) realism; **Rea·list** [rea'lɪst] *m* (-en; -en) realist; **rea·li·stisch** [rea'lɪstɪʃ] *adj.* realistic(ally *adv.*)

Rea·li·tät [reali'tɛ:t] *f* (-; -en) **1.** *no pl.* reality; ***in der ~*** in real life, in reality; **2.** *pl.* facts

rea·li'täts|be·zo·gen *adj.* realistic; **~fern** *adj.* unrealistic; out of touch with reality; **~fremd** *adj.* out of touch (with reality); **~nah** *adj.* close to reality; realistic

Rea·li'täts·sinn *m* (-[e]s; *no pl.*) sense of reality

rea·li·ter [re'a:litɐ] *adv.* in reality

Re'al·le·xi·kon *n* (specialist) encyclop(a)edia

Rea·lo [re'a:lo] F *m* (-s; -s) *pol.* pragmatic Green

Re'al|po·li,tik *f* realpolitik; **~po,li·ti·ker** *m* political pragmatist; **♀po,li·tisch** *adj.* pragmatic; **~schu·le** *f secondary school leading to intermediate qualification*; junior high school; **~wert** *m* real value

Re'al·zeit *f computer*: real time; **~ver·ar·bei·tung** *f* real-time processing

Re·ani·ma·ti·on [reˀanima'tsĭo:n] *f* (-; -en) ⚕ reanimation

Re·be ['re:bə] *f* (-; -n) a) tendril, shoot, b) vine; *poet.* grape

Re·bell [re'bɛl] *m* (-en; -en) rebel (*a. fig.*); **re·bel·lie·ren** [rebɛ'li:rən] *v/i.* (h) rebel (*a. fig.*); ***~de Studenten*** rebel students; **Re·bel·li·on** [rebɛ'lĭo:n] *f* (-; -en) rebellion; **re·bel·lisch** [re'bɛlɪʃ] *adj.* rebellious (*a. fig.*); ***~ werden*** be up in arms, *children*: start to play up; ***j-n ~ machen*** have s.o. up in arms; ***die Leute*** *etc.* ***~ machen*** *a.* cause an uproar

'Re·ben·saft *lit. m* juice of the vine

Reb|huhn ['re:p-] *n* partridge; **~laus** *f* phylloxera; **~stock** *m* vine

Re·chaud [re'ʃo] *m, n* (-s; -s) warming plate; burner, réchaud

re·chen ['rɛçən] *v/t.* rake (up)

'Re·chen *m* (-s; -) rake

'Re·chen|an·la·ge *f* computer; **~auf·ga·be** *f* sum, problem; **~buch** *n* arithmetic book; **~feh·ler** *m* mistake, miscalculation; **~ge·schwin·dig·keit** *f computer*: computing speed; **~heft** *n* arithmetic book; **~ka·pa·zi·tät** *f computer*: computing capacity; **~künst·ler** *m* mathematical genius; **~ma,schi·ne** *f* calculator

Re·chen·schaft ['rɛçənʃaft] *f* (-; *no pl.*): (***j-m***) ***~ ablegen über*** *acc.* account (to s.o.) for *s.th.*; ***j-m ~ schuldig sein*** be answerable to s.o.; ***j-n zur ~ ziehen*** call s.o. to account (***wegen*** *gen.* for)

'Re·chen·schafts·be·richt *m* report, statement

'Re·chen|schie·ber *m* slide rule; **~stift** *fig. m*: ***den ~ ansetzen*** do one's sums; **~werk** *n computer*: arithmetic unit; **~zen·trum** *n* computer centre (*Am.* center)

Re·cher·che [re'ʃɛrʃə] *f* (-; -n) investigation, inquiry; ***~n anstellen über*** *acc.* investigate, make investigations about (*or* into); **re·cher·chie·ren** [reʃɛr'ʃi:rən] (h) **I.** *v/i.* a) investigate, b) (do) research; **II.** *v/t.* investigate *a case etc.*; research, do research into *a subject etc.*

rech·nen ['rɛçnən] (h) **I.** *v/i.* a) calculate, make a calculation; *ped.* do sums, do one's arithmetic, b) count, c) reckon, estimate, d) charge, e) economize; ***gut ~ können*** be good at figures; ***grob gerechnet*** at a rough estimate (*or* guess); ***das ist großzügig gerechnet*** that's a generous estimate; ***du kannst ja selbst ~!*** work it out for yourself; ***von Montag an gerechnet*** as from Monday; ***er kann nicht ~*** he doesn't know how to handle money; ***wir müssen sehr ~*** we've got to watch the pennies (*or* watch what we spend); ***~ auf*** *acc.* *or* ***mit*** *dat.* reckon (*or* count, rely) on, reckon with, expect; ***ich rechne mit d-r Hilfe*** (***d-m Verständnis***) I'm counting on your help (I hope you'll understand); ***mit mir brauchst du nicht zu ~!*** count me out; ***wir müssen damit ~, daß er geht*** (***daß der Flug Verspätung hat***) we must reckon on his *or* him leaving (on the flight being delayed); ***mit ihm wird man ~ müssen*** he's one to look out for in the future; ***alles rechnet mit e-m Sieg von X*** everyone expects X to win, all the bets are on X winning; ***~ zu*** *dat.* count (*or* rank) among; **II.** *v/t.* a) calculate, work out, b) reckon (on), estimate, c) take into account; ***ich habe zwei Tassen Kaffee für jeden gerechnet*** I've allowed for two cups of coffee each; ***wir ~ für die Fahrt vier Stunden*** we reckon it'll take us four hours, we should make it in four hours; ***die Kinder nicht gerechnet*** not counting the children; ***alles in allem gerechnet*** all in all; ***j-n ~ zu*** *dat.* count (*or* rank, rate) s.o. among; **III.** ♀ *n* (-s; *no pl.*) *ped.* arithmetic

Rech·ner ['rɛçnɐ] *m* (-s; -) **1.** ***er ist ein guter*** (***schlechter***) ***~*** he's good (not very good) at figures; **2.** a) calculator, b) computer

'rech·ner|ge·steu·ert *adj.* computer-controlled; **~ge·stützt** *adj.* computer-aided

rech·ne·risch ['rɛçnərɪʃ] **I.** *adj.* mathematical, arithmetical; **II.** *adv.* mathematically, arithmetically; by way of calculation; ***rein ~ gesehen*** in terms of figures

Rech·nung ['rɛçnʊŋ] *f* (-; -en) **1.** calculation; ***die ~ geht nicht auf*** it doesn't work out; **2.** bill, *Am.* check; † invoice; **auf ~** on account; **j-m et. in ~ stellen** charge s.th. to s.o.'s account; **laut ~** as per invoice; **e-e ~ begleichen** settle an account, pay a check; **die ~ bezahlen** pay the check, F pick up the tab; *fig.* **e-e alte ~ zu begleichen haben** have an account to settle (**mit** *dat.* with); *fig.* **et. in ~ stellen, e-r Sache ~ tragen** take s.th. into account (*or* consideration), make allowances for the fact that ...; **das geht auf m-e ~** I'll see to that, F it's on me; *fig.* **das geht auf s-e ~** that's his doing; *fig.* **die ~ ohne den Wirt machen** get one's sums wrong; **ich werde ihm die ~ präsentieren** I'll make him pay for that; **jetzt bekommt er die ~ für s-e Faulheit präsentiert** now he's having to pay for his laziness; → **Strich, ausstellen** 2

'Rech·nungs|ab·gren·zung *f* deferral; **~be·trag** *m* invoice total; **~buch** *n* accounts book; **~ein·heit** *f* accounting unit; **~hof** *m*, **~kam·mer** *f* audit office; **~jahr** *n* financial (*or* fiscal) year; **~po·sten** *m* item, entry; **~prü·fer** *m* auditor; **~prü·fung** *f* audit; **~sum·me** *f* amount payable; **~we·sen** *n* (-s; *no pl.*) accountancy

recht [rɛçt] **I.** *adj.* **1.** right; **~e Hand** right hand, *fig. a.* right-hand man; **~er Winkel** right angle; **2.** a) right; proper, suitable, b) lawful, legitimate, c) true, real; good; **am ~en Ort** in the right place; **ein ~er Narr** a right fool; **der ~e Augenblick** the right (*or* a suitable) moment; **vom ~en Weg abkommen** lose one's way, *fig.* go off the rails, stray from the straight and narrow; **ich habe keinen ~en Appetit** I don't really feel like eating anything; **so ist's ~** that's right, F that's the stuff; **mir ist's ~** I don't mind, it's all right (*Am.* alright) with me, (it) suits me; **mir ist alles ~** it's all the same to me, I don't mind either way; **ihm ist jedes Mittel ~** he'll stop (F stick) at nothing; **das ist nur ~ und billig** it's only fair (*or* right); **alles was ~ ist!** a) fair's fair, b) you can go too far; **schon ~!** it's all right (*Am.* alright); **was dem einen ~ ist, ist dem andern billig** what's sauce for the goose is sauce for the gander; **nach dem 2en sehen** make sure everything's all right (*Am.* alright); **es war nichts 2es** it wasn't the real thing; → **Recht, Rechte, richtig, Ding** 2, **Licht, schlecht** II; **3.** *pol.* right-wing, rightist; **II.** *adv.* a) properly, b) very, c) rather; **~ daran tun zu** *inf.* do right to *inf.*; **~ enttäuscht** rather disappointed; **~ geschickt** rather (*or* very) clever; **~ gut** quite good (*or* well); **es gefällt mir ~ gut** I quite (*or* rather) like it; **erst ~** all the more (so); **es geschieht ihr ~** it serves her right; **man kann es nicht allen ~ machen** you can't please all men (*or* all the people all of the time); **ich weiß nicht ~** I'm not sure, I really don't know; **wenn ich es mir ~ überlege** when I think about it; **ich werde nicht ~ klug daraus** I don't quite know what to make of it; **wenn ich Sie ~ verstehe** if I understand you rightly; **verstehen Sie mich ~!** don't get me wrong; **ich seh' wohl nicht ~!** am I seeing things?; **ich hör' wohl nicht ~!** say that again; would you mind repeating that?; **du kommst mir gerade ~** just the person I want, *iro.* you're the last person I wanted (to see)

Recht [rɛçt] *n* (-[e]s; -e) a) *no pl.* law, b) right, c) authority; **~ und Ordnung** law and order; **das ~ brechen** (*or* **verletzen**) break the law; **~ muß ~ bleiben** the law's the law, *fig.* fair's fair; **nach geltendem ~** under existing law; **nach deutschem ~** under German law; **et. mit vollem ~ tun** have every right to do s.th.; **von ~s wegen** by rights, ⚖ by law; **~ sprechen** administer justice; **das ~ haben zu** *inf.* have the right (*or* be entitled) to *inf.*, *authorized person*: have power to *inf.*; **2 haben** be right; **j-m 2 geben** concede (*or* admit) that s.o. is right; **da muß ich Ihnen 2 geben** I agree with you there; **im ~ sein, das ~ auf s-r Seite haben** be in the right; **das ~ auf Streik** the right to strike; **gleiches ~ für alle** equal rights for all; **sich selbst ~ verschaffen** take the law into one's own hands; **auf s-m ~ bestehen** assert one's rights; (**wieder**) **zu s-m ~ kommen** come into one's own (again); **ich nehme mir das ~ zu** *inf.* I take it upon myself to *inf.*; **mit welchem ~ tut er das?** what right has he got to do that?; **zu ~** rightly, rightly so

Rech·te[1] ['rɛçtə] *f* (-n; -n) **1.** right hand; **zur ~n** to (*or* on) the right; **zu s-r ~n** to (*or* on) his right; **2.** *boxing*: right; **3.** *pol. the* right, right wing

'Rech·te[2] *m, f* (-n; -n) *pol.* right-winger, rightist

'Recht·eck *n* rectangle

'recht·eckig *adj.* rectangular

Rech·tens ['rɛçtəns]: **~ sein** be perfectly (*or* quite) legal; **es war nicht ~, daß sie ihm kündigten** they weren't right (*or* it wasn't right for them) to give him the sack

'recht·fer·ti·gen (h) **I.** *v/t.* justify, warrant; **nicht zu ~(d)** unjustifiable, indefensible; **das in einen gesetzte Vertrauen ~ wollen** aim to live up to the confidence placed in one; **II.** *v/refl.*: **sich ~** vindicate (*or* justify) o.s.; give an account of o.s.; **'Recht·fer·ti·gung** *f* (-; *no pl.*) justification; **zu m-r ~** in my defen|ce (*Am.* -se); **'Recht·fer·ti·gungs·grund** *m* justification; **was läßt sich als ~ anführen?** what can be said in justification?

'recht·gläu·big *adj.* orthodox

Recht·ha·be·rei [rɛçtha:bə'raɪ] *f* (-; *no pl.*) bigotry; know-it-all attitude

recht·ha·be·risch ['rɛçtha:bərɪʃ] *adj.* self-opinionated, dogmatic(ally *adv.*); **er ist ~** he always insists that he's in the right, *iro.* he's always in the right

'recht·lich I. *adj.* legal; lawful, legitimate; **im ~en Sinne** in the legal sense; **II.** *adv.* legally *etc.*; **~ begründet** legally founded; **~ bindend** legally binding; **~ verpflichtet** bound by law; **er ist ~ verpflichtet zu** *inf.* he is under a legal obligation to *inf.*

'recht·los *adj.* a) without rights, b) outlawed, c) lawless

'recht·mä·ßig *adj.* a) lawful, legal, b) legitimate, rightful *owner, claim, heir etc.*; **'Recht·mä·ßig·keit** *f* (-; *no pl.*) lawfulness, legality; legitimacy

rechts [rɛçts] **I.** *adv.* on the right(-hand side); (to the) right; **~ von** *dat.* to the right of; **~ von ihm** on (*or* to) his right; **~ oben** (**unten**) on the top (bottom) right; **erste Querstraße ~** first turning on the right; **~ abbiegen** turn right; **sich ~ halten, ~ fahren** (**gehen**) keep to the right; **~ überholen** overtake on the right; *pol.* **~ stehen** be on the right, be a right-winger; **II.** *prp.* (*gen.*) on (*or* to) the right of; **~ des Mains** on the right bank of the Main; *pol.* **~ der Mitte** right of cent|re (*Am.* -er)

'Rechts·ab·bie·ger [-apbi:gɐ] *m* (-s; -) car *etc.* (*pl.* traffic *sg.*) turning right

'Rechts·ab·bie·ge·spur *f* right-hand turn(-off) lane

'Rechts|ab,tei·lung *f* legal department; **~an·ge·le·gen·heit** *f* legal matter; **~an·schau·ung** *f* legal view; **~an·spruch** *m* legal claim (**auf** *acc.* on, to), (legal) right (to); title (to)

'Rechts·an·walt *m*, **'Rechts·an·wäl·tin** *f* lawyer, *Brit. a.* solicitor; *Brit.* barrister, *Am.* attorney; **'Rechts·an·walt·schaft** *f the* bar; **'Rechts·an·walts·kam·mer** *f* law society; Bar Association

'Rechts·aus·schuß *m* committee on legal affairs, judiciary committee

Rechts'au·ßen *m* **1.** *soccer*: right wing, outside right; **2.** *pol.* extreme right-winger

'Rechts|be·helf *m* (legal) remedy; **~be·leh·rung** *f* ⚖ **1.** → **Rechtsmittelbelehrung**; **2.** directions *pl.*, *Am.* instruction (of the jury); **3.** *w.s.* legal information; **~be·ra·ter** *m* legal adviser; **~be·ra·tungs·stel·le** *f* legal aid office; **~be·schwer·de** *f* appeal; **~beu·gung** *f* perversion of justice; **~bre·cher** *m* lawbreaker; **~bruch** *m* breach of law

'rechts·bün·dig *adj. typ.* flush right

'recht·schaf·fen I. *adj.* honest, upright; **II.** *adv.* a) honestly, b) F really; **~ leben** live an honest life

'Recht·schaf·fen·heit *f* (-; *no pl.*) uprightness; *formal*: probity

'Recht·schrei·ben *n* (-s; *no pl.*) spelling; **'Recht·schreib·feh·ler** *m* spelling mistake; **'Recht·schrei·bung** *f* (-; *no pl.*) spelling; orthography

'Rechts·drall *m* right-hand twist; *fig. pol.* rightist tendencies *pl.*

'Rechts|ein·wand *m* objection, demurrer; **2er·heb·lich** *adj.* legally relevant

'Rechts·ex·tre,mist *m* right-wing extremist; **'rechts·ex·tre,mi·stisch** *adj.* (of the) extreme right

'rechts·fä·hig *adj.*: **~ sein** have legal capacity

'Rechts|fall *m* (law) case; **~form** *f* legal form; **~fra·ge** *f* legal issue; point of law; **~ge·fühl** *n* sense of justice

'rechts·ge·rich·tet *adj. pol.* right-wing

'Rechts|ge·schäft *n* legal transaction; **~ge·schich·te** *f* history of law; **~grund** *m* legal argument; **~grund·la·ge** *f* legal grounds *pl.*; **2gül·tig** *adj.* valid; legally effective; → **rechtskräftig**; **~gut** *n* legally protected right; **~gut·ach·ten** *n* (legal) opinion, counsel's opinion

'Rechts·ha·ken *m boxing*: right hook

Rechts·hän·der ['rɛçtshɛndɐ] *m* (-s; -) right-hander; **er ist ~** he's right-handed; **'rechts·hän·dig** [-hɛndɪç] *adj.* right-handed *person*; right-hand *blow etc.*

'Rechts·hand·lung *f* legal act

rechts·hän·gig ['rɛçtshɛŋɪç] *adj.* ⚖ pending, sub judice

'rechts·her,um *adv.* clockwise; (to the) right

'Rechts·hil·fe *f* legal aid

'Rechts·kraft *f* (-; *no pl.*) legal force, validity; **'rechts·kräf·tig** *adj.* legal(ly bind-

ing); final *decision etc.*; ~ ***werden*** become effective
'**rechts·kun·dig** *adj.* legally qualified
'**Rechts·kurs** *m* rightist policy (*or* tendencies *pl.*)
'**Rechts·kur·ve** *f* right turn (✈ bank); right-hand bend
'**Rechts·la·ge** *f* legal position (*or* status)
rechts·la·stig ['rɛçtslastɪç] *adj.*: ~ ***sein*** lean to the right, *fig.* lean towards the right, have rightist tendencies (*or* leanings)
'**Rechts·len·ker** *m mot.* right-hand drive
'**Rechts·mit·tel** *n* legal remedy, relief; (right of) appeal; ~ ***einlegen*** lodge an appeal; ~**be·leh·rung** *f* instructions *pl.* on rights of appeal
'**Rechts|nach·fol·ge** *f* legal succession; ~**nach·fol·ger** *m* legal successor; ~**norm** *f* legal norm; ~**ord·nung** *f* legal system
'**rechts·ori·en,tiert** *adj.* rightist; '**Rechts·ori·en,tie·rung** *f* rightist tendencies *pl.*
'**Rechts·par,tei** *f* right-wing party
'**Rechts|pfle·ge** *f* administration of justice; ~**pfle·ger** *m* judicial officer; ~**phi·lo·so,phie** *f* philosophy of law
'**Recht·spre·chung** *f* (-; *no pl.*) **1.** administration of justice; **2.** ***die*** ~ the judiciary
'**rechts·ra·di,kal** *adj.* extreme right wing; '**Rechts·ra·di,ka·le** *m, f* right-wing extremist
'**Rechts·re,form** *f* legal reform
'**Rechts|ruck** *m*, ~**rutsch** *m pol.* swing to the right
'**Rechts·sa·che** *f* (legal) case
'**Rechts·schutz** *m* legal protection; ~**ver·si·che·rung** *f* legal costs insurance
rechts·sei·tig ['rɛçtszaɪtɪç] *adj.* right; on the right(-hand) side; → ***gelähmt***
'**Rechts|si·cher·heit** *f* legal security; ~**spruch** *m civil law*: judg(e)ment, *criminal law*: sentence; verdict *of the jury*
'**Rechts·staat** *m* constitutional state; '**rechts·staat·lich** *adj. and adv.* constitutional(ly); '**Rechts·staat·lich·keit** *f* (-; *no pl.*) rule of law
'**Rechts·stel·lung** *f* legal status (*or* position)
'**Rechts·steue·rung** *f mot.* right-hand drive
'**Rechts|streit** *m* lawsuit, action, litigation; ~**sy,stem** *n* judicial system; ~**ti·tel** *m* legal title; ~**un·gül·tig** *adj.* invalid; ~**un·si·cher·heit** *f* (-; *no pl.*) legal uncertainty; ~**un·wirk·sam** *adj.* (legally) ineffective; ~**ver·bind·lich** *adj.* legally binding (***für*** *acc.* [up]on); ~**ver·dre·her** *contp. m* pettifogging lawyer, F shyster; ~**ver·fah·ren** *n* a) legal procedure, b) (legal) action *or* proceedings *pl.*; ~**ver·hält·nis** *n* legal relationship
'**Rechts·ver·kehr** *m mot.*: ***in Kanada ist*** ~ they drive on the right(-hand side) in Canada
'**Rechts|ver·let·zung** *f* infringement (of a law); ~**ver·tre·ter** *m* legal representative; (authorized) agent; ~**weg** *m* course of law; ***den*** ~ ***beschreiten*** take legal action, go to court; ***der*** ~ ***ist ausgeschlossen*** the judge's decision is final
'**Rechts·wen·dung** *f pol.* shift to the right
'**Rechts·we·sen** *n* (-s; *no pl.*) legal system
'**rechts|wid·rig** *adj.* illegal, unlawful, illicit; ~**wirk·sam** *adj.* → ***rechtskräftig***
'**Rechts|wis·sen·schaft** *f* law, *formal*: jurisprudence; ~**wis·sen·schaft·ler** *m* jurist

'**recht·wink·lig** *adj.* right-angled
'**recht·zei·tig I.** *adv.* (just) in time; on time, punctually; in good time; **II.** *adj.* timely; punctual
Reck [rɛk] *n* (-[e]s; -e) *gym.* horizontal bar
recken ['rɛkən] (*sep.* -k·k-) (h) **I.** *v/t.* stretch; rack; ***den Hals nach et.*** ~ crane one's neck to see s.th., *Am.* rubberneck; **II.** *v/refl.*: ***sich*** ~ ***und strecken*** have a good stretch
Re·cor·der [re'kɔrdɐ] *m* (-s; -) (tape, cassette *or* video) recorder
re·cy·celn [ri'saɪkəln] *v/t.* (h) recycle
Re·cy·cling [ri'saɪklɪŋ] *n* (-s; *-no pl.*) recycling; ~**pa,pier** *n* recycled paper
Re·dak·teur [redak'tøːɐ] *m* (-s; -e [-rə]), **Re·dak·teu·rin** [redak'tøːrɪn] *f* (-; -nen) editor; **Re·dak·ti·on** [redak'tsi̯oːn] *f* (-; -en) **1.** *no pl.* editing, editorial work; **2.** editorial staff, editors *pl.*; **3.** editorial office (*or* department); ***politische*** ~ politics department; **re·dak·tio·nell** [redaktsi̯o'nɛl] **I.** *adj.* editorial; **II.** *adv.*: ~ ***bearbeiten*** edit
Re·dak·ti'ons·schluß *m* copy deadline
Re·de ['reːdə] *f* (-; -n) a) speech; address, b) (manner of) speech, language, c) remark; *ling.* ***(in)direkte*** ~ (in)direct speech; ***die Kunst der*** ~ the art of rhetoric; ***e-e*** ~ ***halten*** make a speech; ***(große)*** ~***n schwingen*** F talk big; ***die*** ~ ***bringen auf*** *acc.* bring *s.th.* up; ***die*** ~ ***kam auf*** *acc.* the conversation turned to; ***gerade war von dir die*** ~ we were just talking about you; ***es war einmal die*** ~, ***daß*** it was said at one time that, there was talk at one time of (*s.o. ger.*); ***der langen*** ~ ***kurzer Sinn*** to cut a long story short, in short; ***davon kann keine*** ~ ***sein*** that's out of the question; ***davon ist nicht die*** ~ that's not what I'm talking about; ***wovon ist die*** ~***?*** what are you (*or* they) talking about?; ***das ist ja m-e*** ~ that's what I've been saying all along; ***j-m in die*** ~ ***fallen*** interrupt s.o. (in mid--speech); ***nichts als*** ~***n!*** it's all just talk; ***ihm verschlug es die*** ~ it left him speechless; ***es ist nicht der*** ~ ***wert*** a) it's hardly worth mentioning, b) don't mention it; ~ ***(und Antwort) stehen*** justify o.s., ***über*** *acc.*: account for, answer for; ***j-n zur*** ~ ***stellen*** confront s.o., take s.o. to task (***wegen*** *gen.* for); ~**du,ell** *n* battle of words; ~**fi,gur** *f* figure of speech; ~**fluß** *m* (-sses; *no pl.*) flow of words; ***j-s*** ~ ***unterbrechen*** interrupt s.o.'s flow; ~**frei·heit** *f* (-; *no pl.*) freedom of speech
'**re·de|ge·wal·tig** *adj.*: ~ ***sein*** be a powerful speaker; ~**ge·wandt** *adj.* articulate; *esp. contp.* glib; ~ ***sein*** *a.* know how to talk, F have the gift of the gab
'**Re·de·kunst** *f* (art of) rhetoric
re·den ['reːdən] **I.** *v/i. and v/t.* (h) speak (***mit*** *dat.* to, with); talk (to, with), chat (to, with); ~ ***über*** *acc.* talk about, discuss; ***über Politik*** ~ talk politics; ***über Gott und die Welt*** ~ talk about everything under the sun; ~ ***wir nicht mehr darüber*** let's forget it; ***man redet über sie*** people are talking about her; ***darüber läßt sich*** ~ it's a possibility; ***im Schlaf*** ~ talk in one's sleep; ***er hat kein Wort geredet*** he didn't say a word, he didn't open his mouth once; ***mit sich selbst*** ~ talk to o.s.; ***er hört sich gern*** ~ he likes the sound of his own voice; ***sie*** ~ ***nicht miteinander*** they're not speaking to each other, they're not on speaking terms; ***sie läßt nicht mit sich*** ~ she won't listen to (anyone); ***unter ... lassen wir gar nicht mit uns*** ~ under ..., we're not interested; ***von ... gar nicht zu*** ~ not to mention ...; ***da wir gerade davon*** ~ as we're on the subject; ***er redet, wie er denkt*** he says (exactly) what he thinks; ***er redet anders, als er denkt*** what he says and what he thinks are two different things; ***du hast gut*** ~ you can talk; ***ich habe mit dir zu*** ~ I'd like a word with you; ***wir*** ~ ***später*** we'll talk about it later; ***kannst du mal mit ihm*** ~***?*** can you have a word with him?, can you try and reason with him?; ***da redet man ja gegen e-e Wand*** it's like talking to a brick wall; ***er macht als Rennfahrer von sich*** ~ he's made a name for himself as a racing driver; ***neulich hat er mit e-m Film von sich*** ~ ***gemacht*** he recently got into the news with a film; ***so lasse ich nicht mit mir*** ~ I won't be spoken to like that; ***er redete sich in Zorn*** he went on and on until he got really angry; **II.** ~ *n* (-s; *no pl.*) talking; talk; ***j-n zum*** ~ ***bringen*** get s.o. to talk; ***mit dem*** ~ ***tut er sich nicht schwer*** he has no problems (*or* inhibitions about) talking; ***all mein*** ~ ***war umsonst*** I may as well have been talking to a brick wall; ~ ***ist Silber, Schweigen ist Gold*** silence is golden
'**Re·dens·art** *f* expression; ***allgemeine*** ~ common saying; ***bloße*** ~***en*** empty phrases (*or* talk)
Re·de·rei [reːdə'raɪ] *f* (-; -en) **1.** *no pl.* endless talk; **2.** → ***Gerede, Geschwätz***
'**Re·de|schlacht** *f* battle of words; ~**schwall** *m* (-([e]s; *no pl.*) torrent of words; ~**strom** *m* (-[e]s; *no pl.*) flow of words; ~**wei·se** *f* (manner of) speech, way of talking; ~**wen·dung** *f* figure of speech; idiom; ***feststehende*** ~ set phrase; ~**zeit** *f* time allowed (*or* allotted); ***die*** ~ ***einhalten*** keep to the time allowed (*or* allotted); ***die*** ~ ***nicht einhalten*** go over time
re·di·gie·ren [redi'giːrən] *v/t.* (h) edit
red·lich ['reːtlɪç] **I.** *adj.* honest; upright; **II.** *adv.*: ***sich*** ~ ***bemühen*** do (*or* give) one's best
Red·ner ['reːdnɐ] *m* (-s; -) speaker; ~**büh·ne** *f* rostrum, speaker's platform; ~**ga·be** *f* gift of rhetoric
Red·ne·rin ['reːdnərɪn] *f* (-; -nen) speaker
red·ne·risch ['reːdnərɪʃ] *adj.* rhetorical
'**Red·ner|li·ste** *f* list of speakers; ~**pult** *n* lectern
red·se·lig ['reːtzeːlɪç] *adj.* talkative, *formal*: loquacious, *esp. contp.* garrulous; '**Red·se·lig·keit** *f* (-; *no pl.*) talkativeness, *formal*: loquacity
Re·duk·ti·on [reduk'tsi̯oːn] *f* (-; -en) reduction
Re·duk·ti'ons|mit·tel *n* ⚗ reducing agent; ~**ofen** *m* smelting furnace
re·du·zie·ren [redu'tsiːrən] (h) **I.** *v/t.* reduce (***auf*** *acc.* to); **II.** *v/refl.*: ***sich*** ~ decrease (***auf*** *acc.* to); **Re·du'zie·rung** *f* (-; -en) reduction
Ree·de ['reːdə] *f* (-; -n) ⚓ roadstead, roads *pl.*; ***auf der*** ~ ***liegen*** be (lying) in the roads; **Ree·der** ['reːdɐ] *m* (-s; -) shipowner; **Ree·de·rei** [reːdə'raɪ] *f* (-; -en) shipping company
re·ell [re'ɛl] *adj.* **1.** honest *person*; solid, sound *firm etc.*; fair, realistic *price etc.*; ~***e Leistung*** solid accomplishment; **2.** real; **3.** F decent

Re·fe·rat [refeˈraːt] *n* (-[e]s; -e) **1.** report, lecture, talk; *ped.* (seminar) paper; ***ein ~ halten → referieren;*** **2.** department

Re·fe·ren·dar [referɛnˈdaːɐ] *m* (-s; -s, -e [-rə]), **Re·fe·ren·da·rin** [referɛnˈdaːrɪn] *f* (-; -nen) **1.** probationary teacher, intern; **2.** junior lawyer; **Re·fe·renˈdar·zeit** *f* probationary period

Re·fe·ren·dum [refeˈrɛndʊm] *n* (-s; -da) referendum

Re·fe·rent [refeˈrɛnt] *m* (-en; -en) **1.** speaker; reporter, ⚖, *parl.* referee; **2.** *adm.* adviser, consultant

Re·fe·renz [refeˈrɛnts] *f* (-; -en) reference; referee; *pl.* credentials

re·fe·rie·ren [refeˈriːrən] *v/i.* (h) report (***über*** *acc.* on); (give a) lecture (on); *esp. univ.* give a paper (on)

re·flek·tie·ren [reflɛkˈtiːrən] (h) **I.** *v/t.* **1.** *phys.* reflect; **2.** ***et. kritisch ~*** consider s.th. very carefully; **II.** *v/i.* **3.** reflect (***über*** *acc.* [up]on); **4.** F ***~ auf*** *acc.* F have one's eye on

Re·flek·tor [reˈflɛktoːɐ] *m* (-s; -en [reflɛkˈtoːrən]) reflector (*a. mot.*)

Re·flex [reˈflɛks] *m* (-es; -e) **1.** *phys.* reflection; **2.** *physiol., psych.* reflex; ***bedingter ~*** conditioned reflex; **~be·we·gung** *f* reflex (action); **~hand·lung** *f* reflex action

Re·fle·xi·on [reflɛˈksi̯oːn] *f* (-; -en) **1.** *phys.* reflection; **2.** reflection (***über*** *acc.* [up]on); **Re·fle·xiˈons·win·kel** *m* angle of reflection

re·fle·xiv [reflɛˈksiːf] *adj. ling.* reflexive

Re·fleˈxiv·pro͵no·men *n* reflexive (pronoun)

Reˈflex·zo·nen·Mas͵sa·ge *f* **1.** reflexology; **2.** zone massage

Re·form [reˈfɔrm] *f* (-; -en) reform

Re·for·ma·ti·on [refɔrmaˈtsi̯oːn] *f* (-; *no pl.*) *hist.* Reformation

Re·for·ma·tiˈons|fest *n*, **~tag** *m eccl.* Reformation Day

Re·for·ma·tor [refɔrˈmaːtoːɐ] *m* (-s; -en [refɔrmaˈtoːrən]) **1.** *hist.* Reformer; **2.** reformer, reformist

reˈform·be·dürf·tig *adj.* in need of reform

Reˈform|be·stre·bun·gen *pl.* reformatory efforts; **~be·we·gung** *f* reform movement

Re·for·mer [reˈfɔrmɐ] *m* (-s; -) reformer, reformist; **re·for·me·risch** [reˈfɔrmərɪʃ] *adj.* reformist

reˈform·freu·dig *adj.* reform-minded

Reˈform·haus *n* health food shop

re·for·mie·ren [refɔrˈmiːrən] *v/t.* (h) reform; **Re·forˈmier·te** [refɔrˈmiːɐtə] *m, f* (-n; -n) *eccl.* reformist

Reˈform·kom·mu͵nis·mus *m* reform communism

Reˈform·kost *f* health food(s *pl.*)

Reˈform|kurs *m* reformist course; **~po·li͵tik** *f* reformist policy (*or* politics *pl.*); **~pro͵gramm** *n* reform package; program(me) of reform; **~vor·ha·ben** *n* proposed reforms *pl.*

Re·frain [rəˈfrɛ̃ː] *m* (-s; -s) refrain, chorus

Re·fu·gi·um [reˈfuːgi̯ʊm] *n* (-s; -gien [-gi̯ən]) sanctuary

Re·gal [reˈgaːl] *n* (-s; -e) shelves *pl.*; **~fach** *n* shelf; **~wand** *f* (large) wall unit; wall-to-wall shelving

Re·gat·ta [reˈgata] *f* (-; Regatten [-reˈgatən]) regatta, boat race

re·ge [ˈreːgə] *adj.* lively, alert; busy; active *a. correspondence, participation etc.*; animated *discussion etc.*; lively, keen *interest etc.*; vivid, fertile *imagination etc.*; ***~ Geschäfte*** brisk (*or* buoyant) trading; ***~ Nachfrage*** brisk demand; ***~ werden*** stir, *emotions*: awaken, be stirred up; ***er ist noch geistig ~*** he's still very much with it (*or* very much on the ball)

Re·gel [ˈreːgəl] *f* (-; -n) **1.** rule; norm; habit; ***in der ~*** as a rule; ***j-n nach allen ~n der Kunst besiegen*** defeat s.o. in style; ***zur ~ werden*** become a rule (*or* habit); ***es sich zur ~ machen zu*** *inf.* make it a rule (*or* habit) to *inf.*, make a habit of *ger.*; **→ *Ausnahme;*** **2.** *physiol.* period; *coll.* periods *pl.*; ***wann kommt d-e ~?*** when's your period due?

ˈre·gel·bar *adj.* controllable, adjustable

ˈRe·gel|blu·tung *f* monthly period; *coll.* menstruation; **~fall** *m* norm; ***im ~*** as a rule; **~kreis** *m* control circuit; **~lei·stung** *f* minimum social security benefit

ˈre·gel·los *adj.* disorderly; irregular, erratic; ***es herrscht ein ~es Durcheinander*** it's absolutely chaotic

ˈRe·gel·lo·sig·keit *f* (-; *no pl.*) disorderliness; irregularity, erratic nature (*gen.* of)

ˈre·gel·mä·ßig I. *adj.* a) regular; periodical, b) orderly, regulated; ***~er Gast*** regular (guest); **II.** *adv.* regularly; always, every time; **ˈRe·gel·mä·ßig·keit** *f* (-; *no pl.*) regularity

re·geln [ˈreːgəln] (h) **I.** *v/t.* a) regulate; adjust, b) see to, settle; **II.** *v/refl.*: ***sich ~*** be regulated *or* governed (***nach*** *dat.* by); ***das wird sich schon ~*** it'll sort itself out; **→ *geregelt***

ˈre·gel·recht I. *adj.* regular, proper; F real; **II.** F *adv.*: ***~ unmöglich*** *etc.* absolutely impossible *etc.*; ***er ist ~ reingefallen*** he really fell for it

ˈRe·gel|stu·di·en·zeit *f* **1.** average period of study; **2.** maximum period of study; **~tech·nik** *f* control engineering

Re·ge·lung [ˈreːgəlʊŋ] *f* (-; -en) **1.** regulation; **2.** a) arrangement, settlement, b) provision; rule

ˈRe·ge·lungs·vor·schlag *m* draft regulation

ˈRe·gel|ver·stoß *m sport*: **→ *Regelwidrigkeit;*** **~͵wi·der·stand** *m* ⚡ variable resistor

ˈre·gel·wid·rig *adj.* irregular; *sport*: against the rules; ***~es Spiel*** foul play; **ˈRe·gel·wid·rig·keit** *f* irregularity; *sport*: infringement, offen|ce (*Am.* -se); foul, unfair play

re·gen [ˈreːgən] (h) **I.** *v/refl.*: ***sich ~*** stir (*a. fig.*), move; ***reg dich!*** move!, F stir those stumps!; ***er regt sich schon lange nicht mehr*** I haven't heard (F had a peep) from him for ages; *lit.* ***kein Lüftchen regte sich*** there wasn't a breath of wind in the air; **II.** *v/t.* move; stir

ˈRe·gen *m* (-s; *no pl.*) rain; ***heute kommt noch ~*** we're in for some rain today; ***wir sind in den ~ gekommen*** we got caught in the rain; *fig.* ***ein warmer ~*** a windfall; ***j-n im ~ stehenlassen*** leave s.o. in the lurch; ***vom ~ in die Traufe kommen*** jump out of the frying pan into the fire; ***auf ~ folgt Sonnenschein*** things always brighten up again; **→ *sauer*** I

ˈre·gen·arm *adj.* dry; 🕮 low-precipitation ...

ˈRe·gen·bo·gen *m* rainbow; **~far·ben** *pl.* colo(u)rs of the rainbow; **2far·ben, 2far·big** *adj.* rainbow-colo(u)red; **~haut** *f anat.* iris; **~pres·se** F *f* trashy (women's) weeklies *pl.*; **~tri͵kot** *n cycling*: rainbow jersey

ˈre·gen·dicht *adj.* rainproof, waterproof

Re·ge·ne·ra·ti·on [regeneraˈtsi̯oːn] *f* (-; *no pl.*) regeneration

Re·ge·ne·ra·tiˈons·fä·hig·keit *f* regenerative powers *pl.*

re·ge·ne·rie·ren [regeneˈriːrən] (h) **I.** *v/t.* regenerate; ***s-e Kräfte ~*** recover one's strength; **II.** *v/refl.*: ***sich ~*** regenerate; recover; **Re·ge·neˈrie·rung** *f* (-; *no pl.*) regeneration

ˈRe·gen|fäl·le *pl.* rainfall *sg.*, showers; **~guß** *m* heavy shower, downpour; **~haut** *f* plastic mac; **~klei·dung** *f* rainwear; **~man·tel** *m* raincoat, F mac; **~men·ge** *f* (amount of) rainfall; **~mes·ser** *m* rain ga(u)ge; **2reich** *adj.* wet; **~schau·er** *m* shower; **~schirm** *m* umbrella; F ***ich bin gespannt wie ein ~*** I can't wait to find out (*or* to hear what he says *etc.*)

Re·gent [reˈgɛnt] *m* (-en; -en), **Re·gen·tin** [reˈgɛntɪn] *f* (-; -nen) sovereign, ruler, monarch; regent

ˈRe·gen|tag *m* rainy day; **~trop·fen** *m* raindrop

Reˈgent·schaft *f* (-; -en) regency

ˈRe·gen|wald *m* rainforest; **~was·ser** *n* rainwater; **~wet·ter** *n* rainy weather; **~wol·ke** *f* (rain)cloud; **~wurm** *m* earthworm; **~zeit** *f* rainy season; *the* rains *pl.*

Re·gie [reˈʒiː] *f* (-; *no pl.*) a) *thea., TV* production; *film*: direction, b) management; administration; ***~ führen*** direct (***bei*** *dat. s.th.*); ***unter der ~ von X*** directed by X; ***~ ...*** *trailer etc.*: Director ...; *fig.* ***et. in eigener ~ machen*** do s.th. oneself (*or* on one's own); ***et. in eigene ~ nehmen*** take personal charge (*or* direct control) of s.th.; **~an·wei·sung** *f* stage direction; **~as·si͵stent** *m film*: assistant director; *thea.* assistant producer; **~feh·ler** *fig. m* mistake, slip-up; **~pult** *n TV* control desk

re·gie·ren [reˈgiːrən] (h) **I.** *v/t.* govern (*a. ling.*), rule; reign over; ***kommunistisch regiert*** communist-ruled; ***demokratisch regiert*** democratically ruled (*or* governed); **II.** *v/i.* rule, govern; reign (*a. fig.*)

Reˈgie·rung *f* (-; -en) a) government, b) term of office, reign; ***unter der ~ von*** (*or gen.*) under; ***an der ~*** in power; ***die ~ übernehmen*** take power, *president etc.*: *a.* take office, *monarch*: ascend (to) the throne; ***an die ~ kommen*** come to power, *president etc.*: *a.* come into office, *monarch*: come to (*or* ascend [to]) the throne; ***an der ~ sein*** be in power, *president etc.*: *a.* be in office

Reˈgie·rungs|ab·kom·men *n* agreement between governments, international agreement; **~an·hän·ger** *m* government supporter; **~an·tritt** *m* coming into power, taking office, accession to the throne; ***bei ~ der Partei*** when the party came to power; ***bei s-m ~*** when he came to power (*or* took office, took over the reign), *monarch*: when he ascended (to) the throne; **~auf·trag** *m* government order; **~be·am·te** *m* government official; **~be·zirk** *m* administrative district; **~bil·dung** *f* formation of a government; **~bünd·nis** *n* coalition; **~chef** *m* head of government; **~de·le·ga·ti͵on** *f* government delegation; **~ebe·ne** *f*: ***auf ~*** on an

intergovernmental level; **~er·klä·rung** *f* government (*or* policy) statement
re'gie·rungs|fä·hig *adj.* in a position to govern the country; ***~e Mehrheit*** working majority; **~feind·lich** *adj.* oppositional, anti-government
Re'gie·rungs|form *f* (form of) government; **Ωfreund·lich** *adj.* pro-government; **~ge·walt** *f* governmental power; **~koa·li·ti͵on** *f* ruling coalition; **~krei·se** *pl.* government circles; **~kri·se** *f* government crisis; **~neu·bil·dung** *f* formation of a new government; ***es kommt zu e-r ~*** there's going to be a change in government; **~par͵tei** *f* ruling party; **~po·li͵tik** *f* government policy; **~rat** *m* senior executive officer; **~sach·ver·stän·di·ge** *m* government expert; **~sitz** *m* seat of government; **~spre·cher** *m* government spokesman; **~͵um·bil·dung** *f* cabinet reshuffle; **~ver·ant·wor·tung** *f*: ***die ~ übernehmen*** take over the responsibility of government, assume power; **~vier·tel** *n* government sector; **~vor·la·ge** *f* (government) bill; **~wech·sel** *m* change of government; **~zeit** *f* → ***Regierung*** b
Re·gime [re'ʒiːm] *n* (-s; - [-ə], -s) regime; **~geg·ner** *m* opponent of the regime; **~kri·ti·ker** *m* dissident
Re·gi·ment [regi'mɛnt] *n* (-[e]s; -er) **1.** *no pl.* government, rule; *fig.* ***das ~ führen*** be the boss, rule the roost; ***sie führt das ~ im Haus*** she wears the trousers (*Am.* pants); ***ein strenges ~ führen*** rule with a rod of iron; **2.** ⚔ regiment
Re·gi'ments·kom·man͵deur *m* regimental commander
Re·gi·on [re'gi̯oːn] *f* (-; -en) region; → ***schweben***
re·gio·nal [regi̯o'naːl] *adj.* regional
Re·gio'nal|aus·ga·be *f* regional issue (*or* edition); **~fern·se·hen** *n* regional (TV) programmes *pl.*, *Am.* local television; **~for·schung** *f* regional studies *pl.*
Re·gio·na·lis·mus [regi̯ona'lɪsmʊs] *m* (-; *no pl.*) regionalism
Re·gio'nal|nach·rich·ten *pl.* regional (*Am.* local) news *sg.*; **~pro͵gramm** *n* regional programmes *pl.*, *Am.* local broadcasting; **~sen·dung** *f* regional programme, *Am.* local broadcast
Re·gis·seur [reʒɪ'søːɐ] *m* (-s; -e [-rə]) *thea.*, *TV* producer; *film:* director
Re·gi·ster [re'gɪstɐ] *n* (-s; -) **1.** index; **2.** register (*a. computer*); **3.** ♪ (*organ*) stop; *fig.* ***alle ~ ziehen*** pull out all the stops; **4.** *typ.* register; **~ton·ne** *f* register ton
Re·gi·stra·tur [regɪstra'tuːɐ] *f* (-; -en [-rən]) a) registry; record office, b) filing cabinet
re·gi·strie·ren [regɪs'triːrən] *v/t.* (h) register (*a. fig.*); record (*a.* ⚙); enter; ***sich polizeilich ~ lassen*** register with the police; *fig.* ***sie registrierte alles genau*** she was taking everything in, she didn't miss a thing; ***es wurde von allen registriert*** everyone noticed (it); ***er hat es gar nicht registriert*** it didn't even register with him; ***Unbehagen bei sich ~*** sense a certain (feeling of) discomfort
Re·gi·strier·kas·se [regɪs'triːɐ-] *f* cash register
Re·gi·strie·rung [regɪs'triːrʊŋ] *f* (-; -en) registration; entry; ⚙ reading(s *pl.*)
Re·gle·ment [reglə'mãː] *n* (-s; -s) regulations *pl.*, rules *pl.*
re·gle·men·tie·ren [reglemɛn'tiːrən] *v/t.* (h) regulate, regiment; ***staatlich reglementierte Wirtschaft*** state-controlled economy; **Re·gle·men'tie·rung** *f* (-; -en) regimentation
Reg·ler ['reːglɐ] *m* (-s; -) ⚙ regulator; ⚡ control (knob)
reg·los ['reːkloːs] *adj.* motionless, still
reg·nen ['reːgnən] *v/impers.* (h) rain; ***es regnet stark*** it's pouring; *fig.* ***es regnete Kirschblüten*** it was raining cherry--blossom petals; ***es regnete Geschenke*** he *etc.* was showered with gifts; ***es regnete Beschwerden*** there was a flood of complaints, he was (they were *etc.*) inundated with complaints
Reg·ner ['reːgnɐ] *m* (-s; -) sprinkler
reg·ne·risch ['reːgnərɪʃ] *adj.* rainy
Re·greß [re'grɛs] *m* (-sses; -sse) ⚖, ✝ redress, recourse; ***gegen j-n ~ nehmen*** have recourse against s.o.; **~an·spruch** *m* claim of recourse
Re·gres·si·on [regrɛ'si̯oːn] *f* (-; -en) regression
re'greß·pflich·tig [-pflɪçtɪç] *adj.* liable to recourse
reg·sam ['reːkzaːm] *adj.* active, alert
re·gu·lär [regu'lɛːɐ] *adj.* regular; usual, normal; legitimate
re·gu·la·tiv [regula'tiːf] *adj.*, Ω *n* (-s; -e [-və]) regulative
Re·gu·la·tor [regu'laːtoːɐ] *m* (-s; -en [regula'toːrən]) regulator
re·gu·lier·bar [regu'liːɐbaːɐ] *adj.* adjustable; **re·gu·lie·ren** [regu'liːrən] *v/t.* (h) a) adjust, set; regulate, b) settle *claim for damages etc.*; **Re·gu'lie·rung** *f* (-; -en) regulation; ⚙ *a.* adjustment; ✝ settlement
Re·gung ['reːgʊŋ] *f* (-; -en) **1.** movement; **2.** stirring *of jealousy etc.*; impulse; ***e-r plötzlichen ~ folgend*** on a sudden impulse; ***keiner menschlichen ~ fähig*** void of all human feeling; ***den ~en des Herzens folgen*** do what one's heart tells one, follow the dictates of one's heart; **'re·gungs·los** *adj. and adv.* motionless, still; ***~ daliegen*** lie there motionless (*or* without stirring)
Reh [reː] *n* (-[e]s; -e) **1.** *zo.* (roe) deer; **2.** *gastr.* venison
Re·ha·bi·li·ta·ti·on [rehabilita'tsi̯oːn] *f* (-; -en) rehabilitation (*a.* ⚕)
Re·ha·bi·li·ta·ti'ons·zen·trum *n* rehabilitation centre (*Am.* center)
re·ha·bi·li·tie·ren [rehabili'tiːrən] *v/t.* (h) rehabilitate; **Re·ha·bi·li'tie·rung** *f* → ***Rehabilitation***
'Reh|bock *m* roebuck; **~bra·ten** *m* roast venison; **~geiß** *f* doe; **~kalb** *n* fawn; **~keu·le** *f gastr.* leg of venison; **~kitz** *n* fawn; **~rücken** *m gastr.* saddle of venison
Rei·bach ['raɪbax] F *m*: ***e-n ~ machen*** F make a haul (*or* killing); ***den ~ teilen*** divide the spoils
Reib·ah·le ['raɪp-] *f* reamer
Rei·be ['raɪbə] *f* (-; -n) ⚙ rasp; *gastr.* grater
Reib·ei·sen ['raɪp-] *n* **1.** *obs.* grater; ***e-e Stimme wie ein ~*** a grating (*or* gravelly) voice; F ***ich habe heute e-e Stimme wie ein ~*** my throat feels like sandpaper today; **2.** F *contp.* F shrew
'Rei·be·ku·chen *m* potato pancake
rei·ben ['raɪbən] (rieb, gerieben, h) **I.** *v/t. and v/i.* a) rub, b) grate; ***sich die Augen (Hände) ~*** rub one's eyes (hands); ***die Schuhe ~*** my shoes are chafing; **II.** *fig. v/refl.*: ***sich an j-m ~*** not to get on with s.o.; ***sich aneinander ~*** F rub each other up the wrong way
Rei·be·rei·en [raɪbə'raɪən] *pl.* friction *sg.*; brushes (***mit*** *dat.* with)
Reib·flä·che ['raɪp-] *f* striking surface
Rei·bung ['raɪbʊŋ] *f* (-; -en) rubbing; ⚙ friction (*a. fig.*)
'Rei·bungs|elek·tri·zi͵tät *f* frictional electricity; **~flä·che** *f* → ***Reibungspunkt***
'rei·bungs·los I. *adj.* smooth; **II.** *adv.*: ***~ verlaufen*** go off smoothly (*or* without a hitch)
'Rei·bungs|punkt *fig. m* cause of friction; **~wär·me** *f* frictional heat; **~͵wi·der·stand** *m* frictional resistance
reich [raɪç] **I.** *adj.* rich (*a. crops, colo[u]r, resources etc.*); wealthy, well-to-do; opulent *meal etc.*; ample, abundant; full *life*; fertile *imagination etc.*; elaborate *ornaments etc.*; ***~ an*** *dat.* rich in; ***~e Auswahl*** wide selection; ***... in ~em Maße*** plenty of ...; ***~ an Erfahrungen sein*** have experienced a lot (in one's life); ***~er an Erfahrungen geworden sein*** have learnt something new; ***ein Sport für ~e Leute*** a rich man's sport; **II.** *adv.* richly; ***~ beschenkt*** loaded with gifts; ***~ heiraten*** marry into money; ***~ illustriert*** richly (*or* lavishly) illustrated
Reich [raɪç] *n* (-[e]s; -e) empire (*a. fig.*); *lit.* realm (*a. fig.*); kingdom; *hist.* ***das Deutsche ~*** the (German) Reich; *hist.* ***das Dritte ~*** the Third Reich; ***das ~ Gottes*** the Kingdom of Heaven; *hist.* ***das ~ der Mitte*** China; *hist.* ***das Weströmische (Oströmische) ~*** the Western (Eastern) Empire; ***das ~ der Natur*** the world of nature; ***das ~ der Phantasie*** the world of fantasy; ***das entstammt dem ~ der Phantasie*** that belongs to the realm of fantasy; → ***Pflanzenreich, Tierreich***
'reich·be·bil·dert *adj.* richly illustrated
Rei·che ['raɪçə] *m* (-n; -n) rich man; ***die ~n*** the rich (*pl.*)
rei·chen ['raɪçən] (h) **I.** *v/i.* **1.** ***~ bis*** *acc.* reach (to), reach (*or* come) up to, reach (*or* go) down to; ***das Wasser reichte ihm bis zu den Schultern*** the water was (*or* came) up to his shoulders; *fig.* ***~ von*** *dat.* ***... bis*** last (*or* stretch) from ... till *or* until; **2.** be enough; ***die Zeit wird nicht ~*** there won't be enough time; ***das Geld muß noch e-e Woche ~*** the money has got to last another week; ***das Gehalt reicht kaum zum Leben*** you can hardly live off a salary like that; ***der Kaffee reicht nicht übers Wochenende*** there isn't enough coffee to see us through the weekend (*or* to last us the weekend); ***der Kuchen soll für sechs Leute ~*** there's got to be enough cake for six people; ***es reicht für alle*** there's enough to go round (*or* for everyone); ***das Licht reicht nicht zum Lesen*** you can't read in that light; ***dazu reicht m-e Geduld nicht*** I haven't got the patience for that (kind of thing); *es waren Hunderte da* - ***das reicht noch gar nicht*** it was a lot more than that; ***das reicht!*** that'll do, *a.* that's enough (of that)!; F ***mir reicht's!*** F I've had enough; F ***jetzt reicht's mir aber!*** F that's done it, that's it now; **II.** *v/t.* offer; *gastr.* serve; ***j-m et. ~*** hand (*or* pass, give) s.o. s.th.; ***reichst du mir bitte das Salz*** could you pass (me) the salt, please; ***nach dem Essen wurden Getränke gereicht*** after the meal drinks

were served; ***sich die Hände ~*** shake hands

'reich·hal·tig [-haltıç] *adj.* **1.** rich *food*; **2.** extensive; ***~e Informationen*** a wealth of information

'reich·lich I. *adj.* ample, plentiful; plenty of *time, food etc.*; liberal, generous *payment*; ***e-e ~e Stunde*** a good hour; **II.** *adv.* a) amply *etc.*; → ***I***, b) F pretty; ***~ versehen sein mit*** *dat.* have plenty of; F ***du kommst ~ spät*** *iro.* you're a bit late(, aren't you?)

'Reichs|ad·ler *m hist.* imperial eagle; **~ap·fel** *m hist.* orb; **~bahn** *f* **1.** *hist.* (German) national railway; **2.** *hist. DDR*: East German railway; **~ge·richt** *n hist.* supreme court of the (German) Reich; **~haupt·stadt** *f hist.* German capital; **~kanz,lei** *f hist.* Chancellery of the Reich; **~kanz·ler** *m hist.* Chancellor of the Reich; **~klein·odi·en** [-klaın'ʔoːdĭən] *pl. hist.* imperial insignia; **~mark** *f hist.* Reichsmark; **~stadt** *f hist.*: ***freie ~*** imperial free city; **~tag** *m hist.* a) Reichstag, b) imperial diet

'Reich·tum *m* (-s; ⸚er [-tyːmɐ]) riches *pl.*, *a. fig.* wealth; *fig.* richness, abundance (***an*** *dat.* of); (great) variety

'Reich·wei·te *f* reach; ⚔, *radio etc.*: range; radius (of action); ***in*** (***außer***) ***~*** within (out of) reach

reif [raıf] *adj.* ripe *fruit etc.*; mature *cheese*, *a. fig. person, judgement etc.*; ⚕ fully developed *boil etc.*; ***~ werden*** → ***reifen***; ***in ~eren Jahren*** at a mature age; ***ein Mann in ~eren Jahren*** a man of mature age; ***im ~en Alter von*** *dat.* at the ripe old age of; ***~ sein für*** *acc.* be ready for; F ***~ fürs Irrenhaus*** F fit for the loony bin; F ***~e Leistung*** a) *sport etc.*: spirited performance, b) *iro.* good show; F ***er ist ~*** F he's in for it

Reif¹ *m* (-[e]s; -e) *lit.* ring; bracelet

Reif² *m* (-[e]s; *no pl.*) white frost, hoarfrost

Rei·fe ['raıfə] *f* (-; *no pl.*) **1.** a) ripeness, b) *fig.* maturity; **2.** → *a.* ***Reifezeugnis***; *ped.* ***mittlere ~*** intermediate high school certificate, *in GB*: GCSEs *pl.*

rei·fen ['raıfən] *v/i.* (sn) a) ripen, b) *fig.* mature (***zu*** *dat.* into), c) ⚕ *boil etc.*: come to a head; ***in j-m ~*** *idea etc.*: start to form in s.o.'s mind; ***zur Gewißheit ~*** grow into certainty

Rei·fen ['raıfən] *m* (-s; -) **1.** hoop; **2.** *mot. etc.* tyre, *Am.* tire; ***e-n ~ wechseln*** change a tyre (*Am.* tire); **~druck** *m* tyre (*Am.* tire) pressure; **~pan·ne** *f* flat tyre (*Am.* tire), puncture, F flat; **~pro,fil** *n* (tyre, *Am.* tire) tread; **~wech·sel** *m* tyre (*Am.* tire) change

'Rei·fe|prü·fung *f* school leaving exam(s *pl.*); → *a.* ***Abitur***; **~zeit** *f* ripening period; *fig.* adolescence, *w.s.* formative years *pl.*; **~zeug·nis** *n* school leaving certificate; *in USA*: (senior high school) graduation diploma, *in GB*: GCE A-levels *pl.*

'Reif·glät·te *f mot.* slippery frost

'reif·lich I. *adj.* careful; ***nach ~er Überlegung*** after careful consideration; **II.** *adv.* carefully; ***das würde ich mir ~ überlegen*** I'd be very careful about making any decisions on that

'Reif·rock *obs. m* crinoline

Rei·fung ['raıfʊŋ] *f* (-; *no pl.*) ripening, maturing; *esp. biol. and* ⚕ maturation

Rei·gen ['raıgən] *m* (-s; -) round dance; ***den ~ eröffnen*** open the ball, *a. fig.* lead off

Rei·he ['raıə] *f* (-; -n) a) row, line, b) row (*of seats*), c) series (*sg.*); row, succession, d) 𝔄 progression, series (*sg.*); (***sich***) ***in e-r ~ aufstellen*** line up; ***in Reih und Glied aufgestellt*** standing neatly in a row; F ***e-e ganze ~ von*** *dat.* a lot of, F a whole string of; ***e-e ~ von Indizien*** some evidence; ***aus den ~en*** *gen.* from among; ***e-n Verräter in den eigenen ~n haben*** have a traitor in one's ranks; *fig.* ***die ~n lichten sich*** the ranks are thinning; ***warten, bis man an die ~ kommt*** wait one's turn; ***wer ist an der ~?*** whose turn is it?; (***immer***) ***der ~ nach*** one after the other; ***er ist an der ~*** it's his turn; ***ich kam außer der ~ dran*** they took me before (it was) my turn; ***erzähl der ~ nach!*** tell it from the beginning, start at the beginning; F ***aus der ~ kommen*** get muddled; F ***et.*** (***wieder***) ***auf die ~ kriegen*** get s.th. sorted out; F ***aus der ~ tanzen*** a) be different, b) step out of line

rei·hen ['raıən] (h) **I.** *v/t.* **1.** line up; **2.** tack; **3.** ***Perlen auf e-e Schnur ~*** string pearls; **II.** *v/refl.*: ***eins reiht sich ans andere*** one thing follows another

'Rei·hen|eck·haus *n* end-of-terrace house; **~fer·ti·gung** *f* serial production; **~fol·ge** *f* order, sequence; ***alphabetische*** (***zeitliche***) ***~*** alphabetical (chronological) order; ***der ~ nach*** in order; ***in ununterbrochener ~*** in succession, in a row

'Rei·hen·haus *n* terrace(d) house, *Am.* row house; **~sied·lung** *f* (terraced) housing estate, *Am.* row house development

'Rei·hen|schal·tung *f* ⚡ series connection; **~un·ter,su·chung** *f* ⚕ mass screening

'rei·hen·wei·se *adv.* **1.** in rows; **2.** *fig.* a) F by the dozen, b) one after the other

Rei·her ['raıɐ] *m* (-s; -) *zo.* heron; *sl.* ***kotzen wie ein ~*** *sl.* spew one's guts out

reih·um [raı'ʔʊm] *adv.* **1.** in turn; **2.** ***et. ~ gehen lassen*** pass s.th. round

Reim [raım] *m* (-[e]s; -e) rhyme; *fig.* ***kannst du dir darauf e-n ~ machen?*** does it make any sense to you?, can you make any sense (*or* make head or tail) of it?; ***ich mache mir so m-n ~ darauf*** I can put two and two together; **rei·men** ['raımən] *v/t., v/i. and v/refl.* (***sich ~***) (h) rhyme (***auf*** *acc.*, ***mit*** *dat.* with); *fig.* ***das reimt sich nicht*** that doesn't make sense; **'reim·los** *adj.* unrhymed

'Reim|paar *n* rhyming couplet; **~sche·ma** *n* rhyme pattern (*or* scheme)

rein¹ [raın] **I.** *adj.* pure (*a.* ⚗, *biol., ling., a. silk, alcohol etc. and fig. nonsense etc.*); clean; clear *skin etc., a. fig. conscience*; *metall.* unalloyed; unadulterated (*a. fig.*); net, clear *profit*; sheer *nonsense etc.*; ***~e Baumwolle*** pure (*or* one-hundred per cent) cotton; F ***~ste Freude*** sheer (*or* pure) joy; ***~e Lüge*** downright (*or* barefaced) lie; F ***~er Wahnsinn*** sheer madness; ***die ~e Wahrheit*** the plain truth, ⚖ the truth, the whole truth, and nothing but the truth; ***~er Zufall*** pure coincidence; ***e-e ~e Arbeitergegend*** a real working-class area; ***~e Mathematik*** pure mathematics; ***e-e ~e Formalität*** a mere formality; F ***der ~ste Komiker*** a real comedian; → ***Luft, Tisch, Vergnügen, Wein, Weste***; **II.** *adv.* purely; F absolutely; ***~ pflanzliches Fett*** pure vegetable fat; ***~ gar nichts*** absolutely nothing (F nil); ***~ unmöglich*** absolutely impossible; ***~ verrückt*** totally mad; ***~ zufällig*** by pure accident (*or* chance), purely by accident (*or* chance); ***aus ~ persönlichen Gründen*** for purely personal reasons; ***et. ~ Persönliches*** a purely personal matter; **III.** *su.* ***ins ~e bringen*** clear up, sort out; ***mit j-m ins ~e kommen*** get things straightened out with s.o.; ***ins ~e kommen*** straighten things out (for o.s.); ***et. ins ~e schreiben*** make a fair copy of s.th.

rein² F *adv.* **1.** → ***herein***; **2.** → ***hinein***; **rein...** *in cpds.* **1.** → *a.* ***herein...***; **2.** → *a.* ***hinein...***

Rei·ne·ma·che·frau ['raınəmaxə-] *f* cleaning lady; **'Rei·ne·ma·chen** *n* (-s; *no pl.*) cleaning

'Rein|er·lös *m*, **~er·trag** *m* net proceeds *pl.*, net (*or* clear) profit

'Rein·fall F *m* F flop, washout; F letdown; **'rein·fal·len** F *v/i.* (*irr.*, *sep.*, sn, → ***fallen***) (*a.* ***drauf ~***) F fall for it

'Rein·ge·winn *m* net profit; → ***erzielen***

'Rein·hal·tung *f*: ***die ~ der Luft*** *etc.* keeping the air *etc.* clean

'rein·hän·gen F *v/refl.* (*sep.*, h): ***sich ~*** throw o.s. into it (*or* s.th.), F give it all one has got; ***sich zu sehr ~*** get too involved, take it (*or* s.th.) too seriously

'rein·hau·en (*sep.*, h) F **I.** *v/i.* **1.** a) F get cracking, get stuck in, b) F dig in; **2.** ***das haut voll rein!*** F that really knocks you for a six; **II.** *v/t.* **3.** ***sich et. ~*** F polish off *the soup etc.*, F knock back *a few beers etc.*; **4.** ***j-m e-e ~*** F clobber s.o.

'Rein·heit *f* (-; *no pl.*) purity, pureness, cleanness *etc.*; → ***rein¹***

'Rein·heits|ge·bot *n* purity requirement; **~grad** *m* purity standard

rei·ni·gen ['raınıgən] *v/t.* (h) clean; cleanse; wash; ⚗, ⚙ purify *air, water etc.*; clean up *lake etc.*.; ***sich selbst ~*** *river etc.*: clean itself; ***chemisch ~*** dry-clean; ***zum ♀ bringen*** take to the cleaners; *fig.* ***die Atmosphäre ~*** clear the air; ***sich von e-m Verdacht ~*** clear o.s. of a suspicion

Rei·ni·ger ['raınıgɐ] *m* (-s; -) cleaning agent, cleaner; cleanser

Rei·ni·gung ['raınıgʊŋ] *f* (-; -en) **1.** *no pl.* cleaning *etc.*; → ***reinigen***; **2.** (dry) cleaners *pl.*; ***chemische ~*** dry cleaning; ***in der ~ sein*** *clothes*: be at the cleaners

'Rei·ni·gungs|creme *f* cleansing cream; **~kraft** *f* (-; *no pl.*) cleaning (*or* cleansing) power *or* action; **~mit·tel** *n* cleaning agent, household cleaner

'Rein·kul,tur *f* pure culture; F *fig.* ***Kitsch in ~*** pure unadulterated rubbish

'rein·le·gen F *v/t.* → ***hereinlegen***

'rein·lich *adj.* clean; cleanly; neat, tidy; **'Rein·lich·keit** *f* (-; *no pl.*) cleanliness; neatness, tidiness

'Rein·ma·che... → ***Reinemache...***

'rein·ras·sig *adj. zo.* pedigree, pure-bred *dog etc.*; thoroughbred *horse*

'rein|rei·ßen F *v/t.* (*irr.*, *sep.*, h, → ***reißen***) **1.** F get *s.o.* into a real mess; **2.** F set *s.o.* back a fair bit; **~rie·chen** F *v/i.* (*irr.*, *sep.*, h, → ***riechen***) → ***reinschnuppern***; **~schlit·tern** F *v/i.* (*sep.*, sn): ***in et. ~*** get o.s. involved in (*or* with) s.th.; ***plötzlich war ich da reingeschlittert*** before I knew it I had got myself involved; **~schnup·pern** F *fig. v/i.* (*sep.*, h): ***in et. ~*** have a brief look at s.th., get a taste of s.th.

'Rein·schrift *f* fair copy
'rein|sei·den *adj.* pure silk; **~sil·bern** *adj.* pure silver
'Rein·ver·dienst *m* net earnings *pl.*
re·in·ve·stie·ren [reˀɪnvɛs'tiːrən] *v/t.* (h) ✝ reinvest, plough (*Am.* plow) back
'rein·wa·schen *fig. v/t.* (*irr.*, *sep.*, h, → ***waschen***) whitewash, clear
'rein·weg F *adv.* absolutely, completely
'rein·wür·gen F *v/t.* (*sep.*, h) **1.** force down; **2.** ***j-m eins ~*** F let s.o. know about it
Reis¹ [raɪs] *n* (-es; -e ['raɪzə]) ⚘ twig
Reis² [raɪs] *m* (-es ['raɪzəs]; *no pl.*) rice; **~an·bau** *m* (-[e]s; *no pl.*) growing (*or* cultivation) of rice; **~auf·lauf** *m* baked rice pudding; **~beu·tel** *m* boil-in-the-bag rice; **~brei** *m* rice pudding
Rei·se ['raɪzə] *f* (-; -n) trip; journey, ⚓ voyage (*all* ***nach*** *dat.* to); tour (***in*** *dat.* of); ***wie war die Ungarnreise?*** how was your trip to Hungary?; ***gute ~!*** have a pleasant journey!, have a good trip!; ***viel auf ~n sein*** do a lot of travel(l)ing; ***er ist mal wieder auf ~n*** he's off on his trips again; ***wohin geht die ~?*** where are you off to?; *fig.* ***e-e ~ in die Vergangenheit*** a journey into the past, a walk down memory lane; **~an·den·ken** *n* souvenir; **~apo,the·ke** *f* first-aid kit; **~be·darf** *m* travel(l)ing requisites *pl.*; **~be·glei·ter** *m* **1.** travel companion; **2.** → ***Reiseleiter***; **~be·kannt·schaft** *f* travel(l)ing acquaintance; ***sie ist e-e ~*** I met her when I was on holiday; **~be·schrän·kun·gen** *pl.* travel restrictions, restrictions on travel; **~be·schrei·bung** *f* travelogue; travel diary; **~bü,ro** *n* travel agency (*or* agent['s]); **~bus** *m* coach; **~decke** *f* travel(l)ing rug; **~di·plo,mat** *m* shuttle diplomat; **~di·plo·ma,tie** *f* shuttle diplomacy; **~fie·ber** *n* holiday fever; **~füh·rer** *m* a) guide(book), b) (travel) guide; courier; **~ge·fähr·te** *m* travel companion
'Rei·se·ge·päck *n* baggage, luggage; **~ver·si·che·rung** *f* baggage insurance
'Rei·se|ge·schwin·dig·keit *f* cruising speed; **~ge·sell·schaft** *f* **1.** (tourist) party; **2.** tour operator; **~grup·pe** *f* tourist party; **~kof·fer** *m* suitcase; **~ko·sten** *pl.* travel expenses; **~krank·heit** *f* travel sickness; **~land** *n* tourist country (*or* destination); **~lei·ter** *m* courier; (travel) guide; **~lek,tü·re** *f* holiday reading; something to read on the trip; **~li·te·ra,tur** *f* **1.** travel writing (*or* literature, books *pl.*); **2.** → ***Reiselektüre***
'Rei·se·lust *f*: ***mich packt mal wieder die ~!*** F I've got itchy feet again
'rei·se·lu·stig *adj.*: ***er ist sehr ~*** he's a keen travel(l)er
'rei·se·mü·de *adj.* travel-weary
rei·sen ['raɪzən] **I.** *v/i.* (sn) a) travel (***nach*** *dat.* to); make a trip (to), b) go, leave; ***~ nach*** *dat. a.* go to; ***ins Ausland ~*** go abroad; ***wir ~ am Sonntag*** we leave on Sunday; **II.** ♀ *n* (-s; *no pl.*) travel(l)ing; travel; → ***bilden*** 6
Rei·sen·de ['raɪzəndə] *m, f* (-n; -n) **1.** travel(l)er; ***die ~n werden gebeten zu*** *inf.* passengers are requested to *inf.*; **2.** → ***Handlungsreisende***
'Rei·se|paß *m* passport; **~pro,spekt** *m* travel brochure; **~rou·te** *f* route, itinerary; **~ruf** *m* emergency call, police message; **~scheck** *m* traveller's cheque, *Am.* traveler's check; **~schreib·ma,schi·ne** *f* portable typewriter; **~schrift·stel·ler** *m* travel writer; **~spe·sen** *pl.* travel(l)ing (*or* travel) expenses; **~ta·sche** *f* travel(l)ing bag, holdall, *Am.* carryall; **~,un·ter·la·gen** *pl.* travel documents; **~ver·an·stal·ter** *m* tour operator(s *pl.*); **~ver·kehr** *m* holiday traffic; **~vor·be·rei·tun·gen** *pl.* holiday preparations, preparations for the trip (*or* holiday); ***die ~ machen mich immer fertig*** getting everything ready for the trip always exhausts me; **~wecker** *m* travel(l)ing alarm clock; **~wel·le** *f* wave of holidaymakers; **~wet·ter** *n* **1.** holiday weather; **2.** weather for travel(l)ing; **~wet·ter·be·richt** *m* holiday weather report; **~zeit** *f* holiday season; ***die beste ~*** the best time to travel; **~ziel** *n* **1.** destination; **2.** ***Spanien ist ein beliebtes ~*** a lot of people go to Spain for their holiday(s)
'Reis·feld *n* paddy (*or* rice) field
Rei·sig ['raɪzɪç] *n* (-s; *no pl.*) brushwood
'Reis|korn *n* grain of rice; **~mehl** *n* rice flour; **~pa,pier** *n* rice paper
Reiß·aus [raɪs'ˀaʊs] F *m*: ***~ nehmen*** take to one's heels, F clear off
Reiß·brett ['raɪs-] *n* drawing board
'Reis·schüs·sel *f* rice bowl; *fig.* ***die ~ Asiens*** the rice bowl of Asia
rei·ßen ['raɪsən] (riß, gerissen, h) **I.** *v/t.* **1.** a) tear, b) tear, pull, rip, c) snatch, d) drag, pull, *flood*: sweep, e) ⚕ rupture; ***e-e Seite aus e-m Buch ~*** tear (*or* rip) a page out of a book; ***j-m et. aus der Hand ~*** snatch s.th. away from s.o. (*or* out of s.o.'s hand); ***sich die Kleider vom Leibe ~*** tear (*or* rip) off one's clothes; ***sich e-n Splitter in den Finger ~*** get a splinter into one's finger; ***aus dem Schlaf gerissen werden*** be rudely awakened; ***aus s-n Illusionen gerissen werden*** F come down to earth with a bump; ***die Macht an sich ~*** seize power; ***die Führung an sich ~*** *sport*: take the lead, *w.s.* take over, take command; ***sie war hin und her gerissen*** a) she couldn't make up her mind, b) F she was thrilled to bits; F ***das reißt mich nicht gerade vom Hocker*** F I can't say I'm thrilled, it's nothing to write home about; → ***Witz, Zote***; **2.** *zo.* kill; **II.** *v/i.* **3.** a) tear; *chain, string etc.*: break, b) *lips*: chap, c) *fog*: lift suddenly; ***~ an*** *dat.* tear (*or* tug) at; ***da riß ihm die Geduld*** his patience gave out (on him); → ***Strang, Strick***; **III.** *v/refl.* **4.** *fig.* ***sich ~ um*** *acc.* fight (*or* squabble) over; ***ich reiße mich nicht darum*** I can do without (it); ***ich reiße mich nicht darum, ihn kennenzulernen*** I'm not exactly dying to get to know him; **IV.** ♀ *n* (-s; *no pl.*) **5.** tearing *etc.*; → ***reißen***; **6.** F ⚕ rheumatics; **'rei·ßend** *adj.* a) torrential *river*, b) searing *pain*, c) *zo.* rapacious, d) → ***Absatz*** 3
Rei·ßer ['raɪsɐ] F *m* (-s; -) **1.** thriller; **2.** F winner, money-spinner; **rei·ße·risch** ['raɪsərɪʃ] *adj.* sensational *headlines*; loud *colo(u)rs, advertising etc.*
reiß·fest ['raɪs-] *adj.* tearproof
'Reiß·fe·stig·keit *f* (-; *no pl.*) **1.** resistance to tearing; **2.** ⚙ tensile strength
Reiß·lei·ne ['raɪs-] *f* ripcord *of parachute*
Reiß·ver·schluß ['raɪs-] *m* zipper, *Brit.* zip; ***mach den ~ an d-r Jacke zu*** (***auf***) zip up (unzip) your jacket; **~sy,stem** *n mot.* alternate filtering-in system
Reiß·wolf ['raɪs-] *m* shredder
Reiß·zwecke ['raɪs-] *f* drawing pin, *Am.* thumbtack
'Reis·wein *m* rice wine, sake
Reit·an·zug ['raɪt-] *m* riding habit
rei·ten ['raɪtən] (ritt, geritten) **I.** *v/i.* (sn) ride; ***gut*** (***schlecht***) ***~*** be a good (bad) rider; ***im Galopp ~*** (ride at a) gallop; **II.** *v/t.* (h) ride; ***ein Rennen ~*** ride (in) a race; ***sich wund ~*** get saddle-sore; *fig.* ***ein Thema zu Tode ~*** flog a subject to death; → ***Teufel*** *etc.*; **III.** ♀ *n* (-s; *no pl.*) riding; **'rei·tend** *adj.* on horseback
Rei·ter ['raɪtɐ] *m* (-s; -) **1.** rider, horseman; → ***blau*** 1; **2.** ⚙ rider; **3.** *card index*: rider, tab; **Rei·te·rei** [raɪtə'raɪ] *f* (-; *no pl.*) **1.** ⚔ cavalry; **2.** riding; **Rei·te·rin** ['raɪtərɪn] *f* (-; -nen) rider, horsewoman; **'rei·ter·los** *adj.* riderless; *adv. a.* without a rider
'Rei·ter|re·gi,ment *n hist.* cavalry regiment; **~stand·bild** *n* equestrian statue
Reit|ger·te ['raɪt-] *f* riding crop; **~ho·se** *f*: (***e-e ~*** a pair of) (riding) breeches *pl.*; **~kap·pe** *f* riding cap; **~kunst** *f* horsemanship; **~leh·rer** *m* riding instructor; **~peit·sche** *f* riding whip; **~pferd** *n* saddle (*or* riding) horse; **~schu·le** *f* riding school; **~sport** *m* riding, equestrian sport(s *pl.*); **~stall** *m* riding stable; **~stie·fel** *m* riding boot; **~tier** *n* riding animal, mount; **~tur,nier** *n* horse show; **~,un·ter·richt** *m* riding lessons *pl.*; **~weg** *m* bridle path
Reiz [raɪts] *m* (-es; -e) **1.** *physiol., psych. and fig.* stimulus, *pl.* stimuli; **2.** appeal, attraction; charm; ***der ~ des Neuen*** the novelty (appeal); ***der ~ des Verbotenen*** the lure of forbidden fruit; ***s-n ~ verlieren*** begin to pall (***für*** *acc.* on); ***der ~*** (***an der Sache***) ***liegt in*** what is so fascinating about it is; ***darin liegt gerade der ~*** that's the whole fun of it; ***ich kann dem Film keinen ~ abgewinnen*** I can't (*or* I fail to) see anything in that film; **3.** charm; ***s-e ~e spielen lassen*** display one's charms
'reiz·bar *adj.* irritable, touchy, F uptight; irascible; ***er ist so ~*** he'll fly into a temper at the slightest thing
rei·zen ['raɪtsən] (h) **I.** *v/t.* **1.** annoy, rile; provoke; → ***gereizt***; **2.** ⚕ irritate; **3.** (a)rouse *curiosity, interest etc.*; stimulate, whet *s.o.'s appetite*; tickle *the palate*; lure, tempt; ***es reizte ihn, et. ganz Neues zu machen*** he was tempted to do s.th. completely different; ***es würde mich ~ zu*** *inf.* I wouldn't mind *ger.*, I'd love to *inf.*; F ***das kann mich nicht ~*** that doesn't appeal to me in the slightest, *sl.* it doesn't grab me (at all); **4.** *card game*: bid; **II.** *v/i.* **5.** ⚕ irritate the skin (*or* eyes *etc.*), be an irritant; **6.** *card game*: bid; **'rei·zend** *adj.* charming, delightful; ***~es Mädchen*** lovely (little) girl; ***das ist ja ~!*** how charming!, *iro.* charming(, I must say)!; ***das ist ja ~ von Ihnen*** how nice of you
'Reiz|hu·sten *m* dry cough; **~kli·ma** *n* bracing climate
'reiz·los *adj.* uninteresting, boring
'Reiz|mit·tel *n* **1.** ⚕ stimulant; **2.** → ***Reizthema*** 2; **~schwel·le** *f* stimulus threshold; **~stoff** *m* irritant; **~the·ma** *n* **1.** explosive topic, emotive issue; *pol. a.* gut issue; **2.** touchy subject; ***das ist für sie ein ~*** that's a touchy subject with her, that always gets her going; **~the·ra,pie** *f* ⚕ stimulation therapy; **~über,flu·tung** *f* a) stimulus satiation, b) media saturation

Rei·zung ['raɪtsʊŋ] *f* (-; -en) a) irritation (*a.* ⚕), b) provocation, c) stimulation
'reiz·voll *adj.* **1.** charming; **2.** tempting; ***e-e ~e Aufgabe*** an interesting task
'Reiz|wä·sche *f* sexy underwear; **~wort** *n* emotive (*psych.* test) word; ***Geld war bei ihr ein ~*** money was a touchy subject with her
re·ka·pi·tu·lie·ren [rekapitu'li:rən] *v/i. and v/t.* (h) recapitulate, sum up; ***ich rekapituliere*** to sum up (the main points again)
re·keln ['re:kəln] *v/refl.* (h): ***sich ~*** a) stretch, b) sprawl, lounge around, loll (about)
Re·kla·ma·ti·on [reklama'tsĭo:n] *f* (-; -en) complaint; *esp. sport*: protest
Re·kla·me [re'kla:mə] *f* (-; *no pl.*) a) advertising, b) advertisement, F ad, *Brit. a.* advert; *TV, radio*: *a.* commercial, *coll.* commercials *pl.*; ***~ machen für*** *acc.* advertise, promote, *fig.* F plug; **~ta·fel** *f* billboard, *Brit. a.* hoarding
re·kla·mie·ren [rekla'mi:rən] (h) **I.** *v/t.* complain about *s.th.*; *a.* take *s.th.* back to the shop; query *check etc.*; enquire (*or* inquire) about *goods etc. not received*; **II.** *v/i.* complain, make (*or* lodge) a complaint; *esp. sport*: protest
re·kon·stru·ie·ren [rekɔnstru'i:rən] *v/t.* (h) reconstruct; **Re·kon·struk·ti·on** [rekɔnstrʊk'tsĭo:n] *f* (-; -en) reconstruction
re·kon·va·les·zent [rekɔnvalɛs'tsɛnt] *adj.*, **Re·kon·va·les'zent** *m* (-en; -en) convalescent; **Re·kon·va·les·zenz** [rekɔnvalɛs'tsɛnts] *f* (-; *no pl.*) convalescence
Re·kord [re'kɔrt] *m* (-[e]s; -e [də]) record; *w.s. a.* record (*or* all-time) high; ***e-n ~ aufstellen*** (***brechen***) set up (break) a record; ***e-n ~ halten*** hold a record; ***alle ~e brechen*** break all records; ***der ~ liegt bei*** the record is (*or* stands at); **~be·such** *m* record attendance; **~ern·te** *f* bumper crop; **~hal·ter** *m* record holder; **~hoch** *n stock exchange etc.*: record (*or* all-time) high; **~in·ha·ber** *m* record holder; **~lei·stung** *f* **1.** outstanding performance; **2.** record-beating performance; **~mar·ke** *f* record; **~tief** *n stock exchange etc.*: record (*or* all-time) low; **~ver·such** *m* attempt on the record; **~zeit** *f* record time
Re·krut [re'kru:t] *m* (-en; -en) ⚔ recruit (*a. fig.*); **Re'kru·ten·aus·bil·dung** *f* training of recruits
re·kru·tie·ren [rekru'ti:rən] (h) **I.** *v/t.* ⚔ recruit (*a. fig.*); **II.** *fig. v/refl.*: ***sich ~ aus*** *dat.* be made up of; **Re·kru'tie·rung** *f* (-; -en) recruitment, recruiting
rek·tal [rɛk'ta:l] *adj.* ⚕ rectal
Rek·ti·on [rɛk'tsĭo:n] *f* (-; -en) *ling.* government; case governed by a verb *etc.*
Rek·tor ['rɛkto:ɐ] *m* (-s; -en [rɛk'to:rən]) a) *ped.* headmaster, *Am.* principal, b) *univ.* vice-chancellor, principal, *Am.* president
Rek·to·rat [rɛkto'ra:t] *n* (-[e]s; -e) **1.** headmastership; *univ.* vice-chancellorship, principalship, *Am.* presidency; **2.** headmaster's office; *univ.* vice-chancellor's (*or* principal's, *Am.* president's) office
Rek·to·rin [rɛk'to:rɪn] *f* (-; -nen) a) *ped.* head(mistress), b) → ***Rektor*** b
Rek·tum ['rɛktʊm] *n* (-s; Rekta ['rɛkta]) *anat.* rectum
re·kur·siv [rekʊr'zi:f] *adj.* ⩯, *ling.* recursive

Re·lais [rə'lɛ:] *n* (-; - [rə'lɛ:s]) ⚡ relay; **~sta·ti,on** *f* relay station
Re·la·ti·on [rela'tsĭo:n] *f* (-; -en) a) relation(ship), b) proportion, ratio; ***das steht in keiner ~ zu s-m Einkommen*** it's out of all proportion to his income
re·la·tio·nal [relatsĭo'na:l] *adj. computer*: relational
re·la·tiv [rela'ti:f] **I.** *adj.* relative; **II.** *adv.* relatively, comparatively; ***das trifft nur ~ zu*** that's only partially true; ***es verlief ~ gut*** it went reasonably (*or* relatively) well; **re·la·ti·vie·ren** [relati'vi:rən] *v/t.* (h) **1.** put into perspective, see in perspective; **2.** qualify *remark etc.*
Re·la·ti·vi·tät [relativi'tɛ:t] *f* (-; *no pl.*) relativity; **Re·la·ti·vi'täts·theo,rie** *f* theory of relativity
Re·la'tiv|pro,no·men *n* relative pronoun; **~satz** *m* relative clause
re·le·vant [rele'vant] *adj.* relevant (***für*** *acc.* to), pertinent (to); **Re·le·vanz** [rele'vants] *f* relevance (***für*** *acc.* to, for)
Re·li·ef [re'lĭɛf] *n* (-s; -s) relief; **~glo·bus** *m* raised-relief globe; **~kar·te** *f* relief map
Re·li·gi·on [reli'gĭo:n] *f* (-; -en) **1.** religion (*a. fig.*); faith; **2.** *no pl.* → ***Religionsunterricht***
Re·li·gi'ons|aus·übung *f* religious practice (*or* practise); ***freie ~*** freedom of worship; **~be·kennt·nis** *n* confession; **~er·satz** *m* substitute religion; **~frei·heit** *f* (-; *no pl.*) freedom of worship; **~ge·mein·schaft** *f* confession; religious community; **~krieg** *m* religious war; **~leh·re** *f* religious education; **~leh·rer** *m* RI (= religious instruction) teacher, RE (= religious education) teacher; **~stif·ter** *m* founder of a (*or* the) religion; **~streit** *m* religious controversy; **~,un·ter·richt** *m ped.* religious instruction, RI; religious education, RE; **~wis·sen·schaft** *f* (comparative) theology
re·li·gi·ös [reli'gĭø:s] *adj.* religious; pious, devout; **Re·li·gio·si·tät** [religĭozi'tɛ:t] *f* (-; *no pl.*) religiousness, religion, piety
Re·likt [re'lɪkt] *n* (-[e]s; -e) **1.** relic (*gen.* of; ***aus*** *dat.* from, of); F leftover (from); ***das ist noch ein ~ aus s-r Armeezeit*** *a.* that goes back to his army days; **2.** *biol.* relict
Re·ling ['re:lɪŋ] *f* (-; *no pl.*) ⚓ railing
Re·li·qui·ar [relikvi'a:ɐ] *n* (-s; -e [-rə]) reliquary; **Re·li·quie** [re'li:kvĭə] *f* (-; -n) relic
Re'li·qui·en|schrein *m* reliquary; **~ver·eh·rung** *f* worship of relics
Re·make ['ri:meɪk] *n* (-s; -s) *film*: remake
re·mi·li·ta·ri·sie·ren [remilitari'zi:rən] *v/t.* (h) remilitarize, rearm
Re·mi·li·ta·ri'sie·rung *f* (-; *no pl.*) remilitarization, rearmament
Re·mi·nis·zenz [reminɪs'tsɛnts] *f* (-; -en) reminiscence (***an*** *acc.* of); memento (of)
Re·mis [rə'mi:] **I.** *n* (-; - [rə'mi:s]) draw; **II.** ♘ *adj.*: ***die Partie endete ~*** the game ended in a draw
Re·mit·ten·de [remɪ'tɛndə] *f* (-; -n) return
Rem·mi·dem·mi ['rɛmi'dɛmi] F *n* (-s; *no pl.*) wild celebration; ***~ machen*** a) F make a racket (*sl.* a hell of a noise), b) have a wild time of it; ***hier herrscht ~!*** F this is where it's at!
Re·mou·la·de [remu'la:də] *f* (-; -n) remoulade; tartar sauce
Rem·pe·lei [rɛmpə'laɪ] *f* (-; -en) jostling; *sport*: pushing; **rem·peln** ['rɛmpəln] *v/t.* (h) jostle, bump into, F barge into; *sport*: push, give *s.o.* a push, F shove

REM-Pha·se ['rɛmfa:zə] *f* (-; -n) REM (= rapid eye movement) phase
Ren [rɛn, re:n] *n* (-s; -s) *zo.* reindeer
Re·nais·sance [rənɛ'sã:s] *f* (-; -n) **1.** *no pl. hist.* Renaissance; **2.** renaissance, revival; **~mensch** *m* (*a.* ***der ~***) Renaissance man
Ren·dez·vous [rãde'vu:] *n* (-; - [-'vu:s]) **1.** date, rendezvous; ***heimliches ~*** *esp. iro.* tryst; **2.** *space travel*: docking; **~ma,nö·ver** *n space travel*: docking manoeuvre (*Am.* maneuver)
Ren·di·te [rɛn'di:tə] *f* (-; -n) ♆ yield, profit
Re·ne·gat [rene'ga:t] *m* (-en; -en) renegade
Re·ne·klo·de [renə'klo:də] *f* (-; -n) ♧ greengage
re·ni·tent [reni'tɛnt] *adj.* refractory
Renn|bahn ['rɛn-] *f* racecourse, *Am.* racetrack; *horse racing*: *a.* turf; *mot.* circuit, speedway; *running*: track; **~boot** *n* speedboat
ren·nen ['rɛnən] (rannte, gerannt) **I.** *v/i.* (sn) run; race; rush, tear; ***~ gegen*** *acc.* run into; ***er rennt bei jeder Kleinigkeit zu s-r Mutter*** he goes running to his mother for every little thing; F ***er rennt zu jedem Popkonzert*** he goes to every pop concert that comes along, he can't miss any pop concert; F ***er mußte die ganze Nacht ~*** he was up all night running to the toilet (*Am.* bathroom); *fig.* ***ins Verderben ~*** rush headlong into disaster; → ***Wette***; **II.** *v/t.* (h) → ***Haufen***
'Ren·nen *n* (-s; -) **1.** *no pl.* run(ning); **2.** a) race; *a.* race meeting, *pl.* races, b) heat; ***totes ~*** dead heat; ***aus dem ~ fallen*** drop out of the running; ***j-n aus dem ~ werfen*** put s.o. out of the running; ***das ~ machen*** come in first, *fig.* come out on top; *fig.* ***er liegt noch gut im ~*** he's still going strong, he's still in the running; ***das ~ ist gelaufen*** it's all over
Ren·ner ['rɛnɐ] *m* (-s; -) **1.** → ***Rennpferd***; **2.** F hit; ♆ winner; ***das Buch wird ein ~*** we're *etc.* onto a winner with that book
Ren·ne·rei [rɛnə'raɪ] F *f* (-; -en) running around; ***diese ~!*** all this running around from place to place
Renn|fah·rer ['rɛn-] *m* racing driver (*or* cyclist); **~läu·fer** *m* professional skier, racer; **~len·ker** *m* drop(ped) handlebars *pl.*; **~ma,schi·ne** *f* racer; **~pferd** *n* racehorse; **~platz** *m* racecourse, *the* turf; **~rad** *n* racing cycle, racer; **~schu·he** *pl.* spikes; **~ski** *m* racing ski; **~sport** *m* racing; **~wa·gen** *m* racing car
Re·nom·mee [renɔ'me:] *n* (-s; -s) reputation; fame, renown; ***ein gutes ~ haben*** have a good name (*or* reputation)
re·nom·mie·ren [renɔ'mi:rən] *v/i.* (h) boast (***mit*** *dat.* of)
Re·nom·mier|mar·ke [renɔ'mi:ɐ-] *f* prestige label; **~stück** *n* showpiece
re·nom·miert [renɔ'mi:ɐt] *adj.* famous, noted (***wegen*** *gen.* for); (highly) acclaimed; *a.* prestigious *institute etc.*
re·no·vieren [reno'vi:rən] *v/t.* (h) renovate, F do up; redecorate *room*; **Re·no'vie·rung** *f* (-; -en) renovation; redecoration
ren·ta·bel [rɛn'ta:bəl] *adj.* ♆ profitable, viable; *w.s.* worthwhile; **Ren·ta·bi·li·tät** [rɛntabili'tɛ:t] *f* (-; *no pl.*) profitability, viability
Ren·ta·bi·li'täts|gren·ze *f*, **~schwel·le** *f* breakeven point

Ren·te ['rɛntə] *f* (-; -n) **1.** pension; ***in ~ gehen*** retire; **2.** ✝ a) revenue, b) annuity, c) interest
'**Ren·ten|al·ter** *n*: ***das ~*** retirement age; **~an·pas·sung** *f* adjustment of pensions (to wages and prices); **~an·spruch** *m* pension claim; **~ba·sis** *f* annuity claim; **~be·rech·nung** *f* calculation of pensions; **&be·rech·tigt** *adj.* entitled to a pension; pensionable *age*; **~er·hö·hung** *f* pension increase; **~markt** *m* ✝ bond market; **~pa,pie·re** *pl.* ✝ fixed-interest bonds; **~re,form** *f* pension(s) reform; **~ver·si·che·rung** *f* pension scheme; **~wer·te** *pl.* ✝ fixed-interest securities
Ren·tier ['rɛntiːɐ] *n zo.* reindeer; caribou
ren·tie·ren [rɛn'tiːrən] *v/refl.*: ***sich ~*** (h) → ***lohnen*** I
Rent·ner ['rɛntnɐ] *m* (-s; -), **Rent·ne·rin** ['rɛntnərɪn] *f* (-; -nen) (old age) pensioner, senior citizen; '**Rent·ner·streß** *m* retirement stress
re·or·ga·ni·sie·ren [reˀɔrgani'ziːrən] *v/t.* (h) reorganize
re·pa·ra·bel [repa'raːbəl] *adj.* reparable
Re·pa·ra·tio·nen [repara'tsĭoːnən] *pl.*, **Re·pa·ra·ti'ons·zah·lung** *f* reparations (*pl.*)
Re·pa·ra·tur [repara'tuːɐ] *f* (-; -en [-rən]) repair(s *pl.*); ***in ~*** in for repair, being repaired; ***et. zur ~ geben*** have s.th. repaired; **&an·fäl·lig** *adj.*: **~ *sein*** keep breaking down; **~an·fäl·lig·keit** *f* (-; *no pl.*) tendency to break down; breakdown record; **~an·lei·tung** *f* service manual; instructions *pl.* for repair; **&be·dürf·tig** *adj.*: (***dringend ~***) in need of (urgent) repair; **~ko·sten** *pl.* (cost *sg.* of) repairs; **~werft** *f* repair yard; **~werk·statt** *f* workshop; garage; **~schnell·dienst** *m* fast repair service, while-you-wait repair service
re·pa·rie·ren [repa'riːrən] *v/t.* (h) repair, mend, F fix; ***das ist nicht mehr zu ~*** it can't be repaired, it's beyond repair
Re·per·toire [repɛr'tŏaːɐ] *n* (-s; -s) repertoire (*a. fig.*); **~stück** *n* repertory play; **~thea·ter** *n* repertory theat|re (*Am. a.* -er)
re·pe·tie·ren [repe'tiːrən] (h) **I.** *v/t.* revise; **II.** *v/i. ped.* repeat a year
Re·pe·tier·ge·wehr [repe'tiːɐ-] *n* repeating rifle, repeater
Re·pe·ti·ti·on [repeti'tsĭoːn] *f* (-; -en) repetition; **Re·pe·ti·tor** [repe'tiːtoːɐ] *m* (-s; -en [repeti'toːrən]) *univ.* coach; **Re·pe·ti·to·ri·um** [repeti'toːrĭʊm] *n* (-s; -ien) *univ.* revision course
Re·plik [re'pliːk] *f* (-; -en) **1.** reply (*a.* ⚖), rejoinder; **2.** *art*: replica
Re·port [re'pɔrt] *m* (-[e]s; -e) report
Re·por·ta·ge [repɔr'taːʒə] *f* (-; -n) report, *a. sport*: commentary; ***die ~n über*** *acc.* ***...*** *a.* coverage of ...
Re·por·ter [re'pɔrtɐ] *m* (-s; -), **Re·por·te·rin** [re'pɔrtərɪn] *f* (-; -nen) reporter
re·prä·sen·ta·bel [reprɛzɛn'taːbəl] *adj.* presentable; impressive, prestigious
Re·prä·sen·tant [reprɛzɛn'tant] *m* (-en; -en) representative; exponent *of a theory etc.*; **Re·prä·sen'tan·ten·haus** *n USA*: *parl.* House of Representatives
Re·prä·sen·ta·ti·on [reprɛzɛnta'tsĭoːn] *f* (-; -en) representation; ***der ~ dienen*** have a representational function; ***sehr auf ~ bedacht sein*** *firm etc.*: be very concerned with its image
Re·prä·sen·ta·ti'ons|auf·wand *m* entertainment expenses *pl.*; **~bau** *m* (-[e]s; -ten) prestige building; **~fi,gur** *f* figurehead; **~pflich·ten** *pl.* representational duties; **~wa·gen** *m* prestige car
re·prä·sen·ta·tiv [reprɛzɛnta'tiːf] *adj.* a) *a. pol.* representative (***für*** *acc.* of), b) impressive, imposing; prestige ..., status *car etc.*; ***das Modell ist ihm nicht ~ genug*** that model isn't flashy enough for him
Re·prä·sen·ta'tiv|er·he·bung *f* controlled sampling; **~sy,stem** *n pol.* representative government
re·prä·sen·tie·ren [reprɛzɛn'tiːrən] (h) **I.** *v/t.* represent; be a calling card for; **II.** *v/i.* act in a representative capacity; ***gut ~ können*** be a good ambassador (*or* hostess *etc.*)
Re·pres·sa·lie [reprɛ'saːlĭə] *f* (-; -n) reprisal; retaliation (*a. pl.*); ***~n ergreifen gegen*** *acc.* take reprisals on, retaliate against
Re·pres·si·on [reprɛ'sĭoːn] *f* (-; -en) **1.** *pol.* suppression; repression; **2.** *psych.* repression; **re·pres·si'ons·frei** *adj.* free of suppression
re·pres·siv [reprɛ'siːf] *adj.* repressive
Re·print [re'prɪnt] *m* (-s; -s) reprint
Re·pri·se [re'priːzə] *f* (-; -n) **1.** *thea.* revival; *film*: rerun, *TV a.* repeat; *record*: re-release, reissue; **2.** ♪ recapitulation
re·pri·va·ti·sie·ren [reprivati'ziːrən] *v/t.* (h) reprivatize, denationalize
Re·pri·va·ti'sie·rung *f* (-; -en) reprivatization, denationalization
Re·pro·duk·ti·on [reprodʊk'tsĭoːn] *f* (-; -en) reproduction; **re·pro·du·zie·ren** [reprodu'tsiːrən] *v/t.* (h) reproduce
Rep·til [rɛp'tiːl] *n* (-s; Reptilien [rɛp'tiːlĭən]) *zo.* reptile
Rep'ti·li·en·fonds *m pol.* secret funds *pl.*
Re·pu·blik [repu'bliːk] *f* (-; -en) republic
Re·pu·bli·ka·ner [republi'kaːnɐ] *m* (-s; -) **1.** republican; **2.** *USA*: *parl.* Republican; **3.** *Germany*: *pol.* Republican; ***die ~*** the Republican Party; **re·pu·bli·ka·nisch** [republi'kaːnɪʃ] *adj.* **1.** republican; **2.** *USA*: *parl.* Republican; **3.** *Germany*: *pol.* Republican
Re·qui·em ['reːkviɛm] *n* (-s; -s) requiem (mass)
Re·qui·sit [rekvi'ziːt] *n* (-s; -en) **1.** requisite; **2.** *pl.* (stage) props; **Re·qui·si·te** [rekvi'ziːtə] *f thea.* **1.** props (department); **2.** → **Re·qui'si·ten·kam·mer** *f* props room; **Re·qui·si·teur** [rekvizi'tøːɐ] *m* (-s; -e [-rə]) props man
Re·ser·vat [rezɛr'vaːt] *n* (-[e]s; -e) **1.** (nature) reserve; **2.** (*Indian*) reservation; **3.** ⚖ prerogative, preserve
Re·ser·ve [re'zɛrvə] *f* (-; -n) **1.** reserve supply; ✝ ***stille ~n*** hidden reserves; ***in ~ halten*** keep in reserve; **2.** *sport*: reserve team; **4.** ⚔ reserves *pl.*; **5.** *fig.* reserve; ***j-n aus der ~ locken*** bring s.o. out of his (*or* her) shell, draw s.o. out; **~bank** *f* (-; ⸚e) *sport*: (substitutes') bench; **~ka,ni·ster** *m* spare petrol can, jerry can; **~of·fi,zier** *m* ⚔ reserve officer; **~rad** *n* spare (wheel); **~rei·fen** *m* spare (tyre, *Am.* tire); **~spie·ler** *m sport*: reserve, substitute; **~tank** *m* reserve tank; **~trup·pen** *pl.* ⚔ reserves
re·ser·vie·ren [rezɛr'viːrən] *v/t.* (h) (*a.* ~ ***lassen***) reserve; book
re·ser·viert [rezɛr'viːɐt] *adj.* reserved (*a. fig.*); ***sich ~ verhalten*** keep one's distance
Re·ser'vie·rung *f* (-; -en) reservation
Re·ser·vist [rezɛr'vɪst] *m* (-en; -en) ⚔ reservist
Re·ser·voir [rezɛr'vŏaːɐ] *n* (-s; -e [-rə]) reservoir (*a. fig.*)
Re·si·denz [rezi'dɛnts] *f* (-; -en) **1.** residence; **2.** → **~stadt** *f* seat of (royal) power
re·si·die·ren [rezi'diːrən] *v/i.* (h) reside
Re·si·gna·ti·on [rezɪgna'tsĭoːn] *f* (-; *no pl.*) resignation
re·si·gnie·ren [rezɪ'gniːrən] *v/i.* (h) give up; resign; **re·si·gniert** [rezɪ'gniːɐt] *adj.* resigned(ly *adv.*); ***ein ~es Lächeln*** a smile of resignation
re·si·stent [rezɪs'tɛnt] *adj.* ⚕ resistant (***gegen*** *acc.* to); **Re·si·stenz** [rezɪs'tɛnts] *f* (-; *no pl.*) ⚕ resistance (***gegen*** *acc.* to)
re·so·lut [rezo'luːt] *adj.* resolute, determined; forceful; **Re·so'lut·heit** *f* (-; *no pl.*) resoluteness, determination; forcefulness
Re·so·lu·ti·on [rezolu'tsĭoːn] *f* (-; -en) resolution
Re·so·nanz [rezo'nants] *f* (-; -en) resonance; *fig.* response; *fig.* ***der Plan fand keine ~*** the plan didn't meet with any response; **~bo·den** *m* sounding board; **~kör·per** *m* sound box; **~sai·te** *f* sympathetic string
re·sor·bier·bar [rezɔr'biːɐbaːɐ] *adj.* absorbable; ***nicht ~*** non-absorbable
re·sor·bie·ren [rezɔr'biːrən] *v/t.* (h) (re)-absorb
re·so·zia·li·sie·ren [rezotsĭali'ziːrən] *v/t.* (h) rehabilitate; **Re·so·zia·li'sie·rung** *f* (-; -en) rehabilitation
Re·spekt [re'spɛkt] *m* (-[e]s; *no pl.*) respect (***vor*** *dat.* for); **~ *haben vor*** *dat.* respect; ***großen ~ haben vor*** *dat.* have great respect for, hold *s.o.* in great respect, stand in awe of; ***die haben ganz schön ~ vor ihm*** *a.* they wouldn't dare put a foot wrong when he's around; ***aus ~ gegenüber*** *dat.* out of respect for, *formal*: in deference to; ***sich bei j-m ~ verschaffen*** teach s.o. to respect one; ***bei allem ~*** with all due respect; → ***einflößen***
re·spek·ta·bel [respɛk'taːbəl] *adj.* respectable (*a. fig.*)
Re'spekt·frist *f* ✝ period of grace
re·spek·tie·ren [respɛk'tiːrən] *v/t.* (h) respect
re·spek·ti·ve [respɛk'tiːvə] *adv.* **1.** and ... respectively; ***sie wurden nach Indonesien ~ Australien geschickt*** they were sent to Indonesia and Australia respectively; **2.** or (alternatively); (either ...) or (..., as the case may be); **3.** or rather; **4.** and
re'spekt·los *adj.* disrespectful
Re'spekts·per,son *f* figure of authority; person in authority
re'spekt·voll *adj.* respectful
Res·sen·ti·ment [rɛsãti'mãː] *n* (-s; -s) ill feeling, hard feelings *pl.*, resentment; prejudice; ***persönliches ~*** personal grudge
Res·sort [rɛ'soːɐ] *n* (-s; -s) department; *pol.* portfolio; province, purview, preserve; ***das fällt nicht in mein ~*** that is not (within) my province; **~chef** *m*, **~lei·ter** *m* head of department
Res·sour·cen [rɛ'sʊrsən] *pl.* **1.** resources; **2.** funds
Rest [rɛst] *m* (-[e]s; -e) rest; 𝔄 remainder; ⚗, ⚙, ⚖ residue; *pl.* ✝ remainders, rem-

nants; *gastr.* leftovers; remains *of a castle etc., a. fig. of a civilization etc.*; **sterbliche ~e** (mortal) remains; **der letzte ~** the last bit(s *pl.*); **der letzte ~ an Kraft** one's last ounce of strength; **das ist mein letzter ~ Zucker** that's the last of my sugar; **von den hundert Mark ist nur noch ein kleiner ~ übrig** there's very little left of the hundred marks; **die ~e sozialer Gerechtigkeit** the last vestiges of social justice; **wenn du e-n ~ von Anstand hättest** if you had the least bit of decency; F *fig.* **das gab ihm den ~** that finished him (off)

'Rest|al·ko·hol *m* residual alcohol; **~auf·la·ge** *f* remaindered stock

Re·stau·rant [rɛsto'rã:] *n* (-s; -s) restaurant; **er ißt oft im ~** he eats out a lot

Re·stau·ra·ti·on [rɛstaʊra'tsǐo:n] *f* (-; -en) *pol., art*: restoration; **Re·stau·ra·ti'ons·ar·bei·ten** *pl.* restoration work *sg.*; **Re·stau·ra·tor** [rɛstaʊ'ra:to:ɐ] *m* (-s; -en [-ra'to:rən]), **Re·stau·ra·to·rin** [rɛstaʊra'to:rɪn] *f* (-; -nen) restorer

re·stau·rie·ren [rɛstaʊ'ri:rən] *v/t.* (h) restore; **Re·stau'rie·rung** *f* (-; -en) restoration

'Rest|be·stand *m* remaining stock; **~be·trag** *m* balance, outstanding sum

'Re·ste·es·sen *n* leftovers *pl.*

'Rest·for·de·rung *f* residual claim

re·sti·tu·ie·ren [restitu'i:rən] *v/t.* (h) restore; **Re·sti·tu·ti·on** [restitu'tsǐo:n] *f* (-; -en) restitution

'rest·lich *adj.* remaining; **der ~e Zucker** (**Abend**) the rest of the sugar (evening)

'rest·los I. *adj.* complete, total; **zu s-r ~en Zufriedenheit** to his complete satisfaction; **II.** *adv.* completely, totally, absolutely; **~ zufrieden** *a.* entirely (*or* perfectly) satisfied; **~ glücklich** perfectly happy; F **~ erledigt** F done for, absolutely whacked; F **ich bin ~ bedient** I've had enough, F I've had about as much as I can take, that's finished me off

'Rest·po·sten *m* ✝ remainders *pl.*

Re·strik·ti·on [restrɪk'tsǐo:n] *f* (-; -en) restriction; **j-m** (**e-r Sache**) **~en auferlegen** place restrictions on s.o. (s.th.)

re·strik·tiv [restrɪk'ti:f] *adj.* restrictive; **~e Finanzpolitik** tight monetary policy

'Rest|ri·si·ko *n* residual risk; **es bleibt ein ~** an element of risk remains; **~span·nung** *f* ⚡ residual voltage; **~stra·fe** *f* remaining sentence, *the* rest of the sentence; **~strom** *m* ⚡ residual (*or* leakage) current; **~sum·me** *f* balance; **~ur·laub** *m* holiday carried over, unused holiday, *formal*: residual holiday entitlement; **ich habe noch** (**zehn Tage**) **~** *a.* I've still got (ten days') holiday owing to me; **~wär·me** *f* residual heat; **~zah·lung** *f* final payment (*or* instal[l]ment); payment of the balance

Re·sul·tat [rezʊl'ta:t] *n* (-[e]s; -e) result, outcome; *sport*: score, results *pl.*

re·sul·tie·ren [rezʊl'ti:rən] *v/i.* (h): **~ aus** *dat.* result from; **~ in** *dat.* end up in

Re·sü·mee [rezy'me:] *n* (-s; -s) summary, résumé; **re·sü·mie·ren** [rezy'mi:rən] *v/t. and v/i.* (h) sum up, summarize, recapitulate

re·tar·die·ren [retar'di:rən] *v/t.* (h) delay, retard; **~des Moment** *thea.* retarding element, *fig.* delaying factor

re·tar·diert [retar'di:ɐt] *adj.* retarded, backward

Re·tor·te [re'tɔrtə] *f* (-; -n) retort; **aus der ~** synthetic

Re'tor·ten|ba·by *n* test-tube baby; **~be·fruch·tung** *f* in vitro fertilization; **~stadt** *f* new town, pre-planned city

re·tour [rə'tu:ɐ] *dial. adv.* back; **einmal ... und ~** one return to ..., *Am.* a round-trip ticket to ...

Re'tour·kut·sche F *f* tit for tat; **mit e-r ~ antworten** (*or* **reagieren**) strike back; **das war e-e gute ~!** touché!

re·tro·ak·tiv [retroˀak'ti:f] *adj.* retroactive

Re·tro·spek·ti·ve [retrospɛk'ti:və] *f* (-; -n) **1. in der ~** in retrospect, looking back; **2.** retrospective (exhibition) (*gen.* of)

ret·ten ['rɛtən] (h) **I.** *v/t.* save (*a. fig.*), rescue (**aus** *dat.*, **vor** *dat.* from); recover, *esp.* ⚓ salvage (*a. fig.*); **j-m das Leben ~** save s.o.'s life; **j-n vor dem Ertrinken ~** save s.o. from drowning; **j-n aus e-m brennenden Wagen ~** rescue s.o. from a burning car; F **bist du noch zu ~?** F have you gone completely mad?; F **er ist nicht mehr zu ~** he's a lost cause, he's beyond help; **II.** *v/i. sport*: make a save; **den ~den Einfall haben** come up with the answer, save the day; **III.** *v/refl.*: **sich ~** escape (**vor** *dat.* from); **sich vor Arbeit** *etc.* **nicht mehr ~ können** be snowed under with work *etc.*, be drowning in work *etc.*; *iro.* **rette sich, wer kann!** it's every man for himself

Ret·ter ['rɛtɐ] *m* (-s; -) rescuer, *lit.* deliverer; **ein ~ in der Not** a friend in need, F *iro.* a knight in shining armo(u)r

Ret·tich ['rɛtɪç] *m* (-s; -e) mooli; (white) radish

Ret·tung ['rɛtʊŋ] *f* (-; -en) rescue; escape; recovery, *esp.* ⚓ salvaging; **das war s-e** (**letzte**) **~** that was his salvation (*or* last hope); **es gab keine ~** there was no hope, **für ihn**: *a.* he was past help (*or* beyond salvation)

'Ret·tungs|ak·ti̦on *f* rescue operation (*a. fig.*); ✝ rescue bid; **~an·ker** *m* sheet anchor (*a. fig.*); **~bo·je** *f* lifebuoy; **~boot** *n* lifeboat; **~dienst** *m* rescue service; **~fahr·zeug** *n* rescue vehicle; **~fall·schirm** *m* emergency parachute; **~flug·dienst** *m* air rescue service; **~hub·schrau·ber** *m* rescue helicopter; **~in·sel** *f* (inflatable) life raft; **~lei·ne** *f* lifeline

'ret·tungs·los I. *adj.* hopeless; **II.** *adv.* hopelessly (*a. fig.*), beyond all hope; **~ verloren** *a.* irretrievably lost; **~ verliebt** hopelessly in love, F smitten

'Ret·tungs|mann·schaft *f* rescue team; *pl. a.* relief workers; **~plan** *m* rescue plan; **~ring** *m* **1.** life belt (*Am.* preserver); **2.** F spare tyre (*Am.* tire); **~schlit·ten** *m* rescue sledge, F bloodwagon; **~schwim·men** *n* life saving; **~schwim·mer** *m* lifeguard; **~sta·ti̦on** *f* first-aid post; **~ver·such** *m* rescue attempt, attempt to save s.o.'s life; **~wa·gen** *m* ambulance; **~we·ste** *f* life vest

re·tu·schie·ren [retu'ʃi:rən] *v/t.* (h) touch up

Reue ['rɔʏə] *f* (-; *no pl.*) remorse (**über** *acc.* for), repentance (for); **keine ~ empfinden** feel no remorse

reu·en ['rɔʏən] *v/impers. and v/t.* (h): **es reut mich, ihn beleidigt zu haben** I regret having insulted him; **das Geld** (**die Zeit**) **reut mich** I regret the money (time) wasted

'reue·voll, reu·ig ['rɔʏɪç], **reu·mü·tig** ['rɔʏmy:tɪç] *adj.* repentant, full of remorse, contrite

Reu·se ['rɔʏzə] *f* (-; -n) creel, fish basket

re·üs·sie·ren [reˀʏ'si:rən] *v/i.* (h) be successful

Re·van·che [re'vã:ʃə] *f* (-; -n) revenge; **j-m ~ geben** give s.o. a chance to get even; **~ fordern** challenge s.o. to a return game (*sport*: *a.* match); **~kampf** *m* **1.** *boxing etc.*: return bout; **2.** → **Revanchespiel**; **~krieg** *m* war of revenge; **~po·li̦tik** *f* revanchist policy; **~spiel** *n* return match

re·van·chie·ren [revã:'ʃi:rən] *v/refl.* (h): **sich ~** a) take revenge (**an** *dat.* on), F get one's own back (on), b) return the favo(u)r, pay s.o. back

Re·van·chis·mus [revã'ʃɪsmʊs] *m* (-; *no pl.*) *pol.* revanchism; **Re·van·chist** [revã'ʃɪst] *m* (-en; -en) revanchist; **re·van·chi·stisch** [revã'ʃɪstɪʃ] *adj.* revanchist

Re·ve·renz [reve'rɛnts] *f* (-; -en) reverence, respect, deference; **j-m s-e ~ erweisen** a) show deference to s.o., b) pay s.o. one's respects

Re·vers[1] [re've:ɐ] *n, m* (-; - [re've:ɐs]) lapel

Re·vers[2] [re'vɛrs] *m* (-es; -e [-zə]) reverse

Re·vers[3] [re'vɛrs] *m* (-es; -e [-zə]) (written) declaration

re·ver·si·bel [revɛr'zi:bəl] *adj.* reversible

re·vi·die·ren [revi'di:rən] *v/t.* (h) revise; check; **ich muß m-e Meinung ~** I'll have to revise my opinion (on that)

Re·vier [re'vi:ɐ] *n* (-s; -e [-rə]) **1.** a) (*police*) district, *Am.* (*police*) precinct, b) beat, c) police station; **2.** (*forest*) district, range, beat; **3.** ⚒ area; **4.** hunting ground; **5.** *zo.* territory; **6.** tables *pl. of a waiter etc.*; **7.** *fig.* stamping ground

Re·vi·re·ment [revirə'mã:] *n* (-s; -s) *pol.* reshuffle

Re·vi·si·on [revi'zǐo:n] *f* (-; -en) **1.** check; ✝ audit; (*customs*) examination; **2.** *typ.* final proofreading; **3.** revision, change; **4.** ⚖ appeal; **~ einlegen** lodge an appeal

Re·vi·sio·nis·mus [revizǐo'nɪsmʊs] *m* (-; *no pl.*) revisionism

Re·vi·sor [re'vi:zo:ɐ] *m* (-s; -en [revi'zo:rən]) **1.** *typ.* reviser; **2.** ✝ auditor

Re·vol·te [re'vɔltə] *f* (-; -n) revolt

re·vol·tie·ren [revɔl'ti:rən] *v/i.* (h) revolt; *fig. stomach*: protest, rebel

Re·vo·lu·ti·on [revolu'tsǐo:n] *f* (-; -en) revolution; **re·vo·lu·tio·när** [revolutsǐo'nɛ:ɐ] *adj.*, **Re·vo·lu·tio'när** *m* (-s; -e [-rə]) revolutionary (*a. fig.*)

re·vo·lu·tio·nie·ren [revolutsǐo'ni:rən] *v/t.* (h) *esp. fig.* revolutionize

Re·vo·lu·ti'ons|füh·rer *m* revolutionary leader; **~ge·richt** *n* revolutionary tribunal; **~rat** *m* revolutionary council; **~re·̦gie·rung** *f* revolutionary government

Re·vo·luz·zer [revo'lʊtsɐ] *contp. m* (-s; -) would-be (*or* small-time) revolutionary, radical

Re·vol·ver [re'vɔlvɐ] *m* (-s; -) revolver, gun; **~blatt** F *n* sensational newspaper; **~held** *m* gunslinger; **~lauf** *m* (revolver) barrel; **~schnau·ze** F *f* F motormouth; **~trom·mel** *f* drum magazine

Re·vue [re'vy:] *f* (-; -n [-ən]) *thea.* revue; *fig.* **~ passieren lassen** pass in review; **~film** *m* film musical; **~girl** *n* chorus girl

Re·zen·sent [retsɛn'zɛnt] *m* (-en; -en) critic; **re·zen·sie·ren** [retsɛn'zi:rən] *v/t.* (h) review, write a review on

Re·zen·si·on [retsɛn'zǐo:n] *f* (-, -en) review, write-up; ***gute (schlechte) ~en bekommen*** *a.* get a good (bad) press

Re·zen·si'ons|ex·em,plar *n*, **~stück** *n* review copy

Re·zept [re'tsɛpt] *n* (-[e]s; -e) **1.** ⚕ prescription; *fig.* cure, remedy (***gegen*** *acc.* for); ***nur auf ~ erhältlich*** available on prescription only, *attr.* prescription-only ...; *fig.* ***dafür gibt es kein allgemeines ~*** there's no general rule about that; **2.** *gastr.* recipe; **~block** *m* prescription pad

re'zept·frei I. *adj.* over-the-counter ..., non-prescription ...; **II.** *adv.*: ***et. ~ bekommen*** get s.th. without a prescription (*or* over the counter)

Re'zept·ge·bühr *f* prescription charge

Re·zep·ti·on [retsɛp'tsio:n] *f* (-; -en) **1.** reception (desk); **2.** *no pl.* reception

re'zept·pflich·tig [-pflıçtıç] *adj.* prescribable, available on prescription only; **~e** ***Arzneimittel*** prescription(-only) drugs

Re·zes·si·on [retsɛ'sio:n] *f* (-; -en) ✝ recession

re·zes·siv [retsɛ'si:f] *adj. biol.* recessive

re·zi·pie·ren [retsi'pi:rən] *v/t.* (h) absorb *ideas etc.*; receive *book*

re·zi·prok [retsi'pro:k] *adj.* reciprocal

Re·zi·ta·ti·on [retsita'tsio:n] *f* (-; -en) recitation, recital; reading

Re·zi·ta·tiv [retsita'ti:f] *n* (-s; -e [-və]) ♪ recitative

Re·zi·ta·tor [retsi'ta:to:ɐ] *m* (-s; -en [retsita'to:rən]) reciter

re·zi·tie·ren [retsi'ti:rən] *v/t.* (h) recite

R-Ge·spräch ['ɛr-] *n teleph.* reversed charges (*or* collect) call

Rha·bar·ber [ra'barbɐ] *m* (-s; *no pl.*) *a. fig.* rhubarb

Rhap·so·die [rapzo'di:] *f* (-; -n [-ən]) rhapsody

Rhein·ar,mee ['raın-] *hist. f*: ***die britische ~*** the British Army of the Rhine (*abbr.* BAOR)

Rhein·län·der ['raınlɛndɐ] *m* (-s; -), **Rhein·län·de·rin** ['raınlɛndərın] *f* (-; -nen) Rhinelander; **rhein·län·disch** ['raınlɛndıʃ] *adj.* Rhineland ..., from the Rhineland

Rhein·land-Pfäl·zer ['raınlant'pfɛltsɐ] *m* (-s; -), **'Rhein·land-Pfäl·ze·rin** [-'pfɛltsərın] *f* (-; -nen) man (woman) from the Rhineland-Palatinate; ***~ sein*** *usu.* come from the Rhineland-Palatinate; **'rhein·land-pfäl·zisch** [-'pfɛltsıʃ] *adj.* from the Rhineland-Palatinate; Rhenish

Rhein·wein ['raın-] *m* Rhine wine; hock

Rhe·sus|af·fe ['re:zʊs-] *m* rhesus (monkey); **~fak·tor** *m* rhesus factor

Rhe·to·rik [re'to:rık] *f* (-; *no pl.*) rhetoric; **Rhe·to·ri·ker** [re'to:rikɐ] *m* (-s; -) orator; ***ein ausgezeichneter ~*** a brilliant speaker; **rhe·to·risch** [re'to:rıʃ] **I.** *adj.* rhetorical (*a. question*); **II.** *adv.*: ***er ist ~ sehr begabt*** he has the gift of rhetoric

Rheu·ma ['rɔyma] F *n* (-s; *no pl.*) rheumatism; **'Rheu·ma·decke** *f* thermal blanket (*or* quilt); **Rheu·ma·ti·ker** [rɔy'ma:tikɐ] *m* (-s; -) rheumatic (sufferer); **rheu·ma·tisch** [rɔy'ma:tıʃ] *adj.* rheumatic(ally *adv.*); **Rheu·ma·tis·mus** [rɔyma'tısmʊs] *m* (-; *no pl.*) rheumatism

'Rheu·ma·wä·sche *f* thermal underwear

Rh-Fak·tor [ɛr'ha:-] *m* Rh (*or* rhesus) factor

Rhi·no·ze·ros [ri'no:tserɔs] *n* (-[ses]; -se) **1.** *zo.* rhinoceros, F rhino; **2.** F dumbo, twit

Rh-ne·ga·tiv [ɛr'ha:-] *adj.* Rh (*or* rhesus) negative

Rho·do·den·dron [rodo'dɛndrɔn] *n, m* (-s; -dren) rhododendron

rhom·bisch ['rɔmbıʃ] *adj.* rhombic; **Rhom·bo·id** [rɔmbo'i:t] *n* (-[e]s; -e [-də]) rhomboid; **Rhom·bus** ['rɔmbʊs] *m* (-; -ben) rhombus

Rh-po·si·tiv [ɛr'ha:-] *adj.* Rh (*or* rhesus) positive

Rhyth·mik ['rʏtmık] *f* (-; *no pl.*) rhythmics *pl.*; **rhyth·misch** ['rʏtmıʃ] *adj.* rhythmic(al)

Rhyth·mus ['rʏtmʊs] *m* (-; -men) rhythm; ***im ~ klatschen*** clap in time to the music, clap to the rhythm; **~gi,tar·re** *f* rhythm guitar; **~grup·pe** *f* rhythm section; **~in·stru,ment** *n* rhythm instrument

Ri·bo·nu·kle·in·säu·re [ribonukle'i:n-] *f* ribonucleic acid

Richt·an,ten·ne ['rıçt-] *f* directional aerial (*or* antenna)

rich·ten ['rıçtən] (h) **I.** *v/t.* **1.** direct, turn (***auf*** *acc.* towards, *fig.* to); point *gun, camera etc.* (at); turn *one's eyes* (towards); address *letter, question etc.* (***an*** *acc.* to); direct, level *one's criticism etc.* (at); ***e-e Frage an j-n (den Sprecher) ~*** put a question to s.o. (address a question to the speaker); ***das war gegen dich gerichtet*** that was directed at (*or* intended for, meant for) you; ***gerichtet auf*** *acc.* ⚔ *rocket* targeted on; **2.** *dial.* a) make *bed*, b) tidy up *room*, c) do *one's hair*, d) get *s.th.* ready, prepare; lay *the table*, get *the table* ready, e) repair, fix; see to; **3.** adjust; set *clock etc.* (***nach*** *dat.* by); **4.** straighten; level *metal sheets*; **5.** judge, ⚖ *a.* pass sentence on; **II.** *v/refl.* **6.** ***sich ~ nach*** *dat.* a) comply with *the rules, s.o.'s wishes etc.*, b) depend on, c) take one's cue from, follow *s.o.'s* example; be model(l)ed after (*or* on) *s.th.*; ***sich nach der Mode ~*** follow the fashion; ***sich nach den Vorschriften ~*** keep to the regulations; ***nach der Uhr kannst du dich nicht ~*** you can't go by that clock; ***ich richte mich (ganz) nach Ihnen*** whatever suits you best; **7.** ***sich ~ an*** (*or* ***gegen***) *acc.* be directed (*or* aimed) at; ***mein Verdacht richtet sich gegen ihn*** I suspect him; **III.** *v/i.* judge (***über j-n*** s.o.), pass judg(e)ment (on s.o.)

Rich·ter ['rıçtɐ] *m* (-s; -) judge; ***Oberster ~*** supreme judge; ***Herr ~!*** Your Lordship, *Am.* Your Honor; ***zum ~ ernannt werden*** be called to the bench; ***j-n vor den ~ bringen*** take s.o. to court; *fig.* ***sich zum ~ machen*** (*or* ***aufwerfen***) set o.s. up in judg(e)ment

'Rich·ter·amt *n* judicial office

'rich·ter·lich *adj.* judicial

'Rich·ter·ro·be *f* judge's gown *or* robe(s *pl.*)

'Rich·ter-Ska·la *f* Richter scale; ***das Erdbeben erreichte Stärke acht auf der ~*** the earthquake registered eight on the Richter scale

'Rich·ter|spruch *m* → ***Urteil*** 2; **~stuhl** *m* judge's seat; *fig.* judg(e)ment seat

Richt·fest ['rıçt-] *n* topping-out ceremony

Richt·funk ['rıçt-] *m* directional radio

Richt·ge·schwin·dig·keit ['rıçt-] *f* recommended speed

rich·tig ['rıçtıç] **I.** *adj.* a) right; correct, b) real, genuine; true, c) appropriate; suitable, d) proper, decent; fair, right; **~e** ***Aussprache*** correct pronunciation; ***ein ~er Engländer*** a real (*or* true) Englishman; ***s-e ~e Mutter*** his real mother; ***das ist der ~e Mann!*** he's just the man we *etc.* need; ***es war ~ von dir, daß du ...*** you did right to *inf.*; ***das finde ich nicht ~*** I don't think it's right; F ***so ist's ~!*** F that's the idea; → ***Kopf*** 5; **II.** *adv.* properly, correctly; the right way; F thoroughly, really; ***mach es ~!*** do it properly; ***geht d-e Uhr ~?*** is your watch right?; ***e-e Sache ~ anpacken*** go about s.th. the right way; ***sehe ich das ~?*** am I right?; ***du kommst gerade ~!*** you've come just at the right moment, *iro.* you're the last person I (*or* we) need; F ***ich fand ihn ~ nett*** I thought he was really nice; **III.** *su.* ***das 2e*** the right thing; ***er ist der 2e*** he's the right man; F ***du bist mir der 2e!*** you're a fine one; ***ich hatte drei 2e im Lotto*** I got three right in the lotto; → ***einzig*** II

'rich·tig·ge·hend I. *adj.* **1.** accurate *watch etc.*; **2.** F regular, real; **II.** F *adv.*: ***~ böse*** *etc.* really angry *etc.*

'Rich·tig·keit *f* (-; *no pl.*) correctness; soundness; ***das hat schon s-e ~*** it's all right (*Am.* alright)

'rich·tig·lie·gen *v/i.* (*irr., sep.*, h, → ***liegen***) a) be on the right track, b) F *fig.* be absolutely right; F ***mit d-r Vermutung liegst du richtig*** you guessed right, your hunch was right; ***bei mir liegen Sie richtig*** you've come to the right person; ***er liegt immer richtig*** he always backs the right horse

'rich·tig·stel·len *v/t.* (*sep.*, h) put *s.th.* right, correct, rectify; ***et. ~*** *a.* set the record straight; **'Rich·tig·stel·lung** *f* (-; -en) rectification, correction

Richt·li·nie ['rıçt-] *f* guideline; *pl. a.* (general) directions, instructions

'Richt·li·ni·en·kom·pe,tenz *f esp. pol.* policy-making power(s *pl.*)

Richt|mi·kro,phon ['rıçt-] *n* directional microphone; **~preis** *m* recommended price; **~satz** *m* ✝ standard rate; **~schnur** *fig. f* guiding principle; **~sen·der** *m* beam transmitter; **~strah·ler** *m* **1.** directional (*or* beam) aerial *or* antenna; **2.** → ***Richtsender***

Rich·tung ['rıçtʊŋ] *f* (-; -en) a) direction; way; ⚓, ✈ course, b) *fig.* line of thought; school of thought; *art*: school, c) trend, *pol. a.* tendency, *a. s.o.'s* views *pl.*; *pol.* faction; ***die falsche ~*** the wrong direction (*or* way); ***aus allen ~en*** from all directions, from all around (*or* all over the place); ***in allen ~en*** in all directions; ***in ~ auf*** *acc.* in the direction of, towards; ***in südlicher ~*** south; ***in welche ~ gehen Sie?*** which way (*or* direction) are you going?; ***er kommt aus dieser ~*** he'll be coming from that direction; ***die ~ verlieren*** lose (one's) direction; ***e-e andere ~ einschlagen*** go in a different direction, *fig.* take a different course, change course

'rich·tung·ge·bend *adj.* trend-setting; ***~ sein für*** *acc.* point the way for

'Rich·tungs|än·de·rung *f* change of direction (*or* course) (*a. fig.*); **~kämp·fe** *pl. pol.* (fundamental) policy disputes

'rich·tungs·los *adj.* aimless; ***~ sein*** be drifting; ***die Partei ist ~ geworden*** the party has lost its sense of direction

'Rich·tungs|pfeil *m mot.* lane indication arrow; **~wech·sel** *fig. m* change of course

'rich·tung·wei·send *adj.* landmark *decision etc.*; ***~ sein*** point the way ahead (*or* to the future)

Richt·wert ['rɪçt-] *m* guide number
rieb [ri:p] *pret. of* ***reiben***
rie·chen ['ri:çən] (roch, gerochen, h) **I.** *v/i.* smell (***nach*** *dat.* of); ~ ***an*** *dat.* smell at, sniff at; ***gut*** (***übel***) ~ smell good (bad); ***es riecht nach Gas*** I can smell gas, there's a smell of gas; ***die Luft riecht nach Schnee*** I can smell snow in the air; *fig.* ~ ***nach*** *dat.* smack of; → ***Mund*; II.** *v/t.* smell; scent; ***ich rieche das Parfüm gern*** I like the smell of that perfume; F *fig.* ***ich kann ihn nicht*** ~ I can't stand him; F *fig.* ***er hat es gerochen*** F he got wind of it; F *fig.* ***das konnte ich doch nicht*** ~! how was I to know?; → ***Braten, Lunte*** 1
Rie·cher ['ri:çɐ] F *m* (-s; -) nose; *fig.* ***e-n guten*** ~ ***haben für*** *acc.* have a (good) nose for
Riech|fläsch·chen ['ri:ç-] *n* (bottle of) smelling salts *pl.*; **~nerv** *m* olfactory nerve; **~or,gan** *n* **1.** olfactory organ; **2.** F hooter
Ried [ri:t] *n* (-[e]s; -e ['ri:də]) **1.** reeds *pl.*; **2.** marsh
rief [ri:f] *pret. of* ***rufen***
Rie·ge ['ri:gə] *f* (-; -n) *gym. and fig.* squad
Rie·gel ['ri:gəl] *m* (-s; -) **1.** bolt; latch; ***den*** ~ ***vorlegen*** bolt the door *etc.*; *fig.* ***e-r Sache e-n*** ~ ***vorschieben*** put a stop to s.th.; → ***Schloß***[1]; **2.** strip, *Brit.* row *of chocolate*; **'rie·geln** *v/t.* (h) bolt
Rie·men[1] ['ri:mən] *m* (-s; -) ⚓ oar; *fig.* ***sich in die*** ~ ***legen*** put one's back into it
'Rie·men[2] *m* (-s; -) a) strap; ⚙ belt, b) sling, c) strop, d) (leather) shoelace; *fig.* ***den*** ~ ***enger schnallen*** tighten one's belt; ***sich am*** ~ ***reißen*** pull o.s. together
'Rie·men|an·trieb *m* ⚙ belt drive; **~schei·be** *f* ⚙ pulley
Rie·se ['ri:zə] *m* (-n; -n) giant (*a. fig.*)
rie·seln ['ri:zəln] *v/i.* (sn) *water, sand etc.*: trickle; *rain*: drizzle; *snow*: fall softly; *fig.* ***ein Schauder rieselte ihr über den Rücken*** a shiver ran down her spine
'Rie·sen... *in cpds.* giant ..., gigantic, mammoth ..., colossal; *w.s.* tremendous, superhuman *effort etc.*; **~ap·pe,tit** F *m* huge (*or* tremendous, voracious) appetite; ***ich habe e-n*** ~ I could eat a horse; **~ar·beit** *f* mammoth task; **~ba·by** F *n* huge baby; **~bau** *m* (-[e]s; -ten) gigantic structure (*or* building); **~bla,ma·ge** *f* terrible disgrace; ***das war e-e*** ~ ***für ihn*** he made an absolute fool of himself; **~dumm·heit** *f* F real boo-boo; ***das war e-e*** ~ *a.* that was really stupid; **~ent·täu·schung** *f* big (*or* terrible) disappointment; **~er·folg** *m* huge success, *thea., film*: *a.* F smash hit; **~feh·ler** *m* huge blunder; **~ge·winn** *m* **1.** huge profits *pl.*; **2.** huge winnings *pl.*; ***e-n*** ~ ***erzielen*** win a fortune; **⁓'groß** *adj.* → ***riesig*** I; **~hun·ger** F *m*: ***e-n*** ~ ***haben*** be ravenous; **~kind** *n* **1.** F giant; **2.** exceptionally large baby; **~kon,zern** *m* giant concern (*or* company); **~krach** F *m* **1.** racket; **2.** huge row; ***e-n*** ~ ***machen*** F hit the roof; **~kraft** *f* tremendous strength; ***Riesenkräfte entwickeln*** summon up incredible strength; **~por·ti,on** F *f* extra large portion; ***e-e*** ~ ***Fleisch*** a huge piece of meat; **~rad** *n* Ferris wheel; **~schlan·ge** *f* boa constrictor; **~schritt** *m* giant stride (*or* step); *fig.* ***sich mit*** ~***en nähern*** be approaching fast, be just around the corner; **~schwin·del** F *m* colossal fraud; **~skan,dal** *m* huge (*or* full-blown) scandal; **~sla·lom** *m* giant slalom; **~spaß** *m*: ***e-n*** ~ ***haben*** have a great time; ***die Kinder hatten e-n*** ~ *a.* the children had the time of their lives; **~stern** *m* giant star; **~weib** F *n* **1.** huge woman, F amazon; **2.** F smasher; **~wuchs** *m* gigantism
rie·sig ['ri:zɪç] **I.** *adj.* gigantic, enormous, huge (*all a. fig.*); F ***das ist ja*** ~! that's tremendous!; **II.** F *fig. adv.* tremendously; ***sich*** ~ ***freuen*** be delighted, F be over the moon; ***das amüsierte ihn*** ~ he was greatly amused
Rie·sin ['ri:zɪn] *f* (-; -nen) giantess
Ries·ling ['ri:slɪŋ] *m* (-s; *no pl.*) riesling
riet [ri:t] *pret. of* ***raten***[1] *and* ***raten***[2]
Riff [rɪf] *n* (-[e]s; -e) reef
Rigg [rɪg] *n* (-s; -s), **Rig·gung** ['rɪgʊŋ] *f* (-; -en) ⚓ rigging
ri·go·ros [rigo'ro:s] **I.** *adj.* severe, austere; adamant, unrelenting; **II.** *adv.*: ***et.*** ~ ***ablehnen*** adamantly refuse s.th.; ~ ***durchgreifen*** take drastic action; ~ ***vorgehen gegen*** *acc.* take drastic measures against
Ri·go·ro·sum [rigo'ro:zʊm] *n* (-s; -sa) *univ.* viva (voce)
Rik·scha ['rɪkʃa] *f* (-; -s) ricksha(w)
Ril·le ['rɪlə] *f* (-; -n) groove
Rind [rɪnt] *n* (-[e]s; Rinder ['rɪndɐ]) a) *zo.* cow, bull, *pl.* cattle (*pl.*), b) *gastr.* beef; ***100*** ~***er*** 100 (head of) cattle
Rin·de ['rɪndə] *f* (-; -n) **1.** ⚘ bark; **2.** (*bread*)crust; (*cheese*) rind
Rin·der|bra·ten ['rɪndɐ-] *m* joint of beef; roast beef; **~brust** *f* brisket of beef; **~fi,let** *n* fillet of beef; **~her·de** *f* herd of cattle; **~herz** *n* ox heart; **~len·de** *f* beef tenderloin; **~pest** *f* cattle plague, rinderpest; **~talg** *m* beef dripping; **~wahn·sinn** *m* mad cow disease; **~zucht** *f* cattle farming
'Rind·fleisch *n* beef; **~brü·he** *f* beef tea
'Rind(s)·le·der *n* cowhide
'Rind·vieh *n* **1.** cattle *pl.*; **2.** F blockhead, stupid ass
Ring [rɪŋ] *m* (-[e]s; -e) a) ring (*a.* ☂, ⚘, ⚙, *boxing, circus etc.*), circle, b) ⚙ washer; rubber seal, c) quoit, ring, d) ring road, e) (*spy etc.*) ring, f) book club; ~***e unter den Augen*** bags (*or* circles, [dark] rings) under one's eyes; ~ ***frei!*** *boxing*: seconds out!; *fig.* ***der*** ~ ***ist frei für neue Verhandlungen*** the way is clear for new negotiations; ***der*** ~ ***schließt sich*** the wheel comes full circle; **~bahn** *f* circular railway; **~buch** *n* ring (*or* loose-leaf) binder
Rin·gel ['rɪŋəl] *m* (-s; -) **1.** little ring; **2.** ringlet; **~blu·me** *f* marigold; **~locke** *f* ringlet
rin·geln ['rɪŋəln] (h) **I.** *v/t.* curl *tail etc.*; coil, twine; **II.** *v/refl.*: ***sich*** ~ curl, coil o.s.; wind, meander
'Rin·gel·nat·ter *f* grass snake
Rin·gel·piez ['rɪŋəlpi:ts] F *m* (-es; -e): ~ (***mit Anfassen***) F hop
Rin·gel·rei·hen ['rɪŋəlraɪən] *m* (-s; -) ring-a-ring-o'-roses
'Rin·gel|spiel *Austrian n* roundabout, merry-go-round, *Am.* car(r)ousel; **~söck·chen** *pl.* hooped (ankle) socks; **~socken** *pl.* hooped socks; **~tau·be** *f* wood pigeon
rin·gen ['rɪŋən] (rang, gerungen, h) **I.** *v/t.* **1.** wring; ***verzweifelt die Hände*** ~ wring one's hands (in despair); ***j-m et. aus der Hand*** ~ wrench s.th. from s.o.'s hand; **II.** *v/i.* **2.** wrestle; **3.** *fig.* ~ ***mit*** *dat.* wrestle (*or* grapple) with; ***mit sich*** ~ wrestle with o.s.; ***mit dem Tod*** ~ wrestle with death; ~ ***um*** *acc.* struggle (*or* fight, vie) for; ***um j-s Anerkennung*** *etc.* ~ vie for s.o.'s recognition *etc.*; ***die Verhandlungspartner*** ~ ***seit Stunden um e-e Entscheidung*** the negotiators have been fighting over a decision for hours; ***nach Atem*** ~ gasp for breath; ***nach Fassung*** ~ try to regain one's composure; ***nach Worten*** ~ struggle for words; **III. ⁓** *n* (-s; *no pl.*) wrestling; *fig.* struggle (***um*** *acc.* for)
Rin·ger ['rɪŋɐ] *m* (-s; -) wrestler
'Ring|fahn·dung *f* cordon search; **~fin·ger** *m* ring finger
'ring·för·mig [-fœrmɪç] **I.** *adj.* ring-shaped; **II.** *adv.*: ~ ***umschließen*** encircle
'Ring|gra·ben *m* moat; **~kampf** *m* (-[e]s; -kämpfe) **1.** *no pl.* ***der*** ~ wrestling; **2.** wrestling match (*or* bout); **~kämp·fer** *m* wrestler; **~mau·er** *f* ring wall; **~mus·kel** *m* sphincter muscle; **~rich·ter** *m boxing*: referee
rings [rɪŋs] *adv.* (all) around; ~ ***um*** *acc.* (all) around, all the way round; ~ ***um die Kapelle sind Pappeln*** the chapel is surrounded by poplars
'Ring|schei·be *f* rifle target; **~sen·dung** *f radio, TV*: linkup
'rings·her'um, 'rings·um'her *adv.* **1.** all (a)round, all the way round; ***ein Teich mit e-m Zaun ringsherum*** a pond surrounded by a fence; **2.** on all sides, wherever you look(ed)
'Ring|stra·ße *f* ring road; **~tausch** *m* three-way (*or* four-way *etc.*) exchange (of flats *etc.*); **~vor·le·sung** *f series of lectures held by various speakers*
Rin·ne ['rɪnə] *f* (-; -n) **1.** channel; *geogr.* trough; ***e-e*** ~ ***im Eis freihalten*** keep a passage through the ice open; **2.** gutter
rin·nen ['rɪnən] *v/i.* (rann, geronnen, sn) run, flow; *rain*: fall; *fig.* ***die Zeit rinnt*** (***dahin***) time is slipping by (*or* away)
Rinn·sal ['rɪnza:l] *n* (-[e]s; -e) rivulet; trickle *of blood, sweat etc.*
Rinn·stein ['rɪn-] *m* gutter; *fig.* → ***Gosse***
Ripp·chen ['rɪpçən] *n* (-s; -) rib (of pork)
Rip·pe ['rɪpə] *f* (-; -n) **1.** *anat.*, ⚘, ⚙, ✈, △, *textil.* rib; ***j-m in die*** ~***n stoßen*** give s.o. a dig in the ribs; ***er hat nichts auf den*** ~***n*** he's skin and bones; F ***ich kann es mir nicht aus den*** ~***n schneiden*** I can't just produce it out of thin air; **2.** row (*Am.* strip) *of chocolate*; **3.** ⚙ fin, *mot. a.* gill
'Rip·pen·bruch *m* broken (*or* fractured) rib(s *pl.*)
'Rip·pen·fell *n* pleura; **~ent·zün·dung** *f* ⚕ pleurisy
'Rip·pen|ge·wöl·be *n* △ rib(bed) vault; **~speer** *m* (-s; *no pl.*) *gastr.*: ***Kasseler*** ~ cured pork rib; **~stoß** *m* dig in the ribs, nudge; **~stück** *n* rib cut
Rips [rɪps] *m* (-es; -e) rep
Ri·si·ko ['ri:ziko] *n* (-s; -ken) risk (*a.* ✚); ***auf eigenes*** ~ at one's own risk; ***ein*** ~ ***eingehen*** take a risk (*or* gamble)
'ri·si·ko·be·reit *adj.* prepared to take risks; **'Ri·si·ko·be·reit·schaft** *f* (-; *no pl.*) venturesomeness; daring
'Ri·si·ko|fak·tor *m* risk factor; **⁓freu·dig** *adj.* venturesome; **~grup·pe** *f* high-risk group; **~ka·pi,tal** *n* risk (*or* venture) capital
'ri·si·ko·los *adj.* safe, free of risk
'ri·si·ko·reich *adj.* high-risk ...

ˈRi·si·ko|schwan·ger·schaft *f* high-risk (*or* potential risk) pregnancy; **~zu·schlag** *m insurance*: loading
ris·kant [rɪsˈkant] *adj.* risky; *pred. a.* a risk
ris·kie·ren [rɪsˈkiːrən] *v/t.* (h) risk; ***sein Geld ~ bei*** *dat.* risk one's money on; ***s-e Stellung ~*** risk losing one's job
Ris·pe [ˈrɪspə] *f* (-; -n) ⚘ panicle
riß [rɪs] *pret. of* ***reißen***
Riß [rɪs] *m* (Risses; Risse [ˈrɪsə]) a) tear, b) cleft, fissure, c) crack; ⚕ chap, d) *fig.* rift, rupture; *fig.* ***innerhalb der Partei klafft ein ~*** there's a (deep) rift within the party; ***ihre Freundschaft hat e-n ~ bekommen*** their friendship has taken a beating
ris·sig [ˈrɪsɪç] *adj.* cracked; ⚕ chapped *skin*; **~ *werden*** *material etc.*: tear; *wall etc.*: develop cracks (*or* a crack), crack; *skin*: chap
ˈRiß·wun·de *f* gash, 📖 laceration
Rist [rɪst] *m* (-es; -e) a) instep, b) back of one's hand
ritt [rɪt] *pret. of* ***reiten***
Ritt [rɪt] *m* (-[e]s; -e) ride; ***e-n ~ machen*** go for a ride; *fig.* ***auf einen ~*** in one go
Rit·ter [ˈrɪtɐ] *m* (-s; -) knight; ***j-n zum ~ schlagen*** knight s.o.; F *iro.* ***ein ~ ohne Furcht und Tadel*** F a knight in shining armo(u)r; **~burg** *f* knight's castle
ˈRit·ter·gut *n hist.* manor; **ˈRit·ter·guts·be·sit·zer** *m hist.* lord of the manor
ˈRit·ter·kreuz *n* ⚔ Knight's Cross
ˈrit·ter·lich *adj.* knightly; *fig.* chivalrous, gallant
ˈRit·ter|or·den *m* order of knights; **~roˌman** *m* chivalrous romance (*or* epic); **~rü·stung** *f* suit of armo(u)r
ˈRit·ter·schaft *f* (-; *no pl.*) **1.** *the* knights *pl.*; **2.** knighthood
ˈRit·ter|sporn *m* (-[e]s; -e) ⚘ larkspur; **~stand** *m* (-[e]s; *no pl.*) knighthood; ***in den ~ erheben*** knight; **~zeit** *f* age of chivalry
ritt·lings [ˈrɪtlɪŋs] *adv.* astride (***auf*** *dat. s.th.*)
ˈRitt·mei·ster *m* ⚔ *hist.* (cavalry) captain
Ri·tu·al [riˈtŭaːl] *n* (-s; -e) ritual; **~mord** *m* ritual murder
ri·tu·ell [riˈtŭɛl] *adj.* ritual
Ri·tus [ˈriːtʊs] *m* (-; -Riten [ˈriːtən]) rite
Ritz [rɪts] *m* (-es; -e) scratch
Rit·ze [ˈrɪtsə] *f* (-; -n) crack; gap
Rit·zel [ˈrɪtsəl] *n* (-s; -) ⚙ pinion
rit·zen [ˈrɪtsən] *v/t.* (h) a) scratch, b) cut (*a. glass*), c) carve; → ***geritzt***
Rit·zer [ˈrɪtsɐ] F *m* (-s; -) scratch
Ri·va·le [riˈvaːlə] *m* (-n; -n), **Ri·va·lin** [riˈvaːlɪn] *f* (-; -nen) rival
ri·va·li·sie·ren [rivaliˈziːrən] *v/i.* (h) compete, vie (***mit*** *dat.* with); **~*de Mächte*** *etc.* rival powers *etc.*
Ri·va·li·tät [rivaliˈtɛːt] *f* (-; -en) rivalry
Ri·zi·nus·öl [ˈriːtsinʊs-] *n* castor oil
Rob·be [ˈrɔbə] *f* (-; -n) *zo.* seal
rob·ben [ˈrɔbən] *v/i.* (sn) crawl (on one's stomach)
ˈRob·ben|fang *m* sealing; **~fän·ger** *m* sealer, seal hunter
Ro·be [ˈroːbə] *f* (-; -n) evening dress; robe(s *pl.*)
ro·bo·ten [ˈrɔbɔtən] F *v/i.* (h) slave away
Ro·bo·ter [ˈrɔbɔtɐ] *m* (-s; -) robot (*a. fig.*); **~arm** *m* robotic arm; **~tech·nik** *f* robotics *pl.*
ro·bust [roˈbʊst] *adj.* robust, sturdy, stout; rugged *car etc.*; **Roˈbust·heit** *f* (-; *no pl.*) robustness; stoutness, sturdiness
roch [rɔx] *pret. of* ***riechen***

Ro·cha·de [rɔˈxaːdə] *f* (-; -n) *chess*: castling; *sport*: changing of positions
ro·chie·ren [rɔˈxiːrən] *v/i.* (h) *chess*: castle; *sport*: change positions
rö·cheln [ˈrœçəln] *v/i.* (h) breathe noisily (*formal*: stertorously); wheeze; give the death rattle
Ro·chen [ˈrɔxən] *m* (-s; -) *zo.* ray
Ro·chus [ˈrɔxʊs] F *m*: ***e-n ~ auf j-n haben*** be furious with s.o.
Rock[1] [rɔk] *m* (-[e]s; Röcke [ˈrœkə]) **1.** skirt; ***die Röcke werden kürzer*** hemlines are going up; F ***hinter jedem ~ hersein*** (*or* ***herlaufen***) F chase after anything in a skirt; **2.** *dial.* jacket; **3.** *obs.* uniform
Rock[2] *m* (-[s]; *no pl.*) ♪ rock
Rocken [ˈrɔkən] (*sep.* -k·k-) *m* (-s; -) distaff
rocken [ˈrɔkən] (*sep.* -k·k-) *v/i.* (h) **1.** play rock music; **2.** dance to rock music
Rocker [ˈrɔkɐ] (*sep.* -k·k-) *m* (-s; -) rocker; **~ban·de** *f* gang of rockers
ˈRock|grup·pe *f* rock group (*or* band); **~konˌzert** *n* rock concert
ˈRock·län·ge *f* skirt length
ˈRock|muˌsik *f* rock music, rock; **~oper** *f* rock opera; **~sän·ger** *m* rock singer
ˈRock|schoß *obs. m* coattail; *fig.* ***sich j-m an die Rockschöße hängen*** cling to s.o. (like a leech); ***er hängt an Mutters Rockschößen*** he's tied to his mother's apron strings, *esp. toddler*: he won't let his mother go anywhere without him; **~zip·fel** *fig. m* → ***Rockschoß***
Ro·del [ˈroːdəl] *m* (-s; -) sledge, *Am.* sled, toboggan; **ˈRo·del·bahn** *f* toboggan run; **ˈro·deln** *v/i.* (sn) toboggan; go sledging (*a. Am.* tobogganing); **ˈRo·del·schlit·ten** *m* → ***Rodel***
ro·den [ˈroːdən] *v/t.* (h) **1.** clear; **2.** root out; **3.** ⚒ lift; *a.* dig up *potatoes*, *a.* pull up *turnips etc.*
Rod·ler [ˈroːdlɐ] *m* (-s; -) tobogganist
Ro·dung [ˈroːdʊŋ] *f* (-; -en) clearing; *a.* cleared woodland
Ro·gen [ˈroːgən] *m* (-s; *no pl.*) roe
Rog·gen [ˈrɔgən] *m* (-s; *no pl.*) rye; **~brot** *n* rye bread
roh [roː] *adj.* **1.** *gastr.* raw; → ***Ei*** 1; **2.** rough, uncut *diamonds etc.*; untreated *hides*; crude *worksmanship*; rough *draft etc.*; **3.** rough, coarse; → ***Gewalt***
ˈRoh|bau *m* (-[e]s; -ten) △ shell; ***im ~ fertig*** structurally complete; **~benˌzin** *n* petroleum; **~biˌlanz** *f* ☤ trial balance; **~diaˌmant** *m* rough (*or* uncut) diamond; **~ein·nah·me** *f* ☤ gross receipts *pl.*; **~ei·sen** *n* pig iron
ˈRo·heit *f* (-; -en) **1.** *no pl.* roughness, coarseness; **2.** brutality, brutal act
ˈRo·heits·deˌlikt *n* act of brutality (*or* hooliganism)
ˈRoh|ent·wurf *m* rough draft; **~er·trag** *m* gross yield; **~er·zeug·nis** *n* raw product; **~fa·ser** *f* raw fibre (*Am.* fiber); **~fas·sung** *f* rough draft; **~ge·wicht** *n* gross weight; **~ge·winn** *m* gross profit; **~kost** *f* raw vegetables and fruit *pl.*; **~le·der** *n* untreated leather, rawhide
Roh·ling [ˈroːlɪŋ] *m* (-s; -e) **1.** brute, ruffian; **2.** *metall.* slug; blank
ˈRoh|ma·te·riˌal *n* raw material; **~meˌtall** *n* crude metal; **~milch** *f* untreated milk
ˈRoh·öl *n* crude oil; **~prei·se** *pl.* price *sg.* of crude oil
ˈRoh·proˌdukt *n* raw product

Rohr [roːɐ] *n* (-[e]s; -e [ˈroːrə]) **1.** ⚘ reed; cane; **2.** ⚙ pipe; piping; **3.** F ***volles ~ fahren*** F drive full tilt; **~blatt** *n* ♪ reed; **~bruch** *m* burst pipe
Röhr·chen [ˈrøːɐçən] *n* (-s; -) ⚗ test tube; F ***ins ~ pusten*** (***müssen***) be breath-tested, be breathalyzed
Röh·re [ˈrøːrə] *f* (-; -n) tube; ⚙ pipe; *anat.* duct, canal; ⚗ test tube; ⚡ valve, tube; oven; *hunt.* gallery; F ***in die ~ gucken*** a) *fig.* be left high and dry, b) *TV* F sit in front of (*or* stare at) the box (*Am.* tube)
röh·ren [ˈrøːrən] *v/i.* (h) **1.** *stag*: bell; **2.** F *car etc.*: roar
ˈröh·ren·för·mig [-fœrmɪç] *adj.* tubular
ˈRöh·ren|ho·se(n *pl.*) F *f* F drainpipe trousers *pl.*; **~kno·chen** *m* long bone; **~pilz** *m* boletus
ˈRohr|flö·te *f* reed pipe; **~ge·flecht** *n* canework
Röh·richt [ˈrøːrɪçt] *n* reeds *pl.*
ˈRohr·kol·ben *m* ⚘ cat's tail
ˈRohr·kre·pie·rer [-kreˌpiːrɐ] *m* (-s; -) ⚔ barrel burst; *fig.* damp squib, non-starter
ˈRohr·le·ger [-leːgɐ] *m* (-s; -) pipe fitter
ˈRohr·lei·tung *f* pipe, piping; ⚡ *etc.* conduit; pipeline; mains *pl.*
Röhr·ling [ˈrøːɐlɪŋ] *m* (-s; -e) boletus
ˈRohr|mö·bel *pl.* wicker furniture *sg.*; **~netz** *n* piping, network of pipes (*or* tubes); **~post** *f* pneumatic dispatch, air tube; **~schilf** *n* reed; **~spatz** *m* reed bunting; *fig.* ***schimpfen wie ein ~*** rant and rave; **~stock** *m* cane; **~stuhl** *m* wicker chair; **~zan·ge** *f* pipe wrench; **~zuck·er** *m* cane sugar
ˈRoh·sei·de *f* raw silk
ˈRoh·stoff *m* raw material; **≈arm** *adj.* lacking in raw materials; **~man·gel** *m* shortage of raw materials; **~prei·se** *pl.* price *sg.* of raw materials; **≈reich** *adj.* rich in raw materials
ˈRoh|über̩set·zung *f* rough translation; **~zucker** *m* raw (*or* unrefined) sugar; **~zu·stand** *m* **1.** natural (*or* crude) state; **2.** ***im ~*** *plans etc.* in draft form; ***mein Artikel ist noch im ~*** I've only done a rough version of the article (so far)
Ro·ko·ko [ˈrɔkoko] *n* (-[s]; *no pl.*) rococo; **~zeit** *f* rococo era (*or* period)
Rolla·den [ˈrɔl-] (*sep.* -ll·l-) *m* shutters *pl.*
Roll|bahn [ˈrɔl-] *f* taxiway; runway; **~band** *n* (-[e]s; ⸚er) walkway; **~bild** *n* scroll painting; **~bra·ten** *m* collared beef (*or* pork *etc.*)
Rol·le[1] [ˈrɔlə] *f* (-; -n) **1.** roll (*a. of bills, paper, tobacco etc.*); coil *of wire etc.*; (*papyrus*) scroll; **~ *Garn*** reel of cotton, *Am.* spool of thread; **2.** ⚙ a) roller, cylinder, b) castor, c) pulley; F *fig.* ***völlig von der ~ sein*** have lost one's grip on things, *sport*: be completely out of touch; **3.** *gym.* roll
ˈRol·le[2] *f* (-; -n) *thea. and fig.* role, part; ***kleine ~*** bit part, small role; ***führende ~*** lead; ***s-e ~ lernen*** learn one's part (*or* lines); ***die ~n e-s Stückes besetzen*** cast a play; ***ein Stück mit verteilten ~n lesen*** do a play-reading; ***er ist in s-r ~ völlig aufgegangen*** he was completely taken over by the role; *fig.* ***e-e ~ spielen*** play a part *or* role (***bei*** *dat.*, ***in*** *dat.* in); ***e-e große ~ spielen*** play an important part (*or* role), be a key player, be in an influential position; ***e-e klägliche ~ spielen*** cut a poor figure; ***Spiel mit vertauschten ~n*** reversal of roles; ***das***

spielt keine ~ it doesn't matter, it doesn't make any difference; ***Geld spielt keine ~*** money is no object; ***aus der ~ fallen*** step out of line, forget o.s.

rol·len ['rɔlən] **I.** *v/i.* (sn) roll; *mot. a.* move; ✈ taxi; *fig. thunder*: rumble; 🚂 ***~des Material*** rolling stock; ***Tränen rollten ihm über die Wangen*** tears rolled down his cheeks; F ***die Sache rollt*** F we've got the ball rolling, we're on our way, F it's all systems go; → ***Kopf*** 5; **II.** *v/t.* (h) roll; wheel; ***die Augen ~*** roll one's eyes; ***das R ~*** roll one's r's; F *fig.* ***man kann sie ~*** F she's like a barrel, she's a real roly-poly; **III.** *v/refl.*: ***sich ~*** roll; *paper etc.*: curl; ***sich im Gras ~*** roll around in the grass; **IV.** ≗ *n* (-s; *no pl.*) rolling; ***ins ~ kommen*** start moving, *fig.* get going, get under way; *fig.* ***die Sache ins ~ bringen*** get the ball rolling, get things moving

'Rol·len|be·set·zung *f thea.* **1.** casting; **2.** cast; **~er·war·tung** *f* role expectation; **~fach** *n thea.* (type of) role; ***ins ~ gehen*** become a character actor; **~kon,flikt** *m* role conflict, conflict of roles

'Rol·len·la·ger *n* ⚙ roller bearing

'Rol·len|spiel *n* **1.** role play; **2.** → ***Rollenverhalten***; **~tausch** *m* role swapping, reversal of roles; **~ver·hal·ten** *n* role behavio(u)r; **~ver·tei·lung** *f* **1.** → ***Rollenbesetzung***; **2.** *fig. the* various (*or* respective) roles; ***die traditionelle ~ zwischen Mann und Frau*** the traditional male-female roles

Rol·ler ['rɔlɐ] *m* (-s; -) **1.** scooter; **2.** (rolling) breaker, roller; **3.** roller; **4.** → ***Rollsprung***

Roll|feld ['rɔl-] *n* → ***Rollbahn***; **~film** *m* roll film; **~gut** *n* rolling freight; **~hockey** *n* roller-skate hockey; **~kom,man·do** *n* heavy squad, heavies *pl.*

Roll·kra·gen ['rɔl-] *m* polo neck; **~pull·over** *m* polo-neck (*Am.* turtleneck) jumper *or* sweater; polo neck, *Am.* turtleneck

Roll|kunst·lauf ['rɔl-] *m* figure roller-skating; **~kur** *f* ⚕ *treatment for gastric disorders in which ingested medicine is distributed by slowly rotating the body*; **~mops** *m* rollmop, rolled pickled herring

Rol·lo ['rɔlo] *n* (-s; -s) (roller) blind, *Am.* shade

Roll|schin·ken ['rɔl-] *m* rolled ham; **~schrank** *m* roll-front cabinet; **~schreib·tisch** *m* roll-top desk

Roll·schuh ['rɔl-] *m* roller skate; ***~ laufen*** roller-skate; **~bahn** *f* roller-skating rink; **~läu·fer** *m* roller skater

Roll|sitz ['rɔl-] *m rowing*: sliding seat; **~splitt** *m* loose chippings *pl.*; **~sprung** *m* western roll; **~steg** *m* travelator

Roll·stuhl ['rɔl-] *m* wheelchair; **~fah·rer** *m* **1.** wheelchair patient; ***er ist ~*** he's in (*or* confined to) a wheelchair; **2.** *sport*: wheelchair athlete

Roll·trep·pe ['rɔl-] *f* escalator

Rom [ro:m] *fig.*: ***~ wurde auch nicht an einem Tage erbaut*** Rome wasn't built in a day; ***viele Wege führen nach ~*** there isn't just one way of doing it, that isn't the only way of doing it (*or* going about it); → ***Zustand***

ROM [rɔm] *n* (-[s]; -[s]) *computer*: ROM, read only memory

Ro·man [ro'ma:n] *m* (-s; -e) novel; *coll.* ***~e*** *a.* fiction; ***das gibt es nur in ~en*** it's the stuff of fiction (*or* fairytales); F *fig.* ***erzähl doch keine ~e!*** a) F don't give me the whole saga (*or* spiel), keep to the point, will you, b) F tell me another

Ro·man·cier [romã'sie:] *m* (-s; -s) novelist

Ro'man|fi,gur *f* character (in a novel); **~held** *m* hero (of a *or* the novel); **~hel·din** *f* heroine (of a *or* the novel)

Ro·ma·nik [ro'ma:nɪk] *f* (-; *no pl.*) a) Romanesque (style), b) Romanesque period; **ro·ma·nisch** [ro'ma:nɪʃ] *adj. ling. etc.* Romance *languages etc.*; *art*: Romanesque; **Ro·ma·nist** [roma'nɪst] *m* (-en; -en) student of (*or* lecturer in) Romance languages and literature; **Ro·ma·ni·stik** [roma'nɪstɪk] *f* (-; *no pl.*) Romance languages and literature, *a.* F French (and Italian *etc.*); **Ro·ma·ni·stin** [roma'nɪstɪn] *f* (-; -nen) → ***Romanist***

Ro'man·schrift·stel·ler *m* novel writer, novelist

Ro·man·tik [ro'mantɪk] *f* (-; *no pl.*) **1.** *art etc.*: Romanticism, *the* Romantic movement; **2.** *fig.* romanticism, romance

Ro·man·ti·ker [ro'mantikɐ] *m* (-s; -) Romantic; *fig.* romantic

ro·man·tisch [ro'mantɪʃ] *adj.* romantic(ally *adv.*); *art etc.*: Romantic

Ro·man·ze [ro'mantsə] *f* (-; -n) *poet.*, ♪ *and fig.* romance

Ro'man·zy·klus *m* cycle of novels

Rö·mer¹ ['rø:mɐ] *m* (-s; -) rummer

'Rö·mer² *m* (-s; -) *a. hist.* Roman; **~brief** *m*: *bibl.* ***der ~*** the (*or* St Paul's) Epistle to the Romans, Romans *pl.*

Rö·me·rin ['rø:mərɪn] *f* (-; -nen) → ***Römer***²

'Rö·mer|reich *n hist.*: Roman Empire; **~stra·ße** *f* Roman road; **~topf** *m* (*TM*) chicken brick; **~zeit** *f* (-; *no pl.*) *hist.*: ***die ~*** Roman times *pl.*, Ancient Rome; ***bis in die ~ zurückreichen*** go back to Roman times

'Rom·fahrt *f* pilgrimage to Rome

'ROM-ge·steu·ert *adj. computer*: ROM-controlled, ROM-driven *chip*

rö·misch ['rø:mɪʃ] *adj.* Roman; ***~e Ziffer*** Roman numeral; **~-ka'tho·lisch** *adj.* Roman Catholic

Rom·mé ['rɔme:] *n* (-s; -s) rummy

Ron·dell [rɔn'dɛl] *n* (-s; -e) **1.** ✿ round (*or* circular) flowerbed; **2.** roundabout

Ron·do ['rɔndo] *n* (-s; -s) ♪ rondo

rönt·gen ['rœntgən] *v/t.* (h) x-ray

'Rönt·gen *n* (-s; -) *phys.* roentgen; **~ap·pa,rat** *m* x-ray unit; **~äqui·va,lent** *n* roentgen equivalent man (*abbr.* rem); **~arzt** *m* radiologist; **~auf·nah·me** *f* x-ray; **~be·hand·lung** *f*, **~be·strah·lung** *f* x-ray treatment, radiotherapy; **~bild** *n* x-ray; **~do·sis** *f* x-ray dose; **~durch,leuch·tung** *f* radioscopy, fluoroscopy

Rönt·ge·no·lo·ge [rœntgeno'lo:gə] *m* (-n; -n) radiologist; **Rönt·ge·no·lo·gie** [rœntgenolo'gi:] *f* (-; *no pl.*) radiology

'Rönt·gen|strah·len *pl.* x-rays; **~the·ra,pie** *f* → ***Röntgenbehandlung***; **~un·ter,su·chung** *f* x-ray (examination)

Ro·sa ['ro:za] *n* (-s; -s) pink

'ro·sa, 'ro·sa·far·ben, 'ro·sa·rot *adj.* pink; ***die Dinge durch e-e rosa(rote) Brille sehen*** see the world through rose-colo(u)red (*or* rose-tinted) spectacles *or* glasses

Ro·se ['ro:zə] *f* (-; -n) **1.** ✿ rose; *fig.* ***er ist auch nicht auf ~n gebettet*** his life is no bed of roses; **2.** △ rose window

ro·sé [ro'ze:] *adj.* pale pink

Ro'sé¹ *n* (-s; -s) pale pink

Ro'sé² *m* (-s; -s) rosé (wine)

'Ro·sen|beet *n* bed of roses; **~gar·ten** *m* rose garden; **~holz** *n* rosewood; **~kohl** *m* Brussels sprouts *pl.*; **~kranz** *m eccl.* rosary; ***den ~ beten*** say the Rosary

Ro·sen'mon·tag *m* Monday before Lent

'Ro·sen|öl *n* attar of roses; **~quarz** *m* rose quartz; **~stock** *m* rose tree; **~strauch** *m* rosebush; **~strauß** *m* bunch of roses; **~was·ser** *n* rosewater; **~zucht** *f* rose-growing; **~züch·ter** *m* rose-grower

Ro·set·te [ro'zɛtə] *f* (-; -n) **1.** rosette; **2.** △ rose window; **3.** ⚙ rose

ro·sig ['ro:zɪç] *adj.* rosy (*a. fig.*); *fig.* ***et. in ~en Farben schildern*** paint s.th. in rosy (*or* bright) colo(u)rs, paint a rosy (*or* bright) picture of s.th.; ***~e Zeiten brechen an*** it looks as if there are rosy times ahead; ***es sieht nicht gerade ~ aus*** things are looking pretty grim

Ro·si·ne [ro'zi:nə] *f* (-; -n) raisin; F *fig.* gem; F *fig.* ***(große) ~n im Kopf haben*** have big ideas; F ***sich die ~n herauspicken*** F take the pick of the bunch, pick out the plum jobs (*or* sites *etc.*)

Ro'si·nen|bom·ber F *m hist.* supply plane (*during the Berlin airlift*); **~brot** *n* raisin bread

Ros·ma·rin ['ro:smari:n] *m* (-s; *no pl.*) ✿ rosemary

Roß [rɔs] *n* (Rosses; Rosse, Rösser ['rœsɐ]) horse, *lit.* steed; *fig.* ***sich (moralisch) aufs hohe ~ setzen*** give o.s. airs (take the moral high ground); F ***komm runter von d-m hohen ~*** come down off your high horse; **~äp·fel** F *pl.* F horse droppings; **~brei·ten** *pl. geogr.* horse latitudes

Rös·sel·sprung ['rœsəl-] *m* **1.** *chess*: knight's move; **2.** *type of crossword puzzle based on the knight's move*

'Roß·haar *n* horsehair; **~ma,trat·ze** *f* hair mattress

'Roß|ka,sta·nie *f* horse chestnut; **~kur** *f* drastic cure

'Roß·täu·scher F *m* F con man; **~trick** F *m* confidence trick, F con

Rost¹ [rɔst] *m* (-[e]s; *no pl.*) rust (*a. fig.*); ***~ ansetzen*** get rusty (*a. fig.*); ***von ~ zerfressen*** rust-eaten

Rost² *m* (-[e]s; -e) **1.** grate; grille, grating; **2.** *gastr.* grill

'rost·be·stän·dig *adj.* rustproof

'Rost|bra·ten *m* roast joint; **~brat·wurst** *f* grilled sausage

'rost·braun *adj.* russet

ro·sten ['rɔstən] *v/i.* (h, sn) rust, *a. fig.* get rusty

rö·sten ['rœstən] *v/t.* (h) roast *coffee etc.*, grill *meat etc.*; toast *bread*; fry *potatoes*

Rö·ster ['rœstɐ] *m* (-s; -) toaster

'rost·far·ben *adj.* rust-colo(u)red, russet

'Rost|fleck *m* patch of rust; **~fraß** *m* corrosion

'rost·frei *adj.* rustproof; stainless *steel*

ro·stig ['rɔstɪç] *adj.* rusty (*a. fig.*)

Röst·kar,tof·feln ['rœst-] *pl.* fried potatoes

'Rost·lau·be F *f* F rust bucket

'Rost·schutz *m* rust protection; **~far·be** *f* anti-rust paint; **~mit·tel** *n* anti-rust agent

'Rost·stel·le *f* patch of rust

rot [ro:t] *adj.* red (*a. pol.*); ***≗e Armee*** Red Army; ***~e Gefahr*** communist threat;

2es Kreuz Red Cross; **das 2e Meer** the Red Sea; **der 2e Platz** (**in Moskau** Moscow's) Red Square; **~es Haar haben** *a.* be a redhead; **e-n ~en Kopf bekommen**) get red in the face, b) blush, go red; **auf j-n wie ein ~es Tuch wirken** be like a red rag to a bull for s.o., get s.o.'s blood up, F get s.o.'s goat; **in den ~en Zahlen stehen** be in the red; → **rotsehen, Faden, Karte, Welle**

Rot *n* (-s; -) **1.** red; **2.** red (light); **bei ~** at red; **bei ~ durchfahren** (*or* **über die Ampel fahren**) jump (F shoot) the lights

'Rot·al·gen *pl.* red algae

Ro·ta·ri·er [ro'ta:riɐ] *m* (-s; -) Rotarian

Rot·ar·mist ['ro:tʔarmɪst] *m* (-en; -en) Red Army soldier

Ro·ta·ti·on [rota'tsĭo:n] *f* (-; -en) rotation

Ro·ta·ti'ons|ach·se *f* axis of rotation; **~druck** *m* rotary press printing; **~ma·ˌschi·ne** *f typ.* rotary press

rot·bäckig ['ro:tbɛkɪç] (*sep.* -k·k-) *adj.* red-cheeked, rosy-cheeked

'Rot·barsch *m* rosefish, ocean perch

'rot|blond *adj.* red(dish); **~ sein** have red(dish) hair; **~braun** *adj.* reddish brown; *zo.* chestnut, sorrel ..., bay *horse*

'Rot|bu·che *f* copper beech; **~dorn** *m* (-[e]s; -e) pink hawthorn

Ro·te ['ro:tə] *m, f* (-n; -n) **1.** *pol.* Red, F commie; **2.** redskin; **3.** redhead

Rö·te ['rø:tə] *f* (-; *no pl.*) redness, red; *a.* red glow *in the sky*; flush; **die ~ stieg ihm ins Gesicht** he colo(u)red up, he flushed

Rö·tel ['rø:təl] *m* (-s; -) **1.** *no pl.* red chalk; **2.** red chalk crayon

Rö·teln ['rø:təln] *pl.* ⚕ German measles, 🕮 rubella *sg.*

'Rö·tel·zeich·nung *f* red chalk drawing

rö·ten ['rø:tən] (h) **I.** *v/t.* redden; **II.** *v/refl.*: **sich ~** turn red, redden, flush

'Rot|fil·ter *m, n phot.* red filter; **~fuchs** *m* **1.** red fox; **2.** (*horse*) chestnut, sorrel, bay; **3.** F redhead, F carrot-top; **4.** fox (fur); **2ge·rän·dert** *adj.* red-rimmed; **2glü·hend** *adj.* red-hot; **~glut** *f* red heat; **~gold** *n* red gold

'rot·haa·rig *adj.* red-haired; **'Rot·haa·ri·ge** [-ha:rɪgə] *m, f* (-n; -n) redhead

'Rot|haut *f* redskin; **~hirsch** *m* red deer

ro·tie·ren [ro'ti:rən] *v/i.* (h) rotate, revolve; F *fig.* **er fing an zu ~** F he got into a flap; F **ich bin am 2** F I don't know whether I'm coming or going; **ro'tie·rend** *adj.* rotating, revolving

Rot|käpp·chen ['ro:tkɛpçən] *n* (-s; *no pl.*) (Little) Red Riding Hood; **~kehl·chen** ['ro:tke:lçən] *n* (-s; -) robin (redbreast); **~kohl** *m*, **~kraut** *n* red cabbage

Rot'kreuz|flag·ge *f* Red Cross flag; **~schwe·ster** *f* Red Cross nurse

rot·lackiert ['ro:tlaki:ɐt] (*sep.* -k·k-) *adj.*: **~e Fingernägel** (bright) red fingernails

röt·lich ['rø:tlɪç] *adj.* reddish; *a.* ruddy *face*; **~blond** *adj.* reddish-blond

'Rot·licht *n* (-[e]s; *no pl.*) **1.** red light (*a. phot.*); **2.** red (traffic) light; **bei ~ fahren** jump (F shoot) the lights; **~be·strah·lung** *f* infrared rays *pl.* (*or* treatment); **~lam·pe** *f* infrared lamp; **~sün·der** *m* red light offender; **~vier·tel** *n* red-light district

Ro·tor ['ro:to:ɐ] *m* (-s; Rotoren [ro'to:rən]) rotor

'Rot·schwanz *m zo.* redstart, redtail

'rot·se·hen F *fig. v/i.* (*irr., sep.,* h, → **sehen**) see red

'Rot|stift *m* red pencil (*or* pen); **mit ~ korrigieren** correct (*or* do corrections) in red; *fig.* **den ~ ansetzen** make cuts (**bei** *dat.* in); **dem ~ zum Opfer fallen** *scene, passage etc.*: fall victim to the censors, be cut out, *project, funds etc.*: be axed, come in for the chop; **~tan·ne** *f* spruce

Rot·te ['rɔtə] *contp. f* (-; -n) horde, mob, gang; **'Rot·ten·füh·rer** *m* foreman

Rö·tung ['rø:tʊŋ] *f* (-; -en) reddening

'rot·un·terˌlau·fen *adj.* bloodshot, red *eyes*

rot·wan·gig ['ro:tvaŋɪç] *adj.* red-cheeked, rosy-cheeked

'Rot·wein *m* red wine; claret; **~fleck** *m* (red) wine stain

Rot·welsch ['ro:tvɛlʃ] *n* (-[s]; *no pl.*) thieves' Latin

'Rot|wild *n* red deer; **~wurst** *f* black pudding

Rotz [rɔts] V *m* (-es; *no pl.*) V snot; **~ und Wasser heulen** F bawl one's eyes out; **~ben·gel** V *m sl.* snotty little brat; **~fah·ne** V *f* V snotrag

'rotz'frech F *adj.* F snotty

rot·zig ['rɔtsɪç] V, **'rotz·nä·sig** [-nɛ:zɪç] *adj.* F snotty; *fig. a.* F bolshy

Rouge [ru:ʃ, ru:ʒ] *n* (-s; -s) rouge; **~ auftragen** put (some) rouge on

Rou·la·de [ru'la:də] *f* (-; -n) *gastr.* beef olive

Rou·leau [ru'lo:] *n* (-s; -s) (roller) blind, *Am.* shade

Rou·lett [ru'lɛt] *n* (-[e]s; -e) roulette

Rou'lettisch (*sep.* -tt·t-) *m* roulette table

Rou'lett·spie·ler *m* roulette player

Rou·te ['ru:tə] *f* (-; -n) route

Rou·ti·ne [ru'ti:nə] *f* (-; *no pl.*) routine; practice (*or* practise), experience; **zur ~ werden** become (a matter of) routine; **~an·ge·le·gen·heit** *f* routine matter; **~ar·beit** *f* routine (work); **2mä·ßig I.** *adj.* routine; **~e Untersuchung** routine check-up; **II.** *adv.* routinely, as a matter of routine; **~sa·che** *f* **1.** routine affair (*or* matter); **2. es ist ~** it's a question of routine (*or* practice)

Rou·ti·nier [ruti'nĭe:] *m* (-s; -s) F old hand (*gen.* at); **rou·ti·niert** [ruti'ni:ɐt] *adj.* experienced, seasoned ..., veteran ...

Row·dy ['raʊdi] *m* (-s; -s) lout, hooligan, hoodlum, F hood, lager lout

'Row·dy·tum *n* (-s; *no pl.*) hooliganism

Roya·lis·mus [rŏaja'lɪsmʊs] *m* (-; *no pl.*) royalism; **Roya·list** [rŏaja'lɪst] *m* (-en; -en) royalist

rub·beln ['rʊbəln] *v/t.* (h) rub; rub *s.o.* down

Rü·be ['ry:bə] *f* (-; -n) **1.** turnip; **rote ~** beetroot; **gelbe ~** carrot; **2.** F conk, noddle, nut; **j-m eins über die ~ geben** F conk s.o. (one); **eins auf die ~ kriegen** F get bashed on the nut

Ru·bel ['ru:bəl] *m* (-s; -) rouble; **der ~ rollt!** the money's rolling in

'Rü·ben·zucker *m* beet sugar

rü·ber(...) ['ry:bɐ] F *adv.* **1.** → **herüber(...)**; **2.** → **hinüber(...)**

'rü·ber·fa·xen F *v/t.* (h) fax *s.th.* through (**j-m** to s.o.)

Ru·bi·kon ['ru:bikɔn] *m*: **den ~ überschreiten** cross the Rubicon

Ru·bin [ru'bi:n] *m* (-s; -e) ruby

ru'bin·rot *adj.* ruby(-red)

Ru·brik [ru'bri:k] *f* (-; -en) a) column, b) category, c) rubric; **unter der ~ ...** under the heading *or* category (of)

ruch·bar ['ru:xba:ɐ] *adj.*: **~ werden** become known; **als der Vorfall ~ wurde** *a.* when news of the incident got (a)round, when people found out about the incident

ruch·los ['ru:xlo:s] *adj.* wicked, contemptible; **'Ruch·lo·sig·keit** *f* (-; -en) **1.** *no pl.* profligacy; **2.** wicked act

Ruck [rʊk] *m* (-[e]s; -e) jerk; jolt (*a. fig.*); *pol.* **~ nach links** swing to the left; **mit e-m ~** in one go; *fig.* **sich e-n ~ geben** pull o.s. together

Rück·an·sicht ['rʏk-] *f* rear view

Rück·ant·wort ['rʏk-] *f* reply; **Postkarte mit ~** reply-paid postcard; **~schein** *m* reply coupon

'ruck·ar·tig I. *adj.* jerky; **II.** *adv.* with a jerk; *fig.* suddenly

Rück·be·sin·nung ['rʏk-] *f*: **die ~ auf** *acc.* recalling, thinking back to, turning one's mind back to

rück·be·züg·lich ['rʏk-] *adj. ling.* reflexive; **~es Fürwort** reflexive pronoun

Rück|bil·dung ['rʏk-] *f* ⚕ regression; *biol.* degeneration; *ling.* back formation; **~blen·de** *f film*: flashback

Rück·blick ['rʏk-] *m* review (**auf** *acc.* of); survey (of); **e-n ~ werfen auf** *acc.* look back at; **im ~** in retrospect; **im ~ auf** *acc.* looking back at, casting our eyes back on; **'rück·blickend I.** *adj.* retrospective; **II.** *adv.* in retrospect, looking back

rück·daˌtie·ren ['rʏk-] *v/t.* antedate

Rück·ein·fuhr ['rʏk-] *f* reimportation

rücken ['rʏkən] (*sep.* -k·k-) **I.** *v/t.* (h) move; shift; push (away); **II.** *v/i.* (sn) move; (*a.* **ein Stückchen ~**) move over; **näher ~** a) move closer, move up, b) approach, draw near, loom up; **an j-s Stelle ~** take s.o.'s place; **er ist nicht von der Stelle gerückt** he didn't (*or* wouldn't) budge; → **Blickfeld, greifbar, Leib, Pelz**

Rücken ['rʏkən] (*sep.* -k·k-) *m* (-s; -) **1.** *anat.* back; **~ an ~** back to back; **mit dem Wind im ~** with a following wind; **dabei lief es ihr** (**heiß und**) **kalt über den ~** it sent shivers down her spine; **j-m in den ~ fallen** attack s.o. from behind, *fig.* stab s.o. in the back; **j-n im ~ haben** ⚔ have s.o. in the rear, *fig.* have s.o. behind one (*or* backing one up); *fig.* **j-m den ~ dekken** back s.o. up; **sich den ~ freihalten** cover o.s.; **hinter j-s ~** behind s.o.'s back; **j-m** (**e-r Sache**) **den ~ kehren** turn one's back on s.o. (s.th.); **vor j-m den ~ beugen** bow down to s.o.; **mit dem ~ zur Wand** with one's back to the wall; F **auf den ~ fallen** F be floored; **2.** (*mountain*) ridge; **3.** spine; **~deckung** *f* ⚔ rear cover; *fig.* backing, support; **~flos·se** *f* dorsal fin; **2frei** *adj.* low-backed *dress etc.*; **~la·ge** *f*: **in ~** (lying) on one's back; **in ~ schwimmen** do the backstroke; **~leh·ne** *f* back (rest)

'Rücken·mark *n* spinal cord (*or* marrow); **'Rücken·marks·nerv** *m* spinal nerve

'Rücken|mus·kel *m* back muscle; **~num·mer** *f sport*: number (*on the back of a player's shirt*); **~pan·zer** *m zo.* carapace; **~schmer·zen** *pl.* backache *sg.*, back pains (*or* pain *sg.*); **~schwim·men** *n* backstroke; **~stär·kung** *fig. f* backing, support; **~stück** *n gastr.* chine; saddle *of mutton, venison*; **~stüt·ze** *f* back support

Rück·ent·wick·lung ['rʏk-] *f* retrogression; ⚕ regression; *biol.* degeneration

'Rücken·wind *m* following wind; **~ haben** have the wind behind one

Rück·er·in·ne·rung ['rʏk-] *f* reminiscence
rück·er·stat·ten ['rʏk-] *v/t.* (*only inf. and p.p.* rückerstattet, h) refund, reimburse; '**Rück·er·stat·tung** *f* (-; *no pl.*) refund
Rück·fahr|kar·te ['rʏk-] *f* return ticket, *Am.* round-trip ticket; **~schein·wer·fer** *m* reversing (*Am.* backup) light
Rück·fahrt ['rʏk-[*f* return journey (*or* trip); ***auf der*** ~ on the way back
Rück·fall ['rʏk-] *m* ⚕ relapse (*a. fig.*); ⚖ repeat offen|ce (*Am.* -se); '**rück·fäl·lig** *adj.* ⚖ a) revertible, b) reoffending ..., recidivist ...; ~ ***werden*** reoffend, *fig.* have a relapse; '**Rück·fäl·lig·keit** *f* (-; *no pl.*) ⚖ recidivism
'**Rück·fall|kri·mi·na·li̩tät** *f* ⚖ recidivism; **~quo·te** *f* ⚖ reoffending rate; **~tä·ter** *m* ⚖ reoffending person, recidivist
Rück|fen·ster ['rʏk-] *n mot.* rear window; **~flug** *m* return flight; **~fluß** *m* backflow, return flow; ✝ reflux; **~for·de·rung** *f* reclaim(ing)
Rück·fra·ge ['rʏk-] *f* further inquiry (*or* enquiry), query; ***bei j-m ~ halten*** → '**rück·fra·gen** *v/i.* (*only inf. and p.p.* rückgefragt, h) inquire; ***bei j-m*** ~ check with s.o.
Rück|front ['rʏk-] *f* back, rear; ***die Tür ist auf der*** ~ the door's at the back; **~füh·rung** *f* (-; *no pl.*) **1.** ⚔ return; **2.** repatriation, return; **3.** ⚙ feedback; ~ ***von Abgasen*** *mot.* exhaust gas recirculation; **4.** tracing back (***auf*** *acc.* to)
Rück·ga·be ['rʏk-] *f* (-; *no pl.*) return; *soccer*: back pass; **~recht** *n* right of return; **~schal·ter** *m* return counter
Rück·gang ['rʏk-] *m* (-[e]s; *no pl.*) decline, drop; ***e-n ~ erleben*** experience a decline, go into decline; '**rück·gän·gig** *adj.*: ~ ***machen*** cancel *order etc.*; *a.* annul, rescind *contract etc.*; call off
rück·ge·win·nen ['rʏk-] *v/t.* (*only inf. and p.p.* rückgewonnen, h) recover, *a.* recycle *raw materials etc.*; reclaim *land*
'**Rück·ge·win·nung** *f* (-; *no pl.*) recovery, *a.* recycling *of raw materials etc.*; reclamation *of land*
Rück·glie·de·rung ['rʏk-] *f* (-; *-no pl.*) reintegration
Rück·grat ['rʏk-] *n* (-[e]s; *no pl.*) *anat.* spine, vertebral column; *a. fig.* backbone; *fig.* ***j-m das ~ brechen*** a) break s.o.'s resistance, b) ruin s.o.; ***er hat kein*** ~ he's got no backbone, F he's gutless; ~ ***zeigen*** show some guts; '**rück·grat·los** *adj.* spineless; '**Rück·grat(ver)krüm·mung** *f* curvature of the spine
Rück·griff ['rʏk-] *m* **1.** ***der ~ auf*** *acc.* ***...*** falling back on ..., going back to ...; ***der Stil stellt e-n ~ auf die Gotik dar*** the style goes back to (*or* draws on) Gothic architecture *etc.*; **2.** *computer*: retrieval
Rück·halt ['rʏk-] *m* (-[e]s; *no pl.*) backing, support; ***ohne*** ~ → '**rück·halt·los I.** *adj.* unreserved; open, frank; **II.** *adv.* unreservedly, without reserve; ***er sagte ~ s-e Meinung*** he didn't pull any punches
Rück·hand(schlag *m*) ['rʏk-] *f tennis*: backhand (stroke)
Rück·kampf ['rʏk-] *m* **1.** → ***Rückspiel***; **2.** *boxing etc.*: return fight (*or* bout)
Rück·kauf ['rʏk-] *m* repurchase
'**Rück·kaufs·recht** *n* right of repurchase (*or* redemption)
Rück·kehr ['rʏkke:ɐ] *f* (-; *no pl.*) return (*a. fig.*); ***bei m-r*** ~ on my return, when I got back
Rück·kopp·lung ['rʏk-] *f* feedback
Rück·la·ge ['rʏk-] *f* (-; -n) **1.** ✝ *usu. pl.* reserve(s *pl.*); savings *pl.*; **2.** *no pl. skiing*: backward lean
Rück·lauf ['rʏk-] *m* **1.** (fast) rewind *of a VCR*; *phot.* rewind; **2.** ⚙ return stroke; **3.** reflux; '**rück·läu·fig** *adj.* declining, downward, *a. ast., biol.*, ⚕ retrograde; ✝ **~e *Tendenz*** downward trend
Rück·licht ['rʏk-] *n* rear light, tail-light
rück·lings ['rʏklɪŋs] *adv.* a) backwards, b) from behind, c) on one's back
'**Rück·mel·dung** *f* reporting back; *univ.* re-registration; *radio*: reply; *electron.* feedback
Rück·nah·me ['rʏkna:mə] *f* (-; *no pl.*) taking back; withdrawal *of a remark etc.*; **~au·to̩mat** *m* bottle bank
Rück|paß ['rʏk-] *m sport*: back pass; **~por·to** *n* return postage
Rück·prall ['rʏkpral] *m* (-[e]s; *no pl.*) rebound
Rück·rei·se ['rʏk-] *f* return (journey *or* trip); **~wel·le** *f* homebound wave of traffic
Rück·roll·brem·se ['rʏk-] *f* hill-holder
Rück·ruf ['rʏk-] *m*: *teleph.* ***auf j-s ~ warten*** wait for s.o. to ring (*or* call) back; ***ich erwarte dann Ihren*** ~ I'll be hearing from you then; **~ak·ti̩on** *f* ✝ recall
Rück·run·de ['rʏk-] *f sport* **1.** second half of the season; **2.** return match (*or* leg)
Ruck·sack ['rʊkzak] *m* rucksack; backpack; **~tou̩ris·mus** *m* backpacking; **~tou̩rist** *m* backpacker
Rück·schlag ['rʏk-] *m* **1.** setback; ⚕ relapse; **2.** *sport*: return; **3.** recoil *of gun*; **~ven̩til** *n* check valve
Rück·schluß ['rʏk-] *m*: ***Rückschlüsse ziehen aus*** *dat.* draw conclusions from
Rück·schrei·ben ['rʏk-] *n* reply
Rück·schritt ['rʏk-] *m* (-[e]s; *no pl.*) step back, backward (*or* retrograde) step; '**rück·schritt·lich** *adj.* reactionary
Rück·sei·te ['rʏk-] *f* back, rear; reverse *of coin etc.*; ***siehe ~!*** see overleaf
Rück·sicht ['rʏk-] *f* (-; *no pl.*) consideration (***auf*** *acc.* for); ***aus*** (*or* ***mit***) ***~ auf*** *acc.* out of consideration for; ***ohne ~ auf*** *acc.* regardless of; F ***ohne ~ auf Verluste*** F regardless; ***auf j-n ~ nehmen*** show consideration for s.o.; ***auf et. ~ nehmen*** make allowances for s.th., take s.th. into account; ***keine ~ nehmen auf*** *acc. a.* pay no heed to
'**Rück·sicht·nah·me** [-na:mə] *f* (-; *no pl.*) consideration (***auf*** *acc.* for); ~ ***im Verkehr*** courtesy on the road
'**rück·sichts·los I.** *adj.* inconsiderate (***gegen*** *acc.* towards), thoughtless; ruthless; **II.** *adv.* inconsiderately *etc.*; ~ ***fahren*** drive recklessly; ~ ***vorgehen*** take drastic action *or* measures (***gegen*** *acc.* against)
'**rück·sichts·voll** *adj.* considerate (***gegenüber*** *dat.* towards), thoughtful; gentle; **~es *Verhalten*** thoughtfulness
Rück|sitz ['rʏk-] *m* back seat; *motorcycle*: pillion; **~spie·gel** *m mot.* rear-view mirror; **~spiel** *n sport*: return match (*or* leg); **~spra·che** *f* consultation; ***mit j-m ~ halten*** confer with s.o., talk *s.th.* over with s.o.; ***nach ~ mit*** *dat.* after consulting (*or* talking to)
Rück·spul·au·to̩ma·tik ['rʏkʃpu:l-] *f phot., VCR etc.*: automatic (film) rewind; '**rück·spu·len** *v/t. and v/i.* (*only inf. and p.p.* rückgespult, h) *tape, VCR etc.*: rewind; '**Rück·spul·knopf** *m phot.* winder; '**Rück·spul·ta·ste** *f* rewind key
Rück·stand ['rʏk-] *m* (-[e]s; ⸚e) **1.** remains *pl.*; ⚗ residue, sediment; **2.** *pl.* ✝ outstanding debts; **3.** backlog; ***im ~ sein*** be behind; ***mit der Miete*** *etc.* ***im ~ sein*** be in arrears with one's rent *etc.*; ***mit zwei Toren im ~ sein*** *soccer*: be two goals down; '**rück·stän·dig** *adj.* out-of-date, antiquated, behind the times; backward, underdeveloped; '**Rückstän·dig·keit** *f* (-; *no pl.*) backwardness
Rück·stau ['rʏk-] *m* **1.** ⚙ backwater; **2.** *mot.* tailback
Rück·stell·ta·ste ['rʏk-] *f* backspacer
Rück·stel·lung ['rʏk-] *f* **1.** ✝ a) transfer to reserve (fund), b) reserve; **2.** ⚡, *computer*: reset(ting)
Rück|stoß ['rʏk-] *m* recoil *of a gun*; reaction *of a rocket*; **~strah·ler** *m* reflector; **~strah·lung** *f* reflection; **~strom** *m* **1.** ⚡ reverse current; **2.** ~ ***von Urlaubern*** returning masses of holidaymakers; **~stu·fung** *f* downgrading; **~ta·ste** *f* backspacer
Rück·tritt ['rʏk-] *m* **1.** resignation *from office*; withdrawal *from a contract etc.*; ***s-n ~ erklären*** hand in one's resignation; **2.** → **~brem·se** *f* backpedal (*Am.* coaster) brake
Rück·tritts|ge·bühr ['rʏk-] *f* cancellation charge (*or* fee); **~ge·such** *n* resignation; ***sein ~ einreichen*** tender one's resignation; **~klau·sel** *f* escape clause; **~recht** *n* right to rescind (***vom Vertrag*** the contract)
rück·über̩set·zen ['rʏk-] *v/t.* (*only inf. and p.p.* rückübersetzt, h) translate back (into English *etc.*)
'**Rück·über̩set·zung** *f* retranslation
rück·ver·gü·ten ['rʏk-] *v/t.* (*only inf. and p.p.* rückvergütet, h) refund, reimburse
'**Rück·ver·gü·tung** *f* refund, reimbursement
rück·ver·si·chern (*only inf. and p.p.* rückversichert, h) **I.** *v/t.* reinsure; **II.** *v/refl.*: ***sich*** ~ reinsure o.s.; *fig.* play safe
'**Rück·ver·si·che·rung** *f* reinsurance
Rück·wand ['rʏk-] *f* back; back wall
Rück·wan·de·rer ['rʏk-] *m* returning emigrant; '**Rück·wan·de·rung** *f* remigration
rück·wär·tig ['rʏkvɛrtɪç] *adj.* rear, back
rück·wärts ['rʏkvɛrts] *adv.* backwards; ***von*** ~ from behind, from the back (*or* rear); ***Salto*** ~ backward somersault; *mot.* ~ ***fahren*** back (up), reverse; ~ ***aus der Garage fahren*** back (the car) out of the garage
'**Rück·wärts|be·we·gung** *f* backward movement; *fig.* decline, falling off; **~gang** *m mot.*: (***im*** ~ in) reverse (gear)
'**rück·wärts·ge·hen** *fig. v/i.* (*irr., sep.,* sn, → ***gehen***) be on the decline, *business etc.*: *a.* go down, fall off
Rück·weg ['rʏk-] *m* (-[e]s; *no pl.*) way back (*or* home); ***auf dem*** ~ on the way back (*or* home); ***den ~ antreten*** head for home
'**ruck·wei·se** *adv.* jerkily, in jerks
rück·wir·kend ['rʏk-] *adj.* retroactive; ***die Gehaltserhöhung gilt ~ ab April*** the salary increase will be backdated to April; '**Rück·wir·kung** *f* **1.** repercussion; **2.** ⚖ ***mit ~ vom*** with retroactive effect from
rück·zahl·bar ['rʏk-] *adj.* repayable; redeemable *loan etc.*; '**Rück·zah·lung** *f* repayment; redemption *of a loan etc.*

Rück·zie·her ['rʏktsiːɐ] *m* (-s; -) **1.** climb-down; ***e-n ~ machen*** climb down; **2.** *soccer*: overhead kick
ruck zuck ['rʊk'tsʊk] F *adv.* in no time, in a flash; ***jetzt aber ~!*** F make it snappy!
Rück·zug ['rʏktsuːk] *m* (-[e]s; -züge [-tsyːgə]) retreat, withdrawal; **'Rück·zugs·ge·fecht** *n* ⚔ *and fig.* rearguard action
Rü·de ['ryːdə] *m* (-n; -n) *zo.* **1.** dog; **2.** male (fox *or* wolf)
'rü·de I. *adj.* coarse, uncouth; ***~r Kerl*** *a.* lout, F yob; **II.** *adv.*: ***sich ~ benehmen*** behave rudely, be uncouth
Ru·del ['ruːdəl] *n* (-s; -) herd *of deer etc.*; pack *of wolves*; *fig.* swarm, horde
Ru·der ['ruːdɐ] *n* (-s; -) a) oar, scull, b) helm, wheel, c) rudder; ***das ~ herumwerfen*** *a. fig.* change course; ***aus dem ~ laufen*** *a. fig.* go off course; *fig. pol.* ***am ~ sein*** be in power, be at the helm; ***ans ~ kommen*** come to power, take over at the helm, take over the reins; **~blatt** *n* (oar) blade; rudder blade; **~boot** *n* rowing boat
Ru·de·rer ['ruːdərɐ] *m* (-s; -) rower; oarsman
'Ru·der|gän·ger [-gɛŋɐ] *m* (-s; -) ⚓ helmsman; **~ge·rät** *n* rowing machine; **~haus** *n* ⚓ wheelhouse
Ru·de·rin ['ruːdərɪn] *f* (-; -nen) rower, oarswoman
'Ru·der·klub *m* rowing club
ru·dern ['ruːdɐn] **I.** *v/t.* (h) *and v/i.* (sn) row; *fig.* ***mit den Armen ~*** thrash one's arms around; **II.** ♀ *n* (-s; *no pl.*) rowing
'Ru·der|pin·ne [-pɪnə] *f* (-; -n) tiller; **~re·ˌgat·ta** *f* boat race, (rowing) regatta; **~schlag** *m* oarstroke
Ru·di·ment [rudi'mɛnt] *n* (-[e]s; -e) **1.** remnant; **2.** *biol.* vestigial organ; **3.** *obs. pl.* rudiments; **ru·di·men·tär** [rudimɛn'tɛːɐ] *adj.* rudimentary
ru·fen ['ruːfən] (rief, gerufen, h) **I.** *v/i.* **1.** shout; ***~ nach*** *dat.* call for; ***um Hilfe ~*** cry (*or* call) for help; **2.** *a. fig.* call; ***die Pflicht ruft*** duty calls; ***die Arbeit ruft*** I've got to get back to work, there's work waiting for me; *iro.* ***die Ferne ruft*** wanderlust has taken hold again, F I've got itchy feet; **II.** *v/t.* call (*a. thea., doctor etc.*); ***~ lassen*** send for, *a.* call *the doctor*; ***du kommst (mir) wie gerufen!*** you're just the person I need; → ***Gedächtnis, Leben***; **III.** ♀ *n* (-s; *no pl.*) shouting, calling, shouts *pl.*, calls *pl.*
Ru·fer ['ruːfɐ] *m* (-s; -) person calling; *fig.* ***der ~ in der Wüste*** a voice (crying) in the wilderness
Rüf·fel ['rʏfəl] F *m* (-s; -) F dressing-down, tongue-lashing, wigging; **'rüf·feln** F *v/t.* (h): ***j-n ~*** F give s.o. a dressing-down (*or* tongue-lashing, wigging), bawl s.o. out
'Ruf|mord *m* character assassination; **~na·me** *m* first name; ***wie ist Ihr ~?*** what name are you called by?; **~num·mer** *f* telephone number; **~säu·le** *f* emergency (tele)phone; taxi (tele)phone
'ruf·schä·di·gend *adj.* defamatory *remark etc.*; **'Ruf·schä·di·gung** *f* defamation
'Ruf|wei·te *f*: ***in ~*** within earshot; **~zei·chen** *n teleph.* call sign (*or* signal)
Rü·ge ['ryːgə] *f* (-; -n) rebuke, reprimand; reproach; censure; **'rü·gen** *v/t.* (h) reprimand, rebuke (***wegen*** *gen.* for); criticize; censure, denounce
Ru·he ['ruːə] *f* (-; *no pl.*) rest (*a. phys.*, ⚙); peace (and quiet); peace (of mind); calm, composure; ***~ und Ordnung*** law and order; ***zur ~ kommen*** *pendulum etc.*: come to rest, *person*: settle down; ***~ vor dem Sturm*** calm before the storm; ***ewige ~*** eternal rest; ***in aller ~*** very calmly; ***überlege es dir in aller ~*** take your time over it; ***~ bewahren*** a) keep (one's) cool, b) keep quiet; ***er kann keine ~ finden*** a) he just won't calm down, b) he can't (get to) sleep; ***sich zur ~ begeben*** retire (to bed); ***angenehme ~!*** sleep well; ***zur ~ bringen*** quieten down, calm down; ***~!*** (be) quiet!; ***~, bitte!*** quiet, please; ***gib doch endlich ~!*** can't you be quiet?, give over, will you; ***es herrschte absolute ~*** there wasn't a sound to be heard, there was dead silence; ***er läßt sie nicht in ~*** he keeps pestering her, *child*: *a.* he gives her no peace; ***laß mich in ~!*** leave me alone; ***laß mich damit in ~!*** I don't want to hear about it; ***es ließ ihm keine ~*** he couldn't stop thinking about it; ***er gönnt mir keine ~*** he doesn't give me a minute's rest, he keeps me on the go non-stop; ***sich zur ~ setzen*** retire, go into retirement; ***j-n zur letzten ~ betten*** lay s.o. to rest; F ***immer mit der ~!*** F (take it) easy!, keep your shirt on!; F ***er hat die ~ weg*** a) he's unflappable, b) F he doesn't half take his time; F ***jetzt hat die liebe Seele ~*** peace and quiet at last
'ru·he·be·dürf·tig *adj.* in need of (a) rest
'Ru·he|ge·halt *n*, **~geld** *n* pension
'Ru·he·la·ge *f* → ***Ruhestellung***
'ru·he·los *adj.* restless
'Ru·he·lo·sig·keit *f* (-; *no pl.*) restlessness
ru·hen ['ruːən] *v/i.* (h) rest (*a. the dead*); *fig. work, traffic etc.*: be at a standstill; *negotiations, proceedings etc.*: have been suspended; *volcano*: be dormant; *fig.* ***~ auf*** *dat. look, burden, responsibility etc.*: rest on; ***etwas ~*** have a little rest; ***j-n nicht ~ lassen*** *idea etc.*: give s.o. no peace; ***er ruhte (und rastete) nicht, bis*** he didn't rest until; ***hier ruht*** here lies; ***er ruhe in Frieden*** may he rest in peace; **'ru·hend** *adj.* idle *capital*, dormant *a. volcano*; stationary *traffic*; ***ein in sich ~er Mensch*** an equable person
'ru·hen·las·sen *v/t.* (*irr., sep.*, h, → ***lassen***) forget (about); leave aside; suspend
'Ru·he|pau·se *f* rest, F breather; **~platz** *m* resting place; **~sitz** *m* retirement home; ***sie wählte Bad Tölz als ihren ~*** she retired (*or* decided to retire) to Bad Tölz; **~stand** *m* (-[e]s; *no pl.*) retirement; ***im ~ (i.R.)*** retired; ***in den ~ treten*** retire; ***in den ~ versetzen*** retire, pension off; ***vorgezogener ~*** early retirement; **~stät·te** *f* place of rest; *fig.* ***letzte ~*** last (*or* final) resting place; **~stel·lung** *f* **1.** ⚙ neutral position; ***in ~*** *pendulum etc.*: at rest; **2.** ⚔ ***in ~*** behind the lines; **~stö·rer** *m* disturber of the peace; noisy person; **~stö·rung** *f* disturbance, noise; (***öffentliche ~***) disturbance of the peace; **~strom** *m* ⚡ closed-circuit current; **~tag** *m* closing day; day off; ***Montag ~*** closed (on) Mondays; **~zu·stand** *m* (-[e]s; *no pl.*) state of rest; ***im ~*** (when) at rest
ru·hig ['ruːɪç] **I.** *adj.* quiet (*a. colo[u]r, neighbo[u]rhood etc.*, ✝ *market*), *pred.* still; peaceful; restful; calm (*a. sea*); smooth (*a. crossing*); leisurely (*a. adv.*); steady *hand*; clear *conscience*; ***er ist ein ~er Mensch*** he is a quiet person; ***~er Posten*** F cushy job (*or* number); ***in ~em Ton*** in a calm (tone of) voice; ***~ und gefaßt*** calm and collected; ***~ werden*** quieten down; ***~ bleiben*** keep calm; ***sei ganz ~*** there's no need to worry; ***~!*** quiet!; ***du bist ganz ~!*** I don't want to hear another sound out of you; ***~ Blut!*** just keep calm, calm down; ***ich habe keine ~e Minute*** I don't get a moment's (*or* minute's) peace (*or* rest); **II.** *adv.* quietly *etc.*; ***~ schlafen*** sleep soundly; ***~ wohnen*** live in a quiet area; ***~ verlaufen*** be uneventful, go off smoothly (*or* without a hitch); ***sie sahen ~ zu, wie er den Hund quälte*** they just stood and watched him tormenting the dog; ***du kannst ~ dableiben*** you can stay if you want; ***das können Sie ~ tun*** feel free (to do so); ***du kannst mir ~ glauben*** you can take my word for it; ***du könntest mir ~ die Tür aufmachen*** you might open the door for me
'ru·hig·stel·len *v/t.* (*sep.*, h) ⚕ immobilize
Ruhm [ruːm] *m* (-[e]s; *no pl.*) fame; glory; ***~ erlangen*** win (*or* gain) fame; F ***er hat sich nicht gerade mit ~ bekleckert*** he didn't exactly cover himself in glory
rüh·men ['ryːmən] *v/t.* (h) praise, extol, sing the praises of; ***sich e-r Sache ~*** pride o.s. on s.th.; ***sich e-r Sache ~ können*** boast s.th.
'rüh·mens·wert *adj.* praiseworthy, laudable, commendable, creditable
Ruh·mes|blatt ['ruːməs-] *fig. n*: F ***das war kein ~ für ihn*** he didn't exactly distinguish himself (with that); **~tat** *f* glorious deed
rühm·lich ['ryːmlɪç] *adj.* praiseworthy, hono(u)rable, laudable; ***~e Ausnahme*** notable exception; ***kein ~es Ende nehmen*** come to a bad end
'ruhm·los *adj.* inglorious
'ruhm·reich *adj.* glorious; famous, renowned
Ruhr [ruːɐ] *f* (-; *no pl.*) ⚕ dysentery
Rühr|be·sen ['ryːɐ-] *m* whisk; **~ei·er** *pl.* scrambled eggs
rüh·ren ['ryːrən] (h) **I.** *v/t.* **1.** stir; **2.** move; → ***Finger, Trommel***; **3.** *fig.* touch; move; ***das rührte ihn wenig*** it left him cold; ***ich dachte, mich rührt der Schlag*** I nearly fell over backwards; → ***Donner, gerührt***; **II.** *v/i.* **4.** stir; **5.** ***~ an*** *acc.* touch; *fig.* touch on *s.th.*; *fig.* ***an diesen Punkt darf man bei ihm nicht ~*** it's a sore point with him; ***laß uns nicht an Vergangenes ~*** let's not stir up the past; **6.** ***~ von*** *dat.* come from, stem from; **III.** *v/refl.*: ***sich ~*** **7.** stir, move; ***er rührte sich nicht vom Fleck*** he didn't budge; **8.** *fig.* do something; ***er rührt sich nicht*** he doesn't lift a finger; ***nebenan rührt sich gar nichts*** it's very quiet next door; ***du mußt dich schon ~*** it's up to you to make a move, you'd better get a move on; **9.** *fig.* a) say something, b) *longing etc.*: stir; ***wenn du was willst, mußt du dich ~*** if you want anything, say so (*or* let me *etc.* know); **IV.** ♀ *n*: ***ein menschliches ~ verspüren*** a) be touched with pity, b) *hum.* have to answer the call of nature; **'rüh·rend I.** *adj.* touching, moving; very kind; ***das ist ja ~!*** that's really nice (*or* sweet) of you; **II.** *adv.* touchingly; ***~ besorgt*** (very) solicitous (***um*** *acc.* towards)
rüh·rig ['ryːrɪç] *adj.* active; enterprising; ***~es Treiben*** bustling activity
Rühr|löf·fel ['ryːɐ-] *m* stirring spoon; **~maˌschi·ne** *f* mixer

Rühr·mich·nicht·an ['ry:ʁmıçnıçtˀan] *n* (-; -) ⚘ touch-me-not
rühr·se·lig ['ry:ʁze:lıç] *adj.* sentimental, maudlin; **~es Zeug** F sob stuff; **~e Geschichte** F sob story; **~es Stück** (**Buch** *etc.*) F tearjerker
Rühr|stück ['ryʁ-] *n* sentimental drama; **~teig** *m* batter, cake mixture
Rüh·rung ['ry:rʊŋ] *f* (-; *no pl.*) emotion; **vor ~ nicht sprechen können** be choked (with emotion)
Rühr·werk ['ry:ʁ-] *n* mixer
Ru·in [ru'i:n] *m* (-s; *no pl.*) ruin; *a. s.o.'s* undoing; **vor dem ~ stehen** be on the verge (*or* brink) of ruin; **das ist noch sein ~** that will be the ruin (*or* ruination) of him yet
Rui·ne [ru'i:nə] *f* (-; -n) ruin(s *pl.*); *fig.* wreck; **Rui·nen·land·schaft** *f* **1.** expanse *or* sea of ruins (*or* rubble); **2.** *art*: landscape with ruins
rui·nie·ren [rui'ni:rən] *v/t.* (h) ruin (**sich** o.s.); undermine *the economy etc.*
rui·niert [rui'ni:ʁt] *adj.* ruined
rui·nös [rui'nø:s] *adj.* ruinous
rülp·sen ['rʏlpsən] F *v/i.* (h), **Rülp·ser** ['rʏlpsʁ] F *m* (-s; -) belch, F burp
rum(...) [rʊm] F *adv.* → **herum(...)**
Rum [rʊm] *m* (-s; *no pl.*) rum
Ru·mä·ne [ru'mɛ:nə] *m* (-n; -n), **Ru·mä·nin** [ru'mɛ:nın] *f* (-; -nen), **ru·mä·nisch** [ru'mɛ:nıʃ] *adj.*, **Ru'mä·nisch** *n* (-en; *no pl.*) *ling.* Rumanian, Romanian
Rum·ba ['rʊmba] *f* (-; -s) rumba
'Rum·ku·gel *f* (rum) truffle
Rum·mel ['rʊməl] F *m* (-s; *no pl.*) **1.** (hustle and) bustle; fuss, F to-do; F razz(a)-matazz; **e-n großen ~ um et. machen** make a big fuss (*or* to-do) about s.th.; **2.** fair; → **~platz** *m* fairground
ru·mo·ren [ru'mo:rən] *v/i.* (h) make a noise, bang around; **es rumort in m-m Bauch** (**Kopf**) my stomach's rumbling (my head's spinning); *fig.* **es rumort in der Opposition** there are rumblings in the opposition, there's trouble brewing among the opposition; **es rumorte im Volk** there was growing unrest among the people
Rum·pel·kam·mer ['rʊmpəl-] *f* lumber room; *fig.* **das gehört in die ~** that belongs in the dustbin (*Am.* garbage can), that's (a lot of) garbage (*or* rubbish)
rum·peln ['rʊmpəln] *v/i.* (h) rumble; bang around
Rumpf [rʊmpf] *m* (-[e]s; Rümpfe ['rʏmpfə] a) trunk; torso, b) ⚓ hull, c) ✈ fuselage, body
rümp·fen ['rʏmpfən] *v/t.* (h): **die Nase ~** turn one's nose up (**über** *acc.* at)
Rump·steak ['rʊmpste:k] *n* (-s; -s) *gastr.* rump steak
rums [rʊms] *int.* bang!; **rum·sen** ['rʊmzən] F *v/i.* (h) bang; **mit dem Kopf gegen die Tür ~** bang one's head against (*or* on) the door
Run [ran] *m* (-s; -s) run (**auf** *acc.* on)
rund [rʊnt] **I.** *adj.* a) round (*a. fig. sum, vowel, number*; circular, b) plump, round *cheeks*, c) *fig.* well-rounded; mellow *wine*; perfect *party etc.*; **ein ~es Dutzend** a dozen or so; **ein ~er Geburtstag** a big "O"; **Gespräche am ~en Tisch** round-table talks; **II.** *adv.* about, around, roughly; **~ um** *acc.* (a)round; **~ um die Welt** (a)round the world; **der Motor** (*fig.* **alles**) **läuft ~** the engine's (everything's) running smoothly; **ein Buch ~ um die Raumfahrt** a book all about (*or* on every aspect of) space travel; → **rundgehen, rundheraus, rundweg**
'Rund|bau *m* (-[e]s; -ten) rotunda; **~blick** *m* panorama, panoramic view; **~bo·gen** *m* ⚠ round arch; **~brief** *m* circular
Run·de ['rʊndə] *f* (-; -n) **1.** group, circle, F crowd; **2.** walk; round; beat; F **e-e ~ drehen** a) go for a walk round the block, b) *mot.* go for a spin; **die ~ machen** a) *bottle, news etc.*: go the rounds, b) *doctor*: do one's round; **3.** *sport*: lap; *boxing, wrestling etc.*: round; **die nächste ~ erreichen** get through to the next round; **4.** round; **ich spendiere die nächste ~** I'll stand you (*or* buy) the next round; **5.** *fig.* (**gerade**) **über die ~n kommen** (just about) make it, make ends meet; **et. über die ~n bringen** get s.th. over (and done) with; **j-n über die ~n bringen** tide s.o. over
run·den ['rʊndən] (h) **I.** *v/t.* round; **II.** *v/refl.*: **sich ~** grow round; *fig.* take shape; *fig.* **das Bild rundet sich** things are beginning to fall into shape
'Rund·er·laß *m* circular (note)
'rund·er·neu·ern *v/t.* (*only inf. and p.p.* runderneuert, h) *mot.* retread, *Brit. a.* remould; **runderneuerter Reifen** retread, *Brit. a.* remould
'Rund|fahrt *f* (sightseeing) tour; **~flug** *m* sightseeing flight; **~fra·ge** *f* survey
Rund·funk *m* (-s; *no pl.*) a) broadcasting, radio, b) broadcasting company; **im ~** on the radio (*or* air); **beim ~ sein** work in broadcasting (*or* for radio); **im ~ übertragen** broadcast; **~an·spra·che** *f* radio address; **~an·stalt** *f* broadcasting company; **~emp·fän·ger** *m* radio (receiver); **~ge·bühr** *f* (radio and TV) licen|ce (*Am.* -se) fee; **~hö·rer** *m* **1.** (radio) listener; **2.** → **Rundfunkteilnehmer**; **~netz** *n* radio network; **~or,che·ster** *n* radio orchestra; **~pro,gramm** *n* a) radio program(me); radio program(me)s *pl.*, b) radio program(me) guide; **~sen·der** *m* radio (*or* broadcasting) station; **~sen·dung** *f* broadcast, (radio) program(me); **~spre·cher** *m* (radio) announcer; **~teil·neh·mer** *m* radio set owner; **~über,tra·gung** *f* → **Rundfunksendung**
'Rund·gang *m* round, tour
'rund·ge·hen *v/i.* (*irr., sep.,* sn, → **gehen**) *rumo(u)r etc.*: go the rounds; F **heute geht's wieder rund!** F it's all go
'Rund·ge·spräch *n* round-table discussion
'rund·her'aus *adv.* in plain terms, straight out, flatly, point-blank
'rund·her'um *adv.* **1.** round about, all (a)round; **2.** *fig.* absolutely
'Rund·korn·reis *m* round-grain rice
'Rund·kurs *m sport*: circuit
'rund·lich *adj.* plump, chubby, F dumpy
'Rund|rei·se *f* tour (**durch** *acc.* of); **Asien**~ tour of Asia; **~rücken** *m* hunchback, ⚕ kyphosis; **~schrei·ben** *n* circular (letter); **~sicht·fen·ster** *n* wrap-round window; **~strecke** *f* circuit; **~strick·na·del** *f* circular knitting needle; **~stück** *dial. n* roll; **~tanz** *m* round dance
'rund'um *adv.* **1.** all (a)round; **2.** *fig.* completely; **~ glücklich** *a.* perfectly happy
'Rund'um|er·neue·rung *f* general overhaul; **~schlag** *m* **1.** *sport*: roundhouse (blow); **2.** *fig.* sweeping attack (**gegen** *acc.* on); **zum ~ ausholen** lash out on all sides
Run·dung ['rʊndʊŋ] *f* (-; -en) curve (*a. fig. hum.*)
'rund'weg *adv.*: **~ leugnen** flatly deny; **~ ablehnen** refuse point-blank; **~ falsch** absolutely wrong
Ru·ne ['ru:nə] *f* (-; -n) rune
'Ru·nen|al·pha,bet *n* runic alphabet; **~schrift** *f* runic characters *pl.*, runes *pl.*
Run·kel·rü·be ['rʊŋkəl-] *f* mangel-wurzel
run·ter(...) ['rʊntʁ-] F *adv.* **1.** → **herunter(...)**; **2.** → **hinunter(...)**
'run·ter|hau·en F *v/t.* (*sep.*, h) **1.** **j-m eine ~** F give s.o. a clip round the ears; **ich hau' dir gleich eine runter!** you'll get a clip round the ears if you're not careful; **2.** F knock *s.th.* off; **~ho·len** *v/t.* (*sep.*, h) **1.** get (*or* fetch) *s.th.* down; **2.** V **sich einen ~** V jerk off; **~rut·schen** *v/t.* (*sep.*, sn) → **Buckel**
Run·zel ['rʊntsəl] *f* (-; -n) wrinkle; **~n haben** be wrinkled; **run·ze·lig** ['rʊntsəlıç] *adj.* wrinkled; **'run·zeln** *v/t.* (h) wrinkle; **die Stirn ~** knit one's brow, frown; **runz·lig** ['rʊntslıç] → **runzelig**
Rü·pel ['ry:pəl] *m* (-s; -) lout, F yob
Rü·pe·lei [ry:pə'laı] *f* (-; -en) loutish behavio(u)r
'rü·pel·haft *adj.* uncouth, rude
rup·fen ['rʊpfən] *v/t.* (h) a) pull out, b) pluck *fowl*; F *fig.* **j-n ~** F fleece s.o.; → **Hühnchen**
Rup·fen ['rʊpfən] *m* (-s; *no pl.*) burlap
rup·pig ['rʊpıç] *adj.* gruff
Rü·sche ['ry:ʃə] *f* (-; -n) frill
Ruß [ru:s] *m* (-es; -e) soot; lamp black
Rus·se ['rʊsə] *m* (-n; -n) Russian
Rüs·sel ['rʏsəl] *m* (-s; -) a) *zo.* (*elephant's*) trunk; snout; proboscis, b) F conk, hooter; **~kä·fer** *m* weevil
ru·ßen ['ru:sən] (h) **I.** *v/i. lamp*: smoke; **II.** *v/t.* blacken; **ru·ßig** ['ru:sıç] *adj.* sooty
Rus·sin ['rʊsın] *f* (-; -nen) Russian (woman); **rus·sisch** ['rʊsıʃ] *adj.*, **'Rus·sisch** *n* (-en; *no pl.*) *ling.* Russian
rü·sten ['rʏstən] (h) **I.** *v/t.* **1.** prepare (**zu** *dat.* for); **II.** *v/i.* build up arms (*or* one's arms stockpile); **um die Wette ~** be competing in (*or* be involved in, be in on) the arms race; **III.** *v/refl.*: **sich ~** prepare, get ready (**zu** *dat.*, **für** *acc.* for); arm o.s.; ⚔ arm (o.s.), build up arms (*or* one's arms stockpile); **sich ~ für** *acc. a.* F gear up for; → **gerüstet**
Rü·ster ['rʏstʁ, 'ry:stʁ] *f* (-; -n), **~holz** *n* ⚘ elm
rü·stig ['rʏstıç] *adj.* sprightly; active
ru·sti·kal [rʊsti'ka:l] *adj.* rustic, rural; **~e Möbel** country-style furniture
Rü·stung ['rʏstʊŋ] *f* (-; -en) **1.** ⚔ a) arming, armament, b) armaments *pl.*; **2.** *hist.* armo(u)r
'Rü·stungs|auf·trag *m* armaments contract; **~aus·ga·ben** *pl.* defen|ce (*Am.* -se) spending *sg.*; **~be·schrän·kung** *f* arms limitation; **~be·trieb** *m* armament factory; **~elek,tro·nik** *f* defen|ce (*Am.* -se) electronics *pl.*; **~etat** *m* defen|ce (*Am.* -se) budget; **~fa,brik** *f* armaments factory; **~in·du,strie** *f* armaments industry; **~kon,trol·le** *f* arms control; **~kon,zern** *m* armaments group; **~po·li,tik** *f* arms policy; **~stopp** *m* arms freeze; **~wett·lauf** *m* arms race
Rüst·zeug ['rʏst-] *n* (-[e]s; *no pl.*) **1.** tools *pl.*, equipment; **2.** *fig.* stock-in-trade; qualifications *pl.*; **sie hat nicht das ~ für diesen Posten** *a.* she isn't equipped for the job, F she hasn't got what it takes

Ru·te ['ruːtə] *f* (-; -n) **1.** switch, rod; ***mit eiserner ~ regieren*** rule with a rod of iron; → ***Wünschelrute***; **2.** *zo.* penis; *hunt.* tail, (*fox*) brush
'Ru·ten·bün·del *n hist.* fasces
'Ru·ten·gän·ger [-gɛŋɐ] *m* (-s; -) diviner, dowser
Ruth [ruːt] *f bibl.* Ruth; ***das Buch ~*** (the Book of) Ruth
Rutsch [rʊtʃ] *m* (-[e]s; -e) **1.** a) slide, b) landslide; F ***in einem ~*** in one go; **2.** *hum.* little trip, jaunt; ***guten ~ (ins neue Jahr)!*** Happy New Year!; **~bahn** *f* slide, *Am.* chute; *fig.* skating rink
rut·schen ['rʊtʃən] *v/i.* (sn) a) slide, b) slip; *mot.* skid; *trousers, skirt etc.*: be slipping; ***in die Höhe ~*** *skirt*: ride up; ***ins*** ♀ ***kommen*** start slipping, *car etc.*: go into a skid, start skidding; F ***rutsch mal ein Stück*** F can you move up a bit?; F ***schnell mal ins nächste Dorf ~*** F scoot along to the next village; F ***das Essen will nicht ~*** I just can't get this food down
'rutsch·fest *adj.* non-skid *tyres*; non-slip *sole*; **'Rutsch·fe·stig·keit** *f* traction
rut·schig ['rʊtʃɪç] *adj.* slippery
'Rutsch·par,tie F *f* (downhill) slide
rüt·teln ['rʏtəln] (h) **I.** *v/t.* shake; **II.** *v/i.* shake (*a. fig.*); *car etc.*: jolt; ⚙ vibrate; ***an der Tür ~*** rattle at the door; *fig.* **~ *an*** *dat.* shake; ***daran ist nicht zu ~*** that's the way it is

S

S, s [ɛs] *n* (-; -) S, s
SA [ɛsˈʔaː] *f* (-; *no pl.*) *hist.* SA, (Nazi) stormtroops *pl. or* stormtroopers *pl.*
Saal [zaːl] *m* (-[e]s; Säle [ˈzɛːlə]) a) hall, b) ⚖ courtroom; **~ord·ner** *m* steward; **~schlacht** *f* (pubhouse) brawl; **~schutz** *m* stewards *pl.*
Saar·län·der [ˈzaːɐlɛndɐ] *m* (-s; -), **Saar·län·de·rin** [ˈzaːɐlɛndərɪn] *f* (-; -nen) Saarlander; ***Saarländer(in) sein*** *a.* come from the Saarland; **saar·län·disch** [ˈzaːɐlɛndɪʃ] *adj.* Saarland ..., from the Saarland
Saat [zaːt] *f* (-; -en) **1.** *no pl.* sowing; **2.** seed (*a. fig.*); crops *pl.*; ***die ~ geht auf*** the seed is coming up, *fig.* the results are beginning to show; **~gut** *n* (-[e]s; *no pl.*) seed(s *pl.*); **~kar,tof·fel** *f* seed potato; **~korn** *n* seed (corn); **~krä·he** *f* rook; **~zeit** *f* sowing time
Sab·bat [ˈzabat] *m* (-s; -e) Sabbath; ***am ~, während des ~s*** on the Sabbath
sab·beln [ˈzabəln] F *v/i.* (h) drivel, F blether
sab·bern [ˈzabɐn] F *v/i.* (h) dribble, slaver
Sä·bel [ˈzɛːbəl] *m* (-s; -) sabre (*Am.* saber); *fig.* ***mit dem ~ rasseln*** rattle one's sabre (*Am.* saber); **~bei·ne** F *pl.* bandy (*or* bow) legs; **~fech·ten** *n sport:* sabre (*Am.* saber) fencing; **~hieb** *m* sabre (*Am.* saber) thrust
sä·beln [ˈzɛːbəln] F(h) **I.** *v/i.* F hack away; **II.** *v/t.* F hack (away at)
ˈsä·bel·ras·selnd *adj.* sabre-rattling, *Am.* saber-rattling
Sa·bo·ta·ge [zaboˈtaːʒə] *f* (-; *no pl.*) sabotage; ***~ begehen*** carry out an act (*or* acts) of sabotage; ***die Ursache war vermutlich ~*** it is presumed to have been an act of sabotage; **~akt** *m* act of sabotage
Sa·bo·teur [zaboˈtøːɐ] *m* (-s; -e [-rə]) saboteur; **sa·bo·tie·ren** [zaboˈtiːrən] *v/t.* (h) sabotage (*a. fig.*)
Sac·cha·rin [zaxaˈriːn] *n* (-s; *no pl.*) saccharin(e)
Sach|an·la·gen [ˈzax-] *pl.* ✝ tangible assets, tangibles; **~be·ar·bei·ter** *m:* ***~ für Export*** *etc.* person who deals with exports *etc.*; **~be·schä·di·gung** *f* ⚖ damage to property; **2be·zo·gen** *adj.* pertinent; **~be·zü·ge** *pl.* payment *sg.* (*or* contributions) in kind
Sach·buch [ˈzax-] *n* non-fiction book (*or* work); **~au·tor** *m* non-fiction writer; **~ver·lag** *m* non-fiction publisher(s *pl.*)
sach·dien·lich [ˈzax-] *adj.* relevant, pertinent; helpful; ***~e Hinweise bitte an*** *acc.* ... if you can help us in any way, please ring ...
Sach·dis·kus·si,on [ˈzax-] *f* factual discussion
Sa·che [ˈzaxə] *f* (-; -n) a) thing, b) affair, matter, business, c) job, concern; matter; ⚖ case, *w.s.* cause; F ***m-e ~n*** my things (*or* belongings); ***das ist e-e ~ für sich*** a) that's a completely different matter, b) *iro.* that's another story; ⚖ ***in ~n A. gegen B.*** in the matter of A versus B; F ***in ~n Umwelt*** where the environment is concerned, in questions of environment; ***bei der ~ bleiben*** keep to the point; ***das gehört nicht zur ~*** that's got nothing to do with it; ***die ~ ist*** the thing is, it's like this; ***in eigener ~ sprechen*** speak on one's own behalf; ***wie ist die ~ mit dem Auto ausgegangen?*** how did that car business turn out?; ***die ~ steht gut*** things are looking good; ***die ~ macht sich*** things are (*or* it's) coming along fine; ***das ist so e-e ~*** it's not so easy; ***das ist nicht jedermanns ~*** that's not everybody's cup of tea; ***er versteht s-e ~*** he knows his stuff; ***et. um der ~ willen tun*** do s.th. for its own sake; ***j-m sagen, was ~ ist*** a) put s.o. in the picture, b) tell s.o. what's what; ***er war nicht bei der ~*** he had his mind on other things, he wasn't concentrating; ***für e-e gute ~ kämpfen*** fight for a good cause; ***mit j-m gemeinsame ~ machen*** make common cause with s.o.; ***s-e ~ gut (schlecht) machen*** do a good (bad) job, make a good (bad) job of it; ***s-r ~ sicher sein*** be sure of oneself; ***zur ~ kommen*** get to the point, *w.s.* get down to business (F brass tacks); ***zur ~!*** can we get to the point?; ***das tut nichts zur ~*** that makes no difference; ***das ist s-e ~*** that's his problem (*or* affair); ***das ist nicht m-e ~*** that's got nothing to do with me; ***es ist ~ des Gerichts zu entscheiden, ob*** it is for the court to decide whether; ***es ist Erziehungs2*** *etc.* it's a matter of upbringing *etc.*; ***die ~ ist die, daß*** the point is that; F ***mach keine ~n!*** a) F you're kidding, b) no funny business; F ***~n gibt's(, die gibt's gar nicht)*** would you believe it; F ***was machst du denn für ~n?*** what have you been up to then?; ***was höre ich denn für (schöne) ~n?*** what's this I've been hearing then?; *mot.* F ***mit 160 ~n*** at a hundred (miles an hour); → ***laufen*** 7
ˈSa·chen·recht *n* (-[e]s; *no pl.*) ⚖ law of property
Sach|feh·ler [ˈzax-] *m* factual error; **~fra·ge** *f* factual issue; **2fremd** *adj.* irrelevant, extraneous; **~ge·biet** *n* subject, field; **2ge·mäß** **I.** *adj.* appropriate; proper; **II.** *adv.:* ***~ behandeln*** treat with due (*or* proper) care; **~ka·ta,log** *m* subject catalog(ue); **~ken·ner** *m* expert; **~kennt·nis** *f* expert knowledge; **~kun·de** *f* **1.** expert knowledge; **2.** *ped.* general knowledge; **2kun·dig** *adj.* expert *judgement etc.*; competent, well-informed *person*; ***sich ~ machen*** inform o.s.; **~la·ge** *f* state of affairs, (present) situation, situation at present; ***bei dieser ~*** under these circumstances, the situation being as it is; **~lei·stung** *f* payment (*or* contribution) in kind
sach·lich [ˈzaxlɪç] **I.** *adj.* objective; matter-of-fact, down-to-earth; factual; functional; substantial, material *difference*; ***~ bleiben*** keep to the facts; **II.** *adv.:* ***~ hat er recht*** in essence he's right
säch·lich [ˈzɛçlɪç] *adj. ling.* neuter
ˈSach·lich·keit *f* (-; *no pl.*) objectivity; matter-of-factness; functionalism *of a building etc.*; ***die Neue ~*** the New Realism
ˈSach|man·gel *m* ⚖ material defect; **~re,gi·ster** *n* subject index; **~scha·den** *m* material damage
Sach·se [ˈzaksə] *m* (-n; -n) *a. hist.* Saxon; ***~ sein*** be (a) Saxon, come from Saxony; **säch·seln** [ˈzɛksəln] *v/i.* (h) **1.** speak in (*or* the) Saxon dialect; **2.** have a Saxon accent; **Säch·sin** [ˈzɛksɪn] *f* (-; -nen) → ***Sachse***; **säch·sisch** [ˈzɛksɪʃ] **I.** *adj.* Saxon; *ling.* ***~er Genitiv*** Saxon genitive; **II.** **2** *n* (-en; *no pl.*) Saxon, the Saxon dialect
Sach·spen·de [ˈzax-] *f* donation in kind
sacht [zaxt] **I.** *adj.* soft, gentle; **II.** *adv.* a) softly, gently, b) cautiously, c) gradually; slowly; ***~e!*** gently does it!; F ***immer ~e!*** easy does it!
sach·te [ˈzaxtə] *adv.* → ***sacht*** II
Sach·ver·halt [ˈzaxfɛɐhalt] *m* (-[e]s; -e) facts *pl.*, circumstances *pl.*
Sach·ver·stand [ˈzax-] *m* expertise
ˈSach·ver·stän·di·ge *m,f* (-n; -n) expert; ⚖ expert witness
Sach·ver·stän·di·gen|gut·ach·ten [ˈzax-] *n* expert opinion; **~rat** *m* board of experts
Sach·ver·zeich·nis [ˈzax-] *n* index
Sach·wal·ter [ˈzaxvaltɐ] *m* (-s; -) a) solicitor, counsel, b) administrator; trustee, c) agent, attorney; *fig.* advocate, champion (*gen.* of)
Sach|wert [ˈzax-] *m* real value; *pl.* tangible assets; **~wis·sen** *n* expert knowledge; **~wör·ter·buch** *n* encyclop(a)edia, dictionary *of art etc.*; **~zwang** *m* force of circumstance; practical necessity
Sack [zak] *m* (-[e]s; Säcke [ˈzɛkə]) **1.** sack; *fig.* ***in ~ und Asche*** in sackcloth and ashes; ***ein ~ voller Lügen*** a pack of lies; ***mit ~ und Pack*** bag and baggage; F ***et. im ~ haben*** have s.th. in the bag; F ***j-n in den ~ stecken*** F knock spots off s.o.; F ***in den ~ hauen*** F chuck it; F ***den ~ zubinden*** wrap things up; → ***Katze*** 1; **2.** F ***fauler ~*** *sl.* lazy bastard; **3.** V balls *pl.*; **~bahn·hof** *m* terminus
Säckel [ˈzɛkəl] (*sep.* -k·k-) *m* (-s; -) mon-

eybag; *fig.* ***tief in den ~ greifen*** dig deep into one's pockets
sacken ['zakən] (*sep.* -k·k-) *v/i.* (sn) sink, *ground etc.*: *a.* subside; *person*: slump; ***zu Boden ~*** slump to the ground; ***er sackte in die Knie*** his knees gave way; → ***absacken***
'Sack|gas·se *f* cul-de-sac, dead-end street; *fig.* dead end, *esp. pol. etc.* impasse; *fig.* ***in e-e ~ geraten*** reach a dead end, *talks etc.*: reach deadlock; **~hüp·fen** *n* sack race; **~kleid** *n* sack dress; **~lei·nen** *n* sacking, burlap
Sa·dis·mus [za'dɪsmʊs] *m* (-; *no pl.*) sadism; **Sa·dist** [za'dɪst] *m* (-en; -en) sadist; **sa·di·stisch** [za'dɪstɪʃ] *adj.* sadistic(ally *adv.*)
Sa·do·ma·so ['za:do'ma:zo] F *m* → ***Sadomasochist***; **Sa·do·ma·so'chis·mus** [zado-] *m* sadomasochism; **Sa·do·ma·so'chist** *m* sadomasochist; **sa·do·ma·so'chi·stisch** *adj.* sadomasochistic(ally *adv.*)
sä·en ['zɛ:ən] *v/t. and v/i.* (h) sow (*a. fig.*); → ***gesät***
Sa·fa·ri [za'fa:ri] *f* (-; -s) safari; **~park** *m* wildlife reserve, safari park
Safe [ze:f, seɪf] *m* (-s; -s) safe; safe-deposit box; **~knacker** F *m* safecracker, safebreaker; **~schlüs·sel** *m* key to a (*or* the) safe
Sa·fran ['zafra:n] *m* (-s; -e) saffron
'sa·fran·gelb *adj.* saffron(-colo[u]red)
Saft [zaft] *m* (-[e]s; Säfte ['zɛftə]) juice; ♣ sap; F ⚡ *etc. sl.* juice; *fig.* ***j-n im eigenen ~ schmoren lassen*** let s.o. stew in his (*or* her) own juice; ***ohne ~ und Kraft*** → ***saftlos*** 2
'saft·grün *adj.* sap green, verdant
saf·tig ['zaftɪç] *adj.* a) juicy, succulent, b) lush *meadows, green*, c) *fig.* juicy, spicy *joke etc.*; F steep *prices etc.*; swingeing *cuts*; F ***das sind schon ~e Preise hier*** F they really slap it on here, don't they?; F ***~e Niederlage*** crushing defeat; F ***~e Ohrfeige*** hefty clout round the ears, real box on the ears
'Saft·la·den F *m* F hopeless joint; ***das ist ja ein ~ hier!*** *a.* what a place this is
'saft·los *adj.* **1.** juiceless, dry; **2.** → ***saft- und kraftlos***
'Saft·pres·se *f* fruit press
'Saft·sack *sl. m sl.* jerk
'saft- und 'kraft·los *adj.* weak, insipid, lacklustre; *a.* wishy-washy *speech*; ***~ sein*** *a.* have no sparkle
Sa·ga ['za:ga] *f* (-; -s) saga
Sa·ge ['za:gə] *f* (-; -n) legend; *fig.* rumo(u)r, myth
Sä·ge ['zɛ:gə] *f* (-; -n) saw; **~blatt** *n* saw blade; **~bock** *m* sawhorse; **~dach** *n* sawtooth roof; **~fisch** *m* sawfish; **~ma,schi·ne** *f* machine saw; **~mehl** *n* sawdust; **~mes·ser** *n* serrated knife; **~mühle** *f* sawmill
sa·gen ['za:gən] (h) **I.** *v/t.* say; → ***Dank, Meinung, Wahrheit; j-m et. ~*** say s.th. to s.o., tell s.o. s.th.; ***sag ihm, er soll kommen*** tell him to come; ***da sag' ich nicht nein*** I won't say no; ***das sagt sich so leicht*** (it's) easier said than done; ***das kann ich dir ~!*** you can say that again, I can tell you; ***das kann man wohl ~*** you can say that again; ***sag's frei heraus!*** out with it!; ***unter uns gesagt*** between you and me; ***du sagst es*** you said it; ***sag bloß*** you don't say; ***sag bloß, es regnet*** don't say it's raining; ***das kann jeder ~*** anyone can say that; ***das sagst du so einfach*** it's easy for you to say; ***das kann man nicht so ~*** it's not as simple as that; ***damit ist alles gesagt*** that says it all; ***was ich noch ~ wollte*** what I was going to say, there's something else I wanted to say; ***wer sagt's denn*** what did I tell you; ***ich hab's (dir) ja gleich gesagt!*** I told you so; ***etwas (nichts) zu ~ haben bei*** *dat.* have a (have no) say in *a matter etc.*; ***bei ihr hat er nichts zu ~*** he has no say when she's around; ***du hast mir nichts zu ~*** I won't have you telling me what to do; ***was willst du damit ~?*** what are you getting at?; ***sagt dir das etwas?*** does that mean anything to you?, F does that ring any bells?; ***das Buch (Bild*** *etc.*) ***sagt mir nichts*** the book (picture *etc.*) doesn't mean a thing to me; ***wie sagt man ... auf englisch?*** what's the English for ...?, what's ... in English?, how do you say ... in English?; ***das hat nichts zu ~*** it doesn't mean anything; ***(das ist) schwer zu ~*** it's hard to say; ***es läßt sich nicht ~, ob (was)*** there's no telling whether (what); ***das sagt man nicht*** you shouldn't say things like that; ***ich habe mir ~ lassen*** I've been told; ***er läßt sich nichts ~*** he won't be told, he won't listen to anyone; ***laß dir das gesagt sein*** let that be a warning to you; ***man sagt, er sei im Ausland*** they say he's abroad, he's supposed to be abroad; ***was Sie nicht ~!*** you don't say; ***ich muß schon ~!*** I mean to say, I must say; F ***wem ~ Sie das?*** F you're telling me; ***wie man so (schön) sagt*** as the saying goes; ***~ wir*** *zehn Stück*: (let's) say; ***wer sagt das?*** says who?, who says?; ***(das) sagst du!*** that's what you say, F says you; ***sage und schreibe fünf Autos*** five cars, no less, F five cars, would you believe; ***ich wollte es nur gesagt haben*** I just wanted to mention it; ***es (or damit) ist nicht gesagt, daß*** that doesn't mean (to say) that; ***wie gesagt*** as I said, as I was saying; **II.** ♀ *n*: ***das ~ haben*** have the (final) say (***bei, in*** *dat.* in), F call the shots; ***er hat das ~*** *a.* what he says goes
sä·gen ['zɛ:gən] *v/t. and v/i.* (h) saw; F *fig.* F saw wood
'Sa·gen·ge·stalt *f* mythical (*or* legendary) figure
'sa·gen·haft **I.** *adj.* **1.** F *fig.* F incredible, fantastic; **2.** legendary, mythical; **II.** *adv.*: ***~ teuer*** *etc.* incredibly expensive *etc.*
'Sa·gen·tier *n* mythical beast
'sa·gen·um,wo·ben *adj.* legendary; shrouded in legend
'Sä·ge|spä·ne *pl.* wood shavings; **~werk** *n* sawmill; **~zahn** *m a. electron.* sawtooth
Sa·go ['za:go] *m, n* (-s; *no pl.*) sago; **~baum** *m* sago palm
sah [za:] *pret. of* ***sehen***
Sah·ne ['za:nə] *f* (-; *no pl.*) cream; **~bon,bon** *m, n* toffee, *Am.* taffy; **~eis** *n* ice cream; **~jo·ghurt** *m* cream yoghurt; **~känn·chen** *n* cream jug, *Am.* creamer; **~kä·se** *m* cream cheese; **~quark** *m* cream *or* high-fat quark (*or* curd cheese); **~tor·te** *f* cream gateau
sah·nig ['za:nɪç] *adj.* creamy
Sai·son [zɛ'zõ:, zɛ'zɔŋ] *f* (-; -s) season
sai'son·ab·hän·gig *adj.* seasonal
Sai'son|ar·beit *f* seasonal work; **~ar·bei·ter** *m* seasonal worker; **~ar,ti·kel** *m* seasonal article; **~auf·schlag** *m* seasonal charge (*or* supplement); **~auf·takt** *m*: ***zum ~*** to open (F kick off) the season, *w.s.* to get the season off to a good start; **~aus·ver·kauf** *m* end-of-season sale; **~be·darf** *m* seasonal consumption; **♀be·dingt** *adj.* seasonal; **~be·ginn** *m* beginning of the season; **♀be·rei·nigt** *adj.* seasonally adjusted; **~be·schäf·ti·gung** *f* seasonal employment; **~be·trieb** *m* **1.** seasonal business; **2.** peak-season activity; **~en·de** *n* end of the season; **~ent·las·sun·gen** *pl.* seasonal layoffs; **~ge·schäft** *n* seasonal business; **♀mä·ßig** *adj.* seasonal; **~schwan·kun·gen** *pl.* seasonal fluctuation(s); **~wan·de·rung** *f* seasonal migration
Sai·te ['zaɪtə] *f* (-; -n) string; *fig.* ***andere ~n aufziehen*** take a tougher line
'Sai·ten|hal·ter *m* tailpiece; **~in·stru,ment** *n* string(ed) instrument
Sa·ke ['za:kə] *m* (-; *no pl.*) sake
Sak·ko ['zako] *m, n* (-s; -s) (sports) jacket
sa·kral [za'kra:l] *adj.* **1.** *eccl.* religious, sacred; **2.** *anat.* sacral
Sa'kral·bau *m* (-[e]s; -ten) *eccl.* sacred building; *pl. a.* sacred architecture *sg.*
Sa·kra·ment [zakra'mɛnt] **I.** *n* (-[e]s; -e) *eccl.* sacrament; ***die ~e austeilen (empfangen)*** administer (receive) the sacraments; **II.** *int.* damn!; **sa·kra·men·tal** [zakramɛn'ta:l] *adj.* sacramental
Sa·kri·leg [zakri'le:k] *n* (-[e]s; -e [-gə]) sacrilege; ***ein ~ begehen*** *a. fig.* commit sacrilege
Sa·kri·stan [zakrɪs'ta:n] *m* (-s; -e) sacristan
Sa·kri·stei [zakrɪs'taɪ] *f* (-; -en) vestry
sa·kro·sankt [zakro'zaŋkt] *adj.* sacrosanct
sä·ku·lar [zɛku'la:ɐ] *adj.* secular (*a. ast.*)
sä·ku·la·ri·sie·ren [zɛkulari'zi:rən] *v/t.* (h) secularize; **Sä·ku·la·ri'sie·rung** *f* (-; -en) secularization
Sä·ku·lum ['zɛ:kulʊm] *n* (-s; -la) century
Sa·la·man·der [zala'mandɐ] *m* (-s; -) salamander
Sa·la·mi [za'la:mi] *f* (-; -s) salami; **~tak·tik** *f pol.* salami tactics *pl.*
Sa·lat [za'la:t] *m* (-[e]s; -e) **1.** *gastr.* salad; F *fig.* ***da haben wir den ~!*** F now we're in a right mess; **2.** ♣ lettuce; **~be·steck** *n* salad servers *pl.*; **~gur·ke** *f* cucumber; **~kar,tof·feln** *pl.* potatoes (for potato salad); **~kopf** *m* (head of) lettuce; **~öl** *n* salad oil; **~plat·te** *f gastr.* salad; **~schüs·sel** *f* salad bowl; **~so·ße** *f* salad dressing
Sal·ba·der [zal'ba:dɐ] *m* (-s; -) sanctimonious bore; **Sal·ba·de·rei** [zalba:də'raɪ] *f* (-; -en) F sanctimonious blethering; **sal·ba·dern** [zal'ba:dɐn] *v/i.* (h) prate
Sal·be ['zalbə] *f* (-; -n) ointment, salve
Sal·bei ['zalbaɪ] *m* (-s; *no pl.*), *f* (-; *no pl.*) ♣ sage
sal·ben ['zalbən] *v/t.* (h) *eccl.* anoint
Sal·bung ['zalbʊŋ] *f* (-; -en) anointing, *a. fig.* unction
'sal·bungs·voll *contp. adj.* unctuous
sal·die·ren [zal'di:rən] *v/t.* (h) ✝ balance, settle
Sal·do ['zaldo] *m* (-s; -s, Saldi ['zaldi]) ✝ balance; ***per ~*** on balance (*a. fig.*); **~,über·trag** *m*, **~vor·trag** *m* balance carried forward
Sa·li·ne [za'li:nə] *f* (-; -n) saltworks

Salm [zalm] *m* (-[e]s; -e) *zo.* salmon
Sal·mi·ak [zal'mi̯ak] *m* (-s; *no pl.*) ammonium chloride; **~geist** *m* (-[e]s; *no pl.*) ammonia solution, liquid ammonia; **~pa͵stil·len** *pl.* ammoniac pastilles
Sal·mo·nel·len [zalmo'nɛlən] *pl.* salmonellae; **~ver·gif·tung** *f* salmonella poisoning
Sa·lo·mo ['za:lomo] *m bibl.* Solomon; ***das Hohelied ~s*** the Song of Solomon; ***die Sprüche ~s*** (the Book of) Proverbs
sa·lo·mo·nisch [zalo'mo:nɪʃ] *adj.* Solomonic; *fig.* ***ein ~es Urteil*** a judg(e)ment of Solomon
Sa·lon [za'lõ:, za'lɔŋ] *m* (-s; -s) **1.** a) drawing room, *Am.* parlor, b) ⚓ saloon, c) (*beauty etc.*) salon; **2.** art exhibition
sa'lon·fä·hig *adj.* socially acceptable; presentable *clothes etc.*, respectable *joke etc.*; ***nicht ~*** risqué *joke etc.*, (a bit) near the knuckle
Sa'lon|lö·we *m* society lion, lounge lizard; **~wa·gen** *m* Pullman (car)
sa·lopp [za'lɔp] *adj.* casual; easygoing; *contp.* sloppy; very colloquial, slangy *expression etc.*
Sal·pe·ter [zal'pe:tɐ] *m* (-s; *no pl.*) ⚗ saltpetre, nitre, *Am.* saltpeter, niter
sal'pe·ter·hal·tig *adj.* nitrous, nitric
Sal'pe·ter·säu·re *f* nitric acid
sal·pe·trig [zal'pe:trɪç] *adj.*: ***~e Säure*** nitrous acid
Sal·to ['zalto] *m* (-s; -s, -ti) somersault; ***e-n ~ machen*** (*or* ***drehen***) turn (*or* do) a somersault, ***über*** *acc.*: *a.* somersault over; **~ mor·ta·le** [- mɔr'ta:lə] *m* (- -; -ti -li) death-defying leap
Sa·lut [za'lu:t] *m* (-[e]s; -e) salute; ***sieben Schuß ~*** seven-gun salute; ***~ schießen*** fire a salute; **sa·lu·tie·ren** [zalu'ti:rən] *v/i.* (h) salute (***vor j-m*** s.o.)
Sa'lut·schuß *m* gun salute; ***zehn Salutschüsse*** a ten-gun salute
Sal·ve ['zalvə] *f* (-; -n) ⚔ volley, salvo; round; salute; *fig.* burst *of applause*; peals *pl. of laughter*; ***e-e ~ abgeben*** fire a volley (*or* round)
Salz [zalts] *n* (-es; -e) *a. fig.* salt; ***et. in ~ legen*** salt s.th. down; *fig.* ***nicht das ~ zur Suppe haben*** live in dire poverty; ***das ~ in der Suppe*** that extra something; ***~ auf die Wunde streuen*** rub it in; ***wie e-e Suppe ohne ~*** like ham without eggs; **≈arm** *adj.*: ***~e Kost*** low-salt diet; **~berg·werk** *n* salt mine; **~bre·zel** *f* pretzel
sal·zen ['zaltsən] *v/t.* (salzte, gesalzen, h) salt (*a. fig.*); pickle; *fig.* season; → ***gesalzen***
'Salz|fäß·chen *n* saltcellar, *Am.* salt shaker; **≈frei** *adj.* salt-free, no-salt *diet*; **~ge·bäck** *n* savo(u)ry snacks *pl.*; **~gehalt** *m* salt content; **~gla͵sur** *f* salt glaze; **~gur·ke** *f* cucumber pickled in brine, *Am.* pickle
'salz·hal·tig [-haltɪç] *adj.* saline; salty *food*; ***~ sein*** *a.* contain salt
'Salz·he·ring *m* salted herring
sal·zig ['zaltsɪç] *adj.* salty
'Salz|in·fu·si͵on *f* ⚕ saline drip; **~kar͵tof·feln** *pl.* boiled potatoes; **~korn** *n* grain of salt; **~la·ke** *f*, **~lau·ge** *f* brine
'salz·los *adj.* salt-free, no-salt *diet*
'Salz|lö·sung *f* salt (*or* saline) solution; **~man·deln** *pl.* salted almonds; **~pfan·ne** *f geol.* salt pan; **~pflan·ze** *f* halophyte; **~quel·le** *f* saline spring; **~säu·le** *f*: *fig.* ***zur ~ erstarren*** be (*or* stand) rooted to the spot; **~säu·re** *f* hydrochloric acid; **~see** *m* salt lake; **~stan·ge** *f* salt (*Am.* pretzel) stick; **~stra·ße** *f hist.* salt road; **~streu·er** *m* saltcellar, *Am.* salt shaker; **~was·ser** *n* salt water; **~wü·ste** *f* salt flats *pl.*
SA-Mann [ɛs'ʔa:-] *m hist.* (Nazi) stormtrooper
Sa·ma·ri·ter [zama'ri:tɐ] *m* (-s; -): (***barmherziger ~*** good) Samaritan; **~dien·ste** *pl.*: ***j-m ~ leisten*** be a good Samaritan to s.o.
Sam·ba ['zamba] *f* (-; -s), *m* (-s; -s) samba
Sa·men ['za:mən] *m* (-s; -) **1.** seed (*a. fig.*); **2.** *no pl. physiol.* sperm, semen
'Sa·men|bank *f* (-; -en) ⚕ sperm bank; **~er·guß** *m* ejaculation; **~fa·den** *m* spermatozoon; **~flüs·sig·keit** *f* semen; **~händ·ler** *m* seedsman; **~hand·lung** *f* seed shop; **~lei·ter** *m anat.* vas deferens; **~spen·de** *f* ⚕ sperm donation; **~spen·der** *m* ⚕ sperm donor
'Sa·men·strang *m anat.* spermatic cord; **~un·ter͵bin·dung** *f* ⚕ vasoligature
'Sa·men·zel·le *f* sperm(atozoon)
Sä·me·rei·en [zɛ:mə'raiən] *pl.* seeds
sä·mig ['zɛ:mɪç] *adj.* thick, creamy
Säm·ling ['zɛ:mlɪŋ] *m* (-s; -e) seedling
Sam·mel|ak·ti͵on ['zaməl-] *f* fund-raising campaign (*or* drive); collection; **~album** *n* scrapbook; **~an·schluß** *m teleph.* private branch exchange; party line; **~auf·trag** *m* collective standing order; **~band** *m* (-[e]s; ⸚e) anthology; **~becken** *n* **1.** reservoir, tank; **2.** *geogr.* catchment area; **3.** *fig.* repository (*gen.* of), rallying point (for); **~be·griff** *m* generic term, collective noun; **~be·stel·lung** *f* collective order; **~be·zeich·nung** *f* collective name; **~büch·se** *f* collecting box; **~fahr·schein** *m* 🚌 a) group ticket, b) multiple-ride ticket; **~gut** *n* collective consignment; **~kon·to** *n* collective account; **~la·ger** *n* assembly camp; **~lin·se** *f opt.* convex lens; **~map·pe** *f* folder, file
sam·meln ['zaməln] (h) **I.** *v/t.* **1.** a) collect, b) gather *wood*, pick *mushrooms, berries etc.*, c) canvass for *votes*; **2.** gather *people, a. fig. experience etc.*; → ***gesammelt***; **II.** *v/refl.*: ***sich ~*** **3.** gather, accumulate, collect; *opt.* focus; **4.** assemble, meet; **5.** collect one's thoughts (*a.* ***s-e Gedanken ~***); compose o.s.; **III.** *v/i.* collect money, *a.* pass the hat (a)round *for s.o.*; **IV.** **≈** *n* (-s; *no pl.*) collecting; gathering; ***das ~ von Nachrichten*** newsgathering
'Sam·mel|na·me *m* collective noun; **~num·mer** *f teleph.* collective number; **~platz** *m*, **~punkt** *m* **1.** meeting place, assembly point; **2.** collecting point; **~stecker** *m* universal adapter plug; **~stel·le** *f* → ***Sammelplatz*** 2
Sam·mel·su·ri·um [zaməl'su:ri̯ʊm] *n* (-s; *no pl.*) motley collection, F hotchpotch
'Sam·mel|ta·xi *n* communal taxi; **~trans͵port** *m* mass transportation; ✝ collective transport; **~trieb** *m* collector's instinct; **~vi·sum** *n* group visa; **~werk** *n* compilation; **~wut** *f* collectomania
Samm·ler ['zamlɐ] *m* (-s; -) **1.** collector; **2.** ***~ und Jäger*** hunter-gatherer; **~ob͵jekt** *n*, **~stück** *n* collector's item (*or* piece); **~wert** *m* collector's value
Samm·lung ['zamlʊŋ] *f* (-; -en) **1.** a) collection, b) anthology, c) museum; **2.** *fig.* composure
Sams·tag ['zamsta:k] *m* (-[e]s; -e) Saturday; (***am***) ~ on Saturday; ***langer ~*** Saturday-afternoon opening; ***morgen ist langer ~*** *a.* the shops are open all day tomorrow; **'sams·tags** *adv.* on Saturdays
samt [zamt] **I.** *adv.*: ***~ und sonders*** each and every one of them, F the whole lot; **II.** *prp.* (*dat.*) together with, along with; ***ich geb's dir ~ allem Zubehör für ...*** you can have the lot for ...
Samt [zamt] *m* (-[e]s; -e) velvet; velveteen; ***weich wie ~*** soft as velvet; ***in ~ und Seide gekleidet*** dressed in silks and satins; **'samt·ar·tig** *adj.* velvety; **sam·ten** ['zamtən] *adj.* **1.** velvet; **2.** → ***samtartig***;
'Samt·hand·schuh *m*: *fig.* ***j-n mit ~en anfassen*** handle s.o. with kid gloves;
'Samt·haut *f* velvety skin; *a.* silken complexion; **sam·tig** ['zamtɪç] *adj.* velvety (*a. wine*); **'Samt·kleid** *n* velvet dress
sämt·lich ['zɛmtlɪç] **I.** *adj.* all; ***~e Anwesende(n)*** all those present; ***~e Werke*** the complete works; **II.** *adv.* all; ***sie haben ~ überlebt*** they all (*or* all of them) survived
Sa·na·to·ri·um [zana'to:ri̯ʊm] *n* (-s; -rien) sanatorium, *Am.* sanitarium
Sand [zant] *m* (-[e]s; *no pl.*) sand; ⚓ ***auf ~ laufen*** run aground; *fig.* ***auf ~ bauen*** build on sand (*or* shaky foundations); ***j-m ~ in die Augen streuen*** throw dust in s.o.'s eyes; ***~ ins Getriebe streuen*** throw a spanner (*Am.* monkey wrench) into the works; F ***et. in den ~ setzen*** F muff (*or* bungle) s.th.; ***im ~e verlaufen*** come to nothing (*lit.* naught), *plans etc.*: *a.* F fizzle out; ***Antiken gab es wie ~ am Meer*** there were no end of antiques, antiques were two a penny
San·da·le [zan'da:lə] *f* (-; -n) sandal
San·da·let·te [zanda'lɛtə] *f* (-; -n) high-heeled sandal
'Sand|bahn *f* dirt track; **~bank** *f* (-; ⸚e) sandbank; **~bo·den** *m* sandy soil; **~burg** *f* sandcastle; **~dorn** *m* sallow thorn; **~dü·ne** *f* sand dune
'sand·far·ben *adj.* sandy
'Sand·floh *m* sand flea
san·dig ['zandɪç] *adj.* full of sand, sandy
'Sand·ka·sten *m* sandpit, *Am.* sandbox; ⚔ sandtable; **~spiel** *n* ⚔ sandtable exercise
'Sand|korn *n* grain of sand; **~ku·chen** *m* **1.** *gastr.* Madeira (*Am.* pound) cake; **2.** sand pie; **~mann** *m* (-[e]s; *no pl.*), **~männ·chen** *n* (-s; *no pl.*) sandman; **~pa͵pier** *n* sandpaper (*a.* ***mit ~ abschmirgeln***); **~sack** *m* sandbag; *boxing*: punching bag
'Sand·stein *m* sandstone; **~fi͵gur** *f* sandstone sculpture
'Sand·strahl *m* ⚙ sandblast; **~ge·blä·se** *n* sandblast unit
'Sand|strand *m* sandy beach; **~sturm** *m* sandstorm
sand·te ['zantə] *pret. of* ***senden¹***
'Sand·uhr *f* hourglass
Sand·wich ['zɛntvɪtʃ] *m, n* (-[e]s; -[e]s) sandwich; ***~ mit Käse u. Gurke*** cheese and cucumber sandwich; **~bau·wei·se** *f* sandwich construction
'Sand·wü·ste *f* (sandy) desert
sanft [zanft] **I.** *adj.* soft (*a. voice, music, colo[u]r etc.*), gentle (*a. hill, pressure, manner, eyes etc.*); light *breeze, rain etc.*; easy *death*; ***mit ~er Stimme*** softly, gently, in a soft (*or* gentle) voice; ***mit ~er Gewalt*** using gentle force; ***~e Revolu-***

tion velvet revolution; ***sie ist ein ~es Wesen*** she's a gentle soul; F ***es auf die ~e Tour versuchen*** F try a bit of soft soap; **II.** *adv.*: ~ ***entschlafen*** pass away peacefully; ***ruhe*** ~ rest in peace

Sänf·te ['zɛnftə] *f* (-; -n) sedan (chair)

'Sänf·ten·trä·ger *m* sedan-chair carrier

'Sanft·heit *f* (-; *no pl.*) softness, gentleness; lightness *of rain etc.*; ease *of s.o.'s death*

'Sanft·mut *f* (-; *no pl.*) gentleness, meekness; **sanft·mü·tig** [-myːtɪç] *adj.* gentle, meek

sang [zaŋ] *pret. of* ***singen***

Sang [zaŋ] *m*: F ***mit ~ und Klang durchfallen*** fail miserably

Sän·ger ['zɛŋɐ] *m* (-s; -) **1.** singer; → ***Höflichkeit;*** **2.** *zo.* songbird; **~kna·be** *m* choirboy

San·gui·ni·ker [zaŋgu'iːnikɐ] *m* (-s; -) sanguine person; **san·gui·nisch** [zaŋgu'iːnɪʃ] *adj.* sanguine

'sang- und' klang·los *adv.* quietly, without much ado; unceremoniously; ~ ***verschwinden*** *a.* disappear without a word

sa·nie·ren [za'niːrən] (h) **I.** *v/t.* **1.** redevelop, F clean up *district etc.*; refurbish, F do up *building*; **2.** rehabilitate; **3.** ✝ revitalize; **II.** *v/refl.*: ***sich*** ~ ✝ get back on one's feet again; F *fig.* line one's (own) pockets; **Sa'nie·rung** *f* (-; -en) **1.** refurbishment *of buildings*; redevelopment *of a district*; slum clearance; **2.** rehabilitation; **3.** ✝ revitalization

Sa'nie·rungs|ge·biet *n* (re)development area; **~maß·nah·men** *pl.* **1.** redevelopment; ~ ***einleiten*** begin redevelopment (work); ***im Stadtzentrum sind ~ erforderlich*** the city centre (*Am.* center) is in need of redevelopment; **2.** ✝ rescue package(s); **~pro͵gramm** *n* ✝ rescue package (*or* scheme)

sa·ni·tär [zani'tɛːɐ] *adj.* sanitary; ***~e Anlagen*** → **Sa·ni'tär·an·la·gen** *pl.* sanitary facilities

Sa·ni·tä·ter [zani'tɛːtɐ] *m* (-s; -) ambulance man, first-aid man, medic; ⚔ medical orderly

Sa·ni·täts|dienst [zani'tɛːts-] *m* medical service; **~flug·zeug** *n* air ambulance; **~korps** *n* (*in GB*: Royal) Army Medical Corps; **~raum** *m* first-aid room; **~truppe** *f* → ***Sanitätskorps;*** **~wa·gen** *m* ambulance

sank [zaŋk] *pret. of* ***sinken***

San·k(r)a ['zaŋk(r)a] F *m* (military) ambulance

Sankt [zaŋkt] *adj.* **(*St.*)** Saint (*abbr.* St., St)

Sank·ti·on [zaŋk'tsǐoːn] *f* (-; -en) sanction; ***~en verhängen gegen*** (*or* ***über***) *acc.* impose (*or* place) sanctions on; ***mit ~en drohen*** threaten (to impose) sanctions; **sank·tio·nie·ren** [zaŋktsǐo'niːrən] *v/t.* (h) sanction

Sank·ti'ons|maß·nah·men *pl.*: (~ ***einleiten*** apply) sanctions; **~pa͵ket** *n* package of sanctions

Sankt-Nimmerleins-Tag [zaŋkt'nɪmɐlaɪnstaːk] F *m*: ***bis zum*** ~ F *wait etc.* till kingdom come

sann [zan] *pret. of* ***sinnen***

Sans·krit ['zanskrɪt] *n* (-s; *no pl.*) Sanskrit

Sa·phir ['zafɪr, za'fiːɐ] *m* **1.** sapphire; **2.** (sapphire) stylus

Sar·de ['zardə] *m* (-n; -n) Sardinian

Sar·del·le [zar'dɛlə] *f* (-; -n) anchovy

Sar'del·len·pa·ste *f* anchovy paste

Sar·din ['zardɪn] *f* (-; -nen) Sardinian

Sar·di·ne [zar'diːnə] *f* (-; -n) sardine, pilchard; **Sar'di·nen·büch·se** *f* sardine tin (*Am.* can); ***wie in e-r*** ~ (packed) like sardines

sar·disch ['zardɪʃ] *adj.* Sardinian

Sarg [zark] *m* (-[e]s; Särge ['zɛrgə]) coffin, casket; → ***Nagel;*** **~deckel** *m* coffin lid; **~na·gel** *m* coffin nail; F *fig.* F cancer stick, coffin nail; **~trä·ger** *m* pallbearer

Sa·ri ['zaːri] *m* (-[s]; -s) sari

Sar·kas·mus [zar'kasmʊs] *m* (-; *no pl.*) sarcasm; **sar·ka·stisch** [zar'kastɪʃ] *adj.* sarcastic(ally *adv.*)

Sar·kom [zar'koːm] *n* (-s; -e) ⚕ sarcoma

Sar·ko·phag [zarko'faːk] *m* (-[e]s; -e [-gə]) sarcophagus

saß [zaːs] *pret. of* ***sitzen***

Sa·tan ['zaːtan] *m* (-s; *no pl.*) Satan; *fig.* satan, devil

sa·ta·nisch [za'taːnɪʃ] *adj.* satanic

'Sa·tans|bra·ten F *m* a) cheeky devil (*or* rascal), b) blackguard; **~weib** F *n sl.* bitch

Sa·tel·lit [zatɛ'liːt] *m* (-en; -en) *ast. and pol.* satellite; ***über*** (*or* ***per***) ~ by (*or* via) satellite

Sa·tel'li·ten|bahn *f* satellite('s) orbit; **~bild** *n* satellite picture; **~fern·se·hen** *n* satellite TV; **~fo·to** *n* → ***Satellitenbild;*** **~funk** *m* satellite broadcasting; **~laufbahn** *f* satellite('s) orbit; **~sen·der** *m* satellite (TV) station; **~staat** *m* satellite (state); **~stadt** *f* satellite town; **~technik** *f* satellite technology; **~trä·ger** *m* satellite launcher; **~über͵tra·gung** *f* satellite transmission; **~ver·bin·dung** *f* satellite link

Sa·tin [za'tɛ̃ː] *m* (-s; -s) satin; sateen

Sa·ti·re [za'tiːrə] *f* (-; -n) satire (***auf*** *acc.* on); **~zeit·schrift** *f* satirical magazine

Sa·ti·ri·ker [za'tiːrikɐ] *m* (-s; -) satirist

sa·ti·risch [za'tiːrɪʃ] *adj.* satirical

satt [zat] *adj. and adv.* **1.** full; ***sich ~ essen*** eat one's fill; ***sich ~ essen an*** *dat.* fill o.s. with; ***ich bin davon nicht ~ geworden*** that wasn't enough for me; ***bist du ~?*** have you had enough (to eat)?; ***es fällt ihm schwer, s-e Familie ~ zu bekommen*** he finds it hard to feed his family; ***das macht*** ~ that's very filling; F ***et.*** (***j-n***) ***gründlich ~ bekommen*** (***haben***) get (be) sick and tired of s.th. (s.o.); F ***ich hab' die Sache so*** ~ I'm sick and tired of it, F I'm fed up to the back teeth with it; ***er konnte sich nicht ~ daran sehen*** he couldn't take his eyes off it; ***ich habe mich daran ~ gesehen*** I've seen enough (*or* too much) of it, I've had my fill of that; ***nicht ~ werden zu*** *inf.* never tire of *ger.*; **2.** *fig.* deep, rich *colo(u)rs etc.*, full *sound etc.*; **3.** *contp.* complacent, smug; **4.** F *fig.* impressive; F terrific; ***~e Preise*** steep prices; ***~e 200 km in der Stunde*** 200 km per hour, no less; ***e-e ~e Leistung*** quite a feat, some feat; ***es gab Kuchen*** ~ there was plenty of cake

Sat·tel ['zatəl] *m* (-s; Sättel ['zɛtəl]) **1.** saddle (*a. mot.*); ***ohne ~ reiten*** ride bareback; ***aus dem ~ geworfen werden*** be thrown off (one's horse); *fig.* ***j-n in den ~ heben*** hoist s.o. into the saddle; ***j-n aus dem ~ heben*** oust s.o.; ***fest im ~ sitzen*** be firmly in the saddle; ***sich im ~ halten*** hold (firmly) onto the reins; ***in allen Sätteln gerecht sein*** be a good all-rounder; **2.** *geogr.* saddle; **3.** *anat.* bridge; **4.** *dressmaking*: yoke; **~dach** *n* saddleback (roof); **~decke** *f* saddlecloth; **2fest** *adj.*: *fig.* ~ ***sein in*** *dat.* be well up in, know one's *economics etc.*; **~gurt** *m* girth

sat·teln ['zatəln] *v/t.* (h) saddle

'Sat·tel|na·se *f* saddlenose; **~pferd** *n* saddle horse; **~platz** *m* paddock; **~schlep·per** *m mot.* **1.** articulated lorry, F artic, *Am.* tractor-trailer, rig, F semi; **2.** tractor; **~ta·sche** *f* saddlebag; **~zeug** *n* saddlery; **~zug** *m* → ***Sattelschlepper*** 1

'Satt·heit *f* (-; *no pl.*) **1.** ful(l)ness; sated feeling; **2.** *fig.* richness; ~ ***der Farben*** *a.* depth of colo(u)r; **3.** *contp.* complacency, smugness

sät·ti·gen ['zɛtɪgən] (h) **I.** *v/t.* feed, fill *s.o.*; satisfy (*a. fig.*); ⚗, ✝ saturate; → ***gesättigt;*** **II.** *v/i.* be filling; **'sät·ti·gend** *adj.* filling; **'Sät·ti·gung** *f* (-; *no pl.*) satiety; ⚗, ✝ *and fig.* saturation

'Sät·ti·gungs|grad *m* degree of saturation; **~punkt** *m* ⚗, ✝ *and fig.* saturation point

Satt·ler ['zatlɐ] *m* (-s; -) saddler

Satt·le·rei [zatlə'raɪ] *f* (-; -en) saddlery

'satt·sam *adv.* more than enough; ***es ist ~ bekannt*** it's a well-known fact; ***wir haben es ~ oft gehört*** we've heard it often enough

sa·tu·rie·ren [zatu'riːrən] *v/t.* (h) saturate; **sa·tu·riert** [zatu'riːɐt] *adj.* sated

Sa·tyr ['zaːtʏr] *m* (-s, -n; -n) *myth.* satyr

Satz [zats] *m* (-es; Sätze ['zɛtsə]) **1.** sentence; *ling. a.* clause; **2.** *phls.* principle, tenet; **3.** 𝔄 theorem; ***der ~ des Euklid*** Euclid's theorem; **4.** *no pl. typ.* a) (type)setting, b) composition; **5.** set *of stamps etc.*; **6.** ♪ movement; **7.** sediment, dregs *pl.*; (*coffee*) grounds *pl.*; **8.** *tennis*: set; ***mit 3:2 Sätzen gewinnen*** win 3 sets to 2; **9.** rate; ***zum ~ von*** *dat.* at a rate of; **10.** leap, bound; ***e-n ~ machen*** (take a) leap; ***er war in vier Sätzen oben*** he was upstairs in four bounds; **~an·wei·sung** *f typ.* printing (*or* setting) instructions *pl.*; **~aus·sa·ge** *f ling.* predicate; **~ball** *m tennis*: set point; **~bau** *m* (-[e]s; *no pl.*) sentence construction; **~er·gän·zung** *f ling.* object; **~feh·ler** *m* misprint, printing error; **2fer·tig** *adj. typ.* ready for setting; ~ ***machen*** copy-edit; **~ge·fü·ge** *n* compound sentence; **~ge·gen·stand** *m ling.* subject; **~me·lo͵die** *f* intonation; **~rech·ner** *m typ.* (typesetting) computer; **2reif** *adj. typ.* ready for setting; **~spie·gel** *m typ.* type area; **~teil** *m* part of a sentence; **~tisch** *m* occasional table

Sat·zung ['zatsʊŋ] *f* (-; -en) statute; *pl.* regulations, statutes and articles *of a club etc.*; **'sat·zungs·ge·mäß** *adj.* statutory, (*a. adv.*) in accordance with the statutes

'Satz|zei·chen *n* punctuation mark; *pl. a.* punctuation *sg.*; **~zu͵sam·men·hang** *m* context

Sau [zaʊ] *f* (-; Säue ['zɔʏə]) **1.** *zo.* sow; V ***bluten wie e-e*** ~ bleed like a pig; **2.** F *contp. sl.* swine, *sl.* bitch, slut; ***unter aller*** ~ F lousy; ***et.*** (***j-n***) ***zur ~ machen*** F tear s.th. to pieces (F let s.o. have it); ***die ~ rauslassen*** F let one's hair down, *sl.* have a (real) binge; ***keine ~ war da*** *sl.* not a sod was there; ***hier kennt sich doch keine ~ aus*** how are you supposed to find anything in this place; ***wie e-e gesengte*** ~ like a lunatic, *a.* F *drive etc.* like the clappers; **~ar·beit** F *f* dirty work; *a* tough job

sau·ber ['zaʊbɐ] *adj.* clean (*a. sport*); neat

(*a. fig. solution, plan etc.*); decent; perfect; F *iro.* **~!** F (that's really) great; **~hal·ten** *v/t.* (*irr.*, *sep.*, h, → ***halten***) keep *s.th.* clean

'Sau·ber·keit *f* (-; *no pl.*) cleanliness, cleanness; neatness; *fig.* integrity

'Sau·ber·keits·fim·mel F *m* obsession with cleanliness (*or* hygiene); cleaning mania

säu·ber·lich ['zɔʏbɐlɪç] **I.** *adj.* neat; *fig. a.* clear, clean *distinction etc.*; **II.** *adv.* neatly; ***alles fein ~ ordnen*** a) put everything into its right place, b) make sure everything's neat and tidy

'sau·ber·ma·chen *v/t. and v/i.* (*sep.*, h) clean (up)

'Sau·ber·mann *iro. m* (-[e]s; ¨er) Mr Clean

säu·bern ['zɔʏbɐn] *v/t.* (h) clean; ⚕ cleanse; clear (***von*** *dat.* of); *fig.*, *a. pol.* purge; **Säu·be·rung** ['zɔʏbərʊŋ] *f* (-; -en) **1.** *no pl.* clean(s)ing; clearing; **2.** → ***Säuberungsaktion***

'Säu·be·rungs|ak·ti,on *f pol.* purge; ⚔ mopping-up operation; **~wel·le** *f pol.* series *pl.* (*or* wave) of purges

'sau'blöd F *adj.* → ***saudumm***

'Sau·boh·ne *f* broad bean

Sau·ce ['zo:sə] *f* (-; -n) → ***Soße***

Sau·cie·re [zo'sĭe:rə] *f* (-; -n) sauce boat

Sau·di·ara·ber [zaudi'arabɐ] *m*, **sau·di·ara·bisch** [zaudia'ra:bɪʃ] *adj.* Saudi (Arabian)

'sau'dumm F *adj.* F as thick as they come; really stupid; ***er ist ~*** *a. sl.* he's a real thicko; ***das ist ja ~!*** what a (F bloody) stupid thing to happen

sau·en ['zauən] *v/i.* (h) make a mess

sau·er ['zauɐ] **I.** *adj.* sour; ⚗ acid; *gastr.* pickled; F *fig.* annoyed (***auf*** *acc.* with, at *s.o.*), F mad (at *s.o.*); → ***Drops; saurer Regen*** acid rain; **~ *werden*** a) turn sour, *milk*: *a.* curdle, b) F *fig.* get cross; *fig.* ***ein saures Gesicht machen*** pull a long face; ***das ist ein saures Brot*** it's a hard life; ***es sich ~ werden lassen*** put a lot into it; → ***Apfel, Saures***; **II.** *adv.*: *gastr.* **~ *einlegen*** pickle; ***es stößt mir ~ auf*** *food etc.*: it's giving me a sour taste in my mouth; F *fig.* ***das wird ihm noch ~ aufstoßen*** that won't be the last he hears of it, he'll regret it yet; **~ *reagieren*** a) ⚗ give an acid reaction, b) F *fig.* be annoyed *or* mad (***auf*** *acc.* at); *fig.* ***sein Brot ~ verdienen*** have to work hard for one's money; **~ *verdientes Geld*** hard-earned money; ***das wird mir ~ ankommen*** it's going to be tough

'Sau·er|amp·fer *m* ♣ sorrel; **~bra·ten** *m* sauerbraten; *marinated potroast*

Saue·rei [zauə'raɪ] *f* (-; -en) → ***Schweinerei***

'Sau·er|kir·sche *f* sour cherry; **~kohl** *m*, **~kraut** *n* sauerkraut

Sau·er·län·der ['zauɐlɛndɐ] *m* (-s; -), **Sau·er·län·de·rin** ['zauɐlɛndərɪn] *f* (-; -nen) man (woman) from the Sauerland; **sau·er·län·disch** ['zauɐlɛndɪʃ] *adj.* Sauerland ..., from the Sauerland

säu·er·lich ['zɔʏɐlɪç] *adj.* (slightly) sour (*a. fig.*); *esp.* ⚗ acidulous

'Sau·er·milch *f* sour milk

säu·ern ['zɔʏɐn] *v/t.* (h) a) (make) sour, b) leaven

'Sau·er·rahm *m* sour cream

'Sau·er·stoff *m* (-[e]s; *no pl.*) ⚗ oxygen; **≈arm** *adj.* low in oxygen; rarefied *air*; **~fla·sche** *f* oxygen cylinder; **~ge·rät** *n* oxygen apparatus

'sau·er·stoff·hal·tig [-haltɪç] *adj.* oxygenous

'Sau·er·stoff|man·gel *m* oxygen starvation, ⚕ *a.* anox(a)emia; **~mas·ke** *f* oxygen mask; **~schuld** *f sport*: oxygen debt; **~zelt** *n* oxygen tent; **~zu·fuhr** *f* oxygen supply

'Sau·er·teig *m* sour dough, leaven

'Sau·er·topf F *m* F sourpuss

'sau·er·töp·fisch [-tœpfɪʃ] F *adj.* F grumpy

Säue·rung ['zɔʏərʊŋ] *f* (-; *no pl.*) leavening

Sauf·bru·der ['zauf-] F *m* **1.** → ***Säufer***; **2.** F drinking mate; **sau·fen** ['zaufən] *v/t. and v/i.* (soff, gesoffen, h) a) *zo.* drink, b) V *person*: F booze; F guzzle; **~ *wie ein Loch*** drink like a fish; **Säu·fer** ['zɔʏfɐ] *sl. m* (-s; -) F boozer, *sl.* dipso; **Sau·fe·rei** [zaufə'raɪ] F *f* (-; -en) F boozing; **Säu·ferin** ['zɔʏfərɪn] *f* (-; -nen) → ***Säufer***

'Säu·fer|le·ber F *f* hobnail liver; **~na·se** F *f* drinker's nose; **~stim·me** F *f* F boozy voice

Sauf|ge·la·ge ['zauf-] *sl. n* drinking bout, F booze-up, soak; **~kum,pan** *sl. m* F drinking mate

'Sau'fraß *sl. m* F muck

Sauf·tour ['zauf-] V *f sl.* binge

Saug·bag·ger ['zauk-] *m* suction dredge(r)

sau·gen ['zaugən] (h) **I.** *v/i.* **1.** (*a.* sog, gesogen, h) suck (***an*** *dat.* [at] *s.th.*); *baby*: *a.* suckle (at); **2.** vacuum, do the vacuuming; *der neue Staubsauger* ***saugt gut*** (***schlecht***) picks up the dirt well (doesn't pick up the dirt properly); **II.** *v/t.* **3.** (*a.* sog, gesogen, h) suck; *roots etc.*: absorb (***aus*** *dat.* from), draw (out of); → ***Finger***; **4.** vacuum; pick up; **III.** *v/refl.* (*a.* sog, gesogen, h): ***sich voll Wasser*** *etc.* **~** soak up as much water *etc.* as it can

säu·gen ['zɔʏgən] *v/t.* (h) nurse, breastfeed

Sau·ger ['zaugɐ] *m* (-s; -) **1.** a) dummy, *Am.* pacifier, b) teat, *Am.* nipple; **2.** ⚙ suction apparatus; **3.** → ***Staubsauger***

Säu·ger ['zɔʏgɐ] *m* (-s; -), **Säu·ge·tier** ['zɔʏgə-] *n* mammal

saug·fä·hig ['zauk-] *adj.* absorbent; **'Saug·fä·hig·keit** *f* (-; *no pl.*) absorptive capacity

Saug|fla·sche ['zauk-] *f* feeding bottle; **~glocke** *f* ⚙ suction bell; ⚕ vacuum extractor; **~ha·ken** *m* suction hook; **~he·ber** *m* siphon

Säug·ling ['zɔʏklɪŋ] *m* (-s; -e) baby, *formal*: infant

'Säug·lings|al·ter *n* infancy; ***im ~*** in infancy, at a very young age, in the first few months; **~nah·rung** *f* baby food(s *pl.*); **~pfle·ge** *f* baby care; **~schwe·ster** *f* baby nurse; **~sta·ti,on** *f* neonatal care unit; **~sterb·lich·keit** *f* infant mortality

Saug|napf ['zauk-] *m zo.* sucker; **~re,flex** *m* sucking instinct

'sau'grob F *adj.* F bloody rude (*or* rough)

Saug|rohr ['zauk-] *n* suction pipe; **~rüs·sel** *m zo.* proboscis; **~wir·kung** *f* sucking action

'Sau·hau·fen V *contp. m* F bunch of no-goods

'Sau·igel V *m sl.* dirty swine; **'sau·igeln** V *v/i.* (h) talk smut

säu·isch ['zɔʏɪʃ] F *adj.* dirty, filthy

'sau'kalt F *adj.* F bloody cold

'Sau·kerl V *m sl.* swine, bastard

Säu·le ['zɔʏlə] *f* (-; -n) **1.** column; *a. fig.* pillar; **2.** *mot.* pump

'Säu·len|dia,gramm *n statistics*: bar chart; **~gang** *m* colonnade; **~hal·le** *f* columned hall; portico; **~hei·li·ge** *m* stylite, pillar saint; **~kak·tus** *m* ♣ candelabra cactus; **~ka·pi,tell** *n* capital (of a *or* the pillar); **~ord·nung** *f* (columnal) order; ***korinthische*** *etc.* **~** Corinthian *etc.* order; **~tem·pel** *m* colonnaded temple; **~vor·bau** *m* portico

Sau·lus ['zaulʊs] *m bibl.* Saul; *fig.* ***vom ~ zum Paulus werden*** undergo a Damascus (*or* Pauline) conversion

Saum [zaum] *m* (-[e]s; Säume ['zɔʏmə]) hem; seam; *a. fig.* border, edge

'sau·mä·ßig F **I.** *adj.* F damned *cold etc.*; *sl.* lousy; ***er hatte ~es Pech*** F he was damned (*or* bloody) unlucky; **II.** *adv. sl.* lousily; ***er singt ~*** he's a lousy singer

säu·men¹ ['zɔʏmən] *v/t.* (h) hem; *fig.* line, skirt

'säu·men² *lit. v/i.* (h) *lit.* tarry

säu·mig ['zɔʏmɪç] *adj.* late, tardy; **~er *Zahler*** defaulter

Säum·nis·zu·schlag ['zɔʏmnɪs-] *m* extra charge (for late payment)

'Saum|pfad *m* mule track; **~pferd** *n* packhorse

'saum·se·lig *adj.* slow, sluggish; dawdling; dilatory; negligent; slack

'Saum·tier *n* pack animal

Sau·na ['zauna] *f* (-; -s; Saunen ['zaunən]) sauna; ***in die ~ gehen*** have (*or* go for) a sauna

Säu·re ['zɔʏrə] *f* (-; -n) **1.** *no pl.* a) sourness, *a.* ⚕ acidity, b) *fig.* acrimony; **2.** ⚗ acid; **~at·ten·tä·ter** *m* acid thrower; **~bad** *n* acid bath

'säu·re|be·stän·dig, ~fest *adj.* acid-resistant, acid-proof; **~frei** *adj.* non-acid

'Säu·re|ge·halt *m*, **~grad** *m* acidity

Sau·re'gur·ken·zeit [zaurə-] F *f* off season; silly season

'säu·re·hal·tig [-haltɪç] *adj.* acid, acidic

'Säu·re·man·tel *m* acid layer *of the skin*

Sau·res ['zaurəs] *n*: F ***gib ihm ~!*** F let him have it!, *sl.* sock it to him!

Sau·ri·er ['zaurĭɐ] *m* (-s; -) saurian

Saus [zaus] *m*: ***in ~ und Braus leben*** live on (*or* off) the fat of the land

Sau·se ['zauzə] F *f* (-; -n) F pub crawl; F booze-up; ***e-e ~ machen*** a) go on a pub crawl, b) have a booze-up

säu·seln ['zɔʏzəln] (h) **I.** *v/i. leaves*: rustle, *wind*: murmur, whisper; **II.** *v/t.* murmur

sau·sen ['zauzən] *v/i.* **1.** (h) *wind*: whistle, howl; **2.** (sn) *bullet etc.*: whistle, whiz; **3.** (sn) rush, whiz; **4.** (sn) F ***durch e-e Prüfung ~*** fail (F flunk) an exam; **~las·sen** F *v/t.* (*irr.*, *sep.*, h, → ***lassen***) pass up; give *s.th.* a miss; drop *s.o.*

'Sau|stall *m* **1.** pigsty (*a.* F *fig. room*); **2.** *no pl.* F *fig.* absolute mess, *a* (F bloody) shambles; F *fig.* ***das ist ja ein ~ hier!*** this place is like a pigsty (*or* is an absolute mess, a shambles); **~wet·ter** F *n* filthy (F bloody awful) weather; **~wirt·schaft** F *f* complete chaos, *a* shambles

'sau'wohl F *adv.*: ***ich fühle mich ~*** F I feel really great

Sa·van·ne [za'vanə] *f* (-; -n) savanna(h)

Sa·xo·phon [zakso'fo:n] *n* (-s; -e) saxophone; **Sa·xo·pho·nist** [zaksofo'nɪst] *m* (-en; -en) saxophonist, sax(ophone) player

S-Bahn ['ɛs-] *f* **1.** suburban train, *Am.* rapid transit; **2.** suburban railway, *Am.* rapid transit; **'S-Bahn·hof** *m*, **'S-Bahn--Sta·ti͵on** *f* suburban train (*Am.* rapid transit) station
SB|-La·den [ɛs'be:-] *m* **1.** self-service shop (*Am.* store); **2.** → **~-Markt** *m* (small) supermarket; **~-Tank·stel·le** *f* self-service petrol (*Am.* gas) station
scan·nen ['skɛnən] *v/t.* (h) *computer*: scan; **Scan·ner** ['skɛnɐ] *m* (-s; -) scanner
sch [ʃ] *int.* ssh!, shush!
Scha·be ['ʃa:bə] *f* (-; -n) *zo.* cockroach, *Am.* roach
Scha·be·fleisch ['ʃa:bə-] *n* minced (*Am.* ground) meat, hamburger
scha·ben ['ʃa:bən] *v/t.* (h) scrape (*a.* ⚙); grate, rasp; scratch; shave *skins*
Scha·ber ['ʃa:bɐ] *m* (-s; -) *mot.* scraper
Scha·ber·nack ['ʃa:bɐnak] *m* (-s; *no pl.*) practical joke, prank(s *pl.*); ~ ***treiben*** play pranks, get up to nonsense
schä·big ['ʃɛ:bɪç] *adj.* **1.** shabby, tatty; wretched, miserable; sleazy; **2.** F a) mean, stingy, b) mean, F pathetic *tip etc.*; **3.** mean, rotten, shabby
Schab·kunst ['ʃa:p-] *f* (-; *no pl.*) mezzotint
Scha·blo·ne [ʃa'blo:nə] *f* (-; -n) **1.** stencil; ⚙ template; **2.** *fig.* a) cliché, b) set pattern, fixed routine; ***j-n in e-e ~ pressen*** pigeonhole s.o.
Scha'blo·nen·den·ken *fig. n* stereotyped thinking
scha'blo·nen·haft, scha'blo·nen·mä·ßig *adj.* stereotyped; mechanical; *only attr.* routine(ly *adv.*)
Scha'blo·nen·zeich·nung *f* stencil drawing
Schab·mes·ser ['ʃa:p-] *n* scraping knife
Scha·bracke [ʃa'brakə] (*sep.* -k·k-) *f* (-; -n) **1.** saddle cloth; **2.** pelmet, *Am.* valance
Schach [ʃax] *n* (-s; *no pl.*) **1.** chess; **2.** check; **~!** check!; ~ ***und matt!*** checkmate!; ***j-m ~ bieten*** check s.o., *fig.* make a stand against s.o.; ***in ~ halten*** hold in check (*a. fig.*), *fig. a.* cover *s.o. with a gun*; **3.** → ***Schachspiel*; ~auf·ga·be** *f* chess problem; **~brett** *n* chessboard
'schach·brett·ar·tig I. *adj.* chequered, *Am.* checkered; **II.** *adv.*: ~ ***angelegt*** set out (*or* arranged) like a chessboard
'Schach·brett·mu·ster *n* chequered (*Am.* checkered) pattern; ***im ~*** chequered, *Am.* checkered
'Schach·com͵pu·ter *m* chess computer
Scha·cher ['ʃaxɐ] *contp. m* (-s; *no pl.*), **Scha·che·rei** [ʃaxə'raɪ] F *contp. f* (-; -en) haggling; *esp. pol.* horse trading
'scha·chern *contp. v/i.* (h) haggle (***um*** *acc.* about, over); ~ ***mit*** *dat.* trade *s.th.*
'Schach|fi͵gur *f* chessman, piece; *fig.* pawn; **~groß·mei·ster** *m* chess grandmaster
schach'matt *adj.* (check)mate; *fig.* exhausted, F dead beat; ~ ***setzen*** *a. fig.* checkmate
'Schach|mei·ster *m* chess champion; **~mei·ster·schaft** *f* chess tournament (*or* championship[s *pl.*]); **~par͵tie** *f* game of chess; **~spiel** *n* **1.** *no pl.* (game of) chess; **2.** chess set
Schacht [ʃaxt] *m* (-[e]s; Schächte ['ʃɛçtə]) shaft, ⚒ *a.* pit; manhole
Schach·tel ['ʃaxtəl] *f* (-; -n) box; carton, cardboard box; shoebox; bandbox; packet, *Am.* pack *of cigarettes*; F *fig.* ***alte ~*** F old crow; **~halm** *m* ⚘ horsetail; **~satz** *m ling.* involved period
'Schach|tur͵nier *n* chess tournament; **~uhr** *f* chess clock; **~welt·mei·ster** *m* world chess champion; **~welt·mei·ster·schaft** *f* world chess championships *pl.*; **~zug** *m* move; ***geschickter ~*** *a. fig.* clever move (*or* gambit)
scha·de ['ʃa:də] *pred. adj.*: (***es ist sehr***) ~ it's a (great *or* real) pity, F (it's) too bad; ***wie ~*** what a pity (*or* shame); ***es ist ~ drum*** it's (such) a shame *or* waste; ***~, daß du schon gehen mußt*** (it's a) pity you have to go so soon, *a.* can't you stay a bit longer?; ***dafür ist es*** (***er***) ***zu ~*** it's (he's) too good for that; ***es ist für ihn viel zu ~*** it'd be wasted on him; ***um das*** (***den***) ***ist's nicht ~*** it's (he's) no great loss; ***es ist ~ um ihn*** it's a (real) shame (with him); ***dafür ist er sich zu ~*** he thinks he's above that kind of thing; ***er ist sich für nichts zu ~*** he's not too proud for anything
'Scha·de *m* → ***Schaden***
Schä·del ['ʃɛ:dəl] *m* (-s; -) skull; F ***e-n dicken ~ haben*** be stubborn (as a mule); ***mir brummt der ~*** my head is spinning (*or* throbbing); F ***j-m eins über den ~ geben*** hit s.o. over the head; → ***einschlagen*** 2; **~(ba·sis)bruch** *m* ⚕ fracture of the (base of the) skull; **~decke** *f anat.* cranium; **~höh·le** *f* cranial cavity; **~kno·chen** *m* cranial bone
scha·den ['ʃa:dən] (h) **I.** *v/i.* (*dat.*) damage, harm (*a. reputation, relationship etc.*); be harmful to, *esp. physically, mentally etc.*: have a harmful effect on; be detrimental to; ***das schadet der Gesundheit*** it's bad for your health; ***es schadet mehr, als daß es nützt*** it does more harm than good; ***es kann doch nicht ~*** there's no harm in it, is there?, it won't do any harm, will it?; ***ein Versuch kann nicht ~*** there's no harm in trying; **II.** *v/t.*: ***das schadet nichts*** a) it doesn't do any harm, b) it doesn't matter; ***das schadet ihm nichts*** it won't do him any harm; ***das schadet ihm gar nichts*** it serves him right; ***es würde ihr*** (***gar***) ***nichts ~, wenn sie …*** it wouldn't do her any harm at all to *inf.*, it would do her good to *inf.*; ***was schadet es schon, wenn …*** what does it matter if …
Scha·den ['ʃa:dən] *m* (-s; Schäden ['ʃɛ:dən]) a) damage (***an*** *dat.* to), b) injury, harm, c) disadvantage; loss; defect; ~ ***nehmen*** be damaged, *person, health etc.*: suffer; ***e-n ~ am Knie haben*** have a damaged knee, *esp. after an accident*: have a knee injury; ***zu ~ kommen*** be hurt (*or* injured); ***nicht zu ~ kommen*** not to come to any harm; ***Personen kamen nicht zu ~*** nobody was injured; ***j-m ~ zufügen*** do s.o. harm; ***es soll dein ~ nicht sein*** it won't be to your disadvantage; ***wer den ~ hat, braucht für den Spott nicht zu sorgen*** the laugh's always on the loser; ***durch ~ wird man klug*** once bitten twice shy; F ***ab mit ~*** F good riddance
'Scha·den·er·satz *m* compensation, indemnification; damages *pl.*; ~ ***fordern*** (***leisten, erhalten***) claim (pay, recover) damages; ***auf ~*** (***ver***)***klagen*** sue for damages; **~an·spruch** *m*, **~for·de·rung** *f* claim for damages; **~kla·ge** *f* action for damages; **~lei·stung** *f* compensation
'scha·den·er·satz·pflich·tig [-pflɪçtɪç] *adj.* liable for damages
'Scha·den|fest·stel·lung *f* assessment of damage; **~frei·heits·ra͵batt** *m* no-claim bonus; **~freu·de** *f* (-; *no pl.*) malicious glee, gloating, schadenfreude; **≈froh** *adj.* gloating(ly *adv.*); **~mel·dung** *f* claim
'Scha·dens|be·gren·zung *f* damage limitation; **~fall** *m* claim
'Scha·den·ver·si·che·rung *f* indemnity insurance
schad·haft ['ʃa:thaft] *adj.* a) damaged, b) defective, faulty; *building*: out of repair; leaking *pipes etc.*; decayed *teeth*
schä·di·gen ['ʃɛ:dɪgən] *v/t.* (h) damage, impair (*a. fig.*); harm *s.o.*
'Schä·di·gung *f* (-; -en) damage (*gen.* to), impairment (of), injury (to)
schäd·lich ['ʃɛ:tlɪç] *adj.* harmful, injurious (*dat. or* ***für*** *acc.* to); detrimental (to); bad (for); harmful, noxious *substance, gas etc.*; ***es ist ~ für die Gesundheit*** it's harmful to your health, it's a health hazard
Schäd·ling ['ʃɛ:tlɪŋ] *m* (-s; -e) pest; ⚘ *a.* destructive weed
'Schäd·lings|be·kämp·fung *f* pest control; **~be·kämp·fungs·mit·tel** *n* pesticide
schad·los ['ʃa:tlo:s] *adj.*: ***sich ~ halten*** recoup o.s. (***für*** *acc.* for), ***an*** *dat.*: recoup one's losses from *s.o.*, F make up for it with *s.th.*
Schad·stoff ['ʃa:t-] *m* harmful (*or* noxious) substance, pollutant; **≈arm** *adj.* low-emission, F clean *car*; **~aus·stoß** *m* → ***Schadstoffemission*; ~be·la·stung** *f* pollution level; **~emis·si͵on** *f* noxious emission; *mot.* car emission; **≈frei** *adj.* emission-free; **~nor·men** *pl.*, **~richt·li·ni·en** *pl.* emission standards
Schaf [ʃa:f] *n* (-[e]s; -e) sheep (*a. pl.*); F *fig.* F twit; *fig.* ***schwarzes ~*** black sheep ([***in***] ***der Familie*** of the family); **~bock** *m* ram
Schäf·chen ['ʃɛ:fçən] *n* (-s; -) **1.** lamb; F *fig.* F silly billy; *fig.* ~ ***zählen*** count sheep; ***sein ~ ins trockene bringen*** feather one's nest; **2.** *pl.* → **~wol·ken** *pl.* fleecy (*or* cotton-wool) clouds
'Schäf·chen·wol·ken *pl.* fleecy (*or* cotton-wool) clouds
Schä·fer ['ʃɛ:fɐ] *m* (-s; -) shepherd; **~hund** *m* a) sheepdog, b) Alsatian, German shepherd (dog)
Schä·fe·rin ['ʃɛ:fərɪn] *f* (-; -nen) shepherdess
'Schä·fer·stünd·chen *n* (lovers') tryst
'Schaf·fell *n* sheepskin
schaf·fen[1] ['ʃafən] *v/t.* (schuf, geschaffen, h) create; ***sich Freunde*** (***Feinde***) ~ make friends (enemies); ***er ist zum Lehrer wie geschaffen*** he's a born teacher, he's made to be a teacher; ***er ist für den Posten wie geschaffen*** he's perfect (*or* cut out) for the job
'schaf·fen[2] (h) **I.** *v/t.* **1.** a) create, b) cause *trouble, unrest etc.*, give *s.o. trouble etc.*; ***Ordnung ~*** sort things out, *esp. pol.* establish (some sort of) order; ***Ruhe ~*** get things under control; ***Rat ~*** find a way (out); ***Linderung ~*** bring relief; ***Klarheit ~*** clarify the situation, set the record straight; ***e-n neuen Rekord ~*** set up a new record; ***Platz für j-n ~*** make room for s.o.; **2.** ***ich habe damit nichts zu ~*** I've got nothing to do with it, I wash my hands of it; ***mit ihm will ich nichts zu ~ haben*** I don't want anything to do with him; **3.** take, put;

wie ~ wir das Bett nach oben? how will we get the bed upstairs?; → ***Hals, Weg, Welt***; **4.** manage, *ped.* do *one's homework etc.*; pass *an examination*; ***viel ~*** (manage to) get a lot done; F ***es ~*** F make (*or* do) it; ***das wäre geschafft!*** a) done it!, that's that!, b) made it!; ***et. zeitlich ~*** get s.th. done in time; ***et. geldlich ~*** have the money for s.th.; ***ich schaffe das Essen nicht mehr*** I can't eat any more; ***er schafft es einfach nicht, pünktlich zu sein*** he just can't bring himself to be punctual; ***das hat noch keiner geschafft*** a) that was brilliant, b) that's a new one, c) that's unbeatable, that must be a record; ***ihn schaffst du spielend*** he's no match for you, F you can beat him with your hands tied behind your back; **5.** F ***j-n ~*** take it out of s.o.; get s.o. down; **II.** *v/i.* **6.** be active, work (hard); **7.** *esp. dial.* work; **8.** ***sich zu ~ machen*** potter about, ***an*** *dat.*: busy o.s. with, tinker about with, *b.s. a.* tamper with; ***was habt ihr dort zu ~?*** what d'you think you're doing (*or* you're up to) there?; **9.** ***j-m (schwer) zu ~ machen*** give s.o. a hard time, F play s.o. up; **III.** ≈ *n* (-s; *no pl.*) work(s *pl.*); ***sein künstlerisches ~*** his artistic work, his (works of) art; ***frohes ~!*** good luck, *iro.* don't work too hard; **'schaf·fend** *adj.*: ***der ~e Mensch*** creative man; ***der ~e Geist*** the creative spirit (*or* mind)

'Schaf·fens|drang *m* creative urge; (great) urge to do s.th.; **~kraft** *f* (-; *no pl.*) **1.** creative power; **2.** energy and drive; **~pe·rio·de** *f* artistic period; **~pro͵zeß** *m* creative process

'Schaf·fleisch *n* mutton; ✝ sheepmeat

Schaff·ner ['ʃafnɐ] *m* (-s; -) conductor, 🚂 *Brit. usu.* guard; **Schaff·ne·rin** ['ʃafnərɪn] *f* (-; -nen) conductress

Schaf·fung ['ʃafʊŋ] *f* (-; *no pl.*) creation

'Schaf|gar·be *f* (-; *no pl.*) ⚘ yarrow; **~her·de** *f* flock of sheep; **~hirt** *m* shepherd; **~hür·de** *f* sheepfold, sheepcote; **~le·der** *n* sheepskin

Schäf·lein ['ʃɛːflaɪn] *n* (-s; -) **1.** → ***Schäfchen***; **2.** *pl. fig.* sheep, flock *sg.*

Scha·fott [ʃa'fɔt] *n* (-[e]s; -e) scaffold; ***j-n aufs ~ bringen*** bring s.o. to the scaffold

'Schaf|pferch *m* sheepfold, sheepcote; **~schur** *f* sheepshearing

'Schaf(s)·kä·se *m* sheep's milk cheese, feta cheese

'Schafs·kopf F *fig. m* F blockhead, numskull

'Schaf(s)|milch *f* sheep's milk; **~pelz** *m* sheepskin; *fig.* ***Wolf im ~*** wolf in sheep's clothing

'Schaf·stall *m* sheep shed

Schaft [ʃaft] *m* (-[e]s; Schäfte ['ʃɛftə]) shaft; stock *of a rifle*; leg *of a boot*; ⚘ stalk; **~stie·fel** *pl.* high boots

'Schaf|wei·de *f* sheep pasture; **~wol·le** *f* sheep's wool; **~zucht** *f* sheep farming

Schah [ʃaː] *m* (-s; -s) *hist.* Shah

Scha·kal [ʃa'kaːl] *m* (-s; -e) jackal

Schä·kel ['ʃɛːkəl] *m* (-s; -) ⚙, ⚓ shackle

schä·kern ['ʃɛːkɐn] *v/i.* (h) joke around; flirt

schal [ʃaːl] *adj.* flat *drink*; *fig.* stale; dull, boring

Schal [ʃaːl] *m* (-s; -s, -e) scarf

Schäl·chen ['ʃɛːlçən] *n* (-s; -) (little *or* small) bowl; dessert bowl

Scha·le¹ ['ʃaːlə] *f* (-; -n) shell *of egg, nut etc.*; skin, peel *of apple, potato etc.*, *pl.* peelings; husk; F ***sich in ~ werfen*** (*or* ***schmeißen***) dress up, put on one's finery; *fig.* ***er hat e-e rauhe ~*** he's a rough diamond

'Scha·le² *f* (-; -n) a) bowl; dish, b) (scale)-pan

schä·len ['ʃɛːlən] (h) **I.** *v/t.* peel *potatoes, apples etc.*; shell *peas etc.*; skin *tomatoes*; bark *trees*; **II.** *v/refl.*: **sich ~** *trees*: exfoliate; *skin, paint etc.*: peel (off); ***ich schäl' mich auf dem Rücken*** my back is peeling; ***sich aus der Kleidung ~*** peel off (one's clothes)

'Scha·len|bau(wei·se *f*) *m* ⚙ monocoque (⚠ shell) construction; **~obst** *n* nuts *pl.*; 🕮 indehiscent fruit; **~sitz** *m mot.* bucket seat; **~tier** *n* crustacean

Schalk [ʃalk] *m* (-[e]s; -e) rogue, rascal; ***er hat den ~ im Nacken*** he's always up to tricks; ***ihm schaut der ~ aus den Augen*** he's always got a (mischievous) twinkle in his eye

'schalk·haft *adj.* mischievous

Schall [ʃal] *m* (-[e]s; *no pl.*) sound; ringing, peal *of bells*; echo; ***Name ist ~ und Rauch*** what's in a name?

'schall·ab·sor͵bie·rend *adj.* → ***schalldämpfend***

'Schall|auf·zeich·nung *f* sound recording; **~be·cher** *m* ♪ bell; **~bo·den** *m* ♪ soundboard; **~däm·mung** *f* → ***Schalldämpfung***; **≈dämp·fend I.** *adj.* sound-absorbing; **II.** *adv.*: ***~ wirken*** act as a sound absorber; **~dämp·fer** *m* sound absorber; *mot.* silencer, *Am.* muffler; silencer *of a gun*; ♪ → ***Dämpfer***; **~dämp·fung** *f* sound damping (*or* absorption); ⚠ soundproofing, sound insulation

'schall·dicht *adj.* soundproof (*a. v/t.* ***~ machen***)

'Schall·druck *m* (-[e]s; *no pl.*) sound pressure

'Schallei·ter (*sep.* -ll·l-) *m* sound conductor

schal·len ['ʃalən] *v/i.* (h) resound; ring; boom; **'schal·lend I.** *adj.* resounding; ***~es Gelächter*** loud laughter, peals (*or* hoots) of laughter; ***~e Ohrfeige*** good box on the ears, *fig.* slap in the face; **II.** *adv.*: ***~ lachen*** roar with laughter

'Schall|ge·schwin·dig·keit *f* speed of sound; **~gren·ze** *f* → ***Schallmauer***

'schall·iso͵liert *adj.* soundproof

'Schall|mau·er *f*: (***die ~ durchbrechen*** break the) soundbarrier; **~mes·sung** *f* ⚔ sound ranging; *phys.* sound level measurement; **~pe·gel** *m* noise level

'Schall·plat·te *f* record

'Schall·plat·ten|ar͵chiv *n* record archives *pl.*; **~auf·nah·me** *f* (gramophone) recording; **~ge·schäft** *n* **1.** record shop; **2.** ✝ record business; **~in·du͵strie** *f* record industry; **~pro·duk·ti͵on** *f* **1.** recording; **2.** record production, making records; **~stän·der** *m* record rack; **~ver·trag** *m* recording contract

'schall·schluckend *adj.* sound-absorbing

'Schall|trich·ter *m* **1.** *loudspeaker*: cone; **2.** ♪ bell; **~wand** *f* baffle (board); **~wel·le** *f* sound wave

Schal·mei [ʃal'maɪ] *f* (-; -en) ♪ shawm

Scha·lot·te [ʃa'lɔtə] *f* (-; -n) ⚘ shallot

schalt [ʃalt] *pret. of* ***schelten***

Schalt|an·la·ge ['ʃalt-] *f* switchgear; **~bild** *n* ⚡ circuit diagram; *mot.* gear-changing (*Am.* gearshifting) diagram; **~brett** *n* ⚡ switchboard, control panel; ✈ instrument panel, *mot a.* dashboard

schal·ten ['ʃaltən] (h) **I.** *v/i.* **1.** ⚙, ⚡ switch (***auf*** *acc.* to); shift the lever(s); *mot.* change (*or* shift) gears; ***auf Grün*** *etc.* **~** *traffic light*: turn (*or* change to) green *etc.*; ⚡ ***in Reihe*** (***parallel***) **~** connect in series (in parallel); **~ *zu*** *dat. TV, radio*: switch (*or* go) over to; **2.** F *fig.* get the picture, catch on, F click; ***ich hab' zu langsam*** (*or* ***spät***) ***geschaltet*** I was too slow, I didn't react quick(ly) enough; ***langsam ~*** be slow on the uptake; **3.** act; ***frei ~ und walten können*** be able to do as one likes (*or* pleases); ***j-n ~ und walten lassen*** give s.o. a free hand; **II.** *v/t.* **4.** ⚙ switch, turn; operate; control; *mot.* change, shift *gears*; start *engine*; shift *lever*; (dis)engage *clutch*; ⚡ switch, wire; connect; → ***anschalten, ausschalten***

Schal·ter¹ ['ʃaltɐ] *m* (-s; -) ⚡, ⚙, *mot.* switch; ⚡ cutout

'Schal·ter² *m* (-s; -) *post office, bank etc.*: counter; ✈ desk; 🚂 ticket window; **~be·am·te** *m* counter clerk; man at the counter; 🚂 booking clerk; **~dienst** *m* counter duty; **~hal·le** *f* (main) hall; **~schluß** *m* (-sses; *no pl.*) closing time; ***~ ist um drei*** banks close (*or* the bank closes) at three; **~stun·den** *pl.* business hours

'schalt|faul *adj. mot.* slow to change gears; **~freu·dig** *adj. mot.* quick to change gears

'Schalt|ge·spräch *n* hook-up, link-up; **~he·bel** *m mot.* gear stick, gearshift; ⚙, ✈ control lever; ⚡ switch lever; *fig.* ***an den ~n der Macht sitzen*** hold the reins of power, be sitting at the controls; **~jahr** *n* leap year; **~ka·sten** *m* ⚡ switchbox; **~knüp·pel** *m mot.* gear lever, gearshift, stick shift; **~kreis** *m* ⚡ circuit; **~pau·se** *f* intermission; **~plan** *m* ⚡ circuit diagram; **~pult** *n* control desk; **~stel·le** *f pol.* powerhouse; **~ta·fel** *f* → ***Schaltbrett***; **~tag** *m* intercalary day; **~uhr** *f* timer

Schal·tung ['ʃaltʊŋ] *f* (-; -en) **1.** *mot.* a) gearshift assembly, b) gear change, gearshift; **2.** ⚡ circuitry, connection(s *pl.*), wiring

'Schalt·zen͵tra·le *f* control centre (*Am.* center); *fig.* nerve centre (*Am.* center); *pol.* powerhouse

Scha·lup·pe [ʃa'lʊpə] *f* (-; -n) ⚓ sloop

Schal·wild ['ʃaːl-] *n* hoofed game

Scham [ʃaːm] *f* (-; *no pl.*) **1.** shame; ***keine ~ haben*** have no (sense of) shame; ***voller ~ über et. sein*** be filled with shame at s.th.; ***nur keine falsche ~!*** no need to pretend you're shy, no need to hold back; ***vor ~ erröten*** blush (*or* go red) with shame; **2.** *anat.* genitals *pl.*, private parts *pl.*; ***s-e ~ bedecken*** *a. lit.* cover *or* hide one's shame (*or* nakedness)

Scha·ma·ne [ʃa'maːnə] *m* (-n; -n) shaman; **Scha·ma·nis·mus** [ʃama'nɪsmʊs] *m* (-; *no pl.*) shamanism; **scha·ma·ni·stisch** [ʃama'nɪstɪʃ] *adj.* shamanistic

'Scham|bein *n anat.* pubic bone; **~berg** *m* → ***Schamhügel***

schä·men ['ʃɛːmən] *v/refl.*: **sich ~** be *or* feel ashamed (of o.s.); ***sich ~ wegen*** *gen. or* ***für*** *acc.* be ashamed of (having done) s.th.; ***du solltest dich*** (***was***) ***~!*** you ought to be ashamed of yourself; ***schäm dich!, schämt euch!*** shame on you!; ***er schämt sich nicht zu*** *inf.* he's not ashamed to *inf.*, he has no qualms about *ger.*; ***er schämt sich nicht, es zuzugeben*** he's not ashamed to admit it, he admits it quite openly

'Scham|frist *f* period of grace; **~ge·fühl** *n* (-[e]s; *no pl.*) sense of shame; (sense of) modesty; ***j-s ~ verletzen*** offend s.o.'s sense of decency; **~ge·gend** *f* pubic region; **~haa·re** *pl.* pubic hair *sg.*

'scham·haft I. *adj.* bashful, blushing *girl etc.*; prudish; **II.** *adv.*: ***~ erröten*** blush with shame; *iro.* ***das verschweigst du jetzt ~*** you're keeping very quiet about that (now); **'Scham·haf·tig·keit** *f* (-; *no pl.*) bashfulness; prudishness

'Scham|hü·gel *m anat.* mons veneris; mons pubis; **~lip·pen** *pl. anat.* labia, lips of the vulva

'scham·los *adj.* a) shameless, b) indecent, c) brazen *insult etc.*, barefaced *lie*

Scha·mott [ʃa'mɔt] F *m* (-[e]s; *no pl.*) F junk

Scha·mot·te [ʃa'mɔtə] *f* (-; *no pl.*) fireclay

Scham·pon ['ʃampɔn] *n* (-s; -s), **scham·po·nie·ren** [ʃampo'niːrən] *v/t.* (h) shampoo

Scham·pus ['ʃampʊs] F *m* (-; *no pl.*) F champers, bubbly

'scham·rot *adj.* red with shame (*or* embarrassment); ***~ werden*** blush (with shame), go (very) red (with shame), colo(u)r up; **'Scham·rö·te** *f*: ***die ~ stieg ihm ins Gesicht*** he blushed with shame (*or* embarrassment)

Schan·de ['ʃandə] *f* (-; *no pl.*) disgrace; shame; ***~ machen*** *dat.* be a disgrace to, bring shame on; F ***mach uns keine ~!*** F try not to disgrace us (*or* the family name); ***zu m-r ~ muß ich gestehen*** I'm ashamed to admit; ***zu ihrer ~ muß gesagt werden, daß sie ...*** I'm afraid to admit (*or* to have to say) that she ...; ***es ist e-e ~, wie soviel Papier einfach weggeworfen wird*** it's a disgrace (*or* it's scandalous) to see all that paper just being thrown away

schän·den ['ʃɛndən] *v/t.* (h) **1.** disgrace, dishono(u)r, bring dishono(u)r upon; **2.** desecrate, defile; **3.** *obs.* violate, abuse

Schand·fleck ['ʃant-] *m* a) stain, blot, b) eyesore, c) (architectural) eyesore, carbuncle; ***ein ~ auf s-r Ehre*** *a. hum.* a blot on his escutcheon (*or* in his copybook); ***er ist der ~ der Familie*** he's the black sheep of the family, he's a disgrace to his family; ***ein ~ in der Landschaft*** a blot on the landscape

schänd·lich ['ʃɛntlɪç] *adj.* shameful, disgraceful (*a.* F *fig.*); ignominious; scandalous; ***ein ~er Lohn*** a pittance (of a wage); ***es ist ~, wie*** *a.* it's a disgrace how (*or* to see)

Schand|mal ['ʃant-] *n* → ***Schandfleck***; **~maul** *n* **1.** wicked (*or* malicious) tongue; **2.** wicked (*or* malicious) gossip, slanderer; **~tat** *f* evil deed; F ***er ist zu jeder ~ bereit*** F he's good for a lark

Schän·dung ['ʃɛndʊŋ] *f* (-; -en) **1.** disgrace (*gen.* to); **2.** desecration, defilement (*gen.* of); **3.** *obs.* abuse, violation (*gen.* of)

Schank|er·laub·nis ['ʃaŋk-] *f*, **~kon·zes·si̦on** *f* licen|ce (*Am.* -se) (to sell alcoholic drinks); **~raum** *m*, **~stu·be** *f* (public) bar; **~tisch** *m* bar

Schan·ze ['ʃantsə] *f* (-; -n) **1.** ski jump; **2.** ⚔ entrenchment; **'Schan·zen·re̦kord** *m sport:* hill record

Schar [ʃaːɐ] *f* (-; -en ['ʃaːrən]) (great) crowd, swarms *pl. of people*; flock *of birds*, covey *of partridges*; bevy (*a. fig. of girls etc.*); army *of ants*; host *of angels*; ***e-e ~ von Kindern*** *etc. a.* hordes of children *etc.*; ***in (hellen) ~en*** in droves; ***die Rockfans kamen in ~en an*** *a.* hundreds (*or* thousands) of rock fans flocked there, rock fans came in their hundreds (*or* thousands)

scha·ren ['ʃaːrən] (h) **I.** *v/t.*: ***um sich ~*** rally (round one); **II.** *v/refl.*: ***sich ~*** assemble, rally; ***sich ~ um*** *acc.* crowd round, rally round *s.o.*

'scha·ren·wei·se *adv.* in droves *etc.*; → ***Schar***

scharf [ʃarf] **I.** *adj.* a) sharp (*a. fig.*), b) hot *mustard etc.*, spicy, highly seasoned *food*; strong *alcohol, vinegar etc.*, c) acrid, pungent *smell*; caustic; aggressive *acid etc.*; piercing, shrill *sound etc.*, c) live *munition*, d) abrupt, sharp *descent etc.*, e) *fig.* clear, f) *fig.* severe; hard, g) F randy (*sl.*); ***~es Auge, ~er Blick*** sharp (*or* keen) eye(s), keen eyesight; ***ein ~es Auge haben für*** *acc.* have an eye (*or* a good eye) for; ***~es Gehör*** sharp ears, keen sense of hearing; ***~er Beobachter*** keen observer; ***~e Bestrafung*** severe punishment; ***~er Gegensatz*** stark contrast; ***~er Gegner von*** *dat.* sworn enemy of; ***~e Gesichtszüge*** clear-cut features; ***~er Kampf*** hard fight; ***~e Konkurrenz*** stiff competition; ***~e Kritik*** sharp (*or* severe) criticism; ***~e Kurve*** sharp bend; ***~e Maßnahmen*** strict (*or* stringent) measures; ***~er Protest*** fierce (*or* sharp, vehement) protest; ***schärfsten Protest einlegen*** protest vehemently; ***~er Prüfer*** very strict (F tough) examiner; ***~er Ritt*** fast ride; ***~es Tempo*** hard (*or* sharp) pace; ***~e Umrisse*** clear (*or* sharp) outlines; ***~er Verstand*** keen (*or* incisive) mind; ***~er Wind*** biting (*or* cutting) wind; ***~e Zunge*** sharp tongue; ***die Luft ist ~*** there's a nip (*or* bite) in the air; F ***das ist vielleicht ein ~es Zeug*** it really burns your throat; F ***~e Klamotten (~es Auto)*** F snazzy clothes (car); F ***das ist ja ~*** *sl.* get a load of that; F ***~ sein auf*** *acc.* be keen on, F be wild about; F ***ganz ~ darauf sein zu*** *inf. sl.* be dead keen on *ger.* (*or* to *inf.*); → ***gestochen*** II; **II.** *adv.* sharply *etc.*; sharp; ***~ ablehnen*** flatly reject; ***~ anbraten*** fry to seal; ***~ bremsen*** brake hard, slam on the brakes; ***j-n ~ anfassen müssen*** have to be very strict with s.o.; ***~ bewachen*** keep a close guard (*fig.* watch, eye) on; ***~ aufpassen*** pay close attention; ***~ durchgreifen*** take tough action (***bei*** *dat.* against), ***bei*** *dat.*: *a.* clamp down on; *phot.* ***~ einstellen*** focus; ***~ formuliert*** sharply-worded; ***~ nachdenken*** think hard, have a good think; ***denkt mal ~ nach*** put your thinking caps on (for a minute); ***~ schießen*** shoot with live ammunition; *fig.* ***in der Diskussion wurde ~ geschossen*** there were some sharp exchanges during the discussion; ***~ sehen (hören)*** have sharp eyes (ears); ***~ verurteilen*** severely condemn; ***~ ins Auge fassen*** fix *s.o.* with one's eyes, *fig.* take a close look at *s.o. or s.th.*; ***~ nach rechts (links) gehen*** turn sharp right (left); ***~ rechts (links) fahren*** swerve *or* veer to the right (left); → ***schärfen, scharfmachen***

'Scharf·blick *m* (-[e]s; *no pl.*) perspicacity

'scharf·blickend *adj.* → ***scharfsichtig***

Schär·fe ['ʃɛrfə] *f* (-; *no pl.*) sharpness *etc.*; → ***scharf***; *opt.* definition; *fig.* keenness, acuity; stridency *of an argument etc.*; ***in aller ~*** in all strictness

'Scharf·ein·stel·lung *f* a) focus(s)ing, b) focus(s)ing control

schär·fen ['ʃɛrfən] (h) **I.** *v/t.* sharpen (*a. fig.*); **II.** *fig. v/refl.*: ***sich ~*** sharpen, become keener (*or* more acute)

'Schär·fen·tie·fe *f phot.* depth of field (*or* focus)

'scharf·kan·tig *adj.* sharp-edged

'scharf·ma·chen F *fig. v/t.* (*sep.*, h) **1.** ***~ gegen*** *acc.* set (*or* stir up) against; **2.** *sl.* turn *s.o.* on; **'Scharf·ma·cher** *m pol.* agitator, rabble-rouser, *pl. a.* ginger group *sg.*; **Scharf·ma·che·rei** [-maxə'raɪ] *f* (-; *no pl.*) agitation

'Scharf|rich·ter *m* executioner; **~schie·ßen** *n* ⚔ live shooting; **~schüt·ze** *m* marksman; ⚔ sniper

'scharf·sich·tig [-zɪçtɪç] *adj.* sharp-sighted; *fig.* perspicacious

'Scharf·sinn *m* (-[e]s; *no pl.*) astuteness, shrewdness; *esp. pol.*, ☿ acumen

'scharf·sin·nig *adj.* astute, shrewd

'scharf·um̦ris·sen *adj.* sharply defined; *fig.* clear-cut

'scharf·zün·gig [-tsʏŋɪç] *adj.* sharp-tongued

Schar·lach¹ ['ʃarlax] *m* (-s; *no pl.*) ⚕ scarlet fever

'Schar·lach² *m, n* (-s; *no pl.*) scarlet

'schar·lach·rot *adj.* scarlet

Schar·la·tan ['ʃarlataːn] *m* (-s; -e) charlatan, F fraud, F quack

Schar·müt·zel [ʃar'mʏtsəl] *n* (-s; -) ⚔ *and fig.* skirmish, brush

Schar·nier [ʃar'niːɐ] *n* (-s; -e [-rə]) hinge; **~ge·lenk** *n* hinge(d) joint

Schär·pe ['ʃɛrpə] *f* (-; -n) sash

schar·ren ['ʃarən] *v/t. and v/i.* (h) scrape (***mit den Füßen*** one's feet); scratch (*a. chicken, dog etc.*); *horse:* paw

Schar·te ['ʃartə] *f* (-; -n) **1.** notch, nick; *fig.* ***e-e ~ auswetzen*** make amends; **2.** → ***Schießscharte***

schar·wen·zeln [ʃar'vɛntsəln] *v/i.* (h) bow and scrape; ***um j-n ~*** dance attendance on s.o.

Schasch·lik ['ʃaʃlɪk] *m, n* (-s; -s) kebab

schas·sen ['ʃasən] F *v/t.* (h) kick (F boot) out

Schat·ten ['ʃatən] *m* (-s; -) **1.** *no pl.* shade; ***30 Grad im ~*** 30 degrees in the shade; ***~ spenden*** give (plenty of) shade; ***Licht und ~*** light and shade; ***im ~ stehen*** *a. fig.* be in the shade; ***in den ~ stellen*** put in(to) the shade, *fig. a.* outshine, eclipse, exceed *expectations etc.*; *fig.* ***ein ~ flog über sein Gesicht*** his face darkened; **2.** shadow; ***e-n ~ werfen*** cast a shadow (***auf*** *acc.* on) (*a. fig.*); *fig.* ***große Ereignisse werfen ihre ~ voraus*** great events cast their shadows before; ***nicht der ~ e-s Verdachts*** not the slightest (cause for) suspicion; ***in j-s ~ stehen*** live in s.o.'s shadow; ***e-m ~ nachjagen*** chase butterflies; ***sich vor s-m ~ fürchten*** be frightened of one's own shadow; ***über s-n ~ springen*** overcome o.s.; ***man kann nicht über s-n eigenen ~ springen*** the leopard can't change its spots; ***er ist nur noch ein ~ seiner selbst*** he's a (mere) shadow of his former self; ***die ~ der Vergangenheit*** the spectres (*Am.* specters) (*or* ghosts, shades) of the past; ***der ~ des Todes*** the shadow of death;

j-m wie ein ~ folgen follow s.o. (around) like a shadow; **3.** silhouette, (dark) shape; **4.** ⚕ shadow; **5.** *fig.* shadow; **6.** *fig.* shade; **~bild** *n* shadowgraph; **~bo·xen** *n* shadow-boxing; **~da·sein** *n*: ***ein ~ führen*** (*or* ***fristen***) live in the shadows
'**schat·ten·haft** *adj.* shadowy; *fig.* ***~e Erinnerung*** vague (*or* shadowy) recollection; ***~e Vorstellung*** vague idea
'**Schat·ten·ka·bi,nett** *n pol.* shadow cabinet
'**schat·ten·los** *adj.* without shade
'**Schat·ten|mo,rel·le** *f* morello; **~reich** *n myth.* realm of the shades; **~riß** *m* silhouette; **~sei·te** *f* shady side; *fig.* drawback; ***die ~ des Lebens*** the dark side of life
'**schat·ten·spen·dend** *adj.* shady
'**Schat·ten|spiel** *n* shadow play; **~stel·le** *f radio*: blind spot; **~wirt·schaft** *f* underground (*or* black) economy
schat·tie·ren [ʃa'tiːrən] *v/t.* (h) shade
Schat'tie·rung *f* (-; -en) a) shading, b) shade, hue, c) *fig.* shade, nuance; ***aller ~en*** of all shades (and colo[u]rs)
schat·tig ['ʃatıç] *adj.* shady
Scha·tul·le [ʃa'tʊlə] *f* (-; -n) casket
Schatz [ʃats] *m* (-es; Schätze ['ʃɛtsə]) **1.** treasure; **2.** *fig. pl.* treasures; riches; **3.** ***ein ~ an Erfahrungen*** *etc.* a wealth of experience *etc.*; **4.** love, darling, F sweetie; honey, F hon; F ***du bist ein ~!*** you're an angel (*or* a real dear); **~amt** *n* treasury; **~an·wei·sung** *f* treasury note
schätz·bar ['ʃɛtsbaːɐ] *adj.* assessable; ***schwer ~*** difficult to assess
Schätz·chen ['ʃɛtsçən] F *n* (-s; -) → ***Schatz*** 4
schät·zen ['ʃɛtsən] *v/t.* (h) **1.** estimate, guess; ***ein Bild ~ lassen*** have a picture valued; ***et. auf 1000 Mark ~*** estimate s.th. at 1000 marks; ***zu hoch ~*** overestimate; ***wie alt ~ Sie ihn?*** how old would you say he is?; ***ich hätte ihn älter geschätzt*** I'd have said he's older; ***schätz mal!*** (have a) guess!; ***grob geschätzt*** at a rough guess; **2.** F reckon, F guess; ***ich schätze, es dauert noch drei Tage*** I reckon (*or* I'd say) it's going to take another three days; ***ich schätze, er ist bei s-r Familie*** I imagine he's (*or* he's probably) with his family; **3.** think highly of, hold *s.o.* in high regard (*or* esteem); appreciate; ***ich weiß es zu ~*** a) I can appreciate it, I really appreciate it, b) I know what it's worth; → ***glücklich*** I, ***geschätzt*** 2; **4.** ✝, ⚖ value, assess (***auf*** *acc.* at); **~ler·nen** *v/t.* (*sep.*, h): ***j-n ~*** come (*or* begin) to appreciate what s.o. is worth; ***et. ~*** come *or* begin to appreciate (*or* value) s.th.
'**schät·zens·wert** *adj.* commendable
Schät·zer ['ʃɛtsɐ] *m* (-s; -) valuer; assessor
'**Schatz·grä·ber** [-grɛːbɐ] *m* (-s; -) treasure hunter (*or* seeker); **~in·sel** *f* treasure island; **~kam·mer** *f* treasury, treasure vault; **~kanz·ler** *m* Treasury Secretary, *in GB*: Chancellor of the Exchequer; **~mei·ster** *m* treasurer; *ped.*, *univ.* bursar; **~pa,pie·re** *pl.* treasury certificates
Schätz·preis ['ʃɛts-] *m* estimate, estimated price
'**Schatz|su·che** *f* treasure hunt(ing); ***auf ~ gehen*** go on a treasure hunt, go treasure hunting; **~su·cher** *m* treasure hunter (*or* seeker)
Schät·zung ['ʃɛtsʊŋ] *f* (-; -en) **1.** estimate, guess; **2.** *no pl.* a) appreciation, b) estimation, esteem; **3.** ✝, ⚖ valuation; assessment; '**schät·zungs·wei·se** *adv.* a) roughly, b) I reckon, I would guess, I think; ***~ sieben Millionen Amerikaner*** an estimated seven million Americans; ***~ habe ich 300 Platten*** at a rough guess I'd say I had 300 records, I reckon I've got about 300 records; ***es werden ~ zehn Leute kommen*** there should be about ten people coming; ***wann wirst du es ~ fertig haben?*** when d'you think (*or* reckon) you'll have it ready?
Schätz·wert ['ʃɛts-] *m* estimated (*or* assessed) value
Schau [ʃaʊ] *f* (-; -en) show (*a. TV etc.*), exhibition; *fig.* big show; ***nur zur ~*** only for show; ***zur ~ stellen*** (put on) display, exhibit; *fig.* display, parade; *a.* show off *one's knowledge etc.*; F ***e-e ~ abziehen*** put on a big show; ***mach keine ~!*** a) stop showing off, b) don't make such a fuss, c) stop putting it on; ***alles an ihm ist ~*** he's all show; F ***er macht auf ~*** F he's just out to pull off a show; ***j-m die ~ stehlen*** steal the show from s.o., upstage s.o.; F ***der Wagen ist e-e ~*** the car's super; **~bild** *n* diagram; sketch; **~bu·de** *f* (show) booth; **~büh·ne** *f* stage
Schau·der ['ʃaʊdɐ] *m* (-s; -) shudder; shiver; ***ein ~ lief ihm den Rücken hinunter*** a shiver ran down his spine
'**schau·der·er·re·gend** *adj.* horrific
'**schau·der·haft I.** *adj.* horrible; dreadful (*a. fig.*); **II.** F *adv.* dreadfully
'**schau·dern** *v/i.* (h) shudder (***vor*** *dat.* at); shiver *with cold*; ***mich schaudert bei dem Gedanken*** I shudder at the thought, the thought of it sends shivers down my spine
'**Schau·ef,fekt** *m* visual effect
schau·en ['ʃaʊən] *v/i.* (h) **1.** look (***auf*** *acc.* at); ***~ auf*** *acc.* a) *window etc.*: look (out) onto *the square etc.*, b) *fig.* set great store by *punctuality etc.*; **2.** look *angry*, *sad etc.*; ***was schaust du so?*** what's up?, why are you looking like that?; ***die hat vielleicht geschaut!*** you should have seen (the look on) her face; **3.** *dial.* have a look, look and see, go and see; ***schau mal, ob*** *a.* go and have a look (to see) whether; ***~ nach*** *dat.* check up on, look after, keep an eye on; **4.** *dial.* ***schau, daß ...*** see (to it) that; ***schau, daß du fertig wirst*** *a.* F get a move on; ***die soll ~, daß sie's selber macht*** she can get on with it herself; **5.** *dial.* ***schau*** (***mal***), ***...*** look ..., (you) see ...; **6.** *dial.* ***schau, schau!*** F well, what do you know!
Schau·er ['ʃaʊɐ] *m* (-s; -) **1.** *a. fig.* shower; **2.** → ***Schauder***; '**schau·er·ar·tig** *adj.*: ***~e Regenfälle*** showers, showery spells
'**Schau·er·ge·schich·te** *f* horror (*fig. a.* scare) story
'**schau·er·lich** *adj.* horrible, terrible (*a.* F *fig.*); blood-curdling
'**Schau·er·mann** *m* (-[e]s; -leute) docker, *Am.* longshoreman
'**Schau·er·mär·chen** *n* horror (*fig. a.* scare) story
schau·ern ['ʃaʊɐn] → ***schaudern***
'**Schau·er·ro,man** *m* gothic novel
'**schau·er·voll** *adj.* → ***schauerlich***
Schau·fel ['ʃaʊfəl] *f* (-; -n) a) shovel, spade, scoop, b) dustpan, c) ⚙ paddle; blade *of turbine*, d) *zo.* palm; **schau·feln** ['ʃaʊfəln] *v/t. and v/i.* (h) shovel; dig *hole etc.*; ***Schnee ~*** clear the snow away
'**Schau·fel·rad** *n* ⚙ paddle wheel; bucket wheel *of an excavator*; (*turbine*) blade wheel
'**Schau·fen·ster** *n* shop window; *fig.* showcase; ***im ~*** in the window; **~aus·la·ge** *f* window display; **~bum·mel** *m*: ***e-n ~ machen*** go window-shopping; **~de·ko·ra,teur** *m* window dresser; **~de·ko·ra·ti,on** *f* window decorations *pl.*; **~dieb·stahl** *m* smash-and-grab raid; **~pup·pe** *f* dummy, mannequin; **~re·,kla·me** *f* shop-window advertising
'**Schau|flug** *m* aerial display; **~ge·schäft** *n* show business, F show biz; **~kampf** *m sport*: exhibition fight; **~ka·sten** *m* showcase
Schau·kel ['ʃaʊkəl] *f* (-; -n) **1.** swing; **2.** seesaw; **~be·we·gung** *f* rocking motion
schau·ke·lig ['ʃaʊkəlıç] *adj.* **1.** rough, bumpy *crossing etc.*; **2.** wobbly
schau·keln ['ʃaʊkəln] (h) **I.** *v/i.* **1.** a) swing (*a.* ***sich ~***); sway *in the wind*; *ship, cradle etc.*: rock, b) seesaw; **II.** *v/t.* **2.** swing; rock; **3.** F *fig.* F wangle; ***das ~ wir schon*** we'll manage (*or* wangle) that somehow, we'll see to that (, don't you worry)
'**Schau·kel|pferd** *n* rocking horse; **~po·li,tik** *f* seesaw politics *pl.*; **~stuhl** *m* rocking chair
'**Schau·lau·fen** *n* (-s; -) exhibition skating
'**Schau·lust** *f* (-; *no pl.*) curiosity, *contp.* sensation-seeking; '**schau·lu·stig** *adj.* curious; '**Schau·lu·sti·ge** [-lʊstıgə] *m, f* (-n; -n) onlooker, *contp.* gaper, gawker, sensation-seeker, *Am.* rubberneck, *pl. a.* crowds of onlookers
Schaum [ʃaʊm] *m* (-[e]s; Schäume ['ʃɔymə]) foam (*a.* ⚙); spray; froth (*a. zo.*), head *of beer etc.*; lather; *gastr.* ***zu ~ schlagen*** beat (to a froth); *fig.* ***~ schlagen*** talk big; ***ihm stand der ~ vor dem Mund*** he was foaming (*or* frothing) at the mouth; **~bad** *n* bubble bath; **~be·,ton** *m* aerated concrete; **~bla·se** *f* bubble
schäu·men ['ʃɔymən] *v/i.* (h) foam (*a. beer*), froth; *drinks*: bubble; *soap etc.*: lather; *fig.* ***vor Wut ~*** F foam
'**Schaum|fe·sti·ger** *m* mousse; **~ge·bäck** *n* meringue(s *pl.*)
'**schaum·ge·bremst** *adj.*: ***~e Waschmittel*** low-sud detergents
'**Schaum·gold** *n* Dutch metal (*or* gold)
'**Schaum·gum·mi** *m* foam rubber; **~ma,trat·ze** *f* foam (rubber) mattress
schau·mig ['ʃaʊmıç] *adj.* frothy (*a. beer*); lathery *soap*; foaming *sea*; *gastr.* ***~ schlagen*** beat to a froth, beat until frothy
'**Schaum|kel·le** *f* → ***Schaumlöffel***; **~kro·ne** *f* a) (white) crest, b) head, froth *of beer*; **~löf·fel** *m* skimmer; **~lö·scher** *m*, **~lösch·ge·rät** *n* foam extinguisher
'**Schaum·schlä·ger** *m* **1.** → ***Schneebesen***; **2.** F *fig.* F big mouth, *sl.* wind-up merchant; **Schaum·schlä·ge'rei** F *fig.* *f* (-; *no pl.*) hot air
'**Schaum·stoff** *m* ⚙ foam (rubber); **~ma,trat·ze** *f* foam (rubber) mattress
'**Schaum|tep·pich** *m* foam carpet; **~wein** *m* sparkling wine
'**Schau|packung** *f* dummy (pack); **~platz** *m* scene; venue; ***~ der Handlungen ist ...*** a) the events are set (*or* take place) in ..., b) the story (*or* play, novel *etc.*) is set in ...; **~pro,zeß** *m* show trial
schau·rig ['ʃaʊrıç] *adj.* a) spine-chilling;

weird, F creepy, b) F awful, dreadful, horrific
'**Schau·spiel** *n* **1.** *thea.* play; drama; **2.** *fig.* spectacle, sight; ***ein ~ der Natur*** one of nature's spectacles
'**Schau·spie·ler** *m* actor; *fig. contp.* (play-)actor; **~be·ruf** *m* acting career, career as an actor (*or* actress); acting
Schau·spie·le'rei *f* (-; *no pl.*) acting; *fig.* play-acting
'**Schau·spie·le·rin** *f* actress
'**schau·spie·le·risch** *adj.* theatrical; acting *talent etc.*; ***ihre ~en Leistungen*** her theatrical achievement(s)
schau·spie·lern ['ʃaʊʃpi:lɐn] *fig. v/i.* (h) play-act, put on an act
'**Schau·spiel|haus** *n* theat|re (*Am. a.* -er); **~kunst** *f* dramatic art; **~schu·le** *f* drama school; **~schü·ler** *m* drama student; **~ˌun·ter·richt** *m* drama lessons (*or* classes) *pl.*
Schau|stel·ler ['ʃaʊʃtɛlɐ] *m* (-s; -) (fairground) showman; **~stück** *n* showpiece; perfect example; **~ta·fel** *f* → ***Schaubild;*** **~tur·nen** *n* gymnastic display
Scheck [ʃɛk] *m* (-s; -s) ✝ cheque, *Am.* check (***über*** *acc.* for); → ***ausstellen*** 2; **~be·trug** *m* cheque (*Am.* check) fraud; ***wegen ~s a.*** for signing bad cheques (*Am.* checks); **~be·trü·ger** *m* F cheque (*Am.* check) bouncer
'**Scheck·buch** *n* chequebook, *Am.* checkbook; **~jour·naˌlis·mus** *m* chequebook (*Am.* checkbook) journalism
Schecke ['ʃɛkə] (*sep.* -k·k-) *m* (-n; -n) piebald
'**Scheck|fäl·scher** *m* cheque (*Am.* check) forger; **~for·muˌlar** *n* cheque (*Am.* check) form; **~heft** *n* chequebook, *Am.* checkbook
scheckig ['ʃɛkɪç] (*sep.* -k·k-) *adj.* dappled *horse*; blotchy *skin*
'**Scheck|kar·te** *f* cheque (*or* banker's, *Am.* check) card; **~ver·kehr** *m* cheque (*Am.* check) transactions *pl.*
scheel [ʃe:l] *adv.*: ***j-n ~ ansehen*** look askance at s.o.
Schef·fel ['ʃɛfəl] *m* (-s; -) bushel; *fig.* ***sein Licht unter den ~ stellen*** hide one's light under a bushel; '**schef·feln** F *v/t.* (h) F rake in; ***das Geld ~ a.*** be raking it in
Scheib·chen ['ʃaɪpçən] *n* (-s; -) small (*or* little) slice; '**scheib·chen·wei·se** *fig. adv.* little by little, bit by bit
Schei·be ['ʃaɪbə] *f* (-; -n) **1.** a) disc (*a.* F *record*), b) *gastr.* slice, c) pane; F ***schwarze ~n*** F vinyl; F **~!** F sugar!; ***manche Leute glauben heute noch, die Erde sei e-e ~*** some people still think the earth is flat; *fig.* ***von ihm kannst du dir e-e ~ abschneiden*** you could learn a thing or two from him, you could take a leaf out of his book; → ***einschmeißen***; **2.** target; **3.** *sport*: puck; **4.** ⚙ disc, plate; lamella; (*potter's etc.*) wheel; gasket; washer; **5.** → ***Windschutzscheibe***
'**Schei·ben|brem·se** *f* disc brake; **~brot** *n* sliced bread; **~garˌdi·ne** *f* net curtain; **~han·tel** *f sport*: barbell; **~heiz·an·la·ge** *f* demister; **~ho·nig** *m* **1.** comb honey; **2.** F *int.* → **~klei·ster** F *int.* F sugar!; **~kupp·lung** *f* disc clutch; **~schie·ßen** *n* target practi|ce (*Am.* -se)
'**Schei·ben·wasch·an·la·ge** *f*, '**Schei·ben·wa·scher** [-vaʃɐ] *m* (-s; -) *mot.* windscreen (*Am.* windshield) washer
'**schei·ben·wei·se** *adv.* in slices
'**Schei·ben·wi·scher** *m mot.* windscreen (*Am.* windshield) wiper; **~blatt** *n mot.* windscreen (*Am.* windshield) wiper blade
Scheich [ʃaɪç] *m* (-[e]s; -s, -e) **1.** sheik(h); **2.** F bloke, *sl.* fella; '**Scheich·tum** *n* (-s; ⸚er [-ty:mɐ]) sheik(h)dom
Schei·de ['ʃaɪdə] *f* (-; -n) **1.** *anat.* vagina; **2.** sheath (*a.* ⚘); scabbard; ***das Schwert aus der ~ ziehen*** draw one's sword
schei·den (schied, geschieden) **I.** *v/t.* (h) a) separate (*a.* ⚗), divide, b) ⚖ divorce *a married couple*; dissolve *a marriage*; ***sich ~ lassen*** get a divorce, get divorced; ***sie will sich ~ lassen*** she wants a divorce; **II.** *v/i.* (sn) a) part, b) depart, leave; ***aus dem Dienst ~*** retire from service, resign; ***aus dem Amt ~*** retire from office; ***aus dem Berufsleben ~*** retire from working life; ***aus dem Leben ~*** pass away; **III.** *v/refl.*: ***sich ~*** (h) separate; *fig.* ***hier ~ sich die Geister*** (*or* ***Meinungen***) opinions are divided on that; → ***geschieden***
'**Schei·den·ab·strich** *m* ⚕ (vaginal) smear test
'**schei·dend** *adj.* outgoing *prime minister etc.*
'**Schei·den·ent·zün·dung** *f* ⚕ inflammation of the vagina, vaginitis
'**Schei·de|wand** *f* partition; *fig.* barrier; **~was·ser** *n* ⚗ aqua fortis, nitric acid; **~weg** *m*: *fig.* ***am ~ stehen*** be standing at a crossroads, be faced with a difficult decision
Schei·dung ['ʃaɪdʊŋ] *f* (-; -en) **1.** separation; **2.** ⚖ a) divorce, b) dissolution *of a marriage*; ***die ~ einreichen*** file for divorce; ***in ~ leben*** be separated, be getting a divorce
'**Schei·dungs|an·walt** *m* divorce lawyer; **~grund** *m* grounds *pl.* for divorce; **~kla·ge** *f* libel for divorce; **~proˌzeß** *m* divorce proceedings *pl.* (*or* suit); **~recht** *n* (-[e]s; *no pl.*) divorce legislation; **~rich·ter** *m* divorce judge; **~ur·teil** *n* decree of divorce; **~ver·trag** *m* separation (*or* divorce) agreement
Schein[1] [ʃaɪn] *m* (-[e]s; *no pl.*) light; glow; flash
Schein[2] *m* (-[e]s; -e) **1.** slip; certificate; **2.** (bank) note, bill
Schein[3] *fig. m* (-[e]s; *no pl.*) appearance; air, look; ***et.*** (***nur***) ***zum ~ tun*** pretend to do s.th.; ***den ~ wahren*** keep up appearances; ***dem ~ nach*** (***zu urteilen***) to all appearances; ***der ~ trügt*** appearances are deceptive, you can't always go by appearances
'**Schein...** *in cpds. often* apparent, mock; sham; *a.* ⚖ fictitious; *a.* ⚕ pseudo; **~amaˌteur** *m sport*: shamateur; **~an·griff** *m* feint, *a. fig.* mock attack (***auf*** *acc.* on); **~ar·guˌment** *n* specious argument; **~asyˌlant** *m* non-genuine refugee; *w.s.* economic refugee (*or* migrant)
'**schein·bar I.** *adj.* a) seeming, apparent, b) feigned *interest etc.*, ostensible *cause etc.*; **II.** *adv.* it seems ..., seemingly; on the face of it; ***es hat ihn ~ nicht berührt*** it didn't seem to bother him
'**Schein|blü·te** *f* ✝ sham boom; *fig.* apparent heyday; ***e-e ~ durchlaufen*** go through what seems to be a heyday (*or* boom); **~da·sein** *n* excuse for living; **~ehe** *f* sham marriage
schei·nen[1] ['ʃaɪnən] *v/i.* (schien, geschienen, h) shine; gleam
'**schei·nen**[2] *v/i.* (schien, geschienen, h) seem, appear; ***es scheint mir*** it seems to me, I have the impression; ***er scheint nicht zu wollen, mir scheint, er will nicht*** he doesn't seem to want to; ***es scheint nur so*** it only seems (*or* looks) like it *or* that way; ***er scheint dazusein*** he seems to be there, it looks as if he's there; ***wie es scheint*** as it seems, it seems, it would seem
'**Schein|fir·ma** *f* dummy (*or* bogus) company; **~frie·de** *m* hollow peace; **~ge·fecht** *fig. n* pillow fight; **~ge·schäft** *n* bogus transaction
'**schein·hei·lig** *adj.* hypocritical; **~ *tun*** act the innocent; '**Schein·hei·lig·keit** *f* (-; *no pl.*) hypocrisy; falseness
'**schein·krank** *adj.*: ***~ sein*** pretend to be sick, malinger; '**Schein·kran·ke** *m, f* (-n; -n) malingerer
'**Schein|maˌnö·ver** *n* dummy manoeuvre (*Am.* maneuver); **~schwan·ger·schaft** *f* false pregnancy
'**Schein·tod** *m* suspended animation, apparent death; '**schein·tot** *adj.* in a state of suspended animation, seemingly dead; F ***er ist ja schon ~*** F he's got one foot in the grave already
'**Schein·welt** *f* dream world
'**Schein·wer·fer** *m* floodlight; *thea.* spotlight; searchlight; *mot.* headlight, headlamp; **~licht** *n* spotlight; *fig.* limelight; *fig.* ***im ~ der Öffentlichkeit stehen*** be very much in the public eye (*or* limelight)
'**Scheinˌwi·der·stand** *m* ⚡ apparent resistance (*or* impedance)
Scheiß... ['ʃaɪs-] V *in cpds.* F damn(ed), bloody, V fucking; **~dreck** V *m* → ***Scheiße*** 2
Schei·ße ['ʃaɪsə] V *f* (-; *no pl.*) **1.** V shit; **2.** *fig.* a) *sl.* crap, V bullshit, b) F bloody (*Am.* goddam) mess (*or* nuisance); ***in der ~ sitzen*** F be in the soup; **~!** *sl.* bloody hell!, V shit!
scheiß·egal ['ʃaɪsˀe'ga:l] V *pred. adj.*: ***das ist*** (***mir***) **~!** F I don't give a damn (V shit)!
schei·ßen ['ʃaɪsən] V *v/i.* (schiß, geschissen, h) V shit; ***scheiß drauf!*** F to hell with it!, V fuck it!; ***scheiß auf*** *acc.* ... V sod ...; **Schei·ßer** ['ʃaɪsɐ] V *m* (-s; -) → ***Scheißkerl; kleiner ~*** V little bugger; **Schei·ße·rei** [ʃaɪsə'raɪ] V *f* (-; *no pl.*) the shits *pl.*
'**scheiß'freund·lich** F *adj. sl.* (as) friendly as hell
'**Scheiß|haus** V *n* V shithouse; **~kerl** V *m sl.* (bloody) bastard, turd, *Am.* son of a bitch; **~wet·ter** F *n* F godawful weather; (***so ein***) **~!** *sl.* what bloody awful weather
Scheit [ʃaɪt] *n* (-[e]s; -e): ***~ Holz*** piece of wood; log
Schei·tel ['ʃaɪtəl] *m* (-s; -) parting; ***e-n ~ ziehen*** → ***scheiteln; vom ~ bis zur Sohle*** from top to toe, every inch *a gentleman*; → ***Scheitelpunkt;*** **~käpp·chen** *n* skullcap
schei·teln ['ʃaɪtəln] *v/t.* (h): ***das Haar ~*** make a parting; → ***gescheitelt***
'**Schei·tel·punkt** *m* **1.** & vortex, apex; *ast.* zenith; **2.** *fig.* peak, apex; ***auf dem ~ s-s Ruhms*** at the height (*or* summit) of his fame
Schei·ter·hau·fen ['ʃaɪtɐ-] *m* funeral pyre; *hist.* ***auf dem ~ verbrannt werden*** be burnt at the stake
schei·tern ['ʃaɪtɐn] **I.** *v/i.* (sn) fail (***an*** *dat.* because of), come to grief; *plans etc.*: *a.* come to nothing, be thwarted (***an*** *dat.*

by); *negotiations, marriage etc.*: fail, break down; *business etc.*: fall apart; *sport*: *a.* be defeated (**an** *dat.* by); **daran ist er gescheitert** that was his undoing; **~ lassen** sink; → **gescheitert; II.** ♀ *n* (-s; *no pl.*) failure, breakdown, defeat; → **scheitern; zum ~ bringen** frustrate, thwart; **zum ~ verurteilt** doomed to fail(ure)

Schel·lack [ˈʃɛlak] *m* (-s; -e) shellac

Schel·le [ˈʃɛlə] *f* (-; -n) **1.** bell; *pl.* ♪ sleigh-bells; **2.** ⚙ clamp, clip; **3.** *dial.* clip round the ears; **4.** *pl. card game*: diamonds

ˈ**schel·len** *v/i.* (h) ring (the bell); **es hat geschellt** the doorbell just rang, there's somebody at the door

ˈ**Schel·len|baum** *m* ♪ Turkish crescent, pavillon chinois; **~bu·be** *m* (*playing card*) knave of diamonds; **~kap·pe** *f* fool's cap; **~kö·nig** *m* (*playing card*) king of diamonds; **~trom·mel** *f* tambourine

Schell·fisch [ˈʃɛl-] *m* haddock

Schelm [ʃɛlm] *m* (-[e]s; -e) rogue, rascal

ˈ**Schel·men|ro,man** *m* picaresque novel; **~streich** *m* practical joke, prank

schel·misch [ˈʃɛlmɪʃ] *adj.* roguish, impish

Schel·te [ˈʃɛltə] *f* (-; *no pl.*) telling-off, scolding; *in cpds.* bashing, *e.g.* **Gewerkschaftsschelte** union-bashing; **~ bekommen** get a telling-off (*or* scolding)

schel·ten [ˈʃɛltən] (schalt, gescholten, h) **I.** *v/t. and v/i.* scold (**wegen** *gen.* for); **j-n e-n Taugenichts ~** call s.o. a good-for--nothing; **II.** F *v/refl.*: **und er schilt sich Lehrer** and he calls himself a teacher

Sche·ma [ˈʃeːma] *n* (-s; Schemata [-ta], Schemen [ˈʃeːmən]) a) pattern, system, b) sketch, plan; diagram; **nach e-m bestimmten ~ arbeiten** work according to a fixed (*or* set) pattern; **es läßt sich in kein ~ pressen** it doesn't fit into any pattern (*or* scheme); **nach ~ F** without putting any real thought into it; **ein Aufsatz** *etc.* **nach ~ F** a very cut and dried essay *etc.*; **~brief** *m* sample letter

sche·ma·tisch [ʃeˈmaːtɪʃ] **I.** *adj.* **1.** schematic; **~e Darstellung** *a.* diagram; **2.** mechanical, rote *work etc.*; **II.** *adv.* **3. ~ darstellen** illustrate in (*or* by means of) a diagram, draw a diagram of; **4. ~ arbeiten** *etc.* work *etc.* by rote

sche·ma·ti·sie·ren [ʃematiˈziːrən] *v/t.* (h) schematize

Sche·ma·tis·mus [ʃemaˈtɪsmʊs] *m* (-; -men [-mən]) schematism

Sche·mel [ˈʃeːməl] *m* (-s; -) (foot)stool

Sche·men [ˈʃeːmən] *m* (-s; -) **1.** silhouette, outline; shadow; **man sah sie nur als ~** you could only make out their general shape, you could only see them in outline; **2.** spectre (*Am.* specter)

ˈ**sche·men·haft I.** *adj.* shadowy; ghostly; **II.** *adv.*: **sich ~ abzeichnen gegen** *acc.* be outlined (*or* silhouetted) against

Schen·ke [ˈʃɛŋkə] *f* (-; -n) inn, tavern

Schen·kel [ˈʃɛŋkəl] *m* (-s; -) **1.** *anat.* thigh; **sich auf die ~ schlagen** slap one's thighs; **2.** ⩘ side *of an angle*; **3.** leg *of dividers*, shank *of scissors*; **~bruch** *m* ⚕ fractured thigh; **~druck** *m riding*: leg (*or* knee) pressure; **~hals** *m anat.* neck of the femur; **~hil·fe** *f riding*: leg aid; **~kno·chen** *m* femur, thighbone

schen·ken [ˈʃɛŋkən] *v/t.* (h) give (as a present); ⚖ donate; **j-m et. ~** give s.o. s.th. (as a present); **et. geschenkt bekommen** get s.th. (as a present); **j-m et. zum Geburtstag** *etc.* **~** get s.o. a birthday *etc.* present, get s.o. s.th. for his (*or* her) birthday *etc.*; **was soll ich ihm ~?** what should I get (for) him?; **sie ~ sich nichts zu Weihnachten** they don't give each other Christmas presents; **ich möchte nichts geschenkt haben** I don't want any presents, *fig. a.* I don't want any special treatment; *fig.* **sich et. ~** F skip s.th., give s.th. a miss; F **den Film kannst du dir ~!** you can forget that film, you needn't bother about that film; **ihm ist nichts geschenkt worden** he had to fight for everything he's got; **sie schenkten sich nichts** they went at it hammer and tongs, F they had a real go at each other; → **Aufmerksamkeit, Gehör, geschenkt, Glaube, Leben, Vertrauen**

Schen·kung [ˈʃɛŋkʊŋ] *f* (-; -en) gift; ⚖ *usu.* donation (**an** *acc.* to)

ˈ**Schen·kungs|steu·er** *f* capital transfer tax, gift tax; **~ur·kun·de** *f* deed of donation

schep·pern [ˈʃɛpɐn] F *v/i.* (h) rattle, clatter; **da hat's gescheppert** there's been a bit of a smash there; **jetzt hat's gescheppert** *sl.* he's (*or* she's) copped it now

Scher·be [ˈʃɛrbə] *f* (-; -n) **1.** piece (of broken glass *etc.*); *pl. a.* broken glass *sg.* (*or* pottery *sg. etc.*); **in ~n schlagen** smash (to pieces); **in ~n gehen** get broken, *fig. marriage etc.*: break up; *fig.* **die ~n zusammenkehren** pick up the pieces; **es hat ~n gegeben** sparks flew; **2.** potsherd

ˈ**Scher·ben|ge·richt** *n* ostracism; **~haufen** *m* pile of broken glass *etc.*; *fig.* sad remains *pl.*

Scher·blatt [ˈʃeːɐ-] *n* shaving blade

Sche·re [ˈʃeːrə] *f* (-; -n) **1.** (**e-e ~** a pair of) scissors *pl.*; **2.** *zo.* claw, pincer; **3.** *wrestling, gym.* scissors *pl.*; *soccer*: scissors kick; **4.** *fig.* ✝ scissors *pl.*

sche·ren¹ [ˈʃeːrən] *v/t.* (schor, geschoren, h) shear *sheep*; trim; cut *hair*; ✂ clip, prune; **sich e-e Glatze ~** shave one's head, shave all one's hair off

ˈ**sche·ren²** (h) **I.** F *v/t.* **1. das schert mich nicht** that doesn't worry me; **was schert mich das?** what do I care?, F so what?; **II.** F *v/refl.* **2. sich nicht ~ um** *acc.* a) not to care (*or* bother) about, b) (completely) ignore; **ich scher' mich e-n Dreck darum** F I don't give a damn; **3. sich ~** F clear off, *sl.* beat it; **scher dich!** *a.* F get lost!; **scher dich zum Teufel!** *a. sl.* go to hell!

ˈ**Sche·ren|blatt** *n* scissor blade; **~git·ter** *n* ⚙ worm (*or* snake) fence; **~schlag** *m soccer*: scissors kick; **~schlei·fer** *m* knife grinder; **~schnitt** *m* silhouette, cut-out

Sche·re·rei [ʃeːrəˈraɪ] F *f* (-; -en) *a. pl.* trouble; **j-m viel ~en machen** give s.o. no end of trouble; **es gab wieder ~en** there were the usual problems

Scherf·lein [ˈʃɛrflaɪn] *n* (-s; -) mite; **sein ~ beisteuern** give one's mite, *fig.* do one's bit

Scher·ge [ˈʃɛrgə] *m* (-n; -n) henchman

Scher|kopf [ˈʃeːɐ-] *m* shaving head; **~ma,schi·ne** *f* shearing machine; **~mes·ser** *n* shearing knife (*or* blade)

Scherz [ʃɛrts] *m* (-es; -e) joke; **schlechter** (*or* **übler**) **~** bad joke; **~ beiseite** seriously (now), (no,) seriously, though; (**ganz**) **ohne ~** F I'm not kidding, I kid you not; **im ~, zum ~** for fun, as a joke; (**s-n**) **~ treiben mit** *dat.* make fun of; F **mach keine ~e!** F you're kidding; F **und ähnliche ~e** and what have you; **~ar,ti·kel** *m* joke article

Scherz·bold [ˈʃɛrtsbɔlt] *m* (-[e]s; -e [-də]) joker

scher·zen [ˈʃɛrtsən] *v/i.* (h) joke (**über** *acc.* about), make jokes (about); **Sie ~!** you're joking, of course; **mit ihm ist nicht zu ~** he's not to be trifled with; **damit ist nicht zu ~** it's not to be taken lightly; **ich scherze nicht** F I'm not kidding, I kid you not

ˈ**Scherz·fra·ge** *f* riddle, conundrum

ˈ**scherz·haft** *adj.* joking; humorous; funny; **das war nur e-e ~e Frage** it wasn't (meant to be) a serious question

ˈ**Scherz|keks** F *m* joker; **~na·me** *m* nickname

Scher·zo [ˈskɛrtso] *n* (-s; -s, -zi [ˈskɛrtsi]) scherzo

ˈ**Scherz·wort** *n* (-[e]s; -e) witticism, witty comment

scheu [ʃɔʏ] **I.** *adj.* shy; timid; reserved; **~ machen** startle, frighten; **~ werden** *game*: take fright, *horse*: shy (**durch** *acc.* at); F *fig.* **mach mal nicht die Pferde ~!** F keep your shirt on!

Scheu *f* (-; *no pl.*) shyness; timidity; reserve; awe; **sie zeigten keine ~** *animals*: they weren't at all afraid

scheu·chen [ˈʃɔʏçən] *v/t.* (h) scare (off), frighten (away); chase away; chase (after)

scheu·en [ˈʃɔʏən] (h) **I.** *v/i. horse etc.*: shy, take fright; **II.** *v/refl.*: **sich ~, et. zu tun** be afraid of doing (*or* to do) s.th., shy away (*or* shrink) from doing s.th.; **sich nicht ~ zu** *inf.* not to be afraid to *inf.*, *contp.* dare to *inf.*, F have the nerve to *inf.*; **er scheut sich vor nichts** he's not afraid of anything, *contp.* he'd do anything; **III.** *v/t.* shun, avoid; shy away from; **keine Kosten** (**Mühe**) **~** spare no expense (pains); **er scheute den langen Weg nicht** he wasn't put off by the long walk (*or* journey)

Scheu·er|bür·ste [ˈʃɔʏɐ-] *f* scrubbing brush; **~lap·pen** *m* floor cloth; **~lei·ste** *f* skirting (*Am.* base) board; **~mit·tel** *n* scouring agent

scheu·ern [ˈʃɔʏɐn] (h) **I.** *v/t.* **1.** scour, scrub; **2.** chafe; **3.** F **j-m eine ~** F give s.o. a clout round the ears; F **eine gescheuert kriegen** get a clout round the ears; **II.** *v/i. collar etc.*: chafe; **am Hals ~** chafe at the neck

Scheu·er|sand [ˈʃɔʏɐ-] *m* scouring powder; **~tuch** *n* floor cloth

ˈ**Scheu·klap·pen** *pl.* blinkers, *Am.* blinders (*a. fig.*); *fig.* **~ vor den Augen haben** have blinkers on, be blinkered; **mit ~ herumlaufen** (*or* **durchs Leben gehen**) go around with blinkers on; **~men·ta·li,tät** *f* blinkered vision (*or* mentality)

Scheu·ne [ˈʃɔʏnə] *f* (-; -n) barn

ˈ**Scheu·nen|dre·scher** *m*: F **essen wie ein ~** eat like a horse; **~tor** *n* barn door; → **Ochse**

Scheu·sal [ˈʃɔʏzaːl] *n* (-s; -e) monster (*a. fig.*); *fig.* horror, little beast

scheuß·lich [ˈʃɔʏslɪç] **I.** *adj.* horrible, dreadful (*both a.* F *fig.*); *a.* hideous *sight etc.*; *a.* revolting *manners etc.*; F awful, rotten *weather*; F **e-e ~e Erkältung** *etc. a.* the most awful cold *etc.*; **es schmeckt ~** *a.* it tastes something awful; **II.** F *adv.* dreadfully, terribly; **~ kalt** *a.* F rotten cold

Schi(...) [ʃiː] → ***Ski(...)***
Schicht [ʃɪçt] *f* (-; -en) **1.** a) layer; *geol.* stratum (*pl.* strata); ⚒ bed, b) coat(ing), layer *of paint etc.*, c) (*oil*) film, d) *phot.* emulsion, e) *fig.* class, *pl. a.* social strata; ***breite ~en*** large sections *of the population*; ***die gebildete ~*** the educated classes; ***aus allen ~en*** from all walks of life; **2.** shift; ***~ haben, auf ~ sein*** be on shift; ***~ arbeiten*** work (in) shifts; F ***~ machen*** call it a day, F knock off (work); ***~arbeit*** *f* shift work; ***~ar·bei·ter*** *m* shift worker; ***~be·trieb*** *m*: ***im ~ arbeiten*** work in shifts; ***~dienst*** *m* shift work
schich·ten [ˈʃɪçtən] *v/t.* (h) pile up; stack
ˈ**schich·ten·spe͵zi·fisch** *adj.* class-related, class ...
ˈ**Schicht|füh·rer** *m* shift manager; ***~holz*** *n* (-[e]s; *no pl.*) **1.** stacked wood; **2.** ⚙ laminated wood
Schich·tung [ˈʃɪçtʊŋ] *f* (-; -en) layers *pl.*; *geol. and fig.* stratification
ˈ**Schicht|͵un·ter·richt** *m* teaching in shifts; ***~wech·sel*** *m* change of shift; ***um sechs ist ~*** we *etc.* change shifts at six
ˈ**schicht·wei·se** *adv.* **1.** in layers; **2.** in shifts
schick [ʃɪk] *adj.* a) (very) smart, b) trendy
Schick *m* (-[e]s; *no pl.*) a) stylishness, b) style; ***sie hat ~*** she's got style; ***~ in die Sache bringen*** put the final touch(es) to it
schicken [ˈʃɪkən] (*sep.* -k·k-) (h) **I.** *v/t.* **1.** send (***an*** *acc.*, ***nach, zu*** *dat.* to); ***nach j-m ~*** send for s.o.; ***j-n ins Bett ~*** send s.o. to bed; **II.** *v/refl.* **2.** ***sich ~ für*** *acc.* be befitting for; ***es schickt sich nicht für e-e Dame zu*** *inf. a.* it's not the done thing for a lady to *inf.*, *formal*: it doesn't befit a lady to *inf.*; ***das schickt sich nicht*** it's not done, it's not the done thing (***zu*** *inf.* to *inf.*); **3.** ***sich ~ in*** *acc.* resign o.s. to; **4.** *dial.* ***sich ~*** hurry up; ***schick dich!*** F step on it!
Schicke·ria [ʃɪkəˈriːa] (*sep.* -k·k-) F *f* (-; *no pl.*) F jet set, trendies *pl.*
Schicki·micki [ʃɪkiˈmɪki] (*sep.* -k·k-) F *m* (-s; -s) F trendy type; *pl. a.* trendies, chiceria *sg.*
schick·lich [ˈʃɪklɪç] *adj.* proper, fitting; acceptable; ˈ**Schick·lich·keits·ge·fühl** *n* sense of propriety (*or* decency)
Schick·sal [ˈʃɪkzaːl] *n* (-s; -e) **1.** *no pl.* fate, destiny; ***das ~ herausfordern*** tempt fate (*or* providence); ***das ~ wollte es, daß*** fate would have it that; ***das ~ hat es anders entschieden*** fate had s.th. else in store; ***das ~ hat es gut mit ihr gemeint*** fortune has favo(u)red her; **2.** fate, destiny, lot; ***sein ~ ist besiegelt*** his fate is sealed; ***es war sein ~ zu*** *inf.* he was destined to *inf.*; ***j-n s-m ~ überlassen*** leave (*or* abandon) s.o. to his *or* her fate; ***sich in sein ~ fügen*** submit (*or* resign o.s.) to one's fate; (***das ist***) ***~*** that's the luck of the draw, that's fate, that's hard luck; ***dort spielen sich manche ~e ab*** you can see some really tragic cases there; ˈ**schick·sal·haft** *adj.* fateful
ˈ**Schick·sals|fra·ge** *f* vital (*or* fateful) question; ***~fü·gung*** *f* act of fate (*or* providence); stroke of luck; ***~ge·fähr·te*** *m* companion in distress, fellow sufferer; ***~ge·mein·schaft*** *f* companions *pl.* in distress; ***e-e ~ bilden*** share a common destiny; ***~glau·be*** *m* fatalism; ***&gläu·big*** *adj.* fatalistic; ***~göt·tin*** *f* goddess of fate; *myth.* ***die ~nen*** the (three) Fates; ***~schlag*** *m* (tragic *or* terrible) blow, stroke of fate; ***das war für ihn ein schwerer ~*** *a.* it was a real blow to him; ***Schicksalsschläge hinnehmen müssen*** be buffeted by fate; ***&schwer*** *adj.* fateful; ***~tra͵gö·die*** *f thea.* tragedy of fate; ***~wen·de*** *f* change in fortune; turn of fate
Schick·se [ˈʃɪksə] F *f* (-; -n) F floozy
Schie·be|büh·ne [ˈʃiːbə-] *f thea.* sliding stage; ***~dach*** *n mot.* sliding roof, sunroof; ***~fen·ster*** *n* sliding (*or* sash) window
schie·ben [ˈʃiːbən] (schob, geschoben, h) **I.** *v/t.* **1.** a) push; wheel, b) put *into one's pocket, mouth etc.*; ***wir mußten das Auto ~*** we had to push the car (*or* give the car a push); ***den Riegel vor die Tür ~*** bolt the door; *fig.* ***e-e Arbeit von einem Tag auf den anderen ~*** put off work from one day to the next; ***ihn muß man immer erst ~*** he always needs a push (F kick in the backside); → ***Bank***[1] 1, ***Wache***; **2.** *fig.* ***et. auf j-n ~*** (try to) blame s.o. for s.th., (try to) push s.th. onto s.o.; → ***Schuld***; **3.** *fig.* ***et.*** (***weit***) ***von sich ~*** deny all responsibility for s.th., claim innocence in the matter; **II.** *v/i.* **4.** push; ***kannst du mal ~?*** will you have a push?, will you push the buggy *etc.* for a bit?; **5.** push, shove; **6.** *fig.* ***~ mit*** *dat.* traffic in, push *drugs*; **III.** *v/refl.*: ***sich nach vorn ~*** push (one's way) to the front, *sport*: move to the top; ***sich durch die Menge ~*** push one's way through the crowd; ***sich nach oben ~*** slide up, work one's way up; ***Wolken schoben sich vor die Sonne*** clouds moved in front of the sun
Schie·ber [ˈʃiːbɐ] *m* (-s; -) **1.** ⚙ slide; **2.** pusher; **3.** F racketeer; black marketeer; **4.** one-step; **5.** bedpan
Schie·be·reg·ler [ˈʃiːbə-] *m radio etc.*: slide control
ˈ**Schie·ber|ge·schäft** *n* racket; *pl. a.* racketeering *sg.*; ***~e machen*** racketeer; ***~müt·ze*** *f* peaked cap
Schie·be|sitz [ˈʃiːbə-] *m* sliding seat; ***~tür*** *f* sliding door; ***~wind*** *m* ✈ tailwind; *sport*: following wind
Schieb·kar·re(n *m*) [ˈʃiːp-] *f* → ***Schubkarre(n)***
Schieb·leh·re [ˈʃiːp-] *f* (-; -n) cal(l)iper rule
Schie·bung [ˈʃiːbʊŋ] *fig. f* (-; -en) manipulation, string-pulling; F put-up job, *sport*: *a.* F fix; ***es war ~*** *a.* it was rigged
schied [ʃiːt] *pret. of* ***scheiden***
schied·lich [ˈʃiːtlɪç] **I.** *adj.* amicable; **II.** *adv.* amicably
Schieds·ge·richt [ˈʃiːts-] *n* court of arbitration, arbitration board; ***internationales ~*** international tribunal; *sport etc.*: jury; ***e-e Sache dem ~ unterbreiten*** submit a dispute to arbitration
ˈ**schieds·ge·richt·lich** **I.** *adj.* arbitral; **II.** *adv.* by arbitration
ˈ**Schieds·ge·richts|hof** *m* court of arbitration; ***Haager ~*** Hague Tribunal; ***~klau·sel*** *f* arbitration clause
Schieds·rich·ter [ˈʃiːts-] *m* **1.** *soccer, boxing etc.*: referee; *tennis*: umpire; **2.** *in competitions*: judge, *pl.* jury; **3.** ✝, ⚖ arbitrator; ***~ball*** *m* drop ball; ***~be·lei·di·gung*** *f* verbal abuse of a *or* the referee (*tennis*: umpire); ***wegen ~*** *a.* for insulting a (*or* the) referee (*tennis*: umpire); ***~ge·spann*** *n soccer*: referee and linesmen
ˈ**schieds·rich·ter·lich** **I.** *adj.* arbitral; **II.** *adv.*: ***~ entscheiden*** settle by arbitration
schieds·rich·tern [ˈʃiːtsrɪçtɐn] *v/i.* (h) arbitrate; *sport*: referee, *tennis*: umpire
Schieds|spruch [ˈʃiːts-] *m* arbitral award, arbitration; ***e-n ~ fällen*** make an award; ***~ver·fah·ren*** *n* arbitration proceedings *pl.*
schief [ʃiːf] **I.** *adj.* crooked, not straight; lop-sided, F skew-whiff; *fig.* distorted; warped; ***~e Absätze*** worn-down heels; ***~e Schultern*** sloping shoulders; ***der &e Turm von Pisa*** the Leaning Tower of Pisa; *fig.* ***~er Blick*** mistrustful look; ***~er Vergleich*** lame comparison; ***~es Bild*** false picture, distorted view; ***ein ~es Gesicht machen*** pull a wry face; → ***Bahn*** 1, ***Ebene, Licht***; **II.** *adv.* crookedly *etc.*; *den Hut etc.* ***~ aufsetzen*** tilt, cock; ***das Bild hängt ~*** the picture isn't hanging straight, the picture's lop-sided (F a bit skew-whiff); *fig.* ***~ ansehen*** look askance at *s.o.*, misjudge *s.th.*
Schie·fer [ˈʃiːfɐ] *m* (-s; -) **1.** slate; shale, schist; **2.** *dial.* splinter; ***&blau*** *adj.* slate-blue; ***~bruch*** *m* slate quarry; ***~dach*** *n* slate(d) roof; ***&far·ben*** *adj.* slate-colo(u)red; ***&grau*** *adj.* slate-grey (*Am.* -gray); ***~plat·te*** *f* slate; ***~ta·fel*** *f* slate
ˈ**schief|ge·hen** F *v/i.* (*irr.*, *sep.*, sn, → ***gehen***) go wrong; ***es ist total schiefgegangen*** everything went wrong, F it was a disaster; *hum.* ***es wird schon ~!*** it'll (*or* you'll) be all right (*Am.* alright); ***~gewickelt*** F *fig. adj.*: ***~ sein*** be very much mistaken; ***da bist du aber ~*** *a.* F you're completely up the pole there; ***~la·chen*** F *v/refl.* (*sep.*, h): ***sich ~*** F kill o.s. (laughing), crease up; ***~lie·gen*** F *v/i.* (*irr.*, *sep.*, h, → ***liegen***) be wrong; ***da liegst du total schief*** F you're way off there; ***~tre·ten*** *v/t.* (*irr.*, *sep.*, h, → ***treten***) wear down *heels*; ***~wink·lig*** *adj.* oblique-angled
Schiel·au·ge [ˈʃiːl-] *n*: ***ein ~ haben*** squint, have a squint (in one eye); *fig.* ***~n machen nach*** *dat.* ogle at
ˈ**schiel·äu·gig** [-ɔʏgɪç] *adj.* squinting, squint-eyed; cross-eyed
schie·len [ˈʃiːlən] *v/i.* (h) squint, have a squint; be cross-eyed; F *fig.* peer *round a corner etc.*, squint *through a keyhole etc.*; *fig.* ***~ auf*** *acc.* (*or* ***nach*** *dat.*) squint at, sneak a glance at, ogle (at); ***~ nach*** *dat.* hanker after, have one's eye on *a job etc.*
schien [ʃiːn] *pret. of* ***scheinen***[1] *and* ***scheinen***[2]
Schien·bein [ˈʃiːn-] *n* shin(bone), 🕮 tibia; ***~schüt·zer*** *m sport*: shin guard (*or* pad); ***~ver·let·zung*** *f* shin injury
Schie·ne [ˈʃiːnə] *f* (-; -n) **1.** ⚙ bar, rail; *fig.* track; **2.** *pl.* 🚂 rails, track; ***aus den ~n springen*** be derailed, jump the rails
schie·nen [ˈʃiːnən] *v/t.* (h) ⚕ put in a splint (*or* in splints)
ˈ**Schie·nen·bus** *m* railcar
ˈ**schie·nen|ge·bun·den** *adj.* railbound; ***~gleich*** *adj.*: 🚂 ***~er Übergang*** level (*Am.* grade) crossing
ˈ**Schie·nen|netz** *n* railway (*Am.* railroad) network *or* system; ***~räu·mer*** [-rɔʏmɐ] *m* (-s; -) rail (*or* obstruction) guard; ***~strang*** *m* stretch of track; ***~ver·kehr*** *m* rail traffic; ***~weg*** *m* railway (*Am.* railroad) line; ***auf dem ~*** by railroad
schier[1] [ʃiːɐ] *adv.* almost; virtually; ***~ un-***

möglich virtually (*or* well-nigh) impossible
schier² *adj.* pure; *fig.* sheer, complete *madness etc.*; ***~er Blödsinn*** *a.* utter nonsense
Schier·ling [ˈʃiːɐlɪŋ] *m* (-s; -e) ♣ hemlock; ˈ**Schier·lings·be·cher** *m* (cup of) hemlock; *fig.* ***den ~ trinken*** poison o.s., *lit.* drain the hemlock cup
Schieß|be·fehl [ˈʃiːs-] *m* order to fire (*or* shoot); **~bu·de** *f* shooting gallery; **~bu·den·fi͵gur** *f* target (doll); F *fig.* ***er sieht aus wie e-e ~*** he looks as if he's run away from a circus; **~ei·sen** F *n sl.* shooting iron
schie·ßen [ˈʃiːsən] (schoß, geschossen) **I.** *v/i.* **1.** (h) shoot (*a. sport*), fire; open fire; ***~ auf*** *acc.* shoot (*or* fire) at *s.o.*; ***gut ~*** a) be a good shot, b) *sport*: have a good shot (on one), c) *gun*: shoot well; ***wild um sich ~*** shoot around wildly; ***aufs Tor ~*** *sport*: shoot at goal; ***links ~*** *sport*: a) be a left-footer (*or* left-hander), b) take a left-foot (*or* left-hand) shot; *fig.* ***gegen j-n ~*** have a go at s.o.; F ***schieß in den Wind!*** F scram!; F ***~ Sie los!*** fire away!; → ***Pistole***; **2.** (sn) *fig.* shoot; ***~ durch*** *acc. pain*: shoot through *one's arm etc.*; ***plötzlich schoß mir der Gedanke durch den Kopf*** the thought suddenly occurred to me (*or* flashed into my mind); ***~ aus*** *dat. blood, water*: shoot (*or* gush) from *or* out of; ***das Blut schoß ihr ins Gesicht*** the blood rushed to her face; ***er kam um die Ecke geschossen*** he shot round the corner, *mot. a.* he came zooming round the corner; ***in die Höhe ~*** *plant, child etc.*: shoot up; → ***Boden, Kraut, Pilz***; **3.** (h) *sl.* shoot, mainline; **II.** *v/t.* (h) a) shoot (*a. phot.*); blast, b) *sport*: kick; ***sich e-e Kugel durch den Kopf ~*** put a bullet through one's head; ***ein Tor ~*** score a goal; ***e-n Teddybären ~*** shoot o.s. a teddy bear; ***e-n Satelliten in die Umlaufbahn ~*** launch a satellite into orbit; *fig.* ***Blicke auf j-n ~*** look daggers at s.o.; **III.** ♀ *n* (-s; *no pl.*) shooting match; F ***es (er) ist zum ~*** F it's (he's) a (real) scream
ˈ**schie·ßen·las·sen** F *v/t.* (*irr.*, *sep.*, h, → ***lassen***) drop, F scupper
Schie·ße·rei [ʃiːsəˈraɪ] *f* (-; -en) gunfight, gun battle; shoot-out; random shooting; endless shooting
Schieß|ge·wehr [ˈʃiːs-] *n* bang-bang gun; **~hund** *m*: F ***aufpassen wie ein ~*** watch like a hawk; **~platz** *m* ⚔ (shooting) range; **~pul·ver** *n* gunpowder; **~schar·te** *f* embrasure, loophole; crenel; **~schei·be** *f* target; **~sport** *m* shooting; **~stand** *m* shooting range; **~übung** *f* target practi|ce (*Am.* -se)
ˈ**schieß·wü·tig** *adj.* trigger-happy
Schiet [ʃiːt] *dial. m* (-s; *no pl.*) → ***Scheiße***
Schi·fah·ren [ˈʃiː-] *n* → ***Skilauf(en)***
Schiff [ʃɪf] *n* (-[e]s; -e) **1.** ship; boat; ***auf dem ~*** on board ship; **2.** △ nave; aisle
ˈ**Schiffahrt** (*sep.* -ff·f-) *f* (-; *no pl.*) navigation; shipping
ˈ**Schiffahrts|ge·sell·schaft** *f* shipping company; **~kun·de** *f* navigation; **~li·nie** *f* shipping line; **~mu͵se·um** *n* maritime museum; **~weg** *m* shipping route (*or* lane)
ˈ**schiff·bar** *adj.* navigable; ***~ machen*** canalize
ˈ**Schiff·bau** *m* (-[e]s; *no pl.*) shipbuilding (industry); ˈ**Schiff·bau·er** *m* (-s; -) shipbuilder
ˈ**Schiff·bruch** *m* shipwreck (*a. fig.*); *fig.* ***~ erleiden*** founder, ***mit*** *dat.*: come a cropper with *s.th.*; ˈ**schiff·brü·chig** *adj.* shipwrecked; ˈ**Schiff·brü·chi·ge** [-brʏçɪgə] *m, f* (-n; -n) shipwrecked person, *a.* castaway
Schiff·chen [ˈʃɪfçən] *n* (-s; -) **1.** little boat; **2.** ⚙ shuttle; **3.** ⚔ forage cap
schif·fen [ˈʃɪfən] V *v/i.* (h) a) V have a slash, b) *sl.* piss down
Schif·fer [ˈʃɪfɐ] *m* (-s; -) sailor; navigator; skipper; boatman; **~kla͵vier** *n* accordion; **~kno·ten** *m* sailor's knot
ˈ**Schiffs|arzt** *m* ship's doctor; **~aus·flug** *m* boat trip; **~bauch** *m* ship's belly; **~be·sat·zung** *f* (ship's) crew; **~brand** *m* fire on a ship; **~brücke** *f* bridge
ˈ**Schiff·schau·kel** *f* swing boat
ˈ**Schiffs|ei·gen·tü·mer** *m* shipowner; **~flag·ge** *f* ship's flag (*or* colo[u]rs *pl.*); ⚔ ensign; **~jour͵nal** *n* logbook; **~jun·ge** *m* ship's boy; **~ka·ta͵stro·phe** *f* disaster at sea; **~koch** *m* ship's cook; **~kü·che** *f* galley; **~la·dung** *f* shipload; cargo, freight; **~mann·schaft** *f* (ship's) crew; **~mo͵dell** *n* model ship; **~of·fi͵zier** *m* (ship's) officer; **~pas͵sa·ge** *f* passage (on a ship); **~rei·se** *f* **1.** boat trip, cruise; sea journey (*or* voyage); **2.** (sea) crossing; **~schrau·be** *f* (ship's) propeller; **~ta·ge·buch** *n* log book; **~tau·fe** *f* christening (*or* naming) of a ship; **~un·fall** *m* shipping accident; (ship) collision; **~ver·kehr** *m* shipping; **~werft** *f* shipyard; **~zwie·back** *m* (ship's) biscuit
Schi·it [ʃiˈiːt] *m* (-en; -en), **Schii·tin** [ʃiˈiːtɪn] *f* (-; -nen), **schi·itisch** [ʃiˈiːtɪʃ] *adj.* Shiite
Schi·ka·ne [ʃiˈkaːnə] *f* (-; -n) **1.** *a. pl.* harassment; ***et. aus reiner ~ machen*** do s.th. out of sheer spite; **2.** *motor racing*: chicane; **3.** F *fig.* ***mit allen ~n (ausgestattet)*** with all the trimmings, *kitchen, house etc.* with all the mod cons
schi·ka·nie·ren [ʃikaˈniːrən] *v/t.* (h) harass; pick on *s.o.*
Schild¹ [ʃɪlt] *n* (-[e]s; -er [ˈʃɪldɐ]) a) sign, signpost; road (*or* street) sign, b) nameplate; firm's name, fascia, c) label, tag
Schild² [ʃɪlt] *m* (-[e]s; -e [ˈʃɪldə]) ⚔, *phys.* shield; *fig.* ***etwas im ~e führen*** be up to something, be hatching something
ˈ**Schild·bür·ger** *m* Gothamite; *w.s.* simpleton; **~streich** *m* piece of bungling, F cock-up
ˈ**Schild·drü·se** *f* thyroid gland
ˈ**Schild·drü·sen|hor͵mon** *n* thyroxin(e); **~͵über·funk·ti͵on** *f* hyperthyroidism; overactive thyroid
schil·dern [ˈʃɪldɐn] *v/t.* (h) describe; relate; outline, sketch; ***j-m et. ~*** *a.* tell s.o. (about) s.th.; ***et. in düsteren Farben ~*** paint a gloomy picture of s.th.; ***detailliert ~*** give a detailed account of
Schil·de·rung [ˈʃɪldərʊŋ] *f* (-; -en) description; account
Schil·der·wald [ˈʃɪldɐ-] *m* jungle of road signs
ˈ**Schild·knor·pel** *m anat.* thyroid cartilage
ˈ**Schild·krö·te** *f* a) tortoise, b) turtle
ˈ**Schild·krö·ten·sup·pe** *f* turtle soup
ˈ**Schild·laus** *f* scale insect
Schild·patt [ˈʃɪltpat] *n* (-[e]s; *no pl.*) tortoiseshell
ˈ**Schild·wa·che** *obs. f* ⚔ a) sentry, b) sentry-go
Schilf [ʃɪlf] *n* (-[e]s; -e) ♣ reed(s *pl.*); ***im ~*** among the reeds; **~mat·te** *f* rush mat; **~rohr** *n* → ***Schilf***
Schil·ler·locke [ˈʃɪlɐ-] *f gastr.* **1.** (*rolled*) *strip of smoked dogfish*; **2.** cream horn
schil·lern [ˈʃɪlɐn] *v/i.* (h) shimmer; sparkle; ***ins Rötliche ~*** have a reddish tinge;
ˈ**schil·lernd** *adj.* **1.** iridescent, opalescent; *textil.* shot; **2.** *fig.* equivocal, ambiguous; ***~e Persönlichkeit*** a) colo(u)rful personality, b) *b.s.* elusive character
Schil·ling [ˈʃɪlɪŋ] *m* (-s; -e) schilling (*Austrian currency*)
schil·pen [ˈʃɪlpən] *v/i.* (h) chirp
Schi·mä·re [ʃiˈmɛːrə] *f* (-; -n) chimera; **schi·mä·risch** [ʃiˈmɛːrɪʃ] *adj.* chimeric(al)
Schim·mel¹ [ˈʃɪməl] *m* (-s; -) white horse
Schim·mel² [ˈʃɪməl] *m* (-s; *no pl.*) ♣ mo(u)ld, mildew
schim·me·lig [ˈʃɪməlɪç] *adj.* mo(u)ldy, mildewy
ˈ**schim·meln** *v/i.* (h, sn) go mo(u)ldy (*or* mildewy)
ˈ**Schim·mel·pilz** *m* mo(u)ld
Schim·mer [ˈʃɪmɐ] *m* (-s; *no pl.*) **1.** glimmer, gleam, shimmer (*a. textil.*); **2.** *fig.* ***ein ~ Hoffnung*** a glimmer (*or* flicker) of hope; ***~ e-s Lächelns*** flicker of a smile; F ***er hat keinen (blassen) ~*** F he hasn't got the foggiest (*or* a clue) (***von*** *dat.* about), ***von*** *dat.*: *a.* he doesn't know the first thing about
ˈ**schim·mern** *v/i.* (h) gleam, glimmer, shimmer; *moonlight etc.*: shine
Schim·pan·se [ʃɪmˈpanzə] *m* (-n; -n) chimpanzee, F chimp
Schimpf [ʃɪmpf] *m*: ***mit ~ und Schande*** ignominiously; ***j-m e-n ~ antun*** insult s.o.
schimp·fen [ˈʃɪmpfən] (h) **I.** *v/i.* scold, rail; ***~ über*** *acc.* complain about; ***auf j-n ~*** complain about s.o.; ***mit j-m ~*** tell s.o. off; ***bitte nicht ~!*** please don't shout at me!; **II.** *v/t.*: ***er schimpfte ihn e-n Lügner*** he called him a liar; **III.** F *v/refl.*: ***und so was schimpft sich Lehrer*** and he calls himself a teacher
ˈ**Schimpf·ka·no͵na·de** *f* volley (*or* torrent, stream) of abuse; ***e-e ~ loslassen*** let fly with (F let rip) a stream of abuse
ˈ**schimpf·lich** *adj.* ignominious, shameful; *a.* humiliating
ˈ**Schimpf|na·me** *m*: ***j-m ~n geben, j-n mit ~n belegen*** call s.o. names; **~wort** *n* (-[e]s; ⸚er) **1.** *pl.* abuse *sg.*; **2.** swearword; ***Schimpfwörter gebrauchen*** use bad language, swear
Schin·del [ˈʃɪndəl] *f* (-; -n) shingle; **~dach** *n* shingle roof
schin·den [ˈʃɪndən] (schindete, geschunden, h) **I.** *v/t.* **1.** a) drive *s.o.* hard, b) maltreat, abuse; **2.** *obs.* flay, skin *animal*; **3.** F scrounge *meal etc.*; ***Zeit ~*** play for time; ***Eindruck ~*** try to impress; ***bei j-m Mitleid ~*** try to make s.o. feel sorry for one; **II.** *v/refl.*: ***sich ~ (und plagen)*** slave away; **Schin·der** [ˈʃɪndɐ] *m* (-s; -) slave driver; **Schin·de·rei** [ʃɪndəˈraɪ] *f* (-; -en) exploitation, slavery; drudgery; ***das war e-e ~!*** F that was a real grind
Schind·lu·der [ˈʃɪntluːdɐ] *n*: *fig.* ***mit j-m ~ treiben*** F play (merry) hell with s.o.; ***mit s-r Gesundheit ~ treiben*** play havoc with one's health

Schind·mäh·re ['ʃɪntmɛ:rə] F *f* (-; -n) F nag

Schin·ken ['ʃɪŋkən] *m* (-s; -) **1.** *gastr.* ham; **2.** F a) great daub, b) fat tome; **~brot** *n* ham sandwich, (piece of) bread with ham; **~bröt·chen** *n* ham roll; **~nu·deln** *pl. noodles with pieces of ham*; **~speck** *m* bacon; **~wurst** *f* ham sausage

Schin·to·is·mus [ʃɪnto'ɪsmʊs] *m* (-; *no pl.*) Shintoism; **Schin·to·ist** [ʃɪnto'ɪst] *m* (-en; -en) Shintoist; **schin·toi·stisch** [ʃɪnto'ɪstɪʃ] *adj.* Shintoist, Shinto ...

Schip·pe ['ʃɪpə] *f* (-; -n) shovel; spade; F *fig.* ***j-n auf die ~ nehmen*** F pull s.o.'s leg, have s.o. on; F ***e-e ~ ziehen*** (*or* ***machen***) pout

'**schip·pen** *v/t.* (h) shovel; ***e-e Grube ~*** dig a hole; ***Schnee ~*** clear the snow away

Schi·ri ['ʃi:ri] F *m* (-s; -s) F ref

Schirm [ʃɪrm] *m* (-[e]s; -e) a) umbrella, b) parasol, sun shade, c) (*lamp*)shade, d) parachute, e) peak, f) *TV etc.* screen, g) shield, screen; **~bild(auf·nah·me** *f*) *n* ⚕ x-ray; **~herr** *m* patron; **~herr·schaft** *f* patronage; ***unter der ~ von*** *dat.* under the patronage (*or* auspices) of; ***die ~ übernehmen*** (agree to) become patron; **~hül·le** *f* umbrella cover; **~müt·ze** *f* peaked cap; **~stän·der** *m* umbrella stand

Schi·rok·ko [ʃi'rɔko] *m* (-s; -s) sirocco

Schis·ma ['ʃɪsma] *n* (-s; -mata, Schismen ['ʃɪsmən]) schism; **Schis·ma·ti·ker** [ʃɪs'ma:tikɐ] *m* (-s; -) schismatic, schismatist; **schis·ma·tisch** [ʃɪs'ma:tɪʃ] *adj.* schismatic

'**Schi·sprin·gen** *n* → ***Skispringen***

schiß [ʃɪs] *pret. of* ***scheißen***

Schiß V *m* (-sses; *no pl.*) **1.** V shit; **2.** *fig.* ***~ haben*** F be scared stiff, V have the shits; ***~ kriegen*** F get the jitters, V get the shits

schi·zo·id [ʃitso'i:t] *adj. psych.* schizoid

schi·zo·phren [ʃitso'fre:n] *adj.* **1.** *psych.* schizophrenic; **2.** *fig.* a) completely contradictory, b) absurd, F crazy; **Schi·zo·phre·ne** [ʃitso'fre:nə] *m, f* (-n; -n) *psych.* schizophrenic; **Schi·zo·phre·nie** [ʃitsofre'ni:] *f* (-; *no pl.*) schizophrenia

Schlab·ber... ['ʃlabɐ-] *in cpds.* sloppy *dress, skirt etc.*; **schlab·be·rig** ['ʃlabərɪç] F *adj.* → ***labberig;*** **schlab·bern** ['ʃlabɐn] F (h) **I.** *v/i.* slobber; slurp; **II.** *v/t.* slurp

Schlacht [ʃlaxt] *f* (-; -en) *a. fig.* battle (***bei*** *dat.* of; *fig.* ***um*** *acc.* over, for); ***j-m e-e ~ liefern*** *a. fig.* do battle with s.o., battle against s.o.; ***in die ~ ziehen*** go into battle; **~bank** *f* (-; ¨-e) shambles *pl.*; *fig.* ***j-n (wie ein Lamm) zur ~ führen*** lead s.o. (like a lamb) to the slaughter; ***er ließ sich wie ein Lamm zur ~ führen*** he went like a lamb to the slaughter

schlach·ten ['ʃlaxtən] *v/t. and v/i.* (h) **1.** kill, slaughter *animals*; **2.** *fig.* massacre, slaughter; F attack, devour *box of chocolates etc.*; → ***Sparschwein***

'**Schlach·ten·bumm·ler** *m sport*: fan, supporter

Schlach·ter ['ʃlaxtɐ] *m* (-s; -) butcher

Schläch·ter ['ʃlɛçtɐ] *m* (-s; -) *a. fig.* butcher

Schlach·te·rei [ʃlaxtə'raɪ] *f* (-; -en) butcher's (shop)

Schläch·te·rei [ʃlɛçtə'raɪ] *f* (-; -en) **1.** butcher's shop; **2.** *fig.* massacre, slaughter, bloodbath

'**Schlacht|feld** *n* battlefield; *fig.* ***hier sieht es aus wie auf e-m ~*** this place looks as if a bomb has hit it (*or* as if it's been hit by a bomb); **~fest** *n social gathering at which meat and sausages from freshly slaughtered pigs are served*; **~ge·tüm·mel** *n*, **~ge·wühl** *n a. fig.* melee; *fig.* ***mitten im ~*** in the thick of it; ***sich ins ~ werfen*** enter (*or* join) the fray; **~hof** *m* slaughterhouse, abattoir; **~mes·ser** *n* butcher's knife; **~op·fer** *n* a) sacrifice, b) sacrificial animal; **~ord·nung** *f* battle formation; **~plan** *m* plan of action (*a. fig.*); **~plat·te** *f gastr. bacon and sausages served with sauerkraut*; **≈reif** *adj.* ready for killing (*or* the slaughter); **~ruf** *m a. fig.* battle (*or* war) cry; **~schiff** *n* battleship; **~tier** *n* animal for slaughter

Schlach·tung ['ʃlaxtʊŋ] *f* (-; -en) kill(ing)

'**Schlacht·vieh** *n* animals *pl.* for slaughter; beef cattle *pl.*

Schlacke ['ʃlakə] (*sep.* -k·k-) *f* (-; -n) **1.** *metall.* slag, *a. fig.* dross; *geol.* (volcanic) slag; cinders *pl.*; **2.** *pl.* ⚕ roughage *sg.*, fibre (*Am.* fiber) *sg.*

'**Schlacken|di**ˌ**ät** *f*, **~kost** *f* high-fibre (*Am.* -fiber) diet; **≈frei** *adj.* non-clinkering

schlackern ['ʃlakɐn] (*sep.* -k·k-) *v/i.* (h) wobble; *loose dress etc.*: flap; **~de Knie** trembling knees; F *fig.* ***ich habe nur noch mit den Ohren geschlackert*** I couldn't believe my ears, I thought I was hearing things; ***da schlackert man nur noch mit den Ohren*** you just can't believe it, it's mind-boggling

Schlaf [ʃla:f] *m* (-[e]s; *no pl.*) sleep (*a. fig.*); ***im ~*** *a. fig.* in one's sleep; ***e-n leichten (festen) ~ haben*** be a light (sound) sleeper; ***er findet keinen ~*** he can't sleep, he can't get to sleep at nights; ***in tiefem ~ liegen*** be fast asleep; ***aus dem ~ gerissen werden*** wake up with a start, be rudely awakened; ***in den ~ singen (wiegen)*** lull (rock) to sleep; ***sich den ~ aus den Augen wischen*** rub the sleep from one's eyes; ***j-n um den ~ bringen*** give s.o. sleepless nights, rob s.o. of his (*or* her) sleep; ***der ~ vor Mitternacht*** the hours (of sleep) before midnight; ***vom ~ übermannt*** overcome by sleep; → ***Gerechte;*** **~an·zug** *m*: (***ein ~*** a pair of) pyjamas (*Am.* pajamas) *pl.*; **~au·gen** *pl.* sleeping eyes *of a doll*; *mot.* visored headlights

Schläf·chen ['ʃlɛ:fçən] *n* (-s; -) nap, F snooze; catnap, F forty winks; ***ein ~ machen*** take a nap, F have forty winks (*or* a snooze)

'**Schlaf·couch** *f* convertible sofa (*or* settee), bed settee

Schlä·fe ['ʃlɛ:fə] *f* (-; -n) temple; ***graue ~n haben*** be greying (*Am.* graying) at the temples

'**Schlaf·ebe·ne** *f* sleep stage

schla·fen ['ʃla:fən] *v/i.* (schlief, geschlafen, h) sleep, be asleep; *fig. a.* not to pay attention; ***fest ~*** be fast (*or* sound) asleep, sleep like a log (*or* top); ***gut (schlecht) ~*** sleep well (badly), be a sound (poor) sleeper; ***~ gehen, sich ~ legen*** go to bed, F turn in; ***j-n ~ legen*** put s.o. to bed; ***lange ~*** have a (good,) long sleep; ***sonntags länger ~*** have a (good) lie-in on Sundays; ***bis weit in den Tag hinein ~*** sleep to all hours; ***sich gesund ~*** sleep o.s. back to health; ***~ Sie gut!*** sleep well!; ***~ Sie darüber!*** sleep on it; ***es ließ ihn nicht ~*** it gave him no peace, it wouldn't let him rest; ***mit offenen Augen ~*** a) be dog-tired, b) daydream; F ***schlaf nicht!*** wake up!, F wakey, wakey!; *fig.* ***nicht ~*** be on one's toes; ***Entschuldigung, jetzt habe ich geschlafen*** sorry, I was miles away; ***bei j-m ~*** sleep (*or* spend the night) at s.o.'s place, stay overnight with s.o. (*or* at s.o.'s place); ***mit j-m ~*** sleep with s.o.; ***mit jedem ~*** sleep around

'**Schla·fen·ge·hen** *n* (-s; *no pl.*): ***vor dem ~*** before one goes to bed, just before bedtime

'**Schla·fens·zeit** *f* bedtime; ***es ist ~*** it's time for (*or* to go to) bed

'**Schlaf·ent·zug** *m* sleep deprivation

Schlä·fer ['ʃlɛ:fɐ] *m* (-s; -) sleeper; ***er ist ein unruhiger ~*** he's very restless in bed

schlaff [ʃlaf] *adj.* flabby *skin, muscles etc.*; limp, weak *body etc., a. handshake*; slack *rope etc., a.* drooping *sail*; *fig.* lax *discipline, morale etc.*; lifeless, F dead boring *party etc.*; sluggish; F **~er Typ** wimp; F **~es Glied** F drooping member

'**Schlaf|for·scher** *m* sleep researcher; **~for·schung** *f* sleep research; **~gast** *m* overnight guest; **~ge·le·gen·heit** *f* place to sleep; ***wir haben genügend ~en*** we've got plenty of sleeping space; ***~ bieten für*** *acc.* sleep *three persons etc.*

Schla·fitt·chen [ʃla'fɪtçən] F *n*: ***j-n beim ~ nehmen*** collar s.o.; *fig.* take s.o. to task

'**Schlaf|ko·je** *f* berth (*a.* 🚂, ✈); ⚓ bunk; **~krank·heit** *f* sleeping sickness; **~kur** *f* ⚕ sleep therapy; **~lern·me**ˌ**tho·de** *f* hypnop(a)edia; **~lied** *n* lullaby

'**schlaf·los** *adj.* sleepless

'**Schlaf·lo·sig·keit** *f* (-; *no pl.*) sleeplessness, ⚕ insomnia

'**Schlaf|man·gel** *m* lack of sleep; **~mit·tel** *n* barbiturate; sleeping pill (*or* tablet); F *fig.* ***das ist ja das reinste ~*** it's enough to send you to sleep, F talk about soporific

'**Schlaf·müt·ze** F *f* sleepyhead; F dope, *int.* dozy; '**schlaf·müt·zig** [-mʏtsɪç] F *adj.* F dop(e)y

'**Schlaf·quar**ˌ**tier** *n* sleeping quarters *pl.*

schläf·rig ['ʃlɛ:frɪç] *adj.* sleepy (*a. voice, eyes*), drowsy

'**Schlaf|ri·tu**ˌ**al** *n* bedtime ritual; **~rock** *m* dressing gown; *gastr.* ***Apfel im ~*** baked apple dumpling; **~saal** *m* dormitory

'**Schlaf·sack** *m* sleeping bag; **~tou**ˌ**rist** *m* backpacker

'**Schlaf|ses·sel** *m* ✈ *etc.* reclining seat; **~stadt** *f* dormitory town; **~stät·te** *f*, **~stel·le** *f* place to sleep; **~stö·run·gen** *pl.* disturbed sleep *sg.*; sleep disorders; ***unter ~ leiden*** *a.* have trouble sleeping; **~sucht** *f* (-; *no pl.*) narcolepsy; **≈süch·tig** *adj.* narcoleptic; ***~ sein*** *a.* suffer from narcolepsy; **~ta**ˌ**blet·te** *f* sleeping pill (*or* tablet); **~tier** *n* soft (*or* cuddly) toy; **~trunk** *m* sleeping draught; F nightcap

'**schlaf·trun·ken** *adj.* drowsy, half-asleep ..., *pred.* half asleep; dop(e)y, still half asleep

'**Schlaf·wa·gen** *m* 🚂 sleeper, sleeping car; **~fuß·ball** F *m* slow-motion football

'**schlaf·wan·deln** *v/i.* (h, sn) sleepwalk; '**Schlaf·wand·ler** *m* (-s; -) sleepwalker, somnambulist; '**schlaf·wand·le·risch** [-vandlərɪʃ] *adj.*: ***mit ~er Sicherheit*** as to the manner born, as if he'd *etc.* been doing it all his *etc.* life

'**Schlaf·zen·trum** *n* sleep centre (*Am.* center)

ˈ**Schlaf·zim·mer** *n* bedroom; **~blick** F *m* **1.** F bedroom (*or* come-hither) eyes *pl.*; **2.** come-hither look; **~ein·rich·tung** *f* bedroom furniture; **~schrank** *m* bedroom wardrobe (*or* cupboard)

Schlag [ʃlaːk] *m* (-[e]s; Schläge [ˈʃlɛːgə]) **1.** a) blow (*a. fig.*), punch, F whack, slap, smack, tap, b) thump, thud, c) lash *of the whip*, d) (electric) shock, e) *sport*: stroke, *golf, tennis etc.*: *a.* shot, f) chime, *a.* stroke *of a clock*; beat (*a.* ⚕); clap (of thunder), g) ⚔ strike; ***Schläge bekommen*** *a. fig.* get a (good) hiding (*or* drubbing); ***~ ins Gesicht*** *a. fig.* slap in the face; ***j-m e-n ~ versetzen*** deal s.o. a blow, *fig. a.* hit s.o. hard; ***zum entscheidenden ~ ausholen*** *a. fig.* move in for the kill; *fig.* ***~ ins Wasser*** F flop, washout; ***~ ins Kontor*** nasty shock (*or* surprise); ***~ auf ~*** in quick succession; ***dann ging es ~ auf ~*** then things started happening (fast); ***auf einen*** (*or* ***mit einem***) ~ a) in one go, b) suddenly, from one moment to the next; ***~ sechs Uhr*** on the stroke of six; F ***er tat keinen ~*** he didn't lift a finger; F ***sie hat e-n ~*** F she's got a screw loose somewhere; **2.** F ⚕ stroke; ***e-n ~ bekommen*** have a stroke; *fig.* ***sie waren wie vom ~ getroffen*** they just stood gaping; ***mich trifft der ~!*** F don't give me a heart attack; ***ich dachte, mich trifft der ~*** F I nearly died (*or* had a heart attack); **3.** → ***Hühnerschlag, Taubenschlag***; **4.** *no pl. fig.* stock, breed (*both a. zo.*), sort; ***vom gleichen ~ sein*** be made of the same stuff, *contp.* be tarred with the same brush; ***Leute s-s ~es*** men of his stamp; ***Männer vom gleichen ~*** birds of a feather; ***vom alten ~*** of the old school; **5.** F helping

ˈ**Schlag|ab·tausch** *m* **1.** *fig.* (hefty) exchange; ***erster ~*** (bit of a) skirmish; ***es kam zu e-m ~ zwischen ihnen*** they clashed (*or* crossed swords, came to blows) (***über*** *acc.* over); **2.** *boxing*: exchange of blows; **~ader** *f* artery; **~anfall** *m* (***e-n ~ bekommen*** have a) stroke

ˈ**schlag·ar·tig I.** *adj.* sudden, abrupt; **II.** *adv.* suddenly, all of a sudden, from one minute (*or* day) to the next

ˈ**Schlag|ball(spiel** *n*) *m* rounders (*sg.*); **~baum** *m* barrier; **~boh·rer** *m* hammer drill

schla·gen [ˈʃlaːgən] (schlug, geschlagen, h) **I.** *v/t.* (h) a) hit, beat (*a. gastr.*), punch, F whack, slap, smack; whip, b) fell, cut down *trees*, c) bang, slam *door etc.*, d) *fig.* beat, defeat, *sl.* lick; ***sich*** (***gegenseitig***) ~ (have a) fight, ***um*** *acc.*: fight over; ***sich geschlagen geben*** admit defeat, give up; ***ich gebe mich geschlagen*** *a.* F okay, you win; ***~ an*** *acc.* throw at *the wall etc.*; ***den Kopf ~ an*** *dat.* hit (*or* bump, knock, bang) one's head on *or* against; ***e-e Notiz ans Brett ~*** put a notice up on the board, pin a notice (up) onto the board; ***mit et. ~ auf*** (***gegen***) *acc.* bang s.th. on (against) *s.th.*; ⚘ ***auf den Preis ~*** add on to the price; ***j-n zu Boden ~*** knock s.o. down, floor s.o.; ***die Augen zu Boden ~*** cast one's eyes down; *gastr.* ***et. durch ein Sieb ~*** pass s.th. through a sieve; ***e-n Nagel ~ in*** *acc.* drive a nail into; ***ein Loch in die Wand ~*** knock a hole into the wall; ***ein Ei in die Pfanne ~*** bang an egg into the pan; ***in Papier ~*** wrap up; ***die Zähne ~ in*** *acc.* *animal*: sink its teeth into; ***j-m et. aus der Hand ~*** knock s.th. out of s.o.'s hand; ***sich et. aus dem Kopf*** (*or* ***Sinn***) ~ put s.th. out of one's mind, F forget (about) s.th.; ***die Uhr schlug zehn*** the clock struck ten; → ***Alarm, Brücke, Flucht*** 1, ***geschlagen, Glocke, Kapital*** I, ***Kreuz*** I, ***Schaum, Waffe, Wurzel***; **II.** *v/i.* hit (s.o. *or* s.th.), strike; *heart etc.*: beat, throb; *clock*: strike; *door etc.*: bang, slam; *sail*: flap; *wheel*: run untrue; *horse*: kick; *nightingale*: sing; ***~ an*** (*or* ***gegen***) *acc.* hit, *rain*: beat against; *waves*: beat (*or* crash) against; ***gegen die Tür ~*** hammer at the door; ***mit dem Kopf an*** (*or* ***gegen***) ***et.*** ~ (sn) hit (*or* bump, knock, bang) one's head against s.th.; ***j-m auf die Finger ~*** rap s.o.'s knuckles; *fig.* ***~ auf*** *acc.* (sn) affect; ***die Erkältung ist ihm auf den Magen geschlagen*** *a.* the cold settled on his stomach; ***~ aus*** (sn) *flames*: leap out of, *smoke*: pour from (*or* out of); ***mit den Flügeln ~*** beat its wings; ***sein Puls schlägt regelmäßig*** his pulse is regular; ***~ nach*** *dat.* a) hit out at *s.o.*, b) (sn) take after *s.o.*; ***um sich ~*** lash out (in all directions), thrash about; *fig.* ***die Arbeit*** *etc.* ***schlägt mir auf den Magen*** the work *etc.* is making me ill (*or* is giving me ulcers); **III.** *v/refl.* (h): ***sich ~*** (have a) fight (***mit*** *dat.* with); *fig.* ***sich gut ~*** hold one's own, give a good account of o.s.; ***sich auf j-s Seite ~*** side with s.o., *w.s.* go over to s.o.; ˈ**schla·gend** *adj.* **1.** *fig.* apt; convincing, very sound; cogent *reasons*; irrefutable; ***~er Beweis*** *a.* conclusive evidence; **2.** *univ.* ***~e Verbindung*** duel(l)ing fraternity

Schla·ger [ˈʃlaːgɐ] *m* (-s; -) ♪ pop song; hit (song *or* tune); *thea.* box-office hit; ⚘ winner, sales hit; bestseller; *fig.* hit, sensation

Schlä·ger [ˈʃlɛːgɐ] *m* (-s; -) **1.** thug; **2.** *sport*: bat; (*tennis*) racket, racquet; (*golf*) club; (*hockey*) stick; **3.** *cricket*: batsman; *baseball*: batter; **4.** *boxing*: fighter; **~ban·de** *f* gang of thugs

Schlä·ge·rei [ʃlɛːgəˈraɪ] *f* (-; -en) fight(ing), brawl, F punch-up; free-for-all

ˈ**Schla·ger|fe·sti·val** *n* song contest; **~kom·po˛nist** *m* pop composer; **~me·lo˛die** *f* pop tune (*or* melody); **~mu˛sik** *f* pop music; **~pa˛ra·de** *f* hit parade; **~sän·ger** *m* pop singer; **~spiel** *n sport*: match of the day; **~text** *m* (pop) lyrics *pl.*; words *pl.* of a (*or* the) song

ˈ**Schlä·ger·typ** *m* thug, F bruiser, bully boy

ˈ**Schla·ger·wett·be·werb** *m* song contest

ˈ**schlag·fer·tig** *adj.* quick-witted, F quick on the return, quick off the mark; ***~ sein*** *a.* always come up with an answer just like that, be good at repartee; ***~e Antwort*** good retort (*or* answer)

ˈ**Schlag·fer·tig·keit** *f* (-; *no pl.*) quick-wittedness; talent for repartee; ***sie ist für ihre ~ bekannt*** she's known for her repartee

ˈ**Schlag·in·stru˛ment** *n* ♪ percussion instrument; *pl. a.* percussion *sg.*

ˈ**Schlag·kraft** *f* (-; *no pl.*) *boxing*: punch; ⚔ fighting strength; *fig.* clout; force *of an argument*; ˈ**schlag·kräf·tig** *adj.* **1.** powerful; **2.** *fig.* → ***schlagend*** 1

ˈ**Schlag·licht** *n* (-[e]s; -er) *phot., art*: highlight; *fig.* ***ein ~ werfen auf*** *acc.* show up, spotlight, highlight

ˈ**schlag·licht·ar·tig** *fig.* **I.** *adj.*: ***~e Erhellung*** spotlighting; **II.** *adv.*: ***~ erhellen*** show in a cold light

ˈ**Schlag|loch** *n* pothole; **~mann** *m* (-[e]s; ⸚er) *cricket*: batsman; *baseball*: batter; *rowing*: stroke; **~obers** [ˈʃlaːkˀoːbɐs] *Austrian n* (-; *no pl.*), **~rahm** *m* → ***Schlagsahne***; **~ring** *m* knuckleduster, *Am.* brass knuckles *pl.*; **~sah·ne** *f gastr.* (whipped) cream; **~schat·ten** *m* shadow; **~sei·te** *f* ⚓ list; ***~ haben*** a) list, b) F *fig.* F be a bit unsteady on one's feet, be reeling; **≗stark** *adj. boxing*: hard-hitting; ***~ sein*** pack a powerful punch

ˈ**Schlag·stock** *m* **1.** baton, truncheon, *Am.* nightstick; **2.** ♪ drumstick; **~einsatz** *m* baton charge

ˈ**Schlag|uhr** *f* chiming clock; **~wech·sel** *m boxing*: exchange of blows; **~werk** *n* striking mechanism, strike *of a clock etc.*

ˈ**Schlag·wet·ter** *pl.* ⚒ **1.** firedamp *sg.*; **2.** → **~ex·plo·si˛on** *f* firedamp explosion

ˈ**Schlag·wort** *n* catchword; *fig. a.* slogan; **~ka·ta˛log** *m* subject catalog(ue)

ˈ**Schlag·zei·le** *f*: (***große ~*** banner) headline; ***~n machen*** make (*or* hit) the headlines; ***für ~n sorgen*** make headlines; ***das wird für ~n sorgen*** that'll make good headline material (F stuff)

ˈ**Schlag·zeug** *n* (-s; -e) ♪ drums *pl.*; percussion (instruments *pl.*); ***~ spielen*** a) play (the) drums, b) play percussion

ˈ**Schlag·zeu·ger** [-tsɔʏgɐ] *m* (-s; -) ♪ drummer; percussionist

schlak·sig [ˈʃlaːksɪç] *adj.* lanky, gangling

Schla·mas·sel [ʃlaˈmasəl] F *m* (-s; *no pl.*) mess; F dog's breakfast; ***da haben wir den ~!*** now we're in a real (F right) mess

Schlamm [ʃlam] *m* (-[e]s; -e, Schlämme [ˈʃlɛmə]) mud; sludge; silt

ˈ**Schlammas·sen** (*sep.* -mm·m-) *pl.* sea *sg.* of mud

ˈ**Schlamm|bad** *n* ⚕ mudbath; **~bo·den** *m* muddy soil; **~flut** *f* river (*or* sea) of sludge *or* mud

schlam·mig [ˈʃlamɪç] *adj.* muddy

Schlämm·krei·de [ˈʃlɛm-] *f* whiting

ˈ**Schlamm|la˛wi·ne** *f* mudslide; **~packung** *f* ⚕ mudpack; **~schlacht** *f* **1.** *pol. etc.* mudslinging; **2.** *soccer*: mudbath

Schlam·pe [ˈʃlampə] F *f* (-; -n) slut, *sl.* slag; ˈ**schlam·pen** F *v/i.* (h) **1.** be slovenly, be sloppy; **2.** a) be a slovenly worker, b) do a slovenly (*or* sloppy) job; *esp. ped. a.* be careless; ***die haben wieder einmal geschlampt*** they made a mess of things (*or* F botched things up) again

Schlam·pe·rei [ʃlampəˈraɪ] F *f* (-; -en) **1.** *no pl.* slovenliness, sloppiness; carelessness; **2.** mess, careless (*or* slovenly, sloppy) work, slovenly (*or* sloppy) job

schlam·pig [ˈʃlampɪç] F *adj.* a) slovenly, sloppy; *a.* slipshod *work etc.*, b) slovenly, frowzy, untidy; slatternly

schlang [ʃlaŋ] *pret. of* **schlingen**[1] *and* **schlingen**[2]

Schlan·ge [ˈʃlaŋə] *f* (-; -n) **1.** snake; *bibl.* serpent; *fig.* (***falsche***) ~ snake in the grass; **2.** *fig.* a) queue, line, b) line (of cars); ***e-e lange ~*** *a.* a long line of people; ***~ stehen, sich in e-e ~ stellen*** queue (up), stand in line, line up (***all um*** *acc.*, ***nach*** *dat.* for)

schlän·geln [ˈʃlɛŋəln] *v/refl.* (h): ***sich ~*** wriggle; *path*: wind, *river*: *a.* meander; ***sich ~ durch*** *acc.* wriggle through *a gap etc.*, weave (*or* worm) one's way through *a crowd etc.*

'Schlan·gen|be·schwö·rer *m* (-s; -) snake charmer; **~biß** *m* snakebite; **~fraß** F *m* F muck; **~gift** *n* snake venom (*or* poison); **~gru·be** *f* snake pit (*a. fig.*); **~haut** *f* snakeskin; **~le·der** *n* snakeskin; **~li·nie** *f* wavy (F wiggly) line; *mot.* ***in ~n fahren*** weave, zigzag (along the road); **~mensch** *m* contortionist

'Schlan·ge·ste·hen *n* having to queue up (*or* stand in line); F ***dieses ewige ~!*** this endless queuing up (*or* standing in line)

schlank [ʃlaŋk] *adj.* slim; slender; ***~ werden*** a) slim, b) lose weight; ***~ machen*** *dress etc.*: make *s.o.* look slim; ***Obst*** *etc.* ***macht ~*** you don't (*or* won't) put any weight on with fruit *etc.*; → ***Linie*** 5

'Schlank·heits|fim·mel F *m* obsession with one's figure; **~kur** *f* (slimming) diet; ***e-e ~ machen*** go (*or* be) on a diet

'schlank·ma·chend *adj.*: ***~e Kleidung*** *etc.* clothes *etc.* that make one look slimmer (F that hide one's extra pounds)

'Schlank·ma·cher *m* slimming agent

'schlank·weg *adv.* point-blank

schlapp [ʃlap] *adj.* **1.** F washed-out; listless; weak; limp *body etc.*; **2.** slack *rope*

Schlap·pe ['ʃlapə] *f* (-; -n) setback; ***e-e ~ einstecken müssen*** suffer a setback

schlap·pen ['ʃlapən] F (h) **I.** *v/i. shoes*: flap; *person*: shuffle along; **II.** *v/t.* lap (up); **'Schlap·pen** *m* (-s; -) slipper

'Schlapp·hut *m* slouch hat

'schlapp·ma·chen F *v/i.* (*sep.*, h) a) slow down, F hit a low; F wilt, b) give up, c) F flake out; ***in der Hitze ~*** *a.* succumb to the heat; ***viele haben schlappgemacht*** *a.* a lot of them couldn't stand the pace; ***nicht ~!*** a) no slacking!, b) come on, you can do it!; **'Schlapp·ma·cher** F *m* slacker

'Schlapp|ohr *n* floppy ear; **~schwanz** F *m* weakling, F wimp, drip

Schla·raf·fen|land [ʃla'rafən-] *n* (-[e]s; *no pl.*) (land of) Cockaigne; *fig. a.* land of milk and honey; **~le·ben** *n* life of luxury, F cushy life

schlau [ʃlaʊ] **I.** *adj.* clever; crafty; F ***aus ihm werde ich nicht ~*** I can't make him out; F ***daraus werde ich nicht ~*** I can't make head or tail of it; F ***~es Buch*** F bible (***über*** *acc.* on); *contp.* ***ein ganz 2er*** → ***Schlauberger*; II.** *adv.*: ***das hat er sich ~ ausgedacht!*** very clever (indeed)

'Schlau·ber·ger [-bɛrgɐ] F *m* (-s; -) F clever dick, smart aleck, smarty pants

Schlauch [ʃlaʊx] *m* (-[e]s; Schläuche ['ʃlɔʏçə]) **1.** a) tube, b) hose, c) *mot. etc.* (inner) tube; F ***auf dem ~ stehen*** F be (completely) clueless; **2.** F hard slog; ***das war ein ~!*** *a.* F that was tough going; **3.** *fig.* F ***das Zimmer ist ein ~*** the room's like a tunnel; **~boot** *n* rubber dinghy; life raft, *Am.* inflatable (boat)

schlau·chen ['ʃlaʊxən] F (h) **I.** *v/t.* take it out of *s.o.*; ⚔ *sl.* give *s.o.* hell; → ***geschlaucht*; II.** *v/i.*: ***das schlaucht ganz schön*** F it really takes it out of you

'schlauch·los *adj. mot.* tubeless

'Schlauch|rei·fen *m* tyre (*Am.* tire) with an inner tube; **~trom·mel** *f* hose reel

Schläue ['ʃlɔʏə] *f* (-; *no pl.*) cleverness, shrewdness; cunning

schlau·er·wei·se ['ʃlaʊɐvaɪzə] *adv.* cleverly (enough); ***~ hat er nichts gesagt*** he was smart enough not to say anything

Schlau·fe ['ʃlaʊfə] *f* (-; -n) loop

'Schlau·kopf F *m*, **'Schlau·mei·er** [-maɪɐ] F *m* (-s; -) → ***Schlauberger***

Schla·wi·ner [ʃla'viːnɐ] F *m* (-s; -) rogue; rascal

schlecht [ʃlɛçt] **I.** *adj.* bad (*comp.* **~er** worse, *sup.* **~est** worst), *a.* poor *eyesight, health, memory, quality, performance etc.*; wicked; stale *air*; ***nicht ~!*** not bad; ***~er Absatz*** poor sales; ***~e Aussichten*** poor (*or* dim) prospects, glum outlook; ***~es Essen*** awful (F rotten) food; ***~er Flug*** bumpy (*or* uncomfortable) flight; ***~e Führung*** bad conduct; ***e-e ~e Nachricht*** bad news (*sg.*); ***~e Zeiten*** bad (*or* hard) times; ***~ sein in*** *dat.* be bad (*or* poor) at *s.th.*; ***~ werden*** go off; ***die Milch ist ~*** the milk has gone (*or* is) off; ***~er werden*** get worse, deteriorate; ***du bist ein ~er Lügner*** you're a hopeless liar; ***e-n ~en Augenblick wählen*** pick a bad (*or* the wrong) moment; ***mir ist ~*** I feel sick; ***es kann einem ~ dabei werden*** it's enough to make you sick; → ***Laune*** 1, ***Tag*; II.** *adv.* bad(ly); ***~ reden von*** *dat.* talk negatively about, run *s.o.*, *s.th.* down, say nasty things about; ***~ aussehen*** a) look bad, b) look ill; ***~ riechen*** smell bad; ***er hört (sieht) ~*** he can't hear (see) very well (he's got bad eyesight); ***ich bin auf ihn ~ zu sprechen*** don't talk to me about him; ***~ dran sein*** be badly off; ***es steht ~ um ihn*** a) things aren't looking too good for him, b) ⚕ he's in a bad way; ***damit würde ich mich nur ~er stellen*** I'd be worse off than (I was) before; ***es bekam ihm ~*** a) *food etc.*: it didn't agree with him, b) *fig.* it didn't do him any good; ***er kann es sich ~ leisten zu*** *inf.* he can't really afford to *inf.*; ***er hat nicht ~ gestaunt*** F he wasn't half surprised; ***das kann ich ~ sagen*** I can't really say; ***heute geht es ~*** it's a bit awkward (*or* difficult) today; ***ich verstehe dich ganz ~*** I can hardly hear what you're saying; ***ich kann ~ nein sagen*** a) I can't say no, I find it hard to say no, b) I can hardly (*or* I can't very well) say no; ***Sie wären ~ beraten zu*** *inf.* I wouldn't advise you to *inf.*, I would advise you against *ger.*; ***~ und recht*** after a fashion; ***er hat's mehr ~ als recht getan*** *a.* he made a bit of a rough job of it

Schlech·te ['ʃlɛçtə] *n*: ***sich zum ~n wenden*** take a turn for the worse; ***er redet nur ~s von ihr*** he hasn't got a good word to say about her; ***das ~ daran*** the bad (*or* negative) side of it

schlech·ter·dings ['ʃlɛçtɐ'dɪŋs] *adv.* absolutely, simply

'schlecht·ge·hen *v/i.* (*irr.*, *sep.*, sn, → ***gehen*): *es geht ihm schlecht*** a) he's having a hard time, things aren't looking too good for him, b) ⚕ he's in a bad way, c) he's in a bad way financially, F he's pretty hard up

'schlecht·ge·launt *adj.* grumpy, in a bad mood

'schlecht'hin *adv.* absolutely; per se, as such; ***der Renaissancemensch ~*** the epitome of the Renaissance man, the classic Renaissance man

Schlech·tig·keit ['ʃlɛçtɪçkaɪt] *f* (-; *no pl.*) wickedness; depravity; baseness

'schlecht·ma·chen *v/t.* (*sep.*, h) run *s.o.*, *s.th.* down, F knock (***bei j-m*** in front of s.o.)

'schlecht·sit·zend *adj.* badly-fitting

'schlecht'weg *adv.* → ***schlechthin***

Schlecht'wet·ter|front *f* bad weather front; **~geld** *n* bad weather allowance; **~lan·dung** *f* bad weather landing; **~pe·rio·de** *f* spell of bad weather

schlecken ['ʃlɛkən] (*sep.* -k·k-) *v/t. and v/i.* (h) **1.** lick; lap up; **2.** → ***naschen***

Schlecke·rei [ʃlɛkə'raɪ] (*sep.* -k·k-) *f* (-; -en) **1.** titbit, *Am.* tidbit; F something to tickle one's tastebuds; something sweet, sweet; **2.** *no pl.* constant eating (of sweets *etc.*); ***jetzt hört aber auf mit der ~!*** you've had far too many sweets *etc.* already

Schlecker·maul ['ʃlɛkɐ-] (*sep.* -k·k-) *n*: ***der ist aber ein ~*** he's really got a sweet tooth, *contp.* F he's always stuffing sweets (and cakes) into his mouth

Schle·gel ['ʃleːgəl] *m* (-s; -) **1.** *gastr.* leg; **2.** ♪ drumstick

Schleh·dorn ['ʃleːdɔrn] *m* (-[e]s; -e), **Schle·he** ['ʃleːə] *f* (-; -n) ⚘ sloe (tree), blackthorn; **'Schle·hen·schnaps** *m* sloe gin

Schlei [ʃlaɪ] *m* (-[e]s; -e) → ***Schleie***

schlei·chen ['ʃlaɪçən] (schlich, geschlichen) **I.** *v/i.* (sn) creep, sneak, prowl; tiptoe; crawl (*a. mot.*); ***ins Haus ~*** sneak (*or* slip, steal) into the house; ***ums Haus ~*** creep (*thief*: prowl) around the house; **II.** *v/refl.* (h): ***sich ~*** creep, sneak; F ***schleich dich!*** get out of here!, F scram!; *fig.* ***sich in j-s Vertrauen ~*** worm one's way into s.o.'s confidence

'schlei·chend *adj.* **1.** ⚕ lingering, insidious, chronic; ***~er Tod*** slow death; **2.** ***~e Inflation*** creeping inflation

Schlei·cher ['ʃlaɪçɐ] F *m* (-s; -) F slink(er)

Schleich|han·del ['ʃlaɪç-] *m* illicit trade; **~weg** *m* hidden (*or* secret) path *or* route; *fig.* secret way (*or* means); *fig.* ***auf ~en*** by indirect ways and means; **~wer·bung** *f* surreptitious advertising, F plugging; ***~ machen für*** *acc.* F plug

Schleie ['ʃlaɪə] *f* (-; -n) *zo.* tench

Schlei·er ['ʃlaɪɐ] *m* (-s; -) a) veil, b) haze; *phot.* fog(ging); *eccl.* ***den ~ nehmen*** take the veil; ***alles wie durch e-n ~ sehen*** see everything through a haze; *fig.* ***den ~ (des Geheimnisses) lüften*** lift the veil of secrecy, unveil the secret, F reveal all; ***den ~ des Vergessens über et. breiten*** draw a veil of oblivion over s.th.; **~eu·le** *f* barn owl

'schlei·er·haft *adj.* mysterious; incomprehensible; ***das ist mir (völlig) ~*** it's a (complete) mystery to me

'Schlei·er|kraut *n* (-[e]s; *no pl.*) ⚘ baby's-breath, babies'-breath; **~tanz** *m* veil dance

Schlei·fe ['ʃlaɪfə] *f* (-; -n) **1.** ribbon; bow; **2.** loop (*a.* ✈, *computer etc.*), horseshoe bend; ***✈ ~n ziehen*** circle (***über*** *dat.* over, above)

schlei·fen¹ ['ʃlaɪfən] *v/t.* (schliff, geschliffen, h) a) sharpen; whet, b) ⚙ grind, abrade, smooth, polish (*a. fig.*), c) cut *glass, gems etc.*, d) ⚔ put through the mill; → ***geschliffen***

'schlei·fen² (h) **I.** *v/t.* **1.** drag (along) (*a.* F *fig.*); lug *suitcase etc.*; F *fig.* ***j-n ins Konzert ~*** drag s.o. along to a concert; **2.** pull down, demolish; **II.** *v/i.* a) *train etc.*: trail (***am Boden*** along the ground), b) rub (***an*** *dat.* against); ***~ lassen*** drag; ***die Füße ~ lassen*** drag one's feet, shuffle (one's feet); *mot.* ***die Kupplung ~ lassen*** let the clutch slip

Schlei·fer ['ʃlaɪfɐ] *m* (-s; -) **1.** ⚙ grinder; (glass) grinder *or* cutter; (gem) cutter; **2.**

♪ slide; **3.** ⚔ slave driver; **Schlei·fe·rei** [ʃlaɪfəˈraɪ] *f* (-; -en) ⚙ grinding shop

ˈ**Schleif|kon,takt** *m* ⚡ sliding contact; **~lack** *m* a) polishing varnish, b) eggshell finish; **~ma,schi·ne** *f* grinding machine, grinder; **~mit·tel** *n* abrasive; **~pa,pier** *n* → ***Schmirgelpapier***; **~rad** *n* grinding (*or* polishing) wheel; **~rie·men** *m* strop; **~ring** *m* ⚡ slip ring; **~schei·be** *f* → ***Schleifrad***; **~spur** *f* trail; **~stein** *m* whetstone; grindstone

Schleim [ʃlaɪm] *m* (-[e]s; -e) **1.** slime; *physiol.* mucus, phlegm; **2.** → ***Schleimsuppe***; **~ab·son·de·rung** *f physiol.* mucous secretion

ˈ**Schleim·beu·tel** *m anat.* bursa; **~ent·zün·dung** *f* ⚕ bursitis; *a.* F housemaid's knee

ˈ**Schleim·drü·se** *f anat.* mucous gland

schlei·men [ˈʃlaɪmən] *v/i.* (h) **1.** *physiol.* produce mucus; **2.** F *contp.* F suck up (to people), toady up to people; **Schlei·mer** [ˈʃlaɪmɐ] F *contp. m* (-s; -) F toady

ˈ**Schleim·haut** *f anat.* mucous membrane

schlei·mig [ˈʃlaɪmɪç] *adj.* slimy (*a. fig. contp.*), mucous; viscous

ˈ**schleim·lö·send I.** *adj.* expectorant; **II.** *adv.*: ***es wirkt*** ~ F it'll loosen up your *etc.* cough

ˈ**Schleim·schei·ßer** V *m* → ***Schleimer***

ˈ**Schleim·sup·pe** *f* gruel

schlem·men [ˈʃlɛmən] (h) **I.** *v/i.* gormandize; have a feast (*sl.* blowout); **II.** *v/t.* feast on, regale o.s. on; **Schlem·mer** [ˈʃlɛmɐ] *m* (-s; -) bon vivant; gourmet; **Schlem·me·rei** [ʃlɛməˈraɪ] *f* (-; *no pl.*) gormandizing, gluttony

ˈ**Schlem·mer|lo,kal** *n* gourmet restaurant; **~mahl** *n* feast, *sl.* blowout

schlen·dern [ˈʃlɛndɐn] *v/i.* (sn) saunter, stroll; *contp.* crawl (along)

Schlen·der|schritt [ˈʃlɛndɐ-] *m*: ***im ~ daherkommen*** come sauntering (F moseying) along; **~spa,zier·gang** *m* leisurely stroll

Schlen·dri·an [ˈʃlɛndriaːn] F *m* (-s; *no pl.*) **1.** humdrum routine, rut; ***gegen den alten ~ ankämpfen*** try and get some action into the place; ***in den alten ~ zurückfallen*** fall back into one's old ways (*or* the old rut); **2.** dawdling; muddling through

Schlen·ker [ˈʃlɛŋkɐ] *m* (-s; -) **1.** *mot. etc.* swerve; ***e-n ~ machen*** swerve; **2.** F detour; **3.** F digression

ˈ**schlen·kern** (h) **I.** *v/t.* swing; **II.** *v/i.*: ***mit den Armen*** *etc.* ~ swing one's arms *etc.*; ***mit den Beinen ~*** *a.* dangle one's legs

schlen·zen [ˈʃlɛntsən] *v/t.* (h) *sport*: scoop

Schlepp [ʃlɛp] *m* (-s; *no pl.*): ***in ~ nehmen*** → ***Schlepptau***; **~an·gel** *f* troll; **~an·ker** *m* sea anchor; **~damp·fer** *m* tug

Schlep·pe [ˈʃlɛpə] *f* (-; -n) train

schlep·pen [ˈʃlɛpən] (h) **I.** *v/t.* drag (*a. fig. s.o.*), *a.* lug *suitcase etc.*; ⚓, ✈, *mot.* tow; F ***Kunden ~*** tout; F *fig.* ***j-n ins Konzert ~*** drag s.o. along to a concert; **II.** *v/refl.*: ***sich ~*** a) *negotiations etc.*: drag on (***seit Monaten*** *etc.* for months *etc.*), b) drag o.s. (along); trudge, plod (along); ***sich mit e-m schweren Koffer ~*** lug a heavy case around; *fig.* ***sich ~ mit*** *dat.* a) be weighed down by *one's problems, grief etc.*, b) be battling with *a cold etc.*

ˈ**schlep·pend I.** *adj.* a) sluggish, slow (*a.* ✝), b) labo(u)red; slow, drawling *speech*, c) tedious; ***mit ~en Schritten gehen*** shuffle along, drag one's feet; **II.** *adv.*: ***nur ~ vorangehen*** *work etc.*: make very slow progress, inch along, *talks etc.*: be very slow to get off the ground; ***~ beginnen*** get off to a slow start

Schlep·per [ˈʃlɛpɐ] *m* (-s; -) **1.** tractor; ⚓ tug; **2.** F tout

ˈ**Schlepp|fahr·zeug** *n* breakdown van, *Am.* tow truck; **~flug·zeug** *n* towplane; **~kahn** *m* barge (in tow), lighter; **~lift** *m* T-bar (lift), drag lift, ski tow; **~netz** *n* dragnet; trawl (net); **~schiff** *n* tug; **~seil** *n* towrope; **~start** *m* ✈ towed takeoff; **~tau** *n* towrope; ***ins ~ nehmen*** (***im ~ haben***) *a. fig.* take (have) in tow; *fig.* ***im ~ folgte ...*** in its (*or* their) wake came ...; **~zug** *m* ⚓ train of barges

Schle·si·er [ˈʃleːzi̯ɐ] *m* (-s; -), **Schle·sie·rin** [ˈʃleːzi̯ərɪn] *f* (-; -nen) Silesian; ***Schlesier sein*** be (a) Silesian, come from Silesia; **schle·sisch** [ˈʃleːzɪʃ] **I.** *adj.* Silesian; **II.** ♀ *n* (-en; *no pl.*) *ling.* Silesian

Schles·wig|-Hol·stei·ner [ˈʃleːsvɪçˈhɔlʃtaɪnɐ] *m* (-s; -), **~-Hol·stei·ne·rin** [-ˈhɔlʃtaɪnərɪn] *f* (-; -nen) man (*f* woman) from Schleswig-Holstein; ***Schleswig-Holsteiner sein*** *a.* come from Schleswig-Holstein; **♀-hol·stei·nisch** [-ˈhɔlʃtaɪnɪʃ] *adj.* Schleswig-Holstein ..., from Schleswig-Holstein

Schleu·der [ˈʃlɔʏdɐ] *f* (-; -n) **1.** catapult, *Am.* slingshot; **2.** spin-drier; **3.** ⚙ a) centrifuge, b) extractor, separator; **~gang** *m* spin; **~ge·fahr** *f road sign*: Slippery Road; **~ho·nig** *m* strained (*or* extracted) honey; **~ma,schi·ne** *f* ⚙ a) centrifuge, b) extractor, separator

schleu·dern [ˈʃlɔʏdɐn] **I.** *v/t.* (h) **1.** fling, hurl; sling; **2.** spin-dry; **3.** ⚙ a) centrifuge, b) strain, extract; **II.** *v/i.* (sn) *mot.* skid, swerve; **III.** ♀ *n*: ***ins ~ kommen*** (go into a) skid, start skidding, *fig.* start floundering; *fig.* ***j-n ins ~ bringen*** throw s.o. (completely)

ˈ**Schleu·der|preis** *m* giveaway (*or* cut-rate) price; ***zu ~en verkaufen*** F sell dirt cheap, throw away, dump; **~sitz** *m* ✈ ejection (*or* ejector) seat; *fig.* hot seat; **~trau·ma** *n* ⚕ whiplash; **~wa·re** *f* give-away articles *pl.*; F *contp.* cheap stuff; **~wä·sche** *f*: ***ist das ~?*** are those clothes for spinning?

schleu·nig [ˈʃlɔʏnɪç] **I.** *adj.* quick, prompt, speedy; hasty; **II.** *adv.* quickly, promptly; ˈ**schleu·nigst** *adv.* at once, without further ado; ***aber ~!*** on the double!; ***tu das ~ weg!*** put that away quick (*or* right now)

Schleu·se [ˈʃlɔʏzə] *f* (-; -n) sluice; *a. fig.* floodgate; lock; *fig.* ***der Himmel öffnete s-e ~n*** the floodgates of heaven opened

ˈ**schleu·sen** *v/t.* (h) **1.** ⚓ lock; **2.** *fig.* channel *s.th.*; steer *s.o.*, herd *a crowd*; ***über die Grenze*** (***durch den Zoll***) ~ smuggle (*or* get) across the border (through customs)

ˈ**Schleu·sen|tor** *n* floodgate; **~trep·pe** *f* flight of locks; **~wär·ter** *m* lockkeeper; sluice keeper

schlich [ʃlɪç] *pret. of* ***schleichen***

Schli·che [ˈʃlɪçə] *pl.* tricks; ***j-m auf die ~ kommen*** find s.o. out, get wise to s.o.('s tricks); ***die kennen alle ~*** they know all the tricks (in the book)

schlicht [ʃlɪçt] **I.** *adj.* a) plain, simple, b) modest, unassuming, unpretentious, c) artless, ingenuous; ***~er Bericht*** straightforward account; ***~e Eleganz*** simple elegance; ***~es Essen*** a) plain food, b) simple (*or* frugal) meal; ***~es Gemüt*** a) simple (*or* naive) mentality, b) simple soul; ***~er Glaube*** simple faith; ***~e Menschen*** simple people; ***~e Schönheit*** unadorned beauty; ***~es Wesen*** a) simple nature, b) simple person; ***in ~en Verhältnissen leben*** be (*or* live) in straitened circumstances; **II.** *adv.*: ***~ und einfach*** (*or* ***~ und ergreifend***) ***falsch*** *etc.* absolutely (*or* purely and simply) wrong *etc.*, ***unsinnig***: utter (*or* pure, sheer, absolute) nonsense; ***ich hab's ~ und ergreifend vergessen*** F I clean forgot (it)

schlich·ten [ˈʃlɪçtən] (h) **I.** *v/t. fig.* settle *dispute etc.*; settle by arbitration; **II.** *v/i.*: ***zwischen zwei Parteien zu ~ versuchen*** mediate between two parties, try to smooth out the differences between two parties; **Schlich·ter** [ˈʃlɪçtɐ] *m* (-s; -) mediator, troubleshooter; arbitrator

ˈ**Schlicht·heit** *f* (-; *no pl.*) plainness, simplicity *etc.*; → ***schlicht*** I

Schlich·tung [ˈʃlɪçtʊŋ] *f* (-; -en) arbitration, settlement

ˈ**Schlich·tungs|aus·schuß** *m* arbitration (*or* conciliation) committee; **~stel·le** *f* board (*or* court) of arbitration; **~ver·fah·ren** *n* arbitration proceedings *pl.*; **~ver·such** *m* attempt at arbitration

ˈ**schlichtˈweg** *adv.* absolutely, purely and simply

Schlick [ʃlɪk] *m* (-[e]s; *no pl.*) sludge

schlief [ʃliːf] *pret. of* ***schlafen***

Schlie·re [ˈʃliːrə] *f* (-; -n) **1.** ⚙ streak, glass bubble; **2.** streak *on windowpane etc.*

schließ·bar [ˈʃliːsbaːɐ] *adj.* lockable

Schlie·ße [ˈʃliːsə] *f* (-; -n) fastening; clasp

schlie·ßen [ˈʃliːsən] (schloß, geschlossen, h) **I.** *v/t.* **1.** close (*a.* ⚡), shut; lock; bolt; shut (*or* close) down *shop, business etc.*; *fig.* form, enter into *an alliance etc.*; reach, come to *an agreement etc.*; ***e-n Hund an die Kette ~*** put a dog on the chain; ***das Geld in die Schublade ~*** lock the money away (*or* up) in the drawer; *fig.* ***et. ~ an*** *acc.* follow s.th. up with *s.th.*; → ***Freundschaft, Frieden, Herz, Lücke, Vertrag***; **2.** close, end, conclude; wind up *speech etc.* (***mit den Worten*** by saying); **3.** conclude (***aus*** *dat.* from); ***kann ich daraus ~, daß*** *a.* do I take it that; **II.** *v/i.* **4.** shut, close; close (*or* shut) down, F fold up *business etc.*; ***der Schlüssel schließt nicht*** the key's jamming; ***das Schloß schließt etwas schwer*** the lock's a bit stiff; ***das Fenster schließt schlecht*** the window won't close properly; ***die Tür schließt von selbst*** the door closes by itself; **5.** (come to a) close; ***~ mit*** *dat. stock exchange*: close at; ***mit den Worten ... ~*** wind up by saying ...; **6.** ***von e-r Sache ~ auf*** *acc.* infer *s.th.* from s.th.; ***von sich auf andere ~*** judge others by o.s.; ***auf et. ~ lassen*** suggest (*or* point to) s.th.; ***es läßt darauf ~, daß*** it would suggest (*or* point to the fact) that; **III.** *v/refl.*: ***sich ~*** close, shut; *wound*: close (up); *fig.* ***an den Vortrag schloß sich ein Dokumentarfilm*** the lecture was followed by a documentary; → ***Kreis***

Schlie·ßer [ˈʃliːsɐ] *m* (-s; -) **1.** doorkeeper; **2.** jailer; **3.** ⚙ catch

Schließ·fach [ˈʃliːs-] *n* a) 🚂 *etc.* (left-luggage) locker, b) post office box, PO box, c) safe deposit box

schließ·lich ['ʃliːslɪç] *adv.* **1.** finally, eventually, in the end; at last; ~ ***und endlich*** when all is said and done; **2.** after all; ~ ***bist du schon 18*** you 'are 18 after all, F I mean, you 'are 18
Schließ·mus·kel ['ʃliːs-] *m anat.* sphincter (muscle)
Schlie·ßung ['ʃliːsʊŋ] *f* (-; *no pl.*) closing (*a.* ⚡), shutting; closure (*a.* ⚡), shutdown, closing down *of a shop, business etc.*
Schließ·win·kel ['ʃliːs-] *m mot.* dwell angle
schliff [ʃlɪf] *pret. of* ***schleifen***[1]
Schliff *m* (-[e]s; -e) ⚙ **1.** *no pl.* a) grinding; sharpening, b) cutting *of glass, gem etc.*; **2.** cut; *fig.* polish; ***der letzte*** ~ the final touch; ***e-r Sache den letzten ~ geben*** put the finishing touch(es) to s.th.; ***ihm fehlt noch der*** ~ he's still a bit rough and ready; ***ihm fehlt jeder*** ~ he has no refinement
schlimm [ʃlɪm] *adj.* a) bad; evil, wicked, b) bad, serious; terrible; *a.* nasty *cold, wound etc.*; ***~er Finger*** (***Hals***) sore finger (throat); ***~er Husten*** bad (*or* nasty) cough; ***das ist ja e-e ~e Sache*** that's awful (*or* terrible); ***es ist schon*** ~ isn't it awful; ***das war*** ~ it was awful (*or* terrible); ***ist das denn so ~?*** what's so bad about it?; ***die letzte Zeit war*** ~ it's been tough going lately; ***~e Zeiten*** hard times; ***mit ihm wird es noch ein ~es Ende nehmen*** he'll come to a bad end; ***es sieht ~ aus*** it looks (pretty) bad; ***das ist halb so ~!*** it's not as bad as all that, it's nothing to get upset about, it doesn't matter, don't worry about it; ***ist es ~, wenn ich nicht komme?*** would it be awful of me not to come (*or* a nuisance if I didn't come)?; ***~er*** worse; ***~er machen, ~ werden*** → ***verschlimmern***; ***~er kann es nicht mehr werden*** things can hardly get any worse; ***es wird immer ~er*** things are going from bad to worse; ***um so ~er*** so much the worse; ***das Schlimm(st)e an der Sache ist ...*** the awful (worst) thing about it is ...; ***sich zum ♀en wenden*** take a turn for the worse; ***ich sehe nichts ♀es darin*** I don't see anything wrong in it; ***es gibt Schlimmeres*** things could be worse, worse things happen at sea; ***am ~sten*** worst of all; ***auf das Schlimmste gefaßt sein*** be prepared for the worst; ***das Schlimmste haben wir hinter uns*** we've got over the worst; ***im ~sten Falle*** → **schlimm·sten·falls** ['ʃlɪmstən'fals] *adv.* if the worst comes to the worst; ~ ***verlierst du die Anzahlung*** *etc. a.* the worst that can happen is for you to lose your deposit *etc.*
Schlin·ge ['ʃlɪŋə] *f* (-; -n) loop; noose; ⚕ sling; *hunt.* snare, *fig. a.* trap; ***den Arm in der ~ tragen*** have one's arm in a sling; ***~n legen*** set snares; *fig.* ***sich aus der ~ ziehen*** wriggle out of it; ***j-m die ~ um den Hals legen*** place a noose around s.o.'s neck; ***bei j-m die ~ zuziehen*** tighten the noose around s.o.'s neck
Schlin·gel ['ʃlɪŋəl] *m* (-s; -) rascal, F scalywag, *Am.* scallawag
schlin·gen[1] ['ʃlɪŋən] (schlang, geschlungen, h) **I.** *v/t.* tie; wrap (***um*** *acc.* around); ***die Arme um j-s Hals*** ~ fling one's arms around s.o.'s neck; **II.** *v/refl.*: ***sich ~ um*** *acc.* wind (*or* twine, coil) (itself) around
'**schlin·gen**[2] (schlang, geschlungen, h) **I.** *v/t.* gulp down, F gobble; → ***hinunterschlingen, verschlingen***; **II.** *v/i.* bolt one's food, F gobble
Schlin·ger·be·we·gung ['ʃlɪŋɐ-] *f* rolling motion
schlin·gern ['ʃlɪŋɐn] *v/i.* (h) ⚓ roll, lurch; *fig.* stagger, totter
Schling·pflan·ze ['ʃlɪŋ-] *f* ⚘ climbing plant, creeper
Schlips [ʃlɪps] *m* (-es; -e) tie; F *fig.* ***j-m auf den ~ treten*** tread on s.o.'s toes; ***sich auf den ~ getreten fühlen*** F be miffed; ***j-n am ~ fassen*** take s.o. to task
Schlit·ten ['ʃlɪtən] *m* (-s; -) sledge, *Am.* sled; sleigh; *sport*: *a.* toboggan; F ***toller*** ~ F flash car; ~ ***fahren*** go sledging (*or* tobogganing); *fig.* ***mit j-m ~ fahren*** haul s.o. over the coals; **~fahrt** *f* sleigh-ride; **~hund** *m* husky, sledge (*Am.* sled) dog; **~par,tie** *f* sleigh-ride
schlit·tern ['ʃlɪtɐn] *v/i.* (sn) slide (***in*** *acc.* into) (*a. fig.*); *a.* slip, *mot.* skid; ***ins ♀ kommen*** start to slip, *mot.* (start to) skid, go into a skid
Schlitt·schuh ['ʃlɪt-] *m* ice-skate; ~ ***laufen*** (*or* ***fahren***) ice-skate, go ice-skating; **~bahn** *f* ice-rink; **~lau·fen** *n* ice-skating; **~läu·fer** *m* ice-skater
Schlitz [ʃlɪts] *m* (-es; -e) **1.** slit; **2.** fly; **3.** slot
'**Schlitz·au·ge** *n a. contp.* slit-eye
'**schlitz·äu·gig** [-ɔʏgɪç] *adj.* slit-eyed
schlit·zen ['ʃlɪtsən] *v/t.* (h) slit
'**Schlitz·ohr** F *n* F sly dog; F crook; ***er ist ein richtiges*** ~ he never misses a trick; '**schlitz·oh·rig** [-oːrɪç] F *adj.* crafty, sly
'**Schlitz|schrau·be** *f* slotted screw; **~verschluß** *m phot.* focal-plane shutter
schloh·weiß ['ʃloː'vaɪs] *adj.* snow-white
schloß [ʃlɔs] *pret. of* ***schließen***
Schloß[1] [ʃlɔs] *n* (-sses; Schlösser ['ʃlœsɐ]) lock; padlock; clasp; ***ins ~ fallen*** slam shut; *fig.* ***hinter ~ und Riegel sitzen*** be (sitting) behind bars; ***j-n hinter ~ und Riegel bringen*** put s.o. behind bars (F in clink)
Schloß[2] *n* (-sses; Schlösser ['ʃlœsɐ]) castle; palace; mansion, *in France*: château; **~an·la·ge** *f* castle (*or* palace) grounds *pl.*
'**schloß·ar·tig** *adj.* palatial
'**Schloß·be·sich·ti·gung** *f* tour of the (*or* a) castle *or* palace
Schlos·ser ['ʃlɔsɐ] *m* (-s; -) a) locksmith, b) (car) mechanic, c) mechanic, fitter
Schlos·se·rei [ʃlɔsə'raɪ] *f* (-; -en) **1.** locksmith's *etc.* shop; **2.** *no pl.* locksmith's *etc.* trade
'**Schlos·ser|hand·werk** *n* → ***Schlosserei*** 2; **~mei·ster** *m* master locksmith *etc.*; → ***Schlosser***; **~werk·statt** *f* → ***Schlosserei*** 1
'**Schloß|fas,sa·de** *f* castle (*or* palace) front *or* façade; **~füh·rung** *f* guided tour of a (*or* the) castle *or* palace; **~gar·ten** *m* castle (*or* palace) gardens *pl. or* grounds *pl.*; **~gra·ben** *m* moat; **~herr** *m* lord of the castle; **~hund** *m*: F ***heulen wie ein*** ~ howl (one's head off); **~ka,pel·le** *f* castle (*or* palace, *often* royal) chapel; **~kon,zert** *n* concert in a palace (*or* castle); **~park** *m* castle (*or* palace) grounds *pl.*; **~rui·ne** *f* ruined castle; ruins *pl.* of a (*or* the) castle, castle ruins *pl.*; **~tor** *n* castle (*or* palace) entrance, entrance to a (*or* the) castle *or* palace; **~vogt** *m* castellan; **~wa·che** *f* palace guard
Schlot [ʃloːt] *m* (-[e]s; -e) chimney (*a. geol.*), smokestack; F ***rauchen*** (*or* ***qualmen***) ***wie ein*** ~ smoke like a chimney
schlot·te·rig ['ʃlɔtərɪç] *adj.* a) shaky, wobbly; doddery, *attr. a.* doddering, b) baggy *clothes*
schlot·tern ['ʃlɔtɐn] *v/i.* (h) a) shake, tremble, shiver *with cold*, b) *clothes etc.*: hang loose(ly), flap; ***vor Angst*** ~ tremble with fear; ***mit ~den Knien*** with shaking knees; ***mir schlotterten die Knie*** my knees were knocking (*or* were like jelly); ***~de Hosen*** baggy trousers
Schlucht [ʃlʊxt] *f* (-; -en) ravine, gorge; canyon; gully
schluch·zen ['ʃlʊxtsən] **I.** *v/i.* (h) sob; F ***schluchz!*** F sniff!; *fig.* ***~de Geigen*** *etc.* sighing violins *etc.*; **II.** ♀ *n* (-s; *no pl.*) sobbing, sobs *pl.*; **Schluch·zer** ['ʃlʊxtsɐ] *m* (-s; -) sob
Schluck [ʃlʊk] *m* (-[e]s; -e) gulp, mouthful; sip; F swig; ***ein ~ Kaffee*** (***Wein***) some (*or* a drop of) coffee (wine); ***ich möchte e-n ~ zu trinken*** I'd like something to drink
'**Schluck·auf** *m* (-s; *no pl.*) hiccups *pl.*; ~ ***haben*** have (the) hiccups
'**Schluck·be·schwer·den** *pl.* difficulty *sg.* (in) swallowing; ***er hat ~*** *a.* he can't swallow very well
Schlück·chen ['ʃlʏkçən] *n* (-s; -) sip, F drop, *a.* F wee dram; ***trinkst du noch ein ~?*** will you have another drop?
'**schlück·chen·wei·se** *adv.*: ~ ***trinken*** sip
schlucken ['ʃlʊkən] (*sep.*, -k·k-) (h) **I.** *v/t.* swallow (*a. fig.*), *fig. a.* take *rebuke etc.*; *fig.* swallow up *firm etc.*, *a.* F *money etc.*; *phys.* absorb; F guzzle *petrol*; F ***einen ~ gehen*** F go for a tipple; **II.** *v/i.* swallow; ***da mußte ich erst einmal*** ~ I had to swallow hard
Schlucker ['ʃlʊkɐ] (*sep.* -k·k-) *m* (-s; -): F ***armer*** ~ poor devil (*sl.* bastard)
'**Schluck|imp·fung** *f* oral vaccination; **~specht** F *m* F boozer
'**schluck·wei·se** *adv.* in sips, slowly
schlu·dern ['ʃluːdɐn] *v/i.* (h) → ***schlampen***; **Schlu·dri·an** ['ʃluːdriaːn] F *m* (-s; -e) **1.** messy (*or* chaotic) person; **2.** *no pl.* sloppiness, slovenliness; ***hier ist der ~ eingerissen*** things have got pretty chaotic in here; **schlu·drig** ['ʃluːdrɪç] *adj.* slovenly, sloppy
schlug [ʃluːk] *pret. of* ***schlagen***
Schlum·mer ['ʃlʊmɐ] *m* (-s; *no pl.*) sleep, *lit.* slumber; **~lied** *n* lullaby
schlum·mern ['ʃlʊmɐn] *v/i.* (h) sleep, *lit.* slumber; *fig. a.* lie dormant
'**schlum·mernd** *fig. adj.* dormant, *a.* latent *illness, talent etc.*
'**Schlum·mer|rol·le** *f* bolster; **~stünd·chen** *n* nap
Schlumpf [ʃlʊmpf] *m* (-[e]s; Schlümpfe ['ʃlʏmpfə]) **1.** smurf; **2.** F *fig.* dwarf, F midget
Schlund [ʃlʊnt] *m* (-[e]s; Schlünde ['ʃlʏndə]) **1.** *anat.* (back of the) throat, 🕮 pharynx; *zo.* maw; **2.** *fig.* (yawning) chasm; ***der ~ der Hölle*** the jaws of hell
Schlupf [ʃlʊpf] *m* (-[e]s; *no pl.*) ⚙ slip
schlüp·fen ['ʃlʏpfən] *v/i.* (sn) **1.** slip (***aus*** *dat.* out of); **2.** ~ ***in*** *acc.* slip into *one's coat etc.*; ~ ***aus*** *dat.* slip out of *s.th.*, slip *s.th.* off; **3.** *zo.* hatch (out)
Schlüp·fer ['ʃlʏpfɐ] *m* (-s; -) (***ein*** ~ a pair of) underpants (*or* pants) *pl.*
'**Schlupf·loch** *n* a) gap, b) hideout
schlüpf·rig ['ʃlʏpfrɪç] *adj.* slippery (*a. fig.*); *fig.* risqué, off-colo(u)r *joke etc.*
'**Schlupf·win·kel** *m* **1.** hideout; *w.s.* haunt; **2.** *zo.* hiding place

schlur·fen ['ʃlʊrfən] *v/i.* (sn) shuffle, drag one's feet; *w.s.* slouch

schlür·fen ['ʃlʏrfən] *v/t. and v/i.* (h) slurp; sip

Schluß [ʃlʊs] *m* (-sses; Schlüsse ['ʃlʏsə]) **1.** end; conclusion; ending *of a book, film etc.*; *parl.* closing, closure, *Am.* cloture *of a debate*; ✝ closing time; (*copy*) deadline; ***am ~ e-s Jahres*** at the end (*or* close) of a year, after a year; ***~ für heute!*** that's all for today; ***~ damit!*** stop it!, that'll do (now)!; ***und damit ~!*** and that's that, and that's the end of that; ***~ mit dem Unsinn!*** stop that nonsense, enough of that nonsense; ***am ~*** a) at the end, b) in the end; ***irgendwann muß mal ~ sein*** you've got to call a halt somewhere; ***~ machen*** a) finish work, F knock off (for the day), b) put an end to it all; ***machen wir ~ für heute*** let's call it a day; ***~ machen mit*** *dat.* stop, *a.* give up *smoking etc.*, finish with *s.o.*; ***zum ~*** a) finally, to finish off, b) in the end; ***bis zum ~ bleiben*** stay to the end; ***zum ~ kommen*** come to a close; ***zum ~ möchte ich noch sagen*** in conclusion may I say; **2.** conclusion; ***e-n ~ ziehen*** draw a conclusion, conclude (***aus*** *dat.* from); ***zu dem ~ kommen*** (*or* ***gelangen***), ***daß*** come to the conclusion that, decide that; → ***voreilig, Weisheit***; **~ab·rech·nung** *f* final account; **~ab·stim·mung** *f* final vote; **~ak₁kord** *m* ♪ final chord; **~akt** *m thea.* final act (*a. fig.*), last act; closing ceremony; **~ak·te** *f pol.* final act; **~be·mer·kung** *f* final comment, concluding remark; **~bi₁lanz** *f* annual balance sheet; *fig.* ***wenn ich die ~ ziehe*** in the final analysis

Schlüs·sel ['ʃlʏsəl] *m* (-s; -) a) key (*a. fig.*), b) ♪ clef, c) ratio formula, d) ⚙ spanner, (adjustable) wrench, *Am.* (monkey) wrench; **~bart** *m* bit, ward; **~be·griff** *m* **1.** key concept; **2.** key term (*or* word)

'**Schlüs·sel·bein** *n* collarbone, 📖 clavicle; **~bruch** *m* fractured (*or* broken) collarbone

'**Schlüs·sel|blu·me** f cowslip, primrose; **~brett** *n* key rack; **~bund** *m, n* bunch of keys; **~dienst** *m* locksmith; **~er·leb·nis** *n* crucial (*or* formative) experience; **2fer·tig** *adj.* ready for occupancy, ready to move into; *esp.* ✝ turnkey ...; **~fi₁gur** *f* key figure; *pol. etc. a.* key player; **~ge·walt** *f* (-; *no pl.*) *R.C.* power of the keys; ⚖ wife's agency (in domestic matters); **~in·du₁strie** *f* key industry; **~kind** F *n* latchkey child; **~loch** *n* keyhole; ***durchs ~ gucken*** peep through the keyhole; **~po·si·ti₁on** *f* key position; **~reiz** *m psych.* key stimulus; **~ring** *m* key ring; **~rol·le** *f* key (*or* crucial) role; **~ro₁man** *m* roman-à-clef; **~stel·lung** *f* key position (*a.* ⚔); ***Mann in e-r ~*** key man; **~sze·ne** *f* crucial scene; **~₁über·ga·be** *f* completion; **~wort** *n* (-[e]s; ¨er) a) key word, b) combination *of a lock*

'**Schluß·fei·er** *f* celebration; *ped.* speech day, *Am.* commencement; *sport*: closing ceremony

'**schluß·fol·gern** *v/i. and v/t.* (h): ***~ aus*** *dat.* conclude (*or* infer) from; '**Schluß·fol·ge·rung** *f* conclusion, inference

'**Schluß·for·mel** *f letter*: complimentary close; *contract*: final clause

schlüs·sig ['ʃlʏsɪç] *adj.* **1.** logical; *a.* sound *argument*; ***~er Beweis*** conclusive evidence; **2.** ***sich ~ werden*** make up one's mind (***über*** *acc.* about), decide (about, on, as to); ***sich ~ sein*** have decided, have made up one's mind

'**Schlüs·sig·keit** *f* (-; *no pl.*) conclusiveness

'**Schluß|ka₁pi·tel** *n* final (*or* last) chapter; **~kom·mu·ni₁qué** *n* final communiqué; **~kurs** *m stock exchange*: closing price, final quotation (*gen.* for); closing rate (for *foreign currency*); **~läu·fer** *m sport*: anchor (man); ***als ~ laufen*** run the last leg; **~licht** *n* **1.** *mot. etc.* tail-light; **2.** *fig. sport*: F tailender, bottom-of-the-table team; F *fig.* ***das ~ bilden*** bring up the rear; **~mann** *m* (-[e]s; ¨er) **1.** → ***Schlußläufer***; **2.** *soccer etc.*: goalkeeper, F goalie; **~no₁tie·run·gen** *pl. stock exchange*: closing rates; **~pfiff** *m* final whistle; **~plä·doy·er** *n* summing up, final speech; **~punkt** *m*: *fig.* ***e-n ~ unter e-e Sache setzen*** forget about s.th.; **~re·de** *f* final speech (*or* address), F wind-up speech; **~re·so·lu·ti₁on** *f* final resolution; **~run·de** *f* final(s *pl.*); **~satz** *m* a) concluding (*or* closing) sentence, b) ♪ final movement, c) *tennis*: final set; **~sprung** *m* hop; **~strich** *m* final stroke; *fig.* ***e-n ~ ziehen*** consider the matter closed, ***unter*** *acc.*: *a.* forget about *s.th.*; **~sze·ne** *f* final scene; **~ver·kauf** *m* (end-of-season) sale; **~wort** *n* (-[e]s; -e) closing words *pl.*; closing speech; epilogue; summary; **~ze·re·mo₁nie** *f a. sport*: closing ceremony

Schmach [ʃmaːx] *f* (-; *no pl.*) a) disgrace, shame, b) insult, affront, outrage; humiliation; ***et. als ~ empfinden*** find s.th. humiliating; ***sich mit ~ (und Schande) bedecken*** disgrace o.s., bring disgrace on o.s.

schmach·ten ['ʃmaxtən] *v/i.* (h) **1.** languish (***vor*** *dat.* with); ***vor Durst ~*** be parched with thirst; **2.** yearn, languish, pine (***nach*** *dat.* for); ***j-n ~ lassen*** keep s.o. on tenterhooks, F let s.o. sweat it out; '**schmach·tend** *adj.* languishing, yearning; '**Schmacht·fet·zen** F *m* F weepie, tearjerker

schmäch·tig ['ʃmɛçtɪç] *adj.* of slight build; delicate, frail; ***~er Körperbau*** slight frame

'**Schmacht·locke** F *f* kiss-curl, *Am.* spit curl

'**schmach·voll** *adj.* shameful, ignominious; humiliating

schmack·haft ['ʃmakhaft] *adj.* tasty, *lit.* savo(u)ry *dish*; *fig.* ***j-m et. ~ machen*** make s.th. sound appealing to s.o., whet s.o.'s appetite for s.th.

Schmäh [ʃmɛː] *Austrian* F *m* (-s; -[s]) **1.** F con; **2.** (*Viennese etc.*) patter

'**Schmäh·brief** *m* defamatory letter

schmä·hen ['ʃmɛːən] (h) **I.** *v/t.* revile; disparage, F run down; **II.** *v/i.* blaspheme

schmäh·lich ['ʃmɛːlɪç] **I.** *adj.* → ***schmachvoll***; **II.** *adv.* badly; ***~ versagen*** fail miserably; ***j-n ~ im Stich lassen*** leave s.o. in the lurch

'**Schmäh|re·de** *f* defamatory speech, diatribe; ***~n gegen j-n führen*** heap abuse on s.o., run s.o. down; **~ruf** *m* shout of abuse; ***~e gegen j-n ausstoßen*** call s.o. names; **~schrift** *f* diatribe; lampoon

Schmä·hung ['ʃmɛːʊŋ] *f* (-; -en) *a. pl.* invective, vituperation; blasphemy; calumny

schmal [ʃmaːl] *adj.* narrow *face, eyes etc.*; thin *lips etc.*, slim *hands, hips etc.*; *fig.* meagre (*Am.* meager); poor; *fig.* ***~es Buch*** (*or* ***Büchlein***) slim volume; ***er ist ~er geworden*** he's lost weight; ***er ist ~ geworden*** *a.* he's gone thin

'**schmal·brü·stig** [-brʏstɪç] *adj.* **1.** narrow-chested; **2.** *fig.* narrow(-minded) *views etc.*, hidebound; lowbrow *book etc.*

schmä·lern ['ʃmɛːlərn] *v/t.* (h) a) curtail, reduce, diminish, b) impair (*a. rights*), detract from; belittle, do *s.th.* down

Schmä·le·rung ['ʃmɛːlərʊŋ] *f* (-; -en) a) curtailment, reduction, b) impairment; belittlement; → ***schmälern***

'**Schmal·film** *m* cine-film, 8mm film; **~ka·me·ra** *f* cine-camera; **~pro₁jek·tor** *m* cine-projector, 8mm projector

'**schmal·hüf·tig** [-hʏftɪç] *adj.* slim-hipped

'**schmal·lip·pig** [-lɪpɪç] *adj.* thin-lipped

'**Schmal·sei·te** *f* short side, narrow end

'**Schmal·spur** *f* narrow ga(u)ge; **~...** *in cpds.* F *fig.* small-time; **~bahn** *f* light railway

'**schmal·spu·rig** [-ʃpuːrɪç] *adj.* narrow-ga(u)ge ...

'**schmal·wüch·sig** [-vyːksɪç] *adj.* of slim build, very slim

Schmalz[1] [ʃmalts] *n* (-es; *no pl.*) lard; F *fig.* ***~ in den Knochen haben*** F have plenty of brawn; F ***das hat viel ~ gekostet*** F that took a bit of muscle

Schmalz[2] F *m* (-es; *no pl.*) F schmaltz

'**Schmalz·brot** *n* bread and dripping

schmal·zig ['ʃmaltsɪç] F *fig. adj.* sentimental, F schmaltzy

Schman·kerl ['ʃmaŋkɐl] *dial. n* (-s; -n) tasty titbit (*Am.* tidbit), delicacy; *fig.* (real) treat, something to savo(u)r

schma·rot·zen [ʃma'rɔtsən] *v/i.* (h) **1.** *zo.*, ♣ be a parasite; ***~ auf*** *dat.* live off; ***... schmarotzt auf*** *dat. a.* ... is a parasite that lives off; **2.** F *fig.* F scrounge, sponge; be a sponger (*or* scrounger, parasite); ***~ bei*** *dat.* sponge off (*or* on), scrounge off (*or* from), live off; ***schmarotzt sie wieder?*** is she on the scrounge again?; **Schma·rot·zer** [ʃma'rɔtsɐ] *m* (-s; -) **1.** *zo.*, ♣ parasite; **2.** F *fig.* scrounger, sponger, parasite; **Schma'rot·zer·tum** *n* (-s; *no pl.*) parasitism (*a. fig.*)

Schmar·ren ['ʃmarən] *dial. m* (-s; -) **1.** scrambled pancake; **2.** F *fig.* F rubbish, rot, garbage; ***so ein ~!*** what a load of rubbish *etc.*; ***das geht dich e-n ~ an*** that's none of your (F bloody) business

Schmatz [ʃmats] F *m* (-es; -e) F smacker

schmat·zen ['ʃmatsən] *v/i.* (h) eat noisily; ***schmatz nicht so!*** close your mouth when you're eating; ***er schmatzt furchtbar*** he makes such a noise when he's eating

Schmat·zer ['ʃmatsɐ] F *m* (-s; -) → ***Schmatz***

schmau·chen ['ʃmaʊxən] (h) **I.** *v/i.* puff away; **II.** *v/t.* puff away at

Schmaus [ʃmaʊs] *m* (-es; *no pl.*) feast; *fig.* treat; **schmau·sen** ['ʃmaʊzən] (h) **I.** *v/i.* feast; **II.** *v/t.* feast on, F tuck into

schmecken ['ʃmɛkən] (*sep.* -k·k-) (h) **I.** *v/t.* taste, try; (be able to) taste; ***ich schmecke gar nichts*** I can't taste a thing; **II.** *v/i.*: ***~ nach*** *dat.* taste of, *fig.* smack of; ***gut ~*** taste good; ***es sich ~ lassen*** tuck in; ***laß es dir ~!*** enjoy it, F enjoy!; ***ihm schmeckt es*** a) he likes it, b) he likes his food; ***schmeckt es (dir)?*** do you like it?; ***es schmeckt nach nichts*** it's tasteless, it tastes like nothing; *hum.* ***es schmeckt nach mehr*** F I hope

there's more where that came from; ***das hat aber geschmeckt!*** that was good; ***Nudeln ~ mir immer*** F give me noodles any time; ***es schmeckt mir heute nicht so recht*** I don't really feel like eating today; F *fig.* ***das*** (***die Arbeit***) ***schmeckt ihm nicht*** he doesn't like it (his job); ***das schmeckt mir gar nicht*** *a.* I don't like the sound (*or* look) of that at all
Schmei·che·lei [ʃmaɪçə'laɪ] *f* (-; -en) *a. pl.* flattery
schmei·chel·haft ['ʃmaɪçəlhaft] *adj.* flattering
schmei·cheln ['ʃmaɪçəln] *v/i.* (h) (*dat.*) a) flatter, compliment, b) cajole, c) adulate; F butter up, soft-soap; ***das Foto ist aber geschmeichelt*** it's a very flattering photo (of you *etc.*); ***das schmeichelt s-r Eitelkeit*** it flatters (*or* tickles) his vanity; ***ich schmeichele mir, ein guter Redner zu sein*** I flatter myself that (*or* I like to think) I'm a good speaker; ***du brauchst*** (***mir***) ***gar nicht so zu ~*** flattery will get you nowhere; *fig.* ***~de Musik*** soft music
Schmeich·ler ['ʃmaɪçlɐ] *m* (-s; -) flatterer; ***du ~!*** stop flattering me
schmeich·le·risch ['ʃmaɪçlərɪʃ] *adj.* flattering; *contp.* smooth-tongued, ingratiating
schmei·ßen ['ʃmaɪsən] (schmiß, geschmissen, h) F **I.** *v/t.* throw, F chuck; fling, hurl; *fig.* F chuck (in); ***gerade hat's mich geschmissen*** F I went flying (*or* sprawling) just now; *fig.* ***e-e Runde ~*** stand a round; ***den Laden ~*** run the show; ***die Sache ~*** manage (all right, *Am.* alright), F swing it; ***sie schmeißt schon den Haushalt*** she knows how to run a household; ***die Vorstellung ~*** F muff it; **II.** *v/i.*: ***mit Steinen*** (***nach j-m***) ***~*** throw stones (at s.o.); ***mit Geld um sich ~*** throw one's money around; **III.** *v/refl.*: ***sich aufs Bett*** (***in den Sessel***) ***~*** throw o.s. onto one's bed (drop into the armchair); ***sich in den Mantel ~*** get (*or* dive) into one's coat, throw one's coat on; → ***Schale***
Schmeiß·flie·ge ['ʃmaɪs-] *f* bluebottle
Schmelz [ʃmɛlts] *m* (-es; *no pl.*) **1.** (*a. dental*) enamel; ⚙ glaze; **2.** melodiousness, mellowness
'**schmelz·bar** *adj.* meltable, fusible
Schmel·ze ['ʃmɛltsə] *f* (-; -n) **1.** thaw(ing period); **2.** ⚙ a) smelting, b) molten metal (*or* glass), c) liquid rock
schmel·zen ['ʃmɛltsən] (schmolz, geschmolzen) **I.** *v/i.* (sn) melt (*a. fig.*); dissolve *in a liquid*; liquefy; *fig.* dwindle; **II.** *v/t.* (h) melt, *metall.* smelt; liquefy
'**schmel·zend** *adj.* **1.** melting *snow etc.*; **2.** ♪ mellow *a. voice*, *iro.* dulcet *tones, voice*; *fig.* melting *look*
Schmel·zer ['ʃmɛltsɐ] *m* (-s; -) ⚙ smelter
Schmel·ze·rei [ʃmɛltsə'raɪ] *f* (-; -en) → ***Schmelzhütte***
'**Schmelz|far·be** *f* enamel paint; **⩤flüs·sig** *adj.* molten; **~hüt·te** *f* (iron) foundry; **~kä·se** *m* cheese spread (*or* slices); **~ofen** *m* (s)melting furnace; **~punkt** *m* (s)melting point; **~schwei·ßen** *n* fusion welding; **~si·che·rung** *f* ⚡ fusible cut-out; **~tie·gel** *m* melting pot (*a. fig.*); **~was·ser** *n* melted snow and ice
Schmer·bauch *m* paunch, pot belly
Schmerz [ʃmɛrts] *m* (-es; -en) **1.** pain; ache; ***~en haben*** be in pain; ***ich habe keine ~en*** I don't feel any pain; ***vor ~ aufschreien*** yell with pain; ***von ~en gepeinigt*** racked with pain; ***~en im Kreuz haben*** have a pain in one's back, have (a) backache; F *iro.* ***hast du sonst noch ~en?*** is that all?; **2.** pain; *a. pl.* grief, sorrow, heartache; (***j-m***) ***~ verursachen*** cause (s.o.) pain; ***tiefen ~ empfinden über*** *acc.* be deeply grieved over (*or* about)
'**schmerz·emp·find·lich** *adj.* sensitive to pain
schmer·zen ['ʃmɛrtsən] (h) **I.** *v/i.* hurt; *stomach*, *head*: ache; *wound*: be sore; smart; ***mir ~ alle Glieder*** all my limbs are aching; **II.** *v/t.* hurt (*a. fig.*); ***es schmerzt mich*** *a. fig.* it hurts (me); *fig.* ***es schmerzt mich, das mit ansehen zu müssen*** it hurts to have to stand by and see it happening; ***es schmerzt mich, daß sie nie angerufen hat*** it upsets me to think that she never rang up
'**Schmer·zens|geld** *n* (-[e]s; *no pl.*) compensation (for injuries suffered); **~mann** *m art*: Man of Sorrow(s); **~mut·ter** *f art*: mater dolorosa, Our Lady of Sorrows; **~schrei** *m* scream of pain
'**schmerz·er·füllt** *adj.* deeply grieved
'**Schmerz·for·schung** *f* pain research
'**schmerz·frei** *adj.* a) free of pain, b) painless *treatment etc.*
'**Schmerz|ge·fühl** *n* (sensation of) pain; **~gren·ze** *f* → ***Schmerzschwelle***
'**schmerz·haft** *adj.* painful; *fig. a.* distressing; ***~e Stelle*** sore place (*or* area), tender spot
'**schmerz·lich** *fig.* **I.** *adj.* painful; sad (*loss, memory, smile etc.*); ***~e Pflicht*** sad duty; ***~e Gewißheit*** painful knowledge (*or* certainty); ***~es Verlangen*** (bitter) yearning; **II.** *adv.*: ***j-n ~ vermissen*** miss s.o. badly; ***~ berührt*** sad; ***es hat mich ~ berührt*** it made me very sad
'**schmerz·lin·dernd** *adj.* analgesic (*a. **~es Mittel***); *a.* soothing *ointment*
'**schmerz·los** **I.** *adj.* painless; **II.** *adv.*: F ***mach es kurz und ~*** get it over and done with; F ***das war aber kurz und ~*** that was short and sweet
'**Schmerz|mit·tel** *n* painkiller, analgesic; **~schwel·le** *f* pain threshold
'**schmerz·stil·lend** **I.** *adj.* painkilling; analgesic; ***~es Mittel*** painkiller, analgesic; **II.** *adv.*: ***es wirkt ~*** it will ease the pain
'**Schmerz·ta͵blet·te** *f* → ***Schmerzmittel***
'**schmerz|ver·zerrt** *adj.* contorted with pain; **~voll** *adj.* painful (*a. fig.*)
'**Schmerz·zen·trum** *n* pain centre (*Am.* center)
Schmet·ter·ball ['ʃmɛtɐ-] *m tennis*: smash
Schmet·ter·ling[1] ['ʃmɛtɐlɪŋ] *m* (-s; -e) butterfly
'**Schmet·ter·ling** *n, m* (-s; *no pl.*) *swimming*: butterfly
'**Schmet·ter·lings|netz** *n* butterfly net; **~samm·lung** *f* butterfly collection; **~stil** *m* butterfly (stroke)
schmet·tern ['ʃmɛtɐn] **I.** *v/t.* (h) **1.** smash (***in Stücke*** to pieces); ***~ gegen*** *acc.* hurl at, dash *s.th.* against; **2.** *tennis*: smash; **3.** F belt out *a song etc.*; **II.** *v/i.* **4.** (sn) crash; *door*: slam; **5.** (h) *tennis*: smash; **6.** (h) resound; *voice*: ring (out); *bird*: warble; *trumpets etc.*: blare (out)
Schmet·ter·schlag ['ʃmɛtɐ-] *m tennis*: smash
Schmied [ʃmiːt] *m* (-[e]s; -e [-də]) smith
Schmie·de ['ʃmiːdə] *f* (-; -n) blacksmith's shop, smithy; forge; **~ar·beit** *f* a) forging, b) wrought-iron work
'**Schmie·de·ei·sen** *n* a) forging steel, b) wrought iron; '**schmie·de·ei·sern** *adj.* wrought-iron ...
'**Schmie·de·ham·mer** *m* blacksmith's (*or* forge) hammer
schmie·den ['ʃmiːdən] *v/t.* (h) forge; → ***Eisen, Plan, Ränke***
'**Schmie·de|ofen** *m* forging furnace; **~pres·se** *f* forging press
schmie·gen ['ʃmiːgən] (h) **I.** *v/refl.*: ***sich an j-n ~*** cuddle up to s.o.; ***sich in et. ~*** nestle into s.th., ***in e-e Decke***: cuddle up inside a blanket; ***das Kleid schmiegt sich an ihren Körper*** the dress fits her snugly; **II.** *v/t.*: ***et. ~ in*** (*or* ***an***) *acc.* nestle s.th. into *s.th.*
schmieg·sam ['ʃmiːkzaːm] *adj.* pliant, flexible; soft *leather etc.*; supple, pliable, lithe *body*; *fig.* adaptable
Schmier·dienst ['ʃmiːɐ-] *m* lubrication service
Schmie·re ['ʃmiːrə] *f* (-; -n) **1.** ⚙ grease, lubricant; **2.** muck, F goo; **3.** F second-rate theat|re (*Am. a.* -er); **4.** F ***~ stehen*** keep a lookout
schmie·ren ['ʃmiːrən] (h) **I.** *v/t.* **1.** a) smear, b) ⚙ grease, oil, lubricate, c) butter *bread*; spread *butter etc.*, d) scribble, scrawl; ***sich ein Brot ~*** make o.s. a sandwich; ***schmierst du mir ein Brot mit Käse?*** can you make me a cheese sandwich (*or* some bread with cheese on)?; *fig.* ***wie geschmiert laufen*** run (*or* go) like clockwork; **2.** F ***j-m e-e ~*** paste s.o. one; **3.** F ***j-n ~*** F grease s.o.'s palm; **II.** *v/i.* a) *ballpoint etc.*: smudge, b) *person*: scribble, scrawl
'**Schmie·ren·ko·mö·di͵ant** *m* ham (actor); *fig.* play-actor
Schmie·re·rei [ʃmiːrə'raɪ] *f* (-; -en) smearing; mess
'**Schmier|fä·hig·keit** *f* lubricity; **~fink** F *m* a) F mucky pup; scrawler, b) muckraker; **~geld** *n* bribe money (*a. pl.*), F payoff, payola
schmie·rig ['ʃmiːrɪç] *adj.* a) greasy; grubby; grimy, b) *fig.* smutty; F smarmy
Schmier|in·fek·ti͵on ['ʃmiːɐ-] *f* smear infection; **~kä·se** *m* cheese spread; **~mit·tel** *n* lubricant; **~nip·pel** *m* lubricating nipple; **~öl** *n* lubricating oil, lubricant; **~pa͵pier** *n* rough paper; **~pi͵sto·le** *f* grease gun; **~plan** *m* lubrication chart; **~sei·fe** *f* soft (*or* green) soap; **~stel·le** *f* ⚙ lubrication point
Schmie·rung ['ʃmiːrʊŋ] *f* (-; -en) lubrication
Schmier·zet·tel ['ʃmiːɐ-] *m* scrap of paper, piece of rough paper
Schmin·ke ['ʃmɪŋkə] *f* (-; *no pl.*) makeup (*a. thea.*)
'**schmin·ken** (h) **I.** *v/refl.*: ***sich ~*** **1.** a) put one's (*or* some) makeup on; F *hum.* put one's face on, b) wear makeup; ***sich stark ~*** wear a lot of (*or* heavy) makeup; **II.** *v/t.* **2.** make up; ***sich die Lippen ~*** put (some) lipstick on; ***sich die Augen ~*** put one's (*or* some) eye makeup on, wear eye makeup; **3.** *fig.* colo(u)r *a report etc.*
Schmink|kof·fer ['ʃmɪŋk-] *m* vanity case; **~täsch·chen** *n* makeup bag; **~tisch** *m* dressing table; **~topf** *m* makeup jar
Schmir·gel ['ʃmɪrgəl] *m* (-s; *no pl.*) emery
'**schmir·geln** *v/t.* (h) sandpaper
'**Schmir·gel·pa͵pier** *n* sandpaper
schmiß [ʃmɪs] *pret. of* ***schmeißen***

Schmiß [ʃmɪs] *m* (-sses; -sse) **1.** gash; (duelling) scar; **2.** *no pl.* F *fig.* verve, F zip; ~ ***haben*** have plenty of go; ***die Musik hat*** ~ F that music's got it in it; **schmis·sig** ['ʃmɪsɪç] F *adj.* F zippy, dashing, rousing
Schmö·ker ['ʃmøːkɐ] F *m* (-s; -) *a* good read; s.th. good to read; ***dicker*** ~ thick tome
'**schmö·kern** F *v/i.* (h) **1.** browse; ~ ***in*** *dat.* browse (*or* leaf) through, dip into; **2.** have one's nose in a book, be buried in a book (*or* in books); ***ab und zu schmökert er gern*** he likes a good read now and again; ***ich setz' mich in den Garten und schmökere ein bißchen*** I'm going to sit in the garden and have a little read
schmol·len ['ʃmɔlən] *v/i.* (h) sulk
Schmoll|mund ['ʃmɔl-] *m* pout (*a.* ***e-n*** ~ ***machen***); **~win·kel** *m*: ***sich in den*** ~ ***zurückziehen*** go off in a huff; ***im*** ~ ***sitzen*** be in a huff, be sulking (in a corner somewhere)
schmolz [ʃmɔlts] *pret. of* ***schmelzen***
Schmon·zes ['ʃmɔntsəs] F *m* (-; *no pl.*) F twaddle, tripe, *sl.* bilge
Schmon·zet·te [ʃmɔn'tsɛtə] *contp. f* (-; -n) F slush
Schmor·bra·ten ['ʃmoːɐ-] *m* pot roast
schmo·ren ['ʃmoːrən] (h) **I.** *v/t. gastr.* braise, stew; **II.** *v/i. gastr.* stew; F *fig.* roast, bake; F *fig.* ***j-n*** ~ ***lassen*** F let s.o. stew (in his *or* her own juice), let s.o. sweat it out
Schmor·topf ['ʃmoːɐ-] *m* casserole
Schmu [ʃmuː] F *m* (-s; *no pl.*) swindle; ~ ***machen*** cheat, fiddle
schmuck [ʃmʊk] *adj.* neat; smart, spruce, dapper; pretty
Schmuck [ʃmʊk] *m* (-[e]s; *no pl.*) **1.** jewellery, *Am.* jewelry; **2.** ornamentation, decoration; ornament
schmücken ['ʃmʏkən] (*sep.* -k·k-) (h) **I.** *v/t.* decorate, adorn, deck out; embellish (*a. fig. speech etc.*); **II.** *v/refl.*: ***sich*** ~ dress up
'**Schmuck·käst·chen** *n* jewellery (*Am.* jewelry) box; *fig.* gem; *fig.* ***das Haus ist ein*** ~ it's a gem of a house
'**schmuck·los** *adj.* plain; simple; austere
'**Schmuck|na·del** *f* brooch; **~sa·chen** *pl.* jewellery *sg.*, *Am.* jewelry *sg.*; trinkets; **~stück** *n* piece of jewellery (*Am.* jewelry); *fig.* gem, jewel; **~wa·ren** *pl.* jewellery *sg.*, *Am.* jewelry *sg.*
schmud·de·lig ['ʃmʊdəlɪç] F *adj.* grubby; slovenly; **schmud·deln** ['ʃmʊdəln] F *v/i.* (h) get dirty (*or* soiled)
Schmud·del·wet·ter ['ʃmʊdəl-] F *n* mucky weather
Schmug·gel ['ʃmʊgəl] *m* (-s; *no pl.*) smuggling; ~ ***treiben*** → ***schmuggeln***
Schmug·ge·lei [ʃmʊgə'laɪ] *f* (-; -en) → ***Schmuggel***
'**schmug·geln** (h) **I.** *v/t.* smuggle; *fig. a.* sneak; **II.** *v/i.* smuggle
'**Schmug·gel·wa·re** *f* smuggled goods *pl.*, contraband
Schmugg·ler ['ʃmʊglɐ] *m* (-s; -) smuggler; **~ban·de** *f* ring of smugglers
schmun·zeln ['ʃmʊntsəln] *v/i.* (h) smile (to o.s.), grin
Schmus [ʃmuːs] F *m* (-es; *no pl.*) F rubbish, twaddle
schmu·sen ['ʃmuːzən] F *v/i.* (h) cuddle (***mit j-m*** s.o.); kiss and cuddle, F smooch
Schmutz [ʃmʊts] *m* (-es; *no pl.*) dirt; *fig.* filth, smut; *fig.* ***in den*** ~ ***ziehen*** drag through the mud; ***j-n mit*** ~ ***bewerfen*** sling mud at s.o.; **≈ab·wei·send** *adj.* stain-resistant; **~ar·beit** *f* dirty work; **~bür·ste** *f* cleaning brush
schmut·zen ['ʃmʊtsən] *v/i.* (h) get dirty (*or* soiled); ***leicht*** ~ *a.* soil easily
'**Schmutz|fän·ger** *m* **1.** *mot.* mudflap; **2.** *fig.* dust trap; **~fink** F *m* (-en; -en) F pig; F mucky pup; **~fleck** *m* dirty mark
schmut·zig ['ʃmʊtsɪç] *adj.* dirty, *fig. a.* smutty; ***sich*** ~ ***machen*** get dirty, dirty o.s.; *fig.* **~*e Phantasie*** dirty mind; **~*es Lächeln*** dirty grin; → ***Wäsche***
'**Schmutz|li·te·ra,tur** *f* pornography, smut; **~schicht** *f* layer of dirt; **~stoff** *m* pollutant; **~strei·fen** *m* dirty streak; **~ti·tel** *m typ.* half-title; **~wä·sche** *f* dirty washing; **~zu·la·ge** *f* dirt money
Schna·bel ['ʃnaːbəl] *m* (-s; Schnäbel ['ʃnɛːbəl]) **1.** *zo.* beak, bill; **2.** spout; **3.** F *fig.* mouth, *sl.* trap; F ***halt den*** **~!** shut up!; ***sie spricht, wie ihr der*** ~ ***gewachsen ist*** she doesn't mince her words; ***ihr steht der*** ~ ***nie still*** she never stops talking
schnä·beln ['ʃnɛːbəln] *v/i.* (h) *zo.* bill; *fig.* bill and coo
'**Schna·bel|tas·se** *f* feeding cup; **~tier** *n* duckbilled platypus
schna·bu·lie·ren [ʃnabu'liːrən] F (h) **I.** *v/i.* F have a good munch, munch away; F feed one's face; **II.** *v/t.* F munch, polish off
Schnack [ʃnak] *dial. m* (-[e]s; -s) **1.** chat, F natter; **2.** phrase, saying; **3.** F twaddle
schnacken ['ʃnakən] (*sep.* -k·k-) *dial. v/i.* (h) chat, F natter
schnackeln ['ʃnakəln] (*sep.* -k·k-) *v/i.* (h) **1.** ***mit den Fingern*** ~ snap one's fingers; **2.** F ***bei ihm hat's geschnackelt*** F it finally clicked (with him); **3.** F ***bei ihr hat's geschnackelt*** she's in the family way, *b.s. sl.* she's up the spout
Schna·ke ['ʃnaːkə] *f* (-; -n) daddy-longlegs; mosquito, midge
Schnal·le ['ʃnalə] *f* (-; -n) **1.** buckle, clasp; **2.** F *dial.* ***blöde*** ~ stupid woman; **3.** F tart, hooker; '**schnal·len** *v/t.* (h) **1.** buckle; strap (***auf*** *acc.* onto); ***enger*** ~ tighten; ***weiter*** ~ loosen; → ***Gürtel***; **2.** F get; ***sie hat's nicht geschnallt*** *a.* F it just didn't get through (to her)
'**Schnal·len·schuh** *m* buckled shoe
schnal·zen ['ʃnaltsən] *v/i.* (h): ***mit den Fingern*** ~ snap one's fingers; ***mit der Zunge*** ~ click one's tongue; ***mit der Peitsche*** ~ crack one's whip
Schnäpp·chen ['ʃnɛpçən] F *n* (-s; -) F snip; ***da hast du aber ein*** ~ ***gemacht!*** you got a real snip there
schnap·pen ['ʃnapən] (h) **I.** F *v/t.* **1.** catch, F nab *s.o.*; grab, snatch *s.th.*; (***sich***) ***et.*** ~ grab s.th.; ***j-n am Arm*** ~ grab s.o.'s arm; ***den werde ich mir*** **~!** I'm going to nab him, I'll tell him what's what; **II.** *v/i.* **2.** ~ ***nach*** *dat.* snap (*or* snatch, grab) at; → ***Luft***; **3.** *lock etc.*: click; *scissors*: snip; ***ins Schloß*** ~ snap shut; ***nach hinten*** (***vorne***) ~ snap back (forward); ***nach oben*** ~ spring up (*or* open)
'**Schnapp|mes·ser** *n* switchblade, *Brit.* flick knife; **~schloß** *n* spring lock (*or* catch); **~schuß** *m* snapshot (*a. fig.*), snap; ***e-n*** ~ ***machen von*** *dat.* take a snap of; **~ver·schluß** *m* spring (*or* snap) lock, spring catch
Schnaps [ʃnaps] *m* (-es; Schnäpse ['ʃnɛpsə]) **1.** spirits *pl.*; schnapps; **2.** F drink, F booze, liquor; **~bren·ner** *m* distiller; **~bren·ne·rei** *f* distillery; **~bru·der** F *m* F boozer, dipso; **~bu·de** F *f* F boozer
Schnäps·chen ['ʃnɛpsçən] F *n* (-s; -) F snifter; F quickie
'**Schnaps|dros·sel** F *f* F boozer, dipso; **~fah·ne** F *f*: ***e-e*** ~ ***haben*** F reek of alcohol (*or* drink); **~fla·sche** *f* bottle of brandy (*or* whisk[e]y *etc.*), F bottle of booze; (*empty*) brandy (*or* whisk[e]y *etc.*) bottle; **~glas** *n* shot glass; **~idee** F *f* crazy idea; **~na·se** F *f* drinker's nose; **~zahl** *f* nice number
schnar·chen ['ʃnarçən] *v/i.* (h) snore
Schnar·cher ['ʃnarçɐ] *m* (-s; -) snorer; ***ein*** ~ ***sein*** *a.* snore
schnar·ren ['ʃnarən] *v/i.* (h) **1.** rattle; *bell*: buzz; **2.** rasp
Schnat·ter·gans ['ʃnatɐ-] F *f* F chatterbox
schnat·tern ['ʃnatɐn] *v/i.* (h) *goose*: cackle; *duck*: quack; *fig.* gabble (away), F yak; ***er schnatterte vor Kälte*** his teeth were chattering with cold
schnau·ben ['ʃnaʊbən] *v/i. and v/t.* (h) snort; ***sich*** (***die Nase***) ~ blow one's nose; ***vor Wut*** *etc.* ~ snort with rage *etc.*
schnau·fen ['ʃnaʊfən] *v/i.* (h) a) breathe hard; wheeze; (puff and) pant, b) *dial.* breathe, c) F *mot. etc.*: chug (along); ***wir sind ganz schön ins*** ≈ ***gekommen*** we were puffing and panting
Schnau·fer ['ʃnaʊfɐ] F *m* (-s; -) breath; ***den letzten*** ~ ***tun*** F snuff it, croak
Schnau·ferl ['ʃnaʊfɐl] F *dial. n* (-s; -[n]) a) jalopy, b) veteran car
Schnauz [ʃnaʊts] *dial. m* (-es; Schnäuze ['ʃnɔʏtsə]) moustache, F mo
'**Schnauz·bart** *m* moustache
Schnau·ze ['ʃnaʊtsə] *f* (-; -n) **1.** *zo.* snout; muzzle, nose; **2.** ⚙ nozzle; **3.** V snout (*sl.*), trap (*sl.*); ***e-e große*** ~ ***haben*** have a big mouth (*or* trap); ***die*** ~ ***voll haben*** F be fed up to the back teeth (***von*** *dat.* with); ***halt die*** **~!** F belt up!, *sl.* shut your trap!; ***auf die*** ~ ***fallen*** *a. fig.* fall flat on one's face; ***du kriegst gleich eins auf die*** ~ F you'll have my fist in your jaw if you're not careful; F ***frei nach*** ~ F any old how
schnau·zen ['ʃnaʊtsən] F *v/i.* (h) snap, bark
Schnau·zer ['ʃnaʊtsɐ] *m* (-s; -) **1.** *zo.* schnauzer; **2.** F moustache, F mo
Schnecke ['ʃnɛkə] (*sep.* -k·k-) *f* (-; -n) **1.** snail (*a. gastr.*); slug; *gastr. a.* escargot; ***er ist langsam wie e-e*** ~ he's such a slowcoach (*Am.* slowpoke); F ***j-n zur*** ~ ***machen*** F come down on s.o. like a ton of bricks, have a real go at s.o.; **2.** earphone; **3.** scroll; **4.** *gastr.* Chelsea bun; **5.** ⚙ endless screw, worm
'**Schnecken|an·trieb** *m* ⚙ worm drive; **~för·de·rer** *m* ⚙ screw (*or* worm) conveyor
'**schnecken·för·mig** *adj.* spiral ..., winding ...
'**Schnecken|ge·häu·se** *n*, **~haus** *n* (snail) shell; *fig.* ***sich in sein Schnekkenhaus zurückziehen*** go (*or* withdraw) into one's shell; **~rad** *n* ⚙ worm gear; **~tem·po** *n*: ***im*** ~ at a crawl, at a snail's pace; ***im*** ~ ***fahren*** *a.* crawl along
Schnee [ʃneː] *m* (-s; *no pl.*) **1.** snow; F ***schmelzen wie*** ~ ***an der Sonne*** *money etc.*: trickle away, just disappear; F ***und wenn der ganze*** ~ ***verbrennt*** come hell or high water; F ***das ist doch*** ~ ***von***

gestern F that's old hat; **2.** *gastr.* whipped egg whites *pl.*, froth; **3.** *sl.* snow; **4.** *TV* snow

'Schnee·ball *m* snowball (*a.* ✿); **~schlacht** *f* snowball fight; **~sy͵stem** *n* ✝ snowball (*or* pyramid) sales system

'schnee·be·deckt *adj.* snow-covered, snowy; *a.* snowcapped *mountains*

'Schnee|be·richt *m* snow report; **~be·sen** *m gastr.* whisk; **2blind** *adj.* snow-blind; **~blind·heit** *f* snow blindness; **~brett** *n* windslab; **~bril·le** *f*: (**e-e ~** a pair of) snow goggles *pl.*; **~decke** *f* blanket of snow, snow covering; **~eu·le** *f zo.* snowy owl; **~fall** *m* snowfall; **~flocke** *f* snowflake; **~frä·se** *f* snow blower

'schnee·frei *adj.* **1.** free (*or* clear) of snow; **2. ~ haben** be off school because of the snow

'Schnee·ge·stö·ber *n* snow flurry

'schnee·glatt *adj.*: **~e Fahrbahnen** snow-slippery roads; **'Schnee·glät·te** *f* packed snow; snow-slippery roads *pl.*

'Schnee|glöck·chen *n* ✿ snowdrop; **~gren·ze** *f* snow line; **~huhn** *n* ptarmigan; **~ka͵no·ne** *f* snow cannon; **~ket·ten** *pl.* snow chains; **~kö·nig** *m*: F **sich freuen wie ein ~** F be tickled pink, be (as) pleased as punch; **~ku·gel** *f* snowstorm globe; **~mann** *m* (-[e]s; ⸗er) snowman; **~matsch** *m* slush; **~mensch** *m*: **der ~** the Abominable Snowman

'Schnee·mo·bil ['ʃneːmobiːl] *n* (-s; -e) snowmobile; **~pflug** *m a. skiing*: snowplough, *Am.* snowplow; **~räum·fahr·zeug** *n* snowblower; **~rau·pe** *f* snowcat; **~re·gen** *m* sleet; **~schau·er** *m a. pl.* snow(fall); **~schau·fel** *f* snow shovel; **~schmel·ze** *f* thaw; **~schuh** *m* snowshoe

'schnee·si·cher *adj.*: **~es Gebiet** *etc.* area *etc.* with snow guaranteed

'Schnee|sturm *m* snowstorm, blizzard; **~trei·ben** *n* (light) blizzard(s *pl.*); **~ver·hält·nis·se** *pl.* snow conditions; **~ver·we·hung** *f*, **~we·he** *f* snowdrift; **2'weiß** *adj.* snow-white; (as) white as a sheet; **~wol·ke** *f* snowcloud

Schneid [naɪt] F *m* (-[e]s; *no pl.*) pluck, courage, gumption, F guts *pl.*, *sl.* bottle; **j-m den ~ abkaufen** unnerve s.o.

Schneid·bren·ner ['ʃnaɪt-] *m* blowtorch

Schnei·de ['ʃnaɪdə] *f* (-; -n) (cutting) edge, blade; → **Messer; ~brett** *n* chopping board; **~ma͵schi·ne** *f* cutting machine, cutter

schnei·den ['ʃnaɪdən] (schnitt, geschnitten, h) **I.** *v/t.* a) cut (**aus** *dat.* out of); *a.* mow *grass etc.*; carve *roast etc.*; ⚕ cut, operate on *s.o.*, b) edit *film etc.*, c) spin *a ball*; cut *a corner*; *mot.* cut in on *s.o.*; **sich ~** *lines*: intersect; (**auf Tonband**) **~** tape, record; **in Stücke ~** cut up; F *fig.* **j-n ~** cut s.o. dead; F **hier ist e-e Luft zum 2!** F what a fug!; → **Gesicht, Grimasse, Haar; II.** *v/refl.*: **sich ~** cut o.s.; → **Finger;** *fig.* **da schneidet er sich aber** (**gewaltig**) he's very much mistaken there; **III.** *v/i.* a) *fig. wind*: cut right through one, b) ⚕ operate; **in die Hand ~** *strap etc.*: cut into one's hand; **gut ~** be a good hairdresser (*or* barber); *fig.* **j-m ins Herz ~** cut s.o. to the quick; **'schnei·dend** *adj.* a) sharp *pain*, b) piercing, biting *wind, cold etc.*, c) caustic *reply etc.*, d) piercing, shrill *voice etc.*

Schnei·der ['ʃnaɪdɐ] *m* (-s; -) tailor; dressmaker; F **frieren wie ein ~** be frozen to the bone; F **aus dem ~ sein** be out of the wood(s)

Schnei·de·rei [ʃnaɪdə'raɪ] *f* (-; -en) **1.** *no pl.* tailoring, tailor's trade; dressmaking; **2.** tailor's (*or* dressmaker's) shop

Schnei·de·rin ['ʃnaɪdərɪn] *f* (-; -nen) dressmaker

'Schnei·der|krei·de *f* tailor's chalk; **~mei·ster** *m* master tailor

schnei·dern ['ʃnaɪdɐn] (h) **I.** *v/i.* do tailoring (*or* dressmaking); be a tailor (*or* dressmaker); **II.** *v/t.* make, tailor, sew

'Schnei·der|pup·pe *f* tailor's dummy; **~sitz** *m*: **im ~** cross-legged

'Schnei·de|tisch *m* editing table; **~zahn** *m* incisor

schnei·dig ['ʃnaɪdɪç] *adj.* a) dynamic, F snappy, b) dashing, F snappy, c) *fig.* spirited *tune etc.*

schnei·en ['ʃnaɪən] **I.** *v/impers.* (h): **es schneit** it's snowing; **II.** *v/i.* (sn) F *fig.* **ins Haus ~** F blow in

Schnei·se ['ʃnaɪzə] *f* (-; -n) open strip; ✈ (flying) lane

schnell [ʃnɛl] **I.** *adj.* a) quick, *a.* rapid *pulse, movement etc.*; fast *car, runner etc.*; swift *bird, flight etc.*, b) prompt *action etc.*, speedy *reply etc.*; ✝ quick *sale*, c) sudden, abrupt; hasty; **~e Bedienung** fast (*or* quick, prompt) service, fast waiter (*or* waitress); **~er Blick** quick glance; **~er Umsatz** quick returns, *a.* fast turnover; **in ~er Folge** in quick (*or* rapid) succession; **auf ~stem Wege** as quickly as possible, by the quickest possible means; **~er werden** *runner*: get faster, *train etc.*: pick up speed; **e-e ~e Entscheidung treffen** make a quick decision, **müssen**: *a.* have to make up one's mind fast; **das erfordert ~es Handeln** that calls for swift (*or* immediate) action; (**mach**) **~!** hurry up!, F get a move on!, step on it!; **nicht so ~!** not so fast!, F hang on!; → **Truppe** 1; **II.** *adv.* quickly, fast; rapidly; promptly *etc.*; → **I; ~ denken** do some quick thinking; **~ handeln** act fast (*or* without delay); **das geht ~** it doesn't (*or* won't) take long; **das ist ~ gegangen!** that was quick!; **~er ging es nicht** I *etc.* couldn't do it any faster; **~er geht's bei mir nicht** I'm doing my best, I can't work *etc.* any faster than that; **das geht mir zu ~** things are happening too fast for my liking, I can't keep up; **ich gehe eben ~ zum Bäcker** I'm just going to pop round to the baker's; **komm ~!** come quick(ly)!; **~ reich werden** get rich quick; **so ~ wie möglich** as quickly as possible; **er begreift ~** he's quick (on the uptake); **er liest ~** he's a fast reader; **sein Atem ging ~** he was breathing fast; **sprich nicht so ~!** don't talk so fast, slow down; **wir wurden ~ bedient** the service was fast, we got served fast; **das werden wir ganz ~ haben** we'll have that (done) in no time; **sie ist ~ verärgert** (**beleidigt**) she gets annoyed very quickly (she's quick to take offen|ce [*Am.* -se]); **wie heißt er ~ noch?** what's his name again?; → **nachmachen** 1

'Schnella·ster (*sep.* -ll·l-) *m* high-speed lorry (*or* truck)

'Schnell|bahn *f* → **S-Bahn; ~boot** *n* speedboat; ⚔ high-speed launch; **~dienst** *m* express service; **~drucker** *m* high-speed printer

Schnel·le ['ʃnɛlə] *f* (-; *no pl.*) **1.** → **Schnelligkeit; 2.** F **et. auf die ~ machen** do s.th. quickly, *a.* do a quick job of it, do s.th. in a hurry, rush s.th. (off); **das geht nicht so auf die ~** it takes time, you can't rush it off like that; **wie krieg' ich das Buch auf die ~ her?** how can I get hold of the book fast?; **3.** → **Stromschnelle**

'schnelle·big (*sep.* -ll·l-) *adj.* short-lived; **in unserer ~en Zeit** in these fast-moving times

'Schnell·ein·greif·trup·pe *f* rapid response (*or* deployment) force

schnel·len ['ʃnɛlən] **I.** *v/i.* (sn) shoot (up); **in die Höhe ~** skyrocket; **II.** *v/t.* (h) flick

'Schnell·feu·er *n* ⚔ rapid fire; **~pi͵sto·le** *f* automatic pistol; **~waf·fe** *f* automatic firearm

'schnell·fü·ßig [-fyːsɪç] *adj.* nimble, light-footed, *lit.* fleet

'Schnell|gang *m mot.* overdrive; ⚙ rapid power traverse; **~gast·stät·te** *f* cafeteria, snack bar, fast-food restaurant (F place); **~ge·frier·ver·fah·ren** *n* quick-freeze (method)

'Schnell·ge·richt¹ *n* quick (*or* ready-to-serve) meal; *pl. a.* instant food *sg.*

'Schnell·ge·richt² *n* summary court

'Schnell·hef·ter *m* folder, ring binder

Schnel·lig·keit ['ʃnɛlɪçkaɪt] *f* (-; *no pl.*) quickness; fastness; swiftness; rapidity; promptness; suddenness *etc.*; → **schnell** I; speed, pace; *phys.* velocity; **er macht es mit e-r ~!** he does it so fast (*or* with such speed)

'Schnell|im·biß *m* snack bar, F fast-food place; **~koch·plat·te** *f* high-speed plate; **~koch·topf** *m* pressure cooker; **~kurs** *m* crash course; **~pa͵ket** *n* express parcel (*Am.* package); **~rech·ner** *m* high-speed computer; **~rei·ni·gung** *f* express dry cleaning; **~re·stau͵rant** *n* → **Schnellgaststätte; ~rück·lauf** *m video etc.*: fast rewind; **~schuß** F *fig. m* rush job; instant book

schnell·stens ['ʃnɛlstəns] *adv.* as quickly (*or* soon) as possible

schnellst'mög·lich ['ʃnɛlst-] *adj.* fastest (*or* quickest) possible

'Schnell|stra·ße *f* dual carriageway, *Am.* divided highway; **~trans͵por·ter** *m* express van; **~ver·band** *m* ⚕ first-aid dressing; **~ver·fah·ren** *n* **1.** ⚖ summary proceedings *pl.*; **2.** ⚙ high-speed process; **3.** *et.* **im ~ lernen** do a crash course in; **~ver·kehr** *m* fast(-moving) traffic; **~vor·lauf** *m video etc.*: fast forward

'schnell·wir·kend *adj.*: **~es Mittel** fast-acting tablets *etc.*

'Schnell·zug *m* fast train

Schnep·fe ['ʃnɛpfə] *f* (-; -n) **1.** *zo.* snipe; **2.** F tart, hooker

schnet·zeln ['ʃnɛtsəln] *v/t.* (h) shred

schneu·zen ['ʃnɔʏtsən] *v/refl.* (h): **sich ~** blow one's nose

Schnick·schnack ['ʃnɪkʃnak] F *m* (-s; *no pl.*) **1.** useless rubbish (*or* bits and pieces *pl.*); trappings *pl.*; **2.** F twaddle

schnie·fen ['ʃniːfən] F *v/i.* (h) sniff(le)

schnie·ke ['ʃniːkə] *dial. adj.* F snazzy

schnipp [ʃnɪp] *int.* snip!

Schnipp·chen ['ʃnɪpçən] *n*: **j-m ein ~ schlagen** (manage to) outwit s.o., get the better of s.o.; F give s.o. the slip

schnip·peln ['ʃnɪpəln] F *v/i. and v/t.* (h) cut (**an** *dat.* at)

schnip·pen ['ʃnɪpən] (h) **I.** *v/i.* snip; snap

one's fingers; **II.** *v/t.* flick (off *or* away *etc.*)
schnip·pisch ['ʃnɪpɪʃ] *adj.* saucy
Schnip·sel ['ʃnɪpsəl] *m, n* (-s; -) piece, bit; *a.* scrap *of paper*; '**schnip·seln** *v/t. and v/i.* (h) → ***schnippeln***
schnip·sen ['ʃnɪpsən] *v/t. and v/i.* (h) → ***schnippen***
schnitt [ʃnɪt] *pret. of* **schneiden**
Schnitt [ʃnɪt] *m* (-[e]s; -e) **1.** cutting; *film*: editing; **2.** cut (*a. typ.*), ⚕ *a.* gash, incision; **3.** a) shape, cut, style, b) features *pl.*; **4.** pattern; **5.** ⩓ intersection; **6.** average (*a.* ***im ~ erreichen*** *etc.*); ***im ~*** on average; **7.** ⚙ section(al view); → ***Längsschnitt, Querschnitt***; **8.** F profit; ***e-n guten ~ machen*** F make a packet
'**Schnitt|blu·men** *pl.* cut flowers; **~boh·nen** *pl.* green (*or* string) beans, *Brit. a.* French beans
Schnit·te ['ʃnɪtə] *f* (-; -n) a) slice, b) (open) sandwich
'**schnitt·fest** *adj.* firm
'**Schnitt·flä·che** *f* **1.** ⩓ section; **2.** *gastr.* cut end
schnit·tig ['ʃnɪtɪç] *adj.* sleek, F slick
'**Schnitt|kä·se** *m* cheese slices *pl.*; **~lauch** *m* ♣ chives *pl.*; **~li·nie** *f* ⩓ (line of) intersection; secant; **~men·ge** *f* ⩓ intersection; **~mu·ster** *n* pattern; **~punkt** *m* ⩓ (point of) intersection; **~stär·ke** *f* ⚙ slice thickness; **~stel·le** *f* **1.** *film etc.*: cut; **2.** *computer*: interface; **~wun·de** *f* cut, gash
Schnitz [ʃnɪts] *dial. m* (-es; -e) slice
Schnitz|al,tar [ʃnɪts-] *m* carved altar(piece); **~ar·beit** *f* carving; **~bank** *f* (-; ⸚e) carver's bench
Schnit·zel ['ʃnɪtsəl] *n* (-s; -) **1.** *a. m* piece, bit, scrap (of paper); chip *of wood*; **2.** *gastr.* veal (*or* pork) cutlet; ***Wiener ~*** (wiener)schnitzel; **~jagd** *f* paperchase
schnit·zeln ['ʃnɪtsəln] *v/t.* (h) shred
'**Schnit·zel·werk** *n* shredder
schnit·zen ['ʃnɪtsən] *v/t. and v/i.* (h) carve; → ***Holz***
Schnit·zer ['ʃnɪtsɐ] *m* (-s; -) **1.** (wood *etc.*) carver; **2.** F *fig.* blunder, F boob; gaffe, faux pas; ***grober ~*** real howler (F boob); terrible gaffe
Schnit·ze·rei [ʃnɪtsə'raɪ] *f* (-, -en) (wood *etc.*) carving
schnod·de·rig ['ʃnɔdərɪç] F *adj.* F snotty; cocky *boy*; saucy *girl*
schnö·de ['ʃnøːdə] **I.** *adj.* a) contemptible, despicable, b) contemptuous; → ***Mammon***; **II.** *adv.*: ***j-n ~ behandeln*** treat s.o. with disdain (*or* contempt)
Schnor·chel ['ʃnɔrçəl] *m* (-s; -) snorkel
'**schnor·cheln** *v/i.* (h) snorkel, go snorkel(l)ing
Schnör·kel ['ʃnœrkəl] *m* (-s; -) a) curlicue; scroll, b) flourish (*a. fig.*), squiggle; **~schrift** *f* fancy writing
schnor·ren ['ʃnɔrən] F *v/i. and v/t.* (h) F scrounge (***bei*** *dat.* off, from), sponge (on, off); **Schnor·rer** ['ʃnɔrɐ] F *m* (-s; -) F scrounger, sponger
Schnö·sel ['ʃnøːzəl] F *m* (-s; -) prig, F snot-nose
schnucke·lig ['ʃnʊkəlɪç] (*sep.* -k·k-) F *adj.* cute; nice
Schnüf·fe·lei [ʃnʏfə'laɪ] F *f* (-; *no pl.*) F snooping; **schnüf·feln** ['ʃnʏfəln] (h) **I.** *v/i.* **1.** sniff (***an*** *dat.* at); F sniff glue (*or* solvents); **2.** F *fig.* F snoop around; **II.** F *v/t.* **3.** sniff *glue etc.*; **III.** ♀ F *n* (-s; *no pl.*) **4.** snooping; **5.** F glue-sniffing, *formal*: solvent abuse; **Schnüff·ler** ['ʃnʏflɐ] F *fig. m* (-s; -) F snoop(er)
Schnul·ler ['ʃnʊlɐ] *m* dummy, *Am.* pacifier
Schnul·ze ['ʃnʊltsə] F *f* (-; -n) F tearjerker, *a. pl.* sobstuff; '**Schnul·zen·sän·ger** F *m* F crooner; **schnul·zig** ['ʃnʊltsɪç] F *adj.* F soppy, schmaltzy
Schnup·fen ['ʃnʊpfən] *m* (-s; -) cold, F *the* sniffles
schnup·fen ['ʃnʊpfən] (h) **I.** *v/i.* take snuff; **II.** *v/t.* snort
'**Schnup·fen·mit·tel** *n* cold remedy
Schnupf·ta·bak ['ʃnʊpf-] *m* snuff; '**Schnupf·ta·bak(s)·do·se** *f* snuffbox
Schnupf·tuch ['ʃnʊpf-] *dial. n* handkerchief
schnup·pe ['ʃnʊpə] F *pred. adj.*: ***das ist mir (völlig) ~*** I couldn't care less (F give a damn)
schnup·pern ['ʃnʊpɐn] *v/i. and v/t.* (h) sniff; ***frische Landluft ~*** breathe in the fresh country air
Schnup·per·preis ['ʃnʊpɐ-] F *m* bargain price
Schnur [ʃnuːɐ] *f* (-; Schnüre ['ʃnyːrə]) a) cord; (piece of) string, b) (fishing) line, c) ⚡ flex, lead; (*telephone*) cord
Schnür|band ['ʃnyːɐ-] *n* → ***Schnürsenkel***; **~bo·den** *m thea. the* flies *pl.*
Schnür·chen ['ʃnyːɐçən] *n*: *fig.* ***es klappte wie am ~*** it went like clockwork; ***bei ihm klappt es wie am ~*** he's got it down to a fine art
schnü·ren ['ʃnyːrən] (h) **I.** *v/t.* lace (up); **II.** *v/i.* be too tight, stop the flow of blood
'**schnur·ge'ra·de I.** *adj.* straight as a die, F dead straight; **II.** *adv.* F dead straight
'**schnur·los** *adj.* cordless
'**Schnur·los·te·le·fon** *n* cordless phone
Schnürl·re·gen ['ʃnyːɐl-] *dial. m* drizzle
Schnurr·bart ['ʃnʊr-] *m* moustache
'**schnurr·bär·tig** *adj.* moustached, F *hum.* moustachioed
Schnur·re ['ʃnʊrə] *f* (-; -n) amusing story; farce
schnur·ren ['ʃnʊrən] *v/i.* (h) *zo.* purr; *mot. a.* hum; *wheel, fan etc.*: whirr, *Am.* whir
Schnür|rie·men ['ʃnyːɐ-] *m* strap; **~schuh** *m* lace-up (shoe); **~sen·kel** [-zɛŋkəl] *m* (-s; -) shoelace, shoestring, bootlace; **~stie·fel** *m* lace-up boot
'**schnur'stracks** *adv.* straight; immediately, straightaway; ***~ zugehen auf*** *acc.* go (*or* make) straight for, make a beeline for
schnurz [ʃnʊrts] F *pred. adj.* → ***schnuppe***
Schnu·te ['ʃnuːtə] *dial. f* (-; -n) mouth, F mush; ***e-e ~ machen*** (*or* ***ziehen***) pull a face
schob [ʃoːp] *pret. of* **schieben**
Scho·ber ['ʃoːbɐ] *m* (-s; -) haystack, rick; shed, barn
Schock [ʃɔk] *m* (-[e]s; -s) *a. fig.* shock; ***e-n ~ bekommen*** get a shock; ***e-n ~ haben*** be in a state of shock; ***unter ~ stehen*** be suffering from shock; **~be·hand·lung** *f* shock treatment (*a. fig.*), (electro)shock therapy
schocken ['ʃɔkən] (*sep.* -k·k-) F *v/t.* (h) ⚕ *and fig.* shock; **Schocker** ['ʃɔkɐ] (*sep.* -k·k-) F *m* (-s; -) shocker, F (spine-)chiller
'**Schock·far·be** *f* garish colo(u)r; '**schock·far·ben** *adj.* garish
'**schock·ge·fro·ren** *adj.* shock-frozen
schockie·ren [ʃɔ'kiːrən] (*sep.* -k·k-) *v/t.* (h) shock; ***schockiert über*** *acc.* shocked at; ***ich war richtig schockiert*** *a.* I was really taken aback; **schockie·rend** *adj.* shocking; horrifying; frightening
'**Schock|the·ra,pie** *f* shock treatment (*a. fig.*), (electro)shock therapy; **~wir·kung** *f* **1.** shock effect; **2.** ***unter ~ stehen*** be suffering from shock
scho·fel ['ʃoːfəl] F *adj.* a) mean, F rotten, shabby, b) mean, stingy
Schöf·fe ['ʃœfə] *m* (-n; -n) ⚖ lay assessor
'**Schöf·fen·ge·richt** *n* court of lay assessors
Scho·ko·la·de [ʃoko'laːdə] *f* (-; *no pl.*) chocolate; ***heiße ~*** hot chocolate
scho·ko'la·den *adj.* chocolate ...; **~braun** *adj.* chocolate(-colo[u]red), F chocolatey
Scho·ko'la·den|ei *n* chocolate egg; **~eis** *n* chocolate ice cream, F choc-ice; **~fa,brik** *f* chocolate factory; **~gla,sur** *f* chocolate glazing; **~pud·ding** *m* chocolate pudding; **~sei·te** F *f* a) *s.o.'s* best side, b) sunny side; ***sich von s-r ~ zeigen*** show one's best side
Scho·ko·rie·gel ['ʃoːko-] *m* chocolate bar
Scho·la·stik [ʃo'lastɪk] *f* (-; *no pl.*) scholasticism; **Scho·la·sti·ker** [ʃo'lastikɐ] *m* (-s; -) scholastic; **scho·la·stisch** [ʃo'lastɪʃ] *adj.* scholastic(ally *adv.*)
Schol·le[1] ['ʃɔlə] *f* (-; -n) **1.** clod (of earth); **2.** (ice) floe
'**Schol·le**[2] *f* (-; -n) *zo. a. pl.* plaice
schon [ʃoːn] *adv.* **1.** a) already; before, b) so far; *in questions*: yet, ever, c) even; ***~ damals*** even then; ***~ früher*** before, a long time ago; ***~ immer*** always, all along; ***~ oft*** often (enough); ***~ wieder*** again; ***~ wieder!*** not again!; ***~ nach fünf Minuten*** after only five minutes, five minutes later *he'd already gone etc.*; ***~ von Anfang an*** right from the start, F from the word go; ***es ist ~ 12 Uhr*** it's twelve o'clock already; ***ich habe ~ eins*** I've already got one; ***wenn du ~ (mal) da bist*** since you're here; ***~ am nächsten Tag*** the very next day; ***~ um 6 Uhr waren sie auf*** they were already up at 6 o'clock; ***~ im 16. Jahrhundert*** as early (*or* as far back) as the 16th century, ***gab es die Krankheit:*** the disease was already around in the 16th century; ***das war ~ vor zwanzig Jahren*** that was twenty (whole) years ago; ***wie lange sind Sie ~ hier?*** how long have you been here?; ***hast du ~ (einmal) ...?*** have you ever ...?; ***danke, ich habe ~*** *zu trinken etc.*: no thanks, I'm fine; ***da ist er ja ~ wieder*** he's (*iro.* look who's) back again; ***das kenne ich ~*** I know that, I've seen that before, I've heard that one before; ***das kennen wir ~*** we know all about that, that's an old one; ***ich habe ~ bessere Weine getrunken*** I've tasted better wines in my time; ***ich habe ihn ~ (einmal) gesehen*** I've seen him before somewhere; ***hast du ~ gehört?*** have you heard?; ***sind Sie ~ (einmal) in Spanien gewesen?*** have you ever been to Spain?; ***hast du ~ mit ihm gesprochen?*** have you talked to him yet?; ***ist er ~ da?*** has he come yet?, is he here yet?, is he here already?; ***was, (du bist) ~ zurück?*** what, back already?; ***werden Sie ~ bedient?*** are you being served?; ***ich komme (ja) ~!*** (I'm) coming!; ***da sind wir (ja) ~!*** here we are; ***was gibt es denn ~***

wieder? what is it now (*or* this time)?; ***ich verstehe*** ~ I see; ***er wollte*** ~ ***gehen*** he was about (*or* all set) to go; ***warum willst du*** ~ ***gehen?*** why are you leaving so early?; **2.** ***sie wird's*** ~ ***schaffen*** she'll make it all right (*Am.* alright), *a.* don't worry, she'll make it; ***die Zinsen steigen*** ~ ***noch*** the interest rates are bound to go up, the interest rates will go up, you'll see; ***ich mach's*** ~ leave it to me; ***es wird*** ~ ***gehen*** it'll be all right (*Am.* alright), I'll *etc.* manage (somehow); ***das ist*** ~ ***möglich*** that could be, that's quite possible; ***das läßt sich*** ~ ***machen*** a) we *etc.* might be able to do that, it's doable, b) that's no problem, F no problem; ***wir können*** ~ ***mit ihm reden*** we don't mind talking to him; ***ich kann mir*** ~ ***denken, was ...*** I can (just) imagine what ...; ***er ist*** ~ ***eingebildet*** he's certainly bigheaded; ***das war*** ~ ***Glückssache*** that really was a stroke of luck; ***das ist*** ~ ***e-e große Frechheit!*** that really is a bit much; ~ ***gut!*** a) it's all right (*Am.* alright), never mind, b) that'll do; **3.** ***mach*** ~***!*** F get a move on, will you?; ***komm*** ~***!*** come on, then; ***geh*** ~***!*** go on, then; ***nun sag*** ~***, wie's war*** come on, tell us (*or* me) what it was like; **4.** ~***, aber ...*** yes, but ...; ***sie müßte sich*** ~ ***etwas mehr anstrengen*** she'd have to make more of an effort, of course; ***das ist*** ~ ***wahr, aber*** that's (certainly) true, but, that may be true, but; **5.** ***es ist so*** ~ ***teuer genug*** it's expensive enough as it is; ~ ***gar nicht*** least of all; ***morgen*** ~ ***gar nicht*** least of all tomorrow; **6.** ~ ***s-e Stimme*** just to hear his voice, his voice alone; ~ ***der Name*** the mere (mention of the *or* his *etc.*) name, just to hear the (*or* his *etc.*) name; ~ ***der Anblick*** just to see it; ~ ***der Gedanke*** the very idea, the mere thought (of it); ~ ***deswegen*** if only for that (reason); ~ ***ein Milligramm des Gifts kann tödlich sein*** just (*or* even) one milligram(me) of the poison can kill you; ~ ***wegen*** if only because of, if only for the sake of *the children etc.*; ~ ***weil*** if only because; ~ ***sie zu sehen*** (even) just to see her; ***ein Anruf hätte*** ~ ***genügt*** (just) a phone call would have been enough; **7.** F ***na wenn*** ~***!*** so what; so?; ***was macht das*** ~***?*** what does it matter?; ***was heißt das*** ~***?*** so?, that doesn't mean a thing; ***was verstehst du*** ~ ***davon?*** what do you know about it?; **8.** F ***wenn*** ~***, denn*** ~ in for a penny, in for a pound; if you're going to do something, you may as well do it properly; if a thing's worth doing, it's worth doing well

schön [ʃøːn] **I.** *adj.* a) (very) nice, beautiful, *a.* pretty *woman*, handsome, good-looking *man*, lovely *child*, b) *fig.* good; nice; pleasant; choice; F ~***er heißer Tee*** nice hot (cup of) tea; ***ein*** ~***er Erfolg*** quite a success; ~***e Schrift*** nice handwriting; ***ein paar*** ~***e Stunden*** a few pleasant (*or* happy) hours; ***die*** ~***en Künste*** the fine arts; ~***er Tod*** easy death; ~***es Wetter*** good (*or* nice, *esp. meteor.* fine) weather; ***e-s*** ~***en Tages*** a) one day, b) one of these days; ~***en Dank!*** a) many thanks, b) no thank you, F thanks but no thanks; ~***es Wochenende!*** have a nice weekend!; ***war es*** ~ ***im Urlaub?*** did you have a nice holiday?; F ***ein*** ~***es Stück*** (*or* ***e-e*** ~***e Strecke***) ***laufen*** walk quite a way (*or* distance); F ***ein*** ~***es Stück vorankommen*** make a fair bit of progress; ***er macht nur*** ~***e Worte*** it's all talk with him; ***zu*** ~***, um wahr zu sein*** too good to be true; ~ ***wär's!*** would be nice; ***das ist*** ~ ***von ihm*** that's (very) kind *or* nice of him; ***das ist alles*** ~ ***und gut, aber*** that's all very well, but; ***es war sehr*** ~ it was very nice; F ***das sind mir*** ~***e Sachen*** that's a fine kettle of fish; F ***du bist mir ein*** ~***er Freund*** a fine friend you are; F ***das wäre ja noch*** ~***er!*** F that'd be really great; F ~***!*** all right, *Am.* alright; okay; → ***Aussicht, Bescherung***; **II.** *adv.* (very) nicely, beautifully *etc.*; → ***I***; F very, really, F pretty; ***du hast es*** ~***!*** lucky you!; ~ ***warm*** nice and warm; ~ ***kalt*** F pretty cold; F *iro.* ***jetzt steh' ich*** ~ ***da*** F I look a right fool now; F *iro.* ***da ist er aber*** ~ ***angekommen*** he got more than he had bargained for; F *iro.* ***da wärst du*** ~ ***dumm*** you'd be a fool; ***sei*** ~ ***brav!*** be a good boy (*or* girl) now; ***bleib*** ~ ***ruhig*** you be quiet now, just keep calm now; ***es ist ganz*** ~ ***schwer*** a) that's some weight, b) F it's pretty (*or* not half) difficult; ***du hast mich ganz*** ~ ***erschreckt*** you gave me quite a start; ***ich habe mich*** ~ ***gelangweilt*** F I was bored stiff; F *iro.* ***es kommt noch*** ~***er*** there's more to come; F ***wie man so*** ~ ***sagt*** as they say; ***wie es so*** ~ ***heißt*** as the saying goes

Schon·be·zug [ˈʃoːn-] *m* loose cover, *Am.* slipcover; *mot.* seat cover

Schö·ne[1] [ˈʃøːnə] *f* (-n; -n) beauty, *usu. iro.* lovely lady

ˈSchö·ne *n* (-n; *no pl.*): ***das*** ~ ***daran*** the nice thing about it; → ***anrichten***

scho·nen [ˈʃoːnən] (h) **I.** *v/t.* a) spare, b) take care of, look after *s.th.*; take good care of *s.o.*, c) save *supplies, one's strength etc.*; be easy on *s.o.*; ***j-s Gefühle*** ~ spare s.o.'s feelings; ***ich wollte dich*** ~ I didn't want you to get upset; ***um ihren kranken Mann zu*** ~ to make things easier on her sick husband; **II.** *v/refl.*: ***sich*** ~ take it easy; ***du mußt dich*** ~ you must look after yourself, *a.* you mustn't take on so much

schö·nen [ˈʃøːnən] *v/t.* (h) **1.** clarify, fine *wine etc.*; **2.** brighten *colo(u)rs*; **3.** *fig.* massage *facts etc.*

ˈscho·nend I. *adj.* a) careful, gentle; considerate; indulgent, b) *detergent etc.*: mild; **II.** *adv.*: ***j-m et.*** ~ ***beibringen*** break s.th. to s.o. gently; ~ ***umgehen mit*** look after, take care of, handle *s.o.* with kid gloves, go easy on *s.o.*

Scho·ner[1] [ˈʃoːnɐ] *m* (-s; -) cover; antimacassar

ˈScho·ner[2] *m* (-s; -) ⚓ schooner

ˈschön·fär·ben *fig. v/t.* (*sep.*, h) gloss over; **Schön·fär·be'rei** *f* (-; *no pl.*) glossing over the facts

ˈSchon|frist *f* (period of) grace; ~**gang** *m* **1.** *mot.* overdrive; **2.** ⚙ gentle wash, delicate cycle

ˈSchön·geist *m* (a)esthete, belletrist

ˈschön·gei·stig *adj.* (a)esthetic; ~***e Literatur*** belles-lettres

ˈSchön·heit *f* (-; -en) **1.** *no pl.* beauty; **2.** beauty; ~***en des Landes*** beauty spots

ˈSchön·heits|chir,urg *m* cosmetic (*or* plastic) surgeon; ~**chir·ur,gie** *f* cosmetic (*or* plastic) surgery; ~**creme** *f* beauty cream; ~**farm** *f* beauty farm; ~**feh·ler** *m* blemish; flaw, *fig. a.* snag; ~**fleck** *m* beauty spot; ~**ide,al** *n* ideal of beauty; ~**kö·ni·gin** *f* beauty queen; Miss *America etc.*; ~**kon·kur,renz** *f* beauty contest; ~**kor·rek,tur** *f a. fig.* cosmetic change (*or* improvement); ~**ope·ra·ti,on** *f* cosmetic operation, cosmetic (*or* plastic) surgery; ~**pflä·ster·chen** [-pflɛstɐçən] *n* (-s; -) beauty spot; ~**pfle·ge** *f* beauty care; ~**re·pa·ra,tur** *f* basic repair; *mot.* touch-up job; ~**sa,lon** *m* → ***Kosmetiksalon***; ~**sinn** *m* (-[e]s; *no pl.*) sense of beauty; (a)esthetic sense (*or* sensitivity); ~**wett·be·werb** *m* beauty contest

Schon|kaf,fee [ˈʃoːn-] *m* mild coffee; ~**kli·ma** *n* temperate climate; ~**kost** *f* ⚕ bland diet, light foods *pl.*

Schön·ling [ˈʃøːnlɪŋ] *contp. m* (-s; -e) young adonis

ˈschön·ma·chen (*sep.*, h) **I.** *v/refl.*: ***sich*** ~ a) dress up, F get done up, b) put one's makeup (F face) on; **II.** *v/i. dog*: sit up (and beg)

ˈSchön·red·ner *contp. m* smooth-talker

ˈSchön·schreib·drucker *m* letter-quality printer

ˈSchön·schrift *f*: ***et. in*** ~ ***schreiben*** write s.th. in neat

Schön·tu·er [ˈʃøːntuːɐ] *m* (-s; -) flatterer; **Schön·tue·rei** [ʃøːntuːəˈraɪ] *f* (-; *no pl.*) flattery, F soft soap; **ˈschön·tun** *v/i.* (*sep.*, h): ***j-m*** ~ flatter s.o., play (F suck) up to s.o.

Scho·nung [ˈʃoːnʊŋ] *f* (-; -en) **1.** *no pl.* a) care, careful treatment, b) rest, c) protection, d) indulgence, forbearance; mercy; ***er braucht*** ~ he needs to take things easy; ***zur*** ~ ***der Leser*** so as not to offend (the) readers; **2.** protected forest plantation; preserve

ˈscho·nungs·be·dürf·tig *adj.* in need of rest (*or* care)

ˈscho·nungs·los I. *adj.* unsparing (***gegen*** *acc.* of); merciless, pitiless; *w.s. a.* brutal; **II.** *adv.*: ***j-m*** ~ ***et. sagen*** tell s.o. s.th. straight out

ˈSchon·wasch·gang *m* → ***Schongang*** 2

Schönˈwet·ter|la·ge *f* stable area of high pressure; ~**wol·ke** *f* cumulus cloud

Schon·zeit [ˈʃoːn-] *f hunt.* close season

Schopf [ʃɔpf] *m* (-[e]s; Schöpfe [ˈʃœpfə]) shock *or* mop (of hair); *zo.* tuft, crest; ***j-n beim*** ~ ***packen*** grab s.o. by the scruff of the neck; *fig.* ***die Gelegenheit beim*** ~ ***packen*** seize the opportunity, F jump at the chance; ***man sollte die Gelegenheit beim*** ~ ***packen*** make hay while the sun shines; ***ein Problem beim*** ~ ***packen*** deal head-on with a problem

ˈSchöpf|brun·nen *m* draw well; ~**ei·mer** *m* bucket; ⚙ *a.* scoop

schöp·fen [ˈʃœpfən] *v/t.* (h) **1.** scoop, ladle; draw, bail (out) *water, a boat*; **2.** *fig.* draw, derive *strength, courage etc.* (***aus*** *dat.* from); ***neue Kräfte*** ~ build up one's strength again; → ***Atem, Verdacht, voll*** I; **Schöp·fer**[1] [ˈʃœpfɐ] *m* (-s; -) ladle

ˈSchöp·fer[2] *m* (-s; -) **1.** creator; **2.** *no pl.* the Creator; ~**geist** *m* creative genius

schöp·fe·risch [ˈʃœpfərɪʃ] **I.** *adj.* creative; productive; ***e-e*** ~***e Pause einlegen*** have a break to get back into a creative frame of mind, F *hum.* pause for inspiration; **II.** *adv.*: ~ ***veranlagt sein*** be very creative, have a creative mind

ˈSchöp·fer|kraft *f* creative power; ~**tä·tig·keit** *f* creativity

Schöpf|kel·le [ˈʃœpf-] *f*, ~**löf·fel** *m* ladle; ~**rad** *n* water wheel

Schöp·fung [ˈʃœpfʊŋ] *f* (-; -en) **1.** creation; work; product; **2.** *no pl.* the universe, creation; *bibl. the* Creation; *iro.* ***die Herren der ~*** the lords of creation; → ***Krone*** 2

'**Schöp·fungs|akt** *m* creative act; **~be·richt** *m* story of creation; *bibl.* → **~ge·schich·te** *f*: ***die ~*** Genesis

Schop·pen ['ʃɔpən] *m* (-s; -) glass of wine

schor [ʃoːɐ] *pret. of* ***scheren***[1]

Schorf [ʃɔrf] *m* (-[e]s; -e) ⚕ scab (*a.* ⚘), crust

Schor·le ['ʃɔrlə] *f* (-; -n) spritzer

Schorn·stein ['ʃɔrnʃtaɪn] *m* (-[e]s; -e) chimney, ⚙ *a.* smoke stack; ⚓, 🚂 funnel; *fig.* F ***sein Geld zum ~ hinausjagen*** throw one's money out of the window (*or* down the drain); F ***et. in den ~ schreiben*** say goodbye to s.th.; F ***der ~ muß rauchen*** the money has got to come from somewhere; **~fe·ger** *m* chimney sweep

schoß [ʃɔs] *pret. of* ***schießen***

Schoß [ʃoːs] *m* (-es; Schöße ['ʃøːsə]) a) lap, b) womb, c) *fig.* bosom *of the family etc.*; ***auf j-s ~ sitzen*** *usu.* sit on s.o.'s knee; *fig.* ***die Hände in den ~ legen*** sit back and take things easy, twiddle one's thumbs; ***in den ~ der Familie (Kirche etc.) zurückkehren*** return to the fold; ***es ist ihm in den ~ gefallen*** it just fell into his lap; **~hund** *m* lapdog

Schöß·ling ['ʃœslɪŋ] *m* (-s; -e) ⚘ shoot

Schot [ʃoːt] *f* (-; -en) ⚓ sheet

Scho·te ['ʃoːtə] *f* (-; -n) ⚘ husk, pod

Schott [ʃɔt] *n* (-[e]s; -en) ⚓ bulkhead

Schot·te ['ʃɔtə] *m* (-n; -n) Scot, Scotsman; ***die ~n*** the Scots, the Scottish (people)

'**Schot·ten|mu·ster** *n* tartan; **~müt·ze** *f* tam-o'-shanter, F tammy; **~rock** *m* **1.** kilt; **2.** tartan (*or* plaid) skirt; **~witz** *m* Scottish joke

Schot·ter ['ʃɔtɐ] *m* (-s; *no pl.*) ⚙ gravel; *a.* (road) metal; *geol.* detritus

'**Schot·terdecke** *f* road-metal surface

'**schot·tern** *v/t.* (h) gravel; *a.* metal; 🚂 ballast

'**Schot·ter·stra·ße** *f* gravel road

Schot·tin ['ʃɔtɪn] *f* (-; -nen) Scotswoman, Scot; **schot·tisch** ['ʃɔtɪʃ] *adj.* Scots, Scottish; **2er** ***Whisky*** Scotch (whisky)

schraf·fie·ren [ʃra'fiːrən] *v/t.* (h) hatch; *cartography*: hachure

Schraf'fie·rung *f* (-, -en) hatching; *cartography*: hachures *pl.*

schräg [ʃrɛːk] **I.** *adj.* sloping (*a. roof*), slanting (*a. eyes*); diagonal, *a.* oblique *line*; ***~er Bruch*** oblique fracture; ***~er Blick*** sidelong glance, *fig.* disapproving look; *fig.* ***~e Ansichten*** strange ideas; ***~e Musik*** off-beat music, *w.s.* hot jazz; F ***~er Vogel*** F queer fish; **II.** *adv. cut, put etc.* at an angle; ***~ gestreift*** diagonally striped; ***~ gegenüber*** diagonally opposite; ***~ stehende Augen*** slanting eyes; ***~ parken*** park at an angle; ***j-n ~ ansehen*** give s.o. a sidelong glance, *fig.* look askance at s.o.; ***den Kopf ~ halten*** have one's head tilted (*or* cocked) to one side

'**Schräg·dach** *n* pitched roof

Schrä·ge ['ʃrɛːgə] *f* (-; -n) slant; slope, incline

'**Schräg|fahrt** *f skiing*: traverse; **~heck** *n mot.* fastback; **~la·ge** *f* slant; ✈ bank(ing); ⚓ list; ⚕ oblique presentation; **~par·ken** *n* angle parking; **~schrift** *f* sloping hand(writing); *typ.* italics *pl.*; **~schuß** *m soccer*: diagonal shot

'**Schräg·spur** *f video*: slant track; **~auf·zeich·nung** *f* slanted azimuth recording

'**Schräg·strich** *m* slash, oblique; ***umgekehrter ~*** backslash

Schram·me ['ʃramə] *f* (-; -n) scratch

'**schram·men** *v/t.* (h) a) scratch, scrape, b) *mot.* scratch, scrape (against)

Schrank [ʃraŋk] *m* (-[e]s; Schränke ['ʃrɛŋkə]) **1.** cupboard, closet; wardrobe; **2.** F *fig.* great hulk; **~bett** *n* foldaway bed

Schran·ke ['ʃraŋkə] *f* (-; -n) barrier (*a. fig.*); 🚂 *a.* gate; ⚖ bar; *fig.* bounds *pl.*, limits *pl.*; ***vor den ~n des Gerichts erscheinen*** appear in court; *fig.* ***innerhalb der ~n des Gesetzes*** within the bounds of the law; *dat.* ***~n setzen*** put a limit on *s.th.*; ***e-r Sache sind ~n gesetzt*** there are limits to s.th.; ***(sich) in ~n halten*** keep within bounds, restrain (o.s.); ***j-n in s-e ~n weisen*** put s.o. in his (*or* her) place, cut s.o. down to size; ***j-n in die ~n fordern*** challenge s.o.; ***für j-n (et.) in die ~n treten*** stand up for s.o. (s.th.)

'**Schrank·ele,ment** *n* cupboard unit

'**schran·ken·los** *adj.* 🚂 unguarded; *fig.* boundless, unlimited; *b.s.* unbounded, unbridled

'**Schran·ken·wär·ter** *m* 🚂 gatekeeper

Schrän·ker ['ʃrɛŋkɐ] *sl. m* (-s; -) safe-breaker, safecracker

'**Schrank|fach** *n* compartment; **2fer·tig** *adj.* washed and ironed; **~kof·fer** *m* wardrobe trunk; **~wand** *f* large wall unit, wall-to-wall cupboard

Schran·ze ['ʃrantsə] *contp. f* (-; -n) F toady

Schrat [ʃraːt] *dial. m* (-[e]s; -e) goblin

Schraub·deckel ['ʃraʊp-] *m* screw top

Schrau·be ['ʃraʊbə] *f* (-; -n) screw; bolt; ⚓, ✈ propeller; *sport*: twist, twist (*or* spiral) dive; ***~ und Mutter*** bolt and nut; ***~ ohne Ende*** endless screw, *fig.* vicious (*or* never-ending) spiral; ***e-e ~ anziehen*** tighten a screw; *fig.* ***die ~n fester anziehen*** put the screws on; F ***bei ihm ist e-e ~ locker*** he's got a screw loose somewhere

'**schrau·ben** (h) **I.** *v/t. and v/i.* screw (***an*** *acc.* onto); twist, wind; ***fester (loser) ~*** tighten (loosen) the screw(s) of; ***höher (niedriger) ~*** wind up (down), raise (lower); *fig.* ***niedriger ~*** lower, scale down; → ***geschraubt***; **II.** *v/refl.*: ***sich in die Höhe ~*** spiral upwards; *car etc.*: wind its way up

'**Schrau·ben|bol·zen** *m* bolt; **~dre·her** *m* screwdriver; **~fe·der** *f* coil spring

'**schrau·ben·för·mig** [-fœrmɪç] *adj.* (cork)screw-shaped, spiral, helical

'**Schrau·ben|gang** *m* screw thread; **~ge·trie·be** *n* worm gear; **~ge·win·de** *n* screw thread; **~kopf** *m* screwhead, bolt-head; **~mut·ter** *f* nut; **~sal·to** *m sport*: somersault with twist; **~schlüs·sel** *m* spanner, *Am.* wrench; (adjustable) wrench, *Am.* monkey wrench; **~wel·le** *f* propeller shaft; **~win·de** *f* jackscrew, screw jack; **~zie·her** *m* screwdriver

Schraub|stock ['ʃraʊp-] *m* vice, *Am.* vise; **~stol·len** *m* screw-in stud; **~ver·schluß** *m* screw cap (*or* top)

Schre·ber·gar·ten ['ʃreːbɐ-] *m* allotment (garden)

Schreck [ʃrɛk] *m* (-[e]s; *no pl.*) fright; ***er hat e-n ~ bekommen*** he got a fright, it gave him a fright, it gave him (*or* he got) quite a scare; ***er ist mit dem ~en davongekommen*** he got a fright, that was all; ***zu m-m ~en hörte ich ...*** I was quite taken aback (*or* I was shocked) to hear ...; F ***ach, du ~!*** goodness!, oh no!; F ***~, laß nach!*** F spare me!; → ***einjagen***

schrecken ['ʃrɛkən] (*sep.* -k·k-) (h) **I.** *v/t.* frighten, scare, terrify; **II.** *v/i.* start; ***aus dem Schlaf ~*** wake up with a start

'**Schrecken** (*sep.* -k·k-) *m* (-s; -) **1.** *no pl.* → ***Schreck***; **2.** ***die ~en des Krieges*** *etc.* the horrors of war *etc.*

'**schreckens|blaß, ~bleich** *adj.* pale with fright, (as) white as a sheet

'**Schreckens|bot·schaft** *f* → ***Schrekkensnachricht***; **~herr·schaft** *f* reign of terror; **~nach·richt** *f* terrible news (*sg.*); **~nacht** *f* night of horrors; **~re,gime** *n* reign of terror; **~tat** *f* atrocity; **~wort** *n* (-[e]s; -e) scare word

'**Schreck·ge·spenst** *fig. n* bugbear, spectre (*Am.* specter), nightmare; bogeyman

'**schreck·haft** *adj.* nervous, jumpy

'**Schreck·läh·mung** *f* paralytic shock

'**schreck·lich** **I.** *adj.* awful, terrible, dreadful, horrible; atrocious; ***~er Lärm*** terrible racket; **II.** F *fig. adv.* terribly, dreadfully, so, F incredibly *boring etc.*; ***sich ~ freuen*** *etc.* be terribly pleased *etc.*; ***er würde ~ gern mitkommen*** he'd really love to come, he'd do anything to be able to come; ***es tut mir ~ leid*** I'm so sorry, I really am sorry (about that)

'**Schreck|re·ak·ti,on** *f* shock reaction; **~schrau·be** F *f* virago; scarecrow

'**Schreck·schuß** *m a. fig.* warning shot; **~pi,sto·le** *f* blank (cartridge) pistol

'**Schreck·se,kun·de** *f mot.* reaction time; *w.s.* moment of shock (*or* terror); ***in der ersten ~*** when it first hits you

Schrei [ʃraɪ] *m* (-[e]s; -e) shout, cry; yell; scream; shriek; roar; *zo.* screech(ing), *fig.* call; *fig.* ***~ der Entrüstung*** outcry; ***der ~ nach Rache*** the cry for revenge; F ***der letzte ~*** the latest rage

Schreib|ar·beit ['ʃraɪp-] *f* deskwork, paperwork; **~be·fehl** *m computer*: write command; **~block** *m* writing pad; **~dienst** *m* typing pool

Schrei·be ['ʃraɪbə] F *f* (-; *no pl.*) writing; style

schrei·ben ['ʃraɪbən] *v/t. and v/i.* (schrieb, geschrieben, h) write (***über*** *acc.* on, about); compose; † write out; ⚙ *instrument*: record; ***j-m ~*** write (to) s.o.; F drop s.o. a line; ***j-m et. ~*** write to s.o. about s.th.; ***sich (or einander) ~*** write (to one another), *formal*: correspond; ***et. noch einmal ~*** rewrite s.th.; ***gut ~*** a) have a nice hand, have nice handwriting, b) be a good writer; ***er schreibt e-n guten Stil*** his style's good, he's got a good style; ***(Bücher) ~*** be a writer; ***(richtig) ~*** spell (right *or* correctly); ***falsch ~*** misspell; ***wie schreibt er sich?*** how do you (*or* does he) spell his name?; ***~ an*** *dat.* be working on *s.th.*; ***ins reine ~*** make a fair copy of, write out neatly; ***mit Bleistift*** *etc.* ***~*** write in pencil *etc.*; ***mit der Maschine ~*** type (up); ***s-n Namen unter et. ~*** sign s.th., *formal*: put one's signature to s.th.; ***man schreibt uns aus Hamburg, daß*** we hear (*or* are informed) from Hamburg that; ***der Brief, in dem Sie uns ~, daß*** the letter in which you inform us that; ***wie die Zeitung schreibt*** according to the paper; ***was schreibt die Zeitung?*** what do the papers say?; ***man schrieb das Jahr 1840*** it was in the year 1840; → ***Kamin, Leib, Ohr, Zeile***

ˈ**Schrei·ben** *n* (-s; -) **1.** *no pl.* writing;**2.** letter, note; ***Ihr ~ vom*** your letter of
Schrei·ber [ˈʃraɪbɐ] *m* (-s; -) **1.** writer; ***der ~ dieses Briefes*** the undersigned; **2.** ⚙ recorder; (recording) stylus
Schrei·be·rei [ʃraɪbəˈraɪ] *f* (-; *no pl.*) (endless) writing; paperwork; *contp.* scribbling
Schrei·be·rin [ˈʃraɪbərɪn] *f* (-; -nen) → ***Schreiber*** 1
Schrei·ber·ling [ˈʃraɪbɐlɪŋ] *contp. m* (-s; -e) hack writer
schreib·faul [ˈʃraɪp-] *adj.* lazy about writing letters; ***er ist ziemlich ~*** *a.* he's not the greatest of letter-writers, he hates writing letters
Schreib|fe·der [ˈʃraɪp-] *f* pen; quill; **~feh·ler** *m* spelling mistake; slip of the pen; **~ge·rät** *n* writing utensil; ⚙ recording instrument, recorder; **2ge·schützt** *adj. computer*: write-protected; **~heft** *n* exercise book; **~kopf** *m computer*: write head; **~kraft** *f* (shorthand) typist; *pl. a.* clerical staff *sg.*; **~krampf** *m* writer's cramp; ***ich habe e-n ~*** I've got writer's cramp; **~map·pe** *f* writing case
Schreib·maˌschi·ne [ˈʃraɪp-] *f* typewriter; ***mit der ~ schreiben*** type (up); ***mit der ~ geschrieben*** typewritten, typed, in typescript; ˈ**Schreib·maˌschi·nen·paˌpier** *n* typing paper
Schreib|ma·te·riˌal [ˈʃraɪp-] *n* writing materials *pl.*, stationery; **~meß·ge·rät** *n* registering apparatus; **~paˌpier** *n* writing paper; **~pult** *n* (writing) desk; **~schrift** *f* handwriting; *typ.* script; **~schutz** *m computer*: write (*or* file) protection; **~stu·be** *f* ⚔ orderly room; **~ta·fel** *f* **1.** *hist.* tablet; **2.** slate
Schreib·tisch [ˈʃraɪp-] *m* (writing) desk; **~gar·niˌtur** *f* desk set; **~lam·pe** *f* desk lamp; **~tä·ter** *m* mastermind (*gen.* behind), architect (of, behind), F brains (behind)
Schrei·bung [ˈʃraɪbʊŋ] *f* (-; -en) spelling; ***falsche ~*** misspelling
Schreib|ˌun·ter·la·ge [ˈʃraɪp-] *f* desk pad; **~ver·bot** *n* ban on writing
Schreib·wa·ren [ˈʃraɪp-] *pl.* writing materials, stationery *sg.*; **~abˌtei·lung** *f* stationery department; **~ge·schäft** *n* stationer's, stationery shop; **~händ·ler** *m* stationer('s)
Schreib|wei·se [ˈʃraɪp-] *f* a) spelling, b) style; **~wut** *f* obsession with writing, manic urge to write; writing fit; **~zenˌtra·le** *f* typing pool; **~zeug** *n* writing things *pl.*
schrei·en [ˈʃraɪən] **I.** *v/i. and v/t.* (schrie, geschrieen, h) shout; yell; scream, shriek; squeal; roar (***vor Lachen*** with laughter); *baby*: howl, scream; *zo.* screech; *cock*: crow; ***vor Schmerz ~*** scream with pain; ***sich heiser ~*** shout o.s. hoarse; ***schrei nicht so, ich bin nicht taub*** no need to shout, I'm not deaf; ***~ nach*** *dat.* shout for; *fig.* ***nach Rache ~*** cry out for revenge; ***diese Zustände ~ nach Reform*** these conditions cry out for reform; → ***Himmel***; **II.** 2 *n* (-s; *no pl.*) shouting, shouts *pl. etc.*; → ***I***; F ***es (er) ist zum ~*** F it's (he's) a scream
ˈ**schrei·end** *fig. adj.* garish, gaudy, loud *colo(u)rs*; ***~es Unrecht*** glaring injustice; ***~er Gegensatz*** glaring contrast
Schrei·er [ˈʃraɪɐ] *m* (-s; -), ˈ**Schrei·hals** F *m* loudmouth; brawler; (*baby*) bawler; F noisy brat
ˈ**Schrei·krampf** *m* screaming fit
Schrein [ʃraɪn] *m* (-[e]s; -e) chest; *eccl.* shrine
Schrei·ner [ˈʃraɪnɐ] *m* (-s; -) joiner, carpenter; **Schrei·ne·rei** [ʃraɪnəˈraɪ] *f* (-; -en) joiner's (*or* carpenter's) workshop; ˈ**Schrei·ner·mei·ster** *m* master joiner (*or* carpenter); ˈ**schrei·nern** (h) **I.** *v/i.* do carpentry; **II.** *v/t.* make
schrei·ten [ˈʃraɪtən] *v/i.* (schritt, geschritten, sn) step (***zu*** *dat.* up to); stride; walk; stalk; ***im Zimmer auf und ab ~*** pace up and down the room, pace the floor; *fig.* ***~ zu*** *dat.* proceed to *s.th.*; ***zur Abstimmung ~*** (come to the) vote; ***zum Äußersten ~*** take drastic action; ***zur Tat ~*** set to work, F get cracking
schrie [ʃriː] *pret. of* ***schreien***
schrieb [ʃriːp] *pret. of* ***schreiben***
Schrieb [ʃriːp] F *m* (-s; -e [ˈʃriːbə]) F screed
Schrift [ʃrɪft] *f* (-; -en) **1.** a) writing, b) hand(writing), c) characters *pl.*, letters *pl.*; *typ.* script, type; ***in lateinischer ~*** in Roman characters (*or* letters); ***kyrillische ~*** Cyrillic script; ***chinesische ~*** Chinese characters; *contp.* ***was ist denn das für e-e ~?*** what kind of scrawl is that?; **2.** publication; treatise, paper; work; document; *pl. a.* writings; ***sämtliche ~en Kants*** Kant's complete works; → ***heilig***; **~art** *f* type(face); *computer*: font; **~bild** *n* typeface; **~deutsch** *n* written (*or* standard) German
ˈ**Schrif·ten·rei·he** *f* series
ˈ**Schrift|fäl·scher** *m* (handwriting) forger; **~füh·rer** *m* secretary; clerk; **~ge·lehr·te** *m hist.* scribe; **~grad** *m* type size; **~lei·ter** *obs. m* editor
ˈ**schrift·lich** **I.** *adj.* written, ... in writing; ***~e Prüfung*** written exam(ination); ***darüber habe ich nichts Schriftliches*** I have nothing in writing; **II.** *adv.* in writing; in black and white; ***~ niederlegen*** put down in writing; ***jetzt haben wir es ~*** now we have it in black and white; F ***das kann ich dir ~ geben!*** F I can guarantee you that
ˈ**Schrift|pro·be** *f* handwriting specimen; *typ.* type specimen; **~quel·le** *f* written source (*or* document); **~rol·le** *f* scroll; **~sach·ver·stän·di·ge** *m* handwriting expert; **~satz** *m* **1.** *typ.* composition; **2.** ⚖ statement; **~set·zer** *m typ.* typesetter, compositor; **~spra·che** *f* written (*or* standard) language
ˈ**Schrift·stel·ler** [-ʃtɛlɐ] *m* (-s; -) author, writer; **Schrift·stel·le·rei** [-ʃtɛləˈraɪ] *f* (-; *no pl.*) writing; ˈ**Schrift·stel·le·rin** [-ʃtɛlərɪn] *f* (-; -nen) author, writer; ˈ**schrift·stel·le·risch** [-ʃtɛlərɪʃ] **I.** *adj.* literary; **II.** *adv.* as a writer; ˈ**schrift·stel·lern** [-ʃtɛlɐn] *v/i.* (h) be a writer, be an author; ***nebenbei ~*** write on the side
ˈ**Schrift·stel·ler|na·me** *m* pen name, pseudonym, nom de plume; **~ver·band** *m* writers' union
ˈ**Schrift·stück** *n* paper, document
ˈ**Schrift·tum** *n* (-s; *no pl.*) literature
ˈ**Schrift|ver·kehr** *m*, **~wech·sel** *m* correspondence; **~zei·chen** *n* character, letter; **~zug** *m* a) stroke, b) (hand)writing
schrill [ʃrɪl] *adj.* shrill (*a. fig.*); **schril·len** [ˈʃrɪlən] *v/i. and v/t.* (h) shrill; ***~ durch*** *acc. a.* pierce through
Schrip·pe [ˈʃrɪpə] *dial. f* (-; -n) roll
schritt [ʃrɪt] *pret. of* ***schreiten***
Schritt [ʃrɪt] *m* (-[e]s; -e) **1.** step (*a. fig.*), pace, stride; footstep; *fig.* move, *esp. pl.* measures; ***mit schnellen ~en*** briskly; ***e-n ~ zur Seite tun*** step aside; ***~ halten mit*** *dat.* keep pace with, *fig. a.* keep abreast of; ***~ für ~*** step by step, *fig. a.* little by little, gradually; ***auf ~ und Tritt*** at every turn; ***j-m auf ~ und Tritt folgen*** dog s.o.'s footsteps; ***es sind nur ein paar ~e*** it's not far; *fig.* ***Politik der kleinen ~e*** step-by-step policy; ***der erste ~ zur Besserung*** a first step towards improvement; ***mit großen ~en*** with giant strides (*or* steps); ***den ersten ~ tun*** take the first step, make the first move; ***den zweiten ~ vor dem ersten tun*** put the cart before the horse; ***den entscheidenden ~ tun*** take the (final) plunge; ***wir sind keinen ~ weitergekommen*** we haven't made the slightest bit of progress (*or* any headway at all); ***e-n ~ zu weit gehen*** overstep the mark; ***ich möchte noch e-n ~ weiter gehen*** I'd like to go one step further; F ***j-m drei ~e vom Leibe bleiben*** F give s.o. a wide berth; **2.** pace; ***im ~*** at a walking pace; ***~ fahren!*** dead slow; F ***e-n schnellen ~ am Leib haben*** be a fast walker; ***der hat aber e-n schnellen ~ am Leib!*** *a.* F you've got to run to keep up with him; **3.** *a.* F *anat.* crotch
ˈ**Schrittem·po** (*sep.* -tt·t-) *n* walking speed; ***im ~ fahren*** crawl (along)
ˈ**Schritt|län·ge** *f* inside leg; **~ma·cher** *m sport*: pacemaker (*a.* ⚕ *and fig.*), pacer; *fig.* trendsetter; **~mes·ser** *m* pedometer; **~mo·tor** *m* ⚙ stepper motor
ˈ**schritt·wei·se** *fig.* **I.** *adj.* gradual, step-by-step ...; **II.** *adv.* step by step, gradually, by degrees, little by little; ***~ einstellen*** phase out
schroff [ʃrɔf] *adj.* **1.** jagged; steep, precipitous; **2.** *fig.* gruff; curt, brusque; abrupt; ***~e Ablehnung*** flat refusal; ***~er Gegensatz (Widerspruch)*** glaring contrast (contradiction); ***in ~em Gegensatz stehen zu*** *dat.* contrast sharply with
schröp·fen [ˈʃrœpfən] *fig. v/t.* (h) fleece, milk
Schrot [ʃroːt] *m, n* (-[e]s; *no pl.*) **1.** wholemeal; **2.** small shot, pellets *pl.*, buckshot; **3.** *fig.* ***von altem ~ und Korn*** of the old school; ***ein Sizilianer von echtem ~ und Korn*** a Sicilian born and bred; **~brot** *n* wholemeal bread
schro·ten [ˈʃroːtən] *v/t.* (h) crush; bruise (*a. malt*)
ˈ**Schrot|flin·te** *f* shotgun; **~korn** *n*, **~ku·gel** *f* pellet; **~la·dung** *f* round of shot
Schrott [ʃrɔt] *m* (-[e]s; *no pl.*) **1.** scrap metal; F ***ein Auto zu ~ fahren*** smash up a car; **2.** F junk; **3.** F rubbish; **~au·to** *n* wrecked car; **~ei·sen** *n* scrap iron; **~händ·ler** *m* scrap merchant; **~hau·fen** *m* scrap heap (*a. fig.*); **~platz** *m* scrapyard; **2reif** *adj.* ready for the scrap heap; ***~ sein*** *a.* F have had it; ***~ fahren*** write of, *Am. sl.* total; **~wert** *m* scrap value
schrub·ben [ˈʃrʊbən] *v/t.* (h) scrub
Schrub·ber [ˈʃrʊbɐ] *m* (-s; -) scrubbing brush
Schrul·le [ˈʃrʊlə] *f* (-; -n) **1.** quirk; F cranky idea; **2.** F old crone; **schrul·lig** [ˈʃrʊlɪç] *adj.* cranky; crotchety
schrum·pe·lig [ˈʃrʊmpəlɪç] *adj.* wrinkled; shrivel(l)ed; **schrum·peln** [ˈʃrʊmpəln] *v/i.* (sn) → ***schrumpfen***
schrump·fen [ˈʃrʊmpfən] *v/i.* (sn) shrink (*a.* ⚙, ⚕ *and fig.*); shrivel; *fig.* dwindle

Schrumpf|kopf ['ʃrʊmpf-] *m* shrunken head; **~le·ber** *f* cirrhosis of the liver; **~nie·re** *f* cirrhosis of the kidney

Schrump·fung ['ʃrʊmpfʊŋ] *f* (-; *no pl.*) shrinking; *a.* ⚕, ⚙ shrinkage, contraction; ⚕ atrophy; *fig.* reduction; scaling-down

Schub [ʃu:p] *m* (-[e]s; Schübe ['ʃy:bə]) **1.** *phys.*, ⚙ thrust; shear; **2.** batch; **3.** ⚕ phase, attack; ***in Schüben verlaufend*** intermittent; **~dü·se** *f* thrust nozzle

Schu·ber ['ʃu:bɐ] *m* (-s; -) slipcase

'**Schub|fach** *n* drawer; **~kar·re(n** *m*) *f* wheelbarrow, push cart; **~ka·sten** *m* drawer; **~kraft** *f* thrust; shear(ing) force; **~la·de** *f* drawer

'**Schub·la·den|den·ken** *n* pigeonholing, stereotyped thinking, F categoritis; **~sy͵stem** *n* front drawer loading

Schubs [ʃʊps] F *m* (-es; -e) push, F shove

'**Schub·schiff** *n* pusher tug, pushboat

schub·sen ['ʃʊpsən] *v/t.* (h) push, F shove

'**schub·wei·se** *adv.* **1.** in batches; **2.** by degrees, F in bits and pieces; *arrive*: *a.* F in dribs and drabs

schüch·tern ['ʃʏçtɐn] *adj.* shy; bashful; timid; ***~er Versuch*** hesitant attempt

'**Schüch·tern·heit** *f* (-; *no pl.*) shyness; bashfulness; timidity

schuf [ʃu:f] *pret. of* **schaffen¹**

Schuft [ʃʊft] *m* (-[e]s; -e) F rotter, *sl.* bastard

schuf·ten ['ʃʊftən] *v/i.* (h) slave (*or* sweat) away; *sl.* work one's butt off

Schuf·te·rei [ʃʊftə'raɪ] *f* (-; *no pl.*) drudgery, F hard graft, grind, sweat

schuf·tig ['ʃʊftɪç] *adj.* mean, low, F rotten

Schuh [ʃu:] *m* (-[e]s; -e) shoe (*a.* ⚙); *fig.* ***j-m et. in die ~e schieben*** pin (the blame) for s.th. on s.o.; ***wo drückt*** (***dich***) ***der ~?*** what's the trouble (*or* problem)?; ***wissen, wo der ~ drückt*** know where the problem lies (*or* problems lie); ***umgekehrt wird ein ~ daraus!*** it's the exact opposite; ***wem der ~ paßt***(***, der ziehe ihn sich an***) if the cap fits wear it; **~ab·satz** *m* heel; **~an·zie·her** [-antsi:ɐ] *m* (-s; -) shoehorn; **~band** *n* (-[e]s; ˉer) shoelace, shoestring; **~bür·ste** *f* shoe brush; **~creme** *f* shoe cream, shoe polish, shoeshine; **~fa͵brik** *f* shoe factory; **~ge·schäft** *n* shoe shop; **~grö·ße** *f* shoe size; *fig.* → ***Kragenweite***; **~in·du͵strie** *f* footwear industry; **~kar͵ton** *m* shoebox; **~löf·fel** *m* shoehorn

'**Schuh·ma·cher** *m* shoemaker, cobbler; **Schuh·ma·che'rei** *f* (-; -en) **1.** *no pl.* shoemaking, shoemaker's trade; **2.** shoemaker's shop

'**Schuh|put·zer** *m* shoeshine boy, *Am.* bootblack; **~putz·zeug** *n* shoe-cleaning things *pl.*; **~rie·men** *m* shoelace; **~schrank** *m* shoe cabinet; **~soh·le** *f* sole (of a *or* the shoe); **~span·ner** *m* shoe tree; **~spit·ze** *f* toe (*or* tip) of a *or* the shoe; **~werk** *n* (-[e]s; *no pl.*) footwear; shoes *pl.*, boots and shoes *pl.*; ***festes ~*** a sturdy pair of shoes

Schu·ko·stecker ['ʃu:ko-] *m* safety plug

Schul|ab·gän·ger ['ʃu:l-] *m* school leaver, *Am.* highschool *etc.* graduate; **~ab·schluß** *m* secondary school qualifications *pl.*; **~al·ter** *n* school age; **~amt** *n* education authority; **~an·fän·ger** *m* school beginner, reception child (*or* pupil); **~ar·beit** *f a. pl.* homework; ***~en machen*** do one's homework; ***hast du noch ~en?*** have you still got some homework to do?; **~arzt** *m* school medical officer; **~auf·ga·be** *f* **1.** → ***Schularbeit***; **2.** *dial.* → ***Klassenarbeit***; **~aus·flug** *m* school outing; **~bank** *f* (-; ˉe) desk; F ***die ~ drücken*** go to school; F ***wir haben zusammen die ~ gedrückt*** we were at school together; **~be·ginn** *m* start of school; ***~ ist am 22.*** (***um acht***) school starts on the 22nd (at eight); **~bei·spiel** *n* classic example (***für*** *acc.* of); **~be·such** *m* school attendance; **~bil·dung** *f* school education; ***höhere ~*** secondary education

'**Schul·buch** *n* textbook; **~ver·lag** *m* educational publisher(s *pl.*)

'**Schul|bus** *m* school bus; **~chor** *m* school choir

Schuld [ʃʊlt] *f* (-; -en ['ʃʊldən]) **1.** *no pl.* blame; *bibl.* sin(s *pl.*); ***moralische ~*** moral guilt; ***~ und Sühne*** sin and atonement; ***er ist daran ℒ, ihn trifft die ~ dafür*** he's responsible *or* to blame (for it), it's his fault; ***ohne m-e ~*** through no fault of mine (*or* my own); ***die ~ auf sich nehmen*** take the blame, take responsibility; ***j-m*** *or* ***e-r Sache die ~ geben*** blame s.o. *or* s.th. (for it), blame it on s.o. *or* s.th.; ***die ~*** (***an e-r Sache***) ***auf j-n schieben, j-m die ~*** (***an e-r Sache***) ***zuschieben*** pin the blame on s.o. (for s.th.); ***er war sich s-r ~ bewußt*** he was aware of his wrongdoing; ***ich bin mir keiner ~ bewußt*** I don't feel that I'm in any way to blame; **2.** *usu. pl.* debt (*a. fig.*); liability; ***~en haben, in ~en stekken*** be in debt; → *a.* ***Ohr***; ***~en machen*** run into debt; ***sich in ~en stürzen*** plunge into debt; ***in ~en geraten*** run into debt; ***s-e ~en bezahlen*** pay (*or* settle) one's debts; ***bei j-m ~en haben*** owe s.o. (some) money; ***frei von ~en*** free from (*or* of) debt, unencumbered *property etc.*; *fig.* ***in j-s ~ sein*** (***or stehen***) owe s.o. a debt of gratitude, be deeply indebted to s.o.; **~be·kennt·nis** *n* confession, admission of guilt; **ℒbe·la·den** *adj.* guilt-ridden, weighed down by guilt; **~be·weis** *m* proof *or* evidence of (s.o.'s) guilt

'**schuld·be·wußt** *adj.* **1.** guilty; **2.** ***er war durchaus ~*** he was well aware of what he had done wrong (*or* of his wrongdoing)

'**Schuld·be·wußt·sein** *n* sense of guilt

schul·den ['ʃʊldən] *v/t.* (h): ***j-m et. ~*** owe s.o. s.th. (*a. fig. an explanation, one's life etc.*); ***ich schulde dir noch 10 Mark*** *a.* you still get 10 marks from me; → ***Dank***

Schul·den|ab·kom·men ['ʃʊldən-] *n pol.* debt agreement; **~berg** *m* (huge) debt mountain; **~er·laß** *m* waiving of debts; debt relief; **ℒfrei** *adj.* free from (*or* of) debt; unencumbered *property etc.*; **~last** *f* debt burden; encumbrance; ***große ~*** *a.* heavy debts; **~ma·cher** *m* contractor of debts; **~mas·se** *f* † (aggregate) liabilities *pl.*; **~rück·zah·lung** *f* debt repayment; **~til·gung** *f* liquidation of debts

'**schuld·fä·hig** *adj.* criminally liable

'**Schuld·fä·hig·keit** *f* (-; *no pl.*) criminal liability (*or* responsibility)

'**Schuld|for·de·rung** *f* claim; **~fra·ge** *f*: ***die ~ klären*** establish who is responsible (*or* to blame); **~ge·fühl** *n a. pl.* sense (*or* feeling) of guilt, guilty feeling; guilty conscience; **~ge·ständ·nis** *n* → ***Schuldbekenntnis***

'**schuld·haft** *adj.* culpable; non-accidental

'**Schul·dienst** *m* (-es; *no pl.*) teaching; ***in den ~ treten*** go into teaching; ***im ~ sein*** be a teacher

schul·dig ['ʃʊldɪç] *adj.* **1.** guilty (*gen.* of) (*adv.* guiltily); ⚖ *usu.* at fault, responsible (for); ⚖ ***j-n für ~ befinden*** find s.o. guilty (***e-s Verbrechens*** of a crime; ***e-r Anklage*** on a charge); ***j-n ~ sprechen*** pronounce s.o. guilty; ***das Gericht erkannte auf ~*** the court brought in a verdict of guilty; ***sich ~ bekennen*** plead guilty (***et. getan zu haben*** to doing s.th.); ***sich ~ machen an*** *dat.* be guilty of; ***der ~e Teil*** → ***Schuldige***; ***ich fühle mich ~*** I feel I'm to blame; ***~ geschieden*** divorced as the guilty party; **2.** ***j-m et. ~ sein*** → ***schulden***; ***das bist du ihm ~*** you owe it to him; ***das ist man ihm ~*** that's only his due; ***das bist du dir ~*** you owe it to yourself; (***j-m***) ***die Antwort ~ bleiben*** give (s.o.) no answer; (***j-m***) ***die Antwort nicht ~ bleiben*** hit back (at s.o.); ***Sie sind mir noch e-e Antwort ~*** I'm still waiting for an answer; ***sie blieb ihm nichts ~*** she paid him back in his own coin; ***was bin ich*** (***Ihnen***) ***~?*** how much do I owe you?; ***ich muß dir das Geld ~ bleiben*** I'll have to owe you the money

Schul·di·ge ['ʃʊldɪgə] *m,f* (-n; -n) culprit; ⚖ guilty party, offender

'**Schul·dig·keit** *f* (-; *no pl.*) duty

'**Schul·di͵rek·tor** *m* headmaster, *Am.* principal

'**Schuld|kla·ge** *f* action for debt; **~kom͵plex** *m* guilt complex

'**schuld·los** *adj.* innocent (***an*** *dat.* of), blameless; *a. adv.* without blame

Schuld·ner ['ʃʊldnɐ] *m* (-s; -) debtor; **~land** *n* debtor nation

'**Schuld|recht** *n* ⚖ law of obligations; **~schein** *m* promissory note, IOU (= "I owe you"); **~spruch** *m* ⚖ verdict of guilty, conviction; **~͵über·nah·me** *f* assumption of debt

'**schuld·un·fä·hig** *adj.* not criminally liable; '**Schuld·un·fä·hig·keit** *f* absence of criminal liability (*or* responsibility)

'**Schuld|ver·hält·nis** *n* ⚖ obligation; **~zu·wei·sung** *f* apportioning of blame

Schu·le ['ʃu:lə] *f* (-; -n) school; ***höhere ~*** secondary (*Am.* senior high) school; ***Hohe ~*** *riding*: manège, haute école; ***die Hohe ~ des Kochens*** haute cuisine; ***auf*** (*or* ***in***) ***der ~*** at school; ***zur*** (*or* ***in die***) ***~ gehen*** go to school; ***e-e ~ besuchen*** go to a school; ***in welche ~ geht sie?*** which school does she go to (*or* is she at)?; ***zur ~ kommen*** start school; ***noch zur ~ gehen*** still be at school; ***an e-r ~ unterrichten*** teach at a school; ***aus der ~ kommen*** come back from school; ***die ~ fängt um neun an*** school starts at nine; *fig.* ***er ist bei s-m Onkel in die ~ gegangen*** he learnt from (*or* was trained by) his uncle; ***er ist bei den Impressionisten in die ~ gegangen*** he went through the Impressionist school; ***durch e-e harte ~ gehen*** learn the hard way; ***~ machen*** set a precedent; → ***plaudern, schwänzen***

schu·len ['ʃu:lən] *v/t.* (h) train (*a. fig. one's eyes, memory etc.*); *pol. a.* indoctrinate

Schul·eng·lisch ['ʃu:l-] *n* school English; ***dazu reicht mein ~ nicht*** the English I learnt at school isn't good enough for that

Schü·ler ['ʃy:lɐ] *m* (-s; -) pupil, schoolboy; student; disciple, follower (*a. phls. etc.*); **~aus·tausch** *m* school exchange

Schü·le·rin ['ʃy:lərɪn] *f* (-; -nen) pupil, schoolgirl, student; disciple, follower

'**Schü·ler|lot·se** *m* (*pupil acting as a*) school crossing patrol; **~mit·ver·wal·tung** *f* school council

'**Schü·ler·schaft** *f* (-; *no pl.*) pupils *pl.*

'**Schü·ler|spre·cher** *m* → ***Schulsprecher***; **~zei·tung** *f* school magazine

Schul|fach ['ʃu:l-] *n* subject; **~fei·er** *f* school function; **~fe·ri·en** *pl.* (school) holidays, vacations, vacation *sg.*; **~flug·zeug** *n* trainer (plane); **~fran,zö·sisch** *n* school French; → *a.* ***Schulenglisch***

schul·frei ['ʃu:l-] *adj.*: **~ *haben*** have a (*or* the) day off; ***morgen ist* ~** there's no school tomorrow

Schul|freund ['ʃu:l-] *m* schoolfriend, friend from school, schoolmate; **~funk** *m* school broadcasts *pl.*; **~ge·bäu·de** *n* (school) building; **~ge·län·de** *n* school grounds *pl.*, *Am.* campus; **~geld** *n* (-[e]s; *no pl.*) school fees *pl.*, tuition (fees *pl.*); **~got·tes·dienst** *m* church service at school; assembly; **~heft** *n* exercise book; **~hof** *m* playground, schoolyard

schu·lisch ['ʃu:lɪʃ] *adj.* school ..., educational; **~e *Leistungen*** performance at school

'**Schul|jahr** ['ʃu:l-] *n* school year; **~e** school days; **~jun·ge** *m* schoolboy; **~ka·me,rad** *m* schoolfriend, schoolmate; **~kennt·nis·se** *pl.*: **~ *in Französisch*** *etc.* school(-level) French *etc.*; **~kind** *n* schoolchild (*pl.* schoolchildren); F schoolkid; **~klas·se** *f* class, form, grade; **~land·heim** *n school's field centre* (*Am. center*) *in the country*; **~leh·rer** *m* teacher; **~lei·ter** *m* → ***Schuldirektor***; **~mäd·chen** *n* schoolgirl; **~map·pe** *f* schoolbag; **~me·di,zin** *f* orthodox (school of) medicine; **~mei·nung** *f*: ***die* ~** received opinion

schul·mei·stern ['ʃu:lmaɪstɐn] *contp. v/i. and v/t.* (h) lecture

Schul|or,che·ster ['ʃu:l-] *n* school orchestra; **~ord·nung** *f* school regulations *pl.*

Schul·pflicht ['ʃu:l-] *f* (-; *no pl.*) compulsory education; '**schul·pflich·tig** [-pflɪçtɪç] *adj.* of school age, school-age ...

Schul|po·li,tik ['ʃu:l-] *f* educational policy; **~psy·cho,lo·ge** *m* educational psychologist; **~ran·zen** *m* satchel; **~rat** *m* school inspector; **~sa·chen** *pl.* school things, things for school; ***s-e* ~ *packen*** get one's things ready for school; **~schiff** *n* school (*or* training) ship; **~schluß** *m* (-sses; *no pl.*) end of school (*or* term); ***wann habt ihr heute* ~?** when does school finish today?, when do you get out of school today?

'**Schul·schwän·zer** [-ʃvɛntsɐ] F *m* (-s; -) truant

'**Schul|spei·sung** *f* school meals (*or* lunches) *pl.*; **~spre·cher** *m* head boy; **~streß** *m* pressures *pl.* of school, school stress; **~stun·de** *f* lesson, class, period; **~sy,stem** *n* school system; **~tag** *m* school day; **~ta·sche** *f* schoolbag; satchel

Schul·ter ['ʃʊltɐ] *f* (-; -n) shoulder (*a.* ⚙); **~ *an* ~** shoulder to shoulder (*a. fig.*), *sport*: neck and neck; ***mit den* ~*n zucken*** shrug (one's shoulders); ***j-m bis zur* ~ *reichen*** come up to s.o.'s shoulder; ***j-n an der* ~ *packen*** grab s.o. by the shoulder; *fig.* ***auf j-s* ~*n ruhen*** *responsibility etc.*: rest on s.o.'s shoulders; ***j-n über die* ~ *ansehen*** look down one's nose at s.o.; → ***kalt, leicht*** 4, ***klopfen*** I; **~blatt** *n* shoulder blade; **~brei·te** *f* width of (the) shoulders; **2frei** *adj.* off-the-shoulder, strapless; **~ge·lenk** *n* shoulder joint; **~half·ter** *f, n* shoulder holster; **~hö·he** *f*: (***in* ~** at) shoulder height; **~klap·pe** *f* ⚔ epaulet(te); **2lang** *adj.* shoulder-length

schul·tern ['ʃʊltɐn] *v/t.* (h) **1.** sling *rifle etc.* over one's shoulder; **2.** *wrestling*: shoulder

'**Schul·ter|rie·men** *m* shoulder strap; **~schluß** *m* (-sses; *no pl.*) closing of ranks (***zwischen*** *dat.* between); close alliance (***von*** *dat.* between); ***sich im* ~ *befinden mit*** *dat.* be standing shoulder to shoulder with; ***es kam zu e-m* ~ *zwischen*** *dat.* there was a closing of ranks between

Schul|trä·ger ['ʃu:l-] *m*: **~ *ist* ...** the school is maintained by ...; **~tü·te** *f cardboard cone filled with presents and sweets and given to children on their first day at school*

Schu·lung ['ʃu:lʊŋ] *f* (-; -en) **1.** training, schooling; practi|ce (*Am.* -se); education; *pol. a.* indoctrination; **2.** → '**Schu·lungs·kurs** *m* course (of training)

Schul|uni,form ['ʃu:l-] *f* school uniform; **~,un·ter·richt** *m* tuition, lessons *pl.*, classes *pl.*; **~ver·such** *m* educational experiment; **~weg** *m* way to school; ***er hat e-n langen* ~** he's got a long way to school; **~weis·heit** *f* book learning; **~we·sen** *n* (-s; *no pl.*) school system; **~wis·sen** *n*: ***mein* ~** what I learnt (*or* they taught me) at school; **~wör·ter·buch** *n* school dictionary; **~zeit** *f* school days *pl.*; ***während m-r* ~** back in my school days, when I was at school; **~zeug·nis** *n* (school) report

schum·meln ['ʃʊməln] F *v/i. and v/t.* (h) **1.** cheat; ***das ist geschummelt*** that's cheating; ***es wird nicht geschummelt!*** no cheating!; **2.** ***et.* ~ *in*** *acc.* smuggle into *the house etc.*, slip into *one's pocket etc.*

schum·me·rig ['ʃʊmərɪç] *adj.* dim, dimly lit

Schum·mer·stun·de ['ʃʊmɐ-] *f* → ***Dämmerstunde***

Schund [ʃʊnt] *m* (-[e]s; *no pl.*) trash, rubbish; **~blatt** *n* rag; **~li·te·ra,tur** *f* pulp fiction, trashy novels *pl.*; **~ro,man** *m* trashy novel

Schun·kel·mu,sik ['ʃʊŋkəl-] *f* jolly (*or* singalong) music

schun·keln ['ʃʊŋkəln] *v/i.* (h) rock, sway; sway to the music

Schup·pe ['ʃʊpə] *f* (-; -n) scale; *pl.* dandruff *sg.*, scurf *sg.*; *fig.* ***es fiel mir wie* ~*n von den Augen*** the scales fell from my eyes

'**schup·pen** (h) **I.** *v/t.* scale; **II.** *v/refl.*: ***sich* ~** peel

Schup·pen ['ʃʊpən] *m* (-s; -) shed, shack; ✈ hangar; F joint (*sl.*); F ***riesiger* ~** F huge place; F ***häßlicher* ~** real eyesore; F ***vornehmer* ~** *sl.* fancy joint

'**Schup·pen·flech·te** *f* ⚕ psoriasis

'**schup·pen·för·mig** [-fœrmɪç] *adj.* scale-like, *formal*: squamous

'**Schup·pen·tier** *n zo.* pangolin, scaly anteater

schup·pig ['ʃʊpɪç] *adj.* a) scaly, b) dandruffy; **~es *Haar haben*** *a.* have dandruff

Schur [ʃu:ɐ] *f* (-; -en ['ʃu:rən]) **1.** shearing; clipping; **2.** fleece

schü·ren ['ʃy:rən] *v/t.* (h) poke, rake; *fig.* stir up, *formal*: foment

schür·fen ['ʃʏrfən] (h) **I.** *v/t.* scrape, graze; ***sich das Knie* ~** scrape (*or* graze) one's knee; **II.** *v/i.* ⚒ prospect (***nach*** *dat.* for), dig (for); *fig.* ***tiefer* ~** dig below the surface

Schürf·wun·de ['ʃʏrf-] *f* graze, abrasion

Schür·ha·ken ['ʃy:ɐ-] *m* poker

schu·ri·geln ['ʃu:ri:gəln] F *v/t.* (h) → ***piesacken***

Schur·ke ['ʃʊrkə] *m* (-n; -n) rogue

'**Schur·wol·le** *f*: (***reine* ~** pure) virgin wool

Schurz [ʃʊrts] *m* (-es; -e) apron; loincloth

Schür·ze ['ʃʏrtsə] *f* (-; -n) apron; pinafore, F pinny

schür·zen ['ʃʏrtsən] *v/t.* (h) gather up

'**Schür·zen|band** *n* apron string; **~jä·ger** F *m* womanizer, philanderer; ***er ist ein richtiger* ~** *a.* he's always chasing after women; **~zip·fel** *m*: F *fig.* ***der Mutter am* ~ *hängen*** be tied to one's mother's apron strings

Schuß [ʃʊs] *m* (Schusses; Schüsse ['ʃʏsə]) a) shot (*a. phot.*); *soccer a.* strike, b) bullet; round, c) *textil.* weft, woof, d) *skiing*: schuss (*a.* ***im* ~ *fahren***), e) F *fig.* shot, *sl.* fix; ***e-n* ~ *abgeben*** fire (a shot), *soccer*: shoot; **~ *ins Schwarze*** bull's-eye (*a. fig.*); ***ein* ~** a dash of *sherry etc.*, *fig.* a touch of *irony etc.*; ***Orangensaft*** *etc.* ***mit* ~** spiked orange juice *etc.*; *fig.* **~ *vor den Bug*** warning shot; F ***ein* ~ *in den Ofen*** a complete flop, F a dead loss; F ***er kam nicht zum* ~** he never got a chance; F ***sich e-n* ~ *setzen*** shoot up; F ***den goldenen* ~ *setzen*** F OD (o.s.); F ***in* ~ *bringen*** F knock *s.th.* into shape, *mot.*, ⚙ get *s.th.* working, ⚕ get *s.th.* going again, get *s.o.* into shape (*or* trim); F ***wieder in* ~ *kommen*** shape up again, get back into shape; F ***sich gut in* ~ *halten*** keep in good shape; F ***gut in* ~ *sein*** be in good shape; F ***weit(ab) vom* ~** well out of harm's way, *live etc.* right out of the way; → ***Pulver***; **~bahn** *f* **1.** line of fire; **2.** *phys.* trajectory

'**schuß·be·reit** *adj.* ready to fire (*or* shoot, *a.* F *phot.*); *gun*: *a.* at the ready

Schus·sel ['ʃʊsəl] F *m* (-s; -) F dope; scatterbrain

Schüs·sel ['ʃʏsəl] *f* (-; -n) **1.** bowl; dish; **2.** ⚕ bedpan

schus·se·lig ['ʃʊsəlɪç] F *adj.* F dop(e)y; scatterbrained, F scatty

'**Schuß|fa·den** *m textil.* weft, woof; **~fahrt** *f skiing*: schuss; **~feld** *n* field of fire; *fig.* ***ins* ~ (*der Öffentlichkeit*) *geraten*** come under fire (from the public); **2fest** *adj.* bulletproof; shellproof; **~ge·fecht** *n* gun battle; **~ge·le·gen·heit** *f sport*: chance of a goal; **~li·nie** *f* line of fire; *fig.* ***in die* ~ *geraten*** come under fire (***von*** *dat.* from); ***in j-s* ~ *geraten*** *a.* get into s.o.'s line of fire; ***sich in die* ~ *begeben*** walk right into the firing line; **~mög·lich·keit** *f soccer*: scoring opportunity; ***e-e* ~ *haben*** *a.* be in a striking position; **~po·si·ti,on** *f* shooting position; **~rich·tung** *f* direction of fire; **~waf·fe** *f* firearm; *pl.* small arms; ***von der* ~ *Gebrauch machen*** use one's weapon, shoot; **~wech·sel** *m* exchange of fire, gun battle; *fig.* heated exchange; ***sich e-n ~ liefern*** exchange shots (*or* fire), have a shootout; **~wei·te** *f* range (of fire); ***außer*** (***in***) ~ out of (within) range; **~wun·de** *f* gunshot wound

Schu·ster ['ʃu:stɐ] *m* (-s; -) shoemaker, cobbler; → ***Rappe***; **'schu·stern** *v/i.* (h) **1.** mend shoes; **2.** F *fig.* F bungle, botch it

Schu·te ['ʃu:tə] *f* (-; -n) ⚓ barge, lighter

Schutt [ʃʊt] *m* (-[e]s; *no pl.*) a) rubbish, garbage, b) rubble, debris, ruins *pl.*; *geol.* detritus, c) F *fig.* F (a load of) rubbish (*or* trash, garbage); ***in ~ und Asche legen*** raze to the ground; **~ab·la·de·platz** *m* rubbish (*or* garbage) dump, tip; **~ab·la·ge·rung** *f geol.* detritus

Schütt·be͵ton ['ʃʏt-] *m* cast concrete

Schüt·tel|be·cher ['ʃʏtəl-] *m* shaker; **~frost** *m* shivering fit, F *the* shivers *pl.*; **~läh·mung** *f* Parkinson's disease

schüt·teln ['ʃʏtəln] (h) **I.** *v/t.* shake; ***den Kopf*** ~ shake one's head; ***j-m die Hand*** ~ shake s.o.'s hand, shake hands with s.o.; → ***Ärmel***, ***Öffnen***; **II.** *v/refl.*: ***sich*** ~ shudder (***vor Angst*** *etc.* with fear *etc.*); ***ich mußte mich*** ~ it made me shudder, F it gave me the creeps; F ***er schüttelte sich vor Lachen*** he shook with laughter

Schüt·tel·sieb ['ʃʏtəl-] *n* vibrating screen

schüt·ten ['ʃʏtən] (h) **I.** *v/t.* a) pour (*a.* ⚙), b) spill; ***auf e-n Haufen*** ~ heap up; **II.** F *v/impers.*: ***es schüttet*** it's pouring, *Brit. a.* F it's bucketing (down)

schüt·ter ['ʃʏtɐ] *adj.* thinning *hair*

Schütt·gut ['ʃʏt-] *n* bulk goods *pl.*

'Schutt|hal·de *f* tip; *geol.* talus; **~hau·fen** *m* a) rubbish heap, b) heap of rubble

Schutz [ʃʊts] *m* (-es; *no pl.*) a) protection (***gegen*** *acc.*, ***vor*** *dat.* against, from), ⚙ insulation, b) escort, c) shelter, refuge, d) custody; safeguard; cover, e) preservation, conservation; ***rechtlicher*** ~ legal protection; ***den ~ des Gesetzes genießen*** be protected by law; ~ ***suchen*** look for (a) shelter, *fig.* seek refuge (***vor*** *dat.* from; ***bei*** *dat.* with); ***j-n in ~ nehmen*** protect s.o., come to s.o.'s defen|ce (*Am.* -se), back s.o. up; ***da muß ich ihn in ~ nehmen*** I have to take his side there; ***er nimmt s-e Frau immer in*** ~ he won't let anything be said against his wife; ***im ~e der Nacht*** under cover of darkness; ***zum ~ gegen Erkältungen*** *etc.* to ward off colds *etc.*, to build up one's resistance against colds *etc.*; ***zum ~ gegen Strahlung*** to protect against radiation; ***diese Medizin bietet ~ vor*** *dat.* ... this drug protects against ...; **~an·strich** *m* protective coat(ing); ⚔ camouflage, ⚓ dazzle paint; **~an·zug** *m* protective clothing; **♀be·dürf·tig** *adj.* in need of protection; **~be·häl·ter** *m* special container (for toxic waste *etc.*); **~be·haup·tung** *f* defensive lie; **~blech** *n* guard; *mot.* mudguard, *Am.* fender; **~brief** *m mot.* accident and breakdown cover; **~bril·le** *f*: (***e-e*** ~ a pair of) safety goggles *pl.*; **~bünd·nis** *n* defensive alliance; **~dach** *n* protective roof, shelter; ⚙ canopy; awning

Schüt·ze ['ʃʏtsə] *m* (-n; -n) **1.** (***guter*** ~ good) shot, marksman; ⚔ private; *sport*: scorer; **2.** *ast.* Sagittarius; (***ein***) ~ ***sein*** be (a) Sagittarius (*or* a Sagittarian)

schüt·zen ['ʃʏtsən] (h) **I.** *v/t.* a) protect, defend (***gegen*** *acc.*, ***vor*** *dat.* against, from); guard (against), watch over, b) shelter (from *rain etc.*), c) cover, *w.s.* shield; screen, d) escort, e) preserve, conserve, *a.* protect *the environment*; ***vor Hitze ~!*** store away from heat; ***vor Nässe ~!*** keep dry, keep (*or* store) in a dry place; ***patentrechtlich*** ~ patent; ***urheberrechtlich*** ~ copyright; **~d** protective; *fig.* ***sich ~d vor j-n stellen*** stand up for s.o.; ***s-e ~de Hand über j-n halten*** take s.o. under one's wing; → ***geschützt***; **II.** *v/refl.*: ***sich*** ~ protect o.s. (***gegen*** *acc.*, ***vor*** *dat.* from); ***sich ~ vor*** *dat. a.* guard against

'Schüt·zen|fest *n* **1.** *fair with shooting competition*; **2.** F *sport*: goal spree; **~feu·er** *n* ⚔ rifle (*or* independent) fire

'Schutz·en·gel *m* guardian angel

'Schüt·zen·gra·ben *m* ⚔ trench; **~krieg** *m* trench warfare

'Schüt·zen|hil·fe *fig. f* support, backing; ***j-m ~ leisten*** back s.o. up; **~kö·nig** *m* **1.** champion marksman; **2.** F *sport*: top scorer; **~loch** *n* foxhole; **~pan·zer** *m* armo(u)red personnel carrier; **~ver·ein** *m* rifle association

'Schutz|far·be *f* protective paint; ⚔ → ***Schutzanstrich***; **~fär·bung** *f zo.* protective colo(u)ring, camouflage; **~film** *m* protective layer (*or* coating); **~frist** *f* term of copyright; **~ge·biet** *n* **1.** *pol.* protectorate; **2.** → ***Naturschutzgebiet***; **~ge·bühr** *f* token fee; **~geist** *m* tutelary spirit; **~ge·leit** *n* escort; ⚔ *etc. a.* convoy; **~ge·wahr·sam** *m* protective custody; **~git·ter** *n* safety barrier; ⚡ screen (grid); *mot.* radiator grille; fireguard; **~haft** *f pol.* preventive detention; **~hei·li·ge** *m, f* (-n; -n) patron saint; **~helm** *m* (safety) helmet; hard hat; **~herr** *m* patron; *pol.* protector; **~her·rin** *f* patron(ess); *pol.* protector, protectress; **~herr·schaft** *f* protectorate; **~hül·le** *f* (protective) cover; holder; dust cover (*or* jacket); **~hüt·te** *f* shelter; **~imp·fung** *f* inoculation, vaccination; **~kap·pe** *f* protective cap; **~kar͵ton** *m* slipcase; **~klau·sel** *f* protective clause; **~klei·dung** *f* protective clothing; **~kon͵takt** *m* earthing (*Am.* grounding) contact; **~lei·ste** *f* protective strip

Schütz·ling ['ʃʏtslɪŋ] *m* (-s; -e) charge, protégé(e *f*)

'schutz·los I. *adj.* a) defenceless, *Am.* defenseless, b) without shelter; **II.** *adv.*: ***j-m ~ ausgeliefert sein*** be at s.o.'s mercy

'Schutz|macht *f pol.* protecting power; protector; **~mann** *obs. m* policeman, constable; **~man·tel** *m* ⚙ protective casing; *nucl.* radiation shield; **~mar·ke** *f*: (***eingetragene*** ~ registered) trademark, brand name; **~mas·ke** *f* (protective) mask; **~maß·nah·me** *f* protective (*or* safety) measure; precaution(ary measure); **~mau·er** *f* protective (*or* screen, ⚔ defensive) wall; **~mit·tel** *n* protective agent; ⚕ prophylactic; **~pa͵tron** *m* patron saint; **~po·li͵zei** *f* police *pl.*, constabulary; **~po·li͵zist** *m* policeman, constable; **~raum** *m* air-raid shelter; **~schicht** *f* protective layer (*or* coating); **~schild** *m* (protective) shield; ***lebendiger*** (*or* ***menschlicher***) ~ human shield; **~schirm** *m* (protective) screen, protective umbrella; **~staat** *m* protectorate; **~stoff** *m* ⚕ a) antibody, b) vaccine; **~͵um·schlag** *m* dust cover, (dust) jacket; **~ver·band** *m* **1.** ⚕ protective bandage; **2.** protective association; **~vor·rich·tung** *f* safety device, guard; **~wir·kung** *f* protective action

'Schutz·zoll *m* protective duty; **~po·li͵tik** *f* protectionism

schwab·be·lig ['ʃvabəlɪç] F *adj.* wobbly; flabby

schwab·beln ['ʃvabəln] F *v/i.* (h) wobble

Schwa·be ['ʃva:bə] *m* (-n; -n) Swabian; ~ ***sein*** be (a) Swabian, come from Swabia

schwä·beln ['ʃvɛ:bəln] *v/i.* (h) **1.** speak in (*or* the) Swabian dialect; **2.** have a Swabian accent

'Schwa·ben·streich *m* folly, foolish act

Schwä·bin ['ʃvɛ:bɪn] *f* (-; -nen) → ***Schwabe***; **schwä·bisch** ['ʃvɛ:bɪʃ] **I.** *adj.* Swabian; **II.** ♀ *n* (-en) Swabian (dialect)

schwach [ʃvax] **I.** *adj.* a) weak (*a. argument, eyes, glasses, character, constitution, stomach, nerves, team, market*, ⚗ *solution etc., drink, ling. declension, verb etc.*), *a.* faint *sound, smell, voice, smile, hope etc.*, poor *health, memory, hearing etc.*; low-powered *engine*; low *battery*; slow *pulse*; dim *light*, b) F *fig.* F hopeless; ***~e Ähnlichkeit*** remote resemblance; ***~es Anzeichen*** faint sign; ***~er Beifall*** half-hearted applause; ***~e Beteiligung*** poor turnout; ***~e Erinnerung*** faint (*or* vague, dim) recollection; ***~er Esser*** poor eater; ***das ~e Geschlecht*** the weaker sex; ***~e Leistung*** poor (*or* weak) performance; ***~es Lob*** scant praise; ***~e Seite*** → ***Schwäche*** 2; ***~e Stelle*** weak spot; ***e-e ~e Stunde*** a moment of weakness; ***~er Trost*** small consolation; ***~er Versuch*** feeble attempt; ***~e Vorstellung*** faint idea; ***e-n ~en Willen haben*** be weak-willed; ***~er Wind*** (s)light breeze; ***in Erdkunde ist sie*** ~ geography is her weak subject, she's weak in (*or* not very good at) geography; ~ ***werden*** weaken, *fig. a.* relent; succumb; *fig.* ***er wurde*** ~ *a.* his resistance broke down; F ***bei dem Anblick wurde ich*** ~ F I melted at the sight; ***sich ~ zeigen*** show one's weakness; ***schwächer werden*** weaken (further), grow weaker, ✝ *demand*: fall off, decrease, *eyesight*: fail, *sound, light*: fade; F ***mach mich nicht ~!*** F don't say things like that!; F ***nur nicht ~ werden!*** don't give in!; F ***mir wird ganz ~, wenn ich daran denke*** I go weak in the knees just at the thought (of it); F ~ ***auf der Brust sein*** be out of pocket; **II.** *adv.*: ~ ***spielen*** play badly; ~ ***entwickelt*** underdeveloped; ~ ***dekliniertes Substantiv*** (***Adjektiv***) weak noun (adjective)

'schwach|be·sie·delt *adj.* sparsely populated; **~be·tont** *adj.* weakly stressed; ~ ***sein*** *a.* have a weak stress; **~be·völ·kert** *adj.* sparsely populated

Schwä·che ['ʃvɛçə] *f* (-; -n) **1.** weakness; (feeling of) faintness; exhaustion; **2.** weak point, weakness (*a. of character*), failing, shortcoming; ***menschliche ~n*** human frailty; **3.** weakness (***für*** *acc.* for), soft spot (for *s.o.*); **4.** weakness; bad performance; **~an·fall** *m*: ***e-n ~ haben*** suddenly feel faint, faint, collapse; **~ge·fühl** *n* weak feeling; lack of energy

schwä·chen ['ʃvɛçən] *v/t.* (h) weaken (*a. fig.*); diminish, reduce; undermine *one's health*, *a.* impair *one's eyesight*; ***j-n*** ~ *a.* sap s.o.'s energy

'Schwä·che·zu·stand *m* weak condition, *formal*: debility

'Schwach·heit *f* (-; -en) **1.** *no pl.* weakness (*a. fig.*); **2.** F *fig.* ***bilde dir nur keine ~en ein!*** F don't kid yourself

'**Schwach·kopf** *contp. m* idiot, F blockhead, twit
schwäch·lich ['ʃvɛçlɪç] *adj.* weakly; delicate, frail; vulnerable, sickly; *fig.* weak
Schwäch·ling ['ʃvɛçlɪŋ] *m* (-s; -e) weakling (*a. fig.*)
'**schwach·sich·tig** [-zɪçtɪç] *adj.* weak-sighted
'**Schwach·sinn** *m* (-[e]s; *no pl.*) **1.** F nonsense; ***so ein ~!*** *a.* F what a load of rot, F what a crazy thing to do; **2.** ⚕ feeble-mindedness
'**schwach·sin·nig** *adj.* **1.** F idiotic, inane, F crazy; **2.** ⚕ mentally deficient, feeble-minded; '**Schwach·sin·ni·ge** [-zɪnɪgə] *m, f* (-n; -n) **1.** F moron, nut; **2.** ⚕ imbecile
'**Schwach|stel·le** *f* weak spot; **~strom** *m* ⚡ weak (*or* low-voltage) current
Schwä·chung ['ʃvɛçʊŋ] *f* (-; *no pl.*) weakening
'**schwach·win·dig** *adj. meteor.* light winds
Schwa·den ['ʃva:dən] *m* (-s; -) cloud; patch; ***dicke ~*** dense *or* thick clouds (*or* patches *of fog*)
Schwa·dron [ʃva'dro:n] *f* (-; -en) squadron
schwa·dro·nie·ren [ʃvadro'ni:rən] *v/i.* (h) bluster, F gas (***von*** *dat.* about)
Schwa·fe·lei [ʃva:fə'laɪ] F *f* (-; *no pl.*) F twaddle, blether(ing); **Schwaf·ler** ['ʃva:flɐ] F *m* (-s; -) F gasbag; waffler; **schwa·feln** ['ʃva:fəln] F (h) **I.** *v/i.* F waffle; ***~ von*** *dat.* waffle (on) about, go on about; **II.** *v/t.*: ***was schwafelt er denn wieder?*** F what's he waffling (*or* going) on about now?
Schwa·ger ['ʃva:gɐ] *m* (-s; -, Schwäger ['ʃvɛ:gɐ]) brother-in-law; **Schwä·ge·rin** ['ʃvɛ:gərɪn] *f* (-; -nen) sister-in-law
Schwal·be ['ʃvalbə] *f* (-; -n) swallow; *fig.* ***e-e ~ macht noch keinen Sommer*** one swallow doesn't make a summer
'**Schwal·ben·nest** *n* swallow's nest
'**Schwal·ben·ne·ster·sup·pe** *f* bird's nest soup
'**Schwal·ben·schwanz** *m* **1.** *zo.* swallow-tail; **2.** F swallow-tails *pl.*, swallow-tailed coat
Schwall [ʃval] *m* (-[e]s; -e) huge splash *of water*, surge (*a. of air, gas*); *fig.* flood *of words*; volley, torrent *of abuse*; barrage *of questions etc.*; burst *of music etc.*
schwamm [ʃvam] *pret. of* ***schwimmen***
Schwamm [ʃvam] *m* (-[e]s; Schwämme ['ʃvɛmə]) **1.** *zo. and w.s.* sponge; ***mit e-m ~ abwaschen*** sponge down; *fig.* ***~ drüber!*** (let's) forget it; **2.** dry rot
Schwam·merl ['ʃvamɐl] *dial. n* (-s; -[n]) → ***Pilz***
schwam·mig ['ʃvamɪç] *adj.* **1.** a) spongy, b) flabby *body etc.*; *a.* puffy *face*; **2.** *fig.* woolly *concept etc.*
Schwan [ʃva:n] *m* (-[e]s; Schwäne ['ʃvɛ:nə]) swan; F ***mein lieber ~!*** a) F blimey!, b) F I tell you, c) and I'm not joking
schwand [ʃvant] *pret. of* ***schwinden***
schwa·nen ['ʃva:nən] F *v/i. and v/impers.* (h): ***mir schwant, es schwant mir*** something tells me, I have a feeling; ***mir schwant nichts Gutes*** I have a funny feeling something's gone wrong (*or* something awful is going to happen *etc.*)
'**Schwa·nen|ge·sang** *fig. m* swan song; **~hals** *m* **1.** ⚙ gooseneck; **2.** *fig. hum.* swan neck
schwang [ʃvaŋ] *pret. of* ***schwingen***
Schwang *m*: ***im ~ sein*** be the fashion, F be in
schwan·ger ['ʃvaŋɐ] *adj.* pregnant, *formal*: expectant; ***~ sein*** *a.* be expecting; ***im dritten Monat ~*** three months pregnant; F *fig.* ***~ gehen mit*** *dat.* F be hatching (out) *great plans etc.*
Schwan·ge·re ['ʃvaŋərə] *f* (-n; -n) pregnant woman, expectant mother
'**Schwan·ge·ren|be·ra·tungs·stel·le** *f* antenatal clinic; **~für·sor·ge** *f* antenatal care; **~gym,na·stik** *f* antenatal exercises *pl.*
schwän·gern ['ʃvɛŋɐn] *v/t.* (h) make *s.o.* pregnant; *fig.* impregnate
'**Schwan·ger·schaft** *f* (-; -en) pregnancy; ***während der ~*** during pregnancy, while (one is) pregnant
'**Schwan·ger·schafts|ab·bruch** *m* abortion; **~gym,na·stik** *f* antenatal exercises *pl.*; **~test** *m* pregnancy test; **~un·ter,bre·chung** *f* abortion; **~ver·hü·tung** *f* → ***Empfängnisverhütung***; **~vor·sor·ge·un·ter,su·chung** *f* antenatal; **~zei·chen** *n* sign of pregnancy
Schwank [ʃvaŋk] *m* (-[e]s; Schwänke ['ʃvɛŋkə]) **1.** *thea.* farce; **2.** (amusing) story, anecdote; ***Schwänke aus s-r Jugend*** adventures of one's youth
schwan·ken ['ʃvaŋkən] **I.** *v/i.* (h) **1.** sway; *ground etc.*: *a.* shake, tremble; *boat*: rock (from side to side); **2.** a) sway (from side to side), totter, reel, b) (sn) stagger; **3.** *fig.* a) vacillate, waver, b) vary; alternate; ✝, ⚙ fluctuate; ***ich schwanke noch*** I'm still undecided, I haven't made up my mind yet; ***ich schwanke noch zwischen Malta und Zypern*** I still can't decide whether to go to Malta or Cyprus; ***die Meinungen ~*** opinions are divided; ***er schwankte e-n Augenblick, bevor er ...*** after a moment of indecision he ...; **II.** ♀ *n* (-s; *no pl.*) swaying; variation; fluctuation *etc.*; ***→ I; ins ~ geraten*** *boat*: start to rock, ground: *Boden*: start to sway (*or* shake, tremble), *person*: start to sway (*or* totter), lose one's balance, *a. fig. government etc.*: begin to teeter, *fig. hopes etc.*: be shaken, begin to waver; ***bei dieser Frage geriet sie ins ~*** that question caught her off her guard (*or* slightly flummoxed her, got her slightly flustered)
'**schwan·kend** *adj.* **1.** swaying *etc.*; → ***schwanken*** 1; **2.** *fig.* undecided, irresolute, wavering; unsteady, unstable (*a.* ✝); ***~er Charakter*** unstable personality
'**Schwan·kung** *f* (-; -en) variation (*gen.* in, of); fluctuation (in, of); deviation; ***seelische ~en*** emotional ups and downs
Schwanz [ʃvants] *m* (-es; Schwänze ['ʃvɛntsə]) **1.** *zo.* tail (*a.* ✈ *etc., a. ast.*); *fig.* (tail) end; F ***den ~ einziehen*** F come down a peg or two; F ***mit eingezogenem ~ abziehen*** slink off with one's tail between one's legs; F ***kein ~*** *sl.* not a sod; **2.** *no pl. fig.* string *of questions etc.*; **3.** V prick, cock, dick
schwän·zeln ['ʃvɛntsəln] *v/i.* **1.** (h) wag one's tail; **2.** (sn) mince (along); ***um j-n ~*** F toady (*or* suck up) to s.o.
schwän·zen ['ʃvɛntsən] F *v/t. and v/i.* (h): (***die Schule ~***) play truant (*Am.* hookey); skip, *Brit. a.* F skive
'**Schwanz|en·de** *n zo.* tip of the tail; ✈ tail; *fig.* tail end; **~fe·der** *f* tail feather; **~flos·se** *f* tail fin
'**schwanz·la·stig** [-lastɪç] *adj.* tail-heavy
'**Schwanz·stück** *n gastr.* tail piece; rump
schwap·pen ['ʃvapən] *v/i.* (h, sn) a) slosh (around), b) slop, spill (***auf*** *acc.* onto)
Schwä·re ['ʃvɛ:rə] *f* (-; -n) abscess, boil
'**schwä·ren** *v/i.* (h) fester, *formal*: suppurate
Schwarm [ʃvarm] *m* (-[e]s; Schwärme ['ʃvɛrmə]) **1.** *zo.* swarm *of insects*; flock, flush *of birds*; shoal, school *of fish*; *fig.* crowd, swarm, F herd *of people*; **2.** F *fig.* a) F heartthrob, b) dream
schwär·men ['ʃvɛrmən] *v/i.* **1.** (h, sn) swarm; **2.** (h) enthuse (***von*** *dat.* about), rave ([on] about); dream (of); ***~ für*** *acc.* be mad (F wild, crazy) about; ***für j-n ~*** *a.* F have a crush on s.o.; ***ins ♀ geraten*** go into raptures
Schwär·mer ['ʃvɛrmɐ] *m* (-s; -) **1.** dreamer; romantic; enthusiast, fanatic, *esp. pol. etc.* zealot; **2.** *zo.* hawkmoth; **3.** squib
Schwär·me·rei [ʃvɛrmə'raɪ] *f* (-; -en) a) enthusiasm (***für*** *acc.* for), passion (for), fanaticism (for), b) romantic zeal, c) idolization, worship (of)
Schwär·me·rin ['ʃvɛrmərɪn] *f* (-; -nen) → ***Schwärmer*** 1
schwär·me·risch ['ʃvɛrmərɪʃ] *adj.* a) gushing, effusive, b) enraptured, c) fanatical
'**Schwarm·geist** *m* zealot
Schwar·te ['ʃvartə] *f* (-; -n) **1.** rind, *a. zo.* skin; *gastr.* bacon rind, crackling; **2.** F ***dicke ~*** F fat tome
'**Schwar·ten·ma·gen** *m gastr.* brawn
schwarz [ʃvarts] **I.** *adj.* a) black (*a. coffee, tea*), b) *fig.* brown (as a berry), c) F black, filthy, d) *fig.* black, gloomy, e) illicit, illegal, black *market*, f) F *pol.* conservative; ***♀es Brett*** notice board, bulletin board; ***~er Humor*** black humo(u)r, *thea.* black comedy; ***der ~e Mann*** a) the chimney sweep, b) the bogeyman; ***~e Liste*** black list; ***j-n auf die ~e Liste setzen*** blacklist s.o.; ***♀e Magie*** Black Magic; ***~er Tag*** black day; ***du hast dich im Gesicht ~ gemacht*** you've dirtied your face; *fig.* ***~en Gedanken nachhängen*** a) be plotting revenge, b) be sunk in gloom (and despondency); ***j-m den ♀en Peter zuspielen*** F pass the buck to s.o.; ***sich ~ ärgern*** F be really mad; ***ich hab' mich ~ geärgert*** F I could have kicked myself; ***~ auf weiß*** in black and white, in cold print; ***aus ~ weiß machen wollen*** try to twist things; ***~ werden*** get dirty, *silver*: tarnish, go black, *card game*: not to get a single trick; ***mir wurde ~ vor Augen*** everything went black; ***da kann er warten, bis er ~ wird*** he can wait till he's blue in the face; ***~ von Menschen*** swarming with people; ***~ wie die Nacht*** (as) black as night; ***wieder ~e Zahlen schreiben*** be in the black again; → ***Schaf***; **II.** *adv.*: ***~ (ver)kaufen*** buy (sell) on the black market; ***~ über die Grenze gehen*** cross the border illegally
Schwarz *n* (-[es]; *no pl.*) black; ***in ~ gekleidet*** (dressed) in black, in mourning
'**Schwarz·afri·ka** *n* black Africa
'**schwarz·afri,ka·nisch** *adj.* black African
'**Schwarz·ar·beit** *f* illicit work, F moonlighting; ***et. in ~ machen*** do s.th. on the side (without declaring it)
'**schwarz·ar·bei·ten** *v/i.* (*sep.*, h) work on the side, F moonlight

'**Schwarz·ar·bei·ter** *m* illicit worker, F moonlighter
'**schwarz·äu·gig** [-ɔʏgɪç] *adj.* dark-eyed
'**schwarz|blau** *adj.* bluish black, blue-black; **~braun** *adj.* brownish black
'**Schwarz|bren·ner** *m* moonshiner; **~brot** *n* brown bread; rye bread
'**schwarz·bunt** *adj.* black and white *cattle*; '**Schwarz·bun·te** *f* (-n; -n) Friesian, *Am.* Holstein
Schwar·ze[1] ['ʃvartsə] *m* (-n; -n) **1.** black (man); **2.** F a) Catholic, b) conservative
'**Schwar·ze**[2] *f* (-n; -n) black (woman)
'**Schwar·ze**[3] *n* (-n; *no pl.*) bull's eye; ***ins ~ treffen*** *a. fig.* hit the bull's eye; ***du hast ins ~ getroffen!*** spot on!
Schwär·ze ['ʃvɛrtsə] *f* (-; *no pl.*) **1.** blackness (*a. fig.*); darkness; **2.** newsprint, printer's ink; black dye
'**schwär·zen** *v/t.* (h) blacken (*a. fig.*), black; ***geschwärzt von*** *dat.* black with
'**schwarz·fah·ren** *v/i.* (*irr.*, *sep.*, sn, → ***fahren***) dodge the fare, ride without paying; be a fare dodger; *mot.* drive without a licen|ce (*Am.* -se)
'**Schwarz·fah·rer** *m* fare dodger, F deadhead
'**schwarz|ge·rän·dert** [-gərɛndɐt] *adj.* black-edged *envelope etc.*; dark-rimmed *eyes*; **~ge·streift** *adj.* black-striped, with black stripes; **~grau** *adj.* greyish (*Am.* grayish) black; **~haa·rig** *adj.* black-haired
'**Schwarz·han·del** *m* black market; black marketeering; ***im ~*** on the black market; ***~ treiben*** be a black market operator; '**Schwarz·händ·ler** *m* black marketeer; (ticket) tout
'**schwarz·hö·ren** *v/i.* (*sep.*, h) be a radio-licen|ce (*Am.* -se) dodger, have no radio licen|se (*Brit.* -ce)
'**Schwarz·hö·rer** *m* radio-licen|ce (*Am.* -se) dodger
'**Schwarz·kit·tel** F *m* **1.** *zo.* wild boar; **2.** cleric; **3.** *sport*: referee
schwärz·lich ['ʃvɛrtslɪç] *adj.* blackish
'**schwarz·ma·len** (*sep.*, h) **I.** *v/t.* paint a gloomy picture of; ***alles ~*** always see the gloomy side of things; ***mußt du immer alles ~?*** *a.* do you have to be so pessimistic?; **II.** *v/i.* see the gloomy side of it; always see the gloomy side of things, take a very pessimistic view of things; '**Schwarz·ma·ler** *m* pessimist, prophet of doom; '**Schwarz·ma·le·rei** *f* (-; *no pl.*) pessimism; pessimistic view; pessimistic (*or* gloomy) forecasts *pl.*
'**Schwarz|markt** *m* black market; **~rock** F *m* cleric
'**Schwarz-'Rot-'Gold** *n* (-; *no pl.*) black, red and gold; '**schwarz'rot'gol·den** *adj.* black, red and gold; ***die ~e Fahne*** the black, red and gold (flag)
'**schwarz·schlach·ten** *v/i. and v/t.* (*sep.*, h) slaughter (a pig *etc.*) illegally
'**Schwarz·schlach·tung** *f* illegal slaughtering
'**schwarz·se·hen** *v/i.* (*irr.*, *sep.*, h, → ***sehen***) **1.** be pessimistic (***für*** *acc.* about), take a dim view of things; always look on the dark side of things; ***da sehe ich aber schwarz*** I don't think there's much hope, things don't look too good; ***ich sehe schwarz für ihn*** *a.* I don't see (*or* hold out) much hope for him; **2.** be a TV-licen|ce (*Am.* -se) dodger, have no TV-licen|ce (*Am.* -se)
'**Schwarz·se·her** *m* **1.** pessimist, prophet of doom; **2.** TV-licen|ce (*Am.* -se) dodger; '**schwarz·se·he·risch** *adj.* pessimistic(ally *adv.*), alarmist
'**Schwarz·sen·der** *m* pirate radio station
'**Schwarz·wald...** *in cpds.* Black Forest ...; '**Schwarz·wäl·der** [-vɛldɐ] *adj.*: ***~ Kirschtorte*** Black Forest gateau
schwarz'weiß I. *adj.* black and white, black-and-white ...; **II.** *adv.*: ***~ fotografieren*** take black-and-white pictures
Schwarz'weiß|fern·se·her *m* black-and-white television (set) *or* TV; **~film** *m* black-and-white (*or* monochrome) film; **~fo·to** *n* black-and-white photo (*or* print)
schwarz'weiß·ma·len (*sep.*, h) **I.** *v/i.* present (*or* paint, see) things *or* everything in (terms of) black and white; **II.** *v/t.* paint *s.th.* in black and white; **Schwarz'weiß·ma·le·rei** *f* (-; *no pl.*) seeing (*or* painting) everything in terms of black and white; black-and-white depiction
'**Schwarz|wild** *n coll.* wild boar; **~wurzel** *f* black salsify
Schwatz [ʃvats] *m* (-es; *no pl.*) chat, F natter; **schwat·zen** ['ʃvatsən] (h) **I.** *v/i.* a) chat, F natter, b) drivel, blather, c) gossip, d) F blab; **II.** *v/t.*: ***dummes Zeug ~*** talk a lot of nonsense (F drivel); ***was schwatzt er schon wieder?*** F what's he going (*or* babbling) on about?
schwät·zen ['ʃvɛtsən] *v/i. and v/t.* (h) → ***schwatzen***; **Schwät·zer** ['ʃvɛtsɐ] *m* (-s; -) F gasbag; gossip; **Schwät·ze·rei** [ʃvɛtsə'raɪ] *f* (-; *no pl.*) a) F prattle, drivel, b) gossip, c) F yakking, d) gossiping
'**schwatz·haft** *adj.* talkative; '**Schwatz·haf·tig·keit** *f* (-; *no pl.*) talkativeness
Schwe·be ['ʃveːbə] *f*: ***in der ~ sein*** be undecided (*or* in the balance), ⚖ be pending; ***es ist noch in der ~*** *a.* it hasn't been decided yet; **~bahn** *f* suspension (cable) railway; **~bal·ken** *m gym.* (balance) beam
schwe·ben ['ʃveːbən] *v/i.* **1.** (h) be suspended, hang; hover; **2.** (sn) float, glide (***über*** *acc.* across); soar; **3.** (h) *fig.* be undecided; ***ihm war, als ob er schwebte*** he felt as if he was walking on air; *fig.* ***über den Wolken ~***, ***in höheren Regionen*** (*or* ***Sphären***) ***~*** have one's head in the clouds; ***in Illusionen ~*** live in a world of fantasy; ***noch im Raum ~*** *sound*: linger on; ***es schwebt mir auf der Zunge*** it's on the tip of my tongue; ***j-m vor Augen ~*** → ***vorschweben***; ***in Gefahr ~*** be in danger; ***in Ungewißheit ~*** be (kept) in suspense; ***zwischen Furcht und Hoffnung*** (***Leben und Tod***) ***~*** hover between fear and hope (life and death); → ***Lebensgefahr***; '**schwe·bend** *adj.* **1.** floating, hovering *etc.*; → ***schweben***; ***~en Schrittes daherkommen*** come gliding along; **2.** ⚖ pending
'**Schwe·be·zu·stand** *m* (-[e]s; *no pl.*) state of suspense; limbo; ***im ~ sein*** a) be in (a state of) suspense, b) be in limbo
Schweb·stof·fe ['ʃveːp-] *pl.* ⚗ suspended matter *sg.*
Schwe·de ['ʃveːdə] *m* (-n; -n), **Schwe·din** ['ʃveːdɪn] *f* (-; -nen) Swede
schwe·disch ['ʃveːdɪʃ] **I.** *adj.* Swedish; F *hum.* ***hinter ~en Gardinen*** behind bars; **II.** ♀ *n* (-en) *ling.* Swedish
Schwe·fel ['ʃveːfəl] *m* (-s; *no pl.*) sulphur, *Am.* sulfur; **~bad** *n* **1.** ⚗ sulphur (*Am.* sulfur) bath; **2.** ⚕ sulphur (*Am.* sulfur) springs *pl.*; **~di·oxyd** *n* sulphur (*Am.* sulfur) dioxide; **~ei·sen** *n* iron (*or* ferrous) sulphide (*Am.* sulfide)
'**schwe·fel·hal·tig** [-haltɪç] *adj.* sulphur(e)ous, *Am.* sulfur(e)ous
Schwe·fel'koh·len·stoff *m* carbon disulphide (*Am.* disulfide)
schwe·feln ['ʃveːfəln] *v/t.* (h) ⚗ sulphurate, *Am.* sulfurate, *a.* ⚙ sulphurize, *Am.* sulfurize; fumigate with sulphur (*Am.* sulfur)
'**Schwe·fel|quel·le** *f* sulphur (*Am.* sulfur) spring; **♀sau·er** *adj.* sulphuric, *Am.* sulfuric; sulphate (*Am.* sulfate) of; ***schwefelsaures Ammoniak*** ammonium sulphate (*Am.* sulfate); **~säu·re** *f* sulphuric (*Am.* sulfuric) acid
Schwe·fel'was·ser·stoff *m* hydrogen sulphide (*Am.* sulfide)
schwef·lig ['ʃveːflɪç] *adj.* sulphurous, *Am.* sulfurous
Schweif [ʃvaɪf] *m* (-[e]s; -e) tail (*a. ast.*); *fig.* train
schwei·fen ['ʃvaɪfən] *v/i.* (sn) wander, roam, rove; *fig.* ***den Blick*** (***s-e Gedanken***) ***~ lassen*** let one's gaze (mind) wander; ***s-e Gedanken schweiften in die Vergangenheit*** his thoughts ranged over the past
Schwei·ge|geld ['ʃvaɪgə-] *n* hush money; **~marsch** *m* silent (protest) march; **~mi·nu·te** *f*: (***e-e ~*** a *or* one) minute's silence, (a) one-minute silence (***zu Ehren*** *gen.* in memory of)
schwei·gen ['ʃvaɪgən] *v/i.* (schwieg, geschwiegen, h) a) be (*or* remain) silent; say nothing, not to say anything, not to say a word; F keep mum, b) *noise etc.*: stop, cease; ***plötzlich ~*** *a. guns etc.*: fall silent; ***~ zu*** *dat.* make no comment on *s.th.*; ***~ über*** *acc.* keep silent about; ***auf e-e Frage ~*** say nothing in reply (to a question); ***zu j-s Vorwürfen ~*** not to try and defend o.s. (against s.o.'s reproaches); ***zu e-m Unrecht ~*** not to protest against an injustice; ***schweig bloß davon!*** don't talk about that; ***darüber schweigt das Gesetz*** the law says nothing about that; ***seit heute ~ die Waffen*** arms were laid down today, *lit.* the guns fell silent today; ***ganz zu ~ von*** *dat.* let alone, never mind, to say nothing of; ***kannst du ~?*** can you keep a secret?; ***~ Sie!*** be quiet!, silence!
'**Schwei·gen** *n* (-s; *no pl.*) silence; ***~ bewahren*** keep silent; ***das ~ brechen*** break the silence; ***zum ~ bringen*** reduce to silence, silence (*a.* ⚔), shut up; → ***hüllen***
'**schwei·gend I.** *adj.* silent; *pol.* ***~e Mehrheit*** silent majority; **II.** *adv.*: in silence, without a word; ***~ zuhören*** listen in silence; ***er ging ~ darüber hinweg*** he passed it over in silence
Schwei·ge·pflicht ['ʃvaɪgə-] *f* (-; *no pl.*) professional discretion (*or* secrecy); ***die ärztliche ~*** medical confidentiality; ***der ~ unterliegen*** be bound to professional discretion
Schwei·ger ['ʃvaɪgɐ] *m* (-s; -) taciturn person, man of few words
schweig·sam ['ʃvaɪkzaːm] *adj.* a) quiet; taciturn, uncommunicative, b) discreet; ***du bist heute aber sehr ~*** *a.* you're not saying very much today
'**Schweig·sam·keit** *f* (-; *no pl.*) a) quietness; taciturnity, uncommunicativeness, b) discretion

Schwein [ʃvaɪn] *n* (-[e]s; -e) **1.** a) *zo.* pig, hog; sow, b) *gastr.* pork; **2.** F *contp.* a) (filthy) pig, b) *sl.* swine, bastard; ***kein*** ~ F not a blessed soul, *sl.* not a sod; ***kein ~ hat mir geholfen*** *a.* nobody lifted a finger to help me; ***das glaubt dir doch kein ~*** F you don't think anyone's going to buy that, do you?; ***armes*** ~ poor wretch, *sl.* poor sod (*or* bastard); ~ ***haben*** be lucky (*or* in luck); F ***da hast du aber ~ gehabt!*** F talk about luck!

'**Schwei·ne|ar·beit** F *f* (-; *no pl.*) dirty work; F tough job; **~bauch** *m* pork belly; **~bra·ten** *m* a) joint of pork, b) roast pork; **~fi,let** *n* fillet of pork; **~fleisch** *n* pork; **~fraß** *m*, **~fut·ter** *n* pigfeed; F *fig.* F swill, muck; **~geld** F *n*: ***ein*** ~ F heaps of money, ***verdienen*:** F earn a packet (*or* bomb), rake it in; **~hund** F *m sl.* swine, bastard; ***der innere*** ~ one's baser instincts; **~ko·te,lett** *n* pork chop; **~len·de** *f* pork tenderloin; **~pest** *f* swine fever

Schwei·ne·rei [ʃvaɪnə'raɪ] F *f* (-; -en) **1.** mess; ***das ist ja e-e ~ hier!*** this place looks disgusting (*or* like a pigsty); **2.** ***das ist e-e*** ~ that's disgusting (F really rotten); **3.** dirty joke; obscenity, *pl.* smut *sg.*; **4.** *a. pl.* obscenity, obscene behavio(u)r

'**Schwei·ne|schmalz** *n* lard, dripping; **~schnit·zel** *n* pork cutlet; **~stall** *m* pigsty (*a. fig.*), pigpen, hogpen; **~zucht** *f* pig-breeding, hog-raising; **~züch·ter** *m* pig-breeder, hog-raiser

Schwein·igel ['ʃvaɪnʔi:gəl] F *m* (-s; -) **1.** F dirty pig, mucky pup; **2.** dirty old so-and-so, *sl.* dirty bugger; ***er ist ein*** ~ *a.* he's got a one-track mind

Schwein·ige·lei [ʃvaɪnʔi:gə'laɪ] F *f* (-; -en) dirty joke; obscenity

'**schwein·igeln** F *v/i.* (h) talk smut

schwei·nisch ['ʃvaɪnɪʃ] *adj.* **1.** filthy; **2.** *fig.* dirty, smutty *joke etc.*; disgusting *behavio(u)r etc.*

'**Schwein·kram** F *m* → ***Schweinerei*** 1, 3

'**Schweins|au·gen** *pl.* piggy eyes; **~fuß** *m* → ***Schweinshaxe;*** **~ga,lopp** *m*: F ***im*** ~ double-quick; **~ha·xe** *f* knuckle of pork; **~le·der** *n* pigskin

Schweiß [ʃvaɪs] *m* (-es; *no pl.*) **1.** sweat, *formal*: perspiration; ***in ~ geraten*** get into a sweat; ***ihm stand der ~ auf der Stirn*** there were beads of sweat on his forehead; ***in ~ gebadet*** → ***schweißgebadet;*** ***nach ~ riechen*** smell (of sweat), have b.o. (*or* BO, body odo[u]r); *fig.* ***es hat viel ~ gekostet*** it was hard work (F a hard slog, *sl.* a real sweat); ***im ~e s-s Angesichts*** by the sweat of one's brow; **2.** *hunt.* blood; **~ab·son·de·rung** *f* perspiration; **~aus·bruch** *m*: ***e-n ~ bekommen*** break out into a sweat; **~band** *n* (-[e]s; ⸚er) *sport*: sweatband; **2be·deckt** *adj.* → ***schweißgebadet***

'**Schweiß|bren·ner** *m* ⚙ welding torch; **~bril·le** *f*: (***e-e*** ~ a pair of) welding goggles *pl.*

'**Schweiß·drü·se** *f* sweat gland

schwei·ßen ['ʃvaɪsən] *v/t. and v/i.* ⚙ weld

Schwei·ßer ['ʃvaɪsɐ] *m* (-s; -) ⚙ welder

'**Schweiß|fleck** *m* sweat mark; **~fü·ße** *pl.* sweaty (F smelly) feet; **2ge·ba·det** *adj.* soaked (*or* bathed) in sweat, dripping with sweat; **~ge·ruch** *m* smell of sweat, body odo(u)r; **~hän·de** *pl.* sweaty palms; **~hund** *m hunt.* bloodhound

schwei·ßig ['ʃvaɪsɪç] *adj.* **1.** sweaty; **2.** *hunt.* bleeding *animal etc.*, bloody *scent*

'**Schweiß·naht** *f* ⚙ weld(ed joint), (welding) seam

'**schweiß·naß** *adj.* → ***schweißgebadet***

'**Schweiß|per·le** *f* bead of perspiration; **~po·re** *f* sweat pore; **~stel·le** *f* ⚙ weld

'**schweiß|trei·bend** *adj.* ⚕ sudorific; ~ ***sein*** *a.* make one sweat; **~trie·fend** *adj.* → ***schweißgebadet***

'**Schweiß·trop·fen** *m* bead of sweat (*or* perspiration)

Schwei·ßung ['ʃvaɪsʊŋ] *f* (-; -en) welding; weld

'**schweiß·ver·klebt** *adj.* sticky with sweat

Schwei·zer ['ʃvaɪtsɐ] **I.** *m* (-s; -) Swiss; ***die*** ~ the Swiss (*pl.*); **II.** *adj.* Swiss; **~deutsch** *n*, **2deutsch** *adj. ling.* Swiss German; **~fran·ken** *m* Swiss franc; **~gar·de** *f* Swiss Guard

Schwei·ze·rin ['ʃvaɪtsərɪn] *f* (-; -nen) Swiss (woman); **schwei·ze·risch** ['ʃvaɪtsərɪʃ] *adj.* Swiss

Schwel·brand ['ʃve:l-] *m* smo(u)ldering fire; **schwe·len** ['ʃve:lən] *v/i.* (h) smo(u)lder; *fig. a.* simmer

schwel·gen ['ʃvɛlgən] *v/i.* (h) **1.** ~ ***in*** *dat.* revel in; wallow in; ***in Erinnerungen*** ~ wallow in memories; **2.** indulge o.s., F have a binge

schwel·ge·risch ['ʃvɛlgərɪʃ] *adj.* a) over-indulgent, extravagant, b) voluptuous, c) opulent, sumptuous *meal etc.*

Schwel·le ['ʃvɛlə] *f* (-; -n) threshold (*a. psych. and fig.*), step; 🚂 sleeper, tie; ***sie soll keinen Fuß mehr über m-e ~ setzen*** she'd better not cross my threshold (*or* darken my door) again; *fig.* ~ ***des Bewußtseins*** threshold of consciousness; ***an der ~ e-r neuen Zeit*** on the threshold of a new age; ***an der ~ des Grabes*** at death's door

schwel·len ['ʃvɛlən] (schwoll, geschwollen) **I.** *v/i.* (sn) swell (*a. fig.*); *water*: *a.* rise; → ***geschwollen;*** **II.** *v/t.* (h) swell; fill out, billow *sails*; *fig.* ***die Brust*** ~ puff one's chest out

'**Schwel·len|angst** *f psych.* fear of entering unfamiliar places, fear of the unknown; **~preis** *m* ⚜ threshold price; **~reiz** *m* threshold stimulus; **~wert** *m* threshold value

Schwell·kör·per [ʃvɛl-] *m anat.* erectile tissue

Schwel·lung ['ʃvɛlʊŋ] *f* (-; -en) ⚕ swelling; swollen spot

Schwell·werk ['ʃvɛl-] *n* ♪ swell organ

Schwem·me ['ʃvɛmə] *f* (-; -n) **1.** watering place; **2.** pub, taproom; **3.** ⚜ glut (***an*** *dat.* of); '**schwem·men** *v/t.* (h) wash (***an Land*** ashore); **Schwemm·land** ['ʃvɛm-] *n* (-[e]s; *no pl.*) alluvial land (*or* plain)

Schwen·gel ['ʃvɛŋəl] *m* (-s; -) **1.** clapper, tongue; **2.** handle

Schwenk [ʃvɛŋk] *m* (-[e]s; -e) *film*: pan (shot) (***auf*** *acc.* of), tilt (shot)

'**Schwenk·arm** *m* swivel arm

'**schwenk·bar** *adj.* swivel ..., swivel(l)ing; slewing, sluable *crane etc.*; **schwen·ken** ['ʃvɛŋkən] (h) **I.** *v/t.* a) swing; wave *one's hat etc.*; brandish, flourish *stick etc.*; ⚙ swivel; slew *crane etc.*; *film*: pan *the camera*; shake, *gastr.* toss, b) rinse; **II.** *v/i.* turn, swing (round); ⚔ wheel (about); *movie camera*: pan; ***nach links*** (***rechts***) ~ *car*: turn left (right), swerve (to the) left (right); **Schwen·ker** ['ʃvɛŋkɐ] *m* (-s; -) brandy balloon

'**Schwenk|flü·gel** *m* ✈ swing wing; **~glas** *n* → ***Schwenker;*** **~hahn** *m* swivel tap; **~kar,tof·feln** *pl.* potatoes tossed in butter; **~kran** *m* swivel (*or* slewing) crane

Schwen·kung ['ʃvɛŋkʊŋ] *f* (-; -en) turn, swivel; ⚙ slewing; ⚔ wheel; wheeling manoeuvre (*Am.* maneuver); *film*: pan; *fig.* change of heart, *pol.* change of front, turnabout, about-turn, volte-face

'**Schwenk·vor·rich·tung** *f* swivel mechanism

schwer [ʃve:ɐ] **I.** *adj.* a) heavy (*a. fig. attack, scent, step, storm, losses*), *a.* heavy-going *reading etc.*, b) hard, F tough; difficult, c) bad *accident, illness etc.*, serious *illness, mistake, crime etc.*, d) weighty; oppressive; onerous *office, duty etc.*, d) *gastr.* rich *food etc.*, heavy *wine etc.*; strong *cigar, smell etc.*; ***~er Atem*** labo(u)red breathing; ***~e Erkältung*** bad (*or* heavy) cold; ***e-e ~e Gehirnerschütterung*** severe concussion; F ***~es Geld verdienen*** F make big money, make a packet; F ***~es Geld kosten*** F cost a packet; ***~es Gold*** solid gold; ***~en Herzens*** reluctantly, with a heavy heart; F ***~er Junge*** thug, F heavy; ***ich habe e-n ~en Kopf*** my head's throbbing; ***~e Körperverletzung*** grievous bodily harm, GBH; ***~e Maschine*** powerful (*or* heavy) machine; ***~es Schicksal*** hard lot; ***~er Schlaf*** deep (*or* heavy) sleep; ***~er Schock*** bad (*or* severe, terrible) shock; ***~e See*** heavy (*or* rough) seas; ***~er Tag*** hard (F tough) day; ***heute war ein ~er Tag*** *a.* it was hard (F tough) going today; ⚗ ***~es Wasser*** heavy water; ***~e Zeit(en)*** hard times; ***~e Zunge*** heavy tongue; ***wie ~ bist du?*** how much do you weigh?; ***es ist zwei Pfund ~*** it weighs (*or* it's) two pounds; ***ein drei Pfund ~er Braten*** *etc.* a three-pound roast *etc.*; ***ein mehrere Tonnen ~er Kran*** a crane weighing several tons; F ***etliche Millionen ~ sein*** be worth a few million; → ***Begriff*** 1, ***Blei*** 1, ***Geschütz;*** **II.** *adv.* heavily *etc.*; really; badly; ~ ***arbeiten*** work hard; ~ ***atmen*** have difficulty breathing; F ~ ***aufpassen*** watch like a hawk; ***das ist ~ zu beantworten*** there's no easy answer to that, that's a good question; ~ ***beleidigt*** deeply offended, *esp. iro.* mortally wounded; ~ ***bestrafen*** punish severely; ~ ***betrunken*** very drunk, F drunk out of one's mind; ***das ist ~ zu beurteilen*** it's hard to say (*or* judge); ~ ***büßen*** pay dearly; ~ ***enttäuscht*** really (*or* deeply) disappointed; ~ ***erkältet sein*** have a bad (*or* heavy) cold; ***er hat es ~*** he has a hard time (of it); F ***das will ich ~ hoffen!*** I sincerely hope so, you'd *etc.* better!; ~ ***hören*** be hard of hearing; ~ ***leiden*** suffer badly; ***j-m ~ auf der Seele liegen*** prey on s.o.'s mind; F ~ ***reich sein*** F be loaded; ~ ***zu sagen*** hard to say; ***da hat er sich aber ~ getäuscht*** he's very much mistaken there; ~ ***zu verstehen*** difficult to understand, hard to grasp; ***er ist ~ zu verstehen*** it's difficult to hear what he's saying; → ***Magen, schwerfallen***

'**Schwer·ar·beit** *f* (-; *no pl.*) heavy labo(u)r; '**Schwer·ar·bei·ter** *m* heavy labo(u)rer

'**Schwer·ath,let** *m* weight lifter, wrestler, shot putter *etc.*; '**Schwer·ath,le·tik** *f* strength events *pl.*

'schwer·be·hin·dert *adj.* severely handicapped (*or* disabled)
'Schwer·be·hin·der·te *m, f* (-n; -n) handicapped person; **'Schwer·be·hin·der·ten·aus·weis** *m* disabled pass
'schwer·be·la·den *adj. mot. etc.* heavily laden, with a heavy load (✈ *etc.* cargo); *person*: weighed down (**mit** *dat.* with)
'schwer·be·schä·digt *adj.* severely (*or* badly) damaged; ⚕ (severely) disabled
'Schwer·be·schä·dig·te *m, f* (-n; -n) disabled person
'schwer·be·waff·net *adj.* heavily armed
'schwer·blü·tig [-blyːtɪç] *adj.* ponderous
Schwe·re ['ʃveːrə] *f* (-; *no pl.*) weight; *phys. and fig.* gravity; *gastr. and fig.* heaviness; *fig.* seriousness *of an accident, illness etc.*; severity *of punishment etc.*; import, significance; **~feld** *n phys.* gravitational field
'schwe·re·los *adj.* weightless
'Schwe·re·lo·sig·keit *f* (-; *no pl.*) weightlessness
Schwe·re·nö·ter ['ʃveːrənøːtɐ] *m* (-s; -) ladykiller
'schwer·er·zieh·bar *adj.* difficult, recalcitrant; **~es** ***Kind*** *usu.* problem child
'schwer·fal·len *v/i.* (*irr., sep.*, sn, → ***fallen***) be difficult (*dat.* for), not to be easy (for); ***es fällt ihm schwer*** *a.* he finds it hard, it's hard on him; ***auch wenn's dir schwerfällt*** whether you like it or not; ***es fällt mir schwer, Ihnen sagen zu müssen*** I'm afraid I have to tell you
'schwer·fäl·lig *adj.* a) ponderous, slow, sluggish, b) awkward, clumsy, c) *fig.* labo(u)red, F stodgy; heavy-going *book etc.*; **'Schwer·fäl·lig·keit** *f* (-, *no pl.*) ponderousness *etc.*; → ***schwerfällig***
'schwer·ge·prüft *adj.* sorely tried
'Schwer·ge·wicht *n* (-[e]s; *no pl.*) **1.** *sport*: heavyweight; **2.** *fig.* (main) emphasis; ***das ~ lag auf*** *dat.* the emphasis was (*or* fell) on, the focus of attention was on
'Schwer·ge·wicht·ler [-gəvɪçtlɐ] *m* (-s; -) *sport*: heavyweight (*a.* F *fig.*)
'schwer·hö·rig [-høːrɪç] *adj.* hard of hearing; **'Schwer·hö·rig·keit** *f* (-; *no pl.*) difficulty in hearing, partial deafness
'Schwer|in·duˌstrie *f* heavy industry; **~kraft** *f* (-; *no pl.*) *phys.* (force of) gravity; **Ϙkrank** *adj.* seriously (*or* very, extremely) ill; **~la·ster** *m* heavy lorry (*or* truck), juggernaut
'schwer·lich *adv.* hardly, scarcely
'schwer·lös·lich *adj.* ⚗ of low solubility, not easily soluble
'schwer·ma·chen *v/t.* (*sep.*, h): ***j-m et. ~*** make s.th. difficult for s.o.; ***j-m das Leben ~*** give s.o. a hard time
'Schwer·meˌtall *n* heavy metal
'Schwer·mut *f* (-; *no pl.*) melancholy
'schwer·mü·tig [-myːtɪç] *adj.* melancholy; *fig. a.* gloomy *picture, poem etc.*
'schwer·neh·men *v/t.* (*irr., sep.*, h, → ***nehmen***) take *s.th.* seriously (*or* to heart); ***nimm's nicht so schwer*** don't take it to heart
'Schwer·öl *n* heavy oil (*or* fuel)
'Schwer·punkt *m phys.* centre (*Am.* center) of gravity; *fig.* main area; ***der ~ s-r Arbeit liegt in*** *dat.* his work centres (*Am.* centers) *or* focus(s)es on; **~proˌgramm** *n* priority program(me) *or* plan; **~streik** *m* selective (strike) action, pinpoint strike; **~the·ma** *n* main (discussion) topic
Schwert [ʃveːɐt] *n* (-[e]s; -er) **1.** sword; ***das ~ ziehen*** draw one's sword; ***die ~er kreuzen*** cross swords; *fig.* ***das ~ in die Scheide stecken*** bury the hatchet; **2.** centreboard, *Am.* centerboard; **~fisch** *m* swordfish; **~li·lie** *f* ⚘ iris
'Schwer·transˌport *m* **1.** heavy load; **2.** → **'Schwer·transˌpor·ter** *m* heavy lorry (*or* truck), juggernaut
'Schwert|schlucker *m* sword swallower; **~trä·ger** *m zo.* swordtail
'schwer·tun *v/refl.* (**sich ~**) (*irr., sep.*, h, → ***tun***): ***sich ~ mit*** *dat.* have a hard time with *s.th.*, find *s.th.* difficult; ***ich tu' mich mit*** (*or* ***bei***) ***Fremdsprachen schwer*** *a.* I'm not very good at foreign languages; ***er tut sich mit s-r Schwester schwer*** he doesn't get on with his sister
'Schwer·ver·bre·cher *m* dangerous criminal, ⚖ felon
'schwer|ver·dau·lich *adj.* indigestible, heavy; *fig.* heavy(-going); **~ver·dient** *adj.* hard-earned; **~ver·käuf·lich** *adj.* hard to get rid of; † non-selling ...
'schwer·ver·letzt *adj.* seriously hurt (*or* injured); **'Schwer·ver·letz·te** *m, f* (-n; -n) serious casualty; seriously injured person
'schwer|ver·ständ·lich *adj.* difficult (*or* hard) to understand; garbled *message etc.*; **~ver·träg·lich** *adj. drug etc.*: hard on the digestive system
'schwer·ver·wun·det *adj.* seriously wounded; **'Schwer·ver·wun·de·te** *m, f* (-n; -n) major casualty
'Schwer·was·ser *n* ⚗ heavy water; **~reˌak·tor** *m* heavy water reactor
'schwer·wie·gend *adj.* serious; grave *accusation etc.*; momentous *decision etc.*
Schwe·ster ['ʃvɛstɐ] *f* (-; -n) a) sister (*a. fig.*), b) ⚕ (hospital) nurse, sister, c) *eccl.* sister; nun; **Schwe·ster·chen** ['ʃvɛstɐçən] *n* (-s; -) little sister
'Schwe·ster|fir·ma *f*, **~ge·sell·schaft** *f* affiliated company; **~herz** *hum. n* dear sister; *int.* sister dear, F sis
'schwe·ster·lich *adj.* sisterly
'Schwe·stern|hel·fe·rin *f* auxiliary nurse; **~lie·be** *f* sisterly love; **~paar** *n* two sisters *pl.*; ***das ~ X*** the X sisters; **~schu·le** *f* nursing college (*or* school); **~wohn·heim** *n* nurses' home
'Schwe·ster|parˌtei *f* sister party; **~schiff** *n* sister ship
schwieg [ʃviːk] *pret. of* ***schweigen***
Schwie·ger|el·tern ['ʃviːgɐ-] *pl.* parents-in-law; **~mut·ter** *f* mother-in-law, *pl.* mothers-in-law; **~sohn** *m* son-in-law, *pl.* sons-in-law; **~toch·ter** *f* daughter-in-law, *pl.* daughters-in-law; **~va·ter** *m* father-in-law, *pl.* fathers-in-law
Schwie·le ['ʃviːlə] *f* (-; -n) callus; weal
schwie·lig ['ʃviːlɪç] *adj.* callous, horny
schwie·rig ['ʃviːrɪç] *adj.* difficult, *esp. pred. a.* hard; F tough; complicated, intricate; awkward; ***sie ist ~*** she is a difficult person; **~*er Fall*** problem, difficult (*or* problem) case; **~*e Frage*** difficult (*or* tricky) question; **~*es Kind*** difficult (*or* problem) child; **~*e Lage*** difficult (*or* awkward) situation, predicament, F fix; **~*er Punkt***, **~*e Sache*** problem; ***es wurde sehr ~*** things got very difficult; ***das macht alles noch ~er*** that makes things even more difficult, that complicates matters even more; ***in e-m ~en Alter sein*** be at an awkward age; ***das Schwierigste haben wir hinter uns*** the worst is over, we're out of the wood(s)
'Schwie·rig·keit *f* (-; -en) **1.** difficulty; **~*en haben, et. zu tun*** have difficulty (in) doing s.th.; ***j-m ~en machen*** (*or* ***bereiten***) a) be a problem for s.o., cause s.o. problems, b) *person*: make things difficult for s.o.; ***das Gehen machte ihm ~en*** *a.* he found it difficult to walk, he had trouble walking; ***sie haben wegen des Visums ~en gemacht*** they made a fuss about the visa; ***unnötige ~en machen*** complicate matters unnecessarily; ***das bereitete ihm keinerlei ~en*** it was no trouble at all for him, he took it all in his stride; ***auf ~en stoßen*** run into difficulty (*or* difficulties, problems); ***in ~en geraten*** run into trouble; **~*en bekommen*** get into trouble, have trouble (***wegen*** *gen.* because of); ***es ist nicht ohne ~en*** it's not without its difficulties; **2.** → **'Schwie·rig·keits·grad** *m* level (of difficulty)
Schwimm|bad ['ʃvɪm-] *n* swimming pool; indoor pool, swimming baths *pl.*; **~bag·ger** *m* sand dredge(r); **~bahn** *f* lane; **~becken** *n* swimming pool; **~bla·se** *f zo.* air bladder; **~dock** *n* floating dock
Schwimmei·ster ['ʃvɪm-[(*sep.* -mm·m-) *m* swimming champion
schwim·men ['ʃvɪmən] **I.** *v/i.* (schwamm, geschwommen, sn) a) swim (*a. v/t.* [*a.* h] *distance, record etc.*); float, *ship*: be afloat, b) F be swimming, be flooded, c) *fig.* be floundering; **~ *gehen*** go swimming, go for a swim; ***auf dem Rücken ~*** do backstroke; ***Papierschiffe ~ lassen*** float paper boats (on the water); ***über den Kanal ~*** swim (across) the Channel; *fig.* ***in s-m Blut ~*** be lying in a pool of blood; ***ihre Augen schwammen*** (***in Tränen***) her eyes were filled with tears; ***im Geld ~*** be rolling in money; ***im Erfolg*** (***Glück***) **~** wallow in success (good fortune); ***alles schwamm vor s-n Augen*** everything started dancing in front of his eyes; ***er schwimmt oben*** he's got everything going for him, he's riding on the crest of a wave; → ***Strom*** 1; **II. Ϙ** *n* (-s; *no pl.*) swimming; *fig.* ***ins ~ kommen*** *actor etc.*: start floundering, *car etc.*: go into a skid; **'schwim·mend** *adj.* floating; **~*es Haus*** houseboat, floating home; ***in ~em Fett braten*** deep-fry; *fig.* **~*e Konturen*** blurred edges (*or* contours)
Schwim·mer ['ʃvɪmɐ] *m* (-s; -) **1.** swimmer; **2.** *angling*, ⚙, ✈, *mot.* float; **~becken** *n* swimmer's pool; **~venˌtil** *n* float valve
schwimm·fä·hig ['ʃvɪm-] *adj.* buoyant, floatable
Schwimm|fahr·zeug ['ʃvɪm-] *n* amphibious vehicle; **~flos·se** *f zo.* fin; *sport*: flipper; **~flü·gel** *pl.* water wings; **~fuß** *m zo.* webbed foot; **~gür·tel** *m* **1.** swimming belt; **2.** F spare tyre (*Am.* tire); **~hal·le** *f* indoor (swimming) pool; **~haut** *f zo.* webbing; **~kran** *m* floating crane; **~leh·rer** *m* swimming instructor; **~pan·zer** *m* amphibious tank; **~rei·fen** *m* → ***Schwimmgürtel***; **~sport** *m* swimming; **~stil** *m* (swimming) style, stroke; **~ver·ein** *m* swimming club; **~vo·gel** *m* water bird; **~we·ste** *f* life jacket (*or* vest), *Am.* life preserver
Schwin·del ['ʃvɪndəl] *m* (-s; *no pl.*) **1.** dizziness, ⚕ vertigo; dizzy spell; **2.** F swindle, *coll.* swindling; lie, fib; ***den ~ kenne ich*** I know that trick; **3.** F ***der ganze ~***

F the whole caboodle; **~an·fall** *m* dizzy spell; **e-n ~ bekommen** have a dizzy spell, suddenly feel dizzy
Schwin·de·lei [ʃvɪndəˈlaɪ] F *f* (-; -en) swindling; (constant) lying; lies *pl.*
ˈschwin·del·er·re·gend I. *adj.* dizzy, giddy (*a. fig.*); *fig.* staggering *figures, prices etc.*; **II.** *adv.*: **~ hoch** *a. fig.* a) at a dizzying height, b) to dizzying heights; staggering(ly high) *prices etc.*; *fig.* **~ steigen** *prices etc.*: go sky-high, skyrocket
ˈSchwin·del·fir·ma *f* bogus company
ˈschwin·del·frei *adj.*: **~ sein** have a good head for heights; **nicht ~ sein** be afraid of heights
ˈSchwin·del·ge·fühl *n* dizzy feeling, dizziness
ˈSchwin·del|ge·schäft *n* bogus transaction; **~maˌnö·ver** *n* deceitful trick
schwin·deln [ˈʃvɪndəln] (h) **I.** *v/i.* **1.** F tell a fib (*or* lie), tell fibs (*or* lies), fib, lie; **schwindel doch nicht!** stop fibbing *etc.*; **2. mir schwindelt** I feel dizzy; **ihm schwindelte (der Kopf) bei dem Gedanken** his head reeled at the thought; **II.** *v/t.*: F **das ist geschwindelt!** that's a lie!; **III.** *v/refl.*: F **sich durchs Examen ~** bluff one's way through the exam; **ˈschwin·delnd** *adj.* → **schwindelerregend; in ~er Höhe** at a dizzy height
ˈSchwin·del·preis *m* exorbitant (F jacked-up) price
schwin·den [ˈʃvɪndən] **I.** *v/i.* (schwand, geschwunden, sn) *influence, power etc.*: dwindle, diminish; *supplies, money*: dwindle, run low; *strength*: (begin to) fail (*or* dwindle, seep away); *radio station, colo(u)rs, beauty*: fade; *interest*: dwindle, drop off; *suspicion etc*: disappear; **aus dem Gedächtnis ~** fade from memory; **mein Interesse schwand** I lost interest; **sein Lächeln schwand** his face dropped; **ihm schwand der Mut (das Vertrauen, die Hoffnung)** he lost courage (confidence, hope); **ihr schwanden die Sinne** she fainted (*or* passed out); **II.** 2 *n* (-s; *no pl.*) dwindling *etc.*; → **I; das ~ der Hoffnung** *etc.* the dwindling hope *etc.*; **im ~ begriffen** dwindling, *power etc.*: on the wane; **ˈschwin·dend** *adj.* dwindling, diminishing; **~es Interesse** *a.* loss of interest
Schwind·ler [ˈʃvɪndlɐ] F *m* (-s; -) swindler, F con man; liar; **Schwind·le·rin** [ˈʃvɪndlərɪn] F *f* (-; -nen) swindler; liar
schwind·lig [ˈʃvɪndlɪç] *adj. a. fig.* dizzy, giddy; **mir wird ~** I feel dizzy; **mir wird immer ~, wenn** I always get (*or* feel) dizzy when; **mir wurde ~** I (suddenly) felt dizzy, I had a dizzy turn
Schwind·sucht [ˈʃvɪnt-] *obs. f* (-; *no pl.*) ⚕ consumption, tuberculosis
ˈschwind·süch·tig *obs. adj.*, **ˈSchwind·süch·ti·ge** *m, f* (-n; -n) consumptive
Schwin·ge [ˈʃvɪŋə] *f* (-; -n) **1.** *zo.* wing, *poet. a.* pinion; **2.** ⚙ rocker arm
schwin·gen [ˈʃvɪŋən] (schwang, geschwungen, h) **I.** *v/t.* swing; brandish, wield; wave *flag etc.*; → **Rede, Tanzbein; II.** *v/refl.*: **sich ~** swing o.s. (**hinauf** up), jump (**auf** *acc.* onto); **sich in den Sattel ~** swing o.s. into the saddle; **sich ~ über** *acc.* vault over *s.th.*; **sich von Ast zu Ast ~** swing from branch to branch; **sich in die Höhe ~** *eagle etc.*: soar (up) into the air; **III.** *v/i.* swing (*a. gym., skiing etc.*); ⚙ oscillate; *acoustics*: vibrate, resonate; → **geschwungen**
Schwin·ger [ˈʃvɪŋɐ] *m* (-s; -) *boxing*: swing; **wilder ~** haymaker
Schwing|kreis [ˈʃvɪŋ-] *m radio*: oscillating circuit; **~meˌtall** *n* rubber-bonded metal; **~quarz** *m* piezoelectric crystal; **~schlei·fer** *m* sander; **~tor** *n* up-and-over garage door; **~tür** *f* swing door
Schwin·gung [ˈʃvɪŋʊŋ] *f* (-; -en) ⚙ *and acoustics*: vibration; *a.* ⚡ oscillation; *fig.* reverberation; **et. in ~en versetzen** set s.th. vibrating (*a. fig.*)
ˈSchwin·gungs|dämp·fer *m* vibration damper; **~dau·er** *f* period (of oscillation); **2frei** *adj.* free from vibration, non-vibrating; **~freˌquenz** *f* oscillation frequency; **~kreis** *m* oscillating circuit; **~wei·te** *f* amplitude; **~zahl** *f* oscillation frequency
Schwips [ʃvɪps] F *m* (-es; -e): **e-n ~ haben** be (a bit) tipsy (F tiddly); **sich e-n ~ antrinken** get tipsy (F tiddly)
schwir·ren [ˈʃvɪrən] *v/i.* (h, sn) whirr, *Am.* whir; *arrow etc.*: *a.* F whiz(z); *insects*: buzz; *snowflakes*: whirl; *fig.* **von Gerüchten** *etc.* **~** be buzzing with rumo(u)rs *etc.*; **j-m durch den Kopf ~** *figures, thoughts*: spin round in s.o.'s head; **Fragen schwirrten durch den Saal** questions came flying from all directions (of the hall); **überall schwirrten Touristen** the place was swarming with tourists; **mir schwirrte der Kopf** my head was buzzing (*or* spinning)
Schwitz·bad [ˈʃvɪts-] *n* steam bath
schwit·zen [ˈʃvɪtsən] (h) **I.** *v/i.* sweat, *formal*: perspire; *walls*: be damp; *windows*: steam up; F sweat away; **am ganzen Körper ~** be sweating all over, be covered in sweat, be soaked in (*or* with) sweat; **vor Angst** *etc.* **~** sweat with fear *etc.*; F **~ über** *dat.* sweat over *a job etc.*; F **den lasse ich noch ein wenig ~** F I'm going to let him sweat it out for a bit; **II.** *v/t.* sweat (out) *resin etc.*; **et. naß ~** sweat s.th. through, soak s.th.; *fig.* **Blut (und Wasser) ~** sweat blood; **III.** *v/refl.*: **sich naß ~** be soaked in (*or* with) sweat, be dripping with sweat; **IV.** 2 *n* (-s; *no pl.*) sweating; **ins ~ kommen** start sweating, *a. fig.* get into a sweat, *fig. a.* F get into a tizz(y)
Schwitz|ka·sten [ˈʃvɪts-] *m wrestling*: headlock; **~kur** *f* sweating cure; **e-e ~ machen** sweat it out; **~packung** *f* ⚕ hot pack
Schwof [ʃvoːf] F *m* (-[e]s; -e) F hop
schwo·fen [ˈʃvoːfən] F *v/i.* (h) F shake a leg
schwoll [ʃvɔl] *pret. of* **schwellen**
schwor [ʃvoːɐ] *pret. of* **schwören**
schwö·ren [ˈʃvøːrən] *v/i. and v/t.* (schwor, geschworen, h) swear, *fig. a.* vow; ⚖ take the oath; **e-n Eid ~** take an oath; **auf die Bibel ~** swear on the Bible; **sich et. ~** swear s.th. to o.s.; **sich ~, daß man** swear to *inf.*; **ich schwöre es (dir)** I swear (to God); *fig.* **~ auf** *acc.* swear by, *a.* F be sold on *s.th.*; F **ich hätte geschworen, daß** I could have sworn that; → **geschworen**
Schwuch·tel [ˈʃvʊxtəl] *contp. f* (-; -n) *sl.* queen
schwul [ʃvuːl] F *adj.* F gay, *contp.* queer
schwül [ʃvyːl] *adj.* **1.** close, muggy, sultry, humid; oppressive, stifling; **2.** sensuous
Schwü·le [ˈʃvyːlə] *f* (-; *no pl.*) **1.** stifling heat, muggy weather, sultriness; **2.** sensuousness
Schwu·le [ˈʃvuːlə] F *m* (-n; -n) F gay, *contp.* queer; **ˈSchwu·len·treff** F *m* F gay hangout
Schwu·li·tät [ʃvuliˈtɛːt] F *f* (-; -en) F fix, scrape; **in ~en kommen** get into a fix
Schwulst [ʃvʊlst] *m* (-[e]s; *no pl.*) *ling.* bombast, fustian; *a. art*: floridity
schwul·stig [ˈʃvʊlstɪç] *adj.* thick, swollen *lips*
schwül·stig [ˈʃvʏlstɪç] *adj.* bombastic(ally *adv.*), pompous, inflated; *art*: florid
schwumm·rig [ˈʃvʊmrɪç] F *adj.* **1.** → **schwindlig; 2.** *fig.* **mir wird ganz ~, wenn** I get a strange feeling in the pit of my stomach when
Schwund [ʃvʊnt] *m* (-[e]s; *no pl.*) dwindling; loss; shrinkage; *radio*: fading; ⚕ atrophy; **~aus·gleich** *m*, **~re·ge·lung** *f radio*: gain (*or* fading) control
Schwung [ʃvʊŋ] *m* (-[e]s; Schwünge [ˈʃvʏŋə]) **1.** a) swing (*a. gym., skiing*); jump, leap, b) curve, sweep, c) *fig.* speed, force; impetus; energy, drive, F punch, oomph; verve; **~ holen** a) take a running jump, b) take a (big) swing; **mit e-m solchen ~ die Tür zuschlagen, daß ...** shut the door with such force (*or* with such a bang) that ...; *fig.* **in ~ bringen** get *s.o. or s.th.* going; **das bringt dich wieder in ~** that'll get you back on your feet again; F **~ in den Laden bringen** get things going; F **~ in die Sache bringen** liven things up; **in ~ halten** keep *s.th.* going, keep up, look after *s.th.*, F keep *s.th.* in good nick; **(richtig) in ~ kommen** get going, *party, discussion etc.*: *a.* F hot up; **langsam in ~ kommen** *a.* F slowly move into gear, slowly pick up steam; **in ~ sein** be in full swing, F be going great guns; **wenn er erst einmal in ~ ist** once he gets going, once he gets into it (*or* into the swing of things); **2.** F batch, F clutch; F bunch *of people*; F pile *of records, books etc.*
ˈSchwung·fe·der *f zo.* pinion
ˈschwung·haft *adj.* brisk, flourishing *trade*
ˈSchwung·kraft *f* **1.** *phys.* momentum; **2.** *fig.* → **Schwung** 1 c
ˈschwung·los *fig. adj.* lifeless; without (any) life
ˈSchwung·rad *n* ⚙ flywheel
ˈschwung·voll *adj.* full of drive (F go); lively (*a.* ♪), spirited; F punchy *speech etc.*; racy *style*; bold *sketch etc.*; enterprising; **~ sein** F have plenty of oomph
schwupp [ʃvʊp] *int.* hey presto!; **~!, fiel mir die Seife aus der Hand** and whoosh! the soap went flying; **~!, fiel die Tasse auf den Boden** and boing! the cup landed on the floor; **~!, war er weg** before you knew it (*or* before you could blink) he was gone; **ˈschwupp·di·wupp** [-diˈvʊp] *int.* → **schwupp**
Schwur [ʃvuːɐ] *m* (-[e]s; Schwüre [ˈʃvyːrə]) oath; vow; **e-n ~ leisten** take an oath
ˈSchwur·ge·richt *n* **1.** *in Germany, court made up of three professional and two lay judges*; **2.** *in USA and GB*: jury court; *obs.* (court of) assizes *pl.*
ˈSchwur·ge·richts·ver·fah·ren *n* **1.** *in Germany, trial before a court made up of three professional and two lay judges*; **2.** *in USA and GB*: trial by jury
Sci·ence-fic·tion [ˈsaɪəns ˈfɪkʃən] *f* science fiction, F sci-fi, SF; **~-Li·te·raˌtur**

f science fiction (writing); **~-Ro,man** *m* science fiction novel
Scotch·ter·ri·er ['skɔtʃ-] *m* Scotch terrier, F scottie (dog)
Sé·ance [ze'ã:s] *f* (-; -n) séance
sechs [zɛks] *adj.* six; **Sechs** *f* (-; -en) **1.** six; **2.** *bus etc.* (number) six; **3.** *ped.* F; ***e-e ~ schreiben*** get an F
Sechs'ach·tel·takt *m*: (***im ~*** in) six-eight time
'sechs·bän·dig [-bɛndıç] *adj.* six-volume ..., in six volumes
'Sechs·eck *n* hexagon; **'sechs·eckig** *adj.* hexagonal
Sech·ser ['zɛksɐ] F *m* (-s; -) **1.** → ***Sechs***; **2.** ***e-n ~ haben*** *lottery etc.*: have (got) six right
'sechs·fach *adj.* sixfold; ***die ~e Menge*** six times the amount; ***~er Sieger*** six-time winner (*or* champion)
'sechs'hun·dert *adj.* six hundred
'sechs·jäh·rig [-jɛ:rıç] *adj.* **1.** six-year-old ...; **2.** six-year ...; ***ein ~es ...*** *a.* six years of ...; **'Sechs·jäh·ri·ge** [-jɛ:rıgə] *m, f* (-n; -n) six-year-old
'sechs·köp·fig [-kœpfıç] *adj.* *family etc.* of six; ***~e Delegation*** *etc. a.* six-member (*or* six-man) delegation *etc.*
Sechs·lin·ge ['zɛkslıŋə] *pl.* sextuplets
'sechs·mal *adv.* six times
'sechs·mo·na·tig [-mona:tıç] *adj.* **1.** six-month-old *baby*; **2.** six-month ...; ***nach e-m ~en Asienaufenthalt*** after six months (*or* a six-month stay) in Asia
'sechs·mo·nat·lich I. *adj.* six-monthly ..., half-yearly ...; **II.** *adv.* every six months
Sechs'mo·nats·kind *n* ⚕ six-month baby
'Sechs·pfün·der [-pfʏndɐ] *m* (-s; -) six-pound baby *etc.*; (*fish*) six-pounder
'sechs|sei·tig [-zaıtıç] *adj.* hexagonal; **~spu·rig** [-ʃpu:rıç] *adj.* six-lane ...; **~stel·lig** [-ʃtɛlıç] *adj.* six-digit *figure etc.*; **~stöckig** [-ʃtœkıç] (*sep.* -k·k-) *adj.* six-stor(e)y ...; **~stün·dig** [-ʃtʏndıç] *adj.* six-hour(-long) ...
sechst [zɛkst] **I.** *adj.* sixth; ***~es Kapitel*** chapter six; ***am ~en April*** on the sixth of April, on April the sixth; **6. *April*** 6th April, April 6(th); **II.** *adv.*: ***wir waren zu ~*** there were six of us; ***wir gingen zu ~ hin*** six of us went there
Sechs'ta·ge·ren·nen *n* six-day race
'sechs·tä·gig [-tɛ:gıç] *adj.* **1.** six-day(-long) ...; **2.** six-day-old ...
'sechs'tau·send *adj.* six thousand
'Sechs'tau·sen·der *m* (-s; -) six-thousand metre (*Am.* meter) peak
Sechs·te ['zɛkstə] *m, f* (-n; -n) (the) sixth; ***er war ~r*** he was (*or* came) sixth; ***Heinrich VI.*** Henry VI (= Henry the Sixth); ***heute ist der ~*** it's the sixth today
'sechs·tei·lig [-taılıç] *adj.* six-part ..., in six parts
Sechs·tel ['zɛkstəl] *n* (-s; -) sixth
sechs·tens ['zɛkstəns] *adv.* sixth(ly), six, in sixth place
'sechs·wö·chig [-vœçıç] *adj.* **1.** six-week ...; **2.** six-week-old ...
'Sechs·zy,lin·der *m* a) six-cylinder (car), b) six-cylinder engine
sech·zehn ['zɛçtse:n] *adj.* sixteen
'sech·zehnt *adj.* sixteenth
'Sech·zehn·tel *n* (-s; -) sixteenth (part)
'Sech·zehn·tel|no·te *f* ♪ semiquaver, *Am.* sixteenth note; **~pau·se** *f* ♪ semiquaver (*Am.* sixteenth-note) rest
sech·zig ['zɛçtsıç] *adj.* sixty; ***in den ~er Jahren*** in the sixties; ***er ist in den ℒern*** he's in his sixties; **Sech·zi·ger** ['zɛçtsıgɐ] *m* (-s; -), **Sech·zi·ge·rin** ['zɛçtsıgərın] *f* (-; -nen) sexagenarian, man (*f* woman) in his (her) sixties; F sixtysomething
'sech·zig·jäh·rig [-jɛ:rıç] *adj.* **1.** sixty-year-old ...; **2.** sixty-year(-long) ...
sech·zigst ['zɛçtsıçst] *adj.* sixtieth; ***er hat heute s-n Sechzigsten*** he's sixty today, it's his sixtieth birthday today
Se·da·ti·vum [zeda'ti:vʊm] *n* (-s; -va [-va]) *pharm.* sedative
Se·di·ment [zedi'mɛnt] *n* (-[e]s; -e) sediment; **se·di·men·tär** [zedimɛn'tɛ:ɐ] *adj.* sedimentary; **Se·di'ment·ge·stein** *n* sedimentary rock
See¹ [ze:] *f* (-; *no pl.*) sea, ocean; ***an der ~*** by the sea(side); ***an die ~ fahren*** go to the seaside; ***auf ~*** at sea; ***auf hoher ~*** on the high seas; ***in ~ gehen*** (*or* ***stechen***) put to sea, *a.* set sail; ***zur ~ gehen*** go to sea; ***zur ~ fahren*** be a sailor; → ***offen*** I
See² [ze:] *m* (-s; -n ['ze:(ə)n]) lake; ***am ~*** by a (*or* the) lake; ***ein Haus am ~*** *a.* a lakeside home
'See|aal *m* **1.** *zo.* sea eel; conger; **2.** *gastr.* dogfish; **~ad·ler** *m* sea eagle; *a.* ern(e); **~ane,mo·ne** *f zo.* sea anemone; **~bad** *n* seaside resort; **~bär** *m* F *fig.* ***alter ~*** F seadog; **~be·ben** *n* seaquake; **~be·stat·tung** *f* burial at sea; **~blick** *m* view of the sea (*or* lake); ***Zimmer mit ~*** a) room with seaview, b) room overlooking the lake; **~blocka·de** *f* naval blockade
'See-Ele,fant *m* elephant seal
'See·fah·rer *obs. m* sailor, seaman; **~volk** *n* seafaring nation (*or* people)
'See·fahrt *f* (-; -en) **1.** *no pl.* seafaring, navigation; **2.** sea journey (*or* voyage); cruise; passage
'See·fahrts·schu·le *f* nautical college
'see·fest *adj.* **1.** ⚓ seaworthy; **2.** (***nicht***) ***~ sein*** be a good (bad) sailor
'See|fisch *m* salt-water fish; **~fi·sche,rei** *f* (deep-)sea fishing; **~fracht** *f* ✈ sea (*or* ocean) freight; **~fracht·brief** *m* ✈ bill of lading (*abbr.* B/L); **~funk** *m* marine radio; **~gang** *m* (-[e]s; *no pl.*) waves *pl.*; ***hoher ~*** rough seas; **~ge·biet** *n* waters *pl.*; **~ge·fecht** *n* sea (*or* naval) battle; **~ge·mäl·de** *n* seascape; **ℒge·stützt** *adj.* sea-based *missile*; **~gras** *n* eel grass; *for padding*: sea grass; **~gur·ke** *f zo.* sea cucumber; **~ha·fen** *m* seaport; **~han·del** *m* maritime trade; **~hecht** *m* hake; **~herr·schaft** *f* (-; *no pl.*) naval supremacy; **~hö·he** *f* sea level
'See·hund *m zo.* seal; **'See·hund·ba·by** *n* baby seal, seal pup; **'See·hunds·fell** *n* sealskin
'See|igel *m zo.* sea urchin; **~jung·frau** *f* mermaid; **~ka·bel** *n* submarine cable; **~ka,dett** *m* naval cadet; **~kar·te** *f* nautical (*or* sea) chart; **ℒklar** *adj.* ready to sail; **~kli·ma** *n* maritime climate; **ℒkrank** *adj.* seasick; ***leicht ~ werden*** be a bad sailor; **~krank·heit** *f* seasickness; **~krieg** *m* naval war; **~krieg·füh·rung** *f* naval warfare; **~kuh** *f zo.* sea cow; **~lachs** *m* coalfish
See·le ['ze:lə] *f* (-; -n) a) *a. eccl., phls.* soul, b) *no pl.* state of mind, mental (*or* emotional) state; heart; ***e-e gute*** (***treue***) ***~*** a good (faithful) soul; ***e-e ~ von e-m Menschen*** a good soul; ***keine ~*** not a (living) soul; ***zwei ~n und ein Gedanke*** two minds and but a single thought; ***aus tiefster ~*** with all one's heart, *thank s.o.* from the bottom of one's heart; ***in tiefster ~ ergriffen sein*** be deeply moved; ***er ist mit ganzer ~ dabei*** he's in it heart and soul (*or* one hundred percent); ***er ist die ~ des Betriebs*** he's the life and soul of the company; ***j-m auf der ~ liegen*** weigh heavily on s.o.; ***sich et. von der ~ reden*** get s.th. off one's chest; ***sich die ~ aus dem Leib schreien*** shout o.s. hoarse; ***j-m die ~ aus dem Leib fragen*** riddle s.o. with questions; ***er*** (***es***) ***ist mir in tiefster ~ verhaßt*** I absolutely despise him (it); ***es tat ihm in der ~ weh*** it cut him to the quick; ***es tut mir in der ~ weh zu sehen*** it grieves me to see; ***du sprichst mir aus der ~*** that's exactly how I feel (about it), *lit.* my sentiments exactly; ***zwei ~n wohnen in m-r Brust*** I'm completely torn; → ***Herz, Leib*** *etc.*; **2.** bore *of gun*; core *of cable*
'See·len|amt *n R.C.* requiem; **~angst** *f* deep anxiety; **~arzt** *m* psychiatrist; *w.s.* counsel(l)or; **~dra·ma** *n* psychological drama; **~frie·de(n)** *m* peace of mind; **~grö·ße** *f* (-; *no pl.*) magnanimity; **~heil** *n* salvation; **~le·ben** *n* emotional life
'see·len·los *adj.* soulless; unfeeling *person*
'See·len|mas,sa·ge F *f* F pep talk; ***e-e ~ brauchen*** F need bucking up; **~mes·se** *f* requiem; **~not** *f*, **~qual** *f* mental anguish; **~ru·he** *f* peace of mind; *w.s.* calmness, coolness; ***in aller ~*** calmly, without batting an eyelid; **ℒru·hig** *adv.* calmly, coolly, without batting an eyelid; **~stär·ke** *f* strength of mind, fortitude; **~trö·ster** F *m* F bracer; **ℒver·gnügt I.** *adj.* happy as a lark; **II.** *adv.* quite happily; **~ver·käu·fer** F *m* ⚓ F old tub
'see·len·ver·wandt *adj.* congenial; ***~ sein*** be kindred spirits, be soulmates
'See·len·ver·wandt·schaft *f* spiritual kinship
'see·len·voll *adj.* soulful (*a. fig. and iro.*)
'See·len|wan·de·rung *f* transmigration of souls, metempsychosis; **~wär·mer** F *m* (-s; -) → ***Seelentröster***; **~zu·stand** *m* state of mind, emotional (*or* mental) state
'See·leu·te *pl.* sailors, seamen
see·lisch ['ze:lıʃ] **I.** *adj.* mental, psychological; spiritual, emotional; ***~e Belastung*** mental (*or* emotional) strain; ***es ist e-e ~e Belastung*** *a.* it takes it out of you emotionally; ***~es Gleichgewicht*** mental (*or* emotional) equilibrium; ⚖ ***~e Grausamkeit*** mental cruelty; ***~er Tiefpunkt*** emotional low; **II.** *adv.*: ***~ bedingt*** emotional, psychological
'See·lö·we *m zo.* sea lion
Seel·sor·ge ['ze:lzɔrgə] *f* (-; *no pl.*) pastoral care; spiritual welfare
Seel·sor·ger ['ze:lzɔrgɐ] *m* (-s; -) pastor, minister
seel·sor·ge·risch ['ze:lzɔrgərıʃ] *adj.* pastoral
'See|luft *f* (-; *no pl.*) sea air; **~macht** *f* naval (*or* maritime) power
'See·mann *m* (-[e]s; -leute) seaman, sailor
see·män·nisch ['ze:mɛnıʃ] *adj.* nautical *training etc.*; sailor's *expression etc.*
'See·manns|gang *m* (-[e]s; *no pl.*) sailor's walk (*or* gait); **~garn** F *n*: ***ein ~ spinnen*** F spin a yarn; **~heim** *n* sailors' home; **~lied** *n* (sea) shanty
'See|mei·le *f* nautical mile, sea mile; **~mö·we** *f* seagull

'**Seen|kun·de** *f* limnology; **~land·schaft** *f* lake district
'**See·not** *f* (-; *no pl.*) distress (at sea); ***Schiffe in ~*** distressed ships; **~dienst** *m* sea rescue service; **~flug·zeug** *n* → ***Seenotrettungsflugzeug***; **~kreu·zer** *m* sea rescue boat; **~ret·tungs·flug·zeug** *n* air-sea rescue plane (*or* aircraft); **~ruf** *m* distress call (at sea)
'**Seen·plat·te** *f* lake district
'**See|of·fi,zier** *m* naval officer; **~ot·ter** *m* sea otter; **~pferd(chen)** *n* seahorse; **~pro·me,na·de** *f* seafront (*or* lakeside) promenade
'**See·räu·ber** *m* pirate; **See·räu·be'rei** *f* (-; *no pl.*) piracy; '**See·räu·ber·schiff** *n* pirate ship
'**See|recht** *n* (-[e]s; *no pl.*) maritime law; **~rei·se** *f* sea journey (*or* voyage); cruise; (sea) crossing; **~ro·se** *f* ♣ water lily; **~sack** *m* (sailor's) kitbag; **~sand** *m* sea sand; **~schiffahrt** (*sep.* -ff·f-) *f* ocean shipping (*or* navigation); **~schlacht** *f* naval battle; **~schlan·ge** *f zo.* sea serpent; **~schwal·be** *f zo.* sea swallow, tern; **~sei·te** *f* seaward side; **~sieg** *m* naval victory; **~stadt** *f* seaside town; **~stern** *m zo.* starfish; **~stra·ße** *f* sea route, shipping lane; **~streit·kräf·te** *pl.* naval forces; **~stück** *n art*: seascape; **~stütz·punkt** *m* naval base; **~tang** *m* seaweed; **~trans,port** *m* shipment by sea; **2tüch·tig** *adj.* seaworthy; **~ufer** *n* lakeshore, lakeside; ***am ~ a.*** on the shores of a (*or* the) lake; **~un·ge·heu·er** *n myth.* sea monster, monster from the seas; **2un·tüch·tig** *adj.* unseaworthy; **~ver·bin·dung** *f* sea route; **~ver·si·che·rung** *f* marine insurance; **~vo·gel** *m* sea bird; **~volk** *n* seafaring people (*or* nation)
see·wärts ['ze:vɛrts] *adv.* seaward(s)
'**See|was·ser** *n* salt water; **~weg** *m* sea route; ***auf dem ~*** by sea
'**See·wet·ter|be·richt** *m* shipping forecast; **~dienst** *m* maritime weather service
'**See|wind** *m* sea breeze; **~zei·chen** *n* navigational aid; **~zun·ge** *f* sole
Se·gel ['ze:gəl] *n* (-s; -) sail; ***mit vollen ~n*** under full sail, *fig.* full tilt; ***~ hissen*** (*or* ***setzen***) make sail; ***unter ~ gehen*** set sail; ***die ~ streichen*** strike sail, *fig. a.* give in, throw in the towel; → ***Wind***; **~boot** *n* sailing boat, *Am.* sailboat; *sport*: yacht; **~fahrt** *f* sail(ing trip); **~flä·che** *f* sail area
'**Se·gel·flie·gen** *n* gliding
'**Se·gel·flie·ger** *m* glider (pilot)
'**Se·gel·flug** *m* (-[e]s; ⸚e) **1.** glider flight; **2.** *no pl.* gliding; '**Se·gel·flug·platz** *m* gliding field; '**Se·gel·flug·zeug** *n* glider
'**Se·gel|jacht** *f* (sailing) yacht; **2klar** *adj.* ready to sail; **~klub** *m* yachting club; **~ma·cher** *m* sailmaker
se·geln ['ze:gəln] *v/i.* (sn) *and v/t.* (h) sail (*a. fig.*); ✈ glide, *bird*: *a.* soar; F *fig.* ***durchs Examen ~*** F flunk (the exam)
'**Se·gel|oh·ren** F *pl.* F bat ears; **~par,tie** *f* sailing trip; **~re,gat·ta** *f* (sailing) regatta; **~schiff** *n* sailing ship (*or* vessel); **~schu·le** *f* sailing school; **~sport** *m* sailing; **~sur·fen** *n* windsurfing
'**Se·gel·tuch** *n* (-[e]s; *no pl.*) canvas (*a.* ✝), sailcloth; **~schu·he** *pl.* canvas shoes
'**Se·gel|werk** *n* (-[e]s; *no pl.*) sails *pl.*; **~yacht** *f* → ***Segeljacht***
Se·gen ['ze:gən] *m* (-s; -) blessing; *eccl. a.* benediction; boon; *fig.* (rich) yield; abundance; ***den ~ geben*** *priest*: give the benediction; ***den ~ sprechen*** say grace; F ***s-n ~ geben*** give one's blessing (**zu** *dat.* to); ***es ist ein ~, daß*** what a blessing (that), thank God (that); ***ein wahrer ~*** a real blessing; *iro.* ***es war ein wahrer ~, daß sie nicht kam*** it was a mercy she didn't come; ***es ist kein reiner ~*** it's a mixed blessing; ***das bringt keinen ~*** no good will come of it; ***auf s-m Geschäft ruht kein ~*** he's not having much luck with his business; F ***der ganze ~*** F the whole caboodle
'**se·gens·reich** *adj.* beneficial; *life* full of blessings
'**Se·gens·spruch** *m* blessing, *eccl. a.* benediction
Seg·ler ['ze:glɐ] *m* (-s; -) **1.** yachtsman; **2.** → ***Segelschiff, Segelboot***; **3.** → ***Segelflugzeug***; **3.** *zo.* swift; **Seg·le·rin** ['ze:glərɪn] *f* (-; -nen) yachtswoman
Seg·ment [zɛ'gmɛnt] *n* (-[e]s; -e) segment
seg·men·tie·ren [zɛgmɛn'ti:rən] *v/t.* (h) segment
seg·nen ['ze:gnən] *v/t.* (h) bless; make the sign of the cross over; ***Gott segne dich*** God bless you; *fig.* ***das Zeitliche ~*** depart this life; → ***gesegnet***
Seg·nung ['ze:gnʊŋ] *f* (-; -en) blessing, benediction; *fig.* ***~en der Zivilisation*** blessings of civilization
seh·be·hin·dert ['ze:-] *adj.* partially sighted (*or* blind), visually handicapped
'**Seh·be·hin·der·te** *m, f* (-n; -n) partially sighted (*or* blind) person; *pl. the* partially sighted *or* blind (*pl.*)
'**Seh·be·hin·de·rung** *f* eye defect; impaired vision
'**Seh·be·tei·li·gung** *f TV* viewing figures *pl.*, (TV) ratings *pl.*
se·hen ['ze:ən] (sah, gesehen, h) **I.** *v/i.* see; look; ***gut*** (***schlecht***) ~ have good (bad, weak) eyes *or* eyesight; ***ich sehe nicht gut*** I can't see very well; ***auf s-e Uhr ~*** look at one's watch; ***sie konnte kaum aus den Augen ~*** she could hardly keep her eyes open; ***wenn ich recht gesehen habe*** if I saw right, if my eyes weren't deceiving me; ***das Fenster sieht auf die See*** the window looks out onto (*or* faces) the sea; ***~ auf*** *acc.* set great store by, be (very) particular about; ***daraus ist zu ~, daß*** this shows that; ***~ nach*** *dat.* look after; ***nach dem Essen ~*** see to the dinner; ***sieh nur!, ~ Sie mal!*** look!; ***siehe oben*** (***unten***) see above (below); F ***siehe da!*** lo and behold!; F ***sieh mal einer an!*** F well, what do you know!; F ***na, siehst du!*** there you are; what did I tell you?, see?; ***wie ich sehe, ist er nicht hier*** I see he's not here; ***~ Sie, die Sache war so*** you see, it was like this; ***ich will ~, daß ich es dir verschaffe*** I'll see if I can (*or* I'll try to) get it for you; ***sieh*** (***zu***), ***daß es erledigt wird*** see (to it) that it gets done; ***wir werden*** (***schon***) ~ we'll (*or* we shall) see, let's wait and see; ***sehe ich richtig?*** am I seeing things?; ***lassen Sie mich ~*** let me see (*a. fig.*); → ***ähnlich, klarsehen***; **II.** *v/t.* a) see, b) look at, c) notice; ***kann ich das mal ~?*** could I have a look at it?; ***die Dinge ~, wie sie sind*** see things for what they are; ***er hat bessere Tage gesehen*** he's seen better days; ***das werden wir ja ~*** we'll see (about that); ***er sieht einfach alles*** he doesn't miss a thing; ***sich*** (*or* ***einander***) ~ see each other; ***wir ~ uns häufig*** we see quite a lot of each other, we see each other quite often; ***wir ~ uns zum ersten Mal*** we've never met before; ***flüchtig ~*** catch a glimpse of; ***gern ~*** like (to see); ***er sieht es gern, wenn man ihn bedient*** he likes being waited on; ***er sieht es nicht gern, wenn sie ausgeht*** he doesn't like her going out; ***zu ~ sein*** a) show, b) be on show; ***es war*** (***gab***) ***nichts zu ~*** you couldn't see a thing (there was nothing to see); ***niemand war zu ~*** there was nobody in sight; ***ich sah ihn fallen*** I saw him fall; ***ich habe es kommen ~*** I could see it coming; ***ich sehe schon kommen, daß er kündigt*** I can see him handing in his notice; ***sich ~ lassen*** put in an appearance, turn up; ***du hast dich lange nicht ~ lassen*** you haven't shown your face for a long time; ***laß dich mal wieder ~!*** come and see me (*or* us) again some time; ***laß dich hier nie mehr ~!*** don't you dare show your face here again; ***sie kann sich ~ lassen*** she's very attractive, F she's not half bad; ***damit kannst du dich ~ lassen*** that looks quite respectable, *w.s.* that's something to be proud of, that's a feather in your hat; ***sich gezwungen ~ zu*** *inf.* find o.s. compelled to *inf.*; ***ich sehe mich nicht imstande*** (*or* ***in der Lage***) ***zu*** *inf.* I don't see how I can possibly *inf.*; ***ich sehe die Sache anders*** I see it differently; ***er sieht es schon richtig*** he's got the picture, he's got it right; ***du siehst es falsch*** you've got it wrong; ***wie ich die Sache sehe*** as I see it; ***so darf man das nicht ~*** you've got to look at it differently; ***so gesehen*** in that light, from that point of view; ***rechtlich*** *etc.* ***gesehen*** from a legal *etc.* standpoint (*or* point of view), legally *etc.*; ***da sieht man es mal wieder*** it all goes to show; ***hat man so etwas schon gesehen!*** did you ever see the like(s) of it!; F ***oder wie seh' ich das?*** am I right?; ***sie kann ihn nicht mehr ~*** she can't stand (the sight of) him; ***ich sehe in ihm ein ...*** I see him as a ...; **III.** 2 *n* (-s; *no pl.*) a) seeing, b) eyesight; (***nur***) ***vom ~*** (only) by sight; ***ich kenne ihn nur vom ~ a.*** I've never actually spoken to him
'**se·hens·wert,** '**se·hens·wür·dig** *adj.* worth seeing (*or* a visit); worthwhile
'**Se·hens·wür·dig·keit** *f* (-; -en) place of interest; attraction; *pl. a.* sights; ***die ~en besichtigen*** go sightseeing, see the sights
Se·her ['ze:ɐ] *m* (-s; -) seer, prophet; **~blick** *m* (-[e]s; *no pl.*) prophetic vision; **~ga·be** *f* (-; *no pl.*) gift of prophecy, visionary powers *pl.*
Se·he·rin ['ze:ərɪn] *f* (-; -nen) seer, prophetess
se·he·risch ['ze:ərɪʃ] *adj.* prophetic(ally *adv.*), visionary
'**Seh|feh·ler** *m* eye defect; **2ge·stört** *adj.*: ***~ sein*** have an eye defect; **~ge·wohn·hei·ten** *pl. TV* viewing habits; **~hil·fe** *f* seeing aid; **~kraft** *f* (-; *no pl.*), **~lei·stung** *f* vision, (eye)sight; **~loch** *n* pupil
Seh·ne ['ze:nə] *f anat.* tendon, sinew; string *of bow*; ⩓ chord
seh·nen ['ze:nən] **I.** *v/refl.* (h): ***sich ~ nach*** *dat.* long for, yearn for, pine for; ***er sehnte sich danach zu*** *inf.* he was longing to *inf.*, he longed to *inf.*; **II.** 2 *n* (-s; *no pl.*) → ***Sehnsucht***

'Seh·nen|ent·zün·dung *f* tendinitis; **~riß** *m* torn tendon; **~schei·den·ent·zün·dung** *f* tendovaginitis; **~zer·rung** *f* pulled tendon
'Seh·nerv *m* optic nerve
seh·nig ['ze:nɪç] *adj.* sinewy; *person*: *a.* wiry; *gastr.* stringy *meat*
sehn·lich ['ze:nlɪç] **I.** *adj.* ardent, fervent; ***sein ~ster Wunsch wäre ein Eigenheim*** his greatest (*or* most fervent) wish is to have a house of his own; **II.** *adv.* ardently, fervently; ***~ erwarten*** await eagerly; ***wir haben dich ~ erwartet*** *a.* we couldn't wait for you to come
Sehn·sucht ['ze:nzʊxt] *f* (-; ⸚e) longing, yearning (***nach*** *dat.* for); ***~ nach*** *dat. a.* ardent desire for; ***~ haben nach*** *dat.* long (*or* yearn) for; ***mit ~ erwarten*** await eagerly
'sehn·süch·tig, 'sehn·suchts·voll *adj.* longing, yearning; *a.* wistful *look etc.*
Seh|or,gan ['ze:-] *n* organ of sight; **~pro·be** *f* **1.** → ***Sehprüfung***; **2.** eye test chart; **~prü·fung** *f* eye test
sehr [ze:ɐ] *adv.* **1.** *with adj. and adv.*: very; most, extremely; ***~ gern*** with pleasure; ***~ viel*** a lot, much *better, worse etc.*; → ***wohl*** 2; **2.** *with verb*: very much; ***~ vermissen*** miss badly (*or* a lot); ***so ~, daß*** so much that; ***wie ~ auch*** however much, much as; ***ich freue mich ~*** I'm very glad; ***schneit es ~?*** is it snowing a lot?
Seh|rin·de ['ze:-] *f* visual cortex; **~rohr** *n* ⚓ periscope; **~schär·fe** *f* vision, eyesight; ⚕ visual acuity; **~schwä·che** *f* bad eyesight; **~stö·rung** *f* eye defect; **~test** *m* eye test; **~ver·mö·gen** *n* (-s; *no pl.*) vision, eyesight; **~wei·se** *f* (point of) view; **~wei·te** *f* visual range; ***in* (*außer*) *~*** within (out of) sight *or* eyeshot
seicht [zaɪçt] *adj.* shallow (*a. fig.*); *fig. a.* insipid
'Seicht·heit *f* (-; *no pl.*), **Seich·tig·keit** ['zaɪçtɪçkaɪt] *f* (-; *no pl.*) shallowness (*a. fig.*)
Sei·de ['zaɪdə] *f* (-; -n) (***reine ~*** pure) silk
Sei·del ['zaɪdəl] *n* (-s; -) beer mug, (beer) stein
Sei·del·bast ['zaɪdəlbast] *m* (-[e]s; -e) ⚘ daphne
sei·den ['zaɪdən] *adj.* (made of) silk; → ***Faden***
'Sei·den|at·las *m* silk satin; **~band** *n* (-[e]s; ⸚er) silk ribbon; **~bau** *m* (-[e]s; *no pl.*) silkworm breeding, sericulture; **~blu·se** *f* silk blouse; **~fa·den** *m*, **~garn** *n* silk thread; **~glanz** *m* silky sheen; **~kleid** *n* silk dress; **~kra,wat·te** *f* silk tie; **~pa,pier** *n* tissue paper; **~rau·pe** *f* silkworm; **~rau·pen·zucht** *f* silkworm breeding, sericulture; **~schal** *m* silk scarf; **~spin·ner** *m zo.* silk moth; **~spin·ne,rei** *f* silk mill; **~sticke,rei** *f* silk embroidery; **~stoff** *m* silk (fabric); **~stra·ße** *f hist.* Silk Route (*or* Road); **~strumpf** *m* silk stocking
'sei·den'weich *adj.* (as) soft as silk, silky
sei·dig ['zaɪdɪç] *adj.* silky
Sei·fe ['zaɪfə] *f* (-; -n) soap; **'seif·en** *v/t.* (h) soap
'Sei·fen|ar,ti·kel *pl.* → ***Seifenwaren***; **~bad** *n* soap bath; **~bla·se** *f* soap bubble; *fig.* bubble; ***~n machen*** blow bubbles; *fig.* ***wie e-e ~ zerplatzen*** vanish into thin air; ***dann platzte die ~*** then the bubble burst; **~flocken** *pl.* soap flakes; **~ki·ste** *f* soapbox; **~ki·sten·ren·nen** *n* soapbox derby; **~lau·ge** *f* soapsuds *pl.*; **~oper** *f TV* soap opera; **~pul·ver** *n* soap powder; **~scha·le** *f* soap dish; **~schaum** *m* lather; **~spen·der** *m* soap dispenser; **~wa·ren** *pl.* (household soaps and) toiletries; **~was·ser** *n* soapy water
sei·fig ['zaɪfɪç] *adj.* soapy
sei·hen ['zaɪən] *v/t.* (h) strain
Seil [zaɪl] *n* (-[e]s; -e) rope; *mot.* towrope; cable; *circus*: tightrope; *fig.* ***auf dem ~ tanzen*** be walking a tightrope; **~bahn** *f* cable railway; *a.* funicular; **~hüp·fen** *n* skipping
'Seil·schaft *f* (-; -en) **1.** rope team; **2.** *fig. pol.* team, crew; ***die alten ~en sind noch intakt*** the old network (*or* power structure) is still functioning
'Seil|sprin·gen *n* skipping; **~tan·zen** *n* tightrope walking; **~tän·zer** *m* tightrope walker; **~win·de** *f* ⚙ cable winch; **~zie·hen** *n* tug-of-war (*a. fig.*)
sein[1] [zaɪn] *v/i.* (war, gewesen, sn) be; *v/aux.*: *a.* have; ***sind Sie es?*** is that you?; ***ich bin's*** it's me; ***sei(d) nicht so laut!*** don't be so loud, stop making such a noise; ***sei so gut und ...*** do me a favo(u)r and ..., will you?; ***ist was?*** is anything (*or* something) wrong?, what's the problem?; ***was ist mit dir?*** what's the matter (*or* what's wrong) with you?; ***mir ist, als kenne ich ihn schon*** I have a feeling (*or* I'm sure) I know him; ***mir ist nicht nach Arbeiten*** I don't feel like working, I'm not in the mood for work; ***mir ist kalt*** I'm cold, I feel cold; ***so ist das nun mal*** that's the way it is; ***nun, wie ist's?*** well, what about it (then)?; ***wie ist es mit dir?*** what about you?; ***wie ist der Wein?*** what's the wine like?; ***sei er auch noch so reich*** no matter how rich he is, however rich he may be; ***sei es, wie es sei*** be that as it may; ***wenn dem so ist*** if that's the case, in that case; ***wenn du nicht gewesen wärst*** if it hadn't been for you; ***keiner will es gewesen sein*** nobody's claiming responsibility; ***ich bin ihm schon begegnet*** I've met him before; ***die Sonne ist untergegangen*** the sun has gone down; ***er ist beim Lesen*** he's reading; ***die Garage ist im Bau*** the garage is being built; ***die Waren sind zu senden an*** *acc.* the goods are to be sent to; ***es ist ein Jahr* (*her*), *seit*** it's a year since, it was a year ago that; ***er ist aus Mexiko*** he comes from Mexico; ***er ist nach Berlin gegangen*** he has gone to Berlin; ***ich bin bei meinem Anwalt gewesen*** I've been to see my lawyer; ***mit dem Urlaub war nichts*** the holiday didn't work out, the holiday fell through; ***was nicht ist, kann ja noch werden*** there's plenty of time yet; ***ich bin ja nicht so*** I'm not like that; ***laß es ~*** a) leave it alone, b) don't bother; ***laß das ~!*** stop it!; ***muß das ~?*** do you have to?; ***es ist nun an dir zu*** *inf.* it's up to you to ... now; ***was soll das ~?*** what's that supposed to be?; (***das***) ***kann ~*** it's possible, F could be; ***es sei denn*(, *daß*)** unless; ***sei es, daß ... oder daß ...*** whether ... or ...; ***wer ist dort*** (*or* ***am Apparat***)? who's speaking (*or* calling)?; ***ist da jemand?*** is anybody there?; ***warst du mal in London?*** have you ever been to London?; ***wie wär's mit e-r Partie Schach?*** how (*or* what) about a game of chess?; ***und das wäre?*** and what might that be?; ***5 und 2 ist 7*** five and two are (*or* is, make[s]) seven; ***3 mal 7 ist 21*** three times seven is (*or* are, make[s]) twenty-one; ***x sei*** let x be
sein[2] [zaɪn] **I.** *poss. pron.* **1.** *adj.* a) his, her, its; *animal usu.* its, *pet*: his; *ship*: *often* her, b) one's; ***~ Glück machen*** make one's fortune; ***all ~* (*bißchen*) *Geld*** what (little) money he had; ***Se Majestät*** His Majesty; ***es kostet* (*gut*) *~e tausend Dollar*** it'll put you back a good thousand dollars; **2.** *su.* his, hers; ***~er, ~e, ~(e)s, der* (*die, das*) *~(ig)e*** his; ***jedem das Seine*** to each his own; ***das Sein(ig)e tun*** do one's share (F bit), do one's best; **II.** *pers. pron.* (*gen. of er and es*) of him, of her; ***er war ~er nicht mehr mächtig*** he had lost control of himself completely
Sein *n* (-s; *no pl.*) being; existence; ***~ und Schein*** appearance and reality; ***mit allen Fasern s-s ~s*** with every fibre (*Am.* fiber) of his being
sei·ner·seits ['zaɪnɐ'zaɪts] *adv.* as far as he's (*or* he was, she's, she was) concerned; in its turn
sei·ner·zeit ['zaɪnɐtsaɪt] *adv.* then, at that time; in those days
sei·nes'glei·chen ['zaɪnəs-] *pron.* his equals *pl.*, F him and his kind *pl.*, the likes *pl.* of him, his sort *pl.*; one's equals *pl.*, one's own kind *pl.*; its kind *pl.*; ***j-n wie ~ behandeln*** treat s.o. as an (*or* one's) equal; ***er* (*es*) *hat nicht ~*** there is no-one (nothing) like him (it); ***~ suchen*** be hard to match, be unequal(l)ed
sei·net·we·gen ['zaɪnət've:gən] *adv.* **1.** for his sake; **2.** on his behalf; **3.** because of him
sei·ni·ge ['zaɪnɪgə] → ***sein***[2] 2
Seis·mik ['zaɪsmɪk] *f* (-; *no pl.*) *geol.* seismology; **seis·misch** ['zaɪsmɪʃ] *adj.* seismic
Seis·mo·gramm [zaɪsmo'gram] *n* (-[e]s; -e) *geol.* seismogram
Seis·mo·graph [zaɪsmo'gra:f] *m* (-en; -en) *geol.* seismograph
Seis·mo·lo·gie [zaɪsmolo'gi:] *f* (-; *no pl.*) *geol.* seismology; **seis·mo·lo·gisch** [zaɪsmo'lo:gɪʃ] *adj.* seismological
seit [zaɪt] **I.** *prp.* (*dat.*) a) since, b) for; ***~ 1985*** since 1985; ***~ neun Uhr*** since nine o'clock; ***~ gestern*** since yesterday; ***~ m-m Geburtstag*** since my birthday; ***~ dem Mittelalter*** since the Middle Ages; ***~ damals, ~ der Zeit*** → ***seitdem***; ***~ einer Stunde*** for an hour; ***~ drei Wochen*** for (the last) three weeks; ***~ einigen Tagen*** for a few days (now); ***~ langem*** for a long time; ***~ Jahren*** for years; ***~ wann?*** since when?, how long (... for)?; ***~ wann warten Sie schon?*** how long have you been waiting (for)?; ***zum ersten Mal ~ Jahren*** for the first time in years; **II.** *cj.* since; ***es ist ein Jahr her, ~*** it's (been) a year since, it was a year ago that
seit'dem I. *adv.* since then, since that time; *a.* ever since; **II.** *cj.* since; ***~ er die neuen Tabletten nimmt, geht's ihm viel besser*** since he's been taking the new tablets he's been feeling much better; ***~ er umgezogen ist, ruft er nicht mehr an*** since he moved he hasn't rung up at all
Sei·te ['zaɪtə] *f* (-; -n) **1.** page; **2.** side (*a. pol., sport and fig.*); *fig.* ***schwache* (*starke*) *~*** weak (strong) point; *textil.* ***rechte* (*linke*) *~*** right (wrong) side; ***hin-***

tere (***vordere***) ~ back (front) *of a house etc.*; ***die Arme in die ~n gestemmt*** with arms akimbo; ***die ~n wechseln*** *sport*: change ends, *a. fig.* change sides; ***an die*** (*or* ***zur***) ~ ***gehen*** step aside; ***an j-s*** ~ at (*or* by) s.o.'s side, *sitting* next to s.o.; ~ ***an*** ~ side by side; ***auf der*** ~ ***landen*** land on its side; ***sich auf die*** ~ ***legen*** lie (down) on one's side; ***sie ist auf der rechten*** ~ ***gelähmt*** she's paralyzed on her right (side); ***auf der einen*** ~ on the one side (*fig. usu.* hand); ***auf väterlicher*** (***mütterlicher***) ~ on one's father's (mother's) side; ***j-n auf seine*** ~ ***bringen*** (*or* ***ziehen***) win s.o. over to one's side; ***auf welcher*** ~ ***stehst du?*** whose side are you on?; ***auf die ~ schaffen, zur ~ legen*** put aside; F ***j-n auf die*** ~ ***schaffen*** F bump s.o. off; ***nach allen ~n*** in all directions; ***von allen ~n*** from all around, *fig.* on all sides; ***von offizieller*** ~ from official quarters, ***bestätigt werden:*** be officially confirmed; *fig.* ***j-n von der ~ ansehen*** look askance at s.o.; ***j-m nicht von der ~ gehen*** not to leave s.o.'s side, F stick to s.o. like a leech; ***von dieser ~ betrachtet*** seen from that angle (*or* standpoint, point of view), seen in that light; ***von der menschlichen ~ betrachtet*** from a human standpoint (*or* point of view); ***sich von der besten ~ zeigen*** show o.s. at one's best, put one's best foot forward; ***komm mir nicht von der ~*** don't try that one on me; ***von s-r ~ bestehen keine Bedenken*** there are no objections on his part (*or* as far as he's concerned); ***j-m zur ~ stehen*** stand by s.o.; ***ganz neue ~n an j-m entdecken*** discover new sides to s.o.'s character; ***e-r Sache die beste ~ abgewinnen*** make the best (*or* most) of s.th.; ***alles hat zwei ~n*** there are two sides to everything

sei·ten ['zaɪtən] *prp.*: ***auf ~ gen.*** on the part of; ***von ~ gen.*** → ***seitens***

'Sei·ten|al,tar *m* side altar; **~an·ga·be** *f* page reference; **~an·sicht** *f* side view; **~arm** *m geogr.* branch; **~aus·gang** *m* side exit; **~blick** *m* sidelong glance; **~drucker** *m computer*: page printer; **~ein·gang** *m* side entrance; **~fen·ster** *n* side window; **~flä·che** *f* lateral surface (*or* face); **~flü·gel** *m* **1.** ⚠ wing; **2.** side panel *of an altarpiece*; **~for,mat** *n* page format; **~for·ma,tie·rung** *f computer*: page formatting; **~gas·se** *f* side street; backstreet; **~hieb** *m* side cut; *fig.* F sideswipe, dig (***gegen*** *acc.*, ***auf*** *acc.* at); **~la·ge** *f* side (*or* lateral) position; ***in ~*** on one's (*or* its) side

'sei·ten·lang *adj.* lengthy *report etc.*; ***~e Briefe*** *etc.* ***schreiben*** write pages and pages; ***~e Beschwerden*** *etc.* pages and pages of complaints *etc.*

'Sei·ten|län·ge *f* page length; **~lay·out** *n* page layout; **~leh·ne** *f* armrest; **~leit·werk** *n* ✈ rudder (assembly); **~li·nie** *f* **1.** 🚂 branch line; **2.** collateral line; **3.** *sport*: sideline; **~por,tal** *n* side portal (*or* entrance); **~rand** *m* margin; **~riß** *m* ⚙ side elevation; **~ru·der** *n* ✈ rudder

sei·tens ['zaɪtəns] *prp.* (*gen.*) on the part of, from; by

'Sei·ten|schei·tel *m* side parting; **~schiff** *n* (side) aisle; **~schnei·der** *m* wire (*or* side) cutter; **~schritt** *m* side step; **~schutz·lei·ste** *f mot.* side protector; **~schwim·men** *n* sidestroke; **~sprung** *fig. m* (extramarital) affair, F fling; **~ste·chen** *n* stitch (in one's side); **~stra·ße** *f* side street; backstreet; **~strei·fen** *m* verge; hard shoulder, *Am.* shoulder; ~ ***nicht befahrbar*** soft verges (*Am.* shoulder); **~tal** *n* side valley; **~ta·sche** *f* side pocket; **~trakt** *m* side wing; **~tür** *f* side door (*or* entrance); **~,um·bruch** *m* paging, page makeup

'sei·ten·ver·kehrt *adj.* the wrong way round, back to front

'Sei·ten|vor·schub *m* page feed; **~wa·gen** *m* sidecar; **~wahl** *f sport*: choice of ends; **~wand** *f* side wall; **~wech·sel** *m sport*: change of ends (*or* sides); **~weg** *m* side path; *fig.* ***~e gehen*** a) do s.th. in a very roundabout way, b) do s.th. on the side

'sei·ten·wei·se *adv.* pages (and pages) of

'Sei·ten|wind *m* crosswind, side wind; **~zahl** *f* a) page number, b) number of pages

seit'her *adv.* since then (*or* that time); *a.* ... since

'seit·lich I. *adj.* side ..., lateral; ***~er Zusammenstoß*** side-on collision; **II.** *adv.* a) at the side, b) to the side; ~ ***von*** *dat.* to the side of

'Seit·pferd *n gym.* pommel horse

'Seit·rut·schen *n skiing*: side slipping

seit·wärts ['zaɪtvɛrts] *adv.* a) to the side; sideways, b) on the side

Se·kan·te [ze'kantə] *f* (-; -n) ⩓ secant

Se·kret [ze'kreːt] *n* (-[e]s; -e) *physiol.* secretion

Se·kre·tär [zekre'tɛːɐ] *m* (-s; -e [-rə]) **1.** male secretary; assistant; **2.** secretary, bureau; **3.** *zo.* secretary (bird)

Se·kre·ta·ri·at [zekreta'ri̯aːt] *n* (-s; -e) (secretary's) office

Se·kre·tä·rin [zekre'tɛːrɪn] *f* (-; -nen) secretary

Se·kre·ti·on [zekre'tsi̯oːn] *f* (-; -en) ⚕, *geol.* secretion

Sekt [zɛkt] *m* (-[e]s; -e) sparkling wine, sekt, champagne

Sek·te ['zɛktə] *f* (-; -n) sect

'Sek·ten·füh·rer *m* leader of a (*or* the) sect

'Sekt|fla·sche *f* champagne bottle; **~flö·te** *f* champagne flute; **~früh·stück** *n* champagne breakfast; **~glas** *n* champagne glass

Sek·tie·rer [zɛk'tiːrɐ] *m* (-s; -), **sek·tie·re·risch** [zɛk'tiːrərɪʃ] *adj.* sectarian

Sek'tie·rer·tum *n* (-s; *no pl.*) sectarianism

Sek·ti·on [zɛk'tsi̯oːn] *f* (-; -en) **1.** section, division, department; **2.** ⚕ a) dissection, b) autopsy, postmortem

Sek·ti'ons·be·fund *m* ⚕ postmortem findings *pl.*, results *pl.* of a (*or* the) postmortem

'Sekt|kelch *m* champagne glass; **~kel·le·,rei** *f* champagne cellars *pl.*; **~kor·ken** *m* champagne cork; **~kü·bel** *m*, **~küh·ler** *m* champagne bucket

Sek·tor ['zɛktoːɐ] *m* (-s; -en [zɛk'toːrən]) sector; *fig. a.* area, field; **~dia,gramm** *n* pie chart

'Sekt|quirl *m* swizzle stick; **~scha·le** *f* champagne glass (*or* saucer)

Se·kund [ze'kʊnt] *f* (-; -en [-dən]) → ***Sekunde*** 2

Se·kun·da [ze'kʊnda] *f* (-; -den) *ped.* **1.** *obs. sixth and seventh year of grammar school*; **2.** *Austrian* second year (of grammar school); **Se·kun·da·ner** [zekʊn'daːnɐ] *m* (-s; -), **Se·kun·da·ne·rin** [zekʊn'daːnərɪn] *f* (-; -nen) *ped.* **1.** *obs. pupil in the sixth or seventh year of grammar school*; **2.** *Austrian* second year (grammar school) pupil

Se·kun·dant [zekʊn'dant] *m* (-en; -en) second

se·kun·där [zekʊn'dɛːɐ] *adj.* secondary; ***das ist von ~er Bedeutung*** that's not so important, that's not the most important thing

Se·kun'där... *in cpds.* secondary; **~li·te·ra,tur** *f* secondary literature; **~span·nung** *f* ⚡ induced (*or* secondary) voltage; **~strom** *m* ⚡ induced (*or* secondary) current

Se·kun·dar·stu·fe [zekʊn'daːɐ-] *f ped.* secondary school (*Am.* high-school) level; ~ ***II*** *Brit.* sixth form

Se·kun'där·wick·lung *f* ⚡ secondary (winding)

Se·kun·de [ze'kʊndə] *f* (-; -n) **1.** second (*a.* ⩓ *and* ♪); ***zehn Uhr auf die*** ~ ten o'clock on the dot; ***auf die ~ genau ankommen*** arrive right on time (*or* on the dot); F (***eine***) ~***!*** just a second!; **2.** ♪ second; ***große*** (***kleine***) ~ major (minor) second

Se'kun·den|kle·ber *m* superglue, instant glue; **2lang I.** *adj.* lasting (*or* of) several seconds; **II.** *adv.* for (several) seconds; **~schnel·le** *f*: ***in ~*** in a matter of seconds; ***es geschah alles in ~*** it was all over in a matter of seconds; **~zei·ger** *m* second hand

se·kun·die·ren [zekʊn'diːrən] *v/i.* (h) second (***j-m*** s.o.); *fig.* support (s.o.), back (s.o.) up

se·künd·lich [ze'kʏntlɪç] *adv.* every (*or* any) second

sel·be ['zɛlbə] *adj.* same; ***zur ~n Zeit*** at the same time, simultaneously

sel·ber ['zɛlbɐ] *pron.* → ***selbst*** I

selbst [zɛlbst] **I.** *pron.*: ***ich*** ~ I myself; ***er*** ~ he himself *etc.*; ***sie möchte es ~ machen*** she wants to do it herself (*or* on her own); ***er möchte ~ kochen*** *a.* he wants to do his own cooking; ***das muß ich mir ~ ansehen*** I'll have to see that for myself; ***ich habe ihn nicht ~ gesprochen*** I didn't talk to him personally; ***der Autor war ~ anwesend*** the author was there in person (*or* himself); ***er ist nicht mehr er*** ~ he's not himself anymore, he's beside himself; ***mit sich ~ sprechen*** talk to o.s.; ***von*** ~ a) of one's own accord, b) (by) itself; ***es öffnet sich von*** ~ it opens automatically (*or* itself); ***das versteht sich*** (***doch***) ***von*** ~ that goes without saying; ~ ***ist der Mann*** (*or* ***die Frau***)***!*** there's nothing like doing it yourself; ***er war die Höflichkeit*** ~ he was politeness in person (*or* itself); ***er ist die Ruhe*** ~ he's unflappable; ***zu sich ~ kommen*** get back on an even keel; ***ich muß wieder zu mir ~ kommen*** *a.* I need some time to straighten out my thoughts; ***ich komme kaum mehr zu mir*** ~ I hardly get time to think, I hardly get a minute to myself; *du bist ein Idiot* - ~ ***einer!*** it takes one to recognize one; **II.** *adv.* even; ~ ***er*** even he; ~ ***wenn*** even if; **Selbst** *n* (-; *no pl.*) self; ***wieder sein altes ~ sein*** be one's old self again; ***das ~ aufgeben*** give up one's personality

'Selbst|ab·ho·ler *m*: ***Möbel für*** ~ flatpack furniture; **~ach·tung** *f* self-esteem, self-respect; **~ana,ly·se** *f* self-analysis

selb·stän·dig ['zɛlpʃtɛndɪç] **I.** *adj.* independent; self-supporting; self-employed, freelance *journalist, architect etc.*; *pol.* autonomous; ***an ~es Arbeiten gewöhnt*** used to working on one's own; ***sich ~ machen*** a) start up one's own business, *journalist etc.*: go freelance, b) F *fig.* F just walk off; **II.** *adv.* independently; oneself, on one's own; ***~ denken*** think for o.s.; ***~ handeln*** act independently (*or* on one's own initiative)

Selb·stän·di·ge ['zɛlpʃtɛndɪgə] *m, f* (-n; -n) self-employed person; (*journalist etc.*) freelance(r)

'Selb·stän·dig·keit *f* (-; *no pl.*) independence, *pol. a.* sovereignty, autonomy

'Selbst|an·kla·ge *f* self-accusation, self-incrimination; **~an·steckung** *f* ⚕ auto-infection; **~an·zei·ge** *f* self-denunciation; **~auf·op·fe·rung** *f* self-sacrifice; **~auf·zug** *m* self-winding mechanism; **~aus·lö·ser** *m phot.* (self-)timer; **~be·die·nung** *f* (-; *no pl.*) self-service; ***Restaurant mit ~*** self-service restaurant, cafeteria

'Selbst·be·die·nungs|la·den *m* self-service shop (*Am.* store); (small) supermarket; **~re·stau͵rant** *n* self-service restaurant, cafeteria

'Selbst|be·frie·di·gung *f* masturbation; **~be·haup·tung** *f* (-; *no pl.*) self-assertion, self-assertiveness; **~be·herr·schung** *f* self-control; ***die ~ verlieren*** *a.* lose one's temper; **~be·kennt·nis** *n* confession; **~be·kö·sti·gung** *f* self-catering; **~be·mit·lei·dung** *f* self-pity; **~be·ob·ach·tung** *f* (-; *no pl.*) introspection, self-observation; **~be·schei·dung** *f*, **~be·schrän·kung** *f* (-; *no pl.*) self-restraint; **~be·sin·nung** *f* self-contemplation; **~be·stä·ti·gung** *f* (-; *no pl.*) ego-boost; ***zu s-r ~*** to prove oneself, to boost one's confidence (*or* ego); ***das war für ihn e-e ~*** that gave his confidence (*or* ego) a boost; **~be·stäu·bung** *f* ⚘ self-pollination

'Selbst·be·stim·mung *f* (-; *no pl.*) self-determination; **'Selbst·be·stim·mungs·recht** *n* (-[e]s; *no pl.*) (right of) self-determination

'Selbst|be·tei·li·gung *f* percentage excess; **~be·trug** *m* self-deception; ***das ist ~*** you're *etc.* deceiving yourself *etc.*; **~be·weih·räu·che·rung** *f* self-adulation

'selbst·be·wußt *adj.* (self-)confident, self-assured; **'Selbst·be·wußt·sein** *n* self-confidence, self-assurance; *phls.* self-awareness

'selbst·be·zo·gen *adj.* self-centred (*Am.* self-centered), egocentric

'Selbst·be·zo·gen·heit *f* self-centredness (*Am.* self-centeredness), obsession with oneself

'Selbst|bild *n* self-image; *the* way one sees oneself; **~bild·nis** *n* self-portrait; **~bio·gra͵phie** *f* autobiography; **~bräu·ner** [-brɔʏnɐ] *m* (-s; -) self-tanning lotion (*or* cream); **~dar·stel·lung** *f* self-projection; image cultivation; *contp.* showmanship; **~dia͵gno·se** *f computer*: self-diagnosis; **~dis·zi͵plin** *f* (-; *no pl.*) (self-)discipline; **~ein·schät·zung** *f* self-assessment; *one's* image of oneself; *the* way one sees oneself; **~ent·fal·tung** *f* self-development; self-fulfil(l)ment; **~ent·frem·dung** *f phls.* alienation from self

'Selbst·er·fah·rung *f* (-; *no pl.*) self-awareness; **'Selbst·er·fah·rungs·grup·pe** *f* consciousness-raising (*or* self-awareness) group

'Selbst·er·hal·tung *f* self-preservation; **'Selbst·er·hal·tungs·trieb** *m* survival instinct

'Selbst|er·kennt·nis *f* (-; *no pl.*) self-knowledge; **&er·nannt** *adj.* self-styled, self-proclaimed, would-be; *formal*: soi-disant; **~er·nied·ri·gung** *f* self-abasement; **~fah·rer** *m* **1.** self-propelling wheelchair; **2.** ***er ist ~*** he drives himself, he doesn't have a chauffeur; ***Autovermietung für ~*** self-drive car hire

'selbst|ge·backen *adj.* homemade; **~ge·ba·stelt** *adj.* homemade; ***ist das ~?*** did you make that yourself?; **~ge·braut** *adj.* home-brewed

'selbst·ge·dreht *adj.*: ***~e Zigarette*** roll-up; **'Selbst·ge·dreh·te** *f* (-n; -n) roll-up; ***~ rauchen*** roll one's own

'selbst·ge·fäl·lig *adj.* complacent, self-satisfied, smug; **'Selbst·ge·fäl·lig·keit** *f* (-; *no pl.*) complacency, smugness

'Selbst·ge·fühl *n* → ***Selbstwertgefühl***

'selbst·ge·macht *adj.* homemade

'selbst·ge·nüg·sam *adj.* contented, satisfied with one's lot; modest; ***er ist sehr ~*** *a.* he doesn't make any great demands (on life); **'Selbst·ge·nüg·sam·keit** *f* (-; *no pl.*) contentedness; modesty

'selbst·ge·recht *adj.* self-righteous, F holier-than-thou *attitude etc.*

'selbst·ge·schnei·dert *adj.* homemade; ***ist das ~?*** did you make that yourself?

'Selbst·ge·spräch *n* monolog(ue); soliloquy; ***~e führen*** talk to o.s.

'selbst|ge·steckt *adj.*: ***~e Grenzen*** self-imposed limits; **~ge·strickt** *adj.* **1.** homemade; ***ist das ~?*** did you knit that yourself?; **2.** *fig.* homespun

'Selbst·haß *m* self-hate

'selbst·herr·lich *adj.* high-handed; overbearing

'Selbst·hil·fe *f* (-; *no pl.*) self-help; ***zur ~ schreiten*** take matters into one's own hands; **~grup·pe** *f* self-help group

'Selbst|in·duk·ti͵on *f* ⚡ self-induction; **~iro͵nie** *f* self-irony; **~ju͵stiz** *f*: ***~ üben*** take the law into one's own hands

'Selbst·kle·be·fo·lie *f* adhesive foil

'selbst·kle·bend *adj.* (self-)adhesive; self-seal *envelope*

'Selbst·kon͵trol·le *f* self-control; *n.s. and* ⚙ self-check(ing); self-censorship *of the press etc.*

'Selbst·ko·sten·preis *m* cost price; ***zum ~*** at cost (price)

'Selbst·kri͵tik *f* self-criticism

'selbst·kri·tisch *adj.* self-critical; ***er ist sehr ~*** *a.* he's very hard on himself

'Selbst·la·de·pi͵sto·le *f* self-loading pistol, automatic (pistol)

'Selbst|laut *m ling.* vowel; **&leuch·tend** *adj.* luminous; **~lob** *n* self-praise

'selbst·los *adj.* selfless

'Selbst·lo·sig·keit *f* (-; *no pl.*) selflessness

'Selbst·mit·leid *n* self-pity

'Selbst·mord *m* suicide; ***~ begehen*** commit suicide; *fig.* ***das ist doch glatter ~*** that's sheer suicide; F ***~ auf Raten*** slow suicide; **'Selbst·mör·der** *m* suicide (victim); **'selbst·mör·de·risch** *adj.* suicidal; *w.s. a.* breakneck *speed etc.*

'Selbst·mord|ge·dan·ken *pl.*: ***~ haben*** be contemplating suicide; **&ge·fähr·det** *adj.* suicidal; ***~ sein*** have suicidal tendencies, be a potential suicide; **~kan·di͵dat** *m* potential suicide; **~klau·sel** *f* suicide clause; **~kom͵man·do** *n* **1.** suicide mission; **2.** suicide squad; **~ra·te** *f* suicide rate; **~ver·such** *m* attempted suicide; suicide attempt; ***e-n ~ machen*** try (*or* attempt) to commit suicide; ***mißglückter ~*** failed suicide attempt

'Selbst·por͵trät *n* self-portrait

'Selbst·quä·le͵rei *f* self-torment, self-torture; **'selbst·quä·le·risch** *adj.* self-tormenting

'selbst|re·gelnd *adj.* self-regulating; **~rei·ni·gend** *adj.* self-cleaning *oven etc.*; **~schlie·ßend** *adj.* self-closing

'Selbst·schuß *m* spring gun; **~an·la·ge** *f* automatic firing device

Selbst·schutz *m* self-defen|ce (*Am.* -se)

'selbst·si·cher *adj.* self-confident, self-assured, very sure of oneself

'Selbst·si·cher·heit *f* (-; *no pl.*) self-confidence, self-assurance

'Selbst|steue·rung *f* automatic control; **~stu·di·um** *n* self-study, private study; ***im ~*** *acquire etc.* through self-study (*or* private study)

'Selbst·sucht *f* (-; *no pl.*) selfishness, ego(t)ism; **'selbst·süch·tig** *adj.* selfish, self-seeking, egotistic(al), egoistic(al)

'selbst·tä·tig *adj.* automatic(ally *adv.*)

'Selbst|täu·schung *f* self-delusion; **~tor** *n sport*: own goal; **~über͵schät·zung** *f* conceitedness; exaggerated opinion of oneself; ***an ~ leiden*** have a very high opinion of oneself; **~über͵win·dung** *f* will-power; ***es kostete ihn viel ~*** it cost him quite an effort; **~ver·ach·tung** *f* self-contempt; **~ver·ant·wor·tung** *f* personal responsibility; **~ver·bren·nung** *f* self-immolation

'selbst·ver·dient *adj*: ***mit ~em Geld*** with one's hard-earned money

'selbst·ver·ges·sen *adj.* lost in thought, oblivious to the world

'Selbst|ver·lag *m*: ***im ~*** published by the author; **~ver·leug·nung** *f* self-denial; **~ver·pfle·gung** *f* self-catering

'selbst·ver·schul·det *adj.*: ***~e Krise*** crisis of one's own making; ***der Unfall war ~*** he *etc.* caused the accident himself *etc.*

'Selbst·ver·sor·ger *m*: ***sie sind ~*** they're self-sufficient; ***Appartements für ~*** self-catering flats (*a. Am.* apartments)

'selbst·ver·ständ·lich I. *adj.* (perfectly) natural; ***das ist (doch) ~*** *a.* that goes without saying; ***es ist die ~ste Sache der Welt*** it's the most natural thing in the world; ***et. als ~ hinnehmen*** take s.th. for granted; **II.** *adv.* of course, naturally; *do s.th.* as a matter of course; ***~!*** of course!, sure!

'Selbst·ver·ständ·lich·keit *f*: ***es ist doch e-e ~, daß*** it goes without saying that, there's no question that, it's only natural that; ***es ist für sie e-e ~*** *a.* it's a matter of course for her, it's a foregone conclusion for her; ***mit e-r ~*** with a matter-of-factness; ***das war doch e-e ~!*** not at all!; ***er machte es mit e-r solchen ~*** he did it as if it was the most natural thing in the world; ***zwei Wagen sind für sie e-e ~*** they take it for granted that they should have two cars

'Selbst|ver·ständ·nis *n one's* self-image, *the* image one has of oneself; ***nationales ~*** national identity; ***das ~ der Partei*** *a.* the way the party sees itself; **~ver·stüm·me·lung** *f* self-mutilation; **~ver·such** *m* self-experiment; ***e-n ~ machen*** experiment on oneself, use oneself as a

guinea-pig; **~ver·tei·di·gung** *f* self-defen|ce (*Am.* -se); **~ver·trau·en** *n* self-confidence, self-assurance; ***Mangel an ~*** *a.* diffidence
'**Selbst·ver·wal·tung** *f* autonomy, self-government; '**Selbst·ver·wal·tungs·recht** *n* right to autonomy
'**Selbst|ver·wirk·li·chung** *f* (-; *no pl.*) self-realization, *esp. psych.* self-actualization; **~vor·wurf** *m* self-reproach
'**Selbst·wähl·fern·dienst** *m* subscriber trunk dialling, STD, *Am.* direct dialing
'**Selbst·wert·ge·fühl** *n* (-[e]s; *no pl.*) self-esteem; ***ein übertriebenes ~ besitzen*** have an exaggerated opinion of oneself
'**Selbst|zen,sur** *f* (-; *no pl.*) self-censorship; **~zer·flei·schung** *f* self-laceration
'**selbst·zer·stö·re·risch** *adj.* self-destructive
'**Selbst·zeug·nis** *n* self-portrayal
'**selbst·zu·frie·den** *adj.* complacent, smug, self-satisfied; '**Selbst·zu·frie·den·heit** *f* complacency, smugness
'**Selbst|zweck** *m* (-[e]s; *no pl.*) end in itself; ***als ~*** *a.* for its own sake; ***zum ~ werden*** become an end in itself; **~zwei·fel** *m* self-doubt
sel·chen ['zɛlçən] *dial. v/t.* (h) smoke
Selch·fleisch ['zɛlç-] *dial. n* smoked meat
se·lek·tie·ren [zelɛk'ti:rən] *v/t.* (h) select; **Se·lek·ti·on** [zelɛk'tsĭo:n] *f* (-; -en) selection; **se·lek·tiv** [zelɛk'ti:f] *adj.* selective; **Se·lek·ti·vi·tät** [zelɛktivi'tɛ:t] *f* (-; *no pl.*) *radio*: selectivity
Se·len [ze'le:n] *n* (-s; *no pl.*) ⚗ selenium; **~zel·le** *f phys.* selenium cell
se·lig ['ze:lıç] *adj.* **1.** blessed; ***Gott hab ihn ~*** God rest his soul; → ***glauben*** I; **2.** a) thrilled (to bits), overjoyed, b) blissful, c) F tiddly; **3.** *obs.* late, deceased; ***mein ~er Vater*** my late father; '**Se·lig·keit** *f* (-; *no pl.*) **1.** *eccl.* everlasting life, salvation; **2.** perfect happiness, (sheer) bliss
'**se·lig·prei·sen** *v/t.* (*irr.*, *sep.*, h, → ***preisen***) **1.** *eccl.* bless; **2.** ***dafür ist sie seligzupreisen*** she can count herself (very) fortunate
'**se·lig·spre·chen** *v/t.* (*irr.*, *sep.*, h, → ***sprechen***) *eccl.* beatify; '**Se·lig·spre·chung** [-ʃprɛçʊŋ] *f* (-; -en) beatification
Sel·le·rie ['zɛləri] *m* (-s; -[s]), *f* (-; -) celeriac; celery (stalks *pl.*); **~knol·le** *f* celery root; **~salz** *n* celery salt
sel·ten ['zɛltən] **I.** *adj.* a) rare; scarce, b) *fig.* rare, exceptional; F ***~er Vogel*** odd character, F queer fish; F ***~e Sorte*** rare breed; **II.** *adv.* rarely, seldom; ***~ findet man ...*** *a.* you don't often find ...; ***höchst ~*** very rarely, once in a blue moon; ***ein ~ schönes Exemplar*** an exceptionally beautiful specimen, a specimen of rare beauty; ***es kommt ~ vor, daß er ...*** he rarely ...; ***solche Menschen trifft man ~*** *a.* people like that are few and far between, there aren't many of that sort around; ***~ habe ich so e-n schönen Teppich gesehen*** *a.* I can't remember the last time I saw such a beautiful carpet; '**Sel·ten·heit** *f* (-; *no pl.*) **1.** rareness, scarcity; **2.** rarity; '**Sel·ten·heits·wert** *m* (-[e]s; *no pl.*) scarcity value
Sel·ters ['zɛltɐs] *f* (-; *no pl.*), *n* (-; *no pl.*), **~was·ser** *n* (-s; -wässer [-vɛsɐ]) mineral water, seltzer
selt·sam ['zɛltza:m] **I.** *adj.* strange, odd, peculiar; ***es ist schon ~*** it's very strange; ***mir ist ganz ~*** I feel really strange; **II.** *adv.* strangely; ***j-n ~ ansehen*** look at s.o. in a strange way, give s.o. a strange look; ***es hat mich ~ berührt*** it moved me in a strange way; '**selt·sa·mer·wei·se** *adv.* strangely (*or* oddly) enough
'**Selt·sam·keit** *f* (-; -en) **1.** *no pl.* strangeness, oddness, peculiarity; **2.** oddity
Se·man·tik [ze'mantık] *f* (-; *no pl.*) semantics *pl.*; **Se·man·ti·ker** [ze'mantikɐ] *m* (-s; -) semanticist; **se·man·tisch** [ze'mantıʃ] *adj.* semantic(ally *adv.*)
Se·me·ster [ze'mɛstɐ] *n* (-s; -) semester; ***er ist im dritten ~*** he's in his third semester; ***wieviel ~ mußt du noch machen?*** how many semesters have you got to go?; ***während des ~s*** during term-time; **~ar·beit** *f* term paper; **~be·ginn** *m*: (***zu ~*** at the) beginning of the semester; **~en·de** *n*: (***am ~*** at the) end of the semester; **~fe·ri·en** *pl.* vacation *sg.*, F vac
Se·mi·fi,na·le ['ze:mi-] *n* → ***Halbfinale***
Se·mi·ko·lon [zemi'ko:lɔn] *n* (-s; -s) semicolon
Se·mi·nar [zemi'na:ɐ] *n* (-s; -e [-rə]) **1.** *univ.* a) seminar, b) institute, department; **2.** teacher training college; **3.** *eccl.* seminary; **~ar·beit** *f univ.* seminar paper; **~schein** *m* course attendance certificate; ***e-n ~ machen*** F do a seminar
Se·mio·tik [ze'mĭo:tık] *f* (-; *no pl.*) semiotics *pl.*; **Se·mio·ti·ker** [ze'mĭo:tikɐ] *m* (-s; -) semiotician
Se·mit [ze'mi:t] *m* (-en; -en), **Se·mi·tin** [ze'mi:tın] *f* (-; -nen) Semite; **se·mi·tisch** [ze'mi:tıʃ] *adj. a. ling.* Semitic
Sem·mel ['zɛməl] *f* (-; -n) roll; F ***wie warme ~n weggehen*** be selling like hot cakes; **♀blond** *adj.* flaxen(-haired); **~brö·sel** *pl.* breadcrumbs; **~knö·del** *m* bread dumpling; **~mehl** *n* breadcrumbs *pl.*
Se·nat [ze'na:t] *m* (-s; -e) *pol.*, *univ.* senate; *in the USA*: Senate; ⚖ panel
Se·na·tor [ze'na:to:ɐ] *m* (-s; -en [zena'to:rən]) senator; *in the USA*: Senator
Se'nats|aus·schuß *m* senate (*or* Senate) committee; **~be·schluß** *m* decree by the senate (*or* Senate); **~mit·glied** *n* member of the senate (*or* Senate), senator, Senator; **~sit·zung** *f* senate (*or* Senate) meeting; **~spre·cher** *m USA*: Speaker of the Senate
Sen·de|an·la·ge ['zɛndə-] *f* transmitter; **~an·stalt** *f* broadcasting (*or* television) station; **~an,ten·ne** *f* transmitting aerial (*or* antenna); **~be·ginn** *m*: ***~ ist um ...*** the program(me) begins at ...; **~be·reich** *m* transmission range; service area; **~be·trieb** *m* (-[e]s; *no pl.*) radio and television operations *pl.*; **~fol·ge** *f* program(me)s *pl.*; **~fre,quenz** *f* transmitting frequency; **~ge·biet** *n* transmission range; service area; **~lei·ter** *m* producer; **~mast** *m* transmitter mast
sen·den[1] ['zɛndən] *v/t. and v/i.* (sandte, gesandt, h) a) send (***nach*** *dat.* for *s.o.*), b) ⚜ send, forward
'**sen·den**[2] *v/t. and v/i.* (h) transmit, *radio*, *TV*: *a.* broadcast
Sen·de·pau·se ['zɛndə-] *f* intermission, interval; *fig.* silence; *fig.* ***jetzt hast du mal ~!*** F put a sock in it, will you?; ***hoffentlich hat sie bald ~*** F I wish she'd shut up (*or* put a sock in it)
Sen·der ['zɛndɐ] *m* (-s; -) transmitter; radio (*or* broadcasting, television) station
Sen·de·raum ['zɛndə-] *m* studio
'**Sen·der·drif·ten** *n* (-s; *no pl.*) fading
Sen·de|rech·te ['zɛndə-] *pl.* broadcasting rights; **~rei·he** *f* series (*sg.*)
'**Sen·der|netz** *n* transmitter network; **~such·lauf** *m* automatic tuning
Sen·de|schluß ['zɛndə-] *m* closedown; **~stö·rung** *f* break in transmission; **~stu·dio** *n* broadcasting studio; **~turm** *m* radio (*TV* television) tower; **~zei·chen** *n* call sign; **~zeit** *f* broadcasting time, time of transmission; *coll.* air time; ***die ~ überziehen*** overrun; **~zen,tra·le** *f* broadcasting centre (*Am.* center)
Sen·dung ['zɛndʊŋ] *f* (-; -en) **1.** package, *Brit.* parcel; ⚜ consignment; **2.** *radio*, *TV* a) transmission, broadcasting, b) program(me), *radio*: *a.* broadcast; ***auf ~ sein*** be on the air; **3.** *fig.* mission; '**Sen·dungs·be·wußt·sein** *n* sense of mission
Se·ne·ga·le·se [zenega'le:zə] *m* (-n; -n), **Se·ne·ga·le·sin** [zenega'le:zın] *f* (-; -nen), **se·ne·ga·le·sisch** [zenega'le:zıʃ] *adj.*, **Se·ne·ga'le·sisch** *n* (-en) *ling.* Senegalese
Senf [zɛnf] *m* (-[e]s; -e) mustard (*a.* ⚘); F ***s-n ~ dazugeben*** have one's say, F put in one's (own) two bits; F ***wenn ich m-n ~ dazugeben darf*** *a.* if I may offer my humble opinion; **♀far·ben, ♀far·big** *adj.* mustard; **~gas** *n* mustard gas; **~glas** *n* mustard jar; **~gur·ke** *f* gherkin (*pickled with mustard seeds*); **~korn** *n* mustard seed; **~pul·ver** *n* ground mustard seed; **~so·ße** *f* mustard sauce; **~topf** *m* mustard pot
Sen·ge ['zɛŋə] *dial. pl.*: ***~ beziehen*** get a thrashing
sen·gen ['zɛŋən] (h) **I.** *v/t.* singe; **II.** *v/i.* scorch; ***~de Hitze*** scorching heat
se·nil [ze'ni:l] *adj.* senile
Se·ni·li·tät [zenili'tɛ:t] *f* (-; *no pl.*) senility
se·ni·or ['ze:nĭo:ɐ] *adj.* (**sen.**) senior (*abbr.* sen., Sr)
Se·ni·or ['ze:nĭo:ɐ] *m* (-s; -en [ze'nĭo:rən]) **1.** senior (*a. sport*); **2.** *pl.* senior citizens; **~chef** *m* senior partner
Se·nio·ren|heim [ze'nĭo:rən-] *n* → ***Seniorenwohnheim***; **~paß** *m* senior citizen's (rail) pass; **~wohn·heim** *n* retirement home
Se·nio·ri·tät [zenĭori'tɛ:t] *f* (-; *no pl.*) seniority
Senk·blei ['zɛŋk-] *n* plumb line; ⚓ plummet
Sen·ke ['zɛŋkə] *f* (-; -n) *geol.* depression, hollow
sen·ken ['zɛŋkən] (h) **I.** *v/t.* **1.** lower (*a. fig. temperature*, *blood pressure*, *one's voice*); *a.* cast *one's eyes* down; bow *one's head*; *fig.* reduce, cut *taxes*, *prices etc.*; **2.** ⚙ sink *shaft*, *well etc.*; **II.** *v/refl.*: ***sich ~*** **3.** *fig. voice*: drop, *temperature*: *a.* fall; **4.** *wall*: sag; *ground etc.*: give way, subside; *road*: dip, fall off; *water level*: drop, fall
Senk·fuß ['zɛŋk-] *m* fallen arches *pl.*; **~ein·la·ge** *f* arch support
Senk|gru·be ['zɛŋk-] *f* cesspit; **~ka·sten** *m* ⚙ caisson; **~kopf·schrau·be** *f* countersunk screw
senk·recht ['zɛŋkrɛçt] **I.** *adj.* vertical; ⩘ *a.* perpendicular; ***die Mauer ist nicht ~*** *a.* the wall is out of plumb; **II.** *adv. crossword*: down; '**Senk·rech·te** *f* (-n; -n) vertical; ⩘ perpendicular
'**Senk·recht|start** *m* vertical takeoff; **~star·ter** *m* **1.** ✈ vertical takeoff plane, F jump jet; **2.** F *fig.* F whiz(z) kid, high flier
Senk·rücken ['zɛŋk-] *m vet.* swayback

Sen·kung ['zɛŋkʊŋ] *f* (-; -en) **1.** ✝ lowering (*gen.* of *prices etc.*), cut(s *pl.*) (in *wages etc.*); **2.** ⚠ setting *of the foundations*; sagging *of walls, ceiling etc.*; subsidence *of ground, house etc.*; **3.** ⚗ sedimentation
Sen·ne¹ ['zɛnə] *m* (-n; -n) Alpine dairyman
'**Sen·ne²** *f* (-; -n) mountain pasture
Sen·ne·rin ['zɛnərɪn] *f* (-; -nen) dairymaid
Sen·sa·ti·on [zɛnza'tsĭo:n] *f* (-; -en) sensation; *a.* F splash; ***e-e ~ verursachen*** create a sensation, cause *or* create (quite) a stir; ***die Zuschauer wollen ~en sehen*** the audience wants to see some action
sen·sa·tio·nell [zɛnzatsĭo'nɛl] *adj.* sensational
Sen·sa·ti'ons|blatt *n* sensational newspaper; *pl. a.* sensational press *sg.*; **~dar·stel·ler** *m* stuntman; **~gier** *f* sensation-seeking; **~ha·sche·rei** [-haʃəraɪ] *f* (-; *no pl.*) sensationalism; **~jour·na,lis·mus** *m* sensational journalism; **~lü·stern** *adj.* sensation-seeking (*or* -hungry); **~ma·che** *f* sensationalism; **~mel·dung** *f* sensational news, F scoop; **~pres·se** *f* sensational (*or* yellow) press; **~pro,zeß** *m* sensational trial; **~stück** *n* sensation drama
Sen·se ['zɛnzə] *f* (-; -n) scythe; F ***jetzt ist aber ~ (bei mir)!*** that's enough of that! (I've had enough); '**Sen·sen·mann** *m* (-[e]s; *no pl.*) *the* Grim Reaper
sen·si·bel [zɛn'zi:bəl] *adj.* sensitive
sen·si·bi·li·sie·ren [zɛnzibili'zi:rən] *v/t.* (h) sensitize (*a. phot.*); ***j-n ~ für*** *acc.* make s.o. sensitive to; **Sen·si·bi·li·tät** [zɛnzibili'tɛ:t] *f* (-; *no pl.*) sensitivity (*a.* ⚗), sensibility; hypersensitivity
Sen·sor ['zɛnzo:ɐ] *m* (-s; -en [zɛn'zo:rən]) ⚡ sensor; '**Sen·sor·bild·schirm** *m computer*: touch(-sensitive) screen
sen·so·risch [zɛn'zo:rɪʃ] *adj.* sensory
'**Sen·sor·ta·ste** *f* feather touch key, light action key (*pl. a.* controls)
Sen·sua·lis·mus [zɛnzŭa'lɪsmʊs] *m* (-; *no pl.*) sensualism; **Sen·sua·li·tät** [zɛnzŭali'tɛ:t] *f* (-; *no pl.*) sensuality
Sen·tenz [zɛn'tɛnts] *f* (-; -en) aphorism, saying; **sen·ten·zi·ös** [zɛntɛn'tsĭø:s] *adj.* sententious
sen·ti·men·tal [zɛntimɛn'ta:l] *adj.* sentimental; **Sen·ti·men·ta·li·tät** [zɛntimɛntali'tɛ:t] *f* (-; -en) sentimentality; *contp.* F slush; ***aus ~*** for sentimental reasons
se·pa·rat [zepa'ra:t] *adj.* separate
Se·pa'rat·frie·den *m* separate peace
Se·pa·ra·tis·mus [zepara'tɪsmʊs] *m* (-; *no pl.*) *pol.* separatism; **Se·pa·ra·tist** [zepara'tɪst] *m* (-en; -en), **se·pa·ra·ti·stisch** [separa'tɪstɪʃ] *adj.* separatist
Sé·pa·rée [zepa're:] *n* (-s; -s) booth
Se·phar·dim [ze'fardɪm] *pl.* Sephardi(m)
se·phar·disch [ze'fardɪʃ] *adj.* Sephardic
se·pia ['ze:pĭa] *adj.*, '**Se·pia** *f* (-; Sepien) sepia
Sep·sis ['zɛpsɪs] *f* (-; Sepsen [-sən]) sepsis
Sept [zɛpt] *f* (-; -en), **Sep·te** ['zɛptə] *f* (-; -n) → ***Septim*** 1
Sep·tem·ber [zɛp'tɛmbɐ] *m* (-s; -) September; ***im ~*** in September
Sep·tim [zɛp'ti:m] *f* (-; -en) **1.** ♪ seventh; ***große (kleine) ~*** major (minor) seventh; **2.** *fencing*: septime
Sep·ti·me [zɛp'ti:mə] *f* (-; -n) → ***Septim*** 1
sep·tisch ['zɛptɪʃ] *adj.* septic
se·quen·ti·ell [zekvɛn'tsĭɛl] *adj.* sequential; **Se·quenz** [ze'kvɛnts] *f* (-; -en) sequence; *card game*: run, set
Ser·be ['zɛrbə] *m* (-n; -n), **Ser·bin** ['zɛrbɪn] *f* (-; -nen), **ser·bisch** ['zɛrbɪʃ] *adj.* Serbian
ser·bo·kroa·tisch [zɛrbokro'a:tɪʃ] *adj.* Serbian; *ling.* Serbo-Croat(ian)
Se·re·na·de [zere'na:də] *f* (-; -n) ♪ serenade
Se·rie ['ze:rĭə] *f* (-; -n) series (*sg.*); *radio, TV*: *a.* serial; set; ✝ line, range; ***in ~ gehen*** go into production; ***in ~ hergestellt werden*** be mass-produced
se·ri·ell [ze'rĭɛl] *adj.* serial
'**Se·ri·en|aus·stat·tung** *f* standard fittings *pl.*; **~bau** *m* (-[e]s; *no pl.*) serial production; **~brie·fe** *pl.* serial letters, mass mailings; **~fahr·zeug** *n* standard car; **~fer·ti·gung** *f*, **~her·stel·lung** *f* serial production
'**se·ri·en·mä·ßig I.** *adj.* production-line ...; ***~e Ausstattung*** standard fittings *pl.*; **II.** *adv.* in series; as standard; ***~ herstellen*** mass-produce
'**Se·ri·en|num·mer** *f* serial number; **~reif** *adj.* ready to go into (mass) production; **~schal·tung** *f* ⚡ series connection; **~un·fall** *m* pile-up, multiple crash, *Am.* chain accident; **~wa·gen** *m* standard car
'**se·ri·en·wei·se** *adv.* in series
se·ri·ös [ze'rĭø:s] *adj.* serious; respectable; ✝ *a.* reliable, honest, reputable *firm etc.*; **Se·rio·si·tät** [zerĭozi'tɛ:t] *f* (-; *no pl.*) seriousness; respectability; reliability; → ***seriös***
Ser·mon [zɛr'mo:n] *contp. m* (-s; -e) lecture; ***e-n ~ halten über*** *acc. a.* hold forth on
se·ro·po·si·tiv [zero'po:ziti:f] *adj.* seropositive, *aids*: *a.* HIV-positive
Ser·pen·ti·ne [zɛrpɛn'ti:nə] *f* (-; -n) switchback, serpentine (*or* winding) road; double bend
Se·rum ['ze:rʊm] *n* (-s; -ra [-ra]) serum
Ser·vice¹ [zɛr'vi:s] *n* (-; - [-'vi:sə]) dinner (*or* tea, coffee) service
Ser·vice² ['zø:ɐvɪs, 'sœ:vɪs] *m, n* (-; *no pl.*) **1.** service; **2.** ⚙ after-sales service; **3.** *sport*: service, serve
'**ser·vice·freund·lich** *adj.* serviceable
ser·vie·ren [zɛr'vi:rən] (h) **I.** *v/t.* serve; ***et. zum Frühstück ~*** serve s.th. for breakfast; ***Wein zum Essen ~*** serve wine with a (*or* the) meal; ***es ist serviert!*** dinner is served; F *fig.* ***j-m Lügen*** *etc.* ***~*** give s.o. lies *etc.*; **II.** *v/i.* serve; *a.* wait (at table)
Ser·vie·re·rin [zɛr'vi:rərɪn] *f* (-; -nen) waitress
Ser·vier|tisch [zɛr'vi:ɐ-] *m* serving table; **~wa·gen** *m* trolley
Ser·vi·et·te [zɛr'vĭɛtə] *f* (-; -n) serviette, *formal*: (table) napkin; **Ser·vi'et·ten·ring** *m* serviette (*or* napkin) ring
ser·vil [zɛr'vi:l] *adj.* servile; **Ser·vi·li·tät** [zɛrvili'tɛ:t] *f* (-; *no pl.*) servility
Ser·vo|brem·se ['zɛrvo-] *f* servo (*or* power) brake; **~len·kung** *f* power steering, servo(-assisted) steering; **~mo·tor** *m* servo motor
Ser·vus ['zɛrvʊs] *int.* F see you!, so long!
Se·sam ['ze:zam] *m* (-s; -s) sesame; ***~ öffne dich!*** open sesame; **~kern** *m* sesame seed; **~öl** *n* sesame oil
Ses·sel ['zɛsəl] *m* (-s; -) armchair, easy chair; F *fig.* ***an s-m ~ kleben*** cling to one's post (*or* position); F ***nach j-s ~ trachten*** have one's eye on s.o.'s job; **~lift** *m* chair lift
seß·haft ['zɛshaft] *adj.* a) settled, b) resident; ***~ werden*** settle (down)
Set [zɛt] *n, m* (-s; -s) **1.** set; **2.** place mat
Set·ter ['zɛtɐ, 'sɛtə] *m* (-s; -) *zo.* setter
set·zen ['zɛtsən] (h) **I.** *v/t.* **1.** a) put; *a.* place *s.th.*; *a.* sit *s.o.*, b) ⚘ plant, set, c) put up *mast*, set *sail*; pile up *wood etc.*; erect, set up *a monument* (***j-m*** to s.o.); put in, fix *a stove*, d) put (in) *commas etc.*, e) bet, place (***auf*** *acc.* on); move *chessman etc.*, f) *sport*: seed *s.o., a team*; ***j-n an e-e Arbeit ~*** set s.o. to work doing s.th.; ***an Land ~*** put ashore; ***an die Lippen ~*** raise (*or* set) to one's lips; F ***e-n Wagen an die Mauer ~*** drive a car into a wall; ***j-n auf e-e Liste ~*** put s.o. *or* s.o.'s name (down) on a list; ***et. auf j-s Rechnung ~*** charge s.th. to s.o.'s account; ***et. in die Zeitung ~*** put s.th. in the paper; ***ein Gedicht in Musik ~*** set a poem to music; ***Fische in e-n Teich ~*** stock a pond with fish; ***j-n über den Fluß ~*** take s.o. across the river; *fig.* ***j-n über j-n ~*** a) think more (highly) of s.o. than of s.o., b) promote s.o. above s.o.; ***unter Wasser ~*** submerge, flood; ***s-e Unterschrift ~ unter*** *acc.* put one's signature to, sign; → ***Druck¹*** 2, ***Erstaunen, Freiheit, Frist***; → *a.* ***gesetzt***; **2.** *typ.* set; **II.** *v/refl.* **3.** ***sich ~*** a) sit down, b) *fig.* sink; *dregs, dust etc.*: settle; ***sich auf e-n Ast ~*** *bird*: land on (*or* fly onto) a branch; ***sich zu j-m ~*** sit down beside s.o.; ***darf ich mich zu Ihnen ~?*** may I join you?; ***sich ans Fenster ~*** sit down at (*or* by, next to) the window; ***sich an die Arbeit ~*** set to work; ***sich vor j-n ~*** *mot.* cut in on (*or* in front of) s.o.; ***sich aufs Pferd ~*** mount a horse; ***~ Sie sich!*** sit down!, take (*or* have) a seat!; **III.** *v/i.* **4.** ***~ über*** *acc.* jump over, clear *a hurdle*, take *a ditch*; → ***übersetzen²*** II; **5.** a) place one's bet, b) move *one's piece etc.*; ***~ auf*** *acc.* bet on, back; ***ich setze auf ihn!*** he's my man; **IV.** *v/impers.*: F ***gleich setzt es was*** F I can see trouble coming, you just watch your step
Set·zer ['zɛtsɐ] *m* (-s; -) *typ.* compositor, typesetter; **Set·ze·rei** [zɛtsə'raɪ] *f* (-; -en) composing (*or* case) room
Setz|feh·ler ['zɛts-] *m* misprint, typographical error; **~ka·sten** *m* **1.** *typ.* letter case; **2.** ⚘ seedling box
Setz·ling ['zɛtslɪŋ] *m* (-s; -e) **1.** ⚘ seedling; **2.** *pl. zo.* fry (*sg.*)
Setz·ma,schi·ne ['zɛts-] *f* typesetting machine
Seu·che ['zɔʏçə] *f* (-; -n) epidemic (*a. fig.*); *fig. contp. a.* plague
'**seu·chen·ar·tig** *adj. and adv.* epidemic; ***sich ~ ausbreiten*** spread like the plague
'**Seu·chen|be·kämp·fung** *f* epidemic control; **~ge·biet** *n* infested area; **~herd** *m* centre (*Am.* center) of an *or* the epidemic
seufz ['zɔʏfts] F *int.* F sniff!
seuf·zen ['zɔʏftsən] *v/i.* (h) sigh (***über*** *acc.* at, over; ***vor*** *dat.* with); '**seuf·zend** *adv.* with a sigh
Seuf·zer ['zɔʏftsɐ] *m* (-s; -) sigh; ***e-n ~ (der Erleichterung) ausstoßen*** heave a sigh (of relief); **~spal·te** F *f* agony column
Sex [zɛks, sɛks] *m* (-[es]; *no pl.*) sex; **~-Ap·peal** ['zɛksəpi:l, 'sɛks-] *m* (-s; *no pl.*) sex appeal; **~bom·be** F *f* F sex bomb, sexpot; **~film** *m* sex film, F blue movie; **~idol** *n* sex idol (*or* symbol)

Se·xis·mus [zɛˈksɪsmʊs] *m* (-; *no pl.*) sexism; **Se·xist** [zɛˈksɪst] *m* (-en; -en), **se·xi·stisch** [zɛˈksɪstɪʃ] *adj.* sexist

Se·xo·lo·ge [zɛksoˈloːgə] *m* (-n; -n) sexologist; **Se·xo·lo·gie** [zɛksoloˈgiː] *f* (-; *no pl.*) sexology, sex studies *pl.*

ˈ**Sex·shop** [-ʃɔp] *m* (-s; -s) sex shop

Sext [zɛkst] *f* (-; -en) **1.** ♪ sixth; ***große*** (***kleine***) ~ major (minor) sixth; **2.** *eccl.* sext; **3.** *fencing*: sixte

Sex·ta [ˈzɛksta] *f ped.* **1.** *obs. first year of grammar school*; **2.** *Austrian* sixth year (of grammar school); **Sex·ta·ner** [zɛksˈtaːnɐ] *m* (-s; -) *ped.* **1.** *obs. first year grammar school pupil*; **2.** *Austrian* sixth-year (grammar school) pupil, *Brit.* sixth-former; **Sexˈta·ner·bla·se** F *f* weak bladder

Sex·tant [zɛksˈtant] *m* (-en; -en) sextant

Sex·te [ˈzɛkstə] *f* (-; -n) → ***Sext*** 1

Sex·tett [zɛksˈtɛt] *n* (-[e]s; -e) sextet(te)

ˈ**Sex·touˌris·mus** F *m* sex tourism

Se·xu·al... [zɛˈksŭaːl-] *in cpds.* sexual, sex ...; **~deˌlikt** *n* sex offen|ce (*Am.* -se); **~er·zie·hung** *f* sex education; **~ethik** *f* sexual ethics *pl.*; **~for·scher** *m* sex researcher, sexologist; **~for·schung** *f* sex(ual) research, sexology; **~horˌmon** *n* sex hormone

Se·xua·li·tät [zɛksŭaliˈtɛːt] *f* (-; *no pl.*) sexuality

Se·xuˈal|kun·de *f ped.* sex education; **~le·ben** *n* sex life; **~moˌral** *f* sexual ethics *pl.*; **~mord** *m* sex murder; **~obˌjekt** *n* sex object; **~part·ner** *m* sex partner; **~tä·ter** *m* sex offender; **~trieb** *m* sexual drive; **~ver·bre·chen** *n* sex(ual) crime; **~ver·bre·cher** *m* sex offender; **~ver·kehr** *m* sexual intercourse; **~wis·sen·schaft** *f* → ***Sexualforschung***; **~wis·sen·schaft·ler** *m* → ***Sexualforscher***

se·xu·ell [zɛˈksŭɛl] **I.** *adj.* sexual; **II.** *adv.*: ~ ***mißbrauchen*** abuse (sexually)

se·xy [ˈzɛksi, ˈsɛksi] F *adj.* sexy

Se·zes·si·on [zetsɛˈsïoːn] *f* (-; -en) secession; ***Wiener*** ~ Vienna Secession

Se·zes·siˈons|krieg *m* war of secession; **~stil** *m* Secessionist style

se·zie·ren [zeˈtsiːrən] *v/t.* (h) dissect; *fig. a.* analyse, take apart

Se·zier|mes·ser [zeˈtsiːɐ-] *n* scalpel; **~saal** *m* dissecting room

Sham·poo [ˈʃampu] *n* (-s; -s) shampoo

Shift-Ta·ste [ˈʃɪft-] *f computer*: shift key; ***die*** ~ ***drücken*** *a.* press shift

Sho·gun [ˈʃoːgun] *m* (-s; -e) shogun, Shogun

Show [ʃoː, ʃoʊ] *f* (-; -s) → ***Schau***; **~ge·schäft** *n* show business; ***im*** ~ ***sein*** be in show business; **~ma·ster** [ˈʃoːmaːstɐ] *m* (-s; -) host, emcee, MC

Sia·me·se [zïaˈmeːzə] *m* (-n; -n), **Sia·me·sin** [zïaˈmeːzɪn] *f* (-; -nen), **sia·me·sisch** [zïaˈmeːzɪʃ] *adj. hist.* Siamese; *fig.* ***siamesische Zwillinge*** Siamese twins

Si·am·kat·ze [ˈziːam-] *f* Siamese cat

Si·bi·ri·er [ziˈbiːrïɐ] *m* (-s; -), **Si·bi·rie·rin** [ziˈbiːrïərɪn] *f* (-; -nen), **si·bi·risch** [ziˈbiːrɪʃ] *adj.* Siberian; *fig.* ***sibirische Kälte*** arctic temperatures

sich [zɪç] *pron.* a) oneself, yourself; himself, herself, itself; *pl.* themselves; *after prp.*: *usu.* him, her, it, *pl.* them, b) each other, one another; ***das Haus an*** ~ the house itself; ***an*** (***und für***) ~ actually, strictly speaking, when you think about it; ***sie haben kein Geld bei*** ~ they have no money with (*or* on) them; ***er kämpfte*** ~ ***durch die Menge*** he fought his way through the crowd; ***man muß*** ~ ***im klaren darüber sein, daß*** you've got to be aware of the fact that; ***sie blickte um*** ~ she looked around (her); ***hat er die Tür hinter*** ~ ***zugemacht?*** did he shut the door behind him?; ***vor*** ~ ***sah er*** in front of him he saw; ***sie kennen*** ~ they know each other; ***von*** ~ ***aus*** of one's own accord, F off one's own bat; ***er hat es von*** ~ ***aus getan*** *a.* nobody prompted him; ***er lud sie zu*** ~ ***ein*** he invited them to his house; ~ ***die Hände waschen*** wash one's hands; → ***auf*** 2, ***für*** I

Si·chel [ˈzɪçəl] *f* (-; -n) **1.** sickle; **2.** crescent; ˈ**si·chel·för·mig** [-fœrmɪç] *adj.* crescent-shaped

si·cher [ˈzɪçɐ] **I.** *adj.* **1.** secure, safe (***vor*** *dat.* from, *a. fig.*); firm; ***vor Neid ist keiner*** ~ none of us is above envy; ***vor ihm ist keiner*** ~ nobody's safe when he's around; ~ ***ist*** ~***!*** better safe than sorry; → ***Geleit***; **2.** a) certain, sure, b) reliable, safe; ~***er Sieg*** certain victory; ~***e Methode*** safe (F surefire) method; ***das ist der*** ~***e Tod*** that's certain death; ~***es Zeichen*** sure sign; ***soviel ist*** ~: this much is certain -; ***es ist nicht*** ~, ***ob*** we're *etc.* not absolutely sure whether, *a.* it hasn't been decided for sure whether; ***die Stelle ist ihm*** ~ he's got the job in his pocket; → ***Amen, Nummer, Quelle***; **3.** good, practi|ced (*Am.* -sed); reliable; ~***es Auftreten*** aplomb, self-assurance; ~***er Fahrer*** safe (*or* good) driver; ~***er Geschmack*** reliable (*or* sound) taste; ~***e Hand*** sure (*or* steady) hand; ~***er Instinkt*** sure instinct; ~***er Schütze*** sure shot; ~***es Urteil*** unfailing judg(e)ment; **4.** sure, certain; positive, confident; ***e-r Sache*** ~ ***sein*** be sure of s.th.; ***s-r Sache*** ~ ***sein*** be absolutely sure about what one is doing; ***er ist s-r Sache sehr*** ~ he's very sure of himself; ***sind Sie*** (***sich dessen***) ~***?*** are you sure (about that)?; *bist du sicher?* - ***ganz*** ~ (I'm) positive; ***du kannst*** ~ ***sein, daß*** you can be sure (*or* rest assured) that; **II.** *adv.* **5.** securely, safely *etc.*; ~ ***fahren*** be a safe driver; ***et.*** ~ ***aufbewahren*** keep s.th. in a safe place; ***nicht*** ~ ***auf den Beinen stehen*** be a bit wobbly; → ***sichergehen, sicherstellen***; **6.** *a. int.*: (***aber***) ~***!***, (***ganz***) ~***!*** → ***sicherlich***; **7.** ***s-e Vokabeln*** ~ ***können*** have (*or* know) one's vocabulary off pat; **8.** ~ ***auftreten*** have a self-confident manner, be very self-confident

ˈ**si·cher·ge·hen** *v/i.* (*irr.*, *sep.*, sn, → ***gehen***) play safe; make sure; ***um sicherzugehen*** to be on the safe side, to make sure

ˈ**Si·cher·heit** *f* (-; -en) **1.** *no pl.* safety; *a. pol.*, ⚔ security; ***öffentliche*** ~ public safety; *pol.* ***innere*** ~ internal security; ***in*** ~ ***bringen*** get *s.o.* out of danger (*or* into safety), *a.* get *s.th.* into a safe place, rescue; ***sich in*** ~ ***bringen*** get out of danger, ***durch e-n Sprung***: jump to safety; ***in*** ~ ***sein*** be safe (and sound); (***sich***) ***in*** ~ ***wiegen*** lull (o.s.) into a false sense of security; → ***Arbeitsplatz***; **2.** *no pl.* certainty; ***mit*** ~ definitely; ***aber mit*** ~***!*** no doubt about it, F you bet, you can bet your bottom dollar on that; ***ich weiß es mit*** ~ I know for sure (*or* for a fact); ***mit ziemlicher*** ~ almost certainly; ***man kann wohl mit*** ~ ***sagen*** it would be safe to say; ***man kann mit*** ~ ***annehmen*** one may safely assume; **3.** *no pl.* a) (self-)confidence, self-assurance, b) confidence *in English etc.*; **4.** *no pl.* competence; reliability; **5.** security; ✝ cover; ~ ***leisten*** give security, ***für*** *acc.*: secure *a loan*; ⚖ ~ ***stellen*** stand bail

ˈ**Si·cher·heits...** *in cpds. a.* ⚙ safety ...; *pol.*, ⚔, ✝, ⚖ security ...; **~ab·stand** *m* safe distance; ***den*** ~ ***einhalten*** keep a safe distance; **~be·am·te** *m* security man (*or* officer); **~be·auf·trag·te** *m* security officer; **~be·ra·ter** *m pol.* (national) security adviser; **~be·stim·mun·gen** *pl.* safety regulations; ✈ security (control) *sg.*, security regulations; **~bin·dung** *f skiing*: safety binding; **~bü·gel** *m mot.* roll bar; **~deˌbat·te** *f pol.* debate on security; **~de·fi·zit** *n* security gap (*or* breach); lapse in safety provision; **~film** *m* safety film; **~glas** *n* safety (*or* shatterproof) glass; **~grün·de** *pl.*: ***aus*** ~***n*** for reasons of safety, for safety's sake; **~gurt** *m* safety belt, *a.* ✈ seatbelt

ˈ**si·cher·heits·hal·ber** [-halbɐ] *adv.* for safety('s sake), as a precaution; (just) to be on the safe side

ˈ**Si·cher·heits|in·geˌnieur** *m* safety expert; **~ket·te** *f* safety chain; **~klau·sel** *f* escape clause; **~konˌtrol·le** *f* security check; **~koˌpie** *f computer*: backup (copy); **~kräf·te** *pl.* security forces; **~lam·pe** *f* ⚒ safety lamp; **~lei·stung** *f* security; ⚖ bail; **~man·gel** *m* → ***Sicherheitsdefizit***; **~maß·nah·me** *f* safety measure, precaution; *pol.* security measure; **~na·del** *f* safety pin; **~orˌga·ne** *pl.* organs of security; **~pakt** *m* security pact; **~po·liˌzei** *f* security police *pl.*; **~rat** *m*: (~ ***der Vereinten Nationen*** United Nations) Security Council; **~ri·si·ko** *n pol.* security risk; **~schloß** *n* safety (*or* security) lock; **~schwel·le** *f* safety threshold; **~sper·re** *f* security barrier; **~streit·kräf·te** *pl.*, **~trup·pen** *pl.* security forces; **~überˌprü·fung** *f* security check; **~venˌtil** *n* ⚙ safety valve; **~ver·stoß** *m* breach of security; security lapse; **~ver·wah·rung** *f* ⚖ preventive detention; **~vor·keh·rung** *f* safety precaution; *pol. etc.* security measure; ***unter strengen*** ~***en*** amid tight security; **~vor·schrif·ten** *pl.* safety regulations; **~zel·le** *f mot.* safety cell (*or* cage)

ˈ**si·cher·lich** *adv. and int.*: ***er hat's*** ~ ***vergessen*** he must have forgotten (it), he's bound to have forgotten (it), F I bet he's forgotten (it) ; ***er hat*** ~ ***kein Geld*** he probably hasn't got any money; ***sie kommt*** ~ I'm sure she'll come, she's bound to come; ~***!*** of course, sure!

si·chern [ˈzɪçɐn] (h) **I.** *v/t.* **1.** safeguard (***vor*** *dat.*, ***gegen*** *acc.* against); *a.* protect (from); **2.** guarantee; ensure; **3.** *computer*: save; **4.** get, secure; *a.* get hold of *tickets etc.*; **5.** secure *evidence etc.*; **6.** lock *gun*; → ***gesichert***; **II.** *v/refl.*: ***sich*** ~ ***vor*** *dat.* (*or* ***gegen*** *acc.*) protect o.s. from, guard against

ˈ**si·cher·stel·len** *v/t.* (*sep.*, h) **1.** seize; put in safekeeping; **2.** guarantee; *w.s. a.* ensure; ˈ**Si·cher·stel·lung** *f* (-; *no pl.*) **1.** seizure; **2.** guarantee(ing)

Si·che·rung [ˈzɪçərʊŋ] *f* (-; -en) **1.** ⚡ fuse; ⚙ safety device; safety catch *of a gun*; F *fig.* (***bei***) ***ihm ist die*** ~ ***durchgebrannt*** F he blew a fuse; **2.** *no pl.* safeguarding, protection, securing *etc.*; → ***sichern***

'Si·che·rungs|ka·sten *m* ↯ fuse box; **~ver·wah·rung** *f* preventive detention
'si·cher·wir·kend *adj.* reliable, F surefire *method etc.*
Sicht [zɪçt] *f* (-; *no pl.*) **1.** a) visibility, b) view; ***gute*** (***schlechte***) ~ high (low *or* poor) visibility; ***außer*** ~ out of sight; ***in*** ~ (with)in view, within eyeshot; ***in ~ kommen*** come into view; ***von hier hat man e-e weite*** ~ you can see for miles from here; *fig.* ***auf lange*** (*or* ***weite***) ~ on a long-term basis, in the long run; ***auf kurze*** ~ in the short term; ***aus s-r*** ~ from his point of view, as he sees it; ***es ist keine Besserung in*** ~ there's no prospect (*or* hope) of improvement; ***es ist nichts in*** ~ there doesn't seem to be anything coming up (*or* in the offing); **2.** ☤ ***auf*** (*or* ***bei***) ~ at sight; (***zahlbar***) ***sechzig Tage nach*** ~ (payable) at sixty days' sight
'sicht·bar I. *adj.* a) visible; exposed, b) noticeable, perceptible; marked; obvious, evident, clear; ***ohne ~en Erfolg*** *a.* without appreciable success; ~ ***werden*** become visible *etc.*, appear, *fig. a.* become apparent; **II.** *adv.*: ***es*** (***er***) ***hat sich ~ gebessert*** there's been (he's shown) a marked improvement
'Sicht|be·hin·de·rung *f* poor visibility (***durch*** *acc.* due to); **~ein·la·ge** *f banking*: sight deposit
sich·ten ['zɪçtən] *v/t.* (h) **1.** sight; **2.** look (*or* go, sift) through; sort out
'Sicht|fen·ster *n* window; **~flug** *m* ✈ contact flight; **~ge·rät** *n* visual display unit; **~gren·ze** *f* visibility limit; ***die ~ beträgt*** visibility is up (*or* down) to; **~kar·te** *f* travel pass; season ticket
'sicht·lich I. *adj.* visible; **II.** *adv.* visibly; evidently; ***er war ~ nervös*** he was clearly (*or* visibly) nervous, you could tell he was nervous
Sich·tung ['zɪçtʊŋ] *f* (-; *no pl.*) **1.** sighting; **2.** examination; sifting, screening
'Sicht|ver·bin·dung *f* visual contact; **~ver·hält·nis·se** *pl.*: (***gute, schlechte*** ~ high, low) visibility *sg.*; **~ver·merk** *m* **1.** visa; **2.** ☤ endorsement; **~wech·sel** *m* ☤ bill payable on demand; **~wei·te** *f* range of vision; ***in*** ~ (with)in sight, within eyeshot; ***außer*** ~ out of sight
Sicker·gru·be ['zɪkɐ-] (*sep.* -k·k-) *f* soakaway, *Am.* dry well
sickern ['zɪkɐn] (*sep.* -k·k-) *v/i.* (sn) seep, trickle (***aus*** *dat.* out of; ***in*** *acc.* into); *fig.* (*a.* ***an die Öffentlichkeit*** ~) leak out; → *a.* ***durchsickern, einsickern***
Sicker·was·ser ['zɪkɐ-] (*sep.* -k·k-) *n* seeping water; ground water
si·de·risch [zi'de:rɪʃ] *adj. ast.* sidereal
sie [zi:] *pers. pron.* **1.** *3. person f/sg.*: she, *acc.* her; it; **2.** *3. person pl.*: they, *acc.* them; **3.** 2 *address*: you (*a. acc.*); ***zu j-m*** 2 ***sagen*** → ***siezen***
Sie *f* (-; -s) **1.** ***es ist e-e*** ~ *a. zo.* it's a she; **2.** *on towels etc.*: hers
Sieb [zi:p] *n* (-[e]s; -e ['zi:bə]) sieve; strainer; *gastr. a.* colander; ⚙ riddle, screen; ***ein Gedächtnis wie ein*** ~ a memory like a sieve; **~druck** *m typ.* silk-screen print (*or* printing)
sie·ben¹ ['zi:bən] *v/t.* (h) (pass through a) sieve; *gastr. a.* strain, sift; ⚙ riddle, screen; *fig.* sift through; *fig.* ***da wird ganz schön gesiebt*** they have a tough screening procedure, F they really pick and choose
sie·ben² ['zi:bən] *adj.* seven; **'Sie·ben** *f* (-; -[en]) **1.** seven; **2.** *bus etc.* number seven
'sie·ben·bän·dig [-bɛndɪç] *adj.* seven-volume ..., in seven volumes
Sie·ben'bür·ger *m* (-s; -), **Sie·ben'bür·ge·rin** *f* (-; -nen) Transylvanian (German); *ethnic German from Transylvania*; **sie·ben·bür·gisch** [-'bʏrgɪʃ] *adj.* Transylvanian
'Sie·ben·eck *n* heptagon
'sie·ben·eckig *adj.* heptagonal
'sie·ben·fach *adj.* sevenfold; **~e *Menge*** seven times the amount; **~er *Sieger*** seven-time winner (*or* champion)
'sie·ben·ge·scheit F *adj.* F smart-alecky
'Sie·ben·ge·stirn *n the* Pleiades *pl., the* Seven Sisters *pl.*
Sie·ben'hü·gel·stadt *f* (*Rome*) City of the Seven Hills
'sie·ben'hun·dert *adj.* seven hundred
'sie·ben·jäh·rig [-jɛ:rɪç] *adj.* **1.** seven-year-old ...; **2.** seven-year ...; ***ein ~es ...*** *a.* seven years of ...
'sie·ben·köp·fig [-kœpfɪç] *adj. family etc.* of seven; **~e *Delegation*** *etc. a.* seven-member (*or* -man) delegation *etc.*
'sie·ben·mal *adv.* seven times
Sie·ben'mei·len·stie·fel *pl.* seven-league boots
Sie·ben'mo·nats·kind *n* seven-month baby
'Sie·ben·pfün·der [-pfʏndɐ] *m* (-s; -) seven-pound baby *etc.*; seven-pounder
'Sie·ben'sa·chen *pl.* (all one's) things; ***hast du d-e ~ zusammen?*** *a.* F have you got all your bits and pieces (together)?
'Sie·ben·schlä·fer *m* (-s; -) **1.** *zo.* dormouse; **2.** *no pl.* 27th June (*the weather on this day being said to determine that of the next seven weeks*); St Swithin's Day
'sie·ben|stel·lig [-ʃtɛlɪç] *adj.* seven-digit *figure etc.*; **~stöckig** [-ʃtœkɪç] (*sep.* -k·k-) *adj.* seven-stor(e)y ...; **~stün·dig** [-ʃtʏndɪç] *adj.* seven-hour(-long) ...
sie·bent ['zi:bənt] **I.** *adj.* seventh; **~es *Kapitel*** chapter seven; ***am ~en März*** on the seventh of March, on March the seventh; **7. *März*** 7th March, March 7(th); **II.** *adv.*: ***wir waren zu*** ~ there were seven of us; ***wir gingen zu ~ hin*** seven of us went
'sie·ben·tä·gig [-tɛ:gɪç] *adj.* **1.** seven-day(-long) ...; **2.** seven-day-old ...
'sie·ben'tau·send *adj.* seven thousand; **'Sie·ben'tau·sen·der** *m* seven-thousand metre (*Am.* meter) peak
Sie·ben·te ['zi:bəntə] *m, f* (-n; -n) (the) seventh; ***er war ~r*** he was (*or* came) seventh; ***Eduard VII.*** Edward VII (= Edward the Seventh); ***heute ist der*** ~ it's the seventh today
'sie·ben·tei·lig [-taɪlɪç] *adj.* seven-part ..., in seven parts
Sie·ben·tel ['zi:bəntəl] *n* (-s; -) seventh
sie·ben·tens ['zi:bəntəns] *adv.* seventh(ly), seven, in the seventh place
siebt [zi:pt] *etc.* → ***siebent*** *etc.*
Sieb·tel ['zi:ptəl] *n* (-s; -) seventh
sieb·zehn ['zi:ptse:n] *adj.* seventeen; 2 ***und Vier*** pontoon, *Am.* blackjack
'sieb·zehnt *adj.* seventeenth
'Siebzehn·tel *n* (-s; -) seventeenth (part)
sieb·zig ['zi:ptsɪç] *adj.* seventy; ***in den ~er Jahren*** in the seventies; ***sie ist in den Siebzigern*** she's in her seventies
Sieb·zi·ger ['zi:ptsɪgɐ] *m* (-s; -), **Sieb·zi·ge·rin** ['zi:ptsɪgərɪn] *f* (-; -nen) septuagenarian, man (*f* woman) in his (her) seventies, F seventysomething
'sieb·zig·jäh·rig [-jɛ:rɪç] *adj.* **1.** seventy-year-old ...; **2.** seventy-year(-long) ...
sieb·zigst ['zi:ptsɪçst] *adj.* seventieth; ***sie hat heute ihren 2en*** she's seventy today, it's her seventieth birthday today
siech [zi:ç] *obs. adj.* infirm, ailing; ***alt und*** ~ old and infirm; **'Siech·tum** *n* (-s; *no pl.*) infirmity
sie·de'heiß ['zi:də-] *adj.* scalding (hot), boiling hot; **'Sie·de·hit·ze** *f* boiling heat
sie·deln ['zi:dəln] *v/i.* (h) settle
sie·den ['zi:dən] (h) **I.** *v/i.* boil; simmer; *fig. a.* seethe; ***es siedete in ihr*** she was seething (inside *or* with rage, anger); **II.** *v/t.* boil, simmer; **'sie·dend I.** *adj.* boiling; *fig. a.* seething (with); **II.** *adv.*: ~ ***heiß*** scalding (hot), boiling (*gastr.* piping) hot; F ***da fiel mir ~ heiß ein*** it suddenly struck me, I suddenly remembered with a shock
Sie·de·punkt ['zi:də-] *m* boiling point (*a. fig.*); *fig. pol. a.* flashpoint; *fig.* ***den ~ erreichen*** reach boiling point (*or* a flashpoint)
Sied·ler ['zi:dlɐ] *m* (-s; -), **Sied·le·rin** ['zi:dlərɪn] *f* (-; -nen) settler
Sied·lung ['zi:dlʊŋ] *f* (-; -en) **1.** settlement; **2.** housing estate, development
'Sied·lungs|dich·te *f* population density; **~ge·biet** *n* settlement (area); **~po·li·tik** *f* settlement policies *pl.*
Sieg [zi:k] *m* (-[e]s; -e ['zi:gə]) victory; *sport etc.*: *a.* win; *fig.* triumph; ***leichter*** ~ walkover, *Am.* walkaway; ***den ~ davontragen*** carry (*or* win) the day; ***am Ende den ~ davontragen*** win out in the end
Sie·gel ['zi:gəl] *n* (-s; -) seal (*a. fig.*); *fig.* ***ein Buch mit sieben ~n*** a closed book (*dat.* to); ***er hat es mir unter dem ~ der Verschwiegenheit erzählt*** he told me in the strictest confidence, he swore me to secrecy
'Sie·gel·lack *m* sealing wax
'sie·geln *v/t.* (h) seal (*a.* ⚙)
'Sie·gel·ring *m* signet ring
sie·gen ['zi:gən] *v/i.* (h) **1.** win; ~ ***über*** *acc.* defeat, beat; **2.** ⚔ *etc.* win; be victorious (***über*** *acc.* over); *fig. justice etc.*: triumph (over), carry the day; *fig.* ***die Wahrheit siegte*** *a.* truth prevailed (*or* won out in the end)
Sie·ger ['zi:gɐ] *m* (-s; -) **1.** *sport etc.*: winner; *lit.* victor; ***zweiter*** ~ runner-up; **2.** ⚔ victor; *a.* victorious nation; **~eh·rung** *f sport*: presentation ceremony
Sie·ge·rin ['zi:gərɪn] *f* (-; -nen) → ***Sieger*** 1
'Sie·ger|macht *f* victorious power; *pol. hist.* ***die vier Siegermächte*** the four allied powers (*or* allies) *of World War II*; **~mann·schaft** *f sport*: winning team; **~po·dest** *n sport*: victory rostrum; **~po·kal** *m* (winner's) cup; **~po·se** *f* victorious pose; **~ur·kun·de** *f* (winner's) certificate
sie·ges·be·wußt ['zi:gəs-] *adj.* confident of victory; *fig.* confident, *contp.* cocksure
Sie·ges|chan·ce ['zi:gəs-] *f* chance of winning; **~fei·er** *f* victory celebration(s *pl.*)
sie·ges·ge·wiß ['zi:gəs-] *adj.* → ***siegessicher***
Sie·ges|göt·tin ['zi:gəs-] *f* goddess of victory; ***die*** ~ Victory; **~kranz** *m* laurel wreath; **~lor·beer** *lit. m* laurel wreath, victor's laurels *pl.*; **~preis** *m* prize;

~rausch *m* flush of victory; **~säu·le** *f* triumphal (*or* victory) column
sie·ges·si·cher ['zi:gəs-] *adj.* confident of victory; *fig.* confident, *contp.* cocksure
Sie·ges|tor ['zi:gəs-] *n* **1.** triumphal arch(way); **2.** → **~tref·fer** *m* winning goal; **~tro͵phäe** *f* **1.** (winner's) trophy; **2.** scalp, trophy
sie·ges·trun·ken ['zi:gəs-] *adj.* drunk (*or* flushed) with victory, triumphant
Sie·ges|wil·le(n) ['zi:gəs-] *m* will to win (*fig.* succeed); **~zug** *m* triumphal procession; *fig.* triumphant advance; *fig.* ***s-n ~ antreten*** set out to conquer the (film, literary *etc.*) world *etc.*
'sieg·reich *adj.* **1.** *sport etc.*: winning ...; *a. fig.* successful, *lit.* victorious; *adv. ein Turnier etc.* ~ ***beenden*** win, *lit.* emerge victorious from; **2.** victorious *battle etc.*; *a.* triumphant *army*
Siel [zi:l] *m, n* (-[e]s; -e) **1.** floodgate, sluice; **2.** sewer
Sie·le ['zi:lə] *f* (-; -n): *fig.* ***in den ~n sterben*** die with one's boots on
Sie·sta ['zĭesta] *f* (-; -s) siesta, afternoon nap; ~ ***halten*** have a (*or* one's) siesta, have an (*or* one's) afternoon nap
sie·zen ['zi:tsən] *v/t.* (h) address *s.o.* as 'Sie', say 'Sie' to *s.o.*
Si·gel ['zi:gəl] *n* (-s; -) short form, abbreviation; 🕮 grammalog(ue)
Si·gnal [zɪ'gna:l] *n* (-s; -e) signal; sign; ***ein ~ geben*** (give a) signal; *mot.* ~ ***geben*** sound one's horn; ***das ~ für Gefahr*** the danger signal, the signal for danger; ***das ~ zum Angriff*** the signal to attack; *fig.* ***das ~ zum Aufbruch*** the sign (for us *etc.*) to leave; ***alle ~e stehen auf*** *dat.* ... all the pointers are in favo(u)r of ...; ***~e setzen*** point the way to the future; **~an·la·ge** *f* signal(l)ing system; **~aus·fall** *m* dropout; **~brü·cke** *f* 🚂 (signal) gantry; **~far·be** *f* striking colo(u)r; **~flag·ge** *f* signal flag; **~gast** *m* (-[e]s; -en) ⚓ signalman
si·gna·li·sie·ren [zɪgnali'zi:rən] *v/t.* (h) signal; *fig. a.* signalize; be a sign of; *fig.* ***es signalisierte mir, daß*** it signalled to me that, it told me (that), I took it as a sign that
Si'gnal|lam·pe *f*, **~leuch·te** *f* signal lamp; **~mast** *m* signal mast, semaphore; **~stär·ke** *f radio etc.*: signal strength; **~wir·kung** *f*: ~ ***haben*** point the way to the future
Si·gna·tar·macht [zɪgna'ta:ʀ-] *f* signatory (state *or* power)
Si·gna·tur [zɪgna'tu:ʀ] *f* (-; -en [-'tu:rən]) a) signature (*a.* ♪), b) *typ.* signature (mark), nick, c) *library*: shelfmark, *Am.* call number, d) *geogr.* conventional sign
Si·gnet [zɪ'gne:t] *n* (-s; -e) (publisher's) imprint, publisher's mark
si·gnie·ren [zɪ'gni:rən] *v/t.* (h) sign; ***sie wird hinterher ihr neuestes Buch ~*** she'll be signing copies of her latest book afterwards; **si·gniert** [zɪ'gni:ʀt] *adj.* signed; ***~es Exemplar*** signed copy
si·gni·fi·kant [zɪgnifi'kant] *adj.* (highly) significant; significant *characteristics*
Si·gni·fi·kanz [zɪgnifi'kants] *f* (-; *no pl.*) significance, implications *pl.*
Sikh [zi:k] *m* (-[s]; -s) Sikh; **Si·khis·mus** [zi'kɪsmʊs] *m* (-; *no pl.*) Sikhism
Sil·be ['zɪlbə] *f* (-; -n) syllable; *fig.* ***keine ~*** not a word; ***ich verstehe keine ~*** I can't understand a word, it's all Greek to me
'Sil·ben·tren·nung *f* syllabification; word division, hyphenation
'Sil·ben·tren·nungs·pro͵gramm *n computer*: hyphenation program(me)
Sil·ber ['zɪlbʀ] *n* (-s; *no pl.*) **1.** silver; ***aus ~*** (made of) silver; **2.** silver(ware); **~be·steck** *n* silver (cutlery); **~blick** F *m* (-[e]s; *no pl.*) (slight) cast; **~di·stel** *f* ⚘ carline thistle; **~draht** *m* silver wire; **~erz** *n* silver ore; **2far·ben, 2far·big** *adj.* silver(y); **~fisch·chen** *n* silverfish; **~fo·lie** *f* silver foil; **~fuchs** *m* silver fox; **~geld** *n* silver; **~ge·schirr** *n* silver(ware)
'sil·ber·grau *adj.* silver(y)-grey (*Am.* -gray)
'sil·ber·hal·tig [-haltɪç] *adj.* containing silver, 🕮 argentiferous
'sil·ber·hell *adj.* silvery *sound, voice etc.*
'Sil·ber|hoch·zeit *f* silver wedding; **~klang** *poet. m* silvery sound
Sil·ber·ling ['zɪlbʀlɪŋ] *m* (-s; -e) *bibl.* piece of silver
'Sil·ber·me͵dail·le *f* silver medal
'Sil·ber·me͵dail·len·ge·win·ner *m* silver medal(l)ist
'Sil·ber|mö·we *f* silvery gull; **~mün·ze** *f* silver coin
sil·bern ['zɪlbʀn] *adj.* **1.** silver; **2.** *fig.* silvery *voice etc.*
'Sil·ber|pa͵pier *n* silver (*or* tin) foil; **~pap·pel** *f* ⚘ white poplar; **~rei·her** *m* great white heron; **~schmied** *m* silversmith; **~strei·fen** *m*: *fig.* ~ ***am Horizont*** ray of hope; **~wäh·rung** *f* silver standard; **~wa·ren** *pl.* silver(ware) *sg.*
silb·rig ['zɪlbrɪç] *adj.* silvery, silver
Sil·hou·et·te [zi'lŭetə] *f* (-; -n) silhouette, outline; *a.* shadow, dark shape, contours *pl. of a mountain etc.*; skyline *of a city*; ***sich als ~ abzeichnen gegen*** *acc.* be silhouetted (*or* outlined) against
Si·li·kat [zili'ka:t] *n* (-[e]s; -e) ⚗ silicate
Si·li·kon [zili'ko:n] *n* (-s; -e) ⚗ silicone
Si·li·zi·um [zi'li:tsĭʊm] *n* (-s; *no pl.*) ⚗ silicon; **~chip** *m* silicon chip
Si·lo ['zi:lo] *m* (-s; -s) silo; **~fut·ter** *n* silage
Sil·ve·ster [zɪl'vɛstʀ] *m, n* (-s; -) New Year's Eve; ***zu ~*** on New Year's Eve; **~abend** *m* New Year's Eve; **~ball** *m* New Year's Eve ball; **~fei·er** *f* New Year's Eve party; **~nacht** *f* night of New Year's Eve
Sim·mer·ring ['zɪmʀ-] *m* ⚙ shaft seal
sim·pel ['zɪmpəl] **I.** *adj.* a) simple; plain, b) simple(-minded); ***es fehlt an den ~sten Dingen*** some of the most basic things are missing; **II.** 2 F *m* (-s; -) simpleton, F dimwit
Sim·pli·fi·ka·ti·on [zɪmplifika'tsĭo:n] *f* (-; -en) simplification; **sim·pli·fi·zie·ren** [zɪmplifi'tsi:rən] *v/t.* (h) simplify; **Sim·pli·fi'zie·rung** *f* (-; -en) simplification
Sims [zɪms] *m, n* (-es; -e) ledge; △ cornice; mantelpiece
Sim·sa·la·bim [zɪmzala'bɪm] *int.* abracadabra!
Si·mu·lant [zimu'lant] *m* (-en; -en) malingerer
Si·mu·la·tor [zimu'la:to:ʀ] *m* (-s; -en [-la'to:rən]) ⚙ simulator
si·mu·lie·ren [zimu'li:rən] (h) **I.** *v/t.* **1.** sham, feign (illness); **2.** ⚙, ⚔ simulate; **II.** *v/i.* sham, F put it on; malinger
si·mul·tan [zimʊl'ta:n] *adj.* simultaneous
Si·mul'tan|dol·met·schen *n* simultaneous translation; **~dol·met·scher** *m* simultaneous translator; **~schach** *n* simultaneous chess; **~über͵tra·gung** *f radio, TV*: simultaneous broadcast, simulcast
si·ne tem·po·re ['zi:nə 'tɛmpore] *adv.* → ***s.t.***
Sin·fo·nie [zɪnfo'ni:] *f* (-; -n) symphony; **Sin·fo'nie·or͵ches·ter** *n* symphony orchestra; **Sin·fo·ni·et·ta** [zɪnfo'nĭeta] *f* (-; -ten [-tən]) sinfonietta; **sin·fo·nisch** [zɪn'fo:nɪʃ] *adj.* symphonic(ally *adv.*); ***~e Dichtung*** tone poem
Sin·ga·pu·rer ['zɪŋgapu:rʀ] *m* (-s; -), **Sin·ga·pu·re·rin** ['zɪŋgapu:rərɪn] *f* (-; -nen), **sin·ga·pu·risch** ['zɪŋgapu:rɪʃ] *adj.* Singaporean
Sing·dros·sel ['zɪŋ-] *f* song thrush
sin·gen ['zɪŋən] *v/i. and v/t.* (sang, gesungen, h) **1.** sing; *eccl.* chant; ***richtig (falsch) ~*** sing in (out of) tune; ***~der Tonfall*** lilting voice; ***es singt mir im Ohr*** my ears are ringing; F ***das kann ich schon ~*** I suppose I'll never hear the end of that; → ***Blatt*** 1, ***Lied, Schlaf***; **2.** (*only v/i.*) a) buzz, hum, b) F squeal
Sin·gha·le·se [zɪŋga'le:zə] *m* (-n; -n), **Sin·gha·le·sin** [zɪŋga'le:zɪn] *f* (-; -nen), **sin·gha·le·sisch** [zɪŋga'le:zɪʃ] *adj.*, **Sin·gha'le·sisch** *n* (-en) *ling.* Sin(g)halese
Sin·gle¹ ['sɪŋgl] *f* (-; -s) single
'Sin·gle² *n* (-[s]; -[s]) *tennis*: singles *sg.*
'Sin·gle³ *m* (-[s]; -s) single person; single man (*or* woman); *pl.* singles; ***ein ~ sein*** be single, *a.* be a bachelor; **~da·sein** *n*, **~le·ben** *n* life as a single, singlehood; **~lo͵kal** *n* singles bar; **~sze·ne** *f* singles scene
Sing·sang ['zɪŋzaŋ] *m* (-s; *no pl.*) low, monotonous singing; ***man hörte s-n leisen ~*** you could hear him quietly singing away to himself
Sing·stim·me ['zɪŋ-] *f* singing voice
Sin·gu·lar ['zɪŋgula:ʀ] *m* (-s; *no pl.*) *ling.*: (***im ~*** in the) singular
Sing·vo·gel ['zɪŋ-] *m* songbird
sin·ken ['zɪŋkən] *v/i.* (sank, gesunken, sn) a) sink; *ship*: *a.* go down; *high water etc.*: subside; *fog*: descend, come down, b) *fig. prices, temperature etc.*: fall, drop, go down; *influence, reputation etc.*: diminish; *hope*: fade; ***j-m in die Arme ~*** fall into s.o.'s arms; ***zu Boden ~*** sink (*or* drop) to the ground; ***auf die Knie ~*** drop to one's knees; ***ins Bett ~*** fall (*or* collapse) into bed; ***in e-n Sessel ~*** sink (*or* collapse) into an armchair; ***~ lassen*** lower, drop (*a. voice*); ***den Kopf ~ lassen*** hang one's head; *fig.* ***s-e Stimmung sank*** his spirits sank; ***er ist tief gesunken*** he has sunk very low; ***in j-s Achtung ~*** go down in s.o.'s opinion (*or* esteem); → ***Mut, Ohnmacht*** 2, ***Wert***
'sin·kend *adj.* falling *prices, temperature etc.*; ***ein ~es Schiff*** a sinking ship; ***die ~e Sonne*** the setting sun; *fig.* ***~es Glück*** flagging fortunes
Sinn [zɪn] *m* (-[e]s; -e) **1.** sense; ***sechster ~*** sixth sense; ***~e*** a) lust *sg.*, desires, b) consciousness *sg.*; ***s-e fünf ~e beisammenhaben*** have one's wits about one; **2.** *no pl.* a) mind; sense (***für*** *acc.* of), feeling (for), b) sense, meaning, (basic) idea; purpose; ***der ~ des Lebens*** the meaning of life; ***~ und Zweck*** the (whole) object *or* purpose; ***ohne ~ und Verstand*** without rhyme or reason; ***aus den Augen, aus dem ~*** out of sight, out of mind; ***mit j-m eines ~es sein*** be of one mind with s.o., see eye to eye with s.o.; ***~ haben für*** *acc.* (be able to) appreciate; ***sie hat keinen ~ dafür*** she has no appreciation for

that kind of thing; ***dafür habe ich keinen ~*** it doesn't mean anything to me (F do anything for me), F it's not really my thing (*or* my cup of tea); ***~ für Musik** an* ear for music; ***er hat keinen ~ für Musik** a.* he's completely unmusical; ***nur ~ für Geld haben*** only be interested in money; ***~ für das Schöne*** an eye for beauty, a sense of beauty; ***~ für das Ästhetische** an* (a)esthetic sense, (a)esthetic sensitivity; ***~ für Humor*** sense of humo(u)r; ***das ist so recht nach s-m ~*** that's exactly what he likes; ***mir steht der ~ nicht danach*** I don't feel like it; ***bist du von ~en?*** are you out of your (F tiny little) mind?; ***im ~ haben*** have in mind, ***zu** inf.*: plan (*or* intend) to *inf.*; ***im wahrsten ~e des Wortes*** in the true sense of the word, literally; ***im engeren (weiteren) ~e*** in the narrower (wider) sense; ***im ~e des Gesetzes*** *etc.* for the purposes of (*or* as defined by) the law *etc.*; ***et. im ~ behalten*** keep (*or* bear) s.th. in mind; ***sich im gleichen ~e äußern*** express o.s. along the same lines, say more or less the same (thing); ***ganz in m-m ~*** a) that suits me fine, b) just as I would have done; ***in diesem ~e*** with this in mind, in this spirit, *part etc.* on this note; ***es kam mir in den ~*** it occurred to me; ***es kam mir nie in den ~** a.* it never entered my head; ***es will mir nicht aus dem ~*** I can't get it out of my mind; ***das will mir nicht in den ~*** I just can't understand it; ***das gibt keinen ~*** that doesn't make sense; ***das hat keinen ~*** it's no use; ***es hat keinen ~ zu** inf.* there's no point in *ger.*; ***was hat es für e-n ~ zu** inf.* what's the point of (*or* in) *ger.*; ***ich kann keinen ~ darin sehen zu** inf.* I don't see the point of (*or* in) *ger.*; ***das ist der ~ der Sache*** that's the whole point; ***das ist nicht der ~ der Sache*** that's not the object of the exercise; F ***das ist nicht im ~e des Erfinders*** that wasn't the object of the exercise, that's not really what we intended; → ***schlagen*** I, ***schwinden***

'Sinn·bild *n* symbol (**für** *acc.* of); allegory (of); **'sinn·bild·lich** *adj.* symbolic(ally *adv.*); allegorical; ***~e Darstellung*** a) symbolic representation, b) allegory

sin·nen ['zɪnən] (sann, gesonnen, h) **I.** *v/i.* reflect (**über** *acc.* [up]on), think (about); ~ ***auf** acc.* contemplate, plan, *b.s.* plot *revenge*, plan *a murder etc.*; ***was sinnst du?*** what are you pondering over?; → ***gesinnt, gesonnen***; **II.** ⁓ *n* (-s; *no pl.*) reflection; ***sein ~ und Trachten auf et. richten*** concentrate one's thought and wish on s.th.; **'sin·nend** *adj.* pensive, thoughtful

'Sin·nen·freu·de *f* sensual enjoyment, sensuality

'sin·nen·freu·dig, 'sin·nen·froh *adj.* sensuous

'Sin·nen|lust *f* sensual enjoyment, sensuality; **~mensch** *m* sensuous person; **~reiz** *m* sensual stimulus

'sinn·ent·leert *adj.* meaningless, hollow

'sinn·ent·stel·lend *adj.* misleading; ***e-e ~e Übersetzung*** *etc.* a translation *etc.* which distorts the meaning

'Sin·nen·welt *f* material world

'Sin·nes|än·de·rung *f* change of heart; **~art** *f* disposition; way of thinking; (mental) attitude; **~ein·druck** *m* sensation, sense impression; **~nerv** *m* sensory nerve; **~or,gan** *n* sense organ; **~reiz** *m* sensory stimulus; **~täu·schung** *f* hallucination; **~wahr·neh·mung** *f* sensory perception; **~wan·del** *m* change of heart

'sinn·fäl·lig *adj.* obvious; clear; ***~er Vergleich*** apt comparison, good analogy

'Sinn|ge·bung [-ge:bʊŋ] *f* (-; -en) interpretation; **~ge·dicht** *n* epigram

'sinn·ge·mäß I. *adj.* **1.** ***~e Wiedergabe*** *etc.* rough summary *etc.*; **2.** logical; **II.** *adv.*: ***~ schreibt er*** the gist of what he writes is, basically what he writes is; ***~ übersetzt*** *etc.* roughly translated *etc.*

'sinn·ge·treu *adj.* faithful

'sinn·gleich *adj.* synonymous

sin·nie·ren [zɪ'ni:rən] *v/i.* (h) muse, brood, ruminate (**über** *acc.* on, about)

sin·nig ['zɪnɪç] *adj. usu. iro.* clever; appropriate

'sinn·lich *adj.* sensuous (*a. phls.*); F sexy; ***~e Liebe*** sensual love; ***ein ~er Mensch*** a very physical person; → ***Wahrnehmung*** 1; **'Sinn·lich·keit** *f* sensuality, voluptuousness; sensuousness

'sinn·los I. *adj.* pointless, useless, futile, *pred. a.* no use; stupid, senseless; meaningless; ***~e Gewalttätigkeit*** mindless violence; ***es ist ~ zu** inf. a.* there's no point in *ger.*; ***das ist völlig ~*** it doesn't make any sense at all; ***es ist alles so ~*** it's all so meaningless (*or* pointless); **II.** *adv.*: ***sich ~ betrinken*** drink o.s. silly (*or* into a stupor); ***~ betrunken*** blind drunk

'Sinn·lo·sig·keit *f* (-; *no pl.*) futility, pointlessness; senselessness; meaninglessness *etc.*; → ***sinnlos***

'sinn·reich *adj.* **1.** ingenious, clever (*a. iro.*); **2.** profound

'Sinn·spruch *m* aphorism; maxim

'sinn·ver·wandt *adj.* synonymous; ***~es Wort*** synonym

'Sinn·ver·wandt·schaft *f* synonymity

'sinn·ver·wir·rend *adj.* bewildering

'sinn·voll *adj.* **1.** a) sensible, *pred. a.* a good idea; wise, b) practical, useful; ***es wäre nicht sehr ~ zu** inf.* it wouldn't be a very good idea to *inf.*, it would be pointless to *inf.*; ***ökonomisch ~ sein*** make good economic sense; **2.** meaningful

'sinn·wid·rig *adj.* absurd

'Sinn·wid·rig·keit *f* (-; *no pl.*) absurdity

'Sinn·zu,sam·men·hang *m* context

Si·no·lo·ge [zino'lo:gə] *m* (-n; -n) Sinologist; **Si·no·lo·gie** [zinolo'gi:] *f* (-; *no pl.*) Chinese studies *pl.*, Sinology

Sint·flut ['zɪnt-] *f* (-; *no pl.*) deluge, flood (*a. fig.*); *bibl. the* Flood; F ***nach uns die ~!*** après nous le déluge

'sint·flut·ar·tig *adj.* torrential *rain*

Sin·ti ['zɪnti] *pl.* Sinti (gypsies)

Si·nus ['zi:nʊs] *m* (-; - ['zi:nu:s] *and* -se ['zi:nʊsə]) **1.** Å sine; **2.** *anat.* sinus; **~kur·ve** *f* Å sinus curve; **~satz** *m* Å sine theorem; **~schwin·gung** *f phys.* harmonic (*or* sinusoidal) oscillation

Si·phon ['zi:fõ] *m* (-s; -s) **1.** soda siphon; **2.** ⚙ siphon

Sip·pe ['zɪpə] *f* (-; -n) family, F clan; tribe; → ***Sippschaft***

'Sip·pen|for·schung *f* genealogical research; **~haft** *f liability of a family for (political) crimes or actions of one of its members*

Sipp·schaft ['zɪpʃaft] *contp. f* (-; -en) **1.** F clan; ***mit der ganzen ~ ankommen*** come with the whole family (*or* clan) in tow; **2.** F riffraff, rabble

Si·re·ne [zi're:nə] *f* (-; -n) *myth. and* ⚙ siren

Si're·nen|ge·heul *n* wailing (of) sirens *pl.*; ***man hörte das ~** a.* you could hear the sirens wailing; **~ge·sang** *m* siren song

sir·ren ['zɪrən] *v/i.* (h) buzz

Si·rup ['zi:rʊp] *m* (-s; *no pl.*) treacle, *Am.* molasses (*sg.*); syrup

Si·sal ['zi:zal] *m* (-s; *no pl.*) sisal; **~hanf** *m* sisal (hemp); **~tep·pich** *m* sisal mat

Si·sy·phus·ar·beit ['zi:zyfʊs-] *f* Sisyphean task

Sit·te ['zɪtə] *f* (-; -n) **1.** custom; ***~n und Gebräuche*** customs and way of life; ***es ist ~, daß der Ehemann ...*** it is the custom for the husband to *inf.*; ***die ~ verlangt, daß*** tradition (*or* social etiquette) demands that; ***das ist bei uns nicht ~*** we don't do that around here (*or* in these parts); F ***dort herrschen rauhe ~n*** F they're a rough lot; ***was sind denn das für ~n?*** where did you pick that up?, who taught you that?; ***das sind ja ganz neue ~n!*** things have changed around here; ***das verstößt gegen alle ~n*** that goes against all etiquette (*or* public decency); ***lockere ~n*** loose morals; ***hier herrschen strenge ~n*** the rules are tough around here; **2.** *no pl.* F vice squad

'Sit·ten|apo·stel *m* moralizer; **~bild** *n* **1.** ***ein ~ der (damaligen) Zeit*** a portrayal of the customs and morals of the time; **2.** *art*: genre painting; **~de·zer,nat** *n* vice squad, public morals department; **~ge·mäl·de** *n* → ***Sittenbild***; **~ko·dex** *m* moral code, code of ethics, mores *pl.*; **~ko,mö·die** *f* comedy of manners; **~leh·re** *f* ethics *pl.*, moral philosophy

'sit·ten·los *adj.* immoral, dissolute

'Sit·ten·lo·sig·keit *f* (-; *no pl.*) immorality, (complete) lack of morals

'Sit·ten|po·li,zei *f* vice squad; **~pre·di·ger** *m* moralizer; **~rich·ter** *m* moral censor; ***sich zum ~ aufwerfen*** set o.s. up as a moral censor

'sit·ten·streng *adj.* austere; *w.s.* puritanical; **'Sit·ten·stren·ge** *f* austerity; high moral standards *pl.*; *w.s.* puritanism

'Sit·ten|strolch *m* (sexual) molester, sex offender; **~ver·fall** *m* moral decline

'sit·ten·wid·rig *adj.* immoral; ⚖ *a.* unethical

Sit·tich ['zɪtɪç] *m* (-s; -e) *zo.* parakeet

sitt·lich ['zɪtlɪç] *adj.* moral; ethical; ***ihm fehlt die ~e Reife*** he lacks maturity

'Sitt·lich·keit *f* (-; *no pl.*) morality; morals *pl.*

'Sitt·lich·keits|de,likt *n*, **~ver·bre·chen** *n* sex crime, sex offen|ce (*Am.* -se); **~ver·bre·cher** *m* sex offender

sitt·sam ['zɪtza:m] *adj.* demure; chaste, modest; well-behaved; decent; **'Sitt·sam·keit** *f* (-; *no pl.*) demureness; chasteness, modesty; good manners *pl.*; decency

Si·tua·ti·on [zitŭa'tsĭo:n] *f* (-; -en) situation; position; **Si·tua·ti'ons·ko·mik** *f* situational humo(u)r

si·tu·iert [zitu'i:ɐt] *adj.*: ***gut ~ sein*** be well off, be well to do; ***schlecht ~ sein*** be badly off

Sitz [zɪts] *m* (-es; -e) **1.** a) seat (*a. parl. and fig.*), b) seat, headquarters *pl.*, c) (place of) residence, *formal*: domicile; ***die Zuschauer von den ~en reißen*** sweep the audience off their feet; **2.** *no pl.* fit (*a.* ⚙); ***e-n guten ~ haben*** a) *clothes*: fit well, sit well on s.o., b) *riding*: sit (the horse) well; **~bad** *n* hip bath, sitz bath; **~bank** *f* (-; ⸚e) bench; seat; **~blocka·de** *f* sit-in, sit-down demonstration (F demo); **~ecke** *f* corner seating unit

sit·zen ['zɪtsən] *v/i.* (saß, gesessen, h) a) sit; be, b) *clothes*: fit; be on properly, c) *model*: sit (**j-m** for s.o.), d) F do time, e) F hit home (*a. fig.*); **~ in** *dat. firm etc.*: have one's headquarters in; F ***im Gedächtnis ~*** have sunk in; **~ *bleiben*** remain (*or* stay) seated, F *at a dance*: be left out; ***bleiben Sie ~!*** don't get up; stay in your seat(s); → ***sitzenbleiben; bei j-m ~*** sit beside (*or* next to, with) s.o.; ***~ Sie bequem?*** are you comfortable?; ***zu viel ~*** spend too much time sitting (F on one's backside); ***das viele ~ ist nicht gut für dich*** sitting on a chair all day doesn't do you any good; ***lieber zu Hause ~*** prefer to stay at home; ***beim Essen ~*** be having one's dinner (*or* lunch); ***im Parlament ~*** have a seat in Parliament, be an MP (*or* a Member of Parliament); ***im Stadtrat ~*** be on the (town) council; ***im Ausschuß ~*** be on the committee; ***sie ~ immer noch*** they're still in the meeting; ***beim Arzt ~*** be at the doctor's; ***den ganzen Tag in der Kneipe ~*** sit around in the pub all day; ***stundenlang vor dem Fernseher ~*** spend hours (sitting) in front of the television, F be glued to the television for hours; ***ich habe lange daran gesessen*** I spent a lot of time on it; ***er sitzt auf s-m Geld*** he's sitting on his money; ***im Gefängnis ~*** be in jail (F clink); F ***er saß sechs Monate wegen Diebstahl(s)*** F he did six months for theft; ***über den Büchern ~*** be poring over one's books; F ***einen ~ haben*** F have had one too many; ***d-e Krawatte sitzt nicht richtig*** your tie's not straight; ***dein Hut sitzt schief*** your hat's cockeyed (F skew-whiff); ***wo sitzt der Schmerz?*** where does it hurt exactly?; ***da sitzt der Fehler!*** that's where the problem lies; ***die Angst (der Haß) sitzt tief*** the fear (hatred) runs *or* goes deep; ***das hat gesessen!*** that hit home; ***die Vokabeln ~ gut (schlecht)*** he *etc.* knows his *etc.* vocabulary off pat (his vocabulary's shaky, he needs to work on his vocabulary); ***bei ihm sitzt jeder Handgriff*** he knows exactly what he's doing; *e-n Vorwurf etc.* ***nicht auf sich ~ lassen*** not to stand for (*or* take); ***das lasse ich nicht auf mir ~*** *a.* I'm not just going to sit here and take that; → ***Patsche, Tinte***

'sit·zen·blei·ben F *v/i.* (*irr., sep.*, sn, → ***bleiben***) **1.** *ped.* have to repeat a year, stay back a class; **2.** *fig.* **~ *auf*** *dat.* be left with (*or* sitting on) s.th.; **3.** be left on the shelf

'sit·zend *adj.* **1. ~*e Lebensweise (Tätigkeit)*** sedentary life (occupation); **2. ~*e Figur*** seated figure

'sit·zen·las·sen F *v/t.* (*irr., sep.*, h, → ***lassen***) a) leave, desert, walk out on, jilt, b) stand *s.o.* up; let *s.o.* down, leave *s.o.* in the lurch; ***sie ließ ihn einfach sitzen*** *a.* she just didn't turn up

'Sitz|flä·che *f* seat; **~fleisch** F *fig. n* perseverance; stamina; ***er hat (aber) ~*** he doesn't seem to be in a hurry to leave; ***er hat kein ~*** a) he can't sit still, b) he can't stick to anything; **~gar·ni,tur** *f* living-room (*or* three-piece) suite; **~ge·le·gen·heit** *f* seat, place to sit; *pl.* seating *sg.*, seats; **~grup·pe** *f* → ***Sitzgarnitur***; **~kis·sen** *n* (seat) cushion; **~ord·nung** *f* seating arrangement(s *pl.*) *or* plan; **~platz** *m* seat (*a.* ***Sitzplätze bieten für***); **~pol·ster** *n* seat; **~rei·he** *f* row (of seats); **~streik** *m* sit-in, sit-down strike

Sit·zung ['zɪtsʊŋ] *f* (-; -en) meeting, conference; *parl. etc.* session (*a.* ⚕), sitting (*a. art*), ⚖ *a.* hearing; ***auf*** (*or* ***bei, in***) ***e-r ~*** at a meeting

'Sit·zungs|be·richt *m* minutes *pl.* (of the meeting); **~pe·rio·de** *f parl.* session; **~saal** *m* conference hall; *parl.* chamber; **~zim·mer** *n* conference room

'Sitz·ver·tei·lung *f parl.* distribution of seats

Six·ti·nisch [zɪks'tiːnɪʃ] *adj.*: **~*e Kapelle*** Sistine Chapel

Si·zi·lia·ner [zitsi'lia:nɐ] *m* (-s; -), **Si·zi·lia·ne·rin** [zitsi'lia:nərɪn] *f* (-; -nen), **si·zi·lia·nisch** [zitsi'lia:nɪʃ] *adj.* Sicilian

Ska·la ['ska:la] *f* (-; -s, Skalen [-lən]) scale (*a.* ♪); ⚙ *and fig.* range; *radio, mot. etc.* dial; *fig.* ***die ganze ~*** the whole gamut

Ska·len|be·leuch·tung ['ska:lən-] *f* dial light (*or* illumination); illuminated dial; **~ein·tei·lung** *f* graduation; **~rei·ter** *m radio*: station marker

Skalp [skalp] *m* (-s; -e) scalp

Skal·pell [skal'pɛl] *n* (-s; -e) ⚕ scalpel

skal·pie·ren [skal'pi:rən] *v/t.* (h) scalp

Skan·dal [skan'da:l] *m* (-s; -e) scandal (***um*** *acc.* surrounding); disgrace; ***es ist ein ~*** *a.* it's scandalous; **~blatt** *n* scandal sheet; **~nu·del** F *f* glutton for scandal; **~ *X*** scandal-ridden X

skan·da·lös [skanda'lø:s] *adj.* scandalous; shocking, disgraceful

Skan'dal·pres·se *f* gutter press

skan'dal|süch·tig *adj.* scandal-seeking; **~*e Person*** scandalmonger; **~um,wit·tert** *adj.* scandal-ridden, surrounded by scandal

Skan·di·na·vi·er [skandi'na:viɐ] *m* (-s; -), **Skan·di·na·vie·rin** [skandi'na:viərɪn] *f* (-; -nen), **skan·di·na·visch** [skandi'na:vɪʃ] *adj.* Scandinavian

Ska·ra·bä·us [skara'bɛ:ʊs] *m* (-; *no pl.*) scarab

Skat [ska:t] *m* (-[e]s; *no pl.*) skat; **~ *spielen*** (F ***kloppen, dreschen***) play skat; **~abend** *m* **1.** skat night; **2.** *an* evening of skat; **~bru·der** *m* skat mate

Skate·board ['skeɪtbɔːd] *n* (-s; -s) skateboard; **~ *fahren*** (ride a) skateboard; **~fah·ren** *n* skateboarding; **~ *verboten!*** no skateboards

Ska·to·lo·gie [skatolo'gi:] *f* (-; *no pl.*) scatology; **ska·to·lo·gisch** [skato'lo:gɪʃ] *adj.* scatological

'Skat·par,tie *f* round (*or* game) of skat

Ske·lett [ske'lɛt] *n* (-s; -e) skeleton (*a.* ⚙, △); ***zum ~ abgemagert sein*** be (just) skin and bones; **Ske'lett·bau·wei·se** *f* skeleton construction; **ske·let·tie·ren** [skelɛ'ti:rən] *v/t.* (h) skeletonize

Skep·sis ['skɛpsɪs] *f* (-; *no pl.*) scepticism, *Am.* skepticism; doubt; *dat.* ***mit ~ gegenüberstehen*** be sceptical (*Am.* skeptical) about, have one's doubts about;

Skep·ti·ker ['skɛptikɐ] *m* (-s; -) sceptic, *Am.* skeptic; **skep·tisch** ['skɛptɪʃ] *adj.* sceptical, *Am.* skeptical; ***ich bin da ~*** *a.* I'm not so sure (about it)

Skep·ti·zis·mus [skɛpti'tsɪsmʊs] *m* (-; *no pl.*) scepticism, *Am.* skepticism

Sketch [skɛtʃ] *m* (-[es]; -e[s] *or* -s) sketch, skit

Ski [ʃi:] *m* (-s; -, Skier ['ʃi:ɐ]) ski; **~ *laufen*** (*or* ***fahren***) ski, go skiing; **~an·zug** *m* ski(ing) suit; **~as** *n* skiing ace; **~aus·rü·stung** *f* skiing gear (F things *pl.*); **~bin·dung** *f* ski binding; *pl. a.* ski fittings; **~bob** *m* skibob; **~bril·le** *f*: (***e-e ~*** a pair of) skiing goggles *pl.*; **~fah·rer** *m* skier; **~ge·biet** *n* skiing area; **~gym,na·stik** *f* skiing exercises *pl.*; **~hang** *m* ski run; **~ha·serl** [-ha:zɐl] F *dial. n* (-s; -n) F snow (*or* ski) bunny; **~ho·se** *f*: (***e-e ~*** a pair of) skiing trousers *pl.*; **~hüt·te** *f* ski hut; **~kurs** *m* skiing course; **~lauf** *m* (-[e]s; *no pl.*), **~lau·fen** *n* skiing; **~läu·fer** *m* skier; **~leh·rer** *m* skiing instructor; **~lift** *m* ski lift; **~müt·ze** *f* skiing hat (*or* cap)

Skin·head ['skɪnhɛd] *m* (-s; -s) skinhead, F skin

'Ski|pa·ra,dies *n* skier's paradise; **~pi·ste** *f* ski run; **~spit·ze** *f* (ski) tip; **~sport** *m* skiing; **~sprin·gen** *n* ski jumping; **~sprin·ger** *m* ski jumper; **~spur** *f* (ski) track; **~stie·fel** *m* skiing boot; **~stock** *m* ski stick, ski pole; **~trä·ger** *m mot.* ski rack; **~un·fall** *m* skiing accident; **~,un·ter·richt** *m* skiing instruction (*or* lessons *pl.*); **~ur·laub** *m* skiing holiday (*Am.* vacation); **~wachs** *n* skiing wax; **~wan·dern** *n* ski-hiking; **~zir·kus** *m* ski circus (*or* circuit)

Skiz·ze ['skɪtsə] *f* (-; -n) sketch; (rough) outline; **'Skiz·zen·block** *m* sketchpad; **'Skiz·zen·buch** *n* sketchbook; **'skiz·zen·haft I.** *adj.* sketchy, rough; **II.** *adv.*: ***man sah ~ angedeutet*** you could see the rough outlines of; **skiz·zie·ren** [skɪ'tsi:rən] *v/t.* (h) sketch; *fig.* outline; *fig.* ***könnten Sie es kurz ~?*** could you give me a brief outline (of it)?

Skla·ve ['skla:və] *m* (-n; -n) slave (*a. fig.*); *fig.* ***ein ~ s-r Gewohnheiten sein*** be a slave to one's habits; ***j-n zum ~n machen*** make s.o. one's slave

'Skla·ven·ar·beit *f* slave labo(u)r; *fig.* drudgery, slavery

'Skla·ven·hal·ter *m* slave holder; **~ge·sell·schaft** *f* slave-owning society

'Skla·ven|han·del *m* slave trade; **~händ·ler** *m* slave trader; **~markt** *m* slave market; **~trei·ber** *m a. fig.* slavedriver

Skla·ve·rei [skla:və'raɪ] *f* (-; *no pl.*) slavery; *fig. a.* slavedriving; *fig.* ***es ist e-e*** (*or* ***die reinste***) **~** it's sheer slavery, F it's a real sweat

Skla·vin ['skla:vɪn] *f* (-; -nen) slave (*a. fig.*)

skla·visch ['skla:vɪʃ] *adj.* slavish; **~*e Nachahmung*** slavish copy (*or* imitation); ***es ist e-e ~e Nachahmung von ...*** *a.* it has been painted *etc.* in slavish adherence to ...

Skle·ro·se [skle'ro:zə] *f* (-; -n): ⚕ (***multiple ~*** multiple) sclerosis; **skle·ro·tisch** [skle'ro:tɪʃ] *adj.* sclerotic

skon·tie·ren [skɔn'ti:rən] *v/t.* (h) ☤ give a (cash) discount on

Skon·to ['skɔnto] *m, n* (-s; -s) cash discount; ***geben Sie ~?*** do you give a cash discount?

Skoo·ter ['sku:tɐ] *m* (-s; -) dodgem, bumper car

Skor·but [skɔr'bu:t] *m* (-[e]s; *no pl.*) ⚕ scurvy; **skor·bu·tisch** [skɔr'bu:tɪʃ] *adj.* scorbutic

Skor·pi·on [skɔr'pio:n] *m* (-s; -e) **1.** *zo.* scorpion; **2.** *ast.* Scorpio; (***ein***) **~ *sein*** be (a) Scorpio

Skript [skrɪpt] *n* (-[e]s; -en, -s) **1.** *film etc.*: script; **2.** *univ.* lecture notes *pl.*; **~girl** *n film*: continuity girl
Skro·fu·lo·se [skrofu'lo:zə] *f* (-; -n) scrofula
Skru·pel ['skru:pəl] *m* (-s; -) scruple; **~ haben, et. zu tun** have scruples about doing s.th.; **keine ~ haben, et. zu tun** have no scruples (*od.* qualms) about doing s.th.; **keine ~ kennen** have no scruples, be totally unscrupulous; **ohne jeden ~** without the slightest scruple
'skru·pel·los *adj.* unscrupulous
'Skru·pel·lo·sig·keit *f* (-; *no pl.*) unscrupulousness
Skull·boot ['skʊl-] *n sport*: scull; **skul·len** ['skʊlən] *v/i.* (h) scull; **Skul·ler** ['skʊlɐ] *m* (-s; -) sculler
skulp·tie·ren [skʊlp'ti:rən] *v/t.* (h) sculpture, sculpt; **Skulp·tur** [skʊlp'tu:ɐ] *f* (-; -en [-rən]) sculpture
Skulp·tu·ren|ga·le͵rie [skʊlp'tu:rən-] *f* sculpture gallery; **~samm·lung** *f* a) collection of sculptures, b) sculpture collection (*or* museum)
skur·ril [skʊ'ri:l] *adj.* strange, bizarre; absurd; ludicrous
S-Kur·ve ['ɛs-] *f* double bend
Sla·lom ['sla:lɔm] *m* (-s; -s) *sport*: slalom; **e-n ~ fahren** do (*or* take part in) a slalom; *fig. mot.* **~ fahren** weave; **~läu·fer** *m* slalom racer
Slang [slɛŋ] *m* (-s; -s) **1.** slang; **2.** *technical etc.* jargon; **~aus·druck** *m* slang expression
Sla·we ['sla:və] *m* (-n; -n), **Sla·win** ['sla:vɪn] *f* (-; -nen) Slav; **sla·wisch** ['sla:vɪʃ] *adj.* Slav, Slavic; **'Sla·wisch** *n* (-en) *ling.* Slavic; **Sla·wist** [sla'vɪst] *m* (-en; -en) Slavonicist; **Sla·wi·stik** [sla'vɪstɪk] *f* (-; *no pl.*) Slavonic studies *pl.*
Slip [slɪp] *m* (-s; -s) (**ein ~** a pair of) briefs *pl.*, panties *pl.*
Slip·per ['slɪpɐ] *m* (-s; -) slip-on (shoe)
Slo·gan ['slo:gən] *m* (-s; -s) slogan, catchphrase
Slo·wa·ke [slo'va:kə] *m* (-n; -n), **Slo·wa·kin** [slo'va:kɪn] *f* (-; -nen), **slo·wa·kisch** [slo'va:kɪʃ] *adj.*, **Slo'wa·kisch** *n* (-en) *ling.* Slovak
Slo·we·ne [slo've:nə] *m* (-n; -n), **Slo·we·nin** [slo've:nɪn] *f* (-; -nen), **slo·we·nisch** [slo've:nɪʃ] *adj.*, **Slo'we·nisch** *n* (-en) *ling.* Slovene
Slum [slam] *m* (-s; -s) slum(s *pl.*); ghetto; **~be·woh·ner** *m* slum-dweller
Sma·ragd [sma'rakt] *m* (-[e]s; -e [sma'ragdə]) emerald; **sma'ragd·grün** *adj.* emerald (green)
Smog [smɔk] *m* (-s; *no pl.*) smog; **~alarm** *m* smog alert; **~war·nung** *f* smog warning
Smo·king ['smo:kɪŋ] *m* (-s; -s) dinner jacket, *Am.* tuxedo; **~hemd** *n* dress shirt
Snack [snɛk] *m* (-s; -s) snack, bite to eat
Snob [snɔp] *m* (-s; -s) snob; **Sno·bis·mus** [sno'bɪsmʊs] *m* (-; *no pl.*) snobbishness, snobbery; **sno·bi·stisch** [sno'bɪstɪʃ] *adj.* snobbish
so [zo:] **I.** *adv.* a) like this *or* that; so *cold etc.*, as *bad etc.*, b) as much, c) around, about; **nicht ~ kalt** *etc.* not so cold *etc.*, *a.* not as cold *etc.*; **~!** right!; that's that!; **~?** is that right (*or* so)?, really?; **~, ~!** I see, well, well!; *er ist hier* - **~!** is he?; *er braucht Geld* - **~!** does he (now)?; **~ ein** such a; **~ ein Idiot!** what an idiot!; **~ etwas** something (*or* anything) like that; **~ etwas habe ich noch nie gesehen** (**gehört**) I've never seen anything like it (I've never heard such a thing); **danke, es geht schon ~** I can manage, thanks; it's all right (*Am.* alright), thanks; F (**na**) **~ was!** really?, you don't say!, that's strange, would you believe it; *warum fragst du?* - **nur ~** I just wondered; *er war Regisseur* **oder ~** or something like that, or something along those lines; *er hieß Merkl* **oder ~** or something like that, or something to that effect; **... und ~ ...** and so on; **~ ... wie** (*or* **als**) as ... as; **~ weit es reicht** as far as it goes; **doppelt ~ viele** twice as many; **um ~ besser** so much the better, just as well; **um ~ mehr** all the more; **ach ~!** oh(, I see)!; **~ ist es** that's how it is, that's it, F you've got it; **~ ist das Leben** that's life, such is life; **und ~ kam es, daß ...** and so ..., that's how ...; **wie du mir, ~ ich dir** tit for tat; **komm mir nicht ~!** don't speak to me like that; **~ oder ~** one way or another, whichever way you look at it, **verlierst du** *etc.*: *a.* whatever you do you lose *etc.*; **~ geht das nicht** that's just not on, oh no you don't!; **er meint es nicht ~** he doesn't (really) mean it (to be taken) like that; **~ in einer Stunde** in an hour or so, in about an hour; **~ alle acht Tage** every week or so; **~ und ~ oft** every so often; **~ gut wie nichts** next to nothing; **~ geht's, wenn du nicht hörst** that's what comes of not listening; **ich habe ~ das Gefühl, daß** I have a feeling that, something tells me that; **er hat ~ s-e Stimmungen** he has his little moods; **tu doch nicht ~!** stop putting it on; **..., ~ der Präsident** ..., according to the president; ..., so the president maintains; **was treibst du ~?** what are you up to these days?; **wie geht es ihm ~?** how is he then?; **was kostet es denn ~?** what sort of price were you thinking of (*or* are they asking *etc.*)?; **wie findest du ihn denn ~?** what do you think of him then?; **II.** *cj.* a) so;, b) however; **~ schnell ich rannte, ...** however fast I ran, ...; **~ krank er auch ist** however ill he may be; **~ daß** so that, so as to *inf.*; **~ sehr, daß** so much (so) that, to such an extent that
so·bald [zo'balt] *cj.*: **~** (**als**) as soon as, the moment *he arrived etc.*; **~ es Ihnen möglich ist** as soon as possible, ✝ at your earliest convenience
Söck·chen ['zœkçən] *pl.* (ankle) socks
Socke ['zɔkə] (*sep.* -k·k-) *f* (-; -n) sock; F *fig.* **sich auf die ~n machen** F make tracks, *sl.* push off; F **ich muß mich auf die ~n machen** *a.* F I'd better get a move on (*or* get my skates on); F **er war von den ~n** F he nearly fell over backwards (*or* keeled over)
Sockel ['zɔkəl] (*sep.* -k·k-) *m* (-s; -) **1.** base; plinth, pedestal; **2.** ⚡ socket; **3.** ✝ → **~be·trag** *m* basic allowance; **~ren·te** *f* basic pension
So·da¹ ['zo:da] *n* (-s; *no pl.*) soda
'So·da² *f* (-; *no pl.*) ⚗ soda, sodium carbonate
so·dann [zo'dan] *obs. adv.* then, *lit.* thereupon
'So·da·was·ser *n* soda water
Sod·bren·nen ['zo:t-] *n* (-s; *no pl.*) heartburn
So·de ['zo:də] *f* (-; -n) piece of turf, sod
So·do·mie [zodo'mi:] *f* (-; *no pl.*) buggery, bestiality
so·eben [zo'ʔe:bən] *adv.* just (now); right now
So·fa ['zo:fa] *n* (-s; -s) sofa, settee; **~ecke** *f* sofa corner; **~kis·sen** *n* (sofa) cushion
so·fern [zo'fɛrn] *cj.* if, provided (that), as long as; **~ er nicht absagt** provided (*or* as long as) he doesn't call it off, unless(, of course,) he calls it off
soff [zɔf] *pret. of* **saufen**
Sof·fit·te [zɔ'fɪtə] *f* (-; -n) tubular lamp
so·fort [zo'fɔrt] *adv.* straightaway, immediately, at once, right away; **er ging ~ ins Bett** *a.* he went straight to bed; (**ich komme**) **~!** I'll be with you right away (F in a sec); **er kommt ~** *a.* he's on his way; **er war ~ tot** he died instantly (*or* straightaway), it was (an) instant death; **das Kind fing ~ an zu schreien, als ich das Zimmer verließ** the child started screaming the moment (*or* minute) I left the room *or* as soon as I left the room; **~ lieferbar** (**zahlbar**) spot delivery (payment)
So'fort·bild·ka·me·ra *f* instant camera
So'fort·hil·fe *f* emergency relief
so·for·tig [zo'fɔrtɪç] *adj.* immediate; prompt *delivery etc.*; → **Wirkung**
So'fort|maß·nah·men *pl.* immediate steps; emergency measures; **~pro͵gramm** *n pol.* crash program(me)
Soft-Eis ['zɔftʔaɪs] *n* soft ice
Sof·tie ['zɔfti] F *m* (-s; -s) (real) softie
Soft·ware ['zɔftvɛ:ɐ] *f* (-; *no pl.*) software; **~pa͵ket** *n* software package; **~tech·no·lo͵gie** *f* software engineering
sog [zo:k] *pret. of* **saugen**
Sog [zo:k] *m* (-[e]s; *no pl.*) suction; ⚓, ✈ *a.* wake; vortex (*a. fig.*); undertow; *fig.* whirlpool, maelstrom; *fig.* **in den ~ der Großstadt** *etc.* **geraten** get caught up in the maelstrom of big city life *etc.*
so·gar [zo'ga:ɐ] *adv.* even; **sie hat ~ den zweiten Platz erreicht** she made second place, no less; **sehr gut, ~ ausgezeichnet** very good, excellent, in fact
'so·ge·nannt *adj.* so-called; *a.* would-be; **das ~e ...** *a.* what is known as ...
so·gleich [zo'glaɪç] *obs. adv.* → **sofort**
Soh·le ['zo:lə] *f* (-; -n) **1.** sole; *fig.* **auf leisen ~n** on tiptoe, stealthily; **2.** *geogr.* bottom; **3.** ⚒ floor
'soh·len *v/t.* (h) (re)sole
Sohn [zo:n] *m* (-[e]s; Söhne ['zø:nə]) son; **ganz der ~ s-s Vaters** a chip off the old block; **Soh·ne·mann** ['zo:nəman] *hum. m* (-[e]s; ⁼er) son, sonny; **der ~** junior
soi·gniert [zŏan'ji:ɐt] *adj.* elegant; soigné
Soi·ree [zŏa're:] *f* (-; -n) soiree, soirée
So·ja ['zo:ja] *f* (-; *no pl.*), **'So·ja·boh·ne** *f* soybean, soya (bean); **'So·ja·boh·nen·keim·lin·ge** *pl.* soybean sprouts
'So·ja|mehl *n* soybean flour; **~milch** *f* soybean milk; **~öl** *n* soybean oil; **~so·ße** *f* soy(a) sauce; **~spros·sen** *pl.* soybean sprouts
So·kra·ti·ker [zo'kra:tikɐ] *m* (-s; -), **so·kra·tisch** [zo'kra:tɪʃ] *adj.* Socratic
so·lan·ge [zo'laŋə] *cj.* as long as; while; as (*or* so) long as; **~ ich lebe** a) for the rest of my life, b) all my life; **~ er nicht anruft, können wir nichts machen** we can't do anything until he rings up
so·lar [zo'la:ɐ] *adj.* solar
So'lar|bat·te͵rie *f* solar battery; **~ener͵gie** *f* solar energy
So·la·ri·sa·ti·on [zolariza'tsĭo:n] *f* (-; -en) *phot.* solarization

So·la·ri·um [zo'la:rĭʊm] *n* (-s; -rien [-rĭən]) solarium
So'lar|jahr *n* solar year; **~kol|lek·tor** *m* → ***Sonnenkollektor***; **~kraft·werk** *n* solar energy plant, solar power station
So·lar·ple·xus [-'plɛksʊs] *m* (-; *no pl.*) *physiol.* solar plexus
So'lar|tech·nik *f* solar technology; **~wind** *m* solar winds (*or* storms) *pl.*; **~zel·le** *f* solar cell; **~zel·len·bat·te|rie** *f* solar battery
Sol·bad ['zo:l-] *n* **1.** brine bath; **2.** saltwater spa
solch [zɔlç] *pron. and adj.* such, that kind (*or* sort) of, ... like that; ***~einer*** someone (*or* a person) like that; ***~e Menschen*** that kind (*or* sort) of person, people like that; ***als ~er*** as such; ***ich hatte ~e Angst*** I was so scared; ***ich habe ~e Kopfschmerzen*** I've got such a headache; ***es gibt eben ~e und ~e*** it takes all sorts to make a world; ***es gab ~e, die ..., und ~e, die ...*** there were those who ... and those (*or* others) who ...
sol·cher·art ['zɔlçɐ?a:ɐt] **I.** *adj.* such, that kind (*or* sort) of, ... like that, ... of that kind (*or* sort); **II.** *adv.* in that (*or* this) way; *formal*: by that manner of means
sol·cher·lei ['zɔlçɐ'laɪ] *adj.* such, that kind (*or* sort) of, ... of that kind (*or* sort)
Sold [zɔlt] *m* (-[e]s; *no pl.*) ⚔ pay; *fig.* ***in j-s ~ stehen*** be in the employ of s.o., *contp.* be one of s.o.'s mercenaries (*or* hirelings)
Sol·dat [zɔl'da:t] *m* (-en; -en) soldier (*a. zo.*), serviceman; ***er ist ~*** *usu.* he's in the army; ***gedienter ~*** veteran, *Brit.* ex-serviceman; ***der Unbekannte ~*** the Unknown Warrior (*or* Soldier); ***~ werden*** join the army, join up
Sol'da·ten|be·ruf *m* military career (*or* profession), army career, career in the army; **~fried·hof** *m* military (*or* war) cemetery; **~grab** *n* war (*or* soldier's) grave; **~le·ben** *n* army life, life in the army, *a* soldier's life; **~spra·che** *f* forces' (*or* army, soldiers') slang; **~uni|form** *f* soldier's (*or* military) uniform
Sol·da·tes·ka [zɔlda'tɛska] *contp. f* (-; -ken) rabble of soldiers, marauding troops *pl.*
sol·da·tisch [zɔl'da:tɪʃ] *adj.* soldierly; military
Söld·ling ['zœltlɪŋ] *contp. m* (-s; -e) mercenary, hireling
Söld·ner ['zœltnɐ] *m* (-s; -) mercenary; **~heer** *n* army of mercenaries; **~trup·pen** *pl.* mercenary troops
So·le ['zo:lə] *f* (-; -n) saltwater, brine
Sol·ei ['zo:l?aɪ] *n* pickled egg
So·li·dar|ge·mein·schaft [zoli'da:ɐ-] *f* unified community; **~haf·tung** *f* joint (and several) liability
so·li·da·risch [zoli'da:rɪʃ] **I.** *adj.* **1.** united *front etc.*; *a.* concerted *action*; ***sich ~ erklären mit*** *dat.* declare one's solidarity with; **2.** ⚖ joint (and several); **II.** *adv.* **3.** ***~ handeln*** *etc.* act *etc.* in solidarity (***mit*** *dat.* with); **4.** ⚖ jointly and severally
so·li·da·ri·sie·ren [zolidari'zi:rən] *v/refl.* (h): ***sich ~ mit*** *dat.* declare one's solidarity with
So·li·da·ri·tät [zolidari'tɛ:t] *f* (-; *no pl.*) solidarity
So·li·da·ri'täts|be·weis *m* show of solidarity; **~er·klä·rung** *f* declaration of solidarity; **~ge·fühl** *n* feeling of solidarity; **~streik** *m* sympathy strike, *a. pl.* sympathetic action; **~schuld·ner** *m* joint debtor
so·li·de [zo'li:də] **I.** *adj.* respectable; ☤ *a.* well-established *firm etc.*; reasonable *prices etc.*; sound *knowledge etc.*, *a.* firm *basis etc.*; solid, robust, strong *material etc.*; ***e-e ~ Arbeit*** a sound piece of work, (*furniture etc.*) a good, solid piece of workmanship; ***e-e ~ Mahlzeit*** a good square meal; ***~ Möbel*** (good,) solid furniture; ***er ist ~ geworden*** he's settled down; **II.** *adv.*: ***~ gebaut*** well-built, solidly built
So·li·di·tät [zolidi'tɛ:t] *f* (-; *no pl.*) solidity; ☤ soundness; respectability
So·list [zo'lɪst] *m* (-en; -en), **So·li·stin** [zo'lɪstɪn] *f* (-; -nen) a) soloist, b) principal; **so·li·stisch** [zo'lɪstɪʃ] *adj.* soloistic; as a soloist
Soll [zɔl] *n* (-s; *no pl.*) ☤ a) debit, b) (fixed) quota; production quota; target; ***~ und Haben*** debit and credit; **~-Be·stand** *m* ☤ calculated assets *pl.*; authorized supplies *pl.*; **~-Bruch·stel·le** *f* ⚙ predetermined breaking point
sol·len ['zɔlən] *v/i.* (sollte, sollen, h) **1.** be to, be supposed to; ***Mutti sagt, du sollst nach Hause kommen*** you're to come home says mom; ***er soll mich anrufen*** he's to ring me up, tell him to ring me up; ***ich soll erst abwaschen*** I have to (*or* I'm to) do the dishes first; ***du solltest längst im Bett sein*** you're supposed to be in bed, you should have been in bed long ago; ***er sollte um zwei hier sein*** he was supposed to be here at two; ***ich soll dir ausrichten, daß*** I'm to tell you that; ***ich soll dir schöne Grüße von ihm bestellen*** he sends his regards, he asked me to give you his regards; ***soll ich mitkommen?*** shall I come?, do you want me to come?; ***du sollst ihn in Ruhe lassen!*** leave him alone!; ***wie oft soll ich dir das noch sagen?*** how many times do I have to tell you?; *bibl.* ***du sollst nicht töten*** thou shalt not kill; **2.** ***hier soll e-e Turnhalle gebaut werden*** a gymnasium is to be built here, there are plans to build a gymnasium here; ***er soll morgen ankommen*** he's due (*or* supposed) to arrive tomorrow; ***das Buch soll Ihnen dabei helfen*** the book is designed to help you with this; **3.** ***was soll das sein?*** what's that supposed to be?; ***es sollte ein Geschenk werden*** it was supposed (*or* meant) to be a present; ***es sollte ein Witz sein*** it was meant as a joke; ***er sollte Arzt werden*** he was supposed to become a doctor, F the idea was for him to become a doctor; **4.** ***du sollst es schon kriegen*** you'll get it, don't worry; I'll make sure you get it; ***er soll alles haben, was er will*** he's to have whatever he wants, *a.* let him have anything he wants; ***es soll nicht wieder vorkommen*** it won't happen again; ***das soll uns nicht stören*** we won't let that bother us; ***niemand soll sagen, daß*** I don't want it to be said that, never let it be said that; ***der soll nur kommen!*** just let him come!; ***das sollst du mir büßen!*** I'll make you pay for that; ***das soll mir mal einer nachmachen!*** I'd like to see anyone do better; **5.** should, ought to; ***du solltest es mal sehen*** you should (*or* ought to) see it; ***du hättest es sehen ~*** you should (*or* ought to) have seen it; ***man hätte es ihm sagen ~*** he ought to (*or* should) have been told; ***das hättest du sagen ~*** you should (*or* ought to) have said so (*or* said that); ***ich hätte es wissen ~*** I should have known; ***du solltest lieber nach Hause gehen*** I think you'd better(*or* you ought to) go home; ***sie sagte, ich sollte erst zu Ende studieren*** she said I should (*or* I ought to, I was to, I'm to) finish my degree first; ***warum sollte ich*** (***auch***)***?*** why should I?, I don't see why I should; **6.** ***was soll ich tun?*** what shall (*or* should) I do?, what am I supposed to do?; ***er wußte nicht, was er machen sollte*** he didn't know what to do; ***sie wußten nicht, ob sie lachen oder weinen sollten*** they didn't know whether to laugh or cry; ***was soll ich sagen?*** what can I say?, what am I supposed (*or* meant) to say?; **7.** ***falls er kommen sollte*** if he should come, in case he comes; ***falls es irgendwelche Probleme geben sollte*** if there should be (*or* are) any problems; ***sollte er es gewesen sein?*** could it have been him?; ***man sollte annehmen*** you would think; **8.** be supposed to, be said to; ***sie soll sehr reich sein*** she's supposed (*or* said) to be very rich, they say she's very rich; ***er soll es versteckt haben*** he's supposed (*or* said) to have hidden it, they say he's hidden it; ***er soll e-e Autorität auf dem Gebiet sein*** *a.* apparently he's quite an expert on the subject; **9.** be to; ***er sollte den Prozeß gewinnen*** he was to win the case; ***sie sollte e-e berühmte Sängerin werden*** she was (destined) to become a famous singer; ***es hat nicht sein ~*** (*or* ***~ sein***) it wasn't meant to be; ***ein Jahr sollte verstreichen, bis*** it was to be another year before, a whole year was to pass before; ***es sollte alles anders kommen*** things turned out (*or* were to turn out) quite differently; ***er wußte nicht, daß er nie wiederkommen sollte*** he didn't know that he would never return (*or* that he was never to return); **10.** (sollte, gesollt, h) ***was soll das?*** a) what's all this about?, b) what's that for?, c) what's the idea?, what are you playing at?; ***wozu soll das gut sein?*** what's that in aid of?; ***was soll ich damit?*** what am I supposed to do with it?; ***was soll ich hier?*** can somebody tell me what I'm supposed to be doing here?; ***wo soll das hin?*** where's it supposed to go?, where do you want me *etc.* to put it?; ***soll er doch!*** let him; see if I care; ***was soll's*** so what; who cares
'Soll|sei·te *f* ☤ debit side; **~-Stär·ke** *f* ⚔ required strength; **~-Wert** *m* rated (*or* desired) value; set point; **~zin·sen** *pl.* debtor interest *sg.*
so·lo ['zo:lo] *adv.* ♪ solo, F *a.* alone
'So·lo *n* (-s; -s, Soli) solo; **~gei·ger** *m* principal violinist; **~ge·sang** *m* (voice) solo; **~gi|tar·re** *f* solo guitar; **~kar·rie·re** *f* career as a soloist; **~part** *m* ♪ solo (part); **~sän·ger** *m* solo singer, soloist; **~spie·ler** *m* solo player, soloist; **~stim·me** *f* **1.** solo voice; **2.** solo part; **~stück** *n* solo (*a.* ♪); **~tän·zer** *m* **1.** solo dancer; **2.** principal (*or* first) dancer
sol·vent [zɔl'vɛnt] *adj.* solvent
Sol·venz [zɔl'vɛnts] *f* (-; -en) solvency
So·ma·li·er [zo'ma:lĭɐ] *m* (-s; -), **So·ma·lie·rin** [zo'ma:lĭərɪn] *f* (-; -nen), **so·ma·lisch** [zo'ma:lɪʃ] *adj.* Somali

so·mit [zo'mɪt] *adv.* thus, therefore, as a result; so

Som·mer ['zɔmɐ] *m* (-s; -) summer; ***im*** ~ in (the) summer; **~abend** *m* summer evening; **~an·fang** *m* beginning of summer; first day of summer; **~fahr·plan** *m* summer timetable (*Am.* schedule); **~fell** *n zo.* summer coat; **~fe·ri·en** *pl.* summer holidays (*esp. Am.* vacation *sg.*); **~fri·sche** *f* (-; -n) summer resort; **~ger·ste** *f* spring barley; **~halb·jahr** *n* summer (months *pl.*); *ped.* summer term; **~haus** *n* summer house; **~hit·ze** *f* summer heat, heat of summer; **~klei·dung** *f* summer clothing; ✝ summerwear; **~kol·lek·ti͵on** *f* summer collection

'som·mer·lich I. *adj.* summery; summer ...; **II.** *adv.*: ***es wird ~ warm*** we are going to get summer temperatures

'Som·mer|loch F *n* silly season; **~mo·de** *f* summer fashions *pl.*; **~mo·nat** *m* summer month; **~nacht** *f* summer('s) night; **~olym·pia·de** *f* Summer Olympics *pl.*; **~pau·se** *f* summer break; *pol.* summer recess; **~re·gen** *m* summer shower(s *pl.*); **~rei·fen** *m* normal tyre (*Am.* tire); **~sa·chen** *pl.* summer clothes; **~schluß·ver·kauf** *m* summer (*or* June) sales *pl.*; **~schu·he** *pl.* summer shoes; **~se͵me·ster** *n* summer semester (*or* term); **~sitz** *m* summer residence; **~son·nen·wen·de** *f* summer solstice; **~spie·le** *pl.*: ***Olympische ~*** Summer Olympics

'Som·mer·spros·sen *pl.* freckles

'som·mer·spros·sig [-ʃprɔsɪç] *adj.* freckled

'Som·mer|tag *m* summer('s) day; **~thea·ter** *n* **1.** summer theat|re (*Am. a.* -er); **2.** F *esp. pol.* silly season; **~ur·laub** *m* → ***Sommerferien;*** **~wet·ter** *n* summer weather; **~zeit** *f* **1.** summer(time); ***wäh·rend der ~*** in summer(time); **2.** summer time, daylight saving time; ***ab morgen gilt die ~*** we switch to summer time tomorrow, we put the clocks forward tomorrow

som·nam·bul [zɔmnam'buːl] *adj.* somnambulistic; **Som·nam·bu·le** [zɔmnam'buːlə] *m, f* (-n; -n) somnambulist

So·nar [zo'naːɐ] *n* (-s; -e [-rə]), **~ge·rät** *n* sonar

So·na·te [zo'naːtə] *f* (-; -n) sonata

So'na·ten·form *f* sonata form

So·na·ti·ne [zona'tiːnə] *f* (-; -n) sonatina

Son·de ['zɔndə] *f* (-; -n) ⚕ probe (*a. fig.*); *radio, radar, meteor.* sonde; (*space*) probe; ⚒ metal detector

Son·der... ['zɔndɐ-] *in cpds.* special; **~ab·druck** *m* → ***Sonderdruck;*** **~ab·kom·men** *n* special agreement; **~an·fer·ti·gung** *f* special version (*or* model); custom-made car *etc.*; ***es ist e-e ~*** *a.* we *etc.* had it specially made; **~an·ge·bot** *n* special offer; ***et. im ~ kaufen*** get s.th. on special offer; **~auf·trag** *m* special mission; **~aus·füh·rung** *f* → ***Sonderanfer·tigung;*** **~aus·ga·be** *f* **1.** special edition; **2.** *pl.* extra expenses; **~aus·schuß** *m* select committee; (special) task force; **~aus·stat·tung** *f* (optional) extras *pl.*; **~aus·stel·lung** *f* special exhibition

son·der·bar ['zɔndɐbaːɐ] *adj.* strange, odd; ***er ist heute ~*** he's acting very strangely today

son·der·ba·rer·wei·se ['zɔndɐbaːrɐvaɪzə] *adv.* strangely (*or* oddly) enough

'Son·der|be·auf·trag·te *m, f* (-n; -n) special commissioner; **~be·deu·tung** *f* added (*or* additional) meaning; **~be·fehl** *m* special order(s *pl.*); **~be·ga·bung** *f* special ability (*or* aptitude); **~be·hand·lung** *f* special treatment (*a. fig.*); preferential treatment; **~bei·la·ge** *f* (special) supplement; **~bei·trag** *m TV etc.* special report; **~be·richt·er·stat·ter** *m* special correspondent; **~be·stim·mung** *f* special provision (*or* rule, condition); **~be·voll·mäch·tig·te** *m, f* (-n; -n) special agent; *pol.* plenipotentiary; **~bot·schaf·ter** *m* special envoy; **~brief·mar·ke** *f* → ***Sondermarke;*** **~bus** *m* special (*or* extra) bus; **~de·le·ga·ti͵on** *f* special delegation (*or* mission); **~de·po͵nie** *f* special waste dump; **~druck** *m* offprint; **~ein·heit** *f* task force; **~ein·satz** *m* special action (*or* operation, mission); **~er·laub·nis** *f* a) special permission, b) special permit; **~er·mä·ßi·gung** *f* special reduction; **~fahrt** *f* **1.** unscheduled (*or* extra) run; **2.** excursion; **~fall** *m* special case; **~flug** *m* unscheduled (*or* special) flight; **~ge·neh·mi·gung** *f* a) special permission, b) special permit; **~ge·richt** *n* special court; **~ge·setz** *n* special law

son·der·glei·chen ['zɔndɐ'glaɪçən] *adv.* unheard of; ***das ist e-e Frechheit ~*** I've never heard (of) such cheek

'Son·der|gre·mi·um *n* special panel; **~heft** *n* special issue; **~in·ter͵es·sen** *pl.* special interests; **~kin·der·gar·ten** *m* kindergarten for handicapped children; **~klas·se** *f*: F ***der Auftritt*** *etc.* ***war ~*** it was a brilliant performance *etc.*; **~kom͵man·do** *n* special detachment; **~kom·mis·si͵on** *f* special commission; **~kon·to** *n* special account; **~kor·re·spon͵dent** *m* special correspondent

son·der·lich ['zɔndɐlɪç] **I.** *adj.* particular; ***kein ~es Vergnügen*** not much fun; ***ohne ~e Mühe*** without much effort; **II.** *adv.* particularly; ***nicht ~*** not particularly

Son·der·ling ['zɔndɐlɪŋ] *m* (-s; -e) strange (*or* odd) sort

'Son·der|mar·ke *f* special stamp; *pl.* special issue *sg.*; **~ma͵schi·ne** *f* unscheduled (*or* special) flight; ***in e-r ~ eintref·fen*** arrive on a special flight; **~mel·dung** *f* special announcement; **~mis·si͵on** *f* special mission

'Son·der·müll *m* hazardous (*or* special, toxic) waste; **~de·po͵nie** *f* special waste dump

son·dern[1] ['zɔndɐn] *cj.* but; ***er fährt nicht, ~ er fliegt*** he's not driving, he's flying; he's flying, not driving; ***das ist kein Chinesisch, ~ Japanisch*** that's not Chinese, that's (*or* it's) Japanese; ***nicht nur, ~ auch*** not only, (but) also

son·dern[2] ['zɔndɐn] *v/t.* (h) separate

'Son·der|num·mer *f* special issue (*or* edition); **~par͵tei·tag** *m* special party conference; **~preis** *m* special price; ***ich ma·che Ihnen e-n ~*** *a.* I'll make you a special offer; ***T-Shirts zum ~ von*** *dat.* T-shirts on special offer at (*or* for); **~re·ge·lung** *f* special arrangement

son·ders ['zɔndɐs] *adv.* → ***samt*** I

'Son·der|schicht *f* special (*or* extra) shift; **~schu·le** *f* special school; **~sen·dung** *f* special broadcast; **~sit·zung** *f* special session; ***e-e ~ abhalten*** be in special session; **~stel·lung** *f* special position (*or* status); **~stem·pel** *m* special postmark; **~ur·laub** *m* special leave; ⚔ *a.* emergency (*or* compassionate) leave; **~ver·packung** *f* special wrapping (*or* packaging); **~voll·macht** *f* emergency powers *pl.*; **~vor·stel·lung** *f* special performance; **~wunsch** *m* special request; **~zei·chen** *n* special character, symbol; **~zu·be·hör** *n* (optional) extras *pl.*; **~zug** *m* special (*or* excursion) train; **~zu·la·ge** *f* special bonus

son·die·ren [zɔn'diːrən] *v/t.* (h) **1.** sound out; ***die Lage ~*** see how the land lies; **2.** ⚕ probe; **3.** ⚓ sound

Son'die·rung *f* (-; -en) **1.** sounding out; **2.** ⚕ probe; **3.** ⚓ sounding; **4.** *pl.* → **Son'die·rungs·ge·spräch** *n a. pl.* exploratory talks *pl.*

So·nett [zo'nɛt] *n* (-[e]s; -e) sonnet

Sonn·abend ['zɔnʔaːbənt] *m* Saturday; (***am***) ~ on Saturday; **'sonn·abends** *adv.* on Saturday(s)

Son·ne ['zɔnə] *f* (-; -n) a) sun, b) sun(light), c) sun(shine); ***an der ~*** in the sun; ***ich gehe raus an die ~*** I'm going out into the sun(shine) (*or* to get some sun[shine]); ***geh mir aus der ~*** get out of the sun; ***von der ~ beschienen*** sunlit; → ***Platz*** 3; **'son·nen** *v/refl.* (h): ***sich ~*** sun oneself, bask (*or* lie) in the sun; *fig.* ***sich ~ in*** *dat.* bask (*or* revel) in

'Son·nen|ak·ti·vi͵tät *f* solar activity; **~an·be·ter** *m* sun worshipper; **~an·be·tung** *f* sun worship; **≈arm** *adj.* lacking in sunshine; ***es ist e-e ~e Gegend*** you don't get much sun (around there *or* here); **~auf·gang** *m* sunrise; ***bei ~*** at sunrise, when the sun comes up; **~bad** *n*: ***ein ~ nehmen*** sunbathe, (go and) lie in the sun; **~bank** *f* (-; ⸚e) sunbed, sun bench; **~bat·te͵rie** *f* solar battery; **≈be·heizt** *adj.* solar-heated; **~be·strah·lung** *f* (exposure to) sunlight; **~blen·de** *f* **1.** *phot.* lens hood; **2.** *mot.* sun visor; **~blu·me** *f* sunflower

'Son·nen·blu·men|kern *m* sunflower seed; **~öl** *n* sunflower oil

'Son·nen|brand *m* sunburn; ***e-n ~ haben*** have sunburn; ***sich e-n ~ holen*** get sunburnt; **~bräu·ne** *f* (sun)tan; **~bril·le** *f*: (***e-e ~*** a pair of) sunglasses (F shades) *pl.*; **~creme** *f* sun cream; **~dach** *n* sunblind, awning; *mot.* sliding (*or* sun) roof; **~deck** *n* ⚓ sun deck; **~ein·strah·lung** *f* solar radiation; **~ener͵gie** *f* solar energy; **~fer·ne** *f astr.* aphelion; **~fin·ster·nis** *f* eclipse of the sun, solar eclipse; **~fleck** *m* sunspot; **≈ge·bräunt** *adj.* (sun)tanned, bronzed; **~ge·flecht** *n anat.* solar plexus; **≈ge·reift** *adj.* sun-ripened; **~glut** *f* blazing heat (of the sun); **~gott** *m* sun god; **~hit·ze** *f* heat of the sun

'son·nen·hung·rig *adj.* hungry for the sun; sun-seeking *tourists etc.*; **'Son·nen·hung·ri·ge** *m, f* (-n; -n) sun-seeker

'Son·nen|hut *m* sunhat; **~jahr** *n* solar year; **≈'klar** F *adj.* (as) clear as daylight; **~er Beweis** glaring evidence; **~kol͵lek·tor** *m* solar (collector) panel; **~kö·nig** *m hist.*: ***der ~*** the Sun King, le Roi Soleil; **~kraft·werk** *n* solar power plant; **~kult** *m* sun cult; sun worship; **~licht** *n* (-[e]s; *no pl.*): (***bei ~*** in) sunlight; **~lie·ge** *f* → ***Sonnenbank***

'son·nen·los *adj.* sunless

'Son·nen|nä·he *f ast.* perihelion; **~ofen** *m* solar furnace; **~öl** *n* suntan lotion (*or* oil); **~pad·del** *n space travel*: solar panel; **≈reich** *adj.* (very) sunny; ***es ist e-e ~e Gegend*** you get plenty of sunshine

(around there *or* here); **~schein** *m* (-[e]s; *no pl.*) sunshine; **~schirm** *m* sunshade; parasol
'Son·nen·schutz|creme *f* sun (filter) cream; **~fak·tor** *m* (sun) protection factor; **~mit·tel** *n* sunscreen; suntan lotion, sun cream
'Son·nen|sei·te *f* sunny side; ***die ~ des Lebens*** the sunny (*or* bright) side of life; **~spek·trum** *n* solar spectrum; **~stand** *m* position of the sun; **~stich** *m* sunstroke; ***e-n ~ haben*** (***bekommen***) have (get) sunstroke; **~strahl** *m* ray of sunshine, sunbeam, sunray; **~strand** *m* sunny beach; **~stu·dio** *n* solarium, *Am.* tanning salon; **~sy,stem** *n* solar system; **~tag** *m* **1.** sunny day; **2.** *ast.* solar day; **~tempel** *m* temple of the sun; **~tier·chen** *n* heliozoan; **2über,flu·tet** *adj.* sun-drenched; **~uhr** *f* sundial; **~,un·ter·gang** *m*: (***bei*** ~ at) sunset (*or* sundown)
'son·nen·ver·brannt *adj.* a) sunburnt, b) scorched
'Son·nen|wär·me *f* warmth of the sun; **~wen·de** *f* solstice; **~wind** *m phys.* solar wind; **~zeit** *f ast.* solar time; **~zel·le** *f* solar cell
son·nig ['zɔnɪç] *adj.* sunny (*a. fig.*)
Sonn·tag ['zɔnta:k] *m* Sunday; (***am***) ~ on Sunday; **'sonn·täg·lich I.** *adj.* Sunday ...; **II.** *adv.*: ~ ***gekleidet*** dressed in one's Sunday best
'sonn·tags *adv.* on Sunday(s)
'Sonn·tags|an·zug *m one's* Sunday best, *one's* best suit; **~ar·beit** *f* Sunday working; **~aus·flug** *m* Sunday drive (*or* trip); **~aus·flüg·ler** *m* weekend tripper; **~aus·ga·be** *f* Sunday edition; **~bei·la·ge** *f* Sunday supplement; **~bra·ten** *m* Sunday roast; **~dienst** *m*: ~ ***haben*** have to work on Sunday(s); *pharmacy*: be open on Sunday(s); **~fah·rer** *contp. m* Sunday driver; **~ge·sicht** *n*: ***von j-m nur das ~ kennen*** only know s.o. from his (*or* her) good side; **~got·tes·dienst** *m* Sunday service; **~kind** *n*: ***er ist ein*** ~ a) he was born on a Sunday, b) he was born under a lucky star; **~kleid** *n one's* Sunday best; **~ma·ler** *m* Sunday painter; **~schu·le** *f eccl.* Sunday school; **~staat** F *m* F *one's* glad rags *pl.*; **~ver·gnü·gen** *n* Sunday treat; **~zei·tung** *f* Sunday paper
Sonn·wend·fei·er ['zɔnvɛnt-] *f* midsummer festival (*or* celebrations *pl.*)
Son·ny·boy ['zɔnibɔʏ] F *m* (-s; -s) sunshine boy
so·nor [zo'no:ɐ] *adj.* sonorous
sonst [zɔnst] *adv.* a) *a. threateningly*: otherwise, or else, or, b) otherwise, apart from that (*or* him *etc.*), other than that, c) usually, normally, d) some other time; ~ ***kam immer ihr Bruder*** her brother always used to come; ***wer ~?*** who else?; ~ (***noch***) ***wer?*** anybody else?; ***wie*** ~ as usual; ***wie ~?*** how else?; ~ ***einmal*** some other day; ~ ***nirgends*** nowhere else; ***wenn es ~ nichts ist*** if that's all (it is); (***wünschen Sie***) ~ ***noch etwas?*** anything else?; *iro.* ~ ***noch was*** (***gefällig***)***?*** anything else while I'm at it?; ***besser als*** ~ better than usual; ***dieses ~ so ausgezeichnete Wörterbuch*** this otherwise excellent dictionary; ~ ***komme ich*** (***noch***) ***zu spät!*** or (else) I'll be late; ***iß das auf, ~ setzt es was!*** you'd better eat that up, or else!; *iro.* ***was denn ~?*** what do (*or* did) 'you think?
son·stig ['zɔnstɪç] *adj.* other; ***~e Kenntnisse*** further skills; ***s-e ~e Geduld*** his usual patience; ***Sonstiges*** a) Miscellaneous, b) Other (business *or* expenses *etc.*)
'sonst|je·mand F *pron.* somebody (*or* someone) else; anybody, anyone; ***da könnte ja ~ kommen*** anyone could just come along; ***er glaubt, er sei*** ~ F he thinks he's the bee's knees
'sonst·was F *pron.* something else; anything; ***du kannst ~ machen*** you can do whatever you like; ***er kann mir ~ geben*** I don't care what he gives me
'sonst·wer F *pron.* → ***sonstjemand***
'sonst·wie F *adv.* some other way; ***mach es so oder*** ~ do it whichever way you like; F ***er hat mich ~ angeredet*** you should have heard the way he spoke to me
'sonst·wo F *adv.* somewhere else; ***er könnte ~ sein*** he could be anywhere; ***er könnte in China sein oder*** ~ he could be in China for all I know
'sonst·wo·hin F *adv.* somewhere else
so·oft [zo'ʔɔft] *cj.* whenever, every time; ~ ***Sie wollen*** as often as you like; ~ ***ich es ihm sage, er hört einfach nicht*** I can tell him as often as I like, he never listens
Soor [zo:ɐ] *m* (-[e]s; -e), **~pilz** *m* ⚕ thrush
So·phist [zo'fɪst] *m* (-en; -en) sophist; *contp. a.* quibbler; **So·phi·ste·rei** [zofɪstə'raɪ] *f* (-; -en) sophistry; *contp. a.* quibbling, splitting (of) hairs
So·pran [zo'pra:n] *m* (-s; -e) **1.** soprano; ***den ~ singen*** sing soprano, be the soprano; **2.** soprano section, sopranos *pl.*; **~block·flö·te** *f* descant (*Am.* soprano) recorder
So·pra·ni·no·block·flö·te [zopra'ni:no-] *f* sopranino recorder
So·pra·nist [zopra'nɪst] *m* (-en; -en), **So·pra·ni·stin** [zopra'nɪstɪn] *f* (-; -nen) soprano
So'pran·sa·xo,phon *n* soprano saxophone
Sor·be ['zɔrbə] *m* (-n; -n), **Sor·bin** ['zɔrbɪn] *f* (-; -nen) Sorb
Sor·bin·säu·re [zɔr'bi:n-] *f* sorbic acid
sor·bisch ['zɔrbɪʃ] *adj.*, **'Sor·bisch** *n* (-en) *ling.* Sorbian
Sor·ge ['zɔrgə] *f* (-; -n) a) worry, concern (***um*** *acc.* over, about); fear(s *pl.*) (for, about), b) *no pl.* care (for); **~n** worries, problems; ***finanzielle ~n*** financial worries, money problems; ***j-m ~n machen*** a) worry s.o., b) cause s.o. trouble; ***sich ~n machen*** be worried (***um*** *acc.* about); ***du machst dir zu viele ~n*** you worry too much; ***vor ~n graue Haare bekommen*** go grey (*Am.* gray) with worry; ***er ist frei von ~n*** he hasn't got any problems; ***da sind wir*** (***wenigstens***) ***e-e ~ los*** that's one problem less; ***ich komm' aus den ~n nicht heraus*** it's just one problem (*or* thing) after another; ***das ist m-e geringste*** ~ that's the least of my worries; ~ ***tragen für*** *acc.* see to, take care of; ***dafür ~ tragen, daß*** see to it that, make sure (that); → ***sorgen*** II; ***laß das m-e ~ sein*** leave that to me; ***das ist d-e*** ~ that's your problem; ***j-m e-e ~ abnehmen*** take a problem off s.o.'s hands; ***keine ~!*** don't (you) worry; *iro.* ***d-e ~n möchte ich haben!*** if that's all you've got to worry about; *iro.* ***du hast ~n!*** you think 'you've got problems!
sor·gen ['zɔrgən] (h) **I.** *v/refl.*: ***sich*** ~ be worried, worry (***um*** *acc.*, ***wegen*** *gen.* about); **II.** *v/i.*: ~ ***für*** *acc.* a) look after *s.o. or s.th.*, b) provide *s.th.*, take care of *s.o. or s.th.*, see to *s.th.*; ensure; ***für sich selbst*** ~ fend for o.s.; ***er kann für sich selbst ~*** *a.* he can look after himself; ***dafür ~, daß*** see to it that, make sure (that); ***dafür werde ich*** ~ I'll see to that, I'll make sure of that; ***für ihn ist gesorgt*** he's taken care of
'Sor·gen|bre·cher F *m* problem solver, F cure of all ills; **~fal·ten** *pl.* worry lines
'sor·gen·frei *adj.* free from cares (*or* worries); ~ ***sein*** *a.* have no worries
'Sor·gen|kind *n* problem child; *fig. one's* biggest worry, problem number one; **~te·le,fon** *n* helpline
'sor·gen·voll I. *adj.* full of worries; ***~e Miene*** worried look; **II.** *adv.* anxiously, worriedly; ~ ***in die Zukunft blicken*** see the future with (great) concern
'Sor·ge|pflicht *f* parental responsibility; **~recht** *n* (-[e]s; *no pl.*) ⚖ custody (***für*** *acc.* of)
Sorg·falt ['zɔrkfalt] *f* (-; *no pl.*) care; scrupulousness; ***große ~ verwenden auf*** *acc.* take great pains over; ***mit der größten ~*** with painstaking (*or* the utmost) care; ***mehr ~ auf et. verwenden*** take more care over s.th.; **sorg·fäl·tig** ['zɔrkfɛltɪç] **I.** *adj.* careful; conscientious; thorough; **II.** *adv.* carefully *etc.*; with care
sorg·los ['zɔrklo:s] **I.** *adj.* a) free from worries; thoughtless, b) careless; nonchalant, happy-go-lucky, devil-may-care, c) very trusting; ***~e Einstellung*** carefree attitude; ***~es Dasein*** carefree existence; **II.** *adv.* thoughtlessly *etc.*; ~ ***umgehen mit*** *dat.* handle (*or* treat) *s.th.* very casually; ***er geht mit s-n Platten sehr ~ um*** he doesn't care how he treats his records; ~ ***in den Tag hineinleben*** live for the day
Sorg·lo·sig·keit ['zɔrklo:zɪçkaɪt] *f* (-; *no pl.*) carelessness, nonchalance *etc.*; → ***sorglos***
sorg·sam ['zɔrkza:m] **I.** *adj.* careful; solicitous; **II.** *adv. a.* with great care
Sor·te ['zɔrtə] *f* (-; -n) **1.** sort, kind; brand; ✝ quality, grade; ***beste*** (*or* ***erste***) ~ finest (*or* prime) quality; *ein Schwindler etc.* ***übelster*** ~ of the worst kind (*or* sort); ***das ist e-e komische ~*** (***Mensch***) F they're a strange lot; → ***selten*** I; **2.** *pl.* foreign exchange
Sor·tier·band [zɔr'ti:ɐ-] *n* (-[e]s; ¨er) conveyor belt
sor·tie·ren [zɔr'ti:rən] *v/t.* (h) sort (***nach*** *dat.* according to); arrange; ✝ grade; ***alphabetisch*** ~ put into alphabetical order, alphabetize; ***in e-n Schrank*** *etc.* ~ tidy *things* away into a cupboard *etc.*; F ***ich muß erst m-e Gedanken*** ~ I've got to straighten things out in my mind first
Sor·tie·rer [zɔr'ti:rɐ] *m* (-s; -) *a.* ⚙ sorter
Sor'tier·ma,schi·ne *f* sorter, sorting machine
sor·tiert [zɔr'ti:ɐt] *adj.* **1.** ***gut*** ~ well-stocked (***in*** *dat.* with); ***gut ~ sein in*** *dat. a.* have a wide selection (*or* range) of; **2.** select, fine
Sor·ti·ment [zɔrti'mɛnt] *n* (-[e]s; -e) **1.** ✝ range; **2.** retail book trade
Sor·ti·menter [zɔrti'mɛntɐ] *m* (-s; -), **Sor·ti'ments·buch·händ·ler** *m* retail bookseller
SOS [ɛsʔo:'ʔɛs] *n* (-; *no pl.*) SOS; ***ein ~ funken*** send an SOS; **~-Kin·der·dorf** *n home for* (*mainly refugee*) *orphans, struc-*

tured around family units; **~-Ruf** *m* SOS (call *or* message); **~-Si͵gnal** *n* SOS signal
so·sehr [zo'zeːɐ] *cj*.: **~ (auch)** however much, no matter how much; ***~ er sich bemüht*** however hard he tries, he can try as hard as he likes
so·so [zo'zoː] F **I.** *adv*. F so-so; **II.** *int*. well, well!; I see, *reproachfully*: 'I see
So·ße ['zoːsə] *f* (-; -n) a) *gastr*. sauce; gravy; (*salad*) dressing, b) F goo
'So·ßen|löf·fel *m* sauce (*or* gravy) spoon; **~schüs·sel** *f* sauceboat, gravy boat
Sou·bret·te [zu'brɛtə] *f* (-, -n) ♪ soubrette
Souf·flé [zu'fleː] *n* (-s; -s) soufflé
Souf·fleur [zu'fløːɐ] *m* (-s; -e [-rə]) prompter; **~ka·sten** *m* prompt box
Souf·fleu·se [zu'fløːzə] *f* (-; -n) prompter
souf·flie·ren [zu'fliːrən] (h) **I.** *v/t*.: ***j-m et. ~*** prompt s.o. with s.th., *fig*. whisper s.th. to s.o., tell s.o. s.th.; **II.** *v/i*. prompt; be (*or* work as) a prompter
so·und·so ['zoːʔʊntzoː] F **I.** *adv*.: ***~ viel*** so and so much; ***~ viele*** so and so many; ***~ oft*** time and again; **II.** *adj*.: ***nach Paragraph ~*** according to paragraph such and such (*or* XYZ); ***Herr*** ♀ Mr what's--his-name
so·und·so·vielt [zoːʔʊntzo'fiːlt] F *adj*. **1.** ***am ~en März*** on March the nth; ***am Soundsovielten*** on such and such a date; **2.** F umpteenth; ***zum ~en Mal*** for the umpteenth (*or* nth) time
Sou·per [zu'peː] *n* (-s; -s) (evening) dinner
Sou·ta·ne [zu'taːnə] *f* (-; -n) *eccl*. cassock
Sou·ter·rain [zutɛ'rɛ̃ː] *n* (-s; -s) basement; **~woh·nung** *f* basement flat
Sou·ve·nir [zuvə'niːɐ] *n* (-s; -s) souvenir; **~la·den** *m* souvenir shop; **~stand** *m* souvenir stall
sou·ve·rän [zuvə'rɛːn] **I.** *adj*. **1.** unflappable; in complete control (of the situation); ***er blieb ganz ~ a.*** he remained unfazed; ***~e Beherrschung*** commanding knowledge *of French etc*.; ***~es Lächeln*** all-knowing smile; ***~!*** that was classy; **2.** *pol*. sovereign; **II.** *adv*. a) with the greatest of ease; unperturbed, b) in superior style; ***er hat alles ~ gehandhabt a.*** he took it all in his stride, F he handled it like a pro
Sou·ve'rän *m* (-s; -e) sovereign
Sou·ve·rä·ni·tät [zuvərɛni'tɛːt] *f* (-; *no pl*.) sovereignty
so·viel [zo'fiːl] **I.** *cj*.: ***~ ich weiß*** as far as I know; ***~ ich gehört habe*** from what I've heard; **II.** *adj. and adv*. so much; ***~ wie*** as much as; ***~ du willst*** as much as you want (*or* like); ***doppelt ~*** twice as much; ***noch einmal ~*** as much again; ***~ ist gewiß*** one thing is certain; ***~ für heute*** that's it for today
so·weit [zo'vaɪt] **I.** *cj*. **1.** as far as; ***~ ich es beurteilen kann*** as far as I can judge (*or* tell); ***~ er beteiligt ist*** insofar (*or* in so far) as he's involved; **II.** *adv*. **2.** so far; ***~ ganz gut*** not (so) bad; ***es geht ihm ~ gut*** he's (doing) quite well on the whole; **3.** ***wir sind ~*** we're ready (and waiting); ***endlich ist es ~*** we've *etc*. finally made it; ***es ist gleich ~*** we're *etc*. nearly there, any minute now
so·we·nig [zo'veːnɪç] **I.** *adv*.: ***~ wie (or als)*** as little as; ***~ wie möglich*** as little as possible; ***ich bin ~ wie er daran interessiert*** I'm no more interested in it than he is; **II.** *cj*. however little, little as
so·wie [zo'viː] *cj*. **1.** as well as, and, plus; **2.** as soon as, the moment, the minute *she gets here etc*.; just as *he was about to leave etc*.
so·wie·so [zovi'zoː] *adv*. anyway, anyhow, in any case; ***(das) ~!*** that goes without saying, absolutely; ***Herr*** ♀ Mr what's-his-name
So·wjet [zɔ'vjɛt, 'zɔvjɛt] *m* (-s; -s) *hist*. Soviet; ***Oberster ~*** Supreme Soviet; **~bür·ger** *m* Soviet citizen
so·wje·tisch [zɔ'vjɛtɪʃ] *adj*. Soviet
so·wje·ti·sie·ren [zɔvjɛti'ziːrən] *v/t*. (h) sovietize
So·wjet|re͵gie·rung *f hist*. Soviet government; **♀rus·sisch** *adj*. Soviet(-Russian); **~uni͵on** *f hist*. Soviet Union; **~zo·ne** *f hist*. Soviet-occupied zone
so·wohl [zo'voːl] *cj*.: ***~ ... als auch*** both ... and; ... as well as
So·zi ['zoːtsi] *contp*. *m* (-s; -s) Socialist
so·zi·al [zo'tsi̯aːl] **I.** *adj*. a) social, b) socially-minded; ***~e Ausgaben*** social spending; ***~e Einrichtungen*** social services; ***~e Fürsorge*** social (*or* welfare) work; ***~e Gegensätze*** class differences; ***~e Stellung, ~er Rang*** social rank, (social) status; ***~er Wohnungsbau*** council housing; → ***Marktwirtschaft, Netz***; **II.** *adv*.: ***~ denken*** be socially-minded
So·zi'al|ab·ga·ben *pl*. social security contributions; **~amt** *n* social welfare office; **~ar·beit** *f* social (*or* welfare) work; **~ar·bei·ter** *m* social (*or* welfare) worker
So·zi'al·de·mo͵krat *m* social democrat; **So·zi'al·de·mo·kra͵tie** *f* social democracy; **so·zi'al·de·mo͵kra·tisch** *adj*. social democratic
So·zi'al|ein·rich·tun·gen *pl*. social services; **~fall** *m* welfare case; **~fonds** *m* social capital; **~ge·richt** *n* social court; **~ge·schich·te** *f* social history
So·zi'al·hil·fe *f* (-; *no pl*.) income support; **~emp·fän·ger** *m*: ***~ sein*** be on social security
so·zia·li·sie·ren [zotsi̯ali'ziːrən] *v/t*. (h) ✝ nationalize; *psych*. rehabilitate
So·zia·li'sie·rung *f* (-; -en) ✝ nationalization; *psych*. rehabilitation
So·zia·lis·mus [zotsi̯a'lɪsmʊs] *m* (-; *no pl*.) socialism; **So·zia·list** [zotsi̯a'lɪst] *m* (-en; -en), **so·zia·li·stisch** [zotsi̯a'lɪstɪʃ] *adj*. socialist
So·zi'al|ko·sten *pl*. social expenditure *sg*.; **~kri͵tik** *f* social criticism; **♀kri·tisch** *adj*. sociocritical; **~kun·de** *f* (-; *no pl*.) social studies *pl*.; **~la·sten** *pl*. social expenditure *sg*.; **~lei·stun·gen** *pl*. a) social security contributions, b) fringe benefits; **~öko·no͵mie** *f* social economics *pl*.; **♀öko͵no·misch** *adj*. socioeconomic; **~ord·nung** *f* social order; **~päd·ago·ge** *m* social education worker; **~päd·ago·gik** *f* social education; **~part·ner** *pl*. employers and employees, *the* two sides of industry; **~plan** *m* social plan; **~po·li͵tik** *f* social policy (*or* policies *pl*.); **♀po͵li·tisch** *adj*. sociopolitical, social; **~pre·sti·ge** *n* social prestige (*or* standing); **~pro͵dukt** *n* gross national product; **~recht** *n* (-[e]s; *no pl*.) social legislation; **~re·vo·lu·tio͵när** *m* social revolutionary; **~staat** *m* welfare state; **~struk͵tur** *f* social structure
So·zi'al·ver·si·che·rung *f* social security; **So·zi'al·ver·si·che·rungs·bei·trag** *m* social security contribution
So·zi'al|we·sen *n* (-s; *no pl*.) social services *pl*.; **~wirt·schaft** *f* social economics *pl*.; **♀wirt·schaft·lich** *adj*. socioeconomic; **~wis·sen·schaf·ten** *pl*. social sciences; **~wis·sen·schaft·ler** *m* sociologist; **~woh·nung** *f* council flat
So·zio·gramm [zotsi̯o'gram] *n* (-s; -e) sociogram
So·zio·lekt [zotsi̯o'lɛkt] *m* (-[e]s; -e) sociolect
So·zio·lin'gui·stik ['zotsi̯o-] *f* sociolinguistics *pl*.
So·zio·lo·ge [zotsi̯o'loːgə] *m* (-n; -n) sociologist; **So·zio·lo·gie** [zotsi̯olo'giː] *f* (-; *no pl*.) sociology; **so·zio·lo·gisch** [zotsi̯o'loːgɪʃ] *adj*. sociological
So·zius ['zoːtsi̯ʊs] *m* (-; -se) **1.** ✝ partner; **2.** pillion rider; **~fah·rer** *m* → ***Sozius* 2**; **~sitz** *m* pillion seat; ***auf dem ~ mitfahren*** ride pillion
so·zu·sa·gen [zoːtsu'zaːgən] *adv*. as it were, so to speak; ***er ist ~ ... a.*** you might say he's ... (*or* call him ...)
Spach·tel ['ʃpaxtəl] *m* (-s; -) **1.** spatula; **2.** → **~mas·se** *f* filler
spach·teln ['ʃpaxtəln] (h) **I.** *v/t*. ⚙ level out; surface; **II.** F *v/i*. F dig in, tuck in
Spa·gat [ʃpa'gaːt] *m*, *n* (-[e]s; -e) *the* splits *pl*.; ***~ machen*** do the splits
Spa·ghet·ti [ʃpa'gɛti] **1.** *pl*. *gastr*. spaghetti *sg*.; **2.** *contp*. *sl*. *m* (-s; -s) F wop, dago
spä·hen ['ʃpɛːən] *v/i*. (h) peer, peep; ***~ nach*** *dat*. look out for, F keep an eye out for; **Spä·her** ['ʃpɛːɐ] *m* (-s; -) scout; lookout; *fig*. spy
Späh|trupp ['ʃpɛː-] *m* reconnaissance (*or* scouting) party *or* patrol; **~wa·gen** *m* scout car
Spa·lier [ʃpa'liːɐ] *n* (-s; -e [-rə]) ⚘ trellis, espalier; *fig*. rows *pl*.; guard of hono(u)r; ***~ stehen*** form a guard of hono(u)r; **~obst** *n* wall fruit
Spalt [ʃpalt] *m* (-[e]s; -e) crack; gap; slit; ***die Tür e-n ~ offenlassen*** leave the door open slightly (*or* an inch or two, just a bit)
'spalt·bar *adj*. *phys*. fissile, fissionable
'Spalt·breit *m*: ***e-n ~ öffnen*** open slightly (*or* just a bit)
Spal·te ['ʃpaltə] *f* (-; -n) **1.** → ***Spalt***; **2.** *geol*. fissure, cleft, crevice; crevasse; **3.** (*newspaper etc*.) column
spal·ten ['ʃpaltən] (spaltete, gespaltet *or* gespalten, h) **I.** *v/t*. split (*a. phys*.); chop *wood*; ⚗ decompose; *fig*. split (up), divide; ***in zwei Teile ~*** split in two; **II.** *v/refl*.: ***sich ~*** split; *fig*. split (up), be divided (up) (***in*** *acc*. into); → ***gespalten***
spal·te·risch ['ʃpaltərɪʃ] *adj*. fissile, breakaway ...
'Spalt|fuß *m* ⚕ cleft foot; **~pilz** *fig*. *m* (spirit of) discord; **~pro͵dukt** *n phys*. fission product
Spal·tung ['ʃpaltʊŋ] *f* (-; -en) splitting (*a. phys*.); ⚗ separation, decomposition; *phys*. fission; *fig*. split (*a. pol*.); division *of opinions, a country etc*.; *esp. eccl*. schism
Span [ʃpaːn] *m* (-[e]s; Späne ['ʃpɛːnə]) *usu*. *pl*. shavings; filings; *fig*. ***wo gehobelt wird, fallen Späne*** you can't make an omelette without breaking eggs; **'span·ab·he·bend** *adj*.: ***~e Werkzeuge*** cutting tools; ***~e Bearbeitung*** metal cutting
spa·nen ['ʃpaːnən] *v/t*. (h) cut, machine
'Span·fer·kel *n* sucking pig
Span·ge ['ʃpaŋə] *f* (-; -n) a) clasp; buckle, b) hair slide, c) strap, d) bangle, e) ⚕ brace; **'Span·gen·schuh** *m* strap shoe

Spa·ni·er ['ʃpa:niɐ] *m* (-s; -), **Spa·nie·rin** ['ʃpa:niərɪn] *f* (-; -nen) Spaniard
spa·nisch ['ʃpa:nɪʃ] **I.** *adj.* Spanish; **~e Wand** folding screen; *fig.* **das kommt mir ~ vor** that's (very) strange *or* odd; **II.** ♀ *n* (-en) *ling.* Spanish
'**Span·korb** *m* chip basket
'**span·los** *adj.*: **~e Bearbeitung** metal forming
spann [ʃpan] *pret. of* **spinnen**
Spann [ʃpan] *m* (-[e]s; -e) *anat.* instep
'**Spann|be,ton** *m* pre-stressed concrete; **~bettuch** (*sep.* -tt·t-) *n* fitted (*Am.* contour) sheet
Span·ne ['ʃpanə] *f* (-; -n) **1. e-e kurze ~** a short space of time; **e-e ~ von fünf Tagen** a five-day period; **2.** (*profit*) margin, spread; **3.** span
span·nen ['ʃpanən] (h) **I.** *v/t.* stretch; tighten *rope etc.*; flex, tense *muscles*; draw *bow*; ⚙ clamp; bend *spring*; put up *clothesline etc.*; cock *gun, camera*; *fig.* strain *nerves*; **Leinwand auf e-n Rahmen ~** stretch a canvas over a frame; **e-n Bogen (Papier) ~ in** *acc.* put a sheet of paper in(to); **neue Saiten auf e-e Gitarre ~** restring a guitar; **Pferde vor den Wagen ~** harness horses to the carriage; *fig.* **s-e Erwartungen hoch ~** pitch one's expectations high; F **er hat's gespannt** he's caught on, he's got it, the penny's dropped; → **Folter, gespannt; II.** *v/refl.*: **sich ~** stretch (**über** *acc.* across, over); *muscle*: flex; *skin*: be taut (*or* tight); **sich über e-n Fluß ~** span a river; **III.** *v/i. skirt, shoes etc.*: be (too) tight; *skin*: be taut (*or* tight); *fig.* **~ auf** *acc.* a) be anxiously waiting for, b) follow closely, have one's eyes fixed on
'**span·nend I.** *adj.* exciting; suspenseful, full of suspense; captivating, gripping; **der Film war echt ~** *a.* the film had us on (*or* gripping) the edge of our seats; F **mach's nicht so ~!** (come on,) get on with it; **II.** *adv.*: **er schreibt ~** he writes in an exciting style, he knows how to hold your interest; **das Buch ist ~ geschrieben** it's a captivating (*or* an exciting) book
Span·ner[1] ['ʃpanɐ] *m* (-s; -) a) shoe tree, b) press
'**Span·ner**[2] *m* (-s; -) *zo.* geometrid
'**Span·ner**[3] F *m* (-s; -) peeping Tom
Spann|fut·ter ['ʃpan-] *n* ⚙ chuck; **~gar,di·ne** *f* net curtain; **~kraft** *f* elasticity; *phys.* tension; *fig.* energy, vigo(u)r; **~laken** *n* fitted (*Am.* contour) sheet; **~rahmen** *m* ⚙ tenter (frame); **~sä·ge** *f* frame saw; **~tep·pich** *m* wall-to-wall carpet(ing)
Span·nung ['ʃpanʊŋ] *f* (-; -en) **1.** a) ⚙ tension, b) ⚙ stress, c) ⚙ strain, d) ⚙ pressure, e) ⚠ span, f) ⚡ voltage; ⚡ **unter ~** live; **2.** *fig.* a) excitement, tension; tenseness, b) suspense; eager expectation; **j-n mit** (*or* **voll**) **~ erwarten** *etc.* await *etc.* s.o. with bated breath; **voller ~** → **spannend; j-n in ~ halten** keep s.o. in suspense; **3.** *pl. a. pol.* tension *sg.*, strained relations; tense atmosphere; **es herrschen ~en in ihrer Ehe** their marriage is under some strain at the moment, their relationship is rather strained at the moment
'**Span·nungs|ab·fall** *m* ⚡ voltage drop; **~feld** *fig. n* field of tension (*or* conflict); **~ge·biet** *n* → **Spannungsherd**
'**span·nungs·ge·la·den** *adj.* a) (extremely) tense, b) exciting, gripping *book, film etc.*, full of excitement; **~e Situation** *a.* cliffhanger situation
'**Span·nungs|herd** *m pol.* trouble spot, area of tension (*or* conflict), F hot spot; **~kopf·schmer·zen** *pl. a* tension headache *sg.*; **~mes·ser** *m* ⚡ voltmeter; **~mo,ment** *n* suspense factor; **~reg·ler** *m* ⚡ voltage regulator; **~ver·hält·nis** *n* strained relationship (*pol. a.* relations *pl.*); **~wäh·ler** *m* ⚡ voltage selector; **~zu·stand** *m* state of tension
'**Spann·wei·te** *f zo.* spread, span (*a.* ⚠); *fig.* scope, range
'**Span·plat·te** *f* chipboard
Spar|ak·ti,on ['ʃpa:ɐ-] *f* economy drive; **~au·to** *n* economy car; **~brief** *m* savings certificate; **~buch** *n* savings book, bankbook, passbook; **~büch·se** *f* money box; **~bud,get** *n* austerity budget; **~ein·la·gen** *pl.* savings deposits
spa·ren ['ʃpa:rən] (h) **I.** *v/t.* save; **ich habe mir einiges gespart** I've managed to save (up) a bit; **spar dir d-e Worte!** save your breath; **spar dir d-e Ratschläge!** I can do without your advice, thank you very much; **~ Sie sich solche Bemerkungen** you'd be better off keeping such remarks to yourself; **das hättest du dir ~ können** you could have saved yourself the trouble (*or* effort); **II.** *v/i.* a) save, b) cut down (expenses), economize; **~ für** (*or* **auf**) *acc.* save up for *s.th.*; **am falschen Ende ~** save at the wrong end; **~ an** (*or* **mit**) *dat.* be sparing with, stint on, be stingy with; **nicht ~ mit** *dat.* be lavish (*or* very generous) with; *fig.* **nicht mit Lob ~** be lavish in one's praise; **bei j-m nicht mit Lob ~** lavish praise on s.o.; **III.** ♀ *n* (-s; *no pl.*) saving; economizing
Spa·rer ['ʃpa:rɐ] *m* (-s; -), **Spa·re·rin** ['ʃpa:rərɪn] *f* (-; -nen) saver
Spar·flam·me ['ʃpa:ɐ-] *f* low flame; pilot light; F *fig.* **auf ~ kochen** go easy (on the money)
Spar·för·de·rungs·maß·nah·men ['ʃpa:ɐ-] *pl.* savings incentive scheme *sg.*; **~ ergreifen** encourage people to save
Spar·gang ['ʃpa:ɐ-] *m mot.* overdrive; *fig.* **e-n ~ einlegen** cut down on expenses
Spar·gel ['ʃpargəl] *m* (-s; -) ⚘ asparagus; **~ge·richt** *n* asparagus dish; **~spit·zen** *pl.* asparagus tips; **~sup·pe** *f* asparagus soup; **~zeit** *f* asparagus season
Spar|gro·schen ['ʃpa:ɐ-] *m* nest egg; **~gut·ha·ben** *n* savings balance; **~haus·halt** *m* austerity budget
Spar·kas·se ['ʃpa:ɐ-] *f* savings bank
'**Spar·kas·sen·buch** *n* → **Sparbuch**
Spar·kon·to ['ʃpa:ɐ-] *n* savings account
spär·lich ['ʃpɛ:ɐlɪç] **I.** *adj.* scanty, meagre (*Am.* meager); scant *praise, knowledge etc.*; sparse; poor; ✝ slack *demand*; thin *hair*; skimpy *clothes*; **~er Beifall** a trickle of applause; **~es Einkommen** pittance (of a wage); **~e Reste** (a few) scraps; **die Reaktionen waren ~** the response was very thin; **II.** *adv.*: **~ bekleidet** scantily (*or* skimpily) dressed, scantily clad; **~ beleuchtet** poorly (*or* badly) lit; **~ besucht** poorly attended; **~ bevölkert** sparsely (*or* thinly) populated
Spar|maß·nah·men ['ʃpa:ɐ-] *pl.* economy (*or* austerity) measures; **~mo·tor** *m* low-fuel consumption engine; **~pak·kung** *f* economy size (*or* pack); **~pa,ket** *n pol.* cuts package; **~pfen·nig** *m* nest egg; **~po·li,tik** *f* policy of austerity; **~prä·mie** *f* savings premium; **~pro,gramm** *n* **1.** *pol.* cuts (*or* austerity) program(me); **2.** ⚙ economy cycle
Spar·ren ['ʃparən] *m* (-s; -) **1.** rafter; **2.** F *fig.* **e-n ~ locker haben** have a screw loose (somewhere)
spar·ren ['ʃparən] *v/i.* (h) *boxing*: spar; **Spar·ring** ['ʃparɪŋ] *n* (-s; -s) sparring; '**Spar·rings·part·ner** *m* sparring partner
spar·sam ['ʃpa:ɐza:m] **I.** *adj.* economical, thrifty; scant *furnishings etc.*; **~ sein** *detergent etc.*: *a.* go a long way; **~ im Verbrauch** economical; **er ist sehr ~** *usu.* he's (very) careful with his money; **~en Gebrauch von et. machen** use s.th. sparingly, make sparing use of s.th.; **II.** *adv.*: **~ umgehen mit** *dat.* go easy on, be sparing with, save *one's energy etc.*; **~ auftragen** apply sparingly; **~ leben** live very economically; **~ möbliert** scantily furnished; '**Spar·sam·keit** *f* (-; *no pl.*) thrift(iness); economy; frugality, austerity; '**Spar·sam·keits·grund** *m*: **aus Sparsamkeitsgründen** for economic reasons, for reasons of economy
Spar|schwein ['ʃpa:ɐ-] *n* piggy bank; **das ~ schlachten** (**müssen**) (have to) rob the piggy bank; **~strumpf** *m* money sock
spar·ta·nisch [ʃpar'ta:nɪʃ] **I.** *adj.* Spartan; *fig.* spartan, austere; *fig.* **~e Erziehung** (**Verhältnisse**) spartan upbringing (conditions); **II.** *adv.*: **~ leben** lead a spartan life
Spar·te ['ʃpartə] *f* (-; -n) **1.** field, line; **2.** section, column
Spar|ver·trag ['ʃpa:ɐ-] *m* savings agreement; **~zins** *m* interest on savings; **~zu·la·ge** *f* (tax-free) savings bonus
spas·mo·disch [ʃpas'mo:dɪʃ] *adj.* spasmodic(ally *adv.*)
spas·mo·ly·tisch [ʃpasmo'ly:tɪʃ] *adj.* anti-spasmodic
Spaß [ʃpa:s] *m* (-es; Späße ['ʃpɛ:sə]) a) joke, *pl. a.* antics, b) fun; **~ machen** a) be joking, b) be (great) fun; **er hat nur ~ gemacht** he was only joking; **sie versteht keinen ~** she can't take a joke, *w.s.* she won't stand for any nonsense; **in Geldsachen versteht er keinen ~** he counts every penny; **~ beiseite!** seriously, though (*or* now); joking aside; **mach keine Späße!** F you're kidding; **da hört der ~ auf** that's going beyond a joke; **aus ~ wurde Ernst** the fun didn't last very long; **wenn's dir ~ macht** if you really want to; **es macht ihm (großen) ~, er hat s-n ~ daran** he (really) enjoys it, F he gets a (big) kick out of it; **es macht keinen ~** it's no fun; **es macht mir keinen ~ mehr** I'm fed up with it, I don't enjoy it any more; **sich e-n ~ daraus machen zu** *inf.* enjoy *ger.*, F get a kick out of *ger.*; **da ist uns der ~ vergangen** it (really) spoilt things (for us), it put a damper on things; **viel ~!** have fun, enjoy yourself (*or* yourselves); **aus** (*or* **im, zum**) **~** for fun; **nur (so) zum ~** just for the fun of it; **was kostet der (ganze) ~?** how much is that going to set me back?; **ein teurer ~** an expensive business
Späß·chen ['ʃpɛ:sçən] *n* (-s; -) little joke; **ich habe mir ein ~ erlaubt** I was just having a little joke (*or* a bit of fun)
spa·ßen ['ʃpa:sən] *v/i.* (h) joke; **damit ist nicht zu ~** it's no joke (*or* joking matter); **mit ihm ist nicht zu ~** he won't stand for

any nonsense (*or* fun and games), you've got to watch what you say when he's around
spa·ßes·hal·ber ['ʃpa:səshalbɐ] *adv.* (just) for the fun of it
'spaß·haft, spa·ßig ['ʃpa:sıç] *adj.* funny
'Spaß|ma·cher *m* comedian; clown; **~ver·der·ber** [-fɛɐdɛrbɐ] *m* (-s; -) spoilsport; F wet blanket; **~vo·gel** *m* comedian
Spa·sti·ker ['ʃpastikɐ] *m* (-s; -) ⚕ spastic; **spa·stisch** ['ʃpastıʃ] **I.** *adj.* spastic; **II.** *adv.*: **~ gelähmt** spastic
spät [ʃpɛ:t] **I.** *adj.* late; **am ~en Nachmittag** (in the) late afternoon, late in the afternoon; **bis in die ~en Nachtstunden** till late at night; **es ist (wird) ~** it's getting late; **wie ~ ist es?** what time is it?; **gestern abend wurde es ~** it went on (*or* I was *etc.* up) till fairly late last night; **heute abend wird's wieder ~** I'll be home (*or* back) late again tonight, it's going to be late again tonight; **in den ~en dreißiger Jahren** in the late thirties; **ein ~er Rembrandt** a late Rembrandt; **der ~e Goethe** the late(r) Goethe, Goethe in his later works; **II.** *adv.* late; *esp. fig.* at a late hour; *fig.* late (on) in life; **zu ~ kommen** be late (**zu** *dat.* for); **er kam fünf Minuten zu ~** he was five minutes late; **du kommst zu ~** you're too late; **~ in der Nacht** late at night; **von früh bis ~** from morning till night; **~ aufstehen** a) get up late, b) be a late riser; **~ dran sein** be (running) late
spät·abends *adv.* late at night
'Spät|an,ti·ke *f*: **die ~** late antiquity; **~auf·ste·her** *m* late riser; **~aus·sied·ler** *m* late repatriate
'Spät·ba,rock *n, m,* **'spät·ba,rock** *adj.* late Baroque
'Spät·dienst *m*: (**~ haben** be on) late shift
Spa·tel ['ʃpa:təl] *m* (-s; -) spatula
Spa·ten ['ʃpa:tən] *m* (-s; -) spade; **~stich** *m* cut of the spade; *fig.* **den ersten ~ tun** break ground
'Spät·ent·wick·ler *m* late developer
spä·ter ['ʃpɛ:tɐ] **I.** *adj.* a) later (**als** than), b) future; subsequent, ... to come; **ihr ~er Mann** her future husband, her husband-to-be; **II.** *adv.* a) later, b) later on; **früher oder ~** sooner or later; **erst ~ wurde mir klar ...** it was only afterwards (*or* much later) that I realized; **~ wirst du vielleicht anders darüber denken** some day (*or* when you're older) you might see it differently; **was willst du ~ einmal werden?** what do you want to be when you grow up?; **an ~ denken** think of the future; **jetzt, ein Jahr ~** a year on; **bis ~!** see you later
'spä·ter'hin *adv.* later on
spä·te·stens ['ʃpɛ:təstəns] *adv.* ... at the latest; not later than; **du kriegst sie ~ am Freitag** you'll have them (by) Friday at the latest; **er wird ~ in einer Stunde hier sein** *a.* he'll be here within an (*or* the) hour
'Spät·ge·burt *f* ⚕ retarded (*or* post-term) birth
'Spät·go·tik *f* △ late Gothic (style); *in England*: *a.* Perpendicular style; *hist.* late Gothic period; **'spät·go·tisch** *adj.* late Gothic, *in England*: △ *a.* Perpendicular
'Spät·heim·keh·rer *m* late-repatriated prisoner of war, late returnee (from a prisoner-of-war camp)
'Spät·herbst *m* late autumn (*Am.* fall)
'Spät·le·se *f* **1.** spätlese; late vintage wine; **2.** late vintage (*or* harvest)
Spät·ling ['ʃpɛ:tlıŋ] *m* (-s; -e) **1.** late fruit; **2.** latecomer, F afterthought
'Spät·mit·tel·al·ter *n* late Middle Ages *pl.*
'Spät·nach·mit·tag *m* late afternoon; **am ~** → **'spät·nach·mit·tags** *adv.* in the late afternoon, late in the afternoon
'Spät|nach·rich·ten *pl.* late(-night) news *sg.*; **~obst** *n* late fruit; **~pro,gramm** *n radio, TV*: late-night program(me) (*or* show); **~schä·den** *pl.* long-term side effects, delayed effects, ⚕ late sequelae; **~schicht** *f*: (**~ haben** be on) late shift; **~som·mer** *m* late summer; **~vor·stel·lung** *f* late-night performance; **~werk** *n* late(r) work
Spatz [ʃpats] *m* (-en; -en) sparrow; *fig.* F darling, sweetie; *fig.* **essen wie ein ~** pick at one's food; **mit Kanonen auf ~en schießen** break a butterfly on the wheel; **das pfeifen die ~en von allen Dächern** it's all over town, everyone knows about it, it's everybody's secret; **lieber den ~ in der Hand als die Taube auf dem Dach** a bird in hand is worth two in the bush; **'Spat·zen·hirn** F *n* F peabrain; **ein ~ haben** be peabrained, be as thick as two short planks
'Spät|zün·der F *m* **1. ~ sein** be slow on the uptake, be a bit slow; **2.** → **Spätentwickler**; **~zün·dung** *f mot.* retarded ignition
spa·zie·ren [ʃpa'tsi:rən] *v/i.* (sn) walk (around), stroll; **wir waren im Wald ~** we went for a walk in (*or* through) the woods; **~fah·ren** (*irr., sep.,* → **fahren**) **I.** *v/i.* (sn) go for a ride (in the car), go for a run (F spin); **II.** *v/t.* (h) take *s.o.* for a ride (in the car), take *s.o.* for a run (F spin); **~füh·ren** *v/t.* (*sep.,* h) take *s.o.* (out) for a walk; **den Hund ~** *a.* walk the dog; *fig.* **den neuen Mantel** *etc.* **~** take one's new coat *etc.* for a walk, show off one's new coat *etc.*
spa'zie·ren·ge·hen I. *v/i.* (*irr., sep.,* sn, → **gehen**) go for a walk (*or* stroll); **im Park ~** *a.* take a walk (*or* stroll) through *or* in the park; **er geht gern im Wald spazieren** he likes to walk (*or* go for walks) in *or* through the woods; **II.** ℒ *n* (-s; *no pl.*) walking, walks *pl.*
Spa·zier·fahrt [ʃpa'tsi:ɐ-] *f* drive, ride, run, F spin; **kurze ~** *a.* run around the block
Spa·zier·gang [ʃpa'tsi:ɐ-] *m* walk, stroll; *fig.* F doddle; **e-n ~ machen** go for a walk (*or* stroll); **machst du mit uns e-n ~?** are you going to come for a walk with us?; **Spa'zier·gän·ger** [-gɛŋɐ] *m* (-s; -) walker, stroller; *pl. a.* people out on a walk
Spa·zier|stock [ʃpa'tsi:ɐ-] *m* (walking) stick, cane; **~weg** *m* (foot)path, walk
Specht [ʃpɛçt] *m* (-[e]s; -e) woodpecker
Speck [ʃpɛk] *m* (-[e]s; *no pl.*) **1.** bacon (fat); F **ran an den ~!** F let's get stuck in(, then); **mit ~ fängt man Mäuse** good bait catches fine fish; → **Made**; **2.** F flab; **~ ansetzen** F put it on, put on the flab; **~bauch** F *m* fat belly, F pot-belly
speckig ['ʃpɛkıç] (*sep.* -k·k-) *adj.* **1.** greasy; **2.** fat
'Speck|nacken F *m* fat neck; **~schei·be** *f* bacon rasher; **~schwar·te** *f* bacon rind; **~sei·te** *f* side of bacon, flitch
Spe·di·teur [ʃpedi'tø:ɐ] *m* (-s; -e [-rə]) forwarding (⚓ shipping) agent, haulage company; **Spe·di·ti·on** [ʃpedi'tsĭo:n] *f* (-; -en) **1.** forwarding; ⚓ shipping, haulage; **2.** forwarding (⚓ shipping) agency, haulage company; **Spe·di·ti'ons·kauf·mann** *m* forwarding (⚓ shipping) agent
Speer [ʃpe:ɐ] *m* (-[e]s; -e [-rə]) spear; *sport*: javelin; **~spit·ze** *f* tip of a (*or* the) spear; *a. fig.* spearhead; **~wer·fen** *n* (throwing the) javelin; **~wer·fer** *m* javelin thrower; **~wurf** *m* **1.** → **Speerwerfen**; **2.** javelin throw
Spei·che ['ʃpaıçə] *f* (-; -n) **1.** spoke; **2.** *anat.* radius
Spei·chel ['ʃpaıçəl] *m* (-s; *no pl.*) saliva, spittle, F spit; **~bil·dung** *f* salivation; **~drü·se** *f* salivary gland; **~fluß** *m* (-sses; *no pl.*) flow of saliva, salivation; **übermäßiger ~** hypersalivation
'Spei·chel·lecker [-lɛkɐ] (*sep.* -k·k-) *contp. m* (-s; -) F toady, bootlicker
Spei·chel·lecke·rei [-lɛkə'raı] (*sep.* -k·k-) *contp. f* (-; *no pl.*) F toadying, sucking up
spei·cheln ['ʃpaıçəln] *v/i.* (h) salivate
'Spei·chen·rad *n* spoke wheel
Spei·cher ['ʃpaıçɐ] *m* (-s; -) **1.** warehouse; **2.** granary, silo, (grain) elevator; **3.** loft, attic; **4.** *computer*: memory; **~bat·te,rie** *f* accumulator, storage battery; **~bek·ken** *n* reservoir; **~dich·te** *f computer*: bit density; **~funk·ti,on** *f* memory function; **~ka·pa·zi,tät** *f* storage (*computer*: memory) capacity; **~kraft·werk** *n* storage power station
spei·chern ['ʃpaıçɐn] *v/t.* (h) store (*a.* ⚡); *computer*: *a.* save (**auf** *acc. or dat.* onto); ✝ stockpile; *fig.* store up
'Spei·cher|ofen *m* storage heater; **~schutz** *m computer*: memory protection
Spei·che·rung ['ʃpaıçəruŋ] *f* (-; *no pl.*) storage, storing
spei·en ['ʃpaıən] (spie, gespien, h) **I.** *v/t.* spit; *fig.* spew, belch; spout *water*; **Feuer ~** spew (*or* belch) flames, spew fire; **II.** *v/i.* vomit, be sick
Spei·se ['ʃpaızə] *f* (-; -n) a) *a. pl.* food, b) dish; **warme und kalte ~n** hot and cold dishes (*or* meals); **~ap·fel** *m* eating apple, eater; **~eis** *n* ice cream; **~fett** *n* edible (*or* cooking) fat; **~kam·mer** *f* pantry, larder; **~kar·te** *f* menu; **die ~, bitte!** could I (*or* we) have the menu, please; **~lo,kal** *n* eatery, restaurant
spei·sen ['ʃpaızən] (h) **I.** *v/i.* eat, *formal*: dine, *lit. and iro.* sup; **zu Mittag ~** (have) lunch; **zu Abend ~** have dinner, dine; **wir haben sehr gut gespeist** we had an excellent meal; **II.** *v/t.* feed (*a.* ⚙, ⚡)
'Spei·sen|auf·zug *m* dumbwaiter; **~fol·ge** *f* order of courses
Spei·se|öl *n* cooking (*or* salad) oil; **~plan** *m this week's etc.* menu; **~re·ste** *pl.* a) leftovers, b) food particles; **~röh·re** *f anat.* (o)esophagus, F gullet; **~saal** *m* dining hall; *hotel*: dining room; *univ., eccl. etc. a.* refectory; **~schrank** *m* food cupboard; **~ser,vice** *n* dinner service (*or* set); **~wa·gen** *m* 🚃 dining (*or* restaurant) car, diner
Spei·sung ['ʃpaızuŋ] *f* (-; -en) feeding; ⚡ supply
spei·übel ['ʃpaı'ʔy:bəl] *adj.*: **mir ist ~** I feel sick, I think I'm going to be sick; *fig.* **da wird e-m ~, wenn man das hört** it's enough to make you sick, it churns your stomach to hear that kind of thing

Spek·ta·kel[1] [ʃpɛk'taːkəl] F *m* (-s; *no pl.*) **1.** row, F racket; ***e-n ~ machen*** kick up a (real) racket; **2.** rumpus; ***e-n ~ machen*** F kick up a row (*or* rumpus); **3.** F palaver, to-do, fuss; ***so ein ~!*** what a palaver (*or* to-do)!, what a fuss they made!

Spek'ta·kel[2] *n* (-s; -) spectacle; media event

spek·ta·ku·lär [ʃpɛktaku'lɛːɐ] *adj.* spectacular

Spek·tral|ana·ly·se [ʃpɛk'traːl-] *f* spectrum analysis; **~be·reich** *m* spectral range; **~far·be** *f* colo(u)r of the spectrum

Spek·tro·gramm [ʃpɛktro'gram] *n* (-s; -e) spectrogram

Spek·tro·graph [ʃpɛktro'graːf] *m* (-en; -en) spectrograph

Spek·tro·skop [ʃpɛktro'skoːp] *n* (-s; -e) spectroscope

Spek·trum ['ʃpɛktrʊm] *n* (-s; -tren [-trən], -tra [-tra]) spectrum (*a. fig.*); *fig.* range; *fig.* ***großes ~*** a) broad spectrum, b) wide range

Spe·ku·lant [ʃpeku'lant] *m* (-en; -en) speculator

Spe·ku·la·ti·on [ʃpekula'tsĭoːn] *f* (-; -en) **1.** speculation; ***~en anstellen*** speculate; ***das sind ~en*** that's (just) speculation; **2.** *phls.* speculation; **3.** ✝ speculation, venture

Spe·ku·la·ti'ons|ge·schäft *n* speculative transaction; gamble; **~ge·win·ne** *pl.* speculative gains; **~ob͵jekt** *n* object of speculation; **~ver·lu·ste** *pl.* speculative losses

Spe·ku·la·ti·us [ʃpeku'laːtsĭʊs] *m thin, gingery biscuit* (*Am. cookie*) *usually eaten around Christmas time*

spe·ku·la·tiv [ʃpekula'tiːf] *adj.* speculative

spe·ku·lie·ren [ʃpeku'liːrən] *v/i.* (h) speculate (***über*** *acc.* on); ✝ speculate (***in*** *dat.* in), play the stock market; ***~ auf*** *acc.* a) ✝ speculate on, operate for, b) F have one's hopes on; → ***Baisse, Hausse***

Spe·ku·lum ['ʃpeːkulʊm] *n* (-s; -la) ⚕ speculum

Spe·lun·ke [ʃpe'lʊŋkə] *contp. f* (-; -n) F (low) dive

spen·da·bel [ʃpɛn'daːbəl] F *adj.* (very) generous

Spen·de ['ʃpɛndə] *f* (-; -n) donation; contribution; ***bitte e-e kleine ~!*** would you like to give something to charity?

spen·den ['ʃpɛndən] (h) **I.** *v/t.* **1.** give, donate (*a.* ⚕); **2.** give, provide; give out *heat*; **3.** *eccl.* administer; **4.** give *praise etc., lit.* bestow (*dat.* on); ***Trost ~*** offer (some) consolation; → ***Beifall***; **II.** *v/i.* give (*or* donate) money, make a donation (***für*** *acc.* to, in aid of); ***großzügig ~*** give *or* donate freely (*or* generously)

'Spen·den|ak·ti͵on *f* fund-raising (*or* charity) drive; **~auf·ruf** *m* appeal for funds; **~be·schei·ni·gung** *f* receipt for a donation to charity; **~kon·to** *n* donations account; **~samm·lung** *f* → ***Spendenaktion***

Spen·der ['ʃpɛndɐ] *m* (-s; -) **1.** donator; donor (*a.* ⚕); **2.** dispenser; **~aus·weis** *m* ⚕ donor card; **~blut** *n* donor blood; **~herz** *n* donor heart; **~nie·re** *f* donor kidney

spen·die·ren [ʃpɛn'diːrən] F *v/t.* (h): ***j-m et. ~*** treat s.o. to s.th.; ***j-m ein Bier ~*** stand (*or* buy) s.o. a beer; ***ich spendier' den Wein*** I'll buy (*or* supply) the wine;

spen·dier·freu·dig [ʃpɛn'diːɐ-] *adj.* generous; **Spen'dier·ho·sen** F *pl.*: ***die ~ anhaben*** be in a generous mood

Speng·ler ['ʃpɛŋlɐ] *m* (-s; -) panel-beater

Sper·ber ['ʃpɛrbɐ] *m* (-s; -) sparrowhawk

Spe·renz·chen [ʃpe'rɛntsçən] F *pl.*: ***~ machen*** be awkward, cause trouble; make a fuss

Sper·ling ['ʃpɛrlɪŋ] *m* (-s; -e) sparrow

Sper·ma ['ʃpɛrma] *n* (-s; -men [-mən], -mata [-mata]) sperm

Sper·mi·um ['ʃpɛrmĭʊm] *n* (-s; Spermien ['ʃpɛrmĭən]) sperm cell

sperr·an·gel·weit ['ʃpɛr'ʔaŋəl'vaɪt] F *adv.*: ***~ offen*** wide open; ***den Mund ~ aufmachen*** gape, F gawk

Sperr·be·zirk ['ʃpɛr-] *m* restricted (*or* no-go) area

Sper·re ['ʃpɛrə] *f* (-; -n) **1.** a) barrier, b) road block; barricade; **2.** ⚙ lock, locking device; **3.** ✝, ⚓ embargo; blockade; *sport*: suspension; ***e-e ~ verhängen über*** *acc.* impose a ban *etc.* on; **4.** *fig.* ***e-e ~ haben*** have a mental block; ***ich habe e-e ~*** *a.* I can't think

'sper·ren (h) **I.** *v/t.* **1.** block (*officially*: close) *a road etc.* (***für den Verkehr*** to traffic), cordon off; close *a bridge, port etc.*; **2.** shut, close; lock (*a.* ⚙); bolt; **3.** *typ.* space (out); **4.** ✝ embargo; ⚙ cut off *gas, water, telephone etc.*; stop *a check etc.*, *a.* freeze *payments etc.*; block *an account*; *fig.* ban, prohibit; → ***gesperrt***; **5.** *sport*: a) block, obstruct, b) suspend, disqualify; **II.** *fig. v/refl.*: ***sich ~*** ba(u)lk (***gegen*** *acc.* at *s.th.*), resist (*s.th.*)

Sperr|feu·er ['ʃpɛr-] *n* ⚔ barrage; *fig.* ***ins ~ der Kritik geraten*** come under fire; **~frist** *f* waiting period; **~ge·biet** *n* restricted (*or* no-go) area; **~ge·päck** *n* bulky luggage; **~gür·tel** *m* (police) cordon; *pol.* cordon sanitaire; **~gut** *n* bulky goods *pl.*

Sperr·holz ['ʃpɛr-] *n* plywood; **~plat·te** *f* piece (*or* sheet) of plywood

sper·rig ['ʃpɛrɪç] *adj.* bulky; unwieldy

Sperr|klau·sel ['ʃpɛr-] *f* restrictive clause; **~kon·to** *n* blocked account; **~kreis** *m radio*: wave trap; **~mi·no·ri͵tät** *f* blocking minority

Sperr·müll ['ʃpɛr-] *m* bulk(y) rubbish (*or* waste, refuse); **~ab·fuhr** *f* bulk(y) waste pickup

Sperr|schrift ['ʃpɛr-] *f* spaced writing; **~sitz** *m thea.* seat in the stalls (*or* orchestra); **~stun·de** *f* curfew; **~ta·ste** *f* locking button

Sper·rung ['ʃpɛrʊŋ] *f* (-; -en) **1.** obstruction; blocking; *official*: closing (off) *of a road etc.*; **2.** ⚙ locking; **3.** → ***Sperre*** 3

Sperr|ven͵til ['ʃpɛr-] *n* lock(ing) valve; **~ver·merk** *m* ✝ non-negotiability clause; **~vor·rich·tung** *f* ⚙ locking device, catch; **~zo·ne** *f* → ***Sperrgebiet***

Spe·sen ['ʃpeːzən] *pl.* ✝ expenses; F ***außer ~ nichts gewesen*** (it was) a waste of time and energy; **⁓frei** *adj.* free of charge; **~kon·to** *n* expense account; **~rit·ter** *contp. m* expense-account rider

Spe·zi[1] ['ʃpeːtsi] *dial. m* (-s; -[s]) pal, *Am.* buddy

'Spe·zi[2] *f* (-; -[s]) *cola and lemonade mix*

spe·zi·al [ʃpe'tsĭaːl] *obs. adj.* → ***speziell***

Spe·zi'al|aus·bil·dung *f* special(ized) training; **~aus·füh·rung** *f* special model (*or* design); **~ein·heit** *f* special unit, special task force; **~fach** *n* special subject; **~fahr·zeug** *n* special-purpose vehicle; **~fall** *m* special case; **~ge·biet** *n* special field (*or* area), speciality, *Am.* specialty; **~ge·schäft** *n* specialist dealer('s), specialist(s *pl.*)

spe·zia·li·sie·ren [ʃpetsĭali'ziːrən] *v/refl.*: ***sich ~ auf*** *acc.* specialize in *s.th.*

spe·zia·li·siert [ʃpetsĭali'ziːɐt] *adj.*: ***sie sind ~ auf*** *acc.* they specialize in, their speciality (*Am.* specialty) is

Spe·zia·li'sie·rung *f* (-; *no pl.*) specialization

Spe·zia·list [ʃpetsĭa'lɪst] *m* (-en; -en) *a.* ⚕ specialist; ***~ sein in*** *dat.* specialize in

Spe·zia·li·tät [ʃpetsĭali'tɛːt] *f* (-, -en) speciality, *Am.* specialty

Spe·zia·li'tä·ten|ge·schäft *n* delicatessen shop; **~re·stau͵rant** *n* restaurant serving (local *or* national) specialities (*Am.* specialties)

Spe·zi'al|klei·dung *f* special clothing; **~sla·lom** *m skiing*: special slalom; **~trai·ning** *n* special training; **~wis·sen** *n* special(ized) knowledge; **~wör·ter·buch** *n* specialized dictionary

spe·zi·ell [ʃpe'tsĭɛl] **I.** *adj.* special; specific, particular; ***in diesem ~en Fall*** in this particular case; **II.** *adv.* specially, particularly; specifically; ***~ angefertigt*** made-to-measure (*or* -order), custom-made; ***~ gebaut*** purpose-built

Spe·zi·es ['ʃpeːtsĭɛs] *f* (-; - [-eːs]) species; *fig. contp.* breed; ***die menschliche ~*** the human species

Spe·zi·fi·ka·ti·on [ʃpetsifika'tsĭoːn] *f* (-; -en) specification

spe·zi·fisch [ʃpe'tsiːfɪʃ] *adj.* specific(ally *adv.*) (*a.* ⚕); ***~es Gewicht*** specific weight (*phys.* gravity); ***~ sein für*** *acc.* be specific to

spe·zi·fi·zie·ren [ʃpetsifi'tsiːrən] *v/t.* (h) specify; give details of; ***könnten Sie das etwas ~?*** could you be more specific?

Spe·zi·fi'zie·rung *f* (-; -en) specification

Sphä·re ['sfɛːrə] *f* (-; -n) sphere (*a. fig.*); → ***schweben***; **'Sphä·ren·har·mo͵nie** *f* harmony of the spheres

sphä·risch ['sfɛːrɪʃ] *adj.* spherical; ***~e Musik*** music of the spheres

Sphinx [sfɪŋks] *f* (-; Sphingen ['sfɪŋən]) sphinx (*a. fig.*); ***wie e-e ~ lächeln*** give an enigmatic smile

spicken ['ʃpɪkən] (*sep.* -k·k-) (h) **I.** *v/t.* *gastr.* lard; *fig.* interlard; F ***j-n ~*** F grease s.o.'s palm; → ***gespickt***; **II.** F *v/i.* cheat, crib

Spick|na·del ['ʃpɪk-] *f* larding pin; **~zet·tel** F *m* crib, pony

spie [ʃpiː] *pret. of* ***speien***

Spie·gel ['ʃpiːgəl] *m* (-s; -) mirror (*a. fig.*); ⚕ speculum; *opt.*, ⚙ reflector; ⚕ *and fig.* level; ***sich im ~ betrachten*** look at o.s. in the mirror; *fig.* ***j-m e-n ~ vorhalten*** hold a mirror up to s.o.; ***die Ereignisse der Woche im ~ der Presse*** the week's events as seen by the press; F ***das kannst du dir hinter den ~ stecken!*** and don't you forget it!

'Spie·gel·bild *n* mirror image; *fig.* mirror, reflection; *fig.* ***sie ist das ~ ihrer Mutter*** she's the spitting image of her mother; **'spie·gel·bild·lich** *adj.* mirror-image ...

'spie·gel'blank *adj.* shiny, gleaming; *w.s.* F squeaky clean; ***et. ~ putzen*** polish s.th. until it shines

'Spie·gel·ei *n* fried egg, *Am.* fried egg sunny-side up

Spie·gel·fech·te·rei [-fɛçtə'raɪ] *fig. f* (-; -en) shadow-boxing; bluff, eyewash

'spie·gel·frei *adj.* non-glare, anti-dazzle

'Spie·gel·glas *n* mirror glass

'spie·gel'glatt *adj. ocean etc.*: glassy, (as) smooth as glass; *road*: like glass; *floor etc.*: (as) slippery as ice

spie·geln ['ʃpi:gəln] (h) **I.** *v/i.* a) shine, b) reflect the light; dazzle; **II.** *v/t.* reflect (*a. fig.*); **III.** *v/refl.*: ***sich*** ~ be reflected; *fig. a.* be mirrored

'Spie·gel·re͵flex·ka·me·ra *f*: (***einäugige*** ~ single-lens) reflex camera

'Spie·gel|saal *m* hall of mirrors; **~schrank** *m* mirrored wardrobe; **~schrift** *f* mirror writing; *typ.* reflected face; **~te·le͵skop** *n* reflector telescope

Spie·ge·lung ['ʃpi:gəlʊŋ] *f* (-; -en) **1.** reflection; **2.** mirage; **3.** ⚕ endoscopy

Spiel [ʃpi:l] *n* (-[e]s; -e) **1.** a) play(ing); gambling, b) game; *sport*: match, play, c) *fig.* play *a. of colo(u)rs etc.*, d) *thea.*, ♪ playing, performance; ***ein ~ Karten*** a pack (*or* deck) of cards; ***ein ~ des Zufalls*** one of fortune's little tricks; ***~ des Schicksals*** *the* vagaries of fortune; ***ein seltsames ~ der Natur*** a freak of nature; ***ein ~ mit Worten*** a play on words; ***ein ~ mit dem Feuer*** playing with fire; ***ein ~ mit der Liebe*** trifling with love; ***das ~ von Licht und Schatten*** the play of light and shade; ***gefährliches ~*** *soccer*: dangerous play, *fig.* (*a.* ***gewagtes ~***) gamble; ***dem ~ verfallen sein*** be an inveterate gambler; ***freies ~ haben*** have the field to o.s.; ***das ~ aufgeben*** throw in the towel; ***j-m das ~ verderben*** spoil things for s.o.; ***j-s ~ durchschauen*** see through s.o.'s (little) game; ***freies ~ der Kräfte*** free interplay of forces; ***auf dem ~ stehen*** be at stake; ***aufs ~ setzen*** (put at) risk; ***j-n (et.) aus dem ~ lassen*** leave s.o. (s.th.) out of it; ***laß mich aus dem ~*** count me out; ***ein doppeltes ~ mit j-m treiben*** double-cross s.o.; ***sein ~ mit j-m treiben*** play games with s.o.; ***gewonnenes ~ haben*** have the game in one's hand; ***im ~ sein*** *ball*: be in play, *fig.* be involved (***bei*** *dat.* in); ***es war e-e gehörige Portion Glück im ~*** there was a fair bit of luck involved; ***ins ~ bringen*** a) *sport*: bring *s.o.* on, b) *fig.* bring *s.th.* into play, get *s.o.* involved; ***j-n aus dem ~ nehmen*** *sport*: take s.o. off; ***das ~ bestimmen*** *sport*: dictate the match; ***wie steht das ~?*** *sport*: what's the score?; ***leichtes ~ haben*** win hands down, *fig.* have an easy job of it; ***das ~ ist aus*** the game's up; ***genug des grausamen ~s!*** that'll do!; ***die Hand im ~ haben*** have a finger in the pie; → ***abgekartet, Miene, olympisch***; **2.** ⚙ play; clearance; allowance

'Spiel|art *f biol. and fig.* variety; **~au·to͵mat** *m* gaming (*or* amusement) machine; slot machine, F one-armed bandit; **~ball** *m* ball; *tennis*: game ball; *billiards*: cue ball; *fig.* plaything; *fig.* ***ein ~ der Wellen sein*** be at the mercy of the waves; **~bank** *f* (-; -en) (gambling) casino

'spiel·bar *adj.* playable

'Spiel|be·ginn *m* start of play; **~bein** *n* free leg; **~brett** *n* board; **~dau·er** *f* playing time *of a cassette etc.*; → ***Spielzeit***

spie·len ['ʃpi:lən] (h) **I.** *v/i.* **1.** play (*a. fig.*); *waves etc.*: *a.* lap; ***mit dem Bleistift ~*** fiddle (*or* play) around with one's pencil; *fig.* ***mit Worten ~*** play (around) with words; ***in allen Farben ~*** sparkle in all colo(u)rs, iridesce; ***ins Rötliche ~*** have a reddish tinge; **2.** gamble (***um*** *acc.* for); ***falsch ~*** cheat; ***aus Leidenschaft ~*** have a passion for gambling; ***hoch (niedrig) ~*** play for high (low) stakes; ***sich um sein Vermögen ~*** gamble away one's fortune; *fig.* ***mit s-m Leben ~*** gamble with one's life, put one's life at risk; **3.** *sport*: ***gut (schlecht) ~*** play well (badly); ***unentschieden ~ gegen*** draw with; ***A spielte gegen B*** A played B; **4.** *thea.* play, act; *film etc.*: be on (***in*** *dat.* at); ***~ in*** *dat. scene, play*: be set in; ***~ an*** *dat. play*: be on at, *actor*: be (engaged) at; ***heute wird nicht gespielt*** there's no performance tonight; ***der Film spielt schon wochenlang*** the film has been running for weeks; **5.** ♪ ***falsch ~*** play a wrong note (*or* the wrong note[s]); **6.** *fig.* ***mit j-m ~*** play (*or* mess) around with s.o.; ***er läßt nicht mit sich ~*** he's not one to mess around (*or* to be trifled) with; ***mit dem Gedanken ~ zu*** *inf.* toy with the idea of *ger.*; ***mit dem Feuer ~*** play with fire; **7.** *fig.* ***~ lassen*** bring into play; ***s-e Beziehungen ~ lassen*** pull a few strings; ***s-n Charme ~ lassen*** use one's charms, turn on the charm; **II.** *v/t.* **8.** play (*a. chess, cards etc.*); **9.** ♪ ***Klavier*** *etc.* ~ play the piano *etc.*; **10.** ***den Ball zu j-m ~*** *sport*: pass the ball to s.o.; **11.** *thea. etc.* play, act; *fig.* ***den Beleidigten ~*** act (all) offended; ***den Kranken ~*** pretend to be sick; ***bei ihr ist alles nur gespielt*** it's all play-acting (*or* an act) with her; F ***was wird hier gespielt?*** what's going on here?; **12.** *thea. etc.* play, perform; show *a film*; ***was wird heute abend gespielt?*** what's on tonight; **13.** *fig.* ***j-m et. in die Hände ~*** play s.th. into s.o.'s hands; → ***Geige, gespielt, krank, Rolle², Theater, Wand***; **'spie·lend** *fig. adv.*: ~ (***leicht***) easily, effortlessly; ***es ist ~ leicht*** it's child's play, F it's a doddle (*sl.* cinch); ***er ist ~ damit fertiggeworden*** he took it all in his stride; ***~ gewinnen*** win hands down

'Spiel·en·de *n*: ***gegen ~*** towards the end of the game (*or* match); ***nach ~*** after the game (*or* match); ***zehn Minuten vor ~*** ten minutes from time (*or* before the end)

Spie·ler ['ʃpi:lɐ] *m* (-s; -) **1.** player; **2.** gambler

Spie·le·rei [ʃpi:lə'raɪ] *f* (-; -en) **1.** messing (*or* fooling) around; ***Schluß mit der ~!*** *a.* that's enough fun and games; **2.** hobby; ***es ist für sie eher e-e ~*** it's more of a hobby for her, she just does it for the fun of it; **3.** *no pl.* child's play; **4.** ⚙ gadget, gimmick; toy; *pl. a.* bits and pieces

Spie·le·rin ['ʃpi:lərɪn] *f* (-; -nen) → ***Spieler***

spie·le·risch ['ʃpi:lərɪʃ] *adj.* **1.** *sport*: playing ...; *thea.* acting ...; *adv.* ***~ überlegen sein*** be the better player(s); **2.** playful; **3.** ***mit ~er Leichtigkeit*** with the greatest of ease

'Spie·ler·na͵tur *f* born gambler

'Spie·ler-'Trai·ner *m sport*: player-manager

'Spiel·far·be *f cards*: suit

'Spiel·feld *n sport*: field, pitch; *tennis*: court; ***das ~ verlassen*** *a.* go off; **~hälf·te** *f* half (of the pitch, *tennis*: of the court)

'Spiel|fi͵gur *f* piece; **~film** *m* feature (film); **~flä·che** *f* **1.** *thea.* stage floor; **2.** *sport*: pitch, ground, lawn

'spiel·frei *adj. thea.* ***Montag ist ~*** there's no performance on Monday; ***das Wochenende ist ~*** *sport*: there are no matches this weekend

'Spiel|füh·rer *m* (team) captain; **~ge·fähr·te** *m* playmate; **~geld** *n* **1.** stake; **2.** → ***Spielmarke***; **~ge·mein·schaft** *f* syndicate; **~hälf·te** *f sport*: half (of the match *or* game); **~hal·le** *f* amusement arcade; **~höl·le** *f* gambling den; **~ka·me͵rad** *m* pal, playmate; **~kar·te** *f* playing card; **~ka͵si·no** *n* (gambling) casino; **~klas·se** *f sport*: league, division; **~klei·dung** *f sport*: kit, *esp. soccer*: *a.* strip; **~lei·den·schaft** *f* passion for gambling; **~lei·ter** *m* **1.** → ***Regisseur***; **2.** *TV* gameshow host, emcee; quiz master; **3.** *sport*: organizer; **~ma·cher** *m sport*: best player; **~mar·ke** *f* counter, chip; **~mi͵nu·te** *f* minute (of play); ***in der 20. ~*** in the 20th minute; **~pau·se** *f sport*: a) half-time; interval, b) (*summer etc.*) break; **~plan** *m thea. etc.* program(me) (of events); ***auf den ~ setzen*** take up into (*or* include in) the program(me); ***auf dem ~ sein*** be included in the program(me); **~platz** *m* playground; **~rat·te** F *f* (board) games freak; ***sie ist e-e ~*** *a.* she's mad about games; **~raum** *m* elbowroom (*a. fig.*), room to move; *mot. etc.* room for manoeuvre (*Am.* maneuver); ⚙ clearance; ✝ margin; *fig.* scope, latitude; time; leeway; **~re·gel** *f* rule; *fig.* **~n** rules (of the game); ***sich an die ~n halten*** stick to the rules, *a. fig.* play the game; **~run·de** *f* round; **~sa·chen** *pl. a. fig.* toys; **~schuld** *f* gambling debt; **~stand** *m* score; **~stra·ße** *f* playstreet; **~tisch** *m* card (*or* gaming) table; **~trieb** *m* play instinct; **~uhr** *f* musical clock; **~un·ter͵bre·chung** *f* stoppage; **~ver·bot** *n sport*: ban (on playing), suspension; ***~ haben*** have been banned (*or* suspended); **~ver·der·ber** [-fɛɐ̯dɛrbɐ] *m* (-s; -) spoilsport; **~ver·län·ge·rung** *f* extra time

'Spiel·wa·ren *pl.* toys; **~ab͵tei·lung** *f* toy department; *sign*: toys (and games); **~ge·schäft** *n* toy shop (*Am.* store); **~in·du͵strie** *f* toy industry

'Spiel|wei·se *f* style of play(ing); **~werk** *n* ⚙ mechanism; chime *of a clock*; **~wie·se** *f* playing field; F *fig.* playground; **~zeit** *f* **1.** *sport*: playing time; ***nach e-r ~ von 31 Minuten*** 31 minutes into the game; **2.** a) *thea. etc.* season, b) *film*: run, duration; ***der Film hat e-e ~ von zwei Stunden*** the film lasts two hours

Spiel·zeug *n* (-[e]s; *no pl.*) toy(s *pl.*) (*a. fig.*); **~ei·sen·bahn** *f* model railway, train set; **~pi͵sto·le** *f* toy pistol

'Spiel|zim·mer *n* **1.** games room; **2.** playroom; **~zug** *m sport*: move

Spieß [ʃpi:s] *m* (-es; -e) a) spit; skewer, b) *hist.* spear, c) ⚔ *sl.* sarge; *fig.* ***den ~ umdrehen*** turn the tables (***gegen*** *acc.* on); ***schreien wie am ~*** scream blue murder; → ***braten*** I; **~bra·ten** *m* spit roast

'Spieß·bür·ger *m* petty bourgeois; philistine; **'spieß·bür·ger·lich** *adj.* petty bourgeois, (very) middle-class; philistine

spie·ßen ['ʃpi:sən] *v/t.* (h) spear, lance; ***~ in*** *acc.* stick (*or* thrust) into

Spie·ßer ['ʃpi:sɐ] F *m* (-s; -) → ***Spießbürger***

'Spieß·ge·sel·le *m* pal, mate, *esp. contp.* crony

spie·ßig [ˈʃpiːsɪç] F *adj.* → ***spießbürgerlich***
ˈ**Spieß·ru·ten** *pl.*: ~ ***laufen*** run the gauntlet
Spikes [ʃpaɪks] *pl.* **1.** *sport*: spikes; **2.** *mot.* a) studs, b) studded tyres (*Am.* tires); **~rei·fen** *pl.* studded tyres (*Am.* tires)
spi·nal [ʃpiˈnaːl] *adj.* spinal; ***~e Kinderlähmung*** polio(myelitis)
Spi·nat [ʃpiˈnaːt] *m* (-[e]s; *no pl.*) spinach
Spiˈnat·wach·tel *contp. f* F old crone
Spind [ʃpɪnt] *m, n* (-[e]s; -e [-də]) locker
Spin·del [ˈʃpɪndəl] *f* (-; -n) spindle (*a. biol.*, ⚘); △ newel (post); ⚙ hydrometer
ˈ**spin·delˈdürr** *adj.* (as) thin as a rake; spindly, skinny *arms, legs etc.*
Spi·nett [ʃpiˈnɛt] *n* (-[e]s; -e) spinet
Spin·ne [ˈʃpɪnə] *f* (-; -n) **1.** *zo.* spider; **2.** → ***Wäschespinne***
ˈ**spin·neˈfeind** F *adj.*: ***er ist ihr*** ~ F he can't stand (the sight of) her; ***er ist allem Geschwafel*** *etc.* ~ if there's one thing he can't stand it's waffle *etc.*
spin·nen [ˈʃpɪnən] (spann, gesponnen, h) **I.** *v/t.* **1.** spin; *fig.* ***ein Netz von Intrigen*** ~ weave a web of intrigue; **2.** F ***es ist alles gesponnen*** he's (*or* she's) made it all up, F it's a load of rubbish; **II.** *v/i.* **3.** spin; **4.** F a) F be mad (*or* nuts, crazy, off one's nut), b) talk rubbish (F rot); ***du spinnst wohl!*** have you gone mad?, are you crazy?; ***spinn' ich?*** am I imagining things?; ***er fängt an zu*** ~ F he's (slowly) going mad (*or* round the bend, off his rocker)
ˈ**Spin·nen·netz** *n* spider's web; cobweb
Spin·ner [ˈʃpɪnɐ] *m* (-s; -) **1.** spinner; **2.** F crackpot, F screwball; **3.** *zo.* silkworm moth; **Spin·ne·rei** [ʃpɪnəˈraɪ] *f* (-; -en) **1.** a) spinning, b) spinning mill; **2.** F *fig.* crazy (*or* crackpot) idea; fad, craze; nonsense; ***das ist bloß e-e*** ~ ***von ihm*** it's just one of his crazy ideas
Spin·ne·rin [ˈʃpɪnərɪn] *f* (-; -nen) spinner
spin·nert [ˈʃpɪnɐt] *dial. adj.* F mad, crazy
Spinn|ge·we·be [ˈʃpɪn-] *n* cobweb; spider's web; **~rad** *n* spinning wheel; **~rok·ken** *m* distaff; **~stu·be** *f hist.* spinning room
Spinn·we·be [ˈʃpɪnveːbə] *f* (-; -n) cobweb; spider's web
spin·ti·sie·ren [ʃpɪntiˈziːrən] *v/i.* (h) ruminate (***über*** *acc.* on)
Spi·on [ʃpĭoːn] *m* (-s; -e) **1.** spy; **2.** spyhole, peephole
Spio·na·ge [ʃpĭoˈnaːʒə] *f* (-; *no pl.*) spying, espionage; ~ ***treiben*** (act as a) spy, ***für*** *acc.*: *a.* be spying (*or* a spy) for; **~ab·wehr** *f* counter-espionage, counter-intelligence; **~afˌfä·re** *f* espionage affair; **~dienst** *m* intelligence (*Brit. a.* secret) service; *in GB*: MI5; **~film** *m* spy film (*or* thriller); **~flug** *m* reconnaissance flight, spying mission; **~flug·zeug** *n* spy plane, F spy in the sky; **~netz** *n* spy network; **~or·ga·ni·sa·tiˌon** *f* spy(ing) organization; **~ring** *m* spy ring; **~roˌman** *m* spy novel (*or* thriller); **~sa·telˌlit** *m* spy satellite, F spy in the sky; **~schiff** *n* spy ship; **~tä·tig·keit** *f* spying activities *pl.*; **~-U-Boot** *n* spy submarine; **~ver·dacht** *m*: ***unter*** ~ ***stehen*** be suspected of being a spy (*or* of having spied *for* ...)
spio·nie·ren [ʃpĭoˈniːrən] *v/i.* (h) spy; *fig.* snoop around, ***in*** *dat.*: *a.* nose around in; ~ ***für*** *acc.* (act as a) spy for, be spying for; → ***ausspionieren***

Spi·ral·boh·rer [ʃpiˈraːl-] *m* ⚙ twist drill
Spi·ra·le [ʃpiˈraːlə] *f* (-; -n) **1.** spiral; 𝒜 helix; **2.** ⚙ coil; **3.** ⚕ coil, IUD; **4.** ⚚ (*price etc.*) spiral
Spi·ral·fe·der *f* coil spring; mainspring
spi·ral·för·mig [ʃpiˈraːlfœrmɪç] *adj.* spiral, spiral-shaped, helical
Spi·ral|ka·bel [ʃpiˈraːl-] *n* coiled cord; **~ne·bel** *m ast.* spiral nebula
Spi·ri·tis·mus [ʃpiriˈtɪsmʊs] *m* (-; *no pl.*) spiritualism, spiritism; **Spi·ri·tist** [ʃpiriˈtɪst] *m* (-en; -en) spiritualist; **spi·ri·ti·stisch** [ʃpiriˈtɪstɪʃ] *adj.* spiritualist
spi·ri·tu·ell [ʃpiriˈtŭɛl] *adj.* spiritual
Spi·ri·tuo·sen [ʃpiriˈtŭoːzən] *pl.* spirits, *Am.* liquor *sg.*
Spi·ri·tus [ˈʃpiːritʊs] *m* (-; *no pl.*) spirit; **~ko·cher** *m* spirit stove; **~lam·pe** *f* spirit lamp
Spi·tal [ʃpiˈtaːl] *n* (-s; Spitäler [ʃpiˈtɛːlɐ]) *Austrian, Swiss*: hospital
spitz [ʃpɪts] **I.** *adj.* **1.** pointed; sharp *pencil etc.*; 𝒜 acute *angle*; ***et. mit ~en Fingern anfassen*** pick s.th. up with (a look of) disgust; **2.** *fig.* pinched, peaky; **3.** *fig.* pointed, sarcastic; sharp *tongue*; ***~e Bemerkung*** pointed (*or* cutting) remark, F dig; **4.** F *fig.* ~ ***sein auf*** *acc.* have one's eye on; ***er ist*** ~ ***wie Nachbars Lumpi*** F he's a randy old goat (*sl.* git); **II.** *adv.*: ~ ***zusammenlaufen*** taper off
Spitz [ʃpɪts] *m* (-es; -e) *zo.* Pomeranian, spitz
ˈ**Spitz·bart** *m* goatee (beard)
ˈ**spitz·bär·tig** *adj.* with a goatee (beard)
ˈ**Spitz·bauch** *m* paunch, F beer belly
ˈ**spitz·be·kom·men** F *v/t.* (*irr.*, *sep.*, h, → ***bekommen***) find out; F cotton on to, get wise to (***daß*** the fact that)
ˈ**Spitz·bo·gen** *m* pointed arch
ˈ**Spitz·bu·be** *m* scoundrel; rascal
ˈ**spitz·bü·bisch** [-byːbɪʃ] *adj.* impish, mischievous
ˈ**Spitz·dach** *n* pointed roof
Spit·ze[1] [ˈʃpɪtsə] *f* (-; -n) **1.** a) point, b) *geogr.* peak, top, summit, c) (*tree*) top, d) *a. anat.* tip; end, e) toe, f) spire, g) (cigarette) holder; mouthpiece, h) front; head *of a column etc.*; ⚔ (spear)head; *sport*: lead; *soccer*: striker, i) *fig.* peak, high; top (*or* maximum) speed, j) top position; management; **~n** *der Partei etc.*: F top brass; ***die ~n der Gesellschaft*** the leading figures (F lights) of society; ***die*** ~ ***des Eisbergs*** *a. fig.* the tip of the iceberg; ***an der*** ~ ***des Staates*** (***Konzerns*** *etc.*) at the head of the state (company *etc.*); ***an der*** ~ ***sein*** have reached the top of the ladder; ***an die*** ~ ***kommen*** take over the lead, *pol.* take over the reins of power; ***an der*** ~ ***der Entwicklung*** *etc.* ***stehen*** be in the vanguard of progress *etc.*; ***an der*** ~ ***der Tabelle*** at the top of the table; ***an der*** ~ ***liegen*** *sport*: a) be in the lead, b) be at the top; ***sich an die*** ~ ***setzen*** a) take the lead, b) go to the top; ***s-e*** ~ ***erreichen*** (reach its) peak; ***die höchste*** ~ ***erreichen*** reach an all-time high; F ***es ist einsame*** ~ F it's brilliant; ***et. auf die*** ~ ***treiben*** carry s.th. too far; ~ ***auf Knopf stehen*** be touch and go; ***j-m die*** ~ ***bieten*** stand up to s.o.; ***j-s Worten die*** ~ ***nehmen*** take the sting out of s.o.'s words; ***j-s Argumenten die*** ~ ***abbrechen*** take the wind out of s.o.'s sails; **2.** *fig.* barb, sideswipe, F dig (***gegen*** *acc.* at)
Spit·ze[2] [ˈʃpɪtsə] *f* (-; -n) lace

spit·ze [ˈʃpɪtsə] F *adj. and int.* F great, super, magic
Spit·zel [ˈʃpɪtsəl] *m* (-s; -) informer, F stool pigeon, *sl.* nark; ⚚ company spy; snooper; ˈ**spit·zeln** *v/i.* (h) spy; snoop around
spit·zen [ˈʃpɪtsən] (h) **I.** *v/t.* sharpen *pencil etc.*; ***den Mund*** ~ purse one's lips; ***die Ohren*** ~ prick up one's ears (*a. fig.*); **II.** *dial. v/i. and v/refl.*: (***sich***) ~ ***auf*** *acc.* have one's eye on *s.th.*
ˈ**Spit·zen...** *in cpds. often* top ..., front-rank ..., top-flight ...; ⚚ top ..., first-rate..., first-class ...; ⚙ peak ...; **~au·to** *n* → ***Spitzenwagen***; **~be·darf** *m* peak demand; **~be·la·stung** *f* peak load
ˈ**Spit·zen|blu·se** *f* lace blouse; **~deck·chen** *n* lace doily
ˈ**Spit·zen|ein·kom·men** *n* top income; **~er·zeug·nis** *n* top-quality product; **~fa·briˌkat** *n* top-quality make (*or* brand); **~form** *f* top form; **~ge·rät** *n* top(-of-the-range) model; **~ge·schwin·dig·keit** *f* top speed; **~ge·spräch** *n* top-level talks *pl.*; **~grup·pe** *f* top bracket; *sport*: leaders *pl.*; ***in die*** ~ ***aufrücken*** *sport*: join the leaders
ˈ**Spit·zen·hös·chen** *n* lace panties *pl.*
ˈ**Spit·zen|kan·diˌdat** *m* leading (*or* number one) candidate, front runner; **~klas·se** *f* top class; ***ein Cognac*** *etc.* ***der*** ~ a high-quality (*or* fine) cognac *etc.*; ***ein Läufer*** (***Auto***) *etc.* ***der*** ~ a top-class runner (car) *etc.*; ***er gehört zur internationalen*** ~ he's among the world's leading pianists (*or* swimmers *etc.*)
ˈ**Spit·zen|klöp·pe·lei** *f* lacemaking; **~klöpp·le·rin** *f* lacemaker
ˈ**Spit·zen|kön·ner** *m* top expert; *sport*: top-class athlete; **~kraft** *f* highly qualified worker; ⚚ top-level executive; *pl.* top management (*or* executives); **~last** *f* peak load; **~lei·stung** *f* outstanding performance (*or* achievement); *sport*: record; ⚙ peak output; *mot.* peak performance; ⚡ peak power; **~lohn** *m* top wage(s *pl.*); **~ma·na·ger** *m* top (*or* leading) executive; **~mann·schaft** *f* top team; **~mar·ke** *f* brand leader; **~moˌdell** *n* top-of-the-line (*or* -range) model; **~poˌli·ti·ker** *m* leading (*or* high-ranking, front-rank, top) politician; **~po·si·tiˌon** *f* top position; **~preis** *m* top price; **~qua·liˌtät** *f* top quality; **~rei·ter** *m* a) *sport and fig.*: front runner, b) best-selling (*or* most popular, number one) car *etc.*, c) most popular (*or* top-rated) film *etc.*; number one hit; **~spie·ler** *m* top player; **~sport·ler** *m* top sportsman; **~stel·lung** *f* top position; **~steu·er·satz** *m* maximum tax rate; **~tanz** *m* toe dance
ˈ**Spit·zen·ta·schen·tuch** *n* lace(-edged) handkerchief
ˈ**Spit·zen|tech·no·loˌgie** *f* high tech(nology); **~ver·band** *m* central (*or* umbrella) organization; **~ver·die·ner** *m* top earner; **~wa·gen** *m* top-of-the-range (F super) car; **~wein** *m* vintage (*or* fine) wine; **~wert** *m* peak value; **~zeit** *f* **1.** *sport*: best (*or* record) time; **2.** peak period
Spit·zer [ˈʃpɪtsɐ] *m* (-s; -) (pencil) sharpener
ˈ**spitz·fin·dig** *adj.* oversubtle; pedantic; hair-splitting ...; ***e-e ~e Unterscheidung*** a very fine distinction
ˈ**Spitz·fin·dig·keit** *f* (-; -en) subtlety; ***das ist e-e*** ~ that's splitting hairs

'Spitz·gie·bel *m* pointed gable
'spitz·ha·ben F *v/t.* (*irr.*, *sep.*, h, → ***haben***) F have cottoned on to, have got wise to (***daß*** the fact that)
'Spitz|hacke *f* pickaxe, *Am.* pickax; **~keh·re** *f* **1.** hairpin bend; **2.** *skiing*: kick turn
'spitz·krie·gen F *v/t.* F cotton on to, get wise to (***daß*** the fact that)
'Spitz|mar·ke *f typ.* (side) head; **~maus** *f* **1.** *zo.* shrew; **2.** F weasel-face; **~na·me** *m* nickname; **~we·ge·rich** *m* ♃ ribwort
'spitz·wink·lig *adj.* ⩓ acute
'spitz·zün·gig [-tsʏŋɪç] *adj.* sharp-tongued
Spleen [ʃpliːn] *m* (-s; -s) cranky idea; strange habit; ***du hast wohl e-n ~!*** F you must be off your nut!; **splee·nig** ['ʃpliːnɪç] *adj.* F cranky; ***~er Typ*** F crank, weirdo
splei·ßen ['ʃplaɪsən] *v/t.* (h) ⚓ splice
splen·did [ʃplɛn'diːt] *adj.* generous
Splint [ʃplɪnt] *m* (-[e]s; -e) ⚙ cotter pin
Splitt [ʃplɪt] *m* (-s; *no pl.*) (loose) chippings *pl.*
split·ten ['ʃplɪtən] *v/t.* (h) ✝, *pol.* split
Split·ter ['ʃplɪtɐ] *m* (-s; -) splinter; fragment; **~bom·be** *f* fragmentation bomb; **~bruch** *m* ⚕ chip fracture
'split·ter'fa·ser'nackt F *adj.* stark naked, *sl.* starkers; ***er war ~ a.*** F he didn't have a stitch on
'split·ter·frei *adj.* shatterproof
'Split·ter·grup·pe *f pol.* splinter (*or* breakaway) group
split·te·rig ['ʃplɪtərɪç] *adj.* splintery
split·tern ['ʃplɪtɐn] *v/i.* (sn) *and v/t.* (h) splinter; shatter
'split·ter'nackt F *adj.* stark naked
'Split·ter·par,tei *f pol.* splinter party
Split·ting ['ʃplɪtɪŋ] *n* (-s; *no pl.*) ✝ splitting; *pol.* vote-splitting
Spoi·ler ['ʃpɔʏlɐ] *m* (-s; -) *mot.* spoiler
spon·sern ['ʃpɔnzɐn] *v/t.* (h), **Spon·sor** ['ʃpɔnzɐ] *m* (-s; -en [ʃpɔn'zoːrən]) sponsor
spon·tan [ʃpɔn'taːn] **I.** *adj.* spontaneous; off-the-cuff, spur-of-the-moment *decision*; **II.** *adv.* spontaneously; on the spur of the moment; **Spon·ta·nei·tät** [ʃpɔntanei'tɛːt] *f* (-; *no pl.*) spontaneity
Spon'tan|kauf *m* impulse purchase; *pl.* impulse buying *sg.*; **~käu·fer** *m* impulse buyer; **~ur·laub** *m* impulse holiday
spo·ra·disch [ʃpo'raːdɪʃ] **I.** *adj.* sporadic; **II.** *adv.* sporadically; every once in a while
Spo·re ['ʃpoːrə] *f* (-; -n) ♃ spore
Spo·ren ['ʃpoːrən] *pl.* → ***Sporn***
'Spo·ren·tier·chen *n zo.* **1.** *pl.* sporozoa; **2.** sporozoon
Sporn [ʃpɔrn] *m* (-[e]s; Sporen ['ʃpoːrən]) spur (*a. zo. and fig.*); ✈ tail skid; *e-m Pferd* ***die Sporen geben*** → ***spornen***; *fig.* ***sich die Sporen verdienen*** win one's spurs
spor·nen ['ʃpɔrnən] *v/t.* (h) spur
'sporn·streichs [-ʃtraɪçs] *obs. adv.* straightaway, *formal*: post-haste
Sport [ʃpɔrt] *m* (-[e]s; *no pl.*) sport (*a. fig.*), sports *pl.*; *ped. a.* physical education; *fig.* hobby; ***die Welt des ~s*** the world of sport; ***~ treiben*** do a lot of sport(s); **~ab·zei·chen** *n* sports (achievement) badge; **~ang·ler** *m* angler; **~an·la·ge** *f* sports grounds *pl.*; **~an·zug** *m* casual suit; **~art** *f* sport; **~ar,ti·kel** *pl.* sports articles; **~arzt** *m* sports physician; **~aus·rü·stung** *f* sports equipment; **2be·gei·stert** *adj.* keen on sports, sports-mad; ***~ sein*** *a.* be a sports fan; **~bei·la·ge** *f* sports (*or* sporting) page(s *pl.*); **~be·klei·dung** *f* sportswear; **~be·richt** *m* sports report (*or* news); **~be·richt·er·stat·ter** *m* sports correspondent
spor·teln ['ʃpɔrtəln] F *v/i.* (h) do a bit of sport (on the side)
'Sport|er·eig·nis *n* sports event; **~fest** *n* sports meet (*ped.* day); **~fi·scher** *m* angler; **~flie·ger** *m* amateur pilot; **~flug·zeug** *n* sports plane, two-seater; **~freund** *m* **1.** sports fan; **2.** (keen) sportsman; **3.** sports pal; **~geist** *m* (-[e]s; *no pl.*) sportsmanship, sense of fairness; ***keinen ~ haben*** be very unsporting; ***zeig mal d-n ~!*** where's your good sportsmanship; **~ge·rät** *n* piece of apparatus; *pl.* apparatus *sg.*; **~ge·richt** *n* sports tribunal; **~ge·schäft** *n* sports shop (*Am.* store); **~hal·le** *f* gymnasium, F gym; **~hemd** *n* sports (*Am.* sport) shirt; **~herz** *n* ⚕ athlete's heart; **~hoch·schu·le** *f* college of physical education; **~in·ter,nat** *n* special sports boarding school; **~in·va,li·de** *m* sports invalid
spor·tiv [ʃpɔr'tiːf] *adj.* sporty
'Sport|jacke *f* sports jacket; **~jour·na,list** *m* sports journalist, sportswriter; **~klei·dung** sportswear; **~klub** *m* sports club; **~kor·re·spon,dent** *m* sports correspondent; **~leh·rer** *m* sports instructor; *ped.* PE (= physical education) teacher
Sport·ler ['ʃpɔrtlɐ] *m* (-s; -) sportsman, athlete; **~herz** *n* ⚕ athlete's heart
Sport·le·rin ['ʃpɔrtlərɪn] *f* (-; -nen) sportswoman, athlete
'sport·lich I. *adj.* sports *event*, sporting *event*; athletic *man*, *appearance etc.*; sporty *woman etc.*, *a.* casual *clothes*; *fig.* sporting, sportsmanlike; ***~ sein*** *usu.* do a lot of sports, be keen on sports; **II.** *adv.*: ***sich ~ betätigen*** do sport(s)
'Sport|me·di,zin *f* sports medicine; **~mel·dung** *f* sports item; ***e-e ~ a.*** some sports news; **~nach·rich·ten** *pl.* sports news *sg.*; **~platz** *m* sports grounds *pl.*; sports field, athletic track; **~re·dak,teur** *m* sports editor; **~re·por,ta·ge** *f* sports report; **~re,por·ter** *m* sports reporter; **~schuh** *m* **1.** sports shoe; **2.** casual shoe; **~sei·te** *f* sports (*or* sporting) page; **~sen·dung** *f* sports program(me), sportscast
'Sports|freund F *m* **1.** F mate; **2.** → ***Sportfreund***; **~ka,no·ne** F *f* F (sports) ace
'Sport|sta·di·on *n* sports stadium; **~stun·de** *f* sports lesson; **~tau·chen** *n* skin (*or* scuba) diving; **~tau·cher** *m* skin (*or* scuba) diver; **~teil** *m* sports (*or* sporting) section; **~über,tra·gung** *f* sports broadcast, sportscast; **~un·fall** *m* sports accident; **~,un·ter·richt** *m* **1.** sports lesson(s *pl.*); **2.** *the* teaching of sport; sport education; **~ver·an·stal·tung** *f* sporting (*or* sports) event, sports meet(ing); **~ver·band** *m* sports association; **~ver·ein** *m* athletics club, sports club; **~ver·let·zung** *f* sports injury; **~wa·gen** *m* **1.** *mot.* sports car; **2.** pushchair, *Am.* stroller; **~zei·tung** *f* sports magazine; **~zen·trum** *n* sports centre (*Am.* center)
Spot [spɔt, ʃpɔt] *m* (-s; -s) **1.** commercial; **2.** → ***Spotlight***
'Spot·light [-laɪt] *n* (-s; -s) spotlight, F spot
'Spot·markt *m* ✝ spot market
Spott [ʃpɔt] *m* (-[e]s; *no pl.*) mockery, ridicule; teasing; *b.s.* scorn; ***j-n*** (***et.***) ***dem ~ preisgeben*** make s.o. (s.th.) a laughing stock, *formal*: hold s.o. (s.th.) up to ridicule; ***j-n mit Hohn und ~ überschütten*** heap scorn on s.o.; **~bild** *n* mockery
'spott'bil·lig *adj.* dirt cheap
'Spott·dros·sel *f* mocking-bird
Spöt·te·lei [ʃpœtə'laɪ] *f* (-; -en) mockery; gibe, jibe; **spöt·teln** ['ʃpœtəln] *v/i.* (h) mock, gibe (***über*** *acc.* at)
spot·ten ['ʃpɔtən] *v/i.* (h) laugh (***über*** *acc.* at); make fun (of); *fig.* ***jeder Beschreibung ~*** defy (*or* beggar) description; ***es spottet jeder Beschreibung*** *a.* I can't find words to describe it
Spöt·ter ['ʃpœtɐ] *m* (-s; -) mocker
Spöt·te·rei [ʃpœtə'raɪ] *f* (-; -en) → ***Spott***
Spöt·te·rin ['ʃpœtərɪn] *f* (-; -nen) → ***Spötter***
'Spott|fi,gur *f* joke figure, butt of ridicule; **~ge·dicht** *n* satirical poem; **~geld** *n* ridiculous(ly low) sum (*or* price); ***das ist ja ein ~ a.*** F that's peanuts; ***für ein ~ a.*** for next to nothing
spöt·tisch ['ʃpœtɪʃ] *adj.* mocking; sneering; derisive, derisory
'Spott|lied *n* satirical song; **~na·me** *m* (nasty) nickname; **~preis** *m* ridiculous(ly low) price, giveaway price; ***zum ~*** dirt cheap, for next to nothing; **~vo·gel** *m zo.* mockingbird; *fig.* mocker, scoffer
sprach [ʃpraːx] *pret. of* ***sprechen***
Sprach|at·las ['ʃpraːx-] *m* linguistic atlas; **~aus·ga·be** *f computer*: speech (*or* voice) output; **~bar·rie·re** *f* language barrier; **2be·gabt** *adj.* good at languages, linguistically talented; **~be·ga·bung** *f* gift (*or* talent) for languages, linguistic talent; **2be·hin·dert** *adj.*: ***~ sein*** have a speech defect
Spra·che ['ʃpraːxə] *f* (-; -n) a) language (*a. fig.*), *esp. lit.* tongue, b) *no pl.* speech; language, way of speaking, c) articulation, diction; ***alte ~n*** ancient languages; ***in deutscher ~*** in German; ***Publikationen*** *etc.* ***in deutscher ~*** German-language publications *etc.*; ***der ~ nach kommt er aus Berlin*** judging by his accent he comes from Berlin; ***die gleiche ~ sprechen*** *a. fig.* speak the same language; *fig.* ***e-e andere ~ sprechen*** tell a different story; ***e-e deutliche ~ sprechen*** speak for itself (*or* themselves); ***et. zur ~ bringen*** bring s.th. up, raise (*or* moot) s.th.; ***zur ~ kommen*** come up; ***die ~ verlieren*** lose one's speech; ***hast du die ~ verloren?*** have you lost your tongue?; ***heraus mit der ~!*** (come on,) out with it!; ***endlich fand er die ~ wieder*** he finally found his tongue again; ***mir blieb die ~ weg*** I was speechless; → ***beherrschen*** 3, ***herausrücken*** II, ***verschlagen***[1] 4
Sprach|ebe·ne ['ʃpraːx-] *f* speech level, register; **~ein·ga·be** *f computer*: speech (*or* voice) input; **~emp·fin·den** *n* feeling for (the) language
'Spra·chen|ge·wirr *n* confusion of tongues; **~schu·le** *f* language school
Sprach|er·ken·nung ['ʃpraːx-] *f computer*: speech (*or* voice) recognition; **~er·werb** *m* language acquisition; **~fa,mi·lie** *f* family of languages; ***die germanische ~*** the Germanic (family of) languages; **~feh·ler** *m* ⚕ speech impediment (*or* defect); **~for·scher** *m* linguist;

~for·schung *f* linguistic studies *pl.* (*or* research); **~füh·rer** *m* phrasebook; **~ge·biet** *n* speech area; ***deutsches*** **~** (a) German-speaking area; **~ge·brauch** *m* usage; ***im allgemeinen*** **~** in everyday usage; **~ge·fühl** *n* (-[e]s; *no pl.*) feeling for (the) language; **~ge·mein·schaft** *f* speech community; **~ge·misch** *n* linguistic mix, mixture of languages; **~ge·ˌnie** *n* linguistic genius; **~ge·schich·te** *f* **1.** history of language, language history; history of the language; **2.** linguistic history; **~ge·sell·schaft** *f a. hist.* language society; **~ge·setz** *n* linguistic law

ˈsprach·ge·stört *adj.* ⚕ aphasic; **~** ***sein*** *usu.* have a speech disorder (*or* impediment)

ˈSprach·ge·walt *f* (-; *no pl.*) eloquence; **ˈsprach·ge·wal·tig** *adj.* eloquent

ˈsprach·ge·wandt *adj.* a) articulate, b) proficient in languages; **~** ***sein*** *esp. contp. a.* F have the gift of the gab

ˈSprach|gren·ze *f* language (*or* linguistic) boundary; **~in·sel** *f* linguistic island; **~ken·ner** *m* linguist; **~kennt·nis·se** *pl.* knowledge *sg.* of languages; knowledge *sg.* of a (*or* the) language; ***englische*** **~** knowledge (*or* command) of English; ***gute englische*** **~** ***erwünscht*** good command of English desirable; **~kom·pe·ˌtenz** *f* linguistic ability (*or* performance); **~kulˌtur** *f* linguistic sophistication (*or* standards *pl.*); **~kunst** *f* (-; *no pl.*) literary artistry; way with words; **~künst·ler** *m* word genius; ***ein*** **~** ***sein*** *a.* have a way with words; **~kurs** *m* language course; **~laˌbor** *n* language laboratory (F lab); **~laut** *m* speech sound; **~leh·re** *f* a) grammar, b) grammar (book); **~leh·rer** *m* language teacher; **~len·kung** *f* language manipulation; manipulation of a (*or* the) language

ˈsprach·lich I. *adj.* language ..., linguistic; grammatical; stylistic; **~er** ***Fehler*** language mistake, mistake in the language; **~e** ***Kommunikation*** verbal communication, communicating through language; **II.** *adv.* linguistically *etc.*; from a language point of view

sprach·los [ˈʃpraːxloːs] *adj.* speechless; ***da war er*** **~** it left him speechless; ***ich bin*** **~** I don't know what to say

Sprach|me·loˌdie [ˈʃpraːx-] *f* speech melody, intonation; **~min·der·heit** *f* linguistic minority; **~niˌveau** *n* level of language; **~norm** *f* linguistic norm(s *pl.*); prescribed usage; **~pfle·ge** *f* maintaining linguistic standards; purism; **~phi·lo·soˌphie** *f* philosophy of language; **~psy·cho·loˌgie** *f* psychology of language; **~raum** *m* → ***Sprachgebiet***; **~re·ˌform** *f* language (*or* linguistic) reform(s *pl.*); reforming a (*or* the) language; **~re·ge·lung** *f pol.* official version; ***nach offizieller*** **~** ***...*** the official version is ...; **~rei·se** *f* language tour; **~rohr** *n* megaphone; *fig.* mouthpiece; organ; **~schnit·zer** F *fig. m* (linguistic) howler; solecism; malapropism; **≈schöp·fe·risch** *adj.* linguistically creative; **~schran·ke** *f* language barrier; **~schu·le** *f* language school; **~schwie·rig·kei·ten** *pl.* difficulty with a (*or* the) language; **~stö·rung** *f* speech impediment; **~stu·di·um** *n* language studies *pl.*; *univ.* language degree, degree in languages; **~taˌlent** *n* **1.** gift (*or* talent) for languages; **2.** (good) linguist; ***sie ist ein*** **~** *a.* she has a way with words; **~ˌun·ter·richt** *m* language teaching; ***englischer*** **~** English lessons; **~ver·ar·bei·tung** *f computer*: speech (*or* voice) processing; **~ver·glei·chung** *f* comparative linguistics *sg.*; **~ver·hal·ten** *n* speech behavio(u)r; **~ver·mö·gen** *n* (-s; *no pl.*) faculty of speech; **~wis·sen·schaft** *f* linguistics *sg.*; **~wis·sen·schaft·ler** *m* linguist; **≈wis·sen·schaft·lich** *adj.* linguistic(ally *adv.*); **~zen·trum** *n anat.* speech centre (*Am.* center)

sprang [ʃpraŋ] *pret. of* ***springen***

Spray [ʃpreː] *m, n* (-s; -s) spray; **~de·odoˌrant** *n* deodorant spray; **~do·se** *f* spray can

spray·en [ˈʃpreːən] *v/t. and v/i.* (h) spray

Spray·er [ˈʃpreːɐ] *m* (-s; -) spray artist

Sprech|akt [ˈʃprɛç-] *m* speech act; **~an·la·ge** *f* intercom; entryphone; **~bla·se** *f* (speech) balloon, bubble; **~chor** *m* **1.** chorus; ***im*** **~** ***rufen*** chant; **2.** chorus, chant, chanted slogan; **3.** *usu.* chorus of demonstrators

spre·chen [ˈʃprɛçən] (sprach, gesprochen, h) **I.** *v/t. and v/i.* a) speak (***mit*** *dat.* to, with; ***zu*** *dat.* to), talk, b) speak (***über*** *acc.*, ***von*** *dat. usu.* about), *a.* give a speech *or* talk (***über*** *acc.* on), c) say *a prayer etc.*; pronounce; read *the news etc.*, d) see, talk to *s.o.*; ***im Fernsehen*** **~** speak on television; ***et. auf Tonband*** **~** record s.th. on tape; ***s-e ersten Worte*** **~** *baby*: say its first few words; ***er spricht nicht viel*** he doesn't say much; **~** ***für*** *acc.* speak for (*or* on behalf of), put in a good word for, plead for, argue in favo(u)r of; **~** ***gegen*** *acc.* argue (*or* speak out) against; ***das spricht für ihn*** that says something for him; ***das spricht für s-e Unschuld*** that would seem to indicate he's innocent; ***das spricht für sich selbst*** it speaks for itself; ***vieles spricht dafür*** there's much to be said for it, ***daß***: it seems very likely that; ***alles spricht dafür, daß sie es war*** all the evidence points to the fact that it was her (*or* towards her having done it); ***vieles spricht dagegen*** there are lots of reasons against (*or* not to *etc.*), ***daß***: it seems very unlikely that; ***was spricht dafür?*** give me some good reasons why (we should do it *etc.*); ***was spricht dagegen?*** is there any reason why we shouldn't do it *etc.?*; ***man spricht davon, daß er bankrott sei*** there's talk of his being bankrupt; ***jeder spricht davon*** everybody's talking about it, it's the talk of the town; ***er spricht nicht gern darüber*** he doesn't like to talk about it; ***j-n zu*** **~** ***wünschen*** wish to see s.o.; ***ich muß erst mit m-m Anwalt*** **~** I'll have to see my lawyer (*Brit. a.* solicitor) first; ***kann ich Sie kurz*** **~?** can I have a (quick) word with you?; ***für ihn bin ich nicht zu*** **~** I'm not in for him, if he calls I'm not here; ***ich bin heute für niemanden zu*** **~** I'm not available (*or* in) for anybody today; I'm not here today, no matter who calls; ***sie*** **~** ***nicht miteinander*** they're not talking (*or* speaking) to each other, they're not on speaking terms; ***sie ist nicht gut auf ihn zu*** **~** he's in her bad books; ***das Urteil*** **~** pronounce judg(e)ment; ***über Politik*** (***Geschäfte***) **~** talk politics (business); ***sprich mal mit ihm darüber*** have a word with him about it; ***mit sich selbst*** **~** talk to oneself; ***von etwas anderem*** **~** change the subject; ***wir kamen auf Indien zu*** **~** the subject of India came up; ***vor e-r großen Zuhörerzahl*** **~** speak before (*or* to) a large audience; ***unter uns gesprochen*** between you and me; ***da wir gerade von ...*** **~** talking of ...; ***aus s-n Worten spricht der Neid*** you can tell he's jealous by the way he speaks, there's envy in every word; ***die Kosten, sprich Anschaffung und Versicherung, ...*** the costs, i.e. (*or* that is to say) purchase and insurance, ...; ***allgemein gesprochen*** generally speaking; ***sprich!*** spit it out!; ***wir*** **~** ***uns noch!*** you haven't heard the last of this; → ***Anzeichen, Band***[2]***, Recht, schuldig***; **II.** **≈** *n* (-s; *no pl.*) speaking, talking; ***j-n zum*** **~** ***bringen*** get s.o. to talk, make s.o. talk; ***das*** **~** ***fällt ihm schwer*** he finds it hard to speak (*or* talk); **ˈspre·chend** *fig. adj.* (very) expressive; convincing; **~es** ***Beispiel*** graphic illustration

Spre·cher [ˈʃprɛçɐ] *m* (-s; -) a) speaker; announcer, b) newsreader, newscaster, c) narrator, d) spokesman, spokesperson (*gen.* for); *parl.* Speaker

Sprech·er·zie·hung [ˈʃprɛç-] *f* speech training

ˈsprech·faul *adj.* **1.** (very) taciturn; *contp.* too lazy to open one's mouth; **2.** **~** ***sein*** *child*: be a late (*or* lazy) talker

Sprech·funk [ˈʃprɛç-] *m* **1.** radiotelephony (*abbr.* R/T); ***über*** **~** ***in Verbindung stehen mit*** *dat.* be in radio contact with; **2.** → **~ge·rät** *n* radiotelephone; walkie-talkie

Sprech|ge·rät [ˈʃprɛç-] *n* → ***Sprechanlage***; **~ge·sang** *m* sprechgesang, speech song; **~mu·schel** *f* mouthpiece; **~pro·be** *f* sound check; **~pup·pe** *f* talking doll; **~plat·te** *f* spoken-word record; **~rhyth·mus** *m ling.* speech rhythm; **~rol·le** *f thea.* speaking part; **~stim·me** *f* (speaking) voice

Sprech·stun·de [ˈʃprɛç-] *f* office hours *pl.*; ⚕ consulting (*or* surgery) hours *pl.*, *Am.* office hours *pl.*; ***wann hat er*** **~?** when are his surgery (*or* office) hours?, ⚕ *a.* when does he have surgery?; ***ich soll zu ihr in die*** **~** she wants to see me (personally), ⚕ *a.* she wants me to come to the surgery; **ˈSprech·stun·den·hil·fe** *f* doctor's assistant; (doctor's) receptionist

Sprech|übung [ˈʃprɛç-] *f* speech (*or* elocution) exercise; **~ˌun·ter·richt** *m* elocution lessons *pl.*; **~werk·zeu·ge** *pl.* speech organs, organs of speech; **~zeit** *f* **1.** *prison etc.*: visiting time; **2.** *teleph.* call time; **3.** → ***Sprechstunde***; **~zim·mer** *n* consulting room, surgery, (doctor's *etc.*) office

sprei·zen [ˈʃpraɪtsən] (h) **I.** *v/t.* spread, straddle; **II.** *v/refl.*: ***sich*** **~** a) play hard to get, b) give o.s. airs; → ***gespreizt***

Spreiz|fuß [ˈʃpraɪts-] *m* splayfoot; **~ho·se** *f* ⚕ T-splint

Spreng|ar·bei·ten [ˈʃprɛŋ-] *pl.* blasting operations; **~bom·be** *f* high-explosive (*abbr.* HE) bomb, demolition bomb

Spren·gel [ˈʃprɛŋəl] *m* (-s; -) parish; diocese

spren·gen[1] [ˈʃprɛŋən] *v/t.* (h) **1.** sprinkle, spray; water; **2.** burst open; *a.* force *a door etc.*; break *a chain etc.*; blast; blow up; **3.** *fig.* break up *meeting etc.*; disperse *a crowd*; break *the bank*; → ***Rahmen*** I

ˈspren·gen[2] *v/i.* (sn) gallop, ride hard

Spren·ger [ˈʃprɛŋɐ] *m* (-s; -) sprinkler
Spreng|kap·sel [ˈʃprɛŋ-] *f* detonator; **~kom,man·do** *n* demolition squad; bomb disposal unit; **~kopf** *m* warhead; **~kör·per** *m* explosive (device); **~kraft** *f* explosive force; **~la·dung** *f* explosive charge; **~mei·ster** *m* blaster; **~satz** *m* explosive charge
Spreng·stoff [ˈʃprɛŋ-] *m* explosive; *fig.* dynamite; **~an·schlag** *m*, **~at·ten·tat** *n* bomb attack; **~mu·ni·ti,on** *f* explosive ammunition; **~pa,ket** *n* parcel bomb; **~tä·ter** *m* bomb layer, bomber
Spreng·trupp [ˈʃprɛŋ-] *m* → ***Spreng-kommando***
Spren·gung [ˈʃprɛŋʊŋ] *f* (-; -en) **1.** blasting; **2.** *fig.* breaking-up, dispersion
Spreng|wa·gen [ˈʃprɛŋ-] *m* sprinkler truck; **~wir·kung** *f* explosive effect
Spren·kel [ˈʃprɛŋkəl] *m* (-s; -) spot, speck(le)
ˈ**spren·keln** *v/t.* (h) spot, speck(le)
Spreu [ʃprɔʏ] *f* (-; *no pl.*) chaff; *a. fig.* ***die ~ vom Weizen trennen*** separate the grain (*or* wheat) from the chaff
Sprich·wort [ˈʃprɪç-] *n* (-[e]s; ⸚er) proverb, (proverbial) saying; ***wie das ~ sagt*** as the saying goes
ˈ**sprich·wört·lich** *adj.* proverbial (*a. fig.*); ***ihre Gastfreundschaft ist ~*** they're a byword for hospitality; ***sein Geiz ist schon ~*** he's got a real reputation for being mean; ***das war die ~e Katze im Sack*** it was (a case of) your proverbial pig in a poke
sprie·ßen [ˈʃpriːsən] *v/i.* (sproß, gesprossen, sn) shoot (up), come up; germinate; *fig.* awaken, burgeon
Spring|blen·de [ˈʃprɪŋ-] *f phot.* automatic diaphragm; **~brun·nen** *m* fountain
sprin·gen [ˈʃprɪŋən] (sprang, gesprungen, sn) **I.** *v/i.* a) jump (*a. riding, skiing etc.*); leap; hop, skip; *animal*: pounce; *sport*: vault; *ball etc.*: bounce; *water, blood*: spurt, b) F run, dash; jump, c) act as stand-in, be standing in, d) *string*: break; ***~ von*** *dat.* come off, pop off; ***vom Pferd ~*** dismount, jump (*or* leap) off one's horse; ***vom fahrenden Zug ~*** jump out of a moving train; ***zur Seite ~*** jump out of the way; ***aus den Gleisen ~*** jump the rails (*or* track); ***j-m an den Hals ~*** go for s.o. (*or* s.o.'s throat); ***in tausend Stücke ~*** smash into smithereens; ***die Tasse ist gesprungen*** the cup is cracked; ***von e-m Thema zum anderen ~*** jump around from one subject to another; ***j-n für sich ~ lassen*** have s.o. at one's beck and call; ***sie braucht nur zu winken, dann springt er schon*** he's at her beck and call; F ***Geld ~ lassen*** F fork out (*or* cough up) money; ***etwas ~ lassen*** be generous; ***et. für j-n ~ lassen*** treat s.o. to s.th.; → ***Auge*** 1, ***Klinge, Punkt, Stück***; **II.** ≈ *n* (-s; *no pl.*) jumping; *sport*: pole-vaulting; *swimming*: diving
Sprin·ger [ˈʃprɪŋɐ] *m* (-s; -) **1.** *sport*: jumper; *swimming*: diver; **2.** *chess*: knight; **3.** stand-in
Spring|flut [ˈʃprɪŋ-] *f* spring tide; **~form** *f gastr.* springform
Spring·ins·feld [ˈʃprɪŋˀɪnsfɛlt] *m* harum-scarum
Spring|kraut [ˈʃprɪŋ-] *n* ⚘ touch-me-not; ≈**le'ben·dig** *adj.* full of beans; **~maus** *f* jerboa; **~mes·ser** *n* flick knife, *Am.* switchblade; **~pferd** *n* show jumper; **~rei·ten** *n* show jumping; **~rei·ter** *m* show jumper; **~rol·lo** *n* roller blind; **~seil** *n* skipping rope
Sprint [ʃprɪnt] *m* (-s; -s), **sprin·ten** [ˈʃprɪntən] *v/i.* (sn) sprint; **Sprin·ter** [ˈʃprɪntɐ] *m* (-s; -) sprinter
Sprit [ʃprɪt] *m* (-s; *no pl.*) **1.** F juice, *esp. Am.* gas; ***~ tanken*** fill up with petrol (*Am.* gas); **2.** spirit; **~ver·brauch** *m* petrol (*Am.* gas) consumption
Spritz|ap·pa,rat [ˈʃprɪts-] *m* spray gun; **~be,ton** *m* gun(ned) concrete; **~beu·tel** *m* piping bag; **~blech** *n mot.* splashboard; **~dü·se** *f* spray nozzle
Sprit·ze [ˈʃprɪtsə] *f* (-; -n) a) syringe (*a.* ⚕), b) ⚕ injection, F jab; F *fig.* shot in the arm, cash injection, c) hose, d) F sub-machine gun; ***e-e ~ bekommen*** get (*or* have, be given) an injection; F *fig.* ***der erste Mann an der ~ sein*** be at the controls; *sl.* ***an der ~ hängen*** *sl.* be on the needle
sprit·zen [ˈʃprɪtsən] **I.** *v/t.* (h) **1.** squirt; spray; ***naß ~*** spray (with water), *a.* make *s.th. or s.o.* wet; ***sich et. aufs Hemd ~*** spatter (*or* splash, spray) s.th. on one's shirt, spatter *etc.* one's shirt with s.th.; **2.** ⚘ a) spray, sprinkle (***mit*** *dat.* with), b) water *plants, garden etc.*; **3.** a) ⚕ inject; give *s.o.* an injection, b) *sl.* shoot (up), mainline; ***sich ~*** give o.s. an injection, inject o.s.; ***sich ~ lassen*** go for (*or* have, get) an injection; **4.** mix with (soda) water; **5.** spray *car etc.*; **6.** ⚙ die-cast *metal*; inject *plastic*; **II.** *v/i.* (sn) **7.** *water etc.*: splash, spray, *blood*: spurt, gush; *heated oil etc.*: spray; **8.** (h) a) ⚕ give (s.o.) an injection, b) F shoot up (*sl.*), mainline (*sl.*); **9.** F zoom, nip (***nach*** *dat.*, ***zu*** *dat.* round to)
Sprit·zer [ˈʃprɪtsɐ] *m* (-s; -) **1.** splash, drop; dash; **2.** spray *of scent etc.*; **3.** splash; ***voller ~ (Farb≈) sein*** be spattered (with paint)
Spritz|fahrt [ˈʃprɪts-] F *f* → ***Spritztour***; **~ge·bäck** *n* shortbread biscuits (*Am.* cookies) *pl.*; **~guß** *m* ⚙ a) die-casting, b) injection mo(u)lding
sprit·zig [ˈʃprɪtsɪç] *adj.* **1.** crisp, tangy *wine*; **2.** *fig.* sparkling, witty *play etc.*; *dialog(ue) etc.* full of sparkling wit; F zippy (*a. sport*); **3.** F nippy *car etc.*
Spritz|lack [ˈʃprɪts-] *m* spray paint; **~mit·tel** *n* spray; **~pi,sto·le** *f* spray gun; **~tour** F *f* spin, jaunt (through the countryside); ***e-e ~ machen*** go for a spin (*or* jaunt [through the countryside])
sprö·de [ˈʃprøːdə] *adj.* **1.** brittle (*a. nails, hair*); rough, chapped *skin*; grating *voice*; **2.** stand-offish; demure *girl*
Sprö·dig·keit [ˈʃprøːdɪçkaɪt] *f* (-; *no pl.*) **1.** brittleness; **2.** aloofness; demureness
sproß [ʃprɔs] *pret. of* ***sprießen***
Sproß [ʃprɔs] *m* (Sprosses; Sprosse) **1.** ⚘ shoot; **2.** *fig.* offspring, *lit.* scion; F ***das ist unser jüngster ~*** he's our youngest, F he's the latest addition
Spros·se [ˈʃprɔsə] *f* (-; -n) **1.** rung (*a. fig.*); **2.** window bar; **3.** *hunt.* tine
spros·sen [ˈʃprɔsən] *v/i.* (sn) → ***sprießen***
ˈ**Spros·sen|fen·ster** *n* lattice window; **~lei·ter** *f* ladder; **~wand** *f gym.* wall bars *pl.*
Sprößling [ˈʃprœslɪŋ] F *m* (-s; -e) offspring, *sl.* sprog; *a.* F junior; → *a.* ***Sproß*** 2
Sprot·te [ˈʃprɔtə] *f* (-; -n) sprat
Spruch [ʃprʊx] *m* (-[e]s; Sprüche [ˈʃprʏçə]) saying; dictum; aphorism, maxim; epigram; (*bible*) quotation, verse; saying (from the Bible); slogan; *sport*: ruling; ⚖ judg(e)ment, sentence, verdict; F (***große***) ***Sprüche machen*** (*or* ***klopfen***) talk big, *sl.* shoot one's mouth off; F (***das sind***) ***alles Sprüche!*** it's all talk, it's just hot air; → ***Salomo(n)***
ˈ**Spruch·band** *n* (-[e]s; ⸚er) banner; △ banderole
Sprü·che|klop·fer [ˈʃprʏçə-] F *m*, **~ma·cher** F *m* big talker
Sprüch·lein [ˈʃprʏçlaɪn] *n* (-s; -): ***sein ~ hersagen*** say one's little piece (*or* party piece), F come out with the usual spiel
ˈ**spruch·reif** *adj.*: ***die Sache ist noch nicht ~*** it's not official yet
Spru·del [ˈʃpruːdəl] *m* (-s; -) a) (sparkling) water, (sparkling) mineral water, b) lemonade
spru·deln [ˈʃpruːdəln] *v/i.* (h, sn) *spring etc.*: bubble; bubble up (***aus*** *dat.* out of, from), gush (out of); *gastr.* bubble (away); *drink*: fizz, be fizzy; ***aus der Flasche ~*** fizz (*or* spurt) out of the bottle; *fig.* ***~ vor*** *dat.* bubble (over) with *enthusiasm etc.*; ***die Worte sprudelten ihm aus dem Mund*** the words came gushing out; ˈ**spru·delnd** *fig. adj.* effervescent
Sprüh·do·se [ˈʃpryː-] *f* spray can, aerosol (can)
sprü·hen [ˈʃpryːən] (h) **I.** *v/t.* spray; sprinkle; **II.** *v/i.* spray; *sparks*: fly; *fig. eyes*: flash (***vor*** *dat.* with); *fig.* ***vor Ideen ~*** be bubbling over with ideas; ***vor Temperament ~*** be a livewire, *esp. sport*: be a bundle of energy; ***von Geist ~*** sparkle with wit; ˈ**sprü·hend** *adj.* **1.** ***~e Gischt*** spray, foam; **2.** *fig.* bubbling, bubbly, effervescent *mood etc.*; sparkling *wit etc.*
Sprüh|ne·bel [ˈʃpryː-] *m* (Scotch) mist; **~re·gen** *m* drizzle
Sprung [ʃprʊŋ] *m* (-[e]s; Sprünge [ˈʃprʏŋə]) **1.** jump (*a. sport*); leap; *gym.* vault; *swimming*: dive; *fig.* ***~ ins Ungewisse*** (*or* ***Wasser***) leap in the dark; ***großer ~ vorwärts*** great leap forward; ***ein großer ~ nach vorn sein*** be a great advance (***gegenüber*** *dat.* on); ***e-n ~ machen*** take a leap; ***den ~ wagen*** take the plunge; ***auf dem ~ sein, et. zu tun*** be about to do s.th., be on the point of doing s.th.; ***auf e-n ~ vorbeikommen*** drop in (***bei*** *dat.* on), F pop round (and see s.o.); ***sie ist immer auf dem ~*** she's always on the go (F hop); ***es ist nur ein ~ bis dorthin*** it's only a stone's throw from here, it's just down the road (*or* round the corner); ***j-m auf die Sprünge kommen*** find s.o. out, F get wise to s.o.('s tricks *or* game); ***j-m auf die Sprünge helfen*** help s.o. along, give s.o. a leg up; ***dir werd' ich auf die Sprünge helfen!*** we'll soon see about that!; ***j-s Gedächtnis auf die Sprünge helfen*** jog s.o.'s memory; ***Sprünge machen*** jump from one subject to another, jump all over the place; ***damit kann er keine großen Sprünge machen*** he won't be able to go far on that; **2.** crack; flaw; **~bal·ken** *m sport*: takeoff board; **~bek·ken** *n* diving pool; **~bein** *n* ankle-bone; *sport*: takeoff leg; ≈**be·reit** *adj. and adv.* a) ready to jump, b) F all set to go; **~brett** *n* **1.** springboard; *swimming*: *a.* diving board; **2.** *fig.* springboard (***für*** *acc.* for), stepping stone (to); jumping-off place; **~deckel** *m* watch cap

'Sprung·fe·der *f* (coil) spring; **~ma,trat·ze** *f* spring mattress
'Sprung|ge·lenk *n anat.* ankle joint; *zo.* hock; **~gru·be** *f sport*: pit
'sprung·haft I. *adj.* erratic (*a.* ✝), flighty; ✝ spasmodic; **~er Anstieg** sharp rise (*or* increase), jump (*gen.* in *prices etc.*); **II.** *adv. increase etc.* by leaps and bounds
'Sprung|kraft *f* (-; *no pl.*) *sport*: takeoff power; **~lauf** *m sport*: ski-jump(ing); **~schan·ze** *f* ski jump; **~seil** *n* skipping rope; **~stab** *m* pole; **~tuch** *n* safety sheet; **~turm** *m* diving platforms *pl.*
'sprung·wei·se *adv.* in jumps; *fig.* by leaps and bounds; in (*or* by) fits and starts
'Sprung·wei·te *f* jumping distance
Spucke ['ʃpʊkə] (*sep.* -k·k-) F *f* (-; *no pl.*) spittle, F spit; *fig.* ***ein bißchen ~*** F a bit of elbow grease; ***da blieb mir die ~ weg*** I just gulped, my jaw dropped
'spucken (*sep.* -k·k-) (h) **I.** *v/i.* a) spit, b) F be sick, F throw up, c) F *engine*: splutter; ***~ nach*** *dat.* spit at; ***j-m ins Gesicht ~*** spit in s.o.'s face; F ***ich muß ~*** I'm going to be sick; *fig.* ***in die Hände ~*** roll up one's sleeves; ***j-m in die Suppe ~*** put a spoke in s.o.'s wheel; F ***ich spuck' drauf!*** F to hell with it; **II.** *v/t.* spit (out); spit, cough up *blood etc.*; *volcano*: spew *lava*; F *fig.* ***große Töne ~*** talk big, *sl.* shoot one's mouth off
Spuck|napf ['ʃpʊk-] *m* spittoon, cuspidor; **~tü·te** *f* sick bag
Spuk [ʃpu:k] *m* (-[e]s; *no pl.*) **1.** strange happenings *pl.*; ***nächtlicher ~*** things that go bump in the night; ***der ~ beginnt um Mitternacht*** the ghosts come out at midnight; ***an ~ glauben*** believe in ghosts; **2.** apparition, spectre (*Am.* specter); **3.** *fig.* nightmare; ***es erschien wie ein ~*** it all seemed like a bad dream
spu·ken ['ʃpu:kən] *v/i.* (h) **1.** ***es spukt*** (***in dem Haus*** *etc.*) the house *etc.* is haunted; ***hier hat es mal gespukt*** *a.* there used to be ghosts in this house *etc.*; ***~ durch*** *acc.* haunt, walk *the castle etc.*; **2.** *fig.* ***die Idee spukt bei ihm im Kopf*** he's obsessed with the idea; ***der Gedanke spukt noch immer in den Köpfen*** people still believe in it, people still haven't given up the idea, the idea still hasn't been laid to rest; F ***bei dir spukt's wohl!*** F have you gone off your nut?
'Spuk|er·schei·nung *f* apparition; **~ge·schich·te** *f* ghost story; **~haus** *n* haunted house
Spül|becken ['ʃpy:l-] *n* sink; **~bür·ste** *f* washing-up brush
Spu·le ['ʃpu:lə] *f* (-; -n) spool, reel; bobbin; ⚡ coil
Spü·le ['ʃpy:lə] *f* (-; -n) sink unit
spu·len ['ʃpu:lən] *v/t.* (h) spool, reel (***auf*** *acc.* onto)
spü·len ['ʃpy:lən] (h) **I.** *v/t.* **1.** rinse; **2.** wash (up) *the dishes*; **3.** ***an Land ~*** wash ashore, wash up; **II.** *v/i.* **4.** wash up, do the washing up, do the dishes; **5.** flush, pull the chain
'Spu·len(ton·band)ge·rät *n* open-reel tape deck
Spü·ler ['ʃpy:lɐ] *m* (-s; -), **Spü·le·rin** ['ʃpy:lərɪn] *f* (-; -nen) dishwasher, washer-up, F washer-upper
Spül|gang ['ʃpy:l-] *m* rinse (cycle); **~ka·sten** *m* cistern; **~klo,sett** *n* water closet; **~lap·pen** *m* dishcloth, washing-up cloth
Spül·ma,schi·ne ['ʃpy:l-] *f* dishwasher
'spül·ma,schi·nen·fest *adj.* dishwasher-safe
Spül|mit·tel ['ʃpy:l-] *n* washing-up liquid, detergent; **~tuch** *n* dishcloth
Spü·lung ['ʃpy:lʊŋ] *f* (-; -en) **1.** rinse; ⚕ irrigation; douche; ⚙, *mot.* flushing, scavenging; **2.** a) flush, b) cistern
Spül·was·ser ['ʃpy:l-] *n* a) rinsing water, b) washing-up water, dishwater (*a. contp.*)
Spul·wurm ['ʃpu:l-] *m* roundworm
Spund [ʃpʊnt] *m* (-[e]s; -e [-də]) **1.** spigot; **2.** tongue; **3.** F ***junger ~*** (young) whippersnapper
Spur [ʃpu:ɐ] *f* (-; -en ['ʃpu:rən]) a) track(s *pl.*); trail, *hunt. a.* scent, b) *mot.* lane, c) skidmarks *pl.*, d) 🚂 ga(u)ge, track(s *pl.*), e) ⚙ groove; track, f) trace (*a. fig.*), *gastr.* dash; *mot.* ***linke*** (***rechte***) ***~*** left-hand (right-hand) lane; ***die ~ halten*** keep in lane; ***die ~ wechseln*** switch lanes; ⚙ ***~ halten*** keep track; ***e-e ~ aufnehmen*** pick up a trail; *fig.* ***~en des Alters*** signs of age; ***~en des Krieges*** traces left behind by the war, scars of the war; ***~en e-r alten Kultur*** traces (*or* remnants) of an ancient civilization; ***j-m auf die ~ kommen*** get onto s.o.('s trail); ***e-r Sache auf die ~ kommen*** get onto s.th., track s.th. down; ***j-m auf der ~ sein*** be on s.o.'s trail, be after s.o.; ***auf der falschen ~ sein*** be on the wrong track, be barking up the wrong tree; ***j-n von der ~ ablenken*** put (*or* throw) s.o. off the scent; ***j-n auf die richtige ~ bringen*** put s.o. on the right track; ***keine ~en hinterlassen*** leave no trace (*criminal*: traces, evidence); ***s-e ~en hinterlassen*** leave its mark; ***s-e ~en verwischen*** cover up one's tracks; ***vom Täter fehlt jede ~*** there are no clues as to who did it; ***die ~ führt nach*** *dat.* ***...*** the trail leads (*or* takes us) to ...; ***auf j-s ~en wandeln*** follow in s.o.'s tracks; ***keine ~ von Anständigkeit*** *etc.* not a scrap of decency *etc.*, not the least bit of decency *etc.*; F ***keine ~!*** not at all!, F no way!; → ***heiß***
spür·bar ['ʃpy:ɐba:ɐ] **I.** *adj.* a) noticeable, perceptible; marked, distinct, b) considerable; tangible; ***~ werden*** make itself felt; ***es gab e-e ~e Erleichterung*** you could feel (*or* sense) the relief; ***die Auswirkungen werden auf Jahre hinaus ~ sein*** the effects will be felt for years to come; **II.** *adv.* a) noticeably, b) considerably; ***es ist ~ kälter geworden*** it's noticeably colder (today), it's turned quite chilly (today)
spu·ren ['ʃpu:rən] *v/i.* (h) **1.** *skiing*: lay a track; **2.** F toe the line
spü·ren ['ʃpy:rən] *v/t.* (h) feel; sense; notice; ***ich hab' nichts gespürt*** I didn't feel a thing; ***ich spürte Scham*** I felt a sense of shame; ***ich hab's am eigenen Leib gespürt*** I went through it all myself, I experienced it first-hand; ***jetzt spüre ich den Wein*** the wine's beginning to take effect now (*or* is slowly going to my head now); ***jetzt spüre ich den langen Flug*** (***die schlaflosen Nächte***) the long flight is beginning to make itself felt *or* take its toll (those sleepless nights are beginning to take their toll); ***ich spüre mein Alter*** I can tell I'm getting old, F it's old age creeping up on me; ***ich spüre es in den Knochen*** I can feel it in my bones; ***ich spüre sämtliche Knochen*** I feel as if every single bone in my body is aching; F ***ich spür's wieder im Rücken*** F my back's playing me up again; ***zu ~ bekommen*** find out what *s.th.* is like, get a taste of *s.o.'s anger etc.*; ***du wirst es noch zu ~ bekommen*** it'll all come back on you; ***hast du nicht gespürt, wie ...?*** didn't you notice how ...?, couldn't you tell how ...?; ***es war deutlich zu ~*** it was obvious; ***von Haß*** *etc.* ***war nichts zu ~*** there was no sign (*or* trace) of hatred *etc.*; ***von Kooperation war nichts zu ~*** nobody seemed to be interested in cooperation; ***ich hab' ihn m-e Enttäuschung schon ~ lassen*** I made no attempt to hide my disappointment
'Spu·ren|ele,ment *n* trace element; **~me,tall** *n* trace metal; **~si·che·rung** *f* **1.** securing of evidence; **2.** forensic squad
Spür·hund ['ʃpy:ɐ-] *m* **1.** tracker dog, sniffer dog; **2.** *fig.* sleuth
'spur·los *adv.* without (leaving a) trace; ***~ verschwinden*** vanish into thin air, disappear without trace; ***es ist nicht ~ an ihm vorübergegangen*** it's left its mark (on him)
Spür|na·se ['ʃpy:ɐ-] *f* **1.** good nose; *fig.* nose; **2.** snooper; **~sinn** *m* (-[e]s; *no pl.*) **1.** *zo.* sense of smell; **2.** *fig.* nose, instinct; ***er hat e-n ~ dafür*** he's got a nose (*or* an instinct) for that kind of thing, he can sniff that kind of thing out very quickly
Spurt [ʃpʊrt] *m* (-[e]s; -s) sprint, spurt, (quick) burst; ***e-n ~ einlegen*** put on a sprint; ***zum ~ ansetzen*** make a dash for it; **spur·ten** ['ʃpʊrtən] *v/i.* (sn) **1.** sprint; **2.** F sprint; ***~ zu*** *dat. a.* dash to; ***ich bin ganz schön gespurtet*** F I really had to step on it, you should have seen me run
'Spur|wech·sel *m mot.* changing lanes; **~wei·te** *f* 🚂 ga(u)ge; *mot.* wheel track; *tires*: tread
Squash [skvɔʃ] *n* (-; *no pl.*) squash; **~center** *n* squash centre (*Am.* center), squash courts *pl.*; **~spiel** *n* game of squash; **~spie·ler** *m* squash player
Sri·lan·ker [sri'laŋkɐ] *m* (-s; -), **Sri·lan·ke·rin** [sri'laŋkərɪn] *f* (-; -nen), **sri·lan·kisch** [sri'laŋkɪʃ] *adj.* Sri Lankan
SS [ɛs'ʔɛs] *f* (-; *no pl.*) *hist.* SS; *elite corps of the Nazi party*; **~-Mann** *m* member of the SS
st [st] *int.* pst!; ssh!
s.t. [ɛs'te:] *adv.* (= ***sine tempore***): ***18 Uhr ~*** 6 p.m. sharp
Staat¹ [ʃta:t] *m* (-[e]s; -en) **1.** state; country, nation; ***~ im ~*** state within a state; ***von ~s wegen*** by government decree; ***beim ~ arbeiten*** be employed by the government, be a civil servant; **2.** *zo.* colony
Staat² *m* (-[e]s; *no pl.*) a) pomp, splendo(u)r, b) finery; ***großen ~ machen*** a) roll out the red carpet, b) dress up (specially); ***mit et. ~ machen*** flaunt s.th. around; ***damit kannst du keinen ~ machen*** F that's nothing to write home about
'Staa·ten|bund *m* confederacy, confederation (of states); **~bünd·nis** *n* alliance (of states); **~ge·mein·schaft** *f* community of states
'staa·ten·los *adj.* stateless
'Staa·ten·lo·se *m, f* (-n; -n) stateless person
'staat·lich I. *adj.* state(-)..., government(-)..., national; nationalized, state-owned *industries etc.*; **~e Mittel** govern-

ment funds; **II.** *adv.*: ~ ***anerkannt*** officially recognized; ~ ***gefördert*** state-sponsored; ~ ***gelenkt*** (*or* ***geleitet***) state-control(l)ed, state-run; ~ ***geprüft*** certified

'Staats|af,fä·re *f* **1.** affair of state; **2.** F *fig.* ***e-e ~ aus et. machen*** make a big affair (out) of s.th., F make a big thing out of s.th.; **~akt** *m* **1.** act of state; **2.** state occasion (*or* ceremony); **~ak·ti,on** *f* → ***Staatsaffäre*** 2; **~amt** *n* office of state, public office; **~an·ge·hö·ri·ge** *m*, *f* (-n; -n) citizen, national; ***britischer ~r*** *a.* a British subject; ***sie ist deutsche ~*** she's a German citizen (*or* national); **~an·ge·hö·rig·keit** *f*: (***doppelte ~*** dual) nationality, citizenship; ***er hat die französische ~*** he has French nationality (*or* citizenship); **~an·ge·le·gen·heit** *f* affair of state; **~an·lei·he** *f* government loan; government bond (*pl.* *a.* securities, stocks); **~an·walt** *m* ⚖ public prosecutor, district attorney (*abbr.* DA); **~an·walt·schaft** *f* **1.** public prosecutor's office, district attorney's office; **2.** (body of) public prosecutors *pl.*; **~ap·pa,rat** *m* state machinery; **~ar,chiv** *n* state archives *pl.*; *in GB*: Public Record Office; **~auf·fas·sung** *f* concept of the state; **~aus·ga·ben** *pl.* public expenditure *sg.*, government spending *sg.*; **~bahn** *f* national railway (*Am.* railroad); **~bank** *f* (-; -en) state (*or* national) bank; **~ban,kett** *n* state (*or* official) banquet; **~bank,rott** *m* national bankruptcy; **~be·am·te** *m* civil servant; **~be·gräb·nis** *n* state funeral; **~be·such** *m* state visit; **~be·trieb** *m* state-owned enterprise; **~bi·blio,thek** *f* national (*or* state) library

'Staats·bür·ger *m* citizen; **~kun·de** *f* civics *pl.*; civic studies *pl.*; **~rech·te** *pl.* civil rights

'Staats·bür·ger·schaft *f* → ***Staatsangehörigkeit***

'Staats|chef *m* head of state; **~die·ner** *m* civil servant; *hum.* servant of the state; **~dienst** *m* civil (*or* public) service; ***im ~ sein*** be a civil servant

'staats·ei·gen *adj.* state-owned; **'Staats·ei·gen·tum** *n* government (*or* state) property; public (*or* state) ownership

'Staats|ein·nah·men *pl.* public revenue *sg.*; **~emp·fang** *m* official reception; **~ex,amen** *n* state examination(s *pl.*); ***sein ~ machen*** *a.* take one's degree; **~far·ben** *pl.* national colo(u)rs; **~fei·er·tag** *m* national holiday; **~feind** *m* public enemy; **2feind·lich** *adj.* subversive; **~fi,nan·zen** *pl.* public finances; **~flag·ge** *f* national flag; **~form** *f* form of government; **~ge·biet** *n* state territory; ***französisches*** *etc.* ~ French *etc.* territory; ***sich auf britischem ~ befinden*** be on British territory; **2ge·fähr·dend** *adj.* subversive; **~ge·fan·ge·ne** *m* prisoner of state, political prisoner; **~ge·fäng·nis** *n* state prison; **~ge·heim·nis** *n* state secret; F *fig.* ***das ist ein*** (***kein***) ~ that's top secret (it's no great secret); **~gel·der** *pl.* public funds; **~ge·schäf·te** *pl.* state affairs; *the* running *sg.* of the state; ***die ~ führen*** run the (affairs of) state, govern the country; **~ge·walt** *f* (-; *no pl.*) **1.** state authority; **2.** executive body of the state; ***gesetzgebende ~*** legislature; ***vollziehende ~*** executive; ***richterliche ~*** judiciary; **~gren·ze** *f* frontier, border; **~grün·dung** *f* founding of a (*or* the) state; **~haus·halt** *m* (national) budget; **~hil·fe** *f* government (*or* state) aid; **~ho·heit** *f* sovereignty; **~in·ter,es·se** *n* interests *pl.* of the state, public interest; **~in·ter·ven·ti,on** *f* state (*or* government) intervention; **~kanz,lei** *f* state chancellery; **~ka,ros·se** *f* state carriage; **~kas·se** *f* (public) treasury, public purse; *in GB*: *the* Exchequer; *in the USA*: *the* Federal Treasury; **~kir·che** *f* established (*or* state) church; **~ko·sten** *pl.*: ***auf ~*** at (the) public expense; **~kun·de** *f* political science; **~län·de·rei·en** *pl.* public land *sg.*; **~macht** *f* (-; *no pl.*) state power

'Staats·mann *m* (-[e]s; ⸚er) statesman

'staats·män·nisch [-mɛnɪʃ] *adj.* statesmanlike

'Staats|ma·schi·ne,rie *f* state machinery; **~mi,ni·ster** *m* secretary of state, *Am.* secretary; **~mi·ni,ste·ri·um** *n* ministry, *Am.* department; **~mit·tel** *pl.* public funds; **~mo·no,pol** *n* state monopoly; **~ober·haupt** *n* head of state; sovereign; **~oper** *f* national (*or* state) opera; **~or,gan** *n* instrument of state; **~pa,pie·re** *pl.* → ***Staatsanleihe***; **~par,tei** *f* (sole) ruling party; **2po,li·tisch** *adj.* national political ...; **~e *Angelegenheiten*** matters of state; **~po·li,zei** *f* state police; **~prä·si,dent** *m* (state) president; **~prü·fung** *f* state examination(s *pl.*); *adm.* civil service examination(s *pl.*); **~rä,son** *f*: (***aus Gründen der ~*** for) reasons *pl.* of state; **~rat** *m* **1.** council of state; *in GB*: Privy Council; **2.** council(l)or of state; *in GB*: Privy Councillor

'Staats·recht *n* (-[e]s; *no pl.*) constitutional law; public law; **'staats·recht·lich** *adj. and adv.* under (*or* relating to) constitutional law, constitutional; under (*or* relating to) public law

'Staats|re·li·gi,on *f* state religion; **~ru·der** *n* helm of (the) state; ***das ~ fest in der Hand haben*** have a firm hold over (*or* grip on) the country; **~schul·den** *pl.* national (*or* public) debt *sg.*; **~se·kre,tär** *m* minister of state, *Am.* undersecretary

'Staats·si·cher·heit *f* national (*or* state) security; **'Staats·si·cher·heits·dienst** *m* (*a. hist. DDR*) state security service

'Staats|so·zia,lis·mus *m* state socialism; **~spra·che** *f* official (state) language; **~streich** *m* coup (d'état); ***die Regierung durch e-n ~ stürzen*** overthrow the government by coup; **~sub·ven·ti,on** *f* government subsidy (*or* grant); **~thea·ter** *n* state theat|re (*Am. a.* -er); **~trau·er** *f* national mourning; **~trau·er·tag** *m* national day of mourning; **~ver·bre·chen** *n* political crime; **~ver·bre·cher** *m* political offender; **~ver·dros·sen·heit** *f* disillusionment with the state (*or* with politics); political apathy; **~ver·fas·sung** *f* (political) constitution; **~ver·schul·dung** *f* national (*or* public) debt; **~ver·trag** *m* (international) treaty; **~we·sen** *n* state, *formal*: body politic; **~wis·sen·schaft** *f* political science; **~wohl** *n* public welfare (*or* weal); **~zu·ge·hö·rig·keit** *f* nationality, citizenship; **~zu·schuß** *m* government subsidy (*or* grant)

Stab [ʃta:p] *m* (-[e]s; Stäbe ['ʃtɛ:bə]) **1.** a) stick, staff; *eccl.* crosier, crozier; (*magic*) wand; ♪, ⚔, *sport*: baton, *sport*: *a.* pole, b) rod; bar; *fig.* ***den ~ über j-n brechen*** condemn s.o. (outright); **2.** staff *sg.*; team, F squad; **3.** ⚔ a) staff officers *pl.*, b) headquarters *pl.*; **~an,ten·ne** *f* rod aerial (*or* antenna)

Stäb·chen ['ʃtɛ:pçən] *n* (-s; -) **1.** *dim. of Stab*; **2.** chopstick; **3.** jackstraw; **4.** *anat.* rod; **5.** ⚕ (rod-shaped) bacillus, rod; **6.** F ciggy

'Stab|hoch·sprin·ger *m* pole-vaulter; **~hoch·sprung** *m* pole-vaulting

sta·bil [ʃta'bi:l] **I.** *adj.* a) stable (*a.* ⚕, *pol.*, ✝ *prices, currencies etc.*); steady, b) solid, sturdy; robust; ~ ***bleiben*** *prices etc.*: *a.* hold steady; **II.** *adv.*: ~ ***gebaut*** solidly built, solid

Sta·bi·li·sa·tor [ʃtabili'za:to:ɐ] *m* (-s; -en [-za'to:rən]) stabilizer; **sta·bi·li·sie·ren** [ʃtabili'zi:rən] *v/t.* (h) stabilize (*a. v/refl.*: ***sich ~***); **Sta·bi·li'sie·rung** *f* (-; *no pl.*) stabilization

Sta·bi·li'sie·rungs|flä·che *f* ✈ stabilizer; **~flos·se** *f* ✈, ⚓ stabilizer; **~maß·nah·men** *pl.* stabilization measures, moves to stabilize the economy (*or* the political situation *etc.*); **~po·li,tik** *f* policy of stabilization

Sta·bi·li·tät [ʃtabili'tɛ:t] *f* (-; *no pl.*) a) stability, b) sturdiness; **Sta·bi·li'täts·po·li,tik** *f* ✝ policy of stability

'Stab·reim *m* alliteration

'Stabs|arzt *m* ⚔ captain (medical corps); **~chef** *m* ⚔ chief of staff; **~feld·we·bel** *m* ⚔ warrant officer class II (*abbr.* WO II), *Am.* master sergeant; **~of·fi,zier** *m* ⚔ field (*or* staff) officer

'Stab|,über·ga·be *f*, **~wech·sel** *m sport*: baton change

stach [ʃta:x] *pret. of* ***stechen***

Sta·chel ['ʃtaxəl] *m* (-s; -n) **1.** ⚘ prickle, thorn; **2.** *zo.* spine, quill *of a porcupine etc.*; sting *of a bee etc.*; **3.** ⚙ spike; point; barb; **4.** *fig.* a) sting, b) spur; ***der ~ des Ehrgeizes trieb sie an*** she was goaded (*or* spurred on) by ambition; *dat.* ***den ~ nehmen*** take the sting out of *s.th.*; ***wider den ~ löcken*** kick against the pricks; **~bart** F *m* prickly (*or* spiky) beard; **~bee·re** *f* gooseberry

'Sta·chel·beer|mar·me,la·de *f* gooseberry jam; **~strauch** *m* gooseberry bush

'Sta·chel·draht *m* barbed wire; **~ver·hau** *m* barbed wire entanglement; **~zaun** *m* barbed wire fence

'Sta·chel·hals·band *n* spiked collar

'Sta·chel·häu·ter [-hɔytɐ] *m* (-s; -) *zo.* echinoderm

sta·che·lig ['ʃtaxəlɪç] *adj.* prickly (*a.* ⚘); *zo.* spiny; *fig.* bristly *chin, beard etc.*

sta·cheln ['ʃtaxəln] *v/t.* (h) spur on; goad

'Sta·chel·schwein *n* porcupine

stach·lig ['ʃtaxlɪç] *adj.* → ***stachelig***

Sta·del ['ʃta:dəl] *dial. m* (-s; -) barn

Sta·di·on ['ʃta:dĭɔn] *n* (-s; Stadien ['ʃta:dĭən]) stadium; **~spre·cher** *m* stadium announcer

Sta·di·um ['ʃta:dĭʊm] *n* (-s; Stadien ['ʃta:dĭən]) stage, phase; ***in diesem ~*** in (*or* during) this phase, at (*or* during) this stage; ***alle Stadien durchlaufen*** go through all the stages; → ***vorgerückt***

Stadt [ʃtat] *f* (-; Städte ['ʃtɛ:tə]) a) town; city, b) *no pl.* municipality; ***in der ~*** in town; ***in die ~ gehen*** go to town, *Am.* go downtown; ***bei der ~ arbeiten*** work for the council (*or* corporation); ***die ~ Köln*** a) the city of Cologne, b) Cologne City Council; ***die Ewige ~*** the Eternal City; ***die Heilige ~*** the Holy City; ***die Gol-***

dene ~ the Golden City (of Prague); **~ar͵chiv** *n* municipal archives *pl.*

stadt'aus·wärts *adv.* out of town

'Stadt|au·to·bahn *f* urban motorway (*Am.* expressway); **~bahn** *f* urban railway (*Am.* railroad); **＆be·kannt** *adj.* known all over town; **~be·völ·ke·rung** *f* **1.** urban population; **2.** town's (*or* city's) inhabitants *pl.*; **~be·woh·ner** *m* → ***Städter***; **~be·zirk** *m* municipal district; *in New York and London*: borough; **~bi·blio͵thek** *f* public (*or* municipal) library; **~bild** *n* townscape, cityscape; ***das ~ hat sich stark geändert*** the (face of the) town *or* city has changed a lot; **~bum·mel** *m*: (***e-n ~ machen*** go for a) stroll through town

Städt·chen ['ʃtɛːtçən] *n* (-s; -) small town

'Stadt·di͵rek·tor *m* town commissioner, *Am.* city manager

Städ·te·bau ['ʃtɛːtə-] *m* (-[e]s; *no pl.*) urban development; **'städ·te·bau·lich** *adj.* town (*or* urban) planning ...; **~e *Planung*** town (*or* urban) planning

Städ·te|bund ['ʃtɛːtə-] *m hist.* league of cities (*or* towns); **~füh·rer** *m* city guide

stadt'ein·wärts *adv.* into town

Städ·te|part·ner·schaft ['ʃtɛːtə-] *f a. pl.* twinning; ***zwischen München und Edinburgh besteht e-e ~*** Munich and Edinburgh are twinned (*or* twin towns); **~pla·nung** *f* town (*or* urban) planning

Städ·ter ['ʃtɛːtɐ] *m* (-s; -) city dweller, urbanite, F townie, *contp.* city slicker

'Stadt|fahrt *f* ride into (*or* around the) town; ***das Auto ist für ~en gut geeignet*** the car is ideal for getting about (*or* around) town; **~flucht** *f* exodus from the cities, flight to the country; ***die ~ hat zugenommen*** more and more people are leaving the big cities (and moving to the country); **~füh·rer** *m* city guide; **~ge·biet** *n* municipal area; ***im ~ a.*** in the city area; **~ge·spräch** *n* **1.** *teleph.* → ***Ortsgespräch***; **2.** *fig.* ***~ sein*** be the talk of the town; ***zum ~ werden*** become the talk of the town; **~gren·ze** *f* city limits *pl.*; **~gue͵ril·la** *m* urban guer(r)illa; **~hal·le** *f* municipal hall; **~haus** *n* town house; **~in·dia·ner** *m* urban hippy; **~in·ne·re** *n* city (*or* town) centre (*Am.* center); downtown (area); ***diese Straße führt direkt ins ~*** this road takes you straight to the city cent|er (*Brit.* -re) *etc.*

städ·tisch ['ʃtɛːtɪʃ] **I.** *adj.* urban, town ..., city ..., metropolitan; *esp. adm.* municipal; **II.** *adv.*: ***~ verwaltet*** run by the town (*or* city), municipally run (*or* control[l]ed)

'Stadt|kern *m* town (*or* city) cent|re (*Am.* -er); heart of the town; downtown area; **~kind** *n* **1.** town (*or* city) child; **2.** → ***Städter***; **~klatsch** *m* town gossip; **~kli·ma** *n* urban (*or* town) climate; **~le·ben** *n* city life; **~luft** *f* (-; *no pl.*) city air; **~mau·er** *f* city (*or* town) wall; **~mensch** *m* city person, urbanite, F townie; **~mit·te** *f* town *or* city centre (*Am.* center); downtown area; **＆nah** *adj.* (*a. adv.* ***~ gelegen***) close to town (*or* the city); **~nä·he** *f*: ***in ~*** (***gelegen***) close to town (*or* the city); **~park** *m* municipal (*or* public) park; **~plan** *m* town (*or* city) map; **~pla·nung** *f* → ***Städteplanung***

'Stadt·rand *m* outskirts *pl.* of (the) town *or* the city; ***am ~*** on the outskirts of town (*or* the city), ***leben***: *a.* live in suburbia; **~sied·lung** *f* suburban estate (*Am.* development)

'Stadt|rat *m* **1.** town (*or* municipal) council; **2.** town (*Am.* city) council(l)or; **~re·gi͵on** *f* conurbation; **~rund·fahrt** *f* city sightseeing tour; **~sa͵nie·rung** *f* urban renewal; slum clearance; **~staat** *m* city state

'Stadt·strei·cher *m* city vagrant; *contp.* tramp; *pl. a.* street people

Stadt·strei·che·rei [-ʃtraiçə'rai] *f* (-; *no pl.*) urban vagrancy

'Stadt·strei·che·rin [-ʃtraiçərɪn] *f* (-; -nen) bag lady; → *a.* ***Stadtstreicher***

'Stadt|teil *m* district; *w.s.* part of town; **~tor** *n* town (*or* city) gate, entrance to the town (*or* city); **~vä·ter** *hum. pl.* city fathers; **~ver·kehr** *m* city traffic, traffic in the city (*or* cities); **~ver·wal·tung** *f* municipal authorities *pl.*; **~vier·tel** *n* district, part of town; **~wap·pen** *n* city's (*or* town's) coat of arms; **~wer·ke** *pl.* town (*or* city) department *sg.* of works; municipal utilities; **~woh·nung** *f* flat (*or* apartment) in town (*or* in the city); **~zen·trum** *n* → ***Stadtmitte***

Sta·fet·te [ʃta'fɛtə] *f* (-; -n) relay

Staf·fa·ge [ʃta'faːʒə] *f* (-; *no pl.*) **1.** *a* facade, *a* (big) sham; **2.** *art*: staffage

Staf·fel ['ʃtafəl] *f* (-; -n) **1.** *sport*: a) relay (race), b) relay team; **2.** ⚔, ✈ squadron

Staf·fe·lei [ʃtafə'lai] *f* (-; -en) easel

'Staf·fel|lauf *m* relay race; ***~ der Männer*** (***Damen***) men's (women's) relay; **~mie·te** *f* graduated rent

staf·feln ['ʃtafəln] *v/t.* (h) grade, graduate *wages, prices, rates etc.*; stagger *working hours*; → ***gestaffelt***

'Staf·fel|prei·se *pl.* graduated (*or* sliding-scale) prices; **~schwim·men** *n* relay swimming; **~stab** *m* baton

Staf·fe·lung ['ʃtafəlʊŋ] *f* (-; -en) ✈, *sport etc.*: staggering; ⚚ graduation; progressive rates *pl.*; differential(s *pl.*)

'Staf·fel|wett·be·werb *m* relay (race); **~zin·sen** *pl.* graduated interest *sg.*

staf·fie·ren [ʃta'fiːrən] *v/t.* (h) → ***ausstaffieren***

Stag [ʃtaːk] *n* (-[e]s; -e ['ʃtaːgə]) ⚓ stay

Stag·fla·ti·on [ʃtakfla'tsi̯oːn] *f* (-; *no pl.*) ⚚ stagflation

Sta·gna·ti·on [ʃtagna'tsi̯oːn] *f* (-; -en) stagnation; **sta·gnie·ren** [ʃta'gniːrən] *v/i.* (h) stagnate; remain stagnant; **sta'gnie·rend** *adj.* stagnant

'Stag·se·gel *n* ⚓ staysail

stahl [ʃtaːl] *pret. of* ***stehlen***

Stahl [ʃtaːl] *m* (-[e]s; Stähle ['ʃtɛːlə]) steel; *fig.* ***Nerven aus ~*** nerves of steel; **~ar·bei·ter** *m* steelworker; **~bau** *m* (-[e]s; -ten) steel(-girder) construction; **~be·sen** *m* ♪ (wire) brushes *pl.*; **~be͵ton** *m* reinforced concrete, ferro-concrete; **＆blau** *adj.* steel blue; **~blech** *n* sheet steel; **~bril·le** *f*: (***e-e ~*** a pair of) steel-rimmed glasses *pl.*; **~bür·ste** *f* wire brush

stäh·len ['ʃtɛːlən] *v/t.* (h) steel (***sich*** o.s.)

stäh·lern ['ʃtɛːlɐn] *adj.* steel ..., made of steel; *fig.* steely (*a. look*); *grip, muscles etc.* of steel

'Stahl|fe·der *f* steel spring; **~ge·rüst** *n* girder construction; **＆grau** *adj.* steel grey (*Am.* gray); **~gür·tel·rei·fen** *m* steel-braced radial; **＆'hart** *adj.* (as) hard as steel; **~helm** *m* steel helmet; **~in·du͵strie** *f* steel industry; **~kam·mer** *f* strongroom; **~ko·cher** *m* steelworker; **~kon·struk·ti͵on** *f* → ***Stahlbau***; **~man·tel·ge·schoß** *n* steel jacket bullet

'Stahl·rohr *n* steel tube; **~mö·bel** *pl.* tubular steel furniture *sg.*

'Stahl|roß *hum. n* bike; **~sai·te** *f* ♪ steel (*or* wire) string; **~schrank** *m* steel cabinet; **~seil** *n* steel cable; **~stich** *m* steel engraving; **~trä·ger** *m* steel girder; **~wa·ren** *pl.* steel goods; **~werk** *n* steelworks *pl.*, steel mill; **~wol·le** *f* steel wool

sta·ken ['ʃtaːkən] *v/i. and v/t.* (h) punt; **'Sta·ken** *m* (-s; -) punt pole

Sta·ke·ten·zaun [ʃta'keːtən-] *m* picket fence

stak·ka·to [ʃta'kaːto] *adj. and adv.*, **＆** *n* (-s; -s, -ti) ♪ staccato

stak·sen ['ʃtaːksən] F *v/i.* (sn) stalk, strut

Sta·lag·mit [ʃtala'gmiːt] *m* (-s, -en; -e[n]) *geol.* stalagmite

Sta·lak·tit [ʃtalak'tiːt] *m* (-s, -en; -e[n]) *geol.* stalactite

Sta·li·nis·mus [ʃtali'nɪsmʊs] *m* (-; *no pl.*) Stalinism; **Sta·li·nist** [ʃtali'nɪst] *m* (-en; -en), **sta·li·ni·stisch** [ʃtali'nɪstɪʃ] *adj.* Stalinist

Sta·lin·or·gel ['ʃtaːliːn-] F *f* multiple rocket launcher

Stall [ʃtal] *m* (-[e]s; Ställe ['ʃtɛlə]) **1.** a) stable; cowshed, barn; pigsty, pigpen, b) *fig.* stable; *motor racing*: team, c) F *fig.* F hole; F *fig.* ***aus e-m guten ~*** from a good stable; ***ein ganzer ~ voll*** a whole horde of; → ***Pferd***; **2.** F flies *pl.*, fly; **~bur·sche** *m* → ***Stallknecht***; **~dün·ger** *m* manure; **~ha·se** *m* rabbit; **~knecht** *m* stable boy; **~mei·ster** *m* equerry

Stal·lung ['ʃtalʊŋ] *f* (-; -en) stabling; *pl. a.* stables

'Stall·wa·che *f*: *fig.* ***~ halten*** hold the fort

Stamm [ʃtam] *m* (-[e]s; Stämme ['ʃtɛmə]) **1.** (*tree*) trunk; **2.** tribe; stock, lineage, family, line; **3.** *biol.* phylum; ⚘ strain; *zo.* breed; **4.** *ling.* root, stem; **5.** a) permanent staff, b) regular customers *pl.*, c) *sport*: regular players *pl.*; **~ak·tie** *f* ⚚ ordinary share, *pl. a.* common stock *sg.*; **~baum** *m* family tree; *zo.* pedigree; *biol.* phylogenetic tree; **~buch** *n* family register; **~burg** *f* ancestral castle, family seat; **~da͵tei** *f computer*: master file; **~ein·la·ge** *f* ⚚ original investment, *partner's* capital share

stam·meln ['ʃtaməln] (h) **I.** *v/i.* stammer; ⚕ *a.* stutter; **II.** *v/t.* stammer (out)

'Stamm·el·tern *pl.* progenitors

stam·men ['ʃtamən] *v/i.* (h): ***~ von*** (*or* ***aus***) *dat.* come from; date from, go back to; ***diese Gläser ~ noch von der Großmutter*** these glasses used to be my grandmother's; ***die Formulierung*** (***Zeichnung***) ***stammt von ihm*** that's his wording (drawing); *iro.* ***das stammt nicht von mir!*** I had nothing to do with that

'Stam·mes|be·wußt·sein *n* (feeling of) tribal identity; **~füh·rer** *m*, **~fürst** *m* → ***Stammeshäuptling***; **~ge·schich·te** *f biol.* phylogeny; **＆ge·schicht·lich** *adj. biol.* phylogen(et)ic; **~häupt·ling** *m* (tribal) chieftain; **~kun·de** *f* ethnology; **~sit·te** *f* tribal custom (*or* tradition); **~zu·ge·hö·rig·keit** *f* tribal identity

'Stamm|form *f ling.* principal form; **~gast** *m* habitué (***in*** *dat.*, ***bei*** *dat.* of), F regular (at); **~ge·richt** *n* standard dish; **~hal·ter** *m* son and heir; **~haus** *n* ⚚ parent firm

stäm·mig ['ʃtɛmɪç] *adj.* stocky, thickset; sturdy *legs*

'Stamm|ka·pi,tal *n* ✝ joint stock; **~knei·pe** F *f* F watering hole, favo(u)rite haunt, *sl.* hangout; *Brit. a.* local; **~kun·de** *m* regular customer (*or* patron); **~kund·schaft** *f* regulars *pl.*, regular customers (*or* patrons) *pl.*; **~lo,kal** *n* → ***Stammkneipe; ~per·so,nal*** *n* permanent (*or* skeleton) staff *sg.*; **~platz** *m one's* usual seat; *fig.* ~ ***in e-r Mannschaft*** *etc.* firm place in a team *etc.*; **~pu·bli·kum** *n* regular guests (*or* customers *etc.*) *pl.*; *thea. etc.* regular audience; F regulars *pl.*; **~sil·be** *f ling.* root syllable; **~sitz** *m* ancestral seat; ✝ headquarters *pl.*; **~spie·ler** *m* regular (player); **~ta·fel** *f* genealogical table

'Stamm·tisch *m* a) regulars' table, b) round of regulars; ***Montags habe ich*** ~ on Mondays I meet my friends down at the pub; **~bru·der** *m* drinking companion (F mate); **~po·li,tik** *contp. f* alehouse (*Am.* cracker-barrel) politics *pl.*; **~po,li·ti·ker** *contp. m* alehouse (*Am.* cracker-barrel) politician; **~stra,te·ge** *m* armchair strategist

'Stamm|va·ter *m* progenitor; **~vo,kal** *m* root vowel; **~wäh·ler** *m* standing voter, F party diehard

stamp·fen ['ʃtampfən] (h) **I.** *v/i.* **1.** stamp; stomp; ***mit dem Fuß*** ~ stamp one's foot; F ***durch die Gegend*** ~ stomp around (like an elephant); **2.** ⚓ pitch; **II.** *v/t.* a) ⚙ tamp, ram (down); stamp (down) *earth etc.*, b) *gastr.* mash *potatoes*; crush *grapes etc.*, c) *pharm.* pound, crush; → ***kleinstampfen; fig. et. aus dem Boden*** ~ produce s.th. out of thin air; ***ich kann's doch nicht einfach aus dem Boden*** ~ *a.* I can't just wave my magic wand; **Stamp·fer** ['ʃtampfɐ] *m* (-s; -) a) ⚙ tamper, b) *gastr.* masher

stand [ʃtant] *pret. of* ***stehen***

Stand [ʃtant] *m* (-[e]s; Stände ['ʃtɛndə]) **1.** *no pl.* standing position; footing, foothold; ***aus dem*** ~ a) from a standing position, b) *fig.* off the cuff; ***Sprung (Start) aus dem*** ~ standing jump (start); ***keinen (festen)*** ~ ***haben*** a) be wobbly, b) *fig.* have no firm foothold; *fig.* ***e-n schweren*** ~ ***haben*** a) have a hard time of it (***bei j-m*** with s.o.), b) be in a difficult position; **2.** *no pl.* a) state; condition, b) situation, position (*a. ast.*), c) level (*a.* ⚙, ✝), standard, d) number of kilomet|res (*Am.* -ers) clocked up, mileage; reading, e) balance *of account*, f) figure *of sick persons etc.*; *sport*: score; ***den höchsten*** ~ ***erreichen*** reach one's peak (*or* highest level); ***auf den neuesten*** ~ ***bringen*** update, bring *s.th.* up to date; ***der*** ~ ***der Dinge*** the state of affairs; ***nach dem (jetzigen)*** ~ ***der Dinge*** as matters stand (at the moment); ***neuester*** ~ ***(der Technik)*** latest developments (in technology); ***auf dem neuesten*** ~ ***der Technik sein*** be state-of-the-art; **3.** a) *no pl.* social status (*or* position, standing), rank, *formal*: station, b) class, c) profession; ***geistlicher*** ~ *the* clergy; ***die höheren Stände*** the upper classes; *hist.* ***der dritte*** ~ the third estate; ***die drei Stände*** the three orders (*or* estates); ***unter (über) s-m*** ~ ***heiraten*** marry below (above) one's station; **4.** stall, stand; ***e-e Pizza am*** ~ ***essen*** have a (quick) pizza at a stand-up (buffet)

Stan·dard ['ʃtandart] *m* (-s; -s) standard; level; ***das gehört zum*** ~ that's standard; **~ab·wei·chung** *f* standard deviation; **~aus·füh·rung** *f* standard type (*or* model, design); **~aus·rü·stung** *f* standard equipment (*sport*: gear); **~aus·spra·che** *f* standard pronunciation; *in GB*: *a.* received pronunciation

stan·dar·di·sie·ren [ʃtandardi'ziːrən] *v/t.* (h) standardize

Stan·dar·di'sie·rung *f* (-; *no pl.*) standardization

'Stan·dard|schrift *f computer*: standard font; **~spra·che** *f* standard language; **~tanz** *m* standard dance; **~werk** *n* standard work

Stan·dar·te [ʃtan'dartə] *f* (-; -n) standard; guidon; **Stan'dar·ten·trä·ger** *m* standard bearer

'Stand|bein *n* standing leg; **~bild** *n* **1.** *phot.* still; *film, video*: still frame; **2.** statue

Stand-by [ʃtɛnt'baɪ] *n* (-[s]; -s) **1.** ✈ standby; **2.** ~ ***haben*** *doctor etc.*: be on standby; **~-Ta'rif** *m* standby fare; **~-Ticket** *n* standby ticket

Ständ·chen ['ʃtɛntçən] *n* (-s; -) (little) song, F ditty; serenade; ***j-m ein*** ~ ***bringen*** sing s.o. a little song (*or* ditty), serenade s.o.

Stän·de·ord·nung ['ʃtɛndə-] *f hist.* corporative system

Stan·der ['ʃtandɐ] *m* (-s; -) pennant

Stän·der ['ʃtɛndɐ] *m* (-s; -) **1.** stand; rack; **2.** V hard-on (*sl.*)

Stan·des·amt ['ʃtandəs-] *n* registry office

'stan·des·amt·lich *adj.*: ***~e Trauung*** registry office wedding

'Stan·des·be·am·te *m* registrar

Stan·des|be·wußt·sein ['ʃtandəs-] *n* class consciousness; **~dün·kel** *m* class snobbery; F snootiness; **2ge·mäß** *adj. and adv.* in keeping with one's station; **~schran·ken** *pl.* class (*or* social) barriers

Stän·de·staat ['ʃtɛndə-] *m hist.* corporative state

Stan·des,un·ter·schied ['ʃtandəs-] *m* class distinction, difference in class

'stand·fest *adj.* steady; ⚙ stable; ***~e Abwehr*** *sport*: safe defen|ce (*Am.* -se); F *fig.* ***nicht mehr ganz*** ~ a bit tiddly

'Stand·fe·stig·keit *f* steadiness; ⚙ stability; *fig.* → ***Standhaftigkeit***

'Stand|fo·to *n* still; **~fuß·ball** *m*: ~ ***spielen*** play at a walking pace; **~gas** *n mot.* idling mixture (supply); **~geld** *n* stallage; **~ge·rät** *n* console TV set; **~ge·richt** *n* ⚔ drumhead court martial

stand·haft ['ʃtanthaft] **I.** *adj.* a) steadfast; firm, unwavering, staunch *follower etc.*, b) resolute, c) persevering; **II.** *adv.*: ~ ***ablehnen*** firmly refuse

'Stand·haf·tig·keit *f* (-; *no pl.*) steadfastness *etc.*; → ***standhaft***

'stand·hal·ten *v/i.* (*irr.*, *sep.*, h, → ***halten***) hold one's ground (*or* own), stand firm; *dam etc.*: hold out (*dat.* against); withstand *an attack etc.*; stand up to *criticism etc.*; ***j-m (e-r Sache)*** ~ *a.* resist s.o. (s.th.); ***j-s Blick*** ~ resist (*or* sustain) s.o.'s gaze; ***sie konnte ihren neugierigen Blicken nicht*** ~ she couldn't take their inquisitive stares; → ***Vergleich*** 1

stän·dig ['ʃtɛndɪç] **I.** *adj.* a) permanent *address, staff etc.*, b) constant, continual; continuous; steady, c) fixed, regular *income etc.*; established *practise etc.*; ***~er Ausschuß*** standing committee; ***~er Begleiter*** constant companion; ***~er Beirat*** permanent council; ***~er Korrespondent*** resident correspondent; ***unter ~em Druck sein*** be under constant pressure; ***in ~er Sorge leben*** live in a state of constant worry; ***in ~er Verbindung stehen mit*** *dat.* be in regular contact with; **II.** *adv.* permanently; constantly, forever; ***et.*** ~ ***sagen (tun)*** keep saying (doing) s.th.; ***er meckert*** ~ ***über das Essen*** he's always (*or* forever) complaining about the food, he keeps (*or* never stops) complaining about the food

'Stand·licht *n mot.* parking light

'Stand·ort *m* position (*a.* ⚓ *etc.*), location; site *of an industry etc.*; place; ⚔ garrison, *Am.* post; *fig.* position; attitude, standpoint; ***den*** ~ ***bestimmen von*** *dat.* locate; *fig.* ***den*** ~ ***bestimmen*** define one's position, take a clear stand; **~be·stim·mung** *f* location; *radar*: fixing; *fig.* definition of one's position; *fig.* ***e-e*** ~ ***machen*** define one's position, take a clear stand; **~ver·le·gung** *f* relocation; **~vor·teil** *m* ✝ locational advantage; **~wahl** *f* choice of site (*or* location)

'Stand|pau·ke F *f* lecture, *Brit.* F wigging; ***j-m e-e*** ~ ***halten*** give s.o. a lecture (*or* wigging); **~platz** *m* stand, *Brit. a.* taxi rank; **~punkt** *m* point of view, standpoint, stance; ***den*** ~ ***vertreten (or auf dem*** ~ ***stehen, sich auf den*** ~ ***stellen), daß*** take the view (*or* line, stance) that; ***von s-m*** ~ ***aus*** from his point of view; ***vom medizinischen*** ~ ***(aus)*** from a medical point of view (*or* standpoint); ***j-m den*** ~ ***klar machen*** make one's point of view quite clear to s.o.; **~quar,tier** *n* base

'Stand·recht *n* (-[e]s; *no pl.*) ⚔ martial law; **'stand·recht·lich** *adj. and adv.* by order of court martial

'Stand|seil·bahn *f* funicular (railway); **~spur** *f* hard shoulder, *Am.* shoulder; **~uhr** *f* grandfather clock; **~ver·mö·gen** *n* → ***Stehvermögen***

Stan·ge ['ʃtaŋə] *f* (-; -n) pole; rod; rail; post; perch; *ballet etc.*: bar; *gastr.* stick *of cinnamon etc.*; ***Anzug*** *etc.* ***von der*** ~ off-the-peg suit *etc.*, *pred.* suit *etc.* off the peg; ***e-e*** ~ ***Zigaretten*** a carton of cigarettes; F ***e-e*** ~ ***Geld*** F a tidy sum, a packet; F ***e-e*** ~ ***angeben*** F lay it on thick; F ***sie ist e-e lange*** ~ she's like a beanpole; F *fig.* ***bei der*** ~ ***bleiben*** stick it out (to the end), F hang in there; ***j-n bei der*** ~ ***halten*** keep s.o. at it, keep s.o.'s nose to the grindstone; ***j-m die*** ~ ***halten*** back s.o. up, stand (F stick) up for s.o.

'Stan·gen|boh·ne *f* runner (*or* string) bean; **~brot** *n* French stick, baguette; **~sel·le·rie** *m, f* celery (stalks *pl.*); **~spar·gel** *m* asparagus spears *pl.*

stank [ʃtaŋk] *pret. of* ***stinken***

Stän·ke·rer ['ʃtɛŋkərɐ] F *m* (-s; -) troublemaker, stirrer; **stän·kern** ['ʃtɛŋkɐn] F *v/i.* (h) grouse; stir up (*or* make) trouble

Stan·ni·ol ['ʃtanĭoːl] *n* (-s; *no pl.*) tin foil, silver paper

Stan·ze ['ʃtantsə] *f* (-; -n) ⚙ punch, punching machine; **'stan·zen** *v/t.* (h) ⚙ punch; stamp

Sta·pel ['ʃtaːpəl] *m* (-s; -) pile, stack; *computer*: batch; ⚓ stocks *pl.*; ⚓ ***auf*** ~ ***legen*** lay down; ***vom*** ~ ***laufen*** be launched; ***vom*** ~ ***lassen*** a) ⚓ launch, b) *fig.* crack *a*

joke etc., make *a speech*; **~lauf** *m* launching
sta·peln [ˈʃtaːpəln] *v/t.* (h) stack, (*a.* **sich ~**) pile up
ˈ**Sta·pel|ver·ar·bei·tung** *f computer*: batch processing; **~wa·ren** *pl.* staple commodities
ˈ**sta·pel·wei·se** *adv.* in piles; ***bei ihm liegen die Computerhefte ~ herum*** he's got piles (F stacks) of computer magazines lying around (at home)
stap·fen [ˈʃtapfən] *v/i.* (sn) trudge
Stap·fen [ˈʃtapfən] *pl.* footprints
Sta·phy·lo·kok·ken·in·fek·tiˌon [ʃtafyloˈkɔkən-] *f* staphylococcal infection
Sta·phy·lo·kok·kus [ʃtafyloˈkɔkʊs] *m* (-; -ken) staphylococcus
Star¹ [ʃtaːɐ] *m* (s; -e [ˈʃtaːrə]) *zo.* starling
Star² [ʃtaːɐ, staːɐ] *m* (-s; -s) *film etc.*: star, F celeb
Star³ [ʃtaːɐ] *m* (-[e]s; *no pl.*) ⚕: ***grauer ~*** cataract(s *pl.*); ***grüner ~*** glaucoma; ***am ~ operiert werden*** have one's cataracts removed; *fig.* ***j-m den ~ stechen*** remove the scales from s.o.'s eyes, open s.o.'s eyes
ˈ**Star|alˌlü·ren** *pl.* airs (and graces); **~an·walt** *m* top lawyer (*Am. a.* attorney); **~au·tor** *m* best-selling author
starb [ʃtarp] *pret. of* ***sterben***
ˈ**Star|be·set·zung** *f* star cast; ***mit ~*** *a.* star-studded ...; **~di·riˌgent** *m* star conductor; **~gast** *m* star guest
stark [ʃtark] **I.** *adj.* a) strong (*a. ling. and fig.*), *a.* robust, sturdy; powerful *engine etc.*, *a. fig. opponent*, *organization etc.*, b) stout, c) thick *walls etc.*, d) intense; violent; bad; heavy *storm*, *rains*, *cold etc.*, *a. fig. drinker*, *smoker etc.*, e) F great; ***~er Beifall*** loud applause; ***~er Esser*** big eater; ***das ~e Geschlecht*** the stronger sex; ***~es Mittel*** strong medicine (*or* tablets *etc.*); ***~e Nachfrage*** great (*or* heavy) demand; ***~e Schmerzen*** severe pain; ***die Schmerzen sind ~*** *a.* the pain is very bad; ***~e Schmerzen haben*** be in severe pain; *fig.* ***~e Seite*** strong point, strength, forte; ***~e Übertreibung*** gross exaggeration; ***er ist stärker geworden*** he's put on weight; ***e-n ~en Haarwuchs haben*** a) have thick hair, b) have a heavy growth of hair; F ***sich ~ machen für*** *acc.* stand up for; ***den ~en Mann markieren*** try to act tough; ***Politik der ~en Hand*** heavy-handed policy; ***e-e 200 Mann ~e Kompanie*** a company of 200; ***sie waren 200 Mann ~*** they were 200 strong; ***das Buch ist 600 Seiten ~*** the book is 600 pages thick; → ***Blutung, Polizeiaufgebot, Stück***; **II.** *adv.* strongly; ***~ benachteiligt*** severely handicapped; ***~ beschäftigt*** very busy; ***~ betrunken*** very drunk; ***~ erkältet sein*** have a bad cold; ***~ gewürzt*** highly seasoned; ***~ übertrieben*** grossly exaggerated; ***~ ansteigen*** rise sharply; ***~ bluten*** bleed heavily (*or* profusely); ***~ regnen*** rain heavily, pour; ***~ riechen*** have a strong smell, smell strong; ***~ trinken*** (***rauchen***) be a heavy drinker (smoker); ***~ wirken*** have a strong effect; → ***Verdacht***; **~be·fah·ren** *adj.* busy *road etc.*; **~be·haart** *adj.* very hairy; **~be·tont** *adj.* strongly stressed; **~be·völ·kert** *adj.* highly (*or* densely) populated; high-population ...
ˈ**Stark·bier** *n* strong beer; *high-alcohol--content beer*
Stär·ke¹ [ˈʃtɛrkə] *f* (-; -n) **1.** *no pl.* a) strength, ⚗ *a.* concentration; size; ⚙ power, b) intensity; ***Politik der ~*** power politics; **2.** ⚙ thickness, diameter; *opt.* strength; **3.** *fig.* strong point, strength, forte; ***es gehört nicht zu s-n ~n*** it's not one of his strong points (*or* strengths, fortes); → ***Richter-Skala***
ˈ**Stär·ke²** *f* (-; *no pl.*) starch; **~ge·halt** *m* starch content
ˈ**stär·ke·hal·tig** *adj.* starchy; ***~ sein*** *a.* contain starch
ˈ**Stär·ke·mehl** *n* cornflour, *Am.* cornstarch
stär·ken¹ [ˈʃtɛrkən] (h) **I.** *v/t.* strengthen (*a. fig.*); build up *one's health*, *courage etc.*, *a.* boost *one's self-confidence etc.*; increase *s.o.'s influence*, *power etc.*; ***j-m den Rücken ~*** back s.o. up; **II.** *v/refl.*: ***sich ~*** have a bite to eat; have a drink; *lit.* fortify o.s.; ***ich muß mich ~*** *a.* I need s.th. to revive me, *a.* I need a drink
ˈ**stär·ken²** *v/t.* (h) starch
ˈ**stär·kend** *adj.*: ***~es Mittel*** tonic, restorative
ˈ**Stark·strom** *m* ⚡ high-voltage (*or* heavy) current; **~lei·tung** *f* power line; **~tech·nik** *f* heavy current engineering
ˈ**Star·kult** *m* star cult
Stär·kung [ˈʃtɛrkʊŋ] *f* (-; -en) **1.** strengthening; **2.** refreshment; F bracer; ˈ**Stär·kungs·mit·tel** *n* ⚕ tonic, restorative
Star·let [ˈʃtaːɐlɛt, ˈstaːɐlɛt] *n* (-s; -s) starlet
ˈ**Star·ope·ra·tiˌon** *f* ⚕ cataract operation
ˈ**Star·paˌra·de** *f* star gala
ˈ**Star·proˌfil** *n* star (*or* celebrity) profile
starr [ʃtar] **I.** *adj.* **1.** a) stiff, rigid; fixed, b) motionless; ***~er Blick*** fixed (*or* rigid) stare; ⚚ ***~es Budget*** fixed budget; ***~ vor Entsetzen*** paralysed with horror; ***~ vor Staunen*** dumbfounded; ***~ vor Kälte*** numb with cold; ***~ stehenbleiben*** be transfixed, stop dead in one's tracks; **2.** *fig.* rigid *attitude etc.*, *a.* firm *principles etc.*; inflexible, unbending, unyielding; ***~e Regel*** *a.* hard and fast rule; **II.** *adv.* rigidly *etc.*; → ***l***; ***~ festhalten an*** *dat.* adhere rigidly (*or* stubbornly) to *s.th.*
ˈ**Starr·ach·se** *f mot.* rigid axle
Star·re [ˈʃtarə] *f* (-; *no pl.*) stiffness, rigidity
star·ren¹ [ˈʃtarən] *v/i.* (h) stare (***auf*** *acc.* at); ***vor sich hin ~, in die Leere ~*** stare into space
ˈ**star·ren²** *v/i.* (h): ***~ vor*** (*or* ***von***) *dat.* bristle with; ***vor Schmutz ~*** be thick with dirt
ˈ**Star·reˌpor·ter** *m* star reporter
ˈ**Starr·heit** *f* (-; *no pl.*) rigidity; stiffness; inflexibility *etc.*; → ***starr*** I
ˈ**Starr·kopf** *m* stubborn (*or* obstinate) mule; ˈ**starr·köp·fig** [-kœpfɪç] *adj.* stubborn, obstinate
ˈ**Starr·krampf** *m* (-[e]s; *no pl.*) ⚕ tetanus
ˈ**Starr·sinn** *m* (-[e]s; *no pl.*) stubbornness, obstinacy; ˈ**starr·sin·nig** *adj.* stubborn, obstinate
ˈ**Star·rum·mel** F *m* celebrity hype
Start [ʃtart] *m* (-s; -s) start (*a. mot.*, *sport and fig.*), sport: a. starting line; ✈ takeoff; launching, lift-off; ***am ~*** *sport*: at the start, on the starting line; ***fliegender*** (***stehender***) ***~*** *sport*: flying (standing) start; ***e-n guten*** (***schlechten***) ***~ haben*** *sport and fig.*: get off to a good (bad) start; ✈ ***zum ~ freigeben*** clear for takeoff; *fig.* ***~ frei für*** *acc.* ***...*** all clear for (the launching of) ...; ***ein guter ~ ins Leben*** a good start in life; **~aus·rü·stung** *f* basic equipment (*or* kit); **~au·toˌma·tik** *f mot.* automatic choke control
ˈ**Start·bahn** *f* ✈ runway; **~be·feue·rung** *f* runway lighting (*or* lights *pl.*)
ˈ**start·be·reit** *adj.* ready to start; ✈ ready for takeoff; F *fig.* ready to go
ˈ**Start·block** *m* starting block
star·ten [ˈʃtartən] **I.** *v/i.* (sn) start; *sport*: take part (***bei*** *dat.* in), participate (in); ✈ take off; ***zu früh ~*** *sport*: jump the gun; ***~ für*** *acc.* run (*or* race *etc.*) for *Italy etc.*; **II.** *v/t.* (h) start; F *fig. a.* launch; **Star·ter** [ˈʃtartɐ] *m* (-s; -) *mot. and sport*: starter
ˈ**Start|er·laub·nis** *f* ✈ (takeoff) clearance; *sport*: permission to take part; **~geld** *n sport*: entry fee; **~ge·schwin·dig·keit** *f* ✈ takeoff speed
ˈ**Start·hil·fe** *f* ✈ assisted takeoff (*a.* ***Abflug mit ~***); ⚚ initial aid, F start-up cash; ***j-m ~ geben*** *mot.* help s.o. get started, give s.o. a jump start; *fig.* give s.o. a start (in life); **~ka·bel** *n mot.* jump leads *pl.*, *Am.* jumper (cable), booster cable
ˈ**Start|ka·piˌtal** *n* start-up capital; **⚲klar** *adj.* ✈ ready for takeoff; *plane*: in flying condition; **~komˌman·do** *n* starter's order; **~läu·fer** *m* first runner; **~li·nie** *f* starting line; **~loch** *n sport*: starting hole; ***langsam aus den Startlöchern kommen*** get off to a slow start; **~num·mer** *f* number; **~ord·nung** *f* starting order; **~piˌsto·le** *f* starting pistol; **~ram·pe** *f* launch(ing) pad; **~schuß** *m sport*: starting signal; **~siˌgnal** *n* starting (✈ takeoff) signal; *fig.* F go-ahead, green light; **~strecke** *f* ✈ takeoff run; **~turm** *m* launching rail; **~ver·bot** *n sport*: suspension; ✈ grounding; ***e-m Flugzeug ~ erteilen*** ground an aircraft; **~zei·chen** *n* → ***Startsignal***
Sta·si [ˈʃtaːzi] F *f* (-; *no pl.*) *hist. DDR* Stasi, secret police *pl.*; **~-Mit·ar·bei·ter** *m*: (***ehemaliger ~*** former) member of the Stasi
State·ment [ˈsteɪtmənt] *n* (-s; -s) statement; ***ein ~ abgeben*** give a statement (***über*** *acc.* on); make a (*or* an official) statement (on)
Sta·tik [ˈʃtaːtɪk] *f* (-; *no pl.*) *phys.*, ⚡, △ statics *pl.*; *fig.* inertia; **Sta·ti·ker** [ˈʃtaːtɪkɐ] *m* (-s; -) △ structural engineer, stress analyst
Sta·ti·on [ʃtaˈtsi̯oːn] *f* (-; -en) **1.** 🚆 station; stop; ***~ machen in*** *dat.* stop over in (*or* at); ***ich mache bei m-n Eltern ~*** I'll be stopping over at my parents' (place); ***in Kairo zwei Tage ~ machen*** stop over in Cairo for two days, make (*or* have) a two-day stop(over) in Cairo; **2.** *radio*, *meteor. etc.* station; **3.** ⚕ ward; ***auf welcher ~ liegt sie?*** which ward is she in?; ***der Arzt ist auf ~*** the doctor is doing his rounds; **4.** *fig.* stage; **5.** *bibl.* station (of the Cross)
sta·tio·när [ʃtatsi̯oˈnɛːɐ] **I.** *adj.* **1.** a) stationary (*a.* ⚙), b) steady, constant; **2.** ⚕ in-patient ...; ***~e Behandlung*** in-patient treatment; **II.** *adv.*: ***~ behandelter Patient*** in-patient; ***j-n ~ behandeln*** treat s.o. in hospital; ***er muß ~ behandelt werden*** *a.* he'll have to go into hospital (for that)
sta·tio·nie·ren [ʃtatsi̯oˈniːrən] *v/t.* (h) ⚔ station; **Sta·tioˈnie·rung** *f* (-; *no pl.*) stationing
Sta·tioˈnie·rungs|ko·sten *pl.* stationing costs; **~streit·kräf·te** *pl.* stationed forces (*or* troops)

Sta·ti'ons|arzt *m* ward doctor; **~schwe·ster** *f* ward sister; **~ta·ste** *f* preset button; **~vor·ste·her** *m* 🚂 stationmaster

sta·tisch ['ʃtaːtɪʃ] **I.** *adj.* **1.** *phys.* static; ⌂ *a.* structural; **~e Berechnung** structural analysis; **2.** *fig.* static, inert; **II.** *adv.* statically, structurally

Sta·tist [ʃta'tɪst] *m* (-en; -en) *thea., film:* extra; *fig.* bit player; **Sta'ti·sten·rol·le** *f* walk-on part; *fig.* bit part, minor role

Sta·ti·stik [ʃta'tɪstɪk] *f* (-; -en) **1.** *no pl.* statistics *pl.*; **2.** statistical survey; **die ~ zeigt** (the) statistics show, according to the statistics; **e-e ~ aufstellen** a) conduct a survey (**über** *acc.* on), b) compile (a set of) statistics (on); **Sta·ti·sti·ker** [ʃta'tɪstɪkɐ] *m* (-s; -) statistician, statistical expert; **sta·ti·stisch** [ʃta'tɪstɪʃ] **I.** *adj.* statistical; **~e Erhebung** survey; **~es Jahrbuch** annual abstract of statistics; **II.** *adv.*: **~ gesehen** according to the statistics, statistically

Sta·tiv [ʃta'tiːf] *n* (-s; -e [-və]) tripod; **~auf·nah·me** *f* tripod shot; **~bein** *n* (tripod) leg; **~ka·me·ra** *f* stand camera; **~wa·gen** *m* tripod dolly

statt [ʃtat] **I.** *prp.* (*gen.*) instead of; **~ dessen** instead; **aber ~ dessen** instead of which; **II.** *cj.*: **~ zu** *inf.*, **~ daß ...** instead of *ger.*

Statt [ʃtat] *obs. f*: **an j-s ~** in s.o.'s stead

Stät·te ['ʃtɛtə] *f* (-; -n) place; scene; site; **historische ~** historical site; **an historischer ~** *a.* on historical ground; **e-e geweihte ~** a consecrated site, consecrated ground; **~ des Friedens** haven of peace; **~n der Erinnerung (Jugend)** places of the past (of one's youth)

'statt·fin·den *v/i.* (*irr., sep.*, h, → **finden**) take place, be; happen; be held; **die Sitzung findet am Freitag statt** the meeting is (*or* will be) on Friday, *formal*: the meeting will take place on Friday; **das Konzert (die Reise) findet nicht statt** the concert (the trip) has been cancel(l)ed

'statt·ge·ben *v/i.* (*irr., sep.*, h, → **geben**) grant

statt·haft ['ʃtathaft] *adj.* admissible, permissible, legal; **nicht ~** not admissible, *smoking etc.* not permitted

'Statt·hal·ter *m* (-s; -) governor

'Statt·hal·ter·schaft *f* (-; *no pl.*) *hist.* governorship

statt·lich ['ʃtatlɪç] *adj.* a) stately; grand; imposing, impressive, b) well-built ..., *pred.* well built, c) considerable, handsome *sum*; large *family*; **e-e ~e Erscheinung** a commanding figure; **e-e ~e Summe** *a.* F a tidy (little) sum

Sta·tue ['ʃtaːtŭə] *f* (-; -n) statue

'sta·tu·en·haft *adj.* statue-like, statuesque

Sta·tu·et·te [ʃta'tŭɛtə] *f* (-; -n) statuette

sta·tu·ie·ren [ʃtatu'iːrən] *v/t.* (h): **ein Exempel ~** set an (*or* a warning) example; **an j-m ein Exempel ~** make an example of s.o.

Sta·tur [ʃta'tuːɐ] *f* (-; *no pl.*) build; *a. fig.* stature; **von kräftiger ~ sein** be well-built; **von ~ eher klein** (a bit) on the short side

Sta·tus ['ʃtaːtʊs] *m* (-; *no pl.*) **1.** status (*a.* ⚖); **2.** state, status; **~ quo** [- kvoː] *m* (- -; *no pl.*) status quo; **den ~ aufrechterhalten** maintain the status quo; **~sym|bol** *n* status symbol; **~wort** *n computer*: status word

Sta·tut [ʃta'tuːt] *n* (-[e]s; -en) **1.** statute, regulation; **2.** *pl.* ✝ articles of association

Stau [ʃtaʊ] *m* (-[e]s; -s, -e) **1.** *mot.* traffic jam; tailback; **in e-n ~ geraten** get stuck (*or* caught up) in a traffic jam; **im ~ stehen** be stuck (*or* caught up) in a traffic jam; **ein ~ von fünf Kilometer Länge** a five-kilomet|re (*Am.* -er) tailback; **2.** *fig.* accumulation, build-up

Staub [ʃtaʊp] *m* (-[e]s; *no pl.*) dust; powder; ✿ pollen; **~ wischen** dust, do the dusting; **den ~ wischen von** *dat.* dust (down); *fig.* **sich vor j-m in den ~ werfen** a) throw o.s. at s.o.'s feet, b) grovel before s.o. (*or* at s.o.'s feet); F **sich aus dem ~ machen** F clear off, make a (quick) getaway; → **aufwirbeln; ♀be·deckt** *adj.* dusty, dust-covered; thick with dust; **~beu·tel** *m* **1.** ✿ anther; **2.** ⚙ dust bag; **~blatt** *n* ✿ stamen

'Stau·becken *n* reservoir

stau·ben ['ʃtaʊbən] *v/i.* (h) make a lot of dust; **es staubt** there's a lot of dust; F **paß auf, sonst staubt's!** F watch it, or there'll be trouble

stäu·ben ['ʃtɔʏbən] (h) **I.** *v/t.* **1. Mehl** *etc.* **~ über** *acc.* dust *s.th.* with flour *etc.*; **II.** *v/i.* **2.** *water, snow*: spray; **3.** ✿ pollinate

'Staub|fän·ger *m* dust trap; **die Porzellanfiguren sind bloß ~** *a.* those porcelain figures just stand around collecting dust; **~fil·ter** *m* dust filter; **~flocke** *f* piece of fluff; **♀frei** *adj.* dust-free, free of dust; **~ge·fäß** *n* ✿ stamen

stau·big ['ʃtaʊbɪç] *adj.* dusty

'Staub|korn *n* dust particle; speck of dust; **~lap·pen** *m* duster; **~lun·ge** *f* ⚕ silicosis

'staub·sau·gen *v/i. and v/t.* (*sep.*, h) vacuum, *Brit. a.* hoover; **'Staub·sau·ger** *m* vacuum cleaner, *Brit. a.* hoover

'Staub|schicht *f* layer of dust; **~schutz·hau·be** *f* dust cover; **~tuch** *n* duster; **~we·del** *m* feather duster; **~wol·ke** *f* cloud of dust

stau·chen ['ʃtaʊxən] *v/t.* (h) **1.** ram; kick; **2.** shake down; **3.** ⚙ compress, upset; **4.** *fig.* → **zusammenstauchen**

'Stau·damm *m* dam

Stau·de ['ʃtaʊdə] *f* (-; -n) ✿ **1.** herbaceous plant; **2.** shrub

'Stau·den|ge·wächs *n* herbaceous plant; **~sel·le·rie** *m, f* celery (stalks *pl.*)

stau·en ['ʃtaʊən] (h) **I.** *v/t.* **1.** dam up *river etc.*; stop (the flow of) *blood*; **2.** stow (away) *goods*; **II.** *v/refl.*: **sich ~ 3.** *water*: collect, rise; ⚕ congest; **4.** pile up, accumulate; *people etc.*: gather; *traffic*: be(come) congested; *fig. anger etc.*: build up; **die Kinder stauten sich am Eingang** the children were crowding the entrance; **die Autos stauten sich vor dem Tor** there was a long line of cars in front of the gate

Stau·er ['ʃtaʊɐ] *m* (-s; -) ⚓ stevedore

'Stau·mau·er *f* dam

stau·nen ['ʃtaʊnən] (h) **I.** *v/i.* be amazed (**über** *acc.* at); marvel (at); **ich habe gestaunt, wie gut er es gemacht hat** I was amazed at how well he did it; **wir haben nur noch gestaunt** we were amazed, F we just gaped; **da staunst du, was?** I thought that would surprise you, *a.* you didn't think I was capable, did you?; → **Laie; II.** F *v/t.* → **Bauklotz; III.** ♀ *n* (-s; *no pl.*) astonishment, amazement; awe; **j-n in ~ versetzen** amaze s.o., F have s.o. gaping; **sie sind aus dem ~ nicht mehr herausgekommen** they couldn't believe their eyes (*or* ears), F they just gaped; **'stau·nens·wert** *adj.* astonishing, amazing

Stau·pe ['ʃtaʊpə] *f* (-; -n) *vet.* distemper

'Stau·see *m* reservoir

Stau·ung ['ʃtaʊʊŋ] *f* (-; -en) ⚙ buildup (*a. fig.*); ⚕ *and traffic*: *a. pl.* congestion

'Stau·was·ser *n* backwater

Steak [steːk, ʃteːk] *n* (-s; -s) steak

Stea·rin [ʃtea'riːn] *n* (-s; -e) stearin

Stech·ap·fel ['ʃtɛç-] *m* ✿ thorn apple

ste·chen ['ʃtɛçən] (stach, gestochen, h) **I.** *v/i.* **1.** a) *needle, thorn etc.*: prick; *wasp etc.*: sting; *mosquito etc.*: bite, b) stab, c) *sun*: burn; **mit dem Messer nach j-m ~** stab at (*or* attack) s.o. with a knife; *fig.* **in die Nase ~** *smell etc.*: sting in one's nose; **j-m in die Augen ~** strike s.o., catch s.o.'s eye; **2.** *card game*: trump, play a trump; **3.** *show-jumping*: jump off; **4.** *employees*: clock in (*or* out); **5.** → **See** 1; **II.** *v/t.* **6.** a) *needle, thorn etc.*: prick *s.o.*; *wasp etc.*: sting *s.o.*; *mosquito etc.*: bite *s.o.*, b) stab *s.o.*; **7.** cut *peat, asparagus etc.*; **8.** stick *a pig*; spear *eels*; **9.** cut, engrave (**in** *acc.* into); **10.** *card game*: trump; **mit dem König den Buben ~** take (*or* trump) the jack with the king; **11. die Kontrolluhr ~** check in (*or* out); → **gestochen, Hafer; III.** *v/refl.*: **12. sich ~** prick o.s. (**an** *dat.* on; **mit** *dat.* with); **sich in den Daumen ~** prick one's thumb; **IV.** *v/impers.* **13. es sticht mir** (*or* **mich**) **im Rücken** (**in der Seite**) I've got a sharp (*or* stabbing) pain in my back (side), *a.* I've got a stitch in my side; **V.** ♀ *n* (-s; -) **14.** *no pl.* sharp (*or* stabbing) pain; *a.* stitch; **15.** *show-jumping*: jump-off; **'ste·chend** *adj.* piercing *look*; pungent *smell*; sharp, stabbing *pain*

Stech|flie·ge ['ʃtɛç-] *f* stable fly; horsefly; **~gin·ster** *m* ✿ gorse; **~kahn** *m* punt; **~kar·te** *f* clocking-in card; **~mücke** *f* midge, mosquito; **~pad·del** *n* single-bladed paddle; **~pal·me** *f* holly; **~schritt** *m* goosestep; **~uhr** *f* time clock; **~zir·kel** *m* dividers *pl.*

Steck·brief ['ʃtɛk-] *m* "wanted" circular; description, *fig. a.* profile (*gen.* of), fact file (on); **'steck·brief·lich** *adv.*: **~ gesucht werden** be wanted for arrest

Steck·do·se ['ʃtɛk-] *f* ⚡ (wall) socket, power point, outlet

'Steck·do·sen·schutz *m* switch cover

stecken ['ʃtɛkən] (*sep.* -k·k-) (h) **I.** *v/t.* a) put, F pop, stick; slip, b) ⚘ plant, set, c) arrange *flowers*, d) pin; tack; *fig.* **Geld** *etc.* **~ in** *acc.* put money *etc.* into, invest money *etc.* in; **sich die Haare zu e-m Knoten ~** put one's hair up in a knot; **sich e-e Blume ins Haar ~** put (F stick) a flower in one's hair; **den Kopf aus dem Fenster ~** pop one's head out (of) the window; **j-n ins Gefängnis (ins Bett) ~** put s.o. in prison (to bed); **wir ~ dich gleich in den Keller!** you'll be locked up in the cellar if you're not careful; F **wer hat ihm das gesteckt?** who told him (that)?, who passed that on to him?; F **es j-m tüchtig ~** tell s.o. what's what; F **ich weiß nicht, wohin ich ihn ~ soll** I can't place him; → **hineinstecken, Brand** 1, **Nase, Tasche, Ziel; II.** *v/i.* be; be stuck; *bullet, splinter etc.*: be lodged (*or* embedded) in; **der Schlüssel steckt** the key's in the door; *fig.* **vol-**

ler Fehler ~ be full of mistakes; **voller Bosheit (Neugier)** ~ be a spiteful character (F be a nosy old so-and-so); **mitten in der Arbeit** ~ be in the middle of work; **mitten in den Prüfungen** ~ be in the middle of (taking) one's exams; **er steckt immer zu Hause** he never goes out (*or* leaves the house); **in mir steckt e-e Grippe** I think I might be coming down with flu; **wo steckst du denn (so lange)?** where have you been (all this time)?, F where have you been hiding (all this time)?; **wo steckt er bloß immer?** F where does he keep hiding out (*or* hiding himself)?; **dahinter steckt etwas** there's something behind it (all); **da steckt er dahinter** he's at the bottom of it, he's behind it (all); **darin steckt viel Arbeit** a lot of work has gone into it; **zeigen, was in einem steckt** show what one is made of; **in ihm steckt etwas** he's got what it takes, he'll go far (*or* a long way); → **Anfang, Decke, gesteckt, Haut**

Stecken ['ʃtɛkən] (*sep.* -k·k-) *m* (-s; -) stick; → **Dreck**

'stecken·blei·ben *v/i.* (*irr.*, *sep.*, sn, → **bleiben**) get stuck; *fig. a.* dry up, F come unstuck, *thea. a.* forget one's lines; *negotiations etc.*: come to a standstill, reach deadlock; *fig.* **mitten im Satz** ~ break off in mid-sentence; **das Projekt ist in den Anfangsstadien steckengeblieben** the project didn't get beyond the early stages (*lit.* was nipped in the bud); → **Hals**

'stecken·las·sen *v/t.* (*irr.*, *sep.*, h, → **lassen**) leave in; **den Schlüssel** ~ leave the key in the door; F **laß dein Geld nur stecken** this is on me

'Stecken·pferd *n* **1.** hobby; **2.** hobby horse

Stecker ['ʃtɛkɐ] (*sep.* -k·k-) *m* (-s; -) ⚡ plug

Steck|kar·te ['ʃtɛk-] *f computer*: plug-in board; **~kon,takt** *m* ⚡ plug

Steck·ling ['ʃtɛklɪŋ] *m* (-s; -e) ✿ cutting

Steck·na·del ['ʃtɛk-] *f* pin; *fig.* **wie e-e ~ suchen** hunt high and low for; **da sucht man e-e ~ im Heuhaufen** it's like looking for a needle in a haystack; **es war so still, daß man e-e ~ hätte fallen hören können** it was so quiet you could have heard a pin drop

'Steck·na·del·kopf *m* pinhead

'steck·na·del·kopf·groß *adj.* ... the size of (*or* no bigger than) a pinhead

Steck|rü·be ['ʃtɛk-] *f* turnip; **~schlüs·sel** *m* ⚙ socket wrench; **~schuh** *m phot.* accessory shoe; **~schuß** *m* bullet lodged in the body

Steg [ʃteːk] *m* (-[e]s; Stege ['ʃteːgə]) **1.** footbridge; plank; ⚙ catwalk; ⚓ landing stage; gangplank; **2.** bridge *of glasses*; **3.** ♪ bridge; **4.** ⚙ crosspiece, bar; **5.** *typ.* gutter

Steg·reif ['ʃteːkraɪf] *m*: **aus dem** ~ off the cuff; **aus dem ~ spielen** (*or* **dichten** *etc.*) improvise; **e-e Rede aus dem ~ halten** give an impromptu (speech), F ad-lib; **~re·de** *f* impromptu (*or* off-the-cuff) speech

Steh·auf·männ·chen ['ʃteːˀaʊf,mɛnçən] *n* (-s; -) **1.** roly-poly, tumbler; **2.** *fig.* resilient person; **er ist ein richtiges ~** he keeps bouncing back

Steh|aus·schank ['ʃteː-] *m*, **~bier·hal·le** *f* stand-up bar; **~bünd·chen** *n* stand-up collar; **~emp·fang** *m* standing reception

ste·hen ['ʃteːən] (stand, gestanden, h) **I.** *v/i.* **1.** a) stand; be, b) stand still, *a. watch etc.*: have stopped, c) V *penis*: be erect; ~ **in** *dat.* be (written) in; **im Brief steht** the letter says; **wo steht das geschrieben?** where does it say that?, F who says?; **unter der Dusche** ~ be in the shower, be having a shower; **der Kleine kann schon** ~ he can stand up (*or* stand on his own) already; **die Flasche soll ~** the bottle is supposed to stand up; **wo ~ die Gläser?** where are the glasses?; **hier muß ein Komma ~** there should be a comma here; **nach diesem Verb steht der Konjunktiv** that verb takes the subjunctive; **auf e-r Liste** ~ be on a list; **ich kann vor Müdigkeit kaum noch** ~ I'm so tired I can hardly stand on my feet; **plötzlich stand er vor mir** suddenly there he was before me; **der Wein steht kalt** the wine has been chilled; **die Pflanze steht zu dunkel** that plant needs more light; **der Keller steht voll Wasser** the cellar's flooded (*or* full of water); **der Verkehr stand** traffic had come to a standstill; **die Luft steht** a) it's very close, b) the air is thick in here; F **vor Dreck ~** be stiff with dirt; **die Mannschaft (der Plan) steht** the team (the plan) has been decided; **der Termin steht** the date is fixed; **~ auf** *dat.* show, be at; **der Zeiger steht auf Null** the needle is at (*or* on) zero; **das Thermometer steht auf 10 Grad** the thermometer shows (*or* is pointing to) 10 degrees; **wie steht der Dollar?** how high is the dollar?, how does the dollar stand?, what's the dollar worth?; **der Dollar steht bei ...** the dollar stands at (*or* is worth) ...; **höher denn je** ~ have reached an all-time high; **wie steht es?** what's the score?; **es steht 2:1** the score is 2-1 (**für** *acc.* to); F **auf j-n (et.) ~** like (*or* fancy) s.o. (s.th.); F **er steht auf modernen Jazz** he's into modern jazz; **zu ~ kommen auf** *acc.* cost, come to; **auf Diebstahl steht e-e Freiheitsstrafe** theft is punishable by imprisonment; **~ für** *acc.* stand for, represent; **der Name steht für Qualität** the name stands (*or* is a byword) for quality; **er steht dafür, daß das Geld bezahlt wird** he's responsible for seeing that the money is paid; *fig.* **hinter j-m ~** be behind s.o.; **voll hinter j-m** ~ be backing s.o. all the way (*or* up to the hilt); **gut (schlecht) mit j-m ~** (not to) get on (very well) with s.o.; **ihr Sinn steht nach Höherem** she's set her sights higher (than that); *fig.* **über (unter) j-m** ~ be above (below) s.o.; **er steht über solchen Dingen** he's above that kind of thing; **du mußt versuchen, über solchen Dingen zu** ~ you must try not to let that kind of thing bother you; **unter Alkohol** ~ be under the influence of alcohol, have been drinking; **unter Drogen** ~ have been taking drugs, be on drugs; **vor großen Schwierigkeiten ~** face great difficulties; **vor dem Ruin ~** be on the brink of ruin; **er steht vor s-r Abschlußprüfung** he's got his final exams coming up; **zu j-m (et.) ~** stand by s.o. (s.th.); **ich stehe dazu** *a.* I'm sticking by it, I haven't changed my mind (on that); **wie stehst du dazu?** what do you think?; **wo steht er politisch?** what are his political leanings?; **er steht (politisch) links** he's a leftist; **die Sache steht gut** things are looking good; **die Sache muß bis Ende der Woche ~** it's got to be ready (*or* done) by the end of the week; **das Hotel soll Ende Mai ~** the hotel is supposed to be up (*or* ready) by the end of May; **das Ganze steht und fällt mit** *dat.* the whole thing depends on; V **er stand ihm** *penis*: *sl.* he had a hard-on; → **Aufsicht** 1, **Debatte, Einfluß, Sinn; 2.** suit (*dat. s.o.*); **der Hut steht dir gut** this hat (really) suits you; **es steht dir nicht** *a.* it's not you; **II.** *v/t.* → **Mann, Modell, Pate** 1, **Posten; III.** *v/refl.*: **sich gut (schlecht) mit j-m ~** (not to) get on well with s.o.; **er steht sich gut** he's not doing badly; **IV.** *v/impers.*: **es steht zu befürchten, daß** it is to be feared that; **es steht nicht bei mir zu** *inf.* it's not for me to *inf.*, it's not up to me to *inf.*; **es steht (ganz) bei dir** it's up to you, it's your decision; **wie steht's mit e-m Bier?** how about a beer?; **(und) wie steht es mit dir?** how about you?; **V. ♀** *n* (-s; *no pl.*): **er macht alles im ~** he does everything standing; **zum ~ bringen** bring to a stop (*or* standstill), sta(u)nch *bleeding etc.*; **zum ~ kommen** come to a halt (*or* standstill)

'ste·hen·blei·ben *v/i.* (*irr.*, *sep.*, sn, → **bleiben**) a) stop (*a. watch*); ⚙ *a.* come to a standstill (*a. fig.*); *engine*: stall; *heart*: stop beating; *time*: stand still, b) *speaker etc.*: stop (short), c) stay, be left; be left behind; **das Kind ist in der Entwicklung stehengeblieben** the child is (a bit) backward; **soll das so ~?** is it supposed to stay like that?; **wo waren wir stehengeblieben?** where were we?, where did we leave off?; **nicht ~!** move along, please!, keep moving!; **mir ist das Herz fast stehengeblieben** my heart missed (*or* jumped) a beat; **dort scheint die Zeit stehengeblieben zu sein** it's as if time had stood still (*or* the clocks had [been] stopped) there

'ste·hend *adj.* standing; *a.* stagnant *water*; upright; stationary; *fig.* permanent; **~ k.o.** *boxing*: out on one's feet; *fig.* **~er Ausdruck** stock phrase; **~en Fußes** on the spot, straightaway

'ste·hen·las·sen *v/t.* (*irr.*, *sep.*, h, → **lassen**) **1.** a) leave, b) leave behind, c) not to touch, leave (untouched); **er hat s-n Kaffee ~** *a.* he hasn't drunk his coffee; **alles stehen- und liegenlassen** drop everything; **2.** a) leave (in), b) overlook, miss *a mistake etc.*; **3.** (just) leave *s.o.* standing (there); **4. sich e-n Bart ~** grow a beard; **er hat sich e-n Bart ~** *a.* he's sporting a beard

Steh|gei·ger ['ʃteː-] *m* (café) violinist; **~im·biß** *m* stand-up snack bar; **~knei·pe** *f* stand-up bar; **~kra·gen** *m* stand-up collar; **~kur·ven** *pl.* terraces; **~lam·pe** *f* standard (*Am.* floor) lamp; **~lei·ter** *f* step ladder

steh·len ['ʃteːlən] (stahl, gestohlen, h) **I.** *v/i.* steal; **II.** *v/t.* steal (**j-m et.** s.th. from s.o.); *a.* F lift (**aus** *dat.*, **von** *dat.* from); **er hat ihm sein ganzes Geld gestohlen** he stole all his money (from him), he robbed him of all his money; *fig.* **j-m die Zeit ~** waste s.o.'s time; **er hat mir e-n ganzen Tag gestohlen** he wasted a whole day of my time; **j-m den Schlaf (die Ruhe) ~** rob s.o. of his *or* her sleep (peace and quiet); → **gestohlen; III.** *v/refl.*: **sich aus dem Haus ~** steal (*or* sneak) out of the house

Steh|platz ['ʃteː-] *m*: ***e-n ~ bekommen*** have to stand *in the bus etc., thea. etc.*: *a.* get a standing ticket; (***nur noch***) ***Stehplätze*** standing room (only); **~pult** *n* standing desk; **~tri,bü·nen** *pl.* terraces; **~ver·mö·gen** *n* (-s; *no pl.*) stamina; perseverance, staying power

steif [ʃtaɪf] **I.** *adj.* stiff (*a. gastr. and fig.*); *a.* awkward *movements etc.*; *esp. phys.* rigid; firm; V hard *penis*; *fig.* wooden *smile, interpretation etc.*; formal, F (stiff and) starchy; ***~er Hals*** stiff neck; ***~er Gang*** stiff gait; ***~e Haltung*** stiff (*or* rigid) posture; ***er hat ein ~es Bein*** *a.* he can't bend his knee; ***~e Brise*** stiff breeze; ***~er Grog*** strong hot grog; ***~ vor Kälte*** numb with cold; ***~ gefroren*** *a. fig.* frozen stiff; ***~ wie ein Brett*** (as) stiff as a board; ***~ wie ein Stock*** (as) stiff as a poker; ***~ werden*** go stiff, *person*: get stiff, *a. fig.* stiffen; ***ich bin*** (***vom vielen Sitzen***) ***ganz ~ geworden*** I'm all stiff (from sitting around all day); *gastr.* ***~ schlagen*** beat (until stiff); V ***e-n 2en haben*** *sl.* have a hard-on; **II.** *adv.* stiffly *etc.*; ***sich ~ bewegen*** *a.* have (very) stiff *or* wooden movements; *fig.* ***~ und fest behaupten, daß*** insist that, swear that; ***~ und fest glauben, daß*** firmly believe that

'steif·bei·nig [-baɪnɪç] **I.** *adj.* stiff-legged; **II.** *adv.* with stiff legs

'steif·hal·ten *v/t.* (*irr., sep.*, h, → ***halten***): ***halt die Ohren steif!*** chin up!

'Steif·heit *f* (-; *no pl.*) stiffness; *fig. a.* woodenness; starchiness

Steig [ʃtaɪk] *m* (-[e]s; -e ['ʃtaɪgə]) steep (foot)path

'Steig·bü·gel *m* stirrup (*a. anat.*); **~halter** *contp. m pol.* henchman, F stooge; ***j-s ~ sein*** *a.* hoist s.o. to power

Stei·ge ['ʃtaɪgə] *f* (-; -n) crate

'Steig·ei·sen *n* climbing iron; *mountaineering*: *a.* crampon

stei·gen ['ʃtaɪgən] (stieg, gestiegen, sn) **I.** *v/i.* a) go up, climb (up), b) rise, soar; ✈ climb (***auf*** *acc.* to); *fog*: lift, c) *sun, level etc., a. fig. tension etc.*: rise, *temperature etc.*: *a.* go up, *sun*: *a.* come up, d) *fig.* go up, increase; grow; escalate; ✝ *prices etc.*: rise (***bis zu*** to), go up; ***auf e-n Baum ~*** climb (up) a tree; ***auf ein Pferd ~*** mount (*or* get on) a horse; ***vom Pferd ~*** dismount (from a horse), get off a horse; ***auf ein Fahrrad ~*** get on (*or* mount) a bicycle; ***vom Fahrrad ~*** get off (*or* dismount from) a bicycle; ***auf den Thron ~*** ascend the throne; ***aus dem Wasser ~*** come out of the water; ***~ aus*** *dat.* get out of *bed etc.*, get off *a bus etc.*; F ***ins*** (***aus dem***) ***Bett ~*** climb into (get out of) bed; F ***ins Examen ~*** take an exam; ***das Blut stieg ihr ins Gesicht*** the blood rushed to her face; ***Tränen stiegen ihr in die Augen*** tears welled up in her eyes; ***j-m in die Nase ~*** get up (*or* into) s.o.'s nose; ***~ in*** *acc.* climb into *bed etc.*, get into *a bus etc.*; ***e-n Drachen*** (***Ballon***) ***~ lassen*** fly a kite (send a balloon up); F ***heute abend steigt eine Fete*** F there's a party on tonight, there's going to be a party tonight; ***auf die Bremse ~*** slam the brakes on, step on the brakes; ***aufs Gas ~*** step on the accelerator (F gas), *Am.* step on the gas (pedal); → ***Achtung*** 2, ***Dach, Kopf*** 5, ***Wert***; **II.** *v/t.*: ***Treppen ~*** climb stairs; **'stei·gend** *adj. fig.* rising, increasing; growing; mounting; ♈ ***~e Reihe*** ascending series; ***~e Tendenz*** ✝ upward tendency

Stei·ger ['ʃtaɪgɐ] *m* (-s; -) ⚒ pit foreman

stei·gern ['ʃtaɪgɐn] (h) **I.** *v/t.* **1.** a) increase, *a.* put up *the value etc.*, *a.* step up *production, pace etc.*; heighten *effect, tension etc.*, *a.* enhance, boost *effect etc.*, b) improve, enhance, c) aggravate; **2.** *ling.* compare; **II.** *v/refl.*: ***sich ~*** a) increase; grow; rise, go up, mount, b) improve (one's performance); ***er kann sich noch ~*** there's room for improvement yet; **III.** *v/i. at an auction*: bid; raise the amount (***auf*** *acc.* to); **Stei·ge·rung** ['ʃtaɪgərʊŋ] *f* (-; -en) **1.** increase; heightening; enhancement; improvement; aggravation; → ***steigern***; **2.** *ling.* comparison; **'Stei·ge·rungs·ra·te** *f* rate of increase

Steig|fä·hig·keit ['ʃtaɪk-] *f mot.* hill-climbing ability; **~flug** *m* climb(ing flight); **~ge·schwin·dig·keit** *f* climbing speed; **~hö·he** *f* altitude; **~rie·men** *m* stirrup leather

Stei·gung ['ʃtaɪgʊŋ] *f* (-; -en) rise, ascent; 🚗 *etc. a.* gradient; slope; **'Stei·gungs·win·kel** *m* angle of gradient (✈ climb)

steil [ʃtaɪl] **I.** *adj.* steep (*a. fig.*); precipitous; ***~er Abfall*** steep (*or* sharp, sheer) drop; ***~er Aufstieg*** steep ascent, *fig.* (*a.* ***~e Karriere***) meteoric rise; **II.** *adv.* steeply; ***~ ansteigen*** rise steeply, *fig. a.* rise sharply, soar; ***~ abfallen*** slope away steeply, *fig.* drop sharply, plummet; ***dort fällt es ~ ab*** *a.* there's a sharp (*or* steep, sheer) drop at that point; ***~ aufsteigen*** ✈ climb steeply; ***~ aufragend*** soaring

'Steil|flug *m* ✈ vertical flight; **~hang** *m* steep slope; **~heck** *n mot.* wedge-shaped rear; **~kur·ve** *f* steep turn; **~kü·ste** *f* steep coast; **~paß** *m soccer*: through pass; **~ufer** *n* steep bank, bluff

'Steil·wand *f* steep face; **~zelt** *n* frame tent

Stein [ʃtaɪn] *m* (-[e]s; -e) **1.** a) stone (*a.* ⚕); rock; pebble, b) brick, c) *geol.* rock, d) (precious) stone, gem, e) (*tomb*)stone, monument, f) *board game*: piece, g) ♀ stone, kernel; *fig.* ***~ des Anstoßes*** stumbling block; ***der ~ der Weisen*** the philosopher's stone; ***ein Herz aus ~*** a heart of stone; ***zu ~ werden*** turn to stone; ***~ und Bein schwören*** swear by all that is holy; F ***es friert ~ und Bein*** it's absolutely freezing, F it's cold enough to freeze the balls off a brass monkey; ***den ~ ins Rollen bringen*** set the ball rolling; ***den ersten ~ werfen*** cast the first stone; ***mit ~en werfen nach*** *dat.* throw stones at; ***bei j-m e-n ~ im Brett haben*** be in s.o.'s good favo(u)rs; ***j-m ~e in den Weg legen*** place obstacles in s.o.'s path; ***j-m die ~e aus dem Weg räumen*** remove all the obstacles from s.o.'s path; ***es blieb kein ~ auf dem andern*** there wasn't a stone left standing; ***mir fällt ein ~ vom Herzen*** that's (*or* that takes) a load off my mind; → ***Krone*** 1, ***Tropfen***; **2.** *dial.* stein, stone tankard; **~ad·ler** *m* golden eagle; **2'alt** *adj.* ancient; **~axt** *f hist.* stone axe; **~bock** *m* **1.** *zo.* ibex; **2.** *ast.* Capricorn; (***ein***) ***~ sein*** be (a) Capricorn; **~bo·den** *m* **1.** rocky ground; **2.** stone floor; **~boh·rer** *m* rock (⚠ masonry) drill; **~bre·cher** *m* **1.** ⚙ rock crusher; **2.** quarryman; **~bruch** *m* quarry; **~butt** *m zo.* turbot; **~druck** *m* **1.** lithography; **2.** lithograph; **~ei·che** *f* holm oak

stei·nern ['ʃtaɪnɐn] *adj.* stone ...; *fig.* stony; *fig.* ***~es Herz*** heart of stone

'Stein|er·wei·chen *fig. n*: ***zum ~*** heart-rending(ly); ***sie weinte zum ~*** *a.* her crying would have melted a heart of stone; **~flie·se** *f* flagstone; **~frucht** *f* stone fruit; drupe; **~fuß·bo·den** *m* stone floor; **~gar·ten** *m* rock garden; **~gut** *n* (-[e]s; *no pl.*) earthenware, stoneware; **~ha·gel** *m* hail of stones; **2'hart** *adj.* (as) hard as rock; **~hau·fen** *m* pile of stones

stei·nig ['ʃtaɪnɪç] *adj.* stony

stei·ni·gen ['ʃtaɪnɪgən] *v/t.* (h) stone to death; **'Stei·ni·gung** *f* (-; -en) stoning

'Stein·kauz *m zo.* little owlet

'Stein·koh·le *f* hard coal; **Stein·koh·len·berg·werk** *n* coalmine, colliery

'Stein|krug *m* stoneware jug (*Am.* pitcher); stoneware mug, stein; **~mar·der** *m zo.* beech marten

Stein·metz ['ʃtaɪnmɛts] *m* (-en; -en) stonemason

'Stein|obst *n* stone fruit, drupe; **~ope·ra·ti,on** *f* kidney-stone (*or* gallstone *etc.*) operation; **~pilz** *m* cep, boletus; **~plat·te** *f* stone slab; flagstone; **2'reich** F *adj.* F loaded, stinking rich, *pred.* rolling in it; **~salz** *n* rock salt

'Stein·schlag *m* falling rocks *pl.*; **~gefahr** *f*: ***Achtung! ~!*** Danger! Falling rocks!

'Stein|schleu·der *f* sling; catapult, *Am.* slingshot; **~wol·le** *f* rock wool; **~wü·ste** *f* stone desert

'Stein·zeit *f* (-; *no pl.*) Stone Age

'stein·zeit·lich *adj.* Stone Age ...; *fig.* stone-age ...

'Stein·zeit|mensch *m* (*a.* ***die ~en***) Stone Age man; **~me,tho·den** *fig. pl.* stone-age methods

Steiß [ʃtaɪs] *m* (-es; -e) buttocks *pl.*, rump; **~bein** *n* coccyx; **~ge·burt** *f* ⚕ breech delivery; **~la·ge** *f* ⚕ breech presentation

Ste·le ['steːlə, 'ʃteːlə] *f* (-; -n) stele

Stel·la·ge [ʃtɛ'laːʒə] *f* (-; -n) **1.** stand, rack; **2.** ✝ put and call (*abbr.* pac), straddle, *Am.* spread

stel·lar [ʃtɛ'laːɐ] *adj. ast.* stellar

Stell·dich·ein ['ʃtɛldɪçˀaɪn] *n* (-[s]; -[s]) rendezvous, *lit. and iro.* tryst; *sport*: meet; ***sich ein ~ geben*** meet (up), get together

Stel·le ['ʃtɛlə] *f* (-; -n) **1.** place; spot; *a. worn, dirty etc.* patch; point; position; ***undichte ~*** leak; ***wunde ~*** sore, cut; ***entzündete ~*** inflammation; ***empfindliche ~*** tender (*or* sore) spot, *fig.* sensitive (*or* sore) spot; *fig.* ***schwache*** (***verwundbare***) ***~*** weak (vulnerable) spot; ***an anderer ~*** elsewhere, *fig.* at some other point; ***an dieser ~*** here, *fig.* at this point; ***an genau dieser ~*** at this exact (*or* very) spot; ***an erster ~*** firstly; ***an erster ~ stehen*** come first, *matter*: *a.* be top priority; ***an erster ~ der Tagesordnung stehen*** be at the top of the agenda; ***an erster ~ der Tabelle stehen*** be head of the table; ***an erster ~ möchte ich ...*** first and foremost I'd like to ...; ***an ~*** (*gen.*) *or* ***von*** *dat.* in place of, instead of, *esp.* ⚖ in lieu of; (***ich***) ***an deiner ~*** if I were you; ***ich möchte nicht an s-r ~ sein*** I wouldn't like to be in his shoes; ***an die ~ treten von*** *dat.* take the place of; take over from *s.o.*, replace *s.o.*, stand in for *s.o.*; *law etc.*: supersede; ***auf der ~*** straightaway, immediately; ***er war auf der ~ tot*** he died on the spot, he was dead straightaway; *fig.* ***auf der ~ treten*** mark time; ***nicht von der ~ kommen*** not to make any progress, *negotiations etc.*: *a.* be deadlocked; ***ich komme nicht von der ~*** *a.* I'm not getting anywhere; ***sich nicht von der ~ rühren*** not to move (*or* budge); ***er wich nicht von der ~*** he wouldn't budge, he refused to budge; ***zur ~ sein*** be there; ***er ist immer zur ~*** he's always there when you need him; ***sich zur ~ melden*** report (***bei j-m*** to s.o.); **2.** place, *a.* ♪ passage *in a book etc.*; **3.** 𝔄 figure, digit; (decimal) place; ***bis zu drei ~n nach dem Komma*** up to three decimal places; **4.** authority; department, office; **5.** job; position; ***was hat er für e-e ~?*** what kind of job (*or* position) has he got?; ***freie ~*** (job) vacancy

stel·len ['ʃtɛlən] (h) **I.** *v/t.* **1.** ***et. wohin*** *etc.* **~** put (*or* place, set, stand) s.th. somewhere *etc.*; ***kalt ~*** chill; *fig.* ***et. über et. ~*** place s.th. above s.th., value s.th. more highly than s.th.; ***j-n über j-n ~*** promote s.o. above s.o., think more highly of s.o. (than s.o.); ***in den Mittelpunkt ~*** focus (attention) on, make *s.o.* the centre (*Am.* center) of attraction; ***vor e-e Entscheidung gestellt werden*** be faced with a decision; **2.** arrange; **3.** ⚙ set (***auf*** *acc.* on); regulate, adjust; ***leiser*** (*or* ***niedriger***) **~** turn down; ***lauter*** (*or* ***höher***) **~** turn up; ***den Wecker auf sechs ~*** set the alarm for six; **4.** corner; catch; *hunt.* hunt down; **5.** provide (***j-m et.*** s.o. with s.th.), supply *a. troops*; contribute; ⚖ produce *witness etc.*, F come up with; ***dieser Klub stellt die meisten Nationalspieler*** most of the internationals come from this club; **II.** *v/refl.* **6.** ***sich wohin*** *etc.* **~** go and stand somewhere *etc.*; *sport*: position o.s. somewhere *etc.*; **7.** ***sich der Polizei*** *etc.* **~** give o.s. up (*or* surrender) to the police *etc.*; **8.** ***sich e-m Gegner*** *etc.* **~** take on an opponent *etc.*; ***sich e-r Herausforderung ~*** take up (*or* meet) a challenge; ***sich der Kritik*** *etc.* **~** face up to criticism *etc.*; ***die Probleme, die sich uns ~*** the problems we are up against (*or* we face); **9.** ***wie stellt er sich dazu?*** what does he say?; ***sich ~ gegen*** *acc.* oppose; ***sich gut mit j-m ~*** a) get into s.o.'s good books, F get in with s.o., b) keep on s.o.'s right side, stay in s.o.'s good books, F keep in with s.o.; ***sich hinter j-n ~*** back s.o. up; ***sich*** (***schützend***) ***vor j-n ~*** shield s.o.; **10.** ***sich krank ~*** pretend to be ill (*or* sick), *formal*: feign illness; ***stell dich nicht so dumm!*** stop pretending you don't know (*or* understand); ***sich schlafend ~*** pretend to be asleep, F play possum; ***sich tot ~*** pretend to be dead; → ***Abrede*** 2, ***Aussicht*** 2, ***Antrag*** 1, ***Bedingung, Bein, Diagnose, Dienst*** 1, 3, ***Falle, Forderung, Frage, gestellt, Kopf*** 5, ***Rechnung*** 2, ***taub***

'Stel·len|ab·bau *m* reduction in staff, staff reductions *pl.*; **~an·ge·bot** *n* job offer (*or* opening); **~e** vacancies, situations vacant, jobs column; **~an·zei·ge** *f*, **~aus·schrei·bung** *f* job ad(vertisement), employment ad; **~be·schrei·bung** *f* job description (*or* specification); **~be·wer·ber** *m* job applicant; applicant for a (*or* the) job; **~ge·such** *n* job application; **~e** situations wanted

'stel·len·los *adj.* unemployed, jobless

'Stel·len|markt *m* job market; **~nach·weis** *m* **1.** employment agency; **2.** job placement; **~strei·chun·gen** *pl.* job cuts; **~su·che** *f*: (***auf ~ sein*** be) job-hunting; **~su·chen·de** *m, f* (-n; -n) job seeker; **~ver·mitt·lung** *f* employment agency; **~wech·sel** *m* change of job

'stel·len·wei·se *adv.* here and there, in places, in parts; **~ *Regen*** rain in places; ***der Teppich ist ~ abgetreten*** *a.* the carpet has worn (*or* threadbare) patches; ***das Buch ist ~ interessant*** the book has some interesting parts

'Stel·len·wert *m* **1.** 𝔄 place value; **2.** *fig.* rating, (relative) importance; ***e-n hohen ~ haben*** a) rate highly, b) play an important role

...stel·lig [-ʃtɛlɪç] ...-digit; ***zweistellige Zahl*** two-digit figure

Stell|he·bel ['ʃtɛl-] *m* ⚙ adjusting lever; **~ma·cher** *m* cartwright; **~platz** *m* parking space (*Am.* lot); **~rad** *n* regulator; **~schrau·be** *f* ⚙ set screw

Stel·lung ['ʃtɛlʊŋ] *f* (-; -en) **1.** position; **~ *zu*** *dat.* position in relation to; **2.** post, position; ***e-e ~ als Assistent haben*** work as an assistant, have the job of assistant, hold (*or* have) an assistant's post; **3.** position, status; standing; ***soziale ~*** social status (*or* class), position in society, social standing (*or* status); **4.** ⚔ position; front line(s *pl.*); (*gun*) emplacement; ***e-e ~ beziehen*** move into position; ***die ~ halten*** hold the position; ***in ~ bringen*** bring into position, emplace *gun etc.*; **5.** *fig.* position, stance; **~ *beziehen*** take a stand; **~ *nehmen zu*** *dat.* take a stand on *s.th.*, *a.* give one's view on (*or* of) *s.th.*; **~ *nehmen für*** *acc.* stand up for, back (up); **~ *nehmen gegen*** *acc.* oppose, come out against

'Stel·lung·nah·me [-na:mə] *f* (-; -n) opinion (***zu*** *dat.* on); comment, statement (on); ***e-e ~ abgeben*** make a statement (***über*** *acc.* on), comment (on); ***sich e-e ~ vorbehalten*** reserve judg(e)ment, not to commit o.s., decline to comment

'Stel·lungs|be·fehl *m* ⚔ drafting orders *pl.*; **~krieg** *m* static (*or* trench) warfare

'stel·lungs·los *adj.* → ***stellenlos***

'Stel·lungs|su·che *f* → ***Stellensuche***; **~su·chen·de** *m, f* (-n; -n) job seeker; **~spiel** *n sport*: positional play; **~wech·sel** *m* change of position (*or* job)

stell·ver·tre·tend ['ʃtɛl-] **I.** *adj. adm.* acting (***für*** *acc.* for), deputy ...; **~er *Geschäftsführer*** assistant manager; **~er *Vorsitzender*** vice chairman, deputy (*or* acting) chairman; **II.** *adv.*: **~ *für*** *acc.* a) on behalf of, b) standing in for, in place of

Stell·ver·tre·ter ['ʃtɛl-] *m* representative, delegate; *adm.* deputy; substitute (*a.* ⚕); ⚖, ✝ proxy; **~krieg** *m* proxy war

Stell·ver·tre·tung ['ʃtɛl-] *f* representation; substitution; agency; ✝, ⚖ ***in ~*** by proxy

Stell·werk ['ʃtɛl-] *n* 🚂 signal box, *Am.* switch tower

Stelz·bein ['ʃtɛlts-] *n* wooden leg, F peg (leg)

Stel·ze ['ʃtɛltsə] *f* (-; -n) stilt; F *fig.* matchstick leg; ***auf ~n gehen*** walk on stilts, *fig.* be stilted, be wooden; ***wie auf ~n gehen*** walk like a stork; **'stel·zen** *v/i.* (sn) stalk (along)

Stelz|fuß ['ʃtɛlts-] *m* wooden leg, (*a. fig. person*) F peg leg; **~vo·gel** *m* wader, wading bird

Stemm|bo·gen ['ʃtɛm-] *m skiing*: stem turn; **~ei·sen** *n* crowbar; chisel

stem·men ['ʃtɛmən] (h) **I.** *v/t.* **1.** press; heave up; *sport*: lift; ***die Arme in die Seiten gestemmt*** arms akimbo; **2.** ⚙ chisel (out); **3.** F ***einen ~*** F hoist one; **II.** *v/refl.*: ***sich ~ gegen*** *acc.* press (*or* brace o.s.) against *s.th.*; *fig.* resist *s.th.*; *fig.* ***er stemmt sich dagegen*** *a.* F he's dead set against it; **III.** *v/i. skiing*: stem

Stem·pel ['ʃtɛmpəl] *m* (-s; -) a) (rubber) stamp, b) stamp, seal; postmark; hallmark; ✝ brand, trademark, c) ⚙ stamp, punch, d) ♣ pistil; ***den ~ vom 15. tragen*** be postmarked the 15th; *fig.* ***e-r Sache s-n ~ aufdrücken*** leave one's mark (*or* imprint) on s.th.; ***den ~ tragen von*** *dat.* bear the imprint of; **~far·be** *f* stamping ink; **~geld** *n* F dole (money); **~kis·sen** *n* ink (*or* stamp) pad; **~ma,schi·ne** *f* (stamp) cancel(l)ing machine

stem·peln ['ʃtɛmpəln] (h) **I.** *v/t.* stamp; cancel; hallmark; *fig.* **~ *zu*** *dat.* stamp (*or* label) as, brand (as); **II.** *v/i.*: ***bei Arbeitsantritt*** (***Arbeitsende***) **~** clock in (out *or* off); F **~ *gehen*** be on the dole

'Stem·pel|stän·der *m* stamp rack; **~steu·er** *f* stamp duty (*Am.* tax); **~uhr** *f* time clock

Sten·gel ['ʃtɛŋəl] *m* (-s; -) ♣ stalk, stem; F ***fall nicht vom ~!*** take a deep breath, wait for this; F ***ich bin fast vom ~ gefallen*** I nearly fell over backwards

Ste·no ['ʃte:no] *f* (-; *no pl.*) shorthand; **~block** *m* shorthand pad

Ste·no·gramm [ʃteno'gram] *n* (-s; -e) shorthand notes *pl.*

Ste·no·graph [ʃteno'gra:f] *m* (-en; -en) stenographer; **Ste·no·gra·phie** [ʃtenogra'fi:] *f* (-; *no pl.*) shorthand; *formal*: stenography; **ste·no·gra·phie·ren** [ʃtenogra'fi:rən] (h) **I.** *v/i.* write (*or* do) shorthand; **II.** *v/t.* take down in shorthand; **ste·no·gra·phisch** [ʃteno'gra:fɪʃ] **I.** *adj.* shorthand; **II.** *adv.* (in) shorthand

Ste·no·kar·die [ʃtenokar'di:] *f* (-; -n) ⚕ angina pectoris

'Ste·no·kurs *m* shorthand course; ***e-n ~ machen*** take (*or* do) a shorthand course

Ste·no·ty·pi·stin [ʃtenoty'pɪstɪn] *f* (-; -nen) shorthand typist

Sten·tor·stim·me ['ʃtɛnto:ɐ-] *f* stentorian voice

Stenz [ʃtɛnts] F *m* (-es; -e) **1.** fop; **2.** pimp

Stepp|ano·rak ['ʃtɛp-] *m* quilted anorak; **~decke** *f* duvet, *Am.* quilt, comforter

Step·pe ['ʃtɛpə] *f* (-; -n) steppe

step·pen¹ ['ʃtɛpən] *v/t.* (h) backstitch

'step·pen² *v/i.* (h) tap dance

'Step·pen|be·woh·ner *pl.* inhabitants of the steppe(s); ***die ~ Asiens*** the Asian steppe peoples; **~gras** *n* steppe grass; **~land·schaft** *f* steppe(-like) landscape; **~wolf** *m zo.* coyote

Stepp·jacke ['ʃtɛp-] *f* quilted jacket

Stepp·ke ['ʃtɛpkə] *dial. m* (-[s]; -s) F young nipper

Stepp|naht ['ʃtɛp-] *f* backstitch seam; **~stich** *m* backstitch

Step|tanz ['ʃtɛp-] *m* tap dancing; **~tän·zer** *m* tap dancer

Ster·be|bett ['ʃtɛrbə-] *n*: (***auf dem ~*** on one's) deathbed; **~fall** *m* death; ⚖ ***im ~*** in the event of death (*or* decease); **~geld** *n* death grant; **~hil·fe** *f* **1.** euthanasia, mercy killing; **~ *leisten*** carry out euthanasia; **2.** terminal care; **~kli·nik** *f* hospice

ster·ben ['ʃtɛrbən] (starb, gestorben, sn)

I. *v/i.* die (*a. fig.*); pass away (*or* on); ⚖ decease; F *fig. project etc.*: F die a death; *e-s natürlichen Todes* ~ die a natural death; ~ *an dat.* die of *an illness*, die from *a wound*; ~ *für acc.* die for, give one's life for; ~ *über dat.* die in the middle of *one's work etc.*; *fig. vor Scham* (*Neugier etc.*) ~ die of shame (curiosity *etc.*); *wir sind vor Langeweile fast gestorben a.* we were bored to death (*or* tears), F we were bored out of our (tiny little) minds; F *davon stirbst du nicht gleich!* F it won't kill you; F *der ist für mich gestorben* he doesn't exist as far as I'm concerned; *und wenn sie nicht gestorben sind, dann leben sie noch heute* and they all lived happily ever after; II. 2 *n* (-s; *no pl.*) dying, death; *im* ~ *liegen* be dying, *lit.* be at death's door; *im* ~ *sagte er noch ...* just before he died he said ...; *fig. zum* ~ *langweilig* F deadly boring; *zum* ~ *müde* ready to drop, F dog-tired

'ster·bend *adj.* dying; *fig. a.* moribund; **'Ster·ben·de** *m, f* (-n; -n) dying person (*or* man, woman); *pl. a. the* dying (*pl.*)

'Ster·bens·angst *f* mortal terror; ~ *vor dat. a.* mortal fear of; *e-e* ~ *haben vor dat. a.* be terrified of (*or* by); *j-m e-e* ~ *einjagen* put the fear of death into s.o., *lit.* strike s.o. with mortal terror

'ster·bens|elend *adv.*: *sich* ~ *fühlen* feel dreadful, F feel like death warmed up, feel bloody awful; **~krank** *adj.* mortally ill; *sich* ~ *fühlen* F feel like death warmed up; **~lang·wei·lig** *adj.* deadly boring; **~mü·de** *adj.* ready to drop, F dog-tired

'Ster·bens|see·le *f*: *keine* ~ not a (living) soul; **~wort** *n*, **~wört·chen** *n*: *kein* ~ not a word (F peep); *kein* ~ *sagen* not to breathe a word

Ster·be|ra·te ['ʃtɛrbə-] *f* mortality rate; **~sa·kra,men·te** *pl.* last rites; **~stun·de** *f* hour of death; **~ur·kun·de** *f* death certificate; **~zif·fer** *f* mortality rate

sterb·lich ['ʃtɛrplıç] I. *adj.* mortal; *die ~en Überreste, die ~e Hülle* one's mortal remains; II. *fig. adv.* terribly; ~ *verliebt* F smitten; **Sterb·li·che** *m, f* (-n; -n) mortal; *wir gewöhnlichen ~n* we lesser mortals; **'Sterb·lich·keit** *f* (-; *no pl.*) mortality; **'Sterb·lich·keits·zif·fer** *f* mortality rate

ste·reo ['ʃteːreo] *adj.* stereo; *phot.* stereoscopic

'Ste·reo *n* (-s; *no pl.*) stereo; **~an·la·ge** *f* stereo (*or* hi-fi) system, stereo, hi-fi; **~auf·nah·me** *f* stereo recording; **~bild** *n* stereoscopic picture; **~emp·fang** *m* stereo reception; **~fern·se·hen** *n*, **~fern·se·her** *m* stereo TV; **~ge·rät** *n* piece of stereo equipment

Ste·reo·gra·phie [ʃtereogra'fiː] *f* (-; *no pl.*) stereography

Ste·reo·me·trie [ʃtereome'triː] *f* (-; *no pl.*) stereometry

ste·reo·phon [ʃtereo'foːn] *adj.* stereophonic(ally *adv.*); **Ste·reo·pho·nie** [ʃtereofo'niː] *f* (-; *no pl.*) stereophony

'Ste·reo·sen·dung *f* stereo broadcast

Ste·reo·sko·pie [ʃtereosko'piː] *f* (-; *no pl.*) stereoscopy

'Ste·reo·ton *m* stereo sound; *in* ~ (in) stereo

ste·reo·typ [ʃtereo'tyːp] *adj.* 1. *typ.* stereotype ...; 2. *fig.* stereotyped; *~e Antwort* stock reply, stereotyped answer; *~e Redewendung* hackneyed phrase; *~es Lächeln* stereotyped smile

ste·ril [ʃte'riːl] *adj. a. fig.* sterile; *fig. ~e Atmosphäre a.* barren atmosphere; **Ste·ri·li·sa·ti·on** [ʃteriliza'tsi̯oːn] *f* (-; -en) sterilization; **Ste·ri·li·sa·tor** [ʃterili'zaːtoːɐ] *m* (-s; -en [-za'toːrən]) sterilizer; **Ste·ri·li·sier·box** [ʃterili'ziːɐ-] *f* sterilizing unit; **ste·ri·li·sie·ren** [ʃterili'ziːrən] *v/t.* (h) sterilize; *zo. a.* spay; **Ste·ri·li·tät** [ʃterili'tɛːt] *f* (-; *no pl.*) sterility (*a. fig.*)

Stern [ʃtɛrn] *m* (-[e]s; -e) star (*a. fig.*); *mit ~en besät* starry, star-studded; *aufgehender* ~ *a. fig.* rising star; *fig. es geht ein neuer* ~ *auf* there's a new star on the horizon; *lit. unter fremden ~en* under foreign skies; *ein* (*mein*) *guter* ~ a (my) lucky star; *nach den ~en greifen* reach for the stars; *für j-n die ~e vom Himmel holen* go to the milky way for s.o.; *sie ist unter e-m* (*un*)*glücklichen* ~ *geboren* she was born under a lucky (an unlucky) star, she was born (un)lucky; *unter e-m* (*un*)*glücklichen* ~ *stehen* have fortune on one's side (be ill-fated); *das steht noch in den ~en* (*geschrieben*) that's still in the stars; *sein* ~ *ist im Aufgehen* his star is in the ascendant, F he's on the up and up; *sein* ~ *ist im Sinken* his star is on the wane, he's had his day, he's a shooting star; F *~e sehen* see stars; **~anis** *m* star aniseed; **2be·deckt, 2be·sät** *adj.* starry, star-studded; **~bild** *n* constellation

'Stern·chen *n* (-s; -) 1. little star; 2. F starlet; 3. *typ.* asterisk; **~nu·deln** *pl.* star-shaped noodles

'Stern|deu·ter *m* astrologer; **~deu·tung** *f* astrology

'Ster·nen|ban·ner *n* star-spangled banner, Stars and Stripes *pl.*; **~him·mel** *m* starry sky; **2klar** *adj.* starlit, starry; **~licht** *n*, **~schein** *m* starlight, light of the stars; **~zelt** *poet. n* heavenly firmament, starry heavens *pl.*

'Stern·fahrt *f mot.* car rally (*with different starting points*)

'stern·för·mig [-fœrmıç] *adj.* star-shaped, ♀ *a.* stellate; *a.* ⚙ radial

'Stern·gucker F *m* (-s; -) stargazer

'stern'ha·gel'voll F *adj.* F paralytic, *sl.* pissed as a newt

'Stern|hau·fen *m* cluster of stars; **2hell** *adj.* starlit; **~kar·te** *f* celestial chart; **2klar** *adj.* starry, starlit; *~er Himmel a.* clear night sky; **~kun·de** *f* astronomy

'stern·los *adj.* starless

'Stern|marsch *m demonstration march in which marchers converge radially on a central point*; **~mo·tor** *m* radial engine; **~schnup·pe** *f* (-; -n) shooting (*or* falling) star; **~sin·gen** *n carol singing at Epiphany*; **~sin·ger** *m carol singer at Epiphany*; **~stun·de** *f* great moment; decisive turning point; *e-e* ~ *der Menschheit* a great turning point in the history of mankind (*or* civilization); **~war·te** *f* observatory; **~zei·chen** *n* star sign, sign of the zodiac; *welches* ~ *haben Sie?* what's your star sign?, which sign of the zodiac are you?; *er ist im* ~ *des Skorpions geboren* he was born under (the sign of) Scorpio

Sterz [ʃtɛrts] *m* (-es; -e) *zo.* tail

stet [ʃteːt] *adj.* → *stetig*; → *Tropfen*

Ste·tho·skop [ʃteto'skoːp] *n* (-s; -e) ⚕ stethoscope

ste·tig ['ʃteːtıç] *adj.* continual, constant; steady; **'Ste·tig·keit** *f* (-; *no pl.*) constancy, continuity; steadiness; stability

stets [ʃteːts] *adv.* always; constantly, continually

Steu·er[1] ['ʃtɔʏɐ] *n* (-s; -) *mot.* (steering) wheel; ⚓ helm; ✈ controls *pl.*; rudder; *fig. am* ~ *sein* be at the helm (*or* controls); *das* ~ *übernehmen* take over the controls (*or* at the helm); *das* ~ *fest in der Hand haben* be firmly in control; *das* ~ *herumwerfen* alter course (radically)

'Steu·er[2] *f* (-; -n) tax (*auf acc.* on); local tax, *in GB*: community charge, poll tax; duty; assessment; → *erheben* 4; **~ab·kom·men** *n* tax agreement; **~ab·zug** *m* tax deduction; **~ab·zugs·ver·fah·ren** *n* tax deduction at source; **~än·de·rungs·ge·setz** *n* tax amendment law; **~an·reiz** *m* tax incentive; **~auf·kom·men** *n* inland (*Am.* internal) revenue; tax yield; **~auf·schub** *m* tax deferral; **~aus·fall** *m* tax deficit, loss in taxes; **~aus·gleich** *m* tax equalization

'steu·er·bar *adj.* steerable, controllable

'Steu·er·be·fehl *m computer*: control command

'Steu·er|be·frei·ung *f* tax exemption; **2be·gün·stigt** *adj.* tax-deductible; tax-linked *saving*; **~be·hör·de** *f* tax authorities *pl.*; **~be·la·stung** *f* tax burden; **~be·ra·ter** *m* tax adviser; **~be·scheid** *m* tax assessment; **~be·trug** *m* → *Steuerhinterziehung*; **~bi,lanz** *f* tax balance sheet

'Steu·er·bord *n*, **'steu·er·bord(s)** *adv.* ⚓ starboard

'Steu·er|de,likt *n* tax offen|ce (*Am.* -se); **~ein·nah·men** *pl.* → *Steueraufkommen*; **~er·hö·hung** *f* tax increase; **~er·klä·rung** *f* tax return; **~er·laß** *m* tax exemption; **~er·leich·te·rung** *f* tax relief; **~er·mä·ßi·gung** *f* tax allowance; **~er·spar·nis** *f* tax saving; **~fahn·der** *m* tax investigator; **~fahn·dung** *f* (bureau for the) investigation of tax offen|ces (*Am.* -ses); **~flucht** *f* tax evasion; **~flücht·ling** *m* tax fugitive; **2frei** *adj.* tax-free, tax-exempt; duty-free *goods*; **~frei·be·trag** *m* tax-free allowance; **~gel·der** *pl.* tax money *sg.*, taxes

'Steu·er·ge·rät *n* ⚙ control device, controller; *stereo*: receiver

'Steu·er·ge·setz *n* fiscal law

'Steu·er·he·bel *m* ⚙ control lever

'Steu·er|hin·ter,zie·hung *f* tax evasion; **~ho·heit** *f* (-; *no pl.*) tax sovereignty; **~kar·te** *f*: (*Lohn2* wage) tax card; **~klas·se** *f* tax bracket

'Steu·er·knüp·pel *m* ✈ control stick (*or* lever); F joystick

'Steu·er·last *f* tax burden

'steu·er·lich I. *adj.* tax ...; *aus ~en Gründen* for tax purposes; II. *adv.*: ~ *günstig* with low tax liability; ~ *veranlagen* assess for taxation

'Steu·er·mann *m* (-[e]s; -leute) 1. ⚓ helmsman; mate; 2. *rowing*: cox(swain); *mit* (*ohne*) ~ coxed (coxless)

'Steu·er·mar·ke *f* 1. revenue stamp; 2. dog licence disc, *Am.* dog tag

steu·ern ['ʃtɔʏɐn] (h) I. *v/i.* 1. a) ⚓ steer, navigate; pilot, b) *mot.* drive, steer, be at the wheel, c) ✈ navigate, pilot; 2. (sn) ⚓ stand, head (*nach Süden* southward); ~ *nach dat.* be bound for; *fig. heimwärts* ~ head homewards (*or* for home); *wohin steuert Europa?* which direction (*or* where) is Europe headed?; II. *v/t.* a) ⚓ steer, navigate; pilot, b) *mot.* drive, steer,

c) ✈ navigate, pilot, d) ⚙, *computer*: control, e) *fig.* control, run; steer, guide; *fig.* **~d eingreifen in** *acc.* intervene in

'Steu·er|nach·laß *m* tax allowance; **~oa·se** *f* tax haven (*or* shelter); **~pa,ket** *n* tax package; **~pa·ra,dies** *n* → **Steueroase**

'steu·er·pflich·tig [-pflɪçtɪç] *adj.* taxable; dutiable *goods*; **'Steu·er·pflich·ti·ge** *m, f* (-n; -n) taxpayer

'Steu·er·po·li,tik *f* fiscal policy

'Steu·er·pro,gramm *n computer*: control program

'Steu·er|pro·gres·si,on *f* **1.** tax progression; **2.** progressive taxation; **~prü·fer** *m* tax auditor; **~prü·fung** *f* tax audit

'Steu·er|pult *n* ⚡ control desk; *computer*: control panel, console; **~rad** *n* ⚓ *and mot.* (steering) wheel; ✈ control wheel

'Steu·er·recht *n* tax law(s *pl.*); **'steu·er·recht·lich** *adj.* tax law ...; *a. adv.* according to the tax laws

'Steu·er|re,form *f* tax reform(s *pl.*); **~rück·zah·lung** *f* tax rebate

'Steu·er·ru·der *n* ⚓ helm, rudder; ✈ control surface

'Steu·er|satz *m* tax rate; **~schrau·be** *f*: **die ~ anziehen** turn the tax screw; **~schuld** *f* tax(es *pl.*) due, tax liability; *balance*: tax accrued; **~sen·kung** *f* tax cut (*or* reduction); *pl. a.* tax abatement *sg.*; **~ta,bel·le** *f* tax scale

Steue·rung ['ʃtɔyərʊŋ] *f* (-; -en) **1.** *no pl.* steering, ✈ piloting; ⚙, ⚡ *and fig.* control; **2.** control system; *mot.* steering; ✈ controls *pl.*; **'Steue·rungs·me·cha,nis·mus** *m* control mechanism

'Steu·er|ver·an·la·gung *f* tax assessment; **~ver·ge·hen** *n* tax offen|ce (*Am.* -se); **~ver·gün·sti·gung** *f* tax break (*or* concession); *pl. a.* tax relief *sg.*; **~vor·teil** *m* tax benefit (*or* break); **~zah·ler** *m* taxpayer; **~zu·schlag** *m* additional tax; surtax

Ste·ven ['ʃteːvən] *m* (-s; -) ⚓ prow; stern

Ste·ward ['stjuːɐt] *m* (-s; -s) steward

Ste·war·deß ['stjuːɐdɛs] *f* (-; -ssen) stewardess, air hostess

sti·bit·zen [ʃti'bɪtsən] F *v/t.* (h) F pinch, snitch, *sl.* nick

Stich [ʃtɪç] *m* (-[e]s; -e) **1.** a) (*pin*)prick, b) (*bee etc.*) sting; (*mosquito*) bite, c) stab, stab (*or* knife) wound, d) cut *of the spade*; **2.** stabbing pain; **~e haben** have a stitch *in one's side*; *fig.* **es gab mir e-n ~** it really hurt; **3.** *sewing*: stitch; **4.** (*copperplate etc.*) engraving; **5. ein ~ ins Blaue** a tinge of blue, *phot.* a blue cast; *fig.* **er hat e-n ~ ins Rücksichtslose** he's got a ruthless streak; **6.** *card game*: trick; **e-n ~ machen** make a trick; *fig.* **keinen ~ bekommen** *soccer etc.*: not to get a look in, make no mark *during a discussion etc.*; **7.** *fig.* **j-n im ~ lassen** let s.o. down, fail s.o., leave s.o. in the lurch, abandon (*or* desert) s.o., walk out on s.o.; **e-n ~ haben** a) *gastr.* be (slightly) off, b) F *fig.* F be a bit touched; F **du hast wohl e-n ~!** have you gone mad (F off your rocker)?; **~ halten** *argument etc.*: hold water

Sti·che·lei [ʃtɪçə'laɪ] *f* (-; -en) gibe(s *pl.*), dig(s *pl.*), snide remark(s *pl.*)

sti·cheln ['ʃtɪçəln] *v/t. and v/i.* (h) **1.** stitch; **2.** *fig.* gibe, make snide remarks (at)

'stich·fest *adj.* → **hieb- und stichfest**

'Stich·flam·me *f* jet of flame; ⚙ (fine) jet

'stich·hal·tig [-haltɪç] *adj.* sound, well-founded; **seine Theorie ist nicht ~** his theory doesn't hold water

Stich·ling ['ʃtɪçlɪŋ] *m* (-s; -e) *zo.* stickleback

'Stich|pro·be *f* **1.** spot check; ✝ sample audit; **e-e ~ machen** do (*or* carry out) a spot check; **2.** random sample; **e-e ~ machen** take a random sample; **3.** *statistics*: sampling; **~sä·ge** *f* compass (*or* keyhole) saw; **~tag** *m* cutoff date; deadline; **~ver·let·zung** *f* stab wound, knife wound; **~waf·fe** *f* thrust weapon; **~wahl** *f* runoff

'Stich·wort *n* **1.** (*pl.* -wörter) headword, entry; **2.** (*pl.* -worte) *thea.* cue; *fig. a.* key word; **sich ein paar ~e aufschreiben** jot down a few notes; **in ~en festhalten** make a few notes on; **'stich·wort·ar·tig** *adj. and adv.* in note form; **ich habe es ~ notiert** *a.* I've jotted down a few notes

'Stich·wort|re,gi·ster *n*, **~ver·zeich·nis** *n* index

'Stich·wun·de *f* stab (*or* knife) wound

sticken ['ʃtɪkən] (*sep.* -k·k-) *v/t. and v/i.* (h) embroider; **Sticker** ['ʃtɪkɐ] (*sep.* -k·k-) *m* (-s; -) sticker; **Sticke·rei** [ʃtɪkə'raɪ] (*sep.* -k·k-) *f* (-; -en) **1.** *no pl.* embroidery; **2.** piece of embroidery; **Sticke·rin** ['ʃtɪkərɪn] (*sep.* -k·k-) *f* (-; -nen) embroiderer

Stick·garn ['ʃtɪk-] *n* embroidery cotton (*or* silk)

stickig ['ʃtɪkɪç] (*sep.* -k·k-) *adj.* stuffy *room etc.*; close, sticky, muggy

Stick|mu·ster ['ʃtɪk-] *n* embroidery pattern; **~na·del** *f* embroidery needle

Stick·oxid ['ʃtɪk-] *n*, **'Stick·oxyd** *n* ⚗ nitrogen oxide

Stick·rah·men ['ʃtɪk-] *m* tambour (frame)

Stick·stoff ['ʃtɪk-] *m* (-[e]s; *no pl.*) ⚗ nitrogen; **flüssiger ~** liquid nitrogen; **~dün·ger** *m* nitrogenous fertilizer

'stick·stoff·hal·tig [-haltɪç] *adj.* nitrogenous

'Stick·stoff·ver·bin·dung *f* nitrogen compound

stie·ben ['ʃtiːbən] *v/i.* (stob, gestoben, sn) fly (about); spray; **die Funken stoben nur so** the sparks flew; *fig.* **in alle Richtungen ~** scatter in all directions

Stief·bru·der ['ʃtiːf-] *m* stepbrother

Stie·fel ['ʃtiːfəl] *m* (-s; -) boot; *fig.* **das sind zwei Paar ~** they're two completely different things, you can't put them in the same boat; F **s-n alten ~ weitermachen** carry on in the same old groove (*contp.* rut), be doing the same old thing; F **e-n ~ zusammenreden** (**zusammenspielen**) F talk (play) a load of rubbish; F **was redest du da für e-n ~ zusammen?** F what on earth are you going on about?; F **das haut mich aus den ~n** F well blow me; F **das hat ihn aus den ~n gehauen** F he nearly fell over backwards; F **er kann e-n ~ vertragen** he can take his drink, he can hold his liquor

Stie·fe·let·te [ʃtiːfə'lɛtə] *f* (-; -n) ankle boot; bootee

'Stie·fel·knecht *m* bootjack

stie·feln ['ʃtiːfəln] F *v/i.* (sn) F foot it, hoof it; **wir mußten dahin ~** we had to foot it (*or* hoof it) all the way there; → **gestiefelt**

Stief|el·tern ['ʃtiːf-] *pl.* stepparents; **~ge·schwi·ster** *pl.* stepbrother(s) and stepsister(s); **~kind** *n* stepchild (*a. fig.*); **~mut·ter** *f* stepmother (*a. fig.*)

Stief·müt·ter·chen ['ʃtiːf-] *n* ❀ pansy

stief·müt·ter·lich ['ʃtiːf-] *adv.*: *fig.* **~ behandeln** neglect; **sie sind ~ behandelt worden** *a.* they haven't received the attention they deserve, they've been given second-class treatment

Stief|schwe·ster ['ʃtiːf-] *f* stepsister; **~sohn** *m* stepson; **~toch·ter** *f* stepdaughter; **~va·ter** *m* stepfather

stieg [ʃtiːk] *pret. of* **steigen**

Stie·ge ['ʃtiːgə] *f* (-; -n) narrow (*or* steep) staircase *or* stairs *pl.*

Stieg·litz ['ʃtiːglɪts] *m* (-es; -e) goldfinch

Stiel [ʃtiːl] *m* (-[e]s; -e) **1.** handle; broomstick; stem; **Eis am ~** ice lolly; **2.** ❀ stalk; **~au·gen** *pl.* stalk eyes; F *fig.* **~ machen** F goggle, gawk; F **er hat aber ~ gemacht!** he just goggled (*or* gawked), his eyes nearly popped out of his head; **~kamm** *m* tail comb

stier [ʃtiːɐ] *adj.* **1. ~er Blick** glassy (*or* vacant) stare; **2.** F broke, skint

Stier [ʃtiːɐ] *m* (-[e]s; -e ['ʃtiːrə]) **1.** *zo.* bull; **junger ~** bullock; *fig.* **brüllen wie ein ~** bellow (at the top of one's voice); **den ~ bei den Hörnern packen** take the bull by the horns; **2.** *ast.* Taurus; **(ein) ~ sein** be (a) Taurus, be a Taurean

stie·ren ['ʃtiːrən] *v/i.* (h) stare, gape (**auf** *acc.* at); **vor sich hin ~** stare into space

'Stier·kalb *n* bull calf

'Stier·kampf *m* bullfight; **~are·na** *f* bullring

'Stier·kämp·fer *m* bullfighter

'Stier·nacken *m* bull neck; **'stier·nackig** (*sep.* -k·k-) *adj.* bullnecked

Stie·sel ['ʃtiːzəl] F *m* (-s; -) boor, lout; **stie·se·lig** ['ʃtiːzəlɪç] F *adj.* boorish, loutish

stieß [ʃtiːs] *pret. of* **stoßen**

Stift[1] [ʃtɪft] *m* (-[e]s; -e) **1.** ⚙ pin; peg; **2.** a) pencil, b) crayon, colo(u)red pencil, c) felt pen, d) pen, biro (*TM*); **hast du irgendeinen ~?** have you got something to write with?, have you got a pen (of some sort)?; **3.** F (young) apprentice; **4.** F (young) nipper

Stift[2] *n* (-[e]s; -e) **1.** religious foundation (*or* institution); convent; **2.** old people's home

stif·ten ['ʃtɪftən] *v/t.* (h) **1.** a) donate *money etc.*, b) found *a college etc.*, c) provide, supply *the wine etc.*; **2.** cause; **Chaos ~** create (*or* cause) havoc; **Frieden ~** make peace; **Unfrieden ~** cause (*or* make) trouble, *lit.* sow discord; **Unheil ~** cause disaster

'stif·ten·ge·hen F *v/i.* (*irr.*, *sep.*, sn, → **gehen**) F clear off, make o.s. scarce

'Stif·ten·kopf F *m* crew cut

Stif·ter ['ʃtɪftɐ] *m* (-s; -) a) founder, b) donor, sponsor

'Stifts·kir·che *f* **1.** collegiate church; **2.** cathedral

Stif·tung ['ʃtɪftʊŋ] *f* (-; -en) **1.** endowment, donation; **2.** foundation

'Stif·tungs·ur·kun·de *f* deed of foundation

'Stift·zahn *m* pivot tooth

Stig·ma ['ʃtɪgma, 'st-] *n* (-s; -men, -mata) stigma; **die ~ta Christi** the stigmata; **das ~ der Armut tragen, mit dem ~ der Armut behaftet sein** bear the stigma of poverty

stig·ma·ti·sie·ren [ʃtɪgmati'ziːrən, st-] *v/t.* (h) stigmatize, brand (**als** as)

stig·ma·ti·siert [ʃtɪgmati'ziːɐrt, st-] *adj.* branded (**als** as), *a. eccl.* stigmatized

Stil [ʃtiːl, stiːl] *m* (-[e]s; -e) style; **e-e Kirche im spätgotischen ~** a church in late Gothic style; **ein Kavalier alten ~s** a gentleman of the old school; **im gro-**

ßen ~ in (grand) style, on a large scale; ***Betrügereien großen ~s*** large-scale (*or* wholesale) fraud; ***~ haben*** have style; ***das ist nicht mein ~*** that's not my style, that's not the way I like to do things; ***wenn es in dem ~ weitergeht*** if it goes on like that; ***in dem ~ ging die Diskussion weiter*** the discussion continued along those lines (*or* in that vein); **~blü·te** *f* stylistic blunder; F howler; **~bruch** *m* break in style; *fig.* ***das wäre ein ~*** that would be out of style; **~ebe·ne** *f* stylistic register, level of style; **≈echt** *adj.* true to style; in period; **~ele͵ment** *n* stylistic element; **~emp·fin·den** *n* sense of style, stylistic sensitivity; **~epo·che** *f* stylistic era (*or* period); ***die ~ des Rokoko*** the rococo era

Sti·lett [ʃti'lɛt, st-] *n* (-s; -e) stiletto

'Stil|feh·ler *m* stylistic lapse (*or* fault); **~ge·fühl** *n* sense of style, stylistic sensitivity; **≈ge·recht** *adj.* in proper style; appropriate

sti·li·sie·ren [ʃtili'ziːrən, st-] *v/t.* (h) stylize; **sti·li·siert** [ʃtili'ziːɐt, st-] *adj.* stylized

Sti·list [ʃti'lɪst, st-] *m* (-en; -en) stylist (*a. sport*); **Sti·li·stik** [ʃti'lɪstɪk, st-] *f* (-; *no pl.*) **1.** stylistics *pl.*; **2.** style manual

sti·li·stisch [ʃti'lɪstɪʃ, st-] **I.** *adj.* stylistic; ***in ~er Hinsicht*** stylistically, from a stylistic point of view; **II.** *adv.* stylistically; ***~ gut (schlecht) geschrieben*** written in (a) good (bad) style

'Stil·kun·de *f* → ***Stilistik***

still [ʃtɪl] *adj.* a) quiet (*a. fig.*); silent, b) peaceful, c) still, motionless; calm (*a. fig.*), d) secret; ***sei ~!*** (be) quiet!; ***sei ~ davon!*** give over, will you; ***im ~en Einverständnis*** by tacit agreement; ***~es Gebet*** silent prayer; ***~es Glück*** quiet bliss; ***~e Hoffnung*** secret hope; ✝ ***~e Jahreszeit*** dead season; F ***~es Örtchen*** F loo, *Am.* F john; ***der ≈e Ozean*** the Pacific (Ocean); ✝ ***~e Reserven*** hidden reserves; ***in e-r ~en Stunde*** in a quiet moment; ✝ ***~er Teilhaber*** sleeping (*Am.* silent) partner; ***~e Übereinkunft*** tacit understanding; ***~er Verehrer*** secret admirer; ***~er Vorwurf*** silent reproach; ***~e Wasser sind tief*** still waters run deep; ***er ist ein ~es Wasser*** he's a dark horse; ***die ≈en im Lande*** the silent majority; ***im ~en*** a) inwardly, b) secretly; ***im ~en fluchte ich*** I was cursing to myself (*or* inside, under my breath); ***~ werden*** become (*or* go) quiet, calm down; ***plötzlich wurde es ganz ~*** suddenly everything went quiet (*or* there was silence); *fig.* ***um ihn ist es ~ geworden*** you don't hear anything about him these days; → ***Kämmerlein***; **~blei·ben** *v/i.* (*irr.*, *sep.*, sn, → ***bleiben***) keep quiet (*or* still); ***bleib doch mal ~!*** be quiet (*or* keep still), will you

Stil·le ['ʃtɪlə] *f* (-; *no pl.*) silence; hush; quiet, calm; ***die ~ vor dem Sturm*** the calm before the storm; ***in aller ~*** quietly, unnoticed, secretly, without a word to anyone, F without letting on to anyone, on the quiet; ***sie heirateten in aller ~*** the wedding was a very quiet affair, they got married on the quiet; ***in tiefer ~ liegen*** be shrouded in silence; ***die ~ der Nacht*** the dead silence of night; ***in der ~ der Nacht*** in the still(ness) of the night

Stille·ben (*sep.* -ll·l-) *n art:* still life

stille·gen (*sep.* -ll·l-) *v/t.* (*sep.*, h) shut down *firm etc.*; *mot.* lay up; ⚙ put out of operation; ⚓ put out of commission; stop *the traffic*; ⚕ immobilize; *fig.* paralyze; **Stille·gung** (*sep.* -ll·l-) *f* (-; -en) shutdown, closure; stoppage

'Stil·leh·re *f* **1.** stylistics *pl.*; **2.** style manual

stil·len ['ʃtɪlən] (h) **I.** *v/t.* **1.** breastfeed, nurse; **2.** stop, sta(u)nch, ⚕ arrest *a h(a)emorrhage*; **3.** quench *one's thirst*; satisfy (*a. fig.*), take the edge off *one's hunger*; *fig.* satiate; ***s-e Neugier ist jetzt gestillt*** his curiosity has been satisfied; **4.** ease *pain etc.*; **II.** *v/i.* breastfeed, nurse; **III.** ≈ *n* (-s; *no pl.*) breastfeeding

'stil·lend *adj.*: ***~e Mütter*** nursing mothers

'still·ge·legt *adj.* disused *mine*

'Still·hal·te·ab·kom·men *n* standstill agreement; **'still·hal·ten** *v/i.* (*irr.*, *sep.*, h, → ***halten***) keep still; *fig.* keep quiet

'stillie·gen (*sep.* -ll·l-) *v/i.* (*irr.*, *sep.*, h, → ***liegen***) lie still; *fig.* lie dormant; *traffic, business etc.*: be at a standstill; *firm*: be shut down, lie idle

'stil·los I. *adj.* **1.** in bad style (*or* taste), tasteless; **2.** *das Zimmer etc.* ***ist ~*** has no style; **II.** *adv.* in bad style; out of style

'Still·schwei·gen *n* silence (*a.* ⚖); ***~ bewahren*** maintain strict silence (***über*** *acc.* on); ***et. mit ~ übergehen*** pass s.th. over in silence; **'still·schwei·gend I.** *adj.* silent; *fig.* tacit, implicit *agreement*; ***~e Duldung*** tacit consent (*gen.* to), (silent) acquiescence (in), *a.* ⚖ connivance (in); **II.** *adv.* silently, in silence, without a word; *fig.* tacitly; ***et. ~ übergehen*** pass s.th. over in silence; ***~ dulden*** (silently) acquiesce in, tacitly consent to

'still·sit·zen *v/i.* (*irr.*, *sep.*, h, → ***sitzen***) sit still, sit quietly; *fig.* ***er kann nicht ~*** he's always got to be on the go

'Still·stand *m* (-[e]s; *no pl.*) standstill (*a. fig.*), stop(page); ⚕ cardiac arrest; *fig.* stagnation (*a.* ✝); deadlock; ***zum ~ bringen*** *a. fig.* stop (*a.* ⚕), bring to a halt (*or* standstill), put an end (*or* a stop) to *fighting etc.*, end; ***zum ~ kommen*** stop (*a.* ⚕), *a. fig.* come to a halt (*or* standstill), *fighting etc.*: come to a stop (*or* an end), end, *negotiations etc.*: reach deadlock

'still·ste·hen *v/i.* (*irr.*, *sep.*, h, → ***stehen***) **1.** *traffic, business etc.*: be at a standstill; ⚙ lie idle; *fig.* ***die Zeit scheint stillzustehen*** time seems to be standing still; **2.** ⚙ stop (working); *engine*: stop; *heart*: stop (beating); *fig.* ***mein Herz stand still*** my heart stopped (*or* stood still); **3.** ⚔ stand to attention; ***stillgestanden!*** attention!

'still·ver·gnügt I. *adj.* inwardly content (*or* amused); **II.** *adv.*: ***~ lächeln*** smile serenely

'Still·zeit *f* lactation (*or* nursing) period

'Stil|merk·mal *n* stylistic feature; **~mit·tel** *n* stylistic device; **~mö·bel** *pl.* **1.** reproduction furniture *sg.*; **2.** period furniture *sg.*; **~übung** *f* stylistic exercise, exercise in style

'stil·voll I. *adj.* stylish, tasteful; **II.** *adv.* stylishly, tastefully; ***~ eingerichtet*** *a.* furnished in style

'Stil·wör·ter·buch *n* dictionary of (correct) usage, (alphabetically arranged) usage manual

Stimm|ab·ga·be ['ʃtɪm-] *f* voting, vote; **~an·teil** *m* share of the vote; **~band** *n* (-[e]s; ⸚er) *anat.* vocal chord; **≈be·rech·tigt** *adj.* eligible to vote; ***nicht ~*** non-voting ...; **~be·rech·ti·gung** *f* right to vote; → *a.* ***Stimmrecht***; **~bruch** *m* (-[e]s; *no pl.*) breaking of the voice; ***er ist im ~*** his voice is breaking; ***nach dem ~*** after one's voice has broken

Stim·me ['ʃtɪmə] *f* (-; -n) **1.** voice; ***mit lauter (bebender) ~*** in a loud (trembling) voice; ***gut bei ~ sein*** be in good voice; **2.** ♪ a) voice, b) (voice) part, c) part; **3.** *fig.* a) voice, opinion, b) speaker, voice; ***die ~n der Presse*** press comments; ***die ~ des Volkes*** the voice of the people; ***die ~ der Öffentlichkeit*** public opinion; ***es mehren sich die ~n dagegen*** there's mounting opposition (among the public *etc.*); ***es mehren sich die ~n, daß*** more and more people are of the opinion that; **4.** vote; ***e-e ~ haben*** have a vote; ***s-e ~ abgeben*** (cast one's) vote; ***j-m s-e ~ geben*** vote for s.o., give s.o. one's vote; ***~n werben*** canvass (for votes); ***sich der ~ enthalten*** abstain (from voting); → ***abgegeben, entscheidend*** I

stim·men ['ʃtɪmən] (h) **I.** *v/t.* **1.** ♪ tune (***nach*** *dat.* to); ***höher (tiefer) ~*** tune up (down); ***die Instrumente ~*** be tuning up; **2.** *fig.* ***j-n gegen et. ~*** prejudice s.o. against s.th.; ***j-n glücklich ~*** make s.o. happy; ***j-n traurig ~*** sadden s.o., make s.o. sad; ***j-n heiter ~*** put s.o. in a cheerful (*or* good) mood; ***j-n optimistisch ~*** give s.o. cause for optimism; → ***günstig*** I, ***nachdenklich***; **II.** *v/i.* **3.** a) be right, be correct, b) be true; ***stimmt's?*** am I right, is(n't) that right?; ***das stimmt (ganz genau)*** that's (absolutely) right; F ***das stimmt ja hinten und vorne nicht!*** a) F it's a pack of lies, b) F it's all up the creek; ***stimmt so!*** keep the change, that's all right (*Am.* alright); ***da stimmt etwas nicht*** a) there's something wrong here, b) there's something fishy going on (here); ***es stimmt zu dem, was er gesagt hat*** it tallies with what he said; F ***bei dir stimmt's wohl nicht*** have you gone mad?; **4.** ***~ für*** *acc.* vote for (*or* in favo[u]r of); ***~ gegen*** *acc.* vote against; ***mit ja ~*** vote for (*or* in favo[u]r); ***mit nein ~*** vote against

'Stim·men|an·teil *m* percentage of votes; **~aus·zäh·lung** *f* counting of votes, vote count(ing); **~ein·bu·ße** *f* → ***Stimmenverlust***; **~fang** *m* vote catching; **~gewinn** *m* gain (*or* increase) in votes; **~gewirr** *n* babble (*or* confusion) of voices; **~gleich·heit** *f* parity of votes; *parl.* tie; **~mehr·heit** *f* majority of votes; ***einfache ~*** simple majority

Stimm·ent·hal·tung ['ʃtɪm-] *f* abstention

'Stim·men|ver·hält·nis *n* proportion of votes; **~ver·lust** *m* loss of votes, vote loss(es *pl.*); ***starker ~*** heavy vote losses; ***~e erleiden*** lose votes; **~zu·wachs** *m* gain (*or* increase) in votes

Stim·mer ['ʃtɪmɐ] *m* (-s; -) ♪ tuner

Stimm·ga·bel ['ʃtɪm-] *f* ♪ tuning fork

stimm·ge·wal·tig ['ʃtɪm-] *adj.* powerful-voiced; ***~ sein*** have a powerful voice; ***~er Baß*** powerful bass

stim·mig ['ʃtɪmɪç] *adj.* consistent *argument etc.*; *a.* well-rounded *performance etc.*; ***in sich ~ sein*** be consistent within itself, form an intrinsic whole

stimm·haft ['ʃtɪmhaft] *adj. ling.* voiced

Stimm·la·ge ['ʃtɪm-] *f* pitch, register

stimm·lich ['ʃtɪmlɪç] **I.** *adj.* vocal; **II.** *adv.* vocally; ***~ in Form*** in good voice

stimm·los ['ʃtɪmlo:s] *adj. ling.* voiceless, unvoiced
Stimm|or,gan ['ʃtɪm-] *n anat.* vocal organ; **~pfei·fe** *f* pitch pipe; **~recht** *n* (right to) vote; franchise; ***allgemeines ~*** universal suffrage; ***das ~ ausüben*** (exercise one's right to) vote; **~rit·ze** *f anat.* glottis; **~schlüs·sel** *m* ♪ tuning hammer (*or* key); **~,um·fang** *m* vocal range
Stim·mung ['ʃtɪmʊŋ] *f* (-; -en) **1.** mood; **2.** *no pl.* a) morale (*a.* ⚔), b) mood, atmosphere, public sentiment, *the* public mood, c) ⚕ tendency, d) high spirits *pl.*; ***deutschfeindliche ~*** anti-German sentiment (*or* feeling); ***feindselige ~*** (feeling of) animosity; ***das Bild hat ~*** the picture has atmosphere; ***in guter ~*** in good spirits, cheerful, in a good mood; ***in schlechter ~*** in low spirits, depressed, in a bad mood; ***in der ~ sein zu*** *inf.* feel like *ger.*, be in the mood for *ger.* (*or* to *inf.*); ***nicht in der ~ sein zu*** *inf.* not to feel like *ger.*, not to be in the mood for *ger.*; ***~ machen für*** *acc.* work up some enthusiasm for; ***für ~ sorgen, ~ machen*** liven things up (a bit), *a.* put some life into the party; ***in ~ kommen*** get going, *party etc.*: *a.* liven up; → ***gedrückt***
'**Stim·mungs|ba·ro,me·ter** *n* barometer of public opinion; ***das ~ steht auf Null*** (*or* ***ist auf Null gesunken***) everyone's in the doldrums; ***das ~ steigt*** F the (public) mood is on the up; **~bild** *n* **1.** atmospheric (*or* mood) painting; **2.** atmospheric description; **~ka,no·ne** F *f*: ***er ist e-e richtige ~*** he's always the life and soul of the party; **~ma·che** *f* propaganda; **~mu·,sik** *f* singalong music; **~,um·schwung** *m* change of mood; *psych.* mood swing; ⚕ change in trend; *pol.* volte-face
'**stim·mungs·voll** *adj.* atmospheric; evocative *poem*
'**Stim·mungs·wech·sel** *m* → ***Stimmungsumschwung***
Stimm|vieh ['ʃtɪm-] *contp. n* inertia voters *pl.*, F voting fodder; **~wech·sel** *m* → ***Stimmbruch***; **~zet·tel** *m* ballot paper
Sti·mu·lans ['ʃti:mulans, 'st-] *n* (-; Stimulanzien [ʃtimu'lantsǐən, st-]) ⚕ stimulant; *fig. a.* stimulus; ***als ~ wirken*** act as a stimulant (*fig. a.* stimulus), have a stimulating effect; **sti·mu·lie·ren** [ʃtimu'li:rən, st-] *v/t.* (h) stimulate; ***j-n (zu et.) ~*** spur s.o. on (to s.th.); **Sti·mu·lus** ['ʃti:mulʊs, 'st-] *m* (-; -li) stimulus
stink·be'sof·fen ['ʃtɪŋk-] F *adj.* F plastered, *sl.* (completely) sloshed, pissed as a newt
Stink·bom·be ['ʃtɪŋk-] *f* stink bomb
stin·ken ['ʃtɪŋkən] *v/i.* (stank, gestunken, h) **1.** stink (***nach*** *dat.* of), smell (of); ***das stinkt aber!*** what a(n awful) smell (*or* stink, F pong); **2.** F *fig.* ***et. stinkt an der Sache*** there's something fishy about it; ***vor Geld ~*** stink of money, be stinking rich; ***das (er) stinkt mir*** I'm sick of it (him); ***mir stinkt's!*** I'm fed up to the back teeth; ***was mir am meisten stinkt*** F what really gets to me; ***es stinkt mir, daß er so viel mehr verdient*** F the fact that he earns so much more really gets to me; '**stin·kend** *adj.* smelly, stinking; putrid
stink|'faul ['ʃtɪŋk-] F *adj.* bone-idle; **~'fein** F *adj.* F (dead) posh
stin·kig ['ʃtɪŋkɪç] F *adj.*: ***~ sein*** F be in a stinking mood
stink'lang·wei·lig ['ʃtɪŋk-] F *adj.* deadly boring; ***~ sein*** *a.* F be a crushing bore; ***es war ~*** *a.* F we were bored out of our (tiny little) minds
Stink|lau·ne ['ʃtɪŋk-] F *f*: ***e-e ~ haben*** be in a stinker of a mood, be in a stinking mood; **~mor·chel** *f* ♣ stinkhorn
stink|nor'mal ['ʃtɪŋk-] F *adj.* boringly normal; **~'reich** F *adj.* F stinking rich; **~'sau·er** F *adj.* F fuming; ***~ sein auf j-n*** be really mad at s.o.
Stink|tier ['ʃtɪŋk-] *n zo.* skunk; 2'**vor·nehm** F *adj.* F (dead) posh; **~wut** F *f*: ***e-e ~ haben*** F be (absolutely) fuming, ***auf j-n:*** be really mad at s.o.
Sti·pen·di·at [ʃtipɛn'dǐa:t] *m* (-en; -en) scholarship holder; *in cpds.* ... scholar (*i.e.* ***DAAD-~*** DAAD scholar)
Sti·pen·di·um [ʃti'pɛndǐʊm] *n* (-s; -dien) grant; scholarship
Stipp·vi,si·te ['ʃtɪp-] F *f* flying visit (***nach*** *dat.* to), *a.* quick tour (of *Rome etc.*); ***bei j-m e-e ~ machen*** pop round and see s.o., (briefly) drop in on s.o.
Stirn [ʃtɪrn] *f* (-; -en) forehead, *lit.* brow; *fig.* ***die ~ haben zu*** *inf.* F have the cheek (*or* nerve, F brass) to *inf.*; ***j-m (e-r Sache) die ~ bieten*** defy s.o. (s.th.); ***es steht ihm auf der ~ geschrieben*** it's written all over his face; → ***runzeln***; **~an·sicht** *f* front(al) view, front elevation; **~band** *n* (-[e]s; ¨er) headband, sweatband; **~bein** *n anat.* frontal bone; **~fal·te** *f* wrinkle on one's forehead; **~glat·ze** *f* receding hairline; **~höh·le** *f* (frontal) sinus
'**Stirn·höh·len|ent·zün·dung** *f*, **~ka,tarrh** *m* (frontal) sinusitis; **~ver·ei·te·rung** *f* suppurative frontal sinusitis
'**Stirn|locke** *f* forelock, curl at the front (*or* on one's forehead); **~rad** *n* ⚙ spur gear
'**Stirn·run·zeln** *n* frown(ing); '**stirn·run·zelnd** *adv.* frowningly, with a frown
'**Stirn|sei·te** *f* front (side *or* end); **~wand** *f* front (*or* end) wall
stob [ʃto:p] *pret. of* ***stieben***
stö·bern ['ʃtø:bɐn] *v/i.* (h) **1.** rummage around (***nach*** *dat.* for); ***in den Akten ~*** riffle through the files; ***in Büchern nach Hinweisen ~*** hunt down references in books; **2.** *zo.* hunt about (***nach*** *dat.* for); **3.** *dial.* get the place shipshape
sto·chern ['ʃtɔxɐn] *v/i.* (h): ***~ in*** *dat.* poke (about in), poke, stoke (up) *the fire*; ***in den Zähnen ~*** pick one's teeth; ***in s-m Essen ~*** pick at one's food
Stock [ʃtɔk] *m* (-[e]s; Stöcke ['ʃtœkə]) **1.** stick (*a. sport*); *skiing*: *a.* pole; cane; (*billiard*) cue; ♪ baton; ***am ~ gehen*** walk with a stick, F *fig.* be on one's last legs, *a.* be scraping the barrel; **2.** ♣ a) vine, b) stock, c) (flowering) pot plant; ***über ~ und Stein*** up hill and down dale; **3.** *geol.* massif; **4.** floor, stor(e)y; ***im ersten ~ wohnen*** live on the first (*Am.* second) floor; **~ar·beit** *f skiing*: pole work (*or* action)
'**stock|be'sof·fen, ~be'trun·ken** F *adj.* F plastered, *sl.* (completely) sloshed, pissed as a newt
'**Stock·bett** *n* bunk bed
'**stock|'blind** F *adj.* blind as a bat; **~'dumm** F *adj.* F (as) thick as two short planks; **~'dun·kel, ~du·ster** [-'du:stɐ] F *adj.* pitch dark
Stöckel|ab·satz ['ʃtœkəl-] (*sep.* -k·k-) *m* stiletto heel; **~schu·he** *pl.* stilettos
stocken ['ʃtɔkən] (*sep.* -k·k-) **I.** *v/i.* **1.** (h) falter; hesitate; slacken; stop short; ⚕ slacken off; *negotiations etc.*: break down, come to a standstill; *traffic*: be congested; *engine*: stall; *fig.* ***ihm stockte das Herz*** his heart missed a beat; ***ihm stockte der Atem*** he caught his breath; **2.** (sn) ⚕ *blood*: clot, coagulate; *milk*: curdle; *walls etc.*: go mo(u)ldy; *fig.* ***ihr stockte das Blut in den Adern*** her blood froze; **II.** 2 *n*: ***ins ~ geraten*** *speaker*: (begin to) falter; *negotiations etc.*: break down, come to a standstill; *business etc.*: begin to fall off (*or* slacken); *engine*: stall; '**stockend I.** *adj.*: ***~er Atem*** short, sharp breaths; ***~er Herzschlag*** faltering heartbeat; ***~er Gang*** halting gait; ***~e Schritte*** halting (*or* faltering) steps; ***~es Gespräch*** faltering conversation; ***~e Redeweise*** halting speech; ***~er Verkehr*** halting (*or* slow-moving, stop-go) traffic; ⚕ ***~e Geschäfte*** slack (*or* sluggish) trading; ***~e Verhandlungen*** slow-moving (*or* faltering) talks; ***mit ~er Stimme*** in a faltering voice; **II.** *adv.* haltingly; ***wir kommen nur ~ voran*** progress is very sluggish
'**Stock|en·te** *f* mallard; 2'**fin·ster** F *adj.* pitch dark; **~fisch** *m* **1.** dried cod; **2.** F *fig.* F stick
'**Stock·fleck** *m* mo(u)ldy spot, patch of mo(u)ld; '**stock·fleckig** *adj.* mo(u)ldy
'**stock'hei·ser** F *adj.* completely hoarse; ***ich bin ~*** my throat is (absolutely) raw
stockig ['ʃtɔkɪç] (*sep.* -k·k-) *adj.* mo(u)ldy
...stöckig [-ʃtœkɪç] (*sep.* -k·k-) *adj.* ...-stor(e)y, ...-storied
'**stock·kon·ser·va'tiv** F *adj.* ultra-conservative
'**Stock·na·gel** *m* walking-stick plaque
'**stock|'nüch·tern** F *adj.* F stone-cold sober; **~'sau·er** F *adj.* mad, F fuming
'**Stock|schirm** *m* walking-stick umbrella; **~schnup·fen** *m* ⚕ chronic cold
'**stock|'steif** F *adj.* (as) stiff as a poker; **~'taub** F *adj.* stone-deaf
Stockung ['ʃtɔkʊŋ] (*sep.* -k·k-) *f* (-; -en) **1.** (*a. traffic*) holdup, delay; hesitation; *pl.* *a.* congestion; ***ohne ~en verlaufen*** go without a hitch; **2.** a) standstill; deadlock, b) ⚕ stasis, congestion
'**Stock·werk** *n* floor, stor(e)y; *geol.* stratum; ***im ersten ~*** on the first (*Am.* second) floor; ***im oberen ~*** upstairs
Stoff [ʃtɔf] *m* (-[e]s; -e) **1.** material, fabric; cloth; **2.** substance; F stuff (*alcohol*, *drugs*); *fig.* ***aus e-m besseren ~ gemacht*** made of better stuff; **3.** subject matter; *ped.* material, topic; topic(s *pl.*) (for discussion); material (***zu*** *dat.*, ***für*** *acc.* for *a novel etc.*); ***~ zum Nachdenken*** food for thought; **~bahn** *f* length of material; **~bal·len** *m* bale of cloth
Stof·fel ['ʃtɔfəl] F *m* (-s; -) oaf; **stof·fe·lig** ['ʃtɔfəlɪç] F *adj.* boorish, oafish
'**Stoff|mu·ster** *n* pattern; sample; **~pup·pe** *f* rag doll; **~rest** *m* remnant; scrap of material; **~samm·lung** *f* gathering (of) material; **~tier** *n* stuffed animal
'**Stoff·wech·sel** *m* (-s; *no pl.*) metabolism; **~krank·heit** *f* metabolic disease; **~stö·rung** *f* metabolic disorder
stöh·nen ['ʃtø:nən] (h) **I.** *v/i.* **1.** groan (***vor*** *dat.* with); ***vor Lust ~*** moan with pleasure; **2.** moan, complain (***über*** *acc.* about); **3.** *fig.* ***unter dem Gewicht*** *gen.* ***~*** groan under the weight of; **II.** 2 *n* (-s; *no pl.*) groaning; moaning; complaining; ***(ein) leises ~*** soft moaning
Stoi·ker ['ʃto:ikɐ, 'st-] *m* (-s; -) Stoic (philosopher); *fig.* stoic; **sto·isch** ['ʃto:ɪʃ,

'st-] *adj.* Stoic; *fig.* stoic(al); *fig.* **~e Ruhe** stoic calm; **Stoi·zi·smus** [ʃtoi'tsɪsmʊs, st-] *m* (-; *no pl.*) Stoicism; *fig.* stoicism
Sto·la ['ʃto:la, 'st-] *f* stole (*a. eccl.*), wrap
Stol·len ['ʃtɔlən] *m* (-s; -) **1.** ⚒ tunnel; **2.** *gastr.* stollen (cake); **3.** stud
Stol·per·draht ['ʃtɔlpɐ-] *m a. fig.* trip wire
stol·pern ['ʃtɔlpɐn] *v/i.* (sn) trip (up), *a. fig.* stumble; **~ durch (entlang** *etc.*) *acc.* stumble through (along *etc.*); **~ über** *acc.* trip over, trip up on; *fig.* stumble over; stumble across; F bump into *s.o.*; come to grief over *s.th.*; **j-n zum ♀ bringen** *a. fig.* trip s.o. up; **ins ♀ geraten** trip (up), lose one's footing, *fig.* F come a cropper
Stol·per·stein ['ʃtɔlpɐ-] *fig. m* stumbling block (**auf dem Weg zu** *dat.* along the path to)
stolz [ʃtɔlts] *adj.* **1.** proud (**auf** *acc.* of); **darauf kannst du ~ sein** that's something to be proud of; **er war ganz ~ darauf, daß er es alleine geschafft hat** he was really proud at having managed it himself; **ganz ~ hat er s-n neuen Paß vorgezeigt** he proudly presented (*or* showed us *etc.*) his new passport; **2.** *fig.* impressive; **e-e ~e Summe** a tidy (little) sum; **ein ~er Preis** *iro.* not exactly cheap
Stolz *m* (-es; *no pl.*) pride (**auf** *acc.* in); **s-n ~ daransetzen zu** *inf.* make it a point of hono(u)r to *inf.*; **das läßt sein ~ nicht zu** he's too proud for that kind of thing; **er hat keinen ~** he has no (sense of) pride; **er ist der ~ s-r Eltern** he's his parents' pride and joy
'stolz·ge·schwellt *adj.* swollen (*or* bloated, bursting) with pride; **mit ~er Brust** *a.* with one's chest puffed out, **trat er ins Zimmer** *a.* he strutted proudly into the room
stol·zie·ren [ʃtɔl'tsi:rən] *v/i.* (sn) strut, swagger
Stopf·ei ['ʃtɔpf-] *n* darning egg
stop·fen ['ʃtɔpfən] (h) **I.** *v/t.* **1.** darn, mend; **2.** stuff (**in** *acc.* into); **3.** stuff *pillow etc.*; fill *pipe, sausage etc.*; *fig.* **j-m den Mund ~** silence s.o., F shut s.o. up; → **gestopft**; **4.** fill *a gap etc.*, *a.* plug *a hole etc.*; **5.** stuff, fatten; **II.** *v/i.* **6.** be filling; **Reis stopft** *a.* rice fills you up; **7.** ⚕ cause constipation; **das stopft** *a.* that gives you constipation
Stopf|garn ['ʃtɔpf-] *n* darning cotton; **~na·del** *f* darning needle; **~wol·le** *f* darning wool
Stopp [ʃtɔp] *m* (-s; -s) **1.** stop; ✝ ban (**für** *acc.* on); (*wage etc.*) freeze; **2.** *tennis etc.*: drop shot
stopp *int.* stop!
Stop·pel|acker ['ʃtɔpəl-] *m* → **Stoppelfeld**; **~bart** *m* stubbly beard; **~feld** *n* stubble field; **~haar** *n* bristle haircut
stop·pe·lig ['ʃtɔpəlɪç] *adj.* stubbly
Stop·peln ['ʃtɔpəln] *pl.* stubble *sg.*
'stop·peln *v/t.* (h) glean
stop·pen ['ʃtɔpən] (h) **I.** *v/t.* **1.** stop; **die Produktion ~** halt (*or* stop) production; **er war nicht mehr zu ~** there was no stopping him; **2.** time; **ich habe 11 Sekunden gestoppt** I timed it at 11 seconds; **II.** *v/i.* **3.** stop; **4.** time, do the timing; **kannst du für uns ~?** *a.* could you time us?; **Stop·per** ['ʃtɔpɐ] *m* (-s; -) **1.** timekeeper; **2.** doorstop(per)
'Stopp|licht *n mot.* brake light; **~preis** *m* ceiling (*or* stop) price; **~schild** *n* stop sign; **~stra·ße** *f* road with a stop sign, *Am.* stop street; **~ta·ste** *f* stop button; **~uhr** *f* stopwatch
Stöp·sel ['ʃtœpsəl] *m* (-s; -) **1.** stopper; plug (*a.* ⚡); **2.** F *fig.* F shortie; **'stöp·seln** *v/t.* (h) plug (*a.* ⚡)
Stör [ʃtø:ɐ] *m* (-s; -e ['ʃtø:rə]) sturgeon
Stör|ab·stand ['ʃtø:ɐ-] *m* signal-to-noise ratio; **~ak·ti͵on** *f* disruptive action
stör·an·fäl·lig ['ʃtø:ɐ-] *adj.* very sensitive, *a. mot.* temperamental; *radio*: interference-prone, susceptible to interference; *fig.* ✝ susceptible, sensitive; **~ sein** *a.* keep breaking down, *radio*: get a lot of interference; **'Stör·an·fäl·lig·keit** *f* (-; *no pl.*) sensitivity; tendency to develop faults (*or* break down); *radio*: susceptibility to interference; *fig.* susceptibility, sensitivity
Storch [ʃtɔrç] *m* (-[e]s; Störche ['ʃtœrçə]) stork; **~bei·ne** F *pl.* spindly (F matchstick) legs
Stor·chen|gang ['ʃtɔrçən-] *m* (-[e]s; *no pl.*) stalking gait, stalk; **e-n ~ haben** walk like a stork; **~nest** *n* stork's nest
Stör·chin ['ʃtœrçɪn] *f* (-; -nen) female stork
'Storch·schna·bel *m* **1.** stork's bill; **2.** ⚙ pantograph; **3.** ⚘ cranesbill
Stör·dienst ['ʃtø:ɐ-] *m* fault-clearing service; *teleph. a. the* engineers *pl.*
Store [ʃto:ɐ] *m* (-s; -s) net curtain
stö·ren ['ʃtø:rən] (h) **I.** *v/t.* a) disturb; interrupt; *radio*: interfere with, jam *a station etc.*; disrupt *a meeting etc.*, b) distract, c) bother *s.o.*, d) spoil; impair; obstruct; **j-s Pläne ~** upset s.o.'s plans; **das (Gesamt)Bild ~** spoil the effect; **lassen Sie sich nicht ~!** don't let me disturb you; **darf ich Sie kurz ~?** could I bother you for a minute?; **stört es Sie, wenn ich rauche?** do you mind if I smoke?, would it bother you if I smoked?; **das stört mich nicht** I don't mind (that), it doesn't bother me; **er stört mich nicht** he doesn't bother me, he's not in the way; **das stört doch keinen Menschen** that's not going to bother anyone; **das einzige, was mich daran stört** the only thing that bothers me (*or* that I don't like) about it; **was stört dich daran?** what is it you don't like about it?; **er läßt sich durch nichts ~** he doesn't let anything bother him, he's completely unflappable; → **gestört**; **II.** *v/i.* a) be in the way, b) be a nuisance, c) get in the way, interfere, d) spoil the effect, *building etc.*: spoil the view, e) be awkward; **störe ich?** am I disturbing you?; **du störst nur** you're (just) in the way; **„(bitte) nicht ~!"** (please) do not disturb; **III.** *v/refl.*: **sich ~ an** *dat.* take exception to *s.th.*, be bothered by *s.th.*; **ich störe mich nicht daran** it doesn't bother me; **'stö·rend I.** *adj.* a) disturbing, b) distracting, c) irritating, annoying, d) interfering; disruptive; **II.** *adv.*: **~ wirken** be (*or* get) in the way, be a nuisance, have a disruptive effect (**auf** *acc.* on)
'Stö·ren·fried [-fri:t] *m* (-[e]s; -e [-də]) troublemaker
Stö·rer ['ʃtø:rɐ] *m* (-s; -) troublemaker
Stör|fak·tor ['ʃtø:ɐ-] *m* (source of) disturbance; source (*or* element) of interference; nuisance element; **~ge·räusch** *n radio*: *a. pl.* interference; background noise; static; jamming, harmful interference; **~ma͵nö·ver** *n a. pl.* disruptive action
stor·nie·ren [ʃtɔr'ni:rən] *v/t.* (h) ✝ reverse *an entry*; cancel *an order etc.*; **Stor'nie·rung** *f* (-; -en) reversal; cancellation
Stor·no ['ʃtɔrno] *n* (-s; -ni) → **Stornierung**; **~ge·bühr** *f* cancellation fee
stör·risch ['ʃtœrɪʃ] *adj.* stubborn, obstinate; unmanageable, refractory; restive *horse*
Stör|sen·der ['ʃtø:ɐ-] *m* jamming station, jammer; **~si·cher·heit** *f* noise immunity; **~si͵gnal** *n* drop-in, *a. pl.* interference; **~strei·fen** *pl. TV* interference pattern *sg.*
Stö·rung ['ʃtø:rʊŋ] *f* (-; -en) **1.** a) disturbance, b) interruption, c) interference; obstruction; **entschuldigen Sie die ~!** sorry to disturb (*or* bother) you; **2.** ⚙ fault, defect; failure, breakdown; *radio*: *a. pl.* interference, static; jamming, harmful interference; **3.** ⚕ disorder, malfunction; **4.** *meteor.* disturbance
'stö·rungs·an·fäl·lig *adj.* → **störanfällig**
'Stö·rungs·dienst *m* fault-clearing service; *teleph. a. the* engineers *pl.*
'stö·rungs·frei *adj.* **1.** undisturbed, *smooth*; **2.** *radio*: interference-free; ⚙ trouble-free
'Stö·rungs|stel·le *f* → **Stördienst**; **~su·cher** *m teleph.* faultsman; ⚙ troubleshooter; **~ur·sa·che** *f* cause of the trouble (*radio*: interference)
Stoß [ʃto:s] *m* (-es; Stöße ['ʃtø:sə]) **1.** a) push; ⚔ *and fencing*: thrust; stab; punch; kick; butt; poke; dig (in the ribs), nudge, b) jolt, jerk, c) *swimming, rowing, billiards*: stroke; *shot put*: put, d) blast; (*seismic*) shock, e) ⚕ massive dose; **j-m e-n ~ versetzen** give s.o. a push, *fig.* shake s.o. (up); *fig.* **sich** (*or* **s-m Herzen**) **e-n ~ geben** make an effort, force o.s.; **das gab ihm den letzten ~** that was the straw that broke the camel's back; **2.** pile; stack *a. of wood*; batch *of letters*
'stoß·ar·tig *adj.* intermittent (*a.* ⚙, ⚡), sporadic(ally *adv.*)
'Stoß|be·hand·lung *f* ⚕ massive-dose treatment; **~be·trieb** *m* rush hour; peak period (*or* hours *pl.*); **~dämp·fer** *m mot.*, ✈ shock absorber
Stö·ßel ['ʃtø:səl] *m* (-s; -) **1.** pestle; **2.** *mot.* tappet
'stoß·emp·find·lich *adj.* sensitive to shock
sto·ßen ['ʃto:sən] (stieß, gestoßen) **I.** *v/t.* (h) **1.** push; thrust *knife etc.*; punch; kick; nudge, jostle; poke *a stick*; ram; drive; *sport*: put *the shot*; *pharm.* pound; **j-n in die Rippen ~** nudge s.o., give s.o. a dig in the ribs; **j-m das Messer in die Brust ~** plunge a knife into s.o.'s chest; **j-n von sich ~** push s.o. away, *fig.* disown s.o.; **s-e Zehen ~ an** *dat.* stub one's toes on (*or* against); *fig.* **j-n ~ aus** *dat.* turn s.o. out of *his house etc.*, expel s.o. from *his club etc.*; F **es j-m ~** F tell s.o. what's what; → **Bescheid, Kopf** 5, **Nase**; **II.** *v/refl.*: **sich ~** (h) **2.** knock o.s., hurt o.s.; **sich ~ an** *dat.* knock (*or* run, bump) against, *fig.* take offen|ce (*Am.* -se) at, take exception to; *fig.* **an der Unordnung darfst du dich nicht ~** just ignore the mess, don't mind the mess; **III.** *v/i.* **3.** (h) *zo.* butt; **4. ~ an** *acc.* a) (sn) bump into, knock (o.s.) against (*both a.* **~ gegen** *acc.*), b) (h) *fig.* border on, *formal*: abut on; **mit dem Kopf gegen die Tür ~** bump (*or* knock) one's head against *or* on the door; **5.** (sn) *fig.* **~ auf**

acc. a) strike *oil*, b) *road etc.*: lead onto, F hit, c) (happen to) meet *s.o.*, come across *s.o.*, run (*or* bump) into *s.o.*, d) come across, stumble on, discover, e) meet with *resistance etc.*; **6.** (sn) ~ **zu** *dat.* join (up with) *party etc.*; → ***Horn*** 2

'stoß·fest *adj.* shockproof, shock-resistant; **'Stoß·fe·stig·keit** *f* shock resistance

'Stoß|ge·bet *n* quick prayer; ***ein ~ zum Himmel senden*** say a quick prayer; **~ge·schäft** *n* peak-period business; **~kan·te** *f* bottom edge; **~kraft** *f* (-; ⸚e) **1.** ⚙ impact; **2.** *no pl. fig.* impetus, drive, force; thrust; **~rich·tung** *f* ⚔ *and fig.* thrust; *fig.* ***die ~ s-r Attacke ging auf*** *acc.* **...** his assault was aimed at ...; **~seuf·zer** *m* deep (*or* loud) sigh; **≈si·cher** *adj.* shockproof; **~stan·ge** *f mot.* bumper

'Stoß·stan·gen|auf·kle·ber *m* bumper sticker; **~hör·ner** *pl.* (bumper) overriders, *Am.* bumper guards

'Stoß|the·ra,pie *f* ⚕ massive-dose treatment; **~trupp** *m* ⚔ assault party, combat patrol; **~ver·kehr** *m* rush-hour traffic; **~waf·fe** *f* thrust weapon

'stoß·wei·se I. *adj.* intermittent, sporadic; **II.** *adv.* intermittently, sporadically, by fits and starts

'Stoß·wel·le *f a.* ⚕ shock wave

'Stoß·wel·len·the·ra,pie *f* ⚕ shock-wave therapy (*or* treatment)

'Stoß|zahn *m* tusk; **~zeit** *f* peak period; rush hour

Stot·te·rer ['ʃtɔtərɐ] *m* (-s; -) stutterer, stammerer

stot·tern ['ʃtɔtɐn] (h) **I.** *v/i.* stutter, stammer; have a stutter; *mot.* splutter; **II.** *v/t.* stammer, stutter; ***e-e Antwort ~*** stammer out a reply; **III.** ≈ *n* (-s; *no pl.*) stutter(ing), stammer(ing); F *fig.* ***auf ~ kaufen*** F buy on the never-never

Stöv·chen ['ʃtøːfçən] *n* (-s; -) (coffeepot *or* teapot) warmer

stracks [ʃtraks] *adv.* → ***schnurstracks***

Stra·di·va·ri [stradi'vaːri] *f* (-; -[s]) Stradivari(us), F Strad

Straf|ak·te ['ʃtraːf-] *f* case record (*or* file); **~ak·ti,on** *f* punitive action; **~an·dro·hung** *f* threat of punishment; ***unter ~*** under penalty; **~an·stalt** *f* prison, penal institution, penitentiary; **~an·trag** *m* **1.** ***~ stellen*** bring an action, start legal proceedings; **2.** demand for a stated penalty; ***e-n ~ stellen*** demand a stated penalty; **~an·zei·ge** *f* charge; ***~ erstatten gegen*** *acc.* bring a charge against; **~ar·beit** *f ped.* extra (home)work; **~ar·beits·la·ger** *n* hard labo(u)r camp; **~auf·schub** *m* reprieve; **~aus·set·zung** *f* suspension of (*or* suspended) sentence (***zur Bewährung*** on probation); **~bank** *f* (-; ⸚e) *sport*: penalty bench; *ice hockey*: penalty box; ***zwei Minuten auf die ~ müssen*** be sent off for two minutes, get a two minutes penalty

straf·bar ['ʃtraːfbaːɐ] *adj.* punishable, criminal; ***~e Handlung*** (criminal *or* punishable) offen|ce (*Am.* -se); ***~ sein*** be an offen|ce (*Am.* -se); ***sich ~ machen*** commit a (criminal) offen|ce (*Am.* -se), make o.s. liable to prosecution

Straf|be·fehl ['ʃtraːf-] *m* order (of summary punishment); **~be·fug·nis** *f* penal authority; power of sentence; **~be·stim·mung** *f* penal provision (*or* clause)

Stra·fe ['ʃtraːfə] *f* (-; -n) punishment; ⚖ *a.* penalty (*a. sport*); sentence; fine; retribution; ***bei ~ von*** *dat.* on pain (*or* penalty) of; ***zur ~*** as a punishment; ***unter ~ stehen*** be an offen|ce (*Am.* -se); ***et. unter ~ stellen*** make s.th. a punishable offen|ce (*Am.* -se); ***~ zahlen*** pay a fine (*or* penalty); ***das ist die ~ dafür, daß du mir nicht gehorcht hast*** that's what you get for disobeying me; ***~ muß sein*** there's nothing like a bit of discipline; *fig.* ***es ist e-e ~ (für mich) zu*** *inf.* it's a punishment (for me) to *inf.*; → ***abbüßen, antreten*** 4

Straf·ecke ['ʃtraːf-] *f hockey*: penalty corner

stra·fen ['ʃtraːfən] *v/t.* (h) punish; *esp. sport*: penalize (*a. fig.*); fine; F ***mit dieser Familie ist er gestraft genug*** to have a family like that is punishment enough; F ***mit der Stelle bist du wirklich gestraft*** you couldn't have picked a worse (*or* more gruelling *etc.*) job; → ***Lüge, Verachtung***; **'stra·fend** *adj.* punitive; avenging; reproachful, censorious *look*; ***~e Worte*** words of reproach

Straf|ent·las·se·ne ['ʃtraːf-] *m, f* (-n; -n) discharged prisoner; **~er·laß** *m* remission (of sentence); ***allgemeiner ~*** amnesty; ***bedingter ~*** conditional pardon

'straf·er·schwe·rend *adj.* → ***strafverschärfend***

'Straf·ex·pe·di·ti,on *f* punitive campaign

straff [ʃtraf] **I.** *adj.* a) tight; taut *rope, muscles, skin etc.*; smooth *skin*, b) *fig.* concise *style*; tight *control, planning etc.*; strict, rigid *discipline etc.*; ***~er Busen*** firm breasts; ***~e Haltung*** straight posture; ***~e Handlung*** tight (*or* taut) plot; ***~e Unternehmensleitung*** hands-on management; **II.** *adv.* tightly; ***~ anliegen*** fit tightly, be close-fitting; ***~ anziehen*** tighten *rope, screw etc.*, *a.* pull *rope etc.* tight; ***~ organisiert*** tightly organized; ***~ führen*** keep a tight rein on

straf·fäl·lig ['ʃtraːf-] *adj.* guilty of a crime; ***~ werden*** offend, commit an offen|ce (*Am.* -se)

straf·fen ['ʃtrafən] (h) **I.** *v/t.* tighten; *a.* pull *rope etc.* tight; *fig.* tighten up, *a.* tauten *plot etc.*, *a.* streamline *organization etc.*; ***sich die Gesichtshaut (den Busen) ~ lassen*** have a facelift (have one's breasts lifted); **II.** *v/refl.*: ***sich ~*** a) tighten, b) straighten up, draw o.s. up

straf·frei ['ʃtraːf-] **I.** *adj.* exempt from punishment; **II.** *adv. a.* with impunity; → ***ausgehen*** 8; **'Straf·frei·heit** *f* (-; *no pl.*) impunity; immunity (from criminal prosecution); **'Straf·frei·heits·ge·setz** *n* impunity law

Straf·fung ['ʃtrafʊŋ] *f* (-; -en) tightening; tautening *etc.*; → ***straffen***

Straf|ge·bühr ['ʃtraːf-] *f* fine; **~ge·fan·ge·ne** *m, f* (-n; -n) prisoner, convict; **~geld** *n* fine; **~ge·richt** *n* **1.** criminal court, tribunal; **2.** *fig.* punishment, chastisement; ***das göttliche ~*** Divine Judg(e)ment

Straf·ge·setz ['ʃtraːf-] *n* penal law; **~buch** *n* penal code; **~ge·bung** [-geː-bʊŋ] *f* (-; *no pl.*) penal legislation

Straf|ju,stiz ['ʃtraːf-] *f* criminal justice; **~kam·mer** *f* criminal division; **~ko·lo,nie** *f* penal colony

sträf·lich ['ʃtrɛːflɪç] **I.** *adj.* **1.** criminal, punishable; ***~e Vernachlässigung*** criminal neglect; **2.** *fig.* reprehensible; inexcusable, unpardonable; **II.** *adv.* terribly; ***j-n ~ vernachlässigen*** neglect s.o. badly

Sträf·ling ['ʃtrɛːflɪŋ] *m* (-s; -e) prisoner, convict; **'Sträf·lings·klei·dung** *f* prison clothing

Straf|man,dat ['ʃtraːf-] *n* ticket; **~maß** *n* (-es; *no pl.*) penalty, sentence; **~maß·nah·men** *pl.* punitive measures; ***wirtschaftliche ~*** economic sanctions; ***~ ergreifen*** take punitive action, ✝ apply (*or* impose) sanctions

straf·mil·dernd ['ʃtraːf-] **I.** *adj.* mitigating, extenuating *circumstances*; **II.** *adv.*: ***~ wirken*** be considered in mitigation; **'Straf·mil·de·rung** *f* mitigation of sentence, commutation

Straf|mi,nu·te ['ʃtraːf-] *f*: ***er erhielt zwei ~n*** *ice hockey etc.*: he got a two minutes penalty, he was sent off for two minutes; **≈mün·dig** *adj.* criminally liable (*or* responsible); **~nach·laß** *m* reduction of a sentence; **~por·to** *n* excess postage, surcharge; **~pre·digt** *f* lecture; ***j-m e-e ~ halten*** give s.o. a lecture

Straf·pro,zeß ['ʃtraːf-] *m* (criminal) trial, criminal case; **~ord·nung** *f* code of criminal procedure

Straf|punkt ['ʃtraːf-] *m sport*: penalty point; **~raum** *m sport*: penalty area

Straf·recht ['ʃtraːf-] *n* criminal law; **'straf·recht·lich I.** *adj.* penal, criminal, under criminal law; ***~e Verfolgung*** criminal prosecution; **II.** *adv.*: ***~ verfolgen*** prosecute

Straf|re,gi·ster ['ʃtraːf-] *n* criminal records *pl.*; *s.o.'s* criminal record; F *fig.* list of sins (*or* transgressions); **~rich·ter** *m* criminal judge; **~sa·che** *f* criminal case (*or* matter); **~stoß** *m soccer*: penalty kick; ***e-n ~ verhängen*** give a penalty; **~tat** *f* (criminal) offen|ce (*Am.* -se); crime; **~tat·be·stand** *m* statutory offen|ce (*Am.* -se); **~tä·ter** *m* offender; **~,um·wand·lung** *f* commutation (of a sentence); **~ur·teil** *n* sentence; verdict; **~ver·fah·ren** *n* criminal procedure (*or* proceedings *pl.*); **~ver·fol·gung** *f* (criminal) prosecution

straf·ver·schär·fend ['ʃtraːf-] *adj.* aggravating; **'Straf·ver·schär·fung** *f* increase of penalty

straf·ver·set·zen ['ʃtraːf-] *v/t.* (*only inf. and p.p.* strafversetzt, h), **'Straf·verset·zung** *f* transfer for disciplinary reasons

Straf|ver·tei·di·ger ['ʃtraːf-] *m* counsel for the defen|ce (*Am.* -se); **~voll,streck·kung** *f* imprisonment; execution of a sentence; **~voll,zug** *m* execution of (a) sentence; *w.s.* imprisonment; **~voll,zugs·an·stalt** *f* penal institution, penitentiary

straf·wei·se ['ʃtraːf-] *adv.* for disciplinary reasons

Straf|zet·tel ['ʃtraːf-] *m* ticket; **~zin·sen** *pl.* penalty interest *sg.*

Strahl [ʃtraːl] *m* (-[e]s; -en) *a. phys. and fig.* ray; beam; ray (of sunlight), (sun)beam; shaft of (sun)light; flash *of lightning etc.*; jet, stream *of water*; ***kosmische ~en*** cosmic radiation (*or* rays); **~an·trieb** *m* ✈ jet propulsion

Strah·le·mann ['ʃtraːləman] F *m* (-[e]s; ⸚er) F smiley; ***da kommt der ~*** *a.* here comes the man with the big smile

strah·len ['ʃtraːlən] (h) **I.** *v/i.* shine; sparkle (*a. eyes*); *fig.* beam; *face, eyes*: light up; *fig.* ***über das ganze Gesicht ~*** be all smiles, be beaming all over one's face; ***~d (vor Glück)*** radiant (with happiness); **II.** *v/t. a. fig.* radiate

'Strah·len|be·hand·lung *f* radiotherapy, ray treatment; **~be·la·stung** *f* a) exposure to radiation, b) radioactivity level; ***natürliche ~*** natural (background) radiation; **~bre·chung** *f* refraction; **~bün·del** *n*, **~bü·schel** *n phys.* pencil of rays, beam

'strah·lend I. *adj.* **1.** *phys.* radioactive, radiating; **2. *~er Sonnenschein*** bright sunshine; ***~es Sonnenlicht*** bright (*or* streaming) sunlight; ***~es Wetter*** glorious weather; **3.** *fig.* ***~e Augen*** bright (*or* shining) eyes; ***~es Gesicht*** beaming face (*or* expression); ***~es Lächeln*** beaming smile; ***~e Schönheit*** radiant beauty; ***~er Laune sein*** be in great spirits, be in a great mood; **II.** *adv.* **4. *~ vor Freude*** beaming with joy; ***j-n ~ anlächeln*** beam at s.o.; **5. *~ weiß*** gleaming white, pearly white *teeth*; ***~ blaue Augen*** piercing blue eyes; ***~ helles Licht*** brilliant light; ***~ schönes Wetter*** glorious weather

'Strah·len·do·sis *f* radiation dose

'strah·len·för·mig [-fœrmɪç] *adj.* radial

'Strah·len·for·schung *f* radiology

'strah·len·krank *adj.*: ***~ sein*** be suffering from radiation sickness; **'Strah·len·krank·heit** *f* radiation sickness

'Strah·len|kranz *m* halo, nimbus; *fig.* glory; **~meß·ge·rät** *n* radiation meter; **~op·fer** *n* radiation victim; **~schä·di·gung** *f* radiation damage; **~schutz** *m* a) radiation protection, b) (radiation) protection screen; **≈si·cher** *adj.* radiation-proof; **~the·ra̦pie** *f* radiotherapy; **~tier·chen** *n* radiolarian; **~tod** *m* death by radiation; **~über̦wa·chung** *f* monitoring of radiation (levels); **≈ver·seucht** *adj.* contaminated (by radiation)

Strah·ler ['ʃtraːlɐ] *m* (-s; -) **1.** radiator; **2.** spot

strah·lig ['ʃtraːlɪç] *adj.* radial

'Strahl|rohr *n* jet pipe; **~trieb·werk** *n* jet engine

Strah·lung ['ʃtraːlʊŋ] *f* (-; -en) radiation

'Strah·lungs|druck *m* radiation pressure; **~ener̦gie** *f* radiation energy; **~mes·ser** *m* radiation meter; **~wär·me** *f* radiation heat

Sträh·ne ['ʃtrɛːnə] *f* (-; -n) **1.** strand; ***blonde (graue) ~*** blonde (grey, *Am.* gray) streak; **2.** → ***Glückssträhne, Pechsträhne***

sträh·nig ['ʃtrɛːnɪç] *adj.* straggly *hair*

stramm [ʃtram] **I.** *adj.* **1.** tight; taut; **2. *~e Haltung*** straight (*or* erect) posture; ⚔ ***~e Haltung einnehmen*** stand to attention; F *fig.* ***~e Disziplin*** strict discipline; ***~er Katholik*** staunch Catholic; ***~er Sozialist*** staunch (*or* dyed-in-the-wool) socialist; ***~es Tempo*** brisk pace; **3.** robust; sturdy *a. legs*; ***~er Junge*** strapping youth; ***~es Mädchen*** strapping young girl; **4.** F tight; **5.** *gastr.* ***~er Max*** ham and fried egg on bread; **II.** *adv.* tight(ly); ***~ sitzen*** fit tightly; ***~ arbeiten*** work hard; ***~ gehen*** walk briskly

'stramm|ste·hen *v/i.* (*irr., sep.*, h, → ***stehen***) ⚔ stand to attention; **~zie·hen** *v/t.* (*irr., sep.*, h, → ***ziehen***) pull *s.th.* tight; F *fig.* ***j-m die Hosen ~*** give s.o. a good hiding (*or* spanking)

Stram·pel|hös·chen ['ʃtrampəl-] *n*, **~ho·se** *f* rompers *pl.*, stretchsuit

stram·peln ['ʃtrampəln] *v/i.* (h) **1.** kick; thrash about; struggle; **2.** F a) pedal (away), b) F slog away

Strand [ʃtrant] *m* (-[e]s; Strände ['ʃtrɛndə]) beach; (sea)shore; ***am ~*** on the beach (*or* shore); ⚓ ***auf ~ laufen*** run aground; **~an·zug** *m* beach suit; **~bad** *n* swimming area; **~bug·gy** *m* dune buggy; **~burg** *f* sandcastle; **~ca̦fé** *n* seaside café

stran·den ['ʃtrandən] *v/i.* (sn) run aground; *fig.* founder

'Strand|gut *n* (-[e]s; *no pl.*) flotsam and jetsam; **~ha·fer** *m* ♣ marram grass; **~ho̦·tel** *n* beach (*or* seaside) hotel; **~klei·dung** *f* beachwear; **~korb** *m* (wicker) beach chair; **~läu·fer** *m zo.* sandpiper; **~pro·me̦na·de** *f* promenade; **~recht** *n* right of salvage; **~ver·schmut·zung** *f* beach pollution; **~wa·che** *f*, **~wäch·ter** *m* lifeguard

Strang [ʃtraŋ] *m* (-[e]s; Stränge ['ʃtrɛŋə]) a) cord (*a. anat.*); rope; skein, hank, b) 🚂 track, c) *fig.* strand; *fig.* ***wir ziehen alle am selben ~*** we're all in the same boat; ***wenn wir alle an einem ~ ziehen*** if we all get together, if we join forces; ***über die Stränge schlagen*** kick over the traces; ***wenn alle Stränge reißen*** if the worst comes to the worst, if all else fails; ⚖ ***der Tod durch den ~*** death by hanging; ***j-n zum Tod durch den ~ verurteilen*** sentence s.o. to be hanged

stran·gu·lie·ren [ʃtraŋgu'liːrən] *v/t.* (h) **1.** strangle; **2.** ⚕ strangulate

Stran·gu'lie·rung *f* (-; -en) **1.** strangling, strangulation; **2.** ⚕ strangulation

Stra·pa·ze [ʃtra'paːtsə] *f* (-; -n) *a. pl.* strain; ***die ~n des Lebens*** life's difficulties, *iro. a.* the trials and tribulations of life; ***die ~n des Alltags*** the pressures (and worries) of day-to-day living; ***es ist e-e ~*** *a.* it's hard work, F it's tough going; ***sich von den ~n der Arbeit erholen*** recover from the stress and strain of work; ***er war den ~n nicht gewachsen*** he couldn't take (*or* stand up to) the strain

stra·pa·zie·ren [ʃtrapa'tsiːrən] *v/t.* (h) a) strain, be a strain on, be hard on (*a. eyes, nerves, relationship etc.*), *a.* F take it out of *s.o.*; exhaust, wear out, b) tax, test, try *s.o.'s patience etc.*, c) be hard (*or* rough) on *s.o.'s hair, skin etc.*, mistreat, c) overwork, overuse, use (*or* flog) *expression etc.* to death; ***das würde dich zu sehr ~*** that would be too much of a strain on you; ***strapaziert werden*** *a.* F take a beating, have a rough time of it, *esp. car, machine etc.*: *a.* be put through its paces; ***der Sessel ist aber arg strapaziert worden*** that armchair has taken some battering

stra·pa·zier·fä·hig [ʃtrapa'tsiːɐ-] *adj.* **1.** hardwearing *clothes*; *a.* tough *material, shoes, carpet etc.*; ***der Mantel ist sehr ~*** *a.* the coat will take a lot of wear and tear; **2.** *fig.* tough *nerves*

stra·pa·ziert [ʃtrapa'tsiːɐt] *adj.* worn *clothes, carpet etc.*, mistreated *skin, hair*; *fig.* strained, *a.* frayed *nerves*; overtaxed *brain*

stra·pa·zi·ös [ʃtrapa'tsi̯øːs] *adj.* strenuous, F tough; *fig.* taxing, trying

Straps [ʃtraps] *m* (-es; -e) suspender belt, *Am.* garter belt

Straß [ʃtras] *m* (Strasses; *no pl.*) diamanté

Stra·ße ['ʃtraːsə] *f* (-; -n) **1.** road; street; ***die ~ zum Bahnhof*** the road (leading) to the station; ***durch die ~n fahren*** drive through the streets; ***e-e laute ~*** a noisy road (*or* street); ***auf der ~*** a) in the street, b) on the road; ***auf der ~ spielen*** play in the street; ***auf die ~ laufen*** a) run out into the street, b) run onto the road; ***das Postamt ist in der nächsten ~*** the post office is in (*Am.* on) the next street; ***das Zimmer geht zur ~*** the room faces the street; ***an der ~*** at the roadside; ***Verkauf über die ~*** → ***Straßenverkauf***; *fig.* ***auf offener ~*** in broad daylight; ***auf die ~ gehen*** a) go out into the streets, b) walk the streets; ***j-n auf die ~ setzen*** throw s.o. out onto the street(s); ***j-n von der ~ auflesen*** pick s.o. up off the street(s); ***auf der ~ liegen*** (*or* ***sitzen***) a) *unemployed person*: be out on the street(s), b) *homeless person*: be on the streets; ***dort liegt das Geld auf der ~*** the streets are paved with gold there; ***der Mann auf der ~*** the (average) man in the street, *Brit. a.* F the man on the Clapham omnibus; ***Mädchen von der ~*** streetwalker, prostitute; ***Herrschaft der ~*** mob rule; ***der Druck der ~*** pressure from the masses (*or* the population at large); **2.** *geogr.* strait(s *pl.*); ***die ~ von Dover*** the Straits of Dover; ***die ~ von Gibraltar*** *usu.* the Straits of Gibraltar; ***die ~ von Hormuz*** the Strait(s) of Hormuz

'Stra·ßen|an·zug *m* lounge (*Am.* business) suit; **~ar·bei·ten** *pl.* roadworks; **~ar·bei·ter** *m* roadworker

'Stra·ßen·bahn *f* tram, *Am.* streetcar, trolley; **'Stra·ßen·bah·ner** [-baːnɐ] *m* (-s; -) → ***Straßenbahnfahrer*** 1

'Stra·ßen·bahn|fah·rer *m* **1.** tram driver, *Am.* motorman; **2.** tram (*Am.* streetcar) passenger; **~hal·te·stel·le** *f* tram (*Am.* streetcar) stop; **~li·nie** *f* tram line (*or* route), *Am.* streetcar line; **~schaff·ner** *m* tram (*Am.* streetcar) conductor; **~wa·gen** *m* tramcar, *Am.* streetcar

'Stra·ßen|bau *m* (-[e]s; *no pl.*) road construction; **~be·lag** *m* road surface; **~be·leuch·tung** *f* street lighting; **~be·nut·zungs·ge·bühr** *f* road toll; **~ca̦fé** *n* pavement (*Am.* sidewalk) café; **~decke** *f* road surface; **~ecke** *f* street corner; ***an der ~*** on (*or* at) the street corner *or* corner of the street; ***sie wohnt zwei ~n weiter*** she lives two blocks (further) up; **~fe·ger** *m* **1.** → ***Straßenkehrer***; **2.** *TV* blockbuster (series *etc.*); ***die Sendung ist ein ~*** the streets are empty when that program(me) is on; **~fest** *n* street party; **~glät·te** *f* slippery road(s *pl.*); **~gra·ben** *m* (roadside) ditch; **~händ·ler** *m* street vendor (*or* hawker); **~jun·ge** *m* street urchin, guttersnipe; **~kampf** *m* street fight(ing); *pl.* street fighting *sg.*, fighting *sg.* in the street(s); **~kar·te** *f* road map; **~keh·rer** [-keːrɐ] *m* (-s; -), **~kehr·ma̦schi·ne** *f* street sweeper (*or* cleaner); **~kö·ter** F *m* stray dog; **~kreu·zer** F *m* (big) flashy car, *sl.* cruisemobile; **~kreu·zung** *f* crossroads (*sg.*), intersection; **~la·ge** *f mot.* road holding; **~lärm** *m* noise from the street(s); **~la̦ter·ne** *f* street lamp; **~mäd·chen** *n* streetwalker, prostitute; **~mar̦kie·rung** *f* road marking; **~mu·si̦kant** *m* busker; **~na·me** *m* street name; **~netz** *n* road network; **~rand** *m*: (***am ~*** at the) roadside, (on the) kerb (*Am.* curb); **~raub** *m* mugging, street robbery; *hist.* highway robbery; **~räu·ber** *m* mugger; *hist.* highwayman; **~rei·ni·gung** *f* street cleaning; **~ren·nen** *n* road race; **~samm·lung** *f* street collection; **~sän·ger** *m* street singer;

~schild *n* street sign; **~schlacht** *f* street riot; *a. pl.* rioting *sg.* in the street(s); **~schu·he** *pl.* walking shoes; **~sper·re** *f* road block; **~strich** *m* **1.** streetwalking; **2.** red-light district; **~thea·ter** *n* street theat|re (*Am. a.* -er); **~tun·nel** *m* road tunnel; **~über,füh·rung** *f* flyover, overpass; **~un·ter,füh·rung** *f* underpass; **~verhält·nis·se** *pl.* road conditions; **~ver·kauf** *m* **1.** street trading (*or* vending); **2.** *gastr.* a) take-away (*Am.* carry-out) food (*or* snacks *pl. etc.*), food *etc.* to go, b) take-away, *Am.* carryout; **~ver·käu·fer** *m* street vendor; **~ver·kehr** *m* (road) traffic

'Stra·ßen·ver·kehrs|lärm *m* traffic noise; **~ord·nung** *f* traffic regulations *pl.*, *in GB*: Highway Code

'Stra·ßen|ver·zeich·nis *n* index of streets; **~wal·ze** *f* road roller, steamroller; **~zug** *m* street (lined with houses)

'Stra·ßen·zu·stand *m* road condition(s *pl.*); **'Stra·ßen·zu·stands·be·richt** *m* road report

Stra·te·ge [ʃtra'te:gə, st-] *m* (-n; -n) strategist; **Stra·te·gie** [ʃtrate'gi:, st-] *f* (-; -n) strategy; **stra·te·gisch** [ʃtra'te:gɪʃ, st-] *adj.* strategic(ally *adv.*)

Stra·to·sphä·re [ʃtrato'sfɛ:rə, st-] *f* (-; *no pl.*) stratosphere; **Stra·to'sphä·ren·flug·zeug** *n* stratocruiser

sträu·ben ['ʃtrɔʏbən] (h) **I.** *v/refl.*: ***sich*** ~ **1.** *hair*: stand on end, bristle; **2.** *fig.* refuse, F kick up a fuss; kick and struggle; ***sich ~ gegen*** *acc.* resist, fight, struggle against; ***sich ~, et. zu tun*** refuse to do s.th.; ***er sträubte sich dagegen, es zu machen*** *a.* he just wouldn't do it; ***alles in mir sträubt sich, es zu tun*** I can't bring myself to do it; ***die Feder sträubt sich, es zu beschreiben*** I hardly dare put it into words; → ***Haar***; **II.** *v/t.* ruffle (up)

Strauch [ʃtraʊx] *m* (-[e]s; Sträucher ['ʃtrɔʏçɐ]) shrub, bush; **~dieb** *m*: *fig.* ***du siehst aus wie ein ~!*** you look like a tramp

strau·cheln ['ʃtraʊxəln] *v/i.* (sn) *a. fig.* (almost) stumble, trip, lose one's footing; *fig.* stray off the straight and narrow; founder; ***~ an*** *dat.* come to grief over *s.th.*, F come a cropper with *s.th.*

Strauß¹ [ʃtraʊs] *m* (-es; -e) (*a.* ***Vogel ~***) ostrich

Strauß² *m* (-es; Sträuße ['ʃtrɔʏsə]) bunch; spray; bunch of flowers; ***ein ~ Nelken*** a bunch of carnations

Strauß³ *obs. m* (-es; Sträuße ['ʃtrɔʏsə]) fight, struggle; ***e-n ~ mit j-m ausfechten*** (have a) fight with s.o., fight it out with s.o.; F have it out with s.o.

'Strau·ßen|ei *n* ostrich egg; **~fe·der** *f* ostrich feather

Stre·be ['ʃtre:bə] *f* (-; -n), **~bal·ken** *m* ⚠ brace, strut; **~bo·gen** *m* flying buttress

stre·ben ['ʃtre:bən] (h) **I.** *v/i.* **1.** strive (***nach*** *dat.* for); ***~ nach*** *dat. a.* pursue, *formal*: aspire to, *a.* F run after; ***~ zu*** *inf.* strive (*or* aspire) to *inf.*; **2.** F *ped.* F be a swot (*Am.* grind); **3.** ***~ nach*** *dat.* move towards (*or* in the direction of); be drawn to(wards); ***nach dem Licht ~*** *plant*: turn towards the light; ***in die Höhe ~*** soar upwards; **II.** ♀ *n* (-s; *no pl.*) striving (***nach*** *dat.* for), aspiration (to *inf.*); tendency (to, towards); ***~ nach*** *dat. a.* pursuit of; ***das ~ nach Glück*** the pursuit of (*or* search for) happiness; ***sein ganzes ~ ging in Richtung ...*** all his energies and aspirations were directed towards *s.th. or ger.*

'Stre·be·pfei·ler *m* buttress

Stre·ber ['ʃtre:bɐ] *m* (-s; -) a) *ped.* F swot, *Am.* F grind, b) F go-getter; ***er ist ein ~*** *a.* he's very ambitious; **'Stre·ber·na,tur** *f* → ***Streber***; **'Stre·ber·tum** *n* (-s; *no pl.*) a) *ped.* ambitiousness, F swotting, *Am.* F grinding, b) F go-getting (attitude)

streb·sam ['ʃtre:pza:m] *adj.* hardworking, industrious, diligent; ambitious; *ped.* keen; **'Streb·sam·keit** *f* (-; *no pl.*) industriousness, diligence

Streck·bett ['ʃtrɛk-] *n* orthop(a)edic bed

Strecke ['ʃtrɛkə] (*sep.* -k·k-) *f* (-; -n) **1.** a) stretch, b) route, c) *a. sport*: distance, d) ⚡, *teleph.* line; 🚆 section, e) ⚒ roadway; ***die ~ München-Köln*** ✈, 🚆 the Munich-Cologne route, *mot.* the road from Munich to Cologne, the journey from Munich to Cologne; ***die ~ zwischen A. und B.*** the road between A and B, the stretch (of motorway) between A and B; ***e-e lange ~ zurücklegen*** cover a long distance (*or* stretch); ***e-n Teil der ~ zu Fuß gehen*** walk part of the way; ***es ist e-e ganze ~ bis dorthin*** it's quite a distance (*or* way, stretch); ***wir müssen noch e-e ganze ~ fahren*** we've still got quite a way (*or* stretch, distance) to go; ***auf freier ~*** 🚆 between stations, F in the middle of nowhere, on the open road; ***auf e-r ~ von 5 km gesperrt*** closed along a 5 km stretch; ***das Auto blieb in der Mitte der ~ stehen*** the car broke down on the way (*or* in the middle of the road); ***über lange ~n*** *a. fig.* for long stretches; *fig.* ***das Buch ist über lange ~n langweilig*** the book has a lot of long, boring bits (*formal*: a lot of longueurs); ***auf der ~ bleiben*** fall by the wayside, *sport*: *a.* drop out (of the race); **2.** ***zur ~ bringen*** a) *hunt.* kill, shoot down, bag, b) *fig.* hunt down, catch; *w.s.* lay low *one's opponent etc.*

strecken ['ʃtrɛkən] (*sep.* -k·k-) (h) **I.** *v/t.* **1.** stretch; ***s-e Beine*** (***Glieder, Arme***) ***~*** stretch one's legs (limbs, arms); ***die Beine weit von sich ~*** stretch one's legs right out (*or* as far as they will go); ***die Hand*** (*or* ***den Finger***) ***~*** put (F stick) one's hand up; ***den Kopf aus dem Fenster ~*** pop (F stick) one's head out of the window; → ***gestreckt, vier***; **2.** stretch *soup etc.a. fig. lecture etc.*; make *s.th.* last, eke out; F drag out (a bit); **3.** ***die Waffen ~*** lay down arms, surrender, *fig. a.* give in; ***j-n zu Boden ~*** floor s.o., lay s.o. low; **II.** *v/refl.*: ***sich ~*** **4.** stretch (o.s.), have a stretch; ***sich ins Gras ~*** stretch out on the grass; → ***Decke, recken*** II; **5.** *fig.* ***sich in die Länge ~*** go on longer than expected, *contp.* drag on

'Strecken|ar·bei·ter *m* platelayer, *Am.* tracklayer; **~füh·rung** *f* routing; *sport*: course; **~netz** *n* 🚆 railway (*Am.* railroad) network; ✈ (flying) routes *pl.*; **~re,kord** *m sport*: course record; **~wär·ter** *m* linesman, *Am.* trackwalker

'strecken·wei·se *adv.* **1.** in parts; **2.** from time to time

Streck·mus·kel ['ʃtrɛk-] *m anat.* extensor (muscle)

Streckung ['ʃtrɛkʊŋ] (*sep.* -k·k-) *f* (-; -en) **1.** stretching; **2.** fast-growth period

Streck·ver·band ['ʃtrɛk-] *m* ⚕ traction bandage; ***ein Bein*** *etc.* ***im ~*** a leg *etc.* in high traction

Streich [ʃtraɪç] *m* (-[e]s; -e) **1.** prank, trick, (practical) joke; ***dummer ~*** silly (*or* childish) prank; ***j-m e-n*** (***bösen***) ***~ spielen*** play a (nasty) trick on s.o.; *fig.* ***das Wetter hat uns e-n ~ gespielt*** the weather put a spanner in the works; **2.** *lit.* blow; slap; stroke; lash *of the whip*; ***j-m e-n*** (***den tödlichen***) ***~ versetzen*** deal s.o. a blow (the deathblow); ***auf einen ~*** at one blow, *fig.* in one go, in one fell swoop

Strei·chel·ein·heit ['ʃtraɪçəl-] *f* stroke, *pl. a.* stroking *sg.*; pat on the back; ***jeder braucht s-e ~en*** everyone needs a bit of a stroke (*or* a pat on the back) once in a while; ***er hat heute noch keine ~en bekommen*** he hasn't been stroked yet today

strei·cheln ['ʃtraɪçəln] *v/t. and v/i.* (h) stroke; caress; ***j-m übers Haar ~*** stroke s.o.'s hair

strei·chen ['ʃtraɪçən] (strich, gestrichen) **I.** *v/t.* (h) **1.** a) paint, b) spread *butter, sandwich etc.*; ***Salbe*** *etc.* ***~ auf*** *acc.* put ointment *etc.* on, rub ointment *etc.* (gently) on, *formal*: apply ointment *etc.* to; ***die Farbe läßt sich gut ~*** the paint spreads well; ***sich ein Brot ~*** make o.s. a piece of bread; ***et. durch ein Sieb ~*** strain s.th.; → ***gestrichen, frisch*** II; **2.** a) stroke, b) brush *away etc.*; ***sich den Bart ~*** stroke one's beard; (***sich***) ***das Haar aus der Stirn ~*** brush one's hair out of one's face (*or* eyes); **3.** cross out, delete; cut (out); cancel *order etc.*; cut, axe *funds etc.*; freeze, axe *jobs etc.*; waive; ***von der Liste ~*** cross off the list; *fig.* ***et. aus dem Gedächtnis ~*** wipe s.th. out of one's memory; → ***Nichtzutreffendes***; **4.** strike, haul down *sails etc.*; **II.** *v/i.* **5.** (sn) ***~ über*** *acc.* glide over, skim across; *wind*: waft across, sweep across; **6.** (h) ***j-m über das Haar ~*** stroke s.o.'s hair; **7.** (sn) ***j-m um die Beine ~*** *cat etc.*: rub up against s.o.'s legs; **8.** (sn) ***~ durch*** *acc.* roam, wander; ***ums Haus ~*** prowl around the house

Strei·cher ['ʃtraɪçɐ] *m* (-s; -) ♪ string player; ***die ~*** the strings, the string section

'streich·fä·hig *adj.*: ***~ sein*** spread easily

'Streich·fä·hig·keit *f* (-; *no pl.*) spreading property

'streich·fer·tig *adj.* ready for application

'Streich·garn *n* carded yarn

'Streich·holz *n* (-es; -hölzer) match; matchstick; **~heft·chen** *n* matchbook, book of matches; **~schach·tel** *f* matchbox

'Streich|in·stru,ment *n* ♪ string(ed) instrument; **~kä·se** *m* cheese spread; **~mu,sik** *f* music for strings; **~or,ches·ter** *n* string orchestra; **~quar,tett** *n* string quartet; **~quin,tett** *n* string quintet; **~rie·men** *m* strop; **~trio** *n* string trio

Strei·chung ['ʃtraɪçʊŋ] *f* (-; -en) cancellation *of an order etc.*; deletion; cut(s *pl.*), cutting, axing *of funds etc.*; cuts *pl.*, axing (*gen.* [of] *jobs etc.*), freezing (of), cutting down (on *jobs*); ***~en an*** *dat.* cuts in

'Streich·wurst *f* meat (*or* sausage) spread

Streif [ʃtraɪf] *m* (-en; -en) → ***Streifen***

'Streif·band *n* (-[e]s; ⸚er) (postal) wrapper

Strei·fe ['ʃtraɪfə] *f* (-; -n) patrol (*a.* ⚔); ***~ gehen*** go on patrol; *policeman*: be on one's beat

Strei·fen ['ʃtraɪfən] *m* (-s; -) a) stripe;

streak; line, b) strip (*a. film*), *w.s.* film, c) strip (of land), ⚔ sector, d) tape; *mot.* ***weißer*** ~ white line; ***ein heller*** (***schmaler***) ~ ***am Horizont*** a streak (a narrow band) of light on the horizon; ***in*** ~ ***schneiden*** cut into strips; ***e-n*** ~ ***drehen*** make a film

strei·fen ['ʃtraifən] **I.** *v/t.* (h) **1.** touch, brush against; *car*: scrape against; *bullet*: graze; *fig.* touch (up)on *a subject etc.*; ***die Kugel hat ihn am Kopf gestreift*** the bullet grazed the side (*or* top) of his head; **2.** ***den Ring vom Finger*** ~ slip (*or* take) the ring off (one's finger); ***die Kleider vom Leib*** ~ slip out of one's clothes; ***ein T-Shirt über den Kopf*** ~ slip a T-shirt on (over one's head), slip into a T-shirt; ***e-e Wollmütze über den Kopf*** ~ slip a woolly hat over one's head; ***die Krümel von der Hose*** ~ brush the crumbs off one's trousers; ***die Blätter vom Stiel*** ~ strip the leaves off the stalk; ***den Teig von den Fingern*** ~ wipe the dough off one's fingers; *fig.* ***mit dem Blick*** ~ glance at; **II.** *v/i.* (sn) (*a.* ~ ***durch*** *acc.*) wander, roam; ***durch Wälder und Wiesen*** ~ roam the countryside (*or* the woods and the fields)

'Strei·fen|dienst *m* patrol duty; **~gang** *m* (patrol) round

'Strei·fen·mu·ster *n* striped pattern

'Strei·fen·wa·gen *m* (police) patrol car; *in GB*: *a.* panda car; *Am.* patrol (*or* prowl) car

strei·fig ['ʃtraifıç] *adj.* streaky

'Streif|licht *n* ray of light; *phot.* glancing light; *mot.* passing headlights *pl.*; *fig.* sidelight; *fig.* ***interessante*** **~*er*** ***werfen auf*** *acc.* give some interesting sidelights on; ***et. in*** **~*ern*** ***schildern*** give a thumbnail sketch of; **~schuß** *m* a) grazing shot, b) (bullet) graze; ***e-n*** ~ ***bekommen*** be grazed (by a bullet); **~wun·de** *f* (bullet) graze; **~zug** *m* **1.** foray (***in*** *acc.*, ***durch*** *acc.* into); ***Streifzüge durch die Gegend machen*** make a few forays into the surrounding area; **2.** ⚔ foray, raid, incursion; **3.** *fig.* ***literarischer*** ~ literary excursion; ***ein*** ~ ***durch die Geschichte des Films*** a journey through the history of film-making; ***Streifzüge durch die Geschichte*** exploring history, excursions through time

Streik [ʃtraik] *m* (-[e]s; -s) strike; (work) stoppage; walkout; ***wilder*** ~ unofficial (*or* wildcat) strike; ***e-n*** ~ ***ausrufen*** call a strike; ***in den*** ~ ***treten*** go on strike; ***sich im*** ~ ***befinden*** be on strike; ***mit e-m*** ~ ***drohen*** threaten to go on strike; **~ak·ti͵on** *f a. pl.* strike action; **~an·fäl·lig** *adj.* strike-prone; **~an·kün·di·gung** *f* strike warning; **~auf·ruf** *m* strike call, call for a strike, call to strike; **~aus·schuß** *m* strike committee; **~bei·le·gung** *f* settlement of a (*or* the) strike; **~bre·cher** *m* strikebreaker, F blackleg, scab; **~dro·hung** *f* threat of a strike, strike threat

strei·ken ['ʃtraikən] *v/i.* (h) **1.** strike, go (*or* be) on strike; **2.** F *fig.* refuse (to go along with s.th. *etc.*); *car*: refuse to start; *machine, engine etc.*: F be on the blink; *stomach*: protest; ***ich streike!*** I protest; *wenn sich das nicht ändert*, ***streike ich*** I'm opting out; ***der Plattenspieler streikt mal wieder*** F the record player's on the blink (*or* in one of its moods) again; **'Strei·ken·de** *m, f* (-n; -n) striker

'Streik|frei·heit *f* (-; *no pl.*) freedom to strike; **~front** *f* strike front; **~geld** *n* strike pay; **~kas·se** *f* strike fund; **~ko·mi͵tee** *n* strike committee; **~lei·tung** *f* strike committee

'Streik·po·sten *m* picket; ***mit*** ~ ***besetzen***, *a.* ~ ***stehen*** picket; **~ket·te** *f* picket line

'Streik|recht *n* right to strike; **~ver·bot** *n* ban on striking; **~wel·le** *f* wave (*or* series) of strikes

Streit [ʃtrait] *m* (-[e]s; *no pl.*) argument, quarrel (***über*** *acc.*, ***um*** *acc.* about, over); controversy, *pol. a.* dispute; *contp.* squabble; wrangling; row; brawl, fight; ***gelehrter*** ~ scholarly dispute, controversy among scholars; ***ehelicher*** ~ marriage (*or* marital) row; ***in*** ~ ***geraten mit*** *dat.* have an argument with, come to blows with; ***mit j-m im*** ~ ***liegen*** quarrel with s.o., be at loggerheads with s.o.; *fig.* ***miteinander im*** ~ ***liegen*** *emotions*: conflict (*or* be in conflict) with one another; F ***suchst du*** ~***?*** are you looking for trouble?; → ***Zaun***; **~axt** *f* battleaxe; *fig.* ***die*** ~ ***begraben*** bury the hatchet

'streit·bar *adj.* quarrelsome, pugnacious; belligerent

strei·ten ['ʃtraitən] *v/i.* (stritt, gestritten, h) **1.** (*a.* ***miteinander*** *or* ***sich*** ~) argue, quarrel, have an argument (***über*** *acc.* about, over); have a row; fight, have a fight; clash, come to blows; ***sich darüber*** ~, ***ob*** have an argument over (*or* as to) whether; ***sie*** ~ ***sich dauernd*** they fight like cat and dog; ***seid ihr beide wieder am*** ~***?*** *a.* F are you two at it again?; **2.** argue (***über*** *acc.* about, over); ***darüber läßt sich*** ~ that's open to argument, that's a moot point

Strei·ter ['ʃtraitɐ] *m* (-s; -) fighter (***für*** *acc.* for); champion (of)

Strei·te·rei [ʃtraitə'rai] *f* (-; -en) arguing, quarrel(l)ing *etc.*; → ***streiten***

'Streit|fall *m* dispute, conflict; ⚖ case; ***im*** ~ in case of litigation; **~fra·ge** *f* dispute, controversy (***über*** *acc.* over; ***ob*** over whether); (controversial) issue (***ob*** over whether); **~ge·gen·stand** *m* **1.** subject of an (*or* the) argument, bone of contention; **2.** point at issue, subject of a (*or* the) dispute; **3.** ⚖ matter in dispute; **~ge·spräch** *n* debate; **~ham·mel** F *m* quarrel(l)er; ***ein*** ~ ***sein*** *a.* always be looking for an argument

strei·tig ['ʃtraitıç] *adj.* ⚖ litigious; contested, *pred.* in dispute, at issue; ***j-m et.*** ~ ***machen*** dispute s.o.'s right to s.th.; → ***Rang*** 1; **'Strei·tig·kei·ten** *pl.* quarrel(l)ing *sg.*, disputes; → *a.* ***Streit; die*** ~ ***beilegen*** settle one's differences

'Streit·kräf·te *pl.* armed forces; (military) troops

'Streit·lust *f* (-; *no pl.*) belligerence, aggressive nature; **'streit·lu·stig** *adj.* pugnacious, belligerent, aggressive

'Streit|macht *f* **1.** military force; **2.** → ***Streitkräfte***; **~ob͵jekt** *n* → ***Streitgegenstand***; **~punkt** *m* a) point at issue, b) bone of contention; **~sa·che** *f* **1.** ⚖ litigation, lawsuit; **2.** dispute; **~schrift** *f* pamphlet

'Streit·sucht *f* (-; *no pl.*) quarrelsomeness; belligerence; **'streit·süch·tig** *adj.* quarrelsome, cantankerous; belligerent

'Streit·wert *m* ⚖ value in dispute, amount involved

streng [ʃtrɛŋ] **I.** *adj.* severe (*a. dress, hairdo, look, criticism, measure, punishment, winter etc.*); stern (*a. look, face*); harsh, hard; rigid; austere *character, style etc.*; strict *rule, discipline, upbringing, diet etc.*; rigorous *demands, examination etc.*; stringent *rule, measure etc.*; acrid, pungent *smell, taste*; **~*er*** ***Aufbau*** rigid structure *of a drama etc.*; **~*ste*** ***Diskretion*** absolute discretion; **~*er*** ***Katholik*** strict Catholic; **~*e*** ***Sitten*** strict morals; **~*es*** ***Stillschweigen*** strict secrecy; **~*e*** ***Trennung*** strict division (*or* separation); **~*e*** ***Worte*** harsh words; **~*e*** ***Untersuchung*** rigorous investigation; ~ ***sein zu j-m*** be strict with (*or* hard on) s.o.; → ***Regiment*** 1; **II.** *adv.* severely *etc.*; ~ ***geheim*** top secret; ~ ***geschnitten*** *face* with severe features; severely styled *dress etc.*; ~ ***vertraulich*** in strict confidence, *a. adm.* strictly confidential; ***j-n*** ~ ***ansehen*** give s.o. a severe look; ~ ***befolgen, sich*** ~ ***halten an*** *acc.* adhere strictly to; **~*(stens)*** ***verboten*** strictly forbidden (*or* prohibited); ~ ***katholisch sein*** be a strict Catholic; ***j-n*** ~ ***bewachen*** keep s.o. under close watch (*or* surveillance); ~ ***durchgreifen*** take strict measures; ~ ***erziehen*** bring up strictly; ~ ***sachlich betrachtet*** from a strictly objective point of view; ~ ***unterscheiden zwischen*** make a clear(-cut) distinction between; → ***Vorschrift***

Stren·ge ['ʃtrɛŋə] *f* (-; *no pl.*) severity, rigo(u)r; harshness; strictness; stringency *etc.*; → ***streng***

'streng·ge·nom·men *adv.* strictly speaking

'streng·gläu·big *adj.* very orthodox; **~*er*** ***Katholik*** *etc.* strict (*or* orthodox) Catholic *etc.*

'streng·neh·men *v/t.* (*irr.*, *sep.*, h, → ***nehmen***) take *s.th.* seriously

streng·stens ['ʃtrɛŋstəns] *adv.* → ***streng*** II

Strep·to·kok·ken·in·fek·ti͵on [ʃtrɛpto'kɔkən-, st-] *f* streptococcal infection

Strep·to·kok·kus [ʃtrɛpto'kɔkus, st-] *m* (-; -ken) streptococcus; *pl.* streptococci

Streß [ʃtrɛs] *m* (Stresses; *no pl.*) stress; (***schwer***) ***im*** ~ ***sein*** be under (a lot of) pressure; **~be·wäl·ti·gung** *f* coping with stress; stress management

stres·sen ['ʃtrɛsən] F *v/t.* (h) put *s.o.* under stress; *a.* give *s.o.* a hard time; ***die Arbeit streßt mich zur Zeit*** *a.* F work's really getting to me at the moment; → ***gestreßt***

stres·sig ['ʃtrɛsıç] F *adj.* heavy-going

'Streß|op·fer *n* victim of stress; **~si·tua·ti͵on** *f* stress situation

Stretch·ka·bel ['strɛtʃ-] *n* coiled cord

Streu [ʃtrɔy] *f* (-; *no pl.*) litter

streu·en ['ʃtrɔyən] (h) **I.** *v/t.* scatter *sand etc.*, *a.* strew *flowers*; spread *fertilizer etc.*; sow *seeds*; sprinkle *salt, sugar etc.*; grit, salt *roads*; *fig.* distribute, scatter, hand out indiscriminately; **II.** *v/i.* ⚔, *phys.* scatter

Streu·er ['ʃtrɔyɐ] *m* (-s; -) shaker

'Streu|fahr·zeug *n* gritter lorry; **~feu·er** *n* ⚔ scattered (*or* area, sweeping) fire; **~gut** *n* grit; **~licht** *n* (-[e]s; *no pl.*) *phys., phot.* scattered light

streu·nen ['ʃtrɔynən] *v/i.* (h, sn) roam about, stray; **~*der*** ***Hund*** stray dog; **Streu·ner** ['ʃtrɔynɐ] *m* (-s; -) **1.** *zo.* stray; **2.** tramp, vagrant

Streu|salz ['ʃtrɔʏ-] *n* thawing salt; **~sand** *m* dry sand, grit
Streu·sel·ku·chen ['ʃtrɔʏzəl-] *m cake with crumble topping*
Streu·ung ['ʃtrɔʏʊŋ] *f* (-; -en) **1.** scattering *etc.*; → ***streuen*; 2.** deviation; ⚔, *a. statistics etc.*: dispersion, spread; *phys.* scatter(ing), dispersion; ~ ***der Bevölkerung*** population dispersal
Streu·zucker ['ʃtrɔʏ-] *m* granulated sugar
strich [ʃtrɪç] *pret. of* ***streichen***
Strich [ʃtrɪç] *m* (-[e]s; -e) **1.** a) line; dash; ⚙ mark; point, b) stroke (of the brush), c) ♪ stroke; bowing technique, d) region, strip (of land); ***gegen den ~ bürsten*** (***kämmen***) brush (comb) the wrong way; ***mit wenigen ~en*** with a few strokes, *fig.* in brief outlines; ***e-n ~ durch et. machen*** cross s.th. out; *fig.* ***j-m e-n ~ durch die Rechnung machen*** thwart s.o.'s plans; ***e-n*** (***dicken***) ***~ unter et. machen*** (*or* ***ziehen***) make a clean break with s.th., forget s.th.; F ***keinen ~ tun*** (*or* ***machen***) not to do a stroke of work; ***ich hab' daran noch keinen ~ getan*** I haven't touched it yet; F ***ein ~ in der Landschaft sein*** be as thin as a rake; F ***das ging mir gegen den ~*** it went against the grain; F ***nach ~ und Faden*** F good and proper; ***unter dem ~*** all in all, at the end of the day; ***unter dem ~ sein*** *performance etc.*: not to be up to the mark (*or* up to par); **2.** F a) red-light district, b) F prostitution; ***auf den ~ gehen*** walk the streets, F be (*or* go) on the game
'Strich·code *m* bar code; **~le·ser** *m* bar code scanner
stri·cheln ['ʃtrɪçəln] *v/t.* (h) sketch in; hatch; → ***gestrichelt***
Stri·cher ['ʃtrɪçɐ] F *m* (-s; -), **'Strich·junge** F *m* F rent boy
'Strich|li·ste *f* check list; *a. fig.* ***e-e ~ führen*** keep a careful record *or* account (***über*** *acc.* of); **~mäd·chen** F *n* streetwalker, F tart, *Am.* F hooker; **~männ·chen** *n* matchstick man; **~punkt** *m* semicolon
'strich·wei·se *adv.* in parts; ~ ***Regen*** scattered showers
'Strich·zeich·nung *f* line drawing
Strick [ʃtrɪk] *m* (-[e]s; -e) (piece of) rope; cord; *fig.* ***j-m aus e-r Sache e-n ~ drehen*** (***wollen***) use s.th. against s.o.; ***wenn alle ~e reißen*** if the worst comes to the worst; F ***den ~ nehmen*** hang o.s.
Strick·ar·beit ['ʃtrɪk-] *f* knitting
stricken ['ʃtrɪkən] (*sep.* -k·k-) *v/t. and v/i.* (h) knit; **Stricker** ['ʃtrɪkɐ] (*sep.* -k·k-) *m* (-s; -) knitter; **Stricke·rei** [ʃtrɪkə'raɪ] (*sep.* -k·k-) *f* (-; -en) **1.** knitting; **2.** knitting mill; **Stricke·rin** ['ʃtrɪkərɪn] (*sep.* -k·k-) *f* (-; -nen) → ***Stricker***
'Strick|garn *n* knitting yarn; **~heft** *n* knitting magazine; **~jacke** *f* cardigan; **~kleid** *n* knitted dress
'Strick·lei·ter *f* rope ladder
'Strick|ma,schi·ne *f* knitting machine; **~mu·ster** *n* knitting pattern; **~na·del** *f* knitting needle; **~wa·ren** *pl.* knitwear *sg.*; **~we·ste** *f* a) knitted waistcoat, b) cardigan; **~zeug** *n* knitting (things *pl.*)
Strie·gel ['ʃtri:gəl] *m* (-s; -) curry comb
'strie·geln *v/t.* (h) curry; brush; → ***gestriegelt***
Strie·me ['ʃtri:mə] *f* (-; -n), **'Strie·men** *m* (-s; -) weal, welt
strie·zen ['ʃtri:tsən] F *v/t.* (h) harass
strikt [ʃtrɪkt, strɪkt] **I.** *adj.* strict; ***das ~e Gegenteil*** the exact opposite; **II.** *adv.* strictly; ~ ***befolgen*** adhere strictly (*or* rigidly) to; ***es ~ ablehnen zu*** *inf.* flatly refuse to *inf.*
Strip [ʃtrɪp, strɪp] *m* (-s; -s) **1.** → ***Striptease*; 2.** strip
Strip·pe ['ʃtrɪpə] F *f* (-; -n) cord, string; ***j-n an der ~ haben*** F have s.o. on the blower; (***dauernd***) ***an der ~ hängen*** F be on the blower (all day long)
strip·pen ['ʃtrɪpən, 'st-] F *v/i.* (h) strip, perform a striptease, F do a strip; F be a stripper; **Strip·pe·rin** ['ʃtrɪpərɪn, 'st-] F *f* (-; -nen) F stripper
Strip·tease ['ʃtrɪpti:s, 'st-] *m* (-; *no pl.*) striptease; **~lo,kal** *n* striptease club, F strip joint; **~tän·ze·rin** *f* striptease dancer
stritt [ʃtrɪt] *pret. of* ***streiten***
strit·tig ['ʃtrɪtɪç] *adj.* contentious; ***~er Punkt*** point at issue; *w.s. a.* moot point
Stro·bo·skop [ʃtrobo'sko:p, 'st-] *n* stroboscope; **~licht** *n* strobe light
Stroh [ʃtro:] *n* (-[e]s; *no pl.*) straw; thatch; *fig.* ***wie ~ schmecken*** F taste like nothing on earth; ***~ im Kopf haben*** F be as thick as two short planks, have sawdust between one's ears; ***leeres ~ dreschen*** flog a dead horse, talk a lot of hot air, beat the air; **~bal·len** *m* bale of straw; **♀'blond** *adj.* flaxen(-haired); **~blu·me** *f* immortelle; **~dach** *n* thatched roof
'stroh|'dumm *adj.* F as thick as two short planks; **~far·ben, ~far·big** *adj.* straw-colo(u)red
'Stroh·feu·er *n* straw fire; *fig.* flash in the pan
'stroh|ge·deckt *adj.* thatched; **~gelb** *adj.* straw-colo(u)red
'Stroh|halm *m* straw; *fig.* ***nach e-m ~ greifen, sich an e-n ~ klammern*** clutch at straws; **~hut** *m* straw hat
stro·hig ['ʃtro:ɪç] *adj.* dry *oranges etc.*; *hair* like straw
'Stroh|kopf F *m* F blockhead, thicko; **~mann** *m* (-[e]s; ⸗er) **1.** scarecrow, straw man; **2.** *fig.* front (*or* straw) man; **~matte** *f* straw mat; **~sack** *m* straw mattress, palliasse; ***ach du heiliger ~!*** good grief!, goodness gracious!; **♀'trocken** *adj.* (as) dry as a bone, bone-dry; **~wit·we** *f hum.* grass widow; **~wit·wer** *m hum.* grass widower
Strolch [ʃtrɔlç] *m* (-[e]s; -e) **1.** tramp, F bum; **2.** rascal, scamp
'strol·chen ['ʃtrɔlçən] *v/i.* (sn) roam about; ~ ***durch*** *acc.* roam (through)
Strom [ʃtro:m] *m* (-[e]s; Ströme ['ʃtrø:mə]) **1.** a) (large) river, b) torrent, c) current (*a. fig.*), d) (*air*)stream, *fig. a.* stream of traffic; throng of people; ***mit dem*** (***gegen den***) ***~ schwimmen*** swim with (against) the current, *fig.* swim *or* go with (against) the tide; *fig.* ***endloser ~ von Menschen*** (***Autos*** *etc.*) endless stream of people (cars *etc.*); ***ein ~ von Worten*** a flood of words; ***in Strömen fließen*** *champagne etc.*: flow like water; ***es gießt in Strömen*** it's pouring; **2.** a) (electric) current; *w.s.* electricity, b) power (*or* electricity) supply; ***der ~ fiel aus*** there was a power failure; ***unter ~ stehend*** live *wire etc.*; **~ab·fall** *m* ⚡ drop in current; **~ab·neh·mer** *m* **1.** (current) collector; **2.** electricity consumer
strom'ab(wärts) *adv.* downstream, downriver, down the river
strom'auf(wärts) *adv.* upstream, upriver, up the river
'Strom|aus·fall *m* power failure; **~be·darf** *m* electricity requirements *pl.* (*or* consumption); **~ein·heit** *f* unit of power
strö·men ['ʃtrø:mən] *v/i.* (sn) flow; stream, *river*: rush; *rain, blood*: pour, *blood*: *a.* gush; *fig. people*: stream, throng, pour (***aus*** *dat.* out of; ***in*** *acc.* into); **'strö'mend** *adj.*: ***~er Regen*** pouring rain
Stro·mer ['ʃtro:mɐ] F *m* (-s; -) vagrant, tramp; **'stro·mern** F *v/i.* (sn) roam about; ~ ***durch*** *acc.* roam (through)
'Strom|er·zeu·ger *m* (electricity) generator; **~er·zeu·gung** *f* electricity (*or* power) generation; **♀füh·rend** *adj.* ⚡ live; **~ka·bel** *n* electric (*or* power) cable; **~kreis** *m* ⚡ circuit; **~lei·tung** *f* circuit line; **~lei·tungs·mast** *m* (electricity) pylon
'Strom·li·ni·en·form *f* streamlined contours *pl.*, streamlining; *mot. a.* streamlined body; **'strom·li·ni·en·för·mig** [-fœrmɪç] *adj.* streamlined; ~ ***gestalten*** streamline
'Strom|mes·ser *m* ⚡ ammeter; **~netz** *n* power supply network; **~quel·le** *f* ⚡ power source; **~rech·nung** *f* electricity bill; **~schie·ne** *f* ⚡ contact rail; bus bar; **~schnel·le** [-ʃnɛlə] *f* (-; -n) rapid; **~span·nung** *f* ⚡ voltage; **♀spa·rend** *adj.* power-saving; ~ ***sein*** save electricity; **~spei·cher** *m* storage battery; **~sper·re** *f* ⚡ power cut; **~stär·ke** *f* ⚡ current; amperage; **~stoß** *m* ⚡ impulse; *b.s.* electric shock
Strö·mung ['ʃtrø:mʊŋ] *f* (-; -en) **1.** current; (*a. air*)stream; *phys.* flow, flux; **2.** *fig.* current, trend; movement
'Strö·mungs·dia,gramm *n phys.* flow diagram
'Strom|un·ter,bre·cher *m* ⚡ circuit breaker; **~ver·brauch** *m* electricity (*or* power) consumption; **~ver·sor·gung** *f* power (*or* electricity) supply; **~wand·ler** *m* current transformer; **~zäh·ler** *m* electricity meter
Stron·ti·um ['ʃtrɔntsɪʊm, 'st-] *n* (-s; *no pl.*) strontium
Stro·phe ['ʃtro:fə] *f* (-; -n) verse, stanza; strophe
strot·zen ['ʃtrɔtsən] *v/i.* (h): ~ ***von*** (*or* ***vor***) *dat.* be full of, be teeming (F crawling) with *people, lice etc., a.* be bristling (*or* riddled) with *mistakes*; be brimming (*or* bursting) with *health, energy etc.*; ***vor Dreck ~*** be caked with dirt; ***vor Geld ~*** be rolling in money; ***von Juwelen ~*** be dripping with jewel(le)ry
strub·be·lig ['ʃtrʊbəlɪç] *adj.* dishevel(l)ed, tousled; **Strub·bel·kopf** ['ʃtrʊbəl-] *m* a) tousled hair, b) tousle-head, F scarecrow
Stru·del ['ʃtru:dəl] *m* (-s; -) **1.** whirlpool, maelstrom; *fig. a.* vortex; *fig.* ***im ~ der Ereignisse untergehen*** be lost in the whirlpool of events; ***vom ~ der Ereignisse mitgerissen werden*** be caught up in the whirlpool of events; ***sich in den ~ des Karnevals stürzen*** plunge into the carnival fray; **2.** *gastr.* strudel
'stru·deln *v/i.* (h) whirl, swirl
Struk·tur [ʃtrʊk'tu:ɐ] *f* (-; -en) **1.** structure; set-up; ***soziale ~en*** social structures (*or* patterns); **2.** *textil.* texture; **~ana,ly·se** *f* structural analysis

struk'tur·be·dingt *adj.* structural
struk·tu·rell [ʃtrʊktu'rɛl] *adj.* structural
struk·tu·rie·ren [ʃtrʊktu'ri:rən] *v/t.* (h) **1.** structure; **2.** *textil.* texture
Struk·tu'rie·rung *f* (-; -en) structuring
Struk'tur|kri·se *f* structural crisis; **~po·li̦tik** *f* structural policy; **~re̦form** *f* structural reform; **2schwach** *adj.* underdeveloped *area*; developing *country*; **~wan·del** *m* structural change, change in structure
Strumpf [ʃtrʊmpf] *m* (-[e]s; Strümpfe ['ʃtrʏmpfə]) a) sock, b) stocking; ***ein Paar Strümpfe*** a) a pair of socks, b) a pair of stockings (*or* nylons); ***in Strümpfen herumlaufen*** run around in one's stockinged feet; *fig.* ***sein Geld im ~ haben*** keep one's money under the mattress; F ***sich auf die Strümpfe machen*** → ***Socke;*** **~band** *n* (-[e]s; ⸚er) garter; **~hal·ter** *m* suspender, *Am.* garter; **~ho·se** *f* tights *pl.*, panty hose; **~mas·ke** *f* stocking mask; **~wa·ren** *pl.* hosiery *sg.*
Strunk [ʃtrʊŋk] *m* (-[e]s; Strünke ['ʃtrʏŋkə]) stalk; (*tree*) stump
strup·pig ['ʃtrʊpɪç] *adj.* dishevel(l)ed, unkempt; shaggy *dog*; bristly *beard*
Struw·wel·pe·ter ['ʃtrʊvəlpe:tɐ] *m* (-s; -) Shock-headed Peter
Strych·nin [ʃtrʏç'ni:n] *n* (-s; *no pl.*) ⚗ strychnine
Stu·be ['ʃtu:bə] *f* (-; -n): (***gute*** ~ front) room; *fig.* ***immer in der ~ hocken*** be a stay-at-home, sit around at home all the time
'Stu·ben|äl·te·ste *m* (-n; -n) ⚔ room leader; **~ar̦rest** *m* ⚔ confinement to barracks; ***~ haben*** ⚔ be confined to barracks, F be grounded; *child*: have to stay in (one's room); **~dienst** *m* ⚔ barrack-room duty; **~flie·ge** *f* (common) housefly; **~hocker** *m* stay-at-home; **~mäd·chen** *obs. n* chambermaid; **2rein** *adj.* **1.** house-trained; **2.** F *fig.* ***nicht ganz ~*** risqué, F a bit near the knuckle; **~wa·gen** *m* bassinet
Stuck [ʃtʊk] *m* (-[e]s; *no pl.*) stucco
Stück [ʃtʏk] *n* (-[e]s; -e) a) piece; bit, b) stretch, c) slice *of bread*; lump *of sugar*, d) piece (of music); *tape etc.*: track, e) *thea.* play, f) head *of cattle etc.*; ***~ Papier*** piece (*or* scrap) of paper; ***~ Seife*** bar (*or* piece) of soap; ***drei Mark das ~*** three marks each (*or* a piece); ***drei ~ von diesen Äpfeln*** three of these apples; ***ich nehme zwei ~*** I'll take two (of them); ***dem ~ nach verkaufen*** sell by the piece; ***in ~en zu 100 Mark*** in 100 mark notes; ***aus einem ~ geschnitten*** cut from one piece; ***Käse am*** (*or* ***im***) ***~ kaufen*** buy cheese by the piece (*or* unsliced); ***von diesem Buch wurden 10000 ~ verkauft*** 10000 copies of the book were sold; ***~e aus e-m Buch vorlesen*** read passages (*or* extracts) from a book; ***~ Land*** piece (*or* plot) of land, patch; ***ein seltenes ~*** a rare specimen; F ***ein hübsches ~ Geld*** F a tidy (little) sum; F ***freches ~*** F cheeky so-and-so; F ***das ist doch ein starkes ~!*** F that's pretty rich, that's a bit thick; F ***mein bestes ~*** my most prized possession, *a. fig.* my pride and joy; ***~ für ~*** bit by bit; ***in ~e gehen*** (*or* ***springen***) break into pieces; ***in ~e schlagen*** smash to bits; ***ein ~ deutscher Geschichte*** a chapter of German history; ***ein gutes ~ größer*** *etc.* quite a bit bigger *etc.*, a fair bit bigger *etc.*; ***ein gutes ~*** (***Weges***) quite a way (*or* distance); ***ein gutes ~ weiterkommen*** *a. fig.* make a fair bit of headway; ***j-n ein kurzes ~ begleiten*** walk part of the way with s.o.; *fig.* ***in vielen ~en*** in many respects (*or* ways); ***große ~e halten auf*** *acc.* think highly of, think the world of; ***sich große ~e einbilden*** have a very high opinion of oneself; ***aus freien ~en*** of one's own free will, F off one's own bat; ***sich für j-n in ~e reißen lassen*** go through fire and water for s.o.
'Stuck·ar·beit *f* stucco (work)
'Stück|ar·beit *f* piecework; **~ar·bei·ter** *m* pieceworker
Stück·chen ['ʃtʏkçən] *n* (-s; -) small (*or* little) piece (*or* bit); ***j-n ein ~ begleiten*** walk part (*or* a bit) of the way with s.o.; → ***rücken*** I
'Stuck·decke *f* stucco(ed) ceiling
stückeln ['ʃtʏkəln] (*sep.* -k·k-) *v/t.* (h) a) piece together, b) ✝ denominate
Stücke·lung ['ʃtʏkəlʊŋ] (*sep.* -k·k-) *f* (-; -en) ✝ denomination
stücken ['ʃtʏkən] (*sep.* -k·k-) *v/t.* (h) piece together
'Stück|gut *n* ✝ **1.** piece goods *pl.*; **2.** parcel(s *pl.*); **~ko·sten** *pl.* unit cost *sg.* (*or* costs); **~li·ste** *f* parts list; **~lohn** *m* piece rate; **~preis** *m* unit price
'stück·wei·se *adv.* little by little, bit by bit; ✝ by the piece
'Stück|werk *contp. n* patchwork; ***~ sein*** (*or* ***bleiben***) be scrappy, be a scrappy business; **~zahl** *f* number of pieces; **~zin·sen** *pl.* ✝ accrued interest *sg.* (on shares); additional interest *sg.*
Stu·dent [ʃtu'dɛnt] *m* (-en; -en) student; ***~ der Biologie*** biology student, student of biology
Stu'den·ten|aus·tausch *m* student exchange; **~aus·weis** *m* student's identity card (*or* ID); **~be·we·gung** *f* student movement; **~blu·me** *f* ✿ French marigold; **~bu·de** F *f* (student's) digs *pl.*; **~fut·ter** *n assortment of nuts and raisins*; **~ge·mein·de** *f* Protestant (*or* Catholic *etc.*) student community; **~heim** *n* students' hostel, hall of residence, *Am.* dormitory; **~kanz̦lei** *f* student record office; **~pfar·rer** *m* university (*or* college) chaplain
Stu'den·ten·schaft *f* (-; -en) student body, students *pl.*
Stu'den·ten|un·ru·hen *pl.* student unrest *sg.* (*or* riots); **~ver·bin·dung** *f* (students') fraternity; **~wohn·heim** *n* → ***Studentenheim;*** **~zeit** *f* student (*or* university, college) days *pl.*
Stu·den·tin [ʃtu'dɛntɪn] *f* (-; -nen) → ***Student***
stu·den·tisch [ʃtu'dɛntɪʃ] *adj.* student ...
Stu·die ['ʃtu:dĭə] *f* (-; -n) study (*a. art, phot.*); sketch
'Stu·di·en|ab·bre·cher *m* university (*or* college) dropout; **~ab·schluß** *m* final examinations *pl.*, finals *pl.*; degree; ***die Universität ohne ~ verlassen*** leave university without a degree, break off one's studies, drop out of university; ***s-n ~ machen*** take one's final examinations (*or* finals); ***welchen ~ haben Sie?*** what sort of degree have you got?; **~an·fän·ger** *m* university entrant; **~așses·sor** *m* probationary secondary school teacher; **~auf·ent·halt** *m* study trip; **~aus·ga·be** *f* textbook edition; **~be·ra·ter** *m* academic adviser, tutor; **~be·ra·tung** *f* student counsel(l)ing; student advisory service; **~be·wer·ber** *m* university applicant; **~buch** *n* course attendance record; **~di̦rek·tor** *m* deputy head(master), *Am.* vice principal; **~fach** *n* subject (of study); **~fahrt** *f* study trip; **~freund** *m* friend from university (*or* college); **~gang** *m* course of studies; degree; **~ge·büh·ren** *pl.* tuition fees
'stu·di·en·hal·ber [-halbɐ] *adv.* for study purposes
'Stu·di·en|jahr *n* academic year; *pl.* → ***Studienzeit;*** **~kol̦le·ge** *m* fellow student; **~plan** *m* degree course scheme; curriculum, syllabus; **~platz** *m* place at university; **~rat** *m*, **~rä·tin** [-rɛ:tɪn] *f* (-; -nen) secondary school teacher; **~re·fe·ren̦dar** *m* student teacher at a secondary school, intern; **~rei·se** *f* study *or* educational tour (*or* trip); **~zeit** *f* **1.** → ***Studentenzeit;*** **2.** length of a degree (*or* one's studies); ***die ~ für Mathematik*** the length of a mathematics course (*or* degree), the time it takes to get a mathematics degree
stu·die·ren [ʃtu'di:rən] (h) **I.** *v/t.* **1.** study, *w.s. a.* scrutinize; **2.** study; ***er studiert Jura*** he's studying law, he's a law student; **II.** *v/i.* study, go to university (*or* college); ***sie hat studiert*** she's got a degree, she's been to university (*or* college); ***wo hast du studiert?*** where did you study (*or* go to university, college)?
Stu'die·ren·de *m, f* (-n; -n) student
stu·diert [ʃtu'di:ɐt] *adj.* educated; ***~ sein*** *a.* have had a university (*or* an academic) education
Stu'dier·te F *m, f* (-n; -n) university (*or* college) graduate, *w.s.* academic
Stu·dio ['ʃtu:dĭo] *n* (-s; -s) studio; **~auf·füh·rung** *f* studio performance; **~büh·ne** *f* studio; experimental theat|re (*Am. a.* -er); **~mu·si·ker** *m* studio musician
Stu·di·um ['ʃtu:dĭʊm] *n* (-s; Studien ['ʃtu:dĭən]) **1.** *univ. etc.* degree; (course of) studies *pl.*; ***während m-s ~s*** when I was at university (*or* college); ***sich sein ~ verdienen*** work one's way through university (*or* college); ***ein ~ aufnehmen*** start a degree, start at university (*or* college); ***das ~ der Geschichte*** a history degree; **2.** study; **~ ge·ne·ra·le** [genə'ra:lə] *n* BA General, BA in General Studies; general degree
Stu·fe ['ʃtu:fə] *f* (-; -n) a) step; rung (*a. fig.*), b) *geol.* stage; terrace, c) ♪ interval, d) shade, e) (*rocket etc.*) stage, ⚡ *a.* step, f) *a.* ⚔ rank, grade; ⚙ level, standard; ***auf gleicher ~ mit*** *dat.* on a level (*or* par) with; ***auf eine ~ stellen mit*** *dat.* place on a level (*or* par) with; ***sich mit j-m auf eine ~ stellen*** *a.* see oneself as s.o.'s equal; ***die höchste ~ des Erfolgs*** the pinnacle of success; ***die nächste ~ s-r Karriere*** the next step up in his career; ***verschiedene ~n der Entwicklung*** different stages in a development
stu·fen ['ʃtu:fən] *v/t.* (h) **1.** step; *a.* terrace *ground*; **2.** *fig.* graduate
'stu·fen·ar·tig *adj. and adv.* → ***stufenförmig***
'Stu·fen|bar·ren *m* asymmetrical (*Am.* uneven) bars *pl.*; **~dach** *n* stepped roof; **~fol·ge** *fig. f* graduation, sequence of stages
'stu·fen·för·mig [-fœrmɪç] **I.** *adj.* stepped; *fig.* graded, graduated; **II.** *adv.* in steps; *fig.* in stages

'Stu·fen|haar·schnitt *m* layered hairstyle (*or* haircut); **~heck** *n mot.* notchback; **~land·schaft** *f* terraced landscape; **~lei·ter** *f* step ladder; *fig.* ladder; *fig.* ***gesellschaftliche ~*** social ladder

'stu·fen·los *adj. and adv.* ⚙ (*a.* ***~ verstellbar***) infinitely variable

'Stu·fen|plan *m* step-by-step plan; **~py·ra͵mi·de** *f* step(ped) pyramid; **~ra͵ke·te** *f* multistage rocket; **~schnitt** *m* layered hairstyle (*or* haircut)

'stu·fen·wei·se I. *adj.* gradual, progressive; **II.** *adv.* step by step, by degrees; in stages

Stuhl [ʃtu:l] *m* (-[e]s; Stühle ['ʃty:lə]) **1.** chair; (*piano etc.*) stool; ***der elektrische ~*** the electric chair; *eccl.* ***der Heilige ~*** the Holy See; *fig.* ***j-m den ~ vor die Tür setzen*** turn s.o. out, F give s.o. the sack; ***sich zwischen zwei Stühle setzen*** fall between two stools; F ***mich hat es fast vom ~ gehauen*** F I nearly fell over backwards; F ***an j-s ~ sägen*** try to topple s.o.; F ***an s-m ~ kleben*** cling to one's post; **2.** ⚕ a) stool(s *pl.*), b) → ***Stuhlgang***; **~auf·satz** *m* booster seat; **~bein** *n* chairleg, leg of a (*or* the) chair; **~drang** *m* ⚕ urge to empty one's bowels; **~gang** *m* (-[e]s; *no pl.*) ⚕ bowel movement; ***~ haben*** have a bowel movement; ***harten*** (***weichen***) ***~ haben*** have hard (soft) stools; **~leh·ne** *f* back of a (*or* the) chair; **~ver·hal·tung** *f* ⚕ obstipation; **~ver·stop·fung** *f* ⚕ constipation

Stuk·ka·teur [ʃtuka'tø:ɐ] *m* (-s; -e [-rə]) plasterer; **Stuk·ka·tur** [ʃtuka'tu:ɐ] *f* (-; -en [-rən]) stucco (work)

Stul·le ['ʃtulə] F *f* (-; -n) slice of bread (and butter); (open) sandwich

Stul·pe ['ʃtulpə] *f* (-; -n) a) top, b) cuff

stül·pen ['ʃtylpən] *v/t.* (h) turn *s.th.* upside down; turn up; ***et. nach außen ~*** turn s.th. inside out; ***et. auf*** (*or* ***über***) ***et. ~*** put s.th. on (*or* over) s.th.

'Stul·pen|hand·schuh *m* gauntlet glove; **~stie·fel** *m* top boot

Stülp·na·se ['ʃtylp-] *f* turned-up nose

stumm [ʃtum] **I.** *adj.* a) dumb, b) silent (*a. fig.*), *ling. a.* mute; *fig.* ***~ vor*** *dat.* speechless (*or* struck dumb) with *surprise etc.*; ***~e Rolle*** silent (*or* non-speaking) part; ***~er Zeuge*** silent witness; ***~er Vorwurf*** silent reproach; ***~ wie ein Fisch*** (as) silent as the grave; → ***Diener*** 3; **II.** *adv.* silently; ***~ dasitzen*** sit there without saying a word

Stum·mel ['ʃtuməl] *m* (-s; -) a) stump, b) butt, stub *of a cigar etc.*, c) stub *of pencil, candle etc.*

Stum·me ['ʃtumə] *m, f* (-n; -n) mute

'Stumm·film *m* silent film (*or* movie); **~ära** *f,* **~zeit** *f* silent film (*or* movie) era

Stum·pen ['ʃtumpən] *m* (-s; -) cheroot

Stüm·per ['ʃtympɐ] *m* (-s; -) duffer; **Stüm·pe·rei** [ʃtympə'raɪ] *f* (-; -en) a) bungling, incompetence, F botching, b) bad job, F botch(-up); **'stüm·per·haft I.** *adj.* bungling, incompetent, amateurish; ***~e Arbeit*** F botch, botched-up job; **II.** *adv.*: ***~ ausgeführt sein*** be an amateur piece of work, have been done in an amateurish way; **'stüm·pern** *v/i. and v/t.* (h) bungle, F botch (up)

stumpf [ʃtumpf] *adj.* **1.** blunt *knife, pencil etc.*; ***~ werden*** go blunt; **2.** ∡ obtuse *angle*; truncated *cone*; **3.** masculine *rhyme*; **4.** dull *skin, hair etc.*; **5.** *fig.* obtuse, dull; stolid, apathetic; dulled *senses*; ***~er Blick*** dull look; ***~ gegenüber*** *dat.* insensitive to

Stumpf *m* (-[e]s; Stümpfe ['ʃtympfə]) stump; F ***et. mit ~ und Stiel ausrotten*** eradicate s.th. root and branch

'Stumpf·heit *f* (-; *no pl.*) bluntness, dul(l)ness, obtuseness, apathy *etc.*; → ***stumpf***

'Stumpf·sinn *m* (-[e]s; *no pl.*) a) dul(l)ness, apathy, b) mindlessness, monotony *of a job etc.*; **'stumpf·sin·nig** *adj.* a) dull, b) stolid, apathetic, c) dull, tedious, mindless, soul-destroying *work etc.*

'stumpf·win·ke·lig *adj.* obtuse(-angled)

Stun·de ['ʃtundə] *f* (-; -n) a) hour, *fig. a.* moment, b) *ped.* lesson, period; ***~n geben*** give lessons; ***~ nehmen bei*** *dat.* have lessons with; ***was habt ihr in der ersten ~?*** what's your first lesson?; *mot.* ***50 Meilen in der ~*** 50 miles an (*or* per) hour; ***alle zwei ~n*** every two hours, every other hour; ***von drei ~n*** (***Dauer***) three-hour *speech etc.*; ***von ~ zu ~*** with every hour (that passes *or* passed); ***~ um ~ verging*** the hours passed by; ***bis zur ~*** as yet, up till now; ***zu später*** (***früher***) ***~*** late at night (early in the day); ***zu jeder ~*** at any time; ***zur ~*** at the moment; ***bis zur ~*** so far; ***die Gespräche dauern zur ~ noch an*** the foreign ministers *etc.* are still sitting at the negotiating table; ***die ~n zählen*** count the hours (passing by); *fig.* ***s-e ~n sind gezählt*** his days are numbered; ***s-e*** (***große***) ***~ ist gekommen*** his time (*or* hour) has come; ***die ~ der Entscheidung ist gekommen*** the time has come to decide (*or* to make the big decision); ***die ~ der Rache ist gekommen*** the hour of reckoning has come; ***die ~ des Abschieds*** the time to say goodbye (*lit.* take one's leave); ***die ~ der Wahrheit*** the moment of truth; ***in e-r schwachen ~*** in a moment of weakness; ***ein Mann der ersten ~*** a man of the first hour, a pioneer; ***in e-r stillen ~*** at some quiet moment; ***er wußte, was die ~ geschlagen hatte*** he knew what was up (*or* what was in store for him); → ***halb***

stun·den ['ʃtundən] *v/t.* (h) ☤ grant (*or* allow) respite *or* a delay for *s.th.*; (***j-m***) ***die Zahlung ~*** extend the term of payment (to s.o.)

'Stun·den|aus·fall *m ped.* cancel(l)ed classes *pl.*; **~ge·schwin·dig·keit** *f* (average) speed per hour; ***e-e ~ von 40 Meilen*** an average of 40 miles per hour (*abbr.* mph); **~ho͵tel** *n* short-time hotel (*or* motel); **~ki·lo͵me·ter** *pl.* kilomet|res (*Am.* -ers) per hour (*abbr.* kph)

'stun·den·lang I. *adj.* hours of, hour after hour of; lasting (for) hours; **II.** *adv.* for hours (and hours), for hours on end

'Stun·den|lohn *m* hourly wage; **~plan** *m* timetable, *Am.* schedule; **~schlag** *m* striking of the hour; ***mit dem ~ sechs*** on the stroke of six

'stun·den·wei·se *adj. and adv.* by the hour

...-'Stun·den-'Wo·che *f*: ***30~*** *etc.* 30-hour (working) week *etc.*

'Stun·den|zahl *f* workload; *ped. a.* teaching load; **~zei·ger** *m* hour hand

Stünd·lein ['ʃtyntlaɪn] *n* (-s; -): ***sein letztes ~ hat geschlagen*** his last hour has come

stünd·lich ['ʃtyntlıç] **I.** *adj.* **1.** hourly; **II.** *adv.* **2.** every hour; hourly; **3.** any time (now); ***er kann ~ ankommen*** he could be here any hour (now)

Stun·dung ['ʃtunduŋ] *f* (-; -en) ☤ deferment (of payment)

Stunk [ʃtuŋk] F *m* (-s; *no pl.*) row, F stink; ***~ machen*** kick up a row (*or* stink); ***es wird ~ geben*** there'll be trouble (*or* a real stink)

stu·pend [ʃtu'pɛnt, st-] *adj.* stupendous, amazing

Stunt [stant] *m* (-s; -s) stunt; ***e-n ~ ausführen*** do a stunt; **'Stunt·man** [-mɛn] *m* (-s; -men) stunt man

stu·pid [ʃtu'pi:t], **stu·pi·de** [ʃtu'pi:də] *adj.* dull; mindless

Stups [ʃtups] F *m* (-es; -e), **stup·sen** ['ʃtupsən] F *v/t.* (h) prod (*a. fig.*), nudge

'Stups·na·se *f* snub nose; **'stups·na·sig** [-na:zıç] *adj.* snub-nosed

stur [ʃtu:ɐ] **I.** *adj.* a) stubborn, obstinate; pigheaded; unyielding, unwavering; dogged, b) stolid; mindless; ***ein ~es Nein*** a flat no; **II.** *adv.*: ***~ nach Vorschrift*** strictly according to the letter (of the law); **'Stur·heit** *f* (-; *no pl.*) stubbornness, obstinacy *etc.*; → ***stur*** I

Sturm [ʃturm] *m* (-[e]s; Stürme ['ʃtyrmə]) **1.** a) storm; gale; *lit.* tempest, b) ⚔ *and fig.* attack, assault; ***das Barometer steht auf ~*** the barometer is pointing to a storm, *fig.* there's trouble (*or* a storm) brewing; ***~ läuten*** ring the alarm bell, *fig.* lean on the bell; *fig.* ***~ der Entrüstung*** (public) outcry; ***~ des Protests*** (***des Beifalls***) storm of protest (of applause); ***ein ~ des Gelächters*** peals of laughter; ***ein ~ im Wasserglas*** a storm in a teacup, *Am.* a tempest in a teapot; ☤ ***~ auf*** *acc.* rush for *goods*, run on *a bank*; ***~ laufen gegen*** *acc.* be up in arms against; ***im ~ erobern*** take by storm; F ***bei ihnen herrscht ~*** they're having a row; ***~ und Drang*** Sturm und Drang, Storm and Stress; **2.** *sport*: forward line, forwards *pl.*; **~ab͵tei·lung** *f hist.* SA, (Nazi) stormtroops *pl. or* stormtroopers *pl.*; **~an·griff** *m* ⚔ assault; **~bö** *f* squall; **~boot** *n* ⚔ assault boat

stür·men ['ʃtyrmən] (h) **I.** *v/t.* **1.** ⚔ storm (*a. fig.*); ☤ make a run on *a bank etc.*; **II.** *v/i.* **2.** ⚔ *and sport*: attack, *soccer*: *a.* be a striker; **3.** *storm*: rage; **4.** *fig.* storm; charge, tear; **III.** *v/impers.*: ***es stürmt*** there's a gale blowing, it's stormy outside

Stür·mer ['ʃtyrmɐ] *m soccer etc.*: striker; **~rei·he** *f* forward line

'Sturm·flut *f* storm tide

'sturm·frei *adj.*: F ***~e Bude*** F trouble-free digs *pl.*; ***heute abend hab' ich*** (***e-e***) ***~e Bude*** I've got the run of the place tonight, the coast is going to be clear tonight

'Sturm·ge·päck *n* ⚔ combat pack

'sturm·ge·peitscht *adj.* storm-tossed; *a.* storm-lashed *sea*

'Sturm·glocke *f* alarm bell, tocsin

stür·misch ['ʃtyrmıʃ] **I.** *adj.* **1.** stormy *weather etc.*; ***~e See*** stormy (*or* rough) seas; ***~e Überfahrt*** rough crossing; **2.** *fig.* tempestuous, passionate *love, lover etc.*; stormy *love affair, debate etc.*; tumultuous, frenzied *applause etc.*; vehement, violent *protest, reaction etc.*; rapid *development etc.*; ***~e Begrüßung*** rapturous welcome; ***~es Gelächter*** gales of laughter; ***~er Jubel*** wild rejoicing; ☤ ***~e Nachfrage*** huge demand; ***~e Umar-***

mung passionate embrace; ***e-e ~e Zeit*** turbulent times; ***e-e ~e Karriere erleben*** have a stormy career; **II.** *adv.*: ~ ***bitten um*** *acc.* make a violent plea for; ~ ***protestieren*** protest vehemently (*or* violently); ***et. ~ fordern*** clamo(u)r for s.th.; ***man applaudierte ~*** there was a storm of applause; ~ ***begrüßt werden*** be given a rapturous welcome; ***nicht so ~!*** easy does it!, hold your horses!

'Sturm|ke·gel *m* storm cone; **~la͵ter·ne** *f* storm lantern, hurricane lamp; **~lauf** *m* ⚔ assault, attack; *fig. a.* run (***auf*** *acc.* on); **~mö·we** *f* seagull; **~nacht** *f* **1.** stormy night; **2.** night of the storm; **~reihe** *f sport*: forward line, attack; **~schaden** *m* storm damage; **~schritt** *m*: ***im ~*** at the double; **~se·gel** *n* storm sail; **~spit·ze** *f sport*: spearhead (of the attack); **~tief** *n* cyclone; **~vo·gel** *m* (stormy) petrel; **~war·nung** *f* gale warning; **~wol·ke** *f* storm cloud

Sturz¹ [ʃtʊrts] *m* (-es; Stürze ['ʃtʏrtsə]) (sudden) fall; plunge (*a. fig.*); *fig.* (sudden) drop *in temperature etc.*; ✝ slump; ✝ crash; *pol.* (down)fall, overthrow; F ***e-n ~ bauen*** (*or* ***drehen***) have a fall; *fig.* ***es führte zu s-m ~*** it led to (*or* brought about) his downfall

Sturz² [ʃtʊrts] *m* (-es; Stürze ['ʃtʏrtsə]) **1.** ⚙ camber; **2.** ⚠ lintel

'Sturz·bach *m* torrent (*a. fig.*)

'sturz·be'sof·fen, 'sturz·be'trun·ken F *adj.* F (completely) sloshed, plastered

'Sturz·bom·ber *m* dive bomber

stür·zen ['ʃtʏrtsən] **I.** *v/i.* (sn) **1.** fall; *fig. prices etc.*: plunge, plummet; ***schwer ~*** have a bad (*or* heavy) fall; ***vom Fahrrad ~*** fall off one's bicycle; ***aus den Augen ~*** *tears*: stream from s.o.'s eyes; ***aus der Wunde ~*** *blood*: gush from the wound; ***ins Meer ~*** ✈ crash into the sea; *fig.* ***der Minister stürzte über diesen Skandal*** this scandal brought about (*or* led to) the minister's downfall; **2.** *terrain*: drop; ***in die Tiefe ~*** *cliffs etc.*: drop off sharply; ***die Klippen ~ dort 100 Meter in die Tiefe*** there's a sheer drop of 100 metres (*Am.* meters) at that point; **3.** rush, dash; ***ins Zimmer ~*** *a.* burst into the room; ***in j-s Arme ~*** rush (*or* fling o.s.) into s.o.'s arms; **II.** *v/t.* (h) **4.** throw; *fig.* ***j-n ins Elend*** *etc.* ~ plunge s.o. into misery *etc.*; → ***Verderben*; 5.** turn upside down; *gastr.* turn out of the mo(u)ld (*or* tin); ***Nicht ~!*** this side up; **6.** bring down, bring about the downfall of, overthrow *the government etc.*; **III.** *v/refl.* (h) **7.** ***sich ins Wasser ~*** plunge into the water; ***sich vor e-n Zug ~*** throw o.s. in front of a train; *fig.* ***sich in Unkosten ~*** go to great expense, spare no expense; ***sich in die Arbeit ~*** throw o.s. into one's work; → ***Unglück, Verderben*; 8.** ***sich ~ auf*** *acc.* a) rush to(wards) *s.o.*, b) rush at *s.o.*; *zo. a.* pounce on *s.o.*, swoop down on *s.o.*, c) F *fig.* make straight for, F attack; ***sich aufeinander ~*** fall upon each other; F *fig.* ***sich auf die Süßigkeiten ~*** pounce on (F attack) the sweets

'Sturz|flug *m* nosedive; *fig.* crash; **~flut** *f* torrent (of water); tidal wave; torrential downpour; *fig.* torrent; **~ge·burt** *f* ⚕ precipitate labo(u)r; **~helm** *m* crash helmet; **~kampf·bom·ber** *m* dive bomber; **~re·gen** *m* torrential downpour; **~see** *f* breaker

Stuß [ʃtʊs] F *m* (Stusses; *no pl.*) F rubbish, garbage, trash, *sl.* rot; ***so ein ~!*** what a lot (*or* load) of rubbish *etc.*

Stu·te ['ʃtu:tə] *f* (-; -n) mare

'Stu·ten·foh·len *n* filly

Stütz [ʃtʏts] *m* (-es; -e) *gym.* support

'Stütz·bal·ken *m* supporting beam, brace

Stutz·bart ['ʃtʊts-] *m* trimmed beard

Stüt·ze ['ʃtʏtsə] *f* (-; -n) **1.** support, prop; *fig.* support, *a.* backing; mainstay; ***~n der Gesellschaft*** pillars of society; ***sie war mir e-e große ~*** she gave me a lot of support; **2.** F dole (money)

stut·zen¹ ['ʃtʊtsən] *v/t.* (h) a) cut; trim *hair, beard,* b) ✂ prune, lop *tree etc.*; clip, trim *hedge etc.*, c) *zo.* clip *wings*; crop *ears*; dock *tail*

'stut·zen² *v/i.* (h) a) stop short, b) be taken aback, catch one's breath, c) hesitate, d) F do a double take

'Stut·zen *m* (-s; -) **1.** short rifle, carbine; **2.** ⚙ connecting piece; *mot.* (*filler*) neck; **3.** (football) sock

stüt·zen ['ʃtʏtsən] (h) **I.** *v/t.* support (*a.* ✝ *and fig.*); prop up; ⚠ shore up; *fig.* back (up), ✝ *a.* bolster; ***s-e Ellenbogen ~ auf*** *acc.* prop one's elbows on; *fig.* ***et. ~ auf*** *acc.* base s.th. on; ***et. durch Beweise ~*** support (*or* corroborate) s.th. with evidence; **II.** *v/refl.*: ***sich ~ auf*** *acc.* a) rest on, lean on, b) *fig. argument, judgement etc.*: be based on, rest on; draw upon *a source etc.*

Stutz·flü·gel ['ʃtʊts-] *m* baby grand

'Stütz·ge·we·be *n anat.* supporting tissue

stut·zig ['ʃtʊtsɪç] *adj.*: ~ ***werden*** a) be taken aback, b) be puzzled; ***j-n ~ machen*** perplex (*or* puzzle) s.o.; have s.o. wondering; arouse s.o.'s suspicion

'Stütz|kor͵sett *n* support corset; **~mauer** *f* retaining wall; **~pfei·ler** *m* supporting pillar, buttress; **~punkt** *m* **1.** (military) base; **2.** ⚙ fulcrum; **~rad** *n* supporting wheel; **~strumpf** *m* elasticated stocking

Stüt·zung ['ʃtʏtsʊŋ] *f* (-; -en) support, backing *etc.*; → ***stützen***

'Stüt·zungs|ak·ti͵on *f* ✝ support measures *pl.*; **~käu·fe** *pl.* support buying *sg.*

'Stütz·ver·band *m* ⚕ fixed dressing

sty·len ['staɪlən] *v/t.* (h) design; → ***gestylt*; Sty·ling** ['staɪlɪŋ] *n* (-s; *no pl.*) design, styling

Sty·ro·por [ʃtyro'po:ɐ, st-] (*TM*) *n* (-s; *no pl.*) polystyrene, styrofoam (*TM*)

Sua·he·li¹ [zŭa'he:li] *n* (-[s]; *no pl.*) *ling.* Swahili; **Sua'he·li²** *m* (-[s]; -[s]) Swahili

sub·al·tern [zʊpˀal'tɛrn] *adj.* **1.** subordinate *post etc.*; **2.** *contp.* subservient *behavio(u)r etc.*; **Sub·al'ter·ne** *m* (-n; -n) **1.** subordinate; *esp.* ⚔ subaltern; **2.** *contp.* underling

Sub·jekt [zʊp'jɛkt] *n* (-[e]s; -e) **1.** *ling. and phls.* subject; **2.** *contp.* individual, character; ***übles ~*** F nasty piece of work

sub·jek·tiv [zʊpjɛk'ti:f] **I.** *adj.* subjective; ⚖ → ***Tatbestand*; II.** *adv.*: ***zu ~ urteilen*** be too subjective in one's judg(e)ment; ***das siehst du zu ~*** you're looking at it very subjectively (*or* from a very subjective point of view)

Sub·jek·ti·vis·mus [zʊpjɛkti'vɪsmʊs] *m* (-; *no pl.*) *phls.* subjectivism

Sub·jek·ti·vi·tät [zʊpjɛktivi'tɛ:t] *f* (-; *no pl.*) subjectivity

Sub·kon·ti·nent ['zʊp-] *m* subcontinent

Sub·kul͵tur ['zʊp-] *f* subculture

'sub·kul·tu͵rell *adj.* subcultural

sub·ku·tan [zʊpku'ta:n] *adj.* ⚕ subcutaneous

sub·lim [zu'bli:m] *adj.* sensitive; sublime *irony etc.*; **sub·li·mie·ren** [zubli'mi:rən] *v/t.* (h) sublimate; **Sub·li'mie·rung** *f* (-; -en) sublimation

sub·or·di·nie·ren [zʊpˀɔrdi'ni:rən] *v/t.* (h) subordinate

sub·po·lar [zʊppo'la:ɐ] *adj.* subpolar

Sub·skri·bent [zʊpskri'bɛnt] *m* (-en; -en) subscriber; **sub·skri·bie·ren** [zʊpskri'bi:rən] *v/t.* (h) (*a. v/i.*: ~ ***auf*** *acc.*) subscribe to; **Sub·skrip·ti·on** [zʊpskrɪp'tsĭo:n] *f* (-; -en) subscription

Sub·skrip·ti'ons|li·ste *f* subscription list; **~preis** *m* subscription price

sub·stan·ti·ell [zʊpstan'tsĭɛl] *adj.* substantial

Sub·stan·tiv ['zʊpstanti:f] *n* (-s; -e [-və]) *ling.* noun

sub·stan·ti·vie·ren [zʊpstanti'vi:rən] *v/t.* (h) nominalize; **sub·stan·ti·viert** [zʊpstanti'vi:ɐt] *adj.*: ***~es Adjektiv*** nominalized adjective

sub·stan·ti·visch ['zʊpstanti:vɪʃ] **I.** *adj.* nominal; **II.** *adv.* nominally, as a noun

Sub·stanz [zʊp'stants] *f* (-; -en) **1.** substance; **2.** ✝ capital; ***von der ~ leben*** live on one's capital; ***die ~ angreifen*** draw on one's resources; **3.** *fig.* substance; core; ***es fehlt dem an ~*** it lacks substance; F ***das geht an die ~*** F it really takes it out of you

sub'stanz·los *adj.* insubstantial, lacking in substance

Sub'stanz·ver·lust *m* loss of substance; ✝ loss of capital (*or* resources)

sub·sti·tu·ie·ren [zʊpstitu'i:rən] *v/t.* (h) substitute (***A durch B*** B for A)

Sub·sti·tut¹ [zʊpsti'tu:t] *m* (-en; -en) assistant sales manager

Sub·sti'tut² *n* (-s; -e) substitute

Sub·strat [zʊp'stra:t] *n* (-[e]s; -e) substrate

sub·su·mie·ren [zʊpzu'mi:rən] *v/t.* (h) subsume (***unter*** *dat.* under *or dat.*)

Sub·sy͵stem ['zʊp-] *n* subsystem

sub·til [zʊp'ti:l] **I.** *adj.* subtle; ***~er Hinweis*** subtle hint; ***~e Unterscheidung*** subtle distinction; ***das ≈e daran*** the subtle thing about it; **II.** *adv.* subtly

Sub·ti·li·tät [zʊptili'tɛ:t] *f* (-; -en) subtlety; subtle nature

Sub·tra·hend [zʊptra'hɛnt] *m* (-en; -en) ⩲ subtrahend; **sub·tra·hie·ren** [zʊptra'hi:rən] *v/t.* (h) subtract; **Sub·trak·ti·on** [zʊptrak'tsĭo:n] *f* (-; -en) subtraction

Sub·tro·pen ['zʊp-] *pl.* subtropics

'sub·tro·pisch *adj.* subtropical

Sub·un·ter͵neh·mer ['zʊp-] *m* subcontractor

Sub·ven·ti·on [zʊpvɛn'tsĭo:n] *f* (-; -en) subsidy

sub·ven·tio·nie·ren [zʊpvɛntsĭo'ni:rən] *v/t.* (h) subsidize; **sub·ven·tio·niert** [zʊpvɛntsĭo'ni:ɐt] *adj.* subsidized; ***staatlich ~*** subsidized by the state, state-subsidized; **Sub·ven·tio'nie·rung** *f* (-; -en) subsidization

Sub·ver·si·on [zʊpvɛr'zĭo:n] *f* (-; -en) *pol.* subversion

sub·ver·siv [zʊpvɛr'zi:f] *adj.* subversive

Such|ak·ti͵on ['zu:x-] *f* search; **~al·go͵rith·mus** *m computer*: search algorithm; **~an·zei·ge** *f* **1.** missing person bulletin; **2.** wanted ad; **~be·griff** *m computer*: search word; **~dienst** *m* tracing service

Su·che ['zu:xə] *f* (-; *no pl.*) search (***nach***

dat. for); *a.* hunt (for *a criminal etc.*); *fig.* search (for), quest (for), pursuit (of *happiness etc.*); **auf der ~ nach** *dat.* in search of, *fig. a.* in quest of *happiness etc.*; **auf der ~ sein nach** *dat.* be looking (*or* on the lookout) for, be searching for; **nach langer ~** after a long search; **sich auf die ~ machen** start looking (**nach** *dat.* for)

su·chen ['zu:xən] (h) **I.** *v/t.* look for, search for; *lit.* seek; try to trace *a missing person etc.*; hunt for, try to track down *a criminal etc.*; **du wirst gesucht** they're looking for you, F you're wanted; **Pilze ~** look for (*or* pick) mushrooms; **Hilfe (Rat) ~** seek help (advice); **Abenteuer ~** seek adventure; **e-e neue Stelle ~** look for (*or* try to find) a new job; **Streit mit j-m ~** be trying to pick a fight (*or* an argument) with s.o.; **das Weite ~** take to one's heels; **~ Sie jemand?** are you looking for s.o. in particular?, can I help you?; **was ~ Sie hier?** what are you doing here?; **was suchst du hier?** *a.* F what are you after?; **Sie haben hier nichts zu ~** you have no business being here; **das hat hier nichts zu ~** that has no place around here; **ich hab' bei ihm nichts mehr zu ~** I'm through with him; **such nicht die Schuld bei andern** don't try and blame others; **die beiden haben sich gesucht und gefunden** they('ve) found each other; **sich e-n Weg durch die Menge ~** pick one's way through the crowd; **j-n zu verstehen ~** try to understand s.o.; → **gesucht, polizeilich, seinesgleichen**; **II.** *v/i.* look, search (**nach** *dat.* for); **nach Worten ~** search (*or* grope) for words, be at a loss for words; **da kannst du lange ~** you won't find that there; **in allen Taschen (Schränken) ~** search (through) *or* go through all one's pockets (all the cupboards); *bibl.* **suchet, so werdet ihr finden** search and ye shall find

Su·cher ['zu:xɐ] *m* (-s; -) *phot.* viewfinder; **~ka·me·ra** *f* rangefinder camera

Such|funk·ti͵on ['zu:x-] *f computer*: search function; **~hund** *m* tracker (*or* sniffer) dog; **~lauf** *m radio, video etc.*: scanning, search mode (*or* function); **~ vorwärts (rückwärts)** cue (review), forward (reverse) search; **~lauf·ta·ste** *f* cue/review (*or* scan) button; **~li·ste** *f* list of missing persons; *police*: list of wanted persons, wanted list; **~mann·schaft** *f* search party; **~mel·dung** *f* missing person bulletin; police message; **~schein·wer·fer** *m* searchlight

Sucht [zʊxt] *f* (-; Süchte ['zʏçtə]) a) addiction (**nach** *dat.* to *drugs, alcohol etc.*), b) craving (for); mania (for); **das ist bei ihm zur ~ geworden** a) he's become addicted to it, b) it's become an obsession with him; **2er·zeu·gend** *adj.* ⚕ addictive, habit-forming; **~ge·fahr** *f* danger of habit formation; **~gift** *n* addictive drug

süch·tig ['zʏçtɪç] *adj.* **1.** addicted; **heroin~** addicted to heroin; **~ werden** become addicted (**nach** *dat.* to), *sl.* get hooked (on); **~ machen** *drug etc.*: be addictive; **2. ~ sein nach** *dat.* have a craving for, lust after; **er ist ~ danach** *a.* it's like a drug for him; **Süch·ti·ge** ['zʏçtɪgə] *m, f* (-n; -n) addict

'Süch·tig·keit *f* (-; *no pl.*) addiction

'Sucht|kli·nik *f* detoxification centre (*Am.* center); **2krank** *adj.* addicted; **~kran·ke** *m, f* (-n; -n) ⚕ addict; **~mit·tel** *n* addictive drug (*or* substance)

Such·trupp ['zu:x-] *m* search party

Sud [zu:t] *m* (-[e]s; -e ['zu:də]) **1.** *gastr.* a) juice, b) stock; **2.** ⚗ extract

Süd [zy:t] *without art.* south; **von** (*or* **aus**) **~** from the south; **München ~** the south of Munich; **Eingang ~** the south entrance

'Süd·afri'ka·ner *m*, **'süd·afri'ka·nisch** *adj.* South African

'Süd·ame·ri'ka·ner *m*, **'süd·ame·ri'ka·nisch** *adj.* South American

Su·da·ne·se [zuda'ne:zə] *m* (-n; -n), **Su·da·ne·sin** [zuda'ne:zɪn] *f* (-; -nen), **su·da·ne·sisch** [zuda'ne:zɪʃ] *adj.* Sudanese

'Süd·asi'at *m* South Asian; **'süd·asia·tisch** *adj.* South Asian; **im ~en Raum** in South (*or* Southern) Asia

'süd·deutsch *adj.* South German; **im ~en Raum** in the south of Germany, in Southern Germany; **'Süd·deut·sche** *m, f* (-n; -n) South German

Su·de·lei [zu:də'laɪ] F *f* (-; -en) mess

su·deln ['zu:dəln] *v/i. and v/t.* (h) **1.** make a mess; **2.** scribble, scrawl

Sü·den ['zy:dən] *m* (-s; *no pl.*) south; South; **von ~** from the south; **nach ~** south(wards); southbound *traffic, shipping etc.*; **Balkon nach ~** south-facing balcony; **im sonnigen ~** in the sunny Mediterranean

'süd·eng·lisch *adj.* southern (*or* Southern) English

su·de·ten·deutsch [zu'de:tən-] *adj.*, **Su'de·ten·deut·sche** *m, f* (-n; -n) Sudeten German

'Süd·eu·ro'pä·er *m*, **'süd·eu·ro'pä·isch** *adj.* South (*or* Southern) European

'Süd|fen·ster *n* south-facing window, window facing south, window to the south; **~früch·te** *pl.* tropical (*or* southern) fruits; **~halb·ku·gel** *f* southern hemisphere; **~hang** *m* southern (*or* south-facing) slope

'Süd·ko·rea·ner *m*, **'süd·ko·rea·nisch** *adj.* South Korean

'Süd|kü·ste *f* south coast; **an der ~** on the south coast; **~la·ge** *f* southern exposure

Süd·län·der ['zy:tlɛndɐ] *m* (-s; -) Mediterranean type, Latin; **süd·län·disch** ['zy:tlɛndɪʃ] *adj.* Mediterranean *climate etc.*, *a.* Latin *type*, *a. temperament*

'süd·lich I. *adj.* southern, south ...; southerly *wind*; **in ~er Richtung** south(wards); southbound *traffic, shipping etc.*; **II.** *adv.* (to the) south (**von** *dat.* of)

'süd·lichst *adj.* southernmost

'Süd·licht *n* (-[e]s; -er) southern lights *pl.*, aurora australis

Süd'ost *without art.* → **Südosten**

süd'ost·asia·tisch *adj.* Southeast Asian

Süd'osten *m* (**SO**) southeast (*abbr.* SE)

Süd'ost·eu·ro'pä·er *m*, **süd'ost·eu·ro·'pä·isch** *adj.* Southeast European

süd'öst·lich I. *adj.* southeast(ern); southeasterly *wind*; **II.** *adv.* (to the) southeast

'Süd·pol *m* South Pole

'Süd·po͵lar·ge·biet *n* Antarctic

'Süd·po͵lar·kreis *m* Antarctic circle

'Süd·pol·ex·pe·di·ti͵on *f* Antarctic expedition, expedition to the South Pole

'Süd·see *f* (South) Pacific; **~in·sel** *f* Pacific (*or* South Sea) island; **~in·su͵la·ner** *m* Pacific (*or* South Sea) islander

'Süd·sei·te *f* south (*or* southern) side

'Süd·staa·ten *pl.*: **die ~** the Southern States, the South; F *hum.* the Deep South; **'Süd·staat·ler** [-ʃta:tlɐ] *m* (-s; -) **1.** Southerner; **2.** *hist.* Confederate

'Süd·ti·ro·ler *m*, **'süd·ti·ro·le·risch** *adj.* South Tyrolean

süd·wärts ['zy:tvɛrts] *adv.* south(wards)

Süd'west *without art.*, **Süd'we·sten** *m* (**SW**) southwest (*abbr.* SW)

Süd·we·ster [zy:t'vɛstɐ] *m* (-s; -) sou'wester

süd'west·lich I. *adj.* southwest(ern); southwesterly *wind*; **II.** *adv.* (to the) southwest

'Süd·wind *m* south wind

Suff [zʊf] F *m* (-[e]s; *no pl.*) a) alcohol, b) F boozing; **sich dem ~ ergeben** F hit the bottle; **dem ~ verfallen** F on the bottle; **er hat es im ~ gesagt** he'd had a few when he said that

süf·feln ['zʏfəln] *v/i. and v/t.* (h) F tipple, booze

süf·fig ['zʏfɪç] *adj.* palatable; **dieser Wein ist sehr ~** *a.* this wine goes down well

süf·fi·sant [zʏfi'zant] *adj.* smug, complacent

Suf·fix [zʊ'fɪks] *n* (-es; -e) *ling.* suffix

Süff·ler ['zʏflɐ] F *m* (-s; -) F tippler

sug·ge·rie·ren [zʊge'ri:rən] *v/t.* (h) suggest; **j-m et. ~** persuade s.o. of s.th. (*or* that ...), talk s.o. into thinking (*or* believing) that ...

Sug·ge·sti·on [zʊgɛs'tĭo:n] *f* (-; -en) persuasion, suggestion

sug·ge·stiv [zʊgɛs'ti:f] *adj.* suggestive

Sug·ge'stiv·fra·ge *f* leading question

suh·len ['zu:lən] *v/refl.*: **sich ~** (h) wallow (*a. fig.*)

Süh·ne ['zy:nə] *f* (-; *no pl.*) expiation, atonement; penance; **~ leisten für** *acc.* do penance for

'süh·nen *v/t.* (h) expiate, atone for

'Süh·ne|op·fer *n* expiatory sacrifice; **~ter͵min** *m* ⚖ conciliation hearing; **~ver·such** *m* ⚖ attempt at reconciliation

Sui·te ['svi:tə] *f* (-; -n) **1.** suite (of rooms); **2.** ♪ suite

Sui·zid [zui'tsi:t] *m* (-[e]s; -e [-də]) suicide

sui'zid·ge·fähr·det *adj.* suicide-prone; **~ sein** *a.* have suicidal tendencies, be a potential suicide

Su·jet [zy'ʒe:] *n* (-s; -s) *art*: subject

Suk·zes·si·on [zʊktsɛ'sĭo:n] *f* (-; -en) succession; **apostolische ~** apostolic succession; **Suk·zes·si'ons·krieg** *m* war of succession

suk·zes·siv [zʊktsɛ'si:f] *adj.* gradual; **~e Veränderung** *a.* step-by-step change

suk·zes·si·ve [zʊktsɛ'si:və] *adv.* little by little, step by step

Sul·fat [zʊl'fa:t] *n* (-[e]s; -e) ⚗ sulphate, *Am.* sulfate

Sul·fid [zʊl'fi:t] *n* (-[e]s; -e [-də]) ⚗ sulphide, *Am.* sulfide

Sul·fit [zʊl'fi:t] *n* (-[e]s; -e) ⚗ sulphite, *Am.* sulfite

Sul·fon·amid [zʊlfona'mi:t] *n* (-[e]s; -e [-də]) *pharm.* sulphonamide, *Am.* sulfonamide; *pl. a.* sulpha (*Am.* sulfa) drugs

Sul·tan ['zʊlta:n] *m* (-s; -e) sultan

Sul·ta·nat [zʊlta'na:t] *n* (-[e]s; -e) sultanate

Sul·ta·nin [zʊl'ta:nɪn] *f* (-; -nen) sultana

Sul·ta·ni·ne [zʊlta'ni:nə] *f* (-; -n) sultana

Sül·ze ['zʏltsə] *f* (-; -n) jellied meat; aspic

sül·zen ['zʏltsən] F *v/i.* (h) F prattle on; F give a long spiel

sul·zig ['zʊltsɪç] *adj.* slushy

Sülz·ko·te,lett ['zʏlts-] *n* pork chop in aspic
Sulz·schnee ['zʊlts-] *m* slush, F porridge (snow)
Su·me·rer [zu'meːrɐ] *m* (-s; -), **su·me·risch** [zu'meːrɪʃ] *adj.*, **Su'me·risch** *n* (-en; *no pl.*) *hist.* Sumerian
sum·ma·risch [zʊ'maːrɪʃ] **I.** *adj.* summary (*a.* ⚖); **II.** *adv.* summarily
sum·ma sum·ma·rum ['zʊma zʊ'maːrʊm] *adv.* a) *cost etc.* in total, b) all in all, all things considered; ***der Umzug hat ~ DM 11500 gekostet*** the removal costs came to a (grand) total of 11500 marks
Sümm·chen ['zʏmçən] F *n* (-s; -): ***ein hübsches ~*** F a tidy little sum
Sum·me ['zʊmə] *f* (-; -n) sum; (sum) total; amount; *fig.* sum total
sum·men ['zʊmən] (h) **I.** *v/i. insect etc.*: buzz; hum (*a. v/t. a tune*); drone; ***vor sich hin ~*** hum away to oneself; **II.** ♀ *n* (-s; *no pl.*) buzz(ing); hum(ming); buzzing (*or* humming) noise
Sum·mer ['zʊmɐ] *m* (-s; -) ⚡ buzzer
sum·mie·ren [zʊ'miːrən] (h) **I.** *v/t.* add up; **II.** *v/refl.*: ***sich ~*** add (*or* mount) up (***auf*** *acc.*, ***zu*** *dat.* to); ***es summiert sich*** it all adds up
Summ|ton ['zʊm-] *m*, **~zei·chen** *n* buzz, buzzing signal; *teleph.* dialling (*Am.* dial) tone
Sumpf [zʊmpf] *m* (-[e]s; Sümpfe ['zʏmpfə]) marsh; swamp; bog; *fig.* quagmire; **~blü·te** F *fig. f* excrescence; **~bo·den** *m* marshy ground; **~dot·ter·blu·me** *f* marsh marigold
sump·fen ['zʊmpfən] F *v/i.* (h) F live it up
'**Sumpf|fie·ber** *n* ⚕ marsh fever, malaria; **~gas** *n* marsh gas; **~ge·biet** *n* marshland; swampland; **~huhn** *n* **1.** *zo.* crake; **2.** F *hum.* F boozer
sump·fig ['zʊmpfɪç] *adj.* marshy; swampy
'**Sumpf|land** *n* marshland; swampland; **~pflan·ze** *f* marsh plant; **~schild·krö·te** *f* mud turtle; **~vo·gel** *m* wader; **~wie·se** *f* marshy (*or* swampy) meadow
Sums [zʊms] F *m* (-es; *no pl.*) fuss, F carry-on; ***so ein ~*** what a carry-on; ***mach nicht solchen ~*** don't make such a fuss
Sund [zʊnt] *m* (-[e]s; -e [-də]) sound, strait
Sün·de ['zʏndə] *f* (-; -n) sin; ***e-e ~ begehen*** sin, commit a sin; ***e-e ~ gegen den guten Geschmack*** a sin against good taste; ***das ist doch keine ~*** it's no crime
'**Sün·den|ba·bel** *n* den of iniquity, hotbed of vice; **~be·kennt·nis** *n* confession of one's sins; **~bock** *m* scapegoat, F fall guy; ***j-n zum ~ machen*** use s.o. as a scapegoat; **~er·laß** *m* remission of sins, absolution; **~fall** *m* (-[e]s; *no pl.*) *the* Fall (of Man); **~kon·to** *n* → ***Sündenregister***; **~last** *f* burden of one's sins; **~pfuhl** *m* den of iniquity; **~re,gi·ster** F *n* list of sins (*or* transgressions)
Sün·der ['zʏndɐ] *m* (-s; -) sinner; ***armer ~*** poor wretch; F ***du alter ~!*** F you old devil!
sünd·haft ['zʏnthaft] **I.** *adj.* sinful, wicked; F *fig.* ***ein ~er Preis*** a shocking price; **II.** F *fig. adv.*: ***~ teuer*** shockingly expensive
sün·dig ['zʏndɪç] *adj.* sinful; guilty
sün·di·gen ['zʏndɪgən] *v/i.* (h) **1.** sin (***gegen*** *acc.* against); ***an j-m ~*** wrong s.o.; **2.** *fig. hum.* indulge, F sin
su·per ['zuːpɐ] F *adj. and int.* super, F great
Su·per(ben,zin) ['zuːpɐ-] *n* four-star (petrol), *Am.* premium
'**Su·per·ding** F *n* F (real) humdinger
'**su·per·ge·scheit** F *adj.* F incredibly clever; *iro.* F too clever by half; '**Su·per·ge·schei·te** *m, f* (-n; -n) F know-(it-)all
Su·per·in·ten·dent [zuːpɐˀɪntɛn'dɛnt] *m* (-en; -en) dean
'**su·per·klug** F *adj.* F too clever by half
Su·per·la·tiv ['zuːpɐlatiːf] *m* (-s; -e [-və]) *ling.* superlative (degree); *fig.* superlative; ***in ~en reden*** talk in superlatives
'**su·per·leicht** F *adj.* F dead easy; ***~ sein*** *a.* F be a cinch
'**Su·per·macht** *f pol.* superpower
'**Su·per·markt** *m* supermarket; hypermarket
'**su·per·mo,dern** F *adj.* ultramodern, hypermodern
Su·per·no·va [zupɐ'noːva] *f* (-; -vae [-vɛ]) *ast.* supernova
'**su·per·schick** F *adj.* very smart
'**su·per·schnell** F **I.** *adj.* F incredibly fast, *pred.* like greased lightning; **II.** *adv.* F quick as a flash, in no time
'**Su·per·star** *m* superstar
'**Su·per·tan·ker** *m* supertanker
Süpp·chen ['zʏpçən] *n* (-s; -): *fig.* ***sein eigenes ~ kochen*** do one's own thing; ***gern sein ~ am Feuer anderer kochen*** always try and cash in on other people
Sup·pe ['zʊpə] *f* (-; -n) soup; *fig.* ***die ~ auslöffeln müssen*** F have to face the music; ***j-m (sich) e-e schöne ~ einbrocken*** F get s.o. (o.s.) into a nice mess; ***j-m die ~ versalzen*** spoil s.o.'s (*or* all the) fun, F throw a spanner into the works
'**Sup·pen|fleisch** *n* meat for making soup; **~ge·mü·se** *n* vegetables for making soup; **~grün** *n bunch of herbs and vegetables for flavo(u)ring soup*; **~huhn** *n* boiling fowl; **~kel·le** *f* soup ladle; **~kno·chen** *m* soup bone; **~kü·che** *f* soup kitchen; **~löf·fel** *m* soup spoon; **~schüs·sel** *f* soup tureen; **~tas·se** *f* soup cup; **~tel·ler** *m* soup plate; **~ter,ri·ne** *f* (soup) tureen; **~wür·fel** *m* stock cube; **~wür·ze** *f* soup seasoning
Sup·ple·ment [zʊple'mɛnt] *n* (-[e]s; -e) supplement; **sup·ple·men·tär** [zʊplemɛn'tɛːɐ] *adj.* supplementary
Sup·ple'ment|band *m* (-[e]s; ⸚e) supplement(ary volume); **~win·kel** *m* 𝔄 supplementary angle
Su·pra·lei·ter ['zuːpralaɪtɐ] *m* (-s; -) ⚡ supraconductor
su·pra·na·tio'nal [zupra-] *adj.* supranational
Su·pre·mat [zupre'maːt] *m, n* (-[e]s; -e) supremacy
Surf·brett ['søːɐf-] *n* surfboard
sur·fen ['søːɐfən] *v/i.* (h) **1.** surf; **2.** windsurf; **Sur·fer** ['søːɐfɐ] *m* (-s; -) **1.** surfer; **2.** windsurfer
Sur·rea·lis·mus [zʊrea'lɪsmʊs] *m* (-; *no pl.*) surrealism; **Sur·rea·list** [zʊrea'lɪst] *m* (-en; -en) surrealist; **sur·rea·li·stisch** [zʊrea'lɪstɪʃ] *adj.* surrealistic(ally *adv.*), surrealist ...
sur·ren ['zʊrən] *v/i. camera, engine etc.*: whirr, *Am.* whir; hum; *insect*: buzz
Sur·ro·gat [zʊro'gaːt] *n* (-[e]s; -e) substitute, surrogate
su·spekt [zʊs'pɛkt] *adj.* suspect; dubious; ***er ist mir ~*** I'm not so sure about him
sus·pen·die·ren [zʊspɛn'diːrən] *v/t.* (h) suspend
sus·pen·siv [zʊspɛn'ziːf] *adj.*: ***~es Veto*** power of delay
Sus·pen·so·ri·um [zʊspɛn'zoːrĭʊm] *n* (-s; -rien) ⚕ suspensory; *sport*: athletic support
süß [zyːs] *adj.* sweet (*a.* F *fig.*); ***gern ~e Sachen essen*** have a sweet tooth; *fig.* ***~es Lächeln*** sugary smile; F ***~es Ding*** sweet little thing; **Sü·ße**[1] ['zyːsə] *f* (-; *no pl.*) sweetness; '**Sü·ße** *m, f* (-n; -n) F sweetie; **sü·ßen** ['zyːsən] *v/t.* (h) sweeten; add sugar to
'**Süß·holz** *n* liquorice; F ***~ raspeln*** F turn on the old charm
Sü·ßig·kei·ten ['zyːsɪçkaɪtən] *pl.* sweets, *Am.* candy *sg.*; ***gern ~ essen*** have a sweet tooth
'**Süß·kar,tof·fel** *f* sweet potato, yam
'**süß·lich** *adj.* **1.** sweetish, *contp.* sickly sweet; **2.** *fig.* sickly (sweet); mawkish; F ever so sweet *voice etc.*, *a.* sugary *smile*
'**Süß·most** *m* unfermented fruit juice
'**Süß·rahm·but·ter** *f* creamery butter
'**süß'sau·er** *adj.* **1.** *gastr.* sweet and sour; **2.** *fig.* forced *smile etc.*
'**Süß·spei·se** *f* sweet, dessert
'**Süß·stoff** *m* sweetener
'**Süß·wa·ren** *pl.* sweets, *Am.* candy *sg.*; **~ge·schäft** *n* sweet shop, *Am.* candy store
'**Süß·was·ser** *n* fresh (*or* sweet) water; **~fisch** *m* freshwater fish
'**Süß·wein** *m* dessert wine
Swim·ming·pool ['svɪmɪŋpuːl] *m* (-s; -s) (swimming) pool
Swing [svɪŋ] *m* (-[s]; -s) ♪ swing; **~ära** *f* swing era, era of swing
'**Swing·ge·schäft** *n* ✝ swing
Sy·ba·rit [zyba'riːt] *m* (-en; -en) sybarite
sy·ba·ri·tisch [zyba'riːtɪʃ] *adj.* sybaritic
syl·la·bisch [zʏ'laːbɪʃ] *adj.* syllabic(ally *adv.*)
Syl·lo·gis·mus [zʏlo'gɪsmʊs] *m* (-; -men) syllogism; **syl·lo·gi·stisch** [zʏlo'gɪstɪʃ] *adj.* syllogistic(ally *adv.*)
Syl·phe ['zʏlfə] *f* (-; -n) sylph; **Syl·phi·de** [zʏl'fiːdə] *f* (-n; -n) sylph; **syl'phi·den·haft** *adj. and adv.* sylph-like
Sym·bio·se [zʏm'bĭoːzə] *f* (-; -n) symbiosis; **sym·bio·tisch** [zʏm'bĭoːtɪʃ] *adj.* symbiotic(ally *adv.*)
Sym·bol [zʏm'boːl] *n* (-s; -e) symbol (***für*** *acc.* of *or gen.*); sign; badge; **~cha,rak·ter** *m* symbolic character; **~fi,gur** *f* symbolic figure (***für*** *acc.* for *or gen*), symbol (of)
sym'bol·haft *adj.* symbolic(al) (***für*** *acc.* of)
Sym·bo·lik [zʏm'boːlɪk] *f* (-; *no pl.*) symbolism; **sym·bo·lisch** [zʏm'boːlɪʃ] *adj.* symbolic(al) (***für*** *acc.* of); ***~er Beitrag*** token fee; **sym·bo·li·sie·ren** [zʏmboli'ziːrən] *v/t.* (h) symbolize; **Sym·bo·lis·mus** [zʏmbo'lɪsmʊs] *m* (-; *no pl.*) *art*: Symbolism
Sym'bol|kraft *f* (-; *no pl.*) symbolic power; **~spra·che** *f a. computer*: symbolic language
sym'bol·träch·tig *adj.* highly (*or* deeply) symbolic; steeped in symbolism; **Sym'bol·träch·tig·keit** *f* (-; *no pl.*) highly symbolic nature; deep symbolism
Sym·me·trie [zʏme'triː] *f* (-; -n) symmetry (*a. fig.*); **~ach·se** *f* 𝔄 symmetric axis; **~ebe·ne** *f* 𝔄 plane of symmetry
sym·me·trisch [zʏ'meːtrɪʃ] *adj.* symmetric(al)
Sym·pa·thie [zʏmpa'tiː] *f* (-; -n) a) liking;

sympathy, b) support; ***bei aller ~*** much as I like him *etc.*; ***große ~n genießen bei*** *dat.* be very popular among, be well-liked among; ***der Plan hat m-e volle ~*** the plan has my full support (*or* backing); ***ihre ~n liegen bei*** *dat.* her sympathies are (*or* lie) with; **~kund·ge·bung** *f* demonstration of support; **~streik** *m* sympathy (*or* sympathetic) strike; sympathetic action; **~trä·ger** *m* sympathetic figure

Sym·pa·thi·kus [zʏm'pa:tikʊs] *m* (-; *no pl.*) sympathetic nerve

Sym·pa·thi·sant [zʏmpati'zant] *m* (-en; -en) sympathizer

sym·pa·thisch [zʏm'pa:tɪʃ] *adj.* **1.** likeable, (very) pleasant, personable, F (very) nice; *fig.* pleasant, engaging, F nice *smile, voice etc.*; ***er ist mir ~*** I think he's nice, I quite like him; ***er ist mir überhaupt nicht ~*** I just don't like him (F go for him); ***die Sache ist mir nicht ~*** I don't like it; **2.** *physiol.* sympathetic

sym·pa·thi·sie·ren [zʏmpati'zi:rən] *v/i.* (h): ***~ mit*** *dat.* sympathize with; ***mit den Kommunisten*** *etc.* ~ *a.* be a Communist *etc.* sympathizer

Sym·pho·nie(...) [zʏmfo'ni:] → ***Sinfonie(...)***; **sym·pho·nisch** [zʏm'fo:nɪʃ] *adj.* → ***sinfonisch***

Sym·po·si·on [zʏm'po:zĭɔn] *n* (-s; -sien), **Sym·po·si·um** [zʏm'po:zĭʊm] *n* (-s; -sien) symposium

Sym·ptom [zʏmp'to:m] *n* (-s; -e) *a. fig.* symptom (***für*** *acc.* of); ***~e zeigen von*** *dat. a.* show signs of

Sym·pto·ma·tik [zʏmpto'ma:tɪk] *f* (-; *no pl.*) **1.** ⚕ symptoms *pl.*; **2.** symptomatology; **sym·pto·ma·tisch** [zʏmpto'ma:tɪʃ] *adj. a. fig.* symptomatic (***für*** *acc.* of)

Syn·ago·ge [zyna'go:gə] *f* (-; -n) synagogue

Syn·ap·se [zy'napsə] *f* (-; -n) *physiol.* synapse

Syn·äs·the·sie [zynɛste'zi:] *f* (-; -n) syn(a)esthesia

syn·chron [zʏn'kro:n] **I.** *adj.* synchronous; *ling. etc.* synchronic; **II.** *adv.*: ***~ laufen*** (*or* ***gehen, geschaltet sein***) be synchronized

Syn'chron|aus·strah·lung *f TV, radio*: simulcast; **~ge·trie·be** *n mot.* synchromesh (gear)

Syn·chro·ni·sa·ti·on [zʏnkroniza'tsĭo:n] *f* (-; -en) synchronization; *film*: *a.* dubbing; **syn·chro·ni·sie·ren** [zʏnkroni'zi:rən] *v/t.* (h) synchronize; *film*: *a.* dub, F sync; **syn·chro·ni·siert** [zʏnkroni'zi:ɐt] *adj.* synchronized; *film*: *a.* dubbed; ***~e Fassung*** dubbed version; ***der Film ist ~*** the film has been dubbed

Syn'chron|schal·tung *f mot.* synchronized gear change; **~spre·cher** *m* dubber; **~stim·me** *f* **1.** dubbing voice; **2.** dubbed voice

Syn·di·kat [zʏndi'ka:t] *n* (-[e]s; -e) syndicate; ***zu e-m ~ zusammenschließen*** syndicate

Syn·di·kus ['zʏndikʊs] *m* (-; -se, -dizi [-ditsi]) company lawyer, legal adviser, *Am.* corporation counsel

Syn·drom [zʏn'dro:m] *n* (-[e]s; -e) ⚕ *and w.s.* syndrome

syn·er·ge·tisch [zynɛr'ge:tɪʃ] *adj.* synergetic; **Syn·er·gie** [zynɛr'gi:] *f* (-; -n) synergy

Syn·ko·pe [zʏn'ko:pə] *f* (-; -n) **1.** ♪ syncopation; **2.** *ling.* syncope

Syn·kre·tis·mus [zʏnkre'tɪsmʊs] *m* (-; *no pl.*) syncretism; **syn·kre·ti·stisch** [zʏnkre'tɪstɪʃ] *adj.* syncretic

Syn·ode [zy'no:də] *f* (-; -n) synod

Syn·onym [zyno'ny:m] **I.** *n* (-s; -e, Synonyma [zy'no:nyma]) *ling.* synonym; **II.** ♀ *adj.* synonymous (**zu** *dat.* with)

Syn·ony·mik [zyno'ny:mɪk] *f* (-; *no pl.*) **1.** synonymics *pl*; **2.** → **Syn·onym·wör·ter·buch** *n* dictionary of synonyms; thesaurus

Syn·op·se [zy'nɔpsə] *f* (-; -n), **Syn·op·sis** ['zy:nɔpsɪs] *f* (-; -sen) synopsis

Syn·op·ti·ker [zy'nɔptikɐ] *m* (-s; -) Synoptist

syn·op·tisch [zy'nɔptɪʃ] *adj.* synoptic(ally *adv.*); ***die ~en Evangelien*** the synoptic Gospels

Syn·tag·ma [zʏn'tagma] *n* (-s; -men) *ling.* syntagm; **syn·tag·ma·tisch** [zʏnta'gma:tɪʃ] *adj.* syntagmatic(ally *adv.*)

syn·tak·tisch [zʏn'taktɪʃ] *adj. ling.* syntactic(al)

Syn·tax ['zʏntaks] *f* (-; *no pl.*) syntax; **~feh·ler** *m* syntax (*or* syntactical) error

Syn·the·se [zʏn'te:zə] *f* (-; -n) synthesis

Syn·the·si·zer ['zʏntəsaɪzɐ] *m* (-s; -) synthesizer

Syn·the·tik [zʏn'te:tɪk] *f* (-; *no pl.*) synthetic (fibre [*Am.* fiber]), man-made fibre (*Am.* fiber); ***das ist alles ~*** it's all synthetic(s); **syn·the·tisch** [zʏn'te:tɪʃ] **I.** *adj.* synthetic; **II.** *adv.*: ***~ herstellen*** produce synthetically

Sy·phi·lis ['zy:fɪlɪs] *f* (-; *no pl.*) ⚕ syphilis; **Sy·phi·li·ti·ker** [zyfi'li:tikɐ] *m* (-s; -) syphilitic; **sy·phi·li·tisch** [zyfi'li:tɪʃ] *adj.* syphilitic

Sy·rer ['zy:rɐ] *m* (-s; -), **Sy·re·rin** ['zy:rərɪn] *f* (-; -nen), **sy·risch** ['zy:rɪʃ] *adj.* Syrian; **'Sy·risch** *n* (-en; *no pl.*) *hist. ling.* (*a.* ***das ~e***) Syriac

Sy·stem [zʏs'te:m] *n* (-s; -e) a) system; method, b) 🚂 *etc.* system, network; ***mit ~ arbeiten*** work systematically (*or* methodically); ***da ist überhaupt kein ~ drin*** there's absolutely no system to it, it's completely unsystematic; ***dahinter steckt ~*** there's method in (*or* to) it; ***in ein ~ bringen*** systematize; **~ana̦ly·se** *f* systems analysis; **~ana̦ly·ti·ker** *m* systems analyst

Sy·ste·ma·tik [zʏste'ma:tɪk] *f* (-; -en) **1.** system, method; **2.** *no pl.* systematics *pl.*

Sy·ste·ma·ti·ker [zʏste'ma:tikɐ] *m* (-s; -) systematist; *w.s.* systematic person

sy·ste·ma·tisch [zʏste'ma:tɪʃ] *adj.* systematic(ally *adv.*), methodical

sy·ste·ma·ti·sie·ren [zʏstemati'zi:rən] *v/t.* (h) systematize

sy'stem|feind·lich *adj.* subversive; **~im·ma̦nent** *adj.* inherent in a (*or* the) system

sy·ste·misch [zʏs'te:mɪʃ] *adj. biol.* systemic

sy'stem·kon̦form *adj.* (politically) conformist

Sy'stem·kri̦tik *f* criticism of the system

Sy'stem·kri·ti·ker *m* dissident

sy'stem·kri·tisch *adj.* dissident ...

sy'stem·los *adj.* unsystematic, unmethodical

Sy'stem|ver·än·de·rung *f* change in the system; **~zwang** *m* imposed conformism; ***unter ~ leben*** be forced to conform

Sze·na·rio [tse'na:rĭo] *n* (-s; -s) scenario

Sze·ne ['tse:nə] *f* (-; -n) **1.** scene (*a. thea. and fig.*); *thea. and fig.* ***in ~ setzen*** stage; *fig.* ***sich in ~ setzen*** draw attention to o.s., put o.s. into the limelight; ***die ~ betreten*** come on the scene; ***(j-m) e-e ~ machen*** make a scene; **2.** *political, literary* scene; F ***die ~*** alternative society; ***er kennt sich in der ~ aus*** he knows the scene

'Sze·nen|bei·fall *m* spontaneous applause; **~bild** *n* (stage) set, stage setting; **~wech·sel** *m* scene change; *fig.* change of scene

Sze·ne·rie [tsenə'ri:] *f* (-; -n) **1.** *a. thea.* scenery; **2.** *fig.* setting

sze·nisch ['tse:nɪʃ] **I.** *adj.* scenic; ***~e Darstellung*** a) staging, b) stage presentation; **II.** *adv.* scenically; ***~ darstellen*** stage, put on stage

Szep·ter ['stsɛptɐ] *n* (-s; -) sceptre (*Am.* scepter)

Szyl·la ['stsʏla] *f*: ***zwischen ~ und Charybdis*** between Scylla and Charybdis, between the devil and the deep blue sea

T

T, t [teː] *n* (-; -) T, t
Ta·bak ['taːbak] *m* (-s; -e) tobacco; **~ge·schäft** *n* tobacconist's, *Am.* cigar store; **~händ·ler** *m* tobacconist; **~la·den** *m* tobacconist's, *Am.* cigar store; **~mi·schung** *f* blend of tobacco; **~plan·ta·ge** *f* tobacco plantation; **~qualm** *m*, **~rauch** *m* tobacco smoke
'Ta·baks|beu·tel *m* tobacco pouch; **~do·se** *f* tobacco tin; snuffbox
'Ta·bak|steu·er *f* tobacco duty; **~ver·gif·tung** *f* nicotine poisoning; **~wa·ren** *pl.* tobacco products; cigarettes and tobacco; (*sign*) tobacconist
ta·bel·la·risch [tabɛ'laːrɪʃ] *adj.* tabular, tabulated; **ta·bel·la·ri·sie·ren** [tabɛlari'ziːrən] *v/t.* (h) tabulate; **Ta·bel·le** [ta'bɛlə] *f* (-; -n) table; chart; *sport and fig.* league table
Ta'bel·len|en·de *n*: **(am ~** at the) bottom of the league (*or* table); **~er·ste** *m, f* (-n; -n) league leaders *pl.*; **~r sein** *a.* be (at the) top of the table (*or* league); **~form** *f*: **in ~** in tabular form, tabulated; **~füh·rer** *m* → ***Tabellenerste***; **~letz·te** *m, f* (-n; -n) bottom team; **~r sein** *a.* be at the bottom of the table (*or* league); **~spit·ze** *f*: **(an der ~** at the) top of the league (*or* table)
ta·bel·lie·ren [tabɛ'liːrən] *v/t.* (h) tabulate; **Ta·bel·lier·ma·schi·ne** [tabɛ'liːʁ-] *f* tabulator
Ta·ber·na·kel [tabɛr'naːkəl] *m, n* (-s; -) *eccl.* tabernacle
Ta·blett [ta'blɛt] *n* (-[e]s; -s, -e) tray; F *fig.* ***j-m et. auf e-m silbernen ~ servieren*** hand s.th. to s.o. on a platter; F ***soll ich es dir auf e-m silbernen ~ servieren?*** F not good enough for you, is it?; F ***das kommt nicht aufs ~*** that's out of the question
Ta·blet·te [ta'blɛtə] *f* (-; -n) tablet, pill; **Ta'blet·ten·form** *f*: ***in ~*** in tablets, in tablet form; **ta'blet·ten·süch·tig** *adj.* addicted to pills; **~ *sein*** *a.* F be a pill popper; **Ta'blet·ten·süch·ti·ge** *m, f* (-n; -n) pill addict, F pill popper
ta·bu [ta'buː] *adj.* taboo; **~ *sein*** *a.* F be a no-no; ***das Thema ist für sie ~*** it's a taboo topic with her; **Ta'bu** *n* (-s; -s) taboo; ***ein ~ brechen*** break a taboo; **ta'bu·frei** *adj.*: ***~e Gesellschaft*** permissive society; **ta·bui·sie·ren** [tabui'ziːrən] *v/t.* (h) (put under) taboo
ta·bu·la ra·sa ['taːbula 'raːza]: **(*mit et.*) ~ *machen*** make a clean sweep (of it)
Ta·bu·la·tor [tabu'laːtoːʁ] *m* (-s; -en [-la'toːrən]) tabulator
Ta'bu|schran·ke *f* taboo (barrier); ***~n niederreißen*** break down taboos; **~ver·let·zung** *f* breaking (*or* infringement) of a taboo; **~wort** *n* (-[e]s; ⸗er) taboo word

Ta·che·les: ['taxələs] F **~ *reden*** F talk turkey (***mit*** *dat.* with)
Ta·cho ['taxo] F *m* (-s; -s), **Ta·cho·me·ter** [taxo'meːtɐ] *m, n* (-s; -) *mot.* speedometer; **Ta·cho'me·ter·stand** *m* mileometer reading; number of kilomet|res (*Am.* -ers) *or* miles clocked up
Ta·chy·kar·die [taxykar'diː] *f* (-; -n) ⚕ tachycardia
Ta·del ['taːdəl] *m* (-s; -) a) reprimand; reproach; criticism, b) blemish, fault, flaw; ***ihn trifft kein ~*** he's not to blame; ***über jeden ~ erhaben, lit. ohne ~*** beyond (*or* above) reproach; **'ta·del·los** *adj.* flawless, perfect (*a.* F *fig.*); ***das ist doch ~*** *a.* there's nothing wrong with it; **'ta·deln** *v/t.* (h) rebuke, reprove; reprimand, scold; criticize; find fault with, carp at; disapprove of; **'ta·delnd** *adj.* reproachful; **'ta·delns·wert** *adj.* reproachable, reprehensible
Ta·fel ['taːfəl] *f* (-; -n) **1.** a) *ped.* (black)-board, chalkboard, b) notice (*Am.* bulletin) board, c) plate, d) (*stone*) slab; slate; *hist.* tablet; (*wood*) panel; (*commemorative*) plaque; (*tin*) sheet, e) control panel, console, f) bar *of chocolate*; ***et. an die ~ schreiben*** write s.th. (up) on the (black)board; **2.** *lit.* (dinner) table; ***j-n zur ~ bitten*** ask s.o. to table; ***die ~ aufheben*** rise from table; → ***Anzeigetafel***; **~ap·fel** *m* eating (*or* dessert) apple; **~berg** *m* table mountain; **~be·steck** *n* best cutlery (*or* silver); **~bild** *n* panel painting; **⁓fer·tig** *adj.* ready to serve; **~freu·den** *lit. pl.* culinary delights; **~ge·schirr** *n* (best) china; **~glas** *n* sheet glass; plate glass; **~land** *n* (-[e]s; ⸗er) tableland, plateau; **~lap·pen** *m* (blackboard *or* chalkboard) cloth; **~ma·le·rei** *f* panel painting; **~mu·sik** *f* table music
ta·feln ['taːfəln] *v/i.* (h) dine; banquet
tä·feln ['tɛːfəln] *v/t.* (h) panel
'Ta·fel|obst *n* dessert fruit; **~öl** *n* salad oil; **~run·de** *f* (company at) table; ***König Artus und die ~*** King Arthur and the Knights of the Round Table; **~salz** *n* table salt; **~sil·ber** *n* silver(ware)
Tä·fe·lung ['tɛːfəlʊŋ] *f* (-; -en) panel(l)ing, wainscoting
'Ta·fel|was·ser *n* table water; **~wein** *m* table wine
Taft [taft] *m* (-[e]s; -e) taffeta
Tag [taːk] *m* (-[e]s; -e ['taːgə]) **1.** day; ***am*** (*or* ***bei***) ***~e*** a) during the day, in the daytime, b) in daylight; ***dreimal am ~*** three times a day; ***am nächsten ~*** the next day; ***am ~ zuvor*** the day before; ***an jenem ~*** on that (particular) day; ***e-s ~es*** a) one day, b) some day; ***welcher ~ ist heute?*** what day is it today?; ***ein ~ wie jeder andere*** a perfectly ordinary day; ***es wird ~*** it's getting light; ***früh am ~e*** early in the day; ***den ganzen ~*** all day (long); ***den lieben langen ~*** the livelong day; ***~ für ~, ~ um ~*** day after day; ***er wird ~ für ~ besser*** he's getting better every day (*or* from day to day, day by day); ***von ~ zu ~*** from day to day; ***von e-m ~ auf den andern*** from one day to the next, overnight; ***~ und Nacht*** day and night; ***es ist ein Unterschied wie ~ und Nacht*** there's absolutely no comparison; ***ein ~ um den anderen, jeden zweiten ~*** every other day; ***es müßte jeden ~ da sein*** it should be here any day; ***dieser ~e*** a) the other day, b) these days; ***auf*** (*or.* ***für***) ***ein paar ~e*** for a couple of days; ***freier ~*** day off; ***~ der Arbeit*** Labo(u)r Day; ⚒ ***unter ~e*** underground; ***über ~e*** above ground; ***guten ~!*** (good) morning, good afternoon, F hello, hi; *introduction*: how d'you do; (***bei j-m***) ***guten ~ sagen*** pop in and say hello (to s.o.); ***an den ~ bringen*** (***kommen***) bring (come) to light; ***an den ~ legen*** display, show; ***bei ~e besehen*** on closer inspection; ***jetzt wird's ~!*** I don't believe it!; ***er hat bessere ~e gesehen*** he's seen better times (*or* days); ***s-e großen ~e sind vorüber*** he's had his heyday; ***das waren goldene ~e*** those were the days; ***auf den ~*** (***genau***) to the day; ***auf den ~ genau ankommen*** *present etc.*: arrive right on the day; ***bis auf den heutigen ~*** to this day; ***in den ~ hinein leben*** live from day to day; ***in den ~ hinein reden*** F talk off the top of one's head; ***er hat s-n guten*** (***schlechten***) ***~*** he's in a good (bad) mood today; ***heute hab' ich keinen guten ~*** it's not my day today, it's an off day for me today; ***sich e-n guten ~ machen*** have an easy day of it; ***sich ein paar schöne ~e machen*** go off and enjoy o.s. for a couple of days; F ***das dauert ewig und drei ~e*** F it's taking an age and a half; ***es ist noch nicht aller ~e Abend*** it's early days yet; → ***Abend, acht*** I, ***jüngst*** I, ***Tür, vierzehn, zutage***; **2.** F *pl.* ⚕ period; F ***sie hat ihre ~e*** she's got her period, it's that time of the month (for her); F ***wann kriegst du d-e ~e?*** when's your period due?
'tag·ak·tiv *adj. zo.* diurnal
tag'aus *adv.* → ***tagein***
'Tag·blind·heit *f* day blindness
Ta·ge|bau ['taːgə-] *m* (-[e]s; *no pl.*) ⚒ opencast (*Am.* strip) mining; **~blatt** *n* daily (paper); **~buch** *n* diary; **~dieb** *obs. m* idler; **~geld** *n* daily allowance
tag'ein *adv.*: **~, *tagaus*** day in, day out
ta·ge·lang ['taːgə-] **I.** *adj.* lasting for days; endless; **II.** *adv.* for days (and days), for days on end

Ta·ge·lohn ['ta:gə-] *m* daily wage; ***im ~ arbeiten*** work by the day; '**Ta·ge·löh·ner** [-løːnɐ] *m* (-s; -) day labo(u)rer

ta·gen ['ta:gən] *v/i.* (h) **1.** have a meeting (*or* conference), sit (in conference); ⚖, *parl.* be in session; F *fig.* ***bis in den Morgen ~*** F have an all-night conference; **2.** *lit.* ***es tagt*** *lit.* day (*or* dawn) is breaking, day is dawning

Ta·ge·rei·se ['ta:gə-] *f* day's journey

Ta·ges|ab·lauf ['ta:gəs-] *m* day; ***gewöhnlicher ~*** daily (*or* day-to-day) routine; **~an·bruch** *m* daybreak; ***bei ~*** at daybreak, at dawn, at the first light of day; **~aus·flug** *m* day trip; **~be·richt** *m* daily report (*or* bulletin); **~creme** *f* day cream; **~decke** *f* bedspread, counterpane; **~ein·nah·me** *f* day's takings *pl.*; **~er·eig·nis·se** *pl.* events of the day; *TV etc. the* day's *or* today's news *sg.* (and current affairs); ***ein Blick auf die ~*** a look at what's been happening in the news today; **~fahrt** *f* day trip; **~form** *f sport etc.*: form on the day; **~frist** *f*: ***binnen ~*** within a day; **~ge·richt** *n gastr.* dish of the day; **~ge·sche·hen** *n* → ***Tagesereignisse***; **~ge·spräch** *n the* talk of the day; ***... war das ~*** *a.* everyone was talking about ..., ... was topic number one; **~höchst·tem·pe·ra,tu·ren** *pl.* maximum temperatures (of the day); **~kar·te** *f* **1.** day ticket; **2.** *gastr.* menu for the day; today's menu; **~kas·se** *f* **1.** *thea. etc.* box office; **2.** day's takings *pl.*; **~kind** *n* day-care child; **~kopf·ver·brauch** *m* daily per capita consumption; **~kurs** *m* a) (today's *or the* day's) rate of exchange, b) current price; **~lei·stung** *f* daily output

Ta·ges·licht ['ta:gəs-] *n* (-[e]s; *no pl.*) daylight; ***bei ~*** a) in (the) daylight, b) before dark; ***das ~ scheuen*** shun the daylight, *fig.* have s.th. to hide; *fig.* ***ans ~ kommen*** come to light, become known; ***ans ~ bringen*** bring to light, expose, bring out into the open; **~auf·nah·me** *f* daylight shot (*or* exposure); **~film** *m* daylight film; **~pro,jek·tor** *m* overhead projector

Ta·ges|marsch ['ta:gəs-] *m* day's march; **~mut·ter** *f* childminder; **~ord·nung** *f* (*the* day's) agenda; ***(ganz oben) auf der ~ stehen*** be (high) on the agenda; ***zur ~ übergehen*** a) proceed to the order of the day, F get down to business, b) get on with things again; ***wir gingen wieder zur ~ über*** F it was business as usual; *fig.* ***an der ~ sein*** be nothing unusual; ***das ist hier an der ~*** *a.* it happens all the time around here; **~ord·nungs·punkt** *m* item on the agenda; **~pen·sum** *n* daily quota (F stint); **~po·li,tik** *f* day-to-day politics *pl.*; **~preis** *m* current (market) price; **~pres·se** *f* daily press; **~ra·ti,on** *f* daily ration(s *pl.*); **~raum** *m* dayroom; **~rück·fahr·kar·te** *f* day return (ticket); **~satz** *m* a) daily rate, b) daily ration(s *pl.*); **~stät·te** *f* day-care cent|re (*Am.* -er); **~sup·pe** *f gastr.* soup of the day; **~tem·pe·ra,tur** *f* temperature; **~tour** *f* day trip; **~,um·satz** *m* ✝ **1.** daily turnover; **2.** *the* day's turnover; **~zeit** *f* time of day; ***zu jeder ~*** any time of the day; ***zu jeder Tages- und Nachtzeit*** any time of the day or night; ***er ruft zu jeder Tages- und Nachtzeit an*** he'll ring up in the middle of the night if he feels like it; **~zei·tung** *f* daily (newspaper)

Ta·ge·tes [ta'geːtɛs] *f* (-; -) ⚘ French marigold

ta·ge·wei·se ['ta:gə-] *adv.* a) on a day-to-day basis, b) on certain days

Ta·ge·werk ['ta:gə-] *lit. n* (-[e]s; *no pl.*) day's work; ***sein ~ verrichtet haben*** have done one's work for the day

'**Tag·fal·ter** *m* butterfly

'**tag'hell** *adj.* (as) light as day

täg·lich ['tɛːklɪç] **I.** *adj.* a) daily, b) everyday; ***sein ~ Brot verdienen*** earn a living; ***das ist mein ~ Brot*** a) that's my bread and butter, b) it's all part and parcel; ***so wichtig wie das ~e Brot*** as important as the air we breathe; **II.** *adv.* every day, daily; ✝ *a.* per day, per diem; ***zweimal ~*** twice a day; ***sie arbeitet ~ drei Stunden*** she does three hours' work a day, she goes to work for three hours a (*or* every) day

tags [ta:ks] *adv.*: ***~ darauf*** the following day, the day after; ***~ zuvor*** the day before

'**Tag·schicht** *f* day shift; ***~ haben*** be on day shift

tags·über ['ta:ksˀy:bɐ] *adv.* during the day

'**tag'täg·lich I.** *adv.* every day; day in, day out; **II.** *adj.* daily, day-to-day; everyday

'**Tag·traum** *m* daydream; '**tag·träu·men** *v/i.* (h) daydream; fantasize; '**Tag·träu·mer** *m* daydreamer

'**Tag·und'nacht|be·trieb** *m* 24-hour (*or* round-the-clock) service; **~glei·che** *f* equinox

Ta·gung ['ta:gʊŋ] *f* (-; -en) conference, convention

'**Ta·gungs|be·richt** *m* (conference) proceedings *pl.*; **~ort** *m* conference venue

Tai·fun [taɪ'fu:n] *m* (-s; -e) typhoon

Tail·le ['taljə] *f* (-; -n) waist; ***auf ~ gearbeitet*** close-fitting at the waist; **tail·liert** [ta'ji:ɐt] *adj.* waisted

Tai·wa·ne·se [taɪva'ne:zə] *m* (-n; -n), **Tai·wa·ne·sin** [taɪva'ne:zɪn] *f* (-; -nen), **tai·wa·ne·sisch** [taɪva'ne:zɪʃ] *adj.* Taiwanese

Ta·ke·la·ge [takə'la:ʒə] *f* (-; -n) ⚓ rigging

Takt [takt] *m* (-[e]s; -e) **1.** ♪ bar; (*waltz etc.*) time; rhythm; ***3/4-~*** three-four time; ***ein paar ~e*** a couple of bars; ***den ~ schlagen*** beat time; ***den ~ halten, im ~ bleiben*** a) keep time, b) *rowing*: keep stroke; ***aus dem ~*** out of time; ***aus dem ~ kom·men*** lose the beat, *fig.* be put off one's stroke; *fig.* ***j-n aus dem ~ bringen*** put s.o. off his (*or* her) stroke, F throw s.o.; **2.** *mot.* stroke; ⚡ cycle; **3.** *no pl.* → ***Taktgefühl***; **~art** *f* time; **~fre,quenz** *f computer*: clock frequency (*or* rate); **~ge·ber** *m* ♪ metronome; *computer*: clock; **~ge·fühl** *n* (-[e]s; *no pl.*) tact(fulness)

tak·tie·ren [tak'ti:rən] *v/i.* (h) manoeuvre, *Am.* maneuver; ***geschickt ~*** make the right moves, be a good (*or* skilled) tactician

Tak·tik ['taktɪk] *f* (-; -en) tactics *pl.* (*a. sg., fig. nur pl. konstr.*); ***die ~ ändern*** change tactics; **Tak·ti·ker** ['taktikɐ] *m* (-s; -) tactician

'**Takt·im,puls** *m computer*: clock pulse

tak·tisch ['taktɪʃ] **I.** *adj.* tactical (*a. fig.*); **II.** *adv.*: ***~ vorgehen*** use tactics; ***das war ~ geschickt*** that was a clever move, that was good tactics; ***er ist ~ geschickt*** he's a good (*or* skilled) tactician

'**takt·los** *adj.* tactless, indiscreet; ***er ist ein ~er Mensch*** *a.* he has no sense of tact; '**Takt·lo·sig·keit** *f* (-; -en) **1.** *no pl.* tactlessness; **2.** indiscretion; ***das war e-e ~*** that was a tactless thing to say (*or* do)

'**Takt·stock** *m* baton

'**takt·voll** *adj.* tactful, diplomatic, discreet

Tal [ta:l] *n* (-[e]s; Täler ['tɛ:lɐ]) valley; *fig.* ***sich in e-m ~ befinden*** *economy etc.*: be in (*or* have reached) a trough

tal'ab·wärts *adv.* down (in)to the valley

Ta·lar [ta'la:ɐ] *m* (-s; -e [-rə]) ⚖ robe, gown (*a. univ.*); *eccl.* cassock

Ta·lent [ta'lɛnt] *n* (-[e]s; -e) **1.** talent, gift; ***musikalisches ~*** musical talent, a gift for music; **2.** talented person; *pl.* talent *sg.*; ***sie ist ein echtes ~*** she's got a gift, F she's brilliant; **ta·len·tiert** [talɛn'ti:ɐt] *adj.* talented, gifted

Ta'lent|su·che *f* search for (new) talent; **~su·cher** *m* talent scout; *sport*: scout

ta'lent·voll *adj.* talented, gifted

Ta·ler ['ta:lɐ] *m* (-s; -) *hist.* t(h)aler

'**Tal·fahrt** *f* descent; *mot. and skiing*: *a.* downhill run; *fig.* decline, ✝ *a.* downward trend, *a.* (downward) slide *of a currency*

Talg [talk] *m* (-[e]s; *no pl.*) a) *gastr.* suet, b) tallow, c) *physiol.* sebum; **~drü·se** *f anat.* sebaceous gland

Ta·lis·man ['ta:lɪsman] *m* (-s; -e) lucky charm

Talk [talk] *m* (-[e]s; *no pl.*) talcum (powder), talc

'**Tal·kes·sel** *m* valley basin, hollow

Talk·mas·ter ['tɔ:kma:stɐ] *m* (-s; -) chat-show (*Am.* talk-show) host

Talk-Show ['tɔ:kʃo:] *f* chat (*Am.* talk) show

Tal·mi ['talmi] *n* (-s; *no pl.*) pinchbeck; *fig. a.* cheap imitation(s *pl.*); **~glanz** *m* false glitter; **~wa·re** *f* cheap imitation(s *pl.*), fake(s *pl.*)

Tal·mud ['talmu:t] *m* (-s; *no pl.*) Talmud; **tal·mu·disch** [tal'mu:dɪʃ] *adj.* Talmudic; ***~e Weisheiten*** Talmudic sayings, sayings from the Talmud

'**Tal|mul·de** *f* → ***Talkessel***; **~ski** *m* lower ski; **~soh·le** *f* bottom of a (*or* the) valley; *fig.* ✝ trough ; *fig.* ***die ~ erreichen*** bottom out; ***die ~ durchschreiten*** go through a trough; **~sper·re** *f* dam; **~sta·ti,on** *f* base terminal

tal·wärts ['ta:lvɛrts] *adv.* a) downhill, b) downstream; → *a.* ***talabwärts***

Ta·ma·rin·de [tama'rɪndə] *f* (-; -n) ⚘ tamarind

Ta·ma·ris·ke [tama'rɪskə] *f* (-; -n) ⚘ tamarisk

Tam·bu·rin [tambu'ri:n] *n* (-s; -e) ♪ tambourine

Ta·mi·le [ta'mi:lə] *m* (-n; -n), **Ta·mi·lin** [ta'mi:lɪn] *f* (-; -nen), **ta·mi·lisch** [ta'mi:lɪʃ] *adj.*, **Ta'mi·lisch** *n* (-en; *no pl.*) *ling.* Tamil

Tam·pon ['tampɔn, tam'po:n] *m* (-s; -s) tampon; ⚕ swab; **tam·po·nie·ren** [tampo'ni:rən] *v/t.* (h) plug, tampon

Tam·tam [tam'tam] *n* (-s; *no pl.*) a) fuss, F to-do, b) F ballyhoo; ***mit großem ~*** *celebrate etc.* with great fanfare

Tand [tant] *m* (-s; *no pl.*) trinkets *pl.*; rubbish

Tän·de·lei [tɛndə'laɪ] *f* (-; -en) dilly-dallying; flirting; **tän·deln** ['tɛndəln] *v/i.* (h) play around; flirt

Tan·dem ['tandɛm] *n* (-s; -s) tandem; *fig. a.* twosome

Tang [taŋ] *m* (-s; *no pl.*) ⚘ seaweed

Tan·ga·hös·chen ['taŋga-] *n* G-string, cache-sexe
Tan·gen·te [taŋ'gɛntə] *f* (-; -n) **1.** A tangent; **2.** expressway
tan·gen·ti·al [taŋgɛn'tsĭa:l] *adj.* tangential; **Tan·gen·ti'al(ton)arm** *m* linear tracking (tone)arm
tan·gie·ren [taŋ'gi:rən] *v/t.* (h) **1.** affect; ***das tangiert mich nicht*** that has nothing to do with me; **2.** touch on *a subject etc.*; **3.** A be tangent to
Tan·go ['taŋgo] *m* (-s; -s) tango; **~ *tanzen*** (do the) tango
Tank [taŋk] *m* (-s; -s) tank (*a.* ⚔), container; **~deckel** *m mot.* fuel cap
tan·ken ['taŋkən] (h) **I.** *v/t.* fill up with; F *fig.* ***frische Luft ~*** get some (F a lungful of) fresh air; ***Kräfte ~*** build up one's strength; **II.** *v/i.* tank (up); ✈ refuel; F tank up
Tan·ker ['taŋkɐ] *m* (-s; -) ⚓ oil tanker
'Tank|fahr·zeug *n* tanker (lorry *Brit.*); **~flug·zeug** *n* refueller; **~last·zug** *m* tanker (lorry *Brit.*); **~säu·le** *f* petrol (*Am.* gas) pump; **~schiff** *n* tanker; **~stel·le** *f* filling (*or* petrol) station, *Am.* filling (*or* gas) station; **~ver·schluß** *m mot.* fuel cap; **~wa·gen** *m* tanker (lorry *Brit.*); **~wart** *m* petrol pump (*Am.* gas station) attendant
Tan·ne ['tanə] *f* (-; -n) fir (tree)
'Tan·nen|baum *m* **1.** fir (tree); **2.** Christmas tree; **~na·del** *f* fir needle; **~wald** *m* fir wood; **~zap·fen** *m* fir cone
Tan·sa·ni·er [tan'za:nĭɐ] *m* (-s; -), **Tan·sa·nie·rin** [tan'za:nĭərɪn] *f* (-; -nen), **tan·sa·nisch** [tan'za:nɪʃ] *adj.* Tanzanian
Tan·tal ['tantal] *n* (-s; *no pl.*) ⚗ tantalum
Tan·ta·lus·qua·len ['tantalʊs-] *pl.*: ***wir haben ~ erlitten*** it was torture for us, F we went through hell
Tan·te ['tantə] *f* (-; -n) aunt; F *fig.* (***komische ~***) F funny old bird
Tan·te-'Em·ma-La·den F *m* corner shop, *Am.* mom-and-pop store
'tan·ten·haft *adj.* schoolmarmish
Tan·tie·me [tan'tĭe:mə] *f* (-; -n) **1.** share in profits; **2.** *usu. pl.* royalties
Tanz [tants] *m* (-es; Tänze ['tɛntsə]) **1.** dance; ***zum ~ gehen*** go to a dance; ***j-n zum ~ auffordern*** ask s.o. for a dance; ***darf ich um den nächsten ~ bitten?*** may I have the next dance?; **2.** F *fig.* a) song and dance, b) F rigmarole; ***e-n ~ aufführen*** make a song and dance (***wegen*** *gen.* about); F ***e-n ~ mit j-m haben*** F have a set-to with s.o.; **~abend** *m* **1.** dance; **2.** dance show, evening of dance; **~bar** *f* bar with dancing (*or* with a dance band); **~bär** *m* dancing bear; **~bein** *n*: ***das ~ schwingen*** F shake a leg, skip the light fantastic; **~ca͵fé** *n* café with dancing (*or* dance music)
tän·zeln ['tɛntsəln] *v/i.* (h, sn) skip; *horse*: prance
tan·zen ['tantsən] (h) **I.** *v/i.* dance (*a. fig.*); ***es wurde viel getanzt*** there was plenty of dancing; *fig.* ***auf den Wellen ~*** rock (*or* bob up and down) on the waves; ***die Wörter tanzten ihm vor den Augen*** the words were jumping in front of his eyes; → ***Pfeife*** 1; **II.** *v/t.* dance (***e-n Walzer*** a waltz)
Tän·zer ['tɛntsɐ] *m* (-s; -), **Tän·ze·rin** ['tɛntsərɪn] *f* (-; nen) a) dancer, b) ballet dancer; **tän·ze·risch** ['tɛntsərɪʃ] *adj.* dance-like *movement*; dancing *talent*
'Tanz|flä·che *f* dance floor; **~ka͵pel·le** *f* dance band; **~kurs** *m* dancing course; **~leh·rer** *m* dancing instructor; **~lo͵kal** *n* (small) dance hall; **~maus** *f* waltzing mouse; **~mu͵sik** *f* dance music; **~or͵che·ster** *n* dance band; **~part·ner** *m* (dancing) partner; **~saal** *m* dance hall; **~schritt** *m* (dance) step; **~schuh** *m* dancing shoe; **~schu·le** *f* dance school; **~schü·ler** *m* dance student; **~ *sein*** *a.* be taking dancing lessons; **~sport** *m* competition dancing; **~stun·de** *f* dancing class (*or* lesson); ***zur ~ gehen*** a) go to dancing classes, take dancing lessons, b) go to one's dancing class (*or* lesson); **~tee** *m* tea dance, *formal*: thé dansant; **~tur͵nier** *n* dancing contest; **~ver·an·stal·tung** *f* dance
Ta·pet [ta'pe:t] *n*: *fig.* ***et. aufs ~ bringen*** bring s.th. up (for discussion); ***aufs ~ kommen*** be brought up, come up
Ta·pe·te [ta'pe:tə] *f* (-; -n) wallpaper
Ta'pe·ten|bahn *f* strip of wallpaper; **~mu·ster** *n* wallpaper design; **~rol·le** *f* roll of wallpaper; **~tür** *f* concealed door; **~wech·sel** *fig. m* change of scenery
ta·pe·zie·ren [tape'tsi:rən] *v/t.* (h) wallpaper, decorate; ***neu ~*** redecorate
Ta·pe·zie·rer [tape'tsi:rɐ] *m* (-s; -) decorator, paperhanger
Ta·pe·zier|na·gel [tape'tsi:ɐ-] *m* tack; **~tisch** *m* pasteboard
tap·fer ['tapfɐ] **I.** *adj.* brave; valiant; **II.** *adv.*: ***sich ~ schlagen*** (*or* ***halten***) ⚔ fight like a hero (*or* heroes), *fig.* put up a good fight; ***sie hat es ~ ertragen*** she put on a brave front; **'Tap·fer·keit** *f* (-; *no pl.*) bravery; valo(u)r; **'Tap·fer·keits·me͵dail·le** *f* medal for bravery
tap·pen ['tapən] *v/i.* **1.** (sn) pad; **~ *durch*** *acc.* grope one's way through *the room etc.*; ***in e-e Falle ~*** walk (right) into a trap; **2.** (h) grope about (***nach*** *dat.* for); *fig.* ***im dunkeln ~*** grope in the dark
tap·sen ['tapsən] *v/i.* (h) → ***tappen***
tap·sig ['tapsɪç] F *adj.* clumsy
Ta·ra ['ta:ra] *f* (-; Taren) ✝ tare
Ta·ran·tel [ta'rantəl] *f* (-; -n) *zo.* tarantula; *fig.* ***wie von der ~ gestochen sprang er auf*** he jumped up as if something had bitten him
ta·rie·ren [ta'ri:rən] *v/t.* (h) **1.** ✝ tare; **2.** counterbalance
Ta·rif [ta'ri:f] *m* (-s; -e) **1.** scale of charges; **2.** pay scale; ***unter*** (***über***) ***~ bezahlen*** pay below (above) the standard rate; **~ab·schluß** *m* pay (*or* wage) settlement, collective wage agreement; **~aus·ein͵an·der·set·zung** *f* pay dispute; **~au·to·no͵mie** *f* free collective bargaining; **~er·hö·hung** *f* **1.** increase in rates; **2.** increase in pay rates; **~ge·biet** *n subway etc.*: zone; **~grup·pe** *f* salary (*or* wage) bracket; **~kom·mis·si͵on** *f* union bargaining committee; **~kon͵flikt** *m* pay (*or* wage) dispute
ta'rif·lich **I.** *adj.* tariff ...; standard *wage(s)*; **II.** *adv.* according to the tariff; *wage(s)* according to scale
Ta'rif|lohn *m* standard wage(s *pl.*); **~ord·nung** *f* wage scale; **~part·ner** *m* party to a wage agreement; *pl.* union(s) and management; **~po·li͵tik** *f* pay (*or* wages) policy; **~run·de** *f* pay round; **~satz** *m* **1.** tariff rate; **2.** (standard) wage rate; **~ver·ein·ba·rung** *f* → ***Tarifabschluß***; **~ver·hand·lun·gen** *pl.* wage negotiations; **~ver·trag** *m* wage (*or* collective) agreement, wage settlement
Tarn·an·zug ['tarn-] *m* camouflage suit
tar·nen ['tarnən] *v/t.* (h) *esp.* ⚔ camouflage; *fig.* disguise
Tarn|far·be ['tarn-] *f zo.* camouflage; ⚔ camouflage paint; **~kap·pe** *f* magic hood; **~kap·pen·bom·ber** *m* stealth bomber; **~ma͵nö·ver** *n* smokescreen; **~na·me** *m* code name, cover name; **~netz** *n* camouflage netting; **~or·ga·ni·sa·ti͵on** *f* cover organization
Tar·nung ['tarnʊŋ] *f* (-; -en) camouflage (*a. fig.*)
Ta·rock [ta'rɔk] *m, n* (-s; -s) tarot
Tar·tan·bahn ['tartan-] (*TM*) *f sport*: tartan track (*TM*)
Ta·sche *f* a) pocket, b) (*shopping etc.*) bag, handbag, *Am. a.* purse; ***et. in die ~ stecken*** put s.th. in one's pocket; F *fig.* ***et. in der ~ haben*** have s.th. in the bag; ***j-n in die ~ stecken*** be head and shoulders above s.o.; ***er steckt s-e Mitschüler in die ~*** *a.* his classmates are no match for him; ***er steckt die Hände in die ~n*** he doesn't lift a finger, he doesn't do a stroke of work; ***j-m auf der ~ liegen*** live off s.o.; ***in die eigene ~ arbeiten*** line one's (own) pockets; ***et. aus eigener ~ bezahlen*** pay for s.th. out of one's own pocket; ***tief in die ~ greifen müssen*** have to dig deep into one's pockets; ***die Hand auf der ~ haben*** be tightfisted; ***sich in die eigene ~ lügen*** fool o.s.
'Ta·schen·aus·ga·be *f* pocket edition
'Ta·schen·buch *n* **1.** paperback, pocketbook; ***als ~ erscheinen*** come out in paperback; **2.** notebook; **~la·den** *m* paperback bookshop, pocketbook store; **~rei·he** *f* paperback series; **~ver·lag** *m* paperback publishers *pl.*
'Ta·schen|dieb *m* pickpocket; ***vor ~en wird gewarnt!*** beware pickpockets!; **~dieb·stahl** *m* pickpocketing; **~for͵mat** *n* pocket size; ***im ~*** pocket-size(d); **~geld** *n* pocket money, *Am.* allowance; **~ka͵len·der** *m* pocket diary, *Am.* datebook; **~krebs** *m zo.* (common) crab; **~lam·pe** *f* torch, *Am.* flashlight; **~mes·ser** *n* penknife; **~rech·ner** *m* (pocket) calculator; **~schirm** *m* telescopic umbrella
'Ta·schen·spie·ler *m* conjurer; **~trick** *fig. m* piece of juggling; *pl.* sleight of hand *sg.*; ***politischer ~*** piece of political sleight of hand
'Ta·schen|tuch *n* handkerchief, F hankie; **~uhr** *f* fob watch; **~wör·ter·buch** *n* pocket dictionary
Täß·chen ['tɛsçən] *n* (-s; -) *dim. of Tasse*
Tas·se ['tasə] *f* (-; -n) cup; ***e-e ~ Tee*** a cup of tea; F *fig.* ***er hat nicht alle ~n im Schrank*** F he's got a screw loose (somewhere); → ***trübe***
Ta·sta·tur [tasta'tu:ɐ] *f* (-; -en [-rən]) keyboard, keys *pl.*
tast·bar ['tastba:ɐ] *adj.* palpable
Ta·ste ['tastə] *f* (-; -n) key, ⚙ *a.* pushbutton; ***e-e ~ betätigen*** press (*or* hit) a key
ta·sten ['tastən] (h) **I.** *v/i.* a) touch, feel, b) grope, fumble (***nach*** *dat.* for); **II.** *v/refl.*: ***sich ~*** grope one's way; **III.** *v/t.* feel; ⚕ palpate; **'ta·stend** *adj. and adv.* groping(ly); *fig.* **~*er Versuch*** tentative effort; **~*e Schritte*** tentative moves (*or* steps)
'Ta·sten|feld *n* keypad; **~in·stru͵ment** *n* keyboard instrument; **~rei·he** *f* row of keys; **~te·le͵fon** *n* pushbutton telephone

Ta·ster ['tastɐ] *m* (-s; -) *zo.* feeler, antenna; *typ.* keyboard; ⚙ key; pushbutton; scanner, sensor, probe

Tast|haar ['tast-] *n* tactile hair; **~or͵gan** *n* tactile organ; **~sinn** *m* (-[e]s; *no pl.*) sense of touch

tat [taːt] *pret. of* **tun**

Tat [taːt] *f* (-; -en) a) act, *lit.* deed, b) action, c) ⚖ offen|ce (*Am.* -se), crime; **~ *der Verzweiflung*** act of desperation; ***grausame* ~** act of cruelty, cruel thing to do; ***e-e gute* ~ *vollbringen*** do a good deed; ***Mann der* ~** man of action, doer; ***den Worten* ~*en folgen lassen*** suit the action to the words; ***auf frischer* ~ *ertappen*** catch red-handed; ***ich konnte mich zu keiner* ~ *aufraffen*** I couldn't bring myself to do a thing; ***ich nehme den guten Willen für die* ~** it's the thought that counts; ***in der* ~** indeed; ***er hat es in der* ~ *gemacht*** he actually did it; → ***schreiten, umsetzen***

Ta·tar [ta'taːɐ] *n* (-s; *no pl.*) *gastr.* a) raw minced beef, b) steak tartare

'Tat|be·richt *m* ⚖ charge report; **~be·stand** *m* **1.** state of affairs; **2.** ⚖ facts *pl.* of the case; ***objektiver*** (***subjektiver***) **~** physical (mental) elements *pl.* of the offen|ce (*Am.* -se); **~ein·heit** *f*: ⚖ ***in* ~ *mit*** *dat.* in coincidence with

'Ta·ten·drang *m* energy; ***voller* ~ *sein*** F be raring to go

'ta·ten·los I. *adj.* inactive, idle; **II.** *adv.* inactively, idly; **~ *zusehen*** stand by (*or* sit back) and watch; *dat.* **~ *gegenüberstehen*** sit back idly in the face of

Tä·ter ['tɛːtɐ] *m* (-s; -) culprit; ⚖ *and hum.* offender; ***als* ~ *verdächtig sein*** be a suspect; **'Tä·ter·schaft** *f* (-; *no pl.*) perpetration of an offen|ce (*Am.* -se)

tä·tig ['tɛːtɪç] *adj.* active (*a. volcano*); F busy; **~ *sein als*** work as, act as; **~ *sein bei*** *dat.* work for *a firm etc.*, work at *an institute etc.*; **~ *werden*** act

tä·ti·gen ['tɛːtɪgən] *v/t.* (h) ✝ effect, transact, do *business*, conclude *a deal*; make *a purchase*

'Tä·tig·keit *f* (-; -en) a) activity; *anat.*, ⚙ *etc.* action; function, b) occupation, job, profession

'Tä·tig·keits|be·reich *m* field of activity; **~be·richt** *m* progress report; **~merk·mal** *n* occupational characteristic

'Tat·kraft *f* (-; *no pl.*) energy, vigo(u)r; enterprise; **'tat·kräf·tig** *adj.* energetic(ally *adv.*), active; ***~er Mensch*** *a.* doer, F can-do type

tät·lich ['tɛːtlɪç] *adj.* violent; ⚖ ***~e Beleidigung*** assault (and battery); **~ *werden*** become violent; *a.* come to blows

'Tat|mensch *m* man of action, doer; **~mo͵tiv** *n* motive for the crime; **~ort** *m* scene of the crime

tä·to·wie·ren [tɛto'viːrən] *v/t.* (h), **Tä·to·'wie·rung** *f* (-; -en) tattoo

'Tat·sa·che *f* (-; -n) fact; ***den* ~*n ins Auge sehen*** face the facts, be realistic; ***j-n vor vollendete* ~*n stellen*** confront s.o. with a fait accompli; **~ *ist, daß*** the fact (of the matter) is that; ***das ändert nichts an der* ~, *daß*** that doesn't alter the fact that; → ***Boden*** 1, ***nackt***

'Tat·sa·chen|be·richt *m* true story (*or* account); *TV, film etc.*: *a.* documentary; **~ent·schei·dung** *f sport*: referee's decision; **~ro͵man** *m* documentary novel; *pl. coll. a.* faction *sg.*

'tat·säch·lich I. *adj.* real, actual; **II.** *adv.* really; **~?** really?; ***es regnet* ~** it really 's raining

tät·scheln ['tɛtʃəln] *v/t.* (h) pat; stroke

Tat·ter·greis ['tatɐ-] F *m* F old dodderer; **Tat·te·rich** ['tatərɪç] F *m*: ***den* ~ *haben*** have the shakes; **tat·te·rig** ['tatərɪç] F *adj.* F doddery; shaky

'Tat|͵um·stän·de *pl.* circumstances surrounding the case; **~ver·dacht** *m* suspicion (of a criminal act); ***unter*** (***dringendem***) **~ *stehen*** be under suspicion (be a prime suspect); **~ver·däch·ti·ge** *m, f* (-n; -n) suspect; **~waf·fe** *f* weapon involved, *a.* murder weapon

Tat·ze ['tatsə] *f* paw (*a.* F *hand*)

'Tat|zeit *f* time at which the incident took place; ***während der* ~** at the time of the incident; **~zeu·ge** *m* witness to the crime; eye witness

Tau[1] [taʊ] *m* (-s; *no pl.*) dew

Tau[2] *n* (-[e]s; -e) rope; ⚓ *a.* hawser

taub [taʊp] *adj.* **1.** deaf (*fig.* ***gegen*** *acc.*, ***für*** *acc.* to); ***er ist auf dem linken Ohr* ~** he's deaf in his left ear; **~ *werden*** go deaf; ***sich* ~ *stellen*** pretend not to hear, switch off; *fig.* ***auf* ~*e Ohren stoßen*** fall on deaf ears; ***~en Ohren predigen*** talk to the winds; **2.** numb; **~ *werden*** go numb, lose its (*or* their) feeling; **3.** empty *nut etc.*; **Tau·be**[1] ['taʊbə] *m, f* (-n; -n) deaf person (*or* man, woman); ***die* ~*n*** the deaf

Tau·be[2] ['taʊbə] *f* (-; -n) *zo.* pigeon, *rhet.*, *eccl.*, *pol.* dove

'Tau·ben|dreck *m* pigeon droppings *pl.*; **~ei** *n* pigeon's egg; **2grau** *adj.* dove-grey (*Am.* -gray); **~schie·ßen** *n* pigeon shooting; **~schlag** *m* dovecot(e); F *fig.* ***hier geht's zu wie in e-m* ~** it's like Piccadilly Circus around here; **~züch·ter** *m* pigeon breeder

Tau·ber ['taʊbɐ] *m* (-s; -), **Täu·ber** ['tɔʏbɐ] *m* (-s; -), **Täu·be·rich** ['tɔʏbərɪç] *m* (-s; -e) cock pigeon

'Taub·heit *f* (-; *no pl.*) **1.** deafness; **2.** numbness

Täub·ling ['tɔʏplɪŋ] *m* (-s; -e) 🍄 russula

'Taub·nes·sel *f* 🍄 deadnettle

'taub·stumm *adj.* deaf and dumb; **'Taub·stum·me** *m, f* (-n; -n) deaf-mute, deaf and dumb person (*or* man, woman); **'Taub·stum·men·spra·che** *f* deaf-and-dumb language

Tauch·boot ['taʊx-] *n* submarine, submersible (boat)

tau·chen ['taʊxən] **I.** *v/i.* (h, sn) dive (***nach*** *dat.* for); *sport*: *a.* skin-dive; (scuba-)dive; *submarine*: dive, submerge; **II.** *v/t.* (h) dip (***in*** *acc.* in[to]); immerse (in); → ***getaucht***

Tau·cher ['taʊxɐ] *m* (-s; -) diver (*a. zo.*); **~an·zug** *m* diving suit, wetsuit; **~bril·le** *f*: (***e-e* ~** a pair of) diving goggles *pl.*; **~glocke** *f* diving bell; **~helm** *m* diver's helmet; **~krank·heit** *f the* bends *pl.*; **~mas·ke** *f* diving mask

Tauch|fahrt ['taʊx-] *f* dive; **2klar** *adj. submarine*: ready to submerge; **~ku·gel** *f* bathysphere; **~sie·der** [-ziːdɐ] *m* (-s; -) immersion heater; **~sport** *m* skin (*or* scuba) diving; **~sta·ti͵on** *f submarine*: diving station; ***auf* ~ *gehen*** dive, submerge, *fig.* fade from the scene, go into hiding; **~ver·fah·ren** *n metall.* hot dipping process

tau·en ['taʊən] *v/i.* (h, sn) thaw, melt; ***es taut*** it's thawing; ***der Schnee ist von den Dächern getaut*** the snow has melted off the roofs

Tauf|becken ['taʊf-] *n* (baptismal) font; **~buch** *n* baptismal register

Tau·fe ['taʊfə] *f* (-; -n) baptism, christening (*both a. fig.*); ***die* ~ *empfangen*** be baptized (*or* christened); ***aus der* ~ *heben*** stand godfather (*or* godmother) to, *fig.* call into being, launch; **'tau·fen** *v/t.* (h) baptize, christen (*a. fig. ship etc.*); call; ***auf den Namen ...* ~** baptize (*or* christen) ...; **Täu·fer** ['tɔʏfɐ] *m* (-s; -) **1.** → ***Johannes***; **2.** *pl. the* Baptists

Tauf·kleid ['taʊf-] *n* christening dress

Täuf·ling ['tɔʏflɪŋ] *m* (-s; -e) child (*or* person) to be baptized

Tauf|na·me ['taʊf-] *m* Christian (*or* given) name; **~pa·te** *m* godfather; *pl.* godparents; **~pa·tin** *f* godmother; **~re͵gi·ster** *n* baptismal register

'tau·frisch *adj.* dewy; *fig.* fresh; ***sich* ~ *fühlen*** feel as fresh as a daisy; F ***sie ist auch nicht mehr ganz* ~** F she's no spring chicken

Tauf·schein ['taʊf-] *m* baptismal certificate; **~christ** *m* nominal (*or* non-practising) Christian; **~stein** *m* (baptismal) font

tau·gen ['taʊgən] *v/i.* (h): ***nichts* ~** be no good; ***es taugt wenig*** it isn't much good; ***taugt es etwas?*** is it any good?; ***es taugt nicht für Kinder*** it's not meant for children; ***sie taugt nicht zu dieser*** (***or für diese***) ***Arbeit*** she's not suited to (*or* for) this kind of work; ***er taugt nicht zum Redner*** he wasn't cut out for public speaking; ***in der Schule taugt sie nichts*** she's not doing very well at school

Tau·ge·nichts ['taʊgənɪçts] *m* (-[e]s; -e) good-for-nothing

taug·lich ['taʊklɪç] *adj.* suitable (***für*** *acc.*, ***zu*** *dat.* for); *a.* qualified; ⚔ fit (for service); **'Taug·lich·keit** *f* (-; *no pl.*) suitability; ⚔ fitness

Tau·mel ['taʊməl] *m* (-s; *no pl.*) dizziness, giddiness; *fig.* whirl; frenzy, rapture; ***im* ~ *der Freude*** (***Begeisterung***) in a state of rapture (swept away with enthusiasm); ***in den* ~ *der Ereignisse geraten*** get caught up in the whirlwind of events; **tau·me·lig** ['taʊməlɪç] *adj.* dizzy; **'tau·meln** *v/i.* (h, sn) reel, stagger, sway

Tausch [taʊʃ] *m* (-[e]s; *no pl.*) exchange, F swap; ***im* ~ *gegen*** *acc.* in exchange for; ***in* ~ *geben für*** *acc.* swap (*or* exchange) for; ***e-n guten*** (***schlechten***) **~ *machen*** make a good (bad) deal; **tau·schen** ['taʊʃən] *v/t. and v/i.* (h) exchange (*a. fig. looks, words, blows etc.*); F swap; ***ich möchte nicht mit ihm* ~** I wouldn't like to be in his shoes; ***ich möchte mit keinem* ~** I wouldn't like to swap with anyone

täu·schen ['tɔʏʃən] (h) **I.** *v/t.* a) deceive (*a. fig. one's memory, eyes etc.*), b) mislead, lead astray, c) trick, d) disappoint; ***sich* ~ *lassen*** be deceived, be taken in (***von*** *dat.* by); ***wenn mich nicht alles täuscht*** if I'm not very much mistaken; ***wenn mein Gedächtnis mich nicht täuscht*** if my memory serves me well (*or* correctly); **II.** *v/i.* be deceptive; *sport*: feint, fake a blow *etc.*; **III.** *v/refl.*: ***sich* ~** be wrong, be mistaken; ***sich in j-m* ~** be completely wrong about s.o.; ***da habe ich mich noch nie getäuscht*** I've never been wrong on that; ***da täuscht er sich aber!*** he's very much mistaken there;

'täu·schend I. *adj.* deceptive; **~e Ähnlichkeit** striking resemblance; **II.** *adv.*: **j-m (e-r Sache) ~ ähnlich sein** look exactly like s.o. (s.th.); **er sieht s-m Bruder ~ ähnlich** *a.* he's the spit and image (*or* spitting image) of his brother; **es ist e-e ~ echte Nachahmung** it's a very (*or* deceptively) clever imitation, it could fool anyone

'Tausch|ge·schäft *n* exchange deal, F swap; **~ge·sell·schaft** *f* barter society; **~han·del** *m* **1.** → **Tauschgeschäft; 2.** bartering; **~ treiben** barter; **~ob,jekt** *n* object of exchange

Täu·schung ['tɔʏʃʊŋ] *f* (-; -en) a) deception; delusion, b) mistake; fallacy; **arglistige ~** wilful deceit; **optische ~** optical illusion; **sich e-r ~ hingeben** delude o.s.; **sie gaben sich hinsichtlich** *gen.* **... keiner ~ hin** they were under no illusions about ...

'Täu·schungs|ma,nö·ver *n* ⚔ feint; *fig.* diversion; **~ver·such** *m* attempt to deceive (⚖ *a.* defraud)

'Tausch|wa·ren *pl.* barter goods; **~wert** *m* exchange value; **~wirt·schaft** *f* barter economy

tau·send ['taʊzənt] *adj.* a) a (*or* one) thousand, b) thousands of; **~ Mark** a (*or* one) thousand marks; **~ und aber ~** thousands and thousands of; **ich muß noch ~ Dinge erledigen** I've still got a thousand things to do; **~ Dank!** thanks ever so much; **'Tau·send** *n* (-s; -, -e [-də]) thousand; **zu ~en** by the thousands; **in die ~e gehen** run into thousands

Tau·sen·der ['taʊzəndɐ] *m* (-s; -) thousand mark note (*Am.* bill)

tau·sen·der·lei ['taʊzəndɐ'laɪ] *adj.* a thousand different (kinds of)

'tau·send·fach I. *adj.* thousandfold; **in ~er Ausführung** a thousand copies (of ...); **II.** *adv.* a thousand times

'Tau·send·füß·ler [-fyːslɐ] *m* (-s; -) *zo.* centipede; millipede

Tau·send'jahr·fei·er *f* millennial

'tau·send·jäh·rig [-jɛːrɪç] *adj.* thousand-year-old ..., a thousand years old; of a thousand years; **~es Jubiläum** millennial; *hist.* **das ~e Reich** the thousand-year Reich; *bibl.* **das Ωe Reich** the Millennium

'tau·send·mal *adv.* a thousand times

'Tau·send·sas·sa [-sasa] *m* (-s; -s) F amazing guy

tau·sendst ['taʊzəntst] *adj.*, **Tau·send·ste** ['taʊzəntstə] *m, f* (-n; -n) thousandth; **Tau·send·stel** ['taʊzəntstəl] *n* (-s; -) thousandth (part)

Tau·to·lo·gie [taʊtolo'giː] *f* (-; -n) tautology; **tau·to·lo·gisch** [taʊto'loːgɪʃ] *adj.* tautologous, tautological

'Tau·trop·fen *m* dewdrop

'Tau·werk *n* (-[e]s; *no pl.*) ⚓ rigging

'Tau·wet·ter *n* thaw (*a. fig. pol.*)

'Tau·zie·hen *n* (-s; *no pl.*) tug-of-war (**um** *acc.* for) (*a. fig.*)

Ta·ver·ne [ta'vɛrnə] *f* (-; -n) taverna

Ta·xa·me·ter [taksa'meːtɐ] *m, n* (-s; -) taximeter

Ta·xa·tor [ta'ksaːtoːɐ] *m* (-s; -en [taksa'toːrən]) valuer, assessor

Ta·xe ['taksə] *f* (-; -n) **1.** rate; fee; tax; **2.** estimate, valuation; **3.** F → **Taxi**

Ta·xi ['taksi] *n* (-s; -s) taxi, cab; **~!** taxi!; **mit dem ~ fahren** go by taxi (*or* cab), take a taxi (*or* cab)

ta·xie·ren [ta'ksiːrən] *v/t.* (h) a) estimate; ✝, ⚖ value, assess, b) F size *s.o.* up; **Ta'xie·rung** *f* (-; -en) estimate; valuation, assessment

'Ta·xi|fah·rer *m* taxi (*or* cab) driver, F cabby; **~stand** *m* taxi rank (*or* stand), cabstand; **~zen,tra·le** *f* taxi control cent|re (*Am.* -er)

Tax·wert ['taks-] *m* estimated value

Teak|baum ['tiːk-] *m* teak; **~holz** *n* teak; **Tisch aus ~** teak(wood) table

Team [tiːm] *n* (-s; -s) team; **im ~ arbeiten** work in a team; **~ar·beit** *f* (-; *no pl.*) teamwork; **et. in ~ erledigen** do s.th. as a team; **~chef** *m* team manager; **~geist** *m* (-[e]s; *no pl.*) team spirit

Team·work ['tiːmvøɐk] *n* (-s; *no pl.*) → **Teamarbeit**

Tech·nik ['tɛçnɪk] *f* (-; -en) **1.** *no pl.* technology; engineering; **von ~ verstehe ich gar nichts** I don't know the first thing about technical matters, I'm hopeless when it comes to technical things; → **Stand** 2; **2.** technique (*a. w.s. art, sport etc.*); **3.** *no pl.* equipment; mechanics *pl.*

Tech·ni·ker ['tɛçnikɐ] *m* (-s; -), **Tech·ni·ke·rin** ['tɛçnikərɪn] *f* (-; -nen) (technical) engineer; (*a. w.s. artist, athlete etc.*) technician; technologist

Tech·ni·kum ['tɛçnikʊm] *n* (-s; -ka) college of technology

tech·nisch ['tɛçnɪʃ] *adj.* ⚙ engineering *department, process etc.*; (*a. w.s. art, sport etc.*) technical (*a. fig.*); technological; **~e Anlagen** technical facilities (*or* installations), *a.* technology *of a hospital etc.*; **~e Hochschule** college (*or* institute) of technology; **~e Einzelheiten** technicalities; **~er Leiter** technical director; **~e Disziplinen** field events; **~er K.o.** technical knockout; **~es Personal** technical staff; **~e Schwierigkeiten** technical difficulties; **aus (verfahrens)~en Gründen** on technical grounds; **Ωer Überwachungs-Verein → TÜV**

tech·ni·sie·ren [tɛçni'ziːrən] *v/t.* (h) mechanize; **Tech·ni'sie·rung** *f* (-; *no pl.*) mechanization

Tech·no·krat [tɛçno'kraːt] *m* (-en; -en) technocrat; **Tech·no·kra·tie** [tɛçnokra'tiː] *f* (-; *no pl.*) technocracy

Tech·no·lo·ge [tɛçno'loːgə] *m* (-n; -n) technologist

Tech·no·lo·gie [tɛçnolo'giː] *f* (-; -n) technology; **~park** *m* technology (*or* science) park; **~trans,fer** *m* technology transfer

tech·no·lo·gisch [tɛçno'loːgɪʃ] *adj.* technological

Tech·tel·mech·tel [tɛçtəl'mɛçtəl] F *n* (-s; -) F carrying-on; **ein ~ mit j-m haben** be carrying on with s.o.

Ted·dy ['tɛdi] *m* (-s; -s), **~bär** *m* teddy bear

TEE [teːˀeːˀeː] *m* (-[s]; -[s]) 🚂 TEE, Trans-European Express

Tee [teː] *m* (-s; -s) tea; **e-n ~ machen** (*or* **kochen**) make some tea; **e-n ~ trinken** have a cup of tea; **er kommt zum ~** he's coming for tea; *fig.* **abwarten und ~ trinken!** (let's) wait and see; **~beu·tel** *m* teabag; **~blatt** *n* tea leaf; **~büch·se** *f* tea caddy; **~-Ei** *n* infuser; **~ge·bäck** *n* biscuits *pl.*, *Am.* cookies *pl.*; **~ge·schäft** *n* tea seller('s), teashop; **~ge·schirr** *n* tea service, tea set, tea things *pl.*; **~glas** *n* tea glass; **~haus** *n* teahouse; **~kan·ne** *f* teapot; **~kes·sel** *m* kettle; **~kü·che** *f* (tea) kitchen; **~licht** *n* tea warmer candle

'Tee·löf·fel *m* teaspoon; **zwei (gestrichene) ~ voll** two (level) teaspoons(ful); **'tee·löf·fel·wei·se** *adv.* by the teaspoon

'Tee·mi·schung *f* blend of tea

Teen·ager ['tiːneːdʒɐ] *m* (-s; -) teenager; adolescent; *in cpds.* teenage ..., adolescent ...

'Tee·pau·se *f* tea break

Teer [teːɐ] *m* (-[e]s; *no pl.*) tar; **tee·ren** ['teːrən] *v/t.* (h) tar; **~ und federn** tar and feather

'Tee·ro·se *f* tea rose

'Teer|pap·pe *f* tar paper; **~sei·fe** *f* coal-tar soap; **~stra·ße** *f* tarred road

'Tee|ser,vice *n* tea service, tea set; **~sieb** *n* tea strainer; **~stu·be** *f* tearoom; **~tas·se** *f* teacup; **~trin·ker** *m*: **ich bin ~** I drink tea; **~wa·gen** *m* tea trolley

Teich [taɪç] *m* (-[e]s; -e) pond; F *fig.* **der große ~** the herring pond; **über dem großen ~** on the other side of the pond

Teig [taɪk] *m* (-[e]s; -e ['taɪgə]) dough; batter; **tei·gig** ['taɪgɪç] *adj.* doughy, pasty (*both a. fig.*); **'Teig·wa·ren** *pl.* pasta *sg.*, pastas; **verschiedene ~** *usu.* different types of pasta

Teil¹ [taɪl] *m* (-[e]s; -e) **1.** part; **ein ~ davon** part (*or* some) of it; **der größte ~** *gen.* most of, the majority of; **der größere ~ s-s Vermögens** the greater part of his fortune; **nur ein kleiner ~ stimmte dafür** only a minority was in favo(u)r; **der arbeitende ~ der Bevölkerung** the working population; **Faust, Erster ~** Faust Part One; **im ersten ~ des Films** early on in the film, in part one of the film; **zu gleichen ~en** equally; **in zwei ~e zerbrechen** break in two; **aus allen ~en der Welt** from all over the world; **zum ~** partly; **zum großen** (*or* **größten**) **~** largely, for the most part; **ich habe die Arbeit zum größten ~ fertig** I've more or less finished the work; **der Film war zum ~ sehr spannend** the film was very exciting in parts, there were some very exciting bits in the film; **wir sind zum ~ gefahren, zum ~ gelaufen** we drove part of the way and walked the rest; **2.** side; ⚖ party; **beide ~e anhören** hear both sides (of the story); **für beide ~e vorteilhaft** of advantage to both sides, of mutual advantage

Teil² [taɪl] *m, n* (-[e]s; -e) share; **sein ~ beitragen** do one's part (F bit); **ich für mein(en) ~** I for my part, as for me; **ich habe mir so mein ~ gedacht** I didn't (want to) say anything; **er hat sein(en) ~ weg** he got his share, *fig.* he got what was coming to him; **man hat sein(en) ~ zu tragen** it's not an easy life; **dazu gehört ein gut ~ Frechheit** you've got to be pretty cheeky to do that (kind of thing)

Teil³ [taɪl] *n* (-[e]s; -e) *a.* ⚙ part, component, element; **da fehlt ein ~** there's a piece (*or* part) missing

'Teil|an·sicht *f* partial view; **~aspekt** *m* part, aspect; **das ist nur ein ~ des Problems** it's only part (*or* one aspect) of the problem

'teil·bar *adj.* divisible

'Teil|be·trag *m* a) partial amount, b) instal(l)ment; **~be·völ·ke·rung** *f* sub-population

Teil·chen ['taɪlçən] *n* (-s; -) particle (*a. phys.*); **~be·schleu·ni·ger** *m phys.* particle accelerator

tei·len ['taɪlən] (h) **I.** *v/t.* a) divide (**in** *acc.* into); split (up), b) share out, distribute,

c) share *a. fig. s.o.'s views, fate etc.*; ***35 durch 7** ~* divide 35 by 7; ***et. in gleiche Teile** ~* divide s.th. (up) into equal parts; ***in Grade** ~* calibrate, graduate; ***ich teile d-e Meinung** (**nicht**)* I (can't) agree with you (***über*** *acc.* on, about); (***sich***) ***et.*** ~ share (*or* split) s.th., *a.* go halves on s.th.; → ***geteilt***; **II.** *v/refl.*: ***sich*** ~ divide, *party etc.*: *a.* split; *crowd*: split up, separate; *road*: branch out, fork; ***sich in et.*** ~ share (*or* split) s.th., *a.* go halves (on s.th.); ***sich in die Kosten*** ~ share expenses; **III.** *v/i.* share; ***er teilt nicht gern*** he doesn't like sharing

Tei·ler ['taɪlɐ] *m* (-s; -) 𝔄 factor

'Teil|er·folg *m* partial success; **~er·fül·lung** *f* partial fulfil(l)ment; **~er·geb·nis** *n* first results *pl.*; **~ge·biet** *n* (subsidiary) branch

'teil·ha·ben *v/i.* (*irr., sep.*, h, → ***haben***) participate, have a share (***an*** *dat.* in); share (in *s.o.'s joy etc.*); **'Teil·ha·ber** [-ha:bɐ] *m* (-s; -) ✝ partner, associate; ***stiller*** ~ sleeping partner

...tei·lig [-taɪlɪç] *adj. in cpds.* ***zwei~*** in two parts, two-piece *suit etc.*

'Teil·in·va·li·di·tät *f* partial disablement

'Teil·kas·ko·ver·si·che·rung *f mot.* partial coverage insurance

'Teil|lie·fe·rung *f* part delivery; **~lö·sung** *f* partial solution; **~men·ge** *f* 𝔄 subset

'teil·mö·bliert [-mø,bli:ɐt] *adj.* partly furnished

Teil·nah·me ['taɪlna:mə] *f* (-; *no pl.*) **1.** participation (***an*** *dat.* in) (*a.* ⚖); attendance (at *a conference etc.*); **2.** a) interest (***an*** *dat.* in), b) sympathy (with), compassion (for), c) condolences *pl.*; **~be·din·gun·gen** *pl.* conditions of entry

'teil·nah·me·be·rech·tigt *adj.* eligible

teil·nahms·los ['taɪlna:mslo:s] **I.** *adj.* apathetic; indifferent; **II.** *adv.* apathetically *etc.*; ***sie saß vollkommen** ~ **da*** she sat there like part of the furniture; **'Teil·nahms·lo·sig·keit** *f* (-; *no pl.*) apathy; indifference

teil·nahms·voll ['taɪlna:msfɔl] *adj.* sympathetic(ally *adv.*)

'teil·neh·men *v/i.* (*irr., sep.*, h, → ***nehmen***) a) take part (***an*** *dat.* in), participate (in), b) be present (at), attend (*s.th.*), c) *fig.* take an interest (in); sympathize (with); ***er nahm am Zweiten Weltkrieg teil*** he fought (*or* was) in the Second World War

Teil·neh·mer ['taɪlne:mɐ] *m* (-s; -) participant; ***die*** ~ those present; ***~ an der Schlußrunde*** *sport*: finalist(s); **~feld** *n sport*: (field of) competitors *pl.*, participants *pl.*; **~li·ste** *f* list of participants (*sport*: *a.* entrants); **~staat** *m* participating nation; **~zahl** *f* number of participants (*sport*: *a.* entrants)

teils [taɪls] *adv.* partly, in part; ~ ..., ~ ... part(ly) ..., part(ly) ...; F ~, ~ F so-so; *hat es dir gefallen?* - ~, ~ it was okay; ~ ***gut***, ~ ***schlecht*** *film etc.*: good in parts(, hopeless in others); ~ ***bewölkt***, ~ ***heiter*** cloudy with sunny periods; ***sie kamen** ~ **zu Fuß**, ~ **mit dem Fahrrad*** some came on foot, some by bicycle

'Teil|strecke *f* 🚂 section; *bus etc.*: (fare) stage; stage, *a. sport*: leg; **~strich** *m* ⚙ graduation mark; **~stück** *n* fragment; section; **~sy,stem** *n* subsystem

Tei·lung ['taɪlʊŋ] *f* (-; -en) a) division (*a. biol.*, 𝔄); *pol. a.* separation; partition *of a country etc.*, b) distribution; sharing

'Tei·lungs·mas·se *f* ⚖ bankrupt's estate

'teil·wei·se I. *adv.* partially, partly, in part(s); in some cases; **II.** *adj.* partial

'Teil·zah·lung *f* a) part payment, b) instal(l)ment, c) payment by instal(l)ments; ***auf** ~ **kaufen*** buy on instal(l)ments (*or* hire purchase)

'Teil·zah·lungs|bank *f* (-; -en) finance house; **~kauf** *m* hire purchase; **~kre,dit** *m* hire purchase (*Am.* installment) credit

'Teil·zeit|ar·beit *f* (-; *no pl.*) part-time employment; **~be·schäf·tig·te** *m, f* (-n; -n) part-time employee, F part-timer; **~be·schäf·ti·gung** *f* part-time employment

Teint [tɛ̃:] *m* (-s; -s) complexion

Tek·to·nik [tɛk'to:nɪk] *f* (-; *no pl.*) tectonics *pl.*; **tek·to·nisch** [tɛk'to:nɪʃ] *adj.* tectonic; ***~e Verschiebungen*** tectonic (*or* plate) movements

Te·le ['te:lə] F *n* (-[s]; -s) *phot.* F telephoto

'Te·le·brief *m*: ***per*** ~ by fax

Te·le·fax ['te:ləfaks] *n* (-; -[e]) telefax

Te·le·fon [tele'fo:n, 'te:lefo:n] *n* (-s; -e) telephone, phone; ***am*** ~ on the phone; ***ans** ~ **gehen*** answer the phone; ***gehst du mal ans** ~?* *a.* can you get the phone?; ~ ***haben*** have a phone, be on the phone; **~an·ruf** *m* (tele)phone call; **~an·schluß** *m* telephone connection (*or* extension); **~ap·pa,rat** *m* (tele)phone

Te·le·fo·nat [telefo'na:t] *n* (-[e]s; -e) telephone conversation; phone call

Te·le'fon|buch *n* telephone directory, phone book; **~dienst** *m* telephone service; **~ge·bühr** *f* telephone charge; **~ge·spräch** *n* → ***Telefonat***; **~hö·rer** *m* receiver

te·le·fo·nie·ren [telefo'ni:rən] *v/i.* (h) (tele)phone, ring (*or* call) up; ***mit j-m*** ~ *a.* talk to s.o. on the (tele)phone; ***er telefoniert ständig*** he's on the phone all day, he's never off the phone

te·le·fo·nisch [tele'fo:nɪʃ] **I.** *adj.* telephonic; ***~e Mitteilung*** telephone message; **II.** *adv.* by (tele)phone, over the (tele)phone; telephonically; ~ (***nicht***) ***erreichbar*** (not) on the phone

Te·le·fo·nist [telefo'nɪst] *m* (-en; -en), **Te·le·fo·ni·stin** [telefo'nɪstɪn] *f* (-; -nen) (telephone) operator

Te·le'fon|ka·bel *n* (tele)phone cord; **~kar·te** *f* phonecard; **~lei·tung** *f* telephone line; **~netz** *n* telephone network; **~num·mer** *f* (tele)phone number; **~rech·nung** *f* (tele)phone bill; **~schnur** *f* (tele)phone cord; **~seel·sor·ge** *f* help line, crisis line; *in GB*: *a. the* Samaritans *pl.*; **~ter·ror** *m* telephone harassment; **~über,wa·chung** *f* (tele)phone tapping; **~ver·bin·dung** *f* telephone connection; ***e-e** ~ **herstellen*** put a call through; **~ver·mitt·lung** *f* switchboard; **~zel·le** *f* (tele)phone box, call box, *Am.* (tele-) phone booth; **~zen,tra·le** *f* switchboard; ***über die*** ~ through (*or* via) the switchboard

Te·le·fo·to ['te:ləfo:to] *n* (-s; -s) telephoto shot; **Te·le·fo·to·gra'fie** [tele-] *f* **1.** telephotography; **2.** → ***Telefoto***

te·le·gen [tele'ge:n] *adj. TV* telegenic

Te·le·graf [tele'gra:f] *m* (-en; -en) telegraph

Te·le'gra·fen|amt *n* telegraph office; **~lei·tung** *f* telegraph line; **~mast** *m*, **~stan·ge** *f* telegraph pole

Te·le·gra·fie [telegra'fi:] *f* (-; *no pl.*) telegraphy; ***drahtlose*** ~ radiotelegraphy; **te·le·gra·fie·ren** [telegra'fi:rən] *v/t. and v/i.* (h) telegraph, wire; cable

te·le·gra·fisch [tele'gra:fɪʃ] **I.** *adj.* telegraphic; ***~e Überweisung*** telegraphic (*or* cable) transfer; **II.** *adv.* by telegraph, by wire; by cable; telegraphically

Te·le·gra·fist [telegra'fɪst] *m* (-en; -en), **Te·le·gra·fi·stin** [telegra'fɪstɪn] *f* (-; -nen) telegraphist, telegrapher

Te·le·gramm [tele'gram] *n* (-s; -e) telegram; cable(gram); **~adres·se** *f* telegraphic address; **~for·mu,lar** *n* telegram form (*Am.* blank); **~stil** *m* telegraphic style, telegraphese, F shorthand

Te·le·graph(...) → ***Telegraf(...)***

Te·le·ki·ne·se [teleki'ne:zə] *f* (-; *no pl.*) telekinesis; **te·le·ki·ne·tisch** [teleki'ne:tɪʃ] *adj.* telekinetic

Te·le|kol·leg ['te:ləkɔle:k] *n in GB*: *the* Open University; **~kom·mu·ni·ka·ti,on** *f* telecommunications *pl.*; **~ko,pie·rer** *m* facsimile machine, fax (machine)

Te·le·mark ['te:ləmark] *m* (-s; -s) *skiing*: telemark

Te·le·ob·jek·tiv ['te:ləˀɔpjɛkti:f] *n* (-s; -e [-və]) telephoto lens

Te·leo·lo·gie [teleolo'gi:] *f* (-; *no pl.*) teleology; **te·leo·lo·gisch** [teleo'lo:gɪʃ] *adj.* teleological

Te·le·pa·thie [telepa'ti:] *f* (-; *no pl.*) telepathy; **te·le·pa·thisch** [tele'pa:tɪʃ] *adj.* telepathic(ally *adv.*)

Te·le·phon(...) → ***Telefon(...)***

Te·le·pho·to(...) → ***Telefoto(...)***

Te·le·skop [tele'sko:p] *n* (-s; -e) telescope; **~an,ten·ne** *f* telescopic aerial (*or* antenna); **~arm** *m* telescopic arm; **~au·ge** *n* telescope eye

te·le·sko·pisch [tele'sko:pɪʃ] *adj.* telescopic(ally *adv.*)

Te·le·spiel ['te:lə-] *n* TV game

Te·le·text ['te:lə-] *m* teletext

Te·lex ['te:lɛks] *n* (-; -e) telex; **'te·le·xen** *v/t.* (h) telex (***an*** *acc.* to)

Tel·ler ['tɛlɐ] *m* (-s; -) **1.** plate; ***zwei** ~ (**voll**) **Suppe*** two platefuls of soup; **2.** F turntable; **3.** basket *of a ski stick*; **~fleisch** *n gastr.* boiled beef; **~mi·ne** *f* ⚔ anti-tank mine; **~müt·ze** *f* flat cap; beret; **~wär·mer** *m* plate warmer; **~wä·scher** *m* dishwasher

Tel·lur [tɛ'lu:ɐ] *n* (-s; *no pl.*) ⚗ tellurium

Tem·pel ['tɛmpəl] *m* (-s; -) temple; F *fig.* ***j-n zum** ~ **hinausjagen*** F kick s.o. out; **~herr** *m hist.* (Knight) Templar; **~or·den** *m hist.* Order of the Templar(s) (*or* Knights Templar); **~rit·ter** *m* **1.** *hist.* (Knight) Templar; **2.** Knight Templar

Tem·pe·ra ['tɛmpəra] *f* (-; -s), **~far·be** *f* tempera, distemper; **~ma·le,rei** *f* tempera (painting), (painting in) distemper

Tem·pe·ra·ment [tɛmpəra'mɛnt] *n* (-[e]s; -e) **1.** temperament, disposition; ***hitziges*** ~ hot temper; ***ruhiges*** ~ quiet disposition; ***er hat ein ruhiges*** ~ *a.* he's very quiet by nature; **2.** *no pl.* vivacity, vivaciousness; verve; ***er hat*** ~ a) he's very lively, b) he's got a lot of get-up-and-go, c) he's got a fiery temperament; ***er hat kein*** ~ there's no life in him; ***ihr** ~ **ist mit ihr durchgegangen*** she lost control of herself, she lost her temper

tem·pe·ra'ment·los *adj.* spiritless

Tem·pe·ra'ments·sa·che *f*: ***das ist*** ~ it's a matter of temperament, *a.* he *etc.* can't help it, he's *etc.* (just) like that

tem·pe·ra'ment·voll *adj.* very lively, vivacious; fiery; impetuous; *fig.* zippy *car etc.*

Tem·pe·ra·tur [tɛmpəra'tuːɐ] *f* (-; -en [-rən]) temperature; ***bei e-r ~ von 8 Grad*** at (a temperature of) 8 degrees; ***bei ~en um*** *acc.* at temperatures around; ***~en bis zu*** *dat.* temperatures (of) up to; ⚕ ***(erhöhte) ~ haben*** have (*or* be running) a temperature; ***j-s ~ messen*** take s.o.'s temperature; **~an·stieg** *m* rise in temperature(s); **~aus·gleich** *m* temperature balance; **2emp·find·lich** *adj.* temperature-sensitive; **~füh·ler** *m* ⚙ temperature sensor; **~kur·ve** *f* temperature curve; **~mil·de·rung** *f* rise in temperature(s); *meteor. a.* becoming milder; **~reg·ler** *m* thermostat; **~rück·gang** *m* drop in temperature(s); **~schwan·kung** *f* variation (*or* change) in temperature; **~sturz** *m* sudden drop (*or* fall) in temperature; **~ˌun·ter·schied** *m* difference in temperature

tem·pe·rie·ren [tɛmpə'riːrən] *v/t.* (h) temper (*a.* ♪); ***gut temperiert sein*** have the right temperature

Tem·po ['tɛmpo] *n* (-s; -s) **1.** (*pl.* Tempi) ♪ tempo; **2.** speed, rate; ***in rasendem ~*** at breakneck speed; ***in langsamem ~*** at a slow pace; ***an ~ gewinnen*** gather pace, speed up; ***das ~ bestimmen*** (***or angeben***) set the pace; ***das ~ steigern, aufs ~ drücken*** speed things up; F ***der hat vielleicht ein ~ drauf!*** he's going at some speed; ***~!*** F step on it!; **~läu·fer** *m sport*: front runner; **~li·mit** *n* speed limit

Tem·po·mat [tɛmpo'maːt] *m* (-en; -en) *mot.* cruise control

tem·po·rär [tɛmpo'rɛːɐ] *adj.* temporary

Tem·po·stat [tɛmpo'staːt] *m* (-[e]s; -e) *mot.* cruise control

'Tem·po·sün·der *m* speeder

Tem·pus [['tɛmpʊs] *n* (-; Tempora ['tɛmpora]) *ling.* tense

Ten·denz [tɛn'dɛnts] *f* (-; -en) tendency (***zu*** *dat.* towards); trend (*a.* ✝); *contp. pol.* slant; ***die ~ haben zu*** *inf.* have a tendency to *inf.* (*or* towards *ger.*); ✝ ***aufsteigende*** (***absteigende***) ~ upward (downward) trend; *fig.* ***~ aufsteigend*** (***absteigend***) outlook (*or* prospects) bright (dull); **ten·den·zi·ell** [tɛndɛn'tsīɛl] **I.** *adj.*: ***es gibt e-e ~e Besserung*** there are signs of improvement; **II.** *adv.*: ***~ unterscheiden sich die Parteiprogramme nicht*** the broad tendency (*or* outline) of the party manifestos is the same; **ten·den·zi·ös** [tɛndɛn'tsīøːs] *adj.* tendentious

Ten'denz|li·te·raˌtur *f* tendentious literature; **~stück** *n* thesis play; **~wen·de** *f* change in trend

ten·die·ren [tɛn'diːrən] *v/i.* (h) tend (***nach*** *dat.*, ***zu*** *dat.* towards); ***dazu ~ zu*** *inf.* tend to *inf.* (*or* towards *ger.*); *pol.* ***nach rechts*** (***links***) ~ have right-wing (left-wing) tendencies *or* leanings; ✝ ***nach oben*** (***unten***) ~ show an upward (a downward) trend

Ten·ne ['tɛnə] *f* (-; -n) threshing floor

Ten·nis ['tɛnɪs] *n* (-; *no pl.*) tennis; **~arm** *m* ⚕ tennis elbow; **~ball** *m* tennis ball; **~hal·le** *f* covered court; **~klei·dung** *f* tennis kit (*or* whites *pl.*); ✝ tenniswear; **~klub** *m* tennis club; **~maˌschi·ne** *f* ball machine; **~match** *n* tennis match; **~platz** *m* tennis court; **~schlä·ger** *m* tennis racket (*or* racquet); **~schu·he** *pl.* tennis shoes; **~spie·ler** *m* tennis player; **~stun·de** *f* tennis lesson; **~turˌnier** *n* tennis tournament; **~wand** *f* practi|ce (*Am.* -se) wall

Te·nor¹ ['teːnoːɐ] *m* (-s; *no pl.*) tenor; essence, substance; ***den gleichen ~ haben*** be in the same tenor (*or* mode)

Te·nor² [te'noːɐ] *m* (-s; Tenöre [te'nøːrə]) ♪ **1.** tenor (voice *or* part); **2.** tenor (singer *or* player); **~parˌtie** *f* tenor (part); **~stim·me** *f* tenor (voice)

Tep·pich ['tɛpɪç] *m* (-s; -e) carpet; ***den roten ~ ausrollen*** roll out the red carpet, *fig.* give *s.o.* the red carpet treatment; ***fliegender ~*** magic carpet; *fig.* ***unter den ~ kehren*** sweep under the carpet; F ***auf dem ~ bleiben*** be reasonable, be realistic; **~bo·den** *m* fitted carpet, wall-to-wall carpeting; **~bür·ste** *f* carpet brush; **~flie·sen** *pl.* carpet tiles; **~händ·ler** *m* carpet dealer; **~keh·rer** *m* carpet sweeper; **~klop·fer** *m* carpet beater; **~schaum** *m* carpet foam

Ter·min [tɛr'miːn] *m* (-s; -e) **1.** appointment (***bei*** *dat.* with *one's dentist etc.*); date; ⚖ hearing; ***e-n ~ festsetzen*** fix (*or* agree on) a date; ***ich habe mir für morgen e-n ~ geben lassen*** I've got an appointment (*or* they've put me down) for tomorrow; ***viele ~e haben*** have a busy schedule, have a lot of appointments to keep; **2.** deadline; ***der ~ für die Abgabe des Manuskripts*** the deadline for handing in the manuscript; ***letzter*** (*or* ***endgültiger***) ~ final deadline; ***e-n ~ einhalten*** meet a deadline

Ter·mi·nal ['tøːɐmɪnəl, 'tœr-] *m, n* (-s; -s) ✈ *and computer*: terminal

Ter'min|ar·beit *f* scheduled work; **~bör·se** *f* ✝ futures exchange; **~druck** *m* (-[e]s; *no pl.*) time (*or* deadline) pressure; ***unter ~ stehen*** *a.* have a tight schedule

ter'min|ge·bun·den *adj.* tied to a deadline; ***wir sind ~*** *a.* we've got a deadline; **~ge·mäß, ~ge·recht** *adv.* on schedule, on time

Ter'min|ge·schäft *n* ✝ futures trading; **~kaˌlen·der** *m* appointments book, diary; ⚖ cause list, *Am.* calendar; ***e-n vollen ~ haben*** have a busy schedule

ter'min·lich I. *adj.*: ***~e Schwierigkeiten haben*** a) have difficulty meeting a (*or* the) deadline, b) have a very tight schedule; ***aus ~en Gründen*** due to prior commitments; **II.** *adv.*: ***~ hinkommen*** make a (*or* the) deadline; ***ich schaffe es ~ nicht*** I can't manage (*or* fit it in) timewise

Ter'min·markt *m* ✝ futures market

Ter·mi·no·lo·gie [tɛrminolo'giː] *f* (-; -n) terminology; **ter·mi·no·lo·gisch** [tɛrmino'loːgɪʃ] *adj.* terminological

Ter'min|plan *m* (time) schedule; agenda; **~pla·ner** *m* personal organizer; **~pla·nung** *f* scheduling; setting up a time schedule; **~schwie·rig·kei·ten** *pl.*: ***in ~ sein*** have difficulty meeting a (*or* the) deadline; ***wegen ~*** due to prior commitments; **~ver·län·ge·rung** *f* (deadline) extension

Ter·mi·te [tɛr'miːtə] *f* (-; -n) termite

Ter'mi·ten|hü·gel *m* termites' nest; **~staat** *m* colony of termites

Ter·pen·tin [tɛrpɛn'tiːn] *n* (-s; -e) turpentine

Ter·rain [tɛ'rɛ̃ː] *n* (-s; -s) a) terrain, b) plot of land; building site, c) *fig.* ground; *fig.* ***sich auf bekanntem ~ befinden*** be on familiar ground (*or* turf); ***das ~ vorbereiten*** do the groundwork; ***das ~ sondieren*** F see how the land lies

Ter·ra·kot·ta [tɛra'kɔta] *f* (-; -ten) terracotta

Ter·ra·ri·um [tɛ'raːrīʊm] *n* (-s; -rien [-rīən]) terrarium

Ter·ras·se [tɛ'rasə] *f* (-; -n) terrace (*a. geol.*)

ter'ras·sen·för·mig [-fœrmɪç] **I.** *adj.* terraced, in terraces; **II.** *adv.*: ***~ anlegen*** terrace

Ter'ras·sen|gar·ten *m* terraced garden; **~haus** *n* stepped building

Ter·raz·zo [tɛ'ratso] *m* (-[s]; -zi [-tsi]) terrazzo

ter·re·strisch [tɛ'rɛstrɪʃ] *adj.* terrestrial

Ter·ri·er ['tɛrīɐ] *m* (-s; -) terrier

Ter·ri·ne [tɛ'riːnə] *f* (-; -n) tureen

ter·ri·to·ri·al [tɛrito'rīaːl] *adj.* territorial

Ter·ri·to·ri'al|arˌmee *f* territorial army; **~ge·walt** *f* territorial sovereignty; **~gewäs·ser** *pl.* territorial waters; **~ho·heit** *f* territorial sovereignty

Ter·ri·to·ri·um [tɛri'toːrīʊm] *n* (-s; -rien) territory

Ter·ror ['tɛroːɐ] *m* (-s; *no pl.*) a) terror, b) reign of terror, c) terrorism; F ***das ist der reinste ~*** that's terror tactics; F ***~ machen*** F go wild; F ***mach keinen ~!*** there's no need to make such a fuss; **~akt** *m* act of terrorism; **~an·schlag** *m* terrorist attack; **~ban·de** *f* gang of terrorists; **~be·kämp·fung** *f* counter-terrorism, *the* fight against terrorism; **~herr·schaft** *f* (-; *no pl.*) reign of terror

ter·ro·ri·sie·ren [tɛrori'ziːrən] *v/t.* (h) terrorize; **Ter·ro·ris·mus** [tɛro'rɪsmʊs] *m* (-; *no pl.*) terrorism; **Ter·ro·rist** [tɛro'rɪst] *m* (-en; -en) terrorist

Ter·ro'ri·sten|fahn·dung *f* search for terrorists; **~kreis** *m* terrorist circle; **~sze·ne** *f* terrorist scene; **~woh·nung** *f* terrorist flat (*or* hideout)

Ter·ro·ri·stin [tɛro'rɪstɪn] *f* (-; -nen) terrorist; **ter·ro·ri·stisch** [tɛro'rɪstɪʃ] *adj.* terrorist; ***~e Gewalttat*** act of terrorism

'Ter·ror|or·ga·ni·sa·tiˌon *f* terrorist organization; **~reˌgime** *n* terrorist regime; **~wel·le** *f* wave of terrorism

Ter·tia ['tɛrtsīa] *f* (-; -tien [-tsīən]) **1.** *obs.* first year (of grammar school); **2.** *Austrian* third year (of grammar school)

Ter·ti·är [tɛr'tsīɛːɐ] *n* (-s; *no pl.*) *geol.* Tertiary (period)

Terz [tɛrts] *f* (-; -en) **1.** ♪ third; ***große*** (***kleine***) ~ major (minor) third; **2.** *eccl.* terce; **3.** *fencing*: tierce

Ter·zett [tɛr'tsɛt] *n* (-[e]s; -e) ♪ trio, terzetto

Te·sa·film ['teːza-] (*TM*) *m* (-s; *no pl.*) sellotape (*TM*), scotch tape (*TM*)

Test [tɛst] *m* (-s; -s, -e) test; *esp.* ✝ trial

Te·sta·ment [tɛsta'mɛnt] *n* (-[e]s; -e) will, ⚖ last will and testament; *bibl.* ***Altes*** (***Neues***) ~ Old (New) Testament; ***sein ~ machen*** make a will; ***j-n im ~ bedenken*** include (*or* remember) s.o. in one's will

te·sta·men·ta·risch [tɛstamɛn'taːrɪʃ] **I.** *adj.* testamentary; **II.** *adv.* by will; ***~ verfügen*** dispose by will; ***~ festgelegt sein*** be (stated) in the will

Te·sta'ments|er·öff·nung *f* opening of a (*or* the) will; **~vollˌstrecker** *m* executor; administrator; **~vollˌstreckung** *f* execution of a (*or* the) will

'Test|be·trieb *m computer*: test mode; **~bild** *n TV* test card; **~boh·rung** *f* trial drilling

te·sten ['tɛstən] *v/t.* (h) test; ~ **auf** *acc.* test for; **j-n auf s-e Reaktionsfähigkeit** *etc.* ~ test s.o.'s reactions *etc.*
'Test|er·geb·nis *n* result(s *pl.*) of a (*or* the) test; **~fah·rer** *m* test driver; **~fahrt** *f* test drive; **~flug** *m* test flight
te·stie·ren [tɛs'tiːrən] (h) **I.** *v/i.* make a will; **II.** *v/t.* certify, testify; **te·stier·fä·hig** [tɛs'tiːɐ-] *adj.* ⚖ capable of making a will
Te·sto·ste·ron [tɛstoste'roːn] *n* (-s; *no pl.*) testosterone
'Test|per,son *f* test subject; **~pi,lot** *m* test pilot; **~rei·he** *f* series of tests; **~sen·dung** *f TV, radio*: pilot program(me); **~si,gnal** *n* test signal
'Test·stopp *m* ban on (nuclear) tests *or* testing, test ban; **~ver·trag** *m* test ban treaty
'Test|strecke *f* test track; **~strei·fen** *m* ⚕ test strip; **~ver·fah·ren** *n* test(ing) method(s *pl.*)
Te·ta·nus ['teːtanʊs] *m* (-; *no pl.*) tetanus; **~schutz·imp·fung** *f* tetanus vaccination; **~sprit·ze** *f* tetanus injection (F jab)
teu·er ['tɔʏɐ] **I.** *adj.* expensive, dear; *fig.* dear (**j-m** to s.o.); **et. für teures Geld kaufen** pay good money for s.th.; **wie ~ ist es?** how much is it?; **Fleisch ist teurer geworden** meat prices have gone up; F **es ist ganz schön ~** it's not exactly cheap; → **Pflaster** 2, **Spaß**; **II.** *adv.* dear(ly); **et. zu ~ kaufen** pay too much for s.th.; **das kam ihn ~ zu stehen** it cost him a fortune, *fig.* he had to pay dearly for it; → **bezahlen, erkaufen**
Teue·rung ['tɔʏərʊŋ] *f* rise in prices; *pl.* price rises
'Teue·rungs|ra·te *f* rate of price increases; rate of inflation; **~wel·le** *f* wave of price increases; **~zu·la·ge** *f*, **~zu·schlag** *m* cost-of-living allowance (*or* bonus)
Teu·fel ['tɔʏfəl] *m* (-s; -) devil (*a. fig.*); **der ~** the Devil, Satan, F Old Nick; **armer ~** poor devil (*or* wretch); **kleiner ~** little devil; F **~ (auch)!** F blimey!; F **pfui ~!** ugh!, that's disgusting!; F **scher dich zum ~!** F go to hell; F **j-n zum ~ jagen** send s.o. packing; F **wer (wo, was) zum ~?** who (where, what) the devil (*sl.* the hell)?; F **weiß der ~** F God knows; F **kein ~ ist da** *sl.* not a sod has come; F **zum ~ sein** *money etc.*: F have gone down the drain, *engine etc.*: F have had it; F **wie der ~, auf ~ komm raus** *work etc.* like the devil (F like crazy), *run etc.* F like crazy (*sl.* hell); F **in ~s Küche kommen** F get (o.s.) into a right (*sl.* hell of a) mess; F *wenn sie das sieht etc.*, **dann ist der ~ los** F there'll be merry hell, she'll hit (*or* raise) the roof; F **dort ist der ~ los** F it's like all hell let loose there; F **bist du des ~s?** have you gone mad?; F **den ~ werd' ich tun** F I'll be damned (*or* blowed) if I do, *sl.* the hell I will; F **er schert sich den ~ drum** F he doesn't give a damn; **der ~ steckt im Detail** it's the little things that always cause the problems; F **den ~ an die Wand malen** tempt fate; F **ihn reitet der ~** the devil's got into him; **da hat der ~ s-e Hand im Spiel** the whole thing's jinxed; F **es müßte schon mit dem ~ zugehen, wenn es nicht klappen sollte** the worst would really have to come to the worst for it not to work out; **das hieße, den ~ mit dem Beelzebub austreiben** a) that would be out of the frying pan into the fire, b) that would be robbing Peter to pay Paul; **wenn man vom ~ spricht(, dann ist er nicht weit)** speak (*or* talk) of the devil (and he's sure to appear)
'Teu·fels|aus·trei·bung *f* exorcism; **~kerl** F *m* F devil of a guy; **~kreis** *fig. m* vicious circle; **den ~ durchbrechen** get out of a (*or* the) vicious circle; **~weib** F *n* she-devil; **~zeug** F *n* F infernal stuff
teuf·lisch ['tɔʏflɪʃ] **I.** *adj.* devilish, diabolical; fiendish *smile*; **II.** *adv.* devilishly, diabolically; fiendishly; F **~ kalt** *etc.* F hellishly cold *etc.*, *sl.* cold *etc.* as hell
Teu·to·ne [tɔʏ'toːnə] *m* (-n; -n), **Teu·to·nin** [tɔʏ'toːnɪn] *f* (-; -nen) Teuton; **teu·to·nisch** [tɔʏ'toːnɪʃ] *adj. a. fig.* Teutonic
Text [tɛkst] *m* (-[e]s; -e) text (*a. typ.*); wording; passage; ♪ words *pl.*, lyrics *pl.*; *thea.* lines *pl.*, part; *fig.* **j-n aus dem ~ bringen** put s.o. off; **aus dem ~ kommen** lose the thread; F **weiter im ~!** go on!; **~auf·ga·be** *f* **1.** 𝒜 problem; **2.** comprehension test; **~aus·ga·be** *f* text edition; **~bau·stein** *m* text module; **~buch** *n* libretto; **~dich·ter** *m* songwriter; librettist
tex·ten ['tɛkstən] (h) **I.** *v/t.* write (the words for); **II.** *v/i.* a) ♪ write (the) lyrics, b) copywrite; **Tex·ter** ['tɛkstɐ] *m* (-s; -) a) script writer, b) copywriter, c) songwriter
'Text·ge·schich·te *f* textual history
Tex·til|ar·bei·ter [tɛks'tiːl-] *m* textile worker; **~fa,brik** *f* textile factory; **ℒfrei** F *hum. adj.* nude, *pred. a.* F starkers
Tex·ti·li·en [tɛks'tiːlǐən] *pl.* textiles
Tex·til|in·du,strie [tɛks'tiːl-] *f* textile industry; **~wa·ren** *pl.* textiles
'Text|kri,tik *f* textual criticism; **~stel·le** *f* passage (in a *or* the text); **~ver·ar·bei·tung** *f* word processing
'Text·ver·ar·bei·tungs|ge·rät *n* word processor; **~pro,gramm** *n* word processing program; **~sy,stem** *n* **1.** word processing system; **2.** word processor
'Text·ver·gleich *m* comparison of texts
Te·zett ['teːtsɛt] *n*: F **bis ins ~** completely, *know etc.* inside out; down to the last detail (*or* T)
Thai·län·der ['taɪlɛndɐ] *m* (-s; -), **Thai·län·de·rin** ['taɪlɛndərɪn] *f* (-; -nen), **thai·län·disch** ['taɪlɛndɪʃ] *adj.*, **'Thai·län·disch** *n* (-en; *no pl.*) *ling.* Thai
Thea·ter [te'aːtɐ] *n* (-s; -) **1.** theat|re (*Am.* -er); **am (or im) ~** at the theat|re (*Am.* -er); **beim ~ sein** work for the theat|re (*Am.* -er), be an actor (*or* actress); **ins ~ gehen** go to the theat|re (*Am.* -er); **zum ~ gehen** go on the stage; **2.** *no pl. fig. contp.* a) play-acting, b) fuss, F to-do; **~ spielen** put on an act, *esp. sport*: play-act; **mach kein ~!** don't make such a fuss!; **es ist immer das gleiche ~** it's always the same old carry-on; **~abon·ne·ment** *n* theat|re (*Am.* -er) subscription; **~agent** *m* theatrical agent; **~agen,tur** *f* theatrical agency; **~be·such** *m* visit to the theat|re (*Am.* -er); **~be·su·cher** *m* theatregoer, *Am.* theatergoer; **~di,rek·tor** *m* theat|re (*Am.* -er) director; **~don·ner** *m* artificial thunder; *fig.* **alles nur ~!** they're *etc.* just making a lot of noise; **~en,sem·ble** *n* theat|re (*Am.* -er) ensemble; **~freun·de** *pl.* theatregoers, *Am.* theatergoers; **~ge·schich·te** *f* history of the theat|re (*Am.* -er); **~kas·se** *f* (theat|re, *Am.* -er) box office; **~kri·ti·ker** *m* drama critic; **~pro·be** *f* rehearsal; **~pu·bli·kum** *n* theat|re (*Am.* -er) audience; **~stück** *n* play; **~vor·stel·lung** *f* (stage) performance; **~wis·sen·schaft** *f* theory of drama
Thea·tra·lik [tea'traːlɪk] *f* (-; *no pl.*) *contp.* histrionics *pl.*; **thea·tra·lisch** [tea'traːlɪʃ] *adj.* theatrical; *contp. a.* histrionic
The·is·mus [te'ɪsmʊs] *m* (-; *no pl.*) theism; **thei·stisch** [te'ɪstɪʃ] *adj.* theistic
The·ke ['teːkə] *f* (-; -n) a) bar, b) counter
The·ma ['teːma] *n* (-s; Themen ['teːmən]) subject; topic; ♪ theme; **~ Nummer eins** the number one topic, (*sex*) everybody's favo(u)rite topic; **zum ~ kommen** get to the point; **beim ~ bleiben** stick to the point; **das ~ wechseln** change the subject; **wir wollen das ~ begraben** let's not talk about it any more; **das ist für mich kein ~ mehr** I don't want to hear another word about it
The·ma·tik [te'maːtɪk] *f* (-; *no pl.*) subject (matter); ♪ thematic invention
the·ma·tisch [te'maːtɪʃ] **I.** *adj.* thematic; **nach ~en Gesichtspunkten geordnet** arranged according to subject; **II.** *adv.* thematically; **~ ist der Aufsatz interessant** the subject matter of the essay is interesting, the essay is on an interesting subject (*or* topic)
the·ma·ti·sie·ren [temati'ziːrən] *v/t.* (h): **et. ~** make s.th. a subject of discussion (*or* the theme of a book *etc.*)
'The·ma|ver·feh·lung *f*: **wegen ~ durchfallen** be failed for not answering the question (*or* for deviating from the subject); **~wech·sel** *m* change of subject (*or* topic); **~: ...** switching (*or* moving on) to another subject *or* topic now ...
The·men|be·reich ['teːmən-] *m*, **~kreis** *m* subject area; **~stel·lung** *f* formulation (of the topic)
Theo·kra·tie [teokra'tiː] *f* (-; -n) theocracy
Theo·lo·ge [teo'loːgə] *m* (-n; -n) theologian; **Theo·lo·gie** [teolo'giː] *f* (-; -n) theology; **theo·lo·gisch** [teo'loːgɪʃ] *adj.* theological
Theo·rem [teo'reːm] *n* (-s; -e) theorem
Theo·re·ti·ker [teo'reːtikɐ] *m* (-s; -) theorist; **er ist reiner ~** he has a very theoretical approach to things; **theo·re·tisch** [teo'reːtɪʃ] **I.** *adj.* theoretical; *contp.* academic; **II.** *adv.* theoretically, in theory; **~ hat er recht** *a.* he's right in theory;
Theo·rie [teo'riː] *f* (-; -n) theory (*gen.* of; **über** *acc.*, **zu** *dat.* on); **in der ~** in theory; **das ist reine ~** that's all theory; **das ist graue ~** it sounds all right (*Am.* alright) in theory; **e-e ~ aufstellen** put forward a theory; **... - so die ~ ...** - or so the theory goes
The·ra·peut [tera'pɔʏt] *m* (-en; -en) therapist; **The·ra·peu·tik** [tera'pɔʏtɪk] *f* therapeutics *pl.*; **the·ra·peu·tisch** [tera'pɔʏtɪʃ] *adj.* therapeutic(ally *adv.*)
The·ra·pie [tera'piː] *f* (-; -n) therapy; **e-e ~ machen** undergo therapy, undergo (a course of) treatment; **the·ra·pie·ren** [tera'piːrən] *v/t.* (h) treat, give *s.o.* (a course of) treatment, give *s.o.* therapy
Ther·mal|bad [tɛr'maːl-] *n* hot springs *pl.*, thermal spa; **~quel·le** *f* thermal (*or* hot) spring; **~schwimm·bad** *n* thermal baths *pl.*
Ther·me ['tɛrmə] *f* (-; -n) thermal (*or* hot) spring
Ther·mik ['tɛrmɪk] *f* (-; *no pl.*) thermal (current); **ther·misch** ['tɛrmɪʃ] *adj.* thermal

Ther·mo·drucker ['tɛrmo-] *m* thermal printer
Ther·mo·dy'na·mik [tɛrmo-] *f* thermodynamics *pl.*; **ther·mo·dy'na·misch** *adj.* thermodynamic
ther·mo·elek·trisch [tɛrmoˀe'lɛktrɪʃ] *adj.* thermoelectric
Ther·mo|ele·ment ['tɛrmoˀelemɛnt] *n* thermocouple; **~ho·se** *f*: (**e-e ~** a pair of) thermal trousers *pl.*
Ther·mo·me·ter [tɛrmo'me:tɐ] *n* (-s; -s) thermometer; **~stand** *m* thermometer reading
ther·mo|nu·kle'ar [tɛrmo-] *adj.* thermonuclear; **~'pla·stisch** *adj.* thermoplastic
Ther·mos|fla·sche ['tɛrmɔs-] (*TM*) *f* thermos flask (*Am.* bottle) (*TM*); **~kan·ne** *f* thermal coffee pot
Ther·mo·stat [tɛrmo'sta:t] *m* (-s; -e[n]) thermostat
Ther·mo·wä·sche ['tɛrmo-] *f* thermal underwear
The·sau·rus [te'zaʊrʊs] *m* (-; -ri [-ri]) thesaurus; dictionary
The·se ['te:zə] *f* (-; -n) thesis; theory; ***Luthers 95 ~n*** Luther's 95 propositions (*or* theses)
Tho·mas ['to:mas] *m fig.*: ***ungläubiger ~*** doubting Thomas
Tho·ra ['to:ra] *f* (-; *no pl.*) Torah
Thril·ler ['θrɪlɐ] *m* (-s; -) thriller
Throm·bo·se [trɔm'bo:zə] *f* (-; -n) ⚕ thrombosis
Thron [tro:n] *m* (-[e]s; -e) throne (*a. fig.*); ***j-m auf den ~ folgen*** succeed s.o. to the throne; ***vom ~ stoßen*** *a. fig.* dethrone; **~an·wär·ter** *m* heir apparent; **~be·stei·gung** *f* accession to the throne
thro·nen ['tro:nən] *v/i.* (h) be enthroned (*a. fig.*)
'Thron|er·be *m*, **~er·bin** *f* heir to the throne, heir apparent
'Thron·fol·ge *f* succession; **'Thron·fol·ger** [-fɔlgɐ] *m* (-s; -), **'Thron·fol·ge·rin** [-fɔlgərɪn] *f* (-; -nen) successor to the throne
'Thron|räu·ber *m* usurper (of the throne); **~re·de** *f* speech from the throne; *in GB*: Queen's (*or* King's) speech; **~saal** *m* throne room
Thun·fisch ['tu:n-] *m* tuna (fish)
Thü·rin·ger ['ty:rɪŋɐ] **I.** *m* (-s; -), **Thü·rin·ge·rin** ['ty:rɪŋərɪn] *f* (-; -nen) Thuringian; ***~ sein*** be (a) Thuringian, come from Thuringia; **II.** *adj.* Thuringian; ***~ Wald*** Thuringian Forest
thü·rin·gisch ['ty:rɪŋɪʃ] *adj.* Thuringian, from Thuringia
Thy·mi·an ['ty:mĭa:n] *m* (-s; *no pl.*) ⚘ thyme
Thy·mus·drü·se ['ty:mʊs-] *f* thymus (gland)
Tia·ra ['tĭa:ra] *f* (-; Tiaren [-rən]) tiara
Ti·be·ter [ti'be:tɐ] *m* (-s; -), **Ti·be·te·rin** [ti'be:tərɪn] *f* (-; -nen), **ti·be·tisch** [ti'be:tɪʃ] *adj.* Tibetan
Tic [tɪk] *m* (-s; -s) ⚕ tic
Tick [tɪk] *m* (-s; -s) (strange) quirk; F ***e-n ~ haben*** be mad; ***mit dem Frühaufstehen hat er e-n ~*** he's got a thing about getting up early; *in cpds.* ***e-n ...~ haben*** have a thing about ...
ticken ['tɪkən] (*sep.* -k·k-) *v/i.* (h) tick; F ***bei ihm tickt's nicht ganz richtig*** F he's got a screw loose somewhere; **Ticker** ['tɪkɐ] (*sep.* -k·k-) *m* (-s; -) ticker
Ticket ['tɪkət] (*sep.* -k·k-) *n* (-s; -s) ticket
Tick·tack ['tɪk'tak] **I.** *f* (-; -s) tick-tock; **II.** ~ *int.* tick-tock; ~ machen go tick-tock
Ti·de ['ti:də] *f* (-; -n) tide
tief [ti:f] **I.** *adj.* a) deep (*a. fig. voice, colo[u]r, thoughts, forest etc.*); *fig. a.* profound *knowledge etc.*, b) low (*a. sound*); ***~er Fall*** big drop, *fig.* great fall; ***~er Teller*** soup plate; ***~e Schatten*** dark shadows (*or* rings); ***~er Boden*** muddy ground, *soccer etc.*: heavy pitch; ***es liegt ~er Schnee*** there's deep snow; ***aus ~stem Herzen*** from the bottom of one's heart; ***im ~sten Innern*** in one's heart of hearts; ***im ~sten Elend leben*** live in utter squalor; ***im ~sten Winter*** in the dead of winter; ***in ~ster Nacht*** in the dead of night; ***im ~sten Afrika*** in darkest Africa; ***in ~er Trauer*** in deep mourning; ***den ~sten Stand erreicht haben*** a) *sun*: have reached its lowest point, b) ✝ have reached an all-time low; **II.** *adv.* a) deep, b) low, c) far, d) *fig.* deeply; ***zwei Stockwerke ~er*** two floors down; ***~ atmen*** take a deep breath; ***sich ~ bücken*** bend down low, bend right down; ***j-m ~ in die Augen sehen*** look deep into s.o.'s eyes; ***die Sonne steht ~*** the sun is low; ***~ gekränkt (enttäuscht** etc.**) sein*** be deeply hurt (disappointed *etc.*); ***~ in Gedanken*** deep in thought; ***~ in Arbeit (Schulden) stecken*** be up to one's neck in work (debt); ***~ fallen*** fall from a great height, *fig.* sink low; ***er ist ~ gesunken*** he's really come down in the world; ***das geht bei ihr nicht sehr ~*** a) it doesn't make much of an impression on her, b) it's more show than anything with her; ***~ im Süden (Norden)*** far (in the) south (north); ***bis ~ in die Nacht*** till the (wee) small hours; ***bis ~ in den Herbst hinein*** till late (in the) autumn, *Am.* till late (in) fall; ***das läßt ~ blicken*** that's very revealing
Tief *n* (-s; -s) *meteor.* low (*a. fig.*), depression, low-pressure area, cyclone; *fig.* ***sich in e-m ~ befinden*** be having (*or* be going through) a low
'Tief·bau *m* (-[e]s; *no pl.*) civil engineering, *n.s.* underground engineering
'tief|be·lei·digt *adj.* deeply offended; **~be·wegt** *adj.* deeply moved; **~blau** *adj.* deep blue
'Tief·blick *m* (-[e]s; *no pl.*) great insight (*or* perception); **'tief·blickend** *adj.* (very) perceptive
'tief·braun *adj.* deep brown
'Tief·druck *m* (-[e]s; *no pl.*) **1.** *meteor.* low pressure; **2.** *typ.* rotogravure, intaglio printing; **~ge·biet** *n* → ***Tief***
Tie·fe ['ti:fə] *f* (-; -n) depth (*a. phot. and fig.*); *fig.* deep, abyss; deepness, profundity; ***die ~n des Meeres*** the depths of the sea
'Tief·ebe·ne *f* lowland(s *pl.*)
'tief·emp·fun·den *adj.* deep-felt, heartfelt
'Tie·fen|ana͵ly·se *f* depth analysis; **~be·strah·lung** *f* ⚕ deep therapy; **~dis͵kurs** *m* in-depth debate; **~in·ter·view** *n* (in-)depth interview; **~mes·sung** *f* depth sounding; **~psy·cho͵lo·ge** *m* depth psychologist; **~psy·cho·lo͵gie** *f* depth psychology; **~rausch** *m* rapture of the deep; **~reg·ler** *m* bass control; **~schär·fe** *f phot.* depth of field (*or* focus); **~struk͵tur** *f ling.* deep structure; **~wirk·sam** *adj. pharm.* deep-acting; **~wir·kung** *f* deep action; *phot. etc.* three-dimensionality, plasticity
'tief·ernst *adj.* deadly serious
'Tief|flie·ger *m* low-flying plane (*a. pl.* aircraft); F *fig.* ***geistiger ~*** lowbrow; **~flug** *m* low-level flight; *pl. a.* low(-level) flying *sg.*; **~gang** *m* (-[e]s; *no pl.*) ⚓ draught, *Am.* draft; *fig.* depth; **~ga͵ra·ge** *f* underground car park
'tief·ge·frie·ren *v/t.* (*only inf. and p.p.* tiefgefroren, h) deep-freeze
'tief·ge·hend *adj.* deep *wound etc.*; *fig.* thorough; intensive
'tief·ge·kühlt *adj.* (deep-)frozen
'tief·grei·fend *adj.* far-reaching, radical
tief·grün·dig ['ti:fgrʏndɪç] *adj.* deep, profound
'tief·küh·len *v/t.* (*only inf. and p.p.* tiefgekühlt, h) deep-freeze
'Tief·kühl|fach *n* freezing compartment; **~ket·te** *f* cold chain; **~kost** *f* frozen foods *pl.*; **~tru·he** *f* deep-freeze, freezer
'Tief·la·der *m* (-s; -) *mot.* low loader, low-loader vehicle
'Tief·land *n* lowland(s *pl.*)
'tief·lie·gend *adj.* low(-lying); deep-set *eyes, a.* ⚙ sunken; *fig.* deep(-seated)
'Tief|punkt *fig. m* low; ***e-n absoluten ~ erreicht haben*** have reached an all-time low; ***e-n seelischen ~ haben*** be very depressed, be having (*or* be going through) a (real) low; → *a.* ***Tiefstpunkt***; **~schlaf** *m* deep sleep; ***sich im ~ befinden*** be in a deep sleep, be fast asleep; **~schlag** *m boxing*: hit below the belt (*a. fig.*); *fig.* ***das war ein ~*** that was below the belt
'Tief·schnee *m* deep (powder) snow; **~fah·ren** *n skiing*: off-piste (*or* deep powder) skiing
'tief·schür·fend *adj.* probing, penetrating; profound
'tief·schwarz *adj.* deep black, jet-black
'Tief·see *f* deep sea; **~for·schung** *f* deep-sea research; **~gra·ben** *m* (deep-sea) trench
'Tief·sinn *m* (-[e]s; *no pl.*) a) profundity, b) thoughtfulness, reflectiveness, c) melancholy, pensiveness; **'tief·sin·nig** *adj.* a) profound, deep, b) meditative, c) melancholy, pensive
'tief·sit·zend *adj.* chesty *cough*; *fig.* deep-seated *problems etc.*
'Tief·stand *m* (-[e]s; *no pl.*) low; ***absoluter ~*** all-time low
Tief·sta·pe·lei [-ʃta:pə'laɪ] *f* (-; *no pl.*) understatement; modesty, self-effacement; **'tief·sta·peln** *v/i.* (*sep.*, h) understate the case (*or* things); be very modest (*or* self-effacing), be overmodest; **'Tief·stap·ler** *m*: ***ein ~ sein*** like to understate things; be very modest (*or* self-effacing)
'Tief·start *m sport*: crouch start
'tief·ste·hend *adj.* low
Tiefst|kurs ['ti:fst-] *m* lowest rate; **~prei·se** *pl.* rock-bottom prices; **~punkt** *fig. m* nadir; **~tem·pe·ra͵tur** *f* minimum (*or* lowest) temperature; **~wert** *m* **1.** lowest value; **2.** → ***Tiefsttemperatur***
'Tief·tem·pe·ra͵tur·phy͵sik *f* low temperature physics *pl.*
'Tief·tö·ner [-tø:nɐ] *m* (-s; -) woofer
'tief·trau·rig *adj.* desperately sad (*or* unhappy)
Tie·gel ['ti:gəl] *m* (-s; -) **1.** *gastr.* saucepan; **2.** crucible
Tier [ti:ɐ] *n* (-[e]s; -e ['ti:rə]) animal; beast, *fig. a.* brute; F *fig.* ***hohes ~*** F bigwig, big shot; ***das ~ in j-m wecken*** bring out the

animal in s.o., bring out s.o.'s animal instincts; **~art** *f* animal species

'**Tier·arzt** *m* veterinary surgeon, *Am.* veterinarian; F vet; '**tier·ärzt·lich** *adj.* veterinary

'**Tier|asyl** *n* → ***Tierheim***; **~be·stand** *m* animal population; **~freund** *m* animal lover; **~fut·ter** *n* animal food; **~hal·ter** *m* **1.** pet owner; **2.** livestock breeder; **~hal·tung** *f* **1.** keeping of pets; **2.** livestock breeding; **~hand·lung** *f* pet shop; **~heim** *n* home for animals, animal shelter

tie·risch ['ti:rɪʃ] **I.** *adj.* animal ...; *fig. a.* brutish; F *fig.* incredible; **~e *Fette*** animal fats; **~e *Instinkte*** animal instincts; **II.** *adv.*: F *fig.* ~ ***ernst*** deadly serious

'**Tier·kli·nik** *f* veterinary hospital

'**Tier·kör·per·be·sei·ti·gung** *f* animal waste processing

'**Tier·kreis** *m* (-[es; *no pl.*) *ast.* zodiac; **~zei·chen** *n* sign of the zodiac

'**Tier·kun·de** *f* zoology

'**tier·lieb** *adj.* fond of animals; ~ ***sein*** *a.* like animals

'**Tier|markt** *m* Pets and Livestock; **~me·di͵zin** *f* veterinary medicine; **~park** *m* zoo; **~pfle·ger** *m* keeper; **~prä·pa͵ra·tor** *m* taxidermist; **~quä·ler** *m* animal maltreater (*or* abuser); **~quä·le·rei** *f* (-; *no pl.*) cruelty to (*or* mistreatment of) animals *or* pets; **~reich** *n* (-[e]s; *no pl.*) animal kingdom

'**Tier·schutz** *m* protection of animals; '**Tier·schüt·zer** *m* animal welfarist

'**Tier·schutz|ge·biet** *n* wildlife (*or* game) reserve; **~ver·ein** *m* society for the prevention of cruelty to animals

'**Tier|ver·such** *m* animal experiment; **~ver·wer·tung** *f* animal waste processing; **~welt** *f* (-; *no pl.*) animal world; **~zucht** *f* livestock breeding

Ti·ger ['ti:gɐ] *m* (-s; -) tiger; **~au·ge** *n min.* tiger's eye; **~fell** *n* tiger skin; **~fisch** *m* tiger fish; **~hai** *m* tiger shark

Ti·ge·rin ['ti:gərɪn] *f* (-; -nen) tigress

'**Ti·ger·kat·ze** *f* tiger cat

ti·gern ['ti:gɐn] F *v/i.* (sn): ***durch die Straßen*** ~ F traipse through the streets, F mooch around town

Til·de ['tɪldə] *f* (-; -n) tilde, swung dash

tilg·bar ['tɪlkba:ɐ] *adj.* ⚚ redeemable, repayable; **til·gen** ['tɪlgən] *v/t.* (h) a) strike out, *a. typ.* delete; erase (*a. computer*), b) destroy, c) ⚚ pay off *debts*; redeem *loan etc.*, d) *fig.* expiate, wipe out *a disgrace*; blot out *a memory etc.*; **Til·gung** ['tɪlgʊŋ] *f* (-; -en) a) erasure; deletion, b) ⚚ redemption, repayment, c) *fig.* expiation

'**Til·gungs|an·lei·he** *f* ⚚ amortization loan; **~ra·te** *f* ⚚ redemption rate; **~zeit·raum** *m* amortization period

Tim·bre ['tɛ̃:brə] *n* (-s; -s) timbre

ti·men ['taɪmən] *v/t.* (h) time; ***gut*** (***schlecht***) ***getimt*** well-timed (badly timed)

Ti·mer ['taɪmɐ] *m* (-s; -) timer

tin·geln ['tɪŋəln] *v/i.* (h) do small-time acting

Tink·tur [tɪŋk'tu:ɐ] *f* (-; -en [-rən]) tincture

Tin·nef ['tɪnəf] F *m* (-s; *no pl.*) rubbish; F garbage, F rot

Tin·te ['tɪntə] *f* (-; -n) ink; F *fig.* ***in der*** ~ ***sitzen*** F be in the soup

'**Tin·ten|faß** *n* inkpot; **~fisch** *m* squid; octopus; **~fleck** *m* ink blot (*or* stain), blot of ink; **~kil·ler** *m* correction pen; **~klecks** *m* ink blot (*or* stain); blot of ink; **~ku·li** *m* rollerball pen; **~pa͵tro·ne** *f* ink cartridge; **~stift** *m* indelible pencil

'**Tin·ten·strahl·drucker** *m* ink-jet printer

Tip [tɪp] *m* (-s; -s) *sport and fig.*: tip; hint; pointer, lead; tip-off; ***ein sicherer*** ~ a sure bet; ***j-m e-n*** ~ ***geben*** F tip s.o. off, give s.o. a tip-off

Tip·pel·bru·der ['tɪpəl-] *m* tramp, *Am.* hobo; **tip·peln** ['tɪpəln] *v/i.* (sn) tramp

tip·pen ['tɪpən] (h) **I.** *v/i.* **1.** ~ ***an*** *acc.* tap; **2.** F type; **3.** F a) do the lottery, b) do the pools; **4.** F guess; ***ich tippe auf ihn*** F I reckon it's (*or* it'll be) him; ***man tippt darauf, daß*** the betting is (*or* the bets are) that; **II.** F *v/t.* type (up)

Tipp·feh·ler ['tɪp-] *m* typing error, F typo

Tipp·ge·mein·schaft ['tɪp-] *f* betting (*or* lotto) pool

Tip·se ['tɪpsə] F *f* (-; -n) typist

Tipp·ta·ste ['tɪp-] *f* touch button; *pl. a.* (soft-)touch controls

tipp·topp ['tɪp'tɔp] F **I.** *adj.* first class; **II.** *adv.*: ~ ***sauber*** spick and span, spotless; ~ ***gekleidet*** immaculately dressed

Tipp·zet·tel ['tɪp-] *m* lottery (*or* pools) coupon

Ti·ro·ler [ti'ro:lɐ] **I.** *m* (-s; -), **Ti·ro·le·rin** [ti'ro:lərɪn] *f* (-; -nen) Tyrolean, Tyrolese; ~ ***sein*** be (a) Tyrolean, come from (the) Tyrol; **II.** *adj.* → **ti·ro·le·risch** [ti'ro:lərɪʃ] *adj.* Tyrolean, Tyrolese

Tisch [tɪʃ] *m* (-[e]s; -e) table; ***bei*** ~ at table; ***vom*** ~ ***aufstehen*** leave (*or* get up from) the table; ***darf ich zu*** ~ ***bitten?*** shall we sit down at the table?, *often iro.* lunch (*or* dinner) is served; ***essen, was auf den*** ~ ***kommt*** eat what one is given, eat whatever is put before one; ***zu*** ~ ***gehen*** go for (*or* to) lunch; *fig.* ***getrennt von*** ~ ***und Bett*** separated; ***mit et. reinen*** ~ ***machen*** make a clean sweep of it; ***unter den*** ~ ***fallen*** fall flat; ***unter den*** ~ ***fallen lassen*** drop *a matter*; ***j-n unter den*** ~ ***trinken*** drink s.o. under the table; ***vom*** ~ ***wischen*** (***or fegen***) sweep aside; ***ein Thema auf den*** ~ ***bringen*** bring up a matter (for discussion); ***die Sache muß auf dem*** ~ ***bleiben*** (***muß vom*** ~) the matter has got to be thrashed out (settled); *Streitende* ***an einen*** ~ ***bringen*** get *the parties etc.* to agree to talks; ***Entscheidung am grünen*** ~ bureaucratic decision, *sport*: decision by the league authorities

'**Tisch|bein** *n* table-leg; **~be·sen** *m* crumb brush; **~com͵pu·ter** *m* desktop computer; **~da·me** *f* dinner partner; **~decke** *f* tablecloth; **~en·de** *n*: ***am oberen*** (***unteren***) ~ at the head (foot) of the table; **~fer·tig** *adj.* ready-to-serve *food*; **~feu·er·zeug** *n* table lighter; **~fuß·ball** *m* table football; **~ge·bet** *n* grace; ***das*** ~ ***sprechen*** say grace; **~ge·spräch** *n* table talk; **~herr** *m* dinner partner; **~kan·te** *f* edge of a (*or* the) table; **~kar·te** *f* place card; **~lam·pe** *f* table lamp; **~läu·fer** *m* runner

Tisch·lein·deck·dich [tɪʃlaɪn'dɛkdɪç] *n* F cushy set-up

Tisch·ler ['tɪʃlɐ] *m* (-s; -) carpenter, joiner; cabinet-maker; '**Tisch·ler·ar·beit** *f* carpentry, joinery; **Tisch·le·rei** [tɪʃlə'raɪ] *f* (-; -en) **1.** *no pl.* carpentry, joinery; **2.** carpenter's (*or* joiner's) workshop; '**Tisch·ler·mei·ster** *m* master carpenter (*or* joiner); '**tisch·lern** (h) **I.** *v/i.* do carpentry; **II.** *v/t.* make; '**Tisch·ler·plat·te** *f* block board

'**Tisch|ma͵nie·ren** *pl.* table manners; **~nach·bar** *m* neighbo(u)r; ***mein*** ~ the person (*or* man, woman) sitting next to me (at the table); **~ord·nung** *f* seating plan (*or* arrangements *pl.*); **~plat·te** *f* tabletop; **~rech·ner** *m* desk(top) calculator; desktop computer; **~re·de** *f* after-dinner speech, toast; **~schmuck** *m* table decoration(s *pl.*)

'**Tisch·ten·nis** *n* table tennis; **~ball** *m* table tennis (F ping-pong) ball; **~schlä·ger** *m* table tennis bat (*Am.* paddle); **~tisch** *m* table tennis table

'**Tisch|tuch** *n* tablecloth; *fig.* ***das*** ~ ***zwischen sich und j-m zerschneiden*** break (off relations) with s.o.; **~wein** *m* table wine; **~zeit** *f* **1.** mealtime; **2.** lunch hour (*or* break)

Ti·tan¹ [ti'ta:n] *m* (-en; -en) *myth.* Titan; *fig.* titan, giant

Ti'tan² *n* (-s; *no pl.*) ⚗ titanium

Ti·ta·ne [ti'ta:nə] *m* (-n; -n) → ***Titan¹***

Ti·tel ['ti:təl] *m* (-s; -) a) title, b) slogan, motto; ***das Buch trägt den*** ~ the title of the book is; **~an·wär·ter** *m* challenger(s *pl.*) for the title; **~bild** *n* frontispiece; cover picture (*or* illustration, photo); **~blatt** *n* title page

Ti·te·lei [ti:tə'laɪ] *f* (-; -en) *typ.* prelims *pl.*, front matter

'**Ti·tel|ge·schich·te** *f* cover story; **~hal·ter** *m sport*: titleholder; **~held** *m* (eponymous) hero; ***der*** ~ ***dieses Buches*** *a.* the hero of the same name; **~kampf** *m* title match (*boxing*: bout); **~kan·di͵dat** *m* challenger(s *pl.*) for the title; **~me·lo͵die** *f* theme tune; **~mu͵sik** *f* theme music; **~rol·le** *f thea.* title role; **~sei·te** *f* title page; front cover; **~song** *m* title song; **~trä·ger** *m* titleholder(s *pl.*); **~ver·tei·di·ger** *m* titleholder(s *pl.*), defending champion(s *pl.*)

Tit·ten ['tɪtən] V *pl.* V tits, knockers

ti·tu·lie·ren [titu'li:rən] *v/t.* (h) address; ***j-n mit „Idiot"*** ~ call s.o. an idiot

tja [tja] *int.* well

Toast [to:st] *m* (-[e]s; -s) **1.** *gastr.* toast; **2.** toast; ***auf j-n e-n*** ~ ***ausbringen*** propose a toast to s.o.

toa·sten ['to:stən] (h) **I.** *v/t.* toast *bread*; **II.** *v/i.* drink a toast (***auf*** *acc.* to)

Toa·ster ['to:stɐ] *m* (-s; -) toaster

To·bak ['to:bak] *m*: F *fig.* ***das ist starker*** ~! that's strong stuff, F that's a bit thick

to·ben ['to:bən] *v/i.* (h) rave; go (*or* be) wild (***vor*** *dat.* with *enthusiasm etc.*); romp; *fig. storm, sea, battle etc.*: rage

Tob·sucht ['to:p-] *f* (-; *no pl.*) uncontrolled rage; '**tob·süch·tig** *adj.* raving mad; '**Tob·suchts·an·fall** *m* tantrum

Toch·ter ['tɔxtɐ] *f* (-; Töchter ['tœçtɐ]) daughter; **~fir·ma** *f*, **~ge·sell·schaft** *f* ⚚ subsidiary (company); *below 50%*: affiliated company, affiliate

Tod [to:t] *m* (-es ['to:dəs]; *no pl.*) death; ⚖ decease; *esp. fig. lit.* demise; ~ ***durch Ersticken*** (***Verhungern***) death by suffocation (from starvation); ***zu*** **~*e kommen*** die, be killed; ***e-s natürlichen*** **~*es sterben*** die a natural death; ***zu*** **~*e stürzen*** fall to one's death; ***der Arzt konnte nur noch den*** ~ ***feststellen*** by the time the doctor arrived he (*or* she) was dead; ***zum*** **~*e verurteilen*** sentence to death; ***über den*** ~ ***hinaus*** beyond the grave; *fig.* ***das wäre der*** ~ ***der Demokratie*** that would be the end (*or* death) of democracy; ***das war der*** ~ ***für die Firma***

that was the death of the company, that killed the company off; ***e-n tausendfachen ~ sterben, tausend ~e sterben*** die a thousand deaths; ***sich den ~ holen*** catch one's death of cold; ***sich zu ~e arbeiten*** work o.s. to death; ***j-n zu ~e erschrecken (langweilen)*** scare (bore) s.o. to death; ***ich bin zu ~e erschrocken*** I got the shock (*or* fright) of my life; ***sich zu ~e schämen*** be ashamed (*or* embarrassed) to death; ***ich habe mich zu ~e geschämt*** *a.* I wished the earth would open up and swallow me; ***aussehen wie der ~*** look like death warmed up; ***ich kann ihn auf den ~ nicht leiden*** I can't stand the sight of him; ***das kann ich auf den ~ nicht leiden*** I hate it like poison; → ***Leben***

'tod|brin·gend *adj.* deadly, fatal, lethal; **~'elend** *adj.*: ***mir ist ~*** I feel terrible (F really rotten), F *hum.* I think I'm going to die; **~'ernst I.** *adj.* deadly (F dead) serious; **II.** *adv.* in dead earnest

To·des|ah·nung ['to:dəs-] *f* premonition of death; **~angst** *f* fear of death; *fig.* mortal fear; ***Todesängste ausstehen*** be frightened out of one's mind (*or* wits); **~an·zei·ge** *f* obituary; **~er·klä·rung** *f* ⚖ (official) declaration of death; **~fall** *m* death; ***im ~*** in the event of death; **~fol·ge** *f*: ***schwere Körperverletzung mit ~*** grievous bodily harm resulting in death; **~ge·fahr** *f* mortal danger; ***sich in ~ begeben*** risk one's life, put one's life at risk; **~jahr** *n* year of s.o.'s death, year in which s.o. died; **~kampf** *m* throes *pl.* of death; **~kan·di,dat** *m* **1.** doomed man (*or* woman); ***er ist ein ~*** *a.* he hasn't got long to live; **2.** ⚖ condemned man; **2mu·tig** *adj.* intrepid; **~nach·richt** *f* news of s.o.'s death; **~op·fer** *n* casualty; ***Zahl der ~*** death toll; ***der Unfall forderte zwei ~*** the accident claimed two lives; **~qua·len** *pl.* final agony *sg.*; *fig.* ***~ ausstehen*** go through absolute agony; **~schuß** *m* fatal shot; ***e-n ~ abgeben*** *a.* shoot to kill; **~schwa,dron** *f* death squadron; **~sehn·sucht** *f* death wish, longing for death; **~stoß** *m* deathblow (*a. fig.*); ***den ~ versetzen*** deliver the deathblow (*dat.* to); **~stra·fe** *f* capital punishment, death penalty; ***bei ~*** on penalty of death; **~tag** *m* day (*w.s.* anniversary) of s.o.'s death; **~ur·sa·che** *f* cause of death; **~ur·teil** *n* death sentence; *fig.* death warrant; **~ver·ach·tung** *f* defiance of death; ***mit ~*** fearlessly, F *fig.* in a fit of recklessness; **2wür·dig** *lit. adj.* deserving of death; ***~es Verbrechen*** capital crime; **~zeit** *f* time of death; **~zel·le** *f* death cell; *pl. a.* death row *sg.*

'Tod·feind *m* deadly (*or* mortal) enemy; **'Tod·feind·schaft** *f* (-; *no pl.*) deadly hatred

'tod'krank *adj.* fatally (*or* terminally) ill

'tod'lang·wei·lig *adj.* deadly boring

töd·lich ['tø:tlɪç] **I.** *adj.* a) fatal, b) lethal, deadly (*a.* F *fig.*); ***~er Unfall (Schuß)*** fatal accident (shot); ***~e Dosis (Waffe, ~es Gift)*** lethal *or* deadly dose (weapon, poison); ***~e Hilfe*** lethal aid; ***~e Gefahr*** danger to life, *lit.* mortal danger; *fig.* ***mit ~er Sicherheit*** with deadly accuracy; **II.** *adv.*: ***~ verunglücken*** be killed in an accident, have a fatal accident; *fig.* F ***sich ~ langweilen*** be bored to death; F ***~ beleidigt*** mortally offended (*or* wounded)

'tod|'mü·de *adj.* ready to drop, F dog-tired, shattered; **~'schick** F *adj.* really (F dead) smart; **~'si·cher** F **I.** *adj.* F dead sure (*or* certain); F sure-fire *method etc.*; unerring *judgement etc.*; ***~e Sache*** dead certainty, F (dead) cert; **II.** *adv.* F for sure; ***er kommt ~*** *a.* there's no way he can't come

'Tod·sün·de *f* deadly (*or* mortal) sin; F ***es wäre e-e ~ zu*** *inf.* it would be unforgivable (for s.o.) to *inf.*

'tod'trau·rig *adj.* terribly unhappy

'tod'un·glück·lich *adj.* desperately unhappy

Töff·töff ['tœf'tœf] *n* (-s; -s) beep-beep (car)

To·hu·wa·bo·hu [to:huva'bo:hu] *n* (-[s]; -s) complete chaos

Toi·let·te¹ [tŏa'lɛtə] *f* (-; -n) **1.** a) toilet, lavatory, *Am.* bathroom, b) public lavatory (*or* conveniences *pl.*), *Am.* rest rooms *pl.*; ***auf der ~ sein*** be in the toilet *etc.*; **2.** toilet (bowl), lavatory pan

Toi'let·te² *f* (-; *no pl.*) **1.** ***bei der ~ sein*** be getting ready; **2.** *obs.* dress

Toi'let·ten|ar,ti·kel *m* toilet article; *pl. a.* toiletries; **~deckel** *m* toilet lid; **~frau** *f*, **~mann** *m* (-[e]s; ¨er) lavatory attendant; **~pa,pier** *n* toilet paper; **~sa·chen** *pl.* toiletries; F toilet things; **~sei·fe** *f* toilet soap; **~sitz** *m* toilet (*or* lavatory) seat; **~ta·sche** *f* toilet bag; **~tisch** *m* dressing table; **~was·ser** *n* toilet water

toi-toi-toi ['tɔʏ'tɔʏ'tɔʏ] *int.* a) touch wood, b) good luck!, *Brit. a.* F best of British!

To·kio·ter [to'kĭo:tɐ] *m* (-s; -) Tokyoite

to·le·ra·bel [tole'ra:bəl] *adj.* tolerable; F all right, *Am.* alright

to·le·rant [tole'rant] *adj.* tolerant (***gegen*** *acc.* towards, about, of); broadminded (about)

To·le·ranz [tole'rants] *f* (-; *no pl.*) tolerance (*a.* ✗, ⚙) (***gegen*** *acc.* towards, of); **~be·reich** *m* range of tolerance; **~gren·ze** *f* limit of tolerance; ⚙ tolerance (limit); **~schwel·le** *f* tolerance threshold

to·le·rie·ren [tole'ri:rən] *v/t.* (h) tolerate; **To·le'rie·rung** *f* (-; *no pl.*) toleration

toll [tɔl] **I.** *adj.* **1.** F a) F great (*a. iro.*), F fantastic; incredible, amazing, b) awful, terrible; ***er (es) war nicht so ~*** F he (it) wasn't so hot; ***ein ~er Kerl*** F a great guy; F ***es war e-e ~e Sache (ein ~es Ding)*** it was incredible (*or* amazing); **2.** mad, wild; ***ein ~es Treiben*** mad goings-on; **3.** *obs.* rabid; **4.** *obs.* insane, mad; **II.** *adv.* **5.** F ***~ ankommen*** F go down a bomb; **6.** ***wie ~*** like mad; ***es kommt noch ~er*** there's more to come; ***er treibt es zu ~*** he carries things too far; ***es ging ~ zu*** a) things were really wild, it was a wild party *etc.*, b) it was complete (*or* absolute) chaos

'toll·dreist *adj.* (as) bold as brass

Tol·le ['tɔlə] *f* (-; -n) quiff

tol·len ['tɔlən] *v/i.* (h) romp (around)

'Toll·haus *n*: ***hier geht's zu wie im ~!*** it's like a madhouse around (*or* in) here

'Toll·heit *f* (-; -en) **1.** *no pl.* madness; **2.** mad act (*or* thing to do)

'Toll·kir·sche *f* ♣ deadly nightshade, belladonna

'toll·kühn *adj.* daredevil ..., *contp.* reckless, foolhardy; **'Toll·kühn·heit** *f* (-; *no pl.*) daring; recklessness, foolhardiness

'Toll·wut *f* (-; *no pl.*) rabies; **'toll·wü·tig** [-vy:tɪç] *adj.* rabid

Tol·patsch ['tɔlpatʃ] F *m* (-es; -e) F clumsy oaf

Töl·pel ['tœlpəl] *m* (-s; -) **1.** dolt, oaf; **2.** *zo.* gannet; **'töl·pel·haft** *adj.* doltish, oafish

To·ma·hawk ['tɔmaha:k] *m* (-s; -s) tomahawk

To·ma·te [to'ma:tə] *f* (-; -n) tomato; *fig.* ***rot werden wie e-e ~*** go red as a beetroot; F ***du hast wohl ~n auf den Augen?*** open your eyes!

To'ma·ten|ketch·up *m, n* tomato ketchup (*or* sauce); **~mark** *n* tomato purée (*Am.* paste); **~saft** *m* tomato juice; **~stau·de** *f* tomato plant; **~sup·pe** *f* tomato soup

Tom·bo·la ['tɔmbola] *f* (-; -s, -len) raffle

To·mo·gra·phie [tomogra'fi:] *f* (-; -n) tomography

Ton¹ [to:n] *m* (-[e]s; Töne ['tø:nə]) a) sound (*a. film, TV*), tone, ♪ *a.* note, pitch, b) *a. fig.* accent, stress, c) *fig.* tone, d) tone, shade; ***~ in ~*** *clothes* in matching shades; *fig.* ***in den höchsten Tönen reden von*** *dat.* (*or* ***loben***) sing the praises of; F ***große Töne spucken*** F talk big; ***er hat keinen ~ gesagt (or von sich gegeben)*** he didn't say a word (F dickybird); F ***keinen ~ mehr!*** not another word!; F ***hast du (or hat man) Töne?*** F can you believe it?; ***ich verbitte mir diesen ~*** I won't be spoken to like that (*or* in that tone); ***der ~ macht die Musik*** it's not what you say but how you say it; ***den ~ angeben*** a) give the note, b) *fig.* call the tune, c) set the tone; → *a.* ***anschlagen*** 3; *fig.* ***zum guten ~ gehören*** be good form; ***den richtigen ~ treffen*** strike the right note

Ton² [to:n] *m* (-s; -e) *geol.* clay

'Ton·ab·neh·mer *m* cartridge, pickup

to·nal [to'na:l] *adj.* tonal; **To·na·li·tät** [tonali'tɛ:t] *f* (-; *no pl.*) tonality

'ton·an·ge·bend *adj.* leading; trend-setting; ***~ sein*** *a.* set the tone (***bei*** *dat.* of)

'Ton|arm *m* pickup (arm), tonearm; **~art** *f* ♪ key; *fig.* tone; *fig.* ***e-e andere ~ anschlagen*** change one's tune; **~auf·nah·me** *f*, **~auf·zeich·nung** *f* (sound) recording; **~aus·fall** *m* *TV* loss of sound; (sound) dropout

'Ton·band *n* (-[e]s; ¨er) (recording) tape; ***auf ~ aufnehmen*** (record on) tape, record; **~auf·nah·me** *f* tape recording; **~ge·rät** *n* tape recorder

'Ton·bo·den *m* clay(ey) soil

'Ton·dich·tung *f* tone poem

tö·nen¹ ['tø:nən] *v/i.* (h) a) sound, ring; resound, b) F *fig.* hold forth; ***~de Worte*** hollow words

'tö·nen² *v/t.* (h) tint; tone

'Ton·er·de *f* **1.** argillaceous earth; **2.** ⚗ alumina; ***essigsaure ~*** (basic) alumin(i)um acetate

tö·nern ['tø:nɐn] *adj.* a) (of) clay, b) *fig.* hollow *sound*; *fig.* ***auf ~en Füßen stehen*** be on shaky foundations

'Ton|fall *m* (-[e]s; *no pl.*) intonation; **~film** *m* sound film; **~fol·ge** *f* sequence of notes; *w.s.* melody; **~fre,quenz** *f* audio frequency

'Ton|ge·fäß *n* earthenware vessel (*or* bowl *etc.*); **~ge·schirr** *n* pottery, earthenware

'Ton·ge·schlecht *n* ♪ mode

ton·hal·tig ['to:nhaltɪç] *adj.* clayey

'Ton·hö·he *f phys.*, ♪ pitch

To·ni·ka ['to:nika] *f* (-; -ken) ♪ tonic
To·ni·kum ['to:nikum] *n* (-s; -ka) ⚕ tonic
'Ton|in·ge|nieur *m* sound engineer; **~ka|bi·ne** *f film*: sound booth; **~ka·me·ra** *f film*: sound camera
'Ton·klum·pen *m* lump of clay
'Ton|kon|ser·ve *f* sound recording, F *a. pl.* canned music; **~kopf** *m* recording (*or* audio) head; cartridge, pickup; **~la·ge** *f* pitch; **~lei·ter** *f* ♪ scale
'ton·los *adj.* soundless; *fig.* flat *voice*
'Ton|ma·le·rei *f* tone painting; **~mei·ster** *m* sound mixer
Ton·na·ge [tɔ'na:ʒə] *f* (-; -n) ⚓ tonnage
Ton·ne ['tɔnə] *f* (-; -n) **1.** a) barrel, (*a. beer etc.*) cask, (*a. oil*) drum; (*water*) butt, b) dustbin, *Am.* trashcan; **2.** (metric) ton
'Ton·nen|dach *n* ⚠ barrel roof; **~ge·wöl·be** *n* ⚠ barrel vault
'ton·nen·wei·se *adv.* by the ton
'Ton·pfei·fe *f* clay pipe
'Ton|qua·li|tät *f* sound quality; **~quel·le** *f* sound source; **~reg·ler** *m* tone control; **~schnitt** *m* sound editing; **~si|gnal** *n* sound signal
Ton·sil·lek·to·mie [tɔnzılɛkto'mi:] *f* (-; -n) ⚕ tonsillectomy; **Ton·sil·li·tis** [tɔnzı'li:tıs] *f* (-; Tonsillitiden [tɔnzıli'ti:dən] tonsillitis
'Ton|spur *f film*: sound track; **~stö·rung** *f a. pl.* sound interference; **~stu·dio** *n* recording studio; ***im ~ a.*** at the recording studios; **~stu·fe** *f* ♪ pitch
Ton·sur [tɔn'zu:ɐ] *f* (-; -en [-rən]) tonsure; F *fig. a.* monk's patch
'Ton·ta·fel *f* clay tablet
'Ton·tau·be *f* clay pigeon; **'Ton·tau·ben·schie·ßen** *n* clay pigeon shooting, trap-shooting
'Ton|tech·nik *f* sound (*or* audio) engineering; **~tech·ni·ker** *m* sound engineer; **~trä·ger** *m* sound carrier; **~|um·fang** *m* ♪ range
Tö·nung ['tø:nuŋ] *f* (-; -en) tone (*a. phot.*), shade (*both a. fig.*); **'Tö·nungs·mit·tel** *n* rinse
To·nus ['to:nus] *m* (-; Toni) ⚕ tone, tonicity
'Ton|va·se *f* earthenware vase; **~wa·ren** *pl.* pottery *sg.*, earthenware *sg.*
'Ton|wie·der·ga·be *f* sound reproduction
'Ton·zie·gel *m* clay brick
Top·an·ge·bot ['tɔp-] *n* **1.** really good offer; **2.** highest offer (*or* bid)
To·pas [to'pa:s] *m* (-es; -e [-zə]) topaz
Top·ath|let ['tɔp-] *m* top athlete
Topf [tɔpf] *m* (-[e]s; Töpfe ['tœpfə]) pot; saucepan; *fig.* ***alles in einen ~ werfen*** lump everything together, tar everything with the same brush; **~blu·me** *f* potted flower
Töpf·chen ['tœpfçən] *n* (-s; -) **1.** small pot; **2.** F potty; pot, F jerry; ***aufs ~ gehen*** go potty
Töp·fer ['tœpfɐ] *m* (-s; -) potter; **Töp·fe·rei** [tœpfə'rai] *f* (-; -en) **1.** *no pl.* pottery; **2.** potter's workshop; **'töp·fern** (h) **I.** *v/i.* do pottery; go to pottery classes; **II.** *v/t.* make
'Töp·fer|schei·be *f* potter's wheel; **~wa·re** *f* pottery, earthenware
'Topf·hand·schuh *m* oven glove
top·fit ['tɔp'fıt] *adj.* in top form
'Topf|ku·chen *m* → ***Napfkuchen***; **~lap·pen** *m* oven cloth
Top·form ['tɔp-] *f*: ***in ~ sein*** be in top form
'Topf·pflan·ze *f* potted plant
Top·la·der ['tɔpla:dɐ] *m* (-s; -) top loader
Top·ma·nage·ment ['tɔp-] *n* top management; chief executives *pl.*; **'Top·ma·na·ger** *m* top executive
Top·mo|dell ['tɔp-] *n* top model
To·po·gra·phie [topogra'fi:] *f* (-; -n) topography; **to·po·gra·phisch** [topo'gra:fıʃ] *adj.* topographical
To·po·lo·gie [topolo'gi:] *f* (-; -n) topology; **to·po·lo·gisch** [topo'lo:gıʃ] *adj.* topological
Topp [tɔp] *m* (-s; -s, -e[n]) ⚓ top(mast); ***über die ~en geflaggt*** dressed overall; **~se·gel** *n* topsail
Top·zu·stand ['tɔp-] *m*: ***in ~*** in excellent condition
Tor[1] [to:ɐ] *n* (-[e]s; Tore ['to:rə]) **1.** a) gate (*a. fig.*); archway; (*garage etc.*) door, b) gateway (*a. fig.*); **2.** *sport*: goal; ***im ~ stehen*** be in goal; ***vor dem ~*** in the goalmouth; (***immer***) ***noch kein ~*** no score yet; ***ein Spiel auf ein ~*** one-way traffic; **3.** *skiing*: gate
Tor[2] [to:ɐ] *obs. m* (-en; -en ['to:rən]) fool
'Tor|aus *n*: ***ins ~ gehen*** go behind for a goalkick; **~be·reich** *m sport*: goal area; **~bo·gen** *m* archway; **~chan·ce** *f sport*: chance (to score), scoring chance (*or* opportunity); **~dif·fe|renz** *f sport*: goal difference
To·rea·dor [torea'do:ɐ] *m* (-s, -en [-rən]; -e [rə], -en) toreador
'Tor|eck *n*: ***oberes ~*** top corner of the net; **~ein·fahrt** *f* entrance; ***an der ~ a.*** at the gate; **~er·folg** *m* goal
To·re·ro [to're:ro] *m* (-s; -s) torero
To·res·schluß ['to:rəs-] *m*: ***kurz vor ~*** at the last minute
Torf [tɔrf] *m* (-[e]s; *no pl.*) peat; ***~ stechen*** cut peat; **~bo·den** *m*, **~er·de** *f* peaty soil
tor·fig ['tɔrfıç] *adj.* peaty
'Torf|moor *n* peat bog; **~mull** *m* peatdust
'Tor·heit *f* (-; -en) **1.** *no pl.* foolishness, folly; **2.** foolish act, stupid thing to do; ***e-e ~ begehen*** do something foolish (*or* silly, stupid)
'Tor·hü·ter *m sport*: goalkeeper, F goalie
tö·richt ['tø:rıçt] *adj.* a) foolish, b) *fig.* vain *hope*; **tö·rich·ter·wei·se** ['tø:rıçtɐvaizə] *adv.* foolishly, stupidly
'Tor·jä·ger *m sport*: goal-getter
tor·keln ['tɔrkəln] *v/i.* (h, sn) stagger, reel
'Tor|lat·te *f* crossbar; **~lauf** *m* slalom; **~li·nie** *f* goal-line
'tor·los *adj.* goalless
'Tor|mann *m* goalkeeper, F goalie; **~mög·lich·keit** *f* → ***Torchance***
Törn [tœrn] *m* (-s; -s) ⚓ turn
Tor·na·do [tɔr'na:do] *m* (-s; -s) tornado
'Tor|nä·he *f*: ***in ~*** near the goal; **~netz** *n* net
Tor·ni·ster [tɔr'nıstɐ] *m* (-s; -) ⚔ kit bag, (field) pack; *ped.* satchel
tor·pe·die·ren [tɔrpe'di:rən] *v/t.* (h) ⚓ *and fig.* torpedo
Tor·pe·do [tɔr'pe:do] *m* (-s; -s) ⚔ torpedo; **~boot** *n* torpedo boat
'Tor|pfo·sten *m* a) doorpost, b) *sport*: goalpost; **~raum** *m* goal area
'Tor·schluß·pa·nik F *f* a) last-minute panic, b) fear of being left on the shelf, fear of missing the boat
'Tor·schuß *m sport*: shot at goal
'Tor·schüt·ze *m* (goal-)scorer; **'Tor·schüt·zen·kö·nig** *m* top scorer
Tor·si·on [tɔr'zĭo:n] *f* (-; -en) ⚙ torsion, twist
Tor·so ['tɔrzo] *m* (-s; -s, -si [-zi]) torso (*a. fig.*)
Tört·chen ['tœrtçən] *n* (-s; -) tartlet, small tart
Tor·te ['tɔrtə] *f* (-; -n) gateau, layer cake; fruit tart
'Tor·ten|bo·den *m* flan base; **~dia|gramm** *n statistics*: pie chart; **~guß** *m* glaze; **~he·ber** *m* cake server; **~plat·te** *f* cake plate
Tor·tur [tɔr'tu:ɐ] *fig. f* (-; -en [-rən]) ordeal; ***das war e-e ~ a.*** F it was hell
'Tor|ver·hält·nis *n* goal difference; **~wart** *m* goalkeeper, F goalie
to·sen ['to:zən] *v/i.* (h) roar, rage; **'to·send** *adj.*: ***~er Beifall*** thunderous applause; ***et. mit ~em Beifall aufnehmen*** give s.th. a rapturous welcome
tot [to:t] *adj.* a) dead (*a. tree, volcano,* ⚡ *line,* ✝ *inventory, capital, fig. season, language etc.*); *esp.* ⚖ deceased; lifeless (*a. fig.*); extinct *volcano*, b) desolate; deserted, c) dull *colo(u)r etc., a.* lifeless *eyes*; ***~es Rennen a. fig.*** dead heat; ***~es Wissen*** useless knowledge; ***~er Punkt*** a) ⚙ dead cent|re (*Am.* -er), b) *fig.* deadlock, c) *fig.* low point; ***den ~en Punkt erreichen*** a) reach deadlock, b) have a low point; ***den ~en Punkt überwinden*** a) break the deadlock, b) get one's second wind; ***~er Winkel*** blind spot, ⚔ dead angle; ***mehr ~ als lebendig*** more dead than alive; ***halb ~ vor Angst*** petrified (with fear); ***er ist ein ~er Mann*** he's a dead man (*sl.* a goner); F ***den ~en Mann machen*** float (on the water); ***~ umfallen*** drop dead; ***für ~ erklären*** declare dead; ***er war sofort ~*** he died instantly; ***das Kind wurde ~ geboren*** the child was stillborn; F ***ich bin einfach ~*** F I'm dead (*or* finished); F ***~ und begraben*** all over and finished (*or* forgotten); → ***Gleis, Hose***
to·tal [to'ta:l] **I.** *adj.* total, complete; ***~er Krieg*** all-out war; ***~er Konflikt*** full-scale conflict; **II.** *adv.* totally, completely; F ***~ verrückt*** F stark raving mad; F ***~ besoffen*** F paralytic, *sl.* pissed out of one's mind; F ***~ pleite*** F dead broke; F ***~ gut*** F brilliant; F ***du machst es ~ falsch*** you're doing it all wrong
To'tal|aus·fall *m* **1.** ⚡ complete blackout; ⚙ breakdown; **2.** F *esp. sport*: F dead loss; **~aus·ver·kauf** *m* clearance sale, closing-down sale
To·ta·le [to'ta:lə] *f* (-; -n) *film*: full shot
To'tal·er·he·bung *f* universal census
to·ta·li·tär [totali'tɛ:ɐ] *adj.* totalitarian; **To·ta·li·ta·ris·mus** [totalita'rısmus] *m* (-; *no pl.*) totalitarianism
To·ta·li·tät [totali'tɛ:t] *f* (-; *no pl.*) totality
To'tal|ope·ra·ti|on *f* hysterectomy; **~scha·den** *m* total loss; *mot.* write-off
'tot|ar·bei·ten F *v/refl.* (*sep.*, h): ***sich ~*** work o.s. to death; **~är·gern** F *v/refl.* (*sep.*, h): ***sich ~*** be *or* get really annoyed (F mad); ***ich hab' mich totgeärgert*** I could have kicked myself
To·te ['to:tə] *m, f* (-n; -n) dead person, dead man (*f* woman); (dead) body, corpse; ⚔ casualty; ***die ~n*** the dead; ***bei dem Unfall gab es fünf ~*** five people were killed in the accident
To·tem ['to:tɛm] *n* (-s; -s) totem
To·te·mis·mus [tote'mısmus] *m* (-; *no pl.*) totemism
'To·tem·pfahl *m* totem pole

tö·ten ['tø:tən] (h) **I.** *v/t.* kill; *fig. a.* destroy; → ***Nerv***; **II.** *v/refl.*: ***sich*** ~ commit suicide

'To·ten|amt *n* requiem mass; **~bah·re** *f* bier; **~bett** *n* deathbed; **ℒ'blaß, ℒ'bleich** *adj.* deathly pale, (as) white as a sheet; **~fei·er** *f* remembrance ceremony; **~glocke** *f* death knell; **~grä·ber** [-grɛ:bɐ] *m* (-s; -) **1.** gravedigger; **2.** *zo.* burying beetle; **~hal·le** *f* mortuary; **~hemd** *n* shroud; **~kla·ge** *f* **1.** lamentation of the dead; **2.** ♪ dirge; **3.** dirge, lament, threnody; **~kopf** *m* **1.** a) death's head (*a. symbol*), skull, b) skull and crossbones; **2.** *zo.* death's-head moth; **~kult** *m* cult of the dead; **~mas·ke** *f* death mask; **~mes·se** *f* requiem (mass); **~reich** *n* realm of the dead, underworld; Hades; **~schein** *m* death certificate; **~sonn·tag** *m last Sunday before Advent commemorating the dead*; **~stadt** *f* necropolis; **~star·re** *f* rigor mortis; **ℒ'still** *adj.* (as) silent as the grave; **~tanz** *m art*: dance of death, danse macabre; **~tem·pel** *m hist.* funerary temple; **~wa·che** *f* wake, deathwatch

'tot·fah·ren *v/t.* (*irr.*, *sep.*, h, → ***fahren***) run over and kill; ***er hat sie totgefahren*** he ran her over and killed her

'tot·ge·bo·ren *adj.* stillborn; *fig.* abortive *attempt etc.*; **'Tot·ge·burt** *f* stillbirth; stillborn child

'tot|ge·glaubt *adj.* presumed dead; ***sein ~er Onkel*** his uncle who was presumed dead (*or* who[m] everyone believed to be dead); **~ge·sagt** *adj. pred.* presumed (*or* believed to be) dead; *fig.* written off; **~krie·gen** F *v/t.* (*sep.*, h): ***er ist nicht totzukriegen*** he just goes on for ever; **~la·chen** F *v/refl.* (*sep.*, h): ***sich*** ~ F kill o.s. (laughing); ***es ist zum*** ℒ F it's a scream; **~lau·fen** F *fig. v/refl.* (*irr.*, *sep.*, h, → ***laufen***): ***sich*** ~ peter (*or* fizzle) out, play itself out; **~ma·chen** F (*sep.*, h) **I.** *v/t.* kill; *fig.* eliminate, get rid of *of a competitor etc.*; **II.** *v/refl.*: ***sich*** ~ sacrifice o.s.

'Tot·mann·schal·tung *f* dead man's handle

To·to ['to:to] *n*, *m* (-s; *no pl.*) **1.** F tote; **2.** football pools *pl.*; ~ ***spielen*** do the pools; ***im ~ gewinnen*** win the pools; **~schein** *m* pools coupon

'tot|re·den F (*sep.*, h) **I.** *v/t.*: ***j-n*** ~ talk s.o. into the ground; ***et.*** ~ thrash s.th. to death; **II.** *v/refl.*: ***sich*** ~ talk till one is blue in the face; **~rei·ten** F *v/t.* (*irr.*, *sep.*, h, → ***reiten***) flog *topic etc.* to death; **~schie·ßen** *v/t.* (*irr.*, *sep.*, h, → ***schießen***) shoot *s.o.* dead

'Tot·schlag *m* (-[e]s; *no pl.*) ⚖ manslaughter; **'tot·schla·gen** *v/t.* (*irr.*, *sep.*, h, → ***schlagen***) kill, beat (*or* cudgel) to death; F *fig.* ***Zeit*** ~ kill time; F ***den Tag*** ~ get through the day (somehow); F ***er läßt sich lieber ~, als*** he'd rather die than; **'Tot·schlä·ger** *m* **1.** killer; **2.** life preserver, *Am.* blackjack

'tot|schwei·gen *v/t.* (*irr.*, *sep.*, h, → ***schweigen***) hush up; ***et.*** ~ *a.* pretend s.th. never happened; ***j-n*** ~ pretend s.o. doesn't exist; **~stel·len** *v/refl.* (*sep.*, h): ***sich*** ~ play dead (F possum)

Tö·tung ['tø:tʊŋ] *f* (-; -en) killing; ⚖ homicide

'Tö·tungs|ab·sicht *f* intention to kill; **~ver·such** *m* murder attempt, attempted murder

Tou·pet [tu'pe:] *n* (-s; -s) toupee

tou·pie·ren [tu'pi:rən] *v/t.* (h) back-comb

Tour [tu:ɐ] *f* (-; -en ['tu:rən]) a) tour (***durch*** *acc.* of, around); excursion, trip, hike, b) stretch, c) ⚙ revolution, turn, d) F ploy; ***auf ~ gehen*** take the road; ⚙ ***auf ~en*** on speed; ***auf vollen ~en laufen*** go full blast; ***auf ~en bringen*** *mot.* rev up, *fig.* get *s.o. or s.th.* going; ***auf ~en kommen*** *mot.* pick up, rev up, *fig.* get into gear, get going; F ***in einer*** ~ incessantly; F ***komm mir bloß nicht auf diese ~!*** F don't try that one on me; F ***j-m die ~ vermasseln*** queer s.o.'s pitch; → ***krumm, link, sanft***

Tou·ren|rad ['tu:rən-] *n* touring bicycle; **~ski** *m* touring ski; **~ski·fah·ren** *n* off-piste skiing; **~wa·gen** *m* touring car; **~zäh·ler** *m* revolution counter

Tou·ris·mus [tu'rɪsmʊs] *m* (-; *no pl.*) tourism; **~ge·schäft** *n* tourist industry

Tou·rist [tu'rɪst] *m* (-en; -en) tourist

Tou'ri·sten|at·trak·ti͵on *f* tourist attraction; **~ho͵tel** *n* tourist (*or* budget) hotel; **~klas·se** *f* ✈ economy class; **~rum·mel** F *m* hordes *pl.* of tourists; tourist invasion (***in*** *dat.* of); ***da ist der ~ zu groß*** the place is overrun with tourists; **~strom** *m* stream of tourists; ***abseits vom*** ~ off the tourist track

Tou·ri·stik [tu'rɪstɪk] *f* (-; *no pl.*) tourism; **~un·ter͵neh·men** *n* tour operator

Tou·ri·stin [tu'rɪstɪn] *f* (-; -nen) tourist

Tour·nee [tʊr'ne:] *f* (-; -n) tour; ***auf ~ gehen*** (***sein***) go (be) on tour, ***mit e-m Stück***: tour a play

to·xisch ['tɔksɪʃ] *adj.* toxic

Trab [tra:p] *m* (-s; *no pl.*) trot; ***im*** ~ at a trot, F *fig.* quickly; *fig.* ***j-n auf ~ bringen*** get s.o. moving; ***j-n in ~ halten*** keep s.o. on his *or* her toes (*or* on the trot, on the go); ***immer auf ~ sein*** always be on the go

Tra·bant [tra'bant] *m* (-en; -en) *ast.* satellite; **Tra'ban·ten·stadt** *f* satellite town

tra·ben ['tra:bən] *v/i.* (sn) trot

Tra·ber ['tra:bɐ] *m* (-s; -), **~pferd** *n* trotter

'Trab·renn·bahn *f* trotting course; **'Trab·ren·nen** *n* a) trotting, b) trotting race

Tracht [traxt] *f* (-; -en) **1.** dress; traditional (*or* national) costume; ⚔ *etc.* uniform; **2.** → ***Prügel*** 2

trach·ten ['traxtən] **I.** *v/i.* (h): ~ ***nach*** *dat.* strive for (*or* after); (***danach***) ~ ***zu*** *inf.* endeavo(u)r (*or* strive) to *inf.*; ***j-m nach dem Leben*** ~ be out to kill s.o., be after s.o.'s life (F head); **II.** ℒ *n* (-s; *no pl.*) pursuit (***nach*** *dat.* of), striving (after, for)

'Trach·ten|an·zug *m*: (***im*** ~ in) traditional costume; **~kleid** *n* traditional costume (*or* dress); **~look** *m* ethnic (*or* traditional costume) look

träch·tig ['trɛçtɪç] *adj. zo.* pregnant (*a. lit. fig.* ***von*** *dat.* with)

tra·die·ren [tra'di:rən] *v/t.* (h) hand down

Tra·di·ti·on [tradi'tsĭo:n] *f* (-; -en) tradition; ***nach alter*** ~ by tradition; ***zur ~ machen*** make *it* a tradition; ***zur ~ werden*** become a tradition, become established (*or* traditional); **tra·di·tio·nell** [traditsĭo'nɛl] *adj.* traditional

tra·di·ti'ons|be·wußt *adj.* traditionally-minded; ~ ***sein*** *a.* have a sense of tradition; **~ge·mäß** *adj.* in keeping with tradition; **ℒpfle·ge** *f* keeping up *or* upholding (of) traditions; **~reich** *adj.* steeped in tradition, historic

traf [tra:f] *pret. of* ***treffen***

Tra·fik [tra'fɪk] *Austrian f* (-; -en) tobacconist's; **Tra·fi·kant** [trafi'kant] *Austrian m* (-en; -en) tobacconist

Tra·fo ['tra:fo] *m* (-s; -s) ⚡ transformer

Trag·bah·re ['tra:k-] *f* stretcher

trag·bar ['tra:kba:ɐ] *adj.* a) portable *radio etc.*; hand-held *movie camera etc.*, b) *clothes* fit for wear, c) *fig.* acceptable; tolerable; (***finanziell***) ***nicht mehr*** ~ beyond one's means

trä·ge ['trɛ:gə] *adj.* sluggish (*a. w.s. and* ✝); lethargic, listless; drowsy; *phys.* inert (*a. fig.*)

Tra·ge|griff ['tra:gə-] *m* handle; **~korb** *m* a) basket, b) Moses basket

tra·gen ['tra:gən] (trug, getragen, h) **I.** *v/t.* a) carry; take, b) support, c) wear *clothes, glasses etc.*, *a.* have on, d) bear *fruit*, *a. fig. name, responsibility, costs, consequences etc.*; *fig. a.* endure; ***e-n Bart*** *etc.* ~ have (*or* wear, sport) a beard *etc.*; ***et. bei sich*** ~ carry *or* have s.th. on (*od.* with) one; ***e-n Brief zur Post*** ~ take a letter to the post office; ***man trägt die Röcke wieder kürzer*** short skirts are in again; ***diese Schuhe trägt man nicht mehr*** people don't wear those kind of shoes any more; ***das kannst du gut*** ~ it really suits you; ***et. auf e-r Party*** (***in der Kirche*** *etc.*) ~ wear to a party (to church *etc.*); ***die Haare lang*** (***kurz***) ~ wear one's hair long (short); *fig.* ***den Schaden*** ~ pay for the damage; ***wie trägt sie es?*** how's she taking it?, how's she bearing up?; → ***Herz, Rechnung*** 2, ***Trauer, Zins***; **II.** *v/i.* a) ⚘ bear fruit, b) *zo.* be pregnant, c) *ice*: hold; *fig. voice*: carry; ***schwer ~ an*** *dat.* have a hard time carrying; ***schwer zu ~ haben*** be loaded down, *fig.* be weighed down (***an*** *dat.* by); **III.** *v/refl.*: ***sich*** ~ *business etc.*: pay (its way); ***sich leicht*** ~ *bag etc.*: be light, be easy to carry; ***sich gut*** ~ *material*: wear well; ***sich mit der Absicht*** (*or* ***dem Gedanken***) ~ ***zu*** *inf.* be thinking of *ger.*, be considering *ger.*; **'tra·gend** *adj.* a) ⚠ load-bearing *wall*, b) *fig.* main *idea etc.*, *thea. etc. a.* leading *role*, c) powerful *voice*; ***sich selbst*** ~ self-funding

Trä·ger ['trɛ:gɐ] *m* (-s; -) **1.** carrier (*a.* ⚔), bearer (*a. of a name, title etc.*); porter; *fig.* upholder, champion; *univ. etc.* body responsible *for s.th.*; → ***Bauträger, Flugzeugträger, Preisträger***; **2.** (shoulder) strap; → ***Hosenträger***; **3.** ⚙ support; ⚠ supporting beam; girder; **4.** ***ein ~ Bier*** a crate (*Am.* case) of beer; **~fre͵quenz** *f* ✈ carrier frequency; **~kleid** *n* pinafore dress, *Am.* jumper

'trä·ger·los *adj.* strapless *dress etc.*

'Trä·ger|ra͵ke·te *f* booster rocket; **~rock** *m* **1.** skirt with straps; **2.** → ***Trägerkleid***

Tra·ge|ta·sche ['tra:gə-] *f* **1.** carrier bag; **2.** carrycot; **~tuch** *n* sling

trag·fä·hig ['tra:k-] *adj.* **1.** load-bearing; able to carry a load; **2.** *fig.* sound; firm, stable; acceptable *compromise*; **~e *Mehrheit*** working majority; **'Trag·fä·hig·keit** *f* (-; *no pl.*) **1.** load(-carrying) capacity; *bridge*: safe load; *crane*, ✈ lifting capacity; ⚓ tonnage; **2.** *fig.* soundness; stability; acceptability

Trag·flä·che ['tra:k-] *f* ✈ wing; ⚓ hydrofoil; **'Trag·flä·chen·boot** *n* hydrofoil

Trag·flü·gel ['tra:k-] *m* → ***Tragfläche***;

'Trag·flü·gel·boot *n* → ***Tragflächenboot***

Träg·heit ['trɛːkhaɪt] *f* (-; *no pl.*) sluggishness; lethargy, listlessness; drowsiness; *phys.* inertia (*a. fig.*); ⚕ inactivity

'Träg·heits|ge·setz *n phys.* law of inertia; **~mo,ment** *n* moment of inertia

Tra·gik ['traːgɪk] *f* (-; *no pl.*) tragedy; tragic element (*or* aspect); ***die ~ daran*** *a.* the tragic thing about it

Tra·gi·ko·mik [tragi'koːmɪk] *f* (-; *no pl.*) tragicomedy; tragicomic element (*or* aspect); **tra·gi'ko·misch** *adj.* tragicomic(ally *adv.*); **Tra·gi·ko'mö·die** *f* tragicomedy

tra·gisch ['traːgɪʃ] **I.** *adj.* tragic; **II.** *adv.* tragically; ***nimm's nicht so ~!*** don't take it to heart, it's not the end of the world

Trag|kraft ['traːk-] *f* (-; *no pl.*) → ***Tragfähigkeit*** 1; **~last** *f* a) load, burden, b) (load) capacity

Tra·gö·die [tra'gøːdĭə] *f* (-; -n) tragedy; tragic event; ***da spielen sich ~n ab*** they've had some tragic things happen to them; F ***mach nicht gleich e-e ~ draus*** F no need to make a full-scale drama out of it; F ***es ist e-e ~ mit ihr (diesem Computer)*** F it's absolutely hopeless with her (this computer's an absolute disaster); **Tra'gö·di·en·dich·ter** *m* tragedian

Trag|pfei·ler ['traːk-] *m* (load-carrying) pillar; support *of a bridge etc.*; **~rie·men** *m* strap; sling *of a rifle*; **~ta·sche** *f* carrier bag; **~wei·te** *f* (-; *no pl.*) range; *fig.* significance, implications *pl.*; *fig.* ***von großer ~*** significant, of great import, ***sein***: *a.* have far-reaching implications (*or* consequences); ***sie war sich der ~ ihrer Entscheidung nicht bewußt*** *a.* she didn't realize what an effect her decision might (*or* would) have; **~werk** *n* ✈ wing unit

Trai·ner ['trɛːnɐ] *m* (-s; -) trainer, coach; *soccer*: manager; **~bank** *f* (trainer's) bench

trai·nie·ren [trɛ'niːrən] (h) **I.** *v/i.* train, coach (**auf** *acc.* for); **II.** *v/t.* coach *s.o.* (**auf** *acc.* for); ***Hochsprung*** *etc.* **~** practi|se (*Am.* -ce) the (*or* one's) high jump *etc.*; ***das Gedächtnis*** *etc.* **~** train one's memory *etc.*

Trai·ning ['trɛːnɪŋ] *n* (-s; *no pl.*) training

'Trai·nings|an·zug *m* tracksuit; **~ho·se** *f* tracksuit bottoms *pl.*; **~jacke** *f* tracksuit top; **~la·ger** *n* training camp; **~part·ner** *m* training partner; **~platz** *m* practi|ce (*Am.* -se) ground; **~pro,gramm** *n* training program(me) *or* schedule; **~spiel** *n* practi|ce (*Am.* -se) match; **~zeit** *f* practi|ce (*Am.* -se) time

Trakt [trakt] *m* (-[e]s; -e) part, wing

Trak·tat [trak'taːt] *n* (-[e]s; -e) treatise; *eccl.* tract

trak·tie·ren [trak'tiːrən] *v/t.* (h) pester; maltreat; ***mit Schlägen ~*** beat up; ***j-n mit Vorwürfen ~*** F keep getting on at s.o.

Trak·tor ['traktoːɐ] *m* (-s; -en [trak'toːrən]) tractor

träl·lern ['trɛlɐn] *v/t. and v/i.* (h) warble, trill

Tram [tram] *dial. f* (-; -s), **~bahn** *f* tram, *Am.* streetcar

Tram·pel ['trampəl] F *m, n* (-s; -) F elephant; ***das ist ein ~!*** he's like a baby elephant; **'tram·peln** *v/i.* (h, sn) trample; stamp

'Tram·pel|pfad *m* beaten path; **~tier** *n* **1.** *zo.* Bactrian camel; **2.** F clumsy oaf; ***paß auf, du ~!*** look out, clumsy!

tram·pen ['trɛmpən] *v/i.* (sn) hitchhike, F hitch (it); **Tram·per** ['trɛmpɐ] *m* (-s; -), **Tram·pe·rin** ['trɛmpərɪn] *f* (-; -nen) hitchhiker

Tram·po·lin [trampo'liːn] *n* (-s; -e) trampoline

Tramp·schiff ['trɛmp-] *n* tramp steamer

Tran [traːn] *m* (-[e]s; *no pl.*) train oil; F *fig.* ***im ~*** dop(e)y, in a dream; F ***das muß ich im ~ gemacht haben*** a) I must have been drunk, b) I must have been dreaming (*or* in a dream)

Tran·ce ['trãːs(ə)] *f* (-; -n) trance; ***in ~ fallen*** go into a trance; ***in ~ versetzen*** put into a trance; **'tran·ce·ar·tig I.** *adj.* trance-like; **II.** *adv.*: **~ *handeln*** act as if in a trance

Tran·chier·be·steck [trã'ʃiːɐ-] *n*: (***ein ~*** a pair of) carvers *pl.*; **tran·chie·ren** [trã'ʃiːrən] *v/t.* (h) carve, cut; **Tran'chier·mes·ser** *n* carving knife

Trä·ne ['trɛːnə] *f* (-; -n) tear; ***den ~n nahe*** on the verge of tears; ***in ~n ausbrechen*** burst into tears; ***unter ~n*** in tears; ***unter ~n erzählte er uns alles*** he was in tears (*or* he wept) as he told us everything; ***keine ~ wert*** not worth shedding any tears over (*or* getting upset about); ***wir haben ~n gelacht*** we laughed till we cried; F *iro.* ***mir kommen die ~n*** F don't make me weep; → ***aufgelöst*** 2, ***gerührt, nachweinen***

trä·nen ['trɛːnən] *v/i.* (h) water; ***mir ~ die Augen*** my eyes are watering

'trä·nen·blind *adj.* blinded with tears

'Trä·nen·drü·se *f* lachrymal gland; F *fig.* ***das Lied drückt aber auf die ~n*** that song is a real tearjerker

'trä·nen|er·stickt *adj.*: ***mit ~er Stimme*** in a choked voice, choked with tears; **~feucht** *adj.* wet with tears; tear-stained

'Trä·nen·gas *n* (-es; *no pl.*) tear gas; **~pi,sto·le** *f* tear-gas pistol (*or* gun)

'Trä·nen·ka,nal *m* tear duct

'trä·nen·reich *adj.* tearful

'Trä·nen·sack *m* lachrymal sac

'trä·nen·über,strömt I. *adj.* wet with tears; **II.** *adv.* in tears

trank [traŋk] *pret. of* ***trinken***

Trank [traŋk] *m* (-[e]s; Tränke ['trɛŋkə]) drink

Trän·ke ['trɛŋkə] *f* (-; -n) a) watering place, b) drinking trough; **'trän·ken** *v/t.* (h) **1.** water *cattle, plants etc.*; **2.** soak

Trans·ak·ti·on [transʔak'tsĭoːn] *f* (-; -en) transaction

trans·al·pin [transʔal'piːn] *adj.* transalpine

Trans·at·lan·tik... [transʔat'lantɪk-], **trans·at'lan·tisch** *adj.* transatlantic

Trans·fer [trans'feːɐ] *m* (-s; -s) ⚕, ✈, *sport, psych.* transfer

Trans·fe·renz [transfe'rɛnts] *f* (-; -en) *ling.* transference

trans·fe·rie·ren [transfe'riːrən] *v/t.* (h) transfer (**an** *acc.*, **auf** *acc.* to)

Trans'fer|li·ste *f* transfer list; ***auf die ~ setzen*** put up for transfer, put on the transfer list; **~sum·me** *f* transfer fee

Trans·fi·gu·ra·ti·on [transfigura'tsĭoːn] *f* (-; -en) transfiguration

Trans·for·ma·ti·on [transfɔrma'tsĭoːn] *f* (-; -en) transformation; **Trans·for·ma·ti'ons·gram,ma·tik** *f* transformational grammar

Trans·for·ma·tor [transfɔr'maːtoːɐ] *m* (-s; -en [-ma'toːrən]) ⚡ transformer

trans·for·mie·ren [transfɔr'miːrən] *v/t.* (h) *a.* ⚡, ⛏, *psych.* transform

Trans·fu·si·on [transfu'zĭoːn] *f* (-; -en) ⚕ transfusion

Tran·si·stor [tran'zɪstoːɐ] *m* (-s; -en [-zɪs'toːrən]) transistor; **tran'si·stor·be·stückt** *adj.* transistorized, solid-state

tran·si·sto·ri·sie·ren [tranzɪstori'ziːrən] *v/t.* (h) transistorize; **tran·si·sto·ri·siert** [tranzɪstori'ziːɐt] *adj.* transistorized, solid-state

Tran'si·stor|ra·dio *n* transistor (radio); **~zün·dung** *f* electronic ignition

Tran·sit [tran'ziːt] *m* (-s; *no pl.*) transit; **~ab·fer·ti·gung** *f* transit clearance; **~ab·kom·men** *n* transit convention; **~gü·ter** *pl.* ⚕ transit goods; **~hal·le** *f* transit lounge; **~han·del** *m* transit trade

tran·si·tiv ['tranzitiːf] *adj. ling.* transitive

Tran'sit|pas·sa,gier *m*, **~rei·sen·de** *m, f* (-n; -n) transit passenger; ***Transitpassagiere nach*** *dat.* ***...*** transit passengers continuing their flight to ...; **~strecke** *f* transit road (*or* route); **~ver·kehr** *m* transit traffic (⚕ *a.* trade); **~vi·sum** *n* transit visa; **~weg** *m* transit route

tran·skri·bie·ren [transkri'biːrən] *v/t.* (h) transcribe; **Tran·skrip·ti·on** [transkrɪp'tsĭoːn] *f* (-; -en) transcription

Trans·mis·si·on [transmɪ'sĭoːn] *f* (-; -en) ⚙ transmission

trans·pa·rent [transpa'rɛnt] *adj.* transparent (*a. fig.*)

Trans·pa'rent *n* (-[e]s; -e) transparency; banner; **~pa,pier** *n* tracing paper

Trans·pa·renz [transpa'rɛnts] *f* (-; *no pl.*) transparency

Tran·spi·ra·ti·on [transpira'tsĭoːn] *f* (-; *no pl.*) perspiration; **tran·spi·rie·ren** [transpi'riːrən] *v/i.* (h) perspire

Trans·plan·tat [transplan'taːt] *n* (-[e]s; -e) ⚕ transplant, transplanted organ

Trans·plan·ta·ti·on [transplanta'tsĭoːn] *f* (-; -en) a) transplant; (*skin*) graft, b) transplantation, grafting

trans·plan·tie·ren [transplan'tiːrən] *v/t.* (h) transplant, graft

trans·po·nie·ren [transpo'niːrən] *v/t.* (h) transpose (*a.* ♪)

Trans·port [trans'pɔrt] *m* (-[e]s; -e) **1.** transport(ation), conveyance; ***während des ~s*** in transit, en route; **2.** *phot.* winding (mechanism)

trans·por·ta·bel [transpɔr'taːbəl] *adj.* transportable; portable

Trans'port|ar·bei·ter *m* transport worker; **~au·to,ma·tik** *f phot.* automatic winding, automatic (film) advance; **~band** *n* (-[e]s; ⸚er) conveyor belt

Trans·por·ter [trans'pɔrtɐ] *m* (-s; -) → ***Transportfahrzeug, Transportflugzeug, Transportschiff***

Trans·por·teur [transpɔr'tøːɐ] *m* (-s; -e [-rə]) carrier

trans'port·fä·hig *adj.* transportable; *invalid, animal* :fit for transportation; ***die Verletzten sind nicht ~*** *a.* the injured are in no fit state to be moved

Trans'port|fahr·zeug *n* transporter; **~fir·ma** *f* haulage company (*or* contractors *pl.*); **~flug·zeug** *n* **1.** transport plane; **2.** → ***Truppentransporter***; **~he·bel** *m phot.* film advance lever; **~hub·schrau·ber** *m* transport helicopter

trans·por·tie·ren [transpɔr'tiːrən] (h) **I.** *v/t.* transport; move; carry; take; *phot.*

wind on, advance; ***wie soll man das Ding denn ~?*** how are you supposed to move the thing (*or* get the thing out of here)?; **II.** *v/i. phot.* wind on, advance

Trans'port|ko·sten *pl.* transport(ation) charges; ⚓ freight (charges); forwarding charges; **~mit·tel** *n* (means of) transport(ation); **~netz** *n* transport network; **~scha·den** *m* damage in transit; **~schiff** *n* transport ship; ⚔ troopship; **~un·ter·ˌneh·men** *n* haulage company (*or* contractors *pl.*); **~un·terˌneh·mer** *m* haulier, hauler; **~ver·si·che·rung** *f* transport insurance; **~we·sen** *n* (-s; *no pl.*) transportation

trans·se·xu·ell [transzɛ'ksŭɛl] *adj.*, **Trans·se·xu'el·le** *m, f* (-n; -n) transsexual

Trans·sub·stan·tia·ti·on [transzʊpstantsĭa'tsĭoːn] *f* (-; -en) *eccl.* transubstantiation

'Tran·su·se [-zuːzə] F *f* (-; -n) F slowcoach, *Am.* slowpoke

Trans·ve·stit [transvɛs'tiːt] *m* (-en; -en) transvestite

tran·szen·dent [transtsɛn'dɛnt], **tran·szen·den·tal** [transtsɛndɛn'taːl] *adj.* transcendental

Tran·szen·denz [transtsɛn'dɛnts] *f* (-; *no pl.*) transcendence

Tra·pez [tra'peːts] *n* (-es; -e) **1.** ⩘ trapezium, *Am.* trapezoid; **2.** *gym.* trapeze; **~akt** *m* trapeze act; **~künst·ler** *m* trapeze artist

trap·peln ['trapəln] *v/i.* (h, sn) *horse etc.*: clatter; *child etc.*: patter

Trap·pist [tra'pɪst] *m* (-en; -en) Trappist (monk)

Tra·ra [tra'raː] F *n* (-s; *no pl.*) fuss, F to-do; ***viel ~ machen*** make a big (*or* great) fuss *or* to-do (***um*** *acc.* about); ***ohne viel ~*** without much fuss (*or* fanfare)

Tras·se ['trasə] *f* (-; -n) ⚙ location route

trat [traːt] *pret.of* ***treten***

Tratsch [traːtʃ] F *m* (-[e]s; *no pl.*) gossip; **Trat·sche** ['traːtʃə] F *f* (-; -n) F (old) gossip; **trat·schen** ['traːtʃən] F *v/i.* (h) gossip; ***er tratscht viel zuviel*** he's a real (*or* an old) gossip

Trat·to·ria [trato'riːa] *f* (-; -rien) trattoria

trat·zen ['tratsən], **trät·zen** ['trɛtsən] *dial. v/t.* (h) tease

Trau·alˌtar ['traʊ-] *m* altar

Trau·be ['traʊbə] *f* (-; -n) a) bunch of grapes, b) grape, c) *fig.* cluster; *fig.* ***die ~n hängen (j-m) zu hoch*** it's sour grapes

'Trau·ben|le·se *f* grape harvest; **~most** *m* grape must; **~saft** *m* grape juice; **~sor·te** *f* (type of) grape; **~zucker** *m* glucose, dextrose

trau·en¹ ['traʊən] (h) **I.** *v/i.* trust (*dat. s.o. or s.th.*); ***ich traute m-n Ohren (Augen) nicht*** I couldn't believe my ears (eyes); ***ich trau' der Sache nicht*** I don't like the look of it; ***trau, schau, wem*** you can't just trust anyone; ***dem Glück ist nicht zu ~*** fortune is fickle; → ***Friede(n), Weg*; II.** *v/t.*: ***sich et. ~*** have the courage to do s.th., dare to do s.th.; ***er traut sich was!*** he's got a nerve; **III.** *v/refl.*: ***sich ~*** dare; ***ich trau' mich nicht nach Hause*** I daren't go home, I'm scared to go home; ***er traut sich nicht ins Wasser*** he's scared of the water (*or* to jump in); ***du traust dich nur nicht!*** you're just scared

'trau·en² *v/t.* (h) marry; ***sich ~ lassen*** get married, marry

Trau·er ['traʊɐ] *f* (-; *no pl.*) a) sorrow, grief (***um*** *acc.*, ***wegen*** *gen.* over, at); mourning (for), grieving (over, for), b) mourning (period), c) mourning clothes *pl.*; ***in tiefer ~*** in deep mourning; ***tiefe ~ empfinden*** be deeply grieved (***über*** *acc.* at); ***~ tragen*** be dressed in mourning; **~be·flag·gung** *f*: ***es wurde ~ angeordnet*** flags were ordered to be flown at half-mast; **~fall** *m* death, bereavement; **~fei·er** *f* funeral service; **~flor** *m* (black) crepe; **~gä·ste** *pl.* mourners; **~ge·leit** *n* (funeral) cortege; **~got·tes·dienst** *m* funeral service; **~jahr** *n* year of mourning; **~klei·dung** *f* mourning clothes *pl.*; (widow's) weeds *pl.*; ***~ tragen*** be dressed in mourning, be wearing *or* be in (widow's) weeds; **~kloß** F *m* F wet blanket; **~marsch** *m* funeral march; **~mie·ne** F *f* long face, doleful expression; ***e-e ~ aufsetzen*** pull a long face; **~muˌsik** *f* funeral music

trau·ern ['traʊɐn] *v/i.* (h) mourn (***um*** *acc.* for *s.o.*); *w.s.* grieve (for, over); be in mourning

'Trau·er|nach·richt *f* sad news (*sg.*); **~rand** *m* black edge(s *pl.*), black edging (*or* border); ***mit ~*** black-bordered; F *hum.* ***Trauerränder*** black fingernails; **~re·de** *f* funeral oration; **~spiel** *n* tragedy; *fig.* sorry affair; *fig.* ***es ist schon ein ~*** *a.* it's enough to make you weep; **~wei·de** *f* 🌿 weeping willow; **~zeit** *f* time of mourning; **~zug** *m* funeral procession, (funeral) cortege

Trau·fe ['traʊfə] *f* (-; -n) eaves *pl.*; gutter; → ***Regen***

träu·feln ['trɔʏfəln] **I.** *v/t.* (h) let *s.th.* trickle (***in*** *acc.* in); put *drops etc.* (into *eyes, ears etc.*); **II.** *v/i.* (sn) drip, trickle

trau·lich ['traʊlɪç] *adj.* homely, *Am.* homey; cosy, *Am.* cozy

Traum [traʊm] *m* (-[e]s; Träume ['trɔʏmə]) dream (*a.* F *fig.*); ***böser ~*** bad dream; ***im ~*** in a (*or* one's) dream; ***j-m im ~ erscheinen*** appear to s.o. in a dream; ***j-n aus dem ~ reißen*** jolt s.o. out of his (*or* her) dreams; ***es war wie ein ~*** it was like a dream, it was unbelievably beautiful; ***das fällt mir nicht im ~(e) ein*** I wouldn't (even) dream of (doing) it; F ***aus der ~!*** so much for that, that's the end of that(, I suppose); F ***aus der ~ vom Urlaub*** *a.* that's put paid to my holiday prospects; F ***es ist ein ~ von Auto*** F the car's a dream, it's a dream car; ***Träume sind Schäume*** what's in a dream?

Trau·ma ['traʊma] *n* (-s; Traumata) trauma; **trau·ma·tisch** [traʊ'maːtɪʃ] *adj.* traumatic; **Trau·ma·to·lo·gie** [traʊmatolo'giː] *f* (-; *no pl.*) traumatology

'Traum|au·to F *n* dream car; **~be·ruf** F *m* dream job; **~bild** *n* dream vision; dream; **~deu·tung** *f* dream interpretation

träu·men ['trɔʏmən] (h) **I.** *v/i.* a) dream (***von*** *dat.* of, about *or fig.* of), b) daydream; ***schlecht ~*** have a bad dream; *fig.* ***er träumt nur noch*** he's a real daydreamer; ***du träumst wohl!*** a) wakey, wakey!, b) you must be joking; **II.** *v/t.* dream; ***hast du was geträumt?*** did you have any dreams?; ***ich habe was ganz Furchtbares geträumt*** I had a terrible dream; *fig.* ***das hätte ich mir nie ~ lassen*** I never dreamed it was possible;

Träu·mer ['trɔʏmɐ] *m* (-s; -) dreamer; **Träu·me·rei** [trɔʏmə'raɪ] *f* (-; -en) a) (day)dreaming, b) daydream, (*a.* ♪) reverie; **Träu·me·rin** ['trɔʏmərɪn] *f* (-; -nen) dreamer; **träu·me·risch** ['trɔʏmərɪʃ] *adj.* dreamy; wistful; ***~er Mensch*** dreamer

'Traum|faˌbrik *f* dream factory; **~frau** F *f* *the* woman of one's dreams

'traum·haft I. *adj.* **1.** dreamlike; **2.** (absolutely) wonderful; perfect, unbelievable *weather*; **II.** *adv.*: ***~ schön*** absolutely beautiful

'Traum|hoch·zeit F *f* fairytale wedding; **~in·sel** F *f* **1.** *the* island of one's dreams; **2.** beautiful island (in the sun); **~land** *n* dreamland; **~mann** F *m* (-[e]s; ¨er) *the* man of one's dreams; **~no·te** F *f ped. and sport*: perfect mark; **~rei·se** F *f* dream holiday; **~tän·zer** F *m* dreamer; **≈ver·sun·ken** *adj.* lost in (one's) dreams, F away with the fairies; **~vil·la** F *f* dream mansion; **~welt** *f* dream world, *w.s. a.* world of fantasy

trau·rig ['traʊrɪç] *adj.* a) sad (***über*** *acc.* about, at), b) *fig.* sorry *sight, conditions etc.*; sad *duty, remains etc.*; → ***Bilanz; j-n ~ stimmen*** sadden s.o., make s.o. (feel) sad; ***ein ~es Ende nehmen*** come to an unhappy end; ***(das ist) ~ aber wahr*** it's the sad truth, unfortunately that's the way it is; *contp.* ***es ist ~ genug, daß*** it's bad enough that; ***mach kein so ~es Gesicht*** don't look so sad; ***e-e ~e Figur machen*** cut a poor figure; ***die Mannschaft bot e-e ~e Leistung*** the team performed miserably, it was a pathetic performance (on the part of the team); **'Trau·rig·keit** *f* (-; *no pl.*) sadness

Trau|ring ['traʊ-] *m* wedding ring; **~schein** *m* marriage certificate

traut [traʊt] *adj. esp. iro.* homey, *Brit.* homely; ***~es Heim*** home sweet home

Trau·ung ['traʊʊŋ] *f* (-; -en) marriage ceremony; wedding

Trau·zeu·ge ['traʊ-] *m* witness to a (*or* the) marriage

Tra·vel·ler·scheck ['trɛvəlɐ-] *m* traveller's cheque, *Am.* traveler's check

Tra·ve·stie [travɛs'tiː] *f* (-; -n) travesty; **~künst·ler** *m* drag artist; **~show** *f* drag show

Treck [trɛk] *m* (-s; -s) trail

Trecker ['trɛkɐ] (*sep.* -k·k-) *m* (-s; -) tractor

Treff¹ [trɛf] F *m* (-s; -s) **1.** ***e-n ~ vereinbaren*** arrange to meet (somewhere); **2.** → ***Treffpunkt***

Treff² *n* (-s; -s) club(s *pl.*)

tref·fen ['trɛfən] (traf, getroffen, h) **I.** *v/t.* **1.** hit; *fig.* capture *the mood etc.*; ***nicht ~*** miss; ***die Kugel traf ihn an der Schulter*** the bullet hit his shoulder; ***tödlich getroffen*** mortally wounded; *fig.* ***(du hast's) getroffen!*** bull's-eye!, *Brit.* F spot-on!; ***es gut ~*** be lucky (***mit*** *dat.* with); ***die richtige Wahl ~*** make the right choice; ***damit hast du s-n Geschmack genau getroffen*** that's exactly the sort of thing (*or* the style *etc.*) he likes, (*a.* ***du hast genau das Richtige getroffen***) you couldn't have picked a better present *etc.*; ***die richtigen Worte ~*** find (just) the right words; ***da hast du ihn gut getroffen*** that's a good picture of him; → ***Blitz, getroffen*; 2.** concern, *b.s.* affect; hit *s.o. or s.th.* hard; get at; ***der Vorwurf trifft mich nicht*** I don't feel

(I'm) responsible; ***damit kannst du mich nicht*** ~ you can't get to me with that; ***damit hast du ihn wirklich getroffen*** you hit him where it really hurts (with that); → ***Schuld*; 3.** reach; → ***Anstalt*** 2, ***Auswahl*** 1, ***Entscheidung, Ton², Vorkehrung*; 4.** meet *s.o.*; ***sich*** ~ meet, meet up; **II.** *v/i.* **5.** hit; ***nicht*** ~ miss; **6.** ~ ***auf*** *acc.* a) meet with *resistance etc.*, b) come across *s.th.*, stumble on *s.o. or s.th.*, c) strike *oil*, d) *sport*: come up against; **III.** *v/refl.*: ***sich mit j-m*** ~ meet (up with) s.o.; ***das trifft sich gut*** (***schlecht***) that suits me *etc.* fine (that doesn't fit in at all); ***wie es sich so trifft*** as chance would have it; **IV.** ♀ *n* (-s; -) meeting; get-together; *sport*: meet, contest, encounter, match; *fig.* ***Argumente*** *etc.* ***ins*** ~ ***führen*** put forward arguments *etc.*; **'tref·fend I.** *adj.* apt, appropriate; ~***er Vergleich*** good comparison; **II.** *adv.*: ***du hast ihn*** ~ ***beschrieben*** that's a good description (of him), F you've got him down to a T, that just about sums him up

Tref·fer ['trɛfɐ] *m* (-s; -) **1.** hit (*a. fencing, boxing*); direct hit; *soccer*: goal; *fig.* lucky strike; ~ ***erzielen*** score (hits, *soccer*: goals); **2.** winner

'treff·ge·nau *adj.* accurate *weapon*

treff·lich ['trɛflɪç] *lit. adj.* outstanding; exquisite

'Treff·punkt *m* meeting place; place to meet; ***wo ist unser*** ~? where are we meeting?

'treff·si·cher *adj.* accurate; *fig.* unerring, sound; precise; ***er hat ein*** ~***es Urteil*** he's got a good (*or* sound) sense of judg(e)ment, F his judg(e)ments are usually spot-on

Treib·eis ['traɪp-] *n* drift ice, ice floes *pl.*

trei·ben ['traɪbən] (trieb, getrieben, h) **I.** *v/t.* **1.** drive (*a. fig.*); ***die Preise in die Höhe*** ~ force up prices; ***j-n zur Verzweiflung*** ~ drive s.o. to despair; ***ich laß' mich nicht*** ~ I won't be rushed, I refuse to be rushed; **2.** a) ♣ sprout *leaves etc.*, force *plants*, b) make *the dough* rise, c) ⚕ *physiol.* produce *urine etc.*; ***es treibt einem den Schweiß auf die Stirn*** it gets you sweating; **3.** chase *metal*; **4.** do (*a. sports*); ⚖ commit *adultery etc.*; ***was treibst du da?*** what are you up to?; ***was treibst du denn so?*** what are you doing with yourself (*or* what are you up to) these days?; ***treibt es nicht zu toll!*** don't overdo it!; F ***es mit j-m*** ~ F have it off with s.o.; → ***Aufwand, Enge, Spitze¹*** 1, ***Unfug*; II.** *v/i.* **5.** (sn) float, *a. snow, smoke*: drift; ***sich*** ~ ***lassen*** drift (*a. fig.*); ***du kannst die Dinge nicht einfach*** ~ ***lassen*** you can't just let things drift (along); **6.** a) ♣ sprout, b) ⚕ be (*or* act as) a diuretic, c) ferment, work; → ***Kraft*** 1; **7.** ***er treibt immer*** he's always breathing down your neck; **III.** ♀ *n* (-s; *no pl.*) activity; goings-on *pl.* (*a. contp.*); bustle, bustling activity; ***buntes*** ~ *a.* hustle and bustle; ***geschäftiges*** ~ a buzz (*or* flurry) of activity; ***es war ein wildes*** ~ F they were going at it hammer and tongs

Trei·ber ['traɪbɐ] *m* (-s; -) **1.** drover; *hunt.* beater; **2.** F slave-driver

Treib·gas ['traɪp-] *n* fuel gas; propellant

Treib·haus ['traɪp-] *n* hothouse; ~**at·mo·ˌsphä·re** *fig. f* hothouse atmosphere; ~**efˌfekt** *m* greenhouse effect; ~**gas** *n* greenhouse gas; ~**ge·mü·se** *n* hothouse vegetables *pl.*; ~**pflan·ze** *f* hothouse plant

Treib|holz ['traɪp-] *n* (-es; *no pl.*) driftwood; ~**jagd** *f* drive, battue; *fig.* round-up, *pol.* witch-hunt; ~**mit·tel** *n* **1.** ⚙, ⚗ propellant; **2.** *gastr.* raising agent; ~**netz** *n* drift net; ~**rad** *n* driving wheel; ~**rie·men** *m* drive (*or* transmission) belt; ~**sand** *m* quicksand

Treib·stoff ['traɪp-] *m mot. and* ✈ fuel, *esp. rocket*: propellant; ~**tank** *m* fuel tank

Trek·king ['trɛkɪŋ] *n* (-s; -s) **1.** trekking; **2.** trek, trekking tour

Tre·ma ['treːma] *n* (-s; -s, -mata) *ling.* di(a)eresis

Tre·mo·lo ['treːmolo] *n* (-s; -s, -li) ♪ tremolo

Trench·coat ['trɛnʃkoːt] *m* (-s; -s) trench coat

Trend [trɛnt] *m* (-s; -s) trend (***zu*** *dat.* towards); ~**er·mitt·lung** *f* analysis of trends; ~**for·schung** *f* trend research; ~**mel·dung** *f a. pl.* early indications *pl.* (*or* returns *pl.*); predictions *pl.*; exit poll; ~**wen·de** *f* turn of the tide, change in trend

trenn·bar ['trɛnbaːɐ] *adj.* separable; detachable; **'Trenn·bar·keit** *f* (-; *no pl.*) separability

Trenn·di·ät ['trɛn-] *f* → ***Trennkost***

tren·nen ['trɛnən] (h) **I.** *v/t.* a) separate (*a.* ⚙, ⚗); keep *things* separate; segregate *races*, b) divide; *ling.* divide (up), c) detach; cut off (*a. fig.*); sever *arm, leg etc.*, d) undo *seams*, e) *teleph.* cut off, disconnect; ***ihre Ehe wurde getrennt*** their marriage was annulled; ***nur noch ein paar Tage*** ~ ***uns von Weihnachten*** we've only got a few days to go till Christmas; ***uns*** ~ ***Welten*** we're worlds apart; → ***getrennt*; II.** *v/i.*: ~ ***zwischen*** *dat.* distinguish between; ***gut*** ~ *radio*: have good selectivity; **III.** *v/refl.*: ***sich*** ~ a) part company, go one's separate ways, b) say goodbye, c) *partner*: split up (***von*** *dat.* with), *husband, wife*: *a.* separate; ***die Mannschaften trennten sich unentschieden*** the teams had to settle for a draw; ***sich*** ~ ***von*** *dat.* a) part with *s.th.*, b) give up, get away from *an idea etc.*; ***von dem Gedanken wirst du dich*** ~ ***müssen*** *a.* you'll (just) have to rethink; ***ich konnte mich von dem Auto*** (***von ihr, von dem Anblick***) ***nicht*** ~ I couldn't bear to part with the car (I couldn't tear myself away from her, I couldn't take my eyes off it); ***er kann sich von nichts*** ~ he has to hold on to everything; ***hier*** ~ ***sich unsere Wege*** *esp. fig.* this is where we go our separate ways

Trenn|kost ['trɛn-] *f* compatible eating; *the* Hay diet; ~**li·nie** *f* dividing line

trenn·scharf ['trɛn-] *adj.*: ~ ***sein*** *radio*: have good selectivity; **'Trenn·schär·fe** *f radio*: selectivity

Tren·nung ['trɛnʊŋ] *f* (-; -en) a) separation (*a.* ⚙, ⚗); (*racial*) segregation, b) division; *ling.* syllabification; ⚖ ***eheliche*** ~ judicial separation; ***in*** ~ ***leben*** be separated; ***seit ihrer*** ~ since they (got) separated, since they split up

'Tren·nungs|angst *f* fear of separation (*or* being separated); ~**ent·schä·di·gung** *f*, ~**geld** *n* separation allowance; ~**li·nie** *f* dividing line; ~**proˌgramm** *n computer*: hyphenation program; ~**re·geln** *pl.* hyphenation rules; ~**schmerz** *m* (-es; *no pl.*) pain of parting; ~**schock** *m* shock of separation; ~**strich** *m* hyphen; *fig.* ***e-n*** ~ ***ziehen zwischen*** *dat.* draw a clear dividing line between, make a clear distinction between; ~**zei·chen** *n* hyphen

Trenn·wand ['trɛn-] *f* partition

Tren·se ['trɛnzə] *f* (-; -n) snaffle (bit)

trepp'auf [trɛp-] *adv.*: ~, ***treppab*** up and down the stairs

Trep·pe ['trɛpə] *f* (-; -n) **1.** (***eine*** ~ a flight of) stairs *pl. or* steps *pl.*, staircase, stairway; ***zwei*** ~***n hoch*** on the second (*Am.* third) floor; ***die*** ~ ***hinauf*** (***hinunter***) up (down) the stairs; ***er kann kaum die*** ~***n steigen*** he can hardly climb (up) the stairs; **2.** a) stair, b) step

'Trep·pen|ab·satz *m* landing; ~**ge·län·der** *n* banisters *pl.*; ~**haus** *n* staircase, stairs *pl.*; hallway; ***im*** ~ a) on the stairs, b) in the hallway; ~**lift** *m* stair lift; ~**stei·gen** *n* climbing (the) stairs; ~**stu·fe** *f* a) step, b) stair; ~**witz** *m*: ***ein*** ~ ***der Weltgeschichte*** one of history's ironies

Tre·sen ['treːzən] *m* (-s; -) a) bar, b) counter

Tre·sor [tre'zoːɐ] *m* (-s; -e [-rə]) a) safe, b) strongroom, vault; ~**fach** *n* safe deposit box; ~**raum** *m* strongroom; ~**schlüs·sel** *m* a) key to a (*or* the) safe, b) strongroom key

Tres·se ['trɛsə] *f* (-; -n) braid; ⚔ stripe

Tret|au·to ['treːt-] *n* pedal car; ~**boot** *n* pedal boat, pedalo; ~**ei·mer** *m* pedal bin

tre·ten ['treːtən] (trat, getreten) **I.** *v/i.* **1.** (sn) step; ***j-m in den Weg*** ~ block s.o.'s path; ***zu j-m*** ~ walk up to s.o.; ***in ein Zimmer*** ~ go into (*or* walk into, enter) a room; ***man wußte nicht, wohin man*** ~ ***sollte*** you didn't know where to step; ***von e-m Fuß auf den andern*** ~ hop from one leg to the other; *fig.* ***der Mond trat hinter die Wolken*** the moon disappeared behind the clouds; ***die Tränen traten ihm in die Augen*** tears came to (*or* welled up in) his eyes; ***über die Ufer*** ~ *river*: overflow its banks; → ***Dienst*** 6, , ***Kraft*** 2, ***nah*** II, ***näher, Schlips, zutage*; 2.** (h) ~ ***auf*** *acc.* step on *s.th.*, *a. intentionally*: tread on *s.th.*; ***aufs Gas*** ~ step on the gas, F step on it; ***auf die Bremse*** ~ step on the brakes; ***j-m auf den Fuß*** ~ step (*or* tread) on s.o.'s toes (*or* foot); ***nach j-m*** ~ (take a) kick at s.o.; ~ ***gegen*** *acc.* bump into, walk into, kick; ***j-m gegen das Schienbein*** ~ kick s.o. in the shin(s); → ***Hühnerauge, Stelle*; II.** *v/t.* (h) kick; *fig.* (*a.* ***mit Füßen*** ~) trample on; ***sich e-n Dorn in den Fuß*** ~ get a thorn into one's foot

Tret|la·ger ['treːt-] *n* pedal(-crank) bearing; ~**mi·ne** *f* ⚔ anti-personnel mine; ~**müh·le** *f* treadmill (*a. fig.*); ~**rol·ler** *m* scooter

treu [trɔʏ] **I.** *adj.* a) faithful (*dat.* to); loyal (to); devoted (to), b) innocent *look*; (big,) faithful *eyes*; ***nicht*** ~ unfaithful *husband, wife*; ***j-m*** ~ ***bleiben*** be faithful to s.o.; ***sich*** (***s-n Grundsätzen***) ~ ***bleiben*** remain true to o.s. (one's principles); ***s-m Entschluß*** ~ ***bleiben*** stick to (*or* by) one's decision; ***zu*** ~***en Händen übergeben*** hand over for safekeeping; **II.** *adv.* faithfully *etc.*; ***j-m*** ~ ***ergeben sein*** be devoted to s.o.; ~ ***und brav*** faithfully; ***er hat s-r Firma*** ~ ***gedient*** he served his company well

'treu'doof F *adj.* naive, artless

Treue ['trɔʏə] *f* (-; *no pl.*) loyalty, faithfulness (*a. fig.*); fidelity; (**die**) ***eheliche*** ~ faithfulness in marriage, being faithful to one's husband or wife; ***j-m die*** ~ ***halten*** keep faith with s.o.; ***in Treu und Glauben*** in good faith; ~**be·kennt·nis** *n* pledge (*or* oath) of loyalty; ~**eid** *m* oath of allegiance; ~**prä·mie** *f* loyalty bonus; ~**ra͵batt** *m* loyalty discount

'**treu·er·ge·ben** *adj.* loyal, devoted (*dat.* to)

'**Treu·hand** *f* (-; *no pl.*) trust

Treu·hän·der ['trɔʏhɛndɐ] *m* (-s; -) trustee; '**treu·hän·de·risch** [-hɛndərɪʃ] **I.** *adj.* fiduciary; **II.** *adv.* in trust; ~ ***verwalten*** hold in trust

'**Treu·hand|ge·biet** *n* trust territory; ~**ge·sell·schaft** *f* trust company

'**Treu·hand·schaft** *f* (-; *no pl.*) trusteeship; '**Treu·hand·ver·wal·tung** *f pol.* trusteeship; ***unter der*** ~ ***stehen von*** *dat.* be under the trusteeship of

'**treu·her·zig** *adj.* guileless; ingenuous, naive; trusting; '**Treu·her·zig·keit** *f* (-; *no pl.*) guilelessness; naivety, ingenuousness

'**treu·los** *adj.* disloyal (***gegen*** *acc.* to); F *fig.* ~***e Tomate*** F unfaithful thing; '**Treu·lo·sig·keit** *f* (-; *no pl.*) disloyalty

'**treu·sor·gend** *adj.* devoted

Tri·an·gel ['tri:aŋəl] *m, n* (-s; -) ♪ triangle

Tri·as ['tri:as] *f* (-; *no pl.*) *geol.* Triassic, Trias

Tri·ath·lon ['tri:atlɔn] *n* (-s; -s) triathlon

Tri·bun [tri'bu:n] *m* (-en; -en) tribune

Tri·bu·nal [tribu'na:l] *n* (-s; -e) tribunal

Tri·bü·ne [tri'by:nə] *f* (-; -n) rostrum; (grand)stand; *in Moscow*: reviewing stand; **Tri'bü·nen·platz** *m* seat in the stand, stand seat

Tri·but [tri'bu:t] *m* (-[e]s; -e) tribute; *fig.* toll; *fig. dat.* ***s-n*** ~ ***zollen*** pay tribute to *s.o. or s.th.*; ***e-n hohen*** ~ ***an Menschenleben fordern*** take a heavy toll on human lives; **tri'but·pflich·tig** [-pflɪçtɪç] *adj.* tributary (***j-m*** to s.o.)

Tri·chi·ne [trɪ'çi:nə] *f* (-; -n) trichina; **Tri·chi·no·se** [trɪçi'no:zə] *f* (-; -n) trichinosis

Trich·ter ['trɪçtɐ] *m* (-s; -) **1.** funnel; **2.** crater; **3.** F *fig.* ***auf den*** (***richtigen***) ~ ***kommen*** F get it; '**trich·ter·för·mig** [-fœrmɪç] *adj.* funnel-shaped

'**Trich·ter·gram·mo·phon** *hist. n* horn gramophone

Trick [trɪk] *m* (-s; -s) trick, *w.s. a.* ploy; *film*: special effect; ***das ist der ganze*** ~ ***dabei*** that's all there is to it; F ***den*** ~ ***heraushaben*** F have got the knack of it; ~**auf·nah·me** *f* a) *film, phot.* trick shot; *pl.* trick photography *sg.*, b) trick recording; ~**be·trug** *m* deception, trick; ~**be·trü·ger** *m* confidence trickster

'**Trick·film** *m* cartoon (film); ~**zeich·ner** *m* cartoonist, animator

'**Trick|ki·ste** *f* box (*fig.* bag) of tricks; ~**lin·se** *f phot.* special effect filter

'**trick·reich** *adj.* artful

trick·sen ['trɪksən] F (h) **I.** *v/i.* **1.** *sport*: feint, swerve; **2.** cheat; **II.** *v/t.*: ***das werden wir schon*** ~ we'll manage (*or* wangle) it somehow

'**Trick·ski·lauf** *m* freestyle skiing, F hot-dogging

trieb [tri:p] *pret. of* ***treiben***

Trieb [tri:p] *m* (-[e]s; -e [-bə]) **1.** ⚘ young shoot; **2.** driving force; impulse; **3.** urge; desire; sex drive; **4.** ⚙ drive; ~**fe·der** *f* ⚙ mainspring; *fig.* driving force (*gen.* behind)

'**trieb·haft** *adj.* instinctive, impulsive, *a.* sexual(ly motivated); '**Trieb·haf·tig·keit** *f* (-; *no pl.*) animal instincts *pl.*; sexuality

'**Trieb|kraft** *f* propelling (*or* motive) power; *fig.* driving force, *a.* powerhouse (*gen.* behind); ~**le·ben** *n* instinctual (*n.s.* sex) life; ~**mör·der** *m* sex murderer; ~**tä·ter** *m*, ~**ver·bre·cher** *m* sex offender; ~**wa·gen** *m* a) 🚂 railcar, b) tramcar, *Am.* streetcar, c) trolley(-bus)

'**Trieb·werk** *n* ✈ *etc.* engine; ~**scha·den** *m* engine fault

Trief·au·ge ['tri:f-] *n* watery eye; '**trief·äu·gig** [-ɔʏgɪç] *adj.* watery-eyed

trie·fen ['tri:fən] *v/i.* (h) drip (***von*** *dat.* with); *eyes, nose*: run; ~ ***vor*** *dat.* be dripping with, *fig.* ooze

trie·zen ['tri:tsən] F *v/t.* (h) **1.** pick on; **2.** torment

trif·tig ['trɪftɪç] *adj.* sound; weighty; cogent; convincing; ~***er Grund*** good reason

Tri·go·no·me·trie [trigonome'tri:] *f* (-; *no pl.*) trigonometry; **tri·go·no·me·trisch** [trigono'me:trɪʃ] *adj.* trigonometric(al)

Tri·ko·lo·re [triko'lo:rə] *f* (-; -n) tricolo(u)r

Tri·kot[1] [tri'ko:, 'trɪko] *n* (-s; -s) **1.** shirt; **2.** leotard

Tri'kot[2] *m* (-s; -s) tricot

Tri'kot|wä·sche *f* knit underwear; ~**wer·bung** *f* shirt advertising

Tril·ler ['trɪlɐ] *m* (-s; -) ♪ trill; '**tril·lern** *v/i. and v/t.* (h) a) ♪ trill, b) *zo.* warble, c) *referee*: whistle; '**Tril·ler·pfei·fe** *f* (signal[l]ing) whistle

Tril·li·on [trɪ'lĭo:n] *f* (-; -en) trillion, *Am.* quintillion

Tri·lo·gie [trilo'gi:] *f* (-; -n) trilogy

Tri·me·ster [tri'mɛstɐ] *n* (-s; -) term

Trimm-dich-Pfad [trɪm-] *m* fitness trail

trim·men ['trɪmən] (h) **I.** *v/t.* a) trim (*a.* ⚓, ✈), b) F *mot. etc.* F soup up, hype up, c) *sport*: train, get *s.o.* into shape, *a. fig.* get *s.o.* in form; ***j-n auf Ordnung*** *etc.* ~ train s.o. to be tidy *etc.*; ***et. auf alt*** ~ do s.th. up to look old; → ***getrimmt***; **II.** *v/refl.*: ***sich*** ~ keep fit; ***sich auf jugendlich*** ~ try to look younger than one is; → ***getrimmt***; '**Trimm·trab** *m* jogging

trink·bar ['trɪŋkba:ɐ] *adj.* drinkable; ***etwas*** ≈***es*** something to drink; **trin·ken** ['trɪŋkən] *v/t. and v/i.* (trank, getrunken, h) drink; ***ein Bier*** ~ have a beer; ***e-n Tee*** ~ have a cup of tea; ***was*** ~ ***Sie?*** what would you like to drink?, *a.* what'll you have?, F *hum.* what's your poison?; ~ ***auf*** *acc.* drink to *s.o. or s.th.*; ***darauf müssen wir*** (***einen***) ~ we'll have to drink to that, that calls for a drink; ***gern einen*** ~ be fond of (*or* partial to) a drop; ***einen*** ~ ***gehen*** go for a drink (*or* pint); ~ ***wir noch was*** let's have another drink; ***der Wein läßt sich*** ~ this wine isn't (too) bad

Trin·ker ['trɪŋkɐ] *m* (-s; -), **Trin·ke·rin** ['trɪŋkərɪn] *f* (-; -nen) alcoholic, heavy drinker; **Trin·ke·rei** [trɪŋkə'raɪ] *f* (-; *no pl.*) drink(ing); ***er mit s-r*** ~ F him and his drink

'**Trin·ker·le·ber** *f* hobnail liver

trink·fest ['trɪŋk-] *adj.*: ~ ***sein*** hold one's drink (F liquor) well, be able to take a lot; '**Trink·fe·stig·keit** *f* (-; *no pl.*) ability to hold one's drink (F liquor)

trink·freu·dig ['trɪŋk-] *adj.*: ~ ***sein*** like (*or* be fond of) one's drink

Trink|ge·fäß ['trɪŋk-] *n* **1.** *arch(a)eology etc.*: drinking vessel; **2.** something to drink out of; cup; glass; ~**ge·la·ge** *n* drinking bout, F booze-up; ~**geld** *n* tip; *fig. contp.* pittance; ***j-m ein*** ~ ***geben*** *a.* tip s.o.; ***was gibt man hier für*** (***ein***) ~***?*** how much do you tip here?, what sort of tip do you give here?; ~**hal·le** *f* **1.** pump room; **2.** refreshment kiosk; ~**halm** *m* (drinking) straw; ~**kur** *f* mineral cure; ~**lied** *n* drinking song; ~**milch** *f* certified milk; ~**spruch** *m* toast; ***e-n*** ~ ***auf j-n ausbringen*** drink (*or* propose) a toast to s.o.

Trink·was·ser ['trɪŋk-] *n* drinking water; ***kein*** ~ not for drinking; ~**auf·be·rei·tungs·an·la·ge** *f* water purification plant; ~**lei·tung** *f* water main; *w.s.* water supply; ~**ver·sor·gung** *f* drinking water supply, supply of drinking water

Trio ['tri:o] *n* (-s; -s) ♪ trio (*a.* F *fig.*)

Trio·le [tri'o:lə] *f* (-; -n) ♪ triplet

Trip [trɪp] *m* (-s; -s) **1.** trip; **2.** F trip; ***auf e-m*** ~ ***sein*** be on a trip; *fig.* ***von dem*** ~ ***kommt er auch wieder runter*** F he'll get over it, *a.* he'll grow out of it

trip·peln ['trɪpəln] *v/i.* (sn) mince (along); *child*: toddle

Trip·per ['trɪpɐ] *m* (-s; *no pl.*) ⚕ gonorrh(o)ea, F *the* clap

Trip·ty·chon ['trɪptʏçɔn] *n* (-s; -chen, -cha) triptych

trist [trɪst] *adj.* dreary, dismal, depressing *a. prospects etc.*; drab, dull *colo(u)rs*; forlorn *area etc.*

Tritt [trɪt] *m* (-[e]s; -e) a) step; footstep, b) kick, c) stepladder, d) ⚙ treadle, e) *mountaineering*: foothold; ***e-n leichten*** ~ ***haben*** have a light gait; ***e-n schweren*** ~ ***haben*** have a heavy gait (*or* tread), F stomp around; ***im*** ~ in step; ***im falschen*** ~ out of step; ***aus dem*** ~ ***geraten*** fall out of step; *fig.* ***aus dem*** ~ ***geraten sein*** be having a hard time, be going through a bad patch; ***wieder*** ~ ***fassen*** fall in(to) step, *fig.* get back on an even keel; ***j-m e-n*** ~ ***versetzen*** give s.o. a kick; F *fig.* ***j-m e-n*** ~ ***geben*** F give s.o. the push

'**Tritt·brett** *n mot.* running board; ~**fahrer** *contp. m* F freeloader

'**tritt·fest** *adj.* safe; ***ist es*** ~***?*** *a.* will it take the weight?

'**Tritt·lei·ter** *f* stepladder

Tri·umph [tri'ʊmf] *m* (-[e]s; -e) triumph; ***im*** ~ in triumph, triumphantly; *fig.* ~***e feiern*** be very successful, revel in success; **tri·um·phal** [triʊm'fa:l] *adj.* triumphant

Tri'umph·bo·gen *m* triumphal arch

tri·um·phie·ren [triʊm'fi:rən] *v/i.* (h) a) triumph (*a. fig.*), b) gloat; **tri·um'phie·rend** *adj.* triumphant

Tri'umph|säu·le *f* triumphal column; ~**wa·gen** *m hist.* triumphal chariot; ~**zug** *m* triumphal procession; *fig.* ***e-n*** ~ ***antreten durch*** *acc.* set out to conquer

tri·vi·al [tri'vĭa:l] *adj.* trivial; trite *remark*

Tri·vi'al·au·tor *m* popular (fiction) writer, pulp writer

Tri·via·li·tät [trivĭali'tɛ:t] *f* (-; *no pl.*) triviality; triteness

Tri·vi'al|li·te·ra͵tur *f* light fiction; ~**ro͵man** *contp. m* trashy novel

trocken ['trɔkən] (*sep.* -k·k-) **I.** *adj.* dry (*a. fig.*); *geogr. a.* arid; seasoned *wood*; *fig.* dull; ~***e Kälte*** crisp cold; ~ ***werden*** dry (out); *fig.* **~en Auges** callously, without flinching; **da blieb kein Auge ~** we (*or* they) couldn't stop laughing, F we (*or* they) were falling about; F*fig.* **~ sein** F be on the wagon; **auf dem ~en sitzen** a) be completely on the rocks, b) be staring into an empty glass, c) not to know (*or* have no idea) what's going on; **noch nicht ~ hinter den Ohren** still wet behind the ears; → **Kehle** 1, **Schäfchen; II.** *adv.*: **~ nach Hause kommen** get home before the rain really starts (*or* without getting wet); **sich ~ rasieren** dry-shave; **~ aufbewahren** keep in a dry place; *fig.* **~ bemerken** remark drily that ...

'Trocken·bat·te,rie *f* dry cell battery

'Trocken·bee·ren·aus·le·se *f* Trockenbeerenauslese; *choice wine made from grapes left to dry on the vine*

'Trocken|dock *n* ⚓ dry dock; **ins ~ bringen** dry-dock *a ship*; **~ei** *n* egg powder; **~eis** *n* dry ice; **~ele,ment** *n* ⚡ dry cell; **~fut·ter** *n* dry feed, provender; **~ge·biet** *n* dry zone; **~ge·mü·se** *n* dried vegetables *pl.*; **~ge·stell** *n* drying rack; clothes horse; **~ge·wicht** *n* dry weight; **~gür·tel** *m geogr.* dry belt (*or* zone); **~hau·be** *f* (hair)drier

Trocken·heit *f* (-; *no pl.*) dryness (*a. fig.*); drought

'Trocken|klo,sett *n* chemical toilet; **~kurs** *m* dry-ski *etc.* course

'trocken·le·gen *v/t.* (*sep.*, h) **1.** ⚙, ⚒ drain; **2.** change *a baby's* nappies (*Am.* diapers); **'Trocken·le·gung** *f* (-; *no pl.*) drainage

'Trocken|mas·se *f* dry matter; **~milch** *f* dried (*or* powdered) milk; **~obst** *n* dried fruit; **~pe·rio·de** *f* dry spell; **~pres·se** *f phot.* dry press; **~ra,sie·rer** *m* **1.** (electric) shaver; **2.** dry shaver; **≗rei·ben** *v/t.* (*irr.*, *sep.*, h, → **reiben**) rub dry; **~rei·ni·gung** *f* dry cleaning; **~schleu·der** *f* spin-drier; **≗schleu·dern** *v/t.* (*sep.*, h) spin-dry; **~schwim·men** *n* land drill; **~sham·poo** *n* dry shampoo; **~stän·der** *m* clothes horse; drying rack; **≗ste·hen** *v/i.* (irr., sep., h, → **stehen**) *cow*: be dry; **~übung** *f* dry ski *etc.* exercise; *swimming*: *a. pl.* land drill; **~wä·sche** *f* dry washing; **≗wi·schen** *v/t.* (*sep.*, h) wipe *s.th.* dry; **~zeit** *f* dry season

trock·nen ['trɔknən] **I.** *v/t.* (h) dry; **sich die Tränen ~** wipe one's tears away, dry one's tears; **II.** *v/i.* (sn) dry; **langsam ~** take a long time to dry; **die Teller werden schon von alleine ~** just leave the plates to dry; **Trock·ner** ['trɔknɐ] *m* (-s; -) drier

Trod·del ['trɔdəl] *f* (-; -n) tassel

Trö·del ['trø:dəl] *m* (-s; *no pl.*) junk; *contp. a.* rubbish

Trö·de·lei [trø:də'laɪ] *f* (-; *no pl.*) dawdling

'Trö·del|la·den *m* junk shop; **~markt** *m* flea market

trö·deln ['trø:dəln] *v/i.* (h) dawdle

Tröd·ler ['trø:dlɐ] *m* (-s; -) **1.** junk dealer; **2.** dawdler, slowcoach, *Am.* slowpoke

trog [tro:k] *pret. of* **trügen**

Trog [tro:k] *m* (-[e]s; Tröge ['trø:gə]) trough; vat

Tro·glo·dyt [troglo'dy:t] *m* (-en; -en) troglodyte

trol·len ['trɔlən] F *v/refl.* (h): **sich ~** toddle off, shuffle off; **troll dich!** *sl.* push off!

Trom·mel ['trɔməl] *f* (-; -n) drum; ⚙ *a.* cylinder, barrel; *fig.* **für et. die ~ rühren** beat the big drum for s.th., F plug s.th.; **~brem·se** *f* ⚙ drum brake; **~fell** *n* **1.** *anat.* eardrum; **2.** drumskin; **~feu·er** *n* ⚔ barrage (*a. fig. of questions etc.*)

trom·meln ['trɔməln] (h) **I.** *v/i.* drum; *rain*: beat; hammer (**auf** *acc.* at, on); **mit den Fingern ~** drum one's fingers; **II.** *v/t.* drum, beat *time etc.*; **j-n aus dem Bett ~** F knock s.o. up

'Trom·mel|re,vol·ver *m* revolver; **~schlag** *m* drumbeat, beat of the (*or* a) drum; **~stock** *m* drumstick; **~wir·bel** *m* drum roll; ruffle

Tromm·ler ['trɔmlɐ] *m* (-s; -) drummer

Trom·pe·te [trɔm'pe:tə] *f* (-; -n) **1.** ♪ trumpet; **2.** *anat.* tube; **trom'pe·ten** (h) **I.** *v/i.* **1.** ♪ play the trumpet; **2.** *elephant*: trumpet; **3.** F honk one's nose loudly; **II.** *v/t.* **4.** ♪ play *s.th.* on the trumpet; **5.** *fig.* trumpet

Trom'pe·ten|si,gnal *n* trumpet call; **~stoß** *m* trumpet blast

Trom·pe·ter [trɔm'pe:tɐ] *m* (-s; -) trumpeter, trumpet player

Tro·pen ['tro:pən] *pl.* tropics; **~an·zug** *m* tropical suit; **≗fest** *adj.* tropic(s)-proof; **~fie·ber** *n* tropical fever; **~helm** *m* pith helmet; **~in·sti,tut** *n* institute for tropical diseases; **~kli·ma** *n* tropical climate; **~kol·ler** *m* tropical frenzy; **~krank·heit** *f* tropical disease; **~me·di,zin** *f* tropical medicine; **~pflan·ze** *f* tropical plant; **≗taug·lich** *adj.* fit for the tropics

Tropf[1] [trɔpf] *obs. contp. m* (-[e]s; Tröpfe ['trœpfə]) F twit, dimwit; **armer ~** poor wretch

Tropf[2] *m* (-[e]s; -e) ⚕ drip; **am ~ hängen** be on the drip

Tröpf·chen ['trœpfçən] *n* (-s; -) droplet, small drop; **~in·fek·ti,on** *f* ⚕ droplet infection

'tröpf·chen·wei·se *adv.* **1.** in drops, drop by drop; **das Wasser kommt nur ~ durch** the water is just dripping (*or* dribbling) through; **2.** *take medicine etc.* in drops; **3.** *fig.* in dribs and drabs

tröp·feln ['trœpfəln] **I.** *v/i.* **1.** (sn) trickle, dribble, *a. tap*: drip; **2.** (h) **es tröpfelt** it's spitting; **II.** *v/t.* (h) let *s.th.* drip (**auf** *acc.* onto; **in** *acc.* into); put *eardrops etc.* (in)

trop·fen ['trɔpfən] *v/t. and v/i.* → **tröpfeln;** (*only v/i.* [h]) *candle*: drip, gutter; *tap*: drip

Trop·fen ['trɔpfən] *m* (-s; -) drop (*a. fig.*); bead *of sweat*; *pl.* ⚕ drops; *fig.* **edler ~** (drop of the) good stuff; **ein ~ auf den heißen Stein** a drop in the ocean; **steter ~ höhlt den Stein** little strokes fell big oaks; **~fän·ger** *m* dripcatcher

'Trop·fen·form *f* drop shape; **'trop·fen·för·mig** [-fœrmɪç] *adj.* drop-shaped

'trop·fen·wei·se *adv.* → **tröpfchenweise**

'Tropf|fla·sche *f* dropper bottle; **~in·fu·si,on** *f* ⚕ intravenous drip

'tropf·naß *adj.* dripping wet

'Tropf·stein *m* stalactite; stalagmite; **~höh·le** *f* stalactite cave

Tro·phäe [tro'fɛ:ə] *f* (-; -n) trophy

tro·pisch ['tro:pɪʃ] *adj.* tropical

Troß [trɔs] *m* (Trosses; Trosse) retinue, followers *pl.*; **sich im ~ befinden von** *dat.* be a fellow travel(l)er of

Trost [tro:st] *m* (-[e]s; *no pl.*) consolation, comfort; **schwacher ~** cold comfort; **mein einziger ~** my one (*or* only) consolation; *iro.* **das ist ein schöner ~!** some consolation that is; **zum ~** as a (*or* by way of) consolation; **ein ~, daß ...** at least ...; **zum ~ kann ich dir sagen ...** if it's any consolation (to you) ...; **es war ein wirklicher ~** it was a real comfort (to me); **~ suchen** *bei j-m*: look for some consolation (F a shoulder to cry on); **~ suchen in** (*or* **bei**) *dat.* seek comfort (*or* consolation) in *s.th.*; **~ zusprechen** *dat.* → **trösten**; F **du bist wohl nicht** (**recht**) **bei ~!** have you gone mad?; → **finden** I

trö·sten ['trø:stən] (h) **I.** *v/t.* console, comfort; cheer up; **das tröstet mich** that makes me feel better; **II.** *v/refl.*: **sich ~** console o.s.; **sich ~ mit** *dat. a.* comfort o.s. with *s.th.*; **sich mit dem Gedanken ~, daß** draw comfort from the fact that; **tröste dich,** *ihm geht's noch schlimmer etc.* if it's any consolation ...; **sich mit j-m ~** turn to s.o. on the rebound; **'trö·stend** *adj.* comforting, consoling; **~e Worte** *a.* words of comfort, cheering words; **Trö·ster** ['trø:stɐ] *m* (-s; -), **Trö·ste·rin** ['trø:stərɪn] *f* (-; -nen) comforter, consoler; **tröst·lich** ['trø:stlɪç] *adj.* comforting, consoling; cheering

'trost·los *adj.* a) hopeless, depressing *situation etc.*; pathetic; bleak *weather, prospects etc.*, b) cheerless; miserable, desperate; unconsolable; **'Trost·lo·sig·keit** *f* (-; *no pl.*) a) hopelessness *of the situation etc.*, b) wretchedness

'Trost|pfla·ster *n* consolation; something to cheer s.o. up; **~preis** *m* consolation prize; **≗reich** *adj.* consoling, comforting; **~spen·der** *m* comforter

Trö·stung ['trø:stʊŋ] *f* (-; -en) consolation, comfort

Trott [trɔt] *m* (-[e]s; *no pl.*) **1.** trot; **2.** *fig.* (**täglicher ~** everyday) routine; **der alte ~** the same old rut; **in den alten ~ zurückfallen** fall back into one's old ways

Trot·tel ['trɔtəl] F *m* (-s; -) F dope

trot·te·lig ['trɔtəlɪç] F *adj.* F dop(e)y; absent-minded; senile

trot·ten ['trɔtən] *v/i.* (sn) trot (along)

Trot·teur [trɔ'tø:ɐ] *m* (-s; -s) casual (shoe)

Trot·toir [trɔ'tõa:ɐ] *dial. n* (-s; -s, -e [-rə]) pavement, *Am.* sidewalk

trotz [trɔts] *prp.* (*gen.*, F *a. dat.*) in spite of, despite; **~ allem** in spite of everything; **~ alledem** for all that; **~ s-r Vorsicht** in spite of (*or* despite) the care he took, however careful he was; **~ all s-r Bemühungen** *a.* for all his efforts

Trotz [trɔts] *m* (-es; *no pl.*) defiance; stubbornness, obstinacy, pigheadedness; **aus ~** just to be stubborn, out of spite; **j-m zum ~** to spite s.o.; **j-m ~ bieten** defy s.o.; **ihrer Warnung zum ~** in defiance of (*or* flouting) her warning; **~al·ter** *n*: (**im ~** at a) defiant age

'trotz·dem I. *adv.* (but) still, all the same, nevertheless; even so; **sie hat es ~ getan** she still did it, she did it all the same (*or* nevertheless), *a.* she just went ahead and did it; **II.** *cj.* although, even though, despite the fact that

trot·zen ['trɔtsən] *v/i.* (h) (*dat.*) defy, brave *a danger etc.*, resist *s.o.*; be stubborn

trot·zig ['trɔtsɪç] *adj.* defiant; stubborn, pigheaded

Trotz·kist [trɔts'kɪst] *m* (-en; -en) *pol.* Trotskyist

'Trotz|kopf *m* F stubborn old so-and-so; **~pha·se** *f* stubborn (*or* defiant) phase; **~re·ak·ti,on** *f* act of defiance

Trou·ble ['trabəl] F *m* (-s; *no pl.*) trouble; **das gibt ~** there'll be trouble

trüb [try:p], **trü·be** ['try:bə] *adj.* cloudy *liquid*; murky *pond etc.*; clouded, cloudy *mirror*; dull (*a. colo[u]rs*); dim *light*; dull, dreary, dismal *day, weather*; dismal, gloomy *thoughts, mood etc.*; *fig.* ***in e-m trüben Licht erscheinen*** appear in a bad light; ***im trüben fischen*** fish in troubled waters; F ***trübe Tasse*** F wet blanket

Tru·bel ['tru:bəl] *m* (-s; *no pl.*) bustle, tumult, hurly-burly; chaos; F fuss; ***sich in den ~ stürzen*** throw o.s. into the fray

trü·ben ['try:bən] (h) **I.** *v/t.* a) cloud, muddy *liquid etc.*, b) dull; tarnish *silver, mirror etc.*, c) *fig.* blur *sight, mood etc.*; spoil, mar *s.o.'s pleasure etc.*; spoil, dampen *s.o.'s mood*; dull, cloud *s.o.'s mind etc.*; cloud, cast a shadow over *a relationship etc.*; → ***Wässerchen***; **II.** *v/refl.*: ***sich ~*** a) *liquid*: become (*or* go) cloudy, b) become (*or* go) dull, c) *fig. sight etc.*: become blurred; *relations etc.*: cool off (slightly), become (slightly) strained; ***der Himmel trübt sich*** the sky is getting overcast

Trüb·sal ['try:pza:l] *f* (-; *no pl.*) misery; distress; grief, sorrow; ***~ blasen*** mope; **trüb·se·lig** ['try:pze:lıç] *adj.* a) gloomy, b) wretched, miserable, c) dreary, bleak

Trüb·sinn ['try:pzın] *m* (-[e]s; *no pl.*) gloom; mood of dejection; **'trüb·sin·nig** *adj.* gloomy; dejected

Trü·bung ['try:bʊŋ] *f* (-; -en) **1.** clouding; blurring *etc.*; **2.** cloudiness; dullness *etc.*; → ***trüben***

tru·deln ['tru:dəln] **I.** *v/i.* (sn) **1.** ✈ spin; **2.** F ***durch die Stadt*** *etc.* ~ F mosey around town *etc.*; **II.** ♀ *n*: ***ins ~ kommen*** get into a tailspin

Trüf·fel ['trʏfəl] *f* (-; -n) ♣ *and gastr.* truffle

trug [tru:k] *pret. of* ***tragen***

Trug [tru:k] *m* (-[e]s; *no pl.*) **1.** delusion; **2.** *obs.* deceit, fraud; **~bild** *n* **1.** hallucination; **2.** delusion

trü·gen ['try:gən] (trog, getrogen, h) **I.** *v/t.* deceive; ***wenn m-e Augen mich nicht ~*** unless I'm seeing things; ***wenn mich mein Gedächtnis nicht trügt*** if my memory serves me right, if I remember rightly; ***wenn mich nicht alles trügt*** unless I'm very much mistaken; **II.** *v/i.* be deceptive; be misleading; → ***Schein***[3]

trü·ge·risch ['try:gərıʃ] *adj.* deceptive; misleading; deceitful; misguided, wrong *conclusion etc.*; fallacious *argument etc.*; vain, illusory *hope etc.*; treacherous *weather etc.*; ***~es Urteil*** misjudg(e)ment

'Trug·schluß *m* fallacy; non sequitur; ***e-m ~ unterliegen*** be labo(u)ring under a misapprehension

Tru·he ['tru:ə] *f* (-; -n) chest

Trüm·mer ['trʏmɐ] *pl.* ruins; rubble *sg.*, debris *sg.*; fragments; remnants, remains; ✈ wreck(age) *sg.*; ***in ~ gehen*** shatter; ***in ~ schlagen*** smash to pieces; ***in ~ legen*** raze (to the ground); ***in ~n liegen*** be (lying) in ruins; ***unter den ~n*** ✈ among the wreckage; **~feld** *n* field of rubble; *fig.* ***ihr Zimmer sah aus wie ein ~*** her room was like a battlefield (*or* looked as if a bomb had hit it); **~frau** *f hist.* woman who helped to clear away debris in Germany after World War II; **~hau·fen** *m* heap of rubble

Trumpf [trʊmpf] *m* (-[e]s; Trümpfe ['trʏmpfə]) trump (card); ***was ist ~?*** what's trumps?; ***alle Trümpfe in der Hand haben*** have (*fig.* hold) all the trumps; ***e-n ~ ausspielen*** play a trump, *fig.* play one's trump card; *fig.* ***j-m die Trümpfe aus der Hand nehmen*** steal s.o.'s thunder; ***Gesundbleiben*** *etc.* ***ist ~*** keeping healthy *etc.* is in (*or* is the thing, is what it's all about); **'Trumpf·as** *n* ace of trumps; *fig.* ***das ~ der Mannschaft*** the team's trump card; **trump·fen** ['trʊmpfən] *v/i. and v/t.* (h) trump; **'Trumpf·kar·te** *f* trump (card)

Trunk [trʊŋk] *m* (-[e]s; *no pl.*) **1.** drink; **2.** drink(ing); ***sich dem ~ ergeben*** take to drink (F the bottle); ***dem ~ verfallen sein*** a) have taken to drink, *iro.* have succumbed to the demon drink, b) be a drinker, F be on the bottle; **trun·ken** ['trʊŋkən] *adj.* drunken ..., *a. pred.* drunk (*a. fig.* ***von*** *dat.* with); intoxicated, inebriated (*both a. fig.*); **Trun·ken·bold** ['trʊŋkənbɔlt] *m* (-[e]s; -e [-də]) drunkard; **'Trun·ken·heit** *f* (-; *no pl.*) drunkenness; intoxication, inebriation; ⚖ ***~ am Steuer*** drink-driving, drunken driving

'Trun·ken·heits|de,likt *n* drinking (*or* alcohol) offen|ce (*Am.* -se); **~fahrt** *f*: ***wegen e-r ~*** *verhaftet werden etc.* for drink-driving; **~un·fall** *m* drink-driving accident

'Trunk·sucht *f* (-; *no pl.*) alcoholism, dipsomania; **'trunk·süch·tig** *adj.*: ***~ sein*** be an alcoholic; **'Trunk·süch·ti·ge** *m, f* (-n; -n) alcoholic

Trupp [trʊp] *m* (-s; -s) troop (*a. zo.*); ⚔ detachment, *police*: *a.* squad

Trup·pe ['trʊpə] *f* (-; -n) **1.** ⚔ a) troops *pl.*; unit, b) *pl.* troops, forces; *fig.* ***von der schnellen ~ sein*** be a fast worker; **2.** *thea.* company, troupe; **3.** *sport*: team

'Trup·pen|ab·bau *m* reduction in forces; **~ab·zug** *m* troop withdrawal, withdrawal (*or* pull-out) of troops; **~auf·marsch** *m* deployment (*or* buildup) of troops; **~be·we·gun·gen** *pl.* troop movement *sg.*; **~ein·heit** *f* unit; **~füh·rer** *m* commander; **~gat·tung** *f* branch (of the service); **~re·du,zie·rung** *f* reduction of troops; **~rück·zug** *m* troop withdrawal, withdrawal of troops; **~schau** *f* military review; **~stär·ke** *f* troop (*or* military) strength, number of troops; **~trans,port** *m* troop transportation; **~trans,por·ter** *m* ⚓ troopship; ✈ troop carrier; **~übung** *f* field exercise, manoeuvre, *Am.* maneuver; **~übungs·platz** *m* military training area

Trust [trast] *m* (-[e]s; -e, -s) ✝ trust

Trut·hahn ['tru:tha:n] *m* turkey (cock); **'Trut·hen·ne** *f* turkey hen

Tscha·der ['tʃadɐ] *m* (-s; -), **Tscha·de·rin** ['tʃadərın] *f* (-; -nen), **tscha·disch** ['tʃadıʃ] *adj.* Chadian

Tsche·che ['tʃɛçə] *m* (-n; -n), **Tsche·chin** ['tʃɛçın] *f* (-; nen), **tsche·chisch** ['tʃɛçıʃ] *adj.*, **'Tsche·chisch** *n* (-en) *ling.* Czech

Tsche·cho·slo·wa·ke [tʃɛçoslo'va:kə] *m* (-n; -n), **Tsche·cho·slo·wa·kin** [tʃɛçoslo'va:kın] *f* (-; -nen), **tsche·cho·slo·wa·kisch** [tʃɛçoslo'va:kıʃ] *adj. hist.* Czechoslovak, Czechoslovakian

tschüs [tʃʏs, tʃy:s] F *int.* F bye, see you

Tset·se·flie·ge ['tse:tse-] *f* tsetse fly

T-Shirt ['ti:ʃøɐt] *n* (-s; -s) T-shirt, tee-shirt

'T-Trä·ger *m* ⚙ T-beam, T-girder

Tu·ba ['tu:ba] *f* (-; Tuben ['tu:bən]) **1.** ♪ tuba; **2.** → ***Tube*** 2

Tu·be ['tu:bə] *f* (-; -n) **1.** tube; ***e-e ~ Zahnpasta*** a tube of toothpaste; F *fig.* ***auf die ~ drücken*** F step on it; **2.** *anat.* Fallopian tube

Tu·ber·kel [tu'bɛrkəl] *m* (-s; -) ⚕ tubercle, tuberculum; **tu·ber·ku·lös** [tubɛrku'lø:s] *adj.* tubercular

Tu·ber·ku·lo·se [tubɛrku'lo:zə] *f* (-; *no pl.*) tuberculosis; **~kran·ke** *m, f* (-n; -n) TB *or* tuberculosis patient (*or* case)

Tuch [tu:x] *n* (-[e]s) **1.** (*pl.* Tücher ['ty:çɐ]) a) cloth, b) scarf, c) sheet; ***das ist ein rotes ~ für ihn*** it's like a red rag to a bull (for him); **2.** (*pl.* Tuche) *textil.* cloth; **~fa,brik** *f* cloth factory; **~füh·lung** *f* close contact; ***in ~*** shoulder to shoulder; *fig.* ***~ haben mit*** *dat.* be in close contact with, be rubbing shoulders with; ***in ~ kommen mit*** *dat.* come into contact with, get to know; **~han·del** *m* cloth trade; **~händ·ler** *m* draper; **~ma·cher** *m* clothworker

tüch·tig ['tʏçtıç] **I.** *adj.* **1.** capable, able, competent; hard-working; efficient; ***~er Arbeiter*** *a.* good worker; ***~ in*** *dat.* good at (*ger.*); *iro.* ~, ~! not bad (at all); **2.** excellent; **3.** F good, decent; ***e-e ~e Tracht Prügel*** a good hiding; ***ein ~er Schrecken*** a real fright; ***ein ~er Esser*** a good (*or* big) eater; ***e-n ~en Appetit haben*** be really hungry; **II.** F *adv.*: ***~ arbeiten*** work hard; ***~ essen (trinken)*** F put away a fair (*or* decent) amount; ***~ heizen*** turn the heating right up; ***~ schneien*** snow hard; ***~ zulangen*** F tuck in, dig in; **'Tüch·tig·keit** *f* (-; *no pl.*) ability, competence; efficiency; diligence

Tücke ['tʏkə] (*sep.* -k·k-) *f* (-; -n) **1.** *no pl.* spite, maliciousness, malice; deceit, insidiousness; ***er ist voller ~*** you've got to watch him; **2.** wile; *pl. a.* trickery *sg.*; **3.** hidden weakness (*or* danger); ***es hat so s-e ~n*** it's not as easy as it looks, it's a bit tricky (to handle)

tuckern ['tʊkɐn] (*sep.* -k·k-) *v/i.* **1.** (h) *engine etc.*: put-put; **2.** (sn) chug (along)

tückisch ['tʏkıʃ] (*sep.* -k·k-) *adj.* a) malicious, spiteful; insidious (*a.* ⚕), b) dangerous, treacherous

Tue·rei [tu:ə'raı] F *f* (-; *no pl.*) fuss; acting; showing-off; ***was soll denn die ~?*** don't put on like that

Tuff [tʊf] *m* (-s; -e) *geol.* **1.** tuff; **2.** → **~stein** *m* tufa

Tüf·tel·ar·beit ['tʏftəl-] *f*, **Tüf·te·lei** [tʏftə'laı] *f* (-; -en) fiddly work, *a* fiddly job (*or* business); tricky work, *a* tricky business (*or* problem); ***das ist e-e ~*** *a.* this is a real brainteaser; **tüf·te·lig** ['tʏftəlıç] *adj.* **1.** fiddly, tricky; **2.** very exact; fussy *person*; **tüf·teln** ['tʏftəln] *v/i.* (h): ***~ an*** *dat.* fiddle about with, tinker with; try to work (*or* puzzle) out, rack one's brains over *a problem etc.*; **Tüft·ler** ['tʏftlɐ] *m* (-s; -) tinkerer; ***er ist ein ~*** *a.* he likes to fiddle around with things

Tu·gend ['tu:gənt] *f* (-; -en [dən]) virtue; → ***Not***; **'Tu·gend·bold** [-bɔlt] *m* (-[e]s; -e [-də]) paragon of virtue; **'tu·gend·haft** *adj.* virtuous; **'Tu·gend·haf·tig·keit** *f* (-; *no pl.*) virtuousness; integrity; **'Tu·gend·wäch·ter** *iro. m* moral watchdog

Tu·kan ['tu:kan] *m* (-s; -e) *zo.* toucan

Tüll [tʏl] *m* (-s; *no pl.*) tulle; net

Tül·le ['tʏlə] *f* (-; -n) ⚙ socket; spout

'Tüll|gar,di·nen *pl.* net (*or* lace) curtains; **~spit·ze(n** *pl.*) *f* net lace (*sg.*)

Tul·pe ['tʊlpə] *f* (-; -n) **1.** ♣ tulip; **2.** tulip(-shaped) glass

'Tul·pen|beet *n* bed of tulips; **~feld** *n*

tulip field; **~zeit** *f* tulip season; **~zwie·bel** *f* tulip bulb
tum·meln ['tʊməln] *v/refl.* (h): ***sich ~*** **1.** romp around; jump (*or* splash) around *or* about; **2.** F hurry up; ***tummle dich!*** *a.* F get a move on; **Tum·mel·platz** ['tʊməl-] *m* playground; *fig.* stomping ground (*a. zo.*), *pol. a.* hotbed *of extremism etc.*
Tümm·ler ['tʏmlɐ] *m* (-s; -) *zo.* **1.** tumbler; **2.** porpoise
Tu·mor ['tu:mo:ɐ] *m* (-s; -e [tu'mo:rə]) ⚕ tumo(u)r
Tüm·pel ['tʏmpəl] *m* (-s; -) pond; puddle
Tu·mult [tu'mʊlt] *m* (-[e]s; -e) tumult, riot; commotion, uproar; ***für ~ sorgen*** cause a riot; ***es kam zu schweren ~en*** there was heavy rioting; **tu'mult·ar·tig** *adj.* riotous; ***~e Ausschreitungen*** near-rioting; ***~e Szenen*** scenes of uproar (*or* rioting)
tun [tu:n] (tat, getan, h) **I.** *v/t.* a) do, b) put; ***dann tu mal was!*** get on with it then; ***was ist zu ~?*** what is there to be done?, F what's on the agenda?; ***was hat er dir getan?*** what did he do (to you)?; ***ich habe ihm nichts getan*** I didn't do anything (to him), I didn't touch him; ***er wird dir schon nichts ~!*** he won't bite you; ***hast du dir was getan?*** did you hurt yourself?, are you all right (*Am.* alright)?; ***was tut man nicht alles*** the things I do for them *etc.*; F ***was ~? sprach Zeus*** F what to do?, what now?; ***damit ist es nicht getan*** that's not enough, that's not all there is to it, there's more to it than that; ***ein Messer tut's auch*** a knife will do; ***der Anzug tut's noch ein paar Jahre*** there's a few more years wear in that suit; ***das tut nichts zur Sache*** that's got nothing to do with it; ***das tut man nicht!*** you don't do things like that, that (just) isn't done; ***er kann ~ und lassen, was er will*** he can do whatever he likes; ***tu, was du nicht lassen kannst*** well, I can't stop you; well, if you (really) must; ***es zu ~ haben mit*** *dat.* be dealing with, find o.s. up against; ***das hat damit nichts zu ~*** that's (got) nothing to do with it; ***damit hast du nichts zu ~*** that's (got) nothing to do with you; ***du wirst es mit ihm zu ~ bekommen*** you'll be in trouble with him, you'll have him after you; ***und was habe ich damit zu ~?*** and where do I come in(to it)?; → ***getan, leid, weh*** I; **II.** *v/i.*: ***so ~, als ob*** pretend to *inf.* (*or* that ...); ***er tut nur so*** he's only pretending, he's putting it on; ***tu doch nicht so!*** a) stop pretending, F who are you trying to kid, b) stop exaggerating, stop making such a fuss; ***höflich*** *etc.* ***~*** act polite *etc.*; ***ich hab' noch zu ~*** I'm still busy, I've still got a few things to do; ***er hat mit sich selbst genug zu ~*** he's got enough on his plate as it is; ***ich hab' sowieso in der Stadt zu ~*** I'm going to be in town anyway; ***du tätest gut*** (*or* ***wohl***) ***daran, jetzt zu gehen*** it might be a good idea if you went now; → ***guttun***; **III.** *v/refl.*: ***es tut sich was*** a) things are happening, b) F I can hear stirrings
Tun *n* (-s; *no pl.*) (*a.* ***~ und Lassen***) activities *pl.*, movements *pl.*, action(s *pl.*); behavio(u)r
Tün·che ['tʏnçə] *f* (-; -n) whitewash; *fig.* ***es ist nur ~*** it's just a veneer, it's all on the surface, it's just for show; **'tün·chen** *v/t.* (h) whitewash
Tun·dra ['tʊndra] *f* (-; -dren) tundra
tu·nen ['tju:nən] *v/t.* (h) *mot.* tune (up); **Tu·ner** ['tju:nɐ] *m* (-s; -) tuner
Tu·ne·si·er [tu'ne:ziɐ] *m* (-s; -), **Tu·ne·sie·rin** [tu'ne:ziərɪn] *f* (-; -nen), **tu·ne·sisch** [tu'ne:zɪʃ] *adj.* Tunisian
Tu·nicht·gut ['tu:nɪçtgu:t] *m* (-[e]s; -e) good-for-nothing
Tun·ke ['tʊŋkə] *f* (-; -n) sauce; gravy; **'tun·ken** *v/t.* (h) dip
tun·lich ['tu:nlɪç] *adj.* expedient
tun·lichst ['tu:nlɪçst] *adv.* if at all possible; as far as possible; ***er sollte Fette ~ vermeiden*** he is urged to avoid all fats; ***machen Sie es ~ nicht*** I strongly advise you not to do it, you won't do it if you know what's good for you; ***das wirst du ~ bleiben lassen*** you won't do anything of the sort
Tun·nel ['tʊnəl] *m* (-s; -) tunnel; **~bau** *m* tunnel construction; work on a (*or* the) tunnel; **~schacht** *m* tunnel shaft
Tun·te ['tʊntə] F *f* (-; -n) **1.** *contp.* woman; **2.** F fairy
Tüp·fel·chen ['tʏpfəlçən] *n* (-s; -) spot; *fig.* ***das ~ auf dem i*** a) the last straw, b) the icing on the cake; **tüp·feln** ['tʏpfəln] *v/t.* (h) dot, spot; → ***getüpfelt***
tup·fen ['tʊpfən] (h) **I.** *v/t.* **1.** dot; → ***getupft***; **2.** dab; ***Creme*** *etc.* ***~ auf*** *acc.* dab some cream *etc.* on; ***sich den Schweiß vom Gesicht ~*** mop the sweat off one's face; **II.** *v/i.*: ***j-m auf die Schulter*** *etc.* ***~*** tap s.o. on the shoulder *etc.*; **'Tup·fen** *m* (-s; -) dot, spot; **Tup·fer** ['tʊpfɐ] *m* (-s; -) **1.** ⚕ swab; **2.** dot, spot
Tür [ty:ɐ] *f* (-; Türen ['ty:rən]) door; ***in der ~*** in the door(way); ***vor der ~*** at the door; ***~ an ~ wohnen*** live next door to each other; ***von ~ zu ~ gehen*** go (knocking) from door to door; ***an die ~ gehen*** answer the door; ***kannst du mal an die ~ gehen?*** *a.* can you get the door?; F ***da ist die ~!*** you know the way out; F ***mach die ~ von außen zu!*** don't forget to shut the door behind you; ***ich muß mal vor die ~ gehen*** I must just get a breath of fresh air; ***ich komme überhaupt nicht vor die ~*** I'm stuck in the house (*or* flat *etc.*) all day long, I never get out; ***ich bin gerade zur ~ rein*** I just got in this minute; ***Tag der offenen ~*** open day; ***er wohnt e-e ~ weiter*** he lives next door (*or* in the next house, flat *etc.*); *fig.* ***Weihnachten steht vor der ~*** Christmas is just around the corner; *dat.* ***~ und Tor öffnen*** give free reign to *s.th.*; ***die ~ für Verhandlungen offenhalten*** keep an open door for negotiations; F ***mit der ~ ins Haus fallen*** blurt it out; F ***j-n vor die ~ setzen*** turn (*or* throw) s.o. out; F ***zwischen ~ und Angel*** in a hurry, (just) as he was (they were *etc.*) leaving; → ***einrennen, kehren***[1]***, verschlossen, weisen*** I
'Tür·an·gel *f* (door) hinge
Tur·ban ['tʊrba:n] *m* (-s; -e) turban
Tur·bi·ne [tʊr'bi:nə] *f* (-; -n) turbine
Tur'bi·nen|flug·zeug *n* turbojet (aircraft); **~trieb·werk** *n* jet turbine engine
Tur·bo·die·sel ['tʊrbo-] *m* turbo diesel
Tur·bo·la·der ['tʊrbola:dɐ] *m* (-s; -) turbocharger
Tur·bo-Prop-'Flug·zeug ['tʊrbo'prɔp-] *n* turboprop (aircraft)
tur·bu·lent [tʊrbu'lɛnt] **I.** *adj.* turbulent, hectic; **II.** *adv.*: ***es ging ~ zu*** things got quite hectic (*or* heated); **Tur·bu·lenz** [tʊrbu'lɛnts] *f* (-; -en) *a. pl.* turbulence (*a. phys.*)
'Tür|fül·lung *f* door panel; **~griff** *m* door-handle
Tür·ke ['tʏrkə] *m* (-n; -n) **1.** Turk; **2.** F fake; ***e-n ~n bauen*** a) pretend, fake, b) make a blunder; **3.** F Turkish restaurant; ***zum ~n gehen*** F go to a Turkish place; ***hier in der Nähe ist ein ~*** there's a Turkish place near here; **'tür·ken** F *v/t.* (h) fake *documents etc.*; fiddle *figures etc.*; **Tür·kin** ['tʏrkɪn] *f* (-; -nen) Turk(ish woman)
Tür·kis [tʏr'ki:s] *m* (-es; -e) *min.* turquoise; **tür'kis(blau)** *adj.* turquoise
tür·kisch ['tʏrkɪʃ] **I.** *adj.* Turkish; ***~er Honig*** nougat; **II.** ℒ *n* (-en) *ling.* Turkish
'Tür|klin·gel *f* doorbell; **~klin·ke** *f* door-handle; **~klop·fer** *m* knocker
Turm [tʊrm] *m* (-[e]s; Türme ['tʏrmə]) tower (*a. fig.*); (*church*) steeple; *chess*: castle, rook; *bibl.* ***der ~ zu Babel*** the Tower of Babel
Tur·ma·lin [tʊrma'li:n] *m* (-s; -e) *min.* tourmaline
'Turm·bau *m*: *bibl.* ***der ~ zu Babel*** (the building of) the Tower of Babel
Türm·chen ['tʏrmçən] *n* (-s; -) turret
tür·men[1] ['tʏrmən] (h) **I.** *v/t.* pile (up); **II.** *v/refl.*: ***sich ~*** pile up
'tür·men[2] F *v/i.* (sn) F bolt, F scarper, do a bunk
'Turm·fal·ke *m* kestrel
'turm·hoch I. *adj.* huge, towering; **II.** *fig. adv.*: ***j-m ~ überlegen sein*** be head and shoulders above s.o.
'Turm|spit·ze *f* spire; **~sprin·gen** *n* high diving; **~uhr** *f* church clock
Turn·an·zug ['tʊrn-] *m* gym outfit
tur·nen ['tʊrnən] **I.** *v/i.* (h) do gymnastics; *ped. a.* do PE (= physical education), do gym; **II.** ℒ *n* (-s; *no pl.*) gymnastics *pl.*; *ped.* PE (= physical education), gym; **Tur·ner** ['tʊrnɐ] *m* (-s; -), **Tur·ne·rin** ['tʊrnərɪn] *f* (-; -nen) gymnast
Turn|hal·le ['tʊrn-] *f* gymnasium, gym; **~hemd** *n* gym shirt (*or* top); **~ho·se** *f*: (***e-e ~*** a pair of) gym shorts *pl.*
Tur·nier [tʊr'ni:ɐ] *n* (-s; -e [-rə]) **1.** tournament; **2.** *hist.* (jousting) tournament; **~pferd** *n* show horse; **~rei·ter** *m* show jumper; **~sie·ger** *m* winner of a (*or* the) tournament; **~spiel** *n* tournament match; **~tanz** *m* ballroom dancing; **~tän·zer** *m* ballroom dancer
Turn|leh·rer ['tʊrn-] *m* gym instructor (*or* teacher); PE (= physical education) teacher; **~schuh** *m* trainer; **~stun·de** *f* gym lesson, PE (= physical education) lesson; **~übung** *f* (gymnastic) exercise; **~,un·ter·richt** *m* PE (= physical education) lesson(s *pl.*)
Tur·nus ['tʊrnʊs] *m* (-; -se) rota; ***im ~*** → ***turnusmäßig*** II; ***im ~ von drei Wochen*** every three weeks; **'tur·nus·mä·ßig I.** *adj.* rotational; ***im ~en Wechsel*** in rotation; **II.** *adv.* in rotation, by turns; (*a.* ***sich***) ***~ auswechseln*** rotate *staff*
Turn|ver·ein ['tʊrn-] *m* gymnastics club; **~zeug** F *n* gym kit, F gym things *pl.*
'Tür|öff·ner *m* door opener; **~pfo·sten** *m* doorpost; **~rah·men** *m* doorframe; **~schild** *n* doorplate; **~schloß** *n* lock; **~schwel·le** *f* threshold; **~sprech·an·la·ge** *f* entryphone
tur·teln ['tʊrtəln] F *v/i.* (h) F bill and coo

Tur·tel·tau·be ['tʊrtəl-] *f* turtledove; F *fig. pl.* F lovey-doveys

Tusch [tʊʃ] *m* (-[e]s; -e) flourish

Tu·sche ['tʊʃə] *f* (-; -n) Indian ink; watercolo(u)r

Tu·sche·lei [tʊʃə'laɪ] *f* (-; *no pl.*) whispering (behind s.o.'s back); **tu·scheln** ['tʊʃəln] *v/i. and v/t.* (h) whisper (behind s.o.'s back)

tu·schen ['tʊʃən] *v/t. and v/i.* (h) draw in Indian ink; paint in watercolo(u)rs; ***(sich) die Wimpern ~*** put some (*or* one's) mascara on

Tusch|ka·sten ['tʊʃ-] *m* paintbox; **~zeich·nung** *f* Indian ink drawing

Tus·si ['tʊsi] F *contp. f* (-; -s) female, F bird, F chick

tut [tu:t] *int.* beep-beep!, toot-toot!

Tü·te ['ty:tə] *f* (-; -n) **1.** (paper) bag; plastic bag; F ***kommt nicht in die ~!*** F no way; **2.** *gastr.* (ice-cream) cone

tu·ten ['tu:tən] *v/i.* (h) toot, honk, blow one's horn; → ***Ahnung***

TÜV [tʏf] *m* (-; *no pl.*) (*abbr. of* ***Technischer Überwachungs-Verein***) safety standards authority; ***ich muß zum ~*** my MOT's due; ***(nicht) durch den ~ kommen*** get through (fail) one's MOT

'TÜV-ge·prüft *adj.* safety-tested

Typ [ty:p] *m* (-s; -en) **1.** type; ⚙ *a.* model; ***ein Kampfflugzeug vom ~ F117*** an F117 fighter plane; **2.** type; ***ein ruhiger*** *etc.* ***~*** *a.* a quiet *etc.* sort of person; ***er ist nicht der richtige ~*** he's not the right sort of person (for the job *etc.*); ***er (sie) ist nicht mein ~*** he's (she's) not my type; **3.** F guy, bloke; ***das ist ihr neuester ~*** he's her latest (bloke)

Ty·pe ['ty:pə] *f* (-; -n) **1.** *typ. etc.* type; **2.** F character

'Ty·pen|be·zeich·nung *f* ⚙ type designation; **~druck** *m* type printing; **~leh·re** *f biol.* typology

'Ty·pen·rad *n* daisy wheel; **~drucker** *m* daisy-wheel printer

'Ty·pen·schild *n* ⚙ identification plate

Ty·phus ['ty:fʊs] *m* (-; *no pl.*) ⚕ typhoid; **~epi·de·mie** *f* typhoid epidemic; **~er·re·ger** *m* typhoid bacillus; **~kran·ke** *m, f* (-n; -n) typhoid patient (*or* case)

ty·pisch ['ty:pɪʃ] **I.** *adj.* typical (***für*** *acc.* of); ***ein ~es Beispiel*** *a.* a classic example; ***das ist wieder mal ~*** that's just typical(, isn't it); **II.** *adv.*: ***~ englisch!*** that's typically English, F that's the English for you; ***das ist ~ Bernd*** that's just like Bernd, that's Bernd all over

ty·pi·sie·ren [typi'zi:rən] *v/t.* (h) typify; ⚙ standardize

Ty·po·gra·phie [typogra'fi:] *f* (-; -n) typography; **ty·po·gra·phisch** [typo'gra:fɪʃ] *adj.* typographic(al)

Ty·po·lo·gie [typolo'gi:] *f* (-; -n) typology; **ty·po·lo·gisch** [typo'lo:gɪʃ] *adj.* typological

Ty·pus ['ty:pʊs] *m* (-; Typen ['ty:pən]) type

Ty·rann [ty'ran] *m* (-en; -en) tyrant (*a. fig.*), despot; **Ty·ran·nei** [tyra'naɪ] *f* (-; *no pl.*) tyranny, despotism; **Ty'ran·nen·herr·schaft** *f* (-; *no pl.*) tyranny, despotic rule; **ty·ran·nisch** [ty'ranɪʃ] *adj.* tyrannical, despotic; domineering; **ty·ran·ni·sie·ren** [tyrani'zi:rən] *v/t.* (h) tyrannize (*a. fig.*), oppress; *fig.* bully *s.o.*

Ty·ran·no·sau·rus [tyrano'zaʊrʊs] *m* (-; -saurier[-'zaʊrīɐ]) tyrannosaurus

Tyr·rhe·nisch [tʏ're:nɪʃ] *adj*: ***das ~e Meer*** the Tyrrhenian Sea

U

U, u [uː] *n* (-; -) U, u

ˈU-Bahn *f* underground, *in London*: *a. the* tube; *Am.* subway; ***mit der ~ fahren*** go by (*or* take) the underground *etc.*; **~hof** *m* underground (*in London a.* tube, *Am.* subway) station; **~-Netz** *n* underground (*Am.* subway) system; **~-Sta·tiˌon** *f* underground (*in London a.* tube, *Am.* subway) stop; **~-Wa·gen** *m* underground carriage, *Am.* subway car

übel [ˈyːbəl] **I.** *adj.* **1.** bad; horrible, nasty; unpleasant; unsavo(u)ry; foul (*a.* F *weather*); ***üble Geschäfte*** shady dealings; ***übler Ruf*** bad reputation; F ***nicht ~*** not bad; F ***kein übler Gedanke*** not a bad idea; F ***das klingt nicht ~*** that's not a bad idea; F ***~ dran sein*** be in a bad way; F ***ein übler Kerl*** a nasty customer; F ***er ist kein übler Kerl*** he's all right *Am.* alright; ***ein übler Trick*** a nasty trick; **2.** ***mir ist ~*** I feel sick; ***dabei kann einem ~ werden*** it's enough to make you sick; **II.** *adv.* badly; ***~ riechen*** smell (awful), stink; ***es bekam ihr ~*** it didn't do her any good; → ***mitspielen, vermerken, wohl*** 2

Übel *n* (-s; -) a) evil; *the* trouble, b) complaint; ***ein schlimmes ~*** a scourge; ***notwendiges ~*** necessary evil; ***das kleinere ~*** the lesser of the two evils; ***die Wurzel allen ~s*** the root of all evil; ***der Grund*** (*or* ***die Ursache***) ***des ganzen ~s*** the root cause of all the trouble; ***von ~*** no good; ***zu allem ~*** to top it all; → ***doppelt*** I

ˈübel|ge·launt *adj.* bad-tempered, F grumpy; ***~ sein*** *a.* be in a bad (*or* foul) mood; **~ge·sinnt** *adj.* ill-disposed (*dat.* towards)

ˈÜbel·keit *f* (-; *no pl.*) feeling of sickness, sick feeling, nausea

ˈübel·lau·nig *adj.* → ***übelgelaunt***; **ˈÜbel·lau·nig·keit** *f* (-; *no pl.*) bad-temperedness, F grumpiness

ˈübel·neh·men *v/t.* (*irr.*, *sep.*, h, → ***nehmen***) take *s.th.* amiss, take offen|ce (*Am.* -se) at; ***j-m et. ~*** hold s.th. against s.o.; ***du nimmst es mir doch nicht übel, oder?*** you're not offended, are you?

ˈübel·rie·chend *adj.* foul-smelling; foul *breath*

ˈÜbel·tat *iro. f* misdeed; **ˈÜbel·tä·ter** *m* malefactor; *a.* perpetrator (of the crime); *iro.* miscreant

ˈübel·wol·len *v/i.* (*irr.*, *sep.*, h, → ***wollen¹***): ***j-m ~*** be ill-disposed towards s.o., be out to harm s.o., F have it in for s.o.

üben [ˈyːbən] *v/t. and v/i.* (h) ♪, *sport etc.*: practi|se (*Am.* -ce); ⚔ drill; train; ***Geige*** *etc.* ***~*** practi|se (*Am.* -ce) the violin *etc.*; ***fleißig ~*** practi|se (*Am.* -ce) hard; (***sich in***) ***Geduld ~*** exercise (a bit of) patience; ***du mußt dich in Geduld ~*** *a.* you'll just have to be patient; → ***Nachsicht***

über [ˈyːbɐ] **I.** *prp.* a) (*dat.*) over; above; *a.* higher than, b) (*acc.*) over, more than; *adm.* exceeding; beyond, c) (*acc.*) across, d) (*acc.*) over, about, e) (*acc.*) during, while, f) *travel, go etc.* ~ *acc.* via *a town*, g) *speak etc.* ~ *acc.* about; *lecture, treatise etc.* ~ *acc.* on; ***~ die Straße gehen*** cross the street; ***~ Geschäfte*** (***den Beruf, Politik***) ***reden*** talk business (shop, politics); ***nachdenken ~*** *acc.* think about; ***Fehler ~ Fehler*** one mistake after the other; ***Ärger ~ Ärger*** no end of trouble; ***~ m-e Kräfte*** (***hinaus***) beyond my strength; ***das geht ~ m-n Verstand*** it's beyond me, it's above my head; ***~ Nacht*** overnight; ***er ist ~ 70*** (***Jahre alt***) he is past (*or* over) seventy, F he is on the shady side of seventy; ***~ das Wochenende*** over the weekend; ***~ einige Jahre verteilt*** spread over several years; ***~ kurz oder lang*** sooner or later; ***e-e Rechnung ~ 400 Mark*** a bill for 400 marks; ***~ den Büchern sitzen*** sit (*or* pore) over one's books; ***das geht ihm ~ alles*** it means more than anything to him; ***es geht nichts ~*** *acc.* ***...*** there's nothing like ...; ***~ der Arbeit*** (***s-r Lektüre***) ***einschlafen*** fall asleep over one's work (while reading); ***~ all dem Gerede habe ich die Kinder ganz vergessen*** with all this chatting I completely forgot about the children; *fig.* ***~ j-m stehen*** be above s.o.; **II.** *adv.*: ***~ und ~*** all over; ***die ganze Zeit ~*** all along; ***den ganzen Tag*** *etc.* ***~*** throughout the day *etc.*; F ***et. ~ haben*** have had enough of s.th., F be sick and tired of s.th.; → ***übrig, vorüber, überhaben***

ˈüber... *in cpds. usu.* over..., hyper...

ˈüber·akˌtiv *adj.* overactive; **ˈÜber·ak·ti·viˌtät** *f* overactivity

über·all [yːbɐˈʔal] everywhere; *a.* F all over the place; ***~ in*** (*or* ***an, auf***) *dat.* all over *town, the house, the wall, the floor etc.*; ***~ wo*** wherever

über·all·her [yːbɐʔalˈheːɐ] *adv.*: ***von ~*** from all around, F from all over the place; *w.s.* from all four corners of the earth; *fig. criticism etc.* from all sides

über·all·hin [yːbɐʔalˈhɪn] *adv.* everywhere, in all directions, F all over the place; *w.s.* to the four corners of the earth

über·al·tert [yːbɐˈʔaltɐt] *adj.* overaged *population etc.*; ***~ sein*** *firm etc.*: have a high (*or* too high a) percentage of old people; **Über·al·te·rung** [yːbɐˈʔaltərʊŋ] *f* (-; *no pl.*) a) ag(e)ing, b) high percentage of old people *in a firm etc.*

ˈÜber·an·ge·bot *n* ✝ oversupply, glut (***an*** *dat.* of); surplus (of); *w.s.* ***ein ~ an*** *dat.* ***...*** (far) too many (*or* much) ...; ***es herrscht ein ~ an*** *dat.* ***...*** there are far too many ..., there is far too much ...; ***bei dem ~*** *weiß man nicht, was man nehmen soll*: with so many things to choose from

ˈüber·ängst·lich *adj.* over-concerned, overly concerned, too nervous about things; ***er ist ~*** *a.* he's always worried (that) something's going to go wrong; **ˈÜber·ängst·lich·keit** *f* over-concern

über'an·stren·gen (*insep.*, *no* -ge-, h) **I.** *v/t.* overexert, strain; **II.** *v/refl.*: ***sich ~*** overexert o.s., F overdo things; **Über'an·stren·gung** *f* overexertion, strain

über'ant·wor·ten *v/t.* (*insep.*, *no* -ge-, h) hand over (*dat.* to); ***j-m ~*** *a.* commit *s.th. od. s.o.* into s.o.'s hands; **Über'ant·wor·tung** *f* (-; *no pl.*) handing over; committal

über'ar·bei·ten (*insep.*, *no* -ge-, h) **I.** *v/t.* rework, go over *s.th.* (again); revise *book etc.*; **II.** *v/refl.*: ***sich ~*** overwork, F overdo things; **über'ar·bei·tet** *adj.* overworked; ***sie ist ~*** *a.* she's been doing too much, F she's been overdoing things; **Über'ar·bei·tung** *f* (-; -en) **1.** reworking; revision; **2.** *no pl.* overwork, *w.s.* exhaustion

ˈüber·aus *adv.* exceedingly, extremely

über'backen **I.** *v/t.* (*insep.*, no -ge-, h) brown; **II.** *adj.* ... au gratin

ˈÜber·bau *m* (-[e]s; *no pl.*) *phls.*, ▲ superstructure; **über'bau·en** *v/t.* (*insep.*, *no* -ge-, h) build over

ˈüber·be·an·spru·chen *v/t.* (*insep.*, *no* -ge-, h) **1.** overexert, put too great a strain on *s.o.*; *a.* strain *one's eyes etc.*; tax *the imagination*; **2.** ⚙ overstress; overload; **ˈÜber·be·an·spru·chung** *f* (-; *no pl.*) **1.** overexertion, strain; **2.** ⚙ overstressing; overloading

ˈÜber·bein *n* ⚕ exostosis; node

ˈüber·be·kom·men F *v/t.* (*irr.*, *sep.*, h, → ***bekommen***): ***et. ~*** F get sick and tired of s.th.; ***er hat's ~*** *a.* he's had enough (of it)

ˈüber·be·legt *adj.* a) overcrowded, b) oversubscribed *course of lectures etc.*

ˈüber·be·lich·ten *v/t.* (*insep.*, h) *phot.* overexpose; **ˈÜber·be·lich·tung** *f* (-; -en) overexposure

ˈÜber·be·schäf·ti·gung *f* (-; *no pl.*) overemployment

ˈüber·be·setzt *adj.* overstaffed; **ˈÜber·be·set·zung** *f* (-; *no pl.*) overmanning, overstaffing

ˈüber·be·to·nen *v/t.* (*insep.*, h) overemphasize, overplay

ˈüber·be·völ·kert *adj.* overpopulated

ˈüber·be·wer·ten *v/t.* (*insep.*, h) overrate; **ˈÜber·be·wer·tung** *f* (-; *no pl.*) overrating

ˈüber·be·zah·len *v/t.* (*insep.*, h) overpay

über·biet·bar [yːbɐˈbiːtbaːɐ] *adj.*: ***nicht***

(*or* **kaum**) ~ unsurpassable, the height of ...; **über'bie·ten** *v/t.* (*irr.*, *insep.*, h, → **bieten**) a) ✝ outbid, b) break *record* (**um** *acc.* by), c) *fig.* outdo; *fig.* **sich** *gegenseitig* ~ vie with one another (**in** *dat.* in); **kaum zu** ~ unsurpassed; **e-e kaum zu ~de Frechheit** the height of insolence
Über·bleib·sel ['y:bɐblaɪpsəl] *n* (-s; -) remnant (*a. fig.* **aus** *dat.* of, from), *pl. a.* remains; *gastr.* leftovers *pl.*; *fig.* hold-over (**aus** *dat.* from)
über'blen·den *v/t.* and *v/i.* (*insep.*, *no* -ge-, h) *film, phot. etc.* (cross-)fade, fade over; ~ **auf** *acc.* (*or* **zu** *dat.*) fade to, go (*or* pass) over to; **Über'blen·den** *n* (-s; *no pl.*), **Über'blen·dung** *f* (-; -en) fading, fade-over
'**Über·blick** *m* (-[e]s; *no pl.*) a) view; *fig.* overall view, overview (*all* **auf, über** *acc.* of), b) survey; summary, synopsis; *fig.* **e-n ~ über et. gewinnen** get the general idea of s.th.; **den ~ behalten** keep track; **den ~ verlieren** lose track of things, **über** *acc.*: lose track of *s.th.*; **ich habe keinen ~ mehr** *a.* I don't know what's going on any more; **über'blicken** *v/t.* (*insep.*, *no* -ge-, h) **1.** overlook, have a view of; **2.** *fig.* grasp; **die Lage ~** have things under control
'**über·braten** F *v/t.* (*irr.*, *sep.*, h, → **braten**): **j-m eins ~** F give s.o. a wallop
über'brin·gen *v/t.* (*irr.*, *insep.*, *no* -ge-, h, → **bringen**) deliver (**j-m et.** s.th. to s.o.); **Über·brin·ger** [y:bɐ'brɪŋɐ] *m* (-s; -) bearer; **Über'brin·gung** *f* (-; *no pl.*) delivery
über·brück·bar [y:bɐ'brʏkba:ɐ] *adj.* bridgeable; **über·brücken** [y:bɐ'brʏkən] (*sep.* -k·k-) *v/t.* (*insep.*, *no* -ge-, h) **1.** *fig.* bridge *a gap etc.*; fill in *time*; **e-e Zeit der Arbeitslosigkeit** *etc.* ~ tide o.s. over during a period of unemployment *etc.*; **2.** bridge, span; **3.** ⚡ bypass, shunt; **Über'brückung** (*sep.* -k·k-) *f* (-; *no pl.*) **1.** *fig.* bridging; tiding o.s. over (*gen.* during ...); **2.** bridging; **3.** ⚡ bypass, shunting; jumper (wire)
Über'brückungs|(bei)hil·fe *f* temporary assistance, F tide-over; **~kre,dit** *m* bridging loan; **~maß·nah·me** *f* stopgap measure; **~,wi·der·stand** *m* ⚡ shunt resistor
über'bu·chen *v/t.* and *v/i.* (*insep.*, *no* -ge-, h) overbook; **Über'bu·chung** *f* overbooking
über·bür·den [y:bɐ'bʏrdən] *v/t.* (*insep.*, *no* -ge-, h) overburden
über·da·chen [y:bɐ'daxən] *v/t.* (*insep.*, *no* -ge-, h) roof over, build a roof over; cover; **über·dacht** [y:bɐ'daxt] *adj.* covered (over)
über'dau·ern *v/t.* (*insep.*, *no* -ge-, h) outlast; survive *a war etc.*; **die Zeit ~** stand the test of time; **s-e Werke haben ihn überdauert** his works lived on after his death; **über'dau·ernd** *adj.* enduring
über'decken *v/t.* (*insep.*, *no* -ge-, h) **1.** cover (up); **2.** mask, conceal; obscure; drown out *noise etc.*; blanket (over *or* out) *smell, stench*; drown *the taste*
über'deh·nen *v/t.* (*insep.*, *no* -ge-, h) overstretch; stretch, pull *a muscle*; **Über'deh·nung** *f* overstretching; pulling, straining *of a muscle*, strain
über'den·ken *v/t.* (*irr.*, *insep.*, *no* -ge-, h, → **denken**) think *s.th.* over; **neu ~** reassess
'**über·deut·lich** *fig.* **I.** *adj.* unmistakable, all too clear; **II.** *adv.* all too clearly, F loud and clear
über·dies [y:bɐ'di:s] *adv.* besides, moreover
'**über·di·men·sio,nal** *adj.* outsize(d); *w.s.* huge; larger-than-life ..., *pred.* larger than life; **über·di·men·sio·niert** ['y:bɐdimɛnzĭo,ni:ɐt] *adj.* oversized
'**über·do,sie·ren** *v/t.* (*insep.*, h) overdose; **et. ~** *a.* go over the dose (on s.th.); '**Über·do·sis** *f* overdose; **an e-r ~ Heroin sterben** F OD on heroin
über'dre·hen *v/t.* (*insep.*, *no* -ge-, h) overwind *watch etc.*; overspeed *engine*; strip *thread*; **über'dreht** *fig. adj.* **1.** wound up, overexcited; **2.** eccentric, F off-beat *ideas etc.*
'**Über·druck** *m phys.*, ⚙ overpressure; **~ka,bi·ne** *f* pressurized cabin; **~ven,til** *n* pressure relief (*or* safety) valve
Über·druß ['y:bɐdrʊs] *m* (-sses; *no pl.*) weariness; surfeit; **bis zum ~** ad nauseam; **ich mußte es mir bis zum ~ anhören** F I had to listen to it till it was coming out of my ears; **~ge·sell·schaft** *f*: **die ~** sated society
über·drüs·sig ['y:bɐdrʏsɪç] *adj.*: **e-r Sache ~ sein** (**werden**) be (get) tired (*or* weary) of s.th., be(come) sated with s.th.; **e-r Sache ~ werden** *a.* weary of s.th.; **ich bin der Sache ~** *a.* I feel jaded
'**über,durch·schnitt·lich** **I.** *adj.* above-average ..., higher-than-average ...; *pred.* above (*or* higher than) average; *w.s.* outstanding; **II.** *adv.* a) outstandingly (well), b) more (better) than average; ~ **verdienen** have a higher-than-average income; ~ **bezahlt werden** be paid better than the average
über·eck [y:bɐ'ʔɛk] *adv.* diagonally, at an angle
'**Über·ei·fer** *m* overkeenness, overzealousness; '**über·eif·rig** *adj.* overkeen, overzealous
über·eig·nen [y:bɐ'ʔaɪgnən] *v/t.* (*insep.*, *no* -ge-, h): **j-m et. ~** make s.th. over to s.o.; **Über'eig·nung** *f* (-; *no pl.*) ⚖ transference (**an** *acc.* to)
über'ei·len (*insep.*, *no* -ge-, h) **I.** *v/t.* rush; **die Dinge** (*or* **Sache**) ~ rush things; **nichts ~** not to rush things; **e-n Entschluß ~** make a rash decision, decide too soon; **II.** *v/refl.*: **sich ~** rush things; **über'eilt** *adj.* rash, (over)hasty, precipitate; **Über·ei·lung** [y:bɐ'ʔaɪlʊŋ] *f* (-; *no pl.*) rashness, haste; F **nur keine ~!** let's not rush things, now
über·ein'an·der *adv.* **1.** on top of each other (*or* one another), one on top of the other; **2.** *talk etc.* about one another; **~le·gen** *v/t.* (*sep.*, h) put (*or* lay) on top of each other (*or* one another); **~liegen** *v/i.* (*irr.*, *sep.*, h, → **liegen**) lie on top of each other (*or* one another); **~schla·gen** *v/t.* (*irr.*, *sep.*, h, → **schlagen**): **die Beine ~** cross one's legs
über·ein·kom·men [y:bɐ'ʔaɪnkɔmən] *v/i.* (*irr.*, *sep.*, sn, → **kommen**) agree; **wir sind** (**mit ihnen**) **übereingekommen, daß** we have agreed (with them) that; **man ist übereingekommen, daß** it has been agreed that; **Über'ein·kom·men** *n* (-s; -) → **Über·ein·kunft** [y:bɐ'ʔaɪnkʊnft] *f* (-; ⸚e) agreement, understanding, arrangement; settlement; **e-e ~ treffen** reach (*or* come to) an agreement, strike a deal
über'ein·stim·men *v/i.* (*sep.*, h) *figures, statements etc.*: tally, correspond, agree; *colo(u)rs, pattern etc.*: match, go together; *ling.* agree; **mit j-m ~** agree with s.o. (**über** *acc.*, **in** *dat.* on); **über'ein·stimmend** **I.** *adj.* corresponding; concurring *opinions, reports etc.*; unanimous; matching *colo(u)rs*; **II.** *adv. declare etc.* unanimously; ~ **mit** *dat.* in accordance (*or* conformity, agreement) with; **es wurde ~ berichtet, daß** reports agreed that; **es wurde ~ festgestellt, daß** everybody agreed that, there was unanimous agreement that; **Über'ein·stimmung** *f* (-; *no pl.*) agreement; correspondence, concurrence; harmony, accord; unison; ~ **erzielen** come to (*or* reach) an agreement; **in ~ bringen** make *things* tally, get *things* to tally; **in ~ stehen → übereinstimmen; in ~ mit** *dat.* in agreement (*or* accordance, conformity) with, in keeping (*or* line) with; **es besteht** (**keine**) **~ zwischen X und Y** X and Y (don't) agree *or* tally, X and Y are(n't) in agreement
'**über·emp·find·lich** *adj.* hypersensitive, oversensitive (**gegen** *acc.* to); '**Über·emp·find·lich·keit** *f* hypersensitivity, oversensitivity
über·er·nährt ['y:bɐʔɛrnɛ:ɐt] *adj.* overnourished, overfed; '**Über·er·näh·rung** *f* (-; *no pl.*) overnourishment; overfeeding
über'es·sen *v/refl.* (*irr.*, *insep.*, *no* -ge-, h, → **essen**): **sich ~** overeat; **sich übergessen haben** *a.* have had too much (to eat)
'**über·es·sen** *v/t.* (*irr.*, *sep.*, h, → **essen**): **sich et. ~** eat too much (*or* many) of s.th.; **ich hab's mir übergegessen** *a.* F I can't stand the sight of it (*or* them) any more
über'fah·ren *v/t.* (*irr.*, *insep.*, *no* -ge-, h, → **fahren**) **1.** run over, knock down; drive through *a sign etc.*; cross, pass *a line etc.*; **die Ampel ~** shoot the lights; **2.** *fig.* steamroller *s.o.* (into it)
'**über·fah·ren** *v/i.* (*irr.*, *sep.*, sn, → **fahren**) cross over; ~ **über** *acc.* cross
'**Über·fahrt** *f* crossing
'**Über·fall** *m* (-[e]s; ⸚e) attack (**auf** *acc.* on); mugging; ambush (attack) (on); raid (on) (*a.* ⚔), hold-up; assault (on); ⚔ invasion (of, *a.* F *fig. of s.o.'s house etc.*); F *fig.* F descent (on); F *fig.* **e-n ~ auf j-n planen** plan to descend on s.o.; **über'fal·len** *v/t.* (*irr.*, *insep.*, *no* -ge-, h, → **fallen**) attack, mug; waylay (*a.* F *fig.*), ambush *s.o.*; raid *bank*, *a.* ⚔ *country etc.*, hold up *a bank*; assault *s.o.*; ⚔ invade *a country etc.*; F *fig.* F descend on *s.o.*; *fig.* **von Müdigkeit** *etc.* ~ **werden** be overcome by tiredness *etc.*; **plötzlich wurde ich von Müdigkeit ~** *a.* suddenly a feeling of tiredness came over me (*or* hit me); **j-n mit e-r Frage** (**Aufgabe** *etc.*) ~ spring a question (a job *etc.*) on s.o.
'**über·fäl·lig** *adj.* overdue; **längst ~** long overdue; **seit drei Tagen** (*or* **drei Tage**) **~ sein** be three days overdue
'**Über·fall·kom,man·do** *n* riot squad
'**über·fein** *adj.* **1.** highly sensitive *ear etc.*; **2.** fastidious *tastes*; **3.** oversubtle *distinction etc.*; **über·fei·nert** [y:bɐ'faɪnɐt] *adj.* overrefined; **Über·fei·ne·rung** [y:bɐ'faɪnərʊŋ] *f* (-; *no pl.*) overrefinement
über'flie·gen *v/t.* (*irr.*, *insep.*, *no* -ge-, h, → **fliegen**) **1.** fly over; F buzz; **2.** *fig.* glance over, skim (through); **et. mit den**

Augen ~ *a.* run one's eyes over (*or* down *a list etc.*); **3.** *smile etc.*: flit across *s.o.'s* face

'**Über·flie·ger** F *m* F superman

'**über·flie·ßen** *v/i.* (*irr., sep.*, sn, → ***flie-ßen***) overflow (*a. fig.* ***von*** *dat.* with); ~ ***aus*** *dat.* flow over the top of *s.th.*

über·flü·geln [y:bɐ'fly:gəln] *fig. v/t.* (*insep., no* -ge-, h) surpass, outstrip

'**Über·fluß** *m* (-sses; *no pl.*) abundance; surplus; glut (*all* ***an*** *dat.* of); ~ ***haben an*** *dat., et.* ***im*** ~ ***haben*** have plenty of, *a.* abound in *resources, fish etc.*; ***Papier*** *etc.* ***ist im*** ~ ***vorhanden*** there's plenty of paper *etc.* (available); ***zu allem*** ~ as if that wasn't enough, F to top it all; ~**ge·sell·schaft** *f* affluent society

'**über·flüs·sig** *adj.* superfluous, *a.* uncalled-for *remark etc.*; unnecessary; undesired; redundant *workers etc.*; ~ ***machen*** render superfluous *etc.*; ~ ***zu sagen, daß*** needless to say, ...; '**über·flüs·si·ger·wei·se** [-flʏsɪgɐvaɪzə] *adv.* unnecessarily; for no real reason; '**Über·flüs·sig·keit** *f* (-; *no pl.*) superfluousness

über'flu·ten *v/t.* (*insep., no* -ge-, h) *a. fig.* flood, inundate; **Über'flu·tung** *f* (-; -en) flooding; *fig.* inundation

über'for·dern *v/t.* (*insep., no* -ge-, h) expect (*or* demand) too much of *s.o.*, be too much for *s.o.* (to handle), be more than *s.o.* can cope with; overtax, strain *one's body, nerves etc.*; **über'for·dert** *adj.*: ***er ist*** ~ he can't cope, he's taken on too much; ***damit ist er*** ~ it's too much for him, it's expecting too much of him; ***ich fühle mich*** ~ I don't think I can cope (with it) *or* manage (it); **Über'for·de·rung** *f* (-; *no pl.*): ***es ist e-e*** ~ it's (expecting) too much (***für*** *acc.* of *s.o.*)

über·frach·ten [y:bɐ'fraxtən] *v/t.* (*insep., no* -ge-, h) *a. fig.* overload; **über'frach·tet** *fig. adj.* overloaded, weighed down (***mit*** *dat.* with)

über·fragt [y:bɐ'fra:kt] *adj.*: ***da bin ich*** ~ I'm afraid I can't answer that (one) for you, F you've got me there

Über·frem·dung [y:bɐ'frɛmdʊŋ] *f* (-; *no pl.*) foreign infiltration (☤ control)

über'fres·sen F *v/refl.* (*irr., insep., no* -ge-, h, → ***fressen***): ***sich*** ~ overeat; ***sich*** ~ ***an*** *dat.* F stuff o.s. with *s.th.*

über'frie·ren *v/i.* (*irr., insep., no* -ge-, sn, → ***frieren***) freeze over

'**über·füh·ren**[1] *v/t.* (*sep.*, h) take, transport, ✈ *a.* fly

über'füh·ren[2] *v/t.* (*insep., no* -ge-, h) **1.** take, transport, ✈ *a.* fly; **2.** ⚖ find *s.o.* guilty (*gen.* of), convict (of)

Über'füh·rung *f* (-; -en) **1.** transportation; **2.** ⚖ conviction; **3.** flyover, overpass; 🚂 viaduct

'**Über·fül·le** *f* (-; *no pl.*) overabundance, profusion (***von*** *dat.* of); **über'fül·len** *v/t.* (*insep., no* -ge-, h) overcrowd *a place etc.*; **über'füllt** *adj.* (over)crowded; *room, bus etc.*: *a. pred.* crammed full, F (jam)packed; congested *roads*; oversubscribed *course of lectures etc.*; ~***e Vorlesungen*** crowded lecture halls; ~***e Seminare*** crowded seminars; ~***er Luftraum*** congested airspace, crowded air lanes; **Über'fül·lung** *f* (-; *no pl.*) overcrowding; ***wegen*** ~ ***geschlossen*** full up

'**Über·funk·ti̦on** *f* ⚕ hyperactivity; ~ ***der Schilddrüse*** *etc.* hyperactive thyroid *etc.*

über'füt·tern *v/t.* (*insep., no* -ge-, h) overfeed

'**Über·ga·be** *f* (-; *no pl.*) handing-over; ⚔ surrender

'**Über·gang** *m* (-[e]s; ⸚e) **1.** crossing (point); footbridge; 🚂 level (*Am.* grade) crossing; **2.** crossing; **3.** *fig.* transition; interim

'**Über·gangs|be·stim·mun·gen** *pl.* provisional regulations; ~**er·schei·nung** *f* transitional phenomenon (*or* aspect)

'**über·gangs·los** *adv.* without transition, directly; ***sich*** ~ ***aneinanderreihen*** run on from one another (*or* without a break)

'**Über·gangs|lö·sung** *f* interim solution, temporary arrangement; ~**man·tel** *m* in-between coat; ~**pha·se** *f* transitional phase; ~**re·ge·lung** *f* temporary arrangement; ~**re̦gie·rung** *f* caretaker (*or* transitional, interim) government; ~**sta·di·um** *n* transitional stage; ~**stil** *m* transitional style; ~**zeit** *f* transitional period

über'ge·ben (*irr., insep., no* -ge-, h, → ***geben***) **I.** *v/t.* hand over; present; ⚔ *etc.* surrender; ***j-m et.*** ~ hand s.th. over to s.o., present s.o. with s.th., ⚔ *etc.* surrender s.th. to s.o.; entrust s.o. with s.th.; ***e-e Sache dem Gericht*** ~ take a matter to court; ***e-e Brücke*** *etc.* ***dem Verkehr*** ~ open a bridge *etc.* to traffic; **II.** *v/refl.*: ***sich*** ~ vomit, be sick

'**über·gehen**[1] *v/i.* (*irr., sep.*, sn, → ***gehen***) go (*or* pass) over (***zu*** *dat.* to); ~ ***auf*** *acc.* devolve upon *s.o.'s successor etc.*; ~ ***in*** *acc.* pass into, turn into, *colo(u)r, sound etc., a. fig. mood etc.*: blend (*or* merge) into; ***in Schnee*** *etc.* ~ turn to snow *etc.*; ***ineinander*** ~ *colo(u)rs*: blend; ***in j-s Besitz*** ~ pass into s.o.'s possession (*or* hands); ***in andere Hände*** ~ change hands; ***zum nächsten Punkt*** *etc.* ~ pass on (*or* move on, *formal*: proceed) to the next item *etc.*; ~ ***zu*** *dat.* go over to *another party etc.*, defect to *the enemy etc.*; F ***die Augen gingen ihm über*** his eyes nearly popped out of his head

über'ge·hen[2] *v/t.* (*irr., insep., no* -ge-, h, → ***gehen***) a) pass *s.th.* over (***mit Stillschweigen*** in silence), b) disregard; ignore, c) leave out, omit, F skip, d) pass *s.o.* over, leave *s.o.* out; ***sich übergangen fühlen*** feel snubbed (*or* left out)

'**über·ge·nau** *adj.* overscrupulous, F *contp.* picky; '**Über·ge·nau·ig·keit** *f* (-; *no pl.*) overscrupulousness, F *contp.* pickiness

'**über·ge·nug** *adj.* more than enough

'**über·ge·ord·net** *adj.* higher *authority etc.*; *matter etc.* of overriding importance; ***e-r Sache*** ~ ***sein*** have priority over s.th.

'**Über·ge·päck** *n* ✈ excess baggage

'**über·ge·schnappt** F *adj.* F cracked, crazy

'**Über·ge·wicht** *n* (-[e]s; *no pl.*) **1.** overweight; excess weight; ~ ***haben*** be overweight, be over the limit; ***20 Kilo*** ~ ***haben*** be 20 kilos overweight; ***20 Gramm*** ~ ***haben*** be 20 gram(me)s over (the limit); **2.** *fig.* preponderance (***an*** *dat.* of); *pol. etc.* supremacy; predominance; ***das*** ~ ***haben*** predominate, be predominant; ***... haben das*** ~ *a.* there is a preponderance of ...; ***das*** ~ ***gewinnen*** gain the upper hand, come out on top; **3.** ***das*** ~ ***bekommen*** lose one's balance, topple over;

'**über·ge·wich·tig** *adj.* overweight

über'gie·ßen[1] *v/t.* (*irr., insep., no* -ge-, h, → ***gießen***) pour water *etc.* over; douse (***mit*** *dat.* with); *gastr.* baste

'**über·gie·ßen**[2] *v/t.* (*irr., sep.*, h, → ***gießen***) spill

'**über·glück·lich** *adj.* overjoyed, *pred.* F over the moon

'**über·grei·fen** *v/i.* (*irr., sep.*, h, → ***greifen***) **1.** ~ ***auf*** *acc.* *fire, epidemic, panic etc.*: spread to; *fighting*: *a.* spill over into; **2.** *gym.*, ♪ shift; ♪ cross one's hands over; '**über·grei·fend** *adj.* general; comprehensive; global

'**Über·griff** *m* (-[e]s; -e) encroachment, infringement (***auf*** *acc.* on), incursion (into)

'**über·groß** *adj.* outsize(d), oversized; '**Über·grö·ße** *f* (-; -n) outsize

'**über·ha·ben** F *v/t.* (*irr., sep.*, h, → ***haben***) **1.** have on *a coat etc.*; **2.** have left (over); **3.** *fig.* ***e-e Sache*** ~ F be sick and tired of s.th., be fed up with s.th.

über'hand·neh·men *v/i.* (nahm überhand, überhandgenommen, h) increase uncontrollably; get out of hand (*or* control); become rampant; **Über'hand·neh·men** *n* (-s; *no pl.*) uncontrolled spread

'**Über·hang** *m* (-[e]s; ⸚e) **1.** overhang; △ *a.* projection; **2.** *fig.* surplus, excess

'**über·hän·gen**[1] *v/i.* (*irr., sep.*, h, → ***hängen***[1]) overhang; △ project

'**über·hän·gen**[2] *v/t.* (*sep.*, h) hang *s.th.* over; throw *a coat etc.* over one's shoulders

über'häu·fen *v/t.* (*insep., no* -ge-, h): ***j-n*** ~ ***mit*** *dat.* inundate (*or* swamp) s.o. with, heap *hono(u)rs etc.* on s.o., shower s.o. with *presents*

über·haupt [y:bɐ'haʊpt] *adv.* a) generally, on the whole, altogether, b) actually, anyway; besides; ~ ***nicht*** not at all, never; ~ ***nichts*** nothing (at all); ~ ***kein ...*** no ... at all, no ... of any sort; ***sie hat ja*** ~ ***keine Stelle*** *a.* she hasn't even got a job (to speak of); ***wenn*** ~ if at all; ***du hättest es*** ~ ***nicht tun sollen*** you shouldn't have done it in the first place; ***gibt es*** ~ ***e-e Möglichkeit?*** is there any chance at all?; ***und*** ~, ... and, come to that, ...; ***wer*** (***wo*** *etc.*) ***ist er*** ~? who (where *etc.*) is he anyway?; ***hast du*** ~ ***schon was gegessen?*** have you actually had anything to eat yet?; ***er ist*** ~ ***sehr begabt*** of course, he 'is very talented (altogether)

über·heb·lich [y:bɐ'he:plɪç] *adj.* overbearing, arrogant; **Über'heb·lich·keit** *f* (-; *no pl.*) arrogance

über'hei·zen *v/t.* (*insep., no* -ge-, h), **über·hit·zen** [y:bɐ'hɪtsən] *v/t.* (*insep., no* -ge-, h) overheat (*a. fig.*, ☤); ⚙ superheat; **über·hitzt** [y:bɐ'hɪtst] *adj.* overheated; *fig.* ***das ist s-e*** ~***e Phantasie*** it's just his imagination running wild

über·hö·hen [y:bɐ'hø:ən] *v/t.* (*insep., no* -ge-, h) bank; **über·höht** [y:bɐ'hø:t] *adj.* **1.** banked *curve*; **2.** *fig.* excessive *prices, speed etc.*, exorbitant, F ridiculous *prices*; ***mit*** ~***er Geschwindigkeit fahren*** go over (*or* break) the speed limit; **Über'hö·hung** *f* (-; *no pl.*): ~ ***der Preise*** exorbitant price rises (*or* prices)

über'ho·len *v/t.* (*insep., no* -ge-, h) **1.** pass, overtake (*a. fig.*), *fig. a.* outstrip; *fig.* ***sie hat ihn längst überholt*** *a.* she's left him trailing; **2.** ⚙ overhaul, recondition

'**über·ho·len** *v/t.* (*sep.*, h) ferry *s.o.* over

Über·hol|ma̦nö·ver [y:bɐ'ho:l-] *n mot.*

overtaking manoeuvre (*Am.* maneuver); **~spur** *f* passing lane

über·holt [y:bɐ'ho:lt] *adj.* (out)dated, outmoded; *a.* antiquated *ideas etc.*

Über·ho·lung [y:bɐ'ho:lʊŋ] *f* (-; -en) ⚙ overhaul, reconditioning

Über·hol|ver·bot [y:bɐ'ho:l-] *n* "No Passing" (rule *or* sign); **~vor·gang** *m*: ***der*** ~ overtaking; ***vor*** (***nach***) ***dem*** ~ before (after) overtaking; ***während des ~s*** when (*or* while) overtaking

über'hö·ren *v/t.* (*insep.*, *no* -ge-, h) not to hear; miss, not to catch *s.o.'s words etc.*; ignore; ***das will ich überhört haben!*** I didn't hear that

'Über·Ich *n psych.* superego

'über·in·ter·pre,tie·ren *v/t.* (*insep.*, h) overinterpret

'über·ir·disch *adj.* supernatural; celestial, heavenly; *fig.* ***von ~er Schönheit*** of divine beauty

über·kan·di·delt ['y:bɐkandi:dəlt] F *adj.* slightly eccentric (F off-beam)

über'kle·ben *v/t.* (*insep.*, *no* -ge-, h) stick s.th. over *s.th.*; ***die Wand war mit Postkarten überklebt*** the wall was covered with postcards (*or* had postcards stuck all over it)

'über·klug *adj.* F too clever by half

'über·ko·chen *v/i.* (*sep.*, sn) boil over (*a. fig.*)

über'kom·men (*irr.*, *insep.*, *no* -ge-, h, → ***kommen***) **I.** *v/t.*: ***Furcht*** *etc.* ***überkam ihn*** he was overcome by fear *etc.*; **II.** *v/i.*: ***diese Sitte ist uns*** ~ this custom has been handed down (*or* has come down) to us; **III.** *adj.* traditional

'Über·kom·pen·sa·ti,on *f* overcompensation; **'über·kom·pen,sie·ren** (*insep.*, h) **I.** *v/t.* overcompensate for; **II.** *v/i.* overcompensate

'über·kon·fes·sio,nell *adj.* interdenominational

über'kreu·zen *v/refl.* (*insep.*, *no* -ge-, h): ***sich*** ~ coincide, *b.s.* clash

'über·krie·gen F *v/t.* (*irr.*, *sep.*, h, → ***kriegen***) F get fed up with, tire of

'über·kri·tisch *adj.* overcritical, overly critical

über·kro·nen [y:bɐ'kro:nən] *v/t.* (*insep.*, *no* -ge-, h) crown *a tooth*

über·kru·sten [y:bɐ'krʊstən] *v/t.* (*insep.*, *no* -ge-, h) crust over; **über·kru·stet** [y:bɐ'krʊstət] *adj.* covered (**mit** *dat.* in); ***die Schuhe waren mit Dreck*** ~ *a.* the shoes were caked with mud

über'la·den¹ *v/t.* (*irr.*, *insep.*, *no* -ge-, h, → ***laden***) a) overload, b) load down, c) *fig.* clutter

über'la·den² **I.** *p.p. of* ***überladen¹***; **II.** *adj.* overloaded; *fig.* overladen, florid *style*; cluttered

über'la·gern *v/t.* (*insep.*, *no* -ge-, h) overlay; overlap (*a.* ***sich*** ~); *geol.* overlie; *radio*: heterodyne; *stations*: jam; *fig.* ***überlagert von*** *dat.* superimposed *or* displaced by *new problems etc.*; **Über'la·ge·rung** *f* (-; -en) overlapping; *radio*: heterodyning

'Über·land|bus *m* long-distance coach (*Am.* bus); **~fahrt** *f mot.* cross-country trip; **~lei·tung** *f* ⚡ power line; **~lei·tungs·mast** *m* ⚡ grid pylon; **~ver·kehr** *m* long-distance traffic

'über·lang *adj.* overlength; ***~e Spieldauer*** extended play; **'Über·län·ge** *f*: ~ ***haben*** be overlength; ***Film mit*** ~ long film

über·lap·pen [y:bɐ'lapən] *v/t. and v/refl.* (***sich*** ~) (*insep.*, *no* -ge-, h) ⚙ overlap (*a. fig.*); **Über·lap·pung** *f* (-; -en) overlapping

über'las·sen *v/t.* (*irr.*, *insep.*, *no* -ge-, h, → ***lassen***): ***j-m et.*** ~ let s.o. have s.th., leave s.th. to s.o.; ***et. dem Schicksal*** (***Zufall*** *etc.*) ~ leave s.th. to fate (chance *etc.*); ***es j-m*** (*or* ***dem Zufall*** *etc.*) ~ ***zu*** *inf.* leave it to s.o. (*or* to chance *etc.*) to *inf.*; ***j-n sich selbst*** ~ leave s.o. to fend for himself (*or* herself); ***j-n s-m Schicksal*** ~ leave s.o. to his (*or* her) fate; ***sich selbst ~ sein*** be left to one's own devices; ~ ***Sie das mir*** leave that to me; ***das überlasse ich dir*** that's up to you, I'll leave that to you; ***es bleibt ihm ~, was er tun will*** it's up to him what he wants to do; ***sich e-m Gefühl*** *etc.* ~ give o.s. over (*or* abandon o.s.) to a feeling *etc.*

über·la·sten [y:bɐ'lastən] *v/t.* (*insep.*, *no* -ge-, h) **1.** overload (*a.* ⚡, ⚙); **2.** *fig.* strain, put too great a strain on; **über·la·stet** [y:bɐ'lastət] *adj.* **1.** overloaded (*a.* ⚡, ⚙); **2.** *fig.* under strain; overworked; **Über'la·stung** *f* (-; -en) **1.** overload (*a.* ⚡, ⚙), overcharge; **2.** *fig.* strain

'über·lau·fen¹ *v/i.* (*irr.*, *sep.*, sn, → ***laufen***) **1.** run over, boil over; *fig.* ***das Faß zum ~ bringen*** be the last straw; **2.** ⚔ desert; go over (**zu** *dat.* to *the enemy*)

über'lau·fen² **I.** *v/t.* (*irr.*, *insep.*, *no* -ge-, h, → ***laufen***) **1.** overrun; **2.** *fig.* come over *s.o.*; ***es überlief mich*** (***heiß und***) ***kalt*** it sent a shiver down my spine, I went hot and cold; **II.** *adj.* a) overcrowded *area etc.*, b) *doctor etc.* overrun with patients *etc.*

'Über·läu·fer *m* ⚔ deserter; *pol. a.* defector, turncoat, renegade

'Über·lauf|rohr *n* overflow pipe; **~ven,til** *n* overflow valve

über'le·ben **I.** *v/t. and v/i.* (*insep.*, *no* -ge-, h) survive (*a.* F *fig.*); F *fig.* ***das überlebe ich nicht*** *a.* that'll be the death of me; F *fig.* ***du wirst es ~!*** F it won't kill you, you'll survive; **II.** *obs.* *v/refl.*: ***sich*** ~ become dated; **Über'le·ben** *n* (-s; *no pl.*) (***ums ~ kämpfen*** fight for) survival; **Über'le·ben·de** *m, f* (-n; -n) survivor

Über'le·bens|an·zug *m* survival suit; **~chan·ce** *f* chance(s *pl.*) of survival; **~dau·er** *f* period of survival

über'le·bens·fä·hig *adj.* capable of surviving; **Über'le·bens·fä·hig·keit** *f* survivability

'über·le·bens·groß *adj.* larger-than-life ..., *pred.* larger than life

Über'le·bens|kampf *m* fight (*or* struggle) for survival; **~künst·ler** *m* survivor; **~stra·te,gie** *f* survival strategy; **~trai·ning** *n* survival training; **~wil·le** *m* will to survive

über'le·gen¹ (*insep.*, *no* -ge-, h) **I.** *v/t.* (*a.* ***sich*** ~) think about, think *s.th.* over; ***noch einmal*** ~ reconsider; ***es sich wieder*** (*or* ***anders***) ~ change one's mind; ***wenn ich es mir recht überlege*** when I think about it; ***sich et. genau*** ~ think carefully about s.th.; ***das würde ich mir zweimal*** ~ I'd think twice about that (*or* before doing that); **II.** *v/i.* think; ***ohne zu*** ~ without thinking, F like a shot, (*a.* ***ohne lange zu*** ~) without thinking twice; ***überleg noch mal*** you should think about it again, F you should give it a rethink; ***ich würde nicht lange*** ~ I wouldn't waste too much time thinking about it; ***ich hätte nicht lange überlegt*** I wouldn't have given it a second thought

über'le·gen² **I.** *adj.* **1.** superior (*dat.* to; **an** *dat.* in); ***j-m weit ~ sein*** be more than a match for s.o., be head and shoulders above s.o.; → ***zahlenmäßig***; **2.** superior, supercilious; ***~es Lächeln*** (***~e Miene***) superior smile (air); **II.** *adv.* **3.** in superior style; convincingly; ~ ***siegen*** win in style; **4.** in a superior manner, in a supercilious way

'über·le·gen³ *v/t.* (*sep.*, h) **1.** lay *s.th.* over *s.o. or s.th.*, cover *s.o. or s.th.* with *s.th.*; **2.** F put *a child* over one's knee

Über'le·gen·heit *f* (-; *no pl.*) superiority; **Über'le·gen·heits·ge·fühl** *n* (-[e]s; *no pl.*) sense of superiority

über'le·gens·wert *adj.* worth considering

über·legt [y:bɐ'le:kt] **I.** *p.p. of* ***überlegen¹***; **II.** *adj.* a) considered; well-thought-out ..., well-planned ..., *pred.* well thought out, well planned, b) circumspect; **Über'legt·heit** *f* (-; *no pl.*) circumspection

Über·le·gung [y:bɐ'le:gʊŋ] *f* (-; -en) **1.** *no pl.* consideration, reflection; ***bei näherer*** ~ on closer reflection; ***bei nüchterner*** ~ looking at it in a more sober light; ***ohne*** ~ a) without thinking, b) without thinking twice (*a.* ***ohne lange*** ~); ***nach reiflicher*** ~ after due consideration; **2.** consideration; point (of view); ***aus dieser ~ heraus*** for this reason

'über·lei·ten *v/i.* (*sep.*, h) lead (**zu** *dat.* to); **'Über·lei·tung** *f* (-; -en) transition

über'le·sen *v/t.* (*irr.*, *insep.*, *no* -ge-, h, → ***lesen***) **1.** run (*or* skim) through; **2.** overlook

über'lie·fern *v/t.* (*insep.*, *no* -ge-, h) hand down (*dat.* to), pass on (to); ***aus dieser Zeit ist nichts überliefert*** no records of this period have survived; ***es ist*** (***schriftlich***) ***überliefert*** there are (written) records testifying to it; ***es ist überliefert, daß*** a) records indicate that, b) tradition has it that; **über·lie·fert** [y:bɐ'li:fɐt] *adj.* traditional; **Über'lie·fe·rung** *f* (-; -en) **1.** *no pl.* handing down (**an** *acc.* to), passing on (to); transmission *of texts*; **2.** tradition; records *pl.*; *pl.* writings, texts; ***mündliche*** ~ oral legend

über·li·sten [y:bɐ'lɪstən] *v/t.* (*insep.*, *no* -ge-, h) outwit, outsmart

'Über·macht *f* (-; *no pl.*) superiority, superior strength; ***in der ~ sein*** be in a superior position; **'über·mäch·tig** *adj.* **1.** *enemy etc.* superior (in strength); **2.** overpowering *emotion etc.*

über'ma·len *v/t.* (*insep.*, *no* -ge-, h) paint over

über·man·nen [y:bɐ'manən] *v/t.* (*insep.*, *no* -ge-, h) overcome; *w.s.* overwhelm; ***übermannt von*** *dat.* overcome by *sleep* (*or* with *emotion*)

'Über·maß *n* (-es; *no pl.*) excess (**an** *dat.* of), *contp.* overkill (of); ***et. im ~ tun*** do s.th. to excess; ***et. im ~ haben*** have more than enough of s.th.; ***... ist im ~ vorhanden*** there's an overabundance of ...; **'über·mä·ßig** **I.** *adj.* a) excessive; immoderate; exaggerated, b) overabundant; **II.** *adv.* excessively, overly ..., too much; *work, exercise etc. a.* too hard; ~ ***großzügig*** *etc.* ***sein*** *a.* be generous *etc.* to a fault; ~ ***betonen*** overemphasize, emphasize unduly

'Über·mensch *m* superman; **'über·mensch·lich** *adj.* superhuman
über·mit·teln [y:bɐ'mɪtəln] *v/t.* (*insep.*, *no* -ge-, h) transmit, convey (*dat.* to); **Über·mitt·lung** [y:bɐ'mɪtlʊŋ] *f* (-; *no pl.*) transmission
'über·mor·gen *adv.* the day after tomorrow
über·mü·det [y:bɐ'my:dət] *adj.* overtired; **Über·mü·dung** [y:bɐ'my:dʊŋ] *f* (-; *no pl.*) overtiredness
Über·mut ['y:bɐmu:t] *m* (-[e]s; *no pl.*) a) high spirits *pl.*, b) wantonness, c) cockiness; **über·mü·tig** ['y:bɐmy:tɪç] *adj.* a) high-spirited, *pred. a.* in high spirits, b) wanton, c) cocky
'über·nächst *adj. the* next but one; **~e Woche** the week after next
über·nach·ten [y:bɐ'naxtən] *v/i.* (*insep.*, *no* -ge-, h) spend the night (**bei** *dat.* at *s.o.'s place, a. outdoors etc.*), stay overnight (at); **im Freien** ~ *a.* sleep in the open
über·näch·tig(t) [y:bɐ'nɛçtɪç(t)] *adj.* tired (from lack of sleep); bleary-eyed
Über·nach·tung [y:bɐ'naxtʊŋ] *f* (-; -en) overnight stay; **~ mit Frühstück** bed and breakfast; **vier ~en (mit Frühstück)** four nights (with breakfast); **Über'nach·tungs·mög·lich·keit** *f a. pl.* overnight accommodation, F place to stay (for the night)
Über·nah·me ['y:bɐna:mə] *f* (-; *no pl.*) taking over, *esp. pol.*, ✝ takeover; assumption *of office, responsibility etc.*; adoption *of methods, concepts, words etc.*
'über·na·tio,nal *adj.* supranational
'über·na,tür·lich *adj.* supernatural
über'neh·men (*irr.*, *insep.*, *no* -ge-, h, → **nehmen**) **I.** *v/t.* take over; take on *work etc.*, *a.* undertake, take *the responsibility* upon oneself; *pol.*, ✝ take over *an office, the power, a firm etc.*; accept *goods etc.*; adopt *methods, concepts, words etc.*; **er übernahm es zu** *inf.* he undertook to *inf.*, he took it upon himself to *inf.*; **Ideen** *etc.* **einfach ~** *contp.* lift ideas *etc.*; → **Bürgschaft; II.** *v/i.* take over (**von** *dat.* from *s.o.*); **III.** *v/refl.*: **sich ~** a) overdo it (*or* things); take on too much, F bite off more than one can chew, b) overestimate one's capabilities, overplay one's hand, c) overreach o.s., d) overeat; **sich bei der Arbeit (beim Sport** *etc.*) ~ do too much work (sport *etc.*)
'über·ord·nen *v/t.* (*sep.*, h): **j-n j-m (e-r Sache)** ~ set s.o. above s.o. (s.th.); **et. j-m (e-r Sache)** ~ *a.* give priority to s.th. over s.o. (s.th.); → **übergeordnet**
'über·par,tei·lich *adj.* all-party *decision etc.*; non-partisan *newspaper etc.*
über'pin·seln *v/t.* (*insep.*, *no* -ge-, h) paint over
'Über·preis *m* excessive price
'Über·pro·duk·ti,on *f* overproduction
'über·pro·por·tio,nal *adj.* disproportionate (**zu** *dat.* to)
über·prüf·bar [y:bɐ'pry:fba:ɐ] *adj.* checkable; verifiable; **über'prü·fen** *v/t.* (*insep.*, *no* -ge-, h) **1.** a) check, examine; scrutinize; verify; test, b) *pol.* screen, F vet *s.o.*; **2.** reconsider, review; *a.* ⚖ revise; **Über'prü·fung** *f* **1.** examination, scrutiny; check; verification; test; **2.** reconsideration; *a.* ⚖ revision
'Über·qua·li·fi·ka·ti,on *f* overqualification; **'über·qua·li·fi,ziert** *adj.* overqualified

'über·quel·len *v/i.* (*irr.*, *sep.*, sn, → **quellen**) *a. fig.* overflow, brim over (**von** *dat.* with); **'über·quel·lend** *adj.* overflowing
über'que·ren *v/t.* (*insep.*, *no* -ge-, h) cross
über'ra·gen *v/t.* (*insep.*, *no* -ge-, h) **1.** tower above; *a.* be taller than *s.o.*; **2.** *fig.* outclass, outshine (**an** *dat.* in); **über'ra·gend** *fig. adj.* outstanding, brilliant; **durch s-e ~e Persönlichkeit** through sheer force of personality
über·ra·schen [y:bɐ'raʃən] (*insep.*, *no* -ge-, h) **I.** *v/t.* a) surprise; *a.* catch (**bei** *dat. ger.*), b) *storm etc.*: catch *s.o.* out, catch *s.o.* by surprise, c) take *s.o.* by surprise; **vom Regen überrascht werden** be caught in the rain; **II.** *v/impers.*: **es überrascht, daß** it's surprising that; **über'ra·schend** *adj.* a) surprising, b) unexpected, sudden; **~ kommen** come as a surprise (**für** *acc.* to); **über·ra·schen·der·weise** [y:bɐ'raʃəndɐvaɪzə] *adv.* surprisingly; **über·rascht** [y:bɐ'raʃt] **I.** *p.p. of* **überraschen; II.** *adj.* surprised (**von** *dat.* by, at); **sich (nicht) ~ zeigen** show a certain (show no) surprise; **III.** *adv.* with (*or* in) surprise; **Über·ra·schung** [y:bɐ'raʃʊŋ] *f* (-; -en) surprise; **e-e (kleine) ~** a little something; **j-m e-e ~ bereiten** surprise s.o., give s.o. a surprise, have a surprise in store for s.o.; **so e-e ~!** what a surprise!
Über'ra·schungs|an·griff *m* surprise attack; **~ef,fekt** *m* surprise effect; **~er·folg** *m* unexpected success, surprise success (*or* hit); **~mo,ment** *n* element of surprise; **~sieg** *m* unexpected victory (*or* win); **~sie·ger** *m* surprise winner
'über·rea,gie·ren *v/i.* (*insep.*, h) overreact; **'Über·re·ak·ti,on** *f* overreaction (**auf** *acc.* to)
über're·den *v/t.* (*insep.*, *no* -ge-, h) persuade (**zu** *dat.* to), talk *s.o.* round; **j-n zu et. ~** talk s.o. into (doing) s.th.
Über·re·dung [y:bɐ're:dʊŋ] *f* (-; *no pl.*) persuasion
Über're·dungs|ga·be *f* (-; *no pl.*) persuasiveness; **~kunst** *f* **1.** art of persuasion; **2.** *a. pl.* powers *pl.* of persuasion
'über·re·gio,nal *adj.* supraregional; national *newspaper*; nationwide *campaign etc.*
'über·reich I. *adj.* overabundant; lavish; **ein ~es Angebot an** *dat.* a profusion of; **~ sein an** *dat.* have more than enough of, abound in; **in ~em Maß → II.** *adv.* overabundantly; lavishly; overly ...; **j-n ~ beschenken** lavish presents on s.o., shower s.o. with presents
über'rei·chen *v/t.* (*insep.*, *no* -ge-, h) hand *s.th.* (over), present *s.th.* (**j-m** to s.o.)
'über·reich·lich I. *adj.* overabundant, ample; **II.** *adv.* amply; → *a.* **überreich**
Über·rei·chung [y:bɐ'raɪçʊŋ] *f* (-; *no pl.*) presentation
'Über·reich·wei·te *f radio*: overshoot
'über·reif *adj.* overripe; **'Über·reif·e** *f* overripeness
über'rei·zen (*insep.*, *no* -ge-, h) **I.** *v/t.* **1.** irritate *skin etc.*; strain *eyes*; **2.** overexcite; **II.** *v/i. and v/refl.* (**sich ~**) *card game*: overcall; **über·reizt** [y:bɐ'raɪtst] *adj.* overwrought; irritable; on edge; **Über'reizt·heit** *f* (-; *no pl.*) overwrought state; irritability; edginess
über'ren·nen *v/t.* (*irr.*, *insep.*, *no* -ge-, h, → **rennen**) knock down; *esp.* ⚔ overrun; *fig.* bulldoze

'Über·rest *m* remains *pl.*; *pl.* relics *of the past etc.*; → **sterblich** I
über'rie·seln *v/t.* (*insep.*, *no* -ge-, h) **1.** *water etc.*: trickle down on; **2. es** (*or* **ein Schauer**) **überrieselte mich** it sent a shiver down my spine
'Über·roll·bü·gel *m mot.* rollbar
über'rol·len *v/t.* (*insep.*, *no* -ge-, h) ⚔ overrun; *train etc.*: run over; *fig.* steamroller
über'rum·peln *v/t.* (*insep.*, *no* -ge-, h) take *s.o.* unawares (*or* by surprise), throw *s.o.* off (his *or* her) guard; **sich ~ lassen** be caught napping
über·run·den [y:bɐ'rʊndən] *v/t.* (*insep.*, *no* -ge-, h) *sport*: lap; *fig.* outstrip
über·sät [y:bɐ'zɛ:t] *adj.*: **~ mit** *dat.* a) strewn (*or* littered, dotted) with, covered in, b) pitted with
'über·satt *adj.* **1.** more than full; **~ sein** *a.* have eaten more than enough; **2.** *fig.* sated (**von** *dat.* with)
über'sät·ti·gen *v/t.* (*insep.*, *no* -ge-, h) oversaturate, ✝ *a.* glut; ⚗ supersaturate; **über'sät·tigt** *adj.* ✝ glutted; ⚗ supersaturated; *fig.* sated; **Über'sät·ti·gung** *f* (-; *no pl.*) surfeit; ✝ glut(ting); ⚗ supersaturation
über'säu·ern *v/t.* (*insep.*, *no* -ge-, h) overacidify (*a.* ⚕); **Über'säue·rung** *f* (-; *no pl.*) hyperacidity (*a.* ⚕)
'Über·schall *m* ultrasound; **~flug·zeug** *n* supersonic aircraft; **~ge·schwin·dig·keit** *f* supersonic speed; **mit ~ fliegen** travel faster than the speed of sound; **~knall** *m* sonic boom
über·schat·ten [y:bɐ'ʃatən] *v/t.* (*insep.*, *no* -ge-, h) overshadow; *fig.* cast a cloud over; *fig.* **überschattet von** *dat.* clouded by
über'schät·zen (*insep.*, *no* -ge-, h) **I.** *v/t.* overestimate; overrate; **II.** *v/refl.*: **sich ~** have too high an opinion of o.s.; **er überschätzt sich** *a.* he's not as good (*or* clever) as he thinks; **Über'schät·zung** *f* (-; *no pl.*) overestimation; overrating
über·schau·bar [y:bɐ'ʃaʊba:ɐ] *adj.* a) clear; *a.* easy to grasp, b) manageable, c) calculable *risk, consequences etc.*; **in der ~en Zukunft** in the foreseeable future; **~ bleiben** *size, quantity etc.*: keep within reasonable (*or* manageable) limits, *development, situation etc.*: not to get out of hand; **Über'schau·bar·keit** *f* (-; *no pl.*) a) clarity; comprehensibility, b) manageability; **über'schau·en** *fig. v/t.* (*insep.*, *no* -ge-, h) a) have a good idea of, b) have under control; keep track of *developments etc.*; be able to calculate *the risk, consequences etc.*
'über·schäu·men *v/i.* (*sep.*, sn) froth over; *fig.* bubble over (**vor** *dat.* with); fume; **vor Wut ~** *a.* F be foaming at the mouth; **'Über·schäu·men** *n* (-s; *no pl.*) ebullience, exuberance; **'über·schäu·mend** *fig. adj.* ebullient, exuberant
über'schla·fen *v/t.* (*irr.*, *insep.*, *no* -ge-, h, → **schlafen**) sleep on *s.th.*
'Über·schlag *m* **1.** *gym.* somersault, handspring; ✈ loop; **2.** (rough) estimate; **3.** ⚡ flashover
über'schla·gen¹ (*irr.*, *insep.*, *no* -ge-, h, → **schlagen**) **I.** *v/t.* **1.** skip, miss; **2.** calculate roughly, give a rough estimate of; **II.** *v/refl.*: **sich ~ 3.** go head over heels, do a somersault; *car etc.*: overturn; ✈ a) loop the loop, b) nose over; **4.** *voice*: crack; **5.** *fig.* **die Ereignisse überschlugen sich**

things started happening very fast; **6.** *fig.* trip over o.s. *in an attempt to help etc.*

'über·schla·gen² (*irr., sep.*, h, → **schlagen**) **I.** *v/t.* **1.** **die Beine** ~ cross one's legs; **II.** *v/i.* **2.** ⚡ spark (*or* jump) over; **3.** *fig.* **(plötzlich)** ~ **in** *acc.* (suddenly) turn into

'über·schnap·pen *v/i.* (*sep.*, sn) **1.** F flip one's lid; → *a.* **übergeschnappt; 2.** *voice*: crack

über'schnei·den *v/refl.* **(sich ~)** (*irr., insep., no* -ge-, h, → **schneiden**) **1.** overlap; intersect; **2.** *fig.* a) coincide, overlap, b) clash; **Über'schnei·dung** *f* (-; -en) **1.** overlapping; intersection; **2.** *fig.* a) coincidence, b) clash(ing)

über'schrei·ben *v/t.* (*irr., insep., no* -ge-, h, → **schreiben**) **1.** head; **2.** transfer, make *s.th.* over (*dat.* to), sign over (to); **3.** *computer*: overwrite; **Über'schrei·bung** *f* (-; -en) *esp.* ⚖ transference

über'schrei·ten *v/t.* (*irr., insep., no* -ge-, h, → **schreiten**) **1.** cross; **2.** ⚖ violate, infringe; exceed *speed limit etc.*; *fig.* exceed, overstep *the limit etc.*; *sum etc.*: go over, top; **die Milliardengrenze** ~ top the billion (*Brit. a.* the one thousand million) mark; **Über'schrei·tung** *f* (-; -en) **1.** crossing (*gen.* of); **2.** ⚖ violation, infringement; exceeding (*or* breaking) *the speed limit*; *fig.* overstepping *the limit etc.*

'Über·schrift *f* heading, title; headline

'Über·schu·he *pl.* overshoes, galoshes, rubbers

über·schul·det [y:bɐ'ʃʊldət] *adj.* heavily indebted; debt-heavy *country*; ~ **sein** *a.* have heavy debts; **Über'schul·dung** *f* (-; *no pl.*) debt overload, heavy debts *pl.*

'Über·schuß *m* (-sses; ⸚sse) surplus (**an** *dat.* of); profit; **ein** ~ **an** *dat. a.* surplus *goods, energy etc.*; **über·schüs·sig** ['y:bɐʃʏsɪç] *adj.* surplus, excess

über'schüt·ten *v/t.* (*insep., no* -ge-, h): ~ **mit** *dat.* throw *s.th.* over (*or* at) *s.th. or s.o.*, spill *s.th.* (all) over *s.th. or s.o.*; *fig.* **j-n mit Geschenken (Ehren** *etc.*) ~ shower s.o. with presents (hono[u]rs *etc.*), heap presents (hono[u]rs *etc.*) on s.o.

Über·schwang ['y:bɐʃvaŋ] *m* (-[e]s; *no pl.*) exuberance; **im ~ der Gefühle** carried away by one's feelings; **im ~ der Begeisterung** in a wave of enthusiasm

'über·schwap·pen *v/i.* (*sep.*, sn) a) *water etc.*: slop over (the edge), b) *bucket etc.*: slop (over)

über'schwem·men *v/t.* (*insep., no* -ge-, h) flood, ☤ *a.* glut, *fig. a.* inundate; **über·schwemmt** [y:bɐ'ʃvɛmt] *adj.* flooded; ☤ glutted; *fig.* ~ **mit** *dat.* swamped with *requests, visitors etc.*; **Über·schwem·mung** [y:bɐ'ʃvɛmʊŋ] *f* (-; -en) a) flooding, b) flood

Über'schwem·mungs|ge·biet *n* flood area; **~ka·ta,stro·phe** *f* flood disaster

über·schweng·lich ['y:bɐʃvɛŋlɪç] *adj.* effusive, gushing; **'Über·schweng·lich·keit** *f* (-; *no pl.*) effusiveness

'Über·see *without art.*: **in (nach)** ~ overseas; **von** ~ from overseas; **~damp·fer** *m* ocean liner; **~han·del** *m* overseas trade

über·see·isch ['y:bɐze:ɪʃ] *adj.* overseas ...

'Über·see·ver·kehr *m* overseas traffic

über·seh·bar [y:bɐ'ze:ba:ɐ] *adj.* **1.** open *country etc.*; **2.** *fig.* calculable *risk, consequences etc.*; assessable *damage*; clear *situation etc.*; **über'se·hen** *v/t.* (*irr., insep., no* -ge-, h, → **sehen**) **1.** → **überblicken; 2.** *fig.* grasp; assess; **3.** a) overlook, miss, b) ignore, turn a blind eye to; **von j-m ~ werden** escape s.o.'s notice

über'sen·den *v/t.* (*irr., insep., no* -ge-, h, → **senden¹**) send (**j-m et.** s.o. s.th., s.th. to s.o.); **anbei ~ wir ...** enclosed please find ...; **Über'sen·der** *m* (-s; -) sender; **Über'sen·dung** *f* (-; *no pl.*) sending

über·setz·bar [y:bɐ'zɛtsba:ɐ] *adj.* translatable; **Über'setz·bar·keit** *f* (-; *no pl.*) translatability; **über'set·zen¹** *v/t. and v/i.* (*insep., no* -ge-, h) translate (**in** *acc.* into; **aus** *dat.* from); **falsch** ~ translate wrong(ly), mistranslate

'über·set·zen² (*sep.*) **I.** *v/t.* (h) ferry *s.o. or s.th.* across (*or* over); **II.** *v/i.* (sn) ferry across the river *etc.*

Über·set·zer [y:bɐ'zɛtsɐ] *m* (-s; -) translator; **~deutsch** *n*, **~eng·lisch** *n etc.* translat(or)ese

Über·set·ze·rin [y:bɐ'zɛtsərɪn] *f* (-; -nen) translator; **Über·set·zung** [y:bɐ'zɛtsʊŋ] *f* (-; -en) **1.** a) translation (**aus** *dat.* from; **in** *acc.* into), b) version; **2.** ⚙ gear ratio

Über'set·zungs|bü,ro *n* translating agency; **~feh·ler** *m* translating error (*or* mistake); mistranslation

'Über·sicht *f* (-; -en) **1.** *no pl.* overall view, overview; **e-e ~ bekommen** obtain a general idea (**über** *acc.* of); **sich e-e ~ verschaffen** brief o.s. (**über** *acc.* on), F find out what's going on; **die ~ verlieren** lose track of things; **2.** a) survey, b) table, chart

über·sicht·lich ['y:bɐzɪçtlɪç] *adj.* **1.** open *country etc.*; clear *bend*; **2.** *fig.* clear(ly arranged); lucid; **'Über·sicht·lich·keit** *f* (-; *no pl.*) *fig.* clarity; clear arrangement

'Über·sichts|kar·te *f* general map; **~plan** *m* general plan; **~ta,bel·le** *f* (synoptic) chart

'über·sie·deln *v/i.* (*sep.*, sn) move (**nach** *dat.* to)

'Über·sied·ler *m hist.* East German migrant (*to the Federal Republic of Germany*); **~strom** *m* flood of immigrants

'Über·sied·lung *f* move (**nach** *dat.* to)

'über·sinn·lich *adj.* **1.** **~e Wahrnehmung** extrasensory perception, ESP; **~e Fähigkeiten** extrasensory (*or* psychic) powers; **2.** supernatural

über'span·nen *v/t.* (*insep., no* -ge-, h) **1.** span *river etc.*; ▲ vault; cover; **2.** overstretch; ⚙ strain; pull *strings* too tight; **3.** *fig.* carry *demands etc.* too far; → **Bogen** 1; **über·spannt** [y:bɐ'ʃpant] *fig. adj.* **1.** unnatural, affected; highly-strung; hysterical; eccentric; **2.** exaggerated, F over the top, OTT; **Über'spannt·heit** *f* (-, *no pl.*) **1.** unnaturalness, affectedness, affectation; highly-strung nature; hysteria; **2.** exaggeratedness

'Über·span·nung *f* ⚡ excess voltage

'über·spe·zia·li,siert *adj.* overspecialized; **'Über·spe·zia·li,sie·rung** *f* overspecialization

über'spie·len *v/t.* (*insep., no* -ge-, h) **1.** cover *s.th.* up; **et. geschickt** ~ do a good job of covering s.th. up; **2.** record (**auf** *acc.* onto), transfer (to, *a. computer*); **3.** *sport*: outplay; **Über·spie·lung** [y:bɐ'ʃpi:lʊŋ] *f* (-; -en) (re)recording

über'spit·zen *v/t.* (*insep., no* -ge-, h) overdo, exaggerate; overstate *an argument etc.*; **die Sache** ~ take it too far; **über·spitzt** [y:bɐ'ʃpɪtst] *adj.* oversubtle; exaggerated; **Über'spitzt·heit** *f* (-; *no pl.*) oversubtlety; exaggeratedness; **Über·spit·zung** [y:bɐ'ʃpɪtsʊŋ] *f* (-; -en) exaggeration

über'sprin·gen¹ *v/t.* (*irr., insep., no* -ge-, h, → **springen**) **1.** jump (over), clear; **2.** *fig.* skip

'über·sprin·gen² *v/i.* (*irr., sep.*, sn, → **springen**) leap over (*or* across); ⚡ flash; *fig.* ~ **von** *dat.* **... zu** *dat.* flit from ... to

'über·spru·deln *v/i.* (*sep.*, sn) bubble over (*fig.* **vor** *dat.* with); **'über·sprudelnd** *adj.*: **~e Laune** bubbly mood; **~er Witz** bubbling wit; **~es Temperament** frothy temperament

über'sprü·hen¹ *v/t.* (*insep., no* -ge-, h) spray; **et. ~ mit** *dat.* spray s.th. with *s.th.*, spray *s.th.* onto s.th.

'über·sprü·hen² *v/i.* (*sep.*, h): ~ **vor** *dat.* bubble over with

'Über·sprung·hand·lung *f* sparking-over (*or* substitute) activity

'über·staat·lich *adj.* supranational

über'ste·hen¹ *v/t.* (*irr., insep., no* -ge-, h, → **stehen**) get over, recover from *illness etc.*; survive *accident etc.*, *a.* F *exam etc.*, come out of *s.th.* alive; weather, ride out *storm etc.*; ⚕ **das Schlimmste überstanden haben** be out of danger; F **et. überstanden haben** have got s.th. over (and done) with; F **das wäre überstanden!** that's that (over and done with), that's that out of the way; *euphem.* **sie hat es überstanden** she's at rest now

'über·ste·hen² *v/i.* (*irr., sep.*, h, → **stehen**) jut out, project

über·stei·gen *v/t.* (*irr., insep., no* -ge-, h, → **steigen**) **1.** cross, climb over; **2.** *fig.* go beyond, exceed (*a. expectations, understanding etc.*); ☤ *a.* top

über'stei·gern *v/t.* (*insep., no* -ge-, h) a) force up *prices etc.*, b) carry (*or* push) too far, exaggerate; **über·stei·gert** [y:bɐ'ʃtaɪgɐt] *adj.* exaggerated; *psych. a.* hypertrophied *craving for recognition*; **~e Erwartungen** high expectations

über'steu·ern *v/t.* (*insep., no* -ge-, h) *mot.* oversteer; ⚡ overmodulate; **Über'steue·rung** *f* overmodulation

über'stim·men *v/t.* (*insep., no* -ge-, h) outvote; override *veto*

über'strah·len *v/t.* (*insep., no* -ge-, h) **1.** light up, flood; **2.** *fig.* outshine, eclipse

'über·stra·pa,zie·ren *v/t.* (*only inf. and p.p.* überstrapaziert, h) **1.** wear out; *a.* strain *s.o.'s nerves*; **2.** *fig.* flog to death

über'strecken *v/t.* (*insep., no* -ge-, h) overstretch

über'strei·chen *v/t.* (*irr., insep., no* -ge-, h, → **streichen**) **1.** coat (over); paint over; **2.** recoat, repaint

'über·strei·fen *v/t.* (*sep.*, h) slip *s.th.* over

über'strö·men¹ *v/t.* (*insep., no* -ge-, h) flood

'über·strö·men² *v/i.* (*sep.*, sn) **1.** overflow, run over; **2.** *fig.* a) overflow (**vor** *dat.* with), b) spread (**auf** *acc.* to); **'über·strö·mend** *fig. adj.* overflowing, exuberant; *b.s.* effusive, gushing

über·strömt [y:bɐ'ʃtrø:mt] *adj.*: ~ **von** *dat.* flooded with, *a. fig.* inundated with *tourists etc.*; pouring with *sweat etc.*; **sein Gesicht war von Tränen ~** the tears were streaming down his face

'über·stül·pen *v/t.* (*sep.*, h): **(sich) et. ~** put s.th. on, pop s.th. on one's head

'Über·stun·den *pl.* overtime *sg.*; **~ machen** work (*or* do) overtime; **~zuschlag** *m* overtime premium

über'stür·zen (*insep., no* -ge-, h) **I.** *v/t.*

rush; **II.** *v/refl.*: **sich ~** rush things; ***die Ereignisse überstürzten sich*** things started happening very fast; **über·stürzt** [y:bɐˈʃtʏrtst] *adj.* hasty; rash *decision etc.*; **Überˈstürzt·heit** *f* (-; *no pl.*) rashness; **Über·stür·zung** [y:bɐˈʃtʏrtsʊŋ] *f* (-; *no pl.*) rush; ***nur keine ~!*** take it easy, now
ˈüber·taˌrif·lich *adj.*: ***~e Bezahlung*** salary in excess of the agreed scale
über·teu·ern [y:bɐˈtɔʏɐn] *v/t.* (*insep.*, *no* -ge-, h) charge too much for; **über·teu·ert** [y:bɐˈtɔʏɐt] *adj.* overpriced; **Über·teue·rung** [y:bɐˈtɔʏərʊŋ] *f* (-; *no pl.*) exorbitant prices *pl.*; *a.* inflation
über·töl·peln [y:bɐˈtœlpəln] *v/t.* (*insep.*, *no* -ge-, h) dupe, take in
überˈtö·nen *v/t.* (*insep.*, *no* -ge-, h) drown (out)
ˈÜber·topf *m* plant pot holder, cache-pot
Über·trag [ˈy:bɐtra:k] *m* (-[e]s; Überträge [ˈy:bɐtrɛ:gə]) † amount carried over
überˈtrag·bar *adj.* **1.** transferable (***auf*** *acc.* to); ***nicht ~*** non-transferable, † non-negotiable; **2.** ⚕ infectious, catching, contagious *disease*; **Überˈtrag·bar·keit** *f* (-; *no pl.*) **1.** transferability; **2.** ⚕ infectiousness; contagiousness
überˈtra·gen (*irr.*, *insep.*, *no* -ge-, h, → ***tragen***) **I.** *v/t.* **1.** transfer (***auf*** *acc.* to); copy out (***in*** *acc.* into); **2.** ⚙, *phys.*, ⚡ transmit; *radio*, *TV*: *a.* broadcast; **3.** make over (***auf*** *acc.* to *s.o.*), transfer (to); convey *real estate* (to); confer *title*, *an office etc.* ([up]on); delegate *powers etc.* (to); ***Rechte*** *etc.* ***auf j-n ~*** vest s.o. with rights *etc.*; ***et. auf j-s Namen ~*** register s.th. in s.o.'s name; **4.** ***j-m die Ausführung*** *etc.* ***~ von*** *dat.* charge (*or* entrust) s.o. with; **5.** *radio*, *TV*: broadcast; ***im Fernsehen ~*** *a.* televise; ***live ~*** broadcast live; **6.** translate; ***ins Englische*** *etc.* ~ translate into (*or* render in[to]) English *etc.*; **7.** transcribe *shorthand notes*; *computer*: transfer, translate; **8.** apply; **9.** communicate (***auf*** *acc.* to); **10.** ⚕ transplant, graft; **II.** *v/refl.*: **sich ~** *mood*, *panic etc.*: spread (***auf*** *acc.* to); ⚕ *a.* be transmitted (to), be passed on (to); **III.** *adj.* figurative; ***im ~en Sinn*** in the figurative sense
Über·tra·gung [y:bɐˈtra:gʊŋ] *f* (-; -en) **1.** (*all* ***auf*** *acc.* to) transfer (*a.* †); assignment *of rights etc.*; delegation *of powers*; conferment *of an office*; conveyance *of real estate*; **2.** ⚙, *phys.* transmission; **3.** ⚕ transmission; infection; **4.** *radio*, *TV*: broadcast, transmission; **5.** translation (***ins*** *Deutsche etc.* into), rendering (in[to]); transcription; **6.** application
Überˈtra·gungs·wa·gen *m radio*, *TV*: outside broadcast *or* OB van (*or* unit, truck); radio car
überˈtref·fen *v/t.* (*irr.*, *insep.*, *no* -ge-, h, → ***treffen***) excel (***sich selbst*** o.s.), outstrip; surpass, beat (*all* ***an*** *dat.*, ***in*** *dat.* in); go beyond, surpass, exceed *one's fears*, *hope etc.*; ***alle Erwartungen ~*** exceed all expectations; ***die Realität ~*** top reality; ***nur noch übertroffen werden von*** *dat.* be second only to
überˈtrei·ben (*irr.*, *insep.*, *no* -ge-, h, → ***treiben***) **I.** *v/t.* a) overdo *s.th.*; *a.* carry *s.th.* too far, b) exaggerate, overstate; ***es ~*** take things too far (*or* to extremes), F go over the top; → ***übertrieben***; **II.** *v/i.* exaggerate; ***stark ~*** grossly exaggerate, F lay it on thick; ***übertreib nicht so!*** stop exaggerating; **Über·trei·bung** [y:bɐˈtraɪbʊŋ] *f* (-; -en) exaggeration, overstatement
ˈüber·tre·ten¹ *v/i.* (*irr.*, *sep.*, sn, → ***treten***) **1.** pass, step over; *sport*: overstep the board; **2.** *river*: overflow (its banks); **3.** *pol. etc.* go over (***zu*** *dat.* to); *eccl.* convert (to)
überˈtre·ten² *v/t.* (*irr.*, *insep.*, *no* -ge-, h, → ***treten***) **1.** ⚖ violate, infringe; **2.** ***sich den Fuß ~*** sprain one's ankle
Über·tre·tung [y:bɐˈtre:tʊŋ] *f* (-; -en) ⚖ violation, infringement (*gen* of); *a.* offen|ce (*Am.* -se)
über·trie·ben [y:bɐˈtri:bən] **I.** *p.p. of* ***übertreiben***; **II.** *adj.* exaggerated; *esp. behavio(u)r etc.*: *a.* F over the top, OTT; excessive *price*, *demands etc.*; extreme *views etc.*; ***leicht ~*** slightly exaggerated; ***et. in ~em Maße tun*** overdo s.th., go to extremes with s.th.; **II.** *adv.* exaggeratedly; excessively; *generous*, *liberal etc.* to a fault; ***~ reagieren*** overreact
Überˈtrie·ben·heit *f* (-; *no pl.*) exaggeration; excessiveness; extreme nature, extremism
ˈÜber·tritt *m* (-[e]s; -e) *pol.* defection (***zu*** *dat.* to); *eccl.* conversion (to)
überˈtrump·fen *v/t.* (*insep.*, *no* -ge-, h) trump; *fig. a.* outdo, go one better than
überˈtün·chen *v/t.* (*insep.*, *no* -ge-, h) whitewash; *fig. a.* gloss over
ˈüber·ver·si·chern *v/t.* (*insep.*, *no* -ge-, h) overinsure; **ˈÜber·ver·si·che·rung** *f* overinsurance
über·völ·kern [y:bɐˈfœlkɐn] *v/t.* (*insep.*, *no* -ge-, h) overpopulate; **Über·völ·ke·rung** [y:bɐˈfœlkərʊŋ] *f* (-; *no pl.*) overpopulation
ˈüber·voll *adj. glass etc.* too full; full to overflowing (***von*** *dat.* with); *room etc.*: *a.* overcrowded (with)
ˈüber·vor·sich·tig *adj.* overcautious
über·vor·tei·len [y:bɐˈfɔrtaɪlən] *v/t.* (*insep.*, *no* -ge-, h) cheat, F do; **Überˈvor·tei·lung** *f* (-; -en) cheating
überˈwa·chen *v/t.* (*insep.*, *no* -ge-, h) supervise; keep under surveillance; ⚕ *etc.* observe; *radio*, *TV etc.* monitor
überˈwach·sen **I.** *adj.* overgrown (***mit*** *dat.* with); **II.** *v/t.* (*irr.*, *insep.*, *no* -ge-, h, → ***wachsen***) grow all over, cover; spread to
Über·wa·chung [y:bɐˈvaxʊŋ] *f* (-; *no pl.*) supervision; surveillance; observation; monitoring; policing
Überˈwa·chungs|an·la·ge *f* closed-circuit television; **~syˌstem** *n* surveillance (*or* monitoring) system; **~zenˌtra·le** *f* control cent|re (*Am.* -er)
über·wäl·ti·gen [y:bɐˈvɛltɪgən] *v/t.* (*insep.*, *no* -ge-, h) **1.** overpower; **2.** *fig.* overcome; ***überwältigt werden von*** be overwhelmed by *a sight*, *feeling etc.*; **überˈwäl·ti·gend** *fig. adj.* overwhelming (*a. pol. majority*); *a.* breathtaking *beauty*; *iro.* ***nicht ~*** nothing to write home about, F no great shakes; **Überˈwäl·ti·gung** *f* (-; *no pl.*) overpowering (*gen.* of); defeat
ˈüber·wech·seln *v/i.* (*sep.*, sn) **1.** ***~ auf*** *acc.* switch to *another topic etc.*; *pol.* ***auf die andere Seite ~*** go over to the other side; **2.** cross over (***auf*** *acc.*, ***zu*** *dat.* to); ***zur anderen Straßenseite ~*** cross the road; *mot.* ***auf e-e andere Spur ~*** change (*or* switch) lanes
überˈwei·sen *v/t.* (*irr.*, *insep.*, *no* -ge-, h, → ***weisen***) **1.** † transfer *money* (***auf*** *acc.* to *an account*), ***j-m***: transfer *money* to s.o.'s account; remit (*dat.* to *s.o.*); **2.** ⚕ refer *patients* (*dat. or* ***an*** *acc.* to); **Überˈwei·sung** *f* (-; -en) **1.** † transfer, remittance; **2.** ⚕ referral
Überˈwei·sungs|auf·trag *m* remittance order; **~for·muˌlar** *n* transfer form; **~schein** *m* ⚕ letter of referral, referral slip
ˈüber·weit *adj.* too large (*or* big); † extra large; **ˈÜber·wei·te** *f* extra large size
ˈüber·wer·fen¹ *v/t.* (*irr.*, *sep.*, h, → ***werfen***) slip on; throw on *a coat etc.*
überˈwer·fen² *v/refl.* (*irr.*, *insep.*, *no* -ge-, h, → ***werfen***): ***sich mit j-m ~*** fall out with s.o.
überˈwie·gen *v/i.* (*irr.*, *insep.*, *no* -ge-, h, → ***wiegen***) predominate; be predominant; **überˈwie·gend** **I.** *adj.* predominant; prevailing; ***der ~e Teil*** the majority, the greater part, the bulk; ***die ~e Mehrzahl*** the vast majority; ***zum ~en Teil*** → **II.** *adv.* predominantly; *w.s.* mainly, chiefly; for the most part
über·wind·bar [y:bɐˈvɪntba:ɐ] *adj.* surmountable; **über·win·den** [y:bɐˈvɪndən] (*irr.*, *insep.*, *no* -ge-, h, → ***winden***) **I.** *v/t.* overcome *one's fear etc.*; get over *an illness etc.*; *lit.* conquer (*a. fig.*); *fig.* get away from, outgrow; get past ; ***ein Hindernis ~*** clear a hurdle; → *a.* ***überwunden***; **II.** *v/refl.*: ***sich (selbst) ~*** overcome one's inhibitions; force o.s.; ***sich dazu ~ zu*** *inf.* bring (*or* get) o.s. to *inf.*; ***er konnte sich nicht ~, es zu tun*** he couldn't bring himself to do it; ***ich mußte mich (direkt) ~, (um) zu*** *inf.* I had to force myself to *inf.*, I really had to make an effort to *inf.*; ***sich zu e-r Arbeit ~ müssen*** force o.s. to do a job; **Überˈwin·dung** *f* (-; *no pl.*) **1.** defeat; conquest; **2.** (conscious *or* concerted) effort; will-power; ***es kostete mich ~*** I had to force myself
über·win·tern [y:bɐˈvɪntɐn] (*insep.*, *no* -ge-, h) **I.** *v/i.* **1.** spend the winter (***in*** *dat.* in, at); **2.** overwinter; *n.s.* hibernate; **II.** *v/t.* overwinter *plants etc.*; **Über·win·te·rung** [y:bɐˈvɪntərʊŋ] *f* (-; *no pl.*) overwintering
überˈwöl·ben *v/t.* (*insep.*, *no* -ge-, h) vault; *roof etc.*: *a.* form a vault over
überˈwu·chern *v/t.* (*insep.*, *no* -ge-, h) overgrow; **Überˈwu·che·rung** *f* (-; *no pl.*) overgrowth
über·wun·den [y:bɐˈvʊndən] **I.** *p.p. of* ***überwinden***; **II.** *adj.*: ***ein ~er Standpunkt*** an opinion (which) one has outgrown; ***ein ~es Vorurteil*** *etc.* a prejudice *etc.* (which) one has overcome
ˈÜber·wurf *m* **1.** wrap, shawl; **2.** *wrestling*: sit-back
ˈÜber·zahl *f*: ***in der ~ sein*** be in the majority, *w.s.* predominate; ***die Mädchen sind in der ~*** *a.* the girls outnumber the boys; **über·zäh·lig** [ˈy:bɐtsɛ:lɪç] *adj.* surplus ...; spare; ***drei Leute waren ~*** there were three people too many
überˈzeich·nen *v/t.* (*insep.*, *no* -ge-, h) **1.** † oversubscribe; **2.** *fig.* overdraw; **Überˈzeich·nung** *f* **1.** † oversubscription; **2.** *fig.* overdrawing; *w.s.* caricature
überˈzeu·gen (*insep.*, *no* -ge-, h) **I.** *v/t.* convince (***von*** *dat.* of); ***j-n ~, daß*** *a.* persuade s.o. that; ***j-n zu ~ suchen*** reason with s.o.; ***er läßt sich nicht ~*** he won't be persuaded; **II.** *v/i.* be convincing; **III.**

v/refl.: **sich ~** satisfy o.s. (**von** *dat.* as to); go and see (*or* find out) for o.s.; **~ *Sie sich selbst!*** go and see for yourself; ***sich von der Wahrheit e-r Aussage ~*** verify (F check out) a statement; **über'zeu·gend I.** *adj.* convincing (*a. performance etc.*), *a.* conclusive *argument*, *evidence etc.*, *a.* telling *victory*; **~ *sein*** (*or* ***wirken***) *argument etc.*: *a.* carry conviction; ***nicht ~ sein*** (*or* ***wirken***) *a.* lack conviction; **II.** *adv. defeat etc.* convincingly; **über·zeugt** [y:bɐ'tsɔʏkt] *adj.* a) convinced (***von*** *dat.* of), positive (about), b) convinced *Socialist*, *Catholic etc.*; ***von sich selbst*** (***sehr***) ***~ sein*** have a (very) high opinion of o.s.; ***ich bin noch nicht*** (***ganz***) ~ *a.* I'm not (completely) persuaded yet; **Über'zeu·gung** *f* (-; -en) conviction; firm belief; (*political etc.*) convictions *pl.*; ***gemeinsame ~*** shared belief; ***gegen s-e ~ handeln*** go against one's convictions; ***der ~ sein, daß*** be convinced that, *w.s.* be of the opinion that; ***der festen ~ sein, daß*** be firmly (*or* absolutely) convinced that; ***zu der ~ gelangen, daß*** come to the conclusion that, come to believe that; ***wenn Sie wirklich der ~ sind*** if that's what you really believe; ***zu s-r ~ stehen*** have the courage of one's convictions

Über'zeu·gungs|kraft *f* (-; *no pl.*) powers *pl.* of persuasion; persuasiveness, logic *of an argument etc.*; **~tä·ter** *m*: ***er ist ein ~*** he committed the crime out of moral (*or* religious, political) conviction; ***politischer ~*** politically-motivated offender, political criminal

über'zie·hen[1] (*irr.*, *insep.*, *no* -ge-, h, → ***ziehen***) **I.** *v/t.* **1.** a) cover, b) put a pillowslip (*or* pillowcase) on *a cushion*, put a pillowslip (*or* pillowcase) on, c) *gastr.* coat; ***das Bett ~*** make up the bed; ***das Bett frisch ~*** change the sheets (on the bed), put clean sheets on (the bed); ***neu ~*** re-cover *armchair etc.*; **2.** overdo; exaggerate; **3.** go over *the time limit*, break *the deadline*; *radio*, *TV*: overrun (***um*** *acc.* by); ***et. ~*** *a.* go on longer than allowed; **4.** ☤ overdraw *one's account, credit etc.*; **II.** *v/refl. and v/impers.* **5. *sich ~*** *sky*: become overcast; ***es überzieht sich*** it's clouding over; **III.** *v/i.* **6.** ☤ overdraw (one's account *or* credit); **7.** go over the time limit (***um*** *acc.* by); fail to meet the deadline

'über·zie·hen[2] *v/t.* (*irr.*, *sep.*, h, → ***ziehen***) put on, slip over; F ***j-m eins ~*** F land s.o. one

Über·zie·her ['y:bɐtsi:ɐ] *m* (-s; -) **1.** F rubber; **2.** *obs.* overcoat

Über'zie·hung *f* ☤ overdraft; **Über'zie·hungs·kre,dit** *m* overdraft facility

über·zo·gen [y:bɐ'tso:gən] **I.** *p.p. of* ***überziehen***[1]; **II.** *adj.* **1.** *gastr. etc.* coated; **2.** ☤ overdrawn; **3.** exaggerated; F ***total ~*** F over the top, OTT

über·züch·tet [y:bɐ'tsʏçtət] *adj. biol.* overbred; ⚙ *and fig.* oversophisticated; **Über'züch·tung** *f* (-; *no pl.*) *biol.* overbreeding; ⚙ *and fig.* oversophistication

über'zuckern *v/t.* (*insep.*, *no* -ge-, h) sugar over

Über·zug ['y:bɐtsu:k] *m* (-[e]s; Überzüge ['y:bɐtsy:gə]) **1.** a) cover, b) pillowcase, pillowslip; **2.** coat; *gastr.* coating

üb·lich ['y:plɪç] *adj.* usual, customary; conventional; normal, *esp.* ⚙ standard; ***wie ~*** as usual; ***es ist bei uns*** (***so***) ***~, daß*** it's a custom with us that; ***es ist allgemein ~*** (***bei j-m***) ***zu*** *inf.* it's quite normal (for s.o.) to *inf.*; ***das ist allgemein ~*** that's quite normal (*or* common), that's the norm, F that's what they do around here; ***das ist bei ihr so ~*** that's quite usual for her, *contp.* that's her usual way of doing things; **'Üb·li·che** *n*: ***das ~*** the usual thing; **üb·li·cher·wei·se** ['y:plɪçɐvaɪzə] *adv.* usually, normally

'U-Boot *n* submarine; **~-Kom·man,dant** *m* submarine commander; **~-Krieg** *m* submarine war(fare); **~-Stütz·punkt** *m* submarine base

üb·rig ['y:brɪç] *adj.*: **~ *sein*** be left (over); ***das ~e ..., die ~en ...*** the rest of the ..., *a.* the remaining ...; ***die ~en*** the rest (of them); ***das ~e*** the rest (of it); ***alles ~e, alle ~en*** all the rest; ***im ~en*** (as) for the rest; → ***übrigens; et. ~ haben*** have s.th. left; ***keine Zeit ~ haben*** have no time to spare; ***et. ~ haben für*** *acc.* have a soft spot for; ***nichts ~ haben für*** *acc.* not to care much for, *a.* have no time for *s.th.*; ***hätten Sie vielleicht ein paar Minuten*** (***Mark***) ***für mich ~?*** I wonder if you could spare me a couple of minutes (marks)?; ***ein ~es tun*** go out of one's way *to do s.th.*; **~be·hal·ten** *v/t.* (*irr.*, *sep.*, h, → ***behalten***) have *s.th.* left; **~blei·ben** *v/i.* (*irr.*, *sep.*, sn, → ***bleiben***) be left (*dat.* to); *fig.* ***es blieb mir nichts anderes übrig*** (***als zu*** *inf.*) I had no choice (but to *inf.*); ***was blieb mir anderes übrig?*** what (else) could I do?

üb·ri·gens ['y:brɪgəns] *adv.* by the way, incidentally; besides; **~, *was ich noch sagen wollte, ...*** *a.* oh yes, what I was going to say was, ...; ***das schmeckt ~ sehr gut*** it actually tastes very good, it 'does taste very good

'üb·rig·las·sen *v/t.* (*irr.*, *sep.*, h, → ***lassen***) leave (***j-m et.*** s.o. s.th.); ***viel*** (***wenig***) ***zu wünschen ~*** leave much (little) to be desired

Übung ['y:bʊŋ] *f* (-; -en) **1.** practi|ce (*Am.* -se); ***aus der ~ sein*** (***kommen***) be (get) out of practi|ce (*Am.* -se); ***in ~ sein*** be in (good) form; ***in*** (***der***) ***~ bleiben*** keep one's hand in; → ***Meister*; 2.** exercise (*a.* ♪, *gym. etc.*)

'Übungs|auf·ga·be *f* exercise; **~buch** *n* book of exercises; **~flug** *m* practi|ce (*Am.* -se) run; **~ge·län·de** *n* training ground

'übungs·hal·ber [-halbɐ] *adv.* (just) for practi|ce (*Am.* -se); to keep a hand in

'Übungs|hang *m skiing*: nursery slope; **~heft** *n* exercise book; **~platz** *m* ⚔ training area; *sport*: training ground; **~sa·che** *f*: ***das ist reine ~!*** it's all a matter of practi|ce (*Am.* -se) *or* training

UEFA-Po'kal [u'e:fa-] *m* UEFA cup

'U-Ei·sen *n* ⚙ U-iron

Ufer ['u:fɐ] *n* (-s; -) shore; bank; ***ans ~*** ashore; ***am ~*** on the shore, on the edge of the lake, on the banks of the river; ***über die ~ treten*** overflow (its banks); *fig.* ***am sicheren ~*** on terra firma; ***das sichere ~ erreichen*** reach terra firma; F *fig.* ***vom andern ~*** gay, *contp.* F queer; **~be·fe·sti·gung** *f* bank reinforcement; **~bö·schung** *f*, **~damm** *m* embankment

'ufer·los *fig. adj.* boundless; endless *discussions etc.*; extravagant, wild *plans etc.*; ***das führt ins ~e*** where does it (all) end?

Ufo ['u:fo] *n* (-s; -s) UFO, unidentified flying object, *n.s.* F flying saucer

'U-Haft *f* → ***Untersuchungshaft***

Uhr [u:ɐ] *f* (-; Uhren ['u:rən]) clock; watch; ***wieviel ~ ist es?*** what time is it?, what's the time?; ***nach m-r ~ ist es vier*** it's four o'clock by (*or* according to) my watch; ***um vier ~*** at four o'clock; ***um wieviel ~?*** (at) what time?; ***wieviel ~ ungefähr?*** approximately (*or* round about) what time?; ***rund um die ~*** around the clock, ***geöffnet***: open 24 hours, open night and day; *fig.* ***ein Rennen gegen die ~*** a race against the clock (*or* against time); → ***ablaufen*** 4, ***inner***

'Uhr·arm·band *n* watchstrap

Uh·ren|ge·schäft ['u:rən-] *n* watchmaker's shop; **~in·du,strie** *f* (clock and) watch industry

'Uhr|fe·der *f* watch spring; **~glas** *n* watch glass; **~ket·te** *f* watch chain; **~ma·cher** *m* watchmaker, clockmaker; **~werk** *n* watch (*or* clock) mechanism, works *pl.*; ***wie ein ~*** mechanical(ly); ***mit der Regelmäßigkeit e-s ~s*** regular as clockwork

'Uhr·zei·ger *m* (clock *or* watch) hand; **~sinn** *m*: ***im ~*** clockwise; ***entgegen dem ~*** anti-clockwise, *Am.* counter-clockwise

'Uhr·zeit *f* time

Uhu ['u:hu] *m* (-s; -s) eagle owl

Ukrai·ner [ukra'i:nɐ] *m* (-s; -), **Ukrai·ne·rin** [ukra'i:nərɪn] *f* (-; -nen), **ukrai·nisch** [ukra'i:nɪʃ] *adj.* Ukrainian

UKW [u:ka:'ve:] *without art.* VHF (= very high frequency), FM (= frequency modulation); **~-Be·reich** *m* VHF (*or* FM) range; **~-Sen·der** *m* VHF (*or* FM) station

Ulk [ʊlk] *m* (-[e]s; *no pl.*) joke; ***aus ~*** F for a lark; **ul·ken** ['ʊlkən] *v/i.* (h) lark around; joke; **ul·kig** ['ʊlkɪç] *adj.* funny (*a. fig.*)

Ul·me ['ʊlmə] *f* (-; -n) ⚘ elm

ul·ti·ma·tiv [ʊltima'ti:f] **I.** *adj.*: ***~e Forderung*** ultimatum; ***~en Charakter haben*** take the form of an ultimatum; **II.** *adv.* in the form of an ultimatum; **Ul·ti·ma·tum** [ʊlti'ma:tʊm] *n* (-s; -ten) ultimatum; ***j-m ein ~ stellen*** give s.o. an ultimatum

Ul·ti·mo ['ʊltimo] *m* (-s; -s) ☤ last (trading) day of the month; **~ab·rech·nung** *f* end-of-month settlement

Ul·tra ['ʊltra] *m* (-s; -s) *pol.* extremist

ul·tra·hoch·er·hitzt ['ʊltra-] *adj.* longlife *milk*

Ul·tra|'kurz·wel·le [ʊltra-] *f* (-; *no pl.*) *phys.* ultra-short wave; *radio etc.*: very high frequency (*abbr.* VHF), frequency modulation (*abbr.* FM); **~'leicht·flug·zeug** *n* microlight plane

Ul·tra·lin·ke ['ʊltra-] *f* (-n; *no pl.*) *pol.* extreme left

ul·tra·ma·rin [ʊltrama'ri:n] *adj.*, **Ul·tra·ma'rin** *n* (-s; *no pl.*) ultramarine

ul·tra·rot ['ʊltraro:t] *adj.*, **'Ul·tra·rot** *n* (-s; *no pl.*) ultrared, infrared

Ul·tra·schall ['ʊltra-] *m phys.* ultrasound; **~bild** *n* ultrasound image; **~dia,gno·stik** *f* ultrasound diagnostics *pl.*; **~ge·rät** *n* ultrasound scanner; **~the·ra,pie** *f* ultrasound treatment; **~un·ter,su·chung** *f* ultrasound scan, sonogram; **~wel·le** *f* ultrasonic wave

ul·tra·vio·lett ['ʊltraviolɛt] *adj.*, **'Ul·tra·vio·lett** *n* (-s; *no pl.*) ultraviolet

um [ʊm] **I.** *prp.* (*acc.*) a) (a)round, b) about, around, c) at, d) *increase*, *reduce etc.* by, e) for, f) about; ***Schritt ~ Schritt*** step by step; **~ *die Häfte größer*** *etc.* bigger *etc.* by half; **~ *so besser*** so much the better; ~ ***so mehr*** all the more; (so much) the more (***als*** as; ***weil*** because); ~ ***so weniger*** (all) the less; ***je länger ich darüber nachdenke, ~ so weniger gefällt mir die Sache*** the more I think about it the less I like it; ~ ... (*gen.*) ***willen*** for the sake of; → ***drehen*** III, ***handeln*** III; **II.** *cj.*: ~ ***zu*** *inf.* (in order) to *inf.*; ~ ***ehrlich zu sein*** to be honest; **III.** *adv.* about, around *300 marks etc.*; F ~ ***sein*** be over

'um·adres,sie·ren *v/t.* (*sep.*, h) redirect

'um·än·dern *v/t.* (*sep.*, h) change, alter; **'Um·än·de·rung** *f* (-; -en) change, alteration

'um·ar·bei·ten *v/t.* (*sep.*, h) change, modify; remodel *dress etc.*; revise *novel etc.*, *a. film etc.*: adapt; rewrite, recast *text*

um·ar·men [ʊmˈʔarmən] *v/t.* (*insep.*, *no* -ge-, h) embrace, hug (*both a.* ***sich*** ~); **Um'ar·mung** *f* (-; -en) embrace, hug

'Um·bau *m* (-[e]s; -ten) a) conversion; alteration(s *pl.*), b) altered section, c) *fig.* reorganization; ***wegen ~ geschlossen*** closed for renovation; **'um·bau·en¹** (*sep.*, h) **I.** *v/t.* **1.** alter; *rebuild*; ~ ***in*** *acc. a.* turn into; **2.** *fig.* reorganize; **II.** *v/i.* **3.** do (some) alterations; **4.** *thea.*, *film*: change the setting

um'bau·en² *v/t.* (*insep.*, *no* -ge-, h) build around, surround; ***umbauter Raum*** enclosed space

'um·be·hal·ten *v/t.* (*irr.*, *sep.*, h, → ***behalten***) keep *s.th.* on

'um·be·nen·nen *v/t.* (*irr.*, *sep.*, h, → ***benennen***) rename, rechristen (***in*** *acc.* as); **'Um·be·nen·nung** *f* (-; -en) renaming

'um·be·set·zen *v/t. and v/i.* (*sep.*, h) *thea.* recast; *pol.* reshuffle; **'Um·be·set·zung** *f* (-; -en) *thea.* recasting, change of cast; *pol.* reshuffle

'um·bet·ten *v/t.* (*sep.*, h) **1.** move *patient* to another bed; **2.** rebury *s.o.*

'um·bie·gen (*irr.*, *sep.*, → ***biegen***) **I.** *v/t.* (h) bend; turn down *or* up; **II.** *v/i.* (sn) *mot.* turn round, turn back (again)

'um·bil·den *v/t.* (*sep.*, h) a) reshape, remodel, b) reorganize; *pol.* reshuffle; **'Um·bil·dung** *f* (-; -en) a) reshaping, remodel(l)ing, b) reorganization; *pol.* reshuffle

'um·bin·den *v/t.* (*irr.*, *sep.*, h, → ***binden***) tie round; put on *tie*, *apron etc.*

'um·blät·tern (*sep.*, h) **I.** *v/t.* turn over *the page*; **II.** *v/i.* turn (over) the page

'um·blicken *v/refl.* (*sep.*, h): ***sich*** ~ (***in*** *or* ***an e-m Ort*** *etc.*) look *or* have a look (a)round (a place *etc.*)

Um·bra [ˈʊmbra] *f* (-; Umbren) **1.** *ast.* umbra; **2.** *no pl.* → **'Um·bra·braun** *n*, **'um·bra·braun** *adj.* umber

'um·bre·chen¹ (*irr.*, *sep.*, → ***brechen***) **I.** *v/t.* (h) break down *tree etc.*; ⚒ break up *the soil*; **II.** *v/i.* (sn) break

um'bre·chen² *v/t.* (*irr.*, *insep.*, *no* -ge-, h, → ***brechen***) *typ.* make up

'um·brin·gen (*irr.*, *sep.*, h, → ***bringen***) **I.** *v/t.* kill, murder; **II.** *v/refl.*: ***sich*** ~ kill o.s., commit suicide; F *fig.* ***du wirst dich noch ~!*** you'll kill yourself if you're not careful; F ***das bringt mich noch um!*** F that'll be the death of me; F *fig.* ***sich (fast)*** ~ bend over backwards; *iro.* F ***bring dich bloß nicht um!*** don't strain yourself!

'Um·bruch *m* (-[e]s; ⸚e) **1.** (great) upheaval, deep-rooted change; ***sich im ~ befinden*** be going through a time of upheaval; **2.** *no pl. typ.* make-up

'Um·bruchs·zeit *f* time of upheaval

'um·bu·chen (*sep.*, h) **I.** *v/t.* **1.** ✝ transfer (***auf*** *acc.* to); **2.** change *booking*, *date etc.*; **II.** *v/i.* ✈ change one's booking; **'Um·bu·chung** *f* (-; -en) **1.** ✝ transfer (***auf*** *acc.* to); **2.** ✈ change in booking; **'Um·bu·chungs·ge·bühr** *f* alteration fee

'um·den·ken I. *v/i.* (*irr.*, *sep.*, h, → ***denken***) change one's ideas (*or* approach); ~ ***müssen*** have to do some rethinking; **II.** ≗ *n* (-s; *no pl.*) shift in thinking, rethink

'um·deu·ten *v/t.* (*sep.*, h) give a new interpretation to; **'Um·deu·tung** *f* (-; -en) reinterpretation, new interpretation

'um·dis·po,nie·ren (*sep.*, h) **I.** *v/t.* make new arrangements for; **II.** *v/i.* change one's plans

um'drän·gen *v/t.* (*insep.*, *no* -ge-, h) throng around, crowd

'um·dre·hen (*sep.*, h) **I.** *v/t.* turn (round); ***j-m den Arm*** ~ twist s.o.'s arm; → ***Hals, Magen, Mark³, Mund, Spieß***; **II.** *v/i.* turn round, turn back (again); **III.** *v/refl.*: ***sich*** ~ turn round; ***sich nach j-m (et.)*** ~ turn round to look at s.o. (s.th.); *fig.* ***sich auf dem Absatz*** ~ turn on one's heel, turn tail; → ***drehen*** III

Um'dre·hung *f* (-; -en) turn (*a.* ⚙); ⚙, *phys.* revolution, rotation; ***~en pro Minute*** (***U/min***) revolutions per minute (*abbr.* rpm)

Um'dre·hungs|ge·schwin·dig·keit *f* speed of rotation; **~zahl** *f* speed, number of revolutions per minute *etc.*

um·ein·an·der [ʊmʔaɪˈnandɐ] *adv.* a) (a)round each other, b) about each other

'um·er·zie·hen *v/t.* (*irr.*, *sep.*, h, → ***erziehen***) re-educate; **'Um·er·zie·hung** *f* (-; *no pl.*) re-education

um'fah·ren¹ *v/t.* (*irr.*, *insep.*, *no* -ge-, h, → ***fahren***) drive (⚓ sail) (a)round; *a.* round *a cape*; bypass

'um·fah·ren² *v/t.* (*irr.*, *sep.*, h, → ***fahren***) run *s.o.* down (*or* over), knock *s.o. or s.th.* down

'Um·fall F *contp. m* (-[e]s; *no pl.*) about-turn, about-face; **'um·fal·len** *v/i.* (*irr.*, *sep.*, sn, → ***fallen***) **1.** a) fall (down *or* over), b) faint; collapse; ***zum ≗ müde*** ready to drop; → ***tot***; **2.** F *contp.* give in; yield, capitulate; **Um·fal·ler** [ˈʊmfalɐ] F *contp. m* (-s; -) weathercock

'Um·fang *m* (-[e]s; ⸚e) a) circumference, b) girth, c) area, d) extent (*a. of damage etc.*), size; range; scope; ***in vollem ~e*** fully; ***in großem ~e*** on a large scale, large-scale ...; **um'fan·gen** *v/t.* (*irr.*, *insep.*, *no* -ge-, h, → ***fangen***) embrace; *fig.* surround; **'um·fang·reich** *adj.* **1.** extensive *research*, *knowledge etc.*; ***~es Werk*** F hefty tome; **2.** spacious; **3.** F voluminous

um'fas·sen *v/t.* (*insep.*, *no* -ge-, h) **1.** enclose, surround; ⚔ encircle; **2.** put one's arm(s) round; grip; **3.** *fig.* a) contain, comprise, b) cover *period etc.*; **um'fas·send** *adj.* a) comprehensive, extensive, b) complete, full, c) sweeping, drastic; ***~es Geständnis*** full confession

Um'fas·sung *f* (-; -en) enclosure

'Um·feld *n* (-[e]s; *no pl.*) environment, milieu; sphere

um'flie·gen¹ *v/t.* (*irr.*, *insep.*, *no* -ge-, h) fly round *s.th.*

'um·flie·gen² F *v/i.* (*irr.*, *sep.*, sn, → ***fliegen***) fall over

um'flie·ßen *v/t.* (*irr.*, *insep.*, *no* -ge-, h, → ***fließen***) flow round *s.th.*

'um·for·ma,tie·ren *v/t.* (*sep.*, h) *computer*: reformat; **'Um·for·ma,tie·rung** *f* (-; -en) reformatting

'um·for·men *v/t.* (*sep.*, h) reshape; redesign; ⚡ transform, convert; **'Um·for·mer** *m* (-s; -) ⚡ converter, transformer

'um·for·mu,lie·ren *v/t.* (*sep.*, h) reword, rephrase; **'Um·for·mu,lie·rung** *f* (-; -en) rewording, rephrasing

'Um·for·mung *f* (-; -en) reshaping; conversion; transformation

'Um·fra·ge *f* (-; -n) inquiry; (public) opinion poll, survey; ***die ~ hat ergeben, daß*** the results of the survey show that

um·frie·den [ʊmˈfriːdən] *v/t.* (*insep.*, *no* -ge-, h) enclose, fence off, put a fence up (a)round; **Um'frie·dung** *f* (-; -en) enclosure, fence

'um·fül·len *v/t.* (*sep.*, h) pour (*or* put) into another container (*or* jug *etc.*); decant *wine*; ***et.*** ~ *a.* pour s.th. into s.th. else

'um·funk·tio,nie·ren *v/t.* (*sep.*, h) convert (***zu*** *dat.* into); **'Um·funk·tio,nie·rung** *f* (-; *no pl.*) conversion (***zu*** *dat.* into)

'Um·gang *m* (-[e]s; *no pl.*) **1.** a) contact; relations *pl.*, b) company, acquaintances *pl.*, (circle of) friends *pl.*; ~ ***haben*** (*or* ***pflegen***) ***mit*** *dat.* associate with; ***guten (schlechten)*** ~ ***haben*** keep good (bad) company; ***sie ist kein ~ für dich*** she's not your type, *contp.* F she's not the sort of person you ought to be hanging around with; **2.** ***der ~ mit Kindern (Kunden*** *etc.*) dealing with children (customers *etc.*); ***der ständige ~ mit Büchern (Tieren*** *etc.*) having a lot to do with books (animals *etc.*); ***im ~ mit*** *dat.* (in) dealing with; ***geschickt sein im ~ mit*** *dat.* have a way with *children*, *animals etc.*

um·gäng·lich [ˈʊmɡɛŋlɪç] *adj.* affable; easy to get along with; **'Um·gäng·lich·keit** *f* (-; *no pl.*) affability, affableness

'Um·gangs|for·men *pl.* manners; behavio(u)r *sg.* in public; ***j-s*** ~ *a.* the way *sg.* s.o. treats other people; ***er hat keine*** ~ he doesn't know how to behave (towards other people); **~spra·che** *f* colloquial language; ***die englische*** ~ colloquial English; **≗sprach·lich** *adj.* colloquial; **~ton** *m*: ***es herrscht ein guter*** ~ there's a good atmosphere, they get along well with each other; ***die haben e-n ~!*** just listen to the way they talk to each other; ***er fand nicht den richtigen*** ~ he couldn't find the right level of communication

um·gar·nen [ʊmˈɡarnən] *fig. v/t.* (*insep.*, *no* -ge-, h) ensnare

um'ge·ben *v/t.* (*irr.*, *insep.*, *no* -ge-, h, → ***geben***) surround (***sich*** o.s.; ***mit*** *dat.* with); ***mit Mauern (e-m Zaun)*** ~ wall (fence) in; **Um·ge·bung** [ʊmˈɡeːbʊŋ] *f* (-; -en) a) surroundings *pl.*, environs *pl.*; *s.o.'s* environment; neighbo(u)rhood, *w.s. a.* vicinity, b) entourage; ***in der*** ~ *gen.* (*or* ***von*** *dat.*) in the vicinity of, on the outskirts of *a city etc.*, (a)round *Berlin etc.*; ***e-e bekannte*** ~ familiar surroundings

'um·ge·hen¹ *v/i.* (*irr.*, *sep.*, sn, → ***gehen***) **1.** a) go round; *rumo(u)r etc.*: circulate, F go the rounds, b) *ghost*: walk; ***an*** (*or* ***in***) ***e-m Ort*** ~ haunt a place; **2.** ~ ***mit*** *dat.* a) handle; treat *s.o. or s.th.*, b) manage, deal with *s.o. or s.th.*, c) ⚙ use, work; (***gut***) ~

können mit *dat.* know how to handle *etc.*, have a way with, be good with; **ich weiß gar nicht, wie ich damit ~ soll** I don't know what to do with it; → **schonend** II, **sparsam** II; **3. mit dem Gedanken** (*or* **Plan**) **~ zu** *inf.* be thinking of *ger.*, be contemplating *ger.*
um'ge·hen² *v/t.* (*irr.*, *insep.*, *no* -ge-, h, → **gehen**) **1.** go round; bypass (*a.* ⚡); **2.** *fig.* avoid, *a.* ⚖ evade; elude, sidestep, F get round; **es läßt sich nicht ~** there's no getting out of it, **daß er ...**: there's no way he can avoid (*or* get round) *ger.*
'um·ge·hend *adj.* (*and adv.*) immediate(ly)
Um·ge·hung [ʊm'ge:ʊŋ] *f* (-; *no pl.*) bypassing; *fig.* avoidance, *a.* ⚖ evasion; **Um'ge·hungs·stra·ße** *f* bypass; belt, *Brit.* ring road
um·ge·kehrt ['ʊmgəke:ɐt] **I.** *adj.* a) reverse *order*, inverted, b) opposite, contrary; **~!** (no,) it's exactly the other way round; **in ~er Reihenfolge** in reverse order; **II.** *adv.* a) the other way round, b) on the other hand, conversely
'um·ge·stal·ten *v/t.* (*sep.*, h) reshape; ⚙ *etc. a.* redesign; *a.* rearrange; **'Um·ge·stal·tung** *f* (-; -en) reshaping; redesigning; rearrangement
um·ge·stülpt ['ʊmgəʃtʏlpt] *adj.* a) inside-out ..., *pred.* inside out, b) upside-down ..., *pred.* upside down; upturned
um·ge·stürzt ['ʊmgəʃtʏrtst] *adj.* fallen; blown-down; *mot.* overturned
'um·gie·ßen *v/t.* (*irr.*, *sep.*, h, → **gießen**) **1.** → **umfüllen; 2.** *metall.* refound, recast
'um·gra·ben *v/t.* (*irr.*, *sep.*, h, → **graben**) dig (*or* turn) up; break up *the soil*
um'grei·fen *v/t.* (*irr.*, *insep.*, *no* -ge-, h, → **greifen**) **1.** surround; **2.** *fig.* comprise; **3.** grasp; put (*or* get) one's arm(s) round
um'gren·zen *v/t.* (*insep.*, *no* -ge-, h) **1.** surround, enclose, encircle; **2.** *fig.* define; **Um·gren·zung** [ʊm'grɛntsʊŋ] *f* (-; -en) **1.** enclosure; **2.** *fig.* definition
'um·grup,pie·ren *v/t.* (*sep.*, h) regroup; reshuffle; **'Um·grup,pie·rung** *f* (-; -en) regrouping; reshuffling
'um·ha·ben F *v/t.* (*irr.*, *sep.*, h, → **haben**) have on
'um·hacken *v/t.* (*sep.*, h) chop (*or* cut) down *tree etc.*
Um·hang ['ʊmhaŋ] *m* (-[e]s; Umhänge ['umhɛŋə]) cape
'um·hän·gen *v/t.* (*sep.*, h) **1.** put on *shawl etc.*; sling *rifle etc.* over one's shoulder; **2.** rehang, hang *a picture etc.* somewhere else
'Um·hän·ge·ta·sche *f* shoulder bag
'um·hau·en *v/t.* (*irr.*, *sep.*, h, → **hauen**) **1.** fell, cut down; **2.** F *fig.* bowl over, floor; *beer etc.*: knock *s.o.* out; **es hat mich fast umgehauen** *news etc.*: I was floored
um·her [ʊm'he:ɐ] *adv.* (a)round, about; **~blicken** *v/i.* (*sep.*, h) look around; **~irren** *v/i.* (*sep.*, sn) wander around *or* about (lost, like a lost soul), **in** *dat.*: wander around *a place*; **~schlei·chen** *v/i.* (*irr.*, *sep.*, sn, → **schleichen**) sneak (*or* creep) around
um·hin·kön·nen [ʊm'hınkœnən] *v/i.* (konnte umhin, umhingekonnt, h): **ich kann nicht umhin zu** *inf.* I can't help *ger.*, I can't avoid *ger.*
'um·hö·ren *v/refl.* (*sep.*, h): **sich ~** keep one's ears open, ask around

um'hül·len *v/t.* (*insep.*, *no* -ge-, h) wrap up (**mit** *dat.* in), cover (in, with); **um·hüllt** [ʊm'hʏlt] *adj.* enveloped, shrouded (**von** *dat.* in); *fig.* **von e-m Geheimnis ~** shrouded in mystery; **Um·hül·lung** [ʊm'hʏlʊŋ] *f* (-; -en) wrapping
um'ju·beln *v/t.* (*insep.*, *no* -ge-, h) cheer; **um·ju·belt** [ʊm'ju:bəlt] *adj.* **1.** celebrated; **von der Menge ~** *a.* cheered by the crowd; **2.** *fig.* extremely popular (**von** *dat.* with *the public etc.*); **allgemein ~ werden** enjoy popular acclaim, be widely acclaimed
um'kämp·fen *v/t.* (*insep.*, *no* -ge-, h) ⚔ fight for; dispute (*a. fig. privileges etc.*), *fig. a.* contest → **heiß** II
Um·kehr ['ʊmke:ɐ] *f* (-; *no pl.*) **1.** turning back, return; **2.** *fig.* (complete) change; *pol.* about-face, about-turn, volte-face; **um·kehr·bar** ['ʊmke:ɐba:ɐ] *adj.* reversible; **'um·keh·ren** (*sep.*) **I.** *v/i.* (sn) turn back; retrace one's steps; **II.** *v/t.* (h) a) turn *s.th.* round, b) turn *s.th.* upside down, c) turn *s.th.* (inside) out, d) ⚙, ⚡ *and fig.* reverse; **III.** *v/refl.*: **sich ~** (h) turn round; turn on its head; *fig.* reverse; *fig.* **die Situation kehrte sich um** there was a sudden reverse in the situation; **die Verhältnisse kehrten sich um** the tables turned
'Um·kehr·film *m phot.* reversal film
Um·keh·rung ['ʊmke:rʊŋ] *f* (-; -en) reversal; inversion
'um·kip·pen (*sep.*) **I.** *v/t.* (h) **1.** tip over; knock over; **II.** *v/i.* (sn) **2.** tip over; fall over; **3.** F faint, keel over; **4.** switch (completely); **5.** *lake etc.*: die
um'klam·mern *v/t.* (*insep.*, *no* -ge-, h) **1.** clutch onto, hold tight onto; clutch, grip; clasp; **mit den Armen** (**Beinen**) **~** wrap one's arms (legs) (a)round; **2.** squeeze in, close in on, encircle, surround on all sides; **Um·klam·me·rung** [ʊm'klamərʊŋ] *f* (-; -en) **1.** (**tödliche ~** deadly) embrace; **2.** *boxing*: clinch
'um·klapp·bar *adj.* collapsible, folding ...; **'um·klap·pen** *v/t.* (*sep.*, h) turn down, fold (back)
Um·klei·de·ka,bi·ne ['ʊmklaıdə-] *f* (changing) cubicle
'um·klei·den¹ *v/refl.* (*sep.*, h): **sich ~** change (one's clothes), put some other clothes on
um'klei·den² *v/t.* (*insep.*, *no* -ge-, h) cover; ⚙ *etc. a.* sheathe (**mit** *dat.* in)
Um·klei·de·raum ['ʊmklaıdə-] *m thea.* dressing room; *sport*: *a.* changing (*or* locker) room
Um'klei·dung *f* (-; -en) ⚙ *etc.* sheath, sheathing
'um·knicken (*sep.*) **I.** *v/t.* (h) **1.** bend (over); **2.** fold (down); **II.** *v/i.* (sn) **3.** *tree etc.*: bend; *branch etc.*: snap; **4.** (*a.* **mit dem Fuß ~**) twist one's ankle
'um·kom·men *v/i.* (*irr.*, *sep.*, sn, → **kommen**) die, be killed; **et. ~ lassen** let s.th. go to waste; F *fig.* **wir sind vor Hitze** (**Hunger, Langeweile**) **fast umgekommen** we nearly died in the heat (of hunger, of boredom)
'Um·kreis *m* (-es; *no pl.*) **1.** vicinity; **im ~ von** *dat.* within a radius of, for *three miles etc.* around; **2.** *fig.* circle(s *pl.*) surrounding *s.o.*; **ihr engster ~** those closest to her; **3.** *A* circumcircle
um'krei·sen *v/t.* (*insep.*, *no* -ge-, h) circle (round); *ast.* revolve (a)round
'um·krem·peln *v/t.* (*sep.*, h) **1.** a) roll up, b) turn *s.th.* inside out; **2.** turn *s.th.* upside down (*or* on its head); **3.** change completely; F change *s.o.*; **j-n ~ in** *acc.* turn s.o. into; **j-n völlig ~** make a new person (*or* somebody new) out of s.o.
'um·la·den *v/t.* (*irr.*, *sep.*, h, → **laden**) reload (**auf** *acc.*, **in** *acc.* onto)
'Um·la·ge *f*: **die ~ betrug ...** each person had to pay ...
um'la·gern¹ *v/t.* (*insep.*, *no* -ge-, h) throng (a)round; *a. fig.* beleaguer, besiege
'um·la·gern² *v/t.* (*sep.*, h) move (**in** *acc.* [in]to; **nach** *dat.* to), put in another place
'Um·land *n* (-[e]s; *no pl.*) environs *pl.*, hinterland, surrounding countryside
Um·lauf ['ʊmlaʊf] *m* (-[e]s; Umläufe ['ʊmlɔʏfə]) **1.** *no pl.* a) *phys.*, ⚙ rotation, revolution, b) ☤ circulation *of money*; **in ~ bringen** (*or* **setzen**) put in circulation, circulate, issue, float *capital*, *fig.* start, get *a rumo(u)r* going; **im ~ sein** be in circulation, *rumo(u)r*: *a.* be going round; **~bahn** *f* orbit; **auf s-e ~ bringen** put into orbit
'um·lau·fen¹ *v/i.* (*irr.*, *sep.*, sn, → **laufen**) ⚙ *etc.* revolve, rotate; ☤ *and fig.* circulate
um'lau·fen² *v/t.* (*irr.*, *insep.*, *no* -ge-, h, → **laufen**) run (*or* move) around
'Um·lauf|ge·schwin·dig·keit *f* orbiting speed; **~ka·pi,tal** *n* current liabilities *pl.*; **~ver·mö·gen** *n* current assets *pl.*; **~zeit** *f* period (of revolution *etc.*); orbital period *of a satellite*
'Um·laut *m ling.* a) umlaut, (vowel) mutation, b) umlaut, mutated vowel
'um·le·gen *v/t.* (*sep.*, h) **1.** put (*or* lay) down; move (*a. patient*); shift; *teleph.* transfer; **2.** put on *a shawl etc.*; **3.** tuck *hem*; **4.** ⚙ throw *lever etc.*; **5.** *fig.* divide *costs etc.* (**auf** *acc.* among); **6.** *fig.* change, shift *date, appointment etc.* (**auf** *acc.* to); **7.** F bump *s.o.* off; **8.** V lay (*sl.*)
'um·lei·ten *v/t.* (*sep.*, h) divert, detour *traffic etc.*; reroute *shipment etc.*
'Um·lei·tung *f* (-; -en) diversion; rerouting; detour; *sign*: diversion, *Am.* detour; **~ auf die Gegenfahrbahn** contraflow (traffic)
'Um·lei·tungs|schild *n* diversion (*Am.* detour) sign; **~strecke** *f* diversion, detour
'um·len·ken *v/t.* (*sep.*, h) **1.** turn *a car etc.* round; **2.** *fig.* redirect, rechannel; lead in another direction
'um·ler·nen *v/i.* (*sep.*, h) retrain; *fig.* **~ müssen** have to change one's ideas
'um·lie·gend *adj.* surrounding, neighbo(u)ring, ... in the vicinity, round about; **die ~e Gegend** the neighbo(u)rhood, the surrounding area, the surroundings
'Um·luft *f* (-; *no pl.*) circulating air
um·man·teln [ʊm'mantəln] *v/t.* (*insep.*, *no* -ge-, h) ⚙ coat, sheathe (**mit** *dat.* in); **Um'man·te·lung** *f* (-; -en) coat, sheath
um·mau·ern *v/t.* (*insep.*, *no* -ge-, h) wall in, build a wall (a)round
'um·mel·den *v/refl.* (*sep.*, h): **sich ~** register one's (*or* a) change of address
um'mo·deln *v/t.* (*sep.*, h) remodel, reshape; *fig.* change *s.o. etc.*
'um·mün·zen *fig. v/t.* (*sep.*, h) turn (**in** *acc.* into)
um·nach·tet [ʊm'naxtət] *adj.* (*a.* **geistig ~**) mentally deranged; **Um·nach·tung** [ʊm'naxtʊŋ] *f* (-; *no pl.*) (*a.* **geistige ~**) mental derangement

um'ne·beln *v/t.* (*insep.*, *no* -ge-, h) befog; **um·ne·belt** [ʊm'ne:bəlt] *fig. adj.* befuddled

'um·nu·meˌrie·ren *v/t.* (*sep.*, h) renumber; **'Um·nu·meˌrie·rung** *f* (-; *no pl.*) renumbering

'um·ord·nen *v/t.* (*sep.*, h) rearrange; change (*or* rearrange) the order of

'um·or·ga·niˌsie·ren *v/t.* (*sep.*, h) reorganize

'um·packen *v/t.* (*sep.*, h) repack

'um·pflan·zen[1] *v/t.* (*sep.*, h) replant; repot

um'pflan·zen[2] *v/t.* (*insep.*, *no* -ge-, h) put plants around, surround with plants; ***mit Bäumen ~*** plant trees around

'um·pflü·gen *v/t.* (*sep.*, h) plough (*Am.* plow) up

'um·po·len *v/t.* (*sep.*, h) **1.** ⚡ reverse (the polarity of); **2.** F *fig.* change

'um·pro·gramˌmie·ren *v/t.* (*sep.*, h) reprogram(me); **'Um·pro·gramˌmie·rung** *f* (-; -en) reprogramming

'um·quarˌtie·ren *v/t.* (*sep.*, h) move to other accommodation (*or* another room, other rooms *etc.*); F move *a patient*

um'rah·men *v/t.* (*insep.*, *no* -ge-, h) **1.** frame; **2.** *fig.* serve as a setting for; ***musikalisch ~*** provide the music for; **Um'rah·mung** *f* (-; *no pl.*) **1.** a) framing, b) frame; **2.** *fig.* setting, framework

um·ran·den [ʊm'randən] *v/t.* (*insep.*, *no* -ge-, h) border; **um·ran·det** [ʊm'randət] *adj.* bordered, edged (***von*** *dat.* with); ***schwarz ~*** edged in black; **Um'ran·dung** *f* (-; -en) border, edge

um'ran·ken *v/t.* (*insep.*, *no* -ge-, h) twine (itself) round; **um·rankt** [ʊm'raŋkt] *adj.*: ***~ von*** *dat.* entwined with, covered in; ***von Efeu ~*** ivy-covered; *fig.* ***von Legenden ~*** surrounded by legend

um·rän·dert [ʊm'rɛndɐt] *adj.*: ***rot ~e Augen*** red-rimmed eyes, ***haben***: have red rims around one's eyes

'um·räu·men *v/t.* (*sep.*, h) **1.** move (to another place); **2.** rearrange *room etc.*

'um·rech·nen *v/t.* (*sep.*, h) convert (***in*** *acc.* into); ***in Dollar umgerechnet*** in (terms of) dollars; **'Um·rech·nung** *f* (-; *no pl.*) conversion (***in*** *acc.* into)

'Um·rech·nungs|kurs *m* ☤ exchange rate, rate of exchange; **~taˌbel·le** *f* conversion table

'um·rei·ßen[1] *v/t.* (*irr.*, *sep.*, h, → ***reißen***) pull down; knock down

um'rei·ßen[2] *v/t.* (*irr.*, *insep.*, *no* -ge-, h, → ***reißen***) outline; → ***umrissen***

'um·ren·nen *v/t.* (*irr.*, *sep.*, h, → ***rennen***) run (*or* knock) down

um'rin·gen *v/t.* (*insep.*, *no* -ge-, h) form (*or* make) a circle around; throng round, surround (*a. fig.*)

'Um·riß *m* outline (*a. fig.*), contours *pl.*; ***in kräftigen*** (***groben***) ***Umrissen*** in bold (rough) outline; ***in Umrissen schildern*** outline; ***feste Umrisse bekommen*** begin to take shape

um·ris·sen [ʊm'rɪsən] **I.** *p.p. of* ***umreißen***[2]; **II.** *adj.*: ***scharf ~*** sharply outlined

'Um·riß·kar·te *f* skeleton map

'um·rüh·ren *v/t.* (*sep.*, h) stir

um'run·den *v/t.* (*insep.*, *no* -ge-, h) walk (*or* go, drive *etc.*) round

'um·rü·sten (*sep.*, h) **I.** *v/t.* ⚙ adapt (***auf*** *acc.* to); ⚔ re-equip (with); **II.** *v/i.*: ***~ auf*** *acc.* convert to; **'Um·rü·stung** *f* (-; -en) ⚙ adaptation (***auf*** *acc.* to); ⚔ re-equipping (with); *w.s.* conversion (to)

ums [ʊms] (= ***um das***) → ***um***

'um·sat·teln (*sep.*, h) **I.** *v/t.* resaddle; **II.** *fig. v/i.* a) change jobs, b) *univ.* change one's subject, change subjects; ***~ auf*** *acc.* switch to

'Um·satz *m* (-es; ⸚e) ☤ turnover; sales *pl.*; returns *pl.*; **~be·tei·li·gung** *f* a) commission, b) working on a commission basis; ***mit ~***, F ***auf ~*** *be employed etc.* on a commission basis; **~ent·wick·lung** *f* sales trend; **~rück·gang** *m* drop in sales; **~stei·ge·rung** *f* sales increase; **~steu·er** *f* turnover tax

um'säu·men *v/t.* (*insep.*, *no* -ge-, h) hem; *fig.* surround, line *the streets etc.*

'um·schal·ten (*sep.*, h) **I.** *v/t.* **1.** switch (over) (***auf*** *acc.* to); **II.** *v/i.* **2.** switch over (***auf*** *acc.*, ***nach*** *dat.* to); *traffic lights*: change (***auf*** *acc.* to); ***auf Grün*** *etc.* ***~*** *a.* turn green *etc.*; **3.** F *fig.* adjust (***auf*** *acc.* to); **'Um·schal·ter** *m* (-s; -) **1.** ⚡ commutator; **2.** → **'Um·schalt·ta·ste** *f* shift key

'Um·schau *f* (-; *no pl.*) **1.** ***~ halten*** (have a) look around (***nach*** *dat.* for); **2.** review; **'um·schau·en** *v/refl.* (*sep.*, h) → ***umsehen***

'um·schich·ten *v/t.* (*sep.*, h) rearrange; *fig. a.* regroup, reshuffle; **'Um·schich·tung** *f* (-; -en) regrouping; ***gesellschaftliche ~*** shift in social structure

um'schif·fen *v/t.* (*insep.*, *no* -ge-, h) sail (a)round, *a.* round *a cape*; circumnavigate; **Um'schif·fung** *f* (-; *no pl.*) sailing (a)round; rounding; circumnavigation

'Um·schlag *m* (-[e]s; ⸚e) **1.** a) envelope, b) cover, jacket, c) cuff, d) cuff, *Brit.* turn-up, e) ⚕ compress; **2.** ☤ a) handling *of goods*, b) goods *pl.* handled; **3.** *fig.* → ***Umschwung***; **'um·schla·gen** (*irr.*, *sep.*, → ***schlagen***) **I.** *v/i.* (sn) **1.** overturn; *boat etc.*: *a.* capsize; **2.** *fig.* turn, suddenly change, change (abruptly) (*all* ***in*** *acc.* into); *wind*: veer (round); *voice*: crack; **II.** *v/t.* (h) **3.** turn (over) *page etc.*; turn up *sleeves etc.*; turn down *one's collar*; **4.** knock over (*or* down); cut down *tree etc.*; **5.** (*a.* ***sich ~***) put on, wrap (a)round one's neck (*or* shoulders); **6.** ☤ handle; *n.s.* transfer, tran(s)ship

'Um·schlag·platz *m* trading cent|re (*Am.* -er); ⚓ place of tran(s)shipment

um'schlie·ßen *v/t.* (*irr.*, *insep.*, *no* -ge-, h, → ***schließen***) a) surround, enclose, b) clasp, c) embrace, wrap one's arms (a)round, d) *fig.* encompass, embrace

um'schlin·gen *v/t.* (*irr.*, *insep.*, *no* -ge-, h, → ***schlingen***) **1.** embrace; **2.** ⚘ twine itself (a)round; **um·schlun·gen** [ʊm'ʃlʊŋən] **I.** *p.p. of* ***umschlingen***; **II.** *adj.*: ***sich fest ~ halten*** be clasped in a firm embrace; ***vom Meer*** *etc.* ***~*** surrounded by the sea (*or* by water)

um'schmei·cheln *v/t.* (*insep.*, *no* -ge-, h) sweet-talk; *a.* woo *a girl*

'um·schmei·ßen F *v/t.* (*irr.*, *sep.*, h, → ***schmeißen***) → ***umwerfen***

'um·schnal·len *v/t.* (*sep.*, h) buckle (*or* strap) on; put on *belt*

um'schrei·ben[1] *v/t.* (*irr.*, *insep.*, *no* -ge-, h, → ***schreiben***) **1.** circumscribe (*a.* A), paraphrase; express *s.th.* in different terms; **2.** define; (*a.* ***kurz ~***) sum up

'um·schrei·ben[2] *v/t.* (*irr.*, *sep.*, h, → ***schreiben***) **1.** a) rewrite, b) transcribe; **2.** ☤ transfer, make over (***auf*** *acc.* to)

Um'schrei·bung[1] *f* (-; -en) **1.** circumscription, paraphrase; **2.** definition

'Um·schrei·bung[2] *f* (-; -en) **1.** a) rewriting, b) transcription; **2.** ☤ transfer

'Um·schrift *f* (-; -en) **1.** *ling.* transcription; **2.** *no pl.* phonetic transcription

'um·schul·den *v/t.* (*sep.*, h) ☤ convert *loan*; change the terms of debt of *a firm*

'um·schu·len *v/t.* (*sep.*, h) a) move *pupil* to another school, b) retrain

'Um·schu·lung *f* a) transfer to another school, b) retraining

'Um·schu·lungs·kurs *m* retraining course (*or* program[me])

'um·schüt·ten *v/t.* (*sep.*, h) **1.** → ***umgießen*** 1; **2.** spill, knock over

um'schwär·men *v/t.* (*insep.*, *no* -ge-, h) swarm (a)round; *fig.* idolize *s.o.*; **umschwärmt** [ʊm'ʃvɛrmt] *fig. adj.* idolized; (*a.* ***heftig ~***) much-courted; ***~ sein von*** *dat.* be surrounded by, be in great demand with

Um·schwei·fe ['ʊmʃvaɪfə] *pl.*: ***ohne*** (***lange***) ***~*** without further ado, without wasting any (more) time, without much fuss, *say s.th.* straight out; ***keine langen ~ machen*** get (*or* come) straight to the point; ***sie haben sich ohne lange ~ entschieden*** they didn't waste any time deciding; ***et. ohne ~ sagen*** *a.* come straight out with s.th.; ***et. ohne ~ tun*** *a.* get straight down to s.th.

'um·schwen·ken *v/i.* (*sep.*, sn) wheel round; *fig.* veer round; *pol.* do an about-face (*or* about-turn), do a volte-face

'Um·schwung *m* (-[e]s; ⸚e) (sudden) change (*gen.* in, of); *a.* reversal *of opinion etc.*; *esp. pol.* swing; upheaval

um'se·geln *v/t.* (*insep.*, *no* -ge-, h) sail (a)round, *a.* round *a cape*; circumnavigate; **Um·se·ge·lung** [ʊm'ze:gəlʊŋ] *f* (-; -en) sailing (a)round; rounding; circumnavigation

'um·se·hen *v/refl.* (*irr.*, *sep.*, h, → ***sehen***): ***sich ~*** **1.** look (*or* glance) back *or* round; **2.** *fig.* look (a)round (***nach*** *dat.* for), be on the lookout (for); ***sich ~ an*** (*or* ***in***) *dat.* have a look (a)round *a place*; *fig.* ***du wirst dich noch ~!*** you're in for a surprise (or two)

um·sei·tig ['ʊmzaɪtɪç] **I.** *adv.* overleaf; on the reverse (*or* back); **II.** *adj.* ... overleaf

'um·set·zen *v/t.* (*sep.*, h) **1.** *ped.* move (***in*** *acc.*, ***auf*** *acc.* to); **2.** ⚘ transplant; ⚙ change over; convert (***in*** *acc.* into), *phys.*, ⚗ *etc. a.* transform (into); *fig.* implement *plans etc.*; ☤ sell; turn over; ***sein Geld in*** *acc.* ***... ~*** spend one's money on *candy etc.*; ***et. in Bargeld ~*** turn s.th. into cash; ***in die Tat ~*** put into action; ⚗ ***sich ~ in*** *acc.* be converted into

Um·set·zung ['ʊmzɛtsʊŋ] *f* (-; *no pl.*) conversion (***in*** *acc.* into)

'Um·sich·grei·fen *n* (-; *no pl.*) (rapid) spread, proliferation

'Um·sicht *f* (-; *no pl.*) circumspection; **um·sich·tig** ['ʊmzɪçtɪç] *adj.* circumspect; **'Um·sich·tig·keit** *f* (-; *no pl.*) circumspection

'um·sie·deln (*sep.*) **I.** *v/t.* (h) resettle; **II.** *v/i.* (sn) move (to another place); **'Um·sied·ler** *m* (-s; -) resettler; **'Um·sied·lung** *f* (-; *no pl.*) resettlement; move (***nach*** *dat.* to)

'um·sin·ken *v/i.* (*irr.*, *sep.*, sn, → ***sinken***) collapse; faint; ***zum ≈ müde*** ready to drop

um'sonst *adv.* **1.** for nothing, free (of charge); **2.** for nothing; ***es war ~*** it was a waste of time, it was all for nothing;

***nicht** ~* not without (good) reason *did he come here etc.*

um'sor·gen *v/t.* (*insep., no* -ge-, h) look after *s.o.* (solicitously)

um'span·nen¹ *v/t.* (*insep., no* -ge-, h) **1.** reach round; **2.** clasp; **3.** *fig.* cover, span *period etc.*

'um·span·nen *v/t.* (*sep.*, h) ⚡ transform; **'Um·span·ner** *m* (-s; -) transformer

'Um·spann|sta·ti͵on *f*, **~werk** *n* transformer (station)

um'spie·len *v/t.* (*insep., no* -ge-, h) **1.** *soccer*: dribble round; **2.** *fig. smile*: play around (*or* about) *s.o.'s lips*; *waves etc.*: lap around

'um·sprin·gen *v/i.* (*irr., sep.*, sn, → ***springen***) *wind*: veer; *traffic lights*: change (***auf*** *acc.* to); *skiing*: jump-turn; *fig.* ~ ***mit*** *dat.* treat *s.o.*, *a.* handle *s.th.*

'um·spu·len *v/t.* (*sep.*, h) wind onto another reel

um'spü·len *v/t.* (*insep., no* -ge-, h) wash (*or* lap) around

Um·stand ['ʊmʃtant] *m* (-[e]s; Umstände ['ʊmʃtɛndə]) **1.** fact; detail; *pl.* circumstances, conditions, state *sg.* (of affairs); ***äußere Umstände*** external circumstances; ⚖ ***mildernde Umstände*** mitigating circumstances; ***nähere Umstände*** (further) particulars; ***unter Umständen*** possibly, perhaps; if need be; ***unter allen Umständen*** whatever happens, *formal*: at all events; ***unter keinen Umständen*** under no circumstances, on no account (*or* condition); ***unter diesen Umständen*** under the circumstances, as matters stand; F ***in anderen Umständen*** F in the family way; **2.** *usu. pl.* fuss, trouble; ***viel Umstände machen*** make a lot of fuss (***wegen*** *gen.* about); ***(j-m) viel Umstände machen*** cause (s.o.) a lot of trouble, be a lot of trouble (for s.o.); ***machen Sie (sich) keine Umstände!*** don't go to any trouble; ***wenn es Ihnen keine Umstände macht*** if it's no trouble (to you); ***es macht mir überhaupt keine Umstände*** it's no trouble at all; ***ohne viel Umstände*** without much fuss; ***nicht viel Umstände machen mit*** *dat.* make short work of

'um·stän·de·hal·ber *adv.* owing to circumstances; ***...*** ~ ***zu verkaufen*** forced sale: ...

um·ständ·lich ['ʊmʃtɛntlɪç] **I.** *adj.* a) complicated, b) longwinded, c) pedantic(ally *adv.*), d) awkward, e) fussy; ***das ist viel zu*** ~ that's far too much trouble, that's much too complicated; ***~e Methode*** *a.* roundabout way of doing s.th. (*or* it); *iro.* ***~er geht's wohl nicht?*** couldn't you think of a more complicated way of doing it?; **II.** *adv.* awkwardly; fussily *etc.*; → ***I; et.*** ~ ***erzählen*** narrate s.th. at great length, give a longwinded account of s.th.; **'Um·ständ·lich·keit** *f* (-; *no pl.*) a) complicated nature, b) longwindedness, c) pedantry, d) fussiness

'Um·stands|be·stim·mung *f ling.* adverbial phrase; **~kleid** *n* maternity dress; **~krä·mer** *m* F fusspot; **~mo·de** *f* maternity wear; **~wort** *n* (-[e]s; ⸚er) adverb

um'ste·hen *v/t.* (*irr., insep., no* -ge-, h, → ***stehen***) stand round

'um·ste·hend I. *adj.* next *page*; *text etc.* overleaf; ***die Umstehenden*** the bystanders; **II.** *adv.* overleaf

'um·stei·gen *v/i.* (*irr., sep.*, sn, → ***steigen***) **1.** change (***in*** *acc.* [on]to; ***nach*** *dat.* for); change trains (*or* buses *etc.*); **2.** F *fig.* switch (***auf*** *acc.* to), change over (to)

Um·stei·ge·schwung ['ʊmʃtaɪgə-] *m skiing*: step turn

um'stel·len¹ *v/t.* (*insep., no* -ge-, h) surround

'um·stel·len² (*sep.*, h) **I.** *v/t.* **1.** move (round); *a.* move to (*or* put in) a different place; *a. fig.* rearrange, change round; *fig.* regroup; **2.** ⚙ adjust; **3.** *fig.* switch, change over, convert (***von*** *dat.* ***... auf*** *acc.* from ... to); ***auf Computer (Container)*** ~ *a.* computerize (containerize); **II.** *v/refl.* **4.** ***sich*** ~ adapt (o.s.), adjust (o.s.) (***auf*** *acc.* to), *a.* get used to the change (F to it); *a.* change one's attitude (towards); **5.** (*often a. v/i.*) ***(sich)*** ~ ***auf*** *acc.*, ***(sich)*** ~ ***von*** *dat.* ***... auf*** *acc.* change (*esp.* ⚙ switch) over to *a new method etc.*, change (*esp.* ⚙ switch) over from ... to; **'Um·stel·lung** *f* (-; -en) rearrangement; regrouping; adjustment; switch, changeover *etc.*; → ***umstellen²***

'um·stim·men *v/t.* (*sep.*, h) **1.** ♪ retune, tune to another pitch; ~ ***auf*** *acc.* tune to; **2.** *fig.* ***j-n*** ~ bring s.o. round (***auf*** *acc.* to), change s.o.'s mind, persuade s.o. otherwise

'um·sto·ßen *v/t.* (*irr., sep.*, h, → ***stoßen***) **1.** knock down (*or* over); **2.** *fig.* overrule *decision, sentence etc.*; upset *plans etc.*; change *testament*

'um·stricken¹ *v/t.* (*sep.*, h) **1.** reknit; **2.** F *fig.* rethink

um'stricken² *fig. v/t.* (*insep., no* -ge-, h) ensnare

um·strit·ten [ʊm'ʃtrɪtən] *adj.* disputed, *sport etc.*: contested; controversial, contentious *issue etc.*

'um·struk·tu͵rie·ren *v/t.* (*sep.*, h) restructure; **'Um·struk·tu͵rie·rung** *f* (-; -en) restructuring

'um·stül·pen *v/t.* (*sep.*, h) a) turn *s.th.* inside out, b) turn *s.th.* upside down; → ***umgestülpt***

'Um·sturz *m* (-[e]s; ⸚e) coup; ~ ***der Regierung*** *etc.* overthrow of the government *etc.*; ***e-n*** ~ ***planen*** plan a coup, plan to overthrow (*or* the overthrow of) the government *etc.*; **~be·we·gung** *f* subversive movement

'um·stür·zen (*sep.*) **I.** *v/t.* (h) **1.** knock over; **2.** *pol.* overthrow, topple; **II.** *v/i.* (sn) fall down (*or* over); be knocked down; be blown over; → ***umgestürzt***; **Um·stürz·ler** ['ʊmʃtʏrtslɐ] *m* (-s; -) revolutionary, subversive; **um·stürz·le·risch** ['ʊmʃtʏrtslərɪʃ] *adj.* subversive

'Um·sturz·ver·such *m* attempted coup (*or* overthrow of the government *etc.*)

'um·tau·fen *v/t.* (*sep.*, h) *a. fig.* rename, rechristen (***auf*** *acc.* as)

'Um·tausch *m* (-[e]s; *no pl.*) exchange; ***reduzierte Ware ist vom*** ~ ***ausgeschlossen*** reduced articles cannot be exchanged; **'um·tausch·bar** *adj.* exchangeable; **'um·tau·schen** *v/t.* (*sep.*, h) exchange (***gegen*** *acc.* for); *a.* take *goods* back to the shop; ***sie haben es ohne weiteres umgetauscht*** *a.* they gave me another one straightaway; **'Um·tausch·recht** *n* right to exchange goods

um·top·fen ['ʊmtɔpfən] *v/t.* (*sep.*, h) repot

'um·trei·ben *v/t.* (*irr., sep.*, h, → ***treiben***): ***j-n*** ~ give s.o. no rest, haunt s.o.

'Um·trie·be *pl.* machinations, intrigues; (***staatsfeindliche*** ~ subversive) activities

'Um·trunk *m* (-[e]s; *no pl.*) drink; ***e-n*** ~ ***veranstalten*** get a few people (*or* one's colleagues *etc.*) together for a drink

'um·tun F *v/refl.* (*irr., sep.*, h, → ***tun***): ***sich*** ~ a) get to work on s.th., be working on s.th., b) look around (***in*** *dat. a place*); ***sich*** ~ ***nach*** *dat.* look (around) for

'U-Mu͵sik *f* light (*or* popular) music

'um·ver·tei·len *v/t.* (*sep.*, h) redistribute; **'Um·ver·tei·lung** *f* (-; -en) redistribution

'um·wäl·zen *v/t.* (*sep.*, h) **1.** roll over; ⚙ circulate; **2.** *fig.* revolutionize; **'um·wäl·zend** *adj.* revolutionary *discovery etc.*

Um·wälz·pum·pe ['ʊmvɛlts-] *f* ⚙ circulating pump

Um·wäl·zung ['ʊmvɛltsʊŋ] *f* (-; -en) **1.** ⚙ circulation; **2.** *fig. pol. etc.* revolution, upheaval

'um·wan·deln *v/t.* (*sep.*, h) change, transform (***in*** *acc.*, ***zu*** *dat.* into); *phys.*, ⚡ transform, convert (*a. computer*); ⚖ commute *sentence* (into); ***er ist wie umgewandelt*** he's a completely different person, he's a changed man

'Um·wand·lung *f* (-; -en) change; transformation (***in*** *acc.*, ***zu*** *dat.* into); ✝, ⚡ conversion (*a. computer*); ⚖ commutation

'um·wech·seln *v/t.* (*sep.*, h) change (***in*** *acc.* into); ***Dollar in D-Mark*** *etc.* ~ *a.* exchange dollars for deutschmarks *etc.*; **Um·wechs·lung** ['ʊmvɛkslʊŋ] *f* (-; *no pl.*) exchange (***von*** *dat.* ***... in*** *acc.* of ... for, ✝ *a.* of ... into)

'Um·weg *m* (-[e]s; -e) detour; ***e-n*** ~ ***machen*** take the long way round, make a detour; ***kleiner*** ~ little (*or* slight) detour; *fig.* ***auf ~en*** indirectly, in a roundabout way, *b.s.* by devious means; ***ohne ~e*** straight, directly

'um·we·hen¹ *v/t.* (*sep.*, h) blow down (*or* over)

um'we·hen² *v/t.* (*insep., no* -ge-, h) waft around

'Um·welt *f* (-; *no pl.*) **1.** (natural) environment; ***unsere*** ~ *a.* the world in which we live, the world around us; **2.** milieu, background; surroundings *pl.*; **~au·to** *n* clean-fuel car; **~be·auf·trag·te** *m, f* (-n; -n) environmental health officer

'um·welt·be·dingt *adj.* environmental, due to environmental factors; **'Um·welt·be·din·gun·gen** *pl.* environmental factors

'um·welt·be·la·stend *adj.* polluting ..., harmful to the environment; **'Um·welt·be·la·stung** *f a. pl.* (environmental) pollution

'um·welt·be·wußt *adj.* environment-conscious; **'Um·welt·be·wußt·sein** *n* environmental awareness

'Um·welt·bun·des·amt *n* federal environment office

'um·welt·feind·lich *adj.* harmful to the environment; anti-environment *policy etc.*, hostile to the environment

'Um·welt·for·schung *f* ecological research

'um·welt|freund·lich *adj.* environment-friendly; non-polluting; ecologically (*or* environmentally) sound; **~ge·schä·digt** *adj.*: ~ ***sein*** have been damaged (*or* affected) by pollution

'Um·welt|ge·setz·ge·bung *f* environmental legislation; **~gift** *n* pollutant; **~ka·ta͵stro·phe** *f* environmental disaster; **~kri·mi·na·li͵tät** *f* environmental crime, crimes *pl.* against the environment; **~kri·se** *f* ecological crisis; **~lob·by** *f* environment lobby; **~mi‚ni·ster** *m* environment minister, minister of the environment; *in GB*: Environment Secretary, Secretary of State for the Environment; *in the USA*: Administrator of the Environmental Protection Agency; **~mi·ni‚ste·ri·um** *n* ministry of the environment, environment ministry; *in GB*: Department of the Environment; *in the USA*: Environmental Protection Agency; **~mo‚ral** *f* environmental ethics *pl.*; **~po·li‚tik** *f* environmental policy

'um·welt·po‚li·tisch *adj.* ecopolitical

'Um·welt·schä·den *pl.* damage *sg.* to the environment; **'um·welt·schäd·lich** *adj.* ecologically harmful

'Um·welt·schutz *m* conservation, environmental care, pollution control

'Um·welt·schüt·zer [-ʃʏtsɐ] *m* (-s; -) environmentalist, conservationist

'Um·welt·schutz|or·ga·ni·sa·ti‚on *f*, **~ver·band** *m* conservation group

'Um·welt|sün·der *m* (environmental) polluter; **~ter·ro‚ris·mus** *m* environmental terrorism; **~tou‚ris·mus** *m* ecotourism; **~ver·schmut·zung** *f* environmental pollution

'um·welt·ver·träg·lich *adj.* environment-friendly, environmentally compatible

'Um·welt·zer·stö·rung *f* destruction of the environment; *a.* ecocide

'um·wen·den (*irr.*, *sep.*, h, → **wenden**) **I.** *v/t.* turn (over); **II.** *v/refl.*: **sich ~** turn round

um'wer·ben *v/t.* (*irr.*, *insep.*, *no* -ge-, h, → **werben**) court, woo; → **umworben**

'um·wer·fen *v/t.* (*irr.*, *sep.*, h, → **werfen**) **1.** knock down; **2. sich et. ~** throw s.th. on (*or* over one's shoulders); **3.** *fig.* a) upset *plans etc.*, b) F bowl *s.o.* over, F throw; **'um·wer·fend I.** *adj.*: (**einfach ~** absolutely) staggering; **II.** *adv.*: **~ komisch** hilarious, **sein:** *a.* F be a scream

'um·wer·ten *v/t.* (*sep.*, h) re-evaluate; give new meaning to *an idea etc.*; **'Um·wer·tung** *f* (-; -en) re-evaluation

um'wickeln *v/t.* (*insep.*, *no* -ge-, h) wind *some wire etc.* round *s.th.*, tie *some string, a ribbon etc.* round *s.th.*; wrap up (**mit** *dat.* in); ⚕ bandage (with)

um·wit·tert [ʊm'vɪtɐt] *adj.*: **von Geheimnissen ~** shrouded in mystery

um·wöl·ken [ʊm'vœlkən] (*insep.*, *no* -ge-, h) **I.** *v/refl.*: **sich ~ 1.** *lit. sky*: cloud over, become overcast; **2.** *fig. face etc.*: cloud over, darken; **II.** *fig. v/t.* cloud, darken *s.o.'s face*

um·wor·ben [ʊm'vɔrbən] **I.** *p.p. of* **umwerben**; **II.** *adj.* (much) sought-after

'um·wüh·len *v/t.* (*sep.*, h) churn up

um·zäu·nen [ʊm'tsɔʏnən] *v/t.* (*insep.*, *no* -ge-, h) fence in, enclose; **Um'zäu·nung** *f* (-; -en) enclosure, fence, fencing

'um·zie·hen¹ (*irr.*, *sep.*, → **ziehen**) **I.** *v/refl.*: **sich ~** (h) change (one's clothes), put some other clothes on; **II.** *v/t.* (h) change *s.o.'s* clothes; **III.** *v/i.* (sn) move (house *or* flats, *Am.* apartments), relocate

um'zie·hen² *v/t.* (*irr.*, *insep.*, *no* -ge-, h, → **ziehen**): **et. ~ mit** *dat.* surround s.th. with *a wall, a ditch etc.*; put *a wall, a fence etc.* up around s.th., dig *a ditch, a moat etc.* around s.th.

um·zin·geln [ʊm'tsɪŋəln] *v/t.* (*insep.*, *no* -ge-, h) surround, encircle; **Um·zin·ge·lung** [ʊm'tsɪŋəlʊŋ] *f* (-; -en) encirclement

'Um·zug *m* (-[e]s; ⸚e) **1.** parade, procession; **2.** move; relocation

'Um·zugs|ko·sten *pl.* cost *sg.* of moving; relocation expenses; **~pau‚scha·le** *f* relocation package

un·ab·än·der·lich [ʊnˀap'ˀɛndɐlɪç] *adj.* unalterable, irrevocable; **sich ins ~e fü·gen** resign o.s. to the inevitable; **Un·ab'än·der·lich·keit** *f* (-; *no pl.*) unalterability; irrevocable nature (*gen.* of), irrevocability

un·ab·ding·bar [ʊnˀap'dɪŋbaːɐ] *adj.* indispensable; inalienable *rights*; **Un·ab'ding·bar·keit** *f* (-; *no pl.*) indispensability; inalienable nature (*gen.* of *rights*), inalienability

'un·ab·hän·gig *adj.* (*and adv.*) independent(ly) (**von** *dat.* of); **~ von** *dat.* irrespective of; **~ davon, ob** regardless whether; **'Un·ab·hän·gi·ge** *m, f* (-n; -n) *pol.* independent; **'Un·ab·hän·gig·keit** *f* (-; *no pl.*) independence

'Un·ab·hän·gig·keits|be·stre·ben *n*, **~be·stre·bun·gen** *pl.* drive for independence; **~be·we·gung** *f* independence movement; **~kampf** *m* fight for independence; **~krieg** *m* war of independence; **~tag** *m* Independence Day, *the* Fourth of July

'un·ab·kömm·lich *adj.* a) indispensable, b) busy; **sie ist im Moment ~** *a.* she can't get away at the moment

un·ab·läs·sig [ʊnˀap'lɛsɪç] *adj.* incessant, unremitting; unrelenting *efforts etc.*

un·ab·seh·bar [ʊnˀap'zeːbaːɐ] *adj.* a) unforeseeable; incalculable *loss etc.*, b) endless, *a.* interminable; **auf ~e Zeit** for an indefinite period of time, for the foreseeable future; **sich in ~er Ferne befinden** be a(n endlessly) long way off; **in ~er Zukunft** (some time) in the distant future

'un·ab·sicht·lich *adj.* (*and adv.*) unintentional(ly)

un·ab·wend·bar [ʊnˀap'vɛntbaːɐ] *adj.* inevitable, unavoidable; **Un·ab'wend·bar·keit** *f* (-; *no pl.*) inevitability, unavoidable nature (*gen.* of), unavoidability

'un·acht·sam *adj.* a) inattentive, b) careless, negligent, c) inadvertent ...; **'Un·acht·sam·keit** *f* (-; *no pl.*) a) inattentiveness, b) carelessness, negligence, c) inadvertence

'un·ähn·lich *adj.* dissimilar (*dat.* to); **~ sein** *dat. a.* be unlike *s.o. or s.th.*; **'Un·ähn·lich·keit** *f* (-; *no pl.*) dissimilarity (*dat.* to)

un·an·fecht·bar [ʊnˀan'fɛçtbaːɐ] *adj.* incontestable; ⚖ non-appealable, final; **Un·an'fecht·bar·keit** *f* (-; *no pl.*) incontestability

'un·an·ge·bracht *adj.* inappropriate, *pred. a.* out of place, *remark*: *a.* out of turn

un·an·ge·foch·ten ['ʊnˀangəfɔxtən] *adj. and adv.* a) undisputed(ly); unchallenged *champion etc.*, b) unhindered

un·an·ge·mel·det ['ʊnˀangəmɛldət] **I.** *adj.* unannounced; **II.** *adv.* unannounced; without any warning

'un·an·ge·mes·sen *adj.* a) immoderate; unreasonable, out of proportion (*dat.* to), b) unsuitable, inappropriate; inadequate; **'Un·an·ge·mes·sen·heit** *f* (-; *no pl.*) a) immoderacy; unreasonableness, b) inappropriateness, inadequacy

'un·an·ge·nehm I. *adj.* a) unpleasant, disagreeable; *n.s.* nasty, b) awkward; **~e Fragen stellen** ask awkward questions; **das ~e daran ist** the unpleasant thing about it is; **er kann recht ~ werden** he can get quite nasty (at times); **ihm ist es ~, mit ihr reden zu müssen** he hates having to talk to her; **es ist mir furchtbar ~** I hate it; I find it rather unpleasant (*or* embarrassing); **II.** *adv.* unpleasantly, disagreeably *cold etc.*; **~ überrascht werden** have an unpleasant (*or* a nasty) surprise; **~ auffallen** make a bad impression, make a nuisance of o.s.; **j-m ~ auffallen** annoy s.o.; **j-n ~ berühren** give s.o. an awkward feeling; **sich ~ bemerkbar machen** be (quite) unpleasant

'un·an·ge·paßt *adj.* nonconformist; **'Un·an·ge·paßt·heit** *f* (-; *no pl.*) nonconformism; nonconformist behavio(u)r

un·an·ge·ta·stet ['ʊnˀangətastət] *adj.* untouched

un·an·greif·bar [ʊnˀan'graɪfbaːɐ] *adj.* unassailable (*a. fig.*); ⚖ non-appealable; *fig.* invulnerable

un·an·nehm·bar [ʊnˀan'neːmbaːɐ] *adj.* unacceptable

'Un·an·nehm·lich·kei·ten *pl.* trouble *sg.*; **j-m ~ bereiten** cause s.o. trouble; **~ bekommen** run into difficulties

'un·an·sehn·lich *adj.* unsightly; *a.* homely (*or* plain) *person etc.*; **'Un·an·sehn·lich·keit** *f* (-; *no pl.*) unsightliness; homeliness, plainness

'un·an·stän·dig *adj.* indecent; obscene; **~es Wort** *a.* four-letter word; **~e Sprache** *a.* foul language; **'Un·an·stän·dig·keit** *f* (-; *no pl.*) indecency; obscenity

un·an·tast·bar [ʊnˀan'tastbaːɐ] *adj.* unimpeachable; inviolable *rights*; **Un·an'tast·bar·keit** *f* (-; *no pl.*) unimpeachability; inviolability *of rights*

'un·ap·pe‚tit·lich *adj.* unappetizing; *a. fig.* unsavo(u)ry, off-putting

Un·art ['ʊnˀaːɐt] *f* (-; -en) a) bad habit, b) naughtiness; **'un·ar·tig** *adj.* naughty

un·ar·ti·ku·liert ['ʊnˀartikuliːɐt] *adj.* **1.** inarticulate; **2.** unarticulated; **~ bleiben** be left unexpressed; **'Un·ar·ti·ku‚liert·heit** *f* (-; *no pl.*) inarticulateness

'un·äs‚the·tisch *adj.* un(a)esthetic(ally *adv.*); *w.s.* unpleasant, off-putting; ugly

'un·auf·dring·lich *adj.* unobtrusive; **'Un·auf·dring·lich·keit** *f* (-; *no pl.*) unobtrusiveness

'un·auf·fäl·lig *adj.* (*and adv.*) inconspicuous(ly), discreet(ly); unobtrusive(ly); **sich ~ verhalten** keep one's head down, keep a low profile

un·auf·find·bar [ʊnˀaʊf'fɪntbaːɐ] *adj.* not to be found; untraceable

un·auf·ge·for·dert ['ʊnˀaʊfgəfɔrdɐt] **I.** *adj.* unasked-for, unbidden; ✝ unsolicited; **II.** *adv.* of one's own accord, unasked, without being asked, spontaneously

'un·auf·ge·klärt *adj.* unsolved *crimes*; *w.s.* unexplained

'un·auf·ge·schlos·sen *adj.* narrow-minded; **~ sein** *a.* have a closed mind; **~ sein gegenüber** *dat.* be closed to, *a.* have no appreciation of; **'Un·auf·ge·schlos·sen·heit** *f* (-; *no pl.*) narrow-mindedness; closed mind

un·auf·halt·sam [ʊnˀaʊf'haltzaːm] *adj.* unstoppable; inexorable

un·auf·hör·lich [ʊnˀaʊfˈhøːɐlɪç] **I.** *adj.* incessant, continuous; endless; **II.** *adv.* incessantly, continuously; *a. rain etc.* without stopping; ***es regnete** ~ a.* it just kept on raining, the rain just wouldn't let up

un·auf·lös·bar [ʊnˀaʊfˈløːsbaːɐ], **un·auf·lös·lich** [ʊnˀaʊfˈløːslɪç] *adj.* indissoluble; *a.* ⚗, ⚗ insoluble; ***~es Ganzes*** indivisible whole

ˈ**un·auf·merk·sam** *adj.* a) inattentive, b) thoughtless, c) careless; ˈ**Un·auf·merk·sam·keit** *f* (-; *no pl.*) a) inattentiveness, b) thoughtlessness, c) carelessness

ˈ**un·auf·rich·tig** *adj.* insincere, dishonest; ˈ**Un·auf·rich·tig·keit** *f* (-; *no pl.*) insincerity, dishonesty

un·auf·schieb·bar [ʊnˀaʊfˈʃiːpbaːɐ] *adj.* urgent; ***es ist** ~* it has to be dealt with straightaway, *formal*: it brooks no delay

un·aus·bleib·lich [ʊnˀaʊsˈblaɪplɪç] *adj.* inevitable; ***das war** ~ a.* that was bound to happen

un·aus·denk·bar [ʊnˀaʊsˈdɛŋkbaːɐ] *adj.* unimaginable, unthinkable

un·aus·führ·bar [ʊnˀaʊsˈfyːɐbaːɐ] *adj.* impracticable, not feasible, impossible

un·aus·ge·füllt [ˈʊnˀaʊsgəfʏlt] *adj.* **1.** blank *form*; **2.** *fig.* unfulfilled *life etc.*

ˈ**un·aus·ge·gli·chen** *adj.* unbalanced; unstable; ˈ**Un·aus·ge·gli·chen·heit** *f* (-; *no pl.*) imbalance; instability

ˈ**un·aus·ge·go·ren** *adj.* a) not thought through (to the end); unfinished, b) immature; ***~ sein** a.* need time to mature

ˈ**un·aus·ge·schla·fen** *adj.* tired; lacking in sleep; ***du bist noch** ~* you haven't had enough sleep

ˈ**un·aus·ge·spro·chen** *adj.* unspoken, silent

un·aus·lösch·lich [ʊnˀaʊsˈlœʃlɪç] **I.** *adj.* indelible *impression etc.*; inextinguishable, ineradicable *hatred etc.*; **II.** *adv.*: ***~ eingeprägt*** engraved on *s.o.'s* mind

un·aus·sprech·lich [ʊnˀaʊsˈʃprɛçlɪç] **I.** *adj.* inexpressible, ineffable; unspeakable; indescribable; **II.** *adv.* unspeakably; indescribably, ... beyond description

un·aus·steh·lich [ʊnˀaʊsˈʃteːlɪç] *adj.* unbearable, intolerable; detestable; ***es ist mir** ~* I detest it, ***zu** inf.*: I detest having to *inf.*

un·aus·weich·lich [ʊmˀaʊsˈvaɪçlɪç] *adj.* inevitable, unavoidable, inescapable

un·bän·dig [ˈʊnbɛndɪç] *adj.* a) unrestrained, unbridled *hatred, rage etc.*, b) boundless, unbridled *force etc.*, c) enormous, tremendous *thirst, joy etc.*, d) wild; unruly *child etc.*

ˈ**un·bar I.** *adj.* cashless *payment etc.*; non-cash *transaction*; **II.** *adv.*: ***~ bezahlen*** make a cashless payment

ˈ**un·barm·her·zig** *adj.* merciless, pitiless, relentless; ˈ**Un·barm·her·zig·keit** *f* (-; *no pl.*) mercilessness, (complete) lack of mercy (*or* pity)

ˈ**un·be·ab·sich·tigt** *adj.* unintentional; inadvertent ...

un·be·ach·tet [ˈʊnbəˀaxtət] *adj.* unnoticed; unheeded; ***~ lassen*** ignore

un·be·an·stan·det [ˈʊnbəˀanʃtandət] *adj.* unobjected *goods etc.*; unopposed, uncontested *decision etc.*; ***et. ~ lassen*** let s.th. pass

un·be·ant·wor·tet [ˈʊnbəˀantvɔrtət] *adj.* unanswered

un·be·ar·bei·tet [ˈʊnbəˀarbaɪtət] *adj.* original *version etc.*; in its original state; ⚙ *etc.* unworked; untreated

un·be·auf·sich·tigt [ˈʊnbəˀaʊfzɪçtɪçt] *adj.* unsupervised

ˈ**un·be·baut** *adj.* **1.** undeveloped; ***~es Grundstück*** empty site, vacant lot; **2.** ⚘ untilled, idle

ˈ**un·be·dacht** *adj.* thoughtless; unconsidered, ill-considered

un·be·darft [ˈʊnbədarft] F *adj.* naive, simple; uninitiated; inexperienced; ˈ**Un·be·darft·heit** *f* (-; *no pl.*) naivety; inexperience

ˈ**un·be·denk·lich I.** *adj.* safe; harmless; ***sein Zustand ist** ~* his condition gives no cause for concern; **II.** *adv.* safely; without hesitation; ˈ**Un·be·denk·lich·keit** *f* (-; *no pl.*) safeness; harmlessness

ˈ**un·be·deu·tend** *adj.* insignificant; negligible

ˈ**un·be·dingt I.** *adj.* **1.** unconditional; absolute; implicit *trust, obedience*; **2.** *physiol.* unconditional *reflex*; **II.** *adv.* absolutely; really; at all costs, whatever happens; ***den Film muß man ~ gesehen haben*** the film's an absolute must; ***du mußt ~ kommen*** *etc.* you've got to come *etc.*; ***nicht** ~* not necessarily; ˈ**Un·be·dingt·heit** *f* (-; *no pl.*) absoluteness

un·be·ein·druckt [ʊnbəˈˀaɪndrʊkt] *adj.*: ***~ bleiben*** remain unimpressed; ***er war** ~* it made no impression on him; ***er machte ~ weiter*** he went on undeterred

un·be·ein·flußt [ˈʊnbəˀaɪnflʊst] *adj.* uninfluenced; unbias(s)ed

un·be·ein·träch·tigt [ˈʊnbəˀaɪntrɛçtɪçt] *adj.* unimpaired; unaffected (***durch** acc.* by)

un·beˈ**fahr·bar** *adj.* impassable, unnavigable

ˈ**un·be·fan·gen I.** *adj.* **1.** impartial, *a.* ⚖ unbias(s)ed; **2.** uninhibited; natural, free; **II.** *adv.* **3.** without prejudice (*or* bias); impartially; **4.** without any inhibitions, free from inhibition(s of any sort); naturally, freely; ˈ**Un·be·fan·gen·heit** *f* (-; *no pl.*) **1.** impartiality; **2.** naturalness, lack of inhibition

un·be·fe·stigt [ˈʊnbəfɛstɪçt] *adj.* unsurfaced *road*; ***~e Straße** a.* dirt track (*Am.* road)

un·be·fleckt [ˈʊnbəflɛkt] *fig. adj.* unsullied; *eccl.* ***die ♀e Empfängnis*** the Immaculate Conception

ˈ**un·be·frie·di·gend** *adj.* unsatisfactory; ˈ**un·be·frie·digt** *adj.* dissatisfied

ˈ**un·be·fri·stet I.** *adj.* unlimited; **II.** *adv.* for an unlimited (*or* indefinite) period, indefinitely

ˈ**un·be·fugt** *adj.* unauthorized; ˈ**Un·be·fug·te** *m, f* (-n; -n) unauthorized person; ***Zutritt für ~ verboten*** no unauthorized entry

ˈ**un·be·gabt** *adj.* untalented; ˈ**Un·be·gabt·heit** *f* (-; *no pl.*) lack of talent

un·beˈ**geh·bar** *adj.* impassable

un·be·gli·chen [ˈʊnbəglɪçən] *adj.* unpaid *bill*, unsettled *account*

un·beˈ**greif·lich** *adj.* incomprehensible (*dat.* to); inexplicable (to); ***es ist mir völlig** ~* I just can't understand it, F it beats me, ***daß ...***: I just can't understand why (*or* how) ..., it's beyond me how ..., F it beats me how ...; **un·be**ˈ**greif·li·cher·wei·se** *adv.* inexplicably

ˈ**un·be·grenzt I.** *adj.* unlimited; *lit.* boundless; **II.** *adv.* indefinitely; ˈ**Un·be·grenzt·heit** *f* (-; *no pl.*) limitlessness; boundlessness; ***~ der Vorräte*** *etc.* unlimited supplies *etc.*

ˈ**un·be·grün·det** *adj.* unfounded; *a.* baseless *accusation*; ***dein Verdacht*** *etc.* ***ist** ~ a.* there's no cause for your suspicion *etc.*

ˈ**un·be·haart** *adj.* hairless

ˈ**Un·be·ha·gen** *n* (-s; *no pl.*) **1.** (feeling of) unease; **2.** discomfort; queasiness

ˈ**un·be·hag·lich** *adj.* uncomfortable; *fig. a.* uneasy *feeling etc.*; *fig.* ***sich ~ fühlen*** feel uneasy, be ill at ease; ˈ**Un·be·hag·lich·keit** *f* (-; *no pl.*) uncomfortableness; *fig. a.* uneasiness, feeling of unease

un·be·han·delt [ˈʊnbəhandəlt] *adj.* untreated *fruit etc.*

un·be·haust [ˈʊnbəhaʊst] *lit. adj.* homeless

un·be·hel·ligt [ʊnbəˈhɛlɪçt] *adj.* undisturbed; unhindered; ***j-n ~ durchlassen*** let s.o. through (*or* pass) without questioning; ***von j-m ~ bleiben*** be left alone by s.o.; ***hier bist du von den Fans** ~* the fans won't get in your way here

ˈ**un·be·herrscht I.** *adj.* lacking in self-control; uncontrolled *reaction, remark etc.*; ***~ sein*** have no self-control; **II.** *adv. act etc.* without self-control; *scream etc.* without restraint; *eat etc. a.* greedily; ˈ**Un·be·herrscht·heit** *f* (-; *no pl.*) lack of self-control

ˈ**un·be·hin·dert** *adj.* unhindered, unimpeded

un·be·hol·fen [ˈʊnbəhɔlfən] *adj.* **1.** clumsy, awkward *movements etc.*; **2.** helpless, *contp.* hopeless; ˈ**Un·be·hol·fen·heit** *f* (-; *no pl.*) **1.** clumsiness, awkwardness; **2.** helplessness

un·be·irr·bar [ʊnbəˈˀɪrbaːɐ] *adj.* unswerving, single-minded; **Un·be**ˈ**irr·bar·keit** *f* (-; *no pl.*) unswervingness, single-mindedness; **un·be·irrt** [ʊnbəˈˀɪrt] *adj.* single-minded; *act, fight etc.* single-mindedly; ***~ weitermachen*** carry on regardless; ***~ festhalten an** dat.* persist in *one's belief etc.*

ˈ**un·be·kannt** *adj.* unknown (*dat.* to); unfamiliar (to); ⚗ ***die ♀e*** *a. fig.* the unknown; ***~e Größe*** *a. fig.* unknown quantity; ***das war mir** ~* I didn't know that, I wasn't aware of that; ***es ist mir nicht ~, daß*** I'm quite aware that; ***ich bin hier** ~* I'm a stranger here; ***Ort und Zeit sind noch** ~* a time and place have yet to be decided; ⚖ ***gegen ♀*** versus a person (*or* persons) unknown; ˈ**un·be·kann·ter·wei·se** *adv.*: ***grüßen Sie sie ~ von mir*** please give her my regards, even though we haven't met yet

ˈ**un·be·klei·det** *adj.* undressed, with nothing on

ˈ**un·be·küm·mert** *adj.* unconcerned, nonchalant; carefree; ***~e Einstellung** a.* cavalier approach; ˈ**Un·be·küm·mert·heit** *f* (-; *no pl.*) unconcern, lack of concern, nonchalance; carefree attitude (*or* approach, manner)

ˈ**un·be·la·stet** *adj.* **1.** unloaded, without anything on it; unweighted *leg, ski etc.*; ⚙ running idle, unstressed *component etc.*; ***in ~em Zustand*** unloaded, running idle *etc.*; **2.** ☿ unencumbered; **3.** *fig.* free (***von** dat.* from); *n.s.* free from worries; ***~ von** dat.* free from, without (any) *worries etc.*; ***~ von Vorurteilen*** (***Skrupeln*** *etc.*) without prejudice (scruple *etc.*); **4.** *fig.* clean, unblemished; ***~ sein*** have a clean record, not to have blotted one's copybook

'un·be·lebt *adj.* **1.** inanimate; **2.** unfrequented *road etc.*; deserted *area etc.*; dead *town, place etc.*

un·be·leckt ['ʊnbəlɛkt] F *fig. adj.* F clueless; ***von der Kultur*** ~ untouched by civilization

un·be·lehr·bar [ʊnbə'le:ɐba:ɐ] *adj.* stubborn; ***er ist*** ~ he just won't learn; **Un·be'lehr·bar·keit** *f* (-; *no pl.*) stubbornness

un·be·lich·tet ['ʊnbəlɪçtət] *adj. phot.* unexposed

'un·be·liebt *adj.* unpopular (***bei*** *dat.* with); ***er ist sehr*** ~ *a.* not many people like him; **'Un·be·liebt·heit** *f* (-; *no pl.*) unpopularity

un·be·lohnt ['ʊnbəlo:nt] *adj.* unrewarded; ~ ***bleiben*** not to be rewarded

'un·be·mannt *adj.* **1.** unmanned; ✈ pilotless; **2.** F *hum.* without a man; husbandless

un·be·merkt ['ʊnbəmɛrkt] *adj. and adv.* unnoticed, unseen

'un·be·mit·telt *adj.* penniless; ***~e Bürger*** *etc.* citizens *etc.* without means; ***er ist nicht gerade*** ~ he's not exactly poor

'un·be·nom·men *adj.*: ***es bleibt Ihnen*** ~ ***zu*** *inf.* you are at liberty to *inf.*; ***dieses Privileg bleibt Ihnen*** ~ this is your undisputed right (*or* prerogative)

'un·be·nutz·bar *adj.* unusable; *contp.* useless; **'un·be·nutzt** *adj.* **1.** unoccupied; **2.** clean; ***es ist*** ~ *a.* nobody's used it

un·be·ob·ach·tet ['ʊnbəʔo:baxtət] *adj.* unobserved; ***wenn man sich ganz*** ~ ***fühlt*** when you feel you are completely alone

'un·be·quem *adj.* **1.** uncomfortable; **2.** inconvenient; irksome; **3.** awkward, embarrassing *questions etc.*; **'Un·be·quem·lich·keit** *f* (-; -en) **1.** *no pl.* uncomfortableness; **2.** *usu. pl.* inconvenience, trouble; **3.** *no pl.* awkwardness, embarrassing nature (*gen.* of *a question etc.*)

un·be're·chen·bar *adj.* incalculable; *a. fig.* unpredictable; **Un·be're·chen·bar·keit** *f* (-; *no pl.*) unpredictability

'un·be·rech·tigt *adj.* unauthorized; **'un·be·rech·tig·ter·wei·se** *adv.* without good reason; without permission

un·be·rück·sich·tigt [ʊnbə'rʏkzɪçtɪçt] *adj.* unconsidered, not taken into account; ~ ***lassen*** discount, disregard, make no allowance for; ~ ***bleiben*** not to be taken into account, be disregarded

un·be'ru·fen *int.* touch wood!

un·be·rührt ['ʊnbəry:ɐt] *adj.* a) untouched, b) unspoilt; ***~er Boden*** virgin soil; ***ein Stückchen ~e Natur*** a piece of unspoilt countryside; ***~es Mädchen*** virgin; ~ ***lassen*** leave *one's food etc.* untouched; *fig.* ***es ließ sie*** ~ it left her cold

un·be·scha·det [ʊnbə'ʃa:dət] *prp.* (*gen.*) irrespective of, notwithstanding (*s.th.*)

un·be·schä·digt ['ʊnbəʃɛ:dɪçt] *adj.* intact; undamaged

'un·be·schäf·tigt *adj.* a) idle, b) unemployed

'un·be·schei·den *adj.* immodest; extravagant; ***ich hätte e-e ~e Frage*** may I be so bold as to ask ...; **'Un·be·schei·den·heit** *f* (-; *no pl.*) immodesty; extravagance

un·be·schol·ten ['ʊnbəʃɔltən] *adj.* **1.** respectable; **2.** ⚖ ~ ***sein*** have a clean record; **'Un·be·schol·ten·heit** *f* (-; *no pl.*) **1.** good reputation (*or* name); **2.** ⚖ clean record

'un·be·schrankt *adj.*: ***~er Bahnübergang*** open crossing; *sign*: Crossing No Gates

'un·be·schränkt I. *adj.* unrestricted, full; *a.* ⚖ absolute *power etc.*; **II.** *adv.* without restrictions; ~ ***viel(e)*** ... unlimited (amounts *or* numbers of) ...

un·be·schreib·lich [ʊnbə'ʃraɪplɪç] **I.** *adj.* indescribable; ***es ist*** ~ *a.* I (just) can't describe it; **II.** *adv.* indescribably, ... beyond description

'un·be·schrie·ben *adj.* blank; *fig.* ***~es Blatt*** unknown quantity

un·be·schwert ['ʊnbəʃve:ɐt] *adj.* carefree; lighthearted; ~ ***von*** *dat.* free from, unencumbered by; **'Un·be·schwert·heit** *f* (-; *no pl.*) carefree nature; lightheartedness

un·be'se·hen *adv.* a) without seeing (*or* having seen) it, b) safely, c) without hesitation; just like that, without thinking twice; ***das glaube ich*** ~ I can believe that, *w.s.* I don't need any proof of that

'un·be·setzt *adj.* vacant; *a.* unoccupied, free *seat*; *thea.* uncast

'un·be·sie·delt *adj.* unsettled

un·be·sieg·bar [ʊnbə'zi:kba:ɐ] *adj.* invincible; **un·be·siegt** [ʊnbə'zi:kt] *adj.* undefeated

'un·be·son·nen *adj.* thoughtless; rash; *w.s. a.* impulsive; **'Un·be·son·nen·heit** *f* (-; *no pl.*) thoughtlessness; rashness; impulsiveness

'un·be·sorgt I. *adj.* unconcerned (***wegen*** *gen.* about); ***seien Sie*** ~ don't worry; **II.** *adv.* safely; **'Un·be·sorgt·heit** *f* (-; *no pl.*) unconcern, lack of concern

'un·be·spiel·bar *adj. sport*: unplayable *field etc.*; **'un·be·spielt** *adj.* blank, empty *cassette etc.*

'un·be·stän·dig *adj.* unsteady, unstable; *meteor.* changeable; ☤ unsettled *market*; **'Un·be·stän·dig·keit** *f* (-; *no pl.*) instability; *meteor.* changeableness; ☤ unsettledness

un·be·stä·tigt ['ʊnbeʃtɛ:tɪçt] *adj.* unconfirmed; ***~en Meldungen zufolge*** according to unconfirmed reports

'un·be·stech·lich *adj.* **1.** incorruptible; **2.** *fig.* unerring; ***sie ist in ihrem Urteil*** ~ she has an unerring judg(e)ment; **'Un·be·stech·lich·keit** *f* (-; *no pl.*) incorruptibility, integrity

'un·be·stimm·bar *adj.* indefinable; vague, indeterminate; **'un·be·stimmt** *adj.* **1.** vague *feeling, idea etc.*; **2.** uncertain, indefinite (*a. ling.*); ***auf ~e Zeit*** indefinitely; **'Un·be·stimmt·heit** *f* (-; *no pl.*) **1.** vagueness; **2.** uncertainty

un·be·streit·bar [ʊnbə'ʃtraɪtba:ɐ] *adj.* indisputable, unquestionable

un·be·strit·ten ['ʊnbəʃtrɪtən] **I.** *adj.* undisputed, uncontested; **II.** *adv.* indisputably, without doubt

un·be·tei·ligt ['ʊnbətaɪlɪçt] *adj.* **1.** indifferent, unconcerned; **2.** uninvolved; ***Unbeteiligter*** onlooker; ***an e-r Sache*** ~ ***sein*** not to be involved in s.th., ☤ have no interest in s.th.

'un·be·tont *adj.* unstressed

'un·be·trächt·lich *adj.* insignificant, negligible; ***nicht*** ~ quite considerable

un·beug·sam [ʊn'bɔʏkza:m] *fig. adj.* unbending *will, attitude etc.*; *w.s.* uncompromising; tough-minded; ***~er Wille*** *a.* iron will; **Un'beug·sam·keit** *f* (-; *no pl.*) unbending (*or* uncompromising) attitude; unbendingness

'un·be·wacht *adj.* unguarded (*a. fig.*)

'un·be·waff·net *adj.* unarmed

un·be·wäl·tigt ['ʊnbəvɛltɪçt] *adj.* unsurmounted *problem*; undigested *experience etc.*; ***die ~e Vergangenheit*** the past with which people are still coming (*or* trying to come) to terms; ***die Vergangenheit bleibt noch*** ~ people are still trying to (*or* we *etc.* still haven't) come to terms with the past

un·be·wan·dert ['ʊnbəvandɐt] *adj.* inexperienced (***in*** *dat.* in); ignorant (about); ***auf dem Gebiet bin ich*** ~ I'm not very well up in that area, I don't know anything (F the first thing) about that subject

'un·be·weg·lich *adj.* immobile; motionless; *fig.* rigid; → ***Gut*** 1; **'Un·be·weg·lich·keit** *f* (-; *no pl.*) immobility; motionlessness; *fig.* rigidness, rigidity

'un·be·wegt *adj.* expressionless *face etc.*; **'Un·be·wegt·heit** *f* (-; *no pl.*) expressionlessness; lack of expression

un·be·weibt ['ʊnbəvaɪpt] F *hum. adj.* without a woman; wifeless

'un·be·weis·bar *adj.* unprovable; ***es ist*** ~ *a.* it can't be proved; **'Un·be·weis·bar·keit** *f* (-; *no pl.*) unprovability; **'un·be·wie·sen** *adj.* unproven, *pred.* not proved

'un·be·wohn·bar *adj.* uninhabitable; **'Un·be·wohn·bar·keit** *f* (-; *no pl.*) uninhabitability; **'un·be·wohnt** *adj.* uninhabited; unoccupied, vacant *building etc.*

'un·be·wußt *adj.* unconscious (*gen.* of), involuntary, instinctive, mechanical; **'Un·be·wuß·te** *n*: *psych.* ***das*** ~ the unconscious (mind)

un·be'zahl·bar *adj.* unaffordable, far too expensive, beyond one's (*or* anyone's) reach; prohibitive *price etc.*; *fig.* invaluable, priceless (*a.* F); F worth its weight in gold; **'un·be·zahlt** *adj.* unpaid (*a. vacation*)

un·be·zähm·bar [ʊnbə'tsɛ:mba:ɐ] *fig. adj.* uncontrollable

un·be·zif·fert ['ʊnbətsɪfɐt] *adj.* ☤ uncosted

un·be·zwei·fel·bar [ʊnbə'tsvaɪfəlba:ɐ] *adj.* unquestionable

un·be·zwing·bar [ʊnbə'tsvɪŋba:ɐ], **un·be·zwing·lich** [ʊnbə'tsvɪŋlɪç] *adj.* invincible; impregnable *fortress etc.*; *fig.* uncontrollable *emotion etc.*

'un·bieg·sam *adj.* inflexible

Un·bil·den ['ʊnbɪldən] *pl.* rigo(u)rs; ***die*** ~ ***der Witterung*** the inclemency of the weather

'Un·bil·dung *f* (-; *no pl.*) lack of education

'un·bil·lig *adj.* unreasonable, unfair; ⚖ ***~e Härte*** undue hardship

'un·blu·tig I. *adj.* bloodless; ⚕ non-operative; **II.** *adv.* without bloodshed

un·bot·mä·ßig ['ʊnbo:tmɛ:sɪç] *adj.* insubordinate; *w.s.* rebellious, refractory; **'Un·bot·mä·ßig·keit** *f* (-; *no pl.*) insubordination

'un·brauch·bar *adj.* useless, of no use (to s.o.), unsuitable; ⚙ unserviceable; *a.* waste *material*; impracticable, unworkable *plan etc.*; ***für Hausarbeit*** *etc.* ~ ***sein*** be useless when it comes to housework *etc.*; **'Un·brauch·bar·keit** *f* (-; *no pl.*) uselessness; ⚙ unserviceability; impracticability *of a plan etc.*

'un·bü·ro,kra·tisch *adj.* unbureaucratic(ally *adv.*)

'un·christ·lich *adj.* unchristian

und [ʊnt] *cj.* and; **~?** well?; F **na ~?** F so (what)?; F **~ ob!** F you bet!; **~ so weiter(, ~ so fort)** and so on (and so forth); **~ ~ ~** I could go on and on; *er will es nicht* - **~ ich auch nicht** neither (*or* nor) do I, F me neither; *iro.* **ich ~ Tennisspielen?** me play tennis?; **du ~ fleißig?** you hard-working?; **~ wenn (auch)** even if; **... sagte er ~ lächelte** ... he said, smiling; **er fragte ~ fragte** he (just) kept on asking; **wir überlegten ~ überlegten** we racked our brains; **~ wenn du mich zehnmal fragst** however (*or* no matter how) many times you ask me

'Un·dank *m* (-[e]s; *no pl.*) ingratitude, ungratefulness; **~ ernten** get no (*or* very little) thanks *for s.th.*; **'un·dank·bar** *adj.* a) ungrateful, b) thankless *task etc.*; **'Un·dank·bar·keit** *f* (-; *no pl.*) ingratitude, ungratefulness

'un·da,tiert *adj.* undated

un·de·fi·nier·bar [ʊndefi'niːɐbaːɐ] *adj.* indefinable; **Un·de·fi'nier·bar·keit** *f* (-; *no pl.*) indefinability

'un·dehn·bar *adj.* inelastic

un·de·kli·nier·bar [ʊndekli'niːɐbaːɐ] *adj.* indeclinable

un·de·mo'kra·tisch *adj.* undemocratic(ally *adv.*)

un'denk·bar *adj.* unthinkable

un·denk·lich [ʊn'dɛŋklɪç] *adj.*: **seit ~en Zeiten** from (*or* since) time immemorial, ever since I can remember; *w.s.* for ages

'un·deut·lich *adj.* indistinct, not clear; vague; illegible *writing*; **'Un·deut·lich·keit** *f* (-; *no pl.*) indistinctness; vagueness; illegibility

Un·de·zi·me [ʊn'deːtsimə] *f* (-; -n) ♪ eleventh

'un·dicht *adj.* leaking; not tight; not waterproof, not watertight; not airtight; porous; **~ sein** *a.* be leaking; **~e Stelle** *a. fig. pol.* leak

'un·dif·fe·ren,ziert I. *adj.* (too) simple, simplistic; undiscriminating, indiscriminate; wholesale, sweeping *judg(e)ment, statement etc.*; **II.** *adv.* simplistically; indiscriminately; wholesale; **~ urteilen** make a sweeping judg(e)ment; **'Un·dif·fe·ren,ziert·heit** *f* (-; *no pl.*) simplistic nature (*or* attitude, way of thinking); lack of discrimination

Un·ding ['ʊndɪŋ] *n* (-[e]s; *no pl.*) absurdity; **es ist (wäre) ein ~ zu** *inf. a.* it's (it would be) absurd to *inf.*; **das ist doch wirklich ein ~** that really is absurd (*or* ridiculous)

'un·di·plo,ma·tisch *adj.* undiplomatic(ally *adv.*), tactless

'un·dis·zi·pli,niert *adj.* undisciplined; **'Un·dis·zi·pli,niert·heit** *f* (-; *no pl.*) lack of discipline

'un·duld·sam *adj.* intolerant; **'Un·duld·sam·keit** *f* (-; *no pl.*) intolerance

un·durch·dring·lich [ʊndʊrç'drɪŋlɪç] *adj.* **1.** impenetrable; **2.** inscrutable *expression*; **Un·durch'dring·lich·keit** *f* (-; *no pl.*) **1.** impenetrability; **2.** inscrutability

un·durch'führ·bar *adj.* impracticable, unworkable; **Un·durch'führ·bar·keit** *f* (-; *no pl.*) impracticability

'un·durch·läs·sig *adj.* impervious (**für** *acc.* to); impermeable (to); **'Un·durch·läs·sig·keit** *f* (-; *no pl.*) imperviousness; impermeability

un·durch'schau·bar *adj.* inscrutable *expression, smile, intentions etc.*; *w.s.* mysterious, arcane; obscure; **Un·durch'schau·bar·keit** *f* (-; *no pl.*) inscrutability; mysteriousness, mysterious nature (*gen.* of)

'un·durch·sich·tig *adj.* opaque; *fig.* impenetrable; obscure *dealings, plans etc.*; **'Un·durch·sich·tig·keit** *f* (-; *no pl.*) opacity; *fig.* impenetrability; obscurity

'un·eben *adj.* uneven; *a.* rough, bumpy *path etc.*; F *fig.* **nicht ~** not bad; **'Un·eben·heit** *f* (-; -en) **1.** *no pl.* unevenness; bumpiness; **2.** unevenness, uneven spot, F bump

'un·echt *adj.* **1.** not genuine; counterfeit, fake; imitation ..., artificial; *colo(u)rs*: fading, not fast; ℞ improper; **2.** *fig.* not genuine, false, insincere; *a.* artificial *smile etc.*

'un·edel *adj.* base *metals*

'un·ehe·lich *adj.* illegitimate *child*; unmarried *mother*; **'Un·ehe·lich·keit** *f* (-; *no pl.*) illegitimacy

'Un·eh·re *f* (-; *no pl.*) dishono(u)r; **j-m ~ machen** discredit (*or* disgrace) s.o., bring disgrace on s.o.; **'un·eh·ren·haft** *adj.* dishono(u)rable

'un·ehr·er·bie·tig *adj.* disrespectful, irreverent; **'Un·ehr·er·bie·tig·keit** *f* (-; *no pl.*) irreverence

'un·ehr·lich *adj.* a) dishonest, b) insincere; **auf ~e Weise** by dishonest means, dishonestly; **'Un·ehr·lich·keit** *f* (-; *no pl.*) a) dishonesty, b) insincerity

'un·ei·gen·nüt·zig *adj.* unselfish; **'Un·ei·gen·nüt·zig·keit** *f* (-; *no pl.*) unselfishness

'un·ei·gent·lich F *adv.* actually; if I'm *etc.* honest

un·ein·bring·lich [ʊnʔaɪn'brɪŋlɪç] *adj.*: ⚕ **~e Forderungen** uncollectibles

'un·ein·ge·schränkt *adj.* unrestricted, unlimited; absolute *trust etc.*; unqualified, unreserved *praise etc.*; all-out *support etc.*

'un·ein·ge·stan·den *adj.* unacknowledged

'un·ein·ge·weiht *adj.* uninitiated; **für Uneingeweihte** for the uninitiated

'un·ein·heit·lich *adj.* non-uniform, inconsistent; varied; varying; ⚕ irregular *prices etc.*; **'Un·ein·heit·lich·keit** *f* (-; *no pl.*) lack of uniformity, inconsistency; varied nature (*gen.* of); ⚕ irregularity

'un·ei·nig *adj.* divided, disunited; **(sich) ~ sein** be in disagreement, be at issue (**über** *acc.* about, on), be at variance; **ich bin mit mir selbst noch ~** I'm still undecided; **'Un·ei·nig·keit** *f* (-; *no pl.*) dividedness; disagreement; dissension

un·ein·nehm·bar [ʊnʔaɪn'neːmbaːɐ] *adj.* impregnable

un·eins ['ʊnʔaɪns] *adj.*: **~ sein → uneinig; mit sich selbst ~ sein** be at odds with o.s.

'un·ein·sich·tig *adj.* stubborn; **sie ist so ~** *a.* she just won't listen to reason, you can't reason with her; **'Un·ein·sich·tig·keit** *f* (-; *no pl.*) stubbornness, refusal to listen to reason

'un·emp·fäng·lich *adj.* unreceptive, impervious, insensible (*all* **für** *acc.* to); **'Un·emp·fäng·lich·keit** *f* (-; *no pl.*) unreceptiveness, imperviousness, insensibility (*all* **für** *acc.* to)

'un·emp·find·lich *adj.* insensitive (**gegen** *acc.*, **für** *acc.* to); inured (to); *fig.* indifferent (to); **'Un·emp·find·lich·keit** *f* (-; *no pl.*) insensitiveness (**gegen** *acc.*, **für** *acc.* to), lack of sensitivity (towards); *fig.* indifference (to[wards])

un'end·lich I. *adj. phys.*, ℞, ♪ infinite (*a. fig.*); ℞ **~e Größe** (*or* **Zahl**) infinite; **das Unendliche** infinity (*a.* ℞); **~er Kreislauf** recurring spiral; *phot.* **auf ~ einstellen** focus at infinity; **(bis) ins ~e** ad infinitum; **das geht ins ~e** it's never-ending; **II.** *adv.* infinitely; *fig.* exceedingly, F incredibly, F *pleased etc.* no end; **~ klein** infinitesimal; **~ lang** endless; **~ viel(e)** an infinite number (of), an infinite amount (of); *a.* F no end of ...; **~ viel Sorgen** *etc.* no end of trouble *etc.*; **er hat sich ~ bemüht** F he took no end of pains; **Un'end·lich·keit** *f* (-; *no pl.*) **1. die ~** infinity; **2.** endlessness, infinity; **3.** F **e-e ~ warten** wait for ages (F for an age and a half)

un·ent'behr·lich *adj.* indispensable (*dat. or* **für** *acc.* to); **Un·ent'behr·lich·keit** *f* (-; *no pl.*) indispensability

un·ent·deckt ['ʊnʔɛntdɛkt] *adj.* undiscovered

un·ent·gelt·lich [ʊnʔɛnt'gɛltlɪç] *adj. and adv.* free (of charge)

un·ent·rinn·bar [ʊnʔɛnt'rɪnbaːɐ] *adj.* inescapable, ineluctable; **das Schicksal** *etc.* **ist ~** *a.* there's no escaping fate *etc.*; **Un·ent'rinn·bar·keit** *f* (-; *no pl.*) inescapability

'un·ent·schie·den I. *adj.* undecided (*a. person*); open, unsettled *question etc.*; **~es Spiel** tie; **~es Rennen** dead heat, tie; **II.** *adv.*: **~ spielen** draw; **~ enden** end in a draw (*or* tie); **die Mannschaften haben sich (1:1) ~ getrennt** the game ended in a (1-1 [= one to one]) draw; **III. ≈** *n* (-s; -) *sport*: draw, tie; **'Un·ent·schie·den·heit** *f* (-; *no pl.*) undecidedness

'un·ent·schlos·sen *adj.* undecided, irresolute; **~ sein** *a.* waver, hesitate, vacillate; **'Un·ent·schlos·sen·heit** *f* (-; *no pl.*) a) vacillation, hesitation, b) indecision

un·ent'schuld·bar *adj.* inexcusable, unpardonable; **un·ent·schul·digt** ['ʊnʔɛntʃʊldɪçt] *adj.*: **~es Fehlen** unexcused absence; **~ fehlen** be absent without an excuse

un·ent·wegt [ʊnʔɛnt'veːkt] **I.** *adv.* a) untiringly, b) unswervingly, c) incessantly; **er redete ~** *a.* he wouldn't stop talking; **II.** *adj.* ceaseless, untiring; indefatigable; **~er Kämpfer für** *acc.* unswerving (*lit.* steadfast) champion of; **Un·ent'wegt·heit** *f* (-; *no pl.*) a) untiringness, b) unswervingness

un·ent·wirr·bar [ʊnʔɛnt'vɪrbaːɐ] *adj.* inextricable

un·er·bitt·lich [ʊnʔɛɐ'bɪtlɪç] *adj.* relentless (*a. battle*); unrelenting *hatred, enmity etc.*; unmerciful; inexorable *fate*; **Un·er'bitt·lich·keit** *f* (-; *no pl.*) relentlessness; unrelenting nature (*gen.* of); mercilessness; inexorability

'un·er·fah·ren *adj.* inexperienced (**in** *dat.* in), new (to); **'Un·er·fah·ren·heit** *f* inexperience, lack of experience

un·er·find·lich [ʊnʔɛɐ'fɪntlɪç] *adj.* inexplicable; **aus ~en Gründen** for some obscure reason; **es ist mir (völlig) ~** it's a (complete) mystery to me

un·er·forsch·lich [ʊnʔɛɐ'fɔrʃlɪç] *fig. adj.* unfathomable; **un·er·forscht** ['ʊnʔɛrfɔrʃt] *adj.* unexplored, *a. fig.* uncharted *territory*

'un·er·freu·lich *adj.* a) unpleasant, b) annoying; **so was Unerfreuliches!** *a.* what a nuisance; **ich habe e-e ~e Mit-**

teilung zu machen I've got some unpleasant news for you, I'm afraid
un·er·füll·bar [ʊnˀɛɐ'fʏlbaːɐ] *adj.* unrealizable; **un·er·füllt** ['ʊnˀɛɐfʏlt] *adj.* unfulfilled
'un·er·gie·big *adj.* a) unproductive (*a. fig.*); unprofitable, b) unhelpful *source of information etc.*, c) not worth one's while; ***es war ~ a.*** it didn't get us *etc.* any further; ***das Thema ist ~ a.*** the subject leads nowhere; **'Un·er·gie·big·keit** *f* (-; *no pl.*) unproductiveness; unprofitability; F dead-end nature (*gen.* of)
un·er·gründ·lich [ʊnˀɛɐ'grʏntlɪç] *adj.* unfathomable; *fig.* inscrutable
'un·er·heb·lich *adj.* a) insignificant, unimportant; slight, b) irrelevant; **'Un·er·heb·lich·keit** *f* (-; *no pl.*) a) insignificance, b) irrelevance
un·er·hört ['ʊnˀɛɐhøːɐt] *adj.* **1.** outrageous, scandalous; ***~!*** what a cheek!; **2.** F tremendous, incredible; ***sie hatte ein ~es Glück*** she was incredibly lucky; **3.** unheard-of, unprecedented; **4.** unanswered *prayer etc.*; unrequited *love*, *lover etc.*
un·er·kannt ['ʊnˀɛɐkant] **I.** *adj.* unrecognized, unidentified; **II.** *adv.*: ***~ entfliehen*** escape unrecognized (*or* without being recognized)
un·er'klär·lich *adj.* inexplicable; ***es ist ~ a.*** it's a (real) mystery
un·er·läß·lich [ʊnˀɛɐ'lɛslɪç] *adj.* essential, imperative
un·er·laubt ['ʊnˀɛɐlaʊpt] *adj.* unauthorized ..., prohibited, not allowed (*or* permitted); illegal, illicit; ***~e Handlung*** unlawful act, ⚖ tort; → ***Eingriff*** 2; **un·er·laub·ter·wei·se** ['ʊnˀɛɐlaʊptɐvaɪzə] *adv.* without permission
'un·er·le·digt *adj.* **1.** not (yet) dealt with; unfinished; unsettled *problem etc.*; **2.** ☤ a) unpaid, b) outstanding
un·er·meß·lich [ʊnˀɛɐ'mɛslɪç] *adj.* immeasurable, immense, vast; ***~e Weite*** boundless spaces; **Un·er'meß·lich·keit** *f* (-; *no pl.*) immeasurableness, immensity, vastness
un·er·müd·lich [ʊnˀɛɐ'myːtlɪç] *adj.* untiring, indefatigable *person*; *a.* unflagging, unremitting *efforts etc.*
'un·ernst *adj.* not serious, frivolous; **'Un·ernst** *m* (-[e]s; *no pl.*) lack of seriousness, frivolity
'un·er·probt *adj.* untested
'un·er·quick·lich *adj.* unpleasant, unedifying
un·er'reich·bar *adj.* **1.** inaccessible; *a. fig.* out of (*s.o.'s*) reach, beyond *s.o.'s* reach; *fig. a.* unattainable; **2.** ***er war ~*** we *etc.* couldn't get hold of him; **un·er·reicht** [ʊnˀɛɐ'raɪçt] *fig. adj.* unequal(l)ed, unrival(l)ed, second to none; record *performance*
un·er·sätt·lich [ʊnˀɛɐ'zɛtlɪç] *adj.* insatiable (*a. fig.*), voracious; **Un·er'sätt·lich·keit** *f* (-; *no pl.*) insatiability, insatiable appetite (*both a. fig.*), voracity
un·er·schlos·sen ['ʊnˀɛɐʃlɔsən] *adj.* undeveloped *area etc.*; ☤ *a.* untapped *resources, market*
un·er·schöpf·lich [ʊnˀɛɐ'ʃœpflɪç] *adj.* inexhaustible; **Un·er'schöpf·lich·keit** *f* (-; *no pl.*) inexhaustibility; inexhaustible supply *etc.* (*gen.* of)
'un·er·schrocken *adj.* intrepid, undaunted; **'Un·er·schrocken·heit** *f* (-; *no pl.*) intrepidity, intrepid nature (*gen.* of)
un·er·schüt·ter·lich [ʊnˀɛɐ'ʃʏtɐlɪç] **I.** *adj.* unshak(e)able; unflappable; intrepid; ***s-e Ruhe ist ~*** he's imperturbable; **II.** *adv.*: ***~ konservativ*** *etc.* staunchly conservative *etc.*
un·er'schwing·lich **I.** *adj.* (far) too expensive, unaffordable, beyond one's (*or* anyone's) means; prohibitive *price etc.*; **II.** *adv.*: ***~ teuer*** prohibitively expensive
un·er·setz·lich [ʊnˀɛɐ'zɛtslɪç] *adj.* irreplaceable; *a.* irrecoverable *loss*, *a.* irreparable *damage*
un·er·sprieß·lich [ʊnˀɛɐ'ʃpriːslɪç] *adj.* **1.** unprofitable; fruitless; **2.** unpleasant
un·er'träg·lich *adj.* unbearable, intolerable, *formal*: insufferable (*all a. fig. person*); **Un·er'träg·lich·keit** *f* (-; *no pl.*) unbearableness
un·er·wähnt ['ʊnˀɛɐvɛːnt] *adj.* unmentioned; ***~ lassen*** *a.* fail to mention, make no mention of, pass *s.th.* over (in silence)
un·er·war·tet ['ʊnˀɛɐvartət] **I.** *adj.* unexpected; unforeseen; surprise *visitors, attack etc.*; ☤ ***~er Gewinn*** windfall profit; **II.** *adv.* unexpectedly; ***es kam völlig ~ a.*** it took us all (*or* everyone) by surprise
un·er·wi·dert ['ʊnˀɛɐviːdɐt] *adj.* unanswered *letter etc.*; unrequited *love*
'un·er·wünscht *adj.* undesirable, unwelcome; unwanted *child*; ***du bist hier ~*** you're not welcome around here; ***Rauchen ~*** thank you for not smoking; *Vertreterbesuche, Hunde etc.* ***~*** no ... please
'un·fä·hig *adj.* **1.** unable (**zu** *inf.* to *inf.*), incapable (of *ger.*); **2.** incompetent; ***~ zu*** *dat.* unqualified for *an office etc.*; **'Un·fä·hig·keit** *f* (-; *no pl.*) **1.** inability (**zu** *inf.* to *inf.*); **2.** incompetence
'un·fair *adj.* unfair; ***das war ~ a.*** that wasn't fair
Un·fall ['ʊnfal] *m* (-[e]s; Unfälle ['ʊnfɛlə]) accident; ***e-n ~ bauen*** cause (*or* have) an accident; ***bei ~ bitte ich zu verständigen*** in case of accident please inform; ***bei e-m ~ ums Leben kommen*** (***verletzt werden***) be killed (hurt *or* injured) in an accident; ***~arzt*** *m* casualty doctor (*or* officer); ***~chir·ur,gie*** *f* casualty surgery; ***~flucht*** *f* → ***Fahrerflucht***; ***~fol·gen*** *pl.* consequences of an (*or* the) accident; ***an den ~ sterben*** die as a result of the accident
'un·fall·frei **I.** *adj.* accident-free; **II.** *adv.* without an (*or* a single) accident
'Un·fall|ge·fahr *f* danger (*or* risk) of accidents, hazard; ***es besteht erhöhte ~*** there is a high risk of accidents (happening); ***~kli·nik*** *f*, ***~kran·ken·haus*** *n* casualty hospital; ***~me·di,zin*** *f* emergency-room medicine; ***~ren·te*** *f* accident benefit; ***~sta·ti,on*** *f* first-aid station; casualty ward; ***~stel·le*** *f* scene of the accident; ***~tod*** *m* accidental death, death by accident (*formal*: misadventure); ***~to·te*** *m, f* (-n; -n) accident victim; ***Zahl der ~n*** number of road deaths (*or* deaths on the road)
'un·fall·träch·tig *adj.* hazardous
'Un·fall|ver·hü·tung *f* accident prevention; ***~ver·letz·te*** *m, f* (-n; -n) accident casualty; ***~ver·let·zung*** *f* accident injury; ***~ver·si·che·rung*** *f* accident insurance; ***~wa·gen*** *m* **1.** ambulance; **2.** car damaged in an (*or* the) accident; ***~zeu·ge*** *m* witness of the (*or* an) accident; ***~zif·fer*** *f* number of accidents
un'faß·bar *adj.* a) unfathomable, b) incomprehensible; incredible; ***das ist für mich ~*** I just can't believe it
un'fehl·bar **I.** *adj.* infallible (*a. R.C.*); unerring; ***mit ~em Instinkt*** with an unerring instinct; **II.** *adv.* infallibly; for certain; inevitably; **Un'fehl·bar·keit** *f* (-; *no pl.*) infallibility; **Un'fehl·bar·keits·dog·ma** *n* doctrine of papal infallibility
'un·fein *adj.* indelicate *remark, behavio(u)r etc.*; ungentlemanlike, unladylike, *pred. a.* bad form, not nice; crude, crass; ***et. auf ~e Art ausdrücken*** express s.th. rather crudely; ***als ~ gelten*** be considered bad form
'un·fern *prp.* not far from (*gen. or* ***von*** *dat. s.th., a place*)
'un·fer·tig *adj.* unfinished (*a.* ☤), incomplete; ☤ semifinished *products*; *fig.* immature
Un·flat ['ʊnflaːt] *m* (-[e]s; *no pl.*) dirt, filth; **un·flä·tig** ['ʊnflɛːtɪç] *adj.* dirty, obscene
'un·flott F *adj.*: ***nicht ~*** F not bad at all, F natty *clothes etc.*
'un·folg·sam *adj.* disobedient; **'Un·folg·sam·keit** *f* (-; *no pl.*) disobedience
'un·for·ma,tiert *adj. computer*: unformatted
un·för·mig ['ʊnfœrmɪç] *adj.* a) misshapen, b) bulky
'un·förm·lich *adj.* informal; ***es ging ganz ~ zu*** it was quite an informal (*or* a casual) affair
'un·fran,kiert **I.** *adj.* unstamped; **II.** *adv. a.* without a stamp
'un·frei *adj.* **1.** *pol. etc.* not free, subjected; *w.s.* unliberated; **2.** restricted, *a. psych.* inhibited; **3.** ✉ unfranked
'un·frei·wil·lig **I.** *adj.* a) involuntary, b) compulsory, c) unintentional; ***~e Komik*** unintentional humo(u)r; F ***ein ~es Bad nehmen*** F take a ducking; **II.** *adv.* a) involuntarily, b) unintentionally, c) against one's will; ***et. ~ tun*** *a.* be forced to do s.th.
'un·freund·lich *adj.* unfriendly (*a. weather, atmosphere etc.*); unobliging; *fig.* cheerless *room etc.*; **'Un·freund·lich·keit** *f* (-; *no pl.*) unfriendliness, *w.s.* rudeness
'Un·frie·de(n) *m* discord; ***Unfrieden stiften*** sow discord
'un·fri,siert *adj.* **1.** unkempt; **2.** *fig.* F undoctored *report etc.*
'un·frucht·bar *adj.* **1.** infertile, barren; sterile; **2.** *fig.* fruitless *talk etc.*; unproductive *work etc.*; ***auf ~en Boden fallen*** fall on stony ground, ***bei j-m:*** be lost on s.o.; **'Un·frucht·bar·keit** *f* (-; *no pl.*) **1.** infertility, barrenness; sterility; **2.** *fig.* fruitlessness
Un·fug ['ʊnfuːk] *m* (-[e]s; *no pl.*) mischief; nonsense; ***~ treiben*** get (*or* be) up to mischief (*or* no good); ***~ treiben mit*** *dat.* fool around with
un'fühl·bar *adj.* imperceptible
Un·gar ['ʊŋgar] *m* (-n; -n), **Un·ga·rin** ['ʊŋgarɪn] *f* (-; -nen), **un·ga·risch** ['ʊŋgarɪʃ] *adj.*, **'Un·ga·risch** *n* (-en) *ling.* Hungarian
'un·gast·lich *adj.* inhospitable; **'Un·gast·lich·keit** *f* (-; *no pl.*) inhospitableness, inhospitable nature (*gen.* of)
'un·ge·ach·tet *prp.* (*gen.*) regardless of, irrespective of, notwithstanding (*s.th.*); despite
un·ge·ahn·det [ʊngəˈˀaːndət] **I.** *adj.* unpunished; **II.** *adv. a.* with impunity
un·ge·ahnt [ʊngəˈˀaːnt] *adj.* undreamt-of; unexpected

un·ge·bär·dig ['ʊngəbɛːɐrdɪç] *adj.* unruly
un·ge·be·ten ['ʊngəbeːtən] *adj.* uninvited; **~ *kommen*** come unasked, come without being asked (*or* invited)
'un·ge·bil·det *adj.* uneducated
'un·ge·bo·ren *adj.* unborn
'un·ge·bräuch·lich *adj.* unusual; ***es ist ein ~es Wort*** *etc.* it's not a very common word *etc.*
'un·ge·braucht *adj.* unused; clean
'un·ge·bro·chen *fig. adj.* unbroken *will etc.*; unfailing *strength etc.*
un·ge·bühr·lich ['ʊngəbyːɐlɪç] **I.** *adj.* improper, unseemly; undue; **II.** *adv.* unduly; ***sich ~ benehmen*** misbehave, step out of line; **'Un·ge·bühr·lich·keit** *f* (-; *no pl.*) impropriety, unseemliness
'un·ge·bun·den *adj.* **1.** *typ.* unbound, in sheets; **2.** *fig.* unattached, F footloose and fancy-free; **3.** ***~e Rede*** prose; **'Un·ge·bun·den·heit** *f* (-; *no pl.*) freedom
'un·ge·dämpft *adj.* ♪, *phys.* undamped
'un·ge·deckt *adj.* **1.** a) ⚘ uncovered *check etc.*, b) *sport*: unmarked, c) unprotected, exposed; **2.** ***der Tisch ist noch ~*** the table hasn't been laid yet
'un·ge·druckt *adj.* unprinted
'Un·ge·duld *f* (-; *no pl.*) impatience; ***mit ~*** impatiently; ***voller ~*** terribly impatiently; **'un·ge·dul·dig** *adj.* impatient
'un·ge·eig·net *adj.* unsuited (***zu*** *dat.* for), unsuitable (for); *a.* unqualified (for); ***ein ~er Moment*** an inopportune (*or* the wrong) moment; ***sie ist denkbar ~*** she couldn't be less suited
un·ge·fähr ['ʊngəfɛːɐ] **I.** *adj.* approximate; rough; **II.** *adv.* about, approximately, around; more or less; ***~ um elf*** around eleven; ***~ bei der Post*** about where the post office is; F ***so ~*** something like that; ***wo ~?*** whereabouts?, roughly where?; ***wenn ich ~ wüßte, was er will*** if I had some idea of what he wants; ***~ wie ...*** more or less like ..., much like ...; ***nicht von ~*** not without reason, not for nothing; (***wie***) ***von ~*** (as if) by chance
'un·ge·fähr·det **I.** *adj.* safe; out of danger; **II.** *adv.* without danger; out of harm's way
'un·ge·fähr·lich *adj.* harmless, not dangerous; innocuous; ***es ist nicht ganz ~*** it's a bit risky, there's a slight risk involved
'un·ge·fäl·lig *adj.* unobliging; **'Un·ge·fäl·lig·keit** *f* (-; *no pl.*) unobligingness
'un·ge·färbt *adj.* **1.** undyed, not dyed; raw *silk*; **2.** *fig.* undistorted, unadulterated *report etc.*
'un·ge·fe·stigt *adj.* unmo(u)lded *character etc.*, (still) developing *or* maturing
'un·ge·fragt **I.** *adj.* unasked; **II.** *adv. a.* without being asked
un·ge·früh·stückt ['ʊngəfryːʃtʏkt] F *adj.* on an empty stomach, without any breakfast
'un·ge·fü·gig *adj.* refractory
'un·ge·hal·ten *adj.* annoyed (***über*** *acc.* at), indignant (at); **'Un·ge·hal·ten·heit** *f* (-; *no pl.*) annoyance; indignance
un·ge·hei·ßen ['ʊngəhaɪsən] *adj.* unbidden, of one's own accord
'un·ge·heizt *adj.* unheated
'un·ge·hemmt **I.** *adj.* uninhibited; unchecked; **II.** *adv.* freely, without restraint; unchecked
un·ge·heu·chelt ['ʊngəhɔʏçəlt] *adj.* unfeigned, sincere
un·ge·heu·er ['ʊngəhɔʏɐ] **I.** *adj.* enormous, immense; F tremendous, terrific; dreadful, F incredible *pains, racket etc.*; ***ungeheurer Fehler*** colossal mistake; **II.** *adv.* enormously *etc.*; → ***I; sich ~ freuen*** be incredibly pleased, F be over the moon (***über*** *acc.* about); ***es ist ~ wichtig*** it's of the utmost importance, it's tremendously important
'Un·ge·heu·er *n* (-s; -) monster (*a. fig.*)
un·ge·heu·er·lich [ʊngə'hɔʏɐlɪç] *adj.* monstrous; outrageous; **Un·ge'heu·er·lich·keit** *f* (; -en) **1.** *no pl.* monstrousness; **2.** atrocity
un·ge·hin·dert ['ʊngəhɪndɐt] *adj.* unhindered; unchecked
un·ge·ho·belt ['ʊngəhoːbəlt] *adj.* **1.** ⚙ not planed; **2.** *fig.* uncouth; clumsy; **'Un·ge·ho·belt·heit** *f* (-; *no pl.*) uncouthness
'un·ge·hö·rig *adj.* a) improper, unseemly, b) impertinent; **'Un·ge·hö·rig·keit** *f* (-; *no pl.*) impertinence; ***es ist*** (***einfach***) ***e-e ~ zu*** *inf.* it's (sheer) bad manners to *inf.*
'un·ge·hor·sam *adj.* disobedient (***gegenüber*** *dat.* to); **'Un·ge·hor·sam** *m* (-s; *no pl.*) disobedience
un·ge·hört ['ʊngəhøːɐt] *adj.* unheard; ***~ verhallen*** remain unheard, *fig. request etc.*: go unheard
'Un·geist *m* (-[e]s; *no pl.*) evil spirit; evil (*or* pernicious) zeitgeist
un·ge·kämmt ['ʊngəkɛmt] *adj.* uncombed
un·ge·klärt ['ʊngəklɛːɐt] *adj.* **1.** unsettled, (still) open; unsolved *problem etc.*; **2.** ***~e Abwässer*** untreated (*or* raw) sewage
'un·ge·kocht *adj.* uncooked, raw; unboiled
un·ge·kün·digt ['ʊngəkʏndɪçt] *adj.*: ***in ~er Stellung*** in regular employment without notice being given
'un·ge·kün·stelt *adj.* unaffected, natural
un·ge·kürzt ['ʊngəkʏrtst] *adj.* unabridged *text etc.*; uncut *film*; ***~e Fassung*** *film*: long version
'un·ge·la·den *adj.* **1.** uninvited *guest*; **2.** unloaded *gun etc.*; **3.** empty *battery etc.*
'un·ge·le·gen *adj.* inconvenient, inopportune; ***das kommt mir sehr ~*** that doesn't suit me at all, *a.* that's come at an awkward time (for me); ***komme ich ~?*** am I disturbing you?
'Un·ge·le·gen·hei·ten *pl.*: ***j-m ~ machen*** put s.o. out, inconvenience s.o.
'un·ge·leh·rig *adj.* unteachable
un·ge·lenk ['ʊngəlɛŋk] *adj.*, **'un·ge·len·kig** *adj.* clumsy, awkward; stiff
'un·ge·lernt *adj.* unskilled *work, worker*
un·ge·liebt ['ʊngəliːpt] *adj.* unloved
'un·ge·lo·gen *adv.*: ***ich habe ~ 20 Seiten geschafft*** I literally (*or* honestly) managed 20 pages; I managed 20 pages, and I'm not exaggerating (F kidding)
Un·ge·mach ['ʊngəmaːx] *obs. n* (-[e]s; *no pl.*) adversity, hardship
'un·ge·macht *adj.* unmade *bed*
'un·ge·mein **I.** *adj.* enormous, great; **II.** *adv.* tremendously, extremely; ***~ viel***(***e***) a tremendous (*or* an enormous) amount *or* number (of)
un·ge·min·dert ['ʊngəmɪndɐt] *adj.* undiminished
'un·ge·müt·lich *adj.* uncomfortable (*a. fig. situation, feeling etc.*); cheerless *room etc.*; F *fig.* ***~ werden*** get (*or* turn) nasty; F ***es wird langsam ~*** things are turning a bit nasty; **'Un·ge·müt·lich·keit** *f* (-; *no pl.*) uncomfortableness; cheerlessness; ***~ der Atmosphäre*** *etc.* uncomfortable atmosphere *etc.*
'un·ge·nannt *adj.* unnamed; anonymous, nameless *author etc.*
'un·ge·nau *adj.* inexact; imprecise; inaccurate; vague; **'Un·ge·nau·ig·keit** *f* (-; -en) **1.** *no pl.* inexactness; imprecision; inaccuracy; vagueness; **2.** inaccuracy; ***ihr sind einige ~en unterlaufen*** she got a few things slightly wrong
un·ge·niert ['ʊnʒeniːɐt] **I.** *adj.* uninhibited; **II.** *adv.* uninhibitedly; openly; ***völlig ~*** with such aplomb; ***sich ~ hinwegsetzen über*** *acc.* blithely ignore; **'Un·ge·niert·heit** *f* (-; *no pl.*) (complete) lack of inhibition
'un·ge·nieß·bar *adj.* **1.** *gastr.* inedible; undrinkable; **2.** F *fig.* a) impossible (to read *etc.*), b) unbearable, hard to take; ***er ist für mich ~*** *a.* I can't stomach him
'un·ge·normt *adj.* non-standard
'Un·ge·nü·gen *n* (-s; *no pl.*) inadequacy; **'un·ge·nü·gend** *adj.* a) insufficient, not enough, b) inadequate; *ped.* unsatisfactory
un·ge·nutzt ['ʊngənʊtst], **un·ge·nützt** ['ʊngənʏtst] *adj.* unused; unexploited *resources etc.*; dead *capital*; ***e-e Gelegenheit ~ lassen*** let an opportunity slip, pass up an opportunity
'un·ge·ord·net *adj.* a) unsorted, not yet sorted out, b) disordered, disorderly
un·ge·pfla·stert ['ʊngəpflastɐt] *adj.* unpaved
'un·ge·pflegt *adj.* a) neglected, b) untidy, scruffy; **'Un·ge·pflegt·heit** *f* (-; *no pl.*) a) neglected state, b) untidiness, scruffiness
un·ge·prüft ['ʊngəpryːft] *adj.* unchecked
un·ge·puf·fert ['ʊngəpʊfɐt] *adj. computer*: unbuffered
'un·ge·ra·de *adj.* odd *number*
'un·ge·ra·ten *adj.* wayward *child*
un·ge·rech·net ['ʊngərɛçnət] *adj.* not counting ...
'un·ge·recht *adj.* unjust (***gegen*** *acc.* towards), unfair (to[wards]); **'un·ge·rech·ter·wei·se** *adv.* unjustly
'un·ge·recht·fer·tigt *adj.* unjustified, unwarranted; ⚖ ***~e Bereicherung*** unjust enrichment
'Un·ge·rech·tig·keit *f* (-; -en) **1.** *no pl.* injustice (***gegen*** *acc.* to); **2.** ***soziale ~en*** social injustice(s)
'un·ge·re·gelt *adj.* unregulated; irregular (*a. life*); disorderly
un·ge·reimt ['ʊngəraɪmt] *adj.* unrhymed; *fig.* inconsistent, absurd; ***~es Zeug reden*** talk (a lot of) nonsense; **'Un·ge·reimt·heit** *f* (-; -en) inconsistency; *pl. a.* contradictions; ***es ist voller ~en*** *a.* it's completely incongruous
'un·gern *adv.* unwillingly, grudgingly; reluctantly; ***er tut es*** (***äußerst***) ***~*** *a.* he doesn't like to do it (at all); *machst du's also? - ~* I'm not keen(, but I suppose I'll have to)
'un·ge·rührt *fig. adj.* unmoved (***von*** *dat.* by), impassive; indifferent *expression etc.*
un·ge·rupft ['ʊngərʊpft] *adj.*: *fig.* ***~ davonkommen*** (*or* ***bleiben***) get off lightly (*or* scot-free); ***nicht ganz ~ davonkommen*** (*or* ***bleiben***) leave a few hairs behind, not to get away unscathed
'un·ge·sagt *adj.* unsaid
'un·ge·sal·zen *adj.* unsalted
'un·ge·sät·tigt *adj.* ⚗ unsaturated; ***mehrfach ~*** polyunsaturated; ***mehrfach ~e Fettsäuren*** *a.* polyunsaturates

un·ge·säu·ert ['ʊngəzɔʏɐt] *adj.* unleavened *bread*

un·ge·schält ['ʊngəʃɛ:lt] *adj.* unpeeled *apple etc.*; unpolished *rice*

'un·ge·sche·hen *adj.*: **~ *machen*** undo; ***das kann man nicht ~ machen*** it can't be undone

'Un·ge·schick *n* (-[e]s; *no pl.*), **'Un·ge·schick·lich·keit** *f* (-; *no pl.*) ineptitude; clumsiness; **'un·ge·schickt** *adj.* clumsy (*a. fig.*), hamfisted; *fig.* inept; undiplomatic(ally *adv.*), tactless

un·ge·schlacht ['ʊngəʃlaxt] *adj.* **1.** ungainly, hulking *figure*; massive *hands etc.*; **2.** clumsy, awkward; **3.** uncouth, rough

'un·ge·schla·gen *adj.* undefeated, unbeaten

'un·ge·schlif·fen *adj.* **1.** unpolished; uncut, rough *stone etc.*; **2.** *fig.* unpolished, uncouth; **'Un·ge·schlif·fen·heit** *fig. f* (-; *no pl.*) lack of polish; unpolished manner, uncouthness

un·ge·schmä·lert ['ʊngəʃmɛ:lɐt] *adj.* undiminished

un·ge·schminkt ['ʊngəʃmɪŋkt] **I.** *adj.* **1.** without makeup; **~ *sein*** *a.* not to be made up; **2.** *fig.* unvarnished, unadorned, plain *truth*; ***die ~en Tatsachen*** the bare facts; **II.** *adv.*: **~ *ausgedrückt*** in crude terms, to put it crudely

un·ge·schönt ['ʊngəʃø:nt] *adj.* unprettified

'un·ge·scho·ren *adj.* **1.** unshorn; **2.** *fig.* **~ *davonkommen*** (*or* ***bleiben***) get off lightly (*or* scot-free); ***j-n ~ lassen*** leave s.o. in peace, spare s.o.

'un·ge·schrie·ben *adj.*: ***~es Gesetz*** unwritten law

un·ge·schult ['ʊngəʃu:lt] *adj.* untrained (*a. ear etc.*)

'un·ge·schützt *adj.* unprotected; exposed

'un·ge·se·hen *adj.* unseen, unnoticed, without anybody noticing

'un·ge·sel·lig *adj.* unsociable

'un·ge·setz·lich *adj.* illegal, unlawful, illicit; ***für ~ erklären*** declare illegal (*or* unlawful), outlaw

'un·ge·sit·tet *adj.* uncivilized; bad-mannered

un·ge·stalt ['ʊngəʃtalt] *adj.* misshapen

un·ge·stillt ['ʊngəʃtɪlt] *adj.* **1.** unsatisfied *curiosity etc.*; **2.** unappeased, unsatisfied *hunger*; unquenched *thirst*

'un·ge·stört *adj.* a) undisturbed; uninterrupted *proceedings etc.*, b) peaceful *place etc.*, c) peaceful, *adv. a.* in peace; **'Un·ge·stört·heit** *f* (-; *no pl.*) peace and quiet

un·ge·straft ['ʊngəʃtra:ft] **I.** *adj.* unpunished; **~ *davonkommen*** go unpunished; **II.** *adv.* unpunished, with impunity

un·ge·stüm ['ʊngəʃty:m] *adj.* impetuous; vehement; **'Un·ge·stüm** *n* (-s; *no pl.*) impetuosity; vehemence

un·ge·sühnt ['ʊngəzy:nt] *adj.* unpunished, unavenged

'un·ge·sund *adj.* unhealthy; *fig. a.* unwholesome; ***Rauchen ist ~*** *a.* smoking is bad for you (*or* your health)

un·ge·süßt ['ʊngəzy:st] *adj.* unsweetened

'un·ge·tan *adj.*: ***et. ~ lassen*** leave s.th. undone

'un·ge·teilt *adj.* **1.** undivided, whole; **2.** *fig.* undivided *attention etc.*; unanimous *approval*

un·ge·trübt ['ʊngətry:pt] *adj.* **1.** unclouded, clear; **2.** *fig.* perfect, unspoilt; ***~e Freude*** unalloyed joy (*or* happiness)

Un·ge·tüm ['ʊngəty:m] *n* (-s; -e) monster (*a. fig.*)

'un·ge·übt *adj.* untrained, unskilled; **'Un·ge·übt·heit** *f* (-; *no pl.*) lack of training

'un·ge·wandt *adj.* clumsy; inept

'un·ge·wa·schen *adj.* unwashed

'un·ge·wiß *adj.* uncertain; undecided; ***es ist noch ~, ob*** (***wie, wann*** *etc.*) it's still uncertain (as to) whether (how, when *etc.*); ***j-n im ungewissen lassen*** not to let s.o. know, keep s.o. guessing; ***Sprung ins Ungewisse*** leap in the dark; **'Un·ge·wiß·heit** *f* (-; *no pl.*) uncertainty

'un·ge·wöhn·lich *adj.* unusual; exceptional, remarkable

'un·ge·wohnt *adj.* strange *surroundings etc.*; new (***für*** *acc.* to); unusual; ***das ist für mich ganz ~*** *a.* I'm not used to it at all

'un·ge·wollt *adj.* a) unintentional; unintended *effect etc.*, b) involuntary, c) unwanted *pregnancy*

'un·ge·würzt *adj.* unseasoned

un·ge·zählt ['ʊngətsɛ:lt] *adj.* **1.** countless, innumerable; **2.** uncounted

un·ge·zähmt ['ʊngətsɛ:mt] *adj.* **1.** untamed, wild; **2.** *fig.* unbridled *passion*

Un·ge·zie·fer ['ʊngətsi:fɐ] *n* (-s; *no pl.*) vermin (*a. fig.*); **~be·kämp·fung** *f* vermin control

'un·ge·zie·mend *adj.* improper, unseemly

'un·ge·ziert *adj.* unaffected; **'Un·ge·ziert·heit** *f* (-; *no pl.*) unaffectedness

'un·ge·zo·gen *adj.* naughty; cheeky; **'Un·ge·zo·gen·heit** *f* (-; *no pl.*) naughtiness; cheekiness, cheek

un·ge·zü·gelt ['ʊngətsy:gəlt] *fig. adj.* unbridled *passion etc.*; ***~es Temperament*** volatile temper; ***~er Lebensstil*** freewheeling lifestyle

'un·ge·zwun·gen **I.** *adj.* unconstrained, casual; **II.** *adv.* casually, without constraint; **'Un·ge·zwun·gen·heit** *f* (-; *no pl.*) lack of constraint; *a.* casual atmosphere; naturalness

'Un·glau·be *m* (-ns; *no pl.*) disbelief; *eccl.* lack of faith, unbelief; **'un·glaub·haft** *adj.* implausible, unconvincing; *w.s.* unrealistic; **'un·gläu·big** **I.** *adj.* incredulous (*a. look, smile etc.*), *a. eccl.* unbelieving; **II.** *adv.* incredulously; *look etc. at s.o.* in disbelief; **~ *lächeln*** (***schauen*** *etc.*) *a.* give an incredulous smile (look *etc.*); **un'glaub·lich** *adj.* incredible (*a. fig.*), unbelievable; **'un·glaub·wür·dig** *adj.* implausible *statement etc.*; unreliable, untrustworthy *person*; *pol. etc.* not credible; **'Un·glaub·wür·dig·keit** *f* (-; *no pl.*) implausibility; unreliability, untrustworthiness; lack of credibility

'un·gleich **I.** *adj.* a) dissimilar, b) unequal *opportunities etc.*; odd *shoes, gloves etc.*; ***von ~er Länge*** *etc.* of varying length *etc.*; ***~es Paar*** odd pair (*fig.* match); **II.** *adv. with comparative*: far, much, incomparably *better etc.*

'un·gleich·för·mig *adj.* variable; asymmetrical

'Un·gleich·ge·wicht *n* (-[e]s; *no pl.*) (state of) imbalance

'Un·gleich·heit *f* (-; -en) a) dissimilarity, b) inequality *of opportunities etc.*

'un·gleich·mä·ßig *adj.* a) irregular; unsteady *development etc.*, b) uneven *distribution etc.*, c) erratic *handwriting*; **'Un·gleich·mä·ßig·keit** *f* (-; *no pl.*) irregularity; unsteadiness; unevenness; erratic nature (*gen.* of)

Un·glück ['ʊnglʏk] *n* (-[e]s; -e) **1.** accident; *mot.*, ✈ *etc. a.* disaster; *fig.* mishap; ***schweres ~*** serious accident, *w.s.* disaster; **2.** *no pl.* misfortune; bad luck; ***es ist kein ~, daß*** it's no tragedy that; ***in sein ~ rennen, sich ins ~ stürzen*** rush headlong into disaster; ***j-n ins ~ stürzen*** bring disaster (up)on s.o.; ***zu allem ~, um das ~ vollzumachen*** to crown it all; ***ein ~ kommt selten allein*** it never rains but it pours; **3.** *no pl.* distress, misery; **'un·glück·lich** **I.** *adj.* **1.** unfortunate; *a.* unhappy *wording, coincidence etc.*; awkward, clumsy *movement etc.*; unlucky; ***e-e ~e Art haben*** have an awkward manner, *w.s.* keep treading on people's toes; ***e-e ~e Hand haben*** be unlucky (***mit*** *dat.*, ***bei*** *dat.* with, when it comes to), ***mit*** *dat.* have an awkward way of dealing with *business partners etc.*; **2.** unhappy, sad; ***e-e ~e Figur abgeben*** cut a sorry figure; **3.** ***~e Liebe*** unrequited love; **II.** *adv.* **4.** **~ *enden*** (*or* ***ausgehen***) come to an unhappy end, turn out badly, end in disaster; **5.** *express o.s. etc.* in an unfortunate manner, awkwardly; **~ *stürzen*** fall awkwardly, have a bad fall; **~ *ausrutschen*** slip awkwardly; **6.** **~ *verliebt sein*** be crossed in love; **'un·glück·li·cher·wei·se** *adv.* unfortunately

'Un·glücks|bo·te *m* bringer of bad tidings; **~bot·schaft** *f* bad news (*sg.*)

'un·glück·se·lig *adj.* unfortunate; lamentable; ill-fated; star-crossed *lovers*

'Un·glücks|fall *m* misfortune; accident; **~ra·be** F *m* unlucky person; ***er ist ein ~*** *a.* some people are just born unlucky; **~se·rie** *f* spate (*or* series) of accidents; **~tag** *m* fateful (*or* black) day

Un·gna·de ['ʊngna:də] *f* (-; *no pl.*) disfavo(u)r; ***in ~ fallen*** fall from favo(u)r, ***bei*** *dat.*: fall out of favo(u)r with *s.o.*; ***in ~ sein*** be in the doghouse (***bei*** *dat.* with *s.o.*); **'un·gnä·dig** **I.** *adj.* ungracious, unkind; F grumpy; cross; **II.** *adv.*: ***et. ~ aufnehmen*** take s.th. in (*or* with) bad grace

'un·gram,ma·tisch *adj.* ungrammatical

'un·gül·tig *adj.* invalid; null and void; ⚖ inoperative; ☤ not legal tender; *sport*: disallowed *goal*; *pol.* spoilt *vote*; ***für ~ erklären*** declare null and void, annul, *sport*: chalk off *goal*; **'Un·gül·tig·keit** *f* (-; *no pl.*) invalidity; ⚖ *a.* nullity

Un·gunst ['ʊngʊnst] *f* (-; *no pl.*) disfavo(u)r, ill will; ***zu j-s ~en*** to s.o.'s disadvantage; ***das spricht zu s-n ~en*** that tells against him

'un·gün·stig *adj.* unfavo(u)rable *terms etc.*; inconvenient, inopportune *time etc.*; unflattering *hairdo, dress etc.*; unfortunate; ***bei ~em Wetter*** if the weather is bad (F doesn't play along); ***du stehst hier ~*** you haven't picked a very good place to stand

'un·gut *adj.* bad; ***~es Gefühl*** funny feeling; ***ich hatte ein ~es Gefühl dabei*** I had a funny feeling about it; ***nichts für ~!*** no offen|ce (*Am.* -se) meant, no hard feelings

'un·halt·bar *adj.* **1.** untenable *argument etc.*; intolerable *conditions etc.*; **2.** *sport*: unstoppable *shot*; **'Un·halt·bar·keit** *f* untenable nature (*gen.* of *an argument etc.*); intolerability *of conditions etc.*

'un·hand·lich *adj.* unwieldy; **'Un·hand·lich·keit** *f* (-; *no pl.*) unwieldiness
'un·har,mo·nisch *adj.* ♪ *and fig.* discordant, unharmonious; *fig.* clashing *colo(u)rs*
Un·heil ['ʊnhaɪl] *n* (-s; *no pl.*) disaster; harm; ~ **anrichten** wreak havoc
'un·heil·bar I. *adj.* incurable; terminal *cancer, patient*; *fig.* irreparable; **II.** *adv.*: ~ **krank sein** be suffering from an incurable disease, be incurably ill; ⚖ ~ **zerrüttet** *marriage*: irretrievably broken down; **'Un·heil·bar·keit** *f* (-; *no pl.*) incurability
'un·heil·brin·gend *adj.* fatal, baneful
'un·heil·voll *adj.* disastrous, baneful; sinister *look, mood etc.*
'un·heim·lich I. *adj.* **1.** uncanny, weird (*both a. fig.*); **2.** F *fig.* F terrific, fantastic; F incredible *pains, respect etc.*; **ich hatte e-e ~e Angst** I was incredibly scared; **II.** F *fig. adv.* F incredibly; ~ **viel(e)** a terrific amount (of); **sich ~ freuen** be incredibly pleased, F be over the moon
'un·hi,sto·risch *adj.* unhistoric
'un·höf·lich *adj.* impolite, rude; **'Un·höf·lich·keit** *f* (-; *no pl.*) impoliteness, rudeness
Un·hold ['ʊnhɔlt] *m* (-[e]s; -e [-də]) monster
'un·hör·bar *adj.* inaudible; **'Un·hör·bar·keit** *f* (-; *no pl.*) inaudibility
'un·hy,gie·nisch *adj.* unhygienic(ally *adv.*)
Uni ['ʊni] F *f* (-; -s) university
uni ['yni, y'ni:] *adj.* plain; ✝ self-colo(u)red, solid-colo(u)red
uni·form [uni'fɔrm] *adj.* uniform
Uni'form *f* (-; -en) uniform
uni·for·miert [unifɔr'mi:ɐt] *adj.* **1.** uniformed, in uniform; **2.** uniform; **Uni·for'miert·heit** *f* (-; *no pl.*) uniformity
Uni·kat [uni'ka:t] *n* (-[e]s; -e) unique specimen
Uni·kum ['u:nikʊm] *n* (-s; -ka) unique specimen (*a. iro.* **an** *dat.*, **von** *dat.* of); original, real character
uni·la·te·ral [unilate'ra:l] *adj.* unilateral
'un·in·tel·li,gent *adj.* unintelligent
'un·in·ter·es,sant *adj.* uninteresting, not interesting; of no interest (**für** *acc.* to); irrelevant (to); unattractive (for)
'un·in·ter·es,siert *adj.* uninterested (**an** *dat.* in); **'Un·in·ter·es,siert·heit** *f* (-; *no pl.*) lack of interest
Uni·on [u'nǐo:n] *f* (-; -en) union
Uni·sex·mo·de ['u:nizɛks-] *f* unisex fashions *pl.* (*or* look)
uni·so·no [uni'zo:no] *adv.* ♪ in unison; *fig. a.* unanimously
uni·ver·sal [univɛr'za:l] *adj.* universal
Uni·ver'sal... *in cpds.* ⚙ multipurpose; **~er·be** *m*, **~er·bin** *f* sole heir; **~ge,nie** *n* universal genius; F all-rounder
Uni·ver·sa·li·tät [univɛrzali'tɛ:t] *f* (-; *no pl.*) universality
Uni·ver'sal·mit·tel *n* ⚕ *and fig.* universal remedy, panacea, cure-all
uni·ver·sell [univɛr'zɛl] *adj.* universal; ⚙ all-purpose *appliance etc.*
Uni·ver·si·tät [univɛrzi'tɛ:t] *f* (-; -en) university; **die ~ besuchen** go to university; **an der ~** at university; **auf welcher ~ ist er?** which university does he go to?
Uni·ver·si'täts|ab·schluß *m* (university) degree; **~aus·bil·dung** *f* university education; **~ge·län·de** *n* university grounds *pl.*, campus; **~kli·nik** *f* university hospital; **~stadt** *f* university town; **~stu·di·um** *n* **1.** university degree; **2.** studies *pl.* at university
Uni·ver·sum [uni'vɛrzʊm] *n* (-s; *no pl.*) universe
'un·ka·me,rad·schaft·lich *adj.* unsporting; **'Un·ka·me,rad·schaft·lich·keit** *f* unsporting behavio(u)r (*or* attitude)
Un·ke ['ʊŋkə] *f* (-; -n) **1.** *zo.* toad; **2.** F *fig.* Jeremiah; **'un·ken** F (h) **I.** *v/i.* predict the worst, prophesy doom; **II.** *v/t.* gloomily predict *that ...*
'un·kennt·lich *adj.* a) unrecognizable, b) indecipherable *writing*; ~ **machen** a) disfigure, distort, b) deface *text etc.*, c) disguise; **'Un·kennt·lich·keit** *f*: **bis zur ~** beyond recognition, **entstellt**: *a.* completely disfigured
'Un·kennt·nis *f* (-; *no pl.*) ignorance; **in ~** *gen.* unaware of, not knowing (about) *s.th.*; **j-n in ~ lassen** keep s.o. in the dark (**über** *acc.* about); ~ **schützt nicht vor Strafe** ignorance of the law is no excuse
'Un·ken·ruf *m* gloomy prediction, prophecy of doom; **allen ~en zum Trotz** *a.* despite all predictions to the contrary
'un·klar *adj.* a) unclear, not clear, b) indistinct; *fig.* vague, obscure; uncertain; *a.* F woolly, fuzzy *concept etc.*; **mir ist (völlig) ~, wie (wo, was** *etc.*) I've (absolutely) no idea how (where, what *etc.*); **im ~en sein (lassen) über** *acc.* be (leave *s.o.*) in the dark about; **ich bin mir noch im ~en(, ob, wie** *etc.*) I haven't decided yet (whether, how *etc.*); ~ **zu erkennen (sehen) sein** be hard to make out (see); **'Un·klar·heit** *f* (-; *no pl.*) lack of clarity; vagueness, obscurity; uncertainty; **es herrscht ~ darüber, ob** it's not clear whether; **darüber herrscht absolute ~** it's completely unclear (as yet), *w.s.* it's a complete mystery
'un·klug *adj.* unwise, imprudent; **'Un·klug·heit** *f* (-; -en) **1.** *no pl.* imprudence; **2.** imprudent thing to do
'un·kol·le·gi,al *adj.* unsporting
'un·kom·pli,ziert *adj.* uncomplicated (*a. fig.*), simple; **'Un·kom·pli,ziert·heit** *f* (-; *no pl.*) uncomplicatedness, uncomplicated nature (*gen.* of)
'un·kon·trol,lier·bar *adj.* **1.** impossible to check; **2.** uncontrollable; **un·kon·trol·liert** ['ʊnkɔntrɔli:ɐt] **I.** *adj.* uncontrolled; **II.** *adv. a.* uncontrollably
'un·kon·ven·tio,nell *adj.* unconventional
'un·kon·zen,triert *adj.* lacking in concentration; unconcentrated; **er ist ~** he lacks concentration, he isn't concentrating, he hasn't got his mind on the job; **'Un·kon·zen,triert·heit** *f* (-; *no pl.*) lack of concentration
'un·kor,rekt *adj.* incorrect; not proper
'Un·ko·sten *pl.* costs, expenses, expense *sg.*; → **stürzen** 7; **~bei·trag** *m* contribution (towards expenses)
Un·kraut *n* (-[e]s; *no pl.*) weed(s *pl.*); *fig.* ~ **vergeht nicht** ill weeds grow apace; **~be·kämp·fung** *f*, **~ver·til·gung** *f* weed control; **~ver·til·gungs·mit·tel** *n* weed-killer, herbicide
'un·kri·tisch *adj.* uncritical
'un·kul·ti,viert *adj.* a) uncultivated, b) uncultured; **'Un·kul·ti,viert·heit** *f* (-; *no pl.*) (complete) lack of culture
'un·künd·bar *adj.* permanent *post*; irrevocable *agreement etc.*; ✝ irredeemable *loan*; **sie ist ~** F she can't be sacked; **'Un·künd·bar·keit** *f* (-; *no pl.*) permanence; irrevocability; irredeemability
'un·kun·dig *adj.* ignorant (*gen.* of); uninitiated; **e-r Sache ~ sein** have no knowledge of s.th.; **des Lesens ~** unable to read
'un·künst·le·risch *adj.* unartistic(ally *adv.*)
'un·längst *adv.* recently, not so long ago
un·lau·ter ['ʊnlaʊtɐ] *adj.* dishonest, dubious, F shady; ✝ **~er Wettbewerb** unfair competition
'un·leid·lich *adj.* **1.** unbearable, intolerable; **2.** bad-tempered, F grumpy; **in e-r ~en Stimmung sein** be in a foul mood
un'les·bar *adj.* unreadable
'un·le·ser·lich *adj.* illegible; **'Un·le·ser·lich·keit** *f* (-; *no pl.*) illegibility
un·leug·bar ['ʊnlɔʏkba:ɐ] *adj.* undeniable
'un·lieb *adj.*: **es war ihr nicht ~** it suited her fine
'un·lie·bens·wür·dig *adj.* unkind, unobliging
un·lieb·sam ['ʊnli:pza:m] *adj.* disagreeable, unpleasant
'un·li,niert *adj.* unruled
'Un·lo·gik *f* (-; *no pl.*) illogicality; **'un·lo·gisch** *adj.* illogical
un'lös·bar I. *adj.* **1.** insoluble *problem etc.*; **ein ~es Problem** *a.* a problem that can't be solved; **2.** inseparable; *marriage*: indissoluble; **II.** *adv.*: ~ **verflochten** (*or* **verbunden**) inextricably linked; **Un'lös·bar·keit** *f* (-; *no pl.*) **1.** insolubility; **2.** inseparability; indissolubility
un'lös·lich *adj.* ⚗ insoluble
Un·lust ['ʊnlʊst] *f* (-; *no pl.*) **1.** listlessness; **2.** reluctance; **~ge·fühl** *n* (great) reluctance; aversion (**gegenüber** *dat.* to)
'un·ma,nier·lich *adj.* ill-mannered
'un·männ·lich *adj.* effeminate
'Un·mas·se F *f* → **Unmenge**
'un·maß·geb·lich I. *adj.* irrelevant; insignificant; *w.s.* of no consequence; unauthoritative *opinion etc.*; **nach m-r ~en Meinung** in my humble opinion; **II.** *adv.*: ~ **an et. beteiligt sein** play an insignificant part in s.th.; **'Un·maß·geb·lich·keit** *f* (-; *no pl.*) irrelevance; insignificance
'un·mä·ßig I. *adj.* immoderate, excessive; intemperate; **II.** *adv.* excessively, to excess; ~ **stolz** *etc.* inordinately proud *etc.*; **'Un·mä·ßig·keit** *f* (-; *no pl.*) immoderation, extravagance; excess(es *pl.*); intemperance
'Un·men·ge *f* (-; -n) vast amount (*or* number) (**von** *dat.*, **an** *dat.* of)
'Un·mensch *m* (-en; -en) monster, brute; *hum.* **sei kein ~!** have a heart
'un·mensch·lich *adj.* inhuman, cruel; F tremendous; **'Un·mensch·lich·keit** *f* (-; -en) **1.** *no pl.* inhumanity, cruelty; **2.** act of inhumanity (*or* cruelty), inhumane (*or* cruel) act
un'merk·lich *adj.* imperceptible; **fast ~e Änderung** *a.* subtle change
un'meß·bar *adj.* unmeasurable
'un·me,tho·disch *adj.* unmethodical
'un·miß·ver·ständ·lich I. *adj.* unmistakable; unequivocal *answer etc.*; **II.** *adv.* unmistakably; plainly; **j-m ~ sagen, daß** make it perfectly clear (*or* bring it home) to s.o. that, tell s.o. in no uncertain terms that; ~ **zu verstehen geben, daß** make it perfectly clear that, make no bones about the fact that
'un·mit·tel·bar I. *adj.* immediate *impres-*

sions, vicinity etc.; *a.* direct *consequences etc.*; immediate, imminent *danger, task etc.*; ***in ~er Nähe*** *gen.* (*or* ***von*** *dat.*) in the immediate vicinity of, right next to; **II.** *adv.* a) right, directly, b) straight, immediately, directly; ***~ vor*** *dat.* a) right in front of, b) just before; ***~ bevorstehend*** imminent; ***~ darauf*** immediately afterwards, straight after; ***~ erleben*** experience (at) first hand; ***wir haben es ~ erlebt*** *a.* we were (right) there when it happened; '**Un·mit·tel·bar·keit** *f* (-; *no pl.*) immediacy; directness

'**un·mö,bliert** *adj.* unfurnished

'**un·mo,dern** *adj.* dated; ***~ werden*** go out of fashion, become dated; ***schnell ~ werden*** *a.* date quickly

'**un·mög·lich I.** *adj.* impossible (*a.* F *fig. person etc.*); F *fig. a.* dreadful *dress, manners etc.*; (***das ist***) ~ (that's) impossible, F no way; ***zu e-r ~en Stunde*** at an ungodly hour; ***Unmögliches verlangen*** ask the impossible; *fig.* ***sich ~ machen*** a) compromise o.s., b) make a fool of o.s.; **II.** *adv.* not possibly; *behave etc.* abysmally; ***er kleidet sich ~*** he wears the most dreadful clothes; ***das geht ~*** that's impossible (*or* out of the question); '**Un·mög·lich·keit** *f* (-; *no pl.*) impossibility (***zu*** *inf.* of *ger.*)

'**un·mo,ra·lisch** *adj.* immoral

'**un·mo·ti,viert I.** *adj.* unmotivated; unprompted *action etc.*; **II.** *adv.* for no (apparent) reason, F just like that

'**un·mün·dig** *adj.* **1.** under-age ..., *pred.* under age, not of age; **2.** *fig. politically etc.* immature; '**Un·mün·dig·keit** *f* (-; *no pl.*) **1.** ⚖ minority; **2.** *fig.* (mental) immaturity

'**un·mu·si,ka·lisch** *adj.* unmusical

'**un·mu·sisch** *adj.* unartistic

Un·mut ['ʊnmuːt] *m* (-[e]s; *no pl.*) displeasure; annoyance (***über*** *acc.* at); '**un·mu·tig** *adj.* annoyed (***über*** *acc.* at)

un·nach·ahm·lich [ʊnnaːx'ʔaːmlɪç] *adj.* inimitable; **Un·nach·ahm·lich·keit** *f* (-; *no pl.*) inimitability, inimitableness

'**un·nach·gie·big** *adj.* unyielding, intransigent, inflexible; uncompromising; *esp. pol.* hardline ...; ***~e Haltung*** hardline stance (*or* posture); '**Un·nach·gie·big·keit** *f* (-; *no pl.*) unyieldingness, intransigence, inflexibility; uncompromising attitude (*or* stance); *pol.* hardline approach (*or* stance)

'**un·nach·sich·tig** *adj.* strict, severe; '**Un·nach·sich·tig·keit** *f* (-; *no pl.*) strictness, severity

un·nah·bar [ʊn'naːbaːɐ] *adj.* unapproachable; *contp.* aloof; **Un'nah·bar·keit** *f* (-; *no pl.*) unapproachability; aloofness

'**un·na,tür·lich** *adj.* unnatural (*a. fig.*); affected; '**Un·na,tür·lich·keit** *f* (-; *no pl.*) unnaturalness; affectation

'**un·nor,mal** *adj.* not normal, abnormal

'**un·nö·tig** *adj.* unnecessary; superfluous; needless; (***es ist***) ***~ zu sagen, daß*** it goes without saying that; **un·nö·ti·ger·wei·se** ['ʊnnøːtɪgɐvaɪzə] *adv.* unnecessarily, needlessly

un·nütz ['ʊnnʏts] *adj.* useless; pointless; unnecessary; ***~es Gerede*** idle talk; ***~es Zeug*** F useless stuff

UNO ['uːno] *f* (-; *no pl.*) UN

'**un·öko,no·misch** *adj.* uneconomical

'**UNO-'Mit·glied** *n* member of the United Nations (*or* UN)

'**un·or·dent·lich** *adj.* disorderly; untidy; '**Un·or·dent·lich·keit** *f* (-; *no pl.*) disorderliness; untidiness; '**Un·ord·nung** *f* (-; *no pl.*) disorder(liness), *a* mess; ***in ~*** in a mess, in (complete) disarray; ***in ~ bringen*** mess up; ***dort herrscht e-e furchtbare ~*** the place is (in) a terrible mess

'**un·or,ga·nisch** *adj.* inorganic

un·or·ga·ni·siert ['ʊnʔɔrganiziːɐt] *adj.* disorganized; not organized

'**un·or·tho,dox** *adj.* unorthodox

'**UNO-'Voll·ver·samm·lung** *f* UN (*or* United Nations) assembly

'**un·paa·rig** *adj. biol.* unpaired, 📖 azygous

'**un·päd·ago·gisch** *adj.*: (***~ sein*** go) against educational principles

'**un·par·fü,miert** *adj.* non-scented, fragrance-free, aroma-free

'**un·par,tei·isch** *adj.* impartial, unbias(s)ed, disinterested; even-handed

'**Un·par,tei·ische** *m, f* (-n; -n) *sport:* referee

'**un·par,tei·lich** *adj.* impartial, unbias(s)ed; '**Un·par,tei·lich·keit** *f* (-; *no pl.*) impartiality

'**un·pas·send** *adj.* unsuitable; inappropriate, out of place; improper; untimely

un·päß·lich ['ʊnpɛslɪç] *adj.* indisposed, unwell; out of sorts; '**Un·päß·lich·keit** *f* (-; *no pl.*) indisposition

'**Un·per,son** *f* unperson, non-person; '**un·per,sön·lich** *adj.* impersonal (*a. ling.*)

'**un·pfänd·bar** *adj.* unseizable

'**un·po,li·tisch** *adj.* apolitical

'**un·po·pu,lär** *adj.* unpopular

'**un·prak·tisch** *adj.* impractical

un·prak·ti·zier·bar ['ʊnpraktitsiːɐbaːɐ] *adj.* unworkable

'**un·pro·ble,ma·tisch** *adj.* unproblematic(ally *adv.*)

'**un·pro·duk,tiv** *adj.* unproductive; ✝ non-productive

'**un·pro·por·tio,niert** *adj.* disproportionate; out of proportion

'**un·pünkt·lich** *adj.* **1.** late, unpunctual; ***er ist ~*** *a.* he's never on time; **2.** 🚂 *etc.* late; ***der Zug*** *etc.* ***ist ~*** *a.* the train *etc.* isn't (running) on time; '**Un·pünkt·lich·keit** *f* (-; *no pl.*) unpunctuality, lack of punctuality; being (*or* arriving *etc.*) late; ***diese ~!*** they *etc.* never turn up on time, they're *etc.* never on time

'**un·qua·li·fi,ziert** *adj.* unqualified

un·ra·siert ['ʊnraziːɐt] *adj.* unshaven

Un·rast ['ʊnrast] *f* (-; *no pl.*) restlessness

Un·rat ['ʊnraːt] *m* (-[e]s; *no pl.*) garbage, *Brit.* rubbish; *fig.* ***~ wittern*** smell a rat

'**un·ra·tio,nell** *adj.* inefficient

'**un·rat·sam** *adj.* inadvisable

'**un·rea,li·stisch** *adj.* unrealistic(ally *adv.*)

'**un·recht** *adj.* a) wrong, b) inopportune; ***~ haben → Unrecht; etwas Unrechtes tun*** do something wrong; ***zur ~en Zeit*** at the wrong moment (*or* time); '**Un·recht** *n* (-[e]s; *no pl.*) wrong; injustice; ***j-m ein ~ tun*** (***zufügen***) do s.o. an injustice, do s.o. wrong; ***im ~ sein, 2 haben*** be (in the) wrong, *a.* be mistaken; ***sich ins ~ setzen*** put o.s. in the wrong; ***er hat nicht so ganz 2*** there's something in what he says; ***j-m 2 geben*** disagree with s.o., *fig.* prove s.o. wrong; ***ihm ist ~ geschehen*** he has been wronged; ***zu ~*** wrongfully, wrongly, unjustly

'**un·recht·mä·ßig** *adj.* wrongful, unlawful; '**Un·recht·mä·ßig·keit** *f* (-; *no pl.*) wrongfulness, unlawfulness

'**un·red·lich** *adj.* dishonest, underhand ...; '**Un·red·lich·keit** *f* (-; *no pl.*) dishonesty

'**un·re,ell** *adj.* dubious; unfair; dishonest

'**un·re·gel·mä·ßig** *adj.* irregular (*a. pulse etc.*); *w.s.* erratic(ally *adv.*); uneven; '**Un·re·gel·mä·ßig·keit** *f* (-; -en) irregularity (*a. offence, fraud etc.*)

un·re·gier·bar ['ʊnregiːɐbaːɐ] *adj.* ungovernable; '**Un·re·gier·bar·keit** *f* (-; *no pl.*) ungovernability

'**un·reif** *adj.* unripe, *a.* green *fruit*; *fig.* immature; *fig.* ***~er Bursche*** callow youth; '**Un·rei·fe** *f* (-; *no pl.*) immaturity

'**un·rein** *adj.* impure (*a. fig. thoughts etc.*); dirty *linen, water etc., a.* polluted *water, air etc.*; bad *skin*; impure *sound*; ***ins ~e schreiben*** make a rough copy of; '**Un·rein·heit** *f* (-; -en) **1.** *no pl.* impurity; dirtiness; pollution, polluted state; **2.** ⚗ impurity; '**un·rein·lich** *adj.* unclean; '**Un·rein·lich·keit** *f* (-; *no pl.*) uncleanliness

'**un·ren,ta·bel** *adj.* unprofitable; '**Un·ren·ta·bi·li,tät** *f* (-; *no pl.*) unprofitableness

un·rett·bar [ʊn'rɛtbaːɐ] **I.** *adj.* irrecoverable; past recovery; **II.** *adv.*: ***~ verloren*** irretrievably lost; *person*: beyond help

'**un·rich·tig** *adj.* incorrect, wrong; erroneous; '**Un·rich·tig·keit** *f* (-; *no pl.*) incorrectness

Un·ruh ['ʊnruː] *f* (-; -en) balance spring

'**Un·ru·he** *f* (-; *no pl.*) **1.** a) restlessness, b) uneasiness, anxiety; ***in ~ versetzen*** worry, alarm; **2.** a) noise, b) commotion; *pol.* ***~n*** unrest, disturbances; ***~ stiften*** cause a disturbance; ***~herd*** *m* trouble spot; ***~stif·ter*** *m* troublemaker

'**un·ru·hig** *adj.* a) restless (*a. fig. pattern etc.*), b) irregular *pulse, breathing etc.*, uneven; broken, fitful *sleep*, c) rough, choppy *seas*, d) noisy, e) *fig.* uneasy (***wegen*** *gen.* about); anxious, worried; ***~e Zeiten*** troubled times

'**un·rühm·lich** *adj.* inglorious

'**un·rund** *adv.*: ⚙ ***~ laufen*** run untrue

uns [ʊns] *pers. pron.* (*dat. of wir*) (to) us; *refl.* (to) ourselves, *after prp.*: us; ***ein Freund von ~*** a friend of ours; ***unter ~ gesagt*** between you and me; ***wir sehen ~ nie*** we never see each other; ***wir blickten hinter ~*** we looked behind us, we looked back

'**un·sach·ge·mäß** *adj.* improper, inexpert *treatment etc.*

'**un·sach·lich** *adj.* unobjective, subjective; irrelevant; ***wir wollen nicht ~ werden*** let's try and stick to the facts; '**Un·sach·lich·keit** *f* (-; *no pl.*) lack of objectivity

un·sag·bar [ʊn'zaːkbaːɐ], **un·säg·lich** [ʊn'zɛːklɪç] **I.** *adj.* unspeakable, unutterable, inexpressible; **II.** *adv.* unspeakably *etc.*; ... beyond words

'**un·sanft I.** *adj.* a) rough; hard, b) *fig.* bad, rude; ***~es Erwachen*** rude awakening; **II.** *adv.*: ***~ aus dem Schlaf gerissen werden*** be rudely awakened

'**un·sau·ber** *adj.* **1.** dirty (*a. work*); messy; **2.** *fig.* unfair (*a. sport*), underhand ..., *a.* dubious, F shady *business, method etc.*

'**un·schäd·lich** *adj.* harmless; ***~ machen*** render harmless, put *s.o.* out of action; '**Un·schäd·lich·keit** *f* (-; *no pl.*) harmlessness

'un·scharf *adj.* **1.** *phot.* blurred, fuzzy, unsharp, *a.* out of focus; **2.** *fig.* hazy, fuzzy, vague *notions etc.*
un·schätz·bar [ʊnˈʃɛtsbaːɐ] *adj.* invaluable; inestimable *value, significance etc.*
'un·schein·bar *adj.* a) insignificant; inconspicuous, b) unprepossessing, nondescript; **'Un·schein·bar·keit** *f* (-; *no pl.*) insignificance; inconspicuousness; unprepossessing nature (*gen.* of)
'un·schick·lich *adj.* improper, unseemly; indecent; **'Un·schick·lich·keit** *f* (-; -en) **1.** *no pl.* indecency; impropriety, unseemliness; **2.** indecency
un·schlag·bar [ʊnˈʃlaːkbaːɐ] *adj.* unbeatable (**in** *dat.* at, when it comes to); unrival(l)ed; irrefutable *argument, proof etc.*
'un·schlüs·sig *adj.* undecided; ***ich bin mir ~*** (***über*** *acc.*) I haven't made up my mind yet (about)
'un·schön *adj.* a) unlovely, unsightly, b) unfair, unkind, not nice, c) unpleasant; ***~er Anblick*** eyesore
Un·schuld [ˈʊnʃʊlt] *f* (-; *no pl.*) **1.** innocence; purity (of heart *or* mind); F ***~ vom Lande*** F country cousin; ***in aller ~*** quite innocently; ***ich wasche m-e Hände in ~*** I wash my hands of it; **2.** virginity; ***s-e ~ verlieren*** lose one's innocence
'un·schul·dig *adj.* **1.** a) innocent (**an** *dat.* of); not responsible (for *an accident etc.*), b) harmless; ⚖ ***sich für ~ erklären*** plead not guilty; ***er wurde ~ bestraft*** he was punished although he was innocent; **2.** *obs.* untouched, virgin ...
'Un·schulds|be·teue·run·gen *pl.* protestations of innocence; **~be·weis** *m* proof of s.o.'s innocence; **~en·gel** *m*, **~lamm** *n iro.* innocent little angel; **~mie·ne** *f* air of innocence
'un·schulds·voll *adj.* (*and adv.*) innocent(ly); ***~er Blick*** *a.* look of innocence
'un·schwer *adv.* without difficulty
'un·selb·stän·dig *adj.* dependent (on others); helpless; ***er ist so ~*** *a.* he can't do anything on his own; ***Einkommen aus ~er Arbeit*** wage and salary incomes; **'Un·selb·stän·dig·keit** *f* (-; *no pl.*) lack of independence, helplessness
un·ser [ˈʊnzɐ] **I.** *poss. pron.* **1.** *adj.* our; ***e-r ~er Freunde*** a friend of ours; **2.** *su.* ours; ***~er, ~e, ~(e)s, unsrer, unsre, unsres, der*** (***die, das***) ***~e*** *or* ***uns(e)rige*** ours; **II.** *pers. pron.* (*gen. of wir*) of us
un·ser·ei·ner [ˈʊnzɐˀaɪnɐ], **un·ser·eins** [ˈʊnzɐˀaɪns] *indef. pron.* (*a.* ***unseresgleichen***) people like us, F the likes of us, our sort
un·se·ret·we·gen [ˈʊnzərətˈveːgən] *adv.* a) for our sake, on our account, b) because of us
un·se·ri·ge [ˈʊnzərɪgə] *poss. pron.* → ***unser*** 2
'un·se·ri,ös *adj.* dubious *transaction etc.*; *a.* slippery *character*; popular *newspaper etc.*; *scientist, text etc.* not to be taken seriously; ***es ist e-e ~e Schrift*** *etc.* it's not a serious piece of writing *etc.*
'un·si·cher *adj.* a) insecure; unsafe, b) uncertain; unsteady (*a. hands, legs*), c) insecure, unsure of o.s., lacking in self-confidence, d) unsure, uncertain; (***sich***) ***~ sein, ob*** (***wann, wie*** *etc.*) not to be sure (as to) whether (when, how *etc.*); ***~ im Rechnen*** *etc.* shaky on arithmetic *etc.*; ***j-n ~ machen*** make s.o. unsure of himself (*or* herself), rattle s.o.; F ***die Gegend ~ machen*** terrorize the neighbo(u)rhood; ***~ auf den Beinen*** shaky, wobbly; **'Un·si·cher·heit** *f* (-; *no pl.*) insecurity; unsteadiness; uncertainty; ***s-e tiefe ~*** his deep sense of insecurity; **'Un·si·cher·heits·fak·tor** *m* element of uncertainty
'un·sicht·bar *adj.* invisible (**für** *acc.* to); **'Un·sicht·bar·keit** *f* (-; *no pl.*) invisibility
un·sink·bar [ʊnˈzɪŋkbaːɐ] *adj.* unsinkable
Un·sinn [ˈʊnzɪn] *m* (-[e]s; *no pl.*) nonsense; ***~ machen*** fool around; ***~ reden*** (F ***verzapfen***) talk a lot of nonsense (*sl.* rot); ***~!*** nonsense!, F rubbish!, F garbage!; **'un·sin·nig I.** *adj.* a) silly, ridiculous, absurd, b) F incredible *fear etc.*; **II.** F *adv.* terribly, F incredibly
'Un·sit·te *f* a) bad habit, b) nuisance
'un·sitt·lich *adj.* immoral, indecent; **'Un·sitt·lich·keit** *f* (-; -en) **1.** *no pl.* immorality; indecency; **2.** indecency
'un·so,li·de *adj.* **1.** unstable, unsolid; **2.** *fig.* loose *lifestyle etc.*; dubious *firm etc.*
'un·sor,tiert *adj.* unsorted
'un·so·zi,al *adj.* unsocial; antisocial
'un·sport·lich *adj.* a) unathletic, b) unsporting, unsportsmanlike; ***~es Betragen*** unsporting behavio(u)r
uns·ri·ge [ˈʊnzrɪgə] *poss. pron.* → ***unser*** 2
'un·statt·haft *adj.* inadmissible, not allowed; illicit
'un·sterb·lich I. *adj.* **1.** immortal (*a. artist etc.*); undying *love*; **II.** *adv.* **2.** immortally; **3.** F awfully, dreadfully; ***sich ~ blamieren*** make an absolute fool of o.s.; ***~ verliebt*** hopelessly in love (***in*** *acc.* with), F smitten; **'Un·sterb·lich·keit** *f* (-; *no pl.*) immortality; ***in die ~ eingehen*** be immortalized
Un·stern [ˈʊnʃtɛrn] *m* (-[e]s; *no pl.*) unlucky star; ***unter e-m ~ stehen*** be ill-fated
un·stet [ˈʊnʃteːt] **I.** *adj.* changeable, unstable; restless, *a.* unsettled *life*; shifty *look*; *iro.* ***e-n ~en Lebenswandel führen*** lead a varied life; **II.** *adv.* restlessly; **'Un·ste·tig·keit** *f* (-; *no pl.*) changeability, instability; restlessness
un·still·bar [ʊnˈʃtɪlbaːɐ] *adj.* insatiable *hunger*, *a. fig. desire etc.*; unquenchable *thirst*
'Un·stim·mig·keit *f* (-; -en) **1.** discrepancy, inconsistency; **2.** *a. pl.* disagreement, friction
'un·strei·tig *adj.* undeniable, indisputable
un·struk·tu·riert [ˈʊnʃtrʊkturiːɐt] *adj.* unstructured
'Un·sum·me *f* (-; -n) *a. pl.* enormous sum
'un·sym,me·trisch *adj.* asymmetrical
'un·sym,pa·thisch *adj.* unpleasant, unappealing; off-putting; ***er*** (***es***) ***ist mir ~*** I don't like him (it)
'un·sy·ste,ma·tisch *adj.* unsystematic(al)
un·ta·de·lig [ʊnˈtaːdəlɪç] *adj.* **1.** flawless, irreproachable *behavio(u)r*, beyond reproach; **2.** flawless *performance etc.*; immaculate *dress*
'un·ta·len,tiert *adj.* untalented
'Un·tat *f* (-; -en) atrocity, atrocious deed
'un·tä·tig *adj.* inactive; *a.* dormant *volcano*; idle; ***~ herumsitzen*** sit around doing nothing (F twiddling one's thumbs); **'Un·tä·tig·keit** *f* (-; *no pl.*) inactivity; idleness
'un·taug·lich *adj.* unsuitable; *n.s.* incompetent, incapable; ⚔ unfit (for service); ***~ für*** *acc. a.* not suited to; **'Un·taug·lich·keit** *f* (-; *no pl.*) unsuitability; incompetence; ⚔ unfitness
un'teil·bar *adj.* indivisible; **Un'teil·bar·keit** *f* (-; *no pl.*) indivisibility
un·ten [ˈʊntən] *adv.* (down) below; downstairs; F *geogr.* down south; ***nach ~*** down(wards), downstairs; (***dort***) ***~ am See*** down by the lake; ***da ~*** down there; ***ganz ~*** right (down) at the bottom; ***weiter ~*** further down; ***von ~*** from below; ***von oben bis ~*** from top to bottom (*or* toe); ***siehe ~*** see below; ***siehe S.7 ~*** see p.7 bottom; ***sich von ~ hochdienen*** rise from the ranks; ***mit dem Gesicht nach ~*** face down; ***rechts ~*** at the bottom right; F ***er ist bei mir ~ durch*** F I'm through with him; **~er·wähnt, ~ge·nannt** *adj.* undermentioned, ... mentioned below; **~her'um** *adv.*, **~rum** F *adv.* down below; **~ste·hend** *adj.* → ***untenerwähnt***
un·ter [ˈʊntɐ] **I.** *prp.* (*dat.*) a) under, below; underneath, b) among; ***~ dem Bett*** *etc.* ***hervor*** from under the bed *etc.*; ***~ 21*** (***Jahren***) under 21 (years of age); ***einer ~ vielen*** one of many; ***nicht einer ~ hundert*** not one in a hundred; ***~ anderem*** (***u.a.***) among other things; ***~ zehn Mark*** under (*or* less than) ten marks; (***sich***) ***mischen ~*** *acc.* mix with; ***~ Beifall*** amid applause; ***~ Tränen*** in (*or* amid) tears, tearfully; ***~ der Woche*** during the week; ***~ diesem Gesichtspunkt*** from this point of view; ***~ großem Gelächter*** amid great laughter; ***~ s-r Regierung*** under (*or* during) his reign; ***~ sich haben*** be in charge of *a department, 100 workers etc.*; ***was versteht man ~ ...?*** what is meant by ...?; ***„Land ~"*** 'land under water'; → ***Kritik, Würde, uns***; **II.** *adj.* lower
'Un·ter|ab·schnitt *m* subsection; **~ab,tei·lung** *f* subdivision; **~arm** *m* forearm; **~aus·schuß** *m* subcommittee; **~bau** *m* substructure (*a.* 🚂); foundation (*a. fig.*); *fig. a.* base, *esp.* ✝ infrastructure; **~bauch** *m* lower abdomen
un·ter'bau·en *v/t.* (*insep.*, *no* -ge-, h) **1.** ⚙ support (from below); underlay; **2.** *fig.* underpin, shore up *theory etc.*
'un·ter·be·legt *adj. hotel etc.*: not full, not filled to capacity; *w.s.* half-empty; ✝ undersubscribed
'un·ter|be·lich·ten *v/t.* (*insep.*, *no* -ge-, h) *phot.* underexpose; **~be·lich·tet** *adj.* underexposed; F *fig.* ***geistig ~*** a bit dim, *iro.* not exactly bright
'un·ter·be·schäf·tigt *adj.* underworked; **'Un·ter·be·schäf·ti·gung** *f* (-; *no pl.*) ✝ underemployment
'un·ter·be·setzt *adj.* understaffed
'Un·ter·bett *n* underblanket
'un·ter·be·völ·kert *adj.* underpopulated
'un·ter·be·wer·ten *v/t.* (*only inf. and p.p.* unterbewertet, h) undervalue; underrate; **'Un·ter·be·wer·tung** *f* (-; -en) undervaluation; underrating
'un·ter·be·wußt *adj.* subconscious; **'Un·ter·be·wußt·sein** *n* (-s; *no pl.*) subconscious; ***im ~*** subconsciously
'un·ter·be·zah·len *v/t.* (*only inf. and p.p.* unterbezahlt, h) underpay; **'un·ter·be·zahlt** *adj.* underpaid; **'Un·ter·be·zah·lung** *f* (-; *no pl.*) underpayment
'Un·ter·be·zirk *m* subdistrict

un·ter'bie·ten *v/t.* (*irr., insep., no* -ge-, h, → ***bieten***) a) underbid; ✝ undercut *prices*; undersell *competitors*, b) beat *a record*; F *fig.* ***es ist kaum mehr zu ~*** it can hardly get any worse (than that)

un·ter'bin·den *v/t.* (*irr., insep., no* -ge-, h, → ***binden***) put a stop to; prevent; **Un·ter'bin·dung** *f* (-; *no pl.*) stopping, ending; prevention

un·ter'blei·ben *v/i.* (*irr., insep., no* -ge-, sn, → ***bleiben***) not to be done (*or* undertaken); not to take place; ***es hat zu ~*** a) it must stop, b) it mustn't be done, it mustn't happen

Un·ter'bo·den|schutz *m mot.* underseal, *Am.* undercoat; **~wä·sche** *f* undercar wash

un·ter'bre·chen *v/t.* (*irr., insep., no* -ge-, h, → ***brechen***) interrupt; *a.* cut *s.o.* short; *teleph.* cut off; *sport*: hold up *game*; ⚕ terminate *pregnancy*; ⚖ adjourn; ⚡ interrupt; ***die Fahrt*** (*or* ***Reise***) *~* break one's journey

'Un·ter·bre·cher *m* (-s; -) ⚡ interrupter, contact breaker; **~kon,takt** *m* ⚡ make-and-break contact

Un·ter'bre·chung *f* (-; -en) interruption; break; adjournment *etc.*; → ***unterbrechen***; ***ohne ~*** without stopping, nonstop; ***mit ~en*** intermittently; **Un·ter'bre·chungs·ta·ste** *f computer*: break key

un·ter·brei·ten *v/t.* (*insep., no* -ge-, h) submit *offer etc.* (*dat.* to); *a.* put forward *proposal etc.*; **Un·ter'brei·tung** *f* (-; *no pl.*) submission (*gen.* of)

'un·ter·brin·gen *v/t.* (*irr., sep.*, h, → ***bringen***) a) accommodate, put *s.o.* up, b) get *s.o.* a job (***in*** *dat.*, ***bei*** *dat.* with), c) store; put, get (***in*** *dat.* into), d) have *s.th.* accepted (***bei*** *dat.* by), e) F *fig.* place *s.o. or s.th.*; ***j-n ~ in*** *dat.* put s.o. into *a home, hospital etc., ped. etc.* put s.o. in, get s.o. into; ***in dem Asyl*** *etc.* ***kann man 100 Leute ~*** the home *etc.* accommodates a hundred (people); ***die Akten sind im Keller untergebracht*** the files are kept in the cellar; **'Un·ter·brin·gung** *f* (-; *no pl.*) accommodation; housing; *~* ***von*** *dat.* finding a place for *s.th.*, putting *s.th.* away; **'Un·ter·brin·gungs·mög·lich·keit** *f* (-; -en) accommodation

'un·ter·but·tern F *v/t.* (*sep.*, h): ***laß dich nicht ~*** don't let them *etc.* get the better of you

'Un·ter·deck *n* ⚓ lower deck

un·ter·der'hand *adv.* a) secretly, on the quiet, b) illicitly, illegally, c) privately, d) *earn etc.* on the side; *learn etc.* through unofficial channels

un·ter'des·sen *adv.* in the meantime, meanwhile

'Un·ter·do·mi,nan·te *f* ♪ subdominant

'Un·ter·druck *m phys.* subpressure; ⚕ low blood pressure

un·ter'drü·cken *v/t.* (*insep., no* -ge-, h) suppress *feeling, a. opposition, revolt etc.*; *a.* stifle *laughter, sigh, oath etc.*; oppress *people*; **Un·ter'drü·cker** *m* (-s; -) suppressor; oppressor

'Un·ter·druck·kam·mer *f* decompression chamber

Un·ter·drückung [ʊntɐ'drʏkʊŋ] (*sep.* -k·k-) *f* (-; *no pl.*) suppression; oppression

'un·ter,durch·schnitt·lich *adj.* below-average ..., *pred.* below average

un·ter·ein'an·der *adv.* **1.** one below the other; **2.** among each other (*or* themselves, yourselves *etc.*)

'Un·ter·ein·heit *f* subunit

'un·ter·ent·wickelt *adj.* underdeveloped; *a.* backward *child, economy etc.*; *psych.* subnormal; **'Un·ter·ent·wick·lung** *f* underdevelopment

'un·ter·er·nährt *adj.* undernourished, malnourished; **'Un·ter·er·näh·rung** *f* (-; *no pl.*) malnutrition

'Un·ter·fa,mi·lie *f zo.* subfamily

un·ter·fan·gen (*irr., insep., no* -ge-, h, → ***fangen***) **I.** *obs. v/refl.*: ***sich ~ zu*** *inf.* dare (to) *inf.*, venture to *inf.*; **II.** *v/t.* △ underpin; **III.** ♀ *n* (-s; -) venture, undertaking

'un·ter·fas·sen *v/t.* (*sep.*, h): ***j-n ~*** take s.o.'s arm

un·ter'flie·gen *v/t.* (*irr., insep., no* -ge-, h, → ***fliegen***) fly underneath (*or* below)

un·ter'for·dern *v/t.* (*insep., no* -ge-, h) be too undemanding for; ***in dieser Stufe ist er unterfordert*** this level is too easy for him; ***sich unterfordert fühlen*** feel one is not being stretched (*or* challenged)

Un·ter'füh·rung *f* (-; -en) subway, *Am.* underpass

'Un·ter·funk·ti,on *f* ⚕ hypofunction, insufficiency

'Un·ter·gang *m* (-[e]s; *no pl.*) **1.** *ast.* setting; **2.** ⚓ sinking; **3.** *fig.* decline; downfall; fall *of an empire etc.*; extinction *of a civilization etc.*; *a. iro.* ruin; *a.* F *fig.* ***das ist noch sein ~*** that'll be the ruin of him yet; **'Un·ter·gangs·stim·mung** *f* doomsday atmosphere

'un·ter·gä·rig [-gɛːrɪç] *adj.* bottom-fermented

un·ter'ge·ben *adj.*: ***j-m ~ sein*** be subordinate to s.o.; **Un·ter'ge·be·ne** *m, f* (-n; -n) subordinate, inferior; *contp.* underling

'un·ter·ge·hakt [-gəhaːkt] *adv.*: *~* ***gehen*** go arm in arm

'un·ter·ge·hen *v/i.* (*irr., sep.*, sn, → ***gehen***) **1.** *ast.* set; **2.** ⚓ go down (*or* under), sink; **3.** *fig.* a) decline; *empire etc.*: fall; *civilization, people etc.*: die out; perish, b) be lost (***in*** *dat.* in), be swallowed up (by), *words*: *a.* be drowned out (***im Lärm*** by the noise); ***davon geht die Welt nicht unter!*** it's not the end of the world(, you know)

'un·ter·ge·ord·net *adj.* subordinate (*dat.* to); *fig. a.* ancillary (to); secondary *meaning, a.* minor *role*

'Un·ter|ge·schoß *n* basement; **~ge·stell** *n* **1.** support; *mot.* underframe; **2.** F *fig.* F pins *pl.*; F undercarriage; **~ge·wicht** *n*: (*~* ***haben*** be) underweight

un·ter'glie·dern *v/t.* (*insep., no* -ge-, h) subdivide (***in*** *acc.* into); **Un·ter'glie·de·rung** *f* (-; -en) subdivision

un·ter'gra·ben *v/t.* (*irr., insep., no* -ge-, h, → ***graben***) **1.** undermine, hollow out; **2.** *fig.* undermine *s.o.'s health, position etc.*; *a.* erode *s.o.'s confidence etc.*

'Un·ter·gren·ze *f* lower limit

'Un·ter·grund *m* (-[e]s; *no pl.*) a) subsoil, b) △ foundation, c) ⚙ ground(ing), undercoat, c) *pol., art etc.*: underground; *pol.* ***in den ~ gehen*** go underground; **~...** *in cpds.* underground *film, literature etc.*; **~bahn** *f* underground, *in London*: *a. the* tube; *Am.* subway; **~be·we·gung** *f pol.* underground movement

un·ter·grün·dig ['ʊntɐgrʏndɪç] *fig. adj.* under the surface, hidden

'Un·ter·grund·kämp·fer *m* resistance fighter, guer(r)illa

un·ter·halb ['ʊntɐhalp] **I.** *prp.* below, under (*gen. or* ***von*** *dat. s.th.*); **II.** *adv.* underneath

Un·ter·halt ['ʊntɐhalt] *m* (-[e]s; *no pl.*) support, maintenance; livelihood, living; ***für j-s*** (***s-n***) *~* ***aufkommen*** support s.o. (o.s.); ***s-n ~*** (***selbst***) ***verdienen*** earn one's (own) living (***durch*** *acc.* by); ⚖ *~* ***zahlen*** pay alimony; **un·ter'hal·ten** (*irr., insep., no* -ge-, h, → ***halten***) **I.** *v/t.* **1.** maintain *institute etc.*; keep up, keep *s.th.* going; support *one's family etc.*; keep up *correspondence, relationship*; keep *the fire* burning; keep, have *an account*; **2.** entertain, amuse *s.o.*; **II.** *v/refl.*: ***sich ~*** **3.** talk (***mit j-m über et.*** to s.o. about s.th.); ***sich ungestört ~*** have a quiet chat; **4.** enjoy o.s., have a good time; **un·ter'hal·tend** *adj.* → ***unterhaltsam***; **Un·ter'hal·ter** *m*: ***ein guter ~ sein*** a) be very entertaining (*or* amusing), b) be a good conversationalist; **un·ter·halt·sam** [ʊntɐ'haltzaːm] *adj.* entertaining, amusing

'Un·ter·halts|an·spruch *m* maintenance claim; **~bei·hil·fe** *f* maintenance grant; **♀be·rech·tigt** *adj.* entitled to maintenance; **~kla·ge** *f* maintenance action; **~ko·sten** *pl.* maintenance costs

'Un·ter·halts·pflicht *f* obligation to pay maintenance; **'un·ter·halts·pflich·tig** *adj.* obliged to pay maintenance

Un·ter'hal·tung *f* (-; -en) **1.** entertainment; diversion; ***zu j-s ~*** for s.o.'s entertainment (*or* amusement); **2.** conversation, talk, chat; **3.** *no pl.* upkeep, maintenance

Un·ter'hal·tungs|bei·la·ge *f* magazine (section); **~elek,tro·nik** *f* home entertainment products *pl.*, video and audio equipment; **~in·du,strie** *f* entertainments industry; **~ko·sten** *pl.* maintenance costs; **~lek,tü·re** *f*, **~li·te·ra,tur** *f* light reading (*or* fiction); **~mu,sik** *f* light (*or* popular) music; **~or,che·ster** *n* dance band; palm-court orchestra; **~pro,gramm** *n*, **~sen·dung** *f* (light) entertainment program(me); **~wert** *m* entertainment value

un·ter'han·deln *v/i.* (*insep., no* -ge-, h) negotiate; **'Un·ter·händ·ler** *m* (-s; -) negotiator; **Un·ter'hand·lung** *f* (-; -en) negotiations *pl.*, talks *pl.*

'Un·ter·haus *n* (-es; *no pl.*) *pol. in GB*: House of Commons; **~de,bat·te** *f in GB*: House of Commons debate

'Un·ter·hemd *n* vest, *Am.* underhirt

un·ter·höh·len [-høːlən] *v/t.* (unterhöhlte, unterhöhlt, h) **1.** hollow out; **2.** *fig.* undermine, erode; **Un·ter'höh·lung** *f* (-; -en) **1.** hollowing out; **2.** *fig.* undermining, erosion

'Un·ter·holz *n* (-es; *no pl.*) undergrowth

'Un·ter·ho·se *f*: (***e-e ~*** a pair of) underpants *pl.*; pants *pl.*, *Am.* panties *pl.*; (***e-e***) ***lange ~*** (a pair of) longjohns

'un·ter·ir·disch *adj.* subterranean, underground (*both a. fig.*)

un·ter·jo·chen [-'jɔxən] *v/t.* (unterjochte, unterjocht, h) subjugate; **Un·ter'jo·chung** *f* (-; *no pl.*) subjugation

'un·ter·ju·beln F *v/t.* (*sep.*, h): ***j-m et. ~*** pin s.th. on s.o.; palm (*or* fob) s.th. off on s.o.

un·ter·kel·lern [-'kɛlɐn] *v/t.* (unterkellerte, unterkellert, h) build a cellar under

'Un·ter·kie·fer *m* (-s; -) lower jaw
'Un·ter·kleid *n* (-[e]s; -er) → ***Unterrock***
'un·ter·kom·men *v/i.* (*irr.*, *sep.*, sn, → ***kommen***) a) find a place (***in*** *dat.* in); *n.s.* find accommodation (in), b) find a job (***bei*** *dat.* with); ~ ***bei*** *dat. a.* be taken on by *a firm etc.*; F ***so etwas ist mir noch nicht untergekommen*** I've never come across anything like it (*or* the likes of it) before
'Un·ter·kör·per *m* lower part of the body
'un·ter·krie·chen F *v/i.* (*irr.*, *sep.*, sn, → ***kriechen***) find shelter; hide (away)
'un·ter·krie·gen F *v/t.* (*sep.*, h) a) get *s.o.* down, b) make *s.o.* knuckle under; ***laß dich nicht ~!*** don't let it get you down
un·ter'küh·len (*insep.*, *no* -ge-, h) **I.** *v/t.* undercool; ⚙ *a.* supercool; **II.** *v/refl.*: ⚕ ***sich*** ~ get hypothermia; **un·ter'kühlt** *adj.* a) ⚙ undercooled, b) ⚕ suffering from exposure (*or* hypothermia), c) *fig.* very cool, frosty *relations etc.*; cool, subdued *manner etc.*; **Un·ter'küh·lung** *f* (-; -en) ⚕ exposure, hypothermia; ⚙ undercooling, supercooling
Un·ter·kunft ['ʊntɐkʊnft] *f* (-; Unterkünfte ['ʊntɐkʏnftə]) accommodation; ⚔ quarters *pl.*, billet; ~ ***und Verpflegung*** board and lodging
'Un·ter·la·ge *f* (-; -n) **1.** a) padding, b) ⚙ base, support, c) waterproof sheet, d) something to write on; desk pad, e) *fig. financial etc.* basis; F ***e-e gute*** ~ something to soak up the alcohol, a good base, a good lining for your stomach; **2.** *pl.* (supporting) documents, records, material *sg.*
'Un·ter·land *n* (-[e]s; *no pl.*) lowland
Un·ter·laß ['ʊntɐlas] *m*: ***ohne*** ~ incessantly; without a letup
un·ter'las·sen *v/t.* (*irr.*, *insep.*, *no* -ge-, h, → ***lassen***) **1.** refrain from (*ger.*); stop (*ger.*); leave unsaid, drop *a remark etc.*; ***unterlaß diese Bemerkungen, bitte*** *iro.* we can do without your comments, thank you; **2. *es*** ~ ***zu*** *inf.* omit (*or* fail, neglect) to *inf.*; **Un·ter·las·sung** [ʊntɐ'lasʊŋ] *f* (-; -en) omission; neglect
Un·ter'las·sungs|kla·ge *f* action for injunction; **~sün·de** *f usu. iro.* lapse
'Un·ter·lauf *m* (-[e]s; ⁼e) lower course
un·ter'lau·fen (*irr.*, *insep.*, *no* -ge-, sn, → ***laufen***) **I.** *v/t.* avoid, F dodge; **II.** *v/i.* (*a.* ***j-m*** ~) creep in; ***mir ist ein Fehler*** ~ I've made a mistake; ***es können einem leicht Fehler*** ~ it's easy to make mistakes; **III.** *adj.*: ***mit Blut*** ~ bloodshot *eye*
'Un·ter·le·der *n* sole leather
'un·ter·le·gen[1] *v/t.* (*sep.*, h) lay (*or* put) under
un·ter'le·gen[2] (*insep.*, *no* -ge-, h) **I.** *v/t.* **1.** underlay, line, back (***mit*** *dat.* with); **2. *mit Musik*** ~ add music to; **II.** *adj.*: ***j-m*** ~ ***sein*** be inferior to s.o., not to be up to s.o.; ***die ~e Partei*** *etc.* the losing party *etc.*; **Un·ter'le·ge·ne** *m, f* (-n; -n) loser, F underdog; **Un·ter'le·gen·heit** *f* (-; *no pl.*) inferiority (***gegenüber*** *dat.* to)
'Un·ter·leib *m* (-[e]s; -er) abdomen, belly; *a.* womb area; **'Un·ter·leibs·schmer·zen** *pl.* abdominal (*n.s.* period) pains
un·ter'lie·gen *v/i.* (*irr.*, *insep.*, *no* -ge-, sn, → ***liegen***) **1.** be defeated *or* beaten (*dat.* by), *sport*: *a.* lose (to); succumb (to *a temptation etc.*); ***e-r Täuschung*** ~ be deceived, be duped; **2.** be subject to *regulations etc.*; be liable to *taxation etc.*; depend on, be governed by *principles, rules etc.*; ***Schwankungen*** ~ be subject to fluctuation, fluctuate, vary; ***es unterliegt keinem Zweifel, daß*** there is no doubt that
'Un·ter·lip·pe *f* lower lip
un·ter'ma·len *v/t.* (*insep.*, *no* -ge-, h) **1.** prime; **2.** *fig.* provide a background for, lend some colo(u)r to; ~ ***mit*** *dat.* accompany with, liven up with, underscore with; ***et. musikalisch*** ~ provide a musical accompaniment for s.th.; ***et. mit Geräuschen*** ~ provide sound effects for s.th.; ***et. mit Gesten*** ~ reinforce s.th. with gestures; **Un·ter'ma·lung** *fig. f* (-; -en) background; accompaniment
un·ter'mau·ern *v/t.* (*insep.*, *no* -ge-, h) underpin, shore up; *fig. a.* substantiate, corroborate *theory etc.*
'Un·ter·men·ge *f* 𝔄 subset
'un·ter|men·gen, ~mi·schen *v/t.* (*sep.*, h) mix in(to ***unter*** *acc.*, ***in*** *acc.*), add (to)
'Un·ter·mie·te *f* (-; *no pl.*) sublease; ***in*** ~ ***wohnen*** live in lodgings; **'Un·ter·mie·ter** *m* subtenant, lodger
un·ter·mi·nie·ren [ʊntɐmi'niːrən] *v/t.* (unterminierte, unterminiert, h) *a. fig.* undermine; **Un·ter·mi'nie·rung** *f* (-; -en) undermining
un·ter·neh·men *v/t.* (*irr.*, *insep.*, *no* -ge-, h, → ***nehmen***) do; undertake; ***e-n Ausflug*** ~ go on (*or* make) a trip; ***e-n Spaziergang*** ~ go for a walk; ***e-n Versuch*** ~ make (*or* launch) an attempt; ***er unternahm nichts*** he did nothing; ***dagegen muß man etwas*** ~ something has got to be done about it
Un·ter'neh·men *n* (-s; -) **1.** ✝ firm, (business) enterprise, business, concern, company; **2.** enterprise, undertaking; project; ⚔ operation
Un·ter'neh·mens|be·ra·ter *m* management consultant; **~be·ra·tung** *f* management consultancy; **~for·schung** *f* operations research
Un·ter·neh·mer [ʊntɐ'neːmɐ] *m* (-s; -) entrepreneur, (F big) businessman; F operator; employer; industrialist; ***die*** ~ *coll.* the business community; **~geist** *m* (-[e]s; *no pl.*) spirit of enterprise, entrepreneurial spirit; entrepreneurialism
un·ter·neh·me·risch [ʊntɐ'neːmərɪʃ] *adj.* entrepreneurial, enterprise ...; ***~e Leistung*** (great) business achievement; ***~es Risiko*** business risk
Un·ter'neh·mer·tum *n* (-s; *no pl.*) **1.** entrepreneurship; **2.** *the* business community, *the* employers *pl.*; ***freies*** ~ free enterprise
Un·ter·neh·mung [ʊntɐ'neːmʊŋ] *f* (-; -en) → ***Unternehmen***
Un·ter'neh·mungs|geist *m* (-[e]s; *no pl.*), **~lust** *f* (-; *no pl.*) (spirit of) enterprise, initiative, F get-up-and-go
un·ter'neh·mungs·lu·stig *adj.* enterprising; *n.s.* active
'Un·ter·of·fi̩zier *m* non-commissioned officer, NCO; sergeant; ✈ corporal, *Am.* airman 1st class
'un·ter·ord·nen (*sep.*, h) **I.** *v/t.* subordinate (*dat.* to); **II.** *v/refl.*: ***sich*** ~ submit (*dat.* to); → ***untergeordnet***; **'Un·ter·ord·nung** *f* (-; -en) **1.** *no pl.* subordination; **2.** *biol.* suborder
'Un·ter·pfand *n* pledge
'un·ter·pflü·gen *v/t.* (*sep.*, h) plough (*Am.* plow) *s.th.* under (*a. fig.*)
'Un·ter·pri·ma *obs. f* eighth form (*Am.* grade), *Brit.* Lower Sixth
'un·ter·pri·vi·le̩giert *adj.* underprivileged; ***die Unterprivilegierten*** the underprivileged (*pl.*)
Un·ter·re·dung [ʊntɐ'reːdʊŋ] *f* (-; -en) talk; ***mit j-m e-e*** ~ ***führen*** have talks (*or* a talk) with s.o.
un·ter·re·prä·sen·tiert ['ʊntɐreprɛzɛntiːɐt] *adj.* under-represented
Un·ter·richt ['ʊntɐrɪçt] *m* (-[e]s; *no pl.*) a) instruction, teaching, b) lessons *pl.*; *ped. a.* classes *pl.*; ~ ***geben*** teach, give lessons; *ped. a.* hold classes; **un·ter'richten** (unterrichtete, unterrichtet, h) **I.** *v/t.* **1.** teach, instruct; give lessons (*acc.* to *s.o.*; ***in*** *dat.* on); **2.** inform (***von*** *dat.*, ***über*** *acc.* of); ***j-n laufend*** ~ keep s.o. informed (*or* posted); ***falsch*** ~ misinform; **II.** *v/refl.*: ***sich*** ~ ***über*** *acc.* inform o.s. about; acquaint o.s. with; ***unterrichtet sein*** be (well-)informed (***über*** *acc.* about); ***unterrichtete Kreise*** informed circles; **III.** *v/i.* teach; be a teacher
'Un·ter·richts|ein·heit *f* teaching unit; **~er·fah·rung** *f* teaching (*or* classroom) experience; **~fach** *n* (teaching) subject; **~film** *m* educational film
'un·ter·richts·frei *adj.*: ***~e Stunde*** free period; ***~er Tag*** day off school; ***morgen haben wir*** ~ there are no classes (*or* lessons) tomorrow
'Un·ter·richts|ma·te·ri̩al *n* teaching materials *pl.*; **~me̩tho·de** *f* teaching method; **~raum** *m* classroom; **~stoff** *m* → ***Lehrstoff***; **~stun·de** *f* lesson; *ped. a.* class, period; ***fünf ~n in Geschichte*** five class hours of history
Un·ter·rich·tung [ʊntɐ'rɪçtʊŋ] *f* (-; *no pl.*) instruction; informing
'Un·ter·rock *m* slip
un·ter'sa·gen *v/t.* (*insep.*, *no* -ge-, h) *adm.* prohibit; outlaw; ***j-m*** ~, ***et. zu tun*** order s.o. not to do s.th., forbid s.o. to do s.th., *adm.* prohibit s.o. from doing s.th.; ***j-m das Autofahren*** *etc.* ~ order s.o. not to drive *etc.*; ***er hat es mir untersagt*** *a.* he won't let me (do it); ***das Betreten des Raumes ist strengstens untersagt*** it is strictly forbidden to enter the room
'Un·ter·satz *m* (-es; ⁼e) mat; coaster; saucer; F ***fahrbarer*** ~ F wheels
'Un·ter·schall... *in cpds.* subsonic
un·ter·schät·zen *v/t.* (*insep.*, *no* -ge-, h) underestimate, *a.* underrate *s.o.'s ability etc.*; **Un·ter'schät·zung** *f* (-; *no pl.*) underestimation; underrating
un·ter·scheid·bar [ʊntɐ'ʃaitbaːɐ] *adj.* distinguishable; **un·ter·schei·den** (*irr.*, *insep.*, *no* -ge-, h, → ***scheiden***) **I.** *v/t. and v/i.* a) distinguish (***zwischen*** *dat.* between); make a distinction (between), b) distinguish, make out; ***et.*** ~ ***von*** *dat.* ***...*** *a.* tell s.th. from ...; ***sie sind kaum zu*** ~ you can hardly tell the difference; ***zwischen A und B*** ~ ***können*** be able to tell the difference (*or* to distinguish) between A and B; ***das unterscheidet ihn von*** *dat.* ***...*** that sets him apart from ...; **II.** *v/refl.*: ***sich*** ~ differ (***von*** *dat.* from); ***sich dadurch*** ~, ***daß*** differ in *ger.*; ***wie*** (*or* ***worin***) ***unterscheidet sich A von B?*** what's the difference between A and B?, in what way(s) are A and B different (*or* do A and B differ)?; ***A und B*** ~ ***sich nicht*** there's no difference between A and B; **un·ter'schei·dend** *adj.* distinctive, characteristic; **Un·ter'schei·dung** *f* (-; -en) a) differentiation, b) difference, distinction

Un·ter'schei·dungs|merk·mal *n* distinguishing (*or* distinctive) feature *or* mark; **~ver·mö·gen** *n* powers *pl.* of discernment (*or* distinction)
'Un·ter·schen·kel *m* lower leg
'Un·ter·schicht *f* **1.** *geol.* substratum; **2.** lower class(es *pl.*)
'un·ter·schie·ben *v/t.* (*irr.*, *sep.*, h, → ***schieben***) **1.** (*a.* ***unter'schieben***): ***j-m et.*** ~ a) foist s.th. on s.o., b) (falsely) attribute s.th. to s.o., (wrongly) accuse s.o. of (doing) s.th.; **2.** push *s.th.* under(neath) (*dat. s.th.*, *s.o.*); **Unter'schiebung** *f* (-; -en) (wrongful) accusation
Un·ter·schied ['ʊntɐʃiːt] *m* (-[e]s; -e [-də]) difference, distinction; ***e-n ~ machen*** make a distinction, distinguish, discriminate (***zwischen*** *dat.* between); ***ein feiner ~*** a fine (*or* subtle) distinction, a subtle difference; ***die feinen ~e*** the subtle differences; ***ich sehe keinen ~*** I can't see any (*or* the) difference; ***zum ~ von*** *dat.* unlike *s.th. or s.o.*, as distinct from, in contrast to; ***ohne ~*** indiscriminately, without exception; ***das ist ein großer ~*** that makes a big difference; → ***Tag***; **'un·ter·schied·lich I.** *adj.* different; varying, varied; ***~ sein*** vary; ***mit ~em Erfolg*** with varying degrees of success; **II.** *adv.* differently; varyingly *tall, bright etc.*; ***~ groß*** (***gut***) of varying size (quality); ***~ groß*** (***gut***) ***sein*** *a.* vary in size (quality); ***~ reagieren*** vary in their reactions, have varying reactions; ***es wurde ganz ~ aufgenommen*** reactions (to it) varied greatly; ***wir beurteilen das ziemlich ~*** our views on that differ considerably; ***~ behandeln*** treat differently, *n.s.* discriminate against; **'Un·ter·schied·lich·keit** *f* (-; -en) difference (*gen.* between); variableness, varying nature (*gen.* of); **'un·ter·schieds·los I.** *adj.* indiscriminate; **II.** *adv.* indiscriminately, without exception
un·ter'schla·gen *v/t.* (*irr.*, *insep.*, *no* -ge-, h, → ***schlagen***) embezzle *money*; intercept *letter etc.*; suppress *evidence, testament*; *fig.* hold back, keep quiet about, suppress; **Un·ter·schla·gung** [-'ʃlaːgʊŋ] *f* (-; -en) embezzlement; suppression
Un·ter·schlupf ['ʊntɐʃlʊpf] *m* (-[e]s; -e) a) hiding place, F hideout, b) shelter, refuge; *w.s.* somewhere to go; **'un·ter·schlüp·fen** *v/i.* (*sep.*, sn) a) take shelter, b) hide (away); ***~ in*** *dat.* find a place in
un·ter'schrei·ben (*irr.*, *insep.*, *no* -ge-, h, → ***schreiben***) **I.** *v/t.* sign; *fig.* subscribe to; **II.** *v/i.* sign (one's name)
un·ter'schrei·ten *v/t.* (*irr.*, *insep.*, *no* -ge-, h, → ***schreiten***) remain under, fall short of; *a. temperature*: fall below
'Un·ter·schrift *f* (-; -en) signature; ***mit (s)einer ~ versehen*** give one's signature to, sign one's name on (*or* under)
'Un·ter·schrif·ten|ak·ti,on *f*: (***e-e ~ durchführen*** get up a) petition; **~map·pe** *f* signature blotting-book; **~samm·lung** *f* → ***Unterschriftenaktion***
'un·ter·schrifts·be·rech·tigt *adj.* authorized to sign
'Un·ter·schrifts|fäl·schung *f* forging of a signature (*or* signatures); **~pro·be** *f* specimen signature; **2reif** *adj.* ready for signature; **~stem·pel** *m* signature stamp
un·ter·schwel·lig ['ʊntɐʃvɛlɪç] *adj.* underlying; *psych.* subliminal, sub-threshold
'Un·ter·see·boot *n* submarine
un·ter·see·isch ['ʊntɐzeːɪʃ] *adj.* submarine
'Un·ter·sei·te *f* underside, bottom
un·ter'set·zen¹ *v/t.* (*insep.*, *no* -ge-, h) ⚙ reduce
'un·ter·set·zen² *v/t.* (*sep.*, h) put (*or* place) under(neath); **'Un·ter·set·zer** *m* (-s; -) coaster; saucer
un·ter·setzt [ʊntɐ'zɛtst] *adj.* stocky, thickset
Un·ter·set·zung [ʊntɐ'zɛtsʊŋ] *f* (-; -en) ⚙ (gear) reduction
'un·ter·sin·ken *v/i.* (*irr.*, *sep.*, sn, → ***sinken***) sink, go down, go under
'Un·ter·span·nung *f* ⚡ undervoltage
un·ter'spie·len *v/i. and v/t.* (*insep.*, *no* -ge-, h) underact
un·ter'spü·len *v/t.* (*insep.*, *no* -ge-, h) wash away the foundations of; hollow out *river bank etc.*
un·terst ['ʊntɐst] *adj.* lowest, bottom; ***das Unterste zuoberst kehren*** turn everything upside down
Un·ter·stand ['ʊntɐʃtant] *m* (-[e]s; Unterstände [-ʃtɛndə]) shelter, ⚔ *a.* dugout
un·ter'ste·hen¹ (*irr.*, *insep.*, *no* -ge-, h, → ***stehen***) **I.** *v/i.*: ***j-m*** (*or* ***j-s Aufsicht***) ~ be under s.o., be answerable to s.o., ✝ *and adm. a.* report to s.o.; ***e-m Gesetz ~*** be subject to a law; ***e-r Behörde*** *etc.* ~ come under an authority *etc.*; **II.** *v/refl.*: ***sich ~*** dare; ***sich ~ zu*** *inf.* dare (to) *inf.*, have the audacity (*or* nerve, cheek) to *inf.*; ***~ Sie sich!*** don't you dare!; ***was ~ Sie sich?*** how dare you?
'un·ter·ste·hen² *v/i.* (*irr.*, *sep.*, h, → ***stehen***) shelter, take shelter
'un·ter·stel·len¹ (*sep.*, h) **I.** *v/t.* **1.** put (*or* place) under(neath) *s.th.*; **2.** put (***in*** *dat.* in[to]); leave (***bei*** *dat.* at *s.o.'s place*); store (at); **II.** *v/refl.*: ***sich ~*** shelter, take shelter (***vor*** *dat.* from)
un·ter'stel·len² *v/t.* (*insep.*, *no* -ge-, h) **1.** ***j-m ~, daß ...*** allege (*or* imply, insinuate) that s.o. ...; ***j-m e-e Lüge*** (***unlautere Motive*** *etc.*) ~ allege (*or* imply) that s.o. has lied (has dishonest motives *etc.*); ***j-m böse Absichten ~*** impute bad intentions to s.o.; ***j-m et. ~*** allege that s.o. has done (*or* is capable of doing) s.th.; **2.** suppose, assume; ***~ wir einmal*** let's assume (for the sake of argument); ***wenn man dies unterstellt*** granting that this is (*or* was) so; **3.** ***j-m et.*** (***j-n***) ~ put s.o. in charge of s.th. (s.o.); ***j-m unterstellt werden*** be placed under s.o.('s command ⚔); **Un·ter'stel·lung** *f* (-; -en) allegation, insinuation
un·ter'strei·chen *v/t.* (*irr.*, *insep.*, *no* -ge-, h, → ***streichen***) underline, underscore; *fig. a.* emphasize
'Un·ter·strö·mung *f* undercurrent (*a. fig.*)
'Un·ter·stu·fe *f ped.* junior grades *pl.*
un·ter'stüt·zen *v/t.* (*insep.*, *no* -ge-, h) support *s.o., a plan, project etc.*, *a.* back up *candidate etc.*, *a.* give *s.th.* one's backing, *a.* bolster *the economy etc.*; assist, aid *s.o.* (***bei*** *dat.* in); **Un·ter'stüt·zung** *f* (-; -en) a) support; backing; *a. financial* assistance, aid, b) subsidy, (government) aid *or* grant; ***zur ~*** *gen.* in support of; ***~ beziehen*** be on social security; **un·ter'stüt·zungs·be·rech·tigt** *adj.* entitled to relief; **Un·ter'stüt·zungs·kas·se** *f* relief fund
un·ter'su·chen *v/t.* (*insep.*, *no* -ge-, h) examine (*a.* ⚕); inspect; inquire (*or* look) into, investigate (*all a.* ⚖ *and scientifically*); ⚗ *and w.s.* analy|se (*Am.* -ze); test (***auf*** *acc.* for); **Un·ter·su·chung** [ʊntɐ'zuːxʊŋ] *f* (-; -en) examination; ⚕ *a.* checkup; inquiry (*gen.* into), investigation (of) (*both a.* ⚖), test; ⚗ *and w.s.* analysis (of); study (of); *pl.* research *sg.*; ***amtliche ~*** public inquiry
Un·ter'su·chungs|aus·schuß *m* investigating committee; **~be·fund** *m* ⚕ results *pl.* of the test, (test) findings *pl.*; **~be·richt** *m* inquiry report; **~ge·fan·ge·ne** *m, f* (-n; -n) prisoner on remand; **~ge·fäng·nis** *n* remand prison; **~haft** *f* custody, detention (pending trial), *Am.* pretrial detention; ***in ~ sein*** be on remand; **~kom·mis·si,on** *f* board (*or* committee) of inquiry; **~rich·ter** *m* examining magistrate
Un·ter'ta·ge·bau *m* (-[e]s; *no pl.*) underground mining
un·ter·tan ['ʊntɐtaːn] *pred. adj.* subject (*dat* to); ***j-n ~ machen*** subject s.o. (*dat.* to); **'Un·ter·tan** *m* (-s, -en; -en) subject; **un·ter·tä·nig** ['ʊntɐtɛːnɪç] *adj.* subservient (*dat.* to)
'Un·ter·tas·se *f* saucer; → ***fliegend***
'un·ter·tau·chen (*sep.*) **I.** *v/i.* (sn) **1.** dive; *submarine*: submerge; **2.** *fig.* disappear; *criminal etc.*: go underground, go into hiding; **II.** *v/t.* (h) duck *s.o.*
'Un·ter·teil *n, m* lower part, bottom, base
un·ter'tei·len *v/t.* (*insep.*, *no* -ge-, h) divide (up) (***in*** *acc.* into); subdivide (into); **Un·ter'tei·lung** *f* (-; -en) division (***in*** *acc.* into); subdivision (into)
'Un·ter·ti·tel *m* subtitle; *film*: *a.* caption; **un·ter·ti·teln** [ʊntɐ'tiːtəln] *v/t.* (untertitelte, untertitelt, h) subtitle, give subtitles to
'Un·ter·ton *m* undertone (*a. fig.*)
un·ter·tou·rig ['ʊntɐtuːrɪç] *mot.* **I.** *adj.* low-rev ...; **II.** *adv.* at low rev
un·ter'trei·ben (*irr.*, *insep.*, *no* -ge-, h, → ***treiben***) **I.** *v/t.* understate, play down; **II.** *v/i.* understate; **Un·ter·trei·bung** [ʊntɐ'traɪbʊŋ] *f* (-; -en) understatement
un·ter·tun·neln [ʊntɐ'tʊnəln] *v/t.* (untertunnelte, untertunnelt, h) tunnel through
'un·ter·ver·mie·ten *v/t.* (*sep.*, h) sublet; **'Un·ter·ver·mie·ter** *m* subtenant; **'Un·ter·ver·mie·tung** *f* subletting
'un·ter·ver·si·chern *v/t.* (*only inf. and p.p.* unterversichert, h) underinsure; **'un·ter·ver·si·chert** *adj.* underinsured; **'Un·ter·ver·si·che·rung** *f* underinsurance
'un·ter·ver·sorgt [-fɛɐzɔrkt] *adj.* undersupplied; **'Un·ter·ver·sor·gung** *f* (-; -en) undersupply(ing)
un·ter'wan·dern *v/t.* (*insep.*, *no* -ge-, h) *pol.* infiltrate; **Un·ter'wan·de·rung** *f* (-; -en) infiltration
'Un·ter·wä·sche *f* (-; *no pl.*) underwear
Un·ter'was·ser|ar·chäo·lo,gie *f* underwater (*or* marine) arch(a)eology; **~for·scher** *m* marine biologist, aquanaut; **~jagd** *f* subaqua (*or* underwater) fishing; **~ka·me·ra** *f* underwater camera; **~mas,sa·ge** *f* underwater massage; **~sta·ti,on** *f* undersea habitat
un·ter·wegs [ʊntɐ'veːks] *adv.* on the (*or* one's) way; *a.* en route; away, *mot. a.* on the road *on business etc.*; out (and about); ***ich war gestern den ganzen Tag ~*** I was out and about (*or* I was rushing around from one place to another) all day yesterday

un·ter'wei·sen *v/t.* (*irr., insep., no* -ge-, h, → ***weisen***) instruct; **Un·ter'wei·sung** *f* (-; -en) instruction
'Un·ter·welt *f* (-; *no pl.*) underworld (*a. fig.*)
un·ter'wer·fen (*irr., insep., no* -ge-, h, → ***werfen***) **I.** *v/t.* subject *people etc.* (***s-r Herrschaft*** to one's rule), subdue, subjugate; **II.** *v/refl.*: ***sich ~*** submit (*dat.* to); **Un·ter·wer·fung** [ʊntɐ'vɛrfʊŋ] *f* (-; -en) subjection, subjugation; submission; **un·ter·wor·fen I.** *p.p. of* ***unterwerfen***; **II.** *adj.*: ***e-r Sache ~ sein*** be subject to s.th.; ***Launen ~ sein*** *a.* be moody
un·ter·wür·fig [ʊntɐ'vʏrfɪç] *adj.* subservient, obsequious; **Un·ter'wür·fig·keit** *f* (-; *no pl.*) subservience, obsequiousness
un·ter'zeich·nen *v/t. and v/i.* (*insep., no* -ge-, h) sign; **Un·ter'zeich·ner** *m* (-s; -) *the* undersigned; signatory; **Un·ter'zeich·ner·staat** *m* signatory state; **Un·ter·zeich·ne·te** [ʊntɐ'tsaɪçnətə] *m, f* (-n; -n) *the* undersigned; **Un·ter'zeich·nung** *f* (-; -en) signing
'un·ter·zie·hen¹ *v/t.* (*irr., sep.,* h, → ***ziehen***) **1.** put on underneath; **2.** *gastr.* fold in *beaten egg white etc.*; **3.** ⚠ put in *beam etc.* (underneath)
un·ter'zie·hen² (*irr., insep., no* -ge-, h, → ***ziehen***) **I.** *v/refl.* **1.** ***sich e-r Operation*** *etc.* ~ undergo (*or* have) an operation *etc.*; ***sich e-r Prüfung ~*** take an examination; **2.** ***sich der Mühe ~ zu*** *inf.* take the trouble to *inf.*; **II.** *v/t.* put through, submit to *an interrogation tc.*; ***e-r Prüfung ~*** *a.* test, examine; ***j-n e-m Verhör ~*** *a.* interrogate s.o.
'un·tief *adj.* shallow; **'Un·tie·fe** *f* (-; -n) shallow, shoal
'Un·tier *n* monster (*a. fig.*)
un'trag·bar *adj.* intolerable; prohibitive *prices etc.*; **Un'trag·bar·keit** *f* (-; *no pl.*) intolerability
un'trenn·bar *adj.* inseparable; **Un'trenn·bar·keit** *f* (-; *no pl.*) inseparability
'un·treu *adj.* unfaithful, disloyal (*dat.* to); ***~ werden*** *dat.* be unfaithful to, *fig.* break faith with, abandon, give up *one's principles, belief etc.*; **'Un·treue** *f* (-; *no pl.*) unfaithfulness, disloyalty; infidelity (*all* ***gegenüber*** *dat.* to[wards])
un'trink·bar *adj.* undrinkable
un'tröst·lich *adj.* inconsolable, disconsolate; *w.s. a.* deeply sorry; ***ich bin ~!*** how can I ever forgive myself
un·trüg·lich [ʊn'try:klɪç] *adj.* unmistakable, sure *sign, symptom etc.*; ***~es Gefühl für et.*** unerring instinct for s.th.
'un·tüch·tig *adj.* incapable, incompetent; **'Un·tüch·tig·keit** *f* (-; *no pl.*) incompetence
'Un·tu·gend *f* (-; -en) bad habit; vice
'un·ty·pisch *adj.* atypical (***für*** *acc.* of), out of character (for)
'un·übel F *adj.*: ***gar nicht so ~*** not so bad, not bad at all
un·über·biet·bar [ʊnˀy:bɐ'bi:tba:ɐ] *adj.* unparalleled, F hard to beat
un·über·brück·bar [ʊnˀy:bɐ'brʏkba:ɐ] *fig. adj.* unbridgeable *gulf etc.*; irreconcilable, insurmountable *differences etc.*
un·über·hör·bar [ʊnˀy:bɐ'hø:ɐba:ɐ] *adj.* distinct, *pred. a.* loud and clear (*a. adv.*); ***es war ~*** *a.* you couldn't miss it
'un·über·legt I. *adj.* ill-considered; rash; **II.** *adv. act etc.* without thinking (*or* considering); **'Un·über·legt·heit** *f* (-; -en) **1.** *no pl.* rashness; **2.** rash act (*or* action)
un·über'schau·bar *adj.* → ***unübersehbar*** 1, 2
un·über'seh·bar *adj.* **1.** immense, vast; **2.** incalculable *consequences etc.*; **3.** glaring *mistake etc.*
'un·über·sicht·lich *adj.* **1.** ***~e Kurve*** blind corner; ***die Kreuzung*** *etc.* ***ist ~*** it's difficult (*or* impossible) to see what's going on at that crossing *etc.*; **2.** *fig.* unclear; confusing; **'Un·über·sicht·lich·keit** *f* (-; *no pl.*) confusingness, confusion
un·über·treff·lich [ʊnˀy:bɐ'trɛflɪç] *adj.* unsurpassable, matchless
un·über·trof·fen [ʊnˀy:bɐ'trɔfən] *adj.* unsurpassed, unmatched
un·über·wind·lich [ʊnˀy:bɐ'vɪntlɪç] *adj.* invincible; insurmountable, insuperable *difficulties etc.*; **Un·über'wind·lich·keit** *f* (-; *no pl.*) invincibility; insurmountability, insuperability
'un·üb·lich *adj.* unusual, not usual; ***es ist ~ zu*** *inf. a.* you don't usually ...
un·um·gäng·lich [ʊnˀʊm'gɛŋlɪç] *adj.* a) unavoidable; inevitable, b) indispensable, absolutely essential, imperative *to do s.th.*; **Un·um'gäng·lich·keit** *f* (-; *no pl.*) unavoidability, inevitability; indispensability, indispensable nature (*gen.* of)
un·um·schränkt [ʊnˀʊm'ʃrɛŋkt] *adj.* unlimited; *pol.* absolute *powers etc.*; **Un·um'schränkt·heit** *f* (-; *no pl.*) unlimitedness; absolute nature (*gen.* of)
un·um·stöß·lich [ʊnˀʊm'ʃtø:slɪç] *adj.* irrefutable, incontrovertible *fact etc.*; irrevocable *decision etc.*; **Un·um'stöß·lich·keit** *f* (-; *no pl.*) irrefutability, irrefutable nature (*gen.* of), incontrovertibility; irrevocability, irrevocable nature (*gen.* of)
un·um'strit·ten *adj.* undisputed
un·um·wun·den [ʊnˀʊm'vʊndən] **I.** *adj.* open *avowal, acknowledg(e)ment etc.*; frank *manner etc.*; **II.** *adv.* point-blank, straight out
un·un·ter·bro·chen ['ʊnˀʊntɐbrɔxən] **I.** *adj.* a) uninterrupted, *a.* unbroken *line, series etc.*, b) continuous; incessant; **II.** *adv.* uninterruptedly; continuously; incessantly; ***er hat ~ geschrien*** *etc. a.* he wouldn't stop screaming *etc.*
un·ver'än·der·lich *adj.* unchanging, *a. ling.* invariable; constant, stable; **Un·ver'än·der·lich·keit** *f* (-; *no pl.*) unchangingness; stability; **un·ver·än·dert** [ʊnfɛɐ'ˀɛndɐt] *adj.* unchanged, *pred. a.* (just) as it was
un·ver'ant·wort·lich *adj.* irresponsible; **Un·ver'ant·wort·lich·keit** *f* (-; *no pl.*) irresponsibility
un·ver·ar·bei·tet ['ʊnfɛɐˀarbaɪtət] *adj.* **1.** ⚙ unfinished, unprocessed; **2.** *fig.* undigested
un·ver·äu·ßer·lich [ʊnfɛɐ'ˀɔʏsɐlɪç] *adj.* inalienable; **Un·ver'äu·ßer·lich·keit** *f* (-; *no pl.*) inalienability
un·ver·bes·ser·lich [ʊnfɛɐ'bɛsɐlɪç] *adj.* incorrigible, inveterate ..., F hopeless; ***~er Trinker*** *etc.* hardened drinker *etc.*; **Un·ver'bes·ser·lich·keit** *f* (-; *no pl.*) incorrigibility
'un·ver·bil·det *adj.* unspoilt, uncorrupted
'un·ver·bind·lich I. *adj.* **1.** a) non-binding *offer etc.*, without obligation, b) *information etc.* without guarantee (as to correctness); non-committal *comment etc.*; **2.** (very) non-committal; detached; curt; **II.** *adv.* ✝ without obligation; *give one's view etc.* in a non-committal way; *give information etc.* without guarantee; **'Un·ver·bind·lich·keit** *f* (-; *no pl.*) **1.** ✝ freedom from obligation; **2.** non-committal (*or* detached) manner; curtness
'un·ver·bleit *adj.* unleaded, lead-free
'un·ver·blümt I. *adj.* undisguised *view etc.*; outspoken, blunt, forthright *manner etc.*; **II.** *adv.* bluntly, openly; **'Un·ver·blümt·heit** *f* (-; *no pl.*) bluntness (***s-r Redeweise*** with which he speaks)
'un·ver·braucht *adj.* unused; unspent *vigo(u)r etc.*; fresh; *person* full of energy (*or* vigo[u]r)
un·ver·brüch·lich [ʊnfɛɐ'brʏçlɪç] **I.** *adj.* unswerving, steadfast; **II.** *adv.*: ***~ festhalten an*** *dat.*, ***~ stehen zu*** *dat.* keep unswervingly to *one's principles etc.*; stand unswervingly by *one's promise etc.*; **Un·ver'brüch·lich·keit** *f* (-; *no pl.*) unswervingness, steadfastness
'un·ver·bürgt *adj.* unconfirmed
'un·ver·däch·tig *adj.* **1.** unsuspicious; **2.** unsuspected
'un·ver·dau·lich *adj.* indigestible (*a. fig.*); **'Un·ver·dau·lich·keit** *f* (-; *no pl.*) indigestibility (*a. fig.*); **un·ver·daut** ['ʊnfɛɐdaʊt] *adj.* undigested (*a. fig.*)
'un·ver·derb·lich *adj.* non-perishable *goods*
'un·ver·dient *adj.* undeserved; **'un·ver·dien·ter·ma·ßen** *adv.* undeservedly
'un·ver·dor·ben *adj.* unspoilt, *fig. a.* uncorrupted; **'Un·ver·dor·ben·heit** *f* (-; *no pl.*) unspoilt quality *or* nature (*gen.* of)
'un·ver·dros·sen I. *adj.* untiring, indefatigable, unflagging; **II.** *adv.* untiringly, indefatigably, unflaggingly; ***~ weitermachen*** continue undaunted; **'Un·ver·dros·sen·heit** *f* (-; *no pl.*) indefatigability
'un·ver·dünnt *adj.* undiluted; neat, straight *whisky etc.*
un·ver'ein·bar *adj.* incompatible; irreconcilable *differences*; **Un·ver'ein·bar·keit** *f* (-; *no pl.*) incompatibility; irreconcilability, irreconcilable nature (*gen.* of)
un·ver·fälscht ['ʊnfɛɐfɛlʃt] *adj.* unadulterated, pure; *fig. a.* genuine; **'Un·ver·fälscht·heit** *f* (-; *no pl.*) unadulterated quality (*gen.* of), pureness; genuineness
'un·ver·fäng·lich *adj.* harmless, innocuous; **'Un·ver·fäng·lich·keit** *f* (-; *no pl.*) harmlessness, innocuousness
'un·ver·fro·ren *adj.* unabashed, shameless, brazen; **'Un·ver·fro·ren·heit** *f* (-; -en) **1.** *no pl.* brazenness; insolence; **2.** insolence
'un·ver·gäng·lich *adj.* immortal; undying, everlasting, unfading *memory, fame etc.*; **'Un·ver·gäng·lich·keit** *f* (-; *no pl.*) immortality; everlastingness
'un·ver·ges·sen *adj.* unforgotten; **un·ver'geß·lich** *adj.* unforgettable; ***das wird mir ~ bleiben*** I shall never forget it
un·ver'gleich·lich *adj.* incomparable; unrival(l)ed
un·ver·go·ren ['ʊnfɛɐgo:rən] *adj.* unfermented
'un·ver·hält·nis·mä·ßig *adv.* disproportionately; excessively, unreasonably
'un·ver·hei·ra·tet *adj.* unmarried, single
un·ver·hofft ['ʊnfɛɐhɔft] **I.** *adj.* unexpected; ***~ kommt oft*** life is full of surprises; **II.** *adv.* unexpectedly; ***es kam ganz ~*** *a.* I just wasn't expecting it
'un·ver·hoh·len I. *adj.* undisguised,

open; **II.** *adv.* openly; ***et. ~ zeigen*** *a.* make no secret of s.th.
'un·ver·hüllt *adj.* unveiled; bare; *fig.* undisguised
'un·ver·käuf·lich *adj.* **1.** not for sale; ***~es Muster*** free sample, sample not for sale; **2.** unsal(e)able
un·ver·kenn·bar [ʊnfɛɐ'kɛnba:ɐ] **I.** *adj.* unmistakable; ***es ist ~, daß*** it's quite obvious that; **II.** *adv.* unmistakably; ***es ist ~ s-e Handschrift*** it's his handwriting all right (*Am.* alright)
un·ver·langt ['ʊnfɛɐlaŋt] *adj.* unsolicited (*a. adv.* ***~ eingesandt***), not asked for
'un·ver·läß·lich *adj.* unreliable; **Un·ver·läß·lich·keit** *f* (-; *no pl.*) unreliability
un·ver'letz·bar, un·ver'letz·lich *adj.* inviolable; **'Un·ver·letz·bar·keit** *f* (-; *no pl.*), **Un·ver'letz·lich·keit** *f* (-; *no pl.*) inviolability; **'un·ver·letzt** *adj.* unhurt; safe (and sound)
un·ver'meid·bar *adj.* unavoidable; **Un·ver'meid·bar·keit** *f* (-; *no pl.*) unavoidability; **un·ver'meid·lich I.** *adj.* a) inevitable (*a.* F *fig.*), b) unavoidable; inevitable (*a. iro.*); ***sich ins Unvermeidliche fügen*** bow to the inevitable; **II.** *adv. a.* without fail; **Un·ver'meid·lich·keit** *f* (-; *no pl.*) inevitability; unavoidability
un·ver·min·dert ['ʊnfɛɐmɪndɐt] *adj. and adv.* undiminished
'un·ver·mischt *adj.* unmixed, unblended
un·ver·mit·telt ['ʊnfɛɐmɪtəlt] **I.** *adj.* abrupt, sudden; **II.** *adv.*: (***völlig ~*** quite) suddenly *or* abruptly; *happen etc. a.* without (any) warning; ***es kam so ~*** there was absolutely no warning
'Un·ver·mö·gen *n* (-s; *no pl.*) inability, incapacity
'un·ver·mö·gend *adj.* impecunious, without means; ***nicht ~*** fairly well-off
un·ver·mu·tet ['ʊnfɛɐmu:tət] *adj.* (*and adv.*) unexpected(ly)
'Un·ver·nunft *f* (-; *no pl.*) unreasonableness; folly, stupidity; **'un·ver·nünf·tig** *adj.* unreasonable; foolish
un·ver·öf·fent·licht ['ʊnfɛɐʔœfəntlɪçt] *adj.* unpublished
'un·ver·packt *adj.* unpacked, unpackaged; unwrapped
un·ver·rich·te·ter·din·ge ['ʊnfɛɐrɪçtətɐ'dɪŋə] *adv.*: ***~ weggehen*** (***zurückkommen***) come away (come back) without having achieved anything
un·ver·rück·bar [ʊnfɛɐ'rʏkba:ɐ] *adj.* unshak(e)able
'un·ver·schämt I. *adj.* impertinent, insolent, impudent; barefaced *lie etc.*; F outrageous *price, demand etc.*; F (***ein***) ***~es Glück haben*** F be damned lucky; **II.** *adv.*: ***~ lügen*** lie shamelessly; F ***~ teuer*** *etc.* outrageously expensive *etc.*; F ***er sieht ~ gut aus*** he's outrageously (F damned) good-looking; **'Un·ver·schämt·heit** *f* (-; *no pl.*) impertinence, insolence, impudence; ***die ~ haben zu*** *inf.* have the nerve (*or* cheek) to *inf.*
'un·ver·schlos·sen *adj.* **1.** unsealed *letter*; **2.** unlocked *door etc.*
'un·ver·schul·det *adj.*: ***~ in Geldnot geraten*** *etc.* run into financial difficulties *etc.* through no fault of one's own; ***ein ~er Unfall*** an accident for which one is not responsible; **un·ver·schul·de·ter·ma·ßen** ['ʊnfɛɐʃʊldətɐma:sən], **'un·ver·schul·de·ter·wei·se** *adv.* through no fault of one's own
un·ver·se·hens ['ʊnfɛɐze:əns] *adv.* unexpectedly, all of a sudden, suddenly
'un·ver·sehrt *adj.* unhurt, unscathed; intact
'un·ver·söhn·lich *adj.* irreconcilable (*a. differences*); **'Un·ver·söhn·lich·keit** *f* (-; *no pl.*) irreconcilability
un·ver·sorgt ['ʊnfɛɐzɔrkt] *adj.* unprovided for; *area, people etc.* lacking in supplies
'Un·ver·stand *m* (-[e]s; *no pl.*) ignorance; foolishness; **un·ver·stan·den** ['ʊnfɛɐʃtandən] *adj.* misunderstood, not understood; **'un·ver·stän·dig** *adj.* ignorant; *child*: too young to know; stupid, foolish
'un·ver·ständ·lich *adj.* a) unintelligible, b) incomprehensible (*a. fig.*); obscure *reason*; ***das ist mir völlig ~*** a) I just can't understand it, b) it's beyond me (completely), c) I can't make head or tail of it; **'Un·ver·ständ·lich·keit** *f* (-; *no pl.*) unintelligibility; incomprehensibility
'Un·ver·ständ·nis *n* (-ses; *no pl.*) lack of understanding; *art etc.*: lack of appreciation; ***auf ~ stoßen*** find no sympathy
un·ver·stellt ['ʊnfɛɐʃtɛlt] *adj.* undisguised; genuine
'un·ver·steu·ert *adj.* untaxed
'un·ver·sucht *adj.*: ***nichts ~ lassen*** try everything (***um zu*** *inf.* to *inf.*), leave no stone unturned (in one's attempt to *inf.*)
'un·ver·träg·lich *adj.* **1.** indigestible *food*; **2.** quarrelsome; **3.** incompatible (*a.* ⚘); **'Un·ver·träg·lich·keit** *f* (-; *no pl.*) **1.** indigestibility; **2.** quarrelsomeness; **3.** incompatibility
un·ver'tret·bar *adj.* unacceptable *views etc.*
'un·ver·wandt I. *adj.* fixed *look*; **II.** *adv.* fixedly; ***j-n ~ ansehen*** fix one's gaze on s.o.; ***er sah sie ~ an*** *a.* he wouldn't take his eyes off her
un·ver·wech·sel·bar [ʊnfɛɐ'vɛksəlba:ɐ] *adj.* unmistakable
un·ver·wehrt ['ʊnfɛɐve:ɐt] *adj.*: ***es ist*** (*or* ***sei***) ***ihr*** (***völlig***) ***~ zu*** *inf.* she is (completely) at liberty to *inf.*
un·ver'wert·bar *adj.* unusable; **Un·ver'wert·bar·keit** *f* (-; *no pl.*) unusability
un·ver'wund·bar *adj.* invulnerable; **Un·ver'wund·bar·keit** *f* (-; *no pl.*) invulnerability
un·ver·wüst·lich [ʊnfɛɐ'vy:stlɪç] *adj.* indestructible (*a. fig.*); *fig.* inexhaustible *humo(u)r etc.*; *fig.* ***sie ist ~*** *a.* she keeps bouncing back, you can't get her down; **Un·ver'wüst·lich·keit** *f* (-; *no pl.*) indestructibility; inexhaustibility
'un·ver·zagt *adj. and adv.* undaunted; **'Un·ver·zagt·heit** *f* (-; *no pl.*) undauntedness; intrepidity
un·ver'zeih·lich *adj.* inexcusable; unforgivable; ***es ist ~*** *a.* there's no excuse for it
un·ver·zicht·bar [ʊnfɛɐ'tsɪçtba:ɐ] *adj.* indispensable, (absolutely) essential; inalienable *right*; **Un·ver'zicht·bar·keit** *f* (-; *no pl.*) indispensability; inalienability
'un·ver·zins·lich *adj.* non-interest-bearing; ***~es Darlehen*** interest-free loan
'un·ver·zollt *adj.* duty unpaid; ***~e Waren*** uncleared goods
un·ver·züg·lich [ʊnfɛɐ'tsy:klɪç] **I.** *adj.* immediate, prompt; **II.** *adv.* immediately, straightaway, without delay
'un·voll·en·det *adj.* unfinished
'un·voll·kom·men *adj.* imperfect; **'Un·voll·kom·men·heit** *f* (-; -en) imperfection
'un·voll·stän·dig *adj.* incomplete; **'Un·voll·stän·dig·keit** *f* (-; *no pl.*) incompleteness
un·vor·be·rei·tet ['nfo:ɐbəraɪtət] *adj.* unprepared; impromptu *speech*; ***~ reden*** ad-lib; ***~ in e-e Prüfung gehen*** take (*or* do) an exam without any preparation; ***es traf ihn ~*** it came as a complete surprise (*or* shock) to him, it took him unawares
'un·vor·ein·ge·nom·men *adj.* unbias(s)ed, unprejudiced; objective; **'Un·vor·ein·ge·nom·men·heit** *f* impartiality, lack of (*or* freedom from) prejudice; objectivity
un·vor·her·ge·se·hen ['ʊnfo:ɐhe:ɐgəze:ən] **I.** *adj.* unforeseen; unexpected; **II.** *adv.* unexpectedly; ***~ Besuch bekommen*** have unexpected visitors (*or* an unexpected visitor); **un·vor·her·seh·bar** [ʊnfo:ɐ'he:ɐze:ba:ɐ] *adj.* unforeseeable
'un·vor·schrifts·mä·ßig *adj.* improper; *behavio(u)r etc.* contrary to the regulations
'un·vor·sich·tig *adj.* (*and adv.*) careless(ly); imprudent(ly); rash(ly); **'un·vor·sich·ti·ger'wei·se** *adv.* carelessly; ***er hat es ~ liegenlassen*** *a.* he was careless enough to leave it behind; **'Un·vor·sich·tig·keit** *f* (-; *no pl.*) carelessness; imprudence; rashness
un·vor'stell·bar *adj.* unimaginable; unthinkable; incredible
'un·vor·teil·haft I. *adj.* **1.** unbecoming, unflattering *dress, hairdo etc.*; ***für j-n ~ sein*** not to suit s.o.; ***~ aussehen*** look unattractive; **2.** ***~er Kauf*** bad buy; ***~es Geschäft*** bad deal; **II.** *adv.*: ***sich ~ kleiden*** wear the wrong clothes (for one's figure *etc.*); ***sich ~ auswirken*** prove disadvantageous (***für*** *acc.* for), ***für j-n***: *a.* prove to be to s.o.'s disadvantage
un·wäg·bar [ʊn'vɛ:kba:ɐ] *adj.* imponderable; incalculable; **Un'wäg·bar·keit** *f* (-; -en) **1.** *no pl.* imponderability, incalculability; **2.** imponderability
'un·wahr *adj.* untrue, false; **'Un·wahr·heit** *f* (-; -en) **1.** *no pl.* untruthfulness; **2.** untruth, falsehood
'un·wahr·schein·lich I. *adj.* unlikely, improbable; F *fig.* incredible *luck etc.*; **II.** F *adv.*: ***~ gut*** *etc.* F incredibly good *etc.*; **'Un·wahr·schein·lich·keit** *f* (-; *no pl.*) unlikelihood, improbability
un'wan·del·bar *adj.* unchanging, constant; steadfast *love etc.*; **Un'wan·del·bar·keit** *f* (-; *no pl.*) unchangingness, constancy; steadfastness
un·weg·sam ['ʊnve:kza:m] *adj.* difficult, rough *terrain*; virtually impassable *mountains, forest etc.*; **'Un·weg·sam·keit** *f* (-; *no pl.*) roughness; impassability
'un·weib·lich *adj.* unfeminine
un·wei·ger·lich [ʊn'vaɪgɐlɪç] **I.** *adj.* inevitable; **II.** *adv.* without fail, inevitably; ***es führte ~ zu e-r Zinserhöhung*** it led to an inevitable rise in interest rates
'un·weit *prp.* not far from (*gen. a place etc.*)
'Un·we·sen *n* (-s; *no pl.*) dreadful state of affairs; ***sein ~ treiben*** be up to no good, be on the rampage, ***in*** *dat.*: wreak havoc in, terrorize
'un·we·sent·lich I. *adj.* inessential (***für*** *acc.* to); *w.s.* marginal (to); unimportant (for, to), insignificant (to); irrelevant, immaterial (to); negligible; **II.** *adv.* slightly, marginally; negligibly

'**Un·wet·ter** *n* (-s; -) (thunder)storm; **~scha·den** *m a. pl.* storm damage
'**un·wich·tig** *adj.* not important, insignificant; irrelevant; '**Un·wich·tig·keit** *f* (-; -en) **1.** *no pl.* unimportance, insignificance; irrelevance; **2.** triviality, unimportant matter
un·wi·der'leg·bar *adj.* irrefutable, incontrovertible; **Un·wi·der'leg·bar·keit** *f* (-; *no pl.*) irrefutability, incontrovertibility
un·wi·der·ruf·lich [ʊnviːdɐ'ruːflɪç] **I.** *adj.* irrevocable (*a.* ✝); **II.** *adv.* irrevocably; definitely, positively; ***es steht ~ fest, daß*** it's absolutely definite (*or* certain) that; **Un·wi·der'ruf·lich·keit** *f* irrevocability
un·wi·der·spro·chen [ʊnviːdɐ'ʃprɔxən] *adj.*: ***~ bleiben*** stand uncontradicted; ***et. ~ hinnehmen*** take s.th. without contradiction (*or* without a word of protest)
un·wi·der·steh·lich [ʊnviːdɐ'ʃteːlɪç] *adj.* irresistible; compelling; ***~es Verlangen nach Schokolade*** *etc.* irresistible (*or* overpowering) urge to eat chocolate *etc.*, overpowering desire for chocolate *etc.*; **Un·wi·der'steh·lich·keit** *f* (-; *no pl.*) irresistibility
un·wie·der·bring·lich [ʊnviːdɐ'brɪŋlɪç] **I.** *adj.* irretrievable; **II.** *adv.*: ***~ dahin*** irretrievably lost, lost (*or* gone) forever; **Un·wie·der'bring·lich·keit** *f* (-; *no pl.*) irretrievability
'**Un·wil·le** *m* (-ns; *no pl.*) displeasure, anger; '**un·wil·lent·lich** *adv.* unintentionally; '**un·wil·lig** *adj.* (*and adv.*) indignant(ly) (***über*** *acc.* at); unwilling(ly), reluctant(ly)
'**un·will·kom·men** *adj.* unwelcome
'**un·will·kür·lich** **I.** *adj.* involuntary *movement, thought etc.*; instinctive; automatic; **II.** *adv.* involuntarily; instinctively; automatically; ***~ mußte ich an ihn denken*** *etc.* I couldn't help thinking of him *etc.*
'**un·wirk·lich** *adj.* unreal; '**Un·wirk·lich·keit** *f* (-; *no pl.*) unreality
'**un·wirk·sam** *adj.* ineffective; ⚖ a) inoperative, b) null and void; '**Un·wirk·sam·keit** *f* (-; *no pl.*) ineffectiveness; ⚖ inoperativeness
un·wirsch ['ʊnvɪrʃ] *adj.* gruff
un·wirt·lich ['ʊnvɪrtlɪç] *adj.* inhospitable; '**Un·wirt·lich·keit** *f* (-; *no pl.*) inhospitableness
'**un·wirt·schaft·lich** *adj.* uneconomical; unviable; inefficient; '**Un·wirt·schaft·lich·keit** *f* (-; *no pl.*) uneconomicalness; inefficiency; unviability
'**un·wis·send** *adj.* ignorant; *child:* too young to know; '**Un·wis·sen·heit** *f* (-; *no pl.*): (***aus*** ~ out of) ignorance
'**un·wis·sen·schaft·lich** *adj.* unscientific *age, method etc.*; unscholarly *approach, argument etc.*; '**Un·wis·sen·schaft·lich·keit** *f* (-; *no pl.*) unscientific (*or* unscholarly) nature *or* character *etc.* (*gen.* of)
'**un·wis·sent·lich** *adv.* unknowingly, *lit.* unwittingly
'**un·wohl** *adj.* **1.** unwell; ***mir ist ~*** I don't feel well; **2.** uneasy; ***dabei wird mir ganz ~*** it gives me a very uneasy feeling; '**Un·wohl·sein** *n* (-s; *no pl.*) indisposition; feeling of sickness, nausea
'**un·wohn·lich** *adj.* uncomfortable; unhomely, cheerless; '**Un·wohn·lich·keit** *f* (-; *no pl.*) uncomfortableness; unhomeliness, cheerlessness
'**un·wür·dig** *adj.* a) unworthy (*gen.* of), b) undignified, c) disgraceful; degrading; ***das ist seiner ~*** that is beneath him; '**Un·wür·dig·keit** *f* (-; *no pl.*) unworthiness; lack of dignity, undignified manner
'**Un·zahl** *f*: ***e-e ~ von*** a host of, an enormous number of, innumerable, F no end of; **un'zähl·bar** *adj.*, **un·zäh·lig** [ʊn'tsɛːlɪç] *adj.* innumerable, countless, numberless; ***~e*** *a.* scores of
'**un·zart** *adj.* indelicate; rough
Un·ze ['ʊntsə] *f* (-; -n) ounce (*abbr.* oz.)
'**Un·zeit** *f*: ***zur ~*** at an inopportune time; '**un·zeit·ge·mäß** *adj.* a) old-fashioned, dated, behind the times, b) unseasonable, inopportune
'**un·zer·brech·lich** *adj.* unbreakable; '**Un·zer·brech·lich·keit** *f* (-; *no pl.*) unbreakability
un·zer·reiß·bar [ʊntsɛɐ'raɪsbaːɐ] *adj.* untearable, non-tear(ing); **Un·zer'reiß·bar·keit** *f* (-; *no pl.*) untearable (*or* non-tearing) quality (*gen.* of)
un·zer·stör·bar [ʊntsɛɐ'ʃtøːɐbaːɐ] *adj.* indestructible; **Un·zer'stör·bar·keit** *f* (-; *no pl.*) indestructibility
un·zer·trenn·lich [ʊntsɛɐ'trɛnlɪç] *adj.* inseparable; **Un·zer'trenn·lich·keit** *f* (-; *no pl.*) inseparability
'**un·zi·vi·li·siert** *adj.* uncivilized; '**Un·zi·vi·li·siert·heit** *f* (-; *no pl.*) uncivilized nature (*or* state) (*gen.* of); lack of civilization (among)
'**Un·zucht** *f* (-; *no pl.*) ⚖ sexual offen|ce (*Am.* -se), (act of) indecency; ***~ treiben*** fornicate; '**un·züch·tig** *adj.* lewd, lascivious; obscene *gesture, word etc.*
'**un·zu·frie·den** *adj.* dissatisfied, discontented; '**Un·zu·frie·den·heit** *f* (-; *no pl.*) dissatisfaction, discontentment
'**un·zu·gäng·lich** *adj.* inaccessible (*a.* ⚙), unapproachable; *fig.* ***~ für*** *acc.* impervious to, deaf to; '**Un·zu·gäng·lich·keit** *f* (-; *no pl.*) inaccessibility, unapproachability; *fig.* imperviousness (***für*** *acc.* to)
un·zu·läng·lich ['ʊntsuːlɛŋlɪç] *adj.* inadequate; deficient, insufficient; '**Un·zu·läng·lich·keit** *f* (-; -en) **1.** *no pl.* inadequacy; deficiency; **2.** shortcoming, failing
'**un·zu·läs·sig** *adj.* inadmissible; ⚖ undue *influence*; '**Un·zu·läs·sig·keit** *f* (-; *no pl.*) inadmissibility
un·zu'mut·bar *adj.* unreasonable, too much to expect (*or* ask [for]); unacceptable; ***das ist für ihn ~*** you can't expect him to put up with (*or* accept, do *etc.*) that; **Un·zu'mut·bar·keit** *f* (-; -en) **1.** *no pl.* unreasonableness; ***das ist e-e ~*** *a.* that's asking (*or* expecting) too much; **2.** unreasonable demand
'**un·zu·rech·nungs·fä·hig** *adj.* ⚖ non compos mentis, of unsound mind, *Am. a.* incompetent; '**Un·zu·rech·nungs·fä·hig·keit** *f* (-; *no pl.*) diminished responsibility, *Am.* incompetence
un·zu·rei·chend ['ʊntsuːraɪçənt] *adj.* insufficient
'**un·zu,sam·men·hän·gend** *adj.* disconnected, disjointed; incoherent *speech etc.*
'**un·zu·stän·dig** *adj.* not responsible (***für*** *acc.* for); ⚖ ***~ sein*** have no jurisdiction (***für*** *acc.* over)
un·zu·stell·bar ['ʊntsuːʃtɛlbaːɐ] *adj.* 📯 undelivered; ***falls ~, bitte zurück an Absender*** if undelivered, please return to sender
'**un·zu·träg·lich** *adj.* detrimental (*dat.* to); '**Un·zu·träg·lich·keit** *f* (-; -en) detrimental nature *or* effect(s *pl.*) (*gen.* of)
'**un·zu·tref·fend** *adj.* a) incorrect, b) unfounded, c) inapplicable; ***Unzutreffendes bitte streichen!*** delete where inapplicable
'**un·zu·ver·läs·sig** *adj.* unreliable; untrustworthy; '**Un·zu·ver·läs·sig·keit** *f* (-; *no pl.*) unreliability; untrustworthiness
'**un·zweck·mä·ßig** *adj.* inexpedient; unsuitable; '**Un·zweck·mä·ßig·keit** *f* (-; *no pl.*) inexpediency; unsuitability
'**un·zwei·deu·tig** **I.** *adj.* unequivocal, unambiguous; explicit, plain, clear; **II.** *adv.*: ***~ zu verstehen geben, daß*** make it quite clear (*or* plain) that; '**Un·zwei·deu·tig·keit** *f* (-; *no pl.*) unambiguousness; explicitness
'**un·zwei·fel·haft** **I.** *adj.* unquestionable, indubitable; **II.** *adv.* doubtless, without (a) doubt, undoubtedly
üp·pig ['ʏpɪç] **I.** *adj.* a) luxuriant *vegetation etc.*; lush *meadow, foliage etc., a. fig. life*, b) sumptuous, opulent *meal etc.*; rich *food*, c) F full *figure etc.*, voluptuous *body etc.*, d) F good, F big fat *tip, helping etc.*; ***~er Haarwuchs*** (***Bartwuchs***) thick hair (growth of beard); F ***e-e*** (***ziemlich***) ***~e Angelegenheit*** quite an affair; F ***nicht gerade ~*** F not overwhelming(ly much); **II.** *adv. grow etc.* luxuriantly; ***~ speisen*** have a sumptuous meal; ***~ essen*** eat rich foods; F ***j-n ~ beschenken*** shower s.o. with presents; ***~ leben*** live a life of luxury, live off the fat of the land; '**Üp·pig·keit** *f* (-; *no pl.*) a) luxuriance; thick growth; lushness, b) sumptuousness, opulence; richness, c) voluptuousness
Ur... [uːɐ-] *in cpds.* a) original; primeval; first, b) extremely
'**Ur·ab·stim·mung** *f* strike ballot, secret ballot (on strike action)
'**Ur·ahn** *m* (-[e]s, -en; -en) (earliest) ancestor; *pl. a.* forefathers
'**ur·alt** *adj.* ancient, F (as) old as the hills; age-old *problem*; ***seit ~en Zeiten*** from (*or* since) time immemorial; ***aus ~en Zeiten*** from long, long ago, F from way back when
Uran [u'raːn] *n* (-s; *no pl.*) ⚗ uranium; **~an·rei·che·rungs·an·la·ge** *f* uranium enrichment plant; **~bren·ner** *m* uranium pile; **~erz** *n* uranium ore
'**Ur·an·fang** *m* very first beginnings *pl.*; origins *pl.*; '**ur·an·fäng·lich** *adj.* primeval, primordial
'**Ur·angst** *f psych.* primordial fear
uran·hal·tig *adj.* uranium-bearing
Uran|mi·ne *f* uranium mine; **~vor·kom·men** *n* uranium deposit
'**ur·auf·füh·ren** *v/t.* (*only inf. and p.p.* uraufgeführt, h) première; ***die Oper*** *etc.* ***wurde 1924 uraufgeführt*** the opera *etc.* was first performed in 1924; '**Ur·auf·füh·rung** *f* first performance, *a. film:* première
'**Ur·aus·ga·be** *f* first (*or* original) edition
ur·ban [ʊr'baːn] *adj.* urbane
Ur·ba·ni·sa·ti·on [ʊrbaniza'tsi̯oːn] *f* (-; -en) urbanization; **ur·ba·ni·sie·ren** [ʊrbani'ziːrən] *v/t.* (h) urbanize
Ur·ba·ni·stik [ʊrba'nɪstɪk] *f* (-; *no pl.*) town planning (and urban development)

Ur·ba·ni·tät [ʊrbaniˈtɛːt] *f* (-; *no pl.*) urbanity, urbaneness
ur·bar [ˈuːɐbaːɐ] *adj.*: ~ ***machen*** cultivate; clear *forest*; reclaim *desert etc.*; **ˈUr·bar·ma·chung** *f* (-; -en) cultivation; clearing; reclamation
ˈUr·be·deu·tung *f* original meaning
ˈU·rbe·ginn *m* very first beginnings *pl.*; ***von ~ an*** from the very beginning
ˈUr·be·völ·ke·rung *f* (ab)original population (*or* inhabitants *pl.*)
ˈUr·bild *n* model, prototype
ˈUr·chri·sten·tum *n*: ***das ~*** early Christianity
ˈur·deutsch *adj.* German to the core, F as German as you can get
ˈurˈei·gen *adj.*: ***~es Interesse*** vested interest; ***in Ihrem ~sten Interesse*** in your own best interest(s); ***das ist m-e ~ste Angelegenheit*** that's my business and nobody else's
ˈUr·ein·woh·ner *pl.* (ab)original inhabitants (*or* population *sg.*); ***die ~ Australiens*** the Australian aborigines
ˈUr·el·tern *pl.* ancestors
ˈUr·en·kel *m* great-grandson
ˈUr·en·ke·lin *f* great-granddaughter
ˈUr·form *f* archetype
ˈur·geˈmüt·lich *adj.* really cosy (*Am.* cozy)
ˈur·gerˌma·nisch *adj.* Teutonic; *ling.* Proto-Germanic
ˈUr·ge·schich·te *f* (-; *no pl.*): ***die ~*** prehistory; **ˈur·ge·schicht·lich** *adj.* prehistoric
ˈUr·ge·stein *n* primary rocks *pl.*
ˈUr·ge·walt *f* elemental force
ˈUr·groß|el·tern *pl.* great-grandparents; **~mut·ter** *f* great-grandmother; **~va·ter** *m* great-grandfather
Ur·he·ber [ˈuːɐheːbɐ] *m* (-s; -) a) author, b) creator; **ˈUr·he·ber·recht** *n* **1.** copyright (***für*** *acc.*, ***von*** *dat.* on); **2.** *no pl.* copyright law; **ˈur·he·ber·recht·lich I.** *adj.* copyright ...; **II.** *adv.*: ***~ geschützt*** protected by copyright; **ˈUr·he·ber·schaft** *f* (-; *no pl.*) authorship; **ˈUr·he·ber·schutz** *m* copyright protection
ˈUr·hei·mat *f* original home(land)
urig [ˈuːrɪç] *adj.* a) earthy *person, humo(u)r etc.*, b) rustic *pub etc.*, c) unsophisticated; *contp.* unrefined; F ***ein ~er Typ*** an original
Urin [uˈriːn] *m* (-s; *no pl.*) urine; F *fig.* ***ich spür's im ~*** F I've got a gut feeling about it; **Urin·fla·sche** *f* a) urine bottle, b) urinal; **uri·nie·ren** [uriˈniːrən] *v/i.* (h) urinate; **Urin·pro·be** *f* urine specimen
ˈUr·inˌstinkt *m* primeval instinct
Urin·un·terˌsu·chung *f* urine test, urinalysis
ˈUr·knall *m* (-[e]s; *no pl.*) big bang, Big Bang
ˈurˈko·misch *adj.* hilarious
ˈUr·kraft *f* elemental force
Ur·kun·de [ˈuːɐkʊndə] *f* (-; -n) document; deed; certificate, diploma; **ˈur·kun·den·echt** *adj.*: ***~e Tinte*** indelible ink
ˈUr·kun·den|fäl·scher *m* document forger; **~fäl·schung** *f* forgery of documents; ***wegen ~ verurteilt werden*** be sentenced for forging documents
ur·kund·lich [ˈuːɐkʊntlɪç] **I.** *adj.* documentary; authentic; **II.** *adv.* authentically; ***~ belegt*** documented; ***~ erwähnt werden*** be mentioned in a document; ***der Bau wird erstmals im 9. Jahrhundert ~ erwähnt*** the first documentary evidence of the building goes back to the 9th century
ˈUr·land·schaft *f* primeval landscape
Ur·laub [ˈuːɐlaʊp] *m* (-[e]s; -e [-bə]) holidays *pl.*, *esp. Am.* vacation; ⚔ leave; ***auf (im) ~*** on holiday (*or* vacation); ***in ~ gehen*** go on holiday (*or* vacation)
Ur·lau·ber [ˈuːɐlaʊbɐ] *m* (-s; -) holidaymaker, *Am.* vacationer; **~strom** *m* stream of holidaymakers (*or* vacationers)
ˈUr·laubs|an·spruch *m* holiday entitlement, *Am.* vacation privilege; **~fo·to** *n* holiday (*esp. Am.* vacation) snap; **~geld** *n* holiday pay, *Am.* vacation money; **~pa·raˌdies** *n* holiday(makers') paradise; **~reif** *adj.* in (desperate) need of a holiday; **~rei·se** *f* holiday (*esp. Am.* vacation) trip; **~tag** *m* (a day's) holiday (*esp. Am.* vacation); **~ver·tre·tung** *f* **1.** holiday (*esp. Am.* vacation) replacement; ***X ist m-e ~*** X will be standing in for me when I'm on holiday (*esp. Am.* vacation); **2.** holiday (*esp. Am.* vacation) stand-in scheme; ***für j-n ~ machen*** stand in for s.o. while he (*or* she) is on holiday (*esp. Am.* vacation); **~zeit** *f* holiday (*esp. Am.* vacation) season *or* period; **~ziel** *n* vacation spot; tourist destination
ˈUr·mensch *m*: ***der ~*** primitive man
Ur·ne [ˈʊrnə] *f* (-; -n) urn; *pol. a.* ballot box; **ˈUr·nen·bei·set·zung** *f* urn burial
ˈUr·nen·feld *n hist.* urnfield; **ˈUr·nen·fel·der·kulˌtur** *f hist.* Urnfield culture
ˈUr·nen|gang *m* polling, polls *pl.*; ***80% beteiligten sich am ~*** there was an 80% turnout at the polls; **~grab** *n* urn grave
Uro·lo·ge [uroˈloːgə] *m* (-n; -n) urologist; **Uro·lo·gie** [urolоˈgiː] *f* (-; *no pl.*) urology; **uro·lo·gisch** [uroˈloːgɪʃ] *adj.* urological
ˈurˈplötzlich I. *adj.* sudden, totally unexpected; **II.** *adv.* all of a sudden, completely out of the blue
ˈUr·sa·che *f* (-; -n) cause (*gen. or* ***für*** *acc.* of); reason (for); occasion (for); ***ich habe (alle) ~ zu*** *inf.* I have (every) reason to *inf.*; ***er hat keine ~ zu*** *inf.* there's no reason why he should ...; ***keine ~!*** don't mention it, that's all right (*Am.* alright); ***kleine ~, große Wirkung*** from little acorns grow big oaks
ˈUr·sa·chen·for·schung *f* (a)etiology
ˈur·säch·lich *adj.* (*and adv.*) causal(ly); ***sie stehen in ~em Zusammenhang*** they are causally connected; **ˈUr·säch·lich·keit** *f* (-; *no pl.*) causality
ˈUr·schlamm *m*, **ˈUr·schleim** *m* primeval sludge
ˈUr·schrei *m* (-[e]s; *no pl.*) primal scream
ˈUr·schrift *f* original (text *or* copy)
ˈUr·spra·che *f* **1.** original language; ***in der ~*** in the original (language); **2.** protolanguage
Ur·sprung [ˈuːɐʃprʊŋ] *m* (-[e]s; Ursprünge [ˈuːɐʃprʏŋə]) origin(s *pl.*); *w.s.* beginnings *pl.*; ***s-n ~ haben in*** *dat.* originate in (*or* from), stem from, have one's (*or* its) origin(s) in; ***deutschen ~s*** of German origin (*or* extraction), ✝ made in Germany; *das Wort* ***ist griechischen ~s*** is of Greek origin, goes back to Greek, is originally Greek
ur·sprüng·lich [ˈuːɐʃprʏŋlɪç] **I.** *adj.* **1.** original; initial; ***die ~e Begeisterung*** *etc. a.* the enthusiasm *etc.* that was there at the beginning (*or* to start with); **2.** natural, unspoilt; ***~es Gebiet*** wilderness area; **II.** *adv.* originally, at the beginning, to start (off) with; **ˈUr·sprüng·lich·keit** *f* (-; *no pl.*) naturalness; unspoilt quality (*or* state) (*gen.* of)
ˈUr·sprungs·land *n* ✝ country of origin
Ur·ständ [ˈuːɐʃtɛnt] F *f*: ***fröhliche ~ feiern*** rise from the ashes, *contp.* rear its ugly head again
ˈUr·stoff *m* primary matter; ⚗ element
ˈUr·strom·tal *n geol.* glacial valley
Ur·teil [ˈʊrtaɪl] *n* (-[e]s; -e) **1.** a) judg(e)ment; opinion, b) decision; ***sich ein ~ bilden*** form a judg(e)ment (*or* an opinion) (***über*** *acc.* on); ***m-m ~ nach*** in my opinion; ***darüber kann ich mir kein ~ erlauben*** I'm in no position to judge (that); **2.** ⚖ judg(e)ment, ruling, decision; sentence; decree (*of divorce*); → ***ergehen*** 1, ***fällen***; **ur·tei·len** [ˈʊrtaɪlən] *v/i.* (h) judge (***nach*** *dat.* by); ***~ über*** *acc.* judge *s.o. or s.th.*; ***~ über*** *acc. a.* give one's opinion on; ***darüber kann er nicht ~*** he's no judge; ***~ Sie selbst!*** see for yourself; ***nach s-n Worten zu ~*** judging by what he says
ˈUr·teils·be·grün·dung *f* opinion (of the court)
ˈur·teils·fä·hig *adj.* discerning, discriminating; **ˈUr·teils·fä·hig·keit** *f* (-; *no pl.*) ability to judge; powers *pl.* of discernment (*or* discrimination)
ˈUr·teils·fin·dung [-fɪndʊŋ] *f* (-; -en) reaching a (*or* the) verdict
ˈUr·teils|kraft *f* (-; *no pl.*) (powers *pl.* of) judg(e)ment *or* discernment; **~spruch** *m* sentence, verdict; **~ver·kün·dung** *f* pronouncing of judg(e)ment; **~voll·streckung** *f* execution of a (*or* the) sentence
ˈUr·text *m* original text
ˈUr·trieb *m* basic instinct
ur·tüm·lich [ˈuːɐtyːmlɪç] *adj.* a) unspoilt, original, b) primitive, c) archaic; **ˈUr·tüm·lich·keit** *f* (-; *no pl.*) a) unspoilt (*or* original) state (*gen.* of), b) primitiveness, c) archaic character (*gen.* of)
ˈUr·typ *m* (-s; -en) archetype; **ˈur·ty·pisch** *adj.* archetypal; **ˈUr·ty·pus** *m* (-; -pen) → ***Urtyp***
Uru·gua·yer [ˈuːrugvaɪɐ] *m* (-s; -), **Uru·gua·ye·rin** [ˈuːrugvaɪərɪn] *f* (-; -nen), **uru·gua·yisch** [ˈuːrugvaɪɪʃ] *adj.* Uruguayan
Ur·ur... [ˈuːɐʔuːɐ-] *in cpds.* great-great--*grandfather etc.*
ˈUr·va·ter *m* ancestor
ˈUr·viech F *n* (-[e]s; -er) real character
ˈUr·volk *n* a) primitive people (*or* tribe), b) (ab)original inhabitants *pl.* (*or* population)
ˈUr·wald *m* **1.** jungle; F *fig.* ***aus dem ~ stammen*** come from the jungle; **2.** primeval forest
ˈUr·welt *f* primeval world; **ˈur·welt·lich** *adj.* primeval
ur·wüch·sig [ˈuːɐvyːksɪç] *adj.* a) original, unspoilt; natural, b) earthy (*a. humo[u]r etc.*); ***~er Bayer*** picture-book Bavarian; **ˈUr·wüch·sig·keit** *f* (-; *no pl.*) a) original (*or* unspoilt) state (*gen.* of); naturalness, b) earthiness
ˈUr·zeit *f*: ***die ~*** primeval times; *fig.* ***vor ~en*** a long, long time ago; ***seit ~en*** from (*or* since) time immemorial
ˈUr·zeu·gung *f biol.* spontaneous generation
ˈUr·zu·stand *m* original state
Usam·ba·ra·veil·chen [uzamˈbaːra-] *n* ⚘ African violet

US|-Ame·ri,ka·ner [uːˈʔɛs-] *m* American (citizen); **~-ame·ri,ka·nisch** *adj.* US ..., American; **~-Dol·lar** *m* United States (*or* US) dollar; **~-Streit·kräf·te** *pl.*, **~-Trup·pen** *pl.* US armed forces

Usur·pa·ti·on [uzʊrpaˈtsi̯oːn] *f* (-; -en) usurpation; **Usur·pa·tor** [uzʊrˈpaːtoːɐ] *m* (-s; -en [-paˈtoːrən]) usurper; **usur·pa·to·risch** [uzʊrpaˈtoːrɪʃ] *adj.* usurpatory; **usur·pie·ren** [uzʊrˈpiːrən] *v/t.* usurp; *w.s. a.* appropriate *s.th.*

Usus [ˈuːzʊs] *m* (-; *no pl.*) custom, practi|ce (*Am.* -se); ***das ist hier so ~*** it's the custom around here

Uten·si·li·en [utɛnˈziːli̯ən] *pl.* utensils, implements

Ute·rus [ˈuːterʊs] *m* (-; -ri) *anat.* uterus; **~...** *in cpds. often* uterine *smear etc.*

Uti·li·ta·ris·mus [utilitaˈrɪsmʊs] *m* (-; *no pl.*) utilitarianism; **uti·li·ta·ri·stisch** [utilitaˈrɪstɪʃ] *adj.* utilitarian

Uto·pie [utoˈpiː] *f* (-; -n) **1.** impossible dream; **2.** utopia; **uto·pisch** [uˈtoːpɪʃ] *adj.* fanciful, unrealistic; utopian

UV|-Fil·ter [uːˈfaʊ-] *m* UV filter; **~-Licht** *n* (-[e]s; *no pl.*) ultraviolet light; **~-Strah·len** *pl.*, **~-Strah·lung** *f* ultraviolet rays (*pl.*)

Ü-Wa·gen [ˈyː-] *m* → ***Übertragungswagen***

uzen [ˈuːtsən] F *v/t.* (h) F kid *s.o.*, pull *s.o.'s* leg, have *s.o.* on; **Uze·rei** [uːtsəˈraɪ] F *f* (-; -en) F leg-pulling

V

V, v [faʊ] *n* (-; -) V, v
va banque [va'bãːk]: ~ ***spielen*** take a gamble; **Va'banque·spiel** *fig. n* gamble
Va·ga·bund [vaga'bʊnt] *m* (-en; -en [-dən]) vagabond, tramp, *Am.* F bum, hobo; **Va·ga'bun·den·le·ben** *n* vagabond life, life of a vagabond; **va·ga·bun·die·ren** [vagabʊn'diːrən] *v/i.* (h) lead the life of a vagabond, drift from place to place
va·ge ['vaːgə] *adj.* vague; **Vag·heit** ['vaːkhaɪt] *f* (-; *no pl.*) vagueness
Va·gi·na [va'giːna] *f* (-; -nen) vagina; **va·gi·nal** [vagi'naːl] *adj.* vaginal
va·kant [va'kant] *adj.* vacant; **Va·kanz** [va'kants] *f* (-; -en) vacancy
Va·ku·um ['vaːkuʊm] *n* (-s; -en, -a) vacuum (*a. fig.*); **~brem·se** *f* vacuum brake; **~packung** *f* vacuum pack; **~pum·pe** *f* vacuum pump; **2ver·packt** *adj.* vacuum-packed; **2ver·sie·gelt** *adj.* vacuum-sealed; **~ver·sie·ge·lung** *f* vacuum sealing
Vak·zi·ne [vak'tsiːnə] *f* (-; -n) ⚕ vaccine
Va·len·tins·tag ['vaːlɛntiːns-] *m*: ***der*** ~ St Valentine's day
Va·lenz [va'lɛnts] *f* (-; -en) ⚗ *and ling.* valence
Va·lu·ta [va'luːta] *f* (-; -ten) foreign currency; **~klau·sel** *f* exchange clause
Vam·pir ['vampiːɐ] *m* (-s; -e [-rə]) vampire
Va·na·di·um [va'naːdĭʊm] *n* (-s; *no pl.*) vanadium; **~stahl** *m* vanadium steel
Van·da·le *m* **1.** *hist.* → ***Wandale*; 2.** *fig.* vandal; ***wie die ~n*** like vandals; **Van·da·lis·mus** [vanda'lɪsmʊs] *m* (-; *no pl.*) vandalism
Va·nil·le [va'nɪljə, va'nɪlə] *f* (-; *no pl.*) vanilla; **~eis** *n* vanilla ice-cream; **~ge·schmack** *m* vanilla flavo(u)r; **~so·ße** *f* vanilla sauce; **~stan·ge** *f* vanilla pod; **~zucker** *m* vanilla sugar
va·ria·bel [va'rĭaːbəl] *adj.* variable; **Va·ria·bi·li·tät** [varĭabili'tɛːt] *f* (-; *no pl.*) variability; **Va·ria·ble** [va'rĭaːblə] *f* (-n; -n) 𝔄, *computer*: variable; **Va·ria·blen·na·me** *m computer*: variable name
Va·ri·an·te [va'rĭantə] *f* (-; -n) variation (***zu*** *dat.* on); *ling.* variant (*gen.* of)
Va·ria·ti·on [varĭa'tsĭoːn] *f* (-; -en) variation (*gen.* of, on; ♪ ***zu*** *dat.*, ***über*** *acc.* on)
Va·rie·té [varĭe'te] *n* (-s; -s), **~thea·ter** *n* variety theatre, music hall, *Am.* vaudeville theater; **~künst·ler** *m* music-hall entertainer, *Am.* vaudeville performer; **~vor·stel·lung** *f* variety show, *Am.* vaudeville
va·ri·ie·ren [vari'iːrən] *v/i. and v/t.* (h) vary
Va·rio·ob·jek,tiv ['vaːrĭo-] *n phot.* zoom lens
Va·sall [va'zal] *m* (-en; -en) vassal; **Va'sal·len·staat** *m* satellite state
Va·se ['vaːzə] *f* (-; -n) vase
Vas·ek·to·mie [vazɛkto'miː] *f* (-; -n) vasectomy
Va·se·li·ne [vazə'liːnə] (*TM*) *f* (-; *no pl.*) vaseline (*TM*)
va·so·mo·to·risch [vazomo'toːrɪʃ] *adj. physiol.* vasomotor *reflex etc.*
Va·ter ['faːtɐ] *m* (-s; Väter ['fɛːtɐ]) father (*a. fig.*); *eccl.* Father; *zo.* sire; *pl.* fathers, ancestors; ***~ von drei Kindern sein*** be a (*or* the) father of three children, be a father of three; ***die Väter der Stadt*** the city fathers; *hum.* ~ ***Staat*** the State, Uncle Sam; ***wie der ~, so der Sohn*** like father, like son; **~bild** *n psych.* father image; **~bin·dung** *f psych.* father fixation
Vä·ter·chen ['fɛːtɐçən] *n* old man (*or* fellow), *sl.* old geezer; ~ ***Frost*** Jack Frost
'Va·ter|fi,gur *f psych.* father-figure; **~freu·den** *pl.* joys of fatherhood; ~ ***entgegensehen*** be an expectant father; **~kom,plex** *m psych.* father complex
'Va·ter·land *n one's* native country; (*esp. Germany*) *the* Fatherland
va·ter·län·disch ['faːtɐlɛndɪʃ] *adj.* national; patriotic(ally *adv.*)
'Va·ter·lands|lie·be *f* patriotism, love of one's country; **~ver·rä·ter** *m* traitor to one's (*or* the) country
vä·ter·lich ['fɛːtɐlɪç] **I.** *adj.* fatherly, paternal; **II.** *adv.* like a father; **vä·ter·li·cher·seits** ['fɛːtɐlɪçɐzaɪts] *adv.* on one's father's side; paternal *uncle etc.*; **'Vä·ter·lich·keit** *f* (-; *no pl.*) fatherliness
'Va·ter·lie·be *f* paternal love
'va·ter·los *adj.* fatherless
'Va·ter|mord *m*, **~mör·der** *m* parricide
'Va·ter·schaft *f* (-; *no pl.*) paternity, fatherhood; ⚖ ***Feststellung der*** ~ affiliation (order)
'Va·ter·schafts|kla·ge *f* paternity suit (*or* case); **~ur·laub** *m* paternity leave
'Va·ter|stadt *f* hometown; **~stel·le** *f*: ~ ***vertreten bei*** *dat.* act as father to; **~tag** *m* Father's Day; **~un·ser** *n*: (***das ~ beten*** say the) Lord's Prayer
Va·ti ['faːti] F *m* (-s; -s) dad(dy), *Am. a.* pa; Dad(dy), *Am. a.* Pa
Va·ti·kan [vati'kaːn] *m* (-s; *no pl.*) Vatican; **va·ti·ka·nisch** [vati'kaːnɪʃ] *adj.* Vatican ...; ***Vatikanisches Konzil*** Vatican Council; **Va·ti'kan·stadt** *f* (-; *no pl.*) Vatican City
'V-Aus·schnitt *m* V-neck; ***Pullover mit*** ~ V-neck(ed) jumper (*or* sweater)
Ve·ge·ta·ri·er [vege'taːrĭɐ] *m* (-s; -) vegetarian; **ve·ge·ta·risch** [vege'taːrɪʃ] *adj.* vegetarian
Ve·ge·ta·ti·on [vegeta'tsĭoːn] *f* (-; -en) vegetation
ve·ge·ta·tiv [vegeta'tiːf] *adj.* vegetative; ***~es Nervensystem*** autonomic nervous system
ve·ge·tie·ren [vege'tiːrən] *v/i.* (h) vegetate (*a. fig.*)
ve·he·ment [vehe'mɛnt] *adj.* vehement; **Ve·he·menz** [vehe'mɛnts] *f* (-; *no pl.*) vehemence
Ve·hi·kel [ve'hiːkəl] *n* (-s; -) **1.** *contp.* F contraption; **2.** *fig.* vehicle
Veil·chen ['faɪlçən] *n* (-s; -) **1.** ⚘ violet ; F ***blau wie ein*** ~ F drunk as a lord; **2.** F *hum.* black eye
'veil·chen·blau *adj.* violet
Veits·tanz ['faɪts-] *m* (-es; *no pl.*): ⚕ ***der*** ~ St Vitus's Dance
Vek·tor ['vɛktoːɐ] *m* (-s; -en [vɛk'toːrən]) 𝔄 vector; **~rech·nung** *f* vector analysis
Ve·lours¹ [və'luːɐ] *m* (-; - [və'luːɐs]) velour
Ve'lours² *n* (-; - [və'luːɐs]), **~le·der** *n* suede (leather)
Ve'lours·tep·pich *m* velvet-pile carpet
Ve·ne ['veːnə] *f* (-; -n) vein; **'Ve·nen·ent·zün·dung** *f* phlebitis
ve·ne·risch [ve'neːrɪʃ] *adj.* ⚕ venereal
ve·ne·zia·nisch [vene'tsĭaːnɪʃ] *adj.* Venetian
Ve·ne·zo·la·ner [venetso'laːnɐ] *m* (-s; -), **Ve·ne·zo·la·ne·rin** [venetso'laːnərɪn] *f* (-; -nen), **ve·ne·zo·la·nisch** [venetso'laːnɪʃ] *adj.* Venezuelan
ve·nös [ve'nøːs] *adj. physiol.* venous
Ven·til [vɛn'tiːl] *n* (-s; -e) valve (*a.* ♪); *fig.* vent, outlet
Ven·ti·la·ti·on [vɛntila'tsĭoːn] *f* (-; *no pl.*) a) ventilation, b) ventilating system
Ven·ti·la·tor [vɛnti'laːtoːɐ] *m* (-s; -en [-la'toːrən]) ventilator, (electric) fan; ⚙ *a.* blower
ven·ti·lie·ren [vɛnti'liːrən] *fig. v/t.* (h) air *one's views etc.*; weigh up, consider *problem etc.*
Ven'til|klap·pe *f* valve flap; **~steue·rung** *f* valve timing
Ve·nus ['veːnʊs] *f* (-; *no pl.*) *myth.*, *ast.* Venus; **~berg** *m anat.* mons veneris; **~mu·schel** *f* Venus's shell
ver·ab·re·den [fɛɐ'ʔapreːdən] (h) **I.** *v/t.* agree on *s.th.*, arrange; *a.* fix *date*, *place etc.*; ***wie verabredet*** as agreed (on), as arranged; ***ich bin für morgen mit ihm verabredet*** I've arranged to meet him tomorrow; ***ich bin schon verabredet*** I've already arranged to meet (*or* go out with) someone (*or* a friend *etc.*), *a.* I've already got a date; ***verabredete Sache*** put-up job; **II.** *v/refl.*: ***sich mit j-m ~*** a) arrange to meet (*or* go out with) s.o., b) make an appointment with s.o.; **Ver'ab·re·dung** *f* (-; -en) a) agreement, b) date; appointment; ***e-e ~ haben*** have arranged to meet (*or* go out with) someone
ver·ab·rei·chen [fɛɐ'ʔapraɪçən] *v/t.* (h) give (***j-m et.*** s.o. s.th.), *formal*: adminis-

ter (s.th. to s.o.); *hum.* ***j-m e-e Ohrfeige*** (***e-e Tracht Prügel***) ~ give s.o. a clout round the ears (a good hiding)

ver·ab·säu·men [fɛɐ'ˀapzɔʏmən] *v/t.* (h) neglect

ver·ab·scheu·en [fɛɐ'ˀapʃɔʏən] *v/t.* (h) detest, loathe, abhor; **ver'ab·scheu·ens·wert** *adj.* despicable, abhorrent; **Ver'ab·scheu·ung** *f* (-; *no pl.*) loathing (*gen.* of), disgust (for)

ver·ab·schie·den [fɛɐ'ˀapʃiːdən] (h) **I.** *v/t.* **1.** say goodbye to *s.o.*; see *s.o.* off *at the station etc.*; **2.** dismiss; ⚔ retire; **3.** pass *bill etc.*; **II.** *v/refl.*: ***sich*** ~ say goodbye (***von*** *dat.* to); ***ich muß mich jetzt leider*** ~ I'm afraid I have to go (*or* leave) now; **Ver'ab·schie·dung** *f* (-; -en) **1.** dismissal; **2.** passing *of a bill*

ver·ab·so·lu·tie·ren [fɛɐˀapzolu'tiːrən] *v/t.* (h) make *s.th.* (into) an absolute

ver'ach·ten *v/t.* (h) despise, disdain; scorn; defy *danger, death*; F ***nicht zu*** ~ F not to be sneezed (*or* sniffed) at; **ver'ach·tens·wert** *adj.* contemptible, despicable; **Ver·äch·ter** [fɛɐ'ˀɛçtɐ] *m* (-s; -) despiser (*gen.* of); **ver·ächt·lich** [fɛɐ'ˀɛçtlɪç] *adj.* **1.** contemptuous, disdainful, scornful; ~ ***machen*** run *s.o. or s.th.* down; **2.** → ***verachtenswert***; **Ver'ach·tung** *f* (-; *no pl.*) contempt, disdain; scorn; ***j-n mit*** ~ ***strafen*** ignore s.o., treat s.o. with contempt; **ver'ach·tungs·voll** *adj.* contemptuous, disdainful; **ver'ach·tungs·wür·dig** *adj.* despicable, contemptible

ver'al·bern F *v/t.* (h) F kid, pull *s.o.'s* leg

ver·all·ge·mei·nern [fɛɐˀalgə'maɪnɐn] *v/t.* (h) generalize; **Ver·all·ge'mei·ne·rung** *f* (-; -en): (***grobe*** ~ gross) generalization

ver·al·ten [fɛɐ'ˀaltən] *v/i.* (sn) become outdated; go out of fashion (*or* style); **ver·al·tet** [fɛɐ'ˀaltət] *adj.* out-of-date ..., *pred.* out of date; (out)dated; *a.* antiquated *methods etc.*

Ve·ran·da [ve'randa] *f* (-; -den) veranda(h), *Am.* porch

ver·än·der·lich [fɛɐ'ˀɛndɐlɪç] *adj.* changeable (*a. meteor. etc.*); ⚗, *ling.* variable; *contp.* ~***es Wesen*** fickle nature; **Ver'än·der·lich·keit** *f* (-; *no pl.*) changeability; ⚗, *ling.* variability; *contp.* fickleness; **ver'än·dern** (h) **I.** *v/t.* change; *a.* alter *one's look*; reform; **II.** *v/refl.*: ***sich*** ~ a) change, b) change one's job; ***er hat sich sehr verändert*** he's really changed; ***sie will sich*** ~ she's looking for a new job, she wants to move on; **Ver'än·de·rung** *f* (-; -en) change; alteration, modification; (***berufliche*** ~) change of job

ver'äng·sti·gen *v/t.* (h) frighten, scare; **ver·äng·stigt** [fɛɐ'ˀɛŋstɪçt] *adj.* a) frightened, scared, b) timid; **Ver'äng·sti·gung** *f* (-; *no pl.*) a) state of fright, b) timidity

ver'an·kern *v/t.* (h) ⚓, ⚙ anchor (*a. fig.*); *fig.* ***in e-m Gesetz verankert*** embodied in a law; **Ver·an·ke·rung** [fɛɐ'ˀaŋkəruŋ] *f* (-; *no pl.*) anchoring; *fig.* embodiment *in a law*

ver·an·la·gen [fɛɐ'ˀanlaːgən] *v/t.* (h) assess; **ver·an·lagt** [fɛɐ'ˀanlaːkt] *adj.* (naturally) inclined (***für*** *acc.*, ***zu*** *dat.* to); ***künstlerisch*** ~ ***sein*** have artistic talent, have an artistic bent; **Ver'an·la·gung** *f* (-; -en) **1.** disposition; ***es ist*** ~ it's in his (*or* her) nature, he (*or* she) was made that way; **2.** inclination; gift, talent; **3.** ⚕ ***e-e*** ~ ***haben zu*** *dat.* be prone to, suffer from; **4.** *no pl.* assessment

ver·an·las·sen [fɛɐ'ˀanlasən] *v/t.* (veranlaßte, veranlaßt, h) arrange for; ~, ***daß*** see to it that, arrange for *s.th. to be done*; ***j-n zu et.*** ~ *person*: get s.o. to do s.th., *motive*: prompt s.o. to do s.th., make s.o. do s.th.; ***das Nötige*** ~ make the necessary arrangements, take the necessary steps; ***sich veranlaßt fühlen zu*** *inf.* feel bound to *inf.*; **Ver'an·las·sung** *f* (-; *no pl.*) a) occasion, b) cause, reason; motive; ***auf*** ~ ***von*** *dat.* (*or gen.*) at the instigation of, at *s.o.'s* prompting (*or* urging); ~ ***geben zu*** *dat.* give occasion to; ***ohne jede*** ~ (entirely) without provocation; ***er hat keine*** ~ ***zu*** *inf.* there's no reason for him to *inf.*

ver·an·schau·li·chen [fɛɐ'ˀanʃaʊlɪçən] *v/t.* (h) illustrate; ***sich et.*** ~ visualize s.th., picture s.th. (to o.s.); **Ver'an·schau·li·chung** *f* (-; *no pl.*): (***zur*** ~ by way of) illustration

ver·an·schla·gen [fɛɐ'ˀanʃlaːgən] *v/t.* (veranschlagte, veranschlagt, h) estimate (***auf*** *acc.* at); ***zu hoch*** (***niedrig***) ~ overestimate (underestimate), pitch too high (low); **Ver'an·schla·gung** *f* (-; -en) estimate (***auf*** *acc.* of)

ver·an·stal·ten [fɛɐ'ˀanʃtaltən] *v/t.* (h) arrange, organize; mount *an exhibition*; **Ver·an·stal·ter** [fɛɐ'ˀanʃtaltɐ] *m* (-s; -) organizer; *sport*: *a.* promoter; **Ver'an·stal·tung** *f* (-; -en) arrangement, organization; event; (public) function

Ver'an·stal·tungs|ka,len·der *m* calendar of events; ~**ort** *m* venue

ver'ant·wor·ten (h) **I.** *v/t.* answer for, take the responsibility for; ***du mußt es*** ~ you'll have to answer for it (*or* take [the] responsibility); **II.** *v/refl.*: ***sich für et.*** ~ answer for s.th.; ***sich vor j-m*** ~ ***müssen*** have to answer to s.o.

ver·ant·wort·lich [fɛɐ'ˀantvɔrtlɪç] *adj.* **1.** responsible, answerable (***für*** *acc.* for); ***dafür*** ~ ***sein, daß*** be responsible for seeing to it that, have to make sure that; ***j-n*** ~ ***machen*** hold s.o. responsible, *w.s.* blame s.o. (***für*** *acc.* for); ~ ***zeichnen für*** *acc.* a) be responsible for, b) be the author of; **2.** (highly) responsible; **Ver'ant·wort·lich·keit** *f* (-; *no pl.*) **1.** responsibility; **2.** sense of responsibility

Ver·ant·wor·tung [fɛɐ'ˀantvɔrtuŋ] *f* (-; *no pl.*) responsibility; ***auf eigene*** ~ at one's own risk; ~ ***übernehmen*** take (*or* accept) responsibility; ***zur*** ~ ***ziehen*** call to account

ver'ant·wor·tungs·be·wußt *adj.* responsible(-minded); **Ver'ant·wor·tungs·be·wußt·sein** *n* sense of responsibility

ver'ant·wor·tungs·freu·dig *adj.* ready to take responsibility

Ver'ant·wor·tungs·ge·fühl *n* (-[e]s; *no pl.*) sense of responsibility

ver'ant·wor·tungs·los *adj.* irresponsible; **Ver'ant·wor·tungs·lo·sig·keit** *f* (-; *no pl.*) irresponsibility

ver'ant·wor·tungs·voll *adj.* responsible

ver·äp·peln [fɛɐ'ˀɛpəln] F *v/t.* (h) F pull *s.o.'s* leg, have *s.o.* on, kid *s.o.*; F take the mickey out of *s.o.*; ***du willst mich wohl*** ~***!*** are you trying to pull my leg?, are you having me on?

ver'ar·bei·ten *v/t.* (h) **1.** process; make (***zu*** *dat.* into); treat; ***die Seide wird zu Teppichen verarbeitet*** carpets are made from the silk; **2.** *fig.* a) digest, b) put to use, use, take into consideration; ***s-e Erlebnisse zu e-m Roman*** ~ turn one's experiences into a novel; **3.** ⚕ digest; **ver'ar·bei·tend** *adj.*: ~***e Industrie*** manufacturing (*or* processing) industry; **Ver'ar·bei·tung** *f* (-; *no pl.*) **1.** processing; treatment; digestion; use; **2.** workmanship, finish; quality

ver·ar·gen [fɛɐ'ˀargən] *v/t.* (h): ***ich kann es ihm nicht*** ~ I can't blame him (for it) (***daß*** for *ger. or* ***wenn*** if)

ver'är·gern *v/t.* (h) annoy; upset; **ver'är·gert** *adj.* annoyed; upset; **Ver·är·ge·rung** [fɛɐ'ˀɛrgəruŋ] *f* (-; *no pl.*) annoyance

ver·ar·men [fɛɐ'ˀarmən] *v/i.* (sn) become poor (*or* impoverished), be reduced to poverty; **ver'armt** *adj.* impoverished; **Ver'ar·mung** *f* (-; *no pl.*) impoverishment (*a. fig.*)

ver·ar·schen [fɛɐ'ˀarʃən] *sl. v/t.* (h) **1.** *sl.* take the piss out of *s.o.*; **2.** F take *s.o.* for a ride; ***er hat mich verarscht*** *a.* F I've been had

ver·arz·ten [fɛɐ'ˀartstən] F *v/t.* (h) F fix up; see to

ver·ästeln [fɛɐ'ˀɛstəln] *v/refl.* (h): ***sich*** ~ branch out, ramify (*both a. fig.*); **Ver·äste·lung** [fɛɐ'ˀɛstəluŋ] *f* (-; -en) branching out; *fig.* ramifications *pl.*

ver'ät·zen *v/t.* (h) burn; erode; ⚕ cauterize; **Ver'ät·zung** *f* (-; -en) a) burning, ⚕ cauterization, b) burn; erosion

ver·aus·ga·ben [fɛɐ'ˀaʊsgaːbən] *v/refl.* (h): ***sich*** ~ a) overspend, b) overexert o.s., burn o.s. out

ver'äu·ßer·lich *adj.* sal(e)able; ⚖ *etc. a.* alienable; **ver'äu·ßern** *v/t.* (h) alienate; transfer (***an*** *acc.* to); dispose of, sell; **Ver'äu·ße·rung** *f* (-; -en) alienation; disposal, sale

Verb [vɛrp] *n* (-s; Verben ['vɛrbən]) verb; **ver·bal** [vɛr'baːl] *adj.* verbal

Ver'bal·in,ju·rie *f* (-; -n) ⚖ verbal insult

ver·ba·li·sie·ren [vɛrbali'ziːrən] *v/t.* (h) verbalize; **Ver·ba·li'sie·rung** *f* (-; *no pl.*) verbalization

ver·ball·hor·nen [fɛɐ'balhɔrnən] *v/t.* (h) corrupt, distort; **Ver'ball·hor·nung** *f* (-; -en) corruption

Ver·band [fɛɐ'bant] *m* (-[e]s; Verbände [fɛɐ'bɛndə]) **1.** ⚕ dressing, bandage; **2.** association; **3.** ⚔ formation (*a.* ⚓, ✈), unit

Ver'band(s)|ka·sten *m* first-aid box; ~**mull** *m* lint, surgical gauze; ~**päck·chen** *n* set of bandages; ~**stoff** *m* dressing material; ~**wat·te** *f* surgical cotton wool, *Am.* surgical cotton; ~**zeug** *n* dressing material

ver'ban·nen *v/t.* (h) exile; *hist. and fig.* banish; **Ver·bann·te** [fɛɐ'bantə] *m, f* (-n; -n) exile; **Ver'ban·nung** *f* (-; *no pl.*) exile; *hist. and fig.* banishment; ***j-n in die*** ~ ***schicken*** send s.o. into exile

ver·bar·ri·ka·die·ren [fɛɐbarika'diːrən] *v/t.* (h) barricade (***sich*** o.s.)

ver'bau·en *v/t.* (h) **1.** obstruct, block; **2.** a) build up *an area etc.*, b) spoil; **3.** use (up) in building; **4.** build badly, make a mess of; ***das Haus ist völlig verbaut*** the house is a real mess; **5.** *fig.* ***sich*** (***j-m***) ***et.*** ~ spoil one's (s.o.'s) chances of getting (*or* having, gaining *etc.*) s.th.; ***sich die Zukunft*** ~ ruin one's chances for the future

ver·bau·ern [fɛɐ'bauɐn] F *v/i.* (sn) become countrified; **ver'bau·ert** *adj.* countrified
ver·be·am·ten [fɛɐbə'ʔamtən] *v/t.* (h): ***j-n ~*** give s.o. the status of a civil servant
ver'bei·ßen (*irr.*, *no* -ge-, h, → ***beißen***) **I.** *v/t.* suppress *pain, smile etc.*; ***sich das Lachen ~*** force o.s. not to laugh, stifle one's laughter; ***ich konnte mir das Lachen nicht ~*** I couldn't keep a straight face; **II.** *v/refl.*: ***sich ~ in*** *acc. zo.* sink its teeth into *s.th.*; *fig.* become set (*or* bent) on doing *s.th.*; *fig.* ***sich in et. verbissen haben*** a) keep at s.th. doggedly, b) hold onto s.th. grimly; ***er hat sich in s-e Arbeit verbissen*** *a.* he's working obsessively
ver·ber·gen (*irr.*, *no* -ge-, h, → ***bergen***) **I.** *v/t.* hide, conceal (***vor*** *dat.* from); ***sein Gesicht ~ in*** *dat.* bury one's face in; → ***verborgen***; **II.** *v/refl.*: ***sich ~*** a) hide (o.s. *or* itself), b) be hidden
ver'bes·sern (h) **I.** *v/t.* a) improve (*a.* ⚙), b) correct; revise *novel etc.*; ***die Haltbarkeit ~ von*** *dat.* prolong the shelf-life of; **II.** *v/refl.*: ***sich ~*** a) improve, b) correct o.s., c) better o.s.; **Ver'bes·se·rung** *f* (-; -en) a) improvement, b) correction
ver'bes·se·rungs|be·dürf·tig *adj.*: (***sehr ~*** badly) in need of improvement; **~fä·hig** *adj.* capable of improvement
Ver'bes·se·rungs·vor·schlag *m* suggestion for improvement
ver'beu·gen *v/refl.* (h): ***sich ~*** bow (***vor*** *dat.* to); **Ver'beu·gung** *f* (-; -en) bow
ver'beu·len *v/t.* (h) dent
ver'bie·gen (*irr.*, *no* -ge-, h, → ***biegen***) **I.** *v/t.* bend, buckle; **II.** *v/refl.*: ***sich ~*** bend, get bent, buckle; *wood*: warp
ver·bie·stern [fɛɐ'bi:stɐn] F *v/refl.* (h): ***sich ~ in*** *acc.* become set (*or* bent) on doing *s.th.*; **ver'bie·stert** *dial. adj.* **1.** annoyed; **2.** bewildered, distraught
ver'bie·ten (*irr.*, *no* -ge-, h, → ***bieten***) **I.** *v/t.* forbid (***j-m et.*** [***zu tun***] s.o. [to do] s.th.); *adm.* prohibit (***et.*** s.th.; ***j-m et.*** s.o. from doing s.th.); ban; ***er hat es mir verboten*** *usu.* he won't let me; **II.** *v/refl. and v/impers.*: ***es verbietet sich von selbst*** it's out of the question
ver'bil·den *v/t.* (h) a) deform, spoil, b) miseducate; **ver'bil·det** *adj.* a) deformed, b) *w.s.* overrefined, oversophisticated
ver·bild·li·chen [fɛɐ'bɪltlɪçən] *v/t.* (h) illustrate
ver'bil·li·gen (h) **I.** *v/t.* lower the cost of; reduce *goods* (in price); ***verbilligter Tarif*** cheap rate; **II.** *v/refl.*: ***sich ~*** go down (in price); **Ver'bil·li·gung** *f* (-; *no pl.*) a) reduction (in price), b) reduced price
ver'bin·den (*irr.*, *no* -ge-, h, → ***binden***) **I.** *v/t.* **1.** a) tie (together); connect (***mit*** *dat.* with, to), b) ⚙ connect, couple, link, c) ⚗ combine; **2.** ***j-m die Augen ~*** blindfold s.o.; ***mit verbundenen Augen*** blindfolded; **3.** ⚕ dress, bandage *wound*; bandage *s.o.* up; **4.** *teleph.* ***j-n ~*** put s.o. through (***mit*** *dat.* to, *Am.* with); ***falsch verbunden!*** sorry, wrong number; ***ich verbinde*** hold the line, please; **5.** join, unite; combine; associate; ***uns verbindet vieles*** we have a lot in common; ***sich verbunden fühlen mit*** *dat.* feel a rapport with; ***mich verbindet einiges mit dieser Gegend*** I have several ties with this area; ***verbunden mit*** *dat.* combined (*or* coupled) with; ***die damit verbundenen Unkosten*** (***Gefahren***) the cost (dangers) involved; ***eng verbunden sein mit*** *dat.* be bound up with; **6.** → ***verbunden*** 2; **II.** *v/refl.*: ***sich ~*** combine (*a.* ⚗), be combined
ver·bind·lich [fɛɐ'bɪntlɪç] **I.** *adj.* **1.** binding (***für*** *acc.* upon); **2.** obliging; friendly *a. words*; **~(*st*)*en Dank!*** many thanks indeed; **II.** *adv.* **3.** ***~ zusagen*** accept definitely, commit o.s., *w.s.* say definitely (that) one is coming, promise to come; **4.** obligingly; kindly; *iro.* ***danke ~st!*** thanks a lot (*or* a million)!, much obliged!; **Ver'bind·lich·keit** *f* (-; -en) **1.** *no pl.* obligation, liability, commitment; ⚖ binding force *of an agreement etc.*; **2.** ✝ *pl.* liabilities; ***s-n ~en nachkommen*** meet one's liabilities; **3.** a) *no pl.* obligingness, b) *pl.* courtesies
Ver'bin·dung *f* (-; -en) a) union (*a. marriage*), bond, b) *fig.* combination, c) *fig.* association; connection; context, d) *a.* ✝ relations *pl.*, contact (*both* ***zu*** *dat.* with), e) communication; ⚙ *and teleph.* connection, f) junction, ⚙ joint, g) ⚗ compound, h) students' fraternity, student league; ***in ~ mit*** *dat.* combined with; in connection with, in conjunction with; ***e-e ~ eingehen*** join together, unite, combine, ally, form an alliance (*all* ***mit*** *dat.* with); **~*en knüpfen*** make contacts; ***e-e ~ herstellen mit*** *dat.*, ***sich in ~ setzen mit*** *dat.* contact, get in touch with; *radio*: establish communication with; ***in ~ bleiben*** keep in touch; ***die ~ verlieren*** lose touch; *fig.* ***in ~ bringen mit*** *dat.* associate with; ***in ~ stehen mit*** *dat.* be in touch (*or* contact) with *s.o.*, be connected with *s.th.*
Ver'bin·dungs|au·to·bahn *f* motorway link; **~gang** *m* connecting passage; **~ka·bel** *n* connecting cable; **~li·nie** *f* **1.** connecting line; **2.** ⚔ line of communication; **~mann** *m* contact (*a. agent*), liaison man; **~of·fi,zier** *m* liaison officer; **~punkt** *m* junction; **~stel·le** *f* **1.** junction; ⚙ joint; **2.** liaison office; **~stra·ße** *f* connecting road; **~stück** *n* connecting piece; ⚙ union coupling; ⚡ connector; adaptor; **~stu,dent** *m* member of a students' fraternity (*or* student league); **~tür** *f* connecting door
ver·bis·sen [fɛɐ'bɪsən] **I.** *p.p. of* ***verbeißen***; **II.** *adj.* **1.** dogged, grim *determination etc.*; **2.** grim *face etc.*; **Ver'bis·sen·heit** *f* (-; *no pl.*) doggedness, grim determination
ver'bit·ten *v/t.* (*irr.*, *no* -ge-, h, → ***bitten***): ***sich et. ~*** refuse to tolerate (*or* accept) s.th.; ***das verbitte ich mir!, das möchte ich mir verbeten haben!*** I won't have (*or* stand for) that
ver·bit·tern [fɛɐ'bɪtɐn] **I.** *v/t.* (h) embitter; **II.** *v/i.* (sn) grow bitter, become embittered; **ver'bit·tert** *adj.* embittered, bitter; **Ver·bit·te·rung** [fɛɐ'bɪtərʊŋ] *f* (-; *no pl.*) bitterness
ver·blas·sen [fɛɐ'blasən] *v/i.* (sn) grow pale; *colo(u)r etc.*, *a. fig.* fade; *fig.* ***~ gegenüber*** (*or* ***vor*** *dat.*) pale (into insignificance) beside, be dwarfed by; ***~ lassen*** eclipse; **ver'blaßt** *adj.* faded (*a. fig. memories etc.*)
Ver·bleib [fɛɐ'blaɪp] *m* (-[e]s; *no pl.*) whereabouts *pl.*; ***über s-n ~ ist nichts bekannt*** we (*or* they) know nothing of his whereabouts, nobody knows where he is; **ver'blei·ben** *v/i.* (*irr.*, *no* -ge-, sn, → ***bleiben***) remain; ***wie wollen wir ~?*** what shall we do, then?; ***wollen wir so ~, daß ...?*** shall we say ..., then?; ***~ wir so?*** shall we leave it at that, then?; *obs.* ***... ~ wir hochachtungsvoll*** ... (we remain,) Yours faithfully
ver·blei·en [fɛɐ'blaɪən] *v/t.* (h) lead; **ver'bleit** *adj.* leaded
ver'blen·den *v/t.* (h) **1.** *fig.* blind *s.o.*; ***verblendet von*** *dat.* blinded by; **2.** a) ⚠ *etc.* face, b) screen, conceal
Ver·blend·stein [fɛɐ'blɛnt-] *m* face brick
Ver'blen·dung *f* (-; -en) **1.** *fig.* blindness, delusion; **2.** ⚠ facing
ver·bleu·en [fɛɐ'blɔʏən] F *v/t.* (h) give *s.o.* a real thrashing
ver·bli·chen [fɛɐ'blɪçən] *adj.* **1.** faded *colo(u)r etc.*; **2.** *lit.* deceased; **Ver'bli·che·ne** *m, f* (-n; -n) *lit.* deceased
ver·blö·den [fɛɐ'blø:dən] F **I.** *v/i.* (sn) F go daft (*or* goofy) (***bei*** *dat.* with); F go gaga; ***bei dieser Arbeit verblödet man total*** this work is absolutely mind-numbing (*or* moronic); **II.** *v/t.* (h) dull *s.o.'s* mind, stultify, have a stultifying effect on *s.o.*; **ver'blö·det** F *adj.*: ***total ~*** F demented, senile; ***er*** (***sie***) ***ist total ~*** *a.* F he's (she's) gone completely gaga; **Ver'blö·dung** *f* (-; *no pl.*) stultification; ⚕ (senile) dementia; ***zu j-s ~ führen*** have a stultifying effect on s.o., dull s.o.'s mind
ver·blüf·fen [fɛɐ'blʏfən] *v/t.* (h) amaze, astound; dumbfound, stupefy; bewilder; **ver'blüf·fend** *adj.* amazing, startling, incredible; **ver'blüfft** *adj.* amazed, dumbfounded; F *pred.* taken aback; bewildered; **Ver'blüf·fung** *f* (-; *no pl.*) amazement, astonishment; stupefaction; bewilderment
ver'blü·hen *v/i.* (sn) wither; *fig.* fade
ver·blümt [fɛɐ'bly:mt] **I.** *adj.* veiled *expression etc.*, *a. reproch etc.*; euphemistic; **II.** *adv.* euphemistically; ***sich ~ ausdrücken*** express o.s. in a roundabout way
ver'blu·ten *v/i.* (sn) bleed to death
ver'bocken F *v/t.* (h) F bungle, botch (up)
ver'boh·ren *v/refl.* (h): ***sich ~ in*** *acc.* become obsessed with; become bent (*or* set) on *ger.*; **ver·bohrt** [fɛɐ'bo:ɐt] *adj.* pigheaded, stubborn, wrong-headed; **Ver'bohrt·heit** *f* (-; *no pl.*) pigheadedness, stubbornness
ver·bor·gen [fɛɐ'bɔrgən] **I.** *p.p. of* ***verbergen***; **II.** *adj.* a) hidden, concealed, b) secret, c) latent; ***im ~en*** secretly, in secret, ***blühen*** *etc.*: flourish *etc.* in obscurity; ***et. ~ halten*** hide s.th., keep s.th. secret (***vor*** *dat.* from); ***sich ~ halten*** hide, be (*or* stay) in hiding; **Ver'bor·gen·heit** *f* (-; *no pl.*) seclusion
Ver·bot [fɛɐ'bo:t] *n* (-[e]s; -e) prohibition (*gen.* of); ban (***für*** *acc. or gen.* on *imports, a newspaper etc.*); ***ein ~ aussprechen*** impose a ban; **ver·bo·ten** [fɛɐ'bo:tən] **I.** *p.p. of* ***verbieten***; **II.** *adj. pred.* not allowed (*or* permitted); *a. attr.* prohibited, forbidden; illegal, outlawed; ***Rauchen*** (***Skateboardfahren, Fotografieren***) **~!** no smoking (skateboards, photographs); ***streng ~*** strictly prohibited (*or* forbidden); ***es ist ~ zu*** *inf.* you're not allowed to *inf.*, *adm.* it is prohibited (*or* forbidden) to *inf.*; F *fig.* ***~ aussehen*** F look a real sight; **~*e Früchte*** forbidden fruit; → ***betreten*** II; **ver·bo·te·ner·wei·se** [fɛɐ'bo:tənɐ'vaɪzə] *adv.*: ***et. ~ tun***

do s.th. although it is forbidden (*or* not allowed), break the rules (*or* law) in doing s.th.

Ver'bots·schild *n* no parking (*or* no smoking *etc.*) sign; ***diese vielen ~er!*** all these signs telling you you can't do this, that and the other

ver·brä·men [fɛɐ'brɛ:mən] *v/t.* (h) garnish, gloss over

ver·brannt [fɛɐ'brant] **I.** *p.p. of* ***verbrennen***; **II.** *adj.* a) burnt; *a.* burnt-out *house etc.*, *pred.* burnt out, gutted, b) (sun)burnt; ***Politik der ~en Erde*** scorched earth policy

ver'bra·ten (*irr.*, *no* -ge-, → ***braten***) **I.** *v/i.* (sn) *gastr.* get scorched (*or* burnt), F shrivel; **II.** F *v/t.* (h) F a) blow *one's money etc.*, b) F spout *nonsense etc.*; ***et. zu e-m Roman ~*** exploit s.th. in a novel

Ver'brauch *m* (-[e]s; *no pl.*) consumption (***an*** *dat.* of); ***sparsam im ~*** economical; ***e-n hohen (niedrigen) ~ an Energie*** *etc.* ***haben*** have a high (low) energy *etc.* consumption; **ver'brau·chen** (h) **I.** *v/t.* a) use; *a.* consume *energy etc.*, b) use up; spend; **II.** *v/refl.*: ***sich ~*** wear (*or* burn) o.s. out; → ***verbraucht***

Ver·brau·cher [fɛɐ'braʊxɐ] *m* (-s; -) consumer; user; **~be·ra·tung** *f* **1.** consumer advice; **2.** consumer advice cent|re (*Am.* -er); **≈feind·lich** *adj.* user-hostile; **≈freund·lich** *adj.* user-friendly; **~freund·lich·keit** *f* (-; *no pl.*) user-friendliness; **~ge·nos·sen·schaft** *f* consumer cooperative; **~nach·fra·ge** *f* consumer demand; **~schutz** *m* consumer protection; **~ver·band** *m* consumer organization; **~ver·hal·ten** *n* consumer behavio(u)r; **~zeit·schrift** *f* consumer magazine; **~zen,tra·le** *f* consumer advice cent|re (*Am.* -er)

Ver'brauchs·gü·ter *pl.* consumer goods, commodities; **~in·du,strie** *f* consumer goods industry

Ver'brauchs|len·kung *f* consumer control; **~steu·er** *f* excise duty

ver·braucht [fɛɐ'braʊxt] *adj.* a) used up; stale *air*; flat *battery*, b) worn(-out), *pred.* worn (out); *fig.* spent, *a.* worn-out ..., *pred.* worn out, burnt-out ..., *pred.* burnt out

ver'bre·chen *v/t.* (*irr.*, *no* -ge-, h, → ***brechen***): ***etwas ~*** commit a crime; *fig.* ***was hat er verbrochen?*** what has he done?; ***ich habe nichts verbrochen*** I haven't done anything (wrong); *iro.* ***was hast du denn jetzt wieder verbrochen?*** what have you been up to this time?; *iro.* ***wer hat denn diesen Film verbrochen?*** F who cooked up this film?, who's responsible for this film then?; **Ver'bre·chen** *n* (-s; -) crime (*a. fig.*); F *fig.* ***das ist (doch) kein ~!*** that's no crime(, is it?)

Ver'bre·chens|auf·klä·rung *f* crime detection; criminal investigation; *w.s.* (number of) solved crimes *pl.*; **~be·kämp·fung** *f* fight against crime

Ver·bre·cher [fɛɐ'brɛçɐ] *m* (-s; -) criminal; F crook; **~al·bum** *n* rogues' gallery; **~ban·de** *f* gang of criminals, F mob; **~ge·sicht** *n* villain's face

ver·bre·che·risch [fɛɐ'brɛçərɪʃ] *adj.* criminal (*a. fig.*); ***~er Leichtsinn*** criminal negligence

Ver'bre·cher|jagd *f* chase after a criminal (*or* criminals); **~kar,tei** *f* criminal records *pl.*; **~nest** *n* criminals' hideout

Ver'bre·cher·tum *n* (-s; *no pl.*) **1.** crime; **2.** → **Ver'bre·cher·welt** *f* (-; *no pl.*) world of crime, underworld

ver'brei·ten (h) **I.** *v/t.* a) spread, b) broadcast (*a.* F *news*, *secret etc.*), c) *fig.* spread, disseminate *ideas etc.*, d) circulate *paper etc.*, e) give off *light*, *smell*, *a.* emit, radiate *heat*, *a. fig. calm etc*, f) *fig.* cause, bring about; ***Entsetzen*** *etc.* ***unter den Menschen ~*** fill everyone with horror *etc.*; **II.** *v/refl.*: ***sich ~*** spread; *fig.* ***sich ~ über*** *acc.* expatiate on, hold forth on *a subject etc.*; → ***verbreitet***

ver·brei·tern [fɛɐ'braɪtɐn] (h) **I.** *v/t.* widen; **II.** *v/refl.*: ***sich ~*** widen (out); **Ver·brei·te·rung** [fɛɐ'braɪtərʊŋ] *f* (-; -en) widening

ver·brei·tet [fɛɐ'braɪtət] *adj.* a) widespread, common, b) widely read *paper etc.*

Ver·brei·tung [fɛɐ'braɪtʊŋ] *f* (-; *no pl.*) a) spread(ing), dissemination; circulation; emission; radiation; → ***verbreiten,*** b) extent; ***~ finden*** gain currency; **Ver'brei·tungs·ge·biet** *n* area (in which s.th. is to be found); ⚕ dispersal area *of an epidemic etc.*; area affected *by a disaster*, affected area; *radio*, *TV*: broadcasting (*or* service) area

ver'bren·nen (*irr.*, *no* -ge-, → ***brennen***) **I.** *v/t.* (h) burn; scorch; ⚙ incinerate *waste*; cremate; ***sich die Zunge*** *etc.* ***~*** burn (*or* scald) one's tongue *etc.*; → ***Finger, Mund, verbrannt***; **II.** *v/i.* (sn) a) burn; *building etc.*: burn down, be destroyed by fire, be burnt to the ground, be gutted, b) be burnt to death; **III.** *v/refl.* (h): ***sich ~*** burn o.s., get burnt

Ver·bren·nung [fɛɐ'brɛnʊŋ] *f* (-; -en) **1.** burning; ⚗, ⚙ *usu.* combustion; cremation; **2.** burn (***an*** *dat.* on); → ***Grad***

Ver'bren·nungs|ma,schi·ne *f*, **~mo·tor** *m* internal combustion engine; **~ofen** *m* combustion furnace; ⚙ (waste) incinerator; **~vor·gang** *m* process of combustion; **~wär·me** *f* heat of combustion

ver·brie·fen [fɛɐ'bri:fən] *v/t.* (h) document; *w.s.* guarantee; **ver'brieft** *adj.*: ***~es Recht*** vested right

ver'brin·gen *v/t.* (*irr.*, *no* -ge-, h, → ***bringen***) spend *time etc.*; ***das Wochenende*** *etc.* ***~ mit*** *dat.* spend the weekend *etc.* doing *s.th.*

ver·brü·dern [fɛɐ'bry:dɐn] *v/refl.* (h): ***sich ~*** fraternize; **Ver·brü·de·rung** [fɛɐ'bry:dərʊŋ] *f* (-; -en) fraternization

ver'brü·hen *v/t.* (h) scald; ***sich die Hand*** *etc.* ***~*** scald one's hand *etc.*; **Ver'brü·hung** *f* (-; -en) scald

ver'bu·chen *v/t.* (h) ☤ enter (in the books); *fig.* clock up, notch up; ***e-n Erfolg ~ können*** be successful; ***e-n Gewinn ~*** register a gain

ver'bum·meln F *v/t.* (h) **1.** ***die Zeit ~*** waste (one's) time, idle away one's time; **2.** a) miss *an appointment etc.*; (completely) forget (about) *s.th.*, b) lose *s.th.*; **ver'bum·melt** F *adj.* **1.** idling ..., indolent; **2.** F ... gone to seed; **3.** wasted, *time etc.* idled away

Ver·bund [fɛɐ'bʊnt *m* (-[e]s; -e [-də]) **1.** ⚙, ⚗ *etc.* compound; **2.** ☤ *etc.* combine; (integrated) system; **3.** → ***Medienverbund***; **~bau·wei·se** *f* composite construction

ver·bun·den [fɛɐ'bʊndən] **I.** *p.p. of* ***verbinden***; **II.** *adj.* ***j-m ~ sein*** be indebted (*or* beholden) to s.o.; ***ich bin Ihnen sehr ~*** I'm much obliged to you

ver·bün·den [fɛɐ'bʏndən] *v/refl.* (h): ***sich ~*** form an alliance (***mit*** *dat.* with), *a. w.s.* ally o.s. (to, with)

Ver·bun·den·heit [fɛɐ'bʊndənhaɪt] *f* (-; *no pl.*) attachment (***mit*** *dat.* to), bond (with); *w.s.* solidarity (with)

Ver·bün·de·te [fɛɐ'bʏndətə] *m*, *f* (-n; -n) ally (*a. fig.*)

Ver'bund|glas *n* laminated glass; **~netz** *n* ⚡ integrated power grid; **~(pflaster)stein** *m* interlocking paving stone; **~sy,stem** *n* compound system; **~wirtschaft** *f* ☤ integrated economy

ver'bür·gen (h) **I.** *v/t.* guarantee; **II.** *v/refl.*: ***sich ~ für*** *acc.* vouch for, guarantee; ***sich dafür ~, daß ...*** vouch for *s.o.'s honesty etc.*

ver·bür·ger·li·chen [fɛɐ'bʏrgɐlɪçən] **I.** *v/i.* (sn) become gentrified, gentrify; **II.** *v/t.* (h) gentrify; **ver'bür·ger·licht** *adj.* gentrified

ver·bürgt [fɛɐ'bʏrkt] *adj.* authentic(ated); established *fact etc.*

ver'bü·ßen *v/t.* (h): ***s-e Strafe ~*** serve one's sentence; **Ver'bü·ßung** *f*: ***nach*** *etc.* ***~ s-r Strafe*** after *etc.* serving one's sentence

ver'but·tern *v/t.* (h) **1.** turn (*or* make) *cream* into butter; **2.** F use up, *a.* F blow *one's money*

ver·chro·men [fɛɐ'kro:mən] *v/t.* (h) chromium-plate

Ver·dacht [fɛɐ'daxt] *m* (-[e]s; *no pl.*) suspicion; ***~ erregen*** arouse suspicion; ***den ~ lenken*** (*or* ***schieben***) ***auf*** *acc.* cast suspicion on; ***in ~ haben*** suspect; ***in ~ kommen*** be suspected; ***ich habe den (starken) ~, daß*** I have a (strong) suspicion that, I (strongly) suspect that; ***mein ~ fällt auf X*** I'm inclined to suspect X; ***in den ~ kommen*** (*or* ***geraten***) ***zu*** *inf.* be suspected of *ger.*; ***unter dem ~ zu*** *inf.* under suspicion of *ger.*; ***~ schöpfen*** become suspicious (***gegen*** *acc.* of), F smell a rat; ***bei ihm besteht ~ auf Krebs*** he is suspected of having cancer; F ***et. auf ~ hin tun*** F do s.th. on spec; F ***auf ~ hingehen*** *etc.* go there *etc.* on the off-chance

ver·däch·tig [fɛɐ'dɛçtɪç] *adj.* a) suspicious, suspect; dubious, b) suspicious-looking; *a.* shifty(-eyed) *person*; ***sich ~ machen*** arouse suspicion; ***er ist der Tat (dringend) ~*** he is (strongly) suspected of having committed the crime; **verdäch·ti·gen** [fɛɐ'dɛçtɪgən] *v/t.* (h) suspect (*gen.* of); cast suspicion on; **Verdäch·tig·te** [fɛɐ'dɛçtɪçtə] *m*, *f* (-n; -n) suspect; **Ver·däch·ti·gung** [fɛɐ'dɛçtɪgʊŋ] *f* (-; -en) **1.** suspecting, casting suspicion (*gen.* on); **2.** suspicion; ***~en äußern gegen j-n*** cast (*or* throw) suspicion on s.o.

Ver'dachts|grund *m* grounds *pl.* (*or* cause) for suspicion; **~mo,ment** *n* suspicious factor

ver·dam·men [fɛɐ'damən] *v/t.* (h) a) condemn, b) damn, curse; **ver'dam·mens·wert** *adj.* damnable; **Ver·damm·nis** [fɛɐ'damnɪs] *f* (-; *no pl.*) *eccl.*: (***die ewige ~*** eternal) damnation

ver·dammt [fɛɐ'damt] **I.** *adj.* **1.** damned; ***dazu ~ zu*** *inf.* doomed (*or* condemned) to *inf.*; ***zum Nichtstun ~*** condemned to inactivity; ***zum Scheitern ~*** doomed to fail; **2.** F blasted, damn(ed); ***~!*** F damn (it)!, blast!; ***~ noch mal!, ~ und zugenäht!*** F damnation!; V ***~e Scheiße!*** *sl.* bloody hell!, V shit!; **II.** F *adv.* F damn(ed), bloody; ~ ***viel*** *sl.* a (*or* one) hell of a lot; ~ ***wenig*** V bugger all; ***es tut ~ weh*** *sl.* it hurts like hell, it's helluva painful (*or* sore); **Ver'damm·te** *m, f* (-n; -n) damned soul; ***die ~n*** the damned (*pl.*); **Ver'dam·mung** *f* (-; *no pl.*) **1.** condemnation; **2.** *eccl.* (eternal) damnation; **Ver'dam·mungs·ur·teil** *n* condemnation; damning indictment

ver'damp·fen *v/t. and v/i.* evaporate; ⚗, *phys. a.* vaporize; **Ver'damp·fung** *f* (-; -en) evaporation

ver'dan·ken *v/t.* (h): ***j-m et.*** ~ owe s.th. to s.o.; be indebted to s.o. for s.th.; ***e-r Sache zu ~ sein*** be due to s.th.; ***er hat ihr viel zu*** ~ he owes a lot to her; ***das hab' ich dir zu*** ~ I owe it all to you, *a. iro.* it's all thanks to you; ***dir hab' ich zu ~, daß*** it's thanks to you that, *iro. a.* it's your fault that; ***das hast du dir selbst zu ~!*** it's your own fault

ver·darb [fɛɐ'darp] *pret. of* **verderben**

ver·dat·tert [fɛɐ'datɐt] F *adj.* F flabbergasted; F flummoxed

ver·dau·en [fɛɐ'daʊən] *v/t.* (h) digest; *fig. a.* come to terms with; *fig.* ***schwer zu ~*** *a.* hard to swallow; ***er hat es immer noch nicht verdaut*** *a.* he hasn't got over it yet; ***das kann man nicht so schnell*** ~ that will take a bit of digesting (*or* getting used to)

ver·dau·lich [fɛɐ'daʊlɪç] *adj.* digestible; ***leicht*** ~ easily digestible; *fig.* light *reading etc.*; *fig.* ***ein leicht ~es Buch*** light reading; ***schwer*** ~ hard to digest, heavy; *fig.* heavy-going *book etc.*; **Ver'dau·lich·keit** *f* (-; *no pl.*) digestibility

Ver·dau·ung [fɛɐ'daʊʊŋ] *f* (-; *no pl.*) digestion

Ver'dau·ungs|ap·pa,rat *m* digestive system; **~be·schwer·den** *pl.* indigestion *sg.*, digestive trouble *sg.*; **2för·dernd** *adj.* digestive ..., good for the digestion; **~or,gan** *n* digestive organ; **~spa,zier·gang** *m* constitutional; **~stö·rung** *f* indigestion; dyspepsia; **~trakt** *m* digestive tract

Ver'deck *n* (-[e]s; -e) **1.** ⚓ deck; **2.** *mot.* roof, top

ver'decken *v/t.* (h) a) cover (up), b) hide, *a.* ⚙ conceal; → ***Karte***

ver'den·ken *v/t.* (*irr.*, *no* -ge-, h, → **denken**): ***ich kann es ihr nicht*** ~ I can't blame her (for it) (***daß*** for *ger. or* ***wenn*** if)

Ver·derb [fɛɐ'dɛrp] *m* (-s; *no pl.*) **1.** spoilage; **2.** *fig.* corruption; ruin; → ***Gedeih***

ver·der·ben [fɛɐ'dɛrbən] (verdarb, verdorben) **I.** *v/t.* (h) **1.** spoil; ***sich die Augen*** ~ ruin one's eyes; ***ich habe mir den Magen verdorben*** I've got an upset stomach; ***j-m et.*** ~ spoil s.th. for s.o.; ***j-m die Freude*** ~ spoil s.o.'s fun; ***j-m die Laune*** (***Stimmung***) ~ put s.o. out, put a damper on s.o.; ***es mit j-m*** ~ fall out with s.o., get into s.o.'s bad books; ***er will es mit niemandem*** ~ he tries to please everybody; **2.** *fig.* corrupt; **II.** *v/i.* (sn) **3.** *food*: go bad, *esp. meat, milk etc.*: *a.* go off; rot; **4.** *fig.* perish

Ver'der·ben *n* (-s; *no pl.*) ruin(ation), downfall; ***Drogen*** *etc.* ***waren ihr ~*** *a.* drugs *etc.* were her undoing; (***offenen Auges***) ***in sein ~ rennen*** head straight for disaster; ***j-n ins ~ stürzen*** bring disaster on s.o.; → ***blindlings***

ver'der·ben·brin·gend *adj.* fatal, ruinous

ver·derb·lich [fɛɐ'dɛrplɪç] *adj.* **1.** ***~e Waren*** perishable goods, perishables; **2.** *fig.* ruinous, corrupting

Ver·derb·nis [fɛɐ'dɛrpnɪs] *f* (-; *no pl.*) **1.** depravity; **2.** ruin, disaster; **ver·derbt** [fɛɐ'dɛrpt] *adj.* depraved, corrupt; **Ver'derbt·heit** *f* (-; *no pl.*) depravity, corruptness, corruption

ver·deut·li·chen [fɛɐ'dɔʏtlɪçən] *v/t.* (h) make clear (*dat.* to); explain, elucidate; illustrate; **Ver'deut·li·chung** *f* (-; *no pl.*) elucidation; explanation, illustration; ***zur*** ~ *gen.* to elucidate (*or* explain, illustrate) *s.th.*, *w.s.* to make *s.th.* quite clear; ***zur*** ~ by way of explanation (*or* illustration)

ver·deut·schen [fɛɐ'dɔʏtʃən] *v/t.* (h) put into plain words, F translate (into German)

ver'dich·ten (h) **I.** *v/t.* **1.** *phys.* condense, thicken, solidify *gases*; compress; **2.** *fig.* ~ ***zu*** *dat.* condense into; **II.** *v/refl.*: ***sich*** ~ **3.** *fog etc.*: thicken; *phys. a.* condense, *gases*: solidify; **4.** *fig. rumo(u)r, suspicion etc.*: be consolidated; *rumo(u)r*: grow, gain ground (*or* momentum); *impression*: grow (stronger); **Ver'dich·tung** *f* (-; *no pl.*) **1.** *phys.* condensation; *a. mot.* compression; thickening; **2.** *fig.* consolidation; hardening *of an impression*

ver'dicken *v/t. and v/refl.* (***sich*** ~) (h) thicken; **Ver'dickung** (*sep.* -k·k-) *f* (-; -en) thickening

ver'die·nen (h) **I.** *v/t.* **1.** earn, make *money*; ***et. ~ an*** (*or* ***bei*** *dat.*) make money out of; ***ein Vermögen*** ~ make a fortune; ***daran ist nichts zu*** ~ there's no money in it; **2.** *fig.* deserve, merit *praise, criticism etc.*; ***Beachtung*** *etc.* ~ be worthy of note *etc.*, be worth noting *etc.*; ***das hat er*** (***nicht***) ***verdient*** he deserves it (he doesn't deserve it); ***er hat es nicht anders*** (***besser***) ***verdient*** he got what he deserved (he doesn't deserve any better); ***womit habe ich das verdient?*** what have I done to deserve that?; → ***Brot, verdient***; **II.** *v/i.*: ***gut*** ~ earn a good (*or* decent) salary *or* wage; ***er verdient nicht schlecht*** he doesn't do too badly (salarywise *or* wagewise)

Ver·dienst[1] [fɛɐ'diːnst] *m* (-[e]s; -e) a) earnings *pl.*; wages *pl.*; salary, b) gain, profit

Ver'dienst[2] *n* (-[e]s; -e) merit; service; ***sich um et. große ~e erwerben*** render outstanding services to s.th.; ***es ist*** (***allein***) ***sein ~, daß*** it is (entirely) due to him that; ***nach ~ belohnen*** *etc.* reward *etc.* according to merit

Ver'dienst|aus·fall *m* lost earnings *pl.*; **~kreuz** *n* Distinguished Service Cross; **~mög·lich·keit** *f* chance to earn (some) money; **~span·ne** *f* ✝ profit margin

ver'dienst·voll *adj.* a) deserving, meritorious *person*, b) commendable, laudable *deed*; ***~e Person*** *a.* man (*or* woman) of merit

ver·dient [fɛɐ'diːnt] *adj.* **1.** a) deserving; outstanding, *scientist etc.* of (great) merit, b) well-earned *victory etc.*; due, deserved *punishment etc.*; **2.** ***sich um j-n*** (***et.***) ***~ machen*** do *or* render s.o. (s.th.) a great service; **ver·dien·ter·ma·ßen** [fɛɐ'diːntɐ'maːsən] *adv.* deservedly

Ver·dikt [vɛr'dɪkt] *n* (-[e]s; -e) ⚖ *and fig.* verdict

ver·ding·li·chen [fɛɐ'dɪŋlɪçən] *v/t.* (h) concretize; **Ver'ding·li·chung** *f* (-; -en) concretization

ver'dol·met·schen *v/t.* (h) translate, interpret; *fig.* explain, F translate

ver'don·nern F *v/t.* (h) condemn (***zu*** *dat.* to); ***j-n ~, et. zu tun*** make s.o. do s.th.

ver·dop·peln [fɛɐ'dɔpəln] *v/t. and v/refl.* (***sich*** ~) (h) double; redouble *one's efforts etc.*; **Ver·dopp·lung** [fɛɐ'dɔplʊŋ] *f* (-; -en) doubling; redoubling

ver·dor·ben [fɛɐ'dɔrbən] **I.** *p.p. of* **verderben**; **II.** *adj.* spoilt; *gastr.* bad, *esp. meat, milk etc.*: *pred. a.* off; rotten; foul *air*; ⚕ upset *stomach*; *fig.* depraved, corrupt; ***das Essen ist ~*** *a.* the food has gone bad (*or* off); **Ver'dor·ben·heit** *f* (-; *no pl.*) corruption, depravity

ver·dor·ren [fɛɐ'dɔrən] *v/i.* (sn) wither, *a. meadows etc.*: dry up; **ver'dorrt** *adj.* withered, dried up

ver'dö·sen F *v/t.* (h) doze *the day etc.* away; doze through *a meeting etc.*

ver·drah·ten [fɛɐ'draːtən] *v/t.* (h) wire up (*a.* ⚡); **Ver'drah·tung** *f* (-; -en) wiring

ver'drän·gen *v/t.* (h) **1.** edge *s.o.* out (***von*** *dat.* of); *a.* oust *s.o.* (***aus*** *dat.* from *an office etc.*); drive *s.o.* out (of *an area etc.*), *pol.* displace (from); **2.** *fig.* replace, supersede; **3.** *psych.* suppress, repress; **Ver'drän·gung** *f* (-; -en) edging out; ousting; driving out, displacement; *fig.* replacement, supersession; *psych.* suppression, repression; **Ver'drän·gungs·wett·be·werb** *m* predatory competition

ver·drecken [fɛɐ'drɛkən] (*sep.* -k·k-) **I.** *v/t.* (h) dirty, make a mess of; **II.** *v/i.* (sn) get dirty; **ver'dreckt** *adj.* dirty; ***völlig*** ~ filthy dirty

ver'dre·hen *v/t.* (h) twist; *fig. a.* distort *facts, meaning etc.*; ***die Augen*** ~ roll one's eyes; ***den Hals*** ~ crane one's neck round; *fig.* ***j-m den Kopf*** ~ turn s.o.'s head; **ver'dreht** *adj.* a) twisted, b) F (slightly) screwy; *pred.* in a muddle, c) warped, F cranky *ideas, views etc.*; **Ver'dre·hung** *f* (-; -en) twist(ing); *fig.* twisting, distortion *of facts etc.*

ver·drei·fa·chen [fɛɐ'draɪfaxən] *v/t. and v/refl.* (***sich*** ~) (h) treble, triple; **Ver'drei·fa·chung** *f* (-; *no pl.*) trebling, tripling

ver'dre·schen F *v/t.* (*irr.*, *no* -ge-, h, → **dreschen**) give *s.o.* a thrashing

ver·drie·ßen [fɛɐ'driːsən] *v/t.* (verdroß, verdrossen, h) annoy; ***laß dich's nicht*** ~ don't let it get to you; **ver·drieß·lich** [fɛɐ'driːslɪç] *adj.* **1.** annoyed; F grumpy; **2.** irksome; **Ver'drieß·lich·keit** *f* (-; -en) **1.** *no pl.* annoyance; F grumpiness; **2.** *no pl.* irksome nature (*gen.* of); **3.** *pl.* inconveniences, annoying little things

ver'dril·len *v/t.* (h) twist

ver·droß [fɛɐ'drɔs] *pret. of* **verdrießen**

ver·dros·sen [fɛɐ'drɔsən] **I** *p.p. of* **verdrießen**; **II.** *adj.* sullen; peeved; weary, F fed up; **Ver'dros·sen·heit** *f* (-; *no pl.*) sullenness; weariness

ver'drücken F (h) **I.** *v/t.* F put (*or* stow) away, polish off; **II.** *v/refl.*: ***sich*** ~ slip away (unnoticed), disappear

Ver·druß [fɛɐ'drʊs] *m* (-sses; *no pl.*) displeasure; annoyance; ***j-m ~ bereiten*** cause s.o. (a lot of) trouble

ver'duf·ten F *v/i.* (sn) F clear off

ver·dum·men [fɛɐ'dʊmən] **I.** *v/i.* (sn) become stultified; **II.** *v/t.* (h) stultify, dull *s.o.'s* mind; brainwash; **Ver'dum·mung** *f* (-; *no pl.*) stultification

ver·dun·keln [fɛɐ'dʊŋkəln] (h) **I.** *v/t.* darken (*a. room*); ⚔ black out; *fig.* obscure; **II.** *v/refl.*: **sich** ~ darken; *fig. face*: *a.* cloud over; **Ver'dun·ke·lung** *f* (-; -en) **1.** darkening; ⚔ blackout; **2.** ⚖ collusion; **Ver'dun·ke·lungs·ge·fahr** *f* ⚖ danger of collusion

ver·dün·nen [fɛɐ'dʏnən] *v/t.* (h) dilute; ⚙ thin (down) *paint etc.*; **Ver·dün·ner** [fɛɐ'dʏnɐ] *m* (-s; -) ⚙ thinner

ver·dün·ni·sie·ren [fɛɐdʏni'zi:rən] F *v/refl.*: **sich** ~ (h) F do a vanishing trick

Ver·dün·nung [fɛɐ'dʏnʊŋ] *f* (-; *no pl.*) dilution; ⚙ thinning (down) *of paint etc.*; **Ver'dün·nungs·mit·tel** *n* thinner

ver'dun·sten *v/t.* (h) *and v/i.* (sn) evaporate; **Ver·dun·ster** [fɛɐ'dʊnstɐ] *m* (-s; -) humidifier; **Ver'dun·stung** *f* (-; *no pl.*) evaporation

ver'dur·sten *v/i.* (sn) die of thirst

ver·dü·stern [fɛɐ'dy:stɐn] *v/t. and v/refl.* (**sich** ~) (h) darken

ver·dutzt [fɛɐ'dʊtst] *adj.* nonplussed; *pred.* taken aback

ver'eb·ben *fig. v/i.* (sn) subside, ebb away

ver·edeln [fɛɐ'ʔe:dəln] *v/t.* (h) **1.** ⚙ refine; process, finish; **2.** ❀ graft; **3.** *fig.* ennoble; **Ver·ede·lung** [fɛɐ'ʔe:dəlʊŋ] *f* (-; -en) **1.** ⚙ refinement; processing, finishing; **2.** ❀ grafting; **3.** *fig.* ennoblement, ennobling

ver'ehe·li·chen *v/refl.* (h): **sich** ~ (**mit** *dat.*) marry; **Ver'ehe·li·chung** *f* (-; -en) marriage

ver'eh·ren *v/t.* (h) **1.** admire, revere; worship; **2.** **j-m et.** ~ give s.o. s.th. (as a present), *iro.* bequeath s.th. to s.o.

Ver·eh·rer [fɛɐ'ʔe:rɐ] *m* (-s; -), **Ver·eh·re·rin** [fɛɐ'ʔe:rərɪn] *f* (-; -nen) admirer; devotee, F fan; **Ver'eh·rer·post** *f* fan mail

ver·ehrt [fɛɐ'ʔe:ɐt] *adj.* hono(u)red, venerable; **~e Anwesende!** Ladies and Gentlemen!; **Sehr ~er Herr** Dear Sir; *iro.* **Verehrteste!** my dear!

Ver'eh·rung *f* (-; *no pl.*) admiration, reverence; worship; **ver'eh·rungs·wür·dig** *adj.* admirable; venerable

ver·ei·di·gen [fɛɐ'ʔaɪdɪgən] *v/t.* (h) a) swear *s.o.* in(to office), b) make *s.o.* swear an oath (**auf** *acc.* on); **ver·ei·digt** [fɛɐ'ʔaɪdɪçt] *adj.* sworn; **Ver'ei·di·gung** *f* (-; -en) swearing-in (ceremony)

Ver·ein [fɛɐ'ʔaɪn] *m* (-[e]s; -e) **1.** society, association; club; F *hum.* **ein schöner** (**seltsamer**) ~ F a fine (funny) bunch; **2.** **im ~ mit** *dat.* together with, in conjunction with

ver·ein·bar [fɛɐ'ʔaɪnba:ɐ] *adj.* compatible, consistent (**mit** *dat.* with); **nicht** ~ → **unvereinbar**; **ver·ein·ba·ren** [fɛɐ'ʔaɪnba:rən] *v/t.* (h) **1.** agree (up)on, arrange; **2.** reconcile (**mit** *dat.* with); **sich** (**nicht**) ~ **lassen mit** *dat.* be (in)consistent *or* (in)compatible with; **ich kann es mit m-m Gewissen nicht** ~ it goes against my conscience (*or* principles); **Ver'ein·bar·keit** *f* (-; *no pl.*) compatibility (**mit** *dat.* with); **ver·ein·bart** [fɛɐ'ʔaɪnba:ɐt] *adj.* agreed; arranged; **es gilt als ~, daß** it is understood that; **Ver·ein·ba·rung** [fɛɐ'ʔaɪnba:rʊŋ] *f* (-; -en) a) agreement (*a. pol.*), arrangement, b) clause, provision; **laut** ~ as agreed; **nach** ~ by agreement (*or* arrangement, appointment); **e-e ~ treffen** reach an agreement; **Gehalt nach** ~ salary negotiable

ver'ei·nen *v/t.* (h) → **vereinigen, vereint**

ver·ein·fa·chen [fɛɐ'ʔaɪnfaxən] *v/t.* (h) simplify; **ver'ein·fa·chend** *adj.* simplistic(ally *adv.*); **grob** (*or* **stark**) ~ oversimplistic(ally *adv.*); **Ver'ein·fa·chung** *f* (-; -en) simplification

ver·ein·heit·li·chen [fɛɐ'ʔaɪnhaɪtlɪçən] *v/t.* (h) standardize; **Ver'ein·heit·li·chung** *f* (-; -en) standardization

ver'ei·ni·gen *v/t.* (h) (*a.* **sich** ~) a) unite, join; combine (*a.* **in sich** ~); integrate (**in** *dat.* within); ✝ amalgamate, consolidate, merge (**zu** *dat.* into), b) assemble, gather, *esp. pol.*, ⚔ rally; **sich** ~ *geogr.* meet, merge; **ver·ei·nigt** [fɛɐ'ʔaɪnɪçt] *adj.* **1.** united; **Vereinigte Staaten** (**von Amerika**) United States (of America) (*abbr.* US[A]); **2.** ✝ consolidated; **Ver'ei·ni·gung** *f* (-; -en) **1.** uniting, unification, combining *etc.*; → **vereinigen**; **2.** union; association; **3.** ✝ amalgamation, merger

ver·ein·nah·men [fɛɐ'ʔaɪnna:mən] *v/t.* (h) **1.** take in, collect; F *fig.* pocket; **2.** F *fig.* monopolize

ver·ein·sa·men [fɛɐ'ʔaɪnza:mən] *v/i.* (sn) become isolated; grow lonely; **Ver'ein·sa·mung** *f* (-; *no pl.*) (growing) isolation

Ver'eins|bei·trag *m* membership dues *pl.*; **~far·ben** *pl.* club colo(u)rs; **~haus** *n* → **Vereinslokal**; **~kas·se** *f* club funds *pl.*; **~lo,kal** *n* club house

Ver'eins·mei·er [-maɪɐ] F *m* (-s; -) F joiner; **Ver·eins·meie·rei** [-maɪə'raɪ] F *f* (-; *no pl.*) club mania

Ver'eins·mit·glied *n* club member

Ver'eins·we·sen *n* (-s; *no pl.*) clubs(, societies and associations) *pl.*

ver·eint [fɛɐ'ʔaɪnt] *adj.* united; **mit ~en Kräften** in a joint (*or* combined) effort; **die &en Nationen** the United Nations

ver·ein·zelt [fɛɐ'ʔaɪntsəlt] **I.** *adj.* a) isolated, *meteor. a.* scattered, b) occasional, sporadic; **~e Briefe** the odd letter; → **Bewölkung**; **II.** *adv.* a) sporadically, now and then, b) here and there

ver·ei·sen [fɛɐ'ʔaɪzən] **I.** *v/t.* (h) ❊ freeze; **II.** *v/i.* (sn) *roads etc.*: freeze over; ✈, *windows etc.*: ice up; **ver·eist** [fɛɐ'ʔaɪst] *adj.* iced up (*or* over); frozen (over); **Ver'ei·sung** *f* (-; *no pl.*) icing up; freezing (over)

ver·ei·teln [fɛɐ'ʔaɪtəln] *v/t.* (h) thwart, frustrate, foil; prevent *deed etc.*; **Ver'ei·te·lung** *f* (-; *no pl.*) thwarting, frustration; prevention *of a deed etc.*

ver'ei·tern *v/i.* (sn) go septic; **ver·ei·tert** [fɛɐ'ʔaɪtɐt] *adj.* septic; **Ver'ei·te·rung** *f* (-; -en) sepsis

ver·elen·den [fɛɐ'ʔe:lɛndən] *v/i.* (sn) be reduced to poverty; **Ver'elen·dung** *f* (-; *no pl.*) impoverishment

ver'en·den *v/i.* (sn) perish, die

ver·en·gen [fɛɐ'ʔɛŋən] (h) **I.** *v/t.* narrow; **II.** *v/refl.*: **sich** ~ a) (become) narrow, b) *trousers etc.*: taper, c) *blood vessels*: constrict; *pupils*: contract; **Ver'en·gung** *f* (-; -en) a) narrowing, b) constriction; contraction

ver·erb·bar [fɛɐ'ʔɛrpba:ɐ] *adj.* **1.** ⚖ inheritable; **2.** *biol.*, ❊ hereditary; **Ver'erb·bar·keit** *f* (-; *no pl.*) heritability; **ver'er·ben** (h) **I.** *v/t.* **1.** ⚖ leave, (*a. hum. give*) bequeath (*dat.* to); **2.** *biol.*, ❊ pass on (**auf** *acc.* to), transmit (to); **3.** *fig.* pass *or* hand down (**auf** *acc.* to); **II.** *v/refl.* **4.** **sich** ~ *biol.*, ❊ be hereditary, run in the family, **auf** *acc.*: be passed on (*or* be transmitted) to *s.o.*; **5.** ⚖ **sich ~ auf** *acc.* devolve (up)on, fall to; **ver'erb·lich** *adj.* **1.** ⚖ inheritable, hereditary; **2.** *biol.*, ❊ hereditary; **ver·erbt** [fɛɐ'ʔɛrpt] *adj.* **1.** ⚖ inherited; **2.** *biol.*, ❊ hereditary; **Ver·er·bung** [fɛɐ'ʔɛrbʊŋ] *f* (-; *no pl.*) **1.** ⚖ bequeathal (**an** *acc.* to); **2.** *biol.*, ❊ transmission (**auf** *acc.* to); **3.** *fig.* transmission (**auf** *acc.* to), passing *or* handing down (to); **Ver'er·bungs·leh·re** *f* genetics *pl.*

ver·ewi·gen [fɛɐ'ʔe:vɪgən] (h) **I.** *v/t.* a) perpetuate, b) immortalize; **II.** *v/refl.*: **sich** ~ immortalize o.s.; inscribe one's name (**in** *dat.* in; **an** *dat.* on), carve one's name (into); **ver·ewigt** [fɛɐ'ʔe:vɪçt] *adj.* deceased; **Ver'ewi·gung** *f* (-; *no pl.*) a) perpetuation, b) immortalization

ver'fah·ren¹ (*irr.*, *no* -ge-, → **fahren**) **I.** *v/i.* (sn) proceed, act (**nach** *dat.* on); ~ **mit** *dat.* deal with *s.o.*, *a.* handle *s.th.*; **II.** *v/t.* (h) spend *time, money* driving (around); use up *gas*; **III.** *v/refl.*: **sich** ~ (h) take the wrong road; lose one's way, get lost

ver'fah·ren² **I.** *p.p. of* **verfahren¹**; **II.** *adj.* **1.** hopeless, inextricable; **2.** messed up; tangled, muddled; **e-e ~e Geschichte** a (great) muddle

Ver'fah·ren *n* (-s; -) **1.** procedure; method; **2.** ⚖ a) procedure, b) proceedings *pl.*, (law)suit; **das ~ einleiten gegen** *acc.* take proceedings against; **3.** ⚙ process, method; system

Ver'fah·rens·recht *n* (-[e]s; *no pl.*) procedural law; **ver'fah·rens·recht·lich** **I.** *adj.* procedural; **II.** *adv.* in terms of procedural law

Ver'fah·rens|re·gel *f* rule of procedure; **~tech·nik** *f* process engineering; **~tech·ni·ker** *m* process engineer; **~wei·se** *f* procedure; method; approach

Ver'fall *m* (-[e]s; *no pl.*) **1.** decay (*a. fig.*), ruin, *a.* ❊ *and fig.* decline; dilapidation *of a building*; *fig.* fall; degeneracy; corruption; **et. dem ~ preisgeben** let s.th. go to (rack and) ruin; **der ~ hat schon eingesetzt** the rot has set in; **2.** ✝ expiry; maturity *of a bill*; **bei** ~ upon expiry, at maturity

ver'fal·len¹ *v/i.* (*irr.*, *no* -ge-, sn, → **fallen**) **1.** go to ruin; fall into disrepair; *fig.* decline, fall; ❊ waste away; **2.** ✝ expire; *a.* become invalid; **3.** (*dat.*) take to *ger.*, F get hooked on *drugs etc.*, become a slave to *alcohol, drugs etc.*, *a. a woman etc.*; be bewitched by *s.o. or s.th.*; ~ **in** *acc.* a) fall into, b) lapse (*or* slip) back into; **4.** ~ **auf** *acc.* hit (up)on *an idea etc.*; **wie ist er nur darauf ~?** what on earth made him do it?

ver'fal·len² **I.** *p.p. of* **verfallen¹**; **II.** *adj.* **1.** a) decayed; dilapidated, tumbledown *building etc.*, ramshackle, b) emaciated, F *pred.* a wreck; **2.** ✝ expired, invalid, no longer valid; **3.** addicted (*dat.* to *drugs etc.*), F hooked on; *fig.* bewitched by; **der Liebe** ~ F smitten

Ver'falls|da·tum *n* **1.** ✝ expiry date; **2.** *gastr.* best-before (*or* best-by) date, *Am.* pul date; *pharm.* sell-by date; **~er·schei·nung** *f* sign of decay; **~sta·di·um** *n*: (**im** ~ in a) state of decay *or* collapse; **~sym,ptom** *n* sign of decay; **~tag** *m*, **~zeit** *f* expiry date

ver'fäl·schen *v/t.* (h) distort, falsify; adulterate *wine etc.*; **Ver'fäl·schung** *f* (-; -en) distortion, falsification; adulteration *of wine etc.*

ver'fan·gen (*irr.*, *no* -ge-, h, → **fangen**) **I.** *v/refl.* **1.** **sich** ~ get caught; **2.** **sich in**

Widersprüchen *etc.* ~ get caught up (*or* entangled) in a web of contradictions *etc.*; **II.** *v/i.* work; ***das verfängt bei mir nicht*** F that cuts no ice with me

ver·fäng·lich [fɛɐ'fɛŋlɪç] *adj.* awkward *situation etc.*; risky; compromising *letter etc.*; trick *question*; ***du mit d-n ~en Fragen!*** *a.* you're just trying to catch me out

ver'fär·ben (h) **I.** *v/t.* dye, colo(u)r; ***die Socken haben die ganze Wäsche verfärbt*** the dye from the socks has come off onto all the washing; **II.** *v/refl.*: ***sich ~*** discolo(u)r; *a. person*: change colo(u)r; **ver·färbt** [fɛɐ'fɛrpt] *adj.* discolo(u)red; **Ver'fär·bung** *f* (-; -en) discolo(u)ration

ver'fas·sen *v/t.* (h) write; *a.* compose *poem etc.*; draw up *resolution etc.*

Ver·fas·ser [fɛɐ'fasɐ] *m* (-s; -), **Ver·fas·se·rin** [fɛɐ'fasərɪn] *f* (-; -nen) author, writer

Ver'fas·sung *f* (-; -en) **1.** *no pl.* state, condition; state (*or* frame) of mind; ***in guter*** (***schlechter***) ~ a) in good (bad) shape, b) in good (low) spirits; ***nicht in der ~ sein zu*** *inf.* be in no fit state (*or* in no frame of mind) to *inf.*; ***ich bin nicht in der ~ dazu*** *a.* I don't feel up to it; **2.** *pol.* constitution; **ver'fas·sung·ge·bend** *adj.*: ***~e Versammlung*** constituent assembly

Ver'fas·sungs|än·de·rung *f* constitutional amendment; **~be·schwer·de** *f* constitutional complaint; **~bruch** *m* breach of the constitution; **~feind** *m* enemy of the constitution; **⁓feind·lich** *adj.* anticonstitutional; **~ge·richt** *n* constitutional court; **~ge·richts·bar·keit** *f* constitutional jurisdiction; **~kla·ge** *f* constitutional challenge

ver'fas·sungs·mä·ßig *adj.* constitutional

Ver'fas·sungs|or,gan *n* constitutional body; **~recht** *n* constitutional law; **~schutz** *m* **1.** protection of the constitution; **2.** (*a.* ***Bundesamt für ~***) *federal agency for internal security*; **~staat** *m* constitutional state; **⁓treu** *adj.* loyal to the constitution; **~treue** *f* loyalty to the constitution; **⁓wid·rig** *adj.* unconstitutional; **~wid·rig·keit** *f* breach of the constitution

ver'fau·len *v/i.* (sn) decay; *food, wood etc.*: rot

ver'fech·ten *v/t.* (*irr., no* -ge-, h, → ***fechten***) speak out in support of, champion *a cause*, stand up for; maintain *a view*; defend; **Ver'fech·ter** *m* (-s; -) advocate, champion, promoter (*gen.* of)

ver'feh·len *v/t.* miss (***um*** *acc.* by); ***den Beruf verfehlt haben*** have missed one's vocation, F be in the wrong job; ***s-e Wirkung ~*** not to work, be a failure, *plan, joke etc.*: *a.* misfire; ***sich*** (*or* ***einander***) ~ miss each other; → ***Zweck;*** **ver'fehlt** *adj.* wrong, misguided; ***es für ~ halten zu*** *inf.* consider it amiss to *inf.*; **Ver'feh·lung** *f* (-; -en) offen|ce (*Am.* -se)

ver·fein·den [fɛɐ'faɪndən] (h) **I.** *v/refl.*: ***sich ~*** become enemies; *w.s.* fall out (with each other); ***sich mit j-m ~*** a) make an enemy of s.o., b) fall out with s.o.; **II.** *v/t.* make enemies of; ***j-n mit j-m ~*** set s.o. against s.o.; **ver'fein·det** *adj.* hostile; *pred.* at daggers drawn; ***sie sind vollkommen ~*** they're sworn enemies; **Ver'fein·dung** *f* (-; *no pl.*) (growing) hostility; (state of) enmity

ver·fei·nern [fɛɐ'faɪnɐn] (h) **I.** *v/t.* refine, make *s.th.* more sophisticated; ⚙ *a.* improve; *gastr.* round off; **II.** *v/refl.*: ***sich ~*** become refined, become more sophisticated; ⚙ *a.* improve; **Ver·fei·ne·rung** [fɛɐ'faɪnərʊŋ] *f* (-; -en) refinement, (increasing) sophistication; ⚙ *a.* improvement

ver·fe·men [fɛɐ'feːmən] *v/t.* (h) outlaw; *fig.* ostracize; condemn; **Ver'fe·mung** *f* (-; -en) outlawing; *fig.* ostracism, ostracizing; condemnation, condemning

ver'fer·ti·gen *v/t.* (h) make, manufacture; **Ver'fer·ti·gung** *f* (-; *no pl.*) manufacture

ver'fe·sti·gen *v/t.* (h) → ***festigen***

ver'fet·ten *v/i.* (sn) **1.** get (*or* grow) fat, grow (*or* become) obese; **2.** ⚕ *tissue, organ*: become fatty (*or* adipose); **Ver'fet·tung** *f* (-; -en) **1.** ⚕ fatty degeneration, adiposis; **2.** obesity

ver'feu·ern *v/t.* (h) burn; ✕ fire; *w.s.* use up

ver'fil·men *v/t.* (h) make a film of; *a.* adapt *a novel etc.* for the screen; **Ver'fil·mung** *f* (-; -en) a) filming, b) film version, screen adaptation

ver'fil·zen *v/i. and v/refl.* (***sich ~***) (h) *wool*: felt; *hair*: get matted

ver·fin·stern [fɛɐ'fɪnstɐn] (h) **I.** *v/t.* darken; **II.** *v/refl.*: ***sich ~*** darken; *sun, moon*: eclipse; *fig. face*: *a.* cloud over

ver·fla·chen [fɛɐ'flaxən] **I.** *v/t.* (h) flatten; **II.** *v/i.* (sn) *and v/refl.* (***sich ~***) (h) flatten, level off; *fig. conversation, style etc.*: degenerate; *person*: become shallow (*or* superficial); **Ver'fla·chung** *fig. f* (-; *no pl.*) degeneration; (growing) superficiality

ver'flech·ten *v/t. and v/refl.* (***sich ~***) (*irr., no* -ge-, h, → ***flechten***) interweave, intertwine (*both a. fig.*); ✝ integrate; ***et. zu e-r Gesamtheit*** *etc.* ~ weave s.th. into a whole *etc.*; ***ein Zitat*** *etc.* ***in et. ~*** weave a quotation *etc.* into s.th.; ***j-n in et. ~*** involve s.o. (*or* get s.o. involved) in s.th.; → ***verflochten;*** **Ver'flech·tung** *f* (-; -en) interweaving, intertwining; integration; weaving; involvement

ver'flie·gen (*irr., no* -ge-, → ***fliegen***) **I.** *v/i.* (sn) **1.** *scent etc.*: fade (away); *alcohol etc.*: evaporate; **2.** *fig. time*: fly; *memory etc.*: fade; *fear etc.*: vanish, *anger etc.*: *a.* blow over; **II.** *v/refl.*: ***sich ~*** (h) ✈ lose one's bearings, get lost

ver'flie·ßen *v/i.* (*irr., no* -ge-, sn, → ***fließen***) **1.** *colo(u)rs*: run, merge (*a. fig. concepts etc.*); become (*or* get) blurred; ***ineinander ~*** merge (into one another); **2.** *time*: pass (by)

ver·flixt [fɛɐ'flɪkst] F *adj.* F blasted, damn(ed); ***~!*** F blast!, damn (it)!; ***das ~e siebte Jahr*** the seven-year itch

ver·floch·ten [fɛɐ'flɔxtən] **I.** *p.p. of* ***verflechten;*** **II.** *adj.*: ***~ in*** *acc.* intertwined (with)in, entangled in; ***eng ~*** intricate, ***in*** *acc.*: intricately bound in(to)

ver·flos·sen [fɛɐ'flɔsən] **I.** *p.p. of* ***verfließen;*** **II.** F *adj.* ex-...; one-time ...; **Ver·flos·se·ne** [fɛɐ'flɔsənə] F *m, f* (-n; -n) F ex-boyfriend (*f* ex-girlfriend); *a.* F *hum.* old flame

ver'flu·chen *v/t.* (h) curse; **ver'flucht** *adj. and int.* → ***verdammt***

ver·flüch·ti·gen [fɛɐ'flʏçtɪgən] (h) **I.** *v/refl.*: ***sich ~*** evaporate; F *fig.* disappear, *a.* make o.s. scarce; *anger etc.*: blow over; **II.** *v/t.* volatilize

ver·flüs·si·gen [fɛɐ'flʏsɪgən] *v/t. and v/refl.* (***sich ~***) (h) liquefy; *metall.* fuse; **Ver'flüs·si·gung** *f* (-; -en) liquefaction

Ver·folg [fɛɐ'fɔlk] *m*: ***in ~*** *gen.* in pursuance of, *w.s.* in the course of

ver'fol·gen *v/t.* (h) **1.** pursue, chase (*or* run) after *s.o.*; track down *game*; **2.** follow *a scent*; **3.** pursue *a career, policy, an idea, a claim etc.*; **4.** persecute *s.o.*; ⚖ prosecute *s.o.*; **5.** *fig.* dog, plague *s.o.*; persecute *s.o.*; *dream etc.*: haunt *s.o.*; ***vom Pech verfolgt*** dogged by misfortune; **6.** follow up *line of thoughts*; **7.** follow, observe; trace *development etc.*; ***sie verfolgte jede s-r Bewegungen*** she followed his every move

Ver·fol·ger [fɛɐ'fɔlgɐ] *m* (-s; -) pursuer; persecutor

Ver·folg·te [fɛɐ'fɔlktə] *m, f* (-n; -n): (***politisch ~***) victim of (political) persecution

Ver'fol·gung *f* (-; -en) **1.** pursuit; persecution; prosecution *etc.*; → ***verfolgen;*** ***wilde ~*** hot pursuit, wild chase; ***die ~ aufnehmen*** take up the chase (*or* pursuit); **2.** pursuance

Ver'fol·gungs|jagd *f*, **~sze·ne** *f film*: wild chase, pursuit; *mot.* car chase; **~wahn** *m* persecution complex, paranoia; ***an ~ leiden*** *a.* be (a) paranoiac

ver'form·bar *adj.* ⚙ *etc.* workable; **ver'for·men** (h) **I.** *v/refl.*: ***sich ~*** go out of shape; twist; *metall. a.* buckle; *wood*: warp; **II.** *v/t.* deform; ⚙ work, form, shape; **ver'formt** *adj. a.* ⚕ deformed; ⚙ twisted; *metall. a.* buckled; *wood*: warped; **Ver'for·mung** *f* (-; -en) deformation; ⚙ working, forming, shaping

ver·frach·ten [fɛɐ'fraxtən] *v/t.* (h) freight, *Am.* ship (*a.* ⚓); F bundle *s.o.* off; **Ver'frach·ter** *m* (-s; -) shipper, forwarding (*or* shipping) agent(s *pl.*)

ver·fran·zen [fɛɐ'frantsən] F *v/refl.*: ***sich ~*** (h) a) ✈ lose one's bearings, b) get lost

ver·frem·den [fɛɐ'frɛmdən] *v/t.* (h) *a. art etc.*: alienate; **Ver'frem·dung** *f* (-; -en) alienation; **Ver'frem·dungs·ef,fekt** *m* alienation effect

ver'fres·sen F *adj.* greedy; ***~ sein*** be a glutton, F be a greedy pig; **Ver'fres·sen·heit** F *f* (-; *no pl.*) greed, voraciousness, voracity

ver·fro·ren [fɛɐ'froːrən] *adj.* **1.** ***~ sein*** feel the cold (very easily); **2.** frozen (to the bone)

ver·früht [fɛɐ'fryːt] *adj.* premature, (too) early; ***es war ~*** *a.* it came too soon (*or* early)

ver·füg·bar [fɛɐ'fyːkbaːɐ] *adj.* available, at one's disposal; ***frei ~*** freely disposable; ***~es Geld*** available cash, cash in hand; (***frei***) ***~es Einkommen*** disposable (discretionary) income; ***mit allen ~en Mitteln*** with all means at one's disposal; **Ver'füg·bar·keit** *f* (-; *no pl.*) availability

ver'fü·gen (h) **I.** *v/t.* order; ⚖ decree; **II.** *v/i.*: ***~ über*** *acc.* a) have (available *or* at one's disposal), b) have, be provided (*or* equipped) with, c) dispose of *funds etc.*; (***frei***) ***~ können über*** *acc.* be able (*or* free, in a position) to do what one wants with *s.th.*, ***s-e Zeit:*** *a.* be able to divide up one's time as one wants; ***~ Sie über mich*** at your service

Ver'fü·gung *f* (-; -en) decree, order; instruction; disposition; ***freie ~ über*** *acc.* *a.* power freely to dispose of; ***et. zur ~ haben*** have s.th. at one's disposal; ***zur ~ stehen*** be available (*dat.* to), ***j-m:*** *a.* be at s.o.'s disposal; ***j-m et. zur ~ stellen*** place s.th. at s.o.'s disposal; ***s-n Posten***

etc. ***zur ~ stellen*** resign one's post *etc.*; ***sein Amt zur ~ stellen*** *a.* tender one's resignation; ***sich zur ~ stellen*** volunteer (***für*** *acc.* for), ***j-m***: offer one's services to s.o.; ***freundlicherweise zur ~ gestellt von*** *dat.* courtesy of; ***zu Ihrer ~*** at your service; ***Vormittag zur freien ~*** morning at client's *etc.* discretion; → ***einstweilig***
ver'fü·gungs·be·rech·tigt *adj.* authorized to dispose; **Ver'fü·gungs·be·rech·ti·gung** *f* right of disposal
Ver'fü·gungs|ge·walt *f*: ***freie ~*** discretionary power of disposition; control; **~recht** *n* right of disposal
ver'füh·ren (h) **I.** *v/t.* **1.** seduce *s.o.*; **2.** a) entice, tempt *s.o.* (***zu*** *dat.* to; ***et. zu tun*** into doing s.th.), b) *w.s.* lead *s.o.* astray; **II.** *v/i.*: ***zum Diebstahl ~*** be an invitation to steal; ***es verführt zum Kauf*** it makes you tempted to buy (it); **Ver'füh·rer** *m* (-s; -) seducer; **Ver'füh·re·rin** *f* (-; -nen) seductress; **ver·füh·re·risch** [fɛɐ'fyːrərɪʃ] *adj.* **1.** bewitching, seductive; ***~e Schönheit*** ravishing beauty; **2.** enticing, tempting; **Ver'füh·rung** *f* (-; -en) **1.** seduction; **2.** enticement, temptation; **Ver'füh·rungs·kunst** *f* powers *pl.* of persuasion
ver·fünf·fa·chen [fɛɐ'fʏnffaxən] *v/t. and v/refl.* (***sich ~***) (h) quintuple, increase five times; **Ver'fünf·fa·chung** *f* (-; *no pl.*) quintupling, fivefold increase
ver'füt·tern *v/t.* (h) feed
Ver'ga·be *f* (-; *no pl.*) ✝ placing *of orders etc.*; awarding *of prizes*; allocation *of public funds*
ver·gack·ei·ern [fɛɐ'gakʔaɪɐn] F *v/t.* (h): ***j-n ~*** F pull s.o.'s leg, have s.o. on
ver'gaf·fen F *v/refl.* (h): ***sich in j-n ~*** F fall for s.o., go soft on s.o.
ver·gäl·len [fɛɐ'gɛlən] *fig. v/t.* (h) spoil, sour
ver·ga·lop'pie·ren F *v/refl.*: ***sich ~*** (h) **1.** overdo it, F go over the top; **2.** miscalculate
ver'gam·meln F **I.** *v/i.* (sn) rot; *person*: go to seed; ***~ lassen*** let *a building etc.* go to rack and ruin; **II.** *v/t.* (h) idle (*or* fritter) away; **ver'gam·melt** F *adj.* scruffy *person*; run-down *business etc.*; ***~er Typ*** F scruff, F slob
ver·gan·gen [fɛɐ'gaŋən] **I.** *p.p. of* ***verge-hen***; **II.** *adj.* past; ***im ~en Jahr*** last year; ***am ~en Freitag*** last Friday; ***in ~en Zeiten*** in times past, *lit.* in bygone times (*or* days); ***e-e ~e Größe*** a has-been; **Ver'gan·gen·heit** *f* (-; *no pl.*) past (*a. fig.*); *ling.* past tense; ***politische ~*** *s.o.'s* political background; ***e-e Frau mit ~*** a woman with a past; ***in der ~ liegen*** be a thing of the past; ***laßt die ~ ruhen*** let bygones be bygones; → ***angehören***; **Ver'gan·gen·heits·be·wäl·ti·gung** *f* (-; *no pl.*) (*a.* ***die ~***) coming to terms with the past
ver·gäng·lich [fɛɐ'gɛŋlɪç] *adj.* passing ..., transitory, transient; ***es ist alles ~*** nothing lasts (forever); **Ver'gäng·lich·keit** *f* (-; *no pl.*) transience, transitoriness; ***die ~ des Lebens*** the transitoriness of life, life's transitoriness
ver'gä·ren *v/i.* (sn) ferment; **Ver'gä·rung** *f* (-; *no pl.*) fermentation
ver·ga·sen [fɛɐ'gaːzən] *v/t.* (h) **1.** ⚗ gasify; **2.** gas, *a.* send to the gas chambers
Ver·ga·ser [fɛɐ'gaːzɐ] *m* (-s; -) *mot.* carburet(t)or; **~mo·tor** *m* carburet(t)or engine
ver·gaß [fɛɐ'gaːs] *pret. of* ***vergessen***
Ver·ga·sung [fɛɐ'gaːzʊŋ] *f* (-; -en) **1.** ⚗ gasification; **2.** gassing; F ***bis zur (kalten) ~*** ad nauseam; F ***wir haben das Zeug bis zur (kalten) ~ angehört (gegessen*** *etc.*) *a.* F we listened to (ate *etc.*) the stuff till it was coming out of our ears
ver·gat·tern [fɛɐ'gatɐn] *v/t.* (h) **1.** fence up (*or* in); **2.** F ***j-n dazu ~, et. zu tun*** F rope s.o. into doing s.th., make s.o. do s.th.
ver'ge·ben[1] (*irr.*, *no* -ge-, h, → ***geben***) **I.** *v/t.* **1.** give away (***an*** *acc.* to *s.o.*); ✝ place *order etc.* (with); farm out *work*; confer, *formal*: bestow (on); ***ein Amt an j-n ~*** appoint s.o. to an office; ***zu ~*** available; ***Stelle zu ~*** vacancy; **2.** miss, let *an opportunity* slip; *sport*: give away (the chance *v/i.*); **3.** ***sich et. ~*** compromise o.s.; **4.** forgive (***j-m*** s.o.); **II.** *v/refl.*: ***sich ~*** *card game*: misdeal
ver'ge·ben[2] **I.** *p.p. of* ***vergeben***[1]; **II.** *adj.*: ***~ sein*** *job*: be taken, *orders*: have been given out, *seats*: have been taken, F *person*: be spoken for; ***noch nicht ~*** still available, F to be had, *a.* open; ***ich bin morgen leider schon ~*** I'm booked up for tomorrow, I'm afraid
ver·ge·bens [fɛɐ'geːbəns] **I.** *adv.* in vain; **II.** *pred. adj.* in vain; of no avail
ver·geb·lich [fɛɐ'geːplɪç] **I.** *adj.* vain, fruitless, futile, useless; *pred. a.* no use; ***~e Mühe*** a wasted effort, a waste of time; **II.** *adv.* in vain; **Ver'geb·lich·keit** *f* (-; *no pl.*) futility
Ver·ge·bung [fɛɐ'geːbʊŋ] *f* (-; *no pl.*) **1.** forgiveness, pardon; ***j-n um ~ bitten*** ask s.o.'s forgiveness; **2.** → ***Vergabe***
ver·ge·gen·ständ·li·chen [fɛɐ'geːgənʃtɛntlɪçən] *v/t.* (h) concretize; **Ver'ge·gen·ständ·li·chung** *f* (-; -en) concretization
ver·ge·gen·wär·ti·gen [fɛɐ'geːgənvɛrtɪgən] *v/t.* (h): ***sich et. ~*** visualize (*or* picture) s.th.; make s.th. clear to o.s.; ***~ wir uns doch die Auswirkungen*** let's call to mind (*or* be clear about) the implications; **Ver'ge·gen·wär·ti·gung** *f* (-; -en) visualization
ver'ge·hen (*irr.*, *no* -ge-, sn, → ***gehen***) **I.** *v/i.* a) *time, anger etc.*: pass; *pain*: *a.* go away; *anger etc.*: blow over, b) cease (to exist), die, disappear, vanish, *beauty, memory etc.*: *a.* fade; ***wie die Zeit vergeht!*** time (just) flies; ***das vergeht schon wieder*** it'll pass, it won't last; ***es werden Jahre ~, bis*** (*or* ***bevor***) it'll be years before ...; ***dir wird das Lachen bald ~!*** you'll soon be laughing on the other side of your face; ***da wird ihm das Lachen schon ~!*** that'll wipe the grin off his face; ***mir ist der Appetit vergangen*** I've lost my appetite; ***vor Ungeduld*** *etc.* ***~*** be dying of impatience *etc.*; → ***hören*** II; **II.** *v/refl.*: ***sich ~ an*** *dat.* a) assault *s.o.*, b) commit indecent assault on *s.o.*; ***sich ~ gegen*** *acc.* offend against, violate; ***sich gegen ein Gesetz ~*** *a.* commit an offen|ce (*Am.* -se)
Ver'ge·hen *n* (-s; -) offen|ce (*Am.* -se)
ver·gei·sti·gen [fɛɐ'gaɪstɪgən] *v/t.* (h) **1.** intellectualize; **2.** spiritualize; **ver·gei·stigt** [fɛɐ'gaɪstɪçt] *adj.* **1.** cerebral; ***völlig ~ sein*** *a.* move on a very cerebral plane; **2.** spiritual; **Ver'gei·sti·gung** *f* (-; *no pl.*) **1.** intellectualization, raising to an intellectual (*or* a cerebral) plane; **2.** spiritualization
ver'gel·ten *v/t.* (*irr.*, *no* -ge-, h, → ***gelten***) repay; ***j-m et. ~*** repay s.o. for s.th., (*a. b.s.*) pay s.o. back for s.th.; → ***gleich*** 1; **Ver'gel·tung** *f* (-; *no pl.*) repayment; retribution, retaliation
Ver'gel·tungs|maß·nah·me *f* retaliatory measure, reprisal; *pl. a.* retaliation *sg.*; **~schlag** *m* reprisal, retaliatory strike
ver·ge·sell·schaf·ten [fɛɐgə'zɛlʃaftən] *v/t.* (h) nationalize; ✝ convert into a company (*Am.* corporation)
ver·ges·sen [fɛɐ'gɛsən] (vergaß, vergessen, h) **I.** *v/t.* forget; *a.* leave behind; ***s-n Schirm*** *etc.* ***im Restaurant*** *etc.* ***~*** leave one's umbrella *etc.* (behind) in the restaurant *etc.*; ***nicht ~ zu*** *inf.* be careful to *inf.*; ***nicht zu ~ ...*** not forgetting ...; ***ich habe es ~*** *a.* it slipped my mind; ***ich habe ganz ~, wie*** *a.* I forget how; ***das kannst du ~!*** a) forget it, b) it's useless; ***den kannst du ~!*** he's hopeless; ***das werde ich dir nie ~*** I won't ever forget it; ***das wird man ihr nie ~*** *w.s.* she'll never live it down; ***bevor ich's vergesse*** *a.* while I remember; **II.** *v/refl.*: ***sich ~*** forget o.s.; **Ver'ges·sen·heit** *f*: ***in ~ geraten*** fall into oblivion; ***et. der ~ entreißen (anheimgeben)*** rescue s.th. from (consign s.th. to) oblivion
ver·geß·lich [fɛɐ'gɛslɪç] *adj.* forgetful, absent-minded; ***~ sein*** keep forgetting things; **Ver'geß·lich·keit** *f* (-; *no pl.*) forgetfulness, absent-mindedness
ver·geu·den [fɛɐ'gɔʏdən] *v/t.* (h) waste, squander; **Ver'geu·dung** *f* (-; -en) waste; squandering
ver·ge·wal·ti·gen [fɛɐgə'valtɪgən] *v/t.* (h) **1.** ⚖ rape; **2.** *fig.* do violence to, mutilate; **Ver·ge'wal·ti·gung** *f* (-; -en) **1.** ⚖ rape; **2.** *fig.* violation, mutilation
ver·ge·wis·sern [fɛɐgə'vɪsɐn] *v/refl.* (h): ***sich ~*** make sure (***e-r Sache*** of s.th.); check (s.th.)
ver'gie·ßen *v/t.* (*irr.*, *no* -ge-, h, → ***gießen***) **1.** shed *blood, tears*; ***es wird viel Blut vergossen werden*** there will be a great deal of bloodshed; **2.** spill; **3.** *metall.* cast
ver'gif·ten (h) **I.** *v/t.* poison (*a. fig. the atmosphere etc.*); **II.** *v/refl.*: ***sich ~*** poison o.s.; **Ver'gif·tung** *f* (-; -en) poisoning; **Ver'gif·tungs·tod** *m* death by poisoning
ver·gil·ben [fɛɐ'gɪlbən] *v/i.* (sn) yellow, go yellow (at the edges); **ver·gilbt** [fɛɐ'gɪlpt] *adj.* yellowed, yellowing
ver'gip·sen *v/t.* (h) plaster
Ver·giß·mein·nicht [fɛɐ'gɪsmaɪnnɪçt] *n* (-[e]s; -[e]) ✿ forget-me-not(s *pl.*)
ver·git·tern [fɛɐ'gɪtɐn] *v/t.* (h) fix a grate onto; wire in; bar; **Ver·git·te·rung** [fɛɐ'gɪtərʊŋ] *f* (-; -en) grating
ver·gla·sen [fɛɐ'glaːzən] *v/t.* (h) glaze; glass in (*or* up); **ver·glast** [fɛɐ'glaːst] *adj.* glazed (*a. fig. look, eyes etc.*); **Ver'gla·sung** *f* (-; -en) glazing
Ver·gleich [fɛɐ'glaɪç] *m* (-[e]s; -e) **1.** comparison; ***im ~ zu*** *dat.* compared to (*or* with), in comparison with; ***dem ~ (nicht) standhalten*** bear (no) comparison, ***mit*** *dat.*: *a.* (not to) compare with; ***(un)günstig abschneiden im ~ mit*** *dat.* compare (un)favo(u)rably with; ***das ist ja überhaupt kein ~!*** you can't compare, there's just no comparison; ***e-n ~ anstellen*** draw a comparison; → ***hinken***; **2.** *ling.* simile; analogy; **3.** ⚖ (***gütlicher ~*** amicable) agreement; settlement

ver'gleich·bar *adj.* comparable (**mit** *dat.* to, with); ***das ist überhaupt nicht*** ~ you can't compare, there's just no comparison; **Ver'gleich·bar·keit** *f* (-; *no pl.*) comparability

ver'glei·chen (*irr.*, *no* -ge-, h, → ***glei·chen***) **I.** *v/t.* **1.** compare (**mit** *dat.* to, with); ***die Preise*** ~ compare prices; ***es ist nicht zu*** ~ ***mit*** *dat.* you can't compare it with, it doesn't compare with; **2.** synchronize; ***die Uhren*** ~ synchronize watches; **II.** *v/refl.* **3.** ***sich*** ~ ***mit*** *dat.* compare o.s. with; **4.** ⚖ ***sich*** ~ come to an agreement (*or* to terms); **ver'glei·chend** *adj.* comparative *studies*, *literature etc.*

Ver'gleichs|maß·stab *m* standard of comparison; **~mie·te** *f* comparable rent; **~punkt** *m* point of comparison; **~ta'bel·le** *f* comparison chart

ver'gleichs·wei·se *adv.* **1.** comparatively, relatively; **2.** by way of comparison

Ver'gleichs|wert *m* comparative (*or* comparable) value; **~zahl** *f*, **~zif·fer** *f* comparative figure

ver'glim·men *v/i.* (*irr.*, *no* -ge-, sn, → ***glimmen***) die down (*or* away)

ver'glü·hen *v/i.* (sn) **1.** smo(u)lder out; *meteor etc.*: burn out; *rocket*: burn up; **2.** *fig.* die

ver·gnü·gen [fɛɐ'gny:gən] *v/refl.*: ***sich*** ~ (h) enjoy o.s.

Ver'gnü·gen *n* (-s; -) pleasure, enjoyment; fun; ~ ***finden an*** *dat.* find pleasure in *s.th.*, enjoy *s.th.*; ***j-m*** (***großes***) ~ ***machen*** (*or* ***bereiten***) give s.o. (great) pleasure; ***es war mir ein*** ~ it was a pleasure; ***viel*** **~!** *a. iro.* have fun!, enjoy yourself (*or* yourselves)!; ***es war kein*** (***reines***) ~ F it was no picnic (*or* fun and games), it wasn't exactly (great) fun; ***mit*** (***größtem***) ~ with (the greatest) pleasure; (***nur***) ***zum*** ~ (just) for fun; ***aus reinem*** ~ just for the fun of it; ***ein teures*** ~ an expensive business (*or* affair)

ver·gnüg·lich [fɛɐ'gny:klɪç] *adj.* pleasant, enjoyable

ver·gnügt [fɛɐ'gny:kt] *adj.* pleased (**über** *acc.* with); cheerful, F chirpy, *Am.* F chipper

Ver·gnü·gung [fɛɐ'gny:gʊŋ] *f* (-; -en) **1.** pleasure; **2.** *obs.* entertainment

Ver'gnü·gungs|damp·fer *m* pleasure boat; **~fahrt** *f mot.* joy ride; **~in·du'strie** *f* entertainment industry; **~park** *m* amusement park, fun fair; theme park; **~rei·se** *f* pleasure trip; **~steu·er** *f* entertainment tax; **~sucht** *f* hedonism, craving for pleasure; **2süch·tig** *adj.* pleasure-seeking ..., hedonistic; **~vier·tel** *n* entertainments district; red-light district

ver·gol·den [fɛɐ'gɔldən] *v/t.* (h) gild (*a. fig.*); gold-plate; **Ver'gol·dung** *f* (-; -en) **1.** gilding, gold-plating; **2.** gilt, gold-plate, gold-plating

ver'gön·nen *v/t.* (h) grant; ***es war mir vergönnt zu*** *inf.* I had the privilege of *ger.*; ***es war ihm nicht vergönnt zu*** *inf.* it was not for him to *inf.*, he was not (meant) to *inf.*; ***j-m et. nicht*** ~ begrudge s.o. s.th.

ver·göt·tern [fɛɐ'gœtɐn] *fig. v/t.* (h) idolize, worship; **Ver·göt·te·rung** [fɛɐ'gœtərʊŋ] *f* (-; *no pl.*) idolization, worship(ping)

ver'gra·ben *v/t.* (*irr.*, *no* -ge-, h, → ***graben***) *a. fig.* bury; *fig.* ***sich in s-e Bücher*** ~ bury o.s. in one's books

ver'grä·men *v/t.* (h) **1.** offend; upset; ***j-n nicht*** ~ *a.* keep on s.o.'s right side; **2.** *hunt. and fig.* frighten, startle; frighten away, scare off; **ver'grämt** *adj.* careworn

ver·grät·zen [fɛɐ'grɛtsən] F *v/t.* (h) disgruntle, annoy, upset; **ver'grätzt** F *adj.* disgruntled, annoyed, upset

ver'grau·len F *v/t.* (h) put off; frighten off; ***j-m et.*** ~ spoil s.th. for s.o.

ver'grei·fen *v/refl.* (*irr.*, *no* -ge-, h, → ***greifen***) **1.** ***sich*** ~ make a mistake; ♪ play a wrong note; **2.** ***sich*** ~ ***an*** *dat.* a) lay hands on, attack, (sexually) assault *s.o.*, b) misappropriate *s.th.*, c) F *fig.* interfere (*or* fiddle around) with *s.th.*; ***sich*** ~ ***in*** *dat.* choose (*or* use) the wrong *expression, note etc.*, not to find the right *word etc.*; F *fig.* ***sich an der Kasse*** ~ F dip into the till

ver·grei·sen [fɛɐ'graɪzən] *v/i.* (sn) turn (*or* get) senile; *a. population etc.*: age; **Ver'grei·sung** *f* (-; *no pl.*) (progressive) senility; ag(e)ing *a. of the population etc.*

ver·grif·fen [fɛɐ'grɪfən] **I.** *p.p. of* ***vergreifen***; **II.** *adj.* out-of-print ..., *pred.* out of print

ver·grö·bern [fɛɐ'grø:bɐn] *v/t.* (h) **1.** coarsen; **2.** *fig.* oversimplify; **Ver·grö·be·rung** [fɛɐ'grø:bərʊŋ] *f* (-; -en) **1.** coarsening; **2.** *fig.* oversimplification

ver·grö·ßern [fɛɐ'grø:sɐn] (h) **I.** *v/t.* a) enlarge; *phot. a.* blow up; *opt.* magnify, b) expand, extend, c) *mot.*, ✈ extend, stretch, d) widen (*a. fig.*), e) *fig.* increase, add to; **II.** *v/refl.*: ***sich*** ~ grow (*a. fig.*); *a.* expand, be extended; *organ etc.*: become enlarged; widen; *fig.* increase; **ver'grö·ßernd** *adj.*: ***stark ~e Linse*** powerful lens; **Ver·grö·ße·rung** [fɛɐ'grø:sərʊŋ] *f* (-; -en) **1.** enlargement; growth; expansion, extension; widening; *fig.* increase; → ***vergrößern***; **2.** *phot.* enlargement, blow-up; *opt.* magnification

Ver'grö·ße·rungs|ap·pa'rat *m*, **~ge·rät** *n phot.* enlarger; **~glas** *n* magnifying glass; **~spie·gel** *m* magnifying mirror

ver'gucken F *v/refl.* (h) **1.** ***sich*** ~ see wrong; ***hast du dich auch nicht verguckt?*** *a.* are you sure you saw right?; **2.** *fig.* ***sich in j-n*** ~ F fall for s.o., go soft on s.o.

Ver·gün·sti·gung [fɛɐ'gʏnstɪgʊŋ] *f* (-; -en) privilege; (*tax*) allowance; (*social*) benefit; ✝ reduction, *a.* special rate

ver·gü·ten [fɛɐ'gy:tən] *v/t.* (h) **1.** compensate (***j-m et.*** s.o. for s.th.); reimburse, refund *expenses*; indemnify (***j-m*** s.o. for *damages etc.*); compensate for, make good *losses etc.*; **2.** ⚙ improve, refine; *opt.* coat; **ver'gü·tet** *adj.*: ***~es Objektiv*** coated lens; **Ver'gü·tung** *f* (-; -en) **1.** compensation; reimbursement, refund; indemnification; **2.** consideration; fee; **3.** ⚙ improvement, refinement; *opt.* coating

ver·hack·stücken [fɛɐ'hakʃtʏkən] (*sep.* -k·k-) F *v/t.* (h) F tear to bits (*or* pieces, shreds)

ver'haf·ten *v/t.* (h) arrest; ***Sie sind verhaftet!*** you are under arrest!; **ver'haf·tet** *fig. adj.*: ***im Sozialismus*** *etc.* ~ rooted in Socialism *etc.*; ***im System*** *etc.* ~ ***sein*** *a.* be a captive of the system *etc.*; **Ver'haf·tung** *f* (-; -en) arrest; **Ver'haf·tungs·wel·le** *f* wave of arrests

ver'ha·geln *v/i.* (sn) be damaged (*or* destroyed) by hail; → ***Petersilie***; **ver'ha·gelt** F *adj.*: ~ ***aussehen*** F look a right mess (*or* a real sight)

ver'ha·ken (h) **I.** *v/t.* hook together; ***die Hände*** (*or* ***Finger***) ~ clasp one's hands; **II.** *v/refl.*: ***sich*** ~ get caught (**an** *dat.* on)

ver'hal·len *v/i.* (sn) die away; → ***ungehört***

ver'hal·ten (*irr.*, *no* -ge-, h, → ***halten***) **I.** *v/refl.*: ***sich*** ~ a) be, b) behave, act, be; ***sich ruhig*** ~ keep quiet, keep still, *fig.* keep calm; ***ich weiß nicht, wie ich mich*** ~ ***soll*** I'm not sure what to do; ***sich anders*** (***umgekehrt***) ~ be different (be just the reverse); ***die Sache verhält sich ganz anders*** it's a completely different state of affairs; ***wenn es sich so verhält*** if that is the case; ⚒ ***A verhält sich zu B wie C zu D*** A is to B as C is to D; **II.** *v/t.* hold back, retain (*a. urine etc.*); suppress, restrain (*a. laughter etc.*); ***den Atem*** ~ hold one's breath; **III.** *adj.* restrained; stifled *laughter etc.*; subdued *voice*, *colo(u)r*, *mood etc.*; muted *enthusiasm etc.*; ***mit ~er Stimme*** in a subdued voice; **IV.** *adv.* with restraint; in a subdued manner; ~ ***spielen*** *sport*: play a waiting game, *thea.* underact, ♪ hold back

Ver'hal·ten *n* (-s; *no pl.*) behavio(u)r (*a. zo. etc.*), conduct

Ver'hal·tens|for·scher *m* behavio(u)rist; *zo.* ethologist; **~for·schung** *f* behavio(u)rism; *zo.* ethology; **2ge·stört** *adj.* maladjusted; **~maß·re·gel** *f* → ***Verhaltensregel***; **~merk·mal** *n* behavio(u)ral trait (*or* characteristic); **~mu·ster** *n* behavio(u)ral pattern; **~norm** *f* behavio(u)ral norm; **~psy·cho'lo·ge** *m* behavio(u)ral psychologist; **~psy·cho·lo'gie** *f* behavio(u)rism, behavio(u)ral psychology; **~re·gel** *f* rule of etiquette (*or* conduct); *pl. a.* code *sg.* of conduct; **~stö·rung** *f* behavio(u)ral disorder; **~the·ra'pie** *f* behavio(u)r therapy; **~wei·se** *f* behavio(u)r; *psych. a.* behavio(u)r pattern(s *pl.*)

Ver·hält·nis [fɛɐ'hɛltnɪs] *n* (-ses; -se) **1.** proportion; ratio; ***im*** ~ ***wenig*** *etc.* comparatively little *etc.*; ***im*** ~ ***zu*** *dat.* in proportion to, compared with; ***im*** ~ ***von 1:2*** *etc.* in a ratio of 1:2 *etc.*; ***im umgekehrten*** ~ ***zu*** *dat.* in inverse proportion to, inversely proportionate to; ***im entsprechenden*** ~ proportionately, ***stehen zu*** *dat.*: be proportional to; **2.** relationship, relations *pl.* (**zu** *dat.* with); ***in e-m freundlichen*** ~ ***mit*** *dat.* on friendly terms with; ***ich habe kein*** ~ ***dazu*** I can't relate to it, it doesn't mean anything (*or* a thing) to me; → ***gestört***; **3.** relationship, affair; **4.** *pl.* conditions, circumstances; ***unter den*** (***gegebenen***) ***~sen*** under the circumstances; ***in guten*** (***schlechten***) ***~sen leben*** be well-off (badly-off); ***über s-e ~se leben*** live beyond one's means, overspend; ***das geht über m-e ~se*** I can't afford it, it's beyond my means

ver'hält·nis·mä·ßig **I.** *adv.* relatively, reasonably; **II.** *adj.* proportional; ✝ *a.* pro rata ...

Ver'hält·nis|wahl *f parl.* proportional representation; **~wahl·recht** *n* (system of) proportional representation; **~wort** *n* (-[e]s; ⸚er) *ling.* preposition

Ver'hal·tung *f* (-; *no pl.*) ⚕ retention

ver'han·deln (h) **I.** *v/i.* **1.** negotiate (**über** *acc.* about, on); ~ ***über*** *acc. a.* negotiate, discuss *conditions etc.*; **2.** ⚖ a) hold proceedings, b) hold a trial (***gegen*** *acc.*

against); ***über e-e Sache*** (*or* ***e-n Fall***) ~ hear (*or* try) a case; **II.** *v/t.* **3.** negotiate; **4.** ⚖ a) hear, b) try *a case*; **Ver'hand·lung** *f* (-; -en) **1.** negotiations *pl.*; ***in ~en eintreten*** enter into negotiations; **2.** ⚖ a) hearing, b) trial; ***zur ~ kommen*** come up (for trial)

Ver'hand·lungs|ba·sis *f* basis for negotiation(s); ~ ***DM 5000*** 5000 DM or near(est) offer (*abbr.* o.n.o.); **ℒbe·reit** *adj.* willing to negotiate (*or* enter into negotiations); **~be·reit·schaft** *f* readiness to negotiate; **~er·geb·nis** *n* outcome (*or* result) of the negotiations; **ℒfä·hig** *adj.* **1.** ⚖ able (*or* fit) to stand trial; **2.** (***nicht*** ~ non-)negotiable; **~fä·hig·keit** *f* ⚖ ability to stand trial; **~füh·rer** *m* chief negotiator; **~ge·gen·stand** *m* issue, object of negotiation; **~grund·la·ge** *f* basis for negotiation(s); **~part·ner** *m* negotiating partner; **~po·si·ti̦on** *f* bargaining position; **~run·de** *f* **1.** round of negotiations; **2.** ✝ bargaining round; **~tag** *m* ⚖ day of the hearing (*or* trial); **~ter̦min** *m* ⚖ a) hearing (date), b) trial date; **~tisch** *m* negotiating (✝ *a.* bargaining) table; ***am*** ~ at (*or* around) the negotiating table; **~trick** *m* negotiating ploy; **ℒun·fä·hig** *adj.* ⚖ unable to stand trial; **~un·fä·hig·keit** *f* ⚖ inability to stand trial; **~weg** *m*: ***auf dem ~e*** (***beilegen*** settle) by negotiation

ver·han·gen [fɛɐ'haŋən] *adj.* cloudy, overcast; ***~er Himmel*** cloudy sky, overcast skies

ver'hän·gen *v/t.* (h) **1.** cover, drape, veil; **2.** impose *ban, embargo etc.* (***über*** *acc.* on); *sport*: award (to)

Ver·häng·nis [fɛɐ'hɛŋnɪs] *n* (-ses; -se) fate; disaster; ruin; ***j-m zum ~ werden*** be s.o.'s undoing (*or* ruin[ation]), lead to s.o.'s downfall; **ver'häng·nis·voll** *adj.* fateful; fatal

ver·harm·lo·sen [fɛɐ'harmlo:zən] *v/t.* (h) play down; minimize; **Ver'harm·lo·sung** *f* (-; -en) playing down; minimizing, minimization

ver·härmt [fɛɐ'hɛrmt] *adj.* careworn

ver'har·ren *v/i.* (h) **1.** persevere, persist (***auf, bei, in*** *dat.* in); ***bei s-r Meinung*** ~ stick to one's opinion; **2.** remain *motionless etc.*

ver·har·schen [fɛɐ'harʃən] *v/i.* (sn) *snow*: crust over

ver'här·ten *v/t.* (h), *v/i.* (sn) *and v/refl.* (***sich*** ~) (h) *a. fig.* harden; *fig.* ***die Fronten haben sich verhärtet*** positions have become entrenched; **Ver'här·tung** *f* (-; -en) **1.** hardening; **2.** ⚕ callus

ver'has·peln F *fig. v/refl.* (h): ***sich*** ~ get in a muddle, get one's words muddled

ver·haßt [fɛɐ'hast] *adj.* hated, detested; *object*: *a.* hateful, odious (*dat.* to); ***es ist mir*** ~ I hate (*or* loathe) it; ***sich ~ machen*** (***bei j-m***) arouse *or* incur (s.o.'s) hatred

ver'hät·scheln *v/t.* (h) coddle, pamper; **ver'hät·schelt** *adj.* pampered, spoilt; **Ver'hät·sche·lung** *f* (-; *no pl.*) coddling, pampering

Ver·hau [fɛɐ'haʊ] *m* (-[e]s; -e) **1.** entanglement; **2.** F mess; ***das ist ja ein ~!*** what a mess, it's absolute chaos

ver'hau·en F (h) **I.** *v/t.* **1.** beat (up); give *a child* a hiding; **2.** *fig.* make a hash of; F bungle, muff; **II.** *v/refl.*: ***sich*** ~ miscalculate (badly), F get one's sums wrong; ***sich ~ haben*** *a.* F be way off (*or* out)

ver'he·ben *v/refl.* (*irr.*, *no* -ge-, h, → ***heben***): ***sich*** ~ hurt o.s. lifting s.th., *often* twist one's back

ver·hed·dern [fɛɐ'hɛdɐn] F *v/refl.* (h): ***sich ~ 1.*** get caught (up); **2.** *fig.* get in a muddle, get stuck

ver·hee·ren [fɛɐ'he:rən] *v/t.* (h) devastate, lay waste (to); **ver'hee·rend** *fig. adj.* disastrous; dreadful, horrific; **Ver'hee·rung** *f* (-; -en) devastation; ***~en anrichten*** cause (*or* wreak) havoc

ver·heh·len [fɛɐ'he:lən] *lit. v/t.* (h) hide, conceal (*dat.* from)

ver'hei·len *v/i.* (sn) heal up (completely)

ver·heim·li·chen [fɛɐ'haɪmlɪçən] *v/t.* (h) hide, conceal (*dat.* from); keep quiet about; ***j-m et. ~ a.*** keep s.th. (secret) from s.o.; ***er hat es*** (***uns***) ***verheimlicht*** *a.* F he never let on (about it); **Ver'heim·li·chung** *f* (-; -en) concealment; ~ ***e-r Sache*** *a.* keeping s.th. secret

ver'hei·ra·ten (h) **I.** *v/t.* marry (***mit*** *dat.*, ***an*** *acc.* to); **II.** *v/refl.*: ***sich*** ~ marry, get married; ***sich wieder*** ~ marry again, remarry; **ver'hei·ra·tet** *adj.* married (***mit*** *dat.* to) (*a. fig.*); ***ich bin doch nicht mit dir*** ~ we're not married, you know; I'm not your wife (*or* husband), you know; **Ver'hei·ra·tung** *f* (-; -en) marriage

ver'hei·ßen *v/t.* (*irr.*, *no* -ge-, h, → ***heißen***) promise, *a.* hold out the prospect of (*dat.* to *s.o.*); ***nichts Gutes*** ~ augur badly; **Ver'hei·ßung** *f* (-; -en) promise; **ver'hei·ßungs·voll** *adj.*: (***wenig*** ~ un)promising, (in)auspicious

ver'hei·zen *v/t.* (h) **1.** a) burn, use up, b) use as fuel; **2.** F *fig.* send *soldiers etc.* to the slaughter, use *soldiers etc.* as cannon-fodder; *sport etc.*: burn *s.o.* out

ver'hel·fen *v/i.* (*irr.*, *no* -ge-, h, → ***helfen***): ***j-m zu et.*** ~ help s.o. to get s.th.; ***j-m zu e-r Stelle ~ a.*** F give s.o. a leg up; ***j-m zu s-m Glück*** (***zum Erfolg***) ~ help s.o. on the road to happiness (success); ***j-m zum Sieg*** ~ help s.o. win, help s.o. (on the road) to victory

ver·herr·li·chen [fɛɐ'hɛrlɪçən] *v/t.* (h) glorify, exalt; **Ver'herr·li·chung** *f* (-; -en) glorification

ver'het·zen *v/t.* (h) fill with hatred; indoctrinate; poison *s.o.'s* mind; **Ver'het·zung** *f* (-; -en) indoctrination

ver·heult [fɛɐ'hɔʏlt] *adj.* tear-stained *face*; *eyes* red from crying; ~ ***aussehen*** look as if one has been crying

ver'he·xen *v/t.* (h) bewitch, F jinx; **ver'hext** F *adj.*: ***wie*** ~ F as if it were (*or* was) jinxed

ver·him·meln [fɛɐ'hɪməln] F *v/t.* (h) worship, adulate

ver'hin·dern *v/t.* (h) prevent; hinder; (***es***) ~, ***daß j-d et. tut*** prevent (*or* stop) s.o. from doing s.th.; ***wir können es nicht*** ~ there's nothing we can do about it; **ver'hin·dert** *adj.* **1.** ~ ***sein*** be unable to come *etc.* (***wegen*** *gen.* due to); **2.** ***~er Maler*** *etc.* painter *etc.* manqué, would-be painter *etc.*; **Ver'hin·de·rung** *f* (-; -en) prevention

ver·hoh·len *adj.* hidden, concealed

ver'höh·nen *v/t.* (h) deride, mock; *esp. pol.* lampoon

ver·hoh·ne·pi·peln [fɛɐ'ho:nəpi:pəln] F *v/t.* (h) F take the mickey out of *s.o.*

Ver·höh·nung [fɛɐ'hø:nʊŋ] *f* (-; -en) derision, mockery

ver'hö·kern *v/t.* (h) sell off

ver'hol·zen *v/i.* (sn) ⚘ lignify

Ver·hör [fɛɐ'hø:ɐ] *n* (-[e]s; -e [-rə]) interrogation; ⚖ hearing; ***ins ~ nehmen*** cross-examine, interrogate; **ver'hö·ren** (h) **I.** *v/t.* interrogate, F grill; **II.** *v/refl.*: ***sich*** ~ mishear, hear wrong

ver·hornt [fɛɐ'hɔrnt] *adj.* horny *skin etc.*

ver'hül·len *v/t.* (h) **1.** cover; **2.** *fig.* cover up, disguise; conceal; **ver'hül·lend I.** *adj.*: ***~er Ausdruck*** euphemism; **II.** *adv.*: ~ ***ausgedrückt*** put euphemistically; **ver'hüllt** *adj.* **1.** veiled *statue, face etc.*; hidden, concealed; ***von Wolken*** ~ covered in cloud, hidden by cloud(s); **2.** *fig.* veiled, hidden *threats etc.*; disguised; **Ver'hül·lung** *f* (-; -en) **1.** cover(ing); **2.** *fig.* concealment, disguising; disguise

ver·hun·dert·fa·chen [fɛɐ'hʊndɐtfaxən] *v/t. and v/refl.* (***sich*** ~) (h) increase a hundredfold, *formal*: centuple

ver'hun·gern *v/i.* (sn) die of starvation, starve (to death); F ***ich bin am*** ℒ F I'm starving

ver·hun·zen [fɛɐ'hʊntsən] F *v/t.* (h) ruin, spoil; mess up, F botch (up); *sl.* bugger up

ver'hü·ten *v/t.* (h) prevent; **ver'hü·tend** *adj.* preventive; **Ver·hü·ter·li** [fɛɐ'hy:tɐli] F *n* (-s; -[s]) F rubber

ver·hüt·ten [fɛɐ'hʏtən] *v/t.* (h) smelt *ore*; **Ver'hüt·tung** *f* (-; -en) smelting

Ver·hü·tung [fɛɐ'hy:tʊŋ] *f* (-; *no pl.*) prevention (*a.* ⚕); contraception; **Ver'hü·tungs·mit·tel** *n* contraceptive

ver·hut·zelt [fɛɐ'hʊtsəlt] F *adj.* shrivel(l)ed(-up); *a.* wizened *face, person*

ve·ri·fi·zier·bar [verifi'tsi:ɐba:ɐ] *adj.* verifiable; **ve·ri·fi·zie·ren** [verifi'tsi:rən] *v/t.* (h) verify; **Ve·ri·fi'zie·rung** *f* (-; -en) verification

ver·in·ner·li·chen [fɛɐ'ˀɪnɐlɪçən] *v/t.* (h) internalize; turn *s.o.* inward; *w.s.* spiritualize; **ver'in·ner·licht** *adj.* inward-looking; spiritual; **Ver'in·ner·li·chung** *f* (-; -en) internalization; spiritualization

ver'ir·ren *v/refl.* (h): ***sich*** ~ get lost, lose one's way; *fig. thoughts*: stray; ***sich in das falsche Gebäude*** *etc.* ~ *a.* F wander (off) into the wrong building *etc.*; **ver'irrt** *adj.* lost, *zo. a.* stray; *fig.* ***~e Kugel*** stray bullet; **Ver'ir·rung** *fig. f* (-; -en) aberration; ***geschmackliche*** ~ *a.* lapse of taste

ver'ja·gen *v/t.* (h) *a. fig.* chase away

ver'jäh·ren *v/i.* (sn) come under the statute of limitations; **ver·jährt** [fɛɐ'jɛ:ɐt] *adj.* **1.** ⚖ statute-barred; **2.** old; **Ver'jäh·rung** *f* (-; -en) limitation, prescription; **Ver'jäh·rungs·frist** *f* statutory period of limitation

ver'ju·beln F *v/t.* (h) F blow

ver·jün·gen [fɛɐ'jʏŋən] (h) **I.** *v/t.* **1.** a) rejuvenate; make *s.o.* look younger, b) staff with young(er) people; **II.** *v/refl.*: ***sich ~ 2.*** become rejuvenated; become younger-looking; **3.** taper; **Ver'jün·gung** *f* (-; -en) **1.** rejuvenation; **2.** tapering

Ver'jün·gungs|kur *f* rejuvenation cure; **~mit·tel** *n* rejuvenator

ver'ka·beln *v/t.* (h) wire (up); *TV* cable up; ***unsere Straße wird verkabelt*** our street is going to be hooked up to cable TV; **ver'ka·belt** *adj.*: *TV* ~ ***sein*** have (*or* get) cable TV; **Ver'ka·be·lung** *f* (-; -en) **1.** wiring, *TV* cabling; **2.** *w.s.* cable TV; **Ver'ka·be·lungs·plan** *m* wiring diagram

ver·kal·ken *v/i.* (sn) **1.** ⚙ *boiler etc.*: fur up; **2.** ⚕ *arteries*: harden, 🕮 calcify; **3.** F *person*: go senile; **ver'kalkt** *adj.* **1.** ⚙ furred; **2.** ⚕ hardened, 🕮 sclerotic; **3.** F senile, F gaga; ***völlig ~ sein*** *a.* F have gone (completely) gaga

ver·kal·ku·lie·ren [fɛɐkalku'li:rən] *v/refl.* (h): ***sich*** ~ miscalculate (*a. fig.*), F get one's sums wrong

Ver'kal·kung *f* (-; -en) **1.** ⚙ furring up; **2.** ⚕ hardening (of the arteries), (arterio-) sclerosis; **3.** F senility; ***unter ~ leiden*** *a.* be going senile; **Ver'kal·kungs·er·schei·nung** F *f* sign of old age (*or* senility)

ver·kannt [fɛɐ'kant] **I.** *p.p. of* ***verkennen***; **II.** *adj.*: *iro.* ***~es Genie*** undiscovered (*or* unrecognized) genius

ver'kan·ten (h) **I.** *v/t.* **1.** tilt; cant; **2.** edge *skis*; **II.** *v/i.* **3.** *skiing*: edge over; **III.** *v/refl.*: ***sich*** ~ **4.** get wedged (in); **5.** *skis*: edge over

ver·kappt [fɛɐ'kapt] *adj.* hidden; ⚕ undiagnosed; *pol.* closet *Nazi etc.*

ver·kap·seln [fɛɐ'kapsəln] *v/refl.* ***sich*** ~ (h) encapsulate; ⚕ encyst; *fig.* → ***abkapseln***; **Ver'kap·se·lung** *f* (-; -en) encapsulation; ⚕ encystment

ver·ka·tert [fɛɐ'ka:tɐt] F *adj.* F hung-over

Ver·kauf [fɛɐ'kauf] *m* (-[e]s; Verkäufe [fɛɐ'kɔʏfə]) **1.** a) sale, b) selling; ***zum*** ~ for sale; **2.** → ***Verkaufsabteilung***; **ver'kau·fen** (h) **I.** *v/t.* **1.** a) sell (*a. fig. idea etc.*), b) *fig.* sell *s.o.* (down the river); ***zu*** ~ for sale; → ***dumm***; **II.** *v/refl.*: ***sich*** ~ **2.** sell (***gut*** well; ***schlecht*** badly); F *fig.* sell o.s.; F *fig.* ***sich gut*** (***schlecht***) ~ go down well (badly) (***bei*** *dat.* with), be a great success (a flop) (with); F ***er kann sich hervorragend*** ~ he's an excellent showman; **3.** F make a bad buy; ***mit dem Auto habe ich mich verkauft*** that car was a bad buy (for me)

Ver·käu·fer [fɛɐ'kɔʏfɐ] *m* (-s; -) **1.** shop assistant, *Am.* salesclerk; **2.** ⚚ seller; **3.** F *fig.* showman; **Ver·käu·fe·rin** [fɛɐ'kɔʏfərın] *f* (-; -nen) shop assistant, saleslady, *Am.* salesperson

Ver'käu·fer·markt *m* seller's market

ver·käuf·lich [fɛɐ'kɔʏflıç] *adj.* a) for sale, b) sal(e)able; ***leicht*** (***schwer***) ~ easy (hard) to sell

Ver'kaufs|ab,tei·lung *f* sales department; **~ar,ti·kel** *m* article for sale; *pl. a.* sales articles; **~auf·trag** *m* order to sell; **~aus·stel·lung** *f* sales exhibition; **~au·to,mat** *m* vending machine; **~be·din·gun·gen** *pl.* conditions (*or* terms) of sale; **~be·ra·ter** *m* sales consultant; **~bü,ro** *n* sales office; **~er·lös** *m* proceeds *pl.*; **~flä·che** *f* selling area (*or* space); **~för·de·rung** *f* sales promotion; **~ge·spräch** *n*: ***das*** ~ sales talk; **~hit** F *m*, **~knül·ler** F *m* → ***Verkaufsschlager***; **~lei·ter** *m* sales manager; **≈of·fen** *adj.*: ***~er Samstag*** Saturday afternoon opening; all-day (Saturday) shopping; **~per·so,nal** *n* sales staff; **~preis** *m* selling price; **~pro·vi·si,on** *f* sales commission; **~psy·cho·lo,gie** *f* sales psychology; **~raum** *m* salesroom; **~rück·gang** *m* drop in sales; declining sales *pl.*; **~schla·ger** *m* moneyspinner, F absolute hit; **~stand** *m* stand; stall; **~stän·der** *m* display stand; **~stel·le** *f* retail shop (*Am.* store); **~tak·tik** *f* sales pitch; **~wert** *m* market value; **~ziel** *n* sales target; **~zif·fer** *f* sales figure

Ver·kehr [fɛɐ'ke:ɐ] *m* (-s; *no pl.*) **1.** traffic; ***dem ~ übergeben*** open to traffic; ***für den ~ gesperrt*** closed to (all) traffic; *mot.* ***aus dem ~ ziehen*** take off the road; **2.** a) contact, dealings *pl.*; ⚚ business, b) correspondence; ***aus dem ~ ziehen*** phase out *model etc.*, withdraw *bank notes etc.* from circulation; ***in ~ bringen*** issue, ⚚ *a.* offer for sale, market; **3.** (*sexual*) intercourse

ver·keh·ren [fɛɐ'ke:rən] (h) **I.** *v/i.* **1.** *train, bus etc.*: run; ✈ fly, operate; ⚓ ~ ***zwischen*** *dat. a.* ply between; ~ ***in*** *dat.* serve *an area*; **2.** ~ ***in*** *dat.* frequent *bar etc.*; ***bei j-m*** ~ visit s.o. regularly, be a regular visitor to (*or* at) s.o.'s house *etc.*; ~ ***mit*** *dat.* associate (*or* socialize) with *s.o.*; ***viel mit j-m*** ~ see a great deal of s.o.; **3.** ~ ***mit*** *dat.* have (sexual) intercourse with *s.o.*; **II.** *v/t.* twist; ***ins Gegenteil*** ~ reverse; **III.** *v/refl.*: ***sich*** ~ change, turn (***in*** *acc.* into)

Ver'kehrs|ab·lauf *m* flow of traffic; **~ader** *f* arterial road; **~am·pel** *f* traffic lights *pl.*, *Am.* traffic light, stoplight; **~amt** *n* tourist office; **≈arm** *adj.* quiet; **~auf·kom·men** *n* traffic volume, volume of traffic; **~be·hin·de·rung** *f* traffic obstruction; *pl.* traffic holdups (***durch Nebel*** *etc.* due to fog *etc.*); **≈be·ru·higt** *adj.*: ***~e Zone*** reduced-traffic area, area with reduced traffic; **~be·ru·hi·gung** *f* traffic abatement (*or* reduction); **~be·ru·hi·gungs·maß·nah·men** *pl.* traffic calming measures; **~be·trie·be** *pl. public, municipal etc.* transport (services) *sg.*, *Am.* transportation (services) *sg.*; **~cha·os** *n* chaos on the roads, traffic chaos (*or* snarl-up); **~de,likt** *n* traffic offen|ce (*Am.* -se); **~dich·te** *f* traffic density; **~,durch·sa·ge** *f* traffic announcement; **~er·zie·hung** *f* road safety education; **~flug·zeug** *n* airliner, commercial aircraft; **~fluß** *m* traffic flow; **≈frei** *adj.*: ***~e Zone*** traffic-free area, area closed to traffic, pedestrian zone; **~funk** *m* travel news (*sg.*); information for motorists; **~ge·fähr·dung** *f* **1.** endangerment of traffic; **2.** traffic hazard, hazard on the road(s); **≈gün·stig** *adv.*: ~ ***gelegen*** very convenient as far as public transport(ation *Am.*) goes; **~hin·der·nis** *n* traffic obstruction; **~in,farkt** *m* gridlock (*a.* ***der*** ~**)**, complete breakdown of traffic; **~in·sel** *f* traffic island, central refuge; **~kno·ten·punkt** *m* junction; **~kon,trol·le** *f* vehicle spot-check; **~la·ge** *f* situation on the roads; **~lärm** *m* traffic noise; **~mel·dung** *f* traffic announcement (*or* flash); *pl.* traffic report *sg.*, travel news *sg.*; **~mi,ni·ster** *m* minister of transport(ation *Am.*); *in the USA*: Secretary of Transportation; *in GB*: Transport Secretary, Secretary of State for Transport; **~mi·ni,ste·ri·um** *n* ministry of transport; *in the USA*: Department of Transportation (*in GB*: of Transport); **~mit·tel** *n* (means of) transportation; vehicle; ***öffentliches*** ~ public conveyance, *pl.* public transport(ation *Am.*) *sg.*; **~netz** *n* traffic system; road and rail networks *pl.*; **~op·fer** *n* road casualty; ***über 3000*** ~ *a.* over 3000 road deaths (*or* deaths on the road, deaths caused by traffic accidents); **~ord·nung** *f* traffic regulations *pl.*; **~pla·nung** *f* traffic planning; **~po·li,zei** *f* traffic police; **~po·li,zist** *m* traffic policeman; **~re·gel** *f* traffic regulation; **~re·ge·lung** *f* traffic control; **≈reich** *adj.* busy; **~schild** *n* road sign; **≈schwach** *adj.*: ***~e Zeit*** slack period; **≈si·cher** *adj.* roadworthy; **~si·cher·heit** *f* **1.** road safety; **2.** roadworthiness; **~spra·che** *f* lingua franca; **≈stark** *adj.*: ***~e Zeit*** rush hour; **~stau** *m* traffic jam, (traffic) holdup, bottleneck, *a. pl.* congestion; **~stau·ung** *f* congestion; *pl.* congestion *sg.* (on the roads); **~steu·er** *f* ⚚ transfer tax; **~stockung** *f*, **~stö·rung** *f* traffic holdup; *pl. a.* traffic delays, delays in traffic; **~stra·ße** *f* (public) thoroughfare; road open to traffic; **~strei·fe** *f* traffic patrol; **~strom** *m* flow of traffic, traffic flow; **~sün·der** *m* traffic offender; **~sün·der·kar,tei** *f* (central) index of traffic offenders; **≈taug·lich** *adj.* roadworthy; **~taug·lich·keit** *f* roadworthiness; **~teil·neh·mer** *m* road user; **~to·te** *m*, *f* (-n; -n) road casualty; **≈tüch·tig** *adj.* **1.** roadworthy; **2.** fit to drive; **~tüch·tig·keit** *f* **1.** roadworthiness; **2.** *s.o's* fitness to drive; **~un·fall** *m* traffic accident; **~,un·ter·richt** *m* **1.** *ped.* road-safety classes *pl.*; **2.** road sense classes *pl.* (for convicted traffic offenders); **~ver·bin·dung** *f* (road *or* rail) link; ***es gibt keine ~ zu dem Gebiet*** there are no road or rail links to the area; **~ver·bund** *m* (integrated) public transport system; **~ver·ein** *m* tourist office; **~vor·schrift** *f* traffic regulation; **~wacht** *f* road safety association; **~wert** *m* market value; **~we·sen** *n* (-s; *no pl.*) a) transportation; public transport(ation *Am.*), b) transport and communications *pl.*; **≈wid·rig** *adj.* contrary to (*adv.* in violation of) the traffic regulations; **~wid·rig·keit** *f* traffic offen|ce (*Am.* -se); **~zäh·lung** *f* traffic census; **~zei·chen** *n* road sign

ver·kehrt [fɛɐ'ke:ɐt] *adj. and adv.* wrong, *adv. a.* wrongly, the wrong way; ~ ***herum*** the wrong way round, *a.* upside down, back to front, inside out; F ***das ist gar nicht*** ~ that's not such a bad idea at all; F ***an den Verkehrten kommen*** pick the wrong person; ***etwas Verkehrtes sagen*** say something wrong; ***et. ~ machen*** do s.th. wrong; ***et. ~ anpacken*** go about s.th. the wrong way; ~ ***fahren*** take the wrong road (*or* turning); ***wir sind hier*** ~ we're in (*or* we've come to) the wrong place; F ~ ***liegen*** be wrong, be mistaken; **Ver'kehrt·heit** *f* (-; *no pl.*) wrongness

Ver·keh·rung [fɛɐ'ke:rʊŋ] *f* (-; -en) reversal; distortion, twisting; ~ ***ins Gegenteil*** complete reversal

ver'kei·len (h) **I.** *v/t.* wedge tight; **II.** *v/refl.*: ***sich*** ~ get stuck (*or* jammed); ***sich ineinander*** ~ 🚗 *etc.* plough (*Am.* plow) into each other

ver'ken·nen *v/t.* (*irr.*, *no* -ge-, h, → ***kennen***) misjudge; underestimate; fail to appreciate; ***nicht zu*** ~ unmistakable; → ***verkannt***; **Ver'ken·nung** *f* (-; -en) misjudg(e)ment; underestimation; ***in*** (***völliger***) ~ ***der Tatsachen*** *etc.* in (complete) misapprehension of the facts *etc.*

ver'ket·ten (h) **I.** *v/t.* chain up; link (*a. fig.*); *ling.*, *computer*: concatenate; **II.** *v/refl.*: ***sich*** ~ *molecules etc.*: form a chain (*or* chains); *fig.* interlock; **Ver'ket·tung** *f* (-; -en) *ling.*, *computer*: concatenation (*a. fig. of events*)

ver·ket·zern [fɛɐ'kɛtsɐn] *v/t.* (h) brand,

condemn; **Ver·ket·ze·rung** [fɛɐ'kɛtsərʊŋ] *f* (-; -en) branding, condemnation

ver·kit·schen [fɛɐ'kɪtʃən] *v/t.* (h) **1.** kitschify; **2.** F sell (off), turn into cash; **ver'kitscht** *adj.* kitschy

ver'kit·ten *v/t.* (h) cement (*a. fig.*), seal; putty

ver'kla·gen *v/t.* (h) ⚖ sue (**auf** *acc.*, **wegen** *gen.* for), take *s.o.* to court (for)

ver'klam·mern (h) **I.** *v/t.* clip together; ⚠, ⚙ *etc.* brace together; *fig.* lock together, interlock; **II.** *v/refl.*: **sich** (**ineinander**) ~ lock together, interlock; **ver'klam·mert** *adj.*: **ineinander** ~ locked together, interlocked; **Ver·klam·me·rung** [fɛɐ'klamərʊŋ] *f* (-; -en) **1.** clipping (*or* bracing, locking) together; *esp. fig.* interlocking; **2.** clips *pl.*, braces *pl.*

ver'klap·pen *v/t.* (h) dump (into the sea); **Ver'klap·pung** *f* (-; -en) (ocean) dumping, dumping (of) waste into the sea

ver·kla·ren [fɛɐ'kla:rən] F *v/t.* (h) explain

ver'klä·ren *fig.* (h) **I.** *v/t.* transfigure; **II.** *v/refl.*: **sich** ~ be(come) transfigured; *past*: become idealized; **ver·klärt** [fɛɐ'klɛ:ɐt] *adj.* transfigured; beatific *smile, expression etc.*; **Ver'klä·rung** *f* (-; -en) transfiguration

ver·klau·seln [fɛɐ'klaʊzəln], **ver·klau·su·lie·ren** [fɛɐklaʊzu'li:rən] *v/t.* (h) hedge in by clauses; *fig.* express in a roundabout way

ver'kle·ben I. *v/t.* (h) cover, stick s.th. over *s.th.*; ⚕ cover *wound*; **II.** *v/i.* (sn) *and v/refl.* (**sich** ~) (h) a) close (up), b) get sticky, c) clot; stick together; **ver·klebt** [fɛɐ'kle:pt] *adj.* sticky *eyes etc.*; matted *hair*

ver'kleckern F *v/t.* (h) **1.** spill; **2.** *fig.* fritter away, waste *one's time, money etc.*; **3.** spatter

ver'klei·den (h) **I.** *v/t.* **1.** dress *s.o.* up (**als** as); disguise; **2.** ⚙ *etc.* cover; line; (en)case; panel; ⚠ face; **II.** *v/refl.*: **sich** ~ dress up (**als** as); put on a disguise; **Ver'klei·dung** *f* (-; -en) **1.** fancy dress; disguise; **2.** ⚙ covering; lining; facing; panel(l)ing; → **verkleiden** 2

ver·klei·nern [fɛɐ'klaɪnɐn] (h) **I.** *v/t.* reduce (in size), make *s.th.* smaller; scale down (*a. fig.* ✝); *fig.* belittle; **II.** *v/refl.*: **sich** ~ get (*or* grow) smaller; **ver'kleinert** *adj.* reduced (in size); **im** ~**en Maßstab** on a smaller scale; **Ver·klei·ne·rung** [fɛɐ'klaɪnərʊŋ] *f* (-; -en) **1.** reduction (in size); scaling down (*a. fig.* ✝); **2.** *fig.* belittling, belittlement

Ver'klei·ne·rungs|form *f* diminutive; ~**maß·stab** *m* scale (of reduction)

ver'klem·men *v/refl.*: **sich** ~ (h) get stuck; **ver'klemmt** *adj. psych.* inhibited; **Ver'klem·mung** *f* (-; -en) inhibition

ver·klickern [fɛɐ'klɪkɐn] (*sep.* -k·k-) F *v/t.* (h): **j-m et.** ~ put s.o. straight on s.th., put s.o. in the picture about s.th.; **j-m** ~, **wie** let s.o. know how

ver'klin·gen *v/i.* (*irr.*, *no* -ge-, sn, → **klingen**) die away (*a. fig.*)

ver'knacken F *v/t.* (h) sentence (**zu** *dat.* to); **j-n zu e-r Geldstrafe** ~ F slap a fine on s.o.; **j-n zu drei Jahren** ~ F put s.o. inside (*or* in clink) for three years; **verknackt werden wegen** *gen.* F be done for

ver'knack·sen F *v/t.* (h): **sich den Fuß** ~ sprain one's ankle

ver'knal·len F *v/refl.* (h): **sich in j-n** ~ F fall for s.o., go a bundle on s.o., go soft on s.o.; **er hat sich** (*or* **er ist**) **in sie verknallt** *a.* F he's head over heels in love with her

ver·knap·pen [fɛɐ'knapən] (h) **I.** *v/refl.*: **sich** ~ run short, become scarce; **II.** *v/t.* cut down the supply of; **Ver'knap·pung** *f* (-; -en) shortage, scarcity

ver'knaut·schen F *v/t.* (h) crumple (up)

ver'knei·fen F *v/t.* (*irr.*, *no* -ge-, h, → **kneifen**) **1. er konnte sich das Lachen nicht** ~ he couldn't help laughing, he couldn't keep a straight face; **ich konnte mir die Bemerkung nicht** (**kaum**) ~ I couldn't resist saying it, I just had to come out with it (I was biting my lips not to say it); **2. sich et.** ~ do without s.th.;

ver·knif·fen [fɛɐ'knɪfən] **I.** *p.p. of* **verkneifen**; **II.** *adj.* pinched *face, mouth*

ver·knö·chern [fɛɐ'knœçɐn] *v/i.* (sn) ossify (*a. fig.*); **ver'knö·chert** *adj.*: ~**er Kerl** old fossil; **Ver·knö·che·rung** [fɛɐ'knœçərʊŋ] *f* (-; -en) ossification

ver·knor·peln [fɛɐ'knɔrpəln] *v/i.* (sn) become cartilaginous; **Ver'knor·pe·lung** *f* (-; -en) chondrification

ver'kno·ten *v/t.* (h) tie a knot in *handkerchief etc.*; tie *scarf etc.*

ver'knüp·fen *v/t.* (h) tie together; *fig.* link; combine; **ver'knüpft** *fig. adj.*: ~ **mit** *dat.* tied up with; **eng** ~ **sein mit** *dat.* a) be bound up with, b) have close ties with; **Ver'knüp·fung** *fig. f* (-; -en) **1.** linking (**mit** *dat.* up with); **2.** tie(s *pl.*), link(s *pl.*); connection

ver·knu·sen [fɛɐ'knu:zən] F *v/t.* (h): **ich kann ihn** (**es**) **nicht** ~ I can't take (*or* stomach) him (it)

ver'ko·chen *v/i.* (sn) boil away; *potatoes etc.*: overboil; **zu Brei** ~ *contp.* boil down into a mush

ver·koh·len [fɛɐ'ko:lən] *v/t.* (h) **1.** char (*a. v/i.* [sn]); ⚗ carbonize; **2.** F have s.o. on

ver·ko·ken [fɛɐ'ko:kən] *v/t.* (h) coke

ver'kom·men[1] *v/i.* (*irr.*, *no* -ge-, sn, → **kommen**) **1.** *house, business etc.*: go to rack and ruin, F go to the dogs; *garden*: run wild; **2.** go to seed, sink (very) low; **3.** *food*: go bad, *w.s.* go to waste

ver'kom·men[2] **I.** *p.p. of* **verkommen**[1]; **II.** *adj.* **1.** seedy, depraved; **2.** dilapidated *building etc.*; run-down *enterprise, area etc.*; overgrown, wild *garden etc.*; **der Garten ist völlig** ~ *a.* the garden is a wilderness; **Ver'kom·men·heit** *f* (-; *no pl.*) **1.** seediness; depravity; **2.** dilapidated state; run-down condition; wildness

ver·kom·pli'zie·ren *v/t.* (h) complicate, make *s.th.* more complicated than it is; **warum mußt du immer alles** ~? *a.* why do you always have to complicate matters?

ver·kon·su'mie·ren F *v/t.* (h) F put away

ver·kor·ken [fɛɐ'kɔrkən] *v/t.* (h) cork (up)

ver·kork·sen [fɛɐ'kɔrksən] F *v/t.* (h) F make a hash of, bungle; **ver'korkst** F *adj.* upset *stomach*; F screwed up *person*; ~**e Angelegenheit** mess

ver·kör·pern [fɛɐ'kœrpɐn] *v/t.* (h) **1.** embody; typify; **2.** *thea.* play; **ver'kör·pert** *adj.*: **die** ~**e Tugend** *etc.* virtue *etc.* personified (*or* in person), the embodiment (*or* personification) of virtue *etc.*; **Ver·kör·pe·rung** [fɛɐ'kœrpərʊŋ] *f* (-; -en) embodiment; typification

ver·kö·sti·gen [fɛɐ'kœstɪgən] *v/t.* (h) feed; **Ver'kö·sti·gung** *f* (-; -en) **1.** food; **2.** feeding

ver'kra·chen F *v/refl.*: **sich** ~ (h) fall out (with each other); **ver'kracht** F *adj.* a) at daggers drawn, b) failed; ~**e Existenz** (human) wreck

ver·kraf·ten [fɛɐ'kraftən] *v/t.* (h) take; cope with, handle; *a.* come to terms with *loss etc.*; **ich verkrafte es nicht mehr** I can't cope (with it) *or* take it any longer

ver'kral·len *v/refl.* (h): **sich** ~ **in** *acc.* a) *zo.* dig its claws into, b) dig one's fingers (*or* nails) into, *w.s.* clutch at

ver'kramp·fen *v/refl.*: **sich** ~ (h) *muscles*: cramp, get cramp; *hands*: clench (tightly); *person*: tense (*or* seize) up; **ver'krampft** *adj.* cramped *muscles*; tensed up, tense, *fig. a.* uptight; *fig.* forced, artificial *smile etc.*; **Ver'kramp·fung** *f* (-; -en) cramp(s *pl.*); tenseness, tension; contraction, spasm; *fig.* inner tension, uptightness

ver'krat·zen *v/t.* (h) scratch, scrape; **ver'kratzt** *adj.* scratched; **völlig** ~ scratched all over

ver'krie·chen *v/refl.* (*irr.*, *no* -ge-, sn, → **kriechen**): **sich** ~ creep (*or* crawl, slink) away; *fig.* sneak away; go into hiding, *sun*: hide; *fig.* **sich ins Bett** ~ crawl into bed; **sich in s-e Arbeit** ~ immerse o.s. in work

ver'krü·meln F *v/refl.*: **sich** ~ (h) F make o.s. scarce, sneak off

ver'krüm·men (h) **I.** *v/t.* bend, curve, twist; **II.** *v/refl.*: **sich** ~ bend, curve, become distorted (*or* twisted); *wood*: warp; **ver'krümmt** *adj.* bent, curved (*a.* ⚕), twisted; **Ver'krüm·mung** *f* (-; -en) distortion; warp; twist; bend; ~ **der Wirbelsäule** curvature of the spine

ver·krüp·peln [fɛɐ'krʏpəln] **I.** *v/t.* (h) cripple; **II.** *v/i.* (sn) become crippled, *tree*: become stunted; **Ver'krüp·pe·lung** *f* (-; -en) deformation, deformity

ver·kru·sten [fɛɐ'krʊstən] *v/i. and v/refl.* (**sich** ~) (h) crust, become encrusted; ⚕ scab; **von Schmutz verkrustet** caked with dirt (*or* mud); **Ver'kru·stung** *f* (-; -en) encrustation

ver'küh·len *v/refl.*: **sich** ~ (h) catch (a) cold; **Ver'küh·lung** *dial. f* (-; -en) cold

ver'küm·mern *v/i.* (sn) become stunted; *muscles etc.*: atrophy; *plants, a. fig. talent*: wither, wilt; *person*: languish

ver'kün·den *lit. v/t.* (h) → **verkündigen**; **Ver·kün·der** [fɛɐ'kʏndɐ] *m* (-s; -) *eccl.* preacher; *fig.* herald, harbinger; **ver'kün·di·gen** *v/t.* (h) announce; proclaim; ⚖ promulgate *law*; pronounce *sentence*; *eccl.* preach (*or* spread) *the gospel*; prophesy; *fig.* herald *a new epoch etc.*; **Ver'kün·di·gung** *f* (-; -en) announcement; proclamation; ⚖ promulgation; pronouncement; *eccl.* preaching, spreading; prophecy; *fig.* heralding

ver·kün·stelt [fɛɐ'kʏnstəlt] *adj.* oversophisticated, over-elaborate

ver·kup·fern [fɛɐ'kʊpfɐn] *v/t.* (h) copper-plate; **Ver·kup·fe·rung** [fɛɐ'kʊpfərʊŋ] *f* (-; -en) copper-plating

ver'kup·peln *v/t.* (h): **j-n an j-n** ~ marry s.o. off to s.o.

ver'kür·zen (h) **I.** *v/t.* shorten; curtail, cut; reduce; **sich die Zeit** ~ while away the (*or* one's) time; ~ **auf** *acc. sport*: shorten to; **II.** *v/refl.*: **sich** ~ become shorter; shorten; **ver'kürzt** *adj.* shortened; reduced; ~**e Form** short form; ~**e Ausgabe** abridged (*or* shortened) edition; ~**e Lebenserwartung** shortened lifespan; ~**e Arbeitszeit** short time; ~

erscheinen appear foreshortened; **Ver'kür·zung** *f* (-; -en) shortening; curtailment; reduction

ver'la·chen *v/t.* (h) laugh at, scoff at

Ver·la·de|bahn·hof [fɛɐ'la:də-] *m* loading station; **~kran** *m* loading crane

ver'la·den *v/t.* (*irr.*, *no* -ge-, h, → ***laden***) **1.** load (***auf*** *acc.* onto; ***in*** *acc.* into); **2.** F sell *s.o.* (down the river), leave *s.o.* in the lurch; **Ver·la·der** [fɛɐ'la:dɐ] *m* (-s; -) a) carrier, shipping agent(s *pl.*), b) loader

Ver'la·de·ram·pe *f* loading platform

Ver'la·dung *f* (-; -en) loading

Ver·lag [fɛɐ'la:k] *m* (-[e]s; -e [-gə]) publishing house (*or* company), publisher(s *pl.*), publisher's; (***erschienen***) ***im ~ von*** *dat.* published by; ***in ~ nehmen*** publish; ***in*** (*or* ***bei***) ***e-m ~ arbeiten*** work for a publisher's *etc.*, work (*or* be) in publishing

ver'la·gern (h) **I.** *v/t.* **1.** shift *one's weight etc.*, *a. fig. one's interest etc.*; **2.** transfer, move (***nach*** *dat.* to); **II.** *v/refl.*: ***sich ~*** *a. fig.* shift; **Ver'la·ge·rung** *f* (-; -en) **1.** shift(ing); **2.** transfer, removal

Ver'lags|an·stalt *f* publishing house (*or* company); **~buch·han·del** *m* publishing trade; **~buch·händ·ler** *m* publisher; **~buch·hand·lung** *f* publishing house; **~haus** *n* → ***Verlag***; **~ka·ta,log** *m* (publisher's) catalog(ue), publications list; **~lei·ter** *m* (managing) director of a publishing house; **~pro,gramm** *n* publisher's list; **~re·dak,teur** *m* publishing editor; **~ver·zeich·nis** *n* (publisher's) backlist; **~we·sen** *n* (-s; *no pl.*) publishing

ver'lan·gen (h) **I.** *v/t.* a) demand; claim, b) desire, want, ask for, c) ☤ want, ask for, charge, d) require, call for; ***viel ~*** *task etc.*: be very demanding, *person*: *a.* be hard to please; ***die Rechnung ~*** ask for the bill (*Am.* check); ***das ist zuviel verlangt*** that's asking (a bit) too much, that's a tall order; ***das ist doch nicht zuviel verlangt, oder?*** that's not asking too much, is it?, that's not an unreasonable demand, is it?; ***mehr kann man nicht ~*** you can't ask for more; ***Sie werden am Telefon verlangt*** you're wanted on the phone; ***Rechenschaft ~*** demand an explanation; **II.** *v/i.*: ***~ nach*** *dat.* a) ask for; *a.* ask to see *s.o.*, b) long for

Ver'lan·gen *n* (-s; *no pl.*) a) desire; craving, longing (*all* ***nach*** *dat.* for), b) demand; ***auf ~*** by request, ☤ on demand; ***auf ~ von*** *dat.* at the request of; ***kein ~ haben zu*** *inf.* feel no desire (*or* urge) to *inf.*; ***j-n*** (***et.***) ***voll ~ ansehen*** look at s.o. (s.th.) longingly (*or* with great longing)

ver·län·gern [fɛɐ'lɛŋɐn] (h) **I.** *v/t.* a) lengthen; extend *road etc.*, b) prolong, extend *credit*, *run etc.* (*all* ***um*** *acc.* by), c) renew *contract etc.*, d) *gastr.* stretch, e) ₳ produce; *sport*: ***den Ball ~*** help the ball on; **II.** *v/refl.*: ***sich ~*** be extended; **ver'län·gert** *adj.* extended; ***~es Wochenende*** long weekend, *a.* bank holiday weekend; **Ver·län·ge·rung** [fɛɐ'lɛŋərʊŋ] *f* (-; -en) **1.** a) lengthening, b) prolongation, extension, c) renewal, d) ₳ production; **2.** *sport*: a) extra time, b) pass

Ver'län·ge·rungs|ka·bel *n*, **~schnur** *f* ⚡ extension lead (*or* cord); **~stück** *n* extension; **~wo·che** *f* extra week

ver·lang·sa·men [fɛɐ'laŋza:mən] (h) **I.** *v/t.* a) slow down; reduce *speed*, b) slow down, retard *development etc.*; **II.** *v/refl.*: ***sich ~*** slow down, *mot. etc.*: *a.* lose speed; **Ver'lang·sa·mung** *f* (-; -en) a) slowing down; reduction *in speed*, b) slowing down, retardation *of development etc.*

ver·läp·pern [fɛɐ'lɛpɐn] F *v/t.* (h) fritter away *time*, *money etc.*

Ver·laß [fɛɐ'las] *m*: ***es ist kein ~ auf ihn*** you can't rely on him

ver'las·sen¹ (*irr.*, *no* -ge-, h, → ***lassen***) **I.** *v/t.* leave; desert; *fig. courage*, *self-confidence etc.*: desert, fail *s.o.*; ***das Bett ~*** get out of bed, get up again *after an illness*; ***s-e Kräfte verließen ihn*** his strength failed him, his energy drained from him; F ***da verließen sie ihn*** at that point he dried up; **II.** *v/refl.*: ***sich ~ auf*** *acc.* rely (*or* depend, count) on; ***Sie können sich darauf ~*** you can count on it, ***daß***: *a.* you can rest assured that; ***auf ihn*** (***sein Wort***) ***kann man sich ~*** he's as good as his word; F ***verlaß dich drauf!*** take my word for it

ver'las·sen² **I.** *p.p. of* ***verlassen¹***; **II.** *adj.* **1.** abandoned, *lit.* forsaken (***von*** *dat.* by); ***~ aufgefunden werden*** *car etc.*: be found abandoned; **2.** deserted *region*, *house etc.*, desolate; bleak

Ver'las·sen *n*: ⚖ ***böswilliges ~*** wil(l)ful abandonment

Ver'las·sen·heit *f* (-; *no pl.*) **1.** loneliness; forlornness; **2.** bleakness

ver·läß·lich [fɛɐ'lɛslɪç] *adj.* reliable, dependable; **Ver'läß·lich·keit** *f* (-; *no pl.*) reliability, dependability

Ver·laub [fɛɐ'laʊp] *m*: ***mit ~*** (***gesagt, zu sagen***) with all due respect, if you'll forgive me for saying this; ***mit ~*** *obs.* by your leave

Ver'lauf *m* (-[e]s; *no pl.*) course; ***der ~ e-r Sache*** *a.* the way s.th. goes (*or* develops); ***das kommt auf den ~ ...*** (*gen.*) ***an*** that depends on how (*or* on the way) ... goes (*or* develops), that depends on which course ... takes; ***den weiteren ~ abwarten*** wait and see how things go (*or* develop); ***im ~*** *gen.* (*or* ***von*** *dat.*) in the course of; ***nach ~ von*** *dat.* after (a lapse of); ***e-n schlimmen ~ nehmen*** take a bad course; **ver'lau·fen** (*irr.*, *no* -ge-, → ***laufen***) **I.** *v/i.* (sn) **1.** take a ... course, proceed, go; ***normal ~*** take a normal course; **2.** *border*, *path etc.*: run, pass (***entlang*** *dat.* along); **3.** *colo(u)rs etc.*: run; *butter etc.*: *a.* melt; **II.** *v/refl.*: ***sich ~*** (h) **4.** lose one's way, get lost; **5.** *crowd*: scatter; → ***Sand***

ver·laust [fɛɐ'laʊst] *adj.* full of lice, louse-ridden

ver·laut·ba·ren [fɛɐ'laʊtba:rən] *v/t.* (h) make known, announce; **Ver'laut·ba·rung** *f* (-; -en) a) announcement, b) report; (press) release; **ver'lau·ten** *v/i.* (sn) be reported, be disclosed, be released; ***~ lassen*** give to understand, (be heard to) say, hint; ***nichts davon ~ lassen*** not to say a word about it; ***wie verlautet*** as reported

ver'le·ben *v/t.* (h) **1.** spend; ***schöne Tage ~*** have a good time; **2.** use up, *a.* spend *money*

ver·le·ben·di·gen [fɛɐle'bɛndɪgən] *v/t.* (h) **1.** bring to life; **2.** liven up *report*, *tale*

ver·lebt [fɛɐ'le:pt] *adj.* dissipated, burnt-out ..., *pred.* burnt out

ver'le·gen¹ (h) **I.** *v/t.* **1.** move, transfer (*a.* ⚔) (*both* ***nach*** *dat.* to); *phys.* shift; ***s-n Wohnsitz ~*** move (house); **2.** put off (***auf*** *acc.* to, until, till), postpone (to); **3.** lay *cable*, *pipes etc.*; *a.* put down *tiles etc.*; **4.** publish; **5.** mislay; **II.** *v/refl.* **6.** ***ich muß mich ~ haben*** I must have been lying funny; **7.** ***sich ~ auf*** *acc.* take to *ger.*; resort to *lying*, *denying etc.*

ver'le·gen² **I.** *adj.* embarrassed; (***nie***) ***~ um*** *acc.* (never) at a loss for *an answer*, *an excuse etc.*; ***er ist nie um e-e Antwort ~*** *a.* he's always got an answer (at the) ready; ***um Geld ~*** short of money; ***j-n ~ machen*** embarrass *s.o.*; **II.** *adv.* embarrassedly; in embarrassment; ***~ lächeln*** give an embarrassed smile

Ver'le·gen·heit *f* (-; -en) **1.** *no pl.* embarrassment; ***vor ~ schweigen*** *etc.* be silent *etc.* out of embarrassment; ***j-n in ~ bringen*** embarrass s.o., put s.o. on the spot; ***in ~ kommen*** get embarrassed; **2.** difficult spot; predicament; ***in ~ sein*** a) be in a bit of a spot, be in a difficult spot, b) be a bit short (F hard up); ***j-m aus der ~ helfen*** help s.o. out (of a spot); ***in ~ kommen*** run into difficulties; ***in die ~ kommen, et. tun zu müssen*** find o.s. compelled to do s.th.

Ver'le·gen·heits|lö·sung *f* makeshift (*or* compromise) solution; **~pau·se** *f*: ***e-e ~ machen*** be at a loss for words (*or* as to what to say, as to how to react)

Ver·le·ger [fɛɐ'le:gɐ] *m* (-s; -) publisher

Ver·le·gung [fɛɐ'le:gʊŋ] *f* (-; -en) **1.** moving, transfer(ral), shifting (***nach*** *dat.* to); **2.** postponement (***auf*** *acc.* to)

ver'lei·den *v/t.* (h): ***j-m et. ~*** a) spoil s.th. for s.o., b) put s.o. off s.th.; ***es war ihm verleidet*** he had had enough of it

Ver·leih [fɛɐ'laɪ] *m* (-[e]s; -e) hire (*or* rental) company; rental shop; *film*: a) *no pl.* distribution, b) distributors *pl.*

ver'lei·hen *v/t.* (*irr.*, *no* -ge-, h, → ***leihen***) **1.** lend (out), *esp. Am.* loan (out); hire (*Am.* rent) out; **2.** confer *title etc.* (*dat.* on *s.o.*); grant *right*, *privilege etc.* (to); award *prize etc.* (to); **3.** *fig.* ***j-m*** (***e-r Sache***) ***et. ~*** give *or* lend s.o. (s.th.) s.th.; → ***Ausdruck*** 1, ***Kraft*** 1; **Ver·lei·her** [fɛɐ'laɪɐ] *m* (-s; -) lender; *Brit.* hirer; *film*: distributor; **Ver'lei·hung** *f* (-; -en) **1.** lending, hiring, *Am.* rental; **2.** conferment; awarding

ver'lei·men *v/t.* (h) glue (together)

ver'lei·ten *v/t.* (h) lead astray; tempt (***zu*** *dat.* into *crime etc.*); seduce (***zu tun*** into doing); ***j-n zu et. ~*** *a.* talk s.o. into doing s.th.; ***sich ~ lassen*** (allow o.s. to) be tempted *etc.* (***et. zu tun*** into doing s.th.), succumb (to the temptation); ***dies verleitete mich zu der Annahme*** this led me to believe

ver'ler·nen *v/t.* (h) forget; ***das Lachen ~*** forget how to laugh *etc.*

ver'le·sen¹ (*irr.*, *no* -ge-, h, → ***lesen***) **I.** *v/t.* **1.** read out; **2.** clean *lettuce etc.*; **II.** *v/refl.*: ***sich ~*** misread (it), read it wrong; ***sich bei et. ~*** misread s.th.

ver'le·sen² **I.** *p.p. of* ***verlesen¹***; **II.** *adj.* hand-picked

ver·letz·bar [fɛɐ'lɛtsba:ɐ] *adj. a. fig.* vulnerable; (over)sensitive, touchy; **Ver'letz·bar·keit** *f* (-; *no pl.*) *a. fig.* vulnerability; oversensitiveness

ver·let·zen [fɛɐ'lɛtsən] *v/t.* (h) **1.** hurt, injure; *esp. a.* ⚔ wound; ***sich am Arm*** *etc.* ***~*** hurt (*or* injure) one's arm *etc.*; ***Personen wurden dabei nicht verletzt*** there were no casualties; **2.** *fig.* hurt *s.o.*; *a.* wound *s.o.'s feelings etc.*; *a.* offend *s.o.'s pride etc.*; **3.** violate *law, rule etc.*; offend against *rule, good taste etc.*; ***s-e Pflicht*** ~ neglect one's duty; **ver'let·zend** *adj.* hurtful; offensive; cutting *remark*

ver·letz·lich [fɛɐ'lɛtslɪç] *adj.* → ***verletzbar***; **Ver'letz·lich·keit** *f* (-; *no pl.*) → ***Verletzbarkeit***

Ver·letz·te [fɛɐ'lɛtstə] *m, f* (-n; -n) injured person, casualty; ***die ~n*** the injured (*pl.*)

Ver·let·zung [fɛɐ'lɛtsʊŋ] *f* (-; -en) **1.** ⚕ injury; ***sie kam mit leichten ~en davon*** she wasn't seriously hurt; **2.** ⚖ infringement, violation; breach *of contract, duty etc.*; ~ ***der Privatsphäre*** invasion (*or* intrusion) of privacy; ~ ***des Luftraums*** violation of airspace; **Ver'let·zungs·ge·fahr** *f* risk of injury

ver'leug·nen *v/t.* (h) a) deny, b) disown *child etc.*; ***sich ~ lassen*** not to be at home (***vor*** *dat.* to *s.o.*); ***es läßt sich nicht ~, daß*** there's no denying that; **Ver'leug·nung** *f* (-; -en) a) denial, *formal*: disavowal, b) disowning, disownment

ver·leum·den [fɛɐ'lɔʏmdən] *v/t.* (h) slander, *formal*: calumniate; libel; **Ver·leum·der** [fɛɐ'lɔʏmdɐ] *m* (-s; -) slanderer; libel(l)er; **ver·leum·de·risch** [fɛɐ'lɔʏmdərɪʃ] *adj.* slanderous, *formal*: calumnious; libel(l)ous; **Ver'leum·dung** *f* (-; -en) slander, *formal*: calumny; *esp.* ⚖ defamation; libel

Ver'leum·dungs|kam,pa·gne *f* smear campaign; **~kla·ge** *f* action for slander (*or* libel)

ver'lie·ben *v/refl.* (h): ***sich ~*** fall in love (***in*** *acc.* with) (*a. w.s.*); **ver·liebt** [fɛɐ'li:pt] *adj.* a) in love (***in*** *acc.* with), b) amorous *looks etc.*; ***hoffnungslos ~*** *a.* F smitten; → ***Ohr***; **Ver'liebt·heit** *f* (-; *no pl.*) (state of) being in love (***in*** *acc.* with); infatuation (with); *w.s.* love (for)

ver·lie·ren [fɛɐ'li:rən] (verlor, verloren, h) **I.** *v/t.* lose (***an*** *acc.* to); *a.* shed *leaves, hair*; ***zu ~ haben*** stand to lose; ***kein Wort darüber ~*** not to say a word about it; ***du hast hier nichts verloren*** you've got no business being here; → ***Auge*** 1, ***Geduld, Mut, Nerv***; → *a.* ***verloren***; **II.** *v/refl.*: ***sich ~*** a) lose each other, b) *fig. sound etc.*: be lost; *path, trace etc.*: lose itself, disappear; *effect, emotion etc.*: wear off, c) disappear; *crowd*: disperse; ***sich in Gedanken*** (***Träumen*** *etc.*) ~ be lost in thought (reverie *etc.*); **III.** *v/i.* lose (***gegen*** *acc.* to); *fig.* ***er*** (***es***) ***hat sehr verloren*** he (it) isn't what he (it) used to be; ***an Wirkung*** (***Reiz*** *etc.*) ~ lose some of its effect (its *or* one's charm *etc.*); ***an Wert ~*** lose some of its (*or* go down in) value; ***der Roman*** *etc.* ***verliert sehr in der Übersetzung*** the novel *etc.* loses a lot in translation

Ver·lie·rer [fɛɐ'li:rɐ] *m* (-s; -) loser; ***guter*** (***schlechter***) ~ good (bad) loser; **~sei·te** *f*: ***auf der ~ sein*** be on the losing side

Ver·lies [fɛɐ'li:s] *n* (-es; -e [-zə]) dungeon

ver·lo·ben [fɛɐ'lo:bən] *v/refl.* (h): ***sich ~*** get engaged; **Ver·löb·nis** [fɛɐ'lø:pnɪs] *n* (-ses; -se) engagement; **ver·lobt** [fɛɐ'lo:pt] *adj.* engaged; ***fest ~*** *a.* engaged to be married; **Ver'lob·te** *m, f* (-n; -n) fiancé(e *f*); ***die ~n*** the engaged couple; **Ver'lo·bung** *f* (-; -en) engagement

Ver'lo·bungs|fei·er *f* engagement party; **~ring** *m* engagement ring

ver'locken *v/t.* (h) entice, tempt, seduce (***zu tun*** into doing); ***zum Kauf ~*** tempt people into buying; ***es verlockt zum Kauf*** it's tempting (*or* it tempts one) to buy; **ver'lockend** *adj.* tempting, enticing, alluring; **Ver'lockung** *f* (-; -en) lure, enticement; temptation

ver·lo·gen [fɛɐ'lo:gən] *adj.* lying ..., *formal*: mendacious; false; hypocritical; ~ ***sein*** be a liar; ***~er Kerl*** (damned) liar; **Ver'lo·gen·heit** *f* (-; -en) lying; falseness; hypocrisy

ver·lor [fɛɐ'lo:ɐ] *pret. of* ***verlieren***

ver·lo·ren [fɛɐ'lo:rən] **I.** *p.p. of* ***verlieren***; **II.** *adj.* lost (*a. fig.*); forlorn; *gastr.* ***~e Eier*** poached eggs; ***~es Spiel*** losing game; ***auf ~em Posten stehen*** be fighting a losing battle; *bibl.* ***der ~e Sohn*** the Prodigal Son; ***j-n*** (***et.***) ~ ***geben*** give s.o. (s.th.) up for lost; ***sich ~ geben*** give up; ***in den Anblick e-r Sache ~*** lost in contemplation of s.th.; ***es ist noch nicht alles ~*** there's hope yet, *esp. iro.* all is not lost; ***das ist bei ihm ~*** it's lost on him

ver'lo·ren·ge·hen *v/i.* (*irr.*, *sep.*, sn, → ***gehen***) get lost; *fig.* ~ ***in*** *dat.* be swamped by *an oversize suit etc.*; ***an ihm ist ein Schauspieler verlorengegangen*** he would have made a good actor

Ver'lo·ren·heit *f* (-; *no pl.*) forlornness

ver'lö·schen *v/i.* (sn) **1.** *candle, match etc.*: go out; **2.** *fig.* die; fade (away)

ver'lo·sen *v/t.* (h) a) draw lots for, b) raffle (off); **Ver'lo·sung** *f* (-; -en) a) drawing of lots, b) raffle

ver'lö·ten *v/t.* (h) solder up (*or* together)

ver·lot·tern [fɛɐ'lɔtɐn] *v/i.* (sn) go to rack and ruin, *person*: go to seed; **ver'lot·tert** *adj.* → ***verwahrlost***

Ver·lust [fɛɐ'lʊst] *m* (-[e]s; -e) loss (***an*** *dat.* of); *a.* bereavement; (***hohe***) ***~e*** (heavy) losses (⚔ *a.* casualties); ***mit ~ verkaufen*** *etc.* sell *etc.* at a loss; ***mit ~ arbeiten*** *business*: run at a loss; → ***erleiden, Rücksicht***; **~an·zei·ge** *f* notice of (a) loss; **~aus·gleich** *m* loss compensation; **~be·trieb** *m* loss-maker, loss-making concern, losing business; **ᴤbrin·gend** *adj.* losing *business, deal etc.*, loss-making; **~ge·schäft** *n* **1.** losing deal, loss; **2.** → ***Verlustbetrieb***

ver·lu·stie·ren [fɛɐlʊs'ti:rən] *v/refl.* (h): ***sich ~*** amuse o.s.

ver·lu·stig [fɛɐ'lʊstɪç] *adv.*: ***e-r Sache ~ gehen*** forfeit s.th., lose s.th.

Ver'lust|kon·to *n* deficit account; **~li·ste** *f* ⚔ list of casualties; **~mel·dung** *f* report of loss; ⚔ casualty report; **ᴤreich** *adj.* involving heavy losses; **~vor·trag** *m* ☤ loss carried forward

ver'ma·chen *v/t.* (h): ***j-m et. ~*** leave s.o. s.th., ⚖ bequeath s.th. to s.o.

Ver·mächt·nis [fɛɐ'mɛçtnɪs] *n* (-ses; -se) a) will, b) bequest; *fig.* legacy

ver·mäh·len [fɛɐ'mɛ:lən] (h) **I.** *v/refl.*: ***sich ~*** get married (***mit*** *dat.* to); *fig.* unite; **II.** *v/t.* wed, marry (***mit*** *dat.* to); **Ver·mähl·te** [fɛɐ'mɛ:ltə] *f* (-n; -n): ***die ~n*** the newly-married couple; **Ver'mäh·lung** *f* (-; -en) wedding, marriage

ver·ma·le·deit [fɛɐmale'daɪt] *obs. adj.* confounded

ver·männ·li·chen [fɛɐ'mɛnlɪçən] **I.** *v/t.* (h) masculinize; *clothes*: *a.* make *s.o.* look very masculine, give *s.o.* a very masculine look; **II.** *v/i.* (sn) become masculine (*or* masculinized); **ver'männ·licht** *adj.* masculinized; **Ver'männ·li·chung** *f* (-; *no pl.*) masculinization

ver'man·schen F *v/t.* (h) F mess up

ver·mark·ten [fɛɐ'marktən] *v/t.* (h) (put on the) market; *fig.* capitalize on, exploit (commercially); **Ver'mark·tung** *f* (-; *no pl.*) marketing; *fig.* (commercial) exploitation

ver·mas·seln [fɛɐ'masəln] F *v/t.* (h) F make a hash of, mess up, *sl.* screw up

ver·mas·sen [fɛɐ'masən] **I.** *v/i.* (sn) lose its (*or* one's) identity *or* individuality; become a (mere) cipher; *society*: be level(l)ed; **II.** *v/t.* (h) depersonalize; ***Individuen ~*** *a.* take away people's identity; **ver'maßt** *adj.* depersonalized; anonymous *society*; (***die***) ***~e Gesellschaft*** *a.* faceless society; **Ver'mas·sung** *f* (-; *no pl.*) loss of identity, depersonalization; level(l)ing *of society*; (increasing) anonymity

ver'mau·ern *v/t.* (h) wall up (*or* in)

ver'meh·ren (h) **I.** *v/t.* **1.** increase (***um*** *acc.* by); 𝔄 *a.* multiply; **2.** *biol.* breed; **II.** *v/refl.*: ***sich ~*** **3.** increase, 𝔄 *a.* multiply, rise; ***sich ständig ~*** rise steadily; **4.** *biol.* reproduce, multiply, breed; **Ver'meh·rung** *f* (-; *no pl.*) **1.** increase; **2.** *biol.* reproduction, breeding

ver·meid·bar [fɛɐ'maɪtba:ɐ] *adj.* avoidable; **ver'mei·den** *v/t.* (*irr.*, *no* -ge-, h, → ***meiden***) avoid; evade; steer clear of; shun; ***es läßt sich nicht ~*** it can't be helped; **ver·meid·lich** [fɛɐ'maɪtlɪç] *adj.* avoidable; **Ver'mei·dung** *f* (-; *no pl.*) avoidance

ver·meint·lich [fɛɐ'maɪntlɪç] *adj.* a) supposed; alleged, b) imaginary

ver'mel·den *v/t.* (h) announce; report; F *fig.* → ***melden*** 3

ver'men·gen (h) **I.** *v/t.* **1.** mix; **2.** mix up; **II.** *v/refl.*: ***sich ~*** mix

ver·mensch·li·chen [fɛɐ'mɛnʃlɪçən] *v/t.* (h) humanize; present in human form; personify; **Ver'mensch·li·chung** *f* (-; -en) humanization; personification

Ver·merk [fɛɐ'mɛrk] *m* (-[e]s; -e) note; comment; **ver'mer·ken** *v/t.* (h) **1.** a) make a note of, b) note, mention; ***et. am Rande ~*** a) make a note of s.th. in the margin, b) mention s.th. in passing; ***das sei nur am Rande vermerkt*** if I could just add that; ***es sei am Rande vermerkt, daß*** it might be worth just mentioning that, could I just add that; **2.** ***et. übel ~*** take s.th. amiss (*or* in bad part), take offen|ce (*Am.* -se) at s.th.; ***j-m et. übel ~*** be annoyed (*or* angry) at s.o. for s.th.; ***j-m übel ~, daß*** be annoyed (*or* angry) at s.o. for *ger.*; ***er hat es ihm übel vermerkt*** *a.* he's (*or* he was) not amused; ***et. peinlich ~*** note s.th. with some embarrassment

ver'mes·sen[1] (*irr.*, *no* -ge-, h, → ***messen***) **I.** *v/t.* measure; survey *terrain*; **II.** *v/refl.*: ***sich ~ zu*** *inf.* dare (to) *inf.*, presume to *inf.*, have the temerity to *inf.*

ver'mes·sen[2] **I.** *p.p. of* ***vermessen***[1]; **II.** *adj.* presumptuous; **Ver'mes·sen·heit** *f* (-; *no pl.*) presumption

Ver·mes·ser [fɛɐ'mɛsɐ] *m* (-s; -) surveyor

Ver'mes·sung *f* (-; -en) measuring; surveying

Ver'mes·sungs|amt *n* surveyor's office; **~in·ge,nieur** *m* surveyor; **~kun·de** *f* surveying; **~schiff** *n* surveying ship

ver·mie·sen [fɛɐ'mi:zən] F *v/t.* (h): ***j-m et. ~*** spoil s.th. for s.o.

ver'mie·ten *v/t.* (h) rent (out); *Brit. a.* hire out *car etc.*; ***Haus zu ~*** house to let (*Am.* for rent); **Ver'mie·ter** *m* (-s; -) **1.** owner of the flat (*Am.* apartment) *or* house *etc.*; **2.** landlord; **Ver'mie·te·rin** *f* (-; -nen) **1.** → ***Vermieter*** 1; **2.** landlady; **Ver'mie·tung** *f* (-; -en) renting (out); rental; *Brit. a.* hiring (out)

ver'min·dern (h) **I.** *v/t.* a) decrease, reduce; diminish, lessen, b) detract from; **II.** *v/refl.*: ***sich ~*** decrease; diminish, lessen; **Ver'min·de·rung** *f* (-; -en) decrease (*gen.* in), reduction (of, in); lessening (of)

ver·mi·nen [fɛɐ'miːnən] *v/t.* (h) lay mines in (*or* along), mine; **ver'mint** *adj.* full of mines

ver'mi·schen (h) **I.** *v/t.* **1.** mix; blend *colo(u)rs, tea etc.*; **2.** *biol.* interbreed, *zo. a.* cross; **3.** *ling.* mix (up); **II.** *v/refl.*: ***sich ~*** **4.** mix; *colo(u)rs etc.*: *a.* blend; **5.** *biol.* interbreed; **ver'mischt** *adj.* mixed; ***Vermischtes*** miscellaneous items (*or* writings *etc.*), *heading*: miscellaneous, misc.; **Ver'mi·schung** *f* (-; -en) **1.** mixing; blending; **2.** *biol.* interbreeding

ver·mis·sen [fɛɐ'mɪsən] *v/t.* (h) miss; ***ich vermisse m-n Bleistift*** I can't find my pencil, I'm missing my pencil; ***et. ~ lassen*** lack s.th.; **ver'mißt** *adj.* missing (⚔ in action); ***j-n als ~ melden*** report s.o. missing; ***als ~ gemeldet werden*** (*or* ***sein***) be listed as missing; **Ver'miß·te** *m, f* (-n; -n) missing person (⚔ serviceman); ⚔ *a.* MIA (= missing in action); ⚔ *pl. a.* missing personnel *sg.*; **Ver'miß·ten·an·zei·ge** *f* missing person's report; ***e-e ~ aufgeben*** report s.o. missing

ver'mit·teln (h) **I.** *v/t.* a) get, find, *formal*: procure (***j-m*** for s.o.), b) arrange *meeting etc.*, c) give, convey *impression, idea etc.*; impart *knowledge etc.* (***j-m*** to s.o.); **II.** *v/i.* mediate, act as (a) mediator (***bei*** *dat.* in); intervene; **ver'mit·telnd I.** *adj.* conciliatory, mediatory; **II.** *adv.*: ***~ eingreifen*** intervene, mediate

ver·mit·tels(t) [fɛɐ'mɪtəls(t)] *prp.* (*gen., dat.*) by means of

Ver'mitt·ler *m* (-s; -) **1.** mediator, arbitrator; **2.** intermediary, go-between; **3.** ✝ *etc.* agent; negotiator; broker; **~ge·bühr** *f* → ***Vermittlungsgebühr***; **~rol·le** *f* negotiating role; ***e-e ~ spielen*** act as negotiator (*or* mediator)

Ver·mitt·lung [fɛɐ'mɪtlʊŋ] *f* (-; -en) **1.** *no pl.* mediation, arbitration; intervention; **2.** *no pl.* procurement, obtaining; arrangement; ✝ negotiation; placement; ***durch ~*** *gen.* (*or* ***von*** *dat.*) through; ***durch s-e ~*** *a.* through his help (*or* intervention); **3.** agency, office; **4.** *teleph.* (telephone) exchange, *Am.* central office; ✝ switchboard; *w.s.* operator; ***über die ~*** via (*or* through) the switchboard *etc.*

Ver'mitt·lungs|aus·schuß *m* mediation committee; **~ge·bühr** *f*, **~pro·vi·si͜on** *f* commission; brokerage; **~stel·le** *f* agency; **~ver·fah·ren** *n pol.* joint committee procedure; **~ver·such** *m* mediation attempt (*gen.* by), mediation effort (on the part of), attempt at mediation (on the part of)

ver·mö·beln [fɛɐ'mø:bəln] F *v/t.* (h) F clobber

ver'mo·dern *v/i.* (sn) mo(u)lder, decay

ver'mö·gen *v/t.* (*irr., no* -ge-, h, → ***mögen***): ***~ zu*** *inf.* be able to *inf.*; be capable of *ger.*; be in a position to *inf.*

Ver'mö·gen *n* (-s; -) **1.** fortune; ***ein ~ verdienen*** (***kosten***) earn (cost) a fortune; **2.** property; means *pl.*; ✝ assets *pl.*; **3.** *no pl.* ability; power(s *pl.*); ***nach bestem ~*** to the best of one's ability; ***es geht über*** (*or* ***übersteigt***) ***mein ~*** it's beyond my power (***zu*** *inf.* to *inf.*), it goes beyond my power(s); **ver'mö·gend** *adj.* wealthy, well-to-do, (very) well-off

Ver'mö·gens|an·samm·lung *f* accumulation of wealth; **~bil·dung** *f* wealth formation; **~haf·tung** *f* financial liability; **~la·ge** *f* financial situation; **~mas·se** *f* estate, assets *pl.*; principal; **2recht·lich** *adj* under the law of property; **~steu·er** *f* property tax; **~ver·hält·nis·se** *pl.* financial circumstances; **~ver·wal·ter** *m* property administrator; **~ver·wal·tung** *f* property administration; **~wer·te** *pl.* (property) assets

ver'mö·gens·wirk·sam *adj.* capital-creating (*through fiscal grants and tax concessions*), *w.s.* profitable; ***~e Leistung*** *employer's contribution(s) to tax-deductible (employee) savings scheme*

ver·mum·men [fɛɐ'mʊmən] (h) **I.** *v/t.* a) wrap up, b) disguise; **II.** *v/refl.*: ***sich ~*** a) wrap o.s. up (***in*** *acc.* in), b) disguise o.s., wear a mask *at a demonstration*; **Ver'mum·mung** *f* (-; -en) disguise; wearing of masks; **Ver'mum·mungs·ver·bot** *n ban on wearing masks at demonstrations*

ver'murk·sen F *v/t.* (h) F make a hash of, botch (up)

ver·mu·ten [fɛɐ'muːtən] *v/t.* (h) a) assume; expect, b) suspect; ***ich vermute*** *a.* I imagine, I rather think; ***ich vermute ja*** I imagine (*or* expect) so, I would think so; ***das habe ich schon vermutet*** I had an idea that would happen (*or* be the case *etc.*); ***ich vermute sie nebenan*** I imagine (*or* expect) she's next door, she's probably next door; **ver·mut·lich** [fɛɐ'muːtlɪç] *adj.* presumed; probable, likely; **II.** *adv.* presumably; probably; **Ver'mu·tung** *f* (-; -en) presumption (*a.* ⚖); supposition, F guess; expectation; *a. pl.* speculation; ***~en anstellen*** speculate (***über*** *acc.* on)

ver·nach·läs·si·gen [fɛɐ'naːxlɛsɪgən] *v/t.* (h) neglect; ignore; **Ver'nach·läs·si·gung** *f* (-; -en) neglect

ver'na·geln *v/t.* (h) nail (up); nail down *lid etc.*; ***mit Brettern ~*** board up; **ver'na·gelt** F *adj.* F blockheaded

ver'nä·hen *v/t.* (h) sew (*or* stitch) up

ver'nar·ben *v/i.* (sn) scar over; *fig.* heal; **ver·narbt** [fɛɐ'narpt] *adj.* scarred; pockmarked, pitted *face*; **Ver'nar·bung** *f* (-; -en) a) scarring, b) scar(s *pl.*)

ver·narrt [fɛɐ'nart] *adj.*: ***~ in*** *acc.* besotted (*or* infatuated) with, F wild (*or* crazy) about; ***in ein Kind ~ sein*** dote on a child

ver'na·schen *v/t.* **1.** munch, F scoff; **2.** spend *money* on sweets (*Am.* candy); **3.** F ***j-n ~*** *sl.* lay s.o., have it off with s.o.; **ver'nascht** *adj.*: ***~ sein*** always be eating candy (*Brit.* sweets)

ver·ne·beln [fɛɐ'neːbəln] *v/t.* (h) **1.** put a smoke-screen up in; **2.** *fig.* befuddle *mind*; blur *eyes*; obscure *facts*

ver·nehm·bar [fɛɐ'neːmbaːɐ] *adj.* audible, perceptible; **ver'neh·men** *v/t.* (*irr., no* -ge-, h, → ***nehmen***) **1.** hear; *a.* learn; **2.** interrogate, question, ⚖ *a.* examine; ***als Zeuge vernommen werden*** be called into the witness box (*Am.* witness stand); **Ver'neh·men** *n*: ***dem ~ nach*** from what one hears, rumo(u)r has it that, ***ist*** (*or* ***hat***) ***er ...***: *a.* he is said to ...; **ver·nehm·lich** [fɛɐ'neːmlɪç] *adj.* audible, distinct; loud; **Ver'neh·mung** *f* (-; -en) interrogation, questioning, ⚖ *a.* examination; **ver'neh·mungs·fä·hig** *adj.* fit to be questioned

ver'nei·gen *v/refl.* (h): ***sich ~*** bow; *lady*: curtsey (***vor*** *dat.* to); **Ver'nei·gung** *f* (-; -en) bow; curtsey (***vor*** *dat.* to)

ver·nei·nen [fɛɐ'naɪnən] (h) **I.** *v/t.* a) answer no to *s.th.*, b) deny, c) oppose, d) *ling.* negate; **II.** *v/i.* say no, answer in the negative; **Ver'nei·nung** *f* (-; -en) a) negation, b) denial, c) opposition (*gen.* to), d) *ling.* negative

ver·nich·ten [fɛɐ'nɪçtən] *v/t.* (h) destroy (*a. documents*); annihilate; exterminate; wipe out, eradicate; *fig.* dash, shatter *hope etc.*; **ver'nich·tend I.** *adj.* devastating; destructive; *fig.* crushing *blow, defeat*; withering *reply, look*; scathing, devastating, damning *criticism*; ***~es Urteil*** severe condemnation; **II.** *adv.*: ***~ schlagen*** destroy, *sport*: play into the ground; **Ver'nich·tung** *f* (-; -en) destruction, annihilation *etc.*; → ***vernichten***

Ver'nich·tungs|feld·zug *m* campaign of destruction; **~krieg** *m* war of extermination; **~la·ger** *n* extermination camp; **~mit·tel** *n* a) weedkiller, b) insecticide; **~po·ten·ti͜al** *n* destructive potential (*or* capability); **~schlag** *m* **1.** annihilating blow; **2.** *fig.* final blow; ***zum ~ ausholen*** prepare to (*or* be about to) deal the final blow; **~waf·fe** *f* weapon of mass destruction; *pl. coll.* destructive weaponry *sg.*; **~wut** *f* (sheer) vandalism

ver·nickeln [fɛɐ'nɪkəln] (*sep.* -k·k-) *v/t.* (h) nickel-plate; **Ver'nicke·lung** (*sep.* -k·k-) *f* (-; -en) nickel-plating

ver·nied·li·chen [fɛɐ'niːtlɪçən] *v/t.* (h) minimize; play *s.th.* down; **Ver'nied·li·chung** *f* (-; -en) minimization; playing down

ver'nie·ten *v/t.* (h) rivet

Ver·nis·sa·ge [vɛrnɪ'saːʒə] *f* (-; -n) private view, art opening

Ver·nunft [fɛɐ'nʊnft] *f* (-; *no pl.*) reason; ***~ annehmen*** be reasonable, listen to reason, come to one's senses; ***j-n zur ~ bringen*** make s.o. listen to reason, bring s.o. to his (*or* her) senses; (***wieder***) ***zur ~ kommen*** (begin to) listen to reason, (gradually) come to one's senses

ver'nunft·be·gabt *adj.* rational

Ver'nunft·ehe *f* marriage of convenience

Ver·nünf·te·lei [fɛɐnʏnftə'laɪ] *f* (-; -en) *a. pl.* sophistry

ver'nunft·ge·mäß *adj.* rational, reasonable

Ver'nunft|glau·be *m* belief in (human) reason; rationalism; **~grün·de** *pl.* reason *sg.*, rational arguments (*or* considerations); ***aus ~n*** out of plain common sense

ver·nünf·tig [fɛɐ'nʏnftɪç] **I.** *adj.* **1.** reasonable; sensible; level-headed; ***er ist ganz ~*** *a.* F he's got his head screwed on the right way; ***jeder ~e Mensch*** anyone with a bit of sense, anyone in his right mind; ***du wirst schon noch ~ werden*** you'll come to your senses; **2.** rational *arguments etc.*; **3.** F decent, proper; **II.** *adv.* **4.** sensibly; ***~ reden*** talk sense (***mit*** *dat.* to); ***e-e Sache ~ angehen*** be sensible about s.th.; **5.** F properly; ***~ essen*** *a.* eat sensibly; **ver·nünf·ti·ger·wei·se**

[fɛɐ'nʏnftɪgɐ'vaɪzə] *adv.*: ~ ***et. tun*** be sensible enough (*or* have the good sense) to do s.th.; **Ver'nünf·tig·keit** *f* (-; *no pl.*) reasonableness
ver'nunft·los *adj.* irrational; **Ver'nunft·lo·sig·keit** *f* (-; *no pl.*) irrationality
Ver'nunft·mensch *m* rational type
ver'nunft·wid·rig *adj.* irrational; unreasonable; **Ver'nunft·wid·rig·keit** *f* (-; *no pl.*) a) irrationality, b) irrational behavio(u)r (*or* decision *etc.*)
ver·öden [fɛɐ'ʔøːdən] **I.** *v/i.* (sn) become deserted; **II.** *v/t.* (h) ⚕ sclerose, obliterate *blood vessels*; **Ver'ödung** *f* (-; -en) **1.** *no pl.* desertion; **2.** ⚕ obliteration
ver·öf·fent·li·chen [fɛɐ'ʔœfəntlɪçən] *v/t.* (h) publish; release; ***bisher noch nicht veröffentlicht*** previously unpublished (*or* unreleased); **Ver'öf·fent·li·chung** *f* (-; -en) publication
ver'ord·nen *v/t.* (h) **1.** ⚕ prescribe (***j-m*** for s.o.); ***j-m Bettruhe*** (***Bewegung***) ~ order s.o. to stay in bed (advise s.o. to get some physical exercise); ***wenn vom Arzt nicht anders verordnet*** unless otherwise advised by your physician; **2.** ⚖ decree; **Ver'ord·nung** *f* (-; -en) **1.** prescribing; ***nach ~ des Arztes*** as prescribed by one's physician; **2.** ⚖ decree
ver'pach·ten *v/t.* (h) lease (***j-m*** to s.o.); **Ver'päch·ter** *m* (-s; -) lessor; **Ver'pach·tung** *f* (-; -en) leasing
ver'packen *v/t.* (h) pack (up), *esp.* ⚙ package; wrap up; **ver'packt** *adj.* wrapped up; *esp.* ⚙ packaged; ***festlich*** ~ nicely wrapped (up for the occasion); **Ver'packung** *f* (-; -en) **1.** packing; packaging; **2.** → ***Verpackungsmaterial***
Ver'packungs|ge·wicht *n* tare weight; **~ko·sten** *pl.* packing charges; **~ma·te·ri̦al** *n* packaging material; wrapping
ver'päp·peln F *v/t.* (h) pamper, (molly)coddle
ver'pas·sen *v/t.* (h) **1.** miss *bus, train etc.*, *a. fig. opportunity etc.*; **2.** ⚔ fit *uniform etc.*; **3.** F give, F land *s.o.* with *s.th.*; ***j-m e-e*** ~ F land s.o. one
ver'pat·zen F *v/t.* (h) F mess up, botch (up)
ver'pen·nen F (h) **I.** *v/i.* sleep in, oversleep; **II.** *v/t.* sleep through; *fig.* forget; *fig.* ***ich hab's total verpennt*** *a.* F I clean forgot
ver·pe·sten [fɛɐ'pɛstən] *v/t.* (h) pollute; F stink out; *fig.* poison *the atmosphere etc.*
ver'pet·zen F *v/t.* (h) F sneak on *s.o.*
ver'pfän·den *v/t.* (h) pledge (*a. fig.* ***sein Wort*** one's word); mortgage; pawn
ver'pfei·fen F *v/t.* (*irr.*, *no* -ge-, h, → ***pfeifen***) **1.** F blab on *s.o.*, *esp. ped. a.* sneak (*or* tell) on *s.o.*; F cop out on *s.o.*, *sl.* grass on *s.o.*; **2.** let *s.th.* out; ***et.*** ~ *a.* F blab
ver'pflan·zen *v/t.* (h) transplant; **Ver'pflan·zung** *f* (-; -en) transplant
ver'pfle·gen (h) **I.** *v/t.* feed; **II.** *v/refl.*: ***sich*** ~ feed o.s.; ***sich selbst*** ~ cook for o.s.; **Ver'pfle·gung** *f* (-; *no pl.*) **1.** catering; feeding; **2.** food (and drink), refreshments *pl.*; ⚔ rations *pl.*
ver·pflich·ten [fɛɐ'pflɪçtən] (h) **I.** *v/t.* oblige, *esp.* ⚖, ✝ obligate; ***j-n*** (***zu et.***) ~ place an obligation on s.o. (to do s.th.); ***j-n zum Kauf*** *etc.* ~ put s.o. under an obligation to buy *etc.*; ***j-n zur Einhaltung der Regeln*** ~ bind s.o. to the rules; **II.** *v/refl.*: ***sich*** ~ commit o.s. (***zu et.*** to do[ing] s.th.), *a.* ⚖, ✝ undertake (to do s.th.); *esp.* ⚔ sign on (***auf*** *5 Jahre etc.* for); ***sich vertraglich*** ~ sign a contract; **III.** *v/i.*: ***es verpflichtet zum Kauf*** *gen.* you are obliged to buy, you commit yourself to buying; ***es verpflichtet zu nichts*** there's no obligation involved, there are no strings attached; → ***Adel*** 2;
ver'pflich·tet *adj.* obliged (***zu et.*** to do s.th.), under obligation (to do s.th.), bound by contract (to do s.th.); ***gesetzlich ~ sein*** be bound by law (***zu*** *inf.* to *inf.*), be under legal obligation (to *inf.*); ***sich ~ fühlen zu*** *inf.* feel obliged (*or* bound) to *inf.*; ***j-m*** (***sehr***) ***zu Dank ~ sein*** be (deeply) indebted to s.o.; ***j-m gegenüber ~ sein*** be beholden to s.o.
Ver'pflich·tung *f* (-; -en) commitment; (*esp. moral*) obligation; ⚖, ✝ liability; pledge (***zu*** *dat.* of); duty; ~ ***zum Kauf*** *etc.* obligation to buy *etc.*; ***~en gegenüber j-m haben*** be under an obligation to s.o.; ***s-n ~en nachkommen*** meet one's obligations (✝ *a.* liabilities), *pol.* discharge one's commitments
ver'pfu·schen F *v/t.* (h) F bungle, botch (up), make a mess of; **ver'pfuscht** *adj.* ruined, wrecked
ver'pis·sen *sl. v/refl.* (h): ***verpiß dich!*** *sl.* piss off!, V fuck off!
ver'pla·nen (h) **I.** *v/t.* **1.** budget *funds*; plan *one's time*; ***s-e Zeit verplant haben*** be fully booked; ***m-e Urlaubstage habe ich schon verplant*** my holiday is all booked up (with various activities) already; **2.** plan wrong; miscalculate; **II.** *v/refl.*: ***sich*** ~ plan wrong, get one's planning wrong
ver'plap·pern F *v/refl.* (h): ***sich*** ~ F blab (it out), let the cat out of the bag
ver'plau·dern (h) **I.** *v/t.* talk (*or* chat) away *time etc.*; ***den ganzen Abend*** ~ spend the whole evening chatting (away); **II.** *v/refl.*: ***sich*** ~ (completely) forget the time chatting; ***wir haben uns verplaudert*** *a.* we were so busy chatting we forgot to look at our watches
ver·plem·pern [fɛɐ'plɛmpɐn] F *v/t.* (h) waste, fritter away *time, money*
ver·plom·ben [fɛɐ'plɔmbən] *v/t.* (h) seal
ver·polt [fɛɐ'poːlt] *adj.* ⚡ connected the wrong way round
ver·pönt [fɛɐ'pøːnt] *adj.* disapproved-of ..., *pred.* disapproved of; scorned; ~ ***sein*** *a.* be looked down upon; ***... ist hier*** ~ *a.* we (*or* they) don't approve of ... around here
ver'pras·sen *v/t.* (h) squander (***für*** *acc.* on), F blow (on)
ver'prel·len *v/t.* (h) put off; offend, put out
ver'prü·geln *v/t.* (h) beat *s.o.* up, give *s.o.* a thrashing
ver'puf·fen *v/i.* (sn) **1.** *zeal, anger etc.*: fizzle out; *effect, joke etc.*: fall flat; **2.** *flame, gas etc.*: blow up, F go pop; evaporate (*a. fig.*)
ver·pul·vern [fɛɐ'pʊlvɐn] F *v/t.* (h) F blow
ver·pup·pen [fɛɐ'pʊpən] *v/refl.* (h): ***sich*** ~ pupate, change into a chrysalis; **Ver'pup·pung** *f* (-; -en) pupation
ver'pu·sten F *v/refl.*: ***sich*** ~ (h) get one's breath back
Ver'putz *m* (-es; -e) plaster(work); roughcast; **ver'put·zen** *v/t.* (h) **1.** plaster; roughcast; **2.** F *fig.* F put away, polish off
ver'qual·men F *v/t.* (h) **1.** F smoke up *a room etc.*; **2.** spend *one's money* on cigarettes; ***er verqualmt sein ganzes Geld*** *a.* F all his money goes up in smoke;
ver'qualmt F *adj.* smoky, smoke-filled ..., *pred.* filled with smoke
ver'quat·schen F (h) **I.** *v/t.* **1.** → ***verplaudern*** I; **II.** *v/refl.*: ***sich*** ~ **2.** → ***verplaudern*** II; **3.** F blab
ver'quer F **I.** *adj.* **1.** strange, F screwy *ideas etc.*; ***~er Typ*** F weirdo; ***~e Angelegenheit*** mess; **II.** *adv.* wrong; awry; ***mir geht alles*** ~ everything's going wrong (for me)
ver·quicken [fɛɐ'kvɪkən] (*sep.* -k·k-) *v/t.* (h) **1.** amalgamate; **2.** *fig.* connect, bring together; mix up; **ver'quickt** *adj.*: ***eng*** (***miteinander***) ~ closely connected (*or* related); **Ver'quickung** (*sep.* -k·k-) *f* (-; -en) connection (*gen.* between); mixing-up (of)
ver'quir·len *v/t.* (h) whisk (***in*** *acc.* into), beat (*or* mix) with a whisk
ver·quol·len [fɛɐ'kvɔlən] *adj.* warped *wood*; bloated *face*, swollen *eyes etc.*
ver·ram·meln [fɛɐ'raməln] F *v/t.* (h) barricade, block (up)
ver·ram·schen [fɛɐ'ramʃən] F *v/t.* (h) sell off (F dirt cheap), F flog (dirt cheap)
ver·rannt [fɛɐ'rant] **I.** *p.p. of* ***verrennen***; **II.** *fig. adj.*: ~ ***sein in*** *acc.* be set (*or* stuck) on *s.th.*
Ver·rat [fɛɐ'raːt] *m* (-[e]s; *no pl.*) betrayal (***an*** *dat.* of), F sellout (of); ⚖ (*a.* ~ ***am Vaterland***) treason (to); ***an j-m ~ begehen*** (*or* ***üben***) betray s.o.; **ver'ra·ten** (*irr.*, *no* -ge-, h, → ***raten***) **I.** *v/t.* a) betray; *a.* divulge *secret etc.*; give *s.o. or s.th.* away, F *a.* sell *s.o.*; F blab out, let on *that* ..., b) *fig.* betray, reveal; *a.* give away; ~ ***und verkauft sein*** F have been sold down the river; F ***kannst du mir ~ warum?*** can you tell me why?; ***nicht ~!*** don't tell!; **II.** *v/refl.*: ***sich*** ~ give o.s. away
Ver·rä·ter [fɛɐ'rɛːtɐ] *m* (-s; -) traitor (***an*** *dat.* to); **ver·rä·te·risch** [fɛɐ'rɛːtərɪʃ] *adj.* treacherous, traitorous, ⚖ treasonable; *fig.* revealing; telltale ..., giveaway ...
ver·ratzt [fɛɐ'ratst] F *adj.* lost; ~ ***sein*** *a.* be left high and dry
ver'rau·chen **I.** *v/i.* (sn) blow over; **II.** *v/t.* (h) smoke; spend *money* on smoking
ver'räu·chern *v/t.* (h) → ***verqualmen***
ver·raucht [fɛɐ'raʊxt] *adj.* smoky, smoke-filled ..., *pred.* filled with smoke
ver'rau·schen *fig. v/i.* (sn) *enthusiasm, applause etc.*: die down, fade away; **ver'rauscht** *adj. TV* grainy
ver'rech·nen (h) **I.** *v/t.* settle; credit to s.o.'s account; ***et. mit et.*** ~ offset s.th. against s.th.; **II.** *v/refl.*: ***sich*** ~ miscalculate (***um*** *acc.* by), *a. fig.* make a mistake; ***sich*** (***um 10 Dollar***) ***verrechnet haben*** *a.* be (10 dollars) out; F ***sich gründlich verrechnet haben*** F be miles out, *fig.* have made a big mistake; **Ver'rech·nung** *f* (-; -en) settlement; clearing; ***nur zur*** ~ not negotiable
Ver'rech·nungs|kon·to *n* offset account; **~scheck** *m* crossed (*or* non-negotiable) cheque (*Am.* check); **~stel·le** *f* clearing office; **~we·sen** *n* (-s; *no pl.*) clearing
ver'recken *v/i.* (sn) **1.** V die; *hum. sl.* snuff it; *fig. engine etc.*: F conk out; *fig.* ***nicht ums ~!*** not on your life (*Brit. a.* F nelly)!; **2.** *esp. zo.* die, perish; ***Hunderte sind verreckt*** *a.* they were dying (*or* going down) like flies
ver·reg·net [fɛɐ'rɛːgnət] *adj.* rainy; ***un-***

ser Ausflug war ~ our outing was spoilt by rain, it rained throughout our outing
ver'rei·ben *v/t.* (*irr.*, *no* -ge-, h, → ***reiben***) **1.** grind; **2.** spread *ointment etc.*, (***auf*** *dat.*) rub *s.th.* in(to *one's skin*)
ver'rei·sen *v/i.* (sn) go away; ~ ***nach*** *dat.* go to; ***geschäftlich*** ~ go away (*or* off) on a business trip *or* on business; **ver·reist** [fɛɐ'raɪst] *adj.* away (***geschäftlich*** on business)
ver'rei·ßen (*irr.*, *no* -ge-, h, → ***reißen***) **I.** *v/t.* tear *play etc.* to pieces (F bits, shreds), savage, F trash, rubbish, do a hatchet job on; **II.** *v/impers.*: ***es verriß mir das Steuer*** the steering wheel suddenly jerked round hard
ver·ren·ken [fɛɐ'rɛŋkən] (h) **I.** *v/t.* **1.** sprain, twist, dislocate; ***sich den Arm*** ~ sprain (*or* twist, dislocate) one's arm; **2.** F *fig.* ***sich den Hals*** ~ crane one's neck (***nach*** *dat.* to get a glimpse of), *Am.* rubberneck; **II.** *v/refl.*: ***sich*** ~ **3.** sprain (*or* twist, dislocate) one's shoulder *etc.*; **4.** contort o.s., go into contortions; **ver'renkt** *adj.* twisted; ***ich habe e-n*** ~***en Hals*** I've twisted my neck, I've got a crick in my neck; **Ver'ren·kung** *f* (-; -en) **1.** sprain; dislocation; **2.** contortion, gyration; ~***en machen*** go into contortions; ***geistige*** ~***en*** mental acrobatics (*or* gyrations)
ver'ren·nen *fig. v/refl.* (*irr.*, *no* -ge-, h, → ***rennen***): ***sich*** ~ ***in*** *acc.* get stuck in *s.th.*; → ***verrannt***
ver'rich·ten *v/t.* (h) do, carry out; → ***Notdurft***; **Ver'rich·tung** *f* (-; -en) **1.** execution, carrying out; **2.** *pl.* chores, work *sg.*; ***tägliche*** ~***en*** daily chores (*or* routine)
ver'rie·geln *v/t.* (h) bolt, bar
ver·rin·gern [fɛɐ'rɪŋɐn] (h) **I.** *v/t.* decrease, reduce, lower, cut (down); **II.** *v/refl.*: ***sich*** ~ decrease, diminish, go down; **Ver·rin·ge·rung** [fɛɐ'rɪŋərʊŋ] *f* (-; -en) decrease (*gen.* in), reduction (of), lowering (of)
ver'rin·nen *v/i.* (*irr.*, *no* -ge-, sn, → ***rinnen***) a) trickle away, b) *fig. time*: pass, slip away, *hours*: *a.* tick away; *years*: pass by, slip by
Ver·riß [fɛɐ'rɪs] F *m* (-sses; -sse) F slating, hatchet job
ver·ro·hen [fɛɐ'roːən] *v/i.* (sn) become brutalized; coarsen; **Ver'ro·hung** *f* (-; -en) brutalization; coarsening
ver'ro·sten *v/i.* (sn) rust; **ver'ro·stet** *adj.* rusty
ver·rot·ten [fɛɐ'rɔtən] *v/i.* (sn) rot; *w.s. and fig.* → ***verkommen***; **ver'rot·tet** *adj.* **1.** rotten; **2.** *fig.* depraved; decadent; **Ver'rot·tung** *f* (-; *no pl.*) **1.** rotting; **2.** *fig.* depravity; decadence
ver·rucht [fɛɐ'ruːxt] *adj.* wicked; *a.* foul, heinous *crime*; **Ver'rucht·heit** *f* (-; *no pl.*) wickedness; heinousness, foul nature (*gen.* of)
ver'rücken *v/t.* (h) move, shift
verrückt [fɛɐ'rʏkt] *adj.* mad; F *fig. a.* F crazy *fashion etc.*, *a.* F wild *plan etc.*; *fig.* ~ ***nach*** *dat.* (*or* ***auf*** *acc.*) wild about, F nuts on (*or* about); ~***e Idee*** F crazy idea; ***j-n*** ~ ***machen*** drive s.o. mad (F round the bend), get s.o. all confused; ***sich*** ~ ***machen*** get (o.s.) all worked up (F into a lather), F get into a tiz(zy); F ~ ***spielen*** F act up, go berserk; ***wie*** ~ like mad (F crazy); ***ich werd'*** ~! F well blow me!; ***da kann man ja*** ~ ***werden*** → ***Verrückt-werden***; **Ver'rück·te** *m*, *f* (-n; -n) lunatic; madman (*f* madwoman); maniac; **Ver'rückt·heit** *f* (-; -en) **1.** *no pl.* madness; **2.** craze; **3.** mad (F crazy) idea (*or* thing to do *etc.*); **Ver'rückt·wer·den** *n*: ***es ist zum*** ~ it's enough to drive you mad
Ver'ruf *m*: ***in*** ~ ***bringen*** (***kommen***) bring (fall) into disrepute; **ver'ru·fen** *adj.* disreputable; ~ ***sein*** *usu.* have a bad reputation (*or* name)
ver'rüh·ren *v/t.* (h) mix
ver'ru·ßen I. *v/i.* (sn) become (*or* get) sooty; **II.** *v/t.* (h) soot *s.th.* up, cover *s.th.* in soot
ver'rut·schen *v/i.* (sn) slip, get out of place
Vers [fɛrs] *m* (-es; -e ['fɛrzə]) verse (*a. bibl.*), line; ***et. in*** ~***e setzen*** put s.th. into verse; *fig.* ***er kann sich keinen*** ~ ***darauf machen*** he can't make head or tail of it
ver·sach·li·chen [fɛɐ'zaxlɪçən] *v/t.* (h) objectivize; depersonalize
ver·sacken [fɛɐ'zakən] (*sep.* -k·k-) F *v/i.* (sn) **1.** sink (***in*** *acc.* into); **2.** *fig.* F go to the dogs; **3.** *fig.* F get involved in a (big) booze-up, end up boozing (the night away)
ver'sa·gen (h) **I.** *v/i.* fail (*a. person etc.*); ⚙ *a.* break down; *engine*: stall; ***jämmerlich*** ~ fail miserably; ***die Beine versagten ihr*** (***den Dienst***) her legs gave way; ***s-e Stimme versagte*** his voice failed him, he lost his voice; ***sein Gedächtnis versagte*** his memory failed him (*or* let him down); **II.** *v/t.* refuse, deny; ***j-m et.*** ~ refuse (*or* deny) s.o. s.th.; ***j-m den Dienst*** ~ refuse to obey s.o.; ***sich et.*** ~ deny o.s. s.th., forgo s.th.; ***es blieb ihm versagt*** it was denied him, he was denied it, ***zu*** *inf.*: it was denied him to *inf.*, he was not to *inf.*; **Ver'sa·gen** *n* (-s; *no pl.*) failure; ***menschliches*** ~ human error, ✈ *a.* pilot error; **Ver·sa·ger** [fɛɐ'zaːgɐ] *m* (-s; -) failure; ~ ***im Beruf*** professional failure
Ver·sal [vɛr'zaːl] *m* (-s; -lien [-lĭən]), ~**buch·sta·be** *m* capital (letter), uppercase (letter); (***in***) ***Versalien!*** caps
ver'sal·zen *v/t.* (h) **1.** put too much salt in; **2.** F *fig.* spoil; ***j-m et.*** ~ spoil s.th. (*or* things) for s.o.; → ***Suppe***
ver'sam·meln (h) **I.** *v/t.* assemble (*a.* ⚔), gather; ***um sich*** ~ rally *people* round one; **II.** *v/refl.*: ***sich*** ~ assemble, meet; **Ver'samm·lung** *f* (-; -en) meeting, gathering; *parl.* ***gesetzgebende*** ~ legislative assembly
Ver'samm·lungs|frei·heit *f* freedom of assembly; ~**lo,kal** *n*, ~**raum** *m* meeting place; ~**recht** *n* right of assembly; ~**verbot** *n* ban on public assembly (*or* public gatherings)
Ver·sand [fɛɐ'zant] *m* (-[e]s; *no pl.*) **1.** dispatch; shipment; distribution; **2.** → ~**ab,tei·lung** *f* forwarding department; ≈**be·reit** *adj.* ready for dispatch (*or* sending); ~**beu·tel** *m* padded envelope
ver·san·den [fɛɐ'zandən] *v/i.* (sn) silt up; *fig.* peter out
ver'sand·fer·tig *adj.* ready for dispatch (*or* sending)
Ver'sand|ge·schäft *n*, ~**han·del** *m* mail-order business; ~**haus** *n* mail-order company; ~**haus·ka·ta,log** *m* mail-order catalog(ue); ~**ko·sten** *pl.* forwarding expenses; ~**pa,pie·re** *pl.* shipping documents; ~**schein** *m* shipping note
Ver'san·dung *f* (-; *no pl.*) silting(-up)
ver·sau·beu·teln [fɛɐ'zaʊbɔʏtəln] F *v/t.* (h) F a) mess up, b) go and lose
ver·sau·en [fɛɐ'zaʊən] F *v/t.* (h) **1.** mess up; **2.** *fig.* F mess up; ruin, wreck
ver·sau·ern [fɛɐ'zaʊɐn] F *v/i.* (sn) *person*: stagnate; vegetate
ver'sau·fen V *v/t.* (*irr.*, *no* -ge-, h, → ***saufen***) F guzzle (*or* booze) away
ver'säu·men *v/t.* (h) miss *bus, train, opportunity etc.*; neglect *duty*; miss (out on); ~ ***Sie nicht zu*** *inf.* be sure to *inf.*; ***da hast du nichts*** (***was***) ***versäumt!*** you didn't miss much (you really missed something there); ***versäumte Zeit nachholen*** make up for lost time
Ver·säum·nis [fɛɐ'zɔʏmnɪs] *n* (-ses; -se) omission, failure *to do s.th.*; neglect; ~**urteil** *n* ⚖ judg(e)ment by default
ver'scha·chern F *v/t.* (h) sell off, F flog
ver·schach·teln [fɛɐ'ʃaxtəln] *v/t.* (h) **1.** (*a.* ***ineinander*** ~) fit (*or* slot) into each other; **2.** *fig.* complicate, make *s.th.* complicated; **ver'schach·telt** *adj.* **1.** interlocking; **2.** *fig.* complicated, convoluted; ~***er Satz*** involved period
ver'schaf·fen *v/t.* (h) get (***j-m et.*** s.o. s.th.); *a.* find *s.o. a job, an apartment etc.*; ***sich Geld*** ~ get hold of some money; ***sich e-n Vorteil*** ~ gain an advantage; ***sich Respekt*** ~ gain *or* win (some) respect; ***j-m die Möglichkeit*** ~ ***zu*** *inf.* make it possible for s.o. to *inf.*; *iro.* ***was verschafft mir die Ehre?*** what have I done to deserve this hono(u)r?
ver·scha·len [fɛɐ'ʃaːlən] *v/t.* (h) board, panel; ⚠ shutter; **Ver'scha·lung** *f* (-; -en) boarding; casing; ⚠ form(s *pl.*)
ver·schämt [fɛɐ'ʃɛːmt] *adj.* bashful; coy; ~ ***tun*** act coy
ver·schan·deln [fɛɐ'ʃandəln] *v/t.* (h) disfigure; *a.* spoil *the view etc.*; ***es verschandelt den Platz*** (*or* ***die Aussicht*** *etc.*) it's an eyesore; **Ver'schan·de·lung** *f* (-; -en) disfigurement
ver·schan·zen [fɛɐ'ʃantsən] *v/refl.* (h): ***sich*** ~ entrench o.s.; *fig.* ***sich*** ~ ***hinter*** *dat.* entrench o.s. behind *s.th.*, use *s.th.* as a pretext; **Ver'schan·zung** *f* (-; -en) fortifications *pl.*
ver'schär·fen (h) **I.** *v/t.* tighten (up) *measures etc.*; aggravate *situation, tension etc.*; stiffen *sentence etc.*; ***das Tempo*** ~ *mot. etc.* speed up, *w.s.* step up the pace; **II.** *v/refl.*: ***sich*** ~ *situation*: become more critical, F hot up; *tension*: mount, increase; ✝ *recession etc.*: *a.* tighten its grip; **Ver'schär·fung** *f* (-; -en) tightening (up); aggravation *etc.*; → ***verschärfen***
ver'schar·ren *v/t.* (h) bury
ver'schät·zen *v/refl.* (h): ***sich*** ~ misjudge (***um*** *acc.* by), make a mistake; ***sich um ... verschätzt haben*** be out by ...
ver'schau·keln F *v/t.* (h) **1.** F take *s.o.* for a ride; **2.** leave *s.o.* in the lurch
ver'schei·den *v/i.* (*irr.*, *no* -ge-, sn, → ***scheiden***) pass away
ver·schei·ßern [fɛɐ'ʃaɪsɐn] *sl. v/t.* (h) F take the mickey out of *s.o.*; ***willst du mich*** ~? *a. sl.* are you trying to take the mick?
ver'schen·ken *v/t.* (h) give away
ver·scher·beln [fɛɐ'ʃɛrbəln] F *v/t.* (h) sell off cheap, F flog
ver'scher·zen *v/t.* (h): ***sich et.*** ~ forfeit, lose; throw away *opportunity etc.*; ***sich j-s Gunst*** ~ fall out of favo(u)r with s.o.;

du hast es dir mit ihm verscherzt you've spoilt your chances with him
ver'scheu·chen *v/t.* (h) scare off, chase away (*a. fig.*)
ver'scheu·ern F *v/t.* (h) sell off cheap, F flog
ver'schicken *v/t.* (h) dispatch, send, ship; **Ver'schickung** *f* (-; -en) dispatch(ing), sending; shipping
ver·schieb·bar [fɛɐ'ʃi:pba:ɐ] *adj.* adjustable
Ver·schie·be·bahn·hof [fɛɐ'ʃi:bə-] *m* shunting station, *Am.* switchyard
ver'schie·ben (*irr., no* -ge-, h, → ***schieben***) **I.** *v/t.* **1.** shift, move; **2.** put off, postpone (***auf*** *acc.* to, until, till); **3.** sell *s.th.* underhand; **II.** *v/refl.*: ***sich*** ~ **4.** move; slip; **5.** *meeting etc.*: be postponed (***auf*** *acc.* to, until, till); **Ver'schie·bung** *f* (-; -en) **1.** shift(ing), moving; displacement (*a.* ⚔); **2.** postponement (***auf*** *acc.* to, until, till)
ver·schie·den I. *p.p. of* ***verscheiden***; **II.** *adj.* different (***von*** *dat.* from); distinct (from); differing *opinions etc.*; varied; miscellaneous, various; ***Verschiedenes*** various things *pl.*, *esp.* ✝ sundries *pl.*; *heading*: miscellaneous, misc.; ***~er Meinung sein*** disagree (***über*** *acc.* on), differ in opinion (on), ***über et.***: *a.* see s.th. differently; ***das ist*** ~ it depends; ***das ist von Woche zu Woche*** *etc.* ~ that varies from week to week *etc.*; ***aus den ~sten Gründen*** for various (*or* a variety of) reasons; F ***da hört sich doch Verschiedenes auf!*** that really is going a bit too far
ver'schie·den·ar·tig *adj.* different (kinds of ...); various, a variety of ...; **Ver'schie·den·ar·tig·keit** *f* (-; *no pl.*) a) different nature, b) difference, c) variety, diversity
ver·schie·de·ner·lei [fɛɐ'ʃi:dənɐlaı] *adj.* of various kinds, *formal or iro.*: divers
ver'schie·den·far·big *adj.* of different colo(u)rs, *formal*: varicolo(u)red
Ver'schie·den·heit *f* (-; -en) a) dissimilarity, b) diversity, variety, c) difference
ver·schie·dent·lich [fɛɐ'ʃi:dəntlıç] **I.** *adv.* a) repeatedly, several times, b) occasionally; **II.** *adj.* several; repeated
ver'schie·ßen (*irr., no* -ge-, → ***schießen***) **I.** *v/t.* (h) **1.** shoot; ***s-e Munition*** ~ run out of ammunition; → ***Pulver, verschossen*** 2; **2.** *soccer*: miss; **II.** *v/i.* (sn) *colo(u)r*: fade; → ***verschossen*** 1
ver·schif·fen [fɛɐ'ʃıfən] *v/t.* (h) ✝ ship; **Ver'schif·fung** *f* (-; -en) shipment
ver'schim·meln *v/i.* (sn) go mo(u)ldy
Ver·schiß [fɛɐ'ʃıs] *sl. m*: ***in ~ sein*** F be in the doghouse (***bei*** *dat.* with), ***bei j-m***: *a.* be in s.o.'s bad books, *sl.* be on s.o.'s shit list; ***in ~ geraten*** fall out of favo(u)r, ***bei j-m***: get into s.o.'s bad books, *sl.* get onto s.o.'s shit list
ver'schla·fen¹ (*irr., no* -ge-, h, → ***schlafen***) **I.** *v/t.* sleep away *the day etc.*, *a. fig. one's problems etc.*; sleep through *a concert, storm etc.*; *fig.* miss *opportunity etc.*, (completely) forget *an appointment etc.*; ***ich habe es völlig*** ~ *a.* it slipped my mind completely; **II.** *v/i.* oversleep
ver'schla·fen² I. *p.p. of* ***verschlafen¹***; **II.** *adj.* sleepy (*a. fig. town etc.*), F dop(e)y; **Ver'schla·fen·heit** *f* (-; *no pl.*) drowsiness, sleepiness, F dopiness
Ver·schlag [fɛɐ'ʃla:k] *m* (-[e]s; ⸚e [fɛɐ'ʃlɛ:gə]) shed, *contp.* shack
ver'schla·gen¹ *v/t.* (*irr., no* -ge-, h, → ***schlagen***) **1.** nail up; ***mit Brettern*** ~ board up; **2.** mishit *ball*; **4.** ***die Buchseite*** ~ lose one's place; **4.** throw *s.o.* off course; ***~ nach*** *dat.* (*or* ***in*** *acc.*) bring to; ***~ werden nach*** *dat.* (*or* ***in*** *acc.*) end up in, F land in; **5.** ***j-m den Atem*** ~ take s.o.'s breath away; ***es verschlug ihm die Sprache*** he was (left) speechless
ver'schla·gen² I. *p.p. of* ***verschlagen¹***; **II.** *adj.* deceitful, dishonest; ***~er Blick*** (***Typ***) shifty look (character); **II.** *adv.*: ***j-n ~ ansehen*** give s.o. a shifty look; **Ver'schla·gen·heit** *f* (-; *no pl.*) deceitfulness, shiftiness
ver'schlam·pen F **I.** *v/t.* (h) mislay, F go and lose; ***ich hab's völlig verschlampt*** it completely slipped my mind, F I clean forgot (it); **II.** *v/i.* (sn) go to seed; **ver'schlampt** *adj.* slovenly, scruffy, F tatty; messy, *pred. a.* a mess
ver·schlech·tern [fɛɐ'ʃlɛçtɐn] (h) **I.** *v/t.* make worse; *a.* aggravate *situation*; **II.** *v/refl.*: ***sich*** ~ deteriorate, get worse; *performance, quality*: fall off; **Ver·schlech·te·rung** [fɛɐ'ʃlɛçtərʊŋ] *f* (-; -en) deterioration (*gen.* in, of); worsening (of); change for the worse
ver·schlei·ern [fɛɐ'ʃlaıɐn] (h) **I.** *v/t.* **1.** veil (*a. fig.*); **2.** *fig.* disguise; ✝ F doctor *the balance sheet*, cook *the books*; **II.** *v/refl.*: ***sich*** ~ **3.** put a veil on; **4.** *sky*: become hazy; **ver'schlei·ert** *adj.* **1.** veiled (*a. fig.*); **2.** husky *voice*; **3.** *phot.* fogged; **Ver·schleie·rung** [fɛɐ'ʃlaıərʊŋ] *f* (-; -en) **1.** *no pl.* veiling (*a. fig.*); **2.** *fig.* disguising; **Ver'schleie·rungs·tak·tik** *f* (-; *no pl.*) camouflage tactics *pl.*
ver'schlei·fen (*irr., no* -ge-, h, → ***schleifen***) **I.** *v/t.* **1.** ⚙ smooth (down *or* away); **2.** ♪ *and fig.* slur; **II.** *fig. v/refl.*: ***sich*** ~ *differences etc.*: be smoothed (down), disappear
ver·schleimt [fɛɐ'ʃlaımt] *adj.*: ***~ sein*** be blocked with phlegm, have a lot of phlegm; **Ver'schlei·mung** *f* (-; -en) mucous catarrh
Ver·schleiß [fɛɐ'ʃlaıs] *m* (-es; *no pl.*) a) wear and tear, b) consumption (***an*** *dat.* of), consumption rate; ✝ ***geplanter*** ~ built-in (*or* planned) obsolescence; ***e-n großen ~ haben an*** *dat.* get through a lot of *a. fig. girls etc.*; **ver·schlei·ßen** (verschliß, verschlissen) **I.** *v/t.* (h) a) wear out, b) use up, go through; **II.** *v/refl.*: ***sich*** ~ (h) a) wear out, b) wear (*or* burn) o.s. out; **III.** *v/i.* (sn) wear out
Ver'schleiß|er·schei·nung *f* sign of wear; ***⁲fest*** *adj.* wear-resistant; ***~fe·stig·keit*** *f* wear-resistance, resistance to wear and tear; ***~quo·te*** *f* replacement rate; ***~teil*** *n* wearing part
ver'schlep·pen *v/t.* (h) **1.** a) deport; kidnap, abduct *s.o.*, b) carry *s.th.* off; **2.** protract, delay; *parl.* obstruct, stonewall, *esp. Am.* filibuster; **3.** ⚕ transmit *virus etc.*; protract *illness*; ***verschleppte Grippe*** protracted flu; **Ver'schlep·pung** *f* (-; -en) **1.** deportment; kidnap(p)ing; **2.** protraction, delay; **Ver'schlep·pungs·tak·tik** *f* (-; *no pl.*) delaying tactics *pl.*; *parl.* obstructionism, stonewalling, *esp. Am.* filibustering
ver'schleu·dern *v/t.* (h) a) squander, b) ✝ sell off cheaply (F dirt cheap), F flog; dump
ver·schließ·bar [fɛɐ'ʃli:sba:ɐ] *adj.* lockable; **ver'schlie·ßen** (*irr., no* -ge-, h, → ***schließen***) **I.** *v/t.* a) shut, close, b) lock (up), *a.* put under lock and key; bolt; *fig.* ***die Augen*** (***Ohren***) ***~ vor*** *dat.* shut one's eyes (ears) to s.th.; ***sein Herz*** ~ shut (*or* harden) one's heart (***vor*** *dat.* to); **II.** *v/refl.*: ***sich*** ~ *dat.* close one's mind to *s.th.*; ***sich j-m*** ~ hide one's feelings from s.o.
ver·schlimm·bes·sern [fɛɐ'ʃlımbɛsɐn] *v/t.* (h) disimprove; ***et.*** ~ *a.* make an even worse job of it; **Ver'schlimm·bes·se·rung** *f* (-; -en) disimprovement
ver·schlim·mern [fɛɐ'ʃlımɐn] (h) **I.** *v/t.* make *s.th.* worse; *a.* aggravate *situation etc.*, exacerbate; **II.** *v/refl.*: ***sich*** ~ get worse, worsen; **Ver·schlim·me·rung** [fɛɐ'ʃlımərʊŋ] *f* (-; -en) deterioration; worsening; change for the worse
ver'schlin·gen (*irr., no* -ge-, h, → ***schlingen***) **I.** *v/t.* **1.** devour (*a. fig.*); gobble (up), bolt down; *fig.* swallow (up), gobble up *money etc.*; *fig.* ***von der Dunkelheit*** *etc.* ***verschlungen werden*** be engulfed by darkness *etc.*; **2.** intertwine; fold *hands*; **II.** *v/refl.*: ***sich*** ~ intertwine; become entangled; → ***verschlungen***; **Ver'schlin·gung** *f* (-; -en) entanglement; convolution
ver·schliß [fɛɐ'ʃlıs] *pret. of* ***verschleißen***
ver·schlis·sen [fɛɐ'ʃlısən] **I.** *p.p. of* ***verschleißen***; **II.** *adj.* worn, threadbare; F tatty
ver·schlos·sen [fɛɐ'ʃlɔsən] **I.** *p.p. of* ***verschließen***; **II.** *adj.* **1.** closed, shut; locked (up); ***hinter ~en Türen*** behind closed doors; **2.** *fig.* reserved, withdrawn; uncommunicative; ***er ist ziemlich ~*** *a.* he doesn't say much; **Ver'schlos·sen·heit** *f* (-; *no pl.*) reserve; uncommunicativeness
ver'schlucken (h) **I.** *v/t.* swallow (*a. fig.*); *fig. fog etc.*: engulf; **II.** *v/refl.*: ***sich*** ~ choke (***an*** *dat.* on)
ver·schlun·gen [fɛɐ'ʃlʊŋən] **I.** *p.p. of* ***verschlingen***; **II.** *adj.* a) winding *path etc.*; tortuous (*a. fig.*), b) intricate, *esp. contp.* convoluted
Ver·schluß [fɛɐ'ʃlʊs] *m* (-sses; Verschlüsse [fɛɐ'ʃlysə]) **1.** a) stopper, b) clasp; lock; fastener; ⚙ seal; ***unter ~ halten*** keep under lock and key (*customs*: in bond); **2.** *phot.* shutter; **3.** ⚕ occlusion
ver·schlüs·seln [fɛɐ'ʃlysəln] *v/t.* (h) encode, encrypt; **ver'schlüs·selt** *adj.* coded; **Ver'schlüs·se·lung** *f* (-; -en) encoding
Ver'schluß|kap·pe *f* (screw) cap; ***~laut*** *m ling.* plosive; ***~sa·che*** *f pol.* classified document; ***~zeit*** *f phot.* shutter speed
ver'schmach·ten *v/i.* (sn) languish, pine away; (***vor Durst***) ~ be dying of thirst
ver'schmä·hen *v/t.* (h) disdain, spurn; ***verschmähte Liebe*** unrequited love
ver·schmä·lern [fɛɐ'ʃmɛ:lɐn] *v/t. and v/refl.*: (***sich*** ~) (h) narrow; **Ver'schmä·le·rung** *f* (-; -en) narrowing
ver'schmel·zen *v/t.* (*irr., no* -ge-, h, → ***schmelzen***) *and v/i.* (sn) melt; fuse (*a. fig.*); ⚗ amalgamate; blend *colo(u)rs*; ✝, *pol.* merge; *fig.* amalgamate; **Ver'schmel·zung** *f* (-; -en) a) fusion; amalgamation; blend(ing); merging, b) ✝ merger
ver'schmer·zen *v/t.* (h) get over *s.th.*
ver'schmie·ren *v/t.* (h) smear; spread *dirt etc.*; smear up *paper etc.*; use up; ***verschmiert mit*** *dat. a.* covered in (*or* with)

ver·schmitzt [fɛɐ'ʃmɪtst] *adj.* arch, impish; **~es Augenzwinkern** twinkle in s.o.'s eye
ver'schmo·ren *v/t.* (h) *and v/i.* (sn) *gastr.*, ⚡ burn
ver·schmust [fɛɐ'ʃmuːst] F *adj.* cuddly; **~ sein** *usu.* like cuddling
ver'schmut·zen I. *v/t.* (h) dirty; pollute *air, water etc.*; **II.** *v/i.* (sn) get dirty; *air, water* become polluted; **Ver'schmut·zung** *f* (-; -en) **1.** *no pl.* soiling; **2.** dirt, mark; **3.** pollution; **Ver'schmut·zungs·grad** *m* (-[e]s; *no pl.*) pollution level
ver'schnau·fen F *v/refl.* (h): **sich ~** get one's breath back, F have a breather; **Ver'schnauf·pau·se** F *f* F breather
ver'schnei·den *v/t.* (*irr.*, *no* -ge-, h, → **schneiden**) **1.** cut, trim, clip; **2.** cut wrong, F make a mess of; **3.** *zo.* geld; **4.** blend
ver·schneit [fɛɐ'ʃnaɪt] *adj.* snow-covered ..., *pred.* covered in snow; *a.* snowy *day, landscape etc.*; snowed-in
Ver'schnitt *m* (-[e]s; -e) **1.** blend; **2.** scraps *pl.*
ver·schnör·kelt [fɛɐ'ʃnœrkəlt] *adj.* involuted; ornate; fancy *signature*; **Ver'schnör·ke·lung** *f* (-; -en) flourish; ⚠ *a.* curlicue
ver·schnul·zen [fɛɐ'ʃnʊltsən] F *v/t.* (h) sentimentalize
ver·schnupft [fɛɐ'ʃnʊpft] *adj.* **1.** blocked *nose*; **~ sein** have a cold, F have the sniffles; **2.** F *fig.* F miffed, *pred. a.* in a huff; **Ver'schnup·fung** *f* (-; -en) cold
ver'schnü·ren *v/t.* (h) tie up
ver·schol·len [fɛɐ'ʃɔlən] *adj.* a) missing, b) (long-)forgotten; **Ver'schol·le·ne** *m, f* (-n; -n) missing person
ver'scho·nen *v/t.* (h) spare (**j-n mit et.** s.o. s.th.); **verschont bleiben von** *dat.* be spared *s.th.*; **verschone mich mit ...!** spare me your ...!; **verschone mich!** spare me!, I don't want to know about it
ver'schö·nen *v/t.* (h) enhance
ver·schö·nern [fɛɐ'ʃøːnɐn] (h) **I.** *v/t.* **1.** make *s.th.* look nicer, improve the appearance of; embellish; **II.** *v/refl.*: **sich ~ 2.** improve in appearance, grow more beautiful; **3.** *esp. iro.* prettify o.s.; **Ver·schö·ne·rung** [fɛɐ'ʃøːnərʊŋ] *f* (-; -en) improvement (*gen.* in the appearance of); embellishment
Ver'scho·nung *f* (-; *no pl.*) sparing (*gen.* of)
ver·schos·sen [fɛɐ'ʃɔsən] **I.** *p.p. of* **verschießen**; **II.** *adj.* **1.** faded *colo(u)rs*; **2.** F *fig.* **~ sein in** *acc.* F be head over heels in love with, have fallen for, have a crush on
ver·schrän·ken [fɛɐ'ʃrɛŋkən] *v/t.* (h) **1. die Arme** (**Hände**) **~** fold one's arms (hands); **die Beine ~** cross one's legs; **2.** ⚙ cross, join crosswise; interlace
ver'schrau·ben *v/t.* (h) screw (on; **miteinander** together); **Ver'schrau·bung** *f* (-; -en) screws *pl.*
ver'schrecken *v/t.* (h) scare, frighten; **ver'schreckt** *adj.* timid, frightened
ver'schrei·ben (*irr.*, *no* -ge-, h, → **schreiben**) **I.** *v/t.* **1.** ✱ prescribe (**j-m** for s.o.); **sich et. ~ lassen** get a prescription for s.th.; **2.** ⚖ make over (**j-m** to s.o.); **3.** use up *paper etc.*; **II.** *v/refl.* **4. sich ~** make a mistake (in writing); **da habe ich mich wohl verschrieben** that must have been a slip of the pen; **5.** *fig.* **sich e-r Sache ~** devote (*contp.* sell) o.s. to s.th., espouse s.th.; **sich j-m ~** become a devotee of s.o.; **ver'schrei·bungs·pflich·tig** [-pflɪçtɪç] *adj.* prescribable, available on prescription only; **~e Arzneimittel** prescription(-only) drugs
ver'schrei·en *v/t.* (*irr.*, *no* -ge-, h, → **schreien**) **1.** denounce, F slam, trash; **2.** F **verschrei's nicht!** don't speak too soon, don't put the kiss of death on it
ver·schrien [fɛɐ'ʃriːn] **I.** *p.p. of* **verschreien**; **II.** *adj.* notorious; **~ sein** *a.* have a bad name *or* reputation (**als** as), **als Lügner**: *a.* be a notorious liar, be known as a liar (*or* for lying)
ver·schro·ben [fɛɐ'ʃroːbən] *adj.* eccentric, F (a bit) cranky; *a.* weird *ideas etc.*; **~er Mensch** F crank; **Ver'schro·ben·heit** *f* (-; -en) eccentricity
ver·schrot·ten [fɛɐ'ʃrɔtən] *v/t.* (h) scrap; **Ver'schrot·tung** *f* (-; -en) scrapping (*gen.* of)
ver'schrum·peln F *v/i.* (sn) shrivel (up)
ver·schüch·tert [fɛɐ'ʃʏçtɐt] *adj.* shy, intimidated
ver'schul·den (h) **I.** *v/t.* be to blame for; be responsible for; **II.** *v/refl.*: **sich ~** get (*or* run) into debt; **III.** ♀ *n* (-s; *no pl.*) fault; guilt; **durch j-s** (**eigenes**) **~** through s.o.'s (one's own) fault; **ohne mein ~** through no fault of mine; **ver'schul·det** *adj.* in debt; encumbered *property etc.*; **~ sein** *a.* have debts; **Ver'schul·dung** *f* (-; -en) indebtedness; debts *pl.*; encumbrance *of property etc.*
ver·schus·seln [fɛɐ'ʃʊsəln] F *v/t.* (h) a) (F clean) forget, b) (F go and) mislay, c) mess up; **ver'schus·selt** F *adj.* muddle-headed, scatterbrained, F scatty
ver'schüt·ten *v/t.* (h) **1.** spill; **2.** bury (*s.o.* alive)
ver·schütt·ge·hen [fɛɐ'ʃʏt-] F *v/i.* (*irr.*, *sep.*, sn, → **gehen**) disappear
ver·schwä·gert [fɛɐ'ʃvɛːgɐt] *adj.* related by marriage; **Ver·schwä·ge·rung** [fɛɐ'ʃvɛːgərʊŋ] *f* (-; -en) relationship by marriage
ver'schwei·gen *v/t.* (*irr.*, *no* -ge-, h, → **schweigen**) keep *s.th.* (a) secret, hide *s.th.* (**j-m** from s.o.); withhold *s.th.* (from s.o.)
ver'schwei·ßen *v/t.* (h) ⚙ weld together
ver·schwen·den [fɛɐ'ʃvɛndən] *v/t.* (h) waste, squander (**an** *acc.* on) (*both a. fig.*); **Ver·schwen·der** [fɛɐ'ʃvɛndɐ] *m* (-s; -) spendthrift, squanderer; **ver·schwen·de·risch** [fɛɐ'ʃvɛndərɪʃ] **I.** *adj.* a) wasteful, extravagant, *contp. a.* profligate, b) lavish; **~es Leben** extravagant lifestyle; **II.** *adv.*: **~ umgehen mit** *dat.* be lavish with *s.th.*; **Ver'schwen·dung** *f* (-; -en) waste; extravagance; **Ver'schwen·dungs·sucht** *f* (-; *no pl.*) wastefulness, extravagance; **ver'schwen·dungs·süch·tig** *adj.* wasteful, extravagant
ver·schwie·gen [fɛɐ'ʃviːgən] **I.** *p.p. of* **verschweigen**; **II.** *adj.* **1.** discreet; **2.** *fig.* secret, secluded; **~es Plätzchen** secluded spot; **Ver'schwie·gen·heit** *f* (-; *no pl.*) **1.** discretion; **unter dem Mantel der ~ liegen** be under wraps; → **Siegel**; **2.** *fig.* seclusion
ver'schwim·men *v/i.* (*irr.*, *no* -ge-, sn, → **schwimmen**) become blurred; merge; **vor den Augen ~** start blurring before one's eyes; → **verschwommen**
ver'schwin·den (*irr.*, *no* -ge-, sn, → **schwinden**) **I.** *v/i.* **1.** disappear, vanish (**in** *acc.* into); **mein Koffer** *etc.* **ist verschwunden** *a.* my case *etc.* has (*or* is) gone; **j-n** (**et.**) **spurlos ~ lassen** spirit s.o. (s.th.) away; F **et. ~ lassen** F walk off with s.th.; F *fig.* **ich muß mal ~** F I must just pay a visit; *fig.* **~ neben** *dat.* sink into insignificance beside, be dwarfed by; **2.** F make o.s. scarce, F do a bunk; **verschwinde!** F hop it!, scram!; **II.** ♀ *n* (-s; *no pl.*) disappearance; **ver'schwin·dend** *adv.*: **~ klein** microscopic, minuscule; **~ gering** infinitesimal
ver·schwi·stert [fɛɐ'ʃvɪstɐt] *adj.* **1. ~ sein** a) be brother and sister, b) be sisters, c) be brothers; **2.** *fig.* (**eng ~** closely) related (*esp.* ✝ associated); **Ver·schwi·ste·rung** [fɛɐ'ʃvɪstərʊŋ] *f* (-; -en) *fig.* (close) union *or* association
ver'schwit·zen *v/t.* (h) **1.** get *s.th.* soaked with sweat; **2.** F **ich habe es** (**total**) **verschwitzt** F I clean forgot (it); **ver'schwitzt** *adj.* sweaty; *a.* covered in sweat; **völlig ~** *a.* soaked through (*or* in sweat)
ver·schwol·len [fɛɐ'ʃvɔlən] *adj.* swollen; *a.* bloated *face*
ver·schwom·men [fɛɐ'ʃvɔmən] **I.** *p.p. of* **verschwimmen**; **II.** *adj.* **1.** hazy; *a. phot.* blurred; **2.** *fig.* vague, nebulous, woolly *ideas etc.*; dim, hazy *memory etc.*; **~e Vorstellung** hazy (*or* fuzzy) notion; **III.** *adv.*: **sich ~ an et.** (**j-n**) **erinnern können** have a dim (*or* hazy) recollection of s.th. (s.o.); **Ver'schwom·men·heit** *f* (-; *no pl.*) haziness; vagueness *etc.*; → **verschwommen** II
ver·schwo·ren [fɛɐ'ʃvoːrən] **I.** *p.p. of* **verschwören**; **II.** *adj.* sworn
ver'schwö·ren *v/refl.* (*irr.*, *no* -ge-, h, → **schwören**) **1. sich ~** conspire (*a. fig.*), plot (**gegen** *acc.* against; **zu** *inf.* to *inf.*); **sich zu et. ~** conspire to do s.th., plot (to do) s.th.; **2.** *obs. lit.* **sich e-r Sache** (**j-m**) **~** give o.s. over to s.th. (s.o.); **Ver'schwo·re·ne** *m, f* (-n; -n), **Ver·schwö·rer** [fɛɐ'ʃvøːrɐ] *m* (-s; -) conspirator; **Ver'schwö·rer·mie·ne** *f* look of complicity; conspiratorial air; **Ver'schwö·rung** *f* (-; -en) conspiracy, plot
ver'se·hen (*irr.*, *no* -ge-, h, → **sehen**) **I.** *v/t.* **1.** perform *duties etc.*; hold *office*; look after *household etc.*; **2. ~ mit** *dat.* a) supply with, *a.* ⚙ provide with, b) decorate with; **et. mit et. ~** *a.* add s.th. to s.th.; **j-n mit Vollmacht ~** authorize s.o.; **reichlich ~ sein mit** *dat.* have plenty of, have ample *food etc.*; **II.** *v/refl.* **3. sich ~** make a mistake, slip up; **4. ehe man sich's versieht** before you know it; **5. sich ~ mit** *dat.* equip o.s. with, get in a supply (*or* supplies) of, get (hold of); **Ver'se·hen** *n* (-s; -) oversight, mistake; **aus ~** → **ver·se·hent·lich** [fɛɐ'zeːəntlɪç] *adv.* by mistake, inadvertently, mistakenly
ver·sehrt [fɛɐ'zeːɐt] *adj.* disabled, handicapped; **Ver'sehr·te** *m, f* (-n; -n) disabled (*or* handicapped) person; *pl. coll. the* handicapped (*pl.*)
ver·selb·stän·di·gen [fɛɐ'zɛlpʃtɛndɪgən] *v/refl.* (h): **sich ~** a) go independent, b) break free; **Ver'selb·stän·di·gung** *f* (-; -en) a) process of independence, b) independence
ver'sen·den *v/t.* (*irr.*, *no* -ge-, h, → **senden**[1]) send, dispatch, ✝ *a.* ship; **Ver'sen·dung** *f* (-; -en) dispatch; shipment

ver'sen·gen *v/t.* (h) scorch; singe *hair*
ver·senk·bar [fɛɐ'zɛŋkba:ɐ] *adj.* lowerable *a. stage*; *a.* fold-down *table etc.*; retractable *antenna etc.*; **ver'sen·ken** (h) **I.** *v/t.* **1.** ⚓ sink; **2.** lower (***in*** *acc.* into *the ground etc.*); **3.** ⚙, *thea. etc.* lower; *a.* fold down *table etc.*; retract *antenna etc.*; countersink *screw*; **II.** *v/refl.*: ***sich ~ in*** *acc.* immerse o.s. in, become engrossed in *a book etc.*; **Ver'sen·kung** *f* (-; -en) **1.** sinking; **2.** *thea.* trapdoor; **3.** F *fig.* ***spurlos in der ~ verschwinden*** disappear (from the face of the earth), disappear (*or* fade) from the scene; (***wieder***) ***aus der ~ auftauchen*** resurface, reappear, *a.* reappear (*or* re-emerge) on the scene; **4.** *fig.* (inward) contemplation
ver·ses·sen [fɛɐ'zɛsən] *adj.*: **~ *auf*** *acc.* mad about, madly keen on; ***darauf ~ sein, et. zu tun*** be desperate to do s.th.; **Ver'ses·sen·heit** *f* (-; *no pl.*) craze (***auf*** *acc.* for), *a.* craving (for *candy etc.*)
ver'set·zen (h) **I.** *v/t.* **1.** a) shift, move (*a. ped.*); transfer, ⚔ post, b) ⚙ stagger, c) ⚘ transplant, d) ♪ transpose; **2.** pawn; **3.** F stand *s.o.* up; **4.** mix; **5.** ***j-m e-n Schlag ~*** deal s.o. a blow, hit out at s.o.; ***j-m e-n Tritt ~*** give s.o. a kick; **6.** retort; **7.** **~ *in*** *acc.* put *s.o.* into *a position, situation etc.*; ***j-n in e-e andere Zeit ~*** take (*or* transport) s.o. back in time (*or* back to another era); ***j-n an e-n anderen Ort ~*** transport s.o. (*or* carry s.o. off) to a different place; ***j-n in Erstaunen*** (***Verwirrung*** *etc.*) **~** astonish (confuse *etc.*) s.o.; → ***Angst*** I, ***Bewegung*** 1, ***eins*** 4, ***Ruhestand, Schwingung***; **II.** *v/refl.*: ***sich*** (***geistig***) ***nach X ~*** imagine one is in X; ***sich in j-n*** (*or* ***j-s Lage***) **~** put o.s. in s.o.'s place (*or* position, shoes); ***versuch doch mal, dich in ihre Lage zu ~*** *a.* try and see it from her standpoint (*or* point of view, side); **Ver'set·zung** *f* (-; -en) shifting; transfer, posting *etc.*; → ***versetzen***; **Ver'set·zungs·zei·chen** *n* ♪ accidental
ver·seu·chen [fɛɐ'zɔyçən] *v/t.* (h) **1.** contaminate; **2.** ⚕ infect; **Ver'seu·chung** *f* (-; -en) **1.** contamination; **2.** infection
'Vers|form *f* verse form; ***in ~ schreiben*** write in verse (form); **~fuß** *m* (metrical) foot
ver·si·cher·bar [fɛɐ'zɪçɐba:ɐ] *adj.* insurable; **Ver·si·che·rer** [fɛɐ'zɪçərɐ] *m* (-s; -) insurer; **ver'si·chern** *v/t.* (h) **1.** insure (***gegen*** *acc.* against; ***bei*** *dat.* with); **2.** ***j-m et.* ~** assure s.o. (of) s.th.; ***j-m ~, daß*** assure s.o. (that); ***seien Sie versichert, daß*** you may rest assured that, I can assure you that; ***seien Sie dessen versichert*** you can depend on it; ***sich ~*** *gen.* make sure (*or* certain) of *s.th.*; **ver'sichert** *adj.* insured, covered by insurance; ***zu hoch*** (***niedrig***) **~** overinsured (underinsured); **Ver·si·cher·te** [fɛɐ'zɪçɐtə] *m, f* (-n; -n) insured (party); policy holder; **Ver'si·che·rung** *f* (-; -en) **1.** insurance (***über*** *acc.* for, on); ***e-e ~ abschließen*** take out insurance (*or* an insurance policy) (***bei*** *dat.* with); **2.** assurance, guarantee
Ver'si·che·rungs|agent *m* insurance agent; **~agen,tur** *f* insurance agency; **~an·ge·stell·te** *m, f* (-n; -n) insurance clerk; **~an·spruch** *m* insurance claim; **~an·stalt** *f* insurance company; **~bei·trag** *m* (insurance) premium; **~be·trug** *m* insurance fraud; **~dau·er** *f* period of insurance; **~fall** *m* insured event; ***im ~, bei Eintritt des ~s*** should the event insured against occur; **~ge·sell·schaft** *f* insurance company; **~ma·the·ma,tik** *f* actuarial theory; **~ma·the,ma·ti·ker** *m* actuary
Ver'si·che·rungs·neh·mer [-ne:mɐ] *m* (-s; -) insured (party); policy holder
Ver'si·che·rungs·pflicht *f* compulsory insurance; **~gren·ze** *f* taxable wage base
ver'si·che·rungs·pflich·tig [-pflɪçtɪç] *adj.* a) subject to compulsory insurance, b) *person* liable to insurance
Ver'si·che·rungs|po,li·ce *f* (insurance) policy; **~prä·mie** *f* (insurance) premium; **~ri·si·ko** *n* insured risk; **~schein** *m* insurance policy; **~schutz** *m* insurance cover(age); **~schwin·del** *m* insurance fraud; **~sum·me** *f* sum insured; **~trä·ger** *m* underwriter; insurer; **~ver·trag** *m* contract of insurance; **~ver·tre·ter** *m* insurance agent; **~wert** *m* insurable value; **~we·sen** *n* (-s; *no pl.*) insurance (business)
ver'sickern *v/i.* (sn) **1.** seep (away) (***im Sand*** into the sand); **2.** *fig.* fizzle out
ver'sie·ben F *v/t.* (h) **1.** (F clean) forget; ***ich hab's versiebt*** *a.* it slipped my mind completely; **2.** F botch (up)
ver'sie·geln *v/t.* (h) *a.* ⚙ seal
ver'sie·gen *v/i.* (sn) dry up (*a. fig. funds, conversation etc.*); *fig. strength*: ebb, dwindle
ver·siert [vɛr'zi:ɐt] *adj.* experienced; skilled; well-versed (***auf dem Gebiet*** *gen.* in)
ver'sil·bern *v/t.* (h) **1.** ⚙ silver-plate; **2.** F *fig.* turn into cash; **Ver·sil·be·rung** [fɛr'zɪlbərʊŋ] *f* (-; -en) silver-plate, silver-plating
ver'sin·ken *v/i.* (*irr.*, *no* -ge-, sn, → ***sinken***) sink (*a. fig.*) (***in*** *acc.* into); *fig.* **~ *in*** *acc.* lose o.s. in *memories etc.*, *a.* become immersed (*or* absorbed) in *thoughts etc.*; → ***Boden*** 1, ***versunken***
ver·sinn·bild·li·chen [fɛɐ'zɪnbɪltlɪçən] *v/t.* (h) symbolize, represent; **Ver'sinn·bild·li·chung** *f* (-; -en) symbol
Ver·si·on [vɛr'zio:n] *f* (-; -en) version
ver·sippt [fɛɐ'zɪpt] *adj.* (inter)related, related with one another (*or* to each other)
ver·skla·ven [fɛɐ'skla:vən] *v/t.* (h) enslave; **Ver'skla·vung** *f* (-; -en) enslavement
ver·slu·men [fɛɐ'slamən] *v/i.* (sn) turn into a slum (*or* slums); **Ver'slu·mung** *f* (-; -en) urban decay
'Vers·maß *n* metre, *Am.* meter
ver·snobt [fɛɐ'snɔpt] *adj.* snobbish, F snobby
ver·sof·fen [fɛɐ'zɔfən] V *adj.* F boozy *voice etc.*; drunk(en ...); **~er Typ** F dipso
ver·soh·len [fɛɐ'zo:lən] F *fig. v/t.* (h) (*a. **j-m den Hintern** ~*) give *s.o.* a good thrashing
ver·söh·nen [fɛɐ'zø:nən] (h) **I.** *v/t.* reconcile (***mit*** *dat.* with *s.o. or* to *s.th.*); **II.** *v/refl.*: ***sich ~*** be reconciled, *a.* make it up (***mit*** *dat.* with *s.o.*); **ver·söhn·lich** [fɛɐ'zø:nlɪç] *adj.* conciliatory; **~ *stimmen*** placate; **Ver'söhn·lich·keit** *f* (-; *no pl.*) conciliatoriness; **Ver'söh·nung** *f* (-; -en) reconciliation; **Ver'söh·nungs·an·ge·bot** *n* offer of conciliation
ver·son·nen [fɛɐ'zɔnən] *adj.* pensive; lost in thought; dreamy; **Ver'son·nen·heit** *f* (-; *no pl.*) pensiveness; dreaminess
ver'sor·gen *v/t.* (h) a) provide, supply (***mit*** *dat.* with); provide for, support *family etc.*, b) take care of, look after; tend *cattle*, c) ⚕ tend, see to *a wound etc.*; ***gut versorgt*** a) well looked after, b) well provided for; **Ver·sor·ger** [fɛɐ'zɔrgɐ] *m* (-s; -) **1.** breadwinner; *esp. iro.* provider; **2.** supplier; **Ver'sor·gung** *f* (-; *no pl.*) providing (*gen.* of), supplying (*s.th., s.o.*); supply, provision; care; tending; → ***versorgen***; ***ärztliche ~*** medical care
Ver'sor·gungs|an·spruch *m* claim to maintenance; **2be·rech·tigt** *adj.* entitled to maintenance; **~be·rech·ti·gung** *f* right to maintenance; **~be·trieb** *m* (public) utility company; **~eng·paß** *m* supply bottleneck (*or* shortage); **~flug·zeug** *n* supply plane; **~ge·biet** *n* service area; **~gü·ter** *pl.* supplies; **~in·sel** *f* accommodation rig; **~la·ge** *f* supply situation; **~netz** *n* supply network; **~schiff** *n* supply vessel; **~schwie·rig·kei·ten** *pl.* supply problems, problems in getting supplies through; supply bottleneck *sg.*; **~weg** *m* supply line (*or* channel); **~wirt·schaft** *f* (public) utilities *pl.*
ver'spach·teln *v/t.* fill *holes, cracks etc.*; fill in the cracks in *the wall*
ver'span·nen (h) **I.** *v/t.* **1.** ⚙ stay, guy; wire; **2.** ⚕, *psych.* tense (up); **II.** *v/refl.*: ***sich ~*** ⚕, *psych.* get tensed up, tense up; **ver'spannt** *adj.* ⚕, *psych.* tense, tensed up; **Ver'span·nung** *f* (-; -en) **1.** ⚕ tenseness, *psych. a.* tension; **2.** ⚙ stays *pl.*, guys *pl.*
ver·spä·ten [fɛɐ'ʃpɛ:tən] *v/refl.*: ***sich ~*** (h) be late; **ver'spä·tet** *adj.* late; belated *good wishes etc.*; **Ver'spä·tung** *f* (-; -en) delay; (***zwei Minuten***) **~ *haben*** be (two minutes) late; ***mit ~ abfahren*** (***ankommen*** *etc.*) leave (arrive *etc.*) late; ***mit zwei Stunden ~*** two hours late (✈ *etc. a.* behind schedule); ***entschuldigen Sie die ~*** sorry I'm late, *formal*: I do apologize for being late
ver'spei·sen *v/t.* (h) eat, consume
ver·spe·ku'lie·ren (h) **I.** *v/t.* **1.** lose on the stock market; **II.** *v/refl.*: ***sich ~*** **2.** miscalculate; **3.** ✝ lose (all one's money) on the stock market
ver'sper·ren (h) **I.** *v/t.* **1.** bar, obstruct; barricade; ***j-m die Aussicht ~*** obstruct s.o.'s view; **2.** lock up; **II.** *fig. v/refl.*: ***sich ~*** close one's mind (*dat.* to)
ver'spie·geln *v/t.* (h) line (*or* face) with mirrors; **ver'spie·gelt** *adj.* mirrored
ver'spie·len (h) **I.** *v/t.* gamble away *one's money etc.*, *a. fig. one's happiness etc.*; spend *the day etc.* gambling; **II.** *v/i.* lose; ***er hat bei mir verspielt*** F I'm through with him, he's had his chips with me; **III.** *v/refl.*: ***sich ~*** play wrong, hit a (*or* the) wrong note; **ver'spielt** *adj.* playful; **Ver'spielt·heit** *f* (-; *no pl.*) playfulness
ver·spie·ßern [fɛɐ'ʃpi:sɐn] *contp. v/i.* (sn) become gentrified, gentrify; **Ver·spie·ße·rung** [fɛɐ'ʃpi:sərʊŋ] *contp. f* (-; *no pl.*) gentrification
ver·spon·nen [fɛɐ'ʃpɔnən] *adj.* airy-fairy; (*a. **in sich** ~*) wrapped up in a world of one's own; strange, fanciful *idea etc.*; **~ *in*** *acc.* wrapped up in, totally absorbed in; **~ *sein*** *a.* have one's head in the clouds
ver'spot·ten *v/t.* (h) mock; jeer at, scoff at; **Ver'spot·tung** *f* (-; -en) mocking, mockery, derision
ver'spre·chen (*irr.*, *no* -ge-, h, → ***sprechen***) **I.** *v/t.* **1.** promise; ***du hast es mir***

versprochen you promised (to do it), you promised me it (*or* to give it to me); ***er hat mir versprochen, daß er kommen würde*** he promised to come (*or* that he would come); **2.** ***sich et.*** ~ expect s.th., hope for s.th.; ***sich viel*** ~ ***von*** *dat.* have great hopes of; ***ich verspreche mir wenig*** (***nichts***) ***davon*** I don't expect much (anything) to come of it, I don't think much (anything) will come of it; ***er verspricht ein guter Schauspieler zu werden*** he promises to be a good actor; **II.** *v/refl.*: ***sich*** ~ make a mistake, get it wrong; ***ich habe mich*** (***er hat sich*** *etc.*) ***versprochen*** *a.* it was a slip of the tongue; ***sich dauernd*** ~ keep getting one's words muddled; **Ver'spre·chen** *n* (-s; -) promise; ***j-m ein*** ~ ***abnehmen*** make s.o. promise s.th.; **Ver'spre·cher** F *m* (-s; -) slip of the tongue; ***Freudscher*** ~ Freudian slip; **Ver'spre·chung** *f* (-; -en) promise; ***große*** ~***en machen*** make great promises, promise the earth; ***alles*** (***nur***) ~***en!*** promises, promises!

ver'spren·gen *v/t.* (h) **1.** scatter, disperse; chase away; **2.** spray, sprinkle; **ver'sprengt** *adj.* scattered

ver'sprit·zen *v/t.* (h) squirt; spray

ver·spro·che·ner·ma·ßen [fɛɐ'ʃprɔxənɐ'maːsən] *adv.* as promised

ver'sprü·hen *v/t.* (h) spray

ver'spü·ren *v/t.* (h) feel; sense; ***keine Lust*** ~ ***zu*** *inf.* not to feel like *ger.*

'Vers·schmied F *m* versifier

ver·staat·li·chen [fɛɐ'ʃtaːtlɪçən] *v/t.* (h) nationalize; **Ver'staat·li·chung** *f* (-; -en) nationalization

ver·städ·tern [fɛɐ'ʃtɛːtɐn] **I.** *v/t.* (h) urbanize; **II.** *v/i.* (sn) become urbanized; **Ver·städ·te·rung** [fɛɐ'ʃtɛːtərʊŋ] *f* (-; *no pl.*) urbanization

Ver·stand [fɛɐ'ʃtant] *m* (-[e]s; *no pl.*) intellect, mind; (common) sense; (powers *pl.* of) reason; intelligence; powers *pl.* of judg(e)ment; understanding; ***gesunder*** ~ common sense; ***mein*** ~ ***sagt mir*** common sense tells me; ***klarer*** (***kühler***) ~ *a* clear (cool) head; ***scharfer*** ~ keen mind (*or* intellect); ***mit*** ~ intelligently, with a bit of common sense; ***den*** ~ ***verlieren*** go mad; ***j-n um den*** ~ ***bringen*** drive s.o. mad (*or* insane); ***wieder zu*** ~ ***kommen*** come to one's senses; ***das geht über m-n*** ~ that's beyond me; ***hat er denn keinen*** ~***?*** has he got no sense in him (*or* wits about him)?; ***er ist nicht recht bei*** ~ F he's not in his right mind, F he's not all there; ***et. mit*** ~ ***genießen*** savo(u)r s.th.

Ver·stan·des·kraft [fɛɐ'ʃtandəs-] *f* mental powers (*or* faculties) *pl.*, intelligence

ver'stan·des·mä·ßig *adj.* rational

Ver'stan·des|mensch *m* rational type (of person), rationalist; ~**schär·fe** *f* acumen

ver·stän·dig [fɛɐ'ʃtɛndɪç] *adj.* reasonable, sensible; understanding

ver·stän·di·gen [fɛɐ'ʃtɛndɪgən] (h) **I.** *v/t.* inform, let *s.o.* know; **II.** *v/refl.*: ***sich*** ~ communicate (with one another); ***sich mit j-m*** ~ a) make o.s. understood to s.o., communicate with s.o., get across to s.o., b) come to (*or* reach) an agreement with s.o.; ***wir konnten uns nicht*** ~ a) we couldn't communicate, we couldn't get through to each other (*or* understand what we were saying to each other), b) we couldn't agree (on anything), we couldn't come to (*or* reach) an agreement

Ver'stän·dig·keit *f* (-; *no pl.*) reasonableness

Ver'stän·di·gung *f* (-; *no pl.*) **1.** *a. teleph. etc.* communication; **2.** understanding, agreement; **3.** notification; **ver'stän·di·gungs·be·reit** *adj.* open to discussion

Ver'stän·di·gungs|schwie·rig·kei·ten *pl.* communication problems (*or* breakdown *sg.*); ~ ***haben*** have difficulty communicating (*or* getting through to one another); ~**ver·such** *m* attempt at communication (*or* to communicate)

ver·ständ·lich [fɛɐ'ʃtɛntlɪç] *adj.* a) intelligible, understandable; clear, distinct; audible, b) *fig.* understandable (*dat.* to, for); comprehensible (to); ***es ist mir schwer*** (***nicht***) ~ I find it hard (impossible) to understand (*or* grasp); ***es ist mir*** ~ I can understand it; ***schwer*** ~ difficult, complicated; ***j-m et.*** ~ ***machen*** make s.th. clear to s.o.; ***sich*** ~ ***machen*** make o.s. understood (***j-m*** to s.o.), make o.s. heard; **ver·ständ·li·cher·wei·se** [fɛɐ'ʃtɛntlɪçɐ'vaɪzə] *adv.* understandably; **Ver'ständ·lich·keit** *f* (-; *no pl.*) intelligibility; audibility; comprehensibility

Ver·ständ·nis [fɛɐ'ʃtɛntnɪs] *n* (-ses; *no pl.*) understanding (***für*** *acc.* for); appreciation (of); ***nach m-m*** ~ as I see it; ***dafür habe ich*** (***volles***) ~ I can (fully) understand that; ***für solche Leute habe ich kein*** ~ I have no time for people like that; ***dafür fehlt mir jedes*** ~ I just can't understand that; ***j-m*** ~ ***entgegenbringen*** show some understanding for s.o.; ***um*** ~ ***werben*** ask for some understanding, ***bei j-m***: ask s.o. to (try and) understand; ***wir bitten um*** ~ we hope you'll understand, we do apologize, we apologize for any inconvenience caused

ver'ständ·nis·los *adj.* **1.** uncomprehending; ~***er Ausdruck*** blank look, look of incomprehension; **2.** lacking in understanding, unsympathetic (***gegenüber*** towards); ***j-s Problemen*** *etc.* ~ ***gegenüberstehen*** *a.* have no understanding for s.o.'s problems *etc.*; **3.** *art*: lacking in appreciation (***gegenüber*** for); ***e-m Bild*** *etc.* ~ ***gegenüberstehen*** have no appreciation for a painting *etc.*; **Ver'ständ·nis·lo·sig·keit** *f* (-; *no pl.*) **1.** incomprehension; **2.** lack of understanding (***gegenüber*** towards, for); **3.** *art*: lack of appreciation (***gegenüber*** for *a painting etc.*)

ver'ständ·nis·voll *adj.* understanding; sympathetic(ally *adv.*); knowing *look*

ver'stän·kern F *v/t.* (h) F stink up

ver'stär·ken (h) **I.** *v/t.* strengthen; ⚙, ⚔ reinforce; ⚡ boost; *radio, hi-fi*, ♪ amplify; *fig.* increase, boost; add to *an impression etc.*; **II.** *v/refl.*: ***sich*** ~ increase; *suspicion etc.*: grow

Ver·stär·ker [fɛɐ'ʃtɛrkɐ] *m* (-s; -) *hi-fi*, ♪ amplifier; ⚡, *mot.* booster; *opt.*, *phot.* intensifier; ~**an·la·ge** *f* amplifying system (*or* equipment)

ver'stärkt I. *adj.* ⚙ reinforced; *fig.* increased; ***in*** ~***em Maße*** → **II.** *adv.* increasingly; even more; **Ver'stär·kung** *f* (-; -en) **1.** *no pl.* strengthening; ⚙ reinforcement; *hi-fi*, ♪ amplification; ⚡ boosting; *fig.* increase; **2.** *a. pl.* ⚔ *etc.* reinforcements *pl.*

ver'stau·ben *v/i.* (sn) get dusty, gather dust; **ver·staubt** [fɛɐ'ʃtaupt] *adj.* **1.** dusty; ***völlig*** ~ covered in dust; **2.** *fig.* antiquated, F ancient *ideas etc.*

ver'stau·chen *v/t.* (h) sprain; ***sich den Fuß*** ~ sprain one's ankle; **Ver'stau·chung** *f* (-; -en) sprain

ver'stau·en *v/t.* (h) stow away

Ver·steck [fɛɐ'ʃtɛk] *n* (-[e]s; -e) hiding place; *b.s. a.* hideout; ~ ***spielen*** play hide-and-seek; **ver'stecken** (h) **I.** *v/t.* hide (***vor*** *dat.* from), *formal*: conceal (from); **II.** *v/refl.*: ***sich*** ~ hide (***vor*** *dat.* from); ***die Schlüssel*** *etc.* ***hatten sich unter den Zeitungen versteckt*** the keys *etc.* were hidden among the newspapers; F *fig.* ***sich*** ~ ***müssen vor*** (*or* ***neben*** *dat.*) be no match for *s.o.*, not to come up to (*or* come anywhere near) *s.th.*; **Ver'stecken** *n* (-s; *no pl.*), **Ver'steck·spiel** *n* hide-and-seek; *fig.* game of hide-and-seek; **ver'steckt** *adj.* hidden; *fig. a.* veiled *threats etc.*; ***sich*** ~ ***halten*** hide (***vor*** *dat.* from), be (*or* remain) in hiding; ~ ***in*** *dat.* hidden (away) in

ver'ste·hen (*irr.*, *no* -ge-, h, → ***stehen***) **I.** *v/t. and v/i.* a) understand; see, b) know *English, French etc.*, c) interpret, take, d) hear; ***falsch*** ~ misunderstand, get *s.th. or s.o.* wrong, *fig. a.* take *s.th.* in bad part; ***es*** ~ ***zu*** *inf.* know how to *inf.*; ~ ***Sie mich recht!*** don't get me wrong; ***wenn ich*** (***Sie***) ***recht verstehe*** if I've understood (you) correctly (if I get you right); ***verstehe ich recht?*** did I hear right?; ***ich verstehe kein einziges Wort*** I can't understand a word *or* thing (you're *etc.* saying); ***j-m zu*** ~ ***geben, daß*** give s.o. to understand that; ***wollen Sie mir damit zu*** ~ ***geben, daß ...?*** am I to understand (from this) that ...?; ~ ***Sie?*** do you see (what I mean)?; ***ich verstehe!*** I see, I understand; ***ich verstehe vollkommen*** I fully understand, I understand perfectly; ***verstanden?*** (do you) understand?; ***haben Sie mich verstanden?*** do you read me?; ***hab' schon verstanden!*** F okay, I get it, point taken; ***was*** ~ ***Sie unter*** *dat.* ***...?*** what do you understand (*or* mean) by ...?; ***das ist nicht wörtlich zu*** ~ that's not meant (*or* not to be taken) literally; ***wie soll ich das*** ~***?*** how am I supposed to take that?, what are you getting at?; ***das ist als Spaß*** (***Drohung*** *etc.*) ***zu*** ~ that's meant to be (*or* meant as) a joke (threat *etc.*); ***er versteht etwas davon*** he knows a thing or two about it; ***er versteht gar nichts davon*** he doesn't know the first thing about it; ***was verstehst du schon davon?*** what do you know about it?; ***er versteht es, mit Kindern umzugehen*** he has a way with children; ~ ***Sie mich?*** *radio*: do you read me?; **II.** *v/refl.*: ***sich*** ~ understand each other; ***sich gut*** ~ get on well (with each other), ***mit*** *dat.*: get on (well) with; ***sich*** ~ ***auf*** *acc.* know (how to do), (*a.* ***sich gut*** ~ ***auf*** *acc.*) be good at, be a dab hand at, have a way with *animals, children etc.*; ***sich*** ~ ***als*** see o.s. as; ***als was versteht er sich?*** what does he see himself as?; ***das versteht sich*** (***doch***) ***von selbst*** that goes without saying

ver'stei·fen *v/refl.*: ***sich*** ~ (h) **1.** ⚕ stiffen; **2.** *fig.* harden, *positions*: *a.* become entrenched; ✝ tighten; ***sich*** ~ ***auf*** *acc.* become set on (doing) *s.th.*; ***er hat sich darauf versteift*** he's sticking to it(, no matter what anyone says); **Ver'stei-**

fung *f* (-; -en) **1.** ⚕ stiffening; **2.** *fig.* hardening; *a.* entrenchment *of positions*

ver'stei·gen *v/refl.* (*irr., no* -ge-, h, → ***steigen***): ***sich zu der Behauptung ~, daß*** go so far as to claim that

Ver·stei·ge·rer [fɛɐ'ʃtaɪgərɐ] *m* (-s; -) auctioneer; **ver'stei·gern** *v/t.* (h) auction (off); **Ver'stei·ge·rung** *f* (-; -en) **1.** auction; **2.** auctioning

ver'stei·nern *v/i.* (sn) **1.** fossilize; *wood*: petrify; **2.** *fig.* freeze, turn to stone (*a.* ***sich ~***); **ver'stei·nert** *adj.* **1.** fossilized; petrified *wood*; **2.** *fig.* petrified; stony *face*; ***wie ~ dastehen*** be thunderstruck, stand rooted to the spot; ***mit ~em Gesicht*** stony-faced; **Ver·stei·ne·rung** [fɛɐ'ʃtaɪnərʊŋ] *f* (-; -en) a) fossilization; petrifaction *of wood*, b) fossil

ver·stell·bar [fɛɐ'ʃtɛlba:ɐ] *adj.* adjustable; ***Sitz mit ~er Rückenlehne*** reclining seat; **ver'stel·len** (h) **I.** *v/t.* **1.** a) ⚙ shift *lever etc.*; adjust, b) move *furniture etc.*; **2.** block, obstruct *passage, exit etc.*; **3.** disguise *voice, handwriting etc.*; **II.** *fig. v/refl.*: ***sich ~*** pretend, put on an act; dissemble; ***er kann sich gut ~*** he's a good actor; **Ver'stel·lung** *f* (-; -en) **1.** ⚙ shifting; adjustment; **2.** obstruction, blocking; **3.** *fig.* preten|ce (*Am.* -se); (play-)acting, dissimulation; *fig.* ***das ist reine ~*** *a.* it's just one big act

Ver'stel·lungs|kunst *f* (play-)acting; **~künst·ler** *m* (play-)actor

ver'ster·ben *v/i.* (*irr., no* -ge-, sn, → ***sterben***) pass away

ver·steu·er·bar [fɛɐ'ʃtɔʏɐba:ɐ] *adj.* taxable; **ver·steu·ern** [fɛɐ'ʃtɔʏɐn] *v/t.* (h) pay tax on; ***zu versteuernde Einkünfte*** taxable income; **ver'steu·ert** *adj.* tax-paid; *profits etc.* after tax; **Ver·steue·rung** [fɛɐ'ʃtɔʏərʊŋ] *f* (-; -en) payment of tax (*gen.* on)

ver·stie·gen I. *p.p. of* ***versteigen***; **II.** *fig. adj.* eccentric; *a.* high-flown *idea etc.*

ver'stim·men *v/t.* (h) **1.** ♪ put *s.th.* out of tune; **2.** *fig.* put *s.o.* in a bad mood; annoy; **ver'stimmt** *adj.* **1.** ♪ out-of-tune ..., *pred.* out of tune; **2.** *pred.* in a bad mood; annoyed, disgruntled; **3.** ⚕ upset *stomach*; **Ver'stim·mung** *f* (-; -en) **1.** disgruntlement; **2.** ⚕ upset; ***e-e ~*** *a.* slight indigestion

ver·stockt [fɛɐ'ʃtɔkt] *adj.* stubborn, obdurate; impenitent *sinner*; **Ver'stockt·heit** *f* (-; *no pl.*) stubbornness, obduracy; impenitence

ver·stoh·len [fɛɐ'ʃto:lən] **I.** *adj.* furtive (*a. look*), surreptitious; **II.** *adv.* furtively, surreptitiously; ***~ anblicken*** steal (*or* sneak) a glance at, throw a furtive glance at

ver'stop·fen *v/t.* (h) block (up); *a.* clog up *pipes, drains etc.*; congest *streets*; **ver'stopft** *adj.* **1.** blocked (up), *a.* F bunged up *nose*; *a.* clogged up *pipes, drains etc.*; congested, clogged *streets*; **2.** ⚕ constipated; **Ver'stop·fung** *f* (-; -en) **1.** blockage, obstruction; **2.** ⚕ constipation; ***~ haben*** be constipated

ver·stor·ben [fɛɐ'ʃtɔrbən] **I.** *p.p. of* ***versterben***; **II.** *adj.* late, deceased; **Ver'stor·be·ne** *m, f* (-n; -n) *the* deceased; ***die ~n*** the dead (*pl.*)

ver·stört [fɛɐ'ʃtø:ɐt] *adj.* distraught; *a.* wild *look, behavio(u)r etc.*; ***e-n ~en Eindruck machen*** look (rather) distraught; **Ver'stört·heit** *f* (-; *no pl.*) distraught state

Ver·stoß [fɛɐ'ʃto:s] *m* (-es; Verstöße [fɛɐ'ʃtø:sə]) offen|ce (*Am.* -se) (***gegen*** *acc.* against); *a.* violation (of); **ver'sto·ßen** (*irr., no* -ge-, h, → ***stoßen***) **I.** *v/t.* expel (***aus*** *dat.* from), cast out (of); disown, repudiate *child, wife etc.*; **II.** *v/i.*: ***~ gegen*** *acc.* offend against; violate, infringe *law etc.*; ***gegen die Regeln*** (***das Gesetz*** *etc.*) ***~*** *a.* be against (*or* in breach of) the rules (the law *etc.*); **Ver'sto·ße·ne** *m, f* (-n; -n) outcast; **Ver'sto·ßung** *f* (-; -en) expulsion; repudiation *of wife, child etc.*

ver'strah·len *v/t.* (h) **1.** contaminate (with radioactivity); **2.** *fig.* radiate; **ver'strahlt** *adj.* (radioactively) contaminated; **Ver'strah·lung** *f* (-; -en) **1.** (radioactive) contamination; **2.** *fig.* radiation

ver·stre·ben [fɛɐ'ʃtre:bən] *v/t.* (h) strut, brace; **Ver'stre·bung** *f* (-; -en) strut(s *pl.*), brace(s *pl.*)

ver'strei·chen (*irr., no* -ge-, → ***streichen***) **I.** *v/i.* (sn) **1.** *time*: pass (by); *deadline*: expire; **II.** *v/t.* (h) **2.** spread *butter, ointment etc.*; **3.** ⚙ stop up *cracks etc.*

ver'streu·en *v/t.* (h) **1.** scatter; **2.** spill; **ver'streut** *adj.* scattered, dotted about here and there

ver'stricken (h) **I.** *v/t.* ensnare, involve (***in*** *acc.* in); ***verstrickt werden in*** *acc. a.* become enmeshed in *s.th.*; **II.** *v/refl.*: ***sich ~ in*** *acc.* get entangled (*or* involved, caught up) in; ***sich in Lügen*** *etc.* ***~*** get caught up in a web of lies *etc.*; **Ver'strickung** (*sep.* -k·k-) *f* (-; -en) entanglement, involvement (***in*** *acc.* in)

ver'strö·men (h) **I.** *v/t.* give off, exude *smell etc.*; shed *blood*; ***et. über et. ~*** spread s.th. over s.th.; **II.** *lit. v/refl.*: ***sich ~*** spend itself (*or* o.s.)

ver·stüm·meln [fɛɐ'ʃtʏməln] *v/t.* (h) mutilate; *fig.* garble *report etc.*; **Ver'stüm·me·lung** *f* (-; -en) mutilation; *fig.* garbling

ver·stum·men [fɛɐ'ʃtʊmən] *v/i.* (sn) fall silent; *a.* stop talking; *noise etc.*: stop, die away; *fig. rumo(u)rs*: stop, peter out; ***plötzlich verstummte alles*** there was a sudden hush (*or* silence)

Ver·such [fɛɐ'zu:x] *m* (-[e]s; -e) attempt (*a.* ⚖), try; *phys.*, ⚕ *etc.* experiment; *a.* ⚙ test; ***e-n ~ machen*** make an attempt, have a try (F go), carry out an experiment (***an*** *dat.* on); ***e-n ~ machen mit*** *dat.* give *s.o. or s.th.* a try (F go), F give *s.th.* a whirl; ***den ~ machen zu*** *inf.* make an attempt (F have a go) at *ger.*; ***es auf e-n ~ ankommen lassen*** give it a try (F go), take a chance (***mit*** *dat.* on); ***das käme auf e-n ~ an*** we could give it a try (F go); ***e-n*** (***keinen***) ***~ wert sein*** (not to) be worth trying (*or* a try)

ver'su·chen *v/t.* (h) **1.** try; attempt (*a.* ⚖); ***es ~ mit*** *dat.* try *s.th. or ger.*; ***sich ~ an*** *dat.* try one's hand at; ***sein Glück ~*** try one's luck; ***versuch's doch mal!*** F have a go; ***laß mich mal ~!*** let me try (it), F let me have a go; → ***versucht*** 1; **2.** taste, try; **3.** *obs., bibl.* tempt; *lit.* ***versucht sein zu*** *inf.* feel tempted to *inf.*

Ver'su·cher *m* (-s; -) tempter

Ver'suchs|ab,tei·lung *f* experimental department; **~an·la·ge** *f* testing (*or* pilot) plant; **~an·stalt** *f* research institute; **~bal,lon** *m* trial balloon; *fig.* kite; **~ge·län·de** *n* testing site; **~grup·pe** *f* test group; **~ka,nin·chen** *fig. n* guinea pig; **~mo,dell** *n* test model; **~ob,jekt** *n* test object; **~per,son** *f* test person; **~pro,jekt** *n* pilot project (*or* scheme); **~pup·pe** *f mot.* dummy; **~rei·he** *f* series of experiments; **~sta·di·um** *n*: (***noch im ~*** still at the) experimental stage; **~strecke** *f* test track; **~tier** *n* experimental (*or* laboratory) animal

ver'suchs·wei·se *adv.* by way of trial, on a trial basis

Ver'suchs·zweck *m*: ***zu ~en*** for experimental purposes

ver'sucht *adj.* **1.** attempted *murder etc.*; **2.** → ***versuchen*** 3; **Ver'su·chung** *f* (-; -en) temptation; ***in ~ führen*** lead into temptation; ***in ~ kommen*** be tempted

ver·sump·fen [fɛɐ'zʊmpfən] *v/i.* (sn) **1.** become marshy; **2.** F *fig.* F get involved in a (big) booze-up, end up boozing (the night away)

ver'sün·di·gen *v/refl.*: ***sich ~*** (h) sin (***an*** *dat.* against)

ver·sun·ken [fɛɐ'zʊŋkən] **I.** *p.p. of* ***versinken***; **II.** *adj.* sunken, submerged; *fig. times etc.* long past; lost *empire etc.*; ***~ in*** *acc.* absorbed (*or* engrossed) in; → ***Gedanke***; **Ver'sun·ken·heit** *f* (-; *no pl.*) contemplation

ver'sü·ßen *v/t.* (h) sweeten (*a. fig.*); *fig.* make *s.th.* more attractive; → ***Pille***

ver'tä·feln *v/t.* (h) panel; **Ver'tä·fe·lung** *f* (-; -en) panel(l)ing, wainscoting

ver'ta·gen *v/t. and v/refl.* (***sich ~***) (h) adjourn (***auf*** *acc.* until); **Ver'ta·gung** *f* (-; -en) adjournment

ver·tausch·bar [fɛɐ'taʊʃba:ɐ] *adj.* interchangeable; ⚙ replaceable, exchangeable; **ver'tau·schen** *v/t.* (h) a) exchange, trade, F swap (***gegen*** *acc.*, ***mit*** *dat.* for), b) mix up, c) A substitute, d) reverse *roles*; ***die Plätze*** *etc.* ***~*** change (trade, F swap) seats *etc.*; **Ver'tau·schung** *f* (-; -en) a) exchange, b) mix-up

ver·tei·di·gen [fɛɐ'taɪdɪgən] (h) **I.** *v/t.* defend (*a.* ⚖ *v/i., a. sport*); *a.* stand up for; **II.** *v/refl.*: ***sich ~*** defend o.s., *a.* justify o.s.; **Ver·tei·di·ger** [fɛɐ'taɪdɪgɐ] *m* (-s; -) **1.** defender (*a. sport*), *soccer*: *a.* full-back; **2.** *fig.* advocate, upholder; ⚖ ***~ des Angeklagten*** counsel for the defen|ce (*Am.* -se); **Ver'tei·di·gung** *f* (-; *no pl.*) defen|ce (*Am.* -se) (*a.* ⚖, *sport and fig.*); ***zur ~*** *gen.* in defen|ce (*Am.* -se) of, in *s.o.'s* defen|ce (*Am.* -se); ***zu s-r*** (***eigenen***) ***~*** in one's (own) defen|ce (*Am.* -se); ***zu ihrer ~ muß ich sagen*** I have to say (*or* it has to be said) in her defen|ce (*Am.* -se)

Ver'tei·di·gungs|ab·kom·men *n* defen|ce (*Am.* -se) agreement; **~aus·ga·ben** *pl.* defen|ce (*Am.* -se) spending *sg.*; **~aus·schuß** *m* committee for national defen|ce (*Am.* -se); **~bei·trag** *m* defen|ce (*Am.* -se) contribution; **~bünd·nis** *n* defen|ce (*Am.* -se) *or* defensive alliance; **~etat** *m*, **~haus·halt** *m* defen|ce (*Am.* -se) budget; **~krieg** *m* defensive war(fare); **~mi,ni·ster** *m* defen|ce (*Am.* -se) minister, minister for defen|ce (*Am.* -se); *in GB*: Secretary of State for Defence, Defence Secretary; *in the USA*: Secretary of Defense; **~mi·ni,ste·ri·um** *n* ministry of defen|ce (*Am.* -se), defen|ce (*Am.* -se) ministry; *in GB*: Ministry of Defence, Defence Ministry; *in the USA*: Department of Defense; **~po·li,tik** *f* defen|ce (*Am.* -se) policy; **~po·ten·ti,al** *n* defen|ce (*Am.* -se) capabilities *pl.*;

~re·de *f* speech for the defen|ce (*Am.* -se), plea; *w.s.* apology; **~schrift** *f* apology; **~sy|stem** *n* defensive system; **~waf·fe** *f* defensive weapon

ver'teil·bar *adj.* distributable

ver'tei·len (h) **I.** *v/t.* a) distribute (***auf*** *acc.*, ***unter*** *dat.* among) (*a.* ☤), b) share; divide, c) *thea. etc.* cast *roles*, d) spread *colo(u)r etc.*; **~ *über*** *acc.* spread (out) over *a period etc.*; **II.** *v/refl.*: ***sich*** **~** a) spread (***über*** *acc.* over, across; ***unter*** *dat.* among), b) *group etc.*: split up; *crowd etc.*: scatter, disperse; *fog etc.*: dissipate; ***sich ~ auf*** *acc.* be distributed among *the population etc.* (*or* ***in*** *a place etc.*); ***sich in der*** (*or* ***unter die***) ***Menge ~*** mingle (*or* mix) with the crowd; ***sie verteilten sich auf ihre Plätze*** they all sat down at their places (*or* in their seats)

Ver'tei·ler *m* (-s; -) **1.** distributor (*a.* ☤, ⚡, ⚙, *mot.*); retailer; **2.** distribution list; **~do·se** *f* ⚡ junction box; **~fin·ger** *m mot.* distributor arm; **~ka·sten** *m* ⚡ distribution box; **~netz** *n* distribution system (☤ network); **~ring** *m* dealers' ring

ver'teilt *adj.* a) spread out (***über*** *acc.* over, across), b) distributed, shared (***unter*** *dat.* among); → ***Rolle²***

Ver'tei·lung *f* (-; -en) distribution (*a.* ☤); sharing; spread(ing) *etc.*; → ***verteilen***

ver·te·le·fo'nie·ren F *v/t.* (h) spend *hours etc.* on the phone, spend *hours etc.* phoning; spend *one's money etc.* on phone calls, use up *a fortune etc.* on the phone

ver·teu·ern [fɛɐ'tɔʏɐn] (h) **I.** *v/t.* raise the price of; **II.** *v/refl.*: ***sich ~*** go up (in price); **Ver'teue·rung** *f* (-; -en) rise in price(s) *or* costs

ver·teu·feln [fɛɐ'tɔʏfəln] *v/t.* (h) demonize; **ver'teu·felt** F **I.** *adj.* devilish; **II.** *adv.*: **~ *schwer*** (***gutaussehend*** *etc.*) F damn(ed) difficult (good-looking *etc.*); **Ver'teu·fe·lung** *f* (-; -en) demonization; **Ver'teu·fe·lungs·kam|pa·gne** *f* smear campaign

ver·tie·fen [fɛɐ'ti:fən] (h) **I.** *v/t.* **1.** deepen; **2.** *fig.* deepen, heighten; **3.** extend *one's knowledge etc.*; go into *s.th.* further; → ***Gedanke*; II.** *v/refl.* **4. *sich ~*** *impression etc.*: deepen; **5. *sich ~ in*** *acc.* become engrossed (*or* absorbed, immersed) in *a book etc.*, *a.* become wrapped up in *one's work etc.*; go into *s.th.* further (*or* in greater detail), devote o.s. (*or* one's attention) to, steep o.s. in; **ver'tieft** *adj.* **1.** (more) detailed; **~*es Wissen*** *a.* background knowledge; **2.** absorbed, F dead to the world; **~ *in*** *acc.* absorbed (*or* engrossed) by *a book etc.*, immersed in, *a.* wrapped up in *one's work etc.*; **Ver'tie·fung** *f* (-; -en) **1.** a) deepening, b) depression; **2.** *fig.* deepening *of an impression etc.*, *a. of knowledge etc.*, heightening; **3.** *fig.* absorption; engrossment

ver·ti·kal [vɛrti'ka:l] *adj.* vertical

Ver·ti·ka·le [vɛrti'ka:lə] *f* (-; -n) vertical (line)

ver'til·gen *v/t.* (h) **1.** destroy; *a.* kill *insects, weeds*; **2.** F *fig.* F demolish, polish off; **Ver'til·gung** *f* (-; -en) destruction; killing

ver'tip·pen *v/refl.*: ***sich*** **~** (h) a) make a (typing) mistake, b) *computer etc.*: hit the wrong key, *teleph. a.* get the number wrong

ver·to·nen [fɛɐ'to:nən] *v/t.* (h) ♪ set to music; *film*: sound-track, add the sound to; **Ver'to·nung** *f* (-; -en) ♪ setting

ver·trackt [fɛɐ'trakt] F *adj.* tricky; involved, complicated; **Ver'trackt·heit** F *f* (-; -en) tricky (*or* involved, complicated) nature (*gen.* of)

Ver·trag [fɛɐ'tra:k] *m* (-[e]s; Verträge [fɛɐ'trɛ:gə]) contract; *pol. a.* pact, treaty, convention, agreement; ***mündlicher ~*** verbal agreement (*or* contract); ***e-n ~ schließen*** make a contract, *pol.* sign a treaty (*or* an agreement); ***j-n unter ~ nehmen*** sign s.o. on; ***unter ~ stehen*** be on a contract, have signed a contract

ver'tra·gen (*irr.*, *no* -ge-, h, → ***tragen***) **I.** *v/t.* endure; *usu. negative or in questions*: stand, F take; ***dieses Essen kann ich nicht ~*** this food doesn't agree with me, I can't take this food; F ***etwas ~ können*** hold one's liquor well; ***er kann einiges ~*** a) he can take quite a bit, b) F he can put away a fair bit (of alcohol); **II.** *v/refl.*: ***sich*** (***gut***) **~** a) be (very) compatible; *colo(u)rs etc.*: go (well) together, b) get along (well), get on (well [together]); ***sich nicht ~*** a) be incompatible; *colo(u)rs*: clash, b) not to get on (with each other); ***sich wieder ~*** a) make (it) up, b) have made (it) up

ver'trag·lich **I.** *adj.* contractual; **II.** *adv.* by contract; *stipulate etc.* in a contract; **~ *gebunden sein*** have signed a contract; **~ *zu et. verpflichtet sein*** be under contract to do s.th.

ver·träg·lich [fɛɐ'trɛ:klɪç] *adj.* **1.** *gastr.* easily digestible, easy to digest; *pharm.* well-tolerated, *w.s.* kind to the stomach; ***diese Tabletten sind schwer ~*** these tablets can cause (nausea and) stomach upset; **2.** agreeable *climate*; **3.** agreeable, *w.s. a.* F livable-with; **~ *sein*** *a.* be easy to get on with, be an agreeable sort of person; **Ver'träg·lich·keit** *f* (-; *no pl.*) **1.** *gastr.* digestibility; *pharm.* tolerability; **2.** agreeableness *of a climate*; **3.** *s.o.'s* agreeableness; *s.o.'s* agreeable nature

Ver'trags|ab·schluß *m* conclusion of an agreement *etc.*; → ***Vertrag***; **~be·din·gung** *f* condition (*pl. a.* terms) of a (*or* the) contract; **~be·ginn** *m* commencement of a (*or* the) contract; **~be·stim·mun·gen** *pl.* provisions of a (*or* the) contract; **~bruch** *m* breach of contract; **⁀brü·chig** *adj.* defaulting *party etc.*; **~ *werden*** go back on a (*or* the) contract, commit a breach of contract; **~dau·er** *f* term of a (*or* the) contract; **~ent·wurf** *m* draft agreement; **~ge·gen·stand** *m* object of a(n) (*or* the) agreement *or* contract; **⁀ge·mäß** *adv.* according to agreement (*or* contract, the treaty); **~händ·ler** *m* appointed dealer; **~par|tei** *f*, **~part·ner** *m* party to a(n) *or* the contract (*or* agreement, treaty); **~punkt** *m* article of a(n) *or* the contract (*or* agreement, treaty); **~recht** *n* **1.** *no pl.* law of contract; **2.** contractual right; **~stra·fe** *f* (contractual) penalty; **~treue** *f* loyalty to (the terms of) a(n) *or* the contract (*or* agreement, treaty); **~un·ter|zeich·nung** *f* signing of a(n) *or* the contract (*or* agreement, treaty); **~ur·kun·de** *f* deed, indenture; **~ver·hält·nis** *n* contractual relationship; **~ver·let·zung** *f* breach of contract; **~werk** *n* (set of) agreements *pl.*; **~werk·statt** *f* authorized repairers *pl.*; **⁀wid·rig** *adj.* contrary to (the terms of) a(n) *or* the contract (*or* agreement, treaty); **~wid·rig·keit** *f* breach of contract

ver'trau·en *v/i.* (h) trust (***j-m*** s.o.); **~ *auf*** *acc.* trust in; ***bedingungslos ~*** trust implicitly; ***auf die Zukunft ~*** have faith in (*or* believe in) the future

Ver'trau·en *n* (-s; *no pl.*) confidence, trust (***auf*** *acc.* in); faith, belief (***in*** *acc.* in *technology, the future etc.*); ***im ~*** confidentially; ***ganz im ~*** between you and me; ***j-m*** (***ganz***) ***im ~ sagen*** tell s.o. in (strict) confidence; ***im ~ auf*** *acc.* trusting in; (***volles***) **~ *haben zu*** *dat.* have (every) confidence in; ***j-m sein ~ schenken*** place confidence in s.o.; ***j-n ins ~ ziehen*** take s.o. into one's confidence; ***das ~ verlieren zu*** *dat.* lose faith in; ✈ ***danke für Ihr ~*** thank you for choosing (*or* flying) ...; → ***aussprechen*** 3, ***genießen, schleichen***

ver'trau·en·er·weckend *adj.*: **~ *sein*** (*or* ***aussehen***) inspire confidence; ***wenig ~ sein*** (*or* ***aussehen***) not to inspire much confidence, inspire little confidence

Ver'trau·ens|arzt *m* medical examiner; **~ba·sis** *f* foundation of trust; **~be·weis** *m* mark of confidence; **⁀bil·dend** *adj.*: **~*e Maßnahmen*** confidence-building measures; **~bruch** *m* breach of trust, betrayal of s.o.'s trust; indiscretion; **~fra·ge** *f*: *parl.* ***die ~ stellen*** propose a vote of confidence; **~kri·se** *f* crisis of confidence; **~mann** *m* representative; **~miß·brauch** *m* abuse of (s.o.'s) confidence; **~per|son** *f* reliable person; **~sa·che** *f* confidential matter, something confidential; *w.s.* ***das ist ~*** that's a matter (*or* question) of confidence; **⁀se·lig** *adj.* (too) confiding; gullible; **~stel·lung** *f* position of trust; **~ver·hält·nis** *n* bond of trust; **⁀voll** *adj.* trusting; **~vo·tum** *n parl.* vote of confidence; **⁀wür·dig** *adj.* trustworthy

ver·trau·lich [fɛɐ'traʊlɪç] **I.** *adj.* **1.** confidential; ***streng ~!*** strictly confidential!; **2.** familiar, F pally, chummy; **II.** *adv.* **3.** confidentially, in confidence; (***streng***) **~ *behandeln*** treat confidentially (with the strictest confidence), keep *s.th.* (absolutely) secret; **4.** in a very familiar (F pally) way; **Ver'trau·lich·keit** *f* (-; *no pl.* **1.** confidentiality; **2.** familiarity, F palliness, chumminess

ver'träu·men *v/t.* (h) (day)dream away, spend *one's time etc.* (day)dreaming; **ver'träumt** *adj.* dreamy; *a.* sleepy *village etc.*

ver·traut [fɛɐ'traʊt] *adj.* **1.** close (*dat. or* ***mit*** *dat.* to *s.o.*); **2.** familiar (***j-m*** to s.o.); **~ *mit*** *dat.* familiar with *s.th.*; ***sich mit e-r Sache ~ machen*** acquaint (*or* familiarize) o.s. with s.th.; ***sich mit dem Gedanken ~ machen*** get used to the idea (***daß das Geld verloren ist*** *etc.* of the money being lost *etc.*); **Ver'trau·te** *m, f* (-n; -n) confidant(e *f*); **Ver'traut·heit** *f* (-; *no pl.*) **1.** closeness; **2.** familiarity

ver'trei·ben *v/t.* (*irr.*, *no* -ge-, h, → ***treiben***) **1.** drive away; expel (***aus*** *dat.* from), drive out (of); turn out; **2. *sich die Zeit ~*** while away the time; **3.** ☤ sell, market, distribute; **Ver'trei·bung** *f* (-; -en) expulsion (***aus*** *dat.* from)

ver·tret·bar [fɛɐ'tre:tba:ɐ] *adj.* a) justifiable, justified, b) tenable, defensible, c) *w.s.* acceptable, reasonable; **ver'tre·ten** *v/t.* (*irr.*, *no* -ge-, h, → ***treten***) **1.** a) represent, b) stand in for *a colleague etc.*, c) ⚖ appear for, plead for, d) look after *s.o.'s interests etc.*, e) defend, advocate; support, back, f) justify; answer for; ***den Standpunkt ~, daß*** be of (*or* hold) the opinion that; **2.** ***sich die Beine*** (*or* ***Füße***) ~ stretch one's legs; **3.** ***sich den Fuß*** ~ strain one's ankle

Ver·tre·ter [fɛɐ'tre:tɐ] *m* (-s; -) a) representative (*a. fig.*), ✝ *a.* agent, b) sales representative, F (sales) rep; travel(l)ing salesman, c) deputy, stand-in; ⚕ locum; ⚖ proxy, d) advocate, supporter; exponent; **~pro·vi·si͵on** *f* agent's commission

Ver'tre·tung *f* (-; -en) a) representation; ✝ agency, b) substitution; ***in*** ~ *gen.* in place of, standing in for, (signed) for; ***j-s ~ übernehmen*** stand in for s.o.; **ver'tre·tungs·wei·se** *adv.* as a stand--in; ~ ***dasein*** *a.* be standing in (***für*** *acc.* for *s.o.*)

Ver·trieb [fɛɐ'tri:p] *m* (-[e]s; *no pl.*) **1.** sale, marketing; distribution; **2.** sales (and marketing) department

Ver·trie·be·ne [fɛɐ'tri:bənə] *m, f* (-n; -n) displaced person; exile

Ver'triebs|ab͵tei·lung *f* sales (and marketing) department; **~ge·sell·schaft** *f* marketing company; **~ko·sten** *pl.* distribution cost(s); **~lei·ter** *m* sales (*or* marketing) manager; **~netz** *n* distribution (*or* sales) network; **~recht** *n* right of sale; **~weg** *m* distribution channel

ver'trim·men F *v/t.* (h) F give *s.o.* a thrashing

ver'trin·ken *v/t.* (*irr., no* -ge-, h, → ***trinken***) spend on drink

ver'trock·nen *v/i.* (sn) dry up

ver'trö·deln *v/t.* (h) dawdle away, waste

ver'trö·sten *v/t.* (h) a) feed with hopes (***auf*** *acc.* of); console, b) put off (***auf*** *acc.* till, until); **Ver'trö·stun·gen** *pl.* (empty) promises

ver·trot·teln [fɛɐ'trɔtəln] F *v/i.* (sn) F lose one's marbles; F go gaga; **ver'trot·telt** F *adj.* F goofy; senile; ~ ***sein*** *a.* F have gone gaga

ver'tun (*irr., no* -ge-, h, → ***tun***) **I.** *v/t.* waste; give away, pass up, miss *opportunity etc.*; ***Zeit ~ mit*** *dat.* waste time on; **II.** F *v/refl.*: ***sich*** (***schwer***) ~ make a (big) mistake (***bei*** *dat.*, ***mit*** *dat.* with)

ver'tu·schen *v/t.* (h) cover up; hush up; **Ver'tu·schung** *f* (-; -en) cover-up

ver·übeln [fɛɐ'ʔy:bəln] *v/t.* (h) take offen|ce (*Am.* -se) at; ***j-m et.*** ~ *a.* be annoyed at s.o. for s.th.; ***j-m ~, daß er ...*** be annoyed at s.o. for *ger.*, take offen|ce (*Am.* -se) at s.o.('s) *ger.*; ***ich hoffe, du wirst es mir nicht ~, daß*** (*or* ***wenn***) ***ich ...*** *a.* I hope you won't mind my *ger.*; ***ich kann es ihm nicht*** ~ I can't blame him

ver'üben *v/t.* (h) commit *a murder etc.*; carry out *an assassination etc.*

ver'ul·ken *v/t.* (h) make fun of *s.o.*

ver·un·glimp·fen [fɛɐ'ʔʊnglɪmpfən] *v/t.* (h) denigrate, disparage; ***j-n ~*** *a.* blacken s.o.'s name; **Ver'un·glimp·fung** *f* (-; -en) denigration, disparagement

ver·un·glücken [fɛɐ'ʔʊnglʏkən] (*sep.* -k·k-) *v/i.* (sn) **1.** have an accident; (*a.* ***tödlich ~***) be killed in an accident; **2.** *fig.* fail, go wrong; **ver'un·glückt** *adj.* **1.** ***~e Person*** → ***Verunglückte***; **2.** *fig.* unsuccessful; ***~e Sache*** (*or* ***Angelegenheit,*** F ***Geschichte***) *a.* failure, F flop, F hash; **Ver'un·glück·te** *m, f* (-n; -n) casualty, (accident *or* crash) victim

ver·un·rei·ni·gen [fɛɐ'ʔʊnraɪnɪgən] *v/t.* (h) dirty; pollute; contaminate; **Ver'un·rei·ni·gung** *f* (-; -en) **1.** dirtying; pollution, contamination; **2.** impurity, impurities *pl.*

ver·un·si·chern [fɛɐ'ʔʊnzɪçɐn] *v/t* (h) make *s.o.* (feel) unsure of himself (*or* herself), unnerve; throw, F rattle; **ver'un·si·chert** *adj.* unsure (of o.s.), unnerved; **Ver'un·si·che·rung** *f* (-; -en) (feeling of) uncertainty; ***zur ~ der Bevölkerung*** *etc.* ***führen*** cause (a feeling of) unease among the population *etc.*, make the population *etc.* nervous (*or* uneasy)

ver·un·stal·ten [fɛɐ'ʔʊnʃtaltən] *v/t.* (h) deface; mar, disfigure; **Ver'un·stal·tung** *f* (-; -en) defacing; marring, disfigurement

ver·un·treu·en [fɛɐ'ʔʊntrɔʏən] *v/t.* (h) misappropriate, embezzle *funds etc.*; **Ver'un·treu·ung** *f* (-; -en) misappropriation, embezzlement

ver·un·zie·ren [fɛɐ'ʔʊntsi:rən] *v/t.* (h) spoil, mar

ver·ur·sa·chen [fɛɐ'ʔu:ɐzaxən] *v/t.* (h) cause, bring about, give rise to; ***j-m Schwierigkeiten*** *etc.* ~ cause s.o. difficulties *etc.*, create difficulties *etc.* for s.o.; ***j-m Kosten*** ~ put s.o. to expense

Ver·ur·sa·cher [fɛɐ'ʔu:ɐzaxɐ] *m* (-s; -) responsible party; **~prin͵zip** *n* causation principle; polluter pays principle

Ver'ur·sa·chung *f* (-; *no pl.*) causing (*gen.* of)

ver'ur·tei·len *v/t.* (h) condemn (*a. fig.*), sentence (**zu** *dat.* to); **ver'ur·teilt** *adj.* convicted; *a. fig.* condemned; *fig.* ***zum Scheitern ~*** doomed to fail(ure); ***zum Nichtstun ~*** condemned to a life of idleness; **Ver'ur·teil·te** *m, f* (-n; -n) convicted man (*f* woman), ⚖ convict; ***zum Tode ~*** condemned man (*f* woman); **Ver'ur·tei·lung** *f* (-; -en) a) condemnation (*a. fig.*), conviction, b) sentence

ver·viel·fäl·ti·gen [fɛɐ'fi:lfɛltɪgən] *v/t.* (h) duplicate, copy; **Ver'viel·fäl·ti·gung** *f* (-; -en) a) duplication, copying, b) copy; **Ver'viel·fäl·ti·gungs·ap·pa͵rat** *m* duplicator

ver·vier·fa·chen [fɛɐ'fi:ɐfaxən] *v/t. and v/refl.* (***sich ~***) (h) quadruple

ver·voll·komm·nen [fɛɐ'fɔlkɔmnən] *v/t.* (h) perfect; improve (on); **Ver'voll·komm·nung** *f* (-; -en) perfection; improvement

ver·voll·stän·di·gen [fɛɐ'fɔlʃtɛndɪgən] (h) **I.** *v/t.* complete; **II.** *v/refl.*: ***sich ~*** be completed, become complete; **Ver'voll·stän·di·gung** *f* (-; -en) completion

ver'wach·sen[1] *v/i.* (*irr., no* -ge-, sn, → ***wachsen***[1]) **1.** grow together; ⚕ *bones*: unite; *wound*: heal up; **2.** *fig.* grow close (***mit*** *dat.* to), *lit.* become one (with); ***~ zu*** *dat.* grow into *s.th.*

ver'wach·sen[2] **I.** *p.p. of* ***verwachsen***[1]; **II.** *adj.* **1.** deformed, crippled; hunchbacked; **2.** overgrown *garden etc.*; **3.** 🌱 stunted; **4.** *fig.* ***~ mit*** *dat.* deeply rooted in; ***~ sein mit*** *dat. a.* be one with; **Ver'wach·sung** *f* (-; -en) **1.** deformity; **2.** ⚕ fusion

ver'wackeln *v/t.* (h): ***ein Foto ~*** shake the camera (while taking a photo); **ver'wackelt** *adj.* blurred

ver'wäh·len *v/refl.*: ***sich ~*** (h) dial the wrong number; ***ich glaube, Sie haben sich verwählt*** I think you must have (got) the wrong number

ver'wah·ren (h) **I.** *v/t.*: (***sicher ~***) keep (in a safe place); ***et. für j-n ~*** look after s.th. for s.o.; **II.** *fig. v/refl.*: ***sich ~*** protest (***gegen*** *acc.* against)

ver·wahr·lo·sen [fɛɐ'va:ɐlo:zən] *v/i.* (sn) **1.** *house etc.*: be (*or* get) neglected, go to rack and ruin; *garden etc.*: *a.* run wild; **2.** *fig.* go to seed, go off the rails; **ver'wahr·lost** *adj.* **1.** (sadly) neglected, dilapidated *house etc.*; neglected, overgrown *garden etc.*, *garden etc.* run wild; **2.** *fig.* scruffy, seedy; dissolute; **Ver'wahr·lo·sung** *f* (-; *no pl.*) **1.** (total) neglect, state of neglect; *a.* dilapidation *of a house etc.*; **2.** *fig.* (moral) decline; ***die ~ der heutigen Jugend*** the decline of today's youth

Ver'wah·rung *f* (-; *no pl.*) **1.** safekeeping; custody; ***j-m et. in ~ geben*** deposit s.th. with s.o., leave s.th. with s.o. for safekeeping; ***in ~ nehmen*** take charge of; **2.** protest; ***~ einlegen*** protest, enter a protest (***gegen*** *acc.* against)

ver·wai·sen [fɛɐ'vaɪzən] *v/i.* (sn) be orphaned, become (*or* be made) an orphan; **ver·waist** [fɛɐ'vaɪst] *adj.* orphan (*a. fig.*); *fig.* abandoned; deserted; vacant *position etc.*

ver'wal·ten *v/t.* (h) administer; manage; conduct; **Ver·wal·ter** [fɛɐ'valtɐ] *m* (-s; -) administrator; manager; ⚒ estate manager; **Ver'wal·tung** *f* (-; -en) **1.** *no pl.* administration; management; **2.** administrative authority; ***zentrale ~*** administrative headquarters *pl.*, central administration (offices)

Ver'wal·tungs|akt *m* administrative act; **~an·ge·stell·te** *m, f* (-n; -n) administrative assistant; **~ap·pa͵rat** *m* administrative (*or* bureaucratic) machinery; **~auf·ga·ben** *pl.* administrative tasks (*or* duties); **~be·am·te** *m* civil servant; **~be·hör·de** *f* → ***Verwaltung*** 2; **~be·zirk** *m* administrative district; **~dienst** *m* civil service; **~ge·bäu·de** *n* administrative (F admin) building; **~ge·bühr** *f* administration charge; **~ge·richt** *n* administrative court; **~ge·richts·hof** *m* higher administrative court; **~ko·sten** *pl.* administrative overheads (*or* expenses, costs); **~kram** F *m* paperwork; red tape; **~per·so͵nal** *n* administrative staff; **~rat** *m* governing board; **~recht** *n* administrative law; **~sitz** *m* (administrative) headquarters *pl.*; **2tech·nisch** *adj.*: ***aus ~en Gründen*** for administrative reasons; **~weg** *m*: ***auf dem ~e*** through (the) administrative channels

ver'wan·del·bar *adj.* convertible

ver'wan·deln (h) **I.** *v/t.* **1.** change; convert; transform; ⚖ commute (*all* ***in*** *acc.* into); ***~ in*** *acc. a.* turn into; **2.** *soccer*: convert; ***den Strafstoß*** *etc.* ~ score; **II.** *v/refl.*: ***sich ~*** change (***in*** *acc.* into); metamorphose (into); ***sich ~ in*** *acc. a.* turn into; **III.** *v/i. soccer*: score; ***er hätte ~ müssen*** he should have scored

Ver'wand·lung *f* (-; -en) change; conversion; transformation; metamorphosis; **Ver'wand·lungs·künst·ler** *m* quick--change artist

ver·wandt [fɛɐ'vant] *adj.* **1.** related (***mit*** *dat.* to) (*a. fig.*); *fig.* ***~ sein*** be akin (*dat.* to); ***~e Seelen*** (*or* ***Geister***) kindred spirits, soulmates; ***geistig*** (*or* ***seelisch, innerlich***) ***~ sein*** be kindred spirits; **2.** *ling.* cognate (***mit*** *dat.* with), related (to); ***die Wörter sind ~*** *a.* the words go back to (*or* have) the same root

Ver·wand·te [fɛɐ'vantə] *m, f* (-n; -n) rela-

tive, relation; ***der nächste*** ~ the next of kin; **Ver'wand·ten·kreis** *m* (circle of) relatives *pl.*
Ver'wandt·schaft *f* (-; -en) **1.** relationship; *fig.* affinity; ***geistige*** (*or* ***seelische, innere***) ~ *a.* meeting of minds; **2.** *no pl.* relations *pl.*; ***die ganze*** ~ F the whole clan; **ver'wandt·schaft·lich** *adj.* family ...; ~***e Beziehung(en)*** family connections, relationship
Ver'wandt·schafts·grad *m* degree of relationship
ver·wanzt [fɛɐ'vantst] *adj.* **1.** bug-infested, bug-ridden; **2.** *fig.* bugged
ver'war·nen *v/t.* (h) warn, give *s.o.* a warning; *police etc.*: caution, *sport*: *a.* book; **Ver'war·nung** *f* (-; -en) warning; *police etc.*: caution, *sport*: *a.* yellow card
ver'wa·schen *adj.* faded, washed out; *fig.* watery, F wishy-washy
ver'wäs·sern *v/t.* (h) dilute, *a. fig.* water down; **ver'wäs·sert** *adj.* diluted; *a. fig.* watered down, watery
ver'wech·seln *v/t.* (h) confuse, mix up (***mit*** *dat.* with), mistake (for); ***j-n mit e-m andern*** ~ mistake s.o. for s.o. else; ***et. mit et. anderem*** ~ mix s.th. up (*or* confuse s.th.) with s.th. else, mistake s.th. for s.th. else; ***ich habe ihn verwechselt*** I mistook him for s.o. else, I thought he was s.o. else; ***die Hüte*** *etc.* ~ take the wrong hat *etc.*, mix up the hats *etc.*; ***Sie können es gar nicht*** ~ you can't mistake it; ***sie sehen sich zum*** ≈ ***ähnlich*** they're as (a)like as two peas (in a pod); **Ver·wechs·lung** [fɛɐ'vɛksluŋ] *f* (-; -en) mistake; case of mistaken identity, F mix-up
ver·we·gen [fɛɐ've:gən] *adj.* daring, bold; reckless; *fig.* rakish *clothes etc.*; **Ver'we·gen·heit** *f* (-; *no pl.*) daring; recklessness; *fig.* rakishness
ver'we·hen **I.** *v/t.* (h) a) blow away; scatter, b) cover with snow *etc.*; **II.** *v/i.* (sn) be blown over; *fig.* fade (away); **Ver'we·hung** *f* (-; -en) (snow)drift; (sand)drift
ver'weh·ren *v/t.* (h) bar; ***j-m et.*** ~ refuse (*or* deny) s.o. s.th.; ***j-m*** ~, ***et. zu tun*** keep (*or* stop, prevent) s.o. from doing s.th.; ***j-m den Zutritt*** ~ refuse s.o. admittance (***zu*** *dat.* to)
ver·weib·li·chen [fɛɐ'vaɪplıçən] **I.** *v/i.* (sn) become effeminate; **II.** *v/t.* (h) feminize; **ver'weib·licht** *adj.* effeminate; **Ver'weib·li·chung** *f* (-; *no pl.*) **1.** increasing effeminacy; **2.** feminization
ver·weich·li·chen [fɛɐ'vaıçlıçən] **I.** *v/t.* (h) make *s.o.* soft, F turn *s.o.* into a softie; **II.** *v/i.* (sn) go (*or* turn) soft; **ver'weich·licht** *adj.* soft; ~***er Kerl*** F softie, wimp; **Ver'weich·li·chung** *f* (-; *no pl.*) turning soft; *w.s.* F increasing wimpishness; ***es führt zur*** ~ ***der Jugend*** *etc.* F it's turning our youth *etc.* into a bunch of softies
ver'wei·gern (h) **I.** *v/t.* refuse; ***e-n Befehl*** ~ disobey an order; ***j-m s-e Hilfe*** ~ refuse to help s.o.; ***den Kriegsdienst*** ~ refuse to do one's military service, ignore one's conscription orders; ***die Nahrung (Nahrungsaufnahme)*** ~ refuse all food, refuse to eat; **II.** *v/refl.*: ***sich*** ~ refuse to cooperate (*or* go along with s.th.); ***sich der Gesellschaft*** ~ opt out (of society)
Ver'wei·ge·rung *f* (-; -en) refusal
Ver'wei·ge·rungs·fall *m*: ***im*** ~ in case of refusal

ver'wei·len *v/i.* (h) stay; linger; *fig. look etc.*: rest (***auf*** *dat.* on); *thoughts*: linger (***bei*** *dat.* on), dwell (on); ***bei e-m Thema*** ~ dwell on a topic
ver·weint [fɛɐ'vaınt] *adj.* tear-stained *face*; *eyes* red with tears
Ver·weis [fɛɐ'vaıs] *m* (-es; -e [-zə]) **1.** reprimand, reproof, rebuke; ***j-m e-n*** ~ ***erteilen*** reprimand s.o. (***wegen*** *gen.* for); **2.** reference (***auf*** *acc.* to)
ver'wei·sen (*irr.*, *no* -ge-, h, → ***weisen***) **I.** *v/t.* **1.** expel (*a. ped.*); ***j-n des Landes*** ~ *a.* serve s.o. with a deportation; → ***Platz***; **2.** ⚖ remit; **3.** ***j-n*** ~ ***auf*** (*or* ***an*** *acc.*) refer s.o. to; **II.** *v/i.*: ~ ***auf*** *acc.* refer to; point *s.th.* out; ***darf ich auf*** *acc.* ... ~ may I refer you to ...; **Ver'wei·sung** *f* (-; -en) **1.** expulsion; **2.** reference (***auf*** *acc.* to)
ver'wel·ken *v/i.* (sn) *flower*: wilt; *leaves etc.*: wither; *fig. glory etc.*: fade; **ver'welkt** *adj.* wilted, limp *flowers*; withered, dried up *leaves etc.*; *fig.* faded *glory etc.*
ver·welt·li·chen [fɛɐ'vɛltlıçən] *v/t.* (h) secularize; **Ver'welt·li·chung** *f* (-; *no pl.*) secularization
ver·wend·bar [fɛɐ'vɛntba:ɐ] *adj.* usable; applicable; **ver'wen·den** (h) **I.** *v/t.* a) use; apply; utilize, b) spend; ***viel Mühe (Sorgfalt, Zeit)*** ~ ***auf*** *acc.* devote much trouble (care, time) to; **II.** *v/refl.*: ***sich bei j-m für j-n*** ~ approach s.o. on s.o.'s behalf; **Ver'wen·dung** *f* (-; -en) a) use; application; utilization, b) expenditure; ***keine*** ~ ***haben für*** *acc.* have no use for; ***das wird schon irgendwo*** ~ ***finden*** we'll *etc.* find some use for it
Ver'wen·dungs|be·reich *m* range (*or* field) of application; ≈**fä·hig** *adj.* usable; ~**mög·lich·keit** *f* (possible) use *or* application; ***e-e*** ~ *gen.* one way (in which) *s.th.* can be used; ~**wei·se** *f* (manner of) use; ***die*** ~ *gen.* the way (in which) *s.th.* is used; ~**zweck** *m* use, intended purpose
ver'wer·fen (*irr.*, *no* -ge-, h, → ***werfen***) **I.** *v/t.* **1.** reject, dismiss (*a.* ⚖); *a.* turn down *suggestion etc.*; ⚖ quash *sentence*; overrule *bill etc.*; **II.** *v/refl.*: ***sich*** ~ **2.** *wood*: warp; **3.** *geol.* fault
ver·werf·lich [fɛɐ'vɛrflıç] *adj.* reprehensible; abominable; **Ver'werf·lich·keit** *f* (-; *no pl.*) reprehensibility
Ver·wer·fung [fɛɐ'vɛrfuŋ] *f* (-; -en) **1.** rejection; ⚖ a) dismissal, b) quashing, c) overruling; **2.** warp(ing) *of wood*; **3.** *geol.* fault
ver·wert·bar [fɛɐ've:ɐtba:ɐ] *adj.* usable; ☤ realizable; **Ver'wert·bar·keit** *f* (-; *no pl.*) usability; ☤ realizability
ver'wer·ten *v/t.* (h) make use of, utilize, use; turn *experiences etc.* to (good) account; exploit *invention etc.*; ☤ commercialize; realize; ***kannst du das irgendwie*** ~? can you make any use of this?; **Ver'wer·tung** *f* (-; -en) utilization, use; exploitation; commercialization; realization
ver·we·sen [fɛɐ've:zən] *v/i.* (sn) rot; decay; **ver·west** [fɛɐ've:st] *adj.* rotted, putrefied; decayed; ***halb*** ~ rotting, putrefying; decaying; **Ver'we·sung** *f* (-; *no pl.*) (state of) decay; ***in*** ~ ***übergehen*** (begin to) decay; **Ver'we·sungs·ge·ruch** *m* putrid smell, (strong) smell of putrefaction; **Ver'we·sungs·pro,zeß** *m* process of decay
ver'wet·ten *v/t.* (h) bet away, spend on betting; throw away on bets

ver'wickeln (h) **I.** *v/t.* **1.** tangle (up), get *s.th.* tangled; **2.** *fig.* ***j-n*** ~ ***in*** *acc.* involve s.o. in *s.th.*, get s.o. involved (*or* embroiled, caught up) in *s.th.*, drag s.o. into *s.th.*; ***in e-e Sache verwickelt werden*** be(come) *or* get involved (*or* caught up, embroiled) in s.th., F get mixed up in s.th.; **II.** *v/refl.*: ***sich*** ~ ***in*** *acc.* get (o.s.) involved in, get tangled up in *a web of contradictions*; **ver'wickelt** *adj.* **1.** complicated, involved; ~***e Lage*** *a.* imbroglio; **2.** ~ ***in*** *acc.* involved in, caught up in; **Ver'wick·lung** *f* (-; -en) a) entanglement, involvement, b) complexity, complication, c) confusion, tangle, imbroglio; ***diplomatische*** *etc.* ~***en*** diplomatic *etc.* embroilment
ver'wil·dern *v/i.* ♣, *zo.* run wild; *fig. a.* go to seed; **ver'wil·dert** *adj.* a) ♣ overgrown, wild (*a. zo.*), *garden etc.* run wild, b) *fig.* wild, *a.* unruly *children*; dissipated, dissolute; **Ver·wil·de·rung** [fɛɐ'vıldəruŋ] *f* (-; *no pl.*) a) (state of) neglect, b) (increasing) unruliness
ver'win·den *v/t.* (*irr.*, *no* -ge-, h, → ***winden***) get over *s.th.*
ver'wir·ken *v/t.* (h) forfeit
ver·wirk·li·chen [fɛɐ'vırklıçən] (h) **I.** *v/t.* realize *plans, dreams etc.*, *a.* achieve, attain *one's aim etc.*; **II.** *v/refl.*: ***sich*** ~ be realized, materialize; come true; *aim etc.*: be achieved (*or* attained, realized); ***sich selbst*** ~ find one's fulfil(l)ment, ***in*** *dat.*: find fulfil(l)ment in *s.th.*; **Ver'wirk·li·chung** *f* (-; -en) realization, *a.* fulfil(l)ment *of one's dreams etc.*; achievement, attainment *of one's aims etc.*
ver·wir·ren [fɛɐ'vırən] (h) **I.** *v/t.* **1.** confuse, bewilder, perplex *s.o.*; **2.** tangle (up) *wool etc.*; dishevel *hair*; **II.** *v/refl.*: ***sich*** ~ get tangled (up); **ver'wir·rend** *adj.* confusing, bewildering; ~***e Vielfalt*** bewildering variety (*or* choice); **Ver'wirr·spiel** *n* deliberate confusion; ***mit j-m ein*** ~ ***treiben*** keep s.o. guessing; **ver'wirrt** *adj.* confused, bewildered, perplexed; **Ver'wirrt·heit** *f* (-; *no pl.*) → ***Verwirrung*** 1; **Ver'wir·rung** *f* (-; -en) **1.** *no pl.* confusion, bewilderment, perplexity; ***j-n in*** ~ ***bringen*** confuse (*or* bewilder) s.o., throw s.o. into confusion; ***in*** ~ ***geraten*** get (*or* become) confused; ***er war in e-m Zustand geistiger*** ~ he was clearly disturbed; **2.** confusion, muddle; ~ ***stiften*** cause confusion; **Ver'wir·rungs·zu·stand** *m* state of confusion (*or* bewilderment)
ver'wirt·schaf·ten *v/t.* (h) squander away
ver'wi·schen (h) **I.** *v/t.* a) blur, b) smear, c) cover up *traces etc.*; **II.** *v/refl.*: ***sich*** ~ become blurred, blur; *memories*: become hazy
ver·wit·tern [fɛɐ'vıtɐn] *v/i.* (sn) a) weather, b) disintegrate; **ver'wit·tert** *adj.* weather-beaten; **Ver·wit·te·rung** [fɛɐ'vıtəruŋ] *f* (-; -en) a) weathering, b) disintegration
ver·wit·wet [fɛɐ'vıtvət] *adj.* widowed
ver·wöh·nen [fɛɐ'vø:nən] *v/t.* (h) spoil; ***jeder läßt sich hin und wieder gern*** ~ everyone likes to be spoilt (a bit) now and again; ***das Schicksal hat sie nicht verwöhnt*** she hasn't had an easy time of it; **ver'wöhnt** *adj.* spoilt; ***total*** ~ thoroughly spoilt, F spoilt as hell; ***das Kind ist total*** ~ *a.* F he's (*or* she's) a spoilt brat; ***er hat e-n*** ~***en Geschmack*** he has very

fine taste (*contp.* very fussy tastes); **Ver'wöh·nung** *f* (-; *no pl.*) spoiling
ver·wor·fen [fɛɐ'vɔrfən] **I.** *p.p. of* ***verwerfen***; **II.** *adj.* depraved; **Ver'wor·fen·heit** *f* (-; *no pl.*) depravity
ver·wor·ren [fɛɐ'vɔrən] *adj.* **1.** confused, muddled; **2.** involved, intricate; **Ver'wor·ren·heit** *f* (-; *no pl.*) **1.** confusion, confused state (of mind); **2.** intricacy, involved nature (*gen.* of)
ver·wund·bar [fɛɐ'vʊntbaːɐ] *adj.* vulnerable (*a. fig.*); **Ver'wund·bar·keit** *f* (-; *no pl.*) vulnerability (*a. fig.*); **ver·wun·den** [fɛɐ'vʊndən] *v/t.* (h) wound (*a. fig.*); ***sie war am Bein** etc.* ***verwundet*** she had a wounded leg *etc.*
ver'wun·der·lich *adj.* surprising, astonishing; ***es ist nicht ~, daß*** it's no wonder that; **ver'wun·dern** (h) **I.** *v/t.* surprise, astonish; **II.** *v/refl.*: ***sich ~*** be surprised, be astonished, be (quite) taken aback; **ver'wun·dert** *adj.* surprised, astonished, taken aback; **Ver·wun·de·rung** [fɛɐ'vʊndərʊŋ] *f* (-; *no pl.*): **(*zu m-r ~*** to my) surprise, astonishment, amazement; ***ich habe zu m-r ~ erfahren*** *a.* I was quite surprised (*or* amazed) to find out; ***es hat für ~ gesorgt*** it raised a few eyebrows
ver·wun·det [fɛɐ'vʊndət] *adj.* wounded; ***~er Soldat*** *a.* casualty; **Ver'wun·de·te** *m* (-n; -n) casualty, wounded (serviceman *etc.*; *pl. coll. a. the* wounded (*pl.*); **Ver'wun·dung** *f* (-; -en) wound, injury
ver·wun·schen [fɛɐ'vʊnʃən] *adj.* enchanted
ver'wün·schen *v/t.* (h) **1.** curse; **2.** enchant, cast a spell on; **ver'wünscht** *adj.* cursed, confounded; **Ver'wün·schung** *f* (-; -en) **1.** curse; **2.** spell
ver·wursch·teln [fɛɐ'vʊrʃtəln], **ver'wur·steln** F *v/t.* (h) mess up; *a.* muss up *hair*; **ver'wursch·telt, ver'wur·stelt** F *adj.* messed up; *a.* mussed up, dishevel(l)ed *hair*; ***ganz ~*** *pred. a.* F a (right) mess
ver·wur·zelt [fɛɐ'vʊrtsəlt] *adj.* (deeply) rooted (***in*** *dat.* in); ***fest ~*** firmly rooted *or* entrenched (in); ***tief ~*** deeply rooted (*or* ingrained), ***sein:*** *a.* run deep
ver·wü·sten [fɛɐ'vyːstən] *v/t.* (h) lay waste, devastate; **ver'wü·stet** *adj.* devastated, ravaged, *pred. a.* laid waste; **Ver'wü·stung** *f* (-; -en) devastation, *formal*: depredation(s *pl.*); *a.* ravages *pl. of the storm etc.*
ver'za·gen *v/i.* (h) despair (***an*** *dat.* of), lose heart; ***nur nicht ~!*** don't give up, don't despair; **ver·zagt** [fɛɐ'tsaːkt] *adj.* despondent; fainthearted; desperate; **Ver'zagt·heit** *f* (-; *no pl.*) despondency; despair, desperation
ver'zäh·len *v/refl.*: ***sich ~*** (h) miscount
ver·zah·nen [fɛɐ'tsaːnən] *v/t.* (h) interlock (*a. fig.*); ⚙ dovetail; **ver'zahnt** *adj.* (*a.* ***ineinander*** *or* ***miteinander ~***) interlocked (*a. fig.*); **Ver'zah·nung** *f* (-; -en) interlocking (*a. fig.*); ⚙ dovetail connection
ver'zan·ken F *v/refl.*: ***sich ~*** (h) have an argument (***wegen*** *gen.* over, about); ***sie haben sich verzankt*** *a.* they've fallen out (with each other)
ver'zap·fen *v/t.* (h) **1.** F come up with, *a.* F spout *nonsense etc.*; **2.** have on draught (*Am.* draft); **3.** ⚙ mortise; **Ver'zap·fung** *f* (-; -en) ⚙ mortise joint
ver·zär·teln [fɛɐ'tsɛːɐtəln] *v/t.* (h) (molly)coddle, pamper; **ver'zär·telt** *adj.* (molly)coddled; ***~er Typ*** F wimp; **Ver'zär·te·lung** *f* (-; *no pl.*) (molly)coddling, pampering
ver'zau·bern *v/t.* (h) cast a spell on; *fig.* enchant, bewitch; ***~ in*** *acc.* turn into; **ver'zau·bert** *adj.* enchanted
ver·zehn·fa·chen [fɛɐ'tseːnfaxən] *v/t. and v/refl.* (***sich ~***) (h) increase tenfold
Ver·zehr [fɛɐ'tseːɐ] *m* (-s; *no pl.*) consumption; (***nicht***) ***zum ~ geeignet*** (not) fit to eat, (in)edible; **ver·zeh·ren** [fɛɐ'tseːrən] (h) **I.** *v/t.* consume (*a. fig.*), eat; **II.** *fig. v/refl.*: ***sich ~*** eat one's heart out; ***sich ~ nach*** *dat.* yearn for; ***sich vor Gram ~*** pine away; **ver'zeh·rend** *adj.* consuming, devouring; **Ver'zehr·zwang** *m* obligation to order
ver'zeich·nen *v/t.* (h) **1.** note (*or* write) down; *a.* list; ⚙ *and adm.* record, register; ✝ quote; *fig.* record *progress etc.*; notch up *goals, records etc.*; ***~ können, zu ~ haben*** have notched up; ***... waren*** (***nicht***) ***zu ~*** there were (no) ...; ***es konnten keine Fortschritte verzeichnet werden*** there was no progress to be seen; **2.** draw *s.th.* wrong; **3.** *fig.* misrepresent; distort
Ver·zeich·nis [fɛɐ'tsaɪçnɪs] *n* (-ses; -se) list; *adm.* register; catalog(ue); index
Ver'zeich·nung *f* (-; -en) *a. fig.* distortion
ver·zei·hen [fɛɐ'tsaɪən] *v/t. and v/i.* (verzieh, verziehen, h) forgive; excuse, pardon (***j-m et.*** s.o. [for] s.th.); ***~ Sie!*** excuse me!, sorry, *formal*: I ('do) beg your pardon; ***~ Sie bitte, ...*** excuse me, ...; ***~ Sie bitte die Störung*** sorry to disturb you; ***~ Sie die Frage, aber ...*** if you'll forgive my asking, ...; ***das ist nicht zu ~*** there's no excuse for that; **ver·zeih·lich** [fɛɐ'tsaɪlɪç] *adj.* forgivable; **Ver'zei·hung** *f* (-; *no pl.*) forgiveness; pardon; ***~!*** excuse me!, sorry, *formal*: I ('do) beg your pardon; ***~?*** sorry(, could you repeat that)?; ***j-n um ~ bitten*** ask s.o.'s forgiveness; apologize to s.o.
ver'zer·ren (h) **I.** *v/t.* **1.** distort, contort, convulse; **2.** *fig.* distort; **3.** pull *muscle etc.*; sprain *ankle*; **II.** *v/refl.*: ***sich ~*** become distorted, *face*: *a.* contort; **ver'zerrt** *adj.* **1.** distorted, contorted; **2.** *fig.* distorted; *a.* warped *account etc.*; ***~e Darstellung*** *a.* distortion of the facts; **Ver'zer·rung** *f* (-; -en) distortion (*a. fig.*), contortion
ver·zet·teln [fɛɐ'tsɛtəln] (h) **I.** *v/t.* **1.** waste, fritter away; **II.** *v/refl.*: ***sich ~*** **2.** have too many irons in the fire, be doing too many things at the same time; **3.** waste one's time on (*or* get sidetracked by) little things
Ver·zicht [fɛɐ'tsɪçt] *m* (-[e]s; *no pl.*) renunciation, renouncement (***auf*** *acc.* of); abstention (from); abandonment (of); ⚖ waiver, disclaimer; ***~ leisten auf*** *acc.* → **ver·zich·ten** [fɛɐ'tsɪçtən] *v/i.* (h) forego, do without, *formal*: renounce, forswear (*all* ***auf*** *acc. s.th.*); abstain, refrain (from), ⚖ waive, disclaim (*s.th.*); ***~ auf*** *acc.* give up, abandon; turn down *offer etc.*, *a.* refuse *position etc.*; ***auf e-n Gegenschlag ~*** refrain from retaliatory action; ***auf Gewalt ~*** renounce violence, abandon the use of force; ***danke, ich verzichte*** thanks, but no thanks; ***ich kann nicht mehr darauf ~*** I can't do (*or* live) without it any more
Ver'zicht·er·klä·rung *f* ⚖ waiver, disclaimer
ver·zieh [fɛɐ'tsiː] *pret. of* ***verzeihen***
ver'zie·hen[1] *p.p. of* ***verzeihen***
ver'zie·hen[2] (*irr.*, *no* -ge-, → ***ziehen***) **I.** *v/t.* (h) **1.** ***das Gesicht ~*** pull (*or* make) a face, screw up one's face; ***den Mund ~*** grimace, twist one's mouth; → ***Miene***; **2.** spoil *s.o.*; **3.** ⚘ thin out *plants*; **II.** *v/i.* (sn) **4.** move (house); **III.** *v/refl.*: ***sich ~*** (h) **5.** go out of shape; *wood*: warp; **6.** *face*: screw up (***zu*** *dat.* into), contort (into); *mouth*: twist (into); **7.** disappear; *clouds*: *a.* disperse; *storm*: blow over; **8.** F decamp (***nach*** *dat.* to), F make o.s. scarce; ***sich in sein Zimmer ~*** disappear (*or* slink off) into one's (bed)room; ***verzieh dich!*** F get lost!, push off!, scram!
ver'zie·ren *v/t.* (h) decorate; ⚠, ♪ *etc.* ornament; **Ver'zie·rung** *f* (-; -en) decoration; ⚠ *etc.* ornament, *a. pl.* ornamentation; ♪ ornament(s *pl.*)
ver·zin·ken [fɛɐ'tsɪŋkən] *v/t.* (h) galvanize; **Ver'zin·kung** *f* (-; -en) galvanization
ver·zin·nen [fɛɐ'tsɪnən] *v/t.* (h) tin-plate; **Ver'zin·nung** *f* (-; -en) tin-plating
ver·zin·sen [fɛɐ'tsɪnzən] (h) **I.** *v/t.* pay interest on; ***e-n Betrag zu 3% ~*** pay 3 per cent (*or* percent) interest on a sum; ***mit 5% verzinst*** bearing 5 per cent (*or* percent) interest; **II.** *v/refl.*: ***sich ~*** yield (*or* bear) interest; ***sich mit 5% ~*** bear 5 per cent (*or* percent) interest; **ver·zins·lich** [fɛɐ'tsɪnslɪç] *adj.* bearing interest; interest-bearing *loan etc.*; **Ver'zin·sung** *f* (-; -en) a) payment of interest, b) interest rate, c) return
ver·zo·gen [fɛɐ'tsoːgən] **I.** *p.p. of* ***verziehen***[2]; **II.** *adj.* **1.** spoilt, spoiled *child etc.*; **2.** ⚙ out of shape; *wood etc.*: *a.* warped; **3.** ***Empfänger unbekannt ~*** address unknown; ***falls ~, bitte zurück an*** *acc.* if undelivered, please return to
ver'zö·gern (h) **I.** *v/t.* delay; slow down; protract; ***das Spiel ~*** *sport*: hold up the game; **II.** *v/refl.*: ***sich ~*** a) be delayed; be a long time coming, b) slow down; **Ver·zö·ge·rung** [fɛɐ'tsøːgərʊŋ] *f* (-; -en) delay; **Ver'zö·ge·rungs·tak·tik** *f* delaying (*or* stalling) tactics *pl.*
ver·zol·len [fɛɐ'tsɔlən] *v/t.* (h) pay duty on; ***haben Sie etwas zu ~?*** have you anything to declare?; **ver'zollt** *adj.* duty-paid; **Ver'zol·lung** *f* (-; *no pl.*) payment of duty (*gen.* on)
ver·zücken [fɛɐ'tsʏkən] (*sep.* -k·k-) *v/t.* (h) enrapture
ver'zuckern *v/t.* (h) **1.** sugar (over); candy; **2.** put too much sugar in
ver'zückt *adj.* enraptured, in raptures, ecstatic; rapt *look etc.*; **Ver'zückung** (*sep.* -k·k-) *f* (-; -en) rapture, ecstasy; ***in ~ geraten*** go into raptures (***wegen*** *gen.* over)
Ver·zug [fɛɐ'tsuːk] *m* (-[e]s; *no pl.*) delay; ***ohne ~*** without delay, forthwith; ***in ~ geraten*** (***sein***) get (be) behind, ✝ fall into (be in) arrears; ***es ist Gefahr im ~*** danger is looming; **Ver'zugs·zin·sen** *pl.* ✝ interest *sg.* on arrears, default interest *sg.*
ver'zwei·feln *v/i.* (sn) despair (***an*** *dat.* of); ***an der Menschheit*** *etc.* ***~*** lose all faith in mankind *etc.*; ***am ≈ sein*** be desperate; ***es ist zum ≈*** it's enough to drive you to despair (*or* distraction); ***nur nicht ~!*** don't give up, don't despair;

ver'zwei·felt I. *adj.* despairing; desperate; **~e Lage** hopeless (*or* desperate) situation; **~er Versuch** desperate attempt, last-ditch effort; **II.** F *adv.*: **~ ähnlich** (**komisch** *etc.*) desperately alike (funny *etc.*); **Ver·zweif·lung** [fɛɐ'tsvaɪflʊŋ] *f* (-; *no pl.*) despair; desperation; **aus** (**lauter**) **~** in *or* out of (sheer) desperation; **zur ~ bringen** (*or* **treiben**) exasperate, drive to despair (*or* distraction)

Ver'zweif·lungs·tat *f* act of desperation

ver·zwei·gen [fɛɐ'tsvaɪgən] *v/refl.* (h): **sich ~** branch out, *esp. fig.* ramify; **Ver'zwei·gung** *f* (-; -en) branching out; *fig.* ramifications *pl.*

ver·zwickt [fɛɐ'tsvɪkt] F *adj.* tricky, *a.* F knotty *problem etc.*; complicated; **Ver'zwickt·heit** F *f* (-; -en) trickiness; complicated nature (*gen.* of)

Ves·per ['fɛspɐ] *f* (-; -n) *eccl.* vespers *pl.*

Ve·te·ran [vete'ra:n] *m* (-en; -en) **1.** ⚔ *Brit.* ex-serviceman, *Am.* veteran (*a. fig.*); **2.** vintage car

Ve·te·ri·när [veteri'nɛ:ɐ] *m* (-s; -e [-rə]) veterinary surgeon, *Am.* veterinarian, F vet; **~me·di,zin** *f* veterinary medicine

Ve·to ['ve:to] *n* (-s; -s) veto; **(s)ein ~ einlegen** exercise one's power of veto, **gegen** *acc.*: put a veto on, veto; **~recht** *n* power of veto

Vet·ter ['fɛtɐ] *m* (-s; -n) cousin

'Vet·tern·wirt·schaft *f* (-; *no pl.*) nepotism, F cronyism

Ve·xier|bild [vɛ'ksi:ɐ-] *n* picture puzzle; **~spie·gel** *m* distorting mirror

'V-Ge·spräch *n* person-to-person call

VHS ['faʊ'ha'ʔɛs] *f* → **Volkshochschule; ~-Kurs** *m* evening class; **e-n ~ in** *dat.* **... machen** do a course (*or* do evening classes) in ...

Via·dukt [vi̯a'dʊkt] *m* (-[e]s; -e) viaduct

Vi·bra·phon [vibra'fo:n] *n* (-s; -e) ♪ vibraphone, F vibes *pl.*

Vi·bra·ti·on [vibra'tsi̯o:n] *f* (-; -en) vibration; **Vi·bra·tor** [vi'bra:to:ɐ] *m* (-s; -en [vibra'to:rən]) vibrator; **vi·brie·ren** [vi'bri:rən] *v/i.* (h) vibrate

Vi·deo ['vi:deo] *n* (-s; -s) video (*a.* ♪); **~auf·nah·me** *f*, **~auf·zeich·nung** *f* video recording; **~band** *n* (-[e]s; ⸚er) video tape; **~clip** *m* video clip; **~film** *m* video film; **~ge·rät** *n* video (recorder), VCR; **~ka·me·ra** *f* video camera; camcorder; **~kas,set·te** *f* video cassette; **~kon·fe,renz** *f* video conference; **~-Schocker** (*sep.* -k·k-) *m* (-s; -) video nasty; **~spiel** *n* video game; **~text** *m* teletext

Vi·deo·thek [video'te:k] *f* (-; -en) video(-tape) library

'Vi·deo·über,wa·chung *f* closed-circuit TV

Viech [fi:ç] F *n* (-[e]s; -er ['fi:çɐ]) **1.** *zo.* (**verdammtes ~** F blasted) animal; (*esp. dog*) F critter; (F blasted) insect, *Am.* bug; **2.** *fig.* brute; **Vie·che·rei** [fi:çə'raɪ] F *f* (-; -en) F hard graft, (real) grind, *sl.* hell of a job

Vieh [fi:] *n* (-[e]s; *no pl.*) cattle *pl.*, livestock; F beast; *fig.* brute; **j-n wie ein Stück ~ behandeln** treat s.o. like dirt (*or* muck); **~be·stand** *m* livestock; **~fut·ter** *n* fodder, feed; **~händ·ler** *m* cattle dealer; **~her·de** *f* cattle herd

vie·hisch ['fi:ɪʃ] **I.** *adj.* **1.** brutal; **2.** F dreadful; **II.** *adv.* **3. sich ~ benehmen** behave like a brute (*or* brutes); **4.** F **~ betrunken** *etc. sl.* drunk *etc.* as hell

'Vieh|markt *m* cattle market; **~seu·che** *f* rinderpest; **~trei·ber** *m* drover; **~wa·gen** *m* cattle wag(g)on; **~wei·de** *f* (cattle) pasture

'Vieh·zeug F *n* (-[e]s; *no pl.*) **1.** animals *pl.*; F menagerie; **2.** *contp.* (**verdammtes ~** F blasted) animals (*or* insects, *Am.* bugs) *pl.*

'Vieh·zucht *f* stock farming, cattle breeding

viel [fi:l] *adj. and adv.* a lot of; **~e** many; **nicht ~** not much; **nicht ~e** not many; **sehr ~** a great deal (of); **sehr ~e** very many, a lot (of), a great many; **noch einmal so ~** as much again; **~ besser** much better; **ziemlich ~(e)** quite a lot (of); **einer zu ~** one too many; **ein bißchen ~** a bit too much; → *a.* **bißchen** II; **~ zu ~** far too much; **das ~e Geld** all that money; **in ~em** in many ways; **um ~es besser** far (*or* much) better; **das will** (**nicht**) **~ heißen** that's saying a lot (that's not saying much); **was gibt es da noch ~ zu bereden?** what is there to discuss?, I thought we'd settled things; **was soll ich dir noch ~ erzählen?** there's no point in my going into (any great) detail about it

'viel·bän·dig [-bɛndɪç] *adj.* multivolume

'viel|be·fa·hren *adj.* very busy; **~e Straße** *a.* road with heavy traffic; **~be·schäf·tigt** *adj.* very busy; **~be·wun·dert** *adj.* much-admired

'viel·deu·tig [-dɔʏtɪç] *adj.* ambiguous; **'Viel·deu·tig·keit** *f* (-; *no pl.*) ambiguity

'viel·dis·ku,tiert *adj.* much-discussed, widely discussed

Viel·eck ['fi:lʔɛk] *n* (-[e]s; -e) polygon

'Viel·ehe *f* (*a.* **die ~**) polygamy

vie·len·orts ['fi:lənʔɔrts] *adv.* in many places

vie·ler·lei ['fi:lɐlaɪ] *adj.* various, all sorts of, multifarious

vie·ler·orts ['fi:lɐʔɔrts] *adv.* in many places

viel·fach ['fi:lfax] **I.** *adj.* multiple; **die ~e Menge** many times the amount; **auf ~en Wunsch** by popular request; **II.** *adv.* in many cases; frequently; **'Viel·fa·che** *n* (-n; -n) **1.** 𝔄 **das ~** the multiple; **2. um ein ~s** many times over, **besser** *etc.*: many times better *etc.*

Viel·falt ['fi:lfalt] *f* (-; *no pl.*) (great) variety; **viel·fäl·tig** ['fi:lfɛltɪç] *adj.* varied, manifold; **'Viel·fäl·tig·keit** *f* (-; *no pl.*) variety, diversity

'viel·far·big *adj.* multicolo(u)red

'Viel·flie·ger *m* frequent flyer (*or* travel[l]er)

Viel·fraß ['fi:lfra:s] *m* (-es; -e) **1.** *zo.* wolverine; **2.** F glutton

'viel|ge·braucht *adj.* much-used; **~ge·fragt** *adj.* very popular; **~ sein** *a.* be in great demand; **~ge·haßt** *adj.* much-hated; **~ge·kauft** *adj.* frequently bought; **~ge·liebt** *adj.* much-loved; **~ge·nannt** *adj.* often-mentioned, *lit.* oft-mentioned; much-cited *book etc.*; noted, distinguished; **~ge·prie·sen** *adj.* much-praised; **~ge·prüft** *adj.* sorely tried; **~ge·reist** *adj.* widely- (*or* much-)travel(l)ed; **er ist ein ~er Mann** he's done a lot of travel(l)ing (in his time); **~ge·rühmt** *adj.* much-praised; **~ge·schmäht** *adj.* much-maligned, much-reviled

viel·ge·stal·tig ['fi:lgəʃtaltɪç] *adj.* variform; *fig.* multifarious

Viel·göt·te·rei [fi:lgœtə'raɪ] *f* (-; *no pl.*) polytheism

viel·köp·fig ['fi:lkœpfɪç] *adj.* **1.** large *family etc.*; **2.** many-headed *beast etc.*

viel·leicht [fɪ'laɪçt] *adv.* a) perhaps, maybe; possibly; *in questions*: *often* by any chance, b) (round) about; **~ ist er krank** he might (*or* may) be sick; **Sie haben ~ recht** you may be right; **~ kommt er** perhaps he'll come, he may come; **es ist ~ besser, wenn** it might be better if; **hast du ihn ~ gesehen?** have you seen him by any chance?, do you happen to have seen him?; **es waren ~ 20 Leute da** I'd say there were (round) about 20 people there, there would have been - what - 20 people there; F **das war ~ ein Durcheinander!** what a mess (that was), you should have seen the mess; **der hat ~ geschimpft!** you should have heard him shout; **ich war ~ aufgeregt!** what a state I was in, *a.* F talk about (being) nervous; **kannst du ~ mal aufhören!** d'you think you could stop (*or* shut up) for a minute?; **hast du's ~ verloren?** don't tell me you've lost it; **glaubt er ~, daß ich es war?** surely he doesn't think I did it?

viel·mals ['fi:lma:ls] *adv.* many times, often, frequently; **danke ~** many thanks; **sie läßt** (**dich**) **~ grüßen** she sends (you) her best regards; **entschuldige ~, ich bitte ~ um Entschuldigung** I'm terribly sorry

viel'mehr *adv.* rather; on the contrary; **es waren Tausende, oder ~ Zehntausende von Leuten** there were thousands, or rather tens of thousands of people (*or* I should say tens of thousands of people); **es geht ~ darum, ob** it's rather a question of whether

'Viel·red·ner F *m* F gasbag

'viel·sa·gend *adj.* meaningful *look*

viel·schich·tig ['fi:lʃɪçtɪç] *adj.* **1.** multi-layered; **2.** *fig.* complex *problem etc.*; **'Viel·schich·tig·keit** *f* (-; *no pl.*) complexity

'Viel·schrei·ber *contp. m* F hack (writer)

viel·sei·tig ['fi:lzaɪtɪç] **I.** *adj.* a) many-sided; versatile, b) (very) varied; various, a (whole) variety of *possibilities etc.*; interesting *task, job etc.*; **II.** *adv.*: **~ verwendbar** multi-purpose ...; **~ begabt** multitalented; **er ist ~ begabt** *a.* he's very versatile, he has many talents, he's a man of many talents; **~ interessiert sein** have a lot of interests; **et. ~ verwenden** put s.th. to various (*or* a number of) uses; **'Viel·sei·tig·keit** *f* (-; *no pl.*) many-sidedness; versatility; *the* many aspects *pl.* (*gen.* of)

viel·spra·chig ['fi:lʃpra:xɪç] *adj.* polyglot (*a.* **~er Mensch**), multilingual

Viel·staa·te·rei [fi:lʃta:tə'raɪ] *f* (-; *no pl.*) particularism

viel·stim·mig ['fi:lʃtɪmɪç] *adj.* polyphonic

'viel|um,strit·ten *adj.* highly controversial; **~um,wor·ben** *adj.* much sought-after; **~ver·hei·ßend, ~ver·spre·chend** *adj.* (very) promising

'Viel·völ·ker·staat *m* multinational (*or* multiracial) state

Viel·wei·be·rei [fi:lvaɪbə'raɪ] *f* (-; *no pl.*) (*a.* **die ~**) polygamy

Viel·wis·ser ['fi:lvɪsɐ] *contp. m* (-s; -) F know-(it-)all

'Viel·zahl *f* (-; *no pl.*) huge (*or* vast) number; *formal*: multitude

'viel·zi͵tiert *adj.* much-cited

vier [fiːɐ] *adj.* four; ***auf allen ~en (kriechen*** be) on all fours; ***unter ~ Augen*** in private; ***alle ~e von sich strecken*** flop into an armchair (*or* onto the bed *etc.*); → ***Buchstabe***; **Vier** *f* (-; -en ['fiːrən]) a) four, b) *ped.* D, c) (*bus etc.*) (number) four; *ped.* ***e-e ~ schreiben*** get a D

Vier'au·gen·ge·spräch F *n* tête-à-tête, one-to-one conversation

vier·bän·dig ['fiːɐbɛndɪç] *adj.* four-volume ..., in four volumes

Vier·bei·ner ['fiːɐbaɪnɐ] F *m* (-s; -) quadruped, four-legged animal; *hum.* (*dog*) F *our* four-legged friend; **vier·bei·nig** ['fiːɐbaɪnɪç] *adj.* four-legged

vier·blätt·rig ['fiːɐblɛtrɪç] *adj.* four-leafed, four-leaved, four-leaf ...; ***~es Kleeblatt*** four-leaf (*or* -leaved) clover

Vier·eck ['fiːɐʔɛk] *n* (-[e]s; -e) square; **'vier·eckig** *adj.* square

Vie·rer ['fiːrɐ] *m* (-s; -) **1.** *rowing*: four; **2.** → ***Vier***; **~bob** *m* four-seater bob; **~gespräch** *n* four-sided (*or* four-party) talks *pl.*; *pol. hist.* four-power talks *pl.*

vie·rer·lei ['fiːrɐlaɪ] *adj.* four (different) kinds of; *su.* four things

'Vie·rer·takt *m* ♪ four-four time, quadruple time

vier·fach ['fiːɐfax] *adj.* fourfold; ***die ~e Menge*** four times the amount; ***~er Sieger*** four-time winner (*or* champion); **'Vier·fa·che** *n* (-n; *no pl.*): ***das ~*** four times as much; *a.* four times the amount; ***um ein ~s steigen*** quadruple, rise (*or* go up) fourfold

Vier'far·ben·druck *m* four-colo(u)r printing (*or* print)

Vier·fü·ßer ['fiːɐfyːsɐ] *m* (-s; -) *zo.* quadruped; **vier·fü·ßig** ['fiːɐfyːsɪç] *adj.* four-footed; *zo.* quadruped; **Vier·füß·ler** ['fiːɐfyːslɐ] *m* (-s; -) quadruped

'Vier·gang·ge·trie·be *n mot.* four-speed transmission

'Vier·ge·spann *n* four-in-hand; *hist.* quadriga

vier·hän·dig ['fiːɐhɛndɪç] **I.** *adj. zo. and* ♪ four-handed; **II.** *adv.*: ♪ ***~ spielen*** play a duet

'vier'hun·dert *adj.* four hundred

vier·jäh·rig ['fiːɐjɛːrɪç] *adj.* **1.** four-year-old ...; **2.** four-year ...; ***ein ~es ...*** *a.* four years of ...; **Vier·jäh·ri·ge** ['fiːɐjɛːrɪgə] *m, f* (-n; -n) four-year-old

Vier·kant ['fiːɐkant] *m* (-[e]s; -e) ⚙ square; **'Vier·kant...** *in cpds.* square *timber etc.*; **'vier·kan·tig** *adj.* square; **'Vier·kant·schlüs·sel** *m* square box spanner (*Am.* wrench)

vier·köp·fig ['fiːɐkœpfɪç] *adj. family etc.* of four; ***~e Delegation*** *etc. a.* four-member (*or* four-man) delegation *etc.*

Vier·lin·ge ['fiːɐlɪŋə] *pl.* quadruplets, F quads

Vier'mäch·te|ab·kom·men *n hist.* four-power agreement; **~ge·sprä·che** *pl. hist.* four-power talks

'vier·mal *adv.* four times

vier·mo·to·rig ['fiːɐmotoːrɪç] *adj.* four-engine ..., four-engined

'Vier·rad|an·trieb *m mot.* four-wheel drive; **~brem·se** *f* four-wheel brake

vier·räd·rig ['fiːɐrɛːdrɪç] *adj.* four-wheeled, four-wheel ...

vier·sai·tig ['fiːɐzaɪtɪç] *adj.* ♪ four-string ..., four-stringed

'Vier·schan·zen·tour͵nee *f* Four Hills Tournament

vier·schrö·tig ['fiːɐʃrøːtɪç] *adj.* burly

vier·sei·tig ['fiːɐzaɪtɪç] *adj.* four-sided; ⩓ quadrilateral

vier·sil·big ['fiːɐzɪlbɪç] *adj.* four-syllable ...

Vier·sit·zer ['fiːɐzɪtsɐ] *m* (-s; -) four-seater; **vier·sit·zig** ['fiːɐzɪtsɪç] *adj.* four-seater ...

Vier·spän·ner ['fiːɐʃpɛnɐ] *m* (-s; -) four-in-hand

vier·spu·rig ['fiːɐʃpuːrɪç] *adj.* **1.** four-lane *road etc.*; **2.** four-track *tape*

vier·stel·lig ['fiːɐʃtɛlɪç] *adj.* four-digit *number etc.*

Vier'ster·ne|ge·ne͵ral *m* four-star general; **~ho͵tel** *n* four-star hotel

vier·stim·mig ['fiːɐʃtɪmɪç] *adj.* ♪ four-part ..., *pred.* for four voices

vier·stöckig ['fiːɐʃtœkɪç] (*sep.* -k·k-) *adj.* four-stor(e)y ...

viert [fiːɐt] **I.** *adj.* fourth; ***~es Kapitel*** chapter four; ***am ~en Juni*** on the fourth of June; ***4. Juni*** 4th June, June 4(th); **II.** *adv.*: ***wir waren zu ~*** there were four of us; ***wir gingen zu ~ hin*** four of us went there

vier·tä·gig ['fiːɐtɛːgɪç] *adj.* **1.** four-day(-long) ...; **2.** four-day-old ...

'Vier·takt·mo·tor *m* four-stroke engine

'vier'tau·send *adj.* four thousand; **'Vier'tau·sen·der** *m* four-thousand met|re (*Am.* -er) peak

Vier·te ['fiːɐtə] *m, f* (-n; -n) (the) fourth; ***sie war ~*** she was (*or* came) fourth; ***Heinrich IV.*** Henry IV (= Henry the Fourth); ***heute ist der ~*** it's the fourth today

'vier·tei·len *v/t.* (vierteilte, gevierteilt, h) *hist.* (draw and) quarter; F *fig.* ***er würde sich lieber ~ lassen(, als ...)*** he'd rather die (than ...)

vier·tei·lig ['fiːɐtaɪlɪç] *adj.* four-part ..., in four parts

Vier·tel ['fɪrtəl] *n* (-s; -) quarter; ⩓ fourth; ***~ nach vier*** (a) quarter past four, a quarter after (*or* of) four; ***~ vor vier*** (a) quarter to four; **~dre·hung** *f* quarter turn; **~fi͵na·le** *n* quarter final; **~jahr** *n* three months *pl.*, quarter; **~jah·res·schrift** *f* quarterly (journal)

vier·tel·jäh·rig ['fɪrtəljɛːrɪç] *adj.* **1.** three-month ...; **2.** three-month-old ..., three months old; **'vier·tel·jähr·lich I.** *adj.* quarterly; ***~e Kündigung*** three months' notice; **II.** *adv.* quarterly, every three months

'Vier·tel·li·ter *m*: (***ein ~*** [a]) quarter of a litre (*Am.* liter)

vier·teln ['fɪrtəln] *v/t.* (h) quarter

'Vier·tel|no·te *f* ♪ crotchet, *Am.* quarter note; **~pau·se** *f* ♪ crotchet (*Am.* quarter note) rest; **~pfund** *n*: (***ein ~*** [a]) quarter of a pound, (a) quarter; **~stun·de** *f* quarter of an hour

vier·tel·stün·dig ['fɪrtəlʃtʏndɪç] *adj.* fifteen-minute ..., of (*or* lasting) a quarter of an hour; ***e-e ~e Pause*** *etc.* a fifteen-minute break *etc.*, fifteen minutes' (*or* quarter of an hour's) rest *etc.*; **'vier·tel·stünd·lich I.** *adj.* quarter-hourly, occurring every fifteen minutes; ***in ~en Abständen*** every fifteen minutes; **II.** *adv.* every fifteen minutes (*or* quarter of an hour), quarter-hourly

'Vier·tel·ton *m* quarter tone

vier·tens ['fiːɐtəns] *adv.* fourth(ly), four, in fourth place

Vier·und'sech·zig·stel|-No·te *f* ♪ hemidemisemiquaver, *Am.* sixty-fourth note; **~-Pau·se** *f* ♪ hemidemisemiquaver (*Am.* sixty-fourth note) rest

Vie·rung ['fiːrʊŋ] *f* (-; -en) ⩓ crossing, intersection

'Vier·vier·tel·takt *m* ♪ four-four time

vier·wö·chig ['fiːɐvœçɪç] *adj.* **1.** four-week ...; **2.** four-week-old ...

vier·zehn ['fɪrtseːn] *adj.* fourteen; ***in ~ Tagen*** in a fortnight, in two weeks(' time); **'vier·zehnt** *adj.* fourteenth; **'vier·zehn·tä·gig** [-tɛːgɪç] *adj.* two-week(-long) ..., fortnight's ...; ***ein ~er Urlaub*** *a.* two weeks' holiday

Vier·zehn·tel ['fɪrtseːntəl] *n* (-s; -) fourteenth (part)

Vier·zei·ler ['fiːɐtsaɪlɐ] *m* (-s; -) quatrain; **vier·zei·lig** ['fiːɐtsaɪlɪç] *adj.* four-line ...; ***~ sein*** have four lines

vier·zig ['fɪrtsɪç] *adj.* forty; ***in den ~er Jahren*** in the forties; ***er ist in den Vierzigern*** he's in his forties

Vier·zi·ger ['fɪrtsɪgɐ] *m* (-s; -) man in his forties, F fortysomething; **Vier·zi·ge·rin** ['fɪrtsɪgərɪn] *f* (-; -nen) woman in her forties, F fortysomething

'vier·zig·jäh·rig [-jɛːrɪç] *adj.* **1.** forty-year-old ...; **2.** forty-year(-long) ...

vier·zigst ['fɪrtsɪçst] *adj.* fortieth; ***sie hat heute ihren Vierzigsten*** she's forty today, it's her fortieth birthday today

Vier·zig'stun·den·wo·che *f* 40-hour week

Vier'zim·mer·woh·nung *f* three-bedroom(ed) flat (*Am.* apartment)

'Vier·zy͵lin·der F *m* a) four-cylinder (car), b) four-cylinder engine

Vi·et·na·me·se [vĭetna'meːzə] *m* (-n; -n) **1.** Vietnamese; **2.** F Vietnamese restaurant; ***wir gehen zum ~n*** we're going to a Vietnamese (place); **Vi·et·na·me·sin** [vĭetna'meːzɪn] *f* (-; -nen) Vietnamese; **vi·et·na·me·sisch** [vĭetna'meːzɪʃ] *adj.* Vietnamese

Vi·gnet·te [vɪn'jɛtə] *f* (-; -n) **1.** vignette; **2.** *in Switzerland*: *mot.* sticker

Vi·kar [vi'kaːɐ] *m* (-s; -e [-rə]) curate, assistant

Vil·la ['vɪla] *f* (-; Villen) villa; mansion

Vil·len|ge·gend ['vɪlən-] *f*, **~vier·tel** *n* residential area, F posh part of town; **~vor·ort** *m* residential suburb

Vio·la ['vĭoːla] *f* (-; -len) viola

vio·lett [vĭo'lɛt] *adj.*, **Vio'lett** *n* (-[s]; *no pl.*) violet

Vio·li·ne [vĭo'liːnə] *f* (-; -n) violin

Vio·li·nist [vĭoli'nɪst] *m* (-en; -en), **Vio·li·ni·stin** [vĭoli'nɪstɪn] *f* (-; -nen) violinist

Vio'lin|kon͵zert *n* violin concerto; **~schlüs·sel** *m* treble clef; **~so͵na·te** *f* violin sonata

Vio·lon·cel·lo [vĭolɔn'tʃɛlo] *n* (-s; -li) cello

VIP [vɪp] *f* (-; -s) VIP, F top nob; *pl. coll. a.* F *the* top brass (*pl.*)

Vi·per ['viːpɐ] *f* (-; -n) viper

VIP-Lounge ['vɪplaʊndʒ] *f* executive (*or* VIP) lounge

Vi·ri·li·tät [virili'tɛːt] *f* (-; *no pl.*) virility

Vi·ro·lo·ge [viro'loːgə] *m* (-n; -n) virologist; **Vi·ro·lo·gie** [virolo'giː] *f* (-; *no pl.*) virology; **vi·ro·lo·gisch** [viro'loːgɪʃ] *adj.* virological

vir·tu·os [vɪr'tŭoːs] *adj.* virtuoso ..., brilliant; ***ein ~er Klavierspieler*** a virtuoso on the piano; ***e-e ~e Leistung*** a masterly accomplishment (♪ performance), a brilliant feat; **Vir·tuo·se** [vɪr'tŭoːzə] *m* (-n; -n), **Vir·tuo·sin** [vɪr'tŭoːzɪn] *f* (-;

-nen) virtuoso; **Vir·tuo·si·tät** [vɪrtŭozi'tɛːt] *f* (-; *no pl.*) virtuosity, brilliance *of a performance etc.*
vi·ru·lent [viru'lɛnt] *adj.* virulent
Vi·rus ['viːrʊs] *n*, *m* (-; Viren ['viːrən]) virus (*a. computer*); **~er·kran·kung** *f* virus (*or* viral) disease; **~in·fek·ti͵on** *f* virus (*or* viral) infection; **~krank·heit** *f* virus (*or* viral) disease, F virus; **~trä·ger** *m* virus carrier
Vi·sa·frei·heit ['viːza-] *f* (-; *no pl.*) visa exemption
Vi·sa·ge [vi'zaːʒə] F *f* (-; -n) F mug
Vi·sa·pflicht ['viːza-] *f* visa requirement
vis-à-vis [viza'viː] *adv.* opposite (*dat. s.o., s.th., a place etc.*)
Vi·sier [vi'ziːɐ] *n* (-s; -e [-rə]) **1.** visor; *fig.* ***das ~ herunterlassen*** clam up; ***er ließ das ~ herunter*** *a.* the shutters came down; **2.** sight; *fig.* ***et. ins ~ nehmen*** get s.th. (lined up) in one's sights
vi·sie·ren [vi'ziːrən] *v/t.* (h) ⚙ adjust
Vi·si·on [vi'zĭoːn] *f* (-; -en) vision
vi·sio·när [vizĭo'nɛːɐ] *adj.*, **Vi·sio'när** *m* (-s; -e [-rə]) visionary
Vi·si·ta·ti·on [vizita'tsĭoːn] *f* (-; -en) search
Vi·si·te [vi'ziːtə] *f* (-; -n) (doctor's) round; ***auf ~ sein*** be on (*or* doing) one's rounds
Vi'si·ten·kar·te *f* business (*or* call) card; F *iro.* ***er hat s-e ~ hinterlassen*** he's left his usual trail
vi·si·tie·ren [vizi'tiːrən] *v/t.* (h) **1.** search; *a.* frisk *s.o.*; **2.** inspect
vis·kos [vɪs'koːs] *adj.* viscous
Vis·ko·se [vɪs'koːzə] *f* (-; *no pl.*) viscose
Vis·ko·si·tät [vɪskozi'tɛːt] *f* (-; *no pl.*) viscosity
vi·su·ell [vi'zŭɛl] *adj.* visual
Vi·sum ['viːzʊm] *n* (-s; Visa ['viːza]) visa; **~an·trag** *m* visa application; **&frei** *adj.* visa-exempt; **~zwang** *m* (-[e]s; *no pl.*) visa requirement
vi·tal [vi'taːl] *adj.* **1.** energetic; spry; **2.** *fig.* vital, essential; **Vi·ta·li·tät** [vitali'tɛːt] *f* (-; *no pl.*) vitality
Vit·amin [vita'miːn] *n* (-s; -e) vitamin; F *fig.* ***~ B*** contacts, *in GB*: *a.* the old boy network; **&arm** *adj.* low in vitamins; **~be·darf** *m* vitamin requirement; **~ge·halt** *m* vitamin content
vit·amin·hal·tig [vita'miːnhaltɪç] *adj.*: ***(sehr) ~ sein*** contain (plenty of) vitamins
Vit·amin|haus·halt *m* vitamin balance; **~kap·sel** *f* vitamin pill (*or* capsule); **~man·gel** *m* vitamin deficiency; **~man·gel·er·kran·kung** *f* vitamin-deficiency disease; **~prä·pa͵rat** *n* vitamin preparation (*or* compound); **&reich** *adj.* rich in vitamins; **~sprit·ze** *f* vitamin shot; **~stoß** *m* massive dose of vitamins
Vi·tri·ne [vi'triːnə] *f* (-; -n) showcase, display case (*or* cabinet); glass(-fronted) cabinet
Vi·tri·ol [vitri'oːl] *n* (-s; *no pl.*) vitriol
Vi·vi·sek·ti·on [vivizɛk'tsĭoːn] *f* (-; -en) vivisection; **vi·vi·se·zie·ren** [vivize'tsiːrən] *v/t.* (h) vivisect
Vi·ze ['fiːtsə] F *m* (-s; -s) **1.** deputy, F number two; **2.** *sport*: runner-up; **~ad·mi͵ral** *m* vice admiral; **~kanz·ler** *m* vice(-)chancellor; **~kö·nig** *m* viceroy; **~kon·sul** *m* vice(-)consul; **~mei·ster** *m* runner-up; **~prä·si͵dent** *m* vice(-)president; **~prä·si͵dent·schafts·be·wer·ber** *m pol.* running mate; **~welt·mei·ster** *m* runner-up in the World Cup
V-Leu·te ['faʊ-] *pl.* → ***V-Mann***
Vlies [fliːs] *n* (-es; -e ['fliːzə]) fleece (*a. textil.*)
V-Mann ['faʊ-] *m* (-[e]s; -Leute) contact; *a.* informer
Vo·gel ['foːgəl] *m* (-s; Vögel ['føːgəl]) bird (*a.* F *plane*); F ***komischer ~*** odd character, F strange customer; ***er ist ein lustiger ~*** he's good for a laugh; *fig.* ***e-n ~ haben*** F have a screw loose (somewhere); ***j-m den ~ zeigen*** tap one's forehead at s.o.; ***den ~ abschießen*** F take the cake; ***friß ~, oder stirb!*** it's (a case of) sink or swim; F ***der ~ ist ausgeflogen*** the bird has flown; **~bau·er** *n* birdcage; **~beer·baum** *m* rowan (tree); **~bee·re** *f* rowanberry; **~dreck** *m* bird droppings *pl.*; **~ei** *n* bird's egg; **&frei** *adj.* **1.** outlawed; ***für ~ erklären*** outlaw; **2.** *fig.* ***für ~ gehalten werden*** be considered fair game; **~fut·ter** *n* birdseed; **~ge·zwit·scher** *n* twittering of birds; ***am Morgen hört man ~*** *a.* in the mornings you can hear the birds twittering; **~haus** *n* aviary; **~kä·fig** *m* birdcage; **~kir·sche** *f* rowanberry; **~kun·de** *f* ornithology; **~leim** *m* birdlime
vö·geln ['føːgəln] V *v/t. and v/i.* (h) V screw
'Vo·gel|nest *n* bird's nest; **~per·spek͵ti·ve** *f* bird's-eye view; ***... aus (or in) der ~*** a bird's-eye view of ...; ***Aufnahme aus der ~*** high-angle shot; ***et. aus der ~ sehen*** have a bird's-eye view of s.th.; **~ruf** *m* birdcall; **~schar** *f* flock of birds; **~scheu·che** *f* scarecrow (*a. fig.*); *fig. a.* F frump; **~schutz** *m* protection of birds; **~schutz·ge·biet** *n* bird sanctuary; **~stan·ge** *f* perch
'Vo·gel·stel·ler [-ʃtɛlɐ] *m* (-s; -) bird-catcher
'Vo·gel·stim·me *f* birdcall
Vo·gel-'Strauß-Po·li͵tik *f* ostrich policy; ***~ treiben*** hide one's head in the sand
'Vo·gel|war·te *f* ornithological station; **~züch·ter** *m* bird breeder; **~zug** *m* migration of birds
Vög·lein ['føːglaɪn] *n* (-s; -) little bird; F *hum.* birdie
Vogt [foːkt] *m* (-[e]s; Vögte ['føːktə]) *hist.* **1.** overseer; **2.** sheriff; **3.** bailiff; **4.** administrator
Vo·ka·bel [vo'kaːbəl] *f* (-; -n) word; **~heft** *n* vocabulary book
Vo·ka·bu·lar [vokabu'laːɐ] *n* (-s; -e [-rə]) vocabulary
vo·kal [vo'kaːl] *adj.* ♪ vocal
Vo·kal [vo'kaːl] *m* (-s; -e) vowel
vo·ka·lisch [vo'kaːlɪʃ] *adj.* vowel ..., vocalic
Vo'kal|mu͵sik *f* vocal music; **~par͵tie** *f* vocal part; **~so͵list** *m* solo singer; solo voice
Vo·lant [vo'lãː] *m* flounce
Vo·lie·re [vo'lĭeːrə] *f* (-; -n) aviary
Volk [fɔlk] *n* (-[e]s; Völker ['fœlkɐ]) a) people *pl.*; nation, b) *the* masses *pl.*, *contp. a. the* plebs *pl.*; mob, rabble, c) F crowd, F lot, bunch, *contp. a.* F shower; ***das deutsche ~*** the Germans, the German people (*or* nation); ***das arbeitende ~*** the working classes; F ***das junge ~*** the young set, F the young 'uns; ***viel ~(s)*** crowds of people; ***ein Mann aus dem ~*** a man of the people; F ***unters ~ bringen*** a) spread *a rumo(u)r etc.*, b) sell, get rid of *s.th.*; ***sich unters ~ mischen*** mingle with the crowd; → ***auserwählt***
Völk·chen ['fœlkçən] F *fig.* *n* (-s; -) crowd, F lot, bunch; *contp. a.* F shower
Völ·ker|bund ['fœlkɐ-] *m hist.* League of Nations; **~freund·schaft** *f* friendship between nations; **~ge·mein·schaft** *f* community of nations
Völ·ker·kun·de ['fœlkɐ-] *f* ethnology; **'Völ·ker·kund·ler** [-kʊntlɐ] *m* (-s; -) ethnologist; **'völ·ker·kund·lich** [-kʊntlɪç] *adj.* ethnological
Völ·ker·mord ['fœlkɐ-] *m* genocide
Völ·ker·recht ['fœlkɐ-] *n* (-[e]s; *no pl.*) international law; **'Völ·ker·recht·ler** [-rɛçtlɐ] *m* (-s; -) specialist in international law; **'völ·ker·recht·lich I.** *adj.* international; *question, problem etc.* of (*or* relating to) international law; *decision, measures etc.* bound by international law; **II.** *adv.* under (*or* according to) international law; **'Völ·ker·rechts·ver·let·zung** *f* breach of international law
Völ·ker·schaft ['fœlkɐʃaft] *f* (-; -en) people (*sg.*); tribe
Völ·ker|ver·stän·di·gung ['fœlkɐ-] *f* understanding among nations; **~wan·de·rung** *f* migration (of peoples); *fig.* mass exodus, mass migration (***nach*** *dat.* to); ***die (germanische) ~*** the Germanic migrations
'Volks|ab·stim·mung *f* referendum; **~auf·lauf** *m* throng of people, crowd (of people); crowd of onlookers; **~auf·stand** *m* national uprising; **~be·fra·gung** *f* public opinion poll; **~be·geh·ren** *n* petition for a referendum; **~be·lu·sti·gung** *f* (form of) popular entertainment; *fig.* ***et. zu e-r ~ machen*** turn s.th. into a fairground spectacle; **~de·mo·kra͵tie** *f* people's democracy; **~deut·sche** *m, f* (-n; -n) ethnic German; **~dich·ter** *m* popular poet; **&ei·gen** *adj. hist. DDR*: state-owned; ***~er Betrieb (VEB)*** state-owned company; **~ei·gen·tum** *n* public property; **~ein·kom·men** *n* national income; **~emp·fin·den** *n*: ***das ~*** popular feeling, public opinion; **~ent·scheid** *m* referendum; **~ety·mo·lo͵gie** *f* popular etymology; **~feind** *m* public enemy; **&feind·lich** *adj.* subversive; **~fest** *n* festival; funfair; **~fest·stim·mung** *f* carnival atmosphere; **~front** *f pol.* popular (*or* people's) front; **~ge·mur·mel** *n* **1.** *thea.* crowd noises *pl.*; **2.** F *fig.* rumblings *pl.* (among the party *etc.*); **~grup·pe** *f* ethnic group; **~held** *m* mass (*or* folk) hero; **~hoch·schu·le** *f* **1.** adult education program(me); **2.** adult evening classes *pl.*; **~ju͵stiz** *f* mob law; **~kam·mer** *f hist. DDR*: People's Parliament; former East German parliament; **~krank·heit** *f* endemic (*a. iro.* national) disease
'Volks·kun·de *f* ethnic studies *pl.*; **'volks·kund·lich** [-kʊntlɪç] *adj.* ethnic
'Volks|kunst *f* (-; *no pl.*) folk (*or* ethnic) art; **~lied** *n* folk song; **~mär·chen** *n* folk tale; **~me·di͵zin** *f* folk medicine; **~mei·nung** *f*: ***die ~*** public opinion; **~men·ge** *f* crowd; *the* masses *pl.*; **~mund** *m*: (***im ~*** in) common parlance; ***im ~ heißt es, daß*** it's a popular saying that; **~mu͵sik** *f* folk music; **&nah** *adj.* close to the people; popular; *pol.* grass-roots ...; **~nah·rung** *f*, **~nah·rungs·mit·tel** *n* staple (food); **~po·li͵zei** *f hist. DDR*: People's Police; **~po·li͵zist** *m hist. DDR*: member of the People's Police; **~re·de** F *f*: ***~n halten*** F speechify; ***halte keine ~n!*** keep it short!; **~re·pu͵blik** *f* people's republic; ***die ~***

China the People's Republic of China; **~schicht** *f* social class; **~schu·le** *f hist.* elementary school (*for pupils aged 6 to 14*); **~see·le** *f* (-; *no pl.*) **1. *die*** **~** public feeling; ***die*** **~** ***kocht*** (*or* ***ist empört***) public feeling is running high; **2.** national spirit; ***die deutsche*** **~** the German soul (*or* national spirit); **~spra·che** *f* vernacular; **~stim·me** *f* voice of the people; **~stück** *n* folk play; **~tanz** *m* folk dance; **~tracht** *f* national costume (*or* dress); **~trau·er·tag** *m* national day of mourning

volks·tüm·lich ['fɔlksty:mlıç] *adj.* **1.** a) popular, b) for ordinary people; *prices* within everybody's reach, c) folksy; **2.** traditional; folk *art, medicine etc.*; *contp.* folksy *art etc.*

'volks·ver·bun·den *adj.* close to the people; **'Volks·ver·bun·den·heit** *f* (-; *no pl.*) closeness to the people

'Volks|ver·dum·mung *f* brainwashing (of the public); pulling the wool over the people's eyes; **~ver·füh·rer** *m* demagogue; **~ver·het·zung** *f* incitement of the masses; **~ver·samm·lung** *f* **1.** public gathering; mass rally; **2.** people's assembly; **~ver·tre·ter** *m* people's representative; **~ver·tre·tung** *f* representation of the people; **~wei·se** *f* folk melody (*or* tune); **~weis·heit** *f* piece of popular (*or* folk) wisdom

'Volks·wirt *m* economist; **'Volks·wirt·schaft** *f* **1.** (national) economy; **2.** economics *pl.*; **'Volks·wirt·schaft·ler** *m* (-s; -) → ***Volkswirt***; **'volks·wirt·schaft·lich** *adj.* (politico-)economic(ally *adv.*); **'Volks·wirt·schafts·leh·re** *f* economics *pl.*

'Volks|zäh·lung *f* census; **~zorn** *m* wrath of the people; **~zu·ge·hö·rig·keit** *f* nationality; national identity

voll [fɔl] **I.** *adj.* a) full; full up, b) full (up), filled, c) *streets etc.* full of traffic, d) F plastered, *sl.* tight, e) F full, f) *fig.* full (*a. figure*), g) full, whole *amount, sum*; **~(er), ~ von** *dat.* full of, *b.s.* rife with; ***ein Koffer*** (***e-e Kiste*** *etc.*) **~** ***Bücher*** a caseful (boxful *etc.*) of books; ***e-e*** **~*e Stunde*** a full (*or* whole, solid) hour; ***zu jeder*** **~*en Stunde*** every hour on the hour; **~** ***schlagen*** *clock*: strike the full hour; ***sechs*** **~*e Tage*** six whole days; ***ein*** **~*es Dutzend*** a full (*or* whole) dozen; **~*e Beschäftigung*** full (*or* full-time) employment; ***bei*** **~*er Besinnung*** fully conscious; ***er hat es bei*** **~*er Besinnung gesagt*** he was fully aware of what he was saying; ***aus*** **~*er Brust*** (*or* **~*em Halse***) at the top of one's voice; ***ein*** **~*er Erfolg*** a complete success; ***die*** **~*e Wahrheit*** the whole truth, *w.s.* the full story; ***aus dem*** **~*en schöpfen*** draw on plentiful resources; **~** ***und ganz*** completely, *support etc.* wholeheartedly; F ***in die*** **~*en gehen*** F go the whole hog; ***j-n nicht für*** **~** ***nehmen*** not to take s.o. seriously; → ***Fahrt, Hand, Mund, Recht***; **II.** *adv.* fully; **~** ***und ganz*** fully, completely; ***et.*** **~** ***ausnützen*** use s.th. to (one's) full advantage

volla·den (*sep.* -ll·l-) *v/t.* (*irr., sep.*, h, → ***laden***) load up (to the top)

'Voll·aka,de·mi·ker *m* university graduate

voll'auf *adv.* fully, completely; **~** ***zufrieden*** quite (*or* fully) satisfied; **~** ***beschäftigt mit*** *dat.* fully occupied with *s.th.*; ***ich bin mit den Kindern*** **~** ***beschäftigt*** I've got enough on my hands with the children, the children are a full-time job; **~** ***zu tun haben*** have plenty (*or* enough) to do

vollau·fen (*sep.* -ll·l-] *v/i.* (*irr., sep.*, sn, → ***laufen***) fill up; ***et.*** **~** ***lassen*** fill s.th. up; F ***sich*** **~** ***lassen*** F get tanked up

'Voll·au·to,ma·tik *f* fully automatic system; ***mit*** **~** → **'voll·au·to,ma·tisch** *adj.* fully automatic, all-automatic

'voll·au·to·ma·ti·siert [-aʊtomati,zi:ɐt] *adj.* fully automated; **'Voll·au·to·ma·ti·,sie·rung** *f* (-; *no pl.*) full automation

'Voll|bad *n* bath; ***ein*** **~** ***nehmen*** *a.* F sink into the bath(tub); **~bart** *m* beard

'voll·be·packt *adj.* loaded down with luggage, F (absolutely) loaded

'voll·be·schäf·tigt *adj.* fully employed; full-time *employee*; **'Voll·be·schäf·ti·gung** *f* (-; *no pl.*) full employment

'voll·be·setzt *adj.* (completely) full; *a.* fully-booked *hotel etc.*

'Voll·be·sitz *m*: ***im*** **~** ***von*** *dat.* in full possession of; ***im*** **~** ***s-r Sinne sein*** be completely lucid, F be all there; ***im*** **~** ***s-r geistigen Kräfte sein*** be in full possession (*or* command) of one's mental faculties

'Voll·bier *n beer with a high original wort*

'Voll·bild *n typ.* full-page illustration (*or* picture)

'Voll·blut... *fig. in cpds.* full-blooded

'Voll·blut *n* (-[e]s; *no pl.*), **~pferd** *n* thoroughbred

Voll·blü·ter ['fɔlbly:tɐ] *m* (-s; -) thoroughbred; **'voll·blü·tig** [-bly:tıç] *adj.* thoroughbred, *a. fig.* full-blooded

'Voll·brem·sung *f* full braking; ***e-e*** **~** ***machen*** slam on the brakes

voll'brin·gen *v/t.* (*irr., no* -ge-, h, → ***bringen***) accomplish, achieve; perform *deed, miracle etc.*

voll·bu·sig ['fɔlbu:zıç] *adj.* chesty, busty, F bosomy

'Voll·dampf *m*: ***mit*** **~** at full steam; *fig.* F flat out, *drive etc. a.* F full tilt; ***mit*** **~** ***voraus*** full steam ahead

Völ·le·ge·fühl ['fœlə-] *n* full (*or* bloated) feeling

'voll·elek,tro·nisch *adj.* fully electronic (*or* automatic)

voll'en·den *v/t.* (*insep., no* -ge-, h) complete (*a. studies etc.*); finish; **voll'en·det I.** *p.p. of* ***vollenden***; **II.** *adj.* **1.** perfect; accomplished; masterly *performance etc.*; F utter, absolute *nonsense etc.*; **~*e Schönheit*** perfect beauty; **2.** ***Kinder ab dem*** (***bis zum***) **~*en 8. Lebensjahr*** children aged 8 years and over (children up to and including the age of 8); **vol·lends** ['fɔlɛnts] *adv.* completely; **Voll'en·dung** *f* (-; *no pl.*) **1.** completion; ***der*** **~** ***entgegengehen*** be nearing completion; ***nach*** **~** ***des 18. Lebensjahres*** on reaching the age of 18; **2.** perfection

'voll·ent·wickelt *adj.* fully developed; *fig. a.* full-blown

vol·ler ['fɔlɐ] *adj.* **1.** *comp. of voll*: fuller; **2.** → ***voll*** I

Völ·le·rei [fœlə'raı] *f* (-; *no pl.*) gluttony

Vol·ley·ball ['vɔlibal] *m* (-[e]s; *no pl.*), **~spiel** *n* volleyball

'voll·fett *adj.* full-fat; **'Voll·fett·kä·se** *m* full-fat cheese

'voll·fres·sen F *v/refl.* (*irr., sep.*, h, → ***fressen***): ***sich*** **~** F stuff o.s.; ***ich habe mich so vollgefressen*** F I think I'm going to burst

voll'füh·ren *v/t.* (*insep., no* -ge-, h) do; perform *trick etc.*

'Voll·gas *n*: ***mit*** **~** full speed, F *fig.* F full tilt; **~** ***geben*** F put one's foot down (hard)

'voll|ge·fres·sen F *adj.* F stuffed (full); overfed, fat; **~*er Typ*** F fat slob, tub of lard; **~ge·la·den** *adj.* loaded (to the top); *car etc.*: loaded down; **~ge·packt, ~ge'pfropft, ~ge·stopft** *adj.* crammed (full), (F jam)packed, F chock-a-block

'voll·gie·ßen *v/t.* (*irr., sep.*, h, → ***gießen***) fill (up)

'Voll·glat·ze *f*: ***e-e*** **~** ***haben*** be completely bald

'Voll·gum·mi·rei·fen *m* solid tyre (*Am.* tire)

'Voll·idi,ot F *m* complete idiot, F absolute twit (*or* nincompoop), *sl.* headbanger

völ·lig ['fœlıç] **I.** *adj.* a) full, entire, b) complete, total; absolute, sheer *madness, nonsense etc.*; ***das ist mein*** **~*er Ernst*** I'm quite (F dead) serious about it; **II.** *adv.* completely; **~** ***richtig*** perfectly (*or* quite) right; **~** ***unmöglich*** (***verrückt, betrunken*** *etc.*) absolutely impossible (mad, drunk *etc.*); ***ich bin*** **~** ***einverstanden*** that's perfectly all right (*Am.* alright) by me; ***ich bin*** **~** ***Ihrer Meinung*** I agree with you entirely; ***das genügt*** **~** that's (more than) enough, that's fine, that'll do nicely

'voll·in·halt·lich I. *adj.* full, complete; **II.** *adv. agree etc.* fully, on all points

'Voll·in·va,li·de *m* total invalid; **'Voll·in·va·li·di,tät** *f* total disability

voll·jäh·rig ['fɔljɛ:rıç] *adj. pred.* of age; **~** ***werden*** come of age, reach the age of majority; **Voll·jäh·ri·ge** ['fɔljɛ:rıgə] *m, f* (-n; -n) major; **'Voll·jäh·rig·keit** *f* (-; *no pl.*) majority

'voll·kas·ko·ver·si·chert *adj.* with comprehensive insurance; **~** ***sein*** have comprehensive insurance; **'Voll·kas·ko·ver·si·che·rung** *f* comprehensive insurance

voll·kli·ma·ti·siert ['fɔlklimati,zi:ɐt] *adj.* fully air-conditioned

voll'kom·men I. *adj.* **1.** perfect; **2.** perfect, complete, total, absolute; **II.** *adv.* → ***völlig*** II; **Voll'kom·men·heit** *f* (-; *no pl.*) (sheer) perfection

'Voll·korn|brot *n* wholemeal bread; **~mehl** *n* wholemeal flour; **~nu·deln** *pl.* whole wheat pasta *sg.* (*coll.* pastas)

'voll·kot·zen *sl. v/t.* (*sep.*, h) *sl.* spew all over

'Voll·kraft *f*: ***in der*** **~** ***s-r Jahre*** in his prime

'voll·krie·gen F *v/t.* (*sep.*, h) manage to fill *s.th.* (up); ***er kriegt den Hals nicht voll*** he (just) can't get enough

'voll·krit·zeln F *v/t.* (*sep.*, h) scribble all over *s.th.*

'voll·ma·chen (*sep.*, h) **I.** *v/t.* **1.** fill (up); **2.** F (*a.* ***sich et.*** **~**) dirty, mess up; *a.* make a mess on *table, floor etc.*; F ***die Hosen*** **~** fill one's pants; ***sich die Finger mit Marmelade*** **~** get jam all over one's fingers; **II.** F *v/refl.*: ***sich*** **~** fill one's pants

'Voll·macht *f* (-; -en) full power(s *pl.*), authority; ⚖ power of attorney; ***j-m*** **~** ***erteilen*** authorize s.o. (***zu*** *inf.* to *inf.*); **~ge·ber** *m* principal

'Voll·ma,tro·se *m* able-bodied seaman

voll·me·cha·ni·siert ['fɔlmeçani,zi:ɐt] *adj.* fully mechanized

'Voll·milch *f* full-cream milk; **~scho·ko,la·de** *f* milk chocolate

'Voll·mond *m* (-[e]s; *no pl.*) full moon; ***es ist*** ~ there's a full moon tonight; F ***strahlen wie ein*** ~ be beaming all over one's face; **~ge·sicht** F *n* moon face

voll·mun·dig ['fɔlmʊndɪç] *adj.* full(-bodied) *wine*

'Voll·nar,ko·se *f* ⚕ general an(a)esthetic

'voll·packen *v/t.* (*sep.*, h) pack *s.th.* full (***mit*** *dat.* of)

'Voll·pen·si,on *f* (-; *no pl.*) (full) board and lodging, full board, American plan (*abbr.* AP)

'voll|pum·pen (*sep.*, h) **I.** *v/t.* pump *s.th.* up (completely), pump *s.th.* full; ***sich die Lungen*** ~ fill one's lungs (with fresh air); **II.** *v/refl.*: ***sich*** **~*mit*** *dat.* load o.s. up with *s.th.*; F ***sich*** ~ F tank up, *sl.* get tight; **~qual·men** F *v/t.* (*sep.*, h) F smoke up *room etc.*

'Voll·rausch *m* drunken stupor; ***e-n*** ~ ***haben*** be blind drunk; ***sich e-n*** ~ ***antrinken*** F drink o.s. silly

'voll|sau·fen F *v/refl.* (*irr.*, *sep.*, h, → ***saufen***): ***sich*** ~ *sl.* get tight; **~sau·gen** *v/refl.* (*irr.*, *sep.*, h, → ***saugen***): ***sich*** ~ *insect*, *sponge etc.*: suck itself full (***mit*** *dat.* of); *fabric etc.*: become saturated (with); **~schen·ken** *v/t.* (*sep.*, h) fill (up); **~schla·gen** F *v/t. and v/refl.* (*irr.*, *sep.*, h, → ***schlagen***): ***sich*** (***den Bauch***) ~ F make a (real) pig of o.s.

'voll·schlank *adj.*: ~ ***sein*** have a full figure, F be a bit on the plump side; ***für die*** **~*e Frau*** for the fuller figure

'voll|schmie·ren F (*sep.*, h) **I.** *v/t.* smear all over *s.th.*; mess up *dress etc.*; ***et. mit et.*** ~ smear s.th. all over s.th.; **II.** *v/refl.*: ***sich*** ~ get o.s. dirty, get food *etc.* all over o.s.; **~schrei·ben** *v/t.* (*irr.*, *sep.*, h, → ***schreiben***) fill (with writing); ***drei Seiten*** ~ write three full pages; **~schüt·ten** *v/t.* (*sep.*, h) fill (up); **~sprit·zen** (*sep.*, h) **I.** *v/t.* spatter; spray, get *s.o. or s.th.* all wet; ***et. mit et.*** ~ spatter s.th. all over s.th.; **II.** *v/refl.*: ***sich*** ~ spatter o.s.; get o.s. wet

voll·stän·dig ['fɔlʃtɛndɪç] **I.** *adj.* complete; whole, entire; **II.** *adv.* completely; fully; absolutely; **'Voll·stän·dig·keit** *f* (-; *no pl.*) completeness; ***der*** ~ ***halber*** for the sake of completeness

'voll|stel·len F *v/t.* (*sep.*, h) cram (***mit*** *dat.* with), put things all over *a room etc.*; ***das Schlafzimmer mit alten Möbeln*** *etc.* ~ *a.* F stuff the bedroom with old furniture *etc.*; **~stop·fen** *v/t.* (*sep.*, h) **1.** stuff, cram; **2.** *a. v/refl.*: ***sich*** (***den Bauch***) ~ F stuff o.s.

voll·streck·bar [fɔl'ʃtrɛkba:ɐ] *adj.* executable; **voll'strecken** (*insep.*, *no* -ge-, h) **I.** *v/t.* **1.** ⚖ execute *testament*, *sentence etc.*; enforce *law*; **2.** *sport*: convert; **II.** *v/i.* *sport*: score; **Voll·strecker** [fɔl'ʃtrɛkɐ] (*sep.* -k·k-) *m* (-s; -) **1.** ⚖ executor; **2.** *sport*: scorer; **Voll'streckung** *f* (-, -en) execution; **Voll'streckungs·befehl** *m* writ of execution

'voll·tan·ken (*sep.*, h) **I.** *v/i.* fill up; F *fig.* F get tanked up; *mot.* ***bitte*** ~ fill her up (*Am.* fill up), please; **II.** *v/t.* fill up

'voll·tö·nend *adj.* sonorous, rich

voll·tran·si·sto·ri·siert ['fɔltranzɪstori,zi:ɐt] *adj.* fully transistorized

'Voll·tref·fer *m* a) ⚔ direct hit, b) bull's-eye, c) *fig.* (absolute) hit; ***e-n*** ~ ***landen*** hit the bull's-eye, ⚔ score a direct hit, *fig.* score a hit (*or* success); *fig.* ***absoluter*** ~ (*record*) smash hit

'voll·trun·ken *adj.* completely drunk (*or* intoxicated); **'Voll·trun·ken·heit** *f* (-; *no pl.*) (state of) complete drunkenness (*or* intoxication)

'Voll|verb *n* full verb; **~ver·samm·lung** *f* plenary assembly; **~ver·stär·ker** *m* integrated amplifier; **~wai·se** *f* orphan; **~wasch·mit·tel** *n* all-purpose washing powder

voll·wer·tig ['fɔlve:ɐtɪç] *adj.* full, *a.* adequate *meal*; wholesome *food*

'Voll·wert·kost *f* whole foods *pl.*

voll·zäh·lig ['fɔltsɛ:lɪç] **I.** *adj.* complete; **II.** *adv.*: ***sie waren*** ~ ***versammelt*** all were present; **'Voll·zäh·lig·keit** *f* (-; *no pl.*) completeness

voll'zie·hen (*irr.*, *no* -ge-, h, → ***ziehen***) **I.** *v/t.* execute; carry out; *a.* perform *ritual etc.*; consummate *marriage*; **~*de Gewalt*** executive (power); **II.** *v/refl.*: ***sich*** ~ take place, (come to) pass; **Voll·zie·her** [fɔl'tsi:ɐ] *m* (-s; -) executor; **Voll'zie·hung** *f* (-; *no pl.*), **Voll·zug** [fɔl'tsu:k] *m* (-[e]s; *no pl.*) execution

Voll'zugs|an·stalt *f* ⚖ penal institution; **~be·am·te** *m* (prison) warder; **~per·so,nal** *n* (prison) warders *pl. or* staff

Vo·lon·tär [volɔn'tɛ:ɐ] *m* (-s; -e [-rə]) unpaid trainee; **Vo·lon·ta·ri·at** [volɔnta'rĭa:t] *n* (-[e]s; -e) unpaid traineeship (*or* period of training)

Volt [vɔlt] *n* (-[e]s; -) ⚡ volt; **Vol·ta·me·ter** [vɔlta'me:tɐ] *n* (-s; -) voltameter; **Volt·am·pere** [vɔlt'am'pe:ɐ] *n* (-[s]; -) volt-ampere; **Volt·me·ter** ['vɔltme:tɐ] *n* (-s; -) voltmeter

Vo·lu·men [vo'lu:mən] *n* (-s; -, Volumina [vo'lu:mina]) volume; capacity; **~ge·wicht** *n* volume weight; **~pro,zent** *n* per cent (*or* percent) by volume

vo·lu·mi·nös [volumi'nø:s] *adj.* voluminous; substantial; weighty, hefty *book etc.*

Vo·lu·te [vo'lu:tə] *f* (-; -n) △ scroll

vom (= ***von dem***) → ***von***

von [fɔn] *prp.* (*dat.*) **1.** from; off *s.th.*; ~ ***wo*** (***woher***)? where from?; ***et. vom Tisch nehmen*** take s.th. off the table; **2.** from; ~ ***morgen an*** from tomorrow (onwards), as of tomorrow; → ***an*** II; **3.** of; ***die Einfuhr*** ~ ***Weizen*** the import of wheat; ***zwei*** ~ ***uns*** two of us; ***neun*** ~ ***zehn Leuten*** nine out of (*statistics*: in) ten people; ***ein Freund*** ~ ***mir*** a friend of mine; ~ ***dem Apfel essen*** have some of the apple; **4.** from; ~ ***20 DM an*** (*or* ***aufwärts***) from 20 marks up(wards), 20 marks and up(wards); → ***klein*** I; **5.** by; ***ein Gedicht*** ~ ***Schiller*** a poem by Schiller; ***Kinder haben*** ~ have children by; ***das ist nett*** ~ ***ihm*** that's nice of him; ~ ***mir aus*** I don't mind, it's all the same to me, ***kann er gehen***: I don't mind if he goes, I don't mind him going, he can go as far as I'm concerned; → ***selbst*** I; **6.** ***ein Honorar*** ~ ***DM 500*** a fee of 500 marks; ***ein Aufenthalt*** ~ ***drei Wochen*** a three-week stay; ***ein Kind*** ~ ***drei Jahren*** a child of three; ***ein Mann*** ~ ***Charakter*** (***Format***) a man of character (substance); **7.** of, about; ***ich habe*** ~ ***ihm gehört*** I've heard of him; ***er weiß*** ~ ***der Sache*** he knows about it; **8.** of; ***der Herzog*** ~ ***Edinburgh*** the Duke of Edinburgh

von·ein'an·der *adv.* from each other; ***weit*** ~ ***entfernt*** far apart

von·nö·ten [fɔn'nø:tən] *adj.*: ~ ***sein*** be necessary, be called for

von·stat·ten [fɔn'ʃtatən] *adv.*: ~ ***gehen*** take place; go, proceed

Vo·po ['fo:po] F *m* (-s; -s) → ***Volkspolizist***

vor [fo:ɐ] **I.** *prp.* (*dat.*) **1.** a) in front of (*s.o. or s.th.*), b) in the presence of *witnesses etc.*; ~ ***der Tür*** at the door; ~ ***e-m Hintergrund*** against a background; ***das Subjekt steht*** ~ ***dem Verb*** the subject comes before (*or* precedes) the verb; **2.** a) before, b) ago; ***am Tage*** ~ ***...*** (on) the day before ...; ~ ***einigen Tagen*** a few days ago, the other day; (***heute***) ~ ***acht Tagen*** a week ago (today); ***fünf*** (***Minuten***) ~ ***zehn*** five (minutes) to (*or* of) ten; ***et.*** ~ ***sich haben*** have s.th. ahead (*or* coming up); **3.** ~ ***Tatsachen*** (***e-m Problem, e-r Aufgabe*** *etc.*) ***stehen*** be faced (*or* confronted) with facts (a problem, a task *etc.*); ~ ***dem Ruin stehen*** be faced with ruin, be on the verge (*or* brink) of ruin; ***sich verbeugen*** ~ bow (*or* curtsey) to *or* before; ~ ***allem***, ~ ***allen Dingen*** above all; ~ ***sich hin murmeln*** mutter (*or* mumble) to o.s.; ~ ***sich gehen*** go; **4.** with, for, on account of, because of; ~ ***Freude springen*** (***schreien***) jump (shout) for *or* with joy; ~ (***lauter***) ***Lachen konnte ich nichts sagen*** I couldn't speak for laughing; ~ (***lauter***) ***Arbeit*** with all that work, for work; ***zittern*** ~ shake (*or* tremble) with *cold*, *fear etc.*; ~ ***Hunger sterben*** die of hunger; ***sich fürchten*** ~ be afraid of; **5.** *protect*, *hide*, *shelter etc.* from; *warn* against; **II.** *adv.* forward(s); ***er konnte weder*** ~ ***noch zurück*** he couldn't go forward(s) or backward(s), he couldn't move either way

vor'ab *adv.* **1.** to begin with; **2.** in advance; **Vor'ab...** *in cpds.* advance *copy*, *fee etc.*

'Vor·ab·druck *m* (-[e]s; -e) preprint

'Vor·abend *m* eve; ***am*** ~ on the eve (*gen.* of)

'Vor·ah·nung *f* (-; -en) premonition

vor·an [fo'ran] *adv.* at the head (*dat.* of), in front, F up front; (***nur***) **~!** let's go!; *fig.* ***allem*** ~ first and foremost; **vor'an·bringen** *v/t.* (*irr.*, *sep.*, h, → ***bringen***) get *s.th.* going (*or* moving), get on (*or* make headway) with *one's work etc.*; **vor'an·ge·hen** *v/i.* (*irr.*, *sep.*, sn, → ***gehen***) a) lead the way, walk at the head (*dat.* of), b) precede (***e-r Sache*** s.th.); ***gut*** ~ *work etc*: go ahead well; ***es geht schlecht*** (***or nicht recht***) ***voran*** it's not going very well; **vor'an·kom·men** *v/i.* (*irr.*, *sep.*, sn, → ***kommen***) (*a.* ***gut*** ~) make headway (*or* progress); ***gut*** ~ *a.* stride (*or* forge) ahead; ***wir kommen schlecht voran*** we're not making much *or* any headway (*or* progress); ***im Leben*** (***im Beruf***) ~ get on in life (in one's job, careerwise); ***wie kommst du voran?*** how are you getting on?, F how's it going?

'Vor·an·kün·di·gung *f* announcement

'Vor·an·mel·dung *f* booking; ***Gespräch mit*** ~ person-to-person call

'Vor·an·schlag *m* estimate

vor'an·trei·ben *v/t.* (*irr.*, *sep.*, h, → ***treiben***) speed up, F push

'Vor·an·zei·ge *f* announcement (***für*** *acc.* of); preview; *film*: trailer

'Vor·ar·beit *f* groundwork, preparatory work, preparations *pl.* (*all* ***zu*** *dat.* for);

(**gute**) ~ ***leisten*** *esp. fig.* prepare the ground (well); ***nach guter ~ von*** *dat. sport*: after good work by

'vor·ar·bei·ten (*sep.*, h) **I.** *v/t.* do *s.th.* in advance; prepare; **II.** *v/i.* a) work ahead, b) do the groundwork, prepare the ground; **III.** *v/refl.*: ***sich ~*** work one's way forward, forge ahead

'Vor·ar·bei·ter *m* foreman; **'Vor·ar·bei·te·rin** *f* forewoman

vor·aus [fo'raʊs] *adv.* in front; *a. fig.* ahead (*dat.* of); ***im ~*** in advance; ***Kopf ~*** head first; ***s-r Zeit ~ sein*** be ahead of one's time; ***j-m weit ~ sein*** be streets ahead of s.o.; **~ah·nen** *v/t.* (*sep.*, h) see *s.th.* coming; ***ich hab's vorausgeahnt*** I could see it coming, I had a feeling it would happen; **~be·rech·nen** *v/t.* (*sep.*, h) calculate in advance; **~be·stim·men** *v/t.* (*sep.*, h) determine in advance; **~be·zah·len** *v/t.* (*sep.*, h) pay in advance; **2be·zah·lung** *f* advance payment, deposit; **~blicken** *v/i.* (*sep.*, h) → ***voraus-schauen***; **~den·ken** *v/i.* (*irr.*, *sep.*, h, → ***denken***) think (*or* look) ahead; **~ei·len** *v/i.* (*sep.*, sn) hurry on ahead (*dat.* of); be ahead (of *s.th.*)

Vor'aus·ex·em‚plar *n* advance copy

vor'aus|fah·ren *v/i.* (*irr.*, *sep.*, sn, → ***fahren***) drive (on) ahead (*dat.* of); **~ge·hen** *v/i.* (*irr.*, *sep.*, sn, → ***gehen***) **1.** → ***voran-gehen***; **2.** ***im ~den, im vorausgegangenen*** above; *fig.* ***ihr geht der Ruf voraus zu*** *inf.* she's reputed to *inf.*

vor'aus·ge·setzt *conj.*: **~, *daß*** provided (that), on condition that

vor'aus·ha·ben *v/t.* (*irr.*, *sep.*, h, → ***haben***): ***j-m et. ~*** be in a better position than s.o. (*or* have the edge on s.o.) as far as s.th. is concerned; ***j-m e-e Menge Erfahrung*** *etc.* **~** have a lot more experience *etc.* than s.o.

Vor'aus·kas·se *f* ✝ cash in advance

vor'aus·lau·fen *v/i.* (*irr.*, *sep.*, sn, → ***laufen***) run (on) ahead (*dat.* of)

vor'aus·pla·nen (*sep.*, h) **I.** *v/i.* plan ahead; **II.** *v/t.* plan *s.th.* in advance, plan for *s.th.*; **Vor'aus·pla·nung** *f* (-; -en) advance planning

Vor'aus·sa·ge *f* (-; -n) a) prediction, b) *meteor.*, ✝ *etc.* forecast; ***~n machen*** make predictions, try and predict the future; **vor'aus·sa·gen** *v/t.* (*sep.*, h) a) predict, b) forecast

Vor'aus·schau *f* (-; -en) forecast

vor'aus·schau·en *v/i.* (*sep.*, h) look ahead; **vor'aus·schau·end I.** *adj.* far-sighted; **II.** *adv.* *act etc.* with foresight; **~ *können wir sagen*** looking ahead to the future (*or* as far as the future is concerned) we can say

vor'aus·schicken *v/t.* (*sep.*, h) **1.** send on ahead; **2.** *fig.* begin by mentioning *s.th.*; ***ich muß ~, daß*** I should begin by mentioning that, I should mention at the outset that; ***dies vorausgeschickt*** having said that

vor'aus·se·hen *v/t.* (*irr.*, *sep.*, h, → ***sehen***) foresee

vor'aus·set·zen *v/t.* (*sep.*, h) a) assume (*that* ...), take *s.th.* for granted, b) require; ***zuviel ~*** *a.* expect too much; ***et. als bekannt ~*** take it for granted that everyone knows s.th.; **Vor'aus·set·zung** *f* (-; -en) condition, prerequisite (***für*** *acc.* for, of); ***die ~en erfüllen*** meet the requirements; ***unter der ~, daß*** on condition that

Vor'aus·sicht *f* (-; *no pl.*) foresight; ***aller ~ nach*** in all probability; ***nach menschlicher ~*** as far as one (*or* we) can tell *or* foresee; ***in weiser ~*** with great foresight; ***in weiser ~ habe ich mein ganzes Geld mitgenommen*** I had the good sense to take all my money with me

vor'aus·sicht·lich I. *adv.* probably, in all probability; ***er trifft ~ morgen ein*** *a.* he is expected to arrive tomorrow; ***es dauert ~ e-e Woche*** *a.* they *etc.* estimate it will take a week; **II.** *adj.* prospective; expected, anticipated; estimated

'Vor·aus·wahl *f* (-; *no pl.*) preliminary selection (*or* round of selections); ***e-e ~ treffen*** narrow down the choice

vor'aus|wer·fen *v/t.* (*irr.*, *sep.*, h, → ***werfen***) → ***Schatten*** 2; **~wis·sen** *v/t.* (*irr.*, *sep.*, h, → ***wissen***) know (in advance); ***die Zukunft ~*** know what the future holds

vor'aus·zah·len *v/t.* (*sep.*, h) pay in advance; **Vor'aus·zah·lung** *f* (-; -en) advance payment

'Vor·bau *m* (-[e]s; -ten) a) porch, b) projection; F *hum.* ***e-n ganz schönen ~ haben*** F be well-endowed (*or* -stacked)

'vor·bau·en (*sep.*, h) **I.** *v/t.* build on at the front (*dat.* of); **II.** *fig.* *v/i.* take precautions; ***e-r Sache ~*** take precautions against s.th., (try to) prevent s.th.

'Vor·be·dacht *m*: ***mit ~*** intentionally, deliberately, (quite) consciously, with intent; ***ohne ~*** unintentionally, without meaning to, unconsciously, without realizing, without intent

'Vor·be·deu·tung *f* (-; -en) omen

'Vor·be·din·gung *f* (-; -en) condition

Vor·be·halt ['foːɐbəhalt] *m* (-[e]s; -e) reservation; proviso; ***innerer*** (*or* ***stiller***) **~** mental reservation; ***unter dem ~, daß*** provided (that), with the proviso that

'vor·be·hal·ten (*irr.*, *sep.*, h, → ***behalten***) **I.** *v/t.*: ***sich et. ~*** reserve s.th. (for o.s.); ***sich*** (***das Recht***) ***~ zu*** *inf.* reserve the right to *inf.*; **II.** *adj.*: ***j-m ~ sein*** (*or* ***bleiben***) be left to s.o. (***zu*** *inf.* to *inf.*); ***es bleibt der Zukunft ~, ob*** it remains to be seen whether, only time can tell whether; ***Änderungen ~*** subject to change (without notice); ***Irrtümer ~*** errors excepted; ***alle Rechte ~*** all rights reserved

'vor·be·halt·lich *prp.* (*gen.*) subject to

'vor·be·halt·los I. *adj.* unreserved, unconditional; **II.** *adv.* without reservation

'Vor·be·halts·klau·sel *f* proviso clause

'vor·be·han·deln *v/t.* (*sep.*, h) pretreat; pre-process; **'Vor·be·hand·lung** *f* (-; -en) pretreatment

vor·bei [foːɐ'baɪ] *adv.* a) past (*a.* ***~ an*** *dat.*), b) over, past; ***~!*** missed!; ***es ist ~*** it's all over, *iro.* so much for that; ***~ ist ~*** what's past is past; ***das ist jetzt ~, damit ist es jetzt ~*** that's all over and done with now; ***drei Uhr ~*** past (*or* after) three (o'clock); **~be·neh·men** F *v/refl.* (*irr.*, *sep.*, h, → ***benehmen***): ***sich ~*** step out of line; **~brin·gen** *v/t.* (*irr.*, *sep.*, h, → ***bringen***) drop *s.th.* by (*or* in); **~dür·fen** F *v/i.* (*irr.*, *sep.*, h, → ***dürfen***) be allowed to pass; ***darf ich mal vorbei?*** excuse me(, please); **~ei·len** *v/i.* (*sep.*, sn) hurry past; ***an j-m ~*** *a.* pass s.o. in a hurry; **~fah·ren** *v/i.* (*irr.*, *sep.*, sn, → ***fahren***) drive past (***an*** *dat. s.o.*, *s.th.*), pass (*s.o.*, *s.th.*); **~füh·ren** (*sep.*, h) **I.** *v/t.*: ***j-n ~ an*** *dat.* lead s.o. past *s.th.*; ***et. ~ an*** *dat.* run s.th. along *s.th.*; **II.** *v/i.*: ***~ an*** *dat. path etc.*: go (*or* run) past *s.th.*; *fig.* ***daran führt kein Weg vorbei*** there's no getting round it; **~ge·hen** *v/i.* (*irr.*, *sep.*, sn, → ***gehen***) **1.** pass, go past (***an*** *dat. s.o.*, *s.th.*); ***im 2*** in passing; *fig.* ***~ an*** *dat.* pass *s.th.* by, miss; **2.** *shot etc.*: miss (the mark); **3.** pass; *pain*: *a.* go away; **~kom·men** *v/i.* (*irr.*, *sep.*, sn, → ***kommen***) **1.** pass (by), come past; ***~ an*** *dat.* get past (*or* round) *an obstacle etc.*, pass; **2.** F drop by (***bei*** *dat.* at *s.o.'s place*), drop in (on *s.o.*), come by; **~kön·nen** F *v/i.* (*irr.*, *sep.*, h, → ***können***) be able to get past; ***ich kann nicht vorbei*** I can't get past; **~las·sen** *v/t.* (*irr.*, *sep.*, h, → ***lassen***) let *s.o. or s.th.* pass; ***läßt du mich bitte vorbei?*** can I get past, please?; **~lau·fen** *v/i.* (*irr.*, *sep.*, sn, → ***laufen***) run past (***an*** *dat. s.o.*, *s.th.*); **~le·ben** *v/i.* (*sep.*, h): ***aneinander ~*** live separate lives within a marriage; **~mar‚schie·ren** *v/i.* (*sep.*, sn) march past (***an*** *dat. s.o.*, *s.th.*); file past; **~müs·sen** F *v/i.* (*irr.*, *sep.*, h, → ***müssen***) have to pass (*or* get past); **~pla·nen** *v/i.* (*sep.*, h): ***~ an*** *dat.* ignore, leave out of account (when planning s.th.); **~re·den** *v/i.* (*sep.*, h): ***aneinander ~*** talk at cross-purposes; ***an e-m Thema ~*** talk round the subject; **~schie·ßen** *v/i.* (*irr.*, *sep.*, h, → ***schießen***) **1.** miss (the mark); *soccer*: shoot wide; ***~ an*** *dat.* miss *s.o.*, *s.th.*; **2.** F shoot past; **~schlän·geln** *v/refl.* (*sep.*, h): ***sich ~*** squeeze past (***an*** *dat. s.o.*, *s.th.*); **~zie·hen** *v/i.* (*irr.*, *sep.*, sn, → ***ziehen***) pass (***an*** *dat. s.o.*, *s.th.*); ⚔ march past; *clouds etc.*: drift past; ***Erinnerungen*** *etc.* ***zogen*** (***im Geiste***) ***an ihm vorbei*** memories *etc.* went through his mind

'vor·be·la·stet *adj.* *person* with a past; negatively loaded, tainted *word etc.*; ***~ sein*** have a past to contend with; *word*: have negative connotations; ***kriminell*** *etc.* **~** with a criminal *etc.* past (*or* background); ***psychisch ~ sein*** be a psychological case; ***nicht ~*** *a.* innocent (***in e-r Sache*** of s.th.; ***in dieser Beziehung*** in this respect); ***da ist er erblich ~*** it runs in the family; **'Vor·be·la·stung** *f* (-; -en) (dubious) past *or* background; negative connotations *pl. of a word etc.*

'Vor·be·mer·kung *f* (-; -en) preliminary remark

'vor·be·rei·ten (*sep.*, h) **I.** *v/t.* **1.** *a. fig.* prepare (***für*** *acc.*, ***auf*** *acc.* for); **II.** *v/refl.*: ***sich ~*** **2.** prepare o.s., get ready; ***sich ~ auf*** *acc.* prepare (o.s.) for, get ready for, F gear up for; ***sich für den Unterricht ~*** prepare one's lessons (*or* for class); ***sich auf e-e Prüfung ~*** revise for an exam; ***auf et. vorbereitet sein*** be prepared (*or* ready) for s.th.; **3.** be in the offing, be under way; **'vor·be·rei·tend** *adj.* preparatory; **'Vor·be·rei·tung** *f* (-; -en) preparation (***für*** *acc.*, ***auf*** *acc.*, ***zu*** *dat.* for); ***~en treffen*** make preparations, ***zu*** *dat.*: *a.* prepare (for) *s.th.*; ***in ~*** being prepared, in preparation; *fig.* in the pipeline

'Vor·be·rei·tungs|dienst *m* graduate professional training; **~kurs** *m* preparatory course; **~zeit** *f* preparatory phase

'Vor·ber·ge *pl.* foothills

'Vor·be·richt *m* (-[e]s; -e) preliminary report

'Vor·be·scheid *m* (-[e]s; -e) preliminary notice

'Vor·be·sit·zer *m* (-s; -) previous owner

'Vor·be·spre·chung *f* (-; -en) **1.** preliminary discussion (*or* talks *pl.*); **2.** preview *of a book etc.*

'vor·be·stel·len *v/t.* (*sep.*, h) book *tickets etc.* in advance, make an advance booking for *tickets etc.*; book *room, seat etc.* (ahead), reserve; **'Vor·be·stel·lung** *f* (-; -en) advance booking; booking, reservation *of a room etc.*

'vor·be·straft *adj.* previously convicted; **~ *sein*** *a.* have a criminal record; ***einmal*** (***zweimal, mehrmals***) **~ *sein*** have a (two, several) previous conviction(s) (***wegen*** *gen.* for); **'Vor·be·straf·te** *m, f* (-n; -n) previously convicted person

'vor·be·ten *v/t.* (*sep.*, h) recite *a prayer etc.* (***j-m*** to s.o.); F *fig.* ***j-m et.*** **~** explain s.th. to s.o. (in detail), spell s.th. out to s.o.; ***ich hab's ihm doch schon x-mal vorgebetet*** I've spelt it out to him often enough

'Vor·beu·ge·haft *f* preventive detention

'vor·beu·gen (*sep.*, h) **I.** *v/i.* prevent (*dat. s.th.*); guard against, take precautions against; **~ *ist besser als heilen*** prevention is better than cure; **II.** *v/t. and v/refl.* (***sich* ~**) bend forward; **'vor·beu·gend** *adj.* preventive, *esp.* ⚕ *a.* prophylactic; **'Vor·beu·gung** *f* (-; *no pl.*) prevention, *esp.* ⚕ *a.* prophylaxis

'Vor·beu·gungs|maß·nah·me *f* precaution, preventive measure; **~me·di,zin** *f* preventive medicine; **~mit·tel** *n* ⚕ prophylactic; *fig.* preventive

'Vor·bild *n* (-[e]s; -er) a) model, b) example; ***leuchtendes*** **~** shining example; (***sich***) ***j-n zum* ~ *nehmen*** a) take s.o. as an example, take a leaf from s.o.'s book, b) model o.s. on s.o.; ***j-n als* ~ *hinstellen*** hold s.o. up as an example

'vor·bild·lich I. *adj.* exemplary; model *husband etc.*; ideal; **II.** *adv.* exemplarily, in an exemplary manner (*or* fashion); ***sie benimmt sich*** **~** her behavio(u)r is exemplary; ***das hast du* ~ *gemacht*** F you did a brilliant job (of it); **'Vor·bild·lich·keit** *f* (-; *no pl.*) exemplariness, exemplary nature (*gen.* of)

'Vor·bil·dung *f* (-; *no pl.*) (previous) training; educational background

'vor·bin·den *v/t.* (*irr.*, *sep.*, h, → ***binden***) tie (*or* put) *s.th.* on

'Vor·bo·gen *m* (-s; ~) *typ.* front matter

'Vor·bo·te *m* (-n; -n) forerunner; *fig.* harbinger, herald (*gen.* of)

'vor·brin·gen *v/t.* (*irr.*, *sep.*, h, → ***bringen***) a) bring forward *for discussion etc.*; ⚖ produce *evidence etc.*; offer *reason, excuse, opinion etc.*; make *an objection*; propose, put forward *plan etc.*; lodge *a protest*; express *a wish*, b) ⚖ prefer *a charge against s.o.*; plead, c) *w.s.* tell (***j-m et.*** s.o. s.th.)

'vor·buch·sta,bie·ren *v/t.* (*sep.*, h) spell *a word* (out); ***könnten Sie es mir ~?*** could you spell it for me (*or* spell it out to me)?

'Vor·büh·ne *f* (-; -n) *thea.* proscenium

'vor·christ·lich *adj.* pre-Christian; ***... aus ~er Zeit*** dating back to before the time of Christ (*or* to the pre-Christian era)

'Vor·dach *n* (-[e]s; ⸚er) canopy

'vor·da,tie·ren *v/t.* (*sep.*, h) a) antedate, b) postdate

vor'dem *adv.* before; formerly

vor·der ['fɔrdɐ] *adj.* front

'Vor·der|ach·se *f* front axle; **~an·sicht** *f* front view; △ front elevation; **~an·trieb** *m mot.* front-wheel drive

'vor·der·asia·tisch *adj.* Middle (*or* Near) Eastern; Levantine

'Vor·der|aus·gang *m* front exit; **~bein** *n* foreleg; **~deck** *n* foredeck; **~ein·gang** *m* front entrance; **~fuß** *m* forefoot; *zo.* front paw; **~ge·bäu·de** *n* front building

'Vor·der·grund *m* (-[e]s; *no pl.*) foreground; *fig.* ***et. in den* ~ *stellen*** (*or* ***rücken***) give s.th. special emphasis; ***in den* ~ *treten*** (*or* ***rücken***) become the focus of attention, *person*: be thrust into public prominence; ***im* ~ *stehen*** a) be of immediate importance, be urgent, be top priority, b) be in the limelight, be in the foreground *of discussions*; ***sich in den* ~ *stellen*** take cent|re (*Am.* -er) stage

vor·der·grün·dig ['fɔrdɐgrʏndɪç] *adj.* a) superficial, b) transparent, c) simplistic(ally *adv.*), d) naive *sense of humo(u)r etc.*; **'Vor·der·grün·dig·keit** *f* (-; *no pl.*) a) superficiality, b) transparency, c) simplistic nature (*gen.* of), d) naivety

vor·der·hand ['foːɐdeːɐhant] *adv.* for the time being, for the moment

'Vor·der|hand *f zo.* forehand; **~haus** *n* front building; **~hirn** *n anat.* frontal lobes *pl.* of the brain

'Vor·der·la·der [-laːdɐ] *m* (-s; -) muzzle-loader

'Vor·der|lauf *m zo.* foreleg; **~mann** *m* (-[e]s; ⸚er) person in front (of me, him *etc.*); F *fig.* ***et. auf* ~ *bringen*** bring s.th. up to scratch, spruce s.th. up; ***j-n auf* ~ *bringen*** get s.o. into (proper) shape; **~pfo·te** *f zo.* front paw

'Vor·der·rad *n* front wheel; **~ach·se** *f* front axle; **~an·trieb** *m* front-wheel drive

'Vor·der|rei·fen *m* front tyre (*Am.* tire); **~rei·he** *f* front row; **~schin·ken** *m* shoulder of ham; **~sei·te** *f* front; obverse, face *of coin*; **~sitz** *m* front seat

vor·derst ['fɔrdɐst] *adj.* (very) first, ... at the front; **~*e Reihe*** front (*or* first) row; ***die Vordersten*** the ones (right) at the front

'Vor·der|teil *n, m* front (part); **~tür** *f* front door; **~zahn** *m* front tooth; **~zim·mer** *n* front room

'vor·drän·geln F *v/refl.* (*sep.*, h), **'vor·drän·gen** *v/refl.* (*sep.*, h): ***sich*** **~** push forward; push in *a line*, *Brit. a.* jump the queue; *fig.* (*a.* ***sich* ~ *wollen***) try to be the cent|re (*Am.* -er) of attraction

'vor·drin·gen *v/i.* (*irr.*, *sep.*, sn, → ***dringen***) push (*or* forge) ahead; **~ *in*** *acc.* penetrate (*a. fig.*); **~ *zu*** *dat.* reach (*a. fig.*)

'vor·dring·lich I. *adj.* urgent, pressing; top priority; **~*e Aufgabe*** priority assignment; **II.** *adv.*: ***et.* ~ *behandeln*** give s.th. priority; **~ *behandelt werden*** be given priority (treatment); **'Vor·dring·lich·keit** *f* (-; *no pl.*) urgency

'Vor·druck *m* (-[e]s; -e) **1.** form, *Am.* blank; **2.** *typ.* first impression

'vor·ehe·lich *adj.* premarital

'vor·ei·lig *adj.* rash; **~*e Schlüsse ziehen*** jump to conclusions; **'Vor·ei·lig·keit** *f* (-; *no pl.*) rashness

vor·ein'an·der *adv.* **1.** one in front of the other; **2.** ***Achtung*** **~** respect for each other (*or* one another); ***sie fürchten sich*** **~** they're afraid of each other (*or* one another)

'vor·ein·ge·nom·men *adj.* prejudiced, bias(s)ed (***für*** *acc.* in favo[u]r of; ***gegen*** *acc.* against); **'Vor·ein·ge·nom·men·heit** *f* (-; *no pl.*) prejudice(s *pl.*), bias

'vor·ent·hal·ten *v/t.* (*irr.*, *sep.*, h, → ***enthalten***): ***j-m et.*** **~** keep (*or* withhold) s.th. from s.o.; **'Vor·ent·hal·tung** *f* (-; *no pl.*) withholding *of information etc.*

'Vor·ent·schei·dung *f* (-; -en) preliminary decision; ⚖ precedent

vor·erst ['foːɐʔeːɐst] *adv.* for the time being; *a.* at the moment

'vor·ex·er,zie·ren *v/t.* (*sep.*, h) demonstrate (***j-m*** to s.o.)

vor·fa·bri·ziert ['foːɐfabri,tsiːɐt] *adj.* prefabricated (*a. fig.*)

Vor·fahr ['foːɐfaːɐ] *m* (-en; -en [-rən]) ancestor

'vor·fah·ren (*irr.*, *sep.*, → ***fahren***) **I.** *v/i.* (sn) **1.** drive up (to the entrance *etc.*); **~ *bis*** drive up to, drive as far as; *bleib da -* ***ich fahre vor*** I'll drive (*or* bring) the car up (to the entrance); **2.** F drive (on) ahead; **3.** ***j-m*** **~** pass s.o., overtake s.o.; *j-n, ein Fahrzeug* **~ *lassen*** give (right of) way to, *Am.* yield to; **II.** *v/t.* (h) drive *a car* up (to the entrance *etc.*)

'Vor·fahrt *f* (-; *no pl.*) right of way, priority; **~ *beachten!*** give way, *Am.* yield; **~ *geändert*** changed priorities ahead

'vor·fahrt·be·rech·tigt *adj.*: **~ *sein*** have (the) right of way

'Vor·fahrts|schild *n* **1.** give way (*Am.* yield) sign; **2.** right of way sign; **~stra·ße** *f* priority road; *a.* through street

'Vor·fall *m* (-[e]s; ⸚e) **1.** incident; **2.** ⚕ prolapse; **'vor·fal·len** *v/i.* (*irr.*, *sep.*, sn, → ***fallen***) **1.** happen, occur; **2.** ⚕ prolapse, drop

'Vor·feld *n* (-[e]s; *no pl.*) **1.** approach(es *pl.*); ✈ apron; **2.** *fig.* run-up (*gen.* to); ***im* ~ *der Konferenz*** *a.* as the conference approaches (*or* was approaching)

'vor·fer·ti·gen *v/t.* (*sep.*, h) prefabricate; **'Vor·fer·ti·gung** *f* (-; -en) prefabrication

'Vor·film *m* (-[e]s; -e) supporting film

'vor·fi·nan,zie·ren *v/t.* (*sep.*, h) finance in advance; **'Vor·fi·nan,zie·rung** *f* (-; -en) advance financing

'vor·fin·den *v/t.* (*irr.*, *sep.*, h, → ***finden***) find

'vor·flun·kern F *v/t.* (*sep.*, h): ***j-m etwas*** **~** F tell s.o. a lot of rubbish

'Vor·freu·de *f* (-; *no pl.*) (joyful) anticipation; ***die* ~ *auf das Fest*** the excitement at the prospect of the party

'Vor·früh·ling *m*: (***im*** **~** in) early spring

'vor·füh·len *fig.* *v/i.* (*sep.*, h) put one's feelers out; ***bei j-m*** **~** sound s.o. out (***wegen*** *gen.* on)

'vor·füh·ren *v/t.* (*sep.*, h) a) bring forward, b) ⚖ bring *s.o.* before *the judge*, produce *witnesses*, c) show (*a. film*); ✝, ⚙ demonstrate; perform *trick etc.*; *fig.* ***j-n*** **~** make a fool of s.o., *sport*: teach s.o. a lesson; **'Vor·füh·rer** *m* (-s; -) *film*: projectionist; **Vor·führ·raum** ['foːɐfyːɐ-] *m* projection room; **'Vor·füh·rung** *f* (-; -en) presentation; *film*: showing; ✝, ⚙ demonstration; performance *of a trick etc.*; **'Vor·führ·wa·gen** *m* demonstration car, *Am.* demonstrator

'Vor·ga·be *f* (-; -n) **1.** *sport*: handicap, start; **2.** *fig.* guideline, *pl. a.* instructions; **~zeit** *f* time allowed (*or* allotted)

'Vor·gang *m* (-[e]s; ⸚e) **1.** proceedings *pl.*; process; event, occurrence; ***j-n über den* ~ *unterrichten*** tell s.o. (*or* inform s.o. about) what is happening *or* what happened; **2.** file, dossier

Vor·gän·ger ['foːɐgɛŋɐ] *m* (-s; -), **Vor-**

gän·ge·rin ['fo:ɐgɛŋərın] *f* (-; -nen) predecessor
'Vor·gän·ger·mo,dell *n* previous model
'Vor·gar·ten *m* front garden
'vor·gau·keln *v/t.* (*sep.*, h): ***j-m et.*** ~ (try to) get s.o. to believe s.th.; ***j-m ~, daß*** (try to) delude s.o. into thinking (that), (try to) get s.o. to believe (that); ***j-m e-e rosige Zukunft*** *etc.* ~ build up hopes of a rosy future *etc.* in s.o.
'vor·ge·ben *v/t.* (*irr.*, *sep.*, h, → ***geben***) **1.** *sport*: give; **2.** pass *s.th.* to the front; ***j-m et.*** ~ pass s.th. (on) to s.o.; **3.** allege, claim; pretend *to be rich etc.*
'vor·ge·bil·det *adj.*: ~ ***sein*** have some knowledge (***in*** *dat.* of), have had previous training (in); ***juristisch*** *etc.* ~ ***sein*** have had legal *etc.* training
'Vor·ge·bir·ge *n* foothills *pl.*; cape
vor·geb·lich ['fo:ɐge:plıç] *adj.* ostensible
'vor·ge·burt·lich *adj.* prenatal
'vor·ge·faßt *adj.*: ~***e Meinung*** prejudice, preconceived idea (*or* notion); ***e-e*** ~***e Meinung haben*** be prejudiced, be bias(s)ed (***von*** *dat.*, ***gegen*** *acc.* against)
'Vor·ge·fecht *n* preliminary skirmish
'Vor·ge·fühl *n* anticipation; *b.s. a.* presentiment; ***banges*** ~ uneasy feeling, foreboding
'vor·ge·hal·ten I. *p.p. of* ***vorhalten***; **II.** *adj.*: ***mit*** ~***er Pistole*** at gunpoint; *fig.* ***et. hinter der*** ~***en Hand erzählen*** say s.th. in a whisper
'vor·ge·hen *v/i.* (*irr.*, *sep.*, sn, → ***gehen***) **1.** go forward; ~ ***zu*** *dat.* go up to; **2.** F go first, lead the way; **3.** *watch*: be fast; gain *five minutes a day etc.*; **4.** have priority (*dat.* over), be more important (than); **5.** act; take action (***gegen*** *acc.* against); proceed; **6.** happen; ***was geht hier vor?*** what's going on here?; ***was ging wohl in ihm vor?*** I wonder what came over him
'Vor·ge·hen *n* (-s; *no pl.*) a) action, b) procedure; ***sein*** ~ the way he is handling (*or* he handled) things
'vor·ge·la·gert *adj. geogr.* offshore ...; ***e-e der Küste*** ~***e Insel*** an island (just) off the coast
'vor·ge·nannt *adj.* aforementioned
'vor·ge·rückt *adj.*: ***in*** ~***em Alter*** at an advanced age, in advanced years; ***in*** ~***em Stadium*** at an advanced stage; ***zu*** ~***er Stunde*** at a late hour
'vor·ge·schä·digt *adj.*: ~ ***sein*** have been damaged (*or* hurt) before
'Vor·ge·schich·te *f* (-; *no pl.*) **1.** ***die*** ~ prehistory, early history; **2.** (past) history, *the* story so far; *s.o.'s* past life, background; ⚕ case history, 🕮 anamnesis; **'vor·ge·schicht·lich** *adj.* prehistoric
'Vor·ge·schmack *m* foretaste (***auf*** *acc.* of)
'vor·ge·schrit·ten I. *p.p. of* ***vorschreiten***; **II.** *adj.* → ***vorgerückt***
'vor·ge·se·hen *p.p. of* → ***vorsehen***
'Vor·ge·setz·te *m, f* (-n; -n) superior
'Vor·ge·sprä·che *pl.* preliminary talks (*or* discussions)
'vor·ge·stern *adv.* the day before yesterday; F *fig.* ***von*** ~ of yesteryear, antiquated *views etc.*; **'vor·ge·strig** *adj.* **1.** of (*or* from) the day before yesterday; **2.** *fig.* antiquated *views etc.*
'vor·ge·zo·gen I. *p.p. of* ***vorziehen***; **II.** *adj.* early *retirement, elections etc.*
'vor·grei·fen *v/i.* (*irr.*, *sep.*, h, → ***greifen***) act prematurely, F jump the gun; jump ahead; ***e-r Sache*** ~ anticipate s.th.; ***j-m in s-r Entscheidung*** *etc.* ~ anticipate s.o.'s decision *etc.*; ***j-m*** ~ anticipate s.o.'s answer (*or* objections, question *etc.*)
'Vor·griff *m* (-[e]s; *no pl.*) anticipation; ***im*** ~ ***auf*** *acc.* in anticipation of
'vor·ha·ben *v/t.* (*irr.*, *sep.*, h, → ***haben***) **1.** plan, have in mind; ***was haben Sie heute vor?*** what are your plans for today?; ***haben Sie heute abend etwas vor?*** have you got anything planned for tonight?; ***morgen haben wir einiges vor*** a) we've got a lot to do tomorrow, b) we've got a lot on the agenda for tomorrow; ***was hat er jetzt wieder vor?*** F what's he up to now?; ***was hast du mit ihm*** (***damit***) ***vor?*** what are you going to do with him (it)?; ***fest*** ~ ***zu*** *inf.* have firmly decided to *inf.*, be intent on *ger.*; **2.** F have *s.th.* on
'Vor·ha·ben *n* (-s; -) a) intention, purpose, b) plan; project (*a.* ⚠)
'Vor·hal·le *f* (-; -n) entrance hall, vestibule; *thea.*, *hotel*: foyer, lobby
Vor·halt ['fo:ɐhalt] *m* (-[e]s; -e) **1.** ♪ suspension; **2.** *ballistics*: lead
'vor·hal·ten (*irr.*, *sep.*, h, → ***halten***) **I.** *v/t.* **1.** ***j-m et.*** ~ hold s.th. (up) in front of s.o.; ***beim Gähnen*** *etc.* ***die Hand*** ~ put one's hand in front of one's mouth when one yawns *etc.*; → ***vorgehalten***; **2.** *fig.* ***j-m et.*** ~ reproach s.o. with s.th., accuse s.o. of s.th.; **II.** *v/i.* *supply etc.*: last, hold out
'Vor·hal·tung *f* (-; -en) reproach; ***j-m*** ~***en machen*** reproach s.o., *formal*: remonstrate with s.o. (***über*** *acc.* about)
'Vor·hand *f* (-; *no pl.*) **1.** *card game*: lead (*a. fig.*); **2.** *tennis*: forehand
vor·han·den [fo:ɐ'handən] *adj.* a) available, b) extant, in existence; ~ ***sein*** exist; ***es sind*** (*or* ***ist***) ***...*** ~ *a.* there are (*or* is) ...; ***davon ist nichts mehr*** ~ there's nothing of it left; **Vor'han·den·sein** *n* (-s; *no pl.*) existence
'Vor·hand·schlag *m* forehand (shot *or* stroke)
Vor·hang ['fo:ɐhaŋ] *m* (-[e]s; ⸚e [-hɛŋə]) curtain; *pol. hist.* ***der Eiserne*** ~ the Iron Curtain; *thea.* ***zehn Vorhänge haben*** have ten curtain calls
Vor·hän·ge·schloß ['fo:ɐhɛŋə-] *n* padlock
'Vor·hang|stan·ge *f* curtain rod; ~**stoff** *m* curtain material, curtaining
'Vor·haut *f* foreskin, 🕮 prepuce
'vor·hei·zen *v/t.* (*sep.*, h) preheat, heat up
vor·her [fo:ɐ'he:ɐ, 'fo:ɐhe:ɐ] *adv.* before, first; beforehand; ***am Abend*** ~ the evening before, the previous evening; ***drei Tage*** ~ three days before (*or* earlier); ***das hättest du dir*** ~ ***überlegen sollen*** you should have thought about that first (*or* before); ***hättest du das nicht*** ~ ***sagen können?*** couldn't you have said so before (*or* earlier)?
vor'her·be·stim·men *v/t.* (*sep.*, h) **1.** determine in advance; **2.** predestine; ***es war ihr vorherbestimmt, Musikerin zu werden*** she was (pre)destined to become a musician; **Vor'her·be·stim·mung** *f* (-; *no pl.*) **1.** predetermination; **2.** *a. theological*: predestination
vor'her·ge·hen *v/i.* (*irr.*, *sep.*, sn, → ***gehen***) precede (*dat. s.th.*); **vor'her·ge·hend** *adj.* previous; preceding; ***die*** ~***en Ereignisse*** the preceding events, (the) events leading up to it
vor·he·rig [fo:ɐ'he:rıç] *adj.* previous, *a.* preceding *remark etc.*; former *president etc.*; ***ohne*** ~***e Ankündigung*** without prior (*or* any) notice; ***nach*** ~***er Vereinbarung*** after prior arrangement (***mit*** *dat.* with)
'Vor·herr·schaft *f* (-; *no pl.*) (pre)dominance; *pol. a.* supremacy; ~ ***über*** *acc. a.* ascendancy over; ***die*** ~ ***in Asien*** *etc.* dominance over Asia *etc.*
'vor·herr·schen *v/i.* (*sep.*, h) predominate, be (pre)dominant; prevail; **'vor·herr·schend** *adj.* predominant; prevailing *climate etc.*; ***die*** ~***e Meinung*** prevailing opinion, opinion at large
Vor'her·sa·ge *f* (-; -n) prediction; ✝, *meteor.* forecast
vor'her·se·hen *v/t.* (*irr.*, *sep.*, h, → ***sehen***) foresee; ***ich hab's vorhergesehen*** *a.* I could see it coming, I knew it would happen; ***keiner konnte das*** ~ nobody could have foreseen (*or* predicted) that; ***wie vorherzusehen war*** predictably, as was to be expected
'vor·heu·cheln *v/t.* (*sep.*, h) pretend (*dat.* to); ***j-m et.*** ~ try to get s.o. to believe s.th.; ***j-m etwas*** ~ put on an act in front of s.o.
'vor·heu·len F *v/t.* (*sep.*, h): ***j-m etwas*** ~ F give s.o. a sob story; cry on s.o.'s shoulder; ***heul mir nichts vor!*** F I don't want (to hear) any sob stories
vor·hin [fo:ɐ'hın, 'fo:ɐhın] *adv.* earlier on, a (short) while ago (F back); just now
'vor·hin·ein *adv.*: ***im*** ~ a) in advance, b) from the start, (right) at the outset
'Vor·hof *m* **1.** forecourt; **2.** *anat.* a) atrium, auricle, b) vestibule; ~**flim·mern** *n* ⚕ auricular fibrillation
'Vor·höl·le *f*: ***die*** ~ limbo, Limbo
Vor·hut ['fo:ɐhu:t] *f* (-; *no pl.*) ⚔ vanguard (*a. fig.*), advance guard
vo·rig ['fo:rıç] *adj.* previous; *a.* former *president etc.*; last; ~***e Woche*** last week
'Vor·jahr *n* (-[e]s; -e) previous year; ***im*** ~ a) the previous year, b) last year; ***die Rechnungen vom*** ~ a) the previous year's bills, b) last year's bills
vor·jäh·rig ['fo:ɐjɛ:rıç] *adj.* **1.** of (*or* from) the previous year; **2.** last year's ...
'vor·jam·mern *v/t.* (*sep.*, h): ***j-m etwas*** ~ moan to s.o. (***über*** *acc.* about)
'Vor·kämp·fer *m* champion, pioneer
'vor·kau·en *fig.* *v/t.* (*sep.*, h): ***j-m et.*** ~ spoon-feed s.o. with s.th.
'Vor·kaufs·recht *n* (right of) first refusal (***an*** *dat.*, ***bei*** *dat.* on); ***j-m das*** ~ ***einräumen*** give s.o. first refusal (***an*** *dat.* on)
Vor·keh·rung ['fo:ɐke:rʊŋ] *f* (-; -en) a) measure, b) precaution; ~***en treffen*** take measures *or* precautions (***gegen*** *acc.* against), ***für*** *acc.*: arrange (*or* provide) for
'Vor·kennt·nis·se *pl.* previous knowledge *sg.* (***von*** *dat.* of), previous experience *sg.*
'vor·kli·nisch *adj.* preclinical
'vor·knöp·fen F *v/t.* (*sep.*, h): ***sich j-n*** ~ take s.o. to task, F have s.o. on the carpet, F take care of s.o.
'vor·kom·men *v/i.* (*irr.*, *sep.*, sn, → ***kommen***) **1.** a) appear; be found; crop up, b) happen, occur; ***sie kommen im Mittelalter*** (***in Asien*** *etc.*) ***vor*** you find them in the Middle Ages (in Asia *etc.*); ***das kommt schon mal vor*** it happens, it can happen; → ***Familie***; ***so etwas ist mir noch nie vorgekommen*** nothing like that has ever happened to me before; ***das Wort kommt zweimal vor*** the word

appears (*or* occurs) twice, there are two instances of the word; **2. *es kommt mir vor*** it seems to me; ***es kommt mir merkwürdig vor*** it strikes me as strange, it seems (a bit) strange to me; ***es kam mir so vor, als ob*** I had the impression that; ***sich dumm*** *etc.* ~ feel silly *etc.*; ***sich klug*** (***wichtig*** *etc.*) ~ think one is clever (important *etc.*); ***das kommt dir nur so vor*** you're (just) imagining it; F ***wie kommst du mir vor?*** who do you think you are?; **3.** come forward; *ped. a.* come to the front of the class

'Vor·kom·men *n* (-s; -) **1.** *no pl.* occurrence; incidence; existence; **2.** *min.* deposit

Vor·komm·nis ['fo:ɐkɔmnɪs] *n* (-ses; -se) incident, occurrence; ***keine besonderen ~se*** no unusual occurrences, F nothing unusual happening

'Vor·kriegs... *in cpds.* pre-war

vor·la·den *v/t.* (*irr., sep.*, h, → ***laden***) summon; subpoena; **'Vor·la·dung** *f* (-; -en) (writ of) summons *sg.*; subpoena

'Vor·la·ge *f* (-; -n) **1.** model; pattern; ***et. als ~ benutzen*** copy from s.th.; **2.** *no pl.* presentation, submission; ***gegen ~*** *gen.* on presentation of; **3.** *parl.* bill; **4.** *soccer etc.*: pass; **5.** *skiing*: forward lean

'vor·las·sen *v/t.* (*irr., sep.*, h, → ***lassen***) **1.** let *s.o.* go first (*or* in front); let *s.o.* pass; **2.** admit; ***vorgelassen werden*** *a.* be shown in

'Vor·lauf *m* (-[e]s; ⸚e) **1.** *no pl. tape recorder etc.*: fast forward; **2.** *sport*: preliminary heat; **3.** ⚙ forward movement

'Vor·läu·fer *m* (-s; -) *a. fig.* forerunner, precursor

vor·läu·fig ['fo:ɐlɔyfɪç] **I.** *adj.* provisional, temporary; **II.** *adv.* provisionally, temporarily; for the time being; **'Vor·läu·fig·keit** *f* (-; *no pl.*) provisional nature (*gen.* of)

'vor·laut *adj.* pert, cheeky

'vor·le·ben *v/t.* (*sep.*, h): (***j-m***) ***et.*** ~ be a living example of s.th. (for s.o.)

'Vor·le·ben *n* (-s; *no pl.*) past, past life (*or* history)

Vor·le·ge·be·steck ['fo:ɐle:gə-] *n*: (***ein*** ~ a set of) carvers *pl.*, servers *pl.*

'vor·le·gen *v/t.* (*sep.*, h) a) present (*dat.* to); submit (to), b) put on *lock*, c) *gastr.* serve, d) *fig.* set *the pace etc.*; F ***ein scharfes Tempo*** ~ set a brisk pace; ***j-m den Ball*** ~ play the ball to s.o.

Vor·le·ger ['fo:ɐle:gɐ] *m* (-s; -) rug; mat

Vor·le·ge·schloß ['fo:ɐle:gə-] *n* padlock

'vor·leh·nen *v/refl.* (*sep.*, h): ***sich*** ~ lean forward

'Vor·lei·stung *f* (-; -en) **1.** ✝ advance (payment); *a. pl.* outlay; ***e-e ~*** (*or* ***~en***) ***erbringen*** make an advance payment; **2.** *usu. pl.* preliminary work; *w.s.* previous achievements; **3.** *fig. usu. pl.* concessions; ***~en erbringen*** make concessions

'vor·le·sen (*irr., sep.*, h, → ***lesen***) **I.** *v/t.* read (aloud); ***j-m et.*** ~ read s.th. (out) to s.o. (***aus*** *dat.* from); **II.** *v/i.* read (***aus*** *dat.* from); **'Vor·le·sung** *f* (-; -en) lecture (***über*** *acc.* on); ***e-e ~ halten*** give a lecture; ***~en halten über*** *acc.* lecture on; ***e-e ~ besuchen*** go to (*formal*: attend) a lecture

'Vor·le·sungs|be·ginn *m* start (*or* beginning) of term; ~ ***ist am*** *dat.* ***...*** term starts (*or* begins) on ...; **2frei** *adj.*: ***~e Zeit*** vacation (period); **~ver·zeich·nis** *n* program(me) of lectures, *Am.* catalog

vor·letzt ['fo:ɐlɛtst] *adj.* last but one, next to last, *formal*: penultimate; ***~e Nacht*** the night before last; ***am ~en Freitag*** (on the) Friday before last

'Vor·lie·be *f* (-; -n) liking, fondness (***für*** *acc.* of); ***e-e*** (***besondere***) ***~ haben für*** *acc. a.* be (particularly) fond of; ***et. mit ~ tun*** a) be very fond of (doing) s.th., b) have a penchant for (doing) s.th., *w.s.* do s.th. fairly often (*or* quite a lot)

vor·lieb·neh·men [fo:ɐ'li:pne:mən] *v/i.* (*irr., sep.*, h, → ***nehmen***): ~ ***mit*** *dat.* settle for, make do with, be content with

'vor·lie·gen *v/i.* (*irr., sep.*, h, → ***liegen***) **1.** be there; *a.* have arrived; *n.s.* ***j-m*** ~ lie (*or* be) in front of s.o., lie (*or* be) on s.o.'s desk; *results, data etc.*: have been given to s.o.; *application etc.*: have been submitted (to s.o.); ***die Ergebnisse liegen noch nicht vor*** the results haven't come in yet, we haven't received (*or* had) any results so far; ***es liegen keine Gründe vor zu*** *inf.* there are no reasons why *we should do it etc.*; ***da muß ein Irrtum*** ~ there must be some mistake; ***was liegt hier vor?*** what's going on here?; ⚖ ***was liegt gegen ihn vor?*** what is the charge against him?; ***gegen ihn liegt nichts vor*** there's no charge against him; **2.** have to be done (*or* dealt with); be on the agenda; ***was liegt uns vor?*** what's to be done?; ***es liegt ... vor*** a) there is ..., b) here we have ...; **'vor·lie·gend** *adj. case etc.* in hand; *problem etc.* at issue

'vor·lü·gen *v/t.* (*irr., sep.*, h, → ***lügen***): ***j-m etwas*** ~ lie to s.o., F tell s.o. a pack of lies; ***er lügt ihnen vor, er sei ...*** he's lying to them about being ...

vorm [fo:ɐm] F (= ***vor dem***) → ***vor*** 1

'vor·ma·chen *v/t.* (*sep.*, h) **1.** ***j-m et.*** ~ show s.o. how to do s.th., demonstrate s.th. to s.o.; **2.** ***j-m etwas*** ~ fool s.o.; ***sich*** (***selbst***) ***etwas*** ~ deceive (*or* fool) o.s.; ***machen wir uns nichts vor*** let's be honest about this; ***ihm kannst du nichts*** ~ he's no (*or* nobody's) fool; ***ich lasse mir nichts*** ~ I'm not going to let them *etc.* make a fool of me

'Vor·macht *f* (-; *no pl.*), **~stel·lung** *f* supremacy; hegemony (*both* ***in*** *dat.* over); ~ ***in*** *dat. a.* ascendancy over

vor·ma·lig ['fo:ɐma:lɪç] *adj.* former

vor·mals ['fo:ɐma:ls] *adv.* formerly (known as)

'Vor·marsch *m* (-[e]s; ⸚e) advance (*a. fig.*); ***auf dem*** (*or* ***im***) ~ ***sein*** be on the advance, be advancing (***auf*** *acc.* on), *fig.* be gaining ground, be spreading

'vor·mer·ken *v/t.* (*sep.*, h) make a note of *an appointment, order etc.*; reserve (*a.* ~ ***lassen***); put *s.o.'s* name down, F pencil in; earmark *funds*, ✝ target; ***sich ~ lassen*** put one's name down (***für*** *acc.* for), have one's name put down (for); ***sich bei j-m ~ lassen*** make an appointment with s.o.; **'Vor·merk·li·ste** *f* waiting list; **'Vor·mer·kung** *f* (-; -en) a) booking, reservation, b) appointment

'Vor·mie·ter *m* (-s; -) previous tenant

'Vor·mit·tag *m* (-[e]s; -e) morning

vor·mit·täg·lich ['fo:ɐmɪtɛ:klɪç] *adj.* morning ...

'vor·mit·tags *adv.* in the morning(s)

'Vor·mo·nat *m*: (***im*** ~ the) previous month

'Vor·mund *m* (-[e]s; -e, -münder [-mʏndɐ]) guardian; **'Vor·mund·schaft** *f* (-; -en) guardianship; ***unter ~ stehen*** (***stellen***) be placed (place) under the care of a guardian; **'Vor·mund·schafts·ge·richt** *n* guardianship court; *in the USA*: Surrogate's Court; *in GB*: Family Division of the High Court

vorn [fɔrn] *adv.* in front (*a. sport and fig.*), at the front; *sport*: ahead; ***ganz*** ~ a) right in front, b) at the beginning; ***weiter*** ~ a) further up, b) nearer the beginning; ***nach*** ~ forward; ***von*** ~ from the front; ***von ~ anfangen*** start (*or* begin) at the beginning, (*a.* ***wieder von ~ anfangen***) start (all over) again; ***von ~ bis hinten*** a) from front to back, b) from beginning to end; ***noch einmal von*** ~ all over again, let's do that again, let's go back to the beginning again

'Vor·na·me *m* (-n; -n) first (*or* given, Christian) name, *adm. a.* prename

vorn'an *adv.* in (*or* at) the front

vor·ne ['fɔrnə] → ***vorn***

vor·nehm ['fo:ɐne:m] *adj.* a) distinguished; noble, b) classy; elegant, fashionable, smart, F posh; high-class; exclusive; ***~e Gesinnung*** high-mindedness; ***es ist sehr*** ~ *a.* it's got class; ***s-e ~ste Aufgabe*** (***Pflicht*** *etc.*) his chief task (duty *etc.*); ~ ***tun***, F ***auf ~ machen*** put on airs

'vor·neh·men *v/t.* (*irr., sep.*, h, → ***nehmen***) carry out, *a.* make *changes, improvements etc.*; (*a.* ***sich et.*** ~) tackle *s.th.*; get down to *s.th.*; ***sich et.*** ~ a) plan s.th., have (*or* make) plans for s.th., b) take care of (*or* see to) s.th.; ***sich ~ zu*** *inf.* a) decide to *inf.*, resolve to *inf.*, b) plan to *inf.*, intend to *inf.*; ***sich ein Buch*** (***e-e Arbeit***) ~ *a.* set out to read a book (do a job); F ***sich j-n*** ~ a) take s.o. to task, F have s.o. on the carpet, b) F take care of s.o.; ***sich zuviel*** ~ take on too much, F bite off more than one can chew; F ***sich einiges vorgenommen haben*** have taken on quite a job

'Vor·nehm·heit *f* (-; *no pl.*) a) distinguished manner; nobility, b) class(iness); elegance; exclusivity; exclusive atmosphere *etc.*; → ***vornehm***

vor·nehm·lich ['fo:ɐne:mlɪç] *adv.* mainly; first and foremost

Vor·nehm·tue·rei [-tu:ə'raɪ] *f* (-; *no pl.*) airs (and graces) *pl.*

'vor·nehm·tue·risch [-tu:ərɪʃ] *adj.* affected, F snobby, la-di-da; ***~e Art*** affected behavio(u)r, airs (and graces)

'vor·nei·gen *v/refl.* (*sep.*, h): ***sich*** ~ bend (*or* lean) forward

'Vor·ne·ver·tei·di·gung *f* forward defen|ce (*Am.* -se)

vorn·her·ein ['fɔrnhɛraɪn] *adv.*: ***von*** ~ (right) from the beginning (*or* start)

vorn·über [fɔrn'ʔy:bɐ] *adv.* forward; head first

'vor·ord·nen *v/t.* (*sep.*, h) presort, put in some sort of order

Vor·ort ['fo:ɐɔrt] *m* (-[e]s; -e) suburb

'Vor·ort(s)... *in cpds.* suburban

'Vor·ort|ver·kehr *m* suburban traffic; **~zug** *m* local (*or* commuter) train

'Vor·platz *m* (-es; ⸚e) forecourt; square

'Vor·po·sten *m* (-s; -) ⚔ *and fig.* outpost

'vor·pre·schen *v/i.* (*sep.*, sn) rush forward; *fig.* rush ahead; ~ ***in*** *acc.* rush into, *fig. a.* venture into; *usu. fig.* ***zu weit*** ~ venture too far

'Vor·pro,gramm *n* supporting program(me); **'vor·pro·gram,mie·ren** *v/t.* (*sep.*, h) (pre)program(me); **'vor·pro-**

gram,miert *adj.* **1.** (pre)program(m)ed; **2.** *fig.* a) inevitable, b) sure, certain; ***es war ~ a.*** it was bound to happen, it was on the cards; ***die Katastrophe ist ~*** it's program(m)ed for disaster

'Vor·prü·fung *f* (-; -en) preliminary examination; *sport*: trial

'Vor·rang *m* (-[e]s; *no pl.*) a) (position of) pre-eminence, b) priority; ***den ~ haben vor*** *dat.* take precedence (*matter*: *a.* priority) over

vor·ran·gig ['fo:ɐraŋɪç] **I.** *adj.* priority ...; **II.** *adv.*: ***et. ~ behandeln*** give s.th. (top) priority; **'Vor·ran·gig·keit** *f* (-; *no pl.*) priority (***vor*** *dat.* over)

'Vor·rang·stel·lung *f* → ***Vorrang***

Vor·rat ['fo:ɐra:t] *m* (-[e]s; Vorräte ['fo:ɐrɛ:tə]) supply, supplies *pl.*, stocks *pl.*; store; reserves *pl.* (*a. min. and* ✝); ⚔ stockpile; (secret) hoard (*all* ***an*** *dat.* of); *fig.* stock *of anecdotes etc.*; ***et. auf ~ haben*** have s.th. in reserve (✝ in stock), F have a stockpile of s.th.; ***et. auf ~ kaufen*** stock up on s.th.; ***solange der ~ reicht*** while stocks last

vor·rä·tig ['fo:ɐrɛ:tɪç] *adj.* available; ✝ in stock; ***nicht (mehr) ~*** out of stock; ***et. nicht mehr ~ haben*** be (*or* have run) out of s.th.

'Vor·rats|kam·mer *f* pantry, larder; **~la·ger** *n*, **~raum** *m* storeroom; **~schrank** *m* store cupboard; larder

'Vor·raum *m* (-[e]s; ⸚e) anteroom; *thea. etc.*: foyer, lobby

'vor·rech·nen *v/t.* (*sep.*, h) reckon up (***j-m*** for s.o.); enumerate; *fig. a.* list, go through *s.th.*

'Vor·recht *n* (-[e]s; -e) privilege, prerogative

'Vor·re·de *f* (-; -n) **1.** opening words *pl.*; **2.** preface; **'Vor·red·ner** *m* (-s; -) previous speaker

'Vor·rei·ter *fig. m* pioneer, trailblazer; ***den ~ machen bei*** *dat.* blaze the trail for, be the trailblazer for, pioneer *an idea etc.*

'vor·ren·nen *v/i.* (*irr.*, *sep.*, sn, → ***rennen***) run forward; run (on) ahead

'Vor·rich·tung *f* (-; -en) device; appliance

'vor·rü·cken (*sep.*) **I.** *v/t.* (h) move forward (*a. chess etc.*); **II.** *v/i.* (sn) advance (⚔ ***in Richtung auf*** *acc.* on; ***nach*** *dat.* to); ***auf den 3. Platz ~*** *sport*: move up to third place; → ***vorgerückt***

'Vor·ru·he·stand *m* (-[e]s; *no pl.*) early retirement; ***in den ~ treten*** take early retirement

'Vor·ru·he·stands|gel·der *pl.* early retirement benefits; **~re·ge·lung** *f* early retirement law(s *pl.*) *or* policy

'Vor·run·de *f* (-; -n) qualifying round

vors [fo:ɐs] F (= ***vor das***) → ***vor*** 1

'vor·sa·gen (*sep.*, h) **I.** *v/t.*: ***j-m et. ~*** a) *ped.* tell s.o. s.th., whisper s.th. to s.o., b) say s.th. first (for s.o. to repeat); ***sich et. ~*** talk o.s. into believing s.th.; **II.** *v/i.*: ***j-m ~*** tell s.o. the answer, whisper the answer to s.o.

'Vor·sai,son *f* (-; -s) pre-season, off-season, low season; start of the season; **~preis** *m* off-peak price

'Vor·satz (-es; ⸚e) *m* **1.** intention; resolution; ⚖ (criminal) intent; ***mit ~*** on purpose, ⚖ wil(l)fully, with malice aforethought; ⚖ ***mit dem ~ zu*** *inf.* with the intent of *ger.*; ***den ~ fassen zu*** *inf.* resolve to *inf.*, make up one's mind to *inf.*; **2.** → ***Vorsatzgerät***; **3.** → **'Vor·satz·blatt** *n typ.* end paper; **'Vor·satz·ge·rät** *n* attachment

vor·sätz·lich ['fo:ɐzɛtslɪç] **I.** *adj.* intentional, deliberate; ⚖ wil(l)ful; ***~er Mord*** premeditated murder; **II.** *adv.* deliberately, intentionally; ⚖ wil(l)fully, with criminal intent, with malice aforethought

'Vor·satz·lin·se *f phot.* front lens attachment

'vor·schal·ten *v/t.* (*sep.*, h) **1.** ⚙ *etc.* add (*dat.* to), insert; ⚡ connect in series; **2.** *fig.* slot *s.th.* in ahead, bring *s.th.* forward, move *s.th.* up

'Vor·schalt,wi·der·stand *m* ⚡ series resistor

'Vor·schau *f* (-; -en) preview (***auf*** *acc.* of); *film*: trailer(s *pl.*); ***e-e ~ auf das heutige Programm*** a look at today's program(me)

'Vor·schein *m*: ***zum ~ bringen*** bring to light; ***zum ~ kommen*** a) come to light, surface, come to the surface, *a.* be discovered, b) appear

'vor·schicken *v/t.* (*sep.*, h) send forward; send (on) ahead

'vor·schie·ben (*irr.*, *sep.*, h, → ***schieben***) **I.** *v/t.* push (*or* slide, move) forward; stick out; *fig.* use *s.th.* as an excuse; use *s.o.* as a dummy; → ***Riegel***; **II.** *v/refl.*: ***sich ~*** move forward; push (one's way) forward, *Brit.* jump the queue

'Vor·schlag *m* (-[e]s; ⸚e) **1.** suggestion, *a.* ✝ proposal; (piece of) advice; ***auf j-s ~*** on s.o.'s suggestion (*or* advice); **2.** ♪ ***(langer, kurzer) ~*** long, short) appoggiatura; **3.** *typ.* blank space

'vor·schla·gen *v/t.* (*irr.*, *sep.*, h, → ***schlagen***) suggest, propose; recommend; ***~ zu*** *inf.* suggest *etc. ger.*; ***j-m ~, et. zu tun*** suggest (that) s.o. (should) do s.th., suggest to s.o. that he (*or* she) (should) do s.th.; ***ich schlage vor, daß wir zuerst etwas essen*** I suggest we eat something first; ***er schlug vor, daß wir noch warten*** he suggested waiting a bit; ***j-n ~ für*** *acc.* recommend (*or* propose) s.o. for *a job etc.*

'Vor·schlag·ham·mer *m* sledgehammer

'Vor·schluß·run·de *f* semifinal

'vor·schnell *adj.* → ***voreilig***

'vor·schrei·ben *v/t.* (*irr.*, *sep.*, h, → ***schreiben***) **1.** prescribe; ⚖ stipulate; ***ich lasse mir nichts ~*** I won't be dictated to; **2.** write *s.th.* out (*dat.* for)

'vor·schrei·ten *v/i.* (*irr.*, *sep.*, sn, → ***schreiten***) advance

'Vor·schrift *f* (-; -en) a) rule(s *pl.*), regulation(s *pl.*), b) instruction, direction; ***nach ärztlicher ~*** according to doctor's orders; ***(streng) nach ~*** *work etc.* (strictly) to rule; ***Dienst nach ~*** work-to-rule

'vor·schrifts·mä·ßig **I.** *adj.* correct; regulation *uniform, haircut etc.*; ... as ordered, ... as prescribed; **II.** *adv.* a) correctly, according to regulations, b) according to the instructions

'vor·schrifts·wid·rig **I.** *adj.* incorrect; **II.** *adv.* incorrectly, contrary to (the) regulations (*or* instructions)

Vor·schub ['fo:ɐʃu:p] *m* (-[e]s; ⸚e) **1.** ***e-r Sache ~ leisten*** encourage (*or* foster) s.th.; **2.** ⚙ feed

'Vor·schul·al·ter *n* pre-school age; ***Kinder im ~*** pre-school-age children

'Vor·schu·le *f* (-; *no pl.*) nursery school, *Am.* pre-school; **'vor·schu·lisch** *adj.* pre-school ...; **'Vor·schul·kind** *n* **1.** pre-school-age child; **2.** playschool child

'Vor·schuß *m* (-sses; ⸚sse) advance (payment) (***auf*** *acc.* on); **~lor·bee·ren** *pl.* premature praise *sg.*; unearned laurels

'vor·schuß·wei·se *adv.* as an advance

'Vor·schuß·zah·lung *f* advance (payment)

'vor·schüt·zen *v/t.* (*sep.*, h) give (*or* use) as a pretext; ***Krankheit (Arbeit*** *etc.*) ***~*** *a.* pretend to be ill (to have work to do *etc.*); ***~, man sei (habe*** *etc.*) pretend to be (have *etc.*), make out one is (has *etc.*)

'vor·schwär·men *v/t. and v/i.* (*sep.*, h): ***j-m von et. ~*** rave to s.o. about s.th., rave on about s.th. to s.o.; ***j-m ~, daß (wie)*** rave on about the fact that (about how)

'vor·schwe·ben *v/i.* (*sep.*, h): ***mir schwebt etwas ... vor*** I'm thinking of (*or* I could imagine) something ...

'vor·schwin·deln *v/t.* (*sep.*, h): ***j-m etwas ~*** tell s.o. a lot of lies (*or* fibs); ***j-m ~, man sei (würde*** *etc.*) lie to s.o. about being (doing *etc.*)

'vor·se·hen (*irr.*, *sep.*, h, → ***sehen***) **I.** *v/t.* **1.** intend (***für*** *acc.* for), *a.* earmark, set aside *funds etc.* (for); **2.** ***j-n ~ für*** *acc.* have s.o. in mind for *a post etc.*; have chosen (*adm.* designated) s.o. for *an office etc.*; ***j-n ~ als*** intend s.o. to be, plan to make s.o. *departmental head etc.*; ***vorgesehen sein für*** *acc.* be a candidate for; have been chosen (*or* designated) for, be slated for; **3.** a) plan, *a.* schedule, b) plan, design (*all* ***für*** *acc.* for); ***es ist vorgesehen zu*** *inf.* there are plans to *inf.*, they're planning to *inf.*; ***vorgesehen sein zu*** *inf. a.* be supposed to *inf.*; ***der Fahrstuhl ist für acht Personen vorgesehen*** the elevator is designed to take eight people; ***das Spiel ist für Sonntag vorgesehen*** the match is scheduled for (*or* to take place) on Sunday; ***die Sitzung ist für nächste Woche vorgesehen*** the meeting is planned (*or* scheduled) for next week, the meeting has been slated for next week; ***was ist für heute vorgesehen?*** what are the plans for today?, what's on the agenda today?; ***ist für heute (irgend) etwas vorgesehen?*** are there any plans for today?; **4.** ⚖ provide for; ***wie vorgesehen in*** *dat.* as provided for in; ***das Gesetz sieht vor, daß*** the law provides that; **5.** include; ***im Programm sind mehrere Pausen vorgesehen*** the program(me) will include several breaks; **II.** *v/refl.*: ***sich ~*** be careful, watch out (***bei j-m*** with s.o.); ***sich ~, nicht zu*** *inf.* be careful (*or* take care) not to *inf.*

Vor·se·hung ['fo:ɐze:ʊŋ] *f* (-; *no pl.*): ***(die göttliche ~*** divine) providence, Providence

'vor·set·zen (*sep.*, h) **I.** *v/t.* a) move (*or* put) forward, b) move *s.o.* (up) to the front, c) put in front (*dat.* of); ***j-m et. ~*** place (*or* put) s.th. in front of (*or* before) s.o., *gastr.* serve s.o. s.th. (*or* s.th. to s.o.), offer s.o. s.th., *contp.*, *a. fig.* dish s.th. up to s.o.; *fig.* ***was haben die uns diesmal wieder vorgesetzt?*** what have they dished us up this time?, what have they come up with (for us) this time?; **II.** *v/refl.*: ***sich ~*** move (up) to the front, go and sit at the front

Vor·sicht ['fo:ɐzɪçt] *f* (-; *no pl.*) a) caution, b) care; circumspection; ***~!*** careful!, look out!, watch out!; caution!, danger!; *on boxes etc.*: (handle) with care; ***~, bissi-***

ger Hund! beware of the dog; **~, *Glas!*** glass - with care; **~ *Stufe!*** mind the step; ***mit* ~** cautiously; ***mit äußerster* ~** with the utmost caution; ***mit gebotener* ~** with due care (and attention); ***es ist* (*äußerste*) ~ *geboten*** one has to be (extremely) careful; ***zur* ~ *raten*** advise (*or* recommend) caution; ***j-m zur* ~ *raten*** advise (*or* urge) s.o. to be careful; F **~ *ist die Mutter der Porzellankiste*** better safe than sorry; F ***er ist mit* ~ *zu genießen*** F you've got to watch him; ***es ist mit* (*äußerster*) ~ *zu genießen*** you've got to be (extremely) cautious about it, you've got to take it with a (big) pinch of salt; ***was er sagt, ist mit* ~ *zu genießen*** you've got to take everything he says with a pinch of salt

vor·sich·tig ['foːɐzɪçtɪç] **I.** *adj.* careful; cautious; conservative *estimate etc.*; **~ *sein mit s-m Urteil*** *etc.* be cautious about judging *etc.*; ***sei* ~, *daß du nichts fallen läßt*** be careful not to drop anything, mind you don't drop anything; ***da bin ich immer ein bißchen* ~** I'm always a bit wary of that; **II.** *adv.* a) carefully, b) cautiously

'vor·sichts·hal·ber [-halbɐ] *adv.* as a precaution

'Vor·sichts·maß·nah·me *f* (-; -n) precaution(ary measure); **~*n treffen*** take precautions

'Vor·sil·be *f* (-; -n) *ling.* prefix

'vor·sin·gen (*irr.*, *sep.*, h, → ***singen***) **I.** *v/t.*: ***j-m et.* ~** sing s.th. to s.o.; **II.** *v/i.* (have an) audition (*dat.* with *s.o.*); ***j-n* ~ *lassen*** audition s.o., give s.o. an audition

vor·sint·flut·lich ['foːɐzɪntfluːtlɪç] *adj.* pre-Flood ..., *a. fig.* antediluvian

Vor·sitz ['foːɐzɪts] *m* (-es; *no pl.*) chair(manship); ☤ presidency; ***den* ~ *haben*** (*or* ***führen***) be in the chair, *a.* ☤ preside (***bei*** *dat.* over); ***den* ~ *haben bei*** *dat. a.* chair *a meeting etc.*; ***unter dem* ~ *von*** *dat.* (*or gen.*) under the chairmanship of, with ... in the chair, with ... chairing

Vor·sit·zen·de ['foːɐzɪtsəndə] *m, f* (-n; -n) chairman (*f* chairwoman), chairperson; ☤ president

'Vor·sor·ge *f* (-; *no pl.*) provision(s *pl.*); precaution; **~ *treffen*** → **'vor·sor·gen** *v/i.* (*sep.*, h) provide, make provisions (***für*** *acc.* for); **~, *daß*** see to it that; ***für die Zukunft*** *etc.* **~** *a.* plan ahead for the future *etc.*

'Vor·sor·ge·un·ter,su·chung *f* (-; -en) screening (test); *pl. coll.* screening *sg.*

vor·sorg·lich ['foːɐzɔrklɪç] **I.** *adj.* a) precautionary, b) cautious, solicitous; **II.** *adv.* as a precaution(ary measure), to be on the safe side, F just in case

Vor·spann ['foːɐʃpan] *m* (-[e]s; -e) a) introduction; lead-in; *film*: credits *pl.*; pre-titles sequence, b) *of a tape etc.*: leader; **~mu,sik** *f film*: theme music (*or* tune); signature tune

'vor·span·nen *v/t.* (*sep.*, h) harness (*dat.* to); F *fig.* ***j-n* ~** use s.o. (***für*** *acc.* for), ***für et.***: *a.* F get (*or* rope) s.o. in on s.th.

'Vor·spei·se *f* (-; -n) starter, *formal*: hors d'oeuvre; ***was nimmst du als* ~?** *a.* what are you having to start (off) with?

'vor·spie·geln *v/t.* (*sep.*, h): ***j-m et.* ~** delude s.o. into thinking s.th.; **'Vor·spie·ge·lung** *f* (-; -en) preten|ce (*Am.* -se); (***unter***) **~ *falscher Tatsachen*** (under) false preten|ces (*Am.* -ses)

'Vor·spiel *n* (-[e]s; -e) **1.** ♪ prelude (***zu*** *dat.* to); **2.** *thea.* prolog(ue); **3.** *sport*: curtain-raiser; **4.** foreplay; **5.** *fig.* prelude, overture, curtain-raiser (***zu*** *dat.* to)

'vor·spie·len (*sep.*, h) **I.** *v/t.* play (***j-m et.*** s.th. to s.o.); *fig.* ***et.* ~** put s.th. on; (***j-m***) ***etwas* ~** put on an act (for s.o.); **II.** *v/i. thea.*, ♪ (have an) audition (*dat.* with); ***j-n* ~ *lassen*** audition s.o., give s.o. an audition

'vor·spre·chen (*irr.*, *sep.*, h, → ***sprechen***) **I.** *v/t.* **1.** (***j-m***) ***et.* ~** say s.th. (for s.o. to repeat); **2.** recite; **II.** *v/i.* **3.** ***bei j-m* ~** (go to) see s.o.; ***könnten Sie bei uns* ~?** could you come by (and see us)?; **4.** (have an) audition (*dat.* with); ***j-n* ~ *lassen*** audition s.o., give s.o. an audition

'vor·sprin·gen *v/i.* (*irr.*, *sep.*, sn, → ***springen***) a) jump forward, b) *a.* △ project, jut (out); **'vor·sprin·gend** *adj.* projecting; prominent *chin, nose etc.*; ***er hat ein* ~*es Kinn*** *a.* his chin juts out quite a bit

'Vor·sprung *m* (-[e]s; ¨e) **1.** △ projection; ledge; **2.** *sport*: lead (*a. fig.*) (***gegenüber, vor*** *dat.* over); start; ***ein Tor* ~** a one-goal lead; ***mit e-m* ~ *von 2 Sekunden*** by a margin of 2 seconds; ***er hat e-n* ~ *von 3 Runden*** he leads by 3 laps; *fig.* ***e-n* ~ *von 6 Wochen haben*** be ahead by 6 weeks, be 6 weeks ahead; ***j-m* ~ *geben*** give s.o. a (head) start; ***j-m 10 Meter* ~ *geben*** give s.o. a 10-metre (*Am.* -meter) start; ***s-n* ~ *ausbauen*** consolidate one's lead

'vor·spu·len (*sep.*, h) **I.** *v/t.* run *a or the tape* forward *or* on (to the end); **II.** *v/i.* run a (*or* the) tape forward *or* on (to the end)

'Vor·stadt *f* (-; ¨e) suburb; *contp.* suburbia; ***in der* ~** in the suburbs, in a suburb; **'Vor·städ·ter** *m* (-s; -) suburbanite; **'vor·städ·tisch** *adj.* suburban

Vor·stand ['foːɐʃtant] *m* (-[e]s; Vorstände ['foːɐʃtɛndə]) **1.** ☤ (board of) management; managing committee *of a club etc.*; board of governors (*or* trustees) *of an institute etc.*; ***im* ~ *sitzen*** be on the board; **2.** director; chairman (of the board), *Am.* chief executive

'Vor·stands|eta·ge *f* executive suite; *fig.* boardroom(s *pl.*); **~mit·glied** *n* board member (***bei*** *dat.* of), member of the (executive) board *etc.*; → ***Vorstand*** 1; director; **~sit·zung** *f* board meeting; **~vor·sit·zen·de** *m* chairman of the board (of directors), *Am.* chief executive; *pl. a.* top managers, chief executives; **~wahl** *f* board (*pol.* executive) elections *pl.*

'vor·stecken *v/t.* (*sep.*, h) (*a.* ***sich et.*** **~**) put on, *a.* pin on

'vor·ste·hen *v/i.* (*irr.*, *sep.*, h, → ***stehen***) **1.** protrude, jut out; **2.** a) direct, be in charge of, b) preside over, chair *s.th.*; **'vor·ste·hend** *adj.* **1.** preceding, above; **2. ~*e Zähne*** protruding teeth, buckteeth

Vor·ste·her ['foːɐʃteːɐ] *m* (-s; -) a) director, b) governor, *Am.* warden, c) *eccl.* abbot, d) stationmaster; **~drü·se** *f* prostate gland

Vor·steh·hund ['foːɐʃteː-] *m* pointer

vor·stell·bar ['foːɐʃtɛlbaːɐ] *adj.* conceivable, imaginable; **'vor·stel·len** (*sep.*, h) **I.** *v/t.* **1.** move forward; **2.** put *watch* forward (***um*** *acc.* by); **3. *j-n j-m* ~** introduce s.o. to s.o.; ***darf ich Ihnen Herrn Braun* ~?** may I introduce you to Mr Braun?, I'd like you to meet Mr Braun; **4.** ☤ present *new product etc.*; **5.** represent; ***was soll das* ~?** what's that supposed to be?; F ***er stellt etwas vor*** he's not just anybody; ***es stellt etwas vor*** it's quite something; **6. *sich et.* ~** imagine (*or* envisage) s.th.; visualize (*or* picture) s.th.; F ***stell dir vor!*** just imagine!; ***stell dir das einmal vor!*** *a.* can you imagine that (*or* believe it)?; ***stell dir das nicht so leicht vor*** don't think it's so easy, it's not as easy as you think; ***so stelle ich mir e-n Urlaub*** *etc.* ***vor*** that's my idea of (*or* that's what I call) a holiday *etc.*; ***sich unter e-r Sache et.* ~** imagine s.th. to be s.th.; ***sich unter e-m Begriff et.* ~** take an expression to mean s.th.; ***ich stelle mir darunter ... vor*** a) I imagine it to be ..., b) I understand it as (*or* to mean) ...; ***was stellst du dir darunter vor?*** what does it mean to you?; ***ich kann mir darunter nichts* ~** it doesn't mean a thing to me; **II.** *v/refl.*: ***sich* ~** a) introduce o.s., b) present o.s., c) go for an interview; ***darf ich mich* ~, ...** my name's ...; hello, I'm ...; **vor·stel·lig** ['foːɐʃtɛlɪç] *adj.*: **~ *werden bei*** *dat.* apply to; **'Vor·stel·lung** *f* (-; -en) **1.** a) introduction, b) presentation (*a.* ☤), c) interview (***bei*** *dat.* with); **2.** *thea.* performance, show; *film*: show(ing); **3.** idea; *a.* image; ***falsche* ~** wrong idea, misconception; ***sich e-e*** (***klare***) **~ *machen von*** *dat.* form a (clear) picture of, get an (*or* a proper) idea of; ***in m-r* ~** the way I imagine (*or* see) it; ***du hast manchmal komische* ~*en*** you ('do) have some strange ideas; ***du machst dir keine* ~!** you've no idea; ***das geht über alle* ~** the mind boggles; **4. *j-m* ~*en machen*** remonstrate with s.o. (***wegen*** *gen.* about)

'Vor·stel·lungs|ga·be *f* (-; *no pl.*) (*the* gift of) imagination; ***e-e gute* ~ *haben*** *a.* have a lot of imagination; **~ge·spräch** *n* (job) interview, interview for a (*or* the) job; ***zu e-m* ~ *gehen*** go for an interview; **~kraft** *f* (-; *no pl.*) (powers *pl.* of) imagination; ***das übersteigt m-e* ~** the mind boggles, *a.* I can't cope with those kind of figures *etc.*; **~ver·mö·gen** *n* (-s; *no pl.*) → ***Vorstellungskraft***

Vor·stop·per ['foːɐʃtɔpɐ] *m* (-s; -) *soccer*: centre (*Am.* center) back

'Vor·stoß *m* (-es; ¨e) ⚔ thrust, advance; *sport*: attack (*a. fig.*); attempt; venture (*a. fig.*); effort; ***e-n* ~ *unternehmen*** make a thrust *etc.*, F *fig.* try one's luck (***bei j-m*** with s.o.); **'vor·sto·ßen** (*irr.*, *sep.*, → ***stoßen***) **I.** *v/t.* (h) push forward; **II.** *v/i.* (sn) ⚔ *etc.* push ahead (*a. fig.*), advance; *sport*: attack; **~ *in*** *acc.* penetrate (into), *a.* venture into; **~ *nach*** (*or* ***zu***) *dat.* press on as far as, fight one's way through to; **~ *bis*** advance as far as, reach

'Vor·stra·fe *f* (-; -n) previous conviction

'Vor·stra·fen(re,gi·ster *n*) *pl.* (criminal) record *sg.*

'vor·strecken *v/t.* (*sep.*, h) **1.** stretch out; stick out; **2.** advance *money* (***j-m*** s.o.)

'Vor·stu·die *f* (-; -n) preliminary study; (preliminary) sketch

'Vor·stu·fe *f* (-; -n) a) preliminary stage, b) early stage, c) early ancestor

'Vor·tag *m*: (***am* ~** the) previous day, (the) day before; ***am* ~ *der Hochzeit*** *etc.* the day before the wedding *etc.*, *formal*: on the eve of the wedding *etc.*

'vor·ta·sten *v/refl.* (*sep.*, h): ***sich* ~** grope

one's way (forward) (***bis, zu*** *dat.* to; ***in*** *acc.* into)

'vor·täu·schen *v/t.* (*sep.*, h) feign, fake; *a.* simulate *sickness etc.*; ***Angst*** *etc.* ~ pretend to be scared *etc.*; ***etwas*** ~ be (just) pretending; ***j-m et.*** ~ pretend to s.o.; ***sich selbst etwas*** ~ pretend to o.s., delude o.s.; ***es war vorgetäuscht*** he was (*or* they were *etc.*) faking, it was all a fake; **'Vor·täu·schung** *f* (-; -en) preten|ce (*Am.* -se); feigning *sickness*, simulation; ⚖ ***unter*** ~ ***falscher Tatsachen*** under false preten|ces (*Am.* -ses)

Vor·teil ['fɔrtaɪl] *m* (-[e]s; -e) advantage (*a. sport*); profit, benefit; ***die Vor- und Nachteile e-r Sache erwägen*** consider the pros and cons of s.th.; ***zu j-s*** ~ ***sein, j-m von*** ~ ***sein*** be to s.o.'s advantage; ~***e bieten*** have (*or* offer) advantages; ~ ***bringen*** be profitable, pay; ~ ***haben von*** *dat.* benefit from; ***e-n*** ~ ***haben von*** *dat.* derive an advantage from; ***den (zusätzlichen)*** ~ ***haben zu*** *inf.* have the (added) advantage of *ger.*; ***es hat den großen*** ~, ***billig zu sein*** it has the one big advantage of being cheap; ~ ***ziehen aus*** *dat.* profit from *s.th.*; ***auf s-n*** ~ ***bedacht sein*** be out for one's own interests; ***e-n*** ~ ***haben*** (*or* ***im*** ~ ***sein***) ***gegenüber j-m*** have an (*or* the) advantage over s.o., have a head start on s.o.; ***im*** ~ ***sein*** have the advantage, hold the high ground; ***zu d-m eigenen*** ~ in your own interest; ***er hat sich zu s-m*** ~ ***verändert*** he's changed for the better, he's improved

'vor·teil·haft I. *adj.* advantageous (***für*** *acc.* to); positive; ⚚ profitable (***für*** *acc.* to); favo(u)rable; becoming *dress, colo(u)r etc.*; ~ ***aussehen*** (*or* ***wirken***) look good; **II.** *adv.* advantageously *etc.*; → ***I***; ⚚ *sell etc.* at a profit; *dress etc.* to one's (best) advantage; ***sich*** ~ ***auswirken*** a) have a positive effect (***auf*** *acc.* on), b) (prove to) be of advantage (***auf*** *acc.*, ***für*** *acc.* for), ***auf*** (*or* ***für***) ***j-n:*** *a.* be to s.o.'s advantage; ***sich*** ~ ***kleiden*** *a.* make the most of one's figure; ***sich*** ~ ***entwickeln*** develop positively, make a lot of progress

Vor·trag ['foːɐtraːk] *m* (-[e]s; Vorträge ['foːɐtrɛːgə]) **1.** a) talk, b) *univ.* lecture (*both* ***über*** *acc.* on); ***e-n*** ~ ***halten*** give a talk (*or* lecture); **2.** ♪ *etc.* performance; recital; rendering; **3.** ⚚ balance carried forward; **'vor·tra·gen** *v/t.* (*irr.*, *sep.*, h, → ***tragen***) **1.** ♪ *etc.* perform; recite *poem*; **2.** a) lecture on, b) talk about; **3.** report; **4.** state; put forward, present; tell; **5.** carry (up) *or* take *s.th.* to the front; **6.** ⚚ carry forward

'Vor·tra·gen·de *m, f* (-n; -n) **1.** ♪ *etc.* performer; **2.** speaker; *univ. a.* lecturer

'Vor·trags|abend *m* **1.** evening lecture; **2.** ♪ *etc.* recital; ~**be·zeich·nung** *f* ♪ expression mark; ~**kunst** *f* (-; *no pl.*) art of performance (*or* recital); ***j-s*** ~ *a.* s.o.'s skill as a performer (*or* reciter); ~**rei·he** *f* series of lectures (*or* talks), lecture series; ~**rei·se** *f* lecture tour; ~**saal** *m* lecture hall

vor·treff·lich [foːɐ'trɛflɪç] *adj.* excellent, superb; **Vor'treff·lich·keit** *f* (-; *no pl.*) excellence

'vor·trei·ben *v/t.* (*irr.*, *sep.*, h, → ***treiben***) drive *tunnel etc.*

'vor·tre·ten *v/i.* (*irr.*, *sep.*, sn, → ***treten***) **1.** step (*or* come) forward; **2.** protrude, stick out; project

Vor·tritt ['foːɐtrɪt] *m* (-[e]s; *no pl.*) precedence; ***j-m den*** ~ ***lassen*** let s.o. go first, give precedence to s.o.; ***den*** ~ ***haben vor*** *dat.* take precedence over *s.th.*

vor·über [fo'ryːbɐ] *adv.* → ***vorbei***

vor'über|ge·hen *v/i.* (*irr.*, *sep.*, sn, → ***gehen***) → ***vorbeigehen*** 1, 3; ***die schlimme Zeit ist nicht spurlos an ihr vorübergegangen*** the hard time has left its mark on her; ~**ge·hend I.** *adj.* temporary; passing; **II.** *adv.* a) temporarily; for a short time, b) for the time being

'Vor·über,le·gung *f* (-; -en) initial (*or* preliminary) consideration

vor'über·zie·hen *v/i.* (*irr.*, *sep.*, sn, → ***ziehen***) → ***vorbeiziehen***

'Vor·übung *f* (-; -en) preliminary exercise

'Vor·un·ter,su·chung *f* (-; -en) preliminary examination (*a.* ⚕); ⚖ *a.* pre-trial hearings *pl.*

'Vor·ur·teil *n* (-[e]s; -e) prejudice; ***voller*** ~***e*** full of prejudice, very prejudiced

'vor·ur·teils·frei, 'vor·ur·teils·los *adj.* unprejudiced, unbias(s)ed

'Vor·ur·teils·lo·sig·keit *f* (-; *no pl.*) lack of prejudice; unprejudiced attitude

Vor·vä·ter ['foːɐfɛːtɐ] *pl.* forefathers

'Vor·ver·gan·gen·heit *f* (-; *no pl.*) *ling.* pluperfect, past perfect

'Vor·ver·hand·lung *f* (-; -en) **1.** *pl.* preliminary negotiations; **2.** ⚖ preliminary proceedings *pl.*

'Vor·ver·kauf *m* (-[e]s; *no pl.*) advance sales *pl.*; *thea. etc.*: *a.* advance booking; ***im*** ~ in advance; ***Karten im*** ~ ***besorgen*** buy tickets in advance, book in advance

'Vor·ver·kaufs·kas·se *f* advance booking office

'vor·ver·le·gen *v/t.* (*sep.*, h) bring forward; move up; **'Vor·ver·le·gung** *f* (-; -en) earlier scheduling

'Vor·ver·stär·ker *m* (-s; -) pre-amplifier

'Vor·ver·such *m* (-[e]s; -e) pilot test

'Vor·ver·trag *m* (-[e]s; ⸚e) provisional agreement

'vor·vor·ge·stern *adv.* three days ago

vor·vo·rig ['foːɐfoːrɪç] *adj.* ... before last; ***das*** ~***e Mal*** the time before last, the last time but one

'vor·wa·gen *v/refl.* (*sep.*, h): ***sich*** ~ venture forward

'Vor·wahl *f* (-; -en) **1.** *teleph.* dial(l)ing (*or* area) code (***von*** *dat.* for); *a.* prefix (for); **2.** *pol.* preliminary election, *Am.* primary; ***bei den*** ~***en*** in the primaries (*or* preliminary elections); ~**num·mer** *f* → ***Vorwahl*** 1

Vor·wand ['foːɐvant] *m* (-[e]s; Vorwände ['foːɐvɛndə]) pretext, excuse; ***unter dem*** ~ ***zu*** *inf.* (*or* ***daß***) on the pretext of *ger.* (*or* that); ***et. zum*** ~ ***nehmen*** use s.th. as an excuse (*or* a pretext) (***um zu*** *inf.* for *ger.*)

'vor·wär·men *v/t.* (*sep.*, h) warm up

'vor·war·nen *v/t.* (*sep.*, h): ***j-n*** ~ tell (*or* warn) s.o. in advance, give s.o. advance notice (*or* warning); **'Vor·war·nung** *f* (-; -en) advance warning

vor·wärts ['foːɐvɛrts] *adv.* forward; ~***!*** let's go!; ***ein großer Schritt*** ~ a big step forward

'Vor·wärts·be·we·gung *f* (-; -en) forward movement

'vor·wärts·brin·gen *fig. v/t.* (*irr.*, *sep.*, h, → ***bringen***) further, promote; help *s.o. or s.th.* on (***bei*** *dat.* in); advance *s.th.*

'Vor·wärts·gang *m mot.* forward gear

'vor·wärts·ge·hen *fig. v/i.* (*irr.*, *sep.*, sn, → ***gehen***) advance, progress; improve; ***mit s-r Gesundheit*** *etc.* ***geht es vorwärts*** his health *etc.* is looking up

'vor·wärts·kom·men (*irr.*, *sep.*, sn, → ***kommen***) **I.** *v/i.* make headway (*a. fig.*); *fig. a.* get ahead, get on, get somewhere; *fig.* ***ich komme nicht vorwärts*** I'm not getting anywhere, I'm treading water; **II.** ≗ *n* (-s; *no pl.*) progress; success

'vor·wärts·schrei·ten *v/i.* (*irr.*, *sep.*, sn, → ***schreiten***) move forward, stride ahead

'Vor·wä·sche *f* (-; -n) prewash

'vor·wa·schen *v/t.* (*irr.*, *sep.*, h, → ***waschen***) prewash

'Vor·wasch·gang *m* prewash cycle

vor·weg [foːɐ'vɛk] *adv.* **1.** beforehand, in advance; at the outset; from the start; ***e-e Frage*** ~ I have one question before we get going; **2.** at the front, F up front, leading the way

Vor·weg·nah·me [foːɐ'vɛknaːmə] *f* (-; *no pl.*) anticipation; **vor'weg·neh·men** *v/t.* (*irr.*, *sep.*, h, → ***nehmen***) anticipate; ***um es gleich vorwegzunehmen*** to come to the point

'vor·weih·nacht·lich *adj.* pre-Christmas

'Vor·weih·nachts·zeit *f* (-; *no pl.*) Christmas period, F run-up to Christmas

'vor·wei·sen *v/t.* (*irr.*, *sep.*, h, → ***weisen***) produce, show; *fig.* ~ ***können*** possess; ***et.*** (***nichts***) ***vorzuweisen haben*** have s.th. to show for o.s. (have nothing to show)

'vor·welt·lich *adj.* prehistoric; *fig.* antediluvian

'vor·wer·fen *v/t.* (*irr.*, *sep.*, h, → ***werfen***) **1.** ***j-m et.*** ~ accuse s.o. of s.th., reproach s.o. with s.th.; ***j-m*** ~ ***zu*** *inf.* (*or* ***daß***) accuse s.o. of *ger.*, reproach s.o. for *ger.*; ***j-m Geiz*** *etc.* ~ accuse s.o. of stinginess (*or* being stingy) *etc.*; ***ich habe mir nichts vorzuwerfen*** I don't feel in any way responsible; ***ich lasse mir nicht*** ~, ***daß*** I'm not going to be accused of *ger.*, I'm not going to take the blame for *ger.*; **2.** ***e-m Tier et.*** ~ throw s.th. to an animal

'Vor,wi·der·stand *m* (-[e]s; ⸚e) ⚡ series resistor

'vor·wie·gen *v/i.* (*irr.*, *sep.*, h, → ***wiegen***) predominate; **'vor·wie·gend** *adv.* predominantly, mainly, chiefly, largely; for the most part, in the main; ~ ***sonnig*** mainly sunny

'Vor·wis·sen *n* (-s; *no pl.*) previous knowledge; *obs.* ***ohne mein*** ~ without my knowledge (*or* my knowing)

'vor·wit·zig *adj.* cheeky, pert

'Vor·wo·che *f*: (***in der*** ~ the) week before last

'vor·wöl·ben *v/refl.* (*sep.*, h): ***sich*** ~ bulge out; **'Vor·wöl·bung** *f* (-; -en) (outward) bulge

'Vor·wort *n* (-[e]s; -e) foreword, preface; introduction

Vor·wurf ['foːɐvʊrf] *m* (-[e]s; ⸚e) **1.** reproach; accusation; ***j-m Vorwürfe machen*** reproach s.o. (***wegen*** *gen.* for); ***j-m den*** ~ ***machen zu*** *inf.* (*or* ***daß***) accuse s.o. of *ger.*; ***sich Vorwürfe machen*** reproach o.s., blame o.s.; **2.** theme

'vor·wurfs·voll *adj.* reproachful

'vor·zäh·len *v/t.* (*sep.*, h) count out (***j-m*** to s.o.)

'vor·zau·bern *fig. v/t.* (*sep.*, h): ***j-m et.*** ~ conjure s.th. up before s.o.('s eyes)

'Vor·zei·chen *n* (-s; -) **1.** portent; (***gutes,***

***schlechtes* ~** good, bad) omen; **2.** ♪ accidental; ♮ sign; ♯ first sign; *fig.* ***mit umgekehrtem* ~** the other way round
'vor·zeich·nen *v/t.* (*sep.*, h) **1.** trace (out), mark; ***j-m et.* ~** draw s.th. for s.o.; show s.o. how to draw s.th.; **2.** ♪ ***ein Kreuz* (*ein B*) ~** *dat.* put a sharp (a flat) before
vor·zeig·bar ['fo:ɐtsaɪkba:ɐ] *adj.* (quite) presentable
Vor·zei·ge... ['fo:ɐtsaɪgə] *in cpds. usu.* showpiece ...; **~frau** *f* woman to show off with; F ***die ist nur so e-e* ~** she's just for show
'vor·zei·gen *v/t.* (*sep.*, h) show; *a.* produce *passport etc.*
'Vor·zeit *f* (-; *no pl.*) prehistoric era; ***die* ~** prehistoric times; → ***grau*** I
'vor·zei·tig I. *adj.* premature; early; **II.** *adv.* prematurely; early; **~ *sterben*** die before one's time
'vor·zeit·lich *adj.* prehistoric
'Vor·zeit·mensch *m*: ***der* ~** prehistoric man
'vor·zie·hen *v/t.* (*irr.*, *sep.*, h, → ***ziehen***) **1.** a) pull forward; pull out, b) draw *curtains*; **2.** bring forward, move up *appointment etc.*; deal with *s.th.* first, give priority to *a task etc.*; anticipate; → ***vorgezogen***; **3.** prefer (*dat.* to); give *s.o.* special treatment; ***es* ~ *zu*** *inf.* prefer to *inf.*; ***vorzuziehen sein*** be preferable
'Vor·zim·mer *n* anteroom; outer office; **~da·me** *f* receptionist
Vor·zug ['fo:ɐtsu:k] *m* (-[e]s; Vorzüge ['fo:ɐtsy:gə]) priority (***gegenüber, vor*** *dat.* over); advantage; merit; privilege; ***j-m* (*e-r Sache*) *den* ~ *geben*** give preference to s.o. (s.th.); ***den* ~ *haben, daß*** (*or* ***zu*** *inf.*) have the advantage of *ger.*
vor·züg·lich [fo:ɐ'tsy:klɪç] *adj.* a) excellent; *a.* masterly, b) exquisite; first-rate; **Vor'züg·lich·keit** *f* (-; *no pl.*) excellence; excellent quality; exquisiteness
'Vor·zugs|ak·ti·en *pl.* preference shares, *Am.* preferred stock *sg.*; **~be·hand·lung** *f* preferential (F special) treatment; **~milch** *f* full-cream milk, *in GB*: *a.* gold-top milk; **~preis** *m* special price; ***zum* ~ *von*** *dat.* **...** on special offer at ...
'vor·zugs·wei·se *adv.* **1.** preferably; **2.** chiefly, mainly
vo·tie·ren [vo'ti:rən] *v/i.* (h) vote (***für*** *acc.* for)
Vo·tiv|bild [vo'ti:f-] *n* votive picture; **~ga·be** *f* votive gift; **~ta·fel** *f* votive tablet
Vo·tum ['vo:tʊm] *n* (-s; Voten, Vota) vote; ***sein* ~ *abgeben*** vote
Voy·eur [vǒa'jø:ɐ] *m* (-s; -e [-rə]) voyeur, peeping Tom; **Voy·eu·ris·mus** [vǒajø'rɪsmʊs] *m* (-; *no pl.*) voyeurism
vul·gär [vʊl'gɛ:ɐ] *adj.* vulgar; common
Vul'gär·aus·druck *m*, **Vul·ga·ris·mus** [vʊlga'rɪsmʊs] *m* (-; -men) vulgarism, vulgar expression
Vul·ga·ri·tät [vʊlgari'tɛ:t] *f* (-; *no pl.*) vulgarity
Vul'gär|la͵tein *n* Vulgar Latin; **~spra·che** *f* **1.** vernacular, common language, language of the people; **2.** vulgar language; vulgarisms *pl.*
Vul·kan [vʊl'ka:n] *m* (-[e]s; -e) volcano (*a. fig.*); **~aus·bruch** *m* (volcanic) eruption; **~ge·stein** *n* volcanic rock; **~in·sel** *f* volcanic island
vul·ka·nisch [vʊl'ka:nɪʃ] *adj.* volcanic(ally *adv.*)
vul·ka·ni·sie·ren [vʊlkani'zi:rən] *v/t.* (h) vulcanize, *mot. a.* recap
Vul·ka·nit [vʊlka'ni:t] *m* (-s; -e) *geol.* vulcanite

W

W, w [veː] *n* (-; -) W, w

Waa·ge ['vaːɡə] *f* (-; -n) **1.** (***e-e** ~* a pair of) scales *pl.*; (a) scale; ⚙ spirit level; *fig.* ***die ~ halten*** *dat.* counterbalance *s.th.*, be a match for *s.o.*; ***sich die ~ halten*** be more or less equal; **2.** *ast.* Libra; ***~ sein*** be (a) Libra, be a Libran; **3.** *gym.* lever

'waa·ge·recht I. *adj.* horizontal; level; **II.** *adv.* horizontally; *crossword*: across

'Waa·ge·rech·te *f* (-n; -n) horizontal

Waag·scha·le ['vaːk-] *f* (-; -n) scale; *fig.* ***et. in die ~ werfen*** bring s.th. to bear; ***s-e Worte auf die ~ legen*** weigh one's words; ***schwer in die ~ fallen*** *argument*: carry weight; ***du darfst s-e Worte nicht auf die ~ legen*** you mustn't take everything he says at face value

wab·be·lig ['vabəlɪç] *adj.* wobbly; flabby *cheeks etc.*; **wab·beln** ['vabəln] *v/i.* (h) wobble; **wabb·lig** ['vablɪç] → ***wabbelig***

Wa·be ['vaːbə] *f* (-; -n) honeycomb

'Wa·ben|ho·nig *m* comb honey; **~mus·ter** *n* honeycomb pattern

wach [vax] *adj.* **1.** *pred.* awake; *w.s.* stirring (*a. fig.*); ***~ sein*** *a.* have woken up; ***~ werden*** wake up, awake; ***er ist (morgens) nicht wach zu kriegen*** he (just) won't wake up (you can't get him awake in the mornings); ***j-n ~ rütteln*** shake s.o. awake (*or* out of his *or* her sleep); ***sich mühsam ~ halten*** struggle to stay awake; ***die ganze Nacht ~ liegen*** lie awake all night, not to get a wink of sleep all night; **2.** *fig.* ***~er Geist*** lively (*or* keen) mind *or* intellect; ***~es Auge*** alert (*or* watchful) eye; ***~e Erinnerungen*** vivid memories; *fig.* ***~ werden*** prick up one's ears; *feelings etc.*: be aroused

'Wach|ab·lö·sung *f* changing of the guard; *pol. fig.* changeover of governments, change in leadership; **~buch** *n* incident book; **~dienst** *m* guard duty, ⚓ watch; ***~ haben*** be on guard (duty), ⚓ have the watch

Wa·che ['vaxə] *f* (-; -n) **1.** *no pl.* guard, ⚓ watch; ***auf ~*** on guard, ⚓ on watch; ***~ halten*** keep guard, ⚓ be on watch; ⚔ keep watch; F ***~ schieben*** be on guard (*or* sentry) duty, ⚓ be on watch; *fig.* keep a lookout, be the lookout; **2.** guard room; police station; **3.** sentry, guard

wa·chen ['vaxən] *v/i.* (h) (keep) watch (***über*** *acc.* over), guard *s.th. or s.o.*; ***~ über*** *acc. a.* keep an eye on; ***bei j-m ~*** sit up with s.o.

'wach·ha·bend *adj.*: ***~er Offizier*** officer on guard (⚓ on watch)

'wach·hal·ten *fig. v/t.* (*irr.*, *sep.*, h, → ***halten***) keep alive

'Wach|hund *m* watchdog (*a. fig.*); **~mann** *m* **1.** watchman; **2.** *Austrian* policeman; **~mann·schaft** *f* guard, ⚓ watch

Wa·chol·der [va'xɔldɐ] *m* (-s; -) **1.** juniper; **2.** → **~bee·re** *f* juniper berry; **~schnaps** *m spirit made from juniper berries*

'Wach·po·sten *m* guard

'wach|ru·fen *fig. v/t.* (*irr.*, *sep.*, h, → ***rufen***) rouse; bring back *memories etc.*; **~rüt·teln** *fig. v/t.* (*sep.*, h) rouse (***aus*** *dat.* from), shake up (out of); *w.s.* shake *s.o.* into action

Wachs [vaks] *n* (-es; -e) wax; ***bleich wie ~*** (as) white as a sheet (*or* ghost); *fig.* ***~ in j-s Händen sein*** be putty in s.o.'s hands; ***weich wie ~ werden*** *person*: go all soft, *knees*: turn to jelly; ***weich wie ~ sein*** *person*: be like putty; **~ab·druck** *m* wax impression

wach·sam ['vaxzaːm] **I.** *adj.* watchful, vigilant; alert; ***~ sein*** be on one's guard; ***ein ~es Auge haben auf*** *acc.* keep a sharp (*or* watchful) eye on; **II.** *adv.*: ***~ verfolgen*** *a.* watch closely

'Wach·sam·keit *f* (-; *no pl.*) watchfulness; vigilance

'wachs·bleich *adj.* (as) white as a sheet (*od.* ghost)

'Wachs·boh·ne *f* waxbean

wach·sen¹ ['vaksən] *v/i.* (wuchs, gewachsen, sn) grow (*a. fig.*) (***an*** *dat.* in); *fig.* expand; ***sein Haar ~ lassen*** let one's hair grow (long); ***hier wächst viel Weizen*** a lot of wheat is grown in these parts; ***mit s-r Aufgabe ~*** grow with the task; ***sie ist mir ans Herz gewachsen*** I've become very attached to her; → ***gewachsen, Kopf*** 5

'wach·sen² *v/t.* (h) wax (*a. skis*)

wäch·sern ['vɛksɐn] *adj.* wax; *fig.* waxen

'Wachs|farb·stift *m* wax crayon; **~fi,gur** *f* wax figure; *pl. a.* waxwork *sg.*; **~fi,gu·ren·ka·bi,nett** *n* waxworks *pl.*; **~ker·ze** *f* wax candle; **~pa,pier** *n* wax paper; **~ta·fel** *f hist.* wax tablet

'Wachs·tuch *n* (-[e]s; -e) oilcloth; **~tisch·decke** *f* wax tablecloth

Wachs·tum ['vakstuːm] *n* (-s; *no pl.*) growth (*a.* ✝); *a.* increase; expansion; ***im ~ zurückgeblieben*** stunted (in growth); ***geistiges ~*** mental development

'Wachs·tums|be·reich *m* growth area; **Ձför·dernd** *adj.* **1.** ✝ growth-stimulating; **2.** growth-inducing *hormones etc.*; **Ձhem·mend** *adj.* growth-retarding; **~in·du,strie** *f* growth industry; **~kur·ve** *f* growth curve; **~land** *n* growth country; **Ձorien,tiert** *adj.* growth-oriented; **~pha·se** *f* growth period; **~po·li,tik** *f* growth policy; **~ra·te** *f* ✝ growth rate; **~theo,rie** *f* theory of economic growth

'wachs·weich *adj.* (as) soft as wax; *fig.* ***~ sein*** be a real softie

Wäch·te ['vɛçtə] *f* (-; -n) (snow) cornice

Wach·tel ['vaxtəl] *f* (-; -n) quail; F *fig.* ***alte ~*** F old crow; **~ei·er** *pl.* quail's eggs; **~hund** *m* spaniel

Wäch·ter ['vɛçtɐ] *m* (-s; -) guard; (night) watchman; (*parking lot etc.*) attendant

Wacht·mei·ster ['vaxt-] *m* constable, *Am.* patrolman; *address*: Officer

'Wach·traum *m* daydream

'Wach(t)turm *m* watchtower

'Wach- und 'Schließ·ge·sell·schaft *f* security corps

wacke·lig ['vakəlɪç] (*sep.* -k·k-) *adj.* wobbly; *a.* rickety *chair etc.*; loose *tooth, screw etc.*; ***~ stehen*** *business etc.* be very shaky, *government*: *a.* be teetering, *pupil*: be doing badly, *team*: be in danger of being relegated; ***~ auf den Beinen sein*** a) be a bit shaky (F wobbly round the knees), b) F be (getting) doddery, c) be a bit unsteady (on one's legs)

Wackel·kon,takt ['vakəl-] (*sep.* -k·k-) *m* loose contact

wackeln ['vakəln] (*sep.*,-k·k-) *v/i.* (h) a) *chair etc.*: be wobbly; *tooth, screw*: be loose, b) totter; F *fig. government etc.*: be very shaky, be teetering (on the brink); ***mit dem Schwanz ~*** wag its tail; ***mit dem Kopf (den Ohren) ~*** waggle one's head (ears)

Wackel·pud·ding ['vakəl-] (*sep.* -k·k-) *m* jelly

wacker ['vakɐ] (*sep.* -k·k-) **I.** *adj.* honest, upright; brave; **II.** *adv.* bravely; ***sich ~ schlagen*** put up a good show, do well; ***~ standhalten*** hold one's own; ***sie kann ~ essen*** F she puts away a fair amount

Wa·de ['vaːdə] *f* (-; -n) *anat.* calf

'Wa·den|bein *n anat.* calfbone, fibula; **~krampf** *m* cramp in one's calf (*or* leg)

'wa·den·lang *adj.* mid-calf *skirt etc.*

Waf·fe ['vafə] *f* (-; -n) weapon (*a. fig.*); *pl. a.* arms, weaponry *sg.*; ***unter ~n stehen*** be under arms; ***keine ~n tragen*** carry no arms; ***zu den ~n rufen*** call to arms; *fig.* ***j-n mit s-n eigenen ~n schlagen*** beat s.o. at his (*or* her) own game; ***er wurde mit s-n eigenen ~n geschlagen*** *a.* he was hoist with his own petard; → ***greifen*** II, ***strecken***

Waf·fel ['vafəl] *f* (-; -n) waffle; wafer; **~ei·sen** *n* waffle iron

'Waf·fen|ab·kom·men *n* arms agreement; **~ar·se,nal** *n* a) arsenal, b) weaponry, (weapons) stockpile, armo(u)ry; **~be·sitz** *m* possession of (fire)arms; **~be·sitz·kar·te** *f* gun licen|ce (*Am.* -se); **~bru·der** *m* brother in arms; **~de,pot** *n* arms depot; **~em,bar·go** *n* arms embargo; **~gat·tung** *f* branch; **~ge·brauch** *m* use of firearms; **~ge·set·ze** *pl.* gun-control laws; **~ge·walt** *f* (-; *no pl.*): (***mit ~*** by) force of arms; **~han·del** *m* arms trade; **~händ·ler** *m* arms dealer; **~kam·mer** *f* armo(u)ry; **~la·ger** *n* arms cache; **~lie-**

fe·run·gen *pl.* supply *sg.* of arms (**an** *acc.* to)
ˈ**waf·fen·los** *adj.* weaponless, unarmed
ˈ**Waf·fen|ru·he** *f* truce; ceasefire; **~samm·lung** *f* weapons collection; **~schein** *m* gun licen|ce (*Am.* -se); **~schie·ber** F *m* arms broker; **~schmie·de** *f* arms manufacturer; **~schmug·gel** *m* gun-running; **~schmugg·ler** *m* gun-runner; **~still·stand** *m* armistice, *a. fig.* truce
ˈ**Waf·fen·still·stands|ab·kom·men** *n* ceasefire agreement; **~li·nie** *f* ceasefire line
ˈ**Waf·fen|sy͵stem** *n* weapons system, *pl. a.* weaponry *sg.*; **~tech·nik** *f* weapons technology; **~trä·ger** *m* ⚔ weapons carrier; **~übung** *f* military exercise
Wa·ge·mut [ˈva:gəmu:t] *m* (-[e]s; *no pl.*) daring; spirit of adventure; venturesomeness; ˈ**wa·ge·mu·tig** *adj.* daring, bold, plucky, venturesome
wa·gen [ˈva:gən] (h) **I.** *v/t.* venture; *a.* risk *s.th.*; dare (**zu** *inf.* to *inf.*); **es ~** take a chance; **es ~ zu** *inf.* dare to *inf.*; **es ~ mit** *dat.* give *s.th.* a try, F have a shot (*or* crack) at *s.th.*; **wie kannst du es ~(, mir zu widersprechen)?** how dare you (contradict me)?; **wie konnte er es ~?** where does he get the nerve?; **II.** *v/i.*: **wer nicht wagt, der nicht gewinnt** nothing ventured, nothing gained; **frisch gewagt ist halb gewonnen** well begun is half ended; **III.** *v/refl.*: **sich ~, et. zu tun** venture to do s.th.; **er hat sich nicht gewagt** he didn't have the courage (*or* nerve); **er wagte sich nicht aus dem Hause** he didn't venture out of the house; **sie wagte sich nicht auf die Straße** she was (too) scared to go out into the street; → **gewagt**
Wa·gen [ˈva:gən] *m* (-s; -) a) carriage, b) 🚃 carriage, *Am.* car, c) cart; vehicle, d) *mot.* car, e) pram, *Am.* baby carriage, f) trolley, *Am.* shopping cart, g) trolley, *Am.* tea wagon, h) (*street*)car, i) *hist.* chariot, j) *typewriter*: carriage; *ast.* **der Große ~** the Great Bear, the Plough, the Big Dipper, Ursa Major; **der Kleine ~** the Little Bear, the Little Dipper, Ursa Minor; F *fig.* **j-m an den ~ fahren** F sling mud at s.o.
wä·gen [ˈvɛ:gən] *v/t.* (wog *or* wägte, gewogen, h) weigh; **erst ~, dann wagen** look before you leap, think before you act
ˈ**Wa·gen|ab͵teil** *n* 🚃 compartment; **~be·sit·zer** *m mot.* car owner; **~füh·rer** *m* driver; **~he·ber** *m* jack; **~ko͵lon·ne** *f* column of vehicles; **~la·dung** *f* lorry-load, truckload; carload; **~pa͵pie·re** *pl.* car documents; **~park** *m* fleet of cars; car pool; **~pfle·ge** *f* (car) maintenance; **~ren·nen** *n hist.* chariot race; **~schmie·re** *f* cart grease; **~spur** *f* wheel-track; **~stand·an·zei·ger** *m* 🚃 carriage (*Am.* car) position indicator; **~typ** *m* make (of car); **~wä·sche** *f* car wash
Wag·gon [vaˈgõ:] *m* (-s; -s) 🚃 a) (railway) carriage, *Am.* (railroad) car, b) goods waggon, *Am.* freight car
wagˈ**gon·wei·se** *adv.* by the waggonload (*Am.* carload)
wag·hal·sig [ˈva:khalzɪç] *adj.* a) daredevil ..., b) risky *enterprise etc.*
ˈ**Wag·hal·sig·keit** *f* (-; *no pl.*) daredevil attitude
Wag·nis [ˈva:knɪs] *n* (-sses; -sse) venture, risk; hazardous enterprise; **sich auf kein ~ einlassen** take no risks
Wahl [va:l] *f* (-; -en) **1.** *no pl.* a) choice; alternative, option, b) ✝ selection; **erste ~** top quality; **zweite ~** second-rate quality, seconds; **aus freier ~** of one's own free will (*or* choice); **s-e ~ treffen** make one's choice; **die freie ~ haben** be free to choose; **keine** (**andere**) **~ haben** have no alternative *or* choice (**als** but); **in die engere ~ kommen** be short-listed, be a possibility; **der Wagen Ihrer ~** the car of your choice; **vor der ~ stehen, zu** *inf.* be faced with the choice of *ger.*; **wenn ich die ~ hätte** if I could choose, if I had the choice; **die ~ fällt mir schwer** I find it hard to choose, I can't decide; **drei Themen stehen zur ~** there's a choice of three topics, three topics are on offer; **wer die ~ hat, hat die Qual** decisions, decisions!; **2.** *pol. etc.* election; poll(ing); **freie ~en** free elections; **geheime ~en** a secret ballot; **~ durch Handaufheben** vote by (a) show of hands; **~ durch Zurufen** oral vote; **sich zur ~ stellen** stand (*or* run) as a candidate; stand, run; **~en abhalten** hold elections; **zur ~ schreiten** go to the polls
ˈ**Wahl|ab·spra·che** *f* pre-election agreement; **~al·ter** *n* voting age; **~ana͵ly·ti·ker** *m* psephologist; **~an·fech·tung** *f* contesting an election result; **~aus·gang** *m* election results *pl.*; **~aus·schuß** *m* election committee; **~aus·sich·ten** *pl.* chances in an (*or* the) election
wähl·bar [ˈvɛ:lba:ɐ] *adj.* eligible (for election)
ˈ**Wahl·be·nach·rich·ti·gung** *f* polling card
ˈ**wahl·be·rech·tigt** *adj.* eligible (*or* entitled) to vote; ˈ**Wahl·be·rech·tig·te** *m, f* (-n; -n) person entitled (*or* eligible) to vote; *pl. a.* those entitled (*or* eligible) to vote
ˈ**Wahl|be·tei·li·gung** *f* (voter) turnout; **starke** (**schwache**) **~** heavy (light) polling; **~be·trug** *m* electoral fraud; **~be·zirk** *m* ward, *Am.* precinct; **~ein·bu·ßen** *pl. an* electoral setback *sg.*
wäh·len [ˈvɛ:lən] (h) **I.** *v/i.* **1.** choose; **du kannst ~** it's up to you (to choose), the choice is yours; **du hast klug gewählt** you've made a wise choice; **2.** *pol.* go to the polls; **3.** *teleph.* dial (the *or* a number); **II.** *v/t.* **4.** choose; *a.* pick (out), select; **5.** *pol.* elect; vote for; **zum Präsidenten** (**ins Parlament**) **gewählt werden** be elected president (be voted into parliament); **für fünf Jahre gewählt werden** be elected for a period of five years; → **gewählt**
Wäh·ler [ˈvɛ:lɐ] *m* (-s; -) voter; **~fang** *m* vote-catching
ˈ**Wahl|er·folg** *m* election victory; **~er·geb·nis** *n* election results *pl.*, returns *pl.*
Wäh·le·rin [ˈvɛ:lərɪn] *f* (-; -nen) voter
ˈ**Wäh·ler·in·itia͵ti·ve** *f* voters' initiative
wäh·le·risch [ˈvɛ:lərɪʃ] *adj.* choosy, F picky (**in** *dat.* about, when it comes to)
ˈ**Wäh·ler|li·ste** *f* → **Wählerverzeichnis**; **~po·ten·ti͵al** *n* potential vote(s *pl.*) *or* voters *pl.*
ˈ**Wäh·ler·schaft** *f* (-; -en) electorate; constituency, voters *pl.*
ˈ**Wäh·ler|schicht** *f* group of voters; **~stim·me** *f* vote; **~ver·ei·ni·gung** *f* voters' association; **~ver·hal·ten** *n* voter (*or* voting) patterns *pl.*; **~ver·zeich·nis** *n* electoral list; **~wil·le** *m* will of the electorate, mandate
ˈ**Wahl|fach** *n ped.* optional subject, *Am.* elective; **~fäl·schung** *f* vote-rigging, electoral fraud; **~feld·zug** *m* election campaign; **~frei** *adj.* optional; **~er Zugriff** *computer*: random access; **~gang** *m*: (**im ersten ~** at the first) ballot; **~ge·heim·nis** *n* secrecy of the ballot; **~ge·schenk** *n* F campaign goodie; **~hei·mat** *f* adoptive country; **~hel·fer** *m* campaign assistant; **~jahr** *n* election year; **~ka͵bi·ne** *f* polling (*or* voting) booth
ˈ**Wahl·kampf** *m* election campaign; **e-n ~ führen** run an election campaign; **~gel·der** *pl.* campaign funds; **~lei·ter** *m* campaign manager; **~the·ma** *n* campaign issue; **~ver·spre·chen** *n* → **Wahlversprechen**
ˈ**Wahl|kreis** *m* constituency; **~lei·ter** *m* returning officer; **~li·ste** *f* list of candidates, party ticket; **~lo͵kal** *n* polling station; **~lo·ko·mo͵ti·ve** F *f* F vote-getter
ˈ**wahl·los I.** *adj.* indiscriminate; **II.** *adv.* indiscriminately, at random
ˈ**Wahl|ma·ni·pu·la·ti͵on** *f* vote-rigging, electoral fraud; **~mo·dus** *m* → **Wahlverfahren**; **~nie·der·la·ge** *f* election defeat; **~pa͵ro·le** *f* campaign (*or* election) slogan; **~pla͵kat** *n* election poster; **~platt·form** *f* election platform; **~pro͵gramm** *n* election platform (*or* manifesto); **~pro·pa͵gan·da** *f* election propaganda; **~recht** *n* a) electoral law, b) right to vote, franchise, c) eligibility; **allgemeines ~** universal suffrage; **~re·de** *f* electoral address
Wähl·schei·be [ˈvɛ:l-] *f teleph.* dial
ˈ**Wahl|schwin·del** *m* vote-rigging; **~sieg** *m* election victory; **~sie·ger** *m* election winner, winner of the election(s); **~spruch** *m* motto; *pol.* election slogan; **~sy͵stem** *n* electoral system; **~tag** *m* election day
Wähl·ton [ˈvɛ:l-] *m* dialling (*Am.* dial) tone
ˈ**Wahl|ur·ne** *f* ballot box; **zur ~ schreiten** go to the polls; **~ver·an·stal·tung** *f* election rally; **~ver·fah·ren** *n* electoral procedure; **~ver·hal·ten** *n* voting (*or* voter) patterns *pl.*; **~ver·samm·lung** *f* election meeting; **~ver·spre·chen** *n* campaign (*or* election) pledge; **~ver·wandt·schaft** *f* ⚗ *and fig.* elective affinity; **~vor·stand** *m* election committee
ˈ**wahl·wei·se** *adv.*: **es gab ~ Fisch oder Fleisch** there was a choice of fish or meat
ˈ**Wahl·wie·der͵ho·lung** *f teleph.* last number recall, automatic re-dial
Wahn [va:n] *m* (-[e]s; *no pl.*) delusion; madness; mania; **in e-m ~ befangen sein** be labo(u)ring under a delusion; **~bild** *n* delusion; ⚕ hallucination
wäh·nen [ˈvɛ:nən] *lit. v/t.* (h) fancy, imagine; assume, think; **ich wähnte ihn nebenan** I took him to be next door
ˈ**Wahn·idee** *f* delusion; F crazy idea
ˈ**Wahn·sinn** *m* (-[e]s; *no pl.*) madness, insanity (*a. fig.*); **dem ~ verfallen** go insane (*or* mad); **es ist zwar ~, aber es hat Methode** there's method in my *etc.* madness; F **ja ~!** amazing!, F blimey!, *sl.* get a load of that!; → **hell** I
wahn·sin·nig [ˈva:nzɪnɪç] **I.** *adj.* a) mad, insane (*a. fig.*) (**vor** *dat.* with), b) terrible, F incredible *pain, fright etc.*, c) F incredible, F mind-boggling; **~ werden** go mad

(*or* insane); *fig.* **er macht mich ~** F he's driving me spare (*or* potty, up the wall); **II.** F *fig. adv.* F incredibly; *a.* dreadfully; **~ verliebt** madly in love

Wahn·sin·ni·ge ['va:nzɪnɪgə] *m,f* (-n; -n) madman (*f* madwoman); lunatic; **wie ein ~r** like a maniac (*or* lunatic)

Wahn·sinns... ['va:nzɪns-] F *in cpds. often* F incredible, *sl.* mind-blowing; **das sind ja Wahnsinnspreise** *etc. a.* F the prices *etc.* are out of this world; **~idee** F *f* F crazy idea; **~tat** *f* act of madness

'Wahn·vor·stel·lung *f* delusion; idée fixe; ⚕ hallucination

wahn·wit·zig ['va:nvɪtsɪç] *adj.* mad, insane

wahr [va:ɐ] *adj.* a) true; real, b) real, *formal*: veritable; **et. ~ machen** make s.th. come true, carry out *threat, promise etc.*; **~ werden** come true; **der ~e Grund** the real reason; **ein ~es Wunder** a real (*or* true) miracle; **das ist e-e ~e Wohltat** what a relief; **ein ~es Glück, daß sie hier waren** thank goodness they were here; **davon ist kein Wort ~** there's not a word of truth in it, F it's a pack of lies; **das ist ein ~es Wort** that's very true, never a truer word was spoken; ⚖ **so ~ mir Gott helfe** so help me God; **so ~ ich hier stehe!** I swear it, F I kid you not; **was ~ ist, ist ~** truth must out; **das ist schon gar nicht mehr ~** that was a long time ago; **er kommt doch, nicht ~?** he 'is coming, isn't he?; F **das darf doch nicht ~ sein!** I don't believe it; **das ist nicht das Wahre** it's not the real thing (F real McCoy); **es ist etwas Wahres dran** there's something in it, there's an element of truth in (*or* to) it; → **einzig** II, **Sinn**

wah·ren ['va:rən] *v/t.* (h) preserve, maintain, keep *a. a secret etc.*; look after, protect, safeguard *one's interests etc.*; **den Schein ~** keep up appearances; **die Frist ~** meet the deadline; **j-m die Treue ~** keep faith with s.o.; → **Form** 10

wäh·ren ['vɛ:rən] *v/i.* (h) last; **es währte nicht lange, da** it wasn't long before

wäh·rend ['vɛ:rənt] **I.** *prp.* (*gen.*) during; in the course of; **~ der Sitzung** during the meeting; **~ des Abendessens** while we *etc.* were having dinner; **II.** *cj.* while; *a.* whereas; **~ er schlief, räumte ich auf** while he slept (*or* was asleep), I tidied up; **noch ~ er sprach** even as he was speaking

wäh·rend'des·sen *adv.* in the meantime, meanwhile

'wahr·ha·ben *v/t.*: **er wollte es nicht ~** he wouldn't believe it, he refused to accept it

'wahr·haft I. *adj.* true, real; **II.** *adv.* really

wahr·haf·tig [va:ɐ'haftɪç] **I.** *adv.* really; actually, honestly; **er hat es ~ versucht** he actually (*or* honestly) tried to do it; **II.** *adj.* truthful

Wahr·heit ['va:ɐhaɪt] *f* (-; *no pl.*) truth; **in ~** in fact, in reality; **um die ~ zu sagen** to tell (you) the truth; **er nimmt es mit der ~ nicht so genau** he's not the most honest of people; F **j-m die ~ sagen** F give s.o. a piece of one's mind; → **bleiben** 2, **Ehre, nackt, rein**[1] I

'Wahr·heits|fin·dung *f*: **der ~ dienen** help to establish the truth; **~ge·halt** *m* (-[e]s; *no pl.*) truth(fulness)

'wahr·heits|ge·mäß I. *adj.* true, truthful; **II.** *adv.* truthfully, in accordance with the facts; **~ge·treu I.** *adj.* true; *a.* faithful *copy etc.*; **II.** *adv.* truthfully; *copy etc.* faithfully

'Wahr·heits·lie·be *f* love of truth; **'wahr·heits·lie·bend** *adj.* truth-loving

'Wahr·heits·su·che *f* quest for the truth

'wahr·lich *lit. adv.* really, indeed; certainly, definitely; *bibl.* verily; **es ist ~ kein Vergnügen** *a.* it's no picnic(, I can tell you)

wahr·nehm·bar ['va:ɐne:mba:ɐ] *adj.* discernible, perceptible, noticeable

'wahr·neh·men *v/t.* (*irr., sep.,* h, → **nehmen**) **1.** perceive; see, discern; hear, register; *w.s.* notice; **2.** seize, *formal*: avail o.s. of *an opportunity etc.*; look after, protect, safeguard *interests etc.*; observe *a deadline etc.*, keep *an appointment*; keep to, F stick to *a deadline*

'Wahr·neh·mung *f* (-; -en) **1.** (**sinnliche ~** sense) perception; **2.** *no pl.* care (*gen.* of); safeguarding *of interests*

'Wahr·neh·mungs·ver·mö·gen *n* (-s; *no pl.*) perceptive faculty

Wahr·sa·ge·kunst ['va:ɐza:gə-] *f*: **die ~** fortune-telling

'wahr·sa·gen (wahrsagte *or* sagte wahr, wahrgesagt *or* gewahrsagt, h) **I.** *v/t.* prophesy; **II.** *v/i.* tell fortunes; **j-m ~** tell s.o.'s fortune; **aus den Karten** *etc.* **~** read the cards *etc.*; **sich ~ lassen** have one's fortune told

Wahr·sa·ger ['va:ɐza:gɐ] *m* (-s; -), **Wahr·sa·ge·rin** ['va:ɐza:gərɪn] *f* (-; -nen) fortune-teller

wahr·schein·lich [va:ɐ'ʃaɪnlɪç] **I.** *adv.* probably; **~ hat sie's verloren** she's probably lost it; **~ wird er verlieren** *a.* (the) chances are he'll lose; **II.** *adj.* probable, likely; plausible; **Wahr'schein·lich·keit** *f* (-; *no pl.*) probability, likelihood; **aller ~ nach** in all probability, **wird er siegen**: the odds are (*or* it's odds on) that he will win

Wahr'schein·lich·keits·rech·nung *f* theory of probabilities, probability calculus

Wah·rung ['va:rʊŋ] *f* (-; *no pl.*) maintenance; safeguarding, protection *of interests*

Wäh·rung ['vɛ:rʊŋ] *f* (-; -en) currency; → **hart** 1, **weich**

'Wäh·rungs|ab·kom·men *n* monetary agreement; **~aus·gleichs·fonds** *m* equalization fund; **~aus·schuß** *m* monetary committee; **~block** *m* monetary bloc; **~ein·heit** *f* unit of currency; **~fonds** *m* monetary fund; **Internationaler ~** International Monetary Fund, IMF; **~ge·biet** *n* currency area; **~kri·se** *f* monetary crisis; **~po·li,tik** *f* monetary policy; **~re,form** *f* currency reform; **~re,ser·ven** *pl.* currency reserves; **~schlan·ge** *f the* snake; **~schwan·kun·gen** *pl.* currency fluctuations; **~sy,stem** *n* monetary system; **~uni,on** *f* monetary union

'Wahr·zei·chen *n* symbol; *a.* famous landmark; emblem

Wai·se ['vaɪzə] *f* (-; -n) orphan

'Wai·sen|haus *n* orphanage; **~kind** *n* orphan

Wal [va:l] *m* (-[e]s; -e) whale

Wald [valt] *m* (-[e]s; Wälder ['vɛldɐ]) wood(s *pl.*); forest (*a. fig.*); woodland; *fig.* **er sieht den ~ vor lauter Bäumen nicht** he can't see the wood for the trees; F **ich glaub', ich steh' im ~** F well, blow me; **wie man in den ~ hineinruft, so schallt's heraus** you get what you give; **~amei·se** *f* red ant; **~ar·bei·ter** *m* woodsman; **~be·stand** *m* forest stand; **~brand** *m* forest fire; **~erd·bee·re** *f* wild strawberry; **~flä·che** *f* wooded area, woodland; **~fre·vel** *m* offen|ce (*Am.* -se) against the forest laws; **~ge·biet** *n* tract of forest; **weite ~e** huge tracts of forest; **~ge·gend** *f* wooded area, woodland; **~horn** *n* ♪ French horn

wal·dig ['valdɪç] *adj.* wooded

'Wald|kauz *m* tawny owl; **~land** *n* (-[e]s; *no pl.*) woodland; **~lauf** *m* cross-country run; **~lehr·pfad** *m* (forest) nature trail; **~mei·ster** *m* ⚘ woodruff

Wal·dorf|sa,lat ['valdɔrf-] *m gastr.* Waldorf salad; **~schu·le** *f* Rudolf Steiner school

'Wald|rand *m*: (**am ~** at *or* on the) edge of the forest; **~schä·den** *pl.* forest damage *sg.*; **~ster·ben** *n* dying of forests, forest deaths *pl.* (*or* dieback)

'Wald-und-'Wie·sen-... *in cpds.* → **Feld-Wald-und-Wiesen-...**

Wal·dung ['valdʊŋ] *f* (-; -en) wooded area, woodland, forest

'Wald·wie·se *f* forest glade

'Wal·fang *m* (-[e]s; *no pl.*) whaling; **'Wal·fän·ger** *m* (-s; -) *a.* ⚓ whaler; **'Wal·fang·flot·te** *f* whaling fleet

'Wal·fisch F *m* whale

Wal·hall ['valhal] *n* (-s; *no pl.*), **Wal·hal·la** [val'hala] *n* (-[s]; *no pl.*), *f* (-; *no pl.*) *myth.* Valhalla

Wa·li·ser [va'li:zɐ] *m* (-s; -) Welshman; **er ist ~** *usu.* he's Welsh; **Wa·li·se·rin** [va'li:zərɪn] *f* (-; -nen) Welsh woman; **wa·li·sisch** [va'li:zɪʃ] *adj.*, **Wa'li·sisch** *n* (-en) *ling.* Welsh

wal·ken ['valkən] *v/t.* (h) full *cloth*; felt *hats*; mill *hides*

Walk·man ['wɔ:kmən] (*TM*) *m* (-s; -men) personal stereo; Walkman (*TM*) (*pl.* Walkmans)

Wal·kü·re [val'ky:rə] *f* (-; -n) Valkyrie

Wall [val] *m* (-[e]s; Wälle ['vɛlə]) a) dam, embankment, b) rampart, c) *fig.* bulwark

Wal·lach ['valax] *m* (-[e]s; -e) gelding

wal·len ['valən] *v/i.* (sn) **1.** *hair, dress*: flow; **2.** *liquid*: simmer, bubble; *sea*: surge; *fog*: sweep; *fig. blood*: boil

Wal·ler ['valɐ] *m* (-s; -) catfish

wall·fah·ren ['valfa:rən] *v/i.* (wallfahrte, gewallfahrt, sn) go on a pilgrimage

'Wall·fah·rer *m* (-s; -) pilgrim

'Wall·fahrt *f* (-; -en) pilgrimage

'Wall·fahrts|kir·che *f* pilgrimage church; **~ort** *m* place of pilgrimage

'Wall·gra·ben *m* moat

Wal·lo·ne [va'lo:nə] *m* (-n; -n), **wal·lo·nisch** [va'lo:nɪʃ] *adj.* Walloon

Wal·lung ['valʊŋ] *f* (-; -en) **1.** surge of emotion; **j-n in ~ bringen** make s.o.'s blood boil; **2.** ⚕ hot flush

Walm·dach ['valm-] *n* ⚠ hip roof

Wal·nuß ['valnʊs] *f* (-; ⸚sse) **1.** walnut; **2.** → **~baum** *m* walnut (tree)

'wal·nuß·groß *adj.* walnut-sized, ... the size of a walnut

Wal·pur·gis·nacht [val'pʊrgɪs-] *f*: **die ~** Walpurgis night, Walpurgisnacht

Wal·roß ['valrɔs] *n* (-sses; -sse) walrus

wal·ten ['valtən] *v/i.* (h) a) rule, b) prevail, c) be at work; **Gnade** (**Milde**) **~ lassen** show mercy (some leniency); **Sorgfalt ~ lassen** exercise proper care; **Vernunft ~**

lassen allow reason to prevail; → ***Gerechtigkeit*** 1, ***schalten*** 3
Walz·blech ['valts-] *n* sheet metal
Wal·ze ['valtsə] *f* (-; -n) roller (*a. typ.*); ⚙ cylinder; ⚙ *a.* roll; *typewriter*: platen; (*organ*) barrel; **'wal·zen** *v/t.* (h) ⚙ roll
wäl·zen ['vɛltsən] (h) **I.** *v/t.* **1.** roll; ***in Mehl*** ~ roll in flour, flour; ***in Ei und Mehl*** ~ flour and egg; **2.** pore over *one's books etc.*; ***Probleme*** ~ turn problems over in one's mind; **3.** ***die Schuld auf j-n*** ~ shift the blame onto s.o.; **II.** *v/refl.*: ***sich*** ~ roll; *a.* wallow; writhe *with pain*; toss and turn, F thrash about *in bed etc.*; ***sich ~ durch*** *acc.* (***entlang*** *dat. or acc. etc.*) *crowd, avalanche etc.*: churn its way through (along *etc.*)
'wal·zen·för·mig [-fœrmɪç] *adj.* cylindrical
Wal·zer ['valtsɐ] *m* (-s; -) waltz; ~ ***tanzen*** (dance a) waltz
Wäl·zer ['vɛltsɐ] F *m* (-s; -) thick (*or* heavy, huge) tome
'Wal·zer|mu,sik *f* waltz music; **~schritt** *m* waltz step; **~takt** *m* waltz time
Walz|stahl ['valts-] *m* rolled steel; **~werk** *n* rolling mill
Wam·pe ['vampə] F *f* (-; -n) F paunch
Wams [vams] *n* (-es; Wämser ['vɛmzɐ]) jacket; *hist.* doublet
wand [vant] *pret. of* ***winden***
Wand [vant] *f* (-; Wände ['vɛndə]) wall (*a. fig.*); *a.* (*rock*)face; (*cloud*) bank; blanket *of rain*; *fig.* barrier; ~ ***an*** ~ wall to wall; *fig.* ***in s-n eigenen vier Wänden*** within one's own four walls; ***j-n an die ~ drükken*** put s.o. in the shade; ***j-n an die ~ spielen*** steal the show (from s.o.), *sport*: play s.o. into the ground; ***j-n an die ~ stellen*** shoot s.o. (dead), execute s.o.; ***gegen e-e ~ von Vorurteilen anrennen*** come up against a wall of prejudice(s); ***Wände haben Ohren*** walls have ears; ***wenn Wände reden könnten*** if walls could speak; ***bei ihm redet man gegen e-e*** ~ it's like talking to a brick wall (with him); F ***da wackelt die*** ~ it sounds as if they're having a good time; ***sie haben gespielt, daß die Wände wackelten*** they nearly brought the roof down (with their playing); ***es ist, um an den Wänden hochzugehen*** F it's enough to drive you up the wall; → ***Kopf, Teufel***
Wan·da·le [van'da:lə] *m* (-n; -n) **1.** *hist.* Vandal; *fig.* ***wie die ~n*** like Vandals; **2.** *fig.* vandal; **Wan·da·lis·mus** [vanda'lɪsmʊs] *m* (-; *no pl.*) vandalism
'Wand|be·hang *m* wall hanging; **~bild** *n* wall painting, mural
Wan·del ['vandəl] *m* (-s; *no pl.*) change; ***der ~ der Zeiten*** changing times; ***im ~ der Zeiten*** in the course of time, through the ages; ***dem ~ unterliegen*** be subject to change; ***hier muß ~ geschaffen werden*** things can't go on like this any longer; **~an·lei·he** *f* ✝ convertible loan
'wan·del·bar *adj.* changeable, variable
'Wan·del|gang *m*, **~hal·le** *f* covered walk; pump room
wan·deln ['vandəln] **I.** *v/refl.*: ***sich*** ~ (h) change; ***sich ~ in*** *acc.* turn (in)to, *person*: turn into; **II.** *v/t.* (h) change (*a. person*), alter; **III.** *v/i.* (sn) walk, stroll; promenade; **'wan·delnd** *adj.*: ***~es Lexikon*** walking encyclop(a)edia
'Wan·del·ob·li·ga·ti,on *f* ✝ convertible bond
Wan·der|ar·bei·ter ['vandɐ-] *m* migrant worker; **~aus·stel·lung** *f* travel(l)ing exhibition; **~bü·che,rei** *f* travel(l)ing library; **~büh·ne** *f* touring (F fit-up) company; **~bur·sche** *m* travel(l)ing journeyman; **~dü·ne** *f* shifting sand dune
Wan·de·rer ['vandərɐ] *m* (-s; -) wanderer, travel(l)er; hiker, rambler
Wan·der·fal·ke ['vandɐ-] *m* peregrine falcon
Wan·de·rin ['vandərɪn] *f* (-; -nen) → ***Wanderer***
Wan·der|jah·re ['vandɐ-] *pl.* (journeyman's) years of travel; **~klei·dung** *f* hiking gear (*or* outfit); **~le·ben** *n* vagrant (F gypsy) life
wan·dern ['vandɐn] *v/i.* (sn) **1.** walk, hike; go on a walk (*or* hike); **2.** rove; **3.** *animals, people*: migrate; *dunes*: shift; *clouds*: drift; *kidney*: float; *fig. eyes, thoughts*: roam, wander; ***in den Papierkorb*** (***ins Gefängnis*** *etc.*) ~ end up (*or* land) in the waste-paper bin (in prison *etc.*)
Wan·der|nie·re ['vandɐ-] *f* floating kidney; **~pfad** *m* hiking trail; **~po,kal** *m* challenge cup; **~pre·di·ger** *m* itinerant preacher; **~preis** *m* challenge trophy
Wan·der·schaft ['vandɐʃaft] *f* (-; -en) travels *pl.*; ***auf ~ gehen*** (***sein***) take to the road (be on one's travels)
Wan·ders·mann ['vandɐs-] *m* (-[e]s; -leute) wanderer
Wa·nder|stie·fel ['vandɐ-] *pl.* hiking boots; **~tag** *m* school (*or* class) hike; **~trieb** *m* **1.** roving spirit; wanderlust; **2.** *zo.* migratory instinct
Wan·de·rung ['vandərʊŋ] *f* (-; -en) **1.** hike; ***e-e ~ machen*** go on a hike; **~en** travels, wanderings; **2.** migration (*of peoples*); **3.** *zo.* migration; ascent *of salmon etc.*
Wan·der|ver·ein ['vandɐ-] *m* rambling club; **~vo·gel** *m* **1.** bird of passage; **2.** *hist. German Youth Movement*; **3.** *member of the "Wandervogel" 2*; **4.** *fig.* rambler; **~weg** *m* hiking trail; **~wet·ter** *n* ideal weather for hiking (*or* rambling); **~zir·kus** *m* travel(l)ing circus
'Wand|fries *m* mural (*or* wall) frieze; **~ge·mäl·de** *n* mural; **~ha·ken** *m* wall hook; **~ka,len·der** *m* wall calendar; **~kar·te** *f* wall map; **~lam·pe** *f* wall lamp
Wand·ler ['vandlɐ] *m* (-s; -) ⚡ converter
'Wand·leuch·te *f* wall lamp
Wand·lung ['vandlʊŋ] *f* (-; -en) change, *a.* ⚡ transformation; *eccl.* transubstantiation; ⚖ nullification of a (*or* the) sale, *Am. a.* redhibition; **'wand·lungs·fä·hig** *adj.* capable of change; flexible, versatile; **'Wand·lungs·fä·hig·keit** *f* (-; *no pl.*) flexibility, versatility
'Wand|ma·le,rei *f* a) mural painting, b) mural; **~pfei·ler** *m* pilaster; **~schirm** *m* (folding) screen; **~schmie·re,rei** *f a. pl.* graffiti; **~schrank** *m* built-in cupboard (*Am.* closet); *Brit. a.* built-in wardrobe; **~ta·fel** *f* (black)board, chalkboard; white board
wand·te ['vantə] *pret. of* ***wenden***
'Wand|tep·pich *m* tapestry; **~uhr** *f* wall clock; **~ver·klei·dung** *f* a) wall covering, b) panel(l)ing, wainscoting; **~zei·tung** *f* wall newspaper
Wan·ge ['vaŋə] *f* (-; -n) **1.** cheek; **2.** ⚙ cheek; stringboard *of a staircase*
Wan·kel·mo·tor ['vaŋkəl-] *m* Wankel engine
Wan·kel·mut ['vaŋkəlmu:t] *m* (-[e]s; *no pl.*) fickleness, inconstancy; **wan·kel·mü·tig** ['vaŋkəlmy:tɪç] *adj.* fickle
wan·ken ['vaŋkən] *v/i.* **1.** (h) a) stagger, reel; sway; *boat*: rock; *fig. throne etc.*: rock, totter, b) *fig.* waver, falter, vacillate; ***ihm wankten die Knie*** his knees gave (way); ***ins ~ geraten*** begin to sway (*or* rock), *fig. position etc.*: become shaky, become unsure of o.s.; *fig.* ***ins ~ bringen*** shake, rock; ***nicht ~ und nicht weichen*** not to budge (*or* give) an inch
wann [van] *adv.* when; whenever; ***seit ~?*** how long?, since when?; ***bis ~?*** till when?, (for) how long?, by when?; ***von ~ bis ~ war der Dreißigjährige Krieg?*** what are the dates of the Thirty Years' War?; ***von ~ bis ~ arbeitet ihr?*** what are your working hours?
Wan·ne ['vanə] *f* (-; -n) a) tub; bath(tub), b) *mot.* oil sump; **'Wan·nen·bad** *n* bath
Wanst [vanst] F *m* (-[e]s; Wänste ['vɛnstə]) F paunch
Wan·ze ['vantsə] *f* (-; -n) **1.** *zo.* bug, *Am.* bedbug; **2.** F *fig.* F bug
Wap·pen ['vapən] *n* (-s; -) (coat of) arms *pl.*; ***et. im ~ führen*** have (*or* bear) s.th. on one's coat of arms; **~kun·de** *f* heraldry; **~schild** *m* shield, escutcheon; **~spruch** *m* heraldic motto; **~tier** *n* heraldic animal
wapp·nen ['vapnən] *v/refl.*: ***sich*** ~ (h) steel o.s. (***gegen*** *acc.* against); ***sich mit Mut*** *etc.* ~ muster up courage *etc.*; → ***gewappnet***
war [va:ɐ] *pret. of* ***sein***[1]
warb [varp] *pret. of* ***werben***
Wa·re ['va:rə] *f* (-; -n) product; *pl. a.* goods, commodities; ***beste*** ~ best quality
'Wa·ren|ab·kom·men *n* trade agreement; **~ab·satz** *m* sale of goods; **~an·ge·bot** *n* range of items (for sale); **~aus·fuhr** *f* export of goods; **~au·to,mat** *m* vending machine; **~be·stand** *m* stock on hand; **~bör·se** *f* commodity exchange; **~ein·fuhr** *f* import of goods
'Wa·ren·haus *n* department store; **~dieb·stahl** *m* shoplifting; **~kon,zern** *m* department store chain
'Wa·ren|la·ger *n* **1.** warehouse; **2.** → ***Warenbestand***; **~pro·be** *f* sample; **~sen·dung** *f* consignment of goods; 📯 trade sample; **~sor·ti,ment** *n* line of goods; **~test** *m* product test; **~,um·satz** *m* goods turnover; **~,um·schlag** *m* movement of goods; **~ver·zeich·nis** *n* inventory, list of goods; **~zei·chen** *n* trademark
warf [varf] *pret. of* ***werfen***
warm [varm] **I.** *adj.* a) warm (*a. fig. words, reception etc.*); hot (*a. meal, drink etc., a.* ⚙), b) F gay, *contp.* F queer (*a.* ***~er Bruder***), c) *rent* including heating; ***mir ist ~*** I feel (*or* I'm) warm, I'm getting hot; ***schön*** ~ nice and warm; ***sich ~ halten*** keep warm; ~ ***machen*** warm (up); ~ ***werden*** warm up; ***das Essen ~ machen*** heat up the meal (*or* food); ***sich ~ laufen*** do a warm-up run, warm up; *fig.* ***ihm wurde ~ ums Herz*** it made him feel all warm inside, F *hum.* it warmed the cockles of his heart; ***er wird nur langsam*** ~ it takes him a while to warm up (*or* to come out of his shell); ***ich kann nicht mit ihm ~ werden*** I can't warm

to him; ***weder ~ noch kalt*** neither fish nor fowl; **II.** *adv. fig.* warmly; ***sich ~ anziehen*** dress warmly, *fig.* be prepared for the worst; *fig.* ***j-m et. wärmstens empfehlen*** warmly recommend s.th. to s.o.

'Warm·blü·ter [-bly:tɐ] *m* (-s; -) warm-blooded animal

Wär·me ['vɛrmə] *f* (-; *no pl.*) warmth (*a. fig.*); *phys.* heat; **~ab·ga·be** *f* a) heat emission, b) loss of heat; **~aus·deh·nung** *f* thermal expansion; **~aus·tausch** *m* heat exchange; **~aus·tau·scher** [-aʊstaʊʃɐ] *m* (-s; -) heat exchanger; **~be·hand·lung** *f* heat treatment; **~be·la·stung** *f* thermal pollution

'wär·me·be·stän·dig *adj.* heat-resistant

'Wär·me|däm·mung *f* heat (*or* thermal) insulation; **~ein·heit** *f* thermal (*or* caloric) unit; **~ge·wit·ter** *n* heat thunderstorm; **~grad** *m* degree of heat; **~iso,lie·rung** *f* heat (*or* thermal) insulation; **~leh·re** *f* thermodynamics *pl.*; **~lei·ter** *m* heat conductor

wär·men ['vɛrmən] (h) **I.** *v/t.* warm (up), heat (up); ***sich die Füße ~*** warm one's feet; **II.** *v/i.*: ***gut ~*** give off plenty of heat; ***Wolle wärmt*** wool keeps you warm; ***Alkohol wärmt*** alcohol warms you up; **III.** *v/refl.*: ***sich ~*** warm up (***am Feuer*** in front of the fire)

'Wär·me|pum·pe *f* heat pump; **~reg·ler** *m* thermostat; **~spei·cher** *m* heat accumulator; **~stau** *m* buildup of heat; ⚕ hyperthermia; **~strah·lung** *f* heat radiation; **~tech·nik** *f* heat technology; **~ver·lust** *m* heat loss; **~wir·kungs·grad** *m* thermal efficiency

Wärm·fla·sche ['vɛrm-] *f* hot-water bottle

'warm·hal·ten *fig. v/t.* (*irr., sep.*, h, → ***halten***): ***sich j-n ~*** keep in with s.o.

'Warm·hal·te·plat·te *f* plate warmer, hot server

'warm·her·zig *adj.* warmhearted

'warm·lau·fen *v/i.* (*irr., sep.*, sn, → ***laufen***) run hot; *mot.* ***~ lassen*** warm up

'Warm·luft|front *f* warm front; **~hei·zung** *f* hot-air heating

'Warm·mie·te *f* rent including heating

Warm'was·ser|be·rei·ter [-bəraɪtɐ] *m* (-s; -) water heater; **~hahn** *m* hot-water tap; **~hei·zung** *f* hot-water heating (system); **~spei·cher** *m* hot-water tank; **~ver·sor·gung** *f* hot-water supply

Warn|an·la·ge ['varn-] *f* warning device; **~blink·an·la·ge** *f mot.* warning flasher; **~dienst** *m* warning service; **~drei·eck** *n mot.* warning triangle

war·nen ['varnən] (h) **I.** *v/t.* warn (***vor*** *dat.* about, of); ***j-n davor ~ zu*** *inf.* warn s.o. against *ger.*, warn s.o. not to *inf.*; ***ich warne dich*** I warn you, I'm warning you; ***du bist gewarnt*** you've been warned; F ***j-n rechtzeitig ~*** let s.o. know in advance (*or* in good time), give s.o. plenty of warning; F ***keiner hat mich gewarnt*** *a.* I had no idea; **II.** *v/i.* warn (***vor*** *dat.* against); ***davor ~ zu*** *inf.* warn against *ger.*; ***vor Taschendieben wird gewarnt*** beware pickpockets; **'war·nend I.** *adj.* warning; **II.** *adv.*: ***s-e Stimme ~ erheben*** raise one's voice in warning

Warn|leuch·te ['varn-] *f*, **~licht** *n* warning light; **~ruf** *m* warning cry; **~schild** *n* danger sign; **~schuß** *m* warning shot (*a. fig.*); ***e-n ~ abgeben*** fire a warning shot; **~si,gnal** *n* warning signal; **~streik** *m* token (*or* warning) strike

War·nung ['varnʊŋ] *f* (-; -en) warning; ***ohne ~ schießen*** shoot without warning; ***laß dir das e-e ~ sein*** let that be a warning to you

Warn·zei·chen ['varn-] *n* warning sign

War·te ['vartə] *f* (-; -n) vantage point (*a. fig.*); *fig.* ***von hoher ~ aus*** from a lofty standpoint; ***von m-r ~ aus gesehen*** from my point of view

War·te|hal·le ['vartə-] *f* waiting room; ✈ departure lounge; **~li·ste** *f* waiting list; ***auf der ~ stehen*** be on the waiting list

war·ten[1] ['vartən] *v/i.* (h) wait (***auf*** *acc.* for); ***j-n ~ lassen*** keep s.o. waiting; ***worauf*** (F ***auf was***) ***~ wir noch?*** what are we waiting for?; ***kann es noch ein bißchen ~?*** can it wait a bit?; ***mit dem Essen auf j-n ~*** keep dinner waiting for s.o.; ***nicht mit dem Essen auf j-n ~*** start eating without s.o.; ***lange auf sich ~ lassen*** be a long time (in) coming; ***nicht lange auf sich ~ lassen*** not to be long (in) coming; ***warte mal!*** just (*or* wait) a minute!, F hang on!; ***na, warte!*** just you wait!; ***da kannst du lange ~*** you've got a long wait coming, you could be in for a long wait; *iro.* ***auf dich*** (***darauf***) ***haben wir gerade noch gewartet*** you're (that's) all we needed; ***darauf habe ich gewartet*** I was just waiting for it (to happen), I could see it coming

'war·ten[2] *v/t.* (h) ⚙ service

Wär·ter ['vɛrtɐ] *m* (-s; -) a) attendant, b) guard, warder, c) keeper

War·te|raum ['vartə-] *m*, **~saal** *m* waiting room; **~schlei·fe** *f*: ***~n ziehen*** circle (the airport), be in a holding pattern; *fig.* ***sich in der ~ befinden, e-e ~ durchlaufen*** be on the waiting list, have been put on hold; **~zeit** *f* waiting period; ***e-e lange ~*** a long wait; **~zim·mer** *n* waiting room

War·tung ['vartʊŋ] *f* (-; -en) ⚙ maintenance, servicing

'War·tungs|an·lei·tung *f* service manual; **~ar·beit** *f* maintenance work; **~frei** *adj.* ⚙ maintenance-free; **~per·so,nal** *n* maintenance staff; **~tech·ni·ker** *m* service engineer

war·um [va'rʊm] *adv.* why; ***ich weiß nicht ~*** I don't know why; ***~ bloß?*** but why?; ***~ wohl?*** I wonder why; ***nach dem ~ fragen*** ask (the question) why

War·ze ['vartsə] *f* (-; -n) a) ⚕ wart, b) *anat.* nipple; *zo.* teat

'War·zen·schwein *n* warthog

was [vas] **I.** *interrog. pron. and int.* what (*a.* F *for* ***wie bitte?***); ***~ für*** (***ein***) ***...?*** what sort of ...?; ***~ für*** (***ein***) ***...!*** what *nonsense etc.*, what a *noise etc.*; ***~ kostet das?*** how much is it?; F ***~ muß er lügen?*** why does he have to lie?; ***~ weiß ich*** how should I know, F search me; ***~ haben wir gelacht!*** what a laugh we had; ***~ ist das doch schwierig*** this is so hard; **II.** *rel. pron.* what; ***alles, ~ er weiß*** everything he knows; which; ***..., ~ ihn völlig kalt ließ*** which left him cold; ***~ auch immer*** whatever, no matter what; ***~ ihn betrifft*** as for him; **III.** F *indef. pron.* something *bad, good, else etc.*; ***~ Neues?*** any news?, anything new?; ***das ist ~ anderes*** that's different; ***na, so ~*** *esp. iro.* well I never; ***~ du nicht sagst!*** you don't say!; ***hat man so ~ schon gesehen?*** did you ever see the likes of it?; ***ich will dir ~ sagen*** I'll tell you something, I'll tell you what; ***schäm dich ~!*** you ought to be ashamed of yourself

Wasch|an·la·ge ['vaʃ-] *f mot.* **1.** car wash; **2.** windscreen (*Am.* windshield) washer; **~an·lei·tung** *f* washing instructions *pl.*; **~au·to,mat** *m* washing machine, *Am.* washer

wasch·bar ['vaʃba:ɐ] *adj.* washable, fast *colo(u)rs*

Wasch|bär ['vaʃ-] *m* rac(c)oon, *a.* F coon; **~becken** *n* washbasin; **~beu·tel** *m* sponge (*or* toilet) bag; **~brett** *n* washboard

Wä·sche ['vɛʃə] *f* (-; *no pl.*) **1.** a) washing, laundry, b) (table and bed) linen, c) underwear, d) wash; ***große ~*** washday; ***in der ~*** in the wash, being washed, at the laundry; ***die ~ wechseln*** put on fresh underwear, change one's (under)pants; *fig.* ***schmutzige ~ waschen*** wash one's dirty linen in public; F ***da hat er aber dumm aus der ~ geguckt*** you should have seen his face; F ***j-m an die ~ gehen*** F lay into s.o.; **~beu·tel** *m* laundry bag

wasch·echt ['vaʃ-] *adj.* colo(u)rfast, fast *colo(u)rs*; F *fig.* genuine, true-blue, ... to the bone

'Wä·sche|klam·mer *f* clothes peg, *Am.* clothespin; **~korb** *m* laundry (*or* linen) basket; **~lei·ne** *f*: (***an der ~*** on the) clothesline

wa·schen ['vaʃən] (wusch, gewaschen, h) **I.** *v/t.* wash (*a.* ⚒, *metall.*); *a.* launder (*a.* F *fig. money*); ⚙ pan *gold etc.*; **II.** *v/refl.*: ***sich ~*** wash o.s., (have a) wash; ***es wäscht sich leicht*** it washes easily; F *fig.* ***e-e Ohrfeige*** (***e-e Kritik*** *etc.*), ***die sich gewaschen hat*** F a nasty blow (piece of criticism *etc.*)

Wä·scher ['vɛʃɐ] *m* (-s; -) *metall.* washer; panner; **Wä·sche·rei** [vɛʃə'raɪ] *f* (-; -en) **1.** laundry; **2.** laund(e)rette, laundromat; **Wä·sche·rin** ['vɛʃərɪn] *f* (-; -nen) washerwoman, laundress

'Wä·sche|sack *m* laundry bag; **~schleu·der** *f* spin drier; **~schrank** *m* linen cupboard (*Am.* closet); **~spin·ne** *f* telescopic clothesline; **~spren·ger** *m* spray bottle; **~stän·der** *m* clothes horse; **~trock·ner** *m* tumble drier

Wasch|frau ['vaʃ-] *f* washerwoman; **~gang** *m* ⚙ cycle, wash; **~ge·le·gen·heit** *f* washing facilities *pl.*; **~kü·che** *f* **1.** washhouse; **2.** F peasouper; **~lap·pen** *m* **1.** flannel, *Am.* washcloth; **2.** F *fig.* F drip, wimp; **~le·der** *n* chamois (leather)

Wasch·ma,schi·ne ['vaʃ-] *f* washing machine, *Am.* washer; **'wasch·ma,schi·nen·fest** *adj.* machine-washable

Wasch|mit·tel ['vaʃ-] *n*, **~pul·ver** *n* washing powder; **~pro,gramm** *n* washing program(me); **~raum** *m* washroom; **~sa,lon** *m* laund(e)rette, laundromat; **~stra·ße** *f mot.* car wash; **~tag** *m* washday

Wa·schung ['vaʃʊŋ] *f* (-; -en) washing; *esp.* ⚕, *eccl.* ablution

Wasch|voll·au·to,mat ['vaʃ-] *m* fully automatic washing machine (*Am.* washer); **~was·ser** *n* washing water; **~weib** *fig. n* (old) gossip; **~zet·tel** *m* blurb; **~zeug** *n* washing things *pl.*; **~zwang** *m* obsessional washing, 📖 ablutomania

Was·ser ['vasɐ] *n* (-s; -, Wässer ['vɛsɐ]) water (*a.* ⚕); ***fließendes*** (***stehendes***) ***~*** running (stagnant) water; ***~ lassen*** pass water, urinate; ***zu ~ und zu Land*** by land and by water; ***unter ~ setzen*** flood; ***unter ~ stehen*** be under water, be flooded; ***ins ~ gehen*** go into the water, *fig.* drown o.s.; *fig.* ***ein Berliner reinsten ~s*** a Berliner born and bred; ***ein Edelstein reinsten ~s*** a stone of the first water; ***das ist ~ auf s-e Mühle*** that's grist to his mill; ***ins ~ fallen*** *plans etc.*: fall through (*or* flat); ***sich über ~ halten*** keep one's head above water; ***j-n über ~ halten*** tide s.o. over; *fig.* ***das läuft an ihm ab wie ~*** it's like water off a duck's back; ***das ist ja ~ in ein Sieb schöpfen*** it's a complete waste of time; ***sie hat nahe am ~ gebaut*** tears come easily to her; ***bis dahin fließt noch viel ~ den Berg hinunter*** that's a long way off yet; ***die kochen auch nur mit ~*** they're no different from anybody else; ***da läuft einem das ~ im Munde zusammen*** it makes your mouth water; ***er kann ihr nicht das ~ reichen*** he's not a patch on her, he can't hold a candle to her; ***er ist mit allen ~n gewaschen*** he knows every trick in the book; → ***still, Schlag*** 1

'was·ser|ab·sto·ßend, ~ab·wei·send *adj.* water-repellent

'Was·ser|ader *f* water vein; **≈arm** *adj. geogr.* arid; **~auf·be·rei·tung** *f* (waste) water treatment; **~auf·be·rei·tungs·an·la·ge** *f* (waste) water treatment plant; **~bad** *n gastr.* bain-marie; *phot.* water bath; **~ball** *m* **1.** beach ball; **2.** (water polo) ball; **3.** → **~ball·spiel** *n* water polo; **~bau** *m* (-[e]s; *no pl.*) hydraulic engineering; **~bett** *n* water bed; **~bla·se** *f* ⚕ blister; 📖 vesicle; **≈blau** *adj.* clear blue; **~bom·be** *f* depth charge; **~burg** *f* moated castle

Wäs·ser·chen ['vɛsɐçən] *n*: *fig.* ***er sah so aus, als könne er kein ~ trüben*** he looked as if butter wouldn't melt in his mouth

'Was·ser|dampf *m* steam; **≈dicht** *adj.* waterproof; ⚙, ⚓ *a.* watertight; ***~ machen*** waterproof; **~druck** *m* hydraulic pressure; **~ei·mer** *m* bucket, pail; **~ent·här·ter** *m* water softener; **~fahr·zeug** *n* watercraft (*a. pl.*), waterborne vehicle, vessel; **~fall** *m* waterfall; falls *pl.*; cascade; *fig.* ***er redete wie ein ~*** he wouldn't stop talking, he just went on and on; **~far·be** *f* water colo(u)r; **≈fest** *adj.* waterproof; **~fla·sche** *f* water bottle; **~fleck** *m* water stain; **~floh** *m* water flea; **~flug·zeug** *n* seaplane; **~ge·halt** *m* water content; **~geist** *m* (-[e]s; -er) water spirit; **≈ge·kühlt** *adj.* water-cooled; **~geld** F *n* water rate; **~glas** *n* **1.** ⚗ water glass; **2.** tumbler; → ***Sturm***; **~gra·ben** *m* ditch; *sport*: water jump; **~hahn** *m* tap, *Am.* faucet

'was·ser·hal·tig [-haltɪç] *adj.* ⚗ aqueous, hydrous; ***~ sein*** contain water

'Was·ser|här·te *f* water hardness; **~haus·halt** *m* **1.** water resources *pl.*; **2.** *physiol.* water balance; **~heil·kun·de** *f* hydrotherapy; **~huhn** *n* coot

wäs·se·rig ['vɛsərɪç] *adj.* watery; *fig.* ***j-m den Mund ~ machen*** make s.o.'s mouth water (***nach*** *dat.* for), *w.s.* F get s.o. all keen (on) *or* excited (about)

'Was·ser|kes·sel *m* kettle; ⚙ boiler; **~klo͵sett** *n* water closet; **~kopf** *m* **1.** ⚕ hydrocephalus; ***e-n ~ haben*** have water on the brain; **2.** *fig.* bloated bureaucracy; **~kraft** *f* (-; *no pl.*) water power; **~kraft·werk** *n* hydroelectric power plant; **~kreis·lauf** *m* water (*or* hydrological) cycle; **~küh·lung** *f* water cooling (system); ***mit ~*** water-cooled; **~kur** *f* water cure; **~la·che** *f* pool of water; **~lauf** *m* watercourse; **~lei·che** *f* drowned corpse; **~lei·tung** *f* water pipe(s *pl.*); **~li·lie** *f* water lily; **~li·nie** *f* ⚓ water line; **~loch** *n* water hole; **≈lös·lich** *adj.* (water-)soluble; **~man·gel** *m* water shortage; **~mann** *m* (-[e]s; ⸚er) **1.** *no pl. ast.* Aquarius, *the* Water Bearer (*or* Carrier); ***(ein) ~ sein*** be (an) Aquarius, be an Aquarian; **2.** *myth.* water sprite; **~me·͵lo·ne** *f* water melon; **~müh·le** *f* water mill

was·sern ['vasɐn] *v/i.* (h) ✈ touch down on water; *space capsule*: splash down

wäs·sern ['vɛsɐn] *v/t.* (h) water; irrigate *fields etc.*; soak (*a. gastr.*); *phot.* rinse

'Was·ser|ni·xe *f myth.* water nymph; mermaid; **~nym·phe** *f myth.* water nymph; **~ober·flä·che** *f* surface of the water (*or* lake, sea *etc.*); **~pfei·fe** *f* water pipe; **~pflan·ze** *f* aquatic plant; **~pi͵sto·le** *f* water pistol; **~po·li͵zei** *f* → ***Wasserschutzpolizei***; **~rad** *n* water wheel; **~rat·te** *f* water rat; *fig.* keen swimmer; ***e-e ~ sein*** love the water, swim like a fish; **≈reich** *adj. area etc.* with plenty of water (resources); **~rin·ne** *f* gutter; **~rohr** *n* water pipe; **~rutsch·bahn** *f* water chute; **~scha·den** *m* water damage; **~schei·de** *f* watershed, *Am.* divide; **≈scheu** *adj.* scared (*or* frightened, afraid) of water, 📖 hydrophobic; **~schild·krö·te** *f* turtle; **~schlan·ge** *f* water snake; **~schlauch** *m* hose; **~schloß** *n* moated castle; castle in a lake; **~schutz·ge·biet** *n* water reserve; **~schutz·po·li͵zei** *f* river police; harbo(u)r police

'Was·ser·ski[1] *m* (-[s]; -, -er) water ski

'Was·ser·ski[2] *n* (-[s]; *no pl.*) water skiing; ***~ fahren*** water-ski, go water-skiing

'Was·ser|spei·er *m* gargoyle; **~spie·gel** *m* a) surface of the water, b) water level; **~sport** *m* water sports *pl.*; **~spü·lung** *f* flush; cistern; **~stand** *m* water level; **~stands·an·zei·ger** *m* water ga(u)ge; **~stel·le** *f* watering place

'Was·ser·stoff *m* ⚗ hydrogen; **≈blond** F *adj.* peroxide (blonde); **~bom·be** *f* hydrogen bomb, H-bomb; **~per·oxyd** *n* hydrogen peroxide

'Was·ser|strahl *m* jet of water; **~stra·ße** *f* waterway, canal; ***die ~n Frankreichs*** *etc.* the canals and waterways of France *etc.*; **~sucht** *f* (-; *no pl.*) ⚕ dropsy; **~tier** *n* aquatic animal; **~trä·ger** *m* water carrier; F *fig.* dogsbody; **≈trei·bend I.** *adj.* diuretic; **II.** *adv.*: ***~ wirken*** have a diuretic effect; **~trop·fen** *m* drop of water; **~turm** *m* water tower; **~uhr** *f* **1.** *hist.* water clock; **2.** → ***Wasserzähler***

Was·se·rung ['vasərʊŋ] *f* (-; -en) ✈ touchdown on water; splashdown *of a space capsule*

Wäs·se·rung ['vɛsərʊŋ] *f* (-; -en) watering; irrigation *of fields etc.*; soaking (*a. gastr.*); *phot.* rinsing, rinse

'Was·ser|ver·brauch *m* water consumption; **~ver·drän·gung** *f* (water) displacement; **~ver·schmut·zung** *f* water pollution; **~ver·sor·gung** *f* water supply; **~vo·gel** *m* waterbird, *pl. a.* water fowl (*pl.*); **~vor·rat** *m* water supply; **~waa·ge** *f* spirit level, *Am.* level; **~weg** *m* waterway; ***auf dem ~*** by water; **~wel·le** *f* water wave; **~wer·fer** *m a. pl.* water cannon; **~werk** *n, usu. pl.* waterworks *pl.*; **~wirt·schaft** *f* water supply and distribution; **~zäh·ler** *m* water meter; **~zei·chen** *n* watermark

wäß·rig ['vɛsrɪç] *adj.* → ***wässerig***

wa·ten ['va:tən] *v/i.* (sn) wade

Wa·ter·kant ['va:tɐkant] *f* (-; *no pl.*) coast

Wa·ter·loo ['va:tɐlo] *n*: *fig.* ***sein ~ erleben*** meet one's Waterloo

Wat·sche ['va:tʃə] *dial. f* (-; -n) F clip round the ears

wat·scheln ['va:tʃəln] *v/i.* (sn) waddle

'Wat·schen·mann F *fig. m* (-[e]s; ⸚er) scapegoat, F fall guy

Watt[1] [vat] *n* (-s; -) ⚡ watt

Watt[2] *n* (-[e]s; -en) *geol.* mud flats *pl.*

Wat·te ['vatə] *f* (-; *no pl.*) cotton wool, *Am.* cotton; F *fig.* ***j-n in ~ packen*** handle s.o. with kid gloves, mollycoddle s.o.; **~bausch** *m* cotton(-wool) swab

'Wat·ten·meer *n* mud flats *pl.*

'Wat·te·stäb·chen *n* cotton bud

wat·tie·ren [va'ti:rən] *v/t.* (h) pad, line with wadding; quilt; **Wat'tie·rung** *f* (-; -en) padding

'Watt|stun·de *f* ⚡ watt hour; **~zahl** *f* ⚡ wattage

Wat·vo·gel ['va:t-] *m* wader

Wau·wau ['vaʊvaʊ] *m* (-s; -s) bow-wow, doggie

wau wau *int.* bow-wow, woof-woof

WC [ve:'tse:] *n* (-[s]; -[s]) toilet, bathroom, restroom; **~-Becken** *n* toilet bowl; **~-Bür·ste** *f* toilet brush; **~-Rei·ni·ger** *m* toilet cleaner; **~-Sitz** *m* (toddler) trainer seat

we·ben ['ve:bən] (wob, gewoben, h) **I.** *v/t. and v/i.* weave; **II.** *fig. v/refl.*: ***sich ~ um*** *acc.* grow up around; **We·ber** ['ve:bɐ] *m* (-s; -) weaver; **We·be·rei** [ve:bə'raɪ] *f* (-; -en) **1.** *no pl.* weaving; **2.** weaving mill; **We·be·rin** ['ve:bərɪn] *f* (-; -nen) weaver; **'We·ber·knecht** *m zo.* daddy longlegs; **'We·ber·schiff·chen** *n* shuttle

Web|feh·ler ['ve:p-] *m* flaw; F *fig.* ***e-n ~ haben*** F have a screw loose (somewhere), be slightly cracked; **~kan·te** *f* selvage; **~stuhl** *m* loom

Wech·sel ['vɛksəl] *m* (-s; -) **1.** a) change; exchange, b) succession, alternation, c) 🌾 (*crop*) rotation, d) fluctuation; *pol. etc.* changeover, e) *sport*: (baton) change; change of ends; substitution; *skating*: crossing, f) *hunt.* runway, trail, game pass; ***~ der Jahreszeiten*** changing (*or* rotating) seasons; ***~ von Tag und Nacht*** alternation of day and night; ***in buntem ~*** in motley succession; **2.** ✝ bill (of exchange); draft; ***e-n ~ ausstellen*** draw (*or* issue) a bill; **3.** allowance

'Wech·sel|au·to͵mat *m* change machine (*or* dispenser); **~bad** *n* hot and cold baths *pl.*; *fig.* ***durch ein ~ der Gefühle gehen*** be up one minute, down the next; ***j-n e-m ~ aussetzen*** blow hot and cold towards s.o.; **~bank** *f* (-; -en) discount house; **~be·zie·hung** *f* interrelation; ***in ~ stehen mit*** *dat.* be correlated with; **~bür·ge** *m* bill surety; **~bürg·schaft** *f* bill guaranty; **~du·sche** *f* hot and cold shower; **~fäl·le** *pl.* vicissitudes, F ups and downs; ***die ~ des Lebens*** life's vicissitudes, the vicissitudes (F ups and downs) of life; **~fäl·schung** *f* forgery of bills; **~geld** *n* change; ***~ bekommen*** *a.* get (some) money back; **~ge·sang** *m* responsory; **~ge·spräch** *n* dialog(ue); **~ge·trie·be** *n* ⚙ change(-speed) gearbox, *Am.* transmission

'wech·sel·haft *adj.* changeable

'Wech·sel|jah·re *pl.* menopause *sg.*, climacteric *sg.*, change of life *sg.*; ***in den ~n sein*** be going through the menopause (*or* change of life, one's climacteric); **~kre,dit** *m* acceptance (*or* discount) credit; **~kurs** *m* exchange rate, rate of exchange

wech·seln ['vɛksəln] (h) **I.** *v/t.* change (*money, a. oil, tire etc.*); exchange *a. a few words etc.*, b) alternate; ***Geld ~*** get (some) change; ***Dollar in D-Mark ~*** change dollars into deutschmarks; ***die Fahrbahn ~*** change (*or* switch) lanes; ***die Kleider ~*** change (one's clothes); ***das Hemd*** *etc.* **~** put on a clean shirt *etc.*; ***die Schuhe ~*** put on another pair of shoes; ***Unterwäsche zum*** ♀ a change of underwear; ***den Arbeitsplatz*** (***Arzt***) **~** change jobs (doctors), find another job (go to another doctor); ***die Schule ~*** change (*or* switch) schools; ***die Partei ~*** go over to another party, join the other side; ***Briefe mit j-m ~*** correspond with s.o.; ***ein paar Worte mit j-m ~*** have (*or* exchange) a few words with s.o.; ***die Wohnung ~*** move (house), move to another house; ***das Zimmer ~*** change rooms, move to another room; ***sie wechselten Blicke*** they exchanged glances; → ***Besitzer, Thema***; **II.** *v/i.* a) change, b) vary, c) *hunt.* pass; **~ *in*** *acc.* (*or* ***nach*** *dat. etc.*) switch (over) to, move to; ***kannst du ~?*** can you change this?, have you got change for this?; **'wech·selnd** *adj.* varying; changeable; ***mit ~em Erfolg*** with varying degrees of success; → ***Bewölkung***

'Wech·sel|neh·mer [-neːmɐ] *m* (-s; -) payee (of a bill); **~rah·men** *m* interchangeable picture frame; **~rei·te,rei** *f* bill jobbing, F kite flying; **~schal·ter** *m* ⚡ changeover switch; **~schuld** *f* bill debt; **~schuld·ner** *m* bill debtor

'wech·sel·sei·tig [-zaɪtɪç] *adj.* mutual; reciprocal; **'Wech·sel·sei·tig·keit** *f* (-; *no pl.*) reciprocity

'Wech·sel·spiel *n* interplay

'Wech·sel·strom *m* alternating current (*abbr.* AC); **~er·zeu·ger** *m* alternator

'Wech·sel|stu·be *f* exchange booth, bureau de change; **~tier·chen** *n* am(o)eba; **~ver·hält·nis** *n* interrelation(ship)

'wech·sel·voll *adj.* varied, eventful; ***~e Laufbahn*** chequered (*Am.* checkered) career

'Wech·sel·wäh·ler *m* floating voter

'wech·sel·wei·se *adv.* alternately, in turn

'Wech·sel·wir·kung *f* interaction

Wechs·ler ['vɛkslɐ] *m* (-s; -) **1.** → ***Wechselautomat***; **2.** moneychanger; **3.** record changer

Weck·dienst ['vɛk-] *m* alarm call service

wecken ['vɛkən] (*sep.* -k·k-) *v/t.* (h) wake (up), F give *s.o.* a call; rouse (*a. fig.*); *fig.* awaken *memories*, stir up *emotions etc.*; **Wecken** *n* (-s; *no pl.*) **1.** ⚔ reveille; **2.** ***nach dem ~*** after you've *etc.* been woken up; **Wecker** ['vɛkɐ] (*sep.* -k·k-) *m* (-s; -) alarm clock; F *fig.* ***j-m auf den ~ gehen*** get on s.o.'s nerves (F wick)

Weck·ruf ['vɛk-] *m* early morning (*or* alarm) call

We·del ['veːdəl] *m* (-s; -) feather duster; ♣ frond; *zo.* tail, brush; **'we·deln** *v/i.* (h) a) *dog etc.*: wag (***mit dem Schwanz*** its tail), b) *skiing*: wedel, c) **~ *mit*** *dat.* wave *s.th.*

we·der ['veːdɐ] *cj.*: **~ ... *noch*** neither ... nor; ***er rief ~ an, noch schrieb er*** he neither phoned nor wrote; he didn't phone, (and) nor did he write; ***er zeigt ~ Talent noch Begeisterung*** he hasn't got (either) talent or enthusiasm, he has neither talent nor enthusiasm; *haben Sie die Aufnahme mit Bernstein oder Solti?* - **~ *noch*** neither, I'm afraid

Weg [veːk] *m* (-[e]s; Wege ['veːgə]) a) way (*a. direction, a. fig. manner*); path (*a. fig.*), b) route, c) walk; errand, d) course; ***am ~e*** by the wayside; ***auf dem ~e*** on the way; ***das liegt auf m-m ~*** that's on my way, I'll be passing (by) there on my way (home *etc.*); ***j-m über den ~ laufen*** run (*or* bump) into s.o.; ***sich auf den ~ machen*** set off; ***j-n nach dem ~ fragen*** ask s.o. the way; ***j-m e-n ~ abnehmen*** spare s.o. the trip; ***j-m et. mit auf den ~ geben*** give s.o. s.th. to take along; ***aus dem ~e gehen*** get out of the way, step aside, *fig.* steer clear (*gen.* of); ***et. aus dem ~e schaffen*** *a. fig.* get rid of s.th.; ***j-m im ~e stehen*** *a. fig.* be in s.o.'s way; ***j-m in den ~ treten*** bar s.o.'s way, *fig.* get in s.o.'s way; *fig.* ***auf schriftlichem ~e*** in writing; ***auf gesetzlichem ~e*** legally, by legal means; ***auf diplomatischem ~e*** through diplomatic channels; ***der*** (***auf dem***) **~ *zum Erfolg*** (on) the road to success; ***auf dem ~e der Besserung*** on the road to recovery; ***auf dem besten ~(e) sein zu*** *inf.* be well on the way to *ger.*, ***sich zu ruinieren***: be heading for disaster; ***auf diesem ~e*** this way; ***auf dem richtigen ~(e) sein*** be on the right track; ***j-n auf den richtigen ~ bringen*** put s.o. back on the straight and narrow; ***s-e eigenen ~e gehen*** go one's own way(s), F do one's own thing; ***e-r Frage*** (***Entscheidung***) ***aus dem ~e gehen*** evade a question, avoid the issue (avoid making a decision); ***den ~ bereiten*** (*or* ***ebnen***) *dat.* pave the way for *s.o. or s.th.*, *a.* prepare the ground for *s.th.*; ***et. in die ~e leiten*** initiate s.th., start s.th. off, pave the way for s.th.; ***neue ~e in der Kindererziehung*** new approaches in child education; ***neue ~e gehen*** try out new avenues, pursue a different path; ***unsere ~e haben sich getrennt*** we went our different ways; ***hier scheiden sich unsere ~e*** this is where we say goodbye, *fig.* this is where our ways part; ***er wird s-n ~ machen*** he'll go far (*or* go places); ***ich traue ihm nicht über den ~*** I don't trust him an inch, F I wouldn't trust him as far as I can throw him; ***es bleibt kein anderer ~ offen*** there's no choice (*or* alternative); F ***da führt kein ~ dran vorbei*** there's no way round it; ***dem steht nichts im ~e*** there's nothing to stop it; → ***abbringen, bahnen, Mittel*** 1

weg [vɛk] *adv.* away; gone; not in; ***m-e Uhr ist ~*** my watch is (*or* has) gone; *der Zug, die Maschine etc.* ***ist schon ~*** has (already) left; **~ *da!*** get away!; **~ *damit!*** take it away!; ***Finger*** (*or* ***Hände***) **~*!*** hands off!; F ***ich muß ~*** I must be off; F ***nichts wie ~!*** F let's get out of here, *sl.* scram!; F **~ *sein*** a) be out (for the count), b) F be gone, c) F be miles away, be away with the fairies; F ***ganz ~ sein*** F be thrilled to bits, be over the moon; ***ich bin darüber ~*** I've got over it, I'm over it; → ***Fenster***

weg·ar·bei·ten ['vɛk-] *v/t.* (*sep.*, h): ***alles ~*** get through all one's work; ***nicht viel ~*** not to get much work done

weg·be·kom·men ['vɛk-] *v/t.* (*irr.*, *sep.*, h, → ***bekommen***) **1.** a) move, b) get rid of *a cold etc.*; **2.** F get, F land o.s.

'Weg·be·rei·ter [-bəraɪtɐ] *m* (-s; -) pioneer, F trailblazer; ***der ~ sein für*** *acc.* pave the way for, blaze the trail for

weg|bla·sen ['vɛk-] *v/t.* (*irr.*, *sep.*, h, → ***blasen***) blow off (*or* away); ***wie weggeblasen sein*** have completely disappeared; **~blei·ben** *v/i.* (*irr.*, *sep.*, sn, → ***bleiben***) a) stay away, b) be omitted; → ***Spucke***; **~blicken** *v/i.* (*sep.*, h) look away; **~brin·gen** *v/t.* (*irr.*, *sep.*, h, → ***bringen***) a) take away, b) get rid of; **~den·ken** *v/t.* (*irr.*, *sep.*, h, → ***denken***): ***sich et. ~*** imagine s.th. isn't there; ***es ist aus dem Leben nicht mehr wegzudenken*** it's hard to imagine life without it; **~dis·ku,tie·ren** *v/t.* (*sep.*, h) explain away; **~drän·gen** *v/t.* (*sep.*, h) push *s.o.* aside; **~dre·hen** *v/t.* (*sep.*, h) **1.** turn away *one's face*; **2.** turn down *sound*; **~dür·fen** *v/i.* (*irr.*, *sep.*, h, → ***dürfen***) be allowed to go (*or* go out)

We·ge·geld ['veːgə-] *n* **1.** *hist.* road toll; **2.** travel allowance

We·ge·la·ge·rer ['veːgəlaːgərɐ] *m* (-s; -) *hist.* highwayman

we·gen ['veːgən] *prp.* (*gen.*) a) because of, on account of; *a.* due to, as a result of, owing to, b) for the sake of, for; **~ *Mord*(*es*)** for murder; F ***von ~!*** you must be joking!; F ***von ~ faul!*** F lazy, my foot!; → ***Amt, Recht***

We·ge·rich ['veːgərɪç] *m* (-s; -e) ♣ plantain

weg|es·sen ['vɛk-] *v/t.* (*irr.*, *sep.*, h, → ***essen***) eat up; ***er hat mir alles weggegessen*** he ate all my sandwiches *etc.*, F he's eaten me out of house and home; **~fah·ren** (*irr.*, *sep.* → ***fahren***) **I.** *v/t.* (h) take (*or* drive) away; **II.** *v/i.* (sn) leave; **~fal·len** *v/i.* (*irr.*, *sep.*, sn, → ***fallen***) a) be left out, b) become unnecessary, c) be cancel(l)ed; cease; *rule etc.*: be dropped; ***die Klausel*** *etc.* ***ist weggefallen*** the clause *etc.* no longer applies (*or* is no longer valid); **~fe·gen** (*sep.*) **I.** *v/t.* (h) sweep away (*fig.* aside); **II.** *v/i.* (sn): **~ *über*** *acc. wind*: sweep across; **~fi·schen** *v/t.* (*sep.*, h) → ***wegschnappen***; **~füh·ren** *v/t.* (*sep.*, h) lead (*or* take) away, lead off; **~ge·ben** *v/t.* (*irr.*, *sep.*, h, → ***geben***) give away (*a. child*); ***die Wäsche ~*** take (*or* send) the *or* one's washing to the laundry; **~ge·hen** *v/i.* (*irr.*, *sep.*, sn, → ***gehen***) **1.** a) go away, leave, b) go out; *fig.* ***geh mir weg damit!*** I don't want to know about it; **2.** *stains etc.*: come off (*or* out), go away; **3.** *goods*: sell; **4.** *fig.* **~ *über*** *acc.* pass over

weg·ge·tre·ten ['vɛk-] **I.** *p.p. of* ***wegtreten***; **II.** F *adj.*: ***geistig ~*** F away with the fairies

weg|gie·ßen ['vɛk-] *v/t.* (*irr.*, *sep.*, h, → ***gießen***) pour away; **~gucken** *v/i.* (*sep.*, h) → ***wegsehen***; **~ha·ben** *v/t.* (*irr.*, *sep.*, h, → ***haben***) **1.** ***et. ~ wollen*** want to get rid of s.th.; **2.** F ***et. ~*** a) be good at s.th., b) F have got s.th.; F ***er hat es noch nicht weg*** F he hasn't got the hang of it yet; F ***einen ~*** a) F have had one over the eight, b) (*a.* F ***e-n Knacks*** ~) F have a screw loose (somewhere); → ***Fett, Ruhe***; **~hän·gen** *v/t.* (*sep.*, h) hang *s.th.* away; **~ho·len** *v/t.* (*sep.*, h) take away, (come to) fetch; F ***sich e-e Grippe*** *etc.* ~ catch (the) flu *etc.*; **~hö·ren** *v/i.* (*sep.*, h) try not to listen; shut one's ears; ***könnt ihr mal ~?*** could you shut your ears for a minute?; **~ja·gen** *v/t.* (*sep.*, h) chase away, *a.* F send *s.o.* packing; **~kom·men** *v/i.* (*irr.*, *sep.*, sn, → ***kommen***) a) get away; *sport*: get off, b) get (*or* be) lost; *fig.* ***gut*** (***schlecht***) ~ come off well (badly); ~ ***über*** *acc.* get over *s.th.*

'**Weg·kreuz** *n* roadside calvary

weg|krie·gen ['vɛk-] F *v/t.* (*sep.*, h) → ***wegbekommen***; **~las·sen** *v/t.* (*irr.*, *sep.*, h, → ***lassen***) a) let *s.o.* go, b) leave out; **~lau·fen** *v/i.* (*irr.*, *sep.*, sn, → ***laufen***) run away; ***von zu Hause*** ~ run away from home; F ***das läuft mir nicht weg*** F it won't run away; **~le·gen** *v/t.* (*sep.*, h) put aside (*or* away); **~leug·nen** *v/t.* (*sep.*, h) deny; **~ma·chen** (*sep.*, h) **I.** *v/t.* get rid of *s.th.*, *a.* F *a baby*; **II.** F *v/refl.*: ***sich*** ~ F clear off, do a bunk; **~müs·sen** *v/i.* (*irr.*, *sep.*, h, → ***müssen***) have to go; ***ich muß weg*** I must be off (*or* going); **~neh·men** *v/t.* (*irr.*, *sep.*, h, → ***nehmen***) take, take away (***j-m*** from s.o.); remove; *fig.* block *a view etc.*, block out *the sun*; shut out *light, noise etc.*; take up *space, time etc.*; *mot.* ***Gas*** ~ ease off the gas; **~ope,rie·ren** *v/t.* (*sep.*, h) remove, F cut out; **~packen** *v/t.* (*sep.*, h) pack away; **~put·zen** *v/t.* (*sep.*, h) a) wipe off, b) F polish off, put (*or* stow) away *food*; **~ra,die·ren** *v/t.* (*sep.*, h) rub out

'**Weg·rand** *m*: (***am*** ~ by the) wayside

weg|ra·tio·na·li,sie·ren ['vɛk-] *v/t.* (*sep.*, h) rationalize out of existence; **~räu·men** *v/t.* (*sep.*, h) clear away; *fig.* remove; **~rei·ßen** *v/t.* (*irr.*, *sep.*, h, → ***reißen***) tear away (*or* off); tear (*or* pull) down *building etc.*; ***die Brücke*** ~ *river*: tear down (*or* sweep away) the bridge; ***j-m et.*** ~ snatch s.th. (away) from s.o.; **~ren·nen** *v/i.* (*irr.*, *sep.*, sn, → ***rennen***) run away; *a.* run off; **~rücken** *v/t.* (*sep.*, h) *and v/i.* (sn) move away; **~schaf·fen** *v/t.* (*sep.*, h) a) take away, b) get through *one's work etc.*, get *s.th.* out of the way; **~schau·en** *v/i.* (*sep.*, h) → ***wegsehen***; **~sche·ren** F *v/refl.* (*sep.*, h): ***sich*** ~ F clear off; **~schicken** *v/t.* (*sep.*, h) send away; **~schie·ben** *v/t.* (*irr.*, *sep.*, h, → ***schieben***) push away; *a.* push aside *one's plate etc.*; **~schlei·chen** *v/refl.*: ***sich*** ~ (*irr.*, *sep.*, h, → ***schleichen***) sneak away (*or* off); **~schlep·pen** *v/t.* (*sep.*, h) drag off; **~schlie·ßen** *v/t.* (*irr.*, *sep.*, h, → ***schließen***) lock away; **~schmei·ßen** F *v/t.* (*irr.*, *sep.*, h, → ***schmeißen***) throw away; **~schnap·pen** *v/t.* (*sep.*, h) snatch *s.th.* away (***j-m*** from s.o.); steal, *Brit. a.* F pinch *s.o.'s girlfriend etc.*; snatch *s.th.* away from under s.o.'s eyes; **~schüt·ten** *v/t.* (*sep.*, h) dump, pour away; **~se·hen** *v/i.* (*irr.*, *sep.*, h, → ***sehen***) look away; look the other way; ~ ***über*** *acc.* turn a blind eye to *s.th.*; **~set·zen** (*sep.*, h) **I.** *v/t.* put away; **II.** *v/refl.*: ***sich*** ~ move (away); *fig.* ***sich*** ~ ***über*** *acc.* → ***hinwegsetzen***; **~spü·len** *v/t.* (*sep.*, h) wash away (*a. geol.*); **~stecken** *v/t.* (*sep.*, h) **1.** put away; hide; **2.** swallow *an insult etc.*; take *a blow etc.*; ***er kann viel*** ~ he can take a fair bit (of punishment); **~steh·len** *v/refl.*: ***sich*** ~ (*irr.*, *sep.*, h, → ***stehlen***) steal away, sneak away (*or* off); **~ster·ben** *v/i.* (*irr.*, *sep.*, sn, → ***sterben***) **1.** die off; ***zu Tausenden*** *etc.* ~ die (off) in their thousands *etc.*, go down like flies; **2.** ***j-m*** ~ die before s.o.'s eyes, just die; **~sto·ßen** *v/t.* (*irr.*, *sep.*, h, → ***stoßen***) push away

'**Weg·strecke** *f* stretch; distance covered

weg|strei·chen ['vɛk-] *v/t.* (*irr.*, *sep.*, h, → ***streichen***) cross out; **~tau·chen** *v/i.* (*sep.*, sn) **1.** *submarine etc.*: submerge; *person*: disappear under the water; F *fig.* disappear from the scene; **2.** F *fig.* a) switch off, b) nod off; **~trei·ben** (*irr.*, *sep.*, → ***treiben***) **I.** *v/t.* (h) drive away; **II.** *v/i.* (sn) drift away; **~tre·ten** *v/i.* (*irr.*, *sep.*, sn, → ***treten***) step aside; ⚔ break (the) ranks; ~ ***lassen*** dismiss; → ***weggetreten***; **~tun** *v/t.* (*irr.*, *sep.*, h, → ***tun***) put away; **~wei·sen** *v/t.* (*irr.*, *sep.*, h, → ***weisen***) turn away

weg·wei·send ['ve:k-] *fig. adj.* landmark *decision etc.*; ~ ***sein*** point the way to the future; '**Weg·wei·ser** [-vaɪzɐ] *m* (-s; -) **1.** signpost; sign; **2.** guide (***durch*** *acc.* to)

weg|wen·den ['vɛk-] *v/t.* (*irr.*, *sep.*, h, → ***wenden***) (*a.* ***sich*** ~) turn away; ***den Blick*** ~ avert one's gaze (*or* eyes); **~wer·fen** (*irr.*, *sep.*, h, → ***werfen***) **I.** *v/t.* throw away, F bin; **II.** *fig. v/refl.*: ***sich*** ~ waste o.s. (***an*** *acc.* on); degrade o.s.; **~wer·fend** *adj.* dismissive, disdainful *gesture etc.*

Weg·werf|fla·sche ['vɛkvɛrf-] *f* non-returnable bottle; **~ge·schirr** *n* disposable tableware; **~ge·sell·schaft** *f* throwaway society; **~win·del** *f* disposable nappy (*Am.* diaper)

weg|wi·schen ['vɛk-] *v/t.* (*sep.*, h) wipe off; *fig.* dismiss; **~zau·bern** *v/t.* (*sep.*, h) spirit away; **~zie·hen** (*irr.*, *sep.*, → ***ziehen***) **I.** *v/t.* (h) pull away; **II.** *v/i.* (sn) move (to another place); ***wir sind 1989 weggezogen*** we left (*or* moved [away]) in 1989

weh [ve:] *adj.* sore; ~ ***tun*** hurt; ***j-m*** ~ ***tun*** *a. fig.* hurt s.o.; ***mir tut der Finger*** ~ my finger hurts; ***mir tut der Magen*** (***Kopf, Rücken***) ~ I've got a stomach-ache (a headache, [a] backache); ***sich*** ~ ***tun*** hurt o.s.; *lit.* ***mir tut das Herz*** ~ my heart is aching

Weh [ve:] *lit. n* (-[e]s; *no pl.*) pain; *a.* grief

we·he ['ve:ə] *int.*: ~ ***dir, wenn ...!*** you'll be sorry if ...!

We·he ['ve:ə] *f* (-; -n) (*snow, sand*) drift

We·hen ['ve:ən] *pl.* labo(u)r pains, labo(u)r *sg.*; *fig.* travail *sg.*; ***in den*** ~ ***liegen*** be in labo(u)r; ***die*** ~ ***setzten ein*** labo(u)r (*or* the contractions) started

we·hen ['ve:ən] (h) **I.** *v/i.* blow; *flag*: wave, flutter; *fig. scent, sound etc.*: drift, waft; ***der Wind weht eisig*** (***scharf***) there's an icy (a sharp) wind (blowing); **~*de Gewänder*** flowing robes; → ***Wind***; **II.** *v/t.* blow

'**Weh·ge·schrei** *n* wailing (*a. fig.*)

'**Weh·kla·ge** *f* lament; '**weh·kla·gen** *v/i.* (h) wail, lament

weh·lei·dig ['ve:laɪdɪç] *adj.* self-pitying, F snivel(l)ing ...; maudlin; plaintive *voice*; ***sei nicht so*** ~***!*** stop feeling so sorry for yourself, F stop snivel(l)ing

Weh·mut ['ve:mu:t] *f* (-; *no pl.*) melancholy; **weh·mü·tig** ['ve:my:tɪç] *adj.* melancholy; wistful

Wehr¹ [ve:ɐ] *f*: ***sich zur*** ~ ***setzen*** defend o.s., stand up for o.s.

Wehr² [ve:ɐ] *n* (-[e]s; Wehre ['ve:rə]) weir; dam, barrage

'**Wehr|be·auf·trag·te** *m* defen|ce (*Am.* -se) commissioner (of the German Bundestag); **~be·reich** *m* military district

'**Wehr·dienst** *m* (-[e]s; *no pl.*) military service; **≈taug·lich** *adj.* fit for military service; **≈un·taug·lich** *adj.* not fit for military service; **~ver·wei·ge·rer** [-fɛɐvaɪgərɐ] *m* (-s; -) conscientious objector

weh·ren ['ve:rən] *v/refl.* (h): ***sich*** ~ defend o.s., stand up for o.s.; ***sich gegen et.*** ~ resist s.th.; ***sich*** ~ ***zu*** *inf.* refuse to *inf.*; ***er weiß sich zu*** ~ he can handle it; ***ich wehre mich dagegen, daß*** I refuse to accept that; ***sich mit Händen und Füßen*** ~ put up a fierce struggle

'**Wehr|er·satz·dienst** *m* → ***Zivildienst***; **~etat** *m* defen|ce (*Am.* -se) budget

'**wehr·fä·hig** *adj.* fit for military service

'**wehr·los** *adj.* defenceless, *Am.* defenseless; helpless; ***e-r Sache*** ~ ***gegenüberstehen*** be helpless in the face of s.th.; '**Wehr·lo·sig·keit** *f* (-; *no pl.*) defencelessness, *Am.* defenselessness; helplessness

'**Wehr·macht** *f* (-; *no pl.*) *hist.* (German) Armed Forces *pl.*, Wehrmacht

'**Wehr·paß** *m* service record (book)

'**Wehr·pflicht** *f* (-; *no pl.*) conscription, compulsory military service

wehr·pflich·tig ['ve:ɐpflɪçtɪç] *adj.* liable for military service; '**Wehr·pflich·ti·ge** *m* (-n; -n) a) person liable for military service, b) conscript

'**Wehr|tech·nik** *f* defen|ce (*Am.* -se) technology; **~übung** *f* reserve duty training

Weh·weh·chen [ve:'ve:çən] F *n* (-s; -) little complaint; ***er rennt wegen jedem*** ~ ***zum Arzt*** he runs to the doctor with every little thing

Weib [vaɪp] *n* (-[e]s; Weiber ['vaɪbɐ]) a) woman (*a. contp.*), b) wife; ***typisch*** ~***!*** typical woman!; '**Weib·chen** *n* (-s; -) **1.** *zo.* female; **2.** F *obs.* F wifey, missus

Wei·ber|feind ['vaɪbɐ-] *m* woman-hater, misogynist; **~ge·schich·ten** *pl.* amorous affairs (*or* conquests); ***er mit s-n*** ~***!*** *a.* him and his womanizing; **~ge·schwätz** *n* (women's) gossip; **~held** *m* lady-killer; **~herr·schaft** *f* (-; *no pl.*) petticoat government; **~volk** F *n* (-[e]s; *no pl.*) women(folk) *pl.*

wei·bisch ['vaɪbɪʃ] *adj.* effeminate

'**weib·lich** *adj.* female; feminine (*a. ling. and metric*); '**Weib·lich·keit** *f* (-; *no pl.*) **1.** femininity; **2.** ***die*** ~ womanhood; ***die holde*** ~ the fair sex

'**Weibs·bild** *contp. n* woman, female, *a.* F broad

weich [vaɪç] *adj.* a) soft (*a. phot. and fig.*); *a.* smooth, b) *gastr.* tender *meat*; soft-boiled *egg*; cooked *vegetables*; ~ ***machen*** soften; ~ ***werden*** soften (*a. fig.*), *fig.* give in; ***sich*** ~ ***anfühlen*** feel soft, be soft to the touch; ~ ***landen*** have a soft landing; ***mir wurden die Knie*** ~ I went weak in the knees, my knees turned to jelly; *fig.* **~*e Droge*** (***Währung***) soft drug (currency)

Wei·che¹ ['vaɪçə] *f* (-; -n) *anat.* flank, side

'**Wei·che²** *f* (-; -n) 🚂 points *pl.*, *Am.* switch; ***die*** **~*n stellen*** set the points, *Am.* throw the switch, *fig.* point the way ahead, ***für*** *acc.*: point the way for

wei·chen¹ ['vaɪçən] *v/t. and v/i.* (h) soak (*a.* ~ **lassen**)

'**wei·chen²** *v/i.* (wich, gewichen, sn) move; ⚔ retreat; *fig.* give way (*dat.* to), yield (to), make way (for); ***zur Seite*** ~ step aside; ***j-m nicht von der Seite*** ~ not to leave s.o.'s side, *contp.* cling to s.o. like a leech; ***nicht von der Stelle*** ~ not to move (an inch); *fig.* ***die Angst wich von ihr*** her fear left her; ***das Blut wich aus ihren Wangen*** the blood left (*or* drained from) her cheeks

'**Wei·chen|stel·ler** [-ʃtɛlɐ] *m* (-s; -), ~**wär·ter** *m* pointsman, *Am.* switchman

'**weich·ge·kocht** *adj.* soft-boiled *egg*

'**Weich·heit** *f* (-; *no pl.*) softness; *a.* smoothness

'**weich·her·zig** *adj.* soft(-hearted)

'**Weich|holz** *n* softwood; ~**kä·se** *m* soft cheese; cheese spread

'**weich·lich** *adj.* soft; *fig. a.* weak; effeminate; ~***er Typ*** → **Weich·ling** ['vaɪçlɪŋ] *m* (-s; -e) weakling

'**weich·ma·chen** F *fig. v/t.* (*sep.*, h) soften up; '**Weich·ma·cher** *m* (-s; -) ⚙ softener, softening agent; *gastr.* tenderizer

'**Weich|spü·ler** *m* fabric softener; ~**tei·le** *pl. anat.* soft parts; abdomen *sg.*; ~**tier** *n* mollusc, *Am.* mollusk; ~**zeich·ner** *m phot.* soft-focus lens

Wei·de¹ ['vaɪdə] *f* (-; -n) willow

'**Wei·de²** *f* (-; -n) pasture, meadow; ***auf der*** ~ ***sein*** be grazing; '**Wei·de·land** *n* pasture; '**wei·den** (h) **I.** *v/i.* graze; **II.** *v/t.* put out to pasture; **III.** *fig. v/refl.*: ***sich*** ~ ***an*** *dat.* a) revel in, feast one's eyes on *a sight etc.*, b) gloat over

'**Wei·den|baum** *m* willow (tree); ~**ger·te** *f* willow rod (*or* switch); osier, wicker; ~**kätz·chen** *n* ⚘ catkin, pussy willow; ~**korb** *m* wicker basket

'**Wei·de·platz** *m* pasture

weid·ge·recht ['vaɪt-] *adj. and adv.* in accordance with good huntsmanship

weid·lich ['vaɪtlɪç] *adv.* thoroughly, properly

Weid·mann ['vaɪt-] *m* (-[e]s; ⸚er) huntsman; '**Weid·manns·heil** *int.*: ~! good sport!; '**Weid·mes·ser** *n* hunting knife; '**Weid·werk** *n* (-[e]s; *no pl.*) (art of) hunting

wei·gern ['vaɪgɐn] *v/refl.* (h): ***sich*** ~ refuse; **Wei·ge·rung** ['vaɪgərʊŋ] *f* (-; -en) refusal

Weih·bi·schof ['vaɪ-] *m* suffragan (bishop)

Wei·he ['vaɪə] *f* (-; -n) **1.** *eccl.* consecration; ordination; ***j-m die*** ~ ***erteilen*** consecrate (*or* ordain) s.o. in holy orders; ***die heiligen*** ~***n empfangen*** take (holy) orders; *fig. hum.* ***die höheren*** ~***n haben*** have been officially ordained (***zu*** *dat.* as); **2.** *fig.* solemnity; '**wei·hen** *v/t.* (h) consecrate; ordain; ***j-n zum Bischof*** ~ consecrate s.o. bishop; ***j-n zum Priester*** ~ ordain s.o. priest; ***j-m e-e Kirche*** ~ consecrate a church to s.o.; ***j-m ein Buch*** ~ dedicate a book to s.o.; ***sein Leben*** (***sich***) ***e-r Idee*** ~ dedicate *or* devote one's life (o.s.) to an idea; → ***geweiht***

Wei·her ['vaɪɐ] *m* (-s; -) pond

'**Wei·he·stät·te** *f* shrine

'**wei·he·voll** *adj.* solemn

Weih·nach·ten ['vaɪnaxtən] **I.** *n* (-; -) Christmas, F Xmas; ***fröhliche*** (*or* ***frohe***) ~! merry Christmas!, *a.* Season's Greetings; (***zu***) ~ at (*or* over) Christmas; **II.** 2 *v/impers.* (h): ***es weihnachtet sehr*** Christmas is on its way

weih·nacht·lich ['vaɪnaxtlɪç] *adj.* Christmas ..., Christmassy

Weih·nachts|abend ['vaɪnaxts-] *m* Christmas Eve; ~**baum** *m* Christmas tree; ~**ein·käu·fe** *pl.* Chistmas shopping *sg.*; ~**fei·er** *f* Christmas party; ~**fe·ri·en** *pl.* Christmas holiday(s) (*Am.* vacation); ~**fest** *n* Christmas; ~**frei·be·trag** *m* tax-free Christmas allowance; ~**ge·bäck** *n* Christmas biscuits (*Am.* cookies) *pl.*; ~**geld** *n* Christmas bonus; ~**ge·schäft** *n* (pre-)Christmas sales *pl.*; ~**ge·schenk** *n* Christmas present; ~**gra·ti·fi·ka·tiˌon** *f* Christmas bonus; ~**kar·te** *f* Christmas card; ~**krip·pe** *f* Christmas crib; ~**lied** *n* Christmas carol; ~**mann** *m* (-[e]s; ⸚er) **1.** ***der*** ~ Father Christmas, Santa Claus; **2.** F *contp.* F dope, dummy; ~**markt** *m* Christmas fair; ~**paˌpier** *n* Christmas wrapping paper; ~**stern** *m* **1.** Christmas star; **2.** ⚘ poinsettia; ~**stim·mung** *f* festive atmosphere *or* mood (of Christmas); ~**tag** *m*: ***der erste*** ~ Christmas Day; ***der zweite*** ~ Boxing Day, *Am.* the day after Christmas; ~**tel·ler** *m* plate of Christmas goodies; ~**tru·bel** *m* Christmas rush; ~**ver·kehr** *m* Christmas traffic; ~**zeit** *f* Christmas (season)

Weih·rauch ['vaɪraʊx] *m* (-[e]s; *no pl.*) incense

Weih·was·ser ['vaɪvasɐ] *n* (-s; *no pl.*) holy water; ~**becken** *n* font

weil [vaɪl] *cj.* because; since, as

wei·land ['vaɪlant] *hum. adv.* **1.** formerly; ***Herr X,*** ~ ***Lehrer an unserer Schule*** Mr X, quondam teacher at our school; ~ ***sein Mentor*** his quondam mentor; **2.** once; in days of yore

Weil·chen ['vaɪlçən] *n*: ***ein*** ~ (for) a little while

Wei·le ['vaɪlə] *f* (-; *no pl.*) *a* while, *a* time; ***das kann e-e ziemliche*** ~ ***dauern*** that could take a (fair) while *or* a bit of time

wei·len ['vaɪlən] *v/i.* (h) a) stay, b) linger (*a. fig. thoughts*); ***ein Jahr in Spanien*** ~ spend a year in Spain; *euphem.* ***er weilt nicht mehr unter uns*** he is no longer with us

Wei·ler ['vaɪlɐ] *m* (-s; -) hamlet

Wein [vaɪn] *m* (-[e]s; -e) a) wine, b) ⚘ vine, c) vintage; ***ein Glas*** (***e-e Flasche***) ~ a glass (a bottle) of wine; ***bei e-m Glas*** ~ over a glass of wine; ***im*** ~ ***ist Wahrheit*** in vino veritas; ***der Gott des*** ~***es*** the god of wine, Bacchus, Dionysus; ~, ***Weib und Gesang*** wine, women and song; *fig.* ***j-m reinen*** ~ ***einschenken*** be completely open with s.o.; ***junger*** ~ ***in alten Schläuchen*** new wine in old bottles; ~**(an)bau** *m* (-[e]s; *no pl.*) wine growing, *formal*: viniculture; ~**bau·er** *m* (-n; -n) wine grower; ~**bau·ge·biet** *n* wine-growing area

'**Wein·berg** *m* vineyard; ~**schnecke** *f zo.* snail; *gastr.* escargot

'**Wein·brand** *m* (-[e]s; ⸚e) brandy

wei·nen ['vaɪnən] *v/i. and v/t.* (h) cry, weep (***um*** *acc.* over); ~ ***nach*** *dat.* cry for *s.o.*; ***bittere Tränen*** ~ shed bitter tears; ***j-n zum*** 2 ***bringen*** make s.o. cry; ***es ist zum*** 2 it's enough to make you weep

wei·ner·lich ['vaɪnɐlɪç] *adj.* weepy; whining *child, voice etc.*

'**Wein|ern·te** *f* grape harvest; *w.s.* vintage; ~**es·sig** *m* wine vinegar; ~**faß** *n* wine cask; ~**fla·sche** *f* wine bottle; ~**gar·ten** *m* vineyard; ~**ge·gend** *f* wine-growing area; ~**geist** *m* (-[e]s; *no pl.*) ethyl alcohol; ~**glas** *n* wine glass; ~**gott** *m* god of wine; ***der*** ~ the god of wine, Bacchus, Dionysus; ~**gum·mi** *m, n* wine gum; ~**gut** *n* wine-growing estate, winery; ~**händ·ler** *m* wine merchant; ~**handlung** *f* wine shop (*Am.* store); ~**haus** *n* wine tavern

wei·nig ['vaɪnɪç] *adj.* vinous

'**Wein|jahr** *n*: ***ein gutes*** (***schlechtes***) ~ a good (bad) year for wine; ~**kar·te** *f* wine list; ~**kel·ler** *m* wine cellar; vaults *pl.*; ~**kel·leˌrei** *f* winery; ~**kell·ner** *m* wine waiter; ~**kel·ter** *f* wine press; ~**ken·ner** *m* wine connoisseur; ~**korb** *m* wine cradle

'**Wein·krampf** *m* crying fit; ***e-n*** ~ ***bekommen*** start sobbing (*or* weeping) uncontrollably, have a crying fit

'**Wein|lau·ne** *f*: ***in*** ~ after a few glasses of wine; ***sie sind in*** ~ they've been at the wine; ~**le·se** *f* grape harvest; ~**loˌkal** *n* wine bar (*or* tavern); ~**pres·se** *f* wine press; ~**pro·be** *f* wine tasting (session); ~**ran·ke** *f* vine tendril; ~**re·be** *f* (grape)-vine; 2**rot** *adj.* wine-red; ~**schor·le** *f* spritzer; 2**se·lig** *adj.* merry (with wine), *iro.* vinous; ~**stein** *m* tartar; ~**stock** *m* vine; ~**stu·be** *f* wine tavern; ~**trau·be** *f* bunch of grapes; ~**trin·ker** *m* wine drinker; ~**zwang** *m* (-[e]s; *no pl.*) obligation to order wine; wine obligatory; ***es herrscht*** ~ you have to order wine with your meal

wei·se ['vaɪzə] *adj.* wise; ***ein*** ~***s Wort*** a wise saying

Wei·se¹ ['vaɪzə] *f* (-; -n) **1.** way; ***auf diese*** ~ (in) this way; ***auf die e-e oder andere*** ~ one way or another; ***in der*** ~, ***daß*** in such a way that; ***in keiner*** ~ in no way; F ***in keinster*** ~! not at all!; ***in gewisser*** ~ in a way; ***jeder nach s-r*** ~ everyone after his own fashion; → *a.* **Art**; **2.** ♪ tune

'**Wei·se²** *m* (-n; -n) wise man, sage; ***die*** ~***n aus dem Morgenland*** the three Wise Men from the East, the Magi

wei·sen ['vaɪzən] (wies, gewiesen, h) **I.** *v/t.* **1.** ***j-m den Weg*** (*or* ***die Richtung***) ~ show s.o. the way; ***j-m die Tür*** ~ show s.o. the (way to the) door; **2.** ***aus dem Lande*** ~ banish, exile, send into exile; **3.** *fig.* ***von sich*** ~ reject; repudiate *suspicion etc.*; → **Hand**; **II.** *v/i.* **4.** ~ ***auf*** *acc.* a) point at, b) point to *s.th.*; ***nach Süden*** *etc.* ~ point south *etc.*; **5.** *fig.* ~ ***auf*** *acc.* point to(wards); (***mit dem Finger***) ~ ***auf*** *acc.* point to

Weis·heit ['vashaɪt] *f* (-; -en) **1.** *no pl.* wisdom; ***mit s-r*** ~ ***am Ende sein*** be at one's wits' end; ***das war nicht der*** ~ ***letzter Schluß*** that wasn't the cleverest solution (*or* thing to do); ***er hat die*** ~ ***nicht mit Löffeln gegessen*** he's not exactly an Einstein; → ***pachten***; **2.** wise saying, piece of wisdom

'**Weis·heits·zahn** *m* wisdom tooth

weis·ma·chen ['vaɪs-] *v/t.* (*sep.*, h): ***j-m*** ~, ***daß*** persuade s.o. that; ***willst du mir*** ~, ***daß ...?*** are you trying to tell me (that) ...?; ***mir kannst du nichts*** ~ you needn't (*or* no need to) try and fool me

weiß [vaɪs] *adj.* white; ~***es Blatt*** (***Papier***) blank sheet of paper; ~ ***machen*** whiten; ~ ***werden*** turn white; ~***er Fleck auf der Landkarte*** white spot on the map; ~ ***wie die Wand*** (as) white as a sheet; ***das Weiße vom Ei*** the white of an egg; ***das***

Weiße im Auge the whites of one's eyes; ***draußen ist es ~ geworden*** it's been snowing outside; ***du hast dich am Ärmel ~ gemacht*** you've got some white stuff on your sleeve; → ***Magie***
weis·sagen ['vaɪszaːgən] *v/t.* (h) prophesy, foretell; **Weis·sa·ger** ['vaɪszaːgɐ] *m* (-s; -) prophet; **Weis·sa·ge·rin** ['vaɪszaːgərɪn] *f* (-; -nen) prophetess; **Weis·sa·gung** ['vaɪszaːgʊŋ] *f* (-; -en) prophecy
'**Weiß·bier** *n* wheat beer, weissbier
'**weiß·blond** *adj.* ash-blonde
'**weiß·bluten** *v/refl.* (*only inf.*): ***sich ~*** bleed o.s. white; ***j-n bis zum ♀ ausnehmen*** bleed s.o. white; ***bis zum ♀ zahlen müssen*** be bled white
'**Weiß|brot** *n* white bread; **~buch** *n pol.* (government) white paper; **~bu·che** *f* white beech; **~dorn** *m* ♣ whitethorn
Wei·ße¹ ['vaɪsə] *f* (-; -n) **1.** whiteness; **2.** → ***Weißbier***
'**Wei·ße** *m, f* (-n; -n) white; white man (*f* woman); ***die ~n*** the whites
wei·ßen ['vaɪsən] *v/t.* (h) whiten; whitewash
'**Weiß·fisch** *m* whitefish
'**weiß·ge·klei·det** *adj.* dressed in white
'**weiß·glü·hend** *adj.* white-hot
'**Weiß·glut** *f* (-; *no pl.*) white heat (*a. fig.*); *fig.* ***j-n zur ~ bringen*** incense s.o., make s.o. livid (*or* wild with rage), F have s.o. fuming
'**Weiß·gold** *n* white gold
'**weiß·haa·rig** *adj.* white-haired
'**Weiß·herbst** *m* (-[e]s; -e) rosé (wine)
'**Weiß|kohl** *m*, **~kraut** *n* (-[e]s; *no pl.*) (white) cabbage
'**weiß·lich** *adj.* whitish
'**Weiß|ma·cher** *m* whitener; **~nä·he·rin** *f* plain seamstress; **~tan·ne** *f* silver fir; **~wal** *m* white whale, beluga; **~wand·rei·fen** *m mot.* whitewall tyre (*Am.* tire)
'**Weiß·wa·ren** *pl.* linen *sg.*
'**Weiß·wä·sche** *f* whites *pl.*; '**weiß·wa·schen** *fig. v/t.* (*irr., sep.*, h, → ***waschen***) whitewash (***sich*** o.s.)
'**Weiß|wein** *m* white wine; **~wurst** *f* veal sausage
Wei·sung ['vaɪzʊŋ] *f* (-; -en) directive, instructions *pl.*, orders *pl.*; ***ich habe ~ zu*** *inf.* I have been instructed to *inf.*
'**Wei·sungs·be·fug·nis** *f* authority to issue directives
'**wei·sungs|ge·bun·den** *adj.* subject to directives; **~ge·mäß** *adv.* as directed, according to instructions
weit [vaɪt] **I.** *adj.* a) wide; extensive; vast, immense, b) wide, loose *dress etc.*, c) long *way, distance etc.*, d) *fig.* broad *concept etc.*; ***von ~em*** from a distance; ***ich sah sie von ~em kommen*** I could see her coming in the distance; F ***man konnte s-e Fahne von ~em riechen*** F you could smell his breath a mile away; ***in ~en Abständen*** a) widely spaced, b) at long intervals; ***~er Blick über das Land*** commanding view of the countryside (*or* landscape); *fig.* ***~es Gewissen*** elastic conscience; ***ein ~es Herz haben*** have a big heart; ***~er Horizont*** broad outlook; ***im ~esten Sinne*** in the widest sense (of the word); ***~e Teile der Bevölkerung*** large parts of the population; → ***Feld, Kreis***; **II.** *adv.* a) far, wide(ly), b) *fig. with comp.* far *better etc.*; ***~ offen*** wide open; ***~ oben*** high up, *sport*: well-placed (*or* high up) in the table; ***e-e Meile ~ entfernt*** a mile away; ***~ entfernt*** far away; ***~ entfernt von*** *dat.* a long way from, *fig.* a far cry from; *fig.* ***~ davon entfernt zu*** *inf.* far from *ger.*, F not about to *inf.*; ***ich bin ~ davon entfernt, das zu tun!*** I've (absolutely) no intention of doing that; ***kein Mensch*** *etc.* ***~ und breit*** not a soul *etc.* to be seen (*or* as far as the eye could see); *fig.* ***~ und breit der beste*** *etc.* far and away the best *etc.*, the best *etc.* by far; ***~ über sechzig*** well over sixty; ***bei ~em*** far *better etc.*, by far (*or* far and away) *the best etc.*; ***bei ~em nicht so gut*** *etc.* not nearly as good *etc.*; ***~ gefehlt!*** far from it; ***~ gereist*** widely travel(l)ed, ***sein***: *a.* F have been around; ***es ist nicht ~ her mit*** *dat.* ***...*** ... isn't (aren't) up to much; ***~ vom Thema abkommen*** get right off the subject; ***~ nach Mitternacht*** long after midnight; ***das liegt ~ zurück*** that's a long way back, that was a long time ago; ***das Geld reicht nicht ~*** the money won't go far; ***es ~ bringen (im Leben)*** go far, 'go places; ***zu ~ gehen, es zu ~ treiben*** go too far, overshoot the mark; ***das geht zu ~*** that's going too far, F that's a bit much; ***ich bin so ~*** I'm ready; ***wie ~ bist du?*** how far have you got?; ***wenn es so ~ ist*** when the time comes; ***so ~ ist es nun gekommen?*** has it come to that?; ***es ist noch nicht so ~, daß*** things haven't yet come to the point where; ***er ist so ~ genesen, daß er ... kann*** he's recovered to the extent of being able to *inf.*; → ***Weite, weiter***
weit'ab *adv.* far away (***von*** *dat.* from)
'**weit·är·me·lig** [-ɛrməlɪç] *adj.* wide-sleeved
'**weit'aus** *adv.* far, much *better etc.*; ***die ~ schlimmsten*** *etc.* the worst *etc.* by far
'**weit·be·kannt** *adj.* widely-known ..., *pred.* widely known
'**Weit·blick** *m* (-[e]s; *no pl.*) farsightedness; '**weit·blickend** *adj.* farsighted
Wei·te¹ ['vaɪtə] *f* (-; -n) a) width; ⚙ diameter, b) distance, c) expanse; *fig.* range, scope; → ***licht***
'**Wei·te²** *n*: ***das ~ suchen*** take to one's heels, flee
wei·ten ['vaɪtən] *v/t. and v/refl.* (***sich ~***) (h) widen; open *one's eyes* wide; stretch *shoes*; *fig.* widen, broaden
wei·ter ['vaɪtɐ] *comp. adj. and adv.* a) wider, b) further, c) additional(ly *adv.*), further, d) on, forward, e) further(more), moreover; *ein Kleid* ***~ machen*** let out; ***~?*** and then?; ***~!*** go on!, carry on!; ***immer ~*** on and on; ***nichts ~*** nothing else, that's all; ***~ nichts?*** is that all?; ***wenn es ~ nichts ist*** if that's all (it is); ***was geschah ~?*** what happened then (*or* next)?; ***~ niemand*** no-one else; ***und so ~*** and so on; ***bis auf ~es*** for the time being, until further notice; ***ohne ~es*** without further ado, F just like that, easily; ***das hat ~ nichts zu sagen*** it's not significant, *w.s.* it's irrelevant; ***alles Weitere*** the rest, everything else
'**wei·ter·ar·bei·ten** *v/i.* (*sep.*, h) go (*or* carry) on working
'**wei·ter·be·för·dern** *v/t.* (*sep.*, h) forward, send on; redirect; '**Wei·ter·be·för·de·rung** *f* (-; *no pl.*) forwarding; redirecting
'**Wei·ter·be·hand·lung** *f*: (***zur ~*** for) further *or* continuation treatment
'**wei·ter·be·ste·hen I.** *v/i.* (*irr., sep.*, h, → ***bestehen***) continue (to exist); survive; **II.** ♀ *n* (-s; *no pl.*) continued existence; (continuing) survival
'**wei·ter·bil·den** (*sep.*, h) **I.** *v/t.* give *s.o.* further training; ***es bildet einen weiter*** it's all part of one's educational (*or* further) development; **II.** *v/refl.*: ***sich ~*** continue (*or* further) one's studies; do further training; ***sich in Geschichte*** *etc.* ~ further one's knowledge of history *etc.*; '**Wei·ter·bil·dung** *f* (-; *no pl.*) continuing education; further training; continuing process of education (*or* learning); ***berufliche ~*** *a.* extended vocational training
'**wei·ter·brin·gen** *v/t.* (*irr., sep.*, h, → ***bringen***) help; ***das bringt mich nicht weiter*** that's not much help to me
'**wei·ter·den·ken** *v/i.* (*irr., sep.*, h, → ***denken***) think (*or* look) ahead; ***e-n Schritt ~*** take it one step further
Wei·te·re ['vaɪtərə] *n* (-n; *no pl.*) → ***weiter***
'**wei·ter·emp·feh·len** *v/t.* (*irr., sep.*, h, → ***empfehlen***) recommend; ***kannst du's ~?*** can you pass the word on?
'**wei·ter·ent·wickeln** (*sep.*, h) **I.** *v/t.* develop *s.th.* (further); ⚙ *a.* refine; **II.** *v/refl.*: ***sich ~*** develop; ***er hat sich überhaupt nicht weiterentwickelt*** *a.* he hasn't made any progress at all; '**Wei·ter·ent·wick·lung** *f* **1.** a) further development, b) further stage; **2.** derivative
'**wei·ter·er·zäh·len** *v/t.* (*sep.*, h) pass *s.th.* on; ***nicht ~!*** don't tell anyone
'**wei·ter·fah·ren** *v/i.* (*irr., sep.*, sn, → ***fahren***) go on, drive on; '**Wei·ter·fahrt** *f* (-; *no pl.*): (***während der ~*** on the) second leg of the journey
'**wei·ter·flie·gen** *v/i.* (*irr., sep.*, sn, → ***fliegen***) go on, fly on (***nach*** *dat.* to); take off (for); '**Wei·ter·flug** *m* (-[e]s; *no pl.*) → ***Weiterfahrt***
'**wei·ter·füh·ren** *v/t. and v/i.* (*sep.*, h) continue; ***das führt (uns) nicht weiter*** that doesn't get us any further
'**Wei·ter·ga·be** *f* (-; *no pl.*) passing on; *biol.* transmission; '**wei·ter·ge·ben** *v/t.* (*irr., sep.*, h, → ***geben***) pass on; *biol.* transmit
'**wei·ter|ge·hen** *v/i.* (*irr., sep.*, sn, → ***gehen***) go (*or* walk, carry) on; *fig.* continue, go on; take *s.th.* further; ***~!*** move along(, please)!; ***das kann so nicht ~*** things can't go on like this; **~ge·hend** *adj.* further; greater, more far-reaching, broader *implications etc.*; larger *issue*; wider *cooperation, question etc.*
'**wei·ter·hel·fen** *v/i.* (*irr., sep.*, h, → ***helfen***) help *s.o.* (along); ***sich ~*** manage (somehow); ***das hat mir sehr weitergeholfen*** that was a great help; ***sich weiterzuhelfen wissen*** a) be able to look after o.s., b) know what one is doing
'**wei·ter'hin** *adv.* in (*or* for the) future; further(more); ***et. ~ tun*** continue doing (*or* to do) s.th., carry on with (*or* doing) s.th.
'**wei·ter|kämp·fen** *v/i.* (*sep.*, h) continue fighting; **~kom·men** *v/i.* (*irr., sep.*, sn, → ***kommen***) get on, get somewhere, make headway; *sport*: get through (to the next round); ***nicht ~*** F be stuck; ***wir kommen überhaupt nicht weiter*** we're not getting anywhere; **~lau·fen** *v/i.* (*irr., sep.*, sn, → ***laufen***) a) run on, carry on running, b) *fig. business, production etc.*: continue; *contract*: remain valid; *salary etc.*: continue to be paid; ***~ bis*** *contract etc.*: run on until; **~le·ben** *v/i.* (*sep.*, h)

live on, survive (*both a. fig.*); **~lei·ten** *v/t.* (*sep.*, h) pass *s.th.* on; forward *letter etc.*; ***j-n an j-n*** ~ put s.o. onto s.o.; **~le·sen** *v/i. and v/t.* (*irr., sep.*, h, → ***lesen***) go on (reading), carry on reading, continue to read (*or* reading); **~ma·chen** *v/t. and v/i.* (*sep.*, h) carry (*or* go) on, continue; ***genauso*** ~ carry on as before; ***mach nur so weiter!*** keep it up!, *iro.* see where that gets you

'**Wei·ter·rei·se** *f* (-; *no pl.*) continuation (*or* second leg) of the journey; ***auf der*** ~ as we *etc.* continued our *etc.* journey

'**wei·ter|sa·gen** *v/t.* (*sep.*, h) pass *s.th.* on; ***nicht*** ~! don't tell anyone, F keep that under your hat; **~schicken** *v/t.* (*sep.*, h) forward, send *s.o. or s.th.* on; redirect; **~schla·fen** *v/i.* (*irr., sep.*, h, → ***schlafen***) a) sleep on, not to wake up, b) go back to sleep; ***er schlief bis 9 Uhr weiter*** he slept on till 9 o'clock; **~se·hen** *v/i.* (*irr., sep.*, h, → ***sehen***): *warten wir, bis er da ist,* ***dann werden wir*** ~ then we'll see what happens, and we'll take it from there; **~strei·ken** *v/i.* (*sep.*, h) stay on strike

'**wei·ter·ver·ar·bei·ten** *v/t.* (*sep.*, h) process; '**Wei·ter·ver·ar·bei·tung** *f* (-; *no pl.*) processing

'**wei·ter|ver·äu·ßern** *v/t.* (*sep.*, h) resell; **~ver·bin·den** *v/t.* (*irr., sep.*, h, → ***verbinden***) *teleph.* put *s.o.* through (***an*** *acc.* to); **~ver·brei·ten** *v/t.* (*sep.*, h) spread; **~ver·fol·gen** *v/t.* (*sep.*, h) follow up

'**Wei·ter·ver·kauf** *m* (-[e]s; *no pl.*) resale; '**wei·ter·ver·kau·fen** *v/t.* (*sep.*, h) resell

'**wei·ter|ver·mie·ten** *v/t.* (*sep.*, h) sublet; **~wis·sen** *v/i.* (*irr., sep.*, h, → ***wissen***): ***nicht*** ~ a) be stuck *during an exam*, b) be at one's wits' end; ***ich wußte nicht mehr weiter*** *a.* I didn't know what to do; **~wol·len** *v/i.* (*sep.*, h) want to go on; **~wur·steln** F *v/i.* (*sep.*, h) muddle on

wei·test·ge·hend ['vaɪtəst-] *adv.* as far as possible

'**weit|ge·dehnt** *adj.* extensive; **~ge·hend** **I.** *adj.* extensive, far-reaching; wide *support*; **II.** *adv.* to a great extent; largely; **~ge·reist** *adj.* widely-travel(l)ed; **~gespannt** *fig. adj.* broad *expectations etc.*; ***~er Bogen*** broad spectrum; **~ge·steckt** *adj.* long-range, long-term; **~grei·fend** *adj.* far-reaching

weit'her *adv.* from afar

weit'her·ge·holt *adj.*: (***ziemlich*** ~ a bit) far-fetched

'**weit·her·zig** *adj.* broadminded

'**weit'hin** *adv.* far; *fig.* to a large extent

'**weit·läu·fig** [-lɔʏfɪç] **I.** *adj.* **1.** extensive, vast; *a.* rambling *house, garden etc.*; spacious; **2.** distant *relative*; **3.** detailed, *contp.* longwinded; **II.** *adv.* **4.** at great length; **5.** ~ ***verwandt*** distantly related

'**weit·ma·schig** [-maʃɪç] *adj.* wide-meshed

'**weit·räu·mig** [-rɔʏmɪç] *adj.* spacious

'**weit·rei·chend** *adj.* far-reaching; wide-ranging; ⚔ long-range ...

'**Weit·schuß** *m sport*: long-range shot

'**weit·schwei·fig** [-ʃvaɪfɪç] *adj.* longwinded

'**Weit·sicht** *f* (-; *no pl.*) farsightedness; vision; '**weit·sich·tig** [-zɪçtɪç] *adj.* longsighted, *a. fig.* farsighted

'**Weit·sprin·gen** *n* (-s; *no pl.*) long (*Am.* brod) jump; '**Weit·sprin·ger** *m* long-jumper, *Am.* broadjumper; '**Weitsprung** *m* (-[e]s; *no pl.*) → ***Weitspringen***

'**weit·tra·gend** *adj.* ⚔ long-range; *fig.* far-reaching; wide-ranging *consequences etc.*

Wei·tung ['vaɪtʊŋ] *f* (-; -en) widening

'**weit|ver·brei·tet** *adj.* widespread; *a.* widely held *view etc.*; widely read *newspaper etc.*; ***~er Irrtum*** *a.* popular fallacy; **~ver·zweigt** *adj.* intricate, complex

'**Weit·win·kel·ob·jek,tiv** *n* wide-angle lens

Wei·zen ['vaɪtsən] *m* (-s; *no pl.*) wheat; → ***Spreu***; **~bier** *n* wheat beer, weissbier; **~brot** *n* wheat bread; **~keim** *m a. pl.* wheatgerm; **~keim·öl** *n* wheatgerm oil; **~kleie** *f* wheat bran; **~mehl** *n* wheat flour

welch [vɛlç] **I.** *interr. pron.* what?; which?; ***~er?*** which one?; ***~er von den beiden?*** which of the two?; **II.** *rel. pron.* a) who, b) which, that; **III.** *indef. pron.* some, any; *haben Sie Geld?* - ***ja, ich habe ~es*** yes, I have (*or* I've got) some; ***brauchen Sie ~es?*** do you need any?; ***es gibt ~e, die sagen*** there are some who say, some people say; ***~er (auch) immer*** whoever; ***~es (auch) immer*** whichever

wel·cher·lei ['vɛlçɐlaɪ] *adj.* whatever; ***es ist egal, ~ ...*** it doesn't matter what (sort of) ...

welk [vɛlk] *adj.* wilted *flower*, *a.* withered *leaf*; wrinkled *skin*; shrivel(l)ed

wel·ken ['vɛlkən] *v/i.* (sn) *flower*: wilt, *a. leaf*: wither; *skin*: shrivel

Well·blech ['vɛl-] *n* corrugated iron; **~ba,racke** *f* corrugated-iron hut; Nissen (*Am.* Quonset) hut

Wel·le ['vɛlə] *f* (-; -n) a) wave (*a. phys., radio,* ⚡ *etc., a. in hair*), *fig. a.* surge; ripple, b) ⚙ shaft, c) *gym.* circle, d) *fig.* craze; *mot.* ***grüne*** (*or* ***rote***) ~ phased (*or* linked) traffic lights; ***wir haben grüne (rote)*** ~ we've caught the green (red) phase; *fig.* ***~n schlagen*** have reverberations, cause quite a stir; ***die Stimmung schlug hohe ~n*** spirits were high

wel·len ['vɛlən] (h) **I.** *v/t.* wave *hair*; **II.** *v/refl.*: ***sich*** ~ a) *hair*: be wavy, go wavy, b) *terrain*: undulate

'**Wel·len|bad** *n* wave pool; **~band** *n*, **~bereich** *m radio*: wave band; **~bre·cher** *m* breakwater

'**wel·len·för·mig** [-fœrmɪç] *adj.* wavy

'**Wel·len|gang** *m* (-[e]s; *no pl.*) waves *pl.*; ***starker*** ~ heavy seas; **~kamm** *m* crest (of a *or* the wave); **~län·ge** *f radio etc.*: wavelength; *fig.* ***die gleiche ~ haben*** be on the same wavelength; **~li·nie** *f* wavy line; **~rei·ten** *n* surfing; **~rei·ter** *m* surfer; **~sa,lat** F *fig. m* jumbled reception, (strong) interference; **~schlag** *m* breaking (*or* lapping) of (the) waves; **~schliff** *m*: ***Messer mit*** ~ serrated knife; **~sittich** *m* budgerigar, F budgie; **~tal** *n* trough

wel·lig ['vɛlɪç] *adj.* a) wavy *hair*, b) undulating *terrain*

Well·pap·pe ['vɛl-] *f* corrugated cardboard

Wel·pe ['vɛlpə] *m* (-n; -n) pup(py); cub *of wolf, fox*

Welt [vɛlt] *f* (-; -en ['vɛltən]) world (*a. fig.*); ***alle*** ~ everybody; ***aus der ganzen*** ~ from all over (*or* from all four corners of) the world; ***die ~ kennenlernen*** see the world; ***in der ~ herumkommen*** get around; ***die Dritte*** ~ the Third World; ***auf der*** ~ in the world; ***am Ende der*** ~ *live* F at the back of beyond, out in the sticks, *Am. a.* F in the boondocks; → ***Arsch***; ***was (wo*** *etc.*) ***in aller ~ ...?*** what (where *etc.*) on earth ...?; ***nicht um alles in der ~!*** not on your life!; ***allein auf der ~ sein*** be all alone in the world; ***von aller ~ verlassen*** completely forlorn; ***vor aller*** ~ for all the world to see; ***aus der ~ schaffen*** get rid of, settle *problem, quarrel etc.*; ***das ist nicht aus der*** ~ it isn't 'that far away; ***mit sich und der ~ zufrieden sein*** be at one with the world; ***auf die ~ kommen*** be born; *Kinder* ***in die ~ setzen*** bring into the world, *iro.* sire; ***zur ~ bringen*** give birth to; ***er war damals noch gar nicht auf der*** ~ he wasn't even born at that time; ***~en trennen sie*** they're worlds apart; ***e-e ~ für sich*** a world apart (*or* of its own); ***er lebt in e-r anderen*** ~ he lives in a dream world; ***ihre Familie ist ihre ganze*** ~ her family is all the world to her; ***für sie brach e-e ~ zusammen*** the bottom fell out of her world; ***das ist der Lauf der*** ~ that's the way of the world; ***die ~ erobern*** take the world by storm; ***es kostet doch nicht die*** ~ it won't cost the earth; F ***das hat die ~ noch nicht gesehen*** you've never seen the likes of it

'**welt·ab·ge·wandt** *adj.* withdrawn, seclusive

'**Welt|all** *n* universe; **~an·schau·ung** *f* philosophy (of life), outlook on life; ideology; **~aus·stel·lung** *f* world fair, world exposition

'**welt|be·kannt, ~be·rühmt** *adj.* world-famous, world-renowned, famous the world over

'**Welt·best·lei·stung** *f* world best (performance)

'**welt·be·we·gend** *adj.* earth-shattering, seismic *events etc.*; *iro.* ***nichts Weltbewegendes*** F nothing to write home about, no great shakes

'**Welt|bild** *n* (-[e]s; *no pl.*) world view; **~büh·ne** *f* world stage; **~bür·ger** *m* cosmopolitan; **~bür·ger·tum** *n* cosmopolitanism; **~eli·te** *f* world class; **~emp·fän·ger** *m* short-wave receiver

Wel·ten·bumm·ler ['vɛltən-] *m* globetrotter

'**Welt|en·de** *n* end of the world; **~er·eig·nis** *n* event of worldwide importance; earth-shaking event; **≈er·fah·ren** *adj.* worldly-wise; **~er·folg** *m* worldwide success (F hit)

Wel·ter·ge·wicht ['vɛltɐ-] *n* (-[e]s; *no pl.*), '**Wel·ter·ge·wicht·ler** [-gəvɪçtlɐ] *m* (-s; -) *boxing*: welterweight

'**welt·er·schüt·ternd** *adj.* earth-shaking, seismic *events etc.*

'**Welt·flucht** *f* (-; *no pl.*) escapism

'**welt·fremd** *adj.* out-of-touch ..., *pred.* out of touch; inexperienced, naive; unrealistic; starry-eyed; ivory-tower *scientist etc.*

'**Welt|frie·de(n)** *m* world peace; **~geltung** *f* international standing; *an* international reputation; **~ge·richt** *n* (-[e]s; *no pl.*) *eccl. the* Last Judg(e)ment; **~ge·sche·hen** *n*: ***das*** ~ world affairs; **~ge·schich·te** *f* (-; *no pl.*) **1.** ***die*** ~ world history; the history of the world; F ***in der ~ herumreisen*** F travel all over the place; **2.** history of the world, world history; **~ge·sund·heits·tag** *m* World Health Day; **≈ge·wandt** *adj.* urbane; **~han·del** *m* international trade; **~han·dels·ab·kom·men** *n* international trade agreement; **~herr·schaft** *f* (-; *no pl.*) world domination; **~jah·res·best·lei·stung** *f* best performance in the world this year; **~kar·te** *f* map of the world; **~kennt·nis** *f* (-; *no pl.*) knowledge of the world; **~klas·se** *f sport*: world class; **~klas·se·spie·ler** *m* world class player; **~krieg** *m* world war; ***der erste*** (***zweite***) ~ World War I (II), the First (Second) World War; **~la·ge** *f* (-; *no pl.*) world-wide political situation

'welt·lich I. *adj.* worldly, mundane; *eccl.* secular; ***~e Freuden*** worldly (*or* earthly) pleasures; **II.** *adv.*: ~ ***gesinnt*** worldly(-minded)

'Welt|li·te·ra͵tur *f* world literature; **~macht** *f* superpower, world power

'welt·män·nisch [-mɛnɪʃ] *adj.* man-of--the-world *air etc.*

'Welt|mar·ke *f* ✝ world-famous brand; **~markt** *m* world market; **~mei·ster** *m* world champion; **~mei·ster·schaft** *f* world championship(s *pl.*); *soccer*: World Cup; **~mei·ster·schafts...** *in cpds.* → ***WM-...***; **~ni͵veau** *n* international standing

'welt·of·fen *adj.* open-minded; outward--looking; **'Welt·of·fen·heit** *f* (-; *no pl.*) cosmopolitanism, cosmopolitan outlook

'Welt|öf·fent·lich·keit *f*: ***die*** ~ the world public, the world at large; *w.s.* world opinion; **~po·li͵tik** *f* international politics *pl.*; **~pre͵mie·re** *f* world première; **~pres·se** *f* international press; **~rang·li·ste** *f* world rankings *pl.*; **~rang·li·sten·er·ste** *m, f* (-n; -n) *the* world's number one tennis player *etc.*

'Welt·raum *m* (-[e]s; *no pl.*) (outer) space

'Welt·raum... *in cpds. usu.* space; *a.* spaceborn *satellite etc.*; **~la͵bor** *n* spacelab; **~spa͵zier·gang** *m* spacewalk; **~staub** *m* space dust; **~te·le͵skop** *n* space telescope; **~waf·fen** *pl.* space weapons; **~wett·ren·nen** *n* space race; **~zen·trum** *n* space cent|er (*Brit.* -re)

'Welt|reich *n* (world) empire; **~rei·se** *f* world trip, trip around the world; **~rei·sen·de** *m, f* (-n; -n) globetrotter

'Welt·re͵kord *m* world record

'Welt·re͵kord·in·ha·ber *m*, **'Welt·re·kord·ler** [-re͵kɔrtlɐ] *m* (-s; -), **'Welt·re·kord·le·rin** [-re͵kɔrtlərɪn] *f* (-; -nen) world-record holder

'Welt|re·li·gi͵on *f* world religion; **~ruhm** *m* worldwide fame; **~schmerz** *m* world--weariness, weltschmerz; **~sen·sa·ti͵on** *f* world sensation; **~si·cher·heits·rat** *m* Security Council; **~spra·che** *f* universal language

'Welt·stadt *f* metropolis; **'Welt·stadt...** *in cpds.* cosmopolitan; **'welt·städ·tisch** *adj.* cosmopolitan

'Welt|star *m* world star, international star; **~um͵seg·lung** *f* circumnavigation of the globe; **~͵un·ter·gang** *m* end of the world; **~͵un·ter·gangs·stim·mung** *f* atmosphere of gloom and doom, black mood (of despair); **~ur·auf·füh·rung** *f* world première; **~ver·bes·se·rer** [-fɛɐbɛsərɐ] *m* (-s; -) do-gooder; **~wäh·rungs·fonds** *m* International Monetary Fund, IMF; **2weit** *adj.* worldwide; global; → ***Echo***; **~wirt·schaft** *f* world economy; **~wirt·schafts·gip·fel** *m* world economic summit; **~wirt·schafts·kri·se** *f* worldwide economic crisis; **~wun·der** *n*: ***die sieben*** ~ the Seven Wonders of the World; **~zeit** *f* Greenwich Mean Time, GMT

wem [veːm] *rel. pron.* (*dat. of wer*) (to) whom; ***von*** ~ of whom, by whom

wen [veːn] *rel. pron.* (*acc. of wer*) who(m); F somebody

Wen·de ['vɛndə] *f* (-; -n) **1.** *no pl.* a) turning point; turn *of the century*, b) change (***zum Schlechten*** *etc.* for the worse *etc.*); *pol. hist.* ***die*** ~ the fall of Communism (in Eastern Europe), *n.s.* the breaching (*or* opening) of the Wall; ***vor der*** ~ *a.* before the Wall came down; **2.** *sport*: turn; *gym.* front vault; **~hals** *m* **1.** (political) turncoat; *hum.* F quick--change artist; **2.** *zo.* wryneck; **~jacke** *f* reversible jacket; **~kreis** *m* **1.** *geogr.* tropic; **2.** *mot.* (***enger*** ~ tight) turning circle

Wen·del ['vɛndəl] *f* (-; -n) ⚙ spiral; **~trep·pe** *f* winding (*or* spiral) staircase

'Wen·de|ma͵nö·ver *n* turning manoeuvre (*Am.* maneuver); *a.* three-point turn; *fig.* U-turn; ***schwieriges*** ~ tricky manoeuvring (*Am.* maneuvering); **~mar·ke** *f sport*: turning mark

wen·den ['vɛndən] (wendete *or* wandte ['vantə[, gewendet *or* gewandt, h) **I.** *v/t.* **1.** (*only* wendete) turn; turn over *page, roast etc.*; *mot.* turn (round); **2.** ~ ***an*** *acc.* spend *time, money* on; devote *pains etc.* to; ***keinen Blick*** ~ ***von*** *dat.* not to take one's eyes off; → ***drehen*** 1; **II.** *v/i.* (*only* wendete) turn (round); *mot. a.* make a U-turn; ***bitte ~!*** PTO, pto (= please turn over); **III.** *v/refl.*: ***sich*** ~ turn (round); *fig.* ***sich*** ~ ***an*** *acc.* ask *s.o.* (***um*** *acc.* for *s.th.*), turn to *s.o.* (for *help, advice etc.*); *book etc.*: be directed at *beginners etc.*; ***sich*** ~ ***gegen*** *acc.* turn against (*or* on) *s.o.*, oppose, object to *s.th.*; ***sich zum Gehen*** ~ turn to leave; ***sich zum Guten*** (***Schlechten***) ~ take a turn for the better (worse)

'Wen·de|platz *m* turning space; **~punkt** *m* **1.** turning point, watershed; **2.** *ast.* solstice

wen·dig ['vɛndɪç] *adj.* nimble, agile, *a.* nimble-minded; *mot.* manoeuvrable, *Am.* maneuverable; **'Wen·dig·keit** *f* (-; *no pl.*) nimbleness, agility; nimble-mindedness; *mot.* manoeuvrability, *Am.* maneuverability

Wen·dung ['vɛndʊŋ] *f* (-; -en) **1.** a) turn, b) *fig.* change; ***e-e unerwartete*** ~ ***nehmen*** take an unexpected turn; ***e-r Sache e-e neue*** ~ ***geben*** give a new turn to s.th.; ***günstige*** (***unerwartete***) ~ favo(u)rable (unexpected) turn of events; **2.** expression, figure of speech

we·nig ['veːnɪç] *adj. and adv.* little, not much; ***~e*** few, not many, *su.* few (people); ***~er*** less, ℞ minus; *pl.* fewer; ***das ~ste*** the least; ***am ~sten*** (the) least (of all); ***ein*** ~ a little; ***ein*** ~ ***übertrieben*** slightly exaggerated; ***ein*** ~ ***schneller*** a bit quicker; ***immer ~er*** less and less; ***das ~e Geld, das er hat*** what little money he has; ~ ***beliebt*** not very popular; ***nicht*** ~ quite a lot; ***nicht*** ~ ***erstaunt*** rather surprised; ***nicht ~e*** quite a few (people); ***einige ~e*** a few; ***nicht ~er als*** no less than, *pl.* no fewer than; ***~er werden*** decrease; ~ ***bekannt*** little known; ***in ~en Tagen*** in a few days' time; ***mit ~en Worten*** in a few words; ***das ist*** ~ that's not much; ***dazu gehört*** ~ it doesn't take much; ***das hilft mir*** ~ that's not much help to me; ***das stört mich*** ~ it doesn't really bother me; ***e-e*** ~ ***glückliche Wahl*** a rather unfortunate choice; ***danach fragt er*** ~ it doesn't seem to interest him much; ***ein*** ~ ***gelesener Autor*** a little read author; ***das kostet,*** ~ ***gerechnet, tausend Mark*** at a low estimate it will cost a thousand marks; ***wir haben uns in letzter Zeit*** ~ ***gesehen*** we haven't seen much of each other lately; ***das macht*** ~ ***Freude*** it isn't much fun; ***das hat*** ~ ***Sinn*** there's not much point in it; ***mit mehr oder ~er Erfolg*** more or less successfully; ***mit ~em auskommen*** get by on very little; ***das wissen die ~sten*** people just don't realize that; ***~er wäre mehr gewesen*** you can overdo things; ***das ist das ~ste*** that's the least of my worries; ***je ~er davon wissen, desto besser*** we don't want everybody to know about it; F ***sie wird immer ~er*** she'll disappear completely one of these days

'We·nig·keit *f* (-; *no pl.*) small quantity; trifle; F ***meine*** ~ F yours truly

we·nig·stens ['veːnɪçstəns] *adv.* at least; ***wenn ...*** ~ if only ...

wenn [vɛn] *cj.* a) when, whenever, b) if; ⚖ *often* if and when; provided (that), c) as soon as; ~ ***auch, selbst*** ~ even if; ~ ***auch noch so klein*** *etc.* however small *etc.*; ~ ***doch*** (*or* ***nur***) if only; ***außer*** ~ unless, except if; ***immer*** ~ whenever; ~ ***er nicht gewesen wäre*** if it hadn't been for him; ~ ***ich das gewußt hätte*** if I had known (that), had I known (that); ~ ***das so ist*** if that's the case; ~ ***man ihn so reden hört*** to hear him talk; ***und*** ~ ***du noch so sehr bittest*** you can plead as much as you like; ~ ***nicht heute, so doch morgen*** if not today then tomorrow; ~ ***ich das wüßte*** I wish I knew; ~ ***ich einmal groß bin*** when I grow up; ~ ***man bedenkt, daß*** when you think that; ~ ***du das sagst, wird's wohl stimmen*** if you say so; ~ ***es schon sein muß, dann gleich*** if it's got to be done let's get it over and done with; ~ ***nichts dazwischenkommt*** unless something crops up; ~ ***nicht, dann eben nicht*** well, we may as well forget about that; ~ ***das Wörtchen*** ~ ***nicht wär' ...*** if!; ~ ***du erst einmal dort bist*** once you're there; ~ ***man nach ... urteilt*** judging by ...; ~ ***schon!*** so what; ***es war ein neuer,*** ~ ***auch langsamer Versuch*** it was a new, albeit (*or* if) slow, attempt; → ***schon*** 1, 7, 8

Wenn *n*: ***ohne*** ~ ***und Aber*** a) unconditionally, b) no ifs or buts!

wenn'gleich *cj.* although, even though

wer [veːɐ] **I.** *rel. pron.* who; **II.** *interr. pron.* who?; which (one)?; ~ ***von euch?*** which of you?; ⚔ ~ ***da?*** who goes there?; **III.** *indef. pron.* F someone, somebody; *in questions*: *usu.* anyone, anybody; ~ ***auch*** (***immer***) whoever; ~ ***mitkommen möchte,*** *soll sich eintragen*: whoever wants to come, anyone who wants (*or* wishes) to come

Wer·be|ab͵tei·lung ['vɛrbə-] *f* publicity department; **~agen͵tur** *f* advertising agency; **~ak·ti͵on** *f* → ***Werbekampagne***; **~an·ge·bot** *n* special (*or* introductory) offer; **~ant·wort** *f* business reply; **~ar͵ti·kel** *m* promotional article; **~be·ra·ter** *m* advertising consultant; **~ein·nah·men** *pl.* advertising revenue *sg.*; **~fach·mann** *m* advertising expert;

⁓fern·se·hen *n* a) commercial television, b) television (*or* TV) commercials *pl.*; **⁓film** *m* publicity film; **⁓flä·che** *f* advertising space; **⁓fo·to͵graf** *m* commercial photographer; **⁓funk** *m* a) commercial radio (*or* broadcasting), b) radio ads *pl.*, radio commercials *pl.*; **⁓gag** *m* sales gimmick; **⁓ge·schenk** *n* promotional (*or* free) gift; **⁓gra·phik** *f* commercial art; **⁓gra·phi·ker** *m* commercial artist; **⁓idee** *f* publicity idea; **⁓kam͵pa·gne** *f* publicity (*or* advertising) campaign; ; **⁓ko·sten** *pl.* advertising expenditure *sg.*; **⁓kräf·tig** *adj.* → ***werbewirksam***; **⁓lei·ter** *m* publicity manager; **⁓ma·te·ri͵al** *n* promotional material; **⁓mit·tel** *pl.* **1.** advertising media; **2.** promotion allowance *sg.*

wer·ben ['vɛrbən] (warb, geworben, h) **I.** *v/t.* enlist *members etc.*; attract *customers etc.*; ***j-n für et.*** ⁓ win s.o. over to s.th.; **II.** *v/i. pol.* campaign; ✝ advertise; ⁓ ***für*** *acc. a.* promote, F plug *s.th.*; ⁓ ***um*** *acc.* court

Wer·be|pla͵kat ['vɛrbə-] *n* advertisement, advertising poster; **⁓pro͵spekt** *m* advertising (*or* publicity) brochure

Wer·ber ['vɛrbɐ] *m* (-s; -) ✝ canvasser; ⚔ recruiting officer

Wer·be|rum·mel ['vɛrbə-] F *m* hype; **⁓sen·dung** *f* **1.** commercial program(me); **2.** *a. pl.* advertising mail; **⁓slo·gan** *m* advertising slogan; **⁓spot** *m* commercial; **⁓text** *m* advertising slogan; copy; **⁓tex·ter** *m* copywriter; **⁓trä·ger** *m* advertising media; **⁓trick** *m* sales gimmick; publicity stunt; **⁓trom·mel** *f*: *fig.* ***die ⁓ für et. rühren*** promote (F plug) s.th., beat the drum for s.th.; **⁓ver·an·stal·tung** *f* publicity event

wer·be·wirk·sam ['vɛrbə-] *adj.*: ⁓ ***sein*** have commercial (*or* advertising) appeal

Wer·be·zet·tel ['vɛrbə-] *m* (advertising) leaflet

Wer·bung ['vɛrbʊŋ] *f* (-; *no pl.*) advertising; publicity; *fig.* ***e-e*** (***gute***) ⁓ ***für*** *acc.* good publicity for

'Wer·bungs·ko·sten *pl.* professional outlay *sg.*

Wer·de·gang ['veːɐdə-] *m* (-[e]s; *no pl.*) development; history (*a. fig. and* ⚙); personal background

wer·den ['veːɐdən] (wurde, geworden, sn) **I.** *v/i.* get, become; go (*bald, mad, sour etc.*); ***alt*** ⁓ get (*or* grow) old; ***besser*** ⁓ get better, improve; ***blaß*** ⁓ go (*or* turn) pale; ***blind*** ⁓ go blind; ***böse*** ⁓ get angry; ***dick*** ⁓ get fat, put on weight; ***dunkel*** ⁓ get (*lit.* grow) dark; ***gesund*** ⁓ get well; ***grau*** ⁓ go (*or* turn) grey (*Am.* gray); ***kahl*** ⁓ go bald; ***kalt*** ⁓ get cold, *food*: cool off; ***krank*** ⁓ fall *or* get ill (*or* sick); ***müde*** ⁓ get tired; ***naß*** ⁓ get wet; ***reich*** ⁓ get rich; ***rot*** ⁓ go red, blush; ***sauer*** ⁓ go (*or* turn) sour; ***schlecht*** ⁓ go bad (*or* off); ***schlimmer*** ⁓ get worse; ***schwach*** ⁓ get (*or* grow) weak; ***taub*** ⁓ go deaf; ***verrückt*** ⁓ go mad; ***warm*** ⁓ get warm, warm up; ***wütend*** ⁓ get angry (*or* mad); ***katholisch*** ⁓ become a Catholic, turn Catholic; ***es wird Winter*** winter is on its way; ***mir wird kalt*** I'm beginning to feel (*or* get) chilly; ***mir wird schlecht*** I feel sick; ***er ist Erster geworden*** he was (*or* came) first; ***die Vorräte ⁓ immer weniger*** supplies are getting lower and lower; ***was soll nun ⁓?*** what are we going to do now?; ***ich weiß nicht, was ⁓ soll*** I don't know what to do; ***wie wird die Ernte ⁓?*** what kind of harvest are we going to have?; ***aus dem Geschäft ist nichts geworden*** nothing came of the deal; ***was ist aus ihm geworden?*** what's become of him?; ***was will er ⁓?*** what does he want to be?; ***daraus wird nichts*** you can forget about that; ***es wird schon*** ⁓ it'll be all right (*Am.* alright); ***wie sind die Fotos geworden?*** how have the photos turned out?; ***morgen wird es ein Jahr, daß*** tomorrow it'll be a year ago that; ***die Sache wird allmählich*** things are coming along (*or* are beginning to take shape); → ***spät*** I; **II.** *v/aux.*: ***ich werde fahren*** I will (*or* I'll) drive; ***sie wird gleich weinen*** she's going to cry (any minute); ***es wurde getanzt*** they (*or* we) danced, there was dancing; ***ich würde kommen, wenn ...*** I would (*or* I'd) come if ...; ***es wird ihm doch nichts passiert sein?*** I hope nothing has happened to him; ***es wird schon so sein*** (***wie du sagst***) I'm sure you're right; ***ich werde es verloren haben*** I must have lost it; ***jetzt wird aber geschlafen*** (***gearbeitet***)! it's time to sleep (to get down to work), it's time you *or* we went to sleep (got down to work); ***es ist uns gesagt worden*** we've been told; ***geliebt*** ⁓ be loved; ***gebaut*** ⁓ be built, be being built; ***es wird viel gebaut*** there's a lot of building going on; **III.** ♀ *n* (-s; *no pl.*) a) development, growth, progress, b) birth; ***im ⁓ sein*** be in the making; **'wer·dend** *adj.* growing; ***⁓e Mutter*** expectant mother

wer·fen ['vɛrfən] (warf, geworfen, h) **I.** *v/t.* throw (***nach*** *dat.* at; ***zu*** *dat.* to); ✈ drop *bombs*; ***e-e Sechs*** ⁓ throw a six; ***nicht ⁓!*** handle with care; ***ein sehr helles Licht*** ⁓ *lamp*: cast a very bright light; ***Bilder an die Wand*** ⁓ project pictures on (*or* against) the wall; ***Truppen an die Front*** ⁓ dispatch troops to the front; ***Waren auf den Markt*** ⁓ throw goods on the market; ***e-e Skizze aufs Papier*** ⁓ do a quick sketch; ***einige Zeilen aufs Papier*** ⁓ jot down a few lines; ***den Feind aus e-r Stellung*** ⁓ dislodge the enemy; ***et. in die Diskussion*** ⁓ throw s.th. up for discussion; ***von sich*** ⁓ throw off *coat etc.*; → ***Blick*** 1, ***Handtuch, Haufen, Junge²***, ***Schatten***; **II.** *v/i.* throw; ***mit et.*** (***nach j-m***) ⁓ throw s.th. (at s.o.); ***um sich ⁓ mit*** *dat.* throw *one's money* about, bandy about *names etc.*; **III.** *v/refl.*: ***sich*** ⁓ ⚙ buckle, *wood*: warp; ***sich in den Sessel*** ⁓ throw o.s. onto (*or* flop down into) the armchair; ***sich aufs Pferd*** ⁓ leap (*or* jump) into the saddle; ***sich auf j-n*** ⁓ throw o.s. at s.o., dive for s.o.; *fig.* ***sich in s-e Kleider*** ⁓ throw on (*or* jump into) one's clothes; ***sich ⁓ auf*** *acc.* throw o.s. into *painting etc.*; → ***Brust*** 1, ***Hals***

Werft [vɛrft] *f* (-; -en) shipyard; ✈ hangar; **⁓ar·bei·ter** *m* docker

Werg [vɛrk] *n* (-[e]s; *no pl.*) tow; oakum

Werk [vɛrk] *n* (-[e]s; -e) **1.** a) work, b) works *pl.*, c) deed, act; ***gute ⁓e*** good deeds; ***ans ⁓!*** let's get going!; ***am ⁓ sein*** *a. iro.* be at work; ***ans ⁓ gehen*** set to work; ***ein gutes ⁓ tun*** do a good deed; ***es war sein*** ⁓ it was his work (*or* doing); ***behutsam*** (***geschickt***) ***zu ⁓e gehen*** go about it carefully (skil[l]fully); **2.** a) ⚙ works *pl.*, plant, b) company; ***ab*** ⁓ ex works; **3.** works *pl.*, mechanism

'Werk·bank *f* (-; ⸚e) workbench

wer·keln ['vɛrkəln] *v/i.* (h) potter about (***an*** *dat.* with)

wer·ken ['vɛrkən] (h) **I.** *v/i.* a) work; be busy, b) tinker; *ped.* do handicrafts; **II.** ♀ *n* (-s; *no pl.*) arts and crafts *pl.*

Wer·ke·ver·zeich·nis ['vɛrkə-] *n* catalog(ue) of works

'werk·ge·treu *adj. art*: faithful

'Werk|mei·ster *m* foreman; **⁓num·mer** *f* factory serial number; **⁓raum·thea·ter** *n* theat|re (*Am.* -er) workshop

Werks|an·ge·hö·ri·ge [vɛrks-] *m, f* (-n; -n) (works) employee; **⁓arzt** *m* works (*or* company) doctor

'Werk·schutz *m* factory security officers *pl.*

werks·ei·gen ['vɛrks-] *adj.* company ..., company-owned, works ...

Werks|ga·ran͵tie ['vɛrks-] *f* factory warranty; **⁓ge·län·de** *n* works premises; **⁓kan͵ti·ne** *f* works canteen; cafeteria; **⁓lei·ter** *m* works (*or* plant) manager

'Werk·spio͵na·ge *f* industrial espionage

'Werk·statt *f* (-; -stätten) workshop; *mot.* garage; *art*: studio; **'Werk·stät·te** *f* (-; -n) → ***Werkstatt***

'Werk·statt·mon͵ta·ge *f* shop assembly

'Werk·stoff *m* (raw) material; **⁓prü·fer** *m* materials tester

'Werk|stück *n* ⚙ workpiece; **⁓stu͵dent** *m* working student; ⁓ ***sein*** work one's way through university (*or* college)

'Werk·tag *m* working day; **'werk·tags** *adv.* during the week, on weekdays

'werk·tä·tig *adj.* working ..., employed; ⁓ ***sein*** *a.* have a job; ***die Werktätigen*** the working population (*sg.*)

'Werk|treue *f art*: faithful rendition; **⁓͵un·ter·richt** *m ped.* arts and crafts *pl.*; **⁓ver·trag** *m* contract for work; **⁓woh·nung** *f* company flat (*Am.* apartment)

'Werk·zeug *n* (-[e]s; -e) tool (*a. fig.*); instrument; implement; **⁓ka·sten** *m* tool box; **⁓ma·cher** *m* toolmaker; **⁓ma͵schi·ne** *f* machine tool; **⁓ta·sche** *f* tool bag; **⁓schlos·ser** *m* toolmaker

Wer·mut ['veːɐmuːt] *m* (-s; -s) **1.** *gastr.* vermouth; **2.** ⚘ wormwood; **⁓bru·der, ⁓pen·ner** F *m* F wino

'Wer·muts·trop·fen *fig. m* drop of bitterness

wert [veːɐt] *adj.* a) worth, b) *obs.* dear, c) esteemed, valued; ***et. ⁓ sein*** be worth s.th., be worthy of s.th.; ***viel*** ⁓ worth a lot; ***nichts*** ⁓ worthless; ***das ist schon viel*** ⁓ that takes us a great step forward; ***das ist e-n Versuch*** ⁓ it's worth a try; ***es ist viel ⁓ zu wissen, daß*** it's good to know that; ***er hat es nicht für ⁓ gefunden, mich zu informieren*** he didn't consider it necessary to inform me; ***das Buch ist ⁓, daß man es liest*** the book is worth reading; ***er ist es nicht ⁓, daß man ihm hilft*** he doesn't deserve to be helped; F ***ich bin heut' nicht viel*** ⁓ I'm not up to much today; → ***Mühe, Rede***

Wert [veːɐt] *m* (-[e]s; -e) a) value (*a. phys.*, 𝔄, ⚙); importance, b) quality, c) merit; use, d) equivalent, e) ✝ asset; *pl.* assets, securities, stocks, f) ⚕ *liver etc.* count; ***im ⁓e von*** *dat.* to the value of, worth *millions etc.*; ***Waren im ⁓e von 300 Dollar*** 300 dollars worth of goods; ***geistige ⁓e*** spiritual values; ***sie hat innere ⁓e*** she has personal qualities; ***von unschätzbarem*** ⁓ invaluable; (***großen***) ⁓ ***legen auf*** *acc.* attach (great) importance to; ***ich lege ⁓ darauf festzustellen, daß*** I

would greatly stress that; ***im ~ sinken*** (***steigen***) lose (go up) in value; ***et. über*** (***unter***) ***~ verkaufen*** sell s.th. over (under) value; ***das hat keinen praktischen ~*** that's of no practical use (*or* value); F *fig.* ***das hat keinen ~*** it's pointless
'Wert|an·ga·be *f* **1.** declaration of value; **2.** declared value; **~ar·beit** *f* (-; *no pl.*) quality workmanship; **2be·stän·dig** *adj.* of stable (*fig.* lasting) value; stable *currency*; **~brief** *m* insured letter
wer·ten ['veːɐtən] *v/t.* (h) a) evaluate, assess, b) judge; classify; *esp. sport, ped.* rate
Wer·te|ska·la ['veːɐtə-] *f* scale of values; **~sy,stem** *n* system of values
'wert·frei *pred. adj. and adv.* free of any value judg(e)ment
'Wert·ge·gen·stand *m* article of value; *pl.* valuables
'wert·ge·min·dert *pred. adj.* diminished in value
Wer·tig·keit ['veːɐtɪçkaɪt] *f* (-; -en) **1.** ⚗ valency; **2.** significance
'Wert·kar·ten·te·le,fon *n* cardphone
'wert·los *adj.* a) worthless, b) useless; **'Wert·lo·sig·keit** *f* (-; *no pl.*) a) worthlessness, b) uselessness
'Wert|maß·stab *m* standard (of value); **~min·de·rung** *f* depreciation
'wert·neu,tral *adj.* → ***wertfrei***
'Wert|pa,ket *n* insured parcel (*Am.* package); **~pa,pier** *n* ⚕ security; **~sa·chen** *pl.* valuables; **~schät·zung** *f* (-; *no pl.*) esteem (*gen.* for); **~schöp·fung** *f* ⚕ value added; **~sen·dung** *f* consignment with value declared; ✉ insured matter; **~stei·ge·rung** *f* increase in value, appreciation; **~sy,stem** *n* system of values
Wer·tung ['veːɐtʊŋ] *f* (-; -en) a) evaluation, assessment, b) judg(e)ment; *sport*: score
'Wert|ur·teil *n* value judg(e)ment; **~verlust** *m* depreciation; **2voll** *adj.* valuable; **~vor·stel·lung** *f* value; *pl.* value system; **~zei·chen** *n* (postage) stamp; **~zuwachs** *m* appreciation
Wer·wolf ['veːɐvɔlf] *m* (-[e]s; ⁻e) werewolf
We·sen ['veːzən] *n* (-s; -) a) being, creature (*a.* F *person*), b) *no pl.* nature, character, *a. s.o.'s* personality; *phls.* entity; essence; ***heiteres*** *etc.* **~** cheerful *etc.* disposition; ***gekünsteltes ~*** affected manner; ***sie ist ein furchtsames*** (***lebhaftes***) **~** she is a timid creature (lively soul); F ***armes ~*** poor creature (*or* soul); ***viel ~s von et. machen*** make a great fuss about s.th.; ***es liegt im ~*** *gen.* it's in the nature of; ***das entspricht nicht s-m ~*** that's not at all like him, it's completely out of character for him; ***der Mensch als soziales ~*** man as a social being; ***das gehört zum ~ der Demokratie*** that's an intrinsic feature (*or* that's part and parcel) of democracy; ***das ändert nichts am ~ der Sache*** that doesn't alter the situation
'we·sen·los *adj.* **1.** insubstantial, incorporeal; **2.** empty, meaningless
'We·sens·art *f* (-; *no pl.*) nature
'we·sens·fremd *adj.* alien (to one's nature); ***j-m ~ sein*** *a.* be completely foreign to s.o.
'We·sens|merk·mal *n* (basic *or* essential) trait; **~,un·ter·schied** *m* difference in nature (*or* character); **~zug** *m* characteristic, trait
we·sent·lich ['veːzəntlɪç] **I.** *adj.* essential (***für*** *acc.* to), substantial, important; fundamental; ***das Wesentliche*** the essential part, the most important aspect(s); ***nichts Wesentliches*** nothing important, *formal*: nothing of import; ***~er Inhalt*** substance *of a book etc.*; ***keine ~en Änderungen*** no major changes; ***ein ~er Unterschied*** a big (*or* an important) difference; ***kein ~er Unterschied*** no marked change (*or* difference); ***im ~en*** essentially, in the main, on the whole; **II.** *adv.* a) fundamentally, b) considerably; ***~ besser*** *etc.* far better *etc.*; ***sich ~ unterscheiden in*** *dat.* (***von*** *dat.*) differ considerably in (from) *s.th.*; ***wir müssen noch ~ mehr tun*** we must do a great deal more
wes·halb [vɛs'halp] **I.** *interr. adv.* why?; **II.** *cj.* which is why, and so
Wes·pe ['vɛspə] *f* (-; -n) wasp
'Wes·pen|nest *n* wasps' nest; *fig.* ***in ein ~ stechen*** stir up a hornet's nest; **~stich** *m* wasp sting; **~tail·le** *f* wasp waist
wes·sen ['vɛsən] **I.** *interr. pron.* **1.** (*gen. of wer*) whose?; **2.** (*gen. of was*): ***~ wird er beschuldigt?*** what is he accused of?; **II.** *rel. pron.* (*gen. of was*) (of) which; ***das, ~ er beschuldigt wird*** what he is (being) accused of
West [vɛst] *without art.* west; (***in***) ***München ~*** west Munich (in the west of Munich)
West... *in cpds. hist.* West German; **~auto** *n* West German car
'west·deutsch *adj.*, **'West·deut·sche** *m, f* (-n; -n) West German
We·ste ['vɛstə] *f* (-; -n) waistcoat, *Am.* vest; *fig.* ***e-e reine ~ haben*** have a clean record; ***er hat e-e reine ~*** *a.* his slate is clean
We·sten ['vɛstən] *m* (-s; *no pl.*) west; West; *geogr. and pol. the* West; ***nach ~*** west(wards); westbound *traffic etc.*
'We·sten·ta·sche *f* waistcoat (*Am.* vest) pocket; *fig.* ***et. wie s-e ~ kennen*** know s.th. like the back of one's hand
'We·sten·ta·schen·for,mat *n*: ***im ~*** pocket *camera etc.*; *iro.* would-be (*or* small-time) *politician etc.*
We·stern ['vɛstɐn] *m* (-s; -) western, cowboy film, F horse opera
'West·eu·ro,pä·er *m*, **'west·eu·ro,pä·isch** *adj.* West European
West·fa·le [vɛst'faːlə] *m* (-n; -n), **West·fä·lin** [vɛst'fɛːlɪn] *f* (-; -nen) Westphalian; **west·fä·lisch** [vɛst'fɛːlɪʃ] *adj.* Westphalian; ***der Westfälische Friede*** the Peace of Westphalia
'West·geld *n hist.* West German money (*or* currency)
'West·go·te *m* Visigoth; **'west·go·tisch** *adj.* Visigothic
'West·kü·ste *f*: (***an der ~*** on the) west coast
'west·lich I. *adj.* western, west; westerly *wind*; ***in ~er Richtung*** west(wards); westbound *traffic etc.*; **II.** *adv.* (to the) west (***von*** *dat.* of); **'west·lichst** *adj.* westernmost
'West|mäch·te *pl. pol.* Western Powers; **~mark** *f* (-; *no pl.*) *hist.* West German mark
west'öst·lich *adj.*: *pol.* ***~e Beziehungen*** East-West relations
'West·wall *m* (-[e]s; *no pl.*) *hist.* ⚔ Siegfried Line
west·wärts ['vɛstvɛrts] *adv.* west(wards)
'West·wind *m* west wind
wes·we·gen [vɛs'veːgən] → ***weshalb***
Wett·an·nah·me(stel·le) ['vɛt-] *f* betting office
Wett·be·werb ['vɛtbəvɛrp] *m* (-[e]s; -e [-bə]) competition (*a.* ⚕); contest; ⚕ ***freier*** (***unlauterer***) **~** free (unfair) competition; ***in ~ treten*** (***stehen***) ***mit*** *dat.* enter into (be in) competition with
'Wett·be·werbs|be·schrän·kung *f* restraint of trade; **2fä·hig** *adj.* ⚕ competitive; **~fä·hig·keit** *f* (-; *no pl.*) ⚕ competitiveness; **~klau·sel** *f* ⚕ non-competition clause; **~re·geln** *pl.* rules of competition; **~teil·neh·mer** *m* competitor, contestant; **~ver·bot** *n* ⚕ prohibition of competition; **~ver·zer·rung** *f* ⚕ unfair competition
Wett·bü,ro ['vɛt-] *n* betting office
Wet·te ['vɛtə] *f* (-; -n) bet; wager; ***e-e ~ eingehen*** (*or* ***abschließen***) make a bet; ***ich gehe jede ~ ein, daß*** I'll bet you any money (that); ***was gilt die ~?*** what do you (want to) bet?; ***die ~ gilt!*** you're on!; ***um die ~ rennen*** (***schwimmen*** *etc.*) have a race, race each other; F ***um die ~ arbeiten*** *etc.* work *etc.* all out, ***essen*** *etc.*: F eat *etc.* like it's going out of style
Wett·ei·fer ['vɛtˀaɪfɐ] *m* (-s; *no pl.*) competitive drive; rivalry, competition; **'wett·ei·fern** *v/i.* (h) vie, compete (***mit*** *dat.* with *s.o.*; ***um*** *acc.* for *s.th.*)
wet·ten ['vɛtən] *v/t. and v/i.* (h) bet (***mit j-m*** s.o.; ***um*** *acc. s.th.*), F have a flutter; ***~ auf*** *acc.* bet (*or* put one's money) on, *horse racing etc.*: *a.* back; ***ich wette zehn zu eins, daß*** I bet you ten to one (that); F ***~, daß ...?*** F wanna bet?; *fig.* ***so haben wir nicht gewettet*** that wasn't part of the deal
Wet·ter[1] ['vɛtɐ] *n* (-s; *no pl.*) **1.** weather; ***bei diesem ~*** in this (sort of) weather; *fig.* ***gut ~ bei j-m machen*** get s.o. into the right mood; → ***Wind***; **2.** ⚒ ***schlagende ~*** firedamp; **3.** → ***Unwetter***
'Wet·ter[2] *m* (-s; -) better
'Wet·ter|amt *n* meteorological office, F met office; **~aus·sich·ten** *pl.* weather outlook (*or* forecast) *sg.* (***bis Dienstag*** till Tuesday, for tomorrow and Tuesday); **~be·din·gun·gen** *pl.* weather conditions; **~be·ob·ach·tung** *f* meteorological observation; **~be·richt** *m* weather report (*or* forecast); *radio, TV*: *a.* weathercast; **2be·stän·dig** *adj.* weatherproof; **2be·stim·mend** *adj.*: ***~ sein*** determine the weather; **~dienst** *m* weather service; **~ecke** F *f* bad-weather area; **2empfind·lich** *adj.* → ***wetterfühlig***; **~fah·ne** *f* weather vane; **2fest** *adj.* weatherproof; **~frosch** F *m* F weatherman
'wet·ter·füh·lig [-fyːlɪç] *adj.* weather-sensitive, susceptible to the weather; **'Wetter·füh·lig·keit** *f* (-; *no pl.*) sensitivity (*or* susceptibility) to the weather
'Wet·ter|hahn *m* weathercock; **~häus·chen** *n* weather house; **~kar·te** *f* weather map; **~kun·de** *f* meteorology; **~la·ge** *f* weather situation; **~leuch·ten** *n* sheet (*or* heat) lightning; *fig.* ***~ am politischen Horizont*** storm clouds on the political horizon; **~loch** F *n* bad-weather area; **~ma·cher** F *m* F weatherman
'wet·ter·mä·ßig *adj.*: ***wie sieht es ~ aus?*** what's the weather like?
'Wet·ter·mil·de·rung *f* onset of milder weather
wet·tern ['vɛtɐn] F *v/i.* (h) F rant and rave; ***~ gegen*** *acc.* rail (*formal*: fulminate) against

'Wet·ter|pro,phet *m* weather prophet (*or* sage); **~sa·tel,lit** *m* weather (*or* meteorological) satellite, F metsat; **~schacht** *m* ⚒ ventilation shaft; **~schei·de** *f* weather divide; **~sei·te** *f* exposed side; **~sta·ti,on** *f* weather station; **~sturz** *m* sudden drop in temperature; **~,um·schwung** *m* (sudden) change in (the) weather; **~ver·hält·nis·se** *pl.* weather conditions; **~vor,her·sa·ge** *f* weather forecast; *radio, TV*: *a.* weathercast; **~war·te** *f* weather station; **~wech·sel** *m* change in (the) weather

wet·ter·wen·disch ['vɛtɐvɛndɪʃ] *contp. adj.* moody

'Wet·ter|wol·ke *f* storm cloud; **~zei·chen** *n* weather indicator, sign of good (*or* bad) weather; *fig.* **~ am politischen Horizont** political indicator

Wett|fahrt ['vɛt-] *f* race; **~kampf** *m* contest, competition; *sport*: event; **~kämp·fer** *m* competitor, contestant; **~lauf** *m* race; *fig.* **~ mit der Zeit** race against time (*or* the clock); **~läu·fer** *m* runner

wett·ma·chen ['vɛt-] *v/t.* (*sep.*, h) make up for, compensate for (**durch** *acc.* with, by); recoup *money*

Wett|ren·nen ['vɛt-] *n* race (*a. fig.*); **~rü·sten** *n* arms race; **~schwim·men** *n* swimming competition; **~streit** *m* contest; competition

wet·zen ['vɛtsən] **I.** *v/t.* (h) sharpen; grind; *bird.*: scratch, rub *its bill*; **II.** F *v/i.* (sn) F race; **nach Hause ~** race home, F zoom off home

Wetz·stein ['vɛts-] *m* whetstone

Whis·key ['vɪski] *m* (-s; -s) whiskey

Whis·ky ['vɪski] *m* (-s; -s) whisky, *a.* Scotch; **~ (mit) Soda** whisky (*or* Scotch) and soda; **→ pur**

wich [vɪç] *pret. of* **weichen²**

Wich·se ['vɪksə] F *f* (-; -n) **1.** (shoe) polish; **2.** thrashing, hiding; **'wich·sen** *v/t.* (h) **1.** F polish; **2.** V (have a) wank, jerk off; **Wich·ser** ['vɪksɐ] *m* (-s; -) **1.** V wanker; **2.** F jerk (*sl.*)

Wicht [vɪçt] *m* (-[e]s; -e) F midget, *a.* F nipper; *contp.* F blighter

Wich·tel·männ·chen ['vɪçtəlmɛnçən] *n* (-s; -) elf, goblin

wich·tig ['vɪçtɪç] *adj.* important; **et. (sehr) ~ nehmen** take s.th. (very) seriously, attach (great) importance to s.th.; **sich (sehr) ~ nehmen** take o.s. very seriously; **er macht sich gern ~** he likes to think he's important; **es ist mir sehr ~** it's very important to me, it means a lot to me; **das ist nur halb so ~** that's not so important; **nichts Wichtigeres zu tun haben als** have nothing better to do than; **'Wich·tig·keit** *f* (-; *no pl.*) importance (**für** *acc.* for, to); **von höchster ~** of the greatest importance

'Wich·tig·tu·er [-tuːɐ] *m* (-s; -) pompous ass; **Wich·tig·tue·rei** [-tuːə'raɪ] *f* (-; *no pl.*) pompousness, pompous behavio(u)r; **'wich·tig·tue·risch** [-tuːərɪʃ] *adj.* pompous

Wicke ['vɪkə] (*sep.* -k·k-) *f* (-; -n) ⚘ vetch; sweet pea

Wickel ['vɪkəl] (*sep.* -k·k-) *m* (-s; -) ⚕ compress; F *fig.* **j-n beim ~ packen** F a) grab s.o. by the scruff of his (*or* her) neck, b) take s.o. to task; **~ge·stell** *n* changing stand; **~hemd·chen** *n* wrapover vest; **~kind** *n* baby; **~kom,mo·de** *f* changing unit; **~mul·de** *f* changing mat

wickeln ['vɪkəln] (*sep.* -k·k-) (h) **I.** *v/t.* a) wind (*a.* ⚡); tie *bandage etc.*; wrap *blanket etc.*, b) curl *hair*, c) wrap up, d) change *a baby's* nappies (*Am.* diapers); **→ Finger; II.** *v/refl.*: **sich ~ um** *acc.* wind (*or* coil) itself around *s.th.*, *lead etc.*: get twisted round *s.th.*; **sich in e-e Decke ~** wrap o.s. up in a blanket

'Wickel|raum *m* baby-care room; **~rock** *m* wraparound skirt

Wick·ler ['vɪklɐ] *m* (-s; -) curler

Wick·lung ['vɪklʊŋ] *f* (-; -en) ⚡ winding

Wid·der ['vɪdɐ] *m* (-s; -) **1.** *zo.* ram; **2.** *ast.* Aries; **(ein) ~ sein** be (an) Aries

wi·der ['viːdɐ] *prp.* (*acc.*) against, contrary to; **→ Für, Willen**

'wi·der·bor·stig *adj.* **→ widerspenstig**

wi·der'fah·ren *v/i.* (*irr.*, *insep.*, *no* -ge-, sn, **→ fahren**) happen to, *lit.* befall; **ihm ist Unrecht ~** he has been done wrong; **j-m Gerechtigkeit ~ lassen** do justice to s.o., *w.s.* give s.o. his (*or* her) due

'Wi·der·ha·ken *m* barbed hook; barb

'Wi·der·hall *m* (-[e]s; *no pl.*) echo, reverberation(s *pl.*); *fig. a.* response, resonance; *fig.* **großen ~ finden** meet with an enthusiastic response; **es fand keinen ~** there was no reaction (to it); **'wi·der·hal·len** *v/i.* (*sep.*, h) echo, resound (**von** *dat.* with *laughter etc.*)

wi·der·leg·bar [viːdɐ'leːkbaːɐ] *adj.* refutable; **wi·der'le·gen** *v/t.* (*insep.*, *no* -ge-, h) refute, disprove; *a.* explode *a theory*; **diese Erkenntnis widerlegte die ganze Theorie** this discovery defeated the whole theory; **Wi·der'le·gung** *f* (-; -en) refutation

wi·der·lich ['viːdɐlɪç] *adj.* revolting, repulsive

Wi·der·ling ['viːdɐlɪŋ] F *m* (-s; -e) F creep; *a.* F slob

'wi·der·na,tür·lich *adj.* unnatural, perverse

Wi·der·part ['viːdɐpart] *m* (-[e]s; -e) opponent, adversary

'wi·der·recht·lich I. *adj.* illegal, unlawful; **II.** *adv.*: ⚖ **~ betreten** trespass (up)on; **sich et. ~ aneignen** misappropriate s.th.

'Wi·der·re·de *f* (-; -n) contradiction(s *pl.*); F backchat, *Am.* backtalk; **ohne ~** unquestioningly; **keine ~!** no arguments!, no buts!

'Wi·der·ruf *m* (-[e]s; -e) revocation; retraction; ✝ countermand, withdrawal *a. of an order*; **bis auf ~** until further notice

wi·der'ru·fen *v/t.* (*irr.*, *insep.*, *no* -ge-, h, **→ rufen**) revoke; retract, (*a. v/i.*) recant; ⚖ repeal; cancel *order, contract etc.*

Wi·der·sa·cher ['viːdɐzaxɐ] *m* (-s; -) adversary

'Wi·der·schein *m* reflection

wi·der'set·zen *v/refl.* (*insep.*, *no* -ge-, h): **sich ~** oppose, resist (*dat. s.o. or s.th.*); **sich e-m Befehl (Gesetz) ~** disobey an order (a law)

wi·der·setz·lich [viːdɐ'zɛtslɪç] *adj.* refractory; insubordinate

'Wi·der·sinn *m* (-[e]s; *no pl.*) absurdity; **'wi·der·sin·nig** *adj.* absurd, nonsensical

wi·der·spen·stig ['viːdɐʃpɛnstɪç] *adj.* stubborn; rebellious; unruly *hair*; **'Wi·der·spen·stig·keit** *f* (-; *no pl.*) stubbornness; rebelliousness

'wi·der·spie·geln (*sep.*, h) **I.** *v/t.* reflect (*a. fig.*); **II.** *v/refl.*: **sich ~** *a. fig.* be reflected

wi·der'spre·chen *v/i.* (*irr.*, *insep.*, *no* -ge-, h, **→ sprechen**) contradict (**j-m** s.o.; **sich** o.s.); oppose *plan etc.*; **sich** (*or* **einander**) **~** *opinions etc.*: be contradictory, be at variance; **wi·der'spre·chend** *adj.*: **sich ~** contradictory *reports etc.*; conflicting *rules etc.*

'Wi·der·spruch *m* (-[e]s; ⁼e) a) contradiction, b) protest, c) discrepancy; **im ~ stehen zu** *dat.* be inconsistent with, contradict *s.th.*; **et. ohne ~ hinnehmen** accept s.th. without a word of protest; **heftigen ~ bei j-m hervorrufen** provoke vehement protest from s.o.; **sich in Widersprüche verwickeln** keep contradicting o.s., get caught up in a web of contradictions; **es ist ein ~ in sich** it's a contradiction in terms, it's self-contradictory; **er duldet keinen ~** what he says goes; **kein ~!** no arguments!

wi·der·sprüch·lich ['viːdɐʃprʏçlɪç] *adj.* contradictory, inconsistent; conflicting *emotions, rules etc.*

'Wi·der·spruchs·geist *m* (-[e]s; -er) **1.** *no pl.* argumentative spirit; **2.** argumentative person (*or* type)

'wi·der·spruchs·los *adv.* unquestioningly; without a murmur

Wi·der·stand ['viːdɐʃtant] *m* (-[e]s; -stände [-ʃtɛndə]) **1.** *no pl.* a) resistance (*a.* ⚡), opposition, b) ✈ drag; **~ gegen die Staatsgewalt** obstructing the police; **~ leisten** offer resistance, fight back; **auf (heftigen) ~ stoßen** meet with (stiff) opposition; **den ~ aufgeben** give in; **den Weg des geringsten ~es gehen** take the line of least resistance; **gegen den ~ s-r Eltern** against his parents' wishes; **2.** opposition; **et. gegen alle Widerstände durchsetzen** go through with s.th. despite all opposition; **3.** ⚡ resistor

'Wi·der·stands|be·we·gung *f* resistance movement; **2fä·hig** *adj.* resistant (**gegen** *acc.* to); robust (*a.* ⚙); **~fä·hig·keit** *f* (-; *no pl.*) resistance; robustness; **~kämp·fer** *m* resistance fighter; **~kraft** *f* (-; *no pl.*) (powers *pl.* of) resistance

'wi·der·stands·los *adv.* without resistance

'Wi·der·stands|mes·ser *m*, **~meß·ge·rät** *n* ⚡ ohmmeter; **~nest** *n* pocket of resistance; **~or·ga·ni·sa·ti,on** *f* resistance movement

wi·der'ste·hen *v/i.* (*irr.*, *insep.*, *no* -ge-, h, **→ stehen**) resist (*dat. s.th. or ger.*); *a.* put up with; **er konnte der Versuchung nicht ~** *a.* he succumbed to the temptation

wi·der'stre·ben (*insep.*, *no* -ge-, h) **I.** *v/i.* oppose *s.o. or s.th.*; **es widerstrebt mir** it goes against the grain, I hate to have to do it; **II. 2** *n* (-s; *no pl.*) resistance; reluctance; **wi·der'stre·bend** *adv.* reluctantly

'Wi·der·streit *m* (-[e]s; *no pl.*) conflict; **'wi·der·strei·tend** *adj.* conflicting

wi·der·wär·tig ['viːdɐvɛrtɪç] *adj.* repulsive, nasty, F horrible; disgusting *behavio(u)r etc.*; **'Wi·der·wär·tig·keit** *f* (-; -en) repulsiveness; nastiness

Wi·der·wil·le ['viːdɐvɪlə] *m* (-ns; *no pl.*) a) aversion (**gegen** *acc.* to); loathing (for); disgust (at), b) reluctance

'wi·der·wil·lig I. *adj.* unwilling, reluctant; **II.** *adv.* a) reluctantly, b) grudgingly, c) with disgust

'Wi·der·wor·te *pl.*: **keine ~!** F no backchat!, *Am.* no backtalk!

wid·men ['vɪtmən] (h) **I.** *v/t.* dedicate; *a.* devote *one's time, life etc.* (*dat.* to); give *one's attention*; **II.** *v/refl.*: ***sich j-m*** (***e-r Sache***) **~** devote o.s. to s.o. (s.th.); ***sich e-m Problem*** **~** *a.* address a problem

Wid·mung ['vɪtmʊŋ] *f* (-; -en) dedication; ***j-m e-e*** **~** (***ins Buch***) ***schreiben*** write s.o. a dedication

wid·rig ['viːdrɪç] *adj.* adverse

'Wid·rig·keit *f* (-; -en) adversity

wie [viː] **I.** *adv.* **1.** how?, what ... like?; **~** ***alt sind Sie?*** how old are you?; **~** ***sagten Sie?*** (sorry,) what did you say?; **~** ***lange ist das her?*** how long ago is (*or* was) that?; **~** ***war's im Kino?*** how was the film?; **~** ***ist er*** (***so***)***?*** what's he like?; **~** ***ist der neue Wagen?*** what's the new car like?; **~** ***war das mit dem Unfall?*** what exactly happened in the accident?; ***das war doch sehr witzig,*** **~*?*** that was a good joke, wasn't it?; **~*, hat er das wirklich gesagt?*** what, did he really say that?; F **~** ***das?*** F how come?; **~** ***wäre es mit?*** how about?; **2.** **~** ***schön!*** how beautiful!; **~** ***froh war ich!*** how glad I was; **~** ***gut, daß*** lucky for me (*or* you *etc.*) that; ***und*** **~*!*** and how!, F you bet!; **II.** *cj.* **3.** a) *in comparison*: as, *usu.* as ... as, b) such as; like; **~** ***ein Freund*** as (*or* like) a friend; ***ein Mann*** **~** ***er*** a man like him; (***nicht***) ***so alt*** **~** (not) as old as; ***er sieht nicht*** **~** ***50 aus*** he doesn't look fifty; **~** ***gesagt*** as I said (*or* was saying); **~** ***man mir gesagt hat*** as I've been told; **~** ***so oft*** as is often the case; ***in e-m Fall*** **~** ***diesem*** in a case like this; ***auf dem Land*** **~** ***in den kleinen Städten*** both in the country and in the small towns; **~** ***er nun mal ist*** being the type of person he is; → ***gehabt, sagen*** I; **4.** as, when; **~** ***er dies hörte*** when he heard this; **~** ***ich so vorbeiging*** just as I was passing; ***ich sah,*** **~** ***er weglief*** I saw him running away; ***ich hörte,*** **~** ***er es sagte*** I heard him say so (*or* it); **5.** **~** ***sehr er es auch versuchte*** much as he tried; **~** ***sehr ich mich auch bemühte*** however hard I tried, try as I would; **~** ***es scheint*** it seems; **~** (***auch***) ***immer*** however, no matter how; **~** ***dem auch sei*** be that as it may; **~** ***sie auch heißen mögen*** whatever they're called

Wie·de·hopf ['viːdəhɔpf] *m* (-es; -e) *zo.* hoopoe

wie·der ['viːdɐ] *adv.* a) again, b) back, c) in return; **~** ***einmal*** once again; ***schon*** **~** yet again; ***schon*** **~*!*** not again!; **~** ***und*** **~** again and again, over and over again; (***schon***) **~** ***e-e Seite geschrieben*** that's another page written; ***dafür ist er*** **~** ***teuer*** but then he's expensive; ***wo willst du*** **~** ***hin?*** where are you off to this time?; ***was hat er*** **~** ***angestellt?*** what's he been up to this time?

wie·der'an·le·gen *v/t.* (*sep.*, h) reinvest, plough (*Am.* plow) back *money*

Wie·der'auf·bau *m* (-[e]s; *no pl.*) a) reconstruction, b) ☤ recovery; **wie·der'auf·bau·en** *v/t.* (*sep.*, h) rebuild

wie·der'auf·be·rei·ten *v/t.* (*sep.*, h) reprocess; **Wie·der'auf·be·rei·tung** *f* (-, -en) reprocessing; **Wie·der'auf·be·rei·tungs·an·la·ge** *f*: (***atomare*** **~** nuclear waste) reprocessing plant

wie·der'auf·füh·ren *v/t.* (*sep.*, h) *thea.* show again; rerun *film*; give again, do a repeat of *a concert etc.*

wie·der'auf·lad·bar *adj.* ⚡ rechargeable

wie·der'auf·le·ben **I.** *v/i.* (*sep.*, sn) revive; **II.** Ձ *n* (-s; *no pl.*) revival; resurgence *of customs etc.*; **wie·der'auf·le·bend** *adj.* resurgent

Wie·der'auf·nah·me *f* (-; *no pl.*) resumption; *thea.* revival; ⚖ reopening (of a trial); **~ver·fah·ren** *n* ⚖ new hearing; retrial

wie·der'auf·neh·men *v/t.* (*irr.*, *sep.*, h, → ***nehmen***) resume; *thea.* revive; ⚖ reopen; ***Kontakte*** **~** renew ties

wie·der'auf·rich·ten *v/t.* (*sep.*, h) set *s.o.* up again

wie·der'auf·rü·sten *v/t. and v/i.* (*sep.*, h) rearm; **Wie·der'auf·rü·stung** *f* rearmament, rearming

wie·der|'auf·tau·chen *v/i.* (*sep.*, sn) re-emerge, ⚓ *a.* (re)surface; *fig.* come to light again, reappear; *person*: reappear on the scene, resurface, turn up again; **~'auf·tre·ten** *v/i.* (*irr.*, *sep.*, sn, → ***treten***) reappear; **~'aus·füh·ren** *v/t.* (*sep.*, h) re-export

'Wie·der·be·ginn *m* (-s; *no pl.*) recommencement; *ped. etc.*: reopening; **~** ***des Unterrichts*** *etc.* ***ist am ...*** classes *etc.* start again on ...

'wie·der·be·kom·men *v/t.* (*irr.*, *sep.*, h, → ***bekommen***) get *s.th.* back

'wie·der·be·le·ben *v/t.* (*sep.*, h) resuscitate, *a. fig.* revive; **'Wie·der·be·le·bung** *f* (-; *no pl.*) resuscitation; *fig.* revival; **'Wie·der·be·le·bungs·ver·such** *m* resuscitation attempt; *fig.* attempt to revive s.th.

'wie·der·be·schaf·fen *v/t.* (*sep.*, h) replace; **'Wie·der·be·schaf·fung** *f* (-; *no pl.*) replacement

'Wie·der·be·schaf·fungs|ko·sten *pl.* replacement cost *sg.*; **~wert** *m* replacement (*or* as new) value

'wie·der|be·set·zen *v/t.* (*sep.*, h) **1.** ***e-e Stelle*** **~** fill a vacancy; **2.** ⚔ reoccupy; **~brin·gen** *v/t.* (*irr.*, *sep.*, h, → ***bringen***) bring back; return (*dat.* to)

wie·der'ein·füh·ren *v/t.* (*sep.*, h) a) reintroduce; revive *custom etc.*, b) ☤ reimport; **Wie·der'ein·füh·rung** *f* (-; *no pl.*) a) reintroduction; revival, b) ☤ reimportation

Wie·der'ein·glie·de·rung *f* (-; *no pl.*) reintegration (***in*** *acc.* into); ⚖ rehabilitation

wie·der'ein·set·zen *v/t.* (*sep.*, h) a) reinstate *s.o.* (***in*** *acc.* in); restore *s.o.* to the throne, b) restore *rights to s.o.*; **Wie·der'ein·set·zung** *f* (-; *no pl.*) reinstatement; restoration

wie·der'ein·stel·len *v/t.* (*sep.*, h) re-employ *s.o.*, take *s.o.* back; ***j-n*** **~** *a.* give s.o. his (*or* her) job back

Wie·der'ein·tritt *m* (-[e]s; *no pl.*) re-entry (***in*** *acc.* into)

'wie·der·ent·decken *v/t.* (*sep.*, h) rediscover

'Wie·der·er·grei·fung *f* (-; *no pl.*) recapture

'wie·der|er·in·nern *v/refl.*: ***sich*** **~** (*sep.*, h) recall, remember (***an*** *acc. s.o., s.th.*); **~er·ken·nen** *v/t.* (*irr.*, *sep.*, h, → ***erkennen***) recognize; ***nicht wiederzuerkennen*** unrecognizable; maimed *etc.* beyond recognition; ***es ist nicht wiederzuerkennen*** you won't recognize it; **~er·lan·gen** *v/t.* (*sep.*, h) recover, regain *a. weight*; **~er·le·ben** *v/t.* (*sep.*, h) relive, go through *s.th.* again; **~er·obern** *v/t.* (*sep.*, h) recapture

'wie·der·er·öff·nen *v/t.* (*sep.*, h) reopen; ***das Feuer*** **~** reopen fire, start firing again; **'Wie·der·er·öff·nung** *f* reopening

'wie·der·er·schei·nen *v/i.* (*irr.*, *sep.*, sn, → ***erscheinen***) reappear; *newspaper*: resume publication, reappear on the newsstands; **~** ***lassen*** republish

'wie·der·er·stat·ten *v/t.* (*sep.*, h) refund, reimburse *expenses etc.* (*dat.* to); **'Wie·der·er·stat·tung** *f* refund(ing), reimbursement

'wie·der|er·ste·hen *v/i.* (*irr.*, *sep.*, sn, → ***erstehen***) rise again; *fig.* be revived, (*a.* **~** ***lassen***) revive; **~er·wecken** *v/t.* (*sep.*, h) **1.** revive *interest, feeling etc.*; **2.** bring *s.o.* back to life; **~er·zäh·len** *v/t.* (*sep.*, h) **1.** retell; **2.** → ***weitererzählen***; **~fin·den** (*irr.*, *sep.*, h, → ***finden***) **I.** *v/t.* find again; *fig.* regain; ***s-e Sprache*** **~** be able to speak again; ***sich*** (*or* ***einander***) **~** find (one's way back to) each other again; **II.** *v/refl.*: ***sich*** **~** a) find o.s. (***in*** *dat.* in), end up (in), b) turn up again, reappear, resurface, c) recover, get back on an even keel

'Wie·der·ga·be *f* (-; -n) reproduction; *a.* sound; picture; ♪ *etc.* rendering; *tape*: playback; **~kopf** *m* play head; **~qua·li·tät** *f* sound (*or* picture) quality

'wie·der·ge·ben *v/t.* (*irr.*, *sep.*, h, → ***geben***) a) give back, return (*dat.* to), b) reproduce *a. sound*, c) ♪ *etc.* interpret, d) quote; describe; relate

'Wie·der·ge·burt *f* (-; *no pl.*) **1.** rebirth; **2.** *fig.* revival; *art*: *a.* renaissance

'wie·der·ge·win·nen *v/t.* (*irr.*, *sep.*, h, → ***gewinnen***) regain, win (*or* get) back; **'Wie·der·ge·win·nung** *f* (-; *no pl.*) recovery; ⚙ reclamation

'wie·der·grü·ßen *v/t. and v/i.* (*sep.*, h) return s.o.'s greetings; ***grüßen Sie ihn wieder!*** give him mine(, would you?)

wie·der'gut·ma·chen *v/t.* (*sep.*, h) make up for; *a.* recover *loss etc.*; compensate for *damages etc.*; ***das Unrecht*** **~** right the wrongs; ***nicht wiedergutzumachen*** irreparable *damage*; ***wie kann ich es dir*** **~*?*** how can I make it up to you?; **Wie·der'gut·ma·chung** *f* (-; *no pl.*) **1.** amends *pl.*; compensation; **2.** → **Wie·der'gut·ma·chungs·lei·stung** *f* indemnification, restitution payments *pl.*

'wie·der·ha·ben *v/t.* (*irr.*, *sep.*, h, → ***haben***) have *s.th. or s.o.* back again

wie·der'her·stel·len *v/t.* (*sep.*, h) restore (*a. rights etc.*); re-establish *contacts etc.*; ⚕ ***wiederhergestellt*** cured, recovered; **Wie·der'her·stel·lung** *f* (-; *no pl.*) restoration; *a.* restitution *of a right etc.*; ⚕ recovery; renewal, re-establishment *of contacts*

wie·der·hol·bar [viːdɐ'hoːlbaːɐ] *adj.* repeatable; ***es ist nicht*** **~** it can't be repeated; **wie·der'ho·len¹** (*insep.*, *no* -ge-, h) **I.** *v/t.* a) repeat, say *s.th.* again, b) repeat (*a. examination etc.*), do *s.th.* again; rerun *broadcast etc.*, c) sum up; **II.** *v/refl.*: ***sich*** **~** a) repeat o.s., b) repeat itself, happen again, recur; ***das darf sich nicht*** **~** *a.* that mustn't be allowed to happen again

'wie·der·ho·len² *v/t.* (*sep.*, h) fetch back

wie·der'holt **I.** *adj.* repeated; ***trotz*** **~*er Warnung*** despite repeated (*or* several) warnings; **II.** *adv.* repeatedly; time and again; **Wie·der'ho·lung** *f* (-; -en) repetition; repeat, rerun *of a broadcast etc.*; *TV sport*: replay; *ped. etc.* revision

Wie·der'ho·lungs|fall *m*: ***im*** **~** should it

happen again; ⚖ in case of a repeat offen|ce (*Am.* -se); **~imp·fung** *f* ⚕ booster; **~kurs** *m* refresher course; **~prü·fung** *f* repeat examination; **~sen·dung** *f* repeat (broadcast); **~spiel** *n sport*: replay; **~taste** *f* repeat key; **~tat** *f* repeat offen|ce (*Am.* -se); **~tä·ter** *m* ⚖ repeat offender, recidivist; **~traum** *m* recurrent dream; **~zei·chen** *n* ♪ repeat (sign)

'Wie·der·hö·ren *n*: ***auf ~*** goodbye

wie·der·in'stand·set·zen *v/t.* (*sep.*, h) repair; renovate, F do up; **Wie·der·in'stand·set·zung** *f* repair(s *pl.*)

wie·der·käu·en ['vi:dɐkɔyən] (*sep.*, h) **I.** *v/i.* chew the cud; **II.** *fig. v/t.* go on about; keep regurgitating

Wie·der·käu·er ['vi:dɐkɔyɐ] *m* (-s; -) ruminant

Wie·der·kehr ['vi:dɐke:ɐ] *f* (-; *no pl.*) a) return; recurrence, b) anniversary

'wie·der·keh·ren *v/i.* (*sep.*, sn) a) return, come back, b) recur

'wie·der·kom·men *v/i.* (*irr.*, *sep.*, sn, → ***kommen***) a) come again, b) come back, return

'wie·der·lie·ben *v/t.* (*sep.*, h) return *s.o.'s* love

'wie·der·se·hen *v/t.* (*irr.*, *sep.*, h, → ***sehen***) see again, *a.* meet again (*a.* ***sich ~***); **'Wie·der·se·hen** *n* (-s; *no pl.*) reunion; ***auf ~!*** goodbye!, F bye!

'Wie·der·se·hens|fei·er *f* reunion party (*or* celebration); **~freu·de** *f* joy at seeing each other again, joy of being reunited (once more)

'Wie·der·täu·fer *m* Anabaptist

'wie·der·tun *v/t.* (*sep.*, h) do again, repeat

wie·der·um ['vi:dərʊm] *adv.* a) again, b) on the other hand

'wie·der·ver·ei·ni·gen *v/t. and v/refl.* (***sich ~***) (*sep.*, h) reunite

'Wie·der·ver·ei·ni·gung *f* (-; *no pl.*) reunion; *pol. a.* reunification

'Wie·der·ver·fil·mung *f* remake

'wie·der·ver·hei·ra·ten *v/refl.*: ***sich ~*** (*sep.*, h) remarry, marry again (*or* a second *etc.* time)

'wie·der·ver·kau·fen *v/t.* (*sep.*, h) resell

'Wie·der·ver·käu·fer *m* retailer

'Wie·der·ver·kaufs|preis *m* retail price; **~wert** *m* resale value

'wie·der·ver·wend·bar *adj.* reusable

'wie·der·ver·wen·den *v/t.* (*irr.*, *sep.*, h, → ***verwenden***) reuse, reutilize

'Wie·der·ver·wen·dung *f* (-; *no pl.*) reuse

'wie·der·ver·wer·ten *v/t.* (*sep.*, h) recycle; **'Wie·der·ver·wer·tung** *f* recycling

'Wie·der·wahl *f* (-; *no pl.*) re-election (***zum Präsidenten*** to the presidency, as president); ***sich zur ~ stellen*** stand for re-election; ***nach ihrer ~*** after being returned to office (*or* parliament)

'wie·der·wäh·len *v/t.* (*sep.*, h) re-elect

'Wie·der·zu·las·sung *f* (-; *no pl.*) *pol. etc.* unbanning

Wie·ge ['vi:gə] *f* (-; -n) cradle (*a. fig.*); ***von der ~ bis zur Bahre*** from the cradle to the grave; ***s-e ~ stand in Berlin*** he first saw the light of day in Berlin; ***es ist ihm nicht an der ~ gesungen worden, daß*** who would have thought (that); ***das Schicksal hat ihm ... in die ~ gelegt*** he was endowed with ... from birth

'Wie·ge·mes·ser *n* cradle knife

wie·gen¹ ['vi:gən] (wog, gewogen, h) **I.** *v/t.* weigh; ***das ist reichlich (knapp) gewogen*** it's a bit over (under); *fig.* ***gewogen und zu leicht befunden*** weighed and found wanting; **II.** *v/i.* weigh; ***schwerer ~ als*** be heavier than, weigh more than, outweigh; ***was ~ Sie?*** how much do you weigh?; *fig.* ***schwer ~*** carry weight; **III.** *v/refl.*: ***sich ~*** weigh o.s.

'wie·gen² (h) **I.** *v/t.* **1.** rock (***in den Schlaf*** to sleep); **2.** chop; **II.** *v/refl.*: ***sich ~*** sway; *boat*: *a.* rock; *fig.* ***sich in falschen Hoffnungen ~*** delude o.s. with false hopes; → ***Sicherheit*** 1

'Wie·gen|druck *m typ.* incunabulum (*pl.* incunabula), cradle book; **~fest** *lit. n* birthday; **~lied** *n* lullaby

wie·hern ['vi:ɐn] *v/i.* (h) neigh, whinny; ***vor Lachen ~*** bray with laughter; ***~des Gelächter*** braying (laughter)

Wie·ner¹ ['vi:nɐ] *f* (-; -) *gastr.* vienna, wiener

'Wie·ner² *m* (-s; -), **Wie·ne·rin** ['vi:nərɪn] *f* (-; -nen) Viennese; ***Wiener(in) sein*** *usu.* be (*or* come) from Vienna; **wie·ne·risch** ['vi:nərɪʃ] *adj.* Viennese

wie·nern ['vi:nɐn] F *v/t.* (h) polish

wies [vi:s] *pret. of* ***weisen***

Wie·se ['vi:zə] *f* (-; -n) meadow

Wie·sel ['vi:zəl] *n* (-s; -) weasel; → ***flink***

'wie·sel·flink *adj.* fast as lightning, *a.* quick as a flash

wie·seln ['vi:zəln] *v/i.* (sn) scurry

'Wie·sen|blu·me *f* wild flower; **~schaum·kraut** *n* ⚘ lady's smock

wie·so [vi'zo:] *adv.* → ***warum***

wie·viel [vi'fi:l] *interr. adv.* how much?; how many?; ***~ Uhr ist es?*** what's the time?, what time is it?; **wie'viel·mal** *adv.* how many times, how often; **wie'vielt I.** *interr. adv.*: ***zu ~ wart ihr?*** how many of you were there?; **II.** *adj.*: ***der (die, das) ~e ...?*** which ...?; ***das ~e Stück ißt du jetzt?*** how many pieces have you eaten already?; ***den Wievielten haben wir heute?*** what's the date today?; ***zum ~en Male?*** how many times?; ***als ~er ist er ins Ziel gekommen?*** what place did he come?; ***am ~en August hat er Geburtstag?*** when in August is his birthday?

wie·weit [vi'vaɪt] *cj.* → ***inwieweit***

wild [vɪlt] **I.** *adj.* a) wild (*a. fig. look, threat, battle etc.*); *a.* savage; *fig.* furious, F raving; tempestuous, impetuous; *a.* unruly *children*, b) wild, unkempt; ⚕ ***~es Fleisch*** proud flesh; ***~es Parken (Zelten)*** unauthorized parking (camping); ***~e Schießerei*** mad shootout, shooting spree; ***~er Streik*** wildcat strike; ***~e Vermutungen*** wild speculation (*sg.*); ***~ machen*** make *s.o.* mad, F drive *s.o.* wild, frighten *an animal*; F ***den ~en Mann spielen*** F go berserk; ***~ sein auf*** *acc.* F be wild (*or* crazy) about; F ***wie ~*** F like mad; ***~ wachsen*** grow wild; ***~ werden*** a) turn wild, b) get mad, F go wild; F ***das ist halb so ~!*** not to worry; → ***Affe***; **II.** *adv.* wildly; ***~ um sich blicken*** look around wildly; ***~ schreien*** F shout like mad; ***~ lachen*** laugh hysterically; ***~ durcheinanderliegen*** lie in a wild heap; ***~ entschlossen zu*** *inf.* absolutely determined to *inf.*

Wild [vɪlt] *n* (-[e]s; *no pl.*) a) game; head of game; *a. pl. coll.* deer, b) *gastr.* game, venison; **~bach** *m* torrent; **~bahn** *f*: ***in freier ~*** in the wild; **~bra·ten** *m* roast venison; roast of venison

Wild·bret ['vɪltbrɛt] *n* (-s; *no pl.*) game; venison

'Wild|dieb *m* poacher; **~en·te** *f* wild duck

Wil·de ['vɪldə] *m, f* (-n; -n) savage; *fig.* ***wie ein ~r (e-e ~)*** like a madman (madwoman) *or* maniac

Wil·de·rer ['vɪldərɐ] *m* (-s; -) poacher

wil·dern ['vɪldɐn] *v/i.* (h) poach; *dog*: kill game

Wild·fang ['vɪltfaŋ] *m* (-[e]s; ⸚e) little devil

'wild'fremd *adj.* completely strange (*dat.* to); ***~er Mensch*** complete stranger

'Wild|füt·te·rung *f* feeding of game; **~gans** *f* wild goose; **~ge·flü·gel** *n* wildfowl; **~ge·he·ge** *n* game enclosure; **~ge·schmack** *m* gam(e)y taste

'Wild·heit *f* (-; *no pl.*) wildness; savagery; fury *etc.*; → ***wild***

'Wild|hü·ter *m* gamekeeper; **~kat·ze** *f* wild cat; **≈le·bend** *adj.* wild, ... roaming free; **~le·der** *n*, **≈le·dern** *adj.* suede (leather)

Wild·nis ['vɪltnɪs] *f* (-; -se) wilderness (*a. fig.*), *the* wild; *a. fig.* jungle

'Wild|park *m* game (*or* deer) park; **~pa,ste·te** *f* game (*or* venison) pie; **~ra,gout** *n* game stew; **~re·ser,vat** *n* game reserve

'wild·ro'man·tisch *adj.* wildly romantic; ***~e Landschaft*** wild, romantic landscape; ***~e Liebesgeschichte*** wild romance

'Wild|sau *f* wild sow; *fig.* pig; **~schwein** *n* wild boar (*or* sow)

'wild·wach·send *adj.* wild

'Wild·was·ser *n* torrent; ***~... in cpds.*** white-water *canoeing etc.*; **~bahn** *f* flume; **~ren·nen** *n* white-water race; **~(renn)sport** *m* white-water canoeing

'Wild·wech·sel *m* game path, runway

Wild'west *without art. the* Wild West; **~film** *m* western, cowboy film; **~ma,nier** *f*: ***in ~*** western style

'Wild·wuchs *m* (-es; *no pl.*) rank growth; *fig.* proliferation; **'wild·wuchs·ar·tig** *adv.*: ***sich ~ ausbreiten*** proliferate, *city*: sprawl

'Wild·zie·ge *f* wild goat

Wil·le ['vɪlə] *m* (-ns; *no pl.*) will, *phls. a.* volition; *a.* determination; intention; ***böser ~*** ill will; ***es war kein böser ~*** it wasn't intentional, he *etc.* didn't do it out of spite; ***guter ~*** good will (*or* intention); ***letzter ~*** will, ⚖ last will and testament, *w.s.* last (*or* dying) wish; ***aus freiem ~n*** of one's own free will; ***wider ~n, gegen s-n ~n*** against one's will; ***j-m s-n ~n lassen*** let s.o. have his *or* her (own) way; ***s-n (keinen) eigenen ~n haben*** have a (no) mind of one's own; ***s-n guten ~n zeigen*** show one's (*or* some) goodwill; ***den ~n für die Tat nehmen*** take the will for the deed; ***gegen j-s ~n handeln*** act against s.o.'s wishes; ***es fehlt ihm nur der gute ~*** he just has to want to; ***es ist mein fester ~*** I'm absolutely determined, it's my firm intention; ***wo ein ~ ist, ist auch ein Weg*** where there's a will, there's a way; ***beim besten ~n nicht*** much as I'd like to; ***ich kann mich beim besten ~n nicht erinnern*** I can't for the life of me remember; ***wenn es nach s-m ~n ginge*** if he had his way; ***ganz nach d-m ~n*** as you wish; ***j-m zu ~n sein*** obey s.o.'s wishes, submit to s.o., *woman*: give o.s. to s.o.; → ***willens, durchsetzen¹*** I

Wil·len ['vɪlən] *m* (-s; *no pl.*) → ***Wille***

'wil·len *prp.*: ***um*** *gen.* ***... ~*** for the sake of ..., for *s.o.'s* sake; → ***Gott*** 1

'wil·len·los I. *adj.* weak-willed; ***~ sein*** *a.*

have no willpower; ***j-s ~es Werkzeug sein*** be a tool in s.o.'s hands; **II.** *adv.* meekly; ***j-m ~ ausgeliefert sein*** be at s.o.'s mercy; **'Wil·len·lo·sig·keit** *f* (-; *no pl.*) lack of willpower

wil·lens ['vɪləns] *adj.*: ~ ***sein zu*** *inf.* be willing (*or* prepared) to *inf.*; ***ich bin nicht ~ zu*** *inf. a.* I don't see why I should *inf.*

'Wil·lens|akt *m* act of volition; **~an·stren·gung** *f* effort of will; **~äu·ße·rung** *f* **1.** expression of one's will; **2.** ⚖ declaration of intention; **~er·klä·rung** *f* → ***Willensäußerung*** 2; **~frei·heit** *f* (-; *no pl.*) freedom of will; **~kraft** *f* (-; *no pl.*) willpower; *w.s.* strong will; ***durch ~ allein*** through sheer willpower

'wil·lens·schwach *adj.* weak-willed; **'Wil·lens·schwä·che** *f* (-; *no pl.*) weak will

'wil·lens·stark *adj.* strong-willed; **'Wil·lens·stär·ke** *f* (-; *no pl.*) willpower

wil·lent·lich ['vɪləntlɪç] *adj.* (*and adv.*) deliberate(ly)

will·fäh·rig ['vɪlfɛːrɪç] *adj.* compliant; *contp.* obsequious

wil·lig ['vɪlɪç] *adj.* willing, prepared (**zu** *inf.* to *inf.*); eager, keen; ***ein ~es Ohr leihen*** *dat.* lend a willing ear to

wil·li·gen ['vɪlɪgən] *v/i.* (h): ~ **in** *acc.* agree to, consent to; approve of

Will·kom·men [vɪl'kɔmən] *n, m* (-s; *no pl.*) welcome, reception; ***j-m ein herzliches ~ bereiten*** give s.o. a warm welcome, receive s.o. warmly; **will'kom·men** *adj.* welcome (*dat.* to) (*a. fig.*); ***j-n ~ heißen*** welcome s.o.; ***seid ~!*** welcome!; ***du bist hier immer ~*** you'll always be welcome here (*or* find an open door here)

Will·kür ['vɪlkyːɐ] *f* (-; *no pl.*) a) arbitrariness, b) despotism, despotic rule; ***j-s ~ ausgeliefert sein*** be at s.o.'s mercy; **~akt** *m* arbitrary act; **~herr·schaft** *f* (-; *no pl.*) arbitrary rule, despotism

'will·kür·lich *adj.* a) arbitrary (*a.* ⩘), random *selection etc.*, b) voluntary

wim·meln ['vɪməln] *v/i.* (h): ~ **von** *dat.* be swarming (*or* teeming, F crawling) with *ants etc.*; *fig.* be teeming (*or* bristling) with *mistakes etc.*; ***es wimmelte nur so von*** *dat.* the place was teeming with

wim·mern ['vɪmɐn] **I.** *v/i.* (h) whimper; **II.** ♀ *n* (-s; *no pl.*) whimpering

Wim·pel ['vɪmpəl] *m* (-s; -) pennant

Wim·per ['vɪmpɐ] *f* (-; -n) eyelash; *fig.* ***ohne mit der ~ zu zucken*** without batting an eyelid, without flinching

'Wim·pern·tu·sche *f* mascara

'Wim·per·tier·chen *n* ciliate

Wind [vɪnt] *m* (-[e]s; -e ['vɪndə]) wind; ***guter ~, günstiger ~*** fair wind; ***sanfter ~*** (gentle) breeze; ***schwacher bis mäßiger ~ aus Nordost*** light to moderate northeasterly wind; ***~ und Wetter ausgesetzt sein*** be exposed to the weather (*or* elements); ***bei ~ und Wetter*** in all weathers, no matter what the weather; ***dicht am ~ segeln*** sail close to the wind; ***gegen den ~*** into the wind; ***mit dem ~*** down wind; *fig.* ***~ bekommen von*** *dat.* get wind of *s.th.*; F ***viel ~ machen*** a) F make a great big fuss, b) F talk big; ***j-m den ~ aus den Segeln nehmen*** take the wind out of s.o.'s sails; ***in alle ~e zerstreut*** scattered to the four winds; ***in den ~ reden*** waste one's breath; ***in den ~ schlagen*** cast to the winds; ***frischen ~ in die Firma bringen*** shake the company up; ***das ist ~ in s-e Segel*** that's grist to his mill; ***wissen, woher der ~ weht*** know how the wind blows; ***sich den ~ um die Nase*** (*or* ***Ohren***) ***wehen lassen*** go out into the big wide world; → ***Fähnchen, Mantel***

'Wind·beu·tel *m gastr.* cream puff

Win·de[1] ['vɪndə] *f* (-; -n) ⚙ winch, windlass, hoist; capstan

'Win·de[2] *f* (-; -n) ⚘ bindweed

'Wind·ei *n* wind-egg; F *fig.* F washout

Win·del ['vɪndəl] *f* nappy, *Am.* diaper; ***damals lagst du noch in den ~n*** you were still in your nappies (*Am.* diapers) at the time; F *fig.* **(*noch*) *in den ~n stekken*** still be in its infancy (*or* at a very early stage); **~aus·schlag** *m* nappy (*Am.* diaper) rash; **~ein·la·gen** *pl.* nappy (*Am.* diaper) liners

'win·del'weich F *adj.*: ***j-n ~ schlagen*** (*or* ***dreschen***) F beat the living daylights out of s.o., make mincemeat out of s.o.

win·den ['vɪndən] (wand, gewunden, h) **I.** *v/t.* a) wind (**um** *acc.* round), b) make, bind *wreath etc.*; ***in die Höhe ~*** hoist; **II.** *v/refl.*: **sich** ~ *snake etc.*: writhe; *worm*: wriggle; *person*: writhe (**vor** *dat.* with *pain etc.*), *fig.* squirm (with *embarrassment etc.*); *path*: wind (its way along), *river*: *a.* meander; ***sich ~ um*** *acc.* wind (*or* coil) itself round; ***sich ~ durch*** *acc.* weave one's way through *a crowd etc.*; *fig.* ***sich ~ wie ein Aal*** wriggle like an eel; → ***gewunden***

'Wind·ener,gie *f* wind power; **~park** *m* wind farm

Win·des·ei·le ['vɪndəs-] *f*: ***in ~*** at lightning speed, in no time; ***das Gerücht verbreitete sich in ~*** the rumo(u)r spread like wildfire

'Wind|fah·ne *f* weathervane; **~fang** *m* vestibule; **♀ge·schützt** *adj.* sheltered (from the wind); **~hauch** *m* breath of wind; **~ho·se** *f* whirlwind; **~hund** *m zo.* greyhound; F *fig.* F freewheeler

win·dig ['vɪndɪç] *adj.* windy; F *fig.* unreliable *person*; F dodgy; lame *excuse etc.*

'Wind|jacke *f* windcheater; **~jam·mer** *m* (-s; -) ⚓ windjammer; **~ka,nal** *m* wind tunnel; **~kraft·werk** *n* wind power plant; **~licht** *n* storm lantern; **~ma·cher** F *m* → ***Wichtigtuer***; **~ma,schi·ne** *f* blower, fan; **~müh·le** *f* windmill; *fig.* ***gegen ~n kämpfen*** tilt at windmills; **~müh·len·flü·gel** *m* windmill sail; **~pocken** *pl.* ⚕ chickenpox *sg.*; **~rad** *n* wind turbine, windmill; **~räd·chen** *n* pinwheel; **~rich·tung** *f* direction of the wind; **~rös·chen** *n* ⚘ anemone; **~ro·se** *f* compass card (*or* rose); **~sack** *m* windsock, wind sleeve; **~schat·ten** *m* ⚓ lee; ✈ sheltered zone; ***im ~*** *drive, run etc.* in the slipstream (**von** *dat.* of)

'wind·schief *adj.* crooked, *a.* bowed *tree*, F skew-whiff

wind·schlüp·fig ['vɪntʃlʏpfɪç], **'wind·schnit·tig** *adj.* streamlined

'Wind·schutz *m* a) protection from the wind, b) windbreak; **~klap·pe** *f* storm flap; **~schei·be** *f* windscreen, *Am.* windshield

'Wind|sei·te *f* weather side; **~stär·ke** *f* wind force; **~ 1** Beaufort 1

'wind·still *adj.* calm; **'Wind·stil·le** *f* calm, *a.* lull

'Wind·stoß *m* gust (of wind)

'wind·sur·fen *v/i.* (*insep.*, *no* -ge-, h) windsurf; **'Wind·sur·fen** *n* windsurfing

'Wind·tur,bi·ne *f* wind turbine

Win·dung ['vɪndʊŋ] *f* (-; -en) a) bend *of a road etc.*, b) whorl, c) ⚙ worm, thread, d) *pl. anat.* convolutions

Wink [vɪŋk] *m* (-[e]s; -e) sign; wave; *fig.* hint, tip, tip-off; ***ein ~ des Schicksals*** a sign from above; → ***Zaunpfahl***

Win·kel ['vɪŋkəl] *m* (-s; -) **1.** ⩘ angle; ***im rechten ~ zu*** *dat.* at right angles to; → ***spitz, tot***; **2.** corner; place, spot; *fig.* recess *of the heart*; **3.** ⚔ chevron; **~ad·vo,kat** *m* F pettifogger, *Am.* shyster; **~ei·sen** *n* ⚙ angle iron

'win·kel·för·mig [-fœrmɪç] *adj.* angled; *w.s.* L-shaped

'Win·kel|funk·ti,on *f* ⩘ trigonometric function; **~hal,bie·ren·de** *f* (-; -n) ⩘ bisector of an angle

win·ke·lig ['vɪŋkəlɪç] *adj.* **1.** angular; *in cpds. usu.* ⩘ ...-angled; **2.** *room, apartment etc.* full of nooks and crannies; winding *roads, alleys etc.*

'Win·kel|maß *n* square; **~mes·ser** *m* protractor; *surv.* goniometer; **~trä·ger** *m* angle bracket; **~zug** *m* dodge; ***Winkelzüge machen*** do a bit of skil(l)ful dodging

win·ken ['vɪŋkən] *v/i.* (h) **1.** wave, beckon; make a sign, signal (*dat.* to); ***dem Kellner ~*** signal to the waiter; ***e-m Taxi ~*** hail (*or* wave down) a taxi; ***mit dem Taschentuch*** *etc.* ~ wave one's hankie (*or* handkerchief) *etc.*; **2.** *fig. surprise etc.*: be in store (*dat.* for); ***dem Finder winkt e-e hohe Belohnung*** the finder can expect a large reward; ***dem Gewinner winkt ein hoher Geldpreis*** the winner can look forward to a large cash prize

wink·lig ['vɪŋklɪç] *adj.* → ***winkelig***

win·seln ['vɪnzəln] *v/i.* (h) whine

Win·ter ['vɪntɐ] *m* (-s; -): (***im ~*** in) winter; ***über den ~ kommen*** get through the winter; **~abend** *m* winter evening; **~an·fang** *m* beginning of winter; first day of winter; **~aus·rü·stung** *f mot.* winter equipment; **~fahr·plan** *m* winter timetable (*Am.* schedule); **~fell** *n* winter coat; **~fe·ri·en** *pl.* winter holidays (*Am.* vacation *sg.*); **♀fest** *adj.* **1.** winterproof; **2.** ⚘ hardy; ~ ***machen*** winterize; **~gar·ten** *m* winter garden, conservatory; **~ge·trei·de** *n* winter crop; **~halb·jahr** *n* winter (months *pl.*); *ped.* winter term, winter and spring terms *pl.*; **♀hart** *adj.* → ***winterfest*** 2; **~kleid** *n* winter dress; *zo.* winter coat (*or* plumage); ***Landschaft im ~*** winter (*or* snowclad) landscape; **~klei·dung** *f* winter clothes *pl.* (*or* clothing)

'win·ter·lich *adj.* wint(e)ry

'Win·ter|luft *f* wint(e)ry air; **~man·tel** *m* winter coat; **~mo·de** *f* winter fashions *pl.*; **~mo·nat** *m* winter month; **~mor·gen** *m* winter('s) morning; **~nacht** *f* winter('s) night; ***in e-r kalten ~*** on a cold winter's night; **~olym·pia·de** *f* Winter Olympics *pl.*; **~pau·se** *f* winter break; **~quar,tier** *n* winter quarters *pl.*; **~rei·fen** *m mot.* winter (*or* snow) tyre (*Am.* tire); **~sa·chen** *pl.* winter clothes (*or* things); **~schlaf** *m zo.* hibernation; ~ ***halten*** hibernate; **~schluß·ver·kauf** *m* winter (*or* January) sales *pl.*; **~schu·he** *pl.* winter shoes *pl.*; **~se,me·ster** *n* winter semester (*or* term); **~sitz** *m* winter residence; **~son·nen·wen·de** *f* winter solstice; **~speck** F *m extra pounds put on* *in the winter*; **~spie·le** *pl.*: **Olympische ~** Winter Olympics

'**Win·tersport** *m* winter sport(s *pl. coll.*); **~klei·dung** *f* winter sportswear; **~ort** *m* ski resort

'**Win·ter|tag** *m* winter('s) day; **~ur·laub** *m* → **Winterferien**; **~zeit** *f* (-; *no pl.*) **1.** winter(time); **während der ~** in winter(time); **2.** winter time; **ab morgen gilt die ~** we switch to winter time tomorrow

Win·zer ['vɪntsɐ] *m* (-s; -) winegrower, vintner; **~ge·nos·sen·schaft** *f* winegrowers' cooperative

win·zig ['vɪntsɪç] *adj.* (*a.* **~ klein**) tiny, minute, F teeny(-weeny)

Winz·ling ['vɪntslɪŋ] *m* (-s; -e) **1.** tiny man (*or* woman), F midget, *contp.* F half-pint; **2.** tiny tot

Wip·fel ['vɪpfəl] *m* (-s; -) (tree)top

Wip·pe ['vɪpə] *f* (-; -n) seesaw; '**wip·pen** *v/i.* (h) seesaw, rock; **~ mit** wag *its tail etc.*; **auf den Zehenspitzen ~** rock up and down; **mit den Fußspitzen ~** jiggle one's feet; **in den Knien ~** bob up and down; **~der Gang** bouncing gait

Wipp·schal·ter ['vɪp-] *m* ⚡ rocker switch

wir [viːɐ] *pers. pron.* we; **~ beide** both of us, we both ..., the two of us, F us two; **~ drei** the three of us; **~ alle** all of us, we all ...

Wir·bel ['vɪrbəl] *m* (-s; -) **1.** whirl (*a. fig. of events etc.*), swirl; eddy, whirlpool, *a. phys.* vortex; flurry; whirlwind; ⚙ turbulence; *fig.* hurly-burly (of events); F to-do; **mach nicht solchen ~** don't make such a fuss; **es gab damals wegen dieser Affäre e-n großen ~** the affair caused quite a stir at the time; **2.** *anat.* vertebra (*pl.* vertebrae); **3.** (drum) roll; **4.** crown; **5.** (*violin etc.*) peg; **~bruch** *m* fractured vertebra; **~fort·satz** *m anat.* spinous process; **~ge·lenk** *n* **1.** *anat.* vertebral joint; **2.** ⚙ swivel joint

wir·be·lig ['vɪrbəlɪç] *adj.* **1.** dizzy; **2.** *fig.* wild *children etc.*

'**Wir·bel·kno·chen** *m* vertebra (*pl.* vertebrae)

'**wir·bel·los** *adj.* (*a.* **~es Tier**) invertebrate

wir·beln ['vɪrbəln] *v/i.* (sn) *snow, dust etc.*: whirl, swirl; *dancers etc.*: whirl; *drums*: roll; *fig.* **mir wirbelt der Kopf** my head's spinning

'**Wir·bel|säu·le** *f anat.* spine, spinal column; **~säu·len·er·kran·kung** *f* spinal disease; **~sturm** *m* whirlwind; cyclone; tornado; **~tier** *n* vertebrate; **~wind** *m* whirlwind (*a. fig.*)

Wirk·be·reich ['vɪrk-] *m pharm.* effective range

wir·ken ['vɪrkən] (h) **I.** *v/i.* **1.** have an effect (**auf** *acc.* on), be effective, work; take effect; **~ auf** *acc.* a) have a *depressing etc.* effect on *s.o.*, affect *s.o. or s.th.*, b) appeal to; **berauschend ~** have an intoxicating effect; **anregend ~** act as a stimulant; **die Tabletten ~ schnell** the tablets act fast; **die Arznei beginnt zu ~** the medicine is beginning to take effect; **et. auf sich ~ lassen** take s.th. in, soak s.th. up; **das hat gewirkt!** a) that did the trick, b) that hit home; **2.** work (**an** *dat.* at; **bei** *dat.* with, for), be active; **als Lehrer ~** be a teacher, teach; **als Missionar** *etc.* **~** *a.* be active as a missionary *etc.* (*or* in missionary work *etc.*); **3.** look *younger, sad etc.*; **er wirkt schüchtern** he gives the impression of being rather shy; **4.** look good; **das Bild wirkt aus der Nähe überhaupt nicht** that picture looks like nothing from close up; **II.** *v/t.* **5.** → **bewirken, Wunder**; **6.** knit; weave; **III.** ♀ *n* (-s; *no pl.*) work; activity, activities *pl.*; **sein ~ im Bereich** *gen. a.* his contributions to; '**wir·kend** *adj.* active; **langsam ~** slow-acting; **schnell ~** fast-acting; **stark ~** strong, potent

Wir·ker ['vɪrkɐ] *m* (-s; -), **Wir·ke·rin** ['vɪrkərɪn] *f* (-; -nen) knitter; weaver

wirk·lich ['vɪrklɪç] **I.** *adj.* real, actual, true; **das ~e Leben** real life; **II.** *adv.* really, actually; honestly; **~?** really?, *a. iro.* you don't say; **es war ~ gut** it was really good, it really was good; **es tut mir ~ leid** I really am sorry; '**Wirk·lich·keit** *f* (-; *no pl.*) reality; **die rauhe ~** harsh reality, the hard facts (of life); **in ~** a) in reality, b) in fact

'**wirk·lich·keits|fremd** *adj.* unrealistic(ally *adv.*); starry-eyed; **~ge·treu** *adj.* realistic(ally *adv.*); faithful *copy etc.*; **~nah** *adj.* realistic(ally *adv.*), down-to-earth

wirk·sam ['vɪrkzaːm] *adj.* effective; **sehr ~** *a.* very strong *drug etc.*; **~ gegen** *acc.* good for; **~ werden** *law etc.*: take effect (**am ...** from ...), *drug etc.*: (begin to) take effect *or* have an effect; '**Wirk·sam·keit** *f* (-; *no pl.*) effectiveness; *a.* efficacy *of a drug, method etc.*

'**Wirk·stoff** *m* agent, active substance

Wir·kung ['vɪrkʊŋ] *f* (-; -en) effect; impact; **mit ~ vom** with effect from, as from (*or* of); **mit sofortiger ~** as of now; **~ erzielen** have an effect, work; **s-e ~ tun** work, have the desired effect; **s-e ~ verfehlen, ohne ~ bleiben** have no effect, prove ineffective; **Ursache und ~** cause and effect; **er ist sehr auf ~ bedacht** he's out for effect; → **Ursache**

'**Wir·kungs|be·reich** *m* sphere of activity; ⚔ radius of action; ⚖ operation; **~dau·er** *f* effective period; ☂ persistency; **~grad** *m* efficiency; **~kraft** *f* efficacy; **~kreis** *m* sphere of activity

'**wir·kungs·los** *adj.* ineffective; **~ bleiben** have no effect; '**Wir·kungs·lo·sig·keit** *f* (-; *no pl.*) ineffectiveness, ineffectuality

'**wir·kungs·reich** *adj.* highly effective

'**wir·kungs·voll** *adj.* → **wirksam**

'**Wir·kungs·wei·se** *f* mode of operation; mechanism; *pharm.* effect

wirr [vɪr] *adj.* a) confused; bewildered, *contp.* muddle-headed, b) disorderly, chaotic; incoherent *speech*; dishevel(l)ed *hair*, F all over the place; **mir ist ganz ~ im Kopf** my head's spinning; **~es Zeug reden** ramble, rave

Wir·ren ['vɪrən] *pl.* turmoil *sg.*

'**Wirr·kopf** *m* scatterbrain

Wirr·warr ['vɪrvar] *m* (-s; *no pl.*) a) confusion, chaos, F jumble, mess, b) hubbub; **~ von Meinungen** confusion of opinions; **~ von Stimmen** babble of voices; **~ von Vorschriften und Verordnungen** labyrinth (*or* maze) of rules and regulations; **ein ~ von Gedanken** jumbled ideas

Wir·sing ['vɪrzɪŋ] *m* (-s; *no pl.*), **~kohl** *m* savoy (cabbage)

Wirt [vɪrt] *m* (-[e]s; -e) a) host (*a. biol.*), b) landlord, *a.* proprietor; **Wir·tin** ['vɪrtɪn] *f* (-; -nen) a) hostess, b) landlady; *a.* proprietor, proprietress, c) landlord's wife

Wirt·schaft ['vɪrtʃaft] *f* (-; -en) **1.** *no pl.* a) economy, b) trade and industry; **2.** pub, *formal*: public house, *Am.* saloon; **3.** *no pl.* housekeeping; **4.** farmstead; **5.** *no pl.* a) management, b) F *contp.* F mess; F **das ist ja e-e schöne ~** that's a fine state of affairs; '**wirt·schaf·ten** (h) **I.** *v/i.* **1.** a) keep house, b) economize; **gut ~** be a good housekeeper, *w.s.* be economical, know how to do one's sums; **mit Gewinn** (**Verlust**) **~** come out on the plus (minus) side; **in die eigene Tasche ~** line one's own pockets; **2.** be busy; potter around (*or* about); **II.** *v/t.*: **e-e Firma zugrunde ~** run a firm into the ground

Wirt·schaf·te·rin ['vɪrtʃaftərɪn] *f* (-; -nen) housekeeper

Wirt·schaft·ler ['vɪrtʃaftlɐ] *m* (-s; -) economist

'**wirt·schaft·lich** *adj.* **1.** economic(ally *adv.*); financial; **2.** profitable; efficient; **3.** economical; '**Wirt·schaft·lich·keit** *f* (-; *no pl.*) **1.** good management; (economic) efficiency; **2.** profitability; efficiency; **3.** economy, thrift

'**Wirt·schafts|ab·kom·men** *n* economic (*or* trade) agreement; **~auf·schwung** *m* economic upturn (*or* boom); **~ba·ro·ˌme·ter** *n* business barometer; **~be·ra·ter** *m* economic adviser; **~be·zie·hun·gen** *pl.* economic (*or* trade) relations; **~boyˌkott** *m* economic sanctions *pl.* (*or* boycott, embargo); **~ein·heit** *f* economic entity; **~flücht·ling** *m* economic migrant (*or* refugee); **~form** *f* economic system; **~füh·rer** *m* leading industrialist, captain of industry; **~geld** *n* (-[e]s; *no pl.*) housekeeping money; **~ge·mein·schaft** *f* trading partnership, economic union; *hist.* **Europäische ~** European Economic Community (*abbr.* EEC); **~ge·schich·te** *f* history of economics; **~gip·fel** *m* economic summit; **~gü·ter** *pl.* economic goods; **~gymˌna·si·um** *n grammar school emphasizing the study of economics*; **~hil·fe** *f* economic aid; **~jahr** *n* financial year; **~jour·naˌlist** *m* economic journalist; **~ka·piˌtän** F *m* captain of industry; tycoon; **~kraft** *f* (-; *no pl.*) economic power; **~krieg** *m* economic war(fare); **~kri·mi·na·liˌtät** *f* white-collar crime; **~kri·se** *f* economic crisis; **~la·ge** *f* economic situation; **~le·ben** *n* (-s; *no pl.*) economic activity; **~macht** *f* economic power; **~miˌni·ster** *m* minister for economic affairs; *in GB*: Secretary of State for Trade and Industry, Trade and Industry Secretary; *in the USA*: Secretary of Commerce; **~mi·niˌste·ri·um** *n* economics ministry; *in GB*: Department of Trade and Industry; *in the USA*: Department of Commerce; **~miˌse·re** *f* economic plight; **~ord·nung** *f* economic system; **~part·ner** *m* **1.** trading partner; **2.** business partner; **~po·liˌtik** *f* economic policy; ♀**poˌli·tisch** *adj.* economic(ally *adv.*); **~proˌgno·se** *f* economic forecast; **~prü·fer** *m* auditor; **~psy·cho·loˌgie** *f* industrial psychology; **~recht** *n* (-[e]s; *no pl.*) commercial law; **~spioˌna·ge** *f* industrial espionage; **~syˌstem** *n* economy, economic system; **~teil** *m* financial pages *pl.*, business section *of a paper*; **~uniˌon** *f* economic union; **~ver·band** *m* trade association; **~ver·bre·chen** *n coll.* white-collar crime; **~wachs·tum** *n* economic growth; **~wis·sen·schaft** *f* economics *pl.*; **~wis·sen·schaft·ler** *m* economist; **~wun·der** *n* economic miracle; **~zei·tung** *f* business paper; **~zweig**

m branch of industry; sector of the economy
'**Wirts|haus** *n* pub, *formal:* public house; *Am.* saloon; inn; **~leu·te** *pl.* landlord and landlady; **~pflan·ze** *f* host
Wisch [vɪʃ] F *contp. m* (-[e]s; -e) *sl.* bumf, bumph
wi·schen ['vɪʃən] *v/t.* (h) wipe; mop (up); *fig.* ***j-m e-e*** ~ F give s.o. a clip round the ears
Wi·scher ['vɪʃɐ] *m* (-s; -) *mot.* wiper; **~blatt** *n* wiper blade
wi·schi·wa·schi ['vɪʃi'vaʃi] F **I.** *adj.* vague; **II.** ♀ *n* (-s; *no pl.*) F blah(-blah)
'**Wisch|lap·pen** *m*, **~tuch** *n* cloth
Wi·sent ['vi:zɛnt] *n* (-s; -e) bison
Wis·mut ['vɪsmu:t] *n* (-s; *no pl.*) bismuth
wis·pern ['vɪspɐn] (h) **I.** *v/t.* whisper; **II.** *v/i.* whisper, speak (*or* talk) in a whisper
Wiß·be·gier(de) ['vɪs-] *f* (-; *no pl.*) thirst for knowledge, (intellectual) curiosity; '**wiß·be·gie·rig** *adj.* eager to learn (*or* for knowledge); *w.s.* curious
wis·sen ['vɪsən] *v/t. and v/i.* (wußte, gewußt, h) know (***von*** *dat.* about); ~ ***lassen, daß*** let on that; ***j-n et.*** ~ ***lassen*** let s.o. know s.th.; ***ich weiß genau, daß*** I know for a fact that; ***das hätte ich*** ~ ***sollen*** I wish I'd known; ***ich weiß s-n Namen nicht mehr*** I can't remember his name; ***weißt du schon das Neueste?*** have you heard the latest?; ***er weiß immer alles besser*** he always knows better; ***das mußt du selber*** ~ that's up to you; ***woher weißt du das?*** how do you know?; ***sie ist sehr hübsch, aber sie weiß es auch*** she's very pretty and she knows it; ***ich möchte (doch) gern*** ~ I'd (really) like to know; ***ich möchte nicht*** ~***, was sie dafür bezahlt hat*** I wouldn't like to know what she paid for it; ***sie weiß nicht, was sie will*** she doesn't know what she wants; ***er weiß nicht, was er sagt*** he doesn't know what he's talking about; ***man kann nie*** ~ you never know (***bei*** *dat.* with); ***ich weiß nicht recht*** I'm not (so) sure, F I dunno; ***nicht, daß ich wüßte*** not that I know of; ***soviel ich weiß*** as far as I know; ***was weiß ich!*** how should I know?, how am I supposed to know?; ***und was weiß ich noch alles*** and what not; ***als ob es wer weiß was gekostet hätte*** as if it had cost goodness knows how much; ***er hält sich für wer weiß wie klug*** he thinks he's goodness knows how clever; ***ich will von ihm (davon) nichts*** ~ I don't want anything to do with him (it); ***ich will von ihr nichts mehr*** ~ F I'm through with her; ***von Geld wollte er nichts*** ~ he refused to (*or* he wouldn't) accept any money; ***ich werde ihn schon zu finden*** ~ I'll find him all right (*Am.* alright), I'll find him, don't you worry; ***weißt du noch?*** (do you) remember?; → ***Bescheid, heiß*** I, ***helfen, Rat*** 1
'**Wis·sen** *n* (-s; *no pl.*) knowledge; ***ohne mein*** ~ without my knowing; ***meines*** ~***s*** as far as I know; ***nach bestem*** ~ ***und Gewissen*** to the best of one's knowledge and belief
'**wis·send** *adj.* knowing *look etc.*
'**Wis·sens|be·reich** *m* field of knowledge; **~be·rei·che·rung** *f* gain in knowledge
'**Wis·sen·schaft** *f* (-; -en) a) science, b) research, c) (world of) scholarship, academia; ***in der*** ~ ***tätig sein*** work in research; ***die*** ~ ***sagt*** researchers (*or* scientists) claim; ***die*** ~ ***hat bewiesen ...*** *a.* research has proved ...; ***der*** ~ ***hinterlassen*** bequeath to scholarship, leave *organs etc.* to medical science; F ***das ist e-e*** ~ ***für sich*** that's a book with seven seals
Wis·sen·schaft·ler ['vɪsənʃaftlɐ] *m* (-s; -), **Wis·sen·schaft·le·rin** ['vɪsənʃaftlərɪn] *f* (-; -nen) a) academic, b) scientist, c) scholar, d) researcher
'**wis·sen·schaft·lich** *adj.* a) academic, b) methodical; scientific, c) scholarly; ~***e Laufbahn (Diskussion)*** academic career (discussion); ~***er Beweis*** scientific proof (*or* evidence); '**Wis·sen·schaft·lich·keit** *f* (-; *no pl.*) scholarliness; *a.* scholarly standard
'**Wis·sen·schafts|gläu·big·keit** *f* blind faith in science; **~zweig** *m* branch of learning, discipline
'**Wis·sens|drang** *m*, **~durst** *m* thirst for knowledge; **~ge·biet** *n* field of knowledge; **~gut** *n* (-[e]s; *no pl.*) fund of knowledge; **~lücke** *f* gap in one's knowledge; **~stand** *m* (-[e]s; *no pl.*) level (*or* state) of knowledge; ***auf dem neuesten*** ~ up to date; **~stoff** *m* (-[e]s; *no pl.*) (body of) knowledge; **~ver·mitt·lung** *f* transfer of knowledge; **~vor·sprung** *m* advance in knowledge
'**wis·sens·wert** *adj.* worth knowing; ***Wissenswertes*** interesting facts
wis·sent·lich ['vɪsəntlɪç] **I.** *adj.* conscious; wil(l)ful, deliberate; **II.** *adv.* knowingly; deliberately
wit·tern ['vɪtɐn] (h) **I.** *v/t.* scent, smell; *fig.* sense, see *one's chance*; **II.** *v/i.* sniff the air; **Wit·te·rung** *f* (-; *no pl.*) **1.** (***bei dieser*** ~ in this) weather; ***bei günstiger*** ~ weather permitting; ***bei jeder*** ~ in all weathers; **2.** scent; ***die*** ~ ***aufnehmen (verlieren)*** pick up (lose) the scent; *a. fig.* ***e-e feine*** ~ ***haben*** have a good nose
'**wit·te·rungs|be·dingt** *adj.* weather-induced; ~ ***sein*** *a.* be due to (*or* because of) the weather; **~be·stän·dig** *adj.* weatherproof; stainless *steel*
'**Wit·te·rungs|ein·flüs·se** *pl.* influence *sg.* of the weather; weather factors; **~schutz** *m* cold weather protection; **~ˌum·schlag** *m* sudden change in the weather; **~ver·hält·nis·se** *pl.* weather (*or* atmospheric) conditions
Wit·we ['vɪtvə] *f* (-; -n) widow
'**Wit·wen|ren·te** *f* widow's pension; **~ver·bren·nung** *f* sati, ritual burning of widows
Wit·wer ['vɪtvɐ] *m* (-s; -) widower
Witz [vɪts] *m* (-es; -e) **1.** joke; ***alter*** ~ stale joke, F old chestnut; ***das ist ein (ur)alter*** ~ *a.* that's an old one, that's as old as the hills; ~***e machen*** (*or* ***reißen***) tell (F crack) jokes; ***das ist der*** ~ ***an der Sache*** that's the funny thing about it, *w.s.* that's the whole point; F ***das ist der ganze*** ~ that's all there is to it; F ***mach keine*** ~***e!*** you're joking (F kidding); ***das soll wohl ein*** ~ ***sein*** you're joking, of course; is this supposed to be some kind of joke?; ***das ist ja ein*** ~***!*** *iro.* what a laugh; ***diese Bestimmung ist ja wohl ein*** ~ this regulation is ridiculous; **2.** *no pl.* wit(tiness); ~ ***haben*** be very witty
'**Witz·blatt** *n* funny (*or* satirical) magazine; **~fiˌgur** F *f* caricature
Witz·bold ['vɪtsbɔlt] *m* (-[e]s; -e [-də]) joker; *iro.* ***du*** ~***!*** very funny!
Wit·ze·lei [vɪtsə'laɪ] *f* (-; -en) **1.** witticism; **2.** *no pl.* a) joking, b) teasing
wit·zeln ['vɪtsəln] *v/i.* (h) joke (***über*** *acc.* about); ~ ***über*** *acc. a.* poke fun at
wit·zig ['vɪtsɪç] *adj.* witty; funny; *a. iro.* ***sehr*** ~***!*** very funny!
'**witz·los** *adj.* **1.** unwitty, lacking in wit (*or* humo[u]r), unfunny; **2.** F useless (***zu*** *inf. ger.*)
'**Witz·sei·te** *f* humorous page, F *the* funnies *pl.*
WM [ve:'ʔɛm] *f* (-; *no pl.*) world championship(s *pl.*); **~-Run·de** *f* world championship round (*or* leg); *soccer:* round of the World Cup; **~-Spiel** *n* world championship game (*or* match); *soccer:* World Cup match; **~-Turˌnier** *n* world championship (*soccer:* World Cup) tournament
wo [vo:] **I.** *interr. adv. and rel. adv.* where; F ~ ***gibt's denn so was!*** F have you ever seen the likes of it?; **II.** *cj.* when; ***jetzt*** ~ ***...*** now that ...; ~ ***nicht*** if not; ~ ***auch (nur)*** wherever; **III.** F *indef. adv.* somewhere; **IV.** F *int.:* ***i*** ~***!, ach*** ~***!*** no, no; oh, no
wo·an·ders [vo'ʔandɐs] *adv.* somewhere else; anywhere else
wob [vo:p] *pret. of* ***weben***
wo·bei [vo'baɪ] **I.** *rel. adv.:* ***ich las den Brief noch mal,*** ~ ***mir klar wurde ...*** I re-read the letter and realized ...; ***...,*** ~ ***du beachten (aufpassen) mußt, daß*** but you have to remember (watch) that; ~ ***mir einfällt*** which reminds me; **II.** *interr. adv.:* ~ ***bist du gerade?*** what are you doing right now?; ~ ***haben sie ihn ertappt?*** what was he caught doing?, what did they catch him at (*or* doing)?
Wo·che ['vɔxə] *f* (-; -n) week; ***in einer*** ~ in a week('s time); ***jede zweite*** ~ every other week; ***dreimal die*** ~ three times a week; ~ ***um*** ~ week after week; ***unter der*** ~***, die*** ~ ***über*** during the week
'**Wo·chen|ar·beits·zeit** *f* weekly working hours *pl.*; **~bett** *n* (-[e]s; *no pl.*) lying-in (period); ***im*** ~ ***sterben*** die after giving birth (to a *or* one's child); **~bett...** ⚕ *in cpds.* puerperal *fever etc.*; **~blatt** *n* weekly (paper)
'**Wo·chen·end|arˌrest** *m* ⚔ weekend detention; **~aus·flug** *m* weekend trip; **~aus·flüg·ler** *m* weekender; **~aus·ga·be** *f* weekend edition; **~bei·la·ge** *f* weekend supplement
'**Wo·chen·en·de** *n* weekend; ***am*** ~ at (*or* on) the weekend; ***übers*** ~ over the weekend, ***wegfahren***: go away for the weekend
'**Wo·chen·end|ehe** *f* weekend marriage; **~haus** *n usu.* weekend cottage; **~heim·fah·rer** *m* weekly commuter; **~ur·laub** *m* weekend break (*or* trip); **~ver·kehr** *m* weekend traffic
'**Wo·chen·kar·te** *f* weekly season ticket
'**wo·chen·lang** **I.** *adj.* lasting several weeks; ***nach*** ~***em Warten*** after weeks of waiting; **II.** *adv.* for weeks (and weeks), for weeks on end; ***es dauerte*** ~***, bis*** it took weeks before
'**Wo·chen|lohn** *m* weekly wages *pl.*; **~markt** *m* weekly market; **~pfle·ge·rin** *f* visiting nurse; **~schau** *f hist. film:* newsreel
'**Wo·chen·tag** *m* weekday; '**wo·chen·tags** *adv.* on weekdays
wö·chent·lich ['vœçəntlɪç] **I.** *adj.* weekly; week-by-week ...; **II.** *adv.* every week, weekly; ***einmal*** ~ once a week

'wo·chen·wei·se *adv.* week by week; on a weekly basis
Wöch·n·erin ['vœçnərɪn] *f* (-; -nen) woman in childbed; **'Wöch·ne·rin·nen·sta·ti,on** *f* maternity ward
Wod·ka ['vɔtka] *m* (-s; -s) vodka
wo·durch [vo'dʊrç] **I.** *interr. adv.* how?; **II.** *rel. adv.* by (*or* through) which; *formal*: whereby; by means of which; *referring to a whole sentence*: which; **~ bewiesen wird, daß** which proves that
wo·für [vo'fy:ɐ] **I.** *interr. adv.* what (...) for?; **~ halten Sie mich?** who do you think I am?, who do you take me for?; **II.** *rel. adv.* for which, which ... for; **~ ich mich interessiere** what I'm interested in
wog [vo:k] *pret. of* **wiegen¹** *and* **wägen**
Wo·ge ['vo:gə] *f* (-; -n) wave, billow; *fig.* wave, surge; *fig.* **die ~n glätten** pour oil on troubled waters
wo·ge·gen [vo'ge:gən] **I.** *interr. adv.* against what?, what ... against?; **II.** *rel. adv.* against which, which ... against; in return for which; **III.** *cj.* → **wohingegen**
wo·gen ['vo:gən] *v/i.* (h) surge (*a. fig.*); heave; *grainfield*: sway
wo·her [vo'he:ɐ] **I.** *interr. adv. and rel. adv.* where (...) from; **~ wissen Sie das?** how do you know that?; **II.** F *int.*: **~ denn!** nonsense
wo·hin [vo'hɪn] *interr. adv. and rel. adv.* where (... to); **~ geht's?** were are you off to?
wo·hin'ge·gen *cj.* whereas, while
wohl [vo:l] **I.** *adj.* **1.** well; **sich ~ fühlen** a) feel fine, be happy, b) feel at home; **sich bei j-m ~ fühlen** feel comfortable (*or* comfy) with s.o.; **ich fühle mich in s-r Gegenwart nicht ~** I don't feel at ease (*or* I feel uncomfortable) when he's around; **ich fühle mich nicht ~** I don't feel well; **mir ist nicht ~ dabei** I don't feel happy about it; **sie fühlt sich ~ in München** she's quite happy in Munich; **sie ließen sich's ~ sein** they had a good time; → **bekommen** II, **leben** I; **II.** *adv.* **2.** well; **~ oder übel** willy nilly, whether you *etc.* like it or not; **wir müssen es ~ oder übel machen** there's no getting around it; **er weiß das sehr ~** he knows very well; **ich bin mir dessen ~ bewußt** I'm well aware of that; **das kann man ~ sagen!** you can say that again; **das war ~ überlegt** that was well thought out; **ich erinnere mich sehr ~ daran** I remember it well; **ich verstehe dich sehr ~** I understand you perfectly well; **er hätte sehr ~ kommen können** he could easily have come, there was nothing to stop him (from) coming; **3.** possibly; perhaps, maybe; probably; I suppose; **das ist ~ möglich** I suppose that's possible, that's quite possible; **das wird ~ das beste sein** that's probably the best solution; **das wird ~ so sein** very likely; **~ kaum** hardly, I doubt it; **sie wird ~ kaum anrufen** I doubt whether she'll ring up, I don't suppose she'll ring up; *gehst du mit?* - **~ kaum** I doubt it very much; **ich habe ~ nicht richtig gehört** did I hear you right?; **4.** I wonder; **ob er ~ weiß, daß** I wonder if he knows (that); **5. er könnte ~ noch kommen** he might come yet; **6.** about; **ich habe es ihm ~ schon zehnmal gesagt** I must have told him at least ten times; **7.** *was machst du da?* - **was ~?** what does it look like?, what do you think?
Wohl *n* (-[e]s; *no pl.*) welfare, good; well-being, *w.s.* prosperity; **auf j-s ~ trinken** drink to s.o.'s health; **zum ~!** to your health!, F cheers!
wohl'auf *pred. adj.* well, in good health
'wohl·be·dacht *adj.* well-considered
'Wohl·be·fin·den *n* (-s; *no pl.*) well-being; **sich nach j-s ~ erkundigen** ask after s.o., ask how s.o. is
'Wohl·be·ha·gen *n* (-s; *no pl.*) comfort; pleasure; **mit ~** with relish
'wohl|be·hal·ten *adj.* safe (and sound); undamaged; **~be·hü·tet I.** *adj.* well looked-after; very sheltered *upbringing, life etc.*; **II.** *adv.*: **er ist ~ aufgewachsen** he had a very sheltered upbringing; **~be·kannt** *adj.* well-known, *b.s.* notorious
'wohl·do·siert [-do,zi:ɐt] **I.** *adj.* carefully measured; **~e Menge** *a.* well-measured dose; **II.** *fig. adv.*: **j-m et. ~ beibringen** break s.th. to s.o. gently
'wohl·durch,dacht *adj.* well thought-out
'Wohl·er·ge·hen *n* (-s; *no pl.*) welfare, well-being; **das leibliche ~** creature comforts
'wohl·er·zo·gen *adj.* well-behaved; **~ sein** *a.* have been brought up well
'Wohl·fahrt *f* (-; *no pl.*) **1.** F welfare (services *pl.*); **von der ~ leben** live on welfare; **2.** *obs.* welfare, well-being; **3. für die ~** for charity
'Wohl·fahrts|amt *n* → **Sozialamt; ~mar·ke** *f* charity stamp; **~or·ga·ni·sa·ti,on** *f* charity, charitable institution; **~pfle·ge** *f* welfare work; **~staat** *m* welfare state
'Wohl·ge·fal·len *n* (-s; *no pl.*) pleasure, satisfaction (**über** *acc.* at); **sein ~ haben an** *dat.* take great pleasure in; *hum.* **sich in ~ auflösen** a) *conflicts etc.*: be settled amicably, b) *plans etc.*: go up in smoke, c) *book, shirt, a. fig. club etc.*: disintegrate, come apart at the seams, d) vanish (into thin air); **'wohl·ge·fäl·lig I.** *adj.* a) pleasant, agreeable, b) complacent; **II.** *adv.* with pleasure
'wohl·ge·formt *adj.* well-shaped, shapely
'Wohl·ge·fühl *n* (-[e]s; *no pl.*) a) pleasant (*or* pleasurable) sensation *or* feeling, b) feeling (*or* sense) of well-being
'wohl|ge·launt *adj.* cheerful(ly *adv.*); **~ge·lit·ten** *adj.* (always) welcome; **~ge·lun·gen** *adj.* successful; *pred. a.* a (great) success; **~ge·meint** *adj.* well-meant; **~ge·merkt** *adv.* mind you
wohl·ge·mut ['vo:lgəmu:t] *adj.* cheerful(ly *adv.*)
'wohl|ge·nährt *adj.* well-fed; **~ge·ord·net** *adj.* (neat and) tidy; well-organized; **~ auf dem Schreibtisch liegen** be (placed) in neat piles on the desk; **~ge·ra·ten** *adj.* well-behaved *child*; good; **~ sein** *a.* have turned out well
'Wohl·ge·ruch *m* (-[e]s; ⸚e) fragrance; pleasant smell (*or* aroma)
'Wohl·ge·schmack *m* (-[e]s; *no pl.*) pleasant taste
'wohl|ge·setzt *adj.* **1.** well-chosen *words etc.*; well-rounded *speech etc.*; **2.** well-aimed *blow, shot etc.*; **~ge·sinnt** *adj.* well-meaning; **j-m ~ sein** be well-disposed towards s.o.; **~ge·stal·tet** *adj.* well-shaped, shapely
'wohl·ha·bend *adj.* well-to-do, wealthy; well-off
woh·lig ['vo:lɪç] *adj.* pleasant; cosy, *Am.* cozy
'Wohl·klang *m* (-[e]s; *no pl.*) melodiousness; **'wohl·klin·gend** *adj.* melodious; nice-sounding ...; **der Name ist ~** it's a nice-sounding name, the name has a nice ring to it
'Wohl·le·ben *n* (-s; *no pl.*) good living, life of luxury
'wohl·mei·nend *adj.* well-meaning
wohl·pro·por·tio·niert ['vo:lproportsio-,ni:ɐt] *adj.* well-proportioned; well-balanced; symmetrical
'wohl|rie·chend *adj.* fragrant; pleasant-smelling, aromatic; **~schmeckend** *adj.* tasty
'Wohl·sein *n* (-s; *no pl.*) well-being; **(zum) ~!** to your health!
'Wohl·stand *m* (-[e]s; *no pl.*) prosperity, affluence; **zu ~ kommen** gain prosperity, F strike it rich; **im ~ leben** live in prosperity (*or* affluence); F **ist bei dir der ~ ausgebrochen?** have you won the pools or something?
'Wohl·stands|bür·ger *m* member of the affluent society, affluent citizen; **~den·ken** *n* materialistic thinking; **~ge·fäl·le** *n* unequal distribution of wealth; **~ge·sell·schaft** *f* affluent society; **~krank·heit** *f* civilization disease; **~kri·mi·na·li,tät** *f* affluent delinquency
'Wohl·tat *f* (-; -en) **1.** *no pl.* relief; **das ist e-e ~!** what a relief; that does you good; **das ist e-e wahre ~** that really does you good; **2.** good deed; **'wohl·tä·tig** *adj.* charitable; **~e Stiftung** charitable trust; **für e-n ~en Zweck** for a good cause, for charity; **'Wohl·tä·tig·keit** *f* (-; *no pl.*) charity
'Wohl·tä·tig·keits|kon,zert *n* charity concert; **~spiel** *n sport*: charity match; **~ver·an·stal·tung** *f* charity event (*sport*: *a.* fixture); charity (*or* benefit) concert
wohl·tem·pe·riert ['vo:ltɛmpə,ri:ɐt] *adj.* **1.** *pred.* just the right temperature; **2.** ♪ **das Wohltemperierte Klavier** the Well-Tempered Clavier
'wohl·tu·end *adj.* pleasant; soothing; **~e Wärme** pleasant feeling of warmth; **~e Ruhe** a good rest; **'wohl·tun** *v/i.* (*irr., sep.*, h, → **tun**): **j-m ~** do s.o. good; **das tut wohl** that does you good
'wohl|über,legt *adj.* well-considered; **~un·ter,rich·tet** *adj.* (well-)informed; **~ver·dient** *adj.* well-deserved, well-earned
'Wohl·ver·hal·ten *n* (-s; *no pl.*) good behavio(u)r; **bei ~** in case of good conduct
'wohl|ver·stan·den *adv.* → **wohlgemerkt; ~ver·traut** *adj.* very familiar; **~ver·wahrt** *adj.* under lock and key
wohl·weis·lich ['vo:lvaɪslɪç] *adv.* wisely, for good reason; **er hat es ~ verschwiegen** he was careful not to say anything about it
'Wohl·wol·len *n* (-s; *no pl.*) goodwill; favo(u)r; **'wohl·wol·lend** *adj.* kind, benevolent; **e-r Sache ~ gegenüberstehen** take a favo(u)rable view of s.th.
Wohn|an·hän·ger ['vo:n-] *m* caravan, *Am.* trailer, mobile home; **~an·la·ge** *f* housing area; **~bau·pro,jekt** *n* housing project; **~be·reich** *m* living area; **~be·völ·ke·rung** *f* resident population; **~be·zirk** *m* residential area; **~block** *m* block of flats, *Am.* apartment house; **~dich·te**

f population density; **~ein·heit** *f* living unit

woh·nen ['vo:nən] *v/i.* (h) live (***bei*** *dat.* with *s.o.*), *adm.* reside; stay (***bei*** *dat.* with; ***in*** *dat.* at); *fig.* live, *lit.* dwell

Wohn|flä·che ['vo:n-] *f* living space; **~ge·bäu·de** *n* residential building; **~ge·biet** *n*, **~ge·gend** *f* residential area; **~geld** *n* (-[e]s; *no pl.*) housing subsidy; **~ge·mein·schaft** *f* flat-sharing (*Am.* apartment-sharing) community; flat-share; ***in e-r ~ leben*** share a flat (*Am.* an apartment) (with other people); **~gif·te** *pl.* toxic substances (*or* materials) in the home

wohn·haft ['vo:nhaft] *adj.* resident

Wohn|haus ['vo:n-] *n* residential building; **~heim** *n* a) residential home, *Am.* rooming house, b) students' hostel, hall of residence, *Am.* dormitory, c) asylum-seekers' hostel; **~hoch·haus** *n* tower block; **~klo** F *n* F broom cupboard, (cubby-)hole, rabbit hutch, shoebox apartment; **~kü·che** *f* kitchen-(cum-)living room; **~kul,tur** *f* style of living; home décor; **~la·ge** *f* (residential) area; ***in schöner ~*** pleasantly situated; **~land·schaft** *f* landscaped interior

wohn·lich ['vo:nlıç] *adj.* homely, *Am.* homey; cosy, *Am.* cozy

Wohn·ma,schi·ne ['vo:n-] *f* → ***Wohnsilo***

Wohn·mo·bil ['vo:nmobi:l] *n* (-s; -e) camper (van), mobile home, *Am.* motorhome

Wohn·ort ['vo:n-] *m* (place of) residence

Wohn·raum ['vo:n-] *m* **1.** living space; **2.** housing; **3.** *pl.* living quarters; **4.** → ***Wohnzimmer***; **~be·schaf·fung** *f* housing supply; **~ver·mitt·lung** *f*: (***studentische*** **~** students') accommodation service

Wohn-'Schlaf·zim·mer ['vo:n-] *n* bedsitting room, F bedsit(ter)

Wohn|sied·lung ['vo:n-] *f* housing estate (*or* development); **~si·lo** *contp. m* concrete (*or* tower) block; **~sitz** *m* (place of) residence; ***s-n ~ aufschlagen in*** *dat.* make one's home in; ***s-n ~ auf dem Land haben*** live in the country; **~stadt** *f* residential (*or* dormitory) town; **~trakt** *m* accommodation wing; **~turm** *m* **1.** lived-in tower; **2.** tower block

Woh·nung ['vo:nʊŋ] *f* (-; -en) flat, *Am.* apartment

'Woh·nungs|amt *n* housing office; **~auf·lö·sung** *f* giving up of a household

'Woh·nungs·bau *m* (-[e]s; *no pl.*) house building; **~mi,ni·ster** *m* housing minister, minister of housing; *in the USA*: Secretary of Housing and Urban Development; **~pro,gramm** *n* housing scheme

'Woh·nungs|be·set·zer *m* squatter; **~in·ha·ber** *m* tenant; **~knapp·heit** *f* housing shortage

'woh·nungs·los *adj.* homeless; *adm.* without fixed abode

'Woh·nungs|man·gel *m* housing shortage; **~markt** *m* housing market; ***die Lage auf dem ~*** the housing situation; **~not** *f* (-; *no pl.*) housing shortage; **~po·li,tik** *f* housing policy; **~schlüs·sel** *m* key (to the flat, *Am.* apartment)

'Woh·nungs·su·che *f* search for accommodation, F flat-hunting, *Am.* F apartment-hunting; ***das Problem der ~*** the problem of finding somewhere to live; **'woh·nungs·su·chend** *adj.* accommodation-seeking, F flat-hunting, *Am.* F apartment-hunting; **'Woh·nungs·su·chen·de** *m, f* (-n; -n) accommodation seeker, F flat-hunter, *Am.* F apartment-hunter

'Woh·nungs|tausch *m* flat-swap(ping), *Am.* apartment-swap(ping); **~tür** *f* front door; **~wech·sel** *m* moving house (*or* flats, *Am.* apartments), F move

Wohn|ver·hält·nis·se ['vo:n-] *pl.* housing conditions; **~vier·tel** *n* residential area; **~wa·gen** *m* caravan, *Am.* trailer, mobile home; **~wand** *f* wall-to-wall cupboard; **~zim·mer** *n* sitting (*or* living) room

wöl·ben ['vœlbən] (h) **I.** *v/t. a.* ⚙ curve; △ vault; **II.** *v/refl.*: ***sich ~*** arch; bend; *forehead etc.*: bulge; → ***gewölbt***; **Wöl·bung** *f* (-; -en) a) arch; vault; dome, b) curvature

Wolf [vɔlf] *m* (-[e]s; Wölfe ['vœlfə]) **1.** wolf; *fig.* ***mit den Wölfen heulen*** howl with the pack; ***unter die Wölfe geraten*** fall among thieves; **2.** mincer; F *fig.* ***j-n durch den ~ drehen*** put s.o. through the mill; F ***ich bin wie durch den ~ gedreht*** F I'm knackered; → ***Reißwolf***; **3.** ⚕ chafing; ***e-n ~ haben*** be sore

Wöl·fin ['vœlfın] *f* (-; -nen) she-wolf

Wolf·ram ['vɔlfram] *n* (-s; *no pl.*) ⚗ tungsten

'Wolfs|hund *m* Alsatian, German shepherd; ***Irischer ~*** Irish wolfhound; **~hun·ger** *m*: ***e-n ~ haben*** be ravenous; ***ich habe e-n ~*** *a.* I could eat a horse; **~milch** *f* ✿ spurge; **~ra·chen** *m* ⚕ cleft palate; **~ru·del** *n* pack of wolves

Wol·ke ['vɔlkə] *f* (-; -n) cloud (*a. fig.*); *fig.* ***ich bin aus allen ~n gefallen*** it left me speechless, I was flabbergasted; → ***schweben***

'Wol·ken|auf·lö·sung *f* dispersal of clouds; **~band** *n* (-[e]s; ⸚er) band of cloud; **~bank** *f* (-; ⸚e) cloud bank

'wol·ken·be·deckt *adj.* cloudy, overcast

'Wol·ken|bil·dung *f* **1.** buildup of cloud; **2.** cloud formation; **~bruch** *m* cloudburst; **~decke** *f* cloud cover; ***geschlossene ~*** overcast skies; **~fel·der** *pl.* broken cloud cover *sg.*; **~fet·zen** *pl.* scud *sg.*, wispy clouds; **~him·mel** *m* cloudy sky; **~krat·zer** *m* skyscraper; **~kuk·kucks·heim** *n* Cloud-Cuckoo-Land

'wol·ken·los *adj.* cloudless, clear

'Wol·ken|schicht *f* layer of cloud; **~wand** *f* bank of clouds

wol·kig ['vɔlkıç] *adj.* cloudy; *fig.* nebulous, hazy, fuzzy

Woll·decke ['vɔl-] *f* (wool[l]en) blanket

Wol·le ['vɔlə] *f* (-; *no pl.*) wool; F *fig.* ***sich in die ~ kriegen*** fight, squabble

wol·len¹ ['vɔlən] **I.** *v/aux.* (wollte, gewollt, h) a) want, b) be about to, c) claim; ***ich will es mir überlegen*** I'll think about it; ***ich will es (nicht) tun*** I'll (I won't) do it; ***er will alles besser wissen*** he thinks he knows it all; ***willst du bitte damit aufhören*** will you stop that please; ***was ich sagen wollte*** a) what I meant to say, b) what I was going to say; ***ich will wissen, was los ist*** I'd like to know what's going on; ***das will ich meinen*** 'I'll say so; ***das wollte ich gerade sagen*** I was just going to say that; ***was ~ Sie damit sagen?*** what do you mean (by that)?, what are you getting at?; ***er will dich gesehen haben*** he says he saw you, he claims to have seen you; ***keiner will es gewesen sein*** nobody's admitting to (having done) it; *iro.* ***ich will ja nicht so sein*** out of the goodness of my heart; ***wir ~ sehen, wer hier bestimmt*** we'll see who's boss around here; → ***heißen¹*** I; **II.** *v/t. and v/i.* (wollte, gewollt, h) a) want, demand, b) want to, be willing (*or* prepared) to; ***lieber ~*** prefer; ***ich will lieber laufen*** *etc.* I'd rather walk *etc.*; ***et. unbedingt ~*** insist on s.th.; ***nicht ~*** refuse (*a. fig.* to work *etc.*), not to want to; ***ich will nach Hause*** a) I'm on my way home, b) I want to go home; ***er will, daß ich mitkomme*** he wants me to come with him; ***du kannst es, wenn du willst*** you've just got to put your mind to it; ***sie will zum Theater*** she wants to go on the stage; ***was willst du, alles ging gut*** what are you complaining about, it all went well; ***wohin willst du?*** where are you off to?; ***~ Sie bitte e-n Augenblick warten*** would you mind waiting for a minute?; ***was ~ Sie von mir?*** what do you want?; ***was ~ Sie mit e-m Regenschirm?*** what do you want an umbrella for?; ***Verzeihung, das wollte ich nicht!*** sorry, that was unintentional; ***ob er will oder nicht*** whether he likes it or not; ***er weiß nicht, was er will*** he doesn't know what he wants (*or* his own mind); ***er weiß, was er will*** he knows exactly what he wants; ***was willst du noch?*** what more do you want; ***so gern ich es auch will*** much as I'd like to; ***so Gott will*** God willing; ***mach, was du willst!*** do what you like; ***du hast es ja so gewollt*** you asked for it; ***wie du willst*** as you wish; F ***dann ~ wir mal*** let's get going (F cracking) then; ***m-e Beine ~ nicht mehr*** my legs are giving up on me; F ***er will dir was*** F he's got it in for you; F ***dir will ich!*** F you'd better watch it; F ***die Uhr will nicht mehr*** F that clock has given up the ghost; F ***hier ist nichts zu ~*** F nothing doing; → ***gewollt***

'wol·len² *adj.* wool(l)en

Woll|fa·den ['vɔl-] *m* wool(l)en thread; **~garn** *n* wool; **~gras** *n* cotton grass; **~hand·krab·be** *f* Chinese crab; **~hand·schuh** *m* wool(l)en glove

wol·lig ['vɔlıç] *adj.* **1.** wool(l)y; **2.** fuzzy *hair*

Woll|jacke ['vɔl-] *f* cardigan; **~knäu·el** *m, n* ball of wool; **~müt·ze** *f* wool(l)en hat, F wool(l)y hat; **~sa·chen** *pl.* wool(l)ens, wool(l)y clothes; **~schaf** *n* wool sheep; **~socken** *pl.* wool(l)en socks, F wool(l)y socks; **~spin·ne,rei** *f* wool mill; **~stoff** *m* wool, wool(l)en fabric

woll·te ['vɔltə] *pret. of* ***wollen***

Wol·lust ['vɔlʊst] *f* (-; *no pl.*) voluptuousness; sensuality; lust; ***et. mit wahrer ~ tun*** relish s.th., revel in s.th.; **wol·lü·stig** ['vɔlʏstıç] *adj.* voluptuous; lecherous; **'Wol·lüst·ling** *contp. m* (-s; -e) lecher

Woll·wa·ren ['vɔl-] *pl.* wool(l)ens

wo·mit [vo'mıt] **I.** *interr. adv.* what (...) with?; ***~ kann ich dienen?*** what can I do for you?; ***~ hab' ich das verdient?*** what did I do to deserve that?; **II.** *rel. adv.* with which; ***~ ich nicht sagen will*** by which I don't mean to say; ***~ die Sache erledigt war*** which settled the matter

wo·mög·lich [vo'mø:klıç] *adv.* **1.** if possible; **2.** possibly

wo·nach [vo'na:x] **I.** *interr. adv.* after what?; ***~ fragt er?*** what is he asking about?; F ***~ ist dir denn?*** what do you feel like then?; **II.** *rel. adv.* a) after which, whereupon, b) according to which

Won·ne ['vɔnə] *f* (-; -n) delight, bliss; ***e-e wahre ~*** sheer delight, a real treat; F ***mit ~*** with relish; **~ge·fühl** *n* blissful sensation; **~mo·nat** *lit. m*: ***im ~ Mai*** in the merry month of May; **~prop·pen** F *hum. m* bundle of joy

won·nig ['vɔnɪç] *adj.* lovely, sweet

wor·an [vo'ran] **I.** *interr. adv.*: ***~ denkst du (gerade)?*** what are you thinking about?, F (a) penny for your thoughts; ***~ arbeitet er?*** what is he working on (*or* at)?; ***~ liegt es, daß ...?*** how is it that ...?; ***~ hast du ihn erkannt?*** how did you recognize him?; **II.** *rel. adv.* on (*or* at *etc.*) which; ***das, ~ ich dachte*** what I had in mind; ***..., ~ man merkte, daß*** ... which showed that; ***ich weiß nicht, ~ ich bin*** I don't know where I stand, ***mit ihm:*** I don't know where I stand (*or* where I'm at) with him, *w.s.* I don't know what to make of him

wor·auf [vo'raʊf] **I.** *interr. adv.* on what?, what ... on?; ***~ wartest du (noch)?*** what are you waiting for?; **II.** *rel. adv.* a) on which, b) whereupon, upon which; ***~ er antwortete*** to which he replied; ***~ du dich verlassen kannst*** just wait and see; → ***ankommen*** 5

wor·aus [vo'raʊs] **I.** *interr. adv.* where (...) from?, out of what?, from what?; ***~ ist es gemacht?*** what is it made of?; **II.** *rel. adv.* out of which, from which; ***der Stoff, ~ es gemacht ist*** the material it is made of

wor·in [vo'rɪn] **I.** *interr. adv.* in what?, what (...) in?; ***~ liegt der Unterschied?*** what (*or* where) is the difference?; **II.** *rel. adv.* in which

Wort [vɔrt] *n* (-[e]s; Wörter ['vœrtɐ]) a) *ling.* word, b) term, expression, c) (*pl.* Worte) saying, d) word (of hono[u]r); ***sein ~ geben*** give (*or* pledge) one's word; ***j-s ~ darauf haben*** have s.o.'s word on it; ***~ halten*** keep one's word; ***das ~ (Gottes)*** the Word (of God); F ***dein ~ in Gottes Ohr*** let's hope it works out like that; ***j-m (e-r Sache) das ~ reden*** support s.o. (s.th.), back s.o. (s.th.) up; ***viele ~e machen*** talk a lot; ***ein paar ~e mit j-m wechseln*** have a few words with s.o.; ***für j-n ein gutes ~ einlegen*** put in a good word for s.o.; ***das ~ ergreifen*** (begin to) speak; ***das ~ führen*** do the talking; ***das große ~ haben*** (*or* ***führen***) do all the talking, F talk big; ***Sie haben das ~*** over to you; ***das ~ hat Herr X*** Mr X will now speak to you (*or* address you); ***das letzte ~ in*** *dat.* the last word on *a matter*; ***das letzte ~ haben*** a) have the final say, b) have the last word; ***das letzte ~ ist noch nicht gesprochen*** we haven't heard the last of it; ***das ist mein letztes ~*** that's final; ***ohne viel ~e zu machen*** without further ado; ***kein ~ mehr!*** I don't want to hear another word!; ***kein ~ darüber!*** don't breathe a word; ***genug der ~e!*** enough said; ***ich glaube ihm kein ~*** I don't believe a word he says; F ***hast du ~e!*** would you credit it; ***das ist ein ~!*** you're on!; ***man kann sein eigenes ~ nicht verstehen*** you can't hear yourself speak; ***er macht nicht viele ~e*** he doesn't waste his words; ***ich will nicht viele ~e machen*** I'll be brief; ***ein ~ gab das andere*** one thing led to another; ***mir fehlen die ~e*** words fail me, I don't know what to say; ***aufs ~ gehorchen (glauben)*** obey (believe) implicitly; ***auf ein ~!*** can I have a word with you?; ***nicht viel auf j-s ~e geben*** not to set great store by what s.o. says; ***hör auf m-e ~e*** mark my words; ***j-n beim ~ nehmen*** a) take s.o. at his (*or* her) word, b) take s.o. up on s.th.; ***~ für ~*** word for word; ***in ~en*** in letters; ***in ~ und Bild berichten*** give an illustrated report; ***in ~e fassen*** formulate, express (in words); ***j-m ins ~ fallen*** interrupt s.o., F butt in on s.o.; ***e-e Sprache in ~ und Schrift beherrschen*** have a good spoken and written knowledge (*or* command) of a language; ***mit anderen ~en*** in other words, put another way; ***mit 'einem ~*** in a word; ***mit den ~en schließen: ...*** wind up by saying (that) ...; ***er erwähnte es mit keinem ~*** he didn't even give it a mention; ***nach ~en suchen*** search (*or* be at a loss) for words; ***kein ~ herausbringen*** be tongue-tied; ***ums ~ bitten*** ask to speak; ***zu ~ kommen*** have one's say; ***nicht zu ~ kommen*** not to get a word in edgeways; ***zu s-m ~ stehen*** stick by one's word; → ***abschneiden*** 4, ***entziehen*** 1, ***Mund, ringen*** II, ***sparen*** I, ***Tat***

'wort·arm *adj.* **1.** *language* lacking in vocabulary; **2.** → ***wortkarg***; **'Wort·ar·mut** *f* (-; *no pl.*) poor vocabulary

'Wort·art *f ling.* part of speech

'Wort·bil·dung *f* word formation

'Wort·bruch *m* breach of promise; ***e-n ~ begehen*** break one's word; **'wort·brü·chig** *adj.* not true to one's word; ***~ werden*** break one's word

Wört·chen ['vœrtçən] *n* (-s; -): ***ich möchte ein ~ mit dir reden*** I'd like a word with you; → ***mitreden*** II, ***wenn*** I

Wör·ter|buch ['vœrtɐ-] *n* dictionary; **~ver·zeich·nis** *n* list of words, vocabulary

'Wort|fa,mi·lie *f* word family; **~feld** *n* word field; **~fet·zen** *pl.* scraps of conversation; **~fol·ge** *f* word order; **~füh·rer** *m* spokesman; **~ge·fecht** *n* battle of words; **~ge·klin·gel** *contp. n* nice-sounding words

'wort|ge·treu *adj.* word-for-word ...; literal; **~ge·wal·tig** *adj.* powerful *speaker etc.*; **~ge·wandt** *adj.* articulate, eloquent

'Wort|gut *n* (-[e]s; *no pl.*) vocabulary; **~held** *contp. m* loudmouth; **~hül·se** *f* (empty) cliché, meaningless word

'wort·karg *adj.* taciturn; ***er ist ziemlich ~*** *a.* he doesn't say much; **'Wort·karg·heit** *f* (-; *no pl.*) taciturnity

Wort·klau·be·rei [-klaʊbə'raɪ] *f* (-; -en) hairsplitting

'Wort·laut *m* wording; text; ***der Brief hat folgenden ~*** the letter runs as follows

wört·lich ['vœrtlɪç] **I.** *adj.* literal, word-for-word ...; **II.** *adv.* literally (*a. fig.*); *repeat, translate etc.* word for word; ***so hat er ~ gesagt*** those were his exact words

'wort·los I. *adj.*: ***~es Einverständnis*** tacit agreement; **II.** *adv.* without a word

'Wort|mel·dung *f* request to speak; **~prä·gung** *f* coinage; ***neue ~*** recent coinage, newly coined expression (*or* word); neologism

'wort·reich *adj.* **1.** *language* rich in vocabulary; **2.** *contp.* verbose, wordy; **'Wort·reich·tum** *m* (-[e]s; *no pl.*) rich vocabulary

'Wort|sa,lat *m psych.* word salad; **~schatz** *m* (-es; *no pl.*) vocabulary; ***großer ~*** large (*or* wide) vocabulary; ***kleiner ~*** limited vocabulary; **~schöp·fung** *f* coinage; neologism; **~schwall** *m* (-[e]s; *no pl.*) torrent of words; **~spiel** *n* play on words; pun; *pl. coll.* wordplay *sg.*; **~stamm** *m* root, stem (of a *or* the word); **~stel·lung** *f* word order; **~streit** *m* → ***Wortgefecht***; **~ver·dre·her** *contp. m*: ***er ist ein ~*** he twists (*or* distorts) everything you say; **~wahl** *f* choice of words; **~wech·sel** *m* (verbal) exchange, argument

'wort'wört·lich *adj. and adv.* → ***wörtlich***

wor·über [vo'ry:bɐ] **I.** *interr. adv.* a) over (*or* on) what?, what ... over (*or* on)?, b) *fig.* what (...) about (*or* on)?; ***~ lachst du?*** what are you laughing about (*or* at)?; **II.** *rel. adv.* a) over (*or* on) which, b) *fig.* about (*or* on) which; ***~ er ärgerlich war*** which annoyed him

wor·um [vo'rʊm] **I.** *interr. adv.* about what?, what ... about?; ***~ handelt es sich?*** a) what's it about?, b) what's the problem?; **II.** *rel. adv.* about which; for which

wor·un·ter [vo'rʊntɐ] **I.** *interr. adv.* under (*fig.* among) what?, what ... under (*fig.* among)?; **II.** *rel. adv.* under (*fig.* among) which; ***~ ich mir nichts vorstellen kann*** which doesn't mean anything to me; ***~ ich leide*** what (*or* which) I suffer from

wo·von [vo'fɔn] **I.** *interr. adv.* of (*or* from) what?, what (...) from (*or* of)?, about what?, what (...) about?; **II.** *rel. adv.* of (*or* from, about) which

wo·vor [vo'fo:ɐ] **I.** *interr. adv.* in front of what?; *fig.* of what?, what (...) of?; ***~ hast du Angst?*** what are you afraid of?; **II.** *rel. adv.* in front of which; *fig.* of which

wo·zu [vo'tsu:] **I.** *interr. adv.* a) for what?, what (...) for?, b) why?; **II.** *rel. adv.* a) for which, b) why; ***~ ich bereit bin*** what (*or* which) I'm prepared to do

Wrack [vrak] *n* (-s; -s) wreck (*a. fig.*); *fig.* ***menschliches ~*** physical wreck; **~tei·le** *pl.* wreckage *sg.*

wrin·gen ['vrɪŋən] *v/t.* (wrang, gewrungen, h) wring (out)

Wu·cher ['vu:xɐ] *m* (-s; *no pl.*) profiteering; usury; ***~ treiben*** practi|se (*Am.* -ce) usury; **Wu·che·rer** ['vu:xərɐ] *m* (-s; -) profiteer; usurer

'Wu·cher·mie·te *f* rack rent, extortionate rent; *pl. coll.* rack renting *sg.*

wu·chern ['vu:xɐn] *v/i.* **1.** (h, sn) ⚘ grow rampant; ⚕ proliferate (*a. fig.*); *fig. a.* be rampant; **2.** (h) practi|se (*Am.* -ce) usury

'Wu·cher·preis *m* extortionate price

Wu·che·rung ['vu:xərʊŋ] *f* (-; -en) **1.** *no pl.* ⚘ rank growth; **2.** ⚕ excrescence, growth; proliferation

'Wu·cher·zin·sen *pl.* usurious interest *sg.*

wuchs [vu:ks] *pret. of* ***wachsen***[1]

Wuchs [vu:ks] *m* (-es; *no pl.*) a) growth, b) shape; build, physique; ***von kleinem ~*** of small (*or* slight) build; ***von kräftigem ~*** big-built

Wucht [vʊxt] *f* (-; *no pl.*) **1.** force; impact; ***mit voller ~ auf den Rücken fallen*** fall flat on one's back; ***mit voller ~ gegen die Mauer rennen*** run straight into the wall; ***der ~ e-s Angriffs widerstehen*** resist the onslaught; **2.** F good hiding; **3.** F ***das ist 'ne ~*** F it's great, it's fantastic

wuch·ten ['vʊxtən] *v/t.* (h) **1.** heave; drag; **2.** *soccer etc.*: slam

wuch·tig ['vʊxtɪç] *adj.* **1.** heavy; bulky; massive, big *body*; **2.** hard, powerful *punch etc.*
Wühl·ar·beit ['vy:l-] *fig. f* (underground) agitation
wüh·len ['vy:lən] (h) **I.** *v/i.* a) dig; *zo.* burrow (*a.* **sich ~**) (**in** *acc.* into); *pig*: root, **in** *dat.*: grub up, b) *fig.* rummage (**in** *dat.* around in), c) make a mess; thrash around *in one's bed etc.*, d) *fig.* beaver away; *pol.* agitate; (**sich**) **in den Haaren ~** rumple one's hair; **im Schmutz ~** mess about in the mud (*or* dirt), wallow in the mud (*fig.* mire); *fig.* **Haß** *etc.* **wühlte in ihm** hatred *etc.* gnawed at him; → **Wunde; II.** *v/t.* burrow; **s-n Kopf in das Kissen ~** burrow one's head into the pillow; **III.** *v/refl.*: **sich ~ durch** *acc.* a) *tank etc.*: churn through, b) burrow one's way through, *fig.* rummage through *documents etc.*
Wüh·ler ['vy:lɐ] *m* (-s; -) **1.** *zo.* burrower; **2.** *pol.* agitator; **3.** F *fig.* slaver; **er ist ein ~** *a.* he works like a maniac
Wühl|maus ['vy:l-] *f* vole; **~tisch** F *m* bargain counter
Wulst [vʊlst] *m* (-[e]s; Wülste ['vʏlstə]), *f* (-; ⸗e) bulge; ⚙ bead; △ torus
wul·stig ['vʊlstɪç] *adj.* bulging; puffed up; thick, protruding *lips*
'**Wulst·nar·be** *f* thickened scar
wund [vʊnt] *adj.* sore, chafed; raw; **~e Stelle** sore, *fig.* (*a.* **~er Punkt**) sore point; **~ reiben** chafe; **sich die Füße ~ laufen** get sore feet, *fig.* walk one's feet off; *fig.* **sich die Finger ~ schreiben** wear one's fingers to the bone writing; **sich den Mund ~ reden** talk till one is blue in the face; **den Finger auf e-e ~e Stelle legen** touch a sore point
'**Wund|brand** *m* (-[e]s; *no pl.*) gangrene; **~be·hand·lung** *f*: (**zur ~** for the) treatment of wounds
Wun·de ['vʊndə] *f* (-; -n) wound; cut, gash; *fig.* **alte ~n wieder aufreißen** open old sores; **in e-r ~ wühlen** turn a knife in a wound; **die Zeit heilt alle ~n** time is the great healer
Wun·der ['vʊndɐ] *n* (-s; -) miracle; wonder; **~ der Technik** engineering marvel; (**es ist**) **kein ~**(**, daß**) (it's) no wonder (that); **ist es ein ~, daß ...?** is it any wonder that ...?; **auf ein ~ hoffen** be hoping for a miracle; **er ist ein ~ an Ausdauer** he's got amazing stamina; **~ wirken** perform miracles, *fig.* work wonders; **es grenzt an ein ~** it's a near-miracle; **wenn nicht ein ~ geschieht** barring miracles; **er wird sein blaues ~ erleben** he's got a surprise coming, he's in for a (big) surprise; **wie durch ein ~** miraculously; **er glaubt, er sei ♀ wer** F he thinks he's the bee's knees; **er glaubt ♀ was er getan hat** he thinks he's done goodness knows what
'**wun·der·bar** *adj.* wonderful, marvel(l)ous; *a. fig.* miraculous; '**wun·der·ba·rer'wei·se** *adv.* miraculously
'**Wun·der|ding** *n* wonder, marvel; **~dok·tor** *m* miracle doctor; **~dro·ge** *f* miracle drug; **~glau·be** *m*, **~gläu·big·keit** *f* belief in miracles; ♀'**hübsch** *adj.* (absolutely) lovely; **~ker·ze** *f* sparkler; **~kind** *n* child prodigy, wunderkind; **~kna·be** *m* boy wonder; **~kraft** *f* miraculous powers *pl.*, ability to perform miracles; **~lam·pe** *f* magic lamp; **~land** *n* wonderland
'**wun·der·lich** *adj.* strange, peculiar
'**Wun·der·mit·tel** *n* wonder cure (*or* drug)
wun·dern ['vʊndɐn] (h) **I.** *v/t.* surprise; **es wundert mich** I'm surprised; **es würde mich nicht ~, wenn** I wouldn't be at all surprised if; **wen wundert es?** is it any wonder?; **mich wundert gar nichts mehr** nothing surprises me any more; **II.** *v/refl.*: **sich ~** be surprised (**über** *acc.* at); **ich habe mich gewundert, wer das war** I wondered who that was; **du wirst dich ~** you won't believe it; F **ich muß mich doch sehr ~!** I'm surprised at you, you disappoint me; **er konnte sich nicht genug darüber ~** he couldn't get over it
'**wun·der·neh·men** *v/t.* (*irr.*, *sep.*, h, → **nehmen**) astonish, surprise; **es nimmt mich wunder, daß** I'm surprised that
'**wun·der·sam** *adj.* strange, *lit.* wondrous
'**wun·der'schön** *adj.* wonderful, beautiful
'**Wun·der·tat** *f* miracle; '**Wun·der·tä·ter** *m* miracle-worker; '**wun·der·tä·tig** *adj.* miracle-working
'**Wun·der|tier** *n*: **er wurde wie ein ~ angestarrt** they stared at him as if he had come from another planet; **~tü·te** *f* lucky bag
'**wun·der·voll** *adj.* wonderful, marvel(l)ous
'**Wun·der|waf·fe** *f* wonder weapon; **~werk** *n* miracle; *fig. a.* wonder, marvel
'**Wund·fie·ber** *n* wound fever
'**wund·lie·gen** *v/refl.*: **sich ~** (*irr.*, *sep.*, h, → **liegen**) get bedsores
'**Wund|mal** *n* scar; *eccl.* stigma (*pl.* stigmata); **~pfla·ster** *n* adhesive plaster; **~pu·der** *m* antiseptic powder; **~sal·be** *f* antiseptic ointment; **~schmerz** *m* traumatic pain; **~starr·krampf** *m* tetanus
Wunsch [vʊnʃ] *m* (-[e]s; Wünsche ['vʏnʃə]) wish, desire; **auf** (**allgemeinen**) **~** by (popular) request; **auf eigenen ~** at one's own request; **auf ~ schicken wir ...** if requested, we will send you ...; (**je**) **nach ~** as desired; **der ~ nach Freiheit** the desire for freedom; **es ging alles nach ~** everything went as planned; **mit den besten Wünschen** with best wishes; **j-m e-n ~ erfüllen** (**versagen**) fulfil(l) a wish for s.o. (deny s.o. a wish); **ein eigenes Haus war schon immer mein ~** I('ve) always wanted to have a house of my own; **mein einziger ~ ist ...** all I want (*or* wish for) is ...; **haben Sie noch e-n ~?** is there anything else I can do for you?; *iro.* **dein ~ ist mir Befehl** your wish is my command; **der ~ war Vater des Gedankens** the wish was father to the thought; **am Ziel s-r Wünsche sein** have fulfil(l)ed one's every wish (*or* ambition); → **ablesen** 3, **erfüllen** 2, **fromm**
'**Wunsch|bild** *n* ideal; **~den·ken** *n* wishful thinking
Wün·schel·ru·te ['vʏnʃəl-] *f* divining rod; '**Wün·schel·ru·ten·gän·ger** [-ru:təngɛŋɐ] *m* (-s; -) (water) diviner, dowser
wün·schen ['vʏnʃən] *v/t.* (h) wish; want; **sich et. ~** wish for s.th., long for s.th.; **viel zu ~ übriglassen** leave much to be desired; **was ~ Sie?** what can I do for you?; **~ Sie noch etwas?** would you like anything else?; **wie Sie ~** as you wish (*or* like), *iro.* suit yourself; **ich wünsche Ihnen alles Gute** (I wish you) all the best(, then); **ich wünsche dir Erfolg** (**e-e gute Reise**) I wish you success (a good journey); **sie wünscht sich zu Weihnachten e-e Puppe** she wants a doll for Christmas; **alles, was man sich ~ kann** everything one could wish for; **es ist zu ~, daß e-e Lösung gefunden wird** it is to be hoped that a solution can be found; **ich wünsche, nicht gestört zu werden** I don't want (*or* wish) to be disturbed; **ich wünsche, daß hier nicht geraucht wird** I don't want any smoking here; **das wünsche ich m-m schlimmsten Feind nicht** I wouldn't wish that on my worst enemy; → **gewünscht**
'**wün·schens·wert** *adj.* desirable; **das wäre sehr ~** *a.* that would be very (*or* most) welcome
'**wunsch·ge·mäß** *adv.* as requested
'**Wunsch|kan·di,dat** *m* candidate preference; **~kind** *n* planned child; **sie war ihr ~** she was their long-awaited baby; **~kon,zert** *n* request program(me); **~liste** *f* list of presents; *fig.* shopping list
'**wunsch·los** *adv.*: **~ glücklich** perfectly happy
'**Wunsch|part·ner** *m* ideal partner; *a.* F Mr Right; **~traum** *m* dream, great wish; *contp.* pipe dream, pie in the sky; **~vor·stel·lung** *f* ideal; **~zet·tel** *m* Christmas list
wur·de ['vʊrdə] *pret. of* **werden**
Wür·de ['vʏrdə] *f* (-; -n) a) *no pl.* dignity, b) dignity, hono(u)r, c) rank; **akademische ~** academic degree; **priesterliche ~** priestly office; **die ~ e-s Kardinals erlangen** be made cardinal; **die ~ bewahren** preserve (*or* retain) one's dignity; **unter aller ~** beneath contempt; **unter m-r ~** beneath my dignity; F **sie war ganz ~** she was out to impress; **mit ~ alt werden** grow old gracefully; *hum.* **ich werd's mit ~ tragen** I'll try and keep a stiff upper lip
'**wür·de·los** *adj.* undignified
'**Wür·den·trä·ger** *m* (-s; -) dignitary; **geistlicher ~** church dignitary; **geistliche und weltliche ~** dignitaries from church and state
'**wür·de·voll** **I.** *adj.* dignified; **II.** *adv.* with dignity
wür·dig ['vʏrdɪç] **I.** *adj.* worthy (*gen.* of); deserving (of); dignified; **e-r Sache ~ sein** *a.* merit (*or* deserve) s.th.; **er ist dessen nicht ~** he doesn't deserve it; **ein ~er alter Herr** a dignified old gentleman; **ein ~er Nachfolger** a worthy successor; **sich j-s Vertrauens ~ erweisen** prove worthy of s.o.'s confidence; **II.** *adv.*: **j-n ~ vertreten** be a worthy representative of s.o.
wür·di·gen ['vʏrdɪgən] *v/t.* (h) acknowledge, pay tribute to; appreciate; **j-n keines Blickes** (**keiner Antwort**) **~** not to deign to look at s.o. (reply to s.o.)
Wür·di·gung ['vʏrdɪgʊŋ] *f* (-; -en) acknowledg(e)ment, recognition; hono(u)ring; appreciation; **in ~ s-r Verdienste** in recognition of his services *etc.*
Wurf [vʊrf] *m* (-[e]s; Würfe ['vʏrfə]) **1.** throw (*a. sport*); *handball etc.*: *a.* shot; *fig.* lucky strike; *fig.* **großer ~** great success; **2.** *zo.* litter; **3.** folds *pl.*; **~bahn** *f* trajectory; **~dis·zi,plin** *f sport*: throwing event
Wür·fel ['vʏrfəl] *m* (-s; -) a) cube (*a. gastr.*), b) dice; *fig.* **die ~ sind gefallen** the die is cast; **~be·cher** *m* (dice) shaker
'**wür·fel·för·mig** [-fœrmɪç], **wür·fe·lig** ['vʏrfəlɪç] *adj.* a) cubic, cube-shaped, b) chequered, *Am.* checkered

wür·feln ['vʏrfəln] (h) **I.** *v/i.* **1.** throw dice (**um** *acc.* for); play dice; **II.** *v/t.* **2.** throw; **3.** *gastr.* dice, chop up

'**Wür·fel|spiel** *n* **1.** dice game, game of dice; **2.** (board) game involving dice; **~zucker** *m* sugar cubes *pl.*; *coll.* lump sugar, ✝ cube sugar

'**Wurf|ge·schoß** *n* projectile; **~griff** *m* *judo*: throwing grip; **~kör·per** *m* projectile; **~ma|schi·ne** *f* **1.** *hist.* catapult; **2.** *shooting*: trap; **~pfeil** *m* dart; **~pfeil·spiel** *n* darts (*sg.*); **~schei·be** *f* discus; **~sen·dung** *f* ✉ circular; *pl. formal*: *a.* unaddressed advertising matter *sg.*, F junk mail *sg.*; **~speer** *m*, **~spieß** *m* spear; **~tau·be** *f* clay pigeon; **~tau·ben·schie·ßen** *n* clay-pigeon shooting, trap-shooting

Wür·ge|en·gel ['vʏrgə-] *m* angel of death; **~griff** *m* stranglehold (*a. fig.*); **~ma·le** *pl.* strangulation marks

wür·gen ['vʏrgən] (h) **I.** *v/t.* strangle; make *s.o.* choke; *collar etc.*: choke; **II.** *v/i.* choke; retch; **~ an** *dat.* choke on *s.th.*; *fig.* find *criticism etc.* hard to swallow, sweat over *one's work etc.*

Wür·ger ['vʏrgɐ] *m* (-s; -) **1.** strangler; **2.** *zo.* shrike

Wurm¹ [vʊrm] *m* (-[e]s; Würmer ['vʏrmɐ]) *zo.* worm (*a.* ⚘, ⚙); maggot; ***sich krümmen wie ein getretener ~*** squirm like an eel; F *fig.* ***j-m die Würmer aus der Nase ziehen*** winkle everything (F drag it) out of s.o.; F ***da ist der ~ drin*** there's something very wrong with it, *w.s.* there's something fishy about it

Wurm² *m*, *n* (-[e]s; Würmer ['vʏrmɐ]) mite; ***armer ~!*** poor little mite

Würm·chen ['vʏrmçən] *n* (-s; -) → ***Wurm²***

wur·men ['vʊrmən] F *v/t.* (h) rile, rankle with, F get (to)

'**Wurm·fort·satz** *m anat.* vermiform appendix

wur·mig ['vʊrmɪç] *adj.* → ***wurmstichig***

'**Wurm|kur** *f* deworming; **~lei·den** *n* worms *pl.*; **~mit·tel** *n* dewormer

'**wurm·sti·chig** [-ʃtɪçɪç] *adj.* worm-eaten; maggoty

Wurscht [vʊrʃt] F *f* (-; Würschte ['vʏrʃtə]) → ***Wurst***

Wurst [vʊrst] *f* (-; Würste ['vʏrstə]) **1.** sausage; ***mit der ~ nach der Speckseite werfen*** throw a sprat to catch a mackerel; F ***es ist mir*** (***völlig***) ***~*** I couldn't care less, I don't care, F I don't give a damn; F ***jetzt geht's um die ~!*** this is it (now)!; **2.** F *a. pl.* dog's muck; **~brot** *n* sausage-meat sandwich; **~bu·de** *f* hot-dog stand

Würst·chen ['vʏrstçən] *n* (-s; -) **1.** small sausage; ***Wiener ~*** vienna, wiener; ***Frankfurter ~*** frankfurter, F *a.* frank; ***ein Paar ~*** two frankfurters *etc.*; ***warmes ~*** hot dog; **2.** *baby talk*: job; ***ein ~ machen*** do a poo; **3.** F *fig.* (***kleines***) **~** small fry, *a* nobody

Wur·ste·lei [vʊrstə'laɪ] F *f* (-; -en) muddling (through); **wur·steln** ['vʊrstəln] F *v/i.* (h) muddle (one's way) through

'**Wurst|fin·ger** *pl.* fat (*or* pudgy) fingers; **~haut** *f gastr.* sausage skin

wur·stig ['vʊrstɪç] F *adj.* F couldn't-care-less ...; ***er ist ziemlich ~*** F he doesn't really give a damn; '**Wur·stig·keit** F *f* (-; *no pl.*) F couldn't-care-less (*sl.* to-hell-with-it) attitude

'**Wurst|plat·te** *f* platter of cold cuts; **~wa·ren** *pl.* sausages; **~zip·fel** *m* sausage-end

Wür·ze ['vʏrtsə] *f* (-; -n) spice(s *pl.*); flavo(u)r; aroma; fragrance; *fig.* spice; *fig.* ***ohne ~*** insipid

Wur·zel ['vʊrtsəl] *f* (-; -n) **1.** ⚘ root (*a.* ⅍, *ling.*, ⚕ *and fig.*); ⅍ ***zweite*** (***dritte***) ***~*** square (cubic) root; ⅍ ***die ~ e-r Zahl ziehen*** extract the (square) root of a number; ***~n schlagen*** *a. fig.* take root, *fig.* put down roots; F *fig.* ***willst du hier ~n schlagen?*** are you going to stand around here all day?; ***das Übel an der ~ packen*** strike at the root (of this evil); ***et. mit der ~ ausrotten*** eradicate s.th. root and branch; **2.** *dial.* carrot; **~be·hand·lung** *f* ⚕ root treatment; **~fäu·le** *f* ⚘ soft rot; **~ge·mü·se** *n* root vegetables *pl.*; **~ka|nal** *m* root canal *of a tooth*

'**wur·zel·los** *adj.* rootless (*a. fig.*)

wur·zeln ['vʊrtsəln] *v/i.* (h) take root; *fig.* **~ in** *dat.* a) be rooted in, b) stem from, have its roots in

'**Wur·zel|werk** *n* **1.** roots *pl.*; **2.** → ***Suppengrün***; **~zei·chen** *n* ⅍ radical sign

wür·zen ['vʏrtsən] *v/t.* (h) spice, season; *fig.* spice *s.th.* up, add a bit of spice to

wür·zig ['vʏrtsɪç] *adj.* spicy (*a. fig.*), well-seasoned; fruity *wine*

Würz|kräu·ter ['vʏrts-] *pl.* herbs; **~mi·schung** *f* mixed spices *pl.*; **~so·ße** *f* liquid seasoning; **~stoff** *m* seasoning

wusch [vu:ʃ] *pret. of* ***waschen***

wu·sche·lig ['vʊʃəlɪç] *adj.* curly; fuzzy, frizzy; tousled

Wu·schel·kopf ['vʊʃəl-] *m* a) mop of curly (*or* fuzzy, frizzy) hair, b) curly-head

wuß·te ['vʊstə] *pret. of* ***wissen***

Wust [vu:st] *m* (-[e]s; *no pl.*) a) mess, jumble; rubbish, b) mass, pile

wüst [vy:st] *adj.* **1.** deserted, desolate; **2.** chaotic; wild; ***ein ~es Durcheinander*** complete chaos; ***er*** (***es***) ***sieht ja ~ aus*** he looks a real fright (what a mess *or* shambles); **3.** wild; rabid; ***e-e ~e Schlägerei*** F a real set-to; **4.** wild, dissolute; **5.** ***~e Beschimpfungen*** wild abuse, *w.s.* cursing and swearing

Wü·ste ['vy:stə] *f* (-; -n) desert; wilderness; *fig.* ***j-n in die ~ schicken*** F give s.o. the boot

'**Wü·sten|land·schaft** *f* a) desert landscape, b) *fig.* barren landscape; **~sand** *m* desert sands *pl.*; **~schiff** *hum. n* ship of the desert; **~volk** *n* desert tribe (*or* people)

Wüst·ling ['vy:stlɪŋ] *m* (-s; -e) rake, debauchee

Wut [vu:t] *f* (-; *no pl.*) a) rage, fury, b) *reading etc.* mania; ***in ~ geraten*** fly into a rage; ***j-n in ~ bringen*** infuriate s.o., F get s.o. going; ***e-e fürchterliche ~ haben*** be livid, be absolutely furious; ***leicht in ~ geraten*** have a quick temper; F ***vor ~ platzen*** F be hitting the roof; F ***vor ~ kochen*** (*or* ***schäumen***) seethe with rage, fume; F ***e-e ~ auf j-n haben*** F be mad at s.o.; F ***ich habe e-e ~ auf ihn!*** *a.* I could strangle (*or* kill) him; F ***ich krieg' die ~, wenn ich so was sehe*** F it makes me mad to see it; ***mich packt die ~, wenn ich daran denke, daß*** *a.* it makes my blood boil to think that; → ***auslassen*** 6; **~an·fall** *m* fit of rage; **~aus·bruch** *m* angry outburst, outburst of rage; tantrum

'**wut·be·bend** *adj.* trembling with rage

wü·ten ['vy:tən] *v/i.* (h) rage (*a. fire, storm, epidemic etc.*) (***gegen*** *acc.* at, against); *crowd*: riot; *w.s.* create havoc; '**wü·tend** *adj.* **1.** furious, F mad (***auf*** *acc.*, ***über*** *acc.* at); ***~ machen*** infuriate, enrage, F get *s.o.* going; **2.** *fig.* raging *pain etc.*

'**wut·ent·brannt** *adj.* infuriated, furious

Wü·te·rich ['vy:tərɪç] *obs. m* (-[e]s; -e) **1.** hothead; **2.** ruthless tyrant

'**wut·schnau·bend** *adj.* foaming with rage, F foaming at the mouth

'**Wut·schrei** *m* cry (*or* yell) of rage

'**wut·ver·zerrt** *adj. face etc.* distorted with rage

X, Y

X, x [ɪks] *n* (-; -) X, x; ***Herr X*** Mr X; ***x Leute habe ich gefragt*** F I've asked umpteen (*or* dozens of) people; ***j-m ein X für ein U vormachen*** (try to) pull the wool over s.o.'s eyes
'x-Ach·se *f* ⩚ x-axis
Xan·thip·pe [ksan'tɪpə] F *f* (-; -n) F battle-axe; virago, termagant
'X-Bei·ne *pl.* knock-knees; **~ *haben*** be knock-kneed; **x-bei·nig** ['ɪksbaɪnɪç] *adj.* knock-kneed
x-be'lie·big I. *adj.* any ... you like, F any old ...; **II.** *adv.* any (*or* whichever) way you like, F any old way
'X-Chro·mo,som *n* X-chromosome
Xe·non ['kseːnɔn] *n* (-s; *no pl.*) xenon; **~lam·pe** *f* xenon lamp; **~oxy·de** *pl.* xenon oxides
xe·no·phob [kseno'foːp] *adj.* xenophobic; **Xe·no·pho·bie** [ksenofo'biː] *f* (-; *no pl.*) xenophobia
x-fach ['ɪksfax] **I.** *adj.* F umpteen times; ***die ~e Zahl*** n times that number; **II.** *adv.* as often (*or* as many times) as you like; **X-fache** ['ɪksfaxə] *n* (-n; *no pl.*): ***das ~*** F umpteen times as much, umpteen times the amount
x-för·mig ['ɪksfœrmɪç] *adj.* x-shaped
x-mal ['ɪksmaːl] F *adv.* F umpteen times, dozens (*or* hundreds) of times; ***hab' ich's dir nicht schon ~ gesagt?*** *a.* haven't I told you a thousand times?, I don't know how many times I've told you
x-te ['ɪkstə] F *adj.*: ***zum ~n Mal*** F for the umpteenth (*or* nth, hundredth) time
Xy·lo·phon [ksylo'foːn] *n* (-s; -e) ♪ xylophone

Y, y ['ʏpsilɔn] *n* (-; -) Y, y
'y-Ach·se *f* ⩚ y-axis
Yak [jak] *m* (-s; -s) *zo.* yak
Yang [jaŋ] *n* (-[s]; *no pl.*) *phls.* yang
'Y-Chro·mo,som *n* Y-chromosome
Yen [jɛn] *m* (-[s]; -[s]) yen
Ye·ti ['jeːti] *m* (-s; -s) yeti, *the* Abominable Snowman
Yin [jɪn] *n* (-; *no pl.*) *phls.* yin
Yo·ga ['joːga] *m*, *n* (-[s]; *no pl.*) → ***Joga***
Yo·gi ['joːgi] *m* (-s; -s) → ***Jogi***
Yp·si·lon ['ʏpsilɔn] *n* (-[s]; -s) (the letter) Y
Yuc·ca ['jʊka] *f* (-; -s), **~pal·me** *f* ⚘ yucca
Yup·pie ['jʊpi, 'japi] *m* (-s; -s) yuppie
Yup·pi·fi·zie·rung [jʊpifi'tsiːrʊŋ] *f* (-; *no pl.*) yuppification

Z

Z, z [tsɛt] *n* (-; -) Z, z

zack [tsak] F *int.* just like that; before you knew it; before you can (*or* could) say Jack Robinson; **~, war er weg** he was gone just like that *etc.*; **~!, ~!** F chop! chop!

Zack F: **auf ~ sein** F be on the ball; **et. auf ~ bringen** bring s.th. up to scratch (*or* the mark); **j-n auf ~ bringen** shake s.o. up

Zacke ['tsakə] (*sep.* -k·k-) *f* (-; -n) (sharp) point; prong, tine; tooth *of saw, comb etc.*; jagged peak *of a mountain*

Zacken ['tsakən] (*sep.* -k·k-) F *m* (-s; -) **1.** → **Krone** 2; **2.** F conk; **3. e-n ~ haben** F be plastered; **e-n ~ drauf haben** F be going like a bomb (*or* the clappers), be belting along

zacken ['tsakən] (*sep.* -k·k-) *v/t.* (h) indent, notch; serrate; pink; '**zacken·för·mig** [-fœrmɪç] *adj.* serrated; jagged

'**Zacken|li·nie** *f* zigzag (line); **~sche·re** *f* (**e-e ~** a pair of) pinking shears *pl.*

zackig ['tsakɪç] (*sep.* -k·k-) *adj.* **1.** indented; jagged *rocks*; **2. ~e Bewegung** short, sharp movement; **3.** F *fig.* F snappy

zag·haft ['tsa:khaft] **I.** *adj.* a) timid, b) cautious; **II.** *adv.* timidly, gingerly; hesitatingly

zäh [tsɛ:] **I.** *adj.* a) tough *meat: etc., a. fig. person*, b) viscous *liquid*, c) *fig.* dogged; stubborn; **~ wie Leder** *meat* tough as leather, F *fig.* tough as old boots; *fig.* **~er Bursche** F tough sort; **II.** *adv.* doggedly; stubbornly; *fig.* **~ vorankommen** make sluggish progress; '**zäh·flie·ßend** *adj.*: **~er Verkehr** slow-moving traffic

'**zäh·flüs·sig** *adj.* **1.** viscous; **2.** slow-moving *traffic*; '**Zäh·flüs·sig·keit** *f* (-; *no pl.*) viscosity

Zä·hig·keit ['tsɛ:ɪçkaɪt] *f* **1.** a) toughness *of meat etc.*, b) viscosity; **2.** *fig.* a) toughness, b) tenacity, doggedness

Zahl [tsa:l] *f* (-; -en) number; figure (*a. amount, value*); **vierstellige ~** four-digit number; **in großer ~** in large numbers; **~ oder Adler, Kopf oder ~** heads or tails; *lit.* **ohne ~** countless, innumerable; **er wollte keine ~en nennen** he didn't want to give (*or* quote) any figures; **in ~en ausdrücken** quantify; → **gerade** I, **rot, rund** I

'**zahl·bar** *adj.* payable (**an** *acc.* to; **bis** to); **~ bei Lieferung** cash on delivery (*abbr.* COD)

zähl·bar ['tsɛ:lba:ɐ] *adj.* countable

zäh·le·big ['tsɛ:le:bɪç] *adj.* **1.** tough; **2.** *fig.* tenacious *views etc.*

zah·len ['tsa:lən] *v/t. and v/i.* pay (h) (*a. fig.*); **~!** (could I *or* we have) the bill (*Am.* check), please; **was habe ich Ihnen zu ~?** what do I owe you?; **ich zahle das schon** I'll pay for that, leave that to me; **gut (schlecht) ~** pay well (badly); **was hast du dafür gezahlt?** what (*or* how much) did you pay for that?

zäh·len ['tsɛ:lən] *v/t. and v/i.* (h) a) count (*a. fig.*); *sport, card game etc.*: keep (the) score, b) *fig.* have; **~ auf** *acc.* count on; **j-n zu s-n Freunden** *etc.* **~** count s.o. as a friend *etc.* (*or* among one's friends *etc.*); **zu den Besten** *etc.* **~** rank with (*or* among) the best *etc.*, be among (*or* belong to) the best *etc.*; **zu den größten Malern ~** rank among (*or* with) the greatest painters; **der Ort zählt 20 000 Einwohner** the town has 20,000 inhabitants; **sein Vermögen zählt nach Millionen** his fortune runs into millions; **sie zählte 12 Jahre** she was 12 (years old); **er (es) zählt nicht** he (it) doesn't count; **s-e Tage sind gezählt** his days are numbered; **... nicht gezählt** not counting ...; **hier zählt nur Quantität** only quantity counts (*or* matters) here; → **drei** I

'**Zah·len|akro,ba·tik** *f* juggling with figures; **~an·ga·ben** *pl.* figures; **~bei·spiel** *n* numerical example; **~code** *m computer*: numeric code; **~fol·ge** *f* numerical order; **~ge·dächt·nis** *n*: **ein gutes (schlechtes) ~ haben** be good (bad) at remembering figures; **~ko,lon·ne** *f* column of figures; **~kom·bi·na·ti,on** *f* combination (of numbers *or* figures); **~lot·to** *n* → **Lotto**

'**zah·len·mä·ßig I.** *adj.* numerical; **~e Überlegenheit** superiority in numbers, numerical superiority; **II.** *adv.* numerically, in terms of figures; **~ überlegen sein** be superior in numbers, be numerically superior; **dem Gegner** *etc.* **~ überlegen sein** outnumber the enemy *etc.*

'**Zah·len|ma·te·ri,al** *n* figures *pl.*; **~mystik** *f* numerology; **~rei·he** *f* series of numbers, number sequence; **~schloß** *n* combination lock; **~sym,bo·lik** *f* number symbolism; **~sy,stem** *n* numerical system; **~wert** *m* numerical value

Zah·ler ['tsa:lɐ] *m* (-s; -): **pünktlicher (säumiger) ~** prompt (dilatory) payer

Zäh·ler ['tsɛ:lɐ] *m* (-s; -) **1.** counter; ⚙ *a.* meter; **2.** 𝔄 numerator; **3.** *sport*: point; **4.** teller; **~ab·le·sun·gen** *pl.* meter readings; **~stand** *m* meter reading

'**Zahl|gren·ze** *f* fare stage; *subway*: *a.* zone boundary; **~kar·te** *f* postal money order; **~kell·ner** *m* head waiter

'**zahl·los** *adj.* innumerable, countless, endless, an endless number of

'**Zahl·mei·ster** *m* paymaster; ⚓ purser (*both a. fig.*)

'**zahl·reich I.** *adj.* numerous, a large number of, a great many; large *family etc.*; **II.** *adv.*: **~ kommen (vertreten sein)** come (be represented) in large numbers *or* in force; **~ besucht werden** be well attended

'**Zahl|stel·le** *f* paying office; sub-branch *of a bank*; **~tag** *m* pay day; **~tel·ler** *m* money tray

Zah·lung ['tsa:lʊŋ] *f* (-; -en) payment; *a.* settlement *of debts*; **gegen (mangels) ~** against (in default of) payment; **e-e ~ leisten** make a payment; **in ~ geben (nehmen)** offer (take) in part exchange, *a.* trade in *car etc.*

Zäh·lung ['tsɛ:lʊŋ] *f* (-; -en) **1.** count; **2.** census; **3.** ⚙ reading

'**Zah·lungs|ab·kom·men** *n* payments agreement; **~an·wei·sung** *f* order to pay; money order; **~auf·for·de·rung** *f* request for payment; **~auf·schub** *m* respite; **~auf·trag** *m* payment order; **~be·din·gun·gen** *pl.* terms of payment; **~be·fehl** *m* default summons; **~be·frei·ung** *f* exemption from payment; **~bi,lanz** *f* balance of payments; **~de·fi·zit** *n* payments deficit; **~emp·fän·ger** *m* payee

'**zah·lungs·fä·hig** *adj.* able to pay; ☤ solvent; '**Zah·lungs·fä·hig·keit** *f* (-; *no pl.*) ability to pay; ☤ solvency

'**Zah·lungs|frist** *f* term of payment, period allowed for payment; **2kräf·tig** *adj.* solvent, financially sound; **~mit·tel** *n* means (*sg.*) of payment; **gesetzliches ~** legal tender; **~mo·dus** *m* method of payment; **~mo,ral** *f* paying habits *pl.*, payment pattern (*or* behavio[u]r); **e-e gute ~ haben** settle one's bills promptly, pay (up) promptly; **e-e schlechte ~ haben** be slow to settle one's bills (*or* to pay up); **~ort** *m* place of payment; domicile

'**zah·lungs·pflich·tig** [-pflɪçtɪç] *adj.* liable to pay

'**Zah·lungs|rück·stand** *m* arrears *pl.*, backlog of payments; **~schwie·rig·kei·ten** *pl.* financial difficulties, F liquidity problem *sg.*; **~ter,min** *m* payment (deadline)

'**zah·lungs·un·fä·hig** *adj.* unable to pay; ☤ insolvent; '**Zah·lungs·un·fä·hig·keit** *f* (-; *no pl.*) inability to pay; ☤ insolvency

'**Zah·lungs|ver·kehr** *m* payments *pl.*; **~ver·pflich·tung** *f* financial obligation; liability (to pay); **~ver·spre·chen** *n* promise to pay; **~ver·zug** *m* default (of payment); **in ~ geraten** default on one's payments, get (*or* fall) into arrears; **~wei·se** *f* method of payment

Zähl·werk ['tsɛ:lvɛrk] *n* (-[e]s; -e) counter

'**Zahl|wort** *n* (-[e]s; ·̈er) *ling.* numeral; **~zei·chen** *n* figure, numeral

zahm [tsa:m] *adj.* tame (*a. fig.*)

zähm·bar ['tsɛ:mba:ɐ] *adj.* tameable

zäh·men ['tsɛ:mən] *v/t.* (h) **1.** tame; break in *horse*; **2.** *fig.* control, curb *emotions etc.*; tame, subdue, subjugate, conquer

'**Zahm·heit** *f* (-; *no pl.*) tameness (*a. fig.*)

Zäh·mung ['tsɛːmʊŋ] *f* (-; *no pl.*) taming; *fig. a.* subduing, subjugation; → ***zähmen*** 2

Zahn [tsaːn] *m* (-[e]s; Zähne ['tsɛːnə]) **1.** tooth; ⚙ *a.* cog; ***Zähne bekommen*** cut one's teeth; *fig.* ***bis an die Zähne bewaffnet*** armed to the teeth; ***der ~ der Zeit*** the ravages of time; ***j-m auf den ~ fühlen*** sound s.o. out; F ***et. für den hohlen ~*** F chickenfeed; F ***den ~ hab' ich ihm gezogen*** F I knocked that idea out of his head, I've disabused him of that; → ***ausbeißen, dritte, fletschen, knirschen, putzen*** I, ***zusammenbeißen; 2.*** F ***mit e-m tollen ~*** F at a terrific lick; ***e-n ~ zulegen*** F step on it

'**Zahn·arzt** *m* dentist, *formal*: dental surgeon; **~hel·fe·rin** *f* dental assistant

'**zahn·ärzt·lich** *adj.* dental ...

'**Zahn·arzt|pra·xis** *f* dental practice (*or* surgery); **~stuhl** *m* dentist's chair

'**Zahn|be·hand·lung** *f* dental treatment; **~be·lag** *m* plaque; **~bür·ste** *f* toothbrush; **~chir·ur͵gie** *f* dental surgery; **~creme** *f* toothpaste

zäh·ne·flet·schend ['tsɛːnə-] **I.** *adj.* snarling; **II.** *adv. a.* with its teeth bared, showing its teeth

'**Zäh·ne·klap·pern** *n* chattering (of) teeth; '**zäh·ne·klap·pernd** *adv.* with chattering teeth

'**Zäh·ne·knir·schen** *n* teeth-grinding; '**zäh·ne·knir·schend** *fig. adv. agree etc.* grudgingly, F muttering under one's breath

zah·nen ['tsaːnən] *v/i.* (h) cut one's teeth, be teething

'**Zahn|er·satz** *m* dentures *pl.*, *formal*: dental prosthesis; **~fäu·le** *f* dental decay, (dental) caries

'**Zahn·fleisch** *n* gums *pl.*; F *fig.* ***auf dem ~ gehen*** be on one's last legs; **~blu·ten** *n* bleeding (of the) gums; 🕮 pyorrh(o)ea; **~schwund** *m* shrinking (of the) gums; 🕮 pyorrh(o)ea

'**Zahn|fül·lung** *f* filling; **~hals** *m* neck of a (*or* the) tooth; **~heil·kun·de** *f* → ***Zahnmedizin;*** **~klam·mer** *f* brace; **~kli·nik** *f* dental clinic; **~kranz** *m* ⚙ gear rim; **~laut** *m ling.* dental

'**zahn·los** *adj.* toothless

'**Zahn|lücke** *f* gap (in one's teeth); **~me·di͵zin** *f* dentistry; **~pa·sta** *f* toothpaste; **~pfle·ge** *f* dental hygiene, care of one's teeth; **~pro͵the·se** *f* dentures *pl.*, *formal*: dental prosthesis; **~pul·ver** *n* tooth powder

'**Zahn·rad** *n* gear(wheel), cog(wheel); **~an·trieb** *m* gear drive; **~bahn** *f* rack (*or* cog) railway; **~ge·trie·be** *n* gear transmission; pinion gear

'**Zahn|re·gu͵lie·rung** *f* orthodontic treatment; F teeth-straightening job; **~rei·ni·gung** *f* teeth-cleaning; **~schmelz** *m* (dental) enamel; **~schmerzen** *pl.* toothache *sg.*; **~schutz** *m boxing*: gumshield; **~sei·de** *f* dental floss; **~span·ge** *f* brace; **~stein** *m* tartar; **~sto·cher** *m* toothpick; **~tech·nik** *f* dentistry; **~tech·ni·ker** *m* dental technician; **~trans·plan·ta·ti͵on** *f* tooth transplant; **~wal** *m* toothed whale; **~wech·sel** *m* second dentition; **~weh** *n* toothache; **~wur·zel** *f* root (of a *or* the tooth); **~wur·zel·be·hand·lung** *f* root canal work

Zam·pa·no ['tsampano] *m* (-s; -s): ***sich wie der große ~ aufspielen*** F act the big shot; ***da kommt der große ~*** F here comes Mr Great Guy

Zan·der ['tsandɐ] *m* (-s; -) *zo.* pike-perch

Zan·ge ['tsaŋə] *f* (-; -n): (***e-e ~*** a pair of) pliers (*or* tongs) *pl.*; ⚕ forceps; *fig.* ⚔ pincer; *fig.* ***j-n in die ~ nehmen*** F put the screws on s.o., *soccer*: sandwich s.o.; ⚔ ***in die ~ nehmen*** encircle, surround; ***das würde ich nicht mit der ~ anfassen*** I wouldn't touch it with a bargepole

'**Zan·gen|ent·bin·dung** *f*, **~ge·burt** *f* forceps delivery

Zank [tsaŋk] *m* (-[e]s; *no pl.*) quarrel; **~ap·fel** *m* bone of contention

zan·ken ['tsaŋkən] *v/i.* (h) **1.** (*a.* ***sich ~***) quarrel, argue (***um*** *acc.* about, over); **2.** *dial.* scold; ***mit j-m ~*** tell s.o. off

Zan·ke·rei [tsaŋkəˈraɪ] *f* (-; -en) squabbling, quarrel(l)ing, arguing

zän·kisch ['tsɛŋkɪʃ] *adj.* quarrelsome; cantankerous; nagging ...

Zäpf·chen ['tsɛpfçən] *n* (-s; -) **1.** *anat.*, *ling.* uvula; **2.** ⚕ suppository

Zap·fen ['tsapfən] *m* (-s; -) **1.** ⚙ a) plug; peg, pin; tenon, b) spigot, bung, c) pivot, d) journal, stud; **2.** icicle; **3.** ♣ cone; **4.** *anat.* retinal cone; '**zap·fen** *v/t.* (h) **1.** tap, draw *beer etc.*; **2.** ⚠ join with (mortise and) tenon

'**Zap·fen·streich** *m* ⚔ curfew; tatto, *Brit. a. the* last post, *Am.* taps *pl.*

Zap·fer ['tsapfɐ] *m* (-s; -) barman

'**Zapf|hahn** *m* tap, *Am.* faucet; *mot.* hose nozzle; **~pi͵sto·le** *f* nozzle; **~säu·le** *f mot.* petrol (*Am.* gasoline) pump

zap·pe·lig ['tsapəlɪç] *adj.* a) fidgety, restless, b) excited, nervous, F in a flap

zap·peln ['tsapəln] *v/i.* (h) thrash about, struggle; wriggle; jiggle around; ***hör auf zu ~!*** sit still, will you; *fig.* ***j-n ~ lassen*** keep s.o. on tenterhooks

Zap·pel·phi·lipp ['tsapəlfiːlɪp] F *m* (-s; -s, -e) fidget

zap·pen·du·ster ['tsapən'duːstɐ] F *adj.* pitch-dark, pitch-black; *fig.* ***dann wird's ~*** things will look pretty grim

Zar [tsaːɐ] *m* (-en; -en ['tsaːrən]) tsar, czar

Za·ren|herr·schaft ['tsaːrən-] *f* (-; *no pl.*) tsarist (*or* czarist) rule; **~reich** *n*: ***im ~*** under the tsars (*or* czars)

'**Za·ren·tum** *n* (-s; *no pl.*): (*a.* ***das ~***) tsardom, czardom

Za·re·witsch [tsa'reːvɪtʃ] *m* (-[e]s; -e) tsarevitch, czarevitch

Zar·ge ['tsargə] *f* (-; -n) **1.** frame; **2.** side *of a violin etc.*

Za·rin ['tsaːrɪn] *f* (-; -nen) tsarina, czarina

za·ri·stisch [tsa'rɪstɪʃ] *adj.* tsarist, czarist; ***das ~e Rußland*** tsarist (*or* czarist) Russia, Russia under the tsars (*or* czars)

zart [tsaːɐt] **I.** *adj.* a) tender *meat etc.*, *a. fig. heart*; soft *skin etc.*, *a.* delicate *colo(u)r*, b) *fig.* gentle; sensitive; delicate *health etc.*; ***das ~e Geschlecht*** the gentle sex; ***ein ~es Geschöpf*** a delicate creature; ***~e Andeutung*** gentle hint; ***im ~en Alter von*** at the tender age of; ***nichts für ~e Ohren*** not for sensitive ears; **II.** *adv.* tenderly; gently; ***~ umgehen mit*** *dat.* handle with care, *a.* handle *s.o.* with kid gloves

'**zart·be·sai·tet** [-bəzaɪtət] *fig. adj.* delicately strung, highly sensitive

'**zart·bit·ter** *adj.* plain *chocolate*

'**zart·füh·lend** *adj.* discreet, tactful; '**Zart·ge·fühl** *n* (-[e]s; *no pl.*) delicacy (of feeling), tact

'**zart·glied·rig** [-gliːdrɪç] *adj.* delicately-built ..., *pred.* delicately built; *a.* petite

'**Zart·heit** *f* (-; *no pl.*) tenderness; softness; delicacy, delicateness; gentleness

zärt·lich ['tsɛːɐtlɪç] *adj.* affectionate; loving; tender *look etc.*; ***~ werden*** start caressing (one another); '**Zärt·lich·keit** *f* (-; -en) **1.** *no pl.* a) affection, b) tenderness; **2.** caress; ***~en austauschen*** caress (one another); ***j-m ~en ins Ohr flüstern*** whisper sweet nothings into s.o.'s ear

'**zart·ro·sa** *adj.*, '**Zart·ro·sa** *n* delicate pink

Zä·si·um ['tsɛːzɪ̯ʊm] *n* (-s; *no pl.*) c(a)esium

Za·ster ['tsastɐ] F *m* (-s; *no pl.*) *sl.* dosh, brass, bread

Zä·sur [tsɛ'zuːɐ] *f* (-; -en [-rən]) **1.** *metric*, ♪ caesura, break; **2.** *fig.* break; turning point

Zau·ber ['tsaʊbɐ] *m* (-s; *no pl.*) magic; *contp.* mumbo jumbo; *fig.* magic(al quality); (magic) spell; F *fig.* fuss, song and dance; ***den ~ lösen*** break the spell; ***wie durch ~*** as if by magic; *fig.* ***fauler ~*** humbug, mumbo jumbo, a swindle; F ***den ganzen ~*** the whole bag of tricks; ***was kostet der ganze ~?*** F how much is this lot then?; **Zau·be·rei** [tsaʊbə'raɪ] *f* (-; -en) **1.** *no pl.* a) magic, b) sorcery, witchcraft; **2.** conjuring, sleight-of--hand; **Zau·be·rer** ['tsaʊbərɐ] *m* (-s; -) **1.** magician, sorcerer, wizard (*a. fig.*); **2.** → ***Zauberkünstler***

'**Zau·ber|flö·te** *f* magic flute; **~for·mel** *f* spell, charm; *fig.* magic formula; **~glau·be** *m* belief in magic

'**zau·ber·haft** *adj.* charming, enchanting

'**Zau·ber·hand** *f*: ***wie von ~*** as if by magic

Zau·be·rin ['tsaʊbərɪn] *f* (-; -nen) sorceress; *fig. a.* enchantress

'**Zau·ber|ka·sten** *m* conjuring set; **~kraft** *f* magic power; *fig.* magic (power) *of words etc.*; **~kreis** *m* magic circle; **~kunst** *f* (black) magic; witchcraft; **~künst·ler** *m* conjurer, magician; **~kunst·stück** *n* conjuring trick; **~land** *n* magic realm, wonderland; fairyland; **~lehr·ling** *m* sorcerer's apprentice; **~mit·tel** *n* magic cure (*or* potion)

zau·bern ['tsaʊbɐn] (h) **I.** *v/i.* do (*or* perform) magic *or* conjuring tricks; F *fig.* ***ich kann doch nicht ~*** I can't perform miracles, I can't just wave my magic wand; **II.** *v/t.* conjure (up), *fig.* conjure up

'**Zau·ber|spruch** *m* charm, spell; **~stab** *m* magic wand; **~trank** *m* magic potion; **~wort** *n* (-[e]s; -e) magic word (*or* formula); **~wür·fel** *m* magic cube

Zau·de·rer ['tsaʊdərɐ] *m* (-s; -) vacillator, F ditherer; procrastinator; **zau·dern** ['tsaʊdɐn] *v/i.* (h) hesitate (***mit*** *dat.* about), waver, vacillate; temporize, procrastinate

Zaum [tsaʊm] *m* (-[e]s; Zäume ['tsɔʏmə]) bridle; *fig.* ***im ~ halten*** contain, bridle *one's passion etc.*, keep a tight rein on *s.o.*; ***sich im ~ halten*** restrain o.s.

zäu·men ['tsɔʏmən] *v/t.* (h) bridle

'**Zaum·zeug** *n* (-[e]s; *no pl.*) bridle

Zaun [tsaʊn] *m* (-[e]s; Zäune ['tsɔʏnə]) a) fence, b) ⚠ hoarding; *fig.* ***e-n Streit (Krieg) vom ~ brechen*** pick *or* start a fight (start a war); **~gast** *m* onlooker; **~kö·nig** *m zo.* wren; **~lat·te** *f* picket; **~pfahl** *m* fence post; *fig.* ***Wink mit dem ~*** broad hint; **~pfo·sten** *m* fence post

zau·sen ['tsaʊzən] *v/t.* (h) tousle *hair*; buffet *trees*; *fig.* ***vom Leben arg gezaust*** buffeted by fate
Ze·bra ['tse:bra] *n* (-s; -s) zebra; **~strei·fen** *m* zebra crossing
Zech·bru·der ['tsɛç-] F *m* **1.** F boozer; **2.** → ***Zechkumpan***
Ze·che¹ ['tsɛçə] *f* bill, *Am.* check; ***die ~ bezahlen*** F pick up the tab, foot the bill; → ***prellen*** 1
'**Ze·che**² *f* (-; -n) ⚒ mine
ze·chen ['tsɛçən] *v/i.* (h) F booze
'**Ze·chen·stille·gung** (*sep.* -ll·l-) *f* pit closure
Ze·cher ['tsɛçɐ] *m* (-s; -) F boozer
Zech|ge·la·ge ['tsɛç-] *n* carousal, drinking bout; **~kum,pan** *m* F boozing mate
Zech·prel·ler ['tsɛçprɛlɐ] *m* (-s; -) bilk; **Zech·prel·le·rei** [tsɛçprɛlə'raɪ] *f* (-; -en) bilking
Zech·tour ['tsɛç-] *f* F pub crawl
Zecke ['tsɛkə] (*sep.* -k·k-) *f* (-; -n) tick
Ze·der ['tse:dɐ] *f* (-; -n) ♣ cedar
'**Ze·dern·holz** *n* (-es; *no pl.*) cedar(wood)
Zeh [tse:] *m* (-s; -en), **Ze·he**¹ ['tse:ə] *f* (-; -n) toe; ***auf Zehen gehen*** (walk on) tiptoe; *a.* F *fig.* ***j-m auf die Zehen treten*** tread on s.o.'s toes
'**Ze·he**² *f* (-; -n) clove *of garlic*
'**Ze·hen|na·gel** *m* toenail; **~san,da·le** *f* strap sandal; **~spit·ze** *f* tip of one's toe; ***auf ~n*** on tiptoe, ***gehen:*** (walk on) tiptoe
zehn [tse:n] *adj.* ten
Zehn *f* (-; -en) a) ten, b) *bus etc.* (number) ten; '**zehn·bän·dig** [-bɛndɪç] *adj.* ten-volume ..., in ten volumes; **Zeh·ner** ['tse:nɐ] *m* (-s; -) **1.** ten-pfennig piece; **2.** ten-mark note (*Am.* bill)
'**Zeh·ner|club** *m*, **~grup·pe** *f* ⚚ club of ten; **~stel·le** *f* A decimal place
'**zehn·fach** *adj.* tenfold; ***die ~e Menge*** ten times the amount; ***~er Sieger*** ten-time winner (*or* champion)
Zehn'fin·ger·sy,stem *n*: ***das ~*** touch-typing
'**zehn·jäh·rig** [-jɛ:rɪç] *adj.* **1.** ten-year-old ...; **2.** ten-year ...; ***ein ~es ... a.*** ten years of ...; '**Zehn·jäh·ri·ge** [-jɛ:rɪgə] *m, f* (-n; -n) ten-year-old
'**Zehn|kampf** *m* *sport*: decathlon; **~kämp·fer** *m* decathlete
'**zehn·köp·fig** [-kœpfɪç] *adj. family etc.* of ten; ***~e Delegation*** *etc. a.* ten-member (*or* ten-man) delegation *etc.*
'**zehn·mal** *adv.* ten times
Zehn'mark·schein *m* ten-mark note (*Am.* bill)
zehnt [tse:nt] **I.** *adj.* tenth; ***~es Kapitel*** chapter ten; ***am ~en Mai*** on the tenth of May, on May the tenth; ***10. Mai*** 10th May, May 10(th); **II.** *adv.*: ***wir waren zu ~*** there were ten of us; ***wir gingen zu ~ hin*** ten of us went there
'**zehn·tä·gig** [-tɛ:gɪç] *adj.* **1.** ten-day(-long) ...; **2.** ten-day-old ...
zehn'tau·send *adj.* ten thousand; ***die oberen*** ♀ the upper crust
Zehn·te ['tse:ntə] *m, f* (-n; -n) (the) tenth; ***er war ~r*** he was (*or* came) tenth; ***Papst Johannes X.*** Pope John X (= Pope John the Tenth); ***heute ist der ~*** it's the tenth today
'**zehn·tei·lig** ['tse:ntaɪlɪç] *adj.* ten-part ..., in ten parts
Zehn·tel ['tse:ntəl] *n* (-s; -) tenth; **~se,kun·de** *f* tenth of a second; ***um zwei ~n*** by two tenths of a second, by point two of a second
zehn·tens ['tse:ntəns] *adv.* tenth(ly), ten, in tenth place
zeh·ren ['tse:rən] *v/i.* (h) sap one's energy; ***~ an*** *dat.* take it out of, undermine *s.o.'s health etc.*; ***~ von*** *dat.* live on, *fig.* live off *the capital*, draw on *supplies*, *fig.* thrive on *one's memories etc.*
Zei·chen ['tsaɪçən] *n* (-s; -) a) sign (*a. ast.*, ♪, A), b) character; symbol, c) *ling.* mark, d) indication, sign, *esp.* ⚕ symptom (***für*** *acc.* of), e) *radio etc.*: signal; time signal, pips *pl.*; ⚚ ***unser*** (***Ihr***) ~ our (your) reference; ***als ~*** *gen.* as a mark of; ***als ~ der Freundschaft*** as a token (*or* mark) of friendship; ***zum ~*** *gen.* as a sign of; ***es geschehen*** (***noch***) ***~ und Wunder*** wonders will never cease; ***ein ~ der Zeit*** a sign of the times; ***die ~ der Zeit erkennen*** read the signs of the times; ***die ~ stehen auf Sturm*** *pol.* everything is pointing towards a conflict; ***ich sehe das als ein gutes ~*** I see it as a good omen (*or* positive sign); ***im ~*** *gen.* ***stehen*** be marked by; ***die Stadt steht im ~ der kommenden WM*** the town is gearing up for the World Cup; ***unser Jahrhundert steht im ~ der Naturwissenschaften*** our century is the age of science; ***auf ein ~ von*** *dat.* at a sign from; *mot.* ***~ geben*** (*or* ***machen***) signal, give a sign; ***ein ~ geben*** make a sign (*dat.* to), signal (to); ***das ~ zum Aufbruch geben*** give the signal (for everybody) to leave; *ast.* ***im ~ von*** *dat.* under the sign of; ***ein ~ setzen*** point the way to the future; ***wenn nicht alle ~ trügen*** if I'm not very much mistaken
'**Zei·chen|auf·lö·sung** *f computer*: character resolution; **~block** *m* sketch pad; **~brett** *n* drawing board; **~dich·te** *f computer*: character density; **~drei·eck** *n* A set square; **~er·klä·rung** *f* key; *geogr.* legend; signs and symbols *pl.*; **~fe·der** *f* drawing pen; **~feh·ler** *m* punctuation error (*or* mistake); **~ge·rät** *n computer*: plotter; **~kunst** *f* (art of) drawing; **~leh·rer** *m* art teacher; **~pa,pier** *n* drawing paper; **~saal** *m ped.* art room; **~satz** *m typ.* font; **~set·zung** *f* punctuation; **~spra·che** *f* sign language; **~stift** *m* pencil; crayon; **~tisch** *m* drawing board; **~trick·film** *m* (animated) cartoon; **~,un·ter·richt** *m* drawing lessons *pl.*; *ped.* art (class[es *pl.*])
zeich·nen ['tsaɪçnən] (h) **I.** *v/t. and v/i.* **1.** a) draw (***nach*** *dat.* from *life etc.*); *a. fig.* sketch, outline, b) mark, c) plot, d) *fig.* portray, depict; *fig.* ***ein optimistisches Bild ~ von*** *dat.* paint an optimistic picture of; **II.** *v/i.* **2.** sign; *fig.* ***für et. verantwortlich ~*** take (the) responsibility for s.th.; **3.** ⚚ subscribe (***für*** *acc.* to); → ***gezeichnet***; **III.** ♀ *n* (-s; *no pl.*) drawing; *ped.* art
Zeich·ner ['tsaɪçnɐ] *m* (-s; -) **1.** draughtsman, *Am.* draftsman; **2.** ⚚ subscriber; **Zeich·ne·rin** ['tsaɪçnərɪn] *f* (-; -nen) **1.** draughtswoman, *Am.* draftswoman; **2.** ⚚ subscriber
zeich·ne·risch ['tsaɪçnərɪʃ] *adj.*: ***~e Begabung*** talent for drawing
Zeich·nung ['tsaɪçnʊŋ] *f* (-; -en) **1.** drawing (*a.* ⚙); sketch; draft; illustration; *fig.* portrayal, depiction; **2.** marking; grain *of wood*; pattern; **3.** ⚚ subscription (*gen.* to)
'**zeich·nungs·be·rech·tigt** *adj.* authorized to sign; '**Zeich·nungs·voll·macht** *f* authority to sign
Zei·ge·fin·ger ['tsaɪgə-] *m* forefinger, index finger; ***mit dem ~ auf et. deuten*** point one's finger at s.th.; ***mit erhobenem ~ sagte er mir*** wagging his finger at me he told me; *fig.* ***mit erhobenem ~*** with a (strong) moralizing undertone
zei·gen ['tsaɪgən] (h) **I.** *v/t.* a) show (*a. fig.*); indicate, b) present, show, demonstrate; ***j-m die Stadt ~*** show s.o. round the town (*or* city), show s.o. the sights; ***er kann s-e Gefühle nicht ~*** he finds it hard to express his feelings; ***zeig mal, was du kannst!*** come on, show us what you can do; ***zeig mir j-n, der es besser kann*** I'd like to see anyone do better; ***was zeigt die Waage?*** what do the scales say?; ***die Blumen ~ schon Knospen*** the flowers are beginning to show their buds; ***ihm werd' ich's ~!*** I'll show him; **II.** *v/i.*: ***~ auf*** *acc.* point at, point *s.th.* out; *thermometer*: be at; *watch*: say; *compass*: point (to); ***zeig mal*** (***her***) let's see, let's have a look; ***die Erfahrung zeigt, daß*** experience shows (*or* proves) that; **III.** *v/refl.*: ***sich ~*** show; show o.s., appear, turn up; ***es zeigte sich, daß*** it turned out that; ***es wird sich ja ~*** we shall see, time will tell; ***sich freundlich ~*** be friendly; ***sich ~ als*** prove (o.s.) to be; ***sich in der Öffentlichkeit ~*** appear in public, make a public appearance; ***so kann ich mich nicht ~*** I can't go out (*or* let myself be seen) in this state; ***die ersten Sterne zeigten sich*** the first stars appeared; ***früh zeigte sich sein Talent zum Schriftsteller*** he showed an early talent for writing; ***da zeigt sich wieder einmal, daß*** it just goes to show that; → ***erkenntlich*** 2, ***Seite***
Zei·ger ['tsaɪgɐ] *m* (-s; -) ⚙ needle; (*watch*) hand; *computer*: pointer; A index, exponent; ***großer*** (***kleiner***) ~ big (little) hand
Zei·ge·stock ['tsaɪgə-] *m* pointer
Zei·le ['tsaɪlə] *f* (-; -n) a) line (*a. TV*), b) row; ***j-m ein paar ~n schreiben*** drop s.o. a line; ***danke für die netten ~n*** thank you for your (lovely) letter; ***ich habe jede ~ gelesen*** I read every word; ***~ für ~*** line by line; *fig.* ***zwischen den ~n lesen*** read between the lines
'**Zei·len|ab·stand** *m* line spacing; **~bau·wei·se** *f* ribbon development; **~drucker** *m computer*: line printer; **~edi·tor** *m computer*: line editor; ♀**frei** *adj. TV* line-free; **~ho·no,rar** *n* payment per line; ***~ bekommen*** be paid by the line; **~län·ge** *f* line length; **~norm** *f TV* line standard; **~num·mer** *f* line number; **~schal·ter** *m typewriter*: spacer; **~schal·tung** *f computer*: line feed
'**zei·len·wei·se** *adv.* by the line
Zei·sig ['tsaɪzɪç] *m* (-s; -e) *zo.* siskin
Zeit [tsaɪt] *f* a) *no pl.* time, b) *ling.* tense, c) era, age; period of time, d) *sport*: time; ***schwere*** (*or* ***schlechte***) ***~en*** hard times; ***für schlechte ~en sparen*** save up for a rainy day; ***auf ~ spielen*** play for time, temporize; *sport*: ***die ~ nehmen*** time (***von*** *dat. a run etc.*); ***der beste Spieler*** *etc.* ***aller ~en*** the best player *etc.* of all times; ***die gute alte ~*** the good old days; ***das waren noch ~en!*** those were the days; ***das war die schönste ~ m-s Lebens*** those were the best years of my life;

die ~ des Barock the baroque age (*or* era, period); ***die ~ vor dem zweiten Weltkrieg*** the period before the Second World War; ***unsere ~, die heutige ~*** this (*or* the present) day and age; ***ein Märchen aus alten ~en*** a tale from days of yore; ***einige ~ lang*** for a time; ***für alle ~en*** for good; ***die ganze ~ hindurch*** the whole time; ***seit ewigen ~en*** for ages; ***seit der ~*** since then (*or* that time), ever since (then); ***morgen um diese ~*** this time tomorrow; ***in der ~ vom ... bis ...*** in the time between ... and ...; ***ich habe mich in der ~ geirrt*** I got the time wrong; ***in der ~ richte ich mich nach dir*** you suggest the time; ***j-n nach der ~ fragen*** ask s.o. for the time; ***zu jeder ~*** (at) any time; ***in kurzer ~*** a) very quickly, b) very soon, shortly; ***in kürzester ~*** in no time; ***in letzter ~*** lately, recently; ***lange ~*** a long time; ***mit der ~, im Laufe der ~*** in time; ***mit der ~ gehen*** move (*or* keep up) with the times; ***von ~ zu ~*** from time to time, now and then; ***vor der ~*** prematurely, *a. die* before one's time; ***vor langer ~*** long ago, a long time ago; ***das war vor m-r ~*** that was before my time; ***zur ~*** at the moment; ***zur ~*** *gen.* at the time of; ***zu m-r ~*** in my time, when I was at university *etc.*; ***in Goethes ~*** in Goethe's day (and age), at the time of Goethe; ***alles zu s-r ~*** there's a time for everything, one thing after another; ***es ist nicht die ~, um zu*** *inf.* it's not the right time to *inf.* (*or* to be *ger.*); ***zur gleichen ~*** at the same time; ***Herr über s-e ~ sein*** be able to do what one likes with one's time; ***j-m ~ lassen*** give s.o. time; ***sich ~ lassen*** take one's time (***dazu*** over it); ***laß dir ~!*** take your time, *a.* ***das hat ~*** there's no hurry (*or* rush); ***das hat ~ (bis morgen)*** that can wait (till *or* until tomorrow); ***sich die ~ nehmen zu*** *inf.* take time to *inf.*; ***ich gebe dir ~ bis morgen (5 Minuten ~)*** I'll give you till tomorrow (five minutes); ***das dauert s-e ~*** it takes time; ***es wird noch einige ~ dauern, bis*** it'll be some time before; ***mir fehlt die ~*** I (just) haven't got the time; ***hast du ein paar Stunden ~?*** can you spare a couple of hours?; ***sie hat nie ~ für mich*** she never has any time for me; ***es ist (höchste) ~, es ist an der ~*** it's (high) time; ***es ist (höchste) ~, daß er nach Hause kommt*** it's (high) time he came home; ***sie hat es die ganze ~ gewußt*** she knew all along (*or* all the time); ***nur e-e Frage der ~*** just a matter of time; ***s-e beste ~ hinter sich haben*** have had one's day; ***sie hat bessere ~en gesehen*** she's seen better days; ***er nimmt sich kaum ~ zum Essen*** he hardly takes any time off to eat; ***wenn Sie ~ haben*** whenever you like; ***die ~en sind vorbei, wo*** time was when; ***einige ~ verstreichen lassen, bevor*** wait a while before (*ger.*); ***mir wird die ~ nie lang*** I've plenty to keep me occupied; ***auf die ~ achten*** keep an eye on the time (*or* clock); ***die ~ arbeitet für uns*** time is on our side; ***für kommende ~en ist gesorgt*** we're well prepared for times to come; ***~ gewinnen*** gain time; ***sich die ~ vertreiben*** while away the time; ***s-r ~ voraus sein*** be ahead of one's time; ***kommt ~, kommt Rat*** don't worry, it'll sort itself out; ***andere ~en, andere Sitten*** things really have changed, things were very different in those days; ***ach du liebe ~!*** goodness (me)!; → ***schinden, totschlagen, Wunde***

zeit *prp.* (*gen.*): ***~ s-s Lebens*** a) his whole life long, b) for the rest of his life; → ***zeitlebens***

'Zeit|ab·lauf *m* lapse of time (*a.* ⚖); **~ab·schnitt** *m* period (of time); **~ab·stand** *m* interval; ***in regelmäßigen Zeitabständen*** at regular intervals, periodically; **~al·ter** *n* **1.** age, era, epoch; ***in unserem ~*** in our day and age; ***das ~ des Computers*** the age of the computer; ***goldenes ~*** *a. fig.* golden age; **2.** *geol.* period; **~an·ga·be** *f* exact date and time; date; ***ohne ~*** undated; **~an·sa·ge** *f* time check; *teleph.* speaking clock; **~ar·beit** *f* temporary work

'Zeit·auf·wand *m* time involved (*or* needed *for s.th.*); ***e-n ~ von drei Wochen erfordern*** require three weeks to complete (*or* do *etc.*), take three weeks; ***der ~ ist groß*** it involves a lot of time; **'zeit·auf·wen·dig** *adj.* time-consuming

'Zeit|au·to,ma·tik *f phot.* shutter priority; **&be·dingt** *adj.* arising from (*or* rooted in, embedded in, conditioned by) the times; **~be·griff** *m* concept of time; **~bom·be** *f* time bomb (*a. fig.*); *fig.* ***die ~ tickt*** the time bomb is ticking away (quietly); **~dau·er** *f* length of time; duration; **~do·ku,ment** *n* contemporary document, document of the times; **~druck** *m* (-[e]s; *no pl.*) (time) pressure; ***unter ~ stehen*** be pressed for time, be under deadline pressure; **~ein·heit** *f* unit of time; **~ein·tei·lung** *f* division of time; time plan

Zei·ten|fol·ge ['tsaɪtən-] *f ling.* sequence of tenses; **~wen·de** *f* turn of an era

'Zeit|er·schei·nung *f* emanation of the times; **~er·spar·nis** *f* time saving; **~fak·tor** *m* time factor; **~fol·ge** *f* sequence, chronological order (*or* sequence); **~fra·ge** *f* **1.** question of time; **2.** current issue; **~ge·fühl** *n* (-[e]s; *no pl.*) sense of time; **~geist** *m* (-[e]s; *no pl.*) zeitgeist, spirit of the times

'zeit·ge·mäß *adj.* in keeping with the times; modern; current *issues etc.*

'Zeit·ge·nos·se *m* contemporary; F ***ein unangenehmer ~*** F an awkward customer; **'zeit·ge·nös·sisch** [-gənœsɪʃ] *adj.* contemporary; ♪ ***~e Instrumente*** period (*or* historical) instruments

'Zeit|ge·sche·hen *n* current events *pl.*; **~ge·schich·te** *f* (-; *no pl.*) contemporary history; **~ge·schmack** *m* contemporary fashion(s and tastes *pl.*), fashion of the times; **~ge·winn** *m* (-[e]s; *no pl.*) time saving, gain in time; **&gleich I.** *adj.* simultaneous; ***~ sein*** *sport*: record the same time; **II.** *adv.* simultaneously, at the same time; **~grün·de** *pl.*: ***aus ~n*** for lack of time, *formal*: due to prior commitments (*or* engagements); **~gut·ha·ben** *n* time credit, hours *pl.* in hand

zei·tig ['tsaɪtɪç] **I.** *adj.* early; **II.** *adv.* early; in good time

zei·ti·gen ['tsaɪtɪgən] *v/t.* (h) produce, bring forth

'Zeit·kar·te *f* season ticket, *Am.* commuter's ticket

'Zeit·kri,tik *f* social criticism; **'zeit·kri·tisch** *adj.* topical; critical of the times; sociocritical

'Zeit·lang *f*: ***e-e ~*** for a while

zeit·le·bens [tsaɪt'le:bəns] *adv.* all one's life, one's whole life long

'zeit·lich I. *adj.* time *factor etc.*; *a. eccl.* temporal; chronological; ***in großen (kleinen) ~en Abständen*** at long (short) intervals; ***~e Berechnung*** timing; ***aus ~en Gründen*** → ***Zeitgründe***; ***~e Probleme*** problems of time; ***~e Reihenfolge*** sequence; ***das Zeitliche segnen*** a) depart this life, b) F give up the ghost; **II.** *adv.* timewise; chronologically; ***~ zusammenfallen*** coincide; ***~ befristet*** limited, limited-period ...; ***es ist ~ befristet*** *a.* there's a time limit (on it); ***ich schaffe es ~ nicht*** a) I'm not going to make it in time, b) (*a.* ***das paßt mir ~ nicht***) I can't fit it in (timewise)

'zeit·los *adj.* timeless

'Zeit·lu·pe *f*: (***in ~*** in) slow motion

'Zeit·lu·pen|auf·nah·me *f* slow-motion shot; **~tem·po** *n* slow motion; ***im ~*** in slow motion, *fig.* at a snail's pace

'Zeit|man·gel *m* (-s; *no pl.*) lack of time; ***wegen ~s*** due to lack of time; **~mes·sung** *f* **1.** chronometry; **2.** *sport*: timekeeping

'zeit·nah *adj.* topical; ***~e Probleme*** *a.* current issues

Zeit·nah·me ['tsaɪtna:mə] *f* (-; *no pl.*) *sport*: timekeeping; **'Zeit·neh·mer** [-ne:mɐ] *m* (-s; -) *sport*: timekeeper; ✝ time-study man

'Zeit|not *f*: ***in ~ sein*** be pressed for time, be under time pressure, be running out of time; ***in ~ geraten*** start running out of time; ***wir wollen nicht in ~ geraten*** we don't want to have to start rushing things; **~plan** *m* timetable, schedule; **~pla·nung** *f* scheduling; **~punkt** *m* time; moment; ***zu dem ~*** at that (point in) time; ***zum ~*** *gen.* at the time of; ***von diesem ~ an*** from that point (*or* moment) on; ***bis zu diesem ~*** up until that point (in time); ***e-n geeigneten (or den richtigen) ~ abwarten*** wait for the right moment; ***du bist zum richtigen ~ gekommen*** you've come just at the right time; ***jetzt ist nicht der richtige ~*** it's not the right moment; ***wo waren Sie zu dem ~?*** where were you at that time?; ***e-n ~ festlegen*** fix a time

'Zeit·raf·fer [-rafɐ] *m* (-s; *no pl.*) a) time-lapse photography, b) time-lapse motion camera, c) *video*: quick picture search; ***im ~*** in quick motion

'zeit·rau·bend *adj.* time-consuming

'Zeit|raum *m* period (of time); ***ein ~ von*** *dat.* a period of; **~rech·nung** *f* a) calendar, b) era; ***nach christlicher ~*** according to the Christian calendar; ***die christliche ~*** the Christian Era; ***vor (nach) unserer ~*** before the Christian Era (after the birth of Christ); **~schal·ter** *m* time switch

'Zeit·schrift *f* magazine; periodical

'Zeit·schrif·ten|ka·ta,log *m* periodicals catalog(ue); **~le·se·saal** *m* periodicals room; **~ver·le·ger** *m* magazine publisher

'Zeit|sol,dat *m* short-service volunteer; **~span·ne** *f* period (of time); ***innerhalb e-r ~ von*** *dat.* within a space (*or* period) of

'zeit·spa·rend *adj.* time-saving

'Zeit|stra·fe *f sport*: time penalty; **~strö·mung** *f* prevailing trend; **~stück** *n thea.* period play; **~stu·di·en** *pl.* time (and motion) studies; **~ta·fel** *f* chronological table; **~takt** *m teleph.* time unit; **~über,schrei·tung** *f sport*: exceeding the time limit; **~,um·stän·de** *pl.* prevailing circumstances

Zei·tung ['tsaɪtʊŋ] *f* (-; -en) (news)paper; *adm.* gazette; **(die) ~ lesen** read the paper(s); ***in der ~ steht*** the paper says; ***es steht in der ~*** it's in the paper(s); ***ich hab's in der ~ gelesen*** I read it in the papers; ***bei e-r ~ arbeiten*** work for a newspaper; ***e-e Anzeige in die ~ setzen*** place (*or* put) an ad in the papers

'Zei·tungs|abon·ne,ment *n* newspaper subscription; **~an·zei·ge** *f* advertisement, ad, *Brit. a.* advert; **~ar,ti·kel** *m* newspaper article; news story; **~aus·schnitt** *m* newspaper cutting (*or* clipping); **~aus·trä·ger** *m* paper man (*or* boy); newspaper deliverer; **~bei·la·ge** *f* newspaper supplement; **~be·richt** *m* newspaper report; **~en·te** *f* hoax, canard; **~frau** *f* **1.** newspaper lady; **2.** → **~händ·ler** *m* newsagent, *Am.* news dealer; **~in·se,rat** *n* advertisement, ad, *Brit. a.* advert; **~jun·ge** *m* paper boy; **~ki·osk** *m* newspaper kiosk; **~kor·re·spon,dent** *m* newspaper (*or* press) correspondent; **~le·ser** *m* newspaper reader; **~ma,gnat** *m* press baron, newspaper tycoon; **~no,tiz** *f* press item; **~num·mer** *f* copy; ***alte ~*** back number (*or* copy); **~pa,pier** *n* newspaper; newsprint; **~re·dak,teur** *m* newspaper editor; **~stand** *m* newsstand; **~stän·der** *m* magazine rack; **~stil** *m* journalese; **~ver·käu·fer** *m* news vendor; **~ver·le·ger** *m* newspaper publisher; **~we·sen** *n* (-s; *no pl.*) *the* press; **~wis·sen·schaft** *f* journalism

'Zeit|,un·ter·schied *m* time difference; **~ver·geu·dung** *f* waste of time; **~ver·lust** *m* loss of time, delay; ***~e einholen*** make up for lost time, 🚗 *etc.* catch up; **~ver·schie·bung** *f* time shift; ✈ *etc.* time lag; **~ver·schwen·dung** *f* waste of time

'zeit·ver·setzt I. *adj.*: ***~e Übertragung*** recorded broadcast; **II.** *adv.*: ***das Spiel wird ~ übertragen*** the game was recorded earlier (today)

'Zeit·ver·trag *m* fixed-term contract

Zeit·ver·treib ['tsaɪtfɛɐtraɪp] *m* (-[e]s; -e) pastime; ***zum ~*** to pass the time

zeit·wei·lig ['tsaɪtvaɪlɪç] **I.** *adj.* temporary; intermittent; **II.** *adv.* → **'zeit·wei·se** *adv.* occasionally, from time to time, now and then

'Zeit|wert *m* ✝ current value; **~wort** *n* (-[e]s; ¨er) verb; **~zei·chen** *n radio*: time signal; **~zeu·ge** *m* contemporary witness (of events), witness of the times; **~zo·ne** *f* time zone; **~zün·der** *m* time fuse; **~zün·der·bom·be** *f* time bomb

Ze·le·brant [tsele'brant] *m* (-en; -en) celebrant; **ze·le·brie·ren** [tsele'bri:rən] *v/t.* (h) celebrate; F ***et. ~*** make a big affair out of s.th.

Zell|at·mung ['tsɛl-] *f* vesicular breathing; **~bau** *m* (-[e]s; *no pl.*) cell structure; **~bil·dung** *f* cell formation

Zel·le ['tsɛlə] *f* (-; -n) cell (*a. pol.*, ⚖, ⚡); *teleph.* phone box (*Am.* booth)

zel·len·för·mig ['tsɛlənfœrmɪç] *adj* cellular

'Zel·len·ge·nos·se *m* cell mate

Zell|fu·si,on ['tsɛl-] *f* cell fusion; **~ge·we·be** *n* cellular tissue

zel·lig ['tsɛlɪç] *adj.* cellular

Zell|kern ['tsɛl-] *m* cell nucleus; **~mem·,bran** *f* cell membrane

Zel·lo·phan [tsɛlo'fa:n] (*TM*) *n* (-s; *no pl.*) cellophane (*TM*); **~beu·tel** *m* cellophane bag; **~pa,pier** *n* cellophane

Zell·stoff ['tsɛl-] *m* (-[e]s; *no pl.*) **1.** cellulose; pulp; **2.** ⚕ cellulose wadding

Zell|tei·lung ['tsɛl-] *f* cell division, binary fission; **~the·ra,pie** *f* → ***Zellulartherapie***

Zel·lu·lar·the·ra,pie [tsɛlu'la:ɐ-] *f* cell (*or* cellular) therapy

Zel·lu·la·se [tsɛlu'la:zə] *f* (-; -n) cellulase

Zel·lu·li·tis [tsɛlu'li:tɪs] *f* (-; -litiden [tsɛluli'ti:dən]) ⚕ cellulitis

Zel·lu·loid [tsɛlu'lɔʏt] *n* (-[e]s; *no pl.*) celluloid

Zel·lu·lo·se [tsɛlu'lo:zə] *f* (-; *no pl.*) cellulose, wood pulp

Zell|wachs·tum ['tsɛl-] *n* cell growth; **~wand** *f* cell wall; **~wol·le** *f* rayon staple; **~wu·che·rung** *f* cell proliferation

Ze·lot [tse'lo:t] *m* (-en; -en) **1.** *hist.* Zealot; **2.** *fig.* zealot, fanatic; **Ze·lo·tis·mus** [tselo'tɪsmʊs] *m* (-; *no pl.*) zealotry

Zelt [tsɛlt] *n* (-[e]s; -e) tent; marquee; *poet.* canopy; → ***abbrechen*** I, ***aufschlagen*** 7; **~bahn** *f* tent square; tarpaulin; **~bo·den** *m* ground sheet; **~dach** *n* tent roof; △ tetrahedron roof

zel·ten ['tsɛltən] **I.** *v/i.* (h) camp; ***im Garten ~*** camp out in the garden; **II.** ℒ *n* (-s; *no pl.*) camping

'Zelt|la·ger *n* camp; **~mast** *m* tent post; **~pla·ne** *f* tarpaulin; **~platz** *m* campsite, camping site; **~stadt** *f* tent city; **~stan·ge** *f* tent pole

Ze·ment [tse'mɛnt] *m, n* (-[e]s; *no pl.*) cement; **~bo·den** *m* concrete floor

ze·men·tie·ren [tsemɛn'ti:rən] *v/t.* (h) cement (*a. fig.*); ⚙ carburize; *fig.* ✝ solidify

Ze'ment|platz *m tennis*: hard (*or* concrete) court; **~werk** *n* cement factory

Zen [zɛn] *n* (-[s]; *no pl.*) Zen; **~-Bud,dhis·mus** *m* Zen Buddhism

Ze·nit [tse'ni:t] *m* (-[e]s; *no pl.*) zenith; *fig. a.* apex *of one's career etc.*; ***im ~ stehen*** be at (*or* have reached) its (*fig. a.* one's) zenith

zen·sie·ren [tsɛn'zi:rən] *v/t.* (h) censor; *ped.* grade

Zen·sor ['tsɛnso:ɐ] *m* (-s; -en [tsɛn'zo:rən]) censor

Zen·sur [tsɛn'zu:ɐ] *f* (-; -en [tsɛn'zu:rən]) **1.** *no pl.* censorship; ***~ der Presse*** press censorship, censorship of the press; ***der ~ unterliegen*** be subject to censorship; ***die ~ abschaffen*** abolish censorship; ***der ~ zum Opfer fallen*** fall victim to the censors; **2.** *ped.* mark, grade; ***bald gibt es ~en*** (school) reports will be out soon; **~ver·merk** *m* censor's comment

Zen·taur [tsɛn'taʊɐ] *m* (-en; -en [tsɛn'taʊrən]) *myth.* centaur

Zen·ti'li·ter [tsɛnti-] *m, n* centilitre (*Am.* centiliter)

Zen·ti'me·ter [tsɛnti-] *m, n* (-s; -) centimet|re (*Am.* -er); **~maß** *n* tape measure

Zent·ner ['tsɛntnɐ] *m* (-s; -) (metric) hundredweight; **~last** *fig. f* heavy burden; ***e-e ~ fiel mir vom Herzen*** that was a load off my mind

'zent·ner·schwer I. *adj.*: ***~e Säcke*** *etc.* sacks *etc.* weighing a hundredweight and more; F *fig.* ***das ist ja ~!*** F this thing weighs a ton; **II.** *adv.*: *fig.* ***j-m ~ auf der Seele liegen*** weigh heavily on s.o.('s mind)

'zent·ner·wei·se *adv.* by the hundredweight

zen·tral [tsɛn'tra:l] **I.** *adj.* central, *fig. a.* pivotal *problem etc.*; *fig.* ***~er Charakter*** central (*or* main) figure; ***~es Thema*** central (*or* main) issue; **II.** *adv.* centrally; ***~ gelegen*** very central; ***sehr ~ wohnen*** live very central, live right in the cent|re (*Am.* -er) (of town); **~afri,ka·nisch** *adj.* Central African; **~ame·ri,ka·nisch** *adj.* Central American; **~asia·tisch** *adj.* Central Asian

Zen'tral|aus·schuß *m* central committee; **~bank** *f* (-; -en) central bank

Zen·tra·le [tsɛn'tra:lə] *f* (-; -n) a) head office; (*police etc.*) headquarters *pl.*, b) ⚙ control room, c) (telephone) exchange, switchboard

Zen'tral|ein·heit *f computer*: central processing unit, CPU; **~eu·ro,pä·er** *m*, **ℒeu·ro,pä·isch** *adj.* Central European; **~ge·walt** *f* central(ized) power; **~hei·zung** *f* central heating

zen·tra·li·sie·ren [tsɛntrali'zi:rən] *v/t.* (h) centralize; **Zen·tra·li'sie·rung** *f* (-; -en) centralization; **Zen·tra·lis·mus** [tsɛntra'lɪsmʊs] *m pol.* centralism

Zen'tral|ko·mi,tee *n* central committee; **~ner·ven·sy,stem** *n* central nervous system; **~stel·le** *f* → ***Zentrale***; **~ver·band** *m* central association; **~ver·rie·ge·lung** *f mot.* central locking; **~ver·wal·tung** *f* central administration

zen·trie·ren [tsɛn'tri:rən] *v/t.* (h) centre, *Am.* center; **zen·triert** [tsɛn'tri:ɐt] *adj.* centred, *Am.* centered

zen·tri·fu·gal [tsɛntrifu'ga:l] *adj.* centrifugal; **Zen·tri·fu'gal·kraft** *f* centrifugal force; **Zen·tri·fu·ge** [tsɛntri'fu:gə] *f* (-; -n) centrifuge

zen·tri·pe·tal [tsɛntripe'ta:l] *adj.* centripetal

zen·trisch ['tsɛntrɪʃ] *adj.* (con)centric(ally *adv.*)

Zen·trum ['tsɛntrʊm] *n* (-s; Zentren ['tsɛntrən]) centre, *Am.* center; *a.* eye *of a hurricane etc.*; ***das ~*** *Am. a.* downtown; ***im ~ des Interesses stehen*** be the cent|re (*Am.* -er) *or* focus of attention

Zen·tu·rio [tsɛn'tu:rĭo] *m* (-s; -nen [tsɛntu'rĭo:nən]) *hist.* centurion

Zep·pe·lin ['tsɛpəli:n] *m* (-s; -e) zeppelin

Zep·ter ['tsɛptɐ] *n* (-s; -) scept|re (*Am.* -er); *fig.* ***das ~ schwingen*** wield power, F rule the roost

zer'bei·ßen *v/t.* (*irr.*, *no* -ge-, h, → ***bei·ßen***) a) bite to pieces, b) bite through

zer'ber·sten *v/i.* (*irr.*, *no* -ge-, sn, → ***ber·sten***) burst; *glass*: shatter

zer·beult [tsɛɐ'bɔʏlt] *adj.* battered, *a.* dented *metal*

zer·bom·ben [tsɛɐ'bɔmbən] *v/t.* (h) bomb (to pieces); ***zerbombt werden*** be destroyed by bombs, be blitzed

zer·bombt [tsɛɐ'bɔmpt] *adj.* bombed, bomb-shattered

zer'bre·chen *v/t.* (*irr.*, *no* -ge-, h, → ***bre·chen***) *and v/i.* (sn) break; *fig.* (*only v/i.*) *person*: be crushed *or* broken (***an*** *dat.* by); *friendship*: break up; *fig.* ***sich den Kopf ~*** rack one's brains (***über*** *acc.* over)

zer·brech·lich [tsɛɐ'brɛçlɪç] *adj.* **1.** breakable, *a.* fragile *cup etc.*; ***„Vorsicht, ~!"*** fragile, handle with care; **2.** *fig.* a) delicate, fragile *health etc.*, b) delicately built; *a.* dainty *girl etc.*

zer'bröckeln *v/t.* (h) *and v/i.* (sn) crumble (*a. fig.*)

zer'brö·seln *v/t.* (h) *and v/i.* (sn) crumble

zer·dep·pern [tsɛɐ'dɛpɐn] *dial. v/t.* (h) smash

zer'drücken *v/t.* (h) squash, crush; *gastr.* mash; crumple, crease *skirt etc.*

ze·re·bral [tsere'bra:l] *adj.*, **Ze·re'bral...** *in cpds.* cerebral

Ze·re·mo·nie [tseremo'ni:] *f* (-; -n) ceremony; *fig. a.* ritual; **ze·re·mo·ni·ell** [tseremo'niɛl] **I.** *adj.* ceremonial, formal; **II.** ♀ *n* (-s; -e) ceremonial; *fig. a.* ritual

Ze·re·mo·ni·en·mei·ster [tsere'mo:-nĭən-] *m* master of ceremonies

zer'fah·ren *adj.* **1.** rutted *path etc.*; **2.** *fig.* absent-minded, scatterbrained, F scatty

Zer'fall *m* (-[e]s; *no pl.*) **1.** ruin, decay; **2.** *fig.* decline *of a civilization etc.*; *a.* collapse *of an empire etc.*; ***moralischer*** ~ moral decline (*or* decay); **3.** *phys.* disintegration; ⚗ decomposition; **zer'fal·len** (*irr.*, *no* -ge-, sn, → ***fallen***) **I.** *v/i.* **1.** fall apart (*or* to pieces); disintegrate; *building*: collapse, crumble; **2.** *fig. empire etc.*: decline, decay, collapse; **3.** *phys.* disintegrate; ⚗ decompose; **4.** *fig.* ***mit j-m*** ~ fall out with s.o.; **5.** *fig.* ~ ***in*** *acc.* be divided into, fall into; **II.** *adj.* ruined *castle etc.*; tumbledown *building etc.*; ~ ***sein*** *a.* be in ruins, be in a state of decay

Zer'falls|er·schei·nung *f* sign of decay; **~pro͵dukt** *n* decomposition product; *nuclear physics*: daughter product; **~pro͵zeß** *m* process of disintegration (*or* decay) (*a. fig.*); **~stoff** *m* ⚘ by-product, waste product

zer'fet·zen *v/t.* (h) tear in(to) pieces; shred; **zer'fetzt** *adj.* tattered *clothes etc.*; *fig.* mangled *leg etc.*, F torn to shreds

zer'fled·dern I. *v/t.* (h) tatter; **II.** *v/i.* (sn) get tattered; **zer'fled·dert** *adj.* tattered

zer·flei·schen [tsɛɐ'flaɪʃən] (h) **I.** *v/t.* tear to pieces; **II.** *v/refl.*: ***sich*** ~ torment o.s.; tear each other apart

zer'flie·ßen *v/i.* (*irr.*, *no* -ge-, sn, → ***fließen***) melt, dissolve; *paint, ink*: run; *fig. money*: melt in one's hand; *dream*: come to nothing; **~*de Konturen*** blurred contours; *fig.* ***in Tränen*** ~ dissolve into tears; ***vor Mitleid*** *etc.* ~ melt with pity *etc.*

zer'fres·sen I. *v/t.* (*irr.*, *no* -ge-, h, → ***fressen***) eat away (at); ⚗ corrode; **II.** *adj.* moth-eaten; worm-eaten; ⚗ corroded

zer·furcht [tsɛɐ'fʊrçt] *adj.* furrowed; *fig.* **~*e Stirn*** furrowed brow

zer'ge·hen *v/i.* (*irr.*, *no* -ge-, sn, → ***gehen***) dissolve, *a. fig.* melt; *fig.* ***auf der Zunge*** ~ melt in one's mouth

zer'glie·dern *v/t.* (h) **1.** *a. ling.* analy|se (*Am.* -ze); **2.** dissect; **3.** dismember

zer'hacken *v/t.* (h) chop (up *a.* ⚡); *gastr.* mince

zer'hau·en *v/t.* (*irr.*, *no* -ge-, h, → ***hauen***) **1.** chop to pieces; **2.** F break, F smash

zer'kau·en *v/t.* (h) chew (well)

zer·klei·nern [tsɛɐ'klaɪnɐn] *v/t.* (h) chop (up); crush; grind

zer·klüf·tet [tsɛɐ'klʏftət] *adj.* cleft; rugged *mountains, terrain etc.*

zer'knal·len I. *v/i.* (sn) burst; explode; **II.** *v/t.* (h) burst

zer'knaut·schen F *v/t.* (h) crumple, squash (up)

zer'knicken *v/i.* (sn) get bent; snap; **zer'knickt** *adj.* broken; snapped *twig etc.*

zer·knirscht [tsɛɐ'knɪrʃt] *adj.* smitten with remorse; **~*es Gesicht*** hangdog look; **Zer·knir·schung** [tsɛɐ'knɪrʃʊŋ] *f* (-; *no pl.*) remorse(fulness); contrition

zer'knit·tern *v/t.* (h) *and v/i.* (sn) crumple, crease; **zer'knit·tert** *fig. adj.* crushed, crestfallen

zer'knül·len *v/t.* (h) crumple up, screw up, F scrunch up

zer'ko·chen *v/t.* (h) overcook, F cook to pieces

zer'krat·zen I. *v/t.* (h) scratch (to pieces); **II.** *v/i.* (sn) scratch; ***leicht*** ~ scratch (very) easily, be scratch-prone

zer'krü·meln *v/t.* (h) *and v/i.* (sn) crumble

zer'las·sen I. *v/t.* (*irr.*, *no* -ge-, h, → ***lassen***) *gastr.* melt (in the pan); **II.** *adj.* melted *butter etc.*

zer·leg·bar [tsɛɐ'le:kba:ɐ] *adj.* ⚙ easily dismantled; *a.* knock-down *table etc.*; ⚘ divisible; ⚗ decomposable; **zer'le·gen** *v/t.* (h) a) take apart (*or* to pieces); ⚙ *a.* dismantle, disassemble, b) cut up; carve *roast*; *anat.* dissect, c) ⚗ decompose, d) *fig.* analy|se (*Am.* -ze) (*a. ling.*), dissect, *a.* break down *theory etc.*

zer'le·sen *adj.* well-thumbed; dog-eared

zer·lö·chert [tsɛɐ'lœçɐt] *adj.* full of holes, riddled with holes

zer·lumpt [tsɛɐ'lʊmpt] **I.** *adj.* ragged; *a.* tattered *clothes*; **~*es Kind*** ragamuffin; **II.** *adv.*: ~ ***herumlaufen*** go around in rags (and tatters)

zer'mah·len *v/t.* (h) grind

zer·mal·men [tsɛɐ'malmən] *v/t.* (h) crush (*a. fig.*)

zer'man·schen F *v/t.* (h) mash up; **zer'manscht** F *contp. adj.* squashed, mashed up

zer'mar·tern *v/t.* (h): ***sich den Kopf*** ~ rack one's brains

zer·mür·ben [tsɛɐ'mʏrbən] *v/t.* (h) wear down; **zer'mür·bend** *adj.* wearing, nerve-racking; **Zer'mür·bung** *f* (-; *no pl.*) ⚔ attrition; **Zer'mür·bungs·krieg** *m* war of attrition

zer'na·gen *v/t.* (h) gnaw to pieces; *a.* gnaw away at

zer·narbt [tsɛɐ'narpt] *adj.* scarred, covered in scars; *face*: *a.* pitted with scars, *a.* pockmarked

zer'pflücken *v/t.* (h) **1.** pull the petals off *a flower*; pull to pieces; *gastr.* take apart *lettuce etc.*; **2.** *fig.* pull to pieces, F tear to pieces (*or* shreds)

zer'plat·zen *v/i.* (sn) burst; explode; *fig.* ***vor Wut*** *etc.* ~ burst (*or* explode) with anger *etc.*; ***ich bin bald zerplatzt*** I nearly exploded (F hit the roof)

zer'quet·schen *v/t.* (h) crush (*a.* ⚙); squash; *gastr.* mash; **zer'quetscht** *adj.* squashed (up); F *fig.* ***50 Mark und ein paar Zerquetschte*** 50 marks and a bit, just over 50 marks

zer'rau·fen *v/t.* (h) ruffle, tousle *hair*

Zerr·bild ['tsɛɐ-] *n* **1.** distorted image; **2.** *fig.* distortion, distorted view (*or* picture); caricature; travesty

zer'rei·ben (*irr.*, *no* -ge-, h, → ***reiben***) **I.** *v/t.* **1.** grind; ***mit den Fingern*** ~ crush with one's fingers; **2.** *fig.* wipe out; **II.** *fig. v/refl.*: ***sich*** ~ wear o.s. down, F wear o.s. to a frazzle (***vor*** *dat.* with *grief etc.*)

zer'rei·ßen (*irr.*, *no* -ge-, → ***reißen***) **I.** *v/t.* (h) tear up; tear to pieces; *bomb*: blow *s.o.* to pieces; F *fig.* ***et.*** ~ F tear s.th. to pieces (*or* shreds), trash s.th.; F ***j-n*** (***in der Luft***) ~ tear s.o. to shreds; F ***da hätt's mich fast zerrissen*** F I nearly ruptured myself; → ***Maul***; **II.** *v/i.* (sn) tear; *thread, fog, clouds*: break; **III.** *v/refl.*: ***sich*** ~ (h) F nearly kill o.s.; ***sich für et.*** ~ put everything one has (got) into s.th.; ***ich kann mich doch nicht*** ~***!*** I can't be in two places at once

Zer·reiß·pro·be [tsɛɐ'raɪs-] *f* **1.** ⚙ tensile test; **2.** *fig.* test of endurance, ordeal, real test

zer·ren ['tsɛrən] (h) **I.** *v/t.* pull (*a. muscle etc.*); drag; ***sich e-n Muskel*** *etc.* ~ pull a muscle *etc.*; *fig.* ***vor Gericht*** ~ haul before a court; ***et. an die Öffentlichkeit*** ~ bring s.th. to the public's attention, put the public spotlight on s.th.; **II.** *v/i.*: ~ ***an*** *dat.* tug (*or* pull) at; ***an der Leine*** ~ strain at the leash, pull at the lead (*or* leash)

zer'rin·nen *v/i.* (*irr.*, *no* -ge-, sn, → ***rinnen***) melt away; *fig.* vanish, fade; *money*: disappear; *plans*: come to nothing, F go up in smoke; *days, years etc.*: slip away (*or* by)

zer·ris·sen [tsɛɐ'rɪsən] **I.** *p.p. of* ***zerreißen***; **II.** *adj.* torn (*a. fig.*); **Zer'ris·sen·heit** *f* (-; *no pl.*) inner conflict

Zerr·spie·gel ['tsɛɐ-] *m* distorting mirror

Zer·rung ['tsɛrʊŋ] *f* (-; -en) ⚕ pulled muscle (*or* tendon *etc.*)

zer'rup·fen *v/t.* (h) → ***zerpflücken***; **zer'rupft** *adj.*: ***du siehst ja wie ein*** **~*es Huhn aus*** you look as if you've been dragged through a hedge backwards

zer·rüt·ten [tsɛɐ'rʏtən] *v/t.* (h) disrupt *order etc.*; *a.* wreck *a marriage*; ruin, wreck *one's nerves, health etc.*; ***j-n körperlich*** (***seelisch***) ~ make s.o. a physical (nervous) wreck; **zer'rüt·tet** *adj.*: **~*e Ehe*** broken marriage; **~*es Zuhause*** broken home; **~*e Nerven*** shattered nerves; **Zer'rüt·tungs·prin͵zip** *n* ⚖ *principle of (irretrievable) matrimonial breakdown*

zer'sä·gen *v/t.* (h) saw up (into pieces)

zer'schel·len *v/i.* (sn) be smashed (to pieces); ✈ crash; ⚓ be wrecked; ***am Boden*** ~ crash to the floor, smash to pieces on the floor; ***an e-m Berg*** ~ ✈ crash into a mountainside; ***an den Klippen*** ~ ⚓ be smashed (to pieces) against the rocks

zer'schla·gen (*irr.*, *no* -ge-, → ***schlagen***) **I.** *v/t.* (h) smash (to pieces); *fig.* smash; **II.** *v/refl.*: ***sich*** ~ come to nothing, F go up in smoke; *hopes*: *a.* be shattered; **III.** *fig. adj.* shattered

zer·schlis·sen [tsɛɐ'ʃlɪsən] *adj.* **1.** worn--out ..., *pred.* worn out; threadbare; **2.** *fig.* shattered, frayed, F shot

zer'schmel·zen *v/i.* (*irr.*, *no* -ge-, sn, → ***schmelzen***) melt away; *butter*: melt; *fig.* ***vor Mitleid*** *etc.* ~ melt with pity *etc.*

zer'schmet·tern *v/t.* (h) smash (to pieces), shatter; crush, flatten; F *fig.* ***am Boden zerschmettert*** absolutely crushed

zer'schnei·den *v/t.* (*irr.*, *no* -ge-, h, → ***schneiden***) cut up; slice; shred; carve *roast*

zer'schnip·peln F *v/t.* (h) cut up into little pieces

zer'schram·men *v/t.* (h) scrape *one's knees etc.*; scratch *tabletop etc.*; **zer'schrammt** *adj. knees etc.*: covered in cuts and scrapes; scratched *tabletop etc.*, *desktop etc.* full of scratches

zer'set·zen *v/t.* (h) decompose, disintegrate (*both a.* ***sich*** ~); *fig.* corrupt, undermine; **Zer'set·zung** *f* (-; *no pl.*) de-

composition, disintegration; *fig.* corruption; *pol.* subversion
Zer'sied·lung *f* (-; -en) urban sprawl
zer'spal·ten *v/t.* (h) cleave, split
zer'spa·nen *v/t.* (h) cut; **~de Bearbeitung** metal cutting
zer'split·tern *v/t.* (h) *and v/i.* (sn) split; splinter (*bone etc., a. fig. group etc.*); shatter *glass*; *fig.* **s-e Kräfte ~** fritter away one's energies; **zer'split·tert** *adj.* splintered *bone, wood etc.*; shattered *glass*; *fig.* fragmented *group etc.*
zer'spren·gen *v/t.* (h) **1.** blow up; **2.** ⚔ rout
zer'sprin·gen *v/i.* (*irr., no* -ge-, sn, → **springen**) **1.** crack; shatter; *string*: break; **2.** *fig.* **mir zerspringt der Kopf** (**vor Schmerzen**) I've got a splitting headache; **ihr zersprang fast das Herz vor Freude** her heart was bursting with joy
zer'stamp·fen *v/t.* (h) a) trample on; crush, b) pound, c) *gastr.* mash
zer'stäu·ben *v/t.* (h) spray
Zer·stäu·ber [tsɛɐ'ʃtɔʏbɐ] *m* (-s; -) spray, atomizer
zer'ste·chen *v/t.* (*irr., no* -ge-, h, → **stechen**) sting *or* bite *or* prick (all over); pierce
zer'stie·ben *v/i.* (*irr., no* -ge-, sn, → **stieben**) **1.** *water etc.*: spray (in all directions); **2.** *fig.* disperse, scatter
zer·sto·chen [tsɛɐ'ʃtɔxən] **I.** *p.p. of* **zerstechen; II.** *adj.* covered in (mosquito) bites (*or* wasp stings *etc.*), F bitten (*or* stung) to pieces
zer·stör·bar [tsɛɐ'ʃtøːɐbaːɐ] *adj.* destructible; **zer'stö·ren** *v/t.* (h) **1.** destroy; *a.* demolish *building*; **durch Feuer** *etc.* **zerstört werden** be destroyed by fire *etc.*; → **Boden** 1; **2.** spoil, ruin; destroy; **die Natur ~** spoil (*or* destroy) the (*or* one's) natural environment; **3.** destroy *s.o.'s existence, hopes etc.*; ruin, wreck *one's health etc.*; **Zer'stö·rer** *m* (-s; -) ⚓ destroyer; **zer·stö·re·risch** [tsɛɐ'ʃtøːrərɪʃ] *adj.* destructive; **~ wirken** have a destructive effect; **Zer'stö·rung** *f* (-; -en) destruction; ruin; devastation, ravages *pl. of war etc.*
Zer'stö·rungs|trieb *m* (-[e]s; *no pl.*) destructive urge, destructiveness; **~werk** *n* work of destruction; **~wut** *f* vandalism
zer'sto·ßen *v/t.* (*irr., no* -ge-, h, → **stoßen**) crush; pound
Zer'strah·lung *f nuclear physics*: annihilation (of matter)
zer'strei·ten *v/refl.*: **sich ~** (*irr., no* -ge-, h, → **streiten**) fall out (with each other); **sich mit j-m ~** fall out with s.o.
zer'streu·en (h) **I.** *v/t.* **1.** scatter; disperse; *opt. a.* diffuse; **2.** *fig.* dispel, dissipate *suspicions etc.*; **3.** *fig.* divert, amuse; **j-n ~** *a.* take s.o.'s mind off things; **II.** *v/refl.*: **sich ~ 4.** *crowd*: disperse, scatter, break up; **5.** take one's mind off things, **sich mit et. ~** *a.* occupy o.s. with s.th.; **zer'streut** *fig. adj.* distracted; absent-minded, scatterbrained, F scatty; **Zer'streut·heit** *f* (-; *no pl.*) absent-mindedness; **Zer'streu·ung** *f* (-; -en) **1.** *no pl.* dispersion, scattering; *opt. a.* diffusion; dissipation; **2.** diversion; **Zer'streu·ungs·lin·se** *f opt.* diverging lens
zer'stückeln *v/t.* (h) **1.** cut up, cut into pieces; dismember, chop up; **2.** parcel out *land*; **Zer'stücke·lung** *f* (-; *no pl.*) **1.** cutting up; dismemberment; **2.** parcel(l)ing out
zer'tei·len (h) **I.** *v/t.* divide, split (up) (*both* **in** *acc.* into); separate (into); **II.** *v/refl.*: **sich ~** divide up, split up (*both* **in** *acc.* into); *clouds, fog etc.*: disperse; **Zer'tei·lung** *f* (-; -en) division (**in** *acc.* into); separation; dispersal
Zer·ti·fi·kat [tsɛɐtifi'kaːt] *n* (-[e]s; -e) **1.** certificate, diploma; **2.** ✝ certificate
zer'tram·peln *v/t.* (h) trample all over; crush (underfoot), trample underfoot; ruin *the lawn*
zer'tren·nen *v/t.* (h) open the seams of
zer'tre·ten *v/t.* (*irr., no* -ge-, h, → **treten**) crush (underfoot), tread on; ruin *the lawn*
zer·trüm·mern [tsɛɐ'trʏmɐn] *v/t.* (h) **1.** smash (up); smash *window etc.*; wreck, smash up *furniture etc.*; demolish *building*; **j-m den Schädel ~** smash s.o.'s skull (in F); **2.** *phys.* split; **3.** ⚕ break up *kidney stones*
Zer·ve·lat·wurst [tsɛrvə'laːt-] *f* saveloy, cervelat
zer'wüh·len *v/t.* (h) a) churn up *the ground*, b) dishevel *hair*, c) rumple *one's bed*; **zer'wühlt** *adj.* a) churned up, b) dishevel(l)ed; **~es Bett** rumpled bedclothes; **dein Haar ist ganz ~** *a.* F your hair's a mess (*or* all over the place)
Zer·würf·nis [tsɛɐ'vʏrfnɪs] *n* (-ses; -se) quarrel, argument; discord; rift; **eheliche ~se** marital strife
zer'zau·sen *v/t.* (h) ruffle; **zer'zaust** *adj.* tousled, dishevel(l)ed *hair*
Ze·ter ['tseːtɐ]: **~ und Mordio schreien** F scream blue murder; *fig.* raise a (big) hue and cry; **'ze·tern** *v/i.* (h) **1.** nag, rant and rave; **2.** wail
Zet·tel ['tsɛtəl] *m* (-s; -) slip of paper; note; leaflet; **„~ ankleben verboten"** stick no bills; **ein ~, auf dem stand ...** a note saying ...; **~kar'tei** *f* card index; **~kasten** *m* card index (box); **~wirt·schaft** F *f*: **e-e ~ haben** have everything on scraps of paper, have notes jotted down all over the place
Zeug [tsɔʏk] *n* (-[e]s; *no pl.*) stuff; things *pl.*; **dummes ~** nonsense, F rubbish, F garbage; *fig.* **das ~ haben zu** *dat.* have the makings of *a doctor etc.*, be cut out to be *a teacher etc.*; **er hat das ~ dazu** F he's got what it takes; F **was das ~ hält** F like mad; **sich ins ~ legen** put one's back into it; **sich für j-n ins ~ legen** back s.o. up to the hilt; **sich für et. ins ~ legen** go all out for s.th., give s.th. one's all-out support
Zeu·ge ['tsɔʏgə] *m* (-n; -n) witness (*a. fig.*); **~ der Anklage** witness for the prosecution; **vor ~n** in the presence of witnesses; **~ e-s Unfalls sein** witness (*or* be witness to) an accident
zeu·gen¹ ['tsɔʏgən] *v/i.* (h) ⚖ give evidence; **~ für** (**gegen**) *acc.* testify for (against) *s.o. or s.th.*; *fig.* **~ von** *dat.* testify to; **das zeugt nicht gerade von Takt** that isn't exactly a sign of (great) tact
'zeu·gen² *v/t.* (h) **1.** father; F *hum.* sire; *obs., bibl.* beget; **2.** *fig.* generate, create, engender
'Zeu·gen|aus·sa·ge *f* testimony, evidence; **~bank** *f* (-; ⸚e) witness box (*Am.* stand); **~be·ein·flus·sung** *f* interference (*or* tampering) with witnesses; **~be·weis** *m* evidence (of a witness); **~stand** *m* witness box (*Am.* stand); **in den ~ treten** go into the witness box, take the (witness) stand; **~ver·hör** *n*, **~ver·neh·mung** *f* examination of a witness (*or* of witnesses)
'Zeug·haus *hist. n* ⚔ arsenal
Zeu·gin ['tsɔʏgɪn] *f* (-; -nen) witness
Zeug·nis ['tsɔʏknɪs] *n* (-ses; -se) **1.** a) *ped.* report, *Am.* report card, b) reference, c) certificate, diploma; **2.** ⚖ evidence; *fig. a.* testimony (*gen.* to); *esp. fig.* **~ ablegen** bear witness (**für** *acc.* to), **für** *acc.* testify to *s.th.*; *fig.* **ein ~ der Vergangenheit** a record of the past; **~ver·wei·ge·rung** *f* refusal to give evidence
Zeu·gung ['tsɔʏgʊŋ] *f* (-; -en) **1.** fathering; **2.** *biol.* procreation
'Zeu·gungs·akt *m* procreative act
'zeu·gungs·fä·hig *adj.* fertile, able to reproduce; **'Zeu·gungs·fä·hig·keit** *f* (-; *no pl.*) fertility, reproductive capacity
'zeu·gungs·un·fä·hig *adj.* impotent, sterile; **'Zeu·gungs·un·fä·hig·keit** *f* (-; *no pl.*) impotence, sterility
Zi·cho·rie [tsɪ'çoːrĭə] *f* (-; -n) chicory
Zicke ['tsɪkə] (*sep.* -k·k-) F *f* (-; -n) **1.** → **Ziege; 2.** *contp.* F cow; **3.** *pl.* nonsense; **mach keine ~n!** a) don't do anything stupid, b) don't make such a fuss
zickig ['tsɪkɪç] (*sep.* -k·k-) F *adj.* **1.** silly; **2.** prudish, F uptight
Zick·lein ['tsɪklaɪn] *n* (-s; -) kid
Zick·zack ['tsɪktsak] **I.** *m* (-[e]s; -e) zigzag; **im ~ fahren** *etc.* weave, zigzag across the road, veer all over the road; **II.** *adv.*: **2 übers Feld laufen** *etc.* zigzag (*or* weave) across the field; **~kurs** *m* **1.** zigzag path; **im ~ fahren** weave, zigzag; **2.** *fig. pol.* tacking; **~li·nie** *f* zigzag (line)
Zie·ge ['tsiːgə] *f* (-; -n) **1.** (nanny) goat; **2.** F *contp.* F cow; **blöde ~** silly old cow
Zie·gel ['tsiːgəl] *m* (-s; -) a) brick, b) tile; **~bau** *m* (-[e]s; -ten) brick building; **~dach** *n* tiled roof
Zie·ge·lei [tsiːgə'laɪ] *f* (-; -en) brickyard
'Zie·gel|ofen *m* brick kiln; **2rot** *adj.* brick-red; **~stein** *m* brick
'Zie·gen|bart *m* **1.** *zo.* goat's beard; **2.** goatee (beard); **~bock** *m* billy goat; **~fell** *n* goatskin; **~hirt** *m* goatherd; **~kä·se** *m* goat's cheese; **~le·der** *n* kid (leather); **~milch** *f* goat's milk
Zie·gen·pe·ter ['tsiːgənpeːtɐ] F *m* (-s; *no pl.*) ⚕ mumps (*sg.*)
Zieh|brücke ['tsiː-] *f* drawbridge; **~brunnen** *m* draw well
zie·hen ['tsiːən] (zog, gezogen, h) **I.** *v/t.* **1.** a) pull; drag; tug, b) pull out, extract *tooth*, pull up *carrots*, c) take off *one's hat*, d) stretch (*a.* **sich ~ lassen**), e) take *a card*, f) draw, pull out *knife, gun etc.*, g) put up *clothesline*; put *the wiring* in, build, erect *wall etc.*, dig *trench etc.*, h) draw *candles*, i) *sport*: pace *runner*, j) draw *lots etc.*, k) ⩓ draw *a line*, *a.* describe *a circle*, work out *roots*; **ein Boot ans Ufer ~** pull a boat ashore; **j-n am Ärmel ~** tug at s.o.'s sleeve; **j-n an den Haaren** (**Ohren**) **~** pull s.o.'s hair (ears); **Perlen auf e-e Schnur ~** thread beads; **Saiten auf e-e Geige** *etc.* **~** string a violin *etc.*; **Wein auf Flaschen ~** bottle wine; **Aufmerksamkeit** *etc.* **auf sich ~** attract attention *etc.*; **j-s Haß auf sich ~** incur s.o.'s hatred; **j-n auf die Seite ~** take s.o. aside; **j-n auf s-e Seite ~** win s.o. over to one's side; **Zigaretten** (**aus dem Automaten**) **~** get some cigarettes out of the machine; **et. kurz durchs**

Wasser ~ give s.th. a quick rinse; ***j-n ins Gespräch*** ~ draw s.o. into (*or* include s.o. in) the conversation; ***j-n mit sich*** ~ pull s.o. along (with one); ***nach sich*** ~ *fig.* have as a consequence, bring about, cause, result in, involve; ***den Wagen nach links*** ~ pull out to the left; ***die Gardinen vors Fenster*** ~ draw the curtains (across the window); ***e-n Pullover über die Bluse*** ~ put a jumper on over the blouse; ***e-n Ring vom Finger*** ~ take a ring off, slip a ring from one's finger; ***es zieht mich dorthin (zu ihr)*** I feel drawn there (to her); ***es zieht mich nichts in diese Gesellschaft*** I don't feel drawn to these people in any way; → ***Bilanz, Faden, Ferne, Länge, Rat*** 1, ***Schluß*** 2; **2.** ♣ grow; *zo.* breed, rear; **II.** *v/i.* **3.** pull (***an*** *dat.* at); ***der Wagen zieht schlecht*** the car's not pulling properly; ***er zieht schnell*** he's quick on the draw; ***an der Glocke*** ~ pull (*or* ring) the bell; ***an der Leine*** ~ *dog*: pull at the lead (*or* leash), strain at the leash; **4.** (sn) a) wander, rove; *zo.* migrate, b) go (away), leave; ~ ***nach*** *dat.* (***in*** *acc.*) move to (into); ***zu j-m*** ~ go to live with s.o., move in with s.o.; ***die Wolken*** ~ the clouds are moving; ***durch die Welt*** ~ see (*lit.* roam) the world; ***in den Krieg*** ~ go to war; ***nach Süden*** ~ *zo.* move (*or* migrate) south; **5.** *chess*: (make a) move; ***mit dem König*** ~ move the (*or* one's) king; ***wer zieht?*** whose move is it?; **6.** *oven, pipe etc.*: draw (*a. tea, coffee*); ***der Ofen zieht nicht*** the stove isn't drawing; ***den Tee*** *etc.* ~ ***lassen*** let the tea *etc.* stand; ~ ***an*** *dat.* (take a) puff at *one's pipe etc.*; **7.** F ***e-n*** ~ ***lassen*** F let (one) off; **8.** twinge, ache; **9.** go down (well); ***dieses Stück zieht nicht*** the play isn't going down very well; ***diese Ausrede zieht bei mir nicht*** that excuse won't wash with me, F try another one; ***Schmeichelei zieht bei mir nicht*** flattery will get you nowhere, flattery doesn't work with me; **III.** *v/refl.*: ***sich*** ~ **10.** *a.* ***sich*** ~ ***lassen*** stretch, give; **11.** *wood*: warp; *metal*: buckle; **12.** ***sich*** ~ ***durch*** (***über***) *acc.* stretch through (over, across); ***sich*** ~ ***über*** *acc. scar*: go right across; ***sich*** ~ ***um*** *acc. wall etc.*: go right (a)round, enclose; *fig.* ***sich*** ~ ***durch*** *acc. motif, theme etc.*: run through; → ***Affäre, Länge;*** **IV.** *v/impers.* ***hier zieht's*** there's a draught (*Am.* draft); ***es zieht mir im Rücken*** a) I can feel a twinge in my back, b) I can feel a draught (*Am.* draft) on my back

Zieh·harˌmo·ni·ka ['tsiː-] *f* concertina; accordion

Zie·hung ['tsiːʊŋ] *f* (-; -en) drawing (*a.* ✝); *lotto*: draw; *statistics*: sampling

'Zie·hungs·li·ste *f* drawing list

Ziel [tsiːl] *n* (-[e]s; -e) a) destination, b) *sport*: finish(ing line), c) target (*a.* ✝), ⚔ objective; mark, d) *fig.* goal, objective, aim; *sport*: ***durchs*** ~ ***gehen*** cross the finishing line; ***als Sieger (Zweiter) durchs*** ~ ***gehen*** finish first (second); *fig.* ***sein*** ~ ***erreichen, zum*** ~ ***gelangen*** reach one's goal (*or* objective), F get there; ***unser*** ~ ***ist es zu*** *inf.* our goal (*or* aim, objective) is to *inf.*; ***sich ein*** ~ ***setzen*** (*or* ***stecken***) set o.s. a goal *or* target; ***sich das*** ~ ***setzen zu*** *inf.* aim at *ger.*, aim to *inf.*; ***sich ein hohes*** ~ ***setzen*** aim high; ***mit dem*** ~ ***zu*** *inf.* with the aim (*or* objective) of *ger.*; ***über das*** ~ ***hinausschießen*** overshoot the mark, go over the top; ***zum*** ~***e führen*** succeed, be successful; ***nicht zum*** ~***e führen*** fail; ***so wirst du nie zum*** ~ ***kommen*** it'll never work out that way; ***sie läßt sich von ihrem*** ~ ***nicht abbringen*** she won't be deterred; ***er ist weit vom*** ~ he has a long way to go yet; **~an·flug** *m* ✈ approach run (*or* flight); **~bahn·hof** *m* destination; ***was ist Ihr*** ~***?*** which station are you going to?; **~band** *n* (-[e]s; ‥er) *sport*: tape; ***das*** ~ ***durchreißen*** break the tape

'ziel·be·wußt *adj.* purposeful, single-minded; ***er ist sehr*** ~ he knows what he wants (*or* what he's aiming for)

'Ziel·ein·lauf *m sport*: finish; finishing order

zie·len ['tsiːlən] *v/i.* (h) (take) aim (***auf*** *acc.* at); *fig.* ~ ***auf*** *acc.* aim at, have set one's sights on; *remark etc.*: be aimed at; ***darauf*** ~ ***zu*** *inf.* be aimed at *ger.*; → ***gezielt***

'Ziel|fern·rohr *n* telescopic sight; **~flag·ge** *f motor sport*: chequered (*Am.* checkered) flag; **~flug** *m* ✈ homing; **~flug·ha·fen** *m* destination airport; **~ge·ra·de** *f sport*: home stretch (*or* straight); **~grup·pe** *f* target group; *TV etc.* target audience; **~ka·me·ra** *f sport*: photo-finish camera; **~kur·ve** *f sport*: home bend; **~lan·dung** *f* ✈ precision (*or* spot) landing; **~li·nie** *f sport*: finishing line

'ziel·los *adj.* (*and adv.*) aimless(ly)

'Ziel|ort *m* (place of) destination; **~proˌgramm** *n computer*: object (*or* target) program(me); **~punkt** *m* bull's eye; *sport and fig.* goal; **~rich·ter** *m sport*: judge (at the finish); **~schei·be** *f* target; *fig. a.* butt; ***zur*** ~ ***des Spotts werden*** become the target (*or* an object) of ridicule, become a laughing stock

'Ziel·set·zung *f* (-; -en) objective, target; ***man muß e-e klare*** ~ ***haben*** you've got to know what you're aiming for (*or* what you want)

'ziel·si·cher *adj.* accurate, unerring; *fig.* → ***zielstrebig***

'Ziel·spra·che *f* target language

ziel·stre·big ['tsiːlʃtreːbɪç] **I.** *adj.* single-minded, purposeful, determined; **II.** *adv.* single-mindedly *etc.*; with single-mindedness (*or* determination); **'Ziel·stre·big·keit** *f* (-; *no pl.*) single-mindedness, determination

'Ziel|su·cher *m* (-s; -) homing device; **~vor·stel·lung** *fig. f* objective

zie·men ['tsiːmən] *v/i. and v/refl.* (h) → ***geziemen***

ziem·lich ['tsiːmlɪç] **I.** *adj.* considerable; quite a ...; ***ein*** ~***es Durcheinander*** quite a mess; ***es war ein*** ~***er Aufwand*** it was quite an effort, it took a fair bit of effort; ***ich weiß es mit*** ~***er Sicherheit*** I'm fairly (F pretty) sure about it; **II.** *adv.* quite, F pretty; ~ ***gut*** F pretty good; ***et.*** ~ ***ausführlich beschreiben*** depict s.th. in some detail (*or* at some length); ~ ***viel*** quite a lot (of); ~ ***viele*** *a.* quite a few; ***so*** ~ more or less, just about, F pretty much; ***so*** ~ ***dasselbe*** more or less (F pretty much) the same thing; ***er ist so*** ~ ***in m-m Alter*** he's round about my age; ***ich bin so*** ~ ***kaputt*** *a.* F I'm what you might call shattered

zie·pen ['tsiːpən] (h) **I.** *v/i.* **1.** *chick*: cheep; **2.** ***es ziept*** it's pulling; **II.** *v/t.*: ***j-n an den Haaren*** ~ pull (*or* tug at) s.o.'s hair

Zie·rat ['tsiːraːt] *m* (-[e]s; -e) decoration, embellishment

Zier|baum ['tsiːɐ-] *m* ornamental tree; **~buch·sta·be** *m* ornamental letter

Zier·de ['tsiːɐdə] *f* (-; -n) **1.** ornament, decoration; ***nur zur*** ~ just for decoration; **2.** *fig.* showpiece; pride and joy; ***er ist e-e*** ~ ***des Orchesters*** he does the orchestra credit

zie·ren ['tsiːrən] (h) **I.** *v/t.* adorn (*a. fig.*); decorate; *fig.* grace; **II.** *v/refl.*: ***sich*** ~ a) be coy, act coy, b) fuss; ~ ***Sie sich nicht!*** no need to be shy (*or* polite); ***er zierte sich nicht lange*** he didn't need much persuading; ***sie ziert sich nicht*** she doesn't beat about (*or* around) the bush; ***zier dich nicht!*** get to the point; come on, out with it

Zier|fisch ['tsiːɐ-] *m* ornamental fish; **~gar·ten** *m* ornamental garden; **~grä·ser** *pl.* ornamental grasses; **~lei·ste** *f* a) ornamental mo(u)lding (*or* border), b) *mot.* trim, c) vignette

zier·lich ['tsiːɐlɪç] *adj.* delicate; dainty, petite *girl*; *a.* graceful; **'Zier·lich·keit** *f* (-; *no pl.*) delicateness; daintiness; gracefulness

Zier|pflan·ze ['tsiːɐ-] *f* ornamental plant; **~schrift** *f* ornate lettering; **~strauch** *m* ornamental shrub

Zif·fer ['tsɪfɐ] *f* (-; -n) **1.** figure, number; digit; cipher; ***arabische*** (***römische***) ~***n*** Arabic (Roman) numerals; **2.** ⚖ *etc.* clause; item; **~blatt** *n* dial; (clock)face; (watch)face

zig [tsɪç] F *adj.* dozens of, hundreds of, F umpteen

Zi·ga·ret·te [tsigaˈrɛtə] *f* (-; -n) cigarette

Zi·ga'ret·ten|an·zün·der *m* cigarette lighter; **~au·toˌmat** *m* cigarette machine; **~etui** *n* cigarette case; **~faˌbrik** *f* cigarette factory; **~mar·ke** *f* brand of cigarettes; **~pau·se** *f* (break for a) smoke; **~qualm** *m*, **~rauch** *m* cigarette smoke; **~rau·cher** *m* cigarette smoker; **~schach·tel** *f* cigarette packet (*Am.* pack); **~sor·te** *f* brand of cigarettes; **~spit·ze** *f* cigarette holder; **~stum·mel** *m* cigarette end, stub

Zi·ga·ril·lo [tsigaˈrɪlo] *m* (-s; -s) cigarillo

Zi·gar·re [tsiˈgarə] *f* (-; -n) cigar; F *fig.* ***j-m e-e*** ~ ***verpassen*** F give s.o. a rocket

Zi'gar·ren|ab·schnei·der *m* cigar cutter; **~ki·ste** *f* cigar box; **~rauch** *m* cigar smoke; **~rau·cher** *m* cigar smoker; **~sor·te** *f* brand of cigar; **~spit·ze** *f* **1.** cigar holder; **2.** cigar tip; **~stum·mel** *m* cigar end, stub

Zi·geu·ner [tsiˈgɔʏnɐ] *m* (-s; -) gypsy; *fig.* vagabond; **Zi·geu·ne·rin** [tsiˈgɔʏnərɪn] *f* (-; -nen) gypsy (girl *or* woman)

Zi'geu·ner|kaˌpel·le *f* gypsy band; **~la·ger** *n* gypsy camp; **~le·ben** *n* gypsy life; *fig. a. the* life of a vagabond; *fig.* ***ein*** ~ ***führen*** *a.* lead a gypsy life, roam around like a gypsy (*or* gypsies); **~muˌsik** *f* gypsy music

zi·geu·nern [tsiˈgɔʏnɐn] *v/i.* (sn): ***durch die Welt*** ~ roam the world

Zi'geu·ner|schnit·zel *n cutlet in spicy red and green pepper sauce*; **~spra·che** *f*: ***die*** ~ Romany; **~wa·gen** *m* gypsy caravan

zig·fach ['tsɪçfax] F *adj.*: ***die*** ~***e Menge*** F umpteen times the amount; **'Zig·fa·che** F *n* (-n; *no pl.*): ***das*** ~ F umpteen times the amount

zig·mal ['tsɪçmaːl] F *adv.* F umpteen (*or* dozens of) times; a hundred times

'zig·mil|lio·nen F **I.** *adj.* tens of millions of; **II.** ≈ *pl.* tens of millions
'zig·tau·send F **I.** *adj.* tens of thousands of; **II.** ≈**e** *pl.* tens of thousands
Zi·ka·de [tsi'ka:də] *f* (-; -n) cicada; **Zi'ka·den·ge·sang** *m* sound of cicadas
Zim·mer ['tsɪmɐ] *n* (-s; -) room, *a.* lodgings *pl., Brit. a.* F digs *pl.*; ***auf sein ~ gehen*** go (up) to one's room; **~an|ten·ne** *f* indoor aerial (*or* antenna); **~aus·weis** *m hotel*: key card; **~bar** *f* minibar; **~blu·me** *f* indoor (flowering) plant; **~ein·rich·tung** *f* furniture; interior; † ***~en*** interior furnishings; **~flucht** *f* suite (of rooms)
'Zim·mer|ge·sel·le *m* journeyman carpenter; **~hand·werk** *n* carpentry
'Zim·mer|kell·ner *m* room waiter; **~laut·stär·ke** *f* household noise level; **~mäd·chen** *n* (chamber)maid
'Zim·mer·mann *m* (-[e]s; -leute) carpenter
zim·mern ['tsɪmɐn] *v/t.* (h) timber; carpenter (*a. v/i.*); make; *fig.* shape
'Zim·mer|nach·weis *m* accommodation office; **~num·mer** *f* room number; **~pal·me** *f* indoor palm (tree); **~pflan·ze** *f* indoor plant; **~ser·vice** *m* room service; **~su·che** *f* (-; *no pl.*): (***auf ~ sein*** be) room-hunting; **~tem·pe·ra|tur** *f* room temperature; **~thea·ter** *n* small theat|re (*Am.* -er); **~trakt** *m* suite of rooms; **~ver·mitt·lung** *f* accommodation service (*or* office)
zim·per·lich ['tsɪmpɐlɪç] **I.** *adj.* a) oversensitive; squeamish, b) affected, c) F prissy; ***sei nicht so ~*** don't make such a fuss; **II.** *adv.*: ***wenig ~*** none too gently, unscrupulously
Zimt [tsɪmt] *m* (-[e]s; *no pl.*) **1.** cinnamon; **2.** F *fig.* rubbish, *esp. Am.* F garbage; **~ap·fel** *m* custard apple; **~baum** *m* cinnamon tree; **~rin·de** *f* cinnamon bark; **~stan·ge** *f* cinnamon stick; **~stern** *m star-shaped cinnamon biscuit*
Zink[1] [tsɪŋk] *n* (-[e]s; *no pl.*) ⚗ zinc
Zink[2] *m* (-[e]s; -en) ♪ cornett, zink
'Zink·blech *n* sheet zinc; zinc plate
Zin·ke ['tsɪŋkə] *f* (-; -n) a) prong, *a.* tine, b) tooth; **Zin·ken** ['tsɪŋkən] *m* (-s; -) **1.** secret sign; **2.** F beak, conk; **'zin·ken** *v/t.* (h) mark *cards etc.*
'Zink·sal·be *f* zinc ointment
Zinn [tsɪn] *n* (-[e]s; *no pl.*) tin; pewter; **~be·cher** *m* pewter mug
Zin·ne ['tsɪnə] *f* (-; -n) merlon; *pl.* battlements
'Zinn|fi|gur *f* pewter figure; **~fo·lie** *f* tinfoil; **~ge·schirr** *n* pewter(ware); **~krug** *m* pewter mug
Zin·no·ber [tsɪ'no:bɐ] *m* (-s; -) **1.** *min.* cinnabar; **2.** vermilion; **3.** *no pl.* F *fig.* a) F stuff, b) fuss; ≈**rot** *adj.* vermilion
'Zinn·sol|dat *m* tin soldier
Zins [tsɪns] *m* (-es; -en) *a. pl.* interest; ***zu 4% ~en*** at 4% interest; ***hohe ~en*** high interest (rates); ***~en tragen*** bear interest; ***zuzüglich ~en*** plus interest; *fig.* ***et. mit ~en heimzahlen*** return s.th. with interest; **~aus·fall** *m* loss of interest; **~be·la·stung** *f* interest load
'zins·brin·gend *adj.* interest-bearing
'Zins|er·hö·hung *f* increase in interest rates; **~er·trä·ge** *pl.* interest earnings; ***~ aus*** *dat.* ***...*** interest yield on ...
Zin·ses·zins ['tsɪnzəs-] *m* compound interest
'zins·frei *adj.* interest-free
'Zins|fuß *m* interest rate; **~ge·fäl·le** *n* interest rate differential
'zins·gün·stig *adj.* low-interest ...
'zins·los *adj.* interest-free; non-interest-bearing *loan etc.*
'Zins·ni|veau *n* level of interest rates
'zins·pflich·tig [-pflɪçtɪç] *adj.* subject to payment of interest
'Zins|po·li|tik *f* interest rate policy; **~rech·nung** *f* calculation of interest; interest account; **~satz** *m* interest rate; **~schwan·kun·gen** *pl.* fluctuations in the interest rate (*or* in interest rates); **~sen·kung** *f* lowering of interest rates; ≈**tra·gend** *adj.* interest-bearing; **~ver·ein·ba·run·gen** *pl.* terms of interest; **~ver·lust** *m* loss on interest; **~wett·be·werb** *m* interest rate competition; **~wu·cher** *m* usury
Zio·nis·mus [tsĭo'nɪsmʊs] *m* (-; *no pl.*) Zionism; **Zio·nist** [tsĭo'nɪst] *m* (-en; -en) Zionist; **zio·ni·stisch** [tsĭo'nɪstɪʃ] *adj.* Zionist(ic)
Zip·fel ['tsɪpfəl] *m* (-s; -) **1.** corner *of a blanket etc.*; point *of a cap etc.*; (*sausage etc.*) end; tip; **2.** *geol.* promontory, tongue; **3.** F ding-dong; **'Zip·fel·müt·ze** *f* pointed cap; **zip·feln** ['tsɪpfəln] *v/i.* (h) be uneven
Zir·bel|drü·se ['tsɪrbəl-] *f anat.* pineal gland; **~kie·fer** *f* Swiss pine
zir·ka ['tsɪrka] *adv.* about, approximately
Zir·kel ['tsɪrkəl] *m* (-s; -) **1.** *a. fig.* circle; **2.** ⚙ (***ein ~*** a pair of) compasses *pl. or* dividers *pl.*; **~schluß** *m*: ***ein ~*** circular reasoning; **~trai·ning** *n sport*: circuit training
Zir·kon [tsɪr'ko:n] *m* (-s; -e) *min.* zircon
Zir·ko·ni·um [tsɪr'ko:nĭʊm] *n* (-s; *no pl.*) zirconium
Zir·ku·la·ti·on [tsɪrkula'tsĭo:n] *f* (-; -en) †, ⚕ circulation; **zir·ku·lie·ren** [tsɪrku'li:rən] *v/i.* (h) circulate; ***~ lassen*** circulate
Zir·kus ['tsɪrkʊs] *m* (-; -se) **1.** circus; **2.** *no pl.* F *fig.* fuss, F carry-on; ***mach keinen ~!*** don't make such a fuss; **~di|rek·tor** *m* circus director (*or* manager); **~künst·ler** *m* circus artist; **~ma|ne·ge** *f* circus ring; **~num·mer** *f* circus act; **~rei·ter** *m* circus rider; **~zelt** *n* circus tent, big top
zir·pen ['tsɪrpən] *v/i. and v/t.* (h) chirp, cheep
Zir·rho·se [tsɪ'ro:zə] *f* (-; -n) ⚕ cirrhosis
Zir·ro·ku·mu·lus [tsɪro'ku:mulʊs] *m* (-; -li) cirrocumulus; **Zir·ro·stra·tus** [tsɪro'stra:tʊs] *m* (-; -ti) cirrostratus
Zir·rus·wol·ke ['tsɪrʊs-] *f* cirrus cloud
zis·al·pin [tsɪsʔal'pi:n] *adj.* cisalpine
zi·scheln ['tsɪʃəln] *v/i. and v/t.* (h) whisper; hiss
zi·schen ['tsɪʃən] (h) **I.** *v/i.* **1.** hiss; *fat*: sizzle; *lemonade etc.*: fizz; **2.** whiz(z) (*a.* F); **II.** *v/t.* **3.** hiss; **4.** F ***ein Bier ~*** F down (*or* guzzle) a beer; ***e-n ~*** F down one, knock one back
Zisch·laut ['tsɪʃ-] *m ling.* sibilant
Zi·se·lier·ar·beit [tsizə'li:ɐ-] *f* chased work
zi·se·lie·ren [tsizə'li:rən] *v/t.* (h) chase
Zi·ster·ne [tsɪs'tɛrnə] *f* (-; -n) cistern, tank
Zi·ster·zi·en·ser [tsɪstɛr'tsĭɛnzɐ] *m* (-s; -) Cistercian (monk); **Zi·ster·zi·en·se·rin** [tsɪstɛr'tsĭɛnzərɪn] *f* (-; -nen) Cistercian (nun)
Zi·ster·zi'en·ser|klo·ster *n* Cistercian monastery; **~or·den** *m* Cistercian order
Zi·ta·del·le [tsita'dɛlə] *f* (-; -n) citadel
Zi·tat [tsi'ta:t] *n* (-[e]s; -e) quotation, F quote (***aus*** *dat.* from); ***Ende des ~s*** end of quote
Zi'ta·ten|le·xi·kon *n* dictionary of quotations; **~samm·lung** *f* collection (*or* anthology) of quotations
Zi·ther ['tsɪtɐ] *f* (-; -n) zither
zi·tie·ren [tsi'ti:rən] (h) **I.** *v/t.* **1.** quote, cite; ***~ aus*** *dat.* quote from; ***darf ich Sie ~?*** may I quote you?; **2.** summon, *formal*: cite; ***vor Gericht zitiert werden*** be summoned to court; ***zu j-m zitiert werden*** be called into s.o.'s office, *formal*: be summoned before s.o.; **II.** *v/i.* quote; ***ich zitiere: ...*** (and) I quote - ..., open quote - ...
Zi·tro·nat [tsitro'na:t] *n* (-[e]s; *no pl*) candied lemon peel
Zi·tro·ne [tsi'tro:nə] *f* (-; -n) lemon; *fig.* ***j-n ausquetschen wie e-e ~*** squeeze everything out of s.o.
Zi'tro·nen|baum *m* lemon tree; **~creme** *f* lemon mousse; **~fal·ter** *m* brimstone butterfly; ≈**gelb** *adj.* lemon(-colo[u]red); **~li·mo|na·de** *f* lemonade; **~pres·se** *f* lemon squeezer; **~saft** *m* lemon juice; **~säu·re** *f* citric acid; **~scha·le** *f* lemon peel; *gastr. a. the* zest of a lemon; **~schei·be** *f* slice of lemon, lemon slice
Zi·trus·früch·te ['tsi:trʊs-] *pl.* citrus fruits
Zit·ter|aal ['tsɪtɐ-] *m* electric eel; **~gras** *n* trembling grass
zit·te·rig ['tsɪtərɪç] *adj.* → ***zittrig***
zit·tern ['tsɪtɐn] **I.** *v/i. a. fig.* tremble, shake (***vor*** *dat.* with); *a.* shiver; ***am ganzen Körper ~*** tremble from head to foot, tremble all over; *fig.* ***um j-n ~*** fear for s.o.; ***vor j-m (et.) ~*** be terrified of s.o. (s.th.); ***ich hab' ganz schön gezittert*** F I was scared as anything; **II.** ≈ *n* (-s; *no pl.*) trembling, shaking; *a.* shivering, *the* shivers *pl.*; F ***das große ~ kriegen*** F get cold feet; **'zit·ternd** *adj.* trembling, shaking; ***mit ~er Stimme*** *a.* in a tremulous voice
Zit·ter|pap·pel ['tsɪtɐ-] *f* aspen; **~par|tie** F *f* F cliffhanger; F nailbiter; nailbiting game (*or* election *etc.*); ***e-e zweiwöchige ~*** two weeks of nailbiting; **~sieg** F *m* F nailbiting victory; **~spiel** F *n* F cliffhanger, nailbiting game (*or* match)
zitt·rig ['tsɪtrɪç] *adj.* shaky; *a.* tremulous, faltering *voice*; doddery; ***e-e ~e Schrift*** shaky handwriting
Zit·ze ['tsɪtsə] *f* (-; -n) teat
zi·vil [tsi'vi:l] *adj.* **1.** civilian; ***die ~e Luftfahrt*** civil aviation; **2.** reasonable *prices*
Zi'vil *n* (-s; *no pl.*) civilian clothes *pl.* (*or* dress), ⚔ F civvies *pl.*; *police*: plain clothes *pl.*; ***in ~*** *a.* ⚔ F in mufti; ***Polizist in ~*** plainclothes policeman
Zi'vil|be·schäf·tig·te *m, f* (-n; -n) civilian employee (*working for the armed forces*); **~be·völ·ke·rung** *f* civilian population; ***Verluste unter der ~*** civilian casualties; **~cou|ra·ge** *f the* courage of one's convictions; ***er hat ~*** he's not afraid to say what he thinks; **~dienst** *m* (-[e]s; *no pl.*) alternative (*or* community) service (*in lieu of military service*); **~dienst·lei·sten·de** *m* (-n; -n) *conscientious objector conscripted to do community work*; **~ehe** *f* civil marriage; **~fahn·der** *m* plainclothes detective; **~fahn·dung** *f* plainclothes search (*or* dragnet); **~fahr·zeug** *n* unmarked vehicle (*or* police car); **~flug·ha·fen** *m* civil airport; **~flug·zeug** *n* civil aircraft; **~ge·fan·ge·ne** *m, f*

(-n; -n) civilian prisoner (of war), internee; **~ge·richt** *n* civil court; ***Oberstes ~*** High Court of Justice
Zi·vi·li·sa·ti·on [tsiviliza'tsi̯o:n] *f* (-; -en) civilization; **Zi·vi·li·sa·ti'ons·krank·heit** *f* civilization disease
zi·vi·li·sa·ti'ons·mü·de *adj.* tired of modern-day society; world-weary
zi·vi·li·sie·ren [tsivili'zi:rən] *v/t.* (h) civilize; **zi·vi·li·siert** [tsivili'zi:ɐt] *adj.* civilized; **Zi·vi·li'sie·rung** *f* (-; *no pl.*) civilization; **Zi·vi·li'sie·rungs·pro,zeß** *m* process of civilization
Zi·vi·list [tsivi'lɪst] *m* (-en; -en) civilian
Zi'vil|kam·mer *f* ⚖ civil division; **~klei·dung** *f* → ***Zivil***; **~le·ben** *n* civilian life; ***ins ~ zurückkehren*** return to civilian life, F go back to civvy street; **~luft·fahrt** *f*: ***die ~*** civil aviation; **~per,son** *f* civilian; **~pro,zeß** *m* ⚖ civil action; **~recht** *n* civil law; ***gegen das ~ verstoßen*** commit a civil offen|ce (*Am.* -se); **2recht·lich** **I.** *adj.* civil law ..., under civil law; **II.** *adv.* under civil law; ***~ verfolgen*** bring a civil action against, sue; **~re,gie·rung** *f* civilian government; **~schutz** *m* civil defen|ce (*Am.* -se); **~schutz·korps** *n* civil defen|ce (*Am.* -se) organization; militia; **~strei·fe** *f* plainclothes policemen *pl.* (on the beat); **~ver·tei·di·gung** *f* civil defen|ce (*Am.* -se)
Zo·bel ['tso:bəl] *m* (-s; -) **1.** *zo.* sable; **2.** → **'Zo·bel·pelz** *m* **1.** sable (fur); **2.** sable
Zo·fe ['tso:fə] *f* (-; -n) a) lady's maid, b) lady-in-waiting
Zoff [tsɔf] F *m* (-s; *no pl.*) trouble, F strife; ***~ mit j-m haben*** be having a bit of strife with s.o.
zog [tso:k] *pret. of* ***ziehen***
Zö·ge·rer ['tsø:gərɐ] *m* (-s; -) procrastinator, F ditherer; **zö·ger·lich** ['tsø:gɐlɪç] *adj.* hesitant; halting; ***sich ~ geben*** hold back; **zö·gern** ['tsø:gɐn] **I.** *v/i.* (h) hesitate; waver; ***er zögerte nicht zu*** *inf.* he lost no time in *ger.*; ***du darfst nicht zu lange ~*** don't spend too much time thinking about it; ***was zögerst du noch?*** why the hesitation?, what's the problem?; **II.** 2 *n* (-s; *no pl.*) hesitation; ***ohne ~*** unhesitatingly, without (a moment's) hesitation; ***nach anfänglichem ~*** after some hesitation; **'zö·gernd I.** *adj.* hesitating; halting *speech, steps, progress etc.*; **II.** *adv.* hesitatingly; haltingly; ***nur ~ über et. reden*** be reluctant to talk about s.th.
Zög·ling ['tsø:klɪŋ] *m* (-s; -e) pupil; *fig.* protégé
Zö·li·bat [tsøli'ba:t] *n, m* (-[e]s; *no pl.*) celibacy; ***im ~ leben*** be celibate, practi|se (*Am.* -ce) celibacy
Zoll¹ [tsɔl] *m* (-[e]s; Zölle ['tsœlə]) **1.** (customs) duty; **2.** *no pl.* customs *pl.*; ***beim ~ liegen*** be at the customs (office); ***beim ~ arbeiten*** work for (the) customs; ***et. durch den ~ bringen*** get s.th. through customs
Zoll² *m* (-[e]s; -) inch; ***jeder ~ ein Ehrenmann*** every inch a gentleman
'Zoll|ab·fer·ti·gung *f* **1.** customs clearance; **2.** customs; ***es muß durch die ~*** it has to go through customs; **~ab·fer·ti·gungs·ha·fen** *m* port of clearance (*or* entry); **~ab·kom·men** *n* customs (*or* tariff) agreement
Zolla·ger (*sep.* -ll·l-) *n* bonded (*or* customs) warehouse
'Zoll·amt *n* customs office; **'zoll·amt·lich I.** *adj.*: ***~e Abfertigung*** customs clearance; ***~e Untersuchung*** customs inspection; **II.** *adv.*: ***~ abfertigen*** clear through customs; ***~ deklarieren*** declare
'Zoll|be·am·te *m* customs official (*or* officer); **~be·hör·de** *f* customs authorities *pl.*
'Zoll·breit *m*: *fig.* ***keinen ~ weichen*** not to budge (*or* give) an inch
'Zoll·ein·nah·men *pl.* customs revenue *sg.*
zol·len ['tsɔlən] *v/t.* (h): ***j-m Anerkennung ~*** pay tribute to s.o.; ***j-m Dank (Beifall) ~*** thank (applaud) s.o.; ***j-m Bewunderung ~*** express one's admiration for s.o.
'Zoll|er·klä·rung *f* customs declaration; **~fahn·der** *m* customs investigator; **~fahn·dung** *f* **1.** customs investigation; **2.** → **~fahn·dungs·stel·le** *f* customs investigation office; **~for·ma·li,tä·ten** *pl.* customs formalities
'zoll·frei *adj.* duty-free; ***~e Ware*** duty-free goods; **'Zoll·frei·heit** *f* (-; *no pl.*) exemption from duty
'Zoll|ge·biet *n* customs territory; **~ge·büh·ren** *pl.* customs duties; **~ge·setz** *n* customs law; **~grenz·be·zirk** *m* customs district; **~gren·ze** *f* customs frontier; **~ha·fen** *m* port of entry; **~ho·heit** *f* (-; *no pl.*) customs sovereignty; **~in·halts·er·klä·rung** *f* customs declaration; **~in·spek·ti,on** *f* customs inspection; **~kon,trol·le** *f* customs examination (*or* check)
Zöll·ner ['tsœlnɐ] *m* (-s; -) **1.** customs officer; **2.** *bibl.* publican
'Zoll·pa,pie·re *pl.* customs documents
'zoll·pflich·tig [-pflɪçtɪç] *adj.* dutiable, liable to duty
'Zoll|po·li,tik *f* customs policy; **~recht** *n* customs legislation; **~schran·ke** *f* customs barrier; **~stel·le** *f* customs office; **~stock** *m* folding rule; yardstick; **~ta,rif** *m* (customs) tariff; **~uni,on** *f* customs union; **~ver·trag** *m* customs (*or* tariff) agreement; **~vor·schrif·ten** *pl.* customs regulations
Zo·ne ['tso:nə] *f* (-; -n) zone; *geogr. a.* region; *adm. a.* area; *hist. pol.* ***die ~*** East Germany
'Zo·nen|gren·ze *f*: *hist. pol.* ***die ~*** the East German border; **~rand·ge·biet** *n* *hist. pol. border area between East and West Germany*
Zö·no·bit [tsøno'bi:t] *m* (-en; -en) c(o)enobite
Zoo [tso:] *m* (-s; -s) zoo; **~di,rek·tor** *m* zoo director
Zoo·lo·ge [tsoo'lo:gə] *m* (-n; -n) zoologist; **Zoo·lo·gie** [tsoolo'gi:] *f* (-; *no pl.*) zoology; **zoo·lo·gisch** [tsoo'lo:gɪʃ] *adj.* zoological; ***~er Garten*** zoological gardens
Zoom [zu:m] *n* (-s; -s) *phot.* zoom; **'Zoom·auf·nah·me** *f* zoom shot; **zoo·men** ['zu:mən] *v/t. and v/i.* (h) zoom; **'Zoom·ob·jek,tiv** *n* zoom lens
'Zoo·tier *n* zoo animal
Zopf [tsɔpf] *m* (-[e]s; Zöpfe ['tsœpfə]) plait; *a.* pigtail; *fig.* ***ein (alter) ~*** an antiquated custom, F old hat; ***das ist doch ein alter ~!*** F that went out with the ark; ***die alten Zöpfe abschneiden*** get rid of the old practi|ces (*Am.* -ses); **~mu·ster** *n* cable stitch; **~stil** *m* late rococo (style)
Zorn [tsɔrn] *m* (-[e]s; *no pl.*) rage, anger, fury; *rhet.* wrath (*all* ***auf*** *acc.* at); ***in ~ geraten*** fly into a rage; ***ihn packte der ~*** he got really angry (*or* furious)
Zor·nes|aus·bruch ['tsɔrnəs-] *m* fit of anger (*or* rage); **~rö·te** *f* flush of anger
zor·nig ['tsɔrnɪç] *adj.* angry (***auf*** *acc.* at, about *s.th.*, with *s.o.*)
Zo·te ['tso:tə] *f* (-; -n) dirty joke; ***~n reißen*** tell dirty jokes; **zo·tig** ['tso:tɪç] *adj.* dirty, obscene
Zot·te ['tsɔtə] *f* (-; -n) tuft (of hair)
Zot·tel ['tsɔtəl] *f* (-; -n) tuft; *pl.* straggly hair *sg.*; **zot·te·lig** ['tsɔtəlɪç] *adj.* straggly; matted
zu [tsu:] **I.** *prp.* (*dat.*) **1.** a) to, b) at, in, c) for, d) at; ***~ Beginn*** at the beginning; ***~ Berlin*** in (*adm.* at) Berlin; ***3 ~ 1*** three to one, *sport*: *a.* three-one; ***~ deutsch*** in German; ***~ Weihnachten*** *etc.* at Christmas *etc.*; ***wir ziehen zum 15. ein*** we're moving in on the 15th; ***das Gesetz tritt zum 1. September in Kraft*** the law will be in force as of September 1st; ***zur Stunde*** at the moment; ***bis zur Stunde*** up until now, as yet; ***~ m-r Zeit*** in my day; ***~ ebener Erde*** at ground level; ***~ Wasser und ~ Lande*** on land and at sea; ***der Dom ~ Köln*** Cologne Cathedral; ***zum Preis von*** *dat.* at a price of; ***zum Scherz*** for (*or* in) fun; ***zur Stadt*** to town; ***zur Tür hereinkommen*** come in, come through the door; ***j-n zur Bahn bringen*** see s.o. off at (*or* take s.o. to) the station; ***~ Tal*** downhill; ***Liebe (Zuneigung) ~ j-m*** love (affection) for s.o.; ***~ j-m gehen*** go and (*or* to) see s.o.; ***j-n zum Freund (Vater) haben*** have s.o. as a friend (father); ***j-n zum Präsidenten wählen*** elect s.o. president; ***sich ~ j-m setzen*** sit with s.o., join s.o., sit (down) next to s.o.; ***~ et. werden*** turn into s.th., *person*: *a.* become s.th.; ***Brot zum Ei essen*** have bread with one's egg; ***Zukker zum Kaffee nehmen*** take sugar in one's coffee; ***Stoff ~ e-m Kleid*** material for a dress; ***Platz zum Spielen*** room to play (in); ***sie kamen ~ sechst*** six of them came; → ***Beispiel, Erstaunen, Fuß, Haus*** 1; **II.** *adv.* **2.** *with adj. and adv.*: too; ***~ sehr*** too much; ***~ viel*** too much; ***~ sehr betonen*** overemphasize; **3.** closed, shut; ***Tür ~!*** shut the door!; **4.** ***immer*** (*or* ***nur***) ***~!*** go on!; **III.** *cj.*: ***~ sein*** to be; ***ich habe ~ arbeiten*** I've got work to do; ***ich erinnere mich, ihn gesehen ~ haben*** I remember seeing him; ***ein sorgfältig ~ erwägender Plan*** a plan requiring careful consideration; ***die auszuwechselnden Fahrzeugteile*** the parts to be exchanged
zu·al·ler|erst [tsuˀalɐˈˀe:ɐst] *adv.* first of all; **~letzt** [-'lɛtst] *adv.* last of all; **~oberst** [-'ˀo:bɐst] *adv.* **1.** right at the top (***in*** *dat.* of); **2.** *fig.* first and foremost; **~un·terst** [-'ˀʊntɐst] *adv.* **1.** right at the bottom (***in*** *dat.* of); **2.** *fig.* last of all
'zu·bau·en *v/t.* (*sep.*, h) a) build up, b) block, obstruct *a. view etc.*
Zu·be·hör ['tsu:bəhø:ɐ] *n, m* (-[e]s; *no pl.*) accessories *pl.* (*a. phot.*); ⚙ attachment(s *pl.*); fittings *pl.*; ***das ganze ~*** *a.* F all the bits and pieces; **~in·du,strie** *f* accessories industry; **~teil** *n* accessory (part); *pl.* accessories
'zu·bei·ßen *v/i.* (*irr.*, *sep.*, h, → ***beißen***) bite; *dog*: snap
'zu·be·kom·men *v/t.* (*irr.*, *sep.*, h, → ***bekommen***) get *the door etc.* shut; get *blouse etc.* done up

Zu·ber ['tsu:bɐ] *m* (-s; -) tub

'zu·be·rei·ten *v/t.* (*sep.*, h) prepare; ***das Essen*** ~ *a.* make (the) dinner *or* lunch

'Zu·be·rei·tung *f* (-; *no pl.*) preparation; *gastr.* method; ***die*** ~ ***dauert ...*** (the) preparation time is ...

'zu·be·we·gen (*sep.*, h) **I.** *v/t.*: ***et.*** ~ ***auf*** *acc.* move (*or* bring) s.th. towards; **II.** *v/refl.*: ***sich*** ~ ***auf*** *acc.* move (slowly) towards, (slowly) approach

zu·bil·li·gen *v/t.* (*sep.*, h) grant (***j-m et.*** s.o. s.th.); allow (*a.* ⚖ *mitigating circumstances*); ⚖ award

'zu·bin·den *v/t.* (*irr.*, *sep.*, h, → ***binden***) tie up; ***j-m die Augen*** ~ blindfold s.o.

'zu·blei·ben *v/i.* (*irr.*, *sep.*, sn, → ***bleiben***) stay closed (*or* shut)

'zu·blin·zeln *v/i.* (*sep.*, h) wink at *s.o.*

'zu·brin·gen *v/t.* (*irr.*, *sep.*, h, → ***bringen***) **1.** spend *time etc.*; **2.** → ***zubekommen***

Zu·brin·ger ['tsu:brɪŋɐ] *m* (-s; -) feeder; **~bus** *m* feeder bus; airport (*or* transfer) bus; **~dienst** *m* feeder service; **~li·nie** *f* ✈ feeder line; **~stra·ße** *f* feeder road

'zu·but·tern F *v/t.* (*sep.*, h) **1.** F chip in, come up with an extra *million dollars etc.*; **2.** ***zu s-m Einkommen*** *etc.* ***et.*** ~ boost one's income *etc.* (a bit)

Zuc·chi·ni [tsʊ'ki:ni] *pl.* courgettes, *Am.* zucchini

Zucht [tsʊxt] *f* (-; -en) **1.** *no pl. zo.* breeding; culture; ♣ cultivation, growing; **2.** breed, stock; (*bacteria etc.*) culture; **3.** *no pl.* discipline; ~ ***und Ordnung*** strict discipline, law and order; **~bul·le** *m* breeding bull

züch·ten ['tsʏçtən] *v/t.* (h) *zo.* breed (*a. fig.*); ♣ grow; culture *bacteria*, *pearls*; *fig.* cultivate; **Züch·ter** ['tsʏçtɐ] *m* (-s; -) *zo.* breeder; (*bee*)keeper; ♣ grower

'Zucht·haus *obs. n* prison, *Am.* penitentiary; ***zwei Jahre*** ~ two years' imprisonment; ***ins*** ~ ***kommen*** go (*or* be sent) to prison; ***im*** ~ ***sein*** be in prison; ***das wird mit 10 Jahren*** ~ ***bestraft*** that carries a prison sentence of ten years (*or* a ten-year prison sentence)

Zucht·häus·ler ['tsʊxthɔʏslɐ] *m* (-s; -) convict, F con

'Zucht·hengst *m* stud horse, breeding stallion

züch·tig ['tsʏçtɪç] *adj.* virtuous; chaste

züch·ti·gen ['tsʏçtɪgən] *v/t.* (h) punish; **'Züch·ti·gung** *f* (-; -en): (***körperliche*** ~ corporal) punishment

'zucht·los *adj.* undisciplined; disorderly; **'Zucht·lo·sig·keit** *f* (-; *no pl.*) lack of discipline

'Zucht|mit·tel *n* disciplinary measure; **~per·le** *f* cultured pearl; **~stier** *m* breeding bull; **~stu·te** *f* breeding mare; **~tier** *n* stock animal, *pl. a.* breeding stock *sg.*

Züch·tung ['tsʏçtʊŋ] *f* (-; -en) → ***Zucht*** 1, 2

'Zucht·vieh *n* breeding cattle

zuckeln ['tsʊkəln] (*sep.* -k·k-) F *v/i.* (sn) *car*: F chug along; *person*: F trundle along

zucken ['tsʊkən] (*sep.* -k·k-) *v/i.* (h) twitch; wince; *flame, light*: flicker; *lightning*: flash; ***ihm zuckte es in den Beinen*** he was itching for a dance (*or* to dance); ***ein Gedanke zuckte ihr durch den Kopf*** a thought flashed across her mind (*or* suddenly struck her); → ***Achsel, Wimper***

zücken ['tsʏkən] (*sep.* -k·k-) *v/t.* (h) pull out *knife etc.*; *hum.* whip out *one's wallet etc.*

Zucker ['tsʊkɐ] (*sep.* -k·k-) *m* (-s; *no pl.*) **1.** sugar; ***ein Stück*** ~ a lump of sugar; ***ohne*** ~ sugar-free; F *fig.* (***es ist***) ~! F (it's) magic; **2.** F ⚕ diabetes; **~bäcker·stil** *m* gingerbread style; **~brot** *n*: *fig.* ***mit*** ~ ***und Peitsche*** with a carrot and a stick; **~do·se** *f* sugar bowl; **~erb·se** *f* ♣ sugar pea; **~gla,sur** *f*, **~guß** *m* icing, frosting; ***mit*** ~ ***überziehen*** ice, frost

'zucker·hal·tig [-haltɪç] *adj.* containing sugar; ~ ***sein*** contain sugar

'Zucker·hut *m* sugar loaf

zucke·rig ['tsʊkərɪç] (*sep.* -k·k-) *adj.* sugary

'Zucker·kan·dis *m* → ***Kandiszucker***

'zucker·krank *adj.* ⚕ diabetic; ~ ***sein*** have diabetes, be a diabetic; **'Zucker·kran·ke** *m, f* (-n; -n) diabetic; **'Zucker·krank·heit** *f* (-; *no pl.*) diabetes

'Zucker|lecken *n*: ***das ist kein*** ~ it's no fun and games; **~mais** *m* sweetcorn; **~me,lo·ne** *f* sugar melon

zuckern ['tsʊkɐn] (*sep.* -k·k-) *v/t.* (h) sugar; *a.* sprinkle sugar on, sprinkle with sugar; *a.* sweeten

'Zucker|raf·fi·ne,rie *f* sugar refinery; **~rohr** *n* sugarcane; **~rohr·plan,ta·ge** *f* sugarcane plantation; **~rü·be** *f* sugar beet; **~spie·gel** *m* ⚕ blood sugar level; **~stan·ge** *f* stick of rock (*Am.* candy); **~streu·er** *m* sugar caster; **2'süß** *adj.* as sweet as sugar; *fig.* sugary; **~was·ser** *n* sugared water; **~wat·te** *f* candy floss, *Am.* cotton candy; **~zan·ge** *f*: (***e-e*** ~ a pair of) sugar tongs *pl.*; **~zu·satz** *m*: ***ohne*** ~ no (*or* without) added sugar

zuck·rig ['tsʊkrɪç] *adj.* → ***zuckerig***

Zuckung ['tsʊkʊŋ] (*sep.* -k·k-) *f* (-; -en) jerk, twitch; convulsion; contraction; ***nervöse*** **~en** *a.* nervous twitching

'zu·decken *v/t.* (*sep.*, h) cover (up); *fig.* conceal, cover up; inundate with, load down with *work*; *fig.* ***j-n mit Vorwürfen*** ~ heap reproaches on s.o.; ***j-n mit Fragen*** ~ bombard s.o. with questions

zu·dem [tsu'de:m] *adv.* besides, moreover

'zu·den·ken *v/t.* (*irr.*, *sep.*, h, → ***denken***): ***j-m et.*** ~ intend s.th. for s.o., want s.o. to have s.th.

'zu·dre·hen *v/t.* (*sep.*, h) **1.** a) turn off *tap, water etc.*, b) tighten *screw*; **2.** ***j-m den Rücken*** ~ turn one's back to(wards) (*or* on) s.o.; ***j-m das Gesicht*** ~ turn (round) to face (*or* look at) s.o.; ***j-m den Kopf*** ~ turn one's head towards s.o.; *fig.* → ***Hahn*** 2

zu·dring·lich ['tsu:drɪŋlɪç] *adj.* obtrusive, F pushy; ***e-r Frau gegenüber*** ~ ***werden*** make advances (*or* passes) at a woman; **'Zu·dring·lich·keit** *f* (-; -en) **1.** *no pl.* obtrusiveness, F pushiness; **2.** advances *pl.*

'zu·drücken *v/t.* (*sep.*, h) (press) shut; → ***Auge*** 1

'zu·eig·nen *v/t.* (*sep.*, h): ***j-m et.*** ~ dedicate s.th. to s.o.; *esp.* ⚖ ***sich et.*** ~ convert s.th. to one's own use

'zu·ei·len *v/i.* (*sep.*, sn): ~ ***auf*** *acc.* (*or dat.*) rush towards (*or* up to)

zu·ein·an·der [tsuʔaɪ'nandɐ] *adv.* to each other, to one another; **~fin·den** *v/i.* (*irr.*, *sep.*, h, → ***finden***) reach an understanding; **~hal·ten** *v/i.* (*irr.*, *sep.*, h, → ***halten***), **~ste·hen** *v/i.* (*irr.*, *sep.*, h, → ***stehen***) stand (F stick) by each other (*or* one another)

'zu·er·ken·nen *v/t.* (*irr.*, *sep.*, h, → ***erkennen***) award (*a. prize and* ⚖) (*dat.* to); confer (on); grant (***j-m*** s.o.)

zu·erst [tsu'ʔe:ɐst] *adv.* **1.** first; ***er kam*** ~ *a.* he was the first to arrive; ***wer*** ~ ***kommt, mahlt*** ~ first come first served; **2.** first (of all); *a.* to begin (*or* start) with; **3.** (at) first; **4.** first, (for) the first time; ***das wurde*** ~ ***in China eingeführt*** that was first introduced in China

'zu·fah·ren *v/i.* (*irr.*, *sep.*, sn, → ***fahren***) **1.** ~ ***auf*** *acc.* drive to(wards); head (*or* make) for; **2.** ***fahr zu!*** go on!, *iro.* what are you waiting for?

Zu·fahrt ['tsu:fa:ɐt] *f* (-; -en), **'Zu·fahrts·stra·ße** *f* a) access road, b) drive(way); ***die*** ~ ***zum Haus*** the drive(way) leading up to the house

'Zu·fall *m* (-[e]s; ¨-e) chance; coincidence; ***reiner*** ~ pure chance; ***glücklicher*** ~ lucky coincidence; ***unglücklicher*** ~ bit of bad luck; ***das ist*** ~ that's chance (*or* luck); ***durch*** ~ by chance, by accident; ***es dem*** ~ ***überlassen*** leave it to chance; ***nichts blieb dem*** ~ ***überlassen*** nothing was left to chance; ***wie es der*** ~ ***wollte*** as luck would have it; ***es hängt vom*** ~ ***ab, ob*** it's a matter of luck as to whether; ***es ist kein*** ~, ***wenn*** it's no accident that; ***das ist aber ein*** ~! what a coincidence!, *a.* well, fancy meeting you here (*or* you of all people)!

'zu·fal·len *v/i.* (*irr.*, *sep.*, sn, → ***fallen***) **1.** close; ***mir fallen die Augen zu*** I can't keep my eyes open; **2.** *door*: slam shut; **3.** ***j-m*** ~ fall to s.o.; *inheritance etc.*, *formal*: *a.* devolve upon s.o.; ***j-m*** ~ ***zu*** *inf.* fall to s.o.('s lot) to *inf.*; ***ihm ist immer alles zugefallen*** everything has always just fallen into his lap

'zu·fäl·lig I. *adv.* by chance; as luck would have it; ***rein*** ~ purely (*or* quite) by chance; ***er war*** ~ ***zu Hause*** he happened to be at home; ***ich traf ihn*** ~ I happened to bump into him, I just bumped into him; ***weißt du*** ~, ***ob ...?*** do you happen to know whether ...?; ***wenn du*** ~ ***mit ihm sprechen solltest*** if you should happen to be talking to him, if by any chance you might (*or* happen to) be talking to him; **II.** *adj.* accidental; chance ...; incidental; ***es war rein*** ~ it was pure (*or* sheer) coincidence; **zu·fäl·li·ger·wei·se** ['tsu:fɛlɪgɐvaɪzə] *adv.* → ***zufällig*** I

'Zu·falls|aus·wahl *f* random selection (*or* sampling); **~be·kannt·schaft** *f* chance acquaintance; **~fund** *m* lucky find; **~ge·ne,ra·tor** *m computer*: random (number) generator; **~tref·fer** *m* lucky shot, F fluke; *fig.* lucky strike

'zu·flie·gen *v/i.* (*irr.*, *sep.*, sn, → ***fliegen***) **1.** ***j-m*** ~ *bird*: fly to s.o.; *fig.* go out to s.o.; *ideas etc.*: come easily to s.o.; **2.** F *door*: slam shut

'zu·flie·ßen *v/i.* (*irr.*, *sep.*, sn, → ***fließen***) **1.** flow to(wards); **2.** *fig.* go to (*dat. s.o.*); flow into *a fund etc.*; ***j-m et.*** ~ ***lassen*** let s.o. have s.th.

Zu·flucht ['tsu:flʊxt] *f* (-; *no pl.*) **1.** shelter (***vor*** *dat.* from *a storm etc.*); ~ ***suchen*** (***finden***) ***in*** *dat.* seek (find) shelter in; **2.** *fig.* shelter, refuge (***vor*** *dat.* from); ***bei Freunden*** ~ ***suchen*** seek refuge (*or* shelter) among friends; **3.** ~ ***nehmen zu*** *dat.* resort to, *a.* turn to *drugs etc.*; ***m-e letzte*** ~ my last resort; **4.** ~ ***in der Literatur*** *etc.* ***finden*** find solace (*or* an escape) in literature *etc.*

'**Zu·fluchts|ort** *m*, **~stät·te** *f* place of refuge, retreat, sanctuary

'**Zu·fluß** *m* (-sses; ⁼sse) **1.** influx (*a. fig.*); **2.** tributary

'**zu·flü·stern** *v/t.* (*sep.*, h): ***j-m et.*** ~ whisper s.th. to s.o. (*or* into s.o.'s ear)

zu·fol·ge [tsu'fɔlgə] *prp.* (*dat.*) **1.** as a result (*or* consequence) of; **2.** according to; ***Berichte, denen ~ ...*** *a.* reports claiming (that) ...

zu·frie·den [tsu'fri:dən] *adj.* a) content(ed), satisfied (***mit*** *dat.* with); pleased, b) complacent; ***ich bin damit ~*** *a.* I'm quite happy with it, I have no complaints; ***bist du jetzt endlich ~?*** are you quite satisfied (*or* happy) now?; ***du machst ein sehr ~es Gesicht*** you look very satisfied with yourself; ***du kannst ~ sein, daß*** you can be happy (*or* thankful) that; ***sie ist mit nichts ~*** she's never satisfied, there's no pleasing her; ***sie ist mit allem ~*** she's not fussy, she doesn't make any demands; ***glücklich und ~*** perfectly content (*or* happy)

zu'frie·den·ge·ben *v/refl.*: ***sich ~*** (*irr.*, *sep.*, h, → ***geben***) be content (***mit*** *dat.* with), ***mit*** *dat.*: *a.* settle for, (be prepared to) accept; ***damit mußt du dich ~*** *a.* you'll have to learn to put up with it, that's the best we *etc.* can do; ***damit wollte er sich nicht ~*** he wasn't prepared to accept (*or* put up with) that

Zu'frie·den·heit *f* (-; *no pl.*) a) contentment, satisfaction, b) complacency; ***zur allgemeinen ~*** to everyone's satisfaction; ***zur vollsten ~*** to our *etc.* full satisfaction

zu'frie·den|las·sen *v/t.* (*irr.*, *sep.*, h, → ***lassen***) leave *s.o.* alone (*or* in peace); **~stel·len** *v/t.* (*sep.*, h) satisfy; ***schwer zufriedenzustellen*** hard to please; **~stel·lend** *adj.* satisfactory

'**zu·frie·ren** *v/i.* (*irr.*, *sep.*, sn, → ***frieren***) freeze over (*or* up)

'**zu·fü·gen** *v/t.* (*sep.*, h) **1.** add (*dat.* to); **2.** ***j-m et. ~*** cause s.o. s.th.; ***j-m Leid ~*** cause s.o. pain (*or* suffering), hurt s.o.; ***j-m Verluste*** *etc.* ~ inflict losses *etc.* on s.o.; → ***Schaden***

Zu·fuhr ['tsu:fu:ɐ] *f* (-; *no pl.*) **1.** supply; **2.** *meteor.* influx; '**zu·füh·ren** (*sep.*, h) **I.** *v/t.* **1.** supply (*dat.* to), feed (to); ***e-r Sache et. ~*** *a.* supply s.th. with s.th.; **2.** bring (*dat.* to), introduce (to); ***e-r Firma Arbeitskräfte ~*** supply a company with labo(u)r; ***j-n j-m ~*** bring s.o. into contact with s.o., introduce s.o. to s.o.; **3.** ***j-n s-r verdienten Bestrafung ~*** give s.o. his (*or* her) due punishment; ***et. s-r Bestimmung ~*** put s.th. to its proper use; **II.** *v/i.*: ***~ auf*** *acc.* lead to (*a. fig.*); '**Zu·füh·rung** *f* (-; *no pl.*) supply

'**zu·fül·len** *v/t.* (*sep.*, h) fill (up)

Zug [tsu:k] *m* (-[e]s; Züge ['tsy:gə]) **1.** 🚂 train; ***im ~*** on the train; ***mit dem ~*** by train; ***j-n zum ~ bringen*** see s.o. off at the station; *fig.* ***im falschen ~ sitzen*** be barking up the wrong tree; ***der ~ ist abgefahren*** you've (*or* we've, he's *etc.*) missed the boat; **2.** draught, *Am.* draft; ***ich habe ~ bekommen*** I must have been sitting in a draught (*Am.* draft); **3.** a) breath, b) drag, puff (*both* ***an*** *dat.* of, at *one's cigarette etc.*), c) gulp, F swig, *formal*: draught, *Am.* draft (*all* ***aus*** *dat.* from); ***der Ofen hat keinen ~*** the stove isn't drawing; ***e-n tüchtigen ~ aus der Flasche nehmen*** F take a good swig from the bottle; ***sein Glas auf einen ~ leeren*** empty one's glass in one go; ***er hat e-n guten ~*** F he can really down the stuff; *fig.* ***in den letzten Zügen liegen*** a) be breathing one's last, b) be on its last legs; ***in vollen Zügen genießen*** enjoy to the full, make the most of; **4.** pull, tug; **5.** *phys.* tension, pull; ***auf ~ belasten*** subject to tension; **6.** ⚙ hoist; pulley; **7.** a) elastic band, b) strap; drawstring; **8.** a) procession; march; column, b) *zo.* flight, migration *of birds*; ***Hannibals ~ über die Alpen*** Hannibal's crossing of the Alps; F *fig.* ***e-n ~ durch die Gemeinde machen*** F go on a pub crawl; *fig.* ***im ~e*** in progress; ***im ~e des Fortschritts*** *etc.* on the tide of progress *etc.*; ***im ~e der Neuordnung*** in the course of reorganization; ***im besten ~e sein*** a) be well under way, be in full swing, b) be going strong; ***in einem ~e*** *read etc.* in one go; ***dem ~ s-s Herzens folgen*** follow (the dictates of) one's heart; **9.** ⚔ platoon; **10.** *ped.* stream; **11.** team *of oxen etc.*; **12.** *chess etc.*: move (*a. fig.*); ***wer ist am ~?*** whose move is it?; *fig.* ***ein geschickter ~*** a clever move; ***jetzt ist er am ~*** the ball is in his court; ***er kam nicht zum ~e*** he never got a chance (*or* a word in edgeways); ***~ um ~*** a) step by step, b) without delay; **13.** *swimming*: stroke; *rowing*: pull; **14.** stroke (of the pen); *fig.* ***in kurzen Zügen*** in brief outline, briefly, ***schildern***: give a brief outline of, give a thumbnail sketch of; ***in groben Zügen*** in broad outline, roughly; **15.** feature; **16.** trait, characteristic, feature, *esp. contp.* streak; ***e-n leichtsinnigen ~ haben*** have a careless streak; ***das war ein (kein) schöner ~ von ihm*** that says something for him (that reflects badly on him); ***das Bild hat impressionistische Züge*** that picture has impressionist features

'**Zu·ga·be** *f* (-; -n) **1.** ♪, *thea. etc.* encore; ***~!*** encore!; **2.** extra; bonus; **3.** *no pl.* addition; ***unter ~ von*** *dat.* (by) adding; **~stück** *n* encore (piece)

'**Zug·ab|teil** *n* railway (*or* train) compartment

'**Zu·gang** *m* (-[e]s; ⁼e) **1.** a) entrance; *w.s.* access, b) approach, access road, c) *no pl.* *fig.* access, *a* doorway; ***kein ~!*** no admittance; *fig.* ***keinen ~ haben*** (*or* ***finden***) ***zu*** *dat.* have no appreciation (♪ *a.* ear) for *s.th.*; **2.** a) intake *of students etc.*; ⚕ admissions *pl.*, b) *library etc.*: acquisitions *pl.*; **3.** *no pl.* increase

zu·gäng·lich ['tsu:gɛŋlɪç] *adj.* a) accessible (***für*** *acc.* to) (*a. fig.*); *fig.* available, b) approachable; ***~ machen für*** *acc.* open up to; ***allgemein ~*** open to the (general) public; ***schwer ~*** *place etc.* difficult to get to, *documents etc.* difficult to get at (*or* get hold of); ***leicht ~*** easily accessible, *documents etc.* openly accessible, available to the public; *fig.* ***~ für*** *acc.* open to, amenable to *arguments etc.*, willing to listen to *reason*

'**Zu·gangs·stra·ße** *f* access road

'**Zug|aus·kunft** *f* **1.** (information on) train times; **2.** enquiries *pl.*, inquiry *or* information office (*or* desk); **~be·glei·ter** *m* guard, *Am.* conductor; **~brücke** *f* drawbridge

'**zu·ge·ben** *v/t.* (*irr.*, *sep.*, h, → ***geben***) **1.** add; throw in; **2.** a) admit, confess, own up to, b) concede, admit, grant; ***gib's doch zu!*** go on, admit it!; ***man muß ~, daß er*** you have to hand it to him that he; → ***zugegeben***

'**zu·ge·fro·ren** **I.** *p.p. of* ***zufrieren***; **II.** *adj.* frozen over; icebound *harbo(u)r*; *car door etc.*: frozen shut

'**zu·ge·ge·ben** **I.** *p.p. of* ***zugeben***; **II.** *cj.* granted, F okay; ***~, es war nicht sehr geschickt*** granted (*or* okay), it wasn't very clever; **zu·ge·ge·be·ner·ma·ßen** ['tsu:gəge:bənɐ'ma:sən] *adv.* admittedly

zu·ge·gen [tsu'ge:gən] *pred. adj.* present (***bei*** *dat.* at); ***~ sein bei*** *dat.* *a.* attend

'**zu·ge·hen** (*irr.*, *sep.*, sn, → ***gehen***) **I.** *v/i.* **1.** ***~ auf*** *acc.* go up to, make for, head for; *fig.* ***auf j-n ~*** reach out to s.o.; break the ice again with s.o.; ***einer muß auf den anderen ~*** somebody's got to break the ice again (*or* make the first move); ***dem Ende ~*** be drawing to a close; ***auf die Achtzig ~*** be approaching (*or* getting on for) eighty; ***es geht auf den Herbst zu*** autumn is on its way; **2.** ***j-m ~*** *letter etc.*: reach s.o.; ***j-m et. ~ lassen*** have s.th. sent to s.o.; ***die Formulare gehen Ihnen in den nächsten Tagen zu*** you will be receiving the forms in the next few days; **3.** F shut; ***der Reißverschluß geht nicht zu*** I can't do the zip (*Am.* zipper) up; **4.** ***spitz ~*** taper to a point; **5.** *dial.* ***geh zu!*** F get a move on!, step on it!; **II.** *v/impers.* **6.** be; ***es geht dort manchmal etwas wild zu*** things can sometimes get a bit wild there; ***auf der Party ging's zu!*** it was some party!; ***so geht es im Leben manchmal zu*** that's life; ***es müßte seltsam ~, wenn*** it would be very strange if; → ***Ding*** 2

'**zu·ge·hö·rig** *adj.* **1.** accompanying; ***~e Teile*** accessory parts; ***die ~en Gebäude*** the buildings belonging (*or* that belong) to it; **2.** matching, ... to match; **3.** ***sich e-r Gruppe*** *etc.* ***~ fühlen*** feel part of a group *etc.*, feel one belongs to a group *etc.*; '**Zu·ge·hö·rig·keit** *f* (-; *no pl.*) affiliation (***zu*** *dat.* to, with); *pol. etc.* membership (of); '**Zu·ge·hö·rig·keits·ge·fühl** *n* (-[e]s; *no pl.*) sense of belonging (*or* being part of s.th.); feeling of identity (***zu*** *dat.* with)

'**zu·ge·klebt** *adj.* **1.** stuck; **2.** ***mit Plakaten*** *etc.* ***~*** covered in (F plastered with) posters *etc.*

'**zu·ge·knöpft** *fig. adj.* reserved, uncommunicative

Zü·gel ['tsy:gəl] *m* (-s; -) rein; ***ein Pferd am ~ führen*** lead a horse by the rein; ***e-m Pferd in die ~ fallen*** rein a horse in (*or* back); *fig.* ***die ~ anziehen*** tighten the reins; ***die ~ lockern*** loosen the reins; ***bei j-m die ~ kurz halten*** keep a tight rein on s.o.; ***die ~ an sich reißen*** take over control, take over at the helm; ***die ~ (fest) in der Hand haben*** have things (firmly) under control; ***j-m (e-r Sache) die ~ schießen lassen*** give free rein to s.o. (s.th.)

'**zu·ge·las·sen** **I.** *p.p. of* ***zulassen***; **II.** *adj.* admitted; authorized, recognized; *pharm.* approved, licen|sed (*Am.* -ced); *mot. etc.* registered; qualified *doctor etc.*; ⚖ ***~e Gesellschaft*** chartered company; ***für Jugendliche nicht ~*** for adults only

'**zu·ge·lau·fen** **I.** *p.p. of* ***zulaufen***; **II.** *adj.* stray *dog etc.*

'**zü·gel·los** *fig. adj.* a) unrestrained; *a.* unbridled *jealousy, envy etc.*, b) licentious, dissolute; '**Zü·gel·lo·sig·keit** *f* (-;

no pl.) a) (complete) lack of restraint, b) licentiousness

zü·geln ['tsy:gəln] *v/t.* (h) rein (up); *fig.* control, bridle, curb

'**zu·ge·parkt** *adj.* blocked (with parked cars); *road etc.* full of (F choc-a-block with) parked cars; ***die Straße ist ~ a.*** there's not a single parking space in the street

'**Zu·ge·rei·ste** *m, f* (-n; -n) incomer

'**zu·ge·rich·tet** *adj.*: ***übel ~*** in pretty bad shape; ***er (es) war übel ~ a.*** he (it) had taken some beating

'**zu·ge·schneit** *adj.* snowed up

'**zu·ge·schnit·ten I.** *p.p. of* ***zuschneiden***; **II.** *fig. adj.*: ***~ auf*** *acc.* tailored to, designed for

'**zu·ge·sel·len** *v/refl.* (*sep.*, h): ***sich j-m ~*** (go over and) join s.o.

'**zu·ge·spitzt I.** *adj.* **1.** pointed, sharp *stick etc.*; **2.** *fig.* ***~e Bemerkung*** exaggeration, overstatement; ***~e Formulierung*** overstatement; **II.** *adv.*: ***~ gesagt*** to put it in slightly exaggerated (*or* drastic) terms; ***er hat es ~ formuliert*** he overstated the case

zu·ge·stan·de·ner·ma·ßen ['tsu:gəʃtandənɐ'ma:sən] *adv.* admittedly

'**Zu·ge·ständ·nis** *n* (-ses; -se) concession; *a.* acknowledg(e)ment; ***~se machen*** make concessions (*dat.* to); *fig.* make allowances (***an*** *acc.* for)

'**zu·ge·ste·hen** *v/t.* (*irr.*, *sep.*, h, → ***gestehen***) **1.** concede, grant (***j-m et.*** s.o. s.th.); **2.** admit, concede

'**zu·ge·tan I.** *p.p. of* ***zutun***; **II.** *pred. adj.*: ***j-m (e-r Sache) ~ sein*** be fond of s.o. (s.th.); ***dem Wein*** *etc.* ***~ sein*** *a.* be (quite) partial to wine *etc.*

'**zu·ge·wach·sen I.** *p.p. of* ***zuwachsen***; **II.** *adj.* completely overgrown (***mit*** *dat.* with), covered (by, in)

'**zu·ge·wie·sen I.** *p.p. of* ***zuweisen***; **II.** *adj.* assigned; allocated

'**Zu·ge·winn** *m* (-[e]s; -e) increase; ✝ surplus; ***~ge·mein·schaft*** *f* ⚖ community of accrued gain

'**Zug|fe·der** *f* ⚙ tension spring; mainspring; ***~fe·stig·keit*** *f* ⚙ tensile strength

'**zug·frei** *adj.* draught-free, *Am.* draft-free

'**Zug·füh·rer** *m* **1.** 🚂 chief guard, *Am.* conductor; **2.** ⚔ platoon-leader

'**zu·gie·ßen** *v/t.* (*irr.*, *sep.*, h, → ***gießen***) **1.** add; ***darf ich Ihnen noch etwas ~?*** may I fill up your glass (*or* cup *etc.*)?, F may I top you up?; **2.** fill up *gap etc.* (***mit*** *dat.* with)

zu·gig ['tsu:gɪç] *adj.* draughty, *Am.* drafty

zü·gig ['tsy:gɪç] **I.** *adj.* quick, speedy; uninterrupted; **II.** *adv.*: ***~ vorankommen*** make rapid (*or* fast) progress; ***am Zoll*** *etc.* ***~ abgefertigt werden*** be whisked through customs *etc.*

'**Zug·klap·pe** *f* damper

'**Zug·kraft** *f* (-; ⸚e) **1.** *phys.* tractive force; **2.** *no pl. fig.* appeal; draw, attention value *of an advertisement etc.*; *s.o.'s* magnetism; '**zug·kräf·tig** *fig. adj.* popular-appeal ...; F attention-grabbing *ad etc.*; ***~ sein*** have (mass *or* popular) appeal, *film etc.*: be a crowd-puller

zu·gleich [tsu'glaɪç] *adv.* at the same time; together; ***sie ist schön und intelligent ~*** she's both beautiful and intelligent; she's not only beautiful, she's intelligent (*or* she's got intelligence) as well

'**Zug|luft** *f* (-; *no pl.*) draught, *Am.* draft; ***~ma,schi·ne*** *f* traction engine, tractor; ***~mit·tel*** *fig. n* draw, attraction; ***~num·mer*** *f thea. etc.* crowd-puller, big attraction, *a.* draw; ***~per·so,nal*** *n* train staff; ***~pferd*** *n* **1.** draught (*Am.* draft) horse; **2.** *fig.* crowd-puller, big attraction, *a.* draw; ***~pfla·ster*** *n* ⚕ blistering plaster

'**zu·grei·fen** *v/i.* (*irr.*, *sep.*, h, → ***greifen***) **1.** a) make a grab; grab (at) it, b) help o.s., c) *fig.* jump at (*or* grab) the opportunity; ***~ auf*** *acc. computer*: access; ***sofort ~*** accept (*or* say yes) straightaway; ***da hätte ich sofort zugegriffen*** *a.* I wouldn't have thought twice about it; **2.** lend a hand, F chip in

'**Zug|re·stau,rant** *n* restaurant (*or* dining, buffet) car, *Am.* diner; ***~rich·tung*** *f* (-; *no pl.*) direction of travel

'**Zu·griff** *m* (-[e]s; *no pl.*) **1.** (swift) action (***der Polizei*** *etc.* on the part of the police *etc.*); ***sich j-s ~ entziehen*** escape s.o.'s clutches, slip through s.o.'s fingers; **2.** *a. computer, CD-player etc.*: access (***zu*** *dat.*, ***auf*** *acc.* to); '**Zu·griffs·zeit** *f computer, CD-player etc.*: access time

zu·grun·de [tsu'grʊndə] *adv.* **1.** ***~ legen*** take as a basis (*dat.* for), apply; ***er legte s-n Behauptungen ... ~*** he based his allegations on ...; ***~ liegen*** underlie (*dat. s.th.*), be at the root of (*s.th.*); **2.** ***~ gehen*** *enterprise etc.*: go to pieces, go to rack and ruin; *empire*: collapse, decline; *person*: die, *lit.* perish; ***~ gehen an*** *dat.* come to grief with, die of; ***er ist daran ~ gegangen*** a) it was his undoing (*or* ruination), b) it was the death of him; → ***elend*** II; **3.** ***~ richten*** ruin, destroy, F wreck; ***sich (selber) ~ richten*** ruin one's health (*or* nerves), F kill o.s.

zu'grun·de·lie·gend *adj.* underlying

'**Zug|schaff·ner** *m* guard, *Am.* conductor; ***~seil*** *n* tow line; ***~stück*** *n thea.* box-office draw; ***~te·le,fon*** *n* train telephone; ***~tier*** *n* draught (*Am.* draft) animal

'**zu·gucken** F *v/i.* (*sep.*, h) → ***zuschauen***

'**Zug·un·glück** *n* train accident (*or* disaster); train crash

zu·gun·sten [tsu'gʊnstən] *prp.* (*gen. or dat.*) in favo(u)r of; for the benefit of; in aid of

zu·gu·te [tsu'gu:tə] *adv.*: ***j-m et. ~ halten*** give s.o. credit for s.th.; ***j-m s-e Jugend*** *etc.* ***~ halten*** make allowances for s.o.'s age *etc.*; ***~ kommen*** be of benefit to *s.o. or s.th.*, stand *s.o.* in good stead; ***das wird d-r Gesundheit ~ kommen*** it'll be good for your health, it'll do your health the world of good; ***das Geld wird e-m Krankenhaus ~ kommen*** the money will be donated to a hospital; ***j-m et. ~ kommen lassen*** give s.o. s.th.; ***sich etwas ~ tun auf*** *acc.* pride o.s. on

'**Zug|ver·bin·dung** *f* rail connection (*or* link); ***~ver·kehr*** *m* train services *pl.*; ***~ver·spä·tung*** *f* (train) delay; ***~vo·gel*** *m* bird of passage; *fig.* drifter; ***~zeit*** *f zo.* migrating season; ***~zwang*** *m*: ***in ~ geraten*** be forced to make a move; ***unter ~ stehen*** be under pressure to act (*or* make a move); ***j-n unter ~ bringen (*or* setzen)*** force s.o. into action (*or* to make a move)

'**zu·ha·ben** (*irr.*, *sep.*, h, → ***haben***) **I.** *v/i.* be closed; **II.** *v/t.* have *the door etc.* closed

'**zu·hal·ten** (*irr.*, *sep.*, h, → ***halten***) **I.** *v/t.* keep *s.th.* closed (*or* shut); ***sich die Ohren ~*** put (*or* hold) one's hands over one's ears; ***sich die Nase ~*** hold one's nose; **II.** *v/i.*: ***~ auf*** *acc.* make (*or* head) for

Zu·häl·ter ['tsu:hɛltɐ] *m* (-s; -) pimp; **Zu·häl·te·rei** [tsu:hɛltə'raɪ] *f* (-; *no pl.*) pimping

'**zu·hän·gen** *v/t.* (*sep.*, h) hang s.th. over (*or* across) *s.th.*

'**zu·hau·en** F *v/i. and v/t.* (*sep.*, h) → ***zuschlagen***

Zu·hau·se [tsu'haʊzə] *n* (-s; *no pl.*) home; ***sie hat kein ~*** she hasn't got a home

'**zu·hei·len** *v/i.* (*sep.*, sn) heal up

Zu·hil·fe·nah·me [tsu'hɪlfəna:mə] *f*: ***unter (ohne) ~*** *gen. or* ***von*** *dat.* with(out) the aid of

zu·hin·terst [tsu'hɪntɐst] *adv.* right at the back

'**zu·hö·ren** *v/i.* (h) listen (*dat.* to); ***hör mal zu!*** listen, *a.* now you just listen to me; ***genau ~*** listen carefully; ***du hast nicht richtig zugehört*** you haven't been listening

'**Zu·hö·rer** *m* (-s; -) listener; ***~bank*** *f* (-; ⸚e) listeners' bench

'**Zu·hö·re·rin** *f* (-; -nen) listener

'**Zu·hö·rer·kreis** *m* circle of listeners

'**Zu·hö·rer·schaft** *f* (-; *no pl.*) audience; *radio*: *a.* listeners *pl.*

'**zu·ju·beln** *v/i.* (*sep.*, h): ***j-m ~*** cheer s.o.

'**zu·keh·ren** *v/t.* (*sep.*, h) turn *s.th.* towards *s.o. or s.th.*; ***j-m das Gesicht ~*** turn (round) to face (*or* look at) s.o.; ***j-m den Rücken ~*** turn one's back to(wards) (*or* on) s.o.

'**zu·kit·ten** *v/t.* (*sep.*, h) cement (up)

'**zu·klap·pen** (*sep.*) **I.** *v/t.* (h) snap (*or* slam) *s.th.* shut; shut, clap *a book* shut; fold up *knife*; **II.** *v/i.* (sn) snap shut; slam shut

'**zu·kle·ben** *v/t.* (*sep.*, h) **1.** seal *envelope etc.*; **2.** stick *s.th.* over; paste over *a crack*; **3.** cover with, F plaster with; → ***zugeklebt***

'**zu·knal·len** (*sep.*) **I.** *v/t.* (h) slam *a door etc.* (shut); **II.** *v/i.* (sn) slam shut

'**zu·knei·fen** *v/t.* (*irr.*, *sep.*, h, → ***kneifen***): ***den Mund ~*** close one's mouth tight(ly), press one's lips together (tightly); ***die Augen ~*** close one's eyes tightly, screw one's eyes up

'**zu·knöp·fen** *v/t.* (*sep.*, h) button (up)

'**zu·kom·men** *v/i.* (*irr.*, *sep.*, sn, → ***kommen***) **1.** ***auf j-n ~*** a) come up to s.o., *a. fig.* approach s.o., b) *fig.* be in store for s.o.; ***wir werden auf Sie ~*** we'll contact you, we'll get in touch with you; ***wir lassen die Dinge auf uns ~*** we'll wait and see what happens, we'll take things as they come; ***er hatte keine Ahnung, was auf ihn zukam*** he had no idea what he was in for (*or* what was in store for him); **2.** a) fall to *s.o.*; be due to *s.o.*, b) befit *s.o.*; ***das kommt ihm nicht zu*** it's not for him to do *etc.* that; ***dieser Entwicklung*** *etc.* ***kommt große Bedeutung zu*** this is a development *etc.* of great significance; **3.** ***j-m et. ~ lassen*** give s.o. s.th.; *a.* send s.o. s.th.; see to it that s.o. gets s.th.

'**zu·kor·ken** *v/t.* (*sep.*, h) cork up

'**zu·krie·gen** F *v/t.* (*sep.*, h) → ***zubekommen***

Zu·kunft ['tsu:kʊnft] *f* (-; *no pl.*) future; *ling.* future (tense); ***in ~*** in future, for the future, from now on, *lit.* henceforth; ***in naher (nächster) ~*** in the near (immediate) future; ***in ferner (*or* weiter) ~*** in the distant future; ***das liegt noch in weiter***

~ that's a long way off yet; ***ein Blick in die*** ~ a glimpse ahead, a look at the crystal ball; ***e-e große*** ~ (***vor sich***) ***haben*** have a great future ahead (*or* in store for one); ***die*** ~ ***wird es lehren*** time will tell; ***abwarten, was die*** ~ ***bringt*** wait and see what the future has in store; ***j-m die*** ~ ***aus der Hand lesen*** read (the future from) s.o.'s palm; ***das bleibt der*** ~ ***überlassen*** that remains to be seen; ***ein Beruf mit*** ~ a job with a future (*or* with excellent prospects for the future); ***diese Arbeit hat keine*** ~ there's no future in this kind of work; ***dem Computer gehört die*** ~ the future lies with the computer; ***diesem jungen Spieler gehört die*** ~ this young player has the future in his hands

'**zu·künf·tig I.** *adj.* future; *a.* prospective *husband etc.*, ...-to-be; ⚖ expectant; ~***er Vater*** father-to-be; F ***m-e Zukünftige, mein Zukünftiger*** F my intended; ***die*** ~***e Entwicklung*** future developments; ***die*** ~***en Ereignisse*** future events; **II.** *adv.* in future

'**Zu·kunfts|angst** *f* fear of the future; ~**aus·sich·ten** *pl.* future prospects; ~**be·zo·gen I.** *adj.* forward-looking; **II.** *adv.* with a view to the future; ~**er·war·tun·gen** *pl.* future expectations, hopes for the future; ~**for·scher** *m* futurologist; ~**for·schung** *f* futurology; ~**ge·rich·tet** *adj.* forward-looking; ~**glau·be** *m* faith in the future; ~**mu,sik** *fig. f*: ***das ist alles noch*** ~ that's all still up in the air (*or* a long way off); ~**ori·en,tiert** *adj.* forward-looking; ~**per·spek,ti·ve** *f* future outlook, outlook for the future; ~**pes·si,mis·mus** *m* lack of faith in (*or* pessimism with regard to) the future; ~**plä·ne** *pl.* plans for the future; ~**reich** *adj.* promising; ***ein*** ~***er Beruf*** *a.* a career with a (great) future; ~**ro,man** *m* science fiction novel; ~**traum** *m* **1.** dream of the future; **2.** utopian dream; ~**vi·si,on** *f* future vision, vision of the future

'**zu·kunft·wei·send** *adj.* pioneer ...; ~***e Ideen*** *etc. a.* ideas *etc.* that point the way ahead (*or* point to the future)

'**zu·lä·cheln** *v/i.* (*sep.*, h): ***j-m*** ~ smile at s.o., give s.o. a smile

'**Zu·la·ge** *f* (-; -n) **1.** allowance; bonus; **2.** (*salary*) increase

zu·lan·de [tsu'landə] *adv.*: ***bei mir*** ~ where I come from

'**zu·lan·gen** *v/i.* (*sep.*, h) **1.** help o.s.; ***langt zu!*** *a.* F go for it; **2.** knuckle down; ***wir brauchen jemanden, der*** ~ ***kann*** we need someone who's not afraid of some hard physical work; **3.** lend a hand, F chip in

'**zu·las·sen** *v/t.* (*irr.*, *sep.*, h, → ***lassen***) **1.** admit *s.o.*; *adm.* licen|se (*Am.* -ce), *a.* register *car etc.*, *a.* approve *drug etc.*; qualify *doctor etc.*; ***j-n als Rechtsanwalt*** ~ call (*Am.* admit) s.o. to the Bar; ***et. zum Verkauf*** ~ approve s.th. (for sale); ***et. als Beweis*** ~ admit s.th. as evidence; ***zum Studium zugelassen werden*** get a place at university; → ***zugelassen***; **2.** allow; ⚖ approve, authorize; ***ich kann das nicht*** ~ I can't allow that; ***die Tatsachen lassen keinen Zweifel zu*** the facts leave no room for doubt; ***sein Stolz ließ es nicht zu, daß ...*** his pride wouldn't allow him to *inf.* (*or* prevented him from *ger.*); ***verschiedene Deutungen*** ~ be open to different interpretations; **3.** leave *door etc.* shut; not to open *window etc.*

zu·läs·sig ['tsu:lɛsɪç] *adj.* permissible; *adm.* authorized; ~***e Belastung*** safe load; ~***e Höchstgeschwindigkeit*** maximum (permissible) speed; ***das ist nicht*** ~ that is not allowed (*or* permitted, permissible)

Zu·las·sung ['tsu:lasʊŋ] *f* (-; -en) a) permission, b) licensing, c) *mot. etc.* licen|ce (*Am.* -se), registration, d) *univ. etc.* admission

'**Zu·las·sungs|be·schrän·kung** *f a. pl.* restricted admission; ~**num·mer** *f mot.* registration number; ~**pa,pie·re** *pl.* registration papers; ~**prü·fung** *f* entrance exam(ination); ~**schein** *m* licen|ce (*Am.* -se)

'**Zu·lauf** *m* (-[e]s; *no pl.*) **1.** ***großen*** ~ ***haben*** be (very) much in demand, be much sought-after, *a. film etc.*: be very popular; **2.** ⚙ inflow, feed; '**zu·lau·fen** *v/i.* (*irr.*, *sep.*, sn, → ***laufen***) **1.** ~ ***auf*** *acc.* a) run up to *s.o. or s.th.*, b) *road*: lead (up) to; **2.** ***j-m*** ~ *cat etc.*: stray to s.o., *people*: flock to s.o.; → ***zugelaufen***; **3.** *dial.* ***lauf zu!*** run!, F get a move on!, step on it!; **4.** *water etc.*: flow in; ~ ***lassen*** add, run *more water* in; **5.** ***spitz*** ~ taper to a point

'**zu·le·gen** (*sep.*, h) **I.** *v/t.* **1.** ***sich et.*** ~ get (*or* buy) o.s. s.th.; F ***sich e-e Freundin*** *etc.* ~ get (*or* find) o.s. a girlfriend *etc.*; F ***sich e-e Erkältung*** *etc.* ~ F land o.s. (with) a cold *etc.*; **2.** add (*dat.* to); **3.** → ***Zahn*** 2; **II.** F *v/i.* a) F step on it, b) F put it on

zu·lei·de [tsu'laɪdə] *adv.*: ***j-m et.*** ~ ***tun*** harm (*or* hurt) s.o.; → ***Fliege***

'**zu·lei·ten** *v/t.* (*sep.*, h) **1.** let in *water etc.*; ⚙ supply, feed; **2.** pass on to; ***j-m Informationen*** *etc.* ~ *a.* supply s.o. (*or* keep s.o. supplied) with information *etc.*

'**Zu·lei·tung** *f* (-; -en) supply (*gen.* of)

'**Zu·lei·tungs·rohr** *n* supply (*or* feed) pipe

zu·letzt [tsu'lɛtst] *adv.* **1.** last; ***mach das*** ~ do that last (*or* at the end); ***er kommt immer*** ~ he's always the last to arrive; ***bis*** ~ till (*or* to) the (very) end; ***wir blieben bis*** ~ *a.* we sat it out (to the end); ***wir hofften bis*** ~, ***daß*** we hoped to the last that; ***nicht*** ~, ***weil*** not least because; **2.** last, the last time; ***als ich ihn*** ~ ***sah*** when I last saw him; ***wann warst du*** ~ ***beim Zahnarzt?*** when was the last time you were at (*or* you went to) the dentist('s)?; **3.** in the end; ~ ***wollte er doch mitkommen*** in the end he decided to come after all

zu·lie·be [tsu'li:bə] *adv.*: ***j-m*** ~ for s.o.'s sake; ***s-r Ehe*** ~ for the sake of his marriage; ***tu's mir*** ~ do it for me

'**Zu·lie·fe,rant** *m* (outside) supplier

Zu·lie·fer·ar·beit ['tsu:li:fɐ-] *f a. pl.* ancillary work; '**Zu·lie·fer·be·trieb** *m*, **Zu·lie·fe·rer** ['tsu:li:fərɐ] *m* (-s; -) (outside) supplier; '**Zu·lie·fer·in·du,strie** *f* ancillary industry; '**zu·lie·fern** *v/t.* (*sep.*, h) supply; '**Zu·lie·fer·tei·le** *pl.* supplied parts; '**Zu·lie·fe·rung** *f* (-; -en) supply

Zu·lu[1] ['tsu:lu] *m* (-[s]; -[s]) Zulu

'**Zu·lu**[2] *n* (-[s]; *no pl.*) *ling.* Zulu, the Zulu language

'**Zu·lu·stamm** *m* Zulu tribe

zum [tsʊm] (= ***zu dem***) → ***zu*** I

'**zu·ma·chen** (*sep.*, h) **I.** *v/t.* **1.** shut, close *door*, *window etc.*; stop up *gap etc.*; seal *envelope etc.*; button (up), do up *coat etc.*; put down *umbrella*; ***ich habe kein Auge zugemacht*** I didn't sleep a wink; **2.** close down; ***das Geschäft*** ~ *a.* F shut up shop; **II.** *v/i.* **3.** *business*: close; **4.** *store etc.*: close down; **5.** F ***mach zu!*** F get a move on!, step on it!

zu·mal [tsu'ma:l] **I.** *cj.*: ~ (***da*** *or* ***weil***) particularly as (*or* since), F seeing as; **II.** *adv.* particularly, above all, in particular

'**zu·mar,schie·ren** *v/i.* (*sep.*, sn): ~ ***auf*** *acc.* march towards (*or* up to)

'**zu·mau·ern** *v/t.* (*sep.*, h) wall (*or* brick, block) up

zu·meist [tsu'maɪst] *adv.* mostly, for the most part

'**zu·mes·sen** *v/t.* (*irr.*, *sep.*, h, → ***messen***) portion out (*dat.* to); allot (to); *fig.* ***e-r Sache Bedeutung*** ~ attach importance to s.th.

zu·min·dest [tsu'mɪndəst] *adv.* at least; ***du hättest mir*** ~ ***Bescheid geben können*** *a.* the least you could have done is let me know; ***sie sind in Urlaub - glaube ich*** ~ they're on holiday - at least I think they are

'**zu·mi·schen** *v/t.* (*sep.*, h) add (*dat.* to)

zu·mut·bar ['tsu:mu:tba:ɐ] *adj.* not unreasonable, reasonable; ***das ist durchaus*** ~ ***für ihn*** it's not expecting too much of him; ***das ist doch nicht*** ~ that's expecting a bit much (***für*** *acc.* of), ***für ihn***: *a.* you can't expect him to do that; '**Zu·mut·bar·keit** *f* (-; *no pl.*) reasonableness

zu·mu·te [tsu'mu:tə] *adv.*: ***mir ist*** (***nicht***) ***wohl*** ~ I (don't) feel good; ***mir ist nicht danach*** ~ I don't feel like it, I'm not in the mood; ***mir ist nicht zum Lachen*** ~ I'm in no mood for laughter; ***mir war zum Heulen*** ~ I felt like crying

zu·mu·ten ['tsu:mu:tən] *v/t.* (h): ***j-m et.*** ~ expect s.th. of s.o.; ***das kannst du ihr nicht*** ~ you can't expect her to do that; ***sich zuviel*** ~ take on too much, F bite off more than one can chew

'**Zu·mu·tung** *f* (-; -en) imposition; cheek; ***das ist e-e*** ~ that's asking a bit much, F what a nerve, who does he think I am (*or* we are *etc.*)?

zu·nächst [tsu'nɛ:çst] *adv.* **1.** at first, initially; for a while; **2.** first of all, to start with; **3.** for the time being

'**zu·na·geln** *v/t.* (*sep.*, h) nail up; nail down *lid etc.*

'**zu·nä·hen** *v/t.* (*sep.*, h) sew (up)

Zu·nah·me ['tsu:na:mə] *f* (-; -n) increase (*gen. or* ***an*** *dat.* in); ⚔ buildup (of)

'**Zu·na·me** *m* (-ns; -n) surname, last (*or* second) name

Zünd|an·la·ge ['tsʏnt-] *f mot.* ignition system; ~**ein·stel·lung** *f* ignition (*or* injection) timing

zün·den ['tsʏndən] (h) **I.** *v/i.* **1.** catch fire; *wood*: kindle; *match*: light; *engine*, *rocket*: fire; *gas mixture*: ignite; *explosives*: detonate, go off; *lightning*: strike; ***das Streichholz zündet nicht*** the match won't light (*or* strike); **2.** *fig. idea etc.*: arouse enthusiasm; catch on; **II.** *v/t.* light, strike *match*; fire *engine*, *rocket*; detonate, set off *explosives*; **III.** F *v/impers.*: ***bei ihm hat's gezündet*** F the penny has (finally) dropped; '**zün·dend** *fig. adj.* stirring, rousing

Zun·der ['tsʊndɐ] *m* (-s; -) **1.** ***brennen wie*** ~ burn like tinder; **2.** F ***j-m*** ~ ***geben*** F give s.o. (merry) hell; ***es gibt*** ~ F he's in for it

Zün·der ['tsʏndɐ] *m* (-s; -) fuse; detonator

Zünd|flam·me ['tsʏnt-] *f* pilot light; **~fun·ke** *m mot.* (ignition) spark; **~holz** *n*, **~hölz·chen** *n* match; **~holz·schach·tel** *f* matchbox; **~ka·bel** *n mot.* ignition cable; **~ker·ze** *f mot.* spark plug; **~plätt·chen** *n* cap; **~satz** *m* igniting charge; **~schal·ter** *m*, **~schloß** *n mot.* ignition switch; **~schlüs·sel** *m mot.* ignition key; **~schnur** *f* fuse; **~spu·le** *f mot.* ignition coil; **~stein** *m* flint; **~stoff** *m* (-[e]s; *no pl.*) **1.** inflammable matter; **2.** *fig.* dynamite; fuel (**zu** *dat.* for *a discussion etc.*)

Zün·dung ['tsʏndʊŋ] *f* (-; -en) ignition

Zünd·vor·rich·tung ['tsʏnt-] *f* ignition device

'zu·neh·men *v/i.* (*irr.*, *sep.*, h, → **neh·men**) **1.** increase (**an** *dat.* in); *number*: *a.* go up; grow; *days*: get longer; *moon*: wax; *wind*: get stronger, *rain*: get heavier; *pain*: get worse; *applause*: grow (louder); ***die Kälte nimmt zu*** it's getting colder; **2.** put on weight; **'zu·neh·mend I.** *adj.* increasing, growing; ***~er Mond*** waxing moon; ***mit ~em Alter*** as one gets older, with increasing age, with advancing years; ***~e Erkenntnis*** growing realization; ***in ~em Maße → II***; **→ *Bewölkung*; II.** *adv.* increasingly, more and more; ***sich ~ verschlechtern*** get increasingly worse, get worse and worse

'zu·nei·gen (*sep.*, h) **I.** *v/refl.* **1.** ***sich j-m (e-r Sache) ~*** lean towards s.o. (s.th.); **2.** ***sich dem Ende ~*** draw to a close; **II.** *v/i.*: ***der Ansicht ~, daß*** be inclined to think that

'Zu·nei·gung *f* (-; *no pl.*) affection (**für** *acc.*, **zu** *dat.* for)

Zunft [tsʊnft] *f* (-; Zünfte ['tsʏnftə]) **1.** guild; **2.** F *contp.* bunch, shower

zünf·tig ['tsʏnftɪç] **I.** *adj.* real; proper (*a.* F); **II.** *adv.*: ***es ging ~ zu*** they *etc.* were having a good time of it

'Zunft·we·sen *n* (-s; *no pl.*) guilds *pl.*, system of guilds

Zun·ge ['tsʊŋə] *f* (-; -n) **1.** *anat.* tongue (*a. gastr. and fig.*); ***böse (spitze) ~*** malicious (sharp) tongue; ***e-e feine ~ haben*** have a fine palate; ***e-e schwere ~ haben*** slur one's speech (*or* words); ***die ~ herausstrecken*** stick (*or* poke) one's tongue out (*dat.* at), ⚕ put one's tongue out; ***mit der ~ anstoßen*** lisp, have a lisp; ***sich auf die ~ beißen*** bite one's tongue, *fig.* bite one's lips; ***er beißt sich eher die ~ ab, als etwas zu sagen*** he'd rather swallow his tongue than say anything; *fig.* ***sich die ~ abbrechen*** get one's tongue (all) in a twist; ***da bricht man sich ja die ~ ab!*** how are you supposed to get your tongue round that?; ***sich die ~ verbrennen*** open one's mouth too wide; ***mit zwei ~n sprechen*** speak with a forked tongue; ***mir klebt die ~ am Gaumen*** I'm parched; ***s-e ~ an j-m wetzen*** say nasty things about s.o.; ***böse ~n behaupten, daß*** there's some nasty gossip going round that; ***es lag mir auf der ~*** it was on the tip of my tongue; ***es brannte ihm auf der ~, es weiterzusagen*** he was bursting (*or* dying) to tell someone; ***hüte d-e ~!*** mind your tongue!; ***wir werden ihm noch die ~ lockern*** we'll loosen his tongue (*or* get him to talk) yet; **→ *Herz, lösen* 2, *zergehen*; 2.** pointer, needle *of a balance*

zün·geln ['tsʏŋəln] *v/i.* (h) **1.** *snake*: flicker its tongue (in and out); **2.** *flame*: flicker, shoot up; **~ *an*** *dat.* lick

'Zun·gen|akro,ba·tik F *f* contortions *pl.* of the tongue; ***das ist ja die reinste ~!*** F you have to be careful not to strain your tongue (*or* tie your tongue up in knots) trying to pronounce that; **~be·lag** *m* ⚕ coating of the tongue; coated (*or* furred) tongue

'Zun·gen·bre·cher *m* (-s; -) tongue-twister; **'zun·gen·bre·che·risch** [-brɛçərɪʃ] *adj.* tongue-twisting ...

'zun·gen·fer·tig *adj.* articulate, *contp.* glib; ***sie ist sehr ~*** *a.* she's never at a loss for words; **'Zun·gen·fer·tig·keit** *f* (-; *no pl.*) articulacy, *contp.* glibness

'Zun·gen|kuß *m* French kiss; **~laut** *m ling.* lingual (sound); **~schlag** *m* **1.** ***falscher ~*** slip of the tongue; **2.** ⚕ stammer; **3.** ♪ tonguing; **~spit·ze** *f* tip of the tongue; **~wur·zel** *f* base of the tongue

Züng·lein ['tsʏŋlaɪn] *n* (-s; -): *fig.* ***das ~ an der Waage bilden*** tip the scales

zu·nich·te [tsu'nɪçtə] *adv.*: **~ *machen*** destroy, ruin; *a.* shatter *hopes*, put paid to, F scupper *plans etc.*; **~ *werden*** come to nothing (*or* naught)

'zu·nicken *v/i.* (*sep.*, h): ***j-m ~*** nod at s.o., give s.o. a nod; ***j-m freundlich ~*** give s.o. a friendly nod; ***j-m grüßend ~*** nod (at s.o.) in greeting, greet s.o. with a nod

zu·nut·ze [tsu'nʊtsə] *adv.*: ***sich et. ~ machen*** make (good) use of s.th.; take advantage of s.th.

zu·oberst [tsu'oːbɐst] *adv.* a) (right) at the top, b) at the head (of the table)

'zu·ord·nen *v/t.* (*sep.*, h): ***e-r Sache ~*** assign to s.th., class with s.th.; ***den Reptilien*** *etc.* ***zugeordnet werden*** be classified as a reptile *etc.*, belong to the reptile *etc.* family; ***e-m Künstler (e-r Zeit*** *etc.*) **~** ascribe to an artist (a period *etc.*); ***er läßt sich schwer ~*** he's hard to place (*or* categorize)

'zu·packen (*sep.*, h) **I.** *v/i.* **1.** make a grab; grab (at) it; **2.** knuckle down, get down to it; ***jemand, der ~ kann*** someone who's willing to roll up his sleeves, someone who's not afraid of some hard physical work; **II.** *v/t.*: ***j-n ~*** swaddle s.o. in blankets *etc.*; **'zu·packend** *adj.* hands-on ...; ***er hat e-e ~e Art*** he doesn't waste any time (getting things done)

'zu·par·ken *v/t.* (*sep.*, h) block, obstruct; **→ *zugeparkt***

zup·fen ['tsʊpfən] (h) **I.** *v/i.* pull (**an** *dat.* at), tug (at); ***j-n am Ärmel*** *etc.* **~** tug at s.o.'s sleeve *etc.*; **II.** *v/t.* pluck

'Zupf·in·stru,ment *n* plucked instrument

'zu·pfla·stern *v/t.* (*sep.*, h): **~ *mit*** *dat.* cover with, F plaster with; ***sie haben die Stadt mit Betonklötzen zugepflastert*** they've covered every square inch of the town with concrete blocks

'zu·pro·sten *v/i.* (*sep.*, h): ***j-m ~*** raise one's glass to s.o.

zur [tsuːɐ] (= ***zu der***) → ***zu*** I

'zu·ra·ten I. *v/i.* (*irr.*, *sep.*, h, → ***raten***): ***j-m zu et. ~*** advise s.o. to do s.th.; **II.** ℞ *n* (-s; *no pl.*): ***auf sein ~*** on his advice

'zu·rau·nen *v/t.* (*sep.*, h): ***j-m et. ~*** whisper s.th. into s.o.'s ear

'zu·rech·nen *v/t.* (*sep.*, h) **1.** add (**zu** *dat.* to); **2.** ascribe to; **3. → *zuordnen***

'zu·rech·nungs·fä·hig *adj.* accountable, of sound mind; ⚖ *a.* compos mentis; ***ist er ~?*** *a.* can he be held accountable (*or* responsible)?; **'Zu·rech·nungs·fä·hig·keit** *f* (-; *no pl.*) accountability; ⚖ ***verminderte ~*** diminished responsibility

zu·recht|ba·steln [tsu'rɛçt-] *v/t.* (*sep.*, h) rig up (*a.* F *fig.*); **~bie·gen** *v/t.* (*irr.*, *sep.*, h, → ***biegen***) **1.** bend *s.th.* into the right shape; **2.** F *fig.* a) twist *facts etc.* to one's own advantage, b) straighten *s.o.* out; ***die Sache ~*** straighten things out

zu'recht·fin·den *v/refl.* (*irr.*, *sep.*, h, → ***finden***): ***sich ~* 1.** find one's way (around); **2.** *fig.* a) manage, cope (***mit*** *dat.* with *s.th.*), b) F get the hang of it, c) settle in; ***findest du dich zurecht?*** will you be all right (*Am.* alright)?; ***ich find' mich überhaupt nicht mehr zurecht*** I don't know what's going on any more (*or* where to start looking), I'm lost; ***ich find' mich mit diesem System überhaupt nicht zurecht*** I can't make head or tail of this system

zu'recht·kom·men *v/i.* (*irr.*, *sep.*, sn, → ***kommen***) **1.** manage, cope (***mit*** *dat.* with); ***mit j-m ~*** get on with s.o.; ***kommst du zurecht?*** are you (managing) all right (*Am.* alright)?; ***kommen Sie zurecht?*** can I help you?; ***ich komme mit diesem Computer nicht zurecht*** I can't work this computer out; **2.** get there (*or* make it) in time

zu'recht|le·gen *v/t.* (*sep.*, h) **1.** a) put out, b) arrange; **2.** *fig.* ***sich e-e Ausrede*** *etc.* **~** have an excuse *etc.* ready; **~ma·chen** (*sep.*, h) **I.** *v/t.* get *s.th.* ready, prepare; make *bed*; dress *salad etc.*; **II.** *v/refl.*: ***sich ~*** a) get (o.s.) ready, b) do o.s. up; **~rücken** *v/t.* (*sep.*, h) **1.** straighten *s.th.* (out); **2.** *fig.* put *s.th.* straight; ***die Sache ~*** put things (*or* matters) straight; **~schnei·den** *v/t.* (*irr.*, *sep.*, h, → ***schneiden***) cut into shape, cut up; **~set·zen** *v/t.* (*sep.*, h) set right, put straight; put in the right place; **~stau·chen** F *v/t.* (*sep.*, h) haul *s.o.* over the coals; **~stut·zen** *v/t.* (*sep.*, h) **1.** ✂ trim, clip; **2.** F *fig.* ***et. ~*** get s.th. into shape; ***j-n ~*** F cut s.o. down to size

zu'recht·wei·sen *v/t.* (*irr.*, *sep.*, h, → ***weisen***) reprimand, F give *s.o.* a wigging (*or* dressing-down); **Zu'recht·wei·sung** *f* (-; -en) reprimand, rebuke

zu'recht·zim·mern *v/t.* (*sep.*, h) F cobble together

'zu·re·den I. *v/i.* (*sep.*, h): ***j-m (gut) ~*** a) try to persuade s.o., b) coax s.o. into doing it, c) encourage s.o. (to do it); ***ich mußte ihm lange ~*** I really had to work on him; **II.** ℞ *n* (-s; *no pl.*) coaxing, urging; encouragement; ***gütliches ~*** moral suasion; ***erst nach langem ~*** only after a great deal of coaxing *etc.*

'zu·rei·chen *v/t.* (*sep.*, h): ***j-m et. ~*** pass s.o. s.th.

'zu·rei·ten (*irr.*, *sep.*, → ***reiten***) **I.** *v/t.* (h) break in *horse*; **II.** *v/i.* (sn): **~ *auf*** *acc.* ride up to

'zu·rich·ten *v/t.* (*sep.*, h) prepare; ⚙ dress; cut, trim *wood*, *stone*; *textil.* finish; *typ.* get *s.th.* ready; ***übel ~*** injure *s.o.* badly, *a.* beat *s.o.* up badly, make a mess of *s.th.*; **→ *zugerichtet***

'zu·rie·geln *v/t.* (*sep.*, h) bolt

zür·nen ['tsʏrnən] *lit.* *v/i.* (h) be angry ([***mit***] ***j-m*** with s.o.; ***über*** *acc.* at, about)

zur·ren ['tsʊrən] *v/t.* (h) lash, tie

Zur·schau·stel·lung [tsʊr'ʃaʊʃtɛlʊŋ] *f* (-; -en) exhibition; *contp.* parading, flaunting

zu·rück [tsu'rʏk] **I.** *adv.* a) back, backwards, b) behind; ***~!*** a) hold it!, b) stand back!; ***e-n Schritt ~ tun*** go back a step, take a step back(wards); ***11 Punkte*** ~ *sport*: 11 points down; ~ ***an den Absender*** return to sender; ***mit bestem Dank*** ~ returned with thanks; ~ ***sein*** a) *ped.* be (lagging) behind, b) be a late developer, 🚂 be late, c) be a bit backward, d) be behind the times; be backward; **II.** ♀ *n* (-s; *no pl.*): ***es gibt kein*** ~ ***(mehr)*** there's no turning back (now)

zu'rück|be·ge·ben *v/refl.*: ***sich*** ~ (*irr., sep.*, h, → ***begeben***) return, go back; ***sich nach Hause*** ~ return home, go back home, go home again; **~be·glei·ten** *v/t.* (*sep.*, h) see (*or* walk) *s.o.* back (*or* home); **~be·hal·ten** *v/t.* (*irr., sep.*, h, → ***behalten***) **1.** hold onto, keep (back); withhold; **2.** be left with *a scar etc.*; **~be·kom·men** *v/t.* (*irr., sep.*, h, → ***bekommen***) get back; **~be·or·dern** *v/t.* (*sep.*, h) order back; **~be·ru·fen** *v/t.* (*irr., sep.*, h, → ***berufen***) recall; **~bil·den** *v/refl.*: ***sich*** ~ (*sep.*, h) recede; *biol.* regress; **~bin·den** *v/t.* (*irr., sep.*, h, → ***binden***) tie back; **~blei·ben** *v/i.* (*irr., sep.*, sn, → ***bleiben***) **1.** stay behind; **2.** a) *a. ped.* fall behind, be (lagging) behind, b) be backward; → ***zurückgeblieben*** II; **3.** ~ ***hinter*** *dat.* fall short of *expectations etc.*; **4.** be left; remain; **~blen·den** *v/i.* (*sep.*, h) *film*: go back (***auf*** *acc.* to), *a. fig.* flash back (to); **~blicken** *v/i.* (*sep.*, h) look back (***auf*** *acc.* at); *fig.* look back (on); **~brin·gen** *v/t.* (*irr., sep.*, h, → ***bringen***) bring back (***ins Leben*** to life); **~da'tie·ren** (*sep.*, h) **I.** *v/t.* backdate; **II.** *fig. v/i.*: ~ ***auf*** *acc.* date back to; **~den·ken** *v/i.* (*irr., sep.*, h, → ***denken***) think back (***an*** *acc.* to); ~ ***an*** *acc. a.* recall (to memory); **~drän·gen** (*sep.*, h) **I.** *v/t.* drive back; *fig.* restrain; suppress; **II.** *v/i. crowd*: fall back; **~dre·hen** *v/t.* (*sep.*, h) a) turn (*or* put) back, b) turn down *sound etc.*; **~dür·fen** *v/i.* (*irr., sep.*, h, → ***dürfen***) be allowed back; **~ent·wickeln** *v/refl.*: ***sich*** ~ (*sep.*, h) **1.** → ***zurückbilden***; **2.** ☤ be falling off; **~er·in·nern** *v/refl.*: ***sich*** ~ (*sep.*, h) remember, recall (***an*** *acc. s.o. or s.th.*); **~er·obern** *v/t.* (*sep.*, h) recapture; *fig.* win back

zu'rück·er·stat·ten *v/t.* (*sep.*, h) refund, reimburse; **Zu'rück·er·stat·tung** *f* (-; -en) refunding, reimbursement

zu'rück|er·war·ten *v/t.* (*sep.*, h) expect *s.o.* back; **~fah·ren** (*irr., sep.*, → ***fahren***) **I.** *v/i.* (sn) **1.** go back, return; *mot. a.* drive back; **2.** *fig.* recoil, shrink back (***vor*** *dat.* in *terror etc.*); **II.** *v/t.* (h) **3.** drive *s.o. or s.th.* back; **4.** throttle down *engine, fig. production etc.*; **~fal·len** *v/i.* (*irr., sep.*, sn, → ***fallen***) **1.** fall back; **2.** *sport*: fall behind, drop back; **3.** ~ ***in*** *acc.* lapse back into, revert to; → ***Schlendrian*** 1; **4.** ~ ***an*** *acc. property etc.*: revert to *s.o.*; **5.** ~ ***auf*** *acc. disgrace etc.*: reflect on *s.o.*; **~fin·den** *v/i. and v/refl.* (***sich*** ~) (*irr., sep.*, h, → ***finden***) find one's way back (***zu*** *dat.* to) (*a. fig.*); *fig.* ***zu sich selbst*** ~ get back on an even keel; **~flie·gen** *v/i.* (*irr., sep.*, sn, → ***fliegen***) fly back; **~flie·ßen** *v/i.* (*irr., sep.*, sn, → ***fließen***) flow back (*a. fig.* ☤); ~ ***lassen an*** *acc.* feed back to; **~for·dern** *v/t.* (*sep.*, h) ask for *s.th.* back, demand *s.th.* back; **~fra·gen** *v/i.* (*sep.*, h) **1.** ask in reply; **2.** → ***rückfragen***; **~füh·ren** (*sep.*, h) **I.** *v/t.* **1.** lead back; **2.** ***j-n in sein Land*** ~ send s.o. back to his (*or* her) home country, repatriate s.o.; **3.** *fig.* ~ ***auf*** *acc.* reduce to *s.th.*; ***et.*** ~ ***auf*** *acc.* put s.th. down to, attribute s.th. to, explain s.th. by; ***das führt mich auf ein Problem zurück*** that brings me back to (*or* reminds me of) a problem; ***der Unfall ist auf Leichtsinn zurückzuführen*** the accident has been put down to (*or* was due to) carelessness; **II.** *v/i. path etc.*: lead (*or* go) back (***nach*** *dat.* to); **~ge·ben** *v/t.* (*irr., sep.*, h, → ***geben***) **1.** give back, return; ***es gab ihm sein Selbstwertgefühl zurück*** it gave him back his self-esteem; **2.** *soccer*: pass back; **3.** retort; **~ge·blie·ben** **I.** *p.p. of* ***zurückbleiben***; **II.** *adj.* backward, retarded; **~ge·hen** *v/i.* (*irr., sep.*, sn, → ***gehen***) **1.** a) go back, return, b) ⚔ retreat, fall back; ***zwei Schritte*** ~ step two paces back, take two steps back; ☎ ~ ***lassen*** return, send back; **2.** *fig.* ~ ***auf*** *acc.* go back to, *a.* date (*or* hark) back to *the eighteenth century etc.*; ***die Kirche geht auf ein romanisches Kloster zurück*** the church goes back to (*or* can be traced back to, was originally) a Romanesque monastery; **3.** decrease, diminish; drop; *temperature*: go down, drop; *swelling*: go down, recede; *pain*: ease; ☤ *business*: fall off; *prices*: slip, fall, go down

zu'rück·ge·legt *adj.* **1.** **~es Geld** savings; **2.** ***~e Strecke*** distance covered, *mot. etc. a.* mileage

zu'rück·ge·wie·sen **I.** *p.p. of* ***zurückweisen***; **II.** *adj.* rejected; ***~e Flüchtlinge*** refugees turned back at the border *etc.*

zu'rück·ge·win·nen *v/t.* (*irr., sep.*, h, → ***gewinnen***) win back; ⚔ *a.* reconquer, regain (*a. fig. self-confidence etc.*)

zu'rück·ge·zo·gen **I.** *p.p. of* ***zurückziehen***; **II.** *adj.* secluded *life*; withdrawn *person*; **III.** *adv.*: ***er lebt sehr*** ~ he leads a very secluded life, he's cut himself off from society; **Zu'rück·ge·zo·gen·heit** *f* (-; *no pl.*) (life of) seclusion

zu'rück·grei·fen *v/i.* (*irr., sep.*, h, → ***greifen***) **1.** ~ ***auf*** *acc.* fall back on; **2.** ***weiter*** ~ go further back; ***ein wenig*** ~ go back a bit

zu'rück·hal·ten (*irr., sep.*, h, → ***halten***) **I.** *v/t.* **1.** hold back, keep back; detain; ***ich will Sie nicht*** ~ I don't want to keep you; *fig.* ***j-n von e-r Dummheit*** ~ keep s.o. from doing something stupid; **2.** keep back, withhold; **3.** suppress; restrain *anger etc.*; hold back *one's tears*; **II.** *v/refl.*: ***sich*** ~ **4.** be reserved; keep (o.s.) to o.s.; **5.** restrain o.s.; hold back; ***sich*** ~ ***mit*** *dat.* go easy on *food, drink*; **III.** *v/i.*: ~ ***mit*** *dat.* hide *feelings*; withhold *opinion etc.*; **zu'rück·hal·tend** **I.** *adj.* reserved (*a.* ☤); unobtrusive; low-key; ***nicht*** ~ ***sein mit*** *dat.* be unsparing with; **II.** *adv. react etc.* coolly; *replay etc.* cautiously; **Zu'rück·hal·tung** *fig. f* (-; *no pl.*) a) reserve, restraint, b) modesty; ~ ***üben*** keep a low profile, keep one's head down, *pol.* act with restraint; ***s-e*** ~ ***ablegen*** shed all (*or* one's) restraint

zu'rück|ho·len *v/t.* (*sep.*, h) fetch back; ask *s.o.* to come back; **~kau·fen** *v/t.* (*sep.*, h) buy back; **~keh·ren** *v/i.* (*sep.*, sn) return, go (*or* come) back; ***aus der Gefangenschaft*** ~ return from captivity (*or* from the prisoner-of-war camp); *fig.* ***sein Bewußtsein kehrte allmählich zurück*** he gradually regained (*or* recovered) his consciousness; ***zum Ausgangsthema*** ~ get (*or* come) back to the original topic; → ***Schoß***; **~klap·pen** *v/t.* (*sep.*, h) fold back; **~kom·men** *v/i.* (*irr., sep.*, sn, → ***kommen***) come back (*fig.* ***auf*** *acc.* to), return; *fig.* ***auf j-s Angebot*** ~ take s.o. up on an offer, take up s.o.'s offer; ☤ ***wir kommen zurück auf Ihr Schreiben vom ...*** we refer to your letter of ...; **~kön·nen** *v/i.* (*irr., sep.*, h, → ***können***) be able to go back (*or* return); *fig.* ***jetzt kann ich nicht zurück*** I can't go back on my word (*or* decision *etc.*) now; **~kreu·zen** *v/t.* (*sep.*, h) *biol.* backcross; **~las·sen** *v/t.* (*irr., sep.*, h, → ***lassen***) **1.** leave behind (*a. fig.*); **2.** allow *s.o.* to return; **~lau·fen** *v/i.* (*irr., sep.*, sn, → ***laufen***) run back; **~le·gen** (*sep.*, h) **I.** *v/t.* **1.** a) put back, b) put aside, keep (***j-m*** for s.o.), c) *fig.* put aside, save *money*; **2.** lay (*or* lean) back *one's head*; **3.** *fig.* cover (*a. sport*), *a.* walk *a distance etc.*; → ***zurückgelegt*** 2; **II.** *v/refl.*: ***sich*** ~ lie back; **~leh·nen** (*sep.*, h) **I.** *v/t.* lean back; **II.** *v/refl.*: ***sich*** ~ lean back, ***in*** *acc.* settle back into *armchair etc.*; **~lei·ten** *v/t.* (*sep.*, h) lead back; turn back; ☎ return; **~lie·gen** *v/i.* (*irr., sep.*, h, → ***liegen***) **1.** ***das liegt drei Jahre zurück*** that was three years ago; ***liegt es schon so weit zurück?*** was it that long ago?; **2.** *sport*: ***3:0*** ~ be 3-0 (= three-nil) down; ***um fünf Punkte*** ~ be five points down (*or* behind); **~locken** *v/t.* (*sep.*, h) lure back; **~mel·den** *v/refl.*: ***sich*** ~ (*sep.*, h) report back (***bei*** *dat.* to *s.o.*); **~müs·sen** *v/i.* (*irr., sep.*, h, → ***müssen***) have to go back; ***das Buch muß zurück*** the book has to be returned; ***der Schreibtisch muß zurück*** the desk has to be moved back; **~neh·men** *v/t.* (*irr., sep.*, h, → ***nehmen***) **1.** a) take *s.th.* back, b) take back, withdraw, *formal*: recant; revoke, *a.* go back on *a decision, promise, an offer etc.*; cancel *offer etc.*, c) ⚖ withdraw, drop; ***nimmst du das zurück?*** are you going to take that back?; **2.** ⚔ withdraw; **3.** *chess etc.*: take back *a move*; **4.** *mot.* ***Gas*** ~ throttle back; **~pfei·fen** *v/t.* (*irr., sep.*, h, → ***pfeifen***) whistle back *dog*; *fig.* ***j-n*** ~ pull s.o. up short; **~pral·len** *v/i.* (*sep.*, sn) a) rebound; bounce (***von*** *dat.* off), b) recoil, jump back (***vor*** *dat.* from *fright, horror etc.*); **~rech·nen** *v/t.* (*sep.*, h) count back; **~rei·chen** (*sep.*, h) **I.** *v/t.* hand back, return (*a. documents*); **II.** *fig. v/i.*: ~ ***(bis) in*** *acc.* go (*or* date) back to; **~rei·sen** *v/i.* (*sep.*, sn) travel back, return; **~rol·len** *v/t.* (*sep.*, h) *and v/i.* (sn) roll back; **~ru·fen** *v/t.* (*irr., sep.*, h, → ***rufen***) call back; *teleph.* (*a. v/i.*) *a.* ring (*or* phone) back; *fig.* recall *car etc.*; *fig.* ***ins Gedächtnis*** ~ recall (to memory); ***j-n ins Leben*** ~ bring s.o. back to life; **~schal·len** *v/i.* (*sep.*, h) echo (back), resound; **~schal·ten** (*sep.*, h) **I.** *v/t.* switch back; **II.** *v/i. mot.* change (*Am.* shift) down; **~schau·en** *v/i.* (*sep.*, h) look back (***auf*** *acc.* at); *fig.* look back (on); **~scheu·en** *v/i.* (*sep.*, sn) shrink (back) (***vor*** *dat.* from), ba(u)lk (at); ***er scheut vor nichts zurück*** he'll stop at nothing, he'll go to any length(s); **~schicken** *v/t.* (*sep.*, h) send *s.o. or s.th.* back; *a.* return *s.th.*; **~schie·ben** *v/t.* (*irr., sep.*, h, → ***schieben***) push back; **~schla·gen** (*irr., sep.*, → ***schlagen***) **I.** *v/t.* (h) **1.** a) hit *s.o.* back, b) beat off *enemy, attack etc.*; **2.** fold back *blanket etc.*; throw open *coat etc.*; turn down *collar etc.*; **3.** *tennis*:

return *ball*; **II.** *v/i.* **4.** (h) *a. fig.* hit (*or* strike) back; ⚔ *a.* retaliate; **5.** (sn) *flame*: flare back; **6.** (sn) *fig.* ~ ***auf*** *acc.* affect, have a backlash effect on; **~schlep·pen** (*sep.*, h) **I.** *v/t.* drag *s.o. or s.th.* back; **II.** *v/refl.*: ***sich*** ~ drag o.s. back; **~schnel·len** *v/i.* (*sep.*, sn) spring (*or* snap) back; **~schrau·ben** *fig. v/t.* (*sep.*, h) lower; ***s-e Ansprüche*** ~ lower one's sights; **~schrecken** *v/i.* (*sep.*, sn): ~ ***vor*** *dat.* shrink back from; ***er schreckt vor nichts zurück*** he'll stop at nothing, he'll go to any length(s); **~schrei·ben** *v/i.* (*irr.*, *sep.*, h, → ***schreiben***) write back, reply; **~seh·nen** *v/refl.*: ***sich*** ~ (*sep.*, h): ***sich ~ nach*** *dat.* long to be back in *Berlin etc. or* with *s.o.*), long for *one's youth etc.* again; **~sen·den** *v/t.* (*sep.*, h) → ***zurückschicken***

zu'rück·set·zen *v/t.* (*sep.*, h) **1.** put (*or* move) *s.th.* back; back *a car*; **2.** *fig.* slight *s.o.*; **Zu'rück·set·zung** *f* (-; -en) slight; ***et. als ~ empfinden*** take s.th. as a slight

zu'rück|sin·ken *v/i.* (*irr.*, *sep.*, sn, → ***sinken***) sink back (***in*** *acc.* into *a chair etc.*); **~spie·len** *v/t. and v/i.* (*sep.*, h) *sport*: pass (the ball) back; **~sprin·gen** *v/i.* (*irr.*, *sep.*, sn, → ***springen***) **1.** jump back; *ball*: bounce back; **2.** △ recede; **~spu·len** (*sep.*, h) **I.** *v/t.* wind (*or* run) *tape etc.* back (to the beginning), *a. phot.* rewind; **II.** *v/i.* wind (*or* run) the tape back (to the beginning), rewind (the tape); *phot.* rewind the film; **~stecken** (*sep.*, h) **I.** *v/t.* put *s.th.* back; **II.** *fig. v/i.* come down a peg or two; lower one's sights; **~ste·hen** *v/i.* (*irr.*, *sep.*, h, → ***stehen***) **1.** *house etc.*: be set back; **2.** *fig.* ***hinter j-m*** ~ a) be (trailing *or* lagging) behind s.o., b) have to take second place to s.o.; ***sie steht an Begabung nicht hinter ihrer Schwester zurück*** she's every bit as talented as her sister; ***sie mußte immer*** ~ she always came off worst; ***keiner wollte*** ~ nobody wanted to be left out (*or* be the odd man out); ***hinter keinem*** ~ be second to none; **~stel·len** *v/t.* (*sep.*, h) **1.** put back; *a.* turn back *one's watch*; **2.** put aside; ~ ***für*** *acc. a.* keep for *s.o.*; **3.** F *fig.* put *s.th.* on the back burner; **4.** ***die eigenen Interessen*** ~ put one's own interests last; **5.** ⚔ defer; exempt from service; **~sto·ßen** (*irr.*, *sep.*, h, → ***stoßen***) **I.** *v/t.* **1.** push back; **2.** *fig.* disgust; **II.** *v/i.* (*a.* ***mit dem Auto*** ~) reverse, back; **~strah·len** (*sep.*, h) **I.** *v/t.* reflect; **II.** *v/i.* be reflected; **~strö·men** *v/i.* (*sep.*, sn) **1.** *water etc.*: flow back; **2.** *fig. people*: pour back (***in die Stadt*** into town); **~stu·fen** *v/t.* (*sep.*, h) downgrade; *ped.* move *s.o.* down a class; **~tau·meln** *v/i.* (*sep.*, sn) reel (*or* stagger) back; **~te·le·fo͵nie·ren** *v/i.* (*sep.*, h) call (*or* ring, phone) back; **~trei·ben** *v/t.* (*irr.*, *sep.*, h, → ***treiben***) drive back; **~tre·ten** *v/i.* (*irr.*, *sep.*, sn, → ***treten***) **1.** step (*or* stand) back; **2.** step down, stand down, resign; **3.** withdraw (***von*** *dat.* from), back out (of); **4.** *flood*: subside; **5.** △ recede (***von*** *dat.* from); **6.** ~ ***gegenüber*** *dat.* be less important than; **7.** take second place (***hinter*** *dat.* to); **8.** diminish, decline; **~tun** F *v/t.* (*irr.*, *sep.*, h, → ***tun***) → ***zurücklegen*** 1, 2; **~ver·fol·gen** *fig. v/t.* (*sep.*, h) trace back (***zu*** *dat.* to); ***es läßt sich bis ins 13. Jahrhundert*** ~ it can be traced back to the 13th century; **~ver·lan·gen** *v/t.* (*sep.*, h) → ***zurückfordern***; **~ver·set·zen** (*sep.*, h) **I.** *v/t.* **1.** move back; **2.** transfer *s.o.* back; *ped.* move *s.o.* down (a class); **3.** *fig.* take (*or* carry, *lit.* transport) back; ***es versetzt mich sofort in m-e Kindheit zurück*** it takes me straight back to my childhood; **II.** *v/refl.*: ***sich ins Mittelalter*** *etc.* ~ imagine one is living in the Middle Ages *etc.*; **~ver·wan·deln** *v/t.* (*sep.*, h) change back (***in*** *acc.* into); (*a.* ***sich***) ~ ***in*** *acc.* revert to; **~wei·chen** *v/i.* (*irr.*, *sep.*, sn, → ***weichen***) **1.** step back; *crowd*: *a.* move back; shrink back (***vor*** *dat.* from); **2.** ⚔ fall back; **3.** *flood, wood etc.*: recede; **4.** *fig.* recoil (***von*** *dat.* from), back away (from)

zu'rück·wei·sen *v/t.* (*irr.*, *sep.*, h, → ***weisen***) reject, repudiate; turn dow; ⚖ dismiss *an action*; ☤ dishono(u)r *a bill*; turn *s.o.* back; **Zu'rück·wei·sung** *f* (-; -en) rejection; repudiation; dismissal; turning back

zu'rück|wen·den *v/t.* (*irr.*, *sep.*, h, → ***wenden***) (*a.* ***sich*** ~) turn back; **~wer·fen** *v/t.* (*irr.*, *sep.*, h, → ***werfen***) **1.** throw back (*a. one's head*); **2.** a) *opt.* reflect, b) reverberate; **3.** ⚔ repulse; **4.** *fig.* set (*or* throw) back; **~wir·ken** *v/i.*(*sep.*, h): ~ ***auf*** *acc.* have an effect on, react on; **~wol·len** *v/i.* (*sep.*, h) want to go back; **~wün·schen** *v/t.* (*sep.*, h) wish back; **~zah·len** *v/t.* (*sep.*, h) pay back, repay (*a. fig.*); refund, reimburse *expenses*; redeem *loan*; pay off *debts*; ***das kannst du mir nächste Woche*** ~ you can pay me back next week

zu'rück·zie·hen (*irr.*, *sep.*, → ***ziehen***) **I.** *v/t.* (h) **1.** pull back; *a.* draw back *curtain, one's hand*; **2.** withdraw *offer, application etc.*; go back on *a promise etc.*; **3.** ⚔ withdraw, pull out *troops*; **II.** *v/refl.*: ***sich*** ~ (h) **4.** withdraw; ***sich auf sein Zimmer*** ~ go (up) to one's room, slink off to one's room, *w.s.* lock o.s. up in one's room; **5.** ⚔ withdraw, pull out; **6.** ***sich vom Geschäftsleben*** *etc.* ~ retire from business *etc.*; ***sich von der Politik*** ~ *a.* bow out of politics; ***sich von der Bühne*** ~ leave (*or* quit) the stage; ***sich von der Öffentlichkeit*** ~ retire from public life; **7.** ***sich von j-m*** ~ break off contact with s.o., dissociate o.s. from s.o.; **8.** ***sich in sich selbst*** ~ withdraw into one's shell; **9.** ***sich auf s-n alten Standpunkt*** ~ revert (*or* go back) to one's old standpoint; **III.** *v/i.* (sn) move back

Zu·ruf ['tsu:ru:f] *m* (-[e]s; -e) shout; *pl.* cheers, cheering *sg.*; ***durch*** ~ by acclamation (*a. parl.*)

'zu·ru·fen (*irr.*, *sep.*, h, → ***rufen***) **I.** *v/i.*: ***j-m*** ~ call (to) s.o.; **II.** *v/t.*: ***j-m et.*** ~ call s.th. (out) to s.o., shout s.th. to s.o.

Zu·sa·ge ['tsu:za:gə] *f* (-; -n) promise; acceptance; assent; ***s-e ~ geben*** promise, give one's word

'zu·sa·gen (*sep.*, h) **I.** *v/t.* **1.** promise; ***et.*** ~ *a.* undertake to do s.th.; ***s-e Hilfe*** ~ promise to help; ***Hilfe*** ~ *government etc.*: pledge one's aid, promise to send aid; **2.** ***j-m et. auf den Kopf*** ~ tell s.o. s.th. to his (*or* her) face; **II.** *v/i.* **3.** accept the invitation; ***sie haben alle (fest) zugesagt*** they've all said they're coming (they've all promised to come); **4.** ***j-m*** ~ appeal to s.o., *formal*: be to s.o.'s liking (*or* taste); ***ich weiß nicht, ob ihm das Buch (Klima) ~ wird*** I don't know whether he'll like the book (whether it's the right kind of climate for him); ***das sagt mir eher zu*** I prefer that, F that's more up my street

zu·sam·men [tsu'zamən] *adv.* a) together, *a.* jointly, b) (all) together, c) at the same time; ***gehen wir*** ~ let's go together; ***et. ~ besitzen*** own s.th. jointly, be joint owners of s.th.; ~ ***betragen*** make a total of, come to ... all together; ***das macht ...*** ~ that'll be ... all together; ***wir haben ~ 6 Dollar*** we have 6 dollars between us; ***bestellen wir e-n großen Salat*** ~ let's order a large salad between us (*or* for the two of us); ***guten Abend ~!*** evening all!; ***er verdient mehr als alle anderen*** ~ he earns more than the rest of them put together

Zu'sam·men·ar·beit *f* (-; *no pl.*) cooperation, *esp. b.s.* collaboration; teamwork; **zu'sam·men·ar·bei·ten** *v/i.* (*sep.*, h) work together, cooperate

zu'sam·men·backen *v/i.* (*sep.*, h) cake

zu'sam·men·bal·len (*sep.*, h) **I.** *v/t.* make into a ball; screw up *paper*; ***die Hände*** ~ clench one's fists; **II.** *v/refl.*: ***sich*** ~ *clouds etc.*: build up; ⚔ mass together; *fig. disaster etc.*: loom (***über*** *dat.* over); **Zu'sam·men·bal·lung** *f* (-; -en) accumulation; ⚔ massing together; *fig.* concentration

Zu'sam·men·bau *m* (-[e]s; *no pl.*) assembly; **zu'sam·men·bau·en** *v/t.* (*sep.*, h) assemble; put together

zu'sam·men|bei·ßen *v/t.* (*irr.*, *sep.*, h, → ***beißen***): ***die Zähne*** ~ clench (*fig.* grit) one's teeth; **~be·kom·men** *v/t.* (*irr.*, *sep.*, h, → ***bekommen***) get (*or* scrape) together; **~bet·teln** *v/t.* (*sep.*, h): ***das Geld*** ~ go around begging for the money; **~bin·den** *v/t.* (*irr.*, *sep.*, h, → ***binden***) tie together; **~blei·ben** *v/i.* (*irr.*, *sep.*, sn, → ***bleiben***) stay (F stick) together; **~brau·en** (*sep.*, h) **I.** F *v/t.* brew, concoct, F cook up; **II.** *v/refl.*: ***sich*** ~ *storm, quarrel etc.*: be brewing; **~bre·chen** *v/i.* (*irr.*, *sep.*, sn, → ***brechen***) **1.** *building, bridge*: cave in, collapse; **2.** *fig.* collapse; break down (*a.* ⚕); ***sein Kreislauf ist zusammengebrochen*** *a.* he had a circulatory breakdown; **3.** ~ ***über*** *dat. waves*: crash down on; **4.** *fig. economy, firm*: collapse; *attack, plan*: fail; *order, telephone lines, negotiations, theory etc.*: break down; *traffic*: come to a standstill; *fig.* ***m-e Welt ist zusammengebrochen*** my world just caved in; **~brin·gen** *v/t.* (*irr.*, *sep.*, h, → ***bringen***) **1.** a) bring (*or* get, gather) together, b) muster *strength etc.*, c) collect, gather; raise, get (*or* scrape) together; **2.** ***et. ~ mit*** *dat.* bring s.th. into contact with *s.th.*; **3.** *fig.* unite; ***j-n mit j-m*** ~ introduce s.o. to s.o., *a.* get s.o. together with s.o.; ***j-n mit j-m wieder*** ~ reconcile s.o. with s.o.; **4.** F manage; remember; ***er bringt keinen Satz zusammen*** F he can't string a sentence together; ***ich bringe es nicht zusammen zu*** *inf.* I can't bring (*or* get) myself to *inf.*

Zu'sam·men·bruch *m* (-[e]s; ⸚e) breakdown (*a.* ⚕, *pol. etc.*); collapse

zu'sam·men|drän·gen (*sep.*, h) **I.** *v/t.* **1.** crowd together; **2.** *fig.* condense (***auf*** *acc.* to); → ***zusammengedrängt***; **II.** *v/refl.*: ***sich*** ~ **3.** huddle together; **4.** *fig. events etc.*: be concentrated, come thick and fast; **~drücken** *v/t.* (*sep.*, h) a) press together, b) crush, squash; **~fah·ren** (*irr., sep.,* → **fahren**) **I.** F *v/t.* (h) **1.** smash into *a car etc.*, smash up, wreck; **II.** *v/i.* (sn) **2.** *mot. etc.* crash (into each other); **3.** *fig.* jump, start (**vor** *dat.* with *fright etc.*); wince (with *pain*); **~fal·len** *v/i.* (*irr., sep.,* sn, → **fallen**) **1.** *building etc., a. fig. s.o.'s face*: collapse, cave in; *cake etc.*: go down in the middle; *fig. person*: waste away; *fig.* **in sich ~** *plans etc.*: collapse (like a house of cards); **er sah ganz zusammengefallen aus** *a.* F he looked all scrunched up; **2.** coincide, fall on the same day (*or* in the same week *etc.*); **~fal·ten** *v/t.* (*sep.,* h) **1.** fold (up) *blanket etc.*; fold up *newspaper*; **2. die Hände ~** fold one's hands

zu'sam·men·fas·sen (*sep.,* h) **I.** *v/t.* **1.** a) sum up, summarize *speech etc.*, b) condense; **2.** unite, integrate (**in** *acc.* into); **II.** *v/i.* sum up, summarize; **zu'sam·men·fas·send I.** *adj.*: **~er Bericht** *etc.* summary (of events *etc.*), résumé; **~e Wiederholung** recapitulation; **II.** *adv.* in summary, by way of summarizing; **~ läßt sich sagen** in summary it may be said, to sum up one may say

Zu'sam·men·fas·sung *f* (-; -en) a) summary; *a.* abstract, b) condensation, c) *ped.* précis; **~ der Nachrichten** news summary, summary of the news, *the* news in short

zu'sam·men|fe·gen *v/t.* (*sep.,* h) sweep up (*or* together); **~fin·den** *v/refl.*: **sich ~** (*irr., sep.,* h, → **finden**) get together; **~flicken** *v/t.* (*sep.,* h) **1.** patch up (*a.* F *fig. s.o.*); **2.** F *fig.* F cobble together

zu'sam·men·flie·ßen *v/i.* (*irr., sep.,* sn, → **fließen**) *rivers*: flow together, meet, join; *paint*: run (together); *fig.* merge; **Zu'sam·men·fluß** *m* (-sses; ⁼sse) confluence, junction

zu'sam·men|fü·gen (*sep.,* h) **I.** *v/t.* join (together); fit together; **II.** *v/refl.*: **sich ~** fit together; **~füh·ren** *v/t.* (*sep.,* h) bring together; **wieder ~** reunite *families etc.*

zu'sam·men·ge·drängt *adj.* crowded (F squeezed) together; huddled together; **auf engstem Raum ~** crowded into a minimum of space

zu'sam·men·ge·hen *v/i.* (*irr., sep.,* sn, → **gehen**) **1.** *parties, firms etc.*: cooperate; merge; **2.** *colo(u)rs*: match, go together (well); **3.** *lines*: converge, meet; **4.** *dial.* shrink

zu'sam·men·ge·hö·ren *v/i.* (*sep.,* h) belong together; form a pair (*or* set)

zu'sam·men·ge·hö·rig *adj.* **1.** matching *socks etc.*; **2. sich ~ fühlen** feel one belongs together

Zu'sam·men·ge·hö·rig·keit *f* (-; *no pl.*) solidarity; shared identity; **Zu'sam·men·ge·hö·rig·keits·ge·fühl** *n* (feeling of) solidarity; (sense of) togetherness; common (*or* shared) identity; team spirit

zu'sam·men|ge·nom·men I. *p.p. of* **zusammennehmen**; **II.** *adj.*: **alles ~** all in all, all things considered; **~ge·pfercht** *adj.*: **~ in** *dat.* herded into, cooped up in; **~ge·ra·ten** *fig. v/i.* (*irr., sep.,* sn, → **geraten**) clash, come to blows; **~ge·rech·net** *fig. adj.*: **alles ~** all in all, all things considered, taking everything into account; **~ge·schu·stert** F *adj.* F cobbled (*or* thrown) together; piecemeal ...; **~ge·setzt** *adj.* **1. ~ sein aus** *dat.* be made up of; **2.** ⚗, ♪, *ling., pharm.* compound; composite *picture etc.*; **~es Wort** compound (word); **~ge·sun·ken I.** *p.p. of* **zusammensinken**; **II.** *adj.* slumped together, F scrunched up; **~ dasitzen** *a.* F sit there in a heap; **~ge·wür·felt** *adj.*: (**bunt**) **~** motley ..., thrown together; scratch *team etc.*

zu'sam·men·ha·ben *v/t.* (*irr., sep.,* h, → **haben**) have got *a team etc.* together, *a.* have scraped *the money* together

Zu'sam·men·halt *m* (-[e]s; *no pl.*) cohesion (*gen.* of); *fig.* bond (between, within), unity (of); team spirit

zu'sam·men·hal·ten (*irr., sep.,* h, → **halten**) **I.** *v/i.* **1.** hold together (*a. fig.*); *friends*: F stick together; **II.** *v/t.* **2.** hold *s.th.* together (*a. fig.*); hold onto *one's money*; **3.** hold next to each other, hold side by side

Zu'sam·men·hang *m* (-[e]s; ⁼e) a) connection, association *of ideas etc.*, b) continuity, c) context; **es besteht ein ~ zwischen den Ereignissen** the events are connected; **miteinander in ~ bringen** establish a connection (*or* link) between; **im ~ stehen mit** *dat.* be connected with; **nicht im ~ stehen mit** *dat.* have no connection with, have nothing to do with; **in diesem ~** in this connection; **Worte aus ihrem ~ reißen** take words out of their context; **die Dinge im ~ sehen** see things in context; **die größeren Zusammenhänge** the general perspective, *w.s.* the overall scheme (of events *or* things); **der Brief** *etc.* **hat keinen ~** the letter *etc.* is incoherent (*or* doesn't hang together)

zu'sam·men·hän·gen (*irr., sep.,* h, → **hängen**[1]) **I.** *v/i.* **1.** hang together, hang next to each other; **2.** *fig.* be connected, be linked; link up; **es hängt damit zusammen, daß** *a.* it has to do (*or* it ties up) with the fact that; **II.** *v/t.* hang *clothes etc.* (up) together (*or* next to each other); **zu'sam·men·hän·gend I.** *adj.* **1.** coherent (*a. thoughts, speech*); **2.** related, connected; **die damit ~en Fragen** the related issues; **II.** *adv.*: **et. ~ erzählen** give a coherent account of s.th.

zu'sam·men·hang(s)·los *adj.* incoherent, disjointed (*a. speech*), disconnected; *a.* jumbled *sentences*

zu'sam·men|hau·en *v/t.* (*sep.,* h) **1.** smash *s.th.* to pieces; F beat *s.o.* up; **2.** F *fig.* F knock (*or* throw) together; **~hef·ten** *v/t.* (*sep.,* h) **1.** file; **2.** stitch together; tack; **~hei·len** *v/i.* (*sep.,* sn) *wound*: heal (up); *bones*: knit (together); **~ho·len** *v/t.* (*sep.,* h) gather (together); **~kau·ern** *v/refl.*: **sich ~** (*sep.,* h) **1.** squat; cower; **2.** huddle together; **~kau·fen** *v/t.* (*sep.,* h) buy up; **~keh·ren** *v/t.* (*sep.,* h) sweep up (*or* together); **~kit·ten** *v/t.* (*sep.,* h) **1.** stick *s.th.* together; **2.** *fig.* patch up *friendship etc.*

Zu'sam·men·klang *m* (-[e]s; *no pl.*) harmony (*a. fig.*)

zu'sam·men·klapp·bar *adj.* folding ..., collapsible; **zu'sam·men·klap·pen** (*sep.*) **I.** *v/t.* (h) **1.** fold up *chair etc.*; shut *book*, clap *a book* shut; **2. die Hacken ~** click one's heels; **II.** *v/i.* (sn) **3.** *knife, chair*: fold up (*a.* **sich ~ lassen**); *book*: shut; **4.** F *fig.* collapse (**vor** *dat.* from *fatigue etc.*); break down

zu'sam·men|kle·ben *v/t. and v/i.* (*sep.,* h) stick together; **~klin·gen** *v/i.* (*irr., sep.,* h, → **klingen**) **1.** ♪ sound together; **2.** *fig.* be in tune with each other; **~knei·fen** *v/t.* (*irr., sep.,* h, → **kneifen**) → **zukneifen**; **~knül·len** *v/t.* (*sep.,* h) crumple up, screw up, F scrunch up; **~kom·men** *v/i.* (*irr., sep.,* sn, → **kommen**) **1.** gather, meet; get together; **~ mit** *dat.* be in contact with, meet (quite a lot of *business people etc.*); **2.** *money*: be raised; **es kommt einiges zusammen** there's quite a bit of money coming in; **3.** combine; **es ist alles zusammengekommen** everything came together (*or* happened at the same time); **~kop·peln** *v/t.* (*sep.,* h) couple (together); link up, *a.* dock *spaceship*; **~kra·chen** F *v/i.* (*sep.,* sn) **1.** collapse; *building*: *a.* cave in; **2.** *cars, fig. stock exchange*: crash; **~kramp·fen** *v/refl.*: **sich ~** (*sep.,* h) *muscles*: tense up, *a. heart*: seize up; *hands, fingers*: clench tightly; **~krat·zen** *v/t.* (*sep.,* h) scrape together

Zu·sam·men·kunft [tsu'zamənkʊnft] *f* (-; künfte [-kʏnftə]) meeting, get-together; gathering, conference

zu'sam·men|läp·pern F *v/refl.*: **sich ~** (*sep.,* h) add up, mount up; **~lau·fen** *v/i.* (*irr., sep.,* sn, → **laufen**) **1.** *people etc.*: gather; **2.** *lines, streets etc.*: converge, meet; **3.** *colo(u)rs*: run (together); → **spitz, Wasser**

zu'sam·men·le·ben I. *v/i.* (*sep.,* h) live together; **mit j-m ~** live with s.o.; **sie haben viele Jahre glücklich zusammengelebt** they spent many happy years together; **II.** ♀ *n* (-s; *no pl.*) living together, *formal*: cohabitation; **das ~ mit ihm** living with him, life with him

zu·sam·men·leg·bar [tsu'zamənle:kba:ʁ] *adj.* folding ..., collapsible

zu'sam·men·le·gen (*sep.,* h) **I.** *v/t.* **1.** put together; **2.** fold up; **3.** pool; **Geld ~** *a.* club together, F pass the hat round; **4.** combine; centralize; ✝ merge; **II.** *v/i.* club together, F pass the hat round; **wenn wir alle ~** F if everybody chips in

Zu'sam·men·le·gung *f* (-; -en) ✝ merger, fusion; consolidation

zu'sam·men|lü·gen F *v/t.* (*irr., sep.,* h, → **lügen**) make up, F cook up; **was er da zusammenlügt!** the lies he tells; **~na·geln** *v/t.* (*sep.,* h) nail together; **~neh·men** (*irr., sep.,* h, → **nehmen**) **I.** *v/t.* **1.** take together; → **zusammengenommen**; **2.** *fig.* **s-e Gedanken ~** collect one's thoughts; **s-e Kräfte** (**s-n Mut**) **~** muster *or* summon all one's strength (courage); **II.** *v/refl.*: **sich ~** pull o.s. together; **~packen** *v/t. and v/i.* (*sep.,* h) pack up; **ich war gerade am ♀** I was just getting ready to leave (*or* go); *fig.* **er kann ~** he may as well pack his bags and leave; **~pas·sen** *v/i.* (*sep.,* h) *a) clothes, furniture etc.*: go well together; match, b) suit one another; *fig., esp. iro.* **es paßt alles zusammen** it all adds up; **~pfer·chen** *v/t.* (*sep.,* h) herd together (*a. fig.*); *fig.* **~ in** *dat. a.* crowd into, coop up in; → **zusammengepfercht**; **~pral·len** *v/i.* (*sep.,* sn) **1.** a) *cars etc.*: crash, smash into each other, b) run into each other; **~ mit** *dat.* crash (*or* smash *or* run) into; **2.** *fig.* clash, come to blows, cross swords; **~pres·sen** *v/t.* (*sep.,* h) press together; **die Lippen ~** press one's lips together (tightly); **~quet·schen** *v/t.* (*sep.,* h) a) squeeze together, b) squash (up); **~raf·fen** (*sep.,* h) **I.** *v/t.* **1.** snatch up *one's belongings etc.*; **2.** pile up; hoard *money etc.*; **3.** *fig.* muster (up), summon (up), *lit.* gather together *courage etc.*; **4.** gather; **5.** pick up, gather up *skirt etc.*; **II.** F *v/refl.*: **sich** ~ pull o.s. together; **~rau·fen** F *v/refl.*: **sich** ~ (*sep.*, h) work things out with each other, F get it together; **~rech·nen** *v/t.* (*sep.*, h) add up, F tot up; → **zusammengerechnet; ~rei·men** *fig.* (*sep.*, h) **I.** *v/t.*: **sich et.** ~ make sense of s.th.; **II.** *v/refl.*: **sich** ~ make sense; ***wie reimt sich das zusammen?*** how does that fit?; ***wie reimt sich das mit s-n Plänen zusammen?*** how does that fit (*or* tie) in with his plans?; **~rei·ßen** F *v/refl.*: **sich** ~ (*irr.*, *sep.*, h, → **reißen**) pull o.s. together, F get a grip on o.s.; **~rol·len** (*sep.*, h) **I.** *v/t.* roll up; **II.** *v/refl.*: **sich** ~ coil up; *cat etc.*: curl up

zu'sam·men·rot·ten [-rɔtən] *v/refl.*: **sich** ~ (*sep.*, h) gang up; form a mob

zu'sam·men|rücken (*sep.*) **I.** *v/t.* (h) move together (*or* closer); **II.** *v/i.* (sn) move up, sit closer; make room; **~ru·fen** *v/t.* (*irr.*, *sep.*, h, → **rufen**) call together; convene; *parl.* summon; **~sacken** *v/i.* (*sep.*, sn) collapse; **~scha·ren** *v/refl.*: **sich** ~ (*sep.*, h) gather; **~schei·ßen** V *v/t.* (*irr.*, *sep.*, h, → **scheißen**) *sl.* give *s.o.* a bollocking; **~schie·ben** *v/t.* (*irr.*, *sep.*, h, → **schieben**) push (*or* move) together; ⚙ (*a.* **sich** ~) telescope; **~schie·ßen** F *v/t.* (*irr.*, *sep.*, h, → **schießen**): **j-n** ~ F shoot s.o. up, put a bullet through s.o.('s head); **~schla·gen** (*irr.*, *sep.*, → **schlagen**) **I.** *v/t.* (h) **1.** bang together; ***die Hände über dem Kopf*** ~ throw one's hands up *in surprise etc.*; ***die Hacken*** ~ click one's heels; **2.** smash *s.th.* (to pieces); F beat *s.o.* up, F clobber; **II.** *v/i.* (sn): ~ **über** *dat. waves*: crash onto

zu'sam·men·schlie·ßen (*irr.*, *sep.*, h, → **schließen**) **I.** *v/t.* **1.** lock (*or* chain) together; **2.** *fig.* unite; ✝ merge; **3.** ⚡ connect; **II.** *v/refl.*: **sich** ~ unite; join forces, band together; team up; form an alliance; **Zu'sam·men·schluß** *m* (-sses; ¨sse) union (*a. pol.*); ✝ merger

zu'sam·men|schmel·zen (*irr.*, *sep.*, → **schmelzen**) **I.** *v/t.* (h) melt down; **II.** *v/i.* (sn) melt away (*a. fig.*); **~schnei·den** *v/t.* (*irr.*, *sep.*, h, → **schneiden**) *film etc.*: splice; **~schnü·ren** *v/t.* (*sep.*, h) tie up *parcel etc.*; lace up *corset etc.*; *fig.* ***es schnürte ihm die Kehle zusammen*** he was choked; ***es schnürte mir das Herz zusammen*** my heart bled; **~schrau·ben** *v/t.* (*sep.*, h) screw (*or* bolt) together; **~schrecken** *v/i.* (*sep.*, sn) jump, start (**bei** *dat.* at *noise etc.*); **~schrei·ben** *v/t.* (*irr.*, *sep.*, h, → **schreiben**) **1.** write *s.th.* as one word; ***wird das zusammengeschrieben?*** is that one word (or two)?; **2.** scribble down; (***e-n***) ***Unsinn*** ~ write a lot of nonsense; **3.** ***sich ein Vermögen*** ~ make a fortune writing (books); **4.** *contp.* ***das hat er aus anderen Büchern zusammengeschrieben*** he's got it out of (*or* pinched it from) other books; **~schrump·fen** *v/i.* (*sep.*, sn) shrivel (up); *fig.* dwindle, dry up; **~schu·stern** F *v/t.* (*sep.*, h) F cobble (*or* throw, knock) together; **~schwei·ßen** *v/t.* (*sep.*, h) weld together; *fig.* weld, knit together

zu'sam·men·sein I. *v/i.* (*irr.*, *sep.*, sn, → **sein**) **1.** be together; ***das ganze Wochenende*** ~ be together for the whole weekend, spend the whole weekend together; **2.** be going out with each other; ***wie lange sind sie schon zusammen?*** how long have they been together (*or* been going out with each other)?; **II.** ♀ *n* (-s; *no pl.*) **3.** gathering; (*a.* ***geselliges*** ~) get-together; ***gemütliches*** ~ cosy (*Am.* cozy) get-together; **4.** → **Zusammenleben**

zu'sam·men·set·zen (*sep.*, h) **I.** *v/t.* **1.** put together; ⚙ *a.* assemble; compose; *ling. and* ⚗ compound; **2.** sit (*or* put) *pupils etc.* next to each other; **II.** *v/refl.*: **3. sich** ~ a) sit (down) together, b) get together; **4. sich** ~ **aus** *dat.* be made up of, consist of; **Zu'sam·men·set·zung** *f* (-; -en) **1.** composition; ingredients *pl.*; **2.** *ling. and* ⚗ compound; **3.** structure

zu'sam·men|sin·ken *v/i.* (*irr.*, *sep.*, sn, → **sinken**) **1.** *building etc.*: collapse, cave in; **2.** *person*: collapse, slump into a heap (*or* onto the floor), F fold up; **~sit·zen** *v/i.* (*irr.*, *sep.*, h, → **sitzen**) sit next to each other; sit together

Zu'sam·men·spiel *n* (-[e]s; *no pl.*) **1.** teamwork; **2.** *fig.* interplay (***der Kräfte*** of forces); **zu'sam·men·spie·len** *v/i.* (*sep.*, h) **1.** play together; **2.** *fig.* act together

zu'sam·men|stau·chen F *v/t.* (*sep.*, h) F give *s.o.* a dressing-down (*or* roasting), bawl s.o. out; **~stecken** (*sep.*, h) **I.** *v/t.* put together; pin together; *fig.* ***die Köpfe*** ~ put one's heads together; **II.** F *v/i.*: ***immer*** ~ be inseparable, F be as thick as thieves; **~ste·hen** *v/i.* (*irr.*, *sep.*, h, → **stehen**) **1.** stand together (*or* next to each other, side by side); **2.** F *fig.* stick together

zu'sam·men·stel·len *v/t.* (*sep.*, h) **1.** put (*or* move) together; **2.** *fig.* arrange; make (out *or* up), draw up *list, table etc.*; compile, F put together *report, dictionary etc.*; *radio*: *a.* make *program(me)*; pick, come up with *a team*; ***nach Gruppen*** ~ group; ***nach Klassen*** ~ classify; ***nach Farben*** (*or* ***Ausführung***) ~ match

Zu'sam·men·stel·lung *f* (-; -en) **1.** arrangement; drawing up; compilation *etc.*; → **zusammenstellen; 2.** table; survey; list

zu'sam·men|stim·men *v/i.* (*sep.*, h) tally; ***nicht*** ~ *a.* contradict each other, clash; **~stop·peln** *v/t.* (*sep.*, h) piece together; throw together *speech etc.*

Zu'sam·men·stoß *m* (-es; ¨e) **1.** collision; *mot. a.* crash; **2.** *fig.* clash; ***es kam zu schweren Zusammenstößen zwischen den Studenten und der Polizei*** there were heavy clashes between the students and the police; **zu'sam·men·sto·ßen** *v/i.* (*irr.*, *sep.*, sn, → **stoßen**) **1.** collide, crash (into each other); ~ **mit** *dat.* collide with, run into, crash into; **2.** *fig.* clash, come to blows; **3.** *gardens etc.*: meet, adjoin

zu'sam·men|strei·chen *v/t.* (*irr.*, *sep.*, h, → **streichen**) **1.** cut *text etc.* (to length); **2.** slash *funds*; **~strö·men** *v/i.* (*sep.*, sn) flock together; **~stür·zen** *v/i.* (*sep.*, sn) collapse, cave in; **~su·chen** *v/t.* (*sep*, h) get (*or* gather) together, find; **~tra·gen** *v/t.* (*irr.*, *sep.*, h, → **tragen**) gather (*a. fig. information etc.*); compile *notes etc.*

zu'sam·men·tref·fen (*irr.*, *sep.*, sn, → **treffen**) **I.** *v/i.* **1.** meet (**mit j-m** s.o.); **2.** *events*: coincide, take place simultaneously (*or* at the same time); **II.** ♀ *n* (-s; -) **3.** meeting; *b.s.* encounter; **4.** concurrence *of events*

zu'sam·men|trei·ben *v/t.* (*irr.*, *sep.*, h, → **treiben**) round up; **~tre·ten** (*irr.*, *sep.*, → **treten**) **I.** *v/t.* (h) crush *s.th.* underfoot; **II.** *v/i.* (sn) meet; *parl. a.* convene; **~trom·meln** F *v/t.* (*sep.*, h) round up; **~tun** (*irr.*, *sep.*, h, → **tun**) **I.** *v/t.* put together; **II.** *v/refl.*: **sich** ~ join forces, team up; **~wach·sen** *v/i.* (*irr.*, *sep.*, sn, → **wachsen**¹) grow together; *bones*: knit (together); *wound*: heal (up); *towns*: merge; *fig.* grow close; ***er hat zusammengewachsene Augenbrauen*** his eyebrows meet; **~wer·fen** *v/t.* (*irr.*, *sep.*, h, → **werfen**) **1.** throw together; **2.** *fig.* mix up; F lump together; **~wir·ken I.** *v/i.* (*sep.*, h) cooperate, collaborate; interact; **II.** ♀ *n* (-s; *no pl.*) cooperation; interplay *of circumstances*; **~wür·feln** *v/t.* (*sep.*, h) throw together; → **zusammengewürfelt; ~zäh·len** *v/t.* (*sep.*, h) add up; **~zie·hen** (*irr.*, *sep.*, → **ziehen**) **I.** *v/t.* (h) **1.** pull together; *a. phys.* contract; **2.** ⚔ mass *troops*; **3.** → **zusammenzählen; II.** *v/i.* (sn) **4.** move together, move in with each other; **III.** *v/refl.*: **sich** ~ (h) **5.** a) contract (*a. muscle*); *vessel*: constrict, b) narrow; shrink; **6.** *storm, a. fig. disaster*: be brewing; **~zucken** *v/i.* (*sep.*, sn) a) start, jump, b) wince

Zu·satz ['tsu:zats] *m* (-es; ¨e) **1.** addition; ***unter*** ~ ***von*** *dat.* by adding; ***unter*** ~ ***von*** *dat.* ***... mischen*** stir while adding ...; **2.** supplement; admixture; additive; **3.** addendum; postscript; ⚖ amendment; codicil; **~ab·kom·men** *n* supplementary agreement; **~an·trag** *m parl.* supplementary motion; **~bat·te,rie** *f* booster battery; **~er·klä·rung** *f pol.* supplementary declaration; **~fra·ge** *f* follow-up question; **~ge·rät** *n* attachment; adapter, add-on; **~klau·sel** *f* rider; **~ko·sten** *pl.* additional (*or* added) costs; **~last** *f* ⚡ additional load

zu·sätz·lich ['tsu:zɛtslɪç] **I.** *adj.* additional, extra; supplementary; auxiliary; **~e *Arbeit*** extra work; **~e *Belastung*** added burden; **II.** *adv.* in addition; ~ **zu** *dat.* in addition to, over and above; ~ ***noch etwas verdienen*** earn a bit extra; ***ich will nicht noch*** ~ ***auf s-n Hund aufpassen*** I don't want to have to look after his dog on top of it (*or* of everything else)

'Zu·satz|spei·cher *m computer*: extended memory; **~steu·er** *f* surtax; **~stoff** *m* additive; **~ver·si·che·rung** *f* complementary insurance; added protection; **~wer·bung** *f* follow-up advertising; **~zahl** *f* supplementary number

zu·schan·den [tsu'ʃandən] *adv.*: ~ ***machen*** ruin, wreck, destroy, dash *s.o.'s hopes*; ~ ***werden*** *plans etc.*: come to naught

zu·schan·zen ['tsu:ʃantsən] F *v/t.* (*sep.*, h): ***j-m et.*** ~ put s.th. s.o.'s way, *a.* line s.o. up with s.th.

'zu·schar·ren *v/t.* (*sep.*, h) cover up *hole etc.*

'zu·schau·en *v/i.* (*sep.*, h) → **zusehen**

Zu·schau·er ['tsu:ʃaʊɐ] *m* (-s; -) **1.** *sport*: spectator, *pl. a.* crowd; **2.** *TV* viewer; *pl. a.* audience; **3.** *thea. etc.*: member of the audience, *pl.* audience; ***e-r der*** ~ somebody in the audience, a member of the audience; **4.** onlooker, bystander, looker-on; ***unfreiwilliger*** ~ unwilling witness (*gen.* to, of); **~ku,lis·se** *f*, **~men·ge** *f* crowd (of spectators); **~raum** *m* auditorium; **~re·ak·ti,on** *f* audience (*TV a.* viewer) response; *sport*: reaction of the crowd; **~re,kord** *m* record attendance;

~sport *m* spectator sport; **~tri̦bü·ne** *f* (grand)stand; *pl. a.* terraces; **~über̦wa·chung** *f soccer*: crowd control; **~̦um·fra·ge** *f* audience survey; **~zahl** *f a. pl.* **1.** *sport*: number of spectators, crowd; **2.** *TV* number of viewers, viewing figures (*pl.*), (TV) rating; ***geringe ~en*** low ratings, poor audience performance
'**zu·schau·feln** *v/t.* (*sep*, h) fill up
'**zu·schicken** *v/t.* (*sep.*, h) send (*dat.* to); *a.* mail, post (to)
'**zu·schie·ben** *v/t.* (*irr.*, *sep.*, h, → ***schieben***) **1.** close, shut; **2.** ***j-m et.*** ~ push s.th. over to s.o.; **3.** *fig.* ***j-m et.*** ~ pass s.th. on to s.o.; ***j-m die Schuld*** ~ pass (*or* push) the blame onto s.o., lay the blame at s.o.'s door; ***j-m die Verantwortung*** ~ pass (*or* push) the responsibility onto s.o.
'**zu·schie·ßen** (*irr.*, *sep.*, → ***schießen***) **I.** *v/t.* (h) **1.** contribute *money*; ***sie hat mir 1000 Mark für den Wagen zugeschossen*** *a.* she gave me 1000 marks towards the car; **2.** ***j-m e-n Blick*** ~ dart a glance at s.o.; **3.** ***j-m den Ball*** ~ kick (*or* pass) the ball to s.o.; **II.** *v/i.* (sn): ~ ***auf*** *acc.* rush up to
'**Zu·schlag** *m* (-[e]s; ⸗e) **1.** surcharge, extra charge; supplementary fare; surtax; **2.** *auction*: award; ***er erhielt den*** ~ *auction*: the object went to him, ✝ *tender*: he was awarded (*or* he won, he got) the contract
'**zu·schla·gen** (*irr.*, *sep.*, h, → ***schlagen***) **I.** *v/t.* **1.** slam (shut), bang (shut), clap *a book* shut, shut *a book* with a thud; **2.** *fig.* add (*dat.* to), F slap on(to); **3.** ***j-m et.*** ~ *auction*: knock s.th. down to s.o., ✝ *tender*: award s.th. to s.o.; **II.** *v/i.* **4.** *door etc.*: slam (shut), bang (shut); **5.** lash out, F let fly; **6.** *fig.* strike; **7.** F *fig.* F make a killing, grab what one can; ***ich habe sofort zugeschlagen*** F I grabbed it *etc.* straightaway
'**Zu·schlag(s)·kar·te** *f* supplementary ticket; '**zu·schlag(s)·pflich·tig** [-pflɪçtɪç] *adj.* subject to extra charge
'**zu·schlie·ßen** (*irr.*, *sep.*, h, → ***schließen***) **I.** *v/t.* lock *s.th.* (up); **II.** *v/i.* lock up
'**zu·schmei·ßen** F *v/t.* (*irr.*, *sep.*, h, → ***schmeißen***) slam *a door* (shut)
'**zu·schnal·len** *v/t.* (*sep.*, h) buckle (up)
'**zu·schnap·pen** *v/i.* (*sep.*, sn) **1.** *lock etc.*: snap shut; **2.** *dog*: snap (***nach*** *dat.* at)
'**zu·schnei·den** *v/t.* (*irr.*, *sep.*, h, → ***schneiden***) cut up; cut (to size), *w.s. a.* style; → ***zugeschnitten***
'**Zu·schnei·der** *m* (-s; -) cutter
'**zu·schnei·en** *v/t.* (*sep.*, sn) snow up
'**Zu·schnitt** *m* (-[e]s; -e) **1.** cut; *w.s.* style; **2.** *no pl. fig.* a) sort, b) scale, c) calib|re (*Am.* -er); ***ein Mann s-s ~s*** a man of his calib|re (*Am.* -er) *or* standing
'**zu·schnü·ren** *v/t.* (*sep.*, h) tie up; *fig.* → ***zusammenschnüren***
'**zu·schrau·ben** *v/t.* (*sep.*, h) **1.** screw *s.th.* down; **2.** screw shut, put the lid (back) on
'**zu·schrei·ben** *v/t.* (*irr.*, *sep.*, h, → ***schreiben***) **1.** ***j-m et.*** ~ ascribe (*or* attribute) s.th. to s.o., *b.s.* impute s.th. to s.o.; ***j-m zuzuschreiben sein*** be attributable to s.o.; ***das haben wir ihm zuzuschreiben*** *a. iro.* we have him to thank for it; ***j-m die Schuld*** ~ put (*or* place) the blame on s.o. (***an*** *dat.* for); ***das hast du dir selbst zuzuschreiben*** you've only yourself to blame; ***e-r Sache große Bedeutung*** ~ attach great importance to s.th.; **2.** ***j-m e-e Summe*** ~ place a sum to s.o.'s credit
'**zu·schrei·ten** *v/i.* (*irr.*, *sep.*, sn, → ***schreiten***): ~ ***auf*** *acc.* walk (*or* stride) up to; ***tüchtig*** ~ put one's best foot forward
'**Zu·schrift** *f* (-; -en) letter, *a.* reply (*a. to an advertisement*); *adm. a.* communication; ***zahlreiche ~en bekommen*** *a.* receive (*or* get) an overwhelming response
zu·schul·den [tsuˈʃʊldən] *adv.*: ***sich etwas*** ~ ***kommen lassen*** do (something) wrong; ***habe ich mir etwas ~ kommen lassen?*** *a.* am I guilty of some offen|ce (*Am.* -se)?
'**Zu·schuß** *m* (-sses; ⸗sse) allowance; contribution (***zu*** *dat.* towards); subsidy, grant; **~be·trieb** *m* subsidized firm
'**zu·schu·stern** F *v/t.* (*sep.*, h) **1.** → ***zuschanzen***; **2.** ***Geld*** ~ help out with the money
'**zu·schüt·ten** *v/t.* (*sep.*, h) **1.** fill up (*or* in) *a ditch etc.*; fill in, close *a grave*; **2.** F add
'**zu·se·hen** *v/i.* (*irr.*, *sep.*, h, → ***sehen***) **1.** watch (***wie*** how); ***j-m*** ~ watch s.o. (***bei der Arbeit*** *etc.* working, at work *etc.*); ~, ***wie j-d et. macht*** watch s.o. do s.th., watch how s.o. does s.th.; ***ich kann nicht mehr*** ~ I can't look (*a. w.s.* take it) any more; ***wir mußten ~, wie sie den Wagen auseinandernahmen*** we had to just stand and watch them taking the car apart; ***allein vom*** ♀ ***wird mir schlecht*** I feel sick just watching (*or* just to look); **2.** *fig.* sit back (*or* stand by) and watch; **3.** *fig.* ~, ***daß*** see (to it) that, make sure that
zu·se·hends [ˈtsuːzeːənts] *adv.* visibly, noticeably; rapidly, day by day, by the minute; ***die Lage verschlechtert sich*** ~ the situation is getting rapidly worse (*or* is deteriorating rapidly, is deteriorating day by day)
'**Zu·se·her** *m* (-s; -) *Austrian* → ***Zuschauer***
'**zu·sein** F *v/i.* (*irr.*, *sep.*, sn, → ***sein***) **1.** be closed, be shut; **2.** F be plastered, *sl.* be pissed
'**zu·sen·den** *v/t.* (*irr.*, *sep.*, h, → ***senden***) → ***zuschicken***
'**zu·set·zen** (*sep.*, h) **I.** *v/t.* **1.** add (*dat.* to); **2.** lose *time*, *money etc.*; F ***nichts mehr zuzusetzen haben*** have used up all one's reserves, F have run out of steam; **II.** *v/i.*: ***j-m*** ~ press s.o. (hard); pester s.o. (***mit*** *dat.* with *requests*, *questions etc.*); urge s.o. (***zu*** *inf.* to *inf.*); *w.s. heat*, *strain etc.*: take it out of s.o., F get to s.o.; ***sich gegenseitig*** ~ F get at each other's throats
'**zu·si·chern** *v/t.* (*sep.*, h): ***j-m et.*** ~ assure s.o. of s.th., guarantee s.o. s.th.; promise s.o. s.th.; '**Zu·si·che·rung** *f* (-; -en) assurance; promise, pledge
Zu·spät·kom·men·de [tsuˈʃpɛːtkɔmənda] *m, f* (-n; -n) latecomer
'**zu·sper·ren** (*sep.*, h) **I.** *v/t.* shut, lock; **II.** *v/i.* lock up
'**Zu·spiel** *n* (-[e]s; *no pl.*) *sport*: pass(es *pl.*); '**zu·spie·len** *v/t.* (*sep.*, h) **1.** ***j-m et.*** ~ pass s.th. on to s.o.; **2.** (*a. v/i.*) *sport*: ***j-m (den Ball)*** ~ pass (the ball) to s.o.; *fig.* ***j-m den Ball*** ~ give s.o. his (*or* her) cue; ***sich gegenseitig die Bälle*** ~ feed each other lines, work a nice double act
'**zu·spit·zen** (*sep.*, h) **I.** *v/t.* **1.** sharpen *stick etc.*; **2.** *fig.* bring to a head; → ***zugespitzt***; **II.** *v/refl.*: ***sich*** ~ **3.** taper to a point; **4.** *fig.* come to a head
'**zu·spre·chen** (*irr.*, *sep.*, h, → ***sprechen***) **I.** *v/t.* **1.** ⚖ ***j-m et.*** ~ award s.o. s.th. (*a. w.s. a prize*); ***j-m ein Kind*** ~ grant s.o. custody of a child; **2.** ***j-m Mut*** ~ encourage s.o.; ***j-m Trost*** ~ console s.o., comfort s.o.; **II.** *v/i.* **3.** ***j-m gut*** ~ try and reason with s.o.; ***j-m besänftigend*** ~ try and appease s.o. (*or* calm s.o. down); **4.** have (*or* eat, drink) one's fill (*dat.* of), *lit.* partake freely (of); ***dem Essen tüchtig*** ~ F tuck into the food
'**zu·sprin·gen** *v/i.* (*irr.*, *sep.*, sn, → ***springen***) **1.** *lock*: spring (*or* snap) shut; **2.** ***auf j-n*** ~ a) jump towards s.o., b) jump at s.o.
'**Zu·spruch** *m* (-[e]s; *no pl.*) **1.** words *pl.* of encouragement (*or* consolation *etc.*), soothing (*or* friendly *etc.*) words *pl.*; **2.** reception; ***großen ~ finden*** go down (very) well; **3.** ***großen ~ haben*** be very popular, be much sought after
Zu·stand [ˈtsuːʃtant] *m* (-[e]s; Zustände [ˈtsuːʃtɛndə]) a) state (*a. phys.*), condition, b) situation, *esp. b.s.* state of affairs; conditions *pl.*; ***in gutem*** ~ in good condition, *car*, *house*, *tools etc.*: *a.* in good repair (*sl.* nick); ***in schlechtem*** ~ in bad condition (*or* repair); ***in betrunkenem*** ~ (while) under the influence of alcohol; ***in was für e-m ~ befindet er sich?*** what's his condition like?, F what sort of shape is he in?; ***es herrschen chaotische Zustände*** the situation is completely chaotic, it's absolute chaos; F ***das ist doch kein*** ~ it's impossible, something has got to change (*or* be done); F ***hier herrschen Zustände!*** what a state of affairs; F ***das sind ja Zustände wie im alten Rom!*** it's like Sodom and Gomorrha; F ***Zustände kriegen*** F have a fit; F ***da kann man ja Zustände kriegen!*** F it's enough to drive you spare
zu·stan·de [tsuˈʃtandə] *adv.* **1.** ~ ***bringen*** bring about; manage, succeed in doing *s.th.*, F engineer; ***wie hast du das (bloß) ~ gebracht?*** how (on earth) did you manage that?; ***Unmögliches ~ bringen*** achieve the impossible; **2.** ~ ***kommen*** a) come about; be achieved; *agreement etc.*: be reached; *plan*: materialize; *bill*: be passed, b) take place, come off; ***e-e Einigung kam nicht*** ~ no agreement was reached
zu·stän·dig [ˈtsuːʃtɛndɪç] *adj.* relevant, appropriate *authority etc.*; competent; responsible; **~es Gericht** court of competent jurisdiction; ***~e Stelle*** appropriate authority (*or* department); ***wenden Sie sich an die ~e Stelle*** *a.* apply to the department (*or* authority) that deals with such matters; ***dafür bin ich nicht*** ~ that's not my responsibility (*or* job), *formal*: that's not within my province; ***keiner will ~ sein*** F everyone just passes the buck; '**Zu·stän·dig·keit** *f* (-; -en) competence; responsibility; powers *pl.*; ⚖ jurisdiction (***für*** *acc.* over); '**Zu·stän·dig·keits·be·reich** *m* (sphere of) responsibility; ⚖ jurisdiction; ***es fällt nicht in m-n ~*** *formal*: it doesn't fall within my purview
'**Zu·stands|glei·chung** *f phys.* equation of state; **~grö·ße** *f* variable of state; **~verb** *n ling.* stative verb
zu·stat·ten [tsuˈʃtatən] *adv.*: ***j-m (gut, sehr) ~ kommen*** stand s.o. in good stead; come in handy
'**zu·ste·chen** *v/i.* (*irr.*, *sep.*, h, → ***stechen***) attack, plunge the knife *etc.* in

'zu·stecken *v/t.* (*sep.*, h): ***j-m et.*** ~ slip s.o. s.th.

'zu·ste·hen *v/i.* (*irr.*, *sep.*, h, → ***stehen***) **1.** ***es steht ihm*** (***rechtlich***) ***zu*** he is (legally) entitled to it; **2.** ***es steht ihm nicht zu zu*** *inf.* he has no right to *inf.*, it's not for him to *inf.*; ***es steht mir überhaupt nicht zu zu urteilen*** *a.* who am I to judge?

'zu·stei·gen *v/i.* (*irr.*, *sep.*, sn, → ***steigen***) get on, board the train (*or* bus); ***noch jemand zugestiegen?*** 🚂 tickets, please!; ***wo sind Sie zugestiegen?*** where did you get on?, which station (*or* stop) did you get on at?

Zu·stell|amt ['tsu:ʃtɛl-] *n* 📯 delivery office; **~be·zirk** *m* postal zone (*or* district)

'zu·stel·len *v/t.* (*sep.*, h) **1.** block *entry, exit, passage etc.*; **2.** 📯 deliver; **3.** ⚖ serve (***j-m et.*** s.th. on s.o.)

Zu·stel·ler ['tsu:ʃtɛlɐ] *m* (-s; -) postman, *Am.* mailman

Zu·stell·ge·bühr ['tsu:ʃtɛl-] *f* delivery charge

'Zu·stel·lung *f* (-; -en) **1.** 📯 delivery; **2.** ⚖ service

'zu·steu·ern (*sep.*) **I.** F *v/t.* (h) contribute (***zu*** *dat.* to); **II.** *v/i.* (sn): ~ ***auf*** *acc.* a) head for, make (a beeline) for; veer towards, b) *fig.* be aiming at; be driving at, c) *fig.* be heading for, be veering towards *a crisis etc.*

'zu·stim·men *v/i.* (*sep.*, h) agree (*dat.* to *s.th. or* with *s.o.*); *a.* consent (to *s.th.*); approve (of *s.th.*); **~d *nicken*** nod in approval, nod assent; **'Zu·stim·mung** *f* (-; -en) agreement; *a.* consent; approval; ***allgemeine*** ~ ***finden*** meet with unanimous approval

'zu·stop·fen *v/t.* (*sep.*, h) **1.** plug up *hole, one's ears etc.*; **2.** mend, darn *socks etc.*

'zu·stöp·seln *v/t.* (*sep.*, h) stopper; put the stopper (*or* cork) in

'zu·sto·ßen (*irr.*, *sep.*, → ***stoßen***) **I.** *v/t.* (h) **1.** push *s.th.* shut; slam *s.th.* (shut); **II.** *v/i.* **2.** (h) attack; stab, thrust, lunge; **3.** (sn) ***j-m*** ~ happen to s.o.; ***ihm ist etwas zugestoßen*** he's had an accident; *euphem.* ***wenn mir etwas*** ~ ***sollte*** if anything should happen to me

'zu·stre·ben *v/i.* (*sep.*, sn) **1.** head for, make for (***dem Ausgang*** *etc.* the exit *etc.*); **2.** *fig.* aim at, have set one's sights on (*dat. s.th.*)

'Zu·strom *m* (-[e]s; *no pl.*) **1.** a) stream *of visitors, customers etc.*, b) rush, c) influx *of tourists, capital, goods etc.*; **2.** *meteor.* influx, inflow; **'zu·strö·men** *v/i.* (*sep.*, sn) **1.** flow towards; **2.** stream (*or* throng) towards *the exit etc.*; **3.** ***die Ideen strömten ihm nur so zu*** the ideas came flooding to him (*or* into his head)

'zu·stür·men *v/i.* (*sep.*, sn): ~ ***auf*** *acc.* storm (towards), make a rush for

'zu·stür·zen *v/i.* (*sep.*, sn): ~ ***auf*** *acc.* rush towards, descend (up)on

zu·ta·ge [tsu'ta:gə] *adv.* **1.** ~ ***bringen*** (*or* ***fördern***) bring to the surface, *a.* unearth (*a. fig. secret etc.*); F dig out; *fig.* bring to light, uncover; **2.** *fig.* ~ ***treten*** come to light (*or* to the surface), be revealed, *secret*: *a.* be unearthed; **3.** *geol.* ~ ***treten*** outcrop; **4.** ~ ***liegen*** be evident, be manifest, be there for all to see

Zu·tat ['tsu:ta:t] *f* (-; -en) **1.** *pl. gastr.* ingredients; **2.** *pl.* accessories; **3.** *fig.* addition

zu'teil [tsu'taɪl] *pred. adj.*: ***j-m*** ~ ***werden*** be given (*or* granted) to s.o., *lit.* be bestowed on s.o.; ***j-m et.*** ~ ***werden lassen*** grant s.o. s.th.; *iro.* ***mir wurde ein solcher Empfang nie*** ~ I never had the hono(u)r of a reception like that; ***mir ist diese Gelegenheit bisher nicht*** ~ ***geworden*** that opportunity has as yet passed me by

'zu·tei·len *v/t.* (*sep.*, h) give (*dat.* to), *formal*: assign (to), allot (to); allocate (to), appropriate (to); pay out *loan*; ***der Bevölkerung Nahrungsmittel*** ~ ration food out among the population; ***er ist e-r anderen Abteilung zugeteilt worden*** he's been moved to a different department; **'Zu·tei·lung** *f* (-; -en) a) assignment; allotment; allocation; paying out; → ***zuteilen***, b) quota

'zu·tei·lungs·reif *adj.* mature; ~ ***sein*** have matured, be payable

zu·tiefst [tsu'ti:fst] *adv.* most, deeply; ~ ***beleidigt*** deeply offended, *lit. and iro.* mortally wounded, cut to the quick; ***et.*** ~ ***bedauern*** a) deeply regret s.th., b) express one's deep regret at (*or* over) s.th.

'zu·tra·gen (*irr.*, *sep.*, h, → ***tragen***) **I.** *v/t.*: ***j-m et.*** ~ carry (*or* bring) s.th. to s.o., bring s.o. s.th.; *fig. a.* pass s.th. on to s.o.; **II.** *v/refl.*: ***sich*** ~ happen, take place, occur, transpire; ***es trug sich zu, daß*** *lit.* it came to pass that; **'Zu·trä·ger** *m* (-s; -) informant, informer

zu·träg·lich ['tsu:trɛ:klɪç] *adj.* good (*dat.* for), beneficial (to); conducive (to); healthy, good for one's health, *a.* salubrious *climate*; ***j-m nicht*** ~ ***sein*** disagree with s.o.; **'Zu·träg·lich·keit** *f* (-; *no pl.*) beneficial nature (*gen.* of)

'zu·trau·en *v/t.* (*sep.*, h): ***j-m et.*** ~ believe s.o. (to be) capable of (doing) s.th., credit s.o. with s.th.; ***sich zuviel*** ~ overrate o.s., take too much on; ***ich traue es mir*** (***nicht***) ***zu*** I (don't) think I can do it; ***er traut sich überhaupt nichts zu*** he has no confidence in himself; ***man muß es sich nur*** ~ you just have to believe in yourself; ***ich traue ihm nicht viel zu*** I don't think he's up to much; ***ich traue es ihm glatt zu, zuzutrauen wäre es ihm schon*** I wouldn't put it past him; ***das hätte ich ihm nicht zugetraut*** a) I didn't think he was the sort, b) I never knew he had it in him

'Zu·trau·en *n* (-s; *no pl.*) confidence (***zu*** *dat.* in)

zu·trau·lich ['tsu:traʊlɪç] *adj.* confiding, trusting; *w.s.* friendly (*a. animal*); **'Zu·trau·lich·keit** *f* (-; -en) **1.** *no pl.* confiding nature; **2.** confidence

'zu·tref·fen *v/i.* (*irr.*, *sep.*, h, → ***treffen***) be true (***bei*** *dat.*, ***auf*** *acc.*, ***für*** *acc.* of), be right, be correct, be the case; ~ ***auf*** (*or* ***für***) *acc. a.* hold true of, apply to; ***dasselbe trifft auch für dich zu*** the same applies to (*or* goes for) you; ***das dürfte nicht ganz*** ~ that's not quite correct; ***es trifft nicht immer zu*** it doesn't always follow; ***die Beschreibung trifft genau auf ihn zu*** the description fits him perfectly; **'zu·tref·fend** *adj.* correct; *pred. a.* F spot on; appropriate, fitting, *a.* apt *remark etc.*

'zu·trei·ben (*irr.*, *sep.*, → ***treiben***) **I.** *v/i.* (sn): ~ ***auf*** *acc. boat etc.*: drift towards; *fig.* ***e-r Krise*** *etc.* ~ be drifting towards a crisis *etc.*; **II.** *v/t.* (h): ~ ***auf*** *acc.* drive *the game etc.* towards

'zu·trin·ken *v/i.* (*irr.*, *sep.*, h, → ***trinken***) drink to, raise one's glass to

Zu·tritt ['tsu:trɪt] *m* (-[e]s; *no pl.*) access; admission; ~ ***verboten!*** no entry; ~ ***bekommen*** (*or* ***erhalten***), ***sich*** ~ ***verschaffen*** gain admission (*or* admittance) (***zu*** *dat.* to); ***sich gewaltsam*** ~ ***verschaffen*** force one's way in, ***zu e-m Haus***: force one's way into a house, break down the door of a house

'zu·tun *v/t.* (*irr.*, *sep.*, h, → ***tun***) **1.** close, shut; → ***Auge*** 1; **2.** F add

'Zu·tun *n*: ***ohne mein*** ~ a) without any help (*or* encouragement) from me, b) through no fault of my own (*or* mine); ***es geschah ohne mein*** ~ I had nothing to do with it

zu·un·gun·sten [tu'ʔʊngʊnstən] *prp.* (*gen. or von dat.*) to the disadvantage of; *decision etc.*: *a.* against

zu·un·terst [tsu'ʔʊntɐst] *adv.* right at the bottom

'zu·ver·die·nen *v/t.* (*sep.*, h) make *money* on the side; ***ein bißchen*** ~ *a.* make a bit of extra money

zu·ver·läs·sig ['tsu:fɛɐlɛsɪç] *adj.* reliable (*a.* ⚙), dependable; loyal; trustworthy; safe (*a.* ✝, ⚙); ***aus ~er Quelle*** from a reliable source, ***wissen***: have *s.th.* on good authority; ***die ~ste Quelle für*** *acc.* the authority on; ***er ist absolut*** ~ *a.* you can rely (*or* depend) on him totally

'Zu·ver·läs·sig·keit *f* (-; *no pl.*) reliability; dependability; loyalty; trustworthiness; safety; **'Zu·ver·läs·sig·keits·prü·fung** *f* reliability test

Zu·ver·sicht ['tsu:fɛɐzɪçt] *f* (-; *no pl.*) confidence; optimism; ***voller*** (*or* ***der festen***) ~ ***sein, daß*** be (quite) confident that, have every confidence that; ***voller ~ in die Zukunft blicken*** look confidently ahead to the future, look to the future with optimism, have faith in the future; ***s-e*** ~ ***setzen auf*** *acc.* place one's trust in

'zu·ver·sicht·lich *adj.* confident, optimistic(ally *adv.*); **'Zu·ver·sicht·lich·keit** *f* (-; *no pl.*) confidence; optimism; optimistic outlook

zu·viel [tsu'fi:l] *adv.* too much; ***einer*** *etc.* ~ one *etc.* too many; ***viel*** ~ far (*or* much) too much; ***des Guten*** ~ too much of a good thing; ***es wurde ihm*** ~ it got too much for him, it started getting on top of him; ***ein gutes Gehalt wäre*** ~ ***gesagt*** a good salary would be a bit of an overstatement; ***was*** ~ ***ist, ist*** ~! there's a limit to everything, you can only go so far; F ***ich krieg'*** ~! F well blow me!; ***ein*** ♀ ***an*** *dat.* too much (of), an excess (*or* overkill) of

zu·vor [tsu'fo:ɐ] *adv.* a) before, previously, b) first, beforehand; ***kurz*** ~ shortly before; ***am Tage*** ~ the day before, the previous day; ***ich hatte sie nie*** ~ ***gesehen*** I had never seen (*or* set eyes on) her before; ***wie nie*** ~ as never before

zu·vor·derst [tsu'fɔrdɐst] *adv.* right at the front

zu'vor·kom·men *v/i.* (*irr.*, *sep.*, sn, → ***kommen***) a) preempt (*dat. s.o. or s.th.*); *a.* anticipate *question etc.*, b) forestall, head off, ward off *attack etc.*, c) beat *s.o.* to it, F get in first, F pip *s.o.* at the post;

zu'vor·kom·mend *adj.* (very) obliging; accommodating; helpful; courteous; **Zu'vor·kom·men·heit** *f* (-; *no pl.*) obligingness; courtesy

Zu·wachs ['tsu:vaks] *m* (-es; *no pl.*) **1.** increase (***an*** *dat.* in; ***von*** *dat.* of); *esp.* ✝ growth (in); **2.** F ***die Familie hat*** ~ ***be-***

kommen there's been an addition to the family; **3.** F ***et. auf* ~ *kaufen*** buy s.th. on the big side; **'zu·wach·sen** *v/i.* (*irr., sep.*, sn, → ***wachsen*¹**) **1.** become overgrown; → ***zugewachsen*; 2.** ⚕ heal up, close; **3.** *fig. money*: accrue to; *task, responsibility etc.*: fall to (*or* upon), *formal*: devolve upon; **'Zu·wachs·ra·te** *f* growth rate

'Zu·wan·de·rer *m* (-s; -) immigrant; incomer; **'zu·wan·dern** *v/i.* (*sep.*, sn) immigrate; settle in an area *etc.*

zu·we·ge [tsu've:gə] *adv.* **1.** ***et.* ~ *bringen*** bring about s.th.; manage (to do) s.th.; ***es* ~ *bringen zu*** *inf. a.* succeed in *ger.*; **2.** ***gut* ~ *sein*** be in good health (*or* shape); ***noch gut* ~ *sein*** be doing well for one's age

'zu·we·hen (*sep.*) **I.** *v/t.* (h) block; **II.** *v/i.* (sn): ***j-m* ~** blow towards s.o.; *scent etc.*: waft towards (*or* over to) s.o.

zu·wei·len [tsu'vaılən] *adv.* at times, occasionally, now and then

'zu·wei·sen *v/t.* (*irr., sep.*, h, → ***weisen***) assign (*dat.* to)

'zu·wen·den (*irr., sep.*, h, → ***wenden***) **I.** *v/t.* **1.** turn *s.th.* towards *s.o. or s.th.*; ***j-m das Gesicht* ~** turn (round) to face (*or* look at) s.o.; ***j-m den Rücken* ~** turn one's back to(wards) (*or* on) s.o.; **2.** ***j-m Geld*** *etc.* ~ give s.o. money *etc.*; ***j-m Liebe* ~** devote some love (*or* affection) to s.o., show s.o. some love (*or* affection); ***e-r Sache s-e Aufmerksamkeit* ~** turn (*or* devote) one's attention to s.th.; **II.** *v/refl.* **3.** ***sich j-m* (*e-r Sache*) ~** turn to(wards) s.o. (s.th.), turn (round) to face s.o. (s.th); **4.** ***sich* ~** (*dat.*) turn to; devote o.s. to; ***sich ganz e-r Sache* ~** devote o.s. fully to s.th.; **'Zu·wen·dung** *f* (-; -en) **1.** a) allocation (of funds), b) sum; donation, c) bequest; **2.** *no pl.* a) attention, b) (love and) affection

zu·we·nig [tsu've:nıç] *indef. pron.* not enough, too little; *with pl.*: not enough, too few; ***viel* ~** not nearly enough, far too little (*pl.* few); ***einer*** *etc.* ~ one *etc.* short, one *etc.* too few; ***du ißt* ~** you don't eat enough, you need to eat more

'zu·wer·fen *v/t.* (*irr., sep.*, h, → ***werfen***) **1.** ***j-m et.* ~** throw s.o. s.th., throw s.th. (over) to s.o.; **2.** *fig.* ***j-m e-n Blick* ~** glance at s.o., cast (*or* dart) a glance at s.o.; ***j-m e-n bösen* (*verächtlichen*) *Blick* ~** give s.o. a dirty look (flash a look of contempt at s.o.); **3.** slam *or* bang *a door* (shut); **4.** fill up *trench etc.*

zu·wi·der [tsu'vi:dɐ] **I.** *adv.*: ***j-m* ~ *sein*** repulse s.o., revolt s.o., F turn s.o. off; ***es ist mir* ~** *a.* I find it repugnant; ***das Schwimmen*** *etc.* ***ist mir* ~** I detest (*or* loathe, can't stand) swimming *etc.*; **II.** *prp.* (*dat.*) against, contrary to; ***den Vorschriften* ~** *a.* in defiance of the regulations

zu'wi·der·han·deln *v/i.* (*sep.*, h) ***e-r Vorschrift*** *etc.* ~ act against (*or* contrary to) a regulation *etc.*; ***e-m Gesetz* ~** violate (*or* contravene) a law

Zu'wi·der·han·deln·de *m, f* (-n; -n) offender; **Zu'wi·der·hand·lung** *f* (-; -en) ⚖ violation, offen|ce (*Am.* -se) (***gegen*** *acc.* against); non-compliance (with)

zu'wi·der·lau·fen *v/i.* (*irr., sep.*, sn, → ***laufen***) go against, run counter to (*dat. one's interests etc.*); ***dem Verstand* ~** go against all reason

'zu·win·ken *v/i.* (*sep.*, h): ***j-m* ~** wave to (*or* at) s.o.; beckon to s.o. (to come)

'zu·zah·len *v/t.* (*sep.*, h) **1.** pay *s.th.* extra; ***50 Mark* ~** *a.* pay an extra 50 marks; **2.** contribute; ***j-m et. zum neuen Fernseher*** *etc.* ~ give s.o. s.th. towards the new TV set *etc.*

'zu·zäh·len *v/t.* (*sep.*, h) **1.** a) add, b) count; **2.** ~ ***zu*** *dat.* count among

'zu·zie·hen (*irr., sep.*, → ***ziehen***) **I.** *v/t.* (h) **1.** pull (tight); tighten (*a.* ***sich*** ~); draw, close *curtains*; close, pull *a door etc.* to; **2.** *fig.* call in, consult; **3.** ***sich*** *et.* ~ ⚕ get, *formal*: contract; *a.* catch, pick up *a disease etc.*; suffer, *formal*: sustain *an injury*; F land o.s. (with), come away with; **4.** ***sich j-s Haß* (*Zorn*** *etc.*) ~ incur s.o.'s hatred (anger *etc.*); ***sich Unannehmlichkeiten* ~** get (o.s.) into trouble; **II.** *v/refl.*: ***sich*** ~ (h) *sky*: cloud over, become overcast; **III.** *v/i.* (sn) move to a town *etc.*, move there (*or* here)

'Zu·zug *m* (-[e]s; ⸚e) **1.** move; **2.** influx

zu·züg·lich ['tsu:tsy:klıç] *prp.* (*gen.*) plus, not including, exclusive of; ~ ***Mehrwertsteuer*** plus VAT (*or* sales tax)

'Zu·zugs|ra·te *f* rate of immigration; **~stopp** *m* immigration ban

'zu·zwin·kern *v/i.* (*sep.*, h): ***j-m* ~** wink at s.o., give s.o. a wink

zwacken ['tsvakən] (*sep.* -k·k-) F (h) **I.** *v/t.* pinch; **II.** *v/impers.*: ***es zwackt mich im Rücken*** I can feel a twinge in my back; ***es* (*zwickt und*) *zwackt mich überall*** I'm aching all over

zwang [tsvaŋ] *pret. of* ***zwingen***

Zwang [tsvaŋ] *m* (-[e]s; Zwänge ['tsvɛŋə]) compulsion (*a. psych.*); constraint; (moral) obligation; pressure (*a.* ⚕); *psych.* obsession; ***gesellschaftliche* (*politische, wirtschaftliche*) *Zwänge*** social (political, economic) constraints; ***der* ~ *der Verhältnisse*** the force of circumstances; ***der* ~ *der Mode*** the dictates of fashion; ***der* ~ *der Konvention*** the straitjacket of convention; ***e-m inneren* ~ *folgen*** follow an inner compulsion; ***allen* ~ *ablegen*** abandon all restraint; ***sich* ~ *antun*** a) restrain o.s. (from doing s.th.), b) force o.s. (to do s.th.); ***tun Sie sich nur keinen* ~ *an!*** don't stand on ceremony, make yourself at home, *hum.* no need to be shy(, now); *iro.* ***tu dir nur keinen* ~ *an!*** don't mind me; ***unter* ~ *stehen* (*handeln*)** be (act) under duress

zwän·gen ['tsvɛŋən] (h) **I.** *v/t.* force, squeeze (***in*** *acc.* into); **II.** *v/refl.*: ***sich* ~ *in*** *acc.* squeeze (o.s.) into

'zwang·haft *adj.* compulsive, obsessive

'zwang·los *adj.* informal, casual; unconstrained, uninhibited; relaxed; **~*es Treffen*** informal get-together; ***in* ~*er Anordnung*** in loose order; ***in* ~*er Folge*** in no particular (*or* set) order, *appear etc.*: at irregular intervals; **'Zwang·lo·sig·keit** *f* (-; *no pl.*) casualness, informality

'Zwangs|ab·ga·be *f* compulsory charge (*or* levy); **~an·lei·he** *f* mandatory loan; **~ar·beit** *f* forced labo(u)r; **~ar·bei·ter** *m* forced labo(u)rer; **~ar·beits·la·ger** *n* labo(u)r camp; **~auf·ent·halt** *m* detention; enforced stay; **~be·wirt·schaf·tung** *f* (economic) control; **~ein·wei·sung** *f* committal (***in*** *acc.* to)

'zwangs·er·näh·ren *v/t.* (*only inf. and p.p.* zwangsernährt, h) force-feed

'Zwangs·er·näh·rung *f* force-feeding

'Zwangs|hand·lung *f* compulsive act; **~heim·kehr** *f* forced repatriation; **~herr·schaft** *f* (-; *no pl.*) despotism, tyranny; **~idee** *f* obsession; **~jacke** *f* straitjacket (*a. fig.*); **~la·ge** *f* predicament, plight

'zwangs·läu·fig *adj.* inevitable

'Zwangs|li·qui·da·ti͵on *f* enforced liquidation; **~maß·nah·men** *pl.* coercive measures; *pol.* sanctions; **~mit·glied·schaft** *f* compulsory membership; **~mit·tel** *n* means of enforcement; **~neu͵ro·se** *f* obsessional neurosis; **~räu·mung** *f* eviction

'zwangs·ste·ri·li͵sie·ren *v/t.* (*only inf. and p.p.* zwangssterilisiert, h) forcibly sterilize; **'Zwangs·ste·ri·li͵sie·rung** *f* (-; -en) forced sterilization

'zwangs͵um·sie·deln *v/t.* (*only inf. and p.p.* zwangsumgesiedelt, h) displace (***nach*** *dat.* to), (forcibly) remove (to); **'Zwangs͵um·sied·ler** *m* (-s; -) displaced person; **'Zwangs͵um·sied·lung** *f* (-; en) displacement

'Zwangs|͵um·tausch *m* obligatory exchange; **~ver·fah·ren** *n* enforcement procedure; **~ver·gleich** *m* compulsory settlement (in bankruptcy); **~ver·kauf** *m* forced sale

'zwangs·ver·schicken *v/t.* (*only inf. and p.p.* zwangsverschickt, h) deport; **'Zwangs·ver·schickung** *f* (-; -en) deportation

'zwangs·ver·stei·gern *v/t.* (*only inf. and p.p.* zwangsversteigert, h) put *s.th.* up for public auction; **'Zwangs·ver·stei·ge·rung** *f* (-; -en) forced sale

'Zwangs·ver·wal·tung *f* sequestration

'zwangs·voll͵strecken *v/i.* (*only inf. and p.p.* zwangsvollstreckt, h) issue execution (***gegen*** *acc.* against); **'Zwangs·voll͵streckung** *f* (-; -en) compulsory execution

'Zwangs·vor·stel·lung *f* obsession

'zwangs·wei·se I. *adj.* forcible; ~ ***Evakuierung* (*Pensionierung*)** forced evacuation (retirement); ~ ***Einquartierung*** imposed billeting; **II.** *adv.* by force, forcibly; ***sich* ~ *Zugang verschaffen zu*** *dat.* enter *a building etc.* by force

'Zwangs·wirt·schaft *f* (-; *no pl.*) **1.** government control; **2.** command economy

zwan·zig ['tsvantsıç] *adj.* twenty; ***in den* ~*er Jahren*** in the twenties; ***die goldenen Zwanziger*** the golden twenties; ***sie ist in den Zwanzigern*** she's in her twenties

'Zwan·zig *f* (-; -en) **1.** twenty; **2.** *bus etc.* (number) twenty

'zwan·zig·jäh·rig [-jɛ:rıç] *adj.* **1.** twenty-year-old *girl etc.*; **2.** twenty-year(-long) *absence etc.*

Zwan·zig'mark·schein *m* twenty-mark note (*Am.* bill)

zwan·zigst ['tsvantsıçst] *adj.* twentieth; ***sie hat heute ihren Zwanzigsten*** she's twenty today, it's her twentieth birthday today

Zwan·zig·stel ['tsvantsıçstəl] *n* (-s; -) twentieth (part)

zwar [tsva:ɐ] *adv.* **1.** ~ ***..., aber ...*** (it's true) ..., but ...; certainly ..., but ...; ***es ist* ~ *spät, aber ...*** it 'is late, but ...; ***er hat* ~ *angerufen, aber ...*** he 'did ring up, but ...; he rang up all right (*Am.* alright), but ...; ***sie ist* ~ *hübsch, aber ...*** *a.* she may be pretty, but ...; **2.** ***und* ~** namely, in fact; ***er will das Geld haben, und* ~ *sofort*** he wants the money, and he wants it right now; ***wir haben uns in Rom***

getroffen, und ~ letztes Jahr we met in Rome - last year (it was); ***er ist Sänger, und ~ Bariton*** he's a singer - a baritone; he's a singer, that's to say a baritone

Zweck [tsvɛk] *m* (-[e]s; -e) purpose; object, aim; point, use; ***s-n ~ erfüllen*** serve its purpose, *appliance etc.*: *a.* F do its job; ***s-n ~ verfehlen*** defeat its purpose; ***e-n ~ verfolgen*** pursue an object; ***für friedliche ~e*** for peaceful purposes; ***Räume für gewerbliche ~e*** rooms for commercial use; ***dem ~ entsprechende Kleidung*** *etc.* suitable clothing *etc.*; ***Geld für wohltätige ~e spenden*** donate money to charity; ***für e-n guten ~ spenden*** give to a good cause; ***zum ~e*** *gen.* with a view to *s.th. or ger.*, with the object of *ger.*; ***zu diesem ~e*** to this end; ***zu welchem ~e?*** what (...) for?; ***was für e-n ~ soll es haben zu*** *inf.?* what's the point (*or* use) of *ger.?*; F ***das ist*** (***gerade***) ***der ~ der Übung*** that's the whole point, that's the whole object (*or* point) of the exercise; ***es hat keinen ~*** there's no point (***zu*** *inf.* in *ger.*), it's no use (*ger.*); ***das wird wenig ~ haben*** that won't do (*or* be) much good, that won't be any use; ***was hat das alles für e-n ~?*** what's the point (of it all)?; ***Mittel zum ~*** a means to an end; ***der ~ heiligt die Mittel*** the end justifies the means

'Zweck·bau *m* (-[e]s; -ten) ⚠ functional building

'zweck·be·stimmt *adj.* **1.** functional *building etc.*; **2.** earmarked *funds*; **'Zweck·be·stim·mung** *f* (-; *no pl.*) appropriation *of funds*

'zweck·be·tont *adj.* **1.** functional; **2.** utilitarian

'Zweck|bin·dung *f* project tying; earmarking; **~bünd·nis** *n pol. etc.* marriage of convenience; **~den·ken** *n* pragmatism

'zweck·dien·lich *adj.* **1.** useful, expedient; **2.** relevant; ***~e Hinweise*** any information that might help the police with their enquiries (*or* inquiries); **'Zweck·dien·lich·keit** *f* (-; *no pl.*) **1.** expediency; **2.** relevance, pertinence

'zweck·ent·frem·den *v/t.* (h) use for a purpose not intended; misappropriate (*a. funds*); **'zweck·ent·frem·det** *adj.* misappropriated

'zweck·ent·spre·chend *adj.* appropriate, suitable (to its *or* their purpose)

'Zweck·for·schung *f* applied research

'zweck·frei *adj.*: ***~e Forschung*** pure research

'zweck·ge·bun·den *adj.* earmarked *funds*

'zweck·los *adj.* useless, pointless, *pred. a.* no use; ***es ist ~ zu*** *inf.* it's pointless *etc. ger.*, there's no point in *ger.*; ***geschieden*** *etc.* ~ no divorcees *etc.* need apply

'zweck·mä·ßig *adj.* a) suitable; practical; ⚙ functional, b) effective, c) advisable; expedient; **'Zweck·mä·ßig·keit** *f* (-; *no pl.*) a) suitability; practicality; functional nature (*gen.* of), b) effectivity, effectiveness, c) advisability

'Zweck|op·ti,mis·mus *m* calculated optimism; **~pes·si,mis·mus** *m* calculated pessimism

zwecks *prp.* (*gen.*) for the purpose of (*ger.*), with a view to (*ger.*)

'Zweck|spa·ren *n* target (*or* special-purpose) saving; **~ver·mö·gen** *n* special-purpose fund

'zweck·wid·rig *adj.* inappropriate; ***~e Verwendung von Geldern*** misappropriation of funds

zwei [tsvaɪ] *adj.* two; ***wir ~*** the two of us, you and I (*or* me); ***dazu gehören ~*** it takes two, you need two people (for that); ***zu ~en hintereinander*** two by two, in twos; ***für ~ essen*** (***trinken***) eat (drink) for two; ***für ~ arbeiten*** do the work of two

Zwei *f* (-; -en) two; *ped.* B; (*bus etc.*) (number) two; ***e-e ~ schreiben*** get a B

'Zwei·ach·ser [-aksɐ] *m* (-s; -) *mot.* two-axle(d) car (*or* vehicle *etc.*)

'zwei·ar·mig [-armɪç] *adj.* two-armed

'zwei·ato·mig [-a,toːmɪç] *adj.* diatomic

'zwei·äu·gig [-ɔʏgɪç] *adj.* **1.** two-eyed; **2.** *phot.* ***~e Spiegelreflexkamera*** twin-lens reflex camera

'zwei·bän·dig [-bɛndɪç] *adj.* two-volume ..., in two volumes

'Zwei·bei·ner [-baɪnɐ] *m* (-s; -) *hum.* biped; **'zwei·bei·nig** [-baɪnɪç] *adj.* two-legged

'Zwei·bett·zim·mer *n* twin-bedded room, F twin

'zwei·blätt·rig [-blɛtrɪç] *adj.* ♣ two-leafed, two-leaved, two-leaf ...

'zwei·deu·tig [-dɔʏtɪç] *adj.* ambiguous, equivocal; suggestive, off-colo(u)r *joke etc.*; **'Zwei·deu·tig·keit** *f* (-; -en) **1.** *no pl.* ambiguity, equivocal nature (*gen.* of); suggestiveness; **2.** suggestive remark, double entendre

'zwei·di·men·sio,nal *adj.* two-dimensional

Zwei'drit·tel·mehr·heit *f* two-thirds majority

'zwei·ei·ig [-aɪɪç] *adj.* binovular; ***~e Zwillinge*** nonidentical (*or* fraternal) twins; ***sie sind ~e Zwillinge*** *usu.* they're not identical twins

Zwei·er ['tsvaɪɐ] *m* (-s; -) **1.** *rowing*: pair, two(-seater); **2.** → ***Zwei***; **~be·zie·hung** *f* partnership; relationship (between two people); **~bob** *m* two-man bob

zwei·er·lei ['tsvaɪɐ'laɪ] *adj.* two (different) kinds of; *su.* two things; ***das ist ~*** they're two completely different things; ***mit ~ Maß messen*** apply double standards

'Zwei·er·takt *m* duple time

'zwei·fach *adj.* double; ***die ~e Menge*** double the amount; ***~er Sieger*** two-time winner (*or* champion); ***in ~er Ausfertigung*** in duplicate

'Zwei·fa,mi·li·en·haus *n* two-family (*Am.* duplex) house

Zwei'far·ben·druck *m* two-colo(u)r printing (*or* print)

'zwei·far·big *adj.* two-tone

Zwei·fel ['tsvaɪfəl] *m* (-s; -) doubt; uncertainty; ***berechtigter ~*** reasonable doubt; ***große ~*** grave doubts; ***außer ~*** beyond doubt; ***ohne ~*** without (a) doubt, undoubtedly; ***im ~ sein*** be doubtful, have one's doubts (***über*** *acc.* about); ***ich bin im ~, ob ich gehen soll*** I'm in two minds as to whether I should go or not; ***es besteht kein ~ darüber, daß*** there's absolutely no doubt (*or* question) that; ***ich habe nicht den geringsten ~, daß*** I have no doubt whatsoever that; ***ich habe da m-e ~*** I have my doubts, I'm not so sure; ***keinen ~ daran lassen, daß*** make it quite plain that, leave no room for doubt that; ***in ~ ziehen*** (call into) question, throw (*or* call) into doubt; ***~ äußern an*** *dat.* voice one's doubts about; ***et. außer ~ stellen*** remove all trace of doubt from s.th.; ***j-n im ~ lassen über*** *acc.* leave s.o. in doubt as to (*or* wondering about) *s.th.*; ***~ an sich selbst haben*** have lost faith in oneself; ***mir kommen ~*** I'm beginning to have my doubts; → ***geplagt***

Zwei'fel·der·wirt·schaft *f* (-; *no pl.*) ⚒ two-crop rotation

'zwei·fel·haft *adj.* doubtful, dubious; questionable; ***es ist ~, ob*** it's doubtful (*or* uncertain) whether; ***~e Geschäfte*** dubious (*or* shady) transactions; ***ein ~es Vergnügen*** a doubtful (*or* dubious) pleasure; ***von ~em Wert*** of debatable merit; ***es erscheint kaum ~, daß*** there seems little doubt that

'zwei·fel·los *adv.* undoubtedly, without (a) doubt; ***das ist ~ richtig*** I'm sure that's right, there's no doubt about that

zwei·feln ['tsvaɪfəln] *v/i.* (h): ***~ an*** *dat.* doubt *s.o. or s.th.*, have one's doubts about *s.o. or s.th.*, question *s.th.*; ***~, ob*** be uncertain *or* unsure (as to) whether, doubt whether, have one's doubts as to whether; ***daran ist nicht zu ~*** there's no doubt about that (*or* doubting that); ***an sich selbst ~*** have lost faith in oneself; ***du darfst nicht an dir selbst ~*** you mustn't lose faith in yourself, you've got to believe in yourself

'Zwei·fels·fall *m*: ***im ~*** if there's any doubt, if you're *etc.* not sure, *formal*: in case of doubt, F if necessary; ***im ~ sollte man lieber vorsichtig sein*** it's better to err on the side of caution

'zwei·fels·frei **I.** *adj.* free of doubt, absolutely certain; ***ein ~er Beweis*** unequivocal (*or* unimpeachable) evidence; ***die ~e Ursache*** the undoubted cause; **II.** *adv.*: ***~ feststellen*** (***beweisen***) ascertain (prove) beyond doubt

'zwei·fels'oh·ne *adv.* → ***zweifellos***

'zwei·flam·mig [-flamɪç] *adj.* two-flame ...

Zweif·ler ['tsvaɪflɐ] *m* (-s; -) doubter, sceptic, *Am.* skeptic; **zweif·le·risch** ['tsvaɪflərɪʃ] *adj.* sceptical, *Am.* skeptical, doubting ...

'zwei·flü·ge·lig [-flyːgəlɪç] *adj.* **1.** *zo.* two-winged; *formal*: dipterous; **2.** ***~e Tür*** double door; **'Zwei·flüg·ler** [-flyːglɐ] *m* (-s; -) *zo.* dipteron

Zwei'fron·ten·krieg *m* war on two fronts

Zweig [tsvaɪk] *m* (-[e]s; -e ['tsvaɪgə]) branch (*a. fig.*); twig; *ped. etc.*: section, department; → ***grün*** I

'zwei·ge·schlech·tig [-gəʃlɛçtɪç] *adj.* bisexual

'Zwei·ge·spann *n* **1.** carriage and pair; **2.** F *fig.* twosome, duo

'zwei·ge·teilt *adj.* **1.** bipartite; **2.** divided, split

'Zweig·ge·schäft *n* branch

'zwei·glei·sig [-glaɪzɪç] **I.** *adj.* **1.** double-track ..., *pred.* double-tracked; **2.** *fig.* two-track ..., twin-track ...; **II.** *adv.*: *fig.* ***~ fahren*** leave both one's options open, F hedge one's bets

'Zweig|li·nie *f* 🚂 branch line; **~nie·der·las·sung** *f* subsidiary, branch; **~stel·le** *f* branch (office); **~stel·len·lei·ter** *m* branch manager

'zwei·hän·dig [-hɛndɪç] **I.** *adj.* two-handed; ♪ for two hands; **II.** *adv.* with both hands

'Zwei·heit *f* (-; *no pl.*) duality

'zwei·höcke·rig *adj.* two-humped *camel*

'zwei'hun·dert *adj.* two hundred
'Zwei·hun·dert·jahr·fei·er *f* bicentenary, bicentennial
'zwei·jäh·rig [-jɛːrɪç] *adj.* **1.** two-year-old *girl etc.*; **2.** two-year *stay etc.*; ***ein ~es ... a.*** two years of ...; **'Zwei·jäh·ri·ge** [-jɛːrɪɡə] *m, f* (-n; -n) two-year-old
'zwei·jähr·lich I. *adj.* two-yearly, occurring every two years, biennial; **II.** *adv.* every two years, biennially
Zwei'kam·mer·sy,stem *n parl.* bicameral system
'Zwei·kampf *m* duel; ***e-n ~ gewinnen*** *soccer*: win a tackle
'Zwei·ka,nal·ton *m TV* stereo sound; ***mit ~ a.*** with bilingual facility, with two language channels
'zwei·ka·rä·tig [-ka,rɛːtɪç] *adj.* two-carat ...
Zwei'klas·sen·ge·sell·schaft *f* two-tier society
'zwei·köp·fig [-kœpfɪç] *adj.* **1.** two-headed; **2.** *family etc.* of two
'Zwei·kreis·brem·se *f mot.* dual-circuit brake
'zwei·la·gig [-laːɡɪç] *adj.* two-ply
'Zwei·li·ter·fla·sche *f* two-litre (*Am.* two-liter) bottle
Zwei'mäch·te·ab·kom·men *n* bilateral agreement
'zwei·mal *adv.* twice; ***~ am Tag*** twice a day, twice daily; ***~ die Woche*** twice a week; ***~ so groß wie*** twice as big as, twice the size of; ***es sich ~ überlegen*** think twice (before doing it); ***ich hab's mir nicht ~ sagen lassen*** I didn't wait to be told (*or* asked) twice
zwei·ma·lig ['tsvaɪmaːlɪç] *adj.*: ***nach ~er Wiederholung*** after repeating it twice, after two repetitions (*or* repeats); ***nach ~em Klingeln*** after I *etc.* had rung twice; ***nach ~em Versuch*** after two attempts, after the second attempt; ***erst nach ~er Aufforderung machte er es*** he had to be asked twice before he did it
Zwei'mark·stück *n* two-mark piece
'Zwei·ma·ster [-mastɐ] *m* (-s; -) ⚓ two-master
'zwei·mo·na·tig [-monaːtɪç] *adj.* **1.** two-month ...; ***nach e-m ~en Auslandsaufenthalt*** after two months (*or* a two-month stay) abroad; **2.** two-month-old *baby etc.*; **'zwei·mo·nat·lich I.** *adj.* bimonthly ...; **II.** *adv.* bimonthly, every two months, every other month
'zwei·mo·torig [-mo,toːrɪç] *adj.* twin-engined
Zwei·par'tei·en... *in cpds.* bipartisan, two-party; **~sy,stem** *n pol.* two-party system
Zwei'pha·sen... *in cpds.*, **'zwei·pha·sig** [-faːzɪç] *adj.* two-phase
'zwei·po·lig [-poːlɪç] *adj.* two-pole ...; two-pin *plug*
'Zwei·punkt·gurt *m mot.* two-point belt
'Zwei·rad *n* two-wheeled vehicle
'zwei·räd·rig [-rɛːdrɪç] *adj.* two-wheeled
'Zwei·rei·her [-raɪɐ] *m* (-s; -) double-breasted jacket *etc.*; **'zwei·rei·hig** [-raɪɪç] *adj.* **1.** two-rowed; **2.** double-breasted *suit etc.*
Zwei·sam·keit ['tsvaizaːmkaɪt] *lit. f* (-; *no pl.*) togetherness
'zwei·schläf·rig *adj.*: ***~es Bett*** double bed
'zwei·schnei·dig *adj.* double-edged, two-edged (*both a. fig.*); *fig.* ***das ist so e-e ~e Sache*** it cuts both ways, it's a tricky business
'zwei·sei·tig [-zaɪtɪç] **I.** *adj.* **1.** two-sided, double-sided; **2.** two-page *letter etc.*, *article etc.* two pages long; ***~e Anzeige*** double(-page) spread; **3.** *pol.* bilateral *talks, agreement etc.*; **4.** *textil.* reversible; **II.** *adv.*: ***~ beschriftet*** (***bedruckt*** *etc.*) written (printed *etc.*) on both sides *or* on either side
'zwei·sil·big [-zɪlbɪç] *adj.* two-syllable ..., disyllabic; ***~es Wort a.*** disyllable
'Zwei·sit·zer [-zɪtsɐ] *m* (-s; -) *mot.* two-seater (*a.* ✈); roadster; coupé
'zwei·spal·tig [-ʃpaltɪç] **I.** *adj.* two-column ..., two-columned; **II.** *adv.*: ***~ gedruckt*** (printed) in two columns
'zwei·spra·chig [-ʃpraːxɪç] **I.** *adj.* bilingual; *document etc.* in two languages; **II.** *adv.*: ***~ aufwachsen*** grow up bilingually (*or* speaking two languages)
'Zwei·spra·chig·keit *f* (-; *no pl.*) bilingualism
'zwei·spu·rig [-ʃpuːrɪç] *adj.* **1.** two-lane *road etc.*; **2.** 🚂 double-track ..., *pred.* double-tracked; **3.** two-track *tape*; ***es ist ~*** it's a two-track
'Zwei·stär·ken·bril·le *f*: (***e-e ~*** a pair of) bifocals *pl.*
'zwei·stel·lig [-ʃtɛlɪç] *adj.* two-digit *figure etc.*; ***~e Inflation a.*** double-digit inflation
Zwei'ster·ne|ho,tel *n* two-star hotel; **~re·stau,rant** *n* three-star restaurant
'zwei·stim·mig [-ʃtɪmɪç] *adj.* for (*or* in) two voices, two-part ...
'zwei·stöckig [-ʃtœkɪç] *adj.* two-stor(e)y *building etc.*; ***~es Bett*** bunk bed
'zwei·strah·lig [-ʃtraːlɪç] *adj.* ✈ twin-jet *engine etc.*
Zwei'stu·fen|plan *m* two-stage plan; **~ra,ke·te** *f* two-stage rocket (*or* missile)
'zwei·stu·fig [-ʃtuːfɪç] *adj.* two-stage ...
'zwei·stün·dig [-ʃtʏndɪç] *adj.* two-hour(-long) ...
zweit [tsvaɪt] **I.** *adj.* second; ***~es Kapitel*** chapter two; ***am ~en Juli*** on the second of July, on July the second; ***2. Juli*** 2nd July, July 2(nd); ***Zweites Deutsches Fernsehen*** Second Channel of German Television (*abbr.* ***ZDF***); ***jeder ~e*** every other person; ***ein ~er Napoleon*** another Napoleon; → ***Geige, Hand***; **II.** *adv.*: ***zu ~*** in twos, in pairs; ***wir waren zu ~*** there were two of us; ***wir gingen zu ~ hin*** a) two of us went there, b) both of us went there, we both went there (together)
'zwei·tä·gig [-tɛːɡɪç] *adj.* **1.** two-day(-long) ...; **2.** two-day-old ...
'Zwei·tak·ter [-taktɐ] *m* (-s; -), **'Zwei·takt·mo·tor** *m* two-stroke engine
'zweit·äl·test *adj.* second oldest; *in a family*: *a.* second eldest
'zwei'tau·send *adj.* two thousand
'Zwei'tau·sen·der *m* (-s; -) two-thousand metre (*Am.* -meter) peak
'Zweit|aus·fer·ti·gung *f* duplicate; **~be·ruf** *m* second career
'zweit·best *adj.* second-best
'Zweit·be·ste *m, f* (-n; -n) → ***Zweite***
Zwei·te ['tsvaɪtə] *m, f* (-n; -n) (the) second; ***er war ~r*** he was (*or* came) second; ***Richard II.*** Richard II (= Richard the Second); ***heute ist der ~*** it's the second today; ***wie kein zweiter*** like nobody else
'Zweit·ehe *f* second marriage
'Zwei·tei·ler [-taɪlɐ] *m* (-s; -) a) two-piece, b) two-part film, film in two parts; **'zwei·tei·lig** [-taɪlɪç] *adj.* a) two-part ..., in two parts, b) two-piece *suit etc.*
'Zwei·tei·lung *f* division
'Zwei·te(r)-Klas·se|-Ab,teil *n* second-class compartment; **~-Wa·gen** *m* second-class carriage (*or* car)
zwei·tens ['tsvaɪtəns] *adv.* secondly, two, in second place
'zweit·größt *adj.* second largest
'zweit·höchst *adj.* second highest (*or* tallest)
'zweit·klas·sig [-klasɪç] *adj.* second-class; *contp.* second-rate; *sport*: second-division ...
'zweit·längst *adj.* second longest
'Zweit·laut·spre·cher *m* external (loud)-speaker
'zweit·letzt *adj.* last but one, second to last, *formal*: penultimate
'zweit·ran·gig [-raŋɪç] *adj.* of secondary importance, secondary; *contp.* second-rate
'Zweit|schlüs·sel *m* spare key; **~schrift** *f* copy, duplicate; **~stim·me** *f pol.* second vote; **~stu·di·um** *n* second degree; ***ein ~ machen a.*** take another degree; **~wa·gen** *m* second car; **~woh·nung** *f* second home; pied-à-terre; weekend flat (*Am.* apartment)
Zwei·und'drei·ßig·stel|-No·te *f* ♪ demisemiquaver, *Am.* thirty-second note; **~-Pau·se** *f* demisemiquaver (*Am.* thirty-second-note) rest
Zwei'vier·tel·takt *m*: ♪ (***im ~*** in) two-four time
Zwei'weg|box F *f* two-way speaker; **~laut·spre·cher** *m* two-way (loud)-speaker
'zwei·wer·tig [-veːɐrtɪç] *adj.* ⚗ bivalent; ***~es Element*** dyad
'zwei·wö·chent·lich I. *adj.* two-weekly, *esp. Brit.* fortnightly; **II.** *adv.* every two weeks, *esp. Brit.* fortnightly
'zwei·wö·chig [-vœçɪç] *adj.* **1.** two-week *stay etc.*; **2.** two-week-old *baby etc.*
'Zwei·zei·ler [-tsaɪlɐ] *m* (-s; -) distich; couplet; **'zwei·zei·lig** [-tsaɪlɪç] **I.** *adj.* two-line ...; **II.** *adv.*: ***~ geschrieben*** double-spaced
Zwei'zim·mer·woh·nung *f* one-bedroom flat (*Am.* apartment)
'Zwei·zy,lin·der F *m* a) two-cylinder (car), b) two-cylinder engine
Zwerch·fell ['tsvɛrçfɛl] *n* (-[e]s; -e) diaphragm; **~at·mung** *f* abdominal (*or* diaphragmatic) breathing
'zwerch·fell·er·schüt·ternd *adj.* side-splitting
Zwerg [tsvɛrk] *m* (-[e]s; -e ['tsvɛrɡə]) **1.** dwarf (*a. fig.*); gnome; *fig.* midget
zwer·gen·haft ['tsvɛrɡənhaft] *adj.* dwarfish, dwarf-like; diminutive
'Zwerg|ga·le,rie *f* △ dwarf gallery; **~huhn** *n* bantam; **~hund** *m* miniature dog
Zwer·gin ['tsvɛrɡɪn] *f* (-; -nen) *fig.* dwarf, midget
'Zwerg|ka,nin·chen *n* pygmy rabbit; **~kie·fer** *f* dwarf pine; **~maus** *f* harvest mouse; **~pal·me** *f* dwarf palm; **~schu·le** *f* one-classroom school; **~staat** *m* miniature (F tiny) state; **~tan·ne** *f* dwarf conifer; **~volk** *n* pygmy tribe; **~wuchs** *m* dwarfism, 🕮 nanism
Zwet·sche ['tsvɛtʃə] *f* (-; -n) plum
'Zwet·schen|baum *m* plum tree; **~schnaps** *m*, **~was·ser** *n* plum brandy

Zwetsch·ge ['tsvɛtʃgə] *dial. f* (-; -n) plum
Zwickel ['tsvɪkəl] (*sep.* -k·k-) *m* (-s; -) **1.** gusset; **2.** △ spandrel; **3.** F two-mark piece
zwicken ['tsvɪkən] (*sep.* -k·k-) *v/t. and v/i.* (h) pinch; hurt; ***das Hemd zwickt mich*** my shirt is pinching me; ***mein Bauch zwickt (mich)*** I've got a griping pain in my stomach; ***die Gicht zwickt ihn*** he's feeling twinges of gout; *fig.* ***sein Gewissen zwickt ihn*** his conscience is pricking him
Zwicker ['tsvɪkɐ] *m* (-s; -) *opt.* pince-nez
'Zwick·müh·le *f* **1.** *fig.* F catch-22 situation; ***in e-r ~ sein*** *a.* be in a quandary (F fix); **2.** double row
Zwie·back ['tsvi:bak] *m* (-[e]s; -e, -bäcke [-bɛkə]) rusk, *esp. Am.* zwieback
Zwie·bel ['tsvi:bəl] *f* (-; -n) a) onion, b) (*flower*) bulb; **~kup·pel** *f* △ onion dome; **~mu·ster** *n* blue onion pattern; **~ring** *m gastr.* onion ring; **~scha·le** *f* onion skin; **~sup·pe** *f* onion soup; **~turm** *m* △ onion tower
Zwie·ge·spräch ['tsvi:-] *n* dialog(ue)
Zwie·licht ['tsvi:-] *n* (-[e]s; *no pl.*) twilight; *fig.* ***ins ~ geraten*** lay o.s. open to suspicion; **zwie·lich·tig** ['tsvi:lɪçtɪç] *fig. adj.* dubious, shady; *a.* backstreet *affair*; ***~e Gestalt*** shady character
Zwie·spalt ['tsvi:ʃpalt] *m* (-[e]s; -spälte [-ʃpɛltə]) conflict; 🕮 dichotomy; rift; ***im ~ sein*** be in a cleft stick; ***in e-n ~ geraten*** F get o.s. into a fix; ***im ~ mit sich selbst sein*** be in conflict (*or* at odds) with o.s.; **zwie·späl·tig** ['tsvi:ʃpɛltɪç] *adj.* mixed, conflicting; ***mein Eindruck war ~*** I had (*or* I came away with) mixed impressions; ***er ist ein ~er Mensch*** he has a conflicting personality
Zwie·spra·che ['tsvi:-] *f* (-; *no pl.*) dialog(ue); *fig.* ***~ halten mit*** *dat.* commune with
Zwie·tracht ['tsvi:traxt] *f* (-; *no pl.*) discord; divisiveness; ***~ säen*** sow the seeds of discord; ***in ~ leben mit*** *dat.* be at variance (*or* odds) with; ***es herrscht ~ zwischen ihnen*** they're at loggerheads, *iro.* they're not on the best of terms
Zwil·le ['tsvɪlə] *f* (-; -n) catapult, *Am.* slingshot
Zwil·lich ['tsvɪlɪç] *m* (-s; -e) *textil.* drill
Zwil·ling ['tsvɪlɪŋ] *m* (-s; -e) **1.** twin; **2.** *pl. ast.* Gemini; ***(ein) ~ sein*** be (a) Gemini; **3.** double-barrel(l)ed gun
'Zwil·lings|bru·der *m* twin brother; **~ge·schwi·ster** *pl.* twins; twin brothers (*or* sisters); ***die ~ X*** the X twins; *a.* the X brothers (*or* sisters); **~paar** *n* pair of twins; **~rei·fen** *pl. mot.* double tyres (*Am.* tires); **~schwe·ster** *f* twin sister
Zwing·burg ['tsvɪŋ-] *f hist.* stronghold, citadel
Zwin·ge ['tsvɪŋə] *f* (-; -n) ferrule; ⚙ clamp
zwin·gen ['tsvɪŋən] (zwang, gezwungen, h) **I.** *v/t.* **1.** force (***zu*** *inf.* to *inf.*, into *ger.*); ***j-n ~, et. zu tun*** *a.* make s.o. do s.th., coerce s.o. into doing s.th.; ***j-n gegen die Wand (auf den Boden) ~*** force s.o. against the wall (force s.o. to lie down on the floor *or* ground); ***j-n zum Reden ~*** force s.o. to speak, F loosen s.o.'s tongue; ***manche Leute muß man zu ihrem Glück ~*** some people don't know what's good for them; ***das Glück läßt sich nicht ~*** you can't force happiness; ***das läßt sich nicht ~*** you can't force it; ***ich lass' mich nicht ~*** I won't be forced (*or* coerced); ***das zwingt mich zu der Annahme, daß*** I'm forced to conclude that; → ***gezwungen***; **2.** F manage; **II.** *v/i.*: ***~ zu*** *dat.* demand, necessitate; ***die Lage zwingt zu drastischen Maßnahmen*** the situation demands (*or* necessitates) drastic measures; **III.** *v/refl.*: ***sich ~*** force o.s.; ***sich zur Höflichkeit*** *etc.* ***~*** force o.s. to be polite *etc.*; ***sich zur Ruhe ~*** force o.s. to relax; ***sich zu lächeln ~*** force a smile; **'zwin·gend** *adj.* compelling *reason, evidence etc.*; *a.* inescapable *logic*; absolute, urgent *necessity*; cogent, conclusive *argument, evidence etc.*; ***ein ~er Beweis*** compelling (*or* conclusive, unimpeachable) evidence; ***mit e-r ~en Logik*** with compelling logic
Zwin·ger ['tsvɪŋɐ] *m* (-s; -) **1.** ward; **2.** kennel
zwin·kern ['tsvɪŋkɐn] *v/i.* (h) (*a.* ***mit den Augen ~***) a) blink, b) wink
zwir·beln ['tsvɪrbəln] *v/t.* (h) twist, F twiddle
Zwirn [tsvɪrn] *m* (-[e]s; -e) twine, twist
'Zwirns·fa·den *m* thread
zwi·schen ['tsvɪʃən] *prp.* (*dat.*) *a. fig.* a) between, b) among; ***~ ihnen herrscht Streit*** they've fallen out; ***~ ihnen wird es nie zur Einigung kommen*** they'll never come to an agreement
'Zwi·schen·ab·rech·nung *f* † preliminary billing
'Zwi·schen·akt *m thea.* intermission; **~mu͵sik** *f* interlude
'Zwi·schen|ap͵plaus *m* spontaneous applause; **~auf·ent·halt** *m* stop(over); **~aus·weis** *m* † interim return; **~be·mer·kung** *f* interjection; interruption; **~be·richt** *m* interim report; **~be·scheid** *m* provisional reply; **~bi͵lanz** *f* interim balance (sheet); *fig. pol.* mid-term review; *fig.* ***e-e ~ ziehen*** take stock in between; **~blatt** *n* interleaf; **~blu·tung** *f a. pl.* ⚕ irregular bleeding, spotting; **~deck** ⚓ *n*: ***im ~*** between decks; **~decke** *f* false ceiling; **~ding** *n* something in between; ***es ist ein ~*** *a.* it's a bit of both
'zwi·schen'drin *adv.* **1.** in between; (right) in the middle; **2.** a) in between, b) now and then
'zwi·schen·durch *adv.* a) in between; in the meantime, b) now and then; here and there
'Zwi·schen|eis·zeit *f* interglacial period; **~er·geb·nis** *n* provisional result; *sport*: latest results *pl.* (*or* score); **~fall** *m* incident; ***ohne Zwischenfälle*** without a hitch; ***ohne Zwischenfälle verlaufen*** *demonstration*: pass off peacefully (*or* without incident); → ***blutig*** 2; **~fi·nan·͵zie·rung** *f* bridging; interim financing; **~fra·ge** *f* (interpolated) question; *parl. a.* interruption, interpolation; ***darf ich e-e ~ stellen?*** may I throw in a quick question?; **~fut·ter** *n* interlining; **~gas** *n*: *mot.* ***~ geben*** double-clutch; **~ge·richt** *n gastr.* entrée; **~ge·schoß** *n* mezzanine (floor); **~glied** *n* link; **~grö·ße** *f* intermediate size; **~han·del** *m* intermediate trade; **~händ·ler** *m* middleman, intermediary; **~hirn** *n* diencephalon; **~hoch** *n meteor.* ridge of high pressure; **~kie·fer·kno·chen** *m* intermaxillary (bone); **~kre͵dit** *m* interim loan; **~la·ger** *n* intermediate store; intermediate storage site *for toxic waste*; **~la·ge·rung** *f* intermediate storage
'zwi·schen·lan·den *v/i.* (landete zwischen, zwischengelandet, sn) stop over, make a stopover; **'Zwi·schen·lan·dung** *f* stopover; ***~ zum Auftanken*** refuel(l)ing stop; ***ohne ~*** nonstop
'Zwi·schen|lauf *m sport*: intermediate heat; **~lö·sung** *f* interim solution; **~mahl·zeit** *f* snack (between meals); ***ich muß aufhören mit diesen ~en*** I must stop eating (things) between meals
'zwi·schen·mensch·lich *adj.* interpersonal, interhuman; ***~e Beziehungen*** *a.* human relations; ***im ~en Bereich*** where human relations are concerned
'Zwi·schen|pau·se *f* break; *thea. etc.* interval, *Am.* intermission; **~pro͵dukt** *n* intermediate product; **~prü·fung** *f* intermediate exam(ination); **~raum** *m* **1.** a) space (in between); gap, *formal*: interstice, b) *typ.* spacing, c) *a.* ⚙ clearance; **2.** interval; **~rech·nung** *f* interim bill; **~re·ge·lung** *f* interim ruling; **~ring** *m* **1.** *phot.* adapter; extension tube; **2.** ⚙ rubber insert; **~ruf** *m* (loud) interruption; *pl.* heckling *sg.*; ***durch ~e unterbrechen*** heckle; **~ru·fer** *m* heckler; **~run·de** *f sport*: intermediate round; **~sai͵son** *f* in-between season
'zwi·schen·schal·ten *v/t.* (*only inf. and p.p.* zwischengeschaltet, h) ⚡, ⚙ interpose; interconnect; **'Zwi·schen·schal·tung** *f* (-; -en) ⚡, ⚙ interposition
'Zwi·schen|soh·le *f* midsole; **~spei·che·rung** *f computer*: intermediate storage; **~spiel** *n thea.*, ♪ interlude; **~spurt** *m sport*: (sudden) spurt; ***e-n ~ einschalten*** put in a burst of speed
'zwi·schen·staat·lich *adj.* international; intergovernmental; interstate ...
'Zwi·schen|sta·di·um *n* intermediate stage; **~sta·ti͵on** *f* stop, stopover; ***~ machen in*** *dat.* stop over in, make a stop in; **~stecker** *m* ⚡ adapter (plug); **~stock** *m* mezzanine (floor); **~stück** *n* connecting piece; ⚡ adapter; **~stu·fe** *f* intermediate stage; **~sum·me** *f* subtotal; **~teil** *n* connecting piece; **~text** *m film*: inserted caption(s *pl.*); **~tief** *n meteor.* ridge of low pressure; **~ton** *m* **1.** (intermediate) shade; **2.** *fig.* overtone; nuance
'Zwi·schen·trä·ger *contp. m* informant, F telltale; **Zwi·schen·trä·ge·rei** [-trɛgə'raɪ] *contp. f* (-; -en) informing, F taletelling
'Zwi·schen|tür *f* interconnecting door; **~ur·teil** *n* interlocutory judg(e)ment; **~ver·trag** *m* provisional agreement; **~wand** *f* dividing wall; partition; **~wert** *m* intermediate value; **~wirt** *m biol.* intermediate host
'Zwi·schen·zeit *f* **1.** interim, intervening (*or* interim) period; ***in der ~*** in the meantime, meanwhile, in the interim; **2.** *sport*: intermediate time; **'zwi·schen·zeit·lich** *adv.* in the meantime, meanwhile
'Zwi·schen·zeug·nis *n* a) *ped.* intermediate report, b) intermediate reference
Zwist [tsvɪst] *m* (-[e]s; -e) quarrel, dispute; *a.* feud; **Zwi·stig·kei·ten** ['tsvɪstɪçkaɪtən] *pl.* **1.** discord *sg.*; **2.** → ***Zwist***
zwit·schern ['tsvɪtʃɐn] *v/i. and v/t.* (h) twitter, chirp; F ***e-n ~*** F knock one back, F have a quick one
Zwit·ter ['tsvɪtɐ] *m* (-s; -) **1.** hermaphrodite (*a.* ⚥); **2.** *fig.* hybrid, cross between a(n) ... and a(n) ...; **'zwit·ter·haft** *adj.* hermaphroditic; **'Zwit·ter·haf·tig·keit** *f* (-; *no pl.*) hermaphroditism

'Zwit·ter·we·sen *n* (-s; -) **1.** hermaphrodite; **2.** *no pl.* hermaphroditism
zwo [tsvo:] *adj.* → ***zwei***
zwölf [tsvœlf] *adj.* twelve; ***um ~*** (***Uhr***) at twelve (o'clock), *a.* at noon, *a.* at midnight; *fig.* ***fünf Minuten vor ~*** at the eleventh hour; ***es ist fünf Minuten vor ~*** it's the eleventh hour
Zwölf *f* (-; -en) twelve; (*bus etc.*) (number) twelve
Zwölf'fin·ger·darm *m anat.* duodenum; **~ge·schwür** *n* ⚕ duodenal ulcer
'Zwölf·kampf *m gym.* twelve events *pl.* (competition); **'Zwölf·kämp·fer** *m gym.* dodecathlon athlete
Zwölf'mei·len·zo·ne *f* twelve-mile zone
zwölft *adj.* twelfth
Zwölf·tel ['tsvœlftəl] *n* (-s; -) twelfth (part)
'Zwölf·ton|mu͵sik *f* twelve-tone music; **~tech·nik** *f* ♪ twelve-tone technique, duodecaphony
'Zwölf·zy͵lin·der *m* a) twelve-cylinder (car), b) twelve-cylinder engine
Zya·nid [tsy̆a'ni:t] *n* (-s; -e) cyanide
Zy·an·ka·li [tsy̆a:n'ka:li] *n* (-s; *no pl.*) potassium cyanide
zy·klisch ['tsy:klɪʃ] *adj.* cyclic(ally *adv.*)
Zy·klon [tsy'klo:n] *m* (-s; -e), **Zy'klo·ne** [tsy'klo:nə] *f* (-; -n) *meteor.* cyclone
Zy·klop [tsy'klo:p] *m* (-en; -en) Cyclops; **Zy'klo·pen·mau·er** *f* cyclopean masonry (*or* wall)
Zy·klo·tron [tsyklo'tro:n] *n* (-s; -s, -e) cyclotron
Zy·klus ['tsy:klʊs] *m* (-; Zyklen) cycle (*a.* ♪, ⚕); series *of lectures etc.*; ***der ~ der Jahreszeiten*** the revolving seasons, the seasonal cycle
Zy·lin·der [tsy'lɪndɐ] *m* (-s; -) **1.** a) ⚙, ⚙, *a. mot.* cylinder, b) chimney; **2.** top hat; **~block** *m* cylinder block; **~kol·ben** *m* cylinder piston
Zy'lin·der·kopf *m mot.* cylinder head; **~dich·tung** *f* cylinder-head gasket
Zy'lin·der·schloß *n* cylinder lock
zy·lin·drisch [tsy'lɪndrɪʃ] *adj.* cylindrical
Zy·ni·ker ['tsy:nikɐ] *m* (-s; -) cynic; ***alter ~*** arch-cynic; **zy·nisch** ['tsy:nɪʃ] *adj.* cynical; **Zy·nis·mus** [tsy'nɪsmʊs] *m* (-; -men) cynicism
Zy·pres·se [tsy'prɛsə] *f* (-; -n) cypress
Zy·pri·ot [tsypri'o:t] *m* (-en; -en), **Zy·prio·tin** [tsypri'o:tɪn] *f* (-; -nen), **zy·prio·tisch** [tsypri'o:tɪʃ] *adj.* Cypriot
Zy·ste ['tsʏstə] *f* (-; -n) cyst
Zy·to·lo·ge [tsyto'lo:gə] *m* (-n; -n) cytologist; **Zy·to·lo·gie** [tsytolo'gi:] *f* (-; *no pl.*) cytology; **zy·to·lo·gisch** ['tsyto'lo:gɪʃ] *adj.* cytological

German Abbreviations

A

A ***Ampere*** ampere(s *pl.*) (A)
a ***Ar*** are (a)
AA *das* ***Auswärtige Amt*** foreign ministry
a. a. O. ***am angegebenen*** *or* ***angeführten Ort*** in the place cited (loc. cit.)
Abb. ***Abbildung*** illustration (fig.)
Abf. ***Abfahrt*** departure (dep.)
Abg. ***Abgeordnete(r)*** member of parliament
Abk. ***Abkürzung*** abbreviation (abbr.)
ABM ***Arbeitsbeschaffungsmaßnahme(n)*** job creation scheme
ABS ***Antiblockiersystem*** anti-lock (*or* anti-skid) braking system
Abs. ***Absatz*** paragraph (para., par.), *typ.* break; ***Absender*** sender; return address
Abt. ***Abteilung*** department (dept, dpt)
abzgl. ***abzüglich*** less, minus
a. Chr. (n.) ***ante Christum (natum), vor Christus (vor Christi Geburt)*** before Christ (BC)
ACS ***Automobilclub der Schweiz*** Automobile Association of Switzerland
A. D. ***anno Domini, im Jahre des Herrn*** in the year of our Lord (AD)
a. D. ***außer Dienst*** retired (retd); ***an der Donau*** on the Danube
ADAC ***Allgemeiner Deutscher Automobil-Club*** General German Automobile Association
Add. ***Addenda, Ergänzungen*** addenda, supplements, additions
ADFC ***Allgemeiner Deutscher Fahrrad-Club*** General German Cyclists' Association
ad inf. ***ad infinitum, bis ins unendliche, unaufhörlich*** ad infinitum
ad l., ad lib(it). ***ad libitum, nach Belieben*** ad lib(itum)
Adr. ***Adresse*** address
AEG ***Allgemeine Elektrizitäts-Gesellschaft*** General Electric Company
AG ***Aktiengesellschaft*** public limited company (PLC, Plc, plc; Ltd), *Am.* (stock) corporation; ***Arbeitsgruppe*** study group
Agt. ***Agent*** agent; ***Agentur*** agency; agents *pl.*
Ah ***Amperestunde(n)*** ampere-hour(s *pl.*)
ahd. ***althochdeutsch*** Old High German (OHG)
Akad. ***Akademie*** academy, (*Fachschule*) *a.* college
akad. ***akademisch*** academic(al), university ...
Akk. ***Akkusativ*** accusative (case) (acc.)
Akt.-Nr. ***Aktennummer*** file number (file no.)
AKW ***Atomkraftwerk*** nuclear power station *or* plant
akz. ***akzeptiert*** accepted; ✝ *a.* hono(u)red
al. ***alias, auch ... genannt*** alias, otherwise *or* also known as (aka)
Alk. ***Alkohol*** alcohol (alc.)
allg. ***allgemein*** general(ly *adv.*)
allj. ***alljährlich*** annual(ly *adv.*), yearly
alph. ***alphabetisch*** alphabetical(ly *adv.*)
Alu ***Aluminium*** alumin(i)um
AM ***Amplitudenmodulation*** (*Frequenzbereich der Kurz-, Mittel- u. Langwellen*) amplitude modulation (AM)
a. M. ***am Main*** on the Main
am., amer(ik). ***amerikanisch*** American (Am.)
amtl. ***amtlich*** official(ly *adv.*)
Anal. ***Analogie*** analogy (anal.); ***Analyse*** analysis (anal.)
Anh. ***Anhang*** appendix
Ank. ***Ankunft*** arrival (arr.)
Anl. ***Anlage*** enclosure (encl.)
anl. ***anläßlich*** on the occasion of
Anm. d. Red. ***Anmerkung der Redaktion*** editor's comment (Ed., ed.)
anschl. ***anschließend*** following (foll.), subsequent(ly *adv.*)
AOK ***Allgemeine Ortskrankenkasse*** compulsory health insurance scheme
ao. Prof., a. o. Prof. ***außerordentlicher Professor*** reader, senior lecturer, *Am.* associate professor
Apart. ***Apartment*** flatlet, one-room apartment, *Am.* efficiency apartment (apt.)
APO ***Außerparlamentarische Opposition*** extraparliamentary opposition
App. ***Apparat*** *teleph.* extension (ext.)
appr. ***approbiert*** qualified, licenced, *Am.* licensed
Apr. ***April*** April (Apr., Apr)
Arb. ***Arbeit*** work; labo(u)r; ***Arbeiter*** worker, workman, labo(u)rer
Arbg. ***Arbeitgeber*** employer
Arbn. ***Arbeitnehmer*** employee
ARD ***Arbeitsgemeinschaft der öffentlich-rechtlichen Rundfunkanstalten der Bundesrepublik Deutschland*** working pool of the broadcasting corporations of the Federal Republic of Germany
Arge ***Arbeitsgemeinschaft*** work(ing) group; syndicate
a. Rh. ***am Rhein*** on the Rhine
Art. ***Artikel*** article, ✝ *a.* item, commodity
ärztl. ***ärztlich*** medical (med.); doctor's *certificate etc.*
Assist. ***Assistent(in)*** assistant (assnt); ***Assistenz*** assistence
Asta ***Allgemeiner Studentenausschuß*** general students' committee
ASU ***Abgassonderuntersuchung*** exhaust-emission test
A.T. ***Altes Testament*** Old Testament (OT)
atü ***Atmosphärenüberdruck*** atmospheric excess pressure (psi = pounds per square inch)
Aufl. ***Auflage*** edition (ed.)
Auftr.-Nr. ***Auftragsnummer*** order number
Aug. ***August*** August (Aug., Aug)
Ausg. ***Ausgabe*** **1.** edition (ed.); **2.** copy; ***Ausgang*** exit
austr(al). ***australisch*** Australian (Aus.)
Az. ***Aktenzeichen*** file number (file no.); *on letter*: reference (ref.)

B

B ***Bundesstraße*** major road, federal highway
b. ***bei*** at; near (nr); *address*: care of (c/o)
BAB ***Bundesautobahn*** autobahn; motorway, *Am.* highway
BAFöG ***Bundesausbildungsförderungsgesetz*** student financial assistance scheme
Barz(ahl). ***Barzahlung*** cash payment
BAT ***Bundesangestelltentarif*** salary scale for public employees
Bauj. ***Baujahr*** construction year; ... model
b. a. W. ***bis auf Widerruf*** until recalled *or* revoked; until further notice
b. a. w. ***bis auf weiteres*** for the present, until further notice
BB ***Bundesbahn*** federal railway(s)
Bd. ***Band*** volume (vol.); ***Bund*** union; association (assoc.)
Bde. ***Bände*** volumes (vols)
Bd.-Reg. ***Bundesregierung*** Federal Government (Fed. Govt)
bds. ***beiderseits*** on both sides
Beg. ***Beginn*** start, commencement
Begl. ***Beglaubigung*** certification (cert.); ***Begleichung*** settlement, payment; ***Begleitung*** company (→ *dictionary*)
begl. ***beglaubigt*** certified (cert.); ***beglichen*** paid (pd)
beil. ***beiliegend*** enclosed (encl.)
Beisp. ***Beispiel*** example, instance
belg. ***belgisch*** Belgian (Belg.)
Bem. ***Bemerkung*** remark, note, comment
Ber. ***Bericht*** report (rep.), account, commentary; ***Berichtigung*** correction (corr.)
bes. ***besonder*** special, particular (part.); ***besonders*** (e)specially (esp.), particularly (part.); above all
Best. ***Bestellung*** order
Best.-Nr. ***Bestellnummer*** order number (ord. no.)
Betr. ***Betreff, betrifft*** *on letter*: with reference to (Re, re, Re., re.)
betr. ***betreffend, betrifft, betreffs*** con-

cerning, regarding, as to; ✝ *a.* re
Bez. ***Bezahlung*** pay(ment); ***Bezeichnung*** mark; name, term, designation (des.); ***Beziehung*** → *dictionary*; ***Bezirk*** district (dist.)
bez. ***bezahlt*** paid (pd); ***bezüglich*** regarding, concerning, with reference to; ✝ *a.* re
BF, bfr ***belgische(r) Franc(s)*** Belgian franc(s *pl.*) (BF, Bfr)
BGB ***Bürgerliches Gesetzbuch*** (German) Civil Code
Bge. ***Berge*** mountains (mtns)
BGH ***Bundesgerichtshof*** Federal High Court
BGS ***Bundesgrenzschutz*** Federal Border Guard
Bhf. ***Bahnhof*** station (sta., Sta.)
BI ***Bürgerinitiative*** citizens' (action) group, civic action group, civic action
Bib. ***Bibel*** Bible
bildl. ***bildlich*** pictorial, visual(ly *adv.*), graphic(ally *adv.*); figurative(ly *adv.*) (fig.)
biogr. ***biographisch*** biographical(ly *adv.*) (biog.)
biol. ***biologisch*** biological(ly *adv.*) (biol.); organic(ally *adv.*) (org.)
Bj. ***Baujahr*** construction year; ... model
BKB ***Benzinkostenbeteiligung*** share petrol (*Am.* gas) costs
BLZ ***Bankleitzahl*** bank code
BND ***Bundesnachrichtendienst*** Federal Intelligence Service
bot. ***botanisch*** botanic(al) (bot.)
BPA ***Bahnpostamt*** station post office
BP a. ***Bundespatent angemeldet*** Federal Patent pending
Bq ***Becquerel*** becquerel (Bq.)
BR ***Bayerischer Rundfunk*** Bavarian Broadcasting Corporation
Br. ***Breite*** width (W., w.)
bras. ***brasilianisch*** Brazilian (Braz.)
BRD ***Bundesrepublik Deutschland*** Federal Republic of Germany (FRG)
brit. ***britisch*** British (Brit.)
BRK ***Bayerisches Rotes Kreuz*** Bavarian Red Cross
BRT ***Bruttoregistertonne(n)*** gross register ton(s *pl.*) (GRT)
BRZ ***Bruttoraumzahl*** gross register tonnage *or* tons *pl.*
bsd. ***besonders*** (e)specially (esp.), particularly (part.); above all
BSP ***Bruttosozialprodukt*** gross national product (GNP)
btto. ***brutto*** gross (gr.)
Btx, btx ***Bildschirmtext*** viewdata
Bw. ***Bundeswehr*** (German federal) armed forces, Bundeswehr
b. w. ***bitte wenden*** please turn over (PTO, pto)
BWL ***Betriebswirtschaftslehre*** business administration, business economics
BWV ***Bachwerkeverzeichnis*** (*of the works by Johann Sebastian Bach*) Bach Catalog(ue) (BWV)
bzgl. ***bezüglich*** regarding, concerning, with reference to; ✝ *a.* re
bzw. ***beziehungsweise*** respectively (resp.); or rather ...

C

C ***Celsius*** Celsius, centigrade (C)
c ***Cent(s)*** cent(s *pl.*) (c); ***Centime(s)*** centime(s *pl.*) (c)
ca. ***circa, ungefähr, etwa*** about, approximately (approx.), circa (c.)
cand. ***candidatus, Kandidat*** candidate (cand.)
ccm (*obsolete for* **cm³**) ***Kubikzentimeter*** cubic centimet|re(s *pl.*), *Am.* -er(s *pl.*) (cc)
CD ***compact disc, CD*** compact disc (CD)
CDU ***Christlich-Demokratische Union*** Christian Democratic Union
cf. ***confer, vergleiche*** compare (cf., cp., comp.)
chem. ***chemisch*** chemical (chem.)
chir. ***chirurgisch*** surgical (surg.)
christl. ***christlich*** Christian (Chr.)
cl ***Zentiliter*** centilit|re(s *pl.*), *Am.* -er(s *pl.*)
cm ***Zentimeter*** centimet|re(s *pl.*), *Am.* -er(s *pl.*)
cm² ***Quadratzentimeter*** square centimet|re(s *pl.*), *Am.* -er(s *pl.*) (sq.cm., cm^2)
cm³ ***Kubikzentimeter*** cubic centimet|re(s *pl.*), *Am.* -er(s *pl.*) (cc, cm^3)
Co. ✝ *obsolete* ***Compagnie, Kompanie*** company (Co., co.)
c/o ***care of, bei, per Adresse*** (c/o)
cos ***Kosinus*** cosine (cos)
CSFR *hist.* ***Tschechische und Slowakische Föderative Republik*** Czech and Slovak Federal Republic
ČSSR *hist.* ***Tschechoslowakische Sozialistische Republik*** Czechoslovak Socialist Republic
CSU ***Christlich-Soziale Union*** Christian Social Union (*of Bavaria*)
ct ***Cent(s)*** cent(s *pl.*) (ct, *pl.* cts); ***Centime(s)*** centime(s *pl.*) (ct, *pl.* cts)
c. t. ***cum tempore, mit akademischem Viertel*** quarter past the hour
CTA ***chemisch-technische Assistentin*** (chemical) laboratory assistant
CVJM ***Christlicher Verein Junger Menschen*** Young Men's Christian Association (YMCA); Young Women's Christian Association (YWCA)

D

D ***Durchgangszug, Schnellzug*** express (train), fast train
D. ***Deutschverzeichnis*** (*of the works by Franz Schubert*) Deutsch Catalog(ue) (D); ***Doktor der (protestantischen) Theologie*** Doctor of Divinity (DD)
d. Ä. ***der Ältere*** the Elder
DAAD ***Deutscher Akademischer Austauschdienst*** German Academic Exchange Service
DAG ***Deutsche Angestellten-Gewerkschaft*** Trade Union of German Employees
dän. ***dänisch*** Danish (Dan.)
dank. ***dankend*** with thanks; gratefully
dass. ***dasselbe*** the same (thing)
DAT ***digital audio tape*** (*recorders cassette for digital recordings with DAT*)
Dat. ***Dativ*** dative (case) (dat.); ***Datum*** date (d.)
DB ***Deutsche Bahn*** German Railways; ***Deutsche Bundesbank*** German Federal Bank
DBP ***Deutsche Bundespost*** German Federal Postal Services
DBP(a) ***Deutsches Bundespatent (angemeldet)*** German Federal Patent (pending)
dch. ***durch*** through; by; via
ddp ***Deutscher Depeschendienst*** (*German press agency*)
DDR *hist.* ***Deutsche Demokratische Republik*** German Democratic Republic (GDR)
DDT ***Dichlordiphenyltrichloräthan*** dichlorodiphenyltrichloroethane (DDT)
d. E. ***durch Eilboten*** express, *Am.* (by) special delivery
demn. ***demnach*** thus, so, consequently, therefore; according to that, accordingly; ***demnächst*** soon, before long
ders. ***derselbe*** the same
desgl. ***desgleichen*** likewise, the same; similarly
Det. ***Detail*** detail
Dez. ***Dezember*** December (Dec., Dec)
dez. ***dezimal*** decimal
DFB ***Deutscher Fußball-Bund*** German Football Association
DGB ***Deutscher Gewerkschaftsbund*** Federation of German Trade Unions
dgl. ***dergleichen*** such, like that; the like, such a thing; ***desgleichen*** → **desgl.**
d. Gr. ***der*** *or* ***die Große*** the Great
d. h. ***das heißt*** that is (i.e.)
Di. ***Dienstag*** Tuesday (Tue., Tue, Tues., Tues)
d. i. ***das ist*** that is (i.e.)
Dial. ***Dialekt*** dialect (dial.); ***Dialektik*** dialectics (*sg. and pl.*)
dienstl. ***dienstlich*** official, business ...; on business
diesj. ***diesjährig*** this year's ...
DIN ***Deutsches Institut für Normung*** German Institute for Standardization; *obsolete for* **DIN-Norm** (***Deutsche Industrie-Norm***) German Industrial Standard
Din ***Dinar*** dinar(s *pl.*) (Din.)
Dipl. ***Diplom*** diploma (Dip., Dipl.); ***Diplom...*** qualified ...
dipl. ***diplomatisch*** diplomatic; ***diplomiert*** qualified
Dipl.-Ing. ***Diplomingenieur*** qualified engineer
Dipl.-K(au)fm. ***Diplomkaufmann*** business graduate
Dir. ***Direktion*** management; board of directors; manager's office; head office (HO); ***Direktor*** manager; director (dir.); *ped.* headmaster, *Am.* principal; ***Dirigent*** conductor
Diss. ***Dissertation*** (doctoral) thesis
Distr. ***Distrikt*** district (dist.)
d. J. ***der Jüngere*** the Younger; ***dieses Jahres*** of this year
dkg ***Dekagramm*** decagram(s *pl.*), decagrammes(s *pl*)
dkr ***dänische Krone(n)*** Danish crown(s *pl.*)
DM ***Deutsche Mark*** (German) mark(s *pl.*)
d. M(ts). ***d(ies)es Monats*** of the present month, instant (inst.)
DNA ***Deutscher Normenausschuß*** German Committee of Standards
DNS ***Desoxyribonukleinsäure*** deoxyribonucleic acid (DNA)
Do. ***Donnerstag*** Thursday (Th., Th, Thur., Thur, Thurs., Thurs)
d. O. ***der*** *or* ***die*** *or* ***das Obige*** the above-mentioned
do. ***dito*** ditto (do.)
Dolm. ***Dolmetscher(in)*** interpreter
dopp. ***doppelt*** double (dbl., dble); in duplicate
Doz. ***Dozent*** (university) lecturer, *Am.* assistant professor
Do.-Z(i). ***Doppelzimmer*** double (room)
dpa ***Deutsche Presse-Agentur*** German Press Agency

dpp. → ***dopp.***
Dr, dr ***Drachme(n)*** drachma(s *pl.*), *pl. a.* drachmae (dr.)
Dr. ***Doktor*** doctor (Dr.)
d. R. ***der Reserve*** ⚔ reserve ...
d. Red. ***die Redaktion*** the editor(s *pl.*) (Ed., ed., *pl.* eds)
Dr. jur. ***doctor juris, Doktor der Rechte*** Doctor of Laws (LLD)
DRK ***Deutsches Rotes Kreuz*** German Red Cross
Dr. med. ***doctor medicinae, Doktor der Medizin*** Doctor of Medicine (MD)
Dr. phil. ***doctor philosophiae, Doktor der Philosophie*** Doctor of Philosophy (PhD, DPhil)
Dr. rer. nat. ***doctor rerum naturalium, Doktor der Naturwissenschaften*** Doctor of Science (DSc, ScD)
Dr. theol. ***doctor theologiae, Doktor der Theologie*** Doctor of Divinity (DD)
DSB ***Deutscher Sportbund*** German Sports Association
dstl. → ***dienstl.***
dt(sch.) ***deutsch*** German (Ger.)
Dtzd. ***Dutzend*** dozen (doz.)
d. U. ***der Unterzeichnete*** the undersigned
Dupl. ***Duplikat*** duplicate (dupl.); copy
Durchw.(-Nr.) ***Durchwahl(nummer)*** direct dial(l)ing (number)
d. V(er)f. ***der Verfasser, die Verfasserin*** the author
d. v. J. ***des vorigen Jahres*** last year's, of the previous year
DVO ***Durchführungsverordnung*** implementing ordinance
dyn. ***dynamisch*** dynamic(ally *adv.*)
DZ ***Doppelzimmer*** double (room)
dz ***Doppelzentner*** 100 kilogram(me)s

E

E ***Eilzug*** fast train; ***Elektrizität(s...)*** electricity (...); power *station*; ***Erdgeschoß*** ground floor (grd. fl., G), *Am.* first floor (1st fl.); ***Europastraße*** European Highway (*passing through several countries*)
ea. ***ehrenamtlich*** honorary (hon.)
ebd. ***ebenda*** ibidem (ibid., ib.)
EC ***Eurocity(-Zug)*** Euro-city (train)
ECU, Ecu ***European currency unit(s), europäische Währungseinheit(en*** *pl.*) (*ECU*)
Ed. ***Edition, Ausgabe*** edition (ed.)
ed. ***edidit, hat herausgegeben*** edited by (ed.)
EDV ***Elektronische Datenverarbeitung*** electronic data processing (EDP, edp)
EEG ***Elektroenzephalogramm*** electroencephalogram (EEG)
EG ***Europäische Gemeinschaft*** European Community (EC)
e. G. ***eingetragene Gesellschaft*** registered (*Am.* incorporated) company
eGmbH ***eingetragene Genossenschaft mit beschränkter Haftpflicht*** registered cooperative society with limited liability
e. h. ***ehrenhalber*** honoris causa (h.c.)
ehel. ***ehelich*** marital, conjugal, matrimonial; legitimate *child*
ehem. ***ehemalig*** former, ex-...; ***ehemals*** formerly
Ehrw. ***Ehrwürden*** Reverend (Rev.)
eingetr. ***eingetragen*** ⚚ registered (regd), *Am. a.* incorporated (Inc., inc.); ***eingetreten*** entered
Eing.-Dat. ***Eingangsdatum*** date of receipt
Einh. ***Einheit*** unit (*a. teleph.*, ⚔)
einschl. ***einschlägig*** relevant, appropriate; ***einschließlich*** including (incl.), inclusive of (incl.)
Einschr. ***Einschreiben*** registered letter; registered (regd)
Einz.-Z(i). ***Einzelzimmer*** single (room)
EKD ***Evangelische Kirche in Deutschland*** Protestant Church in Germany
EKG, Ekg ***Elektrokardiogramm*** electrocardiogram (ECG, *Am.* EKG)
el(ektr). ***elektrisch*** electric(al) (elec., elect.); *adv.* electrically
Empf. ***Empfänger*** recipient; addressee
empf. ***empfohlen*** recommended (rec.)
engl. ***englisch*** English (Eng.)
Entf. ***Entfernung*** distance
entspr. ***entsprechen(d)*** → *dictionary*
entw. ***entweder*** either
erb. ***erbaut*** built, erected
Erdg. ***Erdgeschoß*** ground floor (grd. fl.), *Am.* first floor (1st fl.)
erf. ***erfolgt*** effected; ***erforderlich*** required (req.), necessary (nec.)
erg. ***ergänze*** complement, supplement, add
erh. ***erhalten*** received (recd, rec'd); preserved, in ... condition
Erl. ***Erläuterung*** explanation; (explanatory) note
erl. ***erlaubt*** permitted, allowed; ***erledigt*** finished, done; settled
erm. ***ermäßigt*** reduced (red.)
Ers. ***Ersatz*** substitute (subst.); replacement; compensation; indemnification; ***Ersuchen*** request (req.)
Erw. ***Erwachsene(r)*** adult(s *pl.*)
Esc. ***Escudo*** escudo (Esc.)
Et. ***Etage*** floor (fl.), stor(e)y
et. al. ***et alii, und andere*** and others (et al.)
Etg. ***Etage*** floor (fl.), stor(e)y
etw. ***etwaig*** any; possible (poss.); ***etwas*** something (s.th.), anything
EU ***Europäische Union*** European Union (EU)
Euratom ***Europäische Atomgemeinschaft*** European Atomic Energy Community (Euratom)
eur(op). ***europäisch*** European (Eur.)
e. V. ***eingetragener Verein*** registered association *or* society, incorporated (inc.)
ev. ***evangelisch*** Protestant (Prot.)
evtl. ***eventuell*** possible (poss.), any; *adv.* possibly (poss.); if necessary (if nec.)
ew. ***einstweilig*** temporary, provisional; ***ewig*** eternal
EWG *hist.* ***Europäische Wirtschaftsgemeinschaft*** European Economic Community (EEC)
EWS ***Europäisches Währungssystem*** European Monetary System (EMS)
Ex. ***Exemplar(e)*** copy, *pl.* copies; sample(s *pl.*)
exkl. ***exklusiv*** exclusive (excl.); select; *adv.* exclusively (excl.); ***exklusive*** exclusive of (excl.), excluding (excl.), not counting, not including (not incl.)
Expl. ***Exemplar(e)*** copy, *pl.* copies; sample(s *pl.*)
Expr. ***Expreß*** express (train)
Exz. ***Exzellenz*** Excellency (Exc.)
EZ ***Einzelzimmer*** single (room)

F

F ***Fahrenheit*** Fahrenheit (F, f)
f., f ***und folgende*** and following *page* (f., f)
Fa. ***Firma*** firm; *address*: Messrs.
Fabr. ***Fabrik*** factory, works (*sg. and pl.*); ***Fabrikat*** make; brand; product (prod.)
Fahrg(est).-Nr. ***Fahrgestellnummer*** chassis number
F(ahr)z. ***Fahrzeug*** vehicle
Fak. ***Fakultät*** faculty (Fac.)
Fam. ***Familie*** family; *address*: Mr & Mrs ... (and family)
FC ***Fußballclub*** football club
FCKW ***Fluorchlorkohlenwasserstoff*** chlorofluorocarbon (CFC)
FD ***Ferndurchgangszug, Fernschnellzug*** long-distance express (train)
FDGB *hist. GDR*: ***Freier Deutscher Gewerkschaftsbund*** Free Federation of German Trade Unions
FDJ *hist. GDR*: ***Freie Deutsche Jugend*** Free German Youth
F.D.P., FDP ***Freie Demokratische Partei*** Liberal Democratic Party; *in Switzerland*: ***Freisinnig-Demokratische Partei*** Liberal Democratic Party
Feb(r). ***Februar*** February (Feb., Feb)
Fewo. ***Ferienwohnung*** holiday flat *or* apartment (apt.)
FF ***französischer Franc*** French franc (FF)
ff., ff ***und folgende*** and following *pages* (ff., ff)
Ffm. ***Frankfurt am Main*** Frankfurt on the Main
FH ***Fachhochschule*** advanced technical college
Fig. ***Figur*** figure (fig.); diagram (diag.)
fig. ***figürlich, figurativ*** figurative(ly *adv.*) (fig.)
Fin. ***Finanz(en)*** finance(s)
fin. ***finanziell*** financial(ly *adv.*) (fin.)
finn. ***finnisch*** Finnish (Fin.)
FKK ***Freikörperkultur*** nudism
Fla ***Fliegerabwehr*** anti-aircraft defen|ce, *Am.* -se
FM ***Frequenzmodulation*** (*Frequenzbereich der Ultrakurzwellen*) frequency modulation (FM)
fm ***Festmeter*** cubic met|re(s *pl.*), *Am.* -er(s *pl.*)
fmdl. ***fernmündlich*** by telephone; telephone ...
Fmk ***Finnmark*** ⚚ fin(n)mark
Föd. ***Föderation*** (con)federation, confederacy (confed.)
folg. ***folgend(e)*** following (foll.); next; subsequent
fortl. ***fortlaufend*** continuous(ly *adv.*), running; consecutively
Forts. ***Fortsetzung*** continuation
Forts. f. ***Fortsetzung folgt*** to be continued (to be contd)
FPÖ ***Freiheitliche Partei Österreichs*** *Austrian liberal-conservative party*
Fr. ***Frau*** Mrs; *esp. in writing*: Ms; ***Franken*** ⚚ (Swiss) franc(s *pl.*) (fr.); ***Freitag*** Friday (Fri., Fri)
frank. ***frankiert*** stamped; prepaid, post paid
frdl. Grüße ***freundliche Grüße*** kind regards (rgds)
Frh., Frhr ***Freiherr*** baron
Frl. ***Fräulein*** Miss
frz. ***französisch*** French (Fr.)
Ft ***Forint*** forint (Ft)

FU ***Freie Universität*** (*Berlin*) Free University
Fut. ***Futur*** future (tense) (fut.)

G

g ***Gramm*** gram(s *pl.*), gramme(s *pl.*) (g)
Gar. ***Garantie*** guarantee
gar. ***garantiert*** guaranteed (gtd, guar.)
gastr. ***gastronomisch*** gastronomic(al); catering *staff etc.*
GAU ***größter anzunehmender Unfall*** maximum credible accident (MCA)
Gde. ***Gemeinde*** municipality; parish
Geb. ***Gebäude*** building (bldg); ***Gebiet*** district (dist.); area; ***Gebirge*** mountains *pl.* (mtns); ***Gebühr(en)*** charge(s *pl.*), fee(s *pl.*), rate(s *pl.*); ***Geburt*** birth
geb. ***gebaut*** built; erected; ***geboren*** born (b.); ***geborene*** *Schmidt etc.* née; ***gebunden*** bound (bd)
Gebr. ***Gebrüder*** Brothers (Bros.)
gebr. ***gebräuchlich*** common, normal; ***gebraucht*** used, second-hand
gef. ***gefallen*** ⚔ killed in action (KIA)
gegr. ***gegründet*** founded; established (estab., est.)
gem. ***gemacht*** made; ***gemäß*** according to; in compliance with; ***gemischt*** mixed
gen. ***genannt*** called, named; (*the*) said, (*the*) above-mentioned; ***genehmigt*** approved; authorized
Gen. ***Genitiv*** genitive (gen.); ***Genossenschaft*** cooperative
Gen.-Dir. ***Generaldirektor*** general manager, chairman, *Am.* president
Gen.-Sekr. ***Generalsekretär*** secretary general
geogr. ***geographisch*** geographic(al) (geog.)
geol. ***geologisch*** geologic(al) (geol.)
geom. ***geometrisch*** geometric(al) (geom.)
gepr. ***geprüft*** tested; checked; certified *document etc.*
Ges. ***Gesellschaft*** ✝ company, *Am. a.* corporation (corp.); society (soc.), association (assoc.); ***Gesetz*** law, act
gesch. ***geschäftlich*** business ...; on business; ***geschieden*** divorced (div.)
geschl. ***geschlossen*** closed; private *performance etc.*
ges. gesch. ***gesetzlich geschützt*** patented; registered (regd)
gest. ***gestorben*** died (d.)
Gestapo ***Geheime Staatspolizei*** *hist.* (*in Nazi-Germany*) secret state police
Gew. ***Gewicht*** weight (wt)
gew. ***gewöhnlich*** usually (usu.)
gez. ***gezeichnet*** signed (sgd)
GG ***Grundgesetz*** *pol.* Basic Law (*constitution of the Federal Republic of Germany*)
ggf(s). ***gegebenenfalls*** should the occasion arise; if necessary (if nec.); if applicable
Ggs. ***Gegensatz*** contrast; opposite (opp.)
ggz. ***gegengezeichnet*** countersigned
gltd. ***geltend*** valid, in effect; current *prices etc.*
gltg. ***gültig*** valid, good; effective, in force
GmbH ***Gesellschaft mit beschränkter Haftung*** private limited (liability) company (*approx.* plc)
gram(m). ***grammatisch*** grammatical
Grdfl. ***Grundfläche*** (surface) area
griech. ***griechisch*** Greek (Gk)
gr.-orth. ***griechisch-orthodox*** Greek Orthodox
GStA ***Generalstaatsanwalt*** prosecutor general
Gült. ***Gültigkeit*** validity
GUS ***Gemeinschaft unabhängiger Staaten*** Commonwealth of Independent States (CIS)
gzj. ***ganzjährig*** all-year ...; all year round

H

H ***Haltestelle*** *bus etc.* stop; *meteor.* ***Hoch*** (***-druckgebiet***) high(-pressure area)
H. ***Heft*** number (No., no.); ***Höhe*** height (H., h., hgt)
h ***Hekto...*** hecto...; ***Uhr*** hours (hrs); *before noon*: a.m., *after noon*: p.m.; ***hora, Stunde*** hour (hr)
ha ***Hektar*** hectare(s *pl.*) (ha)
habil. ***habilitatus, habilitiert*** habilitated
haftb. ***haftbar*** responsible, ⚖ liable
Halbj. ***Halbjahr*** half-year, six months *pl.*
halbj(hl). ***halbjährlich*** half-yearly, semi--annual(ly *adv.*); *adv.* every six months
Hbf. ***Hauptbahnhof*** main (*or* central) station (main sta., cen. *or* cent. sta.)
HC ***Hockeyclub*** hockey club
h. c. ***honoris causa, ehrenhalber*** honoris causa (h.c.), honorary (hon.)
HD-Öl ***Öl für schwere Betriebsbelastung*** heavy-duty oil
...hdt. ***...hundert*** ... hundred (hund.)
helv. ***helvetisch*** Helvetian; Helvetic
herg(est). ***hergestellt*** produced (prod.), made, built
Herst. ***Hersteller*** manufacturer; ***Herstellung*** production (prod.), manufacture (manuf., manufac.)
HF ***Hochfrequenz*** high frequency (HF, h.f.)
hfl (***holländischer***) ***Gulden*** Dutch guilder(s *pl.*) *or* florin(s *pl.*) (*Gld, gld.*)
Hfn ***Hafen*** harbo(u)r
Hft(g). ***Haftung*** liability; guarantee
Hg. ***Herausgeber(in)*** publisher (pub., publ.); editor (Ed., ed.)
hg. ***herausgegeben*** (***von***) published (by) (pub., publ.); edited (by) (ed.)
HGB ***Handelsgesetzbuch*** Commercial Code
Hi-Fi ***höchste Klangtreue*** high fidelity (hi-fi)
hist. ***historisch*** historic(al), *adv.* historically
HIV ***human immune deficiency virus*** (*virus causing aids*)
Hiwi ***Hilfswissenschaftler(in)*** *univ.* assistant
Hj. ***Halbjahr*** half-year, six months *pl.*
HK ***Handelskammer*** Chamber of Commerce
hl ***Hektoliter*** hectolit|re(s *pl.*), *Am.* -er(s *pl.*) (hl)
hl. ***heilig*** holy; ***heilige(r)*** Saint (St, St.) *Peter etc.*
HO *hist. DDR*: ***Handelsorganisation*** *state-owned store, hotel, and restaurant cooperative*
hochd. ***hochdeutsch*** standard *or* High German
höfl. ***höflich(st)*** kindly, politely
holl(änd). ***holländisch*** Dutch
HP ***Halbpension*** half-board
hPa ***Hektopascal*** hectopascal (hPa)
Hpt. ***Haupt...*** main, chief, principal, head ...
HR ***Hessischer Rundfunk*** Hessian Broadcasting Corporation
Hr(eg). ***Handelsregister*** Commercial Register
Hr(n). ***Herr(n)*** Mr
Hrsg. ***Herausgeber(in)*** publisher (pub., publ.); editor (Ed., ed.)
hrsg. ***herausgegeben*** (***von***) published (by) (pub., publ.); edited (by) (ed.)
Hs.-Nr. ***Hausnummer*** house number (hse no.)
HTL ***Höhere Technische Lehranstalt*** polytechnical school
Hubr. ***Hubraum*** cubic capacity
HVertr., H.-Vertr. ***Handelsvertrag*** trade agreement; ***Handelsvertretung*** commercial agency *or* agents *pl.*
HVerw., H.-Verw. ***Hauptverwaltung*** head office (H.O., HO), headquarters *sg. and pl.* (HQ)
Hyp. ***Hypothek*** mortgage
Hz ***Hertz*** hertz *sg. and pl.* (Hz), cycle(s *pl.*) per second (cps, c/s)
hzb. ***heizbar*** heatable; with heating
Hzg. ***Heizung*** heating

I

i *on signs*: ***Information, Auskunft*** information
i. ***im, in*** in (the); ***innen*** inside
I. A., i. A. ***im Auftrag*** per procurationem, by proxy (pp, p.p.)
i. allg. ***im allgemeinen*** generally (gen.), in general; on the whole
i. a. W. ***in anderen Worten*** in other words
ib. → ***ibd.***
i. b. ***im besonderen*** in particular
ibd. ***ibidem, ebenda, -dort*** in the same place (ib., ibid.)
IC ***Intercity(-Zug)*** inter-city (train)
ICE ***Intercity-Expreß*** inter-city express (train)
i. D. ***im Dienst*** on duty; ***im Durchschnitt*** on (an) average
i. d. M(in). ***in der Minute*** per minute
i. d. R. ***in der Regel*** as a rule
i. d. Sek. ***in der Sekunde*** per second (p.s.)
i. d. St(d). ***in der Stunde*** per hour (p.h.)
i. e. ***im einzelnen*** in detail *or* particular; ***id est, das heißt, das ist*** that is (i.e.)
i. e. S. ***im eigentlichen Sinne*** in the true sense (of the word); in the proper sense; ***im engeren Sinne*** in the narrow(er) sense
i. Fa. ***in Firma*** care of (c/o)
IFO ***Institut für Wirtschaftsforschung*** Institute for Economic Research
IG ***Industriegewerkschaft*** industrial union
i. g. ***im ganzen*** on the whole; altogether
i. H. ***im Hause*** on the premises
IHK ***Industrie- und Handelskammer*** Chamber of Industry and Commerce
i. H. v. ***in Höhe von*** (to the amount) of; at the rate of
i. J. ***im Jahre*** in (the year)
i. K. ***in Kürze*** shortly, soon; briefly
ill. ***illustriert*** illustrated (illust., illus.); pictorial
i. M. ***im Monat*** in (the month of) *July etc.*; monthly, per month
Imm. ***Immobilien*** real estate *sg.*, property *sg.*
Imp. ***Imperativ*** imperative (mood) (imp.,

imper.); ***Import*** import(ing); import(s *pl.*) (imp.)

Imperf. ***Imperfekt*** imperfect (tense) (imp.)

Ind. ***Index*** index (ind.); ***Indikativ*** indicative (mood) (ind.); ***Industrie*** industry (ind.)

i. N. d. ***im Namen des*** *or* ***der*** in the name of; on behalf of

Ing. ***Ingenieur*** engineer (eng.)

Inh. ***Inhaber*** owner, proprietor (prop., propr.); holder; ***Inhalt*** contents *pl.* (cont.)

inkl. ***inklusive*** including, inclusive of (incl.)

insb(es). ***insbesondere*** particularly, (e)specially ([e]sp.), in particular

insges. ***insgesamt*** altogether, in all

int. ***intern*** internal(ly *adv.*) (int.); ***international*** international (int., intl)

intern. ***international*** international (int., intl)

Interpol ***Internationale Kriminalpolizeiliche Organisation*** International Criminal Police Organization (Interpol)

IOK ***Internationales Olympisches Komitee*** International Olympic Committee (IOC)

IQ ***Intelligenzquotient*** intelligence quotient (IQ)

IR ***InterRegio*** long-distance express train (*slower than* ***IC, EC*** *and* ***ICE*** *trains*)

i. R. ***im Ruhestand*** retired (ret., retd)

IRK ***Internationales Rotes Kreuz*** International Red Cross (IRC)

ISBN ***internationale Standardbuchnummer*** international standard book number (ISBN)

ital. ***italienisch*** Italian (It., Ital.)

i. ü. ***im übrigen*** incidentally; (as) for the rest; besides

IV ***Industrieverband*** federation of industries

I. v. ***Irrtum vorbehalten*** errors excepted (e.e.)

I. V. ***in Vertretung*** in place of; on behalf of; *in letter*: (signed) for; ***in Vorbereitung*** being prepared, in preparation (in prep.)

IVF ***In-vitro-Fertilisation*** in vitro fertilization (IVF)

IWF ***Internationaler Währungsfonds*** International Monetary Fund (IMF)

J

J ***Joule*** joule(s *pl.*) (J.)

Jan. ***Januar*** January (Jan., Jan)

jap. ***japanisch*** Japanese (Jap.)

Jb. ***Jahrbuch*** yearbook (YB, Y.B.)

Jg. ***Jahrgang*** → *dictionary*

Jgd. ***Jugend*** youth

Jgg. ***Jahrgänge*** *pl. of* ***Jg.*** → *dictionary*

JH ***Jugendherberge*** youth hostel (Y.H.)

Jh. ***Jahrhundert*** century (c., cent.)

jhrl. ***jährlich*** annual(ly *adv.*)

Jr., jr., jun. ***junior, der Jüngere*** junior (Jun., jun., Jur, Jr)

Jul. ***Juli*** July (Jul., Jul)

Jun. ***Juni*** June (Jun., Jun)

jur. ***juristisch*** legal (leg.); juridical (jurid.)

K

Kal. ***Kalender*** calendar; ***Kaliber*** calib|re, *Am.* -er (cal.)

Kan. ***Kanada*** Canada (Can.); ***Kanadier*** Canadian (Can.); ***Kanal*** canal

Kap. ***Kapitel*** chapter (ch.)

Kapt. ***Kapitän*** captain (Capt.)

kart. ***kartoniert*** hardcover

Kat ***Katalysator*** catalytic converter, catalyst (cat.)

Kat. ***Katalog*** catalog(ue) (cat.); ***Kategorie*** category

kath. ***katholisch*** Catholic (Cath.)

kaufm. ***kaufmännisch*** commercial (comm., com.), business ...

KB ***Kilobyte(s)*** kilobyte(s *pl.*) (KB)

kcal ***Kilo(gramm)kalorie(n)*** kilocalorie(s *pl.*), kilogram(me) calorie(s *pl.*) (kcal, Cal.)

Kčs *hist.* ***tschechoslowakische Krone*** (Czechoslovac) crown, koruna

Kennz. ***Kennzeichen*** *mot.* registration (*Am.* license) number; ***Kennziffer*** code number; index (number); *advertisement*: box number

Kfm. ***Kaufmann*** businessman; trader, dealer; agent

kfm. ***kaufmännisch*** commercial (comm., com.), business ...

Kfz ***Kraftfahrzeug*** motor vehicle

Kfz.-Vers. ***Kraftfahrzeugversicherung*** motor (*Am.* automobile) insurance

KG ***Kommanditgesellschaft*** limited partnership

kg ***Kilogramm*** kilogramme(s *pl.*), *Am.* kilogram(s *pl.*) (kg)

kgl. ***königlich*** royal

kHz ***Kilohertz*** kilohertz (kHz), kilocycle(s *pl.*) (per second)

KJ ***Kilojoule*** kilojoule(s *pl.*) (kJ)

k. k. ***kaiserlich-königlich*** imperial and royal

KKW ***Kernkraftwerk*** nuclear power station *or* plant

Kl. ***Klasse*** class (cl.); *ped. Brit. a.* form, *Am. a.* grade; ☤ grade, quality

km ***Kilometer*** kilomet|re(s *pl.*), *Am.* -er(s *pl.*) (km)

km/h, km/st. ***Kilometer pro Stunde*** kilomet|res (*Am.* -ers) per hour (kph)

Komf. ***Komfort*** conveniences *pl.*

komf. ***komfortabel*** comfortable; well-appointed, luxury *flat etc.*

Komp. ⚔ ***Kompanie*** company; ***Komponist*** composer

Konf. ***Konferenz*** conference (conf.); ***Konfession*** (religious) denomination (denom.); ***Konföderation*** confederation, confederacy

Konj. ***Konjugation*** conjugation; ***Konjunktion*** conjunction (conj.); ***Konjunktiv*** subjunctive (subj.)

Konstr. ***Konstruktion*** construction (constr.); design

Konz. ***Konzert*** concert; concerto (conc.); ***Konzern*** group

KP ***Kommunistische Partei*** Communist Party (CP)

KPdSU *hist.* ***Kommunistische Partei der Sowjetunion*** Communist Party of the Soviet Union (CPSU)

kr ***Krone*** ☤ crown

Kr. ***Kreis*** (administrative) district (dist.)

Kripo ***Kriminalpolizei*** criminal investigation department (CID)

Krs. ***Kreis*** (administrative) district (dist.)

Kr.-Vers. ***Krankenversicherung*** health insurance

KSZE ***Konferenz über Sicherheit und Zusammenarbeit in Europa*** Conference on Security and Cooperation in Europe (CSCE)

KT ***Kaution*** deposit

Kt. ***Kanton*** canton

Kto. ***Konto*** (bank) account (a/c)

Kto.-Nr. ***Kontonummer*** account number (a/c no.)

Ktr.-Nr. ***Kontrollnummer*** code number

k. u. k. ***kaiserlich und königlich*** imperial and royal

künstl. ***künstlerisch*** artistic; ***künstlich*** artificial; synthetic

KV ***Köchelverzeichnis*** (*of the works by Wolfgang Amadeus Mozart*) Köchel (catalog[ue]) (K); ***Kraftverkehr*** motor traffic

KV ***Kilovolt*** kilovolt(s *pl.*)

KW ***Kurzwelle*** short wave (SW)

kW ***Kilowatt*** kilowatt(s *pl.*) (kW)

kWh ***Kilowattstunde(n)*** kilowatt-hour(s *pl.*)

KZ ***Konzentrationslager*** concentration camp

kzfr. ***kurzfristig*** short-term ...; *adv.* at short notice

L

L. ***(italienische) Lira*** *or pl.* ***Lire*** lira, *pl.* lire *or* liras; ***Länge*** length (L., l.)

l ***Liter*** lit|re(s *pl.*), *Am.* -er(s *pl.*) (l)

l. ***links*** left (l.); on *or* to the left

Lab. ***Laboratorium*** lab(oratory)

Landkr. ***Landkreis*** district

landw. ***landwirtschaftlich*** agricultural (agric.); farm ...

lat. ***lateinisch*** Latin (Lat.)

l. c. ***loco citato, am angegebenen Ort*** in the place cited (l.c.)

Ldg. ***Ladung*** load, freight; cargo; shipment

led. ***ledig*** unmarried, single (sgl.)

leg. ***legal*** legal(ly *adv.*)

Lekt. ***Lektion*** chapter (ch.), unit; lesson

lfd. ***laufend*** current, running, ongoing; *adv.* continuously, regularly

lfdm., lfd. m. ***laufende Meter*** running met|res, *Am.* -ers

lfd. M. ***laufenden Monats*** of this month

lfd. Nr. ***laufende Nummer*** (serial) number

Lf(r)g. ***Lieferung*** delivery; consignment, shipment

Lf.-Zt., Lfzt. ***Lieferzeit*** delivery period

LG ***Landgericht,*** *Austrian* ***Landesgericht*** district court

lgfr. ***langfristig*** long-term ...

Lit. ***italienische Lira*** *or pl.* ***Lire*** lira, *pl.* lire *or* liras; ***Literatur*** literature (lit.)

lit(er). ***literarisch*** literary (lit.)

liz. ***lizensiert*** licen|sed, *Am.* -ced

LKW, Lkw ***Lastkraftwagen*** lorry, *esp. Am.* truck

loc. cit. ***loco citato, am angegebenen Ort*** in the place cited (loc. cit.)

log ***Logarithmus*** logarithm (log.)

LP ***Langspielplatte*** long-playing record (LP)

LPG *hist. GDR*: ***landwirtschaftliche Produktionsgenossenschaft*** collective farm

LSD ***Lysergsäurediäthylamid*** lysergic acid diethylamide (LSD)

Lsg. ***Lösung*** solution (sol.) (*a.* ⚗)

lt. ***laut*** according to; as per

ltd. ***leitend*** managerial; chief ...

Ltg. ***Leitung*** direction; management; supervision

lux. ***luxemburgisch*** Luxemb(o)urg ...
LW ***Langwelle*** long wave (LW)
lx ***Lux*** lux (lx)

M

M *hist. GDR*: ***Mark*** mark(s *pl.*)
M. ***Magister*** Master (M)
m ***Meter*** met|re(s *pl.*), *Am.* -er(s *pl.*) (m); ***Milli...*** milli... (m)
m. ***männlich*** male (m., m); masculine (m., m, masc.); ***mit*** with (w.)
m² ***Quadratmeter*** square met|re(s *pl.*), *Am.* -er(s *pl.*) (sq.m, m²)
m³ ***Kubikmeter*** cubic met|re(s *pl.*), *Am.* -er(s *pl.*) (cu.m, m³)
MA ***Mittelalter*** *the* Middle Ages *pl.*
M. A. ***Magister Artium*** Master of Arts (MA)
mA ***Milliampere*** milliampere(s *pl.*) (mA)
MAD ***Militärischer Abschirmdienst*** Military Counter-Intelligence Service
Mag. ***Magazin*** → *dictionary*
m. A. n. ***meiner Ansicht nach*** in my opinion
männl. ***männlich*** male (m., m); masculine (m., m, masc.); for men, men's ...
Mar. ***Marine*** ⚔ Navy
masch. ***maschinell*** machine ..., machine-...; mechanical(ly *adv.*); *adv. a.* by machine
math. ***mathematisch*** mathematical (math.)
m. a. W. ***mit anderen Worten*** in other words
Max. ***Maximum*** maximum (max.)
max. ***maximal*** maximum, top ...; *adv.* maximally (max.)
MAZ ***magnetische Bildaufzeichnung*** video tape recording (VTR)
MdB, M. d. B. ***Mitglied des Bundestages*** Member of the Bundestag
MdL, M. d. L. ***Mitglied des Landtages*** Member of the Landtag
mdl. ***mündlich*** oral(ly *adv.*); verbal(ly *adv.*)
MDR ***Mitteldeutscher Rundfunk*** Central German Broadcasting Corporation
m. E. ***meines Erachtens*** in my opinion; as I see it; ***mit Einschränkungen*** with reservations
mech. ***mechanisch*** mechanical(ly *adv.*) (mech.)
med. ***medizinisch*** medical (med.); medicinal
MESZ ***mitteleuropäische Sommerzeit*** Central European Summer Time (CEST)
mex. ***mexikanisch*** Mexican (Mex.)
MEZ ***mitteleuropäische Zeit*** Central European Time (CET)
MG ***Maschinengewehr*** machine gun (MG)
mg ***Milligramm*** milligramme(s *pl.*), *Am.* milligram(s *pl.*) (mg)
mhd. ***mittelhochdeutsch*** Middle High German (MHG)
MHz ***Megahertz*** megahertz (MHz), megacycles per second (Mc/s)
Mi. ***Mittwoch*** Wednesday (Wed., Wed)
Mia. ***Milliarde(n)*** billion, *pl.* billion(s) (bn); *Brit. obs.* thousand million
mil(it). ***militärisch*** military (mil., milit.)
Mill. ***Million(en)*** million, *pl.* million(s) (m)
Min. ***Minimum*** minimum (min.)
Min., min. ***Minute(n)*** minute(s *pl.*) (min.)
min. ***minimal*** minimal; minimum (min.)
Mio. ***Million(en)*** million, *pl.* million(s) (m)
mm ***Millimeter*** millimet|re(s *pl.*), *Am.* -er(s *pl.*) (mm)
Mo. ***Montag*** Monday (Mon., Mon)
m(ö)bl. ***möbliert*** furnished (furn.)
mod. ***modern*** modern (mod.); ***modisch*** fashiona|ble, *adv.* -bly, stylish(ly *adv.*)
mögl. ***möglich*** possible (poss.); practicable, feasible; potential (pot.); ***möglichst ...*** as ... as possible
mot. ***motorisiert*** motorized
MP ***Maschinenpistole*** submachine gun; ***Militärpolizei*** military police (MPs, *inscription*: MP)
Mrd. ***Milliarde(n)*** billion, *pl.* billion(s) (bn); *Brit. obs.* thousand million
Mrz. ***März*** March (Mar., Mar)
MS, Ms. ***Manuskript*** manuscript (MS, ms.)
Mss. ***Manuskripte*** *pl.* manuscripts (MSS, mss.)
mst. ***meist(ens)*** mostly, usually (usu.)
Mt. ***Monat*** month (mth)
MTA ***medizinisch-technische Assistentin*** medical laboratory assistant
mtl. ***monatlich*** monthly
m. ü. M. ***Meter über (dem) Meer(esspiegel)*** met|res (*Am.* -ers) above sea level
MW ***Mittelwelle*** medium wave (MW)
m. W. ***meines Wissens*** as far as I know
MwSt. ***Mehrwertsteuer*** value-added tax (VAT), *esp. Am.* sales tax

N

N ***Nord(en)*** north (N); ***Nahverkehrszug*** local *or* commuter train
n. ***nach*** after; to
näml. ***nämlich*** namely, that is (to say) (viz., i.e.); to be precise
NATO, Nato ***Nordatlantikpakt-Organisation*** North Atlantic Treaty Organization (NATO, Nato)
NB ***notabene*** note well (NB)
n. Br. ***nördlicher Breite*** northern latitude (N lat.); ... degrees north (°N)
n. Chr. ***nach Christus*** anno Domini (AD)
NDR ***Norddeutscher Rundfunk*** Northern German Broadcasting Corporation
neg. ***negativ*** negative(ly *adv.*) (neg.)
neuw. ***neuwertig*** (as good as) new, as new, not used
n. Gr. ***nach Größe*** according to size
nhd. ***neuhochdeutsch*** New High German (NHG)
n. J. ***nächsten Jahres*** of next year, next year's ...
NK ***Nebenkosten*** extra costs (*or* expenses), extras
nkr ***norwegische Krone(n)*** Norwegian crown(s *pl.*) (Nkr)
n. M. ***nächsten Monats*** of next month, next month's ...
nmtl. ***namentlich*** by name; especially (esp.), particularly (part.)
N. N. ***nomen nominandum*** to be appointed; (*a.* **NN**) ***Normalnull*** sea level
NO ***Nordost(en)*** northeast (NE)
nordd(t). ***norddeutsch*** North German (N Ger.)
nördl. ***nördlich*** northern, north; northerly *wind*; *adv.* north (N)
norw. ***norwegisch*** Norwegian (Norw.)
notf. ***notfalls*** if need be, if necessary (if nec.)
notw. ***notwendig*** necessary (nec.)
Nov. ***November*** November (Nov., Nov)
Nr. ***Nummer*** number (No., no.)
Nrn. ***Nummern*** *pl.* numbers (Nos., nos.)
NRW ***Nordrhein-Westfalen*** North Rhine-Westphalia
NS ***Nachschrift*** postscript (PS); ***Nationalsozialismus*** National Socialism; ***nationalsozialistisch*** National Socialist (Nazi)
NSt ***Nebenstelle*** branch; *teleph.* extension (extn)
N. T. ***Neues Testament*** New Testament (NT)
nto. ***netto*** net (nt., nt)
NW ***Nordwest(en)*** northwest (NW)

O

O ***Ost(en)*** east (E)
o. ***oben*** above; ***oder*** or; ***ohne*** without (w/o)
o. a. ***oben angeführt*** above(-mentioned)
o. ä. ***oder ähnlich(es)*** or the like
ÖAMTC ***Österreichischer Automobil-, Motorrad- und Touring-Club*** Austrian Automobile, Motorcycling and Touring Association
OB ***Oberbürgermeister*** mayor; *in GB*: Lord Mayor
o. B. ***ohne Befund*** negative (neg.)
ÖBB ***Österreichische Bundesbahnen*** Austrian Federal Railways
Obb. ***Oberbayern*** Upper Bavaria
obh. ***oberhalb*** above
oblig. ***obligatorisch*** obligatory, compulsory
od. ***oder*** or
OEZ ***osteuropäische Zeit*** Eastern European Time (EET)
öff(tl). ***öffentlich*** public(ly *adv.*); in public
Offz. ***Offizier*** (commissioned) officer (Off.)
OHG ***Offene Handelsgesellschaft*** (general) partnership
ökon. ***ökonomisch*** economic; economical(ly *adv.*) (econ.)
Okt. ***Oktober*** October (Oct., Oct)
ö. L. ***östlicher Länge*** eastern longitude (E long.)
OLG ***Oberlandesgericht*** Higher Regional Court
OP ***Operationssaal*** operating theatre (*Am.* room)
Op. ***Operation*** operation (op.); ♪ ***Opus, Werk*** opus (op.)
op. cit. ***opere citato, im angegebenen Werk*** in the work quoted *or* cited (from)
Opf. ***Oberpfalz*** *the* Upper Palatinate
o. Prof. ***ordentlicher Professor*** (full) professor (Prof., prof.)
ORB ***Ostdeutscher Rundfunk Brandenburg*** East German Broadcasting Corporation Brandenburg
Orch. ***Orchester*** orchestra (Orch., orch.)
ORF ***Österreichischer Rundfunk*** Austrian Broadcasting Corporation
Orig. ***Original*** original (orig.)
orig. ***original*** original (orig.); genuine; ***originell*** original(ly *adv.*) (orig.)
orth. ***orthodox*** *eccl.* Orthodox (Orth.)
örtl. ***örtlich*** local(ly *adv.*)
ostd(t). ***ostdeutsch*** East German (E Ger.)
österr. ***österreichisch*** Austrian (Aus.)

östl. ***östlich*** eastern, east; easterly *wind*; *adv.* east (E)
o. U. ***ohne Unterschied*** indiscriminately; irrespective of *nationality etc.*
ÖVP ***Österreichische Volkspartei*** Austrian People's Party
Oz. ***Ozean*** ocean (Oc., oc.)

P

P, p ***Peso(s)*** peso(s *pl.*) (P, p)
P. ***Pater*** Father (Fr., Fr)
PA ***Patentanmeldung*** patent application; ***Postamt*** post office (PO)
p. A. ***per Adresse, bei*** care of (c/o)
päd. ***pädagogisch*** pedagogical, educational.
p. Adr. → ***p. A.***
Par(agr). ***Paragraph*** ⚖ section (sect.), article (art.); paragraph (para., par.)
Parl. ***Parlament*** parliament (Parl.)
Part. ***Partei*** party; ***Parterre*** ground floor (grd. fl.), *Am.* first floor (1st fl.); ***Partizip*** participle (part.)
Pat. ***Patent*** patent (pat.)
PC ***Personalcomputer*** personal computer (PC, pc)
p. Chr. (n.) ***post Christum (natum), nach Christus (nach Christi Geburt)*** anno Domini (AD)
PDS ***Partei des Demokratischen Sozialismus*** Party of Democratic Socialism
pers. ***persönlich*** personal(ly *adv.*) (pers.); *adv. a.* in person
Pf ***Pfennig*** pfennig(s *pl.*) (Pf., pf.)
Pfd. ***Pfund*** German pound(s *pl.*)
PGiroA *hist.* ***Postgiroamt*** postal giro office; *in GB*: Girobank
PH ***Pädagogische Hochschule*** college of education, *Am.* teachers' college
pharm. ***pharmazeutisch*** pharmaceutical (pharm.)
philol. ***philologisch*** philological(ly *adv.*) (philol.)
philos. ***philosophisch*** philosophical(ly *adv.*) (philos.)
phys. ***physikalisch*** physical(ly *adv.*) (phys.); ***physisch*** physical(ly *adv.*), somatic(ally *adv.*)
PIN ***persönliche Identifikationsnummer*** personal identification number (PIN)
Pkt. ***Paket*** parcel, *Am.* package; ***Punkt*** point (pt)
PKW, Pkw ***Personenkraftwagen*** (motor)car, *Am. a.* auto(mobile)
Pl. ***Platz*** square (Sq.); ***Plural*** plural (pl.)
PLO ***Palästinensische Befreiungsorganisation*** Palestine Liberation Organization (PLO)
PLZ ***Postleitzahl*** postcode, *Am.* zip code
pol. ***politisch*** political(ly *adv.*) (pol.); ***polizeilich*** police ...; *adv.* of (*or* by) the police
poln. ***polnisch*** Polish (Pol.)
port(ug). ***portugiesisch*** Portuguese (Port.)
Pos. ***Position*** position (pos.)
pos. ***positiv*** positive (pos.)
Postf. ***Postfach*** post office box (PO box, POB)
postw. ***postwendend*** by return (of post), by return mail
pp., p. p., ppa, p. pa. ***per procura(tionem), in Vollmacht*** per pro, per proxy (p.p., pp)
PR ***Public Relations, Öffentlichkeitsarbeit*** public relations (PR)
Präs. ***Präsidium*** presidency, chair(manship); executive committee (exec. comm.); headquarters *sg. and pl.* (HQ)
priv. ***privat*** private(ly *adv.*); *adv. a.* in private
Priv.-Doz. ***Privatdozent(in)*** unsalaried lecturer, *Am.* associate professor
Prof. ***Professor*** professor (Prof.)
prot. ***protestantisch*** Protestant (Prot.)
Prov. ***Provinz*** province (Prov., prov.); ***Provision*** commission
prov. ***provisorisch*** provisional (prov.), temporary (temp.)
PS ***Pferdestärke(n)*** horsepower (HP, h.p.); ***Postscript(um), Nachschrift*** postscript (PS, ps.)
Pseud. ***Pseudonym*** pseudonym (pseud.)
psych. ***psychisch*** psychological(ly *adv.*) (psych.); mental(ly *adv.*)
psychol. ***psychologisch*** psychological(ly *adv.*) (psych.)
PTA ***pharmazeutisch-technische Assistentin*** pharmaceutical laboratory assistant
Pta, *pl.* **Ptas** ***Peseta(s pl.), Pesete(n pl.)*** peseta(s *pl.*) (pta, *pl.* ptas)
PTT ***Post, Telefon, Telegraf; Schweizerische Post-, Telefon- und Telegrafenbetriebe*** Swiss Postal, Telephone and Telegraph Services
PVC ***Polyvinylchlorid*** polyvinyl chloride (PVC)

Q

qcm (*obs for* cm²) ***Quadratzentimeter*** square centimet|re(s *pl.*), *Am.* -er(s *pl.*) (sq. cm)
q. e. d. ***quod erat demonstrandum (= was zu beweisen war)*** (QED)
qkm (*obs for* km²) ***Quadratkilometer*** square kilomet|re(s *pl.*), *Am.* -er(s *pl.*) (sq. km)
qm (*obs. for* m²) ***Quadratmeter*** square met|re(s *pl.*), *Am.* -er(s *pl.*) (sq. m)

R

R ***Réaumur*** Réaumur; ***Rand*** (*South African currency*) rand (R)
r. ***rechts*** right (r.); on (*or* to) the right
RA ***Rechtsanwalt*** lawyer, *Brit. a.* solicitor (Sol., Solr); *Brit.* barrister (Bar., Barr.), *Am.* attorney (att., atty)
RAF *FRG*: ***Rote-Armee-Fraktion*** Red Army Faction
RB ***Radio Bremen*** Broadcasting Corporation of Bremen, Radio Bremen
Rbl ***Rubel*** rouble(s *pl.*), ruble(s *pl.*) (Rbl, rbl., R., r.)
rd. ***rund*** about, around, roughly, approximately (approx.)
Rdf. ***Rundfunk*** broadcasting corporation (*or* company); radio
rechtl. ***rechtlich*** legal(ly *adv.*) (leg.)
Ref. ***Referat*** department (Dept., dept), section (sect.)
Reg. ***Regierung*** government (Gov., gov., Govt, govt); ***Regiment*** ⚔ regiment (Regt, Rgt)
Reg.-Bez. ***Regierungsbezirk*** administrative district
Rel. ***Relation*** relation(ship); proportion; ***Religion*** religion (rel.)
rel. ***relativ*** relative(ly *adv.*) (rel.); *adv.* comparatively (comp., compar.); ***religiös*** religious(ly *adv.*) (rel.)
Rep. ***Reparatur*** repair(s *pl.*); ***Republik*** Republic (Rep.)
Reps(e) *FRG*: ***Republikaner*** *pl.* (members of the) Republican Party
res. ✝ ***reserviert*** reserved (res.)
Rest. ***Restaurant*** restaurant
RGW *hist.* ***Rat für gegenseitige Wirtschaftshilfe*** Council for Mutual Economic Assistance (Comecon)
Rh ***Rhesusfaktor positiv, Rh-positiv*** rhesus positive (Rh pos.)
rh ***Rhesusfaktor negativ, Rh-negativ*** rhesus negative (Rh neg.)
RIAS *hist.* ***Rundfunk im*** (*ehemaligen*) ***amerikanischen Sektor*** (*von Berlin*) Radio in the (*former*) American Sector (*of Berlin*)
R. I. P. ***requiescat in pace, er*** (*or* ***sie***) ***ruhe in Frieden*** may he (*or* she) rest in peace (RIP)
rk, r.-k. ***römisch-katholisch*** Roman Catholic (RC)
RNS ***Ribonukleinsäure*** ribonucleic acid (RNA)
Rp. *Switzerland*: ***Rappen*** (Swiss) centime(s *pl.*)
RT ***Registertonne(n)*** register ton(s *pl.*) (reg. t.)
Rückf. ***Rückfahrt*** return journey (*or* trip); journey (*or* way) back
Rücks. ***Rückseite*** back, rear; reverse (rev.); overleaf
rückw. ***rückwärtig*** back ..., rear ...; ***rückwärts*** backwards; ***rückwirkend*** retroactive; retrospective(ly *adv.*); backdated
russ. ***russisch*** Russian (Russ.)

S

S ***Süd(en)*** south (S); ***Schilling*** schilling (S)
S. ***Seite*** page (p.)
s ***Sekunde(n)*** second(s *pl.*) (s, sec.)
SA ***Sturmabteilung*** *hist.* (Nazi) stormtroops *pl. or* stormtroopers *pl.*
Sa. ***Samstag, Sonnabend*** Saturday (Sat., Sat)
s. a. ***siehe auch*** see also
Sakr. ***Sakrament(e)*** sacrament(s *pl.*)
Sanat. ***Sanatorium*** sanatorium, *Am.* sanitarium
Sa.-Nr. ***Sammelnummer*** collective number
SB- ***Selbstbedienungs...*** self-service ...
S-Bahn ***Schnellbahn, Stadtbahn*** suburban train; suburban railway
SBB ***Schweizerische Bundesbahnen*** Swiss Federal Railways
s. Br. ***südlicher Breite*** southern latitude (S lat.); ... degrees south (°S)
SC ***Sportclub*** sports club
schott. ***schottisch*** Scots, Scottish; Scotch *whisky*
schriftl. ***schriftlich*** written; in writing
schwed. ***schwedisch*** Swedish
schweiz. ***schweizerisch*** Swiss
scil. ***scilicet, nämlich*** namely, that is (to say)
SDR ***Süddeutscher Rundfunk*** Southern German Broadcasting Corporation
s. d. ***siehe dort*** see there; ***sine dato, ohne Erscheinungsjahr*** no date (n.d.)
Sdg. ✝ ***Sendung*** consignment, shipment
SDS *hist.* ***Sozialistischer Deutscher Studentenbund*** Association of German Socialist Students

sec. ***Sekunde*(*n*)** second(s *pl.*) (s, sec.)
SED *hist. GDR*: ***Sozialistische Einheitspartei Deutschlands*** Socialist Unity Party of Germany
Sek., sek. ***Sekunde*(*n*)** second(s *pl.*) (s, sec.)
selbst. ***selbständig*** independent; self--employed
Sem. ***Semester*** semester (sem.)
sen. ***senior, der Ältere*** senior (sen., Sen., Sr, Snr)
Sept. ***September*** September (Sept., Sept, Sep., Sep)
sex. ***sexuell*** sexual(ly *adv.*)
SFB ***Sender Freies Berlin*** Broadcasting Corporation of Free Berlin
sFr., sfr ***Schweizer Franken*** Swiss franc(s *pl.*) (SF, Sfr)
Sg. ***Singular*** singular (sing.)
SGB ***Schweizerischer Gewerkschaftsbund*** Federation of Swiss Trade Unions
sign. ***signiert*** signed
sin ⩘ ***Sinus*** sine (sin)
Sing. ***Singular*** singular (sing.)
SJ ***Societatis Jesu, von der Gesellschaft Jesu, Jesuit*** Jesuit
skand. ***skandinavisch*** Scandinavian (Scan., Scand.)
S. Kgl. H. ***Seine Königliche Hoheit*** His Royal Majesty
skr ***schwedische Krone*(*n*)** Swedish crown(s *pl.*) (Kr, Skr)
sm ***Seemeile*(*n*)** nautical mile(s *pl.*) (n.m.)
SMV ***Schülermitverwaltung*** school council
SO ***Südost*(*en*)** southeast (SE)
So. ***Sonntag*** Sunday (Sun., Sun)
s. o. ***siehe oben*** see above
sof. ***sofern*** if, provided (that), as long as; ***sofort*** at once, immediately; ***sofortig*** immediate; prompt
sog(en). ***sogenannt*** so-called
SOS ***save our ship*** (*or* ***souls***) *international distress signal*
sowj(et). ***sowjetisch*** soviet
soz. ***sozial*** social
span. ***spanisch*** Spanish (Span.)
SPD ***Sozialdemokratische Partei Deutschlands*** Social Democratic Party of Germany
spez. ***speziell*** special, particular; *adv. a.* (e)specially ([e]sp.)
SPÖ ***Sozialistische Partei Österreichs*** Austrian Socialist Party
SPS ***Sozialdemokratische Partei der Schweiz*** Social Democratic Party of Switzerland
SR ***Saarländischer Rundfunk*** Broadcasting Corporation of the Saarland
Sr. ***Senior, der Ältere*** senior (Sr, Snr, Sen., sen.)
s. R. ***siehe Rückseite*** see overleaf
SRG ***Schweizerische Radio- und Fernsehgesellschaft*** Swiss Broadcasting Corporation
SS ***Sommersemester*** summer semester; ***Schutzstaffel*** *hist.* SS (*elite corps of the Nazi Party*)
SS. ***Sanctae*** *or* ***Sancti, die Heiligen*** saints (SS.)
SSV ***Sommerschlußverkauf*** summer sales *pl.*
St. ***Sankt, der Heilige*** saint (St, St.); ***Stock*(*werk*)** floor (fl.), stor(e)y; ***Stück*** piece(s *pl.*) (pc., *pl.* pcs)
s. t. ***sine tempore, ohne*** (***akademisches***) ***Viertel, pünktlich*** sharp
staatl. ***staatlich*** state ..., government ...; state-owned; *adv.* officially
Stasi ***Staatssicherheitsdienst*** *hist. GDR*: state security service, Stasi
stat. ***statistisch*** statistical
Std. ***Stunde*(*n*)** hour(s *pl.*) (h., *pl. a.* hrs, *sg. a.* hr)
stdl. ***stündlich*** hourly; every hour
Stdn. ***Stunden*** hours (h., hrs)
Stellg. ***Stellung*** position, (*job a.*) post
stellv. ***stellvertretend*** deputy (dep.), assistant (asst); vice-...; *adv.* on behalf of ...; in place of ...
StGB ***Strafgesetzbuch*** Penal Code
St(.-)Kl. ***Steuerklasse*** tax bracket
StPO ***Strafprozeßordnung*** Code of Criminal Procedure
StR ***Studienrat*** secondary school teacher
Str. ***Straße*** street (St.); road (Rd)
StRin ***Studienrätin*** secondary ıschool teacher
stud. ***studiosus, Student*** student
StVO ***Straßenverkehrsordnung*** (road) traffic regulations *pl.*; *in GB*: Highway Code
s. u. ***siehe unten*** see below
Subj. ***Subjekt*** subject (subj.)
subj. ***subjektiv*** subjective(ly *adv.*) (subj.)
südd(t). ***süddeutsch*** South German (S Ger.)
südl. ***südlich*** southern, south; southerly *wind*; *adv.* south (S)
SV ***Spielvereinigung*** sports association
SVP ***Schweizerische Volkspartei*** Swiss People's Party; ***Südtiroler Volkspartei*** South Tyrolean People's Party
SW ***Südwest*(*en*)** southwest (SW)
SWF ***Südwestfunk*** Southwestern German Broadcasting Corporation
sym. ***symmetrisch*** symmetric(al); *adv.* symmetrically

T

T *meteor.* ***Tief*(*druckgebiet*)** low(-pressure area)
T. ***Teil*** part (pt, p.); ***Tiefe*** depth (D., d.)
t ***Tonne*(*n*** *pl.*) ton(s *pl.*) (t., t); tonne(s *pl.*) (t)
Tab. ***Tabelle*** table (tab.); chart; ***Tabulator*** tabulator (tab.)
t(äg)l. ***täglich*** daily, a (*or* per) day
Tar.-Gr. ***Tarifgruppe*** salary (*or* wage) bracket
Tb(c) ***Tuberkulose*** tuberculosis (TB)
techn. ***technisch*** technical(ly *adv.*) (tech.); technological(ly *adv.*) (technol.)
TEE ***Trans-Europ-Expreß*** Trans-European Express (TEE)
Teiln.-Geb. ***Teilnahmegebühr*** fee; ***Teilnehmergebühr*** (*teleph. etc.*) charge, rate
t(ei)lw. ***teilweise*** partial(ly *adv.*); partly
Tel. ***Telefon*** (tele)phone (tel.)
tel(ef). ***telefonisch*** telephone ...; by (tele)phone
Telegr. ***Telegramm*** telegram (teleg.)
telegr. ***telegrafisch*** telegraphic(ally *adv.*); by telegraph
Tel.-Nr. ***Telefonnummer*** (tele)phone number (tel. no.)
Temp. ***Temperatur*** temperature (temp.)
TH ***Technische Hochschule*** college (*or* institute) of technology
TL ***türkische Lira*** (*pl.* ***Lire***)**,** ***türkisches*** (*pl.* ***türkische***) ***Pfund*** Turkish lira (*pl.* lire *or* liras) (TL); Turkish pound(s *pl.*) (£T)
-tlg. ***-teilig*** ...-part ..., in (*or* consisting of) ... parts; ...-piece *suit etc.*
...tsd. ***...tausend*** ... thousand (thou.)
TU ***Technische Universität*** technical university; college (*or* institute) of technology
türk. ***türkisch*** Turkish (Turk.)
TÜV ***Technischer Überwachungs-Verein*** safety standards authority; technical control board; *in GB*: MOT (= Ministry of Transport) → ***TÜV*** *in the dictionary*
TV ***Television*** television (TV)

U

U ***Umleitung*** diversion; ***U-Bahn*** underground (U), *Am.* subway
u. ***und*** and
u. a. ***und andere*(*s*)** and others (other things); ***unter anderem*** (*or* ***anderen***) among other things, inter alia; among others
u. ä. ***und ähnliche*(*s*)** and the like
U. (*or* **u.**) **A. w. g.** ***um Antwort wird gebeten*** (R.S.V.P., RSVP)
U-Bahn ***Untergrundbahn*** underground (U), *Am.* subway
Überschr. ***Überschrift*** title; headline
übl. ***üblich*** usual, customary, normal (norm.)
U-Boot ***Unterseeboot*** submarine (sub.)
u. d(er)gl. (m.) ***und dergleichen*** (***mehr***) and the like, and so forth
u. d. M. ***unter dem Meeresspiegel*** below sea level
ü. d. M. ***über dem Meeresspiegel*** above sea level
UdSSR *hist.* ***Union der Sozialistischen Sowjetrepubliken*** Union of Soviet Socialist Republics (USSR)
u. E. ***unseres Erachtens*** in our opinion, as we see it; ***unter Einschränkung*** with reservations
u. f(f). ***und folgende*** *sg.* (*pl.*) and following
UFO, Ufo ***unbekanntes Flugobjekt*** unidentified flying object (UFO)
ugs. ***umgangssprachlich*** colloquial(ly *adv.*) (colloq.)
U-Haft ***Untersuchungshaft*** custody, detention (pending trial)
UKW ***Ultrakurzwelle*** ultrashort wave (USW), *approx.* very high frequency (VHF), *Am.* frequency modulation (FM)
ult. ***ultimo*** at the end (*or* on the last day) of the month
Umf. ***Umfang*** circumference (cir., circ.); extent, size; range; dimension
U/min ***Umdrehungen in der*** (***or pro***) ***Minute*** revolutions per minute (r.p.m., rpm)
U-Musik ***Unterhaltungsmusik*** easy listening, light music
ung(ar). ***ungarisch*** Hungarian (Hung.)
Uni F, **Univ.** ***Universität*** university (Univ., univ.)
Unterz. ***Unterzeichnete*(*r*)** *the* undersigned
unverb. ***unverbindlich*** not binding; without obligation; non-committal *statement etc.*
unvollst. ***unvollständig*** incomplete
unz. ***unzählig*** innumerable, countless
Url. ***Urlaub*** holiday(s), *esp. Am.* vacation; ⚔ leave
urspr. ***ursprünglich*** original(ly *adv.*) (orig.)

US(A) ***Vereinigte Staaten (von Amerika)*** United States (of America) (USA, US)
usf. ***und so fort*** and so forth
USt. ***Umsatzsteuer*** turnover tax
u. U. ***unter Umständen*** possibly (poss.), perhaps (perh.); if need be
u. ü. V. ***unter üblichem*** (*or* ***dem üblichen***) ***Vorbehalt*** within the usual reservations
UV ***Ultraviolett*** ultraviolet (UV)
u. v. a. (m.) ***und viele(s) andere (mehr)*** and many more (*or* others); and many other things
u. W. ***unseres Wissens*** as far as we know
Ü-Wagen ***Übertragungswagen*** outside broadcast van *or* unit (OB van *or* unit)
u. zw. ***und zwar*** namely; that is (to say); → ***zwar*** *in the dictionary*

V

V ***Volt*** volt(s *pl.*) (V)
V. ***Vers*** verse (v.), line (l.)
v. ***versus, gegen*** versus (v., vs.); ***von, vom*** of; from; by
VAE ***Vereinigte Arabische Emirate*** United Arab Emirates (UAE)
VB ***Verhandlungsbasis*** or near(est) offer (o.n.o.)
vbdl. ***verbindlich*** binding; obliging
v. Chr. ***vor Christus*** before Christ (BC)
v. D. ***vom Dienst*** on duty; in charge
VDE ***Verein Deutscher Elektrotechniker*** Association of German Electricians
VdK ***Verband der Kriegs- und Wehrdienstopfer, Behinderten und Sozialrentner*** Association of the Victims of War and Military Service, Disabled Persons and Social Insurance Pensioners
VDS ***Vereinigte Deutsche Studentenschaften*** Association of German Student Bodies
VEB *hist. GDR*: ***volkseigener Betrieb*** state-owned enterprise (*or* company)
ver. ***vereinigt*** united
V(er)f. ***Verfasser*** author
v(er)gl. ***vergleiche*** confer (cf.); compare (cp., comp.)
verh. ***verheiratet*** married (m., mar.)
Verk. ***Verkauf*** sale
Verl. ***Verlag*** publishing house (*or* company), publishers *pl.*; ***Verleger*** publisher (publ.)
Vers.-Anst. ***Versicherungsanstalt*** insurance company
vertr. ***vertraglich*** contractual(ly *adv.*), *adv. a.* by contract; ***vertraulich*** confidential (confid.), *adv.* confidentially, in confidence
Verw. ***Verwaltung*** administration (admin), management (mngmt)
verw. ***verwandt*** related *to*; ***verwitwet*** widowed
verz. ***verzeichnet*** listed; registered (regd); recorded
Vet. ***Veteran(en)*** *Brit.* ex-service|man, *pl.* -men, *Am.* veteran(s *pl.*) (vet, *pl.* vets); ***Veterinär*** veterinary surgeon, *Am.* veterinarian (vet, *pl.* vets)
V-Gespräch ***Voranmeldungsgespräch*** person-to-person call
v. g. u. ***vorgelesen, genehmigt, unterschrieben*** read, confirmed, signed
v. H. ***vom Hundert*** per cent, percent (p.c., pc, %)
VHS ***Volkshochschule*** adult education program(me); adult evening classes *pl.*
v. J. ***vorigen Jahres*** of last year, last year's
VL ***vermögenswirksame Leistung(en)*** *employer's contribution(s pl.) to tax-deductible employee savings scheme*
v. l. n. r. ***von links nach rechts*** from left to right
v. M. ***vorigen Monats*** of last month
V-Mann ***Verbindungsmann, Vertrauensmann*** contact; *contp. a.* informer
v. o. ***von oben*** from above
Vollm. ***Vollmacht*** full power(s *pl.*), authority (auth.); ⚖ power of attorney
vollst. ***vollständig*** complete(ly *adv.*), entire(ly *adv.*); full(y *adv.*)
Vopo *hist. GDR*: ***Volkspolizei*** People's Police; ***Volkspolizist*** member of the People's Police
vorl. ***vorläufig*** temporar|y, *adv.* -ily (temp.), provisional(ly *adv.*) (prov.); *adv. a.* for the present
vorm. ***vormalig*** former; ***vormals*** formerly (known as); ***vormittags*** in the morning (a.m., am)
Vors. ***Vorsitzende(r)*** chairperson, chairman (chm., chmn), chairwoman; chair; ✝ president (Pres., pres.); *party, trade union*: leader
VP ***Vollpension*** (full) board and lodging, full board, *Am.* American plan (AP); ***Volkspolizei*** *hist. GDR*: People's Police
VPS ***Video-Programmierungssystem*** video preprogram(m)ing system
VR ***Volksrepublik*** People's Republic
v. T. ***vom Tausend*** per thousand
VW ***Volkswagen*** Volkswagen (VW, F vee-dub)
VWL ***Volkswirtschaftslehre*** economics *pl.*

W

W ***Watt*** watt(s *pl.*) (W); ***West(en)*** west (W)
WAA ***Wiederaufbereitungsanlage*** reprocessing plant
wbl. ***weiblich*** female (fem.), feminine (fem.); women's ...
WC ***Wasserklosett*** toilet (WC)
WDR ***Westdeutscher Rundfunk*** Western German Broadcasting Corporation
WE ***Wärmeeinheit(en)*** thermal *or* caloric unit(s *pl.*)
werkt. ***werktags*** (on) weekdays
westd(t). ***westdeutsch*** West German (W Ger.)
westl. ***westlich*** western, west; westerly *wind*; *adv.* west (W)
WEU ***Westeuropäische Union*** Western European Union (WEU)
WEZ ***westeuropäische Zeit*** Greenwich Mean Time (GMT)
WG ***Wohngemeinschaft*** flat share, flat sharing (community)
WGB ***Weltgewerkschaftsbund*** World Federation of Trade Unions (WFTU)
Whg. ***Wohnung*** apartment (apt.), *Brit. a.* flat
wirtsch. ***wirtschaftlich*** economic (econ.); *adv.* economically; financial(ly *adv.*) (fin.)
wiss. ***wissenschaftlich*** academic(ally *adv.*); scientific(ally *adv.*) (sci.)
w. L. ***westlicher Länge*** Western longitude (W long.); ... degrees West (°W)
WM ***Weltmeisterschaft*** world championship; *soccer*: World Cup
wö. ***wöchentlich*** weekly, every week
WS ***Wintersemester*** winter semester
WSV ***Winterschlußverkauf*** winter sales *pl.*
Wwe. ***Witwe*** widow
Wz. ***Warenzeichen*** trademark (TM)

Z

Z. ***Zahl*** number; ***Zeile*** line (l.); ***Zeit*** time
z. ***zu, zum, zur*** at; to
z. B. ***zum Beispiel*** for instance, for example (e.g.)
z. b. V. ***zur besonderen Verwendung*** for special duty
ZDF ***Zweites Deutsches Fernsehen*** Second Channel of German Television
ZDL ***Zivildienstleistende(r)*** *conscientious objector conscripted to do community work*
zeitgen. ***zeitgenössisch*** contemporary (contemp.)
zeitl. ***zeitlich*** temporal, time ...
zeitw. ***zeitweilig, -weise*** occasionally, from time to time, now and then
Zentr. ***Zentrale*** head office (H.O., HO); headquarters *sg. and pl.* (HQ); control room; ***Zentrum*** cent|re, *Am.* -er
zentr. ***zentral*** central(ly *adv.*); *adv. a.* in the centre (*Am.* center)
ZH ***Zentralheizung*** central heating (centr. heat., cen. heat.)
z. H(d). ***zu Händen*** attention (attn); care of (c/o)
Zi. ***Ziffer*** figure (fig.); number (No., no.); clause; item; ***Zimmer*** room (number) (rm, rm no.)
zit. n. ***zitiert nach ...*** quoted after ...
ziv. ***zivil*** civilian (civ.); civil *aviation* (civ.)
ZK *pol.* ***Zentralkomitee*** central committee
Zl ***Zloty*** zloty, *pl.* zloty(s) (Zl)
Zlg. ***Zahlung*** payment
ZOB ***zentraler Omnibusbahnhof*** bus (*or* coach) station
zool. ***zoologisch*** zoological (zool.)
ZPO ***Zivilprozeßordnung*** code of civil procedure
Zs., *pl.* **Zss.** ***Zeitschrift(en)*** journal (jour.), *pl.* journals; periodical(s *pl.*)
Zstzg. ***Zusammensetzung*** composition (comp.); compound (comp., compd)
z. T. ***zum Teil*** partly, partially (part.)
Ztg. ***Zeitung*** newspaper
Ztr. ***Zentner*** (*metric*) hundredweight(s *pl.*) (cwt)
zuf. ***zufällig*** accidental(ly *adv.*), chance ...; *adv. a.* by chance; ***zufolge*** as a result (*or* consequence) of; according to (acc. to)
z(u)gl. ***zugleich*** at the same time
zul. ***zulässig*** permissible; ⚙ safe *load*; (maximum) permissible *speed*
zur. ***zurück*** back; ~ ***an*** return to
zus. ***zusammen*** together (tog.)
Zuschr. ***Zuschrift*** letter; reply
zust. ***zuständig*** relevant, appropriate *authority*; competent; responsible
z(u)zgl. ***zuzüglich*** plus
zw. ***zwecks*** for the purpose of; with a view to; ***zwischen*** between; among
ZwSt. ***Zweigstelle*** branch (office)
z. Z(t). ***zur Zeit*** at the moment, at present

Geographical Names

The following list contains a selection of place names which are of interest from a geographical or historical viewpoint or from the tourist's perspective. As a general principle only places which are spelled or pronounced differently in English than in German have been given. Names such as *Berlin*, *Portugal* or *Uruguay* are therefore not to be found on the list. With a few exceptions, the official names of countries have also not been given (so *Armenien* is given instead of *Republik Armenien*). A list of German and Austrian *Länder* as well as the Swiss cantons can be found on page 752.

A

Aachen Aachen, Aix-la-Chapelle
Addis Abeba Addis Ababa
Admiralitätsinseln, *die* *the* Admiralty Islands, *the* Admiralties
Adria, *die* *the* Adriatic (Sea)
Afrika Africa
Ägäis, *die* *the* Aegean (Sea)
Ägäischen Inseln, *die* *the* Aegean Islands
Agrigent Agrigento
Ägypten Egypt
Akaba Aqaba, Akaba
Akkra Accra
Akropolis, *die* *the* Acropolis
Albanien Albania
Aleuten, *die* *the* Aleutian Islands
Alexandrien Alexandria
Algerien Algeria
Algier Algiers
Alpen, *die* *the* Alps
Alpenvorland, *das* *the* foothills of the Alps
Amazonas, *der* *the* Amazon
Amerika America
Anatolien Anatolia
Andalusien Andalusia
Anden, *die* *the* Andes
Antarktis, *die* *the* Antarctic, Antarctica
Antillen, *die* *the* Antilles
Antwerpen Antwerp
Äolischen Inseln, *die* *the* Aeolian Islands; → *a.* ***Liparischen Inseln***
Apennin, *der*, Apenninen, *die* *the* Apennines, *the* Apennine Mountains
Apenninenhalbinsel, *die* *the* Apennine Peninsula
Appalachen, *die* *the* Appalachians, *the* Appalachian Mountains
Apulien Apulia
Äquatorialguinea Equatorial Guinea
Arabien Arabia
Aralsee, *der* Lake Aral
Ardennen, *die* *the* Ardennes
Argentinien Argentina, *the* Argentine
Arktis, *die* *the* Arctic
Ärmelkanal, *der* *the* English Channel, *the* Channel
Armenien Armenia
Aserbeidschan Azerbaijan
Asien Asia
Asowsche Meer, *das* *the* Sea of Azov
Assuan Aswan
Assyrien *hist.* Assyria
Athen Athens
Äthiopien Ethiopia
Atlantik, *der* *the* Atlantic (Ocean)
Atlasgebirge, *das* *the* Atlas Mountains
Ätna, *der* Mount Etna
Attika *hist.* Attica
Austerlitz Slavkov ŭ Brna; *hist.* Austerlitz
Australasien Australasia
Australien Australia
Azoren, *die* *the* Azores

B

Babel → ***Turm von Babel***
Babylonien *hist.* Babylonia
Bagdad Baghdad
Baikalsee, *der* Lake Baikal
Balearen, *die* *the* Balearic Islands
Balkan, *der* → **1.** ***Balkanhalbinsel***; **2.** ***Balkanstaaten***; **3.** ***Balkangebirge***
Balkangebirge, *das* *the* Balkan Mountains
Balkanhalbinsel, *die* *the* Balkan Peninsula
Balkanstaaten, *die* *the* Balkan States, *the* Balkans
Baltikum, *das* *the* Baltic (States), *the* Baltics
Bangladesch Bangladesh
Barentssee, *die* *the* Barents Sea
Basel Basel, Basle
Basiliuskathedrale, *die* (*in Moscow*) St Basil's Cathedral
Baskenland, *das* *the* Basque Provinces
Bayerischen Alpen, *die* *the* Bavarian Alps
Bayerische Wald, *der* *the* Bavarian Forest
Bayern Bavaria
Belgien Belgium
Belgrad Belgrade
Benelux-Länder, *die* *the* Benelux Countries
Bengalen Bengal
Beringmeer, *das* *the* Bering Sea
Beringstraße, *die* *the* Bering Strait
Bern Bern(e)
Berner Alpen, *die* *the* Bernese Alps
Berner Oberland, *das* *the* Bernese Oberland
Bessarabien Bessarabia
Bikini, Bikiniatoll, *das* Bikini
Birma *hist.* Burma
Biskaya, *die* → ***Golf von Biskaya***
Blaue Grotte, *die* (*in Capri*) *the* Blue Grotto
Bodensee, *der* Lake Constance
Böhmen Čechy; *hist.* Bohemia
Böhmen und Mähren *hist.* Bohemia-Moravia
Böhmerwald, *der* *the* Bohemian Forest
Bolivien Bolivia
Bosnien Bosnia
Bosnien und Herzegowina Bosnia and Herzegovina
Bosporus, *der* *the* Bosp(h)orus
Botsuana Botswana
Bottnische Meerbusen, *der* *the* Gulf of Bothnia
Bozen Bolzano
Brandenburger Tor, *das* *the* Brandenburg Gate
Brasilien Brazil
Braunschweig Braunschweig, Brunswick
Brenner(paß), *der* *the* Brenner Pass
Breslau Wroclaw; *hist.* Breslau
Bretagne, *die* Brittany
Britischen Überseegebiete, *die* *the* United Kingdom Overseas Territories
Brügge Bruges
Brüssel Brussels
Buchara Bukhara
Bukarest Bucharest
Bukowina, *die* Bukovina, Bucovina
Bulgarien Bulgaria
Bundeshaus, *das* (*in Bonn*) *the* Federal Parliament Building
Bundesrepublik Deutschland, *die* *the* Federal Republic of Germany
Burgund Burgundy
Burgundische Pforte, *die* *the* Belfort Gap
Byzanz *hist.* Byzantium

C

Cevennen, *die* *the* Cévennes
Chania Canea
Charkow Kharkov
Chiemsee, *der* Lake Chiem, *the* Chiemsee
Chinesische Mauer, *die* *the* Great Wall of China
Chinesische Meer, *das* *the* China Sea
Comer See, *der* Lake Como
Cyrenaika, *die* *hist.* Cyrenaica

D

Dalmatien Dalmatia
Damaskus Damascus
Dänemark Denmark

Danzig Gdansk; *hist.* Danzig
Danziger Bucht, *die* *the* Bay (*or* Gulf) of Gdansk (*hist.* Danzig)
Dardanellen, *die* *the* Dardanelles
Daressalam Dar es Salaam
Den Haag The Hague
Deutsche Bucht, *die* *the* German Bay
Deutsche Demokratische Republik, *die* *hist. the* German Democratic Republic
Deutschland Germany
Dithmarschen Ditmarsh
Dnjepr, *der* *the* Dnieper
Dnjestr, *der* *the* Dniester
Dodekanes, *der* *the* Dodecanese
Dogenpalast, *der* (*in Venice*) *the* Doge's Palace
Dolomiten, *die* *the* Dolomites
Dominikanische Republik, *die* *the* Dominican Republic
Donau, *die* *the* Danube
Donez, *der* *the* Donets
Donezbecken, *das* *the* Donets (Basin)
Dover → ***Straße von Dover***
Drau, *die* *the* Drava
Dschibuti Djibouti
Dschidda Jedda
Dünkirchen Dunkirk

E

Eiffelturm, *der* *the* Eiffel Tower
Eismeer, Nördliche, *das* → ***Nordpolarmeer***
Eismeer, Südliche, *das* → ***Südpolarmeer***
Elat Eilat
Elfenbeinküste, *die* *the* Ivory Coast
Elsaß, *das* Alsace
Elsaß-Lothringen *hist.* Alsace-Lorraine
Engadin, *das* *the* Engadine
Engelsburg, *die* (*in Rome*) *the* Castel Sant'Angelo
Eremitage, *die* (*in Leningrad*) *the* Hermitage Museum
Eriwan Yerevan, Erivan
Erzgebirge, *das* *the* Erzgebirge, *the* Ore Mountains
Estland Estonia
Etsch, *die* *the* Adige
Euphrat, *der* *the* Euphrates
Eurasien Eurasia
Europa Europe
Everest, *der* (Mount) Everest

F

Falklandinseln, *die* *the* Falkland Islands, *the* Falklands
Färöer, *die* *the* Faroes, *the* Faroe Islands
Felsendom, *der* (*in Jerusalem*) *the* Dome of the Rock
Ferne Osten, *der*, Fernost *the* Far East
Fidschi Fiji
Fidschiinseln, *die* *the* Fiji Islands
Finnische Meerbusen, *der* *the* Gulf of Finland
Finnland Finland
Flandern Flanders
Florenz Florence
Franken Franconia
Frankfurt (am Main) Frankfurt (on the Main)
Frankfurt (an der Oder) Frankfurt (on the Oder)
Frankreich France
Französisch-Guayana French Guiana
Freiheitsstatue, *die* *the* Statue of Liberty
Freundschaftsinseln, *die* *the* Tonga (*or* Friendly) Islands
Friaul Friuli
Friesischen Inseln, *die* *the* Frisian Islands
Fudschijama, *der* (Mount) Fuji, *a.* Fujiyama
Fünen Fyn

G

Gabun Gabon
Galapagosinseln, *die* *the* Galapagos Islands
Galicien (*in Spain*) *a. hist.* Galicia
Galiläa Galilee
Galizien Galicia
Gallien *hist.* Gaul
Gambia (*the*) Gambia
Gardasee, *der* Lake Garda
Gazastreifen, *der* *the* Gaza Strip
Genezareth → ***See Genezareth***
Genf Geneva
Genfer See, *der* Lake Geneva, Lac Léman
Gent Ghent
Genua Genoa
Georgien Georgia
Gesellschaftsinseln, *die* *the* Society Islands
Gewürzinseln, *die* *the* Spice Islands; → *a.* ***Molukken***
Gizeh (El) Giza; → ***Pyramiden von Gizeh***
Glarner Alpen, *die* *the* Glarus Alps
Golanhöhen, *die* *the* Golan Heights
Goldene Horn, *das* *the* Golden Horn
Golf von Akaba, *der* *the* Gulf of Aqaba (*or* Akaba)
Golf von Bengalen, *der* *the* Bay of Bengal
Golf von Biskaya, *der* *the* Bay of Biscay
Golf von Genua, *der* *the* Gulf of Genoa
Golf von Korinth, *der* *the* Gulf of Corinth
Golf von Neapel, *der* *the* Bay of Naples
Golf von Triest, *der* *the* Gulf of Trieste
Gomorrha *bibl.* Gomorrah, Gomorrha
Göteborg Gothenburg, Göteborg
Grabeskirche, *die* (*in Jerusalem*) *the* Church of the Holy Sepulchre
Graubünden Graubünden, *the* Grisons
Griechenland Greece
Grönland Greenland
Großbritannien Great Britain, Britain
Große Belt, *der* *the* Great Belt
Großen Antillen, *die* *the* Greater Antilles
Großen Seen, *die* *the* Great Lakes
Große Syrte, *die* *the* Gulf of Sidra
Guayana (*region*) Guiana
Guyana (*state*) Guyana

H

Haiderabad Hyderabad
Hannover Hanover
Harz, *der* *the* Harz (Mountains)
Havanna Havana
Hawaii-Inseln, *die* *the* Hawaiian Islands
Hebriden, *die* *the* Hebrides
Helgoland Hel(i)goland
Helgoländer Bucht, *die* *the* Hel(i)goland Bight
Herzegowina *hist.* Herzegovina
Herzogenbusch 's Hertogenbosch
Hessen Hesse(n)
Himalaja, *der* *the* Himalayas
Himmelfahrtsinsel, *die* Ascension Island
Hindukusch, *der* *the* Hindu Kush
Hinterindien Indochina
Hinterpommern *hist.* Eastern Pomerania
Hiroschima Hiroshima
Hoek van Holland Hook of Holland
Holland Holland, *the* Netherlands
Hongkong Hong Kong
Hradschin, *der* (*in Prague*) *the* Hradčany

I

Iberien *hist.* Iberia
Iberische Halbinsel, *die* *the* Iberian Peninsula
Ijsselmeer, *das* Lake Ijssel, Ijsselmeer
Indien India
Indische Ozean, *der* *the* Indian Ocean
Indonesien Indonesia
Innerasien Central Asia
Innere Mongolei, *die* Inner Mongolia
Insel Man, *die* *the* Isle of Man
Inseln über dem Winde, *die* *the* Leeward Islands
Inseln unter dem Winde, *die* *the* Windward Islands
Insel Wight, *die* *the* Isle of Wight
Invalidendom, *der* (*in Paris*) *the* Invalides
Ionische Meer, *das* *the* Ionian Sea
Ionischen Inseln, *die* *the* Ionian Islands
Irak, *der* Iraq
Irische See, *die* *the* Irish Sea
Irland Ireland
Island Iceland
Istrien Istria
Italien Italy

J

Jadebusen, *der* *the* Jade Bay
Jakutsk Yakutsk
Jalta Yalta
Jamaika Jamaica
Jangtse(kiang), *der* *the* Yangtze(-Kiang)
Japanische Meer, *das* *the* Sea of Japan
Jemen, *der* *the* Yemen
Jordanien Jordan
Judäa *hist.* Jud(a)ea
Jugoslawien *hist.* Yugoslavia
Jungferninseln, *die* *the* Virgin Islands
Jütland Jutland

K

Kaimaninseln, *die* *the* Cayman Islands
Kairo Cairo
Kalabrien Calabria
Kalifornien California
Kalkutta Calcutta
Kambodscha Cambodia
Kamerun Cameroon
Kamputschea *obs.* Kampuchea
Kana(a) *bibl.* Cana
Kanaan *hist.* Canaan
Kanada Canada
Kanal, *der* (= *Ärmelkanal*) *the* (English) Channel
Kanalinseln, *die* *the* Channel Islands

Kanaren, *die*, Kanarischen Inseln, *die* *the* Canaries, *the* Canary Islands
Kantabrische Gebirge, *das* *the* Cantabrian Mountains
Kap der Guten Hoffnung, *das* *the* Cape of Good Hope, *a. the* Cape
Kap Hoorn Cape Horn, *a. the* Horn
Kappadokien Cappadocia
Kapstadt Cape Town
Kapverdischen Inseln, *die* *the* Cape Verde Islands
Karatschi Karachi
Karelien Karelia
Karibik, *die* *the* Caribbean
Kärnten Carinthia
Karolinen, *die* *the* Caroline Islands
Karpaten, *die* *the* Carpathians, *the* Carpathian Mountains
Karthago *hist.* Carthage
Kasachstan Kazakhstan
Kaschmir Kashmir
Kaspische Meer, *das* *the* Caspian Sea
Kastilien Castile
Katalonien Catalonia
Katar Qatar
Katharinenkloster, *das* (*in the Sinai Peninsula*) *the* Monastery of St Catherine
Kattowitz Katowice; *hist.* Kattowitz
Kaukasus, *der* *the* Caucasus, *a. the* Caucasus Mountains
Kenia Kenya
Khaiberpaß, *der* *the* Khyber Pass
Kieler Bucht, *die* Kiel Bay
Kiew Kiev
Kilimandscharo, *der* (Mount) Kilimanjaro
Kirgisien Kirghizia
Klagemauer, *die* (*in Jerusalem*) *the* Wailing Wall
Kleinasien Asia Minor
Kleinen Antillen, *die* *the* Lesser Antilles
Köln Cologne
Kölner Dom, *der* Cologne Cathedral
Kolumbien Colombia
Komoren, *die* *the* Comoro Archipelago
Kongo, *der* *the* Congo
Königsberg Kaliningrad; *hist.* Königsberg
Konstantinopel Constantinople
Konstanz Constance
Kopenhagen Copenhagen
Kordilleren, *die* *the* Cordilleras
Korfu Corfu
Korinth Corinth
Korsika Corsica
Kotschinchina Cochin China
Krakatau Krakatoa
Krakau Cracow, Kraków
Kreml, *der* *the* Kremlin
Kreta Crete
Krim, *die* *the* Crimea
Kroatien Croatia
Kuba Cuba
Kurdistan Kurdistan, Kurdestan, Kordestan
Kurilen, *die* *the* Kuril(e) Islands
Kykladen, *die* *the* Cyclades

L

Ladogasee, *der* Lake Ladoga
Laibach Ljubljana
Lappland Lapland
Lateinamerika Latin America
Lausitz, *die* Lusatia
Lemberg Lvov
Lettland Latvia
Levante, *die* *the* Levant
Libanon, *der* (*the*) Lebanon (*usually without the definite article*)
Libyen Libya
Ligurien Liguria
Ligurische Meer, *das* *the* Ligurian Sea
Liparischen Inseln, *die* *the* Lipari Islands
Lissabon Lisbon
Litauen Lithuania
Loire-Schlösser, *die* *the* Châteaux of the Loire
Lombardei, *die* Lombardy
Lothringen Lorraine
Löwen (*in Belgium*) Louvain, Leuven
Lübecker Bucht, *die* *the* Lübeck Bay
Luganer See, *der* Lake Lugano
Lüneburger Heide, *die* *the* Lüneburg Heath
Lüttich Liège
Luxemburg Luxemb(o)urg
Luzern Lucerne

M

Maas, *die* *the* Meuse, *the* Maas
Madagaskar Madagascar
Magellanstraße, *die* *the* Strait(s) of Magellan
Mähren Moravia
Mährische Pforte, *die* *the* Moravian Gate (*or* Gap)
Mailand Milan
Mainfranken → ***Unterfranken***
Makedonien Macedonia
Malaiische Halbinsel, *die* *the* Malay Peninsula, Malaya
Malakka Malacca
Malediven, *die* *the* Maldives
Mallorca Majorca
Mandschurei, *die* Manchuria
Marianen, *die* *the* Marianas
Mark Brandenburg, *die* *the* Brandenburg Marches
Markuskirche, *die* (*in Venice*) St Mark's (Basilica)
Markusplatz, *der* (*in Venice*) St Mark's Square
Marmarameer, *das* *the* Sea of Marmara
Marokko Morocco
Marsfeld, *das* (*in Paris*) *the* Champ-de-Mars; (*in Rome*) *the* Field of Mars
Masuren Masuria
Masurischen Seen, *die* *the* Masurian Lakes
Mauretanien Mauretania
Mecklenburg-Vorpommern Mecklenburg-Western Pomerania
Mekka Mecca
Melanesien Melanesia
Menorca Minorca
Meran Merano
Mesopotamien Mesopotamia
Mexiko Mexico
Mikronesien Micronesia
Millstätter See, *der* Lake Millstatt
Mittelamerika Central America
Mittelasien Central Asia
Mitteldeutschland Central Germany
Mitteleuropa Central Europe
Mittelmeer, *das* *the* Mediterranean (Sea)
Mittlere Osten, *der* *the* Middle East
Moçambique Mozambique
Moldau¹, *die* (*river*) *the* Vltava; *hist. the* Moldau
Moldau², *die* (*region*) Moldavia
Moldavien Moldavia
Mongolei, *die* Mongolia
Mosel, *die* *the* Moselle
Moskau Moscow
Moskwa, *die* *the* Moskva
Mülhausen Mulhouse
München Munich
Myanmar Myanmar (*official name of* ***Birma***)
Mykene Mycenae

N

Nahe Osten, *der* *the* Middle (*or* Near) East
Navarra Navarre
Neapel Naples
Neu-Delhi New Delhi
Neufundland Newfoundland
Neuguinea New Guinea
Neuseeland New Zealand
Newa, *die* *the* Neva
Niagarafälle, *die* *the* Niagara Falls
Niederbayern Lower Bavaria
Niederlande, *die* *the* Netherlands, Holland
Niederösterreich Lower Austria
Niederrhein, *der* *the* Lower Rhine
Niedersachsen Lower Saxony
Niederschlesien *hist.* Lower Silesia
Nikosia Nicosia
Nil, *der* *the* Nile
Nimwegen Nijmegen
Nizza Nice
Nordafrika North Africa
Nordamerika North America
Norddeutsche Tiefebene, *die* *the* North(ern) German Plain
Norddeutschland North(ern) Germany
Nordeuropa North(ern) Europe
Nordfriesischen Inseln, *die* *the* North Frisians
Nordirland Northern Ireland
Nordkap, *das* *the* North Cape
Nordkorea North Korea
Nord-Ostsee-Kanal, *der* *the* Kiel Canal
Nordpol, *der* *the* North Pole
Nordpolarmeer, *das* *the* Arctic Ocean
Nordrhein-Westfalen North Rhine-Westphalia
Nordsee, *die* *the* North Sea
Normandie, *die* Normandy
Norwegen Norway
Nowgorod Novgorod
Nowosibirsk Novosibirsk
Nubien (*a. hist.*) Nubia
Nürnberg Nuremberg

O

Oberbayern Upper Bavaria
Oberengadin, *das* *the* Upper Engadine
Obere See, *der* Lake Superior
Oberfranken Upper Franconia
Oberitalien Northern Italy
Oberösterreich Upper Austria
Oberpfalz, *die* *the* Upper Palatinate
Oberrhein, *der* *the* Upper Rhine
Oberrheinische Tiefebene, *die* *the* Upper Rhine Valley
Oberschlesien *hist.* Upper Silesia
Ölberg, *der* *bibl. the* Mount of Olives
Olymp, *der* (Mount) Olympus
Onegasee, *der* Lake Onega
Oranjefreistaat, *der* *the* Orange Free State
Orinoko, *der* *the* Orinoco
Ostafrika East Africa

Ostasien East Asia
Ostdeutschland 1. Eastern Germany; **2.** *hist. the* German Democratic Republic, East Germany
Ostende Ostend
Osterinsel, *die* Easter Island
Österreich Austria
Österreich-Ungarn *hist.* Austria-Hungary
Osteuropa Eastern Europe
Ostfriesischen Inseln, *die* *the* East Frisians
Ostpreußen *hist.* East Prussia
Ostsee, *die* *the* Baltic (Sea)
Ozeanien Oceania

P

Palästina *bibl., hist.* Palestine
Palatin, *der* (*in Rome*) *the* Palatine
Panamakanal, *der* *the* Panama Canal
Pandschab, *das* *the* Punjab
Papua-Neuguinea Papua New Guinea
Parnaß, *der* Mount Parnassus
Patagonien Patagonia
Pazifik, *der* *the* Pacific (Ocean)
Peloponnes, *der* *or* ***die*** *the* Peloponnese, *the* Peloponnesus
Persien *hist.* Persia
Persische Golf, *der* *the* Persian Gulf
Petersburg, (*St.*) St Petersburg
Petersdom, *der* (*in Rome*) St Peter's (Cathedral)
Peterskirche, *die* (*in Rome*) St Peter's
Petersplatz, *der* (*in Rome*) St Peter's Square
Pfalz, *die* *the* Palatinate
Philippinen, *die* *the* Philippines
Picardie, *die* Picardy
Piemont Piedmont
Piräus Piraeus
Plattensee, *der* Lake Balaton
Po-Ebene, *die* *the* Po Valley
Polarkreis, *der* 1. *the* Arctic Circle; **2.** *the* Antarctic Circle
Polen Poland
Polynesien Polynesia
Pommern Pomorze; *hist.* Pomerania
Pompeji Pompeii
Pontinischen Sümpfe, *die* *the* Pontine Marshes
Pontische Gebirge, *das* *the* Pontic Mountains
Posen Poznán
Prag Prague
Preßburg Bratislava; *hist.* Pressburg
Preußen *hist.* Prussia
Provence, *die* Provence
Pyramiden von Gizeh, *die* *the* Pyramids of Giza
Pyrenäen, *die* *the* Pyrenees
Pyrenäenhalbinsel, *die* *the* Iberian Peninsula

R

Rangun Rangoon
Rätischen Alpen, *die* *the* Rhaetian Alps
Republik Irland, *die* *the* Republic of Ireland
Reval Tallin(n); *hist.* Reval
Rhein, *der* *the* Rhine
Rheinfall, *der* *the* Rhine Falls
Rheingau, *der* *the* Rhinegau
Rheinhessen Rhinehessen
Rheinische Schiefergebirge, *das* *the* Rhenish Slate Mountains
Rheinland, *das* *the* Rhineland
Rheinland-Pfalz Rhineland-Palatinate
Rhodos Rhodes
Rom Rome
Rote Meer, *das* *the* Red Sea
Rote Platz, *der* (*in Moscow*) Red Square
Rubikon, *der* *the* Rubicon
Ruhrgebiet, *das* *the* Ruhr(gebiet)
Rumänien Romania, *a.* Rumania
Rußland Russia

S

Saarland, *das* *the* Saar(land)
Saba *hist.* Sheba
Sabiner Berge, *die* *the* Sabine Hills
Sachalin Sakhalin
Sachsen Saxony
Sachsen-Anhalt Saxony-Anhalt
Sächsische Schweiz, *die* Saxon Switzerland
Salomonen, *die*, Salomonischen Inseln, *die* *the* Solomon Islands
Saloniki Salonika, Saloniki
Sambesi, *der* *the* Zambezi
Sambia Zambia
Samothrake Samothrace
Sankt Gallen St Gallen, *obs.* St Gall
Sankt-Lorenz-Strom, *der* *the* St Lawrence (River)
Sansibar Zanzibar
Sarajewo Sarajevo
Sardinien Sardinia
Saudi-Arabien Saudi Arabia
Savoyen Savoy
Schanghai Shanghai
Schatt el Arab, *der* *the* Shatt-al-Arab
Schiefe Turm von Pisa, *der* *the* Leaning Tower of Pisa
Schlesien 1. (*in Poland*) Slask; *hist.* Silesia; **2.** (*in Czechoslovakia*) Slezsko; *hist.* Silesia
Schottland Scotland
Schwaben Swabia
Schwäbische Alb, *die* *the* Swabian Jura
Schwarze Meer, *das* *the* Black Sea
Schwarzwald, *der* *the* Black Forest
Schweden Sweden
Schweiz, *die* Switzerland
Schweizer Mittelland, *das* *the* Swiss Midlands
Seealpen, *die* *the* Maritime Alps
See Genezareth, *der* *the* Sea of Galilee
Seeland Zealand
Seidenstraße, *die* *hist. the* Silk Road (*or* Route)
Serbien Serbia
Seufzerbrücke, *die* (*in Venice*) *the* Bridge of Sighs
Sevilla Seville
Seychellen, *die* *the* Seychelles
Sibirien Siberia
Siebenbürgen Transylvania
Simbabwe Zimbabwe
Sinaigebirge, *das* Mount Sinai
Sinaihalbinsel, *die* *the* Sinai Peninsula
Singapur Singapore
Sixtinische Kapelle, *die* (*in Rome*) *the* Sistine Chapel
Sizilien Sicily
Skandinavien Scandinavia
Slowakei, *die* Slovakia
Slowenien Slovenia
Sorrent Sorrento
Sowjetunion, *die* *hist. the* Soviet Union
Spanien Spain
Spanische Treppe, *die* (*in Rome*) *the* Spanish Steps
Sporaden, *die* *the* Sporades
Steiermark, *die* Styria
Stephansdom, *der* (*in Vienna*) St Stephen's (Cathedral)
Stettin Szczecin; *hist.* Stettin
Stille Ozean, *der* → *Pazifik*
Straßburg Strasbourg
Straßburger Münster, *das* Strasbourg Minster
Straße von Dover, *die* *the* Strait(s) of Dover
Straße von Gibraltar, *die* *the* Strait(s) of Gibraltar
Stubaier Alpen, *die* *the* Stubai Alps
Südafrika South Africa
Südamerika South America
Sudan, *der* (*the*) Sudan
Südchinesische Meer, *das* *the* South China Sea
Süddeutschland South(ern) Germany
Sudetenland, *das* *hist.* Sudetenland, *a. the* Sudeten
Südeuropa South(ern) Europe
Südkorea South Korea
Südpolarmeer, *das* *the* Antarctic Ocean
Südsee, *die* *the* South Pacific, *the* South Seas
Südseeinseln, *die* *the* Pacific (*or* South Sea) Islands
Südtirol South Tyrol
Südwestafrika South-West Africa
Suezkanal, *der* *the* Suez Canal
Sund, *der* *the* Sound
Swasiland Swaziland
Syrakus Syracuse
Syrien Syria
Szegedin Szeged
Szetschuan Szechuan

T

Tadschikistan Tajikistan
Tafelberg, *der* Table Mountain
Taipeh Taipei
Tajo, *der* *the* Tagus
Tanganjika Tanganyika
Tanganjikasee, *der* Lake Tanganyika
Tanger Tangier
Tansania Tanzania
Tarent Taranto
Tasmanien Tasmania
Tatarei, *die* *hist.* Tartary
Tatra, *die* *the* Tatra Mountains, *a. the* High Tatra
Taurus, *der* *the* Taurus (Mountains)
Teheran Teh(e)ran
Tempelberg, *der* (*in Jerusalem*) *the* Temple Mount
Teneriffa Tenerife
Tessin, *das* Ticino
Teutoburger Wald, *der* *the* Teutoburg Forest, *the* Teutoburger Wald
Theben *hist.* Thebes
Themse, *die* *the* Thames
Thermopylen, *die* Thermopylae
Thessalien Thessaly
Thüringen Thuringia
Thüringer Wald, *der* *the* Thuringian Forest
Tirol (*the*) Tyrol
Tokio Tokyo
Toskana, *die* Tuscany
Tote Meer, *das* *the* Dead Sea
Transkaukasien Transcaucasia
Trient Trento
Triest Trieste
Tripolis Tripoli
Troja Troy

Tschad, *der* Chad
Tschechien *the* Czech Republic
Tschechoslowakei, *die* *hist.* Czechoslovakia
Tunesien Tunisia
Türkei, *die* Turkey
Turkestan Turkestan, Turkistan
Tyrrhenische Meer, *das* *the* Tyrrhenian Sea
Tyrus *hist.* Tyre

U

Uffizien, *die* (*in Florence*) *the* Uffizi
Ulmer Münster, *das* Ulm Minster
Umbrien Umbria
Ungarn Hungary
Unterfranken Lower Franconia
Unteritalien Southern Italy
Uppsala Up(p)sala
Ural, *der* *the* Urals
Usbekistan Uzbekistan

V

Vansee, *der* Lake Van
Vatikan, *der* *the* Vatican
Venedig Venice
Venetien Veneto
Verbotene Stadt, *die* (*in Peking*) *the* Forbidden City
Vereinigte Königreich (von Großbritannien und Nordirland), *das* *the* United Kingdom (of Great Britain and Northern Ireland)
Vereinigten Arabischen Emirate, *die* *the* United Arab Emirates
Vereinigten Staaten (von Amerika), *die* *the* United States (of America)
Vesuv, *der* Vesuvius
Via Appia, *die* *hist. the* Appian Way
Vierwaldstätter See, *der* Lake Lucerne
Vietnam Vietnam, Viet Nam
Vlissingen Flushing
Vogesen, *die* *the* Vosges (Mountains)
Volksrepublik China, *die* *the* People's Republic of China
Vorderasien *the* Middle (*or* Near) East; *hist. the* Levant
Vorderindien *the* Indian Peninsula (and Ceylon)
Vorpommern Western Pomerania

W

Walfischbai, *die* Walvis (*or* Walfish) Bay
Wallis, *das* Valais
Wallonien Wallonie
Warschau Warsaw
Wattenmeer, *das* *the* mud flats (*of the North Sea*)
Weichsel, *die* *the* Vistula
Weiße Haus, *das* (*in Washington DC*) *the* White House
Weißrußland Belarus, B(y)elorussia, White Russia
Westdeutschland 1. Western Germany; **2.** *hist.* → ***Bundesrepublik Deutschland***
Westeuropa West(ern) Europe
Westfalen Westphalia
Westfriesischen Inseln, *die* *the* West Frisians
Westindien *the* West Indies
Westpreußen *hist.* West Prussia
Wien Vienna
Wilna Vilnius
Windhuk Windhoek
Wladiwostok Vladivostok
Wolga, *die* *the* Volga

Y

Ypern Ypres

Z

Zentralafrikanische Republik, *die* *the* Central African Republic
Zuckerhut, *der* (*in Rio de Janeiro*) Sugar Loaf Mountain
Zürich Zurich
Zürichsee, *der*, Züricher See, *der* Lake Zurich
Zypern Cyprus

The Länder of the Federal Republic of Germany

Baden-Württemberg Baden-Württemberg
Bayern Bavaria
Berlin Berlin
Brandenburg Brandenburg
Bremen Bremen
Hamburg Hamburg
Hessen Hesse
Meckenburg-Vorpommern Mecklenburg-Western Pomerania
Niedersachsen Lower Saxony
Nordrhein-Westfalen North Rhine-Westphalia
Rheinland-Pfalz Rhineland-Palatinate
Saarland Saarland
Sachsen Saxony
Sachsen-Anhalt Saxony-Anhalt
Schleswig-Holstein Schleswig-Holstein
Thüringen Thuringia

The Länder of the Republic of Austria

Burgenland Burgenland
Kärnten Carinthia
Niederösterreich Lower Austria
Oberösterreich Upper Austria
Salzburg Salzburg
Steiermark Styria
Tirol Tyrol
Vorarlberg Vorarlberg
Wien Vienna

The Cantons of the Swiss Confederation
(Half cantons in brackets)

Aargau Aargau
Appenzell (Inner-Rhoden; Außer-Rhoden) Appenzell (Inner Rhodes; Outer Rhodes)
Basel Basel, Basle
Bern Bern, Berne
Freiburg, *Fr.* **Fribourg** Fribourg
Genf, *Fr.* **Genève** Geneva
Glarus Glarus
Graubünden Graubünden, Grisons
Jura Jura
Luzern Lucerne
Neuenburg, *Fr.* **Neuchâtel** Neuchâtel
St. Gallen St Gallen, St Gall
Schaffhausen Schaffhausen
Schwyz Schwyz
Solothurn Solothurn
Tessin, *Ital.* **Ticino** Ticino
Thurgau Thurgau
Unterwalden (Obwalden; Nidwalden) Unterwalden (Obwalden; Nidwalden)
Uri Uri
Waadt, *Fr.* **Vaud** Vaud
Wallis, *Fr.* **Valais** Valais, Wallis
Zug Zug
Zürich Zurich

Historical, Biblical and Mythological Names

The following list contains a selection of historical names as well as names from mythology and world literature. As a general principle only names which are spelled differently in English than in German have been given. Where there are variations to the name, the most common version has sometimes been given.

Abälard Abelard
Achill(es) *myth.* Achilles
Ahasver *myth.* Ahasuerus
Aktäon *myth.* Actaeon
Alarich Alaric
Alba, *Herzog von* Duke of Alva (*or* Alba)
Albrecht der Bär Albert the Bear
Alexander der Große Alexander the Great
Alkibiades Alcibiades
Alkmene *myth.* Alcmene
Alkuin Alcuin
Ambrosius, *der heilige* St Ambrose
Amenophis Amenhotep
Anakreon Anacreon
Äneas *myth.* Aeneas
Antäus *myth.* Antaeus
Antonius, *der heilige* St Anthony
Äolus *myth.* Aeolus
Aristoteles Aristotle
Artus, *König* *myth.* King Arthur
Äschylus Aeschylus
Äskulap *myth.* Aesculapius
Äsop Aesop
Athene *myth.* Athena
Augias *myth.* Augeas
August der Starke Augustus the Strong
Augustin(us), *der heilige* St Augustine

Baldur *myth.* Balder, Baldur
Barbarossa → *Friedrich Barbarossa*
Bartholomäus, *der heilige* St. Bartholomew
Basilius Basil
Bathseba *bibl.* Bathsheba
Beda (Venerabilis) (the Venerable) Bede
Belisar Belisarius
Belsazar Belshazzar
Benedikt, *der heilige* St Benedict
Bonifatius Boniface
Bukephalos *myth.* Bucephalus

Cäsar Caesar
Cato der Ältere Cato the Elder
Cato der Jüngere Cato the Younger
Chlodwig Clovis
Christophorus, *der heilige* St Christopher
Christus, *Jesus* Jesus Christ
Chrysostomus, *Johannes* St John Chrysostom
Cupido *myth.* Cupid

Dädalus *myth.* Daedalus
Damokles Damocles
Danae *myth.* Danaë
Danaiden, *die* *myth. the* Danaides
Demokrit Democritus
Diokletian Diocletian
Dionysios Dionysius
Dionysius, *der heilige* St Denis
Dionysos Dionysus, Dionysos
Dioskuren, *die* *myth. the* Dioscuri
Donar *myth.* Donar, Thor
Don Quichotte Don Quijote
Drakon Draco
Dschingis-Khan Genghis Khan

Echnaton Akhenaton, Amenhotep IV
Eduard Edward
Eduard der Bekenner Edward the Confessor
Elektra *myth.* Electra
Elias *bibl.* Elijah
Elisabeth Elizabeth
Empedokles Empedocles
Epiktet Epictetus
Epikur Epicurus
Erich der Rote Eric the Red
Erinnyen, *die* *myth. the* Erin(n)yes
Ermanerich Ermaneric
Esra *bibl.* Ezra
Etzel Attila (the Hun)
Eugen, *Prinz* Prince Eugene
Euklid Euclid
Eumeniden, *die* *myth. the* Eumenides
Euridike *myth.* Eurydice
Ezechiel *bibl.* Ezekiel

Franz Ferdinand Francis Ferdinand
Franz Joseph Francis Joseph
Franz von Assisi, *der heilige* St Francis of Assisi
Friedrich Barbarossa Frederick Barbarossa
Friedrich der Große Frederick the Great
Friedrich der Weise Frederick the Wise
Friedrich Wilhelm der Große Kurfürst Frederick William the Great Elector
Fritz: *der Alte* ~ → *Friedrich der Große*
Furien, *die* *myth. the* Furies

Galilei, *Galileo* Galileo (Galilei)
Ganymed *myth.* Ganymede
Geiserich Geiseric
Georg George
Ghibellinen, *die* *the* Ghibellines
Gracchen, *die* *the* Gracchi
Grazien, *die* *myth. the* Graces
Guelfen, *die* *the* Guelfs
Gustav Adolph Gustavus Adolphus

Habakuk *bibl.* Habakkuk
Habsburger, *die* *the* Hapsburgs
Hadrian Hadrian, Adrian
Heinrich der Löwe Henry the Lion
Heinrich der Seefahrer Henry the Navigator
Hekate *myth.* Hecate, Hekate
Hektor *myth.* Hector
Hekuba *myth.* Hecuba
Helena *myth.* Helen
Hephäst *myth.* Hephaestus, Hephaistos
Herakles *myth.* Heracles, Herakles
Herakliden, *die* *myth. the* Heraclidae
Heraklit Heraclitus
Herkules *myth.* Hercules
Hermann der Cherusker Arminius
Herodes Herod
Herodot Herodotus
Hesekiel Ezekiel
Hesperiden, *die* *the* Hesperides
Hieronymus, *der heilige* St Jerome
Hiob *bibl.* Job
Hippokrates Hippocrates
Hippolytos *myth.* Hippolytus
Horaz Horace
Horen, *die* *myth. the* Horae, *a. the* Hours

Ignatius von Loyola Ignatius (of) Loyola
Ignaz, *der heilige* St Ignatius
Ikarus *myth.* Icarus
Innozenz Innocent
Iokaste *myth.* Jocasta
Iphigenie *myth.* Iphigenia
Isaak *bibl.* Isaac
Iwan der Große Ivan the Great
Iwan der Schreckliche Ivan the Terrible

Jahwe Jahweh, Jahveh
Jakob *bibl.* Jacob; (*kings*) James
Jakobus *bibl.* (St) James
Japhet *bibl.* Japheth
Jehova Jehovah
Jeremia(s) *bibl.* Jeremiah
Jerobeam *bibl.* Jeroboam
Jesaja *bibl.* Isaiah
Johann ohne Land, Johann Ohneland John Lackland
Johanna von Orléans, *die heilige* St Joan of Arc
Johannes der Evangelist *bibl.* John the Evangelist
Johannes der Täufer *bibl.* John the Baptist
Jona(s) *bibl.* Jonah
Josia(s) *bibl.* Josiah
Josua *bibl.* Joshua
Juda *bibl.* Judah
Judas Ischariot *bibl.* Judas Iscariot
Judas Makkabäus Judas Maccabeus
Jungfrau von Orléans, *die* St Joan of Arc

Kadmos *myth.* Cadmus
Kain *bibl.* Cain

Kaiphas *bibl.* Caiaphas
Kallimachos Callimachus
Kalliope *bibl.* Calliope
Karl der Dicke Charles the Fat
Karl der Große Charlemagne, Charles the Great
Karl der Kahle Charles the Bald
Karl der Kühne Charles the Bold
Karl Martell Charles Martel
Kassiodor Cassiodorus
Katharina die Große Catherine the Great
Katharina von Aragonien Catherine of Aragon
Katull Catullus
Klemens Clement
Kleopatra Cleopatra
Klytämnestra *myth.* Clyt(a)emnestra
Knut der Große Canute the Great, King Canute
Kolumbus, *Christoph* Christopher Columbus
Konstantin der Große Constantine the Great
Kopernikus, *Nikolaus* Nicolaus Copernicus
Kronos *myth.* Cronus, Cronos
Krösus Croesus
Kyrill, *der heilige* St Cyril
Kyros der Große Cyrus the Great

Laokoon *myth.* Laocoon
Laren, *die* *myth. the* Lares
Leukippos Leucippus
Livius Livy
Lothar Lothair
Ludwig der Bayer Louis the Bavarian
Ludwig der Deutsche Louis the German
Ludwig der Fromme Louis the Pious
Ludwig der Sonnenkönig Louis the Sun King
Lukas *bibl.* (St) Luke
Lukrez Lucretius
Lukullus Lucullus
Luzifer *myth.* Lucifer
Lykurg Lycurgus
Lysipp Lysippus

Makkabäer, *die* *bibl. the* Maccabees
Malachias *bibl.* Malachi
Maria Magdalena Mary Magdalen
Maria Stuart Mary Queen of Scots, Mary Stuart
Maria Theresia Maria Theresa
Mark Anton Mark Antony
Mark Aurel Marcus Aurelius (Antoninus)
Markus *bibl.* (St) Mark
Matthäus *bibl.* (St) Matthew
Megäre *myth.* Megaera
Menelaos *myth.* Menelaus
Merkur *myth.* Mercury
Methusalem *bibl.* Methuselah
Micha *bibl.* Micah
Minotaurus, *der* *myth. the* Minotaur

Najaden, *die* *myth. the* naiads, *the* naiades
Narziß *myth.* Narcissus
Nausikaa *myth.* Nausicaä
Nebukadnezar *bibl.* Nebuchadnezzar
Nehemia *bibl.* Nehemiah
Neptun *myth.* Neptune
Nereiden, *die* *myth. the* Nereides
Nikodemus *bibl.* Nicodemus
Nikolaus, *der heilige* St Nicholas
Nofretete Nefertiti
Nornen, *die* *myth. the* Norns

Ödipus *myth.* Oedipus
Odoaker Odoacer, Odovacar
Oktavian Octavian
Orest *myth.* Orestes
Origenes Origen
Otto der Große Otto the Great

Parzen, *die* *myth. the* Parcae
Parzival *myth.* Percival
Patroklos *myth.* Patroclus
Paulus *bibl.* (St) Paul
Peisistratos Pisistratus
Penaten, *die* *myth. the* penates
Penthesilea *myth.* Penthesile(i)a
Perikles Pericles
Peter der Große Peter the Great
Petrus *bibl.* (St) Peter
Phäaken, *die* *myth. the* Phaeacians
Phaeton Phaethon
Philipp der Gute Philip the Good
Philipp der Kühne Philip the Bold
Philipp der Lange Philip the Tall
Philipp der Schöne Philip the Fair
Philippus der Evangelist *bibl.* Philip the Evangelist
Phöbe *myth.* Phoebe, Phebe
Phöbus *myth.* Phoebus (Apollo)
Phönix *myth.* Phoenix
Pilatus, *Pontius* Pontius Pilate
Pippin der Kleine Pepin the Short
Plejaden, *die* *myth. the* Pleiades
Plinius Pliny
Polykrates Polycrates
Polyphem *myth.* Polyphemus
Pompejus Pompey (the Great)
Priamos *myth.* Priam
Prokop Procopius
Prokrustes *myth.* Procrustes
Properz Propertius
Ptolemäus Ptolemy

Rahel *bibl.* Rachel
Rebekka *bibl.* Rebecca
Richard Löwenherz Richard (the) Lion-Heart

Sacharja *bibl.* Zechariah
Salomo(n) *bibl.* Solomon
Sara *bibl.* Sarah
Saulus *bibl.* Saul
Seleukiden, *die* *the* Seleucids
Sokrates Socrates
Sophokles Sophocles
Spartakus Spartacus
Stephan Stephen
Sueton Suetonius

Telemach(os) *myth.* Telemachus
Terenz Terence
Thaddäus *bibl.* (St) Jude, Thad(d)eus
Themistokles Themistocles
Theoderich der Große Theodoric (*or* Theoderic) the Great
Theokrit Theocritus
Theophrast Theophrastus
Thomas von Aquin(o), *der heilige* St Thomas Aquinas
Thukydides Thucydides
Timotheus *bibl.* Timothy
Titanen, *die* *myth. the* Titans
Tutanchamun, Tutenchamun Tutankhamen, Thutankhamun

Uranos *myth.* Uranus

Vergil Virgil
Vinzenz Vincent
Vitruv Vitruvius
Vulkan Vulcan

Walküre *myth.* Valkyrie
Wenzel Wencesla(u)s
Widukind Wittekind, *a.* Widukind
Wilhelm William
Wilhelm der Eroberer William the Conqueror
Wilhelm von Oranien William of Orange
Wotan *myth.* Wodan, Woden

Xanthippe Xant(h)ippe
Xenokrates Xenocrates

Zebaoth *bibl.* Sabaoth
Zebedäus *bibl.* Zebedee
Zephanja *bibl.* Zephaniah
Zerberus *myth.* Cerberus

Names of Musical Works

Abschiedssymphonie (*Haydn*) Farewell Symphony
Akademische Festouvertüre (*Brahms*) Academic Festival Overture
Eine Alpensymphonie (*R. Strauss*) An Alpine Symphony
Also sprach Zarathustra (*R. Strauss*) Thus Spake Zarathustra
An der schönen blauen Donau (*Joh. Strauß, Eng. J. Strauss*) The Blue Danube
An die ferne Geliebte (*Beethoven*) To the Immortal Beloved
Auferstehungssymphonie (*Mahler*) Resurrection Symphony
Aus der neuen Welt (*Dvořák*) From the New World, The New World Symphony
Aus meinem Leben (*Smetana*) From my Life

Der Bajazzo (*Leoncavallo*) I Pagliacci
Der Barbier von Sevilla (*Rossini*) The Barber of Seville
Der Bettelstudent (*Millöcker*) The Beggar Student
Bilder einer Ausstellung (*Mussorgsky*) Pictures at an Exhibition

Coriolan(-Ouvertüre) (*Beethoven*) Coriolanus (Overture)
Die Czardasfürstin (*Kálmán*) The Gipsy Princess

Ein deutsches Requiem (*Brahms*) A German Requiem, Brahms' Requiem
Dichterliebe (*Schumann*) Poet's Love
Die Diebische Elster (*Rossini*) The Thieving Magpie
Dissonanzenquartett (*Mozart*) Dissonance Quartet
Dornröschen (*Tschaikowsky, Eng. Tchaikovsky*) Sleeping Beauty
Die Dreigroschenoper (*Weill / Brecht*) The Threepenny Opera

Elias (*Mendelssohn-Bartholdy*) Elijah
Die Entführung aus dem Serail (*Mozart*) The Seraglio, The Abduction from the Seraglio

Fantasiestücke (*Schumann*) Fantasy Pieces
Fausts Verdammnis (*Berlioz*) The Damnation of Faust
Der Feuervogel (*Strawinsky, Eng. Stravinsky*) The Firebird
Feuerwerksmusik (*Händel, Eng. Handel*) Fireworks Music, Music for the Royal Fireworks
Figaros Hochzeit (*Mozart*) The Marriage of Figaro
Die Fingalshöhle (*Mendelssohn-Bartholdy*) Fingal's Cave
Die Fledermaus (*Joh. Strauß, Eng. J. Strauss*) Die Fledermaus (The Bat)
Der Fliegende Holländer (*Wagner*) The Flying Dutchman
Forellenquintett (*Schubert*) Trout Quintet
Frauenliebe und -leben (*Schumann*) Woman's Love and Life
Die Frau ohne Schatten (*R. Strauss*) Die Frau ohne Schatten (The Woman without a Shadow)
Der Freischütz (*Weber*) Der Freischütz
Frühlingssonate (*Beethoven*) Spring Sonata
Frühlingssymphonie (*Schumann*) Spring Symphony
Fürst Igor (*Borodin*) Prince Igor

Geistertrio (*Beethoven*) Ghost Trio, The Ghost
Geschichten aus dem Wienerwald (*Joh. Strauß, Eng. J. Strauss*) Tales from the Vienna Woods
Die Geschöpfe des Prometheus (*Beethoven*) The Creatures of Prometheus
Der Goldene Hahn (*Rimsky-Korsakow, Eng. Rimsky-Korsakov*) The Golden Cockerel
Götterdämmerung (*Wagner*) Götterdämmerung (The Twilight of the Gods)
Gräfin Maritza (*Kálmán*) Countess Maritza
Der Graf von Luxemburg (*Lehár*) The Count of Luxembourg
Gurrelieder (*Schönberg*) Gurrelieder (Songs of Gurra)

Hänsel und Gretel (*Humperdinck*) Hansel and Gretel
Harold in Italien (*Berlioz*) Harold in Italy
Hebridenouvertüre (*Mendelssohn-Bartholdy*) Fingal's Cave, Hebrides Overture
Ein Heldenleben (*R. Strauss*) A Hero's Life
Die Hochzeit des Figaro (*Mozart*) The Marriage of Figaro
Hoffmanns Erzählungen (*Offenbach*) Tales of Hoffmann
Die Hugenotten (*Meyerbeer*) The Huguenots

Im Weißen Rößl (*Benatzky*) The White Horse Inn
Iphigenie auf Tauris (*Gluck*) Iphigenia on Tauris
Die Italienerin in Algier (*Rossini*) L'Italiana in Algeri (The Italian Girl in Algiers)
Italienische Symphonie (*Mendelssohn-Bartholdy*) Italian Symphony
Jagdquartett (*Mozart*) The Hunt, Hunting Quartet
Jagdsymphonie (*Haydn*) La Chasse (The Hunt)
Die Jahreszeiten (*Haydn*) The Seasons
Johannespassion (*J.S. Bach*) St John Passion

Kaiserquartett (*Haydn*) Emperor Quartet
Kaiserwalzer (*Joh. Strauß, Eng. J. Strauss*) Kaiser Waltz
Kegelstatt-Trio (*Mozart*) Kegelstatt Trio (Skittleground Trio)
Kindersymphonie (*Leopold Mozart*) Toy Symphony
Kinderszenen (*Schumann*) Scenes from Childhood
Kindertotenlieder (*Mahler*) Kindertotenlieder (Songs on the Death of Children)
Eine kleine Nachtmusik (*Mozart*) Eine kleine Nachtmusik (A Little Serenade)
Die Kluge (*Orff*) The Wise Woman
Des Knaben Wunderhorn (*Mahler*) Des Knaben Wunderhorn (The Youth's Magic Horn)
Krieg und Frieden (*Prokofjew, Eng. Prokofiev*) War and Peace
Die Krönung der Poppea (*Monteverdi*) The Coronation of Poppea
Krönungskonzert (*Mozart*) Coronation Concerto
Krönungsmesse (*Mozart*) Coronation Mass
Die Kunst der Fuge (*J.S. Bach*) The Art of Fugue

Land des Lächelns (*Lehár*) The Land of Smiles
Das Leben eines Wüstlings (*Strawinsky, Eng. Stravinsky*) The Rake's Progress
Leonoren-Ouvertüre(n) (*Beethoven*) Leonora-Overture(s)
Lerchenquartett (*Haydn*) The Lark
Liebesträume (*Liszt*) Liebesträume
Die Liebe zu den drei Orangen (*Prokofjew, Eng. Prokofiev*) Love for Three Oranges
Lied an die himmlische Freude (*Mahler*) Ode to Heavenly Joy
Lieder eines fahrenden Gesellen (*Mahler*) Songs of a Wayfarer
Das Lied von der Erde (*Mahler*) Song of the Earth
Die Lustigen Weiber von Windsor (*Nicolai*) The Merry Wives of Windsor
Die Lustige Witwe (*Lehár*) The Merry Widow

Die Macht des Schicksals (*Verdi*) The Force of Destiny

Marienvesper (*Monteverdi*) Vespers of the Blessed Virgin
Ein Maskenball (*Verdi*) A Masked Ball
Mathis der Maler (*Hindemith*) Mathias the Painter
Matthäuspassion (*J.S. Bach*) St Matthew Passion
Maurerische Trauermusik (*Mozart*) Masonic Funeral Music
Mein Vaterland (*Smetana*) Ma Vlast (My Fatherland)
Die Meistersinger von Nürnberg (*Wagner*) The Mastersingers of Nuremberg
Der Messias (*Händel, Eng. Handel*) The Messiah
Militärsymphonie (*Haydn*) Military Symphony
Minutenwalzer (*Chopin*) Minute Waltz
Die Moldau (*Smetana*) The Moldau
Mondscheinsonate (*Beethoven*) Moonlight Sonata
Das musikalische Opfer (*J.S. Bach*) The Musical Offering

Eine Nacht auf dem kahlen Berge (*Mussorgsky*) A Night on the Bare Mountain
Nachtstücke (*Schumann*) Nocturnes
Die Nachtwandlerin (*Bellini*) La Sonnambula (The Sleepwalker)
Nelson-Messe (*Haydn*) Nelson Mass
Die Neugierigen Frauen (*Wolf-Ferrari*) The Inquisitive Women
Nußknackersuite (*Tschaikowsky, Eng. Tchaikovsky*) Nutcracker Suite

Odysseus' Heimkehr (*Monteverdi*) The Return of Ulysses
O Haupt voll Blut und Wunden (*hymn*) O sacred Head surrounded
Der Opernball (*Heuberger*) The Opera Ball
Orfeo (*Monteverdi*) L'Orfeo (Orpheus)
Orpheus in der Unterwelt (*Offenbach*) Orpheus in the Underworld
Othello (*Verdi*) Othello, Otello

Pastorale (*Beethoven*) Pastoral (Symphony)
Pathétique (*Tschaikowsky, Eng. Tchaikovsky*) Pathétique
Die Perlenfischer (*Bizet*) The Pearl Fishers
Peter und der Wolf (*Prokofjew, Eng. Prokofiev*) Peter and the Wolf
Petruschka (*Strawinsky, Eng. Stravinsky*) Petrushka
Die Planeten (*Holst*) The Planets, The Planets Suite
Polowetzer Tänze (*Borodin*) Polovtsian Dances
Preußische Quartette (*Haydn, Mozart*) Prussian Quartets
Psalmensymphonie (*Strawinsky, Eng. Stravinsky*) Symphony of Psalms

Quintenquartett (*Haydn*) Fifths Quartet

Der Raub der Lukretia (*Britten*) The Rape of Lucretia
Reformationssymphonie (*Mendelssohn-Bartholdy*) Reformation Symphony
Die Regimentstochter (*Donizetti*) The Daughter of the Regiment
Registerarie (*Mozart, from Don Giovanni*) Catalogue Aria
Reiterquartett (*Haydn*) The Rider, Rider Quartet
Das Rheingold (*Wagner*) Rhinegold
Rheinische Symphonie (*Schumann*) Rhenish Symphony
Der Ring des Nibelungen (*Wagner*) The Ring (of the Nibelung)
Romantische Symphonie (*Bruckner*) Romantic Symphony
Romeo und Julia (*Tschaikowsky, Eng. Tchaikovsky*) Romeo and Juliet
Der Rosenkavalier (*R. Strauss*) Der Rosenkavalier (The Cavalier of the Rose)
Russische Quartette (*Haydn*) Russian Quartets

Le Sacre du Printemps (*Strawinsky, Eng. Stravinsky*) The Rite of Spring
Der Schauspieldirektor (*Mozart*) The Impresario
Schicksalssymphonie (*Beethoven*) Battle Symphony
Der Schmuck der Madonna (*Wolf-Ferrari*) The Jewels of the Madonna
Schneeflöckchen (*Rimsky-Korsakow, Eng. Rimsky-Korsakov*) The Snow Maiden
Die schöne Helena (*Offenbach*) La Belle Hélène
Die schöne Müllerin (*Schubert*) The Fair Maid of the Mill
Die Schöpfung (*Haydn*) The Creation
Schöpfungsmesse (*Haydn*) Creation Mass
Schottische Symphonie (*Mendelssohn-Bartholdy*) Scottish Symphony
Schwanda, der Dudelsackpfeifer (*Weinberger*) Schwanda the Bagpiper
Schwanengesang (*Schubert*) Swan Song
Schwanensee (*Tschaikowsky, Eng. Tchaikovsky*) Swan Lake
Die schweigsame Frau (*R. Strauss*) The Silent Woman
Die sieben letzten Worte unseres Erlösers am Kreuze (*Haydn*) The Seven Last Words (of our Saviour on the Cross)
Slawische Tänze (*Dvořák*) Slavonic Dances
Ein Sommernachtstraum (*Mendelssohn-Bartholdy*) A Midsummer Night's Dream
Sonnenquartette (*Haydn*) Sun Quartets
Spanisches Liederbuch (*Wolf*) Spanish Songbook
Spatzenmesse (*Mozart*) Sparrow Mass
Der Sturm (*Beethoven, piano sonata*) Tempest
Susannens Geheimnis (*Wolf-Ferrari*) Susanna's Secret
Symphonie der Tausend (*Mahler*) Symphony of a Thousand
Symphonie mit dem Paukenschlag (*Haydn*) Surprise Symphony
Symphonie mit dem Paukenwirbel (*Haydn*) Drum-roll Symphony
Symphonische Etüden (*Schumann*) Symphonic Studies

Tiefland (*d'Albert*) Tiefland (Lowlands)
Till Eulenspiegels lustige Streiche (*R. Strauss*) Till Eulenspiegel('s Merry Pranks)
Der Tod und das Mädchen (*Schubert*) Death and the Maiden
Tod und Verklärung (*R. Strauss*) Death and Transfiguration
Die Toteninsel (*Rachmaninow, Eng. Rachmaninov*) The Isle of the Dead
Totentanz (*Saint-Saëns, Liszt*) Danse Macabre (Dance of Death)
Tragische Ouvertüre (*Brahms*) Tragic Overture
Die Trojaner (*Berlioz*) The Trojans
Der Troubadour (*Verdi*) Il Trovatore

Ein Überlebender aus Warschau (*Schönberg*) A Survivor from Warsaw
Die Uhr (*Haydn*) The Clock (Symphony)
Ungarische Rhapsodien (*Liszt*) Hungarian Rhapsodies
Die Unvollendete (*Schubert*) Unfinished Symphony

Der Vampyr (*Marschner*) The Vampire
Die verkaufte Braut (*Smetana*) The Bartered Bride
Verklärte Nacht (*Schönberg*) Transfigured Night
Die Vier Jahreszeiten (*Vivaldi*) The Four Seasons

Die Walküre (*Wagner*) The Valkyrie
Wanderer-Fantasie (*Schubert*) Wanderer Fantasy
Wassermusik (*Händel, Eng. Handel*) Water Music
Weihnachtsoratorium (*J.S. Bach, Schütz*) Christmas Oratorio
Wein, Weib und Gesang (*Joh. Strauß, Eng. J. Strauss*) Wine, Women and Song
Wiener Blut (*Joh. Strauß, Eng. J. Strauss*) Vienna Blood
Der Wildschütz (*Lortzing*) The Poacher
Winterreise (*Schubert*) Winter Journey
Das Wohltemperierte Klavier (*J.S. Bach*) The Well-tempered Clavier
Der wunderbare Mandarin (*Bartók*) The Miraculous Mandarin

Zar und Zimmermann (*Lortzing*) Tsar and Carpenter
Die Zauberflöte (*Mozart*) The Magic Flute
Der Zigeunerbaron (*Joh. Strauß, Eng. J. Strauss*) The Gypsy Baron
Zigeunerliebe (*Lehár*) Gipsy Love

Numerals

Cardinal Numbers

0 null *nought, zero*
1 eins *one*
2 zwei *two*
3 drei *three*
4 vier *four*
5 fünf *five*
6 sechs *six*
7 sieben *seven*
8 acht *eight*
9 neun *nine*
10 zehn *ten*
11 elf *eleven*
12 zwölf *twelve*
13 dreizehn *thirteen*
14 vierzehn *fourteen*
15 fünfzehn *fifteen*
16 sechzehn *sixteen*
17 siebzehn *seventeen*
18 achtzehn *eighteen*
19 neunzehn *nineteen*
20 zwanzig *twenty*
21 einundzwanzig *twenty-one*
22 zweiundzwanzig *twenty-two*
23 dreiundzwanzig *twenty-three*
30 dreißig *thirty*
31 einunddreißig *thirty-one*
40 vierzig *forty*
41 einundvierzig *forty-one*
50 fünfzig *fifty*
51 einundfünfzig *fifty-one*
60 sechzig *sixty*
61 einundsechzig *sixty-one*
70 siebzig *seventy*
71 einundsiebzig *seventy-one*
80 achtzig *eighty*
81 einundachtzig *eighty-one*
90 neunzig *ninety*
91 einundneunzig *ninety-one*
100 hundert *a* (or *one*) *hundred*
101 hundert(und)eins *a hundred and one*
200 zweihundert *two hundred*
300 dreihundert *three hundred*
572 fünfhundert(und)zweiundsiebzig *five hundred and seventy-two*
1000 tausend *a* (or *one*) *thousand*
2000 zweitausend *two thousand*
1 000 000 eine Million *a* (or *one*) *million*
2 000 000 zwei Millionen *two million*
1 000 000 000 eine Milliarde *a* (or *one*) *billion*

Ordinal Numbers

1. erste *first*
2. zweite *second*
3. dritte *third*
4. vierte *fourth*
5. fünfte *fifth*
6. sechste *sixth*
7. sieb(en)te *seventh*
8. achte *eighth*
9. neunte *ninth*
10. zehnte *tenth*
11. elfte *eleventh*
12. zwölfte *twelfth*
13. dreizehnte *thirteenth*
14. vierzehnte *fourteenth*
15. fünfzehnte *fifteenth*
16. sechzehnte *sixteenth*
17. siebzehnte *seventeenth*
18. achtzehnte *eighteenth*
19. neunzehnte *nineteenth*
20. zwanzigste *twentieth*
21. einundzwanzigste *twenty-first*
22. zweiundzwanzigste *twenty-second*
23. dreiundzwanzigste *twenty-third*
30. dreißigste *thirtieth*
31. einunddreißigste *thirty-first*
40. vierzigste *fortieth*
41. einundvierzigste *forty-first*
50. fünfzigste *fiftieth*
51. einundfünfzigste *fifty-first*
60. sechzigste *sixtieth*
61. einundsechzigste *sixty-first*
70. siebzigste *seventieth*
71. einundsiebzigste *seventy-first*
80. achtzigste *eightieth*
81. einundachtzigste *eighty-first*
90. neunzigste *ninetieth*
100. hundertste (*one*) *hundredth*
101. hundert(und)erste *hundred and first*
200. zweihundertste *two hundredth*
300. dreihundertste *three hundredth*
572. fünfhundert(und)zweiundsiebzigste *five hundred and seventy-second*
1000. tausendste (*one*) *thousandth*
2000. zweitausendste *two thousandth*
1 000 000. millionste *millionth*
2 000 000. zweimillionste *two millionth*

Fractional Numbers and other Numerical Values

$\frac{1}{2}$ ein halb *a* (or *one*) *half*
$1\frac{1}{2}$ eineinhalb, anderthalb *one and a half*
$2\frac{1}{2}$ zweieinhalb *two and a half*
$\frac{1}{2}$ Meile *half a mile*
$\frac{1}{3}$ ein Drittel *a* (or *one*) *third*
$\frac{2}{3}$ zwei Drittel *two thirds*
$\frac{1}{4}$ ein Viertel *a* (or *one*) *quarter*, *a* (or *one*) *fourth*
$\frac{3}{4}$ drei Viertel *three quarters*, *three fourths*
$1\frac{1}{4}$ Stunden eineinviertel Stunden *one* (or *an*) *hour and a quarter*
$\frac{1}{5}$ ein Fünftel *a* (or *one*) *fifth*
$3\frac{4}{5}$ drei vier Fünftel *three and four fifths*
0,4 null Komma vier (*nought*) *point four* (*0.4*)
2,5 zwei Komma fünf *two point five* (*2.5*)

einfach *single*
zweifach *double*
dreifach *treble*, *triple*, *threefold*
vierfach *fourfold*, *quadruple*
fünffach *fivefold* etc.

einmal *once*
zweimal *twice*
drei-, vier-, fünfmal etc. *three*, *four*, *five times*
zweimal soviel(e) *twice as much* (*many*)
noch einmal *once more*, *once again*

erstens, zweitens, drittens etc. *firstly*, *secondly*, *thirdly*, *in the first* (*second*, *third*) *place*

$6 + 9 = 15$ sechs und (*or* plus) neun ist fünfzehn *six plus nine is fifteen*, *six and nine are* (or *is*) *fifteen*

$12 - 4 = 8$ zwölf weniger (*or* minus) vier ist acht *twelve minus four is eight*

$2 \cdot 3 = 6$ zweimal drei ist sechs *two threes are six*, *two times three is six* ($2 \times 3 = 6$)

$20 : 5 = 4$ zwanzig (geteilt *or* dividiert) durch fünf ist vier *twenty divided by five is four*, *five into twenty is four* ($20 \div 5 = 4$)

German Weights and Measures

I. Linear Measures

1 mm ***Millimeter*** millimetre
= $\frac{1}{1000}$ metre
= 0.001 yards
= 0.003 feet
= 0.039 inches

1 cm ***Zentimeter*** centimetre
= $\frac{1}{100}$ metre
= 0.39 inches

1 dm ***Dezimeter*** decimetre
= $\frac{1}{10}$ metre
= 3.94 inches

1 m ***Meter*** metre
= 1.094 yards
= 3.28 feet
= 39.37 inches

1 km ***Kilometer*** kilometre
= 1,000 metres
= 1,093.637 yards
= 0.621 British or Statute Miles

1 sm ***Seemeile*** (*international standard*) nautical mile
= 1,852 metres

II. Square Measures

1 mm² ***Quadratmillimeter*** square millimetre
= $\frac{1}{1\,000\,000}$ square metre
= 0.0015 square inches

1 cm² ***Quadratzentimeter*** square centimetre
= $\frac{1}{10\,000}$ square metre
= 0.155 square inches

1 m² ***Quadratmeter*** square metre
= 1.195 square yards
= 10.76 square feet

1 a ***Ar*** are
= 100 square metres
= 119.59 square yards
= 1,076.41 square feet

1 ha ***Hektar*** hectare
= 100 ares
= 10,000 square metres
= 11,959.90 square yards
= 2.47 acres

1 km² ***Quadratkilometer*** square kilometre
= 100 hectares
= 1,000,000 square metres
= 247.11 acres
= 0.386 square miles

III. Cubic Measures

1 cm³ ***Kubikzentimeter*** cubic centimetre
= 1,000 cubic millimetres
= 0.061 cubic inches

1 dm³ ***Kubikdezimeter*** cubic decimetre
= 1,000 cubic centimetres
= 61.025 cubic inches

1 m³ ***Kubikmeter***
1 rm ***Raummeter***
1 fm ***Festmeter*** } cubic metre
= 1,000 cubic decimetres
= 1.307 cubic yards
= 35.31 cubic feet

1 RT ***Registertonne*** register ton
= 2.832 m³
= 100 cubic feet

IV. Measures of Capacity

1 l ***Liter*** litre
= 10 decilitres
= 1.76 pints (*Brit.*)
= 7.04 gills (*Brit.*)
= 0.88 quarts (*Brit.*)
= 0.22 gallons (*Brit.*)
= 2.11 pints (*Am.*)
= 8.45 gills (*Am.*)
= 1.06 quarts (*Am.*)
= 0.26 gallons (*Am.*)

1 hl ***Hektoliter*** hectolitre
= 100 litres
= 22.009 gallons (*Brit.*)
= 2.75 bushels (*Brit.*)
= 26.42 gallons (*Am.*)
= 2.84 bushels (*Am.*)

V. Weights

1 mg ***Milligramm*** milligram(me)
= $\frac{1}{1000}$ gram(me)
= 0.015 grains

1 g ***Gramm*** gram(me)
= $\frac{1}{1000}$ kilogram(me)
= 15.43 grains

1 Pfd ***Pfund*** pound (German)
= $\frac{1}{2}$ kilogram(me)
= 500 gram(me)s
= 1.102 pounds (avdp.)
= 1.34 pounds (troy)

1 kg ***Kilogramm, Kilo*** kilogram(me)
= 1,000 gram(me)s
= 2.204 pounds (avdp.)
= 2.68 pounds (troy)

1 Ztr. ***Zentner*** centner
= 100 pounds (German)
= 50 kilogram(me)s
= 110.23 pounds (avdp.)
= 0.98 British hundredweights
= 1.102 U.S. hundredweights

1 t ***Tonne*** ton
= 1,000 kilogram(me)s
= 0.984 British tons
= 1.102 U.S. tons

Second Part

English-German

By
Heinz Messinger

Vorwort

Neubearbeitung

Wörterbücher aus dem Langenscheidt-Verlag sind unverwechselbar. Sie haben eine lange Tradition, und sie stammen aus einer großen „lexikographischen Werkstatt“: mehrere Teams von qualifizierten Lexikographen und Redakteuren bemühen sich, die Wünsche der Wörterbuchbenutzer zu erfüllen und gleichzeitig bei Neubearbeitungen dem Wandel der Sprachen Rechnung zu tragen.

Dies gilt auch für die vorliegende Neubearbeitung von Langenscheidts „Concise English-German Dictionary“. Im folgenden eine kurze Darstellung der wichtigsten Verbesserungen, die das neue Wörterbuch aufweist:

Benutzerfreundlicher durch neue Schriftarten

Gegenüber dem Vorgänger haben die Wörterbuchseiten der Neubearbeitung an Übersichtlichkeit gewonnen. Dies wurde vor allem durch zwei typographische Änderungen erzielt:

(1) Für die Stichwörter findet jetzt eine Schriftart Verwendung, die sich bisher schon in Langenscheidts „German Universal Dictionary“ bewährt hat. Durch ihre „neue Sachlichkeit“ mit den gleichmäßig starken (serifenlosen) Buchstaben ermöglicht sie ein leichteres Auffinden der Stichwörter.

(2) Systematische Meinungsumfragen bei Lehrern und Schülern haben ergeben, daß die bisher verwandte Schrift für die Wendungen (Anwendungsbeispiele, idiomatische Redensarten und Kollokationen) als zu schwach empfunden wurde. Wir verwenden deshalb in der vorliegenden Neubearbeitung für diese Wendungen eine „halbfette“ Schrift. Im Gegensatz zu der für die Stichwörter verwandten Schrift ist diese „halbfette“ Schrift jedoch eine Kursivschrift (Schrägschrift), so daß sie bei der Stichwortsuche nicht störend wirkt. Die Wendungen werden durch diese Auszeichnungsschrift stärker hervorgehoben – sie sind daher innerhalb eines Stichwortartikels leichter zu finden.

Hochaktuell mit „rumpies“ und „woopies“!

Es versteht sich von selbst, daß bei dieser Neubearbeitung viele neue Wörter aufgenommen wurden, die den augenblicklichen Stand der Sprache widerspiegeln. Nicht nur neue griffige allgemeinsprachliche Ausdrücke wie *rumpie* oder *woopie* sind als Stichwörter vorhanden. Die Vielgestaltigkeit des neuen Wortschatzes zeigt sich auch im Fachwortschatz.

Einige Beispiele: Im Bereich der Technik wurden *pixel, APT* und *Eftpos* aufgenommen; für die Wirtschaft sei *management buy-out,* für den Sport *paraglider* genannt. Auch unerfreuliche staatliche Neuerungen (z. B. *withholding tax*) wurden nicht vergessen.

Umfangreicher nicht nur von A–Z!

Durch die neue typographische Gestaltung war es möglich, noch mehr Stichwörter, Wendungen und Übersetzungen unterzubringen. Dies kam vor allem dem Wörterbuchteil (A–Z) zugute.

Aber auch der Gesamtumfang der Anhänge konnte wesentlich erweitert werden: Die Eigennamen- und Abkürzungsverzeichnisse allein nehmen z. B. 20 engbedruckte Seiten ein.

Stichwort oder Wendung: der „overkill"

Die Anzahl der Stichwörter ist eine Aussage, die sich auf das „Skelett" eines Wörterbuchs bezieht; das sogenannte „Fleisch" sind die Anwendungsbeispiele, die idiomatischen Redensarten und die Kollokationen.

Der Lexikograph hat die Aufgabe, eine Ausgewogenheit zwischen den Stichwörtern und diesen Wendungen herzustellen – denn zuviel Fleisch ist ungesund! Belanglose Stilvarianten und unwichtige Anwendungsbeispiele (die lediglich die Grundübersetzung in einem Satz zeigen, ohne Bedeutungsveränderung) führen zu einem „overkill", einem Übermaß an Beispielen, die das Suchen in einem Stichwortartikel für den Benutzer zur Qual machen.

Idiomatik und Kollokationen in angemessener Anzahl zu bieten, daneben aber nicht die Anzahl der Stichwörter und Übersetzungen zu vermindern – dies ist auch die Grundstruktur der vorliegenden Neubearbeitung. Nur so konnten wir den vielfältigen Bedürfnissen der Wörterbuchbenutzer Rechnung tragen, die durchaus auch das fachsprachliche Wort in einem Wörterbuch dieser Größenordnung erwarten.

Lautschrift und Silbentrennung

Durchweg findet die dem Lernenden heute vertraute Internationale Lautschrift (*English Pronouncing Dictionary,* 14. Auflage) Verwendung. Die Angabe der Silbentrennungsmöglichkeiten in den englischen Stichwörtern wurde – da oft sehr hilfreich – beibehalten.

Great dictionaries don't change – they mature! Wir hoffen, daß dies auch auf die vorliegende Neubearbeitung zutrifft: benutzerfreundliche Neuerungen und Modernität unter Beibehaltung der bewährten Grundstruktur.

LANGENSCHEIDT

Preface

Revised and enlarged edition

Langenscheidt dictionaries are unmistakable. They have a long tradition behind them and come out of a large "lexicographers' workshop" in which teams of experienced dictionary compilers and editors labour with two important goals in mind: to fulfil the needs and expectations of the dictionary user and to keep up with the rapid developments in language today.

These two aims also guided the preparation of the present revised and enlarged edition of Langenscheidt's "Concise English-German Dictionary". Some of its significant innovations are described in the following.

New typefaces for better readability

Two typographical adaptations have produced a clearer visual arrangement of the dictionary page:

(1) Entry words are printed in a typeface that has already proved itself in Langenscheidt's "German Universal Dictionary": the neutral, sans serif letters with their even thickness allow the entry words to be picked out quickly and effortlessly.

(2) Widespread surveys among teachers and pupils have shown that the typeface hitherto used for phraseology (i. e. illustrative phrases, idiomatic expressions and collocations) is not considered emphatic enough. This new edition of the dictionary employs a boldface type for phraseology, and in order to distinguish it from the entry words, it is in italics. Phrases are thus given prominence and can be traced more easily within the dictionary article.

"Rumpies" and "woopies"

It goes without saying that this revised dictionary includes a host of neologisms. Not only does it contain popular expressions such as *rumpie* and *woopie,* but a wide variety of specialized terms has been taken up, too.

From the realm of technology we have *pixel, APT* and *Eftpos,* for example; from economics there is *management buy-out,* from sports we have *paraglider,* and from the legal sphere *withholding tax,* to mention but a few.

Expanded dictionary plus much more

The new typography has allowed the inclusion of more entries, phrases and translations in the dictionary proper, but the appendices, too, have profited from these changes. Twenty closely printed pages, for example, are devoted to proper names and abbreviations alone.

Entry words versus phraseology: the problem of overkill

The entry words in a dictionary might be said to constitute its "skeleton", to which is added the "flesh" in the form of illustrative phrases, idioms and collocations.

The lexicographer's task is to try and strike a balance between the two, taking care not to burden the user with an unhealthy excess of flesh. Superfluous stylistic variants and illustrative phrases which do no more than show the basic meaning of a word in context can quickly lead to "overkill", or a glut of examples which can turn any search for a phrase into a grueling task.

It has thus been a fundamental concern in compiling this dictionary to provide an adequate selection of idioms and collocations without taking away from the number of entries and translations. Only in this way can we hope to fulfill the multifarious needs of our dictionary users, who justifiably expect to find a representative selection of specialized vocabulary in a dictionary of this size.

Pronunciation and word division

The phonetic transcriptions which follow the entry words are based on the now well-known International Phonetic Alphabet (*English Pronouncing Dictionary*, 14th edition). Syllabification marks in the English entry words have been retained as a useful guide to word division.

Great dictionaries don't change – they mature. We trust this goes for the present dictionary too, whose endeavor has been to integrate practical innovations and the latest developments in language into a traditional and well-tried framework.

LANGENSCHEIDT

Contents
Inhaltsverzeichnis

Wie benutzen Sie das Wörterbuch?

Keine Angst vor unbekannten Wörtern!

Das Wörterbuch tut alles, um Ihnen das Nachschlagen und Kennenlernen eines gesuchten Wortes so leicht wie möglich zu machen. Legen Sie diese Einführung daher bitte nicht gleich zur Seite. Folgen Sie uns Schritt für Schritt. Wir versprechen Ihnen, daß Sie mit uns am Ende sagen werden "It isn't as bad as all that, is it?"

Und damit Sie in Zukunft von Ihrem Wörterbuch den besten Gebrauch machen können, wollen wir Ihnen zeigen, wie und wo Sie all die Informationen finden können, die Sie für Ihre Übersetzungen in der Schule und privat, im Beruf, in Briefen oder zum Sprechen brauchen.

Wie und wo finden Sie ein Wort?

Sie suchen ein bestimmtes Wort. Und wir sagen Ihnen erst einmal, daß das Wörterbuch in die Buchstaben von A–Z unterteilt ist. Auch innerhalb der einzelnen Buchstaben sind die Wörter **alphabetisch geordnet:**

ha**y** – ha**z**e
se·cre·tar·**i**·al – sec·re·tar·**y**

Neben den Stichwörtern mit ihren Ableitungen und Zusammensetzungen finden Sie an ihrem alphabetischen Platz auch noch

a) die unregelmäßigen Formen des Komparativs und Superlativs (z.B. **better**, **worst**),
b) die verschiedenen Formen der Pronomina (z.B. **her**, **them**),
c) das Präteritum und Partizip Perfekt der unregelmäßigen Verben (z.B. **came**, **bitten**).

Eigennamen und Abkürzungen haben wir für Sie am Schluß des Buches in einem besonderen Verzeichnis zusammengestellt.

Wenn Sie nun ein bestimmtes englisches Wort suchen, wo fangen Sie damit an? – Sehen Sie sich einmal die fettgedruckten Wörter über den Spalten in den oberen äußeren Ecken auf jeder Seite an. Das sind die sogenannten **Leitwörter**, an de-

How to use this dictionary

This dictionary endeavours to do everything it can to help you find the words and translations you are looking for as quickly and as easily as possible. All the more reason, then, to take a little time to read through these guidelines carefully. We promise that in the end you will agree that using a dictionary properly isn't as bad as all that.

To enable you to get the most out of your dictionary in the long term, you will be shown exactly where and how to find the information that will help you choose the right translation in every situation – whether at school or at home, in your profession, when writing letters, or in everyday conversation.

How to find a word

When you are looking for a particular word it is important to know that the dictionary entries are arranged in strict **alphabetical order:**

ha**y** – ha**z**e
se·cre·tar·**i**·al – sec·re·tar·**y**

Besides the entry words and their derivatives and compounds, the following are also given as individual entries, in alphabetical order:

a) irregular comparative and superlative forms (e.g. **better**, **worst**),
b) the various pronoun forms (e.g. **her**, **them**),
c) the past tense and past participle of irregular verbs (e.g. **came**, **bitten**).

Proper names and abbreviations are given in separate lists at the end of the dictionary.

How then do you go about finding a particular word? Take a look at the words in bold print at the top of each page. These are so-called **catchwords** and they serve as a guide to tracing your word as quickly as possible. The catchword on the top left

nen Sie sich orientieren können. Diese Leitwörter geben Ihnen jeweils (links) das ***erste*** fettgedruckte Stichwort auf der linken Seite des Wörterbuches an bzw. (rechts) das ***letzte*** fettgedruckte Stichwort auf der rechten Seite, z.B.

backhand – bag

Wollen Sie nun das Wort ***badly***, zum Beispiel, suchen, so muß es in unserem Beispiel im Alphabet zwischen ***backhand*** und ***bag*** liegen. Suchen Sie jetzt z.B. das Wort ***effort***. Blättern Sie dazu schnell das Wörterbuch durch, und achten Sie dabei auf die linken und rechten Leitwörter. Welches Leitwort steht Ihrem gesuchten Wort ***effort*** wohl am nächsten? Dort schlagen Sie das Wörterbuch auf (in diesem Fall zwischen ***edition*** und ***ego***). Sie werden so sehr bald die gewünschte Spalte mit *Ihrem Stichwort* finden.

Wie ist das aber nun, wenn Sie auch einmal ein Stichwort nachschlagen wollen, das aus zwei einzelnen Wörtern besteht? Nehmen Sie z.B. ***evening classes*** oder einen Begriff, bei dem die Wörter mit einem Bindestrich (hyphen) miteinander verbunden sind, wie in ***baby-sit(ter)***. Diese Wörter werden wie ein einziges Wort behandelt und dementsprechend alphabetisch eingeordnet. Sollten Sie einmal ein solches zusammengesetztes Wort nicht finden, so zerlegen Sie es einfach in seine Einzelbestandteile und schlagen dann bei diesen an ihren alphabetischen Stellen nach. Sie werden sehen, daß Sie sich auf diese Weise viele Wörter selbst erschließen können.

Beim Nachschlagen werden Sie auch merken, daß viele sogenannte „Wortfamilien" entstanden sind. Das sind Stichwortartikel, die von einem gemeinsamen Stamm oder Grundwort ausgehen und deshalb – aus Gründen der Platzersparnis – in einem Artikel zusammengefaßt sind:

de·pend – **de·pend·a·bil·i·ty** – **de·pend·a·ble** – **de·pend·ance** etc.
door – **'~·bell** – **~ han·dle** – **'~ˌkeep·er** etc.

Wie schreiben Sie ein Wort?

Sie können in Ihrem Wörterbuch wie in einem Rechtschreibwörterbuch nachschlagen, wenn Sie wissen wollen, wie ein Wort richtig geschrieben wird. Sind die **britische** und die **amerikanische Schreibung** eines Stichwortes verschieden, so wird von der amerikanischen Form auf die britische verwiesen:

a·ne·mi·a, **a·ne·mic** *Am.* → ***anaemia, anaemic***
cen·ter *etc. Am.* → ***centre*** *etc.*
col·or *etc. Am.* → ***colour*** *etc.*

gives you the first word on the left-hand page, while that on the top right gives you the last word on the right-hand page, e.g.

backhand – bag

If you are looking for the word ***badly***, for example, you will find it somewhere on this double page between ***backhand*** and ***bag***. Let us take the word ***effort***: flick through the dictionary, keeping an eye open for the catchwords on the top right and left. Find the catchwords which come closest to ***effort*** and look for the word on these pages (in this case those covering ***edition*** to ***ego***). With a little practice you will be able to find the words you are looking for quite quickly.

What about entries comprising two words, such as ***evening classes***, or hyphenated expressions like ***baby-sit(ter)***? Expressions of this kind are treated in the same way as single words and thus appear in strict alphabetical order. Should you be unable to find a compound in the dictionary, just break it down into its components and look these up separately. In this way the meaning of many compound expressions can be derived indirectly.

When using the dictionary you will notice many 'word families', or groups of words stemming from a common root, which have been collated within one article in order to save space:

de·pend – **de·pend·a·bil·i·ty** – **de·pend·a·ble** – **de·pend·ance** etc.
door – **'~·bell** – **~ han·dle** – **'~ˌkeep·er** etc.

Spelling

Where the British and American spelling of a word differs, a cross reference is given from the American to the British form, where the word is treated in full:

a·ne·mi·a, **a·ne·mic** *Am.* → ***anaemia, anaemic***
cen·ter *etc. Am.* → ***centre*** *etc.*
col·or *etc. Am.* → ***colour*** *etc.*

Ein eingeklammertes u oder l in einem Stichwort oder Anwendungsbeispiel kennzeichnet ebenfalls den Unterschied zwischen britischer und amerikanischer Schreibung:

col·o(u)red bedeutet: britisch ***coloured***, amerikanisch ***colored***; **trav·el·(l)er** bedeutet: britisch ***traveller***, amerikanisch ***traveler***.

In seltenen Fällen bedeutet ein eingeklammerter Buchstabe aber auch ganz allgemein zwei Schreibweisen für ein und dasselbe Wort: **lan·o·lin(e)** wird entweder ***lanolin*** oder ***lanoline*** geschrieben.

Für die Abweichungen in der Schreibung geben wir Ihnen für das amerikanische Englisch ein paar einfache Regeln:

Die amerikanische Rechtschreibung

weicht von der britischen hauptsächlich in folgenden Punkten ab:

1. Für **...our** tritt **...or** ein, z. B. hon*or* = honour, lab*or* = labour.
2. **...re** wird zu **...er**, z. B. cent*er* = centre, meag*er* = meagre; ausgenommen sind og*re* und die Wörter auf ...cre, z. B. massa*cre*, a*cre*.
3. Statt **...ce** steht **...se**, z. B. defen*se* = defence, licen*se* = licence.
4. Bei den meisten Ableitungen der Verben auf **...l** und einigen wenigen auf **...p** unterbleibt die Verdoppelung des Endkonsonanten, also travel – trave*l*ed – trave*l*ing – trave*l*er, worship – worshi*p*ed – worshi*p*ing – worshi*p*er. Auch in einigen anderen Wörtern wird der Doppelkonsonant durch einen einfachen ersetzt, z. B. woo*l*en = woollen, carbure*t*or = carburettor.
5. Ein stummes **e** wird in gewissen Fällen weggelassen, z. B. ax = ax*e*, goodby = goodby*e*.
6. Bei einigen Wörtern mit der Vorsilbe **en...** gibt es auch noch die Schreibung **in...**, z. B. *in*close = enclose, *in*snare = ensnare.
7. Der Schreibung **ae** und **oe** wird oft diejenige mit **e** vorgezogen, z. B. an*e*mia = anaemia, diarrh*e*a = diarrhoea.
8. Aus dem Französischen stammende stumme Endsilben werden meist weggelassen, z. B. catalog = catalog*ue*, program = program*me*, prolog = prolog*ue*.
9. Einzelfälle sind: st*a*nch = staunch, m*o*ld = mould, m*o*lt = moult, gr*a*y = grey, pl*ow* = plough, ski*ll*ful = skilful, t*i*re = tyre etc.

A 'u' or 'l' in parentheses in an entry word or phrase also indicates variant spellings:

col·o(u)red means: British ***coloured***, American ***colored***; **trav·el·(l)er** means: British ***traveller***, American ***traveler***.

In a few rare cases a letter in parentheses indicates that there are two interchangeable spellings of the word: thus **lan·o·lin(e)** may be written ***lanolin*** or ***lanoline***.

Here are a few basic guidelines to help you distinguish between British and American spelling:

American spelling

differs from British spelling in the following respects:

1. **...our** becomes **...or** in American, e. g. hon*or* = honour, lab*or* = labour.
2. **...re** becomes **...er**, e. g. cent*er* = centre, meag*er* = meagre; exceptions are og*re* and words ending in ...cre, such as massa*cre*, a*cre*.
3. **...ce** becomes **...se**, e. g. defen*se* = defence, licen*se* = licence.
4. Most derivatives of verbs ending in **...l** and some of verbs ending in **...p** do not double the final consonant: travel – trave*l*ed – trave*l*ing – trave*l*er, worship – worshi*p*ed – worshi*p*ing – worshi*p*er. In certain other words, too, the double consonant is replaced by a single consonant: woo*l*en = woollen, carbure*t*or = carburettor.
5. A silent **e** is sometimes omitted, as in ax = ax*e*, goodby = goodby*e*.
6. Some words with the prefix **en...** have an alternative spelling with **in...**, e. g. *in*close = enclose, *in*snare = ensnare.
7. **ae** and **oe** are often simplified to **e**, e. g. an*e*mia = anaemia, diarrh*e*a = diarrhoea.
8. Silent endings of French origin are usually omitted, e. g. catalog = catalog*ue*, program = program*me*, prolog = prolog*ue*.
9. Further differences are found in the following words: st*a*nch = staunch, m*o*ld = mould, m*o*lt = moult, gr*a*y = grey, pl*ow* = plough, ski*ll*ful = skilful, t*i*re = tyre, etc.

Wie trennen Sie ein Wort?

Die Silbentrennung im Englischen ist für uns Deutsche ein heikles Kapitel. Aus diesem Grunde haben wir Ihnen die Sache erleichtert und geben Ihnen für jedes mehrsilbige englische Wort die Aufteilung in Silben an. Bei mehrsilbigen Stichwörtern müssen Sie nur darauf achten, wo zwischen den Silben ein halbhoher Punkt oder ein Betonungsakzent steht, z.B. **ex·pect**, **ex'pect·ance**. Bei alleinstehenden Wortbildungselementen, wie z.B. **electro-**, entfällt die Angabe der Silbentrennung, weil diese sich je nach der weiteren Zusammensetzung ändern kann.

Die Silbentrennungspunkte haben für Sie den Sinn, zu zeigen, an welcher Stelle im Wort Sie am Zeilenende trennen können. Sie sollten es aber vermeiden, nur einen Buchstaben abzutrennen, wie z.B. in **a·mend** oder **cit·y**. Hier nehmen Sie besser das ganze Wort auf die neue Zeile.

Word division

Word division in English can be a somewhat tricky matter. To make things easier we have marked the divisions of each word containing more than one syllable with a centred dot or an accent, as in **ex·pect**, **ex'pect·ance**. Combining forms which appear as individual entries (e.g. **electro-**) do not have syllabification marks since these depend on the subsequent element(s) of the compound.

Syllabification marks indicate where a word can be divided at the end of a line. The separation of a single letter from the rest of the word, as in **a·mend** or **cit·y**, should, however, be avoided if at all possible. In such cases it is better to bring the entire word forward to the new line.

Was bedeuten die verschiedenen Schriftarten?

Sie finden **fettgedruckt** alle englischen Stichwörter, alle römischen Ziffern zur Unterscheidung der Wortarten (Substantiv, transitives und intransitives Verb, Adjektiv, Adverb etc.) und alle arabischen Ziffern zur Unterscheidung der einzelnen Bedeutungen eines Wortes:

feed ... **I** *v/t.* [*irr.*] **1.** Nahrung zuführen (*dat.*) ...; **II** *v/i.* [*irr.*] **10.** a) fressen (*Tier*) ...; **III** *s.* **12.** Fütterung *f* ...

Sie finden *kursiv*

a) alle Grammatik- und Sachgebietsabkürzungen:
s., *v/t.*, *v/i.*, *adj.*, *adv.*, *hist.*, *pol.* etc.;

b) alle Genusangaben (Angaben des Geschlechtswortes): *m*, *f*, *n*;

c) alle Zusätze, die entweder als Dativ- oder Akkusativobjekt der Übersetzung vorangehen oder ihr als erläuternder Hinweis vor- oder nachgestellt sind:

e·lect ... **1.** *j-n in ein Amt* wählen ...
cut ... **19.** ... *Baum* fällen ...
byte ... *Computer*: Byte *n*
bike ... ‚Maschine' *f* (*Motorrad*) ...

d) alle Erläuterungen bei Wörtern, die keine genaue deutsche Entsprechung haben:

cor·o·ner ... ⚖ Coroner *m* (*richterlicher Beamter zur Untersuchung der Todesursache in Fällen unnatürlichen Todes*) ...

Sie finden in ***halbfetter kursiver Auszeichnungsschrift*** alle Wendungen und Hinweise zur Konstruktion mit Präpositionen:

gain ... ***~ experience*** ...
de·pend ... ***it ~s on you*** ...
de·part ... **1.** (***for*** nach) weg-, fortgehen ...
glance ... **6.** flüchtiger Blick (***at*** auf *acc.*) ...

The different typefaces and their functions

Bold type is used for the English entry words, for Roman numerals separating different parts of speech (nouns, transitive and intransitive verbs, adjectives and adverbs, etc.) and for Arabic numerals distinguishing various senses of a word:

feed ... **I** *v/t.* [*irr.*] **1.** Nahrung zuführen (*dat.*) ...; **II** *v/i.* [*irr.*] **10.** a) fressen (*Tier*) ...; **III** *s.* **12.** Fütterung *f* ...

Italics are used for

a) grammatical abbreviations and subject labels:
s., *v/t.*, *v/i.*, *adj.*, *adv.*, *hist.*, *pol.* etc.;

b) gender labels (masculine, feminine and neuter): *m*, *f*, *n*;

c) any additional information preceding or following a translation (including dative or accusative objects, which are given before the translation):

e·lect ... **1.** *j-n in ein Amt* wählen ...
cut ... **19.** ... *Baum* fällen ...
byte ... *Computer*: Byte *n*
bike ... ‚Maschine' *f* (*Motorrad*) ...

d) definitions of English words which have no direct correspondence in German:

cor·o·ner ... ⚖ Coroner *m* (*richterlicher Beamter zur Untersuchung der Todesursache in Fällen unnatürlichen Todes*) ...

Boldface italics are used for phraseology and for prepositions taken by the entry word:

gain ... ***~ experience*** ...
de·pend ... ***it ~s on you*** ...
de·part ... **1.** (***for*** nach) weg-, fortgehen ...
glance ... **6.** flüchtiger Blick (***at*** auf *acc.*) ...

Sie finden in normaler Schrift
a) alle Übersetzungen;
b) alle kleinen Buchstaben zur weiteren Bedeutungsdifferenzierung eines Wortes oder einer Wendung:

Goth·ic ... **4.** ... a) ba'rock, ro'mantisch, b) Schauer...
give in ... **2.** (***to*** *dat.*) a) nachgeben (*dat.*), b) sich anschließen (*dat.*) ...

Normal type is used for
a) translations of the entry words;
b) small letters marking subdivisions of meaning:

Goth·ic ... **4.** ... a) ba'rock, ro'mantisch, b) Schauer...
give in ... **2.** (***to*** *dat.*) a) nachgeben (*dat.*), b) sich anschließen (*dat.*) ...

Wie sprechen Sie ein Wort aus?

Sie haben das gesuchte Stichwort mit Hilfe der Leitwörter gefunden. Hinter dem Stichwort sehen Sie nun eine Reihe von Zeichen in einer eckigen Klammer. Dies ist die sogenannte Lautschrift. Die Lautschrift beschreibt, wie Sie ein Wort aussprechen sollen. So ist das „th" in ***thin*** ein ganz anderer Laut als das „th" in ***these***. Da die normale Schrift für solche Unterschiede keine Hilfe bietet, ist es nötig, diese Laute mit anderen Zeichen zu beschreiben. Damit *jeder* genau weiß, welches Zeichen welchem Laut entspricht, hat man sich international auf eine Lautschrift geeinigt. Da die Zeichen von der **I**nternational **P**honetic **A**ssociation als verbindlich angesehen werden, nennt man sie auch **IPA-Lautschrift**.

Hier sind nun die Zeichen, ohne die Sie bei unbekannten englischen Wörtern nicht auskommen werden.

Pronunciation

When you have found the entry word you are looking for, you will notice that it is followed by certain symbols enclosed in square brackets. This is the phonetic transcription of the word, which tells you how it is pronounced. As our normal alphabet cannot distinguish between certain crucial differences in sounds (e.g. that between 'th' in ***thin*** and in ***these***), a different system of symbols has to be used. To avoid the confusion of conflicting systems, one phonetic alphabet has come to be used internationally, namely that of the International Phonetic Association. This phonetic system is known by the abbreviation **IPA**. The symbols used in this dictionary are listed and illustrated in the table below:

Die englischen Laute in der Internationalen Lautschrift

[ʌ]	much [mʌtʃ], come [kʌm]	kurzes *a* wie in *Matsch*, *Kamm*
[ɑː]	after ['ɑːftə], park [pɑːk]	langes *a*, etwa wie in *Bahn*
[æ]	flat [flæt], madam ['mædəm]	mehr zum *a* hin als *ä* in *Wäsche*
[ə]	after ['ɑːftə], arrival [ə'raɪvl]	wie das End-*e* in *Berge*, *mache*, *bitte*
[e]	let [let], men [men]	*ä* wie in *hätte*, *Mäntel*
[ɜː]	first [fɜːst], learn [lɜːn]	etwa wie *ir* in *flirten*, aber offener
[ɪ]	in [ɪn], city ['sɪtɪ]	kurzes *i* wie in *Mitte*, *billig*
[iː]	see [siː], evening ['iːvnɪŋ]	langes *i* wie in *nie*, *lieben*
[ɒ]	shop [ʃɒp], job [dʒɒb]	wie *o* in *Gott*, aber offener
[ɔː]	morning ['mɔːnɪŋ], course [kɔːs]	wie in *Lord*, aber ohne *r*
[ʊ]	good [gʊd], look [lʊk]	kurzes *u* wie in *Mutter*
[uː]	too [tuː], shoot [ʃuːt]	langes *u* wie in *Schuh*, aber offener
[aɪ]	my [maɪ], night [naɪt]	etwa wie in *Mai*, *Neid*
[aʊ]	now [naʊ], about [ə'baʊt]	etwa wie in *blau*, *Couch*
[əʊ]	home [həʊm], know [nəʊ]	von [ə] zu [ʊ] gleiten
[eə]	air [eə], square [skweə]	wie *är* in *Bär*, aber kein *r* sprechen
[eɪ]	eight [eɪt], stay [steɪ]	klingt wie *äi*
[ɪə]	near [nɪə], here [hɪə]	von [ɪ] zu [ə] gleiten
[ɔɪ]	join [dʒɔɪn], choice [tʃɔɪs]	etwa wie *eu* in *neu*
[ʊə]	sure [ʃʊə], tour [tʊə]	wie *ur* in *Kur*, aber kein *r* sprechen

[j] [w]	yes [jes], tube [tju:b] way [weɪ], one [wʌn], quick [kwɪk]	wie *j* in *jetzt* sehr kurzes *u* – kein deutsches *w*!
[ŋ] [r] [s]	thing [θɪŋ], English ['ɪŋglɪʃ] room [ru:m], hurry ['hʌrɪ] see [si:], famous ['feɪməs]	wie *ng* in *Ding* nicht rollen! stimmloses *s* wie in *lassen*, *Liste*
[z]	zero ['zɪərəʊ], is [ɪz], runs [rʌnz]	stimmhaftes *s* wie in *lesen*, *Linsen*
[ʃ] [tʃ] [ʒ]	shop [ʃɒp], fish [fɪʃ] cheap [tʃi:p], much [mʌtʃ] television ['telɪvɪʒn]	wie *sch* in *Scholle*, *Fisch* wie *tsch* in *tschüs*, *Matsch* stimmhaftes *sch* wie in *Genie*, *Etage*
[dʒ] [θ] [ð] [v]	just [dʒʌst], bridge [brɪdʒ] thanks [θæŋks], both [bəʊθ] that [ðæt], with [wɪð] very ['verɪ], over ['əʊvə]	wie in *Job*, *Gin* wie *ß* in *Faß*, aber gelispelt wie *s* in *Sense*, aber gelispelt etwa wie deutsches *w*, aber Oberzähne auf Oberkante der Unterlippe
[x]	loch [lɒx]	wie *ch* in *ach*

[:] bedeutet, daß der vorhergehende Vokal lang zu sprechen ist.

[:] indicates that the preceding vowel is long.

Lautsymbole der nichtanglisierten Stichwörter

In nichtanglisierten Stichwörtern, d.h. in Fremdwörtern, die noch nicht als eingebürgert empfunden werden, werden gelegentlich einige Lautsymbole der französischen Sprache verwandt, um die nichtenglische Lautung zu kennzeichnen. Die nachstehende Liste gibt einen Überblick über diese Symbole:

[ɑ̃] ein nasaliertes, offenes a wie im französischen Wort *enfant*.

[ɛ̃] ein nasaliertes, offenes ä wie im französischen Wort *fin*.

[ɔ̃] ein nasaliertes, offenes o wie im französischen Wort *bonbon*.

[œ] ein offener ö-Laut wie im französischen Wort *jeune*.

[ø] ein geschlossener ö-Laut wie im französischen Wort *feu*.

[y] ein kurzes ü wie im französischen Wort *vu*.

[ɥ] ein kurzer Reibelaut, Zungenstellung wie beim deutschen ü („gleitendes ü"). Wie im französischen Wort *muet*.

[ɲ] ein j-haltiges n, noch zarter als in *Champagner*. Wie im französischen Wort *Allemagne*.

Phonetic symbols for foreign loan-words

Occasionally French phonetic symbols have been used to transcribe foreign loan-words whose pronunciation has not been Anglicized:

[ɑ̃] like the e or a in the French *enfant*.

[ɛ̃] like the i in the French *fin*.

[ɔ̃] like the o in the French *bonbon*.

[œ] like the eu in the French *jeune*.

[ø] like the eu in the French *feu*.

[y] like the u in the French *vu*.

[ɥ] like the u in the French *muet*.

[ɲ] like the gn in the French *Champagne*.

Kursive phonetische Zeichen

Ein kursives phonetisches Zeichen bedeutet, daß der Buchstabe gesprochen oder nicht gesprochen werden kann. Beide Aussprachen sind dann im Englischen gleich häufig. Z.B. das kursive *ʊ* in

Phonetic symbols in italics

If a phonetic symbol appears in italics, this means that it may be spoken or not. In such cases, both pronunciations are more or less equally common. The italic *ʊ*, for example, in the phonetic

der Umschrift von molest [məʊ'lest] bedeutet, daß die Aussprache des Wortes mit [ə] oder mit [əʊ] etwa gleich häufig ist.

transcription of molest [məʊ'lest] means that it can be pronounced with [ə] or [əʊ].

Die **Betonung** der englischen Wörter wird durch das Zeichen ˈ für den Hauptakzent bzw. ˌ für den Nebenakzent vor der zu betonenden Silbe angegeben:

on·ion ['ʌnjən] – **dis·loy·al** [ˌdɪs'lɔɪəl]

Bei den zusammengesetzten Stichwörtern ohne Lautschriftangabe wird der Betonungsakzent im zusammengesetzten Stichwort selbst gegeben, z. B. **ˌup'stairs**. Die Betonung erfolgt auch dann im Stichwort, wenn nur ein Teil der Lautschrift gegeben wird, z. B. **ad'min·is·tra·tor** [-treɪtə], **'dog·ma·tism** [-ətɪzəm].

Bei einem Stichwort, das aus zwei oder mehreren einzelnen Wörtern besteht, können Sie die Aussprache bei dem jeweiligen Einzelwort nachschlagen, z. B. **school leav·ing cer·tif·i·cate**.

Primary (or strong) stress is indicated by ˈ preceding the stressed syllable, and secondary (or weak) stress by ˌ preceding the stressed syllable:

on·ion ['ʌnjən] – **dis·loy·al** [ˌdɪs'lɔɪəl]

In the case of compounds without phonetic transcription, the accents are given in the entry word itself, as in **ˌup'stairs**. Stress is also indicated in the entry word if only part of the phonetic transcription is given, as in **ad'min·is·tra·tor** [-treɪtə], **'dog·ma·tism** [-ətɪzəm].

For the pronunciation of entries consisting of more than one word, each individual word should be looked up, as with **school leav·ing cer·tif·i·cate**.

Einige Worte noch zur **amerikanischen Aussprache:**
Amerikaner sprechen viele Wörter anders aus als die Briten. In diesem Wörterbuch geben wir Ihnen aber meistens nur die britische Aussprache, wie Sie sie auch in Ihren Lehrbüchern finden. Ein paar Regeln für die Abweichungen in der amerikanischen Aussprache wollen wir Ihnen hier aber doch geben.

Die amerikanische Aussprache weicht hauptsächlich in folgenden Punkten von der britischen ab:

1. ɑː wird zu (gedehntem) æ(ː) in Wörtern wie *ask* [æ(ː)sk = ɑːsk], *castle* ['kæ(ː)sl = 'kɑːsl], *grass* [græ(ː)s = grɑːs], *past* [pæ(ː)st = pɑːst] etc.; ebenso in *branch* [bræ(ː)ntʃ = brɑːntʃ], *can't* [kæ(ː)nt = kɑːnt], *dance* [dæ(ː)ns = dɑːns] etc.
2. ɒ wird zu ɑ in Wörtern wie *common* ['kɑmən = 'kɒmən], *not* [nɑt = nɒt], *on* [ɑn = ɒn], *rock* [rɑk = rɒk], *bond* [bɑnd = bɒnd] und vielen anderen.
3. juː wird zu uː, z. B. *due* [duː = djuː], *duke* [duːk = djuːk], *new* [nuː = njuː].
4. r zwischen vorhergehendem Vokal und folgendem Konsonanten wird stimmhaft gesprochen, indem die Zungenspitze gegen den harten Gaumen zurückgezogen wird, z. B. *clerk* [klɜːrk = klɑːk], *hard* [hɑːrd = hɑːd]; ebenso im Auslaut, z. B. *far* [fɑːr = fɑː], *her* [hɜːr = hɜː].
5. Anlautendes p, t, k in unbetonter Silbe (nach betonter Silbe) wird zu b, d, g abgeschwächt, z. B. in *property*, *water*, *second*.
6. Der Unterschied zwischen stark- und schwachbetonten Silben ist viel weniger ausgeprägt; längere Wörter haben einen deutlichen Nebenton, z. B. *dictionary* ['dɪkʃəˌnerɪ = 'dɪkʃənrɪ], *ceremony* ['serəˌməʊnɪ = 'serɪmənɪ], *inventory* ['ɪnvənˌtɔːrɪ = 'ɪnvəntrɪ], *secretary* ['sekrəˌterɪ = 'sekrətrɪ].
7. Vor, oft auch nach nasalen Konsonanten (m, n, ŋ) sind Vokale und Diphthonge nasal gefärbt, z. B. *stand*, *time*, *small*.

Was sagen Ihnen die Symbole und Abkürzungen?

Wir geben Ihnen die Symbole und Abkürzungen im Wörterbuch, um Sie davor zu bewahren, durch falsche Anwendung einer Übersetzung in das berühmte „Fettnäpfchen" zu treten.

Die Liste mit den **Abkürzungen** zur Kennzeichnung des Grammatik- und Sachgebietsbereiches finden Sie auf den Seiten 28 und 29.

Die **Symbole** zeigen Ihnen, in welchem Lebens-, Arbeits- und Fachbereich ein Wort am häufigsten benutzt wird.

~ ≗ Tilde; siehe Seite 18.
⚘ Botanik, *botany.*
⚙ Handwerk, *handicraft*; Technik, *engineering.*
⚒ Bergbau, *mining.*
⚔ militärisch, *military term.*
⚓ Schiffahrt, *nautical term.*
☤ Handel u. Wirtschaft, *commercial term.*
🚂 Eisenbahn, *railway, railroad.*
✈ Flugwesen, *aviation.*
📯 Postwesen, *post and telecommunications.*
♪ Musik, *musical term.*
⌂ Architektur, *architecture.*
ϟ Elektrotechnik, *electrical engineering.*
⚖ Rechtswissenschaft, *legal term.*
A Mathematik, *mathematics.*
⚒ Landwirtschaft, *agriculture.*
⚗ Chemie, *chemistry.*
⚕ Medizin, *medicine.*
→ Verweiszeichen; siehe Seite 20.

Ein weiteres Symbol ist das Kästchen: □. Steht es nach einem englischen Adjektiv, so bedeutet das, daß das Adverb regelmäßig durch Anhängung von ***-ly*** an das Adjektiv oder durch Umwandlung von ***-le*** in ***-ly*** oder von ***-y*** in ***-ily*** gebildet wird, z. B.

bald □ = ***baldly***
change·a·ble □ = ***changeably***
bus·y □ = ***busily***

Es gibt auch noch die Möglichkeit, ein Adverb durch Anhängen von ***-ally*** an das Stichwort zu bilden. In diesen Fällen haben wir auch das angegeben:

his·tor·ic (□ *~ally*) = ***historically***

Bei Adjektiven, die auf ***-ic*** und ***-ical*** enden können, wird die Adverbbildung auf folgende Weise gekennzeichnet:

phil·o·soph·ic, **phil·o·soph·i·cal** *adj.* □

d. h. ***philosophically*** ist das Adverb zu beiden Adjektivformen.

Wird bei der Adverbangabe auf das Adverb selbst verwiesen, so bedeutet dies, daß unter diesem Stichwort vom Adjektiv abweichende Übersetzungen zu finden sind:

a·ble □ → ***ably***

Symbols and abbreviations

Symbols and abbreviations indicating subject areas are designed to aid the user in choosing the appropriate translation of a word.

A list of **abbreviations** of grammatical terms and subject areas is given on pp. 28–29.

The pictographic **symbols** indicate the field in which a word is most commonly used.

~ ≗ tilde; see p. 18.
⚘ Botanik, *botany.*
⚙ Handwerk, *handicraft*; Technik, *engineering.*
⚒ Bergbau, *mining.*
⚔ militärisch, *military term.*
⚓ Schiffahrt, *nautical term.*
☤ Handel u. Wirtschaft, *commercial term.*
🚂 Eisenbahn, *railway, railroad.*
✈ Flugwesen, *aviation.*
📯 Postwesen, *post and telecommunications.*
♪ Musik, *musical term.*
⌂ Architektur, *architecture.*
ϟ Elektrotechnik, *electrical engineering.*
⚖ Rechtswissenschaft, *legal term.*
A Mathematik, *mathematics.*
⚒ Landwirtschaft, *agriculture.*
⚗ Chemie, *chemistry.*
⚕ Medizin, *medicine.*
→ cross-reference mark; see p. 20.

A square box □ after an English adjective indicates that the adverb is formed regularly by adding ***-ly***, changing ***-le*** into ***-ly***, or ***-y*** into ***-ily***:

bald □ = ***baldly***
change·a·ble □ = ***changeably***
bus·y □ = ***busily***

Some adverbs are formed by adding ***-ally*** to the adjective. This is indicated by a box followed by the adverbial ending:

his·tor·ic (□ *~ally*) = ***historically***

Adverb forms deriving from adjectives which may end in ***-ic*** or ***-ical*** are given as follows:

phil·o·soph·ic, **phil·o·soph·i·cal** *adj.* □

i. e., ***philosophically*** is the adverb derived from both adjective forms.

If an adjective is followed by a cross-reference to the adverb, this means that the adverb is used in a sense quite different from that of the adjective:

a·ble □ → ***ably***

Was bedeutet das Zeichen ~, die Tilde?

Ein Symbol, das Ihnen ständig in den Stichwortartikeln begegnet, ist ein Wiederholungszeichen, die Tilde (~ ≗).

Zusammengehörige oder verwandte Wörter sind häufig zum Zwecke der Raumersparnis unter Verwendung der Tilde zu Gruppen vereinigt. Die Tilde vertritt dabei entweder das ganze Stichwort oder den vor dem senkrechten Strich (|) stehenden Teil des Stichworts.

drink·ing ... ~ **wa·ter** = ***drinking water***
'head|·light ... **'~·line** = ***headline***

Bei den in halbfetter kursiver Auszeichnungsschrift gesetzten Redewendungen vertritt die Tilde stets das unmittelbar vorhergehende Stichwort, das selbst schon mit Hilfe der Tilde gebildet worden sein kann:

ˌdou·ble|-'act·ing ... **ˌ~-'edged** ...: ***~ sword*** = ***double-edged sword***

Wechselt die Schreibung von klein zu groß oder von groß zu klein, steht statt der einfachen Tilde (~) die Kreistilde (≗):

mid·dle| age ... ≗ **Ag·es** = ***Middle Ages***
Ren·ais·sance ... **2.** ≗ 'Wiedergeburt *f* ... = ***renaissance***

The swung dash, or tilde (~)

A symbol you will repeatedly come across in the dictionary articles is the so-called tilde (~ ≗), which serves as a replacement mark. For reasons of space, related words are often combined in groups with the help of the tilde. In these cases, the tilde replaces either the entire entry word or that part of it which precedes a vertical bar (|):

drink·ing ... ~ **wa·ter** = ***drinking water***
'head|·light ... **'~·line** = ***headline***

In the case of the phrases in boldface italics, the tilde replaces the entry word immediately preceding, which itself may also have been formed with the help of a tilde:

ˌdou·ble|-'act·ing ... **ˌ~-'edged** ...: ***~ sword*** = ***double-edged sword***

If there is a switch from a small initial letter to a capital or vice-versa, the standard tilde (~) appears with a circle (≗):

mid·dle| age ... ≗ **Ag·es** = ***Middle Ages***
Ren·ais·sance ... **2.** ≗ 'Wiedergeburt *f* ... = ***renaissance***

Einige Worte zu den Übersetzungen und Wendungen

Nach dem fettgedruckten Stichwort, der Ausspracheangabe in eckigen Klammern und der Bezeichnung der Wortart kommt als nächstes das, was für Sie wahrscheinlich das Wichtigste ist: **die Übersetzung**.

Die Übersetzungen haben wir folgendermaßen untergliedert: römische Ziffern zur Unterscheidung der Wortarten (Substantiv, Verb, Adjektiv, Adverb etc.), arabische Ziffern zur Unterscheidung der einzelnen Bedeutungen, kleine Buchstaben zur weiteren Bedeutungsdifferenzierung. z. B.

face ... **I** *s.* **1.** Gesicht *n* ...; ***in*** (***the***) ***~ of*** a) angesichts (*gen.*), gegenüber (*dat.*), b) trotz (*gen. od. dat.*) ...; **II** *v/t.* **11.** ansehen ...; **III** *v/i.* ...

Weist ein Stichwort grundsätzlich verschiedene Bedeutungen auf, so wird es mit einer hochgestellten Zahl, dem Exponenten, als eigenständiges Stichwort wiederholt:

chap¹ [tʃæp] *s.* F Bursche *m*, Junge *m* ...
chap² [tʃæp] *s.* Kinnbacken *m* ...
chap³ [tʃæp] **I** *v/t. u. v/i.* rissig machen *od.* werden ...; **II** *s.* Riß *m*, Sprung *m*.

Dies geschieht aber nicht in Fällen, in denen sich die zweite Bedeutung aus der Hauptbedeutung des Grundwortes entwickelt hat.

Translations and phraseology

After the boldface entry word, its phonetic transcription in square brackets, and its part of speech label, we finally come to the most important part of the entry: **the translation(s)**.

Where an entry word has several different meanings, the translations have been arranged as follows: different parts of speech (nouns, verbs, adjectives, adverbs etc.) separated by Roman numerals, different senses by Arabic numerals, and related senses by small letters:

face ... **I** *s.* **1.** Gesicht *n* ...; ***in*** (***the***) ***~ of*** a) angesichts (*gen.*), gegenüber (*dat.*), b) trotz (*gen. od. dat.*) ...; **II** *v/t.* **11.** ansehen ...; **III** *v/i.* ...

Where a word has fundamentally different meanings, it appears as two or more separate entries distinguished by exponents, or raised figures:

chap¹ [tʃæp] *s.* F Bursche *m*, Junge *m* ...
chap² [tʃæp] *s.* Kinnbacken *m* ...
chap³ [tʃæp] **I** *v/t. u. v/i.* rissig machen *od.* werden ...; **II** *s.* Riß *m*, Sprung *m*.

This does not apply to senses which have directly evolved from the primary meaning of the word.

Anwendungsbeispiele in halbfetter kursiver Auszeichnungsschrift werden meist unter den zugehörigen Ziffern aufgeführt. Sind es sehr viele Beispiele, so werden sie in einem eigenen Abschnitt „*Besondere Redewendungen*" zusammengefaßt (siehe Stichwort ***heart***). Eine Übersetzung der Beispiele wird nicht gegeben, wenn diese sich aus der Grundübersetzung von selbst ergibt:

a·like ... **II** *adv.* gleich, ebenso, in gleichem Maße: ***she helps enemies and friends ~***.

Bei sehr umfangreichen Stichwortartikeln werden auch die Zusammensetzungen von **Verben mit Präpositionen oder Adverbien** an das Ende der betreffenden Artikel angehängt, z.B. ***come across***, ***get up***.

Bei den Übersetzungen wird in Fällen, in denen die Aussprache Schwierigkeiten verursachen könnte, die Betonung durch **Akzent(e)** vor der zu betonenden Trennsilbe gegeben. Akzente werden gesetzt bei Wörtern, die nicht auf der ersten Silbe betont werden, z.B. „Bäcke'rei", „je'doch", außer wenn es sich um eine der stets unbetonten Vorsilben handelt, sowie bei Zusammensetzungen mit Vorsilben, deren Betonung wechselt, z.B. „'Mißtrauen", „miß'trauen". Grundsätzlich entfällt der Akzent jedoch bei Verben auf „-ieren" und deren Ableitungen. Bei kursiven Erläuterungen und bei den Übersetzungen von Anwendungsbeispielen werden keine Akzente gesetzt.

Der **verkürzte Bindestrich** (-) steht zwischen zwei Konsonanten, um anzudeuten, daß sie getrennt auszusprechen sind, z.B. „Häus-chen", ebenso in Fällen, die zu Mißverständnissen führen können, z.B. „Erb-lasser".

Wie Sie sicher wissen, gibt es im **britischen und amerikanischen Englisch** hier und da unterschiedliche Bezeichnungen für dieselbe Sache. Ein Engländer sagt z.B. ***pavement***, wenn er den „Bürgersteig" meint, der Amerikaner spricht dagegen von ***sidewalk***. Im Wörterbuch finden Sie die Wörter, die hauptsächlich im britischen Englisch gebraucht werden, mit *Brit.* gekennzeichnet. Die Wörter, die typisch für den amerikanischen Sprachgebrauch sind, werden mit *Am.* gekennzeichnet.

Auf die verschiedenen Wortarten haben wir bereits hingewiesen. Der Eintrag ***dependence*** z.B. ist ein Substantiv (Hauptwort). Dies können Sie daran erkennen, daß hinter der Lautschriftklammer ein kursives *s.* steht. Dementsprechend steht hinter der deutschen Übersetzung „Abhängigkeit" ein kursives *f*, bzw. hinter „Angewiesensein" ein kursives *n*. Diese Buchstaben geben – wie auch das kursive *m* – das **Genus** (Geschlecht) des deutschen Wortes an und kennzeichnen es damit als Substantiv. Die Genusangabe unterbleibt, wenn

Illustrative phrases in boldface italics are generally given within the respective categories of the dictionary article. Where there are a lot af examples, these are found in a separate section entitled "*Besondere Redewendungen*" (see for example the entry ***heart***).

Illustrative phrases whose meaning is self-evident are not translated:

a·like ... **II** *adv.* gleich, ebenso, in gleichem Maße: ***she helps enemies and friends ~***.

In the case of particularly long articles, **verbal phrases** such as ***come across***, ***get up*** etc. are given separately at the end of the main part of the article.

Where the pronunciation of a German translation could be ambiguous or problematical, **accents** are placed before the stressed syllable(s). Accents are also given in words whose initial syllable is unstressed (e.g. 'Bäcke'rei', 'je'doch'), unless it is a generally unstressed prefix. They are further given in compounds in which the accent shifts (e.g. ''Mißtrauen', 'miß'trauen'). Accentuation is not provided for verbs ending in '-ieren' and their derivatives, nor in definitions in italics or translations of phraseology.

A **hyphen** is inserted between two consonants to indicate that they are pronounced separately (e.g. 'Häus-chen') and in words which might be misinterpreted (e.g. 'Erb-lasser').

British and American English occasionally differ in the way they describe things. For ***pavement***, for example, an American would say ***sidewalk***. In the dictionary, words which are predominantly used in British English are marked *Brit.*, and those which are typically American are marked *Am.*

We have already mentioned the different parts of speech. The entry word ***dependence***, for example, is a noun. This is indicated by the letter *s.* in italics following the phonetic transcription in square brackets. The German translations 'Abhängigkeit' and 'Angewiesensein' are followed by an italic *f* and *n* respectively. These letters, together with the italic *m*, indicate the gender of the German noun, i.e. they show whether it is masculine, feminine or neuter. The gender is not given if it can be inferred from the context, e.g. from the

das Genus aus dem Zusammenhang ersichtlich ist, z. B. „scharfes Durchgreifen", und wenn die weibliche Endung in Klammern steht, z. B. „Verkäufer (-in)". Sie unterbleibt auch bei Erläuterungen in kursiver Schrift, wird aber in den Anwendungsbeispielen dann gegeben, wenn sich das Genus der Übersetzungen hier nicht aus der Grundübersetzung ergibt.

Oft wird Ihnen aber auch die folgende Abweichung begegnen:

Unter ***dependant*** finden Sie die Übersetzung „(Fa'milien)Angehörige(r *m*) *f*". „Angehörige" ist weiblich; deshalb steht hinter der Klammer ein *f*. Es besteht aber auch die Möglichkeit, ***dependant*** als „Angehöriger" zu übersetzen – und das ist männlich. Genau das steht in der Klammer: (r *m*), das Endungs-r und *m* = maskulin.

Sie werden bereits gemerkt haben, daß es selten vorkommt, daß nur eine Übersetzung hinter dem jeweiligen Stichwort steht. Meist ist es so, daß ein Stichwort mehrere sinnverwandte Übersetzungen hat, die durch **Komma** voneinander getrennt werden.

Die Bedeutungsunterschiede in den Übersetzungen werden gekennzeichnet:

a) durch das **Semikolon** und die Unterteilung in **arabische Ziffern**:
bal·ance ... **1.** Waage *f* ...; **2.** Gleichgewicht *n* ...
b) durch Unterteilung in **kleine Buchstaben** zur weiteren Bedeutungsdifferenzierung,
c) durch **Erläuterungen** in kursiver Schrift,
d) durch vorangestellte **bildliche Zeichen** und **abgekürzte Begriffsbestimmungen** (siehe das Verzeichnis auf Seite 17 und die Liste mit den Abkürzungen auf den Seiten 28 und 29).

Siehe auch das Kapitel über die verschiedenen Schriftarten auf Seite 13.

Einfache Anführungszeichen bedeuten, daß eine Übersetzung entweder einer niederen Sprachebene angehört:

gov·er·nor ... **4.** F *der* ‚Alte'

oder in figurativer (bildlicher) Bedeutung gebraucht wird:

land·slide ... **1.** Erdrutsch *m*; **2.** ... *fig.* ‚Erdrutsch' *m*

Häufig finden Sie auch bei einem Stichwort oder einem Stichwortartikel ein **Verweiszeichen** (→). Es hat folgende Bedeutungen:

a) Verweis von Stichwort zu Stichwort bei Bedeutungsgleichheit, z. B.
gaun·try → ***gantry***

adjective ending in 'scharfes Durchgreifen', or if the feminine ending is added in brackets, as in 'Verkäufer(in)'. Definitions in italics do not contain gender indications, and they are only given in phraseology where they cannot be derived from the primary translations.

Frequently you will come across translations such as '(Familien)Angehörige(r *m*) *f*' in the article ***dependant***. Here 'Angehörige' is feminine, as indicated by the *f* after the parentheses. But ***dependant*** can also be translated 'Angehöriger', which is masculine. This is indicated by (r *m*) in parentheses, which gives the ending -r and the gender indication *m* to show that it is masculine.

It is quite rare for an entry word to be given just one translation. Usually a word will have several related translations, which are separated by a **comma**.

Different senses of a word are indicated by

a) **semicolons** and **Arabic numerals**:
bal·ance ... **1.** Waage *f* ...; **2.** Gleichgewicht *n* ...
b) **small letters** for related senses,
c) italics for **definitions**,
d) **pictographic symbols** and **abbreviations of subject areas** (see p. 17 and the list of abbreviations on pp. 28–29).

See also the section on p. 13 concerning the different typefaces.

Single quotation marks mean that a translation is either very informal:

gov·er·nor ... **4.** F *der* ‚Alte'

or used in figurative sense:

land·slide ... **1.** Erdrutsch *m*; **2.** ... *fig.* ‚Erdrutsch' *m*

Frequently you will come across an **arrow** (→) after an entry word or elsewhere in a dictionary article. It is used

a) as a cross reference to another entry:
gaun·try → ***gantry***

b) Verweis innerhalb eines Stichwortartikels, z. B.

dice [daɪs] **I** *s. pl. von* ***die***[2] 1 Würfel *pl.*, Würfelspiel *n*: ***play*** **(*at*)** ~ → II ... **II** *v/i.* würfeln, knobeln

c) oft wurde an Stelle eines Anwendungsbeispiels auf ein anderes Stichwort verwiesen, das ebenfalls in dem Anwendungsbeispiel enthalten ist:

square ... **15.** ⩓ a) den Flächeninhalt berechnen von (*od. gen.*), b) *Zahl* quadrieren, ins Qua'drat erheben, c) *Figur* quadrieren; → ***circle*** 1

Das heißt, daß die Wendung ***square the circle*** unter dem Stichwort ***circle*** aufgeführt und dort übersetzt ist.

Runde Klammern werden verwendet

a) zur Vereinfachung der Übersetzung, z. B.

cov·er ... **4.** ... (Bett-, Möbel- *etc.*)Bezug *m* ...

b) zur Raumersparnis bei gekoppelten Anwendungsbeispielen, z. B.

make (**break**) **contact** Kontakt herstellen (unterbrechen) = ***make contact/break contact*** ...

Grammatik auch im Wörterbuch?

Etwas Grammatik wollen wir Ihnen zumuten. Mit diesem letzten Punkt sind Sie, wie wir glauben, für die Arbeit mit *Ihrem Wörterbuch* bestens gerüstet.

Den grammatisch richtigen Gebrauch eines Wortes können Sie häufig den „Zusätzen" entnehmen.

Die **Rektion** von deutschen Präpositionen wird dann angegeben, wenn sie verschiedene Fälle regieren können, z. B. „vor", „über".

Die Rektion von Verben wird nur dann angegeben, wenn sie von der des Grundwortes abweicht oder wenn das englische Verb von einer bestimmten Präposition regiert wird. Folgende Anordnungen sind möglich:

a) wird ein Verb, das im Englischen transitiv ist, im Deutschen intransitiv übersetzt, so wird die abweichende Rektion angegeben:

con·tra·dict ... *v/t.* **1.** ... wider'sprechen (*dat.*) ...

b) gelten für die deutschen Übersetzungen verschiedene Rektionen, so steht die englische Präposition in halbfetter kursiver Auszeichnungsschrift in Klammern vor der ersten Übersetzung, die deutschen Rektionsangaben stehen hinter jeder Einzelübersetzung:

de·scend ... **4.** (***to***) zufallen (*dat.*), 'übergehen, sich vererben (auf *acc.*) ...

b) as a reference within an article:

dice [daɪs] **I** *s. pl. von* ***die***[2] 1 Würfel *pl.*, Würfelspiel *n*: ***play*** **(*at*)** ~ → II ... **II** *v/i.* würfeln, knobeln

c) as a cross reference to another entry which provides an illustrative phrase containing the initial entry word:

square ... **15.** ⩓ a) den Flächeninhalt berechnen von (*od. gen.*), b) *Zahl* quadrieren, ins Qua'drat erheben, c) *Figur* quadrieren; → ***circle*** 1

This tells you that the expression ***square the circle*** and its translation are found in the entry ***circle***.

Parentheses are used

a) to help present the translations as simply as possible:

cov·er ... **4.** ... (Bett-, Möbel- *etc.*)Bezug *m* ...

b) to combine related phrases in order to save space:

make (**break**) **contact** Kontakt herstellen (unterbrechen) = ***make contact/break contact*** ...

Grammar in a dictionary?

A little bit of grammar, we feel, is not amiss in a dictionary, and knowing what to do with the grammatical information available will enable the user to get the most out of this dictionary.

Information on the correct grammatical use of a word is usually appended to the translation(s).

Where a German preposition can govern either the dative or accusative case, the appropriate case is indicated, as with 'vor' and 'über'.

The cases governed by verbs are given only if they deviate from those of the English verb or where an English verb takes a preposition. The following arrangements are possible:

a) where an English transitive verb is rendered intransitively in German, the required case is given:

con·tra·dict ... *v/t.* **1.** ... wider'sprechen (*dat.*) ...

b) where the German translations take varying cases, the appropriate English preposition is given in boldface italics and in brackets preceding the first translation, while the German grammatical indicators follow each individual translation:

de·scend ... **4.** (***to***) zufallen (*dat.*), 'übergehen, sich vererben (auf *acc.*) ...

c) stimmen Präposition und Rektion für alle Übersetzungen überein, so stehen sie in Klammern hinter der letzten Übersetzung:

ob·serve ... **4.** Bemerkungen machen, sich äußern (***on*, *upon*** über *acc.*) ...

Außerdem finden Sie bei den Stichwörtern noch die folgenden **besonderen Grammatikpunkte** aufgeführt:

a) unregelmäßiger Plural:

child ... *pl.* **chil·dren** ...
a·nal·y·sis ... *pl.* **-ses** ... (= *pl.* ***analyses***)

b) unregelmäßige Verben:

give ... **II** *v/t.* [*irr.*] ... **III** *v/i.* [*irr.*] ...
out·grow ... [*irr.* → ***grow***] ...

Der Hinweis *irr.* bedeutet: in der Liste der unregelmäßigen englischen Verben auf Seite 23 und 24 finden Sie die unregelmäßigen Formen.

c) auslautendes ***-c*** wird zu ***-ck*** vor ***-ed***, ***-er***, ***-ing*** und ***-y***:

frol·ic ... **II** *v/i. pret. u. p.p.* **'frol·icked** ...

d) bei unregelmäßigen Steigerungsformen Hinweis auf die Grundform:

bet·ter ... **I** *comp. von* ***good*** ... **III** *comp. von* ***well*** ...
best ... **I** *sup. von* ***good*** ... **II** *sup. von* ***well*** ...

Die vorausgegangenen Seiten zeigen, daß Ihnen das Wörterbuch mehr bietet als nur einfache Wort-für-Wort-Gleichungen, wie Sie sie in den Vokabelspalten von Lehrbüchern finden.

Und nun viel Erfolg bei der Suche nach den lästigen, aber doch so notwendigen Vokabeln!

c) where the English preposition and the German case apply to all translations, they are given in brackets after the final translation:

ob·serve ... **4.** Bemerkungen machen, sich äußern (***on*, *upon*** über *acc.*) ...

The following grammatical information is also provided:

a) irregular plurals:

child ... *pl.* **chil·dren** ...
a·nal·y·sis ... *pl.* **-ses** ... (= *pl.* ***analyses***)

b) irregular verbs:

give ... **II** *v/t.* [*irr.*] ... **III** *v/i.* [*irr.*] ...
out·grow ... [*irr.* → ***grow***] ...

The abbreviation *irr.* means that the principal parts of the verb can be found in the list of irregular verbs on pp. 23–24.

c) final ***-c*** becomes ***-ck*** before ***-ed***, ***-er***, ***-ing*** and ***-y***:

frol·ic ... **II** *v/i. pret. u. p.p.* **'frol·icked** ...

d) irregular comparative and superlative forms include a reference to the base form:

bet·ter ... **I** *comp. von* ***good*** ... **III** *comp. von* ***well*** ...
best ... **I** *sup. von* ***good*** ... **II** *sup. von* ***well*** ...

We hope that this somewhat lengthy introduction has shown you that this dictionary contains a great deal more than simple one-to-one translations, and that you are now well-equipped to make the most of all it has to offer.

Happy word-hunting!

Irregular Verbs
Unregelmäßige Verben

The verb forms are given in the following order: infinitive (in bold print), past tense (after the first dash), past participle (after the second dash).

abide – abode, abided – abode, abided
arise – arose – arisen
awake – awoke, awaked – awoken, awaked

be – was, were – been
bear – bore – borne
beat – beat – beaten, beat
become – became – become
beget – begot – begotten
begin – began – begun
bend – bent – bent
bereave – bereft, bereaved – bereft, bereaved
beseech – besought, beseeched – besought, beseeched
bet – bet, betted – bet, betted
bid – bad(e), bid – bid, bidden
bide – bode, bided – bided
bind – bound – bound
bite – bit – bitten, bit
bleed – bled – bled
blow – blew – blown
break – broke – broken
breed – bred – bred
bring – brought – brought
broadcast – broadcast, broadcasted – broadcast, broadcasted
build – built – built
burn – burnt, burned – burnt, burned
burst – burst – burst
buy – bought – bought

cast – cast – cast
catch – caught – caught
chide – chid, chided – chidden, chid, chided
choose – chose – chosen
cleave – cleft, clove, cleaved – cleft, cloven, cleaved
cling – clung – clung
come – came – come
cost – cost – cost
creep – crept – crept
cut – cut – cut

deal – dealt – dealt
deepfreeze – deepfroze, -freezed – deepfrozen, -freezed
dig – dug – dug
dive – dived, *Am. a.* dove – dived
do – did – done
draw – drew – drawn
dream – dreamt, dreamed – dreamt, dreamed
drink – drank – drunk
drive – drove – driven
dwell – dwelt, dwelled – dwelt, dwelled

eat – ate – eaten

fall – fell – fallen
feed – fed – fed
feel – felt – felt
fight – fought – fought
find – found – found
flee – fled – fled
fling – flung – flung
fly – flew – flown
forbid – forbade, forbad – forbidden
forget – forgot – forgotten, forgot
forgive – forgave – forgiven
forsake – forsook – forsaken
freeze – froze – frozen

get – got – got, *Am.* gotten
gild – gilded, gilt – gilded, gilt
gird – girded, girt – girded, girt
give – gave – given
go – went – gone
grind – ground – ground
grow – grew – grown

hang – hung, hanged – hung, hanged
have – had – had
hear – heard – heard
heave – heaved, hove – heaved, hove
hew – hewed – hewn, hewed
hide – hid – hidden, hid
hit – hit – hit
hold – held – held
hurt – hurt – hurt

inset – inset – inset

keep – kept – kept
kneel – knelt, kneeled – knelt, kneeled
knit – knitted, knit – knitted, knit
know – knew – known

lade – laded – laded, laden
lay – laid – laid
lead – led – led
lean – leant, leaned – leant, leaned
leap – leapt, leaped – leapt, leaped
learn – learnt, learned – learnt, learned
leave – left – left
lend – lent – lent
let – let – let
lie – lay – lain
light – lit, lighted – lit, lighted
lose – lost – lost

make – made – made
mean – meant – meant
meet – met – met
mow – mowed – mown, mowed

outbid – outbid – outbid, outbidden

pay – paid – paid
put – put – put

read – read – read
rend – rent – rent
rid – rid – rid
ride – rode – ridden
ring – rang – rung
rise – rose – risen
rive – rived – rived, riven
run – ran – run

saw – sawed – sawn, sawed
say – said – said
see – saw – seen
seek – sought – sought
sell – sold – sold
send – sent – sent
set – set – set
sew – sewed – sewn, sewed
shake – shook – shaken
shave – shaved – shaved, shaven
shed – shed – shed
shine – shone – shone
shit – shit, shat – shit
shoe – shod, shoed – shod, shoed
shoot – shot – shot
show – showed – shown, showed
shrink – shrank, shrunk – shrunk
shut – shut – shut
sing – sang – sung
sink – sank, sunk – sunk

sit – sat – sat
slay – slew – slain
sleep – slept – slept
slide – slid – slid, slidden
sling – slung – slung
slink – slunk – slunk
slit – slit – slit
smell – smelt, smelled – smelt, smelled
smite – smote – smitten
sow – sowed – sown, sowed
speak – spoke – spoken
speed – sped, speeded – sped, speeded
spell – spelt, spelled – spelt, spelled
spend – spent – spent
spill – spilt, spilled – spilt, spilled
spin – spun, span – spun
spit – spat, *Am. a.* spit – spat, *Am. a.* spit
split – split – split
spoil – spoilt, spoiled – spoilt, spoiled
spread – spread – spread
spring – sprang, *Am. a.* sprung – sprung
stand – stood – stood
stave – staved, stove – staved, stove
steal – stole – stolen
stick – stuck – stuck
sting – stung – stung
stink – stank, stunk – stunk
strew – strewed – strewn, strewed
stride – strode – stridden
strike – struck – struck
string – strung – strung
strive – strove – striven
swear – swore – sworn
sweat – sweat, sweated – sweat, sweated
sweep – swept – swept
swell – swelled – swollen, swelled
swim – swam – swum
swing – swung – swung

take – took – taken
teach – taught – taught
tear – tore – torn
tell – told – told
think – thought – thought
thrive – thrived, throve – thrived, thriven
throw – threw – thrown
thrust – thrust – thrust
tread – trod – trodden, trod

wake – woke, waked – woken, waked
wear – wore – worn
weave – wove – woven
wed – wedded, wed – wedded, wed
weep – wept – wept
wet – wetted, wet – wetted, wet
win – won – won
wind – wound – wound
wring – wrung – wrung
write – wrote – written

Numerals
Zahlwörter

Grundzahlen

0 nought, zero, cipher; *teleph.* 0 [əʊ] *null*
1 one *eins*
2 two *zwei*
3 three *drei*
4 four *vier*
5 five *fünf*
6 six *sechs*
7 seven *sieben*
8 eight *acht*
9 nine *neun*
10 ten *zehn*
11 eleven *elf*
12 twelve *zwölf*
13 thirteen *dreizehn*
14 fourteen *vierzehn*
15 fifteen *fünfzehn*
16 sixteen *sechzehn*
17 seventeen *siebzehn*
18 eighteen *achtzehn*
19 nineteen *neunzehn*
20 twenty *zwanzig*
21 twenty-one *einundzwanzig*
22 twenty-two *zweiundzwanzig*
30 thirty *dreißig*
31 thirty-one *einunddreißig*
40 forty *vierzig*
41 forty-one *einundvierzig*
50 fifty *fünfzig*
51 fifty-one *einundfünfzig*
60 sixty *sechzig*
61 sixty-one *einundsechzig*
70 seventy *siebzig*
71 seventy-one *einundsiebzig*
80 eighty *achtzig*
81 eighty-one *einundachtzig*
90 ninety *neunzig*
91 ninety-one *einundneunzig*
100 a *od.* one hundred *hundert*
101 a hundred and one *hundert(und)eins*
200 two hundred *zweihundert*
300 three hundred *dreihundert*
572 five hundred and seventy-two *fünfhundert(und)zweiundsiebzig*
1000 a *od.* one thousand *(ein)tausend*
1066 ten sixty-six *tausendsechsundsechzig*
1992 nineteen (hundred and) ninety-two *neunzehnhundertzweiundneunzig*
2000 two thousand *zweitausend*
5044 *teleph.* five 0 double four *fünfzig vierundvierzig*
1000000 a *od.* one million *eine Million*
2000000 two million *zwei Millionen*
1000000000 a *od.* one billion *eine Milliarde*

Ordnungszahlen

1. first *erste*
2. second *zweite*
3. third *dritte*
4. fourth *vierte*
5. fifth *fünfte*
6. sixth *sechste*
7. seventh *siebente*
8. eighth *achte*
9. ninth *neunte*
10. tenth *zehnte*
11. eleventh *elfte*
12. twelfth *zwölfte*
13. thirteenth *dreizehnte*
14. fourteenth *vierzehnte*
15. fifteenth *fünfzehnte*
16. sixteenth *sechzehnte*
17. seventeenth *siebzehnte*
18. eighteenth *achtzehnte*
19. nineteenth *neunzehnte*
20. twentieth *zwanzigste*
21. twenty-first *einundzwanzigste*
22. twenty-second *zweiundzwanzigste*
23. twenty-third *dreiundzwanzigste*
30. thirtieth *dreißigste*
31. thirty-first *einunddreißigste*
40. fortieth *vierzigste*
41. forty-first *einundvierzigste*
50. fiftieth *fünfzigste*

Ordnungszahlen

51. fifty-first *einundfünfzigste*
60. sixtieth *sechzigste*
61. sixty-first *einundsechzigste*
70. seventieth *siebzigste*
71. seventy-first *einundsiebzigste*
80. eightieth *achtzigste*
81. eighty-first *einundachtzigste*
90. ninetieth *neunzigste*
100. (one) hundredth *hundertste*
101. hundred and first *hundertunderste*
200. two hundredth *zweihundertste*
300. three hundredth *dreihundertste*
572. five hundred and seventy-second *fünfhundertundzweiundsiebzigste*
1000. (one) thousandth *tausendste*
1950. nineteen hundred and fiftieth *neunzehnhundertfünfzigste*
2000. two thousandth *zweitausendste*
1000000. millionth *millionste*
2000000. two millionth *zweimillionste*

Bruchzahlen und andere Zahlenwerte

$\frac{1}{2}$ one *od.* a half *ein halb*
$1\frac{1}{2}$ one and a half *anderthalb*
$2\frac{1}{2}$ two and a half *zweieinhalb*
$\frac{1}{3}$ one *od.* a third *ein Drittel*
$\frac{2}{3}$ two thirds *zwei Drittel*
$\frac{1}{4}$ one *od.* a quarter, one fourth *ein Viertel*
$\frac{3}{4}$ three quarters, three fourths *drei Viertel*
$\frac{1}{5}$ one *od.* a fifth *ein Fünftel*
$3\frac{4}{5}$ three and four fifths *drei vier Fünftel*
$\frac{5}{8}$ five eighths *fünf Achtel*
$\frac{12}{20}$ twelve twentieths *zwölf Zwanzigstel*
$\frac{75}{100}$ seventy-five hundredths *fünfundsiebzig Hundertstel*
.45 point four five *null Komma vier fünf*
2.5 two point five *zwei Komma fünf*

once *einmal*
twice *zweimal*
three (four) times *drei- (vier)mal*
twice as much (many) *zweimal* od. *doppelt so viel(e)*
firstly (secondly, thirdly), in the first (second, third) place *erstens (zweitens, drittens)*
$7 + 8 = 15$ seven and eight are fifteen *sieben und* od. *plus acht ist fünfzehn*
$9 - 4 = 5$ nine less four is five *neun minus* od. *weniger vier ist fünf*
$2 \times 3 = 6$ twice three is *od.* makes six *zweimal drei ist sechs*
$20 : 5 = 4$ twenty divided by five is four *zwanzig dividiert* od. *geteilt durch fünf ist vier*

British and American Weights and Measures

Britische und amerikanische Maße und Gewichte

Linear Measure
Längenmaße

1 inch	= 2,54 cm
1 foot	= 12 inches = 30,48 cm
1 yard	= 3 feet = 91,44 cm
1 (statute) mile	
	= 1760 yards = 1,609 km
1 hand	= 4 inches = 10,16 cm
1 rod (perch, pole)	
	= 5½ yards = 5,029 m
1 chain	= 4 rods = 20,117 m
1 furlong	= 10 chains
	= 201,168 m

Nautical Measure
Nautische Maße

1 fathom	= 6 feet = 1,829 m
1 cable's length	
	= 100 fathoms = 182,9 m
	⚓⚔ *Brit.* = 608 feet
	= 185,3 m
	⚓⚔ *Am.* = 720 feet
	= 219,5 m
1 nautical mile	
	= 10 cables' length
	= 1,852 km

Square Measure
Flächenmaße

1 square inch	= 6,452 cm^2
1 square foot	= 144 square inches
	= 929,029 cm^2
1 square yard	= 9 square feet
	= 8361,26 cm^2
1 acre	= 4840 square yards
	= 4046,8 m^2
1 square mile	= 640 acres
	= 259 ha = 2,59 km^2
1 square rod (square pole, square perch)	= 30¼ square yards
	= 25,293 m^2
1 rood	= 40 square rods
	= 1011,72 m^2
1 acre	= 4 roods = 4046,8 m^2

Avoirdupois Weight
Handelsgewichte

1 grain		= 0,0648 g
1 dram		= 27.3438 grains
		= 1,772 g
1 ounce		= 16 drams = 28,35 g
1 pound		= 16 ounces = 453,59 g
1 hundredweight		= 1 quintal
	Brit.	= 112 pounds
		= 50,802 kg
	Am.	= 100 pounds
		= 45,359 kg
1 long ton		
	Brit.	= 20 hundredweights
		= 1016,05 kg
1 short ton		
	Am.	= 20 hundredweights
		= 907,185 kg
1 stone		= 14 pounds = 6,35 kg
1 quarter		
	Brit.	= 28 pounds
		= 12,701 kg
	Am.	= 25 pounds
		= 11,339 kg

Troy Weight
Troygewichte

1 grain	= 0,0648 g
1 pennyweight	
	= 24 grains = 1,5552 g
1 ounce	= 20 pennyweights
	= 31,1035 g
1 pound	= 12 ounces
	= 373,2418 g

Cubic Measure
Raummaße

1 cubic inch	= 16,387 cm^3
1 cubic foot	= 1728 cubic inches
	= 0,02832 m^3
1 cubic yard	= 27 cubic feet
	= 0,7646 m^3

British Measure of Capacity
Britische Hohlmaße

Trocken- und Flüssigkeitsmaße

1 gill	= 0,142 l	
1 pint	= 4 gills	= 0,568 l
1 quart	= 2 pints	= 1,136 l
1 gallon	= 4 quarts	= 4,5459 l
1 quarter	= 64 gallons	= 290,935 l

Trockenmaße

1 peck	= 2 gallons	= 9,092 l
1 bushel	= 4 pecks	= 36,368 l

Flüssigkeitsmaße

1 barrel	= 36 gallons	= 163,656 l

American Measure of Capacity
Amerikanische Hohlmaße

Trockenmaße – Dry Measure

1 pint	= 0,5506 l	
1 quart	= 2 pints	= 1,1012 l
1 gallon	= 4 quarts	= 4,405 l
1 peck	= 2 gallons	= 8,8096 l
1 bushel	= 4 pecks	= 35,2383 l

Flüssigkeitsmaße – Liquid Measure

1 gill	= 0,1183 l	
1 pint	= 4 gills	= 0,4732 l
1 quart	= 2 pints	= 0,9464 l
1 gallon	= 4 quarts	= 3,7853 l
1 barrel	= 31.5 gallons	
	= 119,228 l	
1 hogshead	= 2 barrels	= 238,456 l
1 barrel petroleum		
	= 42 gallons	= 158,97 l

Abbreviations used in the dictionary

Im Wörterbuch verwandte Abkürzungen

a.	auch, *also.*
abbr.	*abbreviation*, Abkürzung.
acc.	*accusative* (*case*), Akkusativ.
act.	*active voice*, Aktiv.
adj.	*adjective*, Adjektiv.
adv.	*adverb*, Adverb.
allg.	allgemein, *generally.*
Am.	*(originally) American English*, (ursprünglich) amerikanisches Englisch.
amer. / amer.	amerikanisch, *American.*
anat.	*anatomy*, Anatomie.
antiq.	*antiquity*, Antike.
Arab.	*Arabic*, arabisch.
ast.	*astronomy*, Astronomie.
art.	*article*, Artikel.
attr.	*attributive*(*ly*), attributiv.
bibl.	*biblical*, biblisch.
biol.	*biology*, Biologie.
Brit.	*in British usage only*, nur im britischen Englisch gebräuchlich.
brit. / brit.	britisch, *British.*
b.s.	*bad sense*, im schlechten Sinne.
bsd.	besonders, *particularly.*
cj.	*conjunction*, Konjunktion.
coll.	*collectively*, als Sammelwort.
comp.	*comparative*, Komparativ.
contp.	*contemptuously*, verächtlich.
dat.	*dative* (*case*), Dativ.
dem.	*demonstrative*, Demonstrativ…
dial.	*dialectal*, dialektisch.
eccl.	*ecclesiastical*, kirchlich, geistlich.
e-e, *e-e*	eine, *a* (*an*).
e-m, *e-m*	einem, *to a* (*an*).
e-n, *e-n*	einen, *a* (*an*).
engS.	im engeren Sinne, *in the narrower sense.*
e-r, *e-r*	einer, *of a* (*an*), *to a* (*an*).
e-s, *e-s*	eines, *of a* (*an*).
et., *et.*	etwas, *something.*
etc.	*et cetera*, usw.
euphem.	*euphemistically*, beschönigend.
F	*familiar*, umgangssprachlich.
f	*feminine*, weiblich.
fenc.	*fencing*, Fechten.
fig.	*figuratively*, im übertragenen Sinne, bildlich.
Fr.	*French*, französisch.
gen.	*genitive* (*case*), Genitiv.
geogr.	*geography*, Geographie.
geol.	*geology*, Geologie.
Ger.	*German*, deutsch.
ger.	*gerund*, Gerundium.
Ggs.	Gegensatz, *antonym.*
her.	*heraldry*, Heraldik, Wappenkunde.
hist.	*historical*, historisch; inhaltlich veraltet.
humor.	*humorously*, scherzhaft.
hunt.	*hunting*, Jagd.
ichth.	*ichthyology*, Ichthyologie, Fischkunde.
impers.	*impersonal*, unpersönlich.
ind.	*indicative* (*mood*), Indikativ.
inf.	*infinitive* (*mood*), Infinitiv.
int.	*interjection*, Interjektion.
interrog.	*interrogative*, Interrogativ…
Ir.	*Irish*, irisch.
iro.	*ironically*, ironisch.
irr.	*irregular*, unregelmäßig.
Ital.	*Italian*, italienisch.
j-d, *j-d*	jemand, *someone.*
j-m, *j-m*	jemandem, *to someone.*
j-n, *j-n*	jemanden, *someone.*
j-s, *j-s*	jemandes, *someone's.*
konkr.	konkret, *concretely.*
konstr.	konstruiert, *construed.*
Lat.	*Latin*, lateinisch.
ling.	*linguistics*, Linguistik, Sprachwissenschaft.
lit.	*literary*, literarisch.
m	*masculine*, männlich.
m-e, *m-e*	meine, *my.*
metall.	*metallurgy*, Metallurgie.

meteor.	*meteorology*, Meteorologie.
min.	*mineralogy*, Mineralogie.
m-m, *m-m*	meinem, *to my*.
m-n, *m-n*	meinen, *my*.
mot.	*motoring*, Auto, Verkehr.
mount.	*mountaineering*, Bergsteigen.
m-r, *m-r*	meiner, *of my*, *to my*.
m-s, *m-s*	meines, *of my*.
mst	meistens, *mostly*, *usually*.
myth.	*mythology*, Mythologie.
n	*neuter*, sächlich.
neg.	*negative*, verneinend.
nom.	*nominative* (*case*), Nominativ.
npr.	*proper name*, Eigenname.
obs.	*obsolete*, veraltet.
od., *od.*	oder, *or*.
opt.	*optics*, Optik.
orn.	*ornithology*, Ornithologie, Vogelkunde.
o.s.	*oneself*, sich.
paint.	*painting*, Malerei.
parl.	*parliamentary term*, parlamentarischer Ausdruck.
pass.	*passive voice*, Passiv.
ped.	*pedagogy*, Pädagogik; Schülersprache.
pers.	*personal*, Personal...
pharm.	*pharmacy*, Pharmazie.
phls.	*philosophy*, Philosophie.
phot.	*photography*, Fotografie.
phys.	*physics*, Physik.
physiol.	*physiology*, Physiologie.
pl.	*plural*, Plural.
poet.	*poetically*, dichterisch.
pol.	*politics*, Politik.
poss.	*possessive*, Possessiv...
p.p.	*past participle*, Partizip Perfekt.
pred.	*predicative(ly)*, prädikativ.
pres.	*present*, Präsens.
pres.p.	*present participle*, Partizip Präsens.
pret.	*preterit(e)*, Präteritum.
pron.	*pronoun*, Pronomen.
prp.	*preposition*, Präposition.
psych.	*psychology*, Psychologie.
R.C.	*Roman-Catholic*, römisch-katholisch.
Redew.	Redewendung, *phrase*.
refl.	*reflexive*, reflexiv.
rel.	*relative*, Relativ...
rhet.	*rhetoric*, Rhetorik.
s.	*substantive*, *noun*, Substantiv.
Scot.	*Scottish*, schottisch.
sculp.	*sculpture*, Bildhauerei.
s-e, *s-e*	seine, *his*, *one's*.
sg.	*singular*, Singular.
sl.	*slang*, Slang.
s-m, *s-m*	seinem, *to his*, *to one's*.
s-n, *s-n*	seinen, *his*, *one's*.
s.o., *s.o.*	*someone*, jemand(en).
sociol.	*sociology*, Soziologie.
sport	*sports*, Sport.
s-r, *s-r*	seiner, *of his*, *of one's*, *to his*, *to one's*.
s-s, *s-s*	seines, *of his*, *of one's*.
s.th., *s.th.*	*something*, etwas.
subj.	*subjunctive* (*mood*), Konjunktiv.
sup.	*superlative*, Superlativ.
surv.	*surveying*, Landvermessung.
tel.	*telegraphy*, Telegrafie.
teleph.	*telephone system*, Fernsprechwesen.
thea.	*theatre*, Theater.
TM	*trademark*, Warenzeichen.
TV	*television*, Fernsehen.
typ.	*typography*, Buchdruck.
u., *u.*	und, *and*.
univ.	*university*, Hochschulwesen; Studentensprache.
V	*vulgar*, vulgär, unanständig.
v/aux.	*auxiliary verb*, Hilfsverb.
vet.	*veterinary medicine*, Tiermedizin.
v/i.	*intransitive verb*, intransitives Verb.
v/refl.	*reflexive verb*, reflexives Verb.
v/t.	*transitive verb*, transitives Verb.
weitS.	im weiteren Sinne, *more widely taken*.
z.B.	zum Beispiel, *for instance*.
zo.	*zoology*, Zoologie.
Zs.-, zs.-	zusammen, *together*.
Zssg(n)	Zusammensetzung(en), *compound word(s)*.

A

A, a [eɪ] **I** *s.* **1.** A *n*, a *n* (*Buchstabe,* ♪ *Note*): ***from A to Z*** von A bis Z; **2. *A*** *ped. Am.* Eins *f* (*Note*); **II** *adj.* **3. *A*** erst; **4. *A*** *Am.* ausgezeichnet.

A 1 [ˌeɪ'wʌn] *adj.* **1.** ⚓ erstklassig (*Schiff*); **2.** F I a, 'prima.

a [eɪ; ə], *vor vokalischem Anlaut* **an** [æn; ən] **1.** ein, eine (*unbestimmter Artikel*): ***a woman***; *manchmal vor pl.*: ***a barracks*** eine Kaserne; ***a bare five minutes*** knappe fünf Minuten; **2.** der-, die-, das'selbe: ***two of a kind*** zwei (von jeder Art); **3.** per, pro, je: ***twice a week*** zweimal wöchentlich *od.* in der Woche; ***fifty pence a dozen*** fünfzig Pence pro *od.* das Dutzend; **4.** einzig: ***at a blow*** auf 'einen Schlag.

Aar·on's rod [ˌeərənz-] *s.* ⚘ **1.** Königskerze *f*; **2.** Goldrute *f*.

a·back [ə'bæk] *adv.* **1.** ⚓ back, gegen den Mast; **2.** nach hinten, zurück; **3.** *fig.* ***taken ~*** bestürzt, verblüfft, sprachlos.

ab·a·cus ['æbəkəs] *pl.* **-ci** [-saɪ] *u.* **-cus·es** *s.* 'Abakus *m*: a) Rechenbrett *n*, -gestell *n*, b) △ Kapi'telldeckplatte *f*.

a·baft [ə'bɑ:ft] ⚓ **I** *prp.* achter, hinter; **II** *adv.* achteraus.

a·ban·don [ə'bændən] **I** *v/t.* **1.** auf-, preisgeben, verzichten auf (*acc.*) (*a.* ✝), entsagen (*dat.*), *Hoffnung* fahrenlassen; **2.** (*a.* ⚓ *Schiff*) aufgeben, verlassen; *Aktion* einstellen; *sport* Spiel abbrechen; **3.** im Stich lassen; *Ehefrau* böswillig verlassen; *Kinder* aussetzen; **4.** (***s.th. to s.o.*** j-m et.) über'lassen, ausliefern; **5. *~ o.s.*** (***to***) sich 'hingeben, sich über'lassen (*dat.*); **II** *s.* [abɑ̃dɔ̃] **6.** Hemmungslosigkeit *f*, Wildheit *f*; ***with ~*** mit Hingabe, wie toll; **a'ban·doned** [-nd] *adj.* **1.** verlassen, aufgegeben; herrenlos; **2.** liederlich; **3.** hemmungslos, wild; **a'ban·don·ment** [-mənt] *s.* **1.** Auf-, Preisgabe *f*, Verzicht *m*; (***to*** an *acc.*) Über'lassung *f*, Abtretung *f*; **2.** (⚖ böswilliges) Verlassen; (Kindes-) Aussetzung *f*; **3.** → ***abandon*** 6.

a·base [ə'beɪs] *v/t.* erniedrigen, demütigen, entwürdigen; **a'base·ment** [-mənt] *s.* Erniedrigung *f*, Demütigung *f*, Verfall *m*.

a·bash [ə'bæʃ] *v/t.* beschämen; in Verlegenheit *od.* aus der Fassung bringen.

a·bate [ə'beɪt] **I** *v/t.* **1.** vermindern, verringern; *Preis etc.* her'absetzen, ermäßigen; **2.** *Schmerz* lindern; *Stolz, Eifer* mäßigen; **3.** ⚖ *Mißstand* beseitigen; *Verfügung* aufheben; *Verfahren* einstellen; **II** *v/i.* **4.** abnehmen, nachlassen; sich legen (*Wind, Schmerz*); fallen (*Preis*); **a'bate·ment** [-mənt] *s.* **1.** Abnehmen *n*, Nachlassen *n*, Verminderung *f*, Linderung *f*; (*Lärm- etc.*)Bekämpfung *f*; **2.** Abzug *m*, (*Preis- etc.*)Nachlaß *m*; **3.** ⚖ Beseitigung *f*, Aufhebung *f*.

ab·a·tis ['æbətɪs] *s. sg. u. pl.* [*pl.* -ti:z] ⚔ Baumverhau *m*.

ab·at·toir ['æbətwɑ:] (*Fr.*) *s.* Schlachthaus *n*.

ab·ba·cy ['æbəsɪ] *s.* Abtswürde *f*; **ab·bess** ['æbes] *s.* Äb'tissin *f*; **ab·bey** ['æbɪ] *s.* **1.** Ab'tei *f*: ***the* ♀ *Brit.*** die Westminsterabtei; **2.** *Brit.* herrschaftlicher Wohnsitz (*frühere Abtei*); **ab·bot** ['æbət] *s.* Abt *m*.

ab·bre·vi·ate [ə'bri:vɪeɪt] *v/t.* (ab)kürzen; **ab·bre·vi·a·tion** [əˌbri:vɪ'eɪʃn] *s.* (*bsd. ling.* Ab)Kürzung *f*.

ABC, Abc [ˌeɪbi:'si:] **I** *s.* **1.** *Am. oft pl.* Abc *n*, Alpha'bet *n*; **2.** *fig.* Anfangsgründe *pl.*; **3.** alpha'betisch angeordnetes Handbuch; **II** *adj.* **4. *the ~ powers*** die ABC-Staaten (*Argentinien, Brasilien, Chile*); **5. *~ weapons*** ABC-Waffen, atomare, biologische u. chemische Waffen; ***~ warfare*** ABC-Kriegführung *f*.

ab·di·cate ['æbdɪkeɪt] **I** *v/t. Amt, Recht etc.* aufgeben, niederlegen; verzichten auf (*acc.*), entsagen (*dat.*); **II** *v/i.* abdanken; **ab·di·ca·tion** [ˌæbdɪ'keɪʃn] *s.* Abdankung *f*, Verzicht *m* (***of*** auf *acc.*); freiwillige Niederlegung (*e-s Amtes etc.*): ***~ of the throne*** Thronverzicht *m*.

ab·do·men ['æbdəmen] *s.* **1.** *anat.* Ab'domen *n*, 'Unterleib *m*, Bauch *m*; **2.** *zo.* ('Hinter)Leib *m* (*von Insekten etc.*); **ab·dom·i·nal** [æb'dɒmɪnl] *adj.* **1.** *anat.* Unterleibs..., Bauch...; **2.** *zo.* Hinterleibs...

ab·duct [æb'dʌkt] *v/t. gewaltsam* entführen; **ab'duc·tion** [-kʃn] *s.* Entführung *f*.

a·beam [ə'bi:m] *adv. u. adj.* ⚓, ✈ querab, dwars.

a·be·ce·dar·i·an [ˌeɪbi:si:'deərɪən] **I** *s.* **1.** Abc-Schütze *m*; **II** *adj.* **2.** alpha'betisch (geordnet); **3.** *fig.* elemen'tar.

a·bed [ə'bed] *adv.* zu *od.* im Bett.

Ab·er·don·i·an [ˌæbə'dəʊnjən] **I** *adj.* aus Aber'deen stammend; **II** *s.* Einwohner (-in) von Aberdeen.

ab·er·ra·tion [ˌæbə'reɪʃn] *s.* **1.** Abweichung *f*; **2.** *fig.* a) Verirrung *f*, Fehltritt *m*, b) (geistige) Verwirrung; **3.** *phys., ast.* Aberrati'on *f*.

a·bet [ə'bet] *v/t.* begünstigen, Vorschub leisten (*dat.*); aufhetzen; anstiften; ⚖ → ***aid*** 1; **a'bet·ment** [-mənt] *s.* Beihilfe *f*, Vorschub *m*; Anstiftung *f*; **a'bet·tor** [-tə] *s.* Anstifter *m*, (Helfers)Helfer *m*, ⚖ *a.* Gehilfe *m*.

a·bey·ance [ə'beɪəns] *s.* Unentschiedenheit *f*, Schwebe *f*: ***in ~*** a) *bsd.* ⚖ in der Schwebe, schwebend unwirksam, b) ⚖ herrenlos (*Grund u. Boden*); ***fall into ~*** zeitweilig außer Kraft treten.

ab·hor [əb'hɔ:] *v/t.* ver'abscheuen; **ab·hor·rence** [əb'hɒrəns] *s.* **1.** Abscheu *m* (***of*** vor *dat.*); **2.** → ***abomination*** 2; **ab·hor·rent** [əb'hɒrənt] *adj.* □ verabscheuungswürdig; abstoßend; verhaßt (***to*** *dat.*).

a·bide [ə'baɪd] [*irr.*] **I** *v/i.* **1.** bleiben, fortdauern; **2. *~ by*** treu bleiben (*dat.*), bleiben bei, festhalten an (*dat.*); sich halten an (*acc.*); sich abfinden mit; **II** *v/t.* **3.** erwarten; **4.** F (*mst neg.*) (v)ertragen, ausstehen: ***I can't ~ him***; **a'bid·ing** [-dɪŋ] *adj.* □ dauernd, beständig.

Ab·i·gail ['æbɪgeɪl] (*Hebrew*) **I** *npr.* **1.** *bibl.* Abi'gail *f*; **2.** *weiblicher Vorname*; **II** *s.* **3.** ♀ (Kammer)Zofe *f*.

a·bil·i·ty [ə'bɪlətɪ] *s.* **1.** Fähigkeit *f*, Befähigung *f*; Können *n*; *psych.* A'bility *f*: ***to the best of one's ~*** nach besten Kräften; ***~ to pay*** ✝ Zahlungsfähigkeit; ***~ test*** Eignungsprüfung *f*; **2.** *mst pl.* geistige Anlagen *pl.*

ab·ject ['æbdʒekt] *adj.* □ **1.** niedrig, gemein; elend; kriecherisch; **2.** *fig.* tiefst, höchst, äußerst: ***~ despair, ~ misery***.

ab·ju·ra·tion [ˌæbdʒʊə'reɪʃn] *s.* Abschwörung *f*; **ab·jure** [əb'dʒʊə] *v/t.* abschwören, (feierlich) entsagen (*dat.*); aufgeben; wider'rufen.

ab·lac·ta·tion [ˌæblæk'teɪʃn] *s.* Abstillen *n e-s Säuglings*.

ab·la·ti·val [ˌæblə'taɪvl] *adj. ling.* Ablativ...; **ab·la·tive** ['æblətɪv] **I** *s.* 'Ablativ *m*; **II** *adj.* Ablativ...

ab·laut ['æblaʊt] (*Ger.*) *s. ling.* Ablaut *m*.

a·blaze [ə'bleɪz] *adv. u. adj.* **1.** *a. fig.* in Flammen, *a. fig.* lodernd: ***set ~*** entflammen; **2.** *fig.* (***with***) a) entflammt (von), b) glänzend (vor *dat.*, von): ***all ~*** Feuer und Flamme.

a·ble ['eɪbl] *adj.* □ → ***ably***; **1.** fähig, geschickt, tüchtig: ***be ~ to*** können, imstande sein zu; ***he was not ~ to get up*** er konnte nicht aufstehen; ***~ to work*** arbeitsfähig; ***~ to pay*** ✝ zahlungsfähig; ***~ seaman*** → ***able-bodied*** 1; **2.** begabt, befähigt; **3.** (vor)'trefflich: ***an ~ speech***; **4.** ⚖ befähigt, fähig; **ˌable-'bod·ied** *adj.* **1.** körperlich leistungsfähig, kräftig: ***~ seaman*** *Brit.* Vollmatrose (*abbr.* ***A.B.***); **2.** ⚔ wehrfähig, (dienst)tauglich.

ab·let ['æblɪt] *s. ichth.* Weißfisch *m*.

a·bloom [ə'blu:m] *adv. u. adj.* in Blüte (stehend), blühend.

ab·lu·tion [ə'blu:ʃn] *s. eccl. u. humor.* Waschung *f*.

a·bly [ˈeɪblɪ] *adv.* geschickt, mit Geschick, gekonnt. **A-B meth·od** *s.* ϟ A-B-Betrieb *m.* **ab·ne·gate** [ˈæbnɪgeɪt] *v/t.* (ab-, ver-) leugnen; aufgeben, verzichten auf (*acc.*); **ab·ne·ga·tion** [ˌæbnɪˈgeɪʃn] *s.* **1.** Ab-, Verleugnung *f*; **2.** Verzicht *m* (**of** auf *acc.*); **3.** *mst* **self-~** Selbstverleugnung *f.* **ab·nor·mal** [æbˈnɔːml] *adj.* □ **1.** ˈabnorˌmal, ˈanomal, ungewöhnlich; geistig behindert; mißgebildet; **2.** ⚙ ˈnormwidrig; **ab·nor·mal·i·ty** [ˌæbnɔːˈmælətɪ] *s.*, **abˈnor·mi·ty** [-mətɪ] *s.* Abnormiˈtät *f*; Anomaˈlie *f.* **a·board** [əˈbɔːd] *adv. u. prp.* ⚓, ✈ an Bord; in (*e-m od. e-n Bus etc.*): **go ~** an Bord gehen, ⚓ *a.* sich einschiffen; **all ~!** a) alle Mann *od.* alle Reisenden an Bord!, b) 🚂 *etc.* alles einsteigen! **a·bode** [əˈbəʊd] **I** *pret. u. p.p. von* **abide**; **II** *s.* Aufenthalt *m*; Wohnort *m*, -sitz *m*; Wohnung *f*: **take one's ~** s-n Wohnsitz aufschlagen; **of no fixed ~** ⚖ ohne festen Wohnsitz. **a·boil** [əˈbɔɪl] *adv. u. adj.* siedend, kochend, in Wallung (*alle a. fig.*). **a·bol·ish** [əˈbɒlɪʃ] *v/t.* **1.** abschaffen, aufheben; **2.** vernichten; **ab·o·li·tion** [ˌæbəʊˈlɪʃn] *s.* Abschaffung *f* (*Am. bsd. der Sklaverei*), Aufhebung *f*, Beseitigung *f*; ⚖ Niederschlagung *f* (*e-s Verfahrens*); **ˌab·oˈli·tion·ism** [-ʃənɪzəm] *s.* Abolitioˈnismus *m*: a) *hist.* (Poliˈtik *f* der) Sklavenbefreiung *f*, b) Bekämpfung *f* e-r bestehenden Einrichtung; **ˌab·oˈli·tion·ist** [-ʃənɪst] *s. hist.* Abolitioˈnist(in). **ˈA-bomb** *s.* Aˈtombombe *f.* **a·bom·i·na·ble** [əˈbɒmɪnəbl] *adj.* □ abscheulich, scheußlich; **aˈbom·i·nate** [-neɪt] *v/t.* verˈabscheuen; **a·bom·i·na·tion** [əˌbɒmɪˈneɪʃn] *s.* **1.** Abscheu *m* (**of** vor *dat.*); **2.** Greuel *m*, Gegenstand *m* des Abscheus: **smoking is her pet ~** F das Rauchen ist ihr ein wahrer Greuel. **ab·o·rig·i·nal** [ˌæbəˈrɪdʒənl] **I** *adj.* □ eingeboren, ureingesessen, ursprünglich, einheimisch; **II** *s.* Ureinwohner *m*; **ab·oˈrig·i·nes** [-dʒəniːz] *s. pl.* **1.** Ureinwohner *pl.*, Urbevölkerung *f*; **2.** *die* ursprüngliche Flora und Fauna. **a·bort** [əˈbɔːt] **I** *v/i.* **1.** ⚕ e-e Fehl- *od.* Frühgeburt haben; **2.** *biol.* verkümmern; **3.** fehlschlagen; **II** *v/t.* **4.** *Raumflug etc.* abbrechen; **aˈbort·ed** [-tɪd] *adj.* → **abortive** 1, 3, 4; **aˌborˈtiˈfa·cient** [-tɪˈfeɪʃənt] *s.* Abtreibungsmittel *n*; **a·bor·tion** [əˈbɔːʃn] *s.* **1.** ⚕ a) Abˈort *m*, Fehl- *od.* Frühgeburt *f*, b) Abtreibung *f*, ˈSchwangerschaftsunterˌbrechung *f*: **procure an ~** e-e Abtreibung vornehmen (**on s.o.** bei j-m); **2.** ˈMißgeburt *f* (*a. fig.*); Verkümmerung *f*; **3.** *fig.* Fehlschlag *m*; **a·bor·tion·ist** [əˈbɔːʃnɪst] *s.* Abtreiber(in); **aˈbor·tive** [-tɪv] *adj.* □ **1.** zu früh geboren; **2.** vorzeitig; **3.** mißˈlungen, erfolg-, fruchtlos: **prove ~** sich als Fehlschlag erweisen; **4.** *biol.* verkümmert; **5.** ⚕ Frühgeburt verursachend; abtreibend. **a·bound** [əˈbaʊnd] *v/i.* **1.** im ˈÜberfluß *od.* reichlich vorˈhanden sein; **2.** ˈÜberfluß haben (**in** an *dat.*); **3.** voll sein, wimmeln (**with** von); **aˈbound·ing** [-dɪŋ] *adj.* reichlich (vorˈhanden); reich (**in** an *dat.*), voll (**with** von).

a·bout [əˈbaʊt] **I** *prp.* **1.** um, um … herum; **2.** umher in (*dat.*): **wander ~ the streets**; **3.** bei, auf (*dat.*), an (*dat.*), um, in (*dat.*): (**somewhere**) **~ the house** irgendwo im Haus; **have you any money ~ you?** haben Sie Geld bei sich?; **look ~ you!** sieh dich um!; **there is nothing special ~ him** an ihm ist nichts Besonderes; **4.** wegen, über (*acc.*), um (*acc.*), von: **talk ~ business** über Geschäfte sprechen; **I'll see ~ it** ich werde danach sehen *od.* mich darum kümmern; **what is it ~?** worum handelt es sich?; **5.** im Begriff, daˈbei: **he was ~ to go out**; **6.** beschäftigt mit: **what is he ~?** was macht er (da)?; **he knows what he is ~** er weiß, was er tut *od.* was er will; **II** *adv.* **7.** umˈher, (ˈrings-, ˈrund)herˌum: **drive ~** umher- *od.* herumfahren; **the wrong way ~** falsch herum; **three miles ~** drei Meilen im Umkreis; **all ~** überall; **a long way ~** ein großer Umweg; **~ face!** *Am.*, **~ turn!** *Brit.* ⚔ (ganze Abteilung) kehrt!; **8.** ungefähr, etwa, um, gegen: **~ three miles** etwa drei Meilen; **~ this time** ungefähr um diese Zeit; **~ noon** um die Mittagszeit, gegen Mittag; **that's just ~ enough!** das reicht (mir gerade)!; **9.** auf, in Bewegung: **be** (**up and**) **~** auf den Beinen sein; **there is no one ~** es ist niemand in der Nähe *od.* da; **smallpox is ~** die Pocken gehen um; **10.** → **bring about** *etc.*; **~-face**, **~-turn** *s.* Kehrtwendung *f*, *fig. a.* (völliger) ˈUmschwung. **a·bove** [əˈbʌv] **I** *prp.* **1.** über (*dat.*), oberhalb (*gen.*): **~ sea level** über dem Meeresspiegel; **~** (**the**) **average** über dem Durchschnitt; **2.** *fig.* über, mehr als; erhaben über (*acc.*): **~ all** vor allem; **you, ~ all others** von allen Menschen gerade du; **he is ~ that** er steht über der Sache, er ist darüber erhaben; **she was ~ taking advice** sie war zu stolz, Rat anzunehmen; **he is not ~ accepting a bribe** er scheut sich nicht, Bestechungsgelder anzunehmen; **~ praise** über alles Lob erhaben; **be ~ s.o.** j-m überlegen sein; **it is ~ me** es ist mir zu hoch, es geht über m-n Verstand; **II** *adv.* **3.** oben, oberhalb; **4.** *eccl.* droben im Himmel: **from ~** von oben, vom Himmel; **the powers ~** die himmlischen Mächte; **5.** über, darˈüber (hinˈaus): **over and ~** obendrein, überdies; **6.** weiter oben, oben…: **~-mentioned**; **7.** nach oben; **III** *adj.* **8.** obig, obenerwähnt: **the ~ remarks**; **IV** *s.* **9.** *das* Obige, *das* Obenerwähnte. **aˌbove|-ˈboard** *adv. u. adj.* **1.** offen, ehrlich; **2.** einwandfrei; **~ˈground** *adj.* **1.** ⚙, ⚒ über Tage, oberirdisch; **2.** *fig.* (noch) am Leben. **A-B pow·er pack** *s.* ϟ Netzteil *n* für Heiz- u. Anˈodenleistung. **ab·ra·ca·dab·ra** [ˌæbrəkəˈdæbrə] *s.* **1.** Abrakaˈdabra *n* (*Zauberwort*); **2.** *fig.* Kauderwelsch *n.* **ab·rade** [əˈbreɪd] *v/t.* abschürfen, ab-, aufscheuern; abnutzen, verschleißen (*a. fig.*); ⚙ *a.* abschleifen. **A·bra·ham** [ˈeɪbrəhæm] *npr. bibl.* ˈAbraham *m*: **in ~'s bosom** (sicher wie) in Abrahams Schoß. **ab·ra·sion** [əˈbreɪʒn] *s.* **1.** Abreiben *n*, Abschleifen *n* (*a.* ⚙); **2.** ⚙ Abrieb *m*;

Abnützung *f*, Verschleiß *m*; **3.** ⚕ (Haut)Abschürfung *f*, Schramme *f*; **abˈra·sive** [-sɪv] **I** *adj.* □ abreibend, abschleifend, Schleif…, Schmirgel…; *fig.* ätzend; **II** *s.* ⚙ Schleifmittel *n.* **ab·re·act** [ˌæbrɪˈækt] *v/t. psych.* abreagieren; **ˌab·reˈac·tion** [-kʃn] *s.* ˈAbreaktiˌon *f.* **a·breast** [əˈbrest] *adv.* Seite an Seite, nebeneinˈander: **four ~**; **~ of** *od.* **with** auf der Höhe *gen. od.* von, neben; **keep ~ of** (*od.* **with**) *fig.* Schritt halten mit. **a·bridge** [əˈbrɪdʒ] *v/t.* **1.** (ab-, ver)kürzen; zs.-ziehen; **2.** *fig.* beschränken, beschneiden; **aˈbridged** [-dʒd] *adj.* (ab-) gekürzt, Kurz…; **aˈbridg(e)·ment** [-mənt] *s.* **1.** (Ab-, Ver)Kürzung *f*; **2.** Abriß *m*, Auszug *m*; gekürzte (Buch-) Ausgabe; **3.** Beschränkung *f.* **a·broad** [əˈbrɔːd] *adv.* **1.** im *od.* ins Ausland, auswärts, draußen: **go ~** ins Ausland reisen; **from ~** aus dem Ausland; **2.** draußen, im Freien: **be ~ early** schon früh aus dem Haus sein; **3.** weit umˈher, überallˈhin: **spread ~** (weit) verbreiten; **the matter has got ~** die Sache ist ruchbar geworden; **a rumo(u)r is ~** es geht das Gerücht; **4.** *fig.* **all ~** a) ganz im Irrtum, b) völlig verwirrt. **ab·ro·gate** [ˈæbrəʊgeɪt] *v/t.* abschaffen, *Gesetz etc.* aufheben; **ab·ro·gation** [ˌæbrəʊˈgeɪʃn] *s.* Abschaffung *f*, Aufhebung *f.* **ab·rupt** [əˈbrʌpt] *adj.* □ **1.** abgerissen, zs.-hanglos (*a. fig.*); **2.** jäh, steil; **3.** kurz angebunden, schroff; **4.** plötzlich, abˈrupt, jäh; **abˈrupt·ness** [-nɪs] *s.* **1.** Abgerissenheit *f*, Zs.-hangslosigkeit *f*; **2.** Steilheit *f*; **3.** Schroffheit *f*; **4.** Plötzlichkeit *f.* **ab·scess** [ˈæbsɪs] *s.* ⚕ Abˈszeß *m*, Geschwür *n*, Eiterbeule *f.* **ab·scis·sion** [æbˈsɪʒn] *s.* Abschneiden *n*, Abtrennung *f.* **ab·scond** [əbˈskɒnd] *v/i.* **1.** sich heimlich daˈvonmachen, flüchten (**from** vor *dat.*); *a.* **~ from justice** sich den Gesetzen *od.* der Festnahme entziehen: **~ing debtor** flüchtiger Schuldner; **2.** sich verstecken. **ab·sence** [ˈæbsəns] *s.* **1.** Abwesenheit *f* (**from** von): **~ of mind** → **absent-mindedness**; **2.** (**from**) Fernbleiben *n* (von), Nichterscheinen *n* (in *dat.*, bei, zu): **~ without leave** ⚔ unerlaubte Entfernung von der Truppe; **3.** (**of**) Fehlen *n* (*gen. od.* von), Mangel *m* (an *dat.*): **in the ~ of** in Ermangelung von (*od. gen.*). **ab·sent I** *adj.* □ [ˈæbsənt] **1.** abwesend, fehlend, nicht vorˈhanden *od.* zuˈgegen: **be ~** fehlen; **2.** geistesabwesend, zerstreut; **II** *v/t.* [æbˈsent] **3.** **~ o.s.** (**from**) fernbleiben (*dat. od.* von), sich entfernen (von, aus); **ab·sen·tee** [ˌæbsənˈtiː] *s.* **1.** Abwesende(r *m*) *f*: **~ ballot**, **~ vote** *pol.* Briefwahl *f*; **~ voter** Briefwähler(in); **2.** (unentschuldigt) Fehlende(r *m*) *f*; **3.** Eigentümer, der nicht auf s-m Grundstück lebt; **ab·sen·tee·ism** [ˌæbsənˈtiːɪzəm] häufiges *od.* längeres (unentschuldigtes) Fehlen (am Arbeitsplatz, in der Schule); **ˌab·sent-ˈmind·ed** *adj.* □ geistesabwesend, zerstreut; **ˌab·sent-ˈmind·ed·ness** [-nɪs] *s.* Geistesabwesenheit *f*, Zerstreutheit *f*.

ab·sinth(e) ['æbsɪnθ] *s.* **1.** ♀ Wermut *m*; **2.** Ab'sinth *m* (*Branntwein*).

ab·so·lute ['æbsəlu:t] **I** *adj.* □ **1.** abso'lut (*a.* ♉, *ling., phys., phls.*): **~ *altitude*** ✈ absolute (Flug)Höhe; **~ *majority*** *pol.* absolute Mehrheit; **~ *temperature*** absolute (*od.* Kelvin)Temperatur; **~ *zero*** absoluter Nullpunkt; **2.** unbedingt, unbeschränkt: **~ *monarchy*** absolute Monarchie; **~ *ruler*** unumschränkter Herrscher; **~ *gift*** Schenkung *f*; **3.** ⚗ rein, unvermischt: **~ *alcohol*** absoluter Alkohol; **4.** rein, völlig, abso'lut, voll'kommen: **~ *nonsense***; **5.** bestimmt, wirklich; 'positiv: **~ *fact*** nackte Tatsache; ***become* ~** ⚖ rechtskräftig werden; **II** *s.* **6.** ***the* ~** das Absolute; **'ab·so·lute·ly** [-lɪ] *adv.* **1.** abso'lut, völlig, vollkommen, 'durchaus; **2.** F abso'lut(!), unbedingt(!), ganz recht(!); **ab·so·lu·tion** [ˌæbsə'lu:ʃn] *s.* **1.** *eccl.* Absoluti'on *f*, Sündenerlaß *m*; **2.** ⚖ Freisprechung *f*; **ab·so·lu·tism** ['æbsəlu:tɪzəm] *s. pol.* Absolu'tismus *m*, unbeschränkte Regierungsform *od.* Herrschergewalt.

ab·solve [əb'zɒlv] *v/t.* **1.** frei-, lossprechen (***of*** von *Sünde*, ***from*** von *Verpflichtung*), entbinden (***from*** von *od. gen.*); **2.** *eccl.* Absoluti'on erteilen (*dat.*)

ab·sorb [əb'sɔ:b] *v/t.* **1.** absorbieren, auf-, einsaugen, (ver)schlucken; *a. fig. Wissen etc.* (in sich) aufnehmen; vereinigen (***into*** mit); **2.** sich einverleiben, trinken; **3.** *fig.* aufzehren, verschlingen, schlucken; ✝ *Kaufkraft* abschöpfen; **4.** *fig.* ganz in Anspruch nehmen *od.* beschäftigen, fesseln; **5.** *phys.* absorbieren, resorbieren, in sich aufnehmen, auffangen, *Schall* schlucken, *Schall, Stoß* dämpfen; **ab'sorbed** [-bd] *adj.* □ *fig.* (***in***) gefesselt (von), vertieft *od.* versunken (in *acc.*): **~ *in thought***; **ab'sorb·ent** [-bənt] **I** *adj.* absorbierend, aufsaugend: **~ *cotton*** ⚕ Verbandwatte *f*; **II** *s.* Absorpti'onsmittel *n*; **ab'sorbing** [-bɪŋ] *adj.* □ **1.** aufsaugend; *fig.* fesselnd, packend; **2.** ⚙, *biol.* Absorptions…, Aufnahme… (*a.* ✝); **ab·sorption** [əb'sɔ:pʃn] *s.* **1.** *a.* ⚡, ♀, ⚙, *biol.*, *phys.* Auf-, Einsaugung *f*, Aufnahme *f*, Absorpti'on *f*; Vereinigung *f*; **2.** Verdrängung *f*, Verbrauch *m*; (*Schall-, Stoß*)Dämpfung *f*; **3.** *fig.* (***in***) Vertieftsein *n* (in *acc.*), gänzliche In'anspruchnahme (durch); **ab·sorp·tive** [əb'sɔ:ptɪv] *adj.* absorp'tiv, Absorptions…, absorbierend, (auf)saug-, aufnahmefähig.

ab·stain [əb'steɪn] *v/i.* **1.** sich enthalten (***from*** *gen.*); **2.** *a.* **~ *from voting*** sich der Stimme enthalten; **ab'stain·er** [-nə] *s. mst* ***total* ~** Absti'nenzler *m*.

ab·ste·mi·ous [æb'sti:mjəs] *adj.* □ enthaltsam, mäßig, fru'gal (*a. Essen*).

ab·sten·tion [æb'stenʃn] *s.* **1.** Enthaltung *f* (***from*** von); **2.** *a.* **~ *from voting*** *pol.* Stimmenthaltung *f*.

ab·sti·nence ['æbstɪnəns] *s.* Absti'nenz *f*, Enthaltung *f* (***from*** von), Enthaltsamkeit *f*: ***total* ~** (völlige) Abstinenz, vollkommene Enthaltsamkeit; ***day of* ~** *R.C.* Abstinenztag *m*; **'ab·sti·nent** [-nt] *adj.* □ enthaltsam, mäßig, absti'nent.

ab·stract[1] ['æbstrækt] **I** *adj.* □ **1.** ab'strakt, theo'retisch, rein begrifflich; **2.** *ling.* ab'strakt (*Ggs. konkret*); **3.** ♉ ab'strakt, rein (*Ggs. angewandt*): **~ *number*** abstrakte Zahl; **4.** → ***abstruse***; **5.** *paint.* ab'strakt; **II** *s.* **6.** *das* Ab'strakte: ***in the* ~** rein theoretisch (betrachtet), an u. für sich; **7.** *ling.* Ab'straktum *n*, Begriffs(haupt)wort *n*; **8.** Auszug *m*, Abriß *m*, Inhaltsangabe *f*, 'Übersicht *f*: **~ *of account*** ✝ Konto-, Rechnungsauszug; **~ *of title*** ⚖ Besitztitel *m*, Eigentumsnachweis *m*.

ab·stract[2] [æb'strækt] *v/t.* **1.** *Geist etc.* ablenken; (ab)sondern, trennen; **2.** abstrahieren; für sich *od.* (ab)gesondert betrachten; **3.** e-n Auszug machen von, kurz zs.-fassen; **4.** ⚗ destillieren; **5.** entwenden; **ab'stract·ed** [-tɪd] *adj.* □ **1.** (ab)gesondert, getrennt; **2.** zerstreut, geistesabwesend; **ab'strac·tion** [-kʃn] *s.* **1.** Abstrakti'on *f*, *a.* ⚗ Absonderung *f*; **2.** *a.* ⚖ Wegnahme *f*, Entwendung *f*; **3.** *phls.* Abstrakti'on *f*, ab'strakter Begriff; **4.** Versunkenheit *f*, Zerstreutheit *f*; **5.** ab'straktes Kunstwerk.

ab·struse [æb'stru:s] *adj.* □ dunkel, schwerverständlich, ab'strus.

ab·surd [əb'sɜ:d] *adj.* □ ab'surd (*a. thea.*), unsinnig, lächerlich; **ab'surd·i·ty** [-dətɪ] *s.* Absurdi'tät *f*, Sinnlosigkeit *f*, Albernheit *f*, Unsinn *m*: ***reduce to* ~** ad absurdum führen.

a·bun·dance [ə'bʌndəns] *s.* **1.** (***of***) 'Überfluß *m* (an *dat.*), Fülle *f* (von), (große) Menge (von): ***in* ~** in Hülle und Fülle; **2.** 'Überschwang *m der Gefühle*; **3.** Wohlstand *m*, Reichtum *m*; **a'bundant** [-nt] *adj.* □ **1.** reichlich (vor'handen); **2.** (***in*** *od.* ***with***) im 'Überfluß besitzend (*acc.*), reich (an *dat.*), reichlich versehen (mit); **3.** ♉ abun'dant; **a'bun·dant·ly** [-ntlɪ] *adv.* reichlich, völlig, in reichem Maße.

a·buse I *v/t.* [ə'bju:z] **1.** miß'brauchen; 'übermäßig beanspruchen; **2.** grausam behandeln, miß'handeln; *Frau* miß'brauchen; **3.** beleidigen, beschimpfen; **II** *s.* [ə'bju:s] **4.** 'Mißbrauch *m*, -stand *m*, falscher Gebrauch; 'Übergriff *m*: **~ *of authority*** ⚖ Amts-, Ermessensmißbrauch; **5.** Miß'handlung *f*; **6.** Kränkung *f*, Beschimpfung *f*, Schimpfworte *pl.*; **a'bu·sive** [-ju:sɪv] *adj.* □ **1.** 'mißbräuchlich; **2.** beleidigend, ausfallend: ***he became* ~**; **~ *language*** Schimpfworte *pl.*; **3.** falsch (angewendet).

a·but [ə'bʌt] *v/i.* angrenzen, -stoßen, (sich) anlehnen (***on***, ***upon***, ***against*** an *acc.*); **a'but·ment** [-mənt] *s.* ⚠ Strebepfeiler *m*, 'Widerlager *n e-r Brücke etc.*; **a'but·tals** [-tlz] *s. pl.* (Grundstücks-) Grenzen *pl*; **a'but·ter** [-tə] *s.* ⚖ Anlieger *m*, Anrainer *m*.

a·bysm [ə'bɪzəm] *s. poet.* Abgrund *m*; **a'bys·mal** [-zml] *adj.* □ abgrundtief, bodenlos, unergründlich (*a. fig.*): **~ *ignorance*** grenzenlose Dummheit; **a·byss** [ə'bɪs] *s.* **1.** *a. fig.* Abgrund *m*, Schlund *m*; **2.** Hölle *f*.

Ab·ys·sin·i·an [ˌæbɪ'sɪnjən] **I** *adj.* abes'sinisch; **II** *s.* Abes'sinier(in).

a·ca·cia [ə'keɪʃə] *s.* **1.** ♀ a) A'kazie *f*, b) *a.* ***false* ~** Gemeine Ro'binie; **2.** A'kazienˌgummi *m*, *n*.

ac·a·dem·i·a [ˌækə'di:mɪə] *s.* die akademische Welt; **ac·a·dem·ic** [ˌækə'demɪk] **I** *adj.* (□ **~*ally***) **1.** aka'demisch, Universitäts…: **~ *dress*** *od.* ***costume*** akademische Tracht; **~ *year*** Studienjahr *n*; **2.** (geistes)wissenschaftlich: **~ *achievement***; ***an* ~ *course***; **3.** a) aka'demisch, (rein) theo'retisch: ***an* ~ *question***, b) unpraktisch, nutzlos; **4.** konventio'nell, traditio'nell; **II** *s.* **5.** Aka'demiker(in); **6.** Universi'tätsmitglied *n* (*Dozent, Student etc.*); **ˌac·a'dem·i·cal** [-kl] **I** *adj.* □ → ***academic*** 1, 2; **II** *s. pl.* aka'demische Tracht; **a·cad·e·mi·cian** [əˌkædə'mɪʃn] *s.* Akade'miemitglied *n*; **a·cad·e·my** [ə'kædəmɪ] *s.* **1.** ♀ Akade'mie *f* (*Platos Philosophenschule*); **2.** a) Hochschule *f*, b) höhere Lehranstalt (*allgemeiner od. spezieller Art*): ***military* ~** Militärakademie *f*, Kriegsschule *f*; ***riding* ~** Reitschule *f*; **3.** Akade'mie *f der Wissenschaften etc.*, gelehrte Gesellschaft.

ac·a·jou ['ækəʒu:] → ***cashew***.

a·can·thus [ə'kænθəs] *s.* **1.** ♀ Bärenklau *m*, *f*; **2.** ⚠ A'kanthus *m*, Laubverzierung *f*.

ac·cede [æk'si:d] *v/i.* **~ *to*** **1.** *e-m Vertrag, Verein etc.* beitreten; *e-m Vorschlag* beipflichten, in *et.* einwilligen; **2.** zu *et.* gelangen; *Amt* antreten; *Thron* besteigen.

ac·cel·er·ant [æk'selərənt] **I** *adj.* beschleunigend; **II** *s.* ⚗ 'positiver Kataly'sator; **ac·cel·er·ate** [æk'seləreɪt] **I** *v/t.* **1.** beschleunigen, die Geschwindigkeit erhöhen von (*od. gen.*); *fig. Entwicklung etc.* beschleunigen, fördern; *et.* ankurbeln; **2.** *Zeitpunkt* vorverlegen; **II** *v/i.* **3.** schneller werden; **ac'cel·er·at·ing** [-reɪtɪŋ] *adj.* Beschleunigungs…: **~ *grid*** ⚡ Beschleunigungs-, Schirmgitter *n*; **ac·cel·er·a·tion** [ækˌselə'reɪʃn] *s.* **1.** *bsd.* ⚙, *phys.*, *ast.* Beschleunigung *f*: **~ *lane*** *mot.* Beschleunigungsspur *f*; **2.** ⚕ Akzelerati'on *f*, Entwicklungsbeschleunigung *f*; **ac'cel·er·a·tor** [-reɪtə] *s.* **1.** *bsd.* ⚙ Beschleuniger *m*, *mot. a.* Gashebel *m*, 'Gaspeˌdal *n*: ***step on the* ~** Gas geben; **2.** *anat.* Sym'pathikus *m*.

ac·cent I *s.* ['æksənt] Ak'zent *m*: a) *ling.* Ton *m*, Betonung *f*, b) *ling.* Tonzeichen *n*, c) Tonfall *m*, Aussprache *f*, d) ♪ Ak'zent(zeichen *n*) *m*, e) *fig.* Nachdruck (***on*** auf *dat.*); **II** *v/t.* [æk'sent] → **ac·cen·tu·ate** [æk'sentjʊeɪt] *v/t.* akzentuieren, betonen: a) her'vorheben (*a. fig.*), b) mit e-m Ak'zent(zeichen) versehen; **ac·cen·tu·a·tion** [ækˌsentjʊ'eɪʃn] *s. allg.* Betonung *f*.

ac·cept [ək'sept] **I** *v/t.* **1.** annehmen: a) entgegennehmen: **~ *a gift***, b) akzeptieren: **~ *a proposal***; **2.** *fig.* akzeptieren: a) *j-n od. et.* anerkennen, *bsd. et.* gelten lassen, b) *et.* 'hinnehmen, sich mit *et.* abfinden; **3.** *j-n* aufnehmen (***into*** in *acc.*); **4.** auffassen, verstehen: → ***accepted***; **5.** ✝ *Auftrag* annehmen; *Wechsel* akzeptieren: **~ *the tender*** den Zuschlag erteilen; **II** *v/i.* **6.** annehmen, zusagen, einverstanden sein; **ac·cept·a·bil·i·ty** [əkˌseptə'bɪlətɪ] *s.* **1.** Annehmbarkeit *f*, Eignung *f*; **2.** Erwünschtheit *f*; **ac'cept·a·ble** [-təbl] *adj.* □ **1.** akzep'tabel, annehmbar, tragbar (***to*** für); **2.** angenehm, will'kommen; **3.** ✝ beleihbar, lom'bardfähig; **ac'cept·ance** [-təns] *s.* **1.** Annahme *f*, Empfang *m*; **2.** Aufnahme *f* (***into*** in *acc.*); **3.** Zusage *f*, Billigung *f*, Anerkennung *f*; **4.** 'Übernahme *f*; **5.** 'Hinnahme *f*; **6.** *bsd.* ✝ Abnahme *f von Waren*: **~ *test*** Abnahmeprüfung *f*; **7.** ✝ a) Annahme *f od.* Anerkennung *f e-s Wechsels*, b) Ak'zept *n*, angenommener Wechsel; **ac·cep·ta·tion** [ˌæksep'teɪʃn] *s. ling.* gebräuchlicher Sinn, landläufige Bedeutung; **ac'cept·ed** [-tɪd] *adj.* allgemein anerkannt; üblich, landläufig: ***in the ~ sense***; **~ *text*** offizieller Text; **ac'cept·er, ac'cep·tor** [-tə] *s.* **1.** Annehmer *m*, Abnehmer *m etc.*; **2.** ✝ Akzep'tant *m*, Wechselnehmer *m*.

ac·cess ['ækses] *s.* **1.** Zugang *m* (*Weg*): **~ *hatch*** ⚓, ✈ Einsteigluke *f*; **~ *road*** *Am.* a) Zufahrtsstraße *f*, b) (Autobahn-)Zubringerstraße *f*; **2.** *fig.* (***to***) Zugang *m* (zu), Zutritt *m* (zu, bei); Gehör *n* (bei); *Computer*: Zugriff (auf *acc*): **~ *to means of education*** Bildungsmöglichkeiten *pl.*; ***easy of ~*** leicht zugänglich; **3.** (Wut-, Fieber- *etc.*)Anfall *m*, Ausbruch *m*; **ac'ces·sa·ry** → ***accessory***; **ac·ces·si·bil·i·ty** [ækˌsesə'bɪlətɪ] *s.* Erreichbarkeit *f*, Zugänglichkeit *f* (*a. fig.*); **ac·ces·si·ble** [æk'sesəbl] *adj.* □ **1.** zugänglich, erreichbar (***to*** für); **2.** *fig.* 'um-, zugänglich; **3.** zugänglich, empfänglich (***to*** für); **ac·ces·sion** [æk'seʃn] *s.* **1.** (***to***) Gelangen *n* (zu *e-r Würde*): **~ *to power*** Machtübernahme *f*; **2.** (***to***) Anschluß *m* (an *acc.*), Beitritt *m* (zu); Antritt *m* (*e-s Amtes*): **~ *to the throne*** Thronbesteigung *f*; **3.** (***to***) Zuwachs *m* (an *dat.*), Vermehrung *f* (*gen.*): ***recent ~s*** Neuanschaffungen; **4.** Wertzuwachs *m*, Vorteil *m*; **5.** (***to***) Erreichung *f e-s Alters*.

ac·ces·so·ry [æk'sesərɪ] **I** *adj.* **1.** zusätzlich, beitragend, Hilfs..., Neben..., Begleit...; **2.** nebensächlich, 'untergeordnet; **3.** teilnehmend, mitschuldig (***to*** an *dat.*); **II** *s.* **4.** Zusatz *m*, Anhang *m*; **5.** *pl.* ⚙ Zubehör(teile *pl.*) *n*, *m*; **6.** *oft pl.* Hilfsmittel *n*, Beiwerk *n*; **7.** ⚖ Teilnehmer *m an e-m Verbrechen*: **~ *after the fact*** Begünstiger *m*, *z. B.* Hehler *m*; **~ *before the fact*** a) Anstifter *m*, b) (Tat-)Gehilfe *m*.

ac·ci·dence ['æksɪdəns] *s. ling.* Formenlehre *f*.

ac·ci·dent ['æksɪdənt] *s.* **1.** Zufall *m*, zufälliges Ereignis: ***by ~*** zufällig; **2.** zufällige Eigenschaft, Nebensächlichkeit *f*; **3.** Unfall *m*, Unglücksfall *m*: ***in an ~*** bei e-m Unfall; **~ *benefit*** Unfallentschädigung *f*; **~*-free*** unfallfrei; **~*-prone*** unfallgefährdet; **4.** Mißgeschick *n*; **ac·ci·den·tal** [ˌæksɪ'dentl] **I** *adj.* □ **1.** zufällig, unbeabsichtigt; nebensächlich; **2.** Unfall...: **~ *death*** Tod *m* durch Unfall; **II** *s.* **3.** ♪ Vorzeichen *n*; **4.** *mst pl. paint.* Nebenlichter *pl.*

ac·claim [ə'kleɪm] **I** *v/t.* **1.** *j-n*, *fig. et.* mit (lautem) Beifall *od.* Jubel begrüßen; *j-m* zujubeln; **2.** jauchzend ausrufen: ***they ~ed him (as) king*** sie riefen ihn zum König aus; **3.** sehr loben; **II** *s.* **4.** Beifall *m*.

ac·cla·ma·tion [ˌæklə'meɪʃn] *s.* **1.** lauter Beifall; **2.** hohes Lob; **3.** *pol.* Abstimmung *f* durch Zuruf: ***by ~*** durch Akklamation.

ac·cli·mate [ə'klaɪmət] *bsd. Am.* → ***acclimatize***; **ac·cli·ma·tion** [ˌæklaɪ'meɪʃn] *s.*, **ac·cli·ma·ti·za·tion** [əˌklaɪmətaɪ'zeɪʃn] *s.* Akklimatisierung *f*, Eingewöhnung *f* (*beide a. fig.*); ⚘ *zo.* Einbürgerung *f*; **ac·cli·ma·tize** [ə'klaɪmətaɪz] *v/t. u. v/i.* (sich) akklimatisieren, (sich) gewöhnen (***to*** an *acc.*) (*a. fig.*).

ac·cliv·i·ty [ə'klɪvətɪ] *s.* Steigung *f*.

ac·co·lade ['ækəʊleɪd] *s.* **1.** Akko'lade *f*: a) Ritterschlag *m*, b) (feierliche) Um'armung. **2.** *fig. Am.* Auszeichnung *f*. **3.** ♪ Klammer *f*.

ac·com·mo·date [ə'kɒmədeɪt] **I** *v/t.* **1.** (***to***) a) anpassen (*dat.*, an *acc.*): **~ *o.s. to circumstances***, b) in Einklang bringen (mit): **~ *facts to theory***; **2.** *j-n* versorgen, *j-m* aushelfen *od.* gefällig sein (***with*** mit): **~ *s.o. with money***; **3.** *Streit* schlichten, beilegen; **4.** 'unterbringen, Platz haben für, fassen; **II** *v/i.* **5.** sich einstellen (***to*** auf *acc.*); **6.** ⚕ sich akkommodieren; **ac'com·mo·dat·ing** [-tɪŋ] *adj.* □ gefällig, entgegenkommend; anpassungsfähig; **ac·com·mo·da·tion** [əˌkɒmə'deɪʃn] *s.* **1.** Anpassung *f* (***to*** an *acc.*); Über'einstimmung *f*; **2.** Über'einkommen *n*, gütliche Einigung; **3.** Gefälligkeit *f*, Aushilfe *f*, geldliche Hilfe; **4.** Versorgung *f* (***with*** mit); **5.** *a. pl.* Einrichtung(en *pl.*) *f*; Bequemlichkeit(en *pl.*) *f*; Räumlichkeit (-en *pl.*) *f*: ***seating ~*** Sitzgelegenheit *f*; **6.** *Brit. sg.*, *Am. mst pl.* (Platz *m* für) 'Unterkunft *f*, -bringung *f*, Quar'tier *n*; **7.** *a.* **~ *train*** *Am.* Per'sonenzug *m*.

ac·com·mo·da·tion| ad·dress *s.* 'Deckaˌdresse *f*; **~ bill, ~ draft** *s.* ✝ Gefälligkeitswechsel *m*; **~ lad·der** *s.* ⚓ Fallreep *n*; **~ road** *s.* Hilfs-, Zufahrtsstraße *f*.

ac·com·pa·ni·ment [ə'kʌmpənɪmənt] *s.* **1.** ♪ Begleitung *f*, *a. fig. iro.* Begleitmusik *f*; **2.** *fig.* Begleiterscheinung *f*; **ac'com·pa·nist** [-pənɪst] *s.* ♪ Begleiter (-in); **ac·com·pa·ny** [ə'kʌmpənɪ] *v/t.* **1.** *a.* ♪ *u. fig.* begleiten; **2.** *fig.* e-e Begleiterscheinung sein von *od. gen.*: ***accompanied by*** *od.* ***with*** begleitet von, verbunden mit; **~*ing address (phenomenon)*** Begleitadresse *f* (-erscheinung *f*); **3.** verbinden (***with*** mit): **~ *the advice with a warning***.

ac·com·plice [ə'kʌmplɪs] *s.* Kom'plice *m*, 'Mittäter(in).

ac·com·plish [ə'kʌmplɪʃ] *v/t.* **1.** *Aufgabe* voll'bringen, voll'enden, erfüllen, *Absicht* ausführen, *Zweck* erreichen, erfüllen, *Ziel* erreichen; **2.** leisten; **3.** ver'vollkommnen, schulen; **ac'com·plished** [-ʃt] *adj.* **1.** 'vollständig ausgeführt; **2.** kultiviert, (fein *od.* vielseitig) gebildet; **3.** voll'endet, per'fekt (*a. iro.*): ***an ~ liar*** ein Erzlügner; **ac'com·plish·ment** [-mənt] *s.* **1.** Ausführung *f*, Voll'endung *f*; Erfüllung *f*; **2.** Ver'vollkommnung *f*; **3.** Voll'kommenheit *f*; Könnerschaft *f*; **4.** *mst pl.* Fertigkeiten *pl.*, Ta'lente *pl.*, Künste *pl.*; **5.** Leistung *f*.

ac·cord [ə'kɔːd] **I** *v/t.* **1.** bewilligen, gewähren, *Lob* spenden; **II** *v/i.* **2.** über'einstimmen, harmonieren, passen; **III** *s.* **3.** Über'einstimmung *f*, Einklang *m*; **4.** Zustimmung *f*; **5.** Über'einkommen *n*, *pol.* Abkommen *n*; ⚖ Vergleich *m*: ***with one ~*** einstimmig, einmütig; ***of one's own ~*** aus eigenem Antrieb, freiwillig; **ac'cord·ance** [-dəns] *s.* Über'einstimmung *f*: ***to be in ~ with*** übereinstimmen mit; ***in ~ with*** in Übereinstimmung mit, gemäß; **ac'cord·ing** [-dɪŋ] **I ~ *as*** *cj.* je nach'dem (wie *od.* ob), so wie; **II ~ *to*** *prp.* gemäß, nach, laut (*gen.*): **~ *to taste*** (je) nach Geschmack; **~ *to directions*** vorschriftsmäßig; **ac'cord·ing·ly** [-dɪŋlɪ] *adv.* demgemäß, folglich; entsprechend.

ac·cor·di·on [ə'kɔːdjən] *s.* Ak'kordeon *n*, 'Zieh-, 'Handharˌmonika *f*.

ac·cost [ə'kɒst] *v/t.* her'antreten an (*acc.*), *j-n* ansprechen.

ac·couche·ment [ə'kuːʃmɑ̃ːŋ] (*Fr.*) *s.* Entbindung *f*, Niederkunft *f*; **ac·cou·cheur** [ˌækuː'ʃɜː; akuʃœːr] *s.* Geburtshelfer *m*; **ac·cou·cheuse** [ˌækuː'ʃɜːz; akuʃøːz] *s.* Hebamme *f*.

ac·count [ə'kaʊnt] **I** *v/t.* **1.** ansehen als, erklären für, betrachten als: **~ *s.o. (to be) guilty***; **~ *o.s. happy*** sich glücklich schätzen; **II** *v/i.* **~ *for* 2.** Rechenschaft ablegen über *acc.*; verantwortlich sein für; **3.** (er)klären, begründen: ***how do you ~ for that?*** wie erklären Sie das?; ***Henry ~s for ten of them*** zehn davon kommen auf H.; ***there is no ~ing for it*** das ist nicht zu begründen, das ist Ansichtssache; (***not***) **~*ed for*** (un)geklärt; **4.** *hunt.* (ab)schießen; *fig. sport* ‚erledigen'; **III** *s.* **5.** Rechnung *f*, Ab-, Berechnung *f*; ✝ *pl.* (Geschäfts)Bücher *pl.*, (Rechnungs-, Jahres)Abschluß *m*; 'Konto *n*: **~*-book*** Konto-, Geschäftsbuch *n*; **~ *current*** *od.* ***current ~*** laufende Rechnung, Kontokorrent *n*; **~ *sales*** Verkaufsabrechnung; **~*s payable*** Verbindlichkeiten, Kreditoren; **~*s receivable*** Außenstände, Debitoren; ***on ~*** auf Abschlag, a conto, als Teilzahlung; ***for ~ only*** nur zur Verrechnung; ***for one's own ~*** auf eigene Rechnung; ***payment on ~*** Anzahlung *f*; ***on one's own ~*** auf eigene Rechnung (u. Gefahr), für sich selber; ***balance an ~*** e-e Rechnung bezahlen, ein Konto ausgleichen; ***carry to a new ~*** auf neue Rechnung vortragen; ***charge to s.o.'s ~*** j-s Konto belasten mit, j-m in Rechnung stellen; ***keep an ~*** Buch führen; ***open an ~*** ein Konto eröffnen; ***place to s.o.'s ~*** j-m in Rechnung stellen; ***render an ~ (for)*** Rechnung (vor)legen (für); **~ *rendered*** vorgelegte Rechnung; ***settle an ~*** e-e Rechnung begleichen; ***settle*** *od.* ***square ~s with, make up one's ~ with*** *a. fig.* abrechnen mit; ***square an ~*** ein Konto ausgleichen; → ***statement*** 5; **6.** Rechenschaft(sbericht *m*) *f*: ***bring to ~*** *fig.* abrechnen mit; ***call to ~*** zur Rechenschaft ziehen; ***give*** *od.* ***render an ~ of*** Rechenschaft ablegen über (*acc.*) → 7; ***give a good ~ of*** *et.* gut erledigen, *Gegner* abfertigen; ***give a good ~ of o.s.*** s-e Sache gut machen, sich bewähren; **7.** Bericht *m*, Darstellung *f*, Beschreibung *f*: ***by all ~s*** nach allem, was man hört; ***give*** *od.* ***render an ~ of*** Bericht erstatten über (*acc.*) → 6; **8.** Liste *f*, Verzeichnis *n*; **9.** 'Umstände *pl.*, Erwägung *f*: ***on ~ of*** um ... willen, wegen; ***on his ~*** seinetwegen; ***on no ~*** keineswegs, unter keinen Umständen; ***leave out of ~*** außer Betracht lassen; ***take ~ of, take into ~*** Rechnung tragen (*dat.*), in Betracht ziehen, berücksichtigen; **10.** Wichtigkeit *f*, Wert *m*: ***of no ~*** ohne Bedeutung; **11.** Vorteil *m*: ***find one's ~ in*** bei *et.* profitieren *od.* auf s-e Kosten kommen; ***turn to*** (***good***) ***~*** (gut) (aus)nutzen, Kapital schlagen aus; **ac·count·a·bil·i·ty** [əˌkaʊntəˈbɪlətɪ] *s.* Verantwortlichkeit *f*; **acˈcount·a·ble** [-təbl] *adj.* □ **1.** verantwortlich, rechenschaftspflichtig (***to*** *dat.*); **2.** erklärlich; **acˈcount·an·cy** [-tənsɪ] *s.* Buchhaltung *f*; Buchführung *f*, Rechnungswesen *n*; *Brit.* Steuerberatung *f*; **acˈcount·ant** [-tənt] *s.* **1.** (*a.* Bilanz)Buchhalter *m*, Rechnungsführer *m*; **2.** (***chartered*** *od.* ***certified ~*** amtlich zugelassener) Buchprüfer *od.* Steuerberater; ***certified public ~*** *Am.* Wirtschaftsprüfer *m*; **3.** *Brit.* Steuerberater *m*; **acˈcount·ing** [-tɪŋ] *s.* **1.** → ***accountancy***; **2.** Abrechnung *f*: ***~ period*** Abrechnungszeitraum *m*; ***~ year*** Geschäftsjahr *n*.

ac·cou·tred [əˈkuːtəd] *adj.* ausgerüstet; **acˈcou·tre·ment** [-təmənt] *s. mst pl.* **1.** Kleidung *f*, Ausstattung *f*; **2.** ⚔ Ausrüstung *f* (*außer Uniform u. Waffen*).

ac·cred·it [əˈkredɪt] *v/t.* **1.** *bsd. e-n Gesandten* akkreditieren, beglaubigen (***to*** bei); **2.** bestätigen, als berechtigt anerkennen; **3.** ***~ s.th. to s.o.*** *od.* ***s.o. with s.th.*** j-m et. zuschreiben.

ac·cre·tion [æˈkriːʃn] *s.* **1.** Zuwachs *m*, Zunahme *f*, Anwachsen *n*; **2.** ⚖ Anwachsung *f* (*Erbschaft*); (Land)Zuwachs *m*; **3.** ⚕ Zs.-wachsen *n*.

ac·cru·al [əˈkruːəl] *s.* †, ⚖ Anfall *m* (*Dividende, Erbschaft etc.*); Entstehung *f* (*Anspruch etc.*); Auflaufen *n* (*Zinsen*); Zuwachs *m*.

ac·crue [əˈkruː] *v/i.* erwachsen, entstehen, zufallen, zukommen (***to*** *dat.*, ***from***, ***out of*** aus): ***~d interest*** aufgelaufene Zinsen *pl*.

ac·cu·mu·late [əˈkjuːmjʊleɪt] **I** *v/t.* ansammeln, anhäufen, aufspeichern (*a.* ⚙), aufstauen; **II** *v/i.* anwachsen, sich anhäufen *od.* ansammeln *od.* akkumulieren, ⚙ sich summieren; auflaufen (*Zinsen*); **ac·cu·mu·la·tion** [əˌkjuːmjʊˈleɪʃn] *s.* Ansammlung *f*, Auf-, Anhäufung *f*, Akkumulation *f*, *a.* ⚙ (Auf-) Speicherung *f*, *a. psych.* (Auf)Stauung *f*: ***~ of capital*** † Kapitalansammlung *f*; ***~ of interest*** Auflaufen *n* von Zinsen; ***~ of property*** Vermögensanhäufung *f*; **acˈcu·mu·la·tive** [-lətɪv] *adj.* (sich) anhäufend *etc.*; Häufungs…, Zusatz…, Sammel…; **acˈcu·mu·la·tor** [-tə] *s.* ⚡ Akkumuˈlator *m*, ˈAkku *m*, (Strom-) Sammler *m*.

ac·cu·ra·cy [ˈækjʊrəsɪ] *s.* Genauigkeit *f*, Sorgfalt *f*, Präzisiˈon *f*; Richtigkeit *f*, Exˈaktheit *f*; **ˈac·cu·rate** [-rət] *adj.* □ **1.** genau; sorgfältig; pünktlich; **2.** richtig, zutreffend, exˈakt.

ac·curs·ed [əˈkɜːsɪd] *adj.*, *a.* **acˈcurst** [-st] *adj.* verflucht, verwünscht, F *a.* ‚verflixt'.

ac·cu·sa·tion [ˌækjuːˈzeɪʃn] *s.* Anklage *f*, An-, Beschuldigung *f*: ***bring an ~ against s.o.*** e-e Anklage gegen j-n erheben; **ac·cu·sa·ti·val** [əˌkjuːzəˈtaɪvl] *adj.* □ *ling.* ˈakkusativisch; **ac·cu·sa·tive** [əˈkjuːzətɪv] *s. a.* ***~ case*** ˈAkkusativ *m*, 4. Fall.

ac·cuse [əˈkjuːz] *v/t. a.* ⚖ anklagen, beschuldigen (***of*** *gen.*; ***before***, ***to*** bei); **acˈcused** [-zd] *s.* a) Angeklagte(r *m*) *f*, b) *die* Angeklagten *pl*; **acˈcus·ing** [-zɪŋ] *adj.* □ anklagend.

ac·cus·tom [əˈkʌstəm] *v/t.* gewöhnen (***to*** an *acc.*): ***be ~ed to do***(***ing***) ***s.th.*** gewohnt sein, et. zu tun, et. zu tun pflegen; ***get ~ed to s.th.*** sich an et. gewöhnen; **acˈcus·tomed** [-md] *adj.* **1.** gewohnt, üblich; **2.** gewöhnt (***to*** an *acc.*, zu *inf.*).

ace [eɪs] **I** *s.* **1.** As *n* (*Spielkarte*): ***an ~ in the hole*** *Am.* F ein Trumpf in petto; **2.** Eins *f* (*Würfel*); **3.** *fig.* ***he came within an ~ of losing*** um ein Haar hätte er verloren; **4.** ⚔ (Flieger)As *n*; **5.** *bsd. sport* ‚Kaˈnone' *f*, As *n*; **6.** *Tennis:* (Aufschlag)As *n*. **II** *adj.* **7.** herˈvorragend, Spitzen…, Star…: ***~ reporter***.

ac·er·bate [ˈæsəbeɪt] *v/t.* er-, verbittern; **a·cer·bi·ty** [əˈsɜːbətɪ] *s.* **1.** Herbheit *f*, Bitterkeit *f* (*a. fig.*); **2.** saurer Geschmack, Säure *f*; **3.** *fig.* Schärfe *f*, Heftigkeit *f*.

ac·e·tate [ˈæsɪteɪt] *s.* **1.** ⚗ Aceˈtat *n*; **2.** *a.* ***~ rayon*** Acetatseide *f*; **a·ce·tic** [əˈsiːtɪk] *adj.* ⚗ essigsauer: ***~ acid*** Essigsäure *f*; **a·cet·i·fy** [əˈsetɪfaɪ] **I** *v/t.* in Essig verwandeln, säuern; **II** *v/i.* sauer werden; **a·cet·y·lene** [əˈsetɪliːn] *s.* ⚗ Acetyˈlen *n*: ***~ welding*** ⚙ Autogenschweißen *n*.

ache [eɪk] **I** *v/i.* **1.** schmerzen, weh tun; Schmerzen haben: ***I am aching all over*** mir tut alles weh; **2.** F sich sehnen (***for*** nach), darˈauf brennen (***to do*** *et.* zu tun); **II** *s.* **3.** (*anhaltender*) Schmerz.

a·chieve [əˈtʃiːv] *v/t.* **1.** zuˈstande bringen, vollˈbringen, schaffen, leisten; **2.** erlangen; *Ziel* erreichen, *Erfolg* erzielen; **aˈchieve·ment** [-mənt] *s.* **1.** Vollˈbringung *f*, Schaffung *f*, Zuˈstandebringen *n*; **2.** Erzielung *f*, Erreichen *n*; **3.** Erringung *f*; **4.** (Groß)Tat *f*, (große) Leistung, Errungenschaft *f*: ***~-oriented*** leistungsorientiert; ***~ test*** *psych.* Leistungstest *m*; **aˈchiev·er** [-və] *s.* j-d, der es zu et. bringt.

A·chil·les [əˈkɪliːz] *npr.* Aˈchill(es) *m*: ***~ heel*** *fig.* Achillesferse *f*; ***~ tendon*** *anat.* Achillessehne *f*.

ach·ing [ˈeɪkɪŋ] *adj.* schmerzend.

ach·ro·mat·ic [ˌækrəʊˈmætɪk] *adj.* (□ ***~ally***) **1.** *phys.*, *biol.* achroˈmatisch, farblos: ***~ lens***; **2.** ♪ diaˈtonisch.

ac·id [ˈæsɪd] **I** *adj.* □ **1.** sauer, scharf (*Geschmack*): ***~ drops*** *Brit.* saure (Frucht)Bonbons, Drops; **2.** *fig.* bissig, beißend: ***~ remark***; **3.** ⚗, ⚙ säurehaltig, Säure…: ***~ bath*** Säurebad *n*; ***~ rain*** saurer Regen; **II** *s.* **4.** ⚗ Säure *f*: ***~-proof*** ⚙ säurefest; **5.** *sl.* LSˈD *n*: ***~-head*** LSD-Süchtiger *m*; **a·cid·i·fy** [əˈsɪdɪfaɪ] *v/t.* (an)säuern; in Säure verwandeln; **a·cid·i·ty** [əˈsɪdətɪ] *s.* **1.** Säure *f*, Schärfe *f*, Säuregehalt *m*; **2.** (ˈüberschüssige) Magensäure; **ac·id re·sist·ance** *s.* Säurefestigkeit *f*; **ac·id test** *s.* **1.** ⚗, ⚡ Scheide-, Säureprobe *f*; **2.** *fig.* strengste Prüfung, Feuerprobe *f*: ***put to the ~*** auf Herz u. Nieren prüfen.

a·cid·u·lat·ed [əˈsɪdjʊleɪtɪd] *adj.* (an-) gesäuert: ***~ drops*** saure Bonbons; **aˈcid·u·lous** [-ləs] *adj.* säuerlich; *fig.* → ***acid*** 2.

ack-ack [ˌækˈæk] *s* ⚔ *sl.* Flak(feuer *n*, -kanone[n *pl.*] *f*) *f*.

ack·em·ma [ækˈemə] *Funkerwort für* ***a.m.*** *Brit. sl.* **I** *adv.* vormittags; **II** *s.* ˈFlugzeugmeˌchaniker *m*.

ac·knowl·edge [əkˈnɒlɪdʒ] *v/t.* **1.** anerkennen; **2.** zugeben, einräumen; **3.** sich bekennen zu; **4.** (dankbar) anerkennen; sich erkenntlich zeigen für; **5.** *Empfang* bestätigen, quittieren; *Gruß* erwidern; **6.** ⚖ *Urkunde* beglaubigen; **acˈknowl·edged** [-dʒd] *adj.* anerkannt; **acˈknowl·edg**(**e**)**·ment** [-mənt] *s.* **1.** Anerkennung *f*; **2.** Ein-, Zugeständnis *n*; **3.** Bekenntnis *n*; **4.** (lobende) Anerkennung; Erkenntlichkeit *f*, Dank *m* (***of*** für); **5.** (Empfangs)Bestätigung *f*; **6.** ⚖ Beglaubigungsklausel *f* (*Urkunde*).

ac·me [ˈækmɪ] *s.* **1.** Gipfel *m*; *fig. a.* Höhepunkt *m*; **2.** ⚕ ˈKrisis *f*.

ac·ne [ˈæknɪ] *s.* ⚕ ˈAkne *f*.

ac·o·lyte [ˈækəʊlaɪt] *s.* **1.** *eccl.* Meßgehilfe *m*, Alˈtardiener *m*; **2.** Gehilfe *m*; Anhänger *m*.

a·corn [ˈeɪkɔːn] *s.* ⚘ Eichel *f*.

a·cous·tic *adj.*, **a·cous·ti·cal** [əˈkuːstɪk(l)] *adj.* □ ⚙, *phys.* aˈkustisch, Schall…, *a.* ⚕ Gehör…, Hör…: ***~ engineering*** Tontechnik *f*; ***~ frequency*** Hörfrequenz *f*; ***~ nerve*** Gehörnerv *m*; **aˈcous·tics** [-ks] *s. pl. phys.* **1.** *mst sg. konstr.* Aˈkustik *f*, Lehre *f* vom Schall; **2.** *pl. konstr.* Aˈkustik *f e-s Raumes*.

ac·quaint [əˈkweɪnt] *v/t.* **1.** (***o.s.*** sich) bekannt (*fig. a.* vertraut) machen (***with*** mit); → ***acquainted***; **2.** *j-m* mitteilen (***with a th.*** et., ***that*** daß); **acˈquaint·ance** [-təns] *s.* **1.** (***with***) Bekanntschaft *f* (mit), Kenntnis *f* (von *od. gen.*): ***make s.o.'s ~*** j-n kennenlernen; ***on closer ~*** bei näherer Bekanntschaft; **2.** Bekanntschaft *f*: a) Bekannte(r *m*) *f*, b) Bekanntenkreis *m*: ***an ~ of mine*** eine(r) meiner Bekannten; **acˈquaint·ed** [-tɪd] *adj.* bekannt: ***be ~ with*** kennen; ***become ~ with*** *j-n od. et.* kennenlernen.

ac·qui·esce [ˌækwɪˈes] *v/i.* **1.** (***in***) sich fügen (in *acc.*), hinnehmen (*acc.*), dulden (*acc.*); **2.** einwilligen; **ˌac·quiˈes·cence** [-sns] *s.* (***in***) Ergebung *f* (in *acc.*); Einwilligung *f* (in *acc.*); Nachgiebigkeit *f* (gegenüber); **ˌac·quiˈes·cent** [-snt] *adj.* □ ergeben, fügsam.

ac·quire [əˈkwaɪə] *v/t.* (käuflich *etc.*) erwerben; erlangen, erreichen, gewinnen; *fig. a. Wissen etc.* erwerben, (er-) lernen, sich aneignen: ***~d taste*** anerzogener *od.* angewöhnter Geschmack; **acˈquire·ment** [-mənt] *s.* **1.** Erwerbung *f*; **2.** (erworbene) Fähig- *od.* Fertigkeit; *pl.* Kenntnisse *pl*.

ac·qui·si·tion [ˌækwɪˈzɪʃn] *s.* **1.** Erwerbung *f*, Erwerb *m*; Kauf *m*, (Neu-) Anschaffung *f*; Errungenschaft *f*; **2.** Gewinn *m*, Bereicherung *f*.

ac·quis·i·tive [əˈkwɪzɪtɪv] *adj.* **1.** auf Erwerb gerichtet, gewinnsüchtig, Erwerbs…; **2.** (lern)begierig; **acˈquis·i·tive·ness** [-nɪs] *s.* Gewinnsucht *f*, Erwerbstrieb *m*.

ac·quit [əˈkwɪt] *v/t.* **1.** *Schuld* bezahlen, *Verbindlichkeit* erfüllen; **2.** entlasten; ⚖ freisprechen (***of*** von); **3.** (***of***) *j-n e-r Verpflichtung* entheben; **4.** ***~ o.s.*** (***of***) *Pflicht etc.* erfüllen; sich *e-r Aufgabe* entledigen: ***~ o.s. well*** s-e Sache gut machen; **ac'quit·tal** [-tl] *s.* **1.** ⚖ Freisprechung *f*, Freispruch *m*; **2.** Erfüllung *f e-r Pflicht*; **ac'quit·tance** [-təns] *s.* **1.** Erfüllung *f e-r Verpflichtung*, Begleichung *f*, Tilgung *f e-r Schuld*; **2.** Quittung *f*.

a·cre ['eɪkə] *s.* Acre *m* (*4047 qm*): ***~s and ~s*** weite Flächen; **a·cre·age** ['eɪkərɪdʒ] *s.* Fläche(ninhalt *m*) *f* (nach Acres).

ac·rid ['ækrɪd] *adj.* □ scharf, ätzend, beißend (*alle fig.*).

ac·ri·mo·ni·ous [ˌækrɪ'məʊnjəs] *adj.* □ *fig.* scharf, bitter, beißend; **ac·ri·mo·ny** ['ækrɪmənɪ] *s.* Schärfe *f*, Bitterkeit *f*.

ac·ro·bat ['ækrəbæt] *s.* Akro'bat *m*; **ac·ro·bat·ic, ac·ro·bat·i·cal** [ˌækrəʊ'bætɪk(l)] *adj.* □ akro'batisch: ***acrobatic flying*** Kunstfliegen *n*; **ac·ro·bat·ics** [ˌækrəʊ'bætɪks] *s. pl. mst sg. konstr.* Akro'batik *f*; akro'batische Kunststücke *pl.*; Kunstflug *m*.

ac·ro·nym ['ækrəʊnɪm] *s. ling.* Akro'nym *n*, Initi'alwort *n*.

a·cross [ə'krɒs] **I** *prp.* **1.** (quer *od.* mitten) durch; **2.** a) (quer) über (*acc.*), b) jenseits (*gen.*), auf der anderen Seite (*gen.*): ***~ the street*** über die Straße *od.* auf der gegenüberliegenden Straßenseite; ***from ~ the lake*** von jenseits des Sees; **II** *adv.* **3.** kreuzweise, über Kreuz; verschränkt; **4.** ***ten feet ~*** zehn Fuß im Durchmesser *od.* breit; **5.** (quer) hin- *od.* herüber, (quer) durch; → ***come across*** *etc.*; **6.** drüben, auf der anderen Seite; **aˌcross-the-'board** *adj.* glo'bal, line'ar: ***~ tax cut.***

a·cros·tic [ə'krɒstɪk] *s.* A'krostichon *n*.

act [ækt] **I** *s.* **1.** Tat *f*, Werk *n*, Handlung *f*, Maßnahme *f*, Akt *m*: ***~ of force*** Gewaltakt; ***~ of God*** ⚖ höhere Gewalt; ***~ of grace*** Gnadenakt; ***~ of state*** (staatlicher) Hoheitsakt; ***~ of war*** kriegerische Handlung; (***sexual***) ***~*** Geschlechts-, Liebesakt; ***catch s.o. in the ~*** j-n auf frischer Tat ertappen; **2.** ⚖ a) *a.* ***~ and deed*** Urkunde *f*, Akte *f*, Willenserklärung *f*, b) Rechtshandlung *f*, c) Tathandlung *f*, d) (Straf)Tat *f*: → ***bankruptcy*** 1; **3.** *mst* ♀ Verordnung *f*, Gesetz *n*: ♀ ***of Parliament*** *Brit.*, ♀ ***of Congress*** *Am.* (verabschiedetes) Gesetz; **4.** ♀***s*** (***of the Apostles***) *pl. bibl.* Apostelgeschichte *f*; **5.** *thea.* Aufzug *m*, Akt *m*; **6.** Stück *n*, (Zirkus)Nummer *f*; **7.** F *fig.* Pose *f*, ‚Tour' *f*: ***put on an ~*** ‚Theater spielen'; **II** *v/t.* **8.** aufführen, spielen; darstellen: ***~ a part*** e-e Rolle spielen; ***~ the fool*** a) sich wie ein Narr benehmen, b) sich dumm stellen; ***~ one's part*** s-e Pflicht tun; ***~ out*** F *et.* durchspielen; **III** *v/i.* **9.** (The'ater) spielen, auftreten; *fig.* ‚The'ater spielen'; **10.** handeln, tätig sein *od.* werden, eingreifen: ***~ as*** fungieren *od.* amtieren *od.* dienen als; ***~ in a case*** in e-r Sache vorgehen; ***~ for s.o.*** für j-n handeln, j-n vertreten; ***~*** (***up***)***on*** handeln *od.* sich richten nach; **11.** (***towards***) sich (*j-m* gegenüber) verhalten; **12.** *a.* ⚗, ⚙ (***on***) (ein)wirken (auf *acc.*); **13.** funktionieren, gehen, arbeiten; **14.** ***~ up*** F a) verrückt spielen (*Person od. Sache*), b) sich aufspielen; **'act·a·ble** [-təbl] *adj. thea.* bühnengerecht; **'act·ing** [-tɪŋ] **I** *adj.* **1.** handelnd, tätig: ***~ on your instructions*** gemäß Ihren Anweisungen; **2.** stellvertretend, amtierend, geschäftsführend: ***the ♀ Consul***; **3.** *thea.* spielend, Bühnen…: ***~ version*** Bühnenfassung *f*; **II** *s.* **4.** Handeln *n*, A'gieren *n*; **5.** *thea.* Spiel(en) *n*, Aufführung *f*; Schauspielkunst *f*.

ac·tion ['ækʃn] *s.* **1.** Handeln *n*, Handlung *f*, Tat *f*, Akti'on *f*: ***man of ~*** Mann *m* der Tat; ***full of ~*** → ***active*** 1; ***course of ~*** Handlungsweise *f*; ***for further ~*** zur weiteren Veranlassung; ***~ committee*** *pol.* Aktionskomitee *n*, (Bürger)Initiative *f*; ***put into ~*** in die Tat umsetzen; ***take ~*** Schritte unternehmen, handeln, et. *in e-r Angelegenheit* tun; ***take ~ against*** vorgehen gegen; → 9; **2.** *a.* ⚙ a) Tätigkeit *f*, Gang *m*, Funktionieren *n*, b) Mecha'nismus *m*, Werk *n*: ***~ of the bowels*** (***heart***) ⚕ Stuhlgang *m* (Herztätigkeit *f*); ***put out of ~*** unfähig *od.* unbrauchbar machen, außer Betrieb setzen; → 10; ***~!*** *Film*: Aufnahme!; **3.** *a.* ⚗, ⚙, *phys.* (Ein)Wirkung *f*, Einfluß *m*; Vorgang *m*, Pro'zeß *m*: ***the ~ of acid on metal*** die Einwirkung der Säure auf Metall; **4.** Handlung *f e-s Dramas*; **5.** Verhalten *n*, Benehmen *n*; **6.** Bewegung *f*, Gangart *f e-s Pferdes*; **7.** *rhet., thea.* Vortragsweise *f*, Ausdruck *m*; **8.** *Kunst u. fig.*: Action *f*, (dra'matisches) Geschehen: ***~ painting*** Action-painting *n*; ***where the ~ is*** F wo was los ist; **9.** ⚖ Klage *f*, Prozeß *m*: ***bring an ~ against*** *j-n* verklagen; ***take ~*** Klage erheben; → 1; **10.** ⚔ Gefecht *n*, Kampf *m*, Einsatz *m*: ***killed*** (***wounded***) ***in ~*** gefallen (verwundet); ***go into ~*** eingreifen, in Aktion treten (*a. fig.*); ***put out of ~*** außer Gefecht setzen (*a. sport etc.*; → 2); ***~ station*** Gefechtsstation *f*; ***~ stations!*** Alarm!; ***he saw ~*** er war im Einsatz *od.* an der Front; **'ac·tion·able** [-ʃnəbl] *adj.* ⚖ (ein-, ver)klagbar; strafbar.

ac·ti·vate ['æktɪveɪt] *v/t* **1.** ⚗, ⚙ aktivieren, in Betrieb setzen, (*a.* radio)ak'tiv machen: ***~d carbon*** Aktivkohle *f*; **2.** ⚔ a) *Truppen* aufstellen, b) *Zünder* scharf machen; **ac·ti·va·tion** [ˌæktɪ'veɪʃn] *s.* Aktivierung *f*.

ac·tive ['æktɪv] *adj.* □ **1.** tätig, emsig, geschäftig, rührig, lebhaft, tatkräftig, ak'tiv: ***an ~ mind*** ein reger Geist; ***~ volcano*** tätiger Vulkan; ***become ~*** in Aktion treten, aktiv werden; **2.** wirklich, tatsächlich: ***take an ~ interest*** reges Interesse zeigen; **3.** *a.* ⚗, ⚕, *biol., phys.* (schnell) wirkend, wirksam, ak'tiv: ***~ current*** Wirkstrom *m*; **4.** ✝ produk'tiv, zinstragend (*Wertpapiere*); rege, lebhaft (*Markt*): ***~ balance*** Aktivsaldo *m*; **5.** ⚔ ak'tiv: ***on ~ service, on the ~ list*** im aktiven Dienst; **6.** *ling.* ak'tiv(isch): ***~ verb*** aktivisch konstruiertes Verb; ***~ voice*** Aktiv *n*, Tatform *f*; **'ac·ti·vist** [-vɪst] *s. pol.* Akti'vist *m*; **ac·tiv·i·ty** [æk'tɪvətɪ] *s.* **1.** Tätigkeit *f*, Betätigung *f*; Rührigkeit *f*; *pl.* Leben *n* u. Treiben *n*, Unter'nehmungen *pl.*, Veranstaltungen *pl.*: ***social activities***; ***political activities*** politische Betätigung(en *pl.*) *f od.* Aktivitäten *od. b.s.* Umtriebe *pl.*; ***in full ~*** in vollem Gang; ***~ holiday*** Aktivurlaub *m*; **2.** Lebhaftigkeit *f*, Beweglichkeit *f*; Betrieb(samkeit *f*) *m*, Aktivi'tät *f*; **3.** Wirksamkeit *f*.

ac·tor ['æktə] *s.* **1.** Schauspieler *m*; **2.** *fig.* Ak'teur *m*, Täter *m* (*a.* ⚖); **'~-ˌman·ag·er** *s.* The'aterdiˌrektor, der selbst Rollen über'nimmt.

ac·tress ['æktrɪs] *s.* Schauspielerin *f*.

ac·tu·al ['æktʃʊəl] *adj.* □ **1.** wirklich, tatsächlich, eigentlich: ***an ~ case*** ein konkreter Fall; ***~ power*** ⚙ effektive Leistung; **2.** gegenwärtig, jetzig: ***~ cost*** ✝ Ist-Kosten *pl.*; ***~ inventory*** (*od.* ***stock***) Ist-Bestand *m*; **ac·tu·al·i·ty** [ˌæktʃʊ'ælətɪ] *s.* **1.** Wirklichkeit *f*; **2.** *pl.* Tatsachen *pl.*, Gegebenheiten *pl.*; **ac·tu·a·lize** ['æktʃʊəlaɪz] **I** *v/t.* **1.** verwirklichen; **2.** rea'listisch darstellen; **II** *v/i.* **3.** sich verwirklichen; **'ac·tu·al·ly** [-lɪ] *adv.* **1.** wirklich, tatsächlich; **2.** augenblicklich, jetzt; **3.** so'gar, tatsächlich (*obwohl nicht erwartet*); **4.** F eigentlich (*unbetont*): ***what time is it ~?***

ac·tu·ar·i·al [ˌæktjʊ'eərɪəl] *adj.* ver'sicherungsstaˌtistisch; **ac·tu·ar·y** ['æktjʊərɪ] *s.* Ver'sicherungsstaˌtistiker *m*, -matheˌmatiker *m*.

ac·tu·ate ['æktjʊeɪt] *v/t.* **1.** in Gang bringen; **2.** antreiben, anreizen; **3.** ⚙ betätigen, auslösen; **ac·tu·a·tion** [ˌæktjʊ'eɪʃn] *s.* Anstoß *m*, Antrieb *m* (*a.* ⚙); ⚙ Betätigung *f*.

a·cu·i·ty [ə'kju:ətɪ] *s.* Schärfe *f* (*a. fig.*); → ***acuteness*** 2.

a·cu·men [ə'kju:men] *s.* Scharfsinn *m*.

ac·u·pres·sure ['ækjʊˌpreʃə] *s.* ⚕ Akupres'sur *f*; **'ac·uˌpunc·ture** [-ˌpʌŋktʃə] ⚕ **I** *s.* Akupunk'tur *f*; **II** *v/t.* akupunktieren; **ˌac·u'punc·tur·ist** [-'pʌŋktʃərɪst] *s.* Akupunk'teur *m*.

a·cute [ə'kju:t] *adj.* □ **1.** scharf; *bsd.* ⩓ spitz: ***~ triangle*** spitzwink(e)liges Dreieck; → ***angle***[1] 1; **2.** scharf (*Sehvermögen*); heftig (*Schmerz, Freude etc.*); fein (*Gehör*); a'kut, brennend (*Frage*); bedenklich: ***~ shortage***; **3.** scharfsinnig, schlau; **4.** schrill, 'durchdringend; **5.** ⚕ a'kut, heftig; **6.** *ling.* ***~ accent*** A'kut *m*; **a'cute·ness** [-nɪs] *s.* **1.** Schärfe *f*, Heftigkeit *f*, A'kutheit *f* (*a.* ⚕); **2.** Scharfsinnigkeit *f*.

ad [æd] *s. abbr. für* ***advertisement***: ***small ~*** Kleinanzeige *f*.

ad·age ['ædɪdʒ] *s.* Sprichwort *n*.

Ad·am ['ædəm] *npr.* 'Adam *m*: ***I don't know him from ~*** F ich kenne ihn überhaupt nicht; ***cast off the old ~*** F den alten Adam ausziehen; ***~'s ale*** F ‚Gänsewein' *m*; ***~'s apple*** Adamsapfel *m*.

ad·a·mant ['ædəmənt] *adj.* **1.** steinhart; **2.** *fig.* unerbittlich, unnachgiebig, eisern (***to*** gegenüber).

a·dapt [ə'dæpt] **I** *v/t.* **1.** anpassen, angleichen (***for, to*** an *acc.*), *a.* ⚙ 'umstellen (***to*** auf *acc.*), zu'rechtmachen: ***~ the means to the end*** die Mittel dem Zweck anpassen; **2.** anwenden (***to*** auf *acc.*); **3.** *Text* bearbeiten: ***~ed from English*** nach dem Englischen bearbeitet; ***~ed from*** (frei) nach; **II** *v/i.* **4.** sich anpassen (***to*** *dat. od.* an *acc.*); **a·dapt·a·bil·i·ty** [əˌdæptə'bɪlətɪ] *s.* **1.** Anpassungsfähigkeit *f* (***to*** an *acc.*); **2.** (***to***) Anwendbarkeit *f* (auf *acc.*), Verwendbarkeit *f* (für, zu); **a'dapt·a·ble** [-təbl] *adj.* **1.** anpassungsfähig (***to*** an *acc.*); **2.** anwendbar (***to*** auf *acc.*); **3.** verwendbar (***to*** für); **ad·ap·ta·tion** [ˌædæp'teɪʃn] *s.* **1.** *a. biol.* Anpassung *f* (***to*** an *acc.*); **2.** Anwendung *f*; **3.** *thea. etc.* Bearbeitung *f* (***from*** nach, ***to*** für);

a'dapt·er [-tə] *s.* **1.** *thea. etc.* Bearbeiter *m*; **2.** *phys.* A'dapter *m*, Anpassungsvorrichtung *f*; **3.** ⚙ Zwischen-, Paß-, Anschlußstück *n*, Vorsatzgerät *n*; ⚡ Zwischenstecker *m*; **a'dap·tive** [-tɪv] *adj.* → ***adaptable*** 1; **a'dap·tor** [-tə] → ***adapter***.

add [æd] **I** *v/t.* **1.** (***to***) hin'zufügen, -rechnen (zu); ⚗ beimischen, zufügen (*dat.*): ***he ~ed that ...*** er fügte hinzu, daß ...; ***~ to this that ...*** hinzu kommt, daß ...; **2.** *a.* ***~ up*** *od.* ***together*** addieren, zs.-zählen; **3.** ✝, 𝔄, ⚙ aufschlagen: ***~ 5% to the price*** 5% auf den Preis aufschlagen; **II** *v/i.* **4.** ***~ to*** hin'zukommen zu, beitragen zu, vermehren (*acc.*); **5.** ***~ up*** a) 𝔄 aufgehen, stimmen (*a. fig.*), b) *fig.* e-n Sinn ergeben, ‚hinhauen'; ***~ up to*** a) sich belaufen auf (*acc.*), b) *fig.* hinauslaufen auf (*acc.*), bedeuten; **add·ed** ['ædɪd] *adj.* vermehrt, erhöht, zusätzlich.

ad·den·dum [ə'dendəm] *pl.* **-da** [-də] *s.* Zusatz *m*, Nachtrag *m*.

ad·der ['ædə] *s. zo.* Natter *f*, Otter *f*, 'Viper *f*: ***common ~*** Gemeine Kreuzotter.

ad·dict I *s.* ['ædɪkt] **1.** Süchtige(r *m*) *f*: ***alcohol*** (***drug***) ***~***; **2.** *humor.* (*Fußball- etc.*)Fan *m*; (*Film- etc.*)Narr *m*; **II** *v/t.* [ə'dɪkt] **3.** ***~ o.s.*** sich hingeben (***to s.th.*** e-r Sache); **4.** *j-n* süchtig machen, *j-n* gewöhnen (***to*** an *Rauschgift etc.*); **III** *v/i.* **5.** süchtig machen; **ad'dic·ted** [-tɪd] *adj.* süchtig, abhängig (***to*** von), verfallen (***to*** *dat.*): ***~ to drugs*** (***television***) drogen- *od.* rauschgift- (fernseh-) süchtig; ***be ~ to films*** (***football***) ein Filmnarr (Fußballfanatiker) sein; **ad·dic·tion** [æ'dɪkʃən] *s.* **1.** Hingabe *f* (to an *acc.*); **2.** Sucht *f*, (*Zustand*) *a.* Süchtigkeit *f*: ***~ to drugs*** (***television***) Drogen- *od.* Rauschgift- (Fernseh)Sucht *f*; **ad·dic·tive** [æ'dɪktɪv] *adj.* suchterzeugend: ***be ~*** süchtig machen; ***~ drug*** Suchtmittel *n*.

add·ing ma·chine ['ædɪŋ] *s.* Ad'dier-, Additi'onsmaˌschine *f*.

ad·di·tion [ə'dɪʃn] *s.* **1.** Hin'zufügung *f*, Ergänzung *f*, Zusatz *m*, Beigabe *f*: ***in ~*** noch dazu, außerdem; ***in ~ to*** außer (*dat.*), zusätzlich zu; **2.** Vermehrung *f* (***to*** *gen.*), (*Familien-, Vermögens- etc.*) Zuwachs *m*: ***recent ~s*** Neuerwerbungen; **3.** 𝔄 Additi'on *f*, Zs.-zählen *n*: ***~ sign*** Pluszeichen *n*; **4.** ✝ Auf-, Zuschlag *m*; **5.** ⚗, ⚙ Zusatz *m*, Beimischung *f*; ⚙ Anbau *m*, Zusatz *m*; **6.** *Am.* neuerschlossenes Baugelände; **ad'di·tion·al** [-ʃənl] *adj.* □ **1.** zusätzlich, ergänzend, weiter(er, -e, -es); **2.** Zusatz..., Mehr..., Extra..., Über..., Nach...: ***~ charge*** ✝ Auf-, Zuschlag *m*; ***~ charges*** ✝ Mehrkosten; ***~ postage*** Nachporto *n*; **ad'di·tion·al·ly** [-ʃnəlɪ] *adv.* zusätzlich, in verstärktem Maße, außerdem; **ad·di·tive** ['ædɪtɪv] **I** *adj.* zusätzlich; **II** *s.* Zusatz *m* (*a.* ⚗).

ad·dle ['ædl] **I** *v/i.* **1.** faul werden, verderben (*Ei*); **II** *v/t.* **2.** *Ei* verderben; **3.** *Verstand* verwirren; **III** *adj.* **4.** unfruchtbar, faul (*Ei*); **5.** verwirrt, kon'fus; **'~-brain** *s.* Hohlkopf *m*; **'~-ˌhead·ed**, **'~-ˌpat·ed** *adj.* **1.** hohlköpfig; **2.** → ***addle*** 5.

ad·dress [ə'dres] **I** *v/t.* **1.** *Worte etc.* richten (***to*** an *acc.*), *j-n* anreden (***as*** als); *Brief* adressieren, richten, schreiben (***to*** an *acc.*); **2.** e-e Ansprache halten an (*acc.*); **3.** *Waren* (ab)senden (***to*** an *acc.*); **4.** ***~ o.s. to*** sich zuwenden (*dat.*), sich an *et.* machen; sich anschicken zu; sich an *j-n* wenden; **II** *s.* **5.** Anrede *f*, Ansprache *f*, Rede *f*; **6.** A'dresse *f*, Anschrift *f*: ***change one's ~*** s-e Adresse ändern, umziehen; ***~ tag*** Kofferanhänger *m*; **7.** Eingabe *f*, Bitt-, Dankschrift *f*, Er'gebenheitsaˌdresse *f*: ***the*** ℒ *Brit. parl.* die Erwiderung des Parlaments auf die Thronrede; **8.** Lebensart *f*, Manieren *pl.*; **9.** Geschick *n*, Gewandtheit *f*; **10.** *pl.* Huldigungen *pl.*: ***pay one's ~es to a lady*** e-r Dame den Hof machen; **ad·dress·ee** [ˌædre'si:] *s.* Adres'sat *m*, Empfänger(in).

ad·duce [ə'dju:s] *v/t. Beweis etc.* bei-, erbringen.

ad·e·noid ['ædɪnɔɪd] ☤ **I** *adj.* die Drüsen betreffend, Drüsen..., drüsenartig; **II** *mst pl.* Po'lypen *pl.* (*in der Nase*); (Rachenmandel)Wucherungen *pl.*

ad·ept ['ædept] **I** *s.* **1.** Meister *m*, Ex'perte *m* (***at, in*** in *dat.*); **2.** A'dept *m*, Anhänger *m* (*e-r Lehre*); **II** *adj.* **3.** erfahren, geschickt (***at, in*** in *dat.*).

ad·e·qua·cy ['ædɪkwəsɪ] *s.* Angemessenheit *f*, Zulänglichkeit *f*; **ad·e·quate** ['ædɪkwət] *adj.* □ **1.** angemessen, entsprechend (***to*** *dat.*); **2.** aus-, 'hinreichend, genügend.

ad·here [əd'hɪə] *v/i.* (***to***) **1.** kleben, haften (an *dat.*); **2.** *fig.* festhalten (an *dat.*), *Regel etc.* einhalten, sich halten (an *e-e Regel etc.*), bleiben (bei *e-r Meinung, e-r Gewohnheit, e-m Plan*), *j-m, e-r Partei, e-r Sache etc.* treu bleiben, halten (zu *j-m*); **3.** angehören (*dat.*); **ad'her·ence** [-ərəns] *s.* (***to***) **1.** (An-, Fest)Haften *n* (an *dat.*); **2.** Anhänglichkeit *f* (an *dat.*); **3.** Festhalten *n* (an *dat.*), Befolgung *f*, Einhaltung (*e-r Regel*); **ad'her·ent** [-ərənt] **I** *adj.* **1.** (an-) haftend, (an)klebend; **2.** *fig.* festhaltend, (fest)verbunden (***to*** mit), anhänglich; **II** *s.* **3.** Anhänger(in).

ad·he·sion [əd'hi:ʒn] *s.* **1.** (An-, Fest)Haften *n*; ⚙ *phys.* Haftvermögen *n*, Klebkraft *f*, Adhäsi'on *f*; **2.** *fig.* → ***adherence*** 2, 3; **3.** Beitritt *m*; Einwilligung *f*; **ad'he·sive** [-sɪv] **I** *adj.* □ **1.** (an)haftend, klebend, gummiert, Klebe...: ***~ plaster*** Heftpflaster *n*; ***~ powder*** Haftpulver *n*; ***~ tape*** a) Heftpflaster *n*, b) Klebstreifen *m*; ***~ rubber*** Klebgummi *m, n*; **2.** gar zu anhänglich, aufdringlich; **3.** ⚙, *phys.* haftend, Adhäsions...: ***~ power*** → ***adhesion*** 1; **II** *s.* **4.** Bindemittel *n*, Klebstoff *m*.

ad hoc [ˌæd'hɒk] (*Lat.*) *adv. u. adj.* ad hoc, (eigens) zu diesem Zweck (gemacht), spezi'ell; Augenblicks..., Adhoc-...

a·dieus, a·dieux [ə'dju:z] *pl.* Lebe'wohl *n*: ***make one's ~*** Lebewohl sagen.

ad in·fi·ni·tum [ˌæd ɪnfɪ'naɪtəm] (*Lat.*) *adv.* endlos, ad infi'nitum.

ad·i·pose ['ædɪpəʊs] **I** *adj.* fett(haltig), Fett...: ***~ tissue*** Fettgewebe *n*; **II** *s.* (Körper)Fett *n*.

ad·it ['ædɪt] *s.* **1.** *bsd.* ⚒ Zugang *m*, Stollen *m*; **2.** *fig.* Zutritt *m*.

ad·ja·cent [ə'dʒeɪsənt] *adj.* □ angrenzend, -liegend, -stoßend (***to*** an *acc.*); benachbart (*dat.*), Nachbar..., Neben...: ***~ angle*** 𝔄 Nebenwinkel *m*.

ad·jec·ti·val [ˌædʒek'taɪvl] *adj.* □ 'adjektivisch; **ad·jec·tive** ['ædʒɪktɪv] **I** *s.* **1.** 'Adjektiv *n*, Eigenschaftswort *n*; **II** *adj.* □ **2.** 'adjektivisch; **3.** abhängig; **4.** *Färberei*: 'adjektiv: ***~ dye*** Beizfarbe *f*; **5.** ⚖ for'mell (*Recht*).

ad·join [ə'dʒɔɪn] **I** *v/t.* **1.** (an)stoßen *od.* (an)grenzen an (*acc.*); **2.** beifügen (***to*** *dat.*); **II** *v/i.* **3.** angrenzen; **ad'join·ing** [-nɪŋ] *adj.* angrenzend, benachbart, Nachbar..., Neben...

ad·journ [ə'dʒɜ:n] **I** *v/t.* **1.** aufschieben, vertagen: ***~ sine die*** ⚖ auf unbestimmte Zeit vertagen; **2.** *Sitzung etc.* schließen; **II** *v/i.* **3.** *a.* ***stand ~ed*** sich vertagen; **4.** den Sitzungsort verlegen (***to*** nach): ***~ to the sitting-room*** F sich ins Wohnzimmer zurückziehen; **ad'journ·ment** [-mənt] *s.* **1.** Vertagung *f*, Verschiebung *f*; **2.** Verlegung *f* des Sitzungsortes.

ad·judge [ə'dʒʌdʒ] *v/t.* **1.** ⚖ entscheiden (über *acc.*), erkennen (für), für *schuldig etc.* erklären, *ein Urteil* fällen: ***~ s.o. bankrupt*** über j-s Vermögen den Konkurs eröffnen; **2.** ⚖, *a. sport* zuerkennen; zusprechen; **3.** verurteilen (***to*** zu).

ad·ju·di·cate [ə'dʒu:dɪkeɪt] **I** *v/t.* **1.** gerichtlich *od.* als Schiedsrichter entscheiden, ein Urteil fällen über (*acc.*): ***~d bankrupt*** Gemeinschuldner *m*; **II** *v/i.* **2.** (zu Recht) erkennen, entscheiden (***upon*** über *acc.*); **3.** als Schieds- *od.* Preisrichter fungieren (***at*** bei); **ad·ju·di·ca·tion** [əˌdʒu:dɪ'keɪʃn] *s.* **1.** richterliche Entscheidung, Urteil *n*; **2.** Zuerkennung *f*; **3.** Kon'kurseröffnung *f*.

ad·junct ['ædʒʌŋkt] *s.* **1.** Zusatz *m*, Beigabe *f*, Zubehör *n*; **2.** *ling.* Attri'but *n*, Beifügung *f*; **ad·junc·tive** [ə'dʒʌŋktɪv] *adj.* □ beigeordnet, verbunden.

ad·ju·ra·tion [ˌædʒʊə'reɪʃn] *s.* **1.** Beschwörung *f*, inständige Bitte; **2.** Auferlegung *f* des Eides; **ad·jure** [ə'dʒʊə] *v/t.* **1.** beschwören, inständig bitten; **2.** *j-m* den Eid auferlegen.

ad·just [ə'dʒʌst] **I** *v/t.* **1.** in Ordnung bringen, ordnen, regulieren, abstimmen; berichtigen; **2.** anpassen (*a. psych.*), angleichen (***to*** *dat.*, an *acc.*); **3.** ***~ o.s.*** (***to***) sich anpassen (*dat.*, an *acc.*) *od.* einfügen (in *acc.*) *od.* einstellen (auf *acc.*); **4.** ✝ *Konto etc.* bereinigen; *Schaden etc.* berechnen, festsetzen; **5.** *Streit* schlichten; **6.** ⚙ an-, einpassen, (ein-, ver-, nach)stellen, richten, regulieren; *a. Gewehr etc.* justieren; **7.** *Maße* eichen; **II** *v/i.* **8.** sich anpassen; **9.** sich einstellen lassen; **ad'just·a·ble** [-təbl] *adj.* □ *bsd.* ⚙ regulierbar, ein-, nach-, verstellbar, Lenk..., Dreh..., Stell...: ***~ speed*** regelbare Drehzahl; **ad'just·er** [-tə] *s.* **1.** j-d der *od.* et. was regelt, ausgleicht, ordnet; Schlichter *m*; **2.** *Versicherung*: Schadenssachverständige(r) *m*; **ad'just·ing** [-tɪŋ] *adj. bsd.* ⚙ (Ein)Stell..., Richt..., Justier...: ***~ balance*** Justierwaage *f*; ***~ lever*** (Ein)Stellhebel *m*; ***~ screw*** Stellschraube *f*; **ad'just·ment** [-tmənt] *s.* **1.** *a.* ✝, *psych. etc.* Anpassung *f* (***to*** an *acc.*); **2.** Regelung *f*, Berichtigung *f*; Abstimmung *f*, Ausgleich *m*; **3.** Schlichtung *f*, Beilegung *f* (*e-s Streits*); **4.** ⚙ Ein-, Nach-, Verstellung *f*; Einstellvorrichtung *f*; Berichtigung *f*; Regulierung *f*; Eichung *f*; **5.** Berechnung *f* von Schadens(ersatz)ansprüchen.

ad·ju·tant ['ædʒʊtənt] *s.* ⚔ Adju'tant *m*; '**~-ˌgen·er·al** *pl.* '**~s-ˌgen·er·al** *s.* ⚔ Gene'raladjuˌtant *m*.

ad-lib [ˌæd'lɪb] **I** *v/i. u. v/t.* F improvisieren, aus dem Stegreif sagen; **II** *adj.* Stegreif..., improvisiert.

ad lib·i·tum [ˌæd 'lɪbɪtəm] (*Lat.*) *adj. u. adv.* ad libitum: a) nach Belieben, b) aus dem Stegreif.

ad·man ['ædmæn] *s.* [*irr.*] F **1.** Anzeigen-, Werbetexter *m*; **2.** Anzeigenvertreter *m*; **3.** *typ.* Akzi'denzsetzer *m*; **ad·mass** ['ædmæs] *s.* **1.** Kon'sumbeeinflussung *f*; **2.** werbungsmanipulierte Gesellschaft.

ad·min ['ædmɪn] *s.* F Verwaltung *f*.

ad·min·is·ter [əd'mɪnɪstə] **I** *v/t.* **1.** verwalten; **2.** ausüben, handhaben: **~ *justice*** (*od.* ***the law***) Recht sprechen; **~ *punishment*** Strafe(n) verhängen; **3.** verabreichen, erteilen (***to*** *dat.*): **~ *medicine*** Arznei (ein)geben; **~ *a shock*** e-n Schrecken einjagen; **~ *an oath*** e-n Eid abnehmen; **~ *the Blessed Sacrament*** das heilige Sakrament spenden; **II** *v/i.* **4.** als Verwalter fungieren; **5.** *obs.* beitragen (***to*** zu); **ad·min·is·trate** [əd'mɪnɪstreɪt] *v/t. u. v/i.* verwalten; **ad·min·is·tra·tion** [ədˌmɪnɪ'streɪʃn] *s.* **1.** (*Betriebs-, Vermögens-, Nachlaß-, etc.*)Verwaltung *f*; **2.** Verwaltung(sbehörde) *f*, Mini'sterium *n*; Staatsverwaltung *f*, Regierung *f*; **3.** *Am.* 'Amtsperiˌode *f* (*bsd. e-s Präsidenten*); **4.** Handhabung *f*, 'Durchführung *f*: **~ *of justice*** Rechtsprechung *f*; **~ *of an oath*** Eidesabnahme *f*; **5.** Aus-, Erteilung *f*; Verabreichung *f* (*Arznei*); Spendung *f* (*Sakrament*); **ad'min·is·tra·tive** [-trətɪv] *adj.* □ verwaltend, Verwaltungs..., Regierungs...: **~ *body*** Behörde *f*, Verwaltungskörper *m*; **ad'min·is·tra·tor** [-treɪtə] *s.* **1.** Verwalter *m*, Verwaltungsbeamte(r) *m*; **2.** ⚖ Nachlaß-, Vermögensverwalter *m*; **ad'min·is·tra·trix** [-treɪtrɪks] *pl.* **-trices** [-trɪsiːz] *s.* (Nachlaß)Verwalterin *f*.

ad·mi·ra·ble ['ædmərəbl] *adj.* □ bewundernswert, großartig.

ad·mi·ral ['ædmərəl] *s.* **1.** Admi'ral *m*: **2 *of the Fleet*** Großadmiral; **2.** *zo.* Admi'ral *m* (*Schmetterling*); '**ad·mi·ral·ty** [-tɪ] *s.* **1.** Admi'ralsamt *n*, -würde *f*; **2.** Admirali'tät *f*: ***Lords Commissioners of 2*** (*od.* ***Board of 2***) *Brit.* Marineministerium *n*; ***First Lord of the 2*** (britischer) Marineminister; **~ *law*** ⚖ Seerecht *n*; **3.** **2** *Brit.* Admiralitätsgebäude *n* (*in London*).

ad·mi·ra·tion [ˌædmə'reɪʃn] *s.* Bewunderung *f* (***of, for*** für): ***she was the ~ of everyone*** sie wurde von allen bewundert.

ad·mire [əd'maɪə] *v/t.* **1.** bewundern (***for*** wegen); **2.** hochschätzen, verehren; **ad'mir·er** [-ərə] *s.* Bewunderer *m*; Verehrer *m*; **ad'mir·ing** [-ərɪŋ] *adj.* □ bewundernd.

ad·mis·si·bil·i·ty [ədˌmɪsə'bɪlətɪ] *s.* Zulässigkeit *f*; **ad·mis·si·ble** [əd'mɪsəbl] *adj.* **1.** *a.* ⚖ zulässig; statthaft; **2.** würdig, zugelassen zu werden; **ad·mis·sion** [əd'mɪʃn] *s.* **1.** Einlaß *m*, Ein-, Zutritt *m*: ***gain* ~** Einlaß finden; **~ *free*** Eintritt frei; **~ *ticket*** Eintrittskarte *f*; **2.** Eintrittserlaubnis *f*; *a.* **~ *fee*** Eintritt(s)geld *n*, -gebühr *f*) *m*; **3.** Zulassung *f*, Aufnahme *f* (*als Mitglied etc.*; *Am. a. e-s Staates in die Union*): **2 *Day*** Jahrestag *m* der Aufnahme in die Union; **4.** Ernennung *f*; **5.** Eingeständnis *n*, Einräumung *f*: ***by*** (*od.* ***on***) ***his own* ~** wie er selbst zugibt *od.* zugab; **6.** ⚙ Eintritt *m*, -laß *m*, Zufuhr *f*: **~ *stroke*** Einlaßhub *m*.

ad·mit [əd'mɪt] **I** *v/t.* **1.** zu-, ein-, vorlassen: **~ *bearer*** dem Inhaber *dieser Karte* ist der Eintritt gestattet; **~ *s.o. into one's confidence*** j-n ins Vertrauen ziehen; **2.** Platz haben für, fassen: ***the theatre* ~*s 800 persons***; **3.** *als Mitglied in e-e Gemeinschaft, Schule etc.* aufnehmen; *in ein Krankenhaus* einliefern, *zu e-m Amt etc.* zulassen: → ***bar*** 10; **4.** gelten lassen, anerkennen, zugeben: ***I* ~ *this to be wrong*** *od.* ***that this is wrong*** ich gebe zu, daß dies falsch ist; **~ *a claim*** e-e Reklamation anerkennen; **5.** ⚖ a) für amtsfähig erklären, b) als rechtsgültig anerkennen; **6.** ⚙ zuführen, einlassen; **II** *v/i.* **7.** **~ *of*** gestatten, *a. weitS. Zweifel etc.* zulassen: ***it* ~*s of no excuse*** es läßt sich nicht entschuldigen; **ad'mit·tance** [-təns] *s.* **1.** Zulassung *f*, Einlaß *m*, Zutritt *m*: ***no* ~** (***except on business***) Zutritt (für Unbefugte) verboten; **2.** Aufnahme *f*; **3.** ϟ Admit'tanz *f*, Scheinleitwert *m*; **ad'mit·ted** [-tɪd] *adj.* □ anerkannt, zugegeben: ***an* ~ *fact***; ***an* ~ *thief*** anerkanntermaßen ein Dieb; **ad'mit·ted·ly** [-tɪdlɪ] *adv.* anerkanntermaßen, zugegeben(ermaßen).

ad·mix [əd'mɪks] *v/t.* beimischen (***with*** *dat.*); **ad'mix·ture** [-tʃə] *s.* Beimischung *f*, Mischung *f*; Zusatz(stoff) *m*.

ad·mon·ish [əd'mɒnɪʃ] **1.** *v/t.* (er-)mahnen, *j-m* dringend raten (***to*** *inf.* zu *inf.*, ***that*** daß); **2.** *j-m* Vorhaltungen machen (***of*** *od.* ***about*** wegen *gen.*); **3.** warnen (***not to*** *inf.* davor, zu *inf. od.* ***of*** vor *dat.*): ***he was* ~*ed not to go*** er wurde davor gewarnt zu gehen; **ad·mo·ni·tion** [ˌædmə'nɪʃn] *s.* **1.** Ermahnung *f*; **2.** Warnung *f*, Verweis *m*; **ad'mon·i·to·ry** [-ɪtərɪ] *adj.* ermahnend, warnend.

ad nau·se·am [ˌæd 'nɔːzɪæm] (*Lat.*) *adv.* (bis) zum Erbrechen.

ad·noun ['ædnaʊn] *s. ling.* Attri'but *n*.

a·do [ə'duː] *s.* Getue *n*, Wirbel *m*, Mühe *f*: ***much* ~ *about nothing*** viel Lärm um nichts; ***without more* ~** ohne weitere Umstände.

a·do·be [ə'dəʊbɪ] *s.* Lehmstein(haus *n*) *m*, Luftziegel *m*, A'dobe *m*.

ad·o·les·cence [ˌædəʊ'lesns] *s.* jugendliches Alter, Adoles'zenz *f*; **ˌad·o'les·cent** [-nt] **I** *s.* Jugendliche(r *m*) *f*, Her'anwachsende(r *m*) *f*; **II** *adj.* her'anwachsend, jugendlich; Jünglings...

A·do·nis [ə'dəʊnɪs] *npr. antiq. u. s. fig.* A'donis *m*.

a·dopt [ə'dɒpt] *v/t.* **1.** adoptieren, (an Kindes Statt) annehmen: **~ *out*** *Am.* zur Adoption freigeben; **2.** *fig.* annehmen, über'nehmen, einführen, sich *ein Verfahren etc.* zu eigen machen; *Handlungsweise* wählen; *Maßregeln* ergreifen; **3.** *pol. e-r Gesetzesvorlage* zustimmen; **4.** **~ *a town*** die Patenschaft für e-e Stadt über'nehmen; **5.** *pol. e-n Kandidaten* (*für die nächste Wahl*) annehmen; **6.** F sti'bitzen; **a'dopt·ed** [-tɪd] *adj. an Kindes Statt* angenommen, Adoptiv...: ***his* ~ *country*** s-e Wahlheimat; **a'dop·tion** [-pʃn] *s.* **1.** Adopti'on *f*, Annahme *f* (an Kindes Statt); **2.** Aufnahme *f in e-e Gemeinschaft*; **3.** *fig.* Annahme *f*, Aneignung *f*, 'Übernahme *f*, Wahl *f*; **a'dop·tive** [-tɪv] → ***adopted***: **~ *parents*** Adoptiveltern.

a·dor·a·ble [ə'dɔːrəbl] *adj.* □ **1.** anbetungswürdig; liebenswert; **2.** allerliebst, entzückend; **ad·o·ra·tion** [ˌædə'reɪʃn] *s.* **1.** *a. fig.* Anbetung *f*, Verehrung *f*; **2.** *fig.* (innige) Liebe, (tiefe) Bewunderung; **a·dore** [ə'dɔː] *v/t.* **1.** anbeten (*a. fig.*); **2.** *fig.* (innig) lieben, (heiß) verehren, (tief) bewundern; **3.** schwärmen für; **a'dor·er** [-rə] *s.* Anbeter(in); Verehrer(in); Bewunderer *m*; **a'dor·ing** [-rɪŋ] *adj.* □ anbetend, bewundernd, schmachtend.

a·dorn [ə'dɔːn] *v/t.* **1.** schmücken, zieren (*a. fig.*); **2.** *fig.* verschöne(r)n, Glanz verleihen (*dat*); **a'dorn·ment** [-mənt] *s.* Schmuck *m*, Verzierung *f*; Zierde *f*, Verschönerung *f*.

ad·re·nal [ə'driːnl] *anat.* **I** *adj.* Nebennieren...: **~ *gland*** → **II** *s.* Nebennierendrüse *f*; **ad·ren·al·in** [ə'drenəlɪn] *s.* Adrena'lin *n*.

A·dri·at·ic [ˌeɪdrɪ'ætɪk] *geogr.* **I** *adj.* adri'atisch: **~ *Sea*** → **II** *s.* ***the* ~** das Adriatische Meer, die 'Adria.

a·drift [ə'drɪft] *adv. u. adj.* **1.** (um'her-)treibend, Wind und Wellen preisgegeben: ***cut* ~** treiben lassen; **2.** *fig.* aufs Geratewohl; hilflos: ***be all* ~** weder aus noch ein wissen; ***cut o.s.* ~** sich losreißen *od.* frei machen *od.* lossagen; ***turn s.o.* ~** j-n auf die Straße setzen.

a·droit [ə'drɔɪt] *adj.* □ geschickt, gewandt; schlagfertig, pfiffig.

ad·u·late ['ædjʊleɪt] *v/t. j-m* schmeicheln, lobhudeln; **ad·u·la·tion** [ˌædjʊ'leɪʃn] *s. niedere* Schmeiche'lei, Lobhude'lei *f*; '**ad·u·la·tor** [-tə] *s.* Schmeichler *m*, Speichellecker *m*; '**ad·u·la·to·ry** [-tərɪ] *adj.* schmeichlerisch, lobhudelnd.

a·dult ['ædʌlt] **I** *adj.* **1.** erwachsen; reif, *fig. a.* mündig; **2.** (nur) für Erwachsene: **~ *film***; **~ *education*** Erwachsenenbildung *f*, *engS.* Volkshochschule *f*; **3.** ausgewachsen (*Tier, Pflanze*); **II** *s.* **4.** Erwachsene(r *m*) *f*.

a·dul·ter·ant [ə'dʌltərənt] *s.* Verfälschungsmittel *n*; **a·dul·ter·ate** [ə'dʌltəreɪt] *v/t.* **1.** *Nahrungsmittel* verfälschen; **2.** *fig.* verschlechtern, verderben; **a·dul·ter·a·tion** [əˌdʌltə'reɪʃn] *s.* Verfälschung *f*, verfälschtes Pro'dukt, Fälschung *f*; **a'dul·ter·er** [-rə] *s.* Ehebrecher *m*; **a'dul·ter·ess** [-rɪs] *s.* Ehebrecherin *f*; **a'dul·ter·ous** [-tərəs] *adj.* □ ehebrecherisch; **a'dul·ter·y** [-rɪ] *s.* Ehebruch *m*.

a·dult·hood ['ædʌlthʊd] *s.* Erwachsensein *n*, Erwachsenenalter *n*.

ad·um·brate ['ædʌmbreɪt] *v/t.* **1.** skizzieren, um'reißen, andeuten; **2.** 'hindeuten auf (*acc.*), vor'ausahnen lassen; **ad·um·bra·tion** [ˌædʌm'breɪʃn] *s.* Andeutung *f*: a) flüchtiger Entwurf, Skizze *f*, b) Vorahnung *f*.

ad va·lo·rem [ˌædvəˈlɔ:rem] (*Lat.*) *adj. u. adv.* dem Wert entsprechend: ~ **duty** Wertzoll *m*.

ad·vance [ədˈvɑ:ns] **I** *v/t.* **1.** vorwärtsbringen, vorrücken (lassen), vorschieben; **2.** a) *Uhr, Fuß* vorstellen, b) *Zeitpunkt* vorverlegen, c) hinˈaus-, aufschieben; **3.** *Meinung, Grund, Anspruch* vorbringen, geltend machen; **4.** a) fördern, verbessern: ~ **one's position**, b) beschleunigen: ~ **growth**; **5.** *pol. Am.* als Wahlhelfer fungieren in (*dat.*); **6.** erheben (*im Amt od. Rang*), befördern (**to the rank of general** zum General); **7.** *Preis* erhöhen; **8.** *Geld* vorˈausbezahlen; vorschießen, leihen; im voraus liefern; **II** *v/i.* **9.** vor-, vorwärtsgehen, vordringen, vormarschieren, vorrücken (*a. fig. Zeit*); **10.** vorˈankommen, Fortschritte machen: ~ **in knowledge**; **11.** *im Rang* aufrücken, befördert werden; **12.** a) zunehmen (**in** an *dat.*), steigen, b) ✝ steigen (*Preis*); teurer werden (*Ware*); **13.** *pol. Am.* a) als Wahlhelfer fungieren, b) Wahlveranstaltungen vorbereiten (**for** für); **III** *s.* **14.** Vorwärtsgehen *n*, Vor-, Anrücken *n*, Vormarsch *m* (*a. fig.*); Vorrücken *n des Alters*; **15.** Aufrücken *n* (*im Amt*), Beförderung *f*; **16.** Fortschritt *m*, Verbesserung *f*; **17.** Vorsprung *m*: **in** ~ a) voraus, b) vorn, c) im voraus, vorher; ~ **section** vorderer Teil; **be in** ~ (e-n) Vorsprung haben (**of** vor *dat.*); **arrive in ~ of the others** vor den anderen ankommen; **order** (*od.* **book**) **in** ~ vor(aus)bestellen; ~ **booking** a) Vor(aus)bestellung *f*, b) Vorverkauf *m*; ~ **censorship** Vorzensur *f*; ~ **copy** *typ.* Vorausexemplar *n*; **18.** *a.* ~ **payment** Vorschuß *m*, Vorˈauszahlung *f*: **in** ~ in pränumerando; **19.** (Preis)Erhöhung *f*; Mehrgebot *n* (*Versteigerung*); **20.** *mst pl.* Entgegenkommen *n*, Vorschlag *m*, erster Schritt (*zur Verständigung*): **make ~s to s.o.** a) j-m entgegenkommen, b) sich an j-n heranmachen, *bsd. e-r Frau* Avancen machen; **21.** ⚔ *Am.* Vorhut *f*, Spitze *f*: ~ **guard** *a. Brit.* Vorhut *f*; **22.** *pol. Am.* Wahlhilfe *f*: ~ **man** Wahlhelfer *m*; **adˈvanced** [-st] *adj.* **1.** vorgerückt (*Alter, Stunde*), vorgeschritten: ~ **in pregnancy** hochschwanger; **2.** fortgeschritten (*Stadium etc.*); fortschrittlich, modern: ~ **opinions**; ~ **students**; ~ **English** Englisch für Fortgeschrittene; **highly** ~ hochentwickelt (*Kultur, Technik*); **3.** gar zu fortschrittlich, exˈtrem, kühn; **4.** ⚔ vorgeschoben, Vor(aus)...; **adˈvancement** [-mənt] *s.* **1.** Förderung *f*; **2.** Beförderung *f*; **3.** Emˈpor-, Weiterkommen *n*, Aufstieg *m*, Fortschritt *m*, Wachstum *n*.

ad·van·tage [ədˈvɑ:ntɪdʒ] **I** *s.* **1.** Vorteil *m*: a) Überˈlegenheit *f*, Vorsprung *m*, b) Vorzug *m*: **to** ~ günstig, vorteilhaft; **have an ~ over** *j-m* gegenüber im Vorteil sein; **you have the ~ of me** ich kenne leider Ihren (werten) Namen nicht; **2.** Nutzen *m*, Gewinn *m*: **take ~ of s.o.** j-n übervorteilen *od.* ausnutzen; **take ~ of s.th.** et. ausnutzen; **derive** *od.* **gain ~ from s.th.** aus et. Nutzen ziehen; **3.** günstige Gelegenheit; **4.** *Tennis etc.*: Vorteil *m*; **II** *v/t.* **5.** fördern, begünstigen; **ad·van·ta·geous** [ˌædvənˈteɪdʒəs] *adj.* ☐ vorteilhaft, günstig, nützlich.

Ad·vent [ˈædvənt] *s.* **1.** *eccl.* Adˈvent *m*, Adˈventszeit *f*; **2.** ♀ Kommen *n*, Erscheinen *n*, Ankunft *f*; **ˈAd·vent·ist** [-tɪst] *s.* Advenˈtist *m*; **ˌad·venˈti·tious** [-ˈtɪʃəs] *adj.* ☐ **1.** (zufällig) hinˈzugekommen; zufällig, nebensächlich: ~ **causes** Nebenursachen; **2.** ⚕, ⚖ zufällig erworben.

ad·ven·ture [ədˈventʃə] **I** *s.* **1.** Abenteuer *n*: a) Wagnis *n*: **life of** ~ Abenteurerleben *n*, b) (tolles) Erlebnis, c) ✝ Spekulatiˈonsgeschäft *n*; ~ **playground** Abenteuerspielplatz *m*; **II** *v/t.* **2.** wagen, gefährden; **3.** ~ **o.s.** sich wagen (**into** in *acc.*); **III** *v/i.* **4.** sich wagen (**on, upon** in, auf *acc.*); **adˈven·tur·er** [-tʃərə] *s.* Abenteurer *m*: a) Wagehals *m*, b) Glücksritter *m*, Hochstapler *m*, c) Spekuˈlant *m*; **adˈven·ture·some** [-tʃəsəm] *adj.* → **adventurous**; **adˈven·tur·ess** [-tʃərɪs] *s.* Abenteu(r)erin *f* (*a. fig. b.s.*); **adˈven·tur·ism** [-tʃərɪzəm] *s.* Abenteurertum *n*; **adˈven·tur·ous** [-tʃərəs] *adj.* ☐ **1.** abenteuerlich: a) waghalsig, verwegen, b) gewagt, kühn (*Sache*); **2.** abenteuerlustig.

ad·verb [ˈædvɜ:b] *s.* Adˈverb *n*, Umstandswort *n*; **ad·ver·bi·al** [ədˈvɜ:bjəl] *adj.* ☐ adverbiˈal: ~ **phrase** adverbiale Bestimmung.

ad·ver·sar·y [ˈædvəsərɪ] *s.* **1.** Gegner (-in), ˈWidersacher(in); **2.** ♀ *eccl.* Teufel *m*; **ad·ver·sa·tive** [ədˈvɜ:sətɪv] *adj.* ☐ *ling.* gegensätzlich, adversaˈtiv: ~ **word**; **ad·verse** [ˈædvɜ:s] *adj.* ☐ **1.** entgegenwirkend, zuˈwider, widrig (**to** *dat.*): ~ **winds** widrige Winde; **2.** gegnerisch, feindlich: ~ **party** Gegenpartei *f*; **3.** ungünstig, nachteilig (**to** für): ~ **decision**; ~ **balance of trade** passive Handelsbilanz; **have an ~ effect** (**up**)**on**, **affect ~ly** sich nachteilig auswirken auf (*acc.*); **4.** ⚖ entgegenstehend: ~ **claim**; **ad·ver·si·ty** [ədˈvɜ:sətɪ] *s.* Mißgeschick *n*, Not *f*, Unglück *n*.

ad·vert **I** *v/i.* [ədˈvɜ:t] hinweisen, sich beziehen (**to** auf *acc.*); **II** *s.* [ˈædvɜ:t] *Brit.* F *für* **advertisement**.

ad·ver·tise, *Am. a.* **ad·ver·tize** [ˈædvətaɪz] **I** *v/t.* **1.** ankündigen, anzeigen, *durch die Zeitung etc.* bekanntmachen: ~ **a post** eine Stellung *öffentlich* ausschreiben; **2.** *fig.* ausposaunen: **you need not ~ the fact** *a.* du brauchst es nicht an die große Glocke zu hängen; **2.** *durch Zeitungsanzeige etc.* Reˈklame machen für, werben für; **II** *v/i.* **3.** inserieren, annoncieren, öffentlich ankündigen: ~ **for** durch Inserat suchen; **4.** werben, Reklame machen; **ad·ver·tise·ment** [ədˈvɜ:tɪsmənt] *s.* **1.** *öffentliche* Anzeige, Ankündigung *f in e-r Zeitung*, Inseˈrat *n*, Anˈnonce *f*: **put an ~ in a paper** ein Inserat in e-r Zeitung aufgeben; **2.** Reˈklame *f*, Werbung *f*; **ˈad·ver·tis·er** [-zə] *s.* **1.** Inseˈrent(in); **2.** Werbeträger *m*; **3.** Werbefachmann *m*; **4.** Anzeiger *m*, Anzeigenblatt *n*; **ˈad·ver·tis·ing** [-zɪŋ] **I** *s.* **1.** Inserieren *n*; Ankündigung *f*; **2.** Reklame *f*, Werbung *f*; **II** *adj.* **3.** Reklame..., Werbe...: ~ **agency** Werbeagentur *f*; ~ **agent** a) Anzeigenvertreter *m*, b) Werbeagent *m*; ~ **campaign** Werbefeldzug *m*; ~ **expert** Werbefachmann *m*; ~ **space** Reklamefläche *f*; **ˈad·ver·tize** *etc.* → **advertise** *etc.*

ad·vice [ədˈvaɪs] *s.* **1.** (*a.* **piece of**) Rat(schlag) *m*; Ratschläge *pl.*: **at** (*od.* **on**) **s.o.'s** ~ auf j-s Rat hin; **take medical** ~ e-n Arzt zu Rate ziehen; **take my** ~ folge meinem Rat; **2.** Nachricht *f*, Anzeige *f*, (schriftliche) Mitteilung; **3.** ✝ Aˈvis *m*, Bericht *m*: **letter of** ~ Benachrichtigungsschreiben *n*; **as per** ~ laut Aufgabe *od.* Bericht.

ad·vis·a·bil·i·ty [ədˌvaɪzəˈbɪlətɪ] *s.* Ratsamkeit *f*; **ad·vis·a·ble** [ədˈvaɪzəbl] *adj.* ☐ ratsam; **ad·vis·a·bly** [ədˈvaɪzəblɪ] *adv.* ratsamerweise.

ad·vise [ədˈvaɪz] **I** *v/t.* **1.** *j-m* raten *od.* empfehlen (**to** *inf.* zu *inf.*); *et.* (an)raten; *j-n* beraten: **he was ~d to go** man riet ihm zu gehen; **2.** ~ **against** warnen vor (*dat.*); *j-m* abraten von; **3.** ✝ benachrichtigen (**of** von, **that** daß), avisieren (**s.o. of s.th.** j-m et.); **II.** *v/i.* **4.** sich beraten (**with** mit); **adˈvised** [-zd] *adj.* ☐ **1.** beraten: **badly** ~; **2.** wohlbedacht, überˈlegt; → **ill-advised**; **well-advised**; **adˈvis·ed·ly** [-zɪdlɪ] *adv.* **1.** mit Bedacht *od.* Überˈlegung; **2.** vorsätzlich, absichtlich; **adˈvis·er** *od.* **adˈvi·sor** [-zə] *s.* **1.** Berater *m*, Ratgeber *m*; **2.** *ped. Am.* ˈStudienberater *m*; **adˈvi·so·ry** [-zərɪ] *adj.* beratend, Beratungs...: ~ **board**, ~ **committee** Beratungsausschuß *m*, Beirat *m*, Gutachterkommission *f*; ~ **body**, ~ **council** Beirat *m*; → **capacity** 6.

ad·vo·ca·cy [ˈædvəkəsɪ] *s.* (**of**) Befürwortung *f*, Empfehlung *f* (*gen.*), Eintreten *n* (für); **ad·vo·cate** **I** *s.* [ˈædvəkət] **1.** Verfechter *m*, Befürworter *m*, Verteidiger *m*, Fürsprecher *m*: **an ~ of peace**; **2.** *Scot. u. hist.* Advoˈkat *m*, (plädierender) Rechtsanwalt: **Lord** ♀ Oberster Staatsanwalt; **3.** *Am.* Rechtsbeistand *m*; **II** *v/t.* [ˈædvəkeɪt] **4.** verteidigen, befürworten, eintreten für.

adze [ædz] *s.* Breitbeil *n*.

Ae·ge·an [i:ˈdʒi:ən] *geogr.* **I** *adj.* äˈgäisch: ~ **Sea** Ägäisches Meer; **II** *s.* **the** ~ die Äˈgäis.

ae·gis [ˈi:dʒɪs] *s. myth.* ˈÄgis *f*; *fig.* Äˈgide *f*, Schirmherrschaft *f*: **under the ~ of**.

Ae·o·li·an [i:ˈəʊljən] *adj.* äˈolisch: ~ **harp** Äolsharfe *f*.

ae·on [ˈi:ən] *s.* Äˈone *f*; Ewigkeit *f*.

aer·ate [ˈeəreɪt] *v/t.* **1.** (*a.* ⚙ be- *od.* ˈdurch- *od.* ent)lüften; **2.** a) mit Kohlensäure sättigen, b) zum Sprudeln bringen; **3.** ⚕ *dem Blut* Sauerstoff zuführen.

aer·i·al [ˈeərɪəl] **I** *adj.* ☐ **1.** Luft..., in der Luft lebend *od.* befindlich, fliegend, hoch: ~ **advertising** Luftwerbung *f*, Himmelsschrift *f*; ~ **cableway** Seilschwebebahn *f*; ~ **camera** Luftbildkamera *f*; ~ **railway** Hänge-, Schwebebahn *f*; ~ **spires** hochragende Kirchtürme; **2.** aus Luft bestehend, leicht, gasförmig, flüchtig; **3.** äˈtherisch, zart: ~ **fancies** Phantastereien; **4.** ✈ Flug(zeug)..., Luft..., Flieger...: ~ **attack** Luft-, Fliegerangriff *m*; ~ **barrage** a) (Luft)Sperr-, Flakfeuer *n*, b) Ballonsperre *f*; ~ **combat** Luftkampf *m*; ~ **map** Luftbildkarte *f*; ~ **navigation** Luftschiffahrt *f*; ~ **survey** Luftbildvermessung *f*; ~ **view** Flugzeugaufnahme *f*,

Luftbild *n*; **5.** ⚙ oberirdisch, Ober..., Frei..., Luft...: **~ *cable*** Luftkabel *n*; **~ *wire*** ϟ Ober-, Freileitung *f*; **6.** ϟ, *Radio, TV*: Antennen...: **~ *wire***; **II** *s.* **7.** ϟ, *Radio, TV*: An'tenne *f*; **'aer·i·al·ist** [-lɪst] *s.* Tra'pezkünstler *m.*

aer·ie, *Am. a.* **aër·ie** ['eərɪ] *s.* **1.** Horst *m* (*Raubvogelnest*); **2.** *fig.* Adlerhorst *m* (*hochgelegener Wohnsitz etc.*).

aer·o ['eərəʊ] **I** *pl.* **-os** *s.* Flugzeug *n*, Luftschiff *n*; **II** *adj.* Luft(schiffahrt)..., Flug(zeug)...: **~ *engine***.

aero- [eərəʊ] *in Zssgn*: Aëro..., Luft...

aer·o·bat·ics [ˌeərəʊ'bætɪks] *s. pl. sg. konstr.* Kunstflug *m*; **'aer·o·drome** [-ədrəʊm] *s. bsd. Brit.* Flugplatz *m.*

aer·o|·dy·nam·ic [ˌeərəʊdaɪ'næmɪk] **I** *adj.* □ aerody'namisch, Stromlinien...; **II** *s. pl. sg. konstr.* Aerody'namik *f*; **'~·dyne** [-əʊdaɪn] *s.* Luftfahrzeug *n* schwerer als Luft; **'~·foil** [-əʊfɔɪl] *s. Brit.* Tragfläche *f*, *a.* Höhen-, Kiel- *od.* Seitenflosse *f*; **'~·gram** [-əʊgræm] *s.* **1.** Funkspruch *m*; **2.** Luftpostleichtbrief *m*; **'~·lite** [-əʊlaɪt] *s.* Aero'lith *m*, Mete'orstein *m.*

aer·ol·o·gy [eə'rɒlədʒɪ] *s. phys.* **1.** Aerolo'gie *f*, Erforschung *f* der höheren Luftschichten; **2.** aero'nautische Wetterkunde; **aer·o·med·i·cine** [ˌeərəʊ'medsɪn] *s.* 'Aero-, 'Luftfahrtmediˌzin *f*; **aer'om·e·ter** [-'ɒmɪtə] *s. phys.* Aero'meter *m*, Luftdichtemesser *m.*

aer·o|·naut ['eərənɔːt] *s.* Aero'naut *m*, Luftschiffer *m*; **~·nau·tic**, **~·nau·ti·cal** [ˌeərə'nɔːtɪk(l)] *adj.* □ aero'nautisch, Flug...; **~·nau·tics** [ˌeərə'nɔːtɪks] *s. pl. sg. konstr.* Aero'nautik *f*: a) *obs.* Luftfahrt *f*, b) Luftfahrtkunde *f*; **~·plane** ['eərəpleɪn] *s. bsd. Brit.* Flugzeug *n*; **~·sol** ['eərəʊsɒl] *s.* **1.** ⚗ Aero'sol *n*; **2.** Spraydose *f*; **~·space** ['eərəʊspeɪs] **I** *s.* Weltraum *m*; **II** *adj.* a) Raumfahrt..., b) (Welt)Raum...; **~·stat** ['eərəʊstæt] *s.* Luftfahrzeug *n* leichter als Luft; **~·stat·ic**, **~·stat·i·cal** [ˌeərəʊ'stætɪk(l)] *adj.* □ aero'statisch; **~·stat·ics** [ˌeərəʊ'stætɪks] *s. pl. sg. konstr.* Aero'statik *f.*

Aes·cu·la·pi·an [ˌiːskjʊ'leɪpjən] *adj.* **1.** Äskulap...; **2.** ärztlich.

aes·thete ['iːsθiːt] *s.* Äs'thet *m*; **aes·thet·ic**, **aes·thet·i·cal** [iːs'θetɪk(l)] *adj.* □ äs'thetisch; **aes·thet·i·cism** [iːs'θetɪsɪzəm] *s.* **1.** Ästheti'zismus *m*; **2.** Schönheitssinn *m*; **aes·thet·ics** [iːs'θetɪks] *s. pl. sg. konstr.* Äs'thetik *f.*

aes·ti·val [iː'staɪvl] *adj.* sommerlich.

ae·ther *etc.* → ***ether*** *etc.*

a·far [ə'fɑː] *adv.* fern: **~ *off*** in der Ferne; ***from* ~** von fern, weither.

af·fa·bil·i·ty [ˌæfə'bɪlətɪ] *s.* Leutseligkeit *f*, Freundlichkeit *f*; **af·fa·ble** ['æfəbl] *adj.* □ leutselig, freundlich, 'umgänglich.

af·fair [ə'feə] *s.* **1.** Angelegenheit *f*, Sache *f*: ***a disgraceful* ~**; ***that is his* ~** das ist seine Sache; ***that is not my* ~** das geht mich nichts an; ***make an* ~ *of s.th.*** et. aufbauschen; ***my own* ~** meine (eigene) Angelegenheit, meine Privatsache; **~ *of honour*** Ehrensache *f*, -handel *m*; **2.** *pl.* Angelegenheiten *pl.*, Verhältnisse *pl.*: ***public* ~*s*** öffentliche Angelegenheiten; ***state of* ~*s*** Lage *f* der Dinge, Sachlage *f*; → ***foreign*** 1; **3.** Af'färe *f*: a) Ereignis *n*, b) Skan'dal *m*, c) (Liebes)Verhältnis *n*; **4.** F Ding *n*, Sache *f*, ‚Appa'rat' *m*: ***the car was a shiny* ~**.

af·fect¹ [ə'fekt] *v/t.* **1.** lieben, e-e Vorliebe haben für, neigen zu, be'vorzugen: **~ *bright colo(u)rs*** lebhafte Farben bevorzugen; ***much* ~*ed by*** sehr beliebt bei; **2.** zur Schau tragen, erkünsteln, nachahmen: ***he* ~*s an Oxford accent*** er redet mit gekünstelter Oxforder Aussprache; ***he* ~*s the freethinker*** er spielt den Freidenker; **3.** vortäuschen: **~ *ignorance***; **~ *a limp*** so tun, als hinke man; **4.** bewohnen, vorkommen in (*dat.*) (*Tiere u. Pflanzen*).

af·fect² [ə'fekt] *v/t.* **1.** betreffen: ***that does not* ~ *me***; **2.** (ein- *od.* sich aus-) wirken auf (*acc.*), beeinflussen, beeinträchtigen, in Mitleidenschaft ziehen, ⚕ *a.* angreifen, befallen: **~ *the health***; **3.** bewegen, rühren, ergreifen.

af·fec·ta·tion [ˌæfek'teɪʃn] *s.* **1.** Affektiertheit *f*, Gehabe *n*; **2.** Verstellung *f*; **3.** Vorliebe (***of*** für).

af·fect·ed¹ [ə'fektɪd] *adj.* □ **1.** affektiert, gekünstelt, geziert; **2.** angenommen, vorgetäuscht; **3.** geneigt, gesinnt.

af·fect·ed² [ə'fektɪd] *adj.* **1.** ⚕ befallen (***with*** *von Krankheit*), angegriffen (*Augen etc.*); **2.** betroffen, berührt; **3.** gerührt, bewegt, ergriffen.

af·fect·ing [ə'fektɪŋ] *adj.* □ ergreifend; **af'fec·tion** [-kʃn] *s.* **1.** *oft pl.* Liebe *f*, (Zu)Neigung *f* (***for, towards*** zu); **2.** Gemütsbewegung *f*, Stimmung *f*; **3.** ⚕ Erkrankung *f*, Leiden *n*; **4.** Einfluß *m*, Einwirkung *f*; **af'fec·tion·ate** [-kʃnət] *adj.* □ gütig, liebevoll, herzlich, zärtlich; **af'fec·tion·ate·ly** [-kʃnətlɪ] *adv.*: ***yours* ~** Dein Dich liebender (*Briefschluß*); **~ *known as Pat*** unter dem Kosenamen Pat bekannt.

af·fi·ci·o·na·do → ***aficionado***.

af·fi·ance [ə'faɪəns] **I** *s.* **1.** Vertrauen *n*; **2.** Eheversprechen *n*; **II** *v/t.* **3.** *j-n od. sich* verloben (***to*** mit).

af·fi·ant [ə'faɪənt] *s. Am.* Aussteller (-in) e-s ***affidavit***.

af·fi·da·vit [ˌæfɪ'deɪvɪt] *s.* ⚖ *schriftliche* beeidigte Erklärung: **~ *of means*** Offenbarungseid *m.*

af·fil·i·ate [ə'fɪlɪeɪt] **I** *v/t.* **1.** *als Mitglied* aufnehmen; **2.** *j-m* die Vaterschaft *e-s Kindes* zuschreiben: **~ *a child on*** (*od.* ***to***); **3.** (***on, upon***) zu'rückführen (auf *acc.*), zuschreiben (*dat.*); **4.** (***to***) verknüpfen, verbinden (mit); angliedern, anschließen (*dat.*, an *acc.*); **II** *v/i.* **5.** sich anschließen (***with*** an *acc.*); **III** *s.* [-ɪɪt] **6.** *Am.* 'Zweigorganisatiˌon *f*, Tochtergesellschaft *f*; **af'fil·i·at·ed** [-tɪd] *adj.* angeschlossen: **~ *company*** Tochter-, Zweiggesellschaft *f*; **af·fil·i·a·tion** [əˌfɪlɪ'eɪʃn] *s.* **1.** Aufnahme *f* (*als Mitglied etc.*); **2.** Zuschreibung *f* der Vaterschaft; **3.** Zu'rückführung *f* (*auf den Ursprung*); **4.** Angliederung *f*; **5.** *oft eccl.* Zugehörigkeit *f*, Mitgliedschaft *f.*

af·fin·i·ty [ə'fɪnətɪ] *s.* **1.** ⚖ Schwägerschaft *f*; **2.** *fig.* a) (Wesens)Verwandtschaft *f*, Affini'tät *f*, b) (Wahl-, Seelen-) Verwandtschaft *f*, gegenseitige Anziehung; **3.** ⚗ Affini'tät *f*, stofflich-'chemische Verwandtschaft.

af·firm [ə'fɜːm] *v/t.* **1.** versichern, beteuern; **2.** bekräftigen; ⚖ *Urteil* bestätigen; **3.** ⚖ an Eides Statt versichern; **af·fir·ma·tion** [ˌæfɜː'meɪʃn] *s.* **1.** Versicherung *f*, Beteuerung *f*; **2.** Bestätigung *f*, Bekräftigung *f*; **3.** ⚖ Versicherung *f* an Eides Statt; **af'firm·a·tive** [-mətɪv] **I** *adj.* □ **1.** bejahend, zustimmend, positiv; **2.** positiv, bestimmt: **~ *action*** *Am.* Aktion *f* gegen die Diskriminierung von Minderheitsgruppen; **II** *s.* **3.** Bejahung *f*: ***answer in the* ~** bejahen.

af·fix **I** *v/t.* [ə'fɪks] **1.** (***to***) befestigen, anbringen (an *dat.*), anheften, ankleben (an *acc.*); **2.** (***to***) beilegen, -fügen (*dat.*), hin'zufügen (zu); *Siegel* anbringen (an *dat.*); *Unterschrift* setzen (unter *acc.*); **II** *s.* ['æfɪks] **3.** *ling.* Af'fix *n*, Anhang *m*, Hin'zufügung *f.*

af·flict [ə'flɪkt] *v/t.* betrüben, quälen, plagen, heimsuchen; **af'flict·ed** [-tɪd] *adj.* **1.** niedergeschlagen, betrübt; **2.** (***with***) leidend (an *dat.*); belastet, behaftet (mit), geplagt (von); **af'flic·tion** [-kʃn] *s.* **1.** Betrübnis *f*, Kummer *m*; **2.** a) Gebrechen, b) *pl.* Beschwerden; **3.** Elend *n*, Not *f*; Heimsuchung *f.*

af·flu·ence ['æflʊəns] *s.* **1.** Fülle *f*, 'Überfluß *m*; **2.** Reichtum *m*, Wohlstand *m*: ***demoralization by* ~** Wohlstandsverwahrlosung *f*; **'af·flu·ent** [-nt] **I** *adj.* □ **1.** reichlich; **2.** wohlhabend, reich (***in*** an *dat.*): **~ *society*** Wohlstandsgesellschaft *f*; **II** *s.* **3.** Nebenfluß *m*; **af·flux** ['æflʌks] *s.* **1.** Zufluß *m*, Zustrom *m* (*a. fig.*); **2.** ⚕ (Blut-) Andrang *m.*

af·ford [ə'fɔːd] *v/t.* **1.** gewähren, bieten; *Schatten* spenden; *Freude* bereiten; **2.** *als Produkt* liefern; **3.** sich leisten, sich erlauben, die Mittel haben für; *Zeit* erübrigen: ***I can't* ~ *it*** ich kann es mir nicht leisten (*a. fig.*); **af'ford·a·ble** *adj.* erschwinglich.

af·for·est·a·tion [æˌfɒrɪ'steɪʃn] *s.* Aufforstung *f.*

af·fran·chise [ə'fræntʃaɪz] *v/t.* befreien (***from*** aus).

af·fray [ə'freɪ] *s.* **1.** Schläge'rei *f*, Kra'wall *m*; **2.** ⚖ Raufhandel *m.*

af·freight [ə'freɪt] *v/t.* ⚓ chartern, befrachten.

af·fri·cate ['æfrɪkət] *s. ling.* Affri'kata *f* (*Verschlußlaut mit folgendem Reibelaut*).

af·front [ə'frʌnt] **I** *v/t.* **1.** beleidigen, beschimpfen; **2.** trotzen (*dat.*); **II** *s.* **3.** Beleidigung *f*, Af'front *m.*

Af·ghan ['æfgæn] **I** *s.* **1.** Af'ghane *m*, Af'ghanin *f*; **2.** Af'ghan *m* (*Teppich*); **II** *adj.* **3.** af'ghanisch.

afi·ci·o·na·do [əˌfɪsjə'nɑːdəʊ] *s.* (*Span.*) begeisterter Anhänger *m*, ‚Fan' *m.*

a·field [ə'fiːld] *adv.* **1.** a) im *od.* auf dem Feld, b) ins *od.* aufs Feld; **2.** in der *od.* in die Ferne, draußen, hin'aus: ***far* ~** weit entfernt; **3.** *bsd. fig.* in die Irre: ***lead s.o.* ~**; ***quite* ~** a) auf dem Holzwege (*Person*), b) ganz falsch (*Sache*).

a·fire [ə'faɪə] *adv. u. adj.* brennend, in Flammen: ***all* ~** *fig.* Feuer und Flamme.

a·flame [ə'fleɪm] → ***afire***.

a·float [ə'fləʊt] *adv. u. adj.* **1.** flott, schwimmend: ***keep* ~** (sich) über Wasser halten (*a. fig.*); **2.** an Bord, auf See; **3.** in 'Umlauf; **4.** im Gange; **5.** über'schwemmt.

a·foot [ə'fʊt] *adv. u. adj.* **1.** zu Fuß, auf den Beinen; **2.** *fig.* a) im Gange, b) im Anzug, im Kommen.

a·fore [əˈfɔː] *obs.* **I** *prp.* vor; **II** *adv.* (nach) vorn; **III** *cj.* ehe, bevor; **~·men·tioned** [əˌfɔːˈmenʃənd], **~·said** [əˈfɔːsed] *adj.* obenerwähnt *od.* -genannt; **~·thought** [əˈfɔːθɔːt] *adj.* vorbedacht; → ***malice*** 3.

a·fraid [əˈfreɪd] *adj.*: ***be ~*** Angst haben, sich fürchten (***of*** vor *dat.*); ***I am ~ (that) he will not come*** ich fürchte, er wird nicht kommen; ***I am ~ I must go*** F leider muß ich gehen; ***I'm ~ so*** leider ja!; ***I shall tell him, don't be ~!*** F (nur) keine Angst, ich werde es ihm sagen!; ***~ of hard work*** F arbeitsscheu; ***be ~ to do*** sich scheuen zu tun.

a·fresh [əˈfreʃ] *adv.* von neuem, von vorn: ***start ~***.

Af·ri·can [ˈæfrɪkən] **I** *s.* **1.** Afriˈkaner (-in); **2.** Neger(in) (*in Amerika lebend*); **II** *adj.* **3.** afriˈkanisch; **4.** afriˈkanischer Abstammung, Neger…

Af·ri·kaans [ˌæfrɪˈkɑːns] *s. ling.* Afriˈkaans(ch) *n*, Kapholländisch *n*; ˌ**Af·ri·ˈkan·(d)er** [-ˈkæn(d)ə] *s.* Afriˈkander *m* (*Weißer mit Afrikaans als Muttersprache*).

Af·ro [ˈæfrəʊ] *pl.* **-ros** *s.* **1.** Afro-Look *m*; **2.** *a.* ***~ hairdo*** ˈAfro-Friˌsur *f*.

ˌ**Af·ro|-Aˈmer·i·can** [ˌæfrəʊ-] *s.* Afroameriˈkaner(in); ˌ**~-ˈA·sian** *adj.* ˈafroasiˈatisch.

aft [ɑːft] *adv.* ⚓ (nach) achtern.

aft·er [ˈɑːftə] **I** *prp.* **1.** nach: ***~ lunch***; ***~ a week***; ***day ~ day*** Tag für Tag; ***the day ~ tomorrow*** übermorgen; ***the month ~ next*** der übernächste Monat; ***~ all*** schließlich, im Grunde, immerhin, (also) doch; ***~ all my trouble*** nach *od.* trotz all meiner Mühe; → ***look after*** *etc.*; **2.** hinter … (*dat.*) (her): ***I came ~ you***; ***shut the door ~ you***; ***the police are ~ you*** die Polizei ist hinter dir her; ***~ you, sir!*** nach Ihnen!; ***one ~ another*** nacheinander; **3.** nach, gemäß: ***named ~ his father*** nach s-m Vater genannt; ***~ my own heart*** ganz nach m-m Herzen *od.* Wunsch; ***a picture ~ Rubens*** ein Gemälde nach (*im Stil von*) Rubens; **II** *adv.* **4.** nachˈher, hinterˈher, daˈnach, später: ***follow ~*** nachfolgen; ***for months ~*** noch monatelang; ***shortly ~*** kurz danach; **III** *adj.* **5.** später, künftig, Nach…: ***in ~ years***; **6.** ⚓ Achter…; **IV** *cj.* **7.** nachˈdem: ***~ he (had) sat down***; **V** *s. pl.* **8.** *Brit.* F Nachspeise *f*: ***for ~s*** zum Nachtisch; ˈ**~·birth** *s.* ⚕ Nachgeburt *f*; ˈ**~ˌburn·er** *s.* ✈ Nachbrenner *m*; ˈ**~-ˌcab·in** *s.* ⚓ ˈHeckkaˌbine *f*; ˈ**~-care** *s.* **1.** ⚕ Nachbehandlung *f*; **2.** ⚖ Resozialisierungshilfe *f*; ˈ**~-crop** *s.* Nachernte *f*; ˈ**~-death** → ***afterlife*** 1; ˈ**~-deck** *s.* ⚓ Achterdeck *n*; ˈ**~-ˌdin·ner** *adj.* nach Tisch: ***~ speech*** Tischrede *f*; ˈ**~-efˌfect** [-ərɪ-] *s.* Nachwirkung *f* (*a.* ⚕), Folge *f*; ˈ**~-glow** *s.* **1.** Nachglühen *n* (*a.* ⚙ *u. fig.*); **2.** a) Abendrot *n*, b) Alpenglühen *n*; ˈ**~-hold** *s.* ⚓ Achterraum *m*; ˈ**~-hours** *s. pl.* Zeit *f* nach Dienstschluß; ˈ**~-life** *s.* **1.** Leben *n* nach dem Tode; **2.** (zu)künftiges Leben; ˈ**~·math** [-mæθ] *s.* **1.** ⚘ Grummet *n*, Spätheu *n*; **2.** *fig.* Nachwirkungen *pl.*; ˌ**~ˈnoon** *s.* Nachmittag *m*: ***in the ~*** am Nachmittag, nachmittags; ***this ~*** heute nachmittag; ***~ of life*** Herbst *m* des Lebens; → ***good*** 1; ˈ**~-pains** *s. pl.* ⚕ Nachwehen *pl.*; ˈ**~-play** *s.* (sexuˈelles) Nachspiel; ˈ**~-sales ser·vice** *s.* ☤ Kundendienst *m*; ˈ**~-ˌsea·son** *s.* ˈNachsaiˌson *f*; ˈ**~-shave lo·tion** *s.* After-shave-Lotion *f*, Rasierwasser *n*; ˈ**~-taste** *s.* Nachgeschmack *m* (*a. fig.*); **~ tax** *adj.* ☤ nach Abzug der Steuern, *a.* Netto…; ˈ**~-thought** *s.* nachträglicher Einfall: ***as an ~*** nachträglich; ˈ**~-ˌtreat·ment** *s.* ⚕, ⚙ Nachbehandlung *f*.

aft·er|·ward [ˈɑːftəwəd] *Am.*, ˈ**~·wards** [-dz] *adv.* später, nachˈher, hinterˈher; ˈ**~·years** *s. pl.* Folgezeit *f*.

a·gain [əˈgen] *adv.* **1.** ˈwieder(um), von neuem, aber-, nochmals: ***come ~!*** komm wieder!; ***~ and ~*** immer wieder; ***now and ~*** hin und wieder; ***be o.s. ~*** wieder gesund *od.* der alte sein; **2.** schon wieder: ***that fool ~*** schon wieder dieser Narr!; ***what's his name ~?*** F wie heißt er doch schnell?; **3.** außerdem, ferner; **4.** noch einmal: ***as much ~*** noch einmal so viel; ***half as much ~*** anderthalbmal so viel; **5.** *a.* ***then ~*** andererseits, daˈgegen, aber: ***these ~ are more expensive***.

a·gainst [əˈgenst] *prp.* **1.** gegen, wider, entgegen: ***~ the law***; ***to run (up) ~ s.o.*** j-n zufällig treffen; **2.** gegen, gegenˈüber: ***my rights ~ the landlord***; ***over ~ the town hall*** gegenüber dem Rathaus; **3.** auf … (*acc.*) zu, an (*dat. od. acc.*), vor (*dat. od. acc.*), gegen: ***~ the wall***; **4.** *a.* ***as ~*** verglichen mit, gegenüber; **5.** in Erwartung (*gen.*), für.

a·gamic [ˌeɪˈgæmɪk] *adj. biol.* aˈgam, geschlechtslos.

a·gape [əˈgeɪp] *adv. u. adj.* gaffend, mit offenem Munde (*vor Staunen*).

a·gar·ic [ˈægərɪk] *s.* ⚘ Blätterpilz *m*, -schwamm *m*; → ***fly agaric***.

ag·ate [ˈægət] *s.* **1.** *min.* Aˈchat *m*; **2.** *Am.* bunte Glasmurmel; **3.** *typ. Am.* Paˈriser Schrift *f*.

a·ga·ve [əˈgeɪvɪ] *s.* ⚘ Aˈgave *f*.

age [eɪdʒ] **I** *s.* **1.** (Lebens)Alter *n*, Altersstufe *f*: ***what is his ~*** *od.* ***what ~ is he?*** wie alt ist er?; ***ten years of ~*** 10 Jahre alt; ***at the ~ of*** im Alter von; ***at his ~*** in seinem Alter; ***be over ~*** über der Altersgrenze liegen; ***act one's ~*** sich s-m Alter entsprechend benehmen; ***be your ~!*** sei kein Kindskopf!; ***a girl your ~*** ein Mädchen deines Alters; ***he does not look his ~*** man sieht ihm sein Alter nicht an; **2.** (Zeit *f* der) Reife: ***full ~*** Volljährigkeit *f*; ***(come) of ~*** mündig *od.* volljährig (werden); ***under ~*** minderjährig; **3.** *a.* ***old ~*** Alter *n*: ***~ before beauty*** Alter kommt vor Schönheit; **4.** Zeit *f*, Zeitalter *n*; Menschenalter *n*, Generatiˈon *f*: ***Ice ~*** Eiszeit; ***the ~ of Queen Victoria***; ***in our ~*** in unserer (*od.* der heutigen) Zeit; ***down the ~s*** durch die Jahrhunderte; **5.** *oft pl.* F lange Zeit, Ewigkeit *f*: ***I haven't seen him for ~s*** ich habe ihn seit e-r Ewigkeit nicht gesehen; **II** *v/t.* **6.** alt machen; **7.** *j-n* um Jahre älter machen; **8.** ⚙ altern, vergüten; *Wein etc.* ablagern lassen; *Käse etc.* reifen lassen; **III** *v/i.* **9.** alt werden, altern; **age brack·et** → ***age group***; **aged** [eɪdʒd] *adj.* … Jahre alt: ***~ twenty***; **a·ged** [ˈeɪdʒɪd] *adj.* bejahrt, betagt; **age group** *s.* Altersklasse *f*, Jahrgang *m*; **age·ing** → ***aging***; **age·less** [ˈeɪdʒlɪs] *adj.* nicht alternd, zeitlos; **age lim·it** *s.* Altersgrenze *f*; ˈ**age·long** *adj.* lebenslänglich, dauernd.

a·gen·cy [ˈeɪdʒənsɪ] *s.* **1.** (wirkende) Kraft *f*, (ausführendes) Orˈgan, Werkzeug *n* (*fig.*); **2.** Tätigkeit *f*, Wirkung *f*; **3.** Vermittlung *f*, Mittel *n*, Hilfe *f*: ***by*** *od.* ***through the ~ of***; **4.** ☤ Agenˈtur *f*: a) (Handels)Vertretung *f*, b) Büˈro *n od.* Amt *n* e-s Aˈgenten; **5.** ⚖ (ˈHandlungs)ˌVollmacht *f*; **6.** (ˈNachrichten-) Agenˌtur *f*; **7.** Geschäfts-, Dienststelle *f*; Amt *n*, Behörde *f*; ***~ busi·ness*** *s.* Kommissiˈonsgeschäft *n*.

a·gen·da [əˈdʒendə] *s.* Tagesordnung *f*.

a·gent [ˈeɪdʒənt] *s.* **1.** Handelnde(r *m*) *f*, Urheber(in): ***free ~*** selbständig Handelnde(r), *weitS. ein* freier Mensch; **2.** ⚗, ⚕, *biol.*, *phys.* ˈAgens *n*, Wirkstoff *m*, (be)wirkende Kraft *od.* Ursache, Mittel *n*, Werkzeug *n*: ***protective ~*** Schutzmittel; **3.** a) ☤ (Handels)Vertreter *m*, Aˈgent *m*, *a.* Makler *m*, Vermittler *m*, b) ⚖ (Handlungs)Bevollmächtigte(r *m*) *f*, (Stell)Vertreter(in); **4.** *pol.* (Geheim)Agent(in).

a·gent pro·vo·ca·teur *pl.* **a·gents pro·vo·ca·teurs** [ˈæʒɑ̃ːŋ prəˌvɒkəˈtɜː] (*Fr.*) *s.* Lockspitzel *m*.

ˈ**age|-old** *adj.* uralt; ˈ**~-worn** *adj.* altersschwach.

ag·glom·er·ate I *v/t. u. v/i.* [əˈglɒməreɪt] **1.** (sich) zs.-ballen, (sich) an- *od.* aufhäufen; **II** *s.* [-rət] **2.** angehäufte Masse, Ballung *f*; **3.** ⚙, *geol.*, *phys.* Agglomeˈrat *n*; **III** *adj.* [-rət] **4.** zs.-geballt, gehäuft; **ag·glom·er·a·tion** [əˌglɒməˈreɪʃn] *s.* Zs.-ballung *f*, Anhäufung *f*; (wirrer) Haufen.

ag·glu·ti·nate I *adj.* [əˈgluːtɪnət] **1.** zs.-geklebt, verbunden; **2.** *ling.* agglutiniert; **II** *v/t.* [-neɪt] **3.** zs.-kleben, verbinden; **4.** *biol.*, *ling.* agglutinieren; **ag·glu·ti·na·tion** [əˌgluːtɪˈneɪʃn] *s.* **1.** Zs.-kleben *n*; aneinˈanderklebende Masse; **2.** *biol.*, *ling.* Agglutinatiˈon *f*.

ag·gran·dize [əˈgrændaɪz] *v/t.* **1.** *Macht, Reichtum* vermehren, -größern, erhöhen; **2.** verherrlichen, ausschmücken, *j-n* erhöhen; **agˈgran·dize·ment** [-dɪzmənt] *s.* Vermehrung *f*, Vergrößerung *f*, Erhöhung *f*, Aufstieg *m*.

ag·gra·vate [ˈægrəveɪt] *v/t.* **1.** erschweren, verschärfen, verschlimmern; verstärken: ***~d larceny*** ⚖ schwerer Diebstahl; **2.** F erbittern, ärgern; ˈ**ag·gra·vat·ing** [-tɪŋ] *adj.* ☐ **1.** erschwerend *etc.*, graˈvierend; **2.** F ärgerlich, aufreizend; **ag·gra·va·tion** [ˌægrəˈveɪʃn] *s.* **1.** Erschwerung *f*, Verschlimmerung *f*, erschwerender ˈUmstand; **2.** F Ärger *m*.

ag·gre·gate [ˈægrɪgət] **I** *adj.* ☐ **1.** angehäuft, vereinigt, gesamt, Gesamt…: ***~ amount*** → II; **2.** zs.-gesetzt, Sammel…; **II** *s.* **3.** Anhäufung *f*; (Gesamt-) Menge *f*; Summe *f*: ***in the ~*** insgesamt; **4.** ϟ, ⚙, *biol.* Aggreˈgat *n*; **III** *v/t.* [-geɪt] **5.** anhäufen, ansammeln; vereinigen (***to*** mit); **6.** sich insgesamt belaufen auf (*acc.*); **ag·gre·ga·tion** [ˌægrɪˈgeɪʃn] *s.* **1.** Anhäufung *f*, Ansammlung *f*; Zs.-fassung *f*; **2.** *phys.* Aggreˈgat *n*: ***state of ~*** Aggregatzustand *m*.

ag·gres·sion [əˈgreʃn] *s.* Angriff *m*, ˈÜberfall *m*; Aggressiˈon *f* (*a. pol. u. psych.*); **agˈgres·sive** [-esɪv] *adj.* ☐ aggresˈsiv: a) streitsüchtig, angriffslustig, b) eˈnergisch, draufgängerisch, dyˈnamisch, forsch; **ag'gres·sor** [-esə] *s.* Angreifer *m.*

ag·grieved [ə'gri:vd] *adj.* **1.** bedrückt, betrübt; **2.** *bsd.* ⚖ geschädigt, beschwert, benachteiligt.

a·ghast [ə'gɑ:st] *adj.* entgeistert, bestürzt, entsetzt (***at*** über *acc.*).

ag·ile ['ædʒaɪl] *adj.* □ flink, be'hend(e) (*Verstand etc.*); **a·gil·i·ty** [ə'dʒɪlətɪ] *s.* Flinkheit *f*, Be'hendigkeit *f*; Aufgewecktheit *f*.

ag·ing ['eɪdʒɪŋ] **I** *s.* **1.** Altern *n*; **2.** ⚙ Alterung *f*, Vergütung *f*; **II** *pres. p. u. adj.* **3.** alternd.

ag·i·o ['ædʒəʊ] *pl.* **ag·i·os** *s.* ☤ 'Agio *n*, Aufgeld *n*; **ag·i·o·tage** ['ædʒətɪdʒ] *s.* Agio'tage *f*.

ag·i·tate ['ædʒɪteɪt] **I** *v/t.* **1.** hin und her bewegen, schütteln; (um)rühren; **2.** *fig.* beunruhigen, auf-, erregen; **3.** aufwiegeln; **4.** erwägen, lebhaft erörtern; **II** *v/i.* **5.** agitieren, wühlen, hetzen; Propa'ganda machen (***for*** für, ***against*** gegen); **'ag·i·tat·ed** [-tɪd] *adj.* □ aufgeregt; **ag·i·ta·tion** [ˌædʒɪ'teɪʃn] *s.* **1.** Erschütterung *f*, heftige Bewegung; **2.** Aufregung *f*, Unruhe *f*; **3.** Agitati'on *f*, Hetze'rei *f*; Bewegung *f*, Gärung *f*; **'ag·i·ta·tor** [-tə] *s.* **1.** Agi'tator *m*, Aufwiegler *m*, Wühler *m*, Hetzer *m*; **2.** ⚙ 'Rührappaˌrat *m*, -werk *n*, -arm *m*;

ag·it·prop [ˌædʒɪt'prɒp] **1.** Agit'prop *f* (*kommunistische Agitation u. Propaganda*); **2.** Agit'propredner *m.*

a·glow [ə'gləʊ] *adv. u. adj. a. fig.* glühend (***with*** von, vor *dat.*).

ag·nate ['ægneɪt] **I** *s.* **1.** A'gnat *m* (*Verwandter väterlicherseits*); **II** *adj.* **2.** väterlicherseits verwandt; **3.** stamm-, wesensverwandt; **ag·nat·ic** *adj.*; **ag·nat·i·cal** [æg'nætɪk(l)] *adj.* □ → ***agnate*** 2, 3.

ag·nos·tic [æg'nɒstɪk] **I** *s.* A'gnostiker *m*; **II** *adj.* → ***agnostical***; **ag'nos·ti·cal** [-kl] *adj.* a'gnostisch; **ag'nos·ti·cism** [-tɪsɪzəm] *s.* Agnosti'zismus *m.*

a·go [ə'gəʊ] *adv. u. adj.* vor'über, her, vor: ***ten years ~*** vor zehn Jahren; ***long ~*** vor langer Zeit; ***long, long ~*** lang, lang ist's her; ***no longer ~ than last month*** erst vorigen Monat.

a·gog [ə'gɒg] *adv. u. adj.* gespannt, erpicht (***for*** auf *acc.*): ***all ~*** ganz aus dem Häuschen, ‚gespannt wie ein Regenschirm'.

ag·o·nize ['ægənaɪz] **I** *v/t.* **1.** quälen, martern; **II** *v/i.* **2.** mit dem Tode ringen; **3.** Höllenqualen leiden; **4.** sich (ab-)quälen, verzweifelt ringen; **'ag·o·niz·ing** [-zɪŋ] *adj.* □ qualvoll, herzzerreißend; **'ag·o·ny** [-nɪ] *s.* **1.** heftiger Schmerz, Höllenqualen *pl.*, Qual *f*, Pein *f*, Seelenangst *f*: ***~ of despair***; ***~ column*** F *Zeitung*: Seufzerspalte *f*; ***pile on the ~*** F ‚dick auftragen'; **2.** ✝ Ringen *n* Christi mit dem Tode; **3.** Todeskampf *m*, Ago'nie *f*.

ag·o·ra·pho·bi·a [ˌægərə'fəʊbjə] *s.* ⚕ Platzangst *f*.

a·grar·i·an [ə'greərɪən] **I** *adj.* **1.** a'grarisch, landwirtschaftlich, Agrar...: ***~ unrest*** Unruhe in der Landwirtschaft; **2.** gleichmäßige Landaufteilung betreffend; **II** *s.* **3.** Befürworter *m* gleichmäßiger Aufteilung des (Acker)Landes.

a·gree [ə'gri:] **I** *v/i.* **1.** (***to***) zustimmen (*dat.*), einwilligen (in *acc.*), beipflichten (*dat.*), genehmigen (*acc.*), einverstanden sein (mit), eingehen (auf *acc.*), gutheißen (*acc.*): ***~ to a plan***; ***I ~ to come with you*** ich bin bereit mitzukommen; ***you will ~ that*** du mußt zugeben, daß; **2.** (***on, upon, about***) sich einigen *od.* verständigen (über *acc.*); vereinbaren, verabreden (*acc.*): ***they ~d about the price***; ***~ to differ*** sich auf verschiedene Standpunkte einigen; ***let us ~ to differ!*** ich fürchte, wir können uns da nicht einigen!; **3.** über'einkommen, vereinbaren (***to*** *inf.* zu *inf.*, ***that*** daß): ***it is ~d*** es ist vereinbart, es steht fest; → ***agreed*** 2; **4.** (***with*** mit) über'einstimmen (*a. ling.*), (sich) einig sein, gleicher Meinung sein: ***I ~ that your advice is best*** auch ich bin der Meinung, daß Ihr Rat der beste ist; → ***agreed*** 1; **5.** sich vertragen, auskommen, zs.-passen, sich vereinigen (lassen); **6.** ***~ with*** *j-m* bekommen, zuträglich sein: ***wine does not ~ with me***; **II** *v/t.* **7.** ☤ *Konten etc.* abstimmen.

a·gree·a·ble [ə'grɪəbl] *adj.* □ → ***agreeably***; **1.** angenehm; gefällig, liebenswürdig; **2.** einverstanden (***to*** mit): ***~ to the plan***; **3.** F bereit, gefügig; **4.** (***to***) über'einstimmend (mit), entsprechend (*dat.*): ***~ to the rules***; **a'gree·a·ble·ness** [-nɪs] *s.* angenehmes Wesen; Annehmlichkeit *f*; **a'gree·a·bly** [-lɪ] *adv.* **1.** angenehm: ***~ surprised***; **2.** einverstanden (***to*** mit); entsprechend (***to*** *dat.*): ***~ to his instructions***.

a·greed [ə'gri:d] *adj.* **1.** einig (***on*** über *acc.*); einmütig: ***~ decisions***; **2.** vereinbart: ***the ~ price***; ***~!*** abgemacht!, einverstanden!; **a'gree·ment** [-mənt] *s.* **1.** a) Abkommen *n*, Vereinbarung *f*, Einigung *f*, Verständigung *f*, Über'einkunft *f*, b) Vertrag *m*, c) (gütlicher) Vergleich: ***by ~*** wie vereinbart; ***come to an ~*** sich einigen, sich verständigen; ***by mutual ~*** in gegenseitigem Einvernehmen; ***~ country*** (***currency***) ☤ Verrechnungsland *n* (-währung *f*); **2.** Einigkeit *f*, Eintracht *f*; **3.** Über'einstimmung *f* (*a. ling.*), Einklang *m*; **4.** Genehmigung *f*, Zustimmung *f*.

ag·ri·cul·tur·al [ˌægrɪ'kʌltʃərəl] *adj.* □ landwirtschaftlich, Landwirtschaft(s)...: ***~ labo(u)rer*** Landarbeiter *m*; ***~ show*** Landwirtschaftsausstellung *f*; **ˌag·ri'cul·tur·al·ist** [-rəlɪst] → ***agriculturist***; **ag·ri·cul·ture** ['ægrɪkʌltʃə] *s.* Landwirtschaft *f*, Ackerbau *m* (u. Viehzucht *f*); **ˌag·ri'cul·tur·ist** [-tʃərɪst] *s.* (Dip'lom)Landwirt *m.*

ag·ro·nom·ics [ˌægrə'nɒmɪks] *s. pl. sg. konstr.* Agrono'mie *f*, Ackerbaukunde *f*; **a·gron·o·mist** [ə'grɒnəmɪst] *s.* Agro'nom *m*, (Dip'lom)Landwirt *m*; **a·gron·o·my** [ə'grɒnəmɪ] → ***agronomics***.

a·ground [ə'graʊnd] *adv. u. adj.* ⚓ gestrandet: ***run ~*** a) auflaufen, stranden, b) auf Grund setzen; ***be ~*** a) aufgelaufen sein, b) *fig.* auf dem trocknen sitzen.

a·gue ['eɪgju:] *s.* Schüttelfrost *m*; (Wechsel)Fieber *n.*

ah [ɑ:] *int.* ah, ach, oh, ha, ei!

a·ha [ɑ:'hɑ:] **I** *int.* a'ha, ha'ha!; **II** *adj.*: ***~ experience*** Aha-Erlebnis *n.*

a·head [ə'hed] *adv. u. adj.* **1.** vorn; vor'aus, vor'an; vorwärts, nach vorn; einen Vorsprung habend, an der Spitze; be'vorstehend: ***right*** (*od.* ***straight***) ***~*** geradeaus; ***the years ~*** (***of us***) die bevorstehenden (*od.* vor uns liegenden) Jahre; ***look*** (***think, plan***) ***~*** vorausschauen (-denken, -planen); ***look ~!*** a) sieh dich vor!, b) *fig.* denk an die Zukunft!; → ***get ahead, go ahead, speed*** 1; **2.** ***~ of*** vor (*dat.*), vor'aus (*dat.*): ***be ~ of the others*** vor den anderen sein *od.* liegen, den anderen voraus sein, (e-n) Vorsprung vor den anderen haben, die anderen übertreffen; ***get ~ of s.o.*** j-n überholen *od.* überflügeln; ***~ of the times*** der *od.* s-r Zeit voraus.

a·hem [m'mm] *int.* hm!

a·hoy [ə'hɔɪ] *int.* ⚓ ho!, a'hoi!

aid [eɪd] **I** *v/t.* **1.** unter'stützen, fördern; *j-m* helfen, behilflich sein (***in*** bei, ***to*** *inf.* zu *inf.*): ***~ and abet*** ⚖ a) Beihilfe leisten (*dat.*), b) begünstigen (*acc.*); **II** *s.* **2.** Hilfe *f* (***to*** für), -leistung *f* (***in*** bei), Unter'stützung *f*: ***he came to her ~*** er kam ihr zu Hilfe; ***by*** *od.* ***with*** (***the***) ***~ of*** mit Hilfe von; ***in ~ of*** zugunsten von (*od. gen.*); **3.** Helfer(in), Beistand *m*, Assis'tent(in); **4.** Hilfsmittel *n*, (Hilfs-)Gerät *n*, Mittel *n*: → ***hearing*** 2.

aide [eɪd] *s.* **1.** Berater *m*; **2.** → **aid(e)-de-camp** [ˌeɪddə'kɑ̃:ŋ] *pl.* **ˌaid(e)s-de-'camp** [ˌeɪdz-] *s.* ⚔ Adju'tant *m.*

aide-mé·moire [ˌeɪdmem'wɑ:] (*Fr.*) *s. sg. u. pl.* **1.** Gedächtnisstütze *f*, No'tiz *f*; **2.** *pol.* Denkschrift *f*.

ai·grette ['eɪgret] *s.* **1.** *orn.* kleiner, weißer Reiher; **2.** Ai'grette *f*, Kopfschmuck *m* (*aus Federn etc.*).

ail [eɪl] **I** *v/t.* schmerzen: ***what ~s you?*** *a. fig.* was hast du denn?; **II** *v/i.* kränkeln.

ai·ler·on ['eɪlərɒn] (*Fr.*) *s.* ✈ Querruder *n.*

ail·ing ['eɪlɪŋ] *adj.* kränklich, leidend; **ail·ment** ['eɪlmənt] *s.* Unpäßlichkeit *f*, Leiden *n.*

aim [eɪm] **I** *v/i.* **1.** zielen (***at*** auf *acc.*, nach); **2.** *mst* ***~ at*** *fig. et.* beabsichtigen, an-, erstreben, bezwecken: ***~ing to please*** zu gefallen suchend; ***be ~ing to do*** *Am.* vorhaben *et.* zu tun; **3.** abzielen (***at*** auf *acc.*): ***that was not ~ed at you*** das war nicht auf dich gemünzt; **II** *v/t.* (***at***) **4.** *Waffe etc., a. Bestrebungen* richten (auf *acc.*); **5.** *Bemerkungen* richten (gegen); **III** *s.* **6.** Ziel *n*, Richtung *f*: ***take ~ at*** zielen auf (*acc.*) *od.* nach; **7.** Ziel *n*, Zweck *m*, Absicht *f*; **'aim·less** [-lɪs] *adj.* □ ziel-, zweck-, planlos.

ain't [eɪnt] V *abbr. für*: ***am not, is not, are not, has not, have not***.

air[1] [eə] **I** *s.* **1.** Luft *f*, Atmo'sphäre *f*, Luftraum *m*: ***by ~*** auf dem Luftwege, mit dem Flugzeug; ***in the open ~*** im Freien; ***hot ~*** *sl.* leeres Geschwätz, blauer Dunst; → ***beat*** 11; ***clear the ~*** die Luft (*fig.* die Atmosphäre) reinigen; ***vanish into thin ~*** *fig.* sich in nichts auflösen; ***change of ~*** Luftveränderung *f*; ***be in the ~*** *fig.* a) in der Luft liegen, b) in der Schwebe sein (*Frage etc.*), c) im Umlauf sein (*Gerücht etc.*); ***be up in the ~*** *fig.* a) (völlig) in der Luft hängen, b) völlig ungewiß sein, c) F ganz aus dem Häuschen sein (***about*** wegen); ***take the ~*** a) frische Luft schöpfen, b) ✈ abheben, aufsteigen; ***walk on ~*** sich wie im Himmel fühlen, selig sein; ***in the ~*** *fig.* (völlig) ungewiß; ***give s.o. the ~*** *Am.* j-n an die (frische) Luft setzen; **2.** Brise *f*, Luftzug *m*, Lüftchen *n*; **3.** ⚒ Wetter *n*: ***foul ~*** schlagende Wetter *pl.*; **4.** *Radio, TV*: ˈÄther *m*: ***on the ~*** im Rundfunk *od.* Fernsehen; ***be on the ~*** a) senden, b) gesendet werden, c) auf Sendung sein (*Person*), d) zu hören *od.* zu sehen sein (*Person*); ***go off the ~*** a) die Sendung beenden (*Person*), b) sein Programm beenden (*Sender*); ***put on the ~*** senden, übertragen; ***stay on the ~*** auf Sendung bleiben; **5.** Art *f*, Stil *m*; **6.** Miene *f*, Aussehen *n*, Wesen *n*: ***an ~ of importance*** e-e gewichtige Miene; **7.** *mst pl.* Getue *n*; ‚Gehabe' *n*, Pose *f*: ***~s and graces*** affektiertes Getue; ***put on*** (*od.* ***give o.s***) ***~s*** vornehm tun; **II** *v/t.* **8.** der Luft aussetzen, lüften; **9.** *Wäsche* trocknen, zum Trocknen aufhängen; **10.** *Getränke* abkühlen; **11.** an die Öffentlichkeit *od.* zur Sprache bringen, äußern: ***~ one's grievances***; **12.** ***~ o.s.*** frische Luft schöpfen; **III** *adj.* **13.** Luft..., pneuˈmatisch.

air² [eə] *s.* ♪ **1.** Lied *n*, Meloˈdie *f*, Weise *f*; **2.** Arie *f*.

air| a·lert *s.* ˈFlieger-, ˈLuftaˌlarm *m*; **~ arm** *s.* ✈ *Brit.* Luftwaffe *f*; **~ bag** *s. mot.* Luftsack *m*; **~ bar·rage** *s.* ✈ Luftsperre *f*; **ˈ~-base** *s.* ✈ Luft-, Flugstützpunkt *m*, Fliegerhorst *m*; **ˈ~-bath** *s.* Luftbad *n*; **~ bea·con** *s.* ✈ Leuchtfeuer *n*; **ˈ~-bed** *s.* ˈLuftmaˌtratze *f*; **ˈ~-ˌblad·der** *s. ichth.* Schwimmblase *f*; **ˈ~-borne** *adj.* **1.** a) im Flugzeug befördert *od.* eingebaut, Bord...: ***~ transmitter*** Bordfunkgerät *n*, b) Luftlande...: ***~ troops***, c) auf dem Luftwege; **2.** in der Luft befindlich, aufgestiegen: ***be ~***; **~ brake** *s.* **1.** ⚙ Luft(druck)bremse *f*; **2.** ✈ Landeklappe *f*: ***~ parachute*** Landefallschirm *m*; **ˈ~-brick** *s.* ⚙ Luftziegel *m*; **ˈ~-bridge** *s.* ✈ **1.** Luftbrücke *f*; **2.** Fluggastbrücke *f*; **~ bub·ble** *s.* Luftblase *f*; **~ bump** *s.* ✈ Bö *f*, aufsteigender Luftstrom; **~ bus** *s.* ✈ Airbus *m*; **~ car·go** *s.* Luftfracht *f*; **~ car·ri·er** *s.* ✈ **1.** Fluggesellschaft *f*; **2.** Charterflugzeug *n*; **~ cas·ing** *s.* ⚙ Luftmantel *m*; **~ cham·ber** *s.* ♀, *zo.*, ⚙ Luftkammer *f*; **~ com·pres·sor** *s.* ⚙ Luftverdichter *m*; **ˈ~-conˌdi·tion** *v/t.* ⚙ mit Klimaanlage versehen, klimatisieren; **ˈ~-conˌdi·tion·ing** *s.* ⚙ Klimatisierung *f*; *a.* ***~ plant*** Klimaanlage *f*; **ˈ~-cooled** *adj.* luftgekühlt; **2 Corps** *s. hist. Am.* Luftwaffe *f*; **~ cor·ri·dor** *s.* ˈLuftˌkorridor *m*, Einflugschneise *f*; **~ cov·er** *s.* Luftsicherung *f*.

ˈair·craft *s.* Flugzeug *n*; *coll.* Luftfahrzeuge *pl.*; **~ car·ri·er** *s.* Flugzeugträger *m*; **~ en·gine** *s.* ˈFlugˌmotor *m*; **~ in·dus·try** *s.* ˈLuftfahrt-, ˈFlugzeugindusˌstrie *f*; **ˈ~·man** [-mən] *s.* [*irr.*] *Brit.* Flieger *m* (*Dienstgrad*); **~ weap·ons** *s. pl.* Bordwaffen *pl.*

air| crash *s.* Flugzeugabsturz *m*; **~ crew** *s.* (Flugzeug)Besatzung *f*; **~ cush·ion** *s. a.* ⚙ Luftkissen *n*; **ˈ~-ˌcush·ion ve·hic·le** *s.* ⚙ Luftkissenfahrzeug *n*; **~ defence**, *Am.* **~ de·fense** *s.* ⚔ Luftschutz *m*, -verteidigung *f*, Fliegerabwehr *f*.

air·drome [ˈeədrəʊm] *s. Am.* Flugplatz *m*.

ˈair|·drop I *s.* a) Fallschirmabwurf *m*, b) ⚔ Luftlandung *f*; **II** *v/t.* a) mit dem Fallschirm abwerfen, b) ⚔ *Fallschirmjäger etc.* absetzen; **ˈ~-dry** *v/t. u. v/i.* lufttrocknen; **ˈ~·field** *s.* Flugplatz *m*; **~ flap** *s.* ⚙ Luftklappe *f*; **ˈ~·foil** *s.* ✈ Tragfläche *f*; **~ force**, **2 Force** *s.* ✈ Luftwaffe *f*, Luftstreitkräfte *pl.*; **ˈ~·frame** *s.* ✈ Flugwerk *n*, (Flugzeug-)Zelle *f*; **ˈ~·freight** *s.* Luftfracht *f*; **ˈ~ˌfreight·er** *s.* **1.** Luftfrachter *m*; **2.** ˈLuftspeditiˌon *f*; **ˈ~·graph** [-grɑːf] *s.* ˈFotoluftpostbrief *m*; **ˌ~-ˈground** *adj.* ✈ Bord-Boden-...; **ˈ~·gun** *s.* Luftgewehr *n*; **~ host·ess** *s.* ✈ (ˈLuft)ˌStewardeß *f*; **ˈ~·house** *s.* Traglufthalle *f*.

air·i·ly [ˈeərɪlɪ] *adv.* ˈleichtˈhin, unbekümmert; **ˈair·i·ness** [-nɪs] *s.* **1.** Luftigkeit *f*; luftige Lage; **2.** Leichtigkeit *f*; Munterkeit *f*; **3.** Leichtfertigkeit *f*; **ˈair·ing** [-rɪŋ] *s.* **1.** (Be)Lüftung *f*, Trocknen *n*: ***give s.th. an ~*** et. lüften; **2.** Spaziergang *m*: ***take an ~*** frische Luft schöpfen; **3.** Äußerung *f*; Erörterung *f*.

air| in·take *s.* ⚙ **1.** Lufteinlaß *m*; **2.** Zuluftstutzen *m*; **~ jack·et** *s.* **1.** Schwimmweste *f*; **2.** ⚙ Luftmantel *m*; **~ jet** *s.* ⚙ Luftstrahl *m*, -düse *f*; **~ lane** *s.* Luftroute *f*.

air·less [ˈeəlɪs] *adj.* **1.** ohne Luft(zug); **2.** dumpf, stickig.

air| let·ter *s.* **1.** Luftpostbrief *m* (*auf Formular*); **2.** *Am.* Luftpostleichtbrief *m*; **~ lev·el** *s.* ⚙ Liˈbelle *f*, Setzwaage *f*; **ˈ~·lift I** *s.* Luftbrücke *f*; **II** *v/t.* über e-e Luftbrücke befördern; **ˈ~·line** *s.* Luft-, Flugverkehrsgesellschaft *f*; **~ liner** *s.* ✈ Verkehrs-, Linienflugzeug *n*; **ˈ~·lock** *s.* ⚙ **1.** Luftschleuse *f*; **2.** Druckstauung *f*; **~ mail** *s.* (***by ~*** mit *od.* per) Luftpost *f*; **ˈ~·man** [-mən] *s.* [*irr.*] Flieger *m*; **ˈ~-meˌchan·ic** *s.* ✈ ˈBordmonˌteur *m*; **ˈ~-ˌmind·ed** *adj.* ✈ luft(fahrt)-, flug(sport)begeistert; **ˈ~-ˌop·er·at·ed** *adj.* ⚙ preßluftbetätigt; **~ par·cel** *Brit.* ˈLuftpostpaˌket *n*; **~ pas·sage** *s.* **1.** *anat.*, *biol.*, Luft-, Atemweg *m*; **2.** ⚙ Luftschlitz *m*; **~ pas·sen·ger** *s.* ✈ Fluggast *m*; **~ pho·to(·graph)** *s.* ✈ Luftbild *n*, -aufnahme *f*; **~ pi·ra·cy** *s.* ˈLuftpiratenˌrie *f*; **~ pi·rate** *s.* ˈLuftpiˌrat *m*; **ˈ~·plane** *s.* ✈ *bsd. Am.* Flugzeug *n*; **ˈ~·plane car·ri·er** *bsd. Am.* → ***aircraft carrier***; **~ pock·et** *s.* Fallbö *f*, Luftloch *n*; **~ pol·lu·tion** *s.* Luftverschmutzung *f*; **ˈ~·port** *s.* ✈ Flughafen *m*; **ˈ~·proof** *adj.* luftbeständig, -dicht; **~ pump** *s.* ⚙ Luftpumpe *f*; **~ raft** *s.* Schlauchboot *n*; **~ raid** *s.* Luftangriff *m*.

ˈair-raid| pre·cau·tions *s. pl.* Luftschutz *m*; **~ shel·ter** *s.* Luftschutzraum *m*, -bunker *m*, -keller *m*; **~ ward·en** *s.* Luftschutzwart *m*; **~ warn·ing** *s.* Luft-, Fliegerwarnung *f*, ˈFliegeraˌlarm *m*.

air| ri·fle *s.* Luftgewehr *n*; **~ route** *s.* ✈ Flugroute *f*; **~ sched·ule** *s.* Flugplan *m*; **ˈ~·screw** *s.* ✈ Luftschraube *f*; **ˈ~-seal** *v/t.* ⚙ luftdicht verschließen; **ˈ~·ship** *s.* Luftschiff *n*; **ˈ~-sick** *adj.* luftkrank; **ˈ~-ˌsick·ness** *s.* Luftkrankheit *f*; **ˈ~·space** *s.* Luftraum *m*; **~ speed** *s.* ✈ (Flug)Eigengeschwindigkeit *f*; **ˈ~·strip** *s.* ✈ **1.** Behelfslandeplatz *m*; **2.** *Am.* Roll-, Start-, Landebahn *f*; **~ tax·i** *s.* ✈ Lufttaxi *n*; **~ tee** *s.* ✈ Landekreuz *n*; **~ ter·mi·nal** *s.* ✈ **1.** Großflughafen *m*; **2.** Terminal *m*, *n*: a) (Flughafen)Abfertigungsgebäude, b) *Brit.* ˈEndstatiˌon *f* der ˈZubringerˌlinie zum und vom Flughafen; **ˈ~·tight** *adj.* **1.** luftdicht; **2.** *fig.* todsicher, völlig klar; **ˌ~-to-ˈair** *adj.* ✈ Bord-Bord-...; **ˌ~-to-ˈground** *adj.* ✈ Bord-Boden-...; **~ traf·fic** *s.* Luft-, Flugverkehr *m*; **ˈ~-ˌtraf·fic con·trol** *s.* ✈ Flugsicherung *f*; **ˈ~-ˌtraf·fic con·trol·ler** *s.* ✈ Fluglotse *m*; **ˈ~-tube** *s.* **1.** ⚙ Luftschlauch *m*; **2.** *anat.* Luftröhre *f*; **~ um·brel·la** *s.* ✈ Luftschirm *m*; **ˈ~·way** *s.* **1.** ⚙, ⚒ Wetterstrecke *f*, Luftschacht *m*; **2.** ✈ a) Luft(verkehrs)weg *m*, Luftroute *f*, b) → ***airline***; **ˈ~ˌwom·an** *s.* [*irr.*] Fliegerin *f*; **ˈ~ˌwor·thi·ness** *s.* ✈ Lufttüchtigkeit *f*.

air·y [ˈeərɪ] *adj.* ☐ → ***airily***; **1.** Luft...; **2.** luftig, *a.* windig; **3.** körperlos; **4.** graziˈös; **5.** lebhaft, munter; **6.** überˈspannt, verstiegen: ***~ plans***; **7.** lässig: ***an ~ manner***; **8.** vornehmtuerisch.

aisle [aɪl] *s.* **1.** ⛪ a) Seitenschiff *n*, -chor *m* (*e-r Kirche*), b) Schiff *n*, Abteilung *f* (*e-r Kirche od. e-s Gebäudes*); **2.** (Mittel)Gang *m* (*zwischen Bänken etc.*); **3.** *fig.* Schneise *f*.

aitch [eɪtʃ] *s.* H *n*, h *n* (*Buchstabe*): ***drop one's ~es*** das H nicht aussprechen (*Zeichen der Unbildung*); **ˈaitch·bone** *s.* **1.** Lendenknochen *m*; **2.** Lendenstück *n* (*vom Rind*).

a·jar [əˈdʒɑː] *adv. u. adj.* **1.** halb offen, angelehnt (*Tür*); **2.** *fig.* im Zwiespalt.

a·kim·bo [əˈkɪmbəʊ] *adv. die Arme* in die Seite gestemmt.

a·kin [əˈkɪn] *adj.* **1.** (bluts- *od.* stamm-) verwandt (***to*** mit); **2.** verwandt; sehr ähnlich (***to*** *dat.*).

al·a·bas·ter [ˈæləbɑːstə] **I** *s. min.* Alaˈbaster *m*; **II** *adj.* alaˈbastern, alaˈbasterweiß, Alabaster...

a·lac·ri·ty [əˈlækrətɪ] *s.* **1.** Munterkeit *f*; **2.** Bereitwilligkeit *f*, Eifer *m*.

A·lad·din's lamp [əˈlædɪnz] *s.* ˈAladins Wunderlampe *f*; *fig.* wunderwirkender ˈTalisman.

à la mode [ˌɑːlɑːˈməʊd] (*Fr.*) *adj.* **1.** à la mode, modisch; **2.** gespickt u. geschmort u. mit Gemüse zubereitet: ***beef ~***; **3.** *Am.* mit (Speise)Eis (serviert): ***cake ~***.

a·larm [əˈlɑːm] **I** *s.* **1.** Aˈlarm *m*, Warnruf *m*, Warnung *f*: ***false ~*** blinder Alarm, falsche Meldung; ***give*** (***raise, sound***) ***the ~*** Alarm geben *od. fig.* schlagen; **2.** a) Weckvorrichtung *f*, b) Wecker *m*; **3.** Aˈlarmvorrichtung *f*; **4.** Lärm *m*, Aufruhr *m*; **5.** Angst *f*, Unruhe *f*, Bestürzung *f*; **II** *v/t.* **6.** alarmieren, warnen; **7.** beunruhigen, erschrecken (***at*** über *acc.*, ***by*** durch): ***be ~ed*** sich ängstigen, bestürzt sein; **~ bell** *s.* Aˈlarm-, Sturmglocke *f*; **~ clock** *s.* Wecker *m* (*Uhr*).

a·larm·ing [əˈlɑːmɪŋ] *adj.* ☐ beunruhigend, beängstigend; **aˈlarm·ist** [-mɪst] **I** *s.* Bangemacher *m*, Schwarzseher *m*, ‚Unke' *f*; **II** *adj.* schwarzseherisch.

a·las [əˈlæs] *int.* ach!, leider!

alb [ælb] *s. eccl.* Albe *f*, Chorhemd *n*.

Al·ba·ni·an [ælˈbeɪnjən] **I** *adj.* alˈbanisch; **II** *s.* Alˈban(i)er(in).

al·ba·tross [ˈælbətrɒs] *s. orn.* ˈAlbatros *m*, Sturmvogel *m*.

al·be·it [ɔːlˈbiːɪt] *cj.* obˈgleich, wenn auch.

al·bert [ˈælbət] *s. a.* ***2 chain*** *Brit.* (kur-

ze) Uhrkette.
al·bi·no [æl'bi:nəʊ] *pl.* **-nos** *s.* Al'bino *m*, 'Kakerlak *m*.
Al·bion ['ælbjən] *npr. poet.* 'Albion *n* (*Britannien od. England*).
al·bum ['ælbəm] *s.* **1.** 'Album *n*, Stammbuch *n*; **2.** (Briefmarken-, Foto-, Schallplatten- *etc.*)Album *n*; **3.** a) 'Schallplattenkas,sette *f*, b) Album *n* (*Langspielplatte*[*n*]); **4.** Gedichtsammlung *etc.* (in Buchform).
al·bu·men ['ælbjʊmɪn] *s.* **1.** *zo.* Eiweiß *n*, Al'bumen *n*; **2.** ♀, ⚗, ⚘ Eiweiß(stoff *m*) *n*, Albu'min *n*; **al·bu·min** ['ælbjʊmɪn] → ***albumen*** 2; **al·bu·mi·nous** [æl'bju:mɪnəs] *adj.* eiweißartig, -haltig.
al·chem·ic *adj.*; **al·chem·i·cal** [æl'kemɪk(l)] *adj.* □ alchi'mistisch; **al·che·mist** ['ælkɪmɪst] *s.* Alchi'mist *m*, Goldmacher *m*; **al·che·my** ['ælkɪmɪ] *s.* Alchi'mie *f*.
al·co·hol ['ælkəhɒl] *s.* 'Alkohol *m*: a) Sprit *m*, 'Spiritus *m*, Weingeist *m*: ***ethyl ~*** Äthylalkohol *m*, b) geistige *od.* alko'holische Getränke *pl.*; **al·co·hol·ic** [,ælkə'hɒlɪk] **I** *adj.* **1.** alko'holisch, 'alkoholartig, -haltig, Alkohol...: ***~ drinks***; ***~ strength*** Alkoholgehalt *m*; **II** *s.* **2.** (Gewohnheits)Trinker(in), Alko'holiker(in); **3.** *pl.* Alko'holika *pl.*, alkoholische Getränke *pl.*; **'al·co·hol·ism** [-lɪzəm] *s.* Alkoho'lismus *m*: a) Trunksucht *f*, b) *durch Trunksucht verursachte Organismusschädigungen*.
al·cove ['ælkəʊv] *s.* Al'koven *m*, Nische *f*; (Garten)Laube *f*, Grotte *f*.
al·de·hyde ['ældɪhaɪd] *s.* ⚗ Alde'hyd *m*.
al·der ['ɔ:ldə] *s.* ♀ Erle *f*.
al·der·man ['ɔ:ldəmən] *s.* [*irr.*] Ratsherr *m*, Stadtrat *m*; **'al·der·man·ry** [-rɪ] *s.* **1.** (von e-m Ratsherrn vertretener) Stadtbezirk; **2.** → **'al·der·man·ship** [-ʃɪp] *s.* Amt *n* e-s Ratsherrn; **al·der·wom·an** ['ɔ:ldə,wʊmən] *s.* [*irr.*] Stadträtin *f*.
ale [eɪl] *s.* Ale *n* (*helles, obergäriges Bier*).
a·leck ['ælɪk] *s. Am.* F → ***smart aleck***.
a·lee [ə'li:] *adv. u. adj.* leewärts.
'ale-house *s.* 'Bierlo,kal *n*.
a·lem·bic [ə'lembɪk] *s.* **1.** Destillierkolben *m*; **2.** *fig.* Re'torte *f*.
a·lert [ə'lɜ:t] **I** *adj.* □ **1.** wachsam, auf der Hut; achtsam: ***~ to*** klar bewußt (*gen.*); **2.** rege, munter; **3.** aufgeweckt, forsch, a'lert; **II** *s.* **4.** (A'larm-)Bereitschaft *f*: ***on the ~*** auf der Hut, in Alarmbereitschaft; **5.** A'larm(si,gnal *n*) *m*, Warnung *f*; **III** *v/t.* **6.** alarmieren, warnen, ⚔ *a.* in A'larmzustand versetzen, *weitS.* mobilisieren: ***~ s.o. to s.th.*** *fig.* j-m et. zum Bewußtsein bringen; **a'lert·ness** [-nɪs] *s.* **1.** Wachsamkeit *f*; **2.** Munterkeit *f*, Flinkheit *f*; **3.** Aufgewecktheit *f*, Forschheit *f*.
A lev·el *s. Brit. ped.* (*etwa*) Abi'tur *n*: ***he has three ~s*** er hat das Abitur in drei Fächern gemacht.
Al·ex·an·drine [,ælɪg'zændraɪn] *s.* Alexan'driner *m* (*Versart*).
al·fal·fa [æl'fælfə] *s.* ♀ Lu'zerne *f*.
al·fres·co [æl'freskəʊ] (*Ital.*) *adj. u. adv.* im Freien: ***~ lunch***.
al·ga ['ælgə] *pl.* **-gae** [-dʒi:] *s.* ♀ Alge *f*, Tang *m*.
al·ge·bra ['ældʒɪbrə] *s.* ⩚ Algebra *f*; **,al·ge'bra·ic** [-reɪk] *adj.* □ alge'braisch: ***~ calculus*** Algebra *f*.
Al·ge·ri·an [æl'dʒɪərɪən] **I** *adj.* al'gerisch; **II** *s.* Al'gerier(in).
Al·gol ['ælgɒl] *s.* ALGOL *n* (*Computersprache*).
a·li·as ['eɪlɪæs] **I** *adv.* 'alias, sonst (... genannt); **II** *s. pl.* **-as·es** angenommener Name, Deckname *m*.
al·i·bi ['ælɪbaɪ] *s.* **1.** ⚖ 'Alibi *n*: ***establish one's ~*** sein Alibi erbringen; **3.** F Ausrede *f*, 'Alibi *n*.
al·ien ['eɪljən] **I** *adj.* **1.** fremd; ausländisch: ***~ subjects*** ausländische Staatsangehörige; **2.** außerirdisch (*Wesen*); **3.** *fig.* andersartig, fernliegend, fremd (***to*** *dat.*); **4.** *fig.* zu'wider, 'unsym,pathisch (***to*** *dat.*); **II** *s.* **5.** Fremde(r *m*) *f*, Ausländer(in): ***enemy ~*** feindlicher Ausländer; ***~s police*** Fremdenpolizei *f*; **6.** nicht naturalisierter Bewohner des Landes; **7.** *fig.* Fremdling *m*; **8.** außerirdisches Wesen; **9.** *ling.* Fremdwort *n*; **'al·ien·a·ble** [-nəbl] *adj.* veräußerlich; über'tragbar; **'al·ien·age** [-nɪdʒ] *s.* Ausländertum *n*; **'al·ien·ate** [-neɪt] *v/t.* **1.** ⚖ veräußern, über'tragen; **2.** entfremden, abspenstig machen (***from*** *dat.*); **al·ien·a·tion** [,eɪljə'neɪʃn] *s.* **1.** ⚖ Veräußerung *f*, Über'tragung *f*; **2.** Entfremdung *f* (*a. psych., pol.*) (***from*** von), Abwendung *f*, Abneigung *f*: ***~ of affections*** ⚖ Entfremdung (ehelicher Zuneigung); **3.** *a.* ***mental ~*** Alienati'on *f*, Psy'chose *f*; **4.** *literarische* Verfremdung: ***~ effect*** Verfremdungs-, V-Effekt *m*; **'al·ien·ist** [-nɪst] *s. obs.* Nervenarzt *m*.
a·light[1] [ə'laɪt] *v/i.* **1.** ab-, aussteigen; **2.** sich niederlassen, sich setzen (*Vogel*), fallen (*Schnee*): ***~ on one's feet*** auf die Füße fallen; **3.** ✈ niedergehen, landen; **4.** (***on***) (zufällig) stoßen (auf *acc.*), antreffen (*acc.*).
a·light[2] [ə'laɪt] *adj.* **1.** → ***ablaze***; **2.** erleuchtet (***with*** von).
a·lign [ə'laɪn] **I** *v/t.* **1.** ausfluchten, in e-e (gerade) 'Linie bringen; in gerader Linie *od.* in Reih und Glied aufstellen; ausrichten (***with*** nach); **2.** *fig.* zu e-r Gruppe (*Gleichgesinnter*) zs.-schließen; **3.** ***~ o.s.*** (***with***) sich anschließen, sich anpassen (an *acc.*); **II** *v/i.* **4.** sich in gerader Linie *od.* in Reih und Glied aufstellen; sich ausrichten (***with*** nach); **a'lign·ment** [-mənt] *s.* **1.** Anordnung *f* in 'einer Linie, Ausrichten *n*; Anpassung *f*: ***in ~ with*** in 'einer Linie *od.* Richtung mit (*a. fig.*); **2.** ⚙ a) Ausfluchten *n*, Ausrichten *n*, b) 'Linien-, Zeilenführung *f*, c) 'Absteckungs,linie *f*, Trasse *f*, Flucht *f*, Gleichlauf *m*; **3.** *fig.* Ausrichtung *f*, Gruppierung *f*: ***~ of political forces***.
a·like [ə'laɪk] **I** *adj.* gleich, ähnlich; **II** *adv.* gleich, ebenso, in gleichem Maße: ***she helps enemies and friends ~***.
al·i·ment ['ælɪmənt] *s.* Nahrung(smittel *n*) *f*; **2.** *et.* Lebensnotwendiges; **al·i·men·ta·ry** [,ælɪ'mentərɪ] *adj.* **1.** nahrhaft; **2.** Nahrungs..., Ernährungs...: ***~ canal*** Verdauungskanal *m*; **al·i·men·ta·tion** [,ælɪmen'teɪʃn] *s.* Ernährung *f*, Unterhalt *m*.
al·i·mo·ny ['ælɪmənɪ] *s.* ⚖ 'Unterhalt(szahlung *f*) *m*.
a·line *etc.* → ***align*** *etc.*
al·i·quant ['ælɪkwənt] *adj.* ⩚ ali'quant, mit Rest teilend; **'al·i·quot** [-kwɒt] *adj.* ⩚ ali'quot, ohne Rest teilend.
a·live [ə'laɪv] *adj.* **1.** lebend, (noch) am Leben: ***the proudest man ~*** der stolzeste Mann der Welt; ***no man ~*** kein Sterblicher; ***man ~!*** F Menschenskind!; **2.** tätig, in voller Kraft *od.* Wirksamkeit, im Gange: ***keep ~*** a) aufrechterhalten, bewahren, b) am Leben bleiben; **3.** lebendig, lebhaft, belebt: ***~ and kicking*** F gesund u. munter; ***look ~!*** F (mach) fix!, paß auf!; **4.** (***to***) empfänglich (für), bewußt (*gen.*), achtsam (auf *acc.*); **5.** voll, belebt, wimmelnd (***with*** von); **6.** ⚡ stromführend, geladen, unter Strom stehend.
al·ka·li ['ælkəlaɪ] ⚗ **I** *pl.* **-lies** *od.* **-lis** *s.* **1.** Al'kali *n*; **2.** (in wäßriger Lösung) stark al'kalisch reagierende Verbindung: ***caustic ~*** Ätzalkali; ***mineral ~*** kohlensaures Natron; **3.** *geol.* kalzinierte Soda; **II** *adj.* **4.** al'kalisch: ***~ soil***; **'al·ka·line** [-laɪn] *adj.* ⚗ al'kalisch, al'kalihaltig, basisch; **al·ka·lin·i·ty** [,ælkə'lɪnətɪ] *s.* ⚗ Alkalini'tät *f*, al'kalische Eigenschaft; **'al·ka·lize** [-laɪz] *v/t.* ⚗ alkalisieren, auslaugen; **'al·ka·loid** [-lɔɪd] ⚗ **I** *s.* Alkalo'id *n*; **II** *adj.* al'kaliartig, laugenhaft.
all [ɔ:l] **I** *adj.* **1.** all, sämtlich, vollständig, ganz: ***~ the wine*** der ganze Wein; ***~ day*** (***long***) den ganzen Tag; ***for ~ that*** dessenungeachtet, trotzdem; ***~ the time*** die ganze Zeit; ***for ~ time*** für immer; ***~ the way*** die ganze Strecke, *fig.* völlig, rückhaltlos; ***with ~ respect*** bei aller Hochachtung; **2.** jeder, jede, jedes (beliebige); alle *pl.*: ***at ~ hours*** zu jeder Stunde; ***beyond ~ question*** fraglos; → ***event*** 3, ***mean***[3] 3; **3.** ganz, rein: ***~ wool*** reine Wolle; → ***all-American***; **II** *s.* **4.** das Ganze, alles; Gesamtbesitz *m*: ***his ~*** a) sein Hab u. Gut, b) sein ein u. alles; **III** *pron.* **5.** alles: ***~ of it*** alles; ***~ of us*** wir alle; ***~'s well that ends well*** Ende gut, alles gut; ***when ~ is said*** (***and done***) F letzten Endes, im Grunde genommen; ***what is it ~ about?*** um was handelt es sich?; ***the best of ~ would be*** das allerbeste wäre; ***in ~*** insgesamt; ***~ in ~*** alles in allem; ***is that ~?*** a) sonst noch et.?, b) F schöne Geschichte!; **IV** *adv.* **6.** ganz, gänzlich, völlig, höchst: ***~ wrong*** ganz falsch, völlig im Irrtum; ***that is ~ very well, but ...*** das ist ja ganz schön u. gut, aber ...; ***he was ~ ears*** (***eyes***) er war ganz Ohr (Auge); ***she is ~ kindness*** sie ist die Güte selber; ***~ the better*** um so besser; ***~ one*** einerlei, gleichgültig; ***~ the same*** a) ganz gleich, gleichgültig, b) gleichwohl, trotzdem, immerhin; → ***above*** 2, ***after*** 1, ***at***[1] 7, ***but*** 13, ***once*** 4b; **7.** *Sport:* ***two ~*** zwei beide, zwei zu zwei;
Zssgn mit adv. u. prp.:
all| a·long a) der ganzen Länge nach, b) F die ganze Zeit, schon immer; ***~ in*** *sl.* ‚fertig', ganz ‚erledigt'; ***~ out*** a) ‚auf dem Holzweg', b) völlig ‚ka'putt', c) mit aller Macht: ***be ~ for s.th.*** mit aller Macht auf et. aussein; → ***go*** 16; ***~ o·ver*** a) *es ist* alles aus, b) gänzlich: ***that is Max ~*** F das sieht Max ähnlich, das ist typisch Max, c) am ganzen Körper, d) über'all(hin); ***~ right*** ganz richtig; in Ordnung(!), schön!, (na) gut!; ***~ round*** 'ringsum'her, über'all; ***~ there***: ***he is***

not ~ F er ist nicht ganz bei Trost; ~ **up**: ***it's ~ with him*** mit ihm ist's aus; **for** ~ a) trotz: ~ ***his smartness***; ~ ***that*** trotzdem, b) so'viel: ~ ***I know***; ~ ***I care*** F das ist mir doch egal!, meinetwegen!; **in** ~ insgesamt.
ˌall|-A'mer·i·can *adj.* rein ameri'kanisch, die ganzen USA vertretend; *Sport*: National…; **ˌ~-a'round** *Am.* → ***all-round***; **'all-ˌau·to'mat·ic** *adj.* ⚙ 'vollautoˌmatisch.
al·lay [ə'leɪ] *v/t.* beschwichtigen, beruhigen; *Streit* schlichten; mildern, lindern, *Hunger, Durst* stillen.
ˌall|-'clear *s.* **1.** Ent'warnung(ssiˌgnal *n*) *f*; **2.** *fig.* ‚grünes Licht'; **'~-ˌdu·ty** *adj.* ⚙ Allzweck…
al·le·ga·tion [ˌælɪ'geɪʃn] *s. unerwiesene* Behauptung, Aussage *f*, Vorbringen *n*; Darstellung *f*.
al·lege [ə'ledʒ] *v/t.* **1.** *Unerwiesenes* behaupten, erklären, vorbringen; **2.** vorgeben, vorschützen; **al'leged** [-dʒd] *adj*; **al'leg·ed·ly** [-dʒɪdlɪ] *adv.* an-, vorgeblich.
al·le·giance [ə'li:dʒəns] *s.* **1.** 'Untertanenpflicht *f*, -treue *f*, -gehorsam *m*: ***oath of*** ~ Treu-, ⚔ Fahneneid *m*; ***change one's*** ~ s-e Staats- *od.* Parteiangehörigkeit wechseln; **2.** (***to***) Treue *f* (zu), Loyali'tät *f*; Bindung *f* (an *acc.*); Ergebenheit *f*, Gefolgschaft *f*.
al·le·gor·ic, al·le·gor·i·cal [ˌælɪ'gɒrɪk(l)] *adj.* ☐ alle'gorisch, (sinn)bildlich; **al·le·go·rize** ['ælɪgəraɪz] **I** *v/t.* allegorisch darstellen; **II** *v/i.* in Gleichnissen reden; **al·le·go·ry** ['ælɪgərɪ] *s.* Allego'rie *f*, Sinnbild *n*, sinnbildliche Darstellung, Gleichnis *n*.
al·le·lu·ia [ˌælɪ'lu:jə] **I** *s.* Halle'luja *n*, Loblied *n*; **II** *int.* halleluja!
al·ler·gic [ə'lɜ:dʒɪk] *adj.* ⚕ *u.* F *fig.* all'ergisch, äußerst empfindlich (***to*** gegen); **al·ler·gy** ['ælədʒɪ] *s.* **1.** ⚘, ⚕, *zo.* Aller'gie *f*, 'Überempfindlichkeit *f*; **2.** F ‚Aller'gie' *f*, 'Widerwille *m* (***to*** gegen).
al·le·vi·ate [ə'li:vɪeɪt] *v/t.* erleichtern, lindern, mildern, (ver)mindern; **al·le·vi·a·tion** [əˌli:vɪ'eɪʃn] *s.* Erleichterung *f etc.*
al·ley ['ælɪ] *s.* **1.** (schmale) Gasse, Verbindungsgang *m*, 'Durchgang *m* (*a. fig.*): ***that's down*** (*od.* ***up***) ***my*** ~ F das ist et. für mich, das ist ganz mein Fall; → ***blind alley***; **2.** Spielbahn *f*; → ***bowling-alley*** *etc.*; **'~·way** *s.* → ***alley*** 1.
All| Fools' Day [ˌɔ:l'fu:lzdeɪ] *s.* der 1. A'pril; ♀ **fours** alle vier (*Kartenspiel*); → ***four*** 2; ~ **Hal·lows** [ˌɔ:l'hæləʊz] *s.* Aller'heiligen *n*.
al·li·ance [ə'laɪəns] *s.* **1.** Verbindung *f*, Verknüpfung *f*; **2.** Bund *m*, Bündnis *n*: ***offensive and defensive*** ~ Schutz- und Trutzbündnis; ***form an*** ~ ein Bündnis schließen; **3.** Heirat *f*, Verwandtschaft *f*, Verschwägerung *f*; **4.** *weitS.* Verwandtschaft *f*; **5.** *fig.* Bund *m*, (Inter'essen)Gemeinschaft *f*; **6.** Über'einkunft *f*; **al·lied** [ə'laɪd; *attr.* 'ælaɪd] *adj.* **1.** verbündet, alliiert (***with*** mit): ***the*** ♀ ***Powers***; **2.** *fig.* (art)verwandt (***to*** mit); **Al·lies** ['ælaɪz] *s. pl.*: ***the*** ~ die Alliierten, die Verbündeten.
al·li·ga·tor ['ælɪgeɪtə] *s. zo.* Alli'gator *m*; 'Kaiman *m*; ~ **pear** *s.* → ***avocado***; ~ **skin** *s.* Kroko'dilleder *n*.
'all|-imˌpor·tant *adj.* äußerst wichtig; **ˌ~-'in, 'all-inˌclu·sive** *adj. bsd. Brit.* alles inbegriffen, Gesamt…, Pauschal…: ~ ***insurance*** Generalversicherung *f*; ~ ***wrestling*** *sport* Catchen *n*.
al·lit·er·ate [ə'lɪtəreɪt] *v/t.* **1.** alliterieren; **2.** im Stabreim dichten; **al·lit·er·a·tion** [əˌlɪtə'reɪʃn] *s.* Alliterati'on *f*, Stabreim *m*; **al'lit·er·a·tive** [-rətɪv] *adj.* ☐ alliterierend.
ˌall|-'mains *adj.* ⚡ Allstrom…, mit Netzanschluß; **ˌ~-'met·al** *adj.* Ganzmetall…
al·lo·cate ['æləʊkeɪt] *v/t.* **1.** ver-, zuteilen, an-, zuweisen (***to*** *dat.*): ~ ***duties***; ~ ***shares*** Aktien zuteilen; **2.** → ***allot*** 3; **3.** den Platz bestimmen für; **al·lo·ca·tion** [ˌæləʊ'keɪʃn] *s.* **1.** Zu-, Verteilung *f*; An-, Zuweisung *f*, Kontin'gent *n*; Aufschlüsselung *f*; **2.** ⚜ Bewilligung *f*, Zahlungsanweisung *f*.
al·lo·cu·tion [ˌæləʊ'kju:ʃn] *s.* feierliche *od.* ermahnende Ansprache.
al·lo·path ['æləʊpæθ] *s.* ⚕ Allo'path *m*; **al·lop·a·thy** [ə'lɒpəθɪ] *s.* ⚕ Allopa'thie *f*.
al·lot [ə'lɒt] *v/t.* **1.** zu-, aus-, verteilen; auslosen; **2.** bewilligen, abtreten; **3.** bestimmen (***to***, ***for*** für *j-n od. e-n Zweck*); **al'lot·ment** [-mənt] *s.* **1.** Ver-, Zuteilung *f*; Anteil *m*; zugeteilte 'Aktien *pl.*; **2.** *Brit.* Par'zelle *f*; (*a.* ~ ***garden***) Schrebergarten *m*; **3.** Los *n*, Schicksal *n*.
ˌall-'out *adj.* **1.** to'tal, um'fassend, Groß…: ~ ***effort***; **2.** kompro'mißlos, radi'kal.
al·low [ə'laʊ] **I** *v/t.* **1.** erlauben, gestatten, zulassen: ***he is not ~ed to go there*** er darf nicht hingehen; **2.** gewähren, bewilligen, gönnen, zuerkennen: ~ ***more time***; ***we are ~ed two ounces a day*** uns stehen täglich zwei Unzen zu; ~ ***an item of expenditure*** e-n Ausgabeposten billigen; **3.** a) zugeben: ***I ~ I was rather nervous***, b) gelten lassen, *Forderung* anerkennen: ~ ***a claim***; **4.** lassen, dulden, ermöglichen: ***you must ~ the soup to get cold*** du mußt die Suppe abkühlen lassen; **5.** *Summe für gewisse Zeit* zuwenden, geben: ***my father ~s me £100 a year*** mein Vater gibt mir jährlich £ 100 (*Zuschuß od. Unterhaltsgeld*); **6.** ab-, anrechnen, abziehen, nachlassen, vergüten: ~ ***a discount*** e-n Rabatt gewähren; ~ ***10% for inferior quality***; **7.** *Am.* a) meinen, b) beabsichtigen; **II** *v/i.* **8.** ~ ***of*** erlauben, zulassen, ermöglichen (*acc.*): ***it ~s of no excuse*** es läßt sich nicht entschuldigen; **9.** ~ ***for*** berücksichtigen, bedenken, in Betracht ziehen, anrechnen (*acc.*): ~ ***for wear and tear***; **al'low·a·ble** [-əbl] *adj.* ☐ **1.** erlaubt, zulässig, rechtmäßig; **2.** abziehbar, -zugsfähig: ~ ***expenses*** ⚜ abzugsfähige Ausgaben; **al'low·ance** [-əns] **I** *s.* **1.** Erlaubnis *f*, Be-, Einwilligung *f*, Anerkennung *f*; **2.** *geldliche* Zuwendung; Zuteilung *f*, Rati'on *f*, Maß *n*; Zuschuß *m*, Beihilfe *f*, Taschengeld *n*: ***weekly*** ~; ***family*** ~ Familienunterstützung *f*; ***dress*** ~ Kleidergeld *n*; **3.** Nachsicht *f*: ***make*** ~ ***for*** berücksichtigen, bedenken, in Betracht ziehen; **4.** Entschädigung *f*, Vergütung *f*: ***expense*** ~ Aufwandsentschädigung; **5.** ⚜ Nachlaß *m*, Ra'batt *m*: ~ ***for cash*** Skonto *m*, *n*; ***tax*** ~ Steuerermäßigung *f*; **6.** ⚙, ⚒ Tole'ranz *f*, Spiel(raum *m*) *n*, zulässige Abweichung; **7.** *sport* Vorgabe *f*; **II** *v/t.* **8.** a) *j-n* auf Rationen setzen, b) *Waren* rationieren.
al·loy I *s.* ['ælɔɪ] **1.** Me'tallegierung *f*; **2.** ⚙ Legierung *f*, Gemisch *n*; **3.** [ə'lɔɪ] *fig.* (Bei)Mischung *f*: ***pleasure without*** ~ ungetrübte Freude; **II** *v/t.* [ə'lɔɪ] **4.** *Metalle* legieren, mischen; **5.** *fig.* beeinträchtigen, verschlechtern.
ˌall|-'par·ty *adj. pol.* Allparteien…; **ˌ~-'pur·pose** *adj.* für jeden Zweck verwendbar, Allzweck…, Universal…: ~ ***outfit***; **ˌ~-'red** *adj. bsd. geogr.* rein 'britisch; **ˌ~-'round** *adj.* all-, vielseitig, Allround…; **ˌ~-'round·er** *s.* Alleskönner *m*; *sport* All'roundsportler *m*, -spieler *m*; ♀ **Saints' Day** [ˌɔ:l'seɪntsdeɪ] *s.* Aller'heiligen *n*; ♀ **Souls' Day** [ˌɔ:l'səʊlzdeɪ] *s.* Aller'seelen *n*; **ˌ~-'star** *adj. thea., sport* nur mit ersten Kräften besetzt: ~ ***cast*** Star-, Galabesetzung *f*; **ˌ~-'steel** *adj.* Ganzstahl…; **ˌ~-ter'rain** *adj. mot.* geländegängig, Gelände…; **ˌ~-'time** *adj.* **1.** bisher unerreicht, *der (die, das) beste etc.* aller Zeiten: ~ ***high*** Höchstleistung *f*, -stand *m*; ~ ***low*** Tiefststand *m*; **2.** hauptberuflich, Ganztags…: ~ ***job***.
al·lude [ə'lu:d] *v/i.* (***to***) anspielen, hinweisen (auf *acc.*); *et.* andeuten, erwähnen.
al·lure [ə'ljʊə] **I** *v/t.* **1.** (an-, ver)locken, gewinnen (***to*** für); abbringen (***from*** von); **2.** anziehen, reizen; **II** *s.* **3.** → **al'lure·ment** [-mənt] *s.* **1.** (Ver)Lokkung *f*; **2.** Lockmittel *n*, Köder *m*; **3.** Anziehungskraft *f*, Zauber *m*, Reiz *m*; **al'lur·ing** [-ərɪŋ] *adj.* ☐ verlockend, verführerisch.
al·lu·sion [ə'lu:ʒn] *s.* (***to***) Anspielung *f*, Hinweis *m* (auf *acc.*); Erwähnung *f*, Andeutung *f* (*gen.*); **al'lu·sive** [-u:sɪv] *adj.* ☐ anspielend, verblümt, vielsagend.
al·lu·vi·al [ə'lu:vjəl] *adj. geol.* angeschwemmt, alluvi'al; **al'lu·vi·on** [-ən] *s.* **1.** *geol.* Anschwemmung *f*; **2.** Alluvi'on *f*, angeschwemmtes Land; **al'lu·vi·um** [-əm] *pl.* **-vi·ums** *od.* **-vi·a** [-vjə] *s. geol.* Al'luvium *n*, Schwemmland *n*.
ˌall|-'wave *adj.* ⚡: ~ ***receiving set*** Allwellenempfänger *m*; **ˌ~-'weath·er** *adj.* ⚙ Allwetter…; **ˌ~-'wheel** *adj.* ⚙, *mot.* Allrad…
al·ly [ə'laɪ] **I** *v/t.* **1.** (*durch Heirat, Verwandtschaft, Ähnlichkeit*) vereinigen, verbinden (***to***, ***with*** mit); **2.** ~ ***o.s.*** sich verbinden *od.* verbünden (***with*** mit); **II** *v/i.* **3.** sich vereinigen, sich verbinden, sich verbünden (***to***, ***with*** mit); → ***allied***; **III** *s.* ['ælaɪ] **4.** Alliierte(r *m*) *f*, Verbündete(r *m*) *f*, Bundesgenosse *m*, Bundesgenossin *f* (*a. fig.*); **5.** ⚘, *zo.* verwandte Sippe.
al·ma·nac ['ɔ:lmənæk] *s.* 'Almanach *m*, Ka'lender *m*, Jahrbuch *n*.
al·might·y [ɔ:l'maɪtɪ] *adj.* **1.** allmächtig: ***the*** ♀ der Allmächtige; **2.** *a. adv.* F ‚riesig', ‚mächtig'.
al·mond ['ɑ:mənd] *s.* ⚘ Mandel *f*; Mandelbaum *m*; **'~-eyed** *adj.* mandeläugig.
al·mon·er ['ɑ:mənə] *s.* **1.** *hist.* 'Almosenpfleger *m*; **2.** *Brit.* Sozi'alarbeiter(in) im Krankenhaus.
al·most ['ɔ:lməʊst] *adv.* fast, beinahe.
alms [ɑ:mz] *s. sg. u. pl.* 'Almosen *n*; **'~·house** *s.* **1.** *Brit.* a) pri'vates Alten-

heim, b) privates Wohnheim für sozi'al Schwache; **2.** *hist.* Armenhaus *n*; '**~·man** [-mən] *s.* [*irr.*] *hist.* 'Almosenempfänger *m*.

al·oe ['æləʊ] *s.* **1.** ⚘ 'Aloe *f*; **2.** *pl. sg. konstr.* ⚕ Aloe *f* (*Abführmittel*).

a·loft [ə'lɒft] *adv.* **1.** *poet.* hoch (oben *od.* hin'auf), em'por, droben, in der *od.* die Höhe; **2.** ⚓ oben, in der *od.* die Takelung.

a·lone [ə'ləʊn] **I** *adj.* al'lein, einsam; → ***leave alone***, ***let alone***, ***let***[1] *Redew.*; **II** *adv.* allein, bloß, nur.

a·long [ə'lɒŋ] **I** *prp.* **1.** entlang, längs; **II** *adv.* **2.** entlang, längs; **3.** vorwärts, weiter: → ***get along***; **4.** zu'sammen (mit), mit, bei sich: ***take ~*** mitnehmen; ***come ~*** komm mit!, ‚komm doch schon!'; ***I'll be ~ in a few minutes*** ich werde in ein paar Minuten da sein; **5.** → ***all along***; **a,long'shore** *adv.* längs der Küste; **a,long'side I** *adv.* **1.** ⚓ längsseits; **2.** *fig.* (***of***, ***with***) verglichen (mit), im Vergleich (zu); **II** *prp.* **3.** längsseits (*gen.*); neben (*dat.*).

a·loof [ə'lu:f] **I** *adv.* fern, abseits, von fern: ***keep ~*** sich fernhalten (***from*** von), Distanz wahren; ***stand ~*** für sich bleiben; **II** *adj.* zu'rückhaltend, reser'viert; **a'loof·ness** [-nɪs] *s.* Zu'rückhaltung *f*, Reser'viertheit *f*, Dis'tanz *f*.

a·loud [ə'laʊd] *adv.* laut, mit lauter Stimme.

alp [ælp] *s.* Alp(e) *f*, Alm *f*.

al·pac·a [æl'pækə] *s.* **1.** *zo.* 'Pako *n*, Al'paka *n*; **2.** a) Al'pakawolle *f*, b) Al'pakastoff *m*.

'**al·pen|·glow** ['ælpən-] *s.* Alpenglühen *n*; '**~·horn** (*Ger.*) *s.* Alphorn *n*; '**~·stock** ['ælpɪn-] (*Ger.*) *s.* Bergstock *m*.

al·pha ['ælfə] *s.* **1.** 'Alpha *n*: ***the ~ and omega*** *fig.* das A u. O; **2.** ***~ particles*** (***rays***) *pl. phys.* 'Alphateilchen (-strahlen) *pl.*; **3.** *univ. Brit.* Eins *f* (*beste Note*): ***~ plus*** hervorragend.

al·pha·bet ['ælfəbɪt] *s.* **1.** Alpha'bet *n*, Abc *n*; **2.** *fig.* Anfangsgründe *pl.*, Abc *n*; **al·pha·bet·ic**, **al·pha·bet·i·cal** [,ælfə'betɪk(l)] *adj.* ☐ alpha'betisch: ***~ order*** alphabetische Reihenfolge.

Al·pine ['ælpaɪn] *adj.* **1.** Alpen...; **2.** al'pin, Hochgebirgs...: ***~ sun*** ⚕ Höhensonne *f*; ***~ combined*** *sport* Alpine Kombination; '**Al·pin·ism** [-pɪnɪzəm] *s.* **1.** Alpi'nismus *m*; **2.** al'piner Skisport; '**Al·pin·ist** [-pɪnɪst] *s.* Alpi'nist(in); **Alps** [ælps] *s. pl. die* Alpen *pl.*

al·read·y [ɔ:l'redɪ] *adv.* schon, bereits.

al·right [,ɔ:l'raɪt] *adv. Brit.* F *od. Am. für* ***all right***.

Al·sa·tian [æl'seɪʃjən] **I** *adj.* **1.** elsässisch; **II** *s.* **2.** Elsässer(in); **3.** *a.* ***~ dog*** (deutscher) Schäferhund.

al·so ['ɔ:lsəʊ] *adv.* auch, ferner, außerdem, ebenfalls; '**al·so-ran** *s.* **1.** *sport Rennteilnehmer* (*a. Pferd*), *der sich nicht plazieren kann*: ***she was an ~*** sie kam unter ‚ferner liefen' ein; **2.** F Versager *m*, Niete *f*.

al·tar ['ɔ:ltə] *s.* Al'tar *m*: ***lead to the ~*** zum Altar führen, heiraten; ***~ boy*** *s.* Mini'strant *m*; ***~ cloth*** *s.* Al'tardecke *f*; '**~-piece** *s.* Al'tarblatt *n*, -gemälde *n*; '**~-screen** *s. reichverzierte* Al'tarrückwand, Re'tabel *n*.

al·ter ['ɔ:ltə] **I** *v/t.* **1.** (ver)ändern, ab-, 'umändern; **2.** *Am. dial. Tiere* kastrieren; **II** *v/i.* **3.** sich (ver)ändern; '**al·ter·a·ble** [-tərəbl] *adj.* veränderlich, wandelbar; **al·ter·a·tion** [,ɔ:ltə'reɪʃn] *s.* **1.** (Ab-, 'Um-, Ver)Änderung *f*; **2.** *a. pl.* 'Umbau *m*.

al·ter·ca·tion [,ɔ:ltə'keɪʃn] *s.* heftige Ausein'andersetzung.

al·ter e·go [,æltər'egəʊ] (*Lat.*) *s.* Alter ego *n*: a) *das* andere Ich, b) *j-s* Busenfreund(in).

al·ter·nate [ɔ:l'tɜ:nət] **I** *adj.* ☐ → ***alternately***; **1.** (mitein'ander) abwechselnd, wechselseitig: ***on ~ days*** jeden zweiten Tag; **2.** ⚔ Ausweich...: ***~ position***; **II** *s.* **3.** *pol. Am.* Stellvertreter *m*; **III** *v/t.* ['ɔ:ltəneɪt] **4.** wechselweise tun; abwechseln lassen, *miteinander* vertauschen; **5.** ⚡, ⚙ peri'odisch verändern; **IV** *v/i.* ['ɔ:ltəneɪt] **6.** abwechseln, alternieren; **7.** ⚡ wechseln; **al'ter·nate·ly** [-lɪ] *adv.* abwechselnd, wechselweise; **al·ter·nat·ing** ['ɔ:ltəneɪtɪŋ] *adj.* abwechselnd, Wechsel...: ***~ current*** ⚡ Wechselstrom *m*; ***~ voltage*** ⚡ Wechselspannung *f*; **al·ter·na·tion** [,ɔ:ltə'neɪʃn] *s.* Abwechslung *f*, Wechsel *m*; **al'ter·na·tive** [-nətɪv] **I** *adj.* ☐ → ***alternatively***; **1.** alterna'tiv, die Wahl lassend, ein'ander ausschließend, nur 'eine Möglichkeit lassend; **2.** ander(er, e, es) (*von zweien*), Ersatz..., Ausweich...: ***~ airport*** Ausweichflughafen *m*; **II** *s.* **3.** Alterna'tive *f*, Wahl *f*: ***have no*** (***other***) ***~*** keine andere Möglichkeit *od.* Wahl *od.* keinen anderen Ausweg haben; **al'ter·na·tive·ly** [-nətɪvlɪ] *adv.* im anderen Falle, ersatz-, hilfsweise; **al·ter·na·tor** ['ɔ:ltəneɪtə] *s.* ⚡ 'Wechselstromma,schine *f*.

al·tho [ɔ:l'ðəʊ] *Am.* → ***although***.

alt-horn ['ælthɔ:n] *s.* ♪ Althorn *n*.

al·though [ɔ:l'ðəʊ] *cj.* ob'wohl, ob'gleich, wenn auch.

al·tim·e·ter ['æltɪmi:tə] *s. phys.* Höhenmesser *m*.

al·ti·tude ['æltɪtju:d] *s.* **1.** Höhe *f* (*bsd. über dem Meeresspiegel, a.* ⛰, ✈, *ast.*): ***~ control*** Höhensteuerung *f*; ***~ flight*** Höhenflug *m*; ***~ of the sun*** Sonnenstand *m*; **2.** *mst pl.* hochgelegene Gegend, (Berg)Höhen *pl.*; **3.** *fig.* Erhabenheit *f*.

al·to ['æltəʊ] *pl.* '**al·tos** (*Ital.*) *s.* ♪ **1.** Alt *m*, Altstimme *f*; **2.** Al'tist(in), Altsänger(in).

al·to·geth·er [,ɔ:ltə'geðə] **I** *adv.* **1.** völlig, gänzlich, ganz u. gar *schlecht etc.*; **2.** insgesamt, im ganzen genommen; **II** *s.* **3.** ***in the ~*** splitternackt.

al·to-re·lie·vo [,æltəʊrɪ'li:vəʊ] (*Ital.*) *s.* 'Hochreli,ef *n*.

al·tru·ism ['æltrʊɪzəm] *s.* Altru'ismus *m*, Nächstenliebe *f*, Uneigennützigkeit *f*; '**al·tru·ist** [-ɪst] *s.* Altru'ist(in); **al·tru·is·tic** [,æltrʊ'ɪstɪk] *adj.* (☐ **~ally**) altru'istisch, uneigennützig, selbstlos.

al·um ['æləm] *s.* ⚗ A'laun *m*.

a·lu·mi·na [ə'lju:mɪnə] *s.* ⚗ Tonerde *f*.

al·u·min·i·um [,ælj'ʊmɪnjəm], *Am.* **a·lu·mi·num** [ə'lu:mɪnəm] *s.* ⚗ Alu'minium *n*.

a·lum·na [ə'lʌmnə] *pl.* **-nae** [-ni:] *s.* ehemalige Stu'dentin *od.* Schülerin; **a'lum·nus** [-nəs] *pl.* **-ni** [naɪ] *s.* ehemaliger Stu'dent *od.* Schüler.

al·ve·o·lar [æl'vɪələ] *adj.* **1.** *anat.* alveo'lär, das Zahnfach betreffend; **2.** *ling.* alveo'lar, am Zahndamm artikuliert; **al·ve·o·lus** [æl'vɪələs] *pl.* **-li** [-laɪ] *s. anat.* Alve'ole *f*: a) Zahnfach *n*, b) Zungenbläs-chen *n*.

al·ways ['ɔ:lweɪz] *adv.* **1.** immer, stets, jederzeit; **2.** F auf jeden Fall, immer'hin.

a·lys·sum ['ælɪsəm] *s.* ⚘ Steinkraut *n*.

am [æm; əm] *1. sg. pres. von* **be**.

a·mal·gam [ə'mælgəm] *s.* **1.** Amal'gam *n*; **2.** *fig.* Mischung *f*, Gemenge *n*, Verschmelzung *f*; **a'mal·gam·ate** [-meɪt] **I** *v/t.* **1.** amalgamieren; **2.** *fig.* vereinigen, verschmelzen; zs.-legen, zs.-schließen, ⚜ fusionieren; **II** *v/i.* **3.** sich amalgamieren; **4.** sich vereinigen, verschmelzen, sich zs.-schließen, ⚜ fusionieren; **a·mal·gam·a·tion** [ə,mælgə'meɪʃn] *s.* **1.** Amalgamieren *n*; **2.** Vereinigung *f*, Verschmelzung *f*, Mischung *f*; **3.** *bsd.* ⚜ Zs.-schluß *m*, Fusi'on *f*.

a·man·u·en·sis [ə,mænjʊ'ensɪs] *pl.* **-ses** [-si:z] *s.* Amanu'ensis *m*, (Schreib)Gehilfe *m*, Sekre'tär(in).

am·a·ranth ['æmərænθ] *s.* **1.** ⚘ Ama'rant *m*, Fuchsschwanz *m*; **2.** *poet.* unverwelkliche Blume; **3.** Ama'rantfarbe *f*, Purpurrot *n*.

am·a·ryl·lis [,æmə'rɪlɪs] *s.* ⚘ Ama'ryllis *f*, Nar'zissenlilie *f*.

a·mass [ə'mæs] *v/t. bsd. Geld etc.* an-, aufhäufen, ansammeln.

am·a·teur ['æmətə] *s.* Ama'teur *m*: a) (Kunst- *etc.*)Liebhaber *m*, b) Amateursportler(in): ***~ flying*** Sportfliegerei *f*, c) Nichtfachmann *m*, *contp.* Dilet'tant *m*, Stümper *m* (***at painting*** im Malen), d) Bastler *m*; **am·a·teur·ish** [,æmə'tɜ:rɪʃ] *adj.* ☐ dilet'tantisch; '**am·a·teur·ism** [-ərɪzəm] *s.* **1.** *sport* Amateu'rismus *m*; **2.** Dilet'tantentum *n*.

am·a·tive ['æmətɪv] *adj.*, '**am·a·to·ry** [-tərɪ] → ***amorous***.

a·maze [ə'meɪz] *v/t.* in Staunen setzen, verblüffen, über'raschen; **a'mazed** [-zd] *adj.*; **a'maz·ed·ly** [-zɪdlɪ] *adv.* erstaunt, verblüfft (***at*** über *acc.*); **a'maze·ment** [-mənt] *s.* (Er)Staunen *n*, Verblüffung *f*, Verwunderung *f*; **a'maz·ing** [-zɪŋ] *adj.* ☐ erstaunlich, verblüffend; unglaublich, ‚toll'.

Am·a·zon ['æməzən] *s.* **1.** *antiq.* Ama'zone *f*; **2.** ♀ *fig.* Ama'zone *f*, Mannweib *n*; **Am·a·zo·ni·an** [,æmə'zəʊnjən] *adj.* **1.** ama'zonenhaft, Amazonen...; **2.** *geogr.* Amazonas...

am·bas·sa·dor [æm'bæsədə] *s.* **1.** *pol.* a) Botschafter *m* (*a. fig.*), b) Gesandte(r) *m*; **2.** Abgesandte(r) *m*, Bote *m* (*a. fig.*): ***~ of peace***; **am·bas·sa·do·ri·al** [æm,bæsə'dɔ:rɪəl] *adj.* Botschafts...; **am'bas·sa·dress** [-drɪs] *s.* **1.** Botschafterin *f*; **2.** Gattin *f* e-s Botschafters.

am·ber ['æmbə] **I** *s.* **1.** *min.* Bernstein *m*; **2.** Gelb *n*, gelbes Licht (*Verkehrsampel*): ***at ~*** bei Gelb; ***the lights were at ~*** die Ampel stand auf Gelb; **II** *adj.* **3.** Bernstein...; **4.** bernsteinfarben.

am·ber·gris ['æmbəgri:s] *s.* (graue) Ambra.

am·bi·dex·trous [,æmbɪ'dekstrəs] *adj.* ☐ **1.** beidhändig; **2.** mit beiden Händen gleich geschickt, *weitS.* ungewöhnlich geschickt; **3.** doppelzüngig, 'hinterhältig.

am·bi·ence ['æmbɪəns] *s. Kunst*: Am-bi'ente *n*, *fig. a.* a) Mili'eu *n*, 'Umwelt *f*, b) Atmo'sphäre *f*; **'am·bi·ent** [-nt] *adj.* um'gebend, um'kreisend; ⚙ Umge-bungs…(*-temperatur etc.*), Neben… (*-geräusch*).

am·bi·gu·i·ty [ˌæmbɪ'gju:ɪtɪ] *s.* Zwei-, Vieldeutigkeit *f*, Doppelsinn *m*; Un-klarheit *f*; **am·big·u·ous** [æm'bɪgjʊəs] *adj.* □ zweideutig; unklar.

am·bit ['æmbɪt] *s.* **1.** 'Umkreis *m*; **2.** a) Um'gebung *f*, b) Grenzen *pl.*; **3.** *fig.* Bereich *m*.

am·bi·tion [æm'bɪʃn] *s.* Ehrgeiz *m*, Am-biti'on *f* (*beide a. Gegenstand des Ehr-geizes*); Streben *n*, Begierde *f*, Wunsch *m* (**of** nach *od. inf.*), Ziel *n*, *pl.* Bestre-bungen *pl.*; **am'bi·tious** [-ʃəs] *adj.* □ **1.** ehrgeizig (*a. Plan etc.*); **2.** strebsam; begierig (**of** nach); **3.** ambiti'ös, an-spruchsvoll.

am·bi·va·lence [ˌæmbɪ'veɪləns] *s. psych., phys.* Ambiva'lenz *f*, Doppel-wertigkeit *f*; *fig.* Zwiespältigkeit *f*; **ˌam-bi'va·lent** [-nt] *adj. bes. psych.* ambiva-'lent.

am·ble ['æmbl] **I** *v/i.* im Paßgang gehen *od.* reiten; *fig.* schlendern; **II** *s.* Paß(-gang) *m* (*Pferd*); *fig.* gemächlicher (Spazier)Gang, Schlendern *n*.

am·bro·si·a [æm'brəʊzjə] *s. antiq.* Am-'brosia *f*, Götterspeise *f* (*a. fig.*); **am-'bro·si·al** [-əl] *adj.* □ am'brosisch; *fig.* köstlich (duftend).

am·bu·lance ['æmbjʊləns] *s.* **1.** Ambu-'lanz *f*, Kranken-, Sani'tätswagen *m*; **2.** ⚔ 'Feldlazaˌrett *n*; **~ bat·tal·ion** *s.* ⚔ 'Krankentransˌportbataiˌlon *n*; **~ box** *s.* Verbandskasten *m*; **~ sta·tion** *s.* Sani-'tätswache *f*, 'Unfallstatiˌon *f*.

am·bu·lant ['æmbjʊlənt] *adj.* ambu'lant: a) wandernd: **~ trade** Wandergewerbe *n*, b) ⚕ gehfähig: **~ patients**; **~ treat-ment** ambulante Behandlung; **'am·bu-la·to·ry** [-ətərɪ] **I** *adj.* **1.** beweglich, (orts)veränderlich; **2.** → **ambulant**; **II** *s.* **3.** Ar'kade *f*, Wandelgang *m*.

am·bus·cade [ˌæmbəs'keɪd], **am·bush** ['æmbʊʃ] **I** *s.* **1.** 'Hinterhalt *m*; **2.** im 'Hinterhalt liegende Truppen *pl.*; **II** *v/i.* **3.** im 'Hinterhalt liegen; **III** *v/t.* **4.** in e-n 'Hinterhalt legen; **5.** aus dem 'Hin-terhalt über'fallen, auflauern (*dat.*).

a·me·ba, a·me·bic *Am.* → **amoeba, amoebic.**

a·mel·io·rate [ə'mi:ljəreɪt] **I** *v/t.* verbes-sern (*bsd.* ✓); **II** *v/i.* besser werden, sich bessern; **a·mel·io·ra·tion** [əˌmi:l-jə'reɪʃn] *s.* (✓ Boden)Verbesserung *f*.

a·men [ˌɑ:'men; ˌeɪ'men] **I** *int.* 'amen!; **II** *s.* 'Amen *n*.

a·me·na·ble [ə'mi:nəbl] *adj.* □ (**to**) **1.** zugänglich (*dat.*): **~ to flattery**; **2.** gefü-gig; **3.** unter'worfen (*dat.*): **~ to a fine**; **4.** verantwortlich (*dat.*).

a·mend [ə'mend] **I** *v/t.* **1.** (ver)bessern, berichtigen; **2.** *Gesetz etc.* (ab)ändern, ergänzen; **II** *v/i.* **3.** sich bessern (*bsd. Betragen*).

a·mende ho·no·ra·ble [amɑ̃:d ɔnɔrabl] (*Fr.*) *s.* öffentliche Ehrenerklärung *od.* Abbitte.

a·mend·ment [ə'mendmənt] *s.* **1.** (*bsd. sittliche*) Besserung; **2.** Verbesserung *f*, Berichtigung *f*, Neufassung *f*; **3.** *bsd.* ⚖, *parl.* (Ab)Änderungs-, Ergänzungs-antrag *m* (*zu e-m Gesetz*), *Am.* 'Zusatz-arˌtikel *m* zur Verfassung, Nachtragsge-setz *n*: **the Fifth ~.**

a·mends [ə'mendz] *s. pl. sg. konstr.* (Schaden)Ersatz *m*, Genugtuung *f*: **make ~** Schadenersatz leisten, es wie-dergutmachen.

a·men·i·ty [ə'mi:nətɪ] *s.* **1.** Annehmlich-keit *f*, angenehme Lage; **2.** Anmut *f*, Liebenswürdigkeit *f*; **3.** *pl.* Konventi'on *f*, Eti'kette *f*; Höflichkeiten *pl.*; **4.** *pl.* (na'türliche) Vorzüge *pl.*, Reize *pl.*, Annehmlichkeiten *pl.*

Am·er·a·sian [ˌæmə'reɪʃjən] *adj. u. s.* (Per'son *f*) ameri'kanisch-asi'atischer Abstammung.

A·mer·i·can [ə'merɪkən] **I** *adj.* **1.** a) ameri'kanisch, b) die USA betreffend: **the ~ navy**; **II** *s.* **2.** a) Ameri'kaner(in), b) Bürger(in) der USA; **3.** Ameri'ka-nisch *n* (*Sprache der USA*); **A·mer·i-ca·na** [əˌmerɪ'kɑ:nə] *s. pl.* Ameri'kana *pl.* (*Schriften etc. über Amerika*).

A·mer·i·can| cloth *s.* Wachstuch *n*; **~ foot·ball** *s. sport* American Football *m* (*rugbyähnliches Spiel*); **~ In·di·an** *s.* In-di'aner(in).

A·mer·i·can·ism [ə'merɪkənɪzəm] *s.* **1.** Ameri'kanertum *n*; **2.** Amerika'nismus *m*: a) ameri'kanische Spracheigentüm-lichkeit, b) ameri'kanischer Brauch; **A·mer·i·can·i·za·tion** [əˌmerɪkənaɪ-'zeɪʃən] *s.* Amerikanisierung *f*; **A·mer-i·can·ize** [ə'merɪkənaɪz] **I** *v/t.* amerika-nisieren; **II** *v/i.* Ameri'kaner *od.* ameri-'kanisch werden.

A·mer·i·can| leath·er → **American cloth**; **~ Le·gion** *s. Am.* Frontkämpfer-bund *m*; **~ or·gan** *s.* ♪ Har'monium *n*; **~ plan** *s. Am.* 'Vollpensiˌon *f*.

Am·er·ind ['æmərɪnd], **Am·er·in·di·an** [ˌæmər'ɪndjən] *s.* ameri'kanischer In-di'aner *od.* 'Eskimo.

am·e·thyst ['æmɪθɪst] *s. min.* Ame'thyst *m*.

a·mi·a·bil·i·ty [ˌeɪmjə'bɪlətɪ] *s.* Freund-lichkeit *f*, Liebenswürdigkeit *f*; **a·mi·a-ble** ['eɪmjəbl] *adj.* □ liebenswürdig, freundlich, gewinnend, reizend.

am·i·ca·ble ['æmɪkəbl] *adj.* □ freund-(schaft)lich, friedlich: **~ settlement** gütliche Einigung; **'am·i·ca·bly** [-lɪ] *adv.* freundschaftlich, in Güte, gütlich.

a·mid [ə'mɪd] *prp.* in'mitten (*gen.*), (mit-ten) in *od.* unter (*dat. od. acc.*); **a'mid·ship(s)** [-ʃɪp(s)] ⚓ **I** *adv.* mitt-schiffs; **II** *adj.* in der Mitte des Schiffes (befindlich); **a'midst** [-st] → **amid.**

a·mine ['æmaɪn] *s.* ⚗ A'min *n*.

amino- [əmi:nəʊ] ⚗ *in Zssgn* Amino…: **~ acid.**

a·miss [ə'mɪs] **I** *adv.* verkehrt, verfehlt, schlecht: **take ~** übelnehmen; **II** *adj.* unpassend, verkehrt, falsch, übel: **there is s.th. ~** etwas stimmt nicht; **it would not be ~** es würde nicht schaden.

am·i·ty ['æmətɪ] *s.* Freundschaft *f*, gutes Einvernehmen.

am·me·ter ['æmɪtə] *s.* ⚡ Am'pereˌmeter *n*, Strom(stärke)messer *m*.

am·mo ['æməʊ] *s. sl.* Muniti'on *f*.

am·mo·ni·a [ə'məʊnjə] *s.* ⚗ Ammo-ni'ak *n*: **liquid ~** (*od.* **~ solution**) Sal-miakgeist *m*; **am'mo·ni·ac** [-nɪæk] *adj.* ammonia'kalisch: (**gum**) **~** Ammoniak-gummi *m, n*; → **sal.**

am·mo·ni·um [ə'məʊnjəm] s. ⚗ Am-'monium *n*; **~ car·bon·ate** *s.* ⚗ Hirschhornsalz *n*; **~ chlo·ride** *s.* ⚗ Am'moniumchloˌrid *n*, 'Salmiak *m*; **~ ni·trate** *s.* ⚗ Am'moniumniˌtrat *n*, Ammoni'aksalˌpeter *m*.

am·mu·ni·tion [ˌæmjʊ'nɪʃn] *s.* Muniti'on *f* (*a. fig.*): **~ belt** Patronengurt *m*; **~ carrier** Munitionswagen *m*; **~ dump** Munitionslager *n*.

am·ne·si·a [æm'ni:zjə] *s.* ⚕ Amne'sie *f*, Gedächtnisschwund *m*.

am·nes·ty ['æmnɪstɪ] **I** *s.* Amne'stie *f*, allgemeiner Straferlaß; **II** *v/t.* begnadi-gen, amnestieren.

a·moe·ba [ə'mi:bə] *s. zo.* A'möbe *f*; **a'moe·bic** [-bɪk] *adj.* a'möbisch: **~ dysentery** Amöbenruhr *f*.

a·mok [ə'mɒk] → **amuck.**

a·mong(st) [ə'mʌŋ(st)] *prp.* (mitten) unter (*dat. od. acc.*), in'mitten (*gen.*), zwischen (*dat. od. acc.*), bei: **who ~ you?** wer von euch?; **a custom ~ the savages** e-e Sitte bei den Wilden; **be ~ the best** zu den Besten gehören; **~ other things** unter anderem; **from among** aus der Zahl (derer), aus … heraus; **they had two pounds ~ them** sie hatten zusammen zwei Pfund.

a·mor·al [ˌeɪ'mɒrəl] *adj.* 'amoˌralisch.

am·o·rist ['æmərɪst] *s.* E'rotiker *m*: a) Herzensbrecher *m*, b) Verfasser *m* von 'Liebesroˌmanen *etc.*

am·o·rous ['æmərəs] *adj.* □ amou'rös: a) e'rotisch, sinnlich, Liebes…, b) lie-bebedürftig, verliebt (**of** in *acc.*); **'am·o·rous·ness** [-nɪs] *s.* amou'röse Art, Verliebtheit *f*.

a·mor·phous [ə'mɔ:fəs] *adj.* a'morph: a) formlos, b) ungestalt, c) *min.* 'unkri-stalˌlinisch.

a·mor·ti·za·tion [əˌmɔ:tɪ'zeɪʃn] *s.* **1.** Amortisierung *f*, Tilgung *f* (*von Schul-den*); **2.** Abschreibung *f* (*von Anlage-werten*); **3.** ⚖ Veräußerung *f* (*von Grundstücken*) an die tote Hand; **a·mor·tize** [ə'mɔ:taɪz] *v/t.* **1.** amortisie-ren, tilgen, abzahlen; **2.** ⚖ an die tote Hand veräußern.

a·mount [ə'maʊnt] **I** *v/i.* **1.** (**to**) sich be-laufen (auf *acc.*), betragen (*acc.*): **his debts ~ to £120**; **2.** hin'auslaufen (**to** auf *acc.*), bedeuten: **it ~s to the same thing** es läuft *od.* kommt auf dasselbe hinaus; **that doesn't ~ to much** das ist unbedeutend; **you'll never ~ to much** F aus dir wird nie etwas werden; **II** *s.* **3.** Betrag *m*, Summe *f*, Höhe *f* (*e-r Sum-me*); Menge *f*: **to the ~ of** bis zur *od.* in Höhe von, im Betrag *od.* Wert von; **net ~** Nettobetrag; **~ carried forward** Übertrag *m*; **4.** *fig.* Inhalt *m*, Ergebnis *n*, Wert *m*, Bedeutung *f*.

a·mour [ə'mʊə] (*Fr.*) *s.* Liebschaft *f*, A'mour *f*, ‚Verhältnis' *n*; **~-pro·pre** [ˌæmʊə'prɒprə] (*Fr.*) *s.* Eigenliebe *f*, Eitelkeit *f*.

amp [æmp] *s.* F **1.** a) → **ampere**, b) → **amplifier**; **2.** ♪ 'E-Giˌtarre *f*.

am·per·age [æm'peərɪdʒ] *s.* ⚡ Strom-stärke *f*, Am'perezahl *f*; **am·pere, am-père** ['æmpeə] (*Fr.*) *s.* ⚡ Am'pere *n*; **~ me·ter** → **ammeter.**

am·per·sand ['æmpəsænd] *s. typ.* das Zeichen & (*abbr. für* **and**).

am·phet·a·mine [æm'fetəmɪn] *s.* ⚗ Ampheta'min *n*.

amphi- [æmfɪ] *in Zssgn* doppelt, zwei…,

zweiseitig, beiderseitig, umher…
Am·phib·i·a [æm'fɪbɪə] *s. pl. zo.* Am'phibien *pl.*, Lurche *pl.*; **am'phibi·an** [-ən] **I** *adj.* **1.** *zo.*, *a.* ⚔, ⚙ am'phibisch, Amphibien…; **II** *s.* **2.** *zo.* Am'phibie *f*, Lurch *m*; **3.** a) Am'phibienflugzeug *n*, b) Am'phibien-, Schwimmfahrzeug *n*, c) ⚔ Schwimmkampfwagen *m*; **am'phib·i·ous** [-əs] *adj.* **1.** → ***amphibian*** 1: ~ ***landing*** amphibische Landung *od.* Operation; ~ ***tank*** → ***amphibian*** 3 c; ~ ***vehicle*** → ***amphibian*** 3 b; **3.** von gemischter Na'tur, zweierlei Wesen habend.
am·phi·the·a·tre, *Am.* **am·phi·the·a·ter** ['æmfɪˌθɪətə] *s.* Am'phitheˌater *n* (*a. fig. Gebäudeteil od. Tal etc. in der Form e-s Amphitheaters*).
am·pho·ra ['æmfərə] *pl.* **-rae** [-riː] *od.* **-ras** (*Lat.*) *s.* Am'phore *f.*
am·ple ['æmpl] *adj.* □ → ***amply***; **1.** weit, groß, geräumig; weitläufig; stattlich (*Figur*), üppig (*Busen*); **2.** ausführlich, um'fassend; **3.** reich(lich), mehr als genug, (vollauf) genügend: ~ ***means*** reich(lich)e Mittel; **'am·ple·ness** [-nɪs] *s.* **1.** Weite *f*, Geräumigkeit *f*; **2.** Reichlichkeit *f*, Fülle *f*.
am·pli·fi·ca·tion [ˌæmplɪfɪ'keɪʃn] *s.* **1.** Erweiterung *f*, Vergrößerung *f*, Ausdehnung *f*; **2.** weitere Ausführung, Weitschweifigkeit *f*, Ausschmückung *f*; **3.** ↯, *Radio, phys.* Vergrößerung *f*, Verstärkung *f*.
am·pli·fi·er ['æmplɪfaɪə] *s.* **1.** *phys.* Vergrößerungslinse *f*; **2.** *Radio, phys.* Verstärker *m*: ~ ***tube*** (*od.* ***valve***) Verstärkerröhre *f*; **am·pli·fy** ['æmplɪfaɪ] **I** *v/t.* **1.** erweitern, vergrößern, ausdehnen; **2.** ausmalen, -schmücken; weitläufig darstellen; näher ausführen *od.* erläutern; **3.** *Radio, phys.* verstärken; **II** *v/i.* **4.** sich weitläufig ausdrücken *od.* auslassen; **'am·pli·tude** [-tjuːd] *s.* **1.** Weite *f*, 'Umfang *m* (*a. fig.*), Reichlichkeit *f*, Fülle *f*; **2.** *phys.* Ampli'tude *f*, Schwingungsweite *f* (*Pendel etc.*).
am·ply ['æmplɪ] *adv.* reichlich.
am·poule ['æmpuːl] *s.* Am'pulle *f*.
am·pul·la [æm'pʊlə] *pl.* **-lae** [-liː] *s.* **1.** *antiq.* Am'pulle *f*, Phi'ole *f*, Salbengefäß *n*; **2.** Blei- *od.* Glasflasche *f der Pilger*; **3.** *eccl.* Krug *m* für Wein u. Wasser (*Messe*); Gefäß *n* für das heilige Öl (*Salbung*).
am·pu·tate ['æmpjʊteɪt] *v/t.* **1.** *Bäume* stutzen; **2.** ⚕ amputieren (*a. fig.*), *ein Glied* abnehmen; **am·pu·ta·tion** [ˌæmpjʊ'teɪʃn] *s.* Amputati'on *f*; **'am·pu·tee** [-tiː] *s.* Ampu'tierte(r *m*) *f*.
a·muck [ə'mʌk] *adv.*: ***run*** ~ Amok laufen, *fig. a.* blindwütig rasen (***at***, ***on***, ***against*** gegen *et.*).
am·u·let ['æmjʊlɪt] *s.* Amu'lett *n*.
a·muse [ə'mjuːz] *v/t.* (***o.s.*** sich) amüsieren, unter'halten, belustigen: ***you ~ me!*** da muß ich (über dich) lachen!; ***be ~d*** sich freuen (***at***, ***by***, ***in***, ***with*** über *acc.*); ***it ~s them*** es macht ihnen Spaß; ***he ~s himself with gardening*** er gärtnert zu s-m Vergnügen; **a'mused** [-zd] *adj.* amüsiert, belustigt, erfreut; **a'muse·ment** [-mənt] *s.* Unter'haltung *f*, Belustigung *f*, Vergnügen *n*, Freude *f*, Zeitvertreib *m*: ***to the ~ of*** zur Belustigung (*gen.*); ~ ***arcade*** *Brit.* Spielsalon *m*; ~ ***park*** Vergnügungspark *m*; **a'mus·ing** [-zɪŋ] *adj.* □ amü'sant, unter'haltsam; 'komisch.
am·yl ['æmɪl] *s.* ⚗ A'myl *n*; **am·y·la·ceous** [ˌæmɪ'leɪʃəs] *adj.* stärkemehlartig, stärkehaltig.
an [æn; ən] *unbestimmter Artikel* (*vor Vokalen od. stummem h*) ein, eine.
an·a·bap·tism [ˌænə'bæptɪzəm] *s.* Ana-bap'tismus *m*; **ˌan·a'bap·tist** [-ɪst] *s.* Wiedertäufer *m*.
an·a·bol·ic [ˌænə'bɒlɪk] *s.* ⚕ Ana'bolikum *n*.
a·nach·ro·nism [ə'nækrənɪzəm] *s.* Anachro'nismus *m*; **a·nach·ro·nis·tic** [əˌnækrə'nɪstɪk] *adj.* (□ ~***ally***) anachro'nistisch.
a·nae·mi·a [ə'niːmjə] *s.* ⚕ Anä'mie *f*, Blutarmut *f*, Bleichsucht *f*; **a'nae·mic** [-mɪk] *adj.* **1.** ⚕ blutarm, bleichsüchtig, an'ämisch; **2.** *fig.* farblos, blaß.
an·aes·the·si·a [ˌænɪs'θiːzjə] *s.* ⚕ **1.** Anästhe'sie *f*, Nar'kose *f*, Betäubung *f*; **2.** Unempfindlichkeit *f* (*gegen Schmerz*); **ˌan·aes'thet·ic** [-'θetɪk] **I** *adj.* (□ ~***ally***) nar'kotisch, betäubend, Narkose…; **II** *s.* Betäubungsmittel *n*; **an·aes·the·tist** [æ'niːsθətɪst] *s.* Anästhe'sist *m*, Nar'kosearzt *m*; **an·aes·the·tize** [æ'niːsθətaɪz] *v/t.* betäuben, narkotisieren.
an·a·gram ['ænəgræm] *s.* Ana'gramm *n*.
a·nal ['eɪnl] *adj. anat.* a'nal, Anal…
an·a·lects ['ænəlekts] *s. pl.* Ana'lekten *pl.*, Lesefrüchte *pl.*
an·al·ge·si·a [ˌænæl'dʒiːzjə] *s.* ⚕ Unempfindlichkeit *f* gegen Schmerz, Schmerzlosigkeit *f*; **ˌan·al'ge·sic** [-'dʒesɪk] **I** *adj.* schmerzlindernd; **II** *s.* schmerzlinderndes Mittel.
an·a·log·ic, **an·a·log·i·cal** [ˌænə'lɒdʒɪk(l)] *adj.* □, **a·nal·o·gous** [ə'næləgəs] *adj.* □ ana'log, ähnlich, entsprechend, paral'lel (***to*** *dat.*); **an·a·logue** ['ænəlɒg] *s.* A'nalogon *n*, Entsprechung *f*: ~ ***computer*** Analogrechner *m*; **a·nal·o·gy** [ə'nælədʒɪ] *s.* **1.** *a. ling.* Analo'gie *f*, Entsprechung *f*: ***on the ~ of*** (*od.* ***by ~ with***) analog, nach, gemäß (*dat.*); **2.** ♣ Proporti'on *f*.
an·a·lyse ['ænəlaɪz] *v/t.* **1.** analysieren: a) ⚗, ♣, *psych. etc.* zergliedern, zerlegen, b) *fig.* genau unter'suchen, c) erläutern, darlegen; **a·nal·y·sis** [ə'næləsɪs] *pl.* **-ses** [-siːz] *s.* **1.** Ana'lyse *f*: a) ⚗ *etc.* Zerlegung *f*, ('kritische) Zergliederung, b) *fig.* gründliche Unter'suchung, Darlegung *f*, Deutung *f*: ***in the last ~*** im Grunde, letzten Endes; **2.** ♣ A'nalysis *f*; **3.** (Psycho)Ana'lyse *f*; **'an·a·lyst** [-lɪst] *s.* **1.** ⚗, ♣ Ana'lytiker(in); *fig.* Unter'sucher(in): ***public ~*** (behördlicher) Lebensmittelchemiker; **2.** Psychoana'lytiker *m*; **3.** Sta'tistiker *m*; **an·a·lyt·ic**, **an·a·lyt·i·cal** [ˌænə'lɪtɪk(l)] *adj.* □ **1.** ana'lytisch: ***analytical chemist*** Chemiker(in); **2.** psychoana'lytisch; **an·a·lyt·ics** [ˌænə'lɪtɪks] *s. pl. sg. konstr.* Ana'lytik *f*.
an·a·lyze *bsd. Am.* → ***analyse***.
an·am·ne·sis [ˌænæm'niːsɪs] *pl.* **-ses** [-siːz] *s.* Anam'nese *f*: a) Wiedererinnerung *f*, b) ⚕ Vorgeschichte *f*.
an·aph·ro·dis·i·ac [æˌnæfrəʊ'dɪzɪæk] ⚕ **I** *adj.* den Geschlechtstrieb hemmend; **II** *s.* Anaphrodi'siakum *n*.
an·ar·chic, **an·ar·chi·cal** [æ'nɑːkɪk(l)] *adj.* □ an'archisch, anar'chistisch, gesetzlos, zügellos.
an·arch·ism ['ænəkɪzəm] *s.* **1.** Anar'chie *f*, Regierungs-, Gesetzlosigkeit *f*; **2.** Anar'chismus *m*; **'an·arch·ist** [-ɪst] **I** *s.* Anar'chist(in), 'Umstürzler *m*; **II** *adj.* anar'chistisch, 'umstürzlerisch.
an·ar·cho- [ænɑːkəʊ] *in Zssgn* Anarcho…: ~***-scene***; ~***-situationist*** Chaote *m*.
an·arch·y ['ænəkɪ] *s.* **1.** → ***anarchism***; **2.** *fig.* 'Chaos *n*.
an·as·tig·mat·ic [əˌnæstɪg'mætɪk] *adj. phys.* anastig'matisch (*Linse*).
a·nath·e·ma [ə'næθəmə] (*Greek*) *s.* **1.** *eccl.* A'nathema *n*, Kirchenbann *m*; *fig.* Fluch *m*, Verwünschung *f*; **2.** *eccl.* Exkommunizierte(r *m*) *f*, Verfluchte(r *m*) *f*; **3.** *fig. etwas* Verhaßtes, Greuel *m*; **a'nath·e·ma·tize** [-ətaɪz] *v/t.* in den Bann tun, verfluchen.
an·a·tom·ic, **an·a·tom·i·cal** [ˌænə'tɒmɪk(l)] *adj.* □ ana'tomisch.
a·nat·o·mist [ə'nætəmɪst] *s.* **1.** Ana'tom *m*; **2.** Zergliederer *m* (*a. fig.*); **a'nat·o·mize** [-maɪz] *v/t.* **1.** ⚕ zerlegen, sezieren; **2.** *fig.* zergliedern; **a'nat·o·my** [-mɪ] *s.* **1.** Anato'mie *f* (*Aufbau, Wissenschaft, Abhandlung*); **2.** F a) ‚Wanst' *m*, Körper *m*, b) ‚Gerippe' *n*, Gestell *n*.
an·ces·tor ['ænsestə] *s.* **1.** Vorfahr *m*, Ahn(herr) *m*, Stammvater *m* (*a. fig.*): ~ ***worship*** Ahnenkult *m*; **2.** *fig.* Vorläufer *m*; **3.** ⚖ Vorbesitzer *m*; **an·ces·tral** [æn'sestrəl] *adj.* der Vorfahren, Ahnen…, angestammt, Erb…, Ur…; **'an·ces·tress** [-trɪs] *s.* Ahnfrau *f*, Stammmutter *f*; **'an·ces·try** [-trɪ] *s.* Abstammung *f*, *hohe* Geburt; Ahnen(reihe *f*) *pl*; *fig.* Vorgänger *pl.*: ~ ***research*** Ahnenforschung *f*.
an·chor ['æŋkə] **I** *s.* **1.** ⚓ Anker *m*: ***at ~*** vor Anker; ***weigh ~*** a) den Anker lichten, b) abfahren; ***cast*** (*od.* ***drop***) ~ ankern, vor Anker gehen; ***ride at ~*** vor Anker liegen; **2.** *fig.* Rettungsanker *m*, Zuflucht *f*; **3.** ⚙ Anker *m*, Schließe *f*, Klammer *f*; **4.** *Radio, TV*: *Am.* a) Mode'rator *m*, Modera'torin *f e-r Nachrichtensendung*, b) Diskussi'onsleiter (-in); **5.** *sport*: a) Schlußläufer(in), b) Schlußschwimmer(in); **II** *v/t.* **6.** verankern, vor Anker legen; **7.** ⚙ *u. fig.* verankern; **8.** *Radio, TV*: *Am.* a) *e-e Nachrichtensendung* moderieren, b) *e-e Diskussion* leiten; **9.** Schlußläufer(in) *od.* -schwimmer(in) *e-r Staffel* sein; **III** *v/i.* **10.** ankern, vor Anker gehen *od.* liegen; **11.** *Radio, TV*: *Am.* Moderator (-in) *od.* Diskussi'onsleiter(in) sein.
an·chor·age ['æŋkərɪdʒ] *s.* **1.** Ankerplatz *m*; **2.** *a.* ~***-dues*** Anker-, Liegegebühr *f*; **3.** fester Halt, Verankerung *f*; **4.** *fig.* → ***anchor*** 2.
an·cho·ress ['æŋkərɪs] *s.* Einsiedlerin *f*; **'an·cho·ret** [-ret], **'an·cho·rite** [-raɪt] *s.* Einsiedler *m*.
'an·chor|·man [-mən] *s.* [*irr.*], **'~wo·man** *s* [*irr.*] → ***anchor*** 4, 5.
an·cho·vy ['æntʃəvɪ] *s. ichth.* An'(s)chovis *f*, Sar'delle *f*.
an·cient ['eɪnʃənt] **I** *adj.* □ **1.** alt, aus alter Zeit, das Altertum betreffend, an'tik: ~ ***Rome***; **2.** uralt (*a. humor.*), altberühmt; **3.** altertümlich; ehemalig; **II** *s.* **4.** ***the ~s*** a) die Alten (*Griechen u. Römer*), b) die (antiken) Klassiker; **5.** Alte(r *m*) *f*, Greis(in); F ‚Olle(r' *m*) *f*;

ˈ**an·cient·ly** [-lɪ] *adv.* vorˈzeiten.

an·cil·lar·y [ænˈsɪlərɪ] *adj.* ˈuntergeordnet (*to dat.*), Hilfs…, Neben…: ~ ***equipment*** Zusatz-, Hilfsgerät *n*; ~ ***industries*** Zulieferbetriebe; ~ ***road*** Nebenstraße *f*.

and [ænd; ən(d)] *cj.* und: ~ ***so forth*** und so weiter; ***there are books ~ books*** es gibt gute und schlechte Bücher; ***nice ~ warm*** schön warm; ~ ***all*** F und so weiter; ***skin ~ all*** mitsamt der Haut; ***a little more ~ …*** es fehlte nicht viel, so …; ***try ~ come*** versuchen Sie zu kommen.

and·i·ron [ˈændaɪən] *s.* Feuer-, Brat-, Kaˈminbock *m*.

An·drew [ˈændruː] *npr.* Anˈdreas *m*: ***St. ~'s cross*** Andreaskreuz *n*.

an·drog·y·nous [ænˈdrɒdʒɪnəs] *adj.* zwitterartig, zweigeschlechtig; ⚘ zwitterblütig.

an·droid [ˈændrɔɪd] *s.* Androˈid(e) *m* (*Kunstmensch*).

an·droph·a·gous [ænˈdrɒfəgəs] *adj.* menschenfressend.

an·dro·pho·bi·a [ˌændrəʊˈfəʊbjə] *s.* Androphoˈbie *f*, Männerscheu *f*.

an·ec·do·tal [ˌænekˈdəʊtl] → ***anecdotic***; **an·ec·dote** [ˈænɪkdəʊt] *s.* Anekˈdote *f*; **an·ec·dot·ic**, **an·ec·dot·i·cal** [ˌænekˈdɒtɪk(l)] *adj.* □ anekˈdotenhaft, anekˈdotisch.

a·ne·mi·a, **a·ne·mic** *Am.* → ***anaemia***, ***anaemic***.

an·e·mom·e·ter [ˌænɪˈmɒmɪtə] *s. phys.* Windmesser *m*.

a·nem·o·ne [əˈnemənɪ] *s.* **1.** ⚘ Aneˈmone *f*; **2.** *zo.* ˈSeeaneˌmone *f*.

an·er·oid [ˈænərɔɪd] *s. phys. a.* ~ ***barometer*** Aneroˈidbaroˌmeter *n*.

an·es·the·si·a *etc. Am.* → ***anaesthesia*** *etc.*

a·new [əˈnjuː] *adv.* von neuem, aufs neue; auf neue Art und Weise.

an·gel [ˈeɪndʒəl] *s.* **1.** Engel *m*: ~ ***of death*** Todesengel; ***rush in where ~s fear to tread*** sich törichter- *od.* anmaßenderweise in Dinge einmischen, an die sich sonst niemand heranwagt; **2.** *fig.* Engel *m* (*Person*): ***be an ~ and …*** sei doch so lieb und …; **3.** *sl.* Geldgeber *m*, fiˈnanzkräftiger ˈHintermann.

ˈ**an·gel|·food** *Am.*, ˈ**~-cake** *s. Art* Bisˈkuitkuchen *m*.

an·gel·ic [ænˈdʒelɪk] *adj.* (□ ***~ally***) engelhaft, -gleich, Engels…

an·gel·i·ca [ænˈdʒelɪkə] *s.* **1.** ⚘ Brustwurz *f* (*als Gewürz*); **2.** kandierte Anˈgelikawurzel.

an·gel·i·cal [ænˈdʒelɪkl] *adj.* □ → ***angelic***.

An·ge·lus [ˈændʒɪləs] *s. eccl.* ˈAngelus (-gebet *n*, -läuten *n*) *m*.

an·ger [ˈæŋgə] **I** *s.* Ärger *m*, Zorn *m*, Wut *f* (***at*** über *acc.*); **II** *v/t.* erzürnen, ärgern.

An·ge·vin [ˈændʒɪvɪn] **I** *adj.* **1.** aus Anˈjou (*in Frankreich*); **2.** die Planˈtagenets betreffend; **II** *s.* **3.** Mitglied *n* des Hauses Planˈtagenet.

an·gi·na [ænˈdʒaɪnə] *s.* ⚕ Anˈgina *f*, Halsentzündung *f*; ~ **pec·to·ris** [ˈpektərɪs] *s.* ⚕ Anˈgina *f* ˈpectoris.

an·gle¹ [ˈæŋgl] **I** *s.* **1.** *bsd.* ⩓ Winkel *m*: ***acute*** (***obtuse***, ***right***) ~ spitzer (stumpfer, rechter) Winkel; ~ ***of incidence*** Einfallswinkel; ***at right ~s to*** im rechten Winkel zu; **2.** ⚙ a) Knie(stück) *n*, b) *pl.* Winkeleisen *pl.*; **3.** Ecke *f*, Vorsprung *m*, spitze Kante; **4.** *fig.* a) Standpunkt *m*, Gesichtswinkel *m*, b) Asˈpekt *m*, Seite *f*: ***consider all ~s of a question***; **5.** *Am.* Meˈthode *f* (*et. zu erreichen*); **6.** *sl.* Trick *m*, ‚Tour' *f*, ‚Masche' *f*; **II** *v/t.* **7.** ˈumbiegen; **8.** *fig.* tendenziˈös färben, verdrehen.

an·gle² [ˈæŋgl] *v/i.* angeln (*a. fig.* ***for*** nach).

an·gled [ˈæŋgld] *adj.* **1.** winklig, *mst in Zssgn*: ***right-~*** rechtwinklig; **2.** *fig.* tendenziˈös.

ˈ**an·gle|-ˌdo·zer** [-ˌdəʊzə] *s.* ⚙ Plaˈnierraupe *f*, Winkelräumer *m*; ˈ**~-park** *v/t. u. v/i. mot.* schräg parken.

an·gler [ˈæŋglə] *s.* **1.** Angler(in); **2.** *ichth.* Seeteufel *m*.

An·gles [ˈæŋglz] *s. pl. hist.* Angeln *pl.*; ˈ**An·gli·an** [-glɪən] **I** *adj.* englisch; **II** *s.* Angehörige(r *m*) *f* des Volksstammes der Angeln.

An·gli·can [ˈæŋglɪkən] *eccl.* **I** *adj.* angliˈkanisch, hochkirchlich; **II** *s.* Angliˈkaner(in).

An·gli·cism [ˈæŋglɪsɪzəm] *s.* **1.** *ling.* Angliˈzismus *m*; **2.** englische Eigenart; ˈ**An·gli·cist** [-ɪst] *s.* Anˈglist(in); ˈ**An·gli·cize** [-saɪz], *a.* ♀ *v/t. u. v/i.* (sich) anglisieren, englisch machen (werden).

an·gling [ˈæŋglɪŋ] *s.* Angeln *n*.

An·glist [ˈæŋglɪst] *s.* Anˈglist(in); **An·gli·stics** [æŋˈglɪstɪks] *s. pl. sg. konstr.* Anˈglistik *f*.

Anglo- [æŋgləʊ] *in Zssgn* Anglo…, anglo…, englisch, englisch und …

ˈ**An·glo|-Aˈmer·i·can** [-əʊ-] **I** *s.* ˈAnglo-Ameriˈkaner(in); **II** *adj.* anglo-ameriˈkanisch; ˈ**~-ˈIn·di·an** [-əʊ-] **I** *s.* Angloˈinder(in); **II** *adj.* angloˈindisch; ˌ**~ˈma·ni·a** [-əʊ-] *s.* Anglomaˈnie *f*; ˈ**~-ˈNor·man** [-əʊ-] **I** *s.* **1.** Anglonorˈmanne *m*; **2.** *ling.* Anglonorˈmannisch *n*; **II** *adj.* **3.** anglonorˈmannisch; ˈ**~·phile** [-əʊfaɪl] **I** *s.* Angloˈphile *m*, Englandfreund *m*; **II** *adj.* angloˈphil, englandfreundlich; ˈ**~·phobe** [-əʊfəʊb] **I** *s.* Angloˈphobe *m*, Englandfeind *m*; **II** *adj.* englandfeindlich; ˌ**~ˈpho·bi·a** [-əʊˈfəʊbjə] *s.* Anglophoˈbie *f*; ˌ**~-ˈSax·on** [-əʊ-] **I** *s.* **1.** Angelsachse *m*; **2.** *ling.* Altenglisch *n*, Angelsächsisch *n*; **3.** F urwüchsiges u. einfaches Englisch; **II** *adj.* **4.** angelsächsisch; ˌ**~-ˈScot** [-əʊ-] *s.* dauernd in England lebender Schotte.

an·go·la [æŋˈgəʊlə], **an·go·ra** [æŋˈgɔːrə], *a.* ♀ *s.* Gewebe *n* aus Anˈgorawolle; ~ **cat** *s. zo.* Anˈgorakatze *f*; ~ **goat** *s. zo.* Anˈgoraziege *f*; ~ **wool** *s.* Anˈgorawolle *f*; Moˈhär *m*.

an·gry [ˈæŋgrɪ] *adj.* □ **1.** (***at***, ***about***) ärgerlich, ungehalten (über *acc.*), zornig, böse (auf *j-n*, über *et.*, ***with*** mit *j-m*): ~ ***young man*** *Literatur*: ‚zorniger junger Mann'; **2.** ⚕ entzündet, schlimm; **3.** *fig.* drohend, stürmisch; finster.

angst [æŋst] *s. psych.* Angst *f*.

ang·strom, *a.* ♀ [ˈæŋstrəm] *s. phys. a.* ~ ***unit*** Angström(einheit *f*) *n*.

an·guish [ˈæŋgwɪʃ] *s.* Qual *f*, Pein *f*, Angst *f*, Schmerz *m*: ~ ***of mind*** Seelenqual(en *pl.*) *f*.

an·gu·lar [ˈæŋgjʊlə] *adj.* □ **1.** winklig, winkelförmig, eckig; Winkel…; **2.** *fig.* knochig, hager; **3.** *fig.* eckig, steif; barsch; **an·gu·lar·i·ty** [ˌæŋgjʊˈlærətɪ] *s.* **1.** Winkligkeit *f*; **2.** *fig.* Eckigkeit *f*, Steifheit *f*.

an·hy·drous [ænˈhaɪdrəs] *adj.* ⚗, *biol.* kalziniert, wasserfrei; getrocknet, Dörr… (*Obst etc.*).

an·il [ˈænɪl] *s.* ⚘ ˈIndigopflanze *f*; Indigo (-farbstoff) *m*.

an·i·line [ˈænɪliːn] *s.* Aniˈlin *n*: ~ ***dye*** Anilinfarbstoff *m*, *weitS.* chemisch hergestellte Farbe.

an·i·mad·ver·sion [ˌænɪmædˈvɜːʃn] *s.* Tadel *m*, Rüge *f*, Kriˈtik *f*; ˌ**an·i·madˈvert** [-ˈvɜːt] *v/i.* (***on***, ***upon***) kritisieren; tadeln, rügen (*acc.*).

an·i·mal [ˈænɪml] **I** *s.* **1.** Tier *n*, ‚Vierfüß(l)er' *m*; tierisches Lebewesen (*Ggs. Pflanze*, F *a. Ggs. Vogel*): ***there's no such ~!*** F so was gibt's ja gar nicht!; **2.** *fig.* Tier *n*, viehischer Mensch, ˈBestie *f*; **II** *adj.* **3.** aniˈmalisch, tierisch (*beide a. fig.*); Tier…: ~ ***kingdom*** Tierreich *n*; ~ ***magnetism*** a) tierischer Magnetismus, b) *bsd. humor.* erotische Anziehungskraft; ~ ***spirits*** *pl.* Lebenskraft *f*, -geister *pl.*, Vitalität *f*.

an·i·mal·cu·le [ˌænɪˈmælkjuːl] *s.* mikroˈskopisch kleines Tierchen: ***infusorial ~s***.

an·i·mal·ism [ˈænɪməlɪzəm] *s.* **1.** Vertiertheit *f*; **2.** Sinnlichkeit *f*; **3.** Lebenstrieb *m*, -kraft *f*; ˈ**an·i·mal·ist** [-ɪst] *s.* Tiermaler(in), -bildhauer(in).

an·i·mate I *v/t.* [ˈænɪmeɪt] **1.** beseelen, beleben, mit Leben erfüllen (*alle a. fig.*); anregen, aufmuntern; **2.** lebendig gestalten: ~ ***a cartoon*** e-n Zeichentrickfilm herstellen; **II** *adj.* [-mət] **3.** belebt, lebend; lebhaft, munter; ˈ**an·i·mat·ed** [-tɪd] *adj.* □ **1.** lebendig, beseelt (***with***, ***by*** von), voll Leben: ~ ***cartoon*** Zeichentrickfilm *m*; **2.** ermutigt; **3.** lebhaft, angeregt; **an·i·ma·tion** [ˌænɪˈmeɪʃn] *s.* **1.** Leben *n*, Feuer *n*, Lebhaftigkeit *f*, Munterkeit *f*; Leben *n* und Treiben *n*; **2.** a) Herstellung *f* von Zeichentrickfilmen, b) (Zeichen)Trickfilm *m*; ˈ**an·i·ma·tor** [-tə] *s.* Zeichner *m* von Trickfilmen.

an·i·mos·i·ty [ˌænɪˈmɒsətɪ] *s.* Feindseligkeit *f*, Erbitterung *f*, Animosiˈtät *f*.

an·i·mus [ˈænɪməs] *s.* **1.** (innewohnender) Geist; **2.** *psych.* Animus *m*; **3.** ⚖ Absicht *f*; **4.** → ***animosity***.

an·ise [ˈænɪs] *s.* ⚘ Aˈnis *m*; ˈ**an·i·seed** [-siːd] *s.* Aˈnis(samen) *m*.

an·i·sette [ˌænɪˈzet] *s.* Aniˈsett *m*, Aˈnisliˌkör *m*.

an·kle [ˈæŋkl] **I** *s. anat.* **1.** (Fuß)Knöchel *m*: ***sprain one's ~*** sich den Fuß verstauchen; **2.** Knöchelgegend *f des Beins*; **II** *v/i.* **3.** F marschieren; ˈ**~·bone** *s.* Sprungbein *n*; ~ **boot** *s.* Halbstiefel *m*; ˌ**~-ˈdeep** *adj.* knöcheltief, bis zu den Knöcheln; ˌ**~-ˈlength** *adj.* knöchellang; ˈ**~-sock** *s.* Knöchelsocke *f*, Söckchen *n*; ˈ**~-strap** *s.* Schuhspange *f*: ~ ***shoes*** Spangenschuhe.

an·klet [ˈæŋklɪt] *s.* **1.** Fußkettchen *n*, -spange *f* (*als Schmuck od. Fessel*); **2.** → ***anklesock***.

an·na [ˈænə] *s.* Anˈna *m* (*ind. Münze*).

an·nal·ist [ˈænəlɪst] *s.* Chroˈnist *m*; **an·nals** [ˈænlz] *s. pl.* **1.** Anˈnalen *pl.*, Jahrbücher *pl.*; **2.** hiˈstorischer Bericht; **3.** *regelmäßig erscheinende* wissenschaftliche Berichte *pl.*; **4.** *a. sg. konstr.* (Jahres)Bericht *m*.

an·neal [əˈniːl] *v/t.* **1.** ⚙ *Metall* ausglühen, anlassen, vergüten, tempern; *Glas* kühlen; **2.** *fig.* härten, stählen.

an·nex I *v/t.* [əˈneks] **1.** (**to**) beifügen (*dat.*), anhängen (an *acc.*); **2.** annektieren, (sich) einverleiben: ***the province was ~ed to France*** Frankreich verleibte sich das Gebiet ein; **3.** **~ to** verknüpfen mit; **4.** F sich aneignen, ‚sich unter den Nagel reißen'; **II** *s.* [ˈæneks] **5.** Anhang *m*, Nachtrag *m*; Anlage *f zum Brief*; **6.** Nebengebäude *n*, Anbau *m*; **an·nex·a·tion** [ˌænekˈseɪʃn] *s.* **1.** Hinˈzufügung *f* (**to** zu); **2.** Annexiˈon *f*, Einverleibung *f* (**to** in *acc.*); **3.** Aneignung *f*; **an·nexe** [ˈæneks] (*Fr.*) → ***annex*** 6; **anˈnexed** [-kst] *adj.* ✝ beifolgend, beigefügt.

an·ni·hi·late [əˈnaɪəleɪt] *v/t.* **1.** vernichten (*a. fig.*); **2.** ⚔ aufreiben; **3.** *sport* vernichtend schlagen; **4.** *fig.* zuˈnichte machen, aufheben; **an·ni·hi·la·tion** [əˌnaɪəˈleɪʃn] *s.* Vernichtung *f*; Aufhebung *f*.

an·ni·ver·sa·ry [ˌænɪˈvɜːsərɪ] *s.* Jahrestag *m*, -feier *f*, jährlicher Gedenktag, Jubiˈläum *n*: ***wedding ~*** Hochzeitstag *m*; ***the 50th ~ of his death*** die 50. Wiederkehr s-s Todestages.

an·no Dom·i·ni [ˌænəʊˈdɒmɪnaɪ] (*Lat.*) im Jahre des Herrn, Anno Domini.

an·no·tate [ˈænəʊteɪt] **I** *v/t. e-e Schrift* mit Anmerkungen versehen, kommentieren; **II** *v/i.* (**on**) Anmerkungen machen (zu), einen Kommenˈtar schreiben (über *acc.*); **an·no·ta·tion** [ˌænəʊˈteɪʃn] *s.* Kommentieren *n*; Anmerkung *f*, Kommenˈtar *m*; **ˈan·no·ta·tor** [-tə] *s.* Kommenˈtator *m*.

an·nounce [əˈnaʊns] **I** *v/t.* **1.** ankündigen; **2.** bekanntgeben, verkünden; **3.** a) *Radio, TV*: ansagen, b) (*über Lautsprecher*) ˈdurchsagen; **4.** *Besucher etc.* melden; **5.** *Geburt etc.* anzeigen, bekanntgeben; **II** *v/i.* **6.** *pol. Am.* seine Kandidaˈtur bekanntgeben (**for** für das Amt *gen.*); **7.** **~ for** *Am.* sich aussprechen für; **anˈnounce·ment** [-mənt] *s.* **1.** Ankündigung *f*; **2.** Bekanntgabe *f*; (*Geburts- etc.*)Anzeige *f*; **3.** a) *Radio, TV*: Ansage *f*, b) (ˈLautsprecher-)ˌDurchsage *f*; **anˈnounc·er** [-sə] *s. Radio, TV*: Ansager(in), Sprecher(in).

an·noy [əˈnɔɪ] *v/t.* **1.** ärgern: ***be ~ed*** sich ärgern (***at s.th.*** über et., ***with s.o.*** über j-n); **2.** belästigen, stören; schikanieren; **anˈnoy·ance** [-ɔɪəns] *s.* **1.** Störung *f*, Belästigung *f*, Ärgernis *n*; Ärger *m*; **2.** Plage(geist *m*) *f*; **anˈnoyed** [-ɔɪd] *adj.* ärgerlich; **anˈnoy·ing** [-ɔɪɪŋ] *adj.* □ ärgerlich (*Sache*), lästig; **anˈnoy·ing·ly** [-ɔɪɪŋlɪ] *adv.* ärgerlicherweise.

an·nu·al [ˈænjʊəl] **I** *adj.* □ **1.** jährlich, Jahres...; **2.** *bsd.* ⚘ einjährig: ***~ ring*** Jahresring *m*; **II** *s.* **3.** jährlich erscheinende Veröffentlichung, Jahrbuch *n*; **4.** einjährige Pflanze; → ***hardy*** 2.

an·nu·i·tant [əˈnjuːɪtənt] *s.* Empfänger (-in) e-r Jahresrente, Rentner(in); **anˈnu·i·ty** [-tɪ] *s.* **1.** (Jahres)Rente *f*; **2.** Jahreszahlung *f*; **3.** ✝ *a.* ***~ bond*** Rentenbrief *m*; **4.** *pl.* ˈRentenpaˌpiere *pl.*

an·nul [əˈnʌl] *v/t.* aufheben, für ungültig erklären, annullieren.

an·nu·lar [ˈænjʊlə] *adj.* □ ringförmig; **ˈan·nu·late** [-leɪt], **ˈan·nu·lat·ed** [-leɪtɪd] *adj.* geringelt, aus Ringen bestehend, Ring...

an·nul·ment [əˈnʌlmənt] *s.* Aufhebung *f*, Nichtigkeitserklärung *f*, Annullierung *f*; ***action for ~*** Nichtigkeitsklage *f*.

an·nun·ci·ate [əˈnʌnʃɪeɪt] *v/t.* verkünden, ankündigen; **an·nun·ci·a·tion** [əˌnʌnsɪˈeɪʃn] *s.* **1.** An-, Verkündigung *f*; **2.** ℒ, *a.* ℒ ***Day*** *eccl.* Maˈriä Verkündigung *f*; **anˈnun·ci·a·tor** [-tə] *s.* ⚡ Siˈgnalanlage *f*, -tafel *f*.

an·ode [ˈænəʊd] *s.* ⚡ Anˈode *f*, ˈpositiver Pol: ***~ potential*** Anodenspannung *f*; ***DC ~*** Anodenruhestrom *m*; **an·od·ize** [ˈænəʊdaɪz] *v/t.* eloxieren.

an·o·dyne [ˈænəʊdaɪn] **I** *adj.* schmerzstillend; *fig.* a) lindernd, beruhigend, b) verwässert, kraftlos; **II** *s.* schmerzstillendes Mittel; *fig.* Beruhigungspille *f*.

a·noint [əˈnɔɪnt] *v/t.* **1.** einölen, einschmieren; **2.** *bsd. eccl.* salben; **aˈnoint·ment** [-mənt] *s.* Salbung *f*.

a·nom·a·lous [əˈnɒmələs] *adj.* □ ˈanomal, abˈnorm; ungewöhnlich, abweichend; **aˈnom·a·ly** [-lɪ] *s.* Anomaˈlie *f*.

a·non [əˈnɒn] *adv.* bald, soˈgleich: ***ever and ~*** immer wieder.

an·o·nym·i·ty [ˌænəˈnɪmətɪ] *s.* Anonymiˈtät *f*; **a·non·y·mous** [əˈnɒnɪməs] *adj.* □ anoˈnym, namenlos, ungenannt; unbekannten Ursprungs.

a·noph·e·les [əˈnɒfɪliːz] *s. zo.* Fiebermücke *f*.

a·no·rak [ˈænəræk] *s.* Anorak *m*.

an·oth·er [əˈnʌðə] *adj. u. pron.* **1.** ein anderer, eine andere, ein anderes (***than*** als): ***~ thing*** etwas anderes; ***one ~*** a) einander, b) uns (euch, sich) gegenseitig; ***one after ~*** einer nach dem andern; ***he is ~ man now*** jetzt ist er ein (ganz) anderer Mensch; **2.** ein zweiter *od.* weiterer *od.* neuer, eine zweite *od.* weitere *od.* neue, ein zweites *od.* weiteres *od.* neues; **3.** *a.* ***yet ~*** noch ein(er, e, es): ***~ cup of tea*** noch eine Tasse Tee; ***~ five weeks*** weitere *od.* noch fünf Wochen; ***tell us ~!*** F das glaubst du doch selbst nicht!; ***you are ~!*** F *iro.* danke gleichfalls!; ***~ Shakespeare*** ein zweiter Shakespeare; ***A.N.Other*** *sport* ein ungenannter (Ersatz)Spieler.

An·schluss [ˈɑːnʃlʊs] (*Ger.*) *s. pol.* Anschluß *m*.

an·swer [ˈɑːnsə] **I** *s.* **1.** Antwort *f*, Entgegnung *f* (**to** auf *acc.*): ***in ~ to*** a) in Beantwortung (*gen.*), b) auf *et.* hin; **2.** *fig.* Antwort *f*, Erwiderung *f*; Reaktiˈon *f* (*alle*: **to** auf *acc.*); **3.** Gegenmaßnahme *f*, -mittel *n*; **4.** ⚖ Klagebeantwortung *f*, Gegenschrift *f*; *weitS.* Rechtfertigung *f*; **5.** Lösung *f* (**to** *e-s Problems etc.*); ⅍ Auflösung *f*: ***he knows all the ~s*** a) ‚er blickt voll durch', b) *contp.* er weiß immer alles besser; **II** *v/i.* **6.** antworten (**to** *j-m*, auf *acc.*): ***~ back*** a) freche Antworten geben, b) widersprechen, sich (*mit Worten*) verteidigen *od.* wehren; **7.** sich verantworten, Rechenschaft ablegen (**for** für); **8.** verantwortlich sein, haften, bürgen (**for** für); **9.** die Folgen tragen, büßen (**for** für): ***you have much to ~ for*** du hast viel auf dem Kerbholz; **10.** *fig.* (**to**) reagieren (auf *acc.*), hören (auf *e-n Namen*); gehorchen, Folge leisten (*dat.*); **11.** ***~ to*** *e-r Beschreibung* entsprechen; **12.** sich eignen, taugen; gelingen (*Plan*); **III** *v/t.* **13.** a) *j-m* antworten, b) *et.* beantworten, antworten auf (*acc.*); **14.** a) sich *j-m gegenüber* verantworten, *j-m* Rechenschaft ablegen (**for** für), b) sich gegen *e-e Anklage etc.* verteidigen; **15.** reagieren *od.* eingehen auf (*acc.*); *e-m Befehl etc.* Folge leisten; sich auf *eine Anzeige etc.* hin melden: ***~ the bell*** (*od.* ***door***) auf das Läuten *od.* Klopfen die Tür öffnen; ***~ the telephone*** den Anruf entgegennehmen, ans Telefon gehen; **16.** *dem Steuer* gehorchen; *Gebet* erhören; *Zweck, Wunsch etc.* erfüllen; *Auftrag etc.* ausführen: ***~ the call of duty*** dem Ruf der Pflicht folgen; **17.** *bsd. Aufgabe* lösen; **18.** *e-r Beschreibung, e-m Bedürfnis* entsprechen; **19.** *j-m* genügen, *j-n* zuˈfriedenstellen; **ˈan·swer·a·ble** [-sərəbl] *adj.* **1.** verantwortlich (**for** für): ***to be ~ to s.o. for s.th.*** j-m für et. bürgen, sich vor j-m für et. verantworten müssen; **2.** (**to**) entsprechend, angemessen, gemäß (*dat.*); **3.** zu beantworten(d).

ant [ænt] *s. zo.* Ameise *f*.

an't [ɑːnt; ænt] → ***ain't***.

ant·ac·id [ˌæntˈæsɪd] *adj. u. s.* ⚕ gegen Magensäure wirkend(es Mittel).

an·tag·o·nism [ænˈtægənɪzəm] *s.* **1.** ˈWiderstreit *m*, Gegensatz *m*, ˈWiderspruch *m* (***between*** zwischen *dat.*); **2.** Feindschaft *f* (**to** gegen); ˈWiderstand *m* (***against, to*** gegen); **anˈtag·o·nist** [-ɪst] *s.* Gegner(in), ˈWidersacher(in); **an·tag·o·nis·tic** [ænˌtægəˈnɪstɪk] *adj.* (□ ***~ally***) gegnerisch, feindlich (**to** gegen); widerˈstreitend (**to** *dat.*); **anˈtag·o·nize** [-naɪz] *v/t.* ankämpfen gegen; sich *j-n* zum Feind machen, *j-n* gegen sich aufbringen.

ant·arc·tic [æntˈɑːktɪk] **I** *adj.* antˈarktisch, Südpol...: ℒ ***Circle*** südlicher Polarkreis; ℒ ***Ocean*** südliches Eismeer; **II** *s.* Antˈarktis *f*.

ˈant-bear *s. zo.* Ameisenbär *m*.

an·te [ˈæntɪ] (*Lat.*) **I** *adv.* vorn, voˈran, b) *zeitlich*: vorher, zuˈvor; **II** *prp.* vor; **III** *s.* F *Poker*: Einsatz *m*: ***raise the ~*** a) den Einsatz (*weitS.* den Preis *etc.*) erhöhen, b) F (das nötige) Geld beschaffen; **IV** *v/t. u. v/i. mst **~ up*** (ein)setzen; *fig. Am.* a) (be)zahlen, ‚blechen', b) (dazu) beisteuern.

ˈant-ˌeat·er *s. zo.* Ameisenfresser *m*.

an·te·ced·ence [ˌæntɪˈsiːdəns] *s.* **1.** Vortritt *m*, -rang *m*; **2.** *ast.* Rückläufigkeit *f*; **ˌan·teˈced·ent** [-nt] **I** *adj.* **1.** vorˈhergehend, früher (**to** als); **II** *s.* **2.** *pl.* Vorgeschichte *f*: ***his ~s*** sein Vorleben; **3.** *fig.* Vorläufer *m*; **4.** *ling.* Beziehungswort *n*.

an·te|·cham·ber [ˈæntɪˌtʃeɪmbə] *s.* Vorzimmer *n*; **~·date** [ˌæntɪˈdeɪt] *v/t.* **1.** vor- *od.* zuˈrückdatieren, ein früheres Datum setzen auf (*acc.*); **2.** vorˈwegnehmen; **3.** *zeitlich* vorˈangehen (*dat.*); **~·di·lu·vi·an** [ˌæntɪdɪˈluːvjən] **I** *adj.* vorsintflutlich (*a. fig.*); **II** *s.* vorsintflutliches Wesen; *contp.* a) rückständige Perˈson, b) ‚Fosˈsil' *n* (*sehr alte Person*).

an·te·lope [ˈæntɪləʊp] *s.* **1.** *zo.* Antiˈlope *f*; **2.** Antiˈlopenleder *n*.

an·te me·rid·i·em [ˌæntɪməˈrɪdɪəm] (*Lat.*) *abbr.* **a.m.** vormittags.

an·te·na·tal [ˌæntɪˈneɪtl] **I** *adj.* pränaˈtal: ***~ care*** Mutterschaftsfürsorge *f*; **II** *s.* F Mutterschaftsvorsorgeuntersuchung *f*.

an·ten·na [ænˈtenə] *s.* **1.** *pl.* **-nae** [-niː]

zo. Fühler *m*; Fühlhorn *n*; *fig.* Gespür *n*, ‚An'tenne' *f*; **2.** *pl.* **-nas** *bsd. Am.* ϟ Antenne *f*.

an·te|·nup·tial [ˌæntɪ'nʌpʃl] *adj.* vorhochzeitlich; **~·pe·nul·ti·mate** [ˌæntɪpɪ'nʌltɪmət] **I** *adj.* drittletzt (*bsd. Silbe*); **II** *s.* drittletzte Silbe.

an·te·ri·or [æn'tɪərɪə] *adj.* **1.** vorder; **2.** vor'hergehend, früher (***to*** als).

an·te-room ['æntɪrʊm] *s.* Vor-, Wartezimmer *n*.

an·them ['ænθəm] *s.* 'Hymne *f*, Cho'ral *m*: ***national ~*** Nationalhymne.

an·ther ['ænθə] *s.* ⚘ Staubbeutel *m*.

'ant-hill *s. zo.* Ameisenhaufen *m*.

an·thol·o·gy [æn'θɒlədʒɪ] *s.* Antholo'gie *f*, (Gedicht)Sammlung *f*.

an·thra·cite ['ænθrəsaɪt] *s. min.* Anthra'zit *m*, Glanzkohle *f*.

an·thrax ['ænθræks] *s.* ⚕ 'Anthrax *m*, Milzbrand *m*.

an·thro·poid ['ænθrəʊpɔɪd] *zo.* **I** *adj.* menschenähnlich, Menschen…; **II** *s.* Menschenaffe *m*; **an·thro·po·log·i·cal** [ˌænθrəpə'lɒdʒɪk(l)] *adj.* □ anthropo'logisch; **an·thro·pol·o·gist** [ˌænθrə'pɒlədʒɪst] *s.* Anthropo'loge *m*; **an·thro·pol·o·gy** [ˌænθrə'pɒlədʒɪ] *s.* Anthropolo'gie *f*; **an·thro·po·mor·phous** [ˌænθrəpəʊ'mɔːfəs] *adj.* anthropo'morph(isch), von menschlicher *od.* menschenähnlicher Gestalt; **an·thro·poph·a·gi** [ˌænθrəʊ'pɒfəgaɪ] *s. pl.* Menschenfresser *pl.*; **an·thro·poph·a·gous** [ˌænθrəʊ'pɒfəgəs] *adj.* menschenfressend.

an·ti ['æntɪ] F **I** *prp.* gegen; **II** *adj.*: ***be ~*** dagegen sein; **III** *s.* Gegner(in).

ˌan·ti|-'air·craft [ˌæntɪ-] *adj.* ⚔ Fliegerabwehr…: ***~ gun*** Flakgeschütz *n*, Fliegerabwehrkanone *f*; **'~·auˌthor·i'tar·i·an** *adj.* antiautori'tär; **ˌ~-'ba·by pill** *s.* ⚕ Anti'babypille *f*; **ˌ~·bal'lis·tic** *adj.* ⚔ antibal'listisch; **ˌ~·bi'ot·ic** [-baɪ'ɒtɪk] **I** *s.* Antibi'otikum *n*; **II** *adj.* antibi'otisch; **'~ˌbod·y** *s.* ⚗, *biol.* 'Antikörper *m*, Abwehrstoff *m*; **ˌ~'cath·ode** *s.* ϟ Antika'thode *f*; **'~·christ** *s. eccl.* 'Antichrist *m*; **ˌ~'chris·tian I** *adj.* christenfeindlich; **II** *s.* Christenfeind(in).

an·tic·i·pate [æn'tɪsɪpeɪt] *v/t.* **1.** vor'ausempfinden, -sehen, -ahnen; **2.** erwarten, erhoffen: ***~d profit*** voraussichtlicher Verdienst; **3.** im vor'aus tun *od.* erwähnen, vor'wegnehmen; *Ankunft* beschleunigen; vor'auseilen (*dat.*); **4.** *j-m od. e-m Wunsch etc.* zu'vorkommen; **5.** *e-r Sache* vorbauen, verhindern; **6.** *bsd.* ☤ vorzeitig bezahlen *od.* verbrauchen; **an·tic·i·pa·tion** [ænˌtɪsɪ'peɪʃn] *s.* **1.** Vorgefühl *n*, Vorahnung *f*, Vorgeschmack *m*; **2.** Ahnungsvermögen *n*, Vor'aussicht *f*; **3.** Erwartung *f*, Hoffnung *f*, Vorfreude *f*; **4.** Zu'vorkommen *n*, Vorgreifen *n*, Vor'wegnahme *f*: ***in ~*** im voraus; **5.** Verfrühtheit *f*: ***payment by ~*** Vorauszahlung *f*; **an'tic·i·pa·to·ry** [-tərɪ] *adj.* **1.** vor'wegnehmend, vorgreifend, erwartend, Vor…; **2.** *ling.* vor'ausdeutend; **3.** *Patentrecht*: neuheitsschädlich: ***~ reference*** Vorwegnahme *f*.

ˌan·ti|'cler·i·cal *adj.* kirchenfeindlich; **ˌ~'cli·max** *s.* (enttäuschendes) Abfallen, Abstieg *m*; *a.* ***sense of ~*** plötzliches Gefühl der Leere *od.* Enttäuschung; **ˌ~'clock·wise** *adv. u. adj.* entgegen dem Uhrzeigersinn: ***~ rotation*** Linksdrehung *f*; **ˌ~·cor'ro·sive** *adj.* rostfest; Rostschutz…

an·tics ['æntɪks] *s. pl.* Possen *pl.*, *fig.* Mätzchen *pl.*, (tolle) Streiche *pl*.

ˌan·ti|'cy·cli·cal *adj.* ☤ anti'zyklisch, konjunk'turdämpfend; **ˌ~'cy·clone** *s. meteor.* Hoch(druckgebiet) *n*; **ˌ~-'dazzle** *adj.* Blendschutz…: ***~ switch*** Abblendschalter *m*; **ˌ~·de'pres·sant** *s.* ⚕ Antidepres'sivum *n*; **'~-dim** *adj.* ⚙ Klar(sicht)…; **ˌ~·dis'tor·tion** *s.* ϟ Entzerrung *f*; **'~·dot·al** [-dəʊtl] *adj.* als Gegengift dienend (*a. fig.*); **'~·dote** [-dəʊt] *s.* Gegengift *n*, -mittel *n* (***against, for, to*** gegen); **ˌ~'fad·ing** ϟ **I** *s.* Schwundausgleich *m*; **II** *adj.* schwundmindernd; **ˌ~-'Fas·cist** *pol.* **I** *s.* Antifa'schist(in); **II** *adj.* antifa'schistisch; **ˌ~'fe·brile** *s.* ⚕ Fiebermittel *n*; **♀'fed·er·al·ist** *s. Am. hist.* Antifödera'list *m*; **'~-freeze I** *adj.* Gefrier-, Frostschutz…; **II** *s.* Frostschutzmittel *n*; **'~-ˌfric·tion** *s.* Schmiermittel *n*: ***~ metal*** Lagermetall *n*; **'~-gas** *adj.* Gasschutz…

an·ti·gen ['æntɪdʒən] *s.* ⚕ Anti'gen *n*, Abwehrstoff *m*.

ˌan·ti|-'glare → ***anti-dazzle***; **ˌ~'ha·lo** *adj. phot.* lichthoffrei; **'~-ˌhe·ro** *s.* Antiheld *m*; **ˌ~·im'pe·ri·al·ist** *s.* Gegner *m* des Imperia'lismus; **'~-ˌin·ter'fer·ence** *adj.* ϟ Entstörungs…, Störschutz…; **'~·jam** *v/t. u. v/i. Radio* entstören; **ˌ~'knock** ⚗, *mot.* **I** *adj.* klopffest; **II** *s.* Anti'klopfmittel *n*.

an·ti|·ma·cas·sar [ˌæntɪmə'kæsə] **I** *s.* Sofa- *od.* Sesselschoner *m*; **II** *adj. fig.* altmodisch; **ˌ~-ma'lar·i·al** *s.* ⚕ Ma'lariamittel *n*; **'~ˌmat·ter** *s. phys.* 'Antimaˌterie *f*; **ˌ~'mis·sile** *s.* ⚔ Antira'ketenraˌkete *f*.

an·ti·mo·ny ['æntɪmənɪ] *s.* ⚗, *min.* Anti'mon *n*.

an·tin·o·my [æn'tɪnəmɪ] *s.* Antino'mie *f*, 'Widerspruch *m*.

ˌan·ti·pa'thet·ic, ˌan·ti·pa'thet·i·cal [-pə'θetɪk(l)] *adj.* □ (***to***) **1.** zu'wider (*dat.*); **2.** abgeneigt (*dat.*); **an·tip·a·thy** [æn'tɪpəθɪ] *s.* Antipa'thie *f*, Abneigung *f* (***against, to*** gegen).

ˌan·ti|-per·son'nel *adj.*: ⚔ ***~ bomb*** Splitterbombe *f*; ***~ mine*** Schützen-, Tretmine *f*; **ˌ~·phlo'gis·tic** [-fləʊ'dʒɪstɪk] **I** *adj.* **1.** ⚗ antiphlo'gistisch; **2.** ⚕ entzündungshemmend; **II** *s.* **3.** ⚕ Antiphlo'gistikum *n*.

an·tiph·o·ny [æn'tɪfənɪ] *s.* Antipho'nie *f*, Wechselgesang *m*.

an·tip·o·dal [æn'tɪpədl] *adj.* anti'podisch, *fig. a.* genau entgegengesetzt; **an·tip·o·de·an** [ænˌtɪpə'diːən] *s.* Anti'pode *m*, Gegenfüßler *m*; **an·tip·o·des** [æn'tɪpədiːz] *s. pl.* **1.** die diame'tral gegen'überliegenden Teile *pl.* der Erde; **2.** *sg. u. pl.* Gegenteil *n*, -satz *m*, -seite *f*.

ˌan·ti|·pol'lu·tion *adj.* umweltschützend; **ˌ~·pol'lu·tion·ist** [-pə'luːʃənɪst] *s.* Umweltschützer *m*; **'~·pope** *s.* Gegenpapst *m*; **ˌ~·py'ret·ic** ⚕ **I** *adj.* fieberverhütend; **II** *s.* Fiebermittel *n*; **ˌ~'py·rin(e)** [-'paɪərɪn] *s.* ⚕ Antipy'rin *n*.

an·ti·quar·i·an [ˌæntɪ'kweərɪən] **I** *adj.* altertümlich; **II** *s.* → **an·ti·quar·y** ['æntɪkwərɪ] *s.* **1.** Altertumskenner *m*, -forscher *m*; **2.** Antiqui'tätensammler *m*, -händler *m*; **an·ti·quat·ed** ['æntɪkweɪtɪd] *adj.* veraltet, altmodisch, über'holt, anti'quiert.

an·tique [æn'tiːk] **I** *adj.* □ **1.** an'tik, alt; **2.** altmodisch, veraltet; **II** *s.* **3.** Antiqui'tät *f*: ***~ dealer*** Antiquitätenhändler *m*; **4.** *typ.* Egypti'enne *f*; **an·tiq·ui·ty** [æn'tɪkwətɪ] *s.* **1.** Altertum *n*, Vorzeit *f*; **2.** die Alten *pl.* (*bsd. Griechen u. Römer*); **3.** *die* Antike; **4.** *pl.* Antiqui'täten *pl.*, Altertümer *pl.*; **5.** (ehrwürdiges) Alter.

ˌan·ti|-'rust *adj.* Rostschutz…; **'~-ˌsab·ba'tar·i·an** *adj. u. s.* der strengen Sonntagsheiligung abgeneigt(e Per'son); **ˌ~-'Sem·ite** *s.* Antise'mit(in); **ˌ~-Se'mit·ic** *adj.* antise'mitisch; **ˌ~-'Sem·i·tism** *s.* Antisemi'tismus *m*; **ˌ~'sep·tic** ⚕ **I** *adj.* (□ ***~ally***) anti'septisch; **II** *s.* Anti'septikum *n*; **ˌ~-'skid** *adj.* ⚙, *mot.* gleit-, schleudersicher, Gleitschutz…; rutschfest; **ˌ~'so·cial** *adj.* 'unsoziˌal, gesellschaftsfeindlich; ungesellig; **ˌ~-'tank** *adj.* ⚔ Panzerabwehr… (*-kanone etc.*), Panzer… (*-sperre etc.*); Panzerjäger…: ***~ battalion***.

an·tith·e·sis [æn'tɪθɪsɪs] *pl.* **-ses** [-siːz] *s.* Anti'these *f*: a) Gegensatz *m*, b) 'Widerspruch *m*; **an·ti·thet·ic, an·ti·thet·i·cal** [ˌæntɪ'θetɪk(l)] *adj.* □ im Widerspruch stehend, gegensätzlich, anti'thetisch; **an'tith·e·size** [-saɪz] *v/t.* in Gegensätzen ausdrücken; in 'Widerspruch bringen.

ˌan·ti|'tox·in *s.* ⚕ Antito'xin *n*, Gegengift *n*; **ˌ~-'trust** *adj.* kar'tell- *u.* mono'polfeindlich, Antitrust…; **ˌ~'un·ion** *adj.* gewerkschaftsfeindlich; **'~·world** *s.* Antiwelt *f*.

ant·ler ['æntlə] *s. zo.* **1.** Geweihsprosse *f*; **2.** *pl.* Geweih *n*.

an·to·nym ['æntənɪm] *s. ling.* Anto'nym *n*.

a·nus ['eɪnəs] *s.* After *m*, Anus *m*.

an·vil ['ænvɪl] *s.* Amboß *m* (*a. anat. u. fig.*).

anx·i·e·ty [æŋ'zaɪətɪ] *s.* **1.** Angst *f*, Unruhe *f*; Bedenken *n*, Besorgnis *f*, Sorge *f* (***for*** um); **2.** ⚕ Angst(gefühl *n*) *f*, Beklemmung *f*: ***~ neurosis*** Angstneurose *f*; ***~ state*** Angstzustand *m*; **3.** starkes Verlangen, eifriges (Be)Streben *n* (***for*** nach); **anx·ious** ['æŋkʃəs] *adj.* □ **1.** ängstlich, bange, besorgt, unruhig (***about*** um, wegen): ***~ about his health*** um s-e Gesundheit besorgt; **2.** *fig.* (***for, to*** *inf.*) begierig (auf *acc.*, nach, zu *inf.*), bestrebt (zu *inf.*), bedacht (auf *acc.*): ***~ for his report*** auf s-n Bericht begierig *od.* gespannt; ***he is ~ to please*** er gibt sich alle Mühe(, es recht zu machen); ***I am ~ to see him*** mir liegt daran, ihn zu sehen; ***I am ~ to know*** ich möchte zu gern wissen, ich bin begierig zu wissen.

an·y ['enɪ] **I** *adj.* **1.** (*fragend, verneinend od. bedingend*) (irgend)ein, (irgend)welch; etwaig; einige *pl.*; etwas: ***have you ~ money on you?*** haben Sie Geld bei sich?; ***if I had ~ hope*** wenn ich irgendwelche Hoffnung hätte; ***not ~*** kein; ***there was not ~ milk in the house*** es war keine Milch im Hause; ***I cannot eat ~ more*** ich kann nichts mehr essen; **2.** (*bejahend*) jeder, jede, jedes (beliebige): ***~ cat will scratch*** jede Katze kratzt; ***~ amount*** jede beliebige Menge, ein ganzer Haufen; ***in ~***

case auf jeden Fall; ***at ~ rate*** jedenfalls, wenigstens; ***at ~ time*** jederzeit; **II** *pron. sg. u. pl.* **3.** irgendein; irgendwelche *pl.*; etwas: ***no money and no prospect of ~*** kein Geld und keine Aussicht auf welches; ***I'm not having ~!*** *sl.* ich pfeife drauf!; ***it doesn't help ~*** *sl.* es hilft einen Dreck; **III** *adv.* **4.** irgend(wie), (noch) etwas: ***~ more?*** noch (etwas) mehr?; ***not ~ more than*** ebensowenig wie; ***is he ~ happier now?*** ist er denn jetzt glücklicher?; → ***if*** 1; **'~bod·y** *pron.* irgend jemand, irgendeine(r), ein beliebiger, eine beliebige: ***~ but you*** jeder andere eher als du; ***is he ~ at all?*** ist er überhaupt jemand (von Bedeutung)?; ***ask ~ you meet*** frage den ersten besten, den du triffst; ***it's ~'s match*** F das Spiel ist (noch) völlig offen; → ***guess*** 7; **'~·how** *adv.* **1.** irgendwie; so gut wie's geht, schlecht und recht; **2.** a) trotzdem, jedenfalls, b) sowie'so, ohne'hin, c) immer'hin: ***you won't be late ~*** jedenfalls wirst du nicht zu spät kommen; ***who wants him to come ~?*** wer will denn überhaupt, daß er kommt?; ***I am going there ~*** ich gehe ohnehin dorthin; **'~·one** → ***anybody***; **'~·place** *Am.* → ***anywhere***; **'~·thing** *pron.* **1.** (irgend) etwas, etwas Beliebiges: ***not ~*** gar nichts; ***not for ~*** um keinen Preis; ***take ~ you like*** nimm, was du willst; ***my head aches like ~*** F mein Kopf schmerzt wie toll; ***for ~ I know*** soviel ich weiß; ***~ goes!*** F alles ist ‚drin'!; **2.** alles: ***~ but*** alles andere (eher) als; **'~·way** *adv.* **1.** irgendwie; **2.** → ***anyhow*** 2; **'~·where** *adv.* **1.** irgendwo (-hin): ***not ~*** nirgendwo; **2.** über'all: ***from ~*** von überall her.

A one → ***A 1.***

a·o·rist ['eərɪst] *s. ling.* Ao'rist *m.*

a·or·ta [eɪ'ɔːtə] *s. anat.* A'orta *f*, Hauptschlagader *f.*

a·pace [ə'peɪs] *adv.* schnell, rasch, zusehends.

A·pach·e *pl.* **-es** *od.* **-e** *s.* **1.** [ə'pætʃɪ] A'pache *m* (*Indianer*); **2.** ♀ [ə'pæʃ] A'pache *m*, 'Unterweltler *m.*

ap·a·nage → ***appanage.***

a·part [ə'pɑːt] *adv.* **1.** einzeln, für sich, (ab)gesondert (***from*** von): ***keep ~*** getrennt *od.* auseinanderhalten; ***take ~*** zerlegen, auseinandernehmen (*a. fig.* F *j-n*); ***~ from*** abgesehen von; **2.** abseits, bei'seite: ***joking ~*** Scherz beiseite.

a·part·heid [ə'pɑːtheɪt] *s.* A'partheid *f*, (Poli'tik *f* der) Rassentrennung *f in Südafrika.*

a·part·ho·tel [əˌpɑːthəʊ'tel] *s. Brit. Eigentumswohnanlage, deren Wohneinheiten bei Abwesenheit der Eigentümer als Hotelsuiten vermietet werden.*

a·part·ment [ə'pɑːtmənt] *s.* **1.** Zimmer *n*; **2.** *Am.* (E'tagen)Wohnung *f*; **3.** *Brit.* große Luxuswohnung; **~ block** *s.*, **~ build·ing** *s.* Mietshaus *n*; **~ ho·tel** *s. Am.* A'parthoˌtel *n* (*das Appartements mit Bedienung u. Verpflegung vermietet*); **~ house** *s.* Mietshaus *n.*

ap·a·thet·ic, ap·a·thet·i·cal [ˌæpə'θetɪk(l)] *adj.* □ a'pathisch, teilnahmslos; **ap·a·thy** ['æpəθɪ] *s.* Apa'thie *f*, Teilnahmslosigkeit *f*; Gleichgültigkeit *f* (***to*** gegen).

ape [eɪp] **I** *s. zo.* (*bsd.* Menschen)Affe *m*; *fig.* a) Nachäffer(in), b) ‚Affe' *m*, ‚Go'rilla' *m*: ***go ~*** ‚überschnappen'; **II** *v/t.* nachäffen.

a·pe·ri·ent [ə'pɪərɪənt] ⚕ **I** *adj.* abführend; **II** *s.* Abführmittel *n.*

a·pé·ri·tif [ɑːˌperɪ'tiːf] *s.* Aperi'tif *m.*

ap·er·ture ['æpəˌtjʊə] *s.* **1.** Öffnung *f*, Schlitz *m*, Loch *n*; **2.** *phot.*, *phys.* Blende *f.*

a·pex ['eɪpeks] *pl.* **'a·pex·es** *od.* **'a·pi·ces** [-pɪsiːz] *s.* **1.** (*a. anat. Lungen- etc.*) Spitze *f*, Gipfel *m*, Scheitelpunkt *m*; **2.** *fig.* Gipfel *m*, Höhepunkt *m.*

a·phe·li·on [æ'fiːljən] *s.* **1.** *ast.* A'phelium *n*; **2.** *fig.* entferntester Punkt.

a·phid ['eɪfɪd], *a.* **a·phis** ['eɪfɪs] *pl.* **'aph·i·des** [-diːz] *s. zo.* Blattlaus *f.*

aph·o·rism ['æfərɪzəm] *s.* Apho'rismus *m*, Gedankensplitter *m*; **'aph·o·rist** [-ɪst] *s.* Apho'ristiker *m.*

aph·ro·dis·i·ac [ˌæfrəʊ'dɪzɪæk] ⚕ **I** *adj.* aphro'disisch, den Geschlechtstrieb steigernd; *weitS.* erotisierend, erregend; **II** *s.* Aphrodi'siakum *n.*

a·pi·ar·i·an [ˌeɪpɪ'eərɪən] *adj.* Bienen(zucht)…; **a·pi·a·rist** ['eɪpjərɪst] *s.* Bienenzüchter *m*, Imker *m*; **a·pi·ar·y** ['eɪpjərɪ] *s.* Bienenhaus *n.*

ap·i·cal ['æpɪkl] *adj.* □ Spitzen…: ***~ angle*** ⚔ Winkel *m* an der Spitze; ***~ pneumonia*** ⚕ Lungenspitzenkatarrh *m.*

a·pi·cul·ture ['eɪpɪkʌltʃə] *s.* Bienenzucht *f.*

a·piece [ə'piːs] *adv.* für jedes Stück, je; pro Per'son, pro Kopf.

ap·ish ['eɪpɪʃ] *adj.* □ **1.** affenartig; **2.** nachäffend; albern, läppisch.

a·plomb [ə'plɒm] (*Fr.*) *s.* **1.** A'plomb *m*, (selbst)sicheres Auftreten, Selbstbewußtsein *n*; **2.** Fassung *f.*

A·poc·a·lypse [ə'pɒkəlɪps] *s.* **1.** *bibl.* Apoka'lypse *f*, Offen'barung *f* Jo'hannis; **2.** ♀ a) Enthüllung *f*, Offen'barung *f*, b) Apoka'lypse *f*, ('Welt)kataˌstrophe *f*; **a·poc·a·lyp·tic** [əˌpɒkə'lɪptɪk] *adj.* (□ ***~ally***) **1.** apoka'lyptisch (*a. fig.*); **2.** *fig.* dunkel, rätselhaft; **3.** *fig.* unheilkündend.

a·poc·ry·pha [ə'pɒkrɪfə] *s. bibl.* Apo'kryphen *pl.*; **a'poc·ry·phal** [-fl] *adj.* apo'kryphisch, von zweifelhafter Verfasserschaft; zweifelhaft; unecht.

ap·o·gee ['æpəʊdʒiː] *s.* **1.** *ast.* Apo'gäum *n*, Erdferne *f*; **2.** *fig.* Höhepunkt *m*, Gipfel *m.*

a·po·lit·i·cal [ˌeɪpə'lɪtɪkl] *adj.* 'apolitisch.

A·pol·lo [ə'pɒləʊ] *npr. myth. u. s. fig.* A'poll(o) *m.*

a·pol·o·get·ic [əˌpɒlə'dʒetɪk] **I** *s.* **1.** Entschuldigung *f*, Verteidigung *f*; **2.** *mst pl. eccl.* Apolo'getik *f*; **II** *adj.* **3.** → **aˌpol·o'get·i·cal** [-kl] *adj.* □ **1.** entschuldigend, rechtfertigend; **2.** kleinlaut, reumütig, schüchtern; **ap·o·lo·gi·a** [ˌæpə'ləʊdʒɪə] *s.* Verteidigung *f*, (Selbst-)Rechtfertigung *f*, Apolo'gie *f*; **a·pol·o·gist** [ə'pɒlədʒɪst] *s.* **1.** Verteidiger(in); **2.** *eccl.* Apolo'get *m*; **a·pol·o·gize** [ə'pɒlədʒaɪz] *v/i.* : ***~ to s.o.*** (***for s.th.***) sich bei j-m (für et.) entschuldigen, j-n (für et.) um Verzeihung bitten; **a·pol·o·gy** [ə'pɒlədʒɪ] *s.* **1.** Entschuldigung *f*, Abbitte *f*; Rechtfertigung *f*: ***make an ~ to s.o.*** (***for s.th***) → ***apologize***; **2.** Verteidigungsrede *f*, -schrift *f*; **3.** F minderwertiger Ersatz: ***an ~ for a meal*** ein armseliges Essen.

ap·o·phthegm → ***apothegm.***

ap·o·plec·tic, ap·o·plec·ti·cal [ˌæpə'plektɪk(l)] *adj.* □ apo'plektisch: a) Schlaganfall…, b) zum Schlaganfall neigend; *fig.* e-m Schlaganfall nahe (vor Wut): ***~ fit, ~ stroke*** → **ap·o·plex·y** ['æpəpleksɪ] *s.* ⚕ Apople'xie *f*, Schlaganfall *m*, (Gehirn)Schlag *m.*

a·pos·ta·sy [ə'pɒstəsɪ] *s.* Abfall *m*, Abtrünnigkeit *f* (*vom Glauben, von e-r Partei etc.*); **a'pos·tate** [-teɪt] **I** *s.* Abtrünnige(r *m*) *f*, Rene'gat *m*; **II** *adj.* abtrünnig; **a'pos·ta·tize** [-tətaɪz] *v/i.* **1.** (***from***) abfallen (von), abtrünnig *od.* untreu werden (*dat.*); **2.** 'übergehen (***from … to*** von … zu).

a·pos·tle [ə'pɒsl] *s.* **1.** *eccl.* A'postel *m*: ***♀s' Creed*** Apostolisches Glaubensbekenntnis; **2.** *fig.* A'postel *m*, Verfechter *m*, Vorkämpfer *m*: ***~ of Free Trade***; **a·pos·to·late** [ə'pɒstəʊlət] *s.* Aposto'lat *n*, A'postelamt *n*, -würde *f*; **ap·os·tol·ic**, *oft* ♀ [ˌæpə'stɒlɪk] *adj.* (□ ***~ally***) apo'stolisch: ***~ succession*** apostolische Nachfolge; ***♀ See*** Heiliger Stuhl.

a·pos·tro·phe [ə'pɒstrəfɪ] *s.* **1.** (feierliche) Anrede; **2.** *ling.* Apo'stroph *m*; **a'pos·tro·phize** [-faɪz] *v/t.* apostrophieren: a) mit e-m Apo'stroph versehen, b) *j-n besonders* ansprechen, sich wenden an (*acc.*).

a·poth·e·car·y [ə'pɒθəkərɪ] *s. obs. bsd. Am.* Apo'theker *m.*

ap·o·thegm ['æpəʊθem] *s.* Denk-, Kern-, Lehrspruch *m*; Ma'xime *f.*

a·poth·e·o·sis [əˌpɒθɪ'əʊsɪs] *s.* **1.** Apothe'ose *f*: a) Vergöttlichung *f*, b) *fig.* Verherrlichung *f*, Vergötterung *f*; **2.** *fig.* Ide'al *n.*

Ap·pa·lach·i·an [ˌæpə'leɪtʃjən] *adj.*: ***~ Mountains*** *die* Appalachen (*Gebirge im Nordosten der USA*).

ap·pal, *Am. a.* **ap·pall** [ə'pɔːl] *v/t.* erschrecken, entsetzen: ***be ~led*** entsetzt sein (***at*** über *acc.*); **ap'pal·ling** [-lɪŋ] *adj.* □ erschreckend, entsetzlich, beängstigend.

ap·pa·nage ['æpənɪdʒ] *s.* **1.** Apa'nage *f e-s Prinzen*; *fig.* Erbteil *n*; Einnahme (-quelle) *f*; **2.** abhängiges Gebiet; **3.** *fig.* Merkmal *n*, Zubehör *n.*

ap·pa·ra·tus [ˌæpə'reɪtəs] *pl.* **-tus** [-təs], **-tus·es** *s.* **1.** Appa'rat *m*, Gerät *n*, Vorrichtung *f*; *coll.* Apparat(e *pl.*) *m* (*a. fig.*), Appara'tur *f*, Maschine'rie *f* (*a. fig.*): ***~ work*** Geräteturnen *n*; **2.** ⚕ Sy'stem *n*, Appa'rat *m*: ***respiratory ~*** Atmungsapparat, Atemwerkzeuge *pl.*

ap·par·el [ə'pærəl] *s.* **1.** Kleidung *f*, Tracht *f*; **2.** *fig.* Gewand *n*, Schmuck *m.*

ap·par·ent [ə'pærənt] *adj.* □ → ***apparently***; **1.** sichtbar; **2.** augenscheinlich, offenbar; ersichtlich, einleuchtend: → ***heir***; **3.** scheinbar, anscheinend, Schein…; **ap'par·ent·ly** [-lɪ] *adv.* anscheinend, wie es scheint; **ap·pa·ri·tion** [ˌæpə'rɪʃən] *s.* **1.** (plötzliches) Erscheinen; **2.** Erscheinung *f*, Gespenst *n*, Geist *m.*

ap·peal [ə'piːl] **I** *v/i.* **1.** (***to***) appellieren, sich wenden (an *acc.*); *j-n od. et.* (als Zeugen) anrufen, sich berufen (auf *acc.*): ***~ to the law*** das Gesetz anrufen; ***~ to history*** die Geschichte als Zeugen anrufen; ***~ to the country*** *pol. Brit.*

(das Parlament auflösen u.) Neuwahlen ausschreiben; **2.** (***to s.o. for s.th.***) (j-n) dringend (um et.) bitten, (j-n um et.) anrufen; **3.** Einspruch erheben; *bsd.* ⚖ Berufung *od.* Revisi'on *od.* Beschwerde einlegen (***against***, ⚖ *mst* ***from*** gegen); **4.** (***to***) wirken (auf *acc.*), reizen (*acc.*), gefallen, zusagen (*dat.*), Anklang finden (bei); **II** *s.* **5.** (***to***) dringende Bitte (an *acc.*, ***for*** um); Aufruf *m*, Mahnung *f* (an *acc.*); Werbung *f* (bei); Aufforderung *f* (*gen.*); **6.** (***to***) Ap'pell *m* (an *acc.*), Anrufung *f* (*gen.*): ~ ***to reason*** Appell an die Vernunft; **7.** (***to***) Verweisung *f* (an *acc.*), Berufung *f* (auf *acc.*); **8.** ⚖ Rechtsmittel *n* (***from*** *od.* ***against*** gegen): a) Berufung *f*, Revisi'on *f*, b) (Rechts)Beschwerde *f*, Einspruch *m*: ***Court of*** ♀ Berufungs- *od.* Revisionsgericht *n*; **9.** (***to***) Wirkung *f*, Anziehung(skraft) *f* (auf *acc.*); ✝, *thea. etc.* Zugkraft *f*; Anklang *m*, Beliebtheit *f* (bei); **ap'peal·ing** [-lɪŋ] *adj.* ☐ **1.** flehend; **2.** ansprechend, reizvoll, gefällig.

ap·pear [ə'pɪə] *v/i.* **1.** erscheinen (*a. von Büchern*), sich zeigen; *öffentlich* auftreten; **2.** erscheinen, sich stellen (*vor Gericht etc.*); **3.** scheinen, den Anschein haben, aussehen, *j-m* vorkommen: ***it ~s to me you are right*** mir scheint, Sie haben recht; ***he ~s to be tired***; ***it does not ~ that*** es liegt kein Anhaltspunkt dafür vor, daß; **4.** sich her'ausstellen: ***it ~s from this*** hieraus ergibt sich *od.* geht hervor; **ap·pearance** [ə'pɪərəns] *s.* **1.** Erscheinen *n*, *öffentliches* Auftreten, Vorkommen *n*: ***make one's ~*** sich einstellen, sich zeigen; ***put in an ~*** (persönlich) erscheinen; **2.** (äußere) Erscheinung, Aussehen *n*, *das* Äußere: ***at first ~*** beim ersten Anblick; **3.** äußerer Schein, (An)Schein *m*: ***there is every ~ that*** es hat ganz den Anschein, daß; ***in ~*** anscheinend; ***to all ~(s)*** allem Anschein nach; ***~s are against him*** der (Augen)Schein spricht gegen ihn; ***keep up*** (*od.* ***save***) ***~s*** den Schein wahren.

ap·pease [ə'pi:z] *v/t.* **1.** *j-n od. j-s Zorn etc.* beruhigen, beschwichtigen; *Streit* schlichten, beilegen; *Leiden* mildern; *Durst etc.* stillen; *Neugier* befriedigen; **2.** *bsd. pol.* (durch Nachgiebigkeit *od.* Zugeständnisse) beschwichtigen; **ap'pease·ment** [-mənt] *s.* Beruhigung *f etc.*; Be'schwichtigung(spoli,tik) *f*; **ap'peas·er** [-zə] *s. pol.* Be'schwichtigungspo,litiker *m*.

ap·pel·lant [ə'pelənt] **I** *adj.* appellierend; **II** *s.* Appel'lant *m*, Berufungskläger(in); Beschwerdeführer(in); **ap'pel·late** [-lət] *adj.* Berufungs...: ~ ***court*** Berufungsinstanz *f*, Revisions-, Appellationsgericht *n*.

ap·pel·la·tion [,æpə'leɪʃn] *s.* Benennung *f*, Name *m*; **ap·pel·la·tive** [ə'pelətɪv] **I** *adj.* ☐ *ling.* appella'tiv: ~ ***name*** Gattungsname *m*; **II** *s. ling.* Gattungsname *m*.

ap·pel·lee [,æpe'li:] *s.* ⚖ Berufungsbeklagte(r *m*) *f*.

ap·pend [ə'pend] *v/t.* **1.** (***to***) befestigen, anbringen (an *dat.*), anhängen (an *acc.*); **2.** hin'zu-, beifügen (***to*** *dat.*, zu): ***to ~ the signature***; ***to ~ a price-list***; **ap'pend·age** [-dɪdʒ] *s.* **1.** Anhang *m*, Anhängsel *n*, Zubehör *n*, *m*; **2.** *fig.* Anhängsel *n*: a) Beigabe *f*, b) (ständiger) Begleiter; **ap·pen·dec·to·my** [,æpen'dektəmɪ] *s.* 'Blinddarmoperati,on *f*; **ap·pen·di·ces** *pl. von* ***appendix***; **ap·pen·di·ci·tis** [ə,pendɪ'saɪtɪs] *s.* ⚕ Blinddarmentzündung *f*; **ap·pen·dix** [ə'pendɪks] *pl.* **-dix·es**, **-di·ces** [-dɪsi:z] *s.* **1.** Anhang *m e-s Buches*; **2.** ⚙ Ansatz *m*; **3.** *anat.* Fortsatz *m*: (***vermiform***) ~ Wurmfortsatz *m*, Blinddarm *m*.

ap·per·tain [,æpə'teɪn] *v/i.* (***to***) gehören (zu), (zu)gehören (*dat.*); *j-m* zustehen, gebühren (*dat.*).

ap·pe·tence ['æpɪtəns], **'ap·pe·ten·cy** [-sɪ] *s.* **1.** Verlangen *n* (***of***, ***for***, ***after*** nach); **2.** instink'tive Neigung; (Na'tur) Trieb *m*.

ap·pe·tite ['æpɪtaɪt] *s.* **1.** (***for***) Verlangen *n*, Gelüst *n* (nach); Neigung *f*, Trieb *m*, Lust *f* (zu), ‚Appe'tit' (auf *acc.*); **2.** Appe'tit *m* (***for*** auf *acc.*), Eßlust *f*: ***have an ~*** Appetit haben; ***take away*** (*od.* ***spoil***) ***s.o.'s ~*** j-m den Appetit nehmen *od.* verderben; ***loss of ~*** Appetitlosigkeit *f*; ~ ***suppressant*** Appetitzügler *m*; **'ap·pe·tiz·er** [-aɪzə] *s.* appe'titanregendes Mittel *od.* Getränk *od.* Gericht, Aperi'tif *m*; **'ap·pe·tiz·ing** [-aɪzɪŋ] *adj.* ☐ appe'titanregend; appe'titlich, lecker (*beide a. fig.*); *fig.* reizvoll, ‚zum Anbeißen'.

ap·plaud [ə'plɔ:d] **I** *v/i.* applaudieren, Beifall spenden; **II** *v/t.* beklatschen, *j-m* Beifall spenden; *fig.* loben, billigen; *j-m* zustimmen; **ap·plause** [ə'plɔ:z] *s.* **1.** Ap'plaus *m*, Beifall(klatschen *n*) *m*: ***break into ~*** in Beifall ausbrechen; **2.** *fig.* Zustimmung *f*, Anerkennung *f*, Beifall *m*.

ap·ple ['æpl] *s.* Apfel *m*: ~ ***of discord*** *fig.* Zankapfel; ~ ***of one's eye*** *anat.* Augapfel (*a. fig.*); **'~-cart** *s.* Apfelkarren *m*: ***upset the*** *od.* ***s.o.'s ~*** *fig.* alle *od.* j-s Pläne über den Haufen werfen; ~ **char·lotte** ['ʃɑ:lət] *s.* 'Apfelchar,lotte *f* (*e-e Apfelspeise*); ~ **dump·ling** *s.* Apfel *m* im Schlafrock; ~ **frit·ters** *s. pl.* (in Teig gebackene) Apfelschnitten *pl.*; **'~-jack** *s. Am.* Apfelschnaps *m*; **'~-pie** *s.* (warmer) gedeckter Apfelkuchen; **'~-pie or·der** *s.* F schönste Ordnung: ***everything is in ~*** alles ‚in Butter' *od.* in bester Ordnung; ~ **pol·ish·er** *s. Am.* F Speichellecker *m*; **'~-sauce** *s.* **1.** Apfelmus *n*; **2.** *Am. sl.* a) ‚Schmus' *m*, Schmeiche'lei *f*, b) *int.* Quatsch!; **'~-tree** *s.* ⚘ Apfelbaum *m*.

ap·pli·ance [ə'plaɪəns] *s.* Gerät *n*, Vorrichtung *f*, Appa'rat *m*.

ap·pli·ca·bil·i·ty [,æplɪkə'bɪlətɪ] *s.* (***to***) Anwendbarkeit *f* (auf *acc.*), Eignung *f* (für); **ap·pli·ca·ble** ['æplɪkəbl] *adj.* ☐ (***to***) anwendbar (auf *acc.*), passend, geeignet (für): ***not ~*** *in Formularen*: nicht zutreffend, entfällt; **ap·pli·cant** ['æplɪkənt] *s.* (***for***) Bewerber(in) (um), Besteller(in) (*gen.*); Antragsteller(in); (Pa'tent)Anmelder(in); **ap·pli·ca·tion** [,æplɪ'keɪʃn] *s.* **1.** ⚕ Auf-, Anlegen *n e-s Verbandes etc.*; Anwendung *f* (***to*** auf *acc.*); **2.** (***to*** für) An-, Verwendung *f*, Gebrauch *m*: ~ ***of poison***; ~ ***of drastic measures***; **3.** (***to***) Anwendung *f*, Anwendbarkeit *f* (auf *acc.*); Beziehung *f* (zu): ***have no ~*** keine Anwendung finden, unangebracht sein, nicht zutreffen; **4.** (***for***) Gesuch *n*, Bitte *f* (um); Antrag *m* (auf *acc.*): ***an ~ for help***; ***make an ~*** ein Gesuch einreichen, e-n Antrag stellen; ~ ***for a patent*** Anmeldung *f* zum Patent; ***samples on ~*** Muster auf Verlangen *od.* Wunsch; **5.** Bewerbung *f* (***for*** um): (***letter of***) ~ Bewerbungsschreiben *n*; **6.** Fleiß *m*, Eifer *m* (***in*** bei): ~ ***in one's studies***; **ap·plied** [ə'plaɪd] *adj.* angewandt: ~ ***chemistry*** (***psychology*** *etc.*); ~ ***art*** Kunstgewerbe *n*, Gebrauchsgraphik *f*.

ap·pli·qué [æ'pli:keɪ] *adj.* aufgelegt, -genäht, appliziert: ~ ***work*** Applikation (-sstickerei) *f*.

ap·ply [ə'plaɪ] **I** *v/t.* **1.** (***to***) auflegen, -tragen, legen (auf *acc.*), anbringen (an, auf *dat.*): ~ ***a plaster to a wound***; **2.** (***to***) a) verwenden (auf *acc.*, für), b) anwenden (auf *acc.*): ~ ***a rule***; ***applied to modern conditions*** auf moderne Verhältnisse angewandt, c) gebrauchen (für): ~ ***the brakes*** bremsen, d) verwerten (zu, für); **3.** *Sinn* richten (***to*** auf *acc.*); **4.** ~ ***o.s.*** sich widmen (***to*** *dat.*): ~ ***o.s. to a task***; **II** *v/i.* **5.** (***to***) sich wenden (an *acc.*, ***for*** wegen), sich melden (bei): ~ ***to the manager***; **6.** (***for***) beantragen (*acc.*); sich bewerben, sich bemühen, ersuchen (um): ~ ***for a job***; **7.** (***for***) (*bsd.* zum Pa'tent) anmelden (*acc.*); **8.** (***to***) Anwendung finden (bei, auf *acc.*), passen, zutreffen (auf *acc.*), gelten (für): ***cross out that which does not ~*** Nichtzutreffendes bitte streichen.

ap·point [ə'pɔɪnt] *v/t.* **1.** ernennen, berufen, an-, bestellen: ~ ***a teacher*** e-n Lehrer anstellen; ~ ***an heir*** e-n Erben einsetzen; ~ ***s.o. governor*** j-n zum Gouverneur ernennen, j-n als Gouverneur berufen; ~ ***s.o. to a professorship*** j-m e-e Professur übertragen; **2.** festsetzen, bestimmen; vorschreiben; verabreden: ~ ***a time***; ***the ~ed day*** der festgesetzte Tag *od.* Termin, der Stichtag; ***the ~ed task*** die vorgeschriebene Aufgabe; **3.** einrichten, ausrüsten: ***a well-~ed house***; **ap·point·ee** [əpɔɪn'ti:] *s.* Ernannte(r *m*) *f*; **ap'point·ment** [-mənt] *s.* **1.** Ernennung *f*, Anstellung *f*, Berufung *f*, Einsetzung *f* (*a. e-s Erben*), Bestellung *f* (*bsd. e-s Vormunds*); ♀(***s***) ***Board*** Behörde *f* zur Besetzung höherer Posten; ***by special ~ to the King*** Königlicher Hoflieferant; **2.** Amt *n*, Stellung *f*; **3.** Festsetzung *f bsd. e-s Termins*; **4.** Verabredung *f*; Zs.-kunft *f*; *geschäftlich, beim Arzt etc.*: Ter'min *m*: ***by ~*** nach Vereinbarung; ***make an ~*** e-e Verabredung treffen; ***keep*** (***break***) ***an ~*** eine Verabredung (nicht) einhalten; ~ ***book*** Terminkalender *m*; **5.** *pl.* Ausstattung *f*, Einrichtung *f e-r Wohnung etc.*

ap·por·tion [ə'pɔ:ʃn] *v/t. e-n Anteil* zuteilen, (proportio'nal *od.* gerecht) ein-, verteilen; *Lob* erteilen, zollen; *Aufgabe* zuteilen; *Schuld* beimessen; *Kosten* 'umlegen; **ap'por·tion·ment** [-mənt] *s.* (gleichmäßige *od.* gerechte) Ver-, Zuteilung, Einteilung *f*; ('Kosten),Umlage *f*.

ap·po·site ['æpəʊzɪt] *adj.* ☐ (***to***) passend (für), angemessen (*dat.*), geeignet (für); angebracht, treffend; **'ap·po·site·ness** [-nɪs] *s.* Angemessenheit *f*; **ap·po·si·tion** [,æpə'zɪʃn] *s.* **1.** Bei-, Hin'zufügung *f*; **2.** *ling.* Appositi'on *f*,

Beifügung *f*.

ap·prais·al [əˈpreɪzl] *s*. (Ab)Schätzung *f*, Taxierung *f*; Schätzwert *m*, *a. ped.* Bewertung *f*; *fig.* Beurteilung *f*, Würdigung *f*; **ap·praise** [əˈpreɪz] *v/t.* (ab-, ein)schätzen, taxieren, bewerten, beurteilen, würdigen; **apˈpraise·ment** [-mənt] → ***appraisal***; **apˈprais·er** [-zə] *s*. (Ab)Schätzer *m*.

ap·pre·ci·a·ble [əˈpriːʃəbl] *adj.* □ merklich, spürbar, nennenswert; **ap·pre·ci·ate** [əˈpriːʃɪeɪt] **I** *v/t.* **1.** (hoch-)schätzen; richtig einschätzen, würdigen, zu schätzen *od.* würdigen wissen; **2.** aufgeschlossen sein für, Gefallen finden an (*dat.*), Sinn haben für: ***~ music***; **3.** dankbar sein für: ***I ~ your kindness***; **4.** (richtig) beurteilen, einsehen, (klar) erkennen: ***~ a danger***; **5.** *bsd. Am.* a) den Wert *e-r Sache* erhöhen, b) aufwerten; **II** *v/i.* **6.** im Wert steigen; **ap·pre·ci·a·tion** [əˌpriːʃɪˈeɪʃn] *s*. **1.** Würdigung *f*, (Wert-, Ein)Schätzung *f*, Anerkennung *f*; **2.** Verständnis *n*, Aufgeschlossenheit *f*, Sinn *m* (***of*** für): ***~ of music***; **3.** richtige Beurteilung, Einsicht *f*; **4.** (kritische) Würdigung, *bsd. günstige* Kriˈtik; **5.** (***of***) Dankbarkeit *f* (für), (dankbare) Anerkennung (*gen.*); **6.** ✝ a) Wertsteigerung *f*, b) Aufwertung *f*; **apˈpre·ci·a·tive** [-ʃjətɪv] *adj.*; **apˈpre·ci·a·to·ry** [-ʃjətərɪ] *adj.* □ (***of***) **1.** anerkennend, würdigend (*acc.*); **2.** verständnisvoll, empfänglich, dankbar (für): ***be ~ of*** zu schätzen wissen.

ap·pre·hend [ˌæprɪˈhend] *v/t.* **1.** ergreifen, festnehmen, verhaften: ***~ a thief***; **2.** *fig.* wahrnehmen, erkennen; begreifen, erfassen; **3.** *fig.* (be)fürchten, ahnen, wittern; **ˌap·preˈhen·sion** [-nʃn] *s*. **1.** Festnahme *f*, Verhaftung *f*; **2.** *fig.* Begreifen *n*, Erfassen *n*; Verstand *m*, Fassungskraft *f*; **3.** Begriff *m*, Ansicht *f*: ***according to popular ~***; **4.** (Vor)Ahnung *f*, Besorgnis *f*: ***in ~ of*** *et.* befürchtend; **ˌap·preˈhen·sive** [-sɪv] *adj.* □ besorgt (***for*** um; ***of*** wegen; ***that*** daß), ängstlich: ***~ for one's life*** um sein Leben besorgt; ***be ~ of dangers*** sich vor Gefahren fürchten.

ap·pren·tice [əˈprentɪs] **I** *s*. Lehrling *m*, Auszubildende(r) *m*; Praktiˈkant(in); *fig.* Anfänger *m*, Neuling *m*; **II** *v/t.* in die Lehre geben: ***be ~d to*** in die Lehre kommen zu, in der Lehre sein bei; **apˈpren·tice·ship** [-tɪʃɪp] *s*. a) *a. fig.* Lehrjahre *pl.*, -zeit *f*, Lehre *f*: ***serve one's ~*** (***with***) in die Lehre gehen (bei), b) Lehrstelle *f*.

ap·prise [əˈpraɪz] *v/t.* in Kenntnis setzen, unterˈrichten (***of*** von).

ap·pro [ˈæprəʊ] *s*.: ***on ~*** ✝ F zur Ansicht, zur Probe.

ap·proach [əˈprəʊtʃ] **I** *v/i.* **1.** sich nähern; (herˈan)nahen, bevorstehen; **2.** *fig.* nahekommen, ähnlich sein (***to*** *dat.*); **3.** ✈ an-, einfliegen; **II** *v/t.* **4.** sich nähern (*dat.*): ***~ the city***; ***~ the end***; **5.** *fig.* nahekommen (*dat.*), (fast) erreichen: ***~ the required sum***; **6.** herˈangehen an (*acc.*): ***~ a task***; **7.** herˈantreten *od.* sich herˈanmachen an (*acc.*): ***~ a customer***, ***~ a girl***; **8.** *j-n* angehen, bitten; sich an *j-n* wenden (***for*** um, ***on*** wegen); **9.** auf *et.* zu sprechen kommen; **III** *s*. **10.** (Heran)Nahen *n* (*a. e-s Zeitpunktes etc.*); Annäherung *f*, Anmarsch *m* (*a.* ⚔), ✈ Anflug *m*; **11.** *fig.* (***to***) Nahekommen *n*, Annäherung *f* (an *acc.*); Ähnlichkeit *f* (mit): ***an ~ to truth*** annähernd die Wahrheit; **12.** Zugang *m*, Zufahrt *f*, Ein-, Auffahrt *f*; *pl.* ⚔ Laufgräben *pl.*; **13.** (***to***) Einführung *f* (in *acc.*), erster Schritt (zu), Versuch *m* (*gen.*): ***a good ~ to philosophy***; ***an ~ to a smile*** der Versuch e-s Lächelns; **14.** *oft pl.* Herantreten *n* (***to*** an *acc.*), Annäherungsversuche *pl.*; **15.** *a.* ***method*** *od.* ***line of ~*** (***to***) a) Art *f* und Weise *f et.* anzupacken, Meˈthode *f*, Verfahren *n*: (***basic***) ***~*** Ansatz *m*, b) Auffassung *f* (*gen.*), Haltung *f*, Einstellung *f* (zu), Stellungnahme *f* (zu); Behandlung *f e-s Themas etc.*; **apˈproach·a·ble** [-tʃəbl] *adj.* zugänglich (*a. fig.*).

ap·pro·ba·tion [ˌæprəʊˈbeɪʃn] *s*. Billigung *f*, Genehmigung *f*; Bestätigung *f*; Zustimmung *f*, Beifall *m*.

ap·pro·pri·ate I *adj.* [əˈprəʊprɪət] □ **1.** (***to***, ***for***) passend, geeignet (für, zu), angemessen (*dat.*), entsprechend (*dat.*), richtig (für); **2.** eigen, zugehörig (***to*** *dat.*); **II** *v/t.* [-ɪeɪt] **3.** verwenden, bereitstellen; *parl. bsd. Geld* bewilligen (***to*** zu, ***for*** für); **4.** sich *et.* aneignen (*a. widerrechtlich*); **ap·pro·pri·a·tion** [əˌprəʊprɪˈeɪʃn] *s*. **1.** Aneignung *f*, Besitzergreifung *f*; **2.** Verwendung *f*, Bereitstellung *f*; *parl.* (Geld)Bewilligung *f*.

ap·prov·a·ble [əˈpruːvəbl] *adj.* zu billigen(d), anerkennenswert; **apˈprov·al** [-vl] *s*. **1.** Billigung *f*, Genehmigung *f*: ***the plan has my ~***; ***on ~*** zur Ansicht, auf Probe; **2.** Anerkennung *f*, Beifall *m*: ***meet with ~*** Beifall finden; **ap·prove** [əˈpruːv] **I** *v/t.* **1.** billigen, gutheißen, anerkennen, annehmen; bestätigen, genehmigen; **2.** ***~ o.s.*** sich erweisen *od.* bewähren (***as*** als); **II** *v/i.* **3.** billigen, anerkennen, gutheißen, genehmigen (***of*** *acc.*): ***~ of s.o.*** j-n akzeptieren; ***be ~d of*** Anklang finden; **apˈproved** [-vd] *adj.* **1.** erprobt, bewährt: ***an ~ friend***; ***in the ~ manner***; **2.** anerkannt: ***~ school*** *Brit. hist.* (staatliche) Erziehungsanstalt; **apˈprov·er** [-və] *s*. ⚖ *Brit.* Kronzeuge *m*; **apˈprov·ing·ly** [-vɪŋlɪ] *adv.* zustimmend, beifällig.

ap·prox·i·mate I *adj.* [əˈprɒksɪmət] □ → ***approximately***; **1.** annähernd, ungefähr; Näherungs… (*-formel, -rechnung, -wert*); **2.** *fig.* sehr ähnlich; **II** *v/t.* [-meɪt] **3.** sich *e-r Menge od. e-m Wert* nähern, nahe- *od.* näherkommen (*dat.*); **III** *v/i.* [-meɪt] **4.** nahe- *od.* näherkommen (*oft mit* ***to*** *dat.*); **apˈprox·i·mate·ly** [-lɪ] *adv.* annähernd, ungefähr, etwa; **ap·prox·i·ma·tion** [əˌprɒksɪˈmeɪʃn] *s*. **1.** Annäherung *f* (***to*** an *acc.*): ***an ~ to the truth*** annähernd die Wahrheit; **2.** 𝔄 a) (An)Näherung *f* (***to*** an *acc.*), b) Näherungswert *m*; annähernde Gleichheit; **apˈprox·i·ma·tive** [-ətɪv] *adj.* □ annähernd.

ap·pur·te·nance [əˈpɜːtɪnəns] *s*. **1.** Zubehör *n*, *m*; **2.** *pl.* ⚖ Reˈalrechte *pl.* (*aus Eigentum an Liegenschaften*); **apˈpur·te·nant** [-nt] *adj.* zugehörig (***to*** *dat.*).

a·pri·cot [ˈeɪprɪkɒt] *s*. Apriˈkose *f*.

A·pril [ˈeɪprəl] *s*. Aˈpril *m*: ***in ~*** im April; ***~ fool*** Aprilnarr *m*; ***~ Fools Day*** der 1. April; ***make an ~ fool of s.o.***, ***~-fool s.o.*** j-n in den April schicken.

a pri·o·ri [ˌeɪpraɪˈɔːraɪ] *adv. u. adj. phls.* **1.** a priˈori, dedukˈtiv; **2.** F mutmaßlich, ohne (Über)ˈPrüfung.

a·pron [ˈeɪprən] *s*. **1.** Schürze *f*; Schurz (-fell *n*) *m*; **2.** Schurz *m von Freimaurern od. engl. Bischöfen*; **3.** ⚙ a) Schutzblech *n*, -haube *f*, b) *mot.* Blech-, Windschutz *m*, c) Schutzleder *n*, Kniedecke *f an Fahrzeugen*; **4.** ✈ (betoniertes) (Hallen)Vorfeld; **5.** *a.* ***~-stage*** *thea.* Vorbühne *f*; **ˈ~-strings** *s. pl.* Schürzenbänder *pl.*; *fig.* Gängelband *n*: ***tied to one's mother's ~*** an Mutters Schürzenzipfel hängend; ***tied to s.o.'s ~*** unter j-s Fuchtel stehend.

ap·ro·pos [ˈæprəpəʊ] **I** *adv.* **1.** angemessen, zur rechten Zeit: ***he arrived very ~*** er kam wie gerufen; **2.** ˈhinsichtlich (***of*** *gen.*): ***~ of our talk***; **3.** aproˈpos, nebenbei bemerkt; **II** *adj.* **4.** passend, angemessen, treffend: ***his remark was very ~***.

apse [æps] *s*. ⚠ ˈApsis *f*.

apt [æpt] *adj.* □ **1.** passend, geeignet; treffend: ***an ~ remark***; **2.** geneigt, neigend (***to*** *inf.* zu *inf.*): ***he is ~ to believe it*** er wird es wahrscheinlich glauben; ***~ to be overlooked*** leicht zu übersehen; ***~ to rust*** leicht rostend; **3.** (***at***) geschickt (in *dat.*), begabt (für): ***an ~ pupil***.

ap·ter·ous [ˈæptərəs] *adj.* **1.** *zo.* flügellos; **2.** ♀ ungeflügelt.

ap·ti·tude [ˈæptɪtjuːd] *s*. (*ped.* Sonder-)Begabung *f*, Befähigung *f*, Taˈlent *n*; Fähigkeit *f*; Auffassungsgabe *f*; Eignung *f* (***for*** für, zu): ***~ test*** *Am.* Eignungsprüfung *f*; **apt·ness** [ˈæptnɪs] *s*. **1.** Angemessenheit *f*, Tauglichkeit *f* (***for*** für, zu); **2.** (***for***, ***to***) Neigung *f* (zu), Eignung *f* (für, zu), Geschicklichkeit *f* (in *dat.*).

aq·ua·cul·ture [ˈækwəkʌltʃə] *s*. ˈAquakulˌtur *f*.

aq·ua for·tis [ˌækwəˈfɔːtɪs] *s*. ⚗ Scheidewasser *n*, Salˈpetersäure *f*.

aq·ua·lung [ˈækwəlʌŋ] *s*. Taucherlunge *f*, Atmungsgerät *n*; **ˈaq·ua·lun·ger** [-ŋə] *s*. Tiefsee-, Sporttaucher(in).

aq·ua·ma·rine [ˌækwəməˈriːn] *s*. **1.** *min.* Aquamaˈrin *m*; **2.** Aquamaˈrinblau *n*.

aq·ua·plane [ˈækwəpleɪn] **I** *s*. **1.** *Wassersport*: Monoski *m*; **II** *v/i.* **2.** Monoski laufen; **3.** *mot.* a) aufschwimmen (*Reifen*), b) ‚schwimmen', die Bodenhaftung verlieren; **ˈaq·ua·plan·ing** *s*. **1.** Monoskilauf *m*; **2.** *mot.* Aquaˈplaning *n*.

aq·ua·relle [ˌækwəˈrel] *s*. Aquaˈrell(maleˌrei *f*) *n*; **ˌaq·uaˈrel·list** [-lɪst] *s*. Aquaˈrellmaler(in).

A·quar·i·an [əˈkweərɪən] *s. ast.* Wassermann *m* (*Person*).

a·quar·i·um [əˈkweərɪəm] *pl.* **-i·ums** *od.* **-i·a** [-ɪə] *s*. Aˈquarium *n*.

A·quar·i·us [əˈkweərɪəs] *s. ast.* Wassermann *m*.

aq·ua show [ˈækwə] *s. Brit.* ˈWasserballˌlett *n*.

a·quat·ic [əˈkwætɪk] **I** *adj.* **1.** Wasser…: ***~ plants***; ***~ sports*** Wassersport *m*; **II** *s*. **2.** *biol.* Wassertier *n*, -pflanze *f*; **3.** *pl.* Wassersport *m*.

aq·ua·tint [ˈækwətɪnt] *s*. Aquaˈtinta *f*, ˈTuschmaˌnier *f*.

aq·ua vi·tae [ˌækwəˈvaɪtiː] *s*. **1.** ⚗ *hist.* ˈAlkohol *m*; **2.** Branntwein *m*.

aq·ue·duct ['ækwɪdʌkt] *s.* Aquä'dukt *m*, *n*.
a·que·ous ['eɪkwɪəs] *adj.* wässerig, wäßrig (*a. fig.*), wasserartig, -haltig.
Aq·ui·la ['ækwɪlə] *s. ast.* Adler *m*.
aq·ui·le·gi·a [ˌækwɪ'li:dʒjə] *s.* ⚘ Ake'lei *f*.
aq·ui·line ['ækwɪlaɪn] *adj.* gebogen, Adler..., Habichts...: **~ nose**.
Ar·ab ['ærəb] **I** *s.* **1.** Araber(in); **2.** Araber *m* (*Pferd*); **3.** → **street Arab**; **II** *adj.* **4.** a'rabisch; **ar·a·besque** [ˌærə'besk] **I** *s.* Ara'beske *f*; **II** *adj.* ara'besk; **A·ra·bi·an** [ə'reɪbjən] **I** *adj.* **1.** a'rabisch: **The ~ Nights** Tausendundeine Nacht; **II** *s.* **2.** → **Arab** 1; **3.** → **Arab** 2; **'Ar·a·bic** [-bɪk] **I** *adj.* a'rabisch: **~ figures** (*od.* **numerals**) arabische Ziffern *od.* Zahlen; **II** *s. ling.* A'rabisch *n*; **'Ar·ab·ist** [-bɪst] *s.* Ara'bist *m*.
ar·a·ble ['ærəbl] **I** *adj.* pflügbar, anbaufähig; **II** *s.* Ackerland *n*.
Ar·a·by ['ærəbɪ] *s. poet.* A'rabien *n*.
ar·au·ca·ri·a [ˌærɔ:'keərɪə] *s.* ⚘ Zimmertanne *f*, Arau'karie *f*.
ar·bi·ter ['ɑ:bɪtə] *s.* **1.** Schiedsrichter *m*; **2.** *fig.* Richter *m* (**of** über *acc.*); **3.** *fig.* Herr *m*, Gebieter *m*; **ar·bi·trage** [ˌɑ:bɪ'trɑ:ʒ] *s.* ✝ Arbi'trage *f*; **ar·bi·tral** ['ɑ:bɪtrəl] *adj.* schiedsrichterlich: **~ award** Schiedsspruch *m*; **~ body** *od.* **court** Schiedsgericht *n*, -stelle *f*; **~ clause** Schiedsklausel *f*; **ar·bi·trar·i·ness** ['ɑ:bɪtrərɪnɪs] *s.* Willkür *f*, Eigenmächtigkeit *f*; **ar·bi·trar·y** ['ɑ:bɪtrərɪ] *adj.* ☐ **1.** willkürlich, eigenmächtig, -willig; **2.** launenhaft; **3.** ty'rannisch; **ar·bi·trate** ['ɑ:bɪtreɪt] **I** *v/t.* **1.** (als Schiedsrichter *od.* durch Schiedsspruch) entscheiden, schlichten, beilegen; **2.** e-m Schiedsspruch unter'werfen; **II** *v/i.* **3.** Schiedsrichter sein; **ar·bi·tra·tion** [ˌɑ:bɪ'treɪʃn] *s.* **1.** Schieds(gerichts)verfahren *n*; Schiedsspruch *m*; Schlichtung *f*: **court of ~** Schiedsgericht *n*, -hof *m*; **~ board** Schiedsstelle *f*; **submit to ~** e-m Schiedsgericht unterwerfen; **settle by ~** schiedsgerichtlich beilegen; **2.** ✝ (**~ of exchange** Wechsel)Arbitrage *f*; **'ar·bi·tra·tor** [-reɪtə] *s.* ⚖ Schiedsrichter *m*, -mann *m*.
ar·bor¹ *Am.* → **arbour**; **2 Day** *Am.* Tag *m* des Baums.
ar·bor² ['ɑ:bə] *s.* ⚙ Achse *f*, Welle *f*; (Aufsteck)Dorn *m*, Spindel *f*.
ar·bo·re·al [ɑ:'bɔ:rɪəl] *adj.* baumartig; Baum...; auf Bäumen lebend; **ar'bo·re·ous** [-ɪəs] *adj.* **1.** baumreich, waldig; **2.** baumartig; Baum...; **ar·bo·res·cent** [ˌɑ:bə'resnt] *adj.* baumartig, verzweigt; **ar·bo·re·tum** [ˌɑ:bə'ri:təm] *pl.* **-ta** [-tə] *s.* Arbo'retum *n*; **ar·bo·ri·cul·ture** ['ɑ:bərɪkʌltʃə] *s.* Baumzucht *f*.
ar·bor vi·tae [ˌɑ:bə'vaɪtɪ] *s.* ⚘ Lebensbaum *m*.
ar·bour ['ɑ:bə] *s.* Laube *f*.
arc [ɑ:k] **I** *s.* **1.** *a.* ✈, ⚙, *ast.* Bogen *m*; **2.** ⚡ (Licht)Bogen *m*: **~ welding** Lichtbogenschweißen *n*; **II** *v/i. a.* **~ over** ⚡ e-n (Licht)Bogen bilden, ‚funken'.
ar·cade [ɑ:'keɪd] *s.* Ar'kade *f*: a) Säulen-, Bogen-, Laubengang *m*, b) Pas'sage *f*; **ar'cad·ed** [-dɪd] *adj.* mit Arkaden (versehen).
Ar·ca·di·a [ɑ:'keɪdjə] *s.* Ar'kadien *n*, ländliches Para'dies *od.* I'dyll; **Ar'ca·di·an** [-ən] *adj.* ar'kadisch, i'dyllisch.
ar·cane [ɑ:'keɪn] *adj.* geheimnisvoll; **ar'ca·num** [-nəm] *pl.* **-na** [-nə] *s.* **1.** *hist.* ⚗ Ar'kanum *n*; Eli'xier *n*; **2.** *mst pl.* Geheimnis *n*, My'sterium *n*.
arch¹ [ɑ:tʃ] **I** *s.* **1.** *mst* ⚠ (Brücken-, Fenster- *etc.*)Bogen *m*; über'wölbter (Ein-, 'Durch)Gang; ('Eisenbahn- *etc.*) Über,führung *f*; Tri'umphbogen *m*; **2.** Wölbung *f*, Gewölbe *n*: **~ of the instep** (Fuß)Rist *m*, Spann *m*; **~ support** Senkfußeinlage *f*; **fallen ~es** Senkfuß *m*; **II** *v/t.* **3.** *a.* **~ over** mit Bogen versehen, über'wölben; **4.** wölben, krümmen: **~ the back** e-n Buckel machen (*Katze*); **III** *v/i.* **5.** sich wölben; sich krümmen.
arch² [ɑ:tʃ] *adj. oft* **arch-** erst, oberst, Haupt..., Erz...; schlimmst, Riesen...: **~ rogue** Erzschurke *m*.
arch³ [ɑ:tʃ] *adj.* ☐ schalkhaft, schelmisch: **an ~ look**.
arch- [ɑ:tʃ] *Präfix bei Titeln etc.*: erst, oberst, Haupt..., Erz...
ar·chae·o·log·ic, ar·chae·o·log·i·cal [ˌɑ:kɪə'lɒdʒɪk(l)] *adj.* ☐ archäo'logisch, Altertums...; **ar·chae·ol·o·gist** [ˌɑ:kɪ'ɒlədʒɪst] *s.* Archäo'loge *m*, Altertumsforscher *m*; **ar·chae·ol·o·gy** [ˌɑ:kɪ'ɒlədʒɪ] *s.* Archäolo'gie *f*, Altertumskunde *f*.
ar·cha·ic [ɑ:'keɪɪk] *adj.* (☐ **~ally**) ar'chaisch: a) altertümlich, b) *bsd. ling.* veraltet, altmodisch; **ar·cha·ism** ['ɑ:keɪɪzəm] *s.* **1.** *ling.* Archa'ismus *m*, veralteter Ausdruck; **2.** *et.* Veraltetes.
arch·an·gel ['ɑ:kˌeɪndʒəl] *s.* Erzengel *m*.
ˌarch|'bish·op [ˌɑ:tʃ-] *s.* Erzbischof *m*; **ˌ~'bish·op·ric** *s.* **1.** Erzbistum *n*; **2.** Amt *n* e-s Erzbischofs; **ˌ~'dea·con** *s.* Archidia'kon *m*; **ˌ~'di·o·cese** *s.* 'Erzdiöˌzese *f*; **ˌ~'du·cal** *adj.* erzherzoglich; **ˌ~'duch·ess** *s.* Erzherzogin *f*; **ˌ~'duch·y** *s.* Erzherzogtum *n*; **ˌ~'duke** *s.* Erzherzog *m*.
arched [ɑ:tʃt] *adj.* gewölbt, gebogen, gekrümmt.
ˌarch-'en·e·my *s.* → **arch-fiend**.
arch·er ['ɑ:tʃə] *s.* **1.** Bogenschütze *m*; **2.** 2 *ast.* Schütze *m*; **'arch·er·y** [-ərɪ] *s.* **1.** Bogenschießen *n*; **2.** *coll.* Bogenschützen *pl*.
ar·che·typ·al ['ɑ:kɪtaɪpl] *adj.* arche'typisch; **'ar·che·type** [-taɪp] *s.* Urform *f*, -bild *n*, Arche'typ(us) *m*.
ˌarch-'fiend [ˌɑ:tʃ-] *s.* Erzfeind *m*: a) Todfeind *m*, b) 'Satan *m*, Teufel *m*.
ar·chi·e·pis·co·pal [ˌɑ:kɪɪ'pɪskəpl] *adj.* erzbischöflich; **ˌar·chi·e'pis·co·pate** [-pɪt] *s.* Amt *n od.* Würde *f* e-s Erzbischofs.
Ar·chi·pel·a·go [ˌɑ:kɪ'pelɪgəʊ] **I** *npr.* Ä'gäisches Meer; **II** 2 *pl.* **-gos** *s.* Archi'pel *m*, Inselmeer *n*, -gruppe *f*.
ar·chi·tect ['ɑ:kɪtekt] **I** *s.* **1.** Archi'tekt (-in); **2.** *fig.* Schöpfer(in), Urheber(in), Archi'tekt *m*: **the ~ of one's fortunes** des eigenen Glückes Schmied; **II** *v/t.* **3.** bauen, entwerfen; **ar·chi·tec·ton·ic** [ˌɑ:kɪtek'tɒnɪk] **I** *adj.* (☐ **~ally**) **1.** architek'tonisch, baulich; **2.** aufbauend, konstruk'tiv, planvoll, schöpferisch, syste'matisch; **II** *s. mst pl. sg. konstr.* **3.** Architek'tonik *f*: a) Baukunst *f* (*als Fach*), b) künstlerischer Aufbau; **ar·chi·tec·tur·al** [ˌɑ:kɪ'tektʃərəl] *adj.* ☐ architek'tonisch, Architektur..., Bau...; **'ar·chi·tec·ture** [-tʃə] *s.* Archi'tek'tur *f*: a) Baukunst *f*; Bauart *f*, Baustil *m*, b) Konstrukti'on *f*; (Auf)Bau *m*, Struk'tur *f*, Anlage *f* (*a. fig.*), c) Bau (-werk *n*) *m*, *coll.* Gebäude *pl.*, Bauten *pl.*
ar·chi·trave ['ɑ:kɪtreɪv] *s.* ⚠ Archi'trav *m*, Tragbalken *m*.
ar·chive ['ɑ:kaɪv] *s. mst pl.* Ar'chiv *n*; Urkundensammlung *f*; **ar·chi·vist** ['ɑ:kɪvɪst] *s.* Archi'var *m*.
arch·ness ['ɑ:tʃnɪs] *s.* Schalkhaftigkeit *f*, Durch'triebenheit *f*.
ˌarch'priest [ˌɑ:tʃ-] *s. eccl. hist.* Erzpriester *m*.
'arch|·way ['ɑ:tʃ-] *s.* ⚠ Bogengang *m*, über'wölbter Torweg; **'~·wise** [-waɪz] *adv.* bogenartig.
'arc|-lamp *s.* ⚡ Bogenlampe *f*; **'~-light** *s.* Bogenlicht *n*, -lampe *f*.
arc·tic ['ɑ:ktɪk] **I** *adj.* **1.** 'arktisch, nördlich, Nord..., Polar...: **2 Circle** Nördlicher Polarkreis; **2 Ocean** Nördliches Eismeer; **~ fox** Polarfuchs *m*; **2.** *fig.* sehr kalt, eisig; **II** *s.* **3.** *die* 'Arktis; **4.** *pl. Am.* gefütterte, wasserdichte 'Überschuhe *pl.*
ar·dent ['ɑ:dənt] *adj.* ☐ **1.** *bsd. fig.* heiß, glühend, feurig: **~ eyes**; **~ love**; **~ spirits** hochprozentige Spirituosen; **2.** *fig.* feurig, heftig, inbrünstig, leidenschaftlich: **~ wish**; **~ admirer** glühender Verehrer; **3.** *fig.* begeistert; **ar·dour**, *Am.* **ar·dor** ['ɑ:də] *s. fig.* **1.** Feuer *n*, Glut *f*, Inbrunst *f*, Leidenschaft *f*; **2.** Eifer *m*, Begeisterung *f* (**for** für).
ar·du·ous ['ɑ:djʊəs] *adj.* ☐ **1.** schwierig, anstrengend, mühsam: **an ~ task**; **2.** ausdauernd, zäh, e'nergisch: **an ~ worker**; **3.** steil, jäh (*Berg etc.*); **'ar·du·ous·ness** [-nɪs] *s.* Schwierigkeit *f*, Mühsal *f*.
are¹ [ɑ:; ə] *pres. pl. u. 2 sg. von* **be**.
are² [ɑ:] *s.* Ar *n* (*Flächenmaß*).
a·re·a ['eərɪə] *s.* **1.** (begrenzte) Fläche, Flächenraum *m od.* -inhalt *m*; Grundstück *n*, Are'al *n*; Ober-, Grundfläche *f*; **2.** Raum *m*, Gebiet *n*, Gegend *f*: **danger ~** Gefahrenzone *f*; **prohibited** (*od.* **restricted**) **~** Sperrzone *f*; **~ code** *teleph. Am.* Vorwahl *f*, Vorwählnummer *f*; **in the Chicago ~** im (Groß-) Raum (von) Chikago; **3.** *fig.* Bereich *m*, Gebiet *n*; **4.** *a.* **~way** Kellervorhof *m*; **5.** ⚔ Operati'onsgebiet *n*: **~ bombing** Bombenflächenwurf *m*; **back ~** Etappe *f*; **forward ~** Kampfgebiet *n*; **6.** *anat.* (*Seh- etc.*)Zentrum *n*; **a·re·al** [-əl] *adj.* Flächen(inhalts)...
a·re·na [ə'ri:nə] *s.* A'rena *f*: a) Kampfplatz *m*, b) 'Stadion *n*, c) *fig.* Schauplatz *m*, Bühne *f*: **political ~**.
aren't [ɑ:nt] F *für* **are not**.
a·rête [æ'reɪt] (*Fr.*) *s.* (Fels)Grat *m*.
ar·gent ['ɑ:dʒənt] **I** *s.* Silber(farbe *f*) *n*; **II** *adj.* silberfarbig.
Ar·gen·tine ['ɑ:dʒəntaɪn], **Ar·gen·tin·e·an** [ˌɑ:dʒən'tɪnɪən] **I** *adj.* argen'tinisch; **II** *s.* Argen'tinier(in).
ar·gil ['ɑ:dʒɪl] *s.* Ton *m*, Töpfererde *f*; **ar·gil·la·ceous** [ˌɑ:dʒɪ'leɪʃəs] *adj.* tonartig, Ton...
ar·gon ['ɑ:gɒn] *s.* ⚗ 'Argon *n*.
Ar·go·naut ['ɑ:gənɔ:t] *s.* **1.** *myth.* Argo'naut *m*; **2.** *Am.* Goldsucher *m* in Kali'fornien (*1848/49*).
ar·got ['ɑ:gəʊ] *s.* Ar'got *n*, Jar'gon *m*, Slang *m*, *bsd.* Gaunersprache *f*.
ar·gu·a·ble ['ɑ:gjʊəbl] *adj.* ☐ disku-

'tabel, vertretbar: ***it is ~*** man könnte mit Recht behaupten; **'ar·gu·a·bly** [-lɪ] *adv.* vertretbarerweise; **ar·gue** ['ɑːgjuː] **I** *v/i.* **1.** argumentieren; Gründe (für *od.* wider) anführen: ***~ for s.th.*** a) für et. eintreten, b) für et. sprechen (*Sache*); ***~ against s.th.*** a) gegen et. Einwände machen, b) gegen et. sprechen (*Sache*); ***don't ~!*** keine Widerrede!; **2.** streiten, rechten (***with*** mit); disputieren (***about*** über *acc.*, ***for*** für, ***against*** gegen, ***with*** mit); **II** *v/t.* **3.** *e-e Angelegenheit* erörtern, diskutieren; **4.** *j-n* über'reden *od.* (durch Argu'mente) bewegen: ***~ s.o. into s.th.*** j-n zu et. überreden; ***~ s.o. out of s.th.*** j-n von et. abbringen; **5.** geltend machen, behaupten: ***~ that black is white***; **6.** begründen, beweisen; folgern (***from*** aus); **7.** verraten, (an)zeigen, beweisen: ***his clothes ~ poverty***; **ar·gu·ment** ['ɑːgjʊmənt] *s.* **1.** Argu'ment *n*, (Beweis)Grund *m*; Beweisführung *f*, Schlußfolgerung *f*; **2.** Behauptung *f*; Entgegnung *f*, Einwand *m*; **3.** Erörterung *f*, Besprechung *f*: ***hold an ~*** diskutieren; **4.** F (Wort)Streit *m*, Ausein'andersetzung *f*; Streitfrage *f*; **5.** 'Thema *n*, (Haupt)Inhalt *m*; **ar·gu·men·ta·tion** [ˌɑːgjʊmen'teɪʃn] *s.* **1.** Beweisführung *f*, Schlußfolgerung *f*; **2.** Erörterung *f*; **ar·gu·men·ta·tive** [ˌɑːgjʊ'mentətɪv] *adj.* □ **1.** streitlustig; **2.** strittig, um'stritten; **3.** 'kritisch; **4.** ***~ of*** hindeutend auf (*acc.*).

Ar·gus ['ɑːgəs] *npr. myth.* 'Argus *m*; **'~-eyed** *adj.* 'argusäugig, wachsam, mit 'Argusaugen.

a·ri·a ['ɑːrɪə] *s.* ♪ 'Arie *f*.

Ar·i·an ['eərɪən] *eccl.* **I** *adj.* ari'anisch; **II** *s.* Ari'aner *m*.

ar·id ['ærɪd] *adj.* □ dürr, trocken, unfruchtbar; *fig.* trocken, öde; **a·rid·i·ty** [æ'rɪdətɪ] *s.* Dürre *f*, Trockenheit *f*, Unfruchtbarkeit *f* (*a. fig.*).

A·ri·es ['eəriːz] *s. ast.* Widder *m*.

a·right [ə'raɪt] *adv.* recht, richtig: ***set ~*** richtigstellen.

a·rise [ə'raɪz] *v/i.* [*irr.*] **1.** (***from, out of***) entstehen, entspringen, her'vorgehen (aus), herrühren, stammen (von); **2.** entstehen, sich ergeben (***from*** aus); sich erheben, erscheinen, auftreten; **3.** aufstehen, sich erheben; **a·ris·en** [ə'rɪzn] *p.p. von* ***arise***.

ar·is·toc·ra·cy [ˌærɪ'stɒkrəsɪ] *s.* **1.** Aristokra'tie *f*, *coll. a.* Adel *m*; **2.** *fig.* E'lite *f*, Adel *m*; **a·ris·to·crat** ['ærɪstəkræt] *s.* Aristo'krat(in); Adlige(r *m*) *f*; *fig.* Pa'trizier(in); **a·ris·to·crat·ic, a·ris·to·crat·i·cal** [ˌærɪstə'krætɪk(l)] *adj.* □ aristo'kratisch, Adels...; *fig.* adlig, vornehm.

a·rith·me·tic [ə'rɪθmətɪk] *s.* Arith'metik *f*, Rechnen *n*, Rechenkunst *f*; **ar·ith·met·ic, ar·ith·met·i·cal** [ˌærɪθ'metɪk(l)] *adj.* □ arith'metisch, Rechen...; **a·rith·me·ti·cian** [əˌrɪθmə'tɪʃn] *s.* Rechner(in), Rechenmeister(in).

ark [ɑːk] *s.* **1.** Arche *f*: ***Noah's ~*** Arche Noah(s); **2.** Schrein *m*: ***℈ of the Covenant*** *bibl.* Bundeslade *f*.

arm¹ [ɑːm] *s.* **1.** *anat.* Arm *m*: ***keep s.o. at ~'s length*** *fig.* sich j-n vom Leibe halten; ***within ~'s reach*** in Reichweite; ***with open ~s*** *fig.* mit offenen Armen; ***fly into s.o.'s ~s*** j-m in die Arme fliegen; ***take s.o. in one's ~s*** j-n in die Arme nehmen; ***infant*** (*od.* ***babe***) ***in ~s*** Säugling *m*; **2.** Fluß-, Meeresarm *m*; **3.** Arm-, Seitenlehne *f*; **4.** Ast *m*, großer Zweig; **5.** Ärmel *m*; **6.** ⚙ Arm *m e-r Maschine etc.*: ***~ of a balance*** Waagebalken *m*; **7.** *fig.* Arm *m des Gesetzes etc.*

arm² [ɑːm] **I** *s.* **1.** ⚔ *mst pl.* Waffe(n *pl.*) *f*: ***do ~s drill*** Gewehrgriffe üben; ***in ~s*** bewaffnet; ***rise in ~s*** zu den Waffen greifen, sich empören; ***up in ~s*** a) in Aufruhr, b) *fig.* in Harnisch, in hellem Zorn; ***by force of ~s*** mit Waffengewalt; ***bear ~s*** a) Waffen tragen, b) als Soldat dienen; ***lay down ~s*** die Waffen strecken; ***take up ~s*** zu den Waffen greifen (*a. fig.*); ***~s dealer*** Waffenhändler *m*; ***~s control*** Rüstungskontrolle *f*; ***~s race*** Wettrüsten *n*; ***ground ~s!*** Gewehr nieder!; ***order ~s!*** Gewehr ab!; ***pile ~s!*** setzt die Gewehre zusammen!; ***port ~s!*** fällt das Gewehr!; ***present ~s!*** präsentiert das Gewehr!; ***slope ~s!*** das Gewehr über!; ***shoulder ~s!*** das Gewehr an Schulter!; ***to ~s!*** zu den Waffen!, ans Gewehr!; → ***passage at arms***; **2.** Waffengattung *f*, Truppe *f*: ***the naval ~*** die Kriegsmarine; **3.** *pl.* Wappen *n*; → ***coat*** 1; **II** *v/t.* **4.** bewaffnen: ***~ed to the teeth*** bis an die Zähne bewaffnet; **5.** ⚙ armieren, bewehren, befestigen, verstärken, *mit Metall* beschlagen; **6.** ⚔ *Munition, Mine* scharf machen; **7.** (aus)rüsten, bereit machen, versehen: ***be ~ed with an umbrella***; ***be ~ed with arguments***; **III** *v/i.* **8.** sich bewaffnen, sich (aus)rüsten.

ar·ma·da [ɑː'mɑːdə] *s.* **1.** ℈ *hist.* Ar'mada *f*; **2.** Kriegsflotte *f*, Luftflotte *f*, Geschwader *n*.

ar·ma·dil·lo [ˌɑːmə'dɪləʊ] *s. zo.* **1.** Arma'dill *n*, Gürteltier *n*; **2.** Apo'thekerassel *f*.

Ar·ma·ged·don [ˌɑːmə'gedn] *s. bibl. u. fig.* Entscheidungskampf *m*.

ar·ma·ment ['ɑːməmənt] *s.* ⚔ **1.** Kriegsstärke *f*, -macht *f e-s Landes*: ***naval ~*** Kriegsflotte *f*; **2.** Bewaffnung *f*, Bestückung *f e-s Kriegsschiffes etc.*; **3.** (Kriegsaus)Rüstung *f*: ***~ race*** Wettrüsten *n*; **ar·ma·ture** ['ɑːməˌtjʊə] *s.* **1.** Rüstung *f*, Panzer *m*; **2.** ⚙ Panzerung *f*, Beschlag *m*, Bewehrung *f*, Armierung *f*, Arma'tur *f*; **3.** ⚡ Anker *m* (*a. e-s Magneten etc.*), Läufer *m*: ***~ shaft*** Ankerwelle *f*; **4.** ⚘, *zo.* Bewehrung *f*.

'arm|·band *s.* Armbinde *f*; **ˌ~-'chair I** *s.* Lehnstuhl *m*, (Lehn)Sessel *m*; **II** *adj.* vom (*od.* am) grünen Tisch; Stammtisch..., Salon...: ***~ strategists***.

armed [ɑːmd] *adj.* **1.** bewaffnet: ***~ conflict***; ***~ neutrality***; ***~ forces*** (Gesamt-)Streitkräfte; ***~ robbery*** schwerer Raub; **2.** ⚔ a) scharf, zündfertig (*Munition etc.*), b) *a.* ⚙ → ***armoured***.

Ar·me·ni·an [ɑː'miːnjən] **I** *adj.* ar'menisch; **II** *s.* Ar'menier(in).

'arm·ful [-fʊl] *s.* Armvoll *m*.

arm·ing ['ɑːmɪŋ] *s.* **1.** Bewaffnung *f*, (Aus)Rüstung *f*; **2.** ⚙ Armierung *f*, Arma'tur *f*; **3.** Wappen *n*.

ar·mi·stice ['ɑːmɪstɪs] *s.* Waffenstillstand *m* (*a. fig.*); ***℈ Day*** *s.* Jahrestag *m* des Waffenstillstandes vom 11. November 1918.

arm·let ['ɑːmlɪt] *s.* **1.** Armbinde *f als Abzeichen*; Armspange *f*; **2.** kleiner Meeres- *od.* Flußarm.

ar·mor *etc. Am.* → ***armour*** *etc.*

ar·mo·ri·al [ɑː'mɔːrɪəl] **I** *adj.* Wappen..., he'raldisch: ***~ bearings*** Wappen(schild *m*, *n*) *n*; **II** *s.* Wappenbuch *n*; **ar·mor·y** ['ɑːmərɪ] *s.* **1.** He'raldik *f*, Wappenkunde *f*; **2.** *Am.* → ***armoury***.

ar·mour ['ɑːmə] *s.* **1.** Rüstung *f*, Panzer *m* (*a. fig.*); **2.** ⚔, ⚙ Panzer(ung *f*) *m*, Armierung *f*; *coll.* Panzerfahrzeuge *pl.*, -truppen *pl.*; **3.** ⚘, *zo.* Panzer *m*, Schutzdecke *f*; **'~-clad** → ***armour-plated***.

ar·moured ['ɑːməd] *adj.* ⚔, ⚙ gepanzert, Panzer...: ***~ cable*** armiertes Kabel, Panzerkabel *n*; ***~ car*** a) Panzerkampfwagen *m*, b) gepanzerter (Geld-)Transportwagen; ***~ infantry*** Panzergrenadiere *pl*; ***~ train*** Panzerzug *m*; **'ar·mour·er** [-ərə] *s.* Waffenschmied *m*; ⚔, ⚓ Waffenmeister *m*.

'ar·mour|-ˌpierc·ing *adj.* panzerbrechend, Panzer...: ***~ ammunition***; **'~-ˌplat·ed** *adj.* gepanzert, Panzer...

ar·mour·y ['ɑːmərɪ] *s.* **1.** Rüst-, Waffenkammer *f* (*a. fig.*), Arse'nal *n*, Zeughaus *n*; **2.** *Am.* a) 'Waffenfaˌbrik *f*, b) Exerzierhalle *f*.

'arm|·pit *s.* Achselhöhle *f*; **'~·rest** *s.* Armlehne *f*, -stütze *f*; **'~-ˌtwist·ing** *s.* F Druckausübung *f*.

ar·my ['ɑːmɪ] *s.* **1.** Ar'mee *f*, Heer *n*; Mili'tär *n*: ***~ contractor*** Heereslieferant *m*; ***join the ~*** Soldat werden; ***~ of occupation*** Besatzungsarmee; ***~ issue*** *die* dem Soldaten gelieferte Ausrüstung, Heereseigentum *n*; **2.** Ar'mee *f* (*als militärische Einheit*); **3.** *fig.* Heer *n*, Menge *f*: ***a whole ~ of workmen***; ***~ chap·lain*** *s.* Mili'tärgeistliche(r) *m*; ***~ corps*** *s.* Ar'meekorps *n*.

ar·ni·ca ['ɑːnɪkə] *s.* ⚕ 'Arnika *f*.

a·ro·ma [ə'rəʊmə] *s.* **1.** A'roma *n*, Duft *m*, Würze *f*; Blume *f* (*Wein*); **2.** *fig.* Würze *f*, Reiz *m*; **ar·o·mat·ic** *adj.* [ˌærəʊ'mætɪk] *adj.* (□ ***~ally***) aro'matisch, würzig, duftig: ***~ bath*** Kräuterbad *n*.

a·rose [ə'rəʊz] *pret. von* ***arise***.

a·round [ə'raʊnd] **I** *adv.* **1.** 'ringsher'um, im Kreise; rundum, nach *od.* auf allen Seiten, über'all: ***I've been ~*** F *fig.* ich kenn' mich aus; **2.** *bsd. Am.* F um'her, (in der Gegend) herum; in der Nähe, da'bei; **II** *prp.* **3.** um, um ... her(um), rund um; **4.** *bsd. Am.* F a) (rings- *od.* in der Gegend) herum; durch, hin und her, b) (nahe) bei, in, c) ungefähr, etwa; **aˌround-the-'clock** *adj.* den ganzen Tag dauernd, 24stündig; Dauer...

a·rouse [ə'raʊz] *v/t.* **1.** *j-n* (auf-)wecken; **2.** *fig.* aufrütteln; *Gefühle etc.* erregen.

ar·que·bus ['ɑːkwɪbəs] → ***harquebus***.

ar·rack ['ærək] *s.* 'Arrak *m*.

ar·raign [ə'reɪn] *v/t.* **1.** ⚖ a) vor Gericht stellen, b) zur Anklage vernehmen; **2.** *öffentlich* beschuldigen, rügen; **3.** *fig.* anfechten; **ar'raign·ment** [-mənt] *s.* ⚖ Vernehmung *f* zur Anklage; *bsd. fig.* Anklage *f*.

ar·range [ə'reɪndʒ] **I** *v/t.* **1.** (an)ordnen; aufstellen; einteilen; ein-, ausrichten; erledigen: ***~ one's ideas*** s-e Gedanken ordnen; ***~ one's affairs*** s-e Angelegenheiten regeln; **2.** verabreden, vereinbaren; festsetzen, planen: ***everything***

had been ~d beforehand; ***an ~d marriage*** e-e (von den Eltern) arrangierte Ehe; **3.** *Streit etc.* beilegen, schlichten; **4.** ♪, *thea.* einrichten, bearbeiten; **II** *v/i.* **5.** sich verständigen (***about*** über *acc.*); **6.** Anordnungen *od.* Vorkehrungen treffen (***for***, ***about*** für, zu, ***to*** *inf.* zu *inf.*); es einrichten, dafür sorgen, veranlassen (***that*** daß): ***~ for the car to be ready***; **7.** sich einigen (***with s.o. about s.th.*** mit j-m über et.); **ar'range·ment** [-mənt] *s.* **1.** (An)Ordnung *f*, Einrichtung *f*, Einteilung *f*, Auf-, Zs.-stellung *f*; Sy'stem *n*; **2.** Vereinbarung *f*, Verabredung *f*, Abmachung *f*: ***make an ~ with s.o.*** mit j-m e-e Verabredung treffen; **3.** Ab-, Über'einkommen *n*; Schlichtung *f*: ***come to an ~*** e-n Vergleich schließen; **4.** *pl.* ***make ~s*** Vorkehrungen *od.* Vorbereitungen *od.* s-e Dispositionen treffen; ***today's ~s*** die heutigen Veranstaltungen; **5.** *thea.* Bearbeitung *f*, ♪ *a.* Arrange'ment *n*.

ar·rant ['ærənt] *adj.* □ völlig, ausgesprochen, ,kom'plett': ***an ~ fool***; ***~ nonsense***; ***an ~ rogue*** ein Erzgauner.

ar·ray [ə'reɪ] **I** *v/t.* **1.** ordnen, aufstellen (*bsd. Truppen*); **2.** ⚖ *Geschworene* aufrufen; **3.** *fig.* aufbieten; **4.** (***o.s.*** sich) kleiden, putzen; **II** *s.* **5.** Ordnung *f*; Schlachtordnung *f*; **6.** ⚖ Geschworenen(liste *f*) *pl.*; **7.** 'Phalanx *f*, stattliche Reihe, Menge *f*, Aufgebot *n*; **8.** Kleidung *f*, Staat *m*, Aufmachung *f*.

ar·rear [ə'rɪə] *s.* a) *mst pl.* Rückstand *m*, *bsd.* Schulden *pl.*: ***~s of rent*** rückständige Miete; ***in ~(s)*** im Rückstand *od.* Verzug, b) *et.* Unerledigtes, Arbeitsrückstände *pl.*

ar·rest [ə'rest] **I** *s.* **1.** Aufhalten *n*, Hemmung *f*, Stockung *f*; **2.** ⚖ a) Verhaftung *f*, Haft *f*: ***under ~*** verhaftet, in Haft, b) Beschlagnahme *f*, c) *a.* ***~ of judgment*** Urteilssistierung *f*; **II** *v/t.* **3.** an-, aufhalten, hemmen, hindern: ***~ progress***; ***~ed growth*** *biol.* gehemmtes Wachstum; ***~ed tuberculosis*** ⚕ inaktive Tuberkulose; **4.** ⚙ feststellen, sperren, arretieren; **5.** ⚖ a) verhaften, b) beschlagnahmen, c) ***~ judgment*** das Urteil vertagen; **6.** *Geld etc.* einbehalten, konfiszieren; **7.** *Aufmerksamkeit etc.* fesseln, festhalten; **ar'rest·ing** [-tɪŋ] *adj.* fesselnd, interes'sant; **ar'restment** [-mənt] *s.* Beschlagnahme *f*.

ar·rière-pen·sée [ˌærɪeə(r)'pɒnseɪ] (*Fr.*) *s.* 'Hintergedanke *m*.

ar·riv·al [ə'raɪvl] *s.* **1.** Ankunft *f*, Eintreffen *n*; *fig.* Gelangen *n* (***at*** zu); **2.** Erscheinen *n*, Auftreten *n*; **3.** a) Ankömmling *m*: ***new ~*** Neuankömmling, Familienzuwachs *m*, b) *et.* Angekommenes; **4.** *pl.* ankommende Züge *pl. od.* Schiffe *pl. od.* Flugzeuge *pl. od.* Per'sonen *pl.*; Zufuhr *f*; ✝ (Waren)Eingänge *pl.*; **ar·rive** [ə'raɪv] *v/i.* **1.** (an-) kommen, eintreffen; **2.** erscheinen, auftreten; **3.** *fig.* (***at***) erreichen (*acc.*), gelangen (zu): ***~ at a decision***; **4.** kommen, eintreten (*Zeit, Ereignis*); **5.** Erfolg haben.

ar·ro·gance ['ærəgəns] *s.* Arro'ganz *f*, Anmaßung *f*, Über'heblichkeit *f*; **'ar·ro·gant** [-nt] *adj.* □ arro'gant, anmaßend, über'heblich; **ar·ro·gate** ['ærəʊgeɪt] *v/t.* **1.** ***~ to o.s.*** sich *et.* anmaßen, *et.* für sich in Anspruch nehmen; **2.** zuschreiben, zuschieben (***s.th. to s.o.*** j-m et.); **ar·ro·ga·tion** [ˌærəʊ'geɪʃn] *s.* Anmaßung *f*.

ar·row ['ærəʊ] *s.* **1.** Pfeil *m*; **2.** Pfeil (-zeichen *n*) *m*; **3.** *surv.* Zähl-, Markierstab *m*; **'ar·rowed** [-əʊd] *adj.* mit Pfeilen *od.* Pfeilzeichen (versehen).

'ar·row|·head *s.* **1.** Pfeilspitze *f*; **2.** (Zeichen *n* der) Pfeilspitze *f* (*brit. Regierungsgut kennzeichnend*); **'~·root** *s.* ⚘ a) Pfeilwurz *f*, b) Pfeilwurzstärke *f*.

arse [ɑːs] **I** *s.* V Arsch *m*; **II** *v/i. sl.* ***~ around*** ,herumspinnen'; **'~·hole** *s.* V ,Arschloch' *n* (*a. fig. contp.*); **~·lick·er** *s.* V ,Arschkriecher' *m*.

ar·se·nal ['ɑːsənl] *s.* **1.** Arse'nal *n* (*a. fig.*), Zeughaus *n*, Waffenlager *n*; **2.** 'Waffen-, Muniti'onsfaˌbrik *f*.

ar·se·nic **I** *s.* ['ɑːsnɪk] Ar'sen(ik) *n*; **II** *adj.* [ɑː'senɪk] ar'senhaltig; Arsen…

ar·sis ['ɑːsɪs] *s.* **1.** *poet.* Hebung *f*, betonte Silbe; **2.** ♪ Aufschlag *m*.

ar·son ['ɑːsn] *s.* ⚖ Brandstiftung *f*; **'ar·son·ist** [-nɪst] *s.* Brandstifter *m*.

art¹ [ɑːt] **I** *s.* **1.** (*bsd.* bildende) Kunst: ***the fine ~s*** die schönen Künste; ***brought to a fine ~*** *fig.* zu e-r wahren Kunst entwickelt; ***work of ~*** Kunstwerk *n*; **2.** Kunst(fertigkeit) *f*, Geschicklichkeit *f*: ***the ~ of the painter***, ***the ~ of cooking***; ***industrial ~(s)*** (*od.* ***~s and crafts***) Kunstgewerbe *n*, -handwerk *n*; ***the black ~*** die Schwarze Kunst, die Zauberei; **3.** *pl. univ.* Geisteswissenschaften *pl.*: ***Faculty of 𝔄s***, *Am.* ***𝔄s Department*** philosophische Fakultät; ***liberal ~s*** humanistische Fächer; → ***master*** 10, ***bachelor*** 2; **4.** *mst pl.* Kunstgriff *m*, Kniff *m*, List *f*, Tücke *f*; **5.** *Patentrecht*: a) Fach(gebiet) *n*, b) Fachkenntnis *f*, c) (***state of the ~*** Stand *m* der) Technik; → ***prior*** 1; **II** *adj.* **6.** Kunst…: ***~ critic***; ***~ director*** a) *thea. etc.* Bühnenmeister *m*, b) *Werbung*: Art-director *m*, künstlerischer Leiter; **7.** künstlerisch, dekora'tiv: ***~ pottery***; **III** *v/t.* **8.** ***~ up*** *sl.* (künstlerisch) ,aufmöbeln'.

art² [ɑːt] *obs. 2. pres. sg. von* ***be***.

ar·te·fact → ***artifact***.

ar·te·ri·al [ɑː'tɪərɪəl] *adj.* **1.** ⚕ arteri'ell, Arterien…: ***~ blood*** Pulsaderblut *n*; **2.** *fig.* ***~ road*** Hauptverkehrsader *f*, Ausfall-, Durchgangs-, Hauptverkehrs-, *a.* Fernverkehrsstraße *f*.

ar·te·ri·o·scle·ro·sis [ɑːˌtɪərɪəʊsklɪə'rəʊsɪs] *s.* ⚕ Arterioskle'rose *f*, Ar'terienverkalkung *f*.

ar·ter·y ['ɑːtərɪ] *s.* **1.** Ar'terie *f*, Puls-, Schlagader *f*; **2.** *fig.* Verkehrsader *f*, *bsd.* Hauptstraße *f*, -fluß *m*: ***~ of traffic***; ***~ of trade*** Haupthandelsweg *m*.

ar·te·sian well [ɑː'tiːzjən] *s.* ar'tesischer (*Am.* tiefer) Brunnen.

art·ful ['ɑːtfʊl] *adj.* □ schlau, listig, verschlagen; **'art·ful·ness** [-nɪs] *s.* List *f*, Schläue *f*, Verschlagenheit *f*.

ar·thrit·ic, **ar·thrit·i·cal** [ɑː'θrɪtɪk(l)] *adj.* ⚕ ar'thritisch, gichtisch; **ar·thri·tis** [ɑː'θraɪtɪs] *s.* ⚕ Ar'thritis *f*; **ar·thro·sis** [ɑː'θrəʊsɪs] *s.* Ar'throse *f*.

Ar·thu·ri·an [ɑː'θʊərɪən] *adj.* (König) Arthur *od.* Artus betreffend, Arthur…, Artus…

ar·ti·choke ['ɑːtɪtʃəʊk] *s.* ⚘ **1.** *a.* ***globe ~*** Arti'schocke *f*; **2.** ***Jerusalem ~*** 'Erdartiˌschocke *f*.

ar·ti·cle ['ɑːtɪkl] **I** *s.* **1.** ('Zeitungs- *etc.*) Arˌtikel *m*, Aufsatz *m*; **2.** Ar'tikel *m*, Gegenstand *m*, Sache *f*; Posten *m*, Ware *f*: ***~ of trade*** Handelsware; ***the genuine ~*** F der ,wahre Jakob'; **3.** Abschnitt *m*, Para'graph *m*, Klausel *f*, Punkt *m*: ***~s of apprenticeship*** Lehrvertrag *m*; ***~s*** (***of association***, *Am.* ***incorporation***) ✝ Satzung *f*; ***the Thirty-nine 𝔄s*** die 39 Glaubensartikel *der Anglikanischen Kirche*; ***according to the ~s*** ✝ satzungsgemäß; **4.** *ling.* Ar'tikel *m*, Geschlechtswort *n*; **II** *v/t.* **5.** vertraglich binden; in die Lehre geben (***to*** bei); **'ar·ti·cled** [-ld] *adj.* **1.** vertraglich gebunden; **2.** in der Lehre (***to*** bei): ***~ clerk*** *Brit.* Anwaltsgehilfe *m*.

ar·tic·u·late **I** *v/t.* [ɑː'tɪkjʊleɪt] **1.** artikulieren, deutlich (aus)sprechen; **2.** gliedern; **3.** *Knochen* zs.-fügen; **II** *adj.* [-lət] **4.** klar erkennbar, deutlich (gegliedert), artikuliert, verständlich (*Wörter etc*); **5.** fähig, sich klar auszudrücken, sich klar ausdrückend; **6.** sich Gehör verschaffend; **7.** ⚕, ⚘, *zo.* gegliedert; **ar'tic·u·lat·ed** [-tɪd] *adj.* ⚙ Gelenk…, Glieder…: ***~ train***; ***~ lorry*** *Brit.* Sattelschlepper *m*; **ar·tic·u·la·tion** [ɑːˌtɪkjʊ'leɪʃn] *s.* **1.** *bsd. ling.* Artikulati'on *f*, deutliche Aussprache; Verständlichkeit *f*; **2.** Anein'anderfügung *f*; **3.** ⚙ Gelenk(verbindung *f*) *n*; **4.** Gliederung *f*.

ar·ti·fact ['ɑːtɪfækt] *s.* Arte'fakt *n*: a) Werkzeug *n od.* Gerät *n bsd. primitiver od. prähistorischer Kulturen*, b) ⚕ 'Kunstproˌdukt *n*; **'ar·ti·fice** [-fɪs] *s.* Kunstgriff *m*; Kniff *m*, List *f*; **ar·tif·i·cer** [ɑː'tɪfɪsə] *s.* **1.** → ***artisan***; **2.** ⚔ a) Feuerwerker *m*, b) Handwerker *m*; **3.** Urheber(in).

ar·ti·fi·cial [ˌɑːtɪ'fɪʃl] *adj.* □ **1.** künstlich, Kunst…: ***~ silk***; ***~ leg*** Beinprothese *f*; ***~ teeth*** künstliche Zähne; ***~ person*** ⚖ juristische Person; **2.** *fig.* gekünstelt, falsch; **ar·ti·fi·ci·al·i·ty** [ˌɑːtɪfɪʃɪ'ælətɪ] *s.* Künstlichkeit *f*; *et.* Gekünsteltes.

ar·til·ler·ist [ɑː'tɪlərɪst] *s.* Artille'rist *m*, Kano'nier *m*.

ar·til·ler·y [ɑː'tɪlərɪ] *s.* **1.** Artille'rie *f*; **2.** *sl.* ,Artille'rie' *f*, Schießeisen *n od. pl.*

ar·ti·san [ˌɑːtɪ'zæn] *s.* (Kunst)Handwerker *m*.

art·ist ['ɑːtɪst] *s.* **1.** a) Künstler(in), *bsd.* Kunstmaler(in), b) → ***artiste***; **2.** *fig.* Künstler(in), Könner(in); **ar·tiste** [ɑː'tiːst] (*Fr.*) *s.* Ar'tist(in), Künstler (-in), Sänger(in), Schauspieler(in), Tänzer(in); **ar·tis·tic**, **ar·tis·ti·cal** [ɑː'tɪstɪk(l)] *adj.* □ **1.** künstlerisch, Künstler…, Kunst…; **2.** kunstverständig; **3.** kunst-, geschmackvoll; **'art·ist·ry** [-trɪ] *s.* **1.** Künstlertum *n*, *das* Künstlerische; **2.** künstlerische Wirkung *od.* Voll'endung; **3.** Kunstfertigkeit *f*.

art·less ['ɑːtlɪs] *adj.* □ **1.** ungekünstelt, na'türlich, schlicht, unschuldig, na'iv; **2.** offen, arglos, ohne Falsch; **3.** unkünstlerisch, stümperhaft.

Art Nou·veau [ˌɑːrnuː'vəʊ] (*Fr.*) *s.* *Kunst*: Art *f* nou'veau, Jugendstil *m*.

ar·tsy ['ɑːtsɪ] → ***arty***.

'art·work *s.* Artwork *n*: a) künstlerische Gestaltung, Illustrati'on(en *pl.*) *f*, Grafik *f*, b) (grafische *etc.*) Gestaltungsmittel *pl.*

art·y ['ɑːtɪ] *adj.* F **1.** (gewollt) künstlerisch *od.* bohemi'enhaft; **2.** ‚kunstbeflissen'; **ˌ~(-and)-'craft·y** *adj.* **1.** *iro.* ‚künstlerisch', mo'dern-verrückt; **2.** → ***arty*** 1.

Ar·y·an ['eərɪən] **I** *s.* **1.** Arier *m*, Indoger'mane *m*; **2.** *ling.* arische Sprachengruppe; **3.** Arier *m*, Nichtjude *m* (*in der Nazi-Ideologie*); **II** *adj.* **4.** arisch; **5.** arisch, nichtjüdisch.

as [æz; əz] **I** *adv.* **1.** (ebenso) wie, so: ***~ usual*** wie gewöhnlich *od.* üblich; ***~ soft ~ butter*** weich wie Butter; ***twice ~ large*** zweimal so groß; ***just ~ good*** ebenso gut; **2.** als: ***he appeared ~ Macbeth***; ***I knew him ~ a child***; ***~ prose style this is bad*** für Prosa ist das schlecht; **3.** wie (z. B.): ***cathedral cities, ~ Ely***; **II** *cj.* **4.** wie, so wie: ***~ follows***; ***do ~ you are told!*** tu, wie man dir sagt!; ***~ I said before***; ***~ you were!*** ⚔ Kommando zurück!; ***~ it is*** unter diesen Umständen, ohnehin; ***~ it were*** sozusagen, gleichsam; **5.** als, in'dem, während: ***~ he entered*** als er eintrat, bei s-m Eintritt; **6.** ob'gleich, wenn auch; wie, wie sehr, so sehr: ***old ~ I am*** so alt wie ich bin; ***try ~ he would*** so sehr er (es) auch versuchte; **7.** da, weil: ***~ you are sorry I'll forgive you***; **III** *pron.* **8.** was, wie: ***~ he himself admits***; → ***such*** 7;

Zssgn mit adv. u. prp.:

as| ... as (eben)so ... wie: ***as fast as I could*** so schnell ich konnte; ***as sweet as can be*** so süß wie möglich; ***as cheap as five pence a bottle*** schon für (*od.* für nur) fünf Pence die Flasche; ***as recently as last week*** noch (*od.* erst) vorige Woche; ***as good as*** so gut wie, sozusagen; ***not as bad as (all) that*** gar nicht so schlimm; ***as fine a song as I ever heard*** ein Lied, wie ich kein schöneres je gehört habe; **~ far as** so'weit (wie), so'viel: ***~ I know*** soviel ich weiß; ***~ Cologne*** bis (nach) Köln; ***as far back as 1890*** schon im Jahre 1890; **~ for** was ... (an)betrifft, bezüglich (*gen.*); **~ from** *vor Zeitangaben*: von ... an, ab, mit Wirkung vom...; **~ if** *od.* **though** als ob, als wenn: ***he talks ~ he knew them all***; **~ long as** a) so'lange (wie): ***~ he stays***, b) wenn (nur); vor'ausgesetzt, daß: ***~ you have enough money***; **~ much** gerade (*od.* eben) das: ***I thought ~***; ***~ again*** doppelt soviel; **~ much as** (*neg. mst* ***not so much as***) a) (eben)soviel wie: ***~ my son***, b) so sehr, so viel: ***did he pay ~ that?*** hat er so viel (dafür) bezahlt?, c) so'gar, über'haupt (*neg.* nicht einmal): ***without ~ looking at him*** ohne ihn überhaupt *od.* auch nur anzusehen; **~ per** laut, gemäß (*dat.*); **~ soon as** → ***soon*** 3; **~ to 1.** → ***as for***; **2.** (als *od.* so) daß: ***be so kind ~ come*** sei so gut und komm; **3.** nach, gemäß (*dat.*); **~ well** → ***well***[1] 11; **~ yet** → ***yet*** 2.

as·bes·tos [æz'bestɒs] *s. min.* As'best *m*: ***~ board*** Asbestpappe *f*.

as·cend [ə'send] **I** *v/i.* **1.** (auf-, em'por-, hin'auf)steigen; **2.** ansteigen, (schräg) in die Höhe gehen: ***the path ~s here***; **3.** *zeitlich* hin'aufreichen, zu'rückgehen (***to*** bis in *acc.*, bis auf *acc.*); **4.** ♪ steigen (*Ton*); **II** *v/t.* **5.** be-, ersteigen: ***~ a river*** e-n Fluß hinauffahren; ***~ the throne*** den Thron besteigen; **as'cend·an·cy**, **as'cend·en·cy** [-dənsɪ] *s.* (***over***) Über'legenheit *f*, Herrschaft *f*, Gewalt *f* (über *acc.*); (bestimmender) Einfluß (auf *acc.*); **as'cend·ant**, **as'cend·ent** [-dənt] **I** *s.* **1.** *ast.* Aufgangspunkt *m e-s Gestirns*: ***in the ~*** *fig.* im Kommen *od.* Aufstieg; **2.** → ***ascendancy***; **3.** Verwandte(r *m*) *f* (*in aufsteigender Linie*); Vorfahr *m*; **II** *adj.* **4.** aufgehend, aufsteigend; **5.** über'legen, (vor)herrschend; **as'cend·ing** [-dɪŋ] *adj.* (auf-) steigend (*a. fig.*): ***~ air current*** Aufwind *m*; **as'cen·sion** [-nʃn] *s.* **1.** Aufsteigen *n* (*a. ast.*), Besteigung *f*; **2.** ***the*** ☊ die Himmelfahrt Christi: ☊ ***Day*** Himmelfahrtstag *m*; **as'cent** [-nt] *s.* **1.** Aufstieg *m* (*a. fig.*), Besteigung *f*; **2.** *bsd.* ⛏, ⚙ Steigung *f*, Gefälle *n*, Abhang *m*; **3.** Auffahrt *f*, Rampe *f*, (Treppen)Aufgang *m*.

as·cer·tain [ˌæsə'teɪn] *v/t.* feststellen, ermitteln; in Erfahrung bringen; **ˌas·cer'tain·a·ble** [-nəbl] *adj.* feststellbar, zu ermitteln(d); **ˌas·cer'tain·ment** [-mənt] *s.* Feststellung *f*, Ermittlung *f*.

as·cet·ic [ə'setɪk] **I** *adj.* (□ ***~ally***) as'ketisch, Asketen...; **II** *s.* As'ket *m*; **as'cet·i·cism** [-ɪsɪzəm] *s.* As'kese *f*; Ka'steiung *f*.

as·cor·bic ac·id [ə'skɔːbɪk] *s.* Askor'binsäure *f*, Vitamin C *n*.

as·crib·a·ble [ə'skraɪbəbl] *adj.* zuzuschreiben(d), beizumessen(d); **as·cribe** [ə'skraɪb] *v/t.* (***to***) zuschreiben, beimessen, beilegen (*dat.*); zu'rückführen (auf *acc.*).

a·sep·sis [æ'sepsɪs] *s.* ⚕ A'sepsis *f*; keimfreie Wundbehandlung; **a'sep·tic** [-ptɪk] *adj.* (□ ***~ally***) a'septisch, keimfrei, ste'ril.

a·sex·u·al [eɪ'seksjʊəl] *adj.* □ *biol.* asexual: a) geschlechtslos (*a. fig.*), b) ungeschlechtlich: ***~ reproduction*** ungeschlechtliche Fortpflanzung.

ash[1] [æʃ] *s.* ⚘ **1.** *a.* ***~-tree*** Esche *f*: ***weeping ~*** Traueresche; **2.** *a.* ***~ wood*** Eschenholz *n*.

ash[2] [æʃ] *s.* **1.** Asche *f* (*a.* ⚗): ***~ bin*** (*Am.* ***can***) Aschen-, Mülleimer *m*; ***~ furnace*** Glasschmelzofen *m*; **2.** *mst pl.* Asche *f*: ***lay in ~es*** niederbrennen; **3.** *pl. fig.* sterbliche 'Überreste *pl.*; Trümmer *pl.*, Staub *m*: ***rise from the ~es*** *fig.* (wie ein Phönix) aus der Asche aufsteigen; **4.** ***win the*** ☊***es*** (*Kricket*) gegen Australien gewinnen.

a·shamed [ə'ʃeɪmd] *adj.* □ sich schämend, beschämt: ***be*** (*od.* ***feel***) ***~ of*** sich *e-r Sache od. j-s* schämen; ***be ~ to*** (*inf.*) sich schämen zu (*inf.*); ***I am ~ that*** es ist mir peinlich, daß; ***you ought to be ~ of yourself!*** du solltest dich schämen!

ash·en[1] ['æʃn] *adj.* ⚘ eschen, aus Eschenholz.

ash·en[2] ['æʃn] *adj.* Aschen...; *fig.* aschfahl, -grau.

Ash·ke·naz·im [ˌæʃkɪ'næzɪm] (*Hebrew*) *s. pl.* As(ch)ke'nasim *pl.*

ash·lar ['æʃlə] *s.* ⚠ Quaderstein *m*.

a·shore [ə'ʃɔː] *adv. u. adj.* ans *od.* am Ufer *od.* Land: ***go ~*** an Land gehen; ***run ~*** a) stranden, auflaufen, b) auf Strand setzen.

'ash|·pit *s.* Aschengrube *f*; **'~·tray** *s.* Aschenbecher *m*; ☊ **Wednes·day** *s.* Ascher'mittwoch *m*.

ash·y ['æʃɪ] *adj.* **1.** aus Asche (bestehend); mit Asche bedeckt; **2.** → ***ashen***[2].

A·sian ['eɪʃn], **A·si·at·ic** [ˌeɪʃɪ'ætɪk] **I** *adj.* asi'atisch; **II** *s.* Asi'at(in).

a·side [ə'saɪd] **I** *adv.* **1.** bei'seite, auf die *od.* zur Seite, seitwärts; abseits: ***step*** (***set***) ***~***; **2.** *thea.* beiseite: ***speak ~***; **3.** ***~ from*** *Am.* abgesehen von; **II** *s.* **4.** *thea.* A'parte *n*, beiseite gesprochene Worte *pl.*; **5.** a) Nebenbemerkung *f*, b) geflüsterte Bemerkung.

as·i·nine ['æsɪnaɪn] *adj.* eselartig, Esels...; *fig.* eselhaft, dumm.

ask [ɑːsk] **I** *v/t.* **1.** a) *j-n* fragen: ***~ the policeman***, b) nach *et.* fragen: ***~ the way***; ***~ the time*** fragen, wie spät es ist; ***~ a question of s.o.*** e-e Frage an j-n stellen; **2.** *j-n* nach *et.* fragen, sich bei *j-m* nach *et.* erkundigen: ***~ s.o. the way***; ***may I ~ you a question?*** darf ich Sie (nach) etwas fragen?; ***~ me another!*** F keine Ahnung!; **3.** *j-n* bitten (***for*** um, ***to*** *inf.* zu *inf.*, ***that*** daß): ***~ s.o. for advice***; ***we were ~ed to believe*** man wollte uns glauben machen; **4.** bitten um, erbitten: ***~ his advice***; ***be there for the ~ing*** umsonst *od.* mühelos zu haben sein; → ***favour*** 2; **5.** einladen, bitten: ***~ s.o. to lunch***; ***~ s.o. in*** j-n hereinbitten; **6.** fordern, verlangen: ***~ a high price***; ***that is ~ing too much!*** das ist zuviel verlangt!; **7.** → ***banns***; **II** *v/i.* **8.** (***for***) bitten (um), verlangen (*acc. od.* nach); fragen (nach), *j-n* zu sprechen wünschen; *et.* erfordern: ***~*** (***s.o.***) ***for help*** (j-n) um Hilfe bitten; ***s.o. has been ~ing for you*** es hat jemand nach Ihnen gefragt; ***the matter ~s for great care*** die Angelegenheit erfordert große Sorgfalt; **9.** *fig.* her'beiführen: ***you ~ed for it*** (*od.* ***for trouble***) du wolltest es ja so haben; **10.** fragen, sich erkundigen (***after***, ***about*** nach, wegen).

a·skance [ə'skæns] *adv.* von der Seite; *fig.* schief, scheel, mißtrauisch: ***look ~ at s.o.*** (*od.* ***s.th.***).

a·skew [ə'skjuː] *adv.* schief, schräg (*a. fig.*).

a·slant [ə'slɑːnt] **I** *adv. u. adj.* schräg, quer; **II** *prp.* quer über *od.* durch.

a·sleep [ə'sliːp] *adv. u. adj.* **1.** schlafend, im *od.* in den Schlaf: ***be ~*** schlafen; ***fall ~*** einschlafen; **2.** *fig.* entschlafen, leblos; **3.** *fig.* schlafend, unaufmerksam; **4.** *fig.* eingeschlafen (*Glied*).

a·slope [ə'sləʊp] *adv. u. adj.* abschüssig, schräg.

a·so·cial [æ'səʊʃəl] *adj.* □ **1.** ungesellig, kon'taktfeindlich; **2.** → ***antisocial***.

asp[1] [æsp] *s. zo.* Natter *f*.

asp[2] [æsp] → ***aspen***.

as·par·a·gus [ə'spærəgəs] *s.* ⚘ Spargel *m*: ***~ tips*** Spargelspitzen.

as·pect ['æspekt] *s.* **1.** Aussehen *n*, Äußere(s) *n*, Erscheinung *f*, Anblick *m*, Gestalt *f*; **2.** Gebärde *f*, Miene *f*; **3.** A'spekt *m* (*a. ast.*), Gesichtspunkt *m*, Seite *f*; Hinsicht *f*, (Be)Zug *m*: ***in its true ~*** im richtigen Licht; **4.** Aussicht *f*, Lage *f*: ***the house has a southern ~*** das Haus liegt nach Süden.

as·pen ['æspən] ⚘ **I** *s.* Espe *f*, Zitterpappel *f*; **II** *adj.* espen: ***tremble like an ~ leaf*** wie Espenlaub zittern.

as·per·gill ['æspədʒɪl], **as·per·gil·lum** [ˌæspə'dʒɪləm] *s. eccl.* Weihwedel *m.*

as·per·i·ty [æ'sperətɪ] *s. bsd. fig.* Rauheit *f*, Schroffheit *f*; Schärfe *f*, Strenge *f*, Herbheit *f*.

as·perse [ə'spɜːs] *v/t.* verleumden, in schlechten Ruf bringen, schlechtmachen, schmähen; **as'per·sion** [-ɜːʃn] *s.* **1.** *eccl.* Besprengung *f*; **2.** Verleumdung *f*, Anwurf *m*, Schmähung *f*: ***cast ~s on*** *j-n* verleumden *od.* mit Schmutz bewerfen.

as·phalt ['æsfælt] **I** *s. min.* As'phalt *m*; **II** *v/t.* asphaltieren.

as·phyx·i·a [æs'fɪksɪə] *s.* ⚕ a) Erstikkung(stod *m*) *f*, b) Scheintod *m*; **as·phyx·i·ant** [əs'fɪksɪənt] **I** *adj.* erstikkend; **II** *s.* erstickender (⚔ Kampf-) Stoff *m*; **as·phyx·i·ate** [əs'fɪksɪeɪt] *v/t.* ersticken: ***be ~d*** ersticken; **as·phyx·i·a·tion** [əsˌfɪksɪ'eɪʃn] *s.* Erstickung *f*.

as·pic ['æspɪk] *s.* A'spik *m*, Ge'lee *n*.

as·pir·ant [ə'spaɪərənt] *s.* (***to, after, for***) Aspi'rant(in), Kandi'dat(in) (für); (eifriger) Bewerber (um): ***~ officer*** Offiziersanwärter *m*.

as·pi·rate ['æspərət] *ling.* **I** *s.* Hauchlaut *m*; **II** *adj.* aspiriert; **III** *v/t.* [-pəreɪt] aspirieren; **as·pi·ra·tion** [ˌæspə'reɪʃn] *s.* **1.** Bestrebung *f*, Aspirati'on *f*, Trachten *n*, Sehnen *n* (***for, after*** nach); **2.** *ling.* Aspirati'on *f*; Hauchlaut *m*; **3.** ⚙, ⚕ An-, Absaugung *f*; **as·pi·ra·tor** ['æspəreɪtə] *s.* ⚙, ⚕ 'Saugappaˌrat *m*; **as·pire** [əs'paɪə] *v/i.* **1.** streben, trachten, verlangen (***to, after*** nach, ***to*** *inf.* zu *inf.*); **2.** *fig.* sich erheben.

as·pi·rin ['æspərɪn] *s.* ⚕ Aspi'rin *n*: ***two ~s*** zwei Aspirintabletten.

as·pir·ing [əs'paɪərɪŋ] *adj.* ☐ hochstrebend, ehrgeizig.

ass¹ [æs] *s. zo.* Esel *m*; *fig.* Esel *m*, Dummkopf *m*: ***make an ~ of o.s.*** sich lächerlich machen.

ass² [æs] *s. Am.* V Arsch *m*.

as·sail [ə'seɪl] *v/t.* **1.** angreifen, über'fallen, bestürmen (*a. fig.*): ***~ a city; ~ s.o. with blows; ~ s.o. with questions*** j-n mit Fragen überschütten; ***~ed by fear*** von Furcht ergriffen; ***~ed by doubts*** von Zweifeln befallen; **2.** (eifrig) in Angriff nehmen; **as'sail·a·ble** [-ləbl] *adj.* angreifbar (*a. fig.*); **as'sail·ant** [-lənt], **as'sail·er** [-lə] *s.* Angreifer(in), Gegner(in); *fig.* 'Kritiker *m*.

as·sas·sin [ə'sæsɪn] *s.* (Meuchel)Mörder (-in); po'litischer Mörder, Atten'täter (-in); **as'sas·si·nate** [-neɪt] *v/t.* (meuchlings) (er)morden; **as·sas·si·na·tion** [əˌsæsɪ'neɪʃn] *s.* Meuchelmord *m*, Ermordung *f*, (politischer) Mord, Atten'tat *n*.

as·sault [ə'sɔːlt] **I** *s.* **1.** Angriff *m* (*a. fig.*), 'Überfall *m* (***upon, on*** auf *acc.*); **2.** ⚔ Sturm *m*: ***carry*** (*od.* ***take***) ***by ~*** erstürmen; ***~ boat*** a) Sturmboot *n*, b) Landungsfahrzeug *n*; ***~ troops*** Stoßtruppen; **3.** ⚖ tätliche Bedrohung *od.* Beleidigung: ***~ and battery*** schwere tätliche Beleidigung, Mißhandlung *f*; ***indecent*** *od.* ***criminal ~*** unzüchtige Handlung (*Belästigung*), Sittlichkeitsvergehen *n*; **II** *v/t.* **4.** angreifen, über'fallen (*a. fig.*); anfallen, tätlich werden gegen; **5.** ⚔ bestürmen (*a. fig.*); **6.** ⚖ tätlich *od.* schwer beleidigen; **7.** vergewaltigen.

as·say [ə'seɪ] **I** *s.* **1.** ⚙, ⚗ Probe *f*, Ana'lyse *f*, Prüfung *f*, Unter'suchung *f*, *bsd.* Me'tall-, Münzprobe *f*: ***~ office*** Prüfungsamt *n*; **II** *v/t.* **2.** *bsd.* (*Edel*)*Metalle* prüfen, unter'suchen; **3.** *fig.* versuchen, probieren; **III** *v/i.* **4.** *Am.* 'Edelmeˌtall enthalten; **as'say·er** [-eɪə] *s.* (Münz-) Prüfer *m*.

as·sem·blage [ə'semblɪdʒ] *s.* **1.** Zs.-kommen *n*, Versammlung *f*; **2.** Ansammlung *f*, Schar *f*, Menge *f*; **3.** ⚙ Zs.-setzen *n*, Mon'tage *f*; **4.** *Kunst*: Assem'blage *f*; **as·sem·ble** [ə'sembl] **I** *v/t.* **1.** versammeln, zs.-berufen; *Truppen* zs.-ziehen; **2.** ⚙ *Teile* zs.-setzen, -bauen, montieren; *Computer*: assemblieren; **II** *v/i.* **3.** sich versammeln, zs.-kommen; *parl.* zs.-treten; **as'sem·bler** [-lə] *s.* **1.** ⚙ Mon'teur *m*; **2.** *Computer*: As'sembler *m*; **as'sem·bly** [-lɪ] *s.* **1.** Versammlung *f*, Zs.-kunft *f*, Gesellschaft *f*: ***~ hall, ~ room*** Gesellschafts-, Ballsaal *m*; **2.** *oft* 𝔄 *pol.* beratende *od.* gesetzgebende Körperschaft; *Am.* 𝔄, *a.* ***General*** 𝔄 'Unterhaus *n* (*in einigen Staaten*): ***~ man*** Abgeordnete(r) (→ 3); **3.** ⚙ Zs.-bau *m*, Mon'tage *f*; *a. Computer*: Baugruppe *f*: ***~ line*** Montage-, Fließband *n*, (Fertigungs)Straße *f*, laufendes Band; ***~ man*** Fließbandarbeiter *m* (→ 2); ***~ plant*** Montagewerk *n*; ***~ shop*** Montagehalle *f*; **4.** ⚔ a) Bereitstellung *f*, b) 'SammelsiˌgnaI *n*: ***~ area*** Bereitstellungsraum *m*.

as·sent [ə'sent] **I** *v/i.* (***to***) zustimmen (*dat.*), beipflichten (*dat.*), billigen (*acc.*); genehmigen (*acc.*); **II** *s.* Zustimmung *f*: ***royal ~*** *pol. Brit.* königliche Genehmigung.

as·sert [ə'sɜːt] *v/t.* **1.** behaupten, erklären; **2.** *Anspruch, Recht* behaupten, geltend machen; 'durchsetzen; bestehen auf (*acc.*); verteidigen, einstehen für: ***~ one's liberties***; **3.** ***~ o.s.*** a) sich behaupten, sich geltend machen *od.* 'durchsetzen, b) sich zu'viel anmaßen; **as·ser·tion** [ə'sɜːʃn] *s.* **1.** Behauptung *f*, Erklärung *f*: ***make an ~*** e-e Behauptung aufstellen; **2.** Geltendmachung *f* *od.* 'Durchsetzung *f* *e-s Anspruches etc.*; **as'ser·tive** [-tɪv] *adj.* ☐ **1.** 'positiv, zur Geltung kommend, ausdrücklich; **2.** anspruchsvoll, anmaßend.

as·sess [ə'ses] *v/t.* **1.** besteuern, zur Steuer einschätzen *od.* veranlagen (***in*** *od.* ***at*** [***the sum of***] mit); **2.** *Steuer, Geldstrafe etc.* auferlegen (***upon*** *dat.*): ***~ed value*** Einheitswert *m*; **3.** *bsd. Wert zur Besteuerung od. e-s Schadens* schätzen, veranschlagen, festsetzen; **4.** *fig. Leistung etc.* bewerten, einschätzen, beurteilen, würdigen; **as'sess·a·ble** [-səbl] *adj.* ☐ **1.** (ab)schätzbar; **2.** (***~ to income tax*** einkommens)steuerpflichtig; **as'sess·ment** [-mənt] *s.* **1.** (Steuer)Veranlagung *f*, Einschätzung *f*, Besteuerung *f*: ***~ notice*** Steuerbescheid *m*; ***rate of ~*** Steuersatz *m*; **2.** Festsetzung *f* e-r Zahlung (*als Entschädigung etc.*), (*Schadens*)Feststellung *f*; **3.** (*Betrag der*) Steuer *f*, Abgabe *f*, Zahlung *f*; **4.** *fig.* Bewertung *f*, Beurteilung *f*, Würdigung *f*; **as'ses·sor** [-sə] *s.* **1.** Steuereinschätzer *m*; **2.** ⚖ (sachverständiger) Beisitzer *m*, Sachverständige(r) *m*.

as·set ['æset] *s.* **1.** ☿ Vermögen(swert *m*, -gegenstand *m*) *n*; *Bilanz*: Ak'tivposten *m*, *pl.* Ak'tiva *pl.*, (Aktiv-, Betriebs)Vermögen *n*; (Kapital)Anlagen *pl.*; Guthaben *n u. pl.*: ***~s and liabilities*** Aktiva u. Passiva; ***concealed*** (*od.* ***hidden***) ***~s*** stille Reserven; **2.** *pl.* ⚖ Vermögen(smasse *f*) *n*, Nachlaß *m*; (***bankrupt's***) ***~s*** Kon'kursmasse *f*; **3.** *fig.* a) Vorzug *m*, -teil *m*, Plus *n*, Wert *m*, b) Gewinn (***to*** für), wertvolle Kraft, guter Mitarbeiter *etc.*

as·sev·er·ate [ə'sevəreɪt] *v/t.* beteuern; **as·sev·er·a·tion** [əˌsevə'reɪʃn] *s.* Beteuerung *f*.

as·si·du·i·ty [ˌæsɪ'djuːətɪ] *s.* Emsigkeit *f*, (unermüdlicher) Fleiß; Dienstbeflissenheit *f*; **as·sid·u·ous** [ə'sɪdjʊəs] *adj.* ☐ **1.** emsig, fleißig, eifrig, beharrlich; **2.** aufmerksam, dienstbeflissen.

as·sign [ə'saɪn] **I** *v/t.* **1.** *Aufgabe etc.* zu-, anweisen, zuteilen, über'tragen (***to s.o.*** j-m); **2.** *j-n zu e-r Aufgabe etc.* bestimmen, *j-n mit et.* beauftragen; *e-m Amt*, ⚔ *e-m Regiment* zuteilen; **3.** *fig. et.* zuordnen (***to*** *dat.*); **4.** *Zeit, Aufgabe* festsetzen, bestimmen; **5.** *Grund etc.* angeben, anführen; **6.** zuschreiben (***to*** *dat.*); **7.** ⚖ (***to***) über'tragen (auf *acc.*), abtreten (an *acc.*); **II** *s.* **8.** ⚖ Rechtsnachfolger(in), Zessio'nar *m*; **as'sign·a·ble** [-nəbl] *adj.* bestimmbar, zuweisbar; zuzuschreiben(d); anführbar; ⚖ über'tragbar; **as·sig·na·tion** [ˌæsɪg'neɪʃn] *s.* **1.** → ***assignment*** 1, 2, 4; **2.** *et.* Zugewiesenes, (Geld)Zuwendung *f*; **3.** Stelldichein *n*; **as·sign·ee** [ˌæsɪ'niː] *s.* ⚖ **1.** → ***assign*** 8; **2.** Bevollmächtigte(r *m*) *f*; Treuhänder *m*: ***~ in bankruptcy*** Konkursverwalter *m*; **as'sign·ment** [-mənt] *s.* **1.** An-, Zuweisung *f*; **2.** Bestimmung *f*, Festsetzung *f*; **3.** Aufgabe *f*, Arbeit *f* (*a. ped.*); Auftrag *m*; *bes. Am.* Stellung *f*, Posten *m*; **4.** ⚖ a) Übertragung *f*, Abtretung *f*, b) Abtretungsurkunde *f*; **as·sign·or** [ˌæsɪ'nɔː] *s.* ⚖ Ze'dent(in), Abtretende(r *m*) *f*.

as·sim·i·late [ə'sɪmɪleɪt] **I** *v/t.* **1.** assimilieren: a) angleichen (*a. ling.*), anpassen (***to, with*** *dat.*), b) *bsd. sociol.* aufnehmen, absorbieren, *a.* gleichsetzen (***to, with*** mit), c) *biol. Nahrung* einverleiben, 'umsetzen; **2.** vergleichen (***to, with*** mit); **II** *v/i.* **3.** sich assimilieren, gleich *od.* ähnlich werden, sich anpassen, sich angleichen; **4.** aufgenommen werden; **as·sim·i·la·tion** [əˌsɪmɪ'leɪʃn] *s.* (***to***) Assimilati'on *f* (an *acc.*): a) *a. sociol.* Angleichung *f* (an *acc.*), Gleichsetzung *f* (mit), b) *biol., sociol.* Aufnahme *f*, Einverleibung *f*, c) *bot.* Photosyn'these *f*, d) *ling.* Assimilierung *f*.

as·sist [ə'sɪst] **I** *v/t.* **1.** *j-m* helfen, beistehen; *j-n od. et.* unter'stützen: ***~ed takeoff*** Abflug *m* mit Starthilfe; **2.** fördern, (*mit Geld*) unter'stützen: ***~ed immigration*** Einwanderung mit (staatlicher) Beihilfe; **II** *v/i.* **3.** Hilfe leisten, mithelfen (***in*** bei): ***~ in doing a job*** bei e-r Arbeit (mit)helfen; **4.** (***at***) beiwohnen (*dat.*), teilnehmen (an *dat.*); **III** *s.* **5.** F → ***assistance***; **6.** *Eishockey etc.*: Vorlage *f*; **as'sist·ance** [-təns] *s.* Hilfe *f*, Unter'stützung *f*, Beistand *m*: ***economic*** (***judicial***) ***~*** Wirtschafts- (Rechts)Hilfe; ***social ~*** Sozialhilfe *f*;

afford (*od.* ***lend***) **~** Hilfe gewähren *od.* leisten; **as'sist·ant** [-tənt] **I** *adj.* **1.** behilflich (***to*** *dat.*); **2.** Hilfs..., Unter..., stellvertretend, zweite(r): **~ *driver*** Beifahrer *m*; **~ *judge*** ⚖ Beisitzer *m*; **II** *s.* **3.** Assi'stent(in), Gehilfe *m*, Gehilfin *f*, Mitarbeiter(in); Angestellte(r *m*) *f*; **4.** Ladengehilfe *m*, -gehilfin *f*, Verkäufer(in).

as·size [ə'saɪz] *s. hist.* **1.** ⚖ (Schwur-) Gerichtssitzung *f*, Gerichtstag *m*; **2.** *℞s pl.* ⚖ *Brit.* As'sisen *pl.*, peri'odische (Schwur)Gerichtssitzungen *pl.* des ***High Court of Justice*** in den einzelnen Grafschaften (*bis 1971*).

as·so·ci·a·ble [ə'səʊʃjəbl] *adj.* (gedanklich) vereinbar (***with*** mit).

as·so·ci·ate [ə'səʊʃɪeɪt] **I** *v/t.* **1.** (***with***) vereinigen, verbinden, verknüpfen (mit); hin'zufügen, angliedern, -schließen, zugesellen (*dat.*): **~*d company*** ☤ *Brit.* Schwestergesellschaft *f*; **2.** *bsd. psych.* assoziieren, (gedanklich) verbinden, in Zs.-hang bringen, verknüpfen; **3.** **~ *o.s.*** sich anschließen (***with*** *dat.*); **II** *v/i.* (***with*** mit) **4.** 'Umgang haben, verkehren; **5.** sich verknüpfen, sich verbinden; **III** *adj.* [-ʃɪət] **6.** eng verbunden, verbündet; verwandt (***with*** mit); **7.** beigeordnet, Mit...: **~ *editor*** Mitherausgeber *m*; **~ *judge*** beigeordneter Richter; **8.** außerordentlich: **~ *member***, **~ *professor***; **IV** *s.* [-ʃɪət] **9.** ☤ Teilhaber *m*, Gesellschafter *m*; **10.** Gefährte *m*, Genosse *m*, Kol'lege *m*, Mitarbeiter *m*; **11.** außerordentliches Mitglied, Beigeordnete(r *m*) *f*; **12.** *Am. univ.* Lehrbeauftragte(r *m*) *f*.

as·so·ci·a·tion [əˌsəʊsɪ'eɪʃn] *s.* **1.** Vereinigung *f*, Verbindung *f*, An-, Zs.-schluß *m*; **2.** Verein(igung *f*) *m*, Gesellschaft *f*; Genossenschaft *f*, Handelsgesellschaft *f*, Verband *m*; **3.** Freundschaft *f*, Kame'radschaft *f*; 'Umgang *m*, Verkehr *m*; **4.** Zs.-hang *m*, Beziehung *f*, Verknüpfung *f*; (Gedanken)Verbindung *f*, (I'deen)Assoziatiˌon *f*: **~ *of ideas***; **~ foot·ball** *s. sport* (Verbands-) Fußball(spiel *n*) *m* (*Ggs. Rugby*).

as·so·nance ['æsənəns] *s.* Asso'nanz *f*, vo'kalischer Gleichklang; **'as·so·nant** [-nt] **I** *adj.* anklingend; **II** *s.* Gleichklang *m*.

as·sort [ə'sɔːt] **I** *v/t.* **1.** sortieren, gruppieren, (passend) zs.-stellen; **2.** ☤ assortieren; **II** *v/i.* **3.** (***with***) passen (zu), über'einstimmen (mit); **4.** verkehren, 'umgehen (***with*** mit); **as'sort·ed** [-tɪd] *adj.* **1.** sortiert, geordnet; **2.** ☤ assortiert, *a. fig.* gemischt, verschiedenartig, allerlei; **as'sort·ment** [-mənt] *s.* **1.** Sortieren *n*, Ordnen *n*; **2.** Zs.-stellung *f*, Sammlung *f*; **3.** *bsd.* ⚖ Sorti'ment *n*, Auswahl *f*, Mischung *f*, Kollekti'on *f*.

as·suage [ə'sweɪdʒ] *v/t.* **1.** erleichtern, lindern, mildern; **2.** besänftigen, beschwichtigen; **3.** *Hunger etc.* stillen.

as·sume [ə'sjuːm] *v/t.* **1.** annehmen, vor'aussetzen, unter'stellen: ***assuming that*** angenommen, daß; **2.** *Amt, Pflicht, Schuld etc.* über'nehmen, (*a. Gefahr*) auf sich nehmen: **~ *office***; **3.** *Gestalt, Eigenschaft etc.* annehmen, bekommen; sich zulegen, sich geben, sich angewöhnen; **4.** sich anmaßen *od.* aneignen: **~ *power*** die Macht ergreifen; **5.** vorschützen, vorgeben, (er)heucheln; **6.** *Kleider etc.* anziehen; **as'sumed** [-md] *adj.* □ **1.** angenommen, vor'ausgesetzt; **2.** vorgetäuscht, unecht: **~ *name*** Deckname *m*; **as'sum·ed·ly** [-mɪdlɪ] *adv.* vermutlich; **as'sum·ing** [-mɪŋ] *adj.* □ anmaßend.

as·sump·tion [ə'sʌmpʃn] *s.* **1.** Annahme *f*, Vor'aussetzung *f*; Vermutung *f*: ***on the ~ that*** in der Annahme, daß; **2.** 'Übernahme *f*, Annahme *f*; **3.** ('widerrechtliche) Aneignung; **4.** Anmaßung *f*; **5.** Vortäuschung *f*; **6.** ℞ (***Day***) *eccl.* Mariä Himmelfahrt *f*.

as·sur·ance [ə'ʃʊərəns] *s.* **1.** Ver-, Zusicherung *f*; **2.** Bürgschaft *f*, Garan'tie *f*; **3.** ☤ (*bsd.* Lebens)Versicherung *f*; **4.** Sicherheit *f*, Gewißheit *f*; Sicherheitsgefühl *n*, Zuversicht *f*; **5.** Selbstsicherheit *f*, -vertrauen *n*; sicheres Auftreten; *b.s.* Dreistigkeit *f*; **as·sure** [ə'ʃʊə] *v/t.* **1.** sichern, sicherstellen, bürgen für: ***this will ~ your success***; **2.** ver-, zusichern: **~ *s.o. of s.th.*** j-n e-r Sache versichern, j-m et. zusichern; **~ *s.o. that*** j-m versichern, daß; **3.** beruhigen; **4.** (***o.s.*** sich) über'zeugen *od.* vergewissern; **5.** *Leben* versichern: **~ *one's life with*** e-e Lebensversicherung abschließen bei *e-r Gesellschaft*; **as·sured** [ə'ʃʊəd] **I** *adj.* □ **1.** ge-, versichert; **2.** a) sicher, über'zeugt, b) selbstsicher, c) beruhigt, ermutigt; **3.** gewiß, zweifellos; **II** *s.* **4.** Versicherte(r *m*) *f*; **as'sur·ed·ly** [-rɪdlɪ] *adv.* ganz gewiß; **as·sured·ness** [ə'ʃʊədnɪs] *s.* Gewißheit *f*; Selbstvertrauen *n*; *b.s.* Dreistigkeit *f*; **as'sur·er** [-rə] *s.* Versicherer *m*.

As·syr·i·an [ə'sɪrɪən] **I** *adj.* as'syrisch; **II** *s.* As'syrer(in).

as·ter ['æstə] *s.* ⚘ Aster *f*.

as·ter·isk ['æstərɪsk] *s. typ.* Sternchen *n*.

a·stern [əs'tɜːn] *adv.* ⚓ **1.** achtern, hinten; **2.** achteraus.

as·ter·oid ['æstərɔɪd] *s. ast.* Astero'id *m* (*kleiner Planet*).

asth·ma ['æsmə] *s.* ⚕ 'Asthma *n*, Atemnot *f*; **asth·mat·ic** [æs'mætɪk] **I** *adj.* (□ **~*ally***) asth'matisch; **II** *s.* Asth'matiker (-in); **asth·mat·i·cal** [æs'mætɪkl] → ***asthmatic*** I.

as·tig·mat·ic [ˌæstɪg'mætɪk] *adj.* (□ **~*ally***) *phys.* astig'matisch; **a·stig·ma·tism** [æ'stɪgmətɪzəm] *s.* Astigma'tismus *m*.

a·stir [ə'stɜː] *adv. u. adj.* **1.** auf den Beinen: a) in Bewegung, rege, b) auf(gestanden), aus dem Bett, munter; **2.** in Aufregung (***with*** über *acc.*, wegen).

as·ton·ish [ə'stɒnɪʃ] *v/t.* **1.** in Erstaunen *od.* Verwunderung setzen; **2.** über'raschen, befremden: ***be ~ed*** erstaunt *od.* überrascht sein (***at*** über *acc.*, ***to*** *inf.* zu *inf.*), sich wundern (***at*** über *acc.*); **as'ton·ish·ing** [-ʃɪŋ] *adj.* □ erstaunlich, überraschend; **as'ton·ish·ing·ly** [-ʃɪŋlɪ] *adv.* erstaunlich(erweise); **as'ton·ish·ment** [-mənt] *s.* Verwunderung *f*, (Er)Staunen *n*, Befremden *n* (***at*** über *acc.*): ***to fill*** (*od.* ***strike***) ***with ~*** in Erstaunen setzen.

as·tound [ə'staʊnd] *v/t.* verblüffen, in Erstaunen setzen, äußerst über'raschen; **as'tound·ing** [-dɪŋ] *adj.* □ verblüffend, höchst erstaunlich.

as·tra·chan → ***astrakhan***.

a·strad·dle [ə'strædl] *adv.* rittlings.

as·tra·khan [ˌæstrə'kæn] *s.* 'Astrachan *m*, Krimmer *m* (*Pelzart*).

as·tral ['æstrəl] *adj.* Stern(en)..., Astral...: **~ *body*** Astralleib *m*; **~ *lamp*** Astrallampe *f*.

a·stray [ə'streɪ] **I** *adv.*: ***go ~*** a) vom Weg abkommen, b) *fig.* auf Abwege geraten, c) *fig.* irre-, fehlgehen, d) das Ziel verfehlen (*Schuß etc.*); ***lead ~*** *fig.* irreführen, verleiten; **II** *adj.* irregehend, abschweifend (*a. fig.*); irrig, falsch.

a·stride [ə'straɪd] *adv., adj. u. prp.* rittlings (***of*** auf *dat.*), mit gespreizten Beinen: ***ride ~*** im Herrensattel reiten; **~ (*of*) *a horse*** zu Pferde; **~ (*of*) *a road*** quer über die Straße.

as·tringe [ə'strɪndʒ] *v/t.* (*a.* ⚕) zs.-ziehen, adstringieren; **as'trin·gent** [-dʒənt] **I** *adj.* □ **1.** ⚕ adstringierend, zs.-ziehend; **2.** *fig.* streng, hart; **II** *s.* **3.** ⚕ Ad'stringens *n*.

as·tri·on·ics [ˌæstrɪ'ɒnɪks] *s. pl. sg. konstr.* Astri'onik *f*, 'Raumfahrtelekˌtronik *f*.

as·tro·dome ['æstrəʊdəʊm] *s.* ✈ Kuppel *f* für astro'nomische Navigati'on;

as·tro·labe ['æstrəʊleɪb] *s. ast.* Astro'labium *n*.

as·trol·o·ger [ə'strɒlədʒə] *s.* Astro'loge *m*, Sterndeuter *m*; **as·tro·log·ic**, **as·tro·log·i·cal** [ˌæstrə'lɒdʒɪk(l)] *adj.* □ astro'logisch; **as·trol·o·gy** [ə'strɒlədʒɪ] *s.* Astrolo'gie *f*, Sterndeutung *f*.

as·tro·naut ['æstrənɔːt] *s.* (Welt-) Raumfahrer *m*, Astro'naut *m*; **as·tro·nau·tics** [ˌæstrə'nɔːtɪks] *s. pl. sg. konstr.* Raumfahrt *f*.

as·tron·o·mer [ə'strɒnəmə] *s.* Astro'nom *m*; **as·tro·nom·ic**, **as·tro·nom·i·cal** [ˌæstrə'nɒmɪk(l)] *adj.* □ **1.** astro'nomisch, Stern..., Himmels...; **2.** *fig.* riesengroß: **~ *figures*** astronomische Zahlen; **as·tron·o·my** [ə'strɒnəmɪ] *s.* Astrono'mie *f*, Sternkunde *f*.

as·tro·phys·i·cist [ˌæstrəʊ'fɪzɪsɪst] *s.* Astro'physiker *m*; **as·tro·phys·ics** [ˌæstrəʊ'fɪzɪks] *s. pl. sg. konstr.* Astrophy'sik *f*.

as·tute [ə'stjuːt] *adj.* □ **1.** scharfsinnig; **2.** schlau, gerissen, raffiniert; **as'tute·ness** [-nɪs] *s.* Scharfsinn *m*; Schlauheit *f*.

a·sun·der [ə'sʌndə] **I** *adv.* ausein'ander, ent'zwei, in Stücke: ***cut s.th. ~***; **II** *adj.* ausein'ander(liegend); *fig.* verschieden.

a·sy·lum [ə'saɪləm] *s.* **1.** A'syl *n*, Heim *n*, (Pflege)Anstalt *f*: (***insane*** *od.* ***lunatic***) **~** Irrenanstalt *f*; **2.** A'syl *n*: a) Freistätte *f*, Zufluchtsort *m*, b) *fig.* Zuflucht *f*, Schutz *m*, c) po'litisches A'syl: ***right of ~*** Asylrecht *n*.

a·sym·met·ric, **a·sym·met·ri·cal** [ˌæsɪ'metrɪk(l)] *adj.* □ asym'metrisch, 'unsymˌmetrisch, ungleichmäßig: ***asymmetrical bars*** *Turnen*: Stufenbarren *m*; **a·sym·me·try** [æ'sɪmətrɪ] *s.* Asymme'trie *f*, Ungleichmäßigkeit *f*.

a·syn·chro·nous [æ'sɪŋkrənəs] *adj.* □ 'asynchron, Asynchron...

at[1] [æt; *unbetont* ət] *prp.* **1.** (*Ort*) an (*dat.*), bei, zu, auf (*dat.*), in (*dat.*): **~ *the corner*** an der Ecke; **~ *the door*** an *od.* vor der Tür; **~ *home*** zu Hause; **~ *the baker's*** beim Bäcker; **~ *school*** in der Schule; **~ *a ball*** bei (*od.* auf) e-m Ball; **~ *Stratford*** in Stratford (***at*** *vor dem Namen jeder Stadt außer London* *u. dem eigenen Wohnort*; *vor den beiden letzteren* **in**); **2.** (*Richtung*) auf (*acc.*), nach, gegen, zu, durch: **point ~ s.o.** auf j-n zeigen; **3.** (*Art u. Weise, Zustand*) in (*dat.*), bei, zu, unter (*dat.*), auf (*acc.*): **~ work** bei der Arbeit; **~ your service** zu Ihren Diensten; **good ~ Latin** gut in Latein; **~ my expense** auf meine Kosten; **~ a gallop** im Galopp; **he is still ~ it** er ist noch dabei *od.* dran *od.* damit beschäftigt; **4.** (*Zeit*) um, bei, zu, auf (*dat.*): **~ 3 o'clock** um 3 Uhr; **~ dawn** bei Tagesanbruch; **~ Christmas** zu Weihnachten; **~ (the age of) 21** im Alter von 21 Jahren; **5.** (*Grund*) über (*acc.*), von, bei: **alarmed ~** beunruhigt über; **6.** (*Preis, Maß*) für, um, zu: **~ 6 dollars**; **charged ~** berechnet mit; **7. ~ all** *in neg. od. Fragesätzen*: über'haupt, gar *nichts etc.*: **is he suitable ~ all?** ist er überhaupt geeignet?; **not ~ all** überhaupt nicht; **not ~ all!** F nichts zu danken!, gern geschehen!

At² [æt] *s. Brit.* ⚔ *hist.* F Angehörige *f* der Streitkräfte.

at·a·vism ['ætəvɪzəm] *s. biol.* Ata'vismus *m*, (Entwicklungs)Rückschlag *m*; **at·a·vis·tic** [ˌætə'vɪstɪk] *adj.* ata'vistisch.

a·tax·i·a [ə'tæksɪə], **a'tax·y** [-ksɪ] *s.* Ata'xie *f*, Bewegungsstörung *f*.

ate [et] *pret. von* **eat**.

at·el·ier ['ætəlɪeɪ] (*Fr.*) *s.* Ateli'er *n*.

a·the·ism ['eɪθɪɪzəm] *s.* Athe'ismus *m*, Gottesleugnung *f*; **'a·the·ist** [-ɪst] *s.* **1.** Athe'ist(in); **2.** gottloser Mensch; **a·the·is·tic** *adj.*; **a·the·is·ti·cal** [ˌeɪθɪ'ɪstɪk(l)] *adj.* □ **1.** athe'istisch; **2.** gottlos.

A·the·ni·an [ə'θiːnjən] **I** *adj.* a'thenisch; **II** *s.* A'thener(in).

a·thirst [ə'θɜːst] *adj.* **1.** durstig; **2.** begierig (**for** nach).

ath·lete ['æθliːt] *s.* **1.** Ath'let *m*: a) Sportler *m*, Wettkämpfer *m*, b) *fig.* Hüne *m*; **2.** *Brit.* 'Leichtathˌlet *m*; **~'s foot** *s.* ⚕ Fußpilz *m*.

ath·let·ic [æθ'letɪk] *adj.* (□ **~ally**) ath'letisch: a) Sport..., b) von athletischem Körperbau, musku'lös, c) sportlich (gewandt); **~ heart** *s.* ⚕ Sportherz *n*.

ath·let·i·cism [æθ'letɪsɪzəm] *s.* → **athletics** 2; **ath'let·ics** [-ɪks] *s. pl. sg. konstr.* **1.** a) Sport *m*, b) *Brit.* 'Leichtathˌletik *f*; **2.** sportliche Betätigung *od.* Gewandtheit, Sportlichkeit *f*.

at-home [ət'həʊm] *s.* (zwangloser) Empfang(stag), At-'home *n*.

a·thwart [ə'θwɔːt] **I** *adv.* **1.** quer, schräg hin'durch; ⚓ dwars (über); **2.** *fig.* verkehrt, ungelegen, in die Quere; **II** *prp.* **3.** (quer) über (*acc.*) *od.* durch; ⚓ dwars (über *acc.*); **4.** *fig.* (ent)gegen.

a·tilt [ə'tɪlt] *adv. u. adj.* **1.** vorgebeugt, kippend; **2.** mit eingelegter Lanze: **run** (*od.* **ride**) **~ at s.o.** *fig.* gegen j-n e-e Attacke reiten.

At·lan·tic [ət'læntɪk] **I** *adj.* at'lantisch; **II** *s.*: **the ~** der At'lantik, der Atlantische Ozean; **~ Char·ter** *s. pol.* At'lantikˌCharta *f*; **~ (standard) time** *s.* At'lantische ('Standard)Zeit (*im Osten Kanadas*).

at·las ['ætləs] *s.* **1.** Atlas *m* (*Buch*); **2.** ⚠ At'lant *m*, Atlas *m* (*Gebälkträger*); **3.** *fig.* Hauptstütze *f*; **4.** *anat.* Atlas *m* (*oberster Halswirbel*); **5.** *großes Papierformat*; **6.** Atlas(seide *f*) *m*.

at·mos·phere ['ætməˌsfɪə] *s.* **1.** Atmo'sphäre *f*, Lufthülle *f*; **2.** Luft *f*: **a moist ~**; **3.** ⚙ Atmo'sphäre *f* (*Druckeinheit*); **4.** *fig.* Atmo'sphäre *f*: a) Um'gebung *f*, b) Stimmung *f*.

at·mos·pher·ic [ˌætməs'ferɪk] *adj.* (□ **~ally**) **1.** atmo'sphärisch, Luft...: **~ pressure** *phys.* Luftdruck; **2.** Witterungs..., Wetter...; **3.** ⚙ mit (Luft-)Druck betrieben; **4.** *fig.* stimmungsvoll, Stimmungs...; **at·mos'pher·ics** [-ks] *s. pl.* **1.** ⚙ atmo'sphärische Störungen *pl.*; **2.** *fig.* (*bsd.* opti'mistische) Atmo'sphäre.

at·oll ['ætɒl] *s. geogr.* A'toll *n*.

at·om ['ætəm] *s.* **1.** *phys.* A'tom *n*: **~ bomb** Atombombe *f*; **~ smashing** Atomzertrümmerung *f*; **~ splitting** Atom(kern)spaltung *f*; **2.** *fig.* A'tom *n*, winziges Teilchen, bißchen *n*: **not an ~ of truth** kein Körnchen Wahrheit.

a·tom·ic [ə'tɒmɪk] *adj. phys.* (□ **~ally**) ato'mar, a'tomisch, Atom...: **~ age** Atomzeitalter *n*; **~ bomb** Atombombe *f*; **~ clock** Atomuhr *f*; **~ decay**, **~ disintegration** Atomzerfall *m*; **~ energy** Atomenergie *f*; **~ fission** Atomspaltung *f*; **~ fuel** Kernbrennstoff *m*; **~ index**, **~ number** Atomzahl *f*; **~ nucleus** Atomkern *m*; **~ pile** Atombatterie *f*, -säule *f*, -meiler *m*; **~-powered** mit Atomkraft getrieben, Atom...; **~ power plant** Atomkraftwerk *n*; **~ weight** Atomgewicht *n*.

a·tom·i·cal [ə'tɒmɪkl] → **atomic**.

a·tom·ics [ə'tɒmɪks] *s. pl. mst sg. konstr.* A'tomphyˌsik *f*.

at·om·ism ['ætəmɪzəm] *s. phls.* Ato'mismus *m*; **at·om·is·tic** [ˌætəʊ'mɪstɪk] *adj.* (□ **~ally**) ato'mistisch.

at·om·ize ['ætəʊmaɪz] *v/t.* **1.** in A'tome auflösen; **2.** *Flüssigkeit* zerstäuben; **3.** in s-e Bestandteile auflösen, atomisieren; **4.** ⚔ mit Atombomben belegen; **'at·om·iz·er** [-maɪzə] *s.* ⚙ Zerstäuber *m*.

at·o·my¹ ['ætəmɪ] *s.* **1.** A'tom *n*; **2.** *fig.* Zwerg *m*, Knirps *m*.

at·o·my² ['ætəmɪ] *s.* F ,Gerippe' *n*.

a·tone [ə'təʊn] *v/i.* (**for**) büßen (für); sühnen, wieder'gutmachen (*acc.*); **a'tone·ment** [-mənt] *s.* **1.** Buße *f*, Sühne *f*, Genugtuung *f* (**for** für): **Day of** ♀ *eccl.* a) Buß- und Bettag *m*, b) Versöhnungstag *m* (*jüd. Feiertag*); **2. the** ♀ *eccl.* das Sühneopfer Christi.

a·ton·ic [æ'tɒnɪk] *adj.* **1.** ⚕ a'tonisch, schlaff, schwächend; **2.** *ling.* a) unbetont, b) stimmlos; **at·o·ny** ['ætənɪ] *s.* ⚕ Ato'nie *f*.

a·top [ə'tɒp] **I** *adv.* oben(auf), zu'oberst; **II** *prp. a.* **~ of** (oben) auf (*dat.*); *fig.* besser als.

a·trip [ə'trɪp] *adj.* ⚓ **1.** gelichtet (*Anker*); **2.** steifgeheißt (*Segel*).

a·tri·um ['ɑːtrɪəm] *pl.* **-a** [-ə] *s.* 'Atrium *n*: a) *antiq.* Hauptraum *m*, b) ⚠ Lichthof *m*, c) *anat.* (*bsd.* Herz)Vorhof *m*, Vorkammer *f*.

a·tro·cious [ə'trəʊʃəs] *adj.* □ scheußlich, gräßlich, grausam, *fig.* F *a.* mise'rabel; **a·troc·i·ty** [ə'trɒsətɪ] *s.* **1.** Scheußlichkeit *f*; **2.** Greuel(tat *f*) *m*; **3.** F a) Ungeheuerlichkeit *f*, (grober) Verstoß, b) ,Greuel' *m*, *et.* Scheußliches.

at·ro·phied ['ætrəfɪd] *adj.* ⚕ atrophiert, geschrumpft, verkümmert (*a. fig.*); **'at·ro·phy** [-fɪ] ⚕ **I** *s.* Atro'phie *f*, Abzehrung *f*, Schwund *m*, Verkümmerung *f* (*a. fig.*); **II** *v/t.* abzehren *od.* verkümmern lassen; **III** *v/i.* schwinden, verkümmern (*a. fig.*).

Ats [æts] *s. pl. Brit. hist.* F *statt* **A.T.S.** ['eɪ'tiː'es] *abbr. für* (**Women's**) **Auxiliary Territorial Service** *Organisation der weiblichen Angehörigen der Streitkräfte*.

at·ta·boy ['ætəbɔɪ] *int. Am.* F bravo!, so ist's recht!

at·tach [ə'tætʃ] **I** *v/t.* **1.** (**to**) befestigen, anbringen (an *dat.*), beifügen (*dat.*), anheften, -binden, -kleben (an *acc.*), verbinden (mit); **2.** *fig.* (**to**) *Sinn etc.* verknüpfen, verbinden (mit); *Wert, Wichtigkeit, Schuld* beimessen (*dat.*), *Namen* beilegen (*dat.*): **~ conditions** (**to**) Bedingungen knüpfen (an *acc.*); → **importance** 1; **3.** *fig.* j-n fesseln, gewinnen, für sich einnehmen: **be ~ed to s.o.** an j-m hängen; **be ~ed** ,in festen Händen sein' (*Mädchen etc.*); **~ o.s.** sich anschließen (**to** *dat.*, an *acc.*); **4.** (**to**) *j-n* angliedern, zuteilen (*dat.*); **5.** ⚖ a) *j-n* verhaften, b) *et.* beschlagnahmen, *Forderung*, *Konto etc.* pfänden; **II** *v/i.* **6.** (**to**) anhaften (*dat.*), verknüpft *od.* verbunden sein (mit): **no blame ~es to him** ihn trifft keine Schuld; **7.** ⚖ als Rechtsfolge eintreten: **liability ~es**; **at'tach·a·ble** [-tʃəbl] *adj.* **1.** anfügbar, an-, aufsteckbar; **2.** *fig.* verknüpfbar (**to** mit); **3.** ⚖ zu beschlagnahmen(d); beschlagnahmefähig, pfändbar.

at·ta·ché [ə'tæʃeɪ] (*Fr.*) *s.* Atta'ché *m*: **commercial ~** Handelsattaché; **~ case** *s.* Aktenkoffer *m*.

at·tached [ə'tætʃt] *adj.* **1.** befestigt, fest, da'zugehörig: **with collar ~** mit festem Kragen; **2.** angeschlossen, zugeteilt; **3.** anhänglich, *j-m* zugetan; **at'tach·ment** [-tʃmənt] *s.* **1.** Befestigung *f*, Anbringung *f*; Anschluß *m*; **2.** Verbindung *f*, Verknüpfung *f*; **3.** Anhängsel *n*, Beiwerk *n*; ⚙ Zusatzgerät *n*; **4.** *fig.* (**to**, **for**) Bindung *f* (an *acc.*); Zugehörigkeit *f* (zu); Anhänglichkeit *f* (an *acc.*), Neigung *f*, Liebe *f* (zu); **5.** ⚖ a) Verhaftung *f*, b) Beschlagnahme *f*, Pfändung *f*, dinglicher Ar'rest: **~ of a debt** Forderungspfändung; **order of ~** Beschlagnahmeverfügung *f*.

at·tack [ə'tæk] **I** *v/t.* **1.** angreifen, über'fallen; **2.** *fig.* angreifen, scharf kritisieren; **3.** *fig. Arbeit etc.* in Angriff nehmen, sich über *Essen etc.* hermachen; **4.** *fig.* befallen (*Krankheit*); angreifen: **acid ~s metals**; **II** *s.* **5.** Angriff *m* (**on** auf *acc.*) (*a.* ⚗ *Einwirkung*), 'Überfall *m*; **6.** *fig.* Angriff *m*, At'tacke *f*, (scharfe) Kri'tik: **be under ~** unter Beschuß stehen; **7.** ⚕ Anfall *m*, At'tacke *f*; **8.** In'angriffnahme *f*; **at'tack·er** [-kə] *s.* Angreifer *m*.

at·tain [ə'teɪn] **I** *v/t. Zweck etc.* erreichen; erlangen; erzielen; **II** *v/i.* (**to**) gelangen (zu), erreichen (*acc.*): **after ~ing the age of 18 years** nach Vollendung des 18. Lebensjahres; **at'tain·a·ble** [-nəbl] *adj.* erreichbar; **at'tain·der** [-ndə] *s.* ⚖ Verlust *m* der bürgerlichen Ehrenrechte u. Einziehung *f* des Vermögens; **at'tain·ment** [-mənt] *s.* **1.** Erreichung *f*, Erwerbung *f*; **2.** *pl.* Kenntnisse *pl.*, Fertigkeiten *pl.*; **at'taint** [-nt] **I** *v/t.* **1.** zum Tode und zur

Ehrlosigkeit verurteilen; **2.** befallen (*Krankheit*); **3.** *fig.* beflecken, entehren; **II** *s.* **4.** Makel *m*, Schande *f*.
at·tar ['ætə] *s.* 'Blumenes,senz *f*, *bsd.* **~ of roses** Rosenöl *n*.
at·tempt [ə'tempt] **I** *v/t.* **1.** versuchen, probieren; **2. ~ s.o.'s life** e-n Mordanschlag auf j-n verüben; **~ed murder** Mordversuch *m*; **3.** in Angriff nehmen, sich wagen *od.* machen an (*acc.*); **II** *s.* **4.** Versuch *m*, Bemühung *f* (**to** *inf.* zu *inf.*): **~ at explanation** Erklärungsversuch; **5.** Angriff *m*: **~ on s.o.'s life** (Mord)Anschlag *m*, Attentat *n* auf j-n.
at·tend [ə'tend] **I** *v/t.* **1.** *j-m* aufwarten; als Diener *od.* dienstlich begleiten; **2.** *bsd. Kranke* pflegen; *ärztlich* behandeln; **3.** *fig.* begleiten: **~ed by** *od.* **with** begleitet von, verbunden mit (*Schwierigkeiten etc.*); **4.** beiwohnen (*dat.*), teilnehmen an (*dat.*); *Vorlesung, Schule, Kirche etc.* besuchen; **5.** ⚙ a) bedienen, b) warten, pflegen, über'wachen; **II** *v/i.* **6.** (**to**) beachten (*acc.*), hören, achten (auf *acc.*): **~ to what I am saying**; **7.** (**to**) sich kümmern (um), sich widmen (*dat.*); ✝ *j-n* bedienen (*im Laden*), abfertigen; **8.** (**to**) sorgen (für); besorgen, erledigen (*acc.*); **9.** ([**up**]**on**) *j-m* aufwarten, zur Verfügung stehen; *j-n* bedienen; **10.** erscheinen, zu'gegen sein (**at** bei); **11.** *obs.* achtgeben; **at'tend·ance** [-dəns] *s.* **1.** Bedienung *f*, Aufwartung *f*, Pflege *f* (**on**, **upon** *gen.*), Dienst(leistung *f*) *m*: **medical ~** ärztliche Hilfe; **hours of ~** Dienststunden; **in ~** diensthabend, -tuend; → **dance** 3; **2.** (**at**) Anwesenheit *f*, Erscheinen *n* (bei), Beteiligung *f*, Teilnahme *f* (an *dat.*), Besuch *m* (*gen.*): **~ list** Anwesenheitsliste *f*; **hours of ~** Besuchszeit *f*; **3.** ⚙ Bedienung *f*; Wartung *f*; **4.** Begleitung *f*, Dienerschaft *f*, Gefolge *n*; **5.** a) Besucher(zahl *f*) *pl.*, b) Besuch *m*, Beteiligung *f*: **in ~ at** anwesend bei; **at'tend·ant** [-dənt] **I** *adj.* **1.** (**on**, **upon**) begleitend (*acc.*), diensttuend (bei); **2.** anwesend (**at** bei); **3.** *fig.* (**upon**) verbunden (mit), zugehörig (*dat.*), Begleit...: **~ circumstances** Begleitumstände; **~ expenses** Nebenkosten; **II** *s.* **4.** Begleiter(in), Gefährte *m*, Gesellschafter(in); **5.** Diener(in), Bediente(r *m*) *f*; Aufseher(in), Wärter (-in); **6.** *pl.* Dienerschaft *f*, Gefolge *n*; **7.** ⚙ Bedienungsmann *m*; **8.** Begleiterscheinung *f*, Folge *f*.
at·ten·tion [ə'tenʃn] *s.* **1.** Aufmerksamkeit *f*, Beachtung *f*: **call ~ to** die Aufmerksamkeit lenken auf (*acc.*); **come to s.o.'s ~** j-m zur Kenntnis gelangen; **pay ~ to** *j-m od. et.* Beachtung schenken; **2.** Berücksichtigung *f*, Erledigung *f*: (**for the**) **~ of** zu Händen von (*od. gen.*); **for immediate ~** zur sofortigen Erledigung; **3.** Aufmerksamkeit *f*, Freundlichkeit *f*; *pl.* Aufmerksamkeiten *pl.*: **pay one's ~s to s.o.** j-m den Hof machen; **4. ~!** Achtung!, ⚔ *a.* stillgestanden!; **stand at** *od.* **to ~** ⚔ stillstehen, Haltung annehmen; **5.** Bedienung *f*, Wartung *f*; **at'ten·tive** [-ntɪv] *adj.* □ (**to**) aufmerksam: a) achtsam (auf *acc.*), b) *fig.* höflich (zu).
at·ten·u·ate **I** *v/t.* [ə'tenjʊeɪt] **1.** dünn *od.* schlank machen; verdünnen; ⚡ dämpfen; **2.** *fig.* vermindern, abschwächen; **II** *adj.* [-jʊət] **3.** verdünnt, vermindert, abgeschwächt, abgemagert; **at·ten·u·a·tion** [ə,tenjʊ'eɪʃn] *s.* Verminderung *f*, Verdünnung *f*, Schwächung *f*, Abmagerung *f*; ⚡ Dämpfung *f*.
at·test [ə'test] **I** *v/t.* **1.** a) beglaubigen, bescheinigen, b) amtlich begutachten *od.* attestieren: **to ~ cattle**; **2.** bestätigen, beweisen; **3.** ⚔ *Br.* vereidigen; **II** *v/i.* **4.** zeugen (**to** für); **at·tes·ta·tion** [,ætes'teɪʃn] *s.* **1.** Bezeugung *f*, Zeugnis *n*, Beweis *m*, Bescheinigung *f*, Bestätigung *f*; **2.** Eidesleistung *f*, Vereidigung *f*.
at·tic¹ ['ætɪk] *s.* **1.** Dachstube *f*, Man'sarde *f*; *pl.* Dachgeschoß *n*; **2.** F *fig.* ‚Oberstübchen' *n*, Kopf *m*.
At·tic² ['ætɪk] *adj.* 'attisch: **~ salt**, **~ wit** attisches Salz, feiner Witz.
at·tire [ə'taɪə] **I** *v/t.* **1.** kleiden, anziehen; **2.** putzen; **II** *s.* **3.** Kleidung *f*, Gewand *n*; **4.** Schmuck *m*.
at·ti·tude ['ætɪtju:d] *s.* **1.** Stellung *f*, Haltung *f*: **strike an ~** e-e Pose annehmen; **2.** *fig.* Haltung *f*: a) Standpunkt *m*, Verhalten *n*: **~ of mind** Geisteshaltung, b) Stellung(nahme) *f*, Einstellung *f* (**to**, **towards** zu, gegenüber); **3.** (*a.* ✈) Lage *f*; **at·ti·tu·di·nize** [,ætɪ'tju:dɪnaɪz] *v/i.* **1.** sich in Posi'tur setzen, posieren; **2.** affektiert tun.
at·tor·ney [ə'tɜ:nɪ] *s.* ⚖ (Rechts)Anwalt *m* (*Am. a.* **~ at law**); Bevollmächtigte(r *m*) *f*, (Stell)Vertreter *m*: **letter** (*od.* **warrant**) **of ~** schriftliche Vollmacht; **power of ~** Vollmacht(surkunde) *f*; **by ~** im Auftrag; **At,tor·ney-'Gen·er·al** *s.* ⚖ *Brit.* Kronanwalt *m*, Gene'ralstaatsanwalt *m*; *Am.* Ju'stizmi,nister *m*.
at·tract [ə'trækt] *v/t.* **1.** anziehen (*a. phys.*); **2.** *fig.* anziehen, anlocken, fesseln, reizen; *Mißfallen etc.* auf sich lenken (*od.* ziehen): **~ attention** Aufmerksamkeit erregen; **~ new members** neue Mitglieder gewinnen; **~ed by the music** von der Musik angelockt; **be ~ed** (**to**) eingenommen sein (für), liebäugeln (mit), sich hingezogen fühlen (zu); **at'trac·tion** [-kʃn] *s.* **1.** *phys.* Anziehungskraft *f*: **~ of gravity** Gravitationskraft *f*; **2.** *fig.* Anziehungskraft *f*, -punkt *m*, Reiz *m*, Attrakti'on *f*; *thea.* ('Haupt)Attrakti,on *f*, Zugstück *n*, -nummer *f*; **at'trac·tive** [-tɪv] *adj.* □ anziehend, *fig. a.* attrak'tiv, reizvoll, fesselnd, verlockend; zugkräftig; **at'trac·tive·ness** [-tɪvnɪs] *s.* Reiz *m*, *das* Attrak'tive.
at·trib·ut·a·ble [ə'trɪbjʊtəbl] *adj.* 'zuzuschreiben(d), beizumessen(d); **at·trib·ute** **I** *v/t.* [ə'trɪbju:t] (**to**) **1.** zuschreiben, beilegen, -messen (*dat.*); *b.s. a.* unter'stellen (*dat.*); **2.** zu'rückführen (auf *acc.*); **II** *s.* ['ætrɪbju:t] **3.** Attri'but *n* (*a. ling.*), Eigenschaft *f*, Merkmal *n*; **4.** (Kenn)Zeichen *n*, Sinnbild *n*; **at·tri·bu·tion** [,ætrɪ'bju:ʃn] *s.* **1.** Zuschreibung *f*; **2.** beigelegte Eigenschaft; **3.** zuerkanntes Recht; **at'trib·u·tive** [-tɪv] **I** *adj.* □ **1.** zugeschrieben, beigelegt; **2.** *ling.* attribu'tiv; **II** *s.* **3.** *ling.* Attri'but *n*.
at·trit·ed [ə'traɪtɪd] *adj.* abgenutzt; **at·tri·tion** [ə'trɪʃn] *s.* **1.** Abrieb *m*, Abnutzung *f*, ⚙ *a.* Verschleiß *m*; **2.** Zermürbung *f*: **war of ~** Zermürbungs-, Abnutzungskrieg *m*.
at·tune [ə'tju:n] *v/t.* ♪ stimmen; *fig.* (**to**) in Einklang bringen (mit), anpassen (*dat.*); abstimmen (auf *acc.*).
a·typ·i·cal [,eɪ'tɪpɪkl] *adj.* □ 'atypisch.
au·ber·gine ['əʊbəʒi:n] *s.* ⚘ Auber'gine *f*.
au·burn ['ɔ:bən] *adj.* ka'stanienbraun (*Haar*).
auc·tion ['ɔ:kʃn] **I** *s.* Aukti'on *f*, Versteigerung *f*: **sell by** (*Am.* **at**) **~**, **put up for** (*od.* **to**, *Am.* **at**) **~** verauktionieren, versteigern; **Dutch ~** Auktion, bei der der Preis so lange erniedrigt wird, bis sich ein Käufer findet; **sale by** (*od.* **at**) **~** Versteigerung; **~ bridge** *Kartenspiel*: Auktionsbridge *n*; **~ room** Auktionslokal *n*; **II** *v/t.* *mst* **~ off** versteigern; **auc·tion·eer** [,ɔ:kʃə'nɪə] **I** *s.* Auktio'nator *m*, Versteigerer *m*, *pl. a.* Aukti'onshaus *n*; **II** *v/t.* → **auction** II.
au·da·cious [ɔ:'deɪʃəs] *adj.* □ kühn: a) verwegen, b) keck, dreist, unverfroren; **au·dac·i·ty** [ɔ:'dæsətɪ] *s.* Kühnheit *f*: a) Verwegenheit *f*, Waghalsigkeit *f*, b) Dreistigkeit *f*, Unverfrorenheit *f*.
au·di·bil·i·ty [,ɔ:dɪ'bɪlətɪ] *s.* Hörbarkeit *f*, Vernehmbarkeit *f*; Lautstärke *f*; **au·di·ble** ['ɔ:dəbl] *adj.* □ hör-, vernehmbar, vernehmlich; ⚙ a'kustisch: **~ signal**.
au·di·ence ['ɔ:djəns] *s.* **1.** Anhören *n*, Gehör *n* (*a.* ⚖): **give ~ to s.o.** j-m Gehör schenken, j-n anhören; **right of ~** ⚖ rechtliches Gehör; **2.** Audi'enz *f* (**of**, **with** bei), Gehör *n*; **3.** 'Publikum *n*: a) Zuhörer(schaft *f*) *pl.*, b) Zuschauer *pl.*, c) Besucher *pl.*, d) Leser(kreis *m*) *pl.*: **~ rating** *Radio*, *TV* Einschaltquote *f*.
audio- [ɔ:dɪəʊ] *in Zssgn* Hör..., Ton..., Audio...: **~ frequency** Tonfrequenz *f*; **~ range** Tonfrequenzbereich *m*.
au·di·on ['ɔ:dɪən] *s.* *Radio*: 'Audion *n*: **~ tube** *Am.*, **~ valve** *Brit.* Verstärkerröhre *f*.
au·di·o·phile ['ɔ:dɪəʊfaɪl] *s.* Hi-Fi-Fan *m*.
au·di·o|·tape ['ɔ:dɪəʊteɪp] *s.* (besprochenes) Tonband; **~·typ·ist** ['ɔ:dɪəʊ,taɪpɪst] *s.* Phonoty'pistin *f*; **~·vis·u·al** [,ɔ:dɪəʊ'vɪzjʊəl] **I** *adj.* *ped.* audiovisu'ell: **~ aids** → **II** *s.* *pl.* audiovisu'elle 'Unterrichtsmittel *pl.*
au·dit ['ɔ:dɪt] **I** *s.* **1.** ✝ (Rechnungs-, Wirtschafts)Prüfung *f*, 'Bücherrevisi,on *f*: **~ year** Prüfungs-, Rechnungsjahr *n*; **2.** *fig.* Rechenschaftslegung *f*; **II** *v/t.* **3.** *Geschäftsbücher* (amtlich) prüfen, revidieren; **'au·dit·ing** [-tɪŋ] *s.* → **audit** 1.
au·di·tion [ɔ:'dɪʃn] **I** *s.* **1.** ⚕ Hörvermögen *n*, Gehör *n*; **2.** *thea.*, ♪ a) Vorsprechen *n od.* -singen *n od.* -spielen *n*, b) Anhörprobe *f*; **II** *v/t.* **3.** *thea. etc. j-n* vorsprechen *od.* vorsingen *od.* vorspielen lassen.
au·di·tor ['ɔ:dɪtə] *s.* **1.** Rechnungs-, Wirtschaftsprüfer *m*, 'Bücherre,visor *m*; **2.** *Am. univ.* Gasthörer(in); **au·di·to·ri·um** [,ɔ:dɪ'tɔ:rɪəm] *s.* Audi'torium *n*, Zuhörer-, Zuschauerraum *m*, Hörsaal *m*; *Am.* Vortragssaal *m*, Festhalle *f*; **'au·di·to·ry** [-tərɪ] **I** *adj.* **1.** Gehör..., Hör...; **II** *s.* **2.** Zuhörer(schaft *f*) *pl.*; **3.** → **auditorium**.
au fait [,əʊ 'feɪ] (*Fr.*) *adj.* auf dem laufenden, vertraut (**with** mit).
au fond [,əʊ 'fɔ̃:ŋ] (*Fr.*) *adv.* im Grunde.
Au·ge·an [ɔ:'dʒi:ən] *adj.* Augias...,

'überaus schmutzig: ***cleanse the ~ stables*** *fig.* die Augiasställe reinigen.
au·ger ['ɔːgə] *s.* ⚙ *großer* Bohrer, Löffel-, Schneckenbohrer *m*; Förderschnecke *f*.
aught [ɔːt] *pron.* (irgend) etwas: ***for ~ I care*** meinetwegen; ***for ~ I know*** soviel ich weiß.
aug·ment [ɔːg'ment] **I** *v/t.* vermehren, vergrößern; **II** *v/i.* sich vermehren, zunehmen; **III** *s.* ['ɔːgmənt] *ling.* Aug'ment *n* (*Vorsilbe in griech. Verben*); **aug·men·ta·tion** [ˌɔːgmen'teɪʃn] *s.* Vergrößerung *f*, Vermehrung *f*, Zunahme *f*, Wachstum *n*, Zuwachs *m*; Zusatz *m*; **aug'ment·a·tive** [-tətɪv] **I** *adj.* vermehrend, verstärkend; **II** *s. ling.* Verstärkungsform *f*.
au gra·tin [ˌəʊ 'grætæ̃ŋ] (*Fr.*) *adj. Küche*: au gra'tin, über'krustet.
au·gur ['ɔːgə] **I** *s. antiq.* 'Augur *m*, Wahrsager *m*; **II** *v/t. u. v/i.* prophe'zeien, ahnen (lassen), verheißen: ***~ ill*** (***well***) ein schlechtes (gutes) Zeichen sein (***for*** für), Böses (Gutes) ahnen lassen; **au·gu·ry** ['ɔːgjʊrɪ] *s.* **1.** Weissagung *f*, Prophe'zeiung *f*; **2.** Vorbedeutung *f*, Anzeichen *n*, Omen *n*; Vorahnung *f*.
au·gust¹ [ɔː'gʌst] *adj.* □ erhaben, hehr, maje'stätisch.
Au·gust² ['ɔːgəst] *s.* Au'gust *m*: ***in ~*** im August.
Au·gus·tan age [ɔː'gʌstən] *s.* **1.** Zeitalter *n* des (Kaisers) Au'gustus; **2.** Blütezeit *f* e-r Nati'on.
Au·gus·tine [ɔː'gʌstɪn], *a.* **~ fri·ar** *s.* Augu'stiner(mönch) *m*.
auld [ɔːld] *adj. Scot.* alt; **~ lang syne** [ˌɔːldlæŋ'saɪn] *s. Scot.* die gute alte Zeit.
aunt [ɑːnt] *s.* Tante *f*; **'aunt·ie** [-tɪ] *s.* F Tantchen *n*; **Aunt Sal·ly** ['sælɪ] *s.* **1.** volkstümliches Wurfspiel; **2.** *fig.* (gute) Zielscheibe *f*, *a.* Haßobjekt *n*.
au pair [ˌəʊ 'peə] **I** *adv.* als Au-'pair-Mädchen (*arbeiten etc.*); **II** *s. a.* ***~ girl*** Au-'pair-Mädchen *n*; **III** *v/i.* als Au-'pair-Mädchen arbeiten.
au·ra ['ɔːrə] *pl.* **-rae** [-riː] *s.* **1.** Hauch *m*, Duft *m*; A'roma *n*; **2.** ⚕ Vorgefühl *n* vor Anfällen; **3.** *fig.* Aura *f*: a) Fluidum *n*, Ausstrahlung *f*, b) Atmo'sphäre *f*, c) 'Nimbus *m*.
au·ral ['ɔːrəl] *adj.* □ Ohr…, Ohren…, Gehör…; Hör…, a'kustisch: ***~ surgeon*** Ohrenarzt *m*.
au·re·o·la [ɔː'rɪəʊlə], **au·re·ole** ['ɔːrɪəʊl] *s.* **1.** Strahlenkrone *f*, Aure'ole *f*; **2.** *fig.* 'Nimbus *m*; **3.** *ast.* Hof *m*.
au·ri·cle ['ɔːrɪkl] *s. anat.* **1.** äußeres Ohr, Ohrmuschel *f*; **2.** Herzvorhof *m*; Herzohr *n*.
au·ric·u·la [ə'rɪkjʊlə] *s.* ⚘ Au'rikel *f*.
au·ric·u·lar [ɔː'rɪkjʊlə] *adj.* □ **1.** Ohren…, Hör…: ***~ confession*** Ohrenbeichte *f*; ***~ tradition*** mündliche Überlieferung; ***~ witness*** Ohrenzeuge *m*; **2.** *anat.* zu den Herzohren gehörig.
au·rif·er·ous [ɔː'rɪfərəs] *adj.* goldhaltig.
au·rist ['ɔːrɪst] *s.* ⚕ Ohrenarzt *m*.
au·rochs ['ɔːrɒks] *s. zo.* Auerochs *m*, Ur *m*.
au·ro·ra [ɔː'rɔːrə] *s.* **1.** *poet.* Morgenröte *f*; **2.** ♀ *myth.* Au'rora *f*; **~ bo·re·a·lis** *s. phys.* Nordlicht *n*.
aus·cul·tate ['ɔːskəlteɪt] *v/t.* ⚕ *Lunge, Herz etc.* abhorchen; **aus·cul·ta·tion** [ˌɔːskəl'teɪʃn] *s.* ⚕ Abhorchen *n*.
aus·pice ['ɔːspɪs] *s.* **1.** (günstiges) Vor-, Anzeichen; **2.** *pl. fig.* Au'spizien *pl.*; Schutzherrschaft *f*: ***under the ~s of …*** unter der Schirmherrschaft von …; **aus·pi·cious** [ɔː'spɪʃəs] *adj.* □ günstig, verheißungsvoll, glücklich; **aus·pi·cious·ness** [ɔː'spɪʃəsnɪs] *s.* günstige Aussicht, Glück *n*.
Aus·sie ['ɒzɪ] F **I** *s.* Au'stralier(in); **II** *adj.* aus'tralisch.
aus·tere [ɒ'stɪə] *adj.* □ **1.** streng, herb; rauh, hart; **2.** einfach, nüchtern; mäßig, enthaltsam, genügsam; **3.** dürftig, karg; **aus·ter·i·ty** [ɒ'sterətɪ] *s.* **1.** Strenge *f*, Ernst *m*; **2.** As'kese *f*, Enthaltsamkeit *f*; **3.** Herbheit *f*; **4.** Nüchternheit *f*, Strenge *f*, Schmucklosigkeit *f*; **5.** Einfachheit *f*, Nüchternheit *f*; **6.** Mäßigung *f*, Genügsamkeit *f*; *Brit.* strenge (wirtschaftliche) Einschränkung, Sparmaßnahmen *pl.* (*in Notzeiten*): ***~ program(me)*** Sparprogramm *n*.
aus·tral ['ɔːstrəl] *adj. ast.* südlich.
Aus·tral·a·sian [ˌɒstrə'leɪʒn] **I** *adj.* au'stralˌasisch; **II** *s.* Au'stralˌasier(in), Bewohner(in) Oze'aniens.
Aus·tral·ian [ɒ'streɪljən] **I** *adj.* au'stralisch; **II** *s.* Au'stralier(in).
Aus·tri·an ['ɒstrɪən] **I** *adj.* österreichisch; **II** *s.* Österreicher(in).
Austro- [ɒstrəʊ] *in Zssgn* österreichisch: ***~-Hungarian Monarchy*** österreichisch-ungarische Monarchie.
au·tar·chic, au·tar·chi·cal [ɔː'tɑːkɪk(l)] *adj.* **1.** selbstregierend; **2.** → ***autarkic***; **au·tarch·y** ['ɔːtɑːkɪ] *s.* **1.** Selbstregierung *f*, volle Souveräni'tät; **2.** → ***autarky*** 1.
au·tar·kic, au·tar·ki·cal [ɔː'tɑːkɪk(l)] *adj.* au'tark, wirtschaftlich unabhängig; **au·tar·ky** ['ɔːtɑːkɪ] *s.* **1.** Autar'kie *f*, wirtschaftliche Unabhängigkeit; **2.** → ***autarchy***.
au·then·tic [ɔː'θentɪk] *adj.* (□ ***~ally***) **1.** au'thentisch: a) echt, verbürgt, b) glaubwürdig, zuverlässig, c) origi'nal, urschriftlich: ***~ text*** maßgebender Text, authentische Fassung; **2.** ⚖ rechtskräftig, -gültig, beglaubigt; **au'then·ti·cate** [-keɪt] *v/t.* **1.** die Echtheit (*gen.*) bescheinigen; **2.** beglaubigen, beurkunden, rechtskräftig machen; **au·then·ti·ca·tion** [ɔːˌθentɪ'keɪʃn] *s.* Beglaubigung *f*, Legalisierung *f*; **au·then·tic·i·ty** [ˌɔːθen'tɪsətɪ] *s.* **1.** Authentizi'tät *f*: a) Echtheit *f*, b) Glaubwürdigkeit *f*; **2.** ⚖ (Rechts)Gültigkeit *f*.
au·thor ['ɔːθə] *s.* **1.** Urheber(in); **2.** 'Autor *m*, Au'torin *f*, Schriftsteller(in), Verfasser(in); **au·thor·ess** ['ɔːθərɪs] *s.* Au'torin *f*, Schriftstellerin *f*, Verfasserin *f*.
au·thor·i·tar·i·an [ɔːˌθɒrɪ'teərɪən] *adj.* autori'tär; **auˌthor·i'tar·i·an·ism** [-nɪzəm] *s. pol.* autori'täres Re'gierungssyˌstem; **au·thor·i·ta·tive** [ɔː'θɒrɪtətɪv] *adj.* □ **1.** gebieterisch, herrisch; **2.** autorita'tiv, maßgebend, -geblich.
au·thor·i·ty [ɔː'θɒrətɪ] *s.* **1.** Autori'tät *f*, (Amts)Gewalt *f*: ***by ~*** mit amtlicher Genehmigung; ***on one's own ~*** aus eigener Machtbefugnis; ***be in ~*** die Gewalt in Händen haben; **2.** 'Vollmacht *f*, Ermächtigung *f*, Befugnis *f* (***for, to*** *inf.* zu *inf.*): ***on the ~ of …*** im Auftrage *od.* mit Genehmigung von (*od. gen.*) …; → 4; **3.** Ansehen *n* (***with*** bei), Einfluß *m* (***over*** auf *acc.*); Glaubwürdigkeit *f*: ***of great ~*** von großem Ansehen; **4.** a) Zeugnis *n e-r Persönlichkeit*, b) Gewährsmann *m*, Quelle *f*, Beleg *m*: ***on good ~*** aus glaubwürdiger Quelle; ***on the ~ of …*** a) nach Maßgabe *od.* auf Grund von (*od. gen.*) …, b) mit … als Gewährsmann; → 2; **5.** Autori'tät *f*, Sachverständige(r *m*) *f*, Fachmann *m* (***on*** auf *e-m Gebiet*): ***he is an ~ on the subject of Law***; **6.** *mst pl.* Behörde *f*, Obrigkeit *f*: ***the local authorities*** die Ortsbehörde(n); **au·thor·i·za·tion** [ˌɔːθəraɪ'zeɪʃn] *s.* Ermächtigung *f*, Genehmigung *f*, Befugnis *f*; **au·thor·ize** ['ɔːθəraɪz] *v/t.* **1.** *j-n* ermächtigen, bevollmächtigen, berechtigen, autorisieren; **2.** *et.* gutheißen, billigen, genehmigen; *Handlung* rechtfertigen; **au·thor·ized** ['ɔːθəraɪzd] *adj.* **1.** autorisiert, bevollmächtigt, befugt; zulässig: ***~ capital*** ✝ autorisiertes Kapital; ***~ person*** Befugte(r *m*) *f*; ***~ to sign*** unterschriftsberechtigt; ♀ ***Version*** *eccl.* engl. Bibelübersetzung von 1611; **2.** ⚖ rechtsverbindlich; **au·thor·ship** ['ɔːθəʃɪp] *s.* **1.** 'Autorschaft *f*, Urheberschaft *f*; **2.** Schriftstellerberuf *m*.
au·tism ['ɔːtɪzm] *s. psych.* Au'tismus *m*.
au·to ['ɔːtəʊ] *Am.* F **I** *pl.* **-tos** *s.* Auto *n*: ***~ graveyard*** Autofriedhof *m*; **II** *v/i.* (mit dem Auto) fahren.
auto- [ɔːtəʊ] *in Zssgn* a) selbsttätig, selbst…, Selbst…, auto…, Auto…, b) Auto…, Kraftfahr…
au·to·bahn ['ɔːtəʊbɑːn] *pl.* **-bahnen** [-nən] (*Ger.*) *s.* Autobahn *f*.
au·to·bi·og·ra·pher [ˌɔːtəʊbaɪ'ɒgrəfə] *s.* Autobio'graph(in); **au·to·bi·o·graph·ic** ['ɔːtəʊˌbaɪəʊ'græfɪk] *adj.* (□ ***~ally***) autobio'graphisch; **ˌau·to·bi'og·ra·phy** [-fɪ] *s.* Autobiogra'phie *f*, 'Selbstbiograˌphie *f*.
au·to·bus ['ɔːtəʊbʌs] *s. Am.* Autobus *m*.
au·to·cade ['ɔːtəʊkeɪd] → ***motorcade***.
au·to·car ['ɔːtəʊkɑː] *s.* Auto(mo'bil) *n*, Kraftwagen *m*.
'au·to-ˌchang·er *s.* Plattenwechsler *m*.
au·toch·thon [ɔː'tɒkθən] *s.* Auto'chthone *m*, Ureinwohner *m*; **au'toch·tho·nous** [-θənəs] *adj.* auto'chthon, ureingesessen, bodenständig.
au·to·cide ['ɔːtəʊsaɪd] *s.* **1.** Selbstvernichtung *f*; **2.** Selbstmord *m* mit dem Auto.
au·to·clave ['ɔːtəʊkleɪv] *s.* **1.** Schnell-, Dampfkochtopf *m*; **2.** ⚗, ⚙ Auto'klav *m*.
au·to·code ['ɔːtəʊkəʊd] *s. Computer*: Autocode *m*.
au·toc·ra·cy [ɔː'tɒkrəsɪ] *s.* Autokra'tie *f*, Selbstherrschaft *f*; **au·to·crat** ['ɔːtəʊkræt] *s.* Auto'krat(in), unumschränkter Herrscher; **au·to·crat·ic, au·to·crat·i·cal** [ˌɔːtəʊ'krætɪk(l)] *adj.* □ auto'kratisch, selbstherrlich, unumˈschränkt.
au·to·cue ['ɔːtəʊkjuː] *s. TV* ‚Neger' *m*.
au·to-da-fé [ˌɔːtəʊdɑː'feɪ] *pl.* **au·tos-da-fé** [ˌɔːtəʊzdɑː'feɪ] *s.* **1.** *hist.* Autoda'fé *n*, Ketzergericht *n*, -verbrennung *f*; **2.** *pol.* (Bücher- *etc.*)Verbrennung *f*.
au·to·di·dact ['ɔːtəʊdɪˌdækt] *s.* Autodi'dakt(in).
au·to·e·rot·ic [ˌɔːtəʊɪ'rɒtɪk] *adj. psych.* autoe'rotisch.

au·tog·a·mous [ɔːˈtɒgəməs] *adj.* ⚘ autoˈgam, selbstbefruchtend.

au·tog·e·nous [ɔːˈtɒdʒɪnəs] *adj. allg.* autoˈgen: **~ *training***; **~ *welding*** ⚙ Autogenschweißen *n*.

au·to·gi·ro [ˌɔːtəʊˈdʒaɪərəʊ] *pl.* **-ros** *s.* ✈ Autoˈgiro *n*, Tragschrauber *m*.

au·to·graph [ˈɔːtəgrɑːf] **I** *s.* **1.** Autoˈgramm *n*, eigenhändige ˈUnterschrift; **2.** eigene Handschrift; **3.** Urschrift *f*; **II** *adj.* **4.** eigenhändig unterˈschrieben: **~ *letter*** Handschreiben *n*; **III** *v/t.* **5.** eigenhändig (unter)ˈschreiben; mit s-m Autoˈgramm versehen: **~*ing session*** Autogrammstunde *f*; **6.** ⚙ autographieren, ˈumdrucken; **au·to·graph·ic** [ˌɔːtəʊˈgræfɪk] *adj.* (☐ **~*ally***) autoˈgraphisch, eigenhändig geschrieben; **au·tog·ra·phy** [ɔːˈtɒgrəfɪ] *s.* **1.** ⚙ Autograˈphie *f*, ˈUmdruck *m*; **2.** Urschrift *f*.

au·to·ig·ni·tion [ˌɔːtəʊɪgˈnɪʃn] *s.* ⚙ Selbstzündung *f*.

au·to·ist [ˈɔːtəʊɪst] *s. Am.* F Autofahrer(in).

au·to·mat [ˈɔːtəʊmæt] *s.* **1.** Autoˈmatenrestauˌrant *n*; **2.** (Verˈkaufs)Autoˌmat *m*; **3.** ⚙ Autoˈmat *m* (*Maschine*); **ˈau·to·mate** [-meɪt] *v/t.* automatisieren; **au·to·mat·ic** [ˌɔːtəˈmætɪk] **I** *adj.* ☐ → ***automatically***; **1.** autoˈmatisch: a) selbsttätig, ⚙ *a.* Selbst…, zwangsläufig, ⚔ *a.* Selbstlade…, b) *fig.* unwillkürlich, meˈchanisch; **II** *s.* **2.** ˈSelbstladepiˌstole *f*, -gewehr *n*; **3.** → ***automat*** 3; **4.** *mot.* Auto *n* mit Autoˈmatik; **au·to·mat·i·cal** [ˌɔːtəˈmætɪkl] → ***automatic*** 1; **au·to·mat·i·cal·ly** [ˌɔːtəˈmætɪkəlɪ] *adv.* autoˈmatisch; ohne weiteres.

au·to·mat·ic| lathe *s.* ⚙ ˈDrehautoˌmat *m*; **~ ma·chine** → ***automat*** 2; **~ pi·lot** *s.* ✈ → ***autopilot***; **~ pis·tol** *s.* ˈSelbstladepiˌstole *f*; **~ start·er** *s.* ⚙ Selbstanlasser *m*.

au·to·ma·tion [ˌɔːtəˈmeɪʃn] *s.* ⚙ Automatiˈon *f*; **au·tom·a·ton** [ɔːˈtɒmətən] *pl.* **-ta** [-tə], **-tons** *s.* Autoˈmat *m*, ˈRoboter *m* (*beide a. fig.*).

au·to·mo·bile [ˈɔːtəməʊbiːl] *s. bsd. Am.* Auto *n*, Automoˈbil *n*, Kraftwagen *m*; **au·to·mo·bil·ism** [ˌɔːtəˈməʊbɪlɪzəm] *s.* Kraftfahrwesen *n*; **au·to·mo·bil·ist** [ˌɔːtəˈməʊbɪlɪst] *s.* Kraftfahrer *m*; **au·to·mo·tive** [ˌɔːtəˈməʊtɪv] *adj.* selbstbewegend, -fahrend; *bsd. Am.* ˈkraftfahrˌtechnisch, Auto(mobil)…, Kraftfahrzeug…

au·ton·o·mous [ɔːˈtɒnəməs] *adj.* autoˈnom, sich selbst regierend; **auˈton·o·my** [-mɪ] *s.* Autonoˈmie *f*, Selbständigkeit *f*.

au·to·pi·lot [ˈɔːtəʊˌpaɪlət] *s.* ✈ Autopiˈlot *m*, autoˈmatische Steuervorrichtung.

au·top·sy [ˈɔːtəpsɪ] **I** *s.* **1.** ⚕ Autopˈsie *f*, Obduktiˈon *f*; **2.** *fig.* kritische Anaˈlyse; **II** *v/t.* **3.** ⚕ e-e Autopˈsie vornehmen an (*dat.*).

au·to·sug·ges·tion [ˌɔːtəʊsəˈdʒestʃən] *s.* Autosuggestiˈon *f*.

au·to·type [ˈɔːtətaɪp] **I** *s. typ.* Autotyˈpie *f*: a) Rasterätzung *f*, b) Fakˈsimileabdruck *m*; **II** *v/t.* mittels Autotypie vervielfältigen.

au·tumn [ˈɔːtəm] *s. bsd. Brit.* Herbst *m* (*a. fig.*): ***the ~ of life***; **au·tum·nal** [ɔːˈtʌmnəl] *adj.* herbstlich, Herbst… (*a. fig.*).

aux·il·ia·ry [ɔːgˈzɪljərɪ] **I** *adj.* **1.** helfend, mitwirkend, Hilfs…: **~ *engine*** Hilfsmotor *m*; **~ *troops*** Hilfstruppen; **~ *verb*** Hilfszeitwort *n*; **2.** ⚔ Behelfs…, Ausweich…; **II** *s.* **3.** Helfer *m*, Hilfskraft *f*, *pl. a.* Hilfspersonal *n*; **4.** *pl.* ⚔ Hilfstruppen *pl.*; **5.** *ling.* Hilfszeitwort *n*.

a·vail [əˈveɪl] **I** *v/t.* **1.** nützen (*dat.*), helfen (*dat.*), fördern; **2. ~ *o.s. of s.th.*** sich e-r Sache bedienen, et. benutzen, Gebrauch von et. machen; **II** *v/i.* **3.** nützen, helfen; **III** *s.* **4.** Nutzen *m*, Vorteil *m*, Gewinn *m*: ***of no ~*** nutzlos; ***of what ~ is it?*** was nützt es?; ***to no ~*** vergeblich; **5.** *pl.* † *Am.* Ertrag *m*; **a·vail·a·bil·i·ty** [əˌveɪləˈbɪlətɪ] *s.* **1.** Vorˈhandensein *n*; **2.** Verfügbarkeit *f*; **3.** *Am.* verfügbare Perˈson *od.* Sache; **4.** ⚖ Gültigkeit *f*; **aˈvail·a·ble** [-ləbl] *adj.* ☐ **1.** verfügbar, erhältlich, vorˈhanden, vorrätig, zu haben(d): ***make ~*** bereitstellen, verfügbar machen; **2.** anwesend, abkömmlich; **3.** benutzbar; statthaft; **4.** ⚖ a) gültig, b) zulässig.

av·a·lanche [ˈævəlɑːnʃ] *s.* Laˈwine *f*, *fig. a.* Unmenge *f*.

av·ant-garde [ˌævɑ̃ːŋˈgɑːd] (*Fr.*) **I** *s. fig.* Aˈvantgarde *f*; **II** *adj.* avantgarˈdistisch; **ˌav·ant-ˈgard·ist(e)** [-dɪst] *s.* Avantgarˈdist(in).

av·a·rice [ˈævərɪs] *s.* Geiz *m*, Habsucht *f*; **av·a·ri·cious** [ˌævəˈrɪʃəs] *adj.* ☐ geizig (***of*** mit), habgierig.

a·ve [ˈɑːvɪ] **I** *int.* **1.** sei gegrüßt!; **2.** leb wohl!; **II** *s.* **3.** ~ ˈAve(-Maˈria) *n*.

a·venge [əˈvendʒ] *v/t.* **1.** rächen (***on, upon*** an *dat.*): **~ *one's friend*** s-n Freund rächen; **~ *o.s.***, ***be ~d*** sich rächen; **2.** *et.* rächen, ahnden; **aˈveng·er** [-dʒə] *s.* Rächer(in); **aˈveng·ing** [-dʒɪŋ] *adj.*: **~ *angel*** Racheengel *m*.

av·e·nue [ˈævənjuː] *s.* **1.** *mst fig.* Zugang *m*, Weg *m* (***to, of*** zu): **~ *to fame*** Weg zum Ruhm; **2.** Alˈlee *f*; **3.** a) Haupt-, Prachtstraße *f*, Aveˈnue *f*, b) (Stadt)Straße *f*.

a·ver [əˈvɜː] *v/t.* **1.** behaupten, als Tatsache hinstellen (***that*** daß); **2.** ⚖ beweisen.

av·er·age [ˈævərɪdʒ] **I** *s.* **1.** ˈDurchschnitt *m*: ***on an*** (*od.* ***the***) **~** im Durchschnitt, durchschnittlich; ***strike an ~*** den Durchschnitt schätzen *od.* nehmen; **2.** ⚓, ⚖ Havaˈrie *f*, Seeschaden *m*: **~ *adjuster*** Dispacheur *m*; ***general ~*** große Havarie; ***particular ~*** besondere (*od.* partikulare) Havarie; ***petty ~*** kleine Havarie; ***under ~*** havariert; **3.** *Börse*: *Am.* ˈAktienindex *m*; **II** *adj.* ☐ **4.** ˈdurchschnittlich; Durchschnitts…: **~ *amount*** Durchschnittsbetrag *m*; **~ *Englishman*** Durchschnittsengländer *m*; ***be only ~*** nur Durchschnitt sein; **III** *v/t.* **5.** den ˈDurchschnitt schätzen (***at*** auf *acc.*) *od.* nehmen von (*od. gen.*); **6.** † anteilsmäßig auf-, verteilen: **~ *one's losses***; **7.** ˈdurchschnittlich betragen, haben, erreichen, verlangen, tun *etc.*: ***I ~ £60 a week*** ich verdiene durchschnittlich £ 60 die Woche; **IV** *v/i.* **8. ~ *out at*** sich im Durchschnitt belaufen auf (*acc.*).

a·ver·ment [əˈvɜːmənt] *s.* **1.** Behauptung *f*; **2.** ⚖ Beweisangebot *n*, Tatsachenbehauptung *f*.

a·verse [əˈvɜːs] *adj.* ☐ **1.** abgeneigt (***to, from*** *dat.*, ***to*** *inf.* zu *inf.*): ***not ~ to a drink***; **~ *from such methods***; **2.** zuˈwider (***to*** *dat.*); **a·ver·sion** [əˈvɜːʃn] *s.* **1.** (***to, for, from***) ˈWiderwille *m*, Abneigung *f* (gegen), Abscheu *m* (vor *dat.*): ***take an ~*** (***to***) e-e Abneigung fassen (gegen); **2.** Unlust *f*, Abgeneigtheit *f* (***to*** *inf.* zu *inf.*); **3.** Gegenstand *m* des Abscheus: ***beer is my pet*** (*od.* ***chief***) **~** Bier ist mir ein Greuel.

a·vert [əˈvɜːt] *v/t.* **1.** abwenden, -kehren: **~ *one's face***; **2.** *fig.* abwenden, -wehren, verhüten.

a·vi·ar·y [ˈeɪvjərɪ] *s.* Vogelhaus *n*, Voliˈere *f*.

a·vi·ate [ˈeɪvɪeɪt] *v/i.* ✈ fliegen; **a·vi·a·tion** [ˌeɪvɪˈeɪʃn] *s.* ✈ Luftfahrt *f*, Flugwesen *n*, Fliegen *n*, Flugsport *m*: **~ *industry*** Flugzeugindustrie *f*; ***Ministry of*** ~ Ministerium *n* für zivile Luftfahrt; **a·vi·a·tor** [ˈeɪvɪeɪtə] *s.* Flieger *m*.

a·vi·cul·ture [ˈeɪvɪkʌltʃə] *s.* Vogelzucht *f*.

av·id [ˈævɪd] *adj.* ☐ (be)gierig (***of*** nach, ***for*** auf *acc.*); *weitS.* leidenschaftlich, begeistert; **a·vid·i·ty** [əˈvɪdətɪ] *s.* Gier *f*, Begierde *f*, Habsucht *f*.

a·vi·on·ics [ˌeɪvɪˈɒnɪks] *s. pl. sg. konstr.* Aviˈonik *f*, ˈFlugelekˌtronik *f*.

a·vi·ta·min·o·sis [ˈeɪˌvaɪtəmɪˈnəʊsɪs] *s.* Vitaˈminmangel(krankheit *f*) *m*.

av·o·ca·do [ˌævəʊˈkɑːdəʊ] *s.* ⚘ Avoˈcato(birne) *f*.

av·o·ca·tion [ˌævəʊˈkeɪʃn] *s. obs.* **1.** (Neben)Beschäftigung *f*; **2.** F (Haupt)Beruf *m*.

a·void [əˈvɔɪd] **1.** (ver)meiden, ausweichen (*dat.*), aus dem Wege gehen (*dat.*), *Pflicht etc.* umˈgehen, *e-r Gefahr* entgehen: **~ *s.o.*** j-n meiden; **~ *doing s.th.*** es vermeiden, et. zu tun; **2.** ⚖ a) aufheben, ungültig machen, b) anfechten; **aˈvoid·a·ble** [-dəbl] *adj.* **1.** vermeidbar; **2.** ⚖ a) annullierbar, b) anfechtbar; **aˈvoid·ance** [-dəns] *s.* **1.** Vermeidung *f* (*Sache*), Meidung *f* (*Person*); Umˈgehung *f*; **2.** ⚖ a) Aufhebung *f*, Nichtigkeitserklärung *f*, b) Anfechtung *f*.

av·oir·du·pois [ˌævədəˈpɔɪz] *s.* **1.** † *a.* **~ *weight*** Handelsgewicht *n* (*1 Pfund = 16 Unzen*): **~ *pound*** Handelspfund *n*; **2.** F ‚Lebendgewicht' *n e-r Person*.

a·vow [əˈvaʊ] *v/t.* (offen) bekennen, (ein)gestehen; rechtfertigen; anerkennen: **~ *o.s.*** sich bekennen, sich erklären; **a·vow·al** [əˈvaʊəl] *s.* Bekenntnis *n*, Geständnis *n*, Erklärung *f*; **a·vowed** [əˈvaʊd] *adj.* ☐ erklärt: ***his ~ principle***; ***he is an ~ Jew*** er bekennt sich offen zum Judentum; **a·vow·ed·ly** [əˈvaʊɪdlɪ] *adv.* eingestandenermaßen.

a·vun·cu·lar [əˈvʌŋkjʊlə] *adj.* **1.** Onkel…; **2.** *iro.* onkelhaft.

a·wait [əˈweɪt] *v/t.* **1.** erwarten (*acc.*), entgegensehen (*dat.*); **2.** *fig. j-n* erwarten: ***a hearty welcome ~s you.***

a·wake [əˈweɪk] **I** *v/t.* [*irr.*] **1.** wecken; **2.** *fig.* erwecken, aufrütteln (***from*** aus): **~ *s.o. to s.th.*** j-m et. zum Bewußtsein bringen; **II** *v/i.* [*irr.*] **3.** auf-, erwachen; **4.** *fig. zu neuer Tätigkeit etc.* erwachen: **~ *to s.th.*** sich e-r Sache bewußt werden; **III** *adj.* **5.** wach; **6.** *fig.* munter, wach(sam), auf der Hut: ***be ~ to s.th.*** sich e-r Sache bewußt sein; **aˈwak·en**

[-kən] → ***awake*** 1–4; **a'wak·en·ing** [-knɪŋ] *s.* Erwachen *n*: ***a rude ~*** *fig.* ein unsanftes Erwachen.

a·ward [ə'wɔ:d] **I** *v/t.* **1.** zuerkennen, zusprechen, ⚖ *a.* (*durch Urteil od. Schiedsspruch*) zubilligen: ***he was ~ed the prize*** der Preis wurde ihm zuerkannt; **2.** gewähren, verleihen, zuwenden, zuteilen; **II** *s.* **3.** ⚖ Urteil *n*, (Schieds)Spruch *m*; **4.** Belohnung *f*, Auszeichnung *f*, (*a.* Film- *etc.*)Preis *m*, (Ordens)Verleihung *f*, ☤ 'Prämie *f*; **5.** ☤ Zuschlag *m* (*auf ein Angebot*), (Auftrags)Vergabe *f*.

a·ware [ə'weə] *adj.* **1.** gewahr (***of*** *gen.*, ***that*** daß): ***be ~*** sich bewußt sein, wissen, (er)kennen; ***become ~ of s.th.*** et. gewahr werden *od.* merken, sich e-r Sache bewußt werden; ***not that I am ~ of*** nicht, daß ich wüßte; **2.** aufmerksam, ‚hellwach'; **a'ware·ness** [-nɪs] *s.* Bewußtsein *n*, Kenntnis *f*.

a·wash [ə'wɒʃ] *adv. u. adj.* ⚓ **1.** über'flutet; **2.** über'füllt (***with*** von).

a·way [ə'weɪ] **I** *adv.* **1.** weg, hin'weg, fort: ***go ~*** weg-, fortgehen; ***~ with you!*** fort mit dir!; **2.** (***from***) entfernt, (weit) weg (von), fern, abseits (*gen.*): ***~ from the question*** nicht zur Frage *od.* Sache gehörend; **3.** fort, abwesend, verreist: ***~ from home*** nicht zu Hause; ***~ on leave*** auf Urlaub; **4.** *bei Verben oft* (drauf)'los: ***chatter ~***; ***work ~***; **5.** *bsd. Am.* bei weitem: ***~ below the average***; **II** *adj.* **6.** *sport* Auswärts…: ***~ match*** → **III** *s.* **7.** *sport* Auswärtsspiel *n*.

awe [ɔ:] **I** *s.* **1.** Ehrfurcht *f*, (heilige) Scheu (***of*** vor *dat.*): ***hold s.o. in ~*** Ehrfurcht vor j-m haben; ***stand in ~ of*** a) e-e heilige Scheu haben *od.* sich fürchten vor (*dat.*), b) e-n gewaltigen Respekt haben vor (*dat.*); **2.** *fig.* Macht *f*, Maje'stät *f*; **II** *v/t.* **3.** (Ehr)Furcht einflößen (*dat.*), einschüchtern; **'awe-in-ˌspir·ing** *adj.* ehrfurchtgebietend, eindrucksvoll; **awe·some** ['ɔ:səm] *adj.* ☐ **1.** furchteinflößend, schrecklich; **2.** → ***awe-inspiring***; **'awe·struck** *adj.* von Ehrfurcht *od.* Scheu *od.* Schrecken ergriffen.

aw·ful ['ɔ:fʊl] *adj.* ☐ **1.** → ***awe-inspiring***; **2.** furchtbar, schrecklich; **3.** F ['ɔ:fl] furchtbar: a) riesig, kolos'sal: ***an ~ lot*** e-e riesige Menge, b) scheußlich, schrecklich: ***an ~ noise***; **aw·ful·ly** ['ɔ:flɪ] *adv.* F furchtbar, schrecklich, äußerst: ***~ cold***; ***~ nice*** furchtbar *od.* riesig nett; ***I am ~ sorry*** es tut mir schrecklich leid; ***thanks ~!*** tausend Dank!; **'aw·ful·ness** [-nɪs] *s.* **1.** Schrecklichkeit *f*; **2.** Erhabenheit *f*.

a·while [ə'waɪl] *adv.* ein Weilchen.

awk·ward ['ɔ:kwəd] *adj.* ☐ **1.** ungeschickt, unbeholfen, linkisch, tölpelhaft: ***feel ~*** verlegen sein; → ***squad*** 1; **2.** peinlich, mißlich, unangenehm: ***an ~ silence*** (***matter***); **3.** unhandlich, schwer zu behandeln, schwierig, lästig, ungünstig, ‚dumm': ***an ~ door to open*** e-e schwer zu öffnende Tür; ***an ~ customer*** ein unangenehmer Zeitgenosse; ***it's a bit ~ on Sunday*** am Sonntag paßt es (mir) nicht so recht; **'awk·ward·ness** [-nɪs] *s.* **1.** Ungeschicklichkeit *f*, Unbeholfenheit *f*; **2.** Peinlichkeit *f*, Unannehmlichkeit *f*; **3.** Lästigkeit *f*.

awl [ɔ:l] *s.* ⚙ Ahle *f*, Pfriem *m*.

awn [ɔ:n] *s.* ⚘ Granne *f*.

awn·ing ['ɔ:nɪŋ] *s.* **1.** ⚓ Sonnensegel *n*; **2.** Wagendecke *f*, Plane *f*; **3.** Mar'kise *f*; 'Baldachin *m*; Vorzelt *n*.

a·woke [ə'wəʊk] *pret. von* ***awake*** I *u.* II; **a'wok·en** *p.p. von* ***awake*** I *u.* II.

a·wry [ə'raɪ] *adv. u. adj.* **1.** schief, krumm: ***look ~*** *fig.* schief *od.* scheel blicken; **3.** *fig.* verkehrt: ***go ~*** fehlgehen (*Person*), schiefgehen (*Sache*).

ax, *mst* **axe** [æks] **I** *s.* **1.** Axt *f*, Beil *n*: ***have an ~ to grind*** eigennützige Zwecke verfolgen, es auf et. abgesehen haben; **2.** F *fig.* a) rücksichtslose Sparmaßnahme, b) Abbau *m*, Entlassung *f*: ***get the ~*** entlassen werden, ‚rausfliegen'; **3.** ♪ *Am. sl.* Instru'ment *n*; **II** *v/t.* **4.** F *fig.* drastisch kürzen *od.* zs.-streichen; *Beamte etc.* abbauen, *Leute* entlassen, ‚feuern'.

ax·i·al ['æksɪəl] *adj.* ☐ ⚙ Achsen…, axi'al.

ax·il ['æksɪl] *s.* ⚘ Blattachsel *f*.

ax·i·om ['æksɪəm] *s.* Ax'iom *n*, allgemein anerkannter Grundsatz: ***~ of law*** Rechtsgrundsatz; **ax·i·o·mat·ic** [ˌæksɪəʊ'mætɪk] *adj.* (☐ ***~ally***) axio'matisch, 'unumˌstößlich, selbstverständlich.

ax·is ['æksɪs] *pl.* **'ax·es** [-si:z] *s.* **1.** ⩚, ⚙, *phys.* Achse *f*, 'Mittelˌlinie *f*: ***~ of the earth*** Erdachse; **2.** *pol.* Achse *f*: ***the*** ♀ die Achse Berlin-Rom-Tokio (*vor dem u. im 2. Weltkrieg*); ***the*** ♀ ***powers*** die Achsenmächte.

ax·le ['æksl] *s.* ⚙ **1.** *a.* ***~-tree*** (Rad-)Achse *f*, Welle *f*; **2.** Angel(zapfen *m*) *f*.

ay → ***aye***.

a·yah ['aɪə] *s. Brit. Ind.* 'Aja *f*, indisches Kindermädchen.

aye [aɪ] **I** *int. bsd.* ⚓ *u. parl.* ja: ***~, ~, Sir!*** zu Befehl!; **II** *s. parl.* Ja *n*, Jastimme *f*: ***the ~s have it*** die Mehrheit ist dafür.

a·za·le·a [ə'zeɪljə] *s.* ⚘ Aza'lee *f*.

az·i·muth ['æzɪməθ] *s. ast.* Azi'mut *m*, Scheitelkreis *m*.

a·zo·ic [ə'zəʊɪk] *adj. geol.* a'zoisch (*ohne Lebewesen*): ***the ~ age***.

Az·tec ['æztek] s. Az'teke *m*.

az·ure ['æʒə] **I** *adj.* a'zur-, himmelblau; **II** *s.* a) A'zur(blau *n*) *m*, b) *poet.* das blaue Himmelszelt.

B

B, b [biː] *s.* **1.** B *n*, b *n* (*Buchstabe*); **2.** ♪ H *n*, h *n* (*Note*): ***B flat*** B *n*, b *n*; ***B sharp*** His *n*, his *n*; **3.** *ped. Am.* Zwei *f* (*Note*); **4.** ***B flat*** *Brit. sl.* Wanze *f*.

baa [bɑː] **I** *s.* Blöken *n*; **II** *v/i.* blöken; **III** *int.* bäh!

Ba·al [ˈbeɪəl] **I** *npr. bibl. Gott* Baal *m*; **II** *s.* Abgott *m*, Götze *m*; ˈ**Ba·al·ism** [-lɪzəm] *s.* Götzendienst *m*.

baas [bɑːs] *s. S. Afr.* Herr *m*.

Bab·bitt [ˈbæbɪt] *s.* **1.** *Am.* (selbstzufriedener) Spießer; **2.** ℒ (***metal***) ⚙ ˈLagerweißmeˌtall *n*.

bab·ble [ˈbæbl] **I** *v/t. u. v/i.* **1.** stammeln; plappern, schwatzen; nachschwatzen, ausplaudern; **2.** plätschern, murmeln (*Bach*); **II** *s.* **3.** Geplapper *n*, Geschwätz *n*; ˈ**bab·bler** [-lə] *s.* **1.** Schwätzer(in); **2.** *orn. e-e* Drossel *f*.

babe [beɪb] *s.* **1.** kleines Kind, Baby *n*, *fig. a.* Naˈivling *m*; → ***arm***[1] 1; **2.** *Am. sl.* ‚Puppe' *f* (*Mädchen*).

Ba·bel [ˈbeɪbl] **I** *npr. bibl.* Babel *n*; **II** *s.* ℒ *fig.* Babel *n*, Wirrwarr *m*, Stimmengewirr *n*.

ba·boo [ˈbɑːbuː] *s. Brit.-Ind.* **1.** Herr *m* (*bei den Hindus*); **2.** Inder *m* mit oberflächlicher engl. Bildung.

ba·boon [bəˈbuːn] *s. zo.* ˈPavian *m*.

ba·by [ˈbeɪbɪ] **I** *s.* **1.** Baby *n*: a) Säugling *m*, b) jüngstes Kind: ***be left holding the ~*** F der Dumme sein, die Sache am Hals haben; **2.** a) ‚Kindskopf' *m*, b) ‚Heulsuse' *f*; **3.** *sl.* ‚Schatz' *m*, ‚Kindchen' *n* (*Mädchen*); **4.** *sl.* Sache *f*: ***it's your ~***; **II** *adj.* **5.** Säuglings…, Baby…, Kinder…; **6.** kindlich, kindisch: ***plead the ~ act*** *Am.* F auf Unreife plädieren; **7.** klein; **~ bond** *s.* † *Am.* Baby-Bond *m*, Kleinschuldverschreibung *f*; **~ bot·tle** *s.* (Saug)Flasche *f*; **~ car** *s.* Klein(st)wagen *m*; **~ car·riage** *s. Am.* Kinderwagen *m*; **~ farm·er** *s. mst contp.* Frau, die gewerbsmäßig Kinder in Pflege nimmt; **~ grand** *s.* ♪ Stutzflügel *m*.

ba·by·hood [ˈbeɪbɪhʊd] *s.* Säuglingsalter *n*; ˈ**ba·by·ish** [-ɪʃ] *adj.* **1.** kindlich; **2.** kindisch.

Bab·y·lon [ˈbæbɪlən] **I** *npr.* ˈBabylon *n*; **II** *s. fig.* (Sünden)Babel *n*; **Bab·y·lo·ni·an** [ˌbæbɪˈləʊnjən] **I** *adj.* babyˈlonisch; **II** *s.* Babyˈlonier(in).

ˈ**ba·by|-ˌmind·er** *s. Brit.* Tagesmutter *f*; ˈ**~-sit** *v/i.* [*irr.* → ***sit***] babysitten; ˈ**~-ˌsit·ter** *s.* Babysitter *m*; **~ snatch·er** *s.* *ältere Person* (*Mann od. Frau*), *die mit einem blutjungen Mädchen od. Mann ein Verhältnis hat*: ***I'm no ~*** ich vergreif' mich doch nicht an kleinen Kindern!; **~ spot** *s.* Baby-Spot *m* (*kleiner Suchscheinwerfer*); **~ talk** *s.* Babysprache *f*.

bac·ca·lau·re·ate [ˌbækəˈlɔːrɪət] *s. univ.* Bakkalaureˈat *n*; **2.** *a.* **~ *sermon*** *Am.* Predigt *f* an die promovierten Stuˈdenten.

bac·ca·ra(t) [ˈbækərɑː] *s.* ˈBakkarat *n* (*Glücksspiel*).

bac·cha·nal [ˈbækənl] **I** *s.* **1.** Bacˈchant (-in); **2.** ausgelassener *od.* trunkener Zecher; **3.** *a. pl.* Bacchaˈnal *n* (*wüstes Gelage*); **II** *adj.* **4.** ˈbacchisch; **5.** bacˈchantisch; **bac·cha·na·li·a** [ˌbækəˈneɪljə] → ***bacchanal*** 3; **bac·cha·na·li·an** [ˌbækəˈneɪljən] **I** *adj.* bacˈchantisch, ausschweifend; **II** *s.* Bacˈchant(in); **bac·chant** [ˈbækənt] **I** *s.* Bacˈchant *m*; *fig.* wüster Trinker *od.* Schwelger; **II** *adj.* bacˈchantisch; **bac·chan·te** [bəˈkæntɪ] *s.* Bacˈchantin *f*; **bac·chic** [ˈbækɪk] → ***bacchanal*** 4 *u.* 5.

bac·cy [ˈbækɪ] *s.* F *abbr. für* **tobacco**.

bach [bætʃ] F **I** *s.* → ***bachelor*** 1; **II** *v/i.* *mst* **~ *it*** ein Strohwitwerdasein führen.

bach·e·lor [ˈbætʃələ] *s.* **1.** Junggeselle *m*; *in Urkunden*: ledig (*dem Namen nachgestellt*); **2.** *univ.* Bakkaˈlaureus *m* (*Grad*): ℒ ***of Arts*** (*abbr.* ***B.A.***) Bakkalaureus der philosophischen Fakultät; ℒ ***of Science*** (*abbr.* ***B.Sc.***) Bakkalaureus der Naturwissenschaften; **~ girl** *s.* Junggesellin *f*.

bach·e·lor·hood [ˈbætʃələhʊd] *s.* **1.** Junggesellenstand *m*; **2.** *univ.* Bakkalaureˈat *n*.

ba·cil·lar·y [bəˈsɪlərɪ] *adj.* **1.** stäbchenförmig; **2.** ⚕ Bazillen…; **ba·cil·lus** [bəˈsɪləs] *pl.* **-li** [-laɪ] *s.* ⚕ Baˈzillus *m* (*a. fig.*).

back[1] [bæk] **I** *s.* **1.** Rücken *m* (*Mensch, Tier*); **2.** ˈHinter-, Rückseite *f* (*Kopf, Haus, Tür, Bild, Brief, Kleid etc*); (Rücken)Lehne *f* (*Stuhl*); **3.** *untere od. abgekehrte Seite*: (*Hand-, Buch-, Messer*)Rücken *m*, ˈUnterseite *f* (*Blatt*), linke Seite (*Stoff*), Kehrseite *f* (*Münze*), Oberteil *m*, *n* (*Bürste*); → ***beyond*** 6; **4.** *rückwärtiger od. entfernt gelegener Teil*: hinterer Teil (*Mund, Schrank, Wald etc.*), ˈHintergrund *m*; Rücksitz *m* (*Wagen*); **5.** Rumpf *m* (*Schiff*); **6.** ***the ℒs*** die Parkanlagen *pl.* hinter den Colleges in Cambridge; **7.** *sport* Verteidiger *m*;

Besondere Redewendungen:

(***at the***) **~ *of*** hinter (*dat.*), hinten in (*dat.*); ***be at the ~ of s.th.*** *fig.* hinter e-r Sache stecken; **~ *to front*** die Rückseite nach vorn, falsch herum; ***have s.th. at the ~ of one's mind*** a) insgeheim an et. denken, b) sich dunkel an et. erinnern; ***turn one's ~ on*** *fig. j-m* den Rücken kehren, *et.* aufgeben; ***behind s.o.'s ~*** hinter j-s Rücken; ***on one's ~*** a) auf dem Körper (*Kleidungsstück*), b) bettlägerig, c) am Boden, hilflos, verloren; ***have one's ~ to the wall*** mit dem Rücken zur Wand stehen; ***break s.o.'s ~*** a) j-m das Kreuz brechen (*a. fig.*), b) j-n ‚fertigmachen' *od.* zugrunde richten; ***break the ~ of s.th.*** das Schwierigste e-r Sache hinter sich bringen; ***put one's ~ into s.th.*** sich bei e-r Sache ins Zeug legen, sich in et. hineinknien; ***put s.o.'s ~ up*** j-n ‚auf die Palme bringen';

II *adj.* **8.** rückwärtig, letzt, hinter, Rück…, Hinter…, Nach…: ***the ~ left-hand corner*** die hintere linke Ecke; **9.** rückläufig; **10.** rückständig (*Zahlung*); **11.** zuˈrückliegend, alt (*Zeitung etc.*); **12.** fern, abgelegen; *fig.* finster; **III** *adv.* **13.** zuˈrück, rückwärts; zurückliegend; (wieder) zurück: ***he is ~ again*** er ist wieder da; ***he is ~ home*** er ist wieder zu Hause; **~ *home*** *Am.* bei uns (zulande); **~ *and forth*** hin und her; **14.** zuˈrück, ˈvorher: ***20 years ~*** vor 20 Jahren; **~ *in 1900*** (schon) im Jahre 1900; **IV** *v/t.* **15.** *Buch* mit e-m Rücken *od. Stuhl* mit e-r Lehne *od.* Rückenverstärkung versehen; **16.** hinten grenzen an (*acc.*), den Hintergrund *e-r Sache* bilden; **17.** *a.* **~ *up*** *j-m* den Rücken dekken *od.* stärken, *j-n* unterˈstützen, eintreten für; **18.** *a.* **~ *up*** zuˈrückbewegen; *Wagen, Pferd, Maschine* rückwärts fahren *od.* laufen lassen: **~ *one's car up*** mit dem Auto zurückstoßen; **~ *a car out of the garage*** e-n Wagen rückwärts aus der Garage fahren; **~ *water*** (*od.* ***the oars***) rückwärts rudern; **~*ed up*** (***with traffic***) *Am.* verstopft (*Straße*); **19.** auf der Rückseite beschreiben; *Wechsel* verantwortlich gegenzeichnen, avalieren; **20.** wetten *od.* setzen auf (*acc.*); **V** *v/i.* **21.** *a.* **~ *up*** sich rückwärts bewegen, zuˈrückgehen *od.* -fahren; **22.** **~ *and fill*** a) ⚓ lavieren, b) *Am.* F unschlüssig sein; **~ down** (**from**), **~ out** (**of**) *v/i.* zuˈrücktreten *od.* sich zuˈrückziehen (von), aufgeben (*acc.*); F sich drücken (vor *dat.*), abspringen (von), ‚aussteigen' (bei), kneifen (vor *dat.*); klein beigeben, ‚den Schwanz einziehen'.

back[2] [bæk] *s.* ⚙, *Brauerei, Färberei etc.*: Bottich *m*.

ˈ**back|·ache** *s.* Rückenschmerzen *pl.*; **~ al·ley** *s. Am.* finsteres Seitengäßchen; ˌ**~-ˈbench·er** *s. parl.* ˈHinterbänkler *m*; ˈ**~·bend** *s. sport* Brücke *f* (aus dem Stand); ˈ**~·bite** *v/t. u. v/i.* [*irr.* → ***bite***] *j-n* verleumden; ˈ**~ˌbit·er** *s.* Verleumder (-in); ˈ**~·bone** *s.* **1.** Rückgrat *n*: ***to the ~*** bis auf die Knochen, ganz u. gar; **2.** *fig.* Rückgrat *n*: a) (Chaˈrakter)Stärke *f*, Mut *m*, b) Hauptstütze *f*; **ˈ~-ˌbreak·ing** *adj*. ‚mörderisch', zermürbend: ***a ~ job***; **ˈ~-ˌburn·er** *adj*. F nebensächlich, zweitrangig; **ˈ~·chat** *s. sl*. **1.** freche Antwort(en *pl.*); **2.** *Brit*. schlagfertiges Hin und Her; **~·cloth** → ***backdrop***; **ˈ~-ˌcou·pled** *adj*. ϟ rückgekoppelt; **ˌ~-ˈdate** *v/t*. **1.** zuˈrückdatieren; **2.** rückwirkend in Kraft setzen; **~ door** *s*. ˈHintertür *f* (*a. fig. Ausweg*); **ˌ~-ˈdoor** *adj*. heimlich, geheim; **ˈ~·down** *s. Am*. F ‚Rückzieher' *m*; **ˈ~·drop** *s*. **1.** *thea*. Proˈspekt *m*; **2.** ˈHintergrund *m*, ˈFolie *f*.

backed [bækt] *adj*. **1.** mit Rücken, Lehne *etc*. (versehen); **2.** gefüttert: ***a curtain ~ with satin***; **3.** *in Zssgn*: ***straight-~*** mit geradem Rücken, geradlehnig.

back·er [ˈbækə] *s*. **1.** Unterˈstützer(in), Helfer(in), Förderer *m*; **2.** ✝ a) (Wechsel)Bürge *m*, b) ˈHintermann *m*, Geldgeber *m*; **3.** Wetter(in).

ˌback|ˈfire I *v/i*. **1.** *mot*. früh-, fehlzünden; **2.** *fig*. fehlschlagen, ‚ins Auge gehen': ***the plan ~d*** der Schuß ging nach hinten los; **II** *s*. **3.** ⚙ Früh-, Fehlzündung *f*; **~ for·ma·tion** *s. ling*. Rückbildung *f*; **~ˈgam·mon** *s*. Backˈgammon *n*, Puffspiel *n*; **ˈ~·ground** *s*. **1.** ˈHintergrund *m*: ***keep in the ~***; **2.** *fig*. ˈHintergrund *m*, ˈHintergründe *pl.*, ˈUmstände *pl.*; ˈUmwelt *f*, Miliˈeu *n*; ˈHerkunft *f*; Werdegang *m*, Vorgeschichte *f*; Bildung *f*, Erfahrung *f*, Wissen *n*: ***educational ~*** Vorbildung *f*; **ˈ~·hand I** *s*. **1.** nach links geneigte Handschrift; **2.** *sport* Rückhand(schlag *m*) *f*; **II** *adj*. **3.** *sport* Rückhand…: ***~ stroke*** Rückhandschlag *m*; **ˌ~ˈhand·ed** *adj*. **1.** nach links geneigt (*Schrift*); **2.** Rückhand…; **3.** zweideutig; unredlich, ˈindiˌrekt; **ˈ~·hand·er** *s*. **1.** a) → ***backhand*** 2, b) Schlag *m* mit dem Handrücken; **2.** F ˈindiˌrekter Angriff; **3.** F ‚Schmiergeld' *n*.

back·ing [ˈbækɪŋ] *s*. **1.** Unterˈstützung *f*, Hilfe *f*; Beifall *m*; *coll*. Unterˈstützer *pl.*, Förderer *pl.*, ˈHintermänner *pl.*; **2.** rückwärtige Verstärkung; (*Rock- etc.*) Futter *n*; Stützung *f*; **3.** ✝ a) Wechselbürgschaft *f*, b) Gegenzeichnen *n*, c) Deckung *f*.

ˈback|·lash *s*. **1.** ⚙ toter Gang, Flankenspiel *n*; **2.** (heftige) Reaktiˈon, Rückwirkung *f*; **ˈ~·log** *s*. **1.** großes Scheit hinten im Kaˈmin; **2.** (*Arbeits-, Auftrags- etc.*)Rückstand *m*, ˈÜberhang *m* (***of*** an *dat.*): ***~ demand*** Nachholbedarf *m*; **3.** Rücklage *f*, Reˈserve *f* (***of*** an *dat.*, von); **~ num·ber** *s*. **1.** alte Nummer *e-r Zeitung etc.*; **2.** *fig*. rückständige *od*. altmodische Perˈson *od*. Sache; **ˈ~-pack I** *s*. Rucksack *m*, Back-Pack *m*; **II** *v/i*. ***~ it*** F (mit dem Rucksack) trampen; **~ pay** *s*. Lohn-, Gehaltsnachzahlung *f*; **ˌ~-ˈped·al** *v/i*. **1.** rückwärtstreten (*Radfahrer*); **2.** F *fig*. e-n ‚Rückzieher' machen; **ˈ~ˌped·al brake** *s*. Rücktrittbremse *f*; **ˈ~·rest** *s*. Rückenstütze *f*; **~ room** *s*. ˈHinterzimmer *n*; **ˈ~-room boy** *s. Brit*. F Wissenschaftler, der an Geˈheimproˌjekten arbeitet; **~ sal·a·ry** → ***back pay***; **~ scratch·ing** *s*. F gegenseitige Unterˈstützung; **~ seat** *s*. Rücksitz *m*: ***back-seat driver*** *fig*. Besserwisser(in); ***take a ~*** *fig*. in den Hintergrund treten.

back·sheesh → ***baksheesh***.

ˌback|ˈside *s*. **1.** F Hintern *m*; **2.** *mst* ***back side*** Kehr-, Rückseite *f*, hintere *od*. linke Seite; **ˈ~·sight** *s*. **1.** ⚙ Visier *n*; **2.** ⚔ (Visier)Kimme *f*; **~ slang** *s*. ˈUmkehrung *f* der Wörter (*beim Sprechen*); **ˌ~ˈslap·per** *s. Am*. joviˈaler *od*. plump-vertraulicher Mensch; **ˌ~ˈslide** *v/i*. [*irr*. → ***slide***] **1.** rückfällig werden; **2.** auf die schiefe Bahn geraten, abtrünnig werden; **ˌ~ˈslid·er** *s*. Rückfällige(r *m*) *f*; **ˈ~·space con·trol** *s*. Rückholtaste *f* (*Tonbandgerät*); **ˌ~ˈspac·er** *s*. Rücktaste *f* (*Schreibmaschine*); **~·stage I** *s*. [ˈbæksteɪdʒ] **1.** *thea*. Gardeˈrobenräume *pl*. u. Bühne *f* hinter dem Vorhang; **II** *adv*. [ˌbækˈsteɪdʒ] **2.** (hinten) auf der Bühne; **3.** hinter dem *od*. den Vorhang, hinter den *od*. die Kuˈlissen (*a. fig.*); **ˌ~ˈstairs** *s*. ˈHintertreppe *f*: ***~ talk*** (bösartige) Anspielungen *pl.*; ***~ influence*** Protektion *f*; **ˈ~·stop** *s*. **1.** *Kricket*: Feldspieler *m*, Fänger *m*; **2.** *Baseball*: Gitter *n* (*hinter dem Fänger*); **3.** *Am*. *Schießstand*: Kugelfang *m*; **ˈ~·stroke** *s*. *sport* **1.** Rückschlag *m des Balls*; **2.** Rückenschwimmen *n*; **ˈ~·swept** *adj*. **1.** ⚙, ✈ nach hinten verjüngt, pfeilförmig; **2.** zuˈrückgekämmt (*Haar*); **~ talk** *s. sl*. unverschämte Antwort(en *pl.*); **ˈ~·track** *v/i. Am*. **1.** denˈselben Weg zuˈrückgehen; **2.** *fig*. a) → ***back down*** (***from***), b) e-e Kehrtwendung machen; **ˈ~·up I** *s*. **1.** Unterˈstützung *f*; **2.** → ***backing*** 2; **3.** *mot. Am*. (Rück)Stau *m*; **4.** *fig*. ‚Rückzieher' *m*; **5.** ⚙ Ersatzgerät *n*; **II** *adj*. **6.** Unterstützungs…, Hilfs…; ⚙ Ersatz…, Reserve…

back·ward [ˈbækwəd] **I** *adj*. **1.** rückwärts gerichtet, Rück(wärts)…; ˈumgekehrt; **2.** hinten gelegen, Hinter…; **3.** langsam, schwerfällig, schleppend; **4.** zuˈrückhaltend, schüchtern; **5.** *in der Entwicklung* zuˈrückgeblieben (*Kind etc.*), rückständig (*Land, Arbeit*); **6.** vergangen; **II** *adv*. **7.** *a*. ***backwards*** [-dz] rückwärts, zuˈrück: ***~ and forwards*** vor u. zurück; **8.** *fig*. ˈumgekehrt; zum Schlechten; **back·ward·a·tion** [ˌbækwəˈdeɪʃn] *s. Brit*. ✝ Deˈport *m*, Kursabschlag *m*; **ˈback·ward·ness** [-nɪs] *s*. **1.** Rückständigkeit *f*; **2.** Langsamkeit *f*, Trägheit *f*; **3.** Widerˈstreben *n*; **ˈback·wards** [-dz] → ***backward*** 7.

ˈback|·wash *s*. **1.** Rückströmung *f*; Kielwasser *n*; **2.** *fig*. Nachwirkung *f*; **ˈ~ˌwa·ter** *s*. **1.** totes Wasser, Stauwasser *n*; **2.** Seitenarm *m e-s Flusses*; **3.** *fig*. a) tiefste Provinz, (kultuˈrelles) Notstandsgebiet, b) Rückständigkeit *f*, Stagnatiˈon *f*; **ˈ~·woods I** *s. pl*. **1.** ˈHinterwälder *pl.*, abgelegene Wälder; *fig*. (tiefste) Proˈvinz; **II** *adj*. **2.** ˈhinterwäldlerisch (*a. fig.*), Provinz…; **3.** *fig*. rückständig; **ˈ~·woods·man** [-mən] *s*. [*irr*.] **1.** ˈHinterwäldler *m* (*a. fig.*); **2.** *Brit. parl*. Mitglied *n* des Oberhauses, das selten erscheint; **~ yard** *s*. ˈHinterhof *m*; *Am. a*. Garten *m* hinter dem Haus.

ba·con [ˈbeɪkən] *s*. Speck *m*: ***~ and eggs*** Speck mit (Spiegel)Ei; ***he brought home the ~*** F er hat es geschafft; ***save one's ~*** F a) mit heiler Haut davonkommen, b) s-e Haut retten.

Ba·co·ni·an [beɪˈkəunjən] *adj*. Sir Francis Bacon betreffend; **~ the·o·ry** *s*. ˈBacon-TheoˌRie *f* (*daß Francis Bacon Shakespeares Werke verfaßt habe*).

bac·te·ri·a [bækˈtɪərɪə] *s. pl*. Bakˈterien *pl.*; **bacˈte·ri·al** [-əl] *adj*. Bakterien…; **bac·te·ri·cid·al** [bækˌtɪərɪˈsaɪdl] *adj*. bakteriˈzid, bakˈterientötend; **bac·te·ri·cide** [bækˈtɪərɪsaɪd] *s*. Bakteriˈzid *n*; **bac·te·ri·o·log·i·cal** [bækˌtɪərɪəˈlɒdʒɪkl] *adj*. □ bakterioˈlogisch; **bac·te·ri·ol·o·gist** [bækˌtɪərɪˈɒlədʒɪst] *s*. Bakterioˈloge *m*; **bac·te·ri·ol·o·gy** [bækˌtɪərɪˈɒlədʒɪ] *s*. Bakˈterienkunde *f*; **bac·te·ri·um** [bækˈtɪərɪəm] *sg. von* ***bacteria***.

Bac·tri·an cam·el [ˈbæktrɪən] *s. zo*. Trampeltier *n*, zweihöckriges Kaˈmel.

bad [bæd] **I** *adj*. □ → ***badly***; **1.** *allg*. schlecht, schlimm: ***~ manners*** schlechte Manieren; ***from ~ to worse*** immer schlimmer; **2.** böse, ungezogen: ***a ~ boy***; ***a ~ lot*** F ein schlimmes Pack; **3.** lasterhaft, schlecht: ***a ~ woman***; **4.** anstößig, häßlich: ***a ~ word***; ***~ language*** a) häßliche Ausdrücke *pl.*, b) lästerliche Reden *pl.*; **5.** unbefriedigend, ungünstig, schlecht: ***~ lighting*** schlechte Beleuchtung; ***~ name*** schlechter Ruf; ***in ~ health*** kränkelnd; ***his ~ German*** sein schlechtes Deutsch; ***he is ~ at mathematics*** er ist in Mathematik schwach; ***~ debts*** ✝ zweifelhafte Forderungen; ***~ title*** mangelhafter Rechtstitel; **6.** unangenehm, schlecht: ***a ~ smell***; ***~ news***; (***that's***) ***too ~!*** F (das ist doch) zu dumm *od*. schade!; ***not*** (***half*** *od*. ***too***) ***~*** (gar) nicht übel; **7.** schädlich: ***~ for the eyes***; ***~ for you***; **8.** schlecht, verdorben (*Fleisch, Ei etc.*): ***go ~*** schlecht werden; **9.** ungültig, falsch (*Münze etc.*); **10.** unwohl, krank: ***he is*** (*od*. ***feels***) ***~***; ***a ~ finger*** ein schlimmer *od*. böser Finger; ***he is in a ~ way*** es geht ihm nicht gut, er ist schlecht d(a)ran; **11.** heftig, schlimm, arg: ***a ~ cold***; ***a ~ crime*** ein schweres Verbrechen; **II** *s*. **12.** *das* Schlechte: ***go to the ~*** F auf die schiefe Bahn geraten; → ***worse*** 4; **13.** ✝ ˈDefizit *n*, Verlust *m*: ***be £5 to the ~*** £5 Defizit haben; **14.** ***be in ~ with s.o.*** *Am*. F bei j-m in Ungnade sein; **III** *adv*. **15.** → ***badly***.

bad·die [ˈbædɪ] *s*. F *Film etc.*: Bösewicht *m*, Schurke *m*.

bad·dish [ˈbædɪʃ] *adj*. ziemlich schlecht.

bad·dy → ***baddie***.

bade [beɪd] *pret. von* ***bid*** 7, 8, 9.

badge [bædʒ] *s*. Ab-, Kennzeichen *n* (*a. fig.*); (Dienst- *etc.*)Marke *f*; ⚔ (Ehren)Spange *f*; *fig*. Merkmal *n*, Stempel *m*.

badg·er [ˈbædʒə] **I** *s*. **1.** *zo*. Dachs *m*; **2.** *Am*. F Bewohner(in) von Wisˈconsin; **II** *v/t*. **3.** hetzen; **4.** *fig*. plagen, ‚piesaken', *j-m* zusetzen.

bad·i·nage [ˈbædɪnɑːʒ] *s*. Neckeˈrei *f*, Schäkeˈrei *f*.

ˈbad·lands *s. pl. Am*. Ödland *n*.

bad·ly [ˈbædlɪ] *adv*. **1.** schlecht, schlimm: ***he is ~*** (*Am. a*. ***bad***) ***off*** es geht ihm schlecht (*mst finanziell*); ***do*** (*od*. ***come off***) ***~*** schlecht fahren (***in*** bei, mit); ***be in ~ with*** (*od*. ***over***) *Am*. F über Kreuz stehen mit; ***feel ~*** (*Am. a*. ***bad***) (***about it***) ein ‚mieses' Gefühl haben (deswegen); **2.** dringend, heftig, sehr: ***~ needed*** dringend nötig; ***~***

wounded schwerverwundet.

bad·min·ton [ˈbædmɪntən] *s.* **1.** *sport* Badminton *n*; **2.** Federballspiel *n*.

ˈ**bad·mouth** *v/t.* F *j-n* übel beschimpfen.

bad·ness [ˈbædnɪs] *s.* **1.** schlechte Beschaffenheit; **2.** Schlechtigkeit *f*, Verderbtheit *f*; Bösartigkeit *f*.

ˌ**bad-ˈtem·pered** *adj.* schlechtgelaunt, übellaunig.

Bae·de·ker [ˈbeɪdɪkə] *s.* Baedeker *m*, Reiseführer *m*; *weitS.* Handbuch *n*.

baf·fle [ˈbæfl] *v/t.* **1.** *j-n* verwirren, verblüffen, narren, täuschen, *j-m* ein Rätsel aufgeben: ***be ~d*** vor e-m Rätsel stehen; **2.** *Plan etc.* durchˈkreuzen, unmöglich machen: ***it ~s description*** es spottet jeder Beschreibung; **~ paint** *s.* ⚔ Tarnungsanstrich *m*; **~ plate** *s.* Ablenk-, Prallplatte *f*; Schlingerwand *f* (*im Kraftstoffbehälter*).

baf·fling [ˈbæflɪŋ] *adj.* □ **1.** verwirrend, vertrackt, rätselhaft; **2.** vereitelnd, hinderlich; **3.** ˈumspringend (*Wind*).

bag [bæg] **I** *s.* **1.** Sack *m*, Beutel *m*, Tüte *f*, (Schul-, Hand- *etc.*)Tasche *f*; *engS.* a) Reisetasche *f*, b) Geldbeutel *m*: ***mixed ~*** *fig.* Sammelsurium *n*; ***~ and baggage*** (mit) Sack u. Pack, mit allem Drum und Dran; ***the whole ~ of tricks*** alles, der ganze Krempel; ***give s.o. the ~*** F j-m den Laufpaß geben; ***be left holding the ~*** *Am.* F die Sache ausbaden müssen; ***that's (just) my ~*** *sl.* das ist genau mein Fall; ***that's not my ~*** *sl.* das ist nicht ‚mein Bier'; ***that's in the ~*** das haben wir (so gut wie) sicher; → ***bone*** 1; **2.** *hunt.* a) Jagdtasche *f*, b) Jagdbeute *f*, Strecke *f*; **3.** (***pair of***) ***~s*** F Hose *f*; **4.** (***old***) **~** *sl.* Weibsbild *n*, ‚alte Ziege'; **II** *v/t.* **5.** in e-n Sack *etc.* tun, ⚙ einsacken, abfüllen; **6.** *hunt.* zur Strekke bringen, fangen (*a. fig.*); **7.** *sl.* a) sich *et.* schnappen, b) ‚klauen', c) *j-n* ‚in die Tasche stecken', besiegen; **8.** bauschen; **III** *v/i.* **9.** sich bauschen.

bag·a·telle [ˌbægəˈtel] *s.* **1.** Bagaˈtelle *f* (*a.* ♪), Kleinigkeit *f*; **2.** ˈTivolispiel *n*.

bag·gage [ˈbægɪdʒ] *s.* **1.** *bsd. Am.* (Reise)Gepäck *n*; **2.** ⚔ Baˈgage *f*, Gepäck *n*, Troß *m*; **3.** V ‚Flittchen' *n*; **4.** F ‚Fratz' *m*, (kleiner) Racker (*Mädchen*); **~ al·low·ance** *s.* ✈ Freigepäck *n*; **~ car** *s. Am.* Gepäckwagen *m*; **~ check** *s. Am.* Gepäckschein *m*; **~ claim** *s.* ✈ Gepäckausgabe *f*; **~ hold** *s. Am.* Gepäckraum *m*; **~ in·sur·ance** *s. Am.* (Reise)Gepäckversicherung *f*.

bag·ging [ˈbægɪŋ] **I** *s.* **1.** Sack-, Packleinwand *f*; **II** *adj.* **2.** sich bauschend; **3.** → **bag·gy** [ˈbægɪ] *adj.* bauschig, zu weit, sackartig herabhängend; ausgebeult (*Hose*).

ˈ**bag|·pipe** *s.* ♪ Dudelsack(pfeife *f*) *m*; ˈ**~ˌpip·er** *s.* Dudelsackpfeifer *m*; ˈ**~ˌsnatch·er** *s.* Handtaschenräuber *m*.

bah [bɑː(ː)] *int.* pah! (*Verachtung*).

bail[1] [beɪl] ⚖ **I** *s.* (*nur sg.*) **1.** a) Bürge *m*: ***find ~*** sich e-n Bürgen verschaffen, b) Bürgschaft *f*, Sicherheitsleistung *f*, Kautiˈon *f*: ***admit to ~*** → 4; ***allow*** (*od.* ***grant***) **~** a) → 4, b) Kaution zulassen; ***be out on ~*** gegen Kaution auf freiem Fuß sein; ***forfeit one's ~*** (*bsd. wegen Nichterscheinens*) die Kaution verlieren; ***go*** (*od.* ***stand***) ***~ for s.o.*** für j-n Sicherheit leisten *od.* Kaution stellen; ***jump ~*** *Am.* F die Kaution ‚sausenlassen' (u. verschwinden); ***release on ~*** → 4; ***surrender to*** (*od.* ***save***) ***one's ~*** vor Gericht erscheinen; **2.** *a.* ***release on ~*** Freilassung *f* gegen Kautiˈon *od.* Sicherheitsleistung *f*; **II** *v/t.* **3.** *mst* **~ *out*** *j-s* Freilassung gegen Kautiˈon erwirken; **4.** *j-n* gegen Kautiˈon freilassen; **5.** *Güter* (*zur treuhänderischen Verwahrung*) übergeben (***to s.o.*** j-m); **6.** **~ *out*** *fig. j-n* retten, *j-m* herˈaushelfen (***of*** aus *dat.*).

bail[2] [beɪl] **I** *v/t.* ⚓ ausschöpfen: **~ *out water*** (***a boat***); **II** *v/i.* **~ *out*** ‚aussteigen': a) ✈ mit dem Fallschirm abspringen, b) *fig.* nicht mehr mitmachen.

bail[3] [beɪl] *s.* Bügel *m*, Henkel *m*.

bail·a·ble [ˈbeɪləbl] *adj.* ⚖ kautiˈonsfähig.

bail·ee [ˌbeɪˈliː] *s.* ⚖ Verwahrer *m* (*e-r beweglichen Sache*), *z.B.* Spediˈteur *m*.

bai·ley [ˈbeɪlɪ] *s. hist.* Außenmauer *f*, Außenhof *m e-r Burg*: ***Old ∼*** *Hauptkriminalgericht in London*.

bail·iff [ˈbeɪlɪf] *s.* **1.** ⚖ a) Gerichtsvollzieher *m*, b) Gerichtsdiener *m*, c) *Am.* Jusˈtizwachtmeister *m*; **2.** *bsd. Brit.* (Guts)Verwalter *m*; **3.** *hist. Brit.* königlicher Beamter.

bail·i·wick [ˈbeɪlɪwɪk] *s.* ⚖ Amtsbezirk *m* e-s ***bailiff***.

bail·ment [ˈbeɪlmənt] *s.* ⚖ (vertragliche) Hinterˈlegung (*e-r beweglichen Sache*), Verwahrung(svertrag *m*) *f*.

bail·or [ˈbeɪlə] *s.* ⚖ Hinterˈleger *m*.

bairn [beən] *s. Scot.* Kind *n*.

bait [beɪt] **I** *s.* **1.** Köder *m*; *fig. a.* Lokkung *f*, Reiz *m*: ***take*** (*od.* ***rise to***) ***the ~*** anbeißen, den Köder schlucken, *fig. a.* auf den Leim gehen; **2.** Rast *f*, Imbiß *m*; **3.** Füttern *n* (*Pferde*); **II** *v/t.* **4.** mit Köder versehen; **5.** *fig.* ködern, (an-)locken; **6.** *obs. Pferde unterwegs* füttern; **7.** mit Hunden hetzen; **8.** *fig. j-n* reizen, quälen, peinigen; ˈ**bait·er** [-tə] *s.* Hetzer *m*, Quäler *m*; ˈ**bait·ing** [-tɪŋ] *s.* **1.** *fig.* Hetze *f*, Quäleˈrei *f*; **2.** Rast *f*.

baize [beɪz] *s.* Boi *m*, *mst grüner* Fries (*Wollstoff für Tischüberzug*).

bake [beɪk] **I** *v/t.* **1.** backen, im (Back-)Ofen braten: ***~d potatoes*** Folien-, Ofenkartoffeln *pl.*; **2.** a) dörren, austrocknen, härten: ***sun-baked ground***, b) *Ziegel* brennen, c) ⚙ *Lack* einbrennen; **II** *v/i.* **3.** backen, braten (*a. fig. in der Sonne*); gebacken werden (*Brot etc.*); **4.** dörren, hart werden; **III** *s.* **5.** *Am.* gesellige Zs.-kunft; ˈ**~·house** *s.* Backhaus *n*, -stube *f*.

ba·ke·lite [ˈbeɪkəlaɪt] *s.* ⚙ Bakeˈlit *n*.

bak·er [ˈbeɪkə] *s.* **1.** Bäcker *m*: ***~'s dozen*** dreizehn; **2.** *Am.* tragbarer Backofen; ˈ**bak·er·y** [-ərɪ] *s.* Bäckeˈrei *f*.

bakh·shish → ***baksheesh***.

bak·ing [ˈbeɪkɪŋ] **I** *s.* Backen *n*; Brennen *n* (*Ziegel*); **II** *adv. u. adj.* glühend heiß; ˈ**~-pow·der** *s.* Backpulver *n*.

bak·sheesh, **bak·shish** [ˈbækʃiːʃ] *s.* ˈBakschisch *n*, Trinkgeld *n*; Bestechungsgeld *n* (*im Orient*).

Ba·la·kla·va (**hel·met**) [ˌbæləˈklɑːvə] *s.* ⚔ *Brit.* (wollener) Kopfschützer.

bal·a·lai·ka [ˌbæləˈlaɪkə] *s.* Balaˈlaika *f* (*russ. Zupfinstrument*).

bal·ance [ˈbæləns] **I** *s.* **1.** Waage *f* (*a. fig.*); **2.** Gleichgewicht *n* (*a. fig.*): **~** (***of mind***) inneres Gleichgewicht, Gelassenheit *f*; ***~ of nature*** Gleichgewicht der Natur; ***~ of power*** (politisches) Gleichgewicht der Kräfte; ***loss of ~*** ⚕ Gleichgewichtsstörungen *pl.*; ***hold the ~*** *fig.* das Zünglein an der Waage bilden; ***turn the ~*** den Ausschlag geben; ***lose one's ~*** das Gleichgewicht *od. fig.* die Fassung verlieren; ***in the ~*** in der Schwebe; ***tremble*** (*od.* ***hang***) ***in the ~*** auf Messers Schneide stehen; **3.** Gegengewicht *n*, Ausgleich *m*; **4.** ***on ~*** alles in allem, ‚unterm Strich'; **5.** → ***balance-wheel***; **6.** ☤ ˈSaldo *m*, Ausgleichsposten *m*, ˈÜberschuß *m*, Guthaben *n*, ˈKontostand *m*; Biˈlanz *f*; Rest (-betrag) *m*: ***adverse ~*** Unterbilanz; **~ *brought*** (*od.* ***carried***) ***forward*** Übertrag *m*, Saldovortrag *m*; (***un***)***favo***(***u***)***rable ~ of trade*** aktive (passive) Handelsbilanz; ***~ due*** Debetsaldo; ***~ at the bank*** Bankguthaben; ***~ in hand*** Kassenbestand *m*; ***~ of payments*** Zahlungsbilanz; ***strike a ~*** den Saldo *od.* (*a. fig.*) die Bilanz ziehen; **7.** Bestand *m*; F (ˈÜber)Rest *m*; **II** *v/t.* **8.** *fig.* (er-, ab)wägen; **9.** (*a.* ***o.s.*** sich) im Gleichgewicht halten; ins Gleichgewicht bringen, ausgleichen; ausbalancieren; ☤ *Rechnung od. Konto* ausgleichen, aufrechnen, saldieren, abschließen: ***~ the cash*** Kasse(nsturz) machen; → ***account*** 5; **10.** *Kunstwerk* harˈmonisch gestalten; **III** *v/i.* **11.** balancieren, *fig. a.* **~ *out*** sich im Gleichgewicht halten (*a. fig.*); **12.** sich (hin u. her) wiegen; *fig.* schwanken; **13.** ☤ sich ausgleichen; **14.** *a.* **~ *out*** ⚙ (sich) einspielen; **~ beam** *s. Turnen*: Schwebebalken *m*.

bal·anced [ˈbælənst] *adj. fig.* (gut) ausgewogen, wohlerwogen, ausgeglichen (*a.* ☤ *u.* ⚡), gleichmäßig: ***~ diet*** ausgeglichene Kost; ***~ judg(e)ment*** wohlerwogenes Urteil.

ˈ**bal·ance|-ˌi·tem** *s.* Biˈlanzposten *m*; ˈ**~-sheet** *s* ☤ Biˈlanz *f*, Rechnungsabschluß *m*: ***first*** (*od.* ***opening***) **~** Eröffnungsbilanz; ˈ**~-wheel** *s.* ⚙ Hemmungsrad *n*, Unruh *f* (*Uhr*).

bal·co·ny [ˈbælkənɪ] *s.* Balˈkon *m* (*a. thea.*).

bald [bɔːld] *adj.* □ **1.** kahl (*ohne Haar, Federn, Laub, Pflanzenwuchs*): ***as ~ as a coot*** völlig kahl; **2.** *fig.* kahl, schmucklos, nüchtern, armselig, dürftig; **3.** *fig.* nackt, unverhüllt, trocken, unverblümt: ***a ~ statement***; **4.** *zo.* weißköpfig (*Vögel*), mit Blesse (*Pferde*).

bal·da·chin, **bal·da·quin** [ˈbɔːldəkɪn] *s.* ˈBaldachin *m*, Thron-, Traghimmel *m*.

bal·der·dash [ˈbɔːldədæʃ] *s.* ‚Quatsch' *m*, Unsinn *m*.

ˈ**bald|·head** *s.* Kahlkopf *m*; ˌ**~-ˈhead·ed** *adj.* kahlköpfig: ***go ~ into*** *sl.* blindlings hineinrennen in (*acc.*).

bald·ing [ˈbɔːldɪŋ] *adj.* kahl werdend; **bald·ness** [ˈbɔːldnɪs] *s.* Kahlheit *f*; *fig.* Dürftigkeit *f*, Nacktheit *f*; ˈ**bald·pate** *s.* **1.** Kahl-, Glatzkopf *m*; **2.** *orn.* Pfeifente *f*.

bale[1] [beɪl] **I** *s.* ☤ Ballen *m*: ***~ goods*** Ballengüter *pl.*, Ballenware *f*; **II** *v/t.* in Ballen verpacken.

bale[2] → ***bail***[2].

ˈ**bale·fire** *s.* **1.** Siˈgnalfeuer *n*; **2.** Freudenfeuer *n*.

bale·ful [ˈbeɪlfʊl] *adj.* □ **1.** unheilvoll (*Einfluß*); **2.** a) bösartig, rachsüchtig,

b) haßerfüllt (*Blick*); **3.** niedergeschlagen.

balk [bɔːk] **I** *s.* **1.** Hindernis *n*; **2.** Enttäuschung *f*; **3.** *dial. u. Am.* Auslassung *f*, Fehler *m*, Schnitzer *m*; **4.** (Furchen-)Rain *m*; **5.** Hindernis *n*, Hemmnis *n*; **6.** △ Hauptbalken *m*; **7.** *Billard*: Quartier *n*; **8.** *Am. Baseball*: vorgetäuschter Wurf; **II** *v/i.* **9.** stocken, stutzen; scheuen (***at*** bei, vor. *dat.*) (*Pferd*); *Reitsport*: verweigern (*acc.*); **10.** *~ at fig.* a) sich sträuben gegen, b) zu'rückschrecken vor (*dat.*); **III** *v/t.* **11.** (ver)hindern, vereiteln: ***~ s.o. of s.th.*** j-n um et. bringen; **12.** ausweichen (*dat.*), um'gehen; **13.** sich entgehen lassen.

Bal·kan ['bɔːlkən] **I** *adj.* Balkan…; **II** *s.*: ***the ~s*** *pl.* die 'Balkanstaaten, der 'Balkan; '**Bal·kan·ize** [-naɪz] *v/t. Gebiet* balkanisieren.

ball[1] [bɔːl] **I** *s.* **1.** Ball *m*, Kugel *f*; Knäuel *m*, *n*, Klumpen *m*, Kloß *m*, Ballen *m*: ***three ~s*** drei Kugeln (*Zeichen des Pfandleihers*); **2.** Kugel *f* (*zum Spiel*); **3.** *sport* a) Ball *m*, b) *Am.* Ballspiel *n*, *bsd.* Baseball(spiel *n*) *m*, c) *Tennis*: Ball *m*, Schlag *m*, d) *Fußball*: Ball *m*, Schuß *m*, e) Wurf *m*: ***be on the ~*** F ‚auf Draht' sein; ***have a lot on the ~*** *Am.* F ‚schwer was los' haben; ***have the ~ at one's feet*** s-e große Chance haben; ***keep the ~ rolling*** das Gespräch *od.* die Sache in Gang halten; ***the ~ is with you*** *od.* ***in your court!*** jetzt bist 'du dran!; ***play ~*** F mitmachen, ‚spuren'; **4.** ⚔ *etc.* Kugel *f*; **5.** (Abstimmungs)Kugel *f*; → ***black ball***; **6.** *ast.* Himmelskörper *m*, Erdkugel *f*; **7.** ***~ of the eye*** Augapfel *m*; ***~ of the foot*** Fußballen *m*; ***~ of the thumb*** Handballen; **8.** *pl.* V → ***balls***; **II** *v/t.* **9.** (*v/i.* sich) zs.-ballen; **10.** ***~ up*** *Am. sl.* a) (völlig) durchein'anderbringen, b) ‚vermasseln': **11.** (*a. v/i.*) V ‚bumsen'.

ball[2] [bɔːl] *s.* (Tanz- *etc.*)Ball *m*: ***open the ~*** a) den Ball (*mst fig.* den Reigen) eröffnen, b) *fig.* die Sache in Gang bringen; ***have a ~*** *Am.* F sich (prima) amüsieren; ***get a ~ out of s.th.*** *Am.* F an et. Spaß haben.

ball[3] [bɔːl] *s.* große Arz'neipille (*für Pferde etc.*).

bal·lad ['bæləd] *s.* Bal'lade *f*; '**bal·lad·**ˌ**mon·ger** *s.* Bänkelsänger *m*; Dichterling *m*; '**bal·lad·ry** [-drɪ] *s.* Bal'ladendichtung *f*.

ˌ**ball-and-'sock·et joint** *s.* ⚙, *anat.* Kugel-, Drehgelenk *n*.

bal·last ['bæləst] **I** *s.* **1.** ⚓, ✈ Ballast *m*, Beschwerung *f*: ***in ~*** in Ballast; **2.** *fig.* (sittlicher) Halt; **3.** ⚙ Schotter *m*, 'Bettungsmateriˌal *n*; **II** *v/t.* **4.** ⚓, ✈ mit Ballast beladen; **5.** *fig. j-m* Halt geben; **6.** ⚙ beschottern.

ball| bear·ing(s *pl.*) *s.* ⚙ Kugellager *n*; '**~·boy** *s. Tennis*: Balljunge *m*.

bal·le·ri·na [ˌbælə'riːnə] *s.* **1.** (Prima-)Balle'rina *f*; **2.** Bal'lettänzerin *f*.

bal·let ['bæleɪ] *s.* **1.** *allg.* Bal'lett *n*; **2.** Bal'lettkorps *n*; ***~ danc·er*** ['bælɪ] *s.* Bal'lettänzer(in); ***~ danc·ing*** ['bælɪ] *s.* Bal'lettanzen *n*; Tanzen *n*.

bal·let·o·mane ['bælɪtəʊmeɪn] *s.* Bal'lettfaˌnatiker(in).

'**ball|-**ˌ**flow·er** *s.* △ Ballenblume *f* (*gotische Verzierung*); ***~ game*** *s.* **1.** *sport* (*Am.* Base)Ballspiel *n*; **2.** *Am.* F a) Situati'on *f*, b) Sache *f*.

bal·lis·tic [bə'lɪstɪk] *adj.* (□ ***~ally***) *phys.*, ⚔ bal'listisch; → ***missile*** 2; **bal'lis·tics** [-ks] *s. pl. mst sg. konstr. phys.*, ⚔ Bal'listik *f*.

ball joint *s. anat.*, ⚙ Kugelgelenk *n*.

bal·lon d'es·sai [balɔ̃ desɛ] (*Fr.*) *s. bsd. fig.* Ver'suchsbalˌlon *m*.

bal·loon [bə'luːn] **I** *s.* **1.** ✈ Bal'lon *m*: ***~ barrage*** ⚔ Ballonsperre *f*; ***when the ~ goes up*** F wenn es losgeht; **2.** Luftballon *m* (*Spielzeug*); **3.** △ (Pfeiler)Kugel *f*; **4.** ⚗ Bal'lon *m*, Rezipi'ent *m*; **5.** *in Comics etc.*: (Sprech-, Denk)Blase *f*; **6.** ***~ (glass)*** 'Kognakschwenker *m*; **7.** *sl. sport* ‚Kerze' *f* (*Hochschuß*); **II** *v/i.* **8.** im Ballon aufsteigen; **9.** sich blähen; **III** *v/t.* **10.** *sl. sport den Ball* ‚in die Wolken jagen'; **11.** aufblasen; *fig.* aufblähen, über'treiben, steigern; **12.** ✝ *Am. Preise* in die Höhe treiben; **IV** *adj.* **13.** aufgebläht: ***~ sleeve*** Puffärmel *m*; **bal·loon·ist** [bə'luːnɪst] *s.* Bal'lonfahrer *m*; **bal·loon tire** (*Brit.* **tyre**) *s.* ⚙ Bal'lonreifen *m*.

bal·lot ['bælət] **I** *s.* **1.** *hist.* Wahlkugel *f*; *weitS.* Stimmzettel *m*; **2.** (geheime) Wahl: ***voting is by ~*** die Wahl ist geheim; ***at the first ~*** im ersten Wahlgang; **3.** Zahl *f* der abgegebenen Stimmen, *weitS.* Wahlbeteiligung *f*; **II** *v/i.* **4.** (geheim) abstimmen; **5.** losen (***for*** um); ***~ box*** *s.* Wahlurne *f*; ***~ pa·per*** *s.* Stimmzettel *m*; ***~ vote*** *s.* Urabstimmung *f* (*bei Lohnkämpfen*).

'**ball|(-point) pen** *s.* Kugelschreiber *m*; ***~ race*** *s.* ⚙ Kugellager-, Laufring *m*; ***~ re·cep·tion*** *s. TV* Ball-, Re'laisempfang *m*; '**~·room** *s.* Ball-, Tanzsaal *m*: ***~ dancing*** Gesellschaftstanz *m*, -tänze *pl.*

balls [bɔːlz] **I** *s. pl.* V **1.** ‚Eier' *pl.* (*Hoden*); **II** *int.* ‚Quatsch'!, Blödsinn!

'**ball-up** *s. Am. sl.* Durchein'ander *n*.

bal·ly·hoo [ˌbælɪ'huː] F **I** *s.* (Re'klame)Rummel *m*, Ballyhoo *n*, *a. weitS.* ‚Tam'tam' *n*, ‚Wirbel' *m*; **II** *v/i. u. v/t.* e-n Rummel machen (um), marktschreierisch anpreisen.

bal·ly·rag ['bælɪræg] *v/t.* mit *j-m* Possen *od.* Schindluder treiben.

balm [bɑːm] *s.* **1.** 'Balsam *m*: a) aro'matisches Harz, b) wohlriechende Salbe, c) *fig.* Trost *m*, *a.* Wohltat *f*; **2.** *fig.* bal'samischer Duft; **3.** ♀ ♀ ***of Gilead*** 'Balsamstrauch *m od.* -harz *n*.

bal·mor·al [bæl'mɒrəl] *s.* Schottenmütze *f*.

balm·y ['bɑːmɪ] *adj.* □ **1.** bal'samisch; **2.** *fig.* mild; heilend; **3.** *Brit. sl.* ‚bekloppt'.

bal·ne·ol·o·gy [ˌbælnɪ'ɒlədʒɪ] *s.* ⚕ Balneolo'gie *f*, Bäderkunde *f*.

ba·lo·ney [bə'ləʊnɪ] → ***boloney***.

bal·sam ['bɔːlsəm] *s.* **1.** → ***balm*** 1; **2.** ♀ a) Springkraut *n*, b) Balsa'mine *f*; **bal·sam·ic** [bɔːl'sæmɪk] *adj.* (□ ***~ally***) **1.** 'balsamartig, Balsam…; **2.** bal'samisch (duftend); **3.** *fig.* mild, sanft; lindernd, heilend.

Balt [bɔːlt] *s.* Balte *m*, Baltin *f*; '**Bal·tic** [-tɪk] **I** *adj.* **1.** baltisch; **2.** Ostsee…; **II** *s.* **3.** *a.* ***~ Sea*** Ostsee *f*.

bal·us·ter ['bæləstə] → ***banister***; **bal·us·trade** [ˌbælə'streɪd] *s.* Balu'strade *f*, Brüstung *f*; Geländer *n*.

bam·boo [bæm'buː] *s.* **1.** ♀ 'Bambus *m*: ***~ curtain*** *pol.* Bambusvorhang *m* (*von Rotchina*); ***~ shoot*** Bambussprosse *f*; **2.** 'Bambusrohr *n*, -stock *m*.

bam·boo·zle [bæm'buːzl] *v/t. sl.* **1.** beschwindeln (***out of*** um), übers Ohr hauen; **2.** foppen, verwirren.

ban [bæn] **I** *v/t.* **1.** verbieten: ***~ a play***; ***~ s.o. from speaking*** j-m verbieten zu sprechen; **2.** *sport j-n* sperren; **II** *s.* **3.** (amtliches) Verbot, Sperre *f* (*a. sport*): ***travel ~*** Reiseverbot; ***lift a ~*** ein Verbot aufheben; **4.** Ablehnung *f* durch die öffentliche Meinung: ***under a ~*** allgemein mißbilligt, geächtet; **5.** ⚖, *eccl.* Bann *m*, Acht *f*: ***under the ~*** in die Acht erklärt, exkommuniziert.

ba·nal [bə'nɑːl] *adj.* ba'nal, abgedroschen, seicht; **ba·nal·i·ty** [bə'nælətɪ] *s.* Banali'tät *f*; **ba·na·lize** [bə'nɑːlaɪz] *v/t.* banalisieren.

ba·nan·a [bə'nɑːnə] *s.* ♀ Ba'nane *f*: ***go ~s*** *sl.* ‚überschnappen'; ***~ plug*** *s.* ϟ Ba'nanenstecker *m*; ***~ re·pub·lic*** *s. iro.* Ba'nanenrepuˌblik *f*.

band[1] [bænd] **I** *s.* **1.** Schar, *f*, Gruppe *f*; Bande *f*: ***~ of robbers*** Räuberbande; **2.** Band *f*, (Mu'sik)Kaˌpelle *f*, ('Tanz-)Orˌchester *n*: ***big ~*** Big Band; → ***beat*** 12; **II** *v/t.* **3.** ***~ together*** (zu e-r Gruppe *etc.*) vereinigen; **III** *v/i.* **4.** ***~ together*** sich zs.-tun, *b.s.* sich zs.-rotten.

band[2] [bænd] **I** *s.* **1.** (flaches) Band; (Heft)Schnur *f*: ***rubber ~*** Gummiband; **2.** Band *n* (*an Kleidern*), Gurt *m*, Binde *f*, (Hosen- *etc.*)Bund *m*, Einfassung *f*; **3.** Band *n*, Ring *m* (*als Verbindung od. Befestigung*), Bauchbinde *f* (*Zigarre*); **4.** ⚕ (Gelenk)Band *n*; Verband *m*; **5.** (Me'tall)Reifen *m*; Ring *m*; Streifen *m*; **6.** ⚙ Treibriemen *m*; **7.** *pl.* Beffchen *n der Geistlichen u. Richter*; **8.** *andersfarbiger od. andersartiger* Streifen, Querstreifen *m*; Schicht *f*; **9.** *Radio*: (Fre'quenz)Band *n*; **II** *v/t.* **10.** mit e-m Band *od.* e-r Binde versehen, zs.-binden; *Am. Vogel* beringen; **11.** mit (e-m) Streifen versehen; **band·age** ['bændɪdʒ] **I** *s.* **1.** ⚕ Verband *m*, Binde *f*, Ban'dage *f*: ***~ case*** Verbandskasten *m*; **2.** Binde *f*, Band *n*; **II** *v/t.* **3.** *Wunde etc.* verbinden, *Bein etc.* bandagieren.

'**band-aid** *Am.* **I** *s.* Heftpflaster *n*; **II** *adj.* F Behelfs…

ban·dan·(n)a [bæn'dænə] *s.* buntes Taschen- *od.* Halstuch.

band|·box ['bændbɒks] *s.* Hutschachtel *f*: ***as if he (she) came out of a ~*** wie aus dem Ei gepellt; '**~-brake** *s.* ⚙ Band-, Riemenbremse *f*.

ban·deau ['bændəʊ] *pl.* **-deaux** [-dəʊz] (*Fr.*) *s.* Haar- *od.* Stirnband *n*.

ban·de·rol(e) ['bændərəʊl] *s.* **1.** langer Wimpel, Fähnlein *n*; **2.** Inschriftenband *n*.

ban·dit ['bændɪt] *pl. a.* **-ti** [bæn'dɪtɪ] *s.* Ban'dit *m*, (Straßen)Räuber *m*, *weitS.* Gangster *m*: ***a banditti*** *coll.* e-e Räuberbande; → ***one-armed***; '**ban·dit·ry** [-trɪ] *s.* Ban'ditentum *n*.

band·mas·ter ['bændˌmɑːstə] *s.* ♪ Ka'pellmeister *m*.

'**ban·dog** *s. Brit.* Kettenhund *m*.

ban·do·leer, **ban·do·lier** [ˌbændəʊ'lɪə] *s.* ⚔ (*um die Brust geschlungener*) Pa'tronengurt.

'**band|-pass fil·ter** *s. Radio*: Bandfilter *n*, *m*; ***~ pul·ley*** *s.* ⚙ Riemenscheibe *f*,

Schnurrad *n*; ~ **saw** *s.* ⚙ Bandsäge *f*; ~ **shell** *s.* (muschelförmiger) Or'chester-ˌpavillon.

bands·man ['bændzmən] *s.* [*irr.*] ♪ 'Musiker *m*, Mitglied *n* e-r (Mu'sik)Kaˌpelle.

'**band|·stand** *s.* Mu'sikˌpavillon *m*; Podium *n*; ~ **switch** *s. Radio*: Fre'quenz-(band)ˌumschalter *m*; '~ˌ**wag·on** *s.* **1.** Wagen *m* mit e-r Mu'sikkaˌpelle; **2.** F *pol.* erfolgreiche Seite *od.* Par'tei: ***climb on the*** ~ mit ‚einsteigen', sich der erfolgversprechenden Sache anschließen; '~·**width** *s. Radio*: Bandbreite *f*.

ban·dy ['bændı] **I** *v/t.* **1.** sich *et.* zuwerfen; **2.** sich *et.* erzählen; **3.** sich (gegenseitig) *Vorwürfe, Komplimente etc.* machen, *Blicke, böse Worte, Schläge etc.* tauschen: ~ ***words*** sich streiten; **4.** *a.* ~ ***about*** *Gerüchte* in 'Umlauf setzen *od.* weitertragen; **5.** *a.* ~ ***about*** *j-s Namen* immer wieder erwähnen: ***his name was bandied about*** *a.* er war ins Gerede gekommen; **II** *s.* **6.** *sport* Bandy *n* (*Abart des Eishockey*).

'**bandy-legged** [-legd] *adj.* O- *od.* säbelbeinig.

bane [beın] *s.* Verderben *n*, Ru'in *m*: ***the*** ~ ***of his life*** der Fluch s-s Lebens; '**bane·ful** [-fʊl] *adj.* □ verderblich, tödlich, schädlich.

bang¹ [bæŋ] **I** *s.* **1.** Bums *m*, Schlag *m*, Krach *m*, Knall *m*: ***go over with a*** ~ *Am.* F ein Bombenerfolg sein; **2.** V ‚Nummer' *f* (*Koitus*); **3.** *sl.* ‚Schuß' *m* (*Rauschgift*); **II** *v/t.* **4.** dröhnend schlagen, knallen mit, *Tür etc.* zuknallen: ~ ***one's head against*** sich den Kopf anschlagen an (*dat.*); ~ ***one's fist on the table*** mit der Faust auf den Tisch schlagen; ~ ***sense into s.o.*** j-m Vernunft einbleuen; ~ ***up*** kaputtmachen, -schlagen, *Auto* zu Schrott fahren; ~***ed(-)up*** zerbeult, (arg) mitgenommen, demoliert; **5.** ~ ***about*** *fig. j-n* he'rumstoßen; **6.** V ‚bumsen', ‚vögeln'; **III** *v/i.* **7.** knallen: a) krachen, b) zuschlagen (*Tür etc.*), c) ballern, schießen: ~ ***at*** an *die Tür etc.* schlagen; ~ ***away*** drauflosballern; ~ ***into*** bumsen *od.* knallen gegen; **8.** V ‚bumsen', ‚vögeln'; **IV** *adv.* **9.** bums: a) mit e-m Knall *od.* Krach, b) F *fig.* ‚zack', genau: ~ ***in the eye***, c) F *fig.* plötzlich: ~ ***off*** *sl.* sofort, ‚zack'; ~ ***on*** *sl.* (haar)genau; **V** *int.* **10.** bums!, peng!

bang² [bæŋ] *s. mst pl.* Pony *m*; 'Ponyfriˌsur *f*.

bang·er ['bæŋə] *s.* **1.** et., das knallt, *z.B.* Knallkörper *m*; ‚Klapperkiste' *f* (*Auto*); **2.** (Brat)Würstchen *n*: ~***s*** *pl.* ***and mash*** Würstchen *pl.* mit Kartoffelbrei.

ban·gle ['bæŋgl] *s.* Armring *m*, -reif *m*; Fußring *m*, -spange *f*.

'**bang|-on** *adv.* F haargenau; genau (richtig); '~-**up** *adv. u. adj. Am. sl.* ‚prima'.

ban·ish ['bænıʃ] *v/t.* **1.** verbannen, ausweisen (***from*** aus); **2.** *fig.* (ver)bannen, verscheuchen, vertreiben: ~ ***care***; '**banish·ment** [-mənt] *s.* **1.** Verbannung *f*, Ausweisung *f*; **2.** *fig.* Vertreiben *n*, Bannen *n*.

ban·is·ter ['bænıstə] *s.* Geländersäule *f*; *pl.* Treppengeländer *n*.

ban·jo ['bændʒəʊ] *pl.* **-jos, -joes** *s.* ♪ Banjo *n*; '**ban·jo·ist** [-əʊıst] *s.* Banjospieler *m*.

bank¹ [bæŋk] **I** *s.* **1.** ✝ Bank *f*, Bankhaus *n*: ***the*** ♀ *Brit.* die Bank von England; ~ ***of deposit*** Depositenbank; ~ ***of issue*** (*od.* ***circulation***) Noten-, Emissionsbank; **2.** (Spiel)Bank *f*: ***break*** (***keep***) ***the*** ~ die Bank sprengen (halten); ***go*** (***the***) ~ Bank setzen; **3.** Vorrat *m*, Re'serve *f*, Bank *f*: → ***blood bank*** *etc.*; **II** *v/i.* **4.** ✝ Geld auf e-r Bank haben: ***I*** ~ ***with ...*** ich habe mein Bankkonto bei ...; **5.** *Glücksspiel*: die Bank halten; **6.** ~ ***on*** *fig.* bauen *od.* s-e Hoffnung setzen auf (*acc.*); **III** *v/t.* **7.** *Geld* bei e-r Bank einzahlen *od.* hinter'legen.

bank² [bæŋk] **I** *s.* **1.** (Erd)Wall *m*, Damm *m*, (Straßen- *etc.*)Böschung *f*; Über'höhung *f e-r Straße*; **2.** Ufer *n*; **3.** (Sand)Bank *f*, Untiefe *f*: ***Dogger*** ♀ Doggerbank; **4.** Bank *f*, Wand *f*, Wall *m*; Zs.-ballung *f*: ~ ***of clouds*** Wolkenbank; ***snow*** ~ Schneewall; **5.** ✈ Querneigung *f in der Kurve*; **II** *v/t.* **6.** eindämmen, mit e-m Wall um'geben; *fig.* dämpfen; **7.** *e-e Straße in der Kurve* über'höhen; **8.** *a.* ~ ***up*** aufhäufen, zs.-ballen; **9.** ✈ in die Kurve legen, in Schräglage bringen; **10.** *a.* ~ ***up*** *ein Feuer* mit Asche belegen; **III** *v/i.* **11.** *a.* ~ ***up*** sich aufhäufen, sich zs.-ballen; **12.** ✈ in die Kurve gehen; **13.** e-e Über'höhung haben (*Straße in der Kurve*).

bank³ [bæŋk] *s.* **1.** Ruderbank *f od.* (Reihe *f* der) Ruderer *pl. in e-r Galeere*; **2.** ⚙ Reihe *f*, Gruppe *f*, Reihenanordnung *f*.

bank·a·ble ['bæŋkəbl] *adj.* ✝ bankfähig, diskontierbar; *fig.* verläßlich, zuverlässig.

bank| ac·count *s.* ✝ 'Bankˌkonto *n*; ~ **bill** → ***bank draft***; ~ **book** *s.* Sparbuch *n*; ~ **clerk** *s.* Bankangestellte(r *m*) *f*, -beamte(r) *m*, -beamtin *f*; ~ **code num·ber** *s.* Bankleitzahl *f*; ~ **dis·count** *s.* 'Bankdisˌkont *m*; ~ **draft** *s.* Bankwechsel *m* (*von e-r Bank auf e-e andere gezogen*).

bank·er ['bæŋkə] *s.* **1.** ✝ Banki'er *m*: ~***'s discretion*** Bankgeheimnis *n*; ~***'s order*** Dauerauftrag *m*; **2.** *Kartenspiel etc.*: Bankhalter *m*.

bank hol·i·day *s.* Bankfeiertag *m*.

bank·ing¹ ['bæŋkıŋ] ✝ **I** *s.* Bankwesen *n*; **II** *adj.* Bank...

bank·ing² ['bæŋkıŋ] *s.* ✈ Schräglage *f*.

bank·ing| ac·count *s.* ✝ 'Bankˌkonto *n*; ~ **charg·es** *s. pl.* Bankgebühren *pl.*; ~ **house** *s.* Bankhaus *n*.

bank| man·ag·er *s.* 'Bankdiˌrektor *m*; ~ **note** *s.* ✝ Banknote *f*; ~ **rate** *s.* ✝ Dis'kontsatz *m*; ~ **re·turn** *s.* Bankausweis *m*; '~-ˌ**rob·ber·y** *s.* Bankraub *m*; '~·**roll** *s. Am.* **1.** Bündel *n* Banknoten; **2.** Geld(mittel *pl.*) *n*.

bank·rupt ['bæŋkrʌpt] **I** *s.* **1.** ⚖ Kon'kurs-, Gemeinschuldner *m*, Bankrot'teur *m*: ~***'s certificate*** Dokument *n* über Einstellung des Konkursverfahrens; ~***'s creditor*** Konkursgläubiger *m*; ~***'s estate*** Konkursmasse *f*; ***declare o.s. a*** ~ (s-n) Konkurs anmelden; **2.** *fig.* bank'rotter *od.* her'untergekommener Mensch; **II** *adj.* **3.** ⚖ bank'rott: ***go*** ~ in Konkurs geraten, Bankrott machen; **4.** *fig.* bank'rott (*a. Politik, Politiker etc.*), ruiniert: ***morally*** ~ moralisch bankrott, sittlich verkommen; ~ ***in intelligence*** bar aller Vernunft; **III** *v/t.* **5.** ⚖ bank'rott machen; **6.** *fig.* zu'grunde richten; '**bank·rupt·cy** [-rəptsı] *s.* **1.** ⚖ Bank'rott *m*, Kon'kurs *m*: ***act of*** ~ Konkurshandlung *f*; ♀ ***Act*** Konkursordnung *f*; ***declaration of*** ~ Konkursanmeldung *f*; ***petition in*** ~ Konkursantrag *m*; ***referee in*** ~ Konkursrichter *m*; **2.** *fig.* Ru'in *m*, Bank'rott *m*.

bank state·ment *s.* ✝ **1.** Bankausweis *m*; **2.** *Brit.* Kontoauszug *m*.

ban·ner ['bænə] **I** *s.* **1.** Banner *n*, Fahne *f*, Heeres-, Kirchen-, Reichsfahne *f*; **2.** *fig.* Banner *n*, Fahne *f*: ***the*** ~ ***of freedom***; **3.** Spruchband *n*, Transpa'rent *n bei politischen Umzügen*; **4.** *a.* ~ ***headline*** 'Balkenˌüberschrift *f*, Schlagzeile *f*; **II** *adj. Am.* **5.** führend, 'prima: ~ ***class*** beste Sorte; '~ˌ**bear·er** *s.* **1.** Fahnenträger *m*; **2.** Vorkämpfer *m*.

banns [bænz] *s. pl. eccl.* Aufgebot *n des Brautpaares vor der Ehe*: ***ask the*** ~ das Aufgebot bestellen; ***publish*** (*od.* ***put up***) ***the*** ~ (***of***) (*das Brautpaar*) kirchlich aufbieten.

ban·quet ['bæŋkwıt] **I** *s.* Ban'kett *n*, Festessen *n*; **II** *v/t.* festlich bewirten; **III** *v/i.* tafeln; '**ban·quet·er** [-tə] *s.* Ban'ketteilnehmer(in).

ban·shee [bæn'ʃiː] *s. Ir.*, *Scot.* Todesfee *f*.

ban·tam ['bæntəm] **I** *s.* **1.** *zo.* 'Bantam-, Zwerghuhn *n*, -hahn *m*; **2.** *fig.* Zwerg *m*, Knirps *m*; **II** *adj.* **3.** klein, ⚙ Klein..., *a.* handlich; '~·**weight** *s. sport* 'Bantamgewicht(ler *m*) *n*.

ban·ter ['bæntə] **I** *v/t.* necken, hänseln; **II** *v/i.* necken, scherzen; **III** *s.* Necke'rei *f*, Scherz(e *pl.*) *m*; '**ban·ter·er** [-ərə] *s.* Spaßvogel *m*.

Ban·tu [ˌbæn'tuː] **I** *pl.* **-tu, -tus** *s.* **1.** 'Bantu(neger) *m*; **2.** 'Bantusprache *f*; **II** *adj.* **3.** Bantu...

ban·zai [ˌbæn'zaı] *int.* Banzai! (*japanischer Hoch- od. Hurraruf*).

ba·o·bab ['beıəʊbæb] *s.* ♀ 'Baobab *m*, Affenbrotbaum *m*.

bap·tism ['bæptızəm] *s.* **1.** *eccl.* Taufe *f*: ~ ***of blood*** Märtyrertod *m*; **2.** *fig.* Taufe *f*, Einweihung *f*, Namensgebung *f*: ~ ***of fire*** ⚔ Feuertaufe; **bap·tis·mal** [bæp'tızml] *adj. eccl.* Tauf...; '**bap·tist** [-ıst] *s. eccl.* **1.** Bap'tist(in); **2.** Täufer *m*: ***John the*** ♀; '**bap·tis·ter·y** [-ıstərı], '**bap·tist·ry** [-ıstrı] *s.* **1.** 'Taufkaˌpelle *f*; **2.** Taufbecken *n*; **bap·tize** [bæp'taız] *v/t. u. v/i. eccl. u. fig.* taufen.

bar [bɑː] **I** *s.* **1.** Stange *f*, Stab *m*: ~***s*** Gitter *n*; ***prison*** ~***s*** Gefängnis *n*; ***behind*** ~***s*** *fig.* hinter Schloß u. Riegel; **2.** Riegel *m*, Querbalken *m*, -holz *n*, -stange *f*; Schranke *f*, Sperre *f*; **3.** *fig.* (***to***) Hindernis *n* (für) (*a.* ⚖), Verhinderung *f* (*gen.*), Schranke *f* (gegen); ⚖ Ausschließungsgrund *m*: ~ ***to progress*** Hemmnis *n* für den Fortschritt; ~ ***to marriage*** Ehehindernis *n*; ***as a*** ~ ***to, in*** ~ ***of*** ⚖ zwecks Ausschlusses (*gen.*); **4.** Riegel *m*, Stange *f*: ***a*** ~ ***of soap*** ein Riegel Seife; ~ ***soap*** Stangenseife *f*; ***a chocolate*** ~ ein Riegel (*a.* e-e Tafel) Schokolade; ***gold*** ~ Goldbarren *m*; **5.** Barre *f*, Sandbank *f* (*am Hafeneingang*); **6.** Strich *m*, Streifen *m*, Band *n*, Strahl *m* (*Farbe, Licht*); **7.** ϟ La'melle *f*; **8.** ♪ a) Taktstrich *m*, b) *ein* Takt; **9.** Streifen *m*, Band *n an e-r Medaille*; Spange *f am Orden*; **10.** ⚖ a) Schranke *f vor der Richterbank*: ***prisoner at the ~*** Angeklagte(r *m*) *f*; ***trial at ~*** *Brit.* Verhandlung *f* vor dem vollen Strafsenat des ***High Court of Justice*** (*z.B. bei Landesverrat*), b) Schranke *f* in den ***Inns of Court***: ***be called*** (*Am.* ***admitted***) ***to the ~*** als Anwalt *od. Brit.* als Barrister (*plädierender Anwalt*) zugelassen werden; ***be at the ~*** Barrister sein; ***read for the ~*** Jura studieren, c) ***the ~*** die (gesamte) Anwaltschaft, *Brit.* die Barristers *pl.*: ***2 Association*** *Am.* (halbamtliche) Anwaltsvereinigung, -kammer; **11.** *parl.*: ***the ~ of the House*** Schranke im brit. Unterhaus (*bis zu der geladene Zeugen vortreten dürfen*); **12.** *fig.* Gericht *n*, Tribu'nal *n*: ***the ~ of public opinion*** das Urteil der Öffentlichkeit; **13.** Bar *f*: a) Bü'fett *n*, Theke *f*, b) Schankraum *m*, Imbißstube *f*; → ***ice-cream bar***; **II** *v/t.* **14.** verriegeln: ***~ in*** (***out***) ein- (aus)sperren; **15.** *a.* ***~ up*** vergittern, mit Schranken um'geben: ***~red window*** Gitterfenster *n*; **16.** versperren: ***~ the way*** (*a. fig.*); **17.** hindern (***from*** an *dat.*); hemmen, auf-, abhalten; **18.** ausschließen (***from*** von; *a.* ⚖), verbieten; → ***barred*** 4; **19.** absehen von; **20.** *Brit. sl.* nicht leiden können; **21.** mit Streifen versehen; **III** *prp.* **22.** außer, abgesehen von: ***~ one*** außer einem; ***~ none*** (alle) ohne Ausnahme.

barb¹ [bɑːb] *s.* **1.** 'Widerhaken *m*; **2.** *fig.* a) Stachel *m*, b) Spitze *f*, spitze Bemerkung, Pfeil *m* des Spottes; **3.** *zo.* Bart (-faden) *m*; Fahne *f e-r Feder*.

barb² [bɑːb] *s.* Berberpferd *n*.

bar·bar·i·an [bɑː'beərɪən] **I** *s.* **1.** Bar'bar *m*; **2.** *fig.* Bar'bar *m*, roher u. ungesitteter Mensch; Unmensch *m*; **II** *adj.* **3.** bar'barisch, unzivilisiert; **4.** *fig.* roh, ungesittet, grausam; **bar·bar·ic** [bɑː'bærɪk] *adj.* (☐ ***~ally***) bar'barisch, wild, roh, ungesittet; **bar·ba·rism** ['bɑːbərɪzəm] *s.* **1.** Barba'rismus *m*, Sprachwidrigkeit *f*; **2.** Barba'rei *f*, 'Unkulˌtur *f*; **bar·bar·i·ty** [bɑː'bærətɪ] *s.* Barba'rei *f*, Roheit *f*, Grausamkeit *f*, Unmenschlichkeit *f*; **bar·ba·rize** ['bɑːbəraɪz] **I** *v/t.* **1.** verrohen *od.* verwildern lassen; **2.** *Sprache, Kunst etc.* barbarisieren, verderben; **II** *v/i.* **3.** verrohen; **bar·ba·rous** ['bɑːbərəs] *adj.* ☐ bar'barisch, roh, ungesittet, grausam.

bar·be·cue ['bɑːbɪkjuː] **I** *s.* **1.** Barbecue *n*: a) Grillfest *n* (*bei dem ganze Tiere gebraten werden*), b) Bratrost *m*, Grill *m*, c) gegrilltes *od.* gebratenes Fleisch; **2.** *Am.* in Essigsoße zubereitete Fleisch- *od.* Fischstückchen; **II** *v/t.* **3.** (auf dem Rost *od.* am Spieß) im ganzen *od.* in großen Stücken) braten; **2.** braten, grillen; **3.** *Am.* in stark gewürzter (Essig)Soße zubereiten; **4.** *Am.* a) dörren, b) räuchern.

barbed [bɑːbd] *adj.* **1.** mit 'Widerhaken *od.* Stacheln (versehen), Stachel...; **2.** *fig.* bissig, spitz: ***~ remarks***; ***~ wire*** *s.* Stacheldraht *m*.

bar·bel ['bɑːbəl] *s. ichth.* Barbe *f*.

'bar·bell *s. sport* Hantel *f mit langer Stange*, Kugelstange *f*.

bar·ber ['bɑːbə] **I** *s.* Bar'bier *m*, ('Her-ren)Friˌseur *m*; **II** *v/t. Am.* rasieren; frisieren.

bar·ber·ry ['bɑːbərɪ] *s.* ⚘ Berbe'ritze *f*.

'bar·ber·shop *s.* **1.** *bsd. Am.* Fri'seurgeschäft *n*; **2.** *a.* ***~ singing*** *Am.* 𝔉 (zwangloses) Singen im Chor.

bar·ber's| itch ['bɑːbəz] *s.* ⚕ Bartflechte *f*; ***~ pole*** *s. spiralig bemalte Stange als Geschäftszeichen der Friseure*.

bar·bi·tal ['bɑːbɪtæl] *s. pharm. Am.* Barbi'tal *n*; ***~ so·di·um*** *s. pharm.* 'Natriumsalz *n* von Barbi'tal.

bar·bi·tone ['bɑːbɪtəʊn] *s. Brit.* → ***barbital***; **bar·bi·tu·rate** [bɑː'bɪtjʊrət] *s. pharm.* ☐ Barbitu'rat *n*; **bar·bi·tu·ric** [ˌbɑːbɪ'tjʊərɪk] *adj. pharm.*: ***~ acid*** Barbitursäure *f*.

bar·ca·rol(l)e ['bɑːkərəʊl] *s.* ♪ Barka'role *f* (*Gondellied*).

bar cop·per *s.* ⚙ Stangenkupfer *n*.

bard [bɑːd] *s.* **1.** Barde *m* (*keltischer Sänger*); **2.** *fig.* Barde *m*, Sänger *m* (*Dichter*): ***2 of Avon*** Shakespeare; **'bard·ic** [-dɪk] *adj.* Barden...; **bard·ol·a·try** [bɑː'dɒlətrɪ] *s.* Shakespeare-vergötterung *f*.

bare [beə] **I** *adj.* ☐ → ***barely***; **1.** nackt, unbekleidet, bloß: ***in one's ~ skin*** splitternackt; **2.** kahl, leer, nackt, unbedeckt: ***~ walls*** kahle Wände; ***the ~ boards*** der nackte Fußboden; ***the larder was ~*** *fig.* es war nichts zu essen im Hause; ***~ sword*** bloßes *od.* blankes Schwert; **3.** ⚘, *zo.* kahl; **4.** unverhüllt, klar: ***lay ~*** zeigen, enthüllen (*a. fig.*); ***the ~ facts*** die nackten Tatsachen; ***~ nonsense*** barer *od.* reiner Unsinn; **5.** (***of***) entblößt (von), arm (an *dat.*), ohne; **6.** knapp, kaum hinreichend: ***~ majority*** a) knappe Mehrheit, b) (***of votes***) einfache Stimmenmehrheit; ***a ~ ten pounds*** gerade noch 10 Pfund; **7.** bloß, al'lein, nur: ***the ~ thought*** der bloße (*od.* allein der) Gedanke; **II** *v/t.* **8.** entblößen, entkleiden; **9.** *fig.* bloßlegen, enthüllen: ***~ one's heart*** sein Herz öffnen (***to*** *j-m*); **'~·back(ed)** [-bæk(t)] *adj. u. adv.* ungesattelt; **'~·faced** [-feɪst] *adj.* ☐ schamlos, frech; **'~·foot** *adj. u. adv.* barfuß; **ˌ~'foot·ed** [-'fʊtɪd] *adj.* barfuß, barfüßig; **ˌ~-'head·ed** [-'hedɪd] *adj. u. adv.* mit bloßem Kopf, barhäuptig; **ˌ~-'legged** [-'legd] *adj.* mit nackten Beinen.

bare·ly ['beəlɪ] *adv.* **1.** kaum, knapp, gerade (noch): ***~ enough time***; **2.** ärmlich, spärlich; **bare·ness** ['beənɪs] *s.* **1.** Nacktheit *f*, Blöße *f*, Kahlheit *f*; **2.** Dürftigkeit *f*.

bare·sark ['beəsɑːk] **I** *s.* Ber'serker *m*; **II** *adv.* ohne Rüstung.

bar·gain ['bɑːgɪn] **I** *s.* **1.** (geschäftliches) Abkommen, Handel *m*, Geschäft *n*: ***a good*** (***bad***) ***~***; **2.** *a.* ***good ~*** vorteilhaftes Geschäft, günstiger Kauf, Gelegenheitskauf *m* (*a. die gekaufte Sache*): ***at £10 it is a*** (***dead***) ***~*** für £10 ist es spottbillig; ***it's a ~!*** abgemacht!, topp!; ***into the ~*** obendrein, noch dazu; ***strike*** *od.* ***make a ~*** ein Abkommen treffen, e-n Handel abschließen; ***make the best of a bad ~*** sich so gut wie möglich aus der Affäre ziehen; ***drive a hard ~*** hart feilschen, ‚mächtig rangehen'; **3.** *Brit. Börse*: (*einzelner*) Abschluß: ***~ for account*** Termingeschäft *n*; **II** *v/i.* **4.** handeln, feilschen (***for, about*** um); **5.** verhandeln, über'einkommen (***for*** über *acc.*, ***that*** daß): ***~ing point*** Verhandlungspunkt *m*; ***~ing position*** Verhandlungsposition *f*; **6.** ***~ for*** rechnen mit, erwarten (*acc.*) (*mst neg.*): ***I did not ~ for that*** darauf war ich nicht gefaßt; ***it was more than we had ~ed for*** damit hatten wir nicht gerechnet; **7.** ***~ on*** *fig.* zählen auf (*acc.*); **III** *v/t.* **8.** (ein)tauschen (***for*** gegen); **9.** ***~ away*** verschachern, *fig. a.* verschenken; ***~ basement*** *s.* Niedrigpreisabteilung *f* im Tiefgeschoß *e-s Warenhauses*; ***~ counter*** *s.* **1.** ✝ Wühltisch *m*; **2.** *fig. pol.* 'Tauschobˌjekt *n*.

bar·gain·er ['bɑːgɪnə] *s.* **1.** Feilscher (-in); **2.** Verhandler *m*; **'bar·gain·ing** [-nɪŋ] *s.* Handeln *n*, Feilschen *n*; Verhandeln *n*: → ***collective bargaining***.

bar·gain| price *s.* Spott-, Schleuderpreis *m*; ***~ sale*** *s.* (Ramsch)Ausverkauf *m*.

barge [bɑːdʒ] **I** *s.* **1.** ⚓ a) flaches Flußod. Ka'nalboot, Lastkahn *m*, b) Bar'kasse *f*, c) Hausboot *n*; **II** *v/i.* **2.** 𝔉 ungeschickt gehen *od.* fahren *od.* sich bewegen, torkeln, stürzen, prallen (***into*** in *acc.*, ***against*** gegen); **3.** ***~ in*** 𝔉 her'einplatzen, sich einmischen; **bar·gee** [bɑː'dʒiː] *s. Brit.* Kahnführer *m*: ***swear like a ~*** fluchen wie ein Landsknecht.

'barge|·man [-mən] *s.* [*irr.*] *Am.* Kahnführer *m*; **'~·pole** *s.* Bootsstange *f*: ***I wouldn't touch him*** (***it***) ***with a ~*** *Brit.* 𝔉 a) den (das) würde ich nicht mal mit e-r Feuerzange anfassen, b) mit dem (damit) will ich nichts zu tun haben.

bar·ic ['beərɪk] *adj.* ⚗ Barium...

bar i·ron *s.* ⚙ Stabeisen *n*.

bar·i·tone ['bærɪtəʊn] *s.* ♪ 'Bariton *m* (*Stimme u. Sänger*).

bar·i·um ['beərɪəm] *s.* ⚗ 'Barium *n*; ***~ meal*** *s.* ⚕ Kon'trastmittel *n*, -brei *m*.

bark¹ [bɑːk] **I** *s.* **1.** ⚘ (Baum)Rinde *f*, Borke *f*; **2.** → ***Peruvian*** I; **3.** ⚙ (Gerber)Lohe *f*; **II** *v/t.* **4.** abrinden; **5.** abschürfen: ***~ one's knees***.

bark² [bɑːk] **I** *v/i.* **1.** bellen, kläffen (*a. fig.*): ***~ at s.o.*** *fig.* j-n anschnauzen; ***~ing dogs never bite*** Hunde, die bellen, beißen nicht; ***~ up the wrong tree*** a) auf dem Holzweg sein, b) an der falschen Adresse sein; **2.** *fig.* ‚bellen' (*husten*); ‚bellen', krachen (*Schußwaffe*); **3.** 𝔉 *Ware* marktschreierisch anpreisen; **II** *s.* **4.** Bellen *n*: ***his ~ is worse than his bite*** er kläfft nur (aber beißt nicht); **5.** *fig.* ‚Bellen' *n* (*Husten*); Krachen *n*.

bark³ [bɑːk] *s.* **1.** ⚓ Bark *f*; **2.** *poet.* Schiff *n*.

'bar|·keep *Am.* 𝔉 → **'~ˌkeep·er** *s.* **1.** Barkellner *m*, -mixer *m*; **2.** Barbesitzer *m*.

bark·er ['bɑːkə] *s.* **1.** Beller *m*, Kläffer *m*; **2.** 𝔉 ‚Anreißer' *m* (*Kundenwerber*); Marktschreier *m*; *Am. a.* Fremdenführer *m*.

bark| pit *s. Gerberei*: Lohgrube *f*; ***~ tree*** *s.* ⚘ 'Chinarindenbaum *m*.

bar·ley ['bɑːlɪ] *s.* ⚘ Gerste *f*: ***French ~***, ***pearl ~*** Perlgraupen *pl.*; ***pot ~*** ungeschälte Graupen *pl.*; **'~·corn** *s.* Gerstenkorn *n*: ***John 2*** *scherzhafte Personifikation* (*der Gerste als Grundstoff*) *von Bier* (*‚Gerstensaft'*) *od. Whisky*; ***~ sug-***

ar *s.* Gerstenzucker *m*; ~ **wa·ter** *s. aromatisiertes Getränk aus Gerstenextrakt*; ~ **wine** *s. ein Starkbier.*
bar line *s.* ♪ Taktstrich *m.*
barm [bɑ:m] *s.* Bärme *f*, (Bier)Hefe *f.*
'**bar**|**·maid** *s. bsd. Brit.* Bardame *f*, -kellnerin *f*; '~**·man** [-mən] *s.* [*irr.*] → ***barkeeper*** 1.
barm·y ['bɑ:mɪ] *adj.* **1.** heftig, gärend, schaumig; **2.** *Brit. sl.* ‚bekloppt': ***go*** ~ überschnappen.
barn [bɑ:n] *s.* **1.** Scheune *f*; **2.** *Am.* (Vieh)Stall *m.*
bar·na·cle¹ ['bɑ:nəkl] *s.* **1.** *orn.* Ber'nikel-, Ringelgans *f*; **2.** *zo.* Entenmuschel *f*; **3.** *fig.* a) ‚Klette' *f* (*lästiger Mensch*), b) (lästige) Fessel.
bar·na·cle² ['bɑ:nəkl] *s.* **1.** *mst pl.* Nasenknebel *m für unruhige Pferde*; **2.** *pl. Brit.* F Kneifer *m*, Zwicker *m.*
barn| **dance** *s. Am.* ländlicher Tanz; ₁~-'**door** *s.*: ***as big as a*** ~ F (so) groß wie ein Scheunentor, nicht zu verfehlen; ₁~-'**door fowl** *s.* Haushuhn *n*; '~**-owl** *s.* Schleiereule *f*; '~**·storm** *v/i.* F ‚auf die Dörfer gehen': a) *thea. etc.* auf Tour'nee (durch die Pro'vinz) gehen, b) *pol.* überall Wahlreden halten; '~₁**storm·er** *s.* F **1.** Wander- *od.* Schmierenschauspieler *m*; **2.** her'umreisender Wahlredner; ~ **swal·low** *s.* Rauchschwalbe *f.*
bar·o·graph ['bærəʊgrɑ:f] *s. phys., meteor.* Baro'graph *m* (*selbstaufzeichnender Luftdruckmesser*).
ba·rom·e·ter [bə'rɒmɪtə] *s.* Baro'meter *n*: a) Wetterglas *n*, Luftdruckmesser *m*, b) *fig.* Grad-, Stimmungsmesser *m*; **bar·o·met·ric** [₁bærəʊ'metrɪk] *adj.* (□ ~***ally***) *phys.* baro'metrisch, Barometer…: ~ ***maximum*** Hoch(druckgebiet) *n*; ~ ***pressure*** Luftdruck *m*; ₁**bar·o·'met·ri·cal** [-'metrɪkl] *adj.* → ***barometric.***
bar·on ['bærən] *s.* **1.** *hist.* Pair *m*, Ba'ron *m*; *jetzt*: Ba'ron *m* (*brit. Adelstitel*); **2.** *nicht-Brit.* Ba'ron *m*, Freiherr *m*; **3.** *fig.* (Indu'strie- *etc.*)Ba₁ron *m*, Ma'gnat *m*; **4.** ~ (***of beef***) *Küche*: doppeltes Lendenstück.
bar·on·age ['bærənɪdʒ] *s.* **1.** *coll. die* Ba'rone *pl.*; **2.** Verzeichnis *n* der Ba'rone; **3.** Rang *m* e-s Ba'rons; '**bar·on·ess** [-nɪs] *s.* **1.** *Brit.* Ba'ronin *f*; **2.** *nicht-Brit.* Ba'ronin *f*, Freifrau *f*; '**bar·on·et** [-nɪt] **I** *s.* Baronet *m* (*brit. Adelstitel*; *abbr.* ***Bart.***); **II** *v/t.* zum Baronet ernennen; '**bar·on·et·age** [-nɪtɪdʒ] *s.* **1.** *coll.* die Baronets *pl.*; **2.** Verzeichnis *n* der Baronets; '**bar·on·et·cy** [-nɪtsɪ] *s.* Titel *m od.* Rang *m* e-s Baronet; **ba·ro·ni·al** [bə'rəʊnjəl] *adj.* **1.** Barons…, freiherrlich; **2.** prunkvoll, großartig; '**bar·o·ny** [-nɪ] *s.* Baro'nie *f* (*Gebiet od. Würde*).
ba·roque [bə'rɒk] **I** *adj.* **1.** ba'rock (*a. von Perlen u. fig.*); **2.** *fig.* prunkvoll; über'steigert; bi'zarr, verschnörkelt; **II** *s.* **3.** *allg.* Ba'rock *n, m.*
'**bar-₁par·lour** *s. Brit.* Schank-, Gaststube *f.*
barque → ***bark³***.
bar·rack ['bærək] **I** *s.* **1.** *mst pl.* Ka'serne *f*: ***a*** ~***s*** e-e Kaserne; → ***confine*** 3; **2.** *mst pl. fig.* 'Mietska₁serne *f*; **II** *v/t.* **3.** in Ka'sernen *od.* Ba'racken 'unterbringen; **4.** F *sport, pol.* auspfeifen, -buhen; **III** *v/i.* **5.** F buhen, pfeifen: ~ ***for*** (lautstark) anfeuern; ~ **square** *s.* ⚔ Ka'sernenhof *m.*
bar·rage¹ ['bærɑ:ʒ] *s.* **1.** ⚔ Sperrfeuer *n*; **2.** ⚔ Sperre *f*: ***creeping*** ~ Feuerwalze *f*; ~ ***balloon*** Sperrballon *m*; **3.** *fig.* über'wältigende Menge: ***a*** ~ ***of questions*** ein Schwall *od.* Kreuzfeuer von Fragen.
bar·rage² ['bærɑ:ʒ] *s.* Talsperre *f*, Staudamm *m.*
bar·ra·try ['bærətrɪ] *s.* **1.** ⚖, ⚓ Baratte'rie *f* (*Veruntreuung*); **2.** ⚖ schika'nöses Prozessieren (*od.* Anstiftung *f* dazu); **3.** Ämterschacher *m.*
barred [bɑ:d] *adj.* **1.** (ab)gesperrt, verriegelt; **2.** gestreift; **3.** ♪ durch Taktstriche abgeteilt; **4.** ⚖ verjährt.
bar·rel ['bærəl] **I** *s.* **1.** Faß *n*, Tonne *f*; *im Ölhandel*: Barrel *n*: ***have s.o. over a*** ~ F j-n in s-r Gewalt haben; ***scrape the*** ~ F den letzten, schäbigen Rest zs.-kratzen; **2.** ⚙ Walze *f*, Rolle *f*, Trommel *f*, Zy'linder *m*, (rundes) Gehäuse; (Gewehr)Lauf *m*, (Geschütz)Rohr *n*; Kolbenrohr *n*; Rumpf *m e-s Dampfkessels*; Tintenbehälter *m e-r Füllfeder*; Walze *f der Drehorgel*; Kiel *m e-r Feder*; Zylinder *m e-r Spritze*; **3.** Rumpf *m e-s Pferdes etc.*; **II** *v/t.* **4.** in Fässer füllen *od.* packen; **III** *v/i.* **5.** F rasen, sausen; ~ **chair** *s.* Lehnstuhl *m* mit hoher runder Lehne; '~**-drain** *s.* ⚙, △ gemauerter runder 'Abzugska₁nal; ~ **house** *s. Am. sl.* Spe'lunke *f*, Kneipe *f.*
bar·rel(l)ed ['bærəld] *adj.* **1.** faßförmig; **2.** in Fässer gefüllt; **3.** …läufig (*Gewehr*).
'**bar·rel**|₁**mak·er** *s.* Faßbinder *m*; '~-₁**organ** *s.* ♪ Drehorgel *f*; ~ **roll** *s.* ✈ Rolle *f* (*im Kunstflug*); ~ **roof** *s.* △ Tonnendach *n*; ~ **vault** *s.* △ Tonnengewölbe *n.*
bar·ren ['bærən] **I** *adj.* □ **1.** unfruchtbar (*Lebewesen, Pflanze etc.*; *a. fig.*); **2.** öde, kahl, dürr; **3.** *fig.* trocken, langweilig, seicht; dürftig; **4.** 'unproduk₁tiv (*Geist*); tot (*Kapital*); **5.** leer, arm (***of*** an *dat.*); **II** *s.* **6.** *mst pl.* Ödland *n*; '**barren·ness** [-nɪs] *s.* **1.** Unfruchtbarkeit *f* (*a. fig.*); **2.** *fig.* Trockenheit *f*, geistige Leere, Dürftigkeit *f*, Dürre *f.*
bar·ri·cade [₁bærɪ'keɪd] **I** *s.* **1.** Barri'kade *f*: ***mount*** (*od.* ***go to***) ***the*** ~***s*** auf die Barrikaden steigen (*a. fig.*); **2.** *fig.* Hindernis *n*; **II** *v/t.* **3.** (ver)barrikadieren, (ver)sperren (*a. fig.*).
bar·ri·er ['bærɪə] *s.* **1.** Schranke *f* (*a. fig.*), Barri'ere *f*, Sperre *f*: ~ ***cream*** Schutzcreme *f*; **2.** Schlag-, Grenzbaum *m*; **3.** *sport* 'Startma₁schine *f*; **4.** *fig.* Hindernis *n* (***to*** für); Mauer *f*; (*Sprach- etc.*)Barri'ere *f*; **5.** ♀ 'Eisbarri₁ere *f* der Ant'arktis: ♀ ***Reef*** Barriereriff *n.*
bar·ring ['bɑ:rɪŋ] *prp.* abgesehen von, ausgenommen: ~ ***errors*** Irrtümer vorbehalten; ~ ***a miracle*** wenn kein Wunder geschieht.
bar·ris·ter ['bærɪstə] *s.* ⚖ **1.** *a.* ~***-at-law*** *Brit.* Barrister *m*, *plädierender* Rechtsanwalt (vor höheren Gerichten); **2.** *Am. allg.* Rechtsanwalt *m.*
'**bar-room** *s.* Schankstube *f.*
bar·row¹ ['bærəʊ] *s.* **1.** 'Tumulus *m*, Hügelgrab *n*; **2.** Hügel *m.*
bar·row² ['bærəʊ] *s.* (Hand-, Schub-, Gepäck-, Obst)Karre(n *m*) *f.*
bar·row³ ['bærəʊ] *s.* ⸗ Bork *m* (*im Ferkelalter kastriertes Schwein*).
bar·row| **boy** *s.*, '~**·man** [-mən] *s.* [*irr.*] Straßenhändler *m*, ‚fliegender Händler'.
bar| **steel** *s.* ⚙ Stangenstahl *m*; '~₁**tender** *s.* → ***barkeeper*** 1.
bar·ter ['bɑ:tə] **I** *v/i.* Tauschhandel treiben; **II** *v/t. im Handel* (ein-, 'um)tauschen, austauschen (***for, against*** gegen): ~ ***away*** verschachern, -kaufen (*a. fig. Ehre etc.*); **III** *s.* Tauschhandel *m*, Tausch *m* (*a. fig.*): ~ ***shop*** Tauschladen *m*; ~ **trans·ac·tion** *s.* ⚕ Tausch(handels)-, Kompensati'onsgeschäft *n.*
bar·y·tone → ***baritone.***
bas·al ['beɪsl] *adj.* □ **1.** an der Basis *od.* Grundfläche befindlich; **2.** *mst fig.* grundlegend: ~ ***metabolism*** ⚕ Grundstoffwechsel *m*; ~ ***metabolic rate*** ⚕ Grundumsatz *m*; ~ ***cell*** *biol.* Basalzelle *f.*
ba·salt ['bæsɔ:lt] *s. geol.* Ba'salt *m*; **ba·sal·tic** [bə'sɔ:ltɪk] *adj.* ba'saltisch, Basalt…
base¹ [beɪs] **I** *s.* **1.** Basis *f*, 'Unterteil *m, n*, Boden *m*; 'Unterbau *m*, -lage *f*; Funda'ment *n*; **2.** Fuß *m*, Sockel *m*; Sohle *f*; **3.** *fig.* Basis *f*: a) Grund(lage *f*) *m*, b) Ausgangspunkt *m*, c) *a.* ~ ***camp mount.*** Basislager *n*; **4.** Grundstoff *m*, Hauptbestandteil *m*; **5.** & Grundlinie *f*, -fläche *f*, -zahl *f*; **6.** ⚗ Base *f*; *Färberei*: Beize *f*; **7.** *sport* a) Grund-, Startlinie *f*, b) Mal *n*: ***not to get to first*** ~ (***with s.o.***) F *fig.* keine Chance haben (bei j-m); **8.** ⚔, ⚓ a) Standort *m*, Stati'on *f*, b) (Operati'ons)Basis *f*, Stützpunkt *m*, c) (Flug)Basis *f*, *Am.* (Flieger)Horst *m*: ***naval*** ~ Flottenstützpunkt, d) E'tappe *f*; **II** *v/t.* **9.** stützen, gründen (***on, upon*** auf *acc.*): ***be*** ~***d on*** beruhen auf (*dat.*), sich stützen auf (*acc.*); ~ ***o.s. on*** sich verlassen auf (*acc.*); **10.** *a.* ⚔ stationieren; → ***based*** 2.
base² [beɪs] *adj.* □ **1.** gemein, niedrig, niederträchtig; **2.** minderwertig; unedel: ~ ***metals***; **3.** falsch, unecht (*Geld*): ~ ***coin*** falsche Münze, *coll.* Falschgeld *n*, *Am.* Scheidemünze *f*; **4.** *ling.* unrein, unklassisch.
'**base·ball** *s. sport* **1.** Baseball(spiel *n*) *m*; **2.** Baseball *m.*
based [beɪst] *adj.* **1.** (***on***) gegründet (auf *acc.*), beruhend (auf *dat.*), mit e-r Grundlage (von); **2.** ⚔ *in Zssgn* mit … als Stützpunkt, stationiert in (*dat.*), *a.* (land- *etc.*)gestützt; **3.** *in Zssgn* mit Sitz in (*dat.*): ***a London-*~ *company.***
base·less ['beɪslɪs] *adj.* grundlos, unbegründet.
base| **line** *s.* **1.** Grundlinie *f* (*a. sport*); **2.** *surv.* Standlinie *f*; **3.** ⚔ Basislinie *f*; ~ **load** *s.* ⚡ Grundlast *f*, -belastung *f*; '~**·man** [-mən] *s.* [*irr.*] *Baseball*: Malhüter *m.*
base·ment ['beɪsmənt] *s.* △ **1.** Kellergeschoß *n*; **2.** Grundmauer(n *pl.*) *f.*
base·ness ['beɪsnɪs] *s.* **1.** Gemeinheit *f*, Niederträchtigkeit *f*; **2.** Minderwertigkeit *f*; **3.** Unechtheit *f.*
ba·ses ['beɪsi:z] *pl. von* ***basis.***
base wal·lah *s.* ⚔ *Brit. sl.* E'tappenschwein *n.*
bash [bæʃ] F **I** *v/t.* **1.** heftig schlagen, einhauen auf (*acc.*) (*a.* F *fig.*): ~ ***in*** a) einschlagen, b) verbeulen; ~ ***up*** a) *j-n* zs.-schlagen, b) *Auto* zu Schrott fahren; **II** *s.* **2.** heftiger Schlag: ***have a*** ~ ***at s.th.*** es mit et. probieren; **3.** Beule *f*

(*am Auto etc.*); **4.** *Brit.* (tolle) Party.
bash·ful ['bæʃfʊl] *adj.* □ schüchtern, verschämt, scheu; zu'rückhaltend; '**bash·ful·ness** [-nɪs] *s.* Schüchternheit *f*, Scheu *f*.
bash·ing ['bæʃɪŋ] *s.* F ‚Senge' *f*, Prügel *pl.*: ***get*** (*od.* ***take***) ***a ~*** Prügel beziehen (*a. fig.*).
bas·ic ['beɪsɪk] **I** *adj.* (□ ***~ally***) **1.** grundlegend, die Grundlage bildend; elemen'tar; Einheits..., Grund...; **2.** ⚗, *geol.*, *min.* basisch; **3.** ⚡ ständig (*Belastung*); **II** *s.* **4.** *pl.* a) Grundlagen *pl.*, b) *das* Wesentliche; **5.** → ***Basic English***; '**bas·i·cal·ly** [-kəlɪ] *adv.* im Grunde, grundsätzlich.
Bas·ic| Eng·lish *s.* Basic English *n* (*vereinfachte Form des Englischen von C. K. Ogden*); ≈ **for·mu·la** *s.* ⚗ Grundformel *f*; ≈ **in·dus·try** *s.* 'Grund(stoff)-, 'Schlüsselindu,strie *f*; ≈ **i·ron** *s.* ⚙ Thomaseisen *n*; ≈ **load** *s.* ⚡ ständige Grundlast; ≈ **ma·ter·i·als** *s. pl.* Grund-, Ausgangsstoffe *pl.*; ≈ **ra·tion** *s.* ⚔ Mindestverpflegungssatz *m*; ≈ **research** *s.* Grundlagenforschung *f*; ≈ **sal·a·ry** *s.* ✝ Grundgehalt *n*; ≈ **size** *s.* ⚙ Sollmaß *n*; ≈ **slag** *s.* ⚗ Thomasschlacke *f*; ≈ **steel** *s.* ⚙ Thomasstahl *m*; ≈ **trai·ning** *s. a.* ⚔ Grundausbildung *f*; ≈ **wage** *s.* ✝ Grundlohn *m*.
bas·il ['bæzl] *s.* ⚘ Ba'silienkraut *n*, Ba'silikum *n*.
ba·sil·i·ca [bə'zɪlɪkə] *s.* △ Ba'silika *f*.
bas·i·lisk ['bæzɪlɪsk] **I** *s.* **1.** Basi'lisk *m* (*Fabeltier*); **2.** *zo.* Legu'an *m*; **II** *adj.* **3.** Basilisken...: ***~ eye***.
ba·sin ['beɪsn] *s.* **1.** (Wasser-, Wasch-*etc.*)Becken *n*, Schale *f*, Schüssel *f*; **2.** Fluß-, Hafenbecken *n*; Schwimmbekken *n*, Bas'sin *n*; **3.** a) Stromgebiet *n*, b) (kleine) Bucht; **4.** Wasserbehälter *m*; **5.** Becken *n*, Einsenkung *f*, Mulde *f*; **6.** (Kohlen- *etc.*)Lager *n od.* Revier *n*.
ba·sis ['beɪsɪs] *pl.* **-ses** [-si:z] *s.* **1.** Basis *f*, Grundlage *f*, Funda'ment *n*: ***~ of discussion*** Diskussionsbasis *f*; ***take as a ~*** zugrunde legen; **2.** Hauptbestandteil *m*; **3.** ⚗ Basis *f*, Grundlinie *f*, -fläche *f*; **4.** ⚔, ⚓ (Operati'ons)Basis *f*, Stützpunkt *m*.
bask [bɑ:sk] *v/i.* sich aalen, sich sonnen (*a. fig.*): ***~ in the sun*** ein Sonnenbad nehmen.
bas·ket ['bɑ:skɪt] *s.* **1.** Korb *m*; **2.** Korb (-voll) *m*; **3.** *Basketball*: a) Korb *m*, b) Treffer *m*, Korb *m*; **4.** (Passa'gier)Korb *m*, Gondel *f* (*e-s Luftballons od. Luftschiffes*); **5.** Säbelkorb *m*; **6.** Tastenfeld *n* (*der Schreibmaschine*); '**~·ball** *s. sport* **1.** Basketball(spiel *n*) *m*; **2.** Basketball *m*; **~ case** *Am.* F **1.** Arm- u. Beinamputierte(r *m*) *f*; **2.** to'tales ‚Wrack'; **~ chair** *s.* Korbsessel *m*; **~ din·ner** *s.* *Am.* Picknick *n*.
bas·ket·ful ['bɑ:skɪtfʊl] *pl.* **-fuls** *s. ein* Korb(voll) *m*.
bas·ket| hilt *s.* Säbelkorb *m*; **~ lunch** *s.* *Am.* Picknick *n*.
bas·ket·ry ['baskɪtrɪ] *s.* Korbwaren *pl.*
Basque [bæsk] **I** *s.* Baske *m*, Baskin *f*; **II** *adj.* baskisch.
bas-re·lief ['bæsrɪ,li:f] *s. sculp.* 'Bas-, 'Flachreli,ef *n*.
bass¹ [beɪs] ♪ **I** *adj.* Baß...; **II** *s.* Baß *m* (*Stimme*, *Sänger*, *Instrument u. Partie*).
bass² [bæs] *pl. mst* **bass** *s. ichth.* Barsch *m*.
bass³ [bæs] *s.* **1.** (Linden)Bast *m*; **2.** Bastmatte *f*.
bas·set ['bæsɪt] *s. zo.* Basset *m* (*ein Dachshund*).
bas·si·net [,bæsɪ'net] *s.* **1.** Korbwiege *f*; Stubenwagen *m*; Korb(kinder)wagen *m* (*mit Verdeck*).
bas·soon [bə'su:n] *s.* ♪ Fa'gott *n*.
bas·so| pro·fun·do ['bæsəʊ prə'fʌndəʊ] (*Ital.*) *s.* ♪ tiefster Baß (*Stimme od. Sänger*); **,~-re'lie·vo** [-rɪ'li:vəʊ] *pl.* **-vos** → ***bas-relief***.
'**bass-re,lief** ['bæs-] → ***bas-relief***.
bass vi·ol [beɪs] *s.* ♪ 'Cello *n*.
'**bass-wood** ['bæs-] *s.* ⚘ **1.** Linde *f*; **2.** Lindenholz *n*.
bast [bæst] *s.* (Linden)Bast *m*.
bas·tard ['bæstəd] **I** *s.* **1.** Bastard *m*, *a.* ⚖ uneheliches Kind; **2.** *biol.* Bastard *m*, Mischling *m*; **3.** *fig.* a) Fälschung *f*, Nachahmung *f*, b) Scheußlichkeit *f*; **4.** a) V ‚Schwein' *n*, ‚Scheißkerl' *m*, b) *iro.* alter Ha'lunke, c) Kerl *m*; **II** *adj.* **5.** unehelich, Bastard...; **6.** *biol.* Bastard...; **7.** *fig.* unecht, falsch; **8.** ab'norm; '**bas·tard·ize** [-daɪz] **I** *v/t.* **1.** ⚖ für unehelich erklären; **2.** verschlechtern, verfälschen; **II** *v/i.* **3.** entarten; '**bas·tard·ized** [-daɪzd] *adj.* entartet, Mischlings..., Bastard...
bas·tard| slip → ***bastard*** 1; **~ ti·tle** *s.* *typ.* Schmutztitel *m*.
bas·tar·dy ['bæstədɪ] *s.* uneheliche Geburt: ***~ procedure*** Verfahren *n* zur Feststellung der (unehelichen) Vaterschaft u. Unterhaltspflicht.
baste¹ [beɪst] *v/t.* **1.** ‚(ver)hauen', verprügeln; **2.** *fig.* beschimpfen, herfallen über (*acc.*).
baste² [beɪst] *v/t.* **1.** *Braten etc.* mit Fett begießen; **2.** *Docht der Kerze* mit geschmolzenem Wachs begießen.
baste³ [beɪst] *v/t.* lose (an)heften.
bast·ing ['beɪstɪŋ] *s.* (Tracht *f*) Prügel *pl.*
bas·tion ['bæstɪən] *s.* ⚔ Ba'stei *f*, Basti'on *f*, Bollwerk *n* (*a. fig.*).
bat¹ [bæt] **I** *s.* **1.** *sport* a) Schlagholz *n*, Schläger *m* (*bsd. Baseball u. Kricket*): ***carry one's ~*** *Kricket*: noch im Spiel sein; ***off one's own ~*** *Kricket u. fig.* selbständig, ohne Hilfe, auf eigene Faust; ***right off the ~*** F auf Anhieb; ***be at*** (***the***) ***~*** am Schlagen sein, dran sein; ***go to ~ for s.o.*** *Baseball*: für j-n einspringen, *fig.* → 6, b) → ***batsman***; **2.** F Stockhieb *m*; **3.** *Brit. sl.* (Schritt)Tempo *n*: ***at a rare ~*** mit e-m ‚Affenzahn'; **4.** *Am. sl.* ‚Saufe'rei' *f*: ***go on a ~*** e-e ‚Sauftour' machen; **II** *v/i.* **5.** a) (mit dem Schlagholz) schlagen, b) am Schlagen sein; → ***batting*** 3; **6.** ***~ for s.o.*** *fig.* für j-n eintreten.
bat² [bæt] *s.* **1.** *zo.* Fledermaus *f*: ***have ~s in the belfry*** verrückt sein, ‚e-n Vogel haben'; → ***blind*** 1; **2.** ✈, ⚔ 'radargelenkte Bombe.
bat³ [bæt] *v/t.*: ***~ the eyes*** mit den Augen blinzeln *od.* zwinkern; ***without ~ting an eyelid*** (*Am.* ***eyelash***) ohne mit der Wimper zu zucken; ***I never ~ted an eyelid*** ich habe kein Auge zugetan.
ba·ta·ta [bə'tɑ:tə] *s.* ⚘ Ba'tate *f*, 'Süßkar,toffel *f*.
batch [bætʃ] *s.* **1.** Schub *m* (*die auf einmal gebackene Menge Brot*): ***a ~ of bread***; **2.** ⚙ a) Schub *m*, b) Satz *m* (*Material*), Charge *f*, Füllung *f*; **3.** Schub *m*; ‚Schwung' *m*: a) Gruppe *f* (*von Personen*), Trupp *m* (*Gefangener*), b) Schicht *f*, Satz *m* (*Muster*), Stapel *m*, Stoß *m* (*Briefe etc.*), Par'tie *f*, Posten *m* (*gleicher Dinge*), *Computer*: Stapel *m*: ***in ~es*** schubweise; '**~-,process** *v/t.* *Computer*: stapelweise verarbeiten.
bate¹ [beɪt] **I** *v/i.* abnehmen, nachlassen; **II** *v/t.* schwächen, *Hoffnung etc.* vermindern, *Neugier etc.* mäßigen, *Forderung etc.* her'absetzen: ***with ~d breath*** mit verhaltenem Atem, gespannt.
bate² [beɪt] *s.* ⚙ *Gerberei*: Ätzlauge *f*.
bate³ [beɪt] *s. Brit. sl.* Wut *f*.
ba·teau [bɑ:'təʊ] *pl.* **-teaux** [-'təʊz] (*Fr.*) *s. Am.* leichtes langes Flußboot; **~ bridge** *s.* Pon'tonbrücke *f*.
bath [bɑ:θ] **I** *pl.* **baths** [-ðz] *s.* **1.** (Wannen)Bad *n*: ***take a ~*** ein Bad nehmen, baden, *Am. sl.* (*bsd. finanziell*) ‚baden gehen'; **2.** Badewasser *n*; **3.** Badewanne *f*: ***enamelled ~***; **4.** Badezimmer *n*; **5.** *mst pl.* a) Badeanstalt *f*, b) Badeort *m*; **6.** ⚗ *phot.* a) Bad *n* (*Behandlungsflüssigkeit*), b) Behälter *m dafür*; **7.** *Brit.*: ***order of the ≈*** Bathorden *m*; ***Knight of the ≈*** Ritter *m* des Bathordens; ***Knight Commander of the ≈*** Komtur *m* des Bathordens; **II** *v/t.* **8.** *Kind etc.* baden; **III** *v/i.* **9.** baden, ein Bad nehmen.
Bath| brick *s.* Me'tallputzstein *m*; **~ bun** *s.* über'zuckertes Kuchenbrötchen; **~ chair** *s.* Rollstuhl *m*.
bathe [beɪð] **I** *Auge*, *Hand*, (*verletzten*) *Körperteil* baden, in Wasser *etc.* tauchen; **2.** ***~d in sunlight*** (***perspiration***) in Sonne (Schweiß) gebadet; ***~d in tears*** in Tränen aufgelöst; **3.** *poet.* bespülen; **II** *v/i.* **4.** (sich) baden; **5.** schwimmen; **6.** (Heil)Bäder nehmen; **7.** *fig.* sich baden *od.* schwelgen (***in*** in *dat.*); **III** *s.* **8.** *bsd. Brit.* Bad *n im Freien*; '**bath·er** [-ðə] *s.* **1.** Badende(r *m*) *f*; **2.** Badegast *m*.
'**bath·house** *s. Am.* **1.** Badeanstalt *f*; **2.** 'Umkleideka,binen *pl.*
bath·ing ['beɪðɪŋ] *s.* Baden *n*; **~ beau·ty** *s.*, **~ belle** *s.* F Badeschönheit *f*; '**~-,cos·tume** → ***bathing-suit***; '**~-,draw·ers** *s. pl.* Badehose *f*; '**~-dress** → ***bathing-suit***; '**~-gown** *s.* Bademantel *m*; '**~-ma,chine** *s. hist.* Badekarren *m* (*fahrbare Umkleidekabine*); '**~-suit** *s.* Badeanzug *m*.
Bath met·al *s.* ⚙ 'Tombak *m*.
ba·thos ['beɪθɒs] *s.* **1.** Abgleiten *n* vom Erhabenen zum Lächerlichen; **2.** Gemeinplatz *m*, Plattheit *f*; **3.** falsches Pathos; **4.** a) Null-, Tiefpunkt *m*, b) Gipfel *m der Dummheit etc.*
'**bath|·robe** *s.* Bademantel *m*; '**~·room** [-rʊm] *s.* Badezimmer *n*; *weitS.* Klo'sett *n*; **~ salts** *s. pl.* Badesalz *n*; ≈ **stone** *s.* Muschelkalkstein *m*; **~ tow·el** *s.* Badetuch *n*; '**~·tub** *s.* Badewanne *f* (*a.* F *Skisport*).
ba·thym·e·try [bə'θɪmɪtrɪ] *s.* Tiefen- *od.* Tiefseemessung *f*.
bath·y·sphere ['bæθɪ,sfɪə] *s.* ⚙ Tiefseetaucherkugel *f*.
ba·tik ['bætɪk] *s.* 'Batik(druck) *m*.
ba·tiste [bæ'ti:st] *s.* Ba'tist *m*.
bat·man ['bætmən] *s.* [*irr.*] ⚔ *Brit.* Offi-

ˈziersbursche *m*.

ba·ton [ˈbætən] *s*. **1.** (Amts-, Komˈmando)Stab *m*: ***Field-Marshal's ~*** Marschallsstab; **2.** ♪ Taktstock *m*, Stab *m*; **3.** *sport* (Staffel)Stab *m*; **4.** *Brit*. Schlagstock *m*, (Poliˈzei)Knüppel *m*.

ba·tra·chi·an [bəˈtreɪkjən] *zo*. **I** *adj*. frosch-, krötenartig; **II** *s*. Baˈtrachier *m*, Froschlurch *m*.

bats·man [ˈbætsmən] *s*. [*irr*.] *Kricket, Baseball etc*.: Schläger *m*, Schlagmann *m*.

bat·tal·ion [bəˈtæljən] *s*. ⚔ Batailˈlon *n*.

bat·tels [ˈbætlz] *s*. *pl*. (*Universität Oxford*) College-Rechnungen *pl*. für Lebensmittel *etc*.

bat·ten¹ [ˈbætn] *v/i*. **1.** fett werden (***on*** von *dat*.), gedeihen; **2.** (***on***) *a*. *fig*. sich mästen (mit), sich gütlich tun (an *dat*.): ***~ on others*** auf Kosten anderer dick u. fett werden.

bat·ten² [ˈbætn] **I** *s*. **1.** Latte *f*, Leiste *f*; **2.** Diele *f*, (Fußboden)Brett *n*; **II** *v/t*. **3.** mit Latten verkleiden *od*. befestigen; **4.** ***~ down the hatches*** a) ⚓ die Luken schalken, b) *fig*. dichtmachen.

bat·ter¹ [ˈbætə] ⚠ **I** *v/i*. sich nach oben verjüngen; **II** *s*. Böschung *f*, Verjüngung *f*, Abdachung *f*.

bat·ter² [ˈbætə] **I** *v/t*. **1.** mit heftigen Schlägen traktieren; (zer)schlagen, demolieren; *Ehefrau, Kind* (ständig) mißhandeln *od*. schlagen *od*. prügeln: ***~ed wives*** mißhandelte (Ehe)Frauen; ***~ down*** (*od*. ***in***) *Tür* einschlagen; **2.** ⚔ *u. weitS*. bombardieren: ***~ down*** zs.-schießen; **3.** beschädigen, zerbeulen, *a*. *j-n* böse zurichten, arg mitnehmen; **II** *v/i*. **4.** heftig *od*. wiederholt schlagen: ***~ at the door*** gegen die Tür hämmern; **ˈbat·tered** [-təd] *adj*. **1.** zerschlagen, zerschmettert, demoliert; **2.** a) abgenutzt, zerbeult, beschädigt, b) *a*. *fig*. arg mitgenommen, übel zugerichtet, c) mißˈhandelt (*Kind etc*.).

ˈbat·ter·ing-ram [ˈbætərɪŋ-] *s*. ⚔ *hist*. (Belagerungs)Widder *m*, Sturmbock *m*.

bat·ter·y [ˈbætərɪ] *s*. **1.** a) ⚔ Batteˈrie *f*, b) ⚓ Geschützgruppe *f*; **2.** ⚡, ⚙ Batteˈrie *f*, Eleˈment *n*; **3.** *fig*. Reihe *f*, Satz *m*, Batteˈrie *f* (*von Maschinen, Flaschen etc*.); **4.** ✓ ˈLegebatteˌrie *f*; **5.** ♪ Batteˈrie *f*, Schlagzeuggruppe *f*; **6.** *Baseball*: Werfer *m* u. Fänger *m*; **7.** ⚖ Tätlichkeit *f*, *a*. Körperverletzung *f*; → ***assault*** 3; ***~ cell*** *s*. Sammlerzelle *f*; **ˈ~-ˌcharg·ing sta·tion** *s*. ⚡ ˈLadestatiˌon *f*; **ˈ~-ˌop·er·at·ed** *adj*. batteriebetrieben, Batterie…; ***~ hen*** *s*. Batteˈriehenne *f*.

bat·ting [ˈbætɪŋ] *s*. **1.** Schlagen *n* *bsd*. *der Rohbaumwolle zu Watte*; **2.** (Baumwoll)Watte *f*; **3.** *Kricket, Baseball etc*.: Schlagen *n*, Schlägerspiel *n*: ***~ average*** *a*. *fig*. Durchschnitt(sleistung *f*) *m*.

bat·tle [ˈbætl] **I** *s*. **1.** Schlacht *f* (***of*** *mst* bei), Gefecht *n*: ***~ of Britain*** Schlacht um England (*2. Weltkrieg*); **2.** *fig*. Kampf *m*, Ringen *n* (***for*** um, ***against*** gegen): ***do ~*** kämpfen, sich schlagen; ***fight a ~*** e-n Kampf führen; ***fight a losing ~ against*** e-n aussichtslosen Kampf führen gegen; ***fight s.o.'s ~*** j-s Sache vertreten; ***give*** (*od*. ***join***) ***~*** e-e Schlacht liefern, sich zum Kampf stellen; ***that is half the ~*** damit ist es schon halb gewonnen; ***line of ~*** Schlachtlinie *f*; ***~ of words*** Wortgefecht *n*; ***~ of wits*** geistiges Duell; **II** *v/i*. **3.** *mst fig*. kämpfen, streiten, fechten (***with*** mit, ***for*** um, ***against*** gegen); ***~ ar·ray*** *s*. ⚔ Schlachtordnung *f*; **ˈ~-ax(e)** *s*. **1.** ⚔ *hist*. Streitaxt *f*; **2.** F ‚alter Drachen‘ (*Frau*); **ˈ~-ˌcruis·er** *s*. ⚔ Schlachtkreuzer *m*; **ˈ~-cry** *s*. Schlachtruf *m* (*a*. *fig*.).

bat·tle·dore [ˈbætldɔː] *s*. **1.** Waschschlegel *m*; **2.** *sport hist*. a) Federballschläger *m*, b) *a*. ***~ and shuttle-cock*** *Art* Federballspiel *n*.

bat·tle| dress *s*. *Brit*. ⚔ Dienst-, Feldanzug *m*; ***~ fa·tigue*** *s*. ˈKriegsneuˌrose *f*; **ˈ~·field**, **ˈ~·ground** *s*. Schlachtfeld *n* (*a*. *fig*.).

bat·tle·ment [ˈbætlmənt] *s*. *mst pl*. (Brustwehr *f* mit) Zinnen *pl*.

bat·tle| or·der *s*. **1.** Schlachtordnung *f*; **2.** Gefechtsbefehl *m*; ***~ piece*** *s*. Schlachtenszene *f* (*in Malerei od. Literatur*); ***~ roy·al*** *s*. erbitterter Kampf (*a*. *fig*.); Massenschlägeˈrei *f*; **ˈ~·ship** *s*. ⚔ Schlachtschiff *n*.

bat·tue [bæˈtuː] (*Fr*.) *s*. **1.** Treibjagd *f*; **2.** (auf e-r Treibjagd erlegte) Strecke; **3.** *fig*. Masˈsaker *n*.

bat·ty [ˈbætɪ] *adj*. *sl*. ‚bekloppt‘.

bau·ble [ˈbɔːbl] *s*. **1.** Nippsache *f*; **2.** (protziger) Schmuck; **3.** (Kinder)Spielzeug *n*; **4.** *fig*. Spieleˈrei *f*, Tand *m*.

baulk [bɔːk] → ***balk***.

Ba·var·i·an [bəˈveərɪən] **I** *adj*. bay(e)risch; **II** *s*. Bayer(in).

bawd [bɔːd] *s*. *obs*. Kupplerin *f*; **ˈbawd·ry** [-drɪ] *s*. **1.** Kuppeˈlei *f*; **2.** Unzucht *f*; **3.** Obszöniˈtät *f*.

bawd·y [ˈbɔːdɪ] *adj*. unzüchtig, unflätig (*Rede*); **ˈ~·house** *s*. Borˈdell *n*.

bawl [bɔːl] **I** *v/i*. schreien, grölen, brüllen, *Am*. *a*. ‚heulen‘ (*weinen*): ***~ at s.o.*** j-n anbrüllen; **II** *v/t*. *a*. ***~ out*** F *j-n* anbrüllen, zs.-stauchen.

bay¹ [beɪ] *s*. **1.** ⚘ *a*. ***~ tree*** Lorbeer (-baum) *m*; **2.** *pl*. a) Lorbeerkranz *m*, b) *fig*. Lorbeeren *pl*., Ehren *pl*.

bay² [beɪ] *s*. **1.** Bai *f*, Bucht *f*, Meerbusen *m*; **2.** Talbucht *f*.

bay³ [beɪ] *s*. **1.** ⚠ Fach *n*, Abteilung *f*, Feld *n* *zwischen Pfeilern, Balken etc*.; Brückenglied *n*, Joch *n*; **2.** ⚠ Fensternische *f*, Erker *m*; **3.** ✈ Abteilung *f* *od*. Zelle *f* im Flugzeugrumpf; **4.** ⚓ ˈSchiffslazaˌrett *n*; **5.** 🚂 *Brit*. Seitenbahnsteig *m*, *bsd*. ˈEndstatiˌon *f* e-s Nebengeleises.

bay⁴ [beɪ] **I** *v/i*. **1.** (dumpf) bellen (*bsd*. *Jagdhund*): ***~ at s.o.*** *od*. ***s.th.*** j-n *od*. et. anbellen; **II** *v/t*. **2.** *obs*. anbellen: ***~ the moon***; **III** *s*. **3.** dumpfes Gebell *der Meute*: ***be*** (*od*. ***stand***) ***at ~*** gestellt sein (*Wild*), *fig*. in die Enge getrieben sein; ***bring to ~*** *Wild* stellen, *fig*. in die Enge treiben; ***keep*** (*od*. ***hold***) ***at ~*** a) sich *j-n* vom Leibe halten, b) *j-n* in Schach halten, fernhalten; *Seuche, Feuer etc*. unter Kontrolle halten; ***turn to ~*** sich stellen (*a*. *fig*.).

bay⁵ [beɪ] **I** *adj*. kaˈstanienbraun (*Pferd*): ***~ horse*** → **II** *s*. Braune(r) *m*.

bay leaf *s*. Lorbeerblatt *n*.

bay·o·net [ˈbeɪənɪt] ⚔ **I** *s*. Bajoˈnett *n*, Seitengewehr *n*: ***at the point of the ~*** mit dem Bajoˈnett, im Sturm; ***fix the ~*** das Seitengewehr aufpflanzen; **II** *v/t*. mit dem Bajoˈnett angreifen *od*. niederstechen; **III** *adj*. ⚙ Bajonett… (*-fassung, -verschluß*).

bay·ou [ˈbaɪuː] *s*. *Am*. sumpfiger Flußarm (*Südstaaten der USA*).

bay| rum *s*. ˈBayrum *m*, Piˈmentrum *m*; ***~ salt*** *s*. Seesalz *n*; **♀ State** *s*. *Am*. (*Beiname von*) Massachusetts; ***~ win·dow*** *s*. **1.** Erkerfenster *n*; **2.** *Am*. *sl*., ‚Vorbau‘ *m*, Bauch *m*; **ˈ~·work** *s*. ⚠ Fachwerk *n*.

ba·zaar [bəˈzɑː] *s*. **1.** (*Orient*) Baˈsar *m*; **2.** ✝ Warenhaus *n*; **3.** ˈWohltätigkeitsbaˌsar *m*.

ba·zoo·ka [bəˈzuːkə] *s*. ⚔ Baˈzooka *f* (*Panzerabwehrwaffe*).

B bat·ter·y *s*. ⚡ Anˈodenbatteˌrie *f*.

be [biː; bɪ] [*irr*.] **I** *v/aux*. **1.** *bildet das Passiv transitiver Verben*: ***I was cheated*** ich wurde betrogen; ***I was told*** man sagte mir; **2.** *lit*., *bildet das Perfekt einiger intransitiver Verben*: ***he is come*** er ist gekommen *od*. da; **3.** *bildet die umschriebene Form* (*continuous od. progressive form*) *der Verben*: ***he is reading*** er liest gerade; ***the house was being built*** das Haus war im Bau; ***what I was going to say*** was ich sagen wollte; **4.** *drückt die* (*nahe*) *Zukunft aus*: ***I am leaving for Paris tomorrow*** ich reise morgen nach Paris (ab); **5.** *mit inf*. *zum Ausdruck der Absicht, Pflicht, Möglichkeit etc*.: ***I am to go*** ich soll gehen; ***the house is to let*** das Haus ist zu vermieten; ***he is to be pitied*** er ist zu bedauern; ***it was not to be found*** es war nicht zu finden; **6.** *Kopula*: ***trees are green*** (die) Bäume sind grün; ***the book is mine*** (***my brother's***) das Buch gehört mir (m-m Bruder); **II** *v/i*. **7.** (vorˈhanden *od*. anwesend) sein, bestehen, sich befinden, geschehen; werden: ***I think, therefore I am*** ich denke, also bin ich; ***to be or not to be*** sein oder nicht sein; ***it was not to be*** es hat nicht sollen sein; ***so ~ it!*** so sei es!, gut so!; ***how is it that …?*** wie kommt es, daß …?; ***what will you be when you grow up?*** was willst du werden, wenn du erwachsen bist?; ***there is no substitute for wool*** für Wolle gibt es keinen Ersatz; **8.** stammen (***from*** aus): ***he is from Liverpool***; **9.** gleichkommen, bedeuten: ***seeing is believing*** was man (selbst) sieht, glaubt man; ***that is nothing to me*** das bedeutet mir nichts; **10.** kosten: ***the picture is £10*** das Bild kostet 10 Pfund; **11.** ***been*** (*p.p.*): ***have you been to Rome?*** sind Sie (je) in Rom gewesen?; ***has anyone been?*** F ist j-d dagewesen?

beach [biːtʃ] **I** *s*. Strand *m*; **II** *v/t*. ⚓ *Schiff* auf den Strand setzen *od*. ziehen; ***~ ball*** *s*. Wasserball *m*; ***~ bug·gy*** *s*. *mot*. Strandbuggy *m*; **ˈ~ˌcomb·er** *s*. **1.** ⚓ F a) Strandgutjäger *m*, b) Herˈumtreiber *m*, c) *fig*. Nichtstuer *m*; **2.** breite Strandwelle; **ˈ~·head** *s*. **1.** ⚔ Lande-, Brückenkopf *m*; **2.** *fig*. Ausgangsbasis *f*; ***~ wear*** *s*. Strandkleidung *f*.

bea·con [ˈbiːkən] **I** *s*. **1.** Leucht-, Siˈgnalfeuer *n*; (Feuer)Bake *f*, Seezeichen *n*; **2.** Leuchtturm *m*; **3.** ✈ Funkfeuer *n*, -bake *f*, Landelicht *n*; **4.** (***traffic***) ***~*** Verkehrsampel *f*, *bsd*. Blinklicht *n* an Zebrastreifen; **5.** *fig*. a) Faˈnal *n*, b) Leitstern *m*, c) ˈWarnsigˌnal *n*; **II** *v/t*. **6.** mit Baken versehen; **7.** *fig*. a) erleuchten, b) *j-n* leiten.

bead [bi:d] **I** *s.* **1.** (Glas-, Stick-, Holz-) Perle *f*; **2.** (*Blei- etc.*)Kügelchen *n*; **3.** *pl. eccl.* Rosenkranz *m*: ***tell one's ~s*** den Rosenkranz beten; **4.** (Schaum-) Bläs-chen *n*, (Tau-, Schweiß- *etc.*)Perle *f*, Tröpfchen *n*; **5.** △ perlartige Verzierung; **6.** ⚙ Wulst *m*; **7.** ⚔ (Perl)Korn *n am Gewehr*: ***draw a ~ on*** zielen auf (*acc.*); **II** *v/t.* **8.** mit Perlen *od.* perlartiger Verzierung *etc.* versehen; **9.** *wie Perlen* aufziehen, aufreihen; **III** *v/i.* **10.** perlen, Perlen bilden; ˈ**bead·ed** [-dɪd] *adj.* **1.** mit Perlen versehen *od.* verziert; **2.** ⚙ mit Wulst; ˈ**bead·ing** [-dɪŋ] *s.* **1.** ˈPerlstickeˌrei *f*; **2.** △ Rundstab *m*; **3.** ⚙ Wulst *m*.

bea·dle [ˈbi:dl] *s.* **1.** *bsd. Brit.* Kirchendiener *m*; **2.** *univ. Brit.* Peˈdell *m*, (Fest- *etc.*)Ordner *m*; **3.** *obs.* Büttel *m*, Gerichtsdiener *m*; ˈ**bea·dle·dom** [-dəm] *s.* büttelhaftes Wesen.

bead mo(u)ld·ing *s.* △ Perl-, Rundstab *m*, Perlleiste *f*.

bead·y [ˈbi:dɪ] *adj.* **1.** mit Perlen verziert; **2.** perlartig; **3.** perlend; **4.** ***~ eyes*** glänzende Knopfaugen.

bea·gle [ˈbi:gl] *s.* **1.** *zo.* Beagle *m* (*Hunderasse*); **2.** *fig.* Spiˈon *m*.

beak¹ [bi:k] *s.* **1.** *zo.* Schnabel *m*; **2.** F (scharfe) Nase, ‚Zinken' *m*; **3.** ⚙ a) Tülle *f*, Ausguß *m*, b) Schnauze *f*, Nase *f*, Röhre *f*.

beak² [bi:k] *s. Brit. sl.* **1.** ‚Kadi' *m* (*Richter*); **2.** *ped.* ‚Rex' *m* (*Direktor*).

beaked [bi:kt] *adj.* **1.** geschnäbelt, schnabelförmig; **2.** vorspringend, spitz.

beak·er [ˈbi:kə] *s.* **1.** Becher *m*; **2.** ⚗ Becherglas *n*.

ˈ**be-all**: ***the ~ and end-all*** F das A und O, das Wichtigste; *j-s* ein und alles.

beam [bi:m] **I** *s.* **1.** △ Balken *m*; Tragbalken *m* (*Haus, Brücke*); *a.* ✈ Holm *m*; **2.** ⚓ a) Deckbalken *m*, b) größte Schiffsbreite: ***in the ~*** in der Breite; ***on the starboard ~*** querab an Steuerbord; **3.** *fig.* F Körperbreite *f e-s Menschen*: ***broad in the ~*** breit (gebaut); **4.** ⚙ a) (Waage)Balken *m*, b) Weberbaum *m*, c) Pflugbaum *m*, d) Spindel *f der Drehbank*; **5.** *zo.* Stange *f am Geweih*; **6.** (Licht)Strahl *m*; (Strahlen)Bündel *n*; *mot.* Fernlicht *n*; **7.** *Funk*: Richt-, Peil-, Leitstrahl *m*: ***ride the ~*** ✈ genau auf dem Leitstrahl steuern; ***on the ~*** a) auf dem richtigen Kurs, b) *fig.* F ‚auf Draht'; ***off the ~*** *fig.* auf dem Holzweg, (völlig) daneben (*abwegig*); **8.** strahlender Blick, Glanz *m*; **II** *v/t.* **9.** ⚙ *Weberei*: *Kette* aufbäumen; **10.** *a. phys.* (aus-) strahlen; **11.** a) ⚡ *Funkspruch* mit Richtstrahler senden, b) *Radio*, *TV*: ausstrahlen; **III** *v/i.* **12.** strahlen, glänzen (*a. fig.*): ***~ (up)on s.o.*** j-n anstrahlen; ***~ing with joy*** freudestrahlend; ***~ aer·i·al***, *bsd. Am.* ***~ an·ten·na*** *s. Radio*: ˈRichtstrahler *m*, -anˌtenne *f*; ˌ**~-ˈends** *s. pl.* **1.** ⚓ ***on her ~*** mit starker Schlagseite, in Gefahr; **2.** *fig.*: ***on one's ~*** ‚pleite'; **~ trans·mis·sion** *s.* Richtsendung *f*; **~ trans·mit·ter** *s.* Richt(strahl)sender *m*.

bean [bi:n] **I** *s.* **1.** ⚘ Bohne *f*: ***full of ~s*** F ‚putzmunter', ‚aufgekratzt'; ***give s.o. ~s*** *sl.* j-m ‚Saures geben' (*j-n schlagen, strafen, schelten*); ***not to know ~s*** *Am. sl.* keine Ahnung haben; ***I haven't a ~*** *sl.* ich habe keinen roten Heller; ***spill the ~s*** *sl.* alles ausplaudern, ‚auspacken'; **2.** bohnenförmiger Samen, (*Kaffee- etc.*)Bohne *f*; **3.** *sl.* a) Kerl *m*, b) ‚Birne' *f* (*Kopf*), c) ‚Grips' *m* (*Verstand*); **II** *v/t.* **4.** *Am. sl. j-m* ‚auf die Rübe hauen'; **~ curd** *s.* ˈBohnengalˌlerte *f* (*Ostasien*); ˈ**~·feast** *s. Brit.* F **1.** *jährliches Festessen für die Belegschaft*; **2.** (feucht)fröhliches Fest.

bean·o [ˈbi:nəʊ] F → ***beanfeast*** 2.

bean| pod *s.* Bohnenhülse *f*; **~ pole** *s.* Bohnenstange *f* (*a.* F *Person*).

bean·y [ˈbi:nɪ] *adj.* F ‚putzmunter', temperaˈmentvoll.

bear¹ [beə] **I** *v/t.* [*irr.*] [*p.p.* ***borne***; ***born*** (*bei Geburt*; → *a.* ***borne*** 2)] **1.** *Lasten etc.* tragen, befördern: ***~ a message*** e-e Nachricht überbringen; → ***borne*** 1; **2.** *fig. Waffen, Namen etc.* tragen, führen; *Datum* tragen; **3.** *fig. Kosten, Verlust, Verantwortung, Folgen etc.* tragen, überˈnehmen; → ***blame*** 4, ***palm²*** 2, ***penalty*** 1; **4.** *fig. Zeichen, Stempel etc.* tragen, zeigen; → ***resemblance***; **5.** zur Welt bringen, gebären: ***~ children***; ***he was born into a rich family*** er kam als Kind reicher Eltern zur Welt; → ***born***; **6.** *fig.* herˈvorbringen: ***~ fruit*** Früchte tragen (*a. fig.*); ***~ interest*** Zinsen tragen; **7.** *fig. Schmerzen etc.* ertragen, (er)dulden, (er)leiden, aushalten; *e-r Prüfung etc.* standhalten: ***~ comparison*** den Vergleich aushalten; *mst neg. od. interrog.*: ***I cannot ~ him*** ich kann ihn nicht leiden *od.* ausstehen; ***I cannot ~ it*** ich kann es nicht ausstehen *od.* aushalten; ***his words won't ~ repeating*** s-e Worte lassen sich unmöglich wiederholen; ***it does not ~ thinking about*** daran mag man gar nicht denken; **8.** *fig.*: ***~ a hand*** zur Hand gehen, helfen (*dat.*); ***~ love (a grudge)*** Liebe (Groll) hegen; ***~ a part in*** e-e Rolle spielen bei; **9.** ***~ o.s.*** sich betragen: ***~ o.s. well***; **II** *v/i.* [*irr.*] **10.** tragen, halten (*Balken, Eis etc.*): ***will the ice ~ today?*** wird das Eis heute tragen?; **11.** Früchte tragen; **12.** Richtung annehmen: ***~ (to the) left*** sich links halten; ***~ to the north*** sich nach Norden erstrekken; **13.** → ***bring*** 1.

Zssgn mit prp.:

bear| a·gainst *v/i.* drücken gegen; ˈWiderstand leisten (*dat.*); **~ on** *od.* **up·on** *v/i.* **1.** sich beziehen auf (*acc.*), betreffen (*acc.*); **2.** einwirken *od.* zielen auf (*acc.*); **3.** drücken *od.* sich stützen auf (*acc.*), lasten auf (*dat.*); **4.** ***bear hard on*** *j-m* sehr zusetzen, *j-n* bedrükken; **5.** ⚔ beschießen; **~ with** *v/i.* Nachsicht üben mit, Geduld haben mit;

Zssgn mit adv.:

bear| a·way I *v/t.* forttragen, -reißen (*a. fig.*); **II** *v/i.* ⚓ absegeln, abfahren; **~ down I** *v/t.* überˈwinden, überˈwältigen; **II** *v/i.*: ***~ on*** a) sich wenden gegen, sich stürzen auf (*acc.*), überwältigen (*acc.*), b) sich (schnell) nähern (*dat.*), zusteuern auf (*acc.*); **~ in** *v/t.*: ***it was borne in upon him*** es wurde ihm klar, es drängte sich ihm auf; **~ out** *v/t.* **1.** bestätigen, bekräftigen: ***bear s.o. out*** j-m recht geben; **2.** unterˈstützen; **~ up I** *v/t.* **1.** stützen, ermutigen; **II** *v/i.* **2.** (***against***) (tapfer) standhalten (*dat.*), die Stirn bieten (*dat.*), mutig ertragen (*acc.*), *weitS.* sich fabelhaft halten; **3.** *Brit.* Mut fassen: ***~!*** Kopf hoch!

bear² [beə] **I** *s.* **1.** *zo.* Bär *m*; **2.** *fig.* a) Bär *m*, Tolpatsch *m*, b) ‚Brummbär' *m*, Ekel *n*; **3.** ♆ ˈBaissespekuˌlant *m*, Baissiˈer *m*: ***~ market*** Baissemarkt *m*; **4.** *ast.*: ***Great(er)*** ♌ Großer Bär; ***Little*** *od.* ***Lesser*** ♌ Kleiner Bär; **II** *v/i.* **5.** ♆ auf Baisse spekulieren; **III** *v/t.* **6.** ♆ ***~ the market*** die Kurse drücken (wollen).

bear·a·ble [ˈbeərəbl] *adj.* □ tragbar, erträglich, zu ertragen(d).

ˈ**bear-bait·ing** *s. hist.* Bärenhetze *f*.

beard [bɪəd] **I** *s.* **1.** Bart *m* (*a. von Tieren*); → ***grow*** 6; **2.** ⚘ Grannen *pl.*; **3.** ⚙ ˈWiderhaken *m* (*an Pfeil, Angel etc.*); **II** *v/t.* **4.** *fig.* mutig entgegentreten, Trotz bieten (*dat.*): ***~ the lion in his den*** sich in die Höhle des Löwen wagen; ˈ**beard·ed** [-dɪd] *adj.* **1.** bärtig; **2.** ⚘ mit Grannen; **3.** ⚙ mit (e-m) ˈWiderhaken; ˈ**beard·less** [-lɪs] *adj.* **1.** bartlos; **2.** ⚘ ohne Grannen; **3.** *fig.* jugendlich, unreif.

bear·er [ˈbeərə] *s.* **1.** Träger(in); **2.** Überˈbringer(in) *e-s Briefes, Schecks etc.*; **3.** ♆ Inhaber(in) *e-s Wechsels etc.*: ***~ bond*** Inhaberobligation *f*; ***~ cheque*** (*Am.* ***check***) Inhaberscheck *m*; ***~ securities*** Inhaberpapiere; ***~ share*** (*od.* ***stock***) Inhaberaktie *f*; → ***payable*** 1; **4.** ⚘ ***a good ~*** ein Baum, der gut trägt; **5.** *her.* Schildhalter *m*.

bear| gar·den *s.* **1.** Bärenzwinger *m*; **2.** *fig.* ‚Tollhaus' *n*; **~ hug** *s.* F heftige Umˈarmung.

bear·ing [ˈbeərɪŋ] **I** *adj.* **1.** tragend; **2.** ⚗, *min.* ... enthaltend, ...haltig; **II** *s.* **3.** (Körper)Haltung *f*: ***of noble ~***; **4.** Betragen *n*, Verhalten *n*: ***his kindly ~***; **5.** (***on***) Bezug *m* (auf *acc.*), Beziehung *f* (zu), Verhältnis *n* (zu), Zs.-hang *m* (mit); Tragweite *f*, Bedeutung *f*: ***have no ~ on*** keinen Einfluß haben auf (*acc.*), nichts zu tun haben mit; ***consider it in all its ~s*** es in s-r ganzen Tragweite *od.* von allen Seiten betrachten; **6.** *pl.* ⚓, ✈, *surv.* Richtung *f*, Lage *f*; Peilung *f*; *fig.* Orientierung *f*: ***take the ~s*** die Richtung *od.* Lage feststellen, peilen; ***take one's ~s*** sich orientieren; ***find*** (*od.* ***get***) ***one's ~s*** sich zurechtfinden; ***lose one's ~s*** die Orientierung verlieren, *fig.* in Verlegenheit *od.* ‚ins Schwimmen' geraten; **7.** Ertragen *n*, Erdulden *n*, Nachsicht *f*: ***beyond (all) ~*** unerträglich; ***there is no ~ with such a fellow*** solch ein Kerl ist unerträglich; **8.** *mst pl.* ⚙ a) (Zapfen-, Achsen- *etc.*)Lager *n*, b) Stütze *f*; **9.** *pl. her.* → ***armorial*** I; **10.** (Früchte)Tragen *n*: ***beyond ~*** ⚘ nicht mehr tragend.

bear·ing| com·pass *s.* ⚓ ˈPeilˌkompaß *m*; **~ line** *s.* ⚓, ✈ ˈPeil-, Viˈsierˌlinie *f*; **~ met·al** *s.* ⚙ ˈLagermeˌtall *n*; **~ pin** *s.* ⚙ Lagerzapfen *m*.

bear·ish [ˈbeərɪʃ] *adj.* **1.** bärenhaft; **2.** *fig.* plump; brummig, unfreundlich; **3.** ♆ flau, Baisse...: ***~ operation*** Baissespekulation *f*.

bear lead·er *s. hist.* Bärenführer *m* (*a. fig. Reisebegleiter*).

ˈ**bear|·skin** *s.* **1.** Bärenfell *n*; **2.** ⚔ Bärenfellmütze *f*; ˈ**~·wood** *s.* ⚘ Kreuz-, Wegdorn *m*.

beast [bi:st] *s.* **1.** *bsd. vierfüßiges u. wildes* Tier: ***~ of burden*** Lasttier; ***~s of***

the forest Waldtiere; ***~ of prey*** Raubtier; ***the ~ in us*** *fig.* das Tier(ische) in uns; **2.** ⚘ Vieh *n* (*Rinder*), *bsd.* Mastvieh *n*; **3.** *fig.* a) bru'taler Mensch, Rohling *m*, 'Bestie *f*, b) ‚Biest' *n*, Ekel *n*;

beast·li·ness ['bi:stlɪnɪs] *s.* **1.** Brutali'tät *f*, Roheit *f*; **2.** F a) Scheußlichkeit *f*, b) Gemeinheit *f*; **beast·ly** ['bi:stlɪ] **I** *adj.* **1.** *fig.* viehisch, bru'tal, roh, gemein; **2.** F ab'scheulich, garstig, eklig, *Person*: *a.* ekelhaft, gemein; **II** *adv.* **3.** F scheußlich, ‚verdammt': ***it was ~ hot.***

beat [bi:t] **I** *s.* **1.** (*regelmäßig wiederholter*) Schlag; Herz-, Puls-, Trommelschlag *m*; Ticken *n* (*Uhr*); **2.** ♪ a) Takt (-schlag) *m*, b) *Jazz*: Beat *m*, 'rhythmischer Schwerpunkt, c) → ***beat music***; **3.** *Versmaß*: Hebung *f*; **4.** *phys.*, *Radio*: Schwebung *f*; **5.** Runde *f od.* Re'vier *n e-s Schutzmanns etc.*: ***be on one's ~*** die Runde machen; ***be off*** (*od.* ***out of***) ***one's ~*** *fig.* nicht in s-m Element sein; ***that is outside my ~*** *fig.* das schlägt nicht in mein Fach *od.* ist mir ungewohnt; **6.** *Am.* (Verwaltungs)Bezirk *m*; **7.** *Am.* F a) *wer od. was alles übertrifft*: ***I've never seen his ~*** der schlägt alles, was ich je gesehen habe, b) (sensatio'nelle) Erst- *od.* Al'leinmeldung *e-r Zeitung*, c) → ***deadbeat***, d) → ***beatnik***; **8.** *hunt.* Treibjagd *f*; **II** *adj.* **9.** F (wie) erschlagen: a) ‚ganz ka'putt', erschöpft, b) verblüfft; **10.** *Am. sl.* 'antikonfor,mistisch, illusi'onslos: ***the 2 Generation*** die Beat generation; **III** *v/t.* [*irr.*] **11.** (*regelmäßig od. häufig*) schlagen; *Teppich etc.* klopfen; *Metall* hämmern *od.* schmieden; *Eier*, *Sahne* (zu Schaum *od.* Schnee) schlagen; *Takt*, *Trommel* schlagen: ***~ a horse*** ein Pferd schlagen; ***~ a path*** e-n Weg (durch Stampfen *etc.*) bahnen; ***~ the wings*** mit den Flügeln schlagen; ***~ the air*** *fig.* vergebliche Versuche machen, gegen Windmühlen kämpfen; ***~ a charge*** *Am. sl.* e-r Strafe entgehen; ***~ s.th. into s.o.'s head*** j-m et. einbleuen; ***~ one's brains*** sich den Kopf zerbrechen; ***~ it*** *sl.* ‚abhauen', ‚verduften'; → ***retreat*** 1; **12.** *Gegner* schlagen, besiegen; über'treffen, -'bieten; zu'viel sein für *j-n*: ***~ s.o. at tennis*** j-n im Tennis schlagen; ***~ the record*** den Rekord brechen; ***to ~ the band*** (*Wendung*) mit aller Macht, wie toll; ***~ s.o. hollow*** j-n vernichtend schlagen; ***~ s.o. to it*** j-m zuvorkommen; ***that ~s me!*** F das ist mir zu hoch!, da komme ich nicht mit!; ***this poster takes some ~ing*** dieses Plakat ist schwer zu überbieten; ***that ~s everything!*** F a) das ist die Höhe!, b) ist ja sagenhaft!; ***can you ~ that!*** F das darf doch nicht wahr sein!; ***the journey ~ me*** die Reise hat mich völlig erschöpft; ***hock ~s claret*** Weißwein ist besser als Rotwein; **13.** *Wild* aufstöbern, treiben: ***~ the woods*** e-e Treibjagd *od.* Suche durch die Wälder veranstalten; **14.** schlagen, verprügeln, (ver)hauen; **15.** abgehen, ‚abklopfen', e-n Rundgang machen um; **IV** *v/i.* [*irr.*] **16.** schlagen (*a. Herz etc.*); ticken (*Uhr*): ***~ at*** (*od.* ***on***) ***the door*** (fest) an die Tür pochen; ***rain ~ on the windows*** der Regen schlug *od.* peitschte gegen die Fenster; ***the hot sun was ~ing down on us*** die heiße Sonne brannte auf uns nieder; **17.** *hunt.* treiben; → ***bush***[1] 1; **18.** ⚓ lavieren: ***~ against the wind*** gegen den Wind kreuzen;

Zssgn mit adv.:

beat| back *v/t.* zu'rückschlagen, -treiben, abwehren; ***~ down*** **I** *v/t.* **1.** *fig.* niederschlagen, unter'drücken; **2.** ✝ a) *den Preis* drücken, b) *j-n* her'unterhandeln (***to*** auf *acc.*); **II** *v/i.* **3.** a) her'unterbrennen (*Sonne*), b) niederprasseln (*Regen*); ***~ off*** *v/t.* *Angriff*, *Gegner* abschlagen, -wehren; ***~ out*** *v/t.* **1.** *Metall* (aus)schmieden, hämmern: ***~ s.o.'s brains*** j-m den Schädel einschlagen; **2.** *Feuer* ausschlagen; **3.** *fig. et.* ‚ausknobeln', her'ausarbeiten; **4.** F *j-n* ausstechen; ***~ up*** *v/t.* **1.** *Eier*, *Sahne* (zu Schaum *od.* Schnee) schlagen; **2.** ⚔ *Rekruten* werben; **3.** *j-n* zs.-schlagen, verprügeln; **4.** *fig.* aufrütteln; **5.** *et.* auftreiben.

beat·en ['bi:tn] *p.p. u. adj.* geschlagen; besiegt; erschöpft; ausgetreten, vielbegangen (*Weg*): ***~ gold*** Blattgold *n*; ***the ~ track*** *fig.* das ausgefahrene Geleise; ***off the ~ track*** a) abgelegen, b) *fig.* ungewohnt; ***~ biscuit*** *Am. ein* Blätterteiggebäck *n.*

beat·er ['bi:tə] *s.* **1.** Schläger *m*, Klopfer *m* (*Person od. Gerät*); Stößel *m*, Stampfe *f*; **2.** *hunt.* Treiber *m.*

be·a·tif·ic [,bi:ə'tɪfɪk] *adj.* **1.** glück'selig; **2.** seligmachend; **be·at·i·fi·ca·tion** [bi:,ætɪfɪ'keɪʃn] *s. eccl.* Seligsprechung *f*; **be·at·i·fy** [bi:'ætɪfaɪ] *v/t.* **1.** beseligen, selig machen; **2.** *eccl.* seligsprechen, beatifizieren.

beat·ing ['bi:tɪŋ] *s.* **1.** Schlagen *n* (*a. Herz*, *Flügel etc.*); **2.** Prügel *pl.*: ***give s.o. a good ~*** j-m e-e tüchtige Tracht Prügel verabreichen, *fig.* j-m e-e böse Schlappe bereiten; ***give the enemy a good ~*** den Feind aufs Haupt schlagen; ***take a ~*** Prügel beziehen, e-e Schlappe erleiden.

be·at·i·tude [bi:'ætɪtju:d] *s.* (Glück)'Seligkeit *f*: ***the 2s*** *bibl.* die Seligpreisungen.

beat mu·sic *s.* 'Beatmu,sik *f.*

beat·nik ['bi:tnɪk] *s. hist.* Beatnik *m*, junger 'Antikonfor,mist.

beau [bəʊ] *pl.* **beaus** *od.* **beaux** [bəʊz] (*Fr.*) *s. obs.* **1.** Beau *m*, Geck *m*; **2.** Liebhaber *m*, ‚Kava'lier' *m.*

beau i·de·al *s.* **1.** ('Schönheits)Ide,al *n*, Vorbild *n*; **2.** vollkommene Schönheit.

beaut [bju:t] *s. sl.* → ***beauty*** 3.

beau·te·ous ['bju:tjəs] *adj. mst poet.* (*äußerlich*) schön.

beau·ti·cian [bju:'tɪʃn] *s.* Kos'metiker (-in).

beau·ti·ful ['bju:təfʊl] **I** *adj.* □ **1.** schön: ***the ~ people*** F die ‚Schickeria'; **2.** wunderbar; **II** *s.* **3.** ***the ~*** das Schöne; die Schönen *pl.*; **'beau·ti·ful·ly** [-təflɪ] *adv.* F schön, wunderbar, ausgezeichnet: ***~ warm*** schön warm; **'beau·ti·fy** [-tɪfaɪ] *v/t.* verschönern, verzieren.

beau·ty ['bju:tɪ] *s.* **1.** Schönheit *f*; **2.** *das* Schön(st)e, *et.* Schönes: ***that is the ~ of it*** das ist das Schönste daran; **3.** a) Prachtstück *n*: ***a ~ of a vase*** ein Gedicht von e-r Vase, b) F ‚tolles Ding' schicke Sache: ***that goal was a ~!*** das Tor war Klasse!; **4.** Schönheit *f*, schöne Per'son (*mst Frau*; *a. Tier*): ***~ queen*** Schönheitskönigin *f*; **5.** *iro.*: ***you are a ~!*** du bist mir ein Schöner *od.* ein Schlimmer!; ***~ con·test*** *s.* Schönheitswettbewerb *m*; ***~ par·lo(u)r***, ***~ sa·lon***, ***~ shop*** *s.* 'Schönheitssa,lon *m*; ***~ sleep*** *s.* Schlaf *m* vor Mitternacht; ***~ spot*** *s.* **1.** Schönheitspflästerchen *n*; **2.** schönes Fleckchen Erde, lohnendes Ausflugsziel.

beaux *pl. von* ***beau.***

bea·ver[1] ['bi:və] **I** *s.* **1.** *zo.* Biber *m*: ***work like a ~*** → 5; **2.** Biberpelz *m*; **3.** ✝ Biber *m* (*filziger Wollstoff*); **4.** *sl.* a) Bart(träger) *m*, b) *Am.* ‚Muschi' *f*; **II** *v/i.* **5.** *mst* ***~ away*** (schwer) schuften.

bea·ver[2] ['bi:və] *s.* ⚔ *hist.* Vi'sier *n*, Helmsturz *m.*

be·bop ['bi:bɒp] *s.* ♪ Bebop *m* (*Jazz*).

be·calm [bɪ'kɑ:m] *v/t.* **1.** beruhigen; **2.** ***be ~ed*** ⚓ in e-e Flaute geraten.

be·came [bɪ'keɪm] *pret. von* ***become.***

be·cause [bɪ'kɒz] **I** *cj.* weil, da; **II** ***~ of*** *prp.* wegen (*gen.*), in'folge von (*od. gen.*).

bêche-de-mer [,beɪʃdə'meə] (*Fr.*) *s. zo.* eßbare Seewalze, 'Trepang *m.*

beck[1] [bek] *s.* Wink *m*, Nicken *n*: ***be at s.o.'s ~ and call*** j-m auf den (leisesten) Wink gehorchen, nach j-s Pfeife tanzen.

beck[2] [bek] *s. Brit.* (Wild)Bach *m.*

beck·on ['bekən] **I** *v/t.* *j-m* (zu)winken, zunicken, *j-n* her'anwinken, *j-m* ein Zeichen geben; **II** *v/i.* winken, *fig. a.* locken.

be·cloud [bɪ'klaʊd] *v/t.* um'wölken, verdunkeln, *fig. a.* vernebeln.

be·come [bɪ'kʌm] [*irr.* → ***come***] **I** *v/i.* **1.** werden: ***~ an actor***, ***~ warmer***, ***what has ~ of him?*** a) was ist aus ihm geworden?, b) F wo steckt er nur?; **II** *v/t.* **2.** sich schicken für, sich (ge)ziemen für: ***it does not ~ you***; **3.** *j-m* stehen, passen zu, *j-n* kleiden (*Hut etc.*); **be'com·ing** [-mɪŋ] *adj.* □ **1.** schicklich, geziemend, anständig; **2.** kleidsam.

bed [bed] **I** *s.* **1.** Bett *n*: ***~ and breakfast*** Übernachtung *f* mit Frühstück; ***his life is no ~ of roses*** er ist nicht auf Rosen gebettet; ***marriage is not always a ~ of roses*** die Ehe hat nicht nur angenehme Seiten; ***die in one's ~*** e-s natürlichen Todes sterben; ***get out of ~ on the wrong side*** mit dem verkehrten *od.* linken Fuß zuerst aufstehen; ***go to ~*** zu Bett *od.* schlafen gehen; ***keep one's ~*** das Bett hüten; ***make the ~*** das Bett machen; ***as you make your ~, so you must lie upon it*** wie man sich bettet, so schläft man; ***put to ~*** *j-n* zu Bett bringen; ***take to one's ~*** sich (krank) ins Bett legen; **2.** Federbett *n*; **3.** Ehebett *n*: ***~ and board*** Tisch *m* u. Bett (*Ehe*); **4.** Lager(statt *f*) *n* (*a. e-s Tieres*): ***~ of straw*** Strohlager; **5.** *fig.* letzte Ruhestätte; **6.** 'Unterkunft *f*: ***~ and breakfast*** Zimmer *n* mit Frühstück; **7.** (Fluß- *etc.*)Bett *n*; **8.** ⚘ Beet *n*; **9.** ⚙, △ Bett *n* (*a. e-r Werkzeugmaschine*), Bettung *f*, 'Unterlage *f*, Schicht *f*: ***~ of concrete*** Betonunterlage *f*; **10.** *geol.*, ⚒ Bett *n*, Schicht *f*, Lage *f*, Lager *n*, Flöz *n* (*Kohle*); **11.** 🚂 'Unterbau *m*; **II** *v/t.* **12.** zu Bett bringen; **13.** ***be bedded*** bettlägerig sein; **14.** *mst* ***~ down*** a) *j-m* das Bett machen, b) *j-n* für die Nacht 'unterbringen, d) *Pferd etc.* mit Streu versorgen; **15.** *mst* ***~ out*** in ein

Beet pflanzen, auspflanzen; **III** *v/i.* **16.** *a.* ~ ***down*** a) ins *od.* zu Bett gehen, b) sein Nachtlager aufschlagen; **17.** (sich ein)nisten (*a. fig.*).

be·dad [bɪ'dæd] *int. Ir.* bei Gott!

be·daub [bɪ'dɔ:b] *v/t.* beschmieren.

be·daz·zle [bɪ'dæzl] *v/t.* blenden.

'bed|·bug *s. zo.* Wanze *f*; ~ **bun·ny** *s.* F ‚Betthäschen' *n*; '~ˌ**cham·ber** *s.* (königliches) Schlafgemach: ***Gentleman*** *od.* ***Groom of the*** ♀ königlicher Kammerherr; ***Lady of the*** ♀ königliche Kammerzofe; '~**·clothes** *s. pl.* Bettwäsche *f*.

bed·ding ['bedɪŋ] **I** *s.* **1.** Bettzeug *n*, Bett *n* u. 'Zubehör *n*, *m*; **2.** (Lager-)Streu *f für Tiere*; **3.** ⚙ Bettung *f*, 'Unterschicht *f*, -lage *f*, Lager *n*; **II** *adj.* **4.** ~ ***plants*** Beetpflanzen (*Blumen etc.*).

be·deck [bɪ'dek] *v/t.* (ver)zieren, schmücken.

be·del(l) [be'del] *s. Brit. univ.* Herold *m*.

be·dev·il [bɪ'devl] *v/t. fig.* **1.** *fig.* verhexen; **2.** a) plagen, peinigen, b) bedrükken, belasten; **3.** *fig.* verwirren, durchein'anderbringen.

be·dew [bɪ'dju:] *v/t.* betauen, benetzen.

'bed|·fast *adj.* bettlägerig; '~ˌ**fel·low** *s.* **1.** 'Schlafkameˌrad *m*, Bettgenosse *m*; **2.** *fig.* Genosse *m*; '~**·gown** *s.* (Frauen)Nachthemd *n*.

be·dim [bɪ'dɪm] *v/t.* trüben.

be·diz·en [bɪ'daɪzn] *v/t.* (über'trieben) her'ausputzen.

bed·lam ['bedləm] *s. fig.* Tollhaus *n*: ***cause a*** ~ e-n Tumult auslösen; '**bed·lam·ite** [-maɪt] *s. obs.* Irre(r *m*) *f*.

Bed·ou·in ['bedʊɪn] **I** *s.* Bedu'ine *m*; **II** *adj.* Beduinen…

'bed|·pan *s.* ⚕ Stechbecken *n*, Bettschüssel *f*; '~**·plate** *s.* ⚙ 'Unterlagsplatte *f*, -gestell *n od.* -rahmen *m*; '~**·post** *s.* Bettpfosten *m*: ***between you and me and the*** ~ F unter uns *od.* im Vertrauen (gesagt).

be·drag·gled [bɪ'drægld] *adj.* **1.** a) verdreckt, b) durch'näßt; **2.** *fig.* verwahrlost.

'bed|ˌrid·den *adj.* bettlägerig; '~**·rock I** *s.* **1.** *geol.* unterste Felsschicht, Grundgestein *n*; **2.** (*mst fig.*) Grundlage *f*: ***get down to*** ~ der Sache auf den Grund gehen; **3.** *fig.* Tiefpunkt *m*; **II** *adj.* **4.** F a) grundlegend, b) (felsen)fest, c) ✝ äußerst, niedrigst: ~ ***price***; '~**·roll** *s.* zs.-gerolltes Bettzeug; '~**·room** [-rʊm] *s.* Schlafzimmer *n*: ~ ***eyes*** F ‚Schlafzimmeraugen'; ~ ***suburb*** Schlafstadt *f*; '~-**setˌtee** *s.* Schlafcouch *f*; '~**-sheet** *s.* Bettlaken *n*.

'bed·side *s.*: ***at the*** ~ am (Kranken-)Bett; ***good*** ~ ***manner*** gute Art, mit Kranken umzugehen; ~ **lamp** *s.* Nachttischlampe *f*; ~ **read·ing** *s.* 'Bettlekˌtüre *f*; ~ **rug** *s.* Bettvorleger *m*; ~ **stor·y** *s.* Gutenachtgeschichte *f*; ~ **ta·ble** *s.* Nachttisch *m*.

'bed|-sit *Brit.* **I** *v/i.* [*irr.*] ein möbliertes Zimmer bewohnen; **II** *s.* → '~-ˌ**sit·ter** *s.*, '~-ˌ**sit·ting·room** *s. Brit.* **1.** möbliertes Zimmer; **2.** Ein'zimmerapparteˌment *n*; '~**·sore** *s.* ⚕ wundgelegene Stelle; '~**·space** *s.* (An)Zahl *f* der Betten (*in Klinik etc.*); '~**·spread** *s.* (Zier-)Bettdecke *f*; Tagesdecke *f*; '~**·stead** *s.* Bettstelle *f*, -gestell *n*; '~**·straw** *s.* ⚘ Labkraut *n*; '~**·tick** *s.* Inlett *n*; '~**·time** *s.* Schlafenszeit *f*; '~-ˌ**wet·ting** *s.* Bettnässen *n*.

bee[1] [bi:] *s.* **1.** *zo.* Biene *f*: ***have a*** ~ ***in one's bonnet*** F ‚e-n Vogel haben'; **2.** *fig.* Biene *f*, fleißiger Mensch; → ***busy*** 2; **3.** *bsd. Am.* a) Treffen *n von Freunden* zur Gemeinschaftshilfe *od.* Unter'haltung: ***sewing*** ~ Nähkränzchen *n*, b) Wettbewerb *m*.

bee[2] [bi:] *s.* B, b *n* (*Buchstabe*).

Beeb [bi:b] *s.*: ***the*** ~ *Brit.* F die BB'C.

beech [bi:tʃ] *s.* ⚘ Buche *f*; Buchenholz *n*; **beech·en** ['bi:tʃən] *adj.* aus Buchenholz, Buchen…

beech| mar·ten *s. zo.* Steinmarder *m*; '~**·mast** *s.* Bucheckern *pl.*; '~**·nut** *s.* Buchecker *f*.

beef [bi:f] *pl.* **beeves** [bi:vz], *a.* **beefs I** *s.* **1.** Mastrind *n*, -ochse *m*, -bulle *m*; **2.** Rindfleisch *n*; **3.** F a) Fleisch *n* (*am Menschen*), b) (Muskel)Kraft *f*; **4.** *sl.* ‚Mecke'rei' *f*, Beschwerde *f*; **5.** *Am. sl.* ‚dufte Puppe'; **II** *v/i.* **6.** *sl.* nörgeln, ‚meckern', sich beschweren; **III** *v/t.* **7.** ~ ***up*** F *et.* ‚aufmöbeln'; '~**·cake** *s. Am. sl.* Bild *n* e-s Muskelprotzen; '~ˌ**eat·er** *s. Brit.* Beefeater *m*, Tower-Wächter *m* (*in London*); ˌ~'**steak** *s.* 'Beefsteak *n*; ~ **tea** *s.* (Rind)Fleisch-, Kraftbrühe *f*, Bouil'lon *f*.

beef·y ['bi:fɪ] *adj.* **1.** fleischig; **2.** F bullig, kräftig.

'bee|·hive *s.* **1.** Bienenstock *m*, -korb *m*; **2.** *fig.* ‚Taubenschlag' *m*; '~ˌ**keep·er** *s.* Bienenzüchter *m*, Imker *m*; '~ˌ**keep·ing** *s.* Bienenzucht *f*, Imke'rei *f*; '~**·line** *s.*: ***make a*** ~ ***for*** schnurgerade auf *et.* losgehen.

Be·el·ze·bub [bi:'elzɪbʌb] **I** *npr.* Be'elzebub *m*; **II** *s.* Teufel *m*.

'bee-ˌmas·ter *s.* → ***beekeeper***.

been [bi:n; bɪn] *p.p. von* ***be***.

beep [bi:p] *s.* **1.** ϟ Piepton *m*; **2.** *mot.* 'Hupsigˌnal *n*.

beer [bɪə] *s.* **1.** Bier *n*: ***two*** ~***s*** zwei Glas Bier; ***life is not all*** ~ ***and skittles*** *Brit.* F das Leben besteht nicht nur aus Vergnügen; → ***small beer***; **2.** bierähnliches Getränk (*aus Pflanzen*); ~ **can** *s.* Bierdose *f*; '~-ˌ**en·gine** *s.* 'Bierˌdruckappaˌrat *m*; '~-ˌ**gar·den** *s.* Biergarten *m*; '~**·house** *s. Brit.* Bierschenke *f*; '~**-mat** *s.* Bierfilz *m*, -deckel *m*; '~**-pull** *s.* (Griff *m* der) Bierpumpe *f*.

beer·y ['bɪərɪ] *adj.* **1.** bierartig; **2.** bierselig; **3.** nach Bier riechend.

beest·ings ['bi:stɪŋz] *s.* Biestmilch *f* (*erste Milch nach dem Kalben*).

bees·wax ['bi:zwæks] *s.* Bienenwachs *n*.

beet [bi:t] *s.* ⚘ **1.** Runkelrübe *f*, Mangold *m*, Bete *f*: ~ ***greens*** Mangoldgemüse *n*; **2.** *Am.* rote Bete.

bee·tle[1] ['bi:tl] *s. zo.* Käfer *m*; → ***blind*** 1.

bee·tle[2] ['bi:tl] **I** *s.* **1.** Holzhammer *m*, Schlegel *m*; **2.** ⚙ a) Erdstampfe *f*, b) 'Stampfkaˌlander *m*; **II** *v/t.* **3.** mit e-m Schlegel bearbeiten, (ein)stampfen; **4.** ⚙ ka'landern.

bee·tle[3] ['bi:tl] **I** *adj.* 'überhängend; **II** *v/i.* vorstehen, 'überhängen.

'bee·tle|-browed *adj.* **1.** mit buschigen Augenbrauen; **2.** finster blickend; '~ˌ**crush·ers** *s. pl.* ‚Elbkähne' *pl.* (*riesige Schuhe*).

'beet|·root *s.* ⚘ **1.** *Brit.* Wurzel *f* der roten Bete; **2.** *Am.* → ***beet*** 1; ~ **sug·ar** *s.* ⚘ Rübenzucker *m*.

beeves [bi:vz] *pl. von* ***beef***.

be·fall [bɪ'fɔ:l] [*irr.* → ***fall***] *obs. od. poet.* **I** *v/i.* sich ereignen; **II** *v/t.* zustoßen, wider'fahren (*dat.*).

be·fit [bɪfɪt] *v/t.* sich ziemen *od.* schicken für; **be'fit·ting** [-tɪŋ] *adj.* ☐ geziemend, schicklich.

be·fog [bɪ'fɒg] *v/t.* **1.** in Nebel hüllen; **2.** *fig.* a) um'nebeln, b) verwirren.

be·fool [bɪ'fu:l] *v/t.* zum Narren haben, täuschen.

be·fore [bɪfɔ:] **I** *prp.* **1.** *räumlich*: vor: ***he sat*** ~ ***me***; ~ ***my eyes***; ***the question*** ~ ***us*** die (uns) vorliegende Frage; **2.** vor, in Gegenwart von: ~ ***witnesses***; **3.** *Reihenfolge*, *Rang*: vor'aus: ***be*** ~ ***the others in class*** den anderen in der Klasse voraus sein; **4.** *zeitlich*: vor, früher als: ~ ***lunch*** vor dem Mittagessen; ***an hour*** ~ ***the time*** e-e Stunde früher *od.* zu früh; ~ ***long*** in Kürze, bald; ~ ***now*** schon früher *od.* vorher; ***the day*** ~ ***yesterday*** vorgestern; ***the month*** ~ ***last*** vorletzten Monat; ***to be*** ~ ***one's time*** s-r Zeit voraus sein; **II** *cj.* **5.** be'vor, ehe: ***he died*** ~ ***I was born***; ***not*** ~ nicht früher *od.* eher als bis, erst als *od.* wenn; **6.** lieber … als daß: ***I would die*** ~ ***I lied***; **III** *adv.* **7.** *räumlich*: vorn, vo'ran: ***go*** ~ vorangehen; ~ ***and behind*** vorn u. hinten; **8.** *zeitlich*: 'vorher, vormals, früher, zu'vor; (schon) früher: ***the year*** ~ das vorige *od.* vorhergehende Jahr, das Jahr zuvor; ***an hour*** ~ e-e Stunde vorher *od.* früher *od.* zuvor; ***long*** ~ lange vorher; ***never*** ~ noch nie (-mals), nie zuvor; **be'fore·hand** *adv.* zu'vor, (im) voraus: ***know s.th.*** ~ et. im voraus wissen; ***be*** ~ ***in one's suspicions*** zu früh e-n Verdacht äußern; **be'fore-ˌmen·tioned** *adj.* vorerwähnt; **be'fore-tax** *adj.* ✝ vor Abzug der Steuern, Brutto…

be·foul [bɪ'faʊl] *v/t.* besudeln, beschmutzen (*a. fig.*).

be·friend [bɪ'frend] *v/t.* *j-m* Freundschaft erweisen; *j-m* behilflich sein, sich *j-s* annehmen.

be·fud·dle [bɪ'fʌdl] *v/t.* ‚benebeln', berauschen.

beg [beg] **I** *v/t.* **1.** *et.* erbitten (***of s.o.*** von j-m), bitten um: ***to*** ~ ***leave*** um Erlaubnis bitten; → ***pardon*** 4; **2.** betteln *od.* bitten um: ***to*** ~ ***a meal***; **3.** *j-n* bitten (***to do s.th.*** et. zu tun); **II** *v/i.* **4.** betteln: ***go*** ~***ging*** a) betteln (gehen), b) keinen Interessenten finden; **5.** (dringend) bitten (***for*** um, ***of s.o. to*** *inf.* j-n zu *inf.*): ~ ***off*** sich entschuldigen, absagen; **6.** sich erlauben: ***I*** ~ ***to differ*** ich erlaube mir, anderer Meinung zu sein; ***I*** ~ ***to inform you*** ✝ *obs.* ich erlaube mir, Ihnen mitzuteilen; **7.** schönmachen, Männchen machen (*Hund*); **8.** → ***question*** 1.

be·gad [bɪ'gæd] *int.* F bei Gott!

be·gan [bɪ'gæn] *pret. von* ***begin***.

be·gat [bɪ'gæt] *obs. pret. von* ***beget***.

be·get [bɪ'get] *v/t.* [*irr.*] **1.** zeugen; **2.** *fig.* erzeugen, her'vorbringen; **be'get·ter** [-tə] *s.* **1.** Erzeuger *m*, Vater *m*; **2.** *fig.* Urheber *m*.

beg·gar ['begə] **I** *s.* **1.** Bettler(in); Arme(r *m*) *f*: ~***s must not be choosers*** arme Leute dürfen nicht wählerisch sein; **2.** F Kerl *m*, Bursche *m*: ***lucky ~*** Glückspilz *m*; ***a naughty little ~*** ein kleiner Schelm; **II** *v/t.* **3.** an den Bettelstab bringen; **4.** *fig.* erschöpfen; über'steigen: ***it ~s description*** a) es spottet jeder Beschreibung, b) es läßt sich nicht mit Worten beschreiben; **'beg·gar·ly** [-lɪ] *adj.* **1.** (sehr) arm; **2.** *fig.* armselig, lumpig; **ˌbeg·gar-my-'neigh·bo(u)r** [-mɪ-] *s.* Bettelmann *m* (*Kartenspiel*); **'beg·gar·y** [-ərɪ] *s.* Bettelarmut *f*: ***reduce to ~*** an den Bettelstab bringen.

be·gin [bɪ'gɪn] [*irr.*] **I** *v/t.* **1.** beginnen, anfangen: ***to ~ a new book***; **2.** (be-)gründen; **II** *v/i.* **3.** beginnen, anfangen: ***~ with s.o.*** *od.* ***s.th*** mit *od.* bei j-m *od.* et. anfangen; ***to ~ with*** (*Wendung*) a) zunächst, b) erstens (einmal); ***~ on s.th.*** et. in Angriff nehmen; ***he began by asking*** zuerst fragte er; ***... began to be put into practice*** ... wurde bald in die Praxis umgesetzt; ***he does not even ~ to try*** er versucht es nicht einmal; ***it doesn't ~ to do him justice*** F es wird ihm nicht annähernd gerecht; **4.** entstehen; **be'gin·ner** [-nə] *s.* Anfänger(in), Neuling *m*: ***~'s luck*** Anfängerglück *n*; **be'gin·ning** [-nɪŋ] *s.* **1.** Anfang *m*, Beginn *m*: ***from the*** (***very***) ***~*** (ganz) von Anfang an; ***the ~ of the end*** der Anfang vom Ende; **2.** Ursprung *m*; **3.** *pl.* a) Anfangsgründe *pl.*, b) Anfänge *pl.*

be·gone [bɪ'gɒn] *int.* fort (mit dir)!

be·go·ni·a [bɪ'gəʊnjə] *s.* Be'gonie *f.*

be·got [bɪ'gɒt] *pret. von* ***beget.***

be·got·ten [bɪ'gɒtn] *p.p. von* ***beget***: ***God's only ~ son*** Gottes eingeborener Sohn.

be·grime [bɪ'graɪm] *v/t.* (*mit Ruß, Rauch etc.*) beschmutzen.

be·grudge [bɪ'grʌdʒ] *v/t.* **1.** ***~ s.o. s.th.*** j-m et. mißgönnen; **2.** *et.* nur ungern geben.

be·guile [bɪ'gaɪl] *v/t.* **1.** täuschen; betrügen (***of*** *od.* ***out of*** um); **2.** verleiten (***into doing*** zu tun); **3.** *Zeit* (angenehm) vertreiben; **4.** betören; **be'guil·ing** [-lɪŋ] *adj.* □ verführerisch, betörend.

be·gun [bɪ'gʌn] *p.p. von* ***begin.***

be·half [bɪ'hɑːf] *s.*: ***on*** (*od.* ***in***) ***~ of*** zugunsten *od.* im Namen *od.* im Auftrag von (*od. gen*), für *j-n*; ***on*** (*od.* ***in***) ***my ~*** zu m-n Gunsten, für mich; ***act on one's own ~*** im eigenen Namen handeln.

be·have [bɪ'heɪv] **I** *v/i.* **1.** sich (gut) benehmen, sich zu benehmen wissen: ***please ~!*** bitte benimm dich!; ***he doesn't know how to ~, he can't ~*** er kann sich nicht (anständig) benehmen; **2.** sich verhalten; funktionieren (*Maschine etc.*); **II** *v/t.* **3.** ***~ o.s.*** sich (gut) benehmen: ***~ yourself!*** beninmm dich!; **be'haved** [-vd] *adj.*: ***he is well-~*** er hat ein gutes Benehmen.

be·hav·io(u)r [bɪ'heɪvjə] *s.* Benehmen *n*, Betragen *n*; Verhalten *n* (*a.* ⚒, ⚙, *phys.*): ***~ pattern*** *psych.* Verhaltensmuster *n*; ***~ therapy*** *psych.* Verhaltenstherapie *f*; ***during good ~*** *Am.* auf Lebenszeit (*Ernennung*); ***be in office on one's good ~*** ein Amt auf Bewährung innehaben; ***be on one's best ~*** sich von seiner besten Seite zeigen; ***put s.o. on his good ~*** j-m einschärfen, sich gut zu benehmen; **be'hav·io(u)r·al** [-ərəl] *adj. psych.* Verhaltens...: ***~ science*** Verhaltensforschung *f*; **be'hav·io(u)r·ism** [-ərɪzəm] *s. psych.* Behavio'rismus *m*.

be·head [bɪ'hed] *v/t.* enthaupten.

be·held [bɪ'held] *pret. u. p.p. von* ***behold.***

be·he·moth [bɪ'hiːmɒθ] **1.** *Bibl.* Behemoth; **2.** *fig.* Ko'loß *m*, Ungeheuer *n*.

be·hest [bɪ'hest] *s. poet.* Geheiß *n*: ***at s.o.'s ~*** auf j-s Geheiß *od.* Befehl *od.* Veranlassung.

be·hind [bɪ'haɪnd] **I** *prp.* **1.** hinter: ***~ the tree*** hinter dem *od.* den Baum; ***he looked ~ him*** er blickte hinter sich; ***be ~ s.o.*** a) hinter j-m stehen, j-n unterstützen, b) j-m nachstehen, hinter j-m zurück sein; ***what is ~ all this?*** was steckt dahinter?; **II** *adv.* **2.** hinten, da'hinter, hinter'her: ***walk ~*** hinterhergehen; **3.** nach hinten, zu'rück: ***to look ~*** zurückblicken; **4.** zu'rück, im Rückstand: ***~ with one's work*** mit s-r Arbeit im Rückstand; ***my watch is ~*** meine Uhr geht nach; → ***time*** 7; **5.** *fig.* da'hinter, verborgen: ***there is more ~*** da steckt (noch) mehr dahinter; **III** *s.* **6.** F ‚Hintern' *m*, Gesäß *n*; **be'hind·hand** *adv. u. pred. adj.* **1.** → ***behind*** 4; **2.** *fig.* rückständig; altmodisch.

be·hold [bɪ'həʊld] **I** *v/t.* [*irr.* → ***hold***] erblicken, anschauen; **II** *int.* siehe da!; **be'hold·en** [-dən] *adj.* verpflichtet, dankbar (***to*** *dat.*); **be'hold·er** [-də] *s.* Beschauer(in), Betrachter(in).

be·hoof [bɪ'huːf] *s. lit.*: ***in*** (*od.* ***to, for, on***) (***the***) ***~ of*** um ... willen; ***on her ~*** zu ihren Gunsten.

be·hoove [bɪ'huːv] *Am.*, **be'hove** [-'həʊv] *Brit. v/t. impers.*: ***it ~s you*** (***to*** *inf.*), a) es obliegt dir *od.* ist deine Pflicht (zu *inf.*), b) es gehört sich für dich (zu *inf.*).

beige [beɪʒ] **I** *s.* Beige *f* (*Wollstoff*); **II** *adj.* beige(farben).

be·ing ['biːɪŋ] *s.* **1.** (Da)Sein *n*: ***in ~*** existierend, wirklich (vorhanden); ***come into ~*** entstehen; ***call into ~*** ins Leben rufen; **2.** *j-s* Wesen *n od.* Sein, Na'tur *f*; **3.** Wesen *n*; Geschöpf *n*: ***living ~*** Lebewesen.

be·la·bo(u)r [bɪ'leɪbə] *v/t.* **1.** (mit den Fäusten *etc.*) bearbeiten, 'durchprügeln; **2.** *fig. j-n* ‚bearbeiten', *j-m* zusetzen.

be·lat·ed [bɪ'leɪtɪd] *adj.* **1.** verspätet; **2.** von der Nacht über'rascht.

be·laud [bɪ'lɔːd] *v/t.* preisen.

be·lay [bɪ'leɪ] *v/t.* [*irr.* → ***lay***] **1.** ⚓ festmachen, *Tau* belegen; **2.** *mount. j-n* sichern.

belch [beltʃ] **I** *v/i.* **1.** aufstoßen, rülpsen; **II** *v/t.* **2.** *Rauch etc.* ausspeien; **III** *s.* **3.** Rülpsen *n*; **4.** *fig.* Ausbruch *m* (*Rauch etc.*).

bel·dam(e) ['beldəm] *s. obs.* Ahnfrau *f*; alte Frau; Vettel *f*, Hexe *f*.

be·lea·guer [bɪ'liːgə] *v/t.* **1.** belagern (*a. fig.*); **2.** *fig.* a) heimsuchen, b) um'geben.

bel es·prit [ˌbel es'priː] *pl.* **beaux es·prits** [ˌbəʊz es'priː] (*Fr.*) *s.* Schöngeist *m*.

bel·fry ['belfrɪ] *s.* **1.** Glockenturm *m*; → ***bat***[2] 1; **2.** Glockenstuhl *m*.

Bel·gian ['beldʒən] **I** *adj.* belgisch; **II** *s.* Belgier(in).

be·lie [bɪ'laɪ] *v/t.* **1.** Lügen erzählen über (*acc.*), *et.* falsch darstellen; **2.** *j-n od. et.* Lügen strafen; **3.** wider'sprechen (*dat.*); **4.** hin'wegtäuschen über (*acc.*); **5.** *Hoffnung etc.* enttäuschen, *e-r Sache* nicht entsprechen.

be·lief [bɪ'liːf] *s.* **1.** *eccl.* Glaube *m*, Religi'on *f*: ***the ~*** das apostolische Glaubensbekenntnis; **2.** (***in***) a) Glaube *m* (an *acc.*): ***beyond ~*** unglaublich, b) Vertrauen *n* (auf *et. od.* zu *j-m*); **3.** Meinung *f*, Anschauung *f*, Über'zeugung *f*: ***to the best of my ~*** nach bestem Wissen u. Gewissen.

be·liev·a·ble [bɪ'liːvəbl] *adj.* glaubhaft;

be·lieve [bɪ'liːv] **I** *v/i.* **1.** glauben (***in*** an *acc.*); **2.** (***in***) Vertrauen haben (zu), viel halten (von): ***I do not ~ in sports*** F ich halte nicht viel von Sport; **II** *v/t.* **3.** glauben, meinen, denken: ***~ it or not*** ob Sie es glauben *od.* nicht!, ganz sicher; ***do not ~ it*** glaube es nicht; ***would you ~ it!*** nicht zu glauben!; ***he is ~d to be a miser*** man hält ihn für e-n Geizhals; **4.** Glauben schenken, glauben (*dat.*): ***~ me*** glaube mir; ***not to ~ one's eyes*** s-n Augen nicht trauen; **be'liev·er** [-və] *s.* **1.** ***be a great*** *od.* ***firm ~ in*** fest glauben an (*acc.*), viel halten von; **2.** *eccl.* Gläubige(r *m*) *f*: ***a true ~*** ein Rechtgläubiger; **be'liev·ing** [-vɪŋ] *adj.* □ gläubig: ***a ~ Christian.***

Be·lish·a bea·con [bɪ'liːʃə] *s. Brit.* (gelbes) Blinklicht *n* an 'Fußgängerˌüberwegen.

be·lit·tle [bɪ'lɪtl] *v/t.* **1.** verkleinern; **2.** her'absetzen, schmälern; **3.** herabsetzen, schmähen; **4.** verharmlosen.

bell[1] [bel] **I** *s.* **1.** Glocke *f*, Klingel *f*, Schelle *f*: ***carry away*** (*od.* ***bear***) ***the ~*** Sieger sein; ***does that name ring a*** (*od.* ***the***) ***~?*** erinnert dich der Name an et.?; ***the ~ has rung*** es hat geklingelt; → ***clear*** 5, ***sound***[1] 1; **2.** *pl.* ⚓ (halbstündige Schläge *pl.* der) Schiffsglocke *f*; **3.** Taucherglocke *f*; **4.** ⚘ glockenförmige Blumenkrone, Kelch *m*; **5.** △ Glocke *f*, Kelch *m* (*am Kapitell*); **II** *v/t.* **6.** ***~ the cat*** *fig.* der Katze die Schelle umhängen.

bell[2] [bel] *v/i.* röhren (*Hirsch*).

bel·la·don·na [ˌbelə'dɒnə] *s.* ⚘ Bella'donna *f* (*a. pharm.*), Tollkirsche *f*.

'bell|-ˌbot·tomed *adj.* unten weit ausladend: ***~ trousers***; **'~·boy** *s. Am.* Ho'telpage *m*; **~ buoy** *s.* ⚓ Glockenboje *f*; **~ but·ton** *s.* ⚡ Klingelknopf *m*.

belle [bel] (*Fr.*) *s.* Schöne *f*, Schönheit *f*: ***~ of the ball*** Ballkönigin *f*.

belles-let·tres [ˌbel'letrə] (*Fr.*) *s. pl. sg. konstr.* Belle'tristik *f*, Unter'haltungslitera̩tur *f*.

'bell|ˌflow·er *s.* ⚘ Glockenblume *f*; **~ found·ry** *s.* Glockengieße'rei *f*; **~ glass** *s.* Glasglocke *f*; **'~·hop** *s. Am.* Ho'telpage *m*.

bel·li·cose ['belɪkəʊs] *adj.* □ kriegslustig, kriegerisch; **bel·li·cos·i·ty** [ˌbelɪ'kɒsətɪ] *s.* **1.** Kriegslust *f*; **2.** → ***belligerence*** 2.

bel·lied ['belɪd] *adj.* bauchig; *in Zssgn* ...bauchig, ...bäuchig.

bel·lig·er·ence [bɪ'lɪdʒərəns] *s.* **1.** Kriegführung *f*; **2.** Kampfeslust *f*, Streitsucht *f*; **bel'lig·er·en·cy** [-rənsɪ] *s.* **1.** Kriegszustand *m*; **2.** → ***belligerence***; **bel'lig·er·ent** [-nt] **I** *adj.* □ **1.** kriegführend: ***the ~ powers***; ***~ rights*** Rechte der Kriegführenden; **2.** *fig.* streitlustig; **II** *s.* **3.** kriegführender Staat.

bell| lap *s. sport* letzte Runde; **'~·man** [-mən] *s.* [*irr.*] öffentlicher Ausrufer; **~ met·al** *s.* ⚙ 'Glockenme,tall *n*, -speise *f*; **'~-mouthed** *adj.* (*a.* ⚔) mit trichterförmiger Öffnung.

bel·low ['beləʊ] **I** *v/t. u. v/i.* brüllen; **II** *s.* Gebrüll *n*.

bel·lows ['beləʊz] *s. pl.* (*a. sg. konstr.*) **1.** ⚙ a) Gebläse *n*, b) *a.* ***pair of ~*** Blasebalg *m*; **2.** Lunge *f*; **3.** *phot.* Balg *m*.

bell| pull *s.* Klingelzug *m*; **~ push** *s.* Klingelknopf *m*; **~ ring·er** *s.* Glöckner *m*; **~ rope** *s.* **1.** Glockenstrang *m*; **2.** Klingelzug *m*; **'~-shaped** *adj.* glockenförmig; **~ tent** *s.* Rundzelt *n*; **'~,weth·er** *s.* Leithammel *m* (*a. fig.*, *mst contp.*).

bel·ly ['belı] **I** *s.* **1.** Bauch *m* (*a. fig.*); 'Unterleib *m*: ***go ~ up*** → 8; **2.** Magen *m*; **3.** *fig.* a) Appe'tit *m*, b) Schlemme'rei *f*; **4.** Bauch *m*, Ausbauchung *f*, Höhlung *f*; **5.** 'Unterseite *f*; **6.** ♪ Reso'nanzboden *m*; Decke *f* (*Saiteninstrument*); **II** *v/i.* **7.** sich (aus)bauchen, (an)schwellen; **8.** ***~ up*** a) ,abkratzen' (*sterben*), b) ,Pleite' machen, ,eingehen'; **'~·ache I** *s.* Bauchweh *n*; **II** *v/i.* F ,meckern', nörgeln; **'~-band** *s.* Bauch-, Sattelgurt *m*; **~ but·ton** *s.* F (Bauch-) Nabel *m*; **~ danc·er** *s.* Bauchtänzerin *f*; **~ flop** *s.* F ,Bauchklatscher' *m*; ✈ Bauchlandung *f*; **'~·ful** *s.*: ***have had a ~ (of)*** F die Nase voll haben (von); **'~·hold** *s.* ✈ Frachtraum *m*; **~ land·ing** *s.* ✈ Bauchlandung *f*; **~ laugh** *s.* F dröhnendes Lachen; **~ tank** *s.* Rumpfabwurfbehälter *m*.

be·long [bı'lɒŋ] *v/i.* **1.** gehören (***to*** *dat.*): ***this ~s to me***; **2.** gehören (***to*** zu), da'zugehören, am richtigen Platz sein: ***this lid ~s to another pot*** dieser Dekkel gehört zu e-m anderen Topf; ***where does this book ~?*** wohin gehört dieses Buch?; ***he does not ~*** er gehört nicht dazu *od.* hierher; **3.** (***to***) sich gehören (für), *j-m* ziemen; **4.** *Am.* a) verbunden sein (***with*** mit), gehören *od.* passen (***with*** zu), b) wohnen (***in*** in *dat.*); **5.** an-, zugehören (***to*** *dat*): ***~ to a club***; **be'long·ings** [-ŋıŋz] *s. pl.* a) Habseligkeiten *pl.*, Habe *f*, Gepäck *n*, b) Zubehör *n*, c) F Angehörige *pl*.

be·lov·ed [bı'lʌvd] **I** *adj.* [*attr. a.* -vıd] (innig) geliebt (***of***, ***by*** von); **II** *s.* [*mst* -vıd] Geliebte(r *m*) *f*.

be·low [bı'ləʊ] **I** *adv.* **1.** unten: ***he is ~*** er ist unten (*im Haus*); ***as stated ~*** wie unten erwähnt; **2.** hin'unter; **3.** *poet.* hie'nieden; **4.** in der Hölle; **5.** (dar-) 'unter, niedriger: ***the class ~***; **6.** strom'ab; **II** *prp.* **7.** unter, 'unterhalb, tiefer als: ***~ the line*** unter der *od.* die Linie; ***~ cost*** unter dem Kostenpreis; ***~ s.o.*** unter j-s Rang, Würde, Fähigkeit *etc.*; ***20 ~*** F 20 Grad Kälte.

belt [belt] **I** *s.* **1.** Gürtel *m*, Gurt *m*: ***hit below the ~*** *Boxen u. fig. j-m* e-n Tiefschlag versetzen; ***that was below the ~*** *a. fig.* das war unter der Gürtellinie *od.* unfair; ***tighten one's ~*** *fig.* den Gürtel enger schnallen; ***the Black ♀*** *Judo*: der Schwarze Gürtel (→ 5); ***under one's ~*** F a) im Magen, b) *fig.* ,in der Tasche', c) hinter sich; **2.** ⚔ Koppel *n*; Gehenk *n*; **3.** ⚓ Panzergürtel *m* (*Kriegsschiff*); **4.** Gürtel *m*, Gebiet *n*, Zone *f*: ***green ~*** Grüngürtel (*um e-e Stadt*); ***cotton ~*** *Am. geogr.* Baumwollgürtel; **5.** *Am.* Gebiet *n* (*in dem ein Typus vorherrscht*): ***the black ~*** vorwiegend von Negern bewohnte Staaten der USA; **6.** ⚙ a) (Treib)Riemen *m*: ***~ drive*** Riemenantrieb *m*, b) *a.* ***conveyer ~*** Förderband *n*, c) Streifen *m*, d) ⚔ (Ma'schinengewehr)Gurt *m*; **II** *v/t.* **7.** um'gürten, mit Riemen befestigen; zs.-halten; **8.** 'durchprügeln; *j-m* ,eine knallen'; **9.** ***~ out*** *sl. Lied* schmettern; **10.** *a.* ***~ down*** *Schnaps etc.* ,kippen'; **III** *v/i.* **11.** ***~ up!*** *sl.* (halt die) Schnauze!; **12.** *sl.* rasen: ***~ down the road***; **~ con·vey·er** *s.* ⚙ Bandförderer *m*; **~ drive** *s.* ⚙ Riemenantrieb *m*; **~ line** *s. Am.* Verkehrsgürtel *m um e-e Stadt*; **~ pul·ley** *s.* ⚙ Riemenscheibe *f*; **~ saw** *s.* Bandsäge *f*; **~ trans·mis·sion** *s.* ⚙ 'Riementransmissi,on *f*; **'~·way** *s. Am.* Um'gehungsstraße *f*.

be·lu·ga [bı'lu:gɑ:] *s. ichth.* Be'luga *f*: a) Weißwal *m*, b) Hausen *m*.

be·moan [bı'məʊn] *v/t.* beklagen, betrauern, beweinen.

be·muse [bı'mju:z] *v/t.* verwirren, benebeln, betäuben; nachdenklich stimmen; **be'mused** [-zd] *adj.* **1.** verwirrt *etc.*; **2.** nachdenklich; gedankenverloren.

bench [ben*t*ʃ] *s.* **1.** Bank *f* (*zum Sitzen*); **2.** ⚖ (*oft* ♀) a) Richterbank *f*, b) Gerichtshof *m*, c) *coll.* Richter *pl.*: ***raised to the ~*** zum Richter ernannt; ***~ and bar*** die Richter u. die Anwälte; ***be on the ~*** Richter sein; **3.** *parl. etc.* Platz *m*, Sitz *m*; **4.** ⚙ a) Werkbank *f*, -tisch *m*, Experimentiertisch *m*: ***carpenter's ~*** Hobelbank, b) Bank *f*, Reihe *f von Geräten*; **5.** *geogr. Am.* a) Riff *n*, b) ter'rassenförmiges Flußufer; **6.** *sport* a) (Teilnehmer-, Auswechsel-, Re'serve-) Bank *f*, b) Ruderbank *f*; **'bench·er** [-tʃə] *s.* **1.** *Brit.* Vorstandsmitglied *n* e-r Anwaltsinnung; **2.** *parl.* → ***backbencher***, ***front-bencher***.

bench| lathe *s.* ⚙ Me'chanikerdrehbank *f*; **~ sci·en·tist** *s.* La'borwissenschaftler *m*; **'~,war·rant** *s.* ⚖ richterlicher Haftbefehl.

bend [bend] **I** *v/t.* [*irr.*] **1.** biegen, krümmen: ***~ out of shape*** verbiegen; **2.** beugen, neigen: ***~ the knee*** a) das Knie beugen, *fig.* sich unterwerfen, b) beten; **3.** *Bogen*, *Feder* spannen; **4.** ⚓ *Tau*, *Segel* festmachen; **5.** *fig.* beugen: ***~ the law*** das Recht beugen; ***~ s.o. to one's will*** sich j-n gefügig machen; **6.** richten, (zu)wenden: ***~ one's steps towards home*** s-e Schritte heimwärts lenken; ***~ o.s.*** (***one's mind***) ***to a task*** sich (s-e Aufmerksamkeit) e-r Sache zuwenden, sich auf e-e Sache konzentrieren; **II** *v/i.* [*irr.*] **7.** sich biegen, sich krümmen, sich winden: ***the road ~s here*** die Straße macht hier e-e Kurve; **8.** sich neigen, sich beugen: ***~ down*** sich niederbeugen, sich bücken; **9.** (***to***) *fig.* sich beugen, sich fügen (*dat.*); **10.** (***to***) sich zuwenden, sich widmen (*dat.*); **III** *s.* **11.** Biegung *f*, Krümmung *f*, Windung *f*, Kurve *f*; **12.** Knoten *m*, Schlinge *f*; **13.** ***drive s.o. round the ~*** *sl.* j-n verrückt machen; **14.** ***the ~s*** *pl.* ⚕ Cais'sonkrankheit *f*; **'bend·ed** [-dıd] *adj.* gebeugt: ***on ~ knees*** kniefällig; **'bend·er** [-də] *s. sl.* ,Saufe'rei' *f*, ,Bummel' *m*; **'bend·ing** [-dıŋ] *adj.* ⚙ Biege...: ***~ pressure***; ***~ test***.

bend sin·is·ter *s. her* Schrägbalken *m*.

be·neath [bı'ni:θ] **I** *adv.* dar'unter, 'unterhalb, (weiter) unten; **II** *prp.* unter, unterhalb (*gen.*): ***~ a tree*** unter e-m Baum; ***it is ~ him*** es ist unter s-r Würde; ***~ notice*** nicht der Beachtung wert; ***~ contempt*** unter aller Kritik.

Ben·e·dic·tine *s.* **1.** [,benı'dıktın] Benedik'tiner *m* (*Mönch*); **2.** [-ti:n] Benedik'tiner *m* (*Likör*).

ben·e·dic·tion [,benı'dıkʃn] *s. eccl.* Segnung *f*, Segen(sspruch) *m*.

ben·e·fac·tion [,benı'fækʃn] *s.* **1.** Wohltat *f*; **2.** Spende *f*, Geschenk *n*; Zuwendungen *pl.*; **3.** wohltätige Stiftung; **ben·e·fac·tor** ['benıfæktə] *s.* **1.** Wohltäter *m*; **2.** Gönner *m*; Stifter *m*; **ben·e·fac·tress** ['benıfæktrıs] *s.* Wohltäterin *f etc.*

ben·e·fice ['benıfıs] *s. eccl.* Pfründe *f*; **'ben·e·ficed** [-st] *adj.* im Besitz e-r Pfründe; **be·nef·i·cence** [bı'nefısns] *s.* Wohltätigkeit *f*; **be·nef·i·cent** [bı'nefısnt] *adj.* □ wohltätig, gütig, wohltuend.

ben·e·fi·cial [,benı'fıʃl] *adj.* □ **1.** (***to***) nützlich, wohltuend, förderlich (*dat.*); vorteilhaft (für); **2.** ⚖ nutznießend: ***~ owner*** unmittelbarer Besitzer, Nießbraucher *m*; **,ben·e'fi·ci·ar·y** [-'fıʃərı] *s.* **1.** Nutznießer(in); Begünstigte(r *m*) *f*; Empfänger(in); **2.** Pfründner *m*.

ben·e·fit ['benıfıt] **I** *s.* **1.** Vorteil *m*, Nutzen *m*, Gewinn *m*: ***for the ~ of*** zum Besten *od.* zugunsten (*gen.*); ***derive ~ from*** Nutzen ziehen aus *od.* haben von; ***give s.o. the ~ of*** j-n in den Genuß *e-r Sache* kommen lassen, j-m *et.* gewähren; ***~ of the doubt*** Rechtswohltat *f* des Grundsatzes ,im Zweifel für den Angeklagten'; ***give s.o. the ~ of the doubt*** im Zweifelsfalle zu j-s Gunsten entscheiden; **2.** ✝ Zuwendung *f*, Beihilfe *f*: a) (*Sozial-*, *Versicherungs- etc.*)Leistung *f*, b) (*Alters- etc.*)Rente *f*, c) (*Arbeitslosen- etc.*)Unter'stützung *f*, d) (*Kranken-*, *Sterbe- etc.*)Geld *n*; **3.** Bene'fiz(vorstellung *f*, *sport* -spiel *n*) *n*, Wohltätigkeitsveranstaltung *f*; **4.** Wohltat *f*, Gefallen *m*, Vergünstigung *f*; **II** *v/t.* **5.** nützen (*dat.*), zu'gute kommen (*dat.*), fördern (*acc.*), begünstigen (*acc.*), *a. j-m* (gesundheitlich) guttun; **III** *v/i.* **6.** (***by***, ***from***) Vorteil haben (von, durch), Nutzen ziehen (aus).

Ben·e·lux ['benılʌks] *s.* Benelux-Länder *pl.* (*Belgien*, *Niederlande*, *Luxemburg*).

be·nev·o·lence [bı'nevələns] *s.* Wohlwollen *n*, Güte *f*; Wohltätigkeit *f*, Wohltat *f*; **be'nev·o·lent** [-nt] *adj.* □ wohl-, mildtätig, gütig; wohlwollend: ***~ fund*** Unterstützungsfonds *m*; ***~ society*** Hilfsverein *m* (auf Gegenseitigkeit).

Ben·gal [,beŋ'gɔ:l] *npr.* Ben'galen *n*: ***~ light*** bengalisches Feuer; **Ben'ga·li** [-lı] **I** *s.* **1.** Ben'gale *m*, Ben'galin *f*; **2.** *ling.* das Ben'galische; **II** *adj.* **3.** ben'galisch.

be·night·ed [bı'naıtıd] *adj.* **1.** von der Dunkelheit über'rascht; **2.** *fig.* a) ,geistig um'nachtet', ,verblödet', b) unbe-

darft.
be·nign [bɪˈnaɪn] *adj.* □ **1.** gütig; **2.** günstig, mild, zuträglich; **3.** ⚕ gutartig; **be·nig·nant** [bɪˈnɪgnənt] *adj.* □ **1.** gütig, freundlich; **2.** günstig, wohltuend; **3.** → ***benign*** 3; **be·nig·ni·ty** [bɪˈnɪgnətɪ] *s.* Güte *f*, Freundlichkeit *f*.
ben·i·son [ˈbenɪzn] *s. poet.* Segen *m*, Gnade *f*.
bent[1] [bent] **I** *pret. u. p.p. von* ***bend*** I *u.* II; **II** *adj.* a) entschlossen (***on doing*** zu tun), b) erpicht (***on*** auf *acc.*), darauf aus (***on doing*** zu tun); **III** *s.* Neigung *f*, Hang *m*, Trieb *m* (***for*** zu); Veranlagung *f*: ***to the top of one's ~*** nach Herzenslust; ***allow full ~*** freien Lauf lassen (*dat.*).
bent[2] [bent] *s.* ⚘ **1.** *a.* ***~ grass*** Straußgras *n*; **2.** Sandsegge *f*.
ˈ**bent·wood** *s.* Bugholz *n*: ***~ chair*** Wiener Stuhl *m*.
be·numb [bɪˈnʌm] *v/t.* betäuben: a) gefühllos machen, b) *fig.* lähmen; **beˈnumbed** [-md] *adj.* betäubt, gelähmt (*a. fig.*), starr, gefühllos.
ben·zene [ˈbenziːn] *s.* ⚗ Benˈzol *n*.
ben·zine [ˈbenziːn] *s.* ⚗ Benˈzin *n*.
ben·zo·ic [benˈzəʊɪk] *adj.* ⚗ Benzoe...: ***~ acid*** Benzoesäure *f*; **ben·zo·in** [ˈbenzəʊɪn] *s.* Benˈzoeˌgummi *n*, *m*, -harz *n*, Benˈzoe *f*.
ben·zol(e) [ˈbenzɒl] *s.* ⚗ Benˈzol *n*; ˈ**ben·zo·line** [-zəʊliːn] → ***benzine***.
be·queath [bɪˈkwiːð] *v/t.* **1.** *Vermögen* hinterˈlassen, vermachen (***to s.o.*** j-m); **2.** überˈliefern, vererben (*fig.*).
be·quest [bɪˈkwest] *s.* Vermächtnis *n*, Hinterˈlassenschaft *f*.
be·rate [bɪˈreɪt] *v/t.* heftig ausschelten, auszanken.
Ber·ber [ˈbɜːbə] **I** *s.* **1.** Berber(in); **2.** *ling.* Berbersprache(n *pl.*) *f*; **II** *adj.* **3.** Berber...
Ber·ber·is [ˈbɜːbərɪs], **ber·ber·ry** [ˈbɜːbərɪ] → ***barberry***.
be·reave [bɪˈriːv] *v/t.* [*irr.*] **1.** berauben (***of*** *gen.*); **2.** hilflos zuˈrücklassen; **beˈreaved** [-vd] *adj.* durch den Tod beraubt, hinterˈblieben: ***the ~*** die (trauernden) Hinterbliebenen; **beˈreave·ment** [-mənt] *s.* schmerzlicher Verlust (*durch Tod*); Trauerfall *m*.
be·reft [bɪˈreft] **I** *pret. u. p.p. von* ***bereave***; **II** *adj.* beraubt (***of*** *gen.*) (*mst fig.*): ***~ of hope*** aller Hoffnung beraubt; ***~ of reason*** von Sinnen.
be·ret [ˈbereɪ] *s.* **1.** Baskenmütze *f*; **2.** ⚔ *Brit.* ˈFelduniˌformmütze *f*.
berg [bɜːg] → ***iceberg***.
ber·ga·mot [ˈbɜːgəmɒt] *s.* **1.** ⚘ Bergaˈmottenbaum *m*; **2.** Bergaˈmottöl *n*; **3.** Bergaˈmotte *f* (*Birnensorte*).
be·rib·boned [bɪˈrɪbənd] *adj.* mit (Ordens)Bändern geschmückt.
ber·i·ber·i [ˌberɪˈberɪ] *s.* ⚕ Beriˈberi *f*, Reisesserkrankheit *f*.
Ber·lin| black [bɜːˈlɪn] *s.* schwarzer Eisenlack; ***~ wool*** *s.* feine Strickwolle.
ber·ry [ˈberɪ] **I** *s.* **1.** ⚘ a) Beere *f*, b) Korn *n*, Kern *m* (*beim Getreide*); **2.** *zo.* Ei *n* (*vom Hummer od. Fisch*); **II** *v/i.* **3.** a) ⚘ Beeren tragen, b) Beeren sammeln.
ber·serk [bəˈsɜːk] *adj. u. adv.* wütend, rasend: ***go ~*** (***with***) rasend werden (vor), *fig. a.* wahnsinnig werden (vor); **berˈserk·er** [-kə] *s. hist.* Berˈserker *m* (*a. fig. Wüterich*): ***~ rage*** Berserkerwut *f*; ***go ~*** wild werden, Amok laufen.
berth [bɜːθ] **I** *s.* **1.** ⚓ (genügend) Seeraum (*an der Küste od. zum Ausweichen*): ***give a wide ~ to*** a) weit abhalten von (*Land*, *Insel etc.*), b) *fig.* um *j-n* e-n Bogen machen; **2.** ⚓ Liegeplatz *m* (*e-s Schiffes am Kai*); **3.** a) ⚓ (Schlaf-) Koje *f*, b) Bett *n* (*Schlafwagen*); **4.** *Brit.* F Stellung *f*, ‚Pöstchen' *n*: ***he has a good ~***; **II** *v/t.* **5.** ⚓ am Kai festmachen; vor Anker legen, docken; **6.** *Brit j-m* einen (Schlaf)Platz anweisen; *j-n* ˈunterbringen; **III** *v/i.* **7.** ⚓ anlegen.
ber·yl [ˈberɪl] *s. min.* Beˈryll *m*; **be·ryl·li·um** [beˈrɪljəm] *s.* ⚗ Beˈryllium *n*.
be·seech [bɪˈsiːtʃ] *v/t.* [*irr.*] *j-n* dringend bitten (***for*** um), ersuchen, anflehen (***to*** *inf.* zu *inf.*, ***that*** daß); **beˈseech·ing** [-tʃɪŋ] *adj.* □ flehend, bittend; **beˈseech·ing·ly** [-tʃɪŋlɪ] *adv.* flehentlich.
be·seem [bɪˈsiːm] *v/t.* sich ziemen *od.* schicken für.
be·set [bɪˈset] [*irr.* → ***set***] *v/t.* **1.** umˈgeben, (von allen Seiten) bedrängen, verfolgen: ***~ with difficulties*** mit Schwierigkeiten überhäuft; **2.** *Straße* versperren; **beˈset·ting** [-tɪŋ] *adj.* **1.** hartnäckig, unausrottbar: ***~ sin*** Gewohnheitslaster *n*; **2.** ständig drohend (*Gefahr*).
be·side [bɪˈsaɪd] *prp.* **1.** neben, dicht bei: ***sit ~ me*** setz dich neben mich; **2.** *fig.* außerhalb (*gen.*), außer, nicht gehörend zu: ***~ the point*** nicht zur Sache gehörig; ***~ o.s.*** außer sich (***with*** vor *dat.*); **3.** im Vergleich zu; **beˈsides** [-dz] **I** *adv.* **1.** außerdem, ferner, überˈdies, noch daˈzu; **2.** *neg.* sonst; **II** *prp.* **3.** außer, neben (*dat.*); **4.** über ... hinˈaus.
be·siege [bɪˈsiːdʒ] *v/t.* **1.** belagern (*a. fig.*); **2.** *fig.* bestürmen, bedrängen.
be·slav·er [bɪˈslævə] *v/t.* **1.** begeifern; **2.** *fig. j-m* lobhudeln.
be·slob·ber [bɪˈslɒbə] *v/t.* **1.** → ***beslaver***; **2.** ‚abschlecken', abküssen.
be·smear [bɪˈsmɪə] *v/t.* beschmieren.
be·smirch [bɪˈsmɜːtʃ] *v/t.* besudeln (*bsd. fig.*).
be·som [ˈbiːzəm] *s.* (Reisig)Besen *m*.
be·sot·ted [bɪˈsɒtɪd] *adj.* □ **1.** töricht, dumm; **2.** (***on***, ***about***) vernarrt (in *acc.*), verrückt (auf *acc.*); **3.** berauscht (***with*** von).
be·sought [bɪˈsɔːt] *pret. u. p.p. von* ***beseech***.
be·spat·ter [bɪˈspætə] *v/t.* **1.** (mit Kot *etc.*) bespritzen, beschmutzen; **2.** *fig.* (mit Vorwürfen *etc.*) überˈschütten.
be·speak [bɪˈspiːk] [*irr.* → ***speak***] *v/t.* **1.** (vorˈaus)bestellen, im voraus bitten um: ***~ a seat*** e-n Platz bestellen; ***~ s.o.'s help*** j-n um Hilfe bitten; **2.** zeigen, zeugen von; **3.** *poet.* anreden.
be·spec·ta·cled [bɪˈspektəkld] *adj.* bebrillt.
be·spoke [bɪˈspəʊk] **I** *pret. von* ***bespeak***; **II** *adj. Brit.* auf Bestellung *od.* nach Maß angefertigt, Maß...: ***~ tailor*** Maßschneider *m*; **beˈspo·ken** [-kən] *p.p. von* ***bespeak***.
be·sprin·kle [bɪˈsprɪŋkl] *v/t.* besprengen, bespritzen, bestreuen.
Bes·se·mer steel [ˈbesɪmə] *s.* ⚙ Bessemerstahl *m*.
best [best] **I** *sup. von* ***good*** *adj.* **1.** best: ***the ~ of wives*** die beste aller (Ehe-) Frauen; ***be ~ at*** hervorragend sein in (*dat.*); **2.** geeignetst; höchst; **3.** größt, meist: ***the ~ part of*** der größte Teil (*gen.*); **II** *sup. von* ***well*** *adv.* **4.** am besten (meisten, passendsten): ***as ~ I can*** so gut ich kann; ***the ~ hated man of the year*** der meist- *od.* bestgehaßte Mann des Jahres; ***~ used*** meistgebraucht; ***you had ~ go*** es wäre das beste, Sie gingen; **III** *v/t.* **5.** überˈtreffen; **6.** F überˈvorteilen; **IV** *s.* **7.** *der* (*die*, *das*) Beste (Passendste *etc.*): ***at ~*** bestenfalls, höchstens; ***with the ~*** mindestens so gut wie jeder andere; ***for the ~*** zum besten; ***do one's*** (***level***) ***~*** sein Bestes geben, sein möglichstes tun; ***be at one's ~*** in bester Verfassung (*od.* Form) sein, *a.* in seinem Element sein; ***that is the ~ of ...*** das ist der Vorteil (*gen. od.* wenn ...); ***give s.o. ~*** sich vor j-m beugen; ***look one's ~*** am vorteilhaftesten *od.* blendend aussehen; ***have*** (*od.* ***get***) ***the ~ of it*** am besten dabei wegkommen; ***make the ~ of*** a) bestens ausnutzen, b) sich abfinden mit, c) *e-r Sache* die beste Seite abgewinnen, das Beste machen aus; ***all the ~!*** alles Gute!, viel Glück!; → ***ability*** 1, ***belief*** 3, ***job***[1] 5.
bes·tial [ˈbestjəl] *adj.* □ **1.** tierisch (*a. fig.*); *fig.* bestiˈalisch, entmenscht, viehisch; **2.** *fig.* gemein, verderbt; **bes·ti·al·i·ty** [bestɪˈælətɪ] *s.* **1.** Bestialiˈtät *f*: a) tierisches Wesen, b) *fig.* bestiˈalische Grausamkeit; **2.** ⚖ Sodoˈmie *f*.
be·stir [bɪˈstɜː] *v/t.*: ***~ o.s.*** sich rühren, sich aufraffen; sich bemühen: ***~ yourself!*** tummle dich!
best man *s.* [*irr.*] *Freund des Bräutigams, der bei der Ausrichtung der Hochzeit e-e wichtige Rolle spielt.*
be·stow [bɪˈstəʊ] *v/t.* **1.** schenken, gewähren, geben, spenden, erweisen, verleihen (***s.th.*** [***up***]***on s.o.*** j-m et.): ***~ one's hand on s.o.*** j-m die Hand fürs Leben reichen; **2.** *obs.* ˈunterbringen; **beˈstow·al** [-əʊəl] *s.* **1.** Gabe *f*, Schenkung *f*, Verleihung *f*; **2.** *obs.* ˈUnterbringung *f*.
be·strew [bɪˈstruː] [*irr.* → ***strew***] *v/t.* **1.** bestreuen; **2.** verstreut liegen auf (*dat.*).
be·strid·den [bɪˈstrɪdn] *p.p. von* ***bestride***; **be·stride** [bɪˈstraɪd] *v/t.* [*irr.*] **1.** rittlings sitzen auf (*dat.*), reiten; **2.** mit gespreizten Beinen stehen auf *od.* über (*dat.*); **3.** überˈspannen, überˈbrücken; **4.** sich (schützend) breiten über (*acc.*); **be·strode** [bɪˈstrəʊd] *pret. von* ***bestride***.
best| sell·er *s.* ˈBestseller *m*, Verkaufsschlager *m* (*Buch etc.*); ˈ**~-ˌsell·ing** *adj.* meistgekauft, Erfolgs..., Bestseller...
bet [bet] **I** *s.* Wette *f*; Wetteinsatz *m*; gewetteter Betrag *od.* Gegenstand: ***the best ~*** F das Beste(, was man tun kann), die sicherste Methode; ***that's a better ~ than*** das ist viel besser *od.* sicherer als...; **II** *v/t. u. v/i.* [*irr.*] wetten, (ein)setzen: ***I ~ you ten pounds*** ich wette mit Ihnen um zehn Pfund; (***I***) ***you ~!*** *sl.* aber sicher!; ***~ one's bottom dollar*** *Am. sl.* den letzten Heller wetten, *a.* sich s-r Sache völlig sicher sein.
be·ta [ˈbiːtə] *s.* ˈBeta *n*: a) *griech. Buchstabe*, b) ⚡, *ast.*, *phys. Symbol für 2. Größe*, c) *ped. Brit.* Zwei *f* (*Note*): ***~ rays*** *phys.* Betastrahlen *pl.*

be·take [bɪˈteɪk] [*irr.* → ***take***] *v/t.*: ~ ***o.s.*** (***to***) sich begeben (nach); s-e Zuflucht nehmen (zu).

be·tel [ˈbiːtl] *s.* ˈBetel *m*; ˈ**~-nut** *s.* ♀ ˈBetelnuß *f*.

bête noire [ˌbeɪtˈnwɑː] (*Fr.*) *s. fig.* Schreckgespenst *n*.

beth·el [ˈbeθl] *s.* **1.** *Brit.* Disˈsenterkaˌpelle *f*; **2.** *Am.* Kirche *f* für Maˈtrosen.

be·think [bɪˈθɪŋk] *v/t.* [*irr.* → ***think***]: ~ ***o.s.*** sich überˈlegen, sich besinnen; sich vornehmen; ~ ***o.s. to do*** sich in den Kopf setzen zu tun.

be·thought [bɪˈθɔːt] *pret. u. p.p. von* ***bethink***.

be·tide [bɪˈtaɪd] *v/i. u. v/t.* (*nur 3. sg. pres. subj.*) (*j-m*) geschehen; *v/t. j-m* zustoßen; → ***woe*** II.

be·times [bɪˈtaɪmz] *adv.* **1.** beiˈzeiten, rechtzeitig; **2.** früh(zeitig).

be·to·ken [bɪˈtəʊkən] *v/t.* **1.** bezeichnen, bedeuten; **2.** anzeigen.

be·took [bɪˈtʊk] *pret. von* ***betake***.

be·tray [bɪˈtreɪ] *v/t.* **1.** Verrat begehen an (*dat.*), verraten (***to*** an *acc.*); **2.** *j-n* hinterˈgehen; *j-m* die Treue brechen: ~ ***s.o.'s trust*** j-s Vertrauen mißbrauchen; **3.** *fig.* offenˈbaren; (*a.* ***o.s.*** sich) verraten; **4.** verleiten (***into***, ***to*** zu); **beˈtray·al** [-eɪəl] *s.* Verrat *m*, Treubruch *m*.

be·troth [bɪˈtrəʊð] *v/t. j-n* (*od.* ***o.s.*** sich) verloben (***to*** mit); **beˈtroth·al** [-ðl] *s.* Verlobung *f*; **beˈtrothed** [-ðd] *s.* Verlobte(r *m*) *f*.

bet·ter¹ [ˈbetə] **I** *comp. von* ***good*** *adj.* **1.** besser: ***I am*** ~ es geht mir (*gesundheitlich*) besser; ***get*** ~ a) besser werden, b) sich erholen; ~ ***late than never*** besser spät als nie; ***go one*** ~ ***than s.o.*** j-n (noch) übertreffen; ~ ***off*** a) besser daran, b) wohlhabender; ***be*** ~ ***than one's word*** mehr tun als man versprach; ***my*** ~ ***half*** m-e bessere Hälfte; ***on*** ~ ***acquaintance*** bei näherer Bekanntschaft; **II** *s.* **2.** *das* Bessere: ***for*** ~ ***for worse*** a) in Freud u. Leid (*Trauformel*), b) was auch geschehe; ***get the*** ~ (***of***) die Oberhand gewinnen (über *acc.*), *j-n* besiegen *od.* ausstechen, *et.* überwinden; **3.** *pl. mit pers. pron.* Vorgesetzte *pl.*, Höherstehende *pl.*, Überˈlegene *pl.*; **III** *comp. von* ***well*** *adv.* **4.** besser: ***I know*** ~ ich weiß es besser; ***think*** ~ ***of it*** sich e-s Besseren besinnen, es sich anders überlegen; ***think*** ~ ***of s.o.*** e-e bessere Meinung von j-m haben; ***so much the*** ~ desto besser; ***you had*** ~ (*od.* F *mst* ***you*** ~) ***go*** es wäre besser, wenn du gingest; ***you'd*** ~ ***not!*** F laß das lieber sein!; ***know*** ~ ***than to ...*** gescheit genug sein, nicht zu ...; **5.** mehr: ***like*** ~ lieber haben; ~ ***loved***; **IV** *v/t.* **6.** *allg.* verbessern; **7.** überˈtreffen; **8.** ~ ***o.s.*** sich (*finanziell*) verbessern, vorwärtskommen; *a.* sich weiterbilden; **V** *v/i.* **9.** besser werden.

bet·ter² [ˈbetə] *s.* Wetter(in).

bet·ter·ment [ˈbetəmənt] *s.* **1.** (Ver-) Besserung *f*; **2.** Wertzuwachs *m* (*bei Grundstücken*), Melioratiˈon *f*.

bet·ting [ˈbetɪŋ] *s. sport* Wetten *n*; ~ **man** *s.* [*irr.*] (regelmäßiger) Wetter; ~ **of·fice** *s.*, ~ **shop** *s.* ˈWettbüˌro *n*.

bet·tor → ***better²***.

be·tween [bɪˈtwiːn] **I** *prp.* **1.** zwischen: ~ ***the chairs*** a) zwischen den Stühlen, b) zwischen die Stühle; ~ ***nine and ten at night*** abends zwischen neun und zehn; **2.** unter: ***they shared the money*** ~ ***them*** sie teilten das Geld unter sich; ~ ***ourselves***, ~ ***you and me*** unter uns (gesagt); ***we had fifty pence*** ~ ***us*** wir hatten zusammen fünfzig Pence; **II** *adv.* **3.** daˈzwischen: ***the space*** ~ der Zwischenraum; ***in*** ~ dazwischen, zwischendurch; ~ **decks** *s. pl. sg. konstr.* ⚓ Zwischendeck *n*; **beˈtween·times**; **beˈtween·whiles** *adv.* zwischendurch.

be·twixt [bɪˈtwɪkst] **I** *adv.* daˈzwischen: ~ ***and between*** halb u. halb, weder das e-e noch das andere; **II** *prp. obs.* zwischen.

bev·el [ˈbevl] ⚙ **I** *s.* **1.** Abschrägung *f*, Schräge *f*; **2.** Fase *f*, Faˈcette *f*; **2.** Schrägmaß *n*; **3.** Kegel *m*, Konus *m*; **II** *v/t.* **4.** abschrägen: ~(***l***)***ed edge*** abgeschrägte Kante; ~(***l***)***ed glass*** facettiertes Glas; **III** *adj.* **5.** abgeschrägt; ~ **cut** *s.* Schrägschnitt *m*; ~ **gear** *s.* ⚙ Kegelrad(getriebe) *n*, konisches Getriebe; ~ **plane** *s.* ⚙ Schräghobel *m*; ~ **wheel** *s.* ⚙ Kegelrad *n*.

bev·er·age [ˈbevərɪdʒ] *s.* Getränk *n*.

bev·y [ˈbevɪ] *s.* Schar *f*, Schwarm *m* (*Vögel*; *a. fig. Mädchen etc.*).

be·wail [bɪˈweɪl] **I** *v/t.* beklagen, betrauern; **II** *v/i.* wehklagen.

be·ware [bɪˈweə] *v/i.* sich in acht nehmen, sich hüten (***of*** vor *dat.*, ***lest*** daß nicht): ~***!*** Achtung!; ~ ***of pickpockets!*** vor Taschendieben wird gewarnt!; ~ ***of the dog!*** Warnung vor dem Hunde!

be·wil·der [bɪˈwɪldə] *v/t.* **1.** irreführen; **2.** verwirren, verblüffen; **3.** bestürzen; **beˈwil·dered** [-əd] *adj.* verwirrt; verblüfft, bestürzt, verdutzt; **beˈwil·der·ing** [-dərɪŋ] *adj.* ☐ verwirrend; **beˈwil·der·ment** [-mənt] *s.* Verwirrung *f*, Bestürzung *f*.

be·witch [bɪˈwɪtʃ] *v/t.* berücken, betören, bezaubern; **beˈwitch·ing** [-tʃɪŋ] *adj.* ☐ berückend *etc.*

bey [beɪ] *s.* Bei *m* (*Titel e-s höheren türkischen Beamten*).

be·yond [bɪˈjɒnd] **I** *prp.* **1.** jenseits: ~ ***the seas*** in Übersee; **2.** außer, abgesehen von: ~ ***dispute*** außer allem Zweifel, unstreitig; **3.** über ... (*acc.*) hinˈaus; mehr als, weiter als: ~ ***the time*** über die Zeit hinaus; ~ ***belief*** unglaublich; ~ ***all blame*** über jeden Tadel erhaben; ~ ***endurance*** unerträglich; ~ ***hope*** hoffnungslos; ~ ***measure*** über die Maßen; ***it is*** ~ ***my power*** es übersteigt m-e Kraft; ~ ***praise*** über alles Lob erhaben; ~ ***repair*** nicht mehr zu reparieren; ~ ***reproach*** untadelig; ***that is*** ~ ***me*** das ist mir zu hoch, das geht über m-n Verstand; ~ ***me in Latin*** weiter als ich in Latein; **II** *adv.* **4.** daˈrüber hinˈaus, jenseits; **5.** weiter weg; **III** *s.* **6.** Jenseits *n*: ***at the back of*** ~ im entlegensten Winkel, am Ende der Welt.

ˈ**B-girl** *s. Am.* Animierdame *f*.

bi·an·nu·al [ˌbaɪˈænjʊəl] *adj.* ☐ halbjährlich, zweimal jährlich.

bi·as [ˈbaɪəs] **I** *s.* **1.** schiefe Seite, schräge Richtung; **2.** schräger Schnitt: ***cut on the*** ~ diagonal geschnitten; **3.** *Bowling*: ˈÜberhang *m* der Kugel; **4.** (***towards***) *fig.* Hang *m*, Neigung *f* (zu); Vorliebe *f* (für); **5.** *fig.* a) Tenˈdenz *f*, b) Vorurteil *n*, c) ⚖ Befangenheit *f*: ***free from*** ~ unvoreingenommen; ***challenge a judge for*** ~ e-n Richter wegen Befangenheit ablehnen; **6.** *Statistik etc.*: Verzerrung *f*: ***cause*** ~ ***to the figures*** die Zahlen verzerren; **7.** ⚡ (Gitter-) Vorspannung *f*; **II** *adj u. adv.* **8.** schräg, schief; **III** *v/t.* **9.** (*mst* ungünstig) beeinflussen; gegen *j-n* einnehmen; ˈ**bi·as(s)ed** [-st] *adj.* voreingenommen; ⚖ befangen; tendenziˈös.

bi·ath·lete [ˌbaɪˈæθliːt] *s. sport* ˈBiathˌlet *m*, ˈBiathlonkämpfer *m*; **biˈath·lon** [-ˈæθlɒn] *s.* ˈBiathlon *n*.

bi·ax·i·al [ˌbaɪˈæksɪəl] *adj.* zweiachsig.

bib [bɪb] **I** *s.* **1.** Lätzchen *n*; **2.** Schürzenlatz *m*; → ***tucker*** 2; **II** *v/i.* **3.** (unmäßig) trinken.

Bi·ble [ˈbaɪbl] *s.* **1.** Bibel *f*; **2.** ♀ *fig.* Bibel *f* (*maßgebendes Buch*); ~ **clerk** *s.* (*in Oxford*) *Student, der in der College-Kapelle während des Gottesdienstes die Bibeltexte verliest*; ~ **thump·er** *s.* Moˈralprediger *m*.

bib·li·cal [ˈbɪblɪkl] *adj.* ☐ biblisch, Bibel...

bib·li·og·ra·pher [ˌbɪblɪˈɒgrəfə] *s.* Biblioˈgraph *m*; **bib·li·o·graph·ic**, **bib·li·o·graph·i·cal** [ˌbɪblɪəʊˈgræfɪk(l)] *adj.* ☐ biblioˈgraphisch; **bib·liˈog·ra·phy** [-fɪ] *s.* Bibliograˈphie *f*; **bib·li·o·ma·ni·a** [ˌbɪblɪəʊˈmeɪnjə] *s.* Bibliomaˈnie *f*, (krankhafte) Bücherleidenschaft; **bib·li·o·ma·ni·ac** [ˌbɪblɪəʊˈmeɪnɪæk] *s.* Büchernarr *m*; **bib·li·o·phil** [ˈbɪblɪəʊfɪl], **bib·li·o·phile** [ˈbɪblɪəʊfaɪl] *s.* Biblioˈphile *m*, Bücherliebhaber(in); **bib·li·o·the·ca** [ˌbɪblɪəʊˈθiːkə] *s.* **1.** Biblioˈthek *f*; **2.** ˈBücherkataˌlog *m*.

bib·u·lous [ˈbɪbjʊləs] *adj.* ☐ **1.** trunksüchtig; **2.** weinselig.

bi·cam·er·al [baɪˈkæmərəl] *adj. pol.* Zweikammer...

bi·car·bon·ate [baɪˈkɑːbənɪt] *s.* ⚗ Bikarboˈnat *n*: ~ ***of soda*** doppel(t)kohlensaures Natrium.

bi·cen·te·nar·y [ˌbaɪsenˈtiːnərɪ] **I** *adj.* zweihundertjährig; **II** *s.* Zweihundertjahrfeier *f*; ˌ**bi·cenˈten·ni·al** [-ˈtenjəl] **I** *adj.* zweihundertjährig; alle zweihundert Jahre eintretend; **II** *s. bsd. Am.* → ***bicentenary*** II.

bi·ceph·a·lous [ˌbaɪˈsefələs] *adj.* zweiköpfig.

bi·ceps [ˈbaɪseps] *s. anat.* ˈBizeps *m*.

bick·er [ˈbɪkə] *v/i.* **1.** (sich) zanken; quengeln; **2.** plätschern (*Fluß*, *Regen*); **3.** zucken; ˈ**bick·er·ing** [-ərɪŋ] *s. a. pl.* Gezänk *n*.

bi·cy·cle [ˈbaɪsɪkl] **I** *s.* Fahrrad *n*, Zweirad *n*; **II** *v/i.* radfahren, radeln; ˈ**bi·cy·cler** [-lə] *Am.*, ˈ**bi·cy·clist** [-lɪst] *Brit. s.* Radfahrer(in).

bid [bɪd] **I** *s.* **1.** a) Gebot *n* (*bei Versteigerungen*), b) † Angebot *n* (*bei öffentlichen Ausschreibungen*), c) *Börse*: Geld *n* (*Nachfrage*): ~ ***and asked*** Geld u. Brief; ***higher*** ~ Mehrgebot; ***highest*** ~ Meistgebot; ***invitation for*** ~***s*** Ausschreibung *f*; **2.** *Kartenspiel*: Reizen *n*, Melden *n*: ***no*** ~ ich passe; **3.** Bemühung *f*, Bewerbung *f* (***for*** um); Versuch *m* (***to*** *inf.* zu *inf.*): ~ ***for power*** Versuch, an die Macht zu kommen; ***make a*** ~ ***for*** sich bemühen um *et. od.* zu *inf.*; **4.** *Am.* F Einladung *f*; **II** *v/t.* [*irr.*] 5 *u.* 6 *pret. u. p.p.* **bid**; 7–9 *pret.* **bade** [beɪd], *p.p. mst* **bid·den** [ˈbɪdn] **5.** bieten (*bei Ver-*

steigerungen): ~ ***up*** *den Preis* in die Höhe treiben; **6.** *Kartenspiel*: melden, reizen; **7.** *Gruß* entbieten; wünschen: ~ ***good morning*** e-n guten Morgen wünschen; ~ ***farewell*** Lebewohl sagen; **8.** *lit. j-m et.* gebieten, befehlen; *j-n et. tun* lassen, heißen: ~ ***him come in*** laß ihn hereinkommen; **9.** *obs.* einladen (***to*** zu); **III** *v/i.* [*irr., pret. u. p.p.* **bid**] **10.** ✝ ein (Preis)Angebot machen; **11.** *Kartenspiel*: melden, reizen; **12.** (***for***) werben, sich bemühen (um); **'bid·den** [-dn] *p.p. von* ***bid***; **'bid·der** [-də] *s.* **1.** Bieter *m* (*bei Versteigerungen*): ***highest*** ~ Meistbietende(r); **2.** Bewerber *m bei Ausschreibungen*; **'bid·ding** [-dɪŋ] *s.* **1.** Gebot *n*, Bieten *n* (*bei Versteigerungen*); **2.** Geheiß *n*: ***do s.o.'s*** ~ tun, was j-d will.

bide [baɪd] *v/t.* [*irr.*] er-, abwarten: ~ ***one's time*** (den rechten Augenblick) abwarten.

bi·en·ni·al [baɪ'enɪəl] **I** *adj.* ☐ **1.** alle zwei Jahre eintretend; **2.** ⚘ zweijährig; **II** *s.* **3.** ⚘ zweijährige Pflanze; **bi'en·ni·al·ly** [-lɪ] *adv.* alle zwei Jahre.

bier [bɪə] *s.* (Toten)Bahre *f.*

biff [bɪf] *sl.* **I** *v/t.* ,hauen', schlagen; **II** *s.* Schlag *m*, Hieb *m*.

bif·fin ['bɪfɪn] *s.* roter Kochapfel.

bi·fo·cal [ˌbaɪ'fəʊkl] **I** *adj.* **1.** Bifokal-, Zweistärken...; **II** *s.* **2.** Bifo'kal-, Zweistärkenlinse *f*; **3.** *pl.* Bifo'kal-, Zweistärkenbrille *f.*

bi·fur·cate ['baɪfəkeɪt] **I** *v/t.* gabelförmig teilen; **II** *v/i.* sich gabeln; **III** *adj.* gegabelt, gabelförmig; **bi·fur·ca·tion** [ˌbaɪfə'keɪʃn] *s.* Gabelung *f.*

big [bɪg] **I** *adj.* **1.** groß, dick; stark, kräftig (*a. fig.*): ***the*** ~ ***toe*** der große Zeh; ~ ***business*** Großunternehmertum *n*, Großindustrie *f*; ~ ***ideas*** F ,große Rosinen im Kopf'; ~ ***money*** ein Haufen Geld; ***a*** ~ ***voice*** e-e kräftige Stimme; **2.** groß, weit: ***get too*** ~ ***for one's boots*** (*od.* ***breeches***) *fig.* ,üppig' *od.* größenwahnsinnig werden; **3.** groß, hoch: ~ ***game*** Großwild *n*, *fig.* hochgestecktes Ziel; **4.** groß, erwachsen: ***my*** ~ ***brother***; **5.** schwanger; *fig.* voll: ~ ***with child*** hochschwanger; ~ ***with fate*** schicksalsschwer; **6.** hochmütig, eingebildet: ~ ***talk*** ,große Töne', Angeberei *f*; **7.** F groß, bedeutend, wichtig, führend: ***the*** ♀ ***Three*** (***Five***) die großen Drei (Fünf) (*führende Staaten, Banken etc.*); **8.** großmütig, edel: ***a*** ~ ***heart***; ***that's*** ~ ***of you*** F das ist sehr anständig von dir; **II** *adv.* **9.** großspurig: ***talk*** ~ ,große Töne spucken', angeben; **10.** *sl.* a) ,mächtig', b) *Am.* tapfer.

big·a·mist ['bɪgəmɪst] *s.* Biga'mist(in); **'big·a·mous** [-məs] *adj.* ☐ biga'mistisch; **'big·a·my** [-mɪ] *s.* Biga'mie *f*, Doppelehe *f.*

big| bang *s. phys.* Urknall *m*; ~ **game** *s.* Großwild *n*; ~ **gun** *s.* F **1.** ,schweres Geschütz'; **2.** → ***bigwig***.

bight [baɪt] *s.* **1.** Bucht *f*; Einbuchtung *f*; **2.** Krümmung *f*; **3.** ⚓ Bucht *f* (*im Tau*).

'big·mouth *s.* F Großmaul *n.*

big·ness ['bɪgnɪs] *s.* Größe *f.*

big·ot ['bɪgət] *s.* **1.** blinder Anhänger, Fa'natiker *m*; **2.** Betbruder *m*, -schwester *f*, Frömmler(in); **'big·ot·ed** [-tɪd] *adj.* bi'gott, fa'natisch, frömmlerisch; **'big·ot·ry** [-trɪ] *s.* **1.** blinder Eifer, Fa'natismus *m*, Engstirnigkeit *f*; **2.** Bigotte'rie *f*, Frömme'lei *f.*

big| shot *s.* → ***bigwig***; ~ **stick** *s.* F *pol.* ,großer Knüppel': ~ ***policy*** Politik *f* des Säbelrasselns; **'~-time** *adj. sl.* ,groß', Spitzen...; **'~-ˌtim·er** *s.* ,Spitzenmann' *m*, ,großer Macher'; ~ **top** *s. Am.* **1.** großes 'Zirkuszelt; **2.** 'Zirkus *m* (*a. fig.*).

'big·wig *s.* ,großes' *od.* ,hohes Tier', Bonze *m.*

bike [baɪk] F **I** *s.* a) (Fahr)Rad *n*, b) ,Maschine' *f* (*Motorrad*); **II** *v/i.* a) radeln, b) (mit dem) Motorrad fahren.

bi·lat·er·al [ˌbaɪ'lætərəl] *adj.* ☐ zweiseitig, bilate'ral: a) ⚖ beiderseitig verbindlich, gegenseitig (*Vertrag etc.*), b) *biol.* beide Seiten betreffend, c) ⚙ doppelseitig (*Antrieb*).

bil·ber·ry ['bɪlbərɪ] *s.* ⚘ Heidel-, Blaubeere *f.*

bile [baɪl] *s.* **1.** ⚕ a) Galle *f*, b) Gallenflüssigkeit *f*; **2.** *fig.* Galle *f*, Ärger *m*.

bilge [bɪldʒ] *s.* **1.** ⚓ Kielraum *m*, Bilge *f*, Kimm *f*; **2.** → ***bilge water***; **3.** *sl.* ,Quatsch' *m*, ,Mist' *m*, Unsinn *m*; ~ **pump** *s.* ⚓ Lenzpumpe *f*; ~ **wa·ter** *s.* ⚓ Bilgenwasser *n.*

bi·lin·e·ar [ˌbaɪ'lɪnɪə] *adj.* doppellinig; ⩓ biline'ar.

bi·lin·gual [baɪ'lɪŋgwəl] *adj.* zweisprachig.

bil·ious ['bɪljəs] *adj.* ☐ **1.** ⚕ Gallen...: ~ ***complaint*** Gallenleiden *n*; **2.** *fig.* gallig, gereizt, reizbar; **'bil·ious·ness** [-nɪs] *s.* **1.** Gallenkrankheit *f*; **2.** *fig.* Gereiztheit *f.*

bilk [bɪlk] **I** *v/t.* prellen, betrügen; **II** *s.*, *a.* **'bilk·er** [-kə] *s.* Betrüger *m.*

bill¹ [bɪl] **I** *s.* **1.** *zo.* a) Schnabel *m*, b) schnabelähnliche Schnauze; **2.** Spitze *f am Anker, Zirkel etc.*; **3.** *geogr.* spitz zulaufende Halbinsel; **4.** *hist.* ⚔ Pike *f*; **5.** → ***billhook***; **II** *v/i.* **6.** (sich) schnäbeln; **7.** *fig., a.* ~ ***and coo*** (mitein'ander) turteln.

bill² [bɪl] **I** *s.* **1.** *pol.* (Gesetzes)Vorlage *f*, Gesetzentwurf *m*: ~ ***of Rights*** a) *Brit.* Staatsgrundgesetz *n*, Freiheitsurkunde *f* (*von 1689*), b) *USA*: die ersten 10 Zusatzartikel zur Verfassung; ***bring in a*** ~ e-n Gesetzentwurf einbringen; **2.** ⚖ *a.* ~ ***of indictment*** Anklageschrift *f*: ***find a true*** ~ die Anklage für begründet erklären; **3.** ✝ *a.* ~ ***of exchange*** Wechsel *m*, Tratte *f*: ~***s payable*** Wechselschulden; ~***s receivable*** Wechselforderungen; ***long***(***-dated***) ~ langfristiger Wechsel; ~ ***after date*** Datowechsel *m*; ~ ***after sight*** Nachsichtwechsel *m*; ~ ***of lading*** Seefrachtbrief *m*, Konnossement *n*, *Am. a.* Frachtbrief *m*; **4.** Rechnung *f*: ~ ***of costs*** Kostenberechnung *f*; ~ ***of sale*** Kauf-, Übereignungsvertrag *m*; F *fig.* ***fill the*** ~ den Ansprüchen genügen; ***sell s.o. a*** ~ ***of goods*** F j-n ,verschaukeln'; **5.** Liste *f*, Schein *m*, Zettel *m*, Pla'kat *n*: ~ ***of fare*** Speisekarte *f*; (***theatre***) ~ Theaterzettel *m*, -programm *n*; (***clean***) ~ ***of health*** Gesundheitszeugnis *n*, -paß *m*, *fig.* Unbedenklichkeitsbescheinigung *f*; **6.** *Am.* Banknote *f*, (Geld)Schein *m*; **II** *v/t.* **7.** ~ ***s.o. for s.th.*** j-m et. in Rechnung stellen *od.* berechnen; **8.** (durch Pla'kate) ankündigen, *thea. etc. a. Am. Darsteller etc.* ,bringen'.

'bill|·board *s.* Anschlagbrett *n*, Re'klamefläche *f*, -tafel *f*: ~ ***advertising*** Plakatwerbung *f*; ~ **case** *s.* ✝ 'Wechselporteˌfeuille *n e-r Bank*; ~ **dis·count** *s.* ✝ 'Wechseldisˌkont *m.*

bil·let¹ ['bɪlɪt] **I** *s.* **1.** ⚔ a) Quartierzettel *m*, b) Quartier *n*: ***in*** ~***s*** privat einquartiert; **2.** 'Unterkunft *f*; **3.** F ,Job' *m*, Posten *m*; **II** *v/t.* **4.** 'unterbringen, einquartieren (***on*** bei).

bil·let² ['bɪlɪt] *s.* **1.** Holzscheit *n*, -klotz *m*; **2.** *metall.* Knüppel *m.*

bil·let-doux [ˌbɪleɪ'du:] (*Fr.*) *s. humor.* Liebesbrief *m.*

'bill|·fold *s. Am.* Scheintasche *f*; **'~·head** *s.* gedrucktes 'Rechnungsformuˌlar; **'~·hook** *s.* ✂ Hippe *f.*

bil·liard ['bɪljəd] **I** *s.* **1.** *pl. mst sg. konstr.* Billard(spiel) *n*; **2.** *Billard*: Karambo'lage *f*; **II** *adj.* **3.** Billard...; ~ **ball** *s.* Billardkugel *f*; ~ **cue** *s.* Queue *n*, Billardstock *m.*

bill·ing ['bɪlɪŋ] *s.* **1.** ✝ a) Rechnungsschreibung *f*, b) Buchung *f*, *a.* (Vor'aus)Bestellung *f*; **2.** *thea.* a) Ankündigung *f*, b) Re'klame *f.*

Bil·lings·gate ['bɪlɪŋzgɪt] **I** *npr. Fischmarkt in London*; **II** ♀ *s.* wüstes Geschimpfe, Unflat *m*: ***talk*** ~ keifen wie ein Fischweib.

bil·lion ['bɪljən] *s.* **1.** Milli'arde *f*; **2.** *Brit. obs.* Billi'on *f.*

'bill|-job·ber *s.* ✝ *Brit.* Wechselreiter *m*; **'~-ˌjob·bing** *s.* ✝ *Brit.* Wechselreite'rei *f.*

bil·low ['bɪləʊ] **I** *s.* **1.** Woge *f* (*a. fig.*); **2.** (Nebel- *etc.*)Schwaden *m*; **II** *v/i.* **3.** wogen; **4.** *a.* ~ ***out*** sich bauschen *od.* blähen; **III** *v/t.* bauschen, blähen; **'bil·low·y** [-əʊɪ] *adj.* **1.** wogend; **2.** gebauscht, gebläht.

'bill|-ˌpost·er, **'~-ˌstick·er** *s.* Pla'kat-, Zettelankleber *m.*

bil·ly ['bɪlɪ] *s. Am.* (Poli'zei)Knüppel *m*; **'~·cock** (**hat**) *s. Brit.* F ,Me'lone' *f* (*steifer Filzhut*); ~ **goat** *s.* F Ziegenbock *m.*

bim·bo ['bɪmbəʊ] *s. sl.* ,Knülch' *m.*

bi·met·al·lism [ˌbaɪ'metəlɪzəm] Bimetal'lismus *m*, Doppelwährung *f* (*Gold u. Silber*).

bi·month·ly [ˌbaɪ'mʌnθlɪ] **I** *adj. u. adv.* **1.** a) zweimonatlich, alle zwei Monate ('wiederkehrend *od.* erscheinend), b) zweimal im Monat (erscheinend); **II** *s.* **2.** zweimonatlich erscheinende Veröffentlichung; **3.** Halbmonatsschrift *f.*

bi·mo·tored [ˌbaɪ'məʊtəd] *adj.* ✈ 'zweimoˌtorig.

bin [bɪn] *s.* **1.** (großer) Behälter, Kasten *m*; *a.* Silo *m*, *n*; **2.** Verschlag *m*; **3.** *sl.* ,Klapsmühle' *f.*

bi·na·ry ['baɪnərɪ] *adj.* ⚗, ⚙, ⩓, *phys.* bi'när, aus zwei Einheiten bestehend: ~ ***digit*** Binärziffer *f*; ~ (***number***) ⩓ Binär-, Dualzahl *f*; ~ (***star***) *ast.* Doppelstern *m*; ~ ***fission*** *biol.* Zellteilung *f.*

bind [baɪnd] **I** *s.* **1.** Band *n*; **2.** ♪ Halte- *od.* Bindebogen *m*; **3.** F ***be in a*** ~ in ,Schwulitäten' sein; ***be in a*** ~ ***for*** *et. od. j-n* dringend brauchen, verlegen sein um; **II** *v/t.* [*irr.*] **4.** binden, an-, 'um-, festbinden, verbinden: ~ ***to a tree*** an e-n Baum binden; ***bound hand and foot*** *fig.* an Händen u. Füßen gebunden; **5.** *Buch* (ein)binden; **6.** *Saum etc.* einfassen; **7.** *Rad etc.* (mit Me'tall) beschlagen; **8.** *Sand etc.* fest *od.* hart machen; zs.-fügen; **9.** (**o.s.** sich) binden (*a. vertraglich*), verpflichten; zwingen: ***~ an apprentice*** *j-n* in die Lehre geben (***to*** bei); ***~ a bargain*** e-n Handel (durch Anzahlung) verbindlich machen; → ***bound***[1] 1; **10.** ⚗, ⚙ binden; **11.** ✱ verstopfen; **II** *v/i.* **12.** binden, fest *od.* hart werden, zs.-halten; ~ **o·ver** *v/t.* ⚖ **1.** zum Erscheinen verpflichten (***to*** vor *e-m Gericht*); **2.** *Brit. j-n* auf Bewährung entlassen; ~ **up** *v/t.* **1.** vereinigen, zs.-binden; *Wunde* verbinden; **2.** *pass.* ***be bound up*** (***in*** *od.* ***with***) a) eng verknüpft sein (mit), b) ganz in Anspruch genommen werden (von).

bind·er [ˈbaɪndə] *s.* **1.** a) (*Buch-, Garben*)Binder(in), b) Garbenbinder *m* (*Maschine*); **2.** Binde *f*, Band *n*, Schnur *f*; **3.** Aktendeckel *m*, ˈUmschlag *m*; **4.** ⚙ Bindemittel *n*; **5.** ✝ Vorvertrag *m*; ˈ**bind·er·y** [-ərɪ] *s.* Buchbindeˈrei *f*.

bind·ing [ˈbaɪndɪŋ] **I** *adj.* **1.** *fig.* bindend, (rechts)verbindlich ([***up***]***on*** für): ***~ force*** bindende Kraft; ***~ law*** zwingendes Recht; **II** *s.* **2.** (Buch)Einband *m*; **3.** a) Einfassung *f*, Borte *f*, b) (Meˈtall-) Beschlag *m* (*Rad*), c) (Ski)Bindung *f*; ~ **a·gent** → ***binder*** 4; ~ **post** *s.* ϟ (Pol-, Anschluß)Klemme *f*.

ˈ**bind·weed** *s.* ⚘ *e-e* Winde *f*.

bine [baɪn] *s.* ⚘ Ranke *f*.

binge [bɪndʒ] *s.* F ‚Sauf- *od.* Freßgelage' *n*: ***go on a ~*** ‚einen draufmachen'.

bin·go [ˈbɪŋgəʊ] *s.* Bingo *n* (*ein Glücksspiel*): ***~!*** F Zack!, Volltreffer!

bin·na·cle [ˈbɪnəkl] *s.* ⚓ ˈKompaßhaus *n*.

bin·oc·u·lar I *adj.* [ˌbaɪˈnɒkjʊlə] binokuˈlar, für beide *od.* mit beiden Augen; **II** *s.* [bɪˈn-] *mst pl.* Fernglas *n*; Opernglas *n*.

bi·no·mi·al [ˌbaɪˈnəʊmjəl] *adj.* **1.** A biˈnomisch, zweigliedrig; **2.** ⚘, *zo.* → ***binominal***.

bi·nom·i·nal [ˌbaɪˈnɒmɪnl] *adj.* ⚘, *zo.* binomiˈnal, zweinamig: ***~ system*** (System *n* der) Doppelbenennung *f*.

bi·nu·cle·ar [ˌbaɪˈnjuːklɪə], **biˈnu·cle·ate** [-ɪət] *adj. phys.* zweikernig.

bi·o·chem·i·cal [ˌbaɪəʊˈkemɪkl] *adj.* □ bioˈchemisch; ˌ**bi·oˈchem·ist** [-ɪst] *s.* Bioˈchemiker *m*; ˌ**bi·oˈchem·is·try** [-ɪstrɪ] *s.* Biocheˈmie *f*.

bi·o·de·gra·dab·le [ˌbaɪəʊdɪˈgreɪdəbl] *adj.* ⚗ (bioˈlogisch) abbaubar.

bi·o·en·er·get·ics [ˈbaɪəʊˌenəˈdʒetɪks] *s. pl. sg. konstr.* Bioenerˈgetik *f*.

bi·o·en·gi·neer·ing [ˈbaɪəʊˌendʒɪˈnɪərɪŋ] *s.* Biotechnik *f*.

bi·og·ra·pher [baɪˈɒgrəfə] *s.* Bioˈgraph *m*; **bi·o·graph·ic, bi·o·graph·i·cal** [ˌbaɪəʊˈgræfɪk(l)] *adj.* □ bioˈgraphisch; **biˈog·ra·phy** [-fɪ] *s.* Biograˈphie *f*, Lebensbeschreibung *f*.

bi·o·log·ic [ˌbaɪəʊˈlɒdʒɪk] *adj.* (□ ***~ally***) → **bi·oˈlog·i·cal** [-kl] *adj.* □ bioˈlogisch: ***~ warfare*** Bakterienkrieg *m*; **bi·ol·o·gist** [baɪˈɒlədʒɪst] *s.* Bioˈloge *m*; **bi·ol·o·gy** [baɪˈɒlədʒɪ] *s.* Bioloˈgie *f*.

bi·ol·y·sis [baɪˈɒləsɪs] *s. biol.* Bioˈlyse *f*.

bi·on·ics [baɪˈɒnɪks] *s. pl. sg. konstr. phys.* Biˈonik *f*.

bi·o·nom·ics [ˌbaɪəʊˈnɒmɪks] *s. pl. sg. konstr. biol.* Ökoloˈgie *f*; **bi·o·phys·ics** [ˌbaɪəʊˈfɪzɪks] *s. pl. sg. konstr.* Biophyˈsik *f*.

bi·o·tope [ˌbaɪəʊˈtəʊp] *s. biol. geogr.* Bioˈtop *m, n*.

bi·par·ti·san [ˌbaɪpɑːtɪˈzæn] *adj.* zwei Parˈteien vertretend, Zweiparteien...; ˌ**bi·par·tiˈsan·ship** [-ʃɪp] *s.* Zugehörigkeit *f* zu zwei Parteien; **bi·par·tite** [ˌbaɪˈpɑːtaɪt] *adj.* **1.** zweiteilig; **2.** *pol.*, ⚖ a) zweiseitig (*Vertrag etc.*), b) in doppelter Ausfertigung (*Dokumente*).

bi·ped [ˈbaɪped] *s. zo.* Zweifüß(l)er *m*.

bi·plane [ˈbaɪpleɪn] *s.* ✈ Doppel-, Zweidecker *m*.

birch [bɜːtʃ] **I** *s.* **1.** a) ⚘ Birke *f*, b) Birkenholz *n*; **2.** (Birken)Rute *f*; **II** *v/t.* **3.** mit der Rute züchtigen; ˈ**birch·en** [-tʃən] *adj.* birken, Birken...; ˈ**birch·ing** [-tʃɪŋ] *s.* (Ruten)Schläge *pl.*; ˈ**birch-rod** → ***birch*** 2.

bird [bɜːd] *s.* **1.** Vogel *m*: ***~ of paradise*** Paradiesvogel; ***~ of passage*** Zugvogel (*a. fig.*); ***~ of prey*** Raub-, Greifvogel; F ***early ~*** Frühaufsteher *m*, wer früh kommt; ***the early ~ catches the worm*** Morgenstund hat Gold im Mund; ***~s of a feather flock together*** gleich u. gleich gesellt sich gern; ***kill two ~s with one stone*** zwei Fliegen mit e-r Klappe schlagen; ***a ~ in the hand is worth two in the bush*** ein Sperling in der Hand ist besser als e-e Taube auf dem Dach; ***fine feathers make fine ~s*** Kleider machen Leute; ***the ~ is*** (*od.* ***has***) ***flown*** *fig.* der Vogel ist ausgeflogen; ***give s.o. the ~*** j-n auspfeifen *od.* ‚abfahren lassen', j-m den Laufpaß geben; F ***a little ~ told me*** mein kleiner Finger hat es mir gesagt; ***tell a child about the ~s and the bees*** ein Kind aufklären; ***that's for the ~s*** F das ist ‚für die Katz'; **2.** a) F ‚Knülch' *m*, Kerl *m*, b) *Brit. sl.* ‚Puppe' *f* (*Mädchen*): ***queer ~*** komischer Kauz; ***old ~*** alter Knabe; ***gay ~*** lustiger Vogel; **3.** *sl.* a) ‚Vogel' *m* (*Flugzeug*), b) *Am.* Rangabzeichen *n e-s Colonel etc.*; ˈ**~·brain** *s.* F ‚Spatzen(ge)hirn' *n*; ~ **cage** *s.* Vogelbauer *n*, -käfig *m*; ˈ**~·call** *s.* Vogelruf *m*; Lockpfeife *f*; ~ **dog** *s.* Hühnerhund *m*; ˈ**~-ˌfan·ci·er** *s.* Vogelliebhaber(in), -züchter(in), -händler(in).

bird·ie [ˈbɜːdɪ] *s.* **1.** Vögelchen *n*; **2.** ‚Täubchen' *n* (*Kosewort*); **3.** *Golf*: ˈBirdie *n* (*1 Schlag unter Par*).

bird| life *s.* Vogelleben *n*, -welt *f*; ˈ**~·lime** *s.* Vogelleim *m*; ˈ**~·man** *s.* [*irr.*] **1.** Vogelkenner *m*; **2.** ✈ F Flieger *m*; ˈ**~-ˌnest·ing** *s.* Ausnehmen *n* von Vogelnestern; ˈ**~·seed** *s.* Vogelfutter *n*.

ˈ**bird's|-eye** [bɜːdz] **I** *s.* **1.** ⚘ Aˈdonisröschen *n*; **2.** Feinschnittabak *m*; **3.** ✝ Pfauenauge(nmuster) *n*; **II** *adj.* **4.** ***~ view*** (Blick *m* aus der) Vogelperspektive *f*, allgemeiner Überblick; ~ **nest** *s.* (*a. eßbares*) Vogelnest.

bird watch·er *s.* Vogelbeobachter *m*.

bi·ro [ˈbaɪərəʊ] *s.* (*TM*) *Brit.* Kugelschreiber *m*.

birth [bɜːθ] *s.* **1.** Geburt *f*; Wurf *m* (*Hunde etc.*): ***give ~ to*** gebären, zur Welt bringen, *fig.* hervorbringen, -rufen; ***by ~*** von Geburt; **2.** Abstammung *f*, Herkunft *f*; *engS.* edle Herkunft; **3.** Ursprung *m*, Entstehung *f*; ~ **cer·tif·i·cate** *s.* Geburtsurkunde *f*; ~ **con·trol** *s.* Geburtenregelung *f*, -beschränkung *f*; ˈ**~·day** *s.* Geburtstag *m*: ***~ honours*** *Brit.* Titelverleihungen zum Geburtstag des Königs *od.* der Königin; ***in one's ~ suit*** im Adams- *od.* Evaskostüm; ***~ party*** Geburtstagsparty *f*; ˈ**~·mark** *s.* Muttermal *n*; ˈ**~·place** *s.* Geburtsort *m*; ~ **rate** *s.* Geburtenziffer *f*: ***falling ~*** Geburtenrückgang *m*; ˈ**~·right** *s.* (Erst-) Geburtsrecht *n*.

bis·cuit [ˈbɪskɪt] **I** *s.* **1.** *Brit.* Keks *m*: ***that takes the ~!*** F a) das ist doch das Allerletzte!, b) das ist (einsame) Spitze!; **2.** *Am.* weiches Brötchen; **3.** → ***biscuit ware***; **II** *adj.* **4.** a) blaßbraun, b) graugelb; ~ **ware** *s.* ⚙ Bisˈkuit *n* (*Porzellan*).

bi·sect [baɪˈsekt] *v/t.* **1.** in zwei Teile zerschneiden; **2.** A halbieren; **bi·sec·tion** [ˌbaɪˈsekʃn] *s.* A Halbierung *f*.

bi·sex·u·al [ˌbaɪˈseksjʊəl] *adj. allg.* bisexuˈell.

bish·op [ˈbɪʃɒp] *s.* **1.** Bischof *m*; **2.** *Schach*: Läufer *m*; **3.** Bischof *m* (*Getränk*); ˈ**bish·op·ric** [-rɪk] *s.* Bistum *n*, Diöˈzese *f*.

bi·son [ˈbaɪsn] *s. zo.* **1.** Bison *m*, amer. Büffel *m*; **2.** euroˈpäischer Wisent.

bis·sex·tile [bɪˈsekstaɪl] **I** *s.* Schaltjahr *n*; **II** *adj.* Schalt...: ***~ day*** Schalttag *m*.

bit[1] [bɪt] *s.* **1.** Gebiß *n* (*am Pferdezaum*): ***take the ~ between one's teeth*** a) durchgehen (*Pferd*), b) störrisch werden (*a. fig.*), c) *fig.* ‚rangehen'; → ***champ***[1]; **2.** *fig.* Zaum *m*, Zügel *m u. pl.*; **3.** ⚙ a) Bohrerspitze *f*, b) Hobeleisen *n*, c) Maul *n* der Zange *etc.*, d) Bart *m* des Schlüssels.

bit[2] [bɪt] *s.* **1.** Stückchen *n*: ***a ~ of bread***; ***a ~*** ein bißchen, ein wenig, leicht; ***a ~ of a ...*** so et. wie ein(e) ...; ***a ~ of a fool*** etwas närrisch; ***~ by ~*** Stück für Stück, allmählich; ***after a ~*** nach e-m Weilchen; ***every ~ as good*** ganz genauso gut; ***not a ~ better*** kein bißchen besser; ***not a ~*** (***of it***) ‚keine Spur', ganz und gar nicht; ***do one's ~*** a) s-e Pflicht tun, b) s-n Beitrag leisten; ***give s.o. a ~ of one's mind*** j-m (gehörig) die Meinung sagen; **2.** kleine Münze: a) *Brit.* F ***threepenny ~***, b) *Am.* F ***two ~s*** 25 Cent; **3.** F ‚Mieze' *f* (*Mädchen*); **4.** *a.* ***~ part*** *thea.* F kleine Rolle: ***~ player***.

bit[3] [bɪt] *s. Computer*: Bit *n*.

bit[4] [bɪt] *pret. von* ***bite***.

bitch [bɪtʃ] **I** *s.* **1.** Hündin *f*; **2.** *a.* ***~ fox*** Füchsin *f*; *a.* ***~ wolf*** Wölfin *f*; **3.** V *contp.* a) Schlampe *f*, b) ‚Miststück' *n*; **4.** *sl.* ‚Scheißding' *n*; **II** *v/t.* **5.** *sl. a.* ***~ up*** ‚versauen'; **III** *v/i.* **6.** *sl.* ‚meckern'; **bitch·y** [ˈbɪtʃɪ] *adj.* F ‚gemein'.

bite [baɪt] **I** *s.* **1.** Beißen *n*, Biß *m*; Stich *m* (*Insekt*): ***put the ~ on s.o.*** *Am. sl.* j-n unter Druck setzen; **2.** Bissen *m*, Happen *m*: ***not a ~ to eat***; **3.** (An-) Beißen *n* (*Fisch*); **4.** ⚙ Fassen *n*, Greifen *n*; **5.** *fig.* a) Bissigkeit *f*, Schärfe *f*, Spitze *f*, b) ‚Biß' *m* (*Aggressivität*): ***the ~ was gone***; **6.** *fig.* Würze *f*, Geist *m*; **II** *v/t.* [*irr.*] **7.** beißen: ***~ one's lips*** sich auf die Lippen (*fig.* auf die Zunge) beißen; ***~ one's nails*** an den Nägeln kauen; ***bitten with a desire*** *fig.* von e-m Wunsch gepackt; ***what's biting you?*** *Am. sl.* was ist mit dir los?; → ***dust*** 1; **8.** beißen, stechen (*Insekt*); **9.** ⚙ fassen, greifen; schneiden in (*acc.*); **10.** ⚗ beizen, zerfressen, angreifen; beschädigen; **11.** F *pass.*: ***be bitten***

hereingefallen sein; ***once bitten twice shy*** gebranntes Kind scheut das Feuer; III *v/i.* [*irr.*] **12.** beißen; **13.** (an-) beißen; *fig.* sich verlocken lassen; **14.** ⚙ fassen, greifen (*Rad, Bremse, Werkzeug*); **15.** *fig.* beißen, schneiden, brennen, stechen, scharf sein (*Kälte, Wind, Gewürz, Schmerz*); **16.** *fig.* beißend *od.* verletzend sein; **~ off** *v/t.* abbeißen: ***~ more than one can chew*** sich zuviel zumuten.

bit·er ['baɪtə] *s.*: ***the ~ bit*** der betrogene Betrüger; ***the ~ will be bitten*** wer andern e-e Grube gräbt, fällt selbst hinein.

bit·ing ['baɪtɪŋ] *adj.* ☐ *a. fig.* beißend, scharf, schneidend.

bit·ten ['bɪtn] *p.p. von* ***bite***.

bit·ter ['bɪtə] I *adj.* ☐ → *a.* 4; **1.** bitter (*Geschmack*); **2.** *fig.* bitter (*Schicksal, Wahrheit, Tränen, Worte etc.*), schmerzlich, hart: ***to the ~ end*** bis zum bitteren Ende; **3.** *fig.* verärgert, böse, verbittert; streng, unerbittlich; rauh, unfreundlich (*a. Wetter*); II *adv.* **4.** *nur:* ***~ cold*** bitter kalt; III *s.* **5.** Bitterkeit *f* (*a. fig.*): ***take the ~ with the sweet*** das Leben (so) nehmen, wie es ist; **6.** *a.* ***~ beer*** *Brit. stark gehopftes Faßbier*; **7.** *pl.* Magenbitter *m.*

bit·tern[1] ['bɪtən] *s. orn.* Rohrdommel *f.*

bit·tern[2] ['bɪtən] *s.* **1.** ⚗ Mutterlauge *f*; **2.** Bitterstoff *m* (*für Bier*).

bit·ter·ness ['bɪtənɪs] *s.* **1.** Bitterkeit *f*; **2.** *fig.* Bitterkeit *f*, Schmerzlichkeit *f*; **3.** *fig.* Verbitterung *f*, Härte *f*, Grausamkeit *f.*

'bit·ter·sweet I *adj.* bittersüß; halbbitter; II *s.* ♀ Bittersüß *n.*

bi·tu·men ['bɪtjʊmɪn] *s.* **1.** *min.* Bi'tumen *n*, Erdpech *n*, As'phalt *m*; **2.** *geol.* Bergteer *m.*

bi·tu·mi·nous [bɪ'tju:mɪnəs] *adj. min.* bitumi'nös, as'phalt-, pechhaltig; **~ coal** *s.* Stein-, Fettkohle *f.*

bi·va·lent ['baɪˌveɪlənt] *adj.* ⚗ zweiwertig.

bi·valve ['baɪvælv] *s. zo.* zweischalige Muschel (*z.B. Auster*).

biv·ouac ['bɪvʊæk] I *s.* 'Biwak *n*; II *v/i.* biwakieren.

bi·week·ly [ˌbaɪ'wi:klɪ] I *adj. u. adv.* **1.** zweiwöchentlich, vierzehntägig, halbmonatlich; **2.** zweimal die Woche; II *s.* **3.** Halbmonatsschrift *f.*

biz [bɪz] *s.* F *für* ***business***.

bi·zarre [bɪ'zɑ:] *adj.* bi'zarr, phan'tastisch, ab'sonderlich.

blab [blæb] I *v/t.* ausplaudern; II *v/i.* schwatzen; III *s.* Schwätzer(in), Klatschbase *f*, -weib *n*; **'blab·ber** [-bə] *s.* Schwätzer(in).

black [blæk] I *adj.* **1.** schwarz (*a. Tee, Kaffee*): ***~ as coal*** (*od.* ***the devil*** *od.* ***ink*** *od.* ***night*** *od.* ***pitch***) kohlrabenpechschwarz; → ***black eye, belt*** 1, 5, ***diamond*** 1; **2.** dunkel: ***~ in the face*** dunkelrot im Gesicht (*vor Aufregung etc.*); **3.** dunkel(häutig): ***~ man*** Schwarzer *m*, Neger *m*; **4.** schwarz, schmutzig: ***~ hands***; **5.** *fig.* dunkel, trübe, düster (*Gedanken, Wetter*); **6.** böse, schlecht: ***~ soul*** schwarze Seele; ***not so ~ as he is painted*** besser als sein Ruf; **7.** ,schwarz', ungesetzlich; **8.** ärgerlich, böse: ***~ look(s)*** böser Blick; ***look ~ at s.o.*** j-n böse anblicken; **9.** schlimm: ***~ despair*** völlige Verzweiflung; **10.** *Am.* eingefleischt; **11.** ,schwarz' (*makaber*): ***~ humo(u)r***; **12.** *TV* schwarz'weiß; II *s.* **13.** Schwarz *n*; **14.** *et.* Schwarzes, schwarzer Fleck: ***wear ~*** Trauer(kleidung) tragen; **15.** Schwarze(r *m*) *f*, Neger(in); **16.** Schwärze *f*, schwarze Schuhkrem; **17.** ***be in the ~*** *bsd.* ✝ a) mit Gewinn arbeiten, b) aus den roten Zahlen heraus sein; III *v/t.* **18.** schwärzen, *Schuhe* wichsen; **~ out** I *v/t.* **1.** (völlig) abdunkeln, *a.* ⚔ verdunkeln; **2.** ⚙ *u. fig.* ausschalten, außer Betrieb setzen; *Funkstation* (durch Störgeräusche) ausschalten; **3.** *j-n* bewußtlos machen; **4.** *fig.* (*a. durch Zensur*) unter'drücken; II *v/i.* **5.** sich verdunkeln; **6.** a) das Bewußtsein verlieren, b) e-n ,Blackout' haben; **7.** ⚙ *etc.* ausfallen.

black Af·ri·ca *s. pol.* Schwarzafrika *n.*

black·a·moor ['blækəˌmʊə] *s. obs.* Neger(in *f*) *m*, Mohr(in *f*) *m.*

black| and blue *adj.*: ***beat s.o. ~*** j-n grün und blau schlagen; **~ and tan** *adj.* schwarz mit braunen Flecken; **~ and white** *s.* **1.** Schwarz'weißzeichnung *f*; **2.** ***in ~*** schwarz auf weiß, schriftlich, gedruckt; **3.** *TV etc.* schwarz'weiß; **~ art** → ***black magic***; **~ ball** *s.* schwarze (Wahl)Kugel; *fig.* Gegenstimme *f*; **'~·ball** *v/t.* gegen *j-n* stimmen, *j-n* ausschließen; **~ bee·tle** *s. zo.* Küchenschabe *f*; **'~·ber·ry** [-bərɪ] *s.* ♀ Brombeere *f*; **'~·bird** *s. orn.* Amsel *f*; **'~·board** *s.* (Schul-, Wand)Tafel *f*; **~ box** *s.* ✈ Flugschreiber *m*; **~ cap** *s.* schwarze Kappe (*des Richters bei Todesurteilen*); **'~·cap** *s. orn.* a) Kohlmeise *f*, b) Schwarzköpfige Grasmücke; **~ cat·tle** *s. zo.* schwarze Rinderrasse; **'~ˌcoat(·ed)** *adj. Brit.*: ***~ worker*** Büroangestellte(r) *m* (*Ggs. Arbeiter*); **'~·cock** *s. orn.* Schwarzes Schottisches Moorhuhn (*Hahn*); ♇ **Coun·try** *s.* Indu'striegebiet *n* von Staffordshire u. Warwickshire; ♇ **Death** *s. der* Schwarze Tod, Pest *f*; **~ dog** *s.* F schlechte Laune.

black·en ['blækən] I *v/t.* **1.** schwärzen; wichsen; **2.** *fig.* anschwärzen: ***~ing the memory of the deceased*** ⚖ Verunglimpfung *f* Verstorbener; II *v/i.* **3.** schwarz werden.

black| eye *s.* ,blaues Auge': ***get away with a ~*** mit e-m blauen Auge davonkommen; **'~·face** *s. typ.* (halb)fette Schrift; **~ flag** *s.* schwarze (Pi'raten-) Flagge; ♇ **Fri·ar** *s. eccl.* Domini'kaner *m*; **~ frost** *s.* strenge, aber trockene Kälte; **~ game** *s. orn.* schwarzes Rebhuhn; **~ grouse** *s. orn.* Birkhuhn *n.*

black·guard ['blægɑ:d] I *s.* Lump *m*, Schuft *m*; II *v/t.* *j-n* beschimpfen; **'black·guard·ly** [-lɪ] *adj.* gemein; unflätig.

'black|·head *s.* ☤ Mitesser *m*; **~ ice** *s.* Glatteis *n.*

black·ie ['blækɪ] *s.* → ***blacky***.

black·ing ['blækɪŋ] *s.* **1.** schwarze (Schuh)Wichse; **2.** (Ofen)Schwärze *f.*

black·ish ['blækɪʃ] *adj.* schwärzlich.

'black|·jack I *s.* **1.** → ***black flag***; **2.** *Am.* Totschläger *m* (*Waffe*); **3.** 'Siebzehnund'vier *n* (*Kartenspiel*); II *v/t.* **4.** *Am.* mit e-m Totschläger zs.-schlagen; **~ lead** [led] *s. min.* Gra'phit *m*, Reißblei *n*; **ˌ~-'lead pen·cil** *s.* Graphitstift *m*; **'~·leg** I *s.* **1.** a) Falschspieler *m*, b) Wettbetrüger *m*; **2.** *Brit.* Streikbrecher *m*; II *v/i.* **3.** als Streikbrecher auftreten; **~ let·ter** *s. typ.* Frak'tur *f*, gotische Schrift; **ˌ~-'let·ter** *adj.*: ***~ day*** schwarzer Tag, Unglückstag *m*; **'~·list** I *s.* schwarze Liste; II *v/t.* *j-n* auf die schwarze Liste setzen; **~ mag·ic** *s.* Schwarze Ma'gie; **'~·mail** I *s.* **1.** ⚖ Erpressung *f*; **2.** Erpressungsgeld *n*; II *v/t.* **3.** *j-n* erpressen, von *j-m* Geld erpressen: ***~ s.o. into s.th*** j-n durch Erpressung zu et. zwingen; **'~ˌmail·er** *s.* Erpresser *m*; ♇ **Ma·ri·a** [mə'raɪə] *s.* F ,Grüne Minna', (Poli'zei)Gefangenenwagen *m*; **~ mark** *s.* schlechte Note, Tadel *m*; **~ mar·ket** *s.* schwarzer Markt, Schwarzmarkt *m*, -handel *m* (***in*** mit); **~ mar·ket·eer** *s.* Schwarzhändler(in); **~ mass** *s.* Schwarze Messe, Teufelsmesse *f*; **~ monk** *s.* Benedik'tiner(mönch) *m.*

black·ness ['blæknɪs] *s.* **1.** Schwärze *f*, Dunkelheit *f*; **2.** *fig.* Verderbtheit *f*, Ab'scheulichkeit *f.*

'black|·out *s.* **1.** *bsd.* ⚔ Verdunkelung *f*; **2.** (*Nachrichten- etc.*)Sperre *f*: ***news ~***; **3.** ☤ a) Blackout *n*, *m* (*kurze Ohnmacht, Bewußtseinsstörung etc.*), b) Bewußtlosigkeit *f*, Ohnmacht *f*; **4.** ⚙ *u. fig.* Ausfall *m*; ϟ to'taler Stromausfall; **5.** *TV* a) Austasten *n*, b) Pro'grammod. Bildausfall *m*; **6.** *phys. etc., a. thea.* Blackout *n*, *m*; ♇ **Prince** *s. der* Schwarze Prinz (*Eduard, Prinz von Wales*); **~ pud·ding** *s. Brit.* Blutwurst *f*; ♇ **Rod** *s.* **1.** oberster Dienstbeamter des brit. Oberhauses; **2.** erster Zere'monienmeister des Hosenbandordens; **~ sheep** *s. fig.* schwarzes Schaf; **'~·shirt** *s.* Schwarzhemd *n* (*italienischer Faschist*); **'~·smith** *s.* (Grob-, Huf)Schmied *m*; **~ spot** *s. mot.* schwarzer Punkt, Gefahrenstelle *f*; **'~·strap** *s. Am.* **1.** *Getränk aus Rum u. Sirup*; **2.** F Rotwein *m* aus dem Mittelmeergebiet; **'~·thorn** *s.* ♀ Schwarz-, Schlehdorn *m*; **~ tie** *s.* **1.** schwarze Fliege; **2.** Smoking *m*; **'~·top** *s.* Asphaltbelag *m od.* -straße *f*; **'~ˌwa·ter fe·ver** *s.* ☤ Schwarzwasserfieber *n*; **~ wid·ow** *s. zo.* Schwarze Witwe (*Spinne*).

black·y ['blækɪ] *s.* F Schwarze(r *m*) *f* (*Neger od. Schwarzhaarige[r]*).

blad·der ['blædə] *s.* **1.** *anat.* (Gallen-, *engS.* Harn)Blase *f*; **2.** (*Fußball- etc.*) Blase *f*; **3.** *zo.* Schwimmblase *f*; **~ wrack** *s.* ♀ Blasentang *m.*

blade [bleɪd] *s.* **1.** ♀ Blatt *n* (*mst poet.*), Spreite *f* (*e-s Blattes*), Halm *m*: ***in the ~*** auf dem Halm; ***~ of grass*** Grashalm; **2.** ⚙ Blatt *n* (*Säge, Axt, Schaufel, Ruder*); **3.** ⚙ a) Flügel *m* (*Propeller*); *Hubschrauber*: Rotor *m*, Drehflügel *m*, b) Schaufel *f* (*Schiffsrad, Turbine*); **4.** ⚙ Klinge *f* (*Messer, Degen etc.*); **5.** → ***shoulder-blade***; **6.** *poet.* a) Degen *m*, Klinge *f*, b) Kämpfer *m*; **7.** F (forscher) Kerl, Bursche *m.*

blae·ber·ry ['bleɪbərɪ] → ***bilberry***.

blah[1] [blɑ:] *a.* **ˌblah-'blah** F I *s.* ,Bla'bla' *n*, Geschwafel *n*; II *v/i.* schwafeln.

blah[2] [blɑ:] F I *adj.* (stink)fad; II *s. pl. Am.* a) Langeweile *f*, b) ,mieses Gefühl'.

blain [bleɪn] *s.* ☤ Pustel *f.*

blam·a·ble ['bleɪməbl] *adj.* ☐ zu tadeln(d), schuldig; **blame** [bleɪm] **I** *v/t.* **1.** tadeln, rügen, *j-m* Vorwürfe machen (***for*** wegen); **2.** (***for***) verantwortlich machen (für), *j-m* die Schuld geben (an *dat.*): ***he is to ~ for it*** er ist daran schuld; ***he has only himself to ~*** das hat er sich selbst zuzuschreiben; ***I cannot ~ him for it*** ich kann es ihm nicht verübeln; **II** *s.* **3.** Tadel *m*, Vorwurf *m*, Rüge *f*; **4.** Schuld *f*, Verantwortung *f*: ***lay*** (*od.* ***put***) ***the ~ on s.o.*** j-m die Schuld geben; ***bear*** (*od.* ***take***) ***the ~*** die Schuld auf sich nehmen; **'blame·less** [-lɪs] *adj.* □ untadelig, schuldlos (***of*** an *dat.*); **'blame·less·ness** [-lɪsnɪs] *s.* Schuldlosigkeit *f*, Unschuld *f*; **'blame,wor·thy** *adj.* tadelnswert, schuldig.

blanch [blɑ:ntʃ] **I** *v/t.* **1.** bleichen, weiß machen; *fig.* erbleichen lassen; **2.** ✓ (*durch Ausschluß von Licht*) bleichen; **3.** *Küche*: *Mandeln etc.* blanchieren, brühen; **4.** ⚙ weiß sieden; brühen; **5.** ***~ over*** *fig.* beschönigen; **II** *v/i.* **6.** erbleichen.

blanc·mange [blə'mɒnʒ] *s.* *Küche*: Pudding *m*.

bland [blænd] *adj.* □ **1.** a) mild, sanft, b) höflich, verbindlich, c) (ein)schmeichelnd; **2.** a) kühl, b) i'ronisch.

blan·dish ['blændɪʃ] *v/t.* schmeicheln, zureden (*dat.*); **'blan·dish·ment** [-mənt] *s.* Schmeiche'lei *f*, Zureden *n*; *pl.* Über'redungskünste *pl.*

blank [blæŋk] **I** *adj.* □ **1.** leer, nicht ausgefüllt, unbeschrieben; Blanko... (*bsd.* ✝): ***a ~ page***; ***a ~ space*** ein leerer Raum; ***~ tape*** Leerband *n*; ***in ~*** blanko; ***leave ~*** frei lassen; ***~ acceptance*** Blankoakzept *n*; ***~ signature*** Blankounterschrift *f*; → ***cheque***; **2.** leer, unbebaut; **3.** blind (*Fenster*, *Tür*); **4.** leer, ausdruckslos; **5.** verdutzt, verblüfft, verlegen: ***a ~ look***; **6.** bar, rein, völlig: ***~ astonishment*** sprachloses Erstaunen; ***~ despair*** helle Verzweiflung; **7.** → ***cartridge*** 1, ***fire*** 13, ***verse*** 3; **II** *s.* **8.** Formblatt *n*, Formu'lar *n*, Vordruck *m*; unbeschriebenes Blatt (*a. fig.*); **9.** leerer *od.* freier Raum (*bsd. für Wort[e] od. Buchstaben*); Lücke *f*, Leere *f* (*a. fig.*): ***leave a ~*** e-n freien Raum lassen (*beim Schreiben etc.*); ***his mind was a ~*** a) er hatte alles vergessen, b) in s-m Kopf herrschte völlige Leere; **10.** *Lotterie*: Niete *f*: ***draw a ~*** a) e-e Niete ziehen, b) *fig.* kein Glück haben; **11.** *bsd. sport* Null *f*; **12.** *das* Schwarze (*Zielscheibe*); **13.** Öde *f*, Nichts *n*; **14.** ⚙ unbearbeitetes Werkstück, Rohling *m*; ungeprägte Münzplatte; **15.** Gedankenstrich *m* (*an Stelle e-s* [*unanständigen*] *Wortes*), ‚Pünktchen' *pl.*; **III** *v/t.* **16.** *mst* ***~ out*** a) verhüllen, auslöschen, b) *fig.* ‚erledigen', abtun; **17.** ***~ out*** *typ.* gesperrt drucken; **18.** *Wort* durch e-n Gedankenstrich *od.* Pünktchen ersetzen; **19.** *TV Brit.* austasten; **20.** *sport* zu Null schlagen.

blan·ket ['blæŋkɪt] **I** *s.* **1.** (wollene) Decke, Bettdecke *f*: ***to get between the ~s*** F in die Federn kriechen; ***born on the wrong side of the ~*** F unehelich; → ***wet*** 1; **2.** *fig.* Decke *f*, Hülle *f*: ***~ of snow*** Schneedecke; **3.** ⚙ 'Filz,unterlage *f*; **II** *v/t.* **4.** zudecken; **5.** ⚓ den Wind abfangen (*dat.*); **6.** *fig.* verdecken, unter'drücken, ersticken, vertuschen; **7.** ⚡, ⚔ abschirmen; **8.** *Radio*: stören, über'lagern; **9.** prellen; **10.** *Am.* zs.-fassen, um'fassen; **III** *adj.* **11.** alles einschließend, gene'rell: ***~ clause*** Generalklausel *f*; ***~ insurance*** Kollektivversicherung *f*; ***~ mortgage*** Gesamthypothek *f*; ***~ policy*** Pauschalpolice *f*; ***~ sheet*** *Am.* Zeitung *f* in Großfolio.

blan·ket·ing ['blæŋkɪtɪŋ] *s.* Stoff *m* für Wolldecken.

blare [bleə] **I** *v/i. u. v/t.* a) schmettern (*Trompete*), b) brüllen, plärren (*a. Radio etc.*); **II** *s.* a) Schmettern *n*, b) Brüllen *n*, Plärren *n*, c) Lärm *m*.

blar·ney ['blɑ:nɪ] F **I** (plumpe) Schmeiche'lei, ‚Schmus' *m*; **II** *v/t. u. v/i.* (*j-m*) schmeicheln.

bla·sé ['blɑ:zeɪ] (*Fr.*) *adj.* gleichgültig, gelangweilt.

blas·pheme [blæs'fi:m] **I** *v/t.* (*engS. Gott*) lästern; schmähen; **II** *v/i.*: ***~ against*** *j-m* fluchen, *j-n* lästern; **blas'phem·er** [-mə] *s.* (Gottes)Lästerer *m*; **blas·phe·mous** ['blæsfəməs] *adj.* □ blas'phemisch; **blas·phe·my** ['blæsfəmɪ] *s.* **1.** Blasphe'mie *f*, (Gottes)Lästerung *f*; **2.** Fluchen *n*.

blast [blɑ:st] **I** *s.* **1.** (heftiger) Windstoß *m*; **2.** ♪ Schmettern *n*, Schall *m*: ***~ of a trumpet*** Trompetenstoß *m*; **3.** Si'gnal *n*, (Heul-, Pfeif)Ton *m*; Tuten *n*; **4.** *fig.* Pesthauch *m*, Fluch *m*; **5.** ⚘ Brand *m*, Mehltau *m*; Verdorren *n*; **6.** ⚙ a) Sprengladung *f*, b) Sprengung *f*; **7.** a) Explosi'on *f*, Detonati'on *f*, b) *a.* ***~ wave*** Druckwelle *f*; **8.** ⚙ Gebläse(luft *f*) *n*: (***at***) ***full ~*** *a. fig.* auf Hochtouren, *a.* mit voller Lautstärke; **9.** F a) heftige At'tacke, b) ‚Anschiß' *m*; **10.** *Am. sl.* Party *f*; **II** *v/t.* **11.** sprengen; **12.** *a.* ⚘ vernichten (*a.* F *sport*), *fig. a.* zu'nichte machen; **13.** ⚔ unter Beschuß nehmen, *fig. a.* heftig attackieren, F ‚anscheißen'; *Science Fiction*: durch Strahler(schuß) töten; **14.** verfluchen: ***~ed*** verflucht; ***~ it!*** verdammt!; ***~ him!*** der Teufel soll ihn holen!; **15.** ***~ off*** in den Weltraum schießen; **III** *v/i.* **16.** sprengen; **17.** ‚knallen': ***~ away at*** ballern auf (*acc.*), *fig.* heftig attackieren; **18.** ***~ off*** abheben (*Rakete*); ***~ fur·nace*** *s.* ⚙ Hochofen *m*; **'~-hole** *s.* ⚙ Sprengloch *n*; **'~-off** *s.* (Ra'keten)Start *m*.

bla·tan·cy ['bleɪtənsɪ] *s.* lärmendes Wesen, Angebe'rei *f*; **'bla·tant** [-nt] *adj.* □ **1.** brüllend; **2.** marktschreierisch, lärmend; **3.** aufdringlich; **4.** offenkundig, ekla'tant: ***~ lie***.

blath·er ['blæðə] **I** *v/i.* ‚(blöd) quatschen'; **II** *s.* ‚Gewäsch' *n*; Quatsch *m*; **'~·skite** [-skaɪt] *s.* F **1.** ‚Quatschkopf' *m*; **2.** → ***blather*** II.

blaze [bleɪz] **I** *s.* **1.** *lodernde* Flamme, Feuer *n*, Glut *f*: ***be in a ~*** in Flammen stehen; **2.** *pl.* Hölle *f*: ***go to ~s!*** *sl.* scher dich zum Teufel!; ***like ~s*** F wie verrückt *od.* toll; ***what the ~s is the matter?*** F was zum Teufel ist denn los?; **3.** Leuchten *n*, Glanz *m* (*a. fig.*): ***~ of noon*** Mittagshitze *f*; ***~ of fame*** Ruhmesglanz *m*; ***~ of colo(u)r*** Farbenpracht *f*; ***~ of publicity*** volles Licht der Öffentlichkeit; **4.** *fig.* (plötzlicher) Ausbruch, Auflodern *n* (*Gefühl*): ***~ of anger*** Wutanfall *m*; **5.** Blesse *f* (*bei Rind od. Pferd*); **6.** Anschalmung *f*, Markierung *f an Waldbäumen*; **II** *v/i.* **7.** (auf)flammen, (auf)lodern, (ent)brennen (*alle a. fig.*): ***~ into prominence*** *fig.* e-n kometenhaften Aufstieg erleben; ***~ with anger*** vor Zorn glühen; ***in a blazing temper*** in heller Wut; **8.** leuchten, strahlen (*a. fig.*); **III** *v/t.* **9.** Bäume anschalmen; → ***trail*** 15;

Zssgn mit adv.:

blaze| a·broad *v/t.* verkünden, 'auspo,saunen; ***~ a·way*** *v/i.* drauf'losschießen; *fig.* F loslegen (***at*** mit *et.*), herziehen (***about*** über *acc.*); ***~ out***, ***~ up*** *v/i.* **1.** auflodern, -flammen; **2.** *fig.* in Wut geraten, (wütend) auffahren.

blaz·er ['bleɪzə] *s.* Blazer *m*, Klub-, Sportjacke *f*.

blaz·ing ['bleɪzɪŋ] *adj.* **1.** lodernd (*a. fig.*); **2.** *fig.* a) schreiend, auffallend: ***~ colo(u)rs***, b) offenkundig, ekla'tant: ***~ lie***, c) *hunt.* warm (*Fährte*); → ***scent*** 3; **3.** F verteufelt; ***~ star*** *s.* Gegenstand *m* allgemeiner Bewunderung.

bla·zon ['bleɪzn] **I** *s.* **1.** a) Wappenschild *m, n* b) Wappenkunde *f*; **2.** lautes Lob; **II** *v/t.* **3.** *Wappen* ausmalen; **4.** *fig.* schmücken, zieren; **5.** *fig.* her'ausstreichen, rühmen; **6.** *mst* ***~ abroad***, ***~ out*** 'auspo,saunen; **'bla·zon·ry** [-rɪ] *s.* **1.** a) Wappenzeichen *n*, b) He'raldik *f*; **2.** *fig.* Farbenschmuck *m*.

bleach [bli:tʃ] **I** *v/t.* bleichen (*a. fig.*); **II** *s.* Bleichmittel *n*; **'bleach·er** [-tʃə] *s.* **1.** Bleicher(in); **2.** *mst pl. Am. sport* 'unüber,dachte Tri'büne.

bleak [bli:k] *adj.* □ **1.** kahl, öde; **2.** ungeschützt, windig (gelegen); **3.** rauh (*Wind, Wetter*); **4.** *fig.* trost-, freudlos, trübe, düster: ***~ prospects*** trübe Aussichten.

blear [blɪə] **I** *adj.* verschwommen, trübe (*a. Augen*); **II** *v/t.* trüben; ***~-eyed*** ['blɪəraɪd] *adj.* **1.** a) mit trüben Augen, b) verschlafen; **2.** kurzsichtig, *fig. a.* einfältig.

bleat [bli:t] *v/i.* **1.** blöken (*Schaf, Kalb*), meckern (*Ziege*); **2.** in weinerlichem Ton reden; **II** *s.* **3.** Blöken *n*, Gemecker *n* (*a. fig.*).

bled [bled] *pret. u. p.p. von* ***bleed***.

bleed [bli:d] [*irr.*] **I** *v/i.* **1.** (ver)bluten (*a. Pflanze*): ***~ to death*** verbluten; **2.** sein Blut vergießen, sterben (***for*** für); **3.** *fig.* (***for***) bluten (um) (*Herz*), (tiefes) Mitleid empfinden (mit); **4.** F ‚bluten' (*zahlen*): ***~ for s.th.*** für et. schwer bluten müssen; **5.** auslaufen, ‚bluten' (*Farbe*); zerlaufen (*Teer etc.*); leck sein, lekken; **6.** *typ.* angeschnitten *od.* bis eng an den Druck beschnitten sein (*Buch, Bild*); **II** *v/t.* **7.** ⚕ zur Ader lassen; **8.** *Flüssigkeit, Dampf etc.* ausströmen lassen, abzapfen: ***~ valve*** Ablaßventil *n*; **9.** ⚙, *bsd. mot. Bremsleitung* entlüften; **10.** F ‚bluten lassen', schröpfen: ***~ white*** *j-n* bis zum Weißbluten auspressen; **'bleed·er** [-də] *s.* **1.** ⚕ Bluter *m*; **2.** F a) Erpresser *m*, b) (blöder *etc.*) Kerl, c) ‚Scheißding' *n*; **3.** ⚙ 'Ablaßven,til *n*; **4.** ⚡ 'Vorbelastungs,widerstand *m*.

bleed·ing ['bli:dɪŋ] **I** *s.* **1.** Blutung *f*, Aderlaß *m* (*a. fig.*): ***~ of the nose*** Nasenbluten *n*; **2.** ⚙ ‚Bluten' *n*, Auslaufen *n* (*Farbe, Teer*); **3.** ⚙ Entlüften *n*; **II** *adj.* **4.** *sl.* verdammt; ***~ heart*** *s.* ⚘ F Flammendes Herz.

bleep [bliːp] I *s.* **1.** Piepton *m*; **2.** → ***bleeper***; II *v/i.* **3.** piepen; '**bleep·er** [-pə] *s.* F ‚Piepser' *m* (*Funkrufempfänger*).

blem·ish ['blemɪʃ] I *v/t.* verunstalten, schaden (*dat.*); *fig.* beflecken; II *s.* Fehler *m*, Mangel *m*; Makel *m*, Schönheitsfehler *m*.

blench¹ [blentʃ] I *v/i.* **1.** verzagen; **2.** zu'rückschrecken (***at*** vor *dat.*); II *v/t.* (ver)meiden.

blench² [blentʃ] → ***blanch*** 6.

blend [blend] I *v/t.* **1.** (ver)mengen, (ver)mischen, verschmelzen; **2.** mischen, mixen; e-e (*Tee-, Tabak-, Whisky*)Mischung zs.-stellen; *Wein etc.* verschneiden; II *v/i.* **3.** (***with***) sich mischen *od.* har'monisch verbinden (mit); **4.** verschmelzen, inein'ander 'übergehen (*Farben*); III *s.* **5.** Mischung *f*, (harmonische) Zs.-stellung (*Getränke, Tabak, Farben*); (*Wein*)Verschnitt *m*; **~ word** *s. ling.* Misch-, Kurzwort *n*.

blende [blend] *s. min.* Blende *f*, *engS.* Zinkblende *f*.

Blen·heim or·ange ['blenɪm] *s. Brit. eine Apfelsorte.*

blent [blent] *obs. pret. u. p.p. von* ***blend.***

bless [bles] *v/t.* **1.** segnen; **2.** segnen, preisen; glücklich machen: ***~ed with*** gesegnet mit (*Talent, Reichtum etc.*); ***I ~ the day I met you*** ich segne *od.* preise den Tag, an dem ich dich kennenlernte; ***~ one's stars*** sich glücklich schätzen; **3.** ***~ o.s.*** sich bekreuzigen;
Besondere Redewendungen:
(***God***) ***~ you!*** a) alles Gute!, b) *beim Niesen*: Gesundheit!; ***well, I'm ~ed!*** F na, so was!; ***I'm ~ed if I know*** F ich weiß es wirklich nicht; ***Mr. Brown, ~ him*** Herr Brown, der Gute; ***~ my soul!*** F du meine Güte!; ***not at all, ~ you!*** *iro.* o nein, mein Verehrtester! *od.* meine Beste!; ***~ that boy, what is he doing there?*** F was zum Kuckuck stellt der Junge dort an?; ***not to have a penny to ~ o.s. with*** keinen roten Heller besitzen.

bless·ed ['blesɪd] I *adj.* **1.** gesegnet, selig, glücklich: ***of ~ memory*** seligen Angedenkens; ***~ event*** freudiges Ereignis (*Geburt e-s Kindes*); **2.** gepriesen, selig, heilig: ***the ~ Virgin*** die Heilige Jungfrau (Maria); **3.** ***the whole ~ day*** F den lieben langen Tag; ***not a ~ soul*** keine Menschenseele; II *s.* **4.** ***the ~*** (***ones***) die Seligen; '**bless·ed·ness** [-nɪs] *s.* Glück'seligkeit *f*, Glück *n*; Seligkeit *f*: ***live in single ~*** Junggeselle sein; '**bless·ing** [-sɪŋ] *s.* Segen *m*, Segnung *f*, Wohltat *f*, Gnade *f*: ***ask a ~*** a) Segen erbitten, b) das Tischgebet sprechen; ***what a ~ that ...*** welch ein Segen, daß ...; ***it turned out to be a ~ in disguise*** es stellte sich im nachhinein als Segen heraus; ***count one's ~s*** dankbar sein für das, was e-m beschert ist; ***give one's ~ to*** s-n Segen geben zu, *fig. a. et.* absegnen.

blest [blest] I *poet. pret. u. p.p. von* ***bless***; II *pred. adj. poet.* → ***blessed***; III *s.*: ***the Isles of the ~*** die Inseln der Seligen.

bleth·er ['bleðə] → ***blather.***

blew [bluː] *pret. von* ***blow¹*** II *u.* III *u.* ***blow³.***

blight [blaɪt] I *s.* **1.** ⚘ Mehltau *m*, Fäule *f*, Brand *m* (*Pflanzenkrankheit*); **2.** *fig.* Gift-, Pesthauch *m*; Vernichtung *f*; Fluch *m*; Enttäuschung *f*, Schatten *m*; **3.** Verwahrlosung *f e-r Wohngegend*; II *v/t.* **4.** *fig.* im Keim ersticken, zu'nichte machen, vereiteln; '**blight·er** [-tə] *s. Brit.* F a) Kerl *m*, ‚Knülch' *m*, b) ‚Mistkerl' *m*, c) ‚Mistding' *n*.

Blight·y ['blaɪtɪ] *s.* ✕ *Brit. sl.* **1.** die Heimat, England *n*; **2.** a) *a.* ***a ~ one*** ‚Heimatschuß' *m*, b) Heimaturlaub *m*.

bli·mey ['blaɪmɪ] *int.* F *Brit.* a) ich werd' verrückt! (*überrascht*), b) verdammt!

blimp¹ [blɪmp] *s.* F **1.** unstarres Kleinluftschiff; **2.** *phot.* schalldichte Kamerahülle.

Blimp² [blɪmp] *s.*: (***Colonel***) ***~*** *Brit.* selbstgefälliger Erzkonservativer.

blind [blaɪnd] I *adj.* ☐ → *a.* 9 **1.** blind: ***~ in one eye*** auf 'einem Auge blind; ***struck ~*** mit Blindheit geschlagen; ***as ~ as a bat*** (*od.* ***beetle***) stockblind; **2.** *fig.* blind, verständnislos (***to*** gegen['über]): ***~ to s.o.'s faults*** j-s Fehlern gegenüber blind; ***~ chance*** blinder Zufall; ***~ with rage*** blind vor Wut; ***~ side*** *fig.* schwache Seite; ***turn a ~ eye*** *fig.* ein Auge zudrücken, *et.* absichtlich übersehen; **3.** unbesonnen: ***~ bargain***; **4.** zweck-, ziellos, leer: ***~ excuse*** Ausrede *f*; **5.** verborgen, geheim: ***~ staircase*** Geheimtreppe; **6.** schwererkennbar: ***~ corner*** unübersichtliche Ecke *od.* Kurve; ***~ copy*** *typ.* unleserliches Manuskript; **7.** ⚠ blind: ***~ window***; **8.** ⚘ blütenlos, taub; II *adv.* **9.** ***~ drunk*** sinnlos betrunken, ‚blau'; *fig.* ***go it ~*** blindlings handeln; III *v/t.* **10.** blenden, blind machen; *j-m* die Augen verbinden: ***~ing rain*** alles verhüllender Regen; **11.** verblenden, täuschen; blind machen (***to*** gegen); **12.** *fig.* verdunkeln, verbergen, vertuschen, verwischen; IV *v/i.* **13.** *Brit. sl.* blind drauf'lossausen; V *s.* **14.** ***the ~*** die Blinden *pl.*; **15.** a) Rolladen *m*, b) Rou'leau *n*, Rollo *n*, c) Mar'kise *f*; → ***Venetian*** I; **16.** *pl.* Scheuklappen *pl.*; **17.** *fig.* a) Vorwand *m*, b) (Vor)Täuschung *f*, c) Tarnung *f*, d) F Strohmann *m*; **18.** *hunt.* Deckung *f*; **19.** *Brit. sl.* Saufe'rei *f*; ***~ al·ley*** *s.* Sackgasse *f* (*a. fig.*); ˌ**~-'al·ley** *adj.*: ***~ occupation*** Stellung *f* ohne Aufstiegsmöglichkeit; **~ coal** *s.* Anthra'zit *m*; **~ date** *s.* F a) Verabredung *f* mit e-r *od.* e-m Unbekannten, b) unbekannter Partner bei e-m solchen Rendezvous.

blind·er ['blaɪndə] *s. Am.* Scheuklappe *f* (*a. fig.*).

blind| flight *s.* ✈ Blindflug *m*; '**~·fold** I *adj. u. adv.* **1.** mit verbundenen Augen: ***~ chess*** Blindschach *n*; **2.** blind(-lings) (*a. fig.*): ***~ rage*** blinde Wut; II *v/t.* **3.** *j-m* die Augen verbinden; **4.** *fig.* blind machen; **~ gut** *s. anat.* Blinddarm *m*; ˌ**~-man's-'buff** [ˌblaɪnd*d*mænz-] *s.* Blindekuh(spiel *n*) *f*.

blind·ness ['blaɪndnɪs] *s.* **1.** Blindheit *f* (*a. fig.*); **2.** *fig.* Verblendung *f*.

blind| shell *s.* ✕ Blindgänger *m*; **~ spot** *s.* **1.** ⚕ blinder Fleck *auf der Netzhaut;* **2.** *fig.* schwacher *od.* wunder Punkt; **3.** *mot.* toter Winkel *im Rückspiegel*; **4.** *Radio*: Empfangsloch *n*; **~ stitch** *s.* blinder (*unsichtbarer*) Stich; '**~·worm** *s. zo.* Blindschleiche *f*.

blink [blɪŋk] I *v/i.* **1.** blinken, blinzeln, zwinkern: ***~ at*** a) *j-m* zublinzeln, b) → 2 *u.* 5; **2.** erstaunt *od.* verständnislos dreinblicken: ***~ at*** *fig.* sich maßlos wundern über (*acc.*); **3.** flimmern, schimmern; II *v/t.* **4.** ***~ one's eyes*** mit den Augen zwinkern; **5.** *et.* ignorieren, die Augen verschließen vor (*dat.*): ***there is no ~ing the fact*** (***that***) es ist nicht zu leugnen (, daß); **6.** *Meldung* blinken; III *s.* **7.** Blinzeln *n*; **8.** (Licht)Schimmer *m*; **9.** flüchtiger Blick; **10.** Augenblick *m*; **11.** ***on the ~*** *sl.* a) de'fekt, nicht in Ordnung, b) ‚am Eingehen' (*Gerät etc.*); '**blink·er** [-kə] I *s.* **1.** *pl.* Scheuklappen *pl.* (*a. fig.*); **2.** *pl.* F Schutzbrille *f*; **3.** F ‚Gucker' *pl.* (*Augen*); **4.** a) Blinklicht *n*, b) *mot.* Blinker *m*; **5.** a) Blinkgerät *n*, b) Blinkspruch *m*; II *v/t.* **6.** *e-m Pferd* Scheuklappen anlegen: ***~ed*** mit Scheuklappen (*a. fig.*); **7.** → ***blink*** 6.

'**blink·ing** [-kɪŋ] *adj. u. adv. Brit. sl.* verdammt.

blip [blɪp] *s.* **1.** Klicken *n*; **2.** *Radar*: 'Echoimˌpuls *m*, -zeichen *n*.

bliss [blɪs] *s.* Freude *f*, Entzücken *n*, (Glück)'Seligkeit *f*, Wonne *f*; '**bliss·ful** [-fʊl] *adj.* ☐ (glück)'selig, völlig glücklich; '**bliss·ful·ness** [-fʊlnɪs] *s.* Wonne *f*.

blis·ter ['blɪstə] I *s.* **1.** ⚕ (*Haut*)Blase *f*, Pustel *f*; **2.** Blase *f* (*auf bemaltem Holz, in Glas etc.*); **3.** ⚕ Zugpflaster *n*; **4.** ✕, ✈ a) Bordwaffen- *od.* Beobachterstand *m*, b) Radarkuppel *f*; II *v/t.* **5.** Blasen her'vorrufen auf (*dat.*); **6.** *fig.* scharf kritisieren, ‚fertigmachen'; **7.** brennenden Schmerz her'vorrufen auf (*dat.*): ***~ing heat*** glühende Hitze; III *v/i.* **8.** Blasen ziehen *od.* ⚙ werfen.

blithe [blaɪð] *adj.* ☐ vergnügt.

blith·er·ing ['blɪðərɪŋ] *adj. Brit.* F verdammt: ***~ idiot*** Vollidiot *m*.

blitz [blɪts] ✕ I *s.* **1.** Blitzkrieg *m*; **2.** schwerer Luftangriff; schwere Luftangriffe *pl.*; II *v/t.* **3.** schwer bombardieren: ***~ed area*** zerbombtes Gebiet; '**~·krieg** [-kriːg] → ***blitz*** 1.

bliz·zard ['blɪzəd] *s.* Schneesturm *m*.

bloat¹ [bləʊt] I *v/t. a.* ***~ up*** aufblasen, -blähen (*a. fig.*); II *v/i. a.* ***~ out*** auf-, anschwellen; '**bloat·ed** [-tɪd] *adj.* aufgebläht (*a. fig.*), (auf)gedunsen.

bloat·er ['bləʊtə] *s.* Räucherhering *m*.

blob [blɒb] *s.* **1.** Tropfen *m*, Klümpchen *n*, Klecks *m*; **2.** *Kricket*: null Punkte; **3.** F ‚Kloß' (*Person*).

bloc [blɒk] *s. pol.* Block *m*: ***sterling ~*** † Sterlingblock

block [blɒk] I *s.* **1.** Block *m*, Klotz *m* (*mst Holz, Stein*): ***on the ~*** zur Versteigerung anstehend, unterm Hammer; **2.** Hackklotz *m*; **3.** ***the ~*** der Richtblock: ***go to the ~*** das Schafott besteigen; **4.** ⚙ Block *m*, Rolle *f*; ***pulley*** 1, ***tackle*** 3; **5.** *typ.* Kli'schee *n*, Druckstock *m*; Prägestempel *m*; **6.** a) *a.* ***~ of flats*** *Brit.* Wohnhaus *n*, b) → ***office block***, c) *Am.* Zeile *f* (*Reihenhäuser*), d) *bsd. Am.* Häuserblock *m*: ***three ~s from here*** drei Straßen weiter; **7.** Block *m*, Masse *f*, Gruppe *f*; *attr.* Gesamt...: ***~ of shares*** Aktienpaket *n*; (***data***) ***~*** *Computer*: (Daten)Block *m*; **8.** Abreißblock *m*: ***scribbling ~*** Notiz-, Schmierblock;

9. *fig.* Klotz *m*, Tölpel *m*; **10.** a) Verstopfung *f*, Hindernis *n*, Stockung *f*, b) Sperre *f*, Absperrung *f*: ***traffic ~*** Verkehrsstockung *f*; ***mental ~*** *fig.* ‚geistige Ladehemmung'; **11.** 🚂 Blockstrecke *f*; **12.** *sport:* a) Sperren *n*, b) *Volleyball etc.*: Block *m*; **II** *v/t.* **13.** (auf e-m Block) formen: ***~ a hat***; **14.** hemmen, hindern, blockieren, *fig. a.* durch'kreuzen: ***~ a bill*** *Brit. pol.* die Beratung e-s Gesetzentwurfs verhindern; **15.** *oft* **~ up** (ab-, ver)sperren, verstopfen, blokkieren: ***road ~ed*** Straße ge-, versperrt; **16.** † *Konto*, ϟ *Röhre*, *Leitung* sperren; † *Kredit etc.* einfrieren: ***~ed account*** Sperrkonto *n*; **17.** *sport* a) *Gegner* sperren, *a. Schlag etc.* abblocken, b) *Ball* stoppen, halten; **~ in** *v/t.* skizzieren, entwerfen; **~ out** *v/t.* **1.** → ***block in***; **2.** *Licht* nehmen (*Bäume etc.*); **3.** *phot. Negativteil* abdecken; **~ up** *v/t.* → ***block*** 15.

block·ade [blɒ'keɪd] **I** *s.* Bloc'kade *f*, (Hafen)Sperre *f*: ***impose a ~*** e-e Blokkade verhängen; ***raise a ~*** e-e Blockade aufheben; ***run the ~*** die Blockade brechen; **II** *v/t.* blockieren, absperren; **block'ad·er** [-də] *s.* Bloc'kadeschiff *n*; **block'ade-ˌrun·ner** *s.* Bloc'kadebrecher *m*.

block| brake *s.* Backenbremse *f*; **'~·buster** *s.* F **1.** ⚔ Minenbombe *f*; **2.** *fig.* ‚Knüller' *m*, ‚Hammer' *m*, tolles Ding; **~ di·a·gram** *s.* ⚙, ϟ 'Blockdiaˌgramm *n*, -schaltbild *n*; **'~·head** *s.* Dummkopf *m*; **'~·house** *s.* Blockhaus *n*; **~ let·ters** *s. pl. typ.* Blockschrift *f*; **~ print·ing** *s.* Handdruck *m*; **~ sys·tem** *s.* **1.** 🚂 'Blocksyˌstem *n*; **2.** ϟ Blockschaltung *f*; **~ vote** *s.* Sammelstimme *f* (*e-e ganze Organisation vertretend*).

bloke [bləʊk] *s.* F Kerl *m*.

blond [blɒnd] *adj.* **1.** blond (*Haar*), hell (*Gesichtsfarbe*); **2.** blond(haarig); **blonde** [blɒnd] *s.* **1.** Blon'dine *f*; **2.** † Blonde *f* (*seidene Spitze*).

blood [blʌd] *s.* **1.** Blut *n*: ***spill ~*** Blut vergießen; ***give one's ~ (for)*** sein Blut (*od.* Leben) lassen (für); ***taste ~*** *fig.* Blut lecken; ***fresh ~*** *fig.* frisches Blut; ***~-and-thunder (story)*** *Brit.* F ‚Reißer' *m* (*Roman*); Schauergeschichte *f*; **2.** *fig.* Blut *n*, Tempera'ment *n*, Wesen *n*: ***it made his ~ boil, his ~ was up*** er kochte vor Wut; ***his ~ froze*** (*od.* ***ran cold***) das Blut erstarrte ihm in den Adern; ***breed*** (*od.* ***make***) ***bad ~*** böses Blut machen; → ***cold blood***, ***curdle*** II; **3.** (edles) Blut, Geblüt; *n* Abstammung *f*; Rasse *f* (*Mensch*), 'Vollblut *n* (*bes. Pferd*): ***prince of the ~ royal*** Prinz *m* von königlichem Geblüt; ***noble ~*** → ***blue blood***; ***related by ~*** blutsverwandt; ***it runs in the ~*** es liegt im Blut *od.* in der Familie; ***~ will out*** Blut bricht sich Bahn; **~ al·co·hol (con·cen·tra·tion)** *s.* Blutalkohol(gehalt) *m*; **~ bank** *s.* ⚕ Blutbank *f*; **~ broth·er** *s.* **1.** leiblicher Bruder; **2.** Blutsbruder *m*; **~ cir·cu·la·tion** *s.* ⚕ Blutkreislauf *m*; **~ clot** *s.* ⚕ Blutgerinnsel *n*; **'~ˌcur·dler** *s.* F ‚Reißer' *m* (*Roman etc.*); **'~ˌcur·dling** *adj.* grauenhaft; **~ do·nor** *s.* ⚕ Blutspender *m*.

blood·ed ['blʌdɪd] *adj.* **1.** Vollblut...; **2.** *in Zssgn* ...blütig.

blood| feud *s.* Blut-, Todfehde *f*; **~ group** *s.* ⚕ Blutgruppe *f*; **~ group·ing** *s.* ⚕ Blutgruppenbestimmung *f*; **'~·guilt** *s.* Blutschuld *f*; **~ heat** *s.* ⚕ Blutwärme *f*, 'Körpertemperaˌtur *f*; **~ horse** *s.* 'Vollblut(pferd) *n*; **'~·hound** *s.* **1.** Schweiß-, Bluthund *m*; **2.** F ‚Schnüffler' *m* (*Detektiv*).

blood·less ['blʌdlɪs] *adj.* ☐ **1.** blutlos, -leer (*a. fig.*); **2.** bleich; **3.** *fig.* kalt; **4.** unblutig (*Kampf etc.*).

'blood|ˌlet·ting *s.* **1.** Aderlaß *m* (*a. fig.*); **2.** → ***bloodshed***; **~ mon·ey** *s.* Blutgeld *n*; **~ poi·son·ing** *s.* ⚕ Blutvergiftung *f*; **~ pres·sure** *s.* ⚕ Blutdruck *m*; **~ re·la·tion** *s.* Blutsverwandte(r *m*) *f*; **~ sam·ple** *s.* ⚕ Blutprobe *f*; **'~·shed** *s.* Blutvergießen *n*; **'~·shot** *adj.* 'blutunterˌlaufen; **~ spec·i·men** *s.* ⚕ Blutprobe *f*; **~ sports** *s.* Hetz-, *bsd.* Fuchsjagd *f*; **'~·stained** *adj.* blutbefleckt (*a. fig.*); **'~·stock** *s.* 'Vollblutpferde *pl.*; **~ stream** *s.* **1.** ⚕ Blut(kreislauf *m*) *n*; **2.** *fig.* Lebensstrom *m*; **'~ˌsuck·er** *s.* Blutsauger *m* (*a. fig.*); **~ sug·ar** *s.* ⚕ Blutzucker *m*; **~ test** *s.* ⚕ Blutprobe *f*, 'Blutunterˌsuchung *f*; **'~ˌthirst·i·ness** *s.* Blutdurst *m*; **'~ˌthirst·y** *adj.* blutdürstig; **~ trans·fu·sion** *s.* ⚕ 'Blutüberˌtragung *f*; **~ typ·ing** *s.* → ***blood grouping***; **~ ves·sel** *s. anat.* Blutgefäß *n*.

blood·y ['blʌdɪ] **I** *adj.* ☐ **1.** blutig, blutbefleckt: ***~ flux*** ⚕ rote Ruhr; **2.** blutdürstig, mörderisch, grausam: ***a ~ battle*** e-e blutige Schlacht; **3.** *Brit. sl.* verdammt, saumäßig, Scheiß... (*oft nur verstärkend*): ***not a ~ soul*** kein Schwanz; ***a ~ fool*** ein Vollidiot *m*; ***~ thing*** ‚Scheißding' *n*; **II** *adv.* **4.** *Brit. sl.* mordsmäßig, verdammt: ***~ awful*** ‚beschissen'; ***you ~ well know*** du weißt ganz genau; ♀ **Ma·ri·a** [mə'raɪə; mə'rɪə] *s. Am. Getränk aus Tequila u. Tomatensaft*; ♀ **Mar·y** ['meərɪ] *s. Getränk aus Wodka u. Tomatensaft*; **ˌ~-'mind·ed** *adj. Br.* F **1.** gemein, ekelhaft; **2.** störrisch, stur.

bloom¹ [bluːm] **I** *s.* **1.** Blüte *f*, Blume *f*: ***in full ~*** in voller Blüte; **2.** *fig.* Blüte (-zeit) *f*, Jugendfrische *f*; **3.** Flaum *m* (*auf Pfirsichen etc.*); **4.** *fig.* Schmelz *m*, Glanz *m*; **II** *v/i.* **5.** (er)blühen (*a. fig.*).

bloom² [bluːm] *metall.* **I** *s.* **1.** Walzblock *m*; **2.** Puddelluppe *f*: ***~ steel*** Puddelstahl *m*; **II** *v/t.* **3.** luppen: ***~ing mill*** Luppenwalzwerk *n*.

bloom·er ['bluːmə] *s. sl.* grober Fehler, Schnitzer *m*, (Stil)Blüte *f*.

bloom·ers ['bluːməz] *s. pl.* a) *obs.* (Damen)Pumphose *f*, b) Schlüpfer *m* mit langem Bein, ‚Liebestöter' *m*.

bloom·ing ['bluːmɪŋ] *pres. p. u. adj.* **1.** blühend (*a. fig.*); **2.** *sl.* → ***bloody*** 3.

blos·som ['blɒsəm] **I** *s.* (*bsd.* Obst)Blüte *f*; Blütenfülle *f*: ***in ~*** in (voller) Blüte; **II** *v/i. a. fig.* blühen, Blüten treiben: **~ (*out*) (*into*)** erblühen, gedeihen (zu).

blot [blɒt] **I** *s.* **1.** (Tinten)Klecks *m*, Fleck *m*; **2.** *fig.* Schandfleck *m*, Makel *m*; → ***escutcheon*** 1; **3.** Verunstaltung *f*, Schönheitsfehler *m*; **II** *v/t.* **4.** *mit Tinte* beschmieren, beklecksen; **5.** ***~ out*** *Schrift* ausstreichen; **6.** ***~ out*** *fig.* a) *Erinnerungen etc.* auslöschen, b) verdunkeln, verhüllen: ***fog ~ted out the view*** Nebel verhüllte die Aussicht; **7.** *mit Löschpapier* (ab)löschen.

blotch [blɒtʃ] **I** *s.* **1.** Fleck *m*, Klecks *m*; **2.** *fig.* → ***blot*** 2; **3.** ⚕ Hautfleck *m*; **II** *v/t.* **4.** beklecksen; **III** *v/i.* **5.** klecksen; **'blotch·y** [-tʃɪ] *adj.* **1.** klecksig; **2.** ⚕ fleckig.

blot·ter ['blɒtə] *s.* **1.** (Tinten)Löscher *m*; **2.** *Am.* Kladde *f*, Berichtsliste *f* (*bsd. der Polizei*).

blot·ting| pad ['blɒtɪŋ] *s.* 'Schreibˌunterlage *f od.* Block *m* aus 'Löschpaˌpier; **~ pa·per** *s.* Löschpapier *n*.

blot·to ['blɒtəʊ] *adj. sl.* ‚sternhagelvoll', ‚stinkbesoffen'.

blouse [blaʊz] *s.* **1.** Bluse *f*; **2.** ⚔ a) Uni'formjacke *f*, b) Feldbluse *f*.

blow¹ [bləʊ] **I** *s.* **1.** Blasen *n*, Luftzug *m*, Brise *f*: ***go for a ~*** an die frische Luft gehen; **2.** Blasen *n*, Schall *m*: ***a ~ on a whistle*** ein Pfiff; **3.** *Am.* F a) Angebe'rei *f*, b) Angeber *m*; **II** *v/i.* [*irr.*] **4.** blasen, wehen, pusten: ***it is ~ing hard*** es weht ein starker Wind; ***~ hot and cold*** *fig.* ‚mal so, mal so' *od.* wetterwendisch sein; **5.** ertönen: ***the horn is ~ing***; **6.** keuchen, schnaufen; **7.** spritzen, blasen (*Wal*); **8.** *Am.* F ‚angeben'; **9.** a) explodieren, b) platzen (*Reifen*), c) ϟ 'durchbrennen (*Sicherung*), d) ausbrechen (*Erdöl etc.*); **III** *v/t.* [*irr.*] **10.** wehen, treiben (*Wind*): ***~n ashore*** auf Strand geworfen; **11.** anfachen: ***~ the fire***; **12.** (an)blasen: ***~ the soup***; **13.** blasen, ertönen lassen: ***~ the horn*** ins Horn stoßen; **14.** auf-, ausblasen: ***~ bubbles*** Seifenblasen machen; ***~ glass*** Glas blasen; ***~ one's nose*** sich die Nase putzen, sich schnauben; ***~ an egg*** ein Ei ausblasen; **15.** *sl. Geld* ‚verpulvern'; **16.** zum Platzen bringen: ***blew itself to pieces*** zersprang in Stücke; → ***top*** 4; **17.** F (*p.p.* ***blowed***) verfluchen: ***~ it!*** verflucht!; ***I'll be ~ed (if) ...!*** zum Teufel (wenn) ...!; **18.** *sl.* a) ‚verpfeifen', verraten, b) aufdecken, c) ‚verduften' aus (*dat.*); **19.** *sl.* ‚vermasseln'; **20.** V *j-m* ‚e-n blasen';

Zssgn mit adv.:

blow| a·way *v/t.* **1.** wegblasen; **2.** F *j-n* ‚wegpusten' (*töten*); **~ down** *v/t.* her'unter-, 'umwehen; **~ in I** *v/i. fig.* auftauchen, her'einschneien; **II** *v/t. Scheiben* eindrücken; **~ off I** *v/i.* **1.** fortwehen; **2.** abtreiben (*Schiff*); **II** *v/t.* **3.** fortblasen; verjagen; **4.** *Dampf etc.* ablassen; → ***steam*** 1; **~ out I** *v/i.* **1.** verlöschen; **2.** platzen; **3.** ϟ 'durchbrennen (*Sicherung*); **II** *v/t.* **4.** *Licht* ausblasen, *Feuer* (aus)löschen; **5.** her'ausblasen, -treiben: ***~ one's brains*** sich e-e Kugel durch den Kopf jagen; **6.** sprengen, zertrümmern; **~ o·ver I** *v/i. fig.* vor'beigehen, sich legen; **II** *v/t.* 'umwehen; **~ up I** *v/t.* **1.** a) (in die Luft) sprengen, b) vernichten, *fig. a.* ruinieren; **2.** aufblasen, -pumpen; *fig. et.* aufbauschen; **3.** *Foto* (stark) vergrößern; **4.** F *j-n* ‚anschnauzen'; **II** *v/i.* **5.** a) in die Luft fliegen, b) explodieren (*a.* F *fig. Person*): ***~ at s.o.*** j-m ‚ins Gesicht springen'; **6.** aus-, losbrechen; **7.** *fig.* eintreten, auftauchen.

blow² [bləʊ] *s.* **1.** Schlag *m*, Streich *m*, Stoß *m*: ***at a*** (*od.* ***one***) ***~*** mit 'einem Schlag *od.* Streich; ***without striking a ~*** *fig.* ohne jede Gewalt(anwendung), mühelos; ***come to ~s*** handgemein werden; ***strike a ~ at*** e-n Schlag führen gegen (*a. fig.*); ***strike a ~*** (***for***) sich einsetzen (für), helfen (*dat.*); **2.** *fig.* (Schicksals)Schlag *m*, Unglück *n*: ***it was a ~ to his pride*** es traf ihn schwer in s-m Stolz.

blow³ [bləʊ] *v/i.* [*irr.*] (auf)blühen, sich entfalten (*a. fig.*).

ˈblow|·ball *s.* ⚘ Pusteblume *f*; **ˈ~-dry** *v/t.* (*j-m* die Haare) fönen; **~ dry·er** *s.* Haartrockner *m*.

blowed [bləʊd] *p.p. von* ***blow¹*** 17.

blow·er [ˈbləʊə] *s.* **1.** Bläser *m*: ***glass-~***; ***~ of a horn***; **2.** ⚙ a) Gebläse *n*, b) *mot.* Vorverdichter *m*; **3.** F Telefon *n*.

ˈblow|·fly *s. zo.* Schmeißfliege *f*; **ˈ~·gun** *s.* **1.** Blasrohr *n*; **2.** ⚙ ˈSpritzpisˌtole *f*; **ˈ~·hard** *s. Am.* F Angeber *m*; **ˈ~·hole** *s.* **1.** Luft-, Zugloch *n*; **2.** Nasenloch *n* (*Wal*); **ˈ~·lamp** *s.* ⚙ Lötlampe *f*.

blown¹ [bləʊn] **I** *p.p. von* ***blow¹*** II *u.* III; **II** *adj.* **1.** *oft* ***~ up*** aufgeblasen, -gebläht (*a. fig.*); **2.** außer Atem.

blown² [bləʊn] **I** *p.p. von* ***blow³***; **II** *adj. a. fig.* blühend, aufgeblüht.

ˈblow|-out *s.* **1.** a) Zerplatzen *n*, b) Reifenpanne *f*; **2.** F Koller *m*, (Wut)Ausbruch *m*; **3.** *sl.* a) große Party, b) (ˈFreß)ˌOrgie *f*; **ˈ~·pipe** *s.* **1.** ⚙ Lötrohr *n*, Schweißbrenner *m*; **2.** Puste-, Blasrohr *n*; **ˈ~·torch** *s.* ⚙ *Am.* Lötlampe *f*; **ˈ~·up** *s.* **1.** Exploˈsion *f*; **2.** *fig.* a) ‚Krach' *m*, b) Koller *m*; **3.** *phot.* Vergrößerung *f*, Großfoto *n*.

blow·y [ˈbləʊɪ] *adj.* windig, luftig.

blowz·y [ˈblaʊzɪ] *adj.* **1.** schlampig (*bsd. Frau*); **2.** rotgesichtig (*Frau*).

blub·ber [ˈblʌbə] **I** *s.* Tran *m*, Speck *m*; **II** *v/i.* heulen, ‚flennen'.

bludg·eon [ˈblʌdʒən] **I** *s.* **1.** Knüppel *m*, Keule *f*; **II** *v/t.* **2.** ˈniederknüppeln; **3.** *j-n* zwingen (***into*** zu).

blue [bluː] **I** *adj.* **1.** blau: ***till you are ~ in the face*** F bis Sie schwarz werden; → ***moon*** 1; **2.** F trübe, schwermütig, traurig: ***feel ~*** niedergeschlagen sein; ***look ~*** trübe aussehen (*Person, Umstände*); **3.** *pol. Brit.* ‚schwarz', konservaˈtiv; **4.** *Brit.* F nicht saˈlonfähig, ordiˈnär: ***~ jokes***; ***~ movie*** Pornofilm *m*; **5.** F schrecklich; → ***funk*** 1, ***murder*** 1; **II** *s.* **6.** Blau *n*, blaue Farbe; **7.** Waschblau *n*; **8.** blaue Kleidung; **9.** *mst poet.* ***the ~*** a) der Himmel, b) das Meer: ***out of the ~*** aus heiterem Himmel, völlig unerwartet; **10.** *pol. Brit.* Konservaˈtive(r *m*) *f*; **11.** ***the dark*** (***light***) ***~s*** *pl. Studenten von Oxford* (*Cambridge*), *die bei Wettkämpfen ihre Universität vertreten*: ***get one's ~*** in die Universitätsmannschaft aufgenommen werden; **12.** *pl.* F Trübsinn *m*: ***have the ~s*** ‚den Moralischen haben'; **13.** *pl.* ♪ Blues *m*; **III** *v/t.* **14.** *Wäsche* bläuen; **15.** *sl. Geld* ‚verjuxen'; ***~ ba·by*** *s.* ⚕ Blue baby *n* (*mit angeborenem Herzfehler*); **ˈ2ˌbeard** *s.* (Ritter) Blaubart *m* (*Frauenmörder*); **ˈ~·bell** *s.* ⚘ **1.** ˈSternhyaˌzinthe *f* (*England*); **2.** *e-e* Glockenblume *f* (*Schottland*); **ˈ~·ber·ry** [-bərɪ] *s.* ⚘ Blau-, Heidelbeere *f*; **~ blood** *s.* **1.** blaues Blut, alter Adel; **2.** Aristoˈkrat(in), Adlige(r *m*) *f*; **~ book** *s.* Blaubuch *n*: a) *Brit. amtliche politische Veröffentlichung*, b) F *Am. Verzeichnis prominenter Persönlichkeiten*; **ˈ~ˌbot·tle** *s.* **1.** *zo.* Schmeißfliege *f*; **2.** ⚘ Kornblume *f*; **3.** F *Brit.* ‚Bulle' *m* (*Polizist*); **ˌ~-ˈcol·lar work·er** *s.* Faˈbrikarbeiter *m*; **ˈ~-eyed** *adj.* blauäugig (*a. fig.*): ***~ boy*** F ‚Liebling' *m des Chefs etc.*; **ˈ~ˌjack·et** *s. fig.* Blaujacke *f*, Maˈtrose *m*; **~ laws** *s. pl. Am.* strenge puriˈtanische Gesetze *pl.* (*bsd. gegen die Entheiligung des Sonntags*).

blue·ness [ˈbluːnɪs] *s.* Bläue *f*.

blue| pen·cil *s.* **1.** Blaustift *m*; **2.** *fig.* Zenˈsur *f*; **ˌ~-ˈpen·cil** *v/t.* **1.** *Manuskript etc.* (mit Blaustift) korrigieren *od.* (zs.-, aus)streichen; **2.** *fig.* zensieren, unterˈsagen; **~ print** *s.* **1.** Blaupause *f*; **2.** *fig.* Plan *m*, Entwurf *m*: ***do you need a ~?*** *iro.* ‚brauchst du e-e Zeichnung'?; **ˈ~-print I** *v/t.* entwerfen, planen; **II** *adj.*: ***~ stage*** Planungsstadium *n*; **~ rib·bon** *s.* blaues Band: a) *des Hosenbandordens*, b) *als Auszeichnung für e-e Höchstleistung, bsd.* ⚓ *das* Blaue Band des ˈOzeans; **ˈ~ˌstock·ing** *s. fig.* Blaustrumpf *m*; **ˈ~-stone** *s.* ⚗ ˈKupfervitriˌol *n*; **ˈ~-throat** *s. orn.* Blaukehlchen *n*; **~ tit** (**-mouse**) *s. orn.* Blaumeise *f*.

bluff¹ [blʌf] **I** *v/t.* **1.** a) *j-n* bluffen, b) ***~ it out*** sich (kühn) herausreden *od.* ‚durchmogeln'; **2.** *et.* vortäuschen; **II** *v/i.* **3.** bluffen; **III** *s.* **4.** Bluff *m*: ***call s.o.'s ~*** j-n zwingen, Farbe zu bekennen.

bluff² [blʌf] **I** *adj.* **1.** ⚓ breit (*Bug*); **2.** schroff, steil (*Felsen, Küste*); **3.** rauh, aber herzlich; gutmütig-derb; **II** *s.* **4.** Steilufer *n*, Klippe *f*.

bluff·er [ˈblʌfə] *s.* Bluffer *m*.

blu·ish [ˈbluːɪʃ] *adj.* bläulich.

blun·der [ˈblʌndə] **I** *s.* **1.** (grober) Fehler, Schnitzer *m*; **II** *v/i.* **2.** e-n (groben) Fehler *od.* Schnitzer machen, e-n Bock schießen; **3.** pfuschen, unbesonnen handeln; **4.** stolpern (*a. fig.*): ***~ into a dangerous situation***; ***~ about*** umhertappen; ***~ on*** *fig.* weiterwursteln; ***~ upon s.th.*** zufällig auf et. stoßen; **III** *v/t.* **5.** verpfuschen, verpatzen; **6.** ***~ out*** herˈausplatzen mit.

blun·der·buss [ˈblʌndəbʌs] *s.* ⚔ *hist.* Donnerbüchse *f*.

blun·der·er [ˈblʌndərə] *s.* Stümper *m*, Pfuscher *m*, Tölpel *m*; **ˈblun·der·ing** [-dərɪŋ] *adj.* stümper-, tölpelhaft, ungeschickt.

blunt [blʌnt] **I** *adj.* ☐ **1.** stumpf: ***~ instrument*** ⚖ stumpfer Gegenstand (*Mordwaffe*); **2.** *fig.* unempfindlich (***to*** gegen); **3.** *fig.* ungeschliffen, derb, ungehobelt (*Manieren etc.*); **4.** schonungslos, offen; schlicht; **II** *v/t.* **5.** stumpf machen, abstumpfen (*a. fig.*); **6.** *Gefühle etc.* mildern, schwächen; **III** *s.* **7.** *pl.* kurze Nähnadeln *pl.*; **ˈblunt·ly** [-lɪ] *adv. fig.* frei herˈaus, grob: ***to put it ~*** um es ganz offen zu sagen; ***refuse ~*** glatt ablehnen; **ˈblunt·ness** [-nɪs] *s.* **1.** Stumpfheit *f* (*a. fig.*); **2.** *fig.* Grobheit *f*; schonungslose Offenheit.

blur [blɜː] **I** *v/t.* **1.** *Schrift* verwischen, verschmieren; *Bild* verschwommen machen; verschleiern; **2.** verdunkeln, verwischen, *Sinne* trüben; **3.** *fig.* besudeln, entstellen; **II** *v/i.* **4.** verschwimmen; **III** *s.* **5.** Fleck *m*, verwischte Stelle; **6.** *fig.* Makel *m*; **7.** undeutlicher *od.* nebelhafter Eindruck; **8.** (huschender) Schatten; **9.** Schleier *m* (*vor den Augen*).

blurb [blɜːb] *s.* F *Buchhandel*: a) ‚Waschzettel' *m*, Klappentext *m*, b) ‚Bauchbinde' *f* (*Reklamestreifen*).

blurred [blɜːd] *adj.* unscharf, verschwommen, verwischt; schattenhaft; *fig.* nebelhaft.

blurt [blɜːt] *v/t.* ***~ out*** (ˈvoreilig *od.* unbesonnen) herˈausplatzen mit, ausschwatzen.

blush [blʌʃ] **I** *v/i.* erröten, rot werden, in Verwirrung geraten (***at, for*** über *acc.*); sich schämen (***to do*** zu tun); **II** *s.* Erröten *n*, (Scham)Röte *f*: ***at first ~*** *obs.* auf den ersten Blick; ***put to*** (***the***) ***~*** *j-n* zum Erröten bringen; **ˈblush·er** [-ʃə] *s.* F Rouge *n*; **ˈblush·ing** [-ʃɪŋ] *adj.* ☐ errötend; *fig.* züchtig.

blus·ter [ˈblʌstə] **I** *v/i.* **1.** brausen, tosen, stürmen; **2.** *fig.* poltern, toben, schimpfen; **3.** prahlen, bramarbasieren: ***~ing fellow*** Bramarbas *m*, Großmaul *n*; **II** *s.* **4.** Brausen *n*, Getöse *f*, Toben *n* (*a. fig.*); **5.** Schimpfen *n*; **6.** Prahlen *n*, ‚große Töne' *pl.*

bo [bəʊ] *int.* hu!: ***he can't say ~ to a goose*** er ist ein Hasenfuß.

bo·a [ˈbəʊə] *s.* **1.** *zo.* Boa *f*, Riesenschlange *f*; **2.** *Mode*: Boa *f*.

boar [bɔː] *s. zo.* Eber *m*, Keiler *m*: ***wild ~*** Wildschwein *n*.

board [bɔːd] **I** *s.* **1.** Brett *n*, Planke *f*; **2.** (*Schach-, Bügel*)Brett *n*: ***~ game*** Brettspiel *n*; ***sweep the ~*** alles gewinnen; **3.** Anschlagbrett *n*; **4.** *ped.* → ***blackboard***; **5.** *sport* a) (Surf)Board *n*, b) *pl.* ‚Bretter' *pl.*, Skier *pl.*; **6.** *pl. fig.* Bretter *pl.*, Bühne *f*: ***tread*** (*od.* ***walk***) ***the ~s*** auf den Brettern stehen, Schauspieler sein; **7.** Tisch *m*, Tafel *f* (*nur in festen Ausdrücken*): → ***above-board***, ***bed*** 3, ***groan*** 2; **8.** Kost *f*, Verpflegung *f*: ***~ and lodging*** Kost und Logis, Wohnung u. Verpflegung; **9.** *fig. oft* 2 Ausschuß *m*, Behörde *f*, Amt *n*: ***2 of Admiralty*** Admiralität *f*; ***2 of Examiners*** Prüfungskommission *f*; ***2 of Governors*** Verwaltungsrat *m*, (Schul- *etc.*)Behörde *f*; ***2 of Trade*** a) *Brit.* Handelsministerium *n*, b) *Am.* Handelskammer *f*; **10.** ***~ of directors***, (*the*) 2 ⚚ Verwaltungsrat *m*, Direktiˈon *f* (*Vorstand u. Aufsichtsrat in einem*); ***~ of management*** ⚚ Vorstand *m e-r AG*; **11.** ⚓ Bord *m*, Bordwand *f* (*nur in festen Ausdrücken*): ***on ~*** a) an Bord *e-s Schiffs, Flugzeugs*, b) im Zug *od.* Bus; ***on ~ a ship*** an Bord e-s Schiffes; ***free on ~*** (*abbr.* ***f.o.b.***) ⚚ frei an Bord (geliefert); ***go by the ~*** über Bord gehen *od.* fallen, *fig. a.* zugrunde gehen, verlorengehen, scheitern; **12.** Pappe *f*: ***in ~s*** kartoniert (*Buch*); **II** *v/t.* **13.** täfeln; mit Brettern bedecken *od.* absperren, dielen, verschalen; **14.** beköstigen, in Kost nehmen *od.* geben (***with*** bei); **15.** a) an Bord *e-s Schiffs od. Flugzeugs* gehen, b) in *e-n Zug etc.* einsteigen, c) ⚔, ⚓ entern; **III** *v/i.* **16.** sich in Kost *od.* Pensiˈon befinden, wohnen (***with*** bei); ***~ out I*** *v/t.* außerhalb in Kost geben; **II** *v/i.* auswärts essen; ***~ up*** *v/t.* mit Brettern vernageln.

board·er [ˈbɔːdə] *s.* **1.** a) Kostgänger (-in), b) Pensiˈonsgast *m*; **2.** Interˈnatsschüler(in).

board·ing [ˈbɔːdɪŋ] *s.* **1.** Bretterverschalung *f*, Dielenbelag *m*, Täfelung *f*; **2.** Kost *f*, Verpflegung *f*; **~ card** *s.* ✈ Bordkarte *f*; **ˈ~·house** *s.* Pensiˈon *f*; **~**

school *s.* Inter'nat *n*, Pensio'nat *n*.

board| meet·ing *s.* Vorstandssitzung *f*; **~ room** *s.* Sitzungssaal *m*; **~ wag·es** *s. pl.* Kostgeld *n des Personals*; **'~·walk** *s. Am.* Plankenweg *m*, (hölzerne) 'Strandprome,nade.

boast [bəʊst] **I** *s.* **1.** Prahle'rei *f*, Großtue'rei *f*; **2.** Stolz *m* (*Gegenstand des Stolzes*): ***it was his proud ~ that ...*** es war sein ganzer Stolz, daß ...; ***he was the ~ of his age*** er war der Stolz s-r Zeit; **II** *v/i.* **3.** (***of, about***) prahlen, großtun (mit): ***he ~s of his riches***; ***it is not much to ~ of*** damit ist es nicht weit her; **4.** (***of***) sich rühmen (*gen.*), stolz sein (auf *acc.*): ***our village ~s of a fine church***; **III** *v/t.* **5.** sich (des Besitzes) *e-r Sache* rühmen, aufzuweisen haben: ***our street ~s the tallest house in the town***; **'boast·er** [-tə] *s.* Prahler(in); **'boast·ful** [-fʊl] *adj.* □ prahlerisch, über'heblich.

boat [bəʊt] **I** *s.* **1.** Boot *n*, Kahn *m*; *allg.* Schiff *n*; Dampfer *m*: ***we are all in the same ~*** *fig.* wir sitzen alle in 'einem Boot; ***miss the ~*** *fig.* den Anschluß verpassen; ***burn one's ~s*** alle Brücken hinter sich abbrechen; **2.** bootförmiges Gefäß, (*bsd.* Soßen)Schüssel *f*; **II** *v/i.* **3.** (in e-m) Boot fahren: ***go ~ing*** e-e Bootsfahrt machen (*mst* rudern).

boat·er ['bəʊtə] *s. Brit.* steifer Strohhut, ‚Kreissäge' *f*.

boat·ing ['bəʊtɪŋ] *s.* Bootfahren *n*; Rudersport *m*; Bootsfahrt *f*.

'boat|·man [-mən] *s.* [*irr.*] Bootsführer *m*, -verleiher *m*; **~ race** *s.* 'Ruderre,gatta *f*; **~·swain** ['bəʊsn] *s.* ⚓ Bootsmann *m*; **~ train** *s.* Zug *m* mit Schiffsanschluß.

bob¹ [bɒb] **I** *s.* **1.** Haarschopf *m*, Büschel *n*; Bubikopf(haarschnitt) *m*; gestutzter Pferdeschwanz; Quaste *f*; **2.** Ruck *m*; Knicks *m*; **3.** *sg. u. pl. obs. Brit.* F Schilling *m*: ***five ~***; ***~ a job*** e-n Schilling für jede Arbeit; **4.** *abbr. für* ***bobsled***; **II** *v/t.* **5.** ruckweise (hin u. her, auf u. ab) bewegen; **6.** *Haare, Pferdeschwanz etc.* kurz schneiden, stutzen: ***~bed hair*** Bubikopf *m*; **III** *v/i.* **7.** sich auf u. ab *od.* hin u. her bewegen, baumeln, tänzeln; **8.** schnappen (***for*** nach); **9.** knicksen; **10.** Bob fahren; **11.** **~ up** (plötzlich) auftauchen: ***~ up like a cork*** *fig.* immer wieder hochkommen, sich nicht unterkriegen lassen.

Bob² [bɒb] *npr.*, *abbr. für* ***Robert***: ***~'s your uncle*** ‚fertig ist die Laube'.

bob·bin ['bɒbɪn] *s.* **1.** ⚙ Spule *f*, (Garn-) Rolle *f*; **2.** ⚡ Indukti'onsspule *f*; **3.** Klöppel(holz *n*) *m*; **'~-lace** *s.* Klöppelspitze *f*.

bob·by ['bɒbɪ] *s. Brit.* F ‚Bobby' *m* (*Polizist*); **~ pin** *s.* Haarklemme *f* (*aus Metall*); **~ socks** *s. pl. Am.* F Söckchen *pl.*; **'~,sox·er** [-,sɒksə] *s. Am.* F *hist.* ‚Backfisch' *m*.

'bob|·sled, **'~·sleigh** *s.* Bob *m* (*Rennschlitten*); **'~·tail** *s.* **1.** Stutzschwanz *m*; **2.** Pferd *n od.* Hund *m* mit Stutzschwanz.

bock (beer) [bɒk] *s.* Bockbier *n*.

bode¹ [bəʊd] **I** *v/t.* ahnen lassen: ***this ~s you no good*** das bedeutet nichts Gutes für dich; **II** *v/i.*: ***~ well*** Gutes versprechen: ***~ ill*** Schlimmes ahnen lassen.

bode² [bəʊd] *pret. von* ***bide***.

bod·ice ['bɒdɪs] *s.* **1.** *allg.* Mieder *n*; **2.** Oberteil *n*.

bod·ied ['bɒdɪd] *adj. in Zssgn* ...gebaut, von ... Körperbau *od.* Gestalt: ***small-~*** klein von Gestalt.

bod·i·less ['bɒdɪlɪs] *adj.* **1.** körperlos; **2.** unkörperlich, wesenlos; **'bod·i·ly** [-ɪlɪ] **I** *adj.* körperlich, leiblich: ***~ injury*** (⚖ ***harm***) Körperverletzung *f*; **II** *adv.* leib'haftig, per'sönlich.

bod·kin ['bɒdkɪn] *s.* **1.** ⚙ Ahle *f*, Pfriem *m*: ***sit ~*** eingepfercht sitzen; **2.** 'Durchzieh-, Schnürnadel *f*; **3.** *obs.* lange Haarnadel.

bod·y ['bɒdɪ] **I** *s.* **1.** Körper *m*, Leib *m*: ***heir of one's ~*** Leibeserbe *m*; ***in the ~*** lebend; ***~ and soul*** mit Leib u. Seele; ***keep ~ and soul together*** Leib u. Seele zs.-halten; **2.** *engS.* Rumpf *m*, Leib *m*: ***one wound in the leg and one in the ~***; **3.** *oft* ***dead ~*** Leiche *f*; **4.** Hauptteil *m*, *das* Wesentliche, Kern *m*, Stamm *m*, Rahmen *m*, Gestell *n*; Rumpf *m* (*Schiff, Flugzeug*); eigentlicher Inhalt, Sub'stanz *f* (*Schriftstück, Rede*): ***car ~*** Karosserie *f*; ***hat ~*** Hutstumpen *m*; **5.** Gesamtheit *f*, Masse *f*: ***in a ~*** zusammen, geschlossen, wie 'ein Mann; ***~ of water*** Wassermasse *f*, -fläche *f*, Gewässer *n*; ***~ of facts*** Tatsachenmaterial *n*; ***~ of laws*** Gesetz(es)sammlung *f*; **6.** Körper(schaft *f*) *m*, Gesellschaft *f*; Gruppe *f*; Gremium *n*: ***~ politic*** a) juristische Person, b) Gemeinwesen *n*; ***diplomatic ~*** diplomatisches Korps; ***governing ~*** Verwaltungskörper *m*; ***a ~ of unemployed*** e-e Gruppe Arbeitsloser; ***student ~*** Studentenschaft *f*; **7.** ⚔ Truppenkörper *m*, Trupp *m*, Ab'teilung *f*; **8.** *phys.* Körper *m*: ***solid ~*** fester Körper; ***heavenly ~*** *ast.* Himmelskörper; **9.** ⚗ Masse *f*, Sub'stanz *f*; **10.** F Bursche *m*, Kerl *m*; **11.** *fig.* Güte *f*, Stärke *f*, Festigkeit *f*, Gehalt *m*, Körper *m* (*Wein*), (Klang-) Fülle *f*; **II** *v/t.* **12.** *mst* ***~ forth*** *fig.* verkörpern; **~ blow** *s. Boxen*: Körperschlag *m*; *fig.* harter Schlag; **~ build** *s. biol.* Körperbau *m*; **~ build·er** *s.* Bodybuilder *m*; **~ build·ing** *s.* Bodybuilding *n*; **'~·check** *s. sport* Bodycheck *m*; **'~·guard** *s.* **1.** Leibwächter *m*; **2.** Leibgarde *f*; **~ lan·guage** *s. psych.* Körpersprache *f*; **'~-,mak·er** *s.* ⚙ Karosse'riebauer *m*; **~ o·do(u)r** *s.* Körpergeruch *m*; **~ plasm** *s. biol.* 'Körper,plasma *n*; **~ search** *s.* 'Leibesvisitati,on *f*; **~ seg·ment** *s. biol.* 'Rumpfseg,ment *n*; **~ serv·ant** *s.* Leib-, Kammerdiener *m*; **~ snatch·er** *s.* ⚖ Leichenräuber *m*; **~ stock·ing**, **~ suit** *s.* Bodystocking *m* (*einteilige Unterkleidung* [*mit Strümpfen*]); **'~·work** *s.* ⚙ Karosse'rie *f*.

bof·fin ['bɒfɪn] *s. Brit. sl.* (Geheim)Wissenschaftler *m*.

Boer ['bəʊə] **I** *s.* Bur(e) *m*, Boer *m* (*Südafrika*); **II** *adj.* burisch: ***~ War*** Burenkrieg *m*.

bog [bɒg] **I** *s.* **1.** Sumpf *m*, Mo'rast *m* (*a. fig.*); Moor *n*; **2.** V Scheißhaus *n*; **II** *v/t.* **3.** im Sumpf versenken; *fig. a.* ***~ down*** zum Stocken bringen, versanden lassen; **III** *v/i.* **4.** *a.* ***~ down*** im Sumpf *od.* Schlamm versinken; *a. fig.* steckenbleiben, sich festfahren, versanden.

bo·gey ['bəʊgɪ] *s.* **1.** *Golf*: a) Par *n*, b) Bogey *n* (*1 Schlag über Par*); **2.** → ***bogy***.

bog·gle ['bɒgl] *v/i.* **1.** (***at***) zu'rückschrecken (vor *dat.*): ***imagination ~s at the thought*** es wird einem schwindlig bei dem Gedanken; **2.** stutzen (***at*** vor, bei *dat.*); zögern (***at doing*** zu tun); **3.** pfuschen.

bog·gy ['bɒgɪ] *adj.* sumpfig.

bo·gie ['bəʊgɪ] *s.* **1.** ⚙ *Brit.* a) Blockwagen *m*, b) 🚂 Dreh-, Rädergestell *n*; **2.** ⚒ *Art* Förderkarren *m*; **3.** → ***bogy***; **~ wheel** *s.* ⚔ (Ketten)Laufrad *n*.

'bog,trot·ter *s. contp.* Ire *m*.

bo·gus ['bəʊgəs] *adj.* falsch, unecht, Schein..., Schwindel...

bo·gy ['bəʊgɪ] *s.* **1.** 'Kobold *m*, 'Popanz *m* **2.** (*a. fig.* Schreck)Gespenst *n*; **~ man** *s.* [*irr.*] **1.** Butzemann *m*, *der* Schwarze Mann (*Kindersprache*); **2.** *fig.* ‚Buhmann' *m*.

Bo·he·mi·an [bəʊ'hi:mjən] **I** *s.* **1.** Böhme *m*, Böhmin *f*; **2.** Bohemi'en *m* (*bsd. Künstler*); **II** *adj.* **3.** böhmisch; **4.** *fig.* bo'hemehaft; **bo'he·mi·an·ism** [-nɪzəm] *s.* Bo'heme *f*, ‚Künstlerleben' *n*.

boil¹ [bɔɪl] *s.* ⚕ Geschwür *n*, Fu'runkel *m*; Eiterbeule *f*.

boil² [bɔɪl] **I** *s.* **1.** Kochen *n*, Sieden *n*: ***bring to the ~*** zum Kochen bringen; ***come to the ~*** zu kochen anfangen, *fig.* F sich zuspitzen, s-n Höhepunkt erreichen; ***come off the ~*** F sich ‚legen' *od.* beruhigen; **2.** Wallen *n*, Wogen *n*, Schäumen *n* (*Gewässer*); **3.** *fig.* Erregung *f*, Wut *f*, Wallung *f*; **II** *v/i.* **4.** kochen, sieden; **5.** wallen, wogen, brausen, schäumen; **6.** *fig.* kochen, schäumen (***with*** vor *Wut*); **III** *v/t.* **7.** kochen (lassen), zum Kochen bringen, ab-, einkochen: ***~ eggs*** Eier kochen; ***to ~ clothes*** Wäsche kochen; ***go ~ your head!*** F häng dich doch auf!; **~ a·way** *v/i.* **1.** verdampfen; **2.** weiterkochen; **~ down I** *v/t.* verdampfen, einkochen; *fig.* zs.-fassen, kürzen; **II** *v/i.*: ***~ to*** hin'auslaufen auf (*acc.*); **~ o·ver** *v/i.* 'überkochen, -laufen, -schäumen (*alle a. fig.*).

boiled| din·ner [bɔɪld] *s. Am.* Eintopf (-gericht *n*) *m*; **~ po·ta·toes** *s. pl.* Salzkartoffeln *pl.*; **~ shirt** *s.* F Frackhemd *n*; **~ sweet** *s.* Bon'bon *m*, *n*.

boil·er ['bɔɪlə] *s.* **1.** Sieder *m*: ***soap ~***; **2.** ⚙ Dampfkessel *m*; **3.** 'Boiler *m*, Heißwasserspeicher *m*; **4.** Siedepfanne *f*; **5.** ***be a good ~*** sich (gut) zum Kochen eignen; **6.** Suppenhuhn *n*; **~ suit** *s.* 'Overall *m*.

boil·ing ['bɔɪlɪŋ] **I** *adj.* kochend, heiß; *fig.* kochend, schäumend (***with rage*** vor Wut); **II** *adv.*: ***~ hot*** kochend heiß; **~ point** *s.* Siedepunkt *m* (*a. fig.*).

bois·ter·ous ['bɔɪstərəs] *adj.* □ **1.** stürmisch, ungestüm, rauh; **2.** ausgelassen, lärmend, turbu'lent; **'bois·ter·ous·ness** [-nɪs] *s.* Ungestüm *n*.

bold [bəʊld] *adj.* □ **1.** kühn, zuversichtlich, mutig, unerschrocken; **2.** keck, verwegen, dreist, frech; anmaßend: ***make ~ to ...*** sich erdreisten *od.* es wagen zu ...; ***make ~ (with)*** sich Freiheiten herausnehmen (gegen); ***as ~ as brass*** F frech wie Oskar, unverschämt; **3.** kühn, gewagt: ***a ~ plan*** **4.** a) kühn (*Entwurf etc.*), b) scharf her'vortretend, ins Auge fallend: ***in ~ outline*** in deutlichen Umrissen; ***a few ~ strokes of the brush*** ein paar kühne Pinselstriche; **5.** steil (*Küste*); **6.** → **'bold-face** *adj. typ.* (halb)fett; **'~-faced** *adj.* **1.** kühn, frech; **2.** *typ.* → ***bold-face***.

bold·ness ['bəʊldnɪs] *s.* **1.** Kühnheit *f*: a) Mut *m*, Beherztheit *f*, b) Keckheit *f*, Dreistigkeit *f*; **2.** scharfes Her'vortreten.

bole [bəʊl] *s.* starker Baumstamm.

bo·le·ro¹ [bə'leərəʊ] *s.* Bo'lero *m* (*spanischer Tanz*).

bo·le·ro² ['bɒlərəʊ] *s.* Bo'lero *m* (*kurzes Jäckchen*).

boll [bəʊl] *s.* ⚘ Samenkapsel *f*.

bol·lard ['bɒləd] *s.* ⚓ Poller *m* (*a. weitS. Sperrpfosten an Verkehrsinseln etc.*).

bol·locks ['bɒləks] *s. pl.* V ‚Eier' *pl.* (*Hoden*).

Bo·lo·gna sau·sage [bə'ləʊnjə] *s. bsd. Am.* Morta'della *f*.

bo·lo·ney [bə'ləʊnɪ] *s.* **1.** *sl.* ‚Quatsch' *m*, Geschwafel *n*; **2.** *bsd. Am.* Morta'della *f*; → ***polony***.

Bol·she·vik ['bɒlʃɪvɪk] **I** *s.* Bolsche'wik *m*; **II** *adj.* bolsche'wistisch; **'Bol·she·vism** [-ɪzəm] *s.* Bolsche'wismus *m*; **'Bol·she·vist** [-ɪst] **I** *s.* Bolsche'wist *m*; **II** *adj.* bolsche'wistisch; **'Bol·she·vize** [-vaɪz] *v/t.* bolschewisieren.

bol·ster ['bəʊlstə] **I** *s.* **1.** Kopfpolster *n* (*unter dem Kopfkissen*), Keilkissen *n*; **2.** Polster *n*, Polsterung *f*, 'Unterlage *f* (*a.* ⚙); **II** *v/t.* **3.** *j-m* Kissen 'unterlegen; **4.** (aus)polstern; **5.** ~ ***up*** unter'stützen, stärken, künstlich aufrechterhalten.

bolt¹ [bəʊlt] **I** *s.* **1.** Schraube *f* (mit Mutter), Bolzen *m*: ~ ***nut*** Schraubenmutter *f*; **2.** Bolzen *m*, Pfeil *m*: ***shoot one's ~*** e-n (letzten) Versuch machen; ***he has shot his ~*** er hat sein Pulver verschossen; ~ ***upright*** kerzengerade; **3.** ⚙ (Tür-, Schloß)Riegel *m*: ***behind ~ and bar*** hinter Schloß u. Riegel; **4.** Schloß *n an Handfeuerwaffen*; **5.** Blitzstrahl *m*: ***a ~ from the blue*** ein Blitz aus heiterem Himmel; **6.** plötzlicher Sprung, Flucht *f*: ***he made a ~ for the door*** er machte e-n Satz zur Tür; ***he made a ~ for it*** F er machte sich aus dem Staube; **7.** *pol. Am.* Abtrünnigkeit *f* von der Poli'tik der eigenen Par'tei; **8.** ✝ a) (Stoff)Ballen *m*, b) (Ta'peten- *etc.*)Rolle *f*; **II** *v/t.* **9.** *Tür etc.* ver-, zuriegeln; **10.** *Essen* hin'unterschlingen; **11.** *Am. pol.* sich von *s-r Partei* lossagen; **III** *v/i.* **12.** 'durchgehen (*Pferd*); **13.** da'vonlaufen, ausreißen, ‚'durchbrennen'.

bolt² [bəʊlt] *v/t. Mehl* sieben.

bolt·er ['bəʊltə] *s.* **1.** 'Durchgänger *m* (*Pferd*); **2.** *pol. Am.* Abtrünnige(r *m*) *f*.

bo·lus ['bəʊləs] *s.* ⚕ Bolus *m*, große Pille.

bomb [bɒm] **I** *s.* **1.** Bombe *f*: ***the*** ♁ die (Atom)Bombe; **2.** ⚙ a) Gasflasche *f*, b) Zerstäuberflasche *f*; **3.** F a) Bombenerfolg *m*, b) Heidengeld *n*, c) *thea. etc. Am.* ‚'Durchfall' *m*, ‚Flop' *m*; **II** *v/t.* **4.** mit Bomben belegen, bombardieren; zerbomben: ***~ed out*** ausgebombt; ***~ed site*** Ruinengrundstück *n*; **5.** ~ ***up*** ✈ mit Bomben beladen; **III** *v/i.* **6.** *sl.* e-e ‚Pleite' sein, *thea.* ‚'durchfallen', *bsd. Am.* (*im Examen*) ‚'durchrasseln'.

bom·bard [bɒm'bɑːd] *v/t.* **1.** ⚔ bombardieren, Bomben werfen auf (*acc.*), beschießen; **2.** *fig.* (***with***) bombardieren, bestürmen (mit); **3.** *phys.* bombardieren, beschießen; **bom·bard·ier** [ˌbɒmbə'dɪə] *s.* ⚔ **1.** *Brit.* Artille'rieˌunteroffiˌzier *m*; **2.** Bombenschütze *m* (*im Flugzeug*); **bom'bard·ment** [-mənt] *s.* Bombarde'ment *n*, Beschießung *f* (*a. phys.*), Belegung *f* mit Bomben, Bombardierung *f*.

bom·bast ['bɒmbæst] *s. fig.* Bom'bast *m*, (leerer) Wortschwall, Schwulst *m*; **bom·bas·tic** [bɒm'bæstɪk] *adj.* (□ ***~ally***) bom'bastisch, schwülstig.

bomb| at·tack *s.* Bombenanschlag *m*; ~ **bay** *s.* ✈ Bombenschacht *m*; ~ **dis·pos·al** *s.* ⚔ Bombenräumung *f*: ~ ***squad*** Bombenräumungs-, Sprengkommando *n*.

bom·be [bɔ̃ːmb] (*Fr.*) *s.* Eisbombe *f*.

bombed [bɒmd] *adj. sl.* **1.** ‚besoffen'; **2.** ‚high' (*im Drogenrausch*).

bomb·er ['bɒmə] *s.* **1.** Bomber *m*, Bombenflugzeug *n*; **2.** Bombenleger *m*.

bomb·ing ['bɒmɪŋ] *s.* Bombenabwurf *m*: ~ ***raid*** Bombenangriff *m*.

'bomb|·proof ⚔ **I** *adj.* bombensicher; **II** *s.* Bunker *m*; ~ **scare** *s.* Bombendrohung *f*; **'~·shell** *s. fig.* Bombe *f*: ***the news came like a ~*** die Nachricht schlug ein wie e-e Bombe.

bo·na fi·de [ˌbəʊnə'faɪdɪ] *adj. u. adv.* **1.** in gutem Glauben, auf Treu u. Glauben: ~ ***owner*** ⚖ gutgläubiger Besitzer; **2.** ehrlich; echt; **ˌbo·na 'fi·des** [-diːz] *s. pl.* guter Glaube, Treu *f* und Glauben *m*, ehrliche Absicht; Rechtmäßigkeit *f*.

bo·nan·za [bəʊ'nænzə] **I** *s.* **1.** *min.* reiche Erzader (*bsd. Edelmetalle*); **2.** F Goldgrube *f*, Glücksquelle *f*, *a.* Fundgrube *f*; **3.** Fülle *f*, Reichtum *m*; **II** *adj.* **4.** sehr einträglich *od.* lukra'tiv.

bon·bon ['bɒnbɒn] *s.* Bon'bon *m*, *n*.

bond [bɒnd] **I** *s.* **1.** *pl. obs.* Fesseln *pl.*: ***in ~s*** in Fesseln, gefangen, versklavt; ***burst one's ~s*** s-e Ketten sprengen; **2.** *sg. od. pl. fig.* Bande *pl.*: ***~s of love***; **3.** Verpflichtung *f*, Bürgschaft *f*; (*a.* 'Haft)Kautiˌon *f*; Vertrag *m*; Urkunde *f*; Garan'tie(schein *m*) *f*: ***enter into a ~*** e-e Verpflichtung eingehen; ***his word is as good as his ~*** er ist ein Mann von Wort; **4.** ✝ a) Schuldschein *m*, b) *öffentliche* Schuldverschreibung, (festverzinsliches) 'Wertpaˌpier *n*, Obligati'on *f*, (Schuld-, Staats)Anleihe *f*: ***industrial ~*** Industrieobligation, -anleihe; → ***mortgage bond***; **5.** ✝ Zollverschluß *m*: ***in ~*** unter Zollverschluß; **6.** ⚠ Verband *m*, Verbindungsstück *n*; **7.** ⚗ a) Bindung *f*, b) Bindemittel *n*, c) Wertigkeit *f*; **8.** → ***bond paper***; **II** *v/t.* **9.** verpfänden; **10.** ✝ unter Zollverschluß legen; **11.** ⚙ *Lack etc.* binden (*a. v/i.*): ***~ing agent*** Bindemittel *n*; **'bond·age** [-dɪdʒ] *s. hist.* Knechtschaft *f*, Sklave'rei *f* (*a. fig.*); *fig. a.* Hörigkeit *f*: ***in the ~ of vice*** dem Laster verfallen; **'bond·ed** [-dɪd] *adj.* ✝: ~ ***debt*** fundierte Schuld; ~ ***goods*** Waren unter Zollverschluß; ~ ***warehouse*** Zollspeicher *m*.

'bond|ˌhold·er *s.* Obligati'onsinhaber *m*; **'~·man** [-mən] *s.* [*irr.*] Sklave *m*, Leibeigene(r) *m*; ~ **mar·ket** *s.* ✝ Rentenmarkt *m*; ~ **pa·per** *s.* Bankpost *f*, 'Post-, 'Banknotenpaˌpier *n*; ~ **slave** *s. fig.* Sklave *m*.

bonds·man ['bɒndzmən] *s.* [*irr.*] **1.** → ***bondman***; **2.** ⚖ a) Bürge *m*, b) *Am.* gewerblicher Kauti'onssteller.

bone [bəʊn] **I** *s.* **1.** Knochen *m*; Bein *n*: ~ ***of contention*** Zankapfel *m*; ***to the ~*** bis auf die Knochen *od.* die Haut, durch u. durch (*naß od. kalt*); ***price cut to the ~*** aufs äußerste reduzierter Preis, Schleuderpreis; ***I feel it in my ~s*** *fig.* ich spüre es in den Knochen (*ahne es*); ***a bag of ~s*** F nur (noch) Haut u. Knochen, ein Skelett; ***my old ~s*** m-e alten Knochen; ***bred in the ~*** angeboren; ***make no ~s about it*** nicht viel Federlesens machen, nicht lange (damit) fackeln; ***have a ~ to pick with s.o.*** ein Hühnchen mit j-m zu rupfen haben; **2.** *pl.* Gebeine *pl.*; **3.** (Fisch-)Gräte *f*; **4.** *pl.* Kor'settstangen *pl.*; **5.** *pl. Am.* a) Würfel *pl.*, b) 'Dominosteine *pl.*; **II** *v/t.* **6.** die Knochen her'ausnehmen aus (*dat.*), *Fisch* entgräten; **III** *v/i.* **7.** *oft* ~ ***up on*** *sl. et.* ‚büffeln', ‚ochsen', ‚pauken'; **IV** *adj.* **8.** beinern, knöchern, aus Bein *od.* Knochen; **'~·black** *s.* **1.** ⚗ Knochenkohle *f*; **2.** Beinschwarz *n* (*Farbe*); ~ **chi·na** *s.* 'Knochenporzelˌlan *n*.

boned [bəʊnd] *adj.* **1.** *in Zssgn* …knochig: ***strong-~*** starkknochig; **2.** *Küche*: a) ohne Knochen: ~ ***chicken***, b) entgrätet: ~ ***fish***.

ˌbone|-'dry *adj.* **1.** staubtrocken; **2.** F völlig ‚trocken': a) streng 'antialkoˌholisch, b) ohne jeden Alko'hol (*Party etc.*); ~ **glue** *s.* Knochenleim *m*; **'~·head** *s. sl.* Holz-, Dummkopf *m*; **'~ˌhead·ed** *adj. sl.* dumm; ~ **lace** *s.* Klöppelspitze *f*; **ˌ~'la·zy** *adj.* F ‚stinkfaul'; ~ **meal** *s.* Knochenmehl *n*.

bon·er ['bəʊnə] *s. Am. sl.* Schnitzer *m*, (grober) Fehler.

'bone|ˌshak·er *s. sl.* ‚Klapperkasten' *m* (*Bus etc.*); **'~·yard** *s. Am.* **1.** Schindanger *m*; **2.** F (*a.* Auto- *etc.*)Friedhof *m*.

bon·fire ['bɒnfaɪə] *s.* **1.** Freudenfeuer *n*; **2.** Feuer *n* im Freien (*zum Unkrautverbrennen etc.*); **3.** *allg.* Feuer *n*, ‚Scheiterhaufen' *m*: ***make a ~ of s.th.*** *et.* vernichten.

bon·ho·mie ['bɒnɒmiː] (*Fr.*) *s.* Gutmütigkeit *f*, Joviali'tät *f*.

bon·kers ['bɒŋkəz] *adj. sl.* verrückt.

bon·net ['bɒnɪt] **I** *s.* **1.** (*bsd.* Schotten)Mütze *f*, Kappe *f*; → ***bee¹*** 1; **2.** (Damen)Hut *m*, (Damen- *od.* Kinder-)Haube *f* (*mst randlos*); **3.** Kopfschmuck *m* der Indi'aner; **4.** ⚙ Schornsteinkappe *f*; **5.** *mot. Brit.* 'Motorhaube *f*; **6.** ⚙ Schutzkappe *f* (*für Ventil, Zylinder etc.*); **II** *v/t.* **7.** *j-m* den Hut über die Augen drücken; **'bon·net·ed** [-tɪd] *adj.* e-e Mütze *etc.* tragend.

bon·ny ['bɒnɪ] *adj. bsd. Scot.* **1.** hübsch, nett (*a. iron.*), *fig.* ‚prima'; **2.** F drall.

bo·nus ['bəʊnəs] *s.* ✝ **1.** 'Bonus *m*, 'Prämie *f*, Gratifikati'on *f*, Sondervergütung *f*, (Sonder)Zulage *f*, Tanti'eme *f*: ***Christmas ~*** Weihnachtsgratifikation; **2.** 'Prämie *f*, 'Extradiviˌdende *f*, Sonderausschüttung *f*: ~ ***share*** Gratisaktie *f*; **3.** *Am.* Dreingabe *f* (*beim Kauf*); **4.** Vergünstigung *f*.

bon·y ['bəʊnɪ] *adj.* **1.** knöchern, Knochen…; **2.** starkknochig; **3.** voll Knochen *od.* Gräten; **4.** knochendürr.

bonze [bɒnz] *s.* Bonze *m* (*buddhistischer Mönch od. Priester*).

boo [buː] **I** *int.* **1.** huh! (*um j-n zu er-*

schrecken); → *a.* **bo**; **2.** buh!, pfui! (*Ausruf der Verachtung*); **II** *s.* **3.** Buh(-ruf *m*) *n*, Pfui(ruf *m*) *n*; **III** *v/i.* **4.** buh! *od.* pfui! schreien, buhen; **IV** *v/t.* **5.** durch Pfui- *od.* Buhrufe verhöhnen; auspfeifen, ausbuhen, niederbrüllen.

boob [bu:b] *sl.* **I** *s.* **1.** ‚Schnitzer' *m*, Fehler *m*; **2.** → ***booby*** 1; **3.** *pl.* ‚Titten' *pl.* (*Brüste*); **II** *v/i.* **4.** e-n ‚Schnitzer' machen, ‚Mist bauen'.

boo-boo ['bu:bu:] *s. Am. sl.* → ***boob*** 1.

boob tube *s. Am. sl. TV* ‚Röhre' *f*, ‚Glotze' *f* (*Fernseher*).

boo·by ['bu:bɪ] *s.* **1.** ‚Dussel' *m*, Trottel *m*; **2.** Letzte(r *m*) *f*, Schlechteste(r *m*) *f* (*in Wettkämpfen etc.*); **3.** *orn.* Tölpel *m*, Seerabe *m*; **~ hatch** *s. Am. sl.* ‚Klapsmühle' *f* (*Irrenanstalt*); **~ prize** *s.* Trostpreis *m*; **~ trap** *s.* (versteckte) Sprengladung *od.* Bombe; *allg.* (*bsd.* Todes)Falle *f*; **'~-trap** *v/t.* a) e-e Bombe *etc.* verstecken in (*dat.*), b) durch e-e versteckte Bombe *etc.* e-n Anschlag verüben auf (*acc.*).

boo·dle ['bu:dl] *s. Am. sl.* **1.** → ***caboodle***; **2.** Falschgeld *n*; **3.** Schmiergelder *pl.*

boo·gie-woo·gie ['bu:gɪˌwu:gɪ] *s.* ♪ Boogie-Woogie *m* (*Tanz*).

boo·hoo [ˌbu:'hu:] **I** *s.* lautes Geschluchze; **II** *v/i.* laut schluchzen, plärren.

book [bʊk] **I** *s.* **1.** Buch *n*: ***be at one's ~s*** über s-n Büchern sitzen; ***without the ~*** auswendig; ***he talks like a ~*** er redet sehr gestelzt; ***the ~ of life*** (***nature***) *fig.* das Buch des Lebens (der Natur); ***a closed ~*** a) ein Buch mit sieben Siegeln, b) e-e erledigte Sache; ***the*** 𝔅 (***of*** 𝔅***s***) die Bibel; ***kiss the*** 𝔅 die Bibel küssen; ***swear on the*** 𝔅 bei der Bibel schwören; ***suit s.o.'s ~*** *fig.* j-m passen *od.* recht sein; ***throw the ~ at s.o.*** F a) j-n (zur Höchststrafe) ‚verdonnern', b) j-n wegen sämtlicher einschlägigen Delikte belangen; ***by the ~*** a) ganz korrekt *od.* genau, b) ‚nach allen Regeln der Kunst'; ***in my ~*** F wie 'ich es sehe; → ***leaf*** 3; **2.** Buch *n* (*Teil e-s Gesamtwerkes*); **3.** † Geschäfts-, Handelsbuch *n*: ***close the ~s*** die Bücher abschließen; ***keep ~s*** Bücher führen; ***be deep in s.o.'s ~s*** bei j-m tief in der Kreide stehen; ***bring to ~*** a) *j-n* zur Rechenschaft ziehen, b) † (ver)buchen; ***be in s.o.'s good*** (***bad*** *od.* ***black***) ***~s*** bei j-m gut (schlecht) angeschrieben sein; **4.** (Schreib)Heft *n*, No'tizblock *m*; **5.** (Namens)Liste *f*, Verzeichnis *n*, Buch *n*: ***visitors' ~*** Gästebuch; ***be on the ~s*** auf der Mitgliedsliste (*univ.* Liste der Immatrikulierten) stehen; **6.** Heft(chen) *n*, Block *m*: ***~ of stamps*** Briefmarkenheft; **7.** Wettbuch *n*: ***you can make a ~ on that!*** F darauf kannst du wetten!; **8.** a) *thea.* Text *m*, b) ♪ Textbuch *n*, Lib'retto *n*; **II** *v/t.* **9.** † (ver)buchen, eintragen; **10.** *j-n* verpflichten, engagieren; **11.** *j-n als* (*Fahr*)*Gast, Teilnehmer etc.* einschreiben, vormerken; **12.** *Platz, Zimmer* bestellen, *a. Überfahrt etc.* buchen; *Eintritts-, Fahrkarte* lösen; *Auftrag* notieren; *Güter, Gepäck* (*zur Beförderung*) aufgeben; *Ferngespräch* anmelden; → ***booked***; **13.** *j-n polizeilich* aufschreiben *od. sport* notieren (***for*** wegen); **III** *v/i.* **14.** eine Fahrkarte *etc.* lösen *od.* nehmen: ***~ through*** (***to***) durchlösen (bis, nach); **15.** Platz *etc.* bestellen; **16.** ***~ in*** sich (*im Hotel*) eintragen: ***~ in at*** absteigen in (*dat.*); **'book·a·ble** [-kəbl] *adj.* im Vorverkauf erhältlich (*Karten etc.*).

'book|ˌbind·er *s.* Buchbinder *m*; **'~ˌbinding** *s.* Buchbinderhandwerk *n*, Buchbinde'rei *f*; **'~·case** *s.* 'Bücherschrank *m*, -reˌgal *n*; **~ cloth** *s.* Buchbinderleinwand *f*; **~ club** *s.* Buchgemeinschaft *f*; **~ cov·er** *s.* 'Buchdecke *f*, -ˌumschlag *m*; **~ debt** *s.* † Buchschuld *f*.

booked [bʊkt] *adj.* **1.** gebucht, eingetragen; **2.** vorgemerkt, bestimmt, bestellt: ***all ~*** (***up***) voll besetzt *od.* belegt, ausverkauft.

book end *s. mst pl.* Bücherstütze *f*.

book·ie ['bʊkɪ] *sl.* → ***bookmaker***.

book·ing ['bʊkɪŋ] *s.* **1.** Buchung *f*, Eintragung *f*; **2.** Bestellung *f*; **~ clerk** *s.* Schalterbeamte(r) *m*, Fahrkartenverkäufer *m*; **~ hall** *s.* Schalterhalle *f*; **~ of·fice** *s.* **1.** Fahrkartenschalter *m*; **2.** *thea. etc.* Kasse *f*; Vorverkaufsstelle *f*; **3.** *Am.* Gepäckschalter *m*.

book·ish ['bʊkɪʃ] *adj.* □ **1.** belesen, gelehrt; **2.** voll Bücherweisheit: ***~ person*** a) Büchernarr *m*, b) Stubengelehrte(r) *m*; ***~ style*** papierener Stil; **'book·ish·ness** [-nɪs] *s.* trockene Gelehrsamkeit.

'book|ˌkeep·er *s.* Buchhalter(in); **'~ˌkeep·ing** *s.* Buchhaltung *f*, -führung *f*: ***~ by single*** (***double***) ***entry*** einfache (doppelte) Buchführung; **~ knowl·edge**, **~ learn·ing** *s.* Buchwissen *n*, Bücherweisheit *f*.

book·let ['bʊklɪt] *s.* Büchlein *n*, Bro'schüre *f*.

'book|ˌmak·er *s.* Buchmacher *m*; **'~·man** [-mən] *s.* [*irr.*] Büchermensch *m*, Gelehrte(r) *m*; **'~·mark** *s.* Lesezeichen *n*; **'~·moˌbile** [-məʊbi:l] *s. Am.* 'Auto-, 'Wanderbücheˌrei *f*; **'~·plate** *s.* Ex'libris *n*; **~ post** *s. Brit.* (***by ~*** als) Büchersendung *f*; **~ prof·it** *s.* † Buchgewinn *m*; **'~-rack** *s.* 'Büchergestell *n*, -reˌgal *n*; **'~-rest** *s.* **1.** Buchstütze *f*; **2.** (kleines) Lesepult; **~ re·view** *s.* Buchbesprechung *f*; **~ re·view·er** *s.* 'BuchˌKritiker *m*; **'~ˌsell·er** *s.* Buchhändler (-in); **'~·shelf** *s.* Bücherbrett *n*, -gestell *n*; **'~·shop** *s.* Buchhandlung *f*; **'~·stack** *s.* Bücherregal *n*; **'~·stall** *s.* **1.** Bücher(verkaufs)stand *m*; **2.** Zeitungsstand *m*; **'~·stand** → ***book-rack***; **'~·store** *s. Am.* Buchhandlung *f*.

book·sy ['bʊksɪ] *adj. Am.* F ‚hochgestochen'.

book| to·ken *s. Brit.* Büchergutschein *m*; **~ trade** *s.* Buchhandel *m*; **~ val·ue** *s.* † Buchwert *m*; **'~·worm** *s. zo. u. fig.* Bücherwurm *m*.

boom¹ [bu:m] **I** *s.* Dröhnen *n*, Donnern *n*, Brausen *n*; **II** *v/i.* dröhnen, donnern, brausen; **III** *v/t. a.* **~ out** dröhnen(d äußern).

boom² [bu:m] *s.* **1.** ⚓ Baum *m* (*Hafen- od. Flußsperrgerät*); **2.** ⚓ Baum *m*, Spiere *f* (*Stange am Segel*); **3.** *Am.* Schwimmbaum *m* (*zum Auffangen des Floßholzes*); **4.** *Film, TV:* (Mikro'phon)Galgen *m*.

boom³ [bu:m] **I** *s.* **1.** Aufschwung *m*; Berühmtheit *f*, *das* Berühmtwerden, Blüte(zeit) *f*; **2.** † Boom *m*: a) ('Hoch-) Konjunkˌtur *f*: ***building ~*** Bauboom, b) Aufschwung *m*, c) *Börse:* Hausse *f*; **3.** Re'klamerummel *m*, aufdringliche Propa'ganda; **II** *v/i.* **4.** e-n (ra'piden) Aufschwung nehmen, in die Höhe schnellen, anziehen (*Preise, Kurse*), blühen: ***~ing*** florierend, blühend; **III** *v/t.* **5.** die Werbetrommel rühren für; *Preise* in die Höhe treiben; **ˌ~-and-'bust** *s. Am.* F außergewöhnlicher Aufstieg, dem e-e ernste Krise folgt.

boom·er·ang ['bu:məræŋ] **I** *s.* Bumerang *m* (*a. fig.*); **II** *v/i. fig.* (***on***) sich als Bumerang erweisen (für), zurückschlagen (auf *acc.*).

boon¹ [bu:n] *s.* **1.** Wohltat *f*, Segen *m*; **2.** Gefälligkeit *f*.

boon² [bu:n] *adj. lit.* freundlich, munter: ***~ companion*** lustiger Kumpan *od.* Zechbruder.

boon·docks ['bu:ndɒks] *s. pl. Am. sl. die* Pro'vinz.

boor [bʊə] *s. fig.* a) ‚Bauer' *m*, ungehobelter Kerl, b) Flegel *m*; **boor·ish** ['bʊərɪʃ] *adj.* □ *fig.* ungehobelt, flegelhaft; **boor·ish·ness** ['bʊərɪʃnɪs] *s.* ungehobeltes Benehmen *od.* Wesen.

boost [bu:st] **I** *v/t.* **1.** hochschieben, -treiben; nachhelfen (*dat.*) (*a. fig.*); **2.** † F a) fördern, Auftrieb geben (*dat.*) (*a. fig.*), *Produktion etc.* ‚ankurbeln', *Preise* in die Höhe treiben: ***~ the morale*** die (*Arbeits- etc.*)Moral heben, b) anpreisen, Re'klame machen für; **3.** ⚙, ⚡ *Druck, Spannung* erhöhen, verstärken; **II** *s.* **4.** Förderung *f*, Erhöhung *f*; Auftrieb *m*; **5.** *fig.* Re'klame *f*.

boost·er ['bu:stə] *s.* **1.** F Förderer *m* Re'klamemacher *m*; Preistreiber *m*; **2.** ⚙, ⚡ 'Zusatz(aggreˌgat *n*, -dyˌnamo *m*, -verstärker *m*) *m*; Kom'pressor *m*; Servomotor *m*; *Rakete:* a) 'Antriebsaggreˌgat *n*, b) Zündstufe *f*, c) 'Trägerraˌkete *f*; **~ bat·ter·y** *s.* ⚡ 'Zusatzbatteˌrie *f*; **~ rock·et** *s.* 'Startraˌkete *f*; **~ shot** *s.* ⚕ Wieder'holungsimpfung *f*.

boot¹ [bu:t] **I** *s.* **1.** (*Am.* Schaft)Stiefel *m*; *pl. Mode:* Boots *pl.*: ***the ~ is on the other leg*** a) der Fall liegt umgekehrt, b) die Verantwortung liegt bei der anderen Seite; ***die in one's ~s*** a) in den Sielen sterben, b) e-s plötzlichen *od.* gewaltsamen Todes sterben; ***get the ~*** *sl.* ‚rausgeschmissen' (*entlassen*) werden; → ***big*** 2; **2.** *Brit. mot.* Kofferraum *m*; **3.** ⚙ Schutzkappe *f*, -hülle *f*; **II** *v/t.* **4.** *sl. j-m* e-n Fußtritt geben; **5.** *sl. fig. j-n* ‚rausschmeißen' (*entlassen*); **6.** F *Fußball* treten; **7.** *Computer: Programm* booten, starten.

boot² [bu:t] *s. nur noch in:* ***to ~*** obendrein, noch dazu.

'boot·black *s. Am.* Schuhputzer *m*.

boot·ed ['bu:tɪd] *adj.* Stiefel tragend: ***~ and spurred*** gestiefelt u. gespornt.

booth [bu:ð] *s.* **1.** (Markt)Bude *f*; (Messe)Stand *m*; **2.** (Fernsprech-, *pol.* Wahl)Zelle *f*; **3.** a) *Radio, TV:* (Über'tragungs)Kaˌbine *f*, b) ('Abhör-) Kaˌbine *f* (*Schallplattengeschäft*); **4.** Nische *f*, Sitzgruppe *f im Restaurant.*

'boot|·jack *s.* Stiefelknecht *m*; **'~·lace** *s. bsd. Brit.* Schnürsenkel *m*.

boot·leg ['bu:tleg] *v/t. u. v/i. Am. sl. bsd. Spirituosen* 'illegal herstellen, schwarz verkaufen, schmuggeln; **'boot·ˌleg·ger** [-gə] *s. Am. sl.* ('Alkohol-)

Schmuggler *m*, (-)Schwarzhändler *m*; **'boot,leg·ging** [-gɪŋ] *s. Am. sl.* ('Alkohol)Schmuggel *m*.

boot·less ['bu:tlɪs] *adj.* □ nutzlos, vergeblich.

'boot|·lick *v/t. u. v/i.* F (vor *j-m*) kriechen; **'~,lick·er** *s.* F ,Kriecher' *m*.

boots [bu:ts] *s. sg.* Hausdiener *m* (*im Hotel*).

'boot|·strap *s.* Stiefelstrippe *f*, -schlaufe *f*: ***pull o.s. up by one's own ~s*** sich aus eigener Kraft hocharbeiten; **~ top** *s.* Stiefelstulpe *f*; **~ tree** *s.* Schuh-, Stiefelleisten *m*.

boot·y ['bu:tɪ] *s.* **1.** (Kriegs)Beute *f*, Raub *m*; **2.** *fig.* Beute *f*, Fang *m*.

booze [bu:z] F **I** *v/i.* ,saufen'; **II** *s.* a) Schnaps *m*, 'Alkohol *m*, b) ,Saufe'rei' *f*, Besäufnis *n*: ***go on*** (*od.* ***hit***) ***the ~*** → I; **boozed** [-zd] *adj.* F ,blau', ,voll', besoffen; **'booz·er** [-zə] *s.* **1.** F Säufer *m*; **2.** *Brit. sl.* Kneipe *f*.

'booze-up → ***booze*** II b.

booz·y ['bu:zɪ] *adj.* F **1.** → ***boozed***; **2.** versoffen.

bo·rac·ic [bə'ræsɪk] *adj.* ⚗ 'boraxhaltig, Bor...: **~ *acid*** Borsäure *f*.

bor·age ['bɒrɪdʒ] *s.* ✿ Borretsch *m*, Gurkenkraut *n*.

bo·rax ['bɔ:ræks] *s.* ⚗ 'Borax *m*.

bor·der ['bɔ:də] **I** *s.* **1.** Rand *m*, Kante *f*; **2.** (*Landes- od. Gebiets*)Grenze *f*; *a.* **~ *area*** Grenzgebiet *n*: ***the* ≗** Grenze *od.* Grenzgebiet zwischen England u. Schottland; ***north of the* ≗** in Schottland; **~ *incident*** Grenzzwischenfall *m*; **3.** Um'randung *f*, Borte *f*, Einfassung *f*, Saum *m*; Zierleiste *f*; **4.** Randbeet *n*, Ra'batte *f*; **II** *v/t.* **5.** einfassen, besetzen; **6.** begrenzen, (um)'säumen: ***a lawn ~ed by trees***; **7.** grenzen an (*acc.*): ***my park ~s yours***; **III** *v/i.* **8.** grenzen (***on*** an *acc.*) (*a. fig.*); **'bor·der·er** [-ərə] *s.* **1.** Grenzbewohner *m*; **2.** **≗s** *pl.* ⚔ 'Grenzregi,ment *n*.

'bor·der|·land *s.* Grenzgebiet *n* (*a. fig.*); **'~·line I** *s.* 'Grenz,linie *f*; *fig.* Grenze *f*; **II** *adj.* auf *od.* an e-r Grenze: **~ *case*** Grenzfall *m*.

bor·dure ['bɔ:,djʊə] *s. her.* 'Schild-, 'Wappenum,randung *f*.

bore¹ [bɔ:] **I** *v/t.* **1.** (durch)'bohren: **~ *a well*** e-n Brunnen bohren; ***to ~ one's way*** *fig.* sich (mühsam) e-n Weg bahnen; **II** *v/i.* **2.** (***for***) bohren, Bohrungen machen (nach); ⚒ schürfen (nach); **3.** ⚙ *bei Holz*: (ins Volle) bohren; *bei Metall*: (aus-, auf)bohren; **4.** sich einbohren (***into*** in *acc.*); **III** *s.* **5.** ⚒ Bohrung *f*, Bohrloch *n*; **6.** ⚔, ⚙ Bohrung *f*, Seele *f*, Ka'liber *n* (*e-r Schußwaffe*).

bore² [bɔ:] **I** *s.* **1.** *et.* Langweiliges *od.* Lästiges *od.* Stumpfsinniges: ***what a ~*** a) wie langweilig, b) wie dumm; ***the book is a ~ to read*** das Buch ist ,stinkfad'; **2.** a) fader Kerl, b) unangenehmer Kerl, (altes) Ekel; **II** *v/t.* **3.** langweilen: ***be ~d*** sich langweilen; ***look ~d*** gelangweilt aussehen.

bore³ [bɔ:] *s.* Springflut *f*.

bore⁴ [bɔ:] *pret. von* ***bear¹***.

bo·re·al ['bɔ:rɪəl] *adj.* nördlich, Nord...; **bo·re·a·lis** [bɔ:rɪ'eɪlɪs] → ***aurora borealis***; **Bo·re·as** ['bɒrɪæs] **I** *npr.* 'Boreas *m*; **II** *s. poet.* Nordwind *m*.

bore·dom ['bɔ:dəm] *s.* **1.** Langeweile *f*, Gelangweiltsein *n*; **2.** Langweiligkeit *f*, Stumpfsinn *m*.

bor·er ['bɔ:rə] *s.* **1.** ⚙ Bohrer *m*; **2.** *zo.* Bohrer *m* (*Insekt*).

bo·ric ['bɔ:rɪk] *adj.* ⚗ Bor...: **~ *acid*** Borsäure *f*.

bor·ing ['bɔ:rɪŋ] *adj.* **1.** bohrend, Bohr...; **2.** langweilig.

born [bɔ:n] **I** *p.p. von* ***bear¹***; **II** *adj.* geboren: **~ *of ...*** geboren von ..., Kind des *od.* der ...; ***a ~ poet***, **~ *a poet*** ein geborener Dichter, zum Dichter geboren; ***a ~ fool*** ein völliger Narr; ***an Englishman ~ and bred*** ein echter Engländer; ***never in all my ~ days*** mein Lebtag (noch) nie.

borne [bɔ:n] *p.p. von* ***bear¹*** **1.** getragen *etc.*: ***lorry-~*** mit (e-m) Lastwagen befördert; **2.** geboren (*in Verbindung mit* ***by*** *und dem Namen der Mutter*): ***Elizabeth I was ~ by Anne Boleyn***.

bor·né ['bɔ:neɪ] (*Fr.*) *adj.* borniert.

bo·ron ['bɔ:rɒn] *s.* ⚗ Bor *n*.

bor·ough ['bʌrə] *s.* **1.** *Brit.* a) Stadt *f od.* im Parla'ment vertretener städtischer Wahlbezirk, b) Stadtteil *m* (*von Groß-London*): **≗ *Council*** Stadtrat *m*; **2.** *Am.* a) Stadt- *od.* Dorfgemeinde *f*, b) Stadtbezirk *m* (*in New York*).

bor·row ['bɒrəʊ] *v/t.* **1.** (aus)borgen, (ent)leihen (***from***, ***of*** von): ***~ed funds*** ✝ Fremdmittel *pl.*; **2.** *fig.* entlehnen, *humor.* ,borgen': ***~ed word*** Lehnwort *n*; **'bor·row·er** [-əʊə] *s.* **1.** Entleiher (-in), Borger(in); **2.** ✝ Kre'ditnehmer (-in); **'bor·row·ing** [-əʊɪŋ] *s.* (Aus)Borgen *n*; Darlehns-, Kre'ditaufnahme *f*, Anleihe *f*: **~ *power*** ✝ Kreditfähigkeit *f*.

Bor·stal (**In·sti·tu·tion**) ['bɔ:stl] *s. Brit. erzieherisch gestaltete Jugendstrafanstalt*: ***Borstal training*** Strafvollzug *m* in e-m ***Borstal***.

bosh [bɒʃ] *s.* F ,Quatsch' *m*.

bos·om ['bʊzəm] *s.* **1.** Busen *m*, Brust *f*, *fig. a.* Herz *n*: **~ *friend*** Busenfreund (-in); ***keep*** (*od.* ***lock***) ***in one's*** (***own***) **~** in s-m Busen verschließen; ***take s.o. to one's ~*** j-n ans Herz drücken; **3.** *fig.* Schoß *m*: ***in the ~ of one's family*** (***the Church***); → ***Abraham***; **4.** Brustteil *m* (*Kleid etc.*); *bsd. Am.* Hemdbrust *f*; **5.** Tiefe *f*, *das* Innere: ***in the ~ of the earth*** im Erdinnern; **'bos·omed** [-md] *adj. in Zssgn* ...busig; **'bos·om·y** [-mɪ] *adj.* vollbusig.

boss¹ [bɒs] **I** *s.* Beule *f*, Buckel *m*, Knauf *m*, Knopf *m*, erhabene Verzierung; ⚙ (*Rad-, Schiffsschrauben*)Nabe *f*; **II** *v/t.* mit Buckeln *etc.* verzieren, bosseln, treiben.

boss² [bɒs] F **I** *s.* **1.** *a.* ***~-man*** Chef *m*, Vorgesetzte(r) *m*, ,Boß' *m*; **2.** *fig.* ,Macher' *m*, ,Boß' *m*, Tonangebende(r) *m*; **3.** *Am. pol.* (Par'tei)Bonze *m*, (-)Boß *m*; **II** *v/t.* **4.** Herr sein über (*acc.*): **~ *the show*** der Chef vom Ganzen sein; **III** *v/i.* **5.** den Chef *od.* Herrn spielen, kommandieren; **6.** **~ *about*** herumkommandieren; **boss·y** ['bɒsɪ] *adj.* F **1.** herrisch, dikta'torisch; **2.** rechthaberisch.

bo·sun ['bəʊsn] → ***boatswain***.

bo·tan·ic, **bo·tan·i·cal** [bə'tænɪk(l)] *adj.* □ bo'tanisch.

bot·a·nist ['bɒtənɪst] *s.* Bo'taniker *m*, Pflanzenkenner *m*; **'bot·a·nize** [-naɪz] *v/i.* botanisieren; **'bot·a·ny** [-nɪ] *s.* Bo'tanik *f*, Pflanzenkunde *f*.

botch [bɒtʃ] **I** *s.* Flickwerk *n*, *fig. a.* Pfuscharbeit *f*: ***make a ~ of s.th*** et. verpfuschen; **II** *v/t.* zs.-schustern *od.* -stoppeln; verpfuschen; **III** *v/i.* pfuschen, stümpern; **'botch·er** [-tʃə] *s.* **1.** Flickschneider *m*, -schuster *m* (*a. fig.*); **2.** Pfuscher *m*, Stümper *m*.

both [bəʊθ] **I** *adj. u. pron.* beide, beides: **~ *my sons*** m-e beiden Söhne; **~ *parents*** beide Eltern; **~ *of them*** sie (*od.* alle) beide; ***you can't have it ~ ways*** du kannst nicht beides *od.* nur eins von beiden haben; **II** *adv. od. cj.*: **~ *... and*** sowohl ... als (auch): **~ *boys and girls***.

both·er ['bɒðə] **I** *s.* **1.** a) Last *f*, Plage *f*, Mühe *f*, Ärger *m*, Schere'rei *f*, b) Aufregung *f*, ,Wirbel' *m*, Getue *n*: ***this boy is a great ~*** dieser Junge ist e-e große Plage; **II** *v/t.* **2.** belästigen, quälen, stören, beunruhigen, ärgern: ***don't ~ me!*** laß mich in Frieden!; ***be ~ed about s.th.*** über et. beunruhigt sein; ***I can't be ~ed with it*** ich kann mich nicht damit abgeben; **~ *one's head about s.th.*** sich über et. den Kopf zerbrechen; **~ (*it*)!** F verflixt!; **III** *v/i.* **3.** (***about***) sich sorgen (um), sich aufregen (über *acc.*); **4.** sich Mühe geben: ***don't ~!*** bemüh dich nicht!; **5.** (***about***) sich kümmern (um), sich befassen (mit), sich Gedanken machen (wegen): ***I shan't ~ about it***; **both·er·a·tion** [,bɒðə'reɪʃn] F **I** *s.* Belästigung *f*; **II** *int.* ,Mist'!

bo-tree ['bəʊtri:] *s. der* heilige Feigenbaum (*Buddhas*).

bot·tle ['bɒtl] **I** *s.* **1.** Flasche *f* (*a.* ⚙): ***wine in ~s*** Flaschenwein *m*; ***bring up on the ~*** *Säugling* mit der Flasche aufziehen; ***be fond of the ~*** gern ,einen heben'; **II** *v/t.* **2.** in Flaschen abfüllen; **3.** *bsd. Brit. Früchte etc.* in Gläsern einmachen; **~ *up*** *v/t.* **1.** *fig. Gefühle etc.* unter'drücken: ***bottled-up*** aufgestaut; **2.** einschließen: **~ *the enemy's fleet***.

bot·tle cap *s.* Flaschenkapsel *f*.

bot·tled ['bɒtld] *adj.* in Flaschen *od.* (Einmach)Gläser (ab)gefüllt: **~ *beer*** Flaschenbier *n*; → ***bottle up*** 1.

'bot·tle|-feed *v/t.* [*irr.*] mit der Flasche aufziehen, aus der Flasche ernähren: ***bottle-fed child***; **~ *gourd*** *s.* ✿ Flaschenkürbis *m*; **'~-green** *adj.* flaschen-, dunkelgrün; **'~-,hold·er** *s.* **1.** *Boxen*: Sekun'dant *m*; **2.** *fig.* Helfershelfer *m*; **~ *imp*** *s.* Flaschenteufelchen *n*; **'~-neck** *s.* Engpaß *m* (*a. fig.*); **'~-nosed** *adj.* mit e-r Säufernase; **'~,par·ty** *s.* Bottle-Party *f* (*zu der jeder Gast e-e Flasche Wein etc. mitbringt*); **~ *post*** *s.* Flaschenpost *f*.

bot·tler ['bɒtlə] *s.* 'Abfüllma,schine *f od.* -betrieb *m*.

'bot·tle-,wash·er *s.* **1.** Flaschenreiniger *m*; **2.** *humor.* Fak'totum *n*, ,Mädchen *n* für alles'.

bot·tom ['bɒtəm] **I** *s.* **1.** *der* unterste Teil, 'Unterseite *f*, Boden *m* (*Gefäß etc.*), Fuß *m* (*Berg, Treppe, Seite etc.*), Sohle *f* (*Brunnen, Tal etc.*): ***~s up! sl.*** ex! (*beim Trinken*); **2.** Boden *m*, Grund *m* (*Gewässer*): ***go to the ~*** versinken; ***send to the ~*** versenken; ***touch ~*** a) auf Grund geraten, b) *fig.* den Tiefpunkt erreichen; ***the ~ has fallen out of the market*** der Markt hat e-n Tiefstand erreicht; **3.** *fig.* Grund(lage *f*) *m*: ***what is at the ~ of it?*** was ist der

Grund dafür?, was steckt dahinter?; ***knock the ~ out of s.th.*** et. gründlich widerlegen; ***get to the ~ of s.th.*** e-r Sache auf den Grund gehen *od.* kommen: ***from the ~ up*** von Grund auf; **4.** *fig. das* Innere, Tiefe *f*: ***from the ~ of my heart*** aus tiefstem Herzen; ***at ~*** im Grunde; **5.** ⚓ Schiffsboden *m*; Schiff *n*: ***~ up(wards)*** kieloben; ***shipped in British ~s*** in brit. Schiffen verladen; **6.** (*Stuhl*)Sitz *m*; **7.** F *der* Hintern, ‚Po (-'po)' *m*: ***smack the boy's ~*** den Jungen ‚versohlen'; ***smooth as a baby's ~*** glatt wie ein Kinderpopo; **8.** (unteres) Ende (*Tisch*, *Klasse*, *Garten*); **II** *adj.* **9.** unterst, letzt, äußerst: ***~ shelf*** unterstes (*Bücher*)Brett; ***~ drawer*** a) unterste Schublade (*a. fig.*), b) *Brit.* Aussteuer (-truhe) *f*; ***~ price*** äußerster Preis; ***~ line*** letzte Zeile; **III** *v/t.* **10.** mit e-m Boden *od.* Sitz versehen; **11.** ergründen; **'bot·tomed** [-md] *adj.*: ***~ on*** beruhend auf (*dat.*); ***double-~*** mit doppeltem Boden; ***cane-~*** mit Rohrsitz (*Stuhl*); **'bot·tom·less** [-lɪs] *adj.* bodenlos (*a. fig.*); unergründlich; unerschöpflich; **'bot·tom·ry** [-rɪ] *s.* ⚓ Bodme'rei(geld *n*) *f*.

bot·u·lism ['bɒtjʊlɪzəm] *s.* ⚕ Botu'lismus *m* (*Fleischvergiftung etc.*).

bou·doir ['bu:dwa:] (*Fr.*) *s.* Bou'doir *n*.

bough [baʊ] *s.* Ast *m*, Zweig *m*.

bought [bɔ:t] *pret. u. p.p. von* ***buy***.

boul·der ['bəʊldə] *s.* Fels-, Geröllblock *m*; *geol.* er'ratischer Block: ***~ period*** Eiszeit *f*.

bou·le·vard ['bu:lvɑ:] *s.* Boule'vard *m*, Prachtstraße *f*, *Am. a.* Hauptverkehrsstraße *f*.

boult → ***bolt***[2].

bounce [baʊns] **I** *v/i.* **1.** springen, (hoch)schnellen, hüpfen: ***the ball ~d***; ***he ~d out of his chair***; ***~ about*** herumhüpfen; **2.** stürzen, stürmen: ***~ into a room***; **3.** auf-, anprallen (***against*** gegen): ***~ off*** abprallen; **4.** ☤ ‚platzen' (*Scheck*); **II** *v/t.* **5.** *Ball* (auf)springen lassen; **6.** *Brit.* F *j-n* drängen (***into*** zu); **7.** *Am. sl. j-n* ‚rausschmeißen' (*a. fig. entlassen*); **III** *s.* **8.** Sprungkraft *f*; **9.** Sprung *m*, Schwung *m*, Stoß *m*; **10.** Unverfrorenheit *f*; **11.** F ‚Schwung' *m*, E'lan *m*; **12.** *Am. sl.* ‚Rausschmiß' *m* (*Entlassung*); **'bounc·er** [-sə] *s.* F **1.** a) Angeber *m*, b) Lügner *m*; **2.** freche Lüge; **3.** a) ‚Mordskerl' *m*, b) ‚Prachtweib' *n*, c) ‚Mordssache' *f*; **4.** *Am.* ‚Rausschmeißer' *m* (*in Nachtlokalen etc.*); **5.** ungedeckter Scheck; **'bounc·ing** [-sɪŋ] *adj.* **1.** stramm (*kräftig*): ***~ baby***; ***~ girl***; **2.** munter, lebhaft; **3.** Mords...

bound[1] [baʊnd] **I** *pret. u. p.p. von* ***bind***; **II** *adj.* **1.** ***be ~ to do*** zwangsläufig *et.* tun müssen; ***he is ~ to tell me*** er ist verpflichtet, es mir zu sagen; ***he is ~ to be late*** er muß ja zu spät kommen; ***he is ~ to come*** er kommt bestimmt; ***I'll be ~*** ich bürge dafür, ganz gewiß; **2.** *in Zssgn* festgehalten *od.* verhindert durch: ***ice-~***; ***storm~***.

bound[2] [baʊnd] *adj.* (***for***) bestimmt, unter'wegs (nach): ***~ for London***; ***homeward (outward) ~*** ⚓ auf der Heimreise (Hin-, Ausreise) (befindlich); ***where are you ~ for?*** wohin reisen *od.* gehen Sie?

bound[3] [baʊnd] **I** *s.* **1.** Grenze *f*, Schranke *f*, Bereich *m*: ***beyond all ~s*** maß-, grenzenlos; ***keep within ~s*** in vernünftigen Grenzen halten; ***set ~s to*** Grenzen setzen (*dat.*), in Schranken halten; ***within the ~s of possibility*** im Bereich des Möglichen; ***out of ~s*** a) *sport* aus, im Aus, b) (***to***) Zutritt verboten (für); **II** *v/t.* **2.** be-, abgrenzen, die Grenze von *et.* bilden; **3.** *fig.* beschränken, in Schranken halten.

bound[4] [baʊnd] **I** *v/i.* **1.** (hoch)springen, hüpfen (*a. fig.*); **2.** lebhaft gehen, laufen; **3.** an-, abprallen; **II** *s.* **4.** Sprung *m*, Satz *m*, Schwung *m*: ***at a single ~*** mit 'einem Satz; ***on the ~*** beim Aufspringen (*Ball*).

bound·a·ry ['baʊndərɪ] *s.* **1.** *a. fig.* Grenze *f*, *a.* ***~ line*** 'Grenzˌlinie *f*; **2.** *fig.* Bereich *m*; **4.** ⚒, *phys.* a) Begrenzung *f*, b) Rand *m*, c) 'Umfang *m*.

bound·en ['baʊndən] *adj.*: ***my ~ duty*** m-e Pflicht u. Schuldigkeit.

bound·er ['baʊndə] *s. sl.* ‚Stromer' *m*, Kerl *m*.

bound·less ['baʊndlɪs] *adj.* □ grenzenlos, unbegrenzt, *fig. a.* 'übermäßig.

boun·te·ous ['baʊntɪəs] *adj.* □ **1.** freigebig, großzügig; **2.** (allzu) reichlich; **'boun·ti·ful** [-tɪfʊl] *adj.* □ → ***bounteous***; **boun·ty** ['baʊntɪ] *s.* **1.** Freigebigkeit *f*; **2.** (milde) Gabe; Spende *f* (*bsd. e-s Herrschers*); **3.** ⚔ Handgeld *n*; **4.** ☤ (*bsd.* Ex'port)ˌPrämie *f*, Zuschuß *m* (***on*** auf, für); **5.** Belohnung *f*.

bou·quet [bʊ'keɪ] *s.* **1.** Bu'kett *n*, (Blumen)Strauß *m*; **2.** A'roma *n*; Blume *f* (*Wein*); **3.** *bsd. Am.* Kompli'ment *n*.

Bour·bon ['bʊəbən] *s.* **1.** *pol. Am.* Reaktio'när *m*; **2.** ≈ ['bɜ:bən] 'Bourbon *m* (*amer. Whiskey aus Mais*).

bour·geois[1] ['bʊəʒwɑ:] *contp.* **I** *s.* Bour'geois *m*; **II** *adj.* bour'geois, (spieß)bürgerlich.

bour·geois[2] [bɜ:'dʒɔɪs] *typ.* **I** *s.* 'Borgis *f*; **II** *adj.* in 'Borgisˌlettern gedruckt.

bourn(e)[1] [bʊən] *s.* (Gieß)Bach *m*.

bourn(e)[2] [bʊən] *s.* **1.** *obs.* Grenze *f*; **2.** *poet.* Ziel *n*; Gebiet *n*, Bereich *m*.

bourse [bʊəs] *s.* ☤ Börse *f*.

bout [baʊt] *s.* **1.** Arbeitsgang *m*; *Fechten*, *Tanz*: Runde *f*: ***drinking ~*** Zecherei *f*; **2.** (Krankheits)Anfall *m*, At'tacke *f*; **3.** Zeitspanne *f*; **4.** Kraftprobe *f*, Kampf *m*; **5.** (*bsd.* Box-, Ring)Kampf *m*.

bo·vine ['bəʊvaɪn] *adj.* **1.** *zo.* Rinder...; **2.** *fig.* (*a. geistig*) träge, schwerfällig, dumm.

bov·ver ['bɒvə] *s. Brit. sl.* Schläge'rei *f* *bsd.* zwischen Rockern: ***~ boots*** Rokker-Stiefel *pl.*

bow[1] [baʊ] **I** *s.* **1.** Verbeugung *f*, Verneigung *f*: ***make one's ~*** a) sich vorstellen, b) sich verabschieden; ***take a ~*** sich verbeugen, sich für den Beifall bedanken; **II** *v/t.* **2.** beugen, neigen: ***~ one's head*** den Kopf neigen; ***~ one's neck*** *fig.* den Nacken beugen; ***~ one's thanks*** sich dankend verneigen; ***~ed with grief*** gramgebeugt; → ***knee*** 1; **3.** biegen: ***the wind has ~ed the branches***; **III** *v/i.* **4.** (***to***) sich verbeugen *od.* verneigen (vor *dat.*), grüßen (*acc.*): ***a ~ing acquaintance*** e-e Grußbekanntschaft; ***on ~ing terms*** auf dem Grußfuße, flüchtig bekannt; ***~ and scrape*** Kratzfüße machen, *fig.* katzbuckeln; **5.** *fig.* sich beugen *od.* unter'werfen (***to*** *dat.*): ***~ to the inevitable*** sich in das Unvermeidliche fügen; ***~ down*** *v/i.* (***to***) **1.** verehren, anbeten (*acc.*); **2.** sich unter'werfen (*dat.*); ***~ in*** *v/t. j-n* unter Verbeugungen hin'eingeleiten; ***~ out*** **I** *v/t. j-n* hin'auskomplimentieren; **II** *v/i.* sich verabschieden.

bow[2] [bəʊ] **I** *s.* **1.** (Schieß)Bogen *m*: ***have more than one string to one's ~*** *fig.* mehrere Eisen im Feuer haben; ***draw the long ~*** *fig.* aufschneiden, übertreiben; **2.** ♪ (*Violin- etc.*)Bogen *m*; **3.** ⚒, ⚙ a) Bogen *m*, Kurve *f*, b) *pl.* 'Bogenˌzirkel *m*; **4.** Bügel *m* (*der Brille*); **5.** Knoten *m*, Schleife *f*; **II** *v/i.* **6.** ♪ den Bogen führen.

bow[3] [baʊ] *s.* ⚓ **1.** *a. pl.* Bug *m*; **2.** Bugmann *m* (*im Ruderboot*).

Bow| bells [bəʊ] *s. pl.* Glocken *pl.* der Kirche ***St. Mary le Bow*** (*London*): ***be born within the sound of ~*** ein echter Cockney sein; ≈ **com·pass(·es)** *s. sg. od. pl.* ⚒, ⚙ → ***bow***[2] 3b.

bowd·ler·ize ['baʊdləraɪz] *v/t. Bücher* (von anstößigen Stellen) säubern; *fig.* verwässern.

bow·els ['baʊəlz] *s. pl.* **1.** *anat.* Darm *m*; Gedärm *n*, Eingeweide *pl.*: ***open ~*** ⚕ offener Leib; ***have open ~*** regelmäßig Stuhlgang haben; **2.** *das* Innere, Mitte *f*: ***the ~ of the earth*** das Erdinnere.

bow·er[1] ['baʊə] *s.* (Garten)Laube *f*, schattiges Plätzchen; *obs.* (Frauen)Gemach *n*.

bow·er[2] ['baʊə] *s.* ⚓ Buganker *m*.

bow·er·y ['baʊərɪ] *s. hist. Am.* Farm *f*, Pflanzung *f*: ***the*** ≈ die Bowery (*heruntergekommene Straße u. Gegend in New York City*).

'bow-head ['bəʊ-] *s. zo.* Grönlandwal *m*.

'bow·ie-knife ['bəʊɪ-] *s.* [*irr.*] 'Bowiemesser *n* (*langes Jagdmesser*).

bowl[1] [bəʊl] *s.* **1.** Napf *m*, Schale *f*; Bowle *f* (*Gefäß*); **2.** Schüssel *f*, Becken *n*; **3.** *poet.* Gelage *n*; **4.** a) (Pfeifen-)Kopf *m*, b) Höhlung *f* (*Löffel etc.*); **5.** *Am.* 'Stadion *n*.

bowl[2] [bəʊl] **I** *s.* **1.** a) (*Bowling-*, *Bowls-*, *Kegel*)Kugel *f*, b) → ***bowls*** 1, c) Wurf *m*; **II** *v/t.* **2.** *allg.* rollen (lassen); *Bowling etc*: *die Kugel* werfen; *Ball* rollen, werfen (*a. Kricket*); *Reifen* schlagen, treiben; **III** *v/i.* **3.** a) bowlen, Bowls spielen, b) bowlen, Bowling spielen, c) kegeln, d) werfen; **4.** *mst* ***~ along*** ‚(da'hin)gondeln' (*Wagen*); ***~ out*** *v/t. Kricket*: *den Schläger* (durch Treffen des Dreistabes) ‚ausmachen'; *fig. j-n* ‚erledigen', schlagen; ***~ o·ver*** *v/t.* 'umwerfen (*a. fig.*).

'bow-legged ['bəʊ-] *adj.* säbel-, O-beinig; **'bow-legs** *s. pl.* Säbel-, O-Beine *pl.*

bowl·er ['bəʊlə] *s.* **1.** a) Bowls-Spieler (-in), b) Bowling-Spieler(in), c) Kegler (-in); **2.** *Kricket*: Werfer *m*; **3.** *a.* ***~ hat*** *Brit.* ‚Me'lone' *f*.

bow·line ['bəʊlɪn] *s.* ⚓ Bu'lin *f*.

bowl·ing ['bəʊlɪŋ] *s.* **1.** Bowling *n*; **2.** Kegeln *n*; ***~ al·ley*** *s.* **1.** Bowlingbahn *f*; **2.** Kegelbahn *f*; ***~ green*** *s. Bowls etc*: Rasenplatz *m*.

bowls [bəʊlz] *s. pl. sg. konstr.* **1.** Bowls (-Spiel) *n*; **2.** Kegeln *n*.

bow|·man ['bəʊmən] *s.* [*irr.*] Bogenschütze *m*; '**~·shot** *s.* Bogenschußweite *f*; '**~·sprit** *s.* ⚓ Bugspriet *m*; ℒ **Street** *npr. Straße in London mit dem Polizeigericht*; '**~·string I** *s.* Bogensehne *f*; **II** *v/t.* erdrosseln; **~ tie** *s.* (Frack)Schleife *f*, Fliege *f*; **~ win·dow** *s.* Erkerfenster *n*.

bow-wow I *int.* [ˌbaʊ'waʊ] wau'wau!; **II** *s.* ['baʊwaʊ] *Kindersprache*: Wau'wau *m* (*Hund*).

box[1] [bɒks] **I** *s.* **1.** Kasten *m*, Kiste *f*; *Brit. a.* Koffer *m*; **2.** Büchse *f*, Schachtel *f*, Etu'i *n*, Dose *f*, Kästchen *n*; **3.** Behälter *m*, (*a. Buch-, Film- etc.*)Kas'sette *f*, Hülse *f*, Gehäuse *n*, Kapsel *f*; **4.** Häus-chen *n*; Ab'teil *n*, Ab'teilung *f*, Loge *f* (*Theater etc.*); ⚖ a) Zeugenstand *m*, b) (Geschworenen)Bank *f*; **5.** Box *f*: a) *Pferdestand*, b) *mot. Einstellplatz in e-r Großgarage*; **6.** Fach *n* (*a. für Briefe etc.*); **7.** Kutschbock *m*; **8.** *Am.* Wagenkasten *m*; **9.** *Baseball*: Standplatz *m* (*des Schlägers*); **10.** a) Postfach *n*, b) → ***box number***, c) Briefkasten *m*; **11.** *pol.* (Wahl)Urne *f*; **12.** *typ.* Kasten *m*, Kästchen (*eingeschobener, umrandeter Text*), Rub'rik *f*; **13.** F ,Kasten' *m* (*Fernsehapparat, Fußballtor etc.*); **II** *v/t.* **14.** in Schachteln, Kasten *etc.* legen, packen, einschließen; **15. ~ *the compass*** a) ⚓ alle Kompaßpunkte aufzählen, b) *fig.* alle Gesichtspunkte vorbringen u. schließlich zum Ausgangspunkt zurückkehren, e-e völlige Kehrtwendung machen; **~ in** *v/t.* **1.** → ***box***[1] 14; **2.** → **~ up** *v/t.* einschließen, -klemmen.

box[2] [bɒks] **I** *s.* **1.** Schlag *m* mit der Hand: **~ *on the ear*** Ohrfeige *f*; **II** *v/t.* **2. ~ *s.o.'s ears*** j-n ohrfeigen; **3.** gegen *j-n* boxen; **III** *v/i.* **4.** *sport* boxen.

box[3] [bɒks] *s.* ⚘ Buchsbaum(holz *n*) *m*.

box| bar·rage *s.* ⚔ Abriegelungsfeuer *n*; '**~·calf** *s.* 'Boxkalf *n* (*Leder*); **~ cam·er·a** *s. phot.* 'Box(ˌkamera) *f*; '**~·car** *s.* 🚂 *Am.* geschlossener Güterwagen.

box·er ['bɒksə] *s.* **1.** *sport* Boxer *m*; **2.** *zo.* Boxer *m* (*Hunderasse*); **3.** ℒ *hist.* Boxer *m* (*Anhänger e-s chinesischen Geheimbundes um 1900*).

box·ing ['bɒksɪŋ] *s.* **1.** *sport* Boxen *n*; **2.** Ver-, Einpacken *n*; ℒ **Day** *s. Brit.* der zweite Weihnachtsfeiertag; **~ gloves** *s. pl.* Boxhandschuhe *pl.*; **~ match** *s. sport* Boxkampf *m*.

'**box|-ˌi·ron** *s.* Bolzen(bügel)eisen *n*; **~ junc·tion** *s. Brit. markierte Kreuzung, in die bei stehendem Verkehr nicht eingefahren werden darf*; '**~ˌkeep·er** *s. thea.* 'Logenschließer(in); **~ num·ber** *s.* 'Chiffre(nummer) *f* (*in Zeitungsanzeigen*); **~ of·fice** *s.* **1.** (The'ater- *etc.*) Kasse *f*; **2. *be good ~*** ein Kassenerfolg *od.* -schlager sein; **3.** Einspielergebnis *n*; '**~-ˌof·fice** *adj.* Kassen...: **~ *success*** *od.* ***draw*** Kassenschlager *m*; '**~·room** *s.* Abstellraum *m*; '**~ˌwal·lah** *s. Brit.-Ind.* **1.** F indischer Hausierer; **2.** *contp.* Handlungsreisende(r) *m*; '**~·wood** →***box***[3].

boy [bɔɪ] **1.** Knabe *m*, Junge *m*, Bursche *m*, ,Mann' *m*: ***the*** (*od.* ***our***) **~*s*** unsere Jung(en)s (*z. B. Soldaten*); ***old ~*** a) ,alter Knabe', b) → ***old boy***; ***a ~ child*** ein Kind männlichen Geschlechts, ein Junge; **~ *singer*** Sängerknabe; **~ *wonder*** *oft iro.* Wunderknabe; **2.** Laufbursche *m*; **3.** Boy *m*, (*bsd.* eingeborener) Diener.

boy·cott ['bɔɪkət] **I** *v/t.* boykottieren; **II** *s.* Boy'kott *m*.

'**boy·friend** *s.* Freund *m* (*e-s Mädchens*).

boy·hood ['bɔɪhʊd] *s.* Knabenalter *n*, Kindheit *f*, Jugend *f*.

boy·ish ['bɔɪɪʃ] *adj.* □ a) jungenhaft: **~ *laughter***, b) knabenhaft.

boy scout *s.* Pfadfinder *m*.

bo·zo ['bəʊzəʊ] *s. Am. sl.* Kerl *m*.

B pow·er sup·ply *s.* ⚡ Ener'gieversorgung *f* des An'odenkreises.

bra [brɑ:] *s.* F *für* ***brassière***: B'H *m*.

brace [breɪs] **I** *s.* **1.** ⚙ Stütze *f*, Strebe *f*, (*a.* ⚕ Zahn)Klammer *f*, Anker *m*, Versteifung *f*; (Trag)Band *n*, Gurt *m*; ⚕ Stützband *n*; **2.** ⚙ Griff *m* der Bohrkurbel: **~ *and bit*** Bohrkurbel *f*; **3.** △, ♪, ⚒, *typ.* (geschweifte) Klammer *f*; **4.** ⚓ Brasse *f*; **5.** (***a pair of***) **~*s*** *pl. Brit.* Hosenträger *m od. pl.*; **6.** (*pl.* ***brace***) ein Paar, zwei (*bsd. Hunde, Kleinwild, Pistolen*; *contp. Personen*); **II** *v/t.* **7.** ⚙ versteifen, -streben, stützen, verankern, befestigen; **8.** ⚙, ♪, *typ.* klammern; **9.** ⚓ brassen; **10.** *fig.* stärken, erfrischen; **11.** *a.* **~ *up*** *s-e Kräfte, s-n Mut* zs.-nehmen; **12. ~ *o.s.*** (***up***) a) → 11, b) ***for s.th.*** sich auf et. gefaßt machen; **brace·let** ['breɪslɪt] *s.* **1.** Armband *n*, -reif *m*, -spange *f*; **2.** *pl. humor.* Handschellen *pl.*; '**brac·er** [-sə] *s. Am.* F Stärkung *f*, *bsd.* Schnäpschen *n*; *fig.* Ermunterung *f*.

bra·chi·al ['breɪkjəl] *adj.* Arm...; '**bra·chi·ate** [-kɪeɪt] *adj.* ⚘ paarweise gegenständig.

brach·y·ce·phal·ic [ˌbrækɪke'fælɪk] *adj.* kurzköpfig.

brac·ing ['breɪsɪŋ] *adj.* stärkend, kräftigend, erfrischend (*bsd. Klima*).

brack·en ['brækən] *s.* **1.** Farnkraut *n*; **2.** farnbewachsene Gegend.

brack·et ['brækɪt] **I** *s.* **1.** ⚙ Träger *m*, Halter *m*; **2.** Kon'sole *f*, Krag-, Tragstein *m*, Stützbalken *m*, Winkelstütze *f*; **3.** Wandarm *m*; **4.** ⚔ Gabel *f* (*Einschießen*); **5.** ⚒, *typ.* (*Am. mst* eckige) Klammer: ***in ~s***; ***square ~s*** eckige Klammern; **6.** Gruppe *f*, Klasse *f*, Stufe *f*: ***lower income ~*** niedrige Einkommensstufe; **II** *v/t.* **7.** einklammern; **8.** *a.* **~ *together*** in dieselbe Gruppe einordnen; auf gleiche Stufe stellen; **9.** ⚔ eingabeln.

brack·ish ['brækɪʃ] *adj.* brackig.

bract [brækt] *s.* ⚘ Deckblatt *n*.

brad [bræd] *s.* ⚙ Nagel *m* ohne Kopf; (Schuh)Zwecke *f*.

Brad·shaw ['brædʃɔ:] *s. Brit.* (Eisenbahn)Kursbuch *n* (*1839–1961*).

brae [breɪ] *s. Scot.* Abhang *m*, Böschung *f*.

brag [bræg] **I** *s.* **1.** Prahle'rei *f*; **2.** → ***braggart*** I; **II** *v/i.* **3.** (***about***, ***of***) prahlen (mit), sich rühmen (*gen.*).

brag·ga·do·ci·o [ˌbrægə'dəʊtʃɪəʊ] *s.* Prahle'rei *f*, Aufschneide'rei *f*.

brag·gart ['brægət] **I** *s.* Prahler *m*, Aufschneider *m*; **II** *adj.* prahlerisch.

Brah·man ['brɑ:mən] *s.* Brah'mane *m*; '**Brah·ma·ni** [-nɪ] *s.* Brah'manin *f*; **Brah·man·ic**, **Brah·man·i·cal** [brɑ:'mænɪk(l)] *adj.* brah'manisch.

Brah·min ['brɑ:mɪn] *s.* **1.** → ***Brahman***; **2.** gebildete, kultivierte Per'son; **3.** *Am. iro.* dünkelhafte(r) Intellektu'elle(r).

braid [breɪd] **I** *v/t.* **1.** *bsd. Haar, Bänder* flechten; **2.** mit Litze, Band, Borte besetzen, schmücken; **3.** ⚙ um'spinnen; **II** *s.* **4.** (*Haar*)Flechte *f*; **5.** Borte *f*, Litze *f*, Tresse *f* (*bsd.* ⚔): ***gold ~*** goldene Tresse(n); '**braid·ed** [-dɪd] *adj.* geflochten; mit Litze *etc.* besetzt; um'sponnen; '**braid·ing** [-dɪŋ] *s.* Litzen *pl.*, Borten *pl.*, Tressen *pl.*, Besatz *m*.

braille [breɪl] *s.* Blindenschrift *f*.

brain [breɪn] **I** *s.* **1.** Gehirn *n*; → ***blow out*** 5; **2.** *fig.* (*oft pl.*) a) ,Köpfchen' *n*, ,Grips' *m*, Verstand *m*, b) Kopf *m* (*Leiter*), *b.s.* ,Drahtzieher' *m*: ***a clear ~*** ein klarer Kopf; ***who is the ~ behind it?*** wessen Idee ist das?; ***have ~s*** intelligent sein, ,Köpfchen' haben; ***have*** (***got***) ***s.th on the ~*** et. dauernd im Kopf haben; ***cudgel*** (*od.* ***rack***) ***one's ~s*** sich den Kopf zerbrechen, sich das Hirn zermartern; ***pick s.o.'s ~s*** a) geistigen Diebstahl an j-m begehen, b) j-n ,ausholen'; **II** *v/t.* **3.** *j-m* den Schädel einschlagen; **~ child** *s.* 'Geistesproˌdukt *n*; **~ drain** *s.* Abwanderung *f* von Wissenschaftlern, Brain-Drain *m*.

brained [breɪnd] *adj.*, *nur in Zssgn* ...köpfig, mit e-m ... Gehirn: ***feeble-~*** schwachköpfig.

'**brain|·fag** *s.* geistige Erschöpfung; **~ fe·ver** *s.* ⚕ Gehirnentzündung *f*.

brain·less ['breɪnlɪs] *adj.* **1.** hirnlos, dumm; **2.** gedankenlos.

'**brain|·pan** *s. anat.* Hirnschale *f*, Schädeldecke *f*; '**~·storm** *s.* **1.** geistige Verwirrung; **2.** verrückter Einfall; **3.** *Am.* F → ***brain wave*** 2 ; '**~ˌstorm·ing** *s.* Brainstorming *n* (*Problemlösung durch Sammeln spontaner Einfälle*).

brains trust [breɪnz] *s.* **1.** *Brit.* Teilnehmer *pl.* an e-r 'Podiumsdiskussiˌon; **2.** → ***brain trust***.

brain| trust *s. Am.* F po'litische *od.* wirtschaftliche Beratergruppe, Brain Trust *m*; **~ trust·er** *s. Am.* F Brain-Truster *m*, Mitglied *n* e-s ***brain trust***; **~ twist·er** *s.* ,(harte) Nuß', schwierige Aufgabe; '**~·wash** *v/t. bsd. pol. j-n* e-r Gehirnwäsche unter'ziehen; *weitS.* verdummen; '**~ˌwash·ing** *s. pol.* Gehirnwäsche *f*; **~ wave** *s.* **1.** Hirn(strom)welle *f*; **2.** F Geistesblitz *m*, ,tolle I'dee'; '**~-ˌwork·er** *s.* Kopf-, Geistesarbeiter *m*.

brain·y ['breɪnɪ] *adj.* gescheit.

braise [breɪz] *v/t. Küche*: schmoren: **~*d beef*** Schmorbraten *m*.

brake[1] [breɪk] **I** *s.* ⚙ Bremse *f*, Hemmschuh *m* (*a. fig.*): ***put on*** (*od.* ***apply***) ***the ~*** bremsen, die Bremse ziehen, *fig. a.* der Sache Einhalt gebieten; **II** *v/t.* bremsen.

brake[2] [breɪk] ⚙ **I** *s.* (*Flachs- etc.*)Breche *f*; **II** *v/t. Flachs etc.* brechen.

brake[3] → ***break*** 11.

brake| block → ***brake shoe***; **~ horse-pow·er** *s.* ⚙ (*abbr.* ***b.h.p.***) Nutz-, Bremsleistung *f*; **~ flu·id** *s.* Bremsflüssigkeit *f*; **~ lin·ing** *s.* Bremsbelag *m*; '**~·man** *Am.* → ***brakesman***; **~ par·a·chute** *s.* ✈ Bremsfallschirm *m*; **~ shoe** *s.* ⚙ Bremsbacke *f*, -klotz *m*.

brakes·man ['breɪksmən] *s.* [*irr.*] 🚂

Brit. Bremser *m.*
brak·ing dis·tance [ˈbreɪkɪŋ] *s. mot.* Bremsweg *m.*
bra·less [ˈbrɑːlɪs] *adj.* F ohne BˈH.
bram·ble [ˈbræmbl] *s.* **1.** ⚘ Brombeerstrauch *m*: ~ ***jelly*** Brombeergelee *n*; **2.** Dornenstrauch *m*, -gestrüpp *n*; ~ **rose** *s.* ⚘ Hundsrose *f.*
bram·bly [ˈbræmblɪ] *adj.* dornig.
bran [bræn] *s.* Kleie *f.*
branch [brɑːntʃ] **I** *s.* **1.** ⚘ Zweig *m*; **2.** *fig.* a) Zweig *m*, (ˈUnter)Abteilung *f*, Sparte *f*, b) Branche *f*, Wirtschafts-, Geschäftszweig *m*, c) *a.* ~ ***of service*** ⚔ Waffen-, Truppengattung *f*; **3.** *fig.* Zweig *m*, ˈLinie *f* (*Familie*); **4.** *a.* ~ ***establishment*** ⚕ Außen-, Zweig-, Nebenstelle *f*, Filiˈale *f*, Niederlassung *f*: ~ ***bank*** Filialbank *f*; **5.** 🚂 Zweigbahn *f*; ˈNebenˌlinie *f*; **6.** *geogr.* a) Arm *m* (*Gewässer*), b) Ausläufer *m* (*Gebirge*), c) *Am.* Nebenfluß *m*, Flüßchen *n*; **II** *adj.* **7.** Zweig..., Tochter..., Filial..., Neben...; **III** *v/i.* **8.** Zweige treiben; **9.** *oft* ~ ***off*** (*od.* ***out***) sich verzweigen, sich ausbreiten; abzweigen: ***here the road ~es*** hier gabelt sich die Straße; ~ **out** *v/i.* s-e Unterˈnehmungen ausdehnen, sich vergrößern; → ***branch*** 9.
bran·chi·a [ˈbræŋkɪə] *pl.* **-chi·ae** [-kiː] *s. zo.* Kieme *f*; ˈ**bran·chi·ate** [-kɪeɪt] *adj. zo.* kiementragend.
branch| line *s.* **1.** 🚂 ˈZweig-, ˈNebenˌlinie *f*, **2.** ˈSeitenˌlinie *f* (*Familie*); ~ **man·ag·er** *s.* Filiˈal-, Zweigstellenleiter *m*; ~ **of·fice** *s.* Filiˈale *f*; ~ **road** *s. Am.* Nebenstraße *f.*
brand [brænd] **I** *s.* **1.** Feuerbrand *m*; *fig.* Fackel *f*; **2.** Brandmal *n* (*auf Tieren, Waren etc.*); **3.** *fig.* Schandmal *n*, -fleck *m*: ~ ***of Cain*** Kainszeichen *n*; **4.** Brand-, Brenneisen *n*; **5.** a) ⚕ (Handels-, Schutz)Marke *f*, Warenzeichen *n*, Markenbezeichnung *f*, Sorte *f*, Klasse *f*: ~ ***name*** Markenname *m*; ***best ~ of tea*** beste Sorte Tee, b) *fig.* ‚Sorte' *f*, Art *f*: ***his ~ of humour***; **6.** ⚘ Brand *m* (*Getreidekrankheit*); **II** *v/t.* **7.** mit e-m Brandmal *od.* -zeichen *od.* ⚕ mit e-r Schutzmarke *etc.* versehen: ***~ed goods*** Markenartikel; **8.** *fig.* brandmarken; **9.** einprägen (***on s.o.'s mind*** j-m).
brand·ing i·ron [ˈbrændɪŋ] → ***brand*** 4.
bran·dish [ˈbrændɪʃ] *v/t.* (*bsd.* drohend) schwingen.
brand·ling [ˈbrændlɪŋ] *s. ichth.* junger Lachs.
brand-new [ˌbrændˈnjuː] *adj.* (funkel-) nagelneu.
bran·dy [ˈbrændɪ] *s.* Weinbrand *m*, Kognak *m*; ˈ**~·ball** *s. Brit.* ˈWeinbrandbonˌbon *m, n.*
bran-new [ˌbrænˈnjuː] → ***brand-new.***
brant [brænt] *s. orn. e-e* Wildgans *f.*
brash [bræʃ] **I** *s.* **1.** *geol.* Trümmergestein *n*; **2.** ⚓ Eistrümmer *pl.*; **II** *adj. Am.* **3.** brüchig, bröckelig; **4.** *fig.* a) (naß)forsch, frech, unverfroren, b) ungestüm, c) grell, aufdringlich.
brass [brɑːs] **I** *s.* **1.** Messing *n*; **2.** *Brit.* ziselierte Gedenktafel (*aus Messing od. Bronze, bsd. in Kirchen*); **3.** Messingzierat *m*; **4.** ♪ ***the ~*** die ˈBlechinstruˌmente *pl.* (*e-s Orchesters*), Blechbläser *pl.*; **5.** F *coll.* ‚hohe Tiere' *pl.*, *a.* hohe Offiˈziere *pl.*: ***top ~*** die höchsten ‚Tiere' (*e-s Konzerns etc.*) *od.* Offiziere; **6.** *Brit. sl.* ‚Moos' *n*, ‚Kies' *m* (*Geld*); **7.** F Unverschämtheit *f*, Frechheit *f*; → ***bold*** 2; **II** *adj.* **8.** Messing...; **III** *v/t.* **9.** mit Messing überˈziehen.
bras·sard [ˈbræsɑːd] *s.* Armbinde *f* (*als Abzeichen*).
brass band *s.* ♪ ˈBlaskaˌpelle *f*; ˈBlechmuˌsik *f*; Miliˈtärkaˌpelle *f.*
bras·se·rie [ˈbræsərɪ] (*Fr.*) *s.* ˈBierstube *f*, -loˌkal *n*; Restauˈrant *n.*
brass| far·thing *s.* F ‚roter Heller': ***I don't care a ~*** das kümmert mich e-n Dreck; ~ **hat** *s.* ⚔ *sl.* ‚hohes Tier', hoher Offiˈzier.
bras·sière [ˈbræsɪə] (*Fr.*) *s.* Büstenhalter *m*, F BˈH *m.*
brass| knuck·les *s. pl. Am.* Schlagring *m*; ~ **plate** *s.* Messingschild *n* (*mit Namen*), Türschild *n*; ~ **tacks** *s. pl.*: ***get down to ~*** zur Sache kommen; ˈ**~·ware** *s.* Messinggeschirr *n*, -gegenstände *pl.*; ~ **winds** *bsd. Am.* → ***brass*** 4.
brass·y [ˈbrɑːsɪ] *adj.* □ **1.** messingartig, -farbig; **2.** blechern (*Klang*); **3.** *fig.* unverschämt, frech.
brat [bræt] *s.* Balg *m, n*, Gör *n*, Racker *m* (*Kind*).
bra·va·do [brəˈvɑːdəʊ] *s.* gespielte Tapferkeit, herˈausforderndes Benehmen.
brave [breɪv] **I** *adj.* □ **1.** tapfer, mutig, unerschrocken: ***as ~ as a lion*** mutig wie ein Löwe; **2.** *obs.* stattlich, ansehnlich; **II** *s.* **3.** *poet.* Tapfere(r) *m*: ***the ~*** *coll.* die Tapferen; **III** *v/t.* **4.** mutig begegnen, trotzen, die Stirn bieten (*dat.*): ***~ death***; ***~ it out*** es (trotzig) durchstehen; **5.** herˈausfordern; ˈ**brav·er·y** [-vərɪ] *s.* **1.** Tapferkeit *f*, Mut *m*; **2.** Pracht *f*, Putz *m*, Staat *m.*
bra·vo¹ [ˌbrɑːˈvəʊ] **I** *int.* ˈbravo!; **II** *pl.* **-vos** *s.* ˈBravo(ruf *m*) *n.*
bra·vo² [ˈbrɑːvəʊ] *s.* ˈBravo *m*, Banˈdit *m.*
bra·vu·ra [brəˈvʊərə] *s.* ♪ *od. fig.* **1.** Braˈvour *f*, Meisterschaft *f*; **2.** Braˈvourstück *n.*
brawl [brɔːl] **I** *s.* **1.** Streiteˈrei *f*, Kraˈkeel *m*, Lärm *m*; **2.** Raufeˈrei *f*, Kraˈwall *m*, ⚖ Raufhandel *m*; **II** *v/i.* **3.** kraˈkeelen, zanken, keifen, lärmen; **4.** rauschen (*Fluß*); ˈ**brawl·er** [-lə] *s.* Raufbold *m*, Kraˈkeeler(in); ˈ**brawl·ing** [-lɪŋ] *s.* **1.** → ***brawl*** 1, 2; **2.** ⚖ *Brit.* Ruhestörung *f bsd. in Kirchen.*
brawn [brɔːn] *s.* **1.** Muskeln *pl.*; **2.** *fig.* Muskelkraft *f*, Stärke *f*; **3.** Preßkopf *m*, (Schweine)Sülze *f*; ˈ**brawn·y** [-nɪ] *adj.* muskuˈlös; *fig.* kräftig, stämmig, stark.
bray¹ [breɪ] **I** *s.* **1.** (*bsd.* Esels)Schrei *m*; **2.** Schmettern *n* (*Trompete*); gellender *od.* ˈdurchdringender Ton; **II** *v/i.* **3.** schreien (*bsd. Esel*); **4.** schmettern; kreischen, gellen.
bray² [breɪ] *v/t.* zerstoßen, -reiben, -stampfen (*im Mörser*).
braze [breɪz] *v/t.* ⚙ (hart)löten.
bra·zen [ˈbreɪzn] **I** *adj.* □ **1.** ehern, bronzen, Messing...; **2.** *fig.* meˈtallisch, grell (*Ton*); **3.** *a.* ***~-faced*** *fig.* unverschämt, frech, schamlos; **II** *v/t.* **4.** ***~ it out*** die Sache ‚frech wie Oskar' durchstehen; ˈ**bra·zen·ness** [-nɪs] *s.* Unverschämtheit *f.*
bra·zier [ˈbreɪzjə] *s.* **1.** Kupferschmied *m*, Gelbgießer *m*; **2.** große Kohlenpfanne.
Bra·zil [brəˈzɪl] → ***brazilwood***; **Braˈzil·ian** [-ljən] **I** *adj.* brasiliˈanisch; **II** *s.* Brasiliˈaner(in).
Bra·zil| nut *s.* ⚘ ˈParanuß *f*; **~·wood** *s.* ⚕ Braˈsil-, Rotholz *n.*
breach [briːtʃ] **I** *s.* **1.** *fig.* Bruch *m*, Überˈtretung *f*, Verletzung *f*, Verstoß *m*: ~ ***of contract*** Vertragsbruch; ~ ***of duty*** Pflichtverletzung; ~ ***of etiquette*** Verstoß gegen den guten Ton; ~ ***of faith*** (*od.* ***trust***) Vertrauensbruch, Untreue *f*; ~ ***of the law*** Übertretung des Gesetzes; ~ ***of the peace*** öffentliche Ruhestörung, Aufruhr *m*, *oft* grober Unfug; ~ ***of promise*** (***to marry***) ⚖ Bruch des Eheversprechens; ~ ***of prison*** Ausbruch *m* aus dem Gefängnis; **2.** *fig.* Bruch *m*, Riß *m*, Zwist *m*; **3.** ⚔ *u. fig.* Bresche *f*, Lücke *f*: ***stand in*** (*od.* ***step into***) ***the ~*** in die Bresche springen, (aus)helfen; **4.** ⚓ Einbruch *m* der Wellen; **5.** ⚙ ˈDurchbruch *m*; **II** *v/t.* **6.** ⚔ e-e Bresche schlagen in (*acc.*), durchˈbrechen; **7.** *Vertrag etc.* brechen.
bread [bred] **I** *s.* **1.** Brot *n*; **2.** *fig.*, *a.* ***daily ~*** (tägliches) Brot, ˈLebensˌunterhalt *m*: ***earn one's ~*** sein Brot verdienen; ***~ and butter*** a) Butterbrot, b) Lebensunterhalt, ‚Brötchen' *pl.*; ***quarrel with one's ~ and butter*** a) mit s-m Los hadern, b) sich ins eigene Fleisch schneiden; ***~ buttered both sides*** großes Glück, Wohlstand *m*; ***know which side one's ~ is buttered*** s-n Vorteil (er)kennen; ***take the ~ out of s.o.'s mouth*** j-n brotlos machen; ***cast one's ~ upon the waters*** et. ohne Aussicht auf Erfolg tun; ***~ and water*** Wasser u. Brot; ***~ and wine*** *eccl.* Abendmahl *n*; **3.** *sl.* ‚Kies' *m*, ‚Kohlen' *pl.* (*Geld*); **II** *v/t.* **4.** *Am. Küche*: panieren.
ˌ**bread|-and-ˈbut·ter** *adj.* F **1.** einträglich, Brot...: ~ ***education*** Brotstudium *n*; **2.** praktisch, sachlich; **3.** ~ ***letter*** Dankesbrief *m* für erwiesene Gastfreundschaft; ˈ**~ˌbas·ket** *s.* **1.** Brotkorb *m*; **2.** *sl.* Magen *m*; ~ **bin** *s.* Brotkasten *m*; ˈ**~·board** *s. Brit.* Brotschneidebrett *n*: ~ ***circuit*** ⚡ Brettschaltung *f*; ˈ**~·crumb I** *s.* **1.** Brotkrume *f*; **2.** *das* Weiche des Brotes (*ohne Rinde*); **II** *v/t.* **3.** *Küche*: panieren; ˈ**~·fruit** *s.* ⚘ **1.** Brotfrucht *f*; **2.** → ***bread tree***; ˈ**~·grain** *s.* Brotgetreide *n*; ˈ**~·line** *s.* Schlange *f* von Bedürftigen (*an die Nahrungsmittel verteilt werden*); ~ **sauce** *s.* Brottunke *f*; ˈ**~·stuffs** *s. pl.* Brotgetreide *n.*
breadth [bredθ] *s.* **1.** Breite *f*, Weite *f*; **2.** ⚙ Bahn *f*, Breite *f* (*Stoff*); **3.** *fig.* Ausdehnung *f*, Größe *f*; **4.** *fig.*, *a. Kunst*: Großzügigkeit *f.*
bread| tree *s.* ⚘ Brotfruchtbaum *m*; ˈ**~ˌwin·ner** *s.* Ernährer *m*, Geldverdiener *m* (*e-r Familie*).
break [breɪk] **I** *s.* **1.** (Ab-, Zer-, ˈDurch)Brechen *n*, Bruch *m* (*a. fig.*), Abbruch *m* (*a. fig. von Beziehungen*), Bruchstelle *f*: ***~ in the voice*** Umschlagen *n* der Stimme; ***~ of day*** Tagesanbruch *m*; ***a ~ with tradition*** ein Bruch mit der Tradition; ***make a ~ for it*** (sich) flüchten, das Weite suchen; **2.** Lücke *f* (*a. fig.*), Zwischenraum *m*; Lichtung *f*; **3.** Pause *f*, Ferien *pl.*; Unterˈbrechung *f* (*a.* ⚡), Aufhören *n*, *fig. u. Metrik*: *a.* Zäˈsur *f*: ***without a ~*** ununterbrochen; ***tea ~*** Teepause; **4.**

Wechsel *m*, Abwechslung *f*; 'Umschwung *m*; Sturz *m* (*Wetter, Preis*); **5.** *typ.* Absatz *m*; **6.** *Billard*: Serie *f*; **7.** *Tennis*: Break *m*, *n* (*Durchbrechen des gegnerischen Aufschlagspiels*); **8.** *Jazz*: Break *m*, *n*; **9.** *Am. sl.* Chance *f*, Gelegenheit *f*: ***bad ~*** ‚Pech' *n*; ***give s.o. a ~*** j-m e-e Chance geben; **10.** *Am. sl.* Schnitzer *m*, Faux'pas *m*; **11.** a) Kremser *m*, b) Wagen *m* zum Einfahren von Pferden; **12.** ⚙ → ***brake***[1]; **II** *v/t.* [*irr.*] **13.** brechen (*a. fig.*), auf-, 'durch-, zerbrechen, ent'zweibrechen: ***~ one's arm*** (sich) den Arm brechen; ***~ s.o.'s heart*** j-m das Herz brechen; ***~ jail*** aus dem Gefängnis ausbrechen; ***~ a seal*** ein Siegel erbrechen; ***~ s.o.'s resistance*** j-s Widerstand brechen; **14.** *Geldschein* kleinmachen, wechseln; **15.** zerreißen, -schlagen, -trümmern, ka'puttmachen: ***I've broken my watch*** m-e Uhr ist kaputt; **16.** unter'brechen (*a.* ⚡), aufheben, -geben: ***~ a journey*** e-e Reise unterbrechen; ***~ the circuit*** ⚡ den Stromkreis unterbrechen; ***~ the silence*** das Schweigen brechen; ***~ a custom*** e-e Gewohnheit aufgeben; **17.** *Vorrat etc.* anbrechen; **18.** *fig.* brechen, verletzen, verstoßen gegen, nicht (ein-) halten: ***~ a contract*** e-n Vertrag brechen; ***~ the law*** das Gesetz übertreten; **19.** *fig.* zu'grunde richten, ruinieren, *a. j-n* ka'puttmachen: ***~ the bank*** die Bank sprengen; **20.** vermindern, abschwächen; **21.** *Tier* zähmen, abrichten; gewöhnen (***to*** an *acc.*): ***~ a horse to harness*** ein Pferd einfahren *od.* zureiten; **22.** *Nachricht* eröffnen: ***~ that news gently to her*** bring ihr diese (*schlechte*) Nachricht schonend bei; **23.** ⚒ pflügen, urbar machen; → ***ground***[1] 1; **24.** *Flagge* aufziehen; **III** *v/i.* [*irr.*] **25.** brechen, zerbrechen, -springen, -reißen, platzen, ent'zwei-, ka'puttgehen: ***glass ~s easily*** Glas bricht leicht; ***the rope broke*** das Seil zerriß; **26.** *fig.* brechen (*Herz, Kraft*); **27.** sich brechen (*Wellen*); **28.** unter'brochen werden; **29.** sich (zer)teilen (*Wolken*); sich auflösen (*Heer*); **30.** nachlassen (*Gesundheit*); zu'grunde gehen (*Geschäft*); vergehen, aufhören; **31.** anbrechen (*Tag*); aufbrechen (*Wunde*); aus-, losbrechen (*Sturm, Gelächter*); **32.** brechen (*Stimme*): ***his voice broke*** *a.* er befand sich im Stimmwechsel, er mutierte; **33.** sich verändern, 'umschlagen (*Wetter*); **34.** † im Preise fallen; **35.** bekannt(gegeben) werden (*Nachricht*); **36.** *Boxen*: brechen;

Zssgn mit adv. u. prp.:

break| a·way *v/i.* **1.** ab-, losbrechen; **2.** sich loßreißen, ausreißen; **3.** sich trennen, sich lossagen, absplittern; **4.** *sport* a) sich absetzen (***from, of*** von), ausreißen, b) *Am.* e-n Fehlstart verursachen; ***~ down*** **I** *v/t.* **1.** niederreißen, abbrechen; **2.** *fig. j-n, j-s Widerstand* brechen; **3.** zerlegen (*a.* ⚙); auflösen; *Statistik*: aufgliedern, -schlüsseln; **II** *v/i.* **4.** zs.-brechen (*a. fig.*); **5.** zerbrechen (*a. fig.*); **6.** versagen, scheitern; stekkenbleiben; *mot. a.* e-e Panne haben; **7.** *fig.* zerfallen (*in einzelne Gruppen etc.*); ***~ e·ven*** *v/i.* † kostendeckend arbeiten; ***~ forth*** *v/i.* **1.** her'vorbrechen; **2.** sich erheben (*Geschrei etc.*); ***~ in*** **I** *v/t.* **1.** einschlagen; **2.** *Tier* abrichten; *Pferd* zureiten; *Auto etc.* einfahren; *Person* einarbeiten; *j-n* gewöhnen (***to*** an *acc.*); **II** *v/i.* **3.** einbrechen: ***~ on*** sich einmischen in (*acc.*), *Unterhaltung etc.* unterbrechen; ***~ in·to*** *v/i.* **1.** einbrechen *od.* -dringen in (*acc.*); **2.** *fig.* in *Gelächter etc.* ausbrechen; **3.** *Vorrat etc.* anbrechen; ***~ off*** *v/t. u. v/i.* abbrechen (*a. fig.*); ***~ out*** *v/i.* ausbrechen (*a. fig.*): ***~ in a rash*** ⚕ e-n Ausschlag bekommen; ***~ through*** **I** *v/t.* (durch)'brechen, über'winden; **II** *v/i.* 'durchbrechen, erscheinen; ***~ up*** **I** *v/t.* **1.** zer-, aufbrechen; zerlegen (*a. hunt. Wild*); *weitS.* zerstören, ka'puttmachen, *fig. a.* zerrütten: ***that breaks me up!*** F ich lach' mich tot!; **2.** abbrechen, *Sitzung etc.* aufheben, *Versammlung, Menge, a. Haushalt* auflösen; **II** *v/i.* **3.** aufgehoben werden, sich auflösen (*Versammlung etc., a. Nebel etc.*); **4.** aufhören; schließen (*Schule etc.*); **5.** zerbrechen (*Ehe etc.*); sich trennen, Schluß machen (*Paar*); zerfallen (*Reich etc.*); **6.** *fig.* zs.-brechen (*Person*); **7.** aufklaren (*Wetter, Himmel*); **8.** aufbrechen (*Straße, Eis*); ***~ with*** *v/i.* brechen *od.* Schluß machen mit (*e-m Freund, e-r Gewohnheit*).

break·a·ble ['breɪkəbl] **I** *adj.* zerbrechlich; **II** *s. pl.* zerbrechliche Ware *sg.*; **'break·age** [-kɪdʒ] *s.* **1.** Bruch(stelle *f*) *m*; **2.** Bruchschaden *m*; **'break·a·way** *s.* **1.** (***from***) *pol.* Absplitterung *f*, Lossagung *f* (von), Bruch *m* (mit): ***~ group*** Splittergruppe *f*; **2.** *sport* a) Ausreißen *n*, b) 'Durchbruch *m*, c) *Am.* Fehlstart *m*.

'break·down *s.* **1.** Zs.-bruch *m*, Scheitern *n*: ***nervous ~*** Nervenzusammenbruch; ***~ of marriage*** ⚖ Zerrüttung *f* der Ehe; **2.** Panne *f*, (Ma'schinen)Schaden *m*, (Betriebs)Störung *f*; ⚡ 'Durchschlag *m*; **3.** Zerlegung *f*, *bsd. statistische* Aufgliederung, Aufschlüsselung *f*, Ana'lyse *f* (*a.* 💻); ***~ ser·vice*** *s. mot. Brit.* Pannendienst *m*; ***~ truck***, ***~ van*** *s. Brit.* Abschleppwagen *m*; ***~ volt·age*** *s.* ⚡ 'Durchschlagspannung *f*.

break·er ['breɪkə] *s.* **1.** Brecher *m* (*bsd. in Zssgn Person od. Gerät*); 'Abbruchsunter,nehmer *m*, Verschrotter *m*; **2.** Abrichter *m*, Dres'seur *m*; **3.** Brecher *m*, Sturzwelle *f*: ***~s*** Brandung *f*.

,break-'e·ven point *s.* † Rentabili'tätsgrenze *f*, Gewinnschwelle *f*.

break·fast ['brekfəst] **I** *s.* Frühstück *n*: ***~ television*** Frühstücksfernsehen *n* (*am frühen Morgen*); ***have ~*** → **II** *v/i.* frühstücken.

'break-in → ***breaking-in***.

break·ing ['breɪkɪŋ] *s.* Bruch *m*: ***~ of the voice*** Stimmbruch, -wechsel *m*; ***~ and entering*** ⚖ Einbruch *m*; **'~-in** *s.* **1.** ⚖ Einbruch *m*; **2.** Abrichten *n*; Zureiten *n*; *mot.* Einfahren *n*; Einarbeitung *f*, Anlernen *n von Personen*; ***~ point*** *s.* ⚙, *phys.* Bruch-, Festigkeitsgrenze *f*: ***to ~*** *fig.* bis zur (totalen) Erschöpfung; ***have reached ~*** kurz vor dem Zs.-bruch stehen; ***~ strength*** *s.* ⚙, *phys.* Bruch-, Reißfestigkeit *f*.

'break|·neck *adj.* halsbrecherisch; **'~·out** *s.* Ausbruch *m* (*aus Gefängnis etc.*); **'~·through** *s. bsd.* ⚔ 'Durchbruch *m* (*a. fig. Erfolg*); **'~·up** *s.* **1.** Zerbrechen *n*, -bersten *n*; Bersten *n* (*von Eis*); **2.** *fig.* Zerrüttung *f*, Zs.-bruch *m*, Zerfall *m*; **3.** Bruch *m* (*e-r Freundschaft etc.*); **4.** Auflösung *f* (*e-r Versammlung etc.*); **'~,wa·ter** *s.* Wellenbrecher *m*.

bream[1] [bri:m] *s. ichth.* Brassen *m*.

bream[2] [bri:m] *v/t.* ⚓ den Schiffsboden reinkratzen u. -brennen.

breast [brest] **I** *s.* **1.** Brust *f*; (*weibliche*) Brust, Busen *m*; **2.** *fig.* Brust *f*, Herz *n*, Busen *m*: ***make a clean ~ of s.th.*** et. gestehen; **3.** Brust(stück *n*) *f e-s Kleides etc.*; **4.** Wölbung *f e-s Berges*; **II** *v/t.* **5.** mutig auf *et.* losgehen; gegen *et.* ankämpfen, mühsam bewältigen: ***~ the waves*** gegen die Wellen ankämpfen; **6.** *sport das Zielband* durch'reißen; **'~·bone** ['brest-] *s.* Brustbein *n*; **,~-'deep** *adj.* brusthoch.

breast·ed ['brestɪd] *adj. in Zssgn* ...brüstig.

'breast|-feed *v/t. u. v/i.* [*irr.*] stillen: ***breast-fed child*** Brustkind *n*; **'~·pin** ['brest-] *s.* Ansteck-, Kra'wattennadel *f*; **'~·stroke** *s. sport* Brustschwimmen *n*; **'~·work** *s.* ⚔, △ Brustwehr *f*.

breath [breθ] *s.* **1.** Atem(zug) *m*: ***bad ~*** (übler) Mundgeruch; ***draw one's first ~*** das Licht der Welt erblicken; ***draw one's last ~*** den letzten Atemzug tun (*sterben*); ***it took my ~ away*** *fig.* es verschlug mir den Atem; ***take ~*** Atem schöpfen (*a. fig.*); ***catch one's ~*** den Atem anhalten; ***save your ~!*** spar dir die Worte!; ***waste one's ~*** *fig.* in den Wind reden; ***out of ~*** außer Atem; ***under one's ~*** leise, im Flüsterton; ***with his last ~*** mit s-m letzten Atemzug, als letztes; ***in the same ~*** im gleichen Atemzug; **2.** *fig.* Spur *f*, Anflug *m*; **3.** Hauch *m*, Lüftchen *n*: ***a ~ of air***; **4.** Duft *m*.

breath·a·lyz·er ['breθəlaɪzə] *s. mot.* Alkoholtestgerät *n*.

breathe [bri:ð] **I** *v/i.* **1.** atmen; *fig.* leben; **2.** Atem holen; *fig.* sich verschnaufen: ***~ again*** (*od.* ***freely***) (erleichtert) aufatmen; **3.** ***~ upon*** anhauchen; *fig.* besudeln; **4.** duften (***of*** nach); **II** *v/t.* **5.** (ein- u. aus)atmen; *fig.* ausströmen: ***~ a sigh*** seufzen; **6.** hauchen, flüstern: ***not to ~ a word*** kein Sterbenswörtchen sagen; **'breath·er** [-ðə] *s.* **1.** Atem-, Verschnaufpause *f* (*a. fig.*): ***take a ~*** sich verschnaufen; **2.** *sport* F ‚Spa'ziergang' *m*; **3.** F Stra'paze *f*; **'breath·ing** [-ðɪŋ] *s.* **1.** Atmen *n*, Atmung *f*; **2.** (Luft)Hauch *m*: ***~ space*** Atempause *f*.

breath·less ['breθlɪs] *adj.* ☐ **1.** außer Atem; atemlos (*a. fig.*); **2.** *fig.* atemberaubend; **3.** windstill.

'breath|,tak·ing *adj.* ☐ atemberaubend; ***~ test*** *s. Brit.* (*an e-m Verkehrsteilnehmer vorgenommener*) Alkoholtest.

bred [bred] *pret. u. p.p. von* ***breed***.

breech [bri:tʃ] *s.* **1.** Hosenboden *m*; **2.** ⚔ Verschluß *m* (*Geschütz, Hinterlader*); ***~ de·liv·er·y*** *s.* ⚕ Steißgeburt *f*.

breech·es ['brɪtʃɪz] *s. pl.* Knie-, Reithose(n *pl.*) *f*, Breeches *pl.*; → ***big*** 1, ***wear*** 1.

'breech,load·er *s.* ⚔ 'Hinterlader *m*.

breed [bri:d] **I** *v/t.* [*irr.*] **1.** her'vorbringen, gebären; **2.** *Tiere* züchten; *Pflan-*

zen züchten, ziehen: ***French-bred*** in Frankreich gezüchtet; **3.** *fig.* her'vorrufen, verursachen, erzeugen: ***war ~s misery***; **4.** auf-, erziehen; ausbilden; **II** *v/i.* [*irr.*] **5.** zeugen, brüten, sich paaren, sich fortpflanzen, sich vermehren; **6.** entstehen; **III** *s.* **7.** Rasse *f*, Zucht *f*, Stamm *m*; **8.** Art *f*, Schlag *m*, Herkunft *f*; **'breed·er** [-də] *s.* **1.** Züchter(in); **2.** Zuchttier *n*; **3.** *a.* ***~ reactor*** *phys.* Brüter *m*, 'Brutreˌaktor *m*; **'breed·ing** [-dɪŋ] *s.* **1.** Fortpflanzung *f*; Züchtung *f*, Zucht *f*: ***~ place*** *fig.* Brutstätte *f*; **2.** Erziehung *f*, Ausbildung *f*; **3.** Benehmen *n*; Bildung *f*, (gute) Lebensart *od.* ‚Kinderstube'.

breeze¹ [bri:z] **I** *s.* **1.** Brise *f*, leichter Wind; **2.** F Krach *m*: a) Lärm *m*, b) Streit *m*; **3.** *Am.* ‚Kinderspiel' *n*, ‚Spaziergang' *m*; **II** *v/i.* **4.** wehen; **5.** F a) ‚schweben' (*Person*), b) sausen.

breeze² [bri:z] *s.* ⚙ Kohlenlösche *f*.

breez·y ['bri:zɪ] *adj.* □ **1.** luftig, windig; **2.** F a) forsch, flott, unbeschwert, b) oberflächlich.

Bren gun [bren] *s.* leichtes Ma'schinengewehr.

brent goose [brent] → ***brant***.

breth·ren ['breðrən] *pl. von* ***brother*** 2.

Bret·on ['bretən] **I** *adj.* bre'tonisch; **II** *s.* Bre'tone *m*, Bre'tonin *f*.

breve [bri:v] *s. typ.* Kürzezeichen *n*.

bre·vet ['brevɪt] ⚔ **I** *s.* Bre'vet *n* (*Offizierspatent zu e-m Titularrang*): ***~ major*** Hauptmann *m* im Range e-s Majors (*ohne entsprechendes Gehalt*); **II** *adj.* Brevet…: ***~ rank*** Titularrang *m*.

bre·vi·ar·y ['bri:vjərɪ] *s.* Bre'vier *n*.

bre·vier [brə'vɪə] *s. typ.* Pe'titschrift *f*.

brev·i·ty ['brevətɪ] *s.* Kürze *f*.

brew [bru:] **I** *v/t.* **1.** *Bier* brauen; **2.** *Getränke* (*a. Tee*) (zu)bereiten; **3.** *fig.* aushecken, -brüten; **II** *v/i.* **4.** brauen, Brauer sein; **5.** sich zs.-brauen, in der Luft liegen, im Anzuge sein (*Gewitter*, *Unheil*); **III** *s.* **6.** Gebräu *n* (*a. fig.*); **brew·age** ['bru:ɪdʒ] *s.* Gebräu *n* (*a. fig.*); **brew·er** ['bru:ə] *s.* Brauer *m*: ***~'s yeast*** Bierhefe *f*; **brew·er·y** ['brʊərɪ] *s.* Braue'rei *f*.

bri·ar → ***brier***.

brib·a·ble ['braɪbəbl] *adj.* bestechlich; **bribe** [braɪb] **I** *v/t.* **1.** bestechen; **2.** *fig.* verlocken; **II** *s.* **3.** Bestechung *f*; **4.** Bestechungsgeld *n*, -geschenk *n*: ***taking (of) ~s*** ⚖ Bestechlichkeit *f*, passive Bestechung, *pol.* Vorteilsnahme *f*; **'brib·er** [-bə] *s.* Bestecher *m*; **'brib·er·y** [-bərɪ] *s.* Bestechung *f*.

bric-à-brac ['brɪkəbræk] *s.* **1.** Antiqui'täten *pl.*; **2.** Nippsachen *pl.*

brick [brɪk] **I** *s.* **1.** Ziegel-, Backstein *m*: ***drop a ~*** F ‚ins Fettnäpfchen treten'; ***swim like a ~*** wie e-e bleierne Ente schwimmen; **2.** (Bau)Klötzchen *n* (*Spielzeug*): ***box of ~s*** Baukasten *m*; **3.** F prima Kerl; **II** *adj.* **4.** Ziegel…, Backstein…: ***red-~ university*** *Brit.* moderne Universität (*ohne jahrhundertealte Tradition*); **III** *v/t.* **5.** mit Ziegelsteinen belegen *od.* pflastern: ***to ~ in*** (*od.* ***up***) zumauern; **'~·bat** *s.* Ziegelbrocken *m* (*bsd. als Wurfgeschoß*); **'~ˌlay·er** *s.* Maurer *m*; **'~ˌlay·ing** *s.* Maure'rei *f*; **'~ˌmak·er** *s.* Ziegelbrenner *m*; **~ tea** *s.* (*chinesischer*) Ziegeltee; **~ wall** *s.* Backsteinmauer *f*; *fig.* Wand *f*: ***see through a ~*** das Gras wachsen hören; **'~·work** *s.* **1.** Mauerwerk *n*; **2.** *pl. sg. konstr.* Ziege'lei *f*.

brid·al ['braɪdl] **I** *adj.* □ bräutlich, Braut…; Hochzeits…; **II** *s. poet.* Hochzeit *f*.

bride [braɪd] *s.* Braut *f* (*am u. kurz vor u. nach dem Hochzeitstage*), Neuvermählte *f*: ***give away the ~*** Brautvater sein.

bride-groom ['braɪdgrʊm] *s.* Bräutigam *m*; **brides·maid** ['braɪdzmeɪd] *s.* Brautjungfer *f*.

bride·well ['braɪdwəl] *s.* Gefängnis *n*, Besserungsanstalt *f*.

bridge¹ [brɪdʒ] **I** *s.* **1.** Brücke *f*: ***burn one's ~s (behind one)*** *fig.* alle Brükken hinter sich abbrechen; ***don't cross your ~s before you come to them*** *fig.* laß doch die Dinge einfach auf dich zukommen; **2.** ⚓ Kom'mandobrücke *f*; **3.** ♪ (Vio'linen- *etc.*)Steg *m*; ⚕ (Zahn-)Brücke *f*; (Brillen)Steg *m*; **4.** *a.* ***~ of the nose*** Nasenrücken *m*; **5.** ('Straßen)Überˌführung *f*; **6.** *Turnen*, *Ringen*: Brücke *f*; **7.** ⚡ (Meß)Brücke *f*; Brückenschaltung *f*; **II** *v/t.* **8.** e-e Brükke schlagen über (*acc.*); **9.** *fig.* über'brücken: ***bridging loan*** † Überbrükkungskredit *m*.

bridge² [brɪdʒ] *s.* Bridge *n* (*Kartenspiel*).

'bridge|·head *s.* ⚔ Brückenkopf *m*; **~ toll** *s.* Brückenmaut *f*; **'~·work** *s.* ⚕ (Zahn)Brücke *f*.

bri·dle ['braɪdl] **I** *s.* **1.** Zaum *m*, Zaumzeug *n*; **2.** Zügel *m*: ***give a horse the ~*** e-m Pferd die Zügel schießen lassen; **II** *v/t.* **3.** *Pferd* (auf)zäumen; **4.** *Pferd* (*a. fig. Leidenschaft etc.*) zügeln, im Zaum halten; **III** *v/i.* **5.** *a.* ***~ up*** (*verächtlich od. stolz*) den Kopf zu'rückwerfen, *weitS.* hochfahren, ärgerlich werden; **6.** Anstoß nehmen (***at*** an *dat.*); **~ hand** *s.* Zügelhand *f* (*Linke des Reiters*); **~ path** *s.* schmaler Reitweg, Saumpfad *m*; **~ rein** *s.* Zügel *m*.

brief [bri:f] **I** *adj.* □ **1.** kurz: ***be ~!*** fasse dich kurz!; **2.** kurz, gedrängt: ***in ~*** kurz (gesagt); **3.** kurz angebunden, schroff; **II** *s.* **4.** (päpstliches) Breve; **5.** ⚖ a) Schriftsatz *m*, b) *Brit.* Beauftragung *f* u. Informierung *f* (*des* ***barrister*** *durch den* ***solicitor***) zur Vertretung vor Gericht, *weitS.* Man'dat *n*, c) *Am.* (schriftliche) Informierung des Gerichts (*durch den Anwalt*): ***abandon*** (*od.* ***give up***) ***one's ~*** sein Mandat niederlegen; ***hold a ~ for s.o.*** ⚖ j-s Sache vertreten, *fig.* für j-n e-e Lanze brechen; ***I hold no ~ for*** ich halte nichts von …; ***hold a watching ~*** j-s Interessen (*bei Gericht*) als Beobachter vertreten; **6.** → ***briefing***; **III** *v/t.* **7.** *j-n* instruieren *od.* einweisen, *j-m* genaue Anweisungen geben; **8.** ⚖ a) *e-m Anwalt* e-e Darstellung des Sachverhalts geben, b) *e-n Anwalt* mit s-r Vertretung beauftragen; **'~·case** *s.* Aktentasche *f*.

brief·ing ['bri:fɪŋ] *s.* **1.** ⚖ Beauftragung *f e-s Anwalts*; **2.** *a.* ⚔ (genaue) Anweisung, Instrukti'on *f*, Einweisung *f*; **3.** ⚔ Lage-, Einsatzbesprechung *f*, Befehlsausgabe *f*; **'brief·less** [-lɪs] *adj.* unbeschäftigt (*Anwalt*); **'brief·ness** [-nɪs] *s.* Kürze *f*.

briefs [bri:fs] *s. pl.* Slip *m* (*kurze Unterhose*).

bri·er ['braɪə] *s.* ⚘ **1.** Dornstrauch *m*; **2.** wilde Rose: ***sweet ~*** Weinrose; **3.** Bruy'èreholz *n*: ***~ (pipe)*** Bruyèrepfeife *f*.

brig [brɪg] *s.* **1.** ⚓ Brigg *f*; **2.** ⚔ F ‚Bau' *m*.

Bri·gade [brɪ'geɪd] *s.* **1.** ⚔ Bri'gade *f*; **2.** (*mst* uniformierte) Vereinigung; *contp.* ‚Verein' *m*; **brig·a·dier** [ˌbrɪgə'dɪə] *s.* ⚔ a) *Brit.* Bri'gadekommanˌdeur *m*, -geneˌral *m*, b) *Am. a.* ***~ general*** Brigadegeneral *m*.

brig·and ['brɪgənd] *s.* Ban'dit *m*, (Straßen)Räuber *m*; **'brig·and·age** [-dɪdʒ] *s.* Räuberunwesen *n*.

bright [braɪt] *adj.* □ **1.** hell, glänzend, blank, leuchtend; strahlend (*Wetter*, *Augen*): ***~ red*** leuchtend rot; **2.** klar, 'durchsichtig; heiter (*Wetter*); **3.** *fig.* ‚hell', gescheit, klug; **4.** munter, fröhlich; **5.** glänzend, berühmt; **6.** günstig; **7.** ⚙ blank, Blank…: ***~ wire***; **'bright·en** [-tn] **I** *v/t.* **1.** hell(er) machen; *a. fig.* auf-, erhellen; **2.** *fig.* a) heiter(er) machen, beleben, b) fröhlich stimmen; **3.** polieren, blank putzen; **II** *v/i.* *oft* ***~ up*** **4.** sich aufhellen (*Gesicht*, *Wetter etc.*), aufleuchten (*Gesicht*); **5.** *fig.* a) sich beleben, b) besser werden (*Aussichten etc.*); **'bright·ness** [-nɪs] *s.* **1.** Glanz *m*, Helle *f*, Klarheit *f*: ***~ control*** *TV* Helligkeitssteuerung *f*; **2.** Aufgewecktheit *f*, Gescheitheit *f*; **3.** Munterkeit *f*.

Bright's dis·ease [braɪts] *s.* ⚕ Brightsche Krankheit *f*, Nierenentzündung *f*.

bril·liance ['brɪljəns], **'bril·lian·cy** [-sɪ] *s.* **1.** Leuchten *n*, Glanz *m*; Helligkeit *f* (*a. TV*); **2.** *fig.* a) Scharfsinn *m*, b) Bril'lanz *f*, (*das*) Her'vorragende; **'bril·liant** [-nt] **I** *adj.* □ **1.** leuchtend, glänzend; **2.** *fig.* bril'lant, glänzend, her'vorragend; **II** *s.* **3.** Bril'lant *m* (*Diamant*); **4.** *typ.* Bril'lant *f* (*Schriftgrad*).

bril·lian·tine [ˌbrɪljən'ti:n] *s.* **1.** Brillan'tine *f*, 'Haarpoˌmade *f*; **2.** *Am.* al'pakaartiger Webstoff.

brim [brɪm] **I** *s.* **1.** Rand *m* (*bsd. Gefäß*); **2.** (Hut)Krempe *f*; **II** *v/i.* **3.** voll sein (***with*** von; *a. fig.*): ***~ over*** übervoll sein, überfließen, -sprudeln; **ˌbrim'ful** [-'fʊl] *adj.* rand-, 'übervoll (*a. fig.*); **brimmed** [-md] *adj.* mit Rand, mit Krempe.

brim·stone ['brɪmstən] *s.* **1.** Schwefel *m*; **2.** → ***~ but·ter·fly*** *s. zo.* Zi'tronenfalter *m*.

brin·dled ['brɪndld] *adj.* gestreift, scheckig.

brine [braɪn] *s.* **1.** Sole *f*, (Salz)Lake *f*; **2.** *poet.* Meer(wasser) *n*; **'~-pan** *s.* Salzpfanne *f*.

bring [brɪŋ] *v/t.* [*irr.*] **1.** bringen, mit-, herbringen, her'beischaffen: ***~ him (it) with you*** bring ihn (es) mit; ***~ before the judge*** vor den Richter bringen; ***~ good luck*** Glück bringen; ***~ to bear*** *Einfluß etc.* zur Anwendung bringen, geltend machen, *Druck etc.* ausüben; **2.** *Gründe*, *Beschuldigung etc.* vorbringen; **3.** her'vorbringen; *Gewinn* einbringen; mit sich bringen, her'beiführen: ***~ into being*** ins Leben rufen, entstehen lassen; ***~ to pass*** zustande bringen; **4.** *j-n* veranlassen, bewegen, dazu bringen (***to*** *inf.* zu *inf.*): ***I can't ~ myself to do it*** ich kann mich nicht dazu

durchringen (, es zu tun);
Zssgn mit adv.:
bring| a·bout *v/t.* **1.** zu'stande bringen; **2.** bewirken, verursachen; **3.** ⚓ wenden; **~ a·long** *v/t.* **1.** → ***bring*** 1; **2.** *fig.* mit sich bringen; **~ back** *v/t.* zu'rück-, *a. fig.* wiederbringen; *fig.* a) *Erinnerungen* wachrufen (***of*** an *acc.*), b) Erinnerungen wachrufen an (*acc.*); **~ down** *v/t.* **1.** *a. Flugzeug* her'unterbringen; **2.** *hunt. Wild* erlegen; **3.** ⚔ *Flugzeug* abschießen; **4.** *sport j-n* ‚legen'; **5.** *Regierung etc.* stürzen, zu Fall bringen; **6.** *Preise* drücken; **7. *~ on one's head*** sich *j-s Zorn* zuziehen; **8. *~ the house*** F a) stürmischen Beifall auslösen, b) Lachstürme entfesseln; **~ forth** *v/t.* **1.** her'vorbringen, gebären; **2.** verursachen, zeitigen; **~ for·ward** *v/t.* **1.** *Wunsch etc.* vorbringen; **2.** ✝ *Betrag* über'tragen: (***amount***) ***brought forward*** Übertrag *m*; **~ in** *v/t.* **1.** hereinbringen; **2.** *Ernte, a.* ✝ *Gewinn, Kapital, a. parl. Gesetzesentwurf* einbringen; **3.** a) *j-n* einschalten, b) *j-n* beteiligen (***on*** an *dat.*); **4.** ⚖ *Schuldspruch etc.* fällen: ***~ a verdict of guilty***; **~ off** *v/t.* **1.** retten; **2.** ‚schaffen', fertigbringen; **~ on** *v/t.* **1.** her'beibringen; **2.** her'beiführen, verursachen; **3.** in Gang bringen; **4.** zur Sprache bringen; **5.** *thea. Stück* ‚bringen', aufführen; **~ out** *v/t.* **1.** a) *Buch, Theaterstück* her'ausbringen, b) ✝ *Waren* auf den Markt bringen; **2.** *Sinn etc.* her'ausarbeiten; **3. *bring s.o. out of himself*** j-n dazu bringen, mehr aus sich her'auszugehen; **4.** *j-n* in die Gesellschaft einführen; **~ o·ver** *v/t.* 'umstimmen, bekehren; **~ round** *v/t.* **1.** *Ohnmächtigen* wieder zu sich bringen, *Patienten* 'durchbringen; **2.** *j-n* umstimmen, ‚her'umkriegen'; **3.** *das Gespräch* bringen (***to*** auf *acc.*); **~ through** *v/t.* *Kranken od. Prüfling* 'durchbringen; **~ to** *v/t.* **1.** *Ohnmächtigen* wieder zu sich bringen; **2.** ⚓ stoppen; **~ up** *v/t.* **1.** *Kind* auf-, erziehen; **2.** zur Sprache bringen; **3.** ⚔ *Truppen* her'anführen; **4.** zum Stillstand bringen; **5.** *et.* (er-) brechen: ***~ one's lunch***; **6. *~ short*** zum Halten bringen; **7.** → ***date²*** 5, ***rear²*** 3.

bring·ing-up [ˌbrɪŋɪŋ'ʌp] *s.* **1.** Auf-, Großziehen *n*; **2.** Erziehung *f*.

brink [brɪŋk] *s.* Rand *m* (*mst fig.*): ***on the ~ of*** am Rande (*e-s Krieges, des Ruins etc.*); ***be on the ~ of the grave*** mit e-m Fuß im Grabe stehen; **'~·man·ship** [-mənʃɪp] *s. pol.* Poli'tik *f* des äußersten 'Risikos.

brin·y ['braɪnɪ] **I** *adj.* salzig, solehaltig; **II** *s. Brit.* F: ***the ~*** die See.

bri·oche [bri:'ɒʃ] (*Fr.*) *s.* Bri'oche *f* (*süßes Hefegebäck*).

bri·quet(te) [brɪ'ket] (*Fr.*) *s.* Bri'kett *n*.

brisk [brɪsk] **I** *adj.* □ **1.** lebhaft, flott, flink; **2.** frisch (*Wind*), lustig (*Feuer*); schäumend (*Wein*); **3.** a) lebhaft, munter, b) forsch, e'nergisch; **4.** ✝ lebhaft, flott; **II** *v/t.* **5.** *mst* ***~ up*** anfeuern, beleben.

bris·ket ['brɪskɪt] *s. Küche*: Brust(stück *n*) *f* (*Rind*).

bris·ling ['brɪslɪŋ] *s. ichth.* Sprotte *f*.

bris·tle ['brɪsl] **I** *s.* **1.** Borste *f*; (Bart-) Stoppel *f*; **II** *v/i.* **2.** sich sträuben (*Haar*); **3.** *a.* ***~ up*** (***with anger***) hochfahren, zornig werden: ***~ with anger***; **4.** (***with***) strotzen, starren, voll sein (von).

bris·tling → ***brisling***.

bris·tly ['brɪslɪ] *adj.* stachelig, rauh; struppig; stoppelig, Stoppel...

Brit [brɪt] *s.* F Brite *m*, Britin *f*.

Bri·tan·nic [brɪ'tænɪk] *adj.* bri'tannisch.

Brit·i·cism ['brɪtɪsɪzəm] *s.* Angli'zismus *m*; **'Brit·ish** [-tɪʃ] **I** *adj.* britisch: ***~ subject*** britischer Staatsangehöriger; **II** *s.*: ***the ~*** die Briten *pl.*; **'Brit·ish·er** [-tɪʃə] *s.* Brite *m*; **'Brit·on** [-tn] *s.* **1.** Brite *m*, Britin *f*; **2.** *hist.* Bri'tannier(in)

brit·tle ['brɪtl] *adj.* **1.** spröde, zerbrechlich; bröckelig; brüchig (*metall etc.*; *a. fig.*); **2.** reizbar.

broach [brəʊtʃ] **I** *s.* **1.** Stecheisen *n*; Räumnadel *f*; **2.** Bratspieß *m*; **3.** Turmspitze *f*; **II** *v/t.* **4.** *Faß* anstechen; **5.** ⚙ räumen; **6.** *fig. Thema* anschneiden.

broad [brɔ:d] **I** *adj.* □ → ***broadly***; **1.** breit: ***it is as ~ as it is long*** *fig.* es ist gehüpft wie gesprungen; **2.** weit, ausgedehnt; weitreichend, um'fassend, voll: ***~ jump*** *sport* Weitsprung *m*; ***in the ~est sense*** im weitesten Sinne; ***in ~ daylight*** am hellichten Tage; **3.** deutlich, ausgeprägt; breit (*Akzent, Dialekt*); → ***hint*** 1; **4.** ungeschminkt, offen, derb: ***a ~ joke*** ein derber Witz; **5.** allgemein, einfach: ***the ~ facts*** die allgemeinen Tatsachen; ***in ~ outline*** in groben Umrissen, in großen Zügen; **6.** großzügig: ***a ~ outlook*** e-e tolerante Auffassung; **7.** *Radio*: unscharf; **II** *s.* **8.** *sl.* a) ‚Weib(sbild)' *n*, b) ‚Nutte' *f*; **~ ar·row** *s.* breitköpfiger Pfeil (*amtliches Zeichen auf brit. Regierungsgut u. auf Sträflingskleidung*); **'~-ax(e)** *s.* **1.** Breitbeil *n*; **2.** *hist.* Streitaxt *f*; **~ beam** *s.* ⚡ Breitstrahler *m*; **~ bean** *s.* ♀ Saubohne *f*.

broad·cast ['brɔ:dkɑ:st] **I** *v/t.* [*irr.* → ***cast***; *pret. u. p.p. a.* ***~ed***] **1.** breitwürfig säen; **2.** *fig. Nachricht* verbreiten, *iro.* 'auspoˌsaunen; **3.** durch Rundfunk *od.* Fernsehen verbreiten, über'tragen, senden, ausstrahlen; **II** *v/i.* **4.** im Rundfunk *od.* Fernsehen auftreten; **5.** senden; **III** *s.* **6.** Rundfunk-, Fernsehsendung *f*, Über'tragung *f*; **IV** *adj.* **7.** Rundfunk..., Fernseh...; **'broad·cast·er** [-tə] *s.* **1.** Rundfunk-, Fernsehsprecher(in); **2.** → ***broadcasting station***.

broad·cast·ing ['brɔ:dkɑ:stɪŋ] **I** *s.* **1.** → ***broadcast*** 6; **2.** a) Rundfunk *m od.* Fernsehen *n*: ***~ area*** Sendebereich *m*, b) Sendebetrieb *m*; **II** *adj.* **3.** Rundfunk..., Fernseh...; **~ sta·tion** *s.* 'Rundfunk-, 'Fernsehstatiˌon *f*, Sender *m*; **~ stu·di·o** *s.* Senderaum *m*, 'Studio *n*.

Broad| Church *s. liberale Richtung in der anglikanischen Kirche*; **'♀·cloth** *s.* feiner Wollstoff.

broad·en ['brɔ:dn] *v/t. u. v/i.* (sich) verbreitern, (sich) erweitern: ***~ one's mind*** *fig.* sich bilden, s-n Horizont erweitern; ***travel(l)ing ~s the mind*** Reisen bildet.

'broad-ga(u)ge *adj.* 🚂 Breitspur...

broad·ly ['brɔ:dlɪ] *adv.* **1.** weitgehend (*etc.*, → ***broad*** I); **2.** allgemein (gesprochen), in großen Zügen.

ˌbroad'mind·ed *adj.* großzügig, tole'rant.

'broad|·sheet *s.* **1.** *typ.* Planobogen *m*; **2.** *hist.* große, einseitig bedruckte Flugschrift; Flugblatt *n*; **'~·side** *s.* **1.** ⚓ Breitseite *f* (*Geschütze u. Salve*): ***fire a ~*** e-e Breitseite abgeben; **2.** F ‚Breitseite' *f*, mas'sive At'tacke; **3.** → ***broadsheet***; **'~·sword** *s.* breites Schwert, 'Pallasch *m*.

bro·cade [brəʊ'keɪd] *s.* ✝ **1.** Bro'kat *m*; **2.** Broka'tell(e *f*) *m*.

bro·chure ['brəʊʃə] *s.* Bro'schüre *f*.

brock·et ['brɒkɪt] *s. hunt.* Spießer *m*, zweijähriger Hirsch.

brogue [brəʊg] *s.* **1.** a) irischer Ak'zent (des Englischen), b) dia'lektisch gefärbte Aussprache; **2.** derber Straßenschuh.

broil¹ [brɔɪl] **I** *v/t.* auf dem Rost braten, grillen; **II** *v/i.* schmoren, braten, kochen (*alle a. fig.*).

broil² [brɔɪl] *s.* Krach *m*, Streit *m*.

broil·er¹ ['brɔɪlə] *s.* **1.** Bratrost *m*; Bratofen *m* mit Grillvorrichtung; **2.** Brathühnchen *n* (*bratfertig*); **3.** F glühend heißer Tag.

broil·er² ['brɔɪlə] *s.* Streithammel *m*.

broil·ing ['brɔɪlɪŋ] *adj. a.* ***~ hot*** glühend heiß.

broke¹ [brəʊk] *pret. von* ***break***.

broke² [brəʊk] *adj.* F pleite: a) bank'rott, ruiniert, b) ‚abgebrannt', ‚blank': ***go ~*** pleite gehen; ***go for ~*** alles riskieren.

bro·ken ['brəʊkən] **I** *p.p. von* ***break***; **II** *adj.* □ → ***brokenly***; **1.** zerbrochen, entzwei, ka'putt; zerrissen; **2.** gebrochen; **3.** unter'brochen (*Schlaf*); angebrochen, unvollständig: ***~ line*** gestrichelte *od.* punktierte Linie; **4.** *fig.* (seelisch) gebrochen: ***a ~ man***; **5.** zerrüttet (*Ehe, Gesundheit*): ***~ home*** zerrüttete Familienverhältnisse *pl.*; **6.** uneben, holperig (*Boden*); zerklüftet (*Gelände*); bewegt (*Meer*); **7.** *ling.* gebrochen: ***~ German***; **ˌ~-'down** *adj.* **1.** ruiniert, unbrauchbar; **2.** erschöpft, geschwächt, zerrüttet, ‚ka'putt'; **3.** zs.-gebrochen (*a. fig.*); **ˌ~-'heart·ed** *adj.* un'tröstlich, (ganz) gebrochen.

bro·ken·ly ['brəʊkənlɪ] *adv.* **1.** stoßweise, mit Unter'brechungen; **2.** mit gebrochener Stimme.

bro·ken| num·ber *s.* ✗ gebrochene Zahl, Bruch *m*; **~ stone** *s.* Splitt *m*, Schotter *m*; **ˌ~-'wind·ed** *adj.* dämpfig, kurzatmig (*Pferd*).

bro·ker ['brəʊkə] *s.* a) (Handels)Makler *m*, (*weitS. a.* Heirats)Vermittler *m*: ***honest ~*** *pol.*, *fig.* ehrlicher Makler, b) (Börsen)Makler *m*, Broker *m* (*der im Kundenauftrag Geschäfte tätigt*); **'bro·ker·age** [-ərɪdʒ] *s.* **1.** Maklergebühr *f*, Cour'tage *f*; **2.** Maklergeschäft *n*.

brol·ly ['brɒlɪ] *s. Brit.* F Schirm *m*.

bro·mide ['brəʊmaɪd] *s.* **1.** ⚗ Bro'mid *n*: ***~ paper*** *phot.* Bromsilberpapier *n*; **2.** *fig.* a) Plattheit *f*, Banali'tät *f*, b) langweiliger Mensch; **'bro·mine** [-mi:n] *s.* ⚗ Brom *n*.

bron·chi ['brɒŋkaɪ], **'bron·chi·a** [-kɪə] *s. pl. anat.* 'Bronchien *pl.*; **'bron·chi·al** [-kjəl] *adj.* Bronchial...; **bron·chi·tis** [brɒŋ'kaɪtɪs] *s.* ⚕ Bron'chitis *f*, Bronchi'alkaˌtarrh *m*.

bron·co ['brɒŋkəʊ] *pl.* **-cos** *s.* kleines, halbwildes Pferd (*Kalifornien*): ***~ buster*** Zureiter *m* (von wilden Pferden).

Bronx cheer [brɒŋks] *s. Am. sl.* ,'Pfeifkon,zert' *n.*

bronze [brɒnz] **I** *s.* **1.** Bronze *f*: ~ ***age*** Bronzezeit *f*; ~ ***medal(l)ist*** Bronzemedaillengewinner(in); **2.** ('Statue *f etc.* aus) Bronze *f*; **II** *v/t.* **3.** bronzieren; **III** *adj.* **4.** bronzefarben, Bronze...; **bronzed** [-zd] *adj.* **1.** bronziert; **2.** (sonnen)gebräunt.

brooch [brəʊtʃ] *s.* Brosche *f*, Spange *f*.

brood [bru:d] **I** *s.* **1.** Brut *f*; **2.** Nachkommenschaft *f*; **3.** *contp.* Brut *f*, Horde *f*; **II** *v/i.* **4.** brüten; **5.** *fig.* (***on, over***) brüten (über *dat.*), grübeln (über *acc.*); **6.** brüten, lasten (*Hitze etc.*); **III** *adj.* **7.** Brut..., Zucht...: ~ ***mare*** Zuchtstute *f*; **'brood·er** [-də] *s.* **1.** Bruthenne *f*; **2.** Brutkasten *m*; **'brood·y** [-dɪ] *adj.* **1.** brütig (*Henne*); **2.** *fig.* brütend, grüblerisch; trübsinnig.

brook¹ [brʊk] *s.* Bach *m*.

brook² [brʊk] *v/t.* erdulden: ***it ~s no delay*** es duldet keinen Aufschub.

broom [bru:m] *s.* **1.** Besen *m*: ***a new ~ sweeps clean*** neue Besen kehren gut; **2.** ⚘ (Besen)Ginster *m*; **'~·stick** ['brʊm-] *s.* Besenstiel *m*.

broth [brɒθ] *s.* (Fleisch-, Kraft)Brühe *f*, Suppe *f*.

broth·el ['brɒθl] *s.* Bor'dell *n*.

broth·er ['brʌðə] *s.* **1.** Bruder *m*: ***~s and sisters*** Geschwister; ***Smith ~s*** ✝ Gebrüder Smith; **2.** *eccl. pl.* ***brethren*** Bruder *m*, Nächste(r) *m*, Mitglied *n* e-r (religi'ösen) Gemeinschaft; **3.** Amtsbruder *m*, Kol'lege *m*: ~ ***in arms*** Waffenbruder; ~ ***student*** Kommilitone, Studienkollege *m*; ~ ***officer*** Regimentskamerad *m*; ***~!*** F Mann!, Mensch!; **,broth·er-'ger·man** *s.* leiblicher Bruder; **'broth·er·hood** [-hʊd] *s.* **1.** Bruderschaft *f*; **2.** Brüderlichkeit *f*; **broth·er-in-law** ['brʌðərɪnlɔ:] *s.* Schwager *m*.

broth·er·ly ['brʌðəlɪ] *adj.* brüderlich.

brough·am ['bru:əm] *s.* **1.** Brougham *m* (*geschlossener, vierrädriger, zweisitziger Wagen*); **2.** *hist. mot.* Limou'sine *f* mit offenem Fahrersitz.

brought [brɔ:t] *pret. u. p.p. von* ***bring***.

brou·ha·ha [bru:'hɑ:hɑ:] *s.* Getue *n*, Wirbel *m*, Lärm *m*.

brow [braʊ] *s.* **1.** (Augen)Braue *f*: ***knit*** (*od.* ***gather***) ***one's ~s*** die Stirn runzeln; **2.** Stirn *f*; **3.** Vorsprung *m*, Abhang *m*, (Berg)Kuppe *f*; **'~·beat** *v/t.* [*irr.* → ***beat***] einschüchtern, tyrannisieren.

brown [braʊn] **I** *adj.* braun: ***do s.o.*** (***up***) ~ F j-n ,anschmieren' *od.* ,reinlegen'; **II** *s.* Braun *n*; **III** *v/t. Haut etc.* bräunen, *Fleisch etc.* (an)bräunen; ⚙ brünieren: ***~ed off*** F ,restlos bedient', ,sauer'; **IV** *v/i.* braun werden; ~ ***bear*** *s. zo.* Braunbär *m*; ~ ***bread*** *s.* Vollkorn- *od.* Schwarzbrot *n*; ~ ***coal*** *s.* Braunkohle *f*.

brown·ie ['braʊnɪ] *s.* **1.** Heinzelmännchen *n*; **2.** *Am.* kleiner Schoko'ladenkuchen mit Nüssen; **3.** ,Wichtel' *m* (*junge Pfadfinderin*).

Brown·ing ['braʊnɪŋ] *s.* Browning *m* (*e-e Pistole*).

'brown|-nose *Am.* V **I** *s.* ,Arschkriecher' *m*; **II** *v/t. j-m* ,in den Arsch kriechen'; ~ ***pa·per*** *s.* 'Packpa,pier *n*; **'~-shirt** *s. hist.* Braunhemd *n* (*SA-Mann od. Nazi*); **'~·stone** *Am.* **I** *s.* brauner Sandstein; **II** *adj.* F wohlhabend, vornehm.

browse [braʊz] *v/i.* **1.** grasen, weiden; *fig.* naschen (***on*** von); **2.** *in Büchern* blättern *od.* schmökern; **3.** *a.* ~ ***around*** sich (unverbindlich) 'umsehen (*in e-m Laden*).

bru·in ['bru:ɪn] *s. poet.* (Meister) Petz *m* (*Bär*).

bruise [bru:z] **I** *v/t.* **1.** *Körperteil* quetschen; *Früchte* anstoßen; **2.** zerstampfen, schroten; **3.** *j-n* grün u. blau schlagen; **II** *v/i.* **4.** e-e Quetschung *od.* e-n blauen Fleck bekommen; **III** *s.* **5.** ⚕ Quetschung *f*, Bluterguß *m*; blauer Fleck; **6.** Druckstelle *f* (*auf Obst*); **'bruis·er** [-zə] *s.* **1.** F Boxer *m*; **2.** a) ,Schläger' *m*, b) ,Schrank' *m* (*Hüne*).

bruit [bru:t] *v/t.*: ~ ***about*** *obs. Gerücht* verbreiten.

Brum·ma·gem ['brʌmədʒəm] F **I** *s.* **1.** *npr.* Birmingham (*Stadt*); **2.** ♀ Schund(-ware *f*) *m* (*bsd. in Birmingham hergestellt*); **II** *adj.* **3.** billig, kitschig, Schund..., unecht.

brunch [brʌntʃ] *s.* F (*aus* ***breakfast*** *u.* ***lunch***) Brunch *m*.

bru·nette [bru:'net] **I** *adj.* brü'nett, dunkelbraun; **II** *s.* Brü'nette *f*.

brunt [brʌnt] *s.* Hauptstoß *m*, -last *f*, volle Wucht *des Angriffs* (*a. fig.*): ***bear the ~*** die Hauptlast tragen.

brush [brʌʃ] **I** *s.* **1.** Bürste *f*; Besen *m*: ***tooth-~*** Zahnbürste *f*; **2.** Pinsel *m*: ***shaving-~***; **3.** a) Pinselstrich *m* (*Maler*), b) Maler *m*, c) ***the ~*** die Malerei; **4.** Bürsten *n*: ***give a ~*** (***to***) *et.* abbürsten; **5.** buschiger Schwanz (*bsd. Fuchs*); **6.** ⚡ (Kon'takt)Bürste *f*; **7.** *phys.* Strahlenbündel *n*; **8.** ⚔ Feindberührung *f*; Schar'mützel *n* (*a. fig.*): ***have a ~ with s.o.*** mit j-m aneinandergeraten; **9.** → ***brushwood***; **II** *v/t.* **10.** bürsten; **11.** fegen: ~ ***away*** (*od.* ***off***) abwischen, -streifen (*a. mit der Hand*); ~ ***off*** *fig. j-n* abwimmeln *od.* abweisen; ~ ***aside*** *fig.* beiseite schieben, abtun; **12.** ~ ***up*** *fig.* ,aufpolieren', auffrischen; **13.** streifen, leicht berühren; **III** *v/i.* **14.** ~ ***against*** streifen (*acc.*); **15.** da'hinrasen: ~ ***past*** vorbeisausen; **'brush·ing** [-ʃɪŋ] *s. mst pl.* Kehricht *m*, *n*; **'brush·less** [-lɪs] *adj.* **1.** ohne Bürste; **2.** ohne Schwanz (*Fuchs*); **'brush·off** *s.* F Abfuhr *f*; **'brush·wood** *s.* **1.** 'Unterholz *n*, Gestrüpp *n*; Busch *m* (*USA u. Australien*); **2.** Reisig *n*.

brusque [brʊsk] *adj.* □ brüsk, barsch, schroff.

Brus·sels ['brʌslz] *npr.* Brüssel *n*; ~ ***lace*** *s.* Brüsseler Spitzen *pl.*; ~ ***sprouts*** [,brʌsl'spraʊts] *s. pl.* Rosenkohl *m*.

bru·tal ['bru:tl] *adj.* □ **1.** viehisch; bru'tal, roh, unmenschlich; **2.** scheußlich; **bru·tal·i·ty** [bru:'tælətɪ] *s.* Brutali'tät *f*, Roheit *f*; **'bru·tal·ize** [-təlaɪz] **I** *v/t.* **1.** zum Tier machen, verrohen lassen; **2.** brutal behandeln; **II** *v/i.* verrohen, zum Tier werden.

brute [bru:t] **I** *s.* (*unvernünftiges*) Tier, Vieh *n*, *fig. a.* Untier *n*, Scheusal *n*: ***the ~ in him*** das Tier in ihm; **II** *adj.* tierisch (*a. = triebhaft, unvernünftig, brutal*); viehisch, roh; hirnlos, dumm; gefühllos: ~ ***force*** rohe Gewalt; **'brut·ish** [-tɪʃ] *adj.* □ → ***brute*** II.

Bry·thon·ic [brɪ'θɒnɪk] *s.* Ursprache *f* der Kelten in Wales, 'Cornwall u. der Bre'tagne.

bub·ble ['bʌbl] **I** *s.* **1.** (*Luft-, Gas-, Seifen*)Blase *f*; **2.** *fig.* Seifenblase *f*; Schwindel(geschäft *n*) *m*: ***prick the ~*** den Schwindel aufdecken; ~ ***company*** Schwindelfirma *f*; **3.** Sprudeln *n*, Brodeln *n*, (Auf)Wallen *n*; **4.** *Am.* Traglufthalle *f*; **II** *v/i.* sprudeln, brodeln, wallen; perlen: ~ ***over*** übersprudeln (*a. fig.* ***with*** vor *dat.*); ~ ***up*** aufsprudeln, in Blasen aufsteigen; ~ ***bath*** *s.* Schaumbad *n*; ~ ***car*** *s.* **1.** Kleinstauto *n*, Ka'binenroller *m*; **2.** Wagen *m* mit kugelsicherer Kuppel; ~ ***gum*** *s.* Bal'lon-, Knallkaugummi *m*.

bu·bo ['bju:bəʊ] *pl.* **-boes** *s.* ⚕ 'Bubo *m* (*Drüsenschwellung*); Beule *f*; **bu·bon·ic** [bju:'bɒnɪk] *adj.*: ~ ***plague*** ⚕ Beulenpest *f*.

buc·ca·neer [,bʌkə'nɪə] **I** *s.* Seeräuber *m*, Freibeuter *m*; **II** *v/i.* Seeräube'rei betreiben.

buck¹ [bʌk] **I** *s.* **1.** *zo.* Bock *m* (*Hirsch, Reh, Ziege etc.*; *a. Turnen*); Rammler *m* (*Hase, Kaninchen*); *engS.* Rehbock *m*; **2.** *obs.* Stutzer *m*, Geck *m*; Lebemann *m*; **3.** *Am. obs. contp.* a) Rothaut *f*, b) Nigger *m*; **4.** *Am. Poker*: *Spielmarke, die e-n Spieler daran erinnern soll, daß er am Geben ist*: ***pass the ~ to*** F *j-m* ,den Schwarzen Peter (*die Verantwortung*) zuschieben'; **II** *v/i.* **5.** bocken (*Pferd, Esel etc.*); **6.** *Am.* F ,meutern', sich sträuben (***at, against*** bei, gegen); **7.** ~ ***up*** F a) sich ranhalten, b) sich zs.-reißen: ~ ***up!*** Kopf hoch!; **III** *v/t.* **8.** *Reiter* durch Bocken abwerfen (wollen); **9.** *Am.* wütend angreifen; angehen gegen; **10.** *a.* ~ ***up*** F aufmuntern: ***greatly ~ed*** hocherfreut; **IV** *adj.* **11.** männlich; **12.** ~ ***private*** ⚔ *Am.* F einfacher Soldat.

buck² [bʌk] *s. Am.* F Dollar *m*.

buck·et ['bʌkɪt] **I** *s.* **1.** Eimer *m*, Kübel *m*: ***champagne ~*** Sektkühler *m*; ***kick the ~*** F ,abkratzen' (*sterben*); **2.** ⚙ a) Schaufel *f e-s Schaufelrades*, b) Eimer *m od.* Löffel *m e-s Baggers*, c) (Pumpen)Kolben *m*; **II** *v/t.* **3.** (aus)schöpfen; **4.** *Pferd* zu'schanden reiten; **III** *v/i.* **5.** F (da'hin)rasen; ~ ***con·vey·or*** *s.* Becherwerk *n*; ~ ***dredg·er*** *s.* Löffelbagger *m*; **'~·ful** [-fʊl] *pl.* **-fuls** *s. ein* Eimer(voll) *m*.

buck·et| seat *s.* **1.** *mot.*, ✈ Klapp-, Notsitz *m*; **2.** *mot.* Schalensitz *m*; ~ ***shop*** *s.* **1.** 'unre,elle Maklerfirma; **2.** ,Klitsche' *f*, kleiner ,Laden'.

'buck|-eye *s. Am.* **1.** ⚘ *e-e* 'Roßka,stanie *f*; **2.** ♀ F Bewohner(in) von Ohio; **'~·horn** *s.* Hirschhorn *n*; **'~·hound** *s. zo.* Jagdhund *m*; **'~,jump·er** *s.* störrisches Pferd.

buck·le ['bʌkl] **I** *s.* **1.** Schnalle *f*, Spange *f*; **2.** ⚔ Koppelschloß *n*; **3.** ⚙ verbogene *od.* verzogene Stelle; **II** *v/t.* **4.** *a.* ~ ***on***, ~ ***up*** an-, 'um-, zuschnallen; **5.** ⚙ (ver)biegen, krümmen; **6.** ~ ***o.s. to*** → 9; **III** *v/i.* **7.** ⚙ sich (ver)biegen *od.* verziehen, sich wölben *od.* krümmen; **8.** nachgeben *unter e-r Last*: ~ (***under***) *fig.* zs.-brechen; **9.** ~ ***down to*** F sich hinter *e-e Aufgabe* ,klemmen'.

buck·ling ['bʌklɪŋ] (*Ger.*) *s.* Bückling *m* (*geräucherter Hering*).

buck·ling strength ['bʌklɪŋ] *s.* ⚙

Knickfestigkeit *f*.
buck·ram ['bʌkrəm] **I** *s.* **1.** Steifleinen *n*; **2.** *fig.* Steifheit *f*, Förmlichkeit *f*; **II** *adj.* **3.** *fig.* steif, for'mell.
'**buck**|**·saw** *s. Am.* Bocksäge *f*; '**~·shot** *s. hunt.* grober Schrot, Rehposten *m*; '**~·skin** *s.* **1.** a) Wildleder *n*, b) *pl.* Lederhose *f*; **2.** Buckskin *m* (*Wollstoff*); '**~·thorn** *s.* ⚘ Kreuzdorn *m*; '**~·tooth** *s.* [*irr.*] vorstehender Zahn; '**~·wheat** *s.* ⚘ Buchweizen *m*.
bu·col·ic [bju:'kɒlɪk] **I** *adj.* (□ **~ally**) **1.** bu'kolisch: a) Hirten..., b) ländlich, i'dyllisch; **II** *s.* **2.** I'dylle *f*, Hirtengedicht *n*; **3.** *humor.* Landmann *m*.
bud [bʌd] **I** *s.* **1.** ⚘ Knospe *f*; Auge *n* (*Blätterknospe*): **be in ~** knospen; **2.** Keim *m*; **3.** *fig.* Keim *m*, Ursprung *m*; → **nip**¹ 2; **4.** unentwickeltes Wesen; **5.** *Am.* F Debü'tantin *f*; **II** *v/i.* **6.** knospen, sprossen; **7.** sich entwickeln *od.* entfalten: **~ding lawyer** angehender Jurist; **III** *v/t.* **8.** ✓ okulieren.
Bud·dha ['bʊdə] *s.* 'Buddha *m*; '**Bud·dhism** [-dɪzəm] *s.* Bud'dhismus *m*; '**Bud·dhist** [-dɪst] **I** *s.* Bud'dhist *m*; **II** *adj.* → **Bud·dhis·tic** [bʊ'dɪstɪk] *adj.* bud'dhistisch.
bud·dy ['bʌdɪ] *s.* F **1.** ‚Kumpel' *m*, ‚Spezi' *m*, Kame'rad *m*; **2.** *Anrede*: Freundchen *n*.
budge [bʌdʒ] *mst neg.* **I** *v/i.* sich (von der Stelle) rühren, sich (im geringsten) bewegen: **~ from** *fig.* von *et.* abrücken; **II** *v/t.* (vom Fleck) bewegen.
budg·er·i·gar ['bʌdʒərɪgɑ:] *s. orn.* Wellensittich *m*.
budg·et ['bʌdʒɪt] **I** *s.* **1.** *bsd. pol.* Bud'get *n*, (Staats)Hauhalt *m*, E'tat *m*, (*a.* pri'vater) Haushaltsplan: **open the ~** das Budget vorlegen; **~ cut** Etatkürzung *f*; **for the low ~** für den schmalen Geldbeutel; **~(-priced)** preisgünstig; **2.** *fig.* Vorrat *m*: **a ~ of news** ein Sack voll Neuigkeiten; **II** *v/t.* **3.** a) *Mittel* bewilligen, vorsehen, *Ausgaben* einplanen; **III** *v/i.* **4.** planen, ein Bud'get machen: **~ for s.th.** et. im Haushaltsplan vorsehen, die Kosten für et. veranschlagen; '**budg·et·ar·y** [-tərɪ] *adj.* Budget..., Etat..., Haushalts...: **~ deficit**.
bud·gie ['bʌdʒɪ] *s.* F *für* **budgerigar**.
buff¹ [bʌf] *s.* **1.** starkes Ochsen- *od.* Büffelleder; **2.** F bloße Haut: **in the ~** im Adams- *od.* Evaskostüm (*nackt*); **3.** Lederfarbe *f*; **4.** F ‚Fex' *m*, Fan *m*: **hi-fi ~**; **II** *adj.* **5.** lederfarben.
buff² [bʌf] *v/t.* ⚙ schwabbeln, polieren.
buf·fa·lo ['bʌfələʊ] *pl.* **-loes**, *Am. a.* **-los I** *s.* **1.** *zo.* Büffel *m*; nordamer. 'Bison *m*; **2.** ⚔ am'phibischer Panzerwagen; **II** *v/t.* **3.** *Am.* F *j-n* täuschen *od.* einschüchtern.
buf·fer ['bʌfə] **I** *s.* ⚙ a) Stoßdämpfer *m*, b) Puffer *m* (*a.* ⚗, *Computer u. fig.*), c) Prellbock (*a. fig.*): **~ solution** ⚗ Pufferlösung *f*; **~ state** *pol.* Pufferstaat *m*; **3.** *a.* **~ memory** *Computer*: Pufferspeicher *m*; **II** *v/t.* **4.** als Puffer wirken gegen; **5.** *Computer*: puffern, zwischenspeichern.
buf·fet¹ ['bʌfɪt] **I** *s.* **1.** Puff *m*, Stoß *m*; Schlag *m* (*a. fig.*); **II** *v/t.* **2.** a) *j-m* e-n Schlag versetzen, b) *j-n od. et.* her'umstoßen: **~ (about)** durchrütteln; **3.** gegen *Wellen etc.* (an)kämpfen.
buf·fet² *s.* **1.** ['bʌfɪt] Bü'fett *n*, Anrichte *f*; **2.** ['bʊfeɪ] Bü'fett *n*: a) Theke *f*, b) *Tisch mit Speisen*, c) Erfrischungsbar *f*, Imbißstube *f*: **~ car** 🚃 Büfettwagen *m*; **~ dinner** kaltes Büfett.
buf·foon [bʌ'fu:n] *s.* **1.** Possenreißer *m*, Hans'wurst *m* (*a. fig. contp.*); **2.** derber Witzbold; **buf'foon·er·y** [-nərɪ] *s.* Possen(reißen *n*) *pl.*
bug [bʌg] **I** *s.* **1.** *zo.* (Bett)Wanze *f*; **2.** *zo. bsd. Am. allgemein* In'sekt *n* (*Ameise, Fliege, Spinne, Käfer*); **3.** F Ba'zillus *m* (*a. fig.*): **the golf ~** die Golfleidenschaft; **4.** ⚙ *Am.* F De'fekt *m*, *mst pl.* ‚Mucken' *pl.*; **5. big ~** F ‚großes' *od.* ‚hohes Tier' (*Person*); **6.** *Am.* F Fan *m*, Fa'natiker *m*: **baseball ~**; **7.** *sl.* ‚Wanze' *f* (*Abhörgerät*); **II** *v/t. sl.* **8.** a) ‚Wanzen' anbringen in *e-m Raum etc.*, b) (heimlich) abhören; **9.** *Am.* F *j-n* nerven: **what's ~ging you?** was hast du denn?
bug·a·boo ['bʌgəbu:] *s.* **1.** → **bugbear**; **2.** ‚Quatsch' *m*.
'**bug**|**·bear** *s.* a) ‚Buhmann' *m*, b) Schreckgespenst *n*; '**~-eyed** *adj.* mit her'vorquellenden Augen.
bug·ger ['bʌgə] **I** *s.* **1.** a) Sodo'mit *m*, b) Homosexu'elle(r) *m*; **2.** V a) ‚Scheißkerl' *m*, b) Kerl *m*, ‚Knülch' *m*, c) ‚Scheißding' *n*; **II** *v/t.* **3.** a) Sodo'mie treiben mit, b) a'nal verkehren mit: **~ (it)!** V Scheiße!; **~ you!** V leck mich!; **4.** a) *j-n* ‚fertigmachen', b) *j-n* ‚nerven'; **5. ~ (up)** V *et.* versauen *od.* vermasseln; **III** *v/i.* **6. ~ around** V he'rumgammeln; **7. ~ off** V ‚abhauen'; '**bug·ger·y** [-ərɪ] *s.* **1.** Sodo'mie *f*, 'widerna͵türliche Unzucht; **2.** Homosexuali'tät *f*.
bug·gy¹ ['bʌgɪ] *s.* **1.** leichter (Pferde-) Wagen; **2.** *mot.* Buggy *m* (*geländegängiges, offenes Freizeitauto*); **3.** *Am.* Kinderwagen *m*.
bug·gy² ['bʌgɪ] *adj.* **1.** verwanzt; **2.** *Am. sl.* ‚bekloppt', verrückt.
'**bug**|**·house** *Am. sl.* **I** *s.* ‚Klapsmühle' *f* (*Nervenheilanstalt*); **II** *adj.* verrückt; '**~-**͵**hunt·er** *s. sl.* In'sektensammler *m*.
bu·gle ['bju:gl] *s.* **1.** Wald-, Jagdhorn *n*; **2.** ⚔ Si'gnalhorn *n*: **sound the ~** ein Hornsignal blasen; '**bu·gle-call** *s.* 'Hornsi͵gnal *n*; '**bu·gler** [-lə] *s.* Hor'nist *m*.
buhl [bu:l] *s.* Einlege-, Boulearbeit *f*.
build [bɪld] **I** *v/t.* [*irr.*] **1.** (er)bauen, errichten: **~ a fire** (ein) Feuer machen; **~ in** a) einbauen (*a. fig.*), b) zubauen; **2.** ⚙ bauen: a) konstruieren, b) herstellen: **~ cars**; **3.** *mst* **~ up** aufbauen, gründen, (er)schaffen: **~ up a business** ein Geschäft aufbauen; **~ up one's health** s-e Gesundheit festigen; **~ up a reputation** sich e-n Namen machen; **~ up a case** *bsd.* ⚖ (Beweis)Material zs.-tragen; **4. ~ up** a) zubauen, vermauern: **~ up a window**, b) *Gelände* aus-, bebauen; **5. ~ up** *fig. j-n* ‚aufbauen' *od.* groß her'ausstellen, Re'klame machen für; **6.** *fig.* gründen, setzen: **~ one's hopes on s.th.**; **II** *v/i.* [*irr.*] **7.** bauen; gebaut werden: **the house is ~ing** das Haus ist im Bau; **8.** *fig.* bauen, sich verlassen (**on** auf *acc.*); **9. ~ (up)** a) sich entwickeln, b) zunehmen, wachsen; **III** *s.* **10.** Bauart *f*, Gestalt *f*; **11.** Körperbau *m*, Fi'gur *f*; **12.** Schnitt *m* (*Kleid*); '**build·er** [-də] *s.* **1.** Erbauer *m*; **2.** Baumeister *m*; **3.** 'Bauunter͵nehmer *m*, Bauhandwerker *m*: **~'s merchant** Baustoffhändler *m*.
build·ing ['bɪldɪŋ] *s.* **1.** Bauen *n*, Bauwesen *n*; **2.** Gebäude *n*, Bau *m*, Bauwerk *n*; **~ block** *s.* **1.** ⚙ *u. fig.* Baustein *m*; **2.** Bauklötzchen *n für Kinder*; **~ con·trac·tor** *s.* 'Bauunter͵nehmer *m*; **~ lease** *s.* ⚖ *Brit.* Baupacht(vertrag *m*) *f*; **~ line** *s.* ⚙ 'Baufluch(͵linie) *f*; **~ lot**, **~ plot**, **~ site** *s.* **1.** Bauplatz *m*, -stelle *f*; **2.** Baugrundstück *n*, Baugelände *n*; **~ own·er** *s.* Bauherr *m*; **~ so·ci·e·ty** *s. Brit.* Bausparkasse *f*.
'**build-up** *s.* **1.** Aufbau *m*, Zs.-stellung *f*; **2.** Zunahme *f*; **3.** ‚Aufbauen' *n*, Re'klame *f*, Propa'ganda *f*; **4.** dra'matische Steigerung.
built [bɪlt] **I** *pret. u. p.p. von* **build** I *u.* II; **II** *adj.* gebaut, geformt: **he is ~ that way** F so ist er eben; **͵~-'in** *adj.* eingebaut (*a. fig.*), Einbau...; '**~-up a·re·a** *s.* **1.** bebautes Gelände; **2.** *Verkehr*: geschlossene Ortschaft.
bulb [bʌlb] **I** *s.* **1.** ⚘ Knolle *f*, Zwiebel *f* (*e-r Pflanze*); **2.** Zwiebelgewächs *n*; **3.** (*Glas- etc.*)Bal'lon *m od.* Kolben *m*; Kugel *f* (*Thermometer*); **4.** ϟ Glühbirne *f*, -lampe *f*; **II** *v/i.* **5.** rundlich anschwellen; Knollen bilden; **bulbed** [-bd] *adj.* knollenförmig; '**bulb·ous** [-bəs] *adj.* knollig, Knollen...: **~ nose**.
Bul·gar ['bʌlgɑ:] *s.* Bul'gare *m*, Bul'garin *f*; **Bul·gar·i·an** [bʌl'geərɪən] **I** *adj.* bul'garisch; **II** *s.* → **Bulgar**.
bulge [bʌldʒ] **I** *s.* **1.** (Aus)Bauchung *f*, (*a.* ⚔ Front)Ausbuchtung *f*; Anschwellung *f*, Beule *f*; Vorsprung *m*, Buckel *m*; Rundung *f*, Bauch *m*, Wulst *m*: **Battle of the** ♀ Ardennenschlacht *f* (*1944*); **2.** ⚓ → **bilge** 1; **3.** Anschwellen *n*, Zunahme *f*, plötzliches Steigen (*bsd. der Börsenkurse*); **4.** *a.* **~ age-group** geburtenstarker Jahrgang; **5. have a ~ on s.o.** *sl.* j-m gegenüber im Vorteil sein; **II** *v/i.* **6.** sich (aus)bauchen, her'vortreten, -ragen, -quellen, sich blähen *od.* bauschen; '**bulg·ing** [-dʒɪŋ] *adj.* (zum Bersten) voll (**with** von).
bulk [bʌlk] **I** *s.* **1.** 'Umfang *m*, Größe *f*, Masse *f*; **2.** große *od.* massige Gestalt; 'Körper͵umfang *m*, -fülle *f*; **3.** Hauptteil *m*, -masse *f*, Großteil *m*, Mehrheit *f*; **4.** ☨ (gekaufte) Gesamtheit; ⚓ (unverpackte) Schiffsladung: **in ~** a) unverpackt, lose, b) in großen Mengen, en gros; **break ~** ⚓ zu löschen anfangen; **~ cargo**, **~ goods** ☨ Schüttgut *n*, Massengüter *pl.*; **~ buying** ☨ Mengeneinkauf *m*; **~ mail** Postwurfsendung *f*; **~ mortgage** *Am.* Fahrnishypothek *f*; **II** *v/i.* **5.** 'umfangreich *od.* sperrig sein; **6.** *fig.* wichtig sein: **~ large** e-e große Rolle spielen; **III** *v/t.* **7.** *bsd. Am.* aufstapeln; '**~·head** *s.* **1.** ⚓ Schott *n*; **2.** ⚙ a) Schutzwand *f*, b) Spant *m*.
bulk·y ['bʌlkɪ] *adj.* **1.** (sehr) 'umfangreich, massig; **2.** sperrig: **~ goods** ☨ Sperrgut *n*.
bull¹ [bʊl] **I** *s.* **1.** *zo.* Bulle *m*, Stier *m*: **like a ~ in a china shop** wie ein Elefant im Porzellanladen; **take the ~ by the horns** den Stier bei den Hörnern packen; **2.** *zo.* (*Elefanten-, Elch-, Waletc.*)Bulle *m*; **3.** ☨ Haussi'er *m*, 'Haussespeku͵lant *m*; **4.** *Am. sl.* ‚Bulle' *m* (*Polizist*); **5.** *ast.* Stier *m*; **6.** → **bull's-eye** 3 *u.* 4; **II** *v/t.* **7.** ☨ Preise in

die Höhe treiben für *et.*: **~ the market** auf Hausse kaufen; **III** *v/i.* **8.** ✝ auf Hausse spekulieren; **IV** *adj.* **9.** männlich; **10.** ✝ steigend, Hausse...: **~ market**.

bull² [bʊl] *s.* (päpstliche) Bulle.

bull³ [bʊl] *s. sl.* **1.** *a.* **Irish ~** ungereimtes Zeug, 'widersprüchliche Behauptung; **2.** Schnitzer *m*, Faux'pas *m*; **3.** *Am.* Quatsch *m*, Blödsinn *m*.

'**bull|-ˌbait·ing** *s.* Stierhetze *f*; '**~·dog I** *s.* **1.** *zo.* Bulldogge *f*; **2.** *Brit. univ.* Begleiter *m* des 'Proctors; **3.** *e-e* Pi'stole *f*; **II** *adj.* **4.** mutig, zäh, hartnäckig; '**~·doze** *v/t.* **1.** planieren, räumen; **2.** F ‚über'fahren', einschüchtern, terrorisieren; zwingen (**into** zu); '**~ˌdoz·er** [-ˌdəʊzə] *s.* **1.** ⚙ Planierraupe *f*, Bulldozer *m*; **2.** *fig.* F → **bully²** 1.

bul·let ['bʊlɪt] *s.* (Gewehr- *etc.*)Kugel *f*, Geschoß *n*: **bite the ~** *fig.* die bittere Pille schlucken; '**~-head** *s.* **1.** Rundkopf *m*; **2.** *Am.* F Dickkopf *m*.

bul·le·tin ['bʊlɪtɪn] *s.* **1.** Bulle'tin *n*: a) Tagesbericht *m* (*a.* ⚔), b) Krankenbericht *m*, c) offizi'elle Bekanntmachung: **~ board** *Am.* schwarzes Brett (*für Anschläge*); **2.** Mitteilungsblatt *n*; **3.** *Am.* Kurznachricht *f*.

'**bul·let-proof** *adj.* kugelsicher.

'**bull|·fight** *s.* Stierkampf *m*; '**~ˌfight·er** *s.* Stierkämpfer *m*; '**~·finch** *s.* **1.** *orn.* Dompfaff *m*; **2.** hohe Hecke; '**~·frog** *s.* *zo.* Ochsenfrosch *m*; ˌ**~-'head·ed** *adj.* starrköpfig.

bul·lion ['bʊljən] *s.* **1.** ungemünztes Gold *od.* Silber: **~ point** ✝ Goldpunkt *m*; **2.** Gold *n od.* Silber *n* in Barren; **3.** Gold-, Silberlitze *f*, -schnur *f*, -troddel *f*.

bull·ish ['bʊlɪʃ] *adj.* **1.** dickköpfig; **2.** ✝ steigend, Hausse...

ˌ**bull-'necked** *adj.* stiernackig.

bull·ock ['bʊlək] *s. zo.* Ochse *m*.

bull| pen *s. Am.* **1.** *sl.* Ba'racke *f* für Holzfäller; **2.** F a) ‚Kittchen' *n*, b) große (Gefängnis)Zelle; **3.** *Baseball*: Übungsplatz *m* für Re'servewerfer; '**~·ring** *s.* 'Stierkampfaˌrena *f*.

bull's-eye ['bʊlzaɪ] *s.* **1.** ⚓, △ Bullauge *n*, rundes Fensterchen; **2.** *a.* **~ pane** Ochsenauge *n*, Butzenscheibe *f*; **3.** Zentrum *n od. das* Schwarze *der Zielscheibe*; **4.** *a. fig.* Schuß *m* ins Schwarze, 'Volltreffer *m*; **5.** 'Blendlaˌterne *f*; **6.** großer runder 'Pfefferminzbonˌbon.

'**bull|·shit** *s. u. int.* V Scheiß(dreck) *m*; **~ ter·ri·er** *s. zo.* 'Bullˌterrier *m*.

bul·ly¹ ['bʊlɪ] *s. a.* **~ beef** Rinderpökelfleisch *n* (in Büchsen).

bul·ly² ['bʊlɪ] **I** *s.* **1.** bru'taler Kerl, ‚Schläger' *m*; Ty'rann *m*; Maulheld *m*; **2.** *obs.* Zuhälter *m*; **3.** *Hockey*: Bully *n*, Anspiel *n*; **II** *v/t.* **4.** tyrannisieren, schikanieren, einschüchtern, piesacken; **III** *adj.* **5.** F ‚prima' (*a. int.*); **IV** *int.* **6.** F bravo!, Klasse!

bul·ly| beef → **bully¹**; '**~·rag** → **ballyrag**.

bul·rush ['bʊlrʌʃ] *s.* ⚘ *große* Binse.

bul·wark ['bʊlwək] *s.* **1.** Bollwerk *n*, Wall *m* (*beide a. fig.*); **2.** ⚓ a) Hafendamm *m*, b) Schanzkleid *n*.

bum¹ [bʌm] *bsd. Brit.* F **1.** ‚Hintern' *m*; **2.** ‚Niete' *f*, ‚Flasche' *f*.

bum² [bʌm] *bsd. Am.* F **I** *s.* **1.** a) ‚Stromer' *m*, ‚Gammler' *m*, He'rumtreiber *m*, b) Tippelbruder *m*, c) Schnorrer *m*, d) Mistkerl *m*; **II** *v/i.* **2.** *mst* **~ around** ‚he'rumgammeln'; **3.** schnorren (**off** bei); **III** *v/t.* **4.** *et.* schnorren (**of** bei, von); **IV** *adj.* **5.** a) ‚mies', schlecht, b) ka'putt.

bum·ble-bee ['bʌmblbiː] *s. zo.* Hummel *f*.

bum·ble·dom ['bʌmbldəm] *s.* Wichtigtue'rei *f* der kleinen Beamten.

bumf [bʌmf] *s. Brit. sl.* **1.** *contp.* ‚Pa'pierkram' *m* (*Akten, Formulare etc.*); **2.** ‚'Klopaˌpier' *n*.

bum·mer ['bʌmə] → **bum²** 1.

bump [bʌmp] **I** *v/t.* **1.** (heftig) stoßen, (an)prallen: **~ one's head** sich den Kopf anstoßen; **I ~ed my head against** (*od.* **on**) **the door** ich stieß *od.* rannte mit dem Kopf gegen die Tür; **~ a car** auf ein Auto auffahren; **2.** *Rudern*: *Boot* über'holen u. anstoßen; **3. ~ off** *sl.* ‚'umlegen', ‚kaltmachen'; **4. ~ up** F *Preise etc.* hochtreiben, *Gehalt etc.* aufbessern; **II** *v/i.* **5.** (**against**, **into**) stoßen, prallen, bumsen (gegen), zs.-stoßen (mit): **~ into** *fig. j-n* zufällig treffen, zufällig stoßen auf (*acc.*); **6.** rütteln, holpern (*Wagen*); **III** *s.* **7.** heftiger Stoß, Bums *m*; **8.** ⚕ Beule *f*, Höcker *m*; **9.** Unebenheit *f* (*Straße*); **10.** Sinn *m* (*für et.*): **~ of locality** Ortssinn; **11.** ✈ (Steig)Bö *f*; **IV** *adv.* **12.** bums!

bump·er ['bʌmpə] *s.* **1.** randvolles Glas (*Wein etc.*); **2.** F *et.* Riesiges: **~ crop** Rekordernte *f*; **~ house** *thea.* volles Haus; **3.** 🚗 *Am.* Puffer *m*; **4.** *mot.* Stoßstange *f*: **~ car** (Auto)Skooter *m*; **~ guard** Stoßstangenhorn *n*; **~ sticker** Autoaufkleber *m*.

bump·kin ['bʌmpkɪn] *s.* Bauernlackel *m*.

'**bump-start** *s. Brit. mot.* **I** *s.* Anschieben *n*; **II** *v/t. Auto* anschieben.

bump·tious ['bʌmpʃəs] *adj.* □ aufgeblasen.

bump·y ['bʌmpɪ] *adj.* **1.** holperig, uneben; **2.** ✈ ‚bockig', böig.

bum| steer *s. Am. sl.*: **give s.o. the ~** j-n ‚verschaukeln'; '**~ˌsuck·er** *s.* V ‚Arschkriecher' *m*.

bun¹ [bʌn] *s.* **1.** süßes Brötchen: **she has a ~ in the oven** *sl.* bei ihr ist was unterwegs; **2.** (Haar)Knoten *m*.

bun² [bʌn] *s. Brit.* Ka'ninchen *n*.

bunch [bʌntʃ] **I** *s.* **1.** Bündel *n* (*a.* ⚡), Bund *n*, Büschel *n*: **~ of flowers** Blumenstrauß *m*; **~ of grapes** Weintraube *f*; **~ of keys** Schlüsselbund; **2.** F a) Haufen *m*, b) ‚Verein' *m*: **the best of the ~** der Beste von allen; **II** *v/t.* **3.** bündeln (*a.* ⚡), zs.-fassen, -binden; falten: **~ed circuit** ⚡ Leitungsbündel *n*; **III** *v/i.* **4.** sich zs.-legen, -schließen; **5.** sich bauschen; '**bunch·y** [-tʃɪ] *adj.* büschelig, bauschig, in Bündeln.

bun·co ['bʌŋkəʊ] *v/t. Am. sl.* ‚reinlegen', betrügen.

bun·dle ['bʌndl] **I** *s.* **1.** Bündel *n*, Bund *n*; Pa'ket *n*; Ballen *m*: **~ of energy** (**nerves**) *fig.* Kraft-(Nerven)Bündel *n*; **2.** *fig.* a) Menge *f*, Haufen *m*, b) F ‚Batzen' *m* Geld; **II** *v/t.* **3.** in Bündel zs.-binden, -packen; **4.** *et. wohin* stopfen; **5.** *mst* **~ off** (*od.* **out**) *j-n* abschieben, (eilig) fortschaffen: **he was ~d into a taxi** er wurde in ein Taxi verfrachtet *od.* gepackt; **III** *v/i.* **6. ~ off** (*od.* **out**) sich packen *od.* da'vonmachen.

bung [bʌŋ] **I** *s.* **1.** Spund(zapfen) *m*, Stöpsel *m*; **2.** ⚔ Mündungspfropfen *m* (*Geschütz*); **II** *v/t.* **3.** verspunden, verstopfen; zupfropfen; **4.** F ‚schmeißen', werfen; **5. ~ up** *Röhre, Öffnung* verstopfen (*mst pass.*): **~ed up** verstopft; **6.** *mst* **~ up** *Am.* F *Auto etc.* schwer beschädigen, verbeulen.

bun·ga·low ['bʌŋgələʊ] *s.* 'Bungalow *m*.

'**bung·hole** *s.* Spund-, Zapfloch *n*.

bun·gle ['bʌŋgl] **I** *v/i.* **1.** stümpern, pfuschen; **II** *v/t.* **2.** verpfuschen; **III** *s.* **3.** Stümpe'rei *f*; **4.** Fehler *m*, ‚Schnitzer' *m*; '**bun·gler** [-lə] *s.* Stümper *m*, Pfuscher *m*; '**bun·gling** [-lɪŋ] *adj.* □ ungeschickt, stümperhaft.

bun·ion ['bʌnjən] *s.* ⚕ entzündeter Fußballen.

bunk¹ [bʌŋk] **I** *s.* a) ⚓ (Schlaf)Koje *f*, b) Schlafstelle *f*, Bett *n*, ‚Falle' *f*: **~ bed** Etagenbett *n*; **II** *v/i.* a) in e-r Koje schlafen, b) *oft* **~ down** F ‚kampieren'.

bunk² [bʌŋk] *abbr. für* **bunkum**.

bunk³ [bʌŋk] *Brit.* F **I** *s.*: **do a ~** → **II** *v/i.* ‚ausreißen', ‚türmen'.

bunk·er ['bʌŋkə] **I** *s.* **1.** ⚓ (Kohlen)Bunker *m*; **2.** ⚔ Bunker *m*, bombensicherer 'Unterstand; **3.** *Golf*: Bunker *m* (*Hindernis*); **II** *v/t.* **4.** ⚓ bunkern; **5.** *Golf*: *Ball* in e-n Bunker schlagen; '**bunk·ered** [-əd] *adj.* F in der Klemme.

bun·kum ['bʌŋkəm] *s.* ‚Blech' *n*, Blödsinn *m*, Quatsch *m*.

bun·ny ['bʌnɪ] *s.* Häs-chen *n* (*a.* F *süßes Mädchen*).

bun·ting¹ ['bʌntɪŋ] *s.* **1.** Flaggentuch *n*; **2.** *coll.* Flaggen *pl.*

bun·ting² ['bʌntɪŋ] *s. orn.* Ammer *f*.

buoy [bɔɪ] **I** *s.* **1.** ⚓ Boje *f*, Bake *f*, Seezeichen *n*; **II** *v/t.* **2.** *a.* **~ out** *Fahrrinne* durch Bojen markieren; **3.** *mst* **~ up** flott erhalten; **4.** *fig.* Auftrieb geben (*dat.*), beleben: **~ed up** hoffnungsvoll; **buoy·an·cy** ['bɔɪənsɪ] *s.* **1.** *phys.* Schwimm-, Tragkraft *f*; **2.** ✈ Auftrieb *m* (*a. fig.*); **3.** *fig.* Schwung *m*, Spann-, Lebenskraft *f*; **buoy·ant** ['bɔɪənt] *adj.* □ **1.** schwimmend, tragend (*Wasser etc.*); **2.** *fig.* schwungvoll, lebhaft; **3.** ✝ steigend; lebhaft.

bur [bɜː] *s.* **1.** ⚘ Klette *f* (*a. fig.*): **cling to s.o. like a ~** *fig.* wie e-e Klette an j-m hängen; **2.** → **burr¹** I.

bur·ble ['bɜːbl] **I** *v/i.* **1.** brodeln, sprudeln; **2.** plappern; **II** *s.* **3.** ⚙, ✈ Wirbel *m*.

bur·bot ['bɜːbət] *s. ichth.* Quappe *f*.

bur·den¹ [bɜːdn] *s.* **1.** Re'frain *m*, Kehrreim *m*; **2.** Hauptgedanke *m*, Kern *m*.

bur·den² ['bɜːdn] **I** *s.* **1.** Last *f*, Ladung *f*; **2.** *fig.* Last *f*, Bürde *f*, (*a.* finanzi'elle) Belastung, Druck *m*: **~ of proof** ⚖ Beweislast; **~ of years** Last der Jahre; **he is a ~ on me** er fällt mir zur Last; **3.** ⚙ Traglast *f*; **4.** ⚓ Tragfähigkeit *f*, Ladung *f*; **II** *v/t.* **5.** belasten: **~ s.o. with s.th.** j-m et. aufbürden; '**bur·den·some** [-səm] *adj.* lästig, drückend.

bur·dock ['bɜːdɒk] *s.* ⚘ Große Klette.

bu·reau ['bjʊərəʊ] *pl.* **-reaus**, **-reaux** [-rəʊz] *s.* **1.** Bü'ro *n*; Geschäfts-, Amtszimmer *n*; **2.** Behörde *f*; **3.** *Brit.* Schreibpult *n*; **4.** *Am.* ('Spiegel)Komˌmode *f*; **bu·reauc·ra·cy** [bjʊə'rɒkrəsɪ] *s.* **1.** Bürokra'tie *f*; **2.** *coll.* Beamtenschaft *f*; '**bu·reau·crat** [-əʊkræt] *s.* Bü-

ro'krat *m*; **bu·reau·crat·ic** [ˌbjʊərəʊ'krætɪk] *adj.* (□ **~ally**) büro'kratisch; **bu·reauc·ra·tize** [bjʊə'rɒkrətaɪz] *v/t.* bürokratisieren.
bu·rette [bjʊə'ret] *s.* ⚗ Bü'rette *f.*
burg [bɜ:g] *s. Am.* F Stadt *f.*
bur·geon ['bɜ:dʒən] **I** *s.* ⚘ Knospe *f*; **II** *v/i.* knospen, (her'vor)sprießen (*a. fig.*).
bur·gess ['bɜ:dʒɪs] *s. hist.* **1.** Bürger *m*; **2.** Abgeordnete(r) *m.*
burgh ['bʌrə] *s. Scot.* Stadt *f* (= *Brit.* ***borough***); **burgh·er** ['bɜ:gə] *s.* **1.** (konserva'tiver) Bürger; **2.** Städter *m.*
bur·glar ['bɜ:glə] *s.* Einbrecher: ***we had ~s last night*** bei uns wurde letzte Nacht eingebrochen; **~ a·larm** *s.* A'larmanlage *f.*
bur·glar·i·ous [bɜ:'gleərɪəs] *adj.* □ Einbruchs..., einbrecherisch; **bur·glar·ize** ['bɜ:gləraɪz] → ***burgle***.
'**bur·glar-proof** *adj.* einbruchsicher.
bur·gla·ry ['bɜ:glərɪ] *s.* (nächtlicher) Einbruch; Einbruchdiebstahl *m*; **bur·gle** ['bɜ:gl] *v/t.* einbrechen in (*acc.*).
bur·go·mas·ter ['bɜ:gəʊˌmɑ:stə] *s.* Bürgermeister *m* (*in Deutschland, Holland etc.*).
bur·gun·dy ['bɜ:gəndɪ] *s. a.* **~ wine** Bur'gunder *m.*
bur·i·al ['berɪəl] *s.* **1.** Begräbnis *n*, Beerdigung *f*; **2.** Leichenfeier *f*; **3.** Ein-, Vergraben *n*; **~ ground** *s.* Begräbnisplatz *m*, Friedhof *m*; **~ mound** *s.* Grabhügel *m*; **~ place** *s.* Grabstätte *f*; **~ ser·vice** *s.* Trauerfeier *f.*
burke [bɜ:k] *v/t. fig.* a) vertuschen, b) vermeiden.
bur·lap ['bɜ:læp] *s.* Sackleinwand *f*, Rupfen *m*, Juteleinen *n.*
bur·lesque [bɜ:'lesk] **I** *adj.* **1.** bur'lesk, possenhaft; **II** *s.* **2.** Bur'leske *f*, Posse *f*; **3.** *Am.* Varie'té *n.*
bur·ly ['bɜ:lɪ] *adj.* stämmig.
Bur·man ['bɜ:mən] *s.* Bir'mane *m*, Bir'manin *f*; **Bur·mese** [ˌbɜ:'mi:z] **I** *adj.* bir'manisch; **II** *s.* a) → ***Burman***, b) Bir'manen *pl.*
burn¹ [bɜ:n] **I** *s.* **1.** verbrannte Stelle; **2.** Brandwunde *f*, -mal *n*; **II** *v/i.* [*irr.*] **3.** (ver)brennen, in Flammen stehen, in Brand geraten: ***the house is ~ing*** das Haus brennt; ***the stove ~s well*** der Ofen brennt gut; ***all the lights were ~ing*** alle Lichter brannten; **4.** *fig.* (ent)brennen, dar'auf brennen (***to*** *inf.* zu *inf.*): ***~ing with anger*** wutentbrannt; ***~ing with love*** von Liebe entflammt; **5.** an-, verbrennen, versengen: ***the meat is ~t*** das Fleisch ist angebrannt; **6.** brennen (*Gesicht, Zunge etc.*); **7.** verbrannt werden, in den Flammen 'umkommen; → 9; **III** *v/t.* [*irr.*] **8.** (ver)brennen: ***our boiler ~s coke***; ***his house was ~t*** sein Haus brannte ab; **9.** ver-, anbrennen, versengen, durch Feuer *od.* Hitze verletzen: ***~ a hole*** ein Loch brennen; ***the soup is ~t*** die Suppe ist angebrannt; ***I have ~t my fingers*** ich habe mir die Finger verbrannt (*a. fig.*); ***~ to death*** verbrennen; → 7; **10.** ⚙ *Porzellan*, (*Holz*)*Kohle*, *Ziegel* brennen; **~ down** *v/t. u. v/i.* ab-, niederbrennen; **~ out I** *v/i.* ausbrennen; ⚡ 'durchbrennen; **II** *v/t.* ausbrennen, -räuchern: ***~ o.s. out*** *fig.* sich kaputtmachen *od.* völlig verausgaben; **~ up I** *v/t.* **1.** ganz verbrennen; **2.** *Am.* F *j-n* wütend machen; **II** *v/i.* **3.** auflodern; **4.** a) ab-, aus-, verbrennen, b) verglühen (*Rakete etc.*).
burn² [bɜ:n] *s. Scot.* Bach *m.*
burn·er ['bɜ:nə] *s.* Brenner *m* (*Person u. Gerät*): ***gas-~***.
burn·ing ['bɜ:nɪŋ] *adj.* brennend, heiß, glühend (*a. fig.*): ***a ~ question*** e-e brennende Frage; **~ glass** *s.* Brennglas *n.*
bur·nish ['bɜ:nɪʃ] **I** *v/t.* **1.** polieren, blank reiben; **2.** ⚙ brünieren; **II** *v/i.* **3.** blank *od.* glatt werden; '**bur·nish·er** [-ʃə] *s.* Polierer *m*, Brünierer *m*;
bur·nouse [bɜ:'nu:z] *s.* 'Burnus *m.*
'**burn·out** *s.* **1.** ⚡ 'Durchbrennen *n*; **2.** Brennschluß *m* (*e-r Rakete*).
burnt| al·monds [bɜ:nt] *s. pl.* gebrannte Mandeln *pl.*; **~ lime** *s.* ⚙ gebrannter Kalk; **~ of·fer·ing** *s. bibl.* Brandopfer *n.*
burp [bɜ:p] **I** rülpsen, aufstoßen, ein ‚Bäuerchen' machen (*Baby*); **II** *v/t. Baby* ein ‚Bäuerchen' machen lassen.
burr¹ [bɜ:] **I** *s.* **1.** ⚙ Grat *m* (*rauhe Kante*); **2.** ⚙ Schleif-, Mühlstein *m*; **3.** ⚕ (Zahn)Bohrer *m*; **II** *v/t.* **4.** ⚙ abgraten.
burr² [bɜ:] **I** *s.* **1.** Zäpfchenaussprache *f* des R; **II** *v/t. u. v/i.* **2.** (das R) schnarren; **3.** undeutlich sprechen.
burr³ [bɜ:] → ***bur*** 1.
'**burr-drill** *s.* ⚙, ⚕ Drillbohrer *m.*
bur·row ['bʌrəʊ] **I** *s.* **1.** (*Fuchs- etc.*)Bau *m*, Höhle *f*; **II** *v/i.* **2.** sich eingraben; **3.** *fig.* sich verkriechen *od.* verbergen; sich vertiefen (***into*** in *acc.*); **III** *v/t.* **4.** *Bau* graben.
bur·sar ['bɜ:sə] *s. univ.* **1.** 'Quästor *m*, Fi'nanzverwalter *m*; **2.** Stipendi'at *m*; '**bur·sa·ry** [-ərɪ] *s. univ.* **1.** Quä'stur *f*; **2.** Sti'pendium *n.*
bur·si·tis [bɜ:'saɪtɪs] *s.* ⚕ Schleimbeutelentzündung *f.*
burst [bɜ:st] **I** *v/i.* [*irr.*] **1.** bersten, (auf-*od.* zer)platzen, (auf-, zer)springen; explodieren; sich entladen (*Gewitter*); aufspringen (*Knospe*); aufgehen (*Geschwür*): ***~ open*** aufplatzen, -springen; **2.** **~ *in* (*out*)** herein-(hinaus)stürmen: ***~ in (up)on*** a) hereinplatzen bei *j-m*, b) sich einmischen in (*acc.*); **3.** *fig.* ausbrechen, her'ausplatzen: ***~ into tears*** in Tränen ausbrechen; ***~ into laughter***, ***~ out laughing*** in Gelächter ausbrechen; ***~ out*** herausplatzen (*sagen*); **4.** *fig.* platzen, bersten (***with*** vor *dat.*); gespannt sein, brennen: ***~ with envy*** vor Neid platzen; ***I am ~ing to tell you*** ich brenne darauf, es dir zu sagen; **5.** zum Bersten voll sein (***with*** von): ***a larder ~ing with food***; ***~ with health (energy)*** vor Gesundheit (Kraft) strotzen; **6.** *a.* ***~ up*** zs.-brechen, bank'rott gehen; **7.** plötzlich sichtbar werden: ***~ into view***; ***~ forth*** hervorbrechen, -sprudeln; ***~ upon s.o.*** j-m plötzlich klarwerden; **II** *v/t.* [*irr.*] **8.** sprengen, auf-, zerbrechen, zum Platzen bringen (*a. fig.*): ***~ open*** sprengen, aufbrechen; ***I have ~ a bloodvessel*** mir ist e-e Ader geplatzt; ***the river ~ its banks*** a) der Fluß trat über die Ufer, b) der Fluß durchbrach die Dämme; ***the car ~ a tyre*** ein Reifen am Wagen platzte; ***~ one's sides with laughter*** sich vor Lachen ausschütten; **9.** *fig.* zum Scheitern bringen, auffliegen lassen, ruinieren; **III** *s.* **10.** Bersten *n*, Platzen *n*, Explosi'on *f*; ⚔ Feuerstoß *m* (*Maschinengewehr*); Auffliegen *n*, Ausbruch *m*: ***~ of laughter*** Lachsalve *f*; ***~ of applause*** Beifallssturm *m*; ***~ of hospitality*** plötzliche Anwandlung von Gastfreundschaft; **11.** Bruch *m*, Riß *m*, Sprung *m* (*a. fig.*); **12.** plötzliches Erscheinen; **13.** *sport* (Zwischen)Spurt *m.*
'**burst-up** *s. sl.* **1.** Bank'rott *m*, Zs.-bruch *m*, Pleite *f*; **2.** Krach *m*, Streit *m*; **3.** Saufe'rei *f.*
bur·y ['berɪ] *v/t.* **1.** begraben, beerdigen; **2.** ein-, vergraben, verschütten, versenken (*a. fig.*): ***buried cable*** ⚙ Erdkabel *n*; **3.** verbergen; **4.** *fig.* begraben, vergessen; **5.** ***~ o.s.*** sich verkriechen; *fig.* sich vertiefen.
bus [bʌs] **I** *pl.* '**bus·es** [-sɪz] *s.* **1.** Omnibus *m*, (Auto)Bus *m*: ***miss the ~*** F den Anschluß (*Gelegenheit*) verpassen; **2.** *sl.* ‚Kiste' *f* (*Auto od. Flugzeug*); **II** *v/i.* **3.** *a.* ***~ it*** mit dem Omnibus fahren; **III** *v/t.* **4.** mit dem Bus transportieren; **~ bar** *s.* ⚡ Sammel-, Stromschiene *f*; **~ boy** *s. Am.* 'Pikkolo *m*, Hilfskellner *m.*
bus·by ['bʌzbɪ] *s.* ⚔ Bärenmütze *f.*
bush¹ [bʊʃ] *s.* **1.** Busch *m*, Strauch *m*: ***beat about the ~*** *fig.* wie die Katze um den heißen Brei herumgehen, um die Sache herumreden; **2.** Gebüsch *n*, Dikkicht *n*; **3.** Busch *m*, Urwald *m*; **4.** (Haar)Schopf *m.*
bush² [bʊʃ] *s.* ⚙ Lagerfutter *n.*
bushed [bʊʃt] *adj.* ‚erledigt', erschöpft.
bush·el¹ ['bʊʃl] *s.* Scheffel *m* (*36,37 l*); → ***light¹*** 1.
bush·el² ['bʊʃl] *v/t. Am. Kleidung* ausbessern, flicken, ändern.
'**bush|-ˌfight·er** *s.* Gue'rillakämpfer *m*; **~ league** *s. bsd. Baseball*: *Am.* F a) untere Spielklasse, b) Pro'vinzliga *f*; '**~-league** *adj. Am.* F Schmalspur...; Provinz...; '**~·man** [-mən] *s.* [*irr.*] **1.** Buschmann *m*; **2.** 'Hinterwäldler *m.*
bush·y ['bʊʃɪ] *adj.* buschig.
busi·ness ['bɪznɪs] *s.* **1.** Geschäft *n*, Tätigkeit *f*, Arbeit *f*, Beruf *m*, Gewerbe *n*: ***what is his ~?*** was ist er von Beruf?; → *a.* 5; ***on ~*** beruflich, geschäftlich; ***~ of the day*** Tagesordnung *f*; **2.** a) Handel *m*, Kaufmannsberuf *m*, Geschäftsleben *n*, b) *a.* ***~ activity*** Ge'schäftsvoˌlumen *n*, 'Umsatz *m*: ***go into ~*** Kaufmann werden; ***be in ~*** Kaufmann sein; ***go out of ~*** das Geschäft *od.* den Beruf aufgeben; ***do good ~ (with)*** gute Geschäfte machen (mit); ***lose ~*** Kundschaft *od.* Aufträge verlieren; ***~ as usual!*** nichts Besonderes!; → ***big*** 1; **3.** Geschäft *n*, Firma *f*, Unter'nehmen *n*, Laden *m*, Ge'schäftsloˌkal *n*; **4.** Aufgabe *f*, Pflicht *f*; Recht *n*: ***make it one's ~ (to*** *inf.*) es sich zur Aufgabe machen (zu *inf.*); ***have no ~ (to*** *inf.*) kein Recht haben (zu *inf.*); ***what ~ had you (to*** *inf.*)***?*** wie kamst du dazu (zu *inf.*)?; ***send s.o. about his ~*** j-m heimleuchten; ***he means ~*** er meint es ernst; **5.** Sache *f*, Angelegenheit *f*: ***that is none of your ~*** das geht dich nichts an; ***mind your own ~*** kümmere dich um d-e eigenen Angelegenheiten; ***what is your ~?*** was ist dein Anliegen?; → *a.* 1; ***what a ~ it is!*** das ist ja e-e schreckliche Geschich-

te!; ***like nobody's ~*** F ‚wie nichts', ‚ganz toll'; ***get down to ~*** zur Sache kommen; **~ ad·dress** *s.* Ge'schäfts-a‚dresse *f*; **~ ad·min·is·tra·tion** → ***business economics***; **~ al·low·ance** *s.* Werbungskosten *pl.*; **~ cap·i·tal** *s.* Be'triebskapi‚tal *n*; **~ card** *s.* Geschäftskarte *f*; **~ col·lege** *s.* Wirtschaftsoberschule *f*; **~ con·sult·ant** *s.* Betriebsberater *m*; **~ cy·cle** *s.* Konjunk'tur(zyklus *m*) *f*; **~ e·co·nom·ics** *s. pl. sg. konstr. Brit.* Betriebswirtschaft (-slehre) *f*; **~ end** *s.* F wesentlicher Teil, *z.B.* Spitze *f e-s Bohrers od. Dolches,* Mündung *f e-s Gewehres*; **~ hours** *s. pl.* Geschäftsstunden *pl.*, -zeit *f*; **~ let·ter** *s.* Geschäftsbrief *m*; **'~·like** *adj.* **1.** geschäftsmäßig, sachlich, nüchtern; **2.** (geschäfts)tüchtig; **~ lunch** *s.* Arbeitsessen *n*; **'~·man** *s.* [*irr.*] Geschäfts-, Kaufmann *m*; **~ prac·tic·es** *s. pl.* Geschäftsmethoden *pl.*, -gebaren *n*; **~ prem·is·es** *s. pl.* Geschäftsräume *pl.*; **~ re·search** *s.* Konjunk'turforschung *f*; **~ suit** *Am.* → ***lounge suit***; **~ trip** *s.* Geschäfts-, Dienstreise *f*; **'~‚wom·an** *s.* [*irr.*] Geschäftsfrau *f*; **~ year** *s.* Geschäftsjahr *n*.

busk¹ [bʌsk] *s.* Kor'settstäbchen *n*.

busk² [bʌsk] *v/i. Brit.* F auf der Straße musizieren *etc.*; **'busk·er** [-kə] *s. Brit.* 'Straßenmusi‚kant *m od.* -akro‚bat *m*.

bus·kin ['bʌskɪn] *s.* **1.** Halbstiefel *m*; **2.** Ko'thurn *m*; **3.** *fig.* Tra'gödie *f*.

'bus·man [-mən] *s.* [*irr.*] Omnibusfahrer *m*: ***~'s holiday*** mit der üblichen Berufsarbeit verbrachter Urlaub.

bus·sing ['bʌsɪŋ] *s. Am. Beförderung von Schülern mit Bussen in andere Schulen, um Rassenintegration zu erreichen.*

bust¹ [bʌst] *s.* Büste *f*: a) Brustbild *n*, Kopf *m* (*aus Marmor, Bronze etc.*), b) *anat.* Busen *m*.

bust² [bʌst] *sl.* **I** *v/i.* **1.** *oft* ***~ up*** ‚ka'puttgehen', ‚eingehen', ✝ *a.* ‚pleite' gehen; **2.** ‚auffliegen', ‚platzen'; **II** *v/t.* **3.** ‚ka'puttmachen': a) sprengen, b) ruinieren; **4.** ‚auffliegen' lassen, zerschlagen; **5.** *Am.* ‚knallen', hauen; **6.** einbrechen in (*acc.*); **7.** einsperren; **8.** ⚔ degradieren; **III** *s.* **9.** Sauftour *f*: ***go on the ~*** ‚einen draufmachen'; **10.** ‚Pleite' *f*, Bank'rott *m*; **11.** Razzia *f*; **IV** *adv.* **12.** ***go ~*** → 1.

bus·tard ['bʌstəd] *s. orn.* Trappe *f*.

bust·er ['bʌstə] *s.* **1.** *sl.* a) ‚Mordsding' *n*, b) Kerl *m*, Bursche *m*, ‚Kumpel' *m*; **2.** *in Zssgn* …knacker *m*: ***safe ~*** Geldschrankknacker; **3.** → ***bust²*** 9.

bus·tle¹ ['bʌsl] *s. hist.* Tur'nüre *f*.

bus·tle² ['bʌsl] **I** *v/i. a.* ***~ about*** geschäftig hin u. her rennen, ‚her'umfuhrwerken', hasten, sich tummeln; **II** *v/t.* ***~ up*** hetzen; **III** *s.* Geschäftigkeit *f*, geschäftiges Treiben, Getriebe *n*, Gewühl *n*; Gehetze *n*; Getue *n*; **'bus·tler** [-lə] *s.* geschäftiger Mensch; **'bus·tling** [-lɪŋ] *adj.* geschäftig.

'bust-up *s.* F ‚Krach' *m*.

bus·y ['bɪzɪ] **I** *adj.* □ **1.** beschäftigt, tätig: ***be ~ packing*** mit Packen beschäftigt sein; ***get ~*** F sich ‚ranmachen'; **2.** geschäftig, rührig, fleißig: ***as ~ as a bee*** bienenfleißig; **3.** belebt (*Straße etc.*); ereignis-, arbeitsreich (*Zeit*); **4.** auf-, zudringlich; **5.** *teleph. Am.* besetzt (*Leitung*): ***~ signal*** Besetztzeichen *n*; **II** *v/t.* **6.** (***o.s.*** sich) beschäftigen (***with, in, at, about*** *ger.* mit); **'~‚bod·y** *s.* ‚Gschaftlhuber' *m*, 'Übereifrige(r) *m*, Wichtigtuer *m*.

bus·y·ness ['bɪzɪnɪs] *s.* Geschäftigkeit *f*.

but [bʌt; bət] **I** *cj.* **1.** aber, je'doch, sondern: ***small ~ select*** klein, aber fein; ***I wished to go ~ I couldn't*** ich wollte gehen, aber ich konnte nicht; ***not only … ~ also*** nicht nur …, sondern auch; **2.** außer, als: ***what could I do ~ refuse*** was blieb mir übrig, als abzulehnen; ***he couldn't ~ laugh*** er mußte einfach lachen; **3.** ohne daß: ***justice was never done ~ someone complained***; **4.** ***~ that*** a) wenn nicht: ***I would do it ~ that I am busy***, b) daß: ***you cannot deny ~ that it was you***, c) daß nicht: ***I am not so stupid ~ that I can learn it*** ich bin nicht so dumm, daß ich es nicht lernen könnte; **5.** ***~ then*** andererseits, immer'hin; **6.** ***~ yet, ~ for all that*** (aber) trotzdem; **II** *prp.* **7.** außer: ***~ that*** außer daß; ***all ~ me*** alle außer mir; → 13; ***anything ~ clever*** alles andere als klug: ***the last ~ one*** der vorletzte; ***the last ~ two*** der drittletzte; **8.** ***~ for*** ohne, wenn nicht: ***~ for the war*** ohne den Krieg, wenn der Krieg nicht (gewesen *od.* gekommen) wäre; **III** *adv.* **9.** nur, bloß: ***~ a child***; ***I did ~ glance*** ich blickte nur flüchtig hin; ***~ once*** nur 'einmal; **10.** erst, gerade: ***he left ~ an hour ago***; **11.** immerhin, wenigstens: ***you can ~ try***; **12.** ***nothing ~, none ~*** nur; **13.** ***all ~*** fast: ***he all ~ died*** er wäre fast gestorben; → 7; **IV** *neg. rel. pron.* **14.** ***few of them ~ rejoiced*** es gab wenige, die sich nicht freuten; **V** *s.* **15.** Aber *n*; → ***if*** 5.

bu·tane ['bju:teɪn] *s.* ⚗ Bu'tan *n*.

butch·er ['bʊtʃə] **I** *s.* **1.** Fleischer *m*, Schlachter *m*, Metzger *m*: ***~'s meat*** Schlachtfleisch *n*; **2.** *fig.* Mörder *m*, Schlächter *m*; **3.** 🚃 *Am.* (Süßwaren- *etc.*)Verkäufer *m*; **II** *v/t.* **4.** schlachten; **5.** *fig.* morden, abschlachten; **'butch·er·ly** [-lɪ] *adj.* blutdürstig; **'butch·er·y** [-ərɪ] *s.* **1.** Schlachterhandwerk *n*; **2.** Schlachthaus *n*, -hof *m*; **3.** *fig.* Gemetzel *n*.

but·ler ['bʌtlə] *s.* **1.** Butler *m*; **2.** Kellermeister *m*.

butt [bʌt] **I** *s.* **1.** (dickes) Ende (*e-s Werkzeugs etc.*); **2.** (*Gewehr*)Kolben *m*; **3.** (*Zigaretten- etc.*)Stummel *m*; **4.** ⚘ unteres Ende (*von Stiel od. Stamm*); **5.** ⚙ Stoß *m*; → ***butt joint***; **6.** ⚔ Kugelfang *m*; *pl.* Schießstand *m*; **7.** *fig.* Zielscheibe *f* (*des Spottes etc.*); **8.** (Kopf- *etc.*)Stoß *m*; **9.** *sl.* ‚Hintern' *m*; **II** *v/t.* **10.** (*bsd.* mit dem Kopf) stoßen; **11.** ⚙ anein'anderfügen; **III** *v/i.* **12.** (an-) stoßen, angrenzen (***on, against*** an *acc.*); **13.** ***~ in*** F sich einmischen: ***~ in on, ~ into*** sich einmischen in (*acc.*); **~ end** *s.* **1.** (Gewehr)Kolben *m*; **2.** dickes Endstück; Ende *n*.

but·ter ['bʌtə] **I** *s.* **1.** Butter *f*: ***melted ~*** zerlassene Butter; ***he looks as if ~ would not melt in his mouth*** er sieht aus, als könnte er nicht bis drei zählen; **2.** (*Erdnuß-, Kakao- etc.*)Butter *f*; **3.** F ‚Schmus' *m*, Schmeiche'lei(en *pl.*) *f*; **II** *v/t.* **4.** mit Butter bestreichen *od.* zubereiten; **5.** ***~ up*** F *j-n* ‚einwickeln', *j-m* schmeicheln; **~ bean** *s.* ⚘ Wachsbohne *f*; **~ churn** *s.* Butterfaß *n* (*zum Buttern*); **'~·cup** *s.* ⚘ Butterblume *f*; **~ dish** *s.* Butterdose *f*; **'~‚fin·gers** *s. pl. sg. konstr.* F Tolpatsch *m*, ‚Tapps' *m*.

but·ter·fly ['bʌtəflaɪ] *s.* **1.** *zo.* Schmetterling *m* (*a. fig. flatterhafter Mensch*); **2.** *sport a.* ***~ stroke*** Schmetterlingsstil *m*; **~ nut** *s.* ⚙ Flügelmutter *f*; **~ valve** *s.* ⚙ Drosselklappe *f*.

but·ter·ine ['bʌtəri:n] *s.* Kunstbutter *f*.

'but·ter|·milk *s.* Buttermilch *f*; **'~·scotch** *s.* Kara'melbon‚bon *m, n*.

but·ter·y ['bʌtərɪ] **I** *adj.* **1.** butterartig, Butter…; **2.** F schmeichlerisch; **II** *s.* **3.** Speisekammer *f*; **4.** *Brit. univ.* Kan'tine *f*.

butt joint *s.* ⚙ Stoßfuge *f*, -verbindung *f*.

but·tock ['bʌtək] *s.* **1.** *anat.* 'Hinterbacke *f*; *mst pl.* 'Hinterteil *n*, Gesäß *n*; **2.** *Ringen*: Hüftschwung *m*.

but·ton ['bʌtn] **I** *s.* **1.** (Kleider)Knopf *m*: ***not worth a ~*** keinen Pfifferling wert; ***not to care a ~ (about)*** F sich nichts machen (aus); ***a ~ short*** F ‚leicht beknackt'; (***boy in***) ***~s*** (Hotel)Page *m*; ***take by the ~*** a) *j-n* fest-, aufhalten, b) sich *j-n* vorknöpfen; **2.** (*Klingel-, Licht- etc.*)Knopf *m*; → ***press*** 2; **3.** Knopf *m* (*Gegenstand*), *z.B.* a) Abzeichen *n*, Pla'kette *f*, b) (Mikro'phon)Kapsel *f*; **4.** ⚘ Knospe *f*, Auge *n*; **5.** *sport sl.* ‚Punkt' *m*, Kinnspitze *f*; **II** *v/t.* **6.** *a.* ***~ up*** (zu-) knöpfen: ***~ one's mouth*** den Mund halten; ***~ed up*** *fig.* a) ‚zugeknöpft' (*Person*), b) ‚in der Tasche', unter Dach und Fach (*Sache*); **III** *v/i.* **7.** sich knöpfen lassen, geknöpft werden; **'~·hole I** *s.* **1.** Knopfloch *n*; **2.** *Brit.* Knopflochsträußchen *n*, Blume *f* im Knopfloch; **II** *v/t.* **3.** *j-n* festhalten (u. auf ihn einreden); **4.** mit Knopflöchern versehen.

but·tress ['bʌtrɪs] **I** *s.* **1.** ⚠ Strebepfeiler *m*, -bogen *m*; **2.** Stütze *f* (*a. fig.*); **II** *v/t. a.* ***~ up*** **3.** (durch Strebepfeiler) stützen; **4.** *fig.* stützen.

'butt-weld *v/t.* ⚙ stumpfschweißen.

bu·tyl ['bju:tɪl] *s.* ⚗ Bu'tyl *n*.

bu·tyr·ic [bju:'tɪrɪk] *adj.* ⚗ Butter…

bux·om ['bʌksəm] *adj.* drall.

buy [baɪ] **I** *s.* **1.** F Kauf *m*, *das* Gekaufte: ***a good ~*** ein günstiger Kauf; **II** *v/t.* [*irr.*] **2.** (an-, ein)kaufen (***of, from*** von, ***at*** bei): ***money cannot ~ it*** es ist für Geld nicht zu haben; ***~ing power*** (überschüssige) Kaufkraft; **3.** *fig.* erkaufen: ***dearly bought*** teuer erkauft; **4.** *j-n* kaufen, bestechen; **5.** loskaufen, auslösen; **6.** *Am. sl. et.* ‚abkaufen', glauben; **7.** ***~ it*** *Brit. sl.* ‚dran glauben müssen'; **III** *v/i.* [*irr.*] **8.** kaufen; **9.** ***~ into*** ✝ sich einkaufen in (*acc.*);

Zssgn mit adv.:

buy| in *v/t.* **1.** sich eindecken mit; **2.** (*auf Auktionen*) zu'rückkaufen; **3.** ***buy o.s. in*** ✝ sich einkaufen; **~ off** *v/t.* → ***buy*** 4; **~ out** *v/t.* **1.** *Teilhaber etc.* auszahlen, abfinden; **2.** *Firma etc.* aufkaufen; **~ o·ver** *v/t.* → ***buy*** 4; **~ up** *v/t.* aufkaufen.

buy·er ['baɪə] *s.* **1.** Käufer(in), Abnehmer(in): ***~-up*** Aufkäufer; ***~s' market*** ✝ Käufermarkt *m*; ***~s' strike*** Käuferstreik *m*; **2.** ✝ Einkäufer(in).

buy-out ['baɪaʊt] *s. a.* ***management ~***

Aufkauf *m* e-r Firma durch deren Manager (*der so neuer Eigentümer wird*).

buzz [bʌz] **I** *v/i.* **1.** summen, brummen, surren, schwirren: **~ *about*** (*od.* ***around***) herumschwirren (*a. fig.*); **~*ing with excitement*** in heller Aufregung; **~ *off*** *sl.* ‚abschwirren', ‚abhauen'; **2.** säuseln, sausen; **3.** murmeln, durcheinˈanderreden; **II** *v/t.* **4.** F a) *j-n* mit dem Summer rufen, b) *teleph. j-n* anrufen; **5.** ✈ a) in geringer Höhe überˈfliegen, b) (bedrohlich) anfliegen; **III** *s.* **6.** Summen *n*, Brummen *n*, Schwirren *n*; **7.** Stimmengewirr *n*; **8.** Gerücht *n*.

buz·zard [ˈbʌzəd] *s. orn.* Bussard *m*.

buzz·er [ˈbʌzə] *s.* **1.** Summer *m*, *bsd.* summendes Inˈsekt; **2.** Summer *m*, Summpfeife *f*; **3.** ϟ Summer *m*; **4.** ⚔ a) ˈFeldteleˌgraph *m*, b) *sl.* Telegraˈphist *m*; **5.** *Am. sl.* Poliˈzeimarke *f*.

buzz saw *s. Am.* Kreissäge *f*.

by [baɪ] **I** *prp.* **1.** (*Raum*) (nahe) bei *od.* an (*dat.*), neben (*dat.*): **~ *the window*** beim *od.* am Fenster; **2.** durch (*acc.*), über (*acc.*), via, an (*dat.*) … entlang *od.* vorˈbei: ***he came ~ Park Road*** er kam über *od.* durch die Parkstraße; ***we drove ~ the park*** wir fuhren am Park entlang; **~ *land*** zu Lande; **3.** (*Zeit*) während, bei: **~ *day*** bei Tage; ***day ~ day*** Tag für Tag; **~ *lamplight*** bei Lampenlicht; **4.** bis (zu *od.* um *od.* spätestens): ***be here ~ 4.30*** sei um 4 Uhr 30 hier; **~ *the allotted time*** bis zum festgesetzten Zeitpunkt; **~ *now*** nunmehr, inzwischen, schon; **5.** (*Urheber*) von, durch: ***a book ~ Shaw*** ein Buch von Shaw; ***settled ~ him*** durch ihn *od.* von ihm geregelt; **~ *nature*** von Natur (aus); **~ *oneself*** aus eigener Kraft, selbst, allein; **6.** (*Mittel*) durch, mit, vermittels: **~ *listening*** durch Zuhören; ***driven ~ steam*** mit Dampf betrieben; **~ *rail*** per Bahn; **~ *letter*** brieflich; **7.** gemäß, nach: **~ *my watch it is now ten*** nach m-r Uhr ist es jetzt zehn; **8.** (*Menge*) um, nach: ***too short ~ an inch*** um einen Zoll zu kurz; ***sold ~ the metre*** meterweise verkauft; **9.** A a) mal: ***3*** (***multiplied***) **~ *4***; ***the size is 9 feet ~ 6*** die Größe ist 9 mal 6 Fuß, b) durch: ***6*** (***divided***) **~ *2***; **10. ~ *the way*** *od.* **~ *the ~*(*e*)** übrigens; **II** *adv.* **11.** daˈbei: ***close ~, hard ~*** dicht dabei; **12. ~ *and large*** im großen u. ganzen; **~ *and ~*** demnächst, nach u. nach; **13.** vorˈbei, -ˈüber: ***pass ~*** vorübergehen; **14.** beiˈseite: ***put ~***.

by- [baɪ] *Vorsilbe* **1.** Neben…, Seiten…; **2.** geheim.

bye [baɪ] **I** *s. sport* a) *Kricket*: durch einen vorˈbeigelassenen Ball ausgelöster Lauf, b) Freilos *n*: ***draw a ~*** ein Freilos ziehen; **II** *adj.* ˈuntergeordnet, Neben…

bye- → ***by-***.

bye-bye **I** *s.* [ˈbaɪbaɪ] *Kindersprache*: ‚Heia' *f*, Bett *n*, Schlaf *m*; **II** *int.* [ˌbaɪˈbaɪ] F Wiedersehen!, Tschüs!

ˈbye-law → ***bylaw***.

ˈby|-eˌlec·tion *s.* Ersatz-, Nachwahl *f*; **ˈ~·gone I** *adj.* vergangen; **II** *s. das* Vergangene: ***let ~s be ~s*** laß(t) das Vergangene ruhen; **ˈ~·law** *s.* **1.** Gemeindeverordnung *f*, -satzung *f*; **2.** *pl.* Staˈtuten *pl.*, Satzung *f*; **3.** ˈDurchführungsverordnung *f*; **ˈ~·line** *s.* **1.** 🚆 ˈNebenˌlinie *f*; **2.** Verfasserangabe *f* (*unter der Überschrift e-s Zeitungsartikels*); **3.** Nebenbeschäftigung *f*; **ˈ~·name** *s.* **1.** Beiname *m*; **2.** Spitzname *m*; **ˈ~·pass I** *s.* **1.** ˈUmleitung *f*, Umˈgehungsstraße *f*; **2.** Nebenleitung *f*; **3.** *Gasbrenner*: Dauerflamme *f*; **4.** ϟ Nebenschluß *m*; **5.** ⚕ Bypass *m*; **II** *v/t.* **6.** ˈumleiten; **7.** umˈgehen (*a. fig.*); **8.** vermeiden, überˈgehen; **ˈ~·path** *s.* Seitenweg *m* (*a. fig.*); **ˈ~·play** *s. thea.* Nebenhandlung *f*; **ˈ~-ˌprod·uct** *s.* ˈNebenproˌdukt *n*, *fig. a.* Nebenerscheinung *f*.

byre [ˈbaɪə] *s. Brit.* Kuhstall *m*.

ˈby|·road *s.* Seiten-, Nebenstraße *f*; **ˈ~ˌstand·er** *s.* Zuschauer(in); **ˈ~·street** → ***byroad***.

byte [baɪt] *s. Computer*: Byte *n*.

ˈby|·way *s.* **1.** Seiten-, Nebenweg *m*; **2.** *fig.* ˈNebenasˌpekt *m*; **ˈ~·word** *s.* **1.** Sprichwort *n*; **2.** (***for***) Inbegriff *m* (*gen.*), Musterbeispiel *n* (für); **3.** Schlagwort *n*.

By·zan·tine [bɪˈzæntaɪn] *adj.* byzanˈtinisch.

C

C, c [siː] *s.* **1.** C *n*, c *n* (*Buchstabe*); **2.** ♪ C *n*, c *n* (*Note*); **3.** *ped. Am.* Drei *f*, Befriedigend *n* (*Note*); **4.** *Am. sl.* ‚Hunderter' *m* (*Banknote*).

cab [kæb] **I** *s.* **1.** a) Droschke *f*, b) Taxi *n*; **2.** a) 🚂 Führerstand *m*, b) Führersitz *m* (*Lastauto*), c) Lenkerhäus-chen *n* (*Kran*); **II** *v/i.* **3.** mit e-r Droschke *od.* e-m Taxi fahren.

ca·bal [kəˈbæl] **I** *s.* **1.** Kaˈbale *f*, Inˈtrige *f*; **2.** Clique *f*, Klüngel *m*; **II** *v/i.* **3.** intrigieren, Ränke schmieden, sich verschwören.

cab·a·ret [ˈkæbəreɪ] *s.* **1.** (*a. politisches*) Kabaˈrett, Kleinkunstbühne *f*: ~ ***performer*** Kabarettist(in); **2.** Restauˈrant *n od.* Nachtklub *m* mit Varieˈtédarbietungen.

cab·bage [ˈkæbɪdʒ] *s.* ⚘ **1.** Kohl(pflanze *f*) *m*: ***become a*** ~ F verblöden, dahinvegetieren; **2.** Kohlkopf *m*; ~ **but·ter·fly** *s. zo.* Kohlweißling *m*; ˈ**~·head** *s.* **1.** Kohlkopf *m*; **2.** F Dummkopf *m*; ˈ**~·white** → ***cabbage butterfly***.

ca(b)·ba·la [kəˈbɑːlə] *s.* ˈKabbala *f*, Geheimlehre *f* (*a. fig.*).

cab·by [ˈkæbɪ] F → ***cab driver***.

cab driv·er *s.* **1.** Droschkenkutscher *m*; **2.** Taxifahrer *m*.

ca·ber [ˈkeɪbə] *s. Scot.* Baumstamm *m*: ***tossing the*** ~ Baumstammwerfen *n*.

cab·in [ˈkæbɪn] *s.* **1.** Häus-chen *n*, Hütte *f*; **2.** ⚓ Kaˈbine *f*, Kaˈjüte *f*; **3.** ✈ Kaˈbine *f*: a) Fluggastraum *m*, b) Kanzel *f*; **4.** *Brit.* 🚂 Stellwerk *n*; ~ **boy** *s.* ⚓ Kaˈbinenˌsteward *m*; ~ **class** *s.* ⚓ Kaˈjütenklasse *f*; ~ **cruis·er** *s.* Kaˈbinenkreuzer *m*.

cab·i·net [ˈkæbɪnɪt] *s.* **1.** *oft* ♀ *pol.* Kabiˈnett *n*: ~ ***council***, ~ ***meeting*** Kabinettssitzung *f*; ~ ***crisis*** Regierungskrise *f*; **2.** (Schau-, Sammlungs-, *a.* Büˈro-, Karˈtei- *etc.*)Schrank *m*, (Wand-)Schränkchen *n*, Viˈtrine *f*; **3.** *Radio etc.*: Gehäuse *n*; **4.** *phot.* Kabiˈnettforˌmat *n*; ˈ**~ˌmak·er** *s.* **1.** Kunsttischler *m*; **2.** *humor.* Miˈnisterpräsiˌdent *m* bei der Regierungsbildung; ˈ**~ˌmak·ing** *s.* ˈKunsttischleˌrei *f*; ♀ **Min·is·ter** *s. pol.* Kabiˈnettsmiˌnister *m*; ~ **size** → ***cabinet*** 4.

cab·in scoot·er *s. mot.* Kaˈbinenroller *m*.

ca·ble [ˈkeɪbl] **I** *s.* **1.** Kabel *n*, Tau *n*, (Draht)Seil *n*; **2.** ⚓ Trosse *f*, Ankertau *n*, -kette *f*; **3.** ϟ (Leitungs)Kabel *n*; **4.** → ***cablegram***; **II** *v/t. u. v/i.* **5.** kabeln, telegraphieren; ~ **car** *Seilbahn*: a) Kaˈbine *f*, b) Wagen *m*; ˈ**~·cast I** *v/t.* [*irr.* → ***cast***] per Kabelfernsehen überˈtragen; **II** *s.* Sendung *f* im Kabelfernsehen.

ca·ble·gram [ˈkeɪblgræm] *s.* Kabel *n*, (ˈÜbersee)Teleˌgramm *n*.

ca·ble rail·way *s.* **1.** Drahtseilbahn *f*; **2.** *Am.* Drahtseil-Straßenbahn *f*.

ca·blese [keɪˈbliːz] *s.* Teleˈgrammstil *m*.

ˈ**ca·ble's-length** [ˈkeɪblz-] *s.* ⚓ Kabellänge *f* (*100 Faden*).

ca·ble| tel·e·vi·sion *s.* Kabelfernsehen *n*; ˈ**~·way** *s.* Drahtseilbahn *f*.

ˈ**cab·man** [-mən] *s.* [*irr.*] → ***cab driver***.

ca·boo·dle [kəˈbuːdl] *s. sl.*: ***the whole*** ~ a) der ganze Klimbim, b) die ganze Sippschaft.

ca·boose [kəˈbuːs] *s.* **1.** ⚓ Komˈbüse *f*, Schiffsküche *f*; **2.** 🚂 *Am.* Dienst-, Bremswagen *m*.

cab rank *s. Brit.* Taxi-, Droschkenstand *m*.

cab·ri·o·let [ˈkæbrɪəleɪ] *s. a. mot.* Kabrioˈlett *n*.

ca'can·ny [ˌkɑːˈkænɪ] *s. Scot.* ✝ Bummelstreik *m*.

ca·ca·o [kəˈkɑːəʊ] *s.* **1.** ⚘ *a.* ***~-tree*** Kaˈkaobaum *m*; **2.** Kaˈkaobohnen *pl.*; ~ **bean** *s.* Kaˈkaobohne *f*; ~ **but·ter** *s.* Kaˈkaobutter *f*.

cache [kæʃ] **I** *s.* geheimes (Waffen- *od.* Proviˈant- *etc.*)Lager, Versteck *n*; **II** *v/t.* verstecken.

ca·chet [ˈkæʃeɪ] *s.* **1.** a) Siegel *n*, b) *fig.* Stempel *m*, Merkmal *n*; **2.** ⚕ Kapsel *f*.

cack·le [ˈkækl] **I** *v/i.* gackern (*a. fig. lachen*), schnattern (*a. fig. schwatzen*); **II** *s.* (*a. fig.*) Gegacker *n*, Geschnatter *n*: ***cut the ~!*** F quatsch nicht!

ca·coph·o·nous [kæˈkɒfənəs] *adj.* ˈmißtönend; **caˈcoph·o·ny** [-nɪ] *s.* Kakophoˈnie *f* (*Mißklang*).

cac·tus [ˈkæktəs] *pl.* **-ti** [-taɪ], **-tus·es** *s.* ⚘ ˈKaktus *m*.

cad [kæd] *s.* **1.** ordiˈnärer Kerl; **2.** gemeiner Kerl.

ca·das·tral [kəˈdæstrəl] *adj.*: ~ ***survey*** Katasteraufnahme *f*.

ca·dav·er·ous [kəˈdævərəs] *adj.* leichenhaft.

cad·die [ˈkædɪ] *s.* a) ˈCaddie *m* (*Golfjunge*), b) → ˈ**~-cart** *s.* ˈCaddie *m* (*Golfschlägerwagen*).

cad·dish [ˈkædɪʃ] *adj.* **1.** proˈletenhaft, **2.** gemein, niederträchtig.

cad·dy[1] → ***caddie***.

cad·dy[2] [ˈkædɪ] *s.* Teedose *f*; ~ **spoon** *s.* Tee-, Meßlöffel *m*.

ca·dence [ˈkeɪdəns] *s.* **1.** (ˈVers-, ˈSprech)ˌRhythmus *m*; **2.** ♪ Kaˈdenz *f*; **3.** Tonfall *m* (*am Satzende*); ˈ**ca·denced** [-st] *adj.* ˈrhythmisch.

ca·det [kəˈdet] *s.* **1.** ⚔ Kaˈdett *m*; **2.** (Poliˈzei- *etc.*)Schüler *m*; **3.** jüngerer Sohn *od.* Bruder; **4.** *in Zssgn a.* Nachwuchs…: ~ ***researcher***; ~ ***nurse*** Lernschwester *f*.

cadge [kædʒ] *v/i. u. v/t.* ‚schnorren'; ˈ**cadg·er** [-dʒə] *s.* ‚Schnorrer' *m*, ‚Nassauer' *m*.

ca·di [ˈkɑːdɪ] *s.* Kadi *m*, Bezirksrichter *m* (*im Orient*).

cad·mi·um [ˈkædmɪəm] *s.* ⚗ ˈKadmium *n*; ˈ**~-ˌplate** *v/t.* ⚙ kadmieren.

ca·dre [ˈkɑːdə] *s.* **1.** Kader *m*: a) ⚔ (Truppen)Stamm *m*, b) *pol.* Führungsgruppe *f*, c) ˈRahmenorganisatiˌon *f*; **2.** *fig.* Grundstock *m*.

ca·du·ce·us [kəˈdjuːsjəs] *pl.* **-ce·i** [-sjaɪ] *s.* Merˈkurstab *m* (*a. ärztliches Abzeichen*).

cae·cum [ˈsiːkəm] *s. anat.* Blinddarm *m*.

Cae·sar [ˈsiːzə] *s.* **1.** ˈCäsar *m* (*Titel römischer Kaiser*); **2.** Autoˈkrat *m*.

Cae·sar·e·an, Cae·sar·i·an [siːˈzeərɪən] *adj.* cäˈsarisch: ~ (***operation*** *od.* ***section***) ⚕ Kaiserschnitt *m*.

Cae·sar·ism [ˈsiːzərɪzəm] *s.* Diktaˈtur *f*, Herrschsucht *f*.

cae·su·ra [siːˈzjʊərə] *s.* Zäˈsur *f*: a) (Vers)Einschnitt *m*, b) ♪ Ruhepunkt *m*.

ca·fé [ˈkæfeɪ] *s.* **1.** a) Caˈfé *n*, b) Restauˈrant *n*; **2.** *Am.* Bar *f*.

caf·e·te·ri·a [ˌkæfɪˈtɪərɪə] *s.* ˈSelbstbedienungsrestauˌrant *n*, Cafeteˈria *f*.

caf·fe·ine [ˈkæfiːn] *s.* ⚗ Koffeˈin *n*; ˈ**~-free** *adj.* koffeˈinfrei.

caf·tan [ˈkæftæn] *s.* ˈKaftan *m* (*a. Damenmode*).

cage [keɪdʒ] **I** *s.* **1.** Käfig *m* (*a. fig.*); (Vogel)Bauer *n*; **2.** Gefängnis *n* (*a. fig.*); **3.** Kriegsgefangenenlager *n*; **4.** Kaˈbine *f e-s Aufzuges*; **5.** ⚒ Förderkorb *m*; **6.** *a.* ⚠ Stahlgerüst *n*; **7.** a) *Baseball*: abgegrenztes Trainingsfeld, b) *Eishockey*: Tor *n*, c) *Basketball*: Korb *m*; **II** *v/t.* **8.** (in e-n Käfig) einsperren; **9.** *Eishockey*: *den Puck* ins Tor schießen; ~ **aer·i·al** *s. Brit.*, ~ **an·ten·na** *s. Am.* ϟ ˈKäfiganˌtenne *f*.

ca·gey [ˈkeɪdʒɪ] *adj.* F **1.** verschlossen; **2.** vorsichtig, berechnend; **3.** ‚gerissen', schlau.

ca·hoot [kəˈhuːt] *s.*: ***be in ~s*** (***with***) F unter e-r Decke stecken (mit).

Cain [keɪn] *s.*: ***raise*** ~ F Krach schlagen.

cairn [keən] *s.* **1.** Steinhaufen *m* (*als Grenz- od. Grabmal*); **2.** *mount.* Steinmann *m*; **3.** *a.* ~ ***terrier*** *zo.* ˈCairn-ˌTerrier *m* (*Hund*).

cais·son [kəˈsuːn] *s.* **1.** ⚙ Caisˈson *m*, Senkkasten *m*; **2.** ⚔ Munitiˈonswagen *m*; ~ **dis·ease** *s.* ⚕ Caisˈsonkrankheit *f*.

ca·jole [kəˈdʒəʊl] *v/t.* *j-m* schmeicheln *od.* schöntun; *j-n* beschwatzen, verleiten (***into*** zu): ~ ***s.th. out of s.o.*** j-m et.

abbetteln; **ca'jol·er·y** [-ləri] *s.* Schmei'che'lei *f*, gutes Zureden; Liebediene'rei *f*.

cake [keɪk] **I** *s.* **1.** Kuchen *m* (*a. fig.*): ***parcel out the ~*** *fig.* den (*finanziellen*) Kuchen verteilen; ***take the ~*** den Preis davontragen, *fig.* den Vogel abschießen; ***that takes the ~!*** F a) das ist (einsame) Spitze!, b) *contp.* das ist die Höhe!; ***be selling like hot ~s*** weggehen wie warme Semmeln; ***you can't eat your ~ and have it!*** du kannst nur eines von beiden tun *od.* haben!, entweder – oder!; ***~s and ale*** Lustbarkeit(en *pl.*) *f*, ‚süßes Leben'; **2.** Kuchen *m* (*Masse*); Tafel *f Schokolade*, Riegel *m Seife etc.*; **3.** (Schmutz- *etc.*)Kruste *f*; **II** *v/i.* **4.** zs.-backen, -ballen, verkrusten: ***~d with filth*** mit e-r Schmutzkruste (überzogen *od.* bedeckt); **~ mix** *s.* Backmischung *f*; **'~·walk** *s.* 'Cakewalk *m* (*Tanz*).

cal·a·bash ['kæləbæʃ] *s.* ♀ Kale'basse *f*: a) Flaschenkürbis *m*, b) *daraus gefertigtes Trinkgefäß*.

ca·lam·i·tous [kə'læmɪtəs] *adj.* □ kata-stro'phal, unheilvoll, Unglücks...

ca·lam·i·ty [kə'læmətɪ] *s.* **1.** Unglück *n*, Unheil *n*, Kata'strophe *f*; **2.** Elend *n*, Mi'sere *f*; **~ howl·er** *s. bsd. Am.* Schwarzseher *m*, 'Panikmacher *m*; **℞ Jane** *s.* F Pechmarie *f*, Unglückswurm *m*.

cal·car·e·ous [kæl'keərɪəs] *adj.* ⚗ kalkartig, Kalk...; kalkhaltig.

cal·cif·er·ous [kæl'sɪfərəs] *adj.* ⚗ kalkhaltig; **cal·ci·fi·ca·tion** [ˌkælsɪfɪ'keɪʃn] *s.* **1.** ⚕ Verkalkung *f*; **2.** *geol.* Kalkablagerung *f*; **cal·ci·fy** ['kælsɪfaɪ] *v/t. u. v/i.* verkalken; **cal·ci·na·tion** [ˌkælsɪ'neɪʃn] *s.* ⚙ Kalzinierung *f*, Glühen *n*; **cal·cine** ['kælsaɪn] *v/t.* ⚙ kalzinieren, (aus)glühen, zu Asche verbrennen.

cal·ci·um ['kælsɪəm] *s.* ⚗ 'Kalzium *n*; **~ car·bide** *s.* ⚗ ('Kalzium)Karˌbid *n*; **~ chlo·ride** *s.* ⚗ Chlor'kalzium *n*; **~ light** *s.* Kalklicht *n*.

cal·cu·la·ble ['kælkjʊləbl] *adj.* berechenbar, kalkulierbar (*Risiko*).

cal·cu·late ['kælkjʊleɪt] **I** *v/t.* **1.** aus-, er-, berechnen; ✝ kalkulieren; **2.** *mst pass.* berechnen, planen; → ***calculated***; **3.** *Am.* F vermuten, glauben; **II** *v/i.* **4.** rechnen; ✝ kalkulieren; **5.** über'legen; **6.** (***upon***) rechnen (mit, auf *acc.*), sich verlassen (auf *acc.*); **'cal·cu·lat·ed** [-tɪd] *adj.* berechnet, gewollt, beabsichtigt: ***~ indiscretion*** gezielte Indiskretion; ***~ risk*** kalkuliertes Risiko; ***~ to deceive*** darauf angelegt zu täuschen; ***not ~ for*** nicht geeignet *od.* bestimmt für; **'cal·cu·lat·ing** [-tɪŋ] *adj.* **1.** (schlau) berechnend, (kühl) über'legend; **2.** Rechen...: ***~ machine***; **cal·cu·la·tion** [ˌkælkjʊ'leɪʃn] *s.* **1.** Kalkulati'on *f*, Berechnung *f*: ***be out in one's ~*** sich verrechnet haben; **2.** Voranschlag *m*; **3.** Über'legung *f*; **4.** *fig.* a) Berechnung *f*, b) Schläue *f*; **'cal·cu·la·tor** [-tə] *s.* **1.** Kalku'lator *m*; **2.** 'Rechentaˌbelle *f*; **3.** 'Rechenmaˌschine *f*, Rechner *m*.

cal·cu·lus ['kælkjʊləs] *pl.* **-li** [-laɪ] *s.* **1.** ⚕ (*Blasen-*, *Gallen-*, *Nieren- etc.*)Stein *m*; **2.** ⅌ a) (*bsd. Differential-*, *Integral-*) Rechnung *f*, Rechnungsart *f*, b) höhere A'nalysis: ***~ of probabilities*** Wahrscheinlichkeitsrechnung.

cal·dron ['kɔ:ldrən] → ***cauldron***.

Cal·e·do·ni·an [ˌkælɪ'dəʊnjən] *poet.* **I** *adj.* kale'donisch (*schottisch*); **II** *s.* Kale'donier *m* (*Schotte*).

cal·e·fac·tion [ˌkælɪ'fækʃn] *s.* Erwärmung *f*, Erhitzung *f*.

cal·en·dar ['kælɪndə] **I** *s.* **1.** Ka'lender *m*; **2.** *fig.* Zeitrechnung *f*; **3.** Jahrbuch *n*; **4.** Liste *f*, Re'gister *n*; **5.** *Brit. univ.* Vorlesungsverzeichnis *n*; **6.** ✝, *Am.* ⚖ Ter'minkaˌlender *m*; **II** *v/t.* **7.** registrieren; **~ month** *s.* Ka'lendermonat *m*.

cal·en·der ['kælɪndə] ⚙ **I** *s.* Ka'lander *m*; **II** *v/t.* ka'landern.

cal·ends ['kælɪndz] *s. pl. antiq.* Ka'lenden *pl.*: ***on the Greek ~*** am St. Nimmerleinstag.

calf¹ [kɑ:f] *pl.* **calves** [-vz] *s.* **1.** Kalb *n* (*der Kuh*, *a. von Elefant*, *Wal*, *Hirsch etc.*): ***with*** (*od.* ***in***) ***~*** trächtig (*Kuh*); **2.** Kalbleder *n*: ***~-bound*** in Kalbleder gebunden (*Buch*); **3.** F ‚Kalb' *n*, ‚Schaf' *n*; **4.** treibende Eisscholle.

calf² [kɑ:f] *pl.* **calves** [-vz] *s.* Wade *f* (*Bein*, *Strumpf etc.*).

'calf|·love *s.* F erste, junge Liebe; **'~'s-foot jel·ly** ['kɑ:vz-] *s.* Kalbsfußsülze *f*; **'~·skin** *s.* Kalbleder *n*.

cal·i·ber *Am.* → ***calibre***; **'cal·i·bered** *Am.* → ***calibred***; **cal·i·brate** ['kælɪbreɪt] *v/t.* ⚙ kalibrieren: a) mit e-r Gradeinteilung versehen, b) eichen; **cal·i·bra·tion** [ˌkælɪ'breɪʃn] *s.* ⚙ Kalibrierung *f*, Eichung *f*; **cal·i·bre** ['kælɪbə] *s.* **1.** ✕ Ka'liber *n*; **2.** ⚙ a) ('Innen)Durchmesser *m*, b) Ka'liberlehre *f*; **3.** *fig.* Ka'liber *n*, For'mat *n*; **'cal·i·bred** [-bəd] *adj.* ...kalibrig.

cal·i·ces ['kælɪsi:z] *pl. von* ***calix***.

cal·i·co ['kælɪkəʊ] **I** *pl.* **-coes**, *Am. a.* **-cos** *s.* **1.** 'Kaliko *m*, (bedruckter) Kat'tun; **2.** *Brit.* weißer *od.* ungebleichter Baumwollstoff; **II** *adj.* **3.** Kattun...; **4.** F bunt.

ca·lif, **cal·if·ate** → ***caliph***, ***caliphate***.

Cal·i·for·ni·an [kælɪ'fɔ:njən] **I** *adj.* kali'fornisch; **II** *s.* Kali'fornier(in).

cal·i·pers ['kælɪpəz] *s. pl.* Greif-, Tastzirkel *m*; ⚙ Tast(er)lehre *f*.

ca·liph ['kælɪf] *s.* Ka'lif *m*; **'cal·iph·ate** [-feɪt] *s.* Kali'fat *n*.

cal·is·then·ics → ***callisthenics***.

ca·lix ['keɪlɪks] *pl.* **cal·i·ces** ['kælɪsi:z] *s. anat.*, *zo.*, *eccl.* Kelch *m*; → ***calyx***.

calk¹ [kɔ:k] **I** *s.* **1.** Stollen *m* (*am Hufeisen*); **2.** Gleitschutzbeschlag *m* (*an der Schuhsohle*); **II** *v/t.* **3.** mit Stollen *od.* Griffeisen versehen.

calk² [kɔ:k] *v/t.* ('durch)pausen.

calk³ [kɔ:k] → ***caulk***.

cal·kin ['kælkɪn] *Brit.* → ***calk¹*** I.

call [kɔ:l] **I** *s.* **1.** Ruf *m* (*a. fig.*); Schrei *m*: ***within ~*** in Rufweite; ***the ~ of duty***; ***the ~ of nature*** *humor.* ‚ein dringendes Bedürfnis'; **2.** (Tele'fon)Anruf *m*, (-)Gespräch *n*: ***give s.o. a ~*** j-n anrufen; → ***local*** 1, ***personal*** 1; **3.** *thea.* Her'vorruf *m*; **4.** Lockruf *m* (*Tier*); *fig.* Ruf *m*, Lockung *f*: ***the ~ of the East***; **5.** Namensaufruf *m*; **6.** Ruf *m*, Berufung *f* (***to*** in *ein Amt etc.*, auf *e-n Lehrstuhl*); **7.** (innere) Berufung, Drang *m*, Missi'on *f*; **8.** Si'gnal *n*; **9.** (Auf)Ruf *m*; (✝ Zahlungs)Aufforderung *f*; ✝ Abruf *m*, Kündigung *f von Geldern*; 'Kaufoptiˌon *f*; *Brit.* Vorprämie *f*, Vorprämiengeschäfte *pl.*; *a.* Nachfrage *f* (***for*** nach): ***~ on shares*** Aufforderung zur Einzahlung auf Aktien; ***at ~***, ***on ~*** auf Abruf *od.* sofort bereit(stehend), ✝ *a.* jederzeit kündbar; ***money at ~*** ✝ Tagesgeld *n*; **10.** a) Veranlassung *f*, Grund *m*, b) Recht *n*: ***he had no ~ to do that***; **11.** In'anspruchnahme *f*: ***many ~s on my time*** starke Beanspruchung m-r Zeit; ***have the first ~*** den Vorrang haben; **12.** kurzer Besuch (***at*** in *e-m Ort*, ***on*** bei *j-m*); ⚓ Anlaufen *n*: ***port of ~*** Anlaufhafen *m*; **II** *v/t.* **13.** *j-n* (her'bei)rufen; *et.* (*a. weitS. Streik*) ausrufen; *Versammlung* einberufen; *teleph.* anrufen; *thea. Schauspieler* her'vorrufen: ***~ into being*** *fig.* ins Leben rufen; **14.** berufen (***to*** in *ein Amt*); **15.** ⚖ a) *Zeugen*, *Sache* aufrufen, b) *als Zeugen* vorladen; **16.** *Arzt*, *Auto* kommen lassen; **17.** nennen, bezeichnen als; **18.** *pass.* heißen (***after*** nach): ***he is ~ed Max***; ***what is it ~ed in English?*** wie heißt es auf englisch?; **19.** nennen, heißen (*lit.*), halten für: ***I ~ that a blunder***; ***we'll ~ it a pound*** wir wollen es bei einem Pfund bewenden lassen; **20.** wecken: ***~ me at 6 o'clock***; **21.** *Kartenspiel*: a) *Farbe* ansagen, b) ***~ s.o.'s hand*** *Poker*: j-n auffordern, s-e Karten vorzuzeigen; **III** *v/i.* **22.** rufen: ***you must come when I ~***; ***duty ~s***; ***he ~ed for help*** er rief um Hilfe; → ***call for***; **23.** *teleph.* anrufen: ***who is ~ing?*** wer ist dort?; **24.** (kurz) vor'beischauen (***on s.o.*** bei j-m); *Zssgn mit prp. u. adv.*:

call| at *v/i.* **1.** besuchen (*acc.*), vorsprechen bei *od.* in (*dat.*), gehen *od.* kommen zu; **2.** ⚓ *Hafen* anlaufen; anlegen in (*dat.*); 🚂 halten in (*dat.*); **~ a·way** *v/t.* ab-, wegrufen; *fig.* ablenken; **~ back I** *v/t.* **1.** zu'rückrufen; **2.** wider'rufen; **II** *v/i.* **3.** *teleph.* zu'rückrufen; **~ down** *v/t.* **1.** *Segen etc.* her'abrufen, -flehen; *Zorn etc.* auf sich ziehen; **2.** *Am.* F ‚zs.-stauchen'; **~ for** *v/i.* **1.** nach *j-m* rufen; *Waren* abrufen; *thea.* her'ausrufen; **2.** *et.* erfordern, verlangen: ***~ courage***; ***your remark was not called for*** Ihre Bemerkung war unnötig; **3.** *j-n od. et.* abholen: ***to be called for*** a) abzuholen(d), b) postlagernd; **~ forth** *v/t.* **1.** her'vorrufen, auslösen; **2.** *Kraft* aufbieten; **~ in I** *v/t.* **1.** her'ein-, her'beirufen; hin'zu-, zu Rate ziehen; **2.** zu'rückfordern; *Geld* kündigen; *Schulden* einfordern; *Banknoten etc.* einziehen; **II** *v/i.* **3.** vorsprechen (***on*** bei *j-m*; ***at*** in *dat.*); **~ off** *v/t.* **1.** ab(be)rufen: ***~ goods*** Waren abrufen; **2.** *fig. et.* abbrechen, absagen, abblasen: ***~ a strike***; **3.** *Aufmerksamkeit*, *Gedanken* ablenken; **~ on** *od.* **up·on** *v/i.* **1.** *j-n* besuchen; bei *j-m* vorsprechen; **2.** *j-n* auffordern; **3.** ***~ s.o. for s.th.*** et. von j-m fordern, sich an j-n um et. wenden; ***I am*** (*od.* ***I feel***) ***called upon*** ich bin *od.* fühle mich genötigt (***to*** *inf.* zu *inf.*); **~ out I** *v/t.* **1.** her'ausrufen; **2.** *Polizei*, *Militär* aufbieten; **3.** *zum Kampf* her'ausfordern; *zum Streik* auffordern; **II** *v/i.* **4.** aufschreien; laut rufen; **~ o·ver** *v/t.* **1.** *Namen* verlesen; **2.** *Zahlen*, *Text* kollationieren; **~ to** *v/i. j-m* zurufen, *j-n* anrufen; **~ up** *v/t.* **1.** auf-, her'beirufen; *teleph.* anrufen; **2.** ✕ einberufen; **3.** *fig.* her'vor-, wachrufen, her'aufbeschwören; **4.** sich ins Gedächtnis zu'rückrufen; **~ up·on** → ***call on***.

call·a·ble [ˈkɔːləbl] *adj.* ✝ kündbar (*Geld*, *Kredit*); einziehbar (*Forderungen etc.*).

ˈ**call|·back** *s.* ✝, ⚙ ˈRückrufaktiˌon *f in die Werkstatt*; ~ **box** *s.* **1.** *Brit.* Fernsprechzelle *f*; **2.** *Am.* a) Postfach *n*, b) Notrufsäule *f*; ˈ**~·boy** *s.* **1.** Hoˈtelpage *m*; **2.** *thea.* Inspiziˈentengehilfe *m*; ~ **but·ton** *s.* Klingelknopf *m*.

called [kɔːld] *adj.* genannt, namens.

call·er [ˈkɔːlə] *s.* **1.** *teleph.* Anrufer(in); **2.** Besucher(in); **3.** Abholer(in).

call| girl *s.* Callgirl *n* (*Prostituierte*); ~ **house** *s. Am.* Borˈdell *n*.

cal·lig·ra·phy [kəˈlɪgrəfɪ] *s.* Kalligraˈphie *f*, Schönschreibkunst *f*.

ˈ**call-in** *s. Radio*, *TV*: Sendung *f* mit teleˈfonischer Publikumsbeteiligung.

call·ing [ˈkɔːlɪŋ] *s.* **1.** Beruf *m*, Geschäft *n*, Gewerbe *n*; **2.** *eccl.* Berufung *f*; **3.** Einberufung *f e-r Versammlung*; ~ **card** *s.* Viˈsitenkarte *f*.

cal·li·pers → ***calipers***.

cal·lis·then·ics [ˌkælɪsˈθenɪks] *s. pl. mst sg. konstr.* Freiübungen *pl.*

call| loan *s.* ✝ täglich kündbares Darlehen; ~ **mon·ey** *s.* ✝ Tagesgeld *n*; ~ **num·ber** *s. teleph.* Rufnummer *f*; ~ **of·fice** *s.* Fernsprechstelle *f*, -zelle *f*.

cal·los·i·ty [kæˈlɒsətɪ] *s.* Schwiele *f*, Hornhautbildung *f*; **cal·lous** [ˈkæləs] **I** *adj.* ☐ schwielig; *fig.* abgebrüht, gefühllos; **II** *v/i.* sich verhärten, schwielig werden; *fig.* abstumpfen; **cal·lous·ness** [ˈkæləsnɪs] *s.* Schwieligkeit *f*; *fig.* Abgebrühtheit *f*, Gefühllosigkeit *f*.

cal·low [ˈkæləʊ] *adj.* **1.** ungefiedert, nackt; **2.** *fig.* ‚grün', unreif.

call| sign, ~ **sig·nal** *s. teleph. etc.* Rufzeichen *n*; ˈ**~-up** *s.* ⚔ a) Einberufung, b) Mobilisierung *f*.

cal·lus [ˈkæləs] *pl.* **-li** [-laɪ] *s.* ⚕ **1.** Knochennarbe *f*; **2.** Schwiele *f*.

calm [kɑːm] **I** *s.* **1.** Stille *f*, Ruhe *f* (*a. fig.*); **2.** Windstille *f*, Flaute *f*; **II** *adj.* ☐ **3.** still, ruhig; friedlich; **4.** windstill; **5.** *fig.* ruhig, gelassen: ~ ***and collected*** ruhig u. gefaßt; **6.** F unverfroren, ‚kühl'; **III** *v/t.* **7.** beruhigen, besänftigen; **IV** *v/i.* **8.** *a.* ~ ***down*** sich beruhigen; ˈ**calm·ness** [-nɪs] *s.* **1.** Ruhe *f*, Stille *f*; **2.** Gemütsruhe *f*, Gelassenheit *f*.

ca·lor·ic [kəˈlɒrɪk] *phys.* **I** *s.* Wärme *f*; **II** *adj.* kaˈlorisch, Wärme…: ~ ***engine*** Heißluftmaschine *f*; **cal·o·rie** [ˈkælərɪ] *s.* Kaloˈrie *f*, Wärmeeinheit *f*; **cal·o·rif·ic** [ˌkæləˈrɪfɪk] *adj.* (☐ **~ally**) Wärme erzeugend; Wärme…, Heiz…; **cal·o·ry** → ***calorie***.

cal·u·met [ˈkæljʊmet] *s.* Kaluˈmet *n*, (indiˈanische) Friedenspfeife.

ca·lum·ni·ate [kəˈlʌmnɪeɪt] *v/t.* verleumden; **ca·lum·ni·a·tion** [kəˌlʌmnɪˈeɪʃn] *s.* Verleumdung *f*; **caˈlum·ni·a·tor** [-tə] *s.* Verleumder(in); **caˈlum·ni·ous** [-ɪəs] *adj.* ☐ verleumderisch; **cal·um·ny** [ˈkæləmnɪ] *s.* Verleumdung *f*.

Cal·va·ry [ˈkælvərɪ] *s.* **1.** *bibl.* ˈGolgatha *n*; **2.** *eccl.* Kalˈvarienberg *m*; **3.** ♀ Bildstock *m*, Marterl *n*; **4.** ♀ *fig.* Marˈtyrium *n*.

calve [kɑːv] *v/i.* **1.** *zo.* kalben; **2.** kalben, Eisstücke abstoßen (*Eisberg*, *Gletscher*).

calves [kɑːvz] *pl. von* ***calf***; ˈ**~-foot jel·ly** → ***calf's-foot jelly***.

Cal·vin·ism [ˈkælvɪnɪzəm] *s. eccl.* Kalviˈnismus *m*; ˈ**Cal·vin·ist** [-ɪst] *s.* Kalviˈnist(in).

ca·lyx [ˈkeɪlɪks] *pl.* ˈ**ca·lyx·es** [-ɪksɪz], ˈ**ca·ly·ces** [-ɪsiːz] *s.* ⚘ (*Blüten*)Kelch *m*; → ***calix***.

cam [kæm] *s.* ⚙ Nocken *m*, Mitnehmer *m*, (Steuer)Kurve *f*: ~ ***gear*** Nockensteuerung *f*, Kurvengetriebe *n*; **~*shaft*** Nocken-, Steuerwelle *f*; **~*-control(l)ed*** nockengesteuert.

ca·ma·ra·de·rie [ˌkæməˈrɑːdərɪ] *s.* Kameˈradschaft(lichkeit) *f*; *b.s.* Kumpaˈnei *f*.

cam·a·ril·la [ˌkæməˈrɪlə] *s.* Kamaˈrilla *f*; ˈHofkaˌbale *f*.

cam·ber [ˈkæmbə] **I** *v/t. u. v/i.* (sich) wölben; **II** *s.* leichte Wölbung, Krümmung *f*; *mot.* (Rad)Sturz *m*; ˈ**cambered** [-əd] *adj.* **1.** gewölbt, geschweift; **2.** gestürzt (*Achse*, *Rad*).

Cam·bo·di·an [kæmˈbəʊdjən] **I** *s.* Kamboˈdschaner(in); **II** *adj.* kamboˈdschanisch.

Cam·bri·an [ˈkæmbrɪən] **I** *s.* **1.** Waˈliser (-in); **2.** *geol.* ˈKambrium *n*; **II** *adj.* **3.** waˈlisisch; **4.** *geol.* ˈkambrisch.

cam·bric [ˈkeɪmbrɪk] *s.* Baˈtist *m*.

came [keɪm] *pret. von* ***come***.

cam·el [ˈkæml] *s.* **1.** *zo.* Kaˈmel *n*: ***Arabian*** ~ Dromedar *n*; → ***Bactrian camel***; **2.** ⚓, ⚙ Kaˈmel *n*, Hebeleichter *m*; **cam·el·eer** [ˌkæmɪˈlɪə] *s.* Kaˈmeltreiber *m*; **cam·el hair** → ***camel's hair***.

ca·mel·li·a [kəˈmiːljə] *s.* ⚘ Kaˈmelie *f*.

cam·el's| hair [ˈkæmlz] *s.* Kaˈmelhaar (-stoff *m*) *n*; ˈ**~-hair** *adj.* Kamelhaar…

cam·e·o [ˈkæmɪəʊ] **I** *s.* Kaˈmee *f*; **II** *adj. fig.* Miniatur…

cam·er·a [ˈkæmərə] *s.* **1.** ˈKamera *f*: a) ˈFotoappaˌrat *m*, b) ˈFilm- *od.* ˈFernsehˌkamera *f*: ***be on*** ~ a) auf Sendung *od.* im Bild sein, b) vor der Kamera stehen; **2.** ***in*** ~ ⚖ unter Ausschluß der Öffentlichkeit, nicht öffentlich; *fig.* geheim; ˈ**~·man** [-mæn] *s.* [*irr.*] **1.** ˈPressefotoˌgraf *m*; **2.** *Film*: ˈKameramann *m*; ~ **ob·scu·ra** [ɒbˈskjʊərə] *s. opt.* ˈLochˌkamera *f*, ˈCamera *f* obˈscura; ˈ**~-shy** *adj.* ˈkamerascheu.

cam·i·knick·ers [ˈkæmɪˌnɪkəz] *s. pl. Brit.* (Damen)Hemdhose *f*.

cam·i·sole [ˈkæmɪsəʊl] *s.* **1.** Bett-, Morgenjäckchen *n*; **2.** (Trachten- *etc.*)Mieder *n*.

cam·o·mile [ˈkæməʊmaɪl] *s.* ⚘ Kaˈmille *f*: ~ ***tea*** Kamillentee *m*.

cam·ou·flage [ˈkæmʊflɑːʒ] **I** *s.* ⚔ Tarnung *f* (*a. fig.*): ~ ***paint*** Tarnanstrich *m*; **II** *v/t.* tarnen, *fig. a.* verschleiern.

camp¹ [kæmp] **I** *s.* **1.** (Zelt-, Ferien)Lager *n*, Lagerplatz *m*, Camp *n*: ***break*** *od.* ***strike*** ~ das Lager abbrechen, aufbrechen; **2.** ⚔ Feld-, Heerlager *n*; **3.** *fig.* Lager *n*, Parˈtei *f*, Anhänger *pl. e-r Richtung*: ***the rival*** ~ das gegnerische Lager; **II** *adj.* **4.** Lager…, Camping…: ~ ***bed*** a) Feldbett *n*, b) Campingliege *f*; **III** *v/i.* **5.** *a.* ~ ***out*** zelten, campen, kampieren.

camp² [kæmp] F **I** *adj.* **1.** a) ‚schwul', ‚tuntenhaft', b) überˈzogen, überˈtrieben, ‚irr', c) verkitscht; **II** *v/i.* **2.** → 4; **III** *v/t.* **3.** *et.* ‚aufmotzen', *thea. etc. a.* überˈziehen, überˈtrieben darstellen, *a.* verkitschen; **4.** ~ ***it up*** a) die Sache ‚aufmotzen', *thea. etc. a.* überˈziehen, b) sich ‚tuntenhaft' benehmen.

cam·paign [kæmˈpeɪn] **I** *s.* **1.** ⚔ Feldzug *m*; **2.** *pol. u. fig.* Schlacht *f*, Kamˈpagne *f*, (*a.* Werbe)Feldzug *m*, Aktiˈon *f*; **3.** *pol.* ˈWahlkampf *m*, -kamˌpagne *f*: ~ ***button*** Wahlkampfplakette *f*; **II** *v/i.* **4.** ⚔ an e-m Feldzug teilnehmen, kämpfen; **5.** *fig.* kämpfen, zu Felde ziehen (***for*** für; ***against*** gegen); **6.** *pol.* a) sich am Wahlkampf beteiligen, im Wahlkampf stehen, b) Wahlkampf machen (***for*** für), c) *Am.* kandidieren; **camˈpaign·er** [-nə] *s.* **1.** Feldzugteilnehmer *m*: ***old*** ~ *fig.* alter Praktikus *od.* Hase; **2.** *fig.* Kämpfer *m* (***for*** für).

cam·pan·u·la [kəmˈpænjʊlə] *s.* ⚘ Glokkenblume *f*.

camp·er [ˈkæmpə] *s.* **1.** Camper(in); **2.** *Am.* a) Wohnanhänger *m*, -wagen *m*, b) ˈWohnmoˌbil *n*.

camp| fe·ver *s.* ⚕ ˈTyphus *m*; ˈ**~-ˌfire** *s.* Lagerfeuer *n*: ~ ***girl*** Pfadfinderin *f*; ~ **fol·low·er** *s.* **1.** Solˈdatenprostituierte *f*; **2.** *pol. etc.* Sympathiˈsant(in), Mitläufer(in); ˈ**~·ground** → ***camping ground***.

cam·phor [ˈkæmfə] *s.* ⚗ Kampfer *m*; ˈ**cam·phor·at·ed** [-əreɪtɪd] *adj.* mit Kampfer behandelt, Kampfer…

cam·phor| ball *s.* Mottenkugel *f*; ˈ**~·wood** *s.* Kampferholz *n*.

camp·ing [ˈkæmpɪŋ] *s.* Camping *n*, Zelten *n*; Kampieren *n*; ~ **ground**, ~ **site** *s.* Zelt-, Campingplatz *m*.

cam·pi·on [ˈkæmpjən] *s.* ⚘ Lichtnelke *f*.

camp meet·ing *s. Am.* religiˈöse Versammlung im Freien; ˈZeltmissiˌon *f*.

cam·po·ree [ˌkæmpəˈriː] *s. Am.* regioˈnales Pfadfindertreffen.

cam·pus [ˈkæmpəs] *s.* Campus *m* (*Gesamtanlage e-r Universität od. Schule*), *weitS.* ‚Uni' *f od.* Gymˈnasium *n*.

ˈ**cam·wood** *s.* Kam-, Rotholz *n*.

can¹ [kæn; kən] *v/aux.* [*irr.*], *pres. neg.* ˈ**can·not 1.** können: ~ ***you do it?***; ***he cannot read***; ***we could do it now*** wir könnten es jetzt tun; ***how could you?*** wie konntest du nur (so etwas tun)?; ~ ***do!*** *sl.* (wird) gemacht!; ***no*** ~ ***do!*** *sl.* das geht nicht!; **2.** dürfen, können: ***you*** ~ ***go away now***.

can² [kæn] **I** *s.* **1.** (Blech)Kanne *f*; (*Öl-*) Kännchen *n*: ***carry the*** ~ *sl.* der Sündenbock sein, dran sein; **2.** (Konˈserven)Dose *f*, (-)Büchse *f*: ~ ***opener*** Büchsenöffner *m*; ***in the*** ~ F ‚abgedreht', ‚im Kasten' (*Film*), *allg.* unter Dach u. Fach; **3.** (Blech)Trinkgefäß *n*; **4.** Kaˈnister *m*; **5.** *Am. sl.* a) ‚Kittchen' *n*, ‚Knast' *m*, b) ‚Klo' *n*, c) ‚Arsch' *m*; **II** *v/t.* **6.** in Büchsen konservieren, eindosen; **7.** F auf Schallplatte *od.* Band aufnehmen; **8.** *Am sl.* a) ‚rausschmeißen', entlassen, b) ‚einlochen', c) aufhören mit.

Ca·na·di·an [kəˈneɪdjən] **I** *adj.* kaˈnadisch; **II** *s.* Kaˈnadier(in).

ca·naille [kəˈnɑːiː] (*Fr.*) *s.* Pöbel *m*.

ca·nal [kəˈnæl] *s.* **1.** Kaˈnal *m* (*für Schifffahrt etc.*): **~*s of Mars*** Marskanäle; **2.** *anat.*, *zo.* Kaˈnal *m*, Gang *m*, Röhre *f*; **ca·nal·i·za·tion** [ˌkænəlaɪˈzeɪʃn] *s.* Kanalisierung *f*; Kaˈnalnetz *n*; **ca·nal·ize** [ˈkænəlaɪz] *v/t.* **1.** kanalisieren, schiffbar machen; **2.** *fig.* (in bestimmte Bahnen) lenken, kanalisieren.

can·a·pé ['kænəpeɪ] (*Fr.*) *s.* Appe'tithappen *m*, belegtes Brot.
ca·nard [kæ'nɑːd] (*Fr.*) *s.* (Zeitungs)Ente *f*, Falschmeldung *f*.
ca·nar·y [kə'neərɪ] **I** *s.* **1.** *a.* ~ **bird** *orn.* Ka'narienvogel *m*; **2.** *a.* ♀ **wine** Ka'narienwein *m*; **II** *adj.* **3.** hellgelb.
can·cel ['kænsl] **I** *v/t.* **1.** (durch-, aus-)streichen; **2.** wider'rufen, aufheben (*a.* ♪), annullieren (*a.* †), rückgängig machen, absagen; † stornieren; **3.** ungültig machen, tilgen; erlassen; *Briefmarke, Fahrschein etc.* entwerten; *fig.* zu'nichte machen; *a.* ~ **out** ausgleichen, kompensieren; **4.** ⅌ heben, streichen; **II** *v/i.* **5.** *mst* ~ **out** sich (gegenseitig) aufheben *od.* ausgleichen **6.** ~ **out** absagen, die Sache abblasen; **III** *s.* **7.** Streichung *f*; **can·cel·la·tion** [ˌkænsə'leɪʃn] *s.* **1.** Streichung *f*; Aufhebung *f*; 'Widerruf *m*; Absage *f*; **2.** † Annullierung *f*, Stornierung *f*: ~ **clause** Rücktrittsklausel *f*; ~ **charge**, ~ **fee** Rücktrittsgebühr *f*; **3.** Entwertung *f* (*Briefmarke etc.*).
can·cer ['kænsə] *s.* **1.** ⚕ Krebs *m*; Karzi'nom *n*; **2.** *fig.* Krebsgeschwür *n*, Übel *n*; **3.** ♀ *ast.* Krebs *m*; '**can·cer·ous** [-sərəs] *adj.* ⚕ a) krebsbefallen: ~ **lung**, b) Krebs…: ~ **tumo(u)r**, c) krebsartig: ~ **growth** *fig.* Krebsgeschwür *n*.
can·de·la·bra [ˌkændɪ'lɑːbrə] *pl.* **-bras**, **can·de'la·brum** [-brəm] *pl.* **-bra**, *Am. a.* **-brums** *s.* Kande'laber *m*; (Arm-, Kron)Leuchter *m*.
can·des·cence [kæn'desns] *s.* Weißglut *f*.
can·did ['kændɪd] *adj.* □ **1.** offen (u. ehrlich), freimütig; **2.** aufrichtig, unvoreingenommen, objek'tiv; **3.** freizügig, (ta'bu)frei: **a** ~ **film**; **4.** *phot.* ungestellt, unbemerkt aufgenommen: ~ **camera** a) Kleinstbildkamera *f*, b) versteckte Kamera; ~ **shot** Schnappschuß *m*.
can·di·da·cy ['kændɪdəsɪ] *s.* Kandida'tur *f*, Bewerbung *f*, Anwartschaft *f*; **can·di·date** ['kændɪdət] *s.* **1.** (**for**) Kandi'dat *m* (für) (*a. fig.*), Bewerber *m* (um), Anwärter (auf *acc.*); **2.** ('Prüfungs-)Kandiˌdat(in); '**can·di·da·ture** [-dətʃə] → **candidacy**.
can·died ['kændɪd] *adj.* **1.** kandiert, über'zuckert: ~ **peel** Zitronat *n*; **2.** *fig. contp.* ‚honigsüß'.
can·dle ['kændl] *s.* **1.** (Wachs- *etc.*)Kerze *f*, Licht *n*: **burn the** ~ **at both ends** *fig.* Raubbau mit s-r Gesundheit treiben; **not to be fit to hold a** ~ **to** das Wasser nicht reichen können (*dat.*); → **game¹** 4; **2.** → **candlepower**; '~ˌ**ber·ry** [-ˌbərɪ] *s.* ♀ Wachsmyrtenbeere *f*; '~-**end** *s.* **1.** Kerzenstummel *m*; **2.** *pl. fig.* Abfälle *pl.*, Krimskrams *m*; '~**·light** *s.* **1.** (**by** ~ bei) Kerzenlicht *n*; **2.** Abenddämmerung *f*.
Can·dle·mas ['kændlməs] *s. R.C.* (Ma'riä) Lichtmeß *f*.
'**can·dle**|ˌ**pow·er** *s. phys.* (Nor'mal)Kerze *f* (*Lichteinheit*); '~**·stick** *s.* (Kerzen-)Leuchter *m*; '~**·wick** *s.* Kerzendocht *m*.
can·do(u)r ['kændə] *s.* **1.** Offenheit *f*, Aufrichtigkeit *f*; **2.** 'Unparˌteilichkeit *f*, Objektivi'tät *f*.
can·dy ['kændɪ] **I** *s.* **1.** Kandis(zucker) *m*; **2.** *Am.* a) Süßigkeiten *pl.*, Kon'fekt *n*, b) *a.* **hard** ~ Bon'bon *m*, *n*; **II** *v/t.* **3.** kandieren, glacieren; mit Zucker einmachen; **4.** *Zucker* kristallisieren lassen; **III** *v/i.* **5.** kristallisieren (*Zucker*); '~**·floss** *s.* Zuckerwatte *f*; ~ **store** *s. Am.* Süßwarengeschäft *n*.
cane [keɪn] **I** *s.* **1.** ♀ (*Bambus-, Zucker-, Schilf*)Rohr *n*; **2.** spanisches Rohr; **3.** Rohrstock *m*; **4.** Spazierstock *m*; **II** *v/t.* **5.** (mit dem Stock) züchtigen *od.* prügeln; **6.** *Stuhl* mit Rohrgeflecht versehen: ~**-bottomed** mit Sitz aus Rohr; ~ **chair** *s.* Rohrstuhl *m*; ~ **sug·ar** *s.* Rohrzucker *m*; '~**·work** *s.* Rohrgeflecht *n*.
ca·nine **I** *adj.* ['keɪnaɪn] Hunde…; *fig. contp.* hündisch; **II** *s.* ['kænaɪn] *anat. a.* ~ **tooth** Eckzahn *m*.
can·ing ['keɪnɪŋ] *s.*: **give s.o. a** ~ → **cane** 5.
can·is·ter ['kænɪstə] *s.* **1.** Ka'nister *m*, Blechdose *f*; **2.** ⚔ *a.* ~ **shot** Kar'tätsche *f*.
can·ker ['kæŋkə] **I** *s.* **1.** ⚕ Mund- *od.* Lippengeschwür *n*; **2.** *vet.* Strahlfäule *f*; **3.** ♀ Rost *m*, Brand *m*; **4.** *fig.* Krebsgeschwür *n*; **II** *v/t.* **5.** *fig.* an-, zerfressen, verderben; **III** *v/i.* **6.** angefressen werden, verderben; '**can·kered** [-əd] *adj.* **1.** ♀ a) brandig, b) (von Raupen) zerfressen; **2.** *fig.* a) bösartig, b) mürrisch; '**can·ker·ous** [-ərəs] *adj.* **1.** → **cankered** 1; **2.** fressend, schädlich, vergiftend.
can·na·bis ['kænəbɪs] *s.* 'Cannabis *m*: a) ♀ Hanf *m*, b) Haschisch *n*.
canned [kænd] *adj.* **1.** konserviert, Dosen…, Büchsen…: ~ **food** Konserven *pl.*; ~ **meat** Büchsenfleisch *n*; **2.** F ‚aus der Konserve': ~ **music**; ~ **film** *TV* Aufzeichnung *f*; **3.** *sl.* ‚blau', betrunken; **4.** stereo'typ, scha'blonenhaft; **can·ner** ['kænə] *s.* **1.** Kon'servenfabriˌkant *m*; **2.** Arbeiter(in) in e-r Kon'servenfaˌbrik; '**can·ner·y** [-ərɪ] *s.* Kon'servenfaˌbrik *f*.
can·ni·bal ['kænɪbl] **I** *s.* Kanni'bale *m*, Menschenfresser *m*; **II** *adj.* kanni'balisch (*a. fig.*); '**can·ni·bal·ism** [-bəlɪzəm] *s.* Kanniba'lismus *m* (*a. zo.*); *fig.* Unmenschlichkeit *f*; **can·ni·bal·is·tic** [ˌkænɪbə'lɪstɪk] *adj.* (□ ~**ally**) kanni'balisch (*a. fig.*); '**can·ni·bal·ize** [-bəlaɪz] *v/t. altes Auto etc.* ‚ausschlachten'.
can·ning ['kænɪŋ] *s.* Kon'servenfabrikaˌtiˌon *f*: ~ **factory** *od.* **plant** → **cannery**.
can·non ['kænən] **I** *s.* **1.** ⚔ a) Ka'none *f*, Geschütz *n*, b) *coll.* Ka'nonen *pl.*, Artille'rie *f*; **2.** Wasserwerfer *m*; **3.** ⚙ Zy'linder *m* um e-e Welle; **4.** *Billard: Brit.* Karambo'lage *f*; **II** *v/i.* **5.** *Billard: Brit.* karambolieren; **6.** (**against**, **into**, **with**) rennen, prallen (gegen), karambolieren (mit); **can·non·ade** [ˌkænə'neɪd] **I** *s.* **1.** Kano'nade *f*; **2.** *fig.* Dröhnen *n*; **II** *v/t.* **3.** beschießen.
'**can·non**|·**ball** *s.* **1.** Ka'nonenkugel *f*; **2.** *Fußball:* F Bombe(nschuß *m*) *f*; '~**-bone** *s. zo.* Ka'nonenbein *n* (*Pferd*); '~-ˌ**fod·der** *s. fig.* Ka'nonenfutter *n*.
can·not ['kænɒt] → **can¹**.
can·nu·la ['kænjʊlə] *s.* ⚕ Ka'nüle *f*.
can·ny ['kænɪ] *adj.* □ *Scot.* **1.** schlau, gerissen; **2.** nett.
ca·noe [kə'nuː] **I** *s.* Kanu *n* (*a. sport*), Paddelboot *n*: ~ **slalom** Kanu-, Wildwasserslalom *m*; **paddle one's own** ~ auf eigenen Füßen stehen, selbständig sein; **II** *v/i.* Kanu fahren, paddeln; **ca'noe·ist** [-uːɪst] *s.* Ka'nute *m*, Ka'nutin *f*.
can·on¹ ['kænən] *s.* **1.** Regel *f*, Richtschnur *f*, Grundsatz *m*, 'Kanon *m*; **2.** *eccl.* 'Kanon *m*: a) ka'nonische Bücher *pl.*, b) 'Meßˌkanon *m*, c) Ordensregeln *pl.*, d) → **canon law**; **3.** ♪ 'Kanon *m*; **4.** *typ.* 'Kanon(schrift) *f*.
can·on² ['kænən] *s. eccl.* Ka'noniker *m*, Dom-, Stiftsherr *m*.
ca·ñon ['kænjən] → **canyon**.
can·on·ess ['kænənɪs] *s. eccl.* Kano'nissin *f*, Stiftsdame *f*.
ca·non·i·cal [kə'nɒnɪkl] **I** *adj.* □ ka'nonisch, vorschriftsmäßig; *bibl.* au'thentisch; **II** *s. pl. eccl.* kirchliche Amtstracht; ~ **books** → **canon¹** 2 a; ~ **hours** *s. pl.* a) regelmäßige Gebetszeiten *pl.*, b) *Brit.* Zeiten *pl.* für Trauungen.
can·on·ist ['kænənɪst] *s.* Kirchenrechtslehrer *m*; **can·on·i·za·tion** [ˌkænənaɪ'zeɪʃn] *s. eccl.* Heiligsprechung *f*; '**can·on·ize** [-naɪz] *v/t. eccl.* heiligsprechen; **can·on law** *s.* ka'nonisches Recht, Kirchenrecht *n*.
ca·noo·dle [kə'nuːdl] *v/t. u. v/i. sl.* ‚schmusen', ‚knutschen'.
can·o·py ['kænəpɪ] **I** *s.* **1.** 'Baldachin *m*, (Bett-, Thron-, Trag)Himmel *m*: ~ **of heaven** Himmelszelt *n*; **2.** Schutz-, Ka'binendach *n*, Verdeck *n*; **3.** Fallschirm (-kappe *f*) *m*; **4.** ⚠ Über'dachung *f*; **II** *v/t.* **5.** über'dachen; *fig.* bedecken.
canst [kænst; kənst] *obs. 2. sg. pres. von* **can¹**.
cant¹ [kænt] **I** *s.* **1.** Fach-, Zunftsprache *f*; **2.** Jar'gon *m*, Gaunersprache *f*; **3.** Gewäsch *n*; **4.** Frömme'lei *f*, scheinheiliges Gerede; **5.** (leere) Phrase(n *pl.*) *f*; **II** *v/i.* **6.** frömmeln, scheinheilig reden; **7.** Phrasen dreschen.
cant² [kænt] **I** *s.* **1.** (Ab)Schrägung *f*, schräge Lage; **2.** Ruck *m*, Stoß *m*; plötzliche Wendung; **II** *v/t.* **3.** (ver)kanten, kippen; **4.** ⚙ abschrägen; **III** *v/i.* **5.** *a.* ~ **over** sich neigen, sich auf die Seite legen; 'umkippen.
can't [kɑːnt] F *für* **cannot**; → **can¹**.
Can·tab ['kæntæb] *abbr. für* **Can·ta·brig·i·an** [ˌkæntə'brɪdʒɪən] *s.* Stu'dent (-in) *od.* Absol'vent(in) der Universi'tät Cambridge (*England*) *od.* der Harvard University (*USA*).
can·ta·loup(e) ['kæntəluːp] *s.* ♀ Kanta'lupe *f*, 'Warzenmeˌlone *f*.
can·tan·ker·ous [kæn'tæŋkərəs] *adj.* □ streitsüchtig.
can·ta·ta [kæn'tɑːtə] *s.* ♪ Kan'tate *f*.
can·teen [kæn'tiːn] *s.* **1.** (Mili'tär-, Be'triebs- *etc.*)Kanˌtine *f*; **2.** ⚔ a) Feldflasche *f*, b) Kochgeschirr *n*; **3.** Besteck-, Silberkasten *m*.
can·ter ['kæntə] **I** *s.* 'Kanter *m*, kurzer Ga'lopp: **win in a** ~ mühelos siegen; **II** *v/i.* im kurzen Galopp reiten.
can·ti·cle ['kæntɪkl] *s. eccl.* Lobgesang *m*: ♀**s** *bibl. das* Hohelied (Salo'monis).
can·ti·le·ver ['kæntɪliːvə] **I** *s.* **1.** ⚠ Kon'sole *f*; **2.** ⚙ freitragender Arm, vorspringender Träger, Ausleger *m*; **II** *adj.* **3.** freitragend; ~ **bridge** *s.* Auslegerbrücke *f*; ~ **wing** *s.* ✈ unverspreizte Tragfläche.
can·to ['kæntəʊ] *pl.* **-tos** *s.* Gesang *m* (*Teil e-r größeren Dichtung*).

can·ton¹ ['kæntɒn] **I** *s.* Kan'ton *m*, (Verwaltungs)Bezirk *m*; **II** *v/t.* in Kan'tone *od.* Bezirke einteilen.

can·ton² ['kæntən] **I** *s.* **1.** *her.* Feld *n*; **2.** Gösch *f* (*Obereck an Flaggen*); **II** *v/t.* **3.** *her.* in Felder einteilen.

can·ton³ [kæn'tu:n] *v/t.* ⚔ einquartieren.

Can·ton·ese [ˌkæntə'ni:z] **I** *adj.* kanto'nesisch; **II** *s.* Bewohner(in) 'Kantons.

can·ton·ment [kæn'tu:nmənt] *s.* ⚔ *oft pl.* Quar'tier *n*, 'Ortsˌunterkunft *f*.

Ca·nuck [kə'nʌk] *s.* a) Ka'nadier(in) (*französischer Abstammung*), b) *Am. contp.* Ka'nadier(in).

can·vas ['kænvəs] *s.* **1.** a) Segeltuch *n*: **~ *shoes*** Segeltuchschuhe, b) *coll.* (*alle*) Segel *pl.*: ***under* ~** unter Segel; **2.** Pack-, Zeltleinwand *f*: ***under* ~** in Zelten; **3.** 'Kanevas *m*, Stra'min *m* (*zum Sticken*); **4.** a) (Maler)Leinwand *f*, b) (Öl)Gemälde *n*.

can·vass ['kænvəs] **I** *v/t.* **1.** gründlich erörtern *od.* prüfen; **2.** a) *pol. Stimmen* werben, b) *Am. Wahlresultate* prüfen, c) ✝ *Aufträge* her'einholen, *Abonnenten*, *Inserate* sammeln; **3.** *Wahlkreis od. Geschäftsbezirk* bereisen, bearbeiten; **4.** um *et.* werben, *j-n od. et.* anpreisen; **II** *v/i.* **5.** e-n Wahlfeldzug veranstalten; **6.** *Am.* 'Wahlresulˌtate prüfen; **7.** werben (***for*** um); **III** *s.* **8.** *pol.* a) Stimmenwerbung *f*, Wahlfeldzug *m*, b) *Am.* Wahl(stimmen)prüfung *f*; **9.** ✝ Kundenwerbung *f*; He'reinholen *n* von Aufträgen; **'can·vass·er** [-sə] *s.* **1.** ✝ Kundenwerber *m*; **2.** *pol.* a) Wahleinpeitscher *m*, b) *Am.* Wahl(stimmen)prüfer *m*; **'can·vass·ing** [-sɪŋ] *s.* **1.** 'Wahlpropaˌganda *f*; **2.** ✝ Kundenwerbung *f*.

can·yon ['kænjən] *s.* 'Cañon *m*, Felsschlucht *f*.

caou·tchouc ['kaʊtʃʊk] *s.* 'Kautschuk *m*, 'Gummi *n*, *m*.

cap¹ [kæp] **I** *s.* **1.** Mütze *f*, Kappe *f*, Haube *f*: **~ *and bells*** Schellen-, Narrenkappe; **~ *in hand*** mit der Mütze in der Hand, demütig; ***if the* ~ *fits wear it*** *fig.* wen's juckt, der kratze sich; ***set one's* ~ *at s.o.*** F hinter j-m her sein, sich j-n zu angeln suchen (*Frau*); **2.** *univ.* Ba'rett *n*: **~ *and gown*** *univ.* Barett u. Talar; **3.** (Sport-, Stu'denten-, Klub-, Dienst)Mütze *f*; **4.** *sport Brit.* Auswahl-, Natio'nalspieler(in): ***get*** *od.* ***win one's* ~** in die Nationalmannschaft berufen werden; **5.** (Schutz-, Verschluß)Kappe *f od.* (-)Kapsel *f*, Deckel *m*, Aufsatz *m*; ⚔ Zündkapsel *f*; **6.** *mot.* (Reifen)Auflage *f*: ***full* ~** Runderneuerung *f*; **7.** ⚕ Pes'sar *n*; **8.** Spitze *f*, Gipfel *m*; **II** *v/t.* **9.** (mit *od.* wie mit e-r Kappe) bedecken; **10.** mit (Schutz-) Kappe, Kapsel, Deckel, Aufsatz *etc.* versehen; *mot. Reifen* runderneuern; **11.** *Brit. univ. j-m* e-n aka'demischen Grad verleihen; **12.** oben liegen auf (*dat.*), krönen (*a. fig. abschließen*); **13.** *fig.* über'treffen, -'trumpfen; **14.** *sport Brit. j-n* in die Natio'nalmannschaft berufen.

cap² [kæp] *abbr. für* ***capital¹*** 2.

ca·pa·bil·i·ty [ˌkeɪpə'bɪlətɪ] *s.* **1.** Fähigkeit *f* (***of*** zu); **2.** Tauglichkeit *f* (***for*** zu); **3.** *a. pl.* Ta'lent *n*, Begabung *f*; **ca·pable** ['keɪpəbl] *adj.* □ **1.** (*Personen*) a) fähig, tüchtig, b) (***of***) fähig (zu *od. gen.*), im'stande (zu *inf.*) (*mst b.s.*): ***legally* ~** rechts-, geschäftsfähig; **2.** (*Sachen*) a) geeignet, tauglich (***for*** zu), b) (***of***) (*et.*) zulassend, (zu *et.*) fähig: **~ *of being divided*** teilbar.

ca·pa·cious [kə'peɪʃəs] *adj.* □ geräumig, weit; um'fassend (*a. fig.*).

ca·pac·i·tance [kə'pæsɪtəns] *s.* ⚡ kapazi'tiver ('Blind)ˌWiderstand, Kapazi'tät *f*; **ca'pac·i·tate** [-teɪt] *v/t.* befähigen, ermächtigen (*a.* ⚖); **ca'pac·i·tor** [-tə] *s.* ⚡ Konden'sator *m*; **ca'pac·i·ty** [-sətɪ] **I** *s.* **1.** (Raum)Inhalt *m*, Fassungsvermögen *n*; Kapazi'tät *f* (*a.* ⚡, *phys.*): ***measure of* ~** Hohlmaß *n*; ***seating* ~** Sitzgelegenheit *f* (***of*** für); ***full to* ~** ganz voll, *thea. etc.* ausverkauft; **2.** Leistungsfähigkeit *f*, Vermögen *n*; **3.** ✝, ⚙ Kapazi'tät *f*, Leistungsfähigkeit *f*, (Nenn)Leistung *f*: ***working to* ~** mit Höchstleistung arbeitend, voll ausgelastet; **4.** *fig.* Auffassungsgabe *f*, *geistige* Fähigkeit; **5.** ⚖ (Geschäfts-, Tes'tier- *etc.*)Fähigkeit *f*: **~ *to sue and to be sued*** Prozeßfähigkeit; **6.** Eigenschaft *f*, Stellung *f*: ***in my* ~ *as*** in m-r Eigenschaft als; ***in an advisory* ~** in beratender Funktion; **II** *adj.* **7.** maxi'mal, Höchst…: **~ *business*** Rekordgeschäft *n*; **8.** *thea. etc.* voll, ausverkauft: **~ *house*; ~ *crowd*** *sport* ausverkauftes Stadion.

ca·par·i·son [kə'pærɪsn] *s.* **1.** Scha'brakke *f*; **2.** *fig.* Aufputz *m*.

cape¹ [keɪp] *s.* Cape *n*, 'Umhang *m*; Schulterkragen *m*.

cape² [keɪp] *s.* Kap *n*, Vorgebirge *n*: ***the* ☉** das Kap der Guten Hoffnung; **☉ *Dutch*** Kapholländisch *n*; **☉ *wine*** Kapwein *m*.

ca·per¹ ['keɪpə] **I** *s.* **1.** Kapri'ole *f*: a) Freuden-, Luftsprung *m*, b) Streich *m*, Schabernack *m*: ***cut* ~*s*** → 3; **2.** F *fig.* ‚Ding' *n*, ‚Spaß' *m*, Sache *f*; **II** *v/i.* **3.** a) Luftsprünge machen, b) he'rumtollen.

ca·per² ['keɪpə] *s.* **1.** ♀ Kapernstrauch *m*; **2.** Kaper *f*.

cap·er·cail·lie [ˌkæpə'keɪlɪ], **ˌcap·er'cail·zie** [-lɪ] *s. orn.* Auerhahn *m*.

ca·pi·as ['keɪpɪæs] *s.* ⚖ Haftbefehl *m* (*bsd. im Vollstreckungsverfahren*).

cap·il·lar·i·ty [ˌkæpɪ'lærətɪ] *s. phys.* Kapillari'tät *f*; **cap·il·lar·y** [kə'pɪlərɪ] **I** *adj.* haarförmig, -fein, kapil'lar: **~ *attraction*** Kapillaranziehung *f*; **~ *tube*** → II; **II** *s. anat.* Kapil'largefäß *n*.

cap·i·tal¹ ['kæpɪtl] **I** *s.* **1.** Hauptstadt *f*; **2.** Großbuchstabe *m*; **3.** ✝ Kapi'tal *n*: a) Vermögen *n*, b) Unter'nehmer(tum *n*) *pl.*: **☉ *and Labo*(*u*)*r***; **4.** Vorteil *m*, Nutzen *m*: ***make* ~ *out of*** aus *et.* Kapital schlagen; **II** *adj.* **5.** ⚖ a) kapi'tal, todeswürdig: **~ *crime*** Kapitalverbrechen *n*, b) Todes…: **~ *punishment*** Todesstrafe *f*; **6.** größt, wichtigst, Haupt…: **~ *city*** Hauptstadt *f*; **~ *ship*** Großkampfschiff *n*; **7.** verhängnisvoll: ***a* ~ *error*** ein Kapitalfehler *m*; **8.** großartig: ***a* ~ *joke*; *a* ~ *fellow*** ein Prachtkerl *m*; **9.** ✝ Kapital…: **~ *fund*** Stamm-, Grundkapital *n*; **10.** **~ *letter*** → 2; **~ *B*** großes B.

cap·i·tal² ['kæpɪtl] *s.* ⚠ Kapi'tell *n*.

cap·i·tal| ac·count *s.* ✝ Kapi'talkonto *n*; **~ as·sets** *s. pl.* Anlagevermögen *n*; **~ ex·pend·i·ture** *s.* Investiti'onsaufwand *m*; **~ flight** *s.* Kapi'talflucht *f*; **~ gains tax** *s.* Kapi'talertragssteuer *f*; **~ goods** *s. pl.* Investiti'onsgüter *pl.*; **'~-inˌten·sive** *adj.* kapi'talintenˌsiv; **~ in·vest·ment** *s.* Kapi'talanlage *f*.

cap·i·tal·ism ['kæpɪtəlɪzəm] *s.* Kapita'lismus *m*; **'cap·i·tal·ist** [-ɪst] **I** Kapita'list *m*; **II** *adj.* → **cap·i·tal·is·tic** [ˌkæpɪtə'lɪstɪk] *adj.* (□ **~*ally***) kapita'listisch; **cap·i·tal·i·za·tion** [ˌkæpɪtəlaɪ'zeɪʃn] *s.* **1.** ✝ *allg.* Kapitalisierung *f*; **2.** Großschreibung *f*; **'cap·i·tal·ize** [-laɪz] **I** *v/t.* **1.** ✝ kapitalisieren; **2.** *fig.* sich *et.* zu'nutze machen; **3.** groß (*mit Großbuchstaben od. mit großen Anfangsbuchstaben*) schreiben; **II** *v/i.* **4.** Kapi'tal anhäufen; **5.** e-n Kapi'talwert haben (***at*** von); **6.** *fig.* Kapital schlagen (***on*** aus).

cap·i·tal| lev·y *s.* ✝ Vermögensabgabe *f*; **~ mar·ket** *s.* Kapi'talmarkt *m*; **~ stock** *s.* ✝ 'Aktienkapiˌtal *n*.

cap·i·ta·tion [ˌkæpɪ'teɪʃn] *s.* **1.** *a.* **~ *tax*** Kopfsteuer *f*; **2.** Zahlung *f* pro Kopf: **~ *grant*** Zuschuß *m* pro Kopf.

Cap·i·tol ['kæpɪtl] *s.* Kapi'tol *n*: a) *im alten Rom*, b) *in Washington*.

ca·pit·u·lar [kə'pɪtjʊlə] *eccl.* **I** *adj.* kapitu'lar, zum Ka'pitel gehörig; **II** *s.* Kapitu'lar *m*, Domherr *m*.

ca·pit·u·late [kə'pɪtjʊleɪt] *v/i.* ⚔ *u. fig.* kapitulieren (***to*** vor *dat*); **ca·pit·u·la·tion** [kəˌpɪtjʊ'leɪʃn] *s.* ⚔ a) Kapitulati'on *f*, 'Übergabe *f*, b) Kapitulati'onsurkunde *f*.

ca·pon ['keɪpən] *s.* Ka'paun *m*; **'ca·pon·ize** [-naɪz] *v/t. Hahn* kastrieren, ka'paunen.

capped [kæpt] *adj.* mit e-r Kappe *od.* Mütze bedeckt: **~ *and gowned*** in vollem Ornat.

ca·price [kə'pri:s] *s.* Ka'price *f*, Laune *f*, Grille *f*; Launenhaftigkeit *f*; **ca'pri·cious** [-ɪʃəs] *adj.* □ launenhaft, launisch; kaprizi'ös; **ca'pri·cious·ness** [-ɪʃəsnɪs] *s.* Launenhaftigkeit *f*; kaprizi'öse Art.

Cap·ri·corn ['kæprɪkɔ:n] *s. ast.* Steinbock *m*.

cap·ri·ole ['kæprɪəʊl] **I** *s.* Kapri'ole *f* (*a. Reiten*), Bock-, Luftsprung *m*; **II** *v/i.* Kapri'olen machen.

cap·si·cum ['kæpsɪkəm] *s.* ♀ 'Paprika *m*, Spanischer Pfeffer.

cap·size [kæp'saɪz] **I** *v/i.* **1.** ⚓ kentern; **2.** *fig.* 'umschlagen; **II** *v/t.* **3.** ⚓ zum Kentern bringen.

cap·stan ['kæpstən] *s.* ⚓ Gangspill *n*, Ankerwinde *f*; **~ lathe** *s.* ⚙ Re'volverdrehbank *f*.

cap·su·lar ['kæpsjʊlə] *adj.* kapselförmig, Kapsel…; **cap·sule** ['kæpsju:l] **I** *s.* **1.** *anat.* (Gelenk- *etc.*)Kapsel *f*, Hülle *f*, Schale *f*; **2.** ♀ a) Kapselfrucht *f*, b) Sporenkapsel *f*; **3.** *pharm.* (Arz'nei-) Kapsel *f*; **4.** (Me'tall-, Verschluß)Kapsel *f*; **5.** (Raum)Kapsel *f*; **6.** ⚗ Abdampfschale *f*; **7.** *fig.* kurze 'Übersicht *od.* Beschreibung *etc.*; **II** *adj.* **8.** *fig.* kurz, gedrängt, Kurz…

cap·tain ['kæptɪn] **I** *s.* **1.** Führer *m*, Oberhaupt *n*: **~ *of industry*** Industriekapitän *m*; **2.** ⚔ a) Hauptmann *m*, b) *Kavallerie*: *hist.* Rittmeister *m*; **3.** ⚓ a) Kapi'tän *m*, Komman'dant *m*, b) *Kriegsmarine*: Kapitän *m* zur See; **4.** 'Flugkapiˌtän *m*; **5.** *sport* ('Mannschafts)Kapiˌtän *m*; **6.** *ped.* Klassensprecher(in); **7.** Vorarbeiter *m*; ⚒ Obersteiger *m*; **8.** *Am.* (Poli'zei-)ˌHauptkommisˌsar *m*; **II** *v/t.* **9.** (an)führen; **'cap·tain·cy** [-sɪ], **'cap·tain·ship** [-ʃɪp] *s.* **1.** ⚔ Hauptmanns-, Kapi'tänsposten *m*, -rang *m*; **2.** Führerschaft *f*.

cap·tion ['kæpʃn] **I** *s.* **1.** a) 'Überschrift *f*, Titel *m*, b) ('Bild)ˌUnterschrift *f*, c) *Film*: 'Untertitel *m*; **2.** ⚖ a) Prä'ambel *f*, b) *Prozeßrecht*: 'Rubrum *n*; **II** *v/t.* **3.** mit e-r Überschrift *etc.* versehen; *Film* unter'titeln.

cap·tious ['kæpʃəs] *adj.* ☐ **1.** verfänglich; **2.** spitzfindig; **3.** krittelig, pe'dantisch.

cap·ti·vate ['kæptɪveɪt] *v/t. fig.* gefangennehmen, fesseln, bestricken, bezaubern; **'cap·ti·vat·ing** [-tɪŋ] *adj. fig.* fesselnd, bezaubernd; **cap·ti·va·tion** [ˌkæptɪ'veɪʃn] *s. fig.* Bezauberung *f*.

cap·tive ['kæptɪv] **I** *adj.* **1.** gefangen, in Gefangenschaft: ***be held ~*** gefangengehalten werden; ***take ~*** gefangennehmen (*a. fig.*); **2.** festgehalten, ‚gefangen': ***~ balloon*** Fesselballon *m*; **3.** *fig.* gefangen, gefesselt (***to*** von); **II** *s.* **4.** Gefangene(r) *m*, *fig. a.* Sklave *m* (***to*** *gen.*); **cap·tiv·i·ty** [kæp'tɪvətɪ] *s.* **1.** Gefangenschaft *f*; **2.** *fig.* Knechtschaft *f*.

cap·tor ['kæptə] *s.* **1.** ***his ~*** der ihn gefangennahm; **2.** ⚓ Kaper *m*; **'cap·ture** [-tʃə] **I** *v/t.* **1.** fangen; gefangennehmen; **2.** ⚔ erobern; erbeuten; **3.** ⚓ kapern, aufbringen; **4.** *fig.* (*a. Stimmung etc., a. phys. Neutronen*) einfangen; erobern, für sich einnehmen, gewinnen, erlangen; an sich reißen; **II** *s.* **5.** Gefangennahme *f*, Fang *m*; **6.** ⚔ Eroberung *f* (*a. fig.*); Erbeutung *f*; Beute *f*; **7.** ⚓ a) Kapern *n*, Aufbringung *f*, b) Prise *f*.

Cap·u·chin ['kæpjʊʃɪn] *s.* **1.** *eccl.* Kapu'ziner(mönch) *m*; **2.** ♀ 'Umhang *m* mit Ka'puze; **3.** *a.* ***~ monkey*** *zo.* Kapu'zineraffe *m*.

car [kɑː] *s.* **1.** Auto *n*, Wagen *m*: ***by ~*** mit dem (*od.* im) Auto; **2.** (Eisenbahn *etc.*)Wagen *m*, Wag'gon *m*; **3.** Wagen *m*, Karren *m*; **4.** (*Luftschiff- etc.*)Gondel *f*; **5.** Ka'bine *f e-s Aufzuges*; **6.** *poet.* Kriegs- *od.* Tri'umphwagen *m*.

ca·rafe [kə'ræf] *s.* Ka'raffe *f*.

car·a·mel ['kærəmel] *s.* **1.** Kara'mel *m*, gebrannter Zucker; **2.** Kara'melle *f* (*Bonbon*).

car·a·pace ['kærəpeɪs] *s. zo.* Rückenschild *m* (*Schildkröte, Krebs*).

car·at ['kærət] *s.* Ka'rat *n*: a) *Juwelen- od. Perlengewicht*, b) *Goldfeingehalt*: ***18-~ gold*** 18karätiges Gold.

car·a·van ['kærəvæn] **I** *s.* **1.** Kara'wane *f* (*a. fig.*); **2.** a) Wohnwagen *m* (*von Schaustellern etc.*), b) *Brit.* Caravan *m*, Wohnwagen *m*, -anhänger *m*: ***~ park*** *od.* ***site*** Campingplatz *m* für Wohnwagen; **II** *v/i.* **3.** im Wohnwagen *etc.* reisen; **'car·a·van·ner** [-nə] *s.* **1.** Reisende(r) in e-r Kara'wane; **2.** *mot. Brit.* Caravaner *m*; **ˌcar·a'van·sa·ry** [-sərɪ], **ˌcar·a'van·se·rai** [-səraɪ] *s.* Karawanse'rei *f*.

car·a·vel ['kærəvel] *s.* ⚓ Kara'velle *f*.

car·a·way ['kærəweɪ] *s.* ♀ Kümmel *m*; ***~ seeds*** *s. pl.* Kümmelkörner *pl.*

car·bide ['kɑːbaɪd] *s.* ⚗ Kar'bid *n*.

car·bine ['kɑːbaɪn] *s.* ⚔ Kara'biner *m*.

car bod·y *s.* ⚙ Karosse'rie *f*.

car·bo·hy·drate [ˌkɑːbəʊ'haɪdreɪt] *s.* ⚗ 'Kohle(n)hyˌdrat *n*.

car·bol·ic ac·id [kɑː'bɒlɪk] *s.* ⚗ Kar'bol(säure *f*) *n*, Phe'nol *n*.

car·bo·lize ['kɑːbəlaɪz] *v/t.* ⚗ mit Kar'bolsäure behandeln.

car·bon ['kɑːbən] *s.* **1.** ⚗ Kohlenstoff *m*; **2.** ⚡ 'Kohle(elekˌtrode) *f*; **3.** a) 'Kohlepaˌpier *n*, b) 'Durchschlag *m*; **car·bo·na·ceous** [ˌkɑːbəʊ'neɪʃəs] *adj.* kohlenstoff-, kohleartig; Kohlen…; **'car·bon·ate** ⚗ **I** *s.* [-nɪt] **1.** kohlensaures Salz: ***~ of lime*** Kalziumkarbonat *n*, Kreide *f*; ***~ of soda*** Natriumkarbonat *n*, kohlensaures Natrium, Soda *f*; **II** *v/t.* [-neɪt] **2.** mit Kohlensäure *od.* Kohlen'dioˌxyd behandeln: ***~d water*** kohlensäurehaltiges Wasser, Sodawasser; **3.** karbonisieren, verkohlen.

car·bon| brush *s.* ⚡ Kohlebürste *f*; **~ cop·y** *s.* **1.** 'Durchschlag *m*, -schrift *f*, Ko'pie *f*; **2.** *fig.* Abklatsch *m*, Dupli'kat *n*; **~ dat·ing** *s.* Radiokar'bonmeˌthode *f*, 'C-'14-Meˌthode *f* (*zur Altersbestimmung*); **~ di·ox·ide** *s.* ⚗ Kohlen'dioˌxyd *n*; **~ fil·a·ment** *s.* ⚡ Kohlefaden *m*.

car·bon·ic [kɑː'bɒnɪk] *adj.* ⚗ kohlenstoffhaltig; Kohlen…; **~ ac·id** *s.* ⚗ Kohlensäure *f*; **~-'ac·id gas** *s.* ⚗ Kohlen'dioˌxyd *n*, Kohlensäuregas *n*; **~ ox·ide** *s.* ⚗ Kohlen('mon)oˌxyd *n*.

car·bon·if·er·ous [ˌkɑːbə'nɪfərəs] *adj.* kohlehaltig, kohleführend: ♀ ***Period*** *geol.* Karbon *n*, Steinkohlenzeit *f*; **car·bon·i·za·tion** [ˌkɑːbənaɪ'zeɪʃn] *s.* **1.** Verkohlung *f*; **2.** Verkokung *f*: ***~ plant*** Kokerei *f*; **'car·bon·ize** [-naɪz] *v/t.* **1.** verkohlen; **2.** verkoken.

car·bon| mi·cro·phone *s.* 'Kohlemikroˌphon *n*; **~ pa·per** *s.* 'Kohlepaˌpier *n* (*a. phot.*); **~ print** *s. typ.* Kohle-, Pig'mentdruck *m*; **~ steel** *s.* Kohlenstoff-, Flußstahl *m*.

car·bo·run·dum [ˌkɑːbə'rʌndəm] *s.* ⚙ Karbo'rundum *n* (*Schleifmittel*).

car·boy ['kɑːbɔɪ] *s.* Korbflasche *f*, ('Glas)Balˌlon *m* (*bsd. für Säuren*).

car·bun·cle ['kɑːbʌŋkl] *s.* **1.** ⚕ Kar'bunkel *m*; **2.** Kar'funkel *m*, geschliffener Gra'nat.

car·bu·ret ['kɑːbjʊret] *v/t.* ⚙ karburieren; *mot.* vergasen; **'car·bu·ret·(t)ed** [-tɪd] *adj.* karburiert; **'car·bu·ret·ter, -ret·tor** [-tə], *Am. mst* **-ret·or** [-reɪtə] *s.* ⚙, *mot.* Vergaser *m*.

car·bu·rize ['kɑːbjʊraɪz] *v/t.* **1.** ⚗ a) mit Kohlenstoff verbinden, b) karburieren; **2.** ⚙ einsatzhärten.

car·cass, **car·case** ['kɑːkəs] *s.* **1.** Ka'daver *m*, (Tier-, Menschen)Leiche *f*; *humor.* ‚Leichnam' *m* (*Körper*); **2.** Rumpf *m* (*e-s geschlachteten Tieres*): ***~ meat*** frisches Fleisch (*Ggs. konserviertes*); **3.** Gerippe *n*, Ske'lett *n*, ⚠ *a.* Rohbau *m*; **4.** ⚙ Kar'kasse *f e-s Gummireifens*; **5.** *fig.* Ru'ine *f*.

car·cin·o·gen [kɑː'sɪnədʒən] *s.* Karzino'gen *n*, Krebserreger *m*; **car·cin·o·gen·ic** [ˌkɑːsɪnə'dʒenɪk] *adj.* karzino'gen, krebserzeugend; **car·ci·nol·o·gy** [ˌkɑːsɪ'nɒlədʒɪ] *s.* ⚕, *a. zo.* Karzinolo'gie *f*; **car·ci·no·ma** [ˌkɑːsɪ'nəʊmə] *pl.* **-ma·ta** [-mətə] *od.* **-mas** *s.* ⚕ Karzi'nom *n*, Krebsgeschwür *n*.

card[1] [kɑːd] *s.* **1.** (*Spiel*)Karte *f*: ***play (at) ~s*** Karten spielen; ***game of ~s*** Kartenspiel *n*; ***a pack of ~s*** ein Spiel Karten; ***house of ~s*** *fig.* Kartenhaus *n*; ***a safe ~*** *fig.* eine sichere Sache, et., auf das (*a.* j-d, auf den) man sich verlassen kann; ***play one's ~s well*** *fig.* geschickt vorgehen; ***put one's ~s on the table*** *fig.* s-e Karten auf den Tisch legen; ***show one's ~s*** *fig.* s-e Karten aufdekken; ***on the ~s*** *fig.* (durchaus) möglich, ‚drin'; **2.** (*Post-, Glückwunsch etc., Geschäfts-, Visiten-, Eintritts-, Einladungs*)Karte *f*; **3.** Mitgliedskarte *f*: ***~-carrying member*** eingeschriebenes Mitglied; **4.** *pl.* ('Arbeits)Paˌpiere *pl.*: ***get one's ~s*** Ⓕ entlassen werden; **5.** ⚙ (Loch)Karte *f*; **6.** *sport* Pro'gramm *n*; **7.** Windrose *f* (*Kompaß*); **8.** Ⓕ ‚Type' *f*, Witzbold *m*.

card[2] [kɑːd] ⚙ **I** *s.* Wollkratze *f*, Krempel *f*; **II** *v/t.* *Wolle* krempeln, kämmen: ***~ed yarn*** Streichgarn *n*.

car·dan| joint ['kɑːdən] *s.* ⚙ Kar'dangelenk *n*; **~ shaft** *s.* ⚙ Kar'dan-, Gelenkwelle *f*.

'card|-ˌbas·ket *s.* Vi'sitenkartenschale *f*; **'~·board I** *s.* **1.** Kar'ton(paˌpier *n*) *m*, Pappe *f*; **II** *adj.* **2.** Karton…, Papp…: ***~ box*** Pappschachtel *f*, Karton *m*; **3.** *fig. contp.* ‚nachgemacht', Pappmaché-…; **~ cat·a·logue** → ***card index***.

card·er ['kɑːdə] *s.* ⚙ **1.** Krempler *m*, Wollkämmer *m*; **2.** 'Krempelmaˌschine *f*.

car·di·ac ['kɑːdɪæk] ⚕ **I** *adj.* **1.** Herz…: ***~ arrest*** Herzstillstand *m*; **II** *s.* **2.** Herzmittel *n*; **3.** 'Herzpatiˌent *m*.

car·di·gan ['kɑːdɪgən] *s.* Strickjacke *f*.

car·di·nal ['kɑːdɪnl] **I** *adj.* **1.** grundsätzlich, grundlegend, hauptsächlich, Haupt…, Kardinal…: ***~ points*** *die* vier (Haupt)Himmelsrichtungen; ***~ principles*** Grundprinzipien; ***~ number*** Kardinalzahl *f*; **2.** *eccl.* Kardinals…; **3.** scharlachrot, hochrot: ***~-flower*** ♀ hochrote Lobelie; **II** *s.* **4.** *eccl.* Kardi'nal *m*; **5.** *orn. a.* ***~-bird*** Kardi'nal *m*; **'car·di·nal·ship** [-ʃɪp] *s.* Kardi'nalswürde *f*.

card in·dex *s.* Karto'thek *f*, Kar'tei *f*; **'card-ˌin·dex** *v/t.* **1.** e-e Kartei anlegen von, verzetteln; **2.** in e-e Kartei eintragen.

card·ing ['kɑːdɪŋ] *s.* ⚙ Krempeln *n*, Kratzen *n* (*Wolle*): ***~ machine*** Krempel-, Kratzmaschine *f*.

cardio- [kɑːdɪəʊ] *in Zssgn* Herz…

car·di·o·gram ['kɑːdɪəʊgræm] *s.* ⚕ Kardio'gramm *n*; **car·di·ol·o·gy** [ˌkɑːdɪ'ɒlədʒɪ] *s.* Kardiolo'gie *f*, Herz(heil)kunde *f*.

card| room *s.* (Karten)Spielzimmer *n*; **'~·sharp**, **'~ˌsharp·er** *s.* Falschspieler *m*; **~ ta·ble** *s.* Spieltisch *m*; **~ trick** *s.* Kartenkunststück *n*; **~ vote** *s.* *Brit.* (*mst gewerkschaftliche*) Abstimmung durch Wahlmänner.

care [keə] **I** *s.* **1.** Sorge *f*, Kummer *m*: ***be free from ~(s)*** keine Sorgen haben; ***without a ~ in the world*** völlig sorgenfrei; **2.** Sorgfalt *f*, Aufmerksamkeit *f*, Vorsicht *f*: ***ordinary ~*** ⚖ verkehrsübliche Sorgfalt; ***with due ~*** mit der erforderlichen Sorgfalt; ***have a ~!*** *Brit.* Ⓕ a) paß doch auf!, b) ich bitte dich!; ***take ~*** a) vorsichtig sein, aufpassen, b) sich Mühe geben, c) darauf achten *od.* nicht vergessen (***to do*** zu tun; ***that*** daß); ***take ~ not to do s.th.*** sich hüten, et. zu tun; et. ja nicht tun; ***take ~ not to drop it!*** laß es ja nicht fallen; ***take ~!*** F mach's gut!; **3.** a) Obhut *f*, Schutz *m*, Fürsorge *f*, Betreuung *f*, (*Kinder- etc.*, *a. Körper- etc.*)Pflege *f*, b) Aufsicht *f*, Leitung *f*: ***~ and custody*** (*od.* ***control***) ⚖ Sorgerecht *n* (***of*** für *j-n*); ***take ~ of*** a) → 6, b) aufpassen auf (*acc.*), c) *et.* erledigen *od.* besorgen; ***take ~ of yourself!*** paß auf dich auf!, mach's gut!; ***that takes ~ of that!*** F das wäre (damit) erledigt!; **4.** Pflicht *f*: ***his special ~s***; **II** *v/i.* **5.** sich sorgen (***about*** über *acc.*, um); **6.** ***~ for*** sorgen für, sich kümmern um, betreuen, pflegen: (***well***) ***~d-for*** (gut)gepflegt; **7.** (***for***) (*j-n*) gern haben *od.* mögen: ***he doesn't ~ for her*** er macht sich nichts aus ihr, er mag sie nicht; ***he does ~*** (***for her***) er mag sie wirklich; **8.** sich etwas daraus machen: ***I don't ~ for whisky*** ich mache mir nichts aus Whisky; ***he ~s a great deal*** es ist ihm sehr daran gelegen, es macht ihm schon etwas aus; ***she doesn't really ~*** in Wirklichkeit liegt ihr nicht viel daran: ***I don't ~ a damn*** (*od.* ***fig, pin, straw***), ***I couldn't ~ less*** es ist mir völlig gleich(gültig) *od.* egal *od.* ‚schnuppe'; ***who ~s?*** na, und?, (und) wenn schon?; ***for all I ~*** meinetwegen, von mir aus; ***for all you ~*** wenn es nach dir ginge; ***I don't ~ to do it now*** ich habe keine Lust, es jetzt zu tun; ***I don't ~ to be seen with you*** ich lege keinen Wert darauf, mit dir gesehen zu werden; ***would you ~ for a drink?*** möchtest du et. zu trinken?; ***we don't ~ if you stay here*** wir haben nichts dagegen *od.* es macht uns nichts aus, wenn du hierbleibst; ***I don't ~ if I do!*** F von mir aus!

ca·reen [kəˈriːn] **I** *v/t.* **1.** ⚓ *Schiff* kielholen; **II** *v/i.* **2.** ⚓ krängen, sich auf die Seite legen; **3.** *fig.* (hin u. her) schwanken, torkeln.

ca·reer [kəˈrɪə] **I** *s.* **1.** Karriˈere *f*, Laufbahn *f*, Werdegang *m*: ***enter upon a ~*** e-e Laufbahn einschlagen; **2.** (*erfolgreiche*) Karriˈere: ***make a ~ for o.s.*** Karriere machen; **3.** (Lebens)Beruf *m*: ***~ diplomat*** Berufsdiplomat *m*; ***~ girl*** *od.* ***woman*** Karrierefrau *f*; ***~s guidance*** *Brit.* Berufsberatung *f*; ***~s officer*** *Brit.* Berufsberater *m*; **4.** gestreckter Gaˈlopp, Karriˈere *f*: ***in full ~*** in vollem Galopp (*a. weitS.*); **II** *v/i.* **5.** galoppieren; **6.** rennen, rasen, jagen; **ca·reer·ist** [kəˈrɪərɪst] *s.* Karriˈeremacher *m*.

ˈcare·free *adj.* sorgenfrei.

care·ful [ˈkeəfʊl] *adj.* □ **1.** vorsichtig, achtsam: ***be ~!*** nimm dich in acht!; ***be ~ to*** *inf.* darauf achten zu *inf.*, nicht vergessen zu *inf.*; ***be ~ not to*** *inf.* sich hüten zu *inf.*; aufpassen, daß nicht; ***be ~ of your clothes!*** gib acht auf deine Kleidung!; **2.** bedacht, achtsam (***of, for, about*** auf *acc.*), ˈumsichtig; **3.** sorgfältig, genau, gründlich: ***a ~ study***; **4.** *Brit.* sparsam; **ˈcare·ful·ness** [-nɪs] *s.* Vorsicht *f*, Sorgfalt *f*; Gründlichkeit *f*; ˈUmsicht *f*.

care·less [ˈkeəlɪs] *adj.* □ **1.** nachlässig, unvorsichtig, unachtsam; leichtsinnig; **2.** (***of, about***) unbekümmert (um), unbesorgt (um), gleichgültig (gegenˈüber): ***~ of danger***; **3.** unbedacht, unbesonnen: ***a ~ remark***; ***a ~ mistake*** ein Flüchtigkeitsfehler; **4.** sorgenfrei, fröhlich: ***~ youth***; **ˈcare·less·ness** [-nɪs] *s.* Nachlässigkeit *f*; Unbedachtheit *f*; Sorglosigkeit *f*, Unachtsamkeit *f*.

ca·ress [kəˈres] **I** *s.* Liebkosung *f*; *pl. a.* Zärtlichkeiten *pl.*; **II** *v/t.* liebkosen; streicheln; *fig. der Haut etc.* schmeicheln; **caˈress·ing** [-sɪŋ] *adj.* □ zärtlich; schmeichelnd.

car·et [ˈkærət] *s.* Einschaltungszeichen *n* (*für Auslassung im Text*).

ˈcare|-ˌtak·er *s.* **1.** a) Hausmeister *m*, b) (Haus- *etc.*)Verwalter *m*; **2.** ***~ government*** geschäftsführende Regierung, ˈÜbergangskabiˌnett *n*; **ˈ~-worn** *adj.* vergrämt, abgehärmt.

Ca·rey Street [ˈkeərɪ] *s.*: ***in ~*** *Brit.* F ‚pleite', bankrott.

ˈcar·fare *s. Am.* Fahrgeld *n*, -preis *m*.

car·go [ˈkɑːgəʊ] *pl.* **-goes**, *Am. a.* **-gos** *s.* ⚓, ✈ Ladung *f*, Fracht(gut *n*) *f*; **~ boat** *s.* ⚓ Frachtschiff *n*; **ˈ~-ˌcar·ry·ing** *adj.* Fracht…, Transport…: ***~ glider*** Lastensegler *m*; **~ hold** *s.* Laderaum *m*; **~ par·a·chute** *s.* Lastenfallschirm *m*; **~ plane** *s.* ✈ Transˈportflugzeug *n*.

ˈcar·hop *s. Am.* Kellner(in) in e-m Drive-ˈin-Restauˌrant.

Car·ib·be·an [ˌkærɪˈbiːən] **I** *adj.* kaˈribisch; **II** *s. geogr.* Kaˈribisches Meer.

car·i·bou, **car·i·boo** [ˈkærɪbuː] *s. zo.* ˈKaribu *m*.

car·i·ca·ture [ˈkærɪkəˌtjʊə] **I** *s.* Karikaˈtur *f* (*a. fig.*); **II** *v/t.* karikieren; **ˈcar·i·caˌtur·ist** [-ʊərɪst] *s.* Karikatuˈrist *m*.

car·i·es [ˈkeərɪiːz] *s.* ⚕ ˈKaries *f*: a) Knochenfraß *m*, b) Zahnfäule *f*.

car·il·lon [ˈkærɪljən] *s.* (Turm)Glockenspiel *n*, ˈGlockenspielmuˌsik *f*.

car·ing [ˈkeərɪŋ] *adj.* liebevoll, mitfühlend; soziˈal (engagiert).

Ca·rin·thi·an [kəˈrɪnθɪən] **I** *adj.* kärntnerisch; **II** *s.* Kärntner(in).

car·i·ous [ˈkeərɪəs] *adj.* ⚕ kariˈös, angefressen, faul.

car| jack *s.* ⚙ Wagenheber *m*; **ˈ~·load** *s.* **1.** Wagenladung *f*; **2.** *Am.* a) Güterwagenladung *f*, b) Mindestladung *f* (*für Frachtermäßigung*); **3.** *Am. fig.* ‚Haufen' *m*, Menge *f*; **ˈ~·man** [-mən] *s.* [*irr.*] **1.** Fuhrmann *m*; **2.** (Kraft)Fahrer *m*; **3.** Spediˈteur *m*.

car·mine [ˈkɑːmaɪn] **I** *s.* Karˈminrot *n*; **II** *adj.* karˈminrot.

car·nage [ˈkɑːnɪdʒ] *s.* Blutbad *n*, Gemetzel *n*.

car·nal [ˈkɑːnl] *adj.* □ fleischlich, sinnlich; geschlechtlich: ***~ knowledge*** ⚖ Geschlechtsverkehr (***of*** mit); **car·nal·i·ty** [kɑːˈnælətɪ] *s.* Fleischeslust *f*, Sinnlichkeit *f*.

car·na·tion [kɑːˈneɪʃn] *s.* **1.** ⚘ (Garten-)Nelke *f*; **2.** Blaßrot *n*.

car·net [ˈkɑːneɪ] *s. mot.* Carˈnet *n*, ˈZollpasˌsierschein *m*.

car·ni·val [ˈkɑːnɪvl] *s.* **1.** ˈKarneval *m*, Fasching *m*; **2.** Volksfest *n*; **3.** ausgelassenes Feiern; **4.** *Am.* (Sport- *etc.*)Veranstaltung *f*.

car·niv·o·ra [kɑːˈnɪvərə] *s. pl. zo.* Fleischfresser *pl.*; **car·ni·vore** [ˈkɑːnɪvɔː] *s. zo.* Fleischfresser *m*, *bsd.* Raubtier *n*; **carˈniv·o·rous** [-rəs] *adj. zo.* fleischfressend.

car·ob [ˈkærəb] *s.* ⚘ Joˈhannisbrot(baum *m*) *n*.

car·ol [ˈkærəl] **I** *s.* **1.** Freuden-, *bsd.* Weihnachtslied *n*; **II** *v/i.* **2.** Weihnachtslieder singen; **3.** jubilieren.

Car·o·lin·gi·an [ˌkærəʊˈlɪndʒɪən] *hist.* **I** *adj.* ˈkarolingisch; **II** *s.* ˈKarolinger *m*.

car·om [ˈkærəm] *bsd. Am.* **I** *s.* **1.** *Billard*: Karamboˈlage *f*; **II** *v/i.* **2.** karambolieren; **3.** abprallen.

ca·rot·id [kəˈrɒtɪd] *s. u. adj. anat.* (die) Halsschlagader (betreffend).

ca·rous·al [kəˈraʊzl] *s.* Trinkgelage *n*, Zecheˈrei *f*; **ca·rouse** [kəˈraʊz] **I** *v/i.* (lärmend) zechen; **II** *s.* → ***carousal***.

carp¹ [kɑːp] *v/i.* (***at***) nörgeln (an *dat.*), kritteln (über *acc.*).

carp² [kɑːp] *s. ichth.* Karpfen *m*.

car·pal [ˈkɑːpl] *anat.* **I** *adj.* Handwurzel…; **II** *s.* Handwurzelknochen *m*.

car park *s.* Parkplatz *m*, -haus *n*: ***underground ~*** Tiefgarage *f*.

car·pel [ˈkɑːpel] *s.* ⚘ Fruchtblatt *n*.

car·pen·ter [ˈkɑːpəntə] **I** *s.* Zimmermann *m*; **II** *v/t. u. v/i.* zimmern; **~ ant** *s. zo.* Holzameise *f*; **~ bee** *s. zo.* Holzbiene *f*.

car·pen·ter's| bench [ˈkɑːpəntəz] *s.* Hobelbank *f*; **~ lev·el** *s.* ⚙ Setzwaage *f*.

car·pen·try [ˈkɑːpəntrɪ] *s.* Zimmerhandwerk *n*; Zimmerarbeit *f*.

car·pet [ˈkɑːpɪt] **I** *s.* **1.** Teppich *m* (*a. fig.*), (*Treppen- etc.*)Läufer *m*: ***be on the ~*** *fig.* a) zur Debatte stehen, auf dem Tapet sein, b) F ‚zs.-gestaucht' werden; ***sweep under the ~*** *a. fig.* unter den Teppich kehren; → ***red carpet***; **II** *v/t.* **2.** mit (*od.* wie mit) e-m Teppich belegen; **3.** *Brit.* F ‚zs.-stauchen'; **~ bag** *s.* Reisetasche *f*; **ˈ~ˌbag·ger** *s. Am.* F **1.** (poˈlitischer) Abenteurer (*ursprünglich nach dem Bürgerkrieg*); **2.** *allg.* Schwindler *m*; **~ bomb·ing** *s.* ⚔ Bombenteppichwurf *m*; **~ dance** *s.* zwangloses Tänzchen; **ˈ~·knight** *s. Brit.* Saˈlonlöwe *m*; **~ sweep·er** *s.* ˈTeppichkehrmaˌschine *f*.

carp·ing [ˈkɑːpɪŋ] **I** *s.* Kritteˈlei *f*; **II** *adj.* □ krittelig: ***~ criticism*** → I.

car| pool *s.* **1.** Fuhrpark *m*; **2.** Fahrgemeinschaft *f*; **ˈ~·port** *s.* Einstellplatz *m* (*im Freien*).

car·pus [ˈkɑːpəs] *pl.* **-pi** [-paɪ] *s. anat.* Handgelenk *n*, -wurzel *f*.

car·rel [ˈkærəl] *s.* Lesenische *f* (*in e-r Bibliothek*).

car·riage [ˈkærɪdʒ] *s.* **1.** Wagen *m*, Kutsche *f*: ***~ and pair*** Zweispänner *m*; **2.** *Brit.* Eisenbahnwagen *m*; **3.** Beförderung *f*, Transˈport *m*: ***~ by sea*** Seetransport; **4.** ☤ Transˈportkosten *pl.*, Fracht(gebühr) *f*; Fuhrlohn *m*, Rollgeld *n*: ***~ paid*** frachtfrei, franko; ***~ forward*** *Brit.* Fracht gegen Nachnahme; **5.** ⚔ Laˈfette *f*; **6.** ✈ Fahrgestell *n*; **7.** a) Karren *m*, Laufbrett *n* (*e-r Druckerpresse*), b) Wagen *m* (*e-r Schreibmaschine etc.*), c) Schlitten *m* (*e-r Werkzeugmaschine*); **8.** (Körper)Haltung *f*, Gang *m*: ***a graceful ~***; **9.** *pol.* ˈDurchbringen *n*, Annahme *f* (*Gesetz etc.*); **ˈcar·riage·a·ble** [-dʒəbl] *adj.* befahrbar.

car·riage| bod·y *s.* Wagenkasten *m*, Karosseˈrie *f*; **ˈ~·drive** *s.* Fahrweg *m*; **ˈ~·road**, **ˈ~·way** *s. Brit.* Fahrbahn *f*.

car·ri·er [ˈkærɪə] *s.* **1.** Überˈbringer *m*, Bote *m*; **2.** Spediˈteur *m*, *a.* ***~s*** *pl.* Spedit̆iˈonsfirma *f*: ***common ~*** ☤ Frachtführer *m*, Transportunternehmer *m*,

-unternehmen *n* (*a.* 🚂, ⚓ *etc.*); **3.** ⚕ ('Krankheits)Über,träger *m*; Keimträger *m*; **4.** ⚗ (Über)'Träger *m*, Kataly'sator *m*; **5.** ⚡ Träger(strom *m*, -welle *f*) *m*; **6.** Träger *m*, Tragbehälter *m*, -netz *n*, -kiste *f*, -gestell *n*; Gepäckhalter *m am Fahrrad*; *mot.* Dachgepäckträger *m*; **7.** ⚙ a) Schlitten *m*, Trans'port *m*, b) Mitnehmer *m*; **8.** *abbr. für* ***aircraft carrier***; '**~·bag** *s.* Tragtasche *f*, -tüte *f*; **~ pi·geon** *s.* Brieftaube *f*; **~ rock·et** *s.* 'Trägerra,kete *f*.

car·ri·on ['kærɪən] *s.* **1.** Aas *n*; **2.** verdorbenes Fleisch; **3.** *fig.* Unrat *m*, Schmutz *m*; **~ bee·tle** *s. zo.* Aaskäfer *m*.

car·rot ['kærət] *s.* **1.** ⚘ Ka'rotte *f*, Mohrrübe *f*: ***~ or stick*** *fig.* Zuckerbrot oder Peitsche; ***hold out a ~ to s.o.*** *fig.* j-n zu ködern versuchen; **2.** F a) *pl.* rotes Haar, b) Rotkopf *m*; '**car·rot·y** [-tɪ] *adj.* **1.** gelbrot; **2.** rothaarig.

car·rou·sel [,kærʊ'zel] *s. bsd. Am.* Karus'sell *n*.

car·ry ['kærɪ] **I** *s.* **1.** Trag-, Schußweite *f*; **2.** Flugstrecke *f* (*Golfball*); **3.** → ***portage*** 2; **II** *v/t.* **4.** tragen: ***~ a burden***; ***~ o.s.*** (*od.* ***one's body***) ***well*** e-e gute (Körper)Haltung haben; **5.** bei sich haben, (an sich) haben: ***~ money about one*** Geld bei sich haben; ***~ in one's head*** im Kopf haben *od.* behalten; ***~ authority*** großen Einfluß ausüben; ***~ conviction*** überzeugen(d sein *od.* klingen); ***~ a moral*** e-e Moral (zum Inhalt) haben; **6.** befördern, bringen; mit sich bringen *od.* führen; (ein)bringen: ***railways ~ goods*** die Eisenbahnen befördern Waren; ***~ a message*** e-e Nachricht überbringen; ***~ interest*** Zinsen tragen *od.* bringen; ***~ insurance*** versichert sein; ***~ consequences*** Folgen haben; **7.** (hin'durch-, he'rum)führen; fortsetzen, ausdehnen: ***~ a wall around the park*** e-e Mauer um den Park ziehen; ***~ to excess*** übertreiben; ***you ~ things too far*** du treibst die Dinge zu weit; **8.** erlangen, gewinnen; erobern (*a.* ⚔): ***~ all before one*** auf der ganzen Linie siegen, vollen Erfolg haben; ***~ the audience with one*** die Zuhörer mitreißen; ***~ an election*** e-e Wahl gewinnen; ***~ a district*** *Am.* e-n Wahlkreis *od.* -bezirk erobern, den Wahlsieg in e-m Bezirk davontragen; **9.** 'durchbringen, -setzen: ***~ a motion*** e-n Antrag durchbringen; ***carried unanimously*** einstimmig angenommen; ***~ one's point*** s-e Ansicht durchsetzen, sein Ziel erreichen; **10.** *Waren* führen; *Zeitungsmeldung* bringen; **11.** *Rechnen*: über'tragen, ‚sich merken': ***~ two*** gemerkt zwei; ***~ to a new account*** ♰ auf neue Rechnung vortragen; **III** *v/i.* **12.** *weit* tragen, reichen (*Stimme*, *Schall*; *Schußwaffen*);

Zssgn mit adv.:

car·ry| a·way *v/t.* **1.** wegtragen; fortreißen (*a. fig.*); **2.** *fig.* hinreißen: a) begeistern, b) verleiten: ***get carried away*** a) in Verzückung geraten, b) die Selbstkontrolle verlieren, sich hinreißen lassen (***into doing*** *et.* zu tun); **~ for·ward** *v/t.* **1.** fortsetzen, vor'anbringen; **2.** ♰ *Summe od. Saldo* vortragen: ***amount carried forward*** a) Vor-, Übertrag *m*, b) *Rechnen*: Transport *m*; **~ off** *v/t.* forttragen, -schaffen; ab-, entführen, verschleppen; *j-n* hinwegraffen (*Krankheit*); *Preis etc.* gewinnen, erringen; **~ on I** *v/t.* **1.** *fig.* fortführen, -setzen; *Plan* verfolgen; *Geschäft* betreiben; *Gespräch* führen; **II** *v/i.* **2.** fortfahren; weitermachen; **3.** fortbestehen; **4.** F a) ein ‚The'ater' *od.* e-e Szene machen, sich schlecht aufführen, es wild *od.* wüst treiben, b) ‚es (*ein Verhältnis*) haben' (***with*** mit); **~ out** *v/t.* aus-, 'durchführen, erfüllen; **~ o·ver** *v/t.* ♰ **1.** → ***carry forward*** 2; **2.** *Waren* übrigbehalten; **3.** *Börse*: prolongieren; **~ through** *v/t.* 'durchführen; *j-m* 'durchhelfen, *j-n* 'durchbringen.

'**car·ry|·all** *s. Am.* **1.** Per'sonen,auto *n* mit Längssitzen; **2.** große (Einkaufs-, Reise)Tasche; '**~·cot** *s.* (Baby)Tragetasche *f*; '**~·,for·ward** *s.* ♰ *Brit.* ('Saldo-) Vortrag *m*, 'Übertrag *m*.

car·ry·ing ['kærɪɪŋ] *s.* Beförderung *f*; Trans'port *m*; **~ a·gent** *s.* Spedi'teur *m*; **~ ca·pac·i·ty** *s.* Lade-, Tragfähigkeit *f*; **,~-'on** *pl.* **,~s-'on** *s.* F **1.** ‚The'ater' *n*: a) Getue *n*, b) Af'färe *f*; **2.** schlechtes Benehmen; **~ trade** *s.* Spediti'onsgewerbe *n*.

,car·ry'o·ver *s.* ♰ **1.** → ***carry-forward***; **2.** *Brit. Börse*: Prolongati'on *f*: ***~ rate*** Reportsatz *m*.

'**car|·sick** *adj.* eisenbahn- *od.* autokrank; '**~-,sick·ness** *s.* Autokrankheit *f*, Übelkeit *f* beim Autofahren.

cart [kɑːt] **I** *s.* (Fracht)Karren *m*, Lieferwagen *m*; Handwagen *m*: ***put the ~ before the horse*** *fig.* das Pferd beim Schwanz aufzäumen; ***in the ~*** *Brit.* F in der Klemme; **II** *v/t.* karren, fördern, fahren: ***~ about*** umherschleppen; '**cart·age** [-tɪdʒ] *s.* Fuhrlohn *m*, Rollgeld *n*.

carte blanche [,kɑːt'blɑ̃ːnʃ] *s.* **1.** ♰ Blan'kett *n*; **2.** *fig.* unbeschränkte Vollmacht: ***have ~*** (völlig) freie Hand haben.

car·tel [kɑː'tel] *s.* **1.** ♰, *a. pol.* Kar'tell *n*; **2.** ⚔ Abkommen *n* über den Austausch von Kriegsgefangenen; **car·tel·i·za·tion** [,kɑːtəlaɪ'zeɪʃn] *s.* ♰ Kartellierung *f*; **car·tel·ize** ['kɑːtəlaɪz] *v/t. u. v/i.* ♰ kartellieren.

cart·er ['kɑːtə] *s.* ('Roll)Fuhrunter,nehmer *m*.

Car·te·sian [kɑː'tiːzjən] **I** *adj.* kartesi'anisch; **II** *s.* Kartesi'aner *m*, Anhänger *m* der Lehre Des'cartes'.

'**cart-horse** *s.* Zugpferd *n*.

Car·thu·sian [kɑː'θjuːzjən] *s.* **1.** Kar'täuser(mönch) *m*; **2.** Schüler *m* der Charterhouse-Schule (*in England*).

car·ti·lage ['kɑːtɪlɪdʒ] *s. anat.*, *zo.* Knorpel *m*; **car·ti·lag·i·nous** [,kɑːtɪ'lædʒɪnəs] *adj.* knorpelig.

'**cart·load** *s.* Wagenladung *f*, Fuhre *f*; *fig.* Haufen *m*.

car·tog·ra·pher [kɑː'tɒgrəfə] *s.* Karto'graph *m*, Kartenzeichner *m*; **car'tog·ra·phy** [-fɪ] *s.* Kartogra'phie *f*.

car·ton ['kɑːtən] *s.* **1.** (Papp)Schachtel *f*, Kar'ton *m*: ***a ~ of cigarettes*** e-e Stange Zigaretten; **2.** das ‚Schwarze' (*der Zielscheibe*).

car·toon [kɑː'tuːn] *s.* **1.** Karika'tur *f*: ***~*** (***film***) Zeichentrickfilm *m*; **2.** *mst pl.* Cartoon(s *pl.*) *m*, Comics-Serie *f*, Bilder(fortsetzungs)geschichte *f*; **3.** *paint.* Kar'ton *m*, Entwurf *m* (*in natürlicher Größe*); **car'toon·ist** [-nɪst] *s.* Karika'tu'rist *m*.

car·touch(e) [kɑː'tuːʃ] *s.* ⩓ Kar'tusche *f* (*Ornament*).

car·tridge ['kɑːtrɪdʒ] *s.* **1.** ⚔ a) Pa'trone *f*, b) *Artillerie*: Kar'tusche *f*: ***blank ~*** Platzpatrone *f*; **2.** *phot.* ('Film)Pa,trone *f* (*Kleinbildkamera*), (-)Kas,sette *f* (*Film- od. Kassettenkamera*); **3.** Tonabnehmer *m*; **4.** ('Füllhalter)Pa,trone *f*; **~ belt** *s.* ⚔ Pa'tronengurt *m*; **~ case** *s.* Pa'tronenhülse *f*; **~ clip** *s.* Ladestreifen *m*; **~ pa·per** *s.* 'Zeichenpa,pier *n*; **~ pen** *s.* Pa'tronenfüllhalter *m*.

'**cart|·wheel** *s.* **I** *s.* **1.** Wagenrad *n*; **2.** ***turn a ~*** *sport* radschlagen; **II** *v/i.* **3.** radschlagen; **4.** sich mehrmals (seitlich) über'schlagen; '**~·wright** *s.* Stellmacher *m*, Wagenbauer *m*.

carve [kɑːv] **I** *v/t.* **1.** (*in*) *Holz* schnitzen, (*in*) *Stein* meißeln: ***~ out of stone*** aus Stein meißeln *od.* hauen; ***~ one's name on a tree*** s-n Namen in e-n Baum einritzen *od.* -schneiden; **2.** mit Schnitze'reien *etc.* verzieren: ***~ the leg of a table***; **3.** *Fleisch* vorschneiden, zerlegen, tranchieren; **4.** *fig. oft* ***~ out*** gestalten: ***~ out a fortune*** ein Vermögen machen; ***~ out a career for o.s.*** sich e-e Karriere aufbauen; **5.** ***~ up*** aufteilen, zerstückeln; **6.** ***~ up*** F *j-n* mit dem Messer übel zurichten; **II** *v/i.* **7.** schnitzen, meißeln; **8.** (Fleisch) vorschneiden.

car·vel ['kɑːvl] → ***caravel***; '**~-built** *adj.* ⚓ kra'weelgebaut.

carv·er ['kɑːvə] *s.* **1.** (Holz)Schnitzer *m*, Bildhauer *m*; **2.** Tranchierer *m*; **3.** a) Tranchiermesser *n*, b) *pl.* Tranchierbesteck *n*; '**carv·er·y** [-ərɪ] *s.* *Lokal, in dem man für e-n Einheitspreis soviel Fleisch essen kann, wie man will*.

carv·ing ['kɑːvɪŋ] *s.* Schnitze'rei *f*, Schnitzwerk *n*; **~ knife** → ***carver*** 3 a.

'**car·wash** *s.* **1.** Autowäsche *f*; **2.** (Auto)Waschanlage *f*.

car·y·at·id [,kærɪ'ætɪd] *s.* ⩓ Karya'tide *f*.

cas·cade [kæ'skeɪd] **I** *s.* **1.** Kas'kade *f*, Wasserfall *m*; **2.** *fig.* Kas'kade *f*, *z.B.* Feuerregen *m* (*Feuerwerk*), Faltenbesatz *m*, Faltenwurf *m* (*Kleidung*), *chem. Tandemanordnung von Gefäßen od. Geräten*; **3.** ⚡ *a.* ***~ connection*** Kas'kade(nschaltung) *f*; **II** *adj.* **4.** ⚡ Kaskaden...(*-motor*, *-verstärker etc.*); **III** *v/i.* **5.** kas'kadenartig her'abstürzen; wellig fallen.

case[1] [keɪs] **I** *s.* **1.** Fall *m*, 'Umstand *m*, Vorfall *m*, Sache *f*, Frage *f*: ***a ~ in point*** ein typischer Fall, ein treffendes Beispiel; ***a ~ of fraud*** ein Fall von Betrug; ***a ~ of conscience*** e-e Gewissensfrage; ***a hard ~*** a) ein schwieriger Fall, b) ein schwerer Gegner, c) F ein ‚schwerer Junge'; ***that alters the ~*** das ändert die Sache *od.* Lage; ***in ~*** im Falle, falls; ***in ~ of*** im Falle von (*od. gen.*); ***in ~ of need*** im Notfall; ***in any ~*** auf jeden Fall, jedenfalls; ***in that ~*** in dem Falle; ***if that is the ~*** wenn das der Fall ist, wenn das zutrifft; ***as the ~ may be*** je nachdem; ***it is a ~ of*** es handelt sich um; ***the ~ is this*** die Sache liegt so; ***state one's ~*** s-e Sache *od.* s-n Standpunkt vortragen *od.* vertreten (*a.* ⚖); → 3; ***come down to ~s*** zur Sache kommen; **2.** ⚖ (Rechts)Fall *m*, Pro'zeß *m*: ***leading ~*** Präzedenzfall; **3.** ⚖ Sachverhalt *m*; Begründung *f*, Be'weismateri͵al *n*; (*a.* begründeter) Standpunkt *e-r Partei*: ***~ for the Crown*** Anklage *f*; ***~ for the defence*** Verteidigung *f*; ***make out a*** (*od.* ***one's***) ***~ for*** (***against***) alle Rechtsgründe *od.* Argumente vorbringen für (gegen); ***he has a strong ~*** er hat schlüssige Beweise, s-e Sache steht günstig; ***he has no ~*** s-e Sache ist unbegründet; ***there is a ~ for s.th.*** et. ist begründet *od.* berechtigt, es gibt triftige Gründe für et.; **4.** *ling.* 'Kasus *m*, Fall *m*,; **5.** ⚕ (Krankheits)Fall *m*; Pati'ent(in): ***two ~s of typhoid*** zwei Typhusfälle *od.* Typhuskranke; ***a mental ~*** F ein Geisteskranker; **6.** *Am.* F komischer Kauz; **II** *v/t.* **7.** ***~ the joint*** *sl.* ‚den Laden ausbaldowern'.

case² [keɪs] **I** *s.* **1.** Kiste *f*, Kasten *m*; Koffer *m*; (*Schmuck*)Kästchen *n*; Schachtel *f*; Behälter *m*; **2.** (*Bücher-, Glas*)Schrank *m*; (*Uhr*)Gehäuse *n*; (*Patronen*)Hülse *f*, (*Samen*)Kapsel *f*; (*Zigaretten*)E'tui *n*; (*Brillen-, Messer*)Futte'ral *n*; (Schutz)Hülle *f* (*für Bücher, Messer etc.*); (*Akten*)Tasche *f*; (*Schreib*)Mappe *f*; (*Kissen*)Bezug *m*, 'Überzug *m*: ***pencil ~*** Federmäppchen *n*; **3.** ⚙ Verkleidung *f*, Einfassung *f*, Mantel *m*, Rahmen *m*; Scheide *f*: ***lower*** (***upper***) ***~*** *typ.* (Setzkasten *m* für) kleine (große) Buchstaben *pl.*; **II** *v/t.* **4.** in ein Gehäuse *od.* Futte'ral *etc.* stecken; **5.** ver-, um'kleiden, um'geben (***in, with*** mit); **6.** *Buchbinderei*: *Buch* einhängen.

'case|·book *s.* **1.** ⚖ kommentierte Entscheidungssammlung; **2.** ⚕ Pati'entenbuch *n*; **~ end·ing** *s. ling.* 'Kasusendung *f*; **'~-͵hard·ened** *adj.* **1.** *metall.* schalenhart, im Einsatz gehärtet; **2.** *fig.* abgehärtet, hartgesotten; **~ his·to·ry** *s.* **1.** Vorgeschichte *f* (*e-s Falles*); **2.** ⚕ Krankengeschichte *f*, Ana'mnese *f*; **3.** typisches Beispiel.

ca·se·in ['keɪsiːɪn] *s.* Kase'in *n*.

case law *s.* ⚖ ‚Fallrecht' *n* (*auf Präzedenzfällen beruhend*).

case·mate ['keɪsmeɪt] *s.* ⚔ Kase'matte *f*.

case·ment ['keɪsmənt] *s.* a) Fensterflügel *m*, b) *a.* ***~-window*** Flügelfenster *n*.

ca·se·ous ['keɪsɪəs] *adj.* käsig, käseartig.

case| shot *s.* ⚔ Schrap'nell *n*, Kar'tätsche *f*; **~ stud·y** *s.* (Einzel)Fallstudie *f*; **'~·work** *s. sociol.* Einzelfallhilfe *f*, sozi'ale Einzelarbeit; **'~͵work·er** *s.* Sozi'alarbeiter(in) (für Individu'albetreuung).

cash¹ [kæʃ] **I** *s.* **1.** (Bar)Geld *n*; **2.** ⚜ Barzahlung *f*, Kasse *f*: ***~ down, for ~*** gegen Barzahlung, in bar; ***~ in advance*** gegen Vorauszahlung; → ***cash and carry***; ***~ at bank*** Bankguthaben *n*; ***~ in hand*** Bar-, Kassenbestand *m*; ***~ on delivery*** per Nachnahme, zahlbar bei Lieferung; ***~ with order*** zahlbar bei Bestellung; ***be in*** (***out of***) ***~*** bei (nicht bei) Kasse sein; ***he is rolling in ~*** er hat Geld wie Heu; **II** *v/t.* **3.** *Scheck etc.* einlösen, -kassieren; **~ in I** *v/t.* **1.** *Poker etc.*: *s-e Spielmarken* einlösen; **II** *v/i.* **2.** F ‚abkratzen', sterben; **3.** F **~ (on)** ‚absahnen' (bei), profitieren (von).

cash² [kæʃ] *s. sg. u. pl.* Käsch *n* (*kleine Münze in Indien u. China*).

cash| ac·count *s.* ⚜ Kassenkonto *n*; **~ and car·ry I** *s.* **1.** Selbstabholung *f* gegen Barzahlung; **2.** Cash-and-carry-Geschäft *n*; **II** *adv.* **3.** (nur) gegen Barzahlung u. Selbstabholung; **͵~-and-'car·ry** *adj.* Cash-and-carry-…; **~ bal·ance** *s.* Kassenbestand *m*; Barguthaben *n*; **~ book** *s.* Kassenbuch *n*; **~ cheque** *s. Brit.* Barscheck *m*; **~ crop** *s.* für den Verkauf bestimmte Anbaufrucht; **~ desk** *s.* Kasse *f im Warenhaus etc.*; **~ dis·count** *s.* 'Barzahlungsra͵batt *m*; **~ dis·pens·er** *s.* 'Geldauto͵mat *m*.

ca·shew [kæ'ʃuː] *s.* **1.** Aca'joubaum *m*; **2.** *a.* ***~ nut*** Aca'jou-, 'Cashewnuß *f*.

cash flow *s.* ⚜ Cash-flow *m*, Kassenzufluß *m*.

cash·ier¹ [kæ'ʃɪə] *s.* Kassierer(in): ***~'s check*** *Am.* Bankscheck *m*; ***~'s desk*** *od.* ***office*** Kasse *f*.

cash·ier² [kə'ʃɪə] *v/t.* ⚔ (unehrenhaft) entlassen.

cash·less ['kæʃlɪs] *adj.* ⚜ bargeldlos.

cash·mere [kæʃ'mɪə] *s.* **1.** 'Kaschmir *m* (*feiner Wollstoff*); **2.** 'Kaschmirwolle *f*.

cash·o·mat ['kæʃəʊmæt] → ***cash dispenser***.

cash| pay·ment *s.* Barzahlung *f*; **~ price** *s.* Bar(zahlungs)preis *m*; **~ reg·is·ter** *s.* Registrierkasse *f*; **~ sale** *s.* Barverkauf *m*; **~ sur·ren·der val·ue** *s.* Rückkaufswert *m* (*e-r Police*); **~ vouch·er** *s.* Kassenbeleg *m*.

cas·ing ['keɪsɪŋ] *s.* **1.** Be-, Um'kleidung *f*, Um'hüllung *f*; **2.** (Fenster)Futter *n*; (Tür)Verkleidung *f*; **3.** Gehäuse *n*, Futte'ral *n*; *mot.* Mantel *m e-s Reifens*; **4.** (Wurst)Darm *m*, (-)Haut *f*.

ca·si·no [kə'siːnəʊ] *pl.* **-nos** *s.* ('Spiel-, Unter'haltungs)Ka͵sino *n*.

cask [kɑːsk] *s.* Faß *n*; (hölzerne) Tonne: ***a ~ of wine*** ein Faß Wein.

cas·ket ['kɑːskɪt] *s.* **1.** (Schmuck)Kästchen *n*; **2.** (Bestattungs)Urne *f*; **3.** *Am.* Sarg *m*.

Cas·pi·an ['kæspɪən] *adj.* kaspisch: ***~ Sea*** Kaspisches Meer.

Cas·san·dra [kə'sændrə] *s. fig.* Kas'sandra *f* (*Unglücksprophetin*).

cas·sa·tion [kæ'seɪʃn] *s.* ⚖ Kassati'on *f*: ***Court of ♀*** Kassationshof *m*.

cas·se·role ['kæsərəʊl] *s.* Kasse'rolle *f*, Schmortopf *m* (mit Griff).

cas·sette [kæ'set] *s.* ('Film-, 'Tonband-*etc.*)Kas͵sette *f*; **~ re·cord·er** *s.* Kas'settenre͵corder *m*.

cas·sock ['kæsək] *s. eccl.* Sou'tane *f*.

cast [kɑːst] **I** *s.* **1.** Wurf *m* (*a. mit Würfeln*); **2.** a) Auswerfen *n* (*Angel, Netz, Lot*), b) Angelhaken *m*; **3.** a) Auswurf *m* (*gewisser Tiere*), *bsd.* Gewölle *n* (*von Raubvögeln*), b) abgestoßene Haut (*Schlange, Insekt*); **4.** ***~ in the eye*** Schielen *n*; **5.** Aufrechnung *f*, Additi'on *f*; **6.** ⚙ Gußform *f*, Abguß *m*, -druck *m*; ⚕ Gipsverband *m*; *fig.* Zuschnitt *m*, Anordnung *f*; **7.** *thea.* (Rollen)Besetzung *f*; Mitwirkende *pl.*; Truppe *f*; **8.** Farbton *m*; *fig.* Anflug *m*; **9.** Typ *m*, Art *f*, Schlag *m*: ***~ of mind*** Geistesart *f*; ***~ of features*** Gesichtsausdruck *m*; **II** *v/t.* [*irr.*] **10.** werfen: ***the die is ~*** die Würfel sind gefallen; ***~ s.th. in s.o.'s teeth*** j-m et vorwerfen; **11.** *Angel, Netz, Anker, Lot* (aus)werfen; **12.** *zo.* a) *Haut, Geweih* abwerfen, b) *Junge* vorzeitig werfen; **13.** *fig. Blick, Licht, Schatten* werfen; *Horoskop* stellen: ***~ the blame*** die Schuld zuschieben (***on*** *dat.*); ***~ a slur*** (***on***) verunglimpfen (*acc.*); ***~ one's vote*** s-e Stimme abgeben; ***~ lots*** losen; **14.** *thea.* a) *Stück* besetzen: ***the play is well ~***, b) *Rollen* besetzen, verteilen: ***he was badly ~*** er war e-e Fehlbesetzung; **15.** *Metall, Statue etc.* gießen; *fig.* formen, bilden, anordnen; **16.** ⚖ *pass.* ***be ~ in costs*** zu den Kosten verurteilt werden; **17.** *a.* ***~ up*** aus-, zs.-rechnen: ***to ~ accounts*** Abrechnung machen; **III** *v/i.* [*irr.*] **18.** sich werfen, sich (ver)ziehen; **19.** die Angel auswerfen.

Zssgn mit adv.:

cast| a·bout, ~ a·round *v/i.* **1.** ***~ for*** suchen nach, *fig. a.* sich 'umsehen nach; **2.** ⚓ um'herlavieren; **~ a·way** *v/t.* **1.** wegwerfen; **2.** verschwenden; **3.** ***be ~*** ⚓ verschlagen werden; **~ back** *v/t.*: ***~ one's mind*** (***to***) zu'rückdenken (an *acc.*); **~ down** *v/t.* **1.** *fig.* entmutigen: ***be ~*** niedergeschlagen sein; **2.** *die Augen* niederschlagen; **~ in** *v/t.*: ***~ one's lot with s.o.*** sein Los mit j-m teilen, sich j-m anschließen; **~ off I** *v/t.* **1.** ab-, wegwerfen; *Kleider etc.* ablegen, ausrangieren; **2.** sich befreien von, sich entledigen (*gen.*); **3.** *Freund etc.* fallenlassen; **4.** *Stricken*: *Maschen* abketten; **5.** *typ.* den 'Umfang (*gen.*) berechnen; **II** *v/i.* **6.** ⚓ ablegen, losmachen; **~ on** *v/t. u. v/i. Stricken*: *die ersten Maschen* aufnehmen; **~ out** *v/t.* vertreiben, ausstoßen; **~ up** *v/t.* **1.** *die Augen* aufschlagen; **2.** anspülen; **3.** → ***cast*** 17.

cas·ta·net [͵kæstə'net] *s.* Kasta'gnette *f*.

'cast·a·way I *s.* **1.** Ausgestoßene(r *m*) *f*; **2.** ⚓ Schiffbrüchige(r *m*) *f* (*a. fig.*); **3.** *et.* Ausrangiertes, *bsd.* abgelegtes Kleidungsstück; **II** *adj.* **4.** ausgestoßen; **5.** ausrangiert (*Möbel etc.*), abgelegt (*Kleider*); **6.** ⚓ schiffbrüchig.

caste [kɑːst] *s.* **1.** (*indische*) Kaste: ***~ feeling*** Kastengeist *m*; **2.** Kaste *f*, Gesellschaftsklasse *f*; **3.** Rang *m*, Stellung *f*, Ansehen *n*: ***lose ~*** an gesellschaftlichem Ansehen verlieren (***with*** bei).

cas·tel·lan ['kæstələn] *s.* Kastel'lan *m*; **'cas·tel·lat·ed** [-leɪtɪd] *adj.* **1.** mit Türmen u. Zinnen; **2.** burgenreich.

cast·er ['kɑːstə] *s.* → ***castor³***.

cas·ti·gate ['kæstɪgeɪt] *v/t.* **1.** züchtigen; **2.** *fig.* geißeln; **3.** *fig. Text* verbessern; **cas·ti·ga·tion** [͵kæstɪ'geɪʃn] *s.* **1.** Züchtigung *f*; **2.** Geißelung *f*; scharfe Kri'tik; **3.** Textverbesserung *f*.

cast·ing ['kɑːstɪŋ] *s.* **1.** ⚙ a) Guß *m*, Gießen *n*, b) Gußstück *n*; *pl.* Gußwaren *pl.*; **2.** ⚠ (roher) Bewurf; **3.** *thea.* Rollenverteilung *f*; **4.** *a.* ***~-up*** Additi'on *f*; **5.** Fischen *n* (*mit dem Netz*); **~ net** *s.* Wurfnetz *n*; **~ vote** *s.* entscheidende Stimme.

cast| i·ron *s.* Gußeisen *n*; **͵~-'i·ron** *adj.* **1.** gußeisern; **2.** *fig.* eisern (*Konstitution, Wille etc.*); hart (*Gesetze etc.*); hieb- u. stichfest (*Alibi*), 'unum͵stößlich, unbeugsam: ***~ constitution*** eiserne Gesundheit.

cas·tle ['kɑːsl] **I** *s.* **1.** Burg *f*, Schloß *n*: ***~s in the air*** (*od.* ***in Spain***) *fig.* Luftschlösser; **2.** *Schach*: Turm *m*; **II** *v/i.* **3.** *Schach*: rochieren; **~ nut** *s.* ⚙ Kronenmutter *f*.

cas·tling ['kɑːslɪŋ] *s. Schach*: Ro'chade *f.*

'cast|·off *s.* **1.** ausrangiertes Kleidungsstück; **2.** *typ.* 'Umfangsberechnung *f*; **ˌ~-'off** *adj.* **1.** abgelegt, ausrangiert: **~ *clothes***; **2.** *et.* Abgelegtes *od.* Weggeworfenes.

Cas·tor¹ ['kɑːstə] *s. ast.* 'Kastor *m.*

cas·tor² ['kɑːstə] *s. vet.* Spat *m.*

cas·tor³ ['kɑːstə] *s.* **1.** (*Salz- etc.*)Streuer *m*; **2.** *pl.* Me'nage *f*, Gewürzständer *m*; **3.** (schwenkbare) Laufrolle.

cas·tor| oil *s.* ⚕ 'Rizinus-, 'Kastoröl *n*; **~ sug·ar** *s.* 'Kastorzucker *m.*

cas·trate [kæ'streɪt] *v/t.* **1.** ⚕, *vet.* kastrieren (*a. fig. iro.*); **2.** *Buch* zensieren; **cas'tra·tion** [-eɪʃn] *s.* Kastrierung *f*, Kastrati'on *f.*

cast steel *s.* Gußstahl *m.*

cas·u·al ['kæʒjʊəl] **I** *adj.* ☐ **1.** zufällig, unerwartet; **2.** gelegentlich, unregelmäßig: **~ *labo(u)r(er)*** Gelegenheitsarbeit(er *m*) *f*; **3.** unbestimmt, ungenau; **4.** lässig: a) nachlässig, gleichgültig, b) ungezwungen, zwanglos, *bsd. Mode*: sa'lopp, sportlich: **~ *wear*** Freizeitkleidung *f*; **5.** beiläufig: ***a ~ remark***; **~ *glance*** flüchtiger Blick; **II** *s.* **6.** a) sportliches Kleidungsstück, Straßenanzug *m*, b) *pl.* Slipper *pl.* (*flache Schuhe*); **7.** *Brit.* a) Gelegenheitsarbeiter *m*, b) gelegentlicher Kunde *od.* Besucher; **'cas·u·al·ism** [-lɪzəm] *s. philos.* Kasua'lismus *m*; **'cas·u·al·ness** [-nɪs] *s.* (Nach)Lässigkeit *f*, Gleichgültigkeit *f.*

cas·u·al·ty ['kæʒjʊəltɪ] *s.* **1.** Unfall *m* (*e-r Person*); **2.** a) Verunglückte(r *m*) *f*, (Unfall)Opfer *n*, b) ⚔ Verwundete(r) *m od.* Gefallene(r) *m*: ***casualties*** Opfer *pl. e-r Katastrophe etc.*, ⚔ *mst* Verluste *pl.*; **~ *list*** Verlustliste *f*; **3.** *a.* **~ *ward*** ⚕ 'Unfallstatiˌon *f.*

cas·u·ist ['kæzjʊɪst] *s.* Kasu'ist *m*; **cas·u·is·tic, cas·u·is·ti·cal** [ˌkæzjʊ'ɪstɪk(l)] *adj.* ☐ **1.** kasu'istisch; **2.** spitzfindig; **'cas·u·ist·ry** [-trɪ] *s.* **1.** Kasu'istik *f*; **2.** Spitzfindigkeit *f.*

cat [kæt] *s.* **1.** *zo.* Katze *f*: ***let the ~ out of the bag*** die Katze aus dem Sack lassen; ***it's raining ~s and dogs*** F es gießt wie mit Kübeln; ***has the ~ got your tongue?*** hat es dir die Sprache verschlagen?; ***wait for the ~ to jump*** *od.* ***see which way the ~ jumps*** *fig.* sehen, wie der Hase läuft; ***that ~ won't jump!*** F so geht's nicht!; ***set the ~ among the pigeons*** für helle Aufregung sorgen; ***think one is the cat's whiskers*** *od.* ***pyjamas*** sich für was Besonderes halten; ***not room to swing a ~*** *sl.* kaum Platz zum Umdrehen; ***they lead a ~-and-dog life*** sie leben wie Hund u. Katze; ***it's enough to make a ~ laugh*** F da lachen ja die Hühner; **2.** *zo. bsd. pl.* (Fa'milie *f* der) Katzen *pl.*; **3.** *fig.* falsche Katze (*Frau*): ***old ~*** alte Hexe; **4.** *Am. sl.* a) 'Jazzfaˌnatiker *m*, b) *a.* ***cool ~*** ‚dufter Typ'; **5.** ⚓ Kattanker *m.*

cat·a·clysm ['kætəklɪzəm] *s.* **1.** *geol.* Kata'klysmus *m*, erdgeschichtliche Kata'strophe; **2.** Über'schwemmung *f*; **3.** *fig.* (gewaltige) 'Umwälzung.

cat·a·comb ['kætəku:m] *s.* Kata'kombe *f.*

cat·a·falque ['kætəfælk] *s.* **1.** Kata'falk *m*; **2.** offener Leichenwagen.

Cat·a·lan ['kætələn] **I** *adj.* kata'lanisch; **II** *s.* Kata'lane *m*, Kata'lanin *f.*

cat·a·lep·sis [ˌkætə'lepsɪs], **cat·a·lep·sy** ['kætəlepsɪ] *s.* ⚕ Starrkrampf *m.*

cat·a·logue, *Am. a.* **cat·a·log** ['kætəlɒg] **I** *s.* **1.** Kata'log *m*; **2.** Verzeichnis *n*, (Preis- *etc.*)Liste *f*; **3.** *Am. univ.* Vorlesungsverzeichnis *n*; **II** *v/t.* **4.** katalogisieren.

ca·tal·y·sis [kə'tælɪsɪs] *s.* ⚗ Kata'lyse *f*; **cat·a·lyst** ['kætəlɪst] *s.* ⚗ *u. fig.* Kataly'sator *m*; **cat·a·lyt·ic** [ˌkætə'lɪtɪk] **I** *adj.* ⚗ kata'lytisch: **~ *converter*** Kataly'sator *m*; **II** *s.* → ***catalyst***; **cat·a·lyze** ['kætəlaɪz] *v/t.* katalysieren (*a. fig.*); **cat·a·lyz·er** ['kætəlaɪzə] → ***catalyst***.

cat·a·ma·ran [ˌkætəmə'ræn] *s.* **1.** ⚓ a) Floß *n*, b) Auslegerboot *n*; **2.** F ‚Kratzbürste' *f*, Xan'thippe *f.*

cat·a·mite ['kætəmaɪt] *s.* Lustknabe *m.*

cat·a·plasm ['kætəplæzəm] *s.* ⚕ 'Breiˌumschlag *m*, Kata'plasma *n.*

cat·a·pult ['kætəpʌlt] **I** *s.* **1.** Kata'pult *m, n*: a) *hist.* 'Wurfmaˌschine *f*, b) (Spiel)Schleuder *f*, c) ✈ Startschleuder *f*; **II** *adj.* **2.** ✈ Schleuder...(*-sitz, -start*); **III** *v/t.* **3.** schleudern, katapultieren (*a.* ✈); **4.** mit e-r Schleuder beschießen.

cat·a·ract ['kætərækt] *s.* **1.** Kata'rakt *m*: a) Wasserfall *m*, b) Stromschnelle *f*, c) *fig.* Flut *f*; **2.** ⚕ grauer Star.

ca·tarrh [kə'tɑː] *s.* ⚕ Ka'tarrh *m*; Schnupfen *m*; **ca'tarrh·al** [-ɑːrəl] *adj.* katar'rhalisch: **~ *syringe*** Nasenspritze *f.*

ca·tas·tro·phe [kə'tæstrəfɪ] *s.* Kata'strophe *f* (*a. im Drama u. geol.*), Verhängnis *n*, Unheil *n*, Unglück *n*; **cat·a·stroph·ic, cat·a·stroph·i·cal** [ˌkætə'strɒfɪk(l)] *adj.* katastro'phal.

'cat|·bird *s. orn.* amer. Spottdrossel *f*; **'~·boat** *s.* ⚓ kleines Segelboot (*mit einem Mast*); **~ bur·glar** *s.* Fas'sadenkletterer *m*, Einsteigdieb *m*; **'~·call I** *s.* a) Buh(ruf *m*) *n*, b) Pfiff *m*; **II** *v/i.* buhen, pfeifen; **III** *v/t. j-n* ausbuhen, -pfeifen.

catch [kætʃ] **I** *s.* **1.** Fangen *n*, Fang *m*; *fig.* Fang *m*, Beute *f*, Vorteil *m*: ***a good ~*** a) ein guter Fang (*beim Fischen u. fig.*), b) e-e gute Partie (*Heirat*); ***no ~*** kein gutes Geschäft; **2.** *Kricket, Baseball*: a) Fang *m*, b) Fänger *m*; **3.** Halter *m*, Griff *m*, Klinke *f*, Haken *m*; **4.** Sperr-, Schließhaken *m*, Schnäpper *m*; Sicherung *f*; Verschluß *m*; **5.** Stocken *n*, Anhalten *n*; **6.** *fig.* a) Haken *m*, Schwierigkeit *f*, b) Falle *f*, Trick *m*, Kniff *m*: ***there is a ~ in it*** die Sache hat e-n Haken; ***~-22*** F gemeiner Trick; **II** *v/t.* [*irr.*] **7.** *Ball, Tier etc.* fangen; *Dieb etc. a.* fassen, ‚schnappen', *a. Blick* erhaschen; *Tropfendes* auffangen; *allg.* erwischen, ‚kriegen': **~ *a train*** e-n Zug erreichen *od.* kriegen; → ***glimpse*** 1, ***sight*** 3; **8.** ertappen, über'raschen (***s.o. at*** j-n bei): **~ *me (doing that)!*** F ich denke (ja) nicht dran!, ‚denkste'!; ***I caught myself lying*** ich ertappte mich beim Lügen; ***caught in a storm*** vom Unwetter überrascht; **9.** ergreifen, packen, *Gewohnheit, Aussprache* annehmen; → ***hold²*** 1; **10.** *fig.* fesseln, pakken, gewinnen; einfangen; → ***eye*** 2, ***fancy*** 5; **11.** *fig.* ‚mitkriegen', verstehen: ***I didn't ~ what you said***; **12.** einholen: ***I soon caught him***; → ***catch up*** 2; **13.** sich holen *od.* zuziehen, angesteckt werden von (*Krankheit etc.*); → ***cold*** 8, ***fire*** 1; **14.** sich zuziehen, *Strafe, Tadel* bekommen: **~ *it*** F ‚sein Fett bekommen'; **15.** streifen, mit *et.* hängenbleiben: ***a nail caught my dress*** mein Kleid blieb an e-m Nagel hängen; **~ *one's finger in the door*** sich den Finger in der Tür klemmen; **16.** a) schlagen: **~ *s.o. a blow*** j-m e-n Schlag versetzen, b) *mit e-m Schlag* treffen *od.* ‚erwischen': ***the blow caught him on the chin***; **III** *v/i.* [*irr.*] **17.** greifen: **~ *at*** greifen *od.* schnappen nach, (*fig. Gelegenheit* gern) ergreifen; → ***straw*** 1; **18.** ⚙ (ein)greifen (*Räder*), einschnappen (*Schloß etc.*); **19.** sich verfangen, hängenbleiben: ***the plane caught in the trees***; **20.** klemmen; **21.** *mot.* anspringen;

Zssgn mit adv.:

catch| on *v/i.* F **1.** ‚kapieren' (***to s.th.*** et.); **2.** Anklang finden, einschlagen; **~ out** *v/t.* **1.** ertappen; **2.** *Kricket*: (durch Fangen des Balles) *den Schläger* ‚ausmachen'; **~ up I** *v/t.* **1.** *j-n* unter'brechen; **2.** *j-n* einholen; **3.** *et.* schnell ergreifen; *Kleid* aufraffen; **4.** ***be caught up in*** a) vertieft sein in (*acc.*), b) verwickelt sein in (*acc.*); **II** *v/i.* **5.** aufholen: **~ *with*** einholen (*a. fig.*); **~ *on*** *od.* ***with*** *et.* auf- *od.* nachholen.

'catch|·all *s. Am.* **1.** Tasche *f od.* Behälter *m* für alles mögliche; **2.** *fig.* Sammelbezeichnung *f*, -begriff *m*; **'~-as-ˌcatch-'can** *s. sport* Catchen *n*; **~ *wrestler*** Catcher *m.*

catch·er ['kætʃə] *s.* Fänger *m*; **'catch·ing** [-tʃɪŋ] *adj.* **1.** ⚕ ansteckend (*a. fig.*); **2.** *fig.* anziehend, fesselnd; **3.** eingängig (*Melodie*); **4.** verfänglich; arglistig.

catch·ment ['kætʃmənt] *s.* **1.** Auffangen *n von Wasser etc.*; **2.** *geol.* Reservo'ir *n*; **~ a·re·a** *s.* Einzugsgebiet *n* (*e-s Flusses; a. fig.*).

'catch|ˌpen·ny I *adj.* Schund...; auf Kundenfang berechnet, Lock..., Schleuder...: **~ *title*** reißerischer Titel; **II** *s.* Schundware *f*, 'Ramscharˌtikel *m*; **'~·phrase** *s.* Schlagwort *n*, (hohle) Phrase; **'~·pole, '~·poll** *s.* Gerichtsdiener *m*; **~ ques·tion** *s.* Fangfrage *f*; **'~·up** → ***ketchup***; **'~·weight** *s. sport* durch keinerlei Regeln beschränktes Gewicht e-s Wettkampfteilnehmers; **'~·word** *s.* **1.** *bsd. thea.* Stichwort *n*; **2.** Schlagwort *n*; **3.** *typ.* a) *hist.* 'Kustos *m*, b) Ko'lumnentitel *m.*

catch·y ['kætʃɪ] *adj.* F **1.** → ***catching*** 2, 3; **2.** unregelmäßig; **3.** schwierig.

cat·e·chism ['kætɪkɪzəm] *s.* **1.** ♀ *eccl.* Kate'chismus *m*; **2.** *fig.* Reihe *f od.* Folge *f* von Fragen; **'cat·e·chist** [-kɪst] *s.* Kate'chet *m*, Religi'onslehrer *m*; **'cat·e·chize** [-kaɪz] *v/t.* **1.** *eccl.* katechisieren; **2.** gründlich ausfragen, examinieren.

cat·e·chu ['kætɪtʃuː] *s.* ⚗ 'Katechu *n.*

cat·e·chu·men [ˌkætɪ'kjuːmen] *s.* **1.** *eccl.* Konfir'mand(in); **2.** *fig.* Neuling *m.*

cat·e·gor·i·cal [ˌkætɪ'gɒrɪkl] *adj.* ☐ kate'gorisch, bestimmt, unbedingt; **cat·e·go·ry** ['kætɪgərɪ] *s.* Katego'rie *f*, Klasse *f*, Gruppe *f.*

ca·ter ['keɪtə] **I** *v/i.* **1.** (***for***) Speisen u. Getränke liefern (für): ***~ing industry***

od. ***trade*** Gaststättengewerbe *n*; **2.** sorgen (***for*** für); **3.** *fig.* befriedigen (***for, to*** *acc.*); etwas bieten (***to*** *dat.*); **II** *v/t.* **4.** mit Speisen u. Getränken beliefern; **'ca·ter·er** [-ərə] *s.* Liefe'rant *m* für Speisen u. Getränke.

cat·er·pil·lar ['kætəpɪlə] *s.* **1.** *zo.* Raupe *f*; **2.** ⚙ (*Warenzeichen*) Raupenfahrzeug *n*.

cat·er·waul ['kætəwɔ:l] **I** *v/i.* **1.** jaulen (*Katze etc.*); **2.** kreischen; keifen; **II** *s.* **3.** Jaulen *n*; **4.** Keifen *n*, Kreischen *n*.

'cat|-eyed *adj.* katzenäugig; *weitS.* im Dunkeln sehend; **'~·fish** *s. ichth.* Katzenfisch *m*, Wels *m*; **'~-foot** *v/i. a.* ***~ it*** F schleichen; **'~·gut** *s.* **1.** Darmsaite *f*; **2.** ⚕ 'Katgut *n*; **3.** *Art* Steifleinen *n*.

ca·thar·sis [kə'θɑ:sɪs] *s.* **1.** *Ästhetik, a. psych.*: 'Katharsis *f*; **2.** ⚕ Abführung *f*.

ca·the·dral [kə'θi:drəl] **I** *s.* Kathe'drale *f*, Dom *m*; **II** *adj.* Dom...: ***~ church*** → I; ***~ town*** → ***city*** 2.

Cath·er·ine-wheel ['kæθərɪnwi:l] *s.* **1.** △ Katha'rinenrad *n* (*Radfenster*); **2.** *Feuerwerk*: Feuerrad *n*; **3.** *sport* ***turn ~s*** radschlagen.

cath·e·ter ['kæθɪtə] *s.* ⚕ Ka'theter *m*.

cath·ode ['kæθəʊd] *s.* ⚡ Ka'thode *f*; **~ ray** *s.* Ka'thodenstrahl *m*; **'~-ray tube** *s.* Ka'thodenstrahlröhre *f*.

cath·o·lic ['kæθəlɪk] **I** *adj.* (□ ***~ally***) **1.** ('all)um,fassend, univer'sal: ***~ interests*** vielseitige Interessen; **2.** großzügig, tole'rant; **3.** ♀ ka'tholisch; **II** *s.* **4.** ♀ Katho'lik(in); **Ca·thol·i·cism** [kə'θɒlɪsɪzəm] *s.* Katholi'zismus *m*; **cath·o·lic·i·ty** [,kæθəʊ'lɪsətɪ] *s.* **1.** Universali'tät *f*; **2.** Großzügigkeit *f*, Tole'ranz *f*; **3.** a) ka'tholischer Glaube, b) ♀ Katholizi'tät *f* (*Gesamtheit der katholischen Kirche*).

cat ice *s.* dünne Eisschicht.

cat·kin ['kætkɪn] *s.* ♀ (Blüten)Kätzchen *n* (*an Weiden etc.*).

'cat|·lick *s.* F ‚Katzenwäsche' *f*; **'~·nap** *s.* ‚Nickerchen' *n*, kurzes Schläfchen.

cat-o'-nine-tails [,kætə'naɪnteɪlz] *s.* neunschwänzige Katze (*Peitsche*).

'cat's|-eye ['kæts-] *s.* **1.** *min.* Katzenauge *n*; **2.** a) Katzenauge *n*, Rückstrahler *m*, b) Leuchtnagel *m*; **'~-paw** *s. fig.* Handlanger *m*, *j-s* Werkzeug *n*.

cat suit *s.* einteiliger Hosenanzug, Overall *m*.

cat·sup ['kætsəp] → ***ketchup***.

cat·tish ['kætɪʃ] *adj.* katzenhaft; *fig.* boshaft, gehässig, gemein.

cat·tle ['kætl] *s. coll.* (*mst pl. konstr.*) **1.** (Rind)Vieh *n*, Rinder *pl.*; **2.** *contp.* Viehzeug *n* (*Menschen*); **~ car** *s.* 🚃 *Am.* Viehwagen *m*; **'~-,feed·er** *s.* ⚙ 'Futterma,schine *f*; **'~-,lead·er** *s.* Nasenring *m*; **'~-,lift·er** *s.* Viehdieb *m*; **~ plague** *s. vet.* Rinderpest *f*; **~ ranch, ~ range** *s.* Viehweide(land *n*) *f*.

cat·ty ['kætɪ] → ***cattish***.

'cat|·walk *s.* **1.** ⚙ Laufplanke *f*, Steg *m*; **2.** *Mode*: Laufsteg *m*; **~ whisk·er** *s.* ⚡ De'tektornadel *f*.

Cau·ca·sian [kɔ:'keɪzjən] **I** *adj.* kau'kasisch; **II** *s.* Kau'kasier(in).

cau·cus ['kɔ:kəs] *s. pol. bsd. Am.* **1.** Par'teiausschuß *m* zur Wahlvorbereitung; **2.** Par'teikonfe,renz *f*, -tag *m*; **3.** Par'teiclique *f*.

cau·dal ['kɔ:dl] *adj. zo.* Schwanz...; **'cau·date** [-deɪt] *adj.* geschwänzt.

caught [kɔ:t] *pret. u. p.p. von* ***catch***.

caul·dron ['kɔ:ldrən] *s.* (großer) Kessel.

cau·li·flow·er ['kɒlɪflaʊə] *s.* ♀ Blumenkohl *m*; **~ ear** *s. Boxen*: ‚Blumenkohlohr' *n*.

caulk [kɔ:k] *v/t.* ⚓ kal'fatern, *a. allg.* abdichten; **'caulk·er** [-kə] *s.* ⚓, ⚙ Kal'faterer *m*.

caus·al ['kɔ:zl] *adj.* □ ursächlich, kau'sal: ***~ connection*** → ***causality*** 2; **cau·sal·i·ty** [kɔ:'zælətɪ] *s.* **1.** Ursächlichkeit *f*, Kausali'tät *f*: ***law of ~*** Kausalgesetz *n*; **2.** Kau'salzu,sammenhang *m*; **cau·sa·tion** [kɔ:'zeɪʃn] *s.* **1.** Verursachung *f*; **2.** Ursächlichkeit *f*; **3.** Kau'salprin,zip *n*; **'caus·a·tive** [-zətɪv] *adj.* □ **1.** kau'sal, begründend, verursachend; **2.** *ling.* 'kausativ.

cause [kɔ:z] **I** *s.* **1.** Ursache *f*: ***~ of death*** Todesursache; **2.** Grund *m*; Veranlassung *f*, Anlaß *m*: ***~ for complaint*** Grund *od.* Anlaß zur Klage; ***~ to be thankful*** Grund zur Dankbarkeit; ***without ~*** ohne (triftigen) Grund, grundlos (*entlassen etc.*); **3.** (gute) Sache: ***fight for one's ~*** für s-e Sache kämpfen; ***make common ~ with*** gemeinsame Sache machen mit; **4.** ⚖ a) (Streit)Sache *f*, Rechtsstreit *m*, Pro'zeß *m*, b) Gegenstand *m*; Rechtsgründe *pl.*: ***~-list*** Terminliste *f*; ***show ~*** s-e Gründe darlegen *od.* dartun (***why*** warum); ***upon good ~ shown*** bei Vorliegen von triftigen Gründen; ***~ of action*** Klagegrund *m*; **5.** Sache *f*, Angelegenheit *f*, Gegenstand *m*, 'Thema *n*, Frage *f*, Pro'blem *n*: ***lost ~*** verlorene *od.* aussichtslose Sache; ***in the ~ of*** um ... (*gen.*) willen, für; **II** *v/t.* **6.** veranlassen, (*j-n et.*) lassen: ***I ~ed him to sit down*** ich ließ ihn sich setzen; ***he ~ed the man to be arrested*** er ließ den Mann verhaften, er veranlaßte, daß der Mann verhaftet wurde; **7.** verursachen, bewirken, her'vorrufen, her'beiführen: ***~ a fire*** e-n Brand verursachen; **8.** bereiten, zufügen: ***~ s.o. a loss*** j-m e-n Verlust zufügen; ***~ s.o. trouble*** j-m Schwierigkeiten bereiten.

cause cé·lè·bre [,kəʊz se'lebrə] (*Fr.*) *s.* Cause *f* célèbre.

cause·less ['kɔ:zlɪs] *adj.* □ grundlos.

cau·se·rie ['kəʊzərɪ] (*Fr.*) *s.* Plaude'rei *f*.

cause·way ['kɔ:zweɪ], *Brit. a.* **'cau·sey** [-zeɪ] *s.* erhöhter Fußweg, Damm *m* (*durch e-n See od. Sumpf*).

caus·tic ['kɔ:stɪk] **I** *adj.* (□ ***~ally***) **1.** ⚗ kaustisch, ätzend, beizend, brennend: ***~ potash*** Ätzkali *n*; ***~ soda*** Ätznatron *n*; ***~-soda solution*** Ätzlauge *f*; **2.** *fig.* ätzend, beißend, sar'kastisch (*Worte etc.*); **II** *s.* **3.** ⚗ Beiz-, Ätzmittel *n*: ***lunar ~*** ⚕ Höllenstein *m*; **caus·tic·i·ty** [kɔ:'stɪsətɪ] *s.* **1.** Ätz-, Beizkraft *f*; **2.** *fig.* Sar'kasmus *m*, Schärfe *f*.

cau·ter·i·za·tion [,kɔ:təraɪ'zeɪʃn] *s.* ⚕, ⚙ (Aus)Brennen *n*; Ätzen *n*; **cau·ter·ize** ['kɔ:təraɪz] *v/t.* **1.** ⚕, ⚙ (aus)brennen, ätzen; **2.** *fig. Gefühl etc.* abstumpfen; **cau·ter·y** ['kɔ:tərɪ] *s.* Brenneisen *n*; Ätzmittel *n*.

cau·tion ['kɔ:ʃn] **I** *s.* **1.** Vorsicht *f*, Behutsamkeit *f*: ***proceed with ~*** Vorsicht walten lassen; **2.** Warnung *f*; *a. sport* Verwarnung; **3.** ⚖ Eides- *od.* Rechtsmittelbelehrung *f*; **4.** ⚔ 'Ankündigungskom,mando *n*; **5.** F a) *et.* Origi'nelles, ‚tolles Ding', b) ulkige ‚Nummer' (*Person*), c) unheimlicher Kerl; **II** *v/t.* **6.** warnen (***against*** vor *dat.*); **7.** verwarnen; **8.** ⚖ belehren (***as to*** über *acc.*); **'cau·tion·ar·y** [-ʃnərɪ] *adj.* warnend, Warnungs...: ***~ tale*** Geschichte *f* mit e-r Moral.

cau·tious ['kɔ:ʃəs] *adj.* □ vorsichtig, behutsam, auf der Hut; **'cau·tious·ness** [-nɪs] → ***caution*** 1.

cav·al·cade [,kævl'keɪd] *s.* Kaval'kade *f*, Reiterzug *m*, *a.* Zug *m* von Autos *etc.*

cav·a·lier [,kævə'lɪə] **I** *s.* **1.** *hist.* Ritter *m*; **2.** Kava'lier *m*; **3.** ♀ *hist.* Roya'list *m* (*Anhänger Karls I. von England*); **II** *adj.* □ **4.** anmaßend, rücksichtslos; **5.** unbekümmert, ‚eiskalt', keck.

cav·al·ry ['kævlrɪ] *s.* ⚔ Kavalle'rie *f*, Reite'rei *f*; **'~·man** [-mən] *s.* [*irr.*] Kavalle'rist *m*.

cave¹ [keɪv] **I** *s.* **1.** Höhle *f*; **2.** *pol. Brit.* a) Abspaltung *f e-s Teils e-r Partei*, b) Sezessi'onsgruppe *f*; **II** *v/t.* **3.** *mst* ***~ in*** eindrücken, zum Einsturz bringen; **III** *v/i.* **4.** *mst* ***~ in*** einstürzen, -sinken; **5.** *mst* ***~ in*** F a) nachgeben, klein beigeben (***to*** *dat.*), b) zs.-brechen, ‚zs.-klappen'; **6.** *pol. Brit.* sich *von der Partei* absondern.

ca·ve² ['keɪvɪ] (*Lat.*) *ped. sl.* **I** *int.* Vorsicht!, Achtung!; **II** *s.*: ***keep ~*** ‚Schmiere stehen', aufpassen.

ca·ve·at ['kævɪæt] *s.* **1.** ⚖ Einspruch *m*, Verwahrung *f*: ***enter a ~*** Verwahrung einlegen; ***~ emptor*** Mängelausschluß *m*; **2.** Warnung *f*.

cave| bear [keɪv] *s. zo.* Höhlenbär *m*; **~ dwell·er** → ***caveman*** 1; **'~·man** [-mæn] *s.* [*irr.*] **1.** Höhlenbewohner *m*, -mensch *m*; **2.** F a) Na'turbursche *m*, ‚Bär' *m*, b) ‚Tier' *n*.

cav·ern ['kævən] *s.* **1.** Höhle *f*; **2.** ⚕ Ka'verne *f*; **'cav·ern·ous** [-nəs] *adj.* **1.** voller Höhlen; **2.** po'rös; **3.** tiefliegend, hohl (*Augen*); eingefallen (*Wangen*); tief (*Dunkelheit*); **4.** ⚕ kaver'nös.

cav·i·ar(e) ['kævɪɑ:] *s.* 'Kaviar *m*: ***~ to the general*** Kaviar fürs Volk.

cav·il ['kævɪl] **I** *v/i.* nörgeln, kritteln (***at*** an *dat.*); **II** *s.* Nörge'lei *f*; **'cav·il·(l)er** [-lə] *s.* Nörgler(in).

cav·i·ty ['kævətɪ] *s.* **1.** (Aus)Höhlung *f*, Hohlraum *m*; **2.** *anat.* Höhle *f*, Raum *m*, Grube *f*: ***abdominal ~*** Bauchhöhle; ***mouth ~*** Mundhöhle; **3.** ⚕ Loch *n* (*im Zahn*).

ca·vort [kə'vɔ:t] *v/i.* F he'rumtollen, -tanzen.

ca·vy ['keɪvɪ] *s. zo.* Meerschweinchen *n*.

caw [kɔ:] **I** *s.* Krächzen *n* (*Rabe, Krähe etc.*); **II** *v/i.* krächzen.

cay·enne [keɪ'en], *a.* **~ pep·per** ['keɪən] *s.* Cay'ennepfeffer *m*.

cay·man ['keɪmən] *pl.* **-mans** *s. zo.* 'Kaiman *m*.

cease [si:s] **I** *v/i.* **1.** aufhören, enden: ***the noise ~d***; **2.** (***from***) ablassen (von), aufhören (mit): ***~ and desist order*** ⚖ *Am.* Unterlassungsanordnung *f*; **II** *v/t.* **3.** aufhören (***doing*** *od.* ***to do*** mit *et. od. et.* zu tun); **4.** einstellen: ***~ fire*** ⚔ das Feuer einstellen; ***~ payment*** ✝ die Zahlungen einstellen; **,cease'fire** *s.* ⚔ **1.** (Befehl *m* zur) Feuereinstellung *f*; **2.** Waffenruhe *f*; **'cease·less** [-lɪs] *adj.* □ unaufhörlich.

ce·dar ['si:də] *s.* **1.** ♀ Zeder *f*; **2.** Ze-

dernholz *n.*
cede [si:d] **I** *v/t.* (***to***) abtreten (*dat. od.* an *acc.*), über'lassen (*dat.*); **II** *v/i.* nachgeben, weichen.
ce·dil·la [sɪ'dɪlə] *s.* Ce'dille *f.*
cee [si:] *s.* C *n*, c *n* (*Buchstabe*).
ceil·ing ['si:lɪŋ] *s.* **1.** Decke *f e-s Raumes*; **2.** ⚓ Innenbeplankung *f*; **3.** Höchstmaß *n*, -grenze *f*, ✝ *a.* Pla'fond *m e-s Kredits*: ~ ***price*** ✝ Höchstpreis *m*; **4.** ✈ a) Gipfelhöhe *f*, b) Wolkenhöhe *f.*
cel·e·brant ['selɪbrənt] *s. eccl.* Zele'brant *m*; **cel·e·brate** ['selɪbreɪt] **I** *v/t.* **1.** *Fest etc.* feiern, begehen; **2.** *j-n* feiern (*preisen*); **3.** *R. C. Messe* zelebrieren, lesen; **II** *v/i.* **4.** feiern; *R. C.* zelebrieren; '**cel·e·brat·ed** [-breɪtɪd] *adj.* gefeiert, berühmt (***for*** für, wegen); **cel·e·bra·tion** [ˌselɪ'breɪʃn] *s.* **1.** Feier *f*; Feiern *n*: ***in*** ~ ***of*** zur Feier (*gen.*); **2.** *R. C.* Zelebrieren *n*, Lesen *n* (*Messe*); **ce·leb·ri·ty** [sɪ'lebrətɪ] *s.* **1.** Berühmtheit *f*, Ruhm *m*; **2.** Berühmtheit *f* (*Person*).
ce·ler·i·ac [sɪ'lerɪæk] *s.* ⚘ Knollensellerie *m, f.*
ce·ler·i·ty [sɪ'lerɪtɪ] *s.* Geschwindigkeit *f.*
cel·er·y ['selərɪ] *s.* ⚘ (Stauden)Sellerie *m, f.*
ce·les·tial [sɪ'lestjəl] **I** *adj.* ☐ **1.** himmlisch, Himmels..., göttlich; selig; **2.** *ast.* Himmels...: ~ ***body*** Himmelskörper *m*; ~ ***map*** Himmelskarte *f*; **3.** ♀ chi'nesisch: ♀ ***Empire*** China (*alter Name*); **II** *s.* **4.** Himmelsbewohner(in), Selige(r *m*) *f*; **5.** ♀ F Chi'nese *m*, Chi'nesin *f*; ♀ **Cit·y** *s. das* Himmlische Je'rusalem.
cel·i·ba·cy ['selɪbəsɪ] *s.* Zöli'bat *n, m*, Ehelosigkeit *f*; '**cel·i·bate** [-bət] **I** *s.* Unverheiratete(r *m*) *f*, Zöliba'tär *m*; **II** *adj.* unverheiratet, zöliba'tär.
cell [sel] *s.* **1.** (*Kloster-, Gefängnis- etc.*) Zelle *f*: ***condemned*** ~ Todeszelle; **2.** *allg., a. biol., phys., pol.* Zelle *f*, *a.* Kammer *f*, Fach *n*: ~ ***division*** Zellteilung *f*; **3.** ⚡ Zelle *f*, Ele'ment *n.*
cel·lar ['selə] *s.* **1.** Keller *m*; **2.** Weinkeller *m*: ***he keeps a good*** ~ er hat e-n guten Keller; '**cel·lar·age** [-ərɪdʒ] *s.* **1.** Keller(räume *pl.*) *m*; **2.** Einkellerung *f*; **3.** Kellermiete *f*; '**cel·lar·er** [-ərə] *s.* Kellermeister *m.*
-celled [seld] *adj. in Zssgn* ...zellig.
cel·list ['tʃelɪst] *s.* ♪ Cel'list(in); **cel·lo** ['tʃeləʊ] *pl.* **-los** *s.* (Violon)'Cello *n.*
cel·lo·phane ['seləʊfeɪn] *s.* ⚙ Zello'phan *n*, Zellglas *n.*
cel·lu·lar ['seljʊlə] *adj.* **1.** zellig, Zell(en)...: ~ ***tissue*** Zellgewebe *n*; ~ ***therapy*** ⚕ Zelltherapie *f*; **2.** netzartig: ~ ***shirt*** Netzhemd *n*; '**cel·lule** [-ju:l] *s.* kleine Zelle.
cel·lu·loid ['seljʊlɔɪd] *s.* ⚙ Zellu'loid *n.*
cel·lu·lose ['seljʊləʊs] *s.* Zellu'lose *f*, Zellstoff *m.*
Cel·si·us ['selsjəs], ~ **ther·mom·e·ter** *s. phys.* 'Celsiusthermoˌmeter *n.*
Celt [kelt] *s.* Kelte *m*, Keltin *f*; '**Celt·ic** [-tɪk] **I** *adj.* keltisch; **II** *s. ling. das* Keltische; '**Celt·i·cism** [-tɪsɪzəm] *s.* Kelti'zismus *m* (*Brauch od. Spracheigentümlichkeit*).
ce·ment [sɪ'ment] **I** *s.* **1.** Ze'ment *m*, (Kalk)Mörtel *m*; **2.** Klebstoff *m*, Kitt *m*; Bindemittel *n*; **3.** a) *biol.* 'Zahnzeˌment *m*, b) ⚕ Ze'ment *m* zur Zahnfüllung; **4.** *fig.* Band *n*, Bande *pl.*; **II** *v/t.* **5.** a) zementieren, b) kitten; **6.** *fig.* festigen, ‚zementieren'; **ce·men·ta·tion** [ˌsi:men'teɪʃn] *s.* **1.** Zementierung *f* (*a. fig.*); **2.** Kitten *n*; **3.** *metall.* Einsatzhärtung *f*; **4.** *fig.* Bindung *f.*
cem·e·ter·y ['semɪtrɪ] *s.* Friedhof *m.*
cen·o·taph ['senəʊtɑ:f] *s.* (leeres) Ehren(grab)mal: ***the*** ♀ *das brit. Ehrenmal in London für die Gefallenen beider Weltkriege.*
cense [sens] *v/t.* (mit Weihrauch) beräuchern; '**cen·ser** [-sə] *s.* (Weih-)Rauchfaß *n.*
cen·sor ['sensə] **I** *s.* **1.** ('Kunst-, 'Schrifttums)ˌZensor *m*; **2.** 'Briefˌzensor *m*; **3.** *antiq.* 'Zensor *m*, Sittenrichter *m*; **II** *v/t.* **4.** zensieren; **cen·so·ri·ous** [sen'sɔ:rɪəs] *adj.* ☐ **1.** 'kritisch, streng; **2.** tadelsüchtig, krittelig; '**cen·sor·ship** [-ʃɪp] *s.* **1.** Zen'sur *f*; **2.** 'Zensoramt *n*; **cen·sur·a·ble** ['senʃərəbl] *adj.* tadelnswert, sträflich; **cen·sure** ['senʃə] **I** *s.* Tadel *m*, Verweis *m*; Kri'tik *f*, 'Mißbilligung *f*: ***motion of*** ~ *parl.* Mißtrauensantrag *m*; → ***vote*** 1; **II** *v/t.* tadeln, miß'billigen, kritisieren.
cen·sus ['sensəs] *s.* 'Zensus *m*, (*bsd.* Volks)Zählung *f*, Erhebung *f*: ***livestock*** ~ Viehzählung *f*; ~-***taker*** Volkszähler *m*; ***take a*** ~ e-e (Volks- *etc.*) Zählung vornehmen.
cent [sent] *s.* **1.** Hundert *n* (*nur noch in*): ***per*** ~ Prozent, vom Hundert; **2.** *Am.* Cent *m* (1/100 *Dollar*): ***not worth a*** ~ keinen (roten) Heller wert.
cen·taur ['sentɔ:] *s.* **1.** *myth.* Zen'taur *m*; **2.** *fig.* Zwitterwesen *n*; **Cen·tau·rus** [sen'tɔ:rəs] *s. ast.* Zen'taur *m.*
cen·te·nar·i·an [ˌsentɪ'neərɪən] **I** *adj.* hundertjährig; **II** *s.* Hundertjährige(r *m*) *f*; **cen·te·nar·y** [sen'ti:nərɪ] **I** *adj.* **1.** hundertjährig; **2.** hundert betragend; **II** *s.* **3.** Jahr'hundert *n*; **4.** Hundert'jahrfeier *f.*
cen·ten·ni·al [sen'tenjəl] **I** *adj.* hundertjährig; **II** *s. bsd. Am.* Hundert'jahrfeier *f.*
cen·ter *etc. Am.* → ***centre*** *etc.*
cen·tes·i·mal [sen'tesɪml] *adj.* ☐ zentesi'mal, hundertteilig.
cen·ti·grade ['sentɪgreɪd] *adj.* hundertteilig, -gradig: ~ ***thermometer*** Celsiusthermometer *n*; ***degree(s)*** ~ Grad Celsius; '**cen·ti·gram(me)** [-græm] *s.* Zenti'gramm *n*; '**cen·tiˌme·tre**, *Am.* '**cen·tiˌme·ter** [-ˌmi:tə] *s.* Zenti'meter *m, n*; '**cen·ti·pede** [-pi:d] *s. zo.* Hundertfüßer *m.*
cen·tral ['sentrəl] **I** *adj.* ☐ **1.** zen'tral (gelegen); **2.** Haupt..., Zentral...: ~ ***office*** Hauptbüro *n*, Zentrale *f*; ~ ***idea*** Hauptgedanke *m*; **II** *s.* **3.** *Am.* a) (Tele'fon)Zenˌtrale *f*, b) Telefo'nist(in) (*in e-r Zentrale*); ♀ **A·mer·i·can** *adj.* 'mittelameriˌkanisch; ~ **cit·y** *s. Am.* Stadtkern *m*, Innenstadt *f*; ♀ **Eu·ro·pe·an time** *s.* 'mitteleuroˌpäische Zeit (*abbr. MEZ*); ~ **heat·ing** *s.* Zen'tralheizung *f.*
cen·tral·ism ['sentrəlɪzəm] *s.* Zentra'lismus *m*, (Sy'stem *n* der) Zentralisierung *f*; '**cen·tral·ist** [-ɪst] *s.* Verfechter *m* der Zentralisierung; **cen·tral·i·za·tion** [ˌsentrəlaɪ'zeɪʃn] *s.* Zentralisierung *f*; '**cen·tral·ize** [-laɪz] *v/t.* (*v/i.* sich) zentralisieren.
cen·tral| lock·ing *s. mot.* Zen'tralverriegelung *f*; ~ **nerv·ous sys·tem** *s. anat.* Zen'tralˌnervensyˌstem *n*; ~ **point** *s.* ⚹ Mittelpunkt *m*; ⚡ Nullpunkt *m*; ♀ **Pow·ers** *s. pl. pol. hist.* Mittelmächte *pl.*; ~ **re·serve** *s. mot. Brit.* Mittelstreifen *m*; ~ **sta·tion** *s.* **1.** ⚓ ('Bord)ZenˌTrale *f*, Kom'mandostand *m*; **2.** Haupt-, Zen'tralbahnhof *m*; **3.** ⚡ Zen'trale *f.*
cen·tre ['sentə] **I** *s.* **1.** 'Zentrum *n*, Mittelpunkt *m* (*a. fig.*): ~ ***of attraction*** *fig.* Hauptanziehungspunkt *m*; ~ ***of gravity*** *phys.* Schwerpunkt *m*; ~ ***of motion*** *phys.* Drehpunkt *m*; ~ ***of trade*** Handelszentrum; **2.** Hauptstelle *f*, -gebiet *n*, Sitz *m*, Herd *m*: ***amusement*** ~ Vergnügungszentrum *n*; ~ ***of interest*** Hauptinteresse *n*; → ***shopping***, ***training centre***; **3.** *pol.* Mitte *f*, 'Mittelparˌtei *f*; **4.** ⚙ Spitze *f*: ~ ***lathe*** Spitzendrehbank *f*; **5.** *sport* Flanke *f*; **6.** (Pra'linen- *etc.*)Füllung *f*; **II** *v/t.* **7.** in den Mittelpunkt stellen (*a. fig.*); konzentrieren, vereinigen (***on***, ***in*** auf *acc.*); ⚙ einmitten, zentrieren; ankörnen: ~ ***the bubble*** die Libelle einspielen lassen; **III** *v/i.* **8.** im Mittelpunkt stehen (*a. fig.*); *fig.* sich drehen (***round*** um); **9.** (***in***, ***on***) sich konzentrieren, sich gründen (auf *acc.*); **10.** *Fußball*: flanken; '~-**bit** *s.* ⚙ 'Zentrumsbohrer *m*; '~-**board** *s.* ⚓ (Kiel)Schwert *n*; ~ **cir·cle** *s. Fußball*: Anstoßkreis *m*; ~ **court** *s. Tennis*: 'Centre Court *m*; ~ **for·ward** *s. Fußball*: Mittelstürmer *m*; ~ **half** *s. Fußball*: 'Vorˌstopper *m*; ~ **par·ty** *s. pol.* 'Mittelparˌtei *f*, 'Zentrum *n*; '~-**piece** *s.* **1.** Mittelstück *n*; **2.** (mittlerer) Tafelaufsatz; **3.** *fig.* Hauptstück *n*; ~ **punch** *s.* ⚙ (An)Körner *m*; ~ **sec·ond** *s.* Zen'tralseˌkundenzeiger *m.*
cen·tric, **cen·tri·cal** ['sentrɪk(l)] *adj.* ☐ zen'tral, zentrisch.
cen·trif·u·gal [sen'trɪfjʊgl] *adj. phys.* zentrifu'gal; Schleuder..., Schwung...: ~ ***force*** Zentrifugal-, Fliehkraft *f*; ~ ***governor*** Fliehkraftregler *m*; **cen·tri·fuge** ['sentrɪfju:dʒ] **I** *s.* Zentri'fuge *f*, Trennschleuder *f*; **II** *v/t.* zentrifugieren, schleudern.
cen·trip·e·tal [sen'trɪpɪtl] *adj.* zentripe'tal: ~ ***force*** Zentripetalkraft *f.*
cen·tu·ple ['sentjʊpl], **cen·tu·pli·cate** [sen'tju:plɪkət] **I** *adj.* hundertfach; **II** *v/t.* verhundertfachen; **III** *s.* (*das*) Hundertfache.
cen·tu·ri·on [sen'tjʊərɪən] *s. antiq.* (*Rom*) ⚔ Zen'turio *m.*
cen·tu·ry ['sentʃʊrɪ] *s.* **1.** Jahr'hundert *n*: ***centuries-old*** jahrhundertealt; **2.** Satz *m od.* Gruppe *f* von hundert; *bsd. Kricket*: 100 Läufe *pl.*; **3.** *Am. sl.* hundert Dollar *pl.*; **4.** *antiq.* (*Rom*) Zen'turie *f*, Hundertschaft *f.*
ce·phal·ic [ke'fælɪk] *adj. anat., zo.* Schädel..., Kopf...; **ceph·a·lo·pod** ['sefələʊpɒd] *s. zo.* Kopffüßer *m*; **ceph·a·lous** ['sefələs] *adj. zo.* mit e-m ... Kopf, ...köpfig.
ce·ram·ic [sɪ'ræmɪk] **I** *adj.* **1.** ke'ramisch; **II** *s.* **2.** Ke'ramik *f* (*einzelnes Produkt*); **3.** *pl. mst sg. konstr.* Ke'ramik *f* (*Technik*); **4.** *pl.* Ke'ramik *f*, ke'ramische Erzeugnisse; **cer·a·mist** ['serəmɪst] *s.* Ke'ramiker *m.*
Cer·ber·us ['sɜ:bərəs] *s. fig.* 'Zerberus *m* (*a. ast.*), grimmiger Wächter: ***sop to***

~ Beschwichtigungsmittel *n*.

ce·re·al ['sɪərɪəl] **I** *adj.* **1.** Getreide…; **II** *s.* **2.** *mst pl.* Zere'alien *pl.*, Getreidepflanzen *pl.*, -früchte *pl.*; **3.** Frühstückskost *f aus Weizen, Hafer etc.*

cer·e·bel·lum [ˌserɪ'beləm] *s. anat.* Kleinhirn *n*; **cer·e·bral** ['serɪbrəl] *adj.* **1.** *anat.* Gehirn…: ~ ***death*** ⚕ Hirntod *m*; **2.** *ling.* alveo'lar; ˌ**cer·e'bra·tion** [-'breɪʃn] *s.* Gehirntätigkeit *f*; Denken *n*, 'Denkproˌzeß *m*; **cer·e·brum** ['serɪbrəm] *s. anat.* Großhirn *n*, Ze'rebrum *n*.

cere·cloth ['sɪəklɒθ] *s.* Wachsleinwand *f*, *bsd. als* Leichentuch *n*.

cere·ment ['sɪəmənt] *s. mst pl.* Leichentuch *n*, Totenhemd *n*.

cer·e·mo·ni·al [ˌserɪ'məʊnjəl] **I** *adj.* □ **1.** feierlich, förmlich; **2.** ritu'ell; **II** *s.* **3.** Zeremoni'ell *n*; ˌ**cer·e'mo·ni·ous** [-jəs] *adj.* □ **1.** → ***ceremonial*** 1 *u.* 2; **2.** 'umständlich, steif; **cer·e·mo·ny** ['serɪmənɪ] *s.* **1.** Zeremo'nie *f*, Feierlichkeit *f*, feierlicher Brauch; Feier *f*; → ***master*** 12; **2.** Förmlichkeit(en *pl.*) *f*: ***without*** ~ ohne Umstände; ***stand on*** ~ a) sehr förmlich sein, b) Umstände machen; **3.** Höflichkeit *f*.

ce·rise [sə'ri:z] *adj.* kirschrot, ce'rise.

cert [sɜ:t] *s. a.* ***dead*** ~ *Brit. sl.* ‚todsichere Sache'.

cer·tain ['sɜ:tn] *adj.* □ **1.** (*von Sachen*) sicher, gewiß, bestimmt: ***it is ~ to happen*** es wird gewiß geschehen; ***I know for*** ~ ich weiß ganz bestimmt; **2.** (*von Personen*) über'zeugt, sicher, gewiß: ***to make ~ of s.th.*** sich e-r Sache vergewissern; **3.** bestimmt, zuverlässig, sicher: ***a ~ cure*** e-e sichere Kur; ***a ~ day*** ein (ganz) bestimmter Tag; **4.** gewiß: ***a ~ Mr. Brown*** ein gewisser Herr Brown; ***for ~ reasons*** aus bestimmten Gründen; '**cer·tain·ly** [-lɪ] *adv.* **1.** sicher, zweifellos, bestimmt; **2.** sicherlich, (aber) sicher *od.* na'türlich; '**cer·tain·ty** [-tɪ] *s.* **1.** Sicherheit *f*, Bestimmtheit *f*, Gewißheit *f*: ***know for a*** ~ mit Sicherheit wissen; **2.** Über'zeugung *f*.

cer·ti·fi·a·ble [ˌsɜ:tɪ'faɪəbl] *adj.* □ **1.** feststellbar; **2.** ⚕ *Brit.* a) meldepflichtig (*Krankheit*), b) geisteskrank, c) F verrückt.

cer·tif·i·cate **I** *s.* [sə'tɪfɪkət] Bescheinigung *f*, At'test *n*, Zeugnis *n*, Schein *m*, Urkunde *f*: ***death*** ~ Sterbeurkunde; ***school*** ~ Schul(abgangs)zeugnis; ***~ of baptism*** Taufschein; ***~ of origin*** † Ursprungszeugnis; ***share*** (*Am.* ***stock***) ~ Aktienzertifikat *n*; → ***health*** 1, ***master*** 7, ***medical*** 1; **II** *v/t.* [-keɪt] *j-m* e-e Bescheinigung *od.* ein Zeugnis geben; *et.* attestieren, bescheinigen: ***~d*** amtlich anerkannt *od.* zugelassen; ***~d bankrupt*** rehabilitierter Konkursschuldner; ***~ engineer*** Diplomingenieur *m*; **cer·ti·fi·ca·tion** [ˌsɜ:tɪfɪ'keɪʃn] *s.* **1.** Bescheinigung *f*; Bestätigung *f* (*Am.* † *a. e-s Schecks*); **2.** (amtliche) Beglaubigung *od.* beglaubigte Erklärung.

cer·ti·fied ['sɜ:tɪfaɪd] *adj.* **1.** bescheinigt, beglaubigt, garantiert: ***~ copy*** beglaubigte Abschrift; **2.** staatlich zugelassen *od.* anerkannt, *Am.* Diplom…; **3.** ⚕ *Brit.* für geisteskrank erklärt; ***~ accountant*** *s.* † *Brit.* konzessionierter Buch- *od.* Steuerprüfer; ***~ cheque***, *Am.* ***check*** *s.* (*als gedeckt*) bestätigter Scheck; ***~ mail*** *s. Am.* eingeschriebene Sendung(en *pl.*) *f*; ***~ milk*** *s.* amtlich geprüfte Milch; ***~ pub·lic ac·count·ant*** *s.* † *Am.* amtlich zugelassener 'Bücherreˌvisor *od.* Wirtschaftsprüfer.

cer·ti·fy ['sɜ:tɪfaɪ] **I** *v/t.* **1.** bescheinigen: ***this is to*** ~ hiermit wird bescheinigt; **2.** beglaubigen; **3.** *Scheck* (als gedeckt) bestätigen (*Bank*); **4.** ***~ s.o.*** (***insane***) ⚖ *Brit.* j-n für geisteskrank erklären; **5.** ⚖ *Sache* verweisen (***to*** an *ein anderes Gericht*); **II** *v/i.* **6.** (***to***) bezeugen (*acc.*).

cer·ti·tude ['sɜ:tɪtju:d] *s.* Sicherheit *f*, Gewißheit *f*.

ce·ru·men [sɪ'ru:men] *s.* Ohrenschmalz *n*.

ce·ruse ['sɪəru:s] *s.* **1.** ⚗ Bleiweiß *n*; **2.** weiße Schminke.

cer·vi·cal [sɜ:'vaɪkl] *anat.* **I** *adj.* Hals…, Nacken…; **II** *s.* Halswirbel *m*.

Ce·sar·e·vitch [sɪ'zɑ:rəvɪtʃ] *s. hist.* Za'rewitsch *m*.

ces·sa·tion [se'seɪʃn] *s.* Aufhören *n*, Ende *n*; Stillstand *m*, Einstellung *f*.

ces·sion ['seʃn] *s.* Abtretung *f*, Zessi'on *f*.

cess·pit ['sespɪt], '**cess·pool** [-pu:l] *s.* **1.** Jauche-, Senkgrube *f*; **2.** *fig.* (Sünden)Pfuhl *m*.

ce·ta·cean [sɪ'teɪʃjən] *zo.* **I** *s.* Wal(-fisch) *m*; **II** *adj.* Wal(fisch)…

ce·tane ['si:teɪn] *s.* ⚗ Ce'tan *n*: ***~ number*** Cetanzahl *f*.

chafe [tʃeɪf] **I** *v/t.* **1.** warmreiben, frottieren; **2.** ('durch)reiben, wund reiben, scheuern; **3.** *fig.* ärgern, reizen; **II** *v/i.* **4.** sich ('durch)reiben, sich wund reiben, scheuern (***against*** an *dat.*); **5.** ⚙ verschleißen; **6.** a) sich ärgern, b) toben, wüten.

chaf·er ['tʃeɪfə] *s. zo.* Käfer *m*.

chaff [tʃɑ:f] **I** *s.* **1.** Spreu *f*: ***separate the ~ from the wheat*** die Spreu vom Weizen scheiden; ***as ~ before the wind*** wie Spreu im Winde; **2.** Häcksel *m, n*; **3.** ✕ 'Störˌfolie *f* (*Radar*); **4.** *fig.* wertloses Zeug; **5.** Necke'rei *f*; **II** *v/t.* **6.** zu Häcksel schneiden; **7.** *fig.* necken, aufziehen; '**~-cut·ter** *s.* ✂ Häckselbank *f*.

chaf·fer ['tʃæfə] **I** *s.* Feilschen *n*; **II** *v/i.* feilschen, schachern.

chaf·finch ['tʃæfɪntʃ] *s.* Buchfink *m*.

chaf·ing dish ['tʃeɪfɪŋ] *s.* Re'chaud *m, n*.

cha·grin ['ʃægrɪn] **I** *s.* **1.** Ärger *m*, Verdruß *m*; **2.** Kränkung *f*; **II** *v/t.* **3.** ärgern, verdrießen: ***~ed*** ärgerlich, gekränkt.

chain [tʃeɪn] **I** *s.* **1.** Kette *f* (*a.* ⚗, ⚡, ⚙, *phys.*): ***~ of office*** Amtskette; **2.** *fig.* Kette *f*, Fessel *f*: ***in ~s*** in Ketten, gefangen; **3.** *fig.* Kette *f*, Reihe *f*: ***~ of events***; **4.** *a.* ***~ of mountains*** Gebirgskette *f*; **5.** † (Laden- *etc.*)Kette *f*; **6.** ⚙ Meßkette *f* (*66 engl. Fuß*); **II** *v/t.* **7.** (an)ketten, mit e-r Kette befestigen: ***~ (up) a dog*** e-n Hund an die Kette legen; ***~ a prisoner*** e-n Gefangenen in Ketten legen; ***~ a door*** e-e Tür durch e-e Kette sichern; **8.** *fig.* (***to***) verketten (mit), ketten *od.* fesseln (an *acc.*); **9.** *Land* mit der Meßkette messen; ***~ armo(u)r*** *s.* Kettenpanzer *m*; ***~ belt*** *s.* ⚙ endlose Kette, 'Kettentransmissiˌon *f*; ***~ bridge*** *s.* Hängebrücke *f*; ***~ drive*** *s.* ⚙ Kettenantrieb *m*; ***~ gang*** *s.* Trupp *m* anein'andergeketteter Sträflinge; '**~·less** ['tʃeɪnlɪs] *adj.* ⚙ kettenlos; ***~ let·ter*** *s.* Kettenbrief *m*; ***~ mail*** → ***chain armo(u)r***; ***~ pump*** *s.* Pater'nosterwerk *n*; ***~ re·ac·tion*** *s. phys. u. fig.* 'Kettenreaktiˌon *f*; '**~-smoke** *v/i. u. v/t.* Kette rauchen; '**~-ˌsmok·er** *s.* Kettenraucher *m*; ***~ stitch*** *s. Nähen*: Kettenstich *m*; ***~ store*** *s.* † Kettenladen *m*.

chair [tʃeə] **I** *s.* **1.** Stuhl *m*, Sessel *m*: ***take a*** ~ sich setzen; **2.** *fig.* Vorsitz *m*: ***be in*** (***take***) ***the*** ~ den Vorsitz führen (übernehmen); ***address the*** ~ sich an den Vorsitzenden wenden; ***leave the*** ~ die Sitzung aufheben; ***~! ~!*** *parl. Brit.* zur Ordnung!; **3.** Lehrstuhl *m*, Profes'sur *f* (***of German*** für Deutsch); **4.** *Am.* F *der* e'lektrische Stuhl; **5.** 🚂 Schienenstuhl *m*; **6.** Sänfte *f*; **II** *v/t.* **7.** (in ein Amt) einsetzen, auf *e-n Lehrstuhl etc.* berufen; **8.** den Vorsitz führen von (*od. gen.*); **9.** ***~ s.o. off*** j-n (im Tri'umph) auf den Schultern (da'von-) tragen; ***~ back*** *s.* Stuhllehne *f*; ***~ bottom*** *s.* Stuhlsitz *m*; '**~-car** *s.* 🚂 Sa'lonwagen *m*; ***~ lift*** *s.* Sesselbahn *f*, -lift *m*.

chair·man ['tʃeəmən] *s.* [*irr.*] **1.** Vorsitzende(r) *m*, Präsi'dent *m*; **2.** Sänftenträger *m*; '**chair·man·ship** [-ʃɪp] *s.* Vorsitz *m*.

chair·o·plane ['tʃeərəpleɪn] *s.* 'Kettenkarusˌsell *n*.

'**chair**|ˌ**per·son** *s.* Vorsitzende(r *m*) *f*; '**~ˌwom·an** *s.* [*irr.*] Vorsitzende *f*.

chaise [ʃeɪz] *s.* Chaise *f*, Halbkutsche *f*; ***~ longue*** [lɔ̃:ŋg] *s.* Chaise'longue *f*, Liegesofa *n*.

chal·cog·ra·pher [kæl'kɒgrəfə] *s.* Kupferstecher *m*.

cha·let ['ʃæleɪ] *s.* Cha'let *n*: a) Sennhütte *f*, b) Landhaus *n*.

chal·ice ['tʃælɪs] *s.* **1.** *poet.* (Trink)Becher *m*; **2.** *eccl.* (Abendmahls)Kelch *m*; **3.** ⚘ Blütenkelch *m*.

chalk [tʃɔ:k] **I** *s.* **1.** *min.* Kreide *f*; **2.** (Zeichen)Kreide *f*, Kreidestift *m*: ***colo(u)red*** ~ Buntstift; ***red*** ~ a) Rötel *m*, b) Rotstift; ***as different as ~ and cheese*** grundverschieden; **3.** Kreidestrich *m*: a) (Gewinn)Punkt *m* (*bei Spielen*), b) *Brit.* (angekreidete) Schuld: ***by a long*** ~ bei weitem; **II** *v/t.* **4.** mit Kreide (be)zeichnen; **5.** ***~ out*** entwerfen; *fig. Weg* vorzeichnen; **6.** ***~ up*** anschreiben; ankreiden, auf die Rechnung setzen: ***~ it up to s.o.*** es j-m ankreiden; ***~ mark*** *s.* Kreidestrich *m*; '**~-pit** *s.* Kreidegrube *f*; '**~-stone** *s.* ⚕ Gichtknoten *m*.

chalk·y ['tʃɔ:kɪ] *adj.* kreidig; kreidehaltig.

chal·lenge ['tʃælɪndʒ] **I** *s.* **1.** Her'ausforderung *f* (*a. sport u. fig.*), Forderung *f* (*zum Duell etc.*); (Auf-, An)Forderung *f*; Aufruf *m*; **2.** ✕ Anruf *m* (*Wachtposten*); **3.** *hunt.* Anschlagen *n* (*Hund*); **4.** *bsd.* ⚖ a) Ablehnung *f* (*e-s Geschworenen od. Richters*), b) Anfechtung *f* (*e-s Beweismittels*); **5.** 'Widerspruch *m*, Kri'tik *f*, Bestreitung *f*, Kampfansage *f*; Angriff *m*; Streitfrage *f*; **6.** Her'ausforderung *f*: a) Bedrohung *f*, kritische Lage, b) Schwierigkeit *f*, Pro'blem *n*, c) (schwierige *od.* lockende) Aufgabe; **7.** ⚕ Immuni'tätstest *m*; **II** *v/t.* **8.** her'ausfordern (*a. sport u. fig.*); zur Rede stellen; aufrufen, -fordern; ⚔ anrufen; **9.** Anforderungen an *j-n* stellen; auf die Probe stellen; **10.** bestreiten, anzweifeln; *bsd.* ⚖ anfechten, *Geschworenen etc.* ablehnen; → ***bias*** 5; **11.** trotzen (*dat.*); angreifen; **12.** *j-n* reizen, lokken, fordern (*Aufgabe*); **13.** *j-m Bewunderung etc.* abnötigen; **ˈchal·lenge·a·ble** [-dʒəbl] *adj.* herˈauszufordern(d); anfechtbar; **chal·lenge cup** *s. sport* ˈWanderpoˌkal *m*; **ˈchal·leng·er** [-dʒə] *s.* Herˈausforderer *m*; **chal·lenge tro·phy** *s.* Wanderpreis *m*; **ˈchal·leng·ing** [-dʒɪŋ] *adj.* □ **1.** herˈausfordernd; **2.** *fig.* lockend *od.* schwierig (*Aufgabe*).

cha·lyb·e·ate [kəˈlɪbɪət] *min.* **I** *adj.* stahl-, eisenhaltig: ~ ***spring*** Stahlquelle *f*; **II** *s.* Stahlwasser *n*.

cham·ber [ˈtʃeɪmbə] *s.* **1.** *obs.* Zimmer *n*, Kammer *f*, Gemach *n*; **2.** *pl. Brit.* a) (*zu vermietende*) Zimmer *pl.*: ***live in ~s*** privat wohnen, b) Geschäftsräume *pl.*; **3.** (*Empfangs*)Zimmer *n* (*im Palast etc.*); **4.** *parl.* a) Pleˈnarsaal *m*, b) Kammer *f*; **5.** *pl. Brit.* a) ˈAnwaltsbüˌro *n*, b) Amtszimmer *n* des Richters: ***in ~s*** in nichtöffentlicher Sitzung; **6.** ⚙ Kammer *f*; Raum *m*; (Gewehr)Kammer *f*; ~ **con·cert** *s.* ˈKammerkonˌzert *n*; ~ **coun·sel** *s. Brit.* (nur) beratender Anwalt.

cham·ber·lain [ˈtʃeɪmbəlɪn] *s.* **1.** Kammerherr *m*; **2.** Schatzmeister *m*.

ˈcham·ber|·maid *s.* Zimmermädchen *n* (*in Hotels*); ~ **mu·sic** *s.* ˈKammermuˌsik *f*; ♀ **of Com·merce** *s.* Handelskammer *f*; ~ **pot** *s.* Nachtgeschirr *n*.

cha·me·le·on [kəˈmiːljən] *s. zo.* Chaˈmäleon *n* (*a. fig.*).

cham·fer [ˈtʃæmfə] **I** *s.* **1.** ⚠ Auskehlung *f*; **2.** ⚙ Schrägkante *f*, Fase *f*; **II** *v/t.* **3.** ⚠ auskehlen; **4.** ⚙ abfasen, abschrägen.

cham·ois [ˈʃæmwɑː] *pl.* ~ [-ɑːz] *s.* **1.** *zo.* Gemse *f*; **2.** *a.* ~ ***leather*** [*mst* ˈʃæmɪ] a) Sämischleder *n*, b) ⚙ Polierleder *n*.

champ[1] [tʃæmp] *v/i. u. v/t.* (heftig *od.* geräuschvoll) kauen: ~ ***at the bit*** a) am Gebiß kauen (*Pferd*), b) *fig.* vor Ungeduld (fast) platzen, c) mit den Zähnen knirschen.

champ[2] [tʃæmp] *sl.* → ***champion*** 3.

cham·pagne [ˌʃæmˈpeɪn] *s.* **1.** Chamˈpagner *m*, Sekt *m*, Schaumwein *m*: ~ ***cup*** Sektkelch *m*, -schale *f*; **2.** Chamˈpagnerfarbe *f*.

cham·pi·on [ˈtʃæmpjən] **I** *s.* **1.** Kämpe *m*, (Turˈnier)Kämpfer *m*; **2.** *fig.* Vorkämpfer *m*, Verfechter *m*, Fürsprecher *m*; **3.** a) *sport* Meister *m*, Titelhalter *m*, b) Sieger *m* (*Wettbewerb*); **II** *v/t.* **4.** verfechten, eintreten für, verteidigen; **III** *adj.* **5.** Meister..., best, preisgekrönt; **ˈcham·pi·on·ship** [-ʃɪp] *s.* **1.** Meisterschaft *f*, -titel *m*; **2.** *pl.* Meisterschaftskämpfe *pl.*, Meisterschaften *pl.*; **3.** Verfechten *n*, Eintreten *n für etwas*.

chance [tʃɑːns] **I** *s.* **1.** Zufall *m*: ***by ~*** zufällig; **2.** Glück *n*; Schicksal *n*; ˈRisiko *n*: ***game of ~*** Glücksspiel *n*; ***take one's ~*** sein Glück versuchen; ***take a*** (*od.* ***one's***) ~ es darauf ankommen lassen, es riskieren; ***take no ~s*** nichts riskieren (wollen); **3.** Chance *f*: a) Glücksfall *m*, (günstige) Gelegenheit: ***the ~ of his lifetime*** die Chance s-s Lebens, e-e einmalige Gelegenheit; ***give him a ~!*** gib ihm e-e Chance!, versuch's mal mit ihm!; → ***main chance***, b) Aussicht *f* (***of*** auf *acc.*): ***stand a ~*** Aussichten haben, c) Möglichkeit *f*, Wahrscheinlichkeit *f*: ***the ~s are that*** aller Wahrscheinlichkeit nach; ***the ~s are against you*** die Umstände sind gegen dich; ***on the*** (***off***) ~ auf gut Glück, ‚auf Verdacht', für den Fall (*daß*); **II** *v/t.* **4.** riskieren: ~ ***it*** es darauf ankommen lassen, es wagen; **III** *v/i.* **5.** (unerwartet) geschehen: ***I ~ed to meet her*** zufällig traf ich sie; **6.** ~ ***upon*** auf *j-n od. et.* stoßen; **IV** *adj.* **7.** zufällig, Zufalls..., gelegentlich, ✝ *a.* Gelegenheits...; unerwartet: ~ ***customers*** Laufkundschaft *f*.

chan·cel [ˈtʃɑːnsl] *s.* ⚠ Alˈtarraum *m*, hoher Chor.

chan·cel·ler·y [ˈtʃɑːnsələrɪ] *s.* ˈBotschafts- *od.* Konsuˈlatskanzˌlei *f*.

chan·cel·lor [ˈtʃɑːnsələ] *s.* **1.** Kanzler *m* (*a. univ.*); *univ. Am.* Rektor *m*; ♀ ***of the Exchequer*** *Brit.* Schatzkanzler *m*, Finanzminister *m*; → ***Lord*** ♀; **2.** Kanzˈleivorstand *m*; **ˈchan·cel·lor·ship** [-ʃɪp] *s.* Kanzleramt *n*, -würde *f*.

chan·cer·y [ˈtʃɑːnsərɪ] *s.* Kanzˈleigericht *n* (*Brit. Gerichtshof des Lordkanzlers*; *Am. Billigkeitsgericht*): ***in ~*** a) unter gerichtlicher Verwaltung, b) F in der Klemme; ***ward in ~*** Mündel *n* unter Amtsvormundschaft; ♀ **Di·vi·sion** *s.* ⚖ *Brit.* Kammer *f* für Billigkeitsrechtsprechung des ***High Court of Justice***.

chan·cre [ˈʃæŋkə] *s.* ⚕ Schanker *m*.

chan·de·lier [ˌʃændəˈlɪə] *s.* Arm-, Kronleuchter *m*, Lüster *m*.

chan·dler [ˈtʃɑːndlə] *s.* Krämer *m*; ♀ **Act** *s. Am.* Konˈkursordnung *f*.

change [tʃeɪndʒ] **I** *v/t.* **1.** (ver)ändern, ˈumändern, verwandeln (***into*** in *acc.*): ~ ***one's lodgings*** umziehen; ~ ***the subject*** das Thema wechseln, von et. anderem reden; ~ ***one's position*** die Stellung wechseln, sich beruflich verändern; → ***mind*** 4, ***colour*** 3; **2.** (ˈum-, ver)tauschen (***for*** gegen), wechseln: ~ ***one's shirt*** ein anderes Hemd anziehen; ~ ***hands*** den Besitzer wechseln; ~ ***places with s.o.*** den Platz mit j-m tauschen; ~ ***trains*** umsteigen; → ***side*** 9; **3.** *Geld*, *Banknoten* (ein)wechseln; *Scheck* einlösen; **4.** *j-m* andere Kleider anziehen; *Säugling* trockenlegen; *Bett* frisch überˈziehen *od.* beziehen; **5.** ⚙ schalten: ~ ***up*** (***down***) hinauf- (herunter)schalten; ~ ***over*** *Betrieb*, *Maschinen etc.* umstellen (***to*** auf *acc.*); **II** *v/i.* **6.** sich (ver)ändern, wechseln; **7.** sich verwandeln (***to*** *od.* ***into*** in *acc.*); **8.** 🚂 *etc.* ˈumsteigen: ***all ~!*** alles umsteigen *od.* aussteigen!; **9.** sich ˈumziehen: ~ ***into evening dress*** sich für den Abend umziehen; **10.** ~ ***to*** ˈübergehen zu: ~ ***to cigars***; **III** *s.* **11.** (Ver)Änderung *f*, Wechsel *m*; Wandlung *f*, Wendung *f*, ˈUmschwung *m*: ***no ~*** unverändert; ~ ***for the better*** Besserung *f*; ~ ***of heart*** Sinnesänderung *f*; ~ ***of life*** Wechseljahre *pl.*; ~ ***of moon*** Mondwechsel; ~ ***of voice*** Stimmwechsel; ~ ***in the weather*** Witterungsumschlag *m*; **12.** Abwechs(e)lung *f*, *et.* Neues; Tausch *m*: ***for a ~*** zur Abwechs(e)lung; ***a ~ of clothes*** Wäsche zum Wechseln; ***you need a ~*** Sie müssen mal ausspannen; **13.** Wechselgeld *n*: (***small***) ~ Kleingeld; ***can you give me ~ for a pound?*** a) können Sie mir auf ein Pfund herausgeben?, b) können Sie mir ein Pfund wechseln?; ***get no ~ out of s.o.*** *fig.* nichts (*keine Auskunft od. keinen Vorteil*) aus j-m herausholen können, bei j-m nicht ‚landen' können; **14.** ♀ *Brit.* Börse *f*; **change·a·bil·i·ty** [ˌtʃeɪndʒəˈbɪlətɪ] *s.* Veränderlichkeit *f*; *fig.* Wankelmut *m*; **ˈchange·a·ble** [-dʒəbl] *adj.* □ **1.** veränderlich; **2.** wankelmütig; **ˈchange·ful** [-fʊl] *adj.* □ veränderlich, wechselvoll; **change gear** *s.* ⚙ Wechselgetriebe *n*; **ˈchange·less** [-lɪs] *adj.* unveränderlich, beständig; **ˈchange·ling** [-lɪŋ] *s.* Wechselbalg *m*; ˈuntergeschobenes Kind; **ˈchangeˌo·ver** *s.* **1.** (***to***) ˈÜbergang *m* (zu), Wechsel *m* (zu), ˈUmstellung *f* (auf *acc.*) (*a.* ⚙ *von Maschinen*, *e-s Betriebs etc.*); **2.** ⚙ ˈUmschaltung *f*; **3.** *sport* (Stab)Wechsel *m*; **ˈchang·er** [-dʒə] *s. in Zssgn* ...wechsler *m* (*Person od. Gerät*); **ˈchang·ing** [-dʒɪŋ] *s.* Wechsel *m*, Veränderung *f*: ~ ***of the guard*** ⚔ Wachablösung *f*; ~ ***room*** Umkleidezimmer *n*; ~ ***cubicle*** Umkleidekabine *f*.

chan·nel [ˈtʃænl] **I** *s.* **1.** Flußbett *n*; **2.** Fahrrinne *f*, Kaˈnal *m*; **3.** Rinne *f*; ˈDurchlaßröhre *f*; **4.** breite Wasserstraße: ***the*** (***English***) ♀ *geogr.* der (Ärmel-) Kanal; **5.** Rille *f*, Riefe *f*; ⚠ Auskehlung *f*; **6.** *fig.* Weg *m*, Kaˈnal *m*: ***~s of trade*** Handelswege, *a.* Absatzgebiete; ***official ~s*** Dienstweg; ***through the usual ~s*** auf dem üblichen Wege; **7.** *Radio*, *TV*: Proˈgramm *n*, Kaˈnal *m*: ~ ***selector*** Kanalwähler *m*; **II** *v/t.* **8.** *fig.* leiten, lenken; **9.** ⚙ furchen, riefeln; ⚠ kannelieren, auskehlen.

chant [tʃɑːnt] **I** *s.* **1.** *eccl.* Kirchengesang *m*, -lied *n*; **2.** Singsang *m*, eintöniger Gesang *od.* Tonfall; **3.** Sprechchor *m* (*als Geschrei*); **II** *v/t.* **4.** *Kirchenlied* singen; **5.** absingen, ˈherleiern; **6.** im Sprechchor rufen.

chan·te·relle [ˌtʃæntəˈrel] *s.* ⚘ Pfifferling *m*.

chan·ti·cleer [ˌtʃæntɪˈklɪə] *s. poet.* Hahn *m*.

chan·try [ˈtʃɑːntrɪ] *s. eccl.* **1.** Stiftung *f* von Seelenmessen; **2.** Voˈtivkaˌpelle *f od.* -alˌtar *m*.

chant·y [ˈtʃɑːntɪ] *s.* Maˈtrosenlied *n*, Shanty *n*.

cha·os [ˈkeɪɒs] *s.* ˈChaos *n*, *fig. a.* Wirrwarr *m*, Durcheinˈander *n*; **cha·ot·ic** [keɪˈɒtɪk] *adj.* (□ ***~ally***) chaˈotisch, wirr.

chap[1] [tʃæp] *s.* F Bursche *m*, Junge *m*: ***a nice ~*** ein netter Kerl; ***old ~*** ‚alter Knabe'.

chap[2] [tʃæp] *s.* Kinnbacken *m* (*bsd. Tier*), *pl.* Maul *n*.

chap[3] [tʃæp] **I** *v/t. u. v/i.* rissig machen *od.* werden: ***~ped hands*** aufgesprungene Hände; **II** *s.* Riß *m*, Sprung *m*.

chap·el [ˈtʃæpl] *s.* **1.** Kaˈpelle *f*; Gotteshaus *n* (der Disˈsenters): ***I am ~*** F ich bin ein Dissenter; **2.** (ˈSeiten)Kaˌpelle *f* in e-r Katheˈdrale; **3.** Gottesdienst *m*; **4.** *typ.* betriebliche Geˈwerkschaftsorganisatiˌon der Drucker; **ˈchap·el·ry** [-rɪ] *s. eccl.* Sprengel *m*.

chap·er·on [ˈʃæpərəʊn] **I** *s.* **1.** Anstandsdame *f*; **2.** Be'gleitper,son *f*; **II** *v/t.* (als Anstandsdame) begleiten.

'chap,fall·en *adj.* niedergeschlagen.

chap·lain ['tʃæplɪn] *s.* **1.** Ka'plan *m*, Geistliche(r) *m* (*an e-r Kapelle*); **2.** Hof-, Haus-, Anstalts-, Mili'tär-, Ma'ri-negeistliche(r) *m*; **'chap·lain·cy** [-sɪ] *s.* Ka'plans-amt *n*, -pfründe *f*.

chap·let ['tʃæplɪt] *s.* **1.** Kranz *m*; **2.** *eccl.* Rosenkranz *m*.

chap·py ['tʃæpɪ] *adj.* rissig, aufgesprungen: **~ hands**.

chap·ter ['tʃæptə] *s.* **1.** Ka'pitel *n* (*Buch u. fig.*): **~ and verse** a) *bibl.* Kapitel u. Vers, b) genaue Einzelheiten; **give ~ and verse** *a.* genau zitieren; **to the end of the ~** bis ans Ende; **2.** *eccl.* 'Dom-, 'Ordenska,pitel *n*; **3.** *Am.* Orts-, 'Untergruppe *f e-r Vereinigung*; **~ house** *s.* **1.** *eccl.* 'Domka,pitel *n*, Stiftshaus *n*; **2.** *Am.* Verbindungshaus *n* (*Studenten*).

char¹ [tʃɑ] *v/t. u. v/i.* verkohlen.

char² [tʃɑː] *s. ichth.* 'Rotfo,relle *f*.

char³ [tʃɑː] *Brit.* **I** *v/i.* **1.** als Putzfrau *od.* Raumpflegerin arbeiten; **II** *s.* **2.** Putzen *n* (*als Lebensunterhalt*); **3.** → **charwoman**.

char-à-banc ['ʃærəbæŋ] *pl.* **-bancs** [-z] *s.* **1.** Kremser *m* (*Kutsche*); **2.** Ausflugsautobus *m*.

char·ac·ter ['kærəktə] *s.* **1.** Cha'rakter *m*, Wesen *n*, Na'tur *f* (*e-s Menschen*): **a bad ~** a) ein schlechter Charakter, b) ein schlechter Kerl; **a strange ~** ein eigenartiger Mensch; **quite a ~** ein Original; **2.** Cha'rakter(stärke *f*) *m*, (ausgeprägte) Per'sönlichkeit: **a man of ~**; **a public ~** e-e bekannte Persönlichkeit; **~ actor** *thea.* Charakterdarsteller *m*; **~ part** *thea.* Charakterrolle *f*; **~ assassination** Rufmord *m*; **~ building** Charakterbildung *f*; **~ defect** Charakterfehler *m*; **3.** Cha'rakter *m*, Gepräge *n*, Eigenart *f*; Merkmal *n*, Kennzeichen *n*; **4.** Stellung *f*, Rang *m*, Eigenschaft *f*: **he came in the ~ of a friend** er kam (in s-r Eigenschaft) als Freund; **5.** Leumund *m*, Ruf *m*, Name *m*: **have a good ~** in gutem Ruf stehen; **~ witness** ⚖ Leumundszeuge *m*; **6.** Zeugnis *n* (*für Personal*): **give s.o. a good ~** a) j-m ein gutes Zeugnis geben, b) gut von j-m sprechen; **7.** *thea.* Per'son *f*, Rolle *f*: **in ~** a) der Rolle gemäß, b) (zs.-)passend; **it is out of ~** es paßt nicht (dazu, zu ihm *etc.*); **8.** *Roman*: Fi'gur *f*, Gestalt *f*; **9.** Schriftzeichen *n* (*a. Computer*), Schrift *f*; Handschrift *f*.

char·ac·ter·is·tic [,kærəktə'rɪstɪk] **I** *adj.* ☐ → **characteristically**; charakte'ristisch, bezeichnend, typisch (**of** für): **~ curve** ⚙ Leistungskurve *f*; **II** *s.* charakte'ristisches Merkmal, Eigentümlichkeit *f*, Kennzeichen *n*, Eigenschaft *f*: (**performance**) **~** ⚙ (Leistungs)Angabe *f*, (-)Kennwert *m*; **,char·ac·ter'is·ti·cal** [-kl] → **characteristic** I; **,char·ac·ter-'is·ti·cal·ly** [-kəlɪ] *adv.* bezeichnenderweise; **char·ac·ter·i·za·tion** [,kærəktəraɪ'zeɪʃn] *s.* Charakterisierung *f*, Kennzeichnung *f*; **char·ac·ter·ize** ['kærəktəraɪz] *v/t.* charakterisieren: a) beschreiben, b) kennzeichnen, charakte'ristisch sein für; **char·ac·ter·less** ['kærəktəlɪs] *adj.* nichtssagend.

cha·rade [ʃə'rɑːd] *s.* **1.** Scha'rade *f* (*Ratespiel mit Verkleidungsszenen*); **2.** *fig.* Farce *f*.

'char·broil *v/t.* auf Holzkohle grillen.

char·coal ['tʃɑːkəʊl] *s.* **1.** Holzkohle *f*; **2.** (Zeichen)Kohle *f*, Kohlestift *m*; **3.** Kohlezeichnung *f*; **~ burn·er** *s.* Köhler *m*, Kohlenbrenner *m*; **~ draw·ing** *s.* Kohlezeichnung *f*.

chard [tʃɑːd] *s.* ⚘ Mangold(gemüse *n*) *m*.

charge [tʃɑːdʒ] **I** *v/t.* **1.** belasten, beladen, beschweren (**with** mit) (*mst fig.*); **2.** *Gewehr etc.* laden; *Batterie* aufladen: (**emotionally**) **~d atmosphere** *fig.* geladene (*od.* angeheizte) Stimmung; **3.** (an)füllen; ⚙, ⚒ beschicken; ⚗ sättigen; **4.** beauftragen, betrauen: **~ s.o. with a task**; **5.** ermahnen: **I ~d him not to forget** ich schärfte ihm ein, es nicht zu vergessen; **6.** Weisungen geben (*dat.*); belehren: **~ the jury** ⚖ den Geschworenen Rechtsbelehrung geben; **7.** zur Last legen, vorwerfen, anlasten (**on** *dat.*): **he ~d the fault on me** er schrieb mir die Schuld zu; **8.** beschuldigen, anklagen (**with** *gen.*): **~ s.o. with murder**; **9.** angreifen, *sport a.* ‚angehen', rempeln; anstürmen gegen: **~ the enemy**; **10.** *Preis etc.* fordern, berechnen: **he ~d (me) a dollar for it** er berechnete (mir) e-n Dollar dafür; **11.** ✝ *j-n* mit *et.* belasten, *j-m et.* in Rechnung stellen: **~ these goods to me** (*od.* **to my account**); **II** *v/i.* **12.** angreifen; stürmen: **the lion ~d at me** der Löwe fiel mich an; **13.** (e-n Preis) fordern, (Kosten) berechnen: **~ too much** zuviel berechnen; **I shall not ~ for it** ich werde es nicht berechnen; **III** *s.* **14.** ⚔, ⚡, *mot.* Ladung *f*; ⚙ (Spreng)Ladung *f*; Füllung *f*, Beschickung *f*; *metall.* Einsatz *m*; **15.** Belastung *f*, Forderung *f* (*beide a.* ✝), Last *f*, Bürde *f*; Anforderung *f*, Beanspruchung *f*: **~** (**on an estate**) (Grundstücks)Belastung; **real ~** Grundschuld *f*; **be a ~ on s.o.** j-m zur Last fallen; **a first ~ on s.th.** e-e erste Forderung an et. (*acc.*); **16.** (*a. pl.*) Preis *m*, Kosten *pl.*, Spesen *pl.*, Unkosten *pl.*; Gebühr *f*: **no ~**, **free of ~** kostenlos, gratis; **~s forward** per Nachnahme; **~s** (**to be**) **deducted** abzüglich der Unkosten; **17.** Aufgabe *f*, Amt *n*, Pflicht *f*, Verantwortung *f*; **18.** Aufsicht *f*, Obhut *f*, Pflege *f*, Sorge *f*; Verwahrung *f*; Verwaltung *f*: **person in ~** verantwortliche Person, Verantwortliche(r), Leiter(in); **be in ~ of** verantwortlich sein für, die Aufsicht *od.* den Befehl führen über (*acc.*), leiten; **have ~ of** in Obhut *od.* Verwahrung haben, betreuen, versorgen; **put s.o. in ~ of** j-m die Leitung *od.* Aufsicht *etc.* übertragen (*gen.*); **take ~** die Leitung *etc.* übernehmen, die Sache in die Hand nehmen; **19.** Gewahrsam *m*: **give s.o. in ~** j-n der Polizei übergeben; **take s.o. in ~** j-n festnehmen; **20.** ⚖ Mündel *m*; Pflegebefohlene(r *m*) *f*, Schützling *m*; *a.* anvertraute Sache; **21.** Befehl *m*, Anweisung *f*, Mahnung *f*; ⚖ Rechtsbelehrung *f*; **22.** Vorwurf *m*, Beschuldigung *f*; ⚖ (Punkt *m* der) Anklage *f*: **on a ~ of murder** wegen Mord; **return to the ~** *fig.* noch einmal ‚einhaken' (*Diskussion*); **23.** Angriff *m*, (An)Sturm *m*; **24. get a ~ out of** *Am. sl.* an *e-r Sache* mächtig Spaß haben; **~ ac·count** *s.* ✝ **1.** ('Kunden)Kre,ditkonto *n*; **2.** Abzahlungskonto *n*.

charge·a·ble ['tʃɑːdʒəbl] *adj.* ☐ **1.** anzurechnen(d), zu Lasten gehen(d) (**to** von); zu berechnen(d) (**on** *dat.*); zu belasten(d) (**with** mit); *teleph.* gebührenpflichtig; **2.** zahlbar; **3.** strafbar.

char·gé (**d'af·faires**) [,ʃɑːʒeɪ(dæ'feə)] *pl.* **char·gés** (**d'af·faires**) [-ʒeɪdæ-'feəz] (*Fr.*) *s. pol.* Geschäftsträger *m*.

'charge-nurse *s.* ⚕ Stati'ons-, Oberschwester *f*.

charg·er ['tʃɑːdʒə] *s.* **1.** ⚔ Dienstpferd *n* (*es Offiziers*); **2.** *poet.* Schlachtroß *n*; **3.** ⚙ Aufgeber *m*.

'charge-sheet *s. Brit.* **1.** polizeiliches Aktenblatt über den Beschuldigten u. die ihm zur Last gelegte Tat; **2.** ⚔ Tatbericht *m*.

char·i·ness ['tʃeərɪnɪs] *s.* **1.** Behutsamkeit *f*; **2.** Sparsamkeit *f*.

char·i·ot ['tʃærɪət] *s. antiq.* zweirädriger Streit- *od.* Tri'umphwagen; **char·i·ot·eer** [,tʃærɪə'tɪə] *s. poet.* Wagen-, Rosselenker *m*.

cha·ris·ma [kə'rɪzmə] *pl.* **-ma·ta** [-mətə] *s. eccl.* 'Charisma *n* (*a. fig. persönliche Ausstrahlung*); **char·is·mat·ic** [,kærɪz'mætɪk] *adj.* charis'matisch.

char·i·ta·ble ['tʃærətəbl] *adj.* ☐ **1.** mild-, wohltätig, karita'tiv, Wohltätigkeits...; **2.** mild, nachsichtig; **'char·i·ta·ble·ness** [-nɪs] *s.* Wohltätigkeit *f*; Güte *f*, Milde *f*, Nachsicht *f*; **char·i·ty** ['tʃærətɪ] *s.* **1.** Nächstenliebe *f*; **2.** Wohltätigkeit *f*; Freigebigkeit *f*: **~ stamp** Wohlfahrtsmarke *f*; **~ begins at home** zuerst kommt die eigene Familie *od.* das eigene Land; → **cold** 3; **3.** Güte *f*; Milde *f*, Nachsicht *f*; **4.** Almosen *n*, milde Gabe; Wohltat *f*, gutes Werk; **5.** Wohlfahrtseinrichtung *f*.

cha·ri·va·ri [,ʃɑːrɪ'vɑːrɪ] *s.* **1.** 'Katzenmu,sik *f*; **2.** Lärm *m*, Getöse *n*.

char·la·dy ['tʃɑː,leɪdɪ] → **charwoman**.

char·la·tan ['ʃɑːlətən] *s.* 'Scharlatan *m*: a) Quacksalber *m*, Marktschreier *m*, b) Schwindler *m*; **'char·la·tan·ry** [-tənrɪ] *s.* Scharlatane'rie *f*.

Charles's Wain [,tʃɑːlzɪz'weɪn] *s. ast.* Großer Bär.

char·ley horse ['tʃɑːlɪ] *s. Am.* F Muskelkater *m*.

char·lock ['tʃɑːlɒk] *s.* ⚘ Hederich *m*.

charm [tʃɑːm] **I** *s.* **1.** Anmut *f*, Charme *m*, (Lieb)Reiz *m*, Zauber *m*: (**feminine**) **~s** weibliche Reize; **~ of style** reizvoller Stil; **turn on the old ~** s-n Charme spielen lassen; **2.** Zauber *m*, Bann *m*; Zauberformel *f*: **it worked like a ~** *fig.* es klappte phantastisch; **3.** Amu'lett *n*, 'Talisman *m*; **II** *v/t.* **4.** bezaubern, reizen, entzücken: **be ~ed to meet s.o.** entzückt *od.* erfreut sein, j-n zu treffen; **~ed with** entzückt von; **5.** be-, verzaubern: **~ed against** gefeit gegen; **~ away** wegzaubern; **III** *v/i.* **6.** bezaubern(d wirken), entzücken; **'charm·er** [-mə] *s.* **1.** *fig.* Zauberer *m*, Zauberin *f*; **2.** a) bezaubernder Mensch, Char'meur *m*, b) reizvolles Geschöpf, ‚Circe' *f*; **'charm·ing** [-mɪŋ] *adj.* ☐ char'mant; *a. Sache*: bezaubernd, entzückend, reizend.

char·nel house ['tʃɑːnl] *s.* Leichen-, Beinhaus *n*.

chart [tʃɑ:t] **I** *s.* **1.** (*bsd.* See-, Himmels)Karte *f*: **~room** ⚓ Kartenhaus *n*; **2.** Ta'belle *f*; **3.** a) graphische Darstellung, *z.B.* (Farb)Skala *f*, (Fieber)Kurve *f*, (Wetter)Karte *f*, b) *bsd.* ⚙ Dia'gramm *n*, Schaubild *n*, Kurve(nblatt *n*) *f*; **II** *v/t.* **4.** auf e-r (See- *etc.*)Karte einzeichnen; **5.** graphisch darstellen, skizzieren; **6.** *fig.* planen, entwerfen.

char·ta ['tʃɑ:tə] → ***Magna C(h)arta***.

char·ter ['tʃɑ:tə] **I** *s.* **1.** Urkunde *f*; Freibrief *m*; Privi'leg *n*; **2.** a) Gründungsurkunde *f*, b) *Am.* Satzung *f* (*e-r AG etc.*), c) Konzessi'on *f*; **3.** *pol.* Charta *f*; **4.** ⚓, ✈ a) Chartern *n*, b) → ***charter party***; **II** *v/t.* **5.** *Bank etc.* konzessionieren: **~ed company** zugelassene Gesellschaft; → ***accountant*** 2; **6.** chartern: a) ⚓, ✈ mieten, b) befrachten; '**char·ter·er** [-ərə] *s.* ⚓ Befrachter *m*.

char·ter| flight *s.* Charterflug *m*; **~ par·ty** *s.* 'Chartepar,tie *f*, Miet-, Frachtvertrag *m*.

char·wom·an ['tʃɑ:,wʊmən] *s.* [*irr.*] Reinemach-, Putzfrau *f*, Raumpflegerin *f*.

char·y ['tʃeərɪ] *adj.* □ **1.** vorsichtig, behutsam (**in**, **of** in *dat.*, bei); **2.** sparsam, zu'rückhaltend (**of** mit).

chase¹ [tʃeɪs] **I** *v/t.* **1.** jagen, nachjagen (*dat.*), verfolgen; **2.** *hunt.* hetzen, jagen; **3.** *fig.* verjagen, vertreiben; **II** *v/i.* **4.** nachjagen (**after** *dat.*); F sausen, rasen; **III** *s.* **5.** Verfolgung *f*: **give ~** die Verfolgung aufnehmen; **give ~ to** → 1; **6.** *hunt.* **the ~** die Jagd; **7.** *Brit.* 'Jagdre,vier *n*; **8.** gejagtes Wild (*a. fig.*) *od.* Schiff *etc.*

chase² [tʃeɪs] **I** *s.* **1.** *typ.* Formrahmen *m*; **2.** Rinne *f*, Furche *f*; **II** *v/t.* **3.** ziselieren, ausmeißeln, punzen: **~d work** getriebene Arbeit; **4.** ⚙ *Gewinde* strehlen, schneiden.

chas·er¹ ['tʃeɪsə] *s.* **1.** Jäger *m*; Verfolger *m*; **2.** ⚓ a) Verfolgungsschiff *n*, (*bsd.* U-Boot-)Jäger *m*, b) Jagdgeschütz *n*; **3.** ✈ Jagdflugzeug *n*; **4.** F ‚Schluck *m* zum Nachspülen'; **5.** *sl.* a) Schürzenjäger *m*, b) mannstolles Weib.

chas·er² ['tʃeɪsə] *s.* ⚙ **1.** Zise'leur *m*; **2.** Gewindestahl *m*; Treibpunzen *m*.

chasm ['kæzəm] *s.* **1.** Kluft *f*, Abgrund *m* (*beide a. fig.*) **2.** Schlucht *f*; **3.** Riß *m*, Spalte *f*; **4.** Lücke *f*.

chas·sis ['ʃæsɪ] *pl.* '**chas·sis** [-sɪz] *s.* **1.** Chas'sis *n*: a) ✈, *mot.* Fahrgestell *n*, b) *Radio*: Grundplatte *f*; **2.** ⚔ La'fette *f*.

chaste [tʃeɪst] *adj.* □ **1.** keusch (*a. fig. schamhaft; anständig, tugendhaft*); rein, unschuldig; **2.** rein, von edler Schlichtheit: **~ style**.

chas·ten ['tʃeɪsn] *v/t.* **1.** züchtigen, strafen; **2.** läutern; **3.** mäßigen, dämpfen; ernüchtern.

chas·tise [tʃæ'staɪz] *v/t.* **1.** züchtigen, strafen; **2.** geißeln, tadeln; **chas·tise·ment** ['tʃæstɪzmənt] *s.* Züchtigung *f*, Strafe *f*.

chas·ti·ty ['tʃæstətɪ] *s.* **1.** Keuschheit *f*: **~ belt** Keuschheitsgürtel *m*; **2.** Reinheit *f*; **3.** Schlichtheit *f*.

chas·u·ble ['tʃæzjʊbl] *s. eccl.* Meßgewand *n*.

chat [tʃæt] **I** *v/i.* plaudern, schwatzen; **II** *v/t.* **~ s.o.** (**up**) F a) auf j-n einreden, b) j-n ‚anquatschen'; **III** *s.* Plaude'rei *f*: **~ show** *Brit.* Talk-Show *f*; **have a ~** → I.

chat·e·laine ['ʃætəleɪn] *s.* **1.** Schloßherrin *f*; **2.** Kastel'lanin *f*; **3.** (Gürtel)Kette *f* (*für Schlüssel etc.*).

chat·tel ['tʃætl] *s.* **1.** *mst pl.* bewegliches Eigentum, Habe *f*: **~ mortgage** Mobiliarhypothek *f*; **~ paper** *Am.* Verkehrspapier *n*; → ***good*** 18; **2.** *mst* **~ slave** Leibeigene(r) *m*.

chat·ter ['tʃætə] **I** *v/i.* **1.** plappern, schwatzen; **2.** schnattern; **3.** klappern (*a. Zähne*), rattern; **4.** plätschern; **II** *s.* **5.** Geplapper *n*, Geschnatter *n*; Klappern *n*; '**chat·ter·box** *s.* Plappermaul *n*; '**chat·ter·er** [-ərə] *s.* Schwätzer(in).

chat·ty ['tʃætɪ] *adj.* **1.** gesprächig; **2.** unter'haltsam (*Person*, *Brief*), im Plauderton (geschrieben *etc.*).

chauf·feur ['ʃəʊfə] (*Fr.*) *s.* Chauf'feur *m*, Fahrer *m*; **chauf·feuse** [ʃəʊ'fɜ:z] *s.* Fahrerin *f*.

chau·vie ['ʃəʊvɪ] *s.* F ‚Chauvie' *m* (→ ***chauvinist*** 2).

chau·vin·ism ['ʃəʊvɪnɪzəm] *s.* Chauvi'nismus *m*; '**chau·vin·ist** [-ɪst] *s.* **1.** Chauvi'nist *m*; **2. male ~** *sociol.* männlicher Chauvinist; **chau·vin·is·tic** [,ʃəʊvɪ'nɪstɪk] *adj.* (□ **~ally**) chauvi'nistisch.

cheap [tʃi:p] **I** *adj.* □ **1.** billig, preiswert: **get off ~** mit e-m blauen Auge davonkommen; **hold ~** wenig halten von; **~ as dirt** spottbillig; **2.** billig, minderwertig; schlecht, kitschig: **~ and nasty** billig u. schlecht; **3.** verbilligt, ermäßigt: **~ fare**; **~ money** billiges Geld; **4.** *fig.* billig, mühelos; **5.** *fig.* ‚billig', schäbig: **feel ~** a) sich ‚billig' *od.* ärmlich vorkommen, b) *sl.* sich elend fühlen; **II** *adv.* **6.** billig; **III** *s.* **7. on the ~** F billig; '**cheap·en** [-pən] *v/t.* (*v/i.* sich) verbilligen; her'absetzen (*a. fig.*): **~ o.s.** sich herabwürdigen; '**cheap·jack I** *s.* billiger Jakob; **II** *adj.* Ramsch...; '**cheap·ness** [-nɪs] *s.* Billigkeit *f* (*a. fig.*); '**cheap·skate** *s. Am. sl.* ‚Knikker' *m*, Geizhals *m*.

cheat [tʃi:t] **I** *s.* **1.** Betrüger(in), Schwindler(in); ‚Mogler(in)'; **2.** Betrug *m*, Schwindel *m*; Moge'lei *f*; **II** *v/t.* **3.** betrügen (**of**, **out of** um); **4.** durch List bewegen (**into** zu); **5.** sich entziehen (*dat.*), ein Schnippchen schlagen (*dat.*): **~ justice**; **III** *v/i.* **6.** betrügen, schwindeln, mogeln.

check [tʃek] **I** *s.* **1.** Schach(stellung *f*) *n*: **in ~** im Schach (stehend); **give ~** Schach bieten; **hold** (*od.* **keep**) **in ~** *fig.* in Schach halten; **2.** Hemmnis *n*, Hindernis *n* (**on** für): **put a ~ upon s.o.** j-m e-n Dämpfer aufsetzen, j-n zurückhalten; **3.** Unter'brechung *f*, Rückschlag *m*: **give a ~ to** Einhalt gebieten (*dat.*); **4.** Kon'trolle *f*, Über'prüfung *f*, Nachprüfung *f*, Über'wachung *f*: **keep a ~ upon s.th.** etwas unter Kontrolle halten; **5.** Kon'trollzeichen *n*, *bsd.* Häkchen *n* (*auf Listen etc.*); **6.** ✝ *Am.* Scheck *m* (**for** über *acc.*); **7.** *bsd. Am.* Kassenschein *m*, -zettel *m*, Rechnung *f* (*im Kaufhaus od. Restaurant*); **8.** Kon'trollabschnitt *m*, -marke *f*, -schein *m*; **9.** *bsd. Am.* Aufbewahrungsschein *m*: a) Garde'robenmarke *f*, b) Gepäckschein *m*; **10.** (*Essens- etc.*)Bon *m*, Gutschein *m*; **11.** a) Schachbrett-, Würfel-, Karomuster *n*, b) Karo *n*, Viereck *n*, c) karierter Stoff; **12.** Spielmarke *f*: **to pass** (*od.* **hand**) **in one's ~s** *Am.* F ‚abkratzen' (*sterben*); **13.** *Eishockey*: Check *m*; **II** *v/t.* **14.** Schach bieten (*dat.*): **~!** Schach!; **15.** hemmen, hindern, aufhalten, eindämmen; **16.** ⚙, *a. fig.* ✝ *etc.* drosseln, bremsen; **17.** zu'rückhalten, bremsen, zügeln, dämpfen: **~ o.s.** (plötzlich) innehalten, sich e-s anderen besinnen; **18.** *Eishockey*: *Gegner* checken; **19.** kontrollieren, über'prüfen, nachprüfen, ‚checken' (**for** auf *e-e Sache* hin): **~ against** vergleichen mit; **20.** *Am.* (*auf e-r Liste etc.*) abhaken, ankreuzen; **21.** *bsd. Am.* a) (zur Aufbewahrung *od.* in der Garde'robe) abgeben, b) (als Reisegepäck) aufgeben; **22.** *bsd. Am.* a) (zur Aufbewahrung) annehmen, b) zur Beförderung (als Reisegepäck) über'nehmen *od.* annehmen; **23.** karieren, mit e-m Karomuster versehen; **III** *v/i.* **24.** a) stimmen, b) (**with**) über'einstimmen (mit); **25.** *oft* **~ up** (**on**) nachprüfen, (*e-e Sache od. j-n*) über'prüfen: **~!** *Am.* F klar!; **26.** *Am.* e-n Scheck ausstellen (**for** über *acc.*); **27.** (plötzlich) inne- *od.* anhalten, stutzen.

Zssgn mit adv.:

check| back *v/i.* rückfragen (**with** bei); **~ in I** *v/i.* **1.** sich anmelden; **2.** ✝ einstempeln; **3.** ✈ einchecken; **II** *v/t.* **4.** anmelden; **5.** ✈ einchecken, abfertigen; **~ off** → ***check*** 20; **~ out I** *v/t.* **1.** → ***check*** 19; **II** *v/i.* **2.** (*aus e-m Hotel*) abreisen; **3.** ✝ ausstempeln; **4.** *Am. sl.* ‚abkratzen'; **~ o·ver** → ***check*** 19; **~ up** → ***check*** 25.

'**check|·back** *s.* Rückfrage *f*; **~ bit** *s. Computer*: Kon'trollbit *n*; '**~·book** → ***chequebook***; '**~·card** *s. Am.* Scheckkarte *f*.

checked [tʃekt] *adj.* kariert: **~ pattern** Karomuster *n*.

check·er ['tʃekə] *etc. Am.* → ***chequer*** *etc.*

'**check·in** *s.* **1.** Anmeldung *f in e-m Hotel*; **2.** ✝ Einstempeln *n*; **3.** ✈ Einchekken *n*: **~ counter** Abfertigungsschalter *m*; **~ time** Eincheckzeit *f*.

check·ing ac·count ['tʃekɪŋ] *s. econ. Am.* Girokonto *n*.

check| list *s.* Kon'trolliste *f*; **~ lock** *s.* kleines Sicherheitsschloß; '**~·mate I** *s.* **1.** (Schach)'Matt *n*, Mattstellung *f*; **2.** *fig.* Niederlage *f*; **II** *v/t.* **3.** (schach)'matt setzen (*a. fig.*); **III** *int.* **4.** schach'matt!; **~ nut** *s.* ⚙ Gegenmutter *f*; '**~-out** *s.* **1.** Abreise *f aus e-m Hotel*; **2.** ✝ Ausstempeln *n*; **3.** *a.* **~ counter** Kasse *f im Kaufhaus*; '**~-out test** *s.* ✝ Tauglichkeitstest *m für ein Produkt*; '**~-,o·ver** → ***checkup*** 1; '**~·point** *s. pol.* Kon'trollpunkt *m* (*an der Grenze*); '**~·room** *s. Am.* **1.** 🚂 Gepäckaufbewahrung(sstelle) *f*; **2.** Garde'robe(nraum *m*) *f*; '**~·up** *s.* **1.** Über'prüfung *f*, Kon'trolle *f*; **2.** ⚕ 'Vorsorgeunter,suchung *f*, Check-up *m*; **~ valve** *s.* ⚙ 'Absperr- *od.* 'Rückschlagven,til *n*.

Ched·dar (**cheese**) ['tʃedə] *s.* 'Cheddarkäse *m*.

cheek [tʃi:k] **I** *s.* **1.** Backe *f*, Wange *f*: **~ by jowl** dicht *od.* vertraulich beisammen; **2.** ⚙ Backe *f*; **3.** F Frechheit *f*, Unverfrorenheit *f*: **have the ~** die Frechheit *od.* Stirn besitzen (**to** *inf.* zu *inf.*); **II** *v/t.* **4.** frech sein zu; '**cheek-**

bone *s.* Backenknochen *m*; **cheeked** [-kt] *adj.* ...wangig, ...bäckig; ˈ**cheek·i·ness** [-kınıs] *s.* F Frechheit *f*; ˈ**cheek·y** [-kı] *adj.* □ frech.

cheep [tʃiːp] **I** *v/t. u. v/i.* piep(s)en; **II** *s.* Pieps(er) *m* (*a. fig.*).

cheer [tʃıə] **I** *s.* **1.** Beifall(sruf) *m*, Hurˈra(ruf *m*) *n*, Hoch(ruf *m*) *n*: ***three ~s for him!*** ein dreifaches Hoch auf ihn!, er lebe hoch, hoch, hoch!; ***to the ~s of*** unter dem Beifall *etc.* (*gen.*); **2.** Ermunterung *f*, Trost *m*: ***words of ~***; ***~s!*** prosit!; **3.** a) gute Laune, vergnügte Stimmung, Fröhlichkeit *f*, b) Stimmung *f*: ***good ~*** → a); ***be of good ~*** guter Laune *od.* Dinge sein, vergnügt sein; ***be of good ~!*** sei guten Mutes!; ***make good ~*** sich amüsieren, *a.* gut essen u. trinken; **II** *v/t.* **4.** Beifall spenden (*dat.*), zujubeln (*dat.*), mit Hoch- *od.* Bravorufen begrüßen, hochleben lassen; **5.** *a.* ***~ on*** anspornen, anfeuern; **6.** *a.* ***~ up*** *j-n* er-, aufmuntern, aufheitern; **III** *v/i.* **7.** Beifall spenden, hoch *od.* hurˈra rufen, jubeln; **8.** *meist* ***~ up*** Mut fassen, (wieder) fröhlich werden: ***~ up!*** Kopf hoch!

cheer·ful [ˈtʃıəfʊl] *adj.* □ **1.** heiter, fröhlich; (*iro.* quietsch)vergnügt; **2.** erfreulich, freundlich; **3.** freudig, gern; ˈ**cheer·ful·ness** [-nıs], **cheer·i·ness** [ˈtʃıərınıs] *s.* Heiterkeit *f*, Frohsinn *m*; **cheer·i·o** [ˌtʃıərıˈəʊ] *int.* F *bsd. Brit.* a) mach's gut!, tschüs!, b) ˈprosit!; ˈ**cheer-ˌlead·er** *s. sport Am.* Einpeitscher *m* (*beim Anfeuern*); **cheer·less** [ˈtʃıəlıs] *adj.* □ freudlos, trüb, trostlos; unfreundlich (*Zimmer*, *Wetter etc.*); **cheer·y** [ˈtʃıərı] *adj.* □ fröhlich, heiter, vergnügt.

cheese [tʃiːz] **I** *s.* **1.** Käse *m*; → ***chalk*** 2; **2.** käseartige Masse; Geˈlee *n*, *m*; **3.** ***big ~*** *sl.* ‚hohes Tier'; **4.** *sl. das* Richtige *od.* einzig Wahre: ***that's the ~!*** so ist's richtig!; ***hard ~!*** schöne Pleite!; **II** *v/t.* **5.** *sl.*: ***~ it!*** ‚hau ab'!; ˈ**~·cake** *s.* **1.** Käsekuchen *m*, -törtchen *n*; **2.** *Am.* Pin-up-Girl *n*, Sexbombe *f* (*Bild*); ˈ**~·cloth** *s.* Mull *m*, Gaze *f*; ˈ**~ˌmon·ger** *s.* Käsehändler *m*; ˈ**~ˌpar·ing** **I** *s.* **1.** wertlose Sache; **2.** Knauseˈrei *f*; **II** *adj.* **3.** knauserig; **~ straws** *s. pl.* Käsestangen *pl.*

chee·tah [ˈtʃiːtə] *s. zo.* ˈGepard *m*.

chef [ʃef] (*Fr.*) *s.* Küchenchef *m*.

chem·i·cal [ˈkemıkl] **I** *adj.* □ chemisch, Chemie...: ***~ agent*** ⚔ Kampfstoff *m*; ***~ engineer*** Chemotechniker *m*; ***~ fibre*** Chemie-, Kunstfaser *f*; ***~ warfare*** chemische Kriegführung; **II** *s.* Chemiˈkalie, chemisches Präpaˈrat.

che·mise [ʃıˈmiːz] **1.** (Damen)Hemd *n*; **2.** *a.* ***~ dress*** Hängekleid *n*.

chem·ist [ˈkemıst] *s.* **1.** *a.* ***analytical ~*** Chemiker *m*; **2.** *Brit. a.* ***dispensing ~*** Apoˈtheker *m*: ***~'s shop*** *Brit.* Apotheke *f*, Drogerie *f*; ˈ**chem·is·try** [-trı] *s.* **1.** Cheˈmie *f*; **2.** chemische Zs.-setzung; **3.** *fig.* Naˈtur *f*, Wirken *n*.

cheque [tʃek] *s.* ✝ *Brit.* Scheck *m* (***for*** über *e-e Summe*): ***blank ~*** Blankoscheck, *fig.* unbeschränkte Vollmacht; ***crossed ~*** Verrechnungsscheck; ***~ account*** *s.* ✝ *Brit.* ˈGiroˌkonto *n*; ˈ**~·book** *s. Brit.* Scheckbuch *n*.

cheq·uer [ˈtʃekə] *Brit.* **I** *s.* **1.** Schach-, Karomuster *n*; **2.** *pl. sg. konstr.* Damespiel *n*; **II** *v/t.* **3.** karieren; **4.** bunt *od.* unregelmäßig gestalten; ˈ**cheq·uer·board** *s. Brit.* Damebrett *n*; ˈ**cheq·uered** [-əd] *adj. Brit.* kariert; *fig.* bunt; wechselvoll, bewegt.

cher·ish [ˈtʃerıʃ] *v/t.* **1.** schätzen, hochhalten; **2.** sorgen für, pflegen; **3.** *Gefühle etc.* hegen; bewahren; **4.** *fig.* festhalten an (*dat.*).

che·root [ʃəˈruːt] *s.* Stumpen *m* (*Zigarre*).

cher·ry [ˈtʃerı] **I** *s.* **1.** ⚘ Kirsche *f* (*Frucht od. Baum*); **2.** *sl.* a) Jungfräulichkeit *f*, b) Jungfernhäutchen *n*; **II** *adj.* **3.** kirschrot; **~ bran·dy** *s.* Cherry Brandy *m*, ˈKirschliˌkör *m*; **~ pie** *s.* **1.** Kirschtorte *f*; **2.** ⚘ Helioˈtrop *n*; **~ stone** *s.* Kirschkern *m*; ˈ**~·wood** *s.* Kirschbaumholz *n*.

cher·ub [ˈtʃerəb] *pl.* **-ubs**, **-u·bim** [-əbım] *s.* **1.** *bibl.* ˈCherub *m*, Engel *m*; **2.** geflügelter Engelskopf; **3.** a) pausbäckiges Kind, b) *fig.* Engel(chen *n*) *m* (*Kind*).

cher·vil [ˈtʃɜːvıl] *s.* ⚘ Kerbel *m*.

Chesh·ire| cat [ˈtʃeʃə] *s.*: ***grin like a ~*** grinsen wie ein Affe; **~ cheese** *s.* ˈChesterkäse *m*.

chess [tʃes] *s.* Schach(spiel) *n*: ***a game of ~*** e-e Partie Schach; ˈ**~·board** *s.* Schachbrett *n*; ˈ**~·man** [-mæn] *s.* [*irr.*] ˈSchachfiˌgur *f*; **~ prob·lem** *s.* Schachaufgabe *f*.

chest [tʃest] *s.* **1.** Kiste *f*, Kasten *m*, Truhe *f*: ***~ of drawers*** Kommode *f*; **2.** kastenartiger Behälter; **3.** Brust(kasten *m*) *f*: ***have a weak ~*** schwach auf der Brust sein; ***~ expander*** Expander *m*; ***~ note*** Brustton *m*; ***~ trouble*** Lungenleiden; ***beat one's ~*** *fig.* sich reuig an die Brust schlagen; ***get s.th. off one's ~*** F sich et. von der Seele schaffen; ***play (one's cards) close to one's ~*** *a. fig.* sich nicht in die Karten gucken lassen; **4.** Kasse *f*, Kassenverwaltung *f*; ˈ**chest·ed** [-tıd] *adj. in Zssgn* ...brüstig.

ches·ter·field [ˈtʃestəfiːld] *s.* **1.** Chesterfield *m* (*Herrenmantel*); **2.** ˈPolsterˌsofa *n*.

chest·nut [ˈtʃesnʌt] **I** *s.* **1.** ⚘ Kaˈstanie *f* (*Frucht, Baum od. Holz*); **2.** Braune(r) *m* (*Pferd*); **3.** alter Witz, ‚alte Kaˈmelle'; **II** *adj.* **4.** kaˈstanienbraun.

chest·y [ˈtʃestı] *adj.* **1.** F tief(sitzend) (*Husten*); **2.** F dickbusig; **3.** *sl.* eingebildet, arroˈgant.

chev·a·lier [ˌʃevəˈlıə] *s.* **1.** (Ordens)Ritter *m*; **2.** *fig.* Kavaˈlier *m*.

chev·ron [ˈʃevrən] *s.* **1.** *her.* Sparren *m*; **2.** ⚔ Winkel *m* (*Rangabzeichen*); **3.** △ Zickzackleiste *f*.

chev·y [ˈtʃevı] → ***chiv(v)y***.

chew [tʃuː] **I** *v/t.* **1.** kauen: ***~ the rag*** *od.* ***fat*** a) ‚quatschen', plaudern, b) ‚mekkern'; → ***cud***; **2.** *fig.* sinnen auf (*acc.*), überˈlegen, brüten; **3.** ***~ over*** F *et.* besprechen; **4.** ***~ up*** *Am. sl. j-n* ‚anscheißen'; **II** *v/i.* **5.** kauen; **6.** F ˈTabak kauen; **7.** nachsinnen, grübeln (***on***, ***over*** über *acc.*); **III** *s.* **8.** Kauen *n*; **9.** Priem *m*; ˈ**chew·ing·gum** [ˈtʃuːıŋ-] *s.* ˈKauˌgummi *m*.

chi·a·ro·scu·ro [kıˌɑːrəsˈkʊərəʊ] *pl.* **-ros** (*Ital*) *s. paint.* Helldunkel *n*.

chic [ʃiːk] **I** *s.* Schick *m*, Eleˈganz *f*, Geschmack *m*; **II** *adj.* schick, eleˈgant.

chi·cane [ʃıˈkeın] **I** *s.* **1.** Schiˈkane *f* (*a. Motorsport*); **2.** *Bridge*: Blatt *n* ohne Trümpfe; **II** *v/t. u. v/i.* **3.** schikanieren; **4.** betrügen (***out of*** um); **chiˈcan·er·y** [-nərı] *s.* Schiˈkane *f*, (*bsd.* Rechts-) Kniff *m*.

chi·chi [ˈʃiːʃiː] *adj.* F **1.** (tod)schick; **2.** *contp.* auf schick gemacht.

chick [tʃık] *s.* **1.** Küken *n* (*a. fig. Kind*); junger Vogel; **2.** *sl.* ‚Biene' *f*, ‚Puppe' *f*.

chick·en [ˈtʃıkın] **I** *s.* **1.** Küken *n*; Hühnchen *n*, Hähnchen *n*: ***count one's ~s before they are hatched*** das Fell des Bären verkaufen, ehe man ihn hat; **2.** Huhn *n*; **3.** Hühnerfleisch *n*; **4.** F ‚Küken' *n*: ***she is no ~*** sie ist auch nicht mehr die Jüngste; **5.** *sl.* Mutprobe-Spiel *n*; **6.** ***give s.o. ~*** ⚔ *sl.* ‚mit j-m Schlitten fahren'; **II** *adj.* **7.** *sl.* feig(e); **III** *v/i.* **8.** *sl.* ‚Schiß' bekommen: ***~ out*** ‚kneifen'; ˈ**~-ˌbreast·ed** *adj.* hühnerbrüstig; **~ broth** *s.* Hühnerbrühe *f*; ˈ**~-feed** *s.* **1.** Hühnerfutter *n*; **2.** *sl.* ‚ein paar Groschen', lächerliche Summe: ***no ~*** kein Pappenstiel; ˈ**~-ˌheart·ed**, ˈ**~-ˌliv·ered** *adj.* feig(e); **~ pox** *s.* ⚕ Windpocken *pl.*; **~ run** *s.* Hühnerauslauf *m*.

ˈ**chick·pea** *s.* ⚘ Kichererbse *f*.

chic·le [ˈtʃıkl], *a.* **~ gum** *s.* (Rohstoff *m* von) ˈKauˌgummi *m*.

chic·o·ry [ˈtʃıkərı] *s.* ⚘ **1.** Ziˈchorie *f*; **2.** Chicorée *m*, *f*.

chid [tʃıd] *pret. u. p.p. von* ***chide***; **chid·den** [-dn] *p.p. von* ***chide***; **chide** [tʃaıd] *v/t. u. v/i.* [*irr.*] schelten, tadeln, (aus-) schimpfen.

chief [tʃiːf] **I** *s.* **1.** Haupt *n*, Oberhaupt *n*, Anführer *m*; Chef *m*, Vorgesetzte(r) *m*; Leiter *m*: ***℞ of Staff*** ⚔ (General-) Stabschef *m*; ***℞ of State*** Staatschef *m*, -oberhaupt *n*; ***in ~*** hauptsächlich; **2.** Häuptling *m*; **3.** *her.* Schildhaupt *n*; **II** *adj.* □ → ***chiefly***; **4.** erst, oberst, höchst; bedeutendst, Ober..., Höchst..., Haupt...: ***~ designer*** Chefkonstrukteur *m*; ***~ mourner*** Hauptleidtragende(r *m*) *f*; ***~ part*** Hauptrolle *f*; **~ clerk** *s.* **1.** Büˈrovorsteher *m*; erster Buchhalter; **2.** *Am.* erster Verkäufer; ℞ **Con·sta·ble** *s.* Poliˈzeipräsiˌdent *m*; **~ en·gi·neer** *s.* **1.** ˈChefingeniˌeur *m*; **2.** ⚓ erster Maschiˈnist; ℞ **Ex·ec·u·tive** *s. Am.* Leiter *m* der Verwaltung, *bsd.* Präsiˈdent *m* der U.S.A.; ℞ **Jus·tice** *s.* Oberrichter *m*.

chief·ly [ˈtʃiːflı] *adv.* hauptsächlich.

chief·tain [ˈtʃiːftən] *s.* Häuptling *m* (*Stamm*); Anführer *m* (*Bande*); ˈ**chief·tain·cy** [-sı] *s.* Stellung *f* e-s Häuptlings.

chif·fon [ˈʃıfɒn] Chifˈfon *m*.

chil·blain [ˈtʃılbleın] *s.* Frostbeule *f*.

child [tʃaıld] *pl.* **chil·dren** [ˈtʃıldrən] *s.* **1.** Kind *n*: ***with ~*** schwanger; ***from a ~*** von Kindheit an; ***be a good ~!*** sei artig!; ***~'s play*** *fig.* ein Kinderspiel (***to*** für); **2.** *fig.* Kind *n*, kindische *od.* kindliche Perˈson; **3.** Kind *n*, Nachkomme *m*: ***the children of Israel***; **4.** *fig.* Kind *n*, Proˈdukt *n*; **5.** Jünger *m*; **~ al·low·ance** *s.* Kinderfreibetrag *m*; ˈ**~bear·ing** *s.* Gebären *n*; ˈ**~·bed** *s.* Kind-, Wochenbett *n*; **~ ben·e·fit** *s. Brit.* Kindergeld *n*; ˈ**~·birth** *s.* Geburt *f*, Entbindung *f*, Niederkunft *f*; **~ care** *s.* Jugendfürsorge *f*; **~ guid·ance** *s.* ˈheilpädaˌgogische Betreuung (des Kindes).

child·hood [ˈtʃaıldhʊd] *s.* Kindheit *f*:

second ~ zweite Kindheit (*Senilität*); **ˈchild·ish** [-dɪʃ] *adj.* □ **1.** kindisch; **2.** kindlich; **ˈchild·ish·ness** [-dɪʃnɪs] *s.* **1.** Kindlichkeit *f*; **2.** kindisches Wesen; **ˈchild·less** [-lɪs] *adj.* kinderlos; **ˈchild-like** *adj.* kindlich; **child mind·er** *s.* Tagesmutter *f*; **child prod·i·gy** *s.* Wunderkind *n*.

chil·dren [ˈtʃɪldrən] *pl. von* ***child***: ***~'s allowance*** Kindergeld; *Radio, TV*: ***~'s hour*** Kinderstunde *f*.

child| wel·fare *s.* Jugendfürsorge *f*: ***~ worker*** Jugendfürsorger(in), Jugendpfleger(in); **~ wife** *s.* Kindweib *n*, sehr junge Ehefrau.

chil·e → ***chilli***.

Chil·e·an [ˈtʃɪlɪən] **I** *s.* Chiˈlene *m*, Chiˈlenin *f*; **II** *adj.* chiˈlenisch.

Chil·e| pine [ˈtʃɪlɪ] *s.* ⚘ Chiletanne *f*, Arauˈkarie *f*; **~ salt·pe·tre**, *Am.* **salt·pe·ter** *s.* ⚗ ˈChilesalˌpeter *m*.

chil·i *Am.* → ***chilli***.

chill [tʃɪl] **I** *s.* **1.** Kältegefühl *n*, Frösteln *n*; (*a.* Fieber)Schauer *m*: ***~ of fear*** eisiges Gefühl der Angst; **2.** Kälte *f*: ***take the ~ off*** leicht anwärmen, überschlagen lassen; **3.** Erkältung *f*: ***catch a ~*** sich erkälten; **4.** *fig.* Kälte *f*, Lieblosigkeit *f*, Entmutigung *f*: ***cast a ~ upon*** → 9; **5.** ⚙ Koˈkille *f*, Gußform *f*; **II** *adj.* **6.** kalt, frostig, kühl (*a. fig.*); entmutigend; **III** *v/i.* **7.** abkühlen; **IV** *v/t.* **8.** (ab)kühlen; erstarren lassen: ***~ed meat*** Kühlfleisch *n*; **9.** *fig.* abkühlen, dämpfen, entmutigen; **10.** ⚙ abschrecken, härten: ***~ed (cast) iron*** Hartguß *m*.

chil·li [ˈtʃɪlɪ] *s.* ⚘ Chili *m*.

chill·i·ness [ˈtʃɪlɪnɪs] *s.* Kälte *f*, Frostigkeit *f* (*beide a. fig.*); **chill·ing** [ˈtʃɪlɪŋ] *adj.* kalt, frostig; *fig.* niederdrückend; **chill·y** [ˈtʃɪlɪ] *adj.* a) kalt, frostig, kühl (*alle a. fig.*), b) fröstelnd: ***feel ~*** frösteln.

Chil·tern Hun·dreds [ˈtʃɪltən] *s. Brit. parl.*: ***apply for the ~*** s-n Sitz im Unterhaus aufgeben.

chi·mae·ra [kaɪˈmɪərə] *s.* **1.** *zo.* a) Chiˈmäre *f*, Seehase *m*, b) Seedrachen *m*; **2.** → ***chimera***.

chime [tʃaɪm] **I** *s.* **1.** *oft pl.* Glockenspiel *n*, Geläut(e) *n*; **2.** *fig.* Einklang *m*, Harmoˈnie *f*; **II** *v/i.* **3.** läuten; ertönen; schlagen (*Uhr*); **4.** *fig.* überˈeinstimmen, harmonieren: ***~ in*** einfallen, -stimmen, *weitS.* sich (ins Gespräch) einmischen; ***~ in with*** a) beipflichten (*dat.*), b) übereinstimmen mit; **III** *v/t.* **5.** läuten, ertönen lassen; *die Stunde* schlagen.

chi·me·ra [kaɪˈmɪərə] *s.* **1.** *myth.* Chiˈmära *f*; **2.** Schiˈmäre *f*: a) Schreckgespenst *n*, b) Hirngespinst *n*; **chiˈmer·i·cal** [-ˈmerɪkl] *adj.* □ schiˈmärisch, phanˈtastisch.

chim·ney [ˈtʃɪmnɪ] *s.* **1.** Schornstein *m*, Schlot *m*, Kaˈmin *m*; Rauchfang *m*: ***smoke like a ~*** F rauchen wie ein Schlot; **2.** (*Lampen*)Zyˈlinder *m*; **3.** a) *geol.* Vulˈkanschlot *m*, b) *mount.* Kaˈmin *m*; **~ cor·ner** *s.* Sitzecke *f* am Kaˈmin; **~ piece** *s.* Kaˈminsims *m*, *n*; **~ pot** *s.* Schornsteinaufsatz *m*: ***~ hat*** F ‚Angströhre' *f* (*Zylinderhut*); **~ stack** *s.* Schornstein(kasten) *m*; **~ sweep (-er)** *s.* Schornsteinfeger *m*.

chimp [tʃɪmp] *s.* F, **chim·pan·zee** [ˌtʃɪmpənˈziː] *s. zo.* Schimˈpanse *m*.

chin [tʃɪn] **I** *s.* Kinn *n*: ***up to the ~*** *fig.* bis über die Ohren; ***take it on the ~*** *fig.* a) schwer einstecken müssen, b) e-e böse ‚Pleite' erleben, c) es standhaft ertragen; (***keep your***) ***~ up!*** halt die Ohren steif!; **II** *v/i. sl.* ‚quasseln'; **III** *v/t.* ***~ o.s.*** (***up***) *Am.* e-n Klimmzug *od.* Klimmzüge machen.

chi·na [ˈtʃaɪnə] **I** *s.* **1.** Porzelˈlan *n*; **2.** (Porzelˈlan)Geschirr *n*; **II** *adj.* **3.** Porzellan…; **♀ bark** *s.* ⚘ Chinarinde *f*; **~ clay** *s. min.* Kaoˈlin *n*, Porzelˈlanerde *f*; **ˈ♀·man** [-mən] *s.* [*irr.*] Chiˈnese *m*; **♀ tea** *s.* chiˈnesischer Tee; **ˈ♀·town** *s.* Chiˈnesenviertel *n*; **ˈ~·ware** *s.* Porzelˈlan(waren *pl.*) *n*.

chinch [tʃɪntʃ] *s. Am.* Wanze *f*.

chin-chin [ˌtʃɪnˈtʃɪn] *int.* (*Pidgin-English*) **1.** a) (guten) Tag!, b) tschüs!; **2.** ˈprosit!, prost!

chine [tʃaɪn] *s.* **1.** Rückgrat *n*, Kreuz *n* (*Tier*); **2.** *Küche*: Kammstück *n*; **3.** (Berg)Grat *m*, Kamm *m*.

Chi·nese [ˌtʃaɪˈniːz] **I** *adj.* **1.** chiˈnesisch; **II** *s.* **2.** Chiˈnese *m*, Chiˈnesin *f*, Chiˈnesen *pl.*; **3.** *ling.* Chiˈnesisch *n*; **~ cab·bage** *s.* ⚘ Chinakohl *m*; **~ lan·tern** *s.* **1.** Lampiˈon *m*, *n*; **2.** ⚘ Lampiˈonpflanze *f*; **~ puz·zle** *s.* **1.** Veˈxier-, Geduldspiel *n*; **2.** *fig.* schwierige Sache.

Chink¹ [tʃɪŋk] *s. sl.* Chiˈnese *m*.

chink² [tʃɪŋk] *s.* **1.** Riß *m*, Ritz *m*, Ritze *f*, Spalt *m*, Spalte *f*: ***the ~ in his ar·mo(u)r*** *fig.* sein schwacher Punkt; **2.** ***~ of light*** dünner Lichtstrahl.

chink³ [tʃɪŋk] **I** *v/i. u. v/t.* klingen *od.* klirren (lassen), klimpern (mit) (*Geld etc.*); **II** *s.* Klirren *n*, Klang *m*.

chin strap *s.* Kinnriemen *m*.

chintz [tʃɪnts] *s.* Chintz *m*, buntbedruckter ˈMöbelkatˌtun; **ˈchintz·y** [-sɪ] *adj.* **1.** Plüsch…; **2.** *fig.* kleinbürgerlich, spießig.

ˈchin·wag I *s.* **1.** Plausch *m*; **2.** Tratsch *m*; **II** *v/i.* **3.** plauschen; **2.** tratschen.

chip [tʃɪp] **I** *s.* **1.** (*Holz- od. Metall*)Splitter *m*, Span *m*, Schnitzel *n*, *m*; Scheibchen *n*; abgebrochenes Stückchen; *pl.* Abfall *m*: ***dry as a ~*** fade, *fig. a.* trokken, ledern; ***a ~ of the old block*** ganz (wie) der Vater; ***have a ~ on one's shoulder*** F sehr empfindlich sein; **2.** angeschlagene Stelle; **3.** *pl.* a) *Brit.* Pommes ˈfrites *pl.*: ***fish and ~s***, b) *Am.* (Karˈtoffel)Chips *pl.*; **4.** Spielmarke *f*: ***when the ~s are down*** *fig.* wenn es hart auf hart geht; ***hand in one's ~s*** *Am. sl.* ‚abkratzen'; ***have had one's ~s*** *sl.* ‚fertig' sein; **5.** *pl. sl.* ‚Zaster' *m* (*Geld*): ***in the ~s*** (gut) bei Kasse; **6.** *Computer*: Chip *m* (*Mikrobaustein*); **II** *v/t.* **7.** (ab)schnitzeln; abraspeln; **8.** *Kante von Geschirr etc.* ab-, anschlagen; *Stückchen* ausbrechen; **9.** F hänseln; **III** *v/i.* **10.** (leicht) abbrechen; **~ in** *v/i.* **1.** sich (in ein Gespräch) einmischen; **2.** F beisteuern (*a. v/t.*); **~ off** *v/i.* abblättern, abbröckeln.

chip| bas·ket *s.* Spankorb *m*; **~ hat** *s.* Basthut *m*; **ˈ~·board** *s.* (Holz)Spanplatte *f*.

chip·muck [ˈtʃɪpmʌk], **ˈchip·munk** [-mʌŋk] *s. zo.* amer. gestreiftes Eichhörnchen.

ˈchip-pan *s. Küche*: Friˈteuse *f*.

Chip·pen·dale [ˈtʃɪpəndeɪl] *s.* Chippendale(stil *m*) *n* (*Möbelstil*).

chip·per [ˈtʃɪpə] *Am.* **I** *v/i.* zwitschern; schwatzen; **II** *adj.* F munter, vergnügt.

chip·ping [ˈtʃɪpɪŋ] *s.* Schnitzel *n*, *m*, abgeschlagenes Stück, angestoßene Ecke; Span *m*; *pl.* Splitt *m*.

chip·py [ˈtʃɪpɪ] **I** *adj.* **1.** angeschlagen (*Geschirr etc.*); schartig; **2.** *fig.* trokken, fade; **3.** *sl.* verkatert; **II** *s.* **4.** *Am. sl.* ‚Flittchen' *n*.

chi·ro·man·cer [ˈkaɪərəʊmænsə] *s.* Handleser *m*; **ˈchi·ro·man·cy** [-sɪ] *s.* Handlesekunst *f*.

chi·rop·o·dist [kɪˈrɒpədɪst] *s.* Fußpfleger(in), Pediˈküre *f*; **chi·rop·o·dy** [-dɪ] *s.* Fußpflege *f*, Pediˈküre *f*.

chirp [tʃɜːp] **I** *v/i. u. v/t.* zirpen, zwitschern; schilpen (*Spatz*); **II** *s.* Gezirp *n*, Zwitschern *n*; **ˈchirp·y** [-pɪ] *adj.* F munter, vergnügt.

chirr [tʃɜː] *v/i.* zirpen (*Heuschrecke*).

chir·rup [ˈtʃɪrəp] *v/i.* **1.** zwitschern; **2.** schnalzen.

chis·el [ˈtʃɪzl] **I** *s.* **1.** Meißel *m*; **2.** ⚙ Beitel *m*, Grabstichel *m*; **II** *v/t.* **3.** meißeln; **4.** *fig.* stiˈlistisch ausfeilen; **5.** *sl.* a) betrügen, ‚reinlegen', b) ergaunern, herˈausschinden; **ˈchis·el(l)ed** [-ld] *adj. fig.* **1.** ausgefeilt: ***~ style***; **2.** scharf geschnitten: ***~ face***; **ˈchis·el·(l)er** [-lə] *s.* F Gauner(in); ‚Nassauer' *m*.

chit¹ [tʃɪt] *s.* Kindchen *n*: ***a ~ of a girl*** ein junges Ding, ein Fratz.

chit² [tʃɪt] *s.* **1.** kurzer Brief; Zettel *m*; **2.** vom Gast abgezeichnete (Speise-) Rechnung.

chit·chat [ˈtʃɪttʃæt] → ***chinwag***.

chit·ter·ling [ˈtʃɪtəlɪŋ] *s. mst pl.* Gekröse *n*, Inneˈreien *pl.* (*bsd. Schwein*).

chiv·al·rous [ˈʃɪvlrəs] *adj.* □ ritterlich, gaˈlant; **ˈchiv·al·ry** [-rɪ] *s.* **1.** Ritterlichkeit *f*; **2.** Tapferkeit *f*; **3.** Rittertum *n*; **4.** Ritterdienst *m*.

chive¹ [tʃaɪv] *s.* ⚘ Schnittlauch *m*.

chive² [tʃaɪv] *sl.* **I** *s.* Messer *n*; **II** *v/t.* (er)stechen.

chiv·(v)y [ˈtʃɪvɪ] *v/t.* **1.** *j-n* herˈumjagen, hetzen; **2.** schikanieren.

chlo·ral [ˈklɔːrəl] *s.* ⚗ Chloˈral *n*: ***~ hydrate*** Chloralhydrat *n*; **ˈchlo·rate** [-reɪt] *s.* ⚗ chlorsaures Salz; **ˈchlo·ric** [-rɪk] *adj.* ⚗ Chlor…: ***~ acid*** Chlorsäure *f*; **ˈchlo·ride** [-raɪd] *s.* ⚗ Chloˈrid *n*, Chlorverbindung *f*: ***~ of lime*** Chlorkalk *m*; **ˈchlo·rin·ate** [-rɪneɪt] *v/t.* chloren, chlorieren; **chlo·rin·a·tion** [ˌklɔːrɪˈneɪʃn] *s.* Chloren *n*; **ˈchlo·rine** [-riːn] *s.* ⚗ Chlor *n*.

chlo·ro·form [ˈklɒrəfɔːm] **I** *s.* ⚗, ⚕ Chloroˈform *n*; **II** *v/t.* chloroformieren; **ˈchlo·ro·phyll** [-fɪl] *s.* ⚘ Chloroˈphyll *n*, Blattgrün *n*.

chlo·ro·sis [kləˈrəʊsɪs] *s.* ⚕, ⚘ Bleichsucht *f*; **chlo·rous** [ˈklɔːrəs] *adj.* chlorig.

choc [tʃɒk] *s.* F *abbr. für* ***chocolate***: ***~ ice*** Eis *n* mit Schokoladenüberzug.

chock [tʃɒk] **I** *s.* **1.** (Brems-, Hemm-) Keil *m*; **2.** ⚓ Klampe *f*; **II** *v/t.* **3.** festkeilen; **4.** *fig.* vollpfropfen; **III** *adv.* **5.** dicht; **~-a-block** [ˌtʃɒkəˈblɒk] *adj.* vollgepfropft; **ˌ~-ˈfull** *adj.* zum Bersten voll.

choc·o·late [ˈtʃɒkələt] **I** *s.* **1.** Schokoˈlade *f* (*a. als Getränk*); **2.** Praˈline *f*: ***~s*** Pralinen, Konfekt *n*; **II** *adj.* **3.** schokoˈladenbraun; **~ cream** *s.* ˈCremepraˌline *f*.

choice [tʃɔɪs] **I** *s.* **1.** Wahl *f*: ***make a ~*** wählen, e-e Wahl treffen; ***take one's ~*** s-e Wahl treffen; ***this is my ~*** dies habe ich gewählt; **2.** freie Wahl: ***at ~*** nach Belieben; ***by*** (*od.* ***for***) ***~*** vorzugsweise; ***from ~*** aus Vorliebe; **3.** (große) Auswahl; Sorti'ment *n*: ***a ~ of colours***; **4.** Wahl *f*, Möglichkeit *f*: ***I have no ~*** ich habe keine (andere) Wahl, *a.* es ist mir einerlei; **5.** Auslese *f*, *das* Beste; **II** *adj.* □ **6.** auserlesen, vor'züglich; ✝ Quali'täts…: ***~ fruit*** feinstes Obst; ***~ words*** a) gewählte Worte, b) *humor.* deftige Sprache; ***~ quality*** ✝ ausgesuchte Qualität; '**choice·ness** [-nɪs] *s.* Erlesenheit *f.*

choir ['kwaɪə] **I** *s.* **1.** (Kirchen-, Sänger-) Chor *m*; **2.** Chor *m*, ('Chor)Em,pore *f*; **II** *v/i. u. v/t.* **3.** im Chor singen; '**~·boy** *s.* Chor-, Sängerknabe *m*; '**~,mas·ter** *s.* Chorleiter *m*; **~ stalls** *s. pl.* Chorgestühl *n.*

choke [tʃəʊk] **I** *s.* **1.** Würgen *n*; **2.** *mot.* Luftklappe *f*, Choke *m*: ***pull out the ~*** den Choke ziehen; **3.** → ***choke coil***; **4.** → ***chokebore***; **II** *v/i.* **5.** würgen; ersticken (*a. fig.*): ***with a choking voice*** mit erstickter Stimme; **III** *v/t.* **6.** ersticken (*a. fig.*); erwürgen; würgen (*a. weitS. Kragen etc.*); **7.** hindern; dämpfen, drosseln (*a.* ⚡, ⚙); **8.** *a.* ***~ up*** a) verstopfen, b) 'vollstopfen; **~ back** *v/t.* **1.** *Lachen etc.* ersticken, unter'drücken; **2.** → ***choke off***; **~ down** *v/t.* **1.** hin'unterwürgen (*a. fig.*); **2.** → ***choke back*** 1; **~ off** *v/t. fig.* ‚abwürgen', nicht aufkommen lassen; *Konjunktur etc.* drosseln; **~ up** → ***choke*** 8.

'**choke|·bore** *s.* ⚙ Chokebohrung *f*; **~ coil** *s.* ⚡ Drosselspule *f*; '**~·damp** *s.* ⚒ Nachschwaden *m.*

chok·er ['tʃəʊkə] *s.* F enger Kragen *od.* Schal; enge Halskette.

chol·er ['kɒlə] *s.* **1.** *obs.* Galle *f*; **2.** *fig.* Zorn *m.*

chol·er·a ['kɒlərə] *s.* ⚕ 'Cholera *f.*

chol·er·ic ['kɒlərɪk] *adj.* cho'lerisch.

cho·les·ter·ol [kə'lestərɒl] *s. physiol.* Choleste'rin *n.*

choose [tʃu:z] **I** *v/t.* [*irr.*] **1.** (aus)wählen, aussuchen: ***to ~ a hat***; ***he was chosen king*** er wurde zum König gewählt; ***the chosen people*** *bibl.* das auserwählte Volk; **2.** belieben (*a. iro.*), (es) vorziehen, lieber wollen; beschließen: ***he chose to go*** er zog es vor *od.* er beschloß fortzugehen; ***do as you ~*** tu, wie *od.* was du willst; **II** *v/i.* [*irr.*] **3.** wählen: ***not much to ~*** kaum ein Unterschied; ***he cannot ~ but come*** er hat keine andere Wahl als zu kommen; '**choos·er** [-zə] *s.* (Aus)Wählende(r *m*) *f*; → ***beggar*** 1; '**choos·y** [-zɪ] *adj.* F wählerisch.

chop¹ [tʃɒp] **I** *s.* **1.** Hieb *m*, Schlag *m* (*a. Karate*); *Boxen, Tennis*: Chop *m*; **2.** *Küche*: Kote'lett *n*; **3.** *pl.* a) (Kinn)Backen *pl.*: ***lick one's ~s*** sich die Lippen lecken, b) *fig.* Maul *n*, Rachen *m*; **II** *v/t.* **4.** (zer)hacken, hauen, spalten: ***~ wood*** Holz hacken; ***~ one's words*** abgehackt sprechen; **5.** *Tennis*: *den Ball* choppen; **~ down** *v/t.* fällen; **~ in** *v/i.* sich einmischen; **~ off** *v/t.* abhauen; **~ up** *v/t.* zer-, kleinhacken.

chop² [tʃɒp] **I** *v/i. a.* ***~ about***, ***~ round*** sich drehen, 'umschlagen (*Wind*): ***~ and change*** s-n Standpunkt dauernd ändern, hin u. her schwanken; **II** *v/t. Worte* wechseln; **III** *s. pl.* ***~s and changes*** ewiges Hin und Her.

chop³ [tʃɒp] *s.* (*Indien u. China*) **1.** Stempel *m*, Siegel *n*; **2.** Urkunde *f*; **3.** (Handels)Marke *f*; **4.** Quali'tät *f*: ***first-~*** erste Sorte, erstklassig.

'**chop·house** *s.* Steakhaus *n.*

chop·per ['tʃɒpə] *s.* **1.** Hackmesser *n*, -beil *n*; **2.** ⚡ Zerhacker *m*; **3.** *Am. sl.* Hubschrauber *m*; **4.** *pl. sl.* Zähne *pl.*

chop·ping¹ ['tʃɒpɪŋ] *adj.* stramm (*Kind*).

chop·ping² ['tʃɒpɪŋ] *s.* Wechsel *m*: ***~ and changing*** ewiges Hin und Her.

chop·ping| block ['tʃɒpɪŋ] *s.* Hackblock *m*, -klotz *m*; **~ board** *s.* Hackbrett *n*; **~ knife** *s.* [*irr.*] Hackmesser *n.*

chop·py ['tʃɒpɪ] *adj.* **1.** kabbelig (*Meer*); **2.** böig (*Wind*); **3.** *fig.* wechselnd; **4.** *fig.* abgehackt.

'**chop|·stick** *s.* Eßstäbchen *n* (*China etc.*); **,~-'su·ey** [-'su:ɪ] *s.* Chop-suey *n* (*chinesisches Mischgericht*).

cho·ral ['kɔ:rəl] *adj.* □ Chor…, im Chor gesungen: ***~ service*** Gottesdienst *m* mit Chorgesang; ***~ society*** Chor *m*;

cho·rale [kɒ'rɑ:l] *s.* Cho'ral *m.*

chord [kɔ:d] *s.* **1.** ♪, *poet.*, *fig.* Saite *f*; **2.** ♪ Ak'kord *m*; *fig.* Ton *m*: ***break into a ~*** e-n Tusch spielen; ***strike the right ~ bei j-m*** die richtige Saite anschlagen; ***does that strike a ~?*** erinnert *dich* das an etwas?; **3.** ⚘ Sehne *f*; **4.** *anat.* Band *n*, Strang *m*; **5.** ✈ Pro'filsehne *f*; **6.** ⚙ Gurt *m.*

chore [tʃɔ:] *s.* **1.** (Haus)Arbeit *f*; **2.** schwierige Aufgabe.

cho·re·a [kɒ'rɪə] *s.* ⚕ Veitstanz *m.*

cho·re·og·ra·pher [,kɒrɪ'ɒgrəfə] *s.* Choreo'graph *m*; **cho·re'og·ra·phy** [-fɪ] *s.* Choreogra'phie *f.*

chor·is·ter ['kɒrɪstə] *s.* **1.** Chorsänger (-in), *bsd.* Chorknabe *m*; **2.** *Am.* Kirchenchorleiter *m.*

chor·tle ['tʃɔ:tl] **I** *v/i.* glucksen(d lachen); **II** *s.* Glucksen *n.*

cho·rus ['kɔ:rəs] **I** *s.* **1.** Chor *m* (*a. antiq.*), Sängergruppe *f*; **2.** Tanzgruppe *f* (*e-r Revue*); **3.** *a. thea.* Chor *m*, gemeinsames Singen: ***~ of protest*** Protestgeschrei *n*; ***in ~*** im Chor (*a. fig.*); **4.** Chorsprecher *m* (*im elisabethanischen Theater*); **5.** (im Chor gesungener) Kehrreim; **6.** Chorwerk *n*; **II** *v/i. u. v/t.* **7.** im Chor singen *od.* sprechen *od.* rufen; **~ girl** *s.* (Re'vue)Tänzerin *f.*

chose [tʃəʊz] *pret. von* ***choose.***

cho·sen ['tʃəʊzn] *p.p. von* ***choose.***

chough [tʃʌf] *s. orn.* Dohle *f.*

chow [tʃaʊ] *s.* **1.** *zo.* Chow-'Chow *m* (*Hund*); **2.** *sl.* ‚Futter' *n*, Essen *n.*

chow·chow [,tʃaʊ'tʃaʊ] (*Pidgin-Englisch*) *s.* **1.** chi'nesische Mixed Pickles *pl. od.* 'Fruchtkonfi,türe *f*; **2.** → ***chow*** 1.

chow·der ['tʃaʊdə] *s. Am. dicke Suppe aus Meeresfrüchten.*

Christ [kraɪst] **I** *s.* der Gesalbte, 'Christus *m*: ***before ~*** (***B.C.***) vor Christi Geburt (*v. Chr.*); **II** *int. sl.* verdammt noch mal!; **~ child** *s.* Christkind *n.*

chris·ten ['krɪsn] *v/t. eccl.*, ⚓ *u. fig.* taufen; '**Chris·ten·dom** [-dəm] *s.* Christenheit *f*; '**chris·ten·ing** [-nɪŋ] **I** *s.* Taufe *f*; **II** *adj.* Tauf…

Chris·tian ['krɪstjən] **I** *adj.* □ **1.** christlich; **2.** F anständig; **II** *s.* **3.** Christ(in); **4.** guter Mensch; **5.** Mensch *m* (*Ggs. Tier*); **~ e·ra** *s.* christliche Zeitrechnung.

Chris·ti·an·i·ty [,krɪstɪ'ænətɪ] *s.* Christentum *n*; **Chris·tian·ize** ['krɪstjənaɪz] *v/t.* zum Christentum bekehren, christianisieren.

Chris·tian| name *s.* Tauf-, Vorname *m*; **~ Sci·ence** *s.* Christian Science *f*; **~ Sci·en·tist** *s.* Anhänger(in) der Christian Science.

Christ·mas ['krɪsməs] *s.* Weihnachten *n u. pl.*: ***at ~*** zu *od.* an Weihnachten; ***merry ~!*** frohe Weihnachten!; **~ bo·nus** *s.* ✝ 'Weihnachtsgratifikati,on *f*; **~ card** *s.* Weihnachtskarte *f*; **~ car·ol** *s.* Weihnachtslied *n*; **~ Day** *s.* der erste Weihnachtsfeiertag; **~ Eve** *s.* der Heilige Abend; **~ pud·ding** *s. Brit.* Plumpudding *m*; '**~·tide**, '**~·time** *s.* Weihnachtszeit *f*; '**~·tree** *s.* Weihnachts-, Christbaum *m.*

Christ·mas·y ['krɪsməsɪ] *adj.* F weihnachtlich.

chro·mate ['krəʊmeɪt] *s.* ⚗ Chro'mat *n*, chromsaures Salz.

chro·mat·ic [krəʊ'mætɪk] *adj.* (□ ***~ally***) **1.** *phys.* chro'matisch, Farben…; **2.** ♪ chromatisch; **chro'mat·ics** [-ks] *s. pl. sg. konstr.* **1.** Farbenlehre *f*; **2.** ♪ Chro'matik *f.*

chrome [krəʊm] **I** *s.* **1.** ⚗ a) Chrom *n*, b) Chromgelb *n*; **2.** Chromleder *n*; **II** *v/t.* **3.** *a.* ***~-plate*** verchromen.

chro·mi·um ['krəʊmjəm] *s.* ⚗ Chrom *n*; **,~-'plat·ed** *adj.* verchromt; **,~-'plat·ing** *s.* Verchromung *f*; **~ steel** *s.* Chromstahl *m.*

chro·mo·lith·o·graph [,krəʊməʊ'lɪθəʊgrɑ:f] *s.* Chromolithogra'phie *f*, Mehrfarbensteindruck *m* (*Bild*); **,chro·mo·li'thog·ra·phy** [-lɪ'θɒgrəfɪ] *s.* Mehrfarbensteindruck *m* (*Verfahren*).

chro·mo·some ['krəʊməsəʊm] *s. biol.* Chromo'som *n*; '**chro·mo·type** [-məʊtaɪp] *s.* **1.** Farbdruck *m*; **2.** Chromoty'pie *f.*

chron·ic ['krɒnɪk] *adj.* (□ ***~ally***) **1.** ständig, (an)dauernd, ‚chronisch'; **2.** *mst* ⚕ chronisch, langwierig; **3.** *sl.* scheußlich.

chron·i·cle ['krɒnɪkl] **I** *s.* **1.** Chronik *f*; **2.** **2s** *pl. bibl.* (*das* Buch der) Chronik *f*; **II** *v/t.* **3.** aufzeichnen; '**chron·i·cler** [-lə] *s.* Chro'nist *m.*

chron·o·gram ['krɒnəʊgræm] *s.* Chrono'gramm *n*; '**chron·o·graph** [-grɑ:f] *s.* Chrono'graph *m*, Zeitmesser *m*; **chron·o·log·i·cal** [,krɒnə'lɒdʒɪkl] *adj.* □ chrono'logisch: ***~ order*** zeitliche Reihenfolge; **chro·nol·o·gize** [krə'nɒlədʒaɪz] *v/t.* chronologisieren; **chro·nol·o·gy** [krə'nɒlədʒɪ] *s.* **1.** Chronolo'gie *f*, Zeitbestimmung *f*; **2.** Zeittafel *f*; **chro·nom·e·ter** [krə'nɒmɪtə] *s.* Chrono'meter *n*; **chro·nom·e·try** [krə'nɒmɪtrɪ] *s.* Zeitmessung *f.*

chrys·a·lis ['krɪsəlɪs] *pl.* **-lis·es** [-lɪsɪz], **chry·sal·i·des** [krɪ'sælɪdi:z] *s. zo.* (*Insekten*)Puppe *f.*

chrys·an·the·mum [krɪ'sænθəməm] *s.* ⚘ Chrysan'theme *f.*

chub [tʃʌb] *s. ichth.* Döbel *m.*

chub·by ['tʃʌbɪ] *adj.* a) pausbäckig, b) rundlich.

chuck¹ [tʃʌk] **I** *s.* **1.** F Wurf *m*; **2.** zärtlicher Griff unters Kinn; **3.** ***give s.o. the ~*** F j-n ‚rausschmeißen' (*entlassen*); **II** *v/t.* **4.** F schmeißen, werfen; **5.** ***~ s.o. under the chin*** j-n unters Kinn fassen; **6.** F a) Schluß machen mit: ***~ it!*** laß das!, b) → ***chuck up***; **~ a·way** *v/t.* F **1.** ‚wegschmeißen'; **2.** *Geld* verschwenden; **3.** *Gelegenheit* ‚verschenken'; **~ out** *v/t.* F ‚rausschmeißen'; **~ up** *v/t.* F *Job etc.* ‚hinschmeißen'.

chuck² [tʃʌk] **I** *s.* **1.** Glucken *n* (*Henne*); **2.** F ‚Schnuckie' *m* (*Kosewort*); **II** *v/i. u. v/t.* **3.** glucken; **III** *int.* **4.** put, put! (*Lockruf für Hühner*).

chuck³ [tʃʌk] ⚙ **I** *s.* Spann- *od.* Bohrfutter *n*; **II** *v/t.* (in das Futter) einspannen.

chuck·er-out [ˌtʃʌkər'aʊt] *s.* F ‚Rausschmeißer' *m* (*in Lokalen etc.*).

chuck·le ['tʃʌkl] **I** *v/i.* **1.** glucksen, in sich hin'einlachen; **2.** sich (insgeheim) freuen (***at, over*** über *acc.*); **3.** glucken (*Henne*); **II** *s.* **4.** leises Lachen, Glucksen *n*; '**~·head** *s.* Dummkopf *m*.

chuffed [tʃʌft] *adj. Brit.* F froh.

chug [tʃʌg], **chug-chug** [ˌtʃʌg'tʃʌg] **I** *s.* Tuckern *n* (*Motor*); **II** *v/i.* tuckern(d fahren).

chuk·ker ['tʃʌkə] *s. Polospiel*: Chukker *m* (*Spielabschnitt*).

chum [tʃʌm] F **I** *s.* **1.** ‚Kumpel' *m*, ‚Spezi' *m*, Kame'rad *m*: ***be great ~s*** dicke Freunde sein; **2.** Stubengenosse *m*; **II** *v/i.* **3.** gemeinsam wohnen (***with*** mit); **4.** ***~ up with s.o.*** sich mit j-m anfreunden; '**chum·my** [-mɪ] *adj.* **1.** ‚dick' befreundet; **2.** gesellig; **3.** *contp.* plump-vertraulich.

chump [tʃʌmp] *s.* **1.** Holzklotz *m*; **2.** dickes Ende (*bsd. Hammelkeule*); **3.** F Dummkopf *m*; **4.** *bsd. Brit. sl.* ‚Kürbis' *m*, ‚Birne' *f* (*Kopf*): ***off one's ~*** (total) verrückt.

chunk [tʃʌŋk] *s.* F **1.** (Holz)Klotz *m*; Klumpen *m*, dickes Stück (*Fleisch etc.*), ‚Runken' *m* (*Brot*); *weitS.* ‚großer Brocken'; **2.** *Am.* a) unter'setzter Mensch, b) kleines, stämmiges Pferd; '**chunk·y** [-kɪ] *adj.* **1.** *Am.* unter'setzt, stämmig; **2.** klobig, klotzig.

church [tʃɜːtʃ] **I** *s.* **1.** Kirche *f*: ***in ~*** in der Kirche, beim Gottesdienst; ***~ is over*** die Kirche ist aus; **2.** Kirche *f*, Religi'onsgemeinschaft *f*, *bsd.* Christenheit *f*; **3.** Geistlichkeit *f*: ***enter the ~*** Geistlicher werden; **II** *adj.* **4.** Kirch(en)...; kirchlich; '**~ˌgo·er** *s.* Kirchgänger(in); ♀ **of Eng·land** *s.* englische Staatskirche, anglikanische Kirche; **~ rate** *s.* Kirchensteuer *f*; ˌ**~'ward·en** *s.* **1.** *Brit.* Kirchenvorsteher *m*: ***~ pipe*** langstielige Tonpfeife; **2.** *Am.* Verwalter *m* der weltlichen Angelegenheiten e-r Kirche; **~ wed·ding** *s.* kirchliche Trauung.

church·y ['tʃɜːtʃɪ] *adj.* F kirchlich (gesinnt).

'**church·yard** *s.* Kirchhof *m*.

churl [tʃɜːl] *s.* **1.** Flegel *m*, Grobian *m*; **2.** Geizhals *m*, Knauser *m*; '**churl·ish** [-lɪʃ] *adj.* ☐ **1.** grob, ungehobelt, flegelhaft; **2.** geizig, knauserig; **3.** mürrisch.

churn [tʃɜːn] **I** *s.* **1.** Butterfaß *n* (*Maschine*); **2.** *Brit.* (große) Milchkanne; **II** *v/t.* **3.** verbuttern; **4.** ('durch)schütteln, aufwühlen; **5.** *fig.* ***~ out*** am laufenden Band produzieren, ausstoßen; **III** *v/i.* **6.** buttern; **7.** schäumen; **8.** sich heftig bewegen.

chute [ʃuːt] *s.* **1.** Stromschnelle *f*, starkes Gefälle; **2.** ⚙ a) Rutsche *f*, b) Schacht *m*, c) Müllschlucker *m*; **3.** Rutsche *f*, Rutschbahn *f* (*auf Spielplätzen etc.*); **4.** Rodelbahn *f*; **5.** F → ***parachute*** 1; ˌ**~-the-'chute(s)** → ***chute*** 3.

chutz·pa(h) ['hʊtspə] *s.* F Chuzpe *f*, Frechheit *f*.

ci·bo·ri·um [sɪ'bɔːrɪəm] *s. eccl.* **1.** 'Hostienkelch *m*, Zi'borium *n*; **2.** Al'tarˌbaldachin *m*.

ci·ca·da [sɪ'kɑːdə], **ci'ca·la** [-ɑːlə] *s. zo.* Zi'kade *f*.

cic·a·trice ['sɪkətrɪs] *s.* Narbe *f*; ♀ Blattnarbe *f*; '**cic·a·triced** [-st] *adj.* ⚕ vernarbt; '**cic·a·trize** [-raɪz] *v/i. u. v/t.* vernarben (lassen).

cic·er·o ['sɪsərəʊ] *s. typ.* Cicero *f* (*Schriftgrad*).

ci·ce·ro·ne [ˌtʃɪʃə'rəʊnɪ] *pl.* **-ni** [-niː] *s.* Cice'rone *m*, Fremdenführer *m*.

ci·der ['saɪdə] *s.* (*Am.* ***hard ~***) Apfelwein *m*: (***sweet***) ***~*** *Am.* Apfelmost *m*.

ci·gar [sɪ'gɑː] *s.* Zi'garre *f*; **~ box** *s.* Zi'garrenkiste *f*; **~ case** *s.* Zi'garreneˌtui *n*, -tasche *f*; **~ cut·ter** *s.* Zi'garrenabschneider *m*.

cig·a·ret(te) [ˌsɪgə'ret] *s.* Ziga'rette *f*; **~ case** *s.* Ziga'retteneˌtui *n*; **~ end** *s.* Ziga'rettenstummel *m*; **~ hold·er** *s.* Ziga'rettenspitze *f* (*Halter*).

cil·i·a ['sɪlɪə] *s. pl.* **1.** (Augen)Wimpern *pl.*; **2.** ♀, *zo.* Wimper-, Flimmerhärchen *pl.*; '**cil·i·ar·y** [-ərɪ] *adj.* Wimper...; '**cil·i·at·ed** [-ɪeɪtɪd] *adj.* ♀, *zo.* bewimpert.

cinch [sɪntʃ] *s.* **1.** *Am.* Sattelgurt *m*; **2.** *sl.* a) ‚todsichere Sache', ‚klarer Fall', b) ‚Kinderspiel' *n*.

cin·cho·na [sɪŋ'kəʊnə] *s.* **1.** ♀ 'Chinarindenbaum *m*; **2.** 'Chinarinde *f*.

cinc·ture ['sɪŋktʃə] **I** *s.* **1.** Gürtel *m*, Gurt *m*; **2.** (Säulen)Kranz *m*; **II** *v/t.* **3.** um'gürten, um'geben.

cin·der ['sɪndə] *s.* **1.** Schlacke *f*: ***burnt to a ~*** verkohlt, völlig verbrannt; **2.** *pl.* Asche *f*.

Cin·der·el·la [ˌsɪndə'relə] *s.* Aschenbrödel *n*, -puttel *n* (*a. fig.*).

cin·der| path *s.* **1.** Schlackenweg *m*; **2.** → **~ track** *s. sport* Aschenbahn *f*.

cine- [sɪnɪ] *in Zssgn* Kino..., Film...: ***~ camera*** (Schmal)Filmkamera *f*; ***~ film*** Schmalfilm *m*; ***~-record*** filmen, mit der Schmalfilmkamera aufnehmen.

cin·e·aste ['sɪnɪæst] *s.* Cine'ast *m*, Filmliebhaber(in).

cin·e·ma ['sɪnɪmə] *s.* **1.** 'Lichtspieltheˌater *n*, 'Kino *n*; **2.** ***the ~*** Film(kunst *f*) *m*; '**~ˌgo·er** *s.* 'Kinobesucher(in).

cin·e·mat·ic [ˌsɪnɪ'mætɪk] *adj.* (☐ ***~ally***) filmisch, Film...; **cin·e·mat·o·graph** [ˌsɪnə'mætəgrɑːf] **I** *s.* Kinemato'graph *m*; **II** *v/t.* (ver)filmen; **cin·e·ma·tog·ra·pher** [ˌsɪnəmə'tɒgrəfə] *s.* 'Kameramann *m*; **cin·e·mat·o·graph·ic** [ˌsɪnəmætə'græfɪk] (☐ ***~ally***) kinemato'graphisch; **cin·e·ma·tog·ra·phy** [ˌsɪnəmə'tɒgrəfɪ] *s.* Kinematogra'phie *f*.

cin·e·ra·ri·um [ˌsɪnə'reərɪəm] *s.* Urnennische *f od.* -friedhof *m*.

cin·er·ar·y ['sɪnərərɪ] *adj.* Aschen...; **~ urn** *s.* Totenurne *f*.

cin·er·a·tor ['sɪnəreɪtə] *s.* Feuerbestattungsofen *m*.

cin·na·bar ['sɪnəbɑː] *s.* Zin'nober *m*.

cin·na·mon ['sɪnəmən] **I** *s.* **1.** Zimt *m*, Ka'neel *m*; **2.** Zimtbaum *m*; **II** *adj.* **3.** zimtfarbig.

cinque [sɪŋk] (*Fr.*) *s.* Fünf *f* (*Würfel od. Spielkarten*); '**~·foil** [-fɔɪl] *s.* **1.** ♀ Fingerkraut *n*; **2.** ⚠ Fünfpaß *m*; ♀ **Ports** ['sɪŋkpɔːts] *s. pl. Gruppe von ursprünglich fünf südenglischen Seestädten.*

ci·on ['saɪən] → ***scion***.

ci·pher ['saɪfə] **I** *s.* **1.** ⚘ *die Ziffer* Null *f*; **2.** (a'rabische) Ziffer, Zahl *f*; **3.** *fig.* a) Null *f* (*Person*), b) Nichts *n*; **4.** Chiffre *f*, Geheimschrift *f*: ***in ~*** chiffriert; **5.** *fig.* Schlüssel *m*, Kennwort *n*; **6.** Mono'gramm *n*; **II** *v/i.* **7.** rechnen; **III** *v/t.* **8.** chiffrieren; **9.** *a.* ***~ out*** be-, ausrechnen; entziffern; *Am.* F ‚ausknobeln'; **~ code** *s.* Codechiffre *f*, Tele'gramm-, Chiffrierschlüssel *m*.

cir·ca ['sɜːkə] *prp.* um (*vor Jahreszahlen*).

Cir·ce ['sɜːsɪ] *npr. myth.* 'Circe *f* (*a. fig. Verführerin*).

cir·cle ['sɜːkl] **I** *s.* **1.** ⚘ Kreis *m*: ***full ~*** im Kreise herum, volle Wendung, wieder da, wo *man* angefangen hat; ***run*** (*a.* ***talk***) ***in ~s*** *fig.* sich im Kreis bewegen; ***square the ~*** ⚘ den Kreis quadrieren (*a. fig. das Unmögliche vollbringen*); → ***vicious circle***; **2.** *ast., geogr.* Kreis *m*; **3.** Kreis *m*, Gruppe *f*: ***~ of friends*** Freundeskreis; → ***upper*** I; **4.** Ring *m*, Kranz *m*, Reif *m*; **5.** Kreislauf *m*, 'Umlauf *m*, Runde *f*; Wiederkehr *f*, 'Zyklus *m*; **6.** *thea.* Rang *m*; **7.** Kreis *m*, Gebiet *n*; **8.** a) *Turnen*: Welle *f*, b) *Hockey*: (Schuß)Kreis *m*; **II** *v/t.* **9.** um'kreisen; um'zingeln; **10.** um'winden; **III** *v/i.* **11.** sich im Kreise bewegen, kreisen; die Runde machen; **12.** ⚔ schwenken.

cir·clet ['sɜːklɪt] *s.* **1.** kleiner Kreis, Reif, Ring; **2.** Dia'dem *n*.

circs [sɜːks] *s. pl.* F *für* ***circumstances***.

cir·cuit ['sɜːkɪt] **I** *s.* **1.** 'Kreisˌlinie *f*, 'Um-, Kreislauf *m*; Bahn *f*; **2.** 'Umkreis *m*; **3.** 'Umweg *m*; **4.** Rundgang *m*, -flug *m*; *mot.* Rennstrecke *f*; **5.** ⚖ a) *Brit. hist.* Rundreise *f* der Richter e-s Bezirks (*zur Abhaltung der* ***assizes***), b) Anwälte *pl.* e-s Gerichtsbezirks, c) Gerichtsbezirk *m*; **6.** ⚡ a) Strom-, Schaltkreis *m*: → ***short*** (***closed***) ***circuit***, b) Schaltung *f*, 'Schaltsyˌstem *n*; **7.** *Am.* (Per'sonen)Kreis *m*; **8.** *sport* ‚Zirkus' *m*: ***the tennis ~***; **II** *v/t.* **9.** um'kreisen; **III** *v/i.* **10.** kreisen; **~ break·er** *s.* ⚡ Ausschalter *m*; **~ di·a·gram** *s.* ⚡ Schaltbild *n*, -plan *m*.

cir·cu·i·tous [sə'kjuːɪtəs] *adj.* ☐ weitschweifig, -läufig: ***~ route*** Umweg *m*; **cir·cuit·ry** ['sɜːkɪtrɪ] *s.* ⚡ **1.** 'Schaltsyˌstem *n*; **2.** Schaltungen *pl.*; **3.** Schaltbild *n*.

cir·cu·lar ['sɜːkjʊlə] **I** *adj.* ☐ **1.** (kreis-)rund, kreisförmig; **2.** Rund..., Kreis..., Ring...; **II** *s.* **3.** a) Rundschreiben *n*, b) (Post)Wurfsendung *f*; '**cir·cu·lar·ize** [-əraɪz] *v/t.* *a.* (Post)Wurfsendungen verschicken an (*acc.*); Fragebogen schicken an (*acc.*); durch (Post)Wurfsendungen werben für.

cir·cu·lar| let·ter → ***circular*** 3a; **~ let·ter of cred·it** *s.* ✝ 'Reisekreˌditbrief *m*; **~ note** *s.* **1.** *pol.* Zirku'larnote *f*; **2.** 'Reisekreˌditbrief *m*; **~ saw** *s.* ⚙ Kreissäge *f*; **~ skirt** *s.* Glockenrock *m*; **~ tick·et** *s.* Rundreisekarte *f*; **~ tour**, **~**

trip *s.* Rundreise *f*, -fahrt *f*.

cir·cu·late ['sɜ:kjʊleɪt] **I** *v/i.* **1.** zirkulieren: a) 'umlaufen, kreisen, b) im 'Umlauf sein, kursieren (*Geld, Gerücht etc.*); **2.** her'umreisen, -gehen; **II** *v/t.* **3.** in Umlauf setzen, zirkulieren lassen.

cir·cu·lat·ing ['sɜ:kjʊleɪtɪŋ] *adj.* zirkulierend, 'umlaufend; ~ **cap·i·tal** *s.* 'Umlauf-, Be'triebskapi,tal *n*; ~ **dec·i·mal** *s.* 𝔄 peri'odischer Dezi'malbruch; ~ **li·brar·y** *s.* 'Leihbüche,rei *f*.

cir·cu·la·tion [,sɜ:kjʊ'leɪʃn] *s.* **1.** Kreislauf *m*, Zirkulati'on *f*; **2.** *physiol.* ('Blut)Zirkulati,on *f*, (-)Kreislauf *m*; **3.** ✝ a) 'Umlauf *m*, Verkehr *m*, b) Verbreitung *f*, Absatz *m*, c) Auflage(nziffer) *f* (*Zeitung etc.*), d) 'Zahlungsmittel,umlauf *m*: ***out of*** ~ außer Kurs (gesetzt); ***put into*** ~ in Umlauf setzen; ***withdraw from*** ~ aus dem Verkehr ziehen (*a. fig.*); **4.** Strömung *f*, 'Durchzug *m*, -fluß *m*; **cir·cu·la·tor** ['sɜ:kjʊleɪtə] *s.* Verbreiter(in); **cir·cu·la·to·ry** [,sɜ:kjʊ'leɪtərɪ] *adj.* zirkulierend, 'umlaufend; *physiol.* Kreislauf...: ~ ***collapse***; ~ ***system*** (Blut)Kreislauf *m*.

cir·cum·cise ['sɜ:kəmsaɪz] *v/t.* **1.** ⚕, *eccl.* beschneiden; **2.** *fig.* läutern; **cir·cum·ci·sion** [,sɜ:kəm'sɪʒn] *s.* **1.** ⚕, *eccl.* Beschneidung *f*; **2.** *fig.* Läuterung *f*; **3.** 𝔖 Fest *n* der Beschneidung Christi; **4.** ***the*** ~ *bibl.* die Beschnittenen *pl.* (*Juden*).

cir·cum·fer·ence [sə'kʌmfərəns] *s.* 'Umkreis *m*, 'Umfang *m*, Periphe'rie *f*;

cir·cum·flex ['sɜ:kəmfleks] *s. a.* ~ ***accent*** *ling.* Zirkum'flex *m*; **cir·cum·ja·cent** [,sɜ:kəm'dʒeɪsənt] *adj.* 'umliegend.

cir·cum·lo·cu·tion [,sɜ:kəmlə'kju:ʃn] *s.* **1.** Um'schreibung *f*; **2.** a) 'Umschweife *pl.*, b) Weitschweifigkeit *f*; **cir·cum·loc·u·to·ry** [,sɜ:kəm'lɒkjʊtərɪ] *adj.* weitschweifig.

cir·cum·nav·i·gate [,sɜ:kəm'nævɪgeɪt] *v/t.* um'schiffen, um'segeln; **cir·cum·nav·i·ga·tion** ['sɜ:kəm,nævɪ'geɪʃn] *s.* Um'segelung *f*; ,**cir·cum'nav·i·ga·tor** [-tə] *s.* Um'segler *m*.

cir·cum·scribe ['sɜ:kəmskraɪb] *v/t.* **1.** a) um'schreiben (*a.* 𝔄), b) definieren; **2.** begrenzen, einschränken; **cir·cum·scrip·tion** [,sɜ:kəm'skrɪpʃn] *s.* **1.** Um'schreibung *f* (*a.* 𝔄) **2.** 'Umschrift *f* (*Münze etc.*); **3.** Begrenzung *f*, Beschränkung *f*.

cir·cum·spect ['sɜ:kəmspekt] *adj.* □ 'um-, vorsichtig; **cir·cum·spec·tion** [,sɜ:kəm'spekʃn] *s.* 'Um-, Vorsicht *f*, Behutsamkeit *f*.

cir·cum·stance ['sɜ:kəmstəns] *s.* **1.** 'Umstand *m*, Tatsache *f*; Ereignis *n*; Einzelheit *f*: ***a fortunate*** ~ ein glücklicher Umstand; **2.** *pl.* 'Umstände *pl.*, Lage *f*, Sachverhalt *m*, Verhältnisse *pl.*: ***in*** (*od.* ***under***) ***the*** ~***s*** unter diesen Umständen; ***under no*** ~***s*** auf keinen Fall; **3.** *pl.* Verhältnisse *pl.*, Lebenslage *f*: ***in good*** ~***s*** gut situiert; **4.** 'Umständlichkeit *f*, Weitschweifigkeit *f*; **5.** Förmlichkeit(en *pl.*) *f*, Umstände *pl.*: ***without*** ~ ohne (alle) Umstände; '**cir·cum·stanced** [-st] *adj.* in e-r ... Lage; ...situiert; gelagert (*Sache*): ***poorly*** ~ in ärmlichen Verhältnissen; ***well timed and*** ~ zur rechten Zeit u. unter günstigen Umständen; **cir·cum·stan·tial** [,sɜ:kəm'stænʃl] *adj.* □ **1.** 'umständlich; **2.** ausführlich, genau; **3.** zufällig; **4.** ~ ***evidence*** ⚖ Indizienbeweis *m*; **cir·cum·stan·ti·ate** [,sɜ:kəm'stænʃɪeɪt] *v/t.* **1.** genau beschreiben; **2.** ⚖ durch In'dizien beweisen.

cir·cum·vent [,sɜ:kəm'vent] *v/t.* **1.** über'listen; **2.** vereiteln, verhindern; **3.** um'gehen; ,**cir·cum'ven·tion** [-nʃn] *s.* **1.** Vereitelung *f*; **2.** Um'gehung *f*.

cir·cum·vo·lu·tion [,sɜ:kəmvə'lju:ʃn] *s.* **1.** 'Umdrehung *f*, 'Umwälzung *f*; **2.** Windung *f*.

cir·cus ['sɜ:kəs] *s.* **1.** a) 'Zirkus *m*, b) 'Zirkustruppe *f*, c) ('Zirkus)Vorstellung *f*, d) A'rena *f*; **2.** *Brit. runder Platz mit Straßenkreuzungen*; **3.** *Brit. sl.* ✕ a) im Kreis fliegende Flugzeugstaffel, b) ‚fliegende' Einheit; **4.** F ‚'Zirkus' *m*, Rummel *m*.

cir·rho·sis [sɪ'rəʊsɪs] *s.* ⚕ Zir'rhose *f*, (*Leber*)Schrumpfung *f*.

cir·rose [sɪ'rəʊs], **cir·rous** ['sɪrəs] *adj.* **1.** ⚘ mit Ranken; **2.** *zo.* mit Haaren *od.* Fühlern; **3.** federartig.

cir·rus ['sɪrəs] *pl.* **-ri** [-raɪ] *s.* **1.** ⚘ Ranke *f*; **2.** *zo.* Rankenfuß *m*; **3.** 'Zirrus *m*, Federwolke *f*.

cis·al·pine [sɪs'ælpaɪn] *adj.* diesseits der Alpen; **cis·at·lan·tic** [sɪsət'læntɪk] *adj.* diesseits des At'lantischen 'Ozeans.

cis·sy → ***sissy***.

Cis·ter·cian [sɪ'stɜ:ʃjən] **I** *s.* Zisterzi'enser(mönch) *m*; **II** *adj.* Zisterzienser...

cis·tern ['sɪstən] *s.* **1.** Wasserbehälter *m*; **2.** Zi'sterne *f*, ('unterirdischer) Regenwasserspeicher.

cit·a·del ['sɪtədəl] *s.* **1.** Zita'delle *f* (*a. fig.*); **2.** Burg *f*; *fig.* Zuflucht *f*.

ci·ta·tion [saɪ'teɪʃn] *s.* **1.** Anführung *f*; **2.** a) Zi'tat *n* (*zitierte Stelle*), b) ⚖ (***of***) Berufung *f* (auf *acc.*), Her'anziehung *f* (*gen.*), c) ⚖ Vorladung *f*; **3.** *bsd.* ✕ ehrenvolle Erwähnung.

cite [saɪt] *v/t.* **1.** zitieren; **2.** (als Beispiel *od.* Beweis) anführen; **3.** ⚖ vorladen; **4.** ✕ lobend erwähnen.

cith·er ['sɪθə] *poet.* → ***zither***.

cit·i·fy ['sɪtɪfaɪ] *v/t.* verstädtern.

cit·i·zen ['sɪtɪzn] *s.* **1.** Bürger *m*, Staatsangehörige(r *m*) *f*: ~ ***of the world*** Weltbürger; **2.** Städter(in); **3.** Einwohner(in): ~***s' band*** CB-Funk *m*; **4.** Zivi'list *m*; '**cit·i·zen·ry** [-rɪ] *s.* Bürgerschaft *f* (*e-s Staates*); '**cit·i·zen·ship** [-ʃɪp] *s.* **1.** Staatsangehörigkeit *f*; **2.** Bürgerrecht *n*.

cit·rate ['sɪtreɪt] *s.* ⚗ Zi'trat *n*.

cit·ric ac·id ['sɪtrɪk] *s.* ⚗ Zi'tronensäure *f*.

cit·ri·cul·ture ['sɪtrɪkʌltʃə] *s.* Anbau *m* von 'Zitrusfrüchten.

cit·rus ['sɪtrəs] *s.* ⚘ 'Zitrusgewächs *n*, -frucht *f*.

cit·y ['sɪtɪ] *s.* **1.** (Groß)Stadt *f*: 𝔖 ***of God*** *fig.* Himmelreich *n*; **2.** *Brit.* inkorporierte Stadt (*mst mit Kathedrale*); **3.** ***the*** 𝔖 die (Londoner) City (*Altstadt od. Geschäftsviertel od. Geschäftswelt*); **4.** *Am.* inkorporierte Stadtgemeinde; 𝔖 **ar·ti·cle** *s.* Börsenbericht *m*; 𝔖 **Com·pa·ny** *s. Brit.* e-e der großen Londoner Gilden; ~ **coun·cil** *s.* Stadtrat *m*; ~ **desk** *s. Brit.* 'Wirtschafts-, *Am.* Lo'kalredakti,on *f*; ~ **ed·i·tor** *s.* **1.** *Am.* Lo'kalredak,teur *m*; **2.** *Brit.* Redak'teur *m* des Handelsteiles; ~ **fa·ther** *s.* Stadtrat *m*; *pl.* Stadtväter *pl.*; ~ **hall** *s.* Rathaus *n*; 𝔖 **man** *s. Brit.* Fi'nanz-, Geschäftsmann *m* der City; ~ **man·ag·er** *s. Am.* 'Stadtdi,rektor *m*; ~ **state** *s.* Stadtstaat *m*.

civ·et (**cat**) ['sɪvɪt] *s. zo.* 'Zibetkatze *f*.

civ·ic ['sɪvɪk] *adj.* (□ ~***ally***) **1.** städtisch, Stadt...; **2.** → ***civil*** 2; ~ **cen·tre**, *Am.* **cen·ter** *s.* Behördenviertel *n*, Verwaltungszentrum *n*.

civ·ics ['sɪvɪks] *s. pl. sg. konstr.* Staatsbürgerkunde *f*.

civ·ies ['sɪvɪz] *bsd. Am.* → ***civvies***.

civ·il ['sɪvl] *adj.* (□ *nur für* 6.) **1.** staatlich: ~ ***affairs*** Verwaltungsangelegenheiten; **2.** (staats)bürgerlich, Bürger...: ~ ***duty***; ~ ***commotion*** Aufruhr *m*, innere Unruhen *pl.*; ~ ***death*** bürgerlicher Tod; ~ ***liberties*** bürgerliche Freiheiten; ~ ***list*** *Brit.* Zivilliste *f*; ~ ***rights*** Bürgerrechte, bürgerliche Ehrenrechte; ~ ***rights activist*** Bürgerrechtler(in); ~ ***rights movement*** Bürgerrechtsbewegung *f*; 𝔖 ***Servant*** Staatsbeamte(r); 𝔖 ***Service*** Staats-, Verwaltungsdienst *m*; ~ ***war*** Bürgerkrieg *m*; → ***disobedience*** 1; **3.** zi'vil (*Ggs. militärisch*): ~ ***aviation*** Zivilluftfahrt *f*; ~ ***defence***, *Am.* ~ ***defense*** Zivilverteidigung *f*, -schutz *m*; ~ ***government*** Zivilverwaltung *f*; ~ ***life*** Zivilleben *n*; **4.** zi'vil (*Ggs. kirchlich*): ~ ***marriage*** Ziviltrauung *f*; **5.** ⚖ zi'vil(rechtlich), bürgerlich: ~ ***case*** *od.* ***suit*** Zivilprozeß *m*; ~ ***code*** Bürgerliches Gesetzbuch; ~ ***year*** bürgerliches Jahr; ~ ***law*** a) römisches *od.* kontinentales Recht, b) Zivilrecht *n*, bürgerliches Recht; **6.** höflich: ~***-spoken*** höflich; ~ **en·gi·neer** *s.* 'Bauingeni,eur *m*; ~ **en·gi·neer·ing** *s.* Tiefbau *m*.

ci·vil·ian [sɪ'vɪljən] **I** *s.* Zivi'list *m*; **II** *adj.* zi'vil, Zivil...: ~ ***life***; ~ ***casualties*** Verluste unter der Zivilbevölkerung; **ci'vil·i·ty** [-lətɪ] *s.* Höflichkeit *f*, Artigkeit *f*.

civ·i·li·za·tion [,sɪvɪlaɪ'zeɪʃn] *s.* Zivilisati'on *f*, Kul'tur *f*; **civ·i·lize** ['sɪvɪlaɪz] *v/t.* zivilisieren; **civ·i·lized** ['sɪvɪlaɪzd] *adj.* **1.** zivilisiert: ~ ***nations*** Kulturvölker; **2.** gebildet, kultiviert.

civ·vies ['sɪvɪz] *s. pl. sl.* Zi'vil(kla,motten *pl.*) *n*; **civ·vy street** ['sɪvɪ] *s. sl.* Zi'villeben *n*.

clack [klæk] **I** *v/i.* **1.** klappern, knallen; **2.** plappern; **II** *s.* **3.** Klappern *n*; **4.** Plappern *n*; **5.** ⚙ (Ven'til)Klappe *f*.

clad [klæd] *adj.* gekleidet.

claim [kleɪm] **I** *v/t.* **1.** fordern, verlangen: ~ ***damages*** Schadenersatz fordern; **2.** a) Anspruch erheben auf (*acc.*), beanspruchen: ~ ***the crown***, b) *fig.* in Anspruch nehmen, erfordern: ~ ***attention***; **3.** für sich in Anspruch nehmen: ~ ***victory***; **4.** (*a.* von sich) behaupten (*a.* ***to*** *inf.* zu *inf.*, ***that*** daß): ~ ***accuracy*** die Richtigkeit behaupten; ***the club*** ~***s 200 members*** der Klub behauptet, 200 Mitglieder zu haben; **5.** zu'rück-, einfordern; *Opfer, Leben* fordern: ***death*** ~***ed him*** der Tod ereilte ihn; **II** *v/i.* **6.** ✝ reklamieren; **7.** ~ ***against s.o.*** j-n verklagen; **III** *s.* **8.** Forderung *f* (***on s.o.*** gegen *od.* an j-n), (*a.* Rechts- *od.* Pa'tent)Anspruch *m*: ~ ***for damages*** Schadensersatzanspruch; ~ ***under a contract*** Anspruch aus e-m Vertrag; ***lay*** (*od.* ***make a***) ~ ***to*** Anspruch erheben auf (*acc.*); ***put in a ~ for*** e-e Forderung auf *et.* stellen; ***make ~s upon*** *fig. j-n od. j-s Zeit* (stark) in Anspruch nehmen; **9.** (An)Recht *n* (***to*** auf *acc.*); **10.** Behauptung *f*; **11.** ✝ Reklamati'on *f*; **12.** Versicherungssumme *f*; Schaden(sfall) *m*; **13.** ⚖ Klage(begehren *n*) *f*; → ***statement*** 4; **14.** ⚒ Mutung *f*; *bsd. Am.* zugeteiltes *od.* beanspruchtes Stück Land; **'claim·a·ble** [-məbl] *adj.* zu beanspruchen(d); **'claim·ant** [-mənt] *s.* **1.** Antragsteller (-in), ⚖ *a.* Kläger(in); (Pa'tent)Anmelder(in); **2.** (***for***) Anwärter(in) (auf *acc.*), Bewerber(in) (für): ***rightful ~*** Anspruchsberechtigte(r).

clair·voy·ance [kleə'vɔıəns] *s.* Hellsehen *n*; **clair'voy·ant** [-nt] **I** *adj.* hellseherisch; **II** *s.* Hellseher(in).

clam [klæm] *s.* **1.** *zo.* eßbare Muschel: ***hard*** *od.* ***round ~*** 'Venusmuschel *f*; **2.** *Am.* F ‚zugeknöpfter' Mensch; **'~·bake** *s. Am.* **1.** Picknick *n*; **2.** große Party; **3.** ‚Gaudi' *f*.

cla·mant ['kleımənt] *adj.* **1.** lärmend, schreiend (*a. fig.*); **2.** dringend.

clam·ber ['klæmbə] *v/i.* (mühsam) klettern, klimmen.

clam·my ['klæmı] *adj.* □ feuchtkalt (u. klebrig), klamm.

clam·or·ous ['klæmərəs] *adj.* □ lärmend, schreiend, laut; tobend; *fig.* lautstark; **clam·o(u)r** ['klæmə] **I** *s.* **1.** *a. fig.* Lärm *m*, (zorniges) Geschrei, Tu'mult *m*; **2.** *bsd. fig.* (Auf)Schrei *m* (***for*** nach); Schimpfen; **3.** Tu'mult *m*; **II** *v/i.* **4.** (laut) schreien (***for*** nach; *a. fig. wütend verlangen*); heftig protestieren; toben; **III** *v/t.* **5.** ***~ down*** niederbrüllen.

clamp¹ [klæmp] *s.* **1.** Haufen *m*; **2.** (Kar'toffel- *etc.*)Miete *f*.

clamp² [klæmp] **I** *s.* **1.** ⚙ Klammer *f*, Krampe *f*, Klemmschraube *f*, Zwinge *f*, ⚡ Erdungsschelle *f*; **2.** *sport* Strammer *m* (*Ski*); **II** *v/t.* **3.** festklammern, -klemmen; befestigen; **4.** *fig. a.* ***~ down*** als Strafe auferlegen; **III** *v/i.* **5.** ***~ down*** *fig.* zuschlagen, einschreiten, scharf vorgehen (***on*** gegen); **'clamp·down** *s.* F scharfes Vorgehen (***on*** gegen).

clan [klæn] *s.* **1.** *Scot.* Clan *m*, Stamm *m*, Sippe *f*; **2.** *fig.* Clan *m*, Sippschaft *f*, Clique *f*.

clan·des·tine [klæn'destın] *adj.* □ heimlich, verstohlen, Schleich...

clang [klæŋ] **I** *v/i.* schallen, klingen, klirren; **II** *v/t.* laut schallen *od.* erklingen lassen; **III** *s.* → ***clango(u)r***; **clang·er** ['klæŋə] *s. sl.* Faux'pas *m*: ***drop a ~*** ‚ins Fettnäpfchen treten'; **clang·or·ous** ['klæŋgərəs] *adj.* □ schallend, schmetternd; klirrend; **clang·o(u)r** ['klæŋgə] → ***clank***.

clank [klæŋk] **I** *s.* Klirren *n*, Gerassel *n*, harter Klang; **II** *v/i. u. v/t.* rasseln *od.* klirren (mit).

clan·nish ['klænıʃ] *adj.* **1.** Sippen...; **2.** stammesbewußt; **3.** (unter sich) zs.-haltend, *contp.* cliquenhaft; **'clan·nish·ness** [-nıs] *s.* **1.** Stammesbewußtsein *n*; **2.** Zs.-halten *n*, *contp.* Cliquenwesen *n*; **clan·ship** ['klænʃıp] *s.* **1.** Vereinigung *f* in e-m Clan; **2.** → ***clannishness*** 1; **clans·man** ['klænzmən] *s.* [*irr.*] Mitglied *n* e-s Clans.

clap¹ [klæp] **I** *s.* **1.** (Hände)Klatschen *n*; **2.** (Beifall)Klatschen *n*; **3.** Klaps *m*; **4.** Knall *m*, Krach *m*: ***~ of thunder*** Donnerschlag *m*; **II** *v/t.* **5.** a) klatschen: ***~ one's hands*** in die Hände klatschen, b) schlagen: ***~ the wings*** mit den Flügeln schlagen; **6.** klopfen; **7.** *j-m* Beifall klatschen; **8.** hastig an-, auflegen *od.* ausführen: ***~ eyes on*** erblicken; ***~ a hat on one's head*** den Hut auf den Kopf stülpen; **9.** ***~ on*** F *j-m et.* ‚aufbrummen'; **III** *v/i.* **10.** (Beifall) klatschen.

clap² [klæp] *s.* V (*a.* ***dose of ~***) Tripper *m*.

'clap|·board I *s.* **1.** *Brit.* Faßdaube *f*; **2.** *Am.* Verschalungsbrett *n*; **II** *v/t.* **3.** *Am.* verschalen; **'~-net** *s.* Fangnetz *n* (*für Vögel etc.*).

clap·per ['klæpə] *s.* **1.** Klöppel *m* (*Glokke*); **2.** Klapper *f*; **3.** Beifallsklatscher *m*; **'~·board** *s. Am. Film*: Klappe *f*.

clap·trap ['klæptræp] **I** *s.* Ef'fekthasche,rei *f*; Klim'bim *m*; Re'klame(rummel *m*) *f*; Gewäsch *n*, Unsinn *m*; **II** *adj.* ef'fekthaschend; hohl.

claque [klæk] *s.* Claque *f*.

clar·en·don ['klærəndən] *s. typ.* halbfette Egypti'enne.

clar·et ['klærət] *s.* **1.** roter Bor'deaux (-wein); *weitS.* Rotwein *m*; **2.** Weinrot *n*; **3.** *sl.* Blut *n*; ***~ cup*** *s.* Rotweinbowle *f*.

clar·i·fi·ca·tion [ˌklærıfı'keıʃn] *s.* **1.** ⚙ (Ab)Klärung *f*, Läuterung *f*; **2.** Aufklärung *f*, Klarstellung *f*; **clar·i·fy** ['klærıfaı] **I** *v/t.* **1.** ⚙ (ab)klären, läutern, reinigen; **2.** (auf-, er)klären; **II** *v/i.* **3.** ⚙ sich (ab)klären; **4.** sich (auf)klären, klar werden.

clar·i·net [ˌklærı'net] *s.* ♪ Klari'nette *f*; **ˌclar·i'net·(t)ist** [-tıst] *s.* Klarinet'tist *m*.

clar·i·on ['klærıən] **I** *s.* **1.** ♪ Cla'rino *n*; **2.** *poet.* Trom'petenschall *m*: ***~ call*** *fig.* Auf-, Weckruf *m*; Fan'fare *f*; ***~ voice*** Trompetenstimme *f*; **II** *v/t.* **3.** laut verkünden, 'auspoˌsaunen.

clar·i·ty ['klærətı] *s. allg.* Klarheit *f*.

clash [klæʃ] **I** *v/i.* **1.** klirren, rasseln; **2.** prallen (***into*** gegen), (*a. feindlich u. fig.*) zs.-prallen, -stoßen (***with*** mit); **3.** *fig.* (***with***) kollidieren: a) (zeitlich) zs.-fallen (mit), b) im 'Widerspruch stehen (zu), unvereinbar sein (mit); **4.** nicht zs.-passen (***with*** mit), sich ‚beißen' (*Farben*); **II** *v/t.* **5.** klirren *od.* rasseln mit; klirrend zs.-schlagen; **III** *s.* **6.** Geklirr *n*, Getöse *n*, Krach *m*; **7.** Zs.-prall *m*, Kollisi'on *f*; **8.** (feindlicher) Zs.-stoß; **9.** (zeitliches) Zs.-fallen; **10.** Kon'flikt *m*, 'Widerstreit *m*.

clasp [klɑ:sp] **I** *v/t.* **1.** ein-, zuhaken, zuschnallen; **2.** fest ergreifen, um'klammern, fest um'fassen; um'ranken: ***~ s.o.'s hand*** j-m die Hand drücken; ***~ s.o. in one's arms*** j-n umarmen; ***~ one's hands*** die Hände falten; **II** *v/i.* **3.** sich die Hand reichen; **III** *s.* **4.** Klammer *f*, Haken *m*; Schnalle *f*, Spange *f*, Schließe *f*; Schloß *n* (*Buch etc.*); **5.** Um'klammerung *f*, Um'armung *f*; Händedruck *m*; **6.** ⚔ (Ordens)Spange *f*; ***~ knife*** *s.* [*irr.*] Klapp-, Taschenmesser *n*.

class [klɑ:s] **I** *s.* **1.** Klasse *f* (*a.* 🚃 *etc.*, ♀, *zo.*), Gruppe *f*; **2.** Klasse *f*, Sorte *f*, Güte *f*, Quali'tät *f*; *engS.* Erstklassigkeit *f*: ***in the same ~ with*** gleichwertig mit; ***in a ~ of one's*** (*od.* ***its***) ***own*** e-e Klasse für sich (*überlegen*); ***no ~*** F minderwertig; **3.** Stand *m*, Rang *m*, Schicht *f*: ***the*** (***upper***) ***~es*** die oberen (Gesellschafts)Klassen; ***pull ~ on s.o.*** F j-n s-e gesellschaftliche Überlegenheit fühlen lassen; **4.** *ped., univ.* a) Klasse *f*: ***top of the ~*** Klassenerste(r), b) 'Unterricht *m*, Stunde *f*: ***a ~ in cookery*** Kochstunde, c) *pl.* 'Kurs(us) *m*, d) Semi'nar *n*, e) *Brit.* Stufe *f* bei der Universi'tätsprüfung: ***take a ~*** e-n ***honours degree*** erlangen; **5.** *univ. Am.* Jahrgang *m*; **II** *v/t.* **6.** klassifizieren: a) in Klassen einteilen, b) einordnen, einstufen: ***~ with*** gleichstellen mit; ***be ~ed as*** angesehen werden als; **'~-book** *s. ped.* **1.** *Brit.* Lehrbuch *n*; **2.** *Am.* Klassenbuch *n*; **'~-ˌcon·scious** *adj.* klassenbewußt; **~ dis·tinc·tion** *s. sociol.* 'Klassenˌunterschied *m*; **~ ha·tred** *s.* Klassenhaß *m*.

clas·sic ['klæsık] **I** *adj.* (□ ***~ally***) **1.** erstklassig, ausgezeichnet; **2.** klassisch, mustergültig, voll'endet; **3.** klassisch: a) griechisch-römisch, b) die klassische Litera'tur *od.* Kunst *etc.* betreffend, c) berühmt, d) edel (*Stil etc.*); **4.** klassisch: a) 'herkömmlich, b) zeitlos; **II** *s.* **5.** Klassiker *m*; **6.** klassisches Werk; **7.** Jünger(in) der Klassik; **8.** *pl.* a) klassische Litera'tur, b) *die* alten Sprachen; **'clas·si·cal** [-kl] *adj.* □ **1.** → ***classic*** 1, 2, 3: ***~ music*** klassische Musik; **2.** a) altsprachlich, b) huma'nistisch (gebildet): ***~ education*** humanistische Bildung; ***the ~ languages*** die alten Sprachen; ***~ scholar*** Altphilologe *m*, Humanist *m*; **'clas·si·cism** [-sızəm] *s.* **1.** Klassi'zismus *m*; **2.** klassische Redewendung; **'clas·si·cist** [-sıst] *s.* Kenner *m od.* Anhänger *m* des Klassischen u. der Klassiker.

clas·si·fi·ca·tion [ˌklæsıfı'keıʃn] *s.* Klassifizierung *f* (*a.* ⚓), Einteilung *f*, -stufung *f*, Anordnung *f*; Ru'brik *f*: (***security***) ***~*** *pol.* a) Geheimhaltungseinstufung *f*, b) Geheimhaltungsstufe *f*; **clas·si·fied** ['klæsıfaıd] *adj.* **1.** klassifiziert, eingeteilt: ***~ advertisements*** Kleinanzeigen (*Zeitung*); ***~ directory*** Branchenverzeichnis *n*; **2.** ⚔, *pol.* geheim, Geheim...: ***~ material***; ***~ information*** Verschlußsache(n *pl.*) *f*; **clas·si·fy** ['klæsıfaı] *v/t.* klassifizieren, einteilen; einstufen; ⚔, *pol.* für geheim erklären.

class·less ['klɑ:slıs] *adj.* klassenlos: ***~ society***.

'class|·mate *s.* 'Klassenkameˌrad(in); **~ room** *s.* Klassenzimmer *n*; **~ war** *s. pol.* Klassenkampf *m*.

class·y ['klɑ:sı] *adj. sl.* ‚Klasse', ‚Klasse...'.

clat·ter ['klætə] **I** *v/i.* **1.** klappern, rasseln; **2.** trappeln, trampeln; **II** *v/t.* **3.** klappern *od.* rasseln mit; **III** *s.* **4.** Klappern *n*, Rasseln *n*, Krach *m*; **5.** Getrappel *n*; **6.** Lärm *m*; Stimmengewirr *n*.

clause [klɔ:z] *s.* **1.** *ling.* Satz(teil *m*, -glied *n*) *m*; **2.** *jur.* a) 'Klausel *f*, Bestimmung *f*, Vorbehalt *m*, b) Absatz *m*, Para'graph *m*.

claus·tro·pho·bi·a [ˌklɔ:strə'fəubjə] *s.* Klaustropho'bie *f*.

clav·i·chord ['klævıkɔ:d] *s.* ♪ Clavi'chord *n*.

clav·i·cle ['klævıkl] *s. anat.* Schlüsselbein *n*.

claw [klɔː] **I** *s.* **1.** *zo.* a) Klaue *f*, Kralle *f* (*beide a. fig.*), b) Schere *f* (*Krebs etc.*), c) Pfote *f* (*a. fig.* F *Hand*): ***get one's ~s into s.o.*** *fig.* j-n in s-e Klauen bekommen; ***pare s.o.'s ~s*** *fig.* j-m die Krallen beschneiden; **2.** ⚙ Klaue *f*, (Greif)Haken *m*; **II** *v/t.* **3.** (zer)kratzen, zerreißen, zerren; **4.** *a.* **~ *hold of*** um'krallen, packen; **5. ~ *back*** *fig.* a) zurückgewinnen, b) zurücknehmen; **III** *v/i.* **6.** kratzen; **7.** reißen, zerren (***at*** an); **8.** pakken, greifen (***at*** nach); **9.** ⚓ **~ *off*** vom Ufer abhalten; **'~-ˌham·mer** *s.* **1.** ⚙ Klauenhammer *m*; **2.** *a.* **~ *coat*** F Frack *m*.

clay [kleɪ] *s.* **1.** Ton *m*, Lehm *m*: **~ *hut*** Lehmhütte *f*; ***feet of ~*** *fig.* tönerne Füße; → ***potter²*** 1; **2.** *fig.* Erde *f*, Staub *m* u. Asche *f*; **3.** → ***clay pipe***; **~ court** *s.* *Tennis*: Rotgrantplatz *m*.

clay·ey ['kleɪɪ] *adj.* lehmig, Lehm…

clay·more ['kleɪmɔː] *s.* *hist.* schottisches Breitschwert.

clay| pi·geon *s.* *sport* Wurf-, Tontaube *f*; **~ pipe** *s.* Tonpfeife *f*; **~ pit** *s.* Lehmgrube *f*.

clean [kliːn] **I** *adj.* □ **1.** rein, sauber; → ***breast*** 2; **2.** sauber, frisch, neu (*Wäsche*); unbeschrieben (*Papier*); **3.** reinlich; stubenrein; **4.** einwandfrei, makellos (*a. fig.*); astfrei (*Holz*); fast fehlerlos (*Korrekturbogen*); → ***copy*** 1; **5.** (*moralisch*) lauter, sauber; anständig, gesittet; schuldlos: **~ *record*** tadelloser Ruf; ***keep it ~!*** keine Ferkeleien!; **~ *living!*** bleib sauber!; ***Mr.*** ♀ Saubermann *m*; **6.** ebenmäßig, von schöner Form; glatt (*Schnitt, Bruch*); **7.** sauber, geschickt (ausgeführt), tadellos; **8.** F ‚sauber' (*ohne Waffen, Schmuggelware etc.*); **II** *adv.* **9.** rein, sauber: ***sweep ~*** rein ausfegen; ***come ~*** F alles gestehen; **10.** rein, glatt, völlig, to'tal: ***I ~ forgot*** ich vergaß ganz; **~ *gone*** a) spurlos verschwunden, b) *sl.* total übergeschnappt; **~ *through the wall*** glatt durch die Wand; **III** *v/t.* **11.** reinigen, säubern; *Kleider* ('chemisch) reinigen; **12.** *Fenster, Schuhe, Zähne* putzen; **IV** *v/i.* **13.** sich reinigen lassen; **~ down** *v/t.* gründlich reinigen; abwaschen; **~ out** *v/t.* **1.** reinigen; **2.** auslesen, -räumen; räumen; **3.** *sl.* a) ‚ausnehmen', ‚schröpfen', b) *Am. a. j-n* ‚fertigmachen'; **4.** F *Kasse etc.* leer machen; *Laden etc.* leer kaufen; **5.** F *Bank etc.* ‚ausräumen'; **~ up** *v/t.* **1.** gründlich reinigen; **2.** aufräumen (mit *fig.*); in Ordnung bringen, erledigen, *fig. a.* bereinigen; *Stadt etc.* säubern; **3.** *sl.* (*v/i.* schwer) einheimsen.

clean| and jerk *s.* *Gewichtheben*: Stoßen *n*; **~ bill of lad·ing** *s.* ✝ reines Konosse'ment; **ˌ~-'bred** *adj.* reinrassig; **ˌ~-'cut** *adj.* **1.** klar um'rissen; klar, deutlich; **2.** regelmäßig; wohlgeformt; **3.** scharf geschnitten: **~ *face***.

clean·er ['kliːnə] *s.* **1.** Reiniger *m* (*Person, Gerät od. Mittel*); Reinemachfrau *f*, Raumpflegerin *f*; (Fenster- *etc.*)Putzer *m*; **2.** *pl.* Reinigung(sanstalt) *f*: ***take s.o. to the ~s*** *sl.* a) j-n total ‚ausnehmen', b) j-n ‚fertigmachen'.

ˌclean|-'hand·ed *adj.* schuldlos; **ˌ~-'limbed** *adj.* wohlproportioniert.

clean·li·ness ['klenlɪnɪs] *s.* Reinlichkeit *f*; **clean·ly** ['klenlɪ] *adj.* □ reinlich.

cleanse [klenz] *v/t.* **1.** (*a. fig.*) reinigen, säubern, reinwaschen (***from*** von); **2.** läutern; **'cleans·er** [-zə] *s.* Reinigungsmittel *n*; **'cleans·ing** [-zɪŋ] *adj.* Reinigungs…: **~ *cream***.

ˌclean|-'shav·en *adj.* glattrasiert; **'~·up** *s.* **1.** (gründliche) Reinigung *f*; **2.** F 'Säuberungsaktiˌon *f*; Ausmerzung *f*; **3.** *Am. sl.* ‚Schnitt' *m*, (großer) Pro'fit.

clear [klɪə] **I** *adj.* □ → ***clearly***; **1.** klar, hell, 'durchsichtig, rein (*a. fig.*): ***a ~ day*** ein klarer Tag; ***as ~ as day(light)***, **~ *as mud*** F sonnenklar; ***a ~ conscience*** ein reines Gewissen; **2.** klar, deutlich; 'übersichtlich; scharf (*Photo, Sprache, Verstand*): ***a ~ head*** ein klarer Kopf; **~ *judgment*** gesundes Urteil; ***be ~ in one's mind*** sich klar darüber sein; ***make o.s. ~*** sich verständlich machen; **3.** klar, offensichtlich; sicher, zweifellos: ***I am quite ~ (that)*** ich bin ganz sicher (daß); **4.** klar, rein; unvermischt; ✝ netto: **~ *amount*** Nettobetrag *m*; **~ *profit*** Reingewinn *m*; **~ *loss*** reiner Verlust; **~ *skin*** reine Haut; **~ *soup*** klare Suppe; **~ *water*** (nur) reines Wasser; **5.** klar, hell (*Ton*): ***as ~ as a bell*** glokkenrein; **6.** frei (***of*** von), offen; unbehindert; ohne: ***keep the roads ~*** die Straßen offenhalten; **~ *of debt*** schuldenfrei; **~ *title*** *jur.* unbestrittenes Recht; ***see one's way ~*** freie Bahn haben; ***keep ~ of*** a) (ver)meiden, b) sich fernhalten von; ***keep ~ of the gates!*** Eingang (*Tor*) freihalten!; ***be ~ of s.th.*** et. los sein; ***get ~ of*** loskommen von; **7.** ganz, voll: ***a ~ month*** ein voller Monat; **8.** ⚙ licht (*Höhe, Weite*); **II** *adv.* **9.** hell; klar, deutlich; **10.** frei, los, fort; **11.** völlig, glatt: **~ *over the fence*** glatt über den Zaun; **III** *s.* **12.** ⚙ lichte Weite; **13.** ***in the ~*** a) frei, her'aus, b) *sport* freistehend, c) aus der Sache heraus, vom Verdacht gereinigt, d) *Funk etc.*: im Klartext; **IV** *v/t.* **14.** *a.* **~ *up*** (auf)klären, erläutern; **15.** säubern, reinigen (*a. fig.*), befreien; losmachen (***of*** von): **~ *the street of snow*** die Straße von Schnee reinigen; **16.** *Saal etc.* räumen, leeren; ✝ *Waren(lager)* räumen (→ 23); *Tisch* abräumen, abdecken; *Straße* freimachen; *Land, Wald* roden: **~ *the way*** Platz machen, den Weg bahnen; **~ *out of the way*** *fig.* beseitigen; **17.** reinigen, säubern: **~ *the air*** *a. fig.* die Atmosphäre reinigen; **~ *one's throat*** sich räuspern; **18.** frei-, lossprechen; entlasten (***of, from*** von *e-m Verdacht etc.*); *Am. j-m* (po'litische) Unbedenklichkeit bescheinigen; *Am.* die Genehmigung für *et.* einholen (***with*** bei): **~ *one's conscience*** sein Gewissen entlasten; **~ *one's name*** s-n Namen reinwaschen; **19.** (knapp *od.* heil) vor'beikommen an (*dat.*): ***my car just ~ed the bus***; **20.** *Hindernis* nehmen, glatt springen über (*acc.*): **~ *the hedge***; **~ *6 feet*** 6 Fuß hoch springen; **21.** Gewinn erzielen, einheimsen: **~ *expenses*** die Unkosten einbringen; **22.** ⚓ a) *Schiff* klarmachen (***for action*** zum Gefecht), b) *Schiff* ausklarieren, c) *Ladung* löschen, d) *aus e-m Hafen* auslaufen; **23.** ✝ bereinigen, bezahlen; verrechnen; *Scheck* einlösen; *Hypothek* tilgen; *Ware* verzollen (→ 16); abfertigen; **V** *v/i.* **24.** sich klären, klar werden; **25.** sich aufklären (*Wetter*): **~ (*away*)** sich verziehen (*Nebel etc.*); **26.** sich klären (*Wein etc.*); **27.** ⚓ a) die 'Zollformaliˌtäten erledigen, b) ausklarieren;

Zssgn mit adv.:

clear| a·way I *v/t.* **1.** wegräumen; beseitigen; **II** *v/i.* **2.** verschwinden; → ***clear*** 25; **3.** (den Tisch) abdecken; **~ off I** *v/t.* **1.** beseitigen, loswerden; **2.** erledigen; **II** *v/i.* **3.** → ***clear out*** 3; **~ out I** *v/t.* **1.** ausräumen, reinigen; **2.** ✝ ausverkaufen; **II** *v/i.* **3.** verschwinden, ‚sich verziehen', ‚abhauen'; **~ up I** *v/t.* **1.** ab-, forträumen; **2.** bereinigen, erledigen; **3.** aufklären, lösen; **II** *v/i.* **4.** sich aufklären (*Wetter*).

clear·ance ['klɪərəns] *s.* **1.** Räumung *f* (*a.* ✝), Beseitigung *f*; Leerung *f*; Freilegung *f*; **2.** a) Rodung *f*, b) Lichtung *f*; **3.** ⚙ lichter Raum, Zwischenraum *m*; Spiel(raum *m*) *n*; *mot. etc.* Bodenfreiheit *f*; **4.** *allg.* Abfertigung *f*, *bsd.* a) ✈ Freigabe *f*, Start- *od.* 'Durchflugerlaubnis *f*, b) ⚓ Auslaufgenehmigung *f* (→ 7); **5.** ✝ a) Tilgung *f*, volle Bezahlung *f*, b) Verrechnung *f* (→ ***clearing*** 2), c) → ***clearance sale***; **6.** ⚓ a) (Ein-, Aus-) Klarierung *f*, Zollabfertigung *f*, b) Zollschein *m*: **~ (*papers*)** Zollpapiere; **7.** *pol. etc.* Unbedenklichkeitsbescheinigung *f*; **~ sale** *s.* *Brit.* (Räumungs)Ausverkauf *m*.

ˌclear|-'cut *adj.* scharf um'rissen; klar, eindeutig; **ˌ~-'head·ed** *adj.* klardenkend, intelli'gent.

clear·ing ['klɪərɪŋ] *s.* **1.** Lichtung *f*, Rodung *f*; **2.** ✝ Clearing *n*, Verrechnungsverkehr *m* (*Bank*); **~ bank** *s.* 'Girobank *f*; ♀ **Hos·pi·tal** *s.* ⚔ *Brit.* 'Feldlazaˌrett *n*; **~ house** *s.* ✝ 'Clearinginstiˌtut *n*, Verrechnungsstelle *f*; **~ of·fice** *s.* Verrechnungsstelle *f*; **~ sys·tem** *s.* ✝ Clearingverkehr *m*.

clear·ly ['klɪəlɪ] *adv.* **1.** klar, deutlich; **2.** **~, *that is wrong*** offensichtlich ist das falsch; **3.** zweifellos, ‚klar'; **clear·ness** ['klɪənɪs] *s.* **1.** Klarheit *f*, Deutlichkeit *f*; **2.** *fig.* Reinheit *f*; Schärfe *f*.

ˌclear|-'sight·ed *adj.* **1.** scharfsichtig; **2.** *fig.* klardenkend, hellsichtig, klug; **'~-starch** *v/t.* *Wäsche* stärken; **'~·way** *s.* *Brit.* Schnellstraße *f*.

cleat [kliːt] *s.* **1.** ⚓ Klampe *f*; **2.** Keil *m*, Pflock *m*; **3.** ⚡ Isolierschelle *f*; **4.** ⚙ Querleiste *f*; **5.** breiter Schuhnagel.

cleav·age ['kliːvɪdʒ] *s.* **1.** Spaltung *f* (*a.* ⚗ *u. fig.*); Spaltbarkeit *f*; **2.** Zwiespalt *m*; **3.** *biol.* (Zell)Teilung *f*; **4.** Brustansatz *m*, Dekolleté *n*.

cleave¹ [kliːv] *v/i.* **1.** kleben (***to*** an *dat.*); **2.** *fig.* (***to***) festhalten (an *dat.*), halten (zu *j-m*), treu bleiben (*dat.*), anhängen (*dat.*).

cleave² [kliːv] **I** *v/t.* [*irr.*] **1.** (zer)spalten; **2.** hauen, reißen; *Weg* bahnen; **3.** *Wasser, Luft etc.* durch'schneiden, (zer)teilen; **II** *v/i.* [*irr.*] **4.** sich spalten, bersten; **'cleav·er** [-və] *s.* Hackmesser *n*, -beil *n*.

clef [klef] *s.* ♪ (Noten)Schlüssel *m*.

cleft¹ [kleft] *pret. u. p.p. von* ***cleave²***.

cleft² [kleft] **I** *s.* Spalte *f*, Kluft *f*, Riß *m*; **II** *adj.* gespalten, geteilt; **~ pal·ate** *s.* Gaumenspalte *f*, Wolfsrachen *m*; **~ stick** *s.*: ***be in a ~*** ‚in der Klemme' sitzen.

clem·a·tis ['klemətɪs] *s.* ⚘ Kle'matis *f.*
clem·en·cy ['klemənsɪ] **I** *s.* Milde *f* (*a. Wetter*), Nachsicht *f*; **II** *adj.* Gnaden… (*-behörde etc.*); '**clem·ent** [-nt] *adj.* □ mild (*a. Wetter*), nachsichtig, gnädig.
clench [klentʃ] **I** *v/t.* **1.** *bsd. Lippen* zs.-pressen; *Zähne* zs.-beißen; *Faust* ballen: ~ **one's fist**; **2.** fest anpacken; (an)spannen (*a. fig.*); **3.** → **clinch** 1, 2, 3; **II** *v/i.* **4.** sich fest zs.-pressen; sich ballen.
cler·gy ['klɜːdʒɪ] *s. eccl.* Geistlichkeit *f*, Klerus *m*, *die* Geistlichen *pl.*: **20** ~ 20 Geistliche; '**~·man** [-mən] *s.* [*irr.*] Geistliche(r) *m.*
cler·ic ['klerɪk] *s.* Kleriker *m*; '**cler·i·cal** [-kl] **I** *adj.* □ **1.** geistlich: ~ **collar** Kragen *m* des Geistlichen; **2.** *pol.* kleri'kal; **3.** Schreib…, Büro…: ~ **error** Schreibfehler *m*; ~ **work** Büroarbeit *f*; **II** *s.* **4.** *pol.* Kleri'kale(r) *m*; '**cler·i·cal·ism** [-kəlɪzəm] *s. pol.* Klerika'lismus *m*, kleri'kale Poli'tik.
cler·i·hew ['klerɪhjuː] *s.* 'Clerihew *n* (*witziger Vierzeiler*).
clerk [klɑːk] **I** *s.* **1.** Sekre'tär *m*; Schriftführer *m*; (Bü'ro)Schreiber *m*: ~ **of the court** Urkundsbeamte(r) *m*; → **articled** 2, **town clerk**; **2.** Bü'roangestellte(r *m*) *f*; Buchhalter(in); (Bank)Beamte(r) *m*, (-)Beamtin *f*; **3.** *Brit.* Vorsteher *m*, Leiter *m*: ~ **of** (**the**) **works** Bauleiter; ~ **of the weather** *fig.* Wettergott, Petrus; **4.** *Am.* a) Verkäufer(in) *im Laden*, b) (Ho'tel)Porti,er *m*, Empfangschef *m*, -dame *f*; **5.** ~ **in holy orders** *eccl.* Geistliche(r) *m*; **II** *v/i.* **6.** als Schreiber *etc. od. Am.* als Verkäufer (-in) tätig sein; '**clerk·ship** [-ʃɪp] *s.* Stellung *f* e-s Bü'roangestellten *etc. od. Am.* Verkäufers.
clev·er ['klevə] *adj.* □ **1.** geschickt, raffiniert (*Person u. Sache*); gewandt: ~ **dick** F ‚Klugscheißer' *m*; **2.** klug, gescheit; begabt (**at** in); **3.** geistreich (*Worte, Buch*); **4.** *a.* '~-'~ *contp.* ‚superklug'; '**clev·er·ness** [-nɪs] *s.* Geschicklichkeit *f*; Klugheit *f etc.*
clew [kluː] **I** *s.* **1.** Knäuel *m, n* (*Garn*); **2.** → **clue** 1, 2; **3.** ⚓ Schothorn *n*; **II** *v/t.* **4.** ~ **up** *Segel* aufgeien; ~ **gar·net** *s.* ⚓ Geitau *n.*
cli·ché ['kliːʃeɪ] *s.* Kli'schee *n*: a) *typ.* Druckstock *m*, b) *fig.* Gemeinplatz *m*, abgedroschene Phrase.
click [klɪk] **I** *s.* **1.** Klicken *n*, Knipsen *n*, Knacken *n*, Ticken *n*; Einschnappen *n*; **2.** ⚙ Schnapp-, Sperrvorrichtung *f*; Sperrhaken *m*, Klinke *f*; **3.** Schnalzen *n*; **II** *v/i.* **4.** klicken, knacken, ticken; **5.** schnalzen; **6.** (zu-, ein)schnappen: ~ **into place** einrasten, *fig.* sein (richtiges) Plätzchen finden; **7.** *sl.* F ‚einschlagen', Erfolg haben (**with** mit); **8.** sofort Gefallen anein'ander finden, *engS.* sich inein'ander ‚verknallen'; **9.** F über'einstimmen (**with** mit); **10. it ~ed** F bei *mir etc.* ‚klingelte' es (*als ich hörte etc.*); **III** *v/t.* **11.** klicken *od.* ticken *od.* knakken *od.* einschnappen lassen: ~ **the door** (**to**) die Tür zuklinken; ~ **one's heels** die Hacken zs.-schlagen; **12.** schnalzen mit: ~ **one's tongue.**
cli·ent ['klaɪənt] *s.* **1.** ⚖ Kli'ent(in), Man'dant(in): ~ (**state**) *pol.* abhängiger Staat; **2.** † Kunde *m*, Kundin *f*; **3.** Pati'ent(in) (*e-s Arztes*); **cli·en·tele** [ˌkliːɑ̃ːn'tel] *s.* **1.** Klien'tel *f*, Kli'enten *pl.*; **2.** Pa'tienten(kreis *m*) *pl.*; **3.** Kunden(kreis *m*) *pl.*, Kundschaft *f.*
cliff [klɪf] *s.* Klippe *f*, Felsen *m*: **go over the** ~ F *fig.* ‚eingehen', pleite gehen; ~ **dwell·ing** *s.* Felsenwohnung *f*; '**~-ˌhang·er** *s.* F **1.** 'Fortsetzungsroˌman *m* (*etc.*), der jeweils im spannendsten Mo'ment abbricht; **2.** äußerst spannende Sache.
cli·mac·ter·ic [klaɪ'mæktərɪk] **I** *adj.* **1.** entscheidend, 'kritisch; **2.** ⚕ klimak'terisch; **II** *s.* **3.** ⚕ Klimak'terium *n*, Wechseljahre *pl.*; **4.** a) kritische Zeit, b) (Lebens)Wende *f.*
cli·mate ['klaɪmɪt] *s.* **1.** 'Klima *n*; **2.** Gegend *f*; **3.** *fig.* (*politisches, Betriebs- etc.*)'Klima *n*, Atmo'sphäre *f*; **cli·mat·ic** [klaɪ'mætɪk] *adj.* (□ **~ally**) kli'matisch; **cli·ma·to·log·ic, cli·ma·to·log·i·cal** [ˌklaɪmətə'lɒdʒɪk(l)] *adj.* □ klimato'logisch; **cli·ma·tol·o·gy** [ˌklaɪmə'tɒlədʒɪ] *s.* Klimatolo'gie *f*, 'Klimakunde *f.*
cli·max ['klaɪmæks] **I** *s.* **1.** Steigerung *f*; **2.** Gipfel *m*, Höhepunkt *m*; 'Krisis *f*; **3.** (sexu'eller) Höhepunkt, Or'gasmus *m*; **II** *v/t.* **4.** auf e-n Höhepunkt bringen; *Laufbahn etc.* krönen; **III** *v/i.* **5.** e-n Höhepunkt erreichen; **6.** e-n Or'gasmus haben.
climb [klaɪm] **I** *s.* **1.** Aufstieg *m*, Besteigung *f*; 'Kletterparˌtie *f*; **2.** ✈ Steigen *n*, Steigflug *m*; **II** *v/i.* **3.** klettern; **4.** steigen (*Straße, Flugzeug*); **5.** (auf-, em'por)steigen, (hoch)klettern (*a. fig. Preise etc.*); **6.** ⚘ sich hin'aufranken; **III** *v/t.* **7.** be-, ersteigen; steigen *od.* klettern auf (*acc.*), erklettern; ~ **down** *v/i.* **1.** hin'untersteigen, -klettern; **2.** *fig.* e-n ‚Rückzieher' machen, klein beigeben; ~ **up** *v/t. u. v/i.* hin'aufsteigen, -klettern.
climb·a·ble ['klaɪməbl] *adj.* ersteigbar; '**climb-down** *s.* F ‚Rückzieher' *m*, Nachgeben *n*; '**climb·er** [-mə] *s.* **1.** Kletterer *m*; Bergsteiger(in); **2.** ⚘ Kletter-, Schlingpflanze *f*; **3.** *orn.* Klettervogel *m*; **4.** F (gesellschaftlicher) Streber, Aufsteiger *m.*
climb·ing| a·bil·i·ty ['klaɪmɪŋ] *s.* **1.** ✈ Steigvermögen *n*; **2.** *mot.* Bergfreudigkeit *f*; ~ **i·rons** *s. pl. mount.* Steigeisen *pl.*
clime [klaɪm] *s. poet.* Gegend *f*, Landstrich *m*; *fig.* Gebiet *n*, Sphäre *f.*
clinch [klɪntʃ] **I** *v/t.* **1.** entscheiden, zum Abschluß bringen; *Handel* festmachen: **that ~ed it** damit war die Sache entschieden; ~ **an argument** den Streit für sich entscheiden; **2.** ⚙ a) sicher befestigen, b) vernieten; **3.** *Boxen*: um'klammern; **II** *v/i.* **4.** *Boxen*: clinchen; **III** *s.* **5.** fester Griff *od.* Halt; **6.** *Boxen*: Clinch *m* (*a. sl. Umarmung*); **7.** ⚙ Vernietung *f*; Niet *m*; '**clinch·er** [-tʃə] *s.* F entscheidender 'Umstand *od.* Beweis *etc.*, Trumpf *m.*
cling [klɪŋ] *v/i.* [*irr.*] **1.** (**to**) *a. fig.* kleben, haften (an *dat.*); anhaften (*dat.*): ~ **together** zs.-halten; **2.** (**to**) *a. fig.* sich klammern (an *j-n, e-e Hoffnung etc.*), festhalten (an *e-r Sitte, Meinung etc.*): ~ **to the text** am Text kleben; **3.** sich (an)schmiegen (**to** an *acc.*); **4.** *fig.* (**to**) hängen (an *dat.*), anhängen (*dat.*); '**cling·ing** [-ŋɪŋ] *adj.* enganliegend, hauteng (*Kleid*).
clin·ic ['klɪnɪk] *s.* **1.** Klinik *f*, (Pri'vat- *od.* Universi'täts)Krankenhaus *n*; **2.** Klinikum *n*, klinischer 'Unterricht; **3.** 'Poliklinik *f*, Ambu'lanz *f*; **4.** *Am.* Fachkurs(us) *m*, Semi'nar *n*; '**clin·i·cal** [-kl] *adj.* □ **1.** klinisch: ~ **instruction** Unterweisung *f* am Krankenbett; ~ **thermometer** Fieberthermometer *n*; **2.** *fig.* nüchtern, kühl analysierend; **clin·i·car** ['klɪnɪkɑː] *s.* Notarztwagen *m*; **cli·ni·cian** [klɪ'nɪʃn] *s.* Kliniker *m.*
clink[1] [klɪŋk] **I** *v/i.* klingen, klimpern, klirren; **II** *v/t.* klingen *od.* klirren lassen: ~ **glasses** (mit den Gläsern) anstoßen; **III** *s.* Klingen *n etc.*
clink[2] [klɪŋk] *s. sl.* ‚Knast' *m*, ‚Kittchen' *n* (*Gefängnis*): **in ~.**
clink·er[1] ['klɪŋkə] *s.* **1.** Klinker *m*, Hartziegel *m*; **2.** Schlacke *f.*
clink·er[2] ['klɪŋkə] *bsd. Am. sl.* **1.** ‚Patzer' *m*; **2.** ‚Pleite' *f* (*Mißerfolg*).
'**clink·er-built** *adj.* ⚓ klinkergebaut.
cli·nom·e·ter [klaɪ'nɒmɪtə] *s.* Neigungs-, Winkelmesser *m.*
Cli·o ['klaɪəʊ] *s. Am. alljährlicher Preis für die beste Leistung im Werbefernsehen.*
clip[1] [klɪp] **I** *v/t.* **1.** abschneiden; *a. fig.* beschneiden; *Schwanz, Flügel, Hecke* stutzen: ~ **s.o.'s wings** *fig.* j-m die Flügel beschneiden; **2.** *Haare* (*mit der Maschine*) schneiden; *Tiere* scheren; **3.** *aus der Zeitung* ausschneiden; *Fahrschein* lochen; **4.** *Silben od. Buchstaben* verschlucken: **~ped speech** a) undeutliche (Aus)Sprache, b) knappe *od.* schneidige Sprechweise; **5.** *j-m* e-n Schlag ‚verpassen'; **6.** F a) *j-n* ‚erleichtern' (**for** um), b) *j-n* ‚neppen'; **II** *s.* **7.** Haarschnitt *m*; **8.** Schur *f*; **9.** Wollertrag *m e-r Schur*; **10.** F Hieb *m*; **11.** F Tempo *n*: **at a good ~** in scharfem Tempo.
clip[2] [klɪp] **I** *s.* **1.** (Bü'ro-, Heft)Klammer *f*, Klemme *f*, Spange *f*, Halter *m*; **2.** ⚔ (*Patronen*)Rahmen *m*, Ladestreifen *m*; **II** *v/t.* **3.** festhalten; befestigen, (an)klammern.
'**clip-joint** *s. sl.* 'Nepploˌkal *n.*
clip·per ['klɪpə] *s.* **1.** ⚓ Klipper *m*, Schnellsegler *m*; **2.** ✈ Clipper *m*; **3.** Renner *m* (*schnelles Pferd*); **4.** *pl.* 'Haarschneide-, 'Schermaˌschine *f*, Schere *f.*
clip·pie ['klɪpɪ] *s.* F *Brit.* Busschaffnerin *f.*
clip·ping ['klɪpɪŋ] *s.* **1.** *Am.* (Zeitungs-) Ausschnitt *m*: ~ **bureau** Zeitungsausschnittsdienst *m*; **2.** *mst pl.* Schnitzel *pl.*, Abfälle *pl.*
clique [kliːk] *s.* Clique *f*, Klüngel *m*; '**cli·quish** [-kɪʃ] *adj.* cliquenhaft.
clit [klɪt] *sl. für* **cli·to·ris** ['klɪtərɪs] *s. anat.* 'Klitoris *f*, Kitzler *m.*
clo·a·ca [kləʊ'eɪkə] *pl.* **-s, -cae** [-kiː] *s.* Klo'ake *f* (*a. zo.*; *a. fig. Sündenpfuhl*).
cloak [kləʊk] **I** *s.* **1.** (loser) Mantel, 'Umhang *m*; **2.** *fig.* Deckmantel *m*: **under the ~ of night** im Schutz der Nacht; **II** *v/t.* **3.** (wie) mit e-m Mantel bedekken; **4.** *fig.* bemänteln, verhüllen; ˌ**~-and-'dag·ger** *adj.* **1.** ‚Mantel-und-Degen-…': ~ **drama**; **2.** Spionage…: ~ **story**; '**~·room** *s.* **1.** Garde'robe *f*; **2.** *Brit.* F Toi'lette *f.*
clob·ber ['klɒbə] *v/t. sl.* **1.** verprügeln,

fig. ‚fertigmachen'; **2.** *sport* ‚über'fahren', ‚vernaschen'.
cloche [kləʊʃ] *s.* **1.** Glasglocke *f* (*für Pflanzen*); **2.** Glocke *f* (*Damenhut*).
clock¹ [klɒk] **I** *s.* **1.** (*Wand-, Turm-, Stand*)Uhr *f*: ***five o'clock*** fünf Uhr; (***a***)***round the ~*** rund um die Uhr, den ganzen Tag (*arbeiten etc.*); ***put the ~ back*** *fig.* das Rad zurückdrehen; **2.** F a) Kon'troll-, Stoppuhr *f*, b) Fahrpreisanzeiger *m* (*Taxi*); **3.** *Computer*: Taktgeber *m*; **4.** F ⚘ Pusteblume *f*; **II** *v/t.* **5.** *bsd. sport* a) (*mit der Uhr*) (ab)stoppen, b) *Zeit* nehmen, c) *Zeit* erreichen; **6.** *a.* ***~ up*** F *Zeit, Zahlen etc.* registrieren; **III** *v/i.* **7.** ***~ in*** *od.* ***on*** (***off*** *od.* ***out***) einstempeln (ausstempeln) (*Arbeitnehmer*).
clock² [klɒk] *s.* (Strumpf)Verzierung *f*.
'**clock|-face** *s.* Zifferblatt *n*; **~ ra·di·o** *s.* 'Radiowecker *m*; '**~-ˌwatch·er** *s.* F Angestellte(r), der *od.* die immer nach der Uhr sieht; '**~·wise** *adj. u. adv.* im Uhrzeigersinn; rechtsläufig, Rechts…: ***~ rotation***; '**~·work** *s.* Uhrwerk *n*: ***like ~*** a) wie am Schnürchen, b) (pünktlich) wie die Uhr; ***~ toy*** mechanisches Spielzeug; ***~ fuse*** ⚔ Uhrwerkzünder *m*.
clod [klɒd] *s.* **1.** Erdklumpen *m*, Scholle *f*; **2.** *fig.* ‚Heini' *m*, Trottel *m*; '**~ˌhop·per** *s.* Bauerntölpel *m*; '**~ˌhop·ping** *adj.* F ungehobelt.
clog [klɒg] **I** *s.* **1.** Holzklotz *m*; **2.** Pan'tine *f*, Holzschuh *m*; **3.** *fig.* Hemmnis *n*, Hindernis *n*; **II** *v/t.* **4.** (be)hindern, hemmen; **5.** verstopfen; **6.** *fig.* belasten, 'vollpfropfen; **III** *v/i.* **7.** sich verstopfen; stocken; **8.** klumpig werden, sich zs.-ballen; **~ dance** *s.* Holzschuhtanz *m*.
clois·ter ['klɔɪstə] **I** *s.* **1.** Kloster *n*; **2.** ⛪ a) Kreuzgang *m*, b) *oft pl.* gedeckter (Säulen)Gang *um e-n Hof*; **II** *v/t.* **3.** in ein Kloster stecken; **4.** *fig.* (*a.* ***o.s.*** sich) von der Welt abschließen; '**clois·tered** [-əd] *adj.* zu'rückgezogen, abgeschieden; '**clois·tral** [-trəl] *adj.* klösterlich.
clone [kləʊn] *n biol.* **I** *s.* Klon *m*; **II** *v/t.* klonen.
close¹ [kləʊs] **I** *adj.* □ → ***closely***; **1.** geschlossen (*a. ling.*): ***~ formation*** (*od.* ***order***) ⚔ (Marsch)Ordnung *f*; ***~ company*** *Brit.*, ***~ corporation*** ✝ *Am.* GmbH *f*; **2.** zu'rückgezogen, abgeschlossen; **3.** verschlossen, verschwiegen, zu'rückhaltend; **4.** verborgen, geheim; **5.** geizig; sparsam; **6.** knapp (*Geld*; *Sieg*): ***~ election*** knapper Wahlsieg; ***~ price*** ✝ scharf kalkulierter Preis; **7.** eng, beschränkt (*Raum*); **8.** nahe, dicht; *fig.* eng, vertraut: ***~ friend***; ***~ combat*** ⚔ Nahkampf *m*; ***~ proximity*** nächste Nähe; ***~ fight*** zähes Ringen, Handgemenge *n*; ***~ finish*** scharfer Endkampf; ***~ shave*** (*od.* ***call***) F knappes Entrinnen; ***that was ~!*** F das war knapp!; ***~ shot*** *phot.* Nahaufnahme *f*; → ***quarter*** 10; **9.** dicht, eng; fest; enganliegend (*Kleid*): ***~ texture*** dichtes Gewebe; ***~ writing*** gedrängte Schrift; **10.** genau, gründlich, streng, eingehend (*Prüfung, Verhör etc.*); scharf (*Aufmerksamkeit, Bewachung*); streng (*Haft*); scharf (*Wettbewerb*); stark (*Ähnlichkeit*); (wort)getreu (*Übersetzung, Abschrift*); **11.** schwül, dumpf; **II** *adv.* **12.** nahe, eng, dicht, gedrängt: ***~ by*** nahe (da)bei; ***~ at hand*** nahe bevorstehend; ***~ to the ground*** dicht am Boden; ***~ on 40*** beinahe 40; ***come ~ to*** *fig.* dicht herankommen an (*acc.*); ***cut ~*** sehr kurz schneiden; ***keep ~*** in der Nähe bleiben; ***keep o.s. ~*** sich zurückhalten; ***press s.o. ~*** j-n (be)drängen; ***run s.o. ~*** j-m fast gleichkommen; **III** *s.* **13.** Einfriedigung *f*, (eingefriedetes) Grundstück; **14.** (Schul)Hof *m*; **15.** Sackgasse *f*; **16.** *Scot.* 'Hausˌdurchgang *m zum Hof*.
close² [kləʊz] **I** *s.* **1.** (Ab)Schluß *m*, Ende *n*: ***bring to a ~*** beendigen; ***draw to a ~*** sich dem Ende nähern; **2.** a) Schlußwort *n*, b) Briefschluß *m*; **3.** ♪ Ka'denz *f*; **II** *v/t.* **4.** *Augen, Tür etc.* schließen, zumachen (→ ***door*** 2, ***eye*** 2); *Straße* sperren; *Loch* verstopfen: ***~ a shop*** a) e-n Laden schließen, b) ein Geschäft aufgeben; ***~ about s.o.*** j-n umschließen *od.* umgeben; **5.** beenden, ab-, beschließen; zum Abschluß bringen, erledigen: ***~ the books*** ✝ die Bücher abschließen; ***~ an account*** ein Konto auflösen; **III** *v/i.* **6.** schließen, geschlossen werden; sich schließen; **7.** enden, aufhören; **8.** sich nähern, her'anrücken; **9.** ***~ with*** a) (handels)einig werden mit *j-m*, sich mit *j-m* einigen (***on*** über *acc.*), b) handgemein mit *j-m* werden; ***~ down*** **I** *v/t.* **1.** schließen; *Geschäft* aufgeben; *Betrieb* stillegen; **II** *v/i.* **2.** schließen; stillgelegt werden; **3.** *Radio, TV*: Sendeschluß haben; **4.** ***~ on*** scharf vorgehen gegen; ***~ in*** *v/i.* (***upon***) her'einbrechen (über *acc.*), sich her'anarbeiten (an *acc.*); ***~ out*** *v/t.* **1.** ✝ a) *Lager* räumen, b) → ***wind up*** 4; **2.** *fig. Am.* abwickeln, erledigen; ***~ up*** **I** *v/t.* (ver)schließen, verstopfen, ausfüllen; **II** *v/i.* näher rücken, aufschließen; sich schließen *od.* füllen.
ˌ**close|-'bod·ied** [ˌkləʊs-] *adj.* enganliegend (*Kleider*); ˌ**~-'cropped** *adj.* kurzgeschoren.
closed| cir·cuit [kləʊzd] *s.* ⚡ geschlossener Stromkreis; '**~-ˌcir·cuit tel·e·vi·sion** *s.* Kurzschluß-, Betriebsfernsehen *n*.
'**close-down** ['kləʊz-] *s.* **1.** Schließung *f*, Stillegung *f*; **2.** *Radio, TV*: Sendeschluß *m*.
closed shop *s.* gewerkschaftspflichtiger Betrieb.
ˌ**close|-'fist·ed** [ˌkləʊs-] *adj.* geizig, knauserig; **~ fit** *s.* enge Paßform; ⚙ Edelpassung *f*; ˌ**~-'fit·ting** *adj.* enganliegend; ˌ**~-'grained** *adj.* feinkörnig (*Holz etc.*); ˌ**~-'hauled** *adj.* ⚓ hart am Winde; ˌ**~-'knit** *adj. fig.* engverbunden; ˌ**~-'lipped** *adj.* verschlossen.
close·ly ['kləʊslɪ] *adv.* **1.** dicht, eng, fest; **2.** aus der Nähe; **3.** genau; **4.** scharf, streng; '**close·ness** [-snɪs] *s.* **1.** Nähe *f*; **2.** Enge *f*, Knappheit *f*; **3.** Dichte *f*, Festigkeit *f*; **4.** Genauigkeit *f*, Schärfe *f*, Strenge *f*; **5.** Verschlossenheit *f*; **6.** Schwüle *f*; **7.** Geiz *m*.
'**close|-out** ['kləʊz-] *s. a.* ***~ sale*** Ausverkauf *m* wegen Geschäftsaufgabe; '**~-range** ['kləʊs-] *adj.* aus nächster Nähe, Nah…; **~ sea·son** [kləʊs] *s. hunt.* Schonzeit *f*.
clos·et ['klɒzɪt] **I** *s.* **1.** kleine Kammer; Gelaß *n*, Kabi'nett *n*; Geheimzimmer *n*: ***~ drama*** Lesedrama *n*; **2.** *Am.* (Wand)Schrank *m*; **3.** ('Wasser)Kloˌsett *n*; **II** *adj.* **4.** pri'vat, geheim; **III** *v/t.* **5.** einschließen: ***be ~ed together with s.o.*** e-e vertrauliche Besprechung mit j-m haben.
close| time [kləʊs] *s. hunt.* Schonzeit *f*; ˌ**~-'tongued** *adj.* verschlossen; '**~-up** *s.* **1.** *Film*: Nah-, Großaufnahme *f*; **2.** *fig.* genaue Betrachtung, scharfes Bild.
clos·ing| date ['kləʊzɪŋ] *s.* letzter Ter'min; **~ price** *s. Börse*: 'Schlußnoˌtierung *f*; **~ speech** *s.* Schlußrede; ⚖ 'Schlußplädoˌyer *n*; **~ time** *s.* **1.** Geschäftsschluß *m*; **2.** Poli'zeistunde *f*.
clo·sure ['kləʊʒə] **I** *s.* **1.** Verschluß *m* (*a. Vorrichtung*); **2.** Schließung *f e-s Betriebs*, Stillegung *f*; **3.** *parl.* Schluß *m* der De'batte: ***apply*** (*od.* ***move***) ***the ~*** Antrag auf Schluß der Debatte stellen; **II** *v/t.* **4.** *Debatte etc.* schließen.
clot [klɒt] **I** *s.* **1.** Klumpen *m*, Klümpchen *n*: ***~ of blood*** Blutgerinnsel *n*; **2.** F ‚Blödmann' *m*; **II** *v/i.* **3.** gerinnen, Klumpen bilden: ***~ted hair*** verklebtes Haar.
cloth [klɒθ] *pl.* **cloths** [-θs] *s.* **1.** Tuch *n*, Stoff *m*; *engS.* Wollstoff *m*: ***~ of gold*** Goldbrokat *m*; → ***coat*** 1, ***whole*** 3; **2.** Tuch *n*, Lappen *m*: ***lay the ~*** den Tisch decken; **3.** geistliche Amtstracht: ***the ~*** die Geistlichkeit; **4.** ⚓ a) Segeltuch *n*, b) Segel *pl.*; **5.** (Buchbinder)Leinwand *f*: ***~ binding*** Leinenband *m*; ***~-bound*** in Leinen gebunden.
clothe [kləʊð] *v/t.* **1.** (an- be)kleiden; **2.** einkleiden, mit Kleidung versehen; **3.** *fig. in Worte* kleiden; **4.** *fig.* einhüllen; um'hüllen.
clothes [kləʊðz] *s. pl.* **1.** Kleider *pl.*, Kleidung *f*; **2.** (Leib-, Bett)Wäsche *f*; **~ hang·er** *s.* Kleiderbügel *m*; '**~·horse** *s.* Wäscheständer *m*; **~ line** *s.* Wäscheleine *f*; '**~-peg**, '**~-pin** *s.* Wäscheklammer *f*; '**~·press** *s.* Wäsche-, Kleiderschrank *m*; **~ tree** *s.* Kleiderständer *m*.
cloth hall *s. hist.* Tuchbörse *f*.
cloth·ier ['kləʊðɪə] *s.* Tuch-, Kleiderhändler *m*; '**cloth·ing** [-ðɪŋ] *s.* Kleidung *f*: ***article of ~*** Kleidungsstück *n*; ***~ industry*** Bekleidungsindustrie *f*.
clo·ture ['kləʊtʃə] *Am.* → ***closure*** 3.
cloud [klaʊd] **I** *s.* **1.** Wolke *f* (*a. fig.*); Wolken *pl.*: ***~ of dust*** Staubwolke; ***have one's head in the ~s*** *fig.* a) in höheren Regionen schweben, b) geistesabwesend sein; ***be on ~ nine*** F im siebten Himmel schweben; → ***silver lining***; **2.** *fig.* Schwarm *m*, Haufen *m*: ***a ~ of flies***; **3.** dunkler Fleck, Fehlstelle *f*; **4.** *fig.* Schatten *m*: ***~ of title*** ⚖ (geltend gemachter) Fehler im Besitz; ***cast a ~ on s.th.*** e-n Schatten auf et. werfen; ***under the ~ of night*** im Schatten der Nacht; ***under a ~*** a) unter Verdacht, b) in Ungnade, c) in Verruf; **II** *v/t.* **5.** be-, um'wölken; **6.** *fig.* verdunkeln, trüben: ***~ the issue*** die Sache vernebeln; **7.** ädern, flecken; **8.** ⚙ *Stoff* moirieren; **III** *v/i.* **9.** *a.* ***~ over*** sich bewölken *od.* um'wölken, sich trüben (*a. fig.*); '**~-burst** *s.* Wolkenbruch *m*; '**~-ˌcuck·oo-land** *s.* Wolken'kuckucksheim *n*.
cloud·ed ['klaʊdɪd] *adj.* **1.** be-, um'wölkt; *fig.* nebelhaft; **2.** trübe, wolkig (*Flüssigkeit etc.*); beschlagen (*Glas*); **3.** gefleckt, geädert; '**cloud·ing** [-dɪŋ] *s.* **1.** Wolkigkeit *f*; Trübung *f* (*a. fig.*); **2.** Wolken-, Moirémuster *n*; '**cloud·less**

[-lɪs] *adj.* □ **1.** wolkenlos; **2.** *fig.* ungetrübt; ˈ**cloud·y** [-dɪ] *adj.* □ **1.** wolkig, bewölkt; **2.** geädert; moiriert (*Stoff*); **3.** trübe (*Flüssigkeit*); unklar, verschwommen; **4.** düster.

clout [klaʊt] F **I** *s.* **1.** Schlag *m*; **2.** *fig.* a) Macht *f*, Einfluß *m*, b) Wucht *f*; **II** *v/t.* **3.** hauen, schlagen; ~ **nail** *s.* (Schuh)Nagel *m*.

clove[1] [kləʊv] *s.* ♀ Gewürznelke *f*.

clove[2] [kləʊv] *s.* ♀ Brut-, Nebenzwiebel *f*: ~ ***of garlic*** Knoblauchzehe *f*.

clove[3] [kləʊv] *pret. von* ***cleave***[2].

clove[4] [kləʊv] *s. Am.* Bergschlucht *f*.

clo·ven [ˈkləʊvn] **I** *p.p. von* ***cleave***[2]; **II** *adj.* gespalten; ~ **foot** → ~ **hoof** *s.* **1.** Huf *m* der Paarhufer; **2.** *fig.* ‚Pferdefuß' *m*: ***show the*** ~ *fig.* den Pferdefuß *od.* sein wahres Gesicht zeigen; ˌ~-ˈ**hoofed** *adj.* **1.** *zo.* paarzehig, -hufig; **2.** teuflisch.

clove pink *s.* ♀ Gartennelke *f*.

clo·ver [ˈkləʊvə] *s.* ♀ Klee *m*: ***be*** (*od.* ***live***) ***in*** ~ ‚in der Wolle' sitzen, üppig leben; ˈ~**-leaf** *s.* Kleeblatt *n*: ~ (***intersection***) Kleeblatt (*Autobahnkreuzung*).

clown [klaʊn] **I** *s.* **1.** Clown *m*, Hansˈwurst *m*, Kasper *m* (*alle a. fig.*); **2.** Bauernlümmel *m*, ˈGrobian *m*; **II** *v/i.* **3.** *a.* ~ ***around*** heˈrumkaspern; ˈ**clown·er·y** [-nərɪ] *s.* **1.** Clowneˈrie *f*; **2.** Posse *f*; ˈ**clown·ish** [-nɪʃ] *adj.* □ **1.** bäurisch, tölpelhaft; **2.** närrisch.

cloy [klɔɪ] *v/t.* **1.** überˈsättigen; **2.** anwidern; **cloy·ing** [ˈklɔɪɪŋ] *adj.* widerlich.

club [klʌb] **I** *s.* **1.** Keule *f*, Knüppel *m*; **2.** *sport* a) Schlagholz *n*, Schläger *m*, b) *a.* ***Indian*** ~ (Schwing)Keule *f*; **3.** Klub *m*: a) Verein *m*, Gesellschaft *f*, b) Klub-, Vereinshaus *n*, c) *fig., a. pol.* Klub *m*; **4.** *Spielkarten*: Treff *n*, Kreuz *n*, Eichel *f*; **II** *v/t.* **5.** mit e-r Keule *od.* mit dem Gewehrkolben schlagen; **6.** *Geld* zs.-legen, -schießen; sich teilen in (*acc.*); **III** *v/i.* **7.** *mst* ~ ***together*** (Geld) zs.-legen, sich zs.-tun; **club·(b)a·ble** [ˈklʌbəbl] *adj.* **1.** klub-, gesellschaftsfähig; **2.** → ˈ**club·by** [-bɪ] *adj.* gesellig.

club| car *s.* 🚃 *Am.* Saˈlonwagen *m*; ˌ~-ˈ**foot** *s.* ⚕ Klumpfuß *m*; ˌ~-ˈ**foot·ed** *adj.* klumpfüßig; ˈ~**·house** → ***club*** 3b; ˈ~**·land** *s.* Klubviertel *n* (*bsd. in London*); ˈ~**·man** [-mən] *s.* [*irr.*] **1.** Klubmitglied *n*; **2.** Klubmensch *m*; ~ **sandwich** *s. Am.* ˈSandwich *n* (*aus drei Lagen bestehend*); ~ **steak** *s.* Clubsteak *n*.

cluck [klʌk] **I** *v/i.* **1.** glucken, locken: ~***ing hen*** Glucke *f*; **II 2.** Glucken *n*; **3.** *Am. sl.* ‚Blödmann' *m*.

clue [klu:] **I 1.** Anhaltspunkt *m*, Fingerzeig *m*, Spur *f*: ***I haven't a*** ~**!** keine Ahnung!; **2.** *fig.* a) Faden *m*, b) Schlüssel *m* (*e-s Rätsels etc.*); **3.** → ***clew*** 1, 3; **II** *v/t.* **4.** ~ ***s.o.*** (***in*** *od.* ***up***) *sl.* j-n ins Bild setzen *od.* informieren.

clump [klʌmp] **I** *s.* **1.** Klumpen *m* (*Erde*), (*Holz*)Klotz *m*; **2.** (Baum)Gruppe *f*; **3.** Doppelsohle *f*; **4.** schwerer Tritt; **II** *v/i.* **5.** trampeln; **III** *v/t.* **6.** zs.-ballen; **7.** doppelt besohlen; **8.** F *j-m* e-n Schlag ‚verpassen'.

clum·si·ness [ˈklʌmzɪnɪs] *s.* Plumpheit *f*: a) Ungeschicklichkeit *f*, b) Unbeholfenheit *f*, Schwerfälligkeit *f*, c) Taktlosigkeit *f*, d) Unförmigkeit *f*; **clum·sy** [ˈklʌmzɪ] *adj.* □ plump: a) ungeschickt, unbeholfen, schwerfällig (*a. Stil*), b) taktlos, c) unförmig.

clung [klʌŋ] *pret. u. p.p. von* ***cling***.

clus·ter [ˈklʌstə] **I** *s.* **1.** ♀ Büschel *n*, Traube *f*; **2.** Haufen *m* (*a. ast.*), Menge *f*, Schwarm *m*, Gruppe *f*; *a.* ⚙ Bündel *n*, traubenförmige Anordnung; **3.** ⚔ *Am.* (Ordens)Spange *f*; **II** *v/i.* **4.** in Büscheln *od.* Trauben wachsen; **5.** sich sammeln *od.* häufen *od.* drängen *od.* ranken (***round*** um); in Gruppen stehen.

clutch[1] [klʌtʃ] **I** *v/t.* **1.** fest (er)greifen, packen; drücken; **2.** ⚙ kuppeln; **II** *v/i.* **3.** (gierig) greifen (***at*** nach); **III** *s.* **4.** fester Griff: ***make a*** ~ ***at*** (gierig) greifen nach; **5.** *pl., mst. fig.* Klauen *pl.*; Gewalt *f*, Macht *f*, Bande *pl.*: ***in*** (***out of***) ***s.o.'s*** ~***es*** in (aus) j-s Klauen *od.* Gewalt; **6.** ⚙ (Schalt-, Ausrück)Kupplung *f*; Kupplungshebel *m*: ***let in the*** ~ einkuppeln; ***disengage the*** ~ auskuppeln; **7.** ⚙ Greifer *m*.

clutch[2] [klʌtʃ] *s.* **1.** Gelege *n*; Brut *f*; **2.** *fig.* F Schwarm *m von Leuten*.

clutch| disk *s.* Kupplungsscheibe *f*; ~ **le·ver** *s.*, ~ **ped·al** *s.* ˈKupplungspeˌdal *n*, -hebel *m*.

clut·ter [ˈklʌtə] **I** *v/t.* **1.** *a.* ~ ***up*** in Unordnung bringen; **2.** ˈvollstopfen, anfüllen, überˈhäufen; umˈherstreuen; **II** *s.* **3.** Wirrwarr *m*.

clys·ter [ˈklɪstə] *s.* ⚕ *obs.* Kliˈstier *n*.

coach [kəʊtʃ] **I** *s.* **1.** Kutsche *f*: ~ ***and four*** Vierspänner *m*; **2.** 🚃 *Brit.* (*Personen*)Wagen *m*; **3.** *mot.* a) (Fern-, Reise)Omnibus *m*, b) *Am.* Limouˈsine *f*, c) → ***coachwork***; **4.** Nachhilfe-, Priˈvatlehrer *m*, Einpauker *m*; **5.** *sport* ˈTrainer *m*, Betreuer *m*; **II** *v/t.* **6.** ˈNachhilfeˌunterricht *od.* Anweisungen geben (*dat.*), instruieren, einarbeiten: ~ ***s.o. in s.th.*** j-m et. einpauken; **7.** *sport* trainieren; **III** *v/i.* **8.** in e-r Kutsche reisen; **9.** Nachhilfeunterricht erteilen; ~ **box** *s.* Kutschbock *m*; ˈ~-ˌ**build·er** *s.* **1.** Stellmacher *m*; **2.** *mot. Brit.* Karosseˈriebauer *m*; ~ **horse** *s.* Kutschpferd *n*; ˈ~**-house** *s.* Wagenschuppen *m*.

coach·ing [ˈkəʊtʃɪŋ] *s.* **1.** Reisen *n* in e-r Kutsche; **2.** ˈNachhilfeˌunterricht *m*; **3.** Unterˈweisung *f*, Anleitung *f*.

ˈ**coach·work** *s. mot.* Karosseˈrie *f*.

co·ac·tion [kəʊˈækʃn] *s.* **1.** Zs.-wirken *n*; **2.** Zwang *m*.

co·ag·u·late [kəʊˈægjʊleɪt] **I** *v/i.* **1.** gerinnen; **2.** flockig *od.* klumpig werden; **II** *v/t.* **3.** gerinnen lassen; **co·ag·u·la·tion** [kəʊˌægjʊˈleɪʃn] *s.* Gerinnen *n*; Flockenbildung *f*.

coal [kəʊl] **I** *s.* **1.** Kohle *f*; *engS.* Steinkohle *f*; *a* (ein) Stück Kohle; **2.** *pl. Brit.* Kohle *f*, Kohlen *pl.*, Kohlenvorrat *m*: ***lay in*** ~***s*** sich mit Kohlen eindecken; ***carry*** ~***s to Newcastle*** *fig.* Eulen nach Athen tragen; ***call*** (*od.* ***haul***) ***s.o. over the*** ~***s*** j-n ‚fertigmachen'; ***heap*** ~***s of fire on s.o.'s head*** *fig.* feurige Kohlen auf j-s Haupt sammeln; **3.** glimmendes Stück Kohle *od.* Holz; **II** *v/t.* **4.** 🚃, ⚓ bekohlen, mit Kohle versorgen, **III** *v/i.* **5.** 🚃, ⚓ Kohle einnehmen, bunkern; ˈ~**-bed** *s. geol.* Kohlenflöz *n*; ˈ~**·box** *s.* Kohlenkasten *m*; ~ **car** *s.* 🚃 *Am.* Kohlenwagen *m*; ˈ~**·dust** *s.* Kohlengrus *m*.

coal·er [ˈkəʊlə] *s.* Kohlenschiff *n*; ˈKohlenzug *m*, -wagˌgon *m*.

co·a·lesce [ˌkəʊəˈles] *v/i.* **1.** verschmelzen, sich verbinden *od.* vereinigen; **2.** *fig.* zs.-passen; ˌ**co·aˈles·cence** [-sns] *s.* Verschmelzung *f*, Vereinigung *f*.

ˈ**coal|·field** *s.* ˈKohlenreˌvier *n*; ~ **gas** *s.* Leuchtgas *n*.

coal·ing sta·tion [ˈkəʊlɪŋ] *s.* ⚓ ˈBunker-, ˈKohlenstatiˌon *f*.

co·a·li·tion [ˌkəʊəˈlɪʃn] *s.* Zs.-schluß *m*, Vereinigung *f*; *pol.* Koalitiˈon *f*; ~ **partner** *s. pol.* Koalitiˈonspartner *m*.

coal| mine *s.* Kohlenbergwerk *n*, Kohlengrube *f*, -zeche *f*; ~ **min·er** *s.* Grubenarbeiter *m*, Bergmann *m*; ~ **min·ing** *s.* Kohlenbergbau *m*; ~ **oil** *s. Am.* Peˈtroleum *n*; ˈ~**·pit** *s.* Kohlengrube *f*; ~ **seam** *s. geol.* Kohlenflöz *n*; ~ **tar** *s.* Steinkohlenteer *m*; ~ **wharf** *s.* ⚓ Bunkerkai *m*.

coarse [kɔ:s] *adj.* □ **1.** grob (*Ggs. fein*): ~ ***texture*** grobes Gewebe; **2.** grobkörnig: ~ ***bread*** Schrotbrot *n*; **3.** *fig.* grob, derb, ungehobelt; unanständig, anstößig; **4.** einfach, gemein: ~ ***fare*** grobe *od.* einfache Kost; ˈ~**-grained** *adj.* **1.** grobkörnig, -faserig; grob (*Gewebe*); **2.** → ***coarse*** 3.

coars·en [ˈkɔ:sn] **I** *v/t.* grob machen, vergröbern (*a. fig.*); **II** *v/i.* grob werden (*bsd. fig.*); ˈ**coarse·ness** [-nɪs] *s.* **1.** grobe Qualiˈtät; **2.** *fig.* Grob-, Derbheit *f*; Unanständigkeit *f*.

coast [kəʊst] **I** *s.* **1.** Küste *f*, Meeresufer *n*: ***the*** ~ ***is clear*** *fig.* die Luft ist rein, die Bahn ist frei; **2.** Küstenlandstrich *m*; **3.** *Am.* a) Rodelbahn *f*, b) (Rodel-) Abfahrt *f*; **II** *v/i.* **4.** ⚓ a) die Küste entlangfahren, b) Küstenschiffahrt treiben; **5.** *Am.* rodeln; **6.** *mit e-m Fahrzeug* (bergˈab) rollen; im Freilauf (*Fahrrad*) *od.* im Leerlauf (*Auto*) fahren: ~ ***on*** *sl.* auf *e-n Trick etc.* ‚reisen'; **7.** *sl.* mühelos vorˈankommen; ˈ**coast·al** [-tl] *adj.* Küsten...

coast·er [ˈkəʊstə] *s.* **1.** ⚓ Küstenfahrer *m* (*bsd. Schiff*); **2.** *Am.* Rodelschlitten *m*; **3.** *Am.* Achterbahn *f*; **4.** Taˈblett *n*, *bsd.* Serviertischchen *n*; ~ **brake** *s.* *Am.* Rücktrittbremse *f*.

coast guard *s.* **1.** *Brit.* Küstenwache *f* (*a.* ⚔); Küstenzollwache *f*; **2.** *Am.* ♀ (staatlicher) Küstenwach- u. Rettungsdienst; **3.** Angehörige(r) *m* von 1 u. 2.

coast·ing [ˈkəʊstɪŋ] *s.* **1.** Küstenschifffahrt *f*; **2.** *Am.* Rodeln *n*; **3.** Bergˈabfahren *n* (*im Freilauf od. bei abgestelltem Motor*); ~ **trade** *s.* Küstenhandel *m*.

ˈ**coast|·line** *s.* Küstenlinie *f*, -strich *m*; ˈ~**·wise** *adj. u. adv.* längs der Küste; Küsten...

coat [kəʊt] **I** *s.* **1.** Jacˈkett *n*, Jacke *f*: ***wear the king's*** ~ *hist.* des Königs Rock tragen (*Soldat sein*); ~ ***and skirt*** (Schneider)Kostüm *n*; ~ ***of arms*** Wappen *n*; ~ ***armo***(***u***)***r*** Familienwappen *n*; ~ ***of mail*** Panzerhemd *n*; ***cut one's*** ~ ***according to one's cloth*** sich nach der Decke strecken; **2.** Mantel *m*: ***turn one's*** ~ sein Mäntelchen nach dem Winde hängen; **3.** Fell *n*, Pelz *m* (*Tier*); **4.** Schicht *f*, Lage *f*; Decke *f*, Hülle *f*, (*a. Farb-, Metall- etc.*)ˈÜberzug *m*, Belag *m*, Anstrich *m*; Bewurf *m*: ***a second*** ~ ***of paint*** ein zweiter Anstrich; **II** *v/t.* **5.** anstreichen, überˈstreichen, -ˈziehen, beschichten: ~ ***with silver*** plattieren; **6.** um'hüllen, -'kleiden, bedecken; auskleiden (***with*** mit); **'coat·ed** [-tɪd] *adj.* **1.** mit e-m (...) Rock *od.* Mantel *od.* Fell (versehen): ***black-~*** schwarzgekleidet; **2.** mit ... über'zogen *od.* gestrichen *od.* bedeckt: ***sugar-~*** mit Zuckerüberzug; **3.** ⚕ belegt (*Zunge*); **coat·ee** ['kəʊti:] *s.* kurzer (Waffen)Rock.

'coat-ˌhang·er *s.* Kleiderbügel *m.*

coat·ing ['kəʊtɪŋ] *s.* **1.** Mantelstoff *m*; **2.** ⚙ Anstrich *m*, 'Überzug *m*, Schicht *f*; Bewurf *m*; **3.** ⚙ Auskleidung *f*, Futter *n*.

coat| stand *s.* Garde'robenständer *m*; **'~-tail** *s.* Rockschoß *m*; **'~-ˌtrail·ing** *adj.* provoka'tiv.

co·au·thor [kəʊ'ɔ:θə] *s.* Mitverfasser *m*, -autor *m*.

coax [kəʊks] **I** *v/t.* **1.** schmeicheln (*dat.*); gut zureden (*dat.*), beschwatzen (***to do*** *od.* ***into doing*** zu tun): ***~ s.th. out of s.o.*** j-m et. abschwatzen; **2.** *et.* mit Gefühl *od.* ‚mit Geduld und Spucke' bringen (***into*** in *acc.*); **II** *v/i.* **3.** schmeicheln.

co·ax·al [ˌkəʊ'æksl], **ˌco'ax·i·al** [-sɪəl] ⩚, ⚙ koaxi'al, kon'zentrisch.

cob [kɒb] *s.* **1.** *a.* ***~ swan*** *orn.* männlicher Schwan; **2.** *zo.* kleineres Reitpferd; **3.** Klumpen *m*, Stück *n* (*z. B.* Kohle); **4.** Maiskolben *m*; **5.** *Brit.* Strohlehm *m* (*Baumaterial*); **6.** → ***cob-loaf***; **7.** → ***cobnut***.

co·balt [kəʊ'bɔ:lt] *s. min.*, ⚗ Kobalt *m*; ***~ blue*** *s.* Kobaltblau *n*; ***~ bomb*** *s.* **1.** ⚔ Kobaltbombe *f*; **2.** ⚕ 'Kobaltkaˌnone *f*.

cob·ble¹ ['kɒbl] **I** *s.* **1.** runder Pflasterstein, Kopfstein *m*; **2.** *pl.* → ***cob coal***; **II** *v/t.* **3.** mit Kopfsteinen pflastern.

cob·ble² ['kɒbl] *v/t. Schuhe* flicken; *fig.* zs.-flicken, zs.-schustern; **'cob·bler** [-lə] *s.* **1.** (Flick)Schuster *m*: ***~'s wax*** Schusterpech *n*; **2.** *fig.* Stümper *m*; **3.** *Am.* Cobbler *m* (*ein Cocktail*).

'cob·ble·stone → ***cobble¹*** 1.

cob coal *s.* Nuß-, Stückkohle *f*.

Cob·den·ism ['kɒbdənɪzəm] *s.* ✝ 'Manchestertum *n*, Freihandelslehre *f*.

co·bel·lig·er·ent [ˌkəʊbɪ'lɪdʒərənt] *s.* mitkriegführender Staat.

'cob|·loaf *s.* rundes Brot; **'~·nut** *s.* ⚘ Haselnuß *f*.

Co·bol ['kəʊbɒl] *s.* COBOL *n* (*Computersprache*).

co·bra ['kəʊbrə] *s. zo.* Brillenschlange *f*, 'Kobra *f*.

cob·web ['kɒbweb] *s.* **1.** Spinn(en)gewebe *n*; Spinnenfaden *m*; **2.** feines, zartes Gewebe; **3.** *fig.* Hirngespinst *n*: ***blow away the ~s*** sich e-n klaren Kopf schaffen; **4.** *fig.* Netz *n*, Schlinge *f*; **5.** *fig.* alter Staub; **'cob·webbed** [-bd], **'cobˌweb·by** [-bɪ] *adj.* voller Spinnweben.

co·ca ['kəʊkə] *s.* 'Koka(blätter *pl.*) *f*.

co·cain(e) [kəʊ'keɪn] *s.* ⚗ Koka'in *n*; **co'cain·ism** [-nɪzəm] *s.* **1.** Koka'invergiftung *f*; **2.** Koka'insucht *f*.

coc·cus ['kɒkəs] *pl.* **-ci** [-kaɪ] *s.* ⚕ 'Kokkus *m*, 'Kokke *f* (*a.* ⚘).

coch·i·neal ['kɒtʃɪni:l] *s.* Kosche'nille (-laus) *f*; Kosche'nille(rot *n*) *f*.

coch·le·a ['kɒklɪə] *s. anat.* Cochlea *f*, Schnecke *f* (*im Ohr*).

cock¹ [kɒk] **I** *s.* **1.** *orn.* Hahn *m*: ***old ~*** F alter Knabe; ***that ~ won't fight*** F a) so geht das nicht, b) das zieht nicht; **2.** Vogelmännchen *n*: ***~ sparrow*** Sperlingsmännchen; **3.** Wetterhahn *m*; **4.** ⚙ (*Absperr*)Hahn *m*; **5.** (*Gewehr- etc.*) Hahn *m*: ***full ~*** Hahn gespannt; ***half ~*** Hahn in Ruh; **6.** Anführer *m*: ***~ of the roost*** (*od.* ***walk***) *oft contp.* der Größte; ***~ of the school*** Anführer *m* unter den Schülern; **7.** Aufrichten *n*: ***~ of the eye*** (bedeutsames) Augenzwinkern; ***give one's hat a saucy ~*** s-n Hut keck aufs Ohr setzen; **8.** V ‚Schwanz' *m* (*Penis*); **9.** F Quatsch *m*; **II** *v/t.* **10.** *Gewehrhahn* spannen; **11.** aufrichten: ***~ one's ears*** die Ohren spitzen; ***~ one's eye at s.o.*** j-n vielsagend *od.* verächtlich ansehen; ***~ one's hat*** den Hut schief *od.* keck aufsetzen; → ***cocked hat***; **12.** ***~ up*** *sl.* ‚versauen'.

cock² [kɒk] *s.* kleiner Heuhaufen.

cock·ade [kɒ'keɪd] *s.* Ko'karde *f*.

cock·a·doo·dle·doo [ˌkɒkədu:dl'du:] *s.* a) Kikeri'ki *n* (*Hahnenschrei*), b) *humor.* Kikeri'ki *m* (*Hahn*).

Cock·aigne [kɒ'keɪn] *s.* Schla'raffenland *n*.

ˌcock-and-'bull sto·ry *s.* Ammenmärchen *n*, Lügengeschichte *f*.

cock·a·too [ˌkɒkə'tu:] *s.* 'Kakadu *m*.

cock·a·trice ['kɒkətraɪs] *s.* Basi'lisk *m*.

Cock·ayne → ***Cockaigne***.

'cock|·boat *s.* ⚓ Jolle *f*; **'~ˌchaf·er** *s.* Maikäfer *m*; **'~·crow** *s.* Hahnenschrei *m*; *fig.* Tagesanbruch *m*.

cocked hat [kɒkt] *s.* Zwei-, Dreispitz *m* (*Hut*): ***knock into a ~*** a) zu Brei schlagen, b) (restlos) ‚fertigmachen'.

cock·er¹ ['kɒkə] → ***cocker spaniel***.

cock·er² ['kɒkə] *v/t.* verhätscheln, verwöhnen: ***~ up*** aufpäppeln.

Cock·er³ ['kɒkə] *npr.*: ***according to ~*** nach Adam Riese, genau.

cock·er·el ['kɒkərəl] *s.* Hähnchen *n*.

cock·er span·iel *s.* 'Cockerˌspaniel *m*.

'cock|·eyed *adj. sl.* **1.** schielend; **2.** (krumm u.) schief; **3.** ‚doof'; **4.** ‚blau' (*betrunken*); **'~ˌfight·ing** *s.* Hahnenkampf *m*: ***that beats ~!*** F das ist 'ne Wucht!

cock·i·ness ['kɒkɪnɪs] *s.* F Großspurigkeit *f*, Anmaßung *f*.

cock·le¹ ['kɒkl] **I** *s.* **1.** *zo.* (eßbare) Herzmuschel: ***that warms the ~s of my heart*** das tut mir gut; **2.** → ***cockle-shell***; **II** *v/i.* **3.** sich bauschen *od.* kräuseln *od.* werfen; **III** *v/t.* **4.** kräuseln.

cock·le² ['kɒkl] → ***corncockle***.

'cock·le|·boat → ***cockboat***; **'~·shell** *s.* **1.** Muschelschale *f*; **2.** ‚Nußschale' *f*, kleines Boot.

cock·ney ['kɒknɪ] *s. oft* ♀ **1.** Cockney *m*, (waschechter) Londoner; **2.** 'Cockney (-diaˌlekt *m*, -aussprache *f*) *n*; **'cock·ney·dom** [-dəm] *s.* **1.** Cockneybezirk *m*; **2.** *coll.* die Cockneys *pl.*; **'cock·ney·ism** [-ɪɪzəm] *s.* Cockneyausdruck *m*.

'cock|·pit *s.* **1.** Hahnenkampfplatz *m*; **2.** *fig.* Kampfplatz *m*; **3.** ⚓, ✈, *mot.* Cockpit *n*; **'~·roach** *s.* (Küchen)Schabe *f*.

cocks·comb ['kɒkskəʊm] *s.* **1.** *zo.* Hahnenkamm *m*; **2.** ⚘ Hahnenkamm *m*; **3.** → ***coxcomb*** 1.

'cock|-shy Wurfziel *n*; *fig.* Zielscheibe *f*; **'~·spur** *s.* **1.** *zo.* Hahnensporn *m*; **2.** ⚘ Hahnen-, Weißdorn *m*; **ˌ~'sure** *adj.* **1.** todsicher, 'vollkommen über'zeugt; **2.** über'trieben selbstsicher, anmaßend; **'~·tail** *s. allg.* Cocktail *m*: ***~ cabinet*** Hausbar *f*; ***~ dress*** Cocktailkleid *n*.

'cock-up *s. Brit. sl.* 'Durcheinander *n*: ***make a ~ of s.th.*** et. vermasseln.

cock·y ['kɒkɪ] *adj.* F großspurig, anmaßend.

co·co ['kəʊkəʊ] *pl.* **-cos I** *s. mst in Zssgn* ⚘ 'Kokospalme *f*; **II** *adj.* Kokos...; aus 'Kokosfasern.

co·coa ['kəʊkəʊ] *s.* **1.** Ka'kao(pulver *n*) *m*; **2.** Ka'kao *m* (*Getränk*); ***~ bean*** *s.* Ka'kaobohne *f*.

co·co·nut ['kəʊkənʌt] *s.* **1.** ⚘ 'Kokosnuß *f*: ***that accounts for the milk in the ~*** F daher der Name!; **2.** *sl.* ‚Kürbis' *m* (*Kopf*); ***~ but·ter*** *s.* 'Kokosbutter *f*; ***~ milk*** *s.* 'Kokosmilch *f*; ***~ palm***, ***~ tree*** *s.* 'Kokospalme *f*.

co·coon [kə'ku:n] **I** *s. zo.* Ko'kon *m*, Puppe *f der Seidenraupe*; *weitS.* Gespinst *n*; ⚔, ⚙ Schutzhülle *f*; **II** *v/t. u. v/i.* (sich) einspinnen *od.* (*fig.*) einhüllen; *Gerät etc.* ‚einmotten'.

co·cotte [kɒ'kɒt] *s.* Ko'kotte *f*.

cod¹ [kɒd] *s. ichth.* Kabeljau *m*, Dorsch *m*: ***dried ~*** Stockfisch *m*; ***cured ~*** Klippfisch *m*.

cod² [kɒd] *v/t. j-n* foppen.

co·da ['kəʊdə] *s.* ♪ 'Koda *f*.

cod·dle ['kɒdl] *v/t.* verhätscheln, verzärteln, verwöhnen: ***~ up*** aufpäppeln.

code [kəʊd] **I** *s.* **1.** *bsd.* ⚖ 'Kodex *m*, Gesetzbuch *n*; *weitS.* Regeln *pl.*: ***~ of hono(u)r*** Ehrenkodex; **2.** ⚓, ⚔ Si'gnalbuch *n*; **3.** (Tele'graphen)Kode *m*, (-)Schlüssel *m*; **4.** a) Code *m* (*a. Computer*), Schlüssel(schrift *f*) *m*, b) Chiffre *f*: ***~ name*** Deckname *m*; ***~ number*** Code-, Kennzahl *f*; ***~ word*** Codewort *n*; **II** *v/t.* **5.** codieren, chiffrieren, verschlüsseln: ***~d message***; ***coding device*** → ***coder***.

co·de·ine ['kəʊdi:n] *s. pharm.* Kode'in *n*.

cod·er ['kəʊdə] *s.* Codiergerät *n*, Codierer *m*, Verschlüßler *m*.

co·de·ter·mi·na·tion ['kəʊdɪˌtɜ:mɪ'neɪʃn] *s.* ✝ (***parity ~*** pari'tätische) Mitbestimmung.

co·dex ['kəʊdeks] *pl.* **'co·di·ces** [-dɪsi:z] *s.* 'Kodex *m*, alte Handschrift (*Bibel, Klassiker*).

'cod|·fish → ***cod¹***; **'~·fish·er** *s.* Kabeljaufischer *m*.

codg·er ['kɒdʒə] *s.* F alter Kauz.

co·di·ces *pl. von* ***codex***.

cod·i·cil ['kɒdɪsɪl] *s.* ⚖ Kodi'zill *n*.

cod·i·fi·ca·tion [ˌkəʊdɪfɪ'keɪʃn] *s.* Kodifizierung *f*; **cod·i·fy** ['kəʊdɪfaɪ] *v/t.* **1.** *bsd.* ⚖ kodifizieren; **2.** *Nachricht* verschlüsseln.

cod·ling¹ ['kɒdlɪŋ] *s.* junger Dorsch.

cod·ling² ['kɒdlɪŋ] *s. ein* Kochapfel *m*; ***~ moth*** *s. zo.* Obstmade *f*.

cod-liv·er oil [ˌkɒdlɪvər'ɔɪl] *s.* Lebertran *m*.

co·driv·er ['kəʊˌdraɪvə] *s.* Beifahrer *m*.

co·ed [ˌkəʊ'ed] *s. ped.* Stu'dentin *f od.* Schülerin *f* e-r gemischten Schule; **co·ed·u·ca·tion** [ˌkəʊedju:'keɪʃn] *s. ped.* Koedukati'on *f*, Gemeinschaftserziehung *f*.

co·ef·fi·cient [ˌkəʊɪ'fɪʃnt] **I** *s.* **1.** ⩚, *phys.* Koeffizi'ent *m*; **2.** mitwirkende Kraft, 'Faktor *m*; **II** *adj.* **3.** mitwirkend.

coe·li·ac ['si:lıæk] *adj. anat.* Bauch...

co·erce [kəʊ'ɜ:s] *v/t.* **1.** nötigen, zwingen (*into* zu); **2.** erzwingen; **co'er·ci·ble** [-sıbl] *adj.* ☐ zu (er)zwingen(d); **co'er·cion** [-'ɜ:ʃn] *s.* **1.** Zwang *m*; Gewalt *f*; ⚖ Nötigung *f*; **2.** *pol.* Zwangsherrschaft *f*; **co'er·cive** [-sıv] **I** *adj.* ☐ zwingend (*a. fig.*), Zwangs...; **II** *s.* Zwangsmittel *n*.

co·es·sen·tial [ˌkəʊı'senʃl] *adj.* wesensgleich.

co·e·val [kəʊ'i:vl] *adj.* ☐ **1.** gleichzeitig; **2.** gleichaltrig; **3.** von gleicher Dauer.

co·ex·ist [ˌkəʊıg'zıst] *v/i.* gleichzeitig *od.* nebenein'ander bestehen *od.* leben, koexistieren; **ˌco·ex'ist·ence** [-təns] *s.* Koexi'stenz *f*; **ˌco·ex'ist·ent** [-tənt] *adj.* gleichzeitig *od.* nebenein'ander bestehend, koexi'stent.

cof·fee ['kɒfı] *s.* **1.** 'Kaffee *m* (*Getränk, Bohnen od. Baum*): ***black*** ~ schwarzer Kaffee; ***white*** ~ Milchkaffee; **2.** 'Kaffeebraun *n*; ~ **bar** *s.* **1.** Ca'fé *n*; **2.** Imbißstube *f*; ~ **bean** *s.* 'Kaffeebohne *f*; ~ **break** *s.* 'Kaffeepause *f*; ~ **grounds** *s. pl.* 'Kaffeesatz *m*; '~·**house** *s.* 'Kaffeehaus *n*; '~ˌ**mak·er** *s. Am.* 'Kaffeemaˌschine *f*; ~ **mill** *s.* 'Kaffeemühle *f*; '~·**pot** *s.* 'Kaffeekanne *f*; ~ **set** *s.* 'Kaffeeserˌvice *n*; ~ **shop** *s. Am. für* ***coffee bar***; ~ **ta·ble** *s.* Couchtisch *m*; ~ **urn** *s.* ('Groß)ˌKaffeemaˌschine *f*.

cof·fer ['kɒfə] **I** *s.* **1.** Kasten *m*, Kiste *f*, Truhe *f*, Kas'sette *f* (*für Wertsachen*); **2.** *pl.* a) Schatz *m*, Gelder *pl.*, b) Schatzkammer *f*, Tre'sor *m*; **3.** ⌂ Deckenfeld *n*, Kas'sette *f*; **4.** → ***cofferdam***; **II** *v/t.* **5.** verwahren; '~·**dam** *s.* ⚙ Kastendamm *m*, Senkkasten *m*, Cais'son *m*.

cof·fin ['kɒfın] **I** *s.* Sarg *m* (*a.* F *schlechtes Schiff*); **II** *v/t.* einsargen; ~ **bone** *s. zo.* Hufbein *n* (*Pferd*); ~ **joint** *s.* Hufgelenk *n* (*Pferd*).

cog[1] [kɒg] *s.* **1.** ⚙ (Rad)Zahn *m*; **2.** *fig.* ***he's just a ~ in the machine*** er ist nur ein Rädchen im Getriebe.

cog[2] [kɒg] **I** *v/t. Würfel* beschweren: ~ ***the dice*** beim Würfeln mogeln; **II** *v/i.* betrügen.

co·gen·cy ['kəʊdʒənsı] *s.* Schlüssigkeit *f*, Triftigkeit *f*; '**co·gent** [-nt] *adj.* ☐ zwingend, triftig.

cogged [kɒgd] *adj.* ⚙ gezahnt, Zahn(rad)...: ~ ***railway*** Zahnradbahn *f*.

cog·i·tate ['kɒdʒıteıt] **I** *v/i.* **1.** (nach-) denken, (nach)sinnen (***upon*** über *acc.*); **2.** *phls.* denken; **II** *v/t.* **3.** ersinnen; **cog·i·ta·tion** [ˌkɒdʒı'teıʃn] *s.* **1.** (Nach)Denken *n*; **2.** Denkfähigkeit *f*; **3.** Gedanke *m*.

co·gnac ['kɒnjæk] *s.* 'Kognak *m*.

cog·nate ['kɒgneıt] **I** *adj.* **1.** (*selten*) (bluts)verwandt; **2.** verwandt (*Wörter etc.*); **3.** *ling.* (sinn)verwandt: ~ ***object*** Objekt *n* des Inhalts; **II** *s.* **4.** ⚖ Blutsverwandte(r *m*) *f*; **5.** verwandtes Wort.

cog·ni·tion [kɒg'nıʃn] *s. bsd. phls.* Erkennen *n*, Wahrnehmung *f*; Kenntnis *f*; **cog·ni·tive** ['kɒgnıtıv] *adj.* kogni'tiv, erkenntnismäßig.

cog·ni·za·ble ['kɒgnızəbl] *adj.* ☐ **1.** erkennbar; **2.** ⚖ a) der Gerichtsbarkeit unter'worfen, b) gerichtlich verfolgbar, c) zu verhandeln(d); '**cog·ni·zance** [-zəns] *s.* **1.** Kenntnis *f*, Erkenntnis *f*; **2.** ⚖ a) Zuständigkeit *f*, b) (richterliche) Verhandlung, c) (richterliches) Erkenntnis, d) *Brit.* Anerkenntnis *n*: ***take ~ of*** sich zuständig mit *e-m Fall* befassen, *weitS.* zur Kenntnis nehmen; ***beyond my ~*** außerhalb m-r Befugnis; **3.** *her.* Ab-, Kennzeichen *n*; '**cog·ni·zant** [-zənt] *adj.* **1.** unter'richtet (***of*** über *acc. od.* von); **2.** *phls.* erkennend.

cog·no·men [kɒg'nəʊmen] *s.* **1.** Fa'milien-, Zuname *m*; **2.** Bei-, *bsd.* Spitzname *m*.

'**cog·wheel** *s.* ⚙ Zahnrad *n*; ~ **drive** *s.* ⚙ Zahnradantrieb *m*; ~ **rail·way** *s.* Zahnradbahn *f*.

co·hab·it [kəʊ'hæbıt] *v/i.* (*bsd.* unverheiratet) zs.-leben; **co·hab·i·ta·tion** [ˌkəʊhæbı'teıʃn] *s.* **1.** Zs.-leben *n*; **2.** Beischlaf *m*, Beiwohnung *f*.

co·heir [ˌkəʊ'eə] *s.* Miterbe *m*; **co·heir·ess** [ˌkəʊ'eərıs] *s.* Miterbin *f*.

co·here [kəʊ'hıə] *v/i.* **1.** zs.-hängen (*a. fig.*); **2.** *fig.* in Zs.-hang stehen; **3.** zs.-halten; **4.** zs.-passen, über'einstimmen (***with*** mit); **5.** *Radio*: fritten; **co'her·ence** [-ıərəns], **co'her·en·cy** [-ıərənsı] *s.* **1.** *phys.* Kohäsi'on *f*; **2.** *fig.* a) Zs.-hang *m*, b) Klarheit *f*, c) Über'einstimmung *f*; **3.** *Radio*: Frittung *f*; **co'her·ent** [-ıərənt] *adj.* ☐ **1.** zs.-hängend (*a. fig.*), -haftend; *phys.* kohä'rent; **2.** einheitlich, verständlich, klar; **3.** über'einstimmend, zs.-passend; **co'her·er** [-ırə] *s. Radio*: Fritter(empfänger) *m*.

co·he·sion [kəʊ'hi:ʒn] *s.* **1.** Zs.-halt *m*, -hang *m* (*a. fig.*); **2.** Bindekraft *f*; **3.** *phys.* Kohäsi'on *f*; **co'he·sive** [-i:sıv] *adj.* ☐ **1.** zs.-haltend *od.* -hängend, *fig. a.* bindend; **2.** Kohäsions...; **co'he·sive·ness** [-i:sıvnıs] *s.* **1.** *phys.* Kohäsi'ons-, Bindekraft *f*; **2.** Festigkeit *f*.

co·hort ['kəʊhɔ:t] *s.* **1.** *antiq.* ⚔ Ko'horte *f*; **2.** Schar *f*, Haufen *m*.

coif [kɔıf] *s.* Kappe *f*, Haube *f*.

coif·feur [kwɑ:'fɜ:] (*Fr.*) *s.* Fri'seur *m*; **coif·fure** [kwɑ:'fjʊə; kwafy:r] (*Fr.*) *s.* Fri'sur *f*.

coil[1] [kɔıl] **I** *v/t.* **1.** *a.* ~ ***up*** auf-, zs.-rollen, winden; **2.** ⚡ wickeln; **II** *v/i.* **3.** *a.* ~ ***up*** sich winden, sich zs.-rollen; **4.** sich schlängeln; **III** *s.* **5.** Rolle *f*, Spi'rale *f* (*a. Pessar*), Knäuel *m, n*; **6.** ⚡ Wicklung *f*; Spule *f*; **7.** Windung *f*; **8.** ⚙ (Rohr)Schlange *f*; **9.** Locke *f*, Wickel *m* (*Haar*).

coil[2] [kɔıl] *s. poet.* Tu'mult *m*, Wirrwarr *m*; Plage *f*: ***mortal ~*** Drang *m od.* Mühsal *f* des Irdischen.

coil| ig·ni·tion *s.* ⚡ Abreißzündung *f*; ~ **spring** *s.* ⚙ Spi'ralfeder *f*.

coin [kɔın] **I** *s.* **1.** a) Münze *f*, Geldstück *n*, b) Münzgeld *n*, c) Geld *n*: ***the other side of the ~*** *fig.* die Kehrseite (der Medaille); ***pay s.o. back in his own ~*** *fig.* es j-m mit gleicher Münze heimzahlen; **II** *v/t.* **2.** a) *Metall* münzen, b) *Münzen* prägen: ***be ~ing money*** F Geld wie Heu verdienen; **3.** *fig. Wort* prägen; '**coin·age** [-nıdʒ] *s.* **1.** Prägen *n*; **2.** *coll.* Münzgeld *n*; **3.** 'Münzsyˌstem *n*; **4.** *fig.* Prägung *f* (*Wörter*); '**coin-box tel·e·phone** *s.* Münzfernsprecher *m*.

co·in·cide [ˌkəʊın'saıd] *v/i.* (***with***) **1.** *örtlich od. zeitlich* zs.-treffen, -fallen (mit); **2.** über'einstimmen, sich decken (mit); genau entsprechen (*dat.*); **co·in·ci·dence** [kəʊ'ınsıdəns] *s.* **1.** Zs.-treffen *n* (*Raum od. Zeit*); **2.** zufälliges Zs.-treffen: ***mere ~*** bloßer Zufall; **3.** Über'einstimmung *f*; **co·in·ci·dent** [kəʊ'ınsıdent] *adj.* ☐ (***with*** mit); **1.** zs.-fallend, -treffend; **2.** über'einstimmend, sich deckend; **co·in·ci·den·tal** [kəʊˌınsı'dentl] *adj.* **1.** → ***coincident*** 2; **2.** zufällig; **3.** *bsd.* ⚙ gleichzeitig.

coin·er ['kɔınə] *s.* **1.** Münzer *m*; **2.** *bsd. Brit.* Falschmünzer *m*; **3.** *fig.* Präger *m*, (Wort)Schöpfer *m*.

coin|-op ['kɔınɒp] F **1.** 'Waschsaˌlon *m*; **2.** Münztankstelle *f*; '~-ˌ**op·er·at·ed** *adj.* Münz...

coir ['kɔıə], *a.* ~ **fi·bre** *s.* 'Kokosfaser *f*; ~ **mat** *s.* 'Kokosmatte *f*.

co·i·tal ['kəʊıtl] *adj.* (den) Geschlechtsverkehr betreffend; **co·i·tion** [kəʊ'ıʃn], '**co·i·tus** [-təs] *s.* 'Koitus *m*, Geschlechtsverkehr *m*.

coke[1] [kəʊk] **I** *s.* **1.** Koks *m*; **2.** *sl.* ‚Koks' *m*, Koka'in *n*; **II** *v/t.* **3.** verkoken.

coke[2] [kəʊk] *s.* F a) ♀ ‚Cola' *f, n*, (*Coca-Cola*), b) Limo'nade *f etc.*

co·ker ['kəʊkə] *s.* ♆ *Brit.* → ***coco***; '~·**nut** *s. sl.* 'Kokosnuß *f*.

col [kɒl] *s.* Gebirgspaß *m*, Joch *n*.

co·la ['kəʊlə] *s.* ♆ 'Kolabaum *m*.

col·an·der ['kʌləndə] *s.* Sieb *n*, 'Durchschlag *m*.

co·la nut *s.* 'Kolanuß *f*.

col·chi·cum ['kɒltʃıkəm] *s.* **1.** ♆ Herbstzeitlose *f*; **2.** *pharm.* 'Colchicum *n*.

cold [kəʊld] **I** *adj.* ☐ **1.** kalt: ***as ~ as ice*** eiskalt; ~ ***meat*** *od.* ***cuts*** kalte Platte, Aufschnitt *m*; ***I feel*** (*od.* ***am***) ~ mir ist kalt, mich friert; **2.** kalt, kühl, ruhig, gelassen; trocken: ***that leaves me ~*** das läßt mich kalt; ~ ***reason*** kalter Verstand; ***the ~ facts*** die nackten Tatsachen; ~ ***scent*** kalte Fährte (*a. fig.*); → ***comfort*** 6, ***print*** 12; **3.** kalt (*Blick, Herz etc.*; *a. Frau*), kühl, frostig, unfreundlich, gefühllos: ***a ~ reception*** ein kühler Empfang; ***give s.o. the ~ shoulder*** → ***cold-shoulder***; ***have*** (***get***) ~ ***feet*** F kalte Füße (*Angst*) haben (kriegen); ***as ~ as charity*** hart wie Stein, lieblos; **4.** kalt (*noch nicht in Schwung*): ~ ***player***, ~ ***motor***; **5.** ‚kalt' (*im Suchspiel u. fig.*); **6.** *Am. sl.* a) bewußtlos, b) (tod)sicher; **II** *s.* **7.** Kälte *f*; Frost *m*: ***leave s.o. out in the ~*** *fig.* a) j-n übergehen *od.* ignorieren *od.* kaltstellen, b) j-n im Stich lassen; **8.** ⚕ Erkältung *f*: ***common ~***, ~ ***in the head*** Schnupfen *m*; ~ ***on the chest*** Bronchialkatarrh *m*; ***catch*** (***a***) ~ sich erkälten.

cold| blood *s. fig.* kaltes Blut, Kaltblütigkeit *f*: ***murder s.o. in ~*** j-n kaltblütig *od.* kalten Blutes ermorden; ˌ~-'**blood·ed** *adj.* ☐ **1.** *zo.* kaltblütig; **2.** kälteempfindlich; **3.** *fig.* kaltblütig (begangen): ~ ***murder***; ~ **cream** *s.* Cold Cream *f, n*; ˌ~-'**drawn** *adj.* ⚙ kaltgezogen; kaltgepreßt; ~ **duck** *s.* kalte Ente (*Getränk*); ~ **front** *s.* Kaltfront *f*; ˌ~-'**ham·mer** *v/t.* ⚙ kalthämmern, -schmieden; ˌ~'**heart·ed** *adj.* ☐ kalt-, hartherzig.

cold·ish ['kəʊldıʃ] *adj.* ziemlich kalt.

cold·ness ['kəʊldnıs] *s.* Kälte *f* (*a. fig.*).

ˌ**cold|-'shoul·der** *v/t.* *j-m* die kalte Schulter zeigen, *j-n* kühl behandeln *od.* abweisen; ~ **steel** *s.* blanke Waffe (*Bajonett etc.*); ~ **stor·age** *s.* Kühllagerung *f*; Kühlraum *m*: ***put in ~*** *fig.* ‚auf Eis legen' (*aufschieben*); ˌ~-**'stor·age** *adj.* Kühl(haus)...; ~ **store** *s.* Kühlhalle *f*; Kühlanlage *f*; Ձ **War** *s. pol.* kalter Krieg; Ձ **War·ri·or** *s. pol.* kalter Krieger; ~ **wave** *s.* **1.** Kältewelle *f*; **2.** Kaltwelle *f* (*Frisur*); ˌ~-**'work·ing** *s.* ⚙ Kaltverformung *f*.

cole [kəʊl] *s.* ⚘ **1.** (*Blätter*)Kohl *m*; **2.** Raps *m*.

co·le·op·ter·a [ˌkɒlɪ'ɒptərə] *s. pl. zo.* Käfer *pl.*

'**cole**|-**seed** *s.* ⚘ Rübsamen *m*; '~·**slaw** *s. Am.* 'Kohlsaˌlat *m*.

col·ic ['kɒlɪk] *s.* ⚕ 'Kolik *f*; '**col·ick·y** [-ɪkɪ] *adj.* ⚕ 'kolikartig.

col·i·se·um [ˌkɒlɪ'sɪəm] *s.* **1.** a) Sporthalle *f*, b) 'Stadion *n*; **2.** Ձ Kolos'seum *n* (*Rom*).

co·li·tis [kɒ'laɪtɪs] *s.* ⚕ Ko'litis *f*, 'Dickdarmkaˌtarrh *m*.

col·lab·o·rate [kə'læbəreɪt] *v/i.* **1.** zs.-, mitarbeiten; **2.** behilflich sein; **3.** *pol.* mit dem Feind zs.-arbeiten, kollaborieren; **col·lab·o·ra·tion** [kəˌlæbə'reɪʃn] *s.* **1.** Zs.-arbeit *f*: ***in ~ with*** gemeinsam mit; **2.** *pol.* Kollaborati'on *f*; **col·lab·o·ra·tion·ist** [kəˌlæbə'reɪʃnɪst] *s. pol.* Kollabora'teur *m*; **col'lab·o·ra·tor** [-tə] *s.* **1.** Mitarbeiter *m*; **2.** *pol.* Kollabora'teur *m*.

col·lage [kɒ'lɑːʒ] *s. Kunst*: Col'lage *f*.

col·lapse [kə'læps] **I** *v/i.* **1.** zs.-brechen, einfallen, einstürzen; **2.** *fig.* zs.-brechen, scheitern, versagen; **3.** (körperlich *od.* seelisch) zs.-brechen, ‚zs.-klappen'; **II** *s.* **4.** Zs.-fallen *n*, Einsturz *m*; **5.** Zs.-bruch *m*, Versagen *n*; Sturz *m*: ***~ of a bank*** Bankkrach *m*; ***~ of prices*** Preissturz *m*; **6.** ⚕ Kol'laps *m*, Zs.-bruch *m*; **col'laps·i·ble** [-səbl] *adj.* zs.-klappbar, Klapp..., Falt...: ***~ boat*** Faltboot *n*; ***~ chair*** Klappstuhl *m*; ***~ hood***, ***~ roof*** Klappverdeck *n*.

col·lar ['kɒlə] **I** *s.* **1.** Kragen *m*: ***double ~***, ***turn-down ~*** (Steh)Umlegekragen; ***stand-up ~*** Stehkragen; ***wing ~*** Eckenkragen; ***get hot under the ~*** F wütend werden; **2.** Halsband *n* (*Tier*); **3.** Kummet *n* (*Pferd etc.*): ***against the ~*** *fig.* angestrengt; **4.** Kolli'er *n*, Halskette *f*; Amts-, Ordenskette *f*; **5.** *zo.* Halsstreifen *m*; **6.** ⚙ Ring *m*, Bund *m*, Man'schette *f*, Muffe *f*; **II** *v/t.* **7.** *sport den Gegner* aufhalten; **8.** *j-n* beim Kragen packen; fassen, festnehmen; **9.** F *et.* ergattern, sich aneignen; **10.** *Fleisch etc.* rollen u. zs.-binden; '~·**bone** *s.* Schlüsselbein *n*; ~ **stud** *s.* Kragenknopf *m*.

col·late [kɒ'leɪt] *v/t.* **1.** *Texte* vergleichen, kollationieren; zs.-stellen (u. vergleichen); **2.** *typ. Fahnen* kollationieren, auf richtige Anzahl prüfen.

col·lat·er·al [kɒ'lætərəl] **I** *adj.* □ **1.** seitlich, Seiten...; **2.** begleitend, paral'lel, zusätzlich, Neben...: ***~ acceptance*** † Avalakzept *n*; ***~ circumstances*** Begleitumstände; ***~ credit*** Lombardkredit *m*; **3.** 'indirekt; **4.** in der Seitenlinie verwandt; **II** *s.* **5.** *a.* ***~ security*** zusätzliche Sicherheit, Nebenbürgschaft *f*; **6.** Seitenverwandte(r *m*) *f*.

col·la·tion [kɒ'leɪʃn] *s.* **1.** Vergleichung *f von Texten*, Über'prüfung *f*; **2.** leichte (Zwischen)Mahlzeit: ***cold ~*** kalter Imbiß.

col·league ['kɒliːg] *s.* Kol'lege *m*, Kol'legin *f*; Mitarbeiter(in).

col·lect¹ [kə'lekt] **I** *v/t.* **1.** *Briefmarken, Bilder etc.* sammeln: ***~ed work(s)*** gesammelte Werke; **2.** versammeln; **3.** einsammeln, auflesen; zs.-bringen, ansammeln; auffangen; **4.** *Sachen od. Personen* (ab)holen: ***we ~ and deliver*** † wir holen ab und bringen zurück; **5.** *fig.* ***~ one's thoughts*** s-e Gedanken sammeln *od.* zs.-nehmen; ***~ courage*** Mut fassen; **6.** ***~ o.s.*** sich fassen; **7.** *Geld etc.* einziehen, (ein)kassieren; **8.** *Pferd* versammeln; **II** *v/i.* **9.** sich versammeln; sich ansammeln; **10.** ***~ on delivery*** † *Am.* per Nachnahme; **III** *adj.* **11.** *Am.* Nachnahme...: ***~ call*** *teleph.* R-Gespräch *n*; **IV** *adv.* **12.** *Am.* gegen Nachnahme: ***telegram sent ~*** Nachnahmetelegramm *n*; ***call ~*** *Am.* ein R-Gespräch führen.

col·lect² ['kɒlekt] *s. eccl.* Kol'lekte *f*, *ein Kirchengebet n*.

col·lect·ed [kə'lektɪd] *adj.* □ *fig.* gefaßt; → ***calm*** 5; **col'lect·ed·ness** [-nɪs] *s. fig.* Sammlung *f*, Gefaßtheit *f*.

col·lect·ing| **a·gent** [kə'lektɪŋ] *s.* † In'kassovertreter *m*; ~ **bar** *s.* ϟ Sammelschiene *f*; ~ **cen·tre** (*Am.* **cen·ter**) *s.* Sammelstelle *f*.

col·lec·tion [kə'lekʃn] *s.* **1.** Sammeln *n*; **2.** Sammlung *f*; **3.** Kol'lekte *f*, (Geld-) Sammlung *f*; **4.** *bsd.* † Einziehung *f*, In'kasso *n*; (Steuer-, *a.* sta'tistische) Erhebung(en *pl.*) *f*: ***forcible ~*** Zwangsbeitreibung *f*; **5.** † Kollekti'on *f*, Auswahl *f*; **6.** Abholung *f*, Leerung *f* (*Briefkasten*); **7.** Ansammlung *f*, Anhäufung *f*; **8.** *Brit.* Steuerbezirk *m*; **9.** *pl. Brit. univ.* Prüfung *f* am Ende des Tri'mesters.

col·lec·tive [kə'lektɪv] **I** *adj.* □ → ***collectively***; **1.** gesammelt, vereint, zs.-gefaßt; gesamt, kollek'tiv, Sammel..., Gemeinschafts...: ***~ (wage) agreement*** Kollektiv-, Tarifvertrag *m*; ***~ guilt*** *pol.* Kollektivschuld *f*; ***~ interests*** Gesamtinteressen; ***~ name*** Sammelbegriff *m*; ***~ order*** † Sammelbestellung *f*; ***~ ownership*** gemeinsamer Besitz *m*; ***~ security*** kollektive Sicherheit; ***~ subscription*** Sammelabonnement *n*; **II** *s.* **2.** *ling. a.* ***~ noun*** Kollek'tivum *n*, Sammelwort *n*; **3.** Gemeinschaft *f*, Gruppe *f*; **4.** *pol.* a) Kollek'tiv *n*, Produkti'onsgemeinschaft *f*, b) → ***collective farm***; ~ **bar·gain·ing** *s.* Ta'rifverhandlungen *pl.* (*zwischen Arbeitgeber[n] u. Gewerkschaften*); ~ **con·sign·ment** *s.* † Sammelladung *f*; ~ **farm** *s.* Kol'chose *f*.

col·lec·tive·ly [kə'lektɪvlɪ] *adv.* insgesamt, gemeinschaftlich, zu'sammen, kollek'tiv.

col·lec·tiv·ism [kə'lektɪvɪzəm] *s.* †, *pol.* Kollekti'vismus *m*; **col'lec·tiv·ist** [-ɪst] *s.* Anhänger *m* des Kollekti'vismus; **col·lec·tiv·i·ty** [ˌkɒlek'tɪvətɪ] *s.* **1.** *das* Ganze; **2.** Gesamtheit *f* des Volkes; **3.** → ***collectedness***; **col·lec·tiv·i·za·tion** [kəˌlektɪvaɪ'zeɪʃn] *s.* Kollektivierung *f*.

col·lec·tor [kə'lektə] *s.* **1.** Sammler *m*: ***~'s item*** Sammlerstück *n*; ***~'s value*** Liebhaberwert *m*; **2.** † (Ein)Kassierer *m*, Einnehmer *m*: ***~ of taxes*** Steuereinnehmer; **3.** Einsammler *m*, Abnehmer *m* (*Fahrkarten*); **4.** ϟ Stromabnehmer *m*, 'Auffangelekˌtrode *f*; **5.** ϟ 'Sammelappaˌrat *m*.

col·leen ['kɒliːn] *s. Ir.* Mädchen *n*.

col·lege ['kɒlɪdʒ] *s.* **1.** College *n* (*Wohngemeinschaft von Dozenten u. Studenten innerhalb e-r Universität*): ***~ of education*** *Brit.* Pädagogische Hochschule; **2.** höhere Lehranstalt, College *n*; Insti'tut *n*, Akade'mie *f* (*oft für besondere Studienzweige*): ***Naval Ձ*** Marineakademie; **3.** (*anmaßender*) *Name mancher Schulen*; **4.** College(gebäude) *n*; **5.** Kol'legium *n*; Vereinigung *f*: ***~ of cardinals*** Kardinalskollegium; ***electoral ~*** Wahlausschuß *m*; ~ **pud·ding** *s.* kleiner 'Plumpudding.

col·leg·er ['kɒlɪdʒə] *s.* **1.** *Brit.* (im College wohnender) Stipendi'at (*in Eton*); **2.** *Am.* → **col·le·gi·an** [kə'liːdʒjən] *s.* Mitglied *n od.* Stu'dent *m* e-s College; höherer Schüler.

col·le·gi·ate [kə'liːdʒɪət] *adj.* □ **1.** College..., Universitäts..., aka'demisch: ***~ dictionary*** Schulwörterbuch *n*; **2.** Kollegial...; ~ **church** *s.* **1.** *Brit.* Kollegi'at-, Stiftskirche *f*; **2.** *Am.* Vereinigung *f* mehrerer Kirchen (*unter gemeinsamem Pastorat*); ~ **school** *s. Brit.* höhere Schule.

col·lide [kə'laɪd] *v/i.* (***with***) kollidieren (mit): a) zs.-stoßen (mit) (*a. fig.*), stoßen (gegen), b) *fig.* im 'Widerspruch stehen (zu).

col·lie ['kɒlɪ] *s. zo.* Collie *m*, schottischer Schäferhund.

col·lier ['kɒlɪə] *s.* **1.** Kohlenarbeiter *m*, Bergmann *m*; **2.** ⚓ a) Kohlenschiff *n*, b) Ma'trose *m* auf e-m Kohlenschiff; **col·lier·y** ['kɒljərɪ] *s.* Kohlengrube *f*, (Kohlen)Zeche *f*.

col·li·mate ['kɒlɪmeɪt] *v/t. ast., phys.* **1.** *zwei Linien* zs.-fallen lassen; **2.** *Fernrohr* einstellen.

col·li·sion [kə'lɪʒn] *s.* **1.** Zs.-stoß *m*, Kollisi'on *f*: ***be on (a) ~ course*** auf Kollisionskurs sein (*a. fig.*); **2.** *fig.* 'Widerspruch *m*, Gegensatz *m*, Kon'flikt *m*.

col·lo·cate ['kɒləʊkeɪt] *v/t.* zs.-stellen, ordnen; **col·lo·ca·tion** [ˌkɒləʊ'keɪʃn] *s.* **1.** Zs.-stellung *f*; **2.** *ling.* Kollokati'on *f*.

col·loc·u·tor ['kɒləkjuːtə] *s.* Gesprächspartner(in).

col·lo·di·on [kə'ləʊdjən] *s.* ⚗ Kol'lodium *n*.

col·loid ['kɒlɔɪd] ⚗ **I** *s.* Kollo'id *n*; **II** *adj.* kolloi'dal, gallertartig.

col·lop ['kɒləp] *s. Scot.* Klops *m*.

col·lo·qui·al [kə'ləʊkwɪəl] *adj.* □ 'umgangssprachlich, famili'är: ***~ English*** Umgangsenglisch *n*; ***~ expression*** → **col'lo·qui·al·ism** [-lɪzəm] *s.* Ausdruck *m* der 'Umgangssprache.

col·lo·quy ['kɒləkwɪ] *s.* (förmliches) Gespräch; Konfe'renz *f*.

col·lo·type ['kɒləʊtaɪp] *s. phot.* **1.** Lichtdruckverfahren *n od.* -platte *f*; **2.** Farbenlichtdruck *m*.

col·lude [kə'luːd] *v/i. obs.* in geheimem Einverständnis stehen; unter 'einer Decke stecken; **col'lu·sion** [-uːʒn] *s.* ⚖ **1.** Kollusi'on *f*, geheimes *od.* betrügerisches Einverständnis; **2.** Verdunkelung *f des Sachverhalts*: ***danger of ~*** Verdunkelungsgefahr *f*; **3.** abgekartete Sache, Schwindel *m*; **col'lu·sive** [-uːsɪv] *adj.* □ geheim *od.* betrügerisch verabredet.

col·ly·wob·bles ['kɒlɪˌwɒblz] *s. pl.*:

***have the* ~** F ein flaues Gefühl in der Magengegend haben.

Co·lom·bi·an [kəˈlɒmbɪən] **I** *adj.* koˈlumbisch; **II** *s.* Koˈlumbier(in).

co·lon¹ [ˈkəʊlən] *s.* Dickdarm *m.*

co·lon² [ˈkəʊlən] *s.* Doppelpunkt *m.*

colo·nel [ˈkɜːnl] *s.* ⚔ Oberst *m*; **ˈcolo·nel·cy** [-sɪ] *s.* Stelle *f od.* Rang *m* e-s Obersten.

co·lo·ni·al [kəˈləʊnjəl] **I** *adj.* □ **1.** koloniˈal, Kolonial...: **2 *Office*** *Brit.* Kolonialministerium *n*; **2 *Secretary*** Kolonialminister *m*; **2.** *Am. hist.* die ersten 13 Staaten der heutigen USA *od.* die Zeit vor 1776 *od.* des 18. Jahrhunderts betreffend; **II** *s.* **3.** Bewohner(in) e-r Koloˈnie; **coˈlo·ni·al·ism** [-lɪzəm] *s.* **1.** Koloniaˈlismus *m*; **2.** koloniˈaler (Wesens)Zug *od.* Ausdruck.

col·o·nist [ˈkɒlənɪst] *s.* Koloˈnist(in), (An)Siedler(in); **col·o·ni·za·tion** [ˌkɒlənaɪˈzeɪʃn] *s.* Kolonisatiˈon *f*, Besiedlung *f*; **ˈcol·o·nize** [-naɪz] **I** *v/t.* **1.** kolonisieren, besiedeln; **2.** ansiedeln; **II** *v/i.* **3.** sich ansiedeln; **4.** e-e Koloˈnie bilden; **ˈcol·o·niz·er** [-naɪzə] *s.* Koloniˈsator *m*, An-, Besiedler *m.*

col·on·nade [ˌkɒləˈneɪd] *s.* **1.** Kolonˈnade *f*, Säulengang *m*; **2.** Alˈlee *f.*

col·o·ny [ˈkɒlənɪ] *s.* **1.** Koloˈnie *f* (*Siedlungsgebiet*): ***the Colonies*** *Am.* die ersten 13 Staaten der heutigen USA; **2.** Gruppe *f* von Ansiedlern: ***the German ~ in Rome*** die deutsche Kolonie in Rom; ***a ~ of artists*** e-e Künstlerkolonie; **3.** *biol.* (*Pflanzen-, Bakterien-, Zellen*)Koloˈnie *f.*

co·loph·o·ny [kəˈlɒfənɪ] *s.* Koloˈphonium *n*, Geigenharz *n.*

col·or *etc. Am.* → ***colour*** *etc.*

Col·o·ra·do bee·tle [ˌkɒləˈrɑːdəʊ] *s. zo.* Karˈtoffelkäfer *m.*

col·o·ra·tu·ra [ˌkɒlərəˈtʊərə] *s.* ♪ **1.** Koloraˈtur *f*; **2.** Koloraˈtursängerin *f*; **~ so·pran·o** *s.* ♪ Koloraˈturso͵pran *m* (*Stimme u. Sängerin*).

col·or·if·ic [ˌkɒləˈrɪfɪk] *adj.* farbgebend; **͵col·orˈim·e·ter** [-ˈrɪmɪtə] *s. phys.* Farbmesser *m*, Koloriˈmeter *n.*

co·los·sal [kəˈlɒsl] *adj.* □ **1.** kolosˈsal, riesig, Riesen..., ungeheuer (*alle a.* F *fig.*); riesenhaft; **2.** F kolosˈsal, eˈnorm; **col·os·se·um** [ˌkɒləˈsɪəm] → ***coliseum***; **Coˈlos·sians** [-ɒʃənz] *s. pl. bibl.* (Brief *m* des Paulus an die) Koˈlosser *pl.*; **coˈlos·sus** [-səs] *s.* **1.** Koˈloß *m*: a) Riese *m*, b) *et.* Riesengroßes; **2.** Riesenstandbild *n.*

col·our [ˈkʌlə] **I** *s.* **1.** Farbe *f*; Färbung *f*; ***what ~ is ...?*** welche Farbe hat ...?; **2.** *mst pl. Malerei*: Farbe *f*, Farbstoff *m*: ***lay on the ~s too thickly*** *fig.* zu dick auftragen; ***paint in bright (dark) ~s*** *fig.* in rosigen (düsteren) Farben schildern; **3.** (*a.* gesunde) Gesichtsfarbe: ***she has little ~*** sie ist blaß; ***change (lose) ~*** die Farbe wechseln (verlieren); → ***off-colo(u)r***; **4.** Hautfarbe *f*: ***~ problem*** Rassenfrage *f*; **5.** Anschein *m*, Anstrich *m*, Vorwand *m*, Deckmantel *m*: ***~ of law*** ⚖ Amtsmißbrauch *m*; ***~ of title*** ⚖ unzureichender Eigentumsanspruch; ***give ~ to*** den Anstrich der Wahrscheinlichkeit geben (*dat.*); ***under ~ of*** unter dem Vorwand *od.* Anschein von; **6.** a) Färbung *f*, Ton *m*, b) Farbe *f*, Lebendigkeit *f*, Koloˈrit *n*: ***lend*** (*od.* ***add***) ***~ to*** beleben, lebendig gestalten, *e-r Sache* Farbe verleihen; ***in one's true ~s*** in s-m wahren Licht; ***local ~*** Lokalkolorit; **7.** ♪ Klangfarbe *f*; **8.** *pl.* Farben *pl.*, Abzeichen *n* (*Klub, Schule, Partei, Jockei*): ***show one's ~s*** a) sein wahres Gesicht zeigen, b) Farbe bekennen; ***to get one's ~s*** sein Mitgliedsabzeichen bekommen; **9.** *pl.* bunte Kleider; **10.** *oft pl.* ⚔ *od. fig.* Fahne *f*, Flagge *f*: ***call to the ~s*** einberufen; ***join the ~s*** Soldat werden; ***with flying ~s*** *fig.* mit fliegenden Fahnen; ***come off with flying ~s*** e-n glänzenden Sieg *od.* Erfolg erzielen; ***nail one's ~s to the mast*** nicht kapitulieren (wollen), standhaft bleiben; ***sail under false ~s*** unter falscher Flagge segeln; ***stick to one's ~s*** e-r Sache treu bleiben; → ***troop*** 6; **11.** *Kartenspiel*: rote u. schwarze Farbe; **II** *v/t.* **12.** färben, kolorieren; anstreichen; **13.** *fig.* färben, e-n Anstrich geben (*dat.*); **14.** a) schönfärben, b) entstellen; **III** *v/i.* **15.** sich (ver)färben; e-e Farbe annehmen; *a.* **~ *up*** erröten.

col·o(u)r·a·ble [ˈkʌlərəbl] *adj.* □ *fig.* **1.** vor-, angeblich; fingiert: ***~ title*** ⚖ unzureichender Eigentumsanspruch; **2.** glaubhaft, plauˈsibel; **ˈcol·o(u)r·ant** [-rənt] *s.* Farbstoff *m.*

col·o(u)r·a·tion [ˌkʌləˈreɪʃn] *s.* Färben *n*; Färbung *f*; Farbgebung *f.*

col·o(u)r| bar *s.* Rassenschranke *f*; **ˈ~-blind** *adj.* farbenblind; **~ chart** *s.* Farbenskala *f*; **ˈ~-code** *v/t.* mit Kennfarben versehen.

col·o(u)red [ˈkʌləd] *adj.* **1.** farbig, bunt (*beide a. fig.*), koloriert; *in Zssgn* ...farbig: ***~ pencil*** Bunt-, Farbstift *m*; ***~ plate*** → ***colo(u)r plate***; **2.** farbig, *Am. bsd.* Neger...: ***a ~ man*** ein Farbiger; **3.** *fig.* gefärbt: a) beschönigt, b) tendenziˈös entstellt; **4.** *fig.* angeblich, falsch; **ˈcol·o(u)r·fast** *adj.* farbecht; **ˈcol·o(u)r·ful** [-əfʊl] *adj.* **1.** farbenfreudig; **2.** *fig.* farbig, bunt, lebhaft, abwechslungsreich; **ˈcol·o(u)r·ing** [-ərɪŋ] **I** *s.* **1.** Farbe *f*, Farbton *m*; **2.** Farbgebung *f*; **3.** Gesichts- (u. Haar)farbe *f*; **4.** *fig.* Anstrich *m*, Färbung *f*; **II** *adj.* **5.** Farb...: ***~ matter*** Farbstoff *m*; **ˈcol·o(u)r·ist** [-ərɪst] *s.* Farbenkünstler *m*, *engS.* Koloˈrist *m*; **ˈcol·o(u)r·less** [-əlɪs] *adj.* □ farblos (*a. fig.*).

col·o(u)r| line *s.* Rassenschranke *f*; **~ pho·tog·ra·phy** *s.* ˈFarbfotogra͵fie *f*; **~ plate** *s.* Farben(kunst)druck *m*; **~ print** *s. ein* Farbendruck *m*; **~ print·ing** *s.* Bunt-, Farbendruck *m* (*Verfahren*); **~ scheme** *s.* Farbgebung *f*, Farbenanordnung *f*; **~ ser·geant** *s.* ⚔ (*etwa*) Oberfeldwebel *m*; **~ set** *s.* Farbfernseher *m*; **~ sup·ple·ment** *s.* Farbbeilage *f* (*Zeitung*); **~ tel·e·vi·sion** *s.* Farbfernsehen *n*; **ˈ~-wash I** *s.* farbige Tünche; **II** *v/t.* farbig tünchen.

colt¹ [kəʊlt] **I** *s.* **1.** Füllen *n*, Fohlen *n*; **2.** *fig.* ‚Grünschnabel' *m*, *sport* F *a.* ‚Fohlen' *n*; **3.** ⚓ Tauende *n*; **II** *v/t.* **4.** mit dem Tauende prügeln.

colt² [kəʊlt] *s.* Colt *m* (*Revolver*).

col·ter [ˈkəʊltə] *Am.* → ***coulter***.

ˈcolts·foot *s.* ⚘ Huflattich *m.*

col·um·bine [ˈkɒləmbaɪn] *s.* **1.** ⚘ Akeˈlei *f*; **2.** 2 *thea.* Kolomˈbine *f.*

col·umn [ˈkɒləm] *s.* **1.** △ Säule *f*, Pfeiler *m*; **2.** (*Rauch-, Wasser-, Luft- etc.*)Säule *f*; **3.** *typ.* (Zeitungs-, Buch)Spalte *f*; Ruˈbrik *f*: ***in double ~s*** zweispaltig; **4.** Spalte *f*, Koˈlumne *f* (*regelmäßig erscheinender Meinungsbeitrag*); **5.** ⚔ Koˈlonne *f*; → ***fifth column***; **6.** Koˈlonne *f*, senkrechte Zahlenreihe; **co·lum·nar** [kəˈlʌmnə] *adj.* säulenartig, -förmig; Säulen...; **ˈcol·um·nist** [-mnɪst] *s.* *Zeitung*: Kolumˈnist(in).

col·za [ˈkɒlzə] *s.* ⚘ Raps *m*: ***~ oil*** Rüb-, Rapsöl *n.*

co·ma¹ [ˈkəʊmə] *pl.* **-mae** [-miː] *s.* **1.** ⚘ Haarbüschel *n* (*an Samen*); **2.** *ast.* Nebelhülle *f e-s Kometen.*

co·ma² [ˈkəʊmə] *s.* ⚕ Koma *n*, tiefe Bewußtlosigkeit: ***be in (fall into) a ~*** im Koma liegen (ins Koma fallen); **ˈco·ma·tose** [-ətəʊs] *adj.* komaˈtös, im Koma (befindlich).

comb [kəʊm] **I** *s.* **1.** Kamm *m*; **2.** ⚙ a) (Wollweber)Kamm *m*, b) (Flachs)Hechel *f*, c) Gewindeschneider *m*, d) ⚡ (Kamm)Stromabnehmer *m*; **3.** *zo.* Hahnenkamm *m*; **4.** Kamm *m* (*Berg; Woge*); **5.** → ***honeycomb*** 1; **II** *v/t.* **6.** *Haar* kämmen; **7.** ⚙ a) *Wolle* kämmen, krempeln, b) *Flachs* hecheln; **8.** *Pferd* striegeln; **9.** *fig.* ˈdurchkämmen, durchˈkämmen, absuchen; **10.** *fig. a.* **~ *out*** a) sieben, sichten, b) aussondern, c) ⚔ ausmustern.

com·bat [ˈkɒmbæt] **I** *v/t.* bekämpfen, kämpfen gegen; **II** *v/i.* kämpfen; **III** *s.* Kampf *m*; Streit *m*; ⚔ *a.* Einsatz *m*: ***single ~*** Zweikampf; **ˈcom·bat·ant** [-bətənt] **I** *s.* **1.** Kämpfer *m*; **2.** ⚔ Frontkämpfer *m*; **II** *adj.* **3.** kämpfend; **4.** ⚔ zur Kampftruppe gehörig; Kampf...

com·bat| car *s.* ⚔ *Am.* Kampfwagen *m*; **~ fa·tigue** *s.* ⚔ *psych.* ˈKriegsneu͵rose *f.*

com·ba·tive [ˈkɒmbətɪv] *adj.* □ **1.** kampfbereit; **2.** kampflustig, streitsüchtig.

com·bat| plane *s.* ✈ *Am.* Kampfflugzeug *n*; **~ sport** *s.* Kampfsport *m*; **~ train·ing** *s.* Gefechtsausbildung *f*; **~ troops** *s. pl.* Kampftruppen *pl.*; **~ u·nit** *s.* ⚔ *Am.* Kampfverband *m.*

combe [kuːm] → ***coomb(e)***.

comb·er [ˈkəʊmə] *s.* **1.** ⚙ a) ˈKrempelma͵schine *f*, b) ˈHechelma͵schine *f*; **2.** Sturzwelle *f.*

comb hon·ey *s.* Scheibenhonig *m.*

com·bi·na·tion [ˌkɒmbɪˈneɪʃn] *s.* **1.** Verbindung *f*, Vereinigung *f*; Zs.-setzung *f*; Kombinatiˈon *f* (*a. sport,* ♞ *etc.*); **2.** Zs.-schluß *m*, Bündnis *n*; *b.s.* Komˈplott *n*; **3.** ✝ *etc.* → ***combine*** 6, 7, 8; **4.** ⚗ Verbindung *f*; **5.** *mot.* Gespann *n*, ˈMotorrad *n* mit Beiwagen; **6.** *mst. pl.* Kombinatiˈon *f*: a) Hemdhose *f*, b) Monˈtur *f*; **7.** ♪ → ***combo***; **~ lock** *s.* ⚙ Kombinatiˈons-, Veˈxierschloß *n*; **~ room** *s. Brit. univ.* Gemeinschaftsraum *m.*

com·bine [kəmˈbaɪn] **I** *v/t.* **1.** verbinden (*a.* ⚗), vereinigen, kombinieren; **2.** in sich vereinigen; **II** *v/i.* **3.** sich verbinden (*a.* ⚗), sich vereinigen; **4.** sich zs.-schließen; **5.** zs.-wirken; **III** *s.* [ˈkɒmbaɪn] **6.** Verbindung *f*, Vereinigung *f*; **7.** ✝ Konˈzern *m*, Verband *m*; **8.** poˈlitische *od.* wirtschaftliche Interˈessengemeinschaft; **9.** *a.* **~ *harvester***

⚒ Mähdrescher *m*.

com·bined [kəm'baɪnd] *adj.* vereinigt, verbunden; vereint, gemeinsam, Gemeinschafts…; kombiniert: **~ arms** ⚔ gemischte Verbände; **~ event** *sport* Mehrkampf *m*.

comb·ings ['kəʊmɪŋz] *s. pl.* ausgekämmte Haare *pl.*

com·bo ['kɒmbəʊ] *s.* Combo *f*, kleine Jazzband.

'**comb-out** *s.* Auskämmen *n*; *fig.* Siebung *f*, Sichtung *f*.

com·bus·ti·bil·i·ty [kəmˌbʌstə'bɪlətɪ] *s.* Brennbarkeit *f*, Entzündlichkeit *f*; **com·bus·ti·ble** [kəm'bʌstəbl] **I** *adj.* **1.** brennbar, leichtentzündlich; **2.** *fig.* erregbar; **II** *s.* **3.** Brenn-, Zündstoff *m*; 'Brennmateriˌal *n*.

com·bus·tion [kəm'bʌstʃən] *s.* Verbrennung *f* (*a.* ⚗, *biol.*): **spontaneous ~** Selbstentzündung *f*; **~ cham·ber** *s.* ⚙ Verbrennungsraum *m*; **~ en·gine**, **~ mo·tor** *s.* ⚙ Ver'brennungsˌmotor *m*.

come [kʌm] **I** *v/i.* [*irr.*] **1.** kommen: **be long in coming** lange auf sich warten lassen; **he came to see us** er besuchte uns, er suchte uns auf; **that ~s on page 4** das kommt auf Seite 4; **~ what may!** komme, was da wolle!; **a year ago ~ March** im März vor e-m Jahr; **as stupid as they ~** dumm wie Bohnenstroh; **the message has ~** die Nachricht ist gekommen *od.* eingetroffen; **I was coming to that** darauf wollte ich gerade hinaus; **~ to that** was das betrifft; **~ again!** F sag's noch mal!; **2.** (dran)kommen, an die Reihe kommen: **who ~s first?**; **3.** kommen, erscheinen, auftreten: **~ and go** a) kommen u. gehen, b) erscheinen u. verschwinden; **love will ~ in time** mit der Zeit wird die Liebe sich einstellen; **~ (to pass)** geschehen, sich ereignen, kommen; **how ~?** wie kommt das?, wieso (denn)?; **4.** kommen, gelangen (**to** zu): **~ to the throne** den Thron besteigen; **~ into danger** in Gefahr geraten; **5.** kommen, abstammen (**of**, **from** von): **he ~s of a good family** er kommt *od.* stammt aus gutem Hause; **I ~ from Leeds** ich stamme aus Leeds; **6.** kommen, 'herrühren (**of** von): **that's what ~s of your hurry** das kommt von deiner Eile; **nothing came of it** es wurde nichts daraus; **7.** sich erweisen: **it ~s expensive** es kommt teuer; **the expenses ~ rather high** die Kosten kommen recht hoch; **it ~s to this that** es läuft darauf hinaus, daß; **it ~s to the same thing** es läuft auf dasselbe hinaus; → *a.* **come to** 4; **8.** *fig.* ankommen (**to s.o.** j-n): **it ~s hard (easy) to me** es fällt mir schwer (leicht); **9.** werden, sich entwickeln, dahin *od.* dazu kommen: **he has ~ to be a good musician** er ist ein guter Musiker geworden; **it has ~ to be the custom** es ist Sitte geworden; **~ to know s.o.** j-n kennenlernen; **I have ~ to believe that** ich bin zu der Überzeugung gekommen, daß; **how did you ~ to do that?** wie kamen Sie dazu, das zu tun?; **~ true** wahr werden, sich erfüllen; **~ undone** auf-, ab-, losgehen, sich lösen: **10.** ⚘ (her'aus)kommen, sprießen, keimen; **11.** erhältlich *od.* zu haben sein: **these shirts ~ in three sizes**; **12. to ~** (*als adj. gebraucht*) (zu)künftig, kommend: **the life to ~** das zukünftige Leben; **for all time to ~** für alle Zukunft; **in the years to ~** in den kommenden Jahren; **13.** *sport etc.* ‚kommen' (*angreifen, stärker werden*); **14.** *sl.* ‚kommen' (*e-n Orgasmus haben*); **II** *v/t.* **15.** F sich aufspielen als, *j-n od. etwas* spielen, her'auskehren: **don't try to ~ the great scholar over me!** versuche nicht, mir gegenüber den großen Gelehrten zu spielen!; **III** *int.* **16.** na (hör mal)!, komm!, bitte!: **~, ~!** a) *a.* **~ now!** nanu!, nicht so wild!, immer langsam!, b) (*ermutigend*) na komm schon!, auf geht's!; **IV** *s.* **17.** V ‚Saft' *m* (*Sperma*);

Zssgn mit prp.:

come| a·cross *v/i.* zufällig treffen *od.* finden, stoßen auf (*acc.*); **~ aft·er** *v/i.* **1.** *j-m* folgen; **2.** *et.* holen kommen; **3.** suchen, sich bemühen um; **~ at** *v/i.* **1.** erreichen, bekommen; **2.** angreifen, auf *j-n* losgehen; **~ by** *v/i.* zu *et.* kommen, bekommen; **~ for** *v/i.* **1.** abholen kommen; **2.** → **come at** 2; **~ in·to** *v/i.* **1.** eintreten in (*acc.*); **2.** *e-m Klub etc.* beitreten; **3.** (*rasch od. unerwartet*) zu *et.* kommen: **~ a fortune** ein Vermögen erben; **~ near** *v/i.* **1.** *fig.* nahekommen (*dat.*); **2. ~ doing (s.th.)** beinahe (et.) tun; **~ on** → **come upon**; **~ o·ver** *v/i.* **1.** über'kommen, beschleichen, befallen: **what has ~ you?** was ist mit dir los?, was fällt dir ein?; **2.** *sl. j-n* reinlegen; **3.** → **come** 15; **~ to** *v/i.* **1.** *j-m* zufallen (*bsd. durch Erbschaft*); **2.** *j-m* zukommen, zustehen: **he had it coming to him** F er hatte das längst verdient; **3.** zum *Bewußtsein etc.* kommen; **4.** kommen *od.* gelangen zu: **what are things coming to?** wohin sind wir (*od.* ist die Welt) geraten?; **when it comes to paying** wenn es ans Bezahlen geht; **5.** sich belaufen auf (*acc.*): **it comes to £100**; → *a.* **come** 7; **~ un·der** *v/i.* **1.** kommen *od.* fallen unter (*acc.*): **~ a law**; **2.** geraten unter (*acc.*); **~ up·on** *v/i.* **1.** *j-n* befallen, über'kommen, *j-m* zustoßen; **2.** über *j-n* 'herfallen; **3.** (*zufällig*) treffen, stoßen auf (*acc.*); **4.** *j-m* zur Last fallen; **~ with·in** → **come under**.

Zssgn mit adv.:

come| a·bout *v/i.* **1.** geschehen, pas'sieren; **2.** entstehen; **3.** ⚓ 'umspringen (*Wind*); **~ a·cross** *v/i.* **1.** her'überkommen; **2.** a) verstanden werden, b) ‚ankommen' (*Rede etc.*), c) ‚rüberkommen' (*Filmszene etc.*); **3. ~ with** F ‚rüberkommen' mit, *Geld etc.* her'ausrükken; **~ a·long** *v/i.* **1.** mitkommen, -gehen: **~!** F ‚dalli'!, komm schon!; **2.** sich ergeben (*Chance etc.*); **3.** F vorankommen, Fortschritte machen; **~ a·part** *v/i.* ausein'anderfallen, in Stücke gehen; **~ a·way** *v/i.* **1.** ab-, losgehen (*Knopf etc.*); **2.** weggehen (*Person*); **~ back** *v/i.* **1.** zu'rückkommen, *a. fig.* 'wiederkehren: **~ to s.th.** auf e-e Sache zurückkommen; **2.** *sl.* ein ‚Comeback' feiern; **3.** wieder einfallen (**to s.o.** j-m); **4.** (*bsd.* schlagfertig) antworten (**at s.o.** j-m); **~ by** *v/i.* vor'beikommen, ‚reinschauen'; **~ down** *v/i.* **1.** her'ab-, her'unterkommen; **2.** (ein)stürzen, fallen; **3.** ✈ niedergehen; **4.** *a.* **~ in the world** *fig.* her'unterkommen (*Person*); **5.** *ped. univ. Brit.* a) die Universi'tät verlassen, b) in die Ferien gehen; **6.** über'liefert werden; **7.** her'untergehen, sinken (*Preis*), billiger werden (*Dinge*); **8.** nachgeben, kleinlaut werden; **9. ~ on** a) sich stürzen auf (*acc.*), b) 'herfallen über (*acc.*), *j-m* ‚aufs Dach steigen'; **10. ~ with** F her'ausrücken mit: **~ handsome(ly)** sich spendabel zeigen; **11. ~ with** erkranken an (*dat.*); **12. ~ to** hin'auslaufen auf (*acc.*); **~ forth** *v/i.* her'vorkommen; **~ for·ward** *v/i.* **1.** her'vortreten; **2.** sich melden (*Zeuge etc.*); **~ home** *v/i.* **1.** nach Hause kommen; **2.** *fig.* Eindruck machen, wirken, ‚einschlagen', ‚ziehen'; **~ in** *v/i.* **1.** her'einkommen: **~!** a) herein!, b) (*Funk*) bitte kommen!; **2.** eingehen, -treffen (*Nachricht, Geld etc.*), ⚓, 🚂 *sport* einlaufen: **~ second** den zweiten Platz belegen; **3.** aufkommen, in Mode kommen: **long skirts ~ again**; **4.** an die Macht kommen; **5.** sich *als nützlich etc.* erweisen: **this will ~ useful**; **6.** Berücksichtigung finden: **where do I ~?** wo bleibe ich?; **that's were you ~** da bist dann du dran; **where does the joke ~?** was ist daran so witzig?; **7. ~ for** a) bekommen, ‚kriegen', b) *Bewunderung etc.* erregen: **~ for it** F ‚sein Fett kriegen'; **~ off** *v/i.* **1.** ab-, losgehen, sich lösen; **2.** *fig.* stattfinden, ‚über die Bühne gehen'; **3.** a) abschneiden: **he came off best**, b) erfolgreich verlaufen, glükken; **4. ~ it!** F hör schon auf damit!; **~ on** *v/i.* **1.** her'ankommen: **~!** a) komm (mit)!, b) komm her!, c) na, komm schon!, los!, d) F na, na!; **2.** beginnen, einsetzen: **it came on to rain** es begann zu regnen; **3.** an die Reihe kommen; **4.** *thea.* a) auftreten, b) aufgeführt werden; **5.** stattfinden; ⚖ verhandelt werden; **6.** a) wachsen, gedeihen, b) vor'ankommen, Fortschritte machen; **~ out** *v/i.* **1.** her'aus-, her'vorkommen, sich zeigen; **2.** *a.* **~ on strike** streiken; **3.** her'auskommen: a) erscheinen (*Bücher*), b) bekanntwerden, ans Licht kommen; **4.** ausgehen (*Haare*), her'ausgehen (*Farbe*); **5.** F werden, sich *gut etc.* entwickeln; *phot. etc. gut etc.* werden (*Bild*); **6.** debü'tieren: a) zum ersten Male auftreten (*Schauspieler*), b) in die Gesellschaft eingeführt werden; **7. ~ with** F mit *et.* her'ausrücken (*sagen*); **8. ~ against** sich aussprechen gegen, den Kampf ansagen (*dat.*); **~ o·ver** *v/i.* **1.** her'überkommen; **2.** 'übergehen (**to** zu); **3.** verstanden werden; **~ round** *v/i.* **1.** ‚vor'beikommen' (*Besucher*); **2.** 'wiederkehren (*Fest, Zeitabschnitt*); **3. ~ to s.o.'s way of thinking** sich zu j-s Meinung bekehren; **4.** → **come to** 1; **~ through** *v/i.* **1.** 'durchkommen (*a. allg. fig. Kranker, Meldung etc.*); **2.** *fig.* a) es ‚schaffen', b) → **come across** 3; **~ to** *v/i.* **1.** a) wieder zu sich kommen, das Bewußtsein 'wiedererlangen, b) sich erholen; **2.** ⚓ vor Anker gehen; **~ up** *v/i.* **1.** her'aufkommen; **2.** her'ankommen: **~ to s.o.** an j-n herantreten; **coming up!** kommt gleich!; **3.** ⚖ zur Verhandlung kommen; **4.** *a.* **~ for discussion** zur Sprache kommen, angeschnitten werden; **5. ~ for** zur *Abstimmung, Entscheidung* kommen; **6.** aufkommen, Mode werden; **7.** *Brit.* sein Studium aufnehmen;

8. *Brit.* nach London kommen; **9. ~ to** a) reichen bis an (*acc.*) *od.* zu, b) erreichen (*acc.*), c) *fig.* her'anreichen an (*acc.*); **10. ~ with** a) *j-n* einholen, b) *fig.* es *j-m* gleichtun; **11. ~ with** ‚da'herkommen' mit, *e-e Idee etc.* präsentieren.

come-at-a·ble [ˌkʌm'ætəbl] *adj.* F **1.** zugänglich; **2.** erreichbar.

'come·back *s.* **1.** *sport, thea. etc.* Come'back *n*: **make** *od.* **stage a ~** ein Comeback feiern; **2.** (schlagfertige) Antwort.

co·me·di·an [kə'mi:djən] *s.* **1.** a) Ko'mödienschauspieler *m*, b) Komiker *m* (*a. contp.*); **2.** Lustspieldichter *m*; **3.** Witzbold *m* (*a. contp.*); **co·me·di·enne** [kəˌmi:dɪ'en] *s.* a) Ko'mödienschauspielerin *f*, b) Komikerin *f*.

com·e·do ['kɒmədəʊ] *pl.* **-dos** *s.* ⚕ Mitesser *m*.

'come·down *s.* **1.** *fig.* Abstieg *m*, Abfall *m* (**from** gegenüber); **2.** F Enttäuschung *f*.

com·e·dy ['kɒmɪdɪ] *s.* **1.** Ko'mödie *f*: a) Lustspiel *n*: **light ~** Schwank *m*, b) *fig.* komische Sache; **2.** Komik *f*.

ˌcome-'hith·er *adj.*: **~ look** F einladender Blick.

come·li·ness ['kʌmlɪnɪs] *s.* Anmut *f*, Schönheit *f*; **'come·ly** ['kʌmlɪ] *adj.* attrak'tiv, hübsch.

'come-on *s. Am. sl.* **1.** Köder *m* (*bsd. für Käufer*); **2.** Schwindler *m*; **3.** Gimpel *m* (*einfältiger Mensch*).

com·er ['kʌmə] *s.* **1.** Ankömmling *m*: **first ~** wer zuerst kommt, *weitS.* (*der od. die*) erste beste; **all ~s** jedermann; **2. he is a ~** F er ist der kommende Mann.

co·mes·ti·ble [kə'mestɪbl] **I** *adj.* genießbar; **II** *s. pl.* Nahrungs-, Lebensmittel *pl.*

com·et ['kɒmɪt] *s. ast.* Ko'met *m*.

come·up·pance [ˌkʌm'ʌpəns] *s.* F wohlverdiente Strafe.

com·fit ['kʌmfɪt] *s. obs.* Zuckerwerk *n*, kan'dierte Früchte *pl.*

com·fort ['kʌmfət] **I** *v/t.* **1.** trösten, *j-m* Trost spenden; **2.** beruhigen; **3.** erfreuen; **4.** *j-m* Mut zusprechen; **5.** *obs.* unter'stützen, *j-m* helfen; **II** *s.* **6.** Trost *m*, Erleichterung *f* (**to** für): **derive** *od.* **take ~ from s.th.** aus etwas Trost schöpfen; **what a ~!** Gott sei Dank!; welch ein Trost!; **he was a great ~ to her** er war ihr ein großer Trost *od.* Beistand; **cold ~** ein schwacher *od.* schlechter Trost; **7.** Wohltat *f*, Labsal *n*, Erquickung *f* (**to** für); **8.** Behaglichkeit *f*, Wohlergehen *n*: **live in ~** ein behagliches u. sorgenfreies Leben führen; **9.** *a. pl.* Kom'fort *m*: **with all modern ~s**; **10.** *a.* **soldiers' ~s** *pl.* Liebesgaben *pl.* (für Sol'daten); **11.** *obs.* Hilfe *f*.

com·fort·a·ble ['kʌmfətəbl] *adj.* (*adv.* **comfortably**) **1.** komfor'tabel, bequem, behaglich, gemütlich: **make o.s. ~** es sich bequem machen; **are you ~?** haben Sie es bequem?, sitzen *od.* liegen *etc.* Sie bequem?; **feel ~** sich wohl fühlen; **2.** bequem, sorgenfrei: **live in ~ circumstances** in guten Verhältnissen leben; **3.** gut, reichlich: **a ~ income**; **4.** *bsd. sport* beruhigend (*Vorsprung etc.*); **5.** ohne Beschwerden (*Patient*); **'com·fort·er** [-tə] *s.* **1.** Tröster *m*: → **Job²**; **2. the** ♀ *eccl.* der Heilige Geist; **3.** *bsd. Brit.* Wollschal *m*; **4.** *Am.* Steppdecke *f*; **5.** *bsd. Brit.* Schnuller *m* (*für Babys*); **'com·fort·ing** [-tɪŋ] *adj.* tröstlich; **'com·fort·less** [-lɪs] *adj.* **1.** unbequem; **2.** trostlos; **3.** unerfreulich.

com·frey ['kʌmfrɪ] *s.* ⚘ Schwarzwurz *f*.

com·fy ['kʌmfɪ] F → **comfortable** 1.

com·ic ['kɒmɪk] **I** *adj.* □ → **comically**; **1.** komisch, Lustspiel…: **~ actor** Komiker *m*; **~ opera** komische Oper; **~ writer** Lustspieldichter *m*; **2.** komisch, humo'ristisch: **~ paper** Witzblatt *n*; **~ strips** Comic strips, Comics; **3.** drollig, spaßig; **II** *s.* **4.** Komiker *m*; **5.** Witzblatt *n*; *pl. Zeitung*: Comics *pl.*; **6.** 'Filmkoˌmödie *f*; **'com·i·cal** [-kəl] *adj.* □ **1.** komisch, ulkig; **2.** F komisch, sonderbar; **com·i·cal·i·ty** [ˌkɒmɪ'kælətɪ] *s.* Spaßigkeit *f*; **'com·i·cal·ly** [-kəlɪ] *adv.* komisch(erweise).

com·ing ['kʌmɪŋ] **I** *adj.* kommend, (zu)künftig: **the ~ man** der kommende Mann; **~ week** nächste Woche; **II** *s.* Kommen *n*, Ankunft *f*; Beginn *m*: **~ of age** Mündigwerden *n*; **the Second** ♀ (**of Christ**) die Wiederkunft Christi.

com·i·ty ['kɒmɪtɪ] *s.* **1.** Höflichkeit *f*; **2. ~ of nations** gutes Einvernehmen der Nationen.

com·ma ['kɒmə] *s.* Komma *n*; **~ ba·cil·lus** *s.* [*irr.*] ⚕ 'Kommabaˌzillus *m*.

com·mand [kə'mɑ:nd] **I** *v/t.* **1.** *j-m* befehlen, gebieten; **2.** gebieten, fordern, verlangen: **~ silence** Ruhe gebieten; **3.** beherrschen, gebieten über (*acc.*): **the hill ~s the plain** der Hügel beherrscht die Ebene; **4.** ⚔ kommandieren: a) *j-m* befehlen, b) *Truppe* befehligen, führen; **5.** *Gefühle, die Lage* beherrschen: **~ o.s.** sich beherrschen; **6.** verfügen über (*acc.*) (*Dienste, Gelder*); **7.** *Vertrauen, Liebe* einflößen: **~ respect** Achtung gebieten; **~ admiration** Bewunderung abnötigen *od.* verdienen; **8.** *Aussicht* gewähren, bieten; **9.** ✝ *Preis* erzielen; *Absatz* finden; **II** *v/i.* **10.** befehlen, herrschen; **11.** ⚔ kommandieren; **III** *s.* **12.** *allg.* Befehl *m*: **by ~** auf Befehl; **13.** ⚔ Kom'mando *n*: a) Befehl *m*: **word of ~** Kommando(wort) *n*, b) (Ober)Befehl *m*, Befehlsgewalt *f*, Führung *f*: **be in ~** a) (**of**) das Kommando führen (über *acc.*), b) *sport* den Gegner beherrschen; **take ~** das Kommando übernehmen; **14.** ⚔ a) Oberkom'mando *n*, Führungsstab *m*, b) Befehls-, Kom'mandobereich *m*; **15.** *fig.* Gewalt *f*, Herrschaft *f* (**of** über *acc.*); Beherrschung *f*, Meisterung *f* (*Gefühle*): **have ~ of** *Fremdsprache etc.* beherrschen; **his ~ of English** s-e Englischkenntnisse *pl.*; **16.** Verfügung *f* (**of** über *acc.*): **at your ~** zu Ihrer Verfügung; **be** (**have**) **at ~** zur Verfügung stehen (haben).

com·man·dant [ˌkɒmən'dænt] *s.* ⚔ Komman'dant *m*, Befehlshaber *m*.

com·mand car *s.* ⚔ *Am.* Befehlsfahrzeug *n*.

com·man·deer [ˌkɒmən'dɪə] *v/t.* **1.** zum Mili'tärdienst zwingen; **2.** ⚔ requirieren, beschlagnahmen; **3.** F ‚organisieren', sich aneignen.

com·mand·er [kə'mɑ:ndə] *s.* **1.** ⚔ Komman'dant *m* (*e-r Festung, e-s Flugzeugs etc.*), Befehlshaber *m*; Komman'deur *m* (*e-r Einheit*), Führer *m*; *Am.* ⚓ Fre'gattenkapiˌtän *m*: **~-in-chief** Oberbefehlshaber; **2.** ♀ **of the Faithful** *hist.* Beherrscher *m* der Gläubigen (*Sultan*); **3.** *hist.* (*Ordens*)Kom'tur *m*; **com'mand·ing** [-dɪŋ] *adj.* □ **1.** herrschend, gebietend; **2.** *die Gegend* beherrschend: **~ point** strategischer Punkt; **3.** ⚔ kommandierend, befehlshabend; **4.** imponierend, eindrucksvoll; **5.** gebieterisch; **com'mand·ment** [-dmənt] *s.* Gebot *n*, Vorschrift *f*: **the Ten** ♀**s** *bibl.* die Zehn Gebote.

com·mand mod·ule *s. Raumfahrt*: Kom'mandokapsel *f*.

com·man·do [kə'mɑ:ndəʊ] *pl.* **-dos** *s.* ⚔ **1.** Kom'mando(truppe *f*, -einheit *f*) *n*: **~ squad**; **~ raid** Kommandoüberfall *m*; **2.** Angehörige(r) *m* e-s Kom'mandos.

com·mand| pa·per *s. pol. Brit.* (*dem Parlament vorgelegter*) Kabi'nettsbeschluß *m*; **~ per·form·ance** *s. thea.* Aufführung *f* auf königlichen Befehl *od.* Wunsch; **~ post** *s.* ⚔ Befehls-, Gefechtsstand *m*.

com·mem·o·rate [kə'meməreɪt] *v/t.* (ehrend) gedenken (*gen.*); erinnern an (*acc.*): **a monument to ~ a victory** ein Denkmal zur Erinnerung an e-n Sieg; **com·mem·o·ra·tion** [kəˌmemə'reɪʃn] *s.* **1.** Gedenk-, Gedächtnisfeier *f*: **in ~ of** zum Gedächtnis an (*acc.*); **2.** *Brit. univ.* Stiftergedenkfest *n* (*Oxford*); **com'mem·o·ra·tive** [-rətɪv] *adj.* Gedächtnis…, Erinnerungs…: **~ issue** Gedenkausgabe *f* (*Briefmarken etc.*); **~ plaque** Gedenktafel *f*.

com·mence [kə'mens] *v/t. u. v/i.* **1.** beginnen, anfangen; ⚖ *Klage* anhängig machen; **2.** *Brit. univ.* promovieren (**M.A.** zum M.A.); **com'mence·ment** [-mənt] *s.* **1.** Anfang *m*, Beginn *m*; **2.** *Am.* (Tag *m* der) Feier *f* der Verleihung aka'demischer Grade; **com'menc·ing** [-sɪŋ] *adj.* Anfangs…: **~ salary**.

com·mend [kə'mend] *v/t.* **1.** empfehlen, loben: **~ me to …** F da lobe ich mir …; **2.** empfehlen, anvertrauen (**to** *dat.*); **3. ~ o.s.** sich (*als geeignet*) empfehlen; **com'mend·a·ble** [-dəbl] *adj.* □ empfehlens-, lobenswert; **com·men·da·tion** [ˌkɒmen'deɪʃn] *s.* **1.** Empfehlung *f*; **2.** Lob *n*; **com'mend·a·to·ry** [-dətərɪ] *adj.* **1.** empfehlend, Empfehlungs…; **2.** lobend.

com·men·sal [kə'mensəl] *s.* **1.** Tischgenosse *m*; **2.** *biol.* Kommen'sale *m*.

com·men·su·ra·ble [kə'menʃərəbl] *adj.* □ **1.** kommensu'rabel, vergleichbar (**with**, **to** mit); **2.** angemessen, im richtigen Verhältnis; **com'men·su·rate** [-rət] *adj.* □ **1.** gleich groß, von gleicher Dauer (**with** wie); **2.** (**with**, **to**) im Einklang stehend (mit), angemessen *od.* entsprechend (*dat.*).

com·ment ['kɒment] **I** *s.* **1.** Be-, Anmerkung *f*, Stellungnahme *f*, Kommen'tar *m* (**on** zu): **no ~!** kein Kommentar!; **2.** Erläuterung *f*, Kommen'tar *m*, Deutung *f*; Kri'tik *f*; **3.** Gerede *n*; **II** *v/i.* **4.** (**on**) kommentieren (*acc.*), Erläuterungen *od.* Anmerkungen machen (zu); **5.** sich (kritisch) äußern (**on** über *acc.*); **'com·men·tar·y** [-tərɪ] *s.* Kommen'tar *m* (**on** zu): **radio ~** Rundfunkkommentar; **'com·men·tate** [-teɪt] *v/i.* → **comment** 4; **'com·men·ta·tor** [-teɪtə] *s.*

allg., *a. TV etc.*: Kommen'tator *m.*

com·merce ['kɒmɜːs] *s.* **1.** Handel *m*, Handelsverkehr *m*; **2.** Verkehr *m*, 'Umgang *m.*

com·mer·cial [kə'mɜːʃl] **I** *adj.* □ **1.** kommerzi'ell (*a. Theaterstück etc.*), kaufmännisch, geschäftlich, gewerblich, Handels..., Geschäfts...; **2.** handeltreibend; **3.** für den Handel bestimmt, Handels...; **4.** a) in großen Mengen erzeugt, b) mittlerer *od.* niederer Quali'tät, c) nicht (ganz) rein (*Chemikalien*); **5.** handelsüblich: **~ *quality***; **6.** *Radio*, *TV*: Werbe...: **~ *television*** a) Werbefernsehen *n*, b) kommerzielles Fernsehen; **II** *s.* **7.** *Radio, TV*: a) von e-m Sponsor finanzierte Sendung, b) Werbespot *m*; **~ al·co·hol** *s.* handelsüblicher Alkohol, Sprit *m*; **~ art** *s.* Werbegraphik *f*; **~ a·vi·a·tion** *s.* Verkehrsluftfahrt *f*; **~ col·lege** *s.* Wirtschafts(ober)schule *f*; **~ cor·re·spond·ence** *s.* 'Handelskorrespon,denz *f*; **~ court** *s.* ⚖ Handelsgericht *n*; **~ ge·og·ra·phy** *s.* 'Wirtschaftsgeogra,phie *f.*

com·mer·cial·ism [kə'mɜːʃəlɪzəm] *s.* **1.** Handels-, Geschäftsgeist *m*; **2.** Handelsgepflogenheit *f*; **3.** kommerzi'elle Ausrichtung; **com·mer·cial·i·za·tion** [kə,mɜːʃəlaɪ'zeɪʃn] *s.* Kommerzialisierung *f*, Vermarktung *f*, kaufmännische Verwertung *od.* Ausnutzung; **com·mer·cial·ize** [kə'mɜːʃəlaɪz] *v/t.* kommerzialisieren, vermarkten, verwerten, ein Geschäft machen aus; in den Handel bringen.

com·mer·cial| let·ter of cred·it *s.* Akkredi'tiv *n*; **~ loan** *s.* 'Warenkre,dit *m*; **~ man** *s.* [*irr.*] Geschäftsmann *m*; **~ pa·per** *s.* 'Inhaberpa,pier *n* (*bsd. Wechsel*); **~ plane** *s.* Verkehrsflugzeug *n*; **~ room** *s. Brit. Hotelzimmer, in dem Handlungsreisende Kunden empfangen können*; **~ school** *s.* Handelsschule *f*; **~ trav·el·(l)er** *s.* Handlungsreisende(r) *m*; **~ trea·ty** *s.* Handelsvertrag *m*; **~ val·ue** *s.* Handels-, Marktwert *m*; **~ ve·hi·cle** *s.* Nutzfahrzeug *n.*

com·mie ['kɒmɪ] *s.* F Kommu'nist(in).

com·mi·na·tion [,kɒmɪ'neɪʃn] *s.* Drohung *f*; *bsd. eccl.* Androhung *f* göttlicher Strafe; *a.* **~ *service*** Bußgottesdienst *m.*

com·mi·nute ['kɒmɪnjuːt] *v/t.* zerkleinern, zerstückeln; zerreiben: **~*d fracture*** ✱ Splitterbruch *m*; **com·mi·nu·tion** [,kɒmɪ'njuːʃn] *s.* **1.** Zerkleinerung *f*; Zerreibung *f*; **2.** ✱ Splitterung *f*; **3.** Abnutzung *f.*

com·mis·er·ate [kə'mɪzəreɪt] **I** *v/t.* *j-n* bemitleiden, bedauern; **II** *v/i.* Mitleid haben (***with*** mit); **com·mis·er·a·tion** [kə,mɪzə'reɪʃn] *s.* Mitleid *n*, Erbarmen *n.*

com·mis·sar [,kɒmɪ'sɑː] *s.* Kommis'sar *m* (*bsd. Rußland*): ***People's*** 𝟐 Volkskommissar; **,com·mis'sar·i·at** [-'seərɪət] *s.* ⚔ a) Intendan'tur *f*, b) Ver'pflegungsorganisati,on *f*; **com·mis·sar·y** ['kɒmɪsərɪ] *s.* **1.** Kommis'sar *m*, Beauftragte(r) *m*; **2.** *eccl.* bischöflicher Kommis'sar; **3.** 'Volkskommis,sar *m*; **4.** *Am.* a) ⚔ Verpflegungsstelle *f*, b) Restau'rant *n im Filmstudio etc.*

com·mis·sion [kə'mɪʃn] **I** *s.* **1.** Auftrag *m*, Vollmacht *f*; **2.** Bestallung *f*; Bestallungsurkunde *f*; **3.** ⚔ Offi'zierspa,tent *n*: ***hold a*** **~** Offizier sein; ***receive one's*** **~** Offizier werden; **4.** (An)Weisung *f*, Aufgabe *f*; **5.** Auftrag *m*, Bestellung *f*; **6.** Amt *n*, Dienst *m*, Tätigkeit *f*, Betrieb *m*: ***put into*** **~** *Schiff* in Dienst stellen (F *a. Maschine etc.*); ***in*** **~** im Dienst, in Betrieb; ***out of*** **~** a) außer Dienst (*bsd. Schiff*), b) außer Betrieb, nicht funktionierend, kaputt; **7.** ✝ a) Kommissi'on *f*: ***have on*** **~** in Kommission *od.* Konsignation haben, b) Provisi'on *f*, Vergütung *f*: **~ *agent*** Kommissionär *m*, Provisionsvertreter *m*; ***goods on*** **~** Kommissionswaren; ***on a*** **~ *basis*** in Kommission, auf Provisionsgrundlage; ***sell on*** **~** gegen Provision verkaufen; **8.** Ausführung *f*, Verübung *f*; → ***sin*** 1; **9.** Kommissi'on *f*, Ausschuß *m*; Vorstand *m* (*Klub*): ***Royal*** 𝟐 *Brit.* Untersuchungsausschuß; **II** *v/t.* **10.** beauftragen, be'vollmächtigen; **11.** *j-m* e-e Bestellung *od.* e-n Auftrag geben; **12.** in Auftrag geben, bestellen: **~ *a statue***; **~*ed work*** Auftragsarbeit *f*; **13.** ⚔ zum Offi'zier ernennen: **~*ed officer*** (durch Patent bestallter) Offizier; **14.** *Schiff* in Dienst stellen.

com·mis·sion·aire [kə,mɪʃə'neə] *s.* **1.** *Brit.* (livrierter) Porti'er; **2.** ✝ *Am.* Vertreter *m*, Einkäufer *m.*

com·mis·sion·er [kə'mɪʃnə] *s.* **1.** Be'vollmächtigte(r) *m*, Beauftragte(r) *m*; **2.** (Re'gierungs)Kommis,sar *m*: ***High*** 𝟐 Hochkommissar; **3.** Leiter *m* des Amtes: **~ *of police*** Polizeichef *m*; 𝟐 ***for Oaths*** (*etwa*) Notar *m*; **4.** ⚖ beauftragter Richter; **5.** a) Mitglied *n* e-r (Re'gierungs)Kommissi,on, Kommis'sar *m*, b) *pl.* Kommissi'on *f*, Behörde *f.*

com·mis·sure ['kɒmɪ,sjʊə] *s.* **1.** Naht *f*; Band *n* (*bsd. anat.*); **2.** *anat.* Nervenstrang *m.*

com·mit [kə'mɪt] *v/t.* **1.** anvertrauen, über'geben, über'tragen: **~ *to the ground*** beerdigen; **~ *to memory*** auswendig lernen; **~ *to paper*** zu Papier bringen; ⚖ **~ *s.o. to prison*** (***to an institution***) j-n in e-e Strafanstalt (Heil- u. Pflegeanstalt) einweisen; **~ *for trial*** dem zuständigen Gericht zur Hauptverhandlung überstellen; **2.** anvertrauen, empfehlen; **3.** *pol.* an e-n Ausschuß über'weisen; **4.** (***to***) *pol. etc.* verpflichten (zu), binden (an *acc.*); festlegen (auf *acc.*) (*alle a.* ***o.s.*** sich): ***be*** **~*ted*** sich festgelegt haben, gebunden sein; **~*ted writer*** engagierter Schriftsteller; **5.** *Verbrechen etc.* begehen, verüben; **6.** (***o.s.*** sich) kompromittieren; **com'mit·ment** [-mənt] *s.* **1.** (***to***) Verpflichtung *f* (zu), Bindung *f* (an *acc.*): ***without*** **~** unverbindlich; **2.** ✝ Verbindlichkeit *f*; *Am. engS.* Börsengeschäft *n*; **3.** → ***committal*** 2; **4.** *fig.* Engage'ment *n*; **com'mit·tal** [-tl] *s.* **1.** → ***commitment*** 1; **2.** 'Übergabe *f*, Über'weisung *f* (***to*** an *acc.*): **~ *to prison*** (***an institution***) Einlieferung *f* in e-e Strafanstalt (Einweisung *f* in e-e Heil- und Pflegeanstalt); **~ *order*** Haftbefehl *m*, Einweisungsbeschluß *m*; **~ *service*** Bestattung(sfeier) *f*; **3.** Verübung *f*, Begehung *f* (*von Verbrechen etc.*).

com·mit·tee [kə'mɪtɪ] *s.* Komi'tee *n*, Ausschuß *m*, Kommissi'on *f*: ***be*** (*od.* ***sit***) ***on a*** **~** in e-m Ausschuß sein; ***the House goes into*** (*od.* ***resolves itself into a***) 𝟐 *parl.* das Haus konstituiert sich als Ausschuß; **~ *stage*** *parl.* Stadium *n* der Ausschußberatung (*zwischen 2. u. 3. Lesung e-s Gesetzentwurfes*); **~*man***, **~*woman*** Komiteemitglied *n.*

com·mo·di·ous [kə'məʊdjəs] *adj.* □ geräumig.

com·mod·i·ty [kə'mɒdətɪ] *s.* ✝ Ware *f*, ('Handels-, *bsd.* Ge'brauchs)Ar,tikel *m*; *oft pl.* Waren *pl.*: **~ *value*** Waren-, Sachwert *m*; **~ dol·lar** *s. Am.* Warendollar *m*; **~ ex·change** *s.* Warenbörse *f*; **~ mar·ket** *s.* **1.** Warenmarkt *m*; **2.** Rohstoffmarkt *m*; **~ pa·per** *s.* Doku'mententratte *f.*

com·mo·dore ['kɒmədɔː] *s.* ⚓ **1.** *allg.* Kommo'dore *m*; **2.** Präsi'dent *m* e-s Jachtklubs; **3.** Leitschiff *n* (*Geleitzug*).

com·mon ['kɒmən] **I** *adj.* □ → ***commonly***; **1.** gemeinsam (*a.* ⅍), gemeinschaftlich: ***make*** **~ *cause*** gemeinsame Sache machen; **~ *ground*** gleiche Grundlage, Gemeinsamkeit *f* (der Interessen *etc.*); ***that's*** **~ *ground*** darüber besteht Einigkeit; **2.** allgemein, öffentlich: **~ *knowledge*** allgemein bekannt; **~ *rights*** Menschenrechte; **~ *talk*** Stadtgespräch *n*; **~ *usage*** allgemein üblich; **3.** gewöhnlich, üblich, häufig, alltäglich: **~ *coin of the realm*** übliche Landesmünze; **~ *event*** normales Ereignis; **~ *sight*** alltäglicher Anblick; ***a very*** **~ *name*** ein sehr häufiger Name; **~ *as dirt*** häufig, gewöhnlich; **4.** einfach, gewöhnlich: **~ *looking*** von gewöhnlichem Aussehen; ***the*** **~ *people*** das (einfache) Volk; **~ *salt*** Kochsalz *n*; **~ *soldier*** einfacher Soldat; **~ *or garden ...*** F Feld-Wald-u.-Wiesen-...; → ***cold*** 8; **5.** gewöhnlich, gemein: **~ *accent*** ordinäre Aussprache; ***the*** **~ *herd*** die große Masse; **~ *manners*** schlechtes Benehmen; **6.** *ling.* **~ *gender*** doppeltes Geschlecht; **~ *noun*** Gattungsname *m*; **II** *s.* **7.** Gemeindeland *n* (*heute oft mit Parkanlage*): (***right of***) **~** Mitbenutzungsrecht *n*; **~ *of pasturage*** Weiderecht *n*; **8.** *fig.* ***in*** **~** gemeinsam; ***in*** **~ *with*** (genau) wie; ***have s.th. in*** **~ *with*** et. gemein haben mit; ***out of the*** **~** außergewöhnlich, besonders; **9.** → ***commons.***

com·mon·al·ty ['kɒmənltɪ] *s. das* gemeine Volk, Allgemeinheit *f.*

com·mon| car·ri·er → ***carrier*** 2; **~ chord** *s.* ♪ Dreiklang *m*; **~ de·nom·i·na·tor** *s.* ⅍ gemeinsamer Nenner (*a. fig.*).

com·mon·er ['kɒmənə] *s.* **1.** Bürger(licher) *m*; **2.** *Brit.* Stu'dent (*Oxford*), der s-n 'Unterhalt selbst bezahlt; **3.** *Brit.* a) Mitglied *n* des 'Unterhauses, b) Mitglied *n* des Londoner Stadtrats.

com·mon| frac·tion *s.* ⅍ gemeiner Bruch; **~ law** *s.* a) *das gesamte angloamerikanische Rechtssystem* (*Ggs.* ***civil law***), b) *obs. das engl. Gewohnheitsrecht*; **,~-'law** *adj.* gewohnheitsrechtlich: **~ *marriage*** Konsensehe *f*, eheähnliches Zs.-leben; **~ *wife*** Lebensgefährtin *f.*

com·mon·ly ['kɒmənlɪ] *adv.* gewöhnlich, im allgemeinen.

Com·mon Mar·ket *s.* ✝ Gemeinsamer Markt.

com·mon·ness ['kɒmənnɪs] *s.* **1.** All'täglichkeit *f*, Häufigkeit *f*; **2.** Gewöhnlichkeit *f*, ordi'näre Art.

'com·mon|·place **I** *s.* **1.** Gemeinplatz *m*, Plati'tüde *f*; **2.** *et.* All'tägliches; **II** *adj.* all'täglich, 'uninteres,sant, abgedroschen, platt; ≈ **Prayer** *s. eccl.* **1.** die angli'kanische Litur'gie; **2.** (***Book of***) ~ Gebetbuch *n* der angli'kanischen Kirche; ~ **room** [rʊm] *s.* **1.** *univ.* Gemeinschaftsraum *m*: a) ***junior*** ~ für Studenten, b) ***senior*** ~ für Dozenten; **2.** *Schule*: Lehrerzimmer *n*.

com·mons ['kɒmənz] *s. pl.* **1.** *das* gemeine Volk, *die* Bürgerlichen: ***the*** ≈ *parl. Brit.* das Unterhaus; **2.** *bsd. Brit. univ.* Gemeinschaftskost *f*, -essen *n*: ***kept on short*** ~ auf schmale Kost gesetzt.

com·mon| school *s.* staatliche Volksschule; ~ **sense** *s.* gesunder Menschenverstand; **,~-'sen·si·cal** [-'sensɪkl] *adj.* vernünftig; ~ **ser·geant** *s.* Richter *m* u. Rechtsberater *m* des Magi'strats der ***City of London***; ~ **stock** *s.* ✝ *Am.* 'Stamm,aktie(n *pl.*) *f*; **'~·weal** *s.* **1.** Gemeinwohl *n*; **2.** → **'~·wealth** *s.* **1.** Gemeinwesen *n*, Staat *m*; **2.** Repu'blik *f*: ***the*** ≈ *Brit. hist.* die engl. Republik unter Cromwell; **3.** ***British*** ≈ (***of Nations***) *das* Commonwealth, *die* Britische Nationengemeinschaft; ≈ ***of Australia*** *der* Australische Staatenbund; **4.** *Am. Bezeichnung für einige Staaten der USA*.

com·mo·tion [kə'məʊʃn] *s.* **1.** Erschütterung *f*, Aufregung *f*; Aufsehen *n*; **2.** Aufruhr *m*, Tu'mult *m*; → ***civil*** 2; **3.** Wirrwarr *m*.

com·mu·nal ['kɒmjʊnl] *adj.* **1.** Gemeinde…, Kommunal…: ~ ***tax***; **2.** Gemeinschafts…; Volks…: ~ ***aerial*** (*bsd. Am.* ***antenna***) *TV* Gemeinschaftsantenne *f*; ~ ***kitchen*** Volksküche *f*; **3.** *Indien*: Volksgruppen betreffend; **'com·mu·nal·ism** [-nəlɪzəm] *s.* Kommuna'lismus *m* (*Regierungssystem nach Gemeindegruppen*); **'com·mu·nal·ize** [-nəlaɪz] *v/t.* in Gemeindebesitz über'führen, kommunalisieren.

com·mu·nard ['kɒmjʊnəd] *s. sociol.* Kommu'narde *m*.

com·mune¹ [kə'mjuːn] *v/i.* **1.** sich vertraulich besprechen: ~ ***with o.s.*** mit sich zu Rate gehen; **2.** *eccl.* kommunizieren, die (heilige) Kommuni'on *od.* das Abendmahl empfangen.

com·mune² ['kɒmjuːn] *s.* Kom'mune *f* (*a. sociol.*).

com·mu·ni·ca·ble [kə'mjuːnɪkəbl] *adj.* □ **1.** mitteilbar; **2.** ⚕ über'tragbar, ansteckend; **com'mu·ni·cant** [-ənt] **I** *s.* **1.** *eccl.* Kommuni'kant(in); **2.** Gewährsmann *m*, Informant(in); **II** *adj.* **3.** mitteilend; **4.** teilhabend; **com'mu·ni·cate** [-keɪt] **I** *v/t.* **1.** mitteilen (***to*** *dat.*); **2.** (*a.* ⚕) über'tragen (***to*** auf *acc.*); **II** *v/i.* **3.** sich besprechen, Gedanken *etc.* austauschen, in Verbindung stehen, kommunizieren (***with*** mit), sich mitteilen (***with*** *dat.*); **4.** sich in Verbindung setzen (***with*** mit); **5.** in Verbindung stehen, zs.-hängen (***with*** mit): ***these two rooms*** ~ diese beiden Räume haben e-e Verbindungstür; **6.** sich mitteilen (*Erregung etc.*) (***to*** *dat.*); **7.** *eccl.* → ***commune¹*** 2.

com·mu·ni·ca·tion [kə,mjuːnɪ'keɪʃn] *s.* **1.** (***to***) *allg.* Mitteilung *f* (an *acc.*): a) Verständigung *f* (*gen. od.* von), b) Über'mittlung *f e-r Nachricht* (an *acc.*), c) Nachricht *f* (an *acc.*), d) Kommunikati'on *f* (*e-r Idee etc.*); **2.** Kommunikati'on *f*, Gedankenaustausch *m*, Verständigung *f*; (Brief-, Nachrichten)Verkehr *m*; Verbindung *f*: ***be in*** ~ ***with s.o.*** mit j-m in Verbindung stehen; **3.** (*a. phys.*) Über'tragung *f*, Fortpflanzung *f* (***to*** auf *acc.*); **4.** Kommunikati'on *f*, Verkehrsweg *m*, Verbindung *f*, 'Durchgang *m*; **5.** *pl.* a) Fernmelde-, Nachrichtenwesen *n* (*a.* ⚔): ~ ***net*** Fernmeldenetz *n*; ~ ***officer*** Fernmeldeoffizier *m*, b) Verbindungswege *pl.*, Nachschublinien *pl.*; **6.** *pl.* Kommunikati'onswissenschaft *f*; ~ **cen·tre** (*Am.* **cen·ter**) *s.* ⚔ 'Fernmeldezen,trale *f*; ~ **cord** *s.* 🚂 Notleine *f*, -bremse *f*; ~ **en·gi·neer·ing** *s.* 'Nachrichten,technik *f*; **~s gap** *s.* Kommunikati'onslücke *f*; **~s sat·el·lite** *s.* 'Nachrichtensatel,lit *m*; ~ **trench** *s.* ⚔ Verbindungs-, Laufgraben *m*.

com·mu·ni·ca·tive [kə'mjuːnɪkətɪv] *adj.* □ mitteilsam, kommunika'tiv; **com'mu·ni·ca·tor** [-keɪtə] *s.* **1.** Mitteilende(r *m*) *f*; **2.** *tel.* (Zeichen)Geber *m*.

com·mun·ion [kə'mjuːnjən] *s.* **1.** Gemeinschaft *f*; **2.** enge Verbindung; 'Umgang *m*: ***hold*** ~ ***with o.s.*** Einkehr bei sich selbst halten; **3.** Religi'onsgemeinschaft *f*; **4.** *eccl.* ≈, *a.* ***Holy*** ≈ (heilige) Kommuni'on, (heiliges) Abendmahl: ≈ ***cup*** Abendmahlskelch *m*; ≈ ***table*** Abendmahlstisch *m*.

com·mu·ni·qué [kə'mjuːnɪkeɪ] (*Fr.*) *s.* Kommuni'qué *n*.

com·mu·nism ['kɒmjʊnɪzəm] *s.* Kommu'nismus *m*; **'com·mu·nist** [-nɪst] **I** *s.* Kommu'nist(in); **II** *adj.* → **com·mu·nis·tic** [,kɒmjʊ'nɪstɪk] *adj.* kommu'nistisch.

com·mu·ni·ty [kə'mjuːnətɪ] *s.* **1.** Gemeinschaft *f*: ~ ***aerial*** (*bsd. Am.* ***antenna***) Gemeinschaftsantenne *f*; ~ ***spirit*** Gemeinschaftsgeist *m*; ~ ***singing*** Gemeinschaftssingen *n*; **2.** Gemeinde *f*, Körperschaft *f*: ***the mercantile*** ~ die Kaufmannschaft; ~ ***centre*** (*Am.* ***center***) Gemeindezentrum *n*; ~ ***chest***, ~ ***fund*** *Am.* Wohlfahrtsfonds *m*; ~ ***home*** *Brit.* Erziehungsheim *n*; **3.** Gemeinwesen *n*: ***the*** ~ a) die Allgemeinheit, das Volk, b) der Staat; ~ ***ownership*** öffentliches Eigentum; **4.** Gemeinschaft *f*, Gemeinsamkeit *f*; Gleichheit *f*: ~ ***of goods*** *od.* ***property*** (eheliche) Gütergemeinschaft; ~ ***of interest*** Interessengemeinschaft; ~ ***of goods acquired during marriage*** Errungenschaftsgemeinschaft; ~ ***of heirs*** ⚖ Erbengemeinschaft.

com·mu·nize ['kɒmjʊnaɪz] *v/t.* **1.** in Gemeineigentum 'überführen, sozialisieren; **2.** kommu'nistisch machen.

com·mut·a·ble [kə'mjuːtəbl] *adj.* **1.** austauschbar, 'umwandelbar; **2.** *durch Geld* ablösbar; **com·mu·tate** ['kɒmjʊteɪt] *v/t.* ⚡ *Strom* a) wenden, b) gleichrichten; **com·mu·ta·tion** [,kɒmjuː'teɪʃn] *s.* **1.** 'Um-, Austausch *m*, 'Umwandlung *f*; **2.** Ablösung *f*, Abfindung *f*; **3.** ⚖ 'Straf,umwandlung *f*, -milderung *f*; **4.** ⚡ 'Umschaltung *f*, Stromwendung *f*; **5.** 🚂 *etc.* Pendelverkehr *m*: ~ ***ticket*** Zeitkarte *f*; **com'mu·ta·tive** [-ətɪv] *adj.* □ **1.** auswechselbar, Ersatz…, Tausch…; **2.** wechselseitig;

com·mu·ta·tor ['kɒmjʊteɪtə] *s.* ⚡ a) Kommu'tator *m*, Pol-, Stromwender *m*, b) Kol'lektor *m*, c) *mot.* Zündverteiler *m*; Gleichrichter *m*; **com·mute** [kə'mjuːt] **I** *v/t.* **1.** ein-, 'umtauschen, auswechseln; **2.** *Zahlung* 'umwandeln (***into*** in *acc.*), ablösen (***for***, ***into*** durch); **3.** ⚖ *Strafe* umwandeln (***to***, ***into*** in *acc.*); **4.** → ***commutate***; **II** *v/i.* **5.** 🚂 *etc.* pendeln; **com'mut·er** [-tə] *s.* **1.** 🚂 *etc.* Zeitkarteninhaber(in), Pendler *m*: ~ ***belt*** Einzugsbereich *m* (*e-r Stadt*); ~ ***train*** Nahverkehrszug *m*; **2.** → ***commutator***.

com·pact¹ ['kɒmpækt] *s.* Pakt *m*, Vertrag *m*.

com·pact² [kəm'pækt] **I** *adj.* □ **1.** kom'pakt, fest, dicht (zs.-)gedrängt; mas'siv: ~ ***car*** → 6; ~ ***cassette*** Kompaktkassette *f*; **2.** gedrungen; **3.** knapp, gedrängt (*Stil*); **II** *v/t.* **4.** zs.-drängen, -pressen, fest verbinden; zs.-fügen: ***~ed of*** zs.-gesetzt aus; **III** *s.* ['kɒmpækt] **5.** Kom'paktpuder(dose *f*) *m*; **6.** *Am.* Kom'paktwagen *m*; **com'pact·ness** [-nɪs] *s.* **1.** Kom'paktheit *f*, Festigkeit *f*; **2.** *fig.* Knappheit *f*, Gedrängtheit *f* (*Stil*).

com·pan·ion¹ [kəm'pænjən] **I** *s.* **1.** Begleiter(in), Gesellschafter(in); *engS.* Gesellschafterin *f e-r Dame*; **2.** Kame'rad(in), Genosse *m*, Genossin *f*, Gefährte *m*, Gefährtin *f*: ***~-in-arms*** Waffenbruder *m*; ~ ***in misfortune*** Leidensgefährte; ***constant*** ~ ‚ständiger Begleiter' (*e-r Dame*); **3.** Gegen-, Seitenstück *n*, Pen'dant *n*: ~ ***volume*** Begleitband *m*; **4.** Handbuch *n*; **5.** Ritter *m*: ≈ ***of the Bath*** Ritter des Bath-Ordens; **II** *v/t.* **6.** begleiten; **III** *v/i.* **7.** verkehren (***with*** mit); **IV** *adj.* **8.** (dazu) passend, da'zugehörig.

com·pan·ion² [kəm'pænjən] *s.* ⚓ **1.** → ***companion hatch***; **2.** Ka'jütstreppe *f*; **3.** Deckfenster *n*.

com·pan·ion·a·ble [kəm'pænjənəbl] *adj.* □ 'umgänglich, gesellig; **com'pan·ion·a·ble·ness** [-nɪs] *s.* 'Umgänglichkeit *f*; **com'pan·ion·ate** [-nɪt] *adj.* kame'radschaftlich: ~ ***marriage*** Kameradschaftsehe *f*.

com·pan·ion| hatch *s.* ⚓ Ka'jütsklappe *f*, -luke *f*; ~ **lad·der** → ***companion²*** 2.

com·pan·ion·ship [kəm'pænjənʃɪp] *s.* **1.** Kame'radschaft *f*; Gesellschaft *f*; **2.** *typ. Brit.* Ko'lonne *f* von Setzern.

com'pan·ion·way → ***companion²*** 2.

com·pa·ny ['kʌmpənɪ] *s.* **1.** Gesellschaft *f*, Begleitung *f*: ***for*** ~ zur Gesellschaft; ***in*** ~ ***with*** in Gesellschaft von, zusammen mit; ***he is good*** ~ man ist gern mit ihm zusammen; ***I am*** (*od.* ***err***) ***in good*** ~ ich bin in guter Gesellschaft (*wenn ich das tue*); ***keep*** (*od.* ***bear***) ***s.o.*** ~ j-m Gesellschaft leisten; ***part*** ~ a) sich trennen (***with*** von), b) uneinig werden; **2.** Gesellschaft *f*, Besuch *m*, Gäste *pl.*: ***have*** ~ Besuch haben; ***be fond of*** ~ die Geselligkeit lieben; ***see much*** ~ a) viel Besuch haben, b) oft in Gesellschaft gehen; **3.** Gesellschaft *f*, 'Umgang *m*: ***avoid bad*** ~ schlechte Gesellschaft meiden; ***keep*** ~ ***with*** verkehren mit; **4.** ✝ (Handels)Gesellschaft *f*, Firma *f*: ~ ***car*** Firmenwagen *m*; ~ ***law*** Gesellschaftsrecht *n*; ~ ***store*** *Am.* betriebseigenes (Laden)Geschäft; ~ ***union*** *Am.*

Betriebsgewerkschaft *f*; **~'s water** Leitungswasser *n*; → **private** 2, **public** 3; **5.** Innung *f*, Zunft *f*, Gilde *f*; **6.** *thea.* Truppe *f*; **7.** ⚔ Kompa'nie *f*; **8.** ⚓ Mannschaft *f*.

com·pa·ra·ble ['kɒmpərəbl] *adj.* □ (**to**, **with**) vergleichbar (mit): **~ period** Vergleichszeitraum *m*; **com·par·a·tive** [kəm'pærətɪv] **I** *adj.* □ **1.** vergleichend: **~ literature** vergleichende Literaturwissenschaft; **2.** Vergleichs…; **3.** verhältnismäßig, rela'tiv; **4.** beträchtlich, ziemlich: **with ~ speed**; **5.** *ling.* komparativ, Komparativ…; **II** *s.* **6.** *a.* **~ degree** Komparativ *m*; **com·par·a·tive·ly** [kəm'pærətɪvlɪ] *adv.* verhältnismäßig, ziemlich.

com·pare [kəm'peə] **I** *v/t.* **1.** vergleichen (**with** mit): **as ~d with** im Vergleich zu; → **note** 2; **2.** vergleichen, gleichstellen, -setzen: **not to be ~d to** (*od.* **with**) nicht zu vergleichen mit; **3.** *ling.* steigern; **II** *v/i.* **4.** sich vergleichen (lassen), e-n Vergleich aushalten (**with** mit): **~ favo(u)rably with** den Vergleich mit … nicht zu scheuen brauchen; besser sein als; **III** *s.* **5. beyond ~** unvergleichlich; **com'par·i·son** [-'pærɪsn] *s.* **1.** Vergleich *m*: **by ~** vergleichsweise; **in ~ with** im Vergleich mit *od.* zu; **bear ~ with** e-n Vergleich aushalten mit; **beyond** (**all**) **~** unvergleichlich; **2.** Ähnlichkeit *f*; **3.** *ling.* Steigerung *f*; **4.** Gleichnis *n*.

com·part·ment [kəm'pɑːtmənt] *s.* **1.** Ab'teilung *f*; Fach *n*, Feld *n*; **2.** 🚃 (Wagen)Abteil *n*; **3.** ⚓ Schott *n*: → **watertight**; **4.** *parl. Brit.* Punkt *m* der Tagesordnung; **com·part·men·tal·ize** [ˌkɒmpɑːt'mentəlaɪz] *v/t. bsd. fig.* (auf)teilen.

com·pass ['kʌmpəs] **I** *s.* **1.** *phys.* Kompaß *m*: **mariner's ~** ⚓ Schiffskompaß; **points of the ~** *die* Himmelsrichtungen; **2.** *pl. oft* **pair of ~es** Zirkel *m*; **3.** 'Umkreis *m*, 'Umfang *m*, Ausdehnung *f* (*a. fig.*): **within the ~ of** innerhalb; **it is beyond my ~** es geht über m-n Horizont; **4.** Bereich *m*, Gebiet *n*; **5.** ♪ 'Umfang *m* (*Stimme etc.*); **6.** Grenzen *pl.*, Schranken *pl.*: **to keep within ~** in Schranken halten; **II** *v/t.* **7.** erreichen, zu'stande bringen; **8.** planen; *b.s.* anzetteln; **9.** → **encompass**; **~ bear·ing** *s.* ⚓ Kompaßpeilung *f*; **~ box** *s.* ⚓ Kompaßgehäuse *n*; **~ card** *s.* ⚓ Kompaßscheibe *f*, Windrose *f*.

com·pas·sion [kəm'pæʃn] *s.* Mitleid *n*, Erbarmen *n* (**for** mit): **to have** (*od.* **take**) **~** (**on**) Mitleid haben (mit), sich erbarmen (*gen.*); **com'pas·sion·ate** [-ʃənət] *adj.* □ mitleidsvoll: **~ allowance** (gesetzlich nicht verankerte Beihilfe als) Härteausgleich *m*; **~ leave** ⚔ Sonderurlaub *m* aus familiären Gründen.

com·pass| nee·dle *s.* Kompaßnadel *f*; **~ plane** *s.* ⚙ Rundhobel *m*; **~ rose** *s.* ⚓ Windrose *f*; **~ saw** *s.* Stichsäge *f*; **~ win·dow** *s.* ⚠ Rundbogenfenster *n*.

com·pat·i·bil·i·ty [kəmˌpætə'bɪlətɪ] *s.* **1.** Vereinbarkeit *f*; **2.** Verträglichkeit *f*; **3.** *Nachrichtentechnik*: Kompatibili'tät *f*; **com·pat·i·ble** [kəm'pætəbl] *adj.* □ **1.** (mitein'ander) vereinbar, im Einklang (**with** mit); **2.** angemessen (**with** *dat.*); **3.** ⚕ verträglich; **4.** *Nachrichtentechnik*: kompa'tibel.

com·pa·tri·ot [kəm'pætrɪət] *s.* Landsmann *m*, -männin *f*.

com·peer [kɒm'pɪə] *s.* **1.** Standesgenosse *m*; Gleichgestellte(r *m*) *f*: **have no ~** nicht seinesgleichen haben; **2.** Kame'rad(in).

com·pel [kəm'pel] *v/t.* **1.** zwingen, nötigen; **2.** *et.* erzwingen; *a. Bewunderung etc.* abnötigen (**from s.o.** j-m); **3. ~ s.o. to s.th.** j-m et. aufzwingen; **com'pel·ling** [-lɪŋ] *adj.* **1.** zwingend, stark; **2.** 'unwiderˌstehlich; verlockend.

com·pen·di·ous [kəm'pendɪəs] *adj.* □ kurz(gefaßt), gedrängt; **com'pen·di·um** [-əm] *pl.* **-ums**, **-a** [-ə] *s.* **1.** Kom'pendium *n*, Handbuch *n*; **2.** Zs.-fassung *f*, Abriß *m*.

com·pen·sate ['kɒmpenseɪt] **I** *v/t.* **1.** *j-n* entschädigen (**for** für, **by** durch), *Am. a.* bezahlen, entlohnen; **2.** *et.* ersetzen, vergüten (**to s.o.** j-m); **3.** aufwiegen, ausgleichen (*a.* ⚙), *bsd. psych. u.* ⚙ kompensieren; **II** *v/i.* **4.** (**for**) ersetzen (*acc.*); Ersatz leisten (für); wettmachen (*acc.*); **5. ~ for** → 3; **6.** sich ausgleichen *od.* aufheben; **com·pen·sa·tion** [ˌkɒmpen'seɪʃn] *s.* **1.** Entschädigung *f*, (Schaden)Ersatz *m*; **2.** *Am.* Vergütung *f*, Entgelt *n*; **3.** Belohnung *f*; **4.** *pl.* Vorteile *pl.*; **5.** ⚖ Abfindung *f*; Aufrechnung *f*; **6.** ⚗, ⚡, ⚙, *psych.* Kompensati'on *f*; **com·pen·sa·tive** [kəm'pensətɪv] *adj.* **1.** entschädigend, Entschädigungs…; vergütend; **2.** Ersatz…; **3.** kompensierend, ausgleichend; **'com·pen·sa·tor** [-tə] *s.* ⚙ Kompen'sator *m*, Ausgleichsvorrichtung *f*; **com·pen·sa·to·ry** [kəm'pensətərɪ] → **compensative**.

com·père ['kɒmpeə] (*Fr.*) *bsd. Brit.* **I** *s.* Conférenci'er *m*, Ansager(in); **II** *v/t. u. v/i.* konferieren, ansagen (bei).

com·pete [kəm'piːt] *v/i.* **1.** in Wettbewerb treten, sich (mit)bewerben (**for** um); **2.** konkurrieren (*a.* ✝), wetteifern, sich messen (**with** mit); sich behaupten; **3.** *sport* am Wettkampf teilnehmen; kämpfen (**for** um).

com·pe·tence ['kɒmpɪtəns], **'com·pe·ten·cy** [-sɪ] *s.* **1.** (**for**) Befähigung *f* (zu), Tauglichkeit *f* (für); **2.** ⚖ a) Kompe'tenz *f*, Zuständigkeit *f*, Befugnis *f*, b) Zurechnungsfähigkeit *f*; **3.** Auskommen *n*; **'com·pe·tent** [-nt] *adj.* □ **1.** (leistungs)fähig, tüchtig; fachkundig, qualifiziert; **2.** ausreichend, angemessen; **3.** ⚖ a) zuständig, befugt, b) zulässig (*Zeuge*), c) zurechnungs-, geschäftsfähig; **4.** statthaft.

com·pe·ti·tion [ˌkɒmpɪ'tɪʃn] *s.* **1.** Wettbewerb *m*, -kampf *m* (**for** um), *sport a.* Ver'anstaltung *f*, Konkur'renz *f*; **2.** ✝ Konkur'renz *f*: a) Wettbewerb *m*: **open** (**unfair**) **~** freier (unlauterer) Wettbewerb, b) Konkur'renzkampf *m*, c) Konkur'renzfirmen *pl.*; **3.** Preisausschreiben *n*; **4.** Gegner *pl.*, Ri'valen *pl.*, Konkur'renz *f*; **com·pet·i·tive** [kəm'petətɪv] *adj.* □ **1.** konkurrierend, Konkurrenz…, Wettbewerbs…: **~ capacity** ✝ Konkurrenzfähigkeit *f*; **~ sport(s)** Kampfsport *m*; **2.** konkur'renz-, wettbewerbsfähig (*Preise etc.*); **com·pet·i·tive·ness** [kəm'petətɪvnɪs] *s.* ✝ Konkur'renz-, Wettbewerbsfähigkeit *f*; **com·pet·i·tor** [kəm'petɪtə] *s.* **1.** Mitbewerber(in) (**for** um); **2.** ✝ Konkur'rent(in); **3.** *sport* Teilnehmer(in), Ri'vale *m*, Ri'valin *f*.

com·pi·la·tion [ˌkɒmpɪ'leɪʃn] *s.* Kompilati'on *f*: a) Zs.-stellung *f*, b) Sammelwerk *n* (*Buch*); **com·pile** [kəm'paɪl] *v/t.* **1.** zs.-stellen, kompilieren; **2.** *Material* zs.-tragen; **com·pil·er** [kəm'paɪlə] *s.* **1.** Bearbeiter(in), Verfasser(in); **2.** *Computer*: Com'piler *m*.

com·pla·cence [kəm'pleɪsns], **com'pla·cen·cy** [-sɪ] *s.* 'Selbstzuˌfriedenheit *f*, -gefälligkeit *f*; **com'pla·cent** [-nt] *adj.* □ 'selbstzuˌfrieden, -gefällig.

com·plain [kəm'pleɪn] *v/i.* **1.** sich beklagen, sich beschweren (**of**, **about** über *acc.*, **to** bei, **that** daß); **2.** klagen (**of** über *acc.*); **3.** ✝ reklamieren: **~ about** *a. et.* beanstanden; **4.** ⚖ a) klagen, b) (Straf)Anzeige erstatten (**of** gegen); **com'plain·ant** [-nənt] *s.* ⚖ Kläger(in); Beschwerdeführer *m*; **com'plaint** [-nt] *s.* **1.** Klage *f*, Beschwerde *f*, Beanstandung *f*: **make a ~ about** Klage führen über (*acc.*); **2.** ⚖ Klage *f*, *a.* Strafanzeige *f*; **3.** ✝ Reklamati'on *f*, Beanstandung *f*; **4.** ⚕ Beschwerde *f*, Leiden *n*.

com·plai·sance [kəm'pleɪzəns] *s.* Gefälligkeit *f*, Willfährigkeit *f*, Höflichkeit *f*; **com'plai·sant** [-nt] *adj.* □ gefällig, entgegenkommend.

com·ple·ment **I** *v/t.* ['kɒmplɪment] **1.** ergänzen, ver'vollständigen: **~ each other** sich (gegenseitig) ergänzen; **II** *s.* [-mənt] **2.** Ergänzung *f*, Ver'vollständigung *f*; **3.** 'Vollständigkeit *f*, -zähligkeit *f*; **4.** *a.* **full ~** volle Anzahl *od.* Menge; ⚓ volle Besatzung; **5.** *ling.* Ergänzung *f*; **6.** A Komple'ment *n*; **com·ple·men·tal** [ˌkɒmplɪ'mentl] *adj.* □, **com·ple·men·ta·ry** [ˌkɒmplɪ'mentərɪ] *adj.* Ergänzungs…, Komplementär… (*a.* A, *Farben*); (sich) ergänzend.

com·plete [kəm'pliːt] **I** *adj.* □ **1.** 'vollständig, voll'kommen, völlig, ganz, kom'plett: **~ with …** samt (*dat.*), … eingeschlossen; **2.** 'vollzählig, sämtlich; **3.** beendet, fertig; **4.** völlig: **a ~ surprise**; **5.** *obs.* per'fekt; **II** *v/t.* **6.** ver'vollständigen, ergänzen; **7.** beenden, abschließen, fertigstellen, erledigen; **8.** voll'enden, ver'vollkommnen; *Formular* ausfüllen; **com'plete·ly** [-lɪ] *adv.*: **~ automatic** vollautomatisch; **com'plete·ness** [-nɪs] *s.* 'Vollständigkeit *f*, Voll'kommenheit *f*; **com'ple·tion** [-iːʃn] *s.* **1.** Voll'endung *f*, Fertigstellung *f*, Abschluß *m*, Ablauf *m*: (**up**)**on ~ of** nach Vollendung *od.* Ablauf von *od. gen.*; **bring to ~** zum Abschluß bringen, fertigstellen; **~ date** Fertigstellungstermin *m*; **2.** Ver'vollständigung *f*; **3.** (Vertrags- *etc.*)Erfüllung *f*; **4.** Ausfüllung *f* (*e-s Formulars*).

com·plex ['kɒmpleks] **I** *adj.* □ **1.** zs.-gesetzt (*a. ling.*); **2.** kompliziert, verwickelt; **II** *s.* **3.** Kom'plex *m* (*a. psych.*), Gesamtheit *f*, *das* Ganze; **4.** (Ge'bäude- *etc.*)Komˌplex *m*; **5.** ⚗ Kom'plexverbindung *f*; **com·plex·ion** [kəm'plekʃn] *s.* **1.** Gesichtsfarbe *f*, Teint *m*; **2.** *fig.* Aussehen *n*, Anstrich *m*, Cha'rakter *m*: **that puts a different ~ on it** das gibt der Sache ein (ganz) anderes Gesicht; **3.** *fig.* Cou'leur *f*, (po'litische) Richtung; **com·plex·i·ty** [kəm'pleksɪtɪ] *s.* **1.** Komplexi'tät *f* (*a.* A), Kompliziertheit *f*, Vielschichtigkeit *f*; **2.** *et.* Kom'plexes.

com·pli·ance [kəm'plaɪəns] *s.* **1.** Einwilligung *f*, Erfüllung *f*; Befolgung *f* (***with*** *gen.*): ***in ~ with*** gemäß; **2.** Willfährigkeit *f*; **com'pli·ant** [-nt] *adj.* □ willfährig.

com·pli·ca·cy ['kɒmplɪkəsɪ] *s.* Kompliziertheit *f*; **com·pli·cate** ['kɒmplɪkeɪt] *v/t.* komplizieren; **'com·pli·cat·ed** [-keɪtɪd] *adj.* kompliziert; **com·pli·ca·tion** [ˌkɒmplɪ'keɪʃn] *s.* **1.** Komplikati'on *f* (*a.* ✱); **2.** Kompliziertheit *f*.

com·plic·i·ty [kəm'plɪsətɪ] *s.* Mitschuld *f*, Mittäterschaft *f*: ***look of ~*** komplizenhafter Blick.

com·pli·ment I *s.* ['kɒmplɪmənt] **1.** Kompli'ment *n*: ***pay s.o. a ~*** j-m ein Kompliment machen; → ***fish*** 8; **2.** Ehrenbezeigung *f*, Lob *n*: ***do s.o. the ~*** j-m die Ehre erweisen (***of*** zu *inf. od. gen.*); **3.** Empfehlung *f*, Gruß *m*: ***my best ~s*** m-e Empfehlung; ***with the ~s of the season*** mit den besten Wünschen zum Fest; **II** *v/t.* [-ment] **4.** (***on***) beglückwünschen (zu); *j-m* Kompli'mente machen (über *acc.*); **com·pli·men·ta·ry** [ˌkɒmplɪ'mentərɪ] *adj.* **1.** höflich, Höflichkeits…; schmeichelhaft: ***~ close*** Gruß-, Schlußformel *f* (*in Briefen*); **2.** Ehren…: ***~ ticket*** Ehren-, Freikarte *f*; ***~ dinner*** Festessen *n*; **3.** Frei…, Gratis…: ***~ copy*** Freiexemplar *n*; ***~ meals*** kostenlose Mahlzeiten.

com·plot ['kɒmplɒt] **I** *s.* Kom'plott *n*, Verschwörung *f*; **II** *v/i.* sich verschwören.

com·ply [kəm'plaɪ] *v/i.* (***with***) *e-r Bitte etc.* nachkommen *od.* entsprechen, erfüllen (*acc.*), *Regel etc.* befolgen, einhalten: ***he would not ~*** er wollte nicht einwilligen.

com·po ['kɒmpəʊ] (*abbr. für* ***composition***) *s.* Putz *m*, Gips *m*, Mörtel *m etc.*

com·po·nent [kəm'pəʊnənt] **I** *adj.* e-n Teil bildend, Teil…: ***~ part*** → **II** *s.* (Bestand)Teil *m*, ⚙ *a.* 'Baueleˌment *n*.

com·port [kəm'pɔ:t] **I** *v/t.* ***~ o.s.*** sich betragen; **II** *v/i.* ***~ with*** passen zu.

com·pos ['kɒmpəs] → ***compos mentis***.

com·pose [kəm'pəʊz] **I** *v/t.* **1.** *mst pass.* zs.-setzen: ***be ~d of*** bestehen aus; **2.** bilden; **3.** entwerfen, ordnen, zurechtlegen; **4.** aufsetzen, verfassen; **5.** ♪ komponieren; **6.** *typ.* setzen; **7.** *Streit* schlichten; *s-e Gedanken* sammeln; **8.** besänftigen: ***~ o.s.*** sich beruhigen, sich fassen; **9.** ***~ o.s.*** sich anschicken (***to*** zu); **II** *v/i.* **10.** schriftstellern, dichten; **11.** komponieren; **com'posed** [-zd] *adj.*, **com'pos·ed·ly** [-zɪdlɪ] *adv.* ruhig, gelassen; **com'pos·ed·ness** [-zɪdnɪs] *s.* Gelassenheit *f*, Ruhe *f*; **com'pos·er** [-zə] *s.* **1.** ♪ Kompo'nist(in); **2.** Verfasser(in).

com·pos·ing [kəm'pəʊzɪŋ] *adj.* **1.** beruhigend, Beruhigungs…; **2.** *typ.* Setz…: ***~ machine***; ***~ room*** Setzerei *f*; ***~ stick*** Winkelhaken *m*.

com·pos·ite ['kɒmpəzɪt] **I** *adj.* □ **1.** zs.-gesetzt (*a.* ⚘), gemischt; vielfältig; Misch…: ***~ construction*** △ Gemischtbauweise *f*; ***~ metal*** Verbundmetall *n*; **2.** ⚘ Korbblütler…; **II** *s.* **3.** Zs.-setzung *f*, Mischung *f*; **4.** ⚘ Korbblütler *m*; ***~ pho·to·graph*** *s.* 'Fotomonˌtage *f*.

com·po·si·tion [ˌkɒmpə'zɪʃn] *s.* **1.** Zs.-setzung *f* (*a. ling.*), Bildung *f*; **2.** Abfassung *f*, Entwurf *m*, Anordnung *f*, Gestaltung *f*, Aufbau *m*; **3.** Satzbau *m*; Stilübung *f*, Aufsatz *m*, *a.* Über'setzung *f*: ***English ~***; **4.** Schrift(werk *n*) *f*, Dichtung *f*; **5.** ♪ Kompositi'on *f*, Mu'sikstück *n*; **6.** *typ.* Setzen *n*, Satz *m*; **7.** *a.* ⚙, ⚗ Zs.-setzung *f*, Verbindung *f*, 'Mischmateriˌal *n*; **8.** Über'einkunft *f*, Abkommen *n*; **9.** ⚖, ✝ Vergleich *m mit Gläubigern*: ***~ proceedings*** (Konkurs)Vergleichsverfahren *n*; **10.** Wesen *n*, Na'tur *f*, Anlage *f*; **com·pos·i·tor** [kəm'pɒzɪtə] *s. typ.* (Schrift)Setzer *m*.

com·pos men·tis [ˌkɒmpəs'mentɪs] (*Lat.*) *adj.* ⚖ bei klarem Verstand, geschäftsfähig.

com·post ['kɒmpɒst] **I** *s.* Mischdünger *m*, Kom'post *m*; **II** *v/t.* kompostieren.

com·po·sure [kəm'pəʊʒə] *s.* (Gemüts-)Ruhe *f*, Gelassenheit *f*, Fassung *f*.

com·pote ['kɒmpɒt] *s.* **1.** Kom'pott *n*; **2.** Kom'pottschale *f*.

com·pound¹ ['kɒmpaʊnd] *s.* **1.** Lager *n*; **2.** Gefängnishof *m*; **3.** (Tier)Gehege *n*.

com·pound² [kəm'paʊnd] **I** *v/t.* **1.** mischen, mengen; zs.-setzen, vereinigen, verbinden; **2.** (zu)bereiten, herstellen; **3.** in Güte *od.* durch Vergleich beilegen; erledigen; **4.** ⚖, ✝ a) in Raten abzahlen, b) durch einmalige Zahlung regeln: ***~ creditors*** Gläubiger befriedigen; **5.** gegen Schadloshaltung auf Strafverfolgung (*gen.*) verzichten; **6.** verschlimmern, steigern; **II** *v/i.* **7.** *a.* ⚖, ✝ sich (durch Abfindung) einigen *od.* vergleichen (***with*** mit, ***for*** über *acc.*); **III** *s.* ['kɒmpaʊnd] **8.** Zs.-setzung *f*, Mischung *f*; Masse *f*; Präpa'rat *n*; **9.** ⚗ Verbindung *f*; **10.** *ling.* Kom'positum *n*; **IV** *adj.* ['kɒmpaʊnd] **11.** zs.-gesetzt (*a.* ⚘, ✱, *ling.*); ⚡, ⚙ Verbund…(*-dynamo, -motor, -stahl etc.*): ***~ eye*** *zo.* Netz-, Facettenauge *n*; ***~ fracture*** ✱ komplizierter Bruch; ***~ fruit*** ⚘ Sammelfrucht *f*; ***~ interest*** Staffel-, Zinseszinsen *pl.*; ***~ sentence*** *ling.* zs.-gesetzter Satz.

com·pre·hend [ˌkɒmprɪ'hend] *v/t.* **1.** um'fassen, einschließen; **2.** begreifen, verstehen; **ˌcom·pre'hen·si·ble** [-nsəbl] *adj.* begreiflich, verständlich; **ˌcom·pre'hen·sion** [-nʃən] *s.* **1.** 'Umfang *m*; **2.** Einbeziehung *f*; **3.** Begriffsvermögen *n*; Verstand *m*; Verständnis *n*, Einsicht *f*: ***quick*** (***slow***) ***of ~*** schnell (schwer) von Begriff; **4.** *bsd. eccl.* Duldung *f* (*anderer Ansichten*); **ˌcom·pre'hen·sive** [-nsɪv] **I** *adj.* □ **1.** um'fassend; inhaltsreich: (***fully***) ***~ insurance*** *mot.* Vollkaskoversicherung *f*; ***~ school*** Gesamtschule *f*; ***go ~*** F a) die Gesamtschule einführen, b) in e-e Gesamtschule umgewandelt werden; **2.** verstehend: ***~ faculty*** Begriffsvermögen *n*; **II** *s.* **3.** *Brit.* Gesamtschule *f*; **ˌcom·pre'hen·sive·ness** [-nsɪvnɪs] *s.* 'Umfang *m*, Weite *f*; Reichhaltigkeit *f*; *das* Um'fassende.

com·press I *v/t.* [kəm'pres] zs.-drükken, -pressen, komprimieren; **II** *s.* ['kɒmpres] ✱ Kom'presse *f*, 'Umschlag *m*; **com'pressed** [-st] *adj.* **1.** komprimiert, zs.-gepreßt: ***~ air*** Preß-, Druckluft *f*; **2.** *fig.* zs.-gefaßt, gedrängt, gekürzt; **com'press·i·ble** [-səbl] *adj.* komprimierbar; **com'pres·sion** [-eʃn] *s.* **1.** Zs.-pressen *n*, -drücken *n*; Verdichtung *f*, Druck *m*; **2.** *fig.* Zs.-drängung *f*; **3.** ⚙ Druck *m*, Kompressi'on *f*: ***~ mo(u)lding*** Formpressen *n*; ***~-mo(u)lded*** formgepreßt (*Plastik*); **com'pres·sive** [-sɪv] *adj.* zs.-pressend, Preß…, Druck…; **com'pres·sor** [-sə] *s.* **1.** ⚙ Kom'pressor *m*, Verdichter *m*; ✈ Lader *m*; **2.** *anat.* Schließmuskel *m*; **3.** ✱ Druckverband *m*.

com·prise [kəm'praɪz] *v/t.* einschließen, um'fassen, enthalten, beinhalten.

com·pro·mise ['kɒmprəmaɪz] **I** *s.* **1.** Kompro'miß *m*, (gütlicher) Vergleich; Über'einkunft *f*; **II** *v/t.* **2.** durch Kompro'miß regeln; **3.** gefährden, aufs Spiel setzen; beeinträchtigen; **4.** (*a.* ***o.s.*** sich) bloßstellen *od.* kompromittieren; **III** *v/i.* **5.** e-n Kompro'miß schließen, zu e-r Über'einkunft gelangen (***on*** über *acc.*).

comp·trol·ler [kən'trəʊlə] *s.* (staatlicher) Rechnungsprüfer: ***2 General*** *Am.* Präsident *m* des Rechnungshofes.

com·pul·sion [kəm'pʌlʃn] *s.* Zwang *m* (*a. psych.*): ***under ~*** unter Zwang *od.* Druck, gezwungen; **com'pul·sive** [-lsɪv] *adj.* □ zwingend, (*a. psych.*) Zwangs…; **com'pul·so·ry** [-lsərɪ] *adj.* □ obliga'torisch, zwangsmäßig, Zwangs…; bindend; Pflicht…: ***~ auction*** ⚖ Zwangsversteigerung *f*; ***~ education*** allgemeine Schulpflicht; ***~ insurance*** Pflichtversicherung *f*; ***~ military service*** allgemeine Wehrpflicht; ***~ purchase*** ⚖ Enteignung *f*; ***~ subject*** *ped.* Pflichtfach *n*.

com·punc·tion [kəm'pʌŋkʃn] *s.* a) Gewissensbisse *pl.*, b) Reue *f*, c) Bedenken *pl.*: ***without ~***.

com·put·a·ble [kəm'pju:təbl] *adj.* berechenbar; **com·pu·ta·tion** [ˌkɒmpju:'teɪʃn] *s.* Berechnung *f*, 'Überschlag *m*, Schätzung *f*; **com·pute** [kəm'pju:t] **I** *v/t.* berechnen, schätzen, veranschlagen (***at*** auf *acc.*); **II** *v/i.* rechnen; **com'put·er** [-tə] *s.* **1.** (Be)Rechner *m*; **2.** ⚡ Com'puter *m*: ***~ centre*** (*Am.* ***center***) Rechenzentrum *n*; ***~ science*** Informatik *f*; ***~-aided*** computergestützt; ***~-control(l)ed*** computergesteuert; **com'put·er·ize** [-təraɪz] *v/t.* a) auf Com'puter 'umstellen, b) mit Com'putern betreiben.

com·rade ['kɒmrɪd] *s.* **1.** Kame'rad *m*, Genosse *m*, Gefährte *m*: ***~-in-arms*** Waffenbruder *m*; **2.** *pol.* Genosse *m*; **'com·rade·ly** [-lɪ] *adj.* kame'radschaftlich; **'com·rade·ship** [-ʃɪp] *s.* Kame'radschaft *f*.

com·sat ['kɒmsæt] → ***communications satellite***.

con¹ [kɒn] *v/t.* (auswendig) lernen, sich (*dat.*) *et.* einprägen.

con² → ***conn***.

con³ [kɒn] **I** *s.* **1.** Neinstimme *f*; **2.** 'Gegenarguˌment *n*; → ***pro¹*** I; **II** *adv.* (da-)'gegen.

con⁴ [kɒn] *sl.* **I** *adj.* **1.** betrügerisch: ***~ game*** → ***confidence game***; ***~ man*** → 3; **II** *v/t.* **2.** ‚reinlegen': ***~ s.o. out of*** j-n betrügen um; ***~ s.o. into doing s.th.*** j-n (durch Schwindel) dazu bringen, et. zu tun; **III** *s.* **3.** Betrüger *m*; Hochstapler *m*; Ga'nove *m*; **4.** Sträfling *m*.

con·cat·e·nate [kɒn'kætɪneɪt] *v/t.* verketten, verknüpfen; **con·cat·e·na·tion** [kɒnˌkætɪ'neɪʃn] *s.* **1.** Verkettung *f*; **2.**

Kette *f*.

con·cave [ˌkɒnˈkeɪv] **I** *adj.* □ **1.** konˈkav, hohl, ausgehöhlt; **2.** ⚙ hohlgeschliffen, Hohl…: **~ lens** Zerstreuungslinse *f*; **~ mirror** Hohlspiegel *m*; **II** *s.* **3.** (Aus)Höhlung *f*, Wölbung *f*; **con·cav·i·ty** [kɒnˈkævətɪ] → **concave** 3.

con·ceal [kənˈsiːl] *v/t.* (**from** vor *dat.*) verbergen: a) (*a.* ⚙) verdecken, kaschieren, b) verhehlen, verschweigen, verheimlichen, *a.* ⚔ verschleiern, tarnen, c) verstecken: **~ed assets** ✝ verschleierte Vermögenswerte, *Bilanz*: unsichtbare Aktiva; **conˈceal·ment** [-mənt] *s.* **1.** Verbergung *f*, Verheimlichung *f*, Geheimhaltung *f*; **2.** Verborgenheit *f*; **3.** Versteck *n*.

con·cede [kənˈsiːd] **I** *v/t.* **1.** zugestehen, einräumen, zugeben, anerkennen (*a.* **that** daß); **2.** gewähren, einräumen: **~ a point** a) in e-m Punkt nachgeben, b) (**to**) *sport dem Gegner* e-n Punkt abgeben; **~ a goal** ein Tor zulassen; **II** *v/i.* **3.** *sport*, *pol.* F sich geschlagen geben; **conˈced·ed·ly** [-dɪdlɪ] *adv.* zugestandenermaßen.

con·ceit [kənˈsiːt] *s.* **1.** Eingebildetheit *f*, Einbildung *f*, (Eigen)Dünkel *m*: **in my own ~** nach m-r Ansicht; **out of ~ with** überdrüssig (*gen.*); **2.** *obs.* guter *od.* seltsamer Einfall; **conˈceit·ed** [-tɪd] *adj.* □ eingebildet, dünkelhaft, eitel.

con·ceiv·a·ble [kənˈsiːvəbl] *adj.* □ denkbar, erdenklich, begreiflich, vorstellbar: **the best plan ~** der denkbar beste Plan; **conˈceiv·a·bly** [-blɪ] *adv.* es ist denkbar, daß; **con·ceive** [kənˈsiːv] **I** *v/t.* **1.** *biol. Kind* empfangen; **2.** begreifen; sich denken *od.* vorstellen: **~ an idea** auf e-n Gedanken kommen; **3.** er-, ausdenken, ersinnen; **4.** *in Worten* ausdrücken; **5.** *Wunsch* hegen, *(Ab)Neigung* fassen, entwickeln; **II** *v/i.* **6.** (**of**) sich *et.* vorstellen; **7.** empfangen (*schwanger werden*); *zo.* aufnehmen (*trächtig werden*).

con·cen·trate [ˈkɒnsəntreɪt] **I** *v/t.* **1.** konzentrieren (**on**, **upon** auf *acc.*): a) zs.-ziehen, -ballen, massieren, b) *Gedanken etc.* richten; **2.** *fig.* zs.-fassen (**in** in *dat.*); **3.** ⚗ a) sättigen, konzentrieren, b) verstärken, *bsd. Metall* anreichern; **II** *v/i.* **4.** sich konzentrieren (*etc.*; → 1); **5.** sich *an e-m Punkt* sammeln; **III** *s.* **6.** ⚗ Konzenˈtrat *n*; **ˈcon·cen·trat·ed** [-tɪd] *adj.* konzentriert; **con·cen·tra·tion** [ˌkɒnsənˈtreɪʃn] *s.* **1.** Konzentrierung *f*, Konzentratiˈon *f*: a) Zs.-ziehung *f*, -fassung *f*, (Zs.-)Ballung *f*, Massierung *f*, (An)Sammlung *f* (*alle a.* ⚔): **~ camp** Konzentrationslager *n*, b) Hinlenkung *f* auf ˈeinen Punkt, c) (geistige) Sammlung, gespannte Aufmerksamkeit; **2.** ⚗ Konzentratiˈon *f*, Dichte *f*, Sättigung *f*.

con·cen·tric [kɒnˈsentrɪk] *adj.* (□ **~al·ly**) konˈzentrisch.

con·cept [ˈkɒnsept] *s.* **1.** Begriff *m*; **2.** Gedanke *m*, Auffassung *f*, Konzeptiˈon *f*; **con·cep·tion** [kənˈsepʃn] *s.* **1.** *biol.* Empfängnis *f*; **2.** Begriffsvermögen *n*, Verstand *m*; **3.** Begriff *m*, Auffassung *f*, Vorstellung *f*: **no ~ of …** keine Ahnung von …; **4.** Gedanke *m*, Iˈdee *f*; **5.** Plan *m*, Anlage *f*, Konˈzept *n*, Entwurf *m*; Schöpfung *f*; **con·cep·tion·al** [kənˈsepʃənl] *adj.* begrifflich, abˈstrakt; **con·cep·tive** [kənˈseptɪv] *adj.* **1.** begreifend, Begriffs…; **2.** ⚕ empfängnisfähig; **con·cep·tu·al** [kənˈseptjʊəl] → **conceptive** 1.

con·cern [kənˈsɜːn] **I** *v/t.* **1.** betreffen, angehen; interessieren, von Belang sein für: **it does not ~ me** *od.* **I am not ~ed** es geht mich nichts an; **to whom it may ~** an alle, die es angeht; Bescheinigung (*Überschrift auf Urkunden*); **his hono(u)r is ~ed** es geht um s-e Ehre; → **concerned** 1; **2.** beunruhigen: **don't let that ~ you** mache dir deswegen keine Sorgen!; → **concerned** 4; **3. ~ o.s.** (**with**, **about**) sich beschäftigen *od.* befassen (mit); sich kümmern (um); **II** *s.* **4.** Angelegenheit *f*, Sache *f*: **that is no ~ of mine** das ist nicht meine Sache, das geht mich nichts an; **5.** ✝ Geschäft *n*, Unterˈnehmen *n*, Betrieb *m*; → **going** 4; **6.** Beziehung *f*: **have no ~ with** nichts zu tun haben mit; **7.** Interˈesse *n* (**for** für, **in** an *dat.*); **8.** Wichtigkeit *f*, Bedeutung *f*; **9.** Unruhe *f*, Sorge *f*; Bedenken *pl.* (**at**, **about**, **for** um, wegen); **10.** F Ding *n*, Geschichte *f*; **conˈcerned** [-nd] *adj.* □ **1.** betroffen, berührt; **2.** (**in**) beteiligt, interessiert (an *dat.*); verwickelt (in *acc.*): **the parties ~** die Beteiligten; **3.** (**with**, **in**) beschäftigt (mit); handelnd (von); **4.** besorgt (**about**, **at**, **for** um, **that** daß), *a.* (poˈlitisch *od.* soziˈal) engagiert; **5.** betrübt, sorgenvoll; **conˈcern·ing** [-nɪŋ] *prp.* betreffend, betreffs, hinsichtlich (*gen.*), was … betrifft, über (*acc.*), wegen.

con·cert I *s.* [ˈkɒnsət] **1.** ♪ Konˈzert *n*: **~ hall** Konzertsaal *m*; **~ pitch** Kammerton *m*; **at ~ pitch** *fig.* in Höchstform; **screw o.s. up to ~ pitch** *fig.* sich enorm steigern; **up to ~ pitch** *fig.* auf der Höhe, in Form; **2.** [-sɜːt] Einvernehmen *n*, Überˈeinstimmung *f*, Harmoˈnie *f*: **in ~ with** im Einvernehmen *od.* gemeinsam mit; **≗ of Europe** *pol. hist.* Europäisches Konzert; **II** *v/t.* [kənˈsɜːt] **3.** *et.* verabreden, vereinbaren; *Kräfte etc.* vereinigen; **4.** planen; **III** *v/i.* [kənˈsɜːt] **5.** zs.-arbeiten; **con·cert·ed** [kənˈsɜːtɪd] *adj.* **1.** gemeinsam, gemeinschaftlich: **~ action** gemeinsames Vorgehen, konzertierte Aktion; **2.** ♪ mehrstimmig arrangiert.

ˈcon·cert|ˌgo·er *s.* Konˈzertbesucher *m*; **~ grand** *s.* Konˈzertflügel *m*.

con·cer·ti·na [ˌkɒnsəˈtiːnə] *s.* Konzerˈtina *f* (*Ziehharmonika*): **~ door** Falttür *f*; **con·cer·to** [kənˈtʃeətəʊ] *pl.* **-tos** *s.* ♪ (ˈSolo)Konˌzert *n*.

con·ces·sion [kənˈseʃn] *s.* **1.** Zugeständnis *n*, Entgegenkommen *n*; **2.** Genehmigung *f*, Erlaubnis *f*, Gewährung *f*; **3.** amtliche *od.* staatliche Konzessiˈon, Priviˈleg *n*: a) Genehmigung *f*: **mining ~** Bergwerkskonzession, b) *Am.* Gewerbeerlaubnis *f*, c) überˈlassenes Siedlungs- *od.* Ausbeutungsgebiet; **con·ces·sion·aire** [kənˌseʃəˈneə] *s.* ✝ Konzessiˈonsinhaber *m*; **conˈces·sion·ar·y** [-ʃnərɪ] *adj.* Konzessions…; bewilligt; **conˈces·sive** [-esɪv] *adj.* **1.** einräumend; **2.** *ling.* **~ clause** Konzesˈsivsatz *m*.

conch [kɒŋk] *s. zo.* (Schale *f* der) See- *od.* Schneckenmuschel *f*; **con·cha** [ˈkɒŋkə] *pl.* **-chae** [-kiː] *s.* **1.** *anat.* Ohrmuschel *f*; **2.** ⚠ Kuppeldach *n*.

con·chy [ˈkɒntʃɪ] *s. Brit. sl.* Kriegs-, Wehrdienstverweigerer *m* (*von* **conscientious objector**).

con·cil·i·ate [kənˈsɪlɪeɪt] *v/t.* **1.** aus-, versöhnen; beschwichtigen; **2.** *Gunst etc.* gewinnen; **3.** ausgleichen; in Einklang bringen; **con·cil·i·a·tion** [kənˌsɪlɪˈeɪʃn] *s.* **1.** Versöhnung *f*, Schlichtung *f*: **~ board** Schlichtungsausschuß *m*; **2.** Ausgleich *m*: **debt ~** Schuldenausgleich; **conˈcil·i·a·tor** [-tə] *s.* Vermittler *m*, Schlichter *m*; **conˈcil·i·a·to·ry** [-ɪətərɪ] *adj.* versöhnlich, vermittelnd, Versöhnungs…

con·cin·ni·ty [kənˈsɪnətɪ] *s.* Feinheit *f*, Eleˈganz *f* (*Stil*).

con·cise [kənˈsaɪs] *adj.* □ kurz, gedrängt, knapp, präˈgnant: **~ dictionary** Handwörterbuch *n*; **conˈcise·ness** [-nɪs] *s.* Kürze *f*, Präˈgnanz *f*.

con·clave [ˈkɒnkleɪv] *s.* **1.** *R.C.* Konˈklave *n*; **2.** geheime Sitzung.

con·clude [kənˈkluːd] **I** *v/t.* **1.** beenden, zu Ende führen; (be-, ab)schließen: **to be ~d** Schluß folgt; **he ~d by saying** zum Schluß sagte er (noch); **2.** *Vertrag etc.* (ab)schließen; **3.** schließen, folgern (**from** aus); **4.** beschließen, entscheiden; **II** *v/i.* **5.** schließen, enden, aufhören (**with** mit); **conˈclud·ing** [-dɪŋ] *adj.* (ab)schließend, End…, Schluß…; **conˈclu·sion** [-uːʒn] *s.* **1.** (Ab)Schluß *m*, Ende *n*: **bring to a ~** zum Abschluß bringen; **in ~** zum Schluß, schließlich; **2.** (*Vertrags- etc.*)Abschluß *m*: **~ of peace** Friedensschluß *m*; **3.** Schluß *m*, (Schluß)Folgerung *f*: **come to the ~** zu dem Schluß *od.* der Überzeugung kommen; **draw a ~** e-n Schluß ziehen; **jump** *od.* **rush to ~s** voreilige Schlüsse ziehen; **4.** Beschluß *m*, Entscheidung *f*; **5.** Ausgang *m*, Folge *f*, Ergebnis *n*; **6. try ~s with** sich *od.* s-e Kräfte messen mit; **conˈclu·sive** [-uːsɪv] *adj.* □ schlüssig, endgültig, entscheidend, überˈzeugend, maßgebend: **~ evidence** ⚖ schlüssiger Beweis; **conˈclu·sive·ness** [-uːsɪvnɪs] *s.* Endgültigkeit *f*, Triftigkeit *f*; Schlüssigkeit *f*, Beweiskraft *f*.

con·coct [kənˈkɒkt] *v/t.* zs.-brauen (*a. fig.*); *fig.* aushecken, sich ausdenken; **conˈcoc·tion** [-kʃn] *s.* **1.** (Zs.-)Brauen *n*, Bereiten *n*; **2.** Mischung *f*, Trank *m*; Gebräu *n*; **3.** *fig.* Aushecken *n*, Ausbrüten *n*; **4.** *fig.* Gebräu *n*; Erfindung *f*: **~ of lies** Lügengewebe *n*.

con·com·i·tance [kənˈkɒmɪtəns], **conˈcom·i·tan·cy** [-sɪ] *s.* **1.** Zs.-bestehen *n*, Gleichzeitigkeit *f*; **2.** *eccl.* Konkomiˈtanz *f*; **conˈcom·i·tant** [-nt] **I** *adj.* □ begleitend, Begleit…, gleichzeitig; **II** *s.* Begleiterscheinung *f*, -umstand *m*.

con·cord [ˈkɒŋkɔːd] *s.* **1.** Eintracht *f*, Einklang *m*; Überˈeinstimmung *f* (*a. ling.*); **2.** ♪ Zs.-klang *m*, Harmoˈnie *f*.

con·cord·ance [kənˈkɔːdəns] *s.* **1.** Überˈeinstimmung *f*; **2.** Konkorˈdanz *f*; **con·cord·ant** [kənˈkɔːdənt] *adj.* □ (**with**) überˈeinstimmend (mit), entsprechend (*dat.*); harˈmonisch (*a.* ♪); **con·cor·dat** [kɒnˈkɔːdæt] *s. eccl.* Konkorˈdat *n*.

con·course [ˈkɒŋkɔːs] *s.* **1.** Zs.-treffen *n*; **2.** Ansammlung *f*, Auflauf *m*, Menge *f*; **3.** a) *Am.* Fahrweg *m od.* Promeˈnadeplatz *m* (*im Park*), b) Bahnhofshalle *f*, c) freier Platz.

con·crete [kən'kri:t] **I** *v/t.* **1.** zu e-r festen Masse verbinden, zs.-ballen *od.* vereinigen; **2.** ['kɒnkri:t] ⚙ betonieren; **II** *v/i.* **3.** sich zu e-r festen Masse verbinden; **III** *adj.* □ ['kɒnkri:t] **4.** kon'kret (*a. ling., phls.,* ♪ *etc.*), greifbar, wirklich, dinglich; **5.** fest, dicht, kom'pakt; **6.** A benannt; **7.** ⚙ betoniert, Beton...; **IV** *s.* ['kɒnkri:t] **8.** kon'kreter Begriff: ***in the ~*** im konkreten Sinne, in Wirklichkeit; **9.** ⚙ Be'ton *m*: **~ *jungle*** Betonwüste *f*; **con'cre·tion** [-i:ʃn] *s.* **1.** Zs.-wachsen *n*, Verwachsung *f*; **2.** Festwerden *n*; Verhärtung *f*, feste Masse; **3.** Häufung *f*; **4.** ⚕ Absonderung *f*, Stein *m*, Knoten *m*; **con·cre·tize** ['kɒnkri:taɪz] *v/t.* konkretisieren.

con·cu·bi·nage [kɒn'kju:bɪnɪdʒ] *s.* Konkubi'nat *n*, wilde Ehe; **con·cu·bine** ['kɒŋkjʊbaɪn] *s.* **1.** Konku'bine *f*, Mä'tresse *f*; **2.** Nebenfrau *f*.

con·cu·pis·cence [kən'kju:pɪsns] *s.* Begierde *f*, Lüsternheit *f*; **con'cu·pis·cent** [-nt] *adj.* lüstern.

con·cur [kən'kɜ:] *v/i.* **1.** zs.-treffen, -fallen; **2.** mitwirken, beitragen (***to*** zu); **3.** (***with s.o., in s.th.***) über'einstimmen, gleicher Meinung sein (mit j-m, in e-r Sache), beipflichten (j-m, e-r Sache); **con'cur·rence** [-'kʌrəns] *s.* **1.** Zs.-treffen *n*; **2.** Mitwirkung *f*; **3.** Zustimmung *f*, Einverständnis *n*; **4.** A Schnittpunkt *m*; **con'cur·rent** [-'kʌrənt] **I** *adj.* □ **1.** gleichzeitig: **~ *condition*** ✝ Zug um Zug zu erfüllende Bedingung; **~ *sentence*** ⚖ gleichzeitige Verbüßung zweier Freiheitsstrafen; **2.** gemeinschaftlich; **3.** mitwirkend; **4.** über'einstimmend; **5.** A durch 'einen Punkt laufend; **II** *s.* **6.** Be'gleit,umstand *m*.

con·cuss [kən'kʌs] *v/t. mst fig.* erschüttern; **con'cus·sion** [-ʌʃn] *s.* (*a.* ⚕ Gehirn)Erschütterung *f*: **~ *fuse*** ⚔ Aufschlagzünder *m*; **~ *spring*** ⚙ Stoßdämpfer *m*.

con·demn [kən'dem] *v/t.* **1.** verdammen, verurteilen, miß'billigen, tadeln: ***his looks ~ him*** sein Aussehen verrät ihn; **2.** ⚖ verurteilen (***to death*** zum Tode); *fig. a.* verdammen (***to*** zu): **~*ed cell*** Todeszelle *f*; → ***cost*** 4; **3.** ⚖ als verfallen erklären, beschlagnahmen; *Am.* (zu öffentlichen Zwecken) enteignen; **4.** verwerfen; für gebrauchsunfähig *od.* unbewohnbar *od.* gesundheitsschädlich *od.* seeuntüchtig erklären; *Schwerkranke* aufgeben: **~*ed building*** abbruchreifes Gebäude; **con'dem·na·ble** [-mnəbl] *adj.* verdammenswert, verwerflich, sträflich; **con·dem·na·tion** [ˌkɒndem'neɪʃn] *s.* **1.** Verurteilung *f* (*a.* ⚖), Verdammung *f*, 'Mißbilligung *f*; **2.** Verwerfung *f*; Untauglichkeitserklärung *f*; **3.** Beschlagnahme *f*; *Am.* Enteignung *f*; **con'dem·na·to·ry** [-mnətərɪ] *adj.* verurteilend; verdammend.

con·den·sa·ble [kən'densəbl] *adj. phys.* kondensierbar; **con·den·sa·tion** [ˌkɒnden'seɪʃn] *s.* **1.** *bsd. phys.* Verdichtung *f*, Kondensati'on *f* (*Gase etc.*); Konzentrati'on *f* (*Licht*); **2.** Zs.-drängung *f*, Anhäufung *f*; **3.** *fig.* Zs.-fassung *f*, (Ab-)Kürzung *f*; **con·dense** [kən'dens] **I** *v/t.* **1.** *bsd. phys. Gase etc.* verdichten, kondensieren, niederschlagen; eindicken: **~*d milk*** Kondensmilch *f*; **2.** *fig.* zs.-drängen, -fassen; zs.-streichen, kürzen; **II** *v/i.* **3.** sich verdichten; flüssig werden; **con·dens·er** [kən'densə] *s.* **1.** ⚡, ⚙, *phys.* Konden'sator *m*; **2.** Kühlrohr *n*.

con·dens·ing| coil [kən'densɪŋ] *s.* ⚙ Kühlschlange *f*; **~ *lens*** *s. opt.* Sammel-, Kondensati'onslinse *f*.

con·de·scend [ˌkɒndɪ'send] *v/i.* **1.** sich her'ablassen, geruhen (***to*** [*mst inf.*] zu [*mst inf.*]); **2.** *b.s.* sich (soweit) erniedrigen (***to do*** zu tun); **3.** leutselig sein (***to*** gegen); **ˌcon·de'scend·ing** [-dɪŋ] *adj.* □ her'ablassend, gönnerhaft; **ˌcon·de'scen·sion** [-nʃn] *s.* Her'ablassung *f*, gönnerhaftes Wesen.

con·dign [kən'daɪn] *adj.* □ gebührend, angemessen (*Strafe*).

con·di·ment ['kɒndɪmənt] *s.* Würze *f*, Gewürz *n*.

con·di·tion [kən'dɪʃn] **I** *s.* **1.** Bedingung *f*, Vor'aussetzung *f*: ***on ~ that*** unter der Bedingung, daß; vorausgesetzt, daß; ***on no ~*** unter keinen Umständen, keinesfalls; ***to make it a ~*** es zur Bedingung machen; **2.** ⚖, ✝ (*Vertrags- etc.*) Bedingung *f*, Bestimmung *f*; Vorbehalt *m*, Klausel *f*; **3.** Zustand *m*, Verfassung *f*, Beschaffenheit *f*; *sport* Kondi'tion *f*, Form *f*: ***out of ~*** in schlechter Verfassung; ***in good ~*** gut in Form (*Person, Pferd etc.*), in gutem Zustand (*Sachen*); **4.** (*a.* Fa'milien)Stand *m*, Stellung *f*, Rang *m*: ***change one's ~*** heiraten; **5.** *pl.* 'Umstände *pl.*, Verhältnisse *pl.*, Lage *f*: ***weather ~s*** Witterung *f*; ***working ~s*** Arbeitsbedingungen; **6.** *Am. ped.* (Gegenstand *m* der) Nachprüfung *f*; **II** *v/t.* **7.** bedingen, bestimmen; regeln, abhängig machen: → ***conditioned***; **8.** *fig.* formen, gestalten; **9.** gewöhnen (***to*** an *acc.*, zu *tun*); **10.** *Tiere* in Form bringen; *Sachen* herrichten, in'stand setzen; ⚙ konditionieren, in den *od.* e-n (*gewünschten*) Zustand bringen; *fig. j-n* programmieren (***to, for*** auf *acc.*); **11.** ✝ (*bsd. Textil*)*Waren* prüfen; **12.** *Am. ped.* e-e Nachprüfung auferlegen (*dat.*); **con'di·tion·al** [-ʃənl] **I** *adj.* □ **1.** (***on***) bedingt (durch), abhängig (von), eingeschränkt (durch); unverbindlich; ✝ unter Eigentumsvorbehalt (*Verkauf*): **~ *discharge*** ⚖ bedingte Entlassung; ***make ~ on*** abhängig machen von; **2.** *ling.* konditio'nal: **~ *clause*** → 3 a; **~ *mood*** → 3 b; **II** *s.* **3.** *ling.* a) Bedingungs-, Konditio'nalsatz *m*, b) Bedingungsform *f*, Konditio'nalis *m*, c) Be'dingungspar,tikel *f*; **con'di·tion·al·ly** [-nəlɪ] *adv.* bedingungsweise; **con'di·tioned** [-nd] *adj.* **1.** (***by***) bedingt (durch), abhängig (von): **~ *reflex*** *psych.* bedingter Reflex; **2.** (so) beschaffen *od.* geartet; in ... Verfassung.

con·do ['kɒndəʊ] *s. Am.* F Eigentumswohnung *f*.

con·do·la·to·ry [kən'dəʊlətərɪ] *adj.* Beileids..., Kondolenz...; **con·dole** [kən'dəʊl] *v/i.* Beileid bezeigen, kondolieren (***with s.o. on s.th.*** j-m zu et.); **con'do·lence** [-əns] *s.* Beileid *n*, Kondo'lenz *f*.

con·dom ['kɒndəm] *s.* Kon'dom *n, m*, Präserva'tiv *n*.

con·do·min·i·um [ˌkɒndə'mɪnɪəm] *s.* **1.** *pol.* Kondo'minium *n*; **2.** *Am.* a) Eigentumswohnanlage *f*, b) *a.* **~ *apartment*** Eigentumswohnung *f*.

con·do·na·tion [ˌkɒndəʊ'neɪʃn] *s.* Verzeihung *f* (*bsd. ehelicher Untreue*); stillschweigende Duldung; **con·done** [kən'dəʊn] *v/t.* verzeihen.

con·dor ['kɒndɔ:] *s. orn.* 'Kondor *m*.

con·duce [kən'dju:s] *v/i.* (***to***) dienen, führen, beitragen (zu); förderlich sein (*dat.*); **con'du·cive** [-sɪv] *adj.* dienlich, förderlich (***to*** *dat.*).

con·duct I *v/t.* [kən'dʌkt] **1.** führen, (ge)leiten; → ***tour*** 1; **2.** (be)treiben, handhaben; führen, leiten, verwalten; **3.** *Feldzug, Krieg, Prozeß etc.* führen; **4.** ♪ dirigieren; **5.** ⚡, *phys.* leiten; **6. ~ *o.s.*** sich betragen *od.* benehmen, sich (auf)führen; **II** *s.* ['kɒndʌkt] **7.** Führung *f*, Leitung *f*, Verwaltung *f*; Handhabung *f*; **8.** *fig.* Führung *f*, Betragen *n*; Verhalten *n*, Haltung *f*: **~ *sheet*** Strafregister(auszug *m*) *n*; **con'duct·ance** [-təns], **con·duct·i·bil·i·ty** [kən,dʌktɪ'bɪlətɪ] *s.* ⚡, *phys.* Leitfähigkeit *f*; **con'duct·i·ble** [-tɪbl] *adj.* ⚡, *phys.* leitfähig; **con'duct·ing** [-tɪŋ] *adj.* ⚡, *phys.* Leit..., Leitungs...: **~ *wire*** Leitungsdraht *m*; **con'duc·tion** [-kʃn] *s. oft* ⚙, *phys.* Leitung *f*, (Zu)Führung *f*, Über'tragung *f*; **con'duc·tive** [-tɪv] *adj. phys.* leitend, leitfähig; **con·duc·tiv·i·ty** [ˌkɒndʌk'tɪvətɪ] *s.* ⚡, *phys.* Leitfähigkeit *f*; **con'duc·tor** [-tə] *s.* **1.** Führer *m*, Leiter *m*; **2.** ♪ Diri'gent *m*; **3.** (Bus- *etc.*)Schaffner *m*; *Am.* 🚂 Zugbegleiter *m*; **4.** ⚡, *phys.* Leiter *m*; Ader *f* (*Kabel*); *Am. a.* Blitzableiter *m*; **con'ductress** [-trɪs] *s.* Schaffnerin *f*.

con·duit ['kɒndɪt] *s.* **1.** Rohrleitung *f*, Röhre *f*; Ka'nal *m* (*a. fig.*); **2.** Leitung *f* (*a. fig.*); **3.** ⚡ a) Rohrkabel *n*, b) Isolierrohr *n* (*für Leitungsdrähte*); **~ *pipe*** *s.* Leitungsrohr *n*.

cone [kəʊn] *s.* **1.** A *u. fig.* Kegel *m*: **~ *of fire*** Feuergarbe *f*; **~ *of rays*** Strahlenbündel *n*; **~ *sugar*** Hutzucker *m*; **2.** ⚙ Kegel *m*, Konus *m* (*a.* ⚡): **~ *drive*** Stufen(scheiben)antrieb *m*; **~ *friction clutch*** Reibungskupplung *f*; **~ *valve*** Kegelventil *n*; **3.** Bergkegel *m*; **4.** ⚘ (Tannen- *etc.*)Zapfen *m*; **5.** Waffeltüte *f für Speiseeis*; **coned** [-nd] *adj.* kegelförmig.

con·fab ['kɒnfæb] F *abbr. für* ***confabulation*** *u.* ***confabulate***; **con·fab·u·late** [kən'fæbjʊleɪt] *v/i.* plaudern; **con·fab·u·la·tion** [kən,fæbjʊ'leɪʃn] *s.* **1.** Plaude'rei *f*; **2.** *psych.* Konfabulati'on *f*.

con·fec·tion [kən'fekʃn] *s.* **1.** Kon'fekt *n*, Süßwaren *pl.*, *mit Zucker* Eingemachtes *n*; **2.** 'Damen,modear,tikel *m* (*Kleid, Hut etc.*); **con'fec·tion·er** [-nə] *s.* Kon'ditor *m*: **~*'s sugar*** *Am.* Puderzucker *m*; **con'fec·tion·er·y** [-nərɪ] *s.* **1.** Süßigkeiten *pl.*, Kon'ditorwaren *pl.*; **2.** Süßwarengeschäft *n*, Kondito'rei *f*.

con·fed·er·a·cy [kən'fedərəsɪ] *s.* **1.** Bündnis *n*, Bund *m*; **2.** Staatenbund *m*; **3.** ♀ *Am.* Konföderati'on *f* (*der Südstaaten im Bürgerkrieg*); **4.** Verschwörung *f*; **con'fed·er·ate** [-rət] **I** *adj.* **1.** verbündet, verbunden, Bundes...: ♀ *Am.* zur Konföderation der Südstaaten gehörig; **2.** mitschuldig; **II** *s.* **3.** Verbündete(r) *m*, Bundesgenosse *m*: ♀ *Am. hist.* Konföderierte(r) *m*, Südstaatler *m*; **4.** Kom'plize *m*, Helfershelfer *m*; **III** *v/t. u. v/i.* [-dəreɪt] **5.** (sich) verbünden *od.* vereinigen *od.* zs.-schließen; **con·fed·er·a·tion** [kənˌfedə'reɪʃn] *s.* **1.** Bund *m*, Bündnis *n*; Zs.-schluß *m*; **2.** Staatenbund *m*: ***Swiss* ~** (Schweizer) Eidgenossenschaft *f*.

con·fer [kən'fɜː] **I** *v/t.* **1.** *Titel etc.* verleihen, er-, zuteilen, über'tragen, *Gunst* erweisen (***on, upon*** *dat.*); **2.** *nur noch Imperativ, abbr.* ***cf.*** vergleiche; **II** *v/i.* **3.** sich beraten, Rücksprache nehmen, verhandeln (***with*** mit); **con·fer·ee** [ˌkɒnfə'riː] *s. Am.* **1.** Konfe'renzteilnehmer *m*; **2.** Empfänger *m e-s Titels etc.*; **con·fer·ence** ['kɒnfərəns] *s.* **1.** Konfe'renz *f*: a) Tagung *f*, Sitzung *f*, Zs.-kunft *f*, b) Besprechung *f*, Beratung *f*, Verhandlung *f*: ***at the* ~** auf der Konferenz *od.* Tagung; ***in* ~** bei e-r Besprechung (***with*** mit); **~ *call*** *teleph.* Sammel-, Konferenzgespräch *n*; **2.** Verband *m*; *Am. sport* Liga *f*; **con'fer·ment** [-mənt] *s.* Verleihung *f* (***on, upon*** an *acc.*).

con·fess [kən'fes] **I** *v/t.* **1.** *Schuld etc.* bekennen, (ein)gestehen; anerkennen, zugeben (*a.* ***that*** daß); **2.** *eccl.* a) beichten, b) *j-m* die Beichte abnehmen; **II** *v/i.* **3.** (***to***) (ein)gestehen (*acc.*), sich schuldig bekennen (*gen. od.* an *dat.*); **4.** *eccl.* beichten; **con'fessed** [-st] *adj.* ☐ zugestanden; erklärt: ***a* ~ *enemy*** ein erklärter Gegner; **con'fess·ed·ly** [-sɪdlɪ] *adv.* zugestandenermaßen; **con'fes·sion** [-eʃn] *s.* **1.** Geständnis *n* (*a.* ⚖), Bekenntnis *n*: ***by*** (*od.* ***on***) ***his own* ~** nach (s-m) eigenen Geständnis; **2.** Einräumung *f*, Zugeständnis *n*; **3.** ⚖ *Zivilrecht*: Anerkenntnis *n*; **4.** *eccl.* Beichte *f*: ***dying* ~** Geständnis *n* auf dem Sterbebett; **5.** *eccl.* Konfessi'on *f*: a) Glaubensbekenntnis *n*, b) Glaubensgemeinschaft *f*; **con'fes·sion·al** [-eʃənl] **I** *adj.* konfessio'nell, Bekenntnis...; Beicht...; **II** *s.* Beichtstuhl *m*; **con'fes·sor** [-sə] *s.* **1.** (Glaubens)Bekenner *m*; **2.** *eccl.* Beichtvater *m*.

con·fet·ti [kən'fetɪ] (*Ital.*) *s. pl. sg. konstr.* Kon'fetti *n*.

con·fi·dant [ˌkɒnfɪ'dænt] *s.* Vertraute(r) *m*, Mitwisser *m*; **ˌcon·fi'dante** [-'dænt] *s.* Vertraute *f*, Mitwisserin *f*.

con·fide [kən'faɪd] **I** *v/i.* **1.** sich anvertrauen; (ver)trauen (***in*** *dat.*); **II** *v/t.* (***to***) **2.** vertraulich mitteilen, anvertrauen (*dat.*); **3.** *j-n* betrauen mit.

con·fi·dence ['kɒnfɪdəns] *s.* **1.** (***in***) Vertrauen *n* (auf *acc.*, zu), Zutrauen *n* (zu): ***have*** (*od.* ***place***) **~ *in s.o.*** zu j-m Vertrauen haben; ***take s.o. into one's* ~** j-n ins Vertrauen ziehen; ***be in s.o.'s* ~** j-s Vertrauen genießen; ***in* ~** vertraulich; **2.** Selbstvertrauen *n*, Zuversicht *f*; Über'zeugung *f*; **3.** vertrauliche Mitteilung, Geheimnis *n*; → ***vote*** 1; **~ *game*** *s.*, **~ *trick*** *s.* **1.** a) (aufgelegter) Schwindel, b) Hochstape'lei *f*; **~ *man*** *s.* [*irr.*], **~ *trick·ster*** *s.* **1.** a) Betrüger *m*, b) Hochstapler *m*; **2.** *weitS.* Ga'nove *m*.

con·fi·dent ['kɒnfɪdənt] *adj.* ☐ **1.** (***of, that***) über'zeugt (von, daß), gewiß, sicher (*gen.*, daß); **2.** vertrauensvoll; **3.** zuversichtlich, getrost; **4.** selbstsicher; **5.** eingebildet, kühn; **con·fi·den·tial** [ˌkɒnfɪ'denʃəl] *adj.* ☐ **1.** vertraulich, geheim; **2.** in'tim, vertraut, Vertrauens...: **~ *agent*** Geheimagent *m*; **~ *clerk*** † Prokurist *m*; **~ *secretary*** Privatsekretär(in); **con·fi·den·tial·ly** [ˌkɒnfɪ'denʃəlɪ] *adv.* im Vertrauen: **~ *speaking*** unter uns gesagt; **con·fid·ing** [kən'faɪdɪŋ] *adj.* ☐ vertrauensvoll, zutraulich.

con·fig·u·ra·tion [kənˌfɪgjʊ'reɪʃn] *s.* **1.** Gestalt(ung) *f*, Bau *m*, Struk'tur *f*; Anordnung *f*, Stellung *f*; **2.** *ast.* Konfigurati'on *f*, A'spekt *m*.

con·fine I *s.* ['kɒnfaɪn] *mst pl.* **1.** Grenze *f*, Grenzgebiet *n*; *fig.* Rand *m*, Schwelle *f*; **II** *v/t.* [kən'faɪn] **2.** begrenzen; be-, einschränken (***to*** auf *acc.*): **~ *o.s. to*** sich beschränken auf; ***be* ~*d to*** beschränkt sein auf (*acc.*); **3.** einsperren, einschließen: **~*d to bed*** bettlägerig; **~*d to one's room*** ans Zimmer gefesselt; ***be* ~*d to barracks*** Kasernenarrest haben, die Kaserne nicht verlassen dürfen; **4.** *pass.* (***of***) niederkommen (mit), entbunden werden (von); **con'fined** [-nd] *adj.* **1.** beschränkt *etc.* (→ ***confine*** 2, 3); **2.** ⚕ verstopft; **con'fine·ment** [-mənt] *s.* **1.** Beschränkung *f* (***to*** auf *acc.*); Beengtheit *f*; Gebundenheit *f*; **2.** Haft *f*, Gefangenschaft *f*; Ar'rest *m*: ***close* ~** strenge Haft; ***solitary* ~** Einzelhaft; **3.** Niederkunft *f*, Wochenbett *n*.

con·firm [kən'fɜːm] *v/t.* **1.** *Nachricht, Auftrag, Wahrheit etc.* bestätigen; **2.** *Entschluß* bekräftigen; bestärken (***s.o. in s.th.*** j-n in e-r Sache); **3.** *Macht etc.* festigen; **4.** *eccl.* konfirmieren; *R.C.* firmen; **con'firm·a·ble** [-məbl] *adj.* zu bestätigen(d); **con·firm·and** ['kɒnfəmænd] *s. eccl.* a) Konfir'mand(in), b) *R.C.* Firmling *m*; **con·fir·ma·tion** [ˌkɒnfə'meɪʃn] *s.* **1.** Bestätigung *f*; Bekräftigung *f*; **2.** Festigung *f*; **3.** *eccl.* Konfirmati'on *f*; *R.C.* Firmung *f*; **con'firm·a·tive** [-mətɪv] *adj.* ☐, **con'firm·a·to·ry** [-mətərɪ] *adj.* bestätigend: **~ *letter*** Bestätigungsschreiben *n*; **con'firmed** [-md] *adj.* fest, hartnäckig, eingewurzelt, unverbesserlich, Gewohnheits...; chronisch: **~ *bachelor*** eingefleischter Junggeselle.

con·fis·cate ['kɒnfɪskeɪt] *v/t.* beschlagnahmen, einziehen, konfiszieren; **con·fis·ca·tion** [ˌkɒnfɪ'skeɪʃn] *s.* Einziehung *f*, Beschlagnahme *f*, Konfiszierung *f*; F Plünderung *f*; **con·fis·ca·to·ry** [kən'fɪskətərɪ] *adj.* konfiszierend, Beschlagnahme...; F räuberisch.

con·fla·gra·tion [ˌkɒnflə'greɪʃn] *s.* Feuersbrunst *f*, (großer) Brand.

con·flict I *s.* ['kɒnflɪkt] **1.** Kon'flikt *m*: a) Zs.-prall *m*, Zs.-stoß *m*, Kampf *m*, Ausein'andersetzung *f*, Kollisi'on *f*, Streit *m*, b) 'Widerstreit *m*, -spruch *m*: ***armed* ~** bewaffnete Auseinandersetzung; ***inner* ~** innerer (*od.* seelischer) Konflikt; **~ *of interests*** Interessenkonflikt, -kollision; **~ *of laws*** Gesetzeskollision, *weitS.* internationales Privatrecht; **II** *v/i.* [kən'flɪkt] **2.** (***with***) kollidieren, im 'Widerspruch *od.* Gegensatz stehen (zu); **3.** sich wider'sprechen; **con·flict·ing** [kən'flɪktɪŋ] *adj.* wider'streitend, gegensätzlich; *a.* ⚖ entgegenstehend, kollidierend.

con·flu·ence ['kɒnflʊəns] *s.* **1.** Zs.-fluß *m*; **2.** Zustrom *m*, Zulauf *m* (*Menschen*); **3.** (Menschen)Menge *f*; **'con·flu·ent** [-nt] **I** *adj.* zs.-fließend, -laufend; **II** *s.* Nebenfluß *m*; **con·flux** ['kɒnflʌks] → ***confluence***.

con·form [kən'fɔːm] **I** *v/t.* **1.** (*a.* ***o.s.*** sich) anpassen (***to*** *dat. od.* an *acc.*); **II** *v/i.* **2.** (***to***) sich anpassen (*dat.*), sich richten (nach); sich fügen (*dat.*); entsprechen (*dat.*); **3.** *eccl. Brit.* sich der engl. Staatskirche unter'werfen; **con'form·a·ble** [-məbl] *adj.* ☐ (***to***) **1.** kon'form, gleichförmig (mit); entsprechend, gemäß (*dat.*); **2.** vereinbar (mit); **3.** fügsam, nachgiebig; **con'form·ance** [-məns] *s.* Anpassung *f* (***to*** an *acc.*); Über'einstimmung *f* (***with*** mit): ***in* ~ *with*** gemäß (*dat.*); **con·for·ma·tion** [ˌkɒnfɔː'meɪʃn] *s.* **1.** Anpassung *f*, Angleichung *f* (***to*** an *acc.*); **2.** Gestalt (-ung) *f*, Anordnung *f*, Bau *m*; **con'form·ism** [-mɪzəm] *s.* Konfor'mismus *m*; **con'form·ist** [-mɪst] *s.* Konfor'mist (-in): a) Angepaßte(r *m*) *f*, b) Anhänger(in) der engl. Staatskirche; **con'form·i·ty** [-mətɪ] *s.* **1.** Gleichförmigkeit *f*, Ähnlichkeit *f*, Über'einstimmung *f*: ***in* ~ *with*** in Übereinstimmung mit, gemäß (*dat.*); **2.** (***to***) Anpassung *f* (an *acc.*); Befolgung *f* (*gen.*); **3.** *hist.* Zugehörigkeit *f* zur englischen Staatskirche.

con·found [kən'faʊnd] *v/t.* **1.** vermengen, verwechseln (***with*** mit); **2.** in Unordnung bringen, verwirren; **3.** bestürzen, verblüffen; **4.** vernichten, vereiteln; **5.** [*a.* ˌkɒn-] F **~ *him!*** zum Teufel mit ihm!; **~ *it!*** verdammt!; **con'found·ed** [-dɪd] F **I** *adj.* ☐ (*a. int.*) verwünscht, verflixt; scheußlich; **II** *adv.*, *a.* **~*ly*** ‚verdammt' (*kalt, etc.*).

con·fra·ter·ni·ty [ˌkɒnfrə'tɜːnətɪ] *s.* **1.** *bsd. eccl.* Bruderschaft *f*, Gemeinschaft *f*; **2.** Brüderschaft *f*; **con·frère** ['kɒnfreə] (*Fr.*) *s.* Amtsbruder *m*, Kol'lege *m*.

con·front [kən'frʌnt] *v/t.* **1.** (*oft* feindlich) gegen'übertreten, -stehen (*dat.*); **2.** mutig begegnen (*dat.*); **3.** **~ *s.o. with*** j-n konfrontieren mit, j-m *et.* entgegenhalten; ***be* ~*ed with*** sich gegenübersehen, gegenüberstehen (*dat.*); **con·fron·ta·tion** [ˌkɒnfrən'teɪʃn] *s.* Gegen'überstellung *f*, (*a. feindliche*) Konfrontati'on.

Con·fu·cian [kən'fjuːʃjən] **I** *adj.* konfuzi'anisch; **II** *s.* Konfuzi'aner(in); **Con'fu·cian·ism** [-nɪzəm] *s.* Konfuzia'nismus *m*.

con·fuse [kən'fjuːz] *v/t.* **1.** verwechseln, durchein'anderbringen (***with*** mit); **2.** verwirren: a) verlegen machen, aus der Fassung bringen, b) in Unordnung bringen; **3.** verworren *od.* undeutlich machen; **con'fused** [-zd] *adj.* ☐ **1.** verwirrt: a) kon'fus, verworren, wirr, b) verlegen, bestürzt; **2.** undeutlich, verworren: **~ *sounds***; **con'fus·ing** [-zɪŋ] *adj.* verwirrend; **con'fu·sion** [-uːʒn] *s.* **1.** Verwirrung *f*, Durchein'ander *n*, Unordnung *f*, Wirrwarr *m*; **2.** Aufruhr *m*, Lärm *m*; **3.** Bestürzung *f*: ***put s.o. to* ~** j-n in Verlegenheit bringen; **4.** Verworrenheit *f*; **5.** geistige Verwirrung; **6.** Verwechslung *f*.

con·fut·a·ble [kən'fjuːtəbl] *adj.* wider'legbar; **con·fu·ta·tion** [ˌkɒnfjuː'teɪʃn] *s.* Wider'legung *f*; **con·fute** [kən'fjuːt] *v/t.* **1.** *et.* wider'legen; **2.** *j-n* wider'legen, e-s Irrtums über'führen.

con·geal [kən'dʒiːl] **I** *v/t.* gefrieren *od.* gerinnen *od.* erstarren lassen (*a. fig.*); **II** *v/i.* gefrieren, gerinnen, erstarren (*a. fig.*); fest werden; **con'geal·ment** [-mənt] → ***congelation*** 1.
con·ge·la·tion [ˌkɒndʒɪ'leɪʃn] *s.* **1.** Gefrieren *n*, Gerinnen *n*, Erstarren *n*, Festwerden *n*; **2.** gefrorene (*etc.*) Masse.
con·ge·ner ['kɒndʒɪnə] *bsd. biol.* **I** *s.* gleichartiges *od.* verwandtes Ding *od.* Wesen; **II** *adj.* (art- *od.* stamm)verwandt (***to*** mit); **con·gen·er·ous** [kən'dʒenərəs] *adj.* gleichartig, verwandt.
con·gen·ial [kən'dʒiːnjəl] *adj.* □ **1.** (***with***) kongeni'al (*dat.*), (geistes)verwandt (mit *od. dat.*); **2.** sym'pathisch, zusagend, angenehm (***to*** *dat.*): ***be ~*** zusagen; **3.** zuträglich (***to*** *dat.*); **4.** freundlich; **5.** passend, angemessen, entsprechend (***to*** *dat.*); **con·ge·ni·al·i·ty** [kənˌdʒiːnɪ'ælətɪ] *s.* **1.** Geistesverwandtschaft *f*; **2.** Zuträglichkeit *f*.
con·gen·i·tal [kən'dʒenɪtl] *adj.* □ angeboren: ***~ defect*** Geburtsfehler *m*; **con'gen·i·tal·ly** [-təlɪ] *adv.* von Geburt (an); von Na'tur.
con·ger ['kɒŋgə], ***~ eel*** [ˌkɒŋgər'iːl] *s.* Meeral *m*.
con·ge·ries [kɒn'dʒɪəriːz] *s. sg. u. pl.* Anhäufung *f*, (wirre) Masse.
con·gest [kən'dʒest] **I** *v/t.* **1.** zs.-drängen, über'füllen, anhäufen, stauen; **2.** *fig.* über'schwemmen; **3.** verstopfen; **II** *v/i.* **4.** sich ansammeln, sich stauen, sich verstopfen; **con'gest·ed** [-tɪd] *adj.* **1.** über'füllt (***with*** von); über'völkert: ***~ area*** Ballungsraum *m*; **2.** ⚕ mit Blut über'füllt; **con'ges·tion** [-tʃn] *s.* **1.** Anhäufung *f*, Andrang *m*, Stauung *f*, Über'füllung *f*: ***~ of population*** Übervölkerung *f*; ***traffic ~*** Verkehrsstauung; **2.** ⚕ Blutandrang *m* (***of the brain*** zum Gehirn), (Gefäß)Stauung *f*.
con·glo·bate ['kɒngləʊbeɪt] **I** *adj.* (zs.-)geballt, kugelig; **II** *v/t. u. v/i.* (sich) zs.-ballen (***into*** zu).
con·glom·er·ate [kən'glɒməreɪt] **I** *v/t. u. v/i.* (sich) zs.-ballen, verbinden, anhäufen; **II** *adj.* [-rət] zs.-geballt; *fig.* zs.-gewürfelt; **III** *s.* [-rət] *fig.* (An)Häufung *f*, Gemisch *n*, zs.-gewürfelte Masse, Konglome'rat *n* (*a. geol.*); **con·glom·er·a·tion** [kənˌglɒmə'reɪʃn] → ***conglomerate*** III.
con·glu·ti·nate [kən'gluːtɪneɪt] **I** *v/t.* zs.-leimen, -kitten; **II** *v/i.* zs.-kleben, -haften; **con·glu·ti·na·tion** [kənˌgluːtɪ'neɪʃn] *s.* Zs.-kleben *n*; Verbindung *f*.
Con·go·lese [ˌkɒŋgəʊ'liːz] *hist.* **I** *adj.* Kongo..., kongo'lesisch; **II** *s.* Kongo'lese *m*, Kongo'lesin *f*.
con·grat·u·late [kən'grætjʊleɪt] *v/t.* *j-m* gratulieren, Glück wünschen; *j-n* beglückwünschen (***on*** zu) (*alle a.* ***o.s.*** sich); **con·grat·u·la·tion** [kənˌgrætjʊ'leɪʃn] *s.* Glückwunsch *m*: ***~s!*** ich gratuliere!; **con'grat·u·la·tor** [-tə] *s.* Gratu'lant(in); **con'grat·u·la·to·ry** [-lətərɪ] *adj.* Glückwunsch..., Gratulations...
con·gre·gate ['kɒŋgrɪgeɪt] *v/t. u. v/i.* (sich) (ver)sammeln.
con·gre·ga·tion [ˌkɒŋgrɪ'geɪʃn] *s.* **1.** (Kirchen)Gemeinde *f*; **2.** Versammlung *f*; **3.** *Brit. univ.* Versammlung *f* des Lehrkörpers *od.* des Se'nats; **ˌcon·gre'ga·tion·al** [-ʃənl] *adj. eccl.* **1.** Gemeinde...; **2.** ♀ unabhängig: ***♀ chapel*** Kapelle *f* der ‚freien' Gemeinden; **ˌCon·gre'ga·tion·al·ism** [-ʃnəlɪzəm] *s. eccl.* Selbstverwaltung *f* der ‚freien' Kirchengemeinden, Independen'tismus *m*; **ˌCon·gre'ga·tion·al·ist** [-ʃnəlɪst] *s.* Mitglied *n* e-r ‚freien' Kirchengemeinde.
con·gress ['kɒŋgres] *s.* **1.** Kon'greß *m*, Tagung *f*; **2.** *pol. Am.* ♀ Kon'greß *m*, gesetzgebende Versammlung; **3.** Geschlechtsverkehr *m*.
con·gres·sion·al [kəŋ'greʃənl] *adj.* **1.** Kongreß...; **2.** *pol. Am.* ♀ Kongreß...: ***♀ medal*** Verdienstmedaille *f*.
'Con·gress·man [-mən] *s.* [*irr.*] *pol.* Mitglied *n* des amer. Repräsen'tantenhauses, Kon'greßabgeordnete(r) *m*.
con·gru·ence ['kɒŋgrʊəns] *s.* **1.** Über'einstimmung *f*; **2.** ⩚ Kongru'enz *f*; **'con·gru·ent** [-nt] *adj.* kongru'ent: a) (***with***) über'einstimmend (mit), entsprechend (*dat.*), b) ⩚ deckungsgleich; **con·gru·i·ty** [kɒŋ'gruːətɪ] *s.* **1.** Über'einstimmung *f*; Angemessenheit *f*; **2.** Folgerichtigkeit *f*; **3.** ⩚ Kongru'enz *f*; **'con·gru·ous** [-ʊəs] *adj.* □ **1.** (***to, with***) übereinstimmend (mit), entsprechend (*dat.*); **2.** folgerichtig; passend.
con·ic ['kɒnɪk] **I** *adj.* → ***conical***; **II** *s. a.* ***~ section*** ⩚ a) Kegelschnitt *m*, b) *pl.* → ***conics***; **'con·i·cal** [-kl] *adj.* □ 'konisch, kegelförmig: ***~ frustrum*** ⩚ Kegelstumpf *m*; **co·nic·i·ty** [kə'nɪsətɪ] *s.* Konizi'tät *f*, Kegelform *f*; **'con·ics** [-ks] *s. pl. sg. konstr.* ⩚ Lehre *f* von den Kegelschnitten.
co·ni·fer ['kɒnɪfə] *s.* ♆ Koni'fere *f*, Nadelbaum *m*; **co·nif·er·ous** [kəʊ'nɪfərəs] *adj.* ♆ a) zapfentragend, b) Nadel...: ***~ tree***.
con·jec·tur·a·ble [kən'dʒektʃərəbl] *adj.* □ zu vermuten(d); **con'jec·tur·al** [-rəl] *adj.* □ mutmaßlich; **con·jec·ture** [kən'dʒektʃə] **I** *s.* **1.** Vermutung *f*, Mutmaßung *f*; (vage) I'dee; **II** *v/t.* **2.** vermuten, mutmaßen; **III** *v/i.* **3.** Mutmaßungen anstellen, mutmaßen.
con·join [kən'dʒɔɪn] *v/t. u. v/i.* (sich) verbinden *od.* vereinigen.
con·joint ['kɒndʒɔɪnt] *adj.* □ verbunden, vereinigt, gemeinsam, Mit...; **'con·joint·ly** [-lɪ] *adv.* zu'sammen, gemeinsam.
con·ju·gal ['kɒndʒʊgl] *adj.* □ ehelich, Ehe..., Gatten...
con·ju·gate ['kɒndʒʊgeɪt] **I** *v/t.* **1.** *ling.* konjugieren, beugen; **II** *v/i.* **2.** *biol.* sich paaren; **III** *adj.* [-gɪt] **3.** verbunden, gepaart; **4.** *ling.* wurzelverwandt; **5.** ⩚ zugeordnet; **6.** ♆ paarig; **IV** *s.* [-gɪt] **7.** *ling.* wurzelverwandtes Wort; **con·ju·ga·tion** [ˌkɒndʒʊ'geɪʃn] *s. ling., biol.,* ⚘ Konjugati'on *f*, *ling. a.* Beugung *f*.
con·junct [kən'dʒʌŋkt] *adj.* □ verbunden, vereint, gemeinsam; **con'junc·tion** [-kʃən] *s.* **1.** Verbindung *f*: ***in ~ with*** zusammen mit; **2.** Zs.-treffen *n*; **3.** *ast., ling.* Konjunkti'on *f*; **con·junc·ti·va** [ˌkɒndʒʌŋk'taɪvə] *s. anat.* Bindehaut *f*; **con'junc·tive** [-tɪv] **I** *adj.* □ **1.** verbindend, Verbindungs...: ***~ tissue*** *anat.* Bindegewebe *n*; **2.** *ling.* 'konjunktivisch: ***~ mood*** Konjunktiv *m*; **II** *s.* **3.** *ling.* 'Konjunktiv *m*; **con'junc·tive·ly** [-tɪvlɪ] *adv.* gemeinsam; **con·junc·ti·vi·tis** [kənˌdʒʌŋktɪ'vaɪtɪs] *s.* ⚕ Bindehautentzündung *f*; **con'junc·ture** [-tʃə] *s.* **1.** Zs.-treffen *n* (*von Umständen*); **2.** 'Umstände *pl.*; **3.** Krise *f*; **4.** *ast.* Konjunkti'on *f*.
con·ju·ra·tion [ˌkɒndʒʊə'reɪʃn] *s.* **1.** feierliche Anrufung; Beschwörung *f*; **2.** a) Zauberformel *f*, b) Zaube'rei *f*.
con·jure[1] [kən'dʒʊə] *v/t.* beschwören, inständig bitten (***to*** *inf.* zu *inf.*).
con·jure[2] ['kʌndʒə] **I** *v/t.* **1.** *Geist etc.* beschwören: ***~ up*** heraufbeschwören (*a. fig.*), zitieren, hervorzaubern; **2.** behexen, (be)zaubern: ***~ away*** wegzaubern, bannen; **II** *v/i.* **3.** zaubern, hexen: ***a name to ~ with*** ein Name, der Wunder wirkt; **'con·jur·er, 'con·jur·or** [-dʒərə] *s.* **1.** Zauberer *m*, Zauberin *f*; **2.** Zauberkünstler *m*, Taschenspieler *m*; **'con·jur·ing trick** [-dʒərɪŋ] *s.* Zauberkunststück *n*.
conk[1] [kɒŋk] *s. sl.* ‚Riecher' *m* (*Nase*); *Am. a.* ‚Birne' (*Kopf*).
conk[2] [kɒŋk] *v/i. sl. mst* ***~ out*** **1.** ‚streiken', ‚den Geist aufgeben' (*Fernseher etc.*), ‚absterben' (*Motor*); **2.** ‚umkippen', ohnmächtig werden; **3.** ‚abkratzen', sterben.
con·ker ['kɒŋkə] *s.* F Ka'stanie *f*.
conn [kɒn] *v/t.* ⚓ *Schiff* steuern.
con·nate ['kɒneɪt] *adj.* **1.** angeboren; **2.** *biol.* verwachsen.
con·nat·u·ral [kə'nætʃrəl] *adj.* □ **1.** (***to***) gleicher Na'tur (wie); verwandt (*dat.*); **2.** angeboren.
con·nect [kə'nekt] **I** *v/t.* **1.** verbinden, verknüpfen (*mst* ***with*** mit): ***be ~ed*** (***with***) in Verbindung (mit) *od.* in Beziehungen (zu) treten *od.* stehen; ***be well ~ed*** *fig.* gute Beziehungen haben; **2.** ⚡ (***to***) anschließen (an *acc.*), verbinden (mit) (*a. teleph.*), zuschalten (*dat.*), Kon'takt herstellen zwischen (*dat.*); **3.** ⚙ (***to***) verbinden, zs.-fügen, koppeln (mit), ankuppeln (an *acc.*); **II** *v/i.* **4.** in Verbindung *od.* Zs.-hang treten *od.* stehen; **5.** 🚂 *etc.* Anschluß haben (***with*** an *acc.*); **6.** *Boxen*: ‚landen' (***with a blow*** e-n Schlag); **con'nect·ed** [-tɪd] *adj.* □ **1.** zs.-hängend; **2.** verwandt: ***~ by marriage*** verschwägert; → ***connect*** 1; **3.** (***with***) beteiligt (an *dat.*, bei), verwickelt (in *acc.*); **con'nect·ed·ly** [-tɪdlɪ] *adv.* zs.-hängend; logisch; **con'nect·ing** [-tɪŋ] *adj.* Binde..., Verbindungs..., Anschluß...: ***~ link*** Bindeglied *n*; ***~ rod*** ⚙ Kurbel-, Pleuelstange *f*; ***~ shaft*** ⚙ Transmissionswelle *f*; ***~ train*** Anschlußzug *m*.
con·nec·tion [kə'nekʃn] *s.* **1.** Verbindung *f*; **2.** ⚙ Verbindung *f*, Bindeglied *n*: ***hot-water ~s*** Heißwasseranlage *f*; **3.** Zs.-hang *m*, Beziehung *f*: ***in this ~*** in diesem Zs.-hang; ***in ~ with*** mit Bezug auf; **4.** per'sönliche Beziehung *od.* Verbindung; Verwandtschaft *f*, Verwandte(r *m*) *f*; **5.** *pl.* gute *od.* nützliche Beziehungen; Bekannten-, Kundenkreis *m*; **6.** ⚙ *allg.* Verbindung *f*, Anschluß *m* (*beide a.* ⚡, 🚂, *teleph. etc.*), Verbindungs-, Bindeglied *n*, ⚡ Schaltung *f*, Schaltverbindung *f*: ***~ plug*** Anschlußstecker *m*; ***catch one's ~*** 🚂 den Anschluß erreichen; ***run in ~ with*** Anschluß haben an (*acc.*); **7.** (*bsd. religiöse*) Gemeinschaft; **con'nec·tive** [-ktɪv] **I** *adj.* verbindend: ***~ tissue*** *anat.* Bin-

de-, Zellgewebe *n*; **II** *s. ling.* Bindewort *n*.

con·nex·ion → ***connection***.

con·ning tow·er ['kɒnɪŋ] *s.* ⚓, ⚔ Kom'mandoturm *m*.

con·niv·ance [kə'naɪvəns] *s.* stillschweigende Duldung *od.* Einwilligung (*a.* ⚖), bewußtes Über'sehen (***at***, ***in*** *gen.*); ⚖ Begünstigung *f*; **con·nive** [kə'naɪv] *v/i.* (***at***) stillschweigend dulden (*acc.*), ein Auge zudrücken (bei), Vorschub leisten (*dat.*).

con·nois·seur [ˌkɒnə'sɜː] (*Fr.*) *s.* (Kunst- *etc.*)Kenner *m*: ~ ***of*** (*od.* ***in***) ***wines*** Weinkenner.

con·no·ta·tion [ˌkɒnəʊ'teɪʃn] *s.* **1.** Mitbezeichnung *f*; (Neben)Bedeutung *f*; **2.** *phls.* Begriffsinhalt *m*; **con·note** [kɒ'nəʊt] *v/t.* mitbezeichnen, (zu'gleich) bedeuten.

con·nu·bi·al [kə'njuːbjəl] *adj.* ☐ ehelich, Ehe…; **con·nu·bi·al·i·ty** [kəˌnjuːbɪ'ælətɪ] *s.* **1.** Ehestand *m*; **2.** eheliche Zärtlichkeiten *pl.*

co·noid ['kəʊnɔɪd] **I** *adj.* kegelförmig; **II** *s.* A a) Kono'id *n*, b) Kono'ide *f* (*Fläche*).

con·quer ['kɒŋkə] **I** *v/t.* **1.** erobern, einnehmen, Besitz ergreifen von; **2.** *fig.* erobern, gewinnen; **3.** besiegen, über'winden; unter'werfen; **4.** *fig.* über'winden, bezwingen, Herr werden über (*acc.*); **II** *v/i.* **5.** siegen; Eroberungen machen; **'con·quer·ing** [-kərɪŋ] *adj.* siegreich; **'con·quer·or** [-kərə] *s.* **1.** Eroberer *m*; Sieger *m*: ***the*** 2 *hist.* Wilhelm der Eroberer; **2.** F Entscheidungsspiel *n*.

con·quest ['kɒŋkwest] *s.* **1.** Eroberung *f*: a) Einnahme *f*: ***the*** 2 *hist.* die normannische Eroberung, b) erobertes Gebiet, c) *fig.* Erringung *f*; **2.** Bezwingung *f*; **3.** *fig.* ‚Eroberung' *f*: ***make a*** ~ ***of s.o.*** j-n erobern.

con·san·guine [kɒn'sæŋgwɪn] *adj.* blutsverwandt; **con·san·guin·i·ty** [ˌkɒnsæŋ'gwɪnətɪ] *s.* Blutsverwandtschaft *f*.

con·science ['kɒnʃəns] *s.* Gewissen *n*: ***guilty*** ~ schlechtes Gewissen; ***for*** ~ ***sake*** um das Gewissen zu beruhigen; ***in all*** ~ F wahrhaftig; ***have s.th. on one's*** ~ ein schlechtes Gewissen haben wegen e-r Sache; ~ **clause** *s.* ⚖ Gewissensklausel *f*; ~ **mon·ey** *s.* ano'nyme Steuernachzahlung; **'~-proof** *adj.* ‚abgebrüht'; **'~-ˌstrick·en** *adj.* von Gewissensbissen gepeinigt, reuevoll.

con·sci·en·tious [ˌkɒnʃɪ'enʃəs] *adj.* ☐ gewissenhaft, Gewissens…: ~ ***objector*** Kriegs-, Wehrdienstverweigerer *m* (*aus Gewissensgründen*); **ˌcon·sci'en·tious·ness** [-nɪs] *s.* Gewissenhaftigkeit *f*.

-conscious [kɒnʃəs] *adj. in Zssgn* …bewußt; …freudig, …begeistert.

con·scious ['kɒnʃəs] *adj.* ☐ **1.** *pred.* bei Bewußtsein; **2.** bewußt: ***be*** ~ ***of*** sich bewußt sein (*gen.*), wissen von; ***be*** ~ ***that*** wissen *od.* überzeugt sein, daß; ***she became*** ~ ***that*** es kam ihr zum Bewußtsein, daß; **3.** wissentlich, bewußt: ***a*** ~ ***liar*** ein bewußter Lügner; **4.** (selbst)bewußt, über'zeugt: ***a*** ~ ***artist*** ein überzeugter Künstler; **5.** denkend: ***man is a*** ~ ***being***; **'con·scious·ly** [-lɪ] *adv.* bewußt, wissentlich; gewollt; **'con·scious·ness** [-nɪs] *s.* **1.** Bewußtsein *n*: ***lose*** ~ das Bewußtsein verlieren; ***regain*** ~ wieder zu sich kommen; **2.** (***of***) Bewußtsein *n* (*gen.*), Wissen *n* (um), Kenntnis *f* (von *od. gen.*): ~***-expanding*** bewußtseinserweiternd (*Droge*); ~***-raising*** Bewußtwerdung *f od.* -machung *f*; **3.** Denken *n*, Empfinden *n*.

con·script ['kɒnskrɪpt] **I** *adj.* zwangsweise eingezogen (*Soldat etc.*) *od.* verpflichtet (*Arbeiter*); **II** *s.* ⚔ Dienst-, Wehrpflichtige(r) *m*; ausgehobener Re'krut; **III** *v/t.* [kən'skrɪpt] *bsd.* ⚔ (zwangsweise) ausheben, einziehen; **con·scrip·tion** [kən'skrɪpʃn] *s.* **1.** *bsd.* ⚔ Zwangsaushebung *f*, Wehrpflicht *f*: ***industrial*** ~ Arbeitsverpflichtung *f*; **2.** *a.* ~ ***of wealth*** (Her'anziehung *f* zur) Vermögensabgabe *f*.

con·se·crate ['kɒnsɪkreɪt] **I** *v/t.* **1.** *eccl.* weihen; **2.** widmen; **3.** heiligen; **II** *adj.* **4.** geweiht, geheiligt; **con·se·cra·tion** [ˌkɒnsɪ'kreɪʃn] *s.* **1.** *eccl.* Weihung *f*, Einsegnung *f*; **2.** Heiligung *f*; **3.** Widmung *f*, Hingabe *f* (***to*** an *acc.*).

con·se·cu·tion [ˌkɒnsɪ'kjuːʃn] *s.* **1.** (Aufein'ander)Folge *f*, Reihe *f*; logische Folge; **2.** *ling.* Wort-, Zeitfolge *f*; **con·sec·u·tive** [kən'sekjʊtɪv] *adj.* ☐ **1.** aufein'anderfolgend, fortlaufend: ***six*** ~ ***days*** sechs Tage hintereinander; **2.** *ling.* ~ ***clause*** Konsekutiv-, Folgesatz *m*; **con·sec·u·tive·ly** [kən'sekjʊtɪvlɪ] *adv.* nachein'ander, fortlaufend.

con·sen·sus [kən'sensəs] *s.* **1.** Über'einstimmung *f* (der Meinungen): ~ ***of opinion*** übereinstimmende Meinung, allseitige Zustimmung; **2.** ⚕ Wechselwirkung *f* (*Organe*).

con·sent [kən'sent] **I** *v/i.* **1.** (***to***) zustimmen (*dat.*), einwilligen (in *acc.*); **2.** sich bereit erklären (***to*** *inf.* zu *inf.*); **II** *s.* **3.** (***to***) Zustimmung *f* (zu), Einwilligung *f* (in *acc.*), Genehmigung *f* (für), Einverständnis *n* (zu): ***age of*** ~ ⚖ (*bsd.* Ehe-) Mündigkeit *f*; ***with one*** ~ einstimmig; ***by common*** ~ mit allgemeiner Zustimmung; → ***silence*** 1; **con'sen·tient** [-nʃənt] *adj.* zustimmend.

con·se·quence ['kɒnsɪkwəns] *s.* **1.** Konse'quenz *f*, Folge *f*, Resul'tat *n*, Wirkung *f*: ***in*** ~ folglich, daher; ***in*** ~ ***of*** infolge von (*od. gen.*), wegen; ***in*** ~ ***of which*** weswegen; ***take the*** ~***s*** die Folgen tragen; ***with the*** ~ ***that*** mit dem Ergebnis, daß; **2.** (Schluß)Folgerung *f*, Schluß *m*; **3.** Wichtigkeit *f*, Bedeutung *f*, Einfluß *m*: ***of no*** ~ ohne Bedeutung, unwichtig; ***a man of*** ~ ein bedeutender *od.* einflußreicher Mann; **4.** *pl. mst sg. konstr.* ein Erzählspiel; **'con·se·quent** [-nt] **I** *adj.* ☐ → ***consequently***; **1.** (***on***) folgend (auf *acc.*), sich ergebend (aus); **2.** *phls.* logisch (richtig); **II** *s.* **3.** Folge(-erscheinung) *f*, Folgerung *f*, Schluß *m*; **4.** *ling.* Nachsatz *m*; **con·se·quen·tial** [ˌkɒnsɪ'kwenʃl] *adj.* ☐ **1.** sich ergebend (***on*** aus): ~ ***damage*** ⚖ Folgeschaden *m*; **2.** logisch (richtig); **3.** 'indiˌrekt; **4.** wichtigtuerisch; **'con·se·quent·ly** [-ntlɪ] *adv.* **1.** folglich, deshalb; **2.** als Folge.

con·serv·an·cy [kən'sɜːvənsɪ] *s.* **1.** Aufsichtsbehörde *f* für Flüsse, Häfen *etc.*; **2.** Forstbehörde *f*: ***nature*** ~ Naturschutz(amt *n*) *m*; **con·ser·va·tion** [ˌkɒnsə'veɪʃn] *s.* **1.** Erhaltung *f*, Bewahrung *f*; Instandhaltung *f*, Schutz *m* (*von Forsten*, *Flüssen*, *Boden*); Na'tur-, Umweltschutz *m*: ~ ***of energy*** *phys.* Erhaltung der Energie; **2.** Haltbarmachung *f*, Konservierung *f*; **con·ser·va·tion·ist** [ˌkɒnsə'veɪʃənɪst] *s.* Na'tur- *od.* 'Umweltschützer *m*.

con·serv·a·tism [kən'sɜːvətɪzəm] *s.* Konserva'tismus *m* (*a. pol.*); **con'serv·a·tive** [-tɪv] **I** *adj.* **1.** erhaltend, konservierend; **2.** konserva'tiv (*a. pol.*, *mst* 2); **3.** zu'rückhaltend, vorsichtig (*Schätzung etc.*); **4.** unauffällig: ~ ***dress***; **II** *s.* **5.** 2 *pol.* Konserva'tive(r) *m*.

con·ser·va·toire [kən'sɜːvətwɑː] (*Fr.*) *s. bsd. Brit.* Konserva'torium *n*, Hochschule *f* für Mu'sik (*etc.*).

con·ser·va·tor [kən'sɜːvətə] *s.* **1.** Konser'vator *m*, Mu'seumsdiˌrektor *m*; **2.** ⚖ *Am.* Vormund *m*; **con'serv·a·to·ry** [-trɪ] *s.* **1.** Treib-, Gewächshaus *n*, Wintergarten *m*; **2.** → ***conservatoire***; **con·serve** [kən'sɜːv] **I** *v/t.* **1.** erhalten, bewahren; beibehalten; **2.** schonen, sparsam 'umgehen mit; **3.** einmachen, konservieren; **II** *s.* **4.** *mst pl.* Eingemachtes *n*, Konfi'türe *f*.

con·sid·er [kən'sɪdə] **I** *v/t.* **1.** nachdenken über (*acc.*), (sich) über'legen, erwägen: ~ ***a plan***; **2.** in Betracht ziehen, berücksichtigen, beachten, bedenken: ~ ***his age!*** bedenken Sie sein Alter!; ***all things*** ~***ed*** wenn man alles in Betracht zieht; → ***considered***, ***considering***; **3.** Rücksicht nehmen auf (*acc.*): ***he never*** ~***s others***; **4.** betrachten *od.* ansehen als, halten für: ~ ***s.o.*** (***to be***) ***a fool*** j-n für e-n Narren halten; ***be*** ~***ed rich*** als reich gelten; ***you may*** ~ ***yourself lucky*** du kannst dich glücklich schätzen; ~ ***yourself at home*** tun Sie, als ob Sie zu Hause wären; ~ ***yourself dismissed!*** betrachten Sie sich als entlassen!; **5.** denken, meinen, annehmen, finden (*a.* ***that*** daß); **II** *v/i.* **6.** nachdenken, über'legen; **con'sid·er·a·ble** [-dərəbl] **I** *adj.* ☐ beträchtlich, erheblich; bedeutend (*a. Person*); **II** *s. bsd. Am.* F e-e Menge, viel.

con·sid·er·ate [kən'sɪdərət] *adj.* ☐ rücksichtsvoll, aufmerksam (***towards***, ***of*** gegen): ***be*** ~ ***of*** Rücksicht nehmen auf (*acc.*); **con'sid·er·ate·ness** [-nɪs] *s.* Rücksichtnahme *f*; **con·sid·er·a·tion** [kənˌsɪdə'reɪʃn] *s.* **1.** Erwägung *f*, Über'legung *f*: ***take into*** ~ in Betracht *od.* Erwägung ziehen; ***leave out of*** ~ außer Betracht lassen, ausklammern; ***the matter is under*** ~ die Sache wird (noch) erwogen *od.* geprüft; ***upon*** ~ nach Prüfung; **2.** Berücksichtigung *f*; Begründung *f*: ***in*** ~ ***of*** in Anbetracht (*gen.*); ***on*** (*od.* ***under***) ***no*** ~ unter keinen Umständen; ***that is a*** ~ das ist ein triftiger Grund; ***money is no*** ~ Geld spielt keine Rolle; **3.** Rücksicht(-nahme) *f* (***for*** auf *acc.*): ***lack of*** ~ Rücksichtslosigkeit *f*; **4.** Entgelt *n*, Entschädigung *f*; (vertragliche) Gegenleistung: ***for a*** ~ gegen Entgelt; **con'sid·ered** [-dəd] *adj. a.* ***well-***~ 'wohlüberˌlegt; **con'sid·er·ing** [-rɪŋ] **I** *prp.* in Anbetracht (*gen.*); **II** *adv.* F den 'Umständen nach.

con·sign [kən'saɪn] *v/t.* **1.** über'geben, über'liefern; **2.** anvertrauen; **3.** bestimmen (***for***, ***to*** für); **4.** ✝ *Waren* a) (***to***) versenden (an *acc.*), zu-, über'senden (*dat.*), verfrachten (an *acc.*), b) in Kommissi'on *od.* Konsignati'on geben, konsignieren; **con·sign·ee** [ˌkɒnsaɪ'ni:] *s.* ✝ **1.** Empfänger *m*, Adres'sat *m*; **2.** *Überseehandel*: Konsigna'tar *m*; **con'sign·ment** [-mənt] *s.* ✝ **1.** a) Über'sendung *f*, b) *Überseehandel*: Konsignati'on *f*: **~ *note*** Frachtbrief *m*; ***in* ~** in Konsignation *od.* Kommission; **2.** a) (Waren)Sendung *f*, b) *Überseehandel*: Konsignati'onsware(n *pl.*) *f*; **con'sign·or** [-nə] *s.* ✝ **1.** Über'sender *m*; **2.** *Überseehandel*: Konsi'gnant *m*.

con·sist [kən'sɪst] *v/i.* **1.** bestehen, sich zs.-setzen (***of*** aus); **2.** bestehen (***in*** in *dat.*); **con'sist·ence** [-təns] → ***consistency*** 1 *u.* 2; **con'sist·en·cy** [-tənsɪ] *s.* **1.** Konsi'stenz *f*, Beschaffenheit *f*; **2.** Festigkeit *f*, Dichtigkeit *f*, Dicke *f*; **3.** Konse'quenz *f*, Folgerichtigkeit *f*; **4.** Stetigkeit *f*; **5.** Über'einstimmung *f*, Vereinbarkeit *f*; **con'sist·ent** [-tənt] *adj.* □ **1.** konse'quent: a) folgerichtig, logisch, b) gleichmäßig, stetig, unbeirrbar (*a. Person*); **2.** über'einstimmend, vereinbar, im Einklang stehend (***with*** mit); **3.** beständig, kon'stant (*Leistung etc.*); **con'sist·ent·ly** [-təntlɪ] *adv.* **1.** im Einklang (***with*** mit); **2.** 'durchweg; **3.** logischerweise.

con·sis·to·ry [kən'sɪstərɪ] *s. eccl.* Konsi'storium *n*.

con·so·la·tion [ˌkɒnsə'leɪʃn] *s.* Trost *m*, Tröstung *f*: ***poor* ~** schwacher Trost; **~ *goal*** *sport* Ehrentor *n*; **~ *prize*** Trostpreis *m*.

con·sole[1] [kən'səʊl] *v/t. j-n* trösten: **~ *o.s.*** sich trösten (***with*** mit).

con·sole[2] ['kɒnsəʊl] *s.* **1.** Kon'sole *f*: a) △ Krag-, Tragstein *m*, b) Wandgestell *n*: **~ (*table*)** Wandtischchen *n*; **2.** (Fernseh-, Mu'sik)Truhe *f*, (Radio)Schrank *m*; **3.** ⚙, ⚡ Schalt-, Steuerpult *n*, Kon'sole *f*.

con·sol·i·date [kən'sɒlɪdeɪt] **I** *v/t.* **1.** (ver)stärken, festigen, *fig. a.* konsolidieren; **2.** vereinigen: a) zs.-legen, zs.-schließen, b) *Truppen* zs.-ziehen; **3.** ✝ a) *Schulden* konsolidieren, fundieren, b) *Aktien*, *a.* ⚖ *Klagen* zs.-legen, c) *Gesellschaften* zs.-schließen; **4.** ⚙ verdichten; **II** *v/i.* **5.** fest werden; sich festigen (*a. fig.*); **con'sol·i·dat·ed** [-tɪd] *adj.* **1.** fest, dicht, kom'pakt; **2.** *bsd.* ✝ vereinigt, konsolidiert: **~ *annuities*** → ***consols***; **~ *debt*** fundierte Schuld; ***2 Fund*** *Brit.* konsolidierter Staatsfonds; **con·sol·i·da·tion** [kənˌsɒlɪ'deɪʃn] *s.* **1.** (Ver)stärkung *f*, Festigung *f* (*beide a. fig.*); **2.** ⚔ a) Zs.-ziehung *f*, b) Ausbau *m*; **3.** ✝ a) Konsolidierung *f*, b) Zs.-legung *f*, Vereinigung *f*, c) Zs.-schluß *m*; **4.** ⚙ Verdichtung *f*; **5.** ⚒ Flurbereinigung *f*.

con·sols ['kɒnsɒlz] *s. pl.* ✝ *Brit.* Kon'sols *pl.*, konsolidierte Staatsanleihen *pl.*

con·som·mé [kən'sɒmeɪ] (*Fr.*) *s.* Consom'mé *f*, *n* (*klare Kraftbrühe*).

con·so·nance ['kɒnsənəns] *s.* **1.** Zs.-, Gleichklang *m*; **2.** ♪ Konso'nanz *f*; **3.** *fig.* Über'einstimmung *f*, Harmo'nie *f*; **'con·so·nant** [-nt] **I** *adj.* □ **1.** ♪ konso'nant; **2.** über'einstimmend, vereinbar (***with*** mit); **3.** gemäß (***to*** *dat.*); **II** *s.* **4.** *ling.* Konso'nant *m*; **con·so·nan·tal** [ˌkɒnsə'næntl] *adj. ling.* konso'nantisch.

con·sort I *s.* ['kɒnsɔ:t] **1.** Gemahl(in); **2.** ⚓ Geleitschiff *n*; **II** *v/i.* [kən'sɔ:t] **3.** (***with***) verkehren (mit), sich gesellen (zu); **4.** (***with***) über'einstimmen (mit), passen (zu); **con·sor·ti·um** [kən'sɔ:tjəm] *s.* **1.** Vereinigung *f*, Gruppe *f*, Kon'sortium *n* (*a.* ✝): **~ *of banks*** Bankenkonsortium; **2.** ⚖ eheliche Gemeinschaft.

con·spi·cu·i·ty [ˌkɒnspɪ'kju:ətɪ] → ***conspicuousness***; **con·spic·u·ous** [kən'spɪkjʊəs] *adj.* □ **1.** deutlich sichtbar; **2.** auffallend: ***be* ~** in die Augen fallen; ***be* ~ *by one's absence*** durch Abwesenheit glänzen; ***make o.s.* ~** sich auffällig benehmen, auffallen; ***render o.s.* ~** sich hervortun; **3.** *fig.* bemerkenswert, her'vorragend; **con·spic·u·ous·ness** [kən'spɪkjʊəsnɪs] *s.* **1.** Deutlichkeit *f*; **2.** Auffälligkeit *f*, Augenfälligkeit *f*.

con·spir·a·cy [kən'spɪrəsɪ] *s.* Verschwörung *f*, Kom'plott *n*: **~ *of silence*** verabredetes Stillschweigen; **~ (*to commit a crime*)** (*strafbare*) Verabredung zur Verübung e-r Straftat; **con'spir·a·tor** [-ətə] *s.* Verschwörer *m*; **con·spir·a·to·ri·al** [kənˌspɪrə'tɔ:rɪəl] *adj.* verschwörerisch, Verschwörungs...; **con·spire** [kən'spaɪə] **I** *v/i.* **1.** sich verschwören; sich (heimlich) zs.-tun; ⚖ sich *zu e-r Tat* verabreden; **2.** *fig.* zs.-wirken, (insgeheim) dazu beitragen, sich verschworen haben; **II** *v/t.* **3.** (heimlich) planen, anzetteln.

con·sta·ble ['kʌnstəbl] *s. bsd. Brit.* Poli'zist *m*, Wachtmeister *m*: ***special* ~** Hilfspolizist; → ***Chief Constable***; **con·stab·u·lar·y** [kən'stæbjʊlərɪ] *s.* Poli'zei(truppe) *f*.

con·stan·cy ['kɒnstənsɪ] *s.* **1.** Beständigkeit *f*, Unveränderlichkeit *f*; **2.** Bestand *m*, Dauer *f*; **3.** *fig.* Standhaftigkeit *f*; Treue *f*; **'con·stant** [-nt] **I** *adj.* □ **1.** (be)ständig, unveränderlich, gleichbleibend, kon'stant; **2.** dauernd, unaufhörlich; stetig, regelmäßig: **~ *rain*** anhaltender Regen; → ***companion***[1] 2; **3.** standhaft, beharrlich, fest; **4.** verläßlich, treu; **5.** ⚗, ⚡, *phys.* kon'stant; **II** *s.* **6.** ⚗, *phys.* kon'stante Größe, Kon'stante *f*.

con·stel·la·tion [ˌkɒnstə'leɪʃn] *s.* **1.** Konstellati'on *f*: a) *ast.* Sternbild *n*, b) *fig.* Gruppierung *f*; **2.** glänzende Versammlung.

con·ster·nat·ed ['kɒnstəneɪtɪd] *adj.* bestürzt, konsterniert; **con·ster·na·tion** [ˌkɒnstə'neɪʃn] *s.* Bestürzung *f*.

con·sti·pate ['kɒnstɪpeɪt] *v/t.* ⚕ verstopfen; **con·sti·pa·tion** [ˌkɒnstɪ'peɪʃn] *s.* ⚕ Verstopfung *f*.

con·stit·u·en·cy [kən'stɪtjʊənsɪ] *s.* **1.** Wählerschaft *f*; **2.** Wahlkreis *m*; **3.** *Am.* F Kundenkreis *m*; **con'stit·u·ent** [-nt] **I** *adj.* **1.** e-n (Bestand)Teil bildend: **~ *part*** Bestandteil *m*; **2.** *pol.* Wähler..., Wahl...: **~ *body*** Wählerschaft *f*; **3.** *pol.* konstituierend, verfassunggebend: **~ *assembly*** verfassunggebende Versammlung; **II** *s.* **4.** Bestandteil *m*; **5.** ⚖ Vollmachtgeber(in); **6.** *pol.* Wähler (-in); **7.** *ling.* Satzteil *m*; **8.** ⚗, *phys.* Kompo'nente *f*.

con·sti·tute ['kɒnstɪtju:t] *v/t.* **1.** ernennen, einsetzen: **~ *s.o. president*** j-n als Präsidenten einsetzen; **2.** *Gesetz* in Kraft setzen; **3.** *oft pol.* gründen, einsetzen, konstituieren: **~ *a committee*** e-n Ausschuß einsetzen; ***the* ~*d authorities*** die verfassungsmäßigen Behörden; **4.** ausmachen, bilden: **~ *a precedent*** e-n Präzedenzfall bilden; ***be so* ~*d that*** so geartet sein, daß.

con·sti·tu·tion [ˌkɒnstɪ'tju:ʃn] *s.* **1.** Zs.-setzung *f*, (Auf)Bau *m*, Beschaffenheit *f*; **2.** Einsetzung *f*, Bildung *f*, Gründung *f*; **3.** Konstituti'on *f*, Körperbau *m*, Na'tur *f*: ***by* ~** von Natur; ***strong* ~** starke Konstitution; **4.** Gemütsart *f*, Wesen *n*, Veranlagung *f*; **5.** *pol.* Verfassung *f*, Grundgesetz *n*, Satzung *f*; **ˌcon·sti'tu·tion·al** [-ʃənl] **I** *adj.* □ **1.** körperlich bedingt, angeboren, veranlagungsgemäß; **2.** *pol.* verfassungsmäßig, rechtsstaatlich, Verfassungs...: **~ *monarchy*** konstitutionelle Monarchie; **~ *state*** Rechtsstaat *m*; **II** *s.* **3.** F (Verdauungs-) Spaziergang *m*; **ˌcon·sti'tu·tion·al·ism** [-ʃnəlɪzəm] *s. pol.* verfassungsmäßige Regierungsform; **ˌcon·sti'tu·tion·al·ist** [-ʃnəlɪst] *s. pol.* Anhänger *m* der verfassungsmäßigen Regierungsform.

con·strain [kən'streɪn] *v/t.* **1.** zwingen, nötigen, drängen: ***be*** (*od.* ***feel***) **~*ed*** sich genötigt sehen; **2.** erzwingen; **3.** einzwängen; einsperren; **con'strained** [-nd] *adj.* □ gezwungen, steif, verkrampft, verlegen, befangen; **con'strain·ed·ly** [-nɪdlɪ] *adv.* gezwungen; **con'straint** [-nt] *s.* **1.** Zwang *m*, Nötigung *f*: ***under* ~** unter Zwang, zwangsweise; **2.** Beschränkung *f*; **3.** a) Befangenheit *f*, b) Gezwungenheit *f*; **4.** Zu'rückhaltung *f*.

con·strict [kən'strɪkt] *v/t.* zs.-ziehen, -pressen, -schnüren, einengen; **con'strict·ed** [-tɪd] *adj.* eingeengt; beschränkt; **con'stric·tion** [-kʃn] *s.* Zs.-ziehung *f*, Einschnürung *f*; Beengtheit *f*; **con'stric·tor** [-tə] *s.* **1.** *anat.* Schließmuskel *m*; **2.** *zo.* 'Boa *f*, Riesenschlange *f*.

con·strin·gent [kən'strɪndʒənt] *adj.* zs.-ziehend.

con·struct [kən'strʌkt] *v/t.* **1.** bauen, errichten; **2.** ⚙, ⚗, *ling.* konstruieren; **3.** *fig.* aufbauen, gestalten, formen; ausarbeiten, entwerfen, ersinnen; **con'struc·tion** [-kʃn] *s.* **1.** (Er)Bauen *n*, Bau *m*, Errichtung *f*: ***under* ~** im Bau; **2.** Bauwerk *n*, Bau *m*, Gebäude *n*; **3.** Bauweise *f*; *fig.* Aufbau *m*, Anlage *f*, Gestaltung *f*, Form *f*; **4.** ⚙, ⚗ Konstrukti'on *f*; **5.** *ling.* Konstrukti'on *f*, Satzbau *m*, Wortfügung *f*; **6.** Auslegung *f*, Deutung *f*: ***put a wrong* ~ *on s.th.*** et. falsch auslegen *od.* auffassen; **con'struc·tion·al** [-kʃənl] *adj.* Bau..., Konstruktions..., baulich; **con'struc·tive** [-tɪv] *adj.* □ **1.** aufbauend, schaffend, schöpferisch, konstruk'tiv; **2.** konstruk'tiv, positiv: **~ *criticism***; **3.** Bau..., Konstruktions...; **4.** a) *a.* ⚖ abgeleitet, angenommen, b) ⚖ mittelbar; **con'struc·tor** [-tə] *s.* Erbauer *m*, Konstruk'teur *m*.

con·strue [kən'stru:] **I** *v/t.* **1.** *ling.* a) *Satz* zergliedern, konstruieren, b) (Wort für Wort) über'setzen; **2.** auslegen; deuten; auffassen; **II** *v/i.* **3.** *ling.* sich konstruieren *od.* zergliedern lassen.

con·sub·stan·ti·al·i·ty [ˈkɒnsəbˌstænʃɪˈælətɪ] *s. eccl.* Wesensgleichheit *f* (*der drei göttlichen Personen*); **con·sub·stan·ti·ate** [ˌkɒnsəbˈstænʃɪeɪt] *v/t.* (*v/i.* sich) zu e-m einzigen Wesen vereinigen; **ˈcon·subˌstan·tiˈa·tion** [-ɪˈeɪʃn] *s. eccl.* Konsubstantiatiˈon *f* (*Mitgegenwart des Leibes u. Blutes Christi beim Abendmahl*).

con·sue·tude [ˈkɒnswɪtjuːd] *s.* Gewohnheit *f*, Brauch *m*; **con·sue·tu·di·nar·y** [ˌkɒnswɪˈtjuːdɪnərɪ] *adj.* gewohnheitsmäßig, Gewohnheits…

con·sul [ˈkɒnsəl] *s.* Konsul *m*: **~-general** Generalkonsul; **ˈcon·su·lar** [-sjʊlə] Konsulats…, Konsular…, konsuˈlarisch: **~ invoice** ⚚ Konsulatsfaktura *f*; **ˈcon·su·late** [-sjʊlət] *s.* Konsuˈlat *n* (*a. Gebäude*): **~-general** Generalkonsulat; **ˈcon·sul·ship** [-ʃɪp] *s.* Amt *n* e-s Konsuls.

con·sult [kənˈsʌlt] **I** *v/t.* **1.** um Rat fragen, befragen, *Arzt etc.* zu Rate ziehen, konsultieren: **~ one's watch** auf die Uhr sehen; **~ the dictionary** im Wörterbuch nachschlagen; **2.** beachten, berücksichtigen: **~ s.o.'s wishes**; **II** *v/i.* **3.** sich beraten *od.* besprechen (**with** mit, **about** über *acc.*); **conˈsult·ant** [-tənt] *s.* **1.** (*Fach-, Betriebs- etc.*)Berater *m*; **2.** ⚕ a) Facharzt *m*, b) fachärztlicher Berater; **con·sul·ta·tion** [ˌkɒnsəlˈteɪʃn] *s.* Beratung *f*, Rücksprache *f* (**on** über *acc.*), Konsultatiˈon *f* (*a.* ⚕): **~ hour** ⚕ Sprechstunde *f*; **conˈsult·a·tive** [-tətɪv] *adj.* beratend; **conˈsult·ing** [-tɪŋ] *adj.* beratend: **~ engineer** technischer (Betriebs)Berater; **~ room** ⚕ Sprechzimmer *n*.

con·sum·a·ble [kənˈsjuːməbl] **I** *adj.* verzehrbar, verbrauchbar, zerstörbar; **II** *s. mst pl.* Verˈbrauchsarˌtikel *m*; **con·sume** [kənˈsjuːm] **I** *v/t.* **1.** verzehren (*a. fig.*), verbrauchen: **be ~d with** *fig.* erfüllt sein von, von *Haß, Verlangen* verzehrt werden, vor *Neid* vergehen; **consuming desire** brennende Begierde; **2.** zerstören: **~d by fire** ein Raub der Flammen; **3.** (auf)essen, trinken; **4.** verschwenden; *Zeit* rauben *od.* benötigen; **II** *v/i.* **5.** *a.* **~ away** sich verzehren (*a. fig.*); sich verbrauchen *od.* abnutzen; **conˈsum·er** [-mə] *s.* Verbraucher *m*, Abnehmer *m*, Konsuˈment *m*: **~ goods** Konsumgüter; **~ resistance** Kaufunlust *f*; **~ society** Konsumgesellschaft *f*; **ultimate ~** Endverbraucher *m*; **conˈsum·er·ism** [-mərɪzəm] *s.* **1.** Verbraucherschutzbewegung *f*; **2.** kritische Verbraucherhaltung.

con·sum·mate **I** *v/t.* [ˈkɒnsəmeɪt] vollˈenden; *bsd. Ehe* vollˈziehen; **II** *adj.* □ [kənˈsʌmɪt] vollˈendet, ˈvollkommen, völlig: **~ skill** höchste Geschicklichkeit; **con·sum·ma·tion** [ˌkɒnsəˈmeɪʃn] *s.* **1.** Vollˈendung *f*, Ziel *n*, Ende *n*; **2.** Erfüllung *f*; **3.** ⚖ Vollˈziehung *f* (*Ehe*).

con·sump·tion [kənˈsʌmpʃn] *s.* **1.** Verbrauch *m*, Konˈsum *m* (**of** an *dat. od.* von); **2.** Verzehrung *f*; Zerstörung *f*; **3.** Verzehr *m*: **unfit for human ~** für menschlichen Verzehr ungeeignet; **for public ~** *fig.* für die Öffentlichkeit bestimmt; **4.** ⚕ *obs.* Schwindsucht *f*; **conˈsump·tive** [-ptɪv] **I** *adj.* □ **1.** verbrauchend, Verbrauchs…; **2.** (ver)zehrend; **3.** ⚕ *obs.* schwindsüchtig; **II** *s.* **4.** ⚕ *obs.* Schwindsüchtige(r *m*) *f*.

con·tact [ˈkɒntækt] **I** *s.* **1.** Berührung *f* (*a.* ⚗), Konˈtakt *m*; ⚔ Feindberührung *f*; **2.** *fig.* Konˈtakt *m*: a) Verbindung *f*, Beziehung *f*, Fühlung *f* (*a.* ⚔), b) Verbindungs-, Gewährsmann *m*, c) *pol.* Konˈtaktmann *m* (*Agent*): **make ~s** Verbindungen anknüpfen; **business ~** Geschäftsverbindung; **3.** ϟ Konˈtakt *m*: a) Anschluß *m*, b) Konˈtaktstück *n*: **make** (**break**) **~** Kontakt herstellen (unterbrechen); **4.** ⚕ Konˈtaktperˌson *f*; **II** *v/t.* **5.** in Berührung kommen mit; Konˈtakt haben mit, berühren; **6.** *fig.* sich in Verbindung setzen mit, Beziehungen *od.* Konˈtakt aufnehmen zu, sich an *j-n* wenden; **~ box** *s.* ϟ Anschlußdose *f*; **~ break·er** *s.* ϟ (ˈStrom-)Unterˌbrecher *m*; **~ flight** *s.* ✈ Sichtflug *m*; **~ lens** *s.* Haft-, Konˈtaktschale *f*, Konˈtaktlinse *f*; **~ light** *s.* ✈ Lande-(bahn)feuer *n*; **ˈ~ˌmak·er** *s.* ϟ Einschalter *m*, Stromschließer *m*; **~ man** *s.* [*irr.*] → **contact** 2 b, c; **~ mine** *s.* ⚔ Tretmine *f*.

con·tac·tor [ˈkɒntæktə] *s.* ϟ (Schalt-)Schütz *n*: **~ switch** Schütz(schalter *m*).

con·tact| print *s. phot.* Konˈtaktabzug *m*; **~ rail** *s.* ϟ Konˈtaktschiene *f*.

con·ta·gion [kənˈteɪdʒən] *s.* **1.** ⚕ a) Ansteckung *f* (*durch Berührung*), b) ansteckende Krankheit; **2.** *fig.* Vergiftung *f*; verderblicher Einfluß; **conˈta·gious** [-dʒəs] *adj.* □ **1.** ⚕ a) ansteckend (*a. fig. Stimmung etc.*), b) infiziert: **~ matter** Krankheitsstoff *m*; **2.** *fig. obs.* verderblich.

con·tain [kənˈteɪn] *v/t.* **1.** enthalten; *fig. a.* beinhalten; **2.** (um)ˈfassen, einschließen, aufnehmen, Raum haben für; **3.** bestehen aus, messen; **4.** zügeln, im Zaum halten, bändigen: **~ one's anger**; **5. ~ o.s.** sich beherrschen *od.* mäßigen: **be unable to ~ o.s. for** sich nicht fassen können vor; **6.** *a.* ⚔ fest-, zuˈrückhalten; ⚔ *Feindkräfte* fesseln, binden; *a. pol.* eindämmen: **~ the attack** den Angriff abriegeln; **~ a fire** e-n Brand unter Kontrolle bringen *od.* eindämmen; **7.** ⚗ teilbar sein durch; **conˈtain·er** [-nə] *s.* **1.** Behälter *m*; Gefäß *n*; Kaˈnister *m*; **2.** ⚚ Conˈtainer *m* (*Großbehälter*): **~ port** Containerhafen *m*; **~ ship** Containerschiff *n*; **conˈtain·er·ize** [-nəraɪz] *v/t.* **1.** auf Conˈtainerbetrieb ˈumstellen; **2.** in Conˈtainern transportieren; **conˈtain·ment** [-mənt] *s. fig.* Eindämmung *f*, In-ˈSchach-Halten *n*: **policy of ~** Eindämmungspolitik *f*.

con·tam·i·nant [kənˈtæmɪnənt] *s.* Verseuchungsstoff *m*; **conˈtam·i·nate** [-neɪt] *v/t.* **1.** verunreinigen; **2.** *a. fig.* infizieren, vergiften, (*a.* radioakˈtiv) verseuchen: **~d area** verseuchtes Gelände; **con·tam·i·na·tion** [kənˌtæmɪˈneɪʃn] *s.* **1.** Verunreinigung *f*; **2.** (*a.* radioakˈtive *etc.*) Verseuchung: **~ meter** Geigerzähler *m*; **3.** *ling.* Kontaminatiˈon *f*.

con·tan·go [kənˈtæŋgəʊ] *s.* ⚚ *Börse*: Reˈport *m* (*Kurszuschlag*).

con·temn [kənˈtem] *v/t. poet.* verachten; **conˈtem·nor** [-nə] *s.* ⚖ j-d der **contempt of court** begeht (→ **contempt** 4).

con·tem·plate [ˈkɒntempleɪt] **I** *v/t.* **1.** (nachdenklich) betrachten; nachdenken über (*acc.*); überˈdenken; **2.** ins Auge fassen, erwägen, beabsichtigen; **3.** erwarten, rechnen mit; **II** *v/i.* **4.** nachsinnen; **con·tem·pla·tion** [ˌkɒntemˈpleɪʃn] *s.* **1.** (nachdenkliche) Betrachtung; **2.** Nachdenken *n*, -sinnen *n*; **3.** *bsd. eccl.* Meditatiˈon *f*, innere Einkehr, Versunkenheit *f*; **4.** Erwägung *f*: **have in ~** → **contemplate** 2; **be in ~** erwogen *od.* geplant werden; **5.** Absicht *f*; **ˈcon·tem·pla·tive** [-tɪv] *adj.* □ **1.** nachdenklich; **2.** beschaulich, besinnlich, kontemplaˈtiv.

con·tem·po·ra·ne·ous [kənˌtempəˈreɪnjəs] *adj.* □ gleichzeitig (**with** mit); **conˌtem·po'ra·ne·ous·ness** [-nɪs] *s.* Gleichzeitigkeit *f*; **con·tem·po·rar·y** [kənˈtempərərɪ] **I** *adj.* **1.** zeitgenössisch: a) heutig, unserer Zeit, b) der damaligen Zeit: **~ history** Zeitgeschichte *f*; **2.** gleichalt(e)rig; **II** *s.* **3.** Zeitgenosse *m*, -genossin *f*; **4.** Altersgenosse *m*, -genossin *f*; **5.** gleichzeitig erscheinende Zeitung, Konkurˈrenz(blatt *n*) *f*.

con·tempt [kənˈtempt] *s.* **1.** Verachtung *f*, Geringschätzung *f*: **feel ~ for s.o.**, **hold s.o. in ~** j-n verachten; **bring into ~** verächtlich machen; → **beneath** II; **2.** Schande *f*, Schmach *f*: **fall into ~** in Schande geraten; **3.** ˈMißachtung *f*; **4. ~** (**of court**) ⚖ ˈMißachtung des Gerichts (*Ungebühr, Nichterscheinen etc.*); **con·tempt·i·bil·i·ty** [kənˌtemptəˈbɪlətɪ] *s.* Verächtlichkeit *f*; **conˈtempt·i·ble** [-təbl] *adj.* □ **1.** verächtlich, verachtenswert, nichtswürdig: **Old ⁓s** *brit. Expeditionskorps in Frankreich 1914*; **2.** gemein, niederträchtig; **conˈtemp·tu·ous** [-tjʊəs] *adj.* □ verachtungsvoll, geringschätzig: **be ~ of s.th.** et. verachten; **conˈtemp·tu·ous·ness** [-tjʊəsnɪs] *s.* Verachtung *f*, Geringschätzigkeit *f*.

con·tend [kənˈtend] **I** *v/i.* **1.** kämpfen, ringen (**with** mit, **for** um); **2.** *mit Worten* streiten, disputieren (**about** über *acc.*, **against** gegen); **3.** wetteifern, sich bewerben (**for** um); **II** *v/t.* **4.** behaupten, geltend machen (**that** daß); **conˈtend·er** [-də] *s.* Kämpfer(in); Bewerber(in) (**for** um); Konkurˈrent(in); **conˈtend·ing** [-dɪŋ] *adj.* **1.** streitend, kämpfend; **2.** widerˈstreitend; **3.** konkurrierend.

con·tent[1] [ˈkɒntent] *s.* **1.** *mst pl.* (*Raum*)Inhalt *m*, Fassungsvermögen *n*; ˈUmfang *m*; **2.** *pl. a. fig.* Inhalt *m* (*Buch etc.*); **3.** *mst* ⚗ Gehalt *m*: **gold ~** Goldgehalt.

con·tent[2] [kənˈtent] **I** *pred. adj.* **1.** zuˈfrieden; **2.** bereit, willens (**to** *inf.* zu *inf.*); **3.** *parl. Brit.* (*nur House of Lords*) einverstanden: **not ~** dagegen; **II** *v/t.* **4.** befriedigen, zuˈfriedenstellen; **5. ~ o.s.** zuˈfrieden sein, sich zufrieden geben *od.* begnügen *od.* abfinden (**with** mit); **III** *s.* **6.** Zuˈfriedenheit *f*, Befriedigung *f*: **to one's heart's ~** nach Herzenslust; **7.** *mst pl. parl. Brit.* Ja-Stimmen *pl.*; **conˈtent·ed** [-tɪd] *adj.* □ zuˈfrieden (**with** mit); **conˈtent·ed·ness** [-tɪdnɪs] *s.* Zuˈfriedenheit *f*.

con·ten·tion [kənˈtenʃn] *s.* **1.** Streit *m*, Zank *m*; **2.** Wortstreit *m*; **3.** Behauptung *f*: **my ~ is that** ich behaupte, daß; **4.** Streitpunkt *m*; **conˈten·tious** [-ʃəs] *adj.* □ **1.** streitsüchtig; **2.** streitig (*a.*

⚖), strittig, um'stritten; **con'ten·tious·ness** [-ʃəsnɪs] *s.* Streitsucht *f.*
con·tent·ment [kən'tentmənt] *s.* Zu'friedenheit *f.*
con·test I *s.* ['kɒntest] **1.** Kampf *m*, Streit *m*; **2.** Wettkampf *m*, -streit *m*, -bewerb *m* (***for*** um); **II** *v/t.* [kən'test] **3.** ⚔ *u. fig.* kämpfen um; **4.** konkurrieren *od.* sich bewerben um; **5.** *pol.* ~ ***a seat*** *od.* ***an election*** für e-e Wahl kandidieren; **6.** bestreiten; *a.* ⚖ *Aussage, Testament, Wahl(ergebnis) etc.* anfechten; **III** *v/i.* [kən'test] **7.** wetteifern (***with*** mit); **con·test·a·ble** [kən'testəbl] *adj.* strittig; anfechtbar; **con·test·ant** [kən'testənt] *s.* **1.** (Wett)Bewerber(in); **2.** Wettkämpfer(in); **3.** Kandi'dat(in); **4.** ⚖ a) streitende Par'tei, b) Anfechter(in); **con·tes·ta·tion** [ˌkɒntes'teɪʃn] *s.* Streit *m*; Dis'put *m.*
con·text ['kɒntekst] *s.* **1.** (*inhaltlicher*) Zs.-hang, Kontext *m*: ***out of*** ~ aus dem Zs.-hang gerissen; **2.** Um'gebung *f*, Mili'eu *n*; **con·tex·tu·al** [kɒn'tekstjʊəl] *adj.* □ dem Zs.-hang gemäß; **con·tex·ture** [kɒn'tekstʃə] *s.* **1.** (Auf)Bau *m*, Gefüge *n*, Struk'tur *f*; **2.** Gewebe *n.*
con·ti·gu·i·ty [ˌkɒntɪ'gjuːətɪ] *s.* **1.** (***to***) Angrenzen *n* (an *acc.*), Berührung *f* (mit); **2.** Nähe *f*, Nachbarschaft *f*; **con·tig·u·ous** [kən'tɪgjʊəs] *adj.* □ (***to***) **1.** angrenzend (an *acc.*), berührend (*acc.*); **2.** nahe, benachbart (*dat.*).
con·ti·nence ['kɒntɪnəns] *s.* Mäßigkeit *f*, (*bsd. sexuelle*) Enthaltsamkeit; **'con·ti·nent** [-nənt] **I** *adj.* □ **1.** mäßig; enthaltsam, keusch; **II** *s.* **2.** Konti'nent *m*, Erdteil *m*; **3.** Festland *n*: ***the*** ♀ *Brit.* das europäische Festland.
con·ti·nen·tal [ˌkɒntɪ'nentl] **I** *adj.* □ **1.** kontinen'tal, Kontinental...: ~ ***shelf*** Festlandsockel *m*; **2.** *mst* ♀ *Brit.* kontinen'tal (*das europäische Festland betreffend*); ausländisch: ~ ***quilt*** *Brit.* Federbett *n*; ~ ***tour*** Europareise *f*; **II** *s.* **3.** Festländer(in); **4.** ♀ *Brit.* Kontinen'taleuroˌpäer(in); **ˌcon·ti'nen·tal·ize** [-təlaɪz] *v/t.* kontinen'talen Cha'rakter geben (*dat.*): ~***d*** *Brit.* ‚europäisiert'.
con·tin·gen·cy [kən'tɪndʒənsɪ] *s.* **1.** Eventuali'tät *f*, Möglichkeit *f*, unvorhergesehener Fall: ~ ***insured against*** Versicherungsfall *m*; **2.** Zufälligkeit *f*, Zufall *m*; **3.** *pl.* ✝ unvorhergesehene Ausgaben *pl.*; **con'tin·gent** [-nt] **I** *adj.* □ **1.** eventu'ell, möglich; zufällig, ungewiß; gelegentlich; **2.** (***on, upon***) abhängig (von), bedingt (durch), verbunden (mit): ~ ***fee*** Erfolgshonorar *n*; ~ ***reserve*** ✝ Sicherheitsrücklage *f*; **II** *s.* **3.** Anteil *m*, Beitrag *m*, Quote *f*, (⚔ 'Truppen)Kontinˌgent *n*; **con'tin·gent·ly** [-ntlɪ] *adv.* möglicherweise.
con·tin·u·al [kən'tɪnjʊəl] *adj.* □ **1.** fortwährend, 'ununterˌbrochen, (an)dauernd, (be)ständig; **2.** immer 'wiederkehrend, (sehr) häufig, oft wieder'holt; **3.** *a.* ⩘ kontinuierlich, stetig; **con'tin·u·al·ly** [-lɪ] *adv.* **1.** fortwährend *etc.*; **2.** immer wieder; **con'tin·u·ance** [-əns] *s.* **1.** → ***continuation*** 1, 2; **2.** Dauer *f*, Beständigkeit *f*; **3.** (Ver)Bleiben *n*; **con'tin·u·ant** [-ənt] *s.* **1.** *ling.* Dauerlaut *m*; **2.** ⩘ Kontinu'ante *f*; **con·tin·u·a·tion** [kənˌtɪnjʊ'eɪʃn] *s.* **1.** Fortsetzung *f* (*a. e-s Romans etc.*), Weiterführung *f*: ~ ***school*** Fortbildungsschule *f*; **2.** Fortbestand *m*, -dauer *f*; **3.** Erweiterung *f*; **4.** Verlängerung(sstück *n*) *f*; **5.** ✝ Prolongati'on *f*; **con·tin·ue** [kən'tɪnjuː] **I** *v/i.* **1.** fortfahren, weitermachen; **2.** fortdauern: a) (an)dauern, anhalten, b) sich fortsetzen, weitergehen, c) (fort)bestehen; **3.** (ver)bleiben: ~ ***in office*** im Amt bleiben; **4.** verbeharren (***in*** bei, in *dat.*); **5.** ~ ***doing***, ~ ***to do*** weiter *od.* auch weiterhin tun; ~ ***talking*** weiterreden; ~ (***to be***) ***obstinate*** eigensinnig bleiben; **II** *v/t.* **6.** fortsetzen, -führen, fortfahren mit: ***to be*** ~***d*** Fortsetzung folgt; **7.** verlängern, weiterführen; **8.** aufrechterhalten; beibehalten, erhalten; belassen; **9.** vertagen; **con'tin·ued** [-juːd] *adj.* □ **1.** → ***continuous*** 1–3: ~ ***existence*** Fortbestand *m*; **2.** in Fortsetzungen erscheinend; **con·ti·nu·i·ty** [ˌkɒntɪ'njuːətɪ] *s.* **1.** Fortbestand *m*, Stetigkeit *f*; **2.** Zs.-hang *m*; enge Verbindung; **3.** 'ununterˌbrochene Folge; **4.** *fig.* roter Faden; **5.** *Film*: Drehbuch *n*; *Radio*, *TV*: Manu'skript *n*: ~ ***girl*** Skriptgirl *n*; ~ ***writer*** a) Drehbuchautor *m*, b) Textschreiber *m.*
con·tin·u·ous [kən'tɪnjʊəs] *adj.* □ **1.** 'ununterˌbrochen, (fort)laufend; zs.-hängend; **2.** unaufhörlich, andauernd, fortwährend; **3.** kontinuierlich (*a.* ⚙, *phys.*): ~ ***function***; **4.** *ling.* progres'siv: ~ ***form*** Verlaufsform *f*; ~ **cur·rent** *s.* ⚡ Gleichstrom *m*; ~ **fire** *s.* ⚔ Dauerfeuer *n*; ~ **op·er·a·tion** *s.* ⚙ Dauerbetrieb *m*; ~ **pap·er** *s.* 'Endlospaˌpier *n*; ~ **per·form·ance** *s. thea.* Non'stopvorstellung *f.*
con·tin·u·um [kɒn'tɪnjʊəm] **1.** ⩘ Kon'tinuum *n*; **2.** → ***continuity*** 3.
con·tort [kən'tɔːt] *v/t.* **1.** (*a. Worte etc.*) verdrehen; **2.** *Gesicht etc.* verzerren, verziehen; **con'tor·tion** [-ɔːʃn] *s.* **1.** Verzerrung *f*; **2.** Verrenkung *f*; **con'tor·tion·ist** [-ɔːʃnɪst] *s.* **1.** Schlangenmensch *m*; **2.** Wortverdreher(in).
con·tour ['kɒnˌtʊə] **I** *s.* Kon'tur *f*, 'Umriß(linie *f*) *m*; **II** *v/t.* um'reißen, den 'Umriß zeichnen von; profilieren; *Straße* e-r Höhenlinie folgen lassen; ~ **chair** *s.* körpergerecht gestalteter Sessel; ~ **lathe** *s.* ⚙ Kopierdrehbank *f*; ~ **line** *s. surv.* Höhenlinie *f*; ~ **map** *s.* Höhenlinienkarte *f.*
con·tra ['kɒntrə] **I** *prp.* gegen, kontra (*acc.*); **II** *adv.* da'gegen; **III** *s.* ✝ Gegen-, 'Kreditseite *f*: ~ ***account*** Gegenrechnung *f.*
'con·tra|·band I *s.* **1.** 'Konterbande *f*, Bann-, Schmuggelware *f*: ~ ***of war*** Kriegskonterbande; **2.** Schmuggel *m*, Schleichhandel *m*; **II** *adj.* **3.** Schmuggel..., gesetzwidrig; **ˌ~·bass** [-'beɪs] *s.* ♪ 'Kontrabaß *m*; **ˌ~·bas'soon** *s.* ♪ 'Kontrafaˌgott *n.*
con·tra·cep·tion [ˌkɒntrə'sepʃn] *s.* Empfängnisverhütung *f*; **ˌcon·tra'cep·tive** [-ptɪv] *adj. u. s.* empfängnisverhütend(es Mittel).
con·tract I *s.* ['kɒntrækt] **1.** *a.* ⚖ Vertrag *m*, Kon'trakt *m*: ***by*** ~ vertraglich; ***under*** ~ a) (***to***) vertraglich verpflichtet (*dat.*), b) ✝ in Auftrag gegeben (*Arbeit*); ~ (***to kill***) Mordauftrag *m*; **2.** Vertragsurkunde *f*; **3.** ✝ (Liefer-, Werk-) Vertrag *m*, (fester) Auftrag: ~ ***note*** Schlußschein *m*, -note *f*; ~ ***processing*** Lohnveredelung *f*; **4.** Ak'kord(arbeit *f*) *m*; **5.** *a.* ***marriage*** ~ Ehevertrag *m*; **6.** a) *a.* ~ ***bridge*** Kontrakt-Bridge *n* (*Kartenspiel*), b) höchstes Gebot; **II** *v/t.* [kən'trækt] **7.** *Muskel* zs.-ziehen; *Stirn* runzeln; **8.** *ling.* zs.-ziehen, verkürzen; **9.** ein-, verengen, be-, einschränken; **10.** *Gewohnheit* annehmen, sich *e-e Krankheit* zuziehen; *Vertrag, Ehe, Freundschaft* schließen; *Schulden* machen; **III** *v/i.* [kən'trækt] **11.** sich zs.-ziehen, (ein)schrumpfen; **12.** enger *od.* kürzer *od.* kleiner werden; **13.** e-n Vertrag schließen, sich vertraglich verpflichten (***to*** *inf.* zu *inf.*, ***for*** zu): ~ ***for s.th.*** et. vertraglich übernehmen; ***as*** ~***ed*** wie (vertraglich) vereinbart; ***the*** ~***ing parties*** die vertragschließenden Parteien; ~ **in** *v/i. pol. Brit.* sich zur Bezahlung des Par'teibeitrages (*für die Labour Party*) verpflichten; ~ **out** *v/i.* sich freizeichnen, sich von der Verpflichtung befreien.
con·tract·ed [kən'træktɪd] *adj.* □ **1.** zs.-gezogen; verkürzt; **2.** *fig.* engherzig; beschränkt; **con'tract·i·ble** [-təbl], **con'trac·tile** [-taɪl] *adj.* zs.-ziehbar.
con·trac·tion [kən'trækʃn] *s.* **1.** Zs.-ziehung *f*; **2.** *ling.* Ver-, Abkürzung *f*; Kurzwort *n*; **3.** Verkleinerung *f*, Einschränkung *f*; **4.** Zuziehung *f* (*Krankheit*); Eingehen *n* (*Schulden*); Annahme *f* (*Gewohnheit*); **con'trac·tive** [-ktɪv] *adj.* zs.-ziehend; **con'trac·tor** [-ktə] *s.* **1.** (*bsd.* 'Bau- *etc.*)Unterˌnehmer *m*; **2.** Unter'nehmer *m* (*Dienst-, Werkvertrag*), (Ver'trags)Liefeˌrant *m*; **3.** *anat.* Schließmuskel *m*; **con'trac·tu·al** [-ktʃʊəl] *adj.* vertraglich, Vertrags...: ~ ***capacity*** ⚖ Geschäftsfähigkeit *f.*
con·tra·dict [ˌkɒntrə'dɪkt] *v/t.* **1.** (*a.* ***o.s.*** sich) wider'sprechen (*dat.*); im 'Widerspruch stehen zu; **2.** *et.* bestreiten, in Abrede stellen; **ˌcon·tra'dic·tion** [-kʃn] *s.* **1.** 'Widerspruch *m*, -rede *f*: ***spirit of*** ~ Widerspruchsgeist *m*; **2.** 'Widerspruch *m*, Unvereinbarkeit *f*: ***in*** ~ ***to*** im Widerspruch zu; ~ ***in terms*** Widerspruch in sich; **3.** Bestreitung *f*; **ˌcon·tra'dic·tious** [-kʃəs] *adj.* □ zum 'Widerspruch geneigt, streitsüchtig; **ˌcon·tra'dic·to·ri·ness** [-tərɪnɪs] *s.* **1.** 'Widerspruch *m*; **2.** 'Widerspruchsgeist *m*; **ˌcon·tra'dic·to·ry** [-tərɪ] **I** *adj.* □ (sich) wider'sprechend, entgegengesetzt; unvereinbar; **II** *s.* 'Widerspruch *m*, Gegensatz *m.*
con·tra·dis·tinc·tion [ˌkɒntrədɪ'stɪŋkʃn] *s.* Gegensatz *m*: ***in*** ~ ***to*** (*od.* ***from***) im Gegensatz zu.
con·trail ['kɒntreɪl] *s.* ✈ Kon'densstreifen *m.*
con·tra·in·di·cate [ˌkɒntrə'ɪndɪkeɪt] *v/t.* ⚕ kontraindizieren.
con·tral·to [kən'træltəʊ] *pl.* **-tos** *s.* ♪ Alt *m*: a) Altstimme *f*, b) Al'tist(in), c) 'Altparˌtie *f.*
con·trap·tion [kən'træpʃn] *s.* F (neumodischer) Appa'rat, (komisches) Ding(s).
con·tra·pun·tal [ˌkɒntrə'pʌntl] *adj.* ♪ 'kontrapunktisch.
con·tra·ri·e·ty [ˌkɒntrə'raɪətɪ] *s.* **1.** Gegensätzlichkeit *f*, Unvereinbarkeit *f*; **2.** 'Widerspruch *m*, Gegensatz *m* (***to*** zu); **con·tra·ri·ly** ['kɒntrərəlɪ] *adv.* **1.** entgegen (***to*** *dat.*); **2.** andererseits; **con-**

tra·ri·ness ['kɒntrərɪnɪs] *s.* **1.** Gegensätzlichkeit *f*, 'Widerspruch *m*; **2.** Widrigkeit *f*, Ungunst *f*; **3.** F [*a.* kən'treər-] 'Widerspenstigkeit *f*, Eigensinn *m*; **con·tra·ri·wise** ['kɒntrərɪwaɪz] *adv.* im Gegenteil; 'umgekehrt; and(e)rerseits.

con·tra·ry ['kɒntrərɪ] **I** *adj.* □ → ***contrarily***; **1.** entgegengesetzt, gegensätzlich, -teilig; **2.** (***to***) wider'sprechend (*dat.*), im 'Widerspruch (zu); gegen (*acc.*), entgegen (*dat.*): ~ ***to expectations*** wider Erwarten; **3.** F [*a.* kən'treərɪ] 'widerspenstig, aufsässig; **II** *adv.* **4.** ~ ***to*** gegen, wider: ***act*** ~ ***to nature*** wider die Natur handeln; **III** *s.* **5.** Gegenteil *n* (***to*** von *od. gen.*): ***on the*** ~ im Gegenteil; ***unless I hear to the*** ~ falls ich nichts Gegenteiliges höre; ***proof to the*** ~ Gegenbeweis *m*.

con·trast I *s.* ['kɒntrɑːst] Kon'trast *m*, Gegensatz *m*: ~ ***control*** *TV* Kontrastregler *m*; ***by*** ~ ***with*** im Vergleich mit; ***in*** ~ ***to*** im Gegensatz zu; ***be a great*** ~ ***to*** grundverschieden sein von; **II** *v/t.* [kən'trɑːst] (***with***) entgegensetzen, gegen'überstellen (*dat.*); vergleichen (mit); **III** *v/i.* [kən'trɑːst] (***with***) e-n Gegensatz bilden (zu), sich scharf unter'scheiden (von); sich abheben, abstechen (von): ~***ing colo(u)rs*** Kontrastfarben; **con·trast·y** [kən'trɑːstɪ] *adj.* kon'trastreich.

con·tra·vene [ˌkɒntrə'viːn] *v/t.* **1.** zu'widerhandeln (*dat.*), verstoßen gegen, über'treten, verletzen; **2.** im 'Widerspruch stehen zu; **3.** bestreiten; ˌ**contra'ven·tion** [-'venʃn] *s.* (***of***) Über'tretung *f* (von *od. gen.*); Verstoß *m*, Zu'widerhandlung *f* (gegen): ***in*** ~ ***of the rules*** entgegen den Vorschriften.

con·tre·temps ['kɔ̃ːntrətɑ̃ːŋ] (*Fr.*) *s.* unglücklicher Zufall, Widrigkeit *f*, ‚Panne' *f*.

con·trib·ute [kən'trɪbjuːt] **I** *v/t.* **1.** beitragen, beisteuern (***to*** zu) (*beide a. fig.*); spenden (***to*** für); ✝ a) *Kapital in e-e Firma* einbringen, b) *Brit. Geld* nachschießen; **2.** *Zeitungsartikel* beitragen; **II** *v/i.* **3.** (***to***) beitragen, e-n Beitrag leisten (zu), mitwirken (an *dat.*, bei): ~ ***to a newspaper*** für e-e Zeitung schreiben; **con·tri·bu·tion** [ˌkɒntrɪ'bjuːʃn] *s.* **1.** Beitragen *n*; **2.** Beitrag *m* (*a. für Zeitung*), Beisteuer *f*, Beihilfe *f* (***to*** zu); Spende *f* (***to*** für): ***make a*** ~ e-n Beitrag liefern; **3.** Mitwirkung *f* (***to*** an *dat.*); **4.** ✝ a) Einlage *f*: ~ ***in kind*** (***cash***) Sach-(Bar-)einlage, b) Nachschuß *m*, c) Sozi'alversicherungsbeitrag *m*: ***employer's*** ~ Arbeitgeberanteil *m*, Sozialleistung *f*; **con'trib·u·tive** [-jʊtɪv] *adj.* → ***contributory*** 1, 2; **con'trib·u·tor** [-jʊtə] *s.* **1.** Beitragende(r *m*) *f*; Beisteuernde(r *m*) *f*; **2.** Mitwirkende(r *m*) *f*; Mitarbeiter(in) (*bsd. Zeitung*); **con'trib·u·to·ry** [-jʊtərɪ] **I** *adj.* **1.** beisteuernd, beitragend (***to*** zu); Beitrags…; **2.** mitwirkend (***to*** an *dat.*, bei); Mit…: ~ ***causes*** ⚖ mitverursachende Umstände; ~ ***negligence*** mitwirkendes Verschulden; **3.** beitragspflichtig; **4.** ✝ *Brit.* nachschußpflichtig; **II** *s.* **5.** Beitrags- *od.* ✝ *Brit.* Nachschußpflichtige(r *m*) *f*.

con·trite ['kɒntraɪt] *adj.* □ zerknirscht, reuevoll; **con·tri·tion** [kən'trɪʃn] *s.* Zerknirschung *f*, Reue *f*.

con·triv·ance [kən'traɪvns] *s.* **1.** Ein-, Vorrichtung *f*; Appa'rat *m*; **2.** Kunstgriff *m*, Erfindung *f*, Plan *m*; **3.** Findigkeit *f*, Scharfsinn *m*; **4.** Bewerkstelligung *f*; **con·trive** [kən'traɪv] **I** *v/t.* **1.** erfinden, ersinnen, (sich) ausdenken, entwerfen; **2.** *Pläne* schmieden, aushecken; **3.** zu'stande bringen; **4.** es fertigbringen, es verstehen, es bewerkstelligen (***to*** *inf.* zu *inf.*); **II** *v/i.* **5.** Pläne *od.* Ränke schmieden; **6.** haushalten, auskommen.

con·trol [kən'trəʊl] **I** *v/t.* **1.** beherrschen, die Herrschaft *od.* Kon'trolle haben über (*acc.*), *et.* in der Hand haben *od.* kontrollieren: ~***ling share*** (*od.* ***interest***) ✝ maßgebliche Beteiligung; **2.** verwalten, beaufsichtigen, über'wachen; *Preise etc.* kontrollieren, nachprüfen; **3.** lenken, steuern, leiten; regeln, regulieren: ***radio***-~***led*** funkgesteuert; ~***led ventilation*** regulierbare Lüftung; **4.** (*a.* ***o.s.*** sich) beherrschen, meistern, im Zaum halten, Einhalt gebieten (*dat.*); zügeln; **5.** in Schranken halten, bekämpfen; **6.** (staatlich) bewirtschaften, planen, binden: ~***led economy*** Planwirtschaft *f*; ~***led prices*** gebundene Preise; ~***led rent*** preisrechtlich gebundene Miete; **II** *s.* **7.** Macht *f*, Gewalt *f*, Herrschaft *f*, Kon'trolle *f* (***of***, ***over*** über *acc.*): ***foreign*** ~ Überfremdung *f*; ***bring under*** ~ Herr werden über (*acc.*); ***have the situation under*** ~ Herr der Lage sein; ***get*** ~ ***over*** in s-e Gewalt bekommen; ***get beyond s.o.'s*** ~ j-m über den Kopf wachsen; ***get out of*** ~ außer Kontrolle geraten; ***have*** ~ ***over*** a) → 1, b) Gewalt haben über (*acc.*); ***keep under*** ~ im Zaume halten; ***lose*** ~ ***over*** die Herrschaft *od.* Gewalt *od.* Kontrolle verlieren über (*acc.*); ***circumstances beyond our*** ~ unvorhersehbare Umstände; **8.** Machtbereich *m*, Verantwortung *f*; **9.** Aufsicht *f*, Kontrolle *f* (***of*** über *acc.*); Leitung *f*, Über'wachung *f*, (Nach)Prüfung *f*; ⚖ (***of***) a) Verfügungsgewalt (über *acc.*), b) (Per'sonen)Sorge *f* (für): ***be in*** ~ ***of s.th.*** et. unter sich haben, et. leiten; ***be under s.o.'s*** ~ j-m unterstellt sein *od.* unterstehen; ***traffic*** ~ Verkehrsregelung *f*; **10.** Bekämpfung *f*, Eindämmung *f*: ***without*** ~ uneingeschränkt, frei; ***beyond*** ~ nicht einzudämmen, nicht zu bändigen; ***be out of*** ~ nicht zu halten sein; ***get under*** ~ eindämmen, bewältigen; ***noise*** ~ Lärmbekämpfung *f*; **11.** *mst pl.* ⚙ a) Steuerung *f*, 'Steueror'gan *n*, b) Reguliervorrichtung *f*, Regler *m*, Kon'trollhebel *m*: ***be at the*** ~***s*** *fig.* an den Hebeln der Macht sitzen; **12.** ⚡, ⚙ Regelung *f*; **13.** *pl.* ✈ Steuerung *f*, Leitwerk *n*; **14.** ✝ a) (*Kapital-*, *Konsum- etc.*) Lenkung *f*, b) (Zwangs)Bewirtschaftung *f*: ***foreign exchange*** ~ Devisenkontrolle *f*; **15.** a) Kon'trolle *f*, Anhaltspunkt *m*, b) Vergleichswert *m*, c) Kon'troll-, Gegenversuch *m*.

con·trol| board *s.* ⚡ Schalttafel *f*; ~ **column** *s.* **1.** ✈ Steuersäule *f*; **2.** ⚙ Lenksäule *f*; ~ **desk** *s.* ⚡ Steuer-, Schaltpult *n*; *Radio, TV*: Re'giepult *n*; ~ **en·gi·neer·ing** *s.* 'Steuerungs-, 'Regel,technik *f*; ~ **ex·per·i·ment** → ***control*** 15 c; ~ **knob** *s.* ⚙, ⚡ Bedienungsknopf *m*.

con·trol·la·ble [kən'trəʊləbl] *adj.* **1.** kontrollierbar, regulierbar, lenkbar; **2.** zu beaufsichtigen(d); zu beherrschen(d); **con'trol·ler** [-lə] *s.* **1.** Kontrol'leur *m*, Aufseher *m*; Leiter *m*; Kon'trollbeˌamte(r) *m*, ✈ *a.* Fluglotse *m*; **2.** Rechnungsprüfer *m* (*Beamter*); **3.** ⚡, ⚙ Regler *m*; *mot.* Fahrschalter *m*; **4.** *sport* Kon'trollposten *m*.

con·trol| le·ver *s. mot.* Schalthebel *m*; ✈ Steuerknüppel *m*; ~ **pan·el** *s.* ⚙ Bedienungsfeld *n*; ~ **post** *s.* ⚔ Kon'trollposten *m*; ~ **room** *s.* **1.** Kon'trollraum *m*, (⚔ Be'fehls)Zenˌtrale *f*; **2.** *Radio, TV*: Re'gieraum *m*; ~ **stick** *s.* ✈ Steuerknüppel *m*; ~ **sur·face** *s.* Steuerfläche *f*; ~ **tow·er** *s.* ✈ Kon'trollturm *m*, Tower *m*.

con·tro·ver·sial [ˌkɒntrə'vɜːʃl] *adj.* □ **1.** strittig, um'stritten: ~ ***subject*** Streitfrage *f*; **2.** po'lemisch; streitlustig; ˌ**con·tro'ver·sial·ist** [-ʃəlɪst] *s.* Po'lemiker *m*; **con·tro·ver·sy** ['kɒntrəvɜːsɪ] *s.* **1.** Kontro'verse *f*, Meinungsstreit *m*; Debatte *f*; Aussprache *f*: ***beyond*** (*od.* ***without***) ~ fraglos, unstreitig; **2.** Streitfrage *f*; **3.** Streit *m*; **con·tro·vert** ['kɒntrəvɜːt] *v/t.* **1.** bestreiten, anfechten; **2.** wider'sprechen (*dat.*); ˌ**con·tro'vert·i·ble** [-ɜːtəbl] *adj.* □ strittig; anfechtbar.

con·tu·ma·cious [ˌkɒntjuː'meɪʃəs] *adj.* □ **1.** 'widerspenstig, halsstarrig; **2.** ⚖ ungehorsam; **con·tu·ma·cy** ['kɒntjʊməsɪ] *s.* **1.** 'Widerspenstigkeit *f*, Halsstarrigkeit *f*; **2.** ⚖ Ungehorsam *m od.* (absichtliches) Nichterscheinen vor Gericht: ***condemn for*** ~ gegen *j-n* ein Versäumnisurteil fällen.

con·tu·me·ly ['kɒntjuːmlɪ] *s.* **1.** Unverschämtheit *f*; **2.** Beleidigung *f*.

con·tuse [kən'tjuːz] *v/t.* ⚕ quetschen: ~***d wound*** Quetschwunde *f*; **con'tu·sion** [-uːʒn] *s.* ⚕ Quetschung *f*.

co·nun·drum [kə'nʌndrəm] *s.* **1.** Scherzfrage *f*, -rätsel *n*; **2.** *fig.* Rätsel *n*.

con·ur·ba·tion [ˌkɒnɜː'beɪʃn] *s.* Ballungsraum *m*, -zentrum *n*, Stadtgroßraum *m*.

con·va·lesce [ˌkɒnvə'les] *v/i.* gesund werden, genesen; ˌ**con·va'les·cence** [-sns] *s.* Rekonvales'zenz *f*, Genesung *f*; ˌ**con·va'les·cent** [-snt] **I** *adj.* genesend, auf dem Wege der Besserung: ~ ***home*** Genesungsheim *n*; **II** *s.* Rekonvales'zent(in).

con·vec·tion [kən'vekʃn] *s. phys.* Konvekti'on *f*; **con'vec·tor** [-ktə] *s. phys.* Konvekti'ons(strom)leiter *m*.

con·vene [kən'viːn] **I** *v/t.* **1.** zs.-rufen, (ein)berufen; versammeln; **2.** ⚖ vorladen; **II** *v/i.* **3.** zs.-kommen, sich versammeln.

con·ven·ience [kən'viːnjəns] *s.* **1.** Annehmlichkeit *f*, Bequemlichkeit *f*: ***all*** (***modern***) ~***s*** alle Bequemlichkeiten *od.* aller Komfort (der Neuzeit); ***at your*** ~ wenn es Ihnen paßt; ***at your earliest*** ~ möglichst bald; ***at one's own*** ~ nach (eigenem) Gutdünken; ***suit your own*** ~ handeln Sie ganz nach Ihrem Belieben; ~ ***food*** Fertignahrung *f*; ~ ***goods*** ✝ *Am.* bequem erhältliche Waren des täglichen Bedarfs; **2.** Vorteil *m*, Nutzen *m*: ***it is a great*** ~ es ist sehr nützlich; → ***flag***[1] 1, ***marriage*** 2; **3.** Angemessenheit *f*, Eignung *f*; **4.** *Brit.* Klo-

'sett *n*: ***public ~*** öffentliche Bedürfnisanstalt; **con'ven·ient** [-nt] *adj.* □ **1.** bequem, geeignet, günstig, passend: ***if it is ~ to you*** wenn es Ihnen paßt; ***it is not ~ for me*** (***to*** *inf.*) es paßt mir schlecht (zu *inf.*); ***make it ~*** es (so) einrichten; **2.** (zweck)dienlich, praktisch, brauchbar; **3.** günstig gelegen.

con·vent ['kɒnvənt] *s.* (*bsd.* Nonnen-) Kloster *n*: ~ (***school***) Klosterschule *f.*

con·ven·ti·cle [kən'ventɪkl] *s. eccl.* Konven'tikel *n.*

con·ven·tion [kən'venʃn] *s.* **1.** Zs.-kunft *f*, (*Am. a.* Par'tei)Versammlung *f*, Kon'vent *m*, (*a.* Be'rufs-, 'Fach)Kon͵greß *m*, (-)Tagung *f*; **2.** *a. pol.* Vertrag *m*, Abkommen *n*, Konventi'on *f* (*a.* ⚔); **3.** *oft pl.* (gesellschaftliche) Konventi'on, Sitte *f*, Gewohnheits- *od.* Anstandsregel *f*, (stillschweigende) Gepflogenheit *od.* Über'einkunft; **con'ven·tion·al** [-ʃənl] *adj.* □ **1.** herkömmlich, konventio'nell (*beide a.* ⚔), üblich, traditio'nell: ~ ***weapons***; ~ ***sign*** (*bsd.* Karten)Zeichen *n*, Symbol *n*; **2.** förmlich, for'mell; **3.** vereinbart, Vertrags...; **4.** *contp.* 'unorigi͵nell; **con'ven·tion·al·ism** [-ʃnəlɪzəm] *s.* Festhalten *n* am Hergebrachten; **con·ven·tion·al·i·ty** [kən͵venʃə'nælətɪ] *s.* **1.** Herkömmlichkeit *f*, Üblichkeit *f*; **2.** Scha'blonenhaftigkeit *f*; **con'ven·tion·al·ize** [-ʃnəlaɪz] *v/t.* konventio'nell machen *od.* darstellen, den Konventi'onen unter'werfen.

con·verge [kən'vɜːdʒ] *v/i.* zs.-laufen, sich (ein'ander) nähern, 𝔄 *u. fig.* konvergieren; **con'ver·gence** [-dʒəns], **con'ver·gen·cy** [-dʒənsɪ] *s.* **1.** Zs.-laufen *n*; **2.** 𝔄 a) Konver'genz *f* (*a. biol.*, *phys.*), b) Annäherung *f*; **con'ver·gent** [-dʒənt] *adj. bsd.* 𝔄 konver'gent; **con'verg·ing** [-dʒɪŋ] *adj.* zs.-laufend, konvergierend: ~ ***lens*** Sammellinse *f*; ~ ***point*** Konvergenzpunkt *m.*

con·vers·a·ble [kən'vɜːsəbl] *adj.* □ unter'haltend, gesprächig; gesellig; **con'ver·sance** [-səns] *s.* Vertrautheit *f* (***with*** mit); **con'ver·sant** [-sənt] *adj.* **1.** bekannt, vertraut (***with*** mit); **2.** geübt, bewandert, erfahren (***with***, ***in*** in *dat.*).

con·ver·sa·tion [͵kɒnvə'seɪʃn] *s.* **1.** Unter'haltung *f*, Gespräch *n*, Konversati'on *f*: ***enter into a ~*** ein Gespräch anknüpfen; **2.** *obs.* (*a.* Geschlechts-) Verkehr *m*; → ***criminal conversation***; **3.** *a.* ~ ***piece*** a) *paint.* Genrebild *n*, b) *thea.* Konversati'onsstück *n*; ͵**con·ver'sa·tion·al** [-ʃənl] *adj.* □ → ***conversationally***; **1.** gesprächig; **2.** Unterhaltungs..., Gesprächs...: ~ ***grammar*** Konversationsgrammatik *f*; ~ ***tone*** Plauderton *m*; ͵**con·ver'sa·tion·al·ist** [-ʃnəlɪst] *s.* gewandter Unter'halter, guter Gesellschafter; ͵**con·ver'sa·tion·al·ly** [-ʃnəlɪ] *adv.* **1.** gesprächsweise; **2.** im Plauderton.

con·ver·sa·zi·o·ne [͵kɒnvəsætsɪ'əʊnɪ] *pl.* **-ni** [-niː], **-nes** (*Ital.*) *s.* **1.** 'Abendunter͵haltung *f*; **2.** lite'rarischer Gesellschaftsabend.

con·verse[1] [kən'vɜːs] *v/i.* sich unter'halten, sprechen (***with*** mit, ***on***, ***about*** über *acc.*).

con·verse[2] ['kɒnvɜːs] **I** *adj.* □ gegenteilig, 'umgekehrt; wechselseitig; **II** *s.* 'Umkehrung *f*; Gegenteil *n*; '**con·verse·ly** [-lɪ] *adv.* 'umgekehrt.

con·ver·sion [kən'vɜːʃn] *s.* **1.** *allg.* 'Um-, Verwandlung *f* (***from*** von, ***into*** in *acc.*); **2.** ☿ a) Konvertierung *f*, 'Umwandlung *f* (*Effekten*, *Schulden*), b) Zs.-legung *f* (*von Aktien*), c) ('Währungs)͵Umstellung *f*, d) (Ge'schäfts-, *a.* Ver'mögens)͵Umwandlung *f*; **3.** 𝔄 a) 'Umrechnung *f* (***into*** in *acc.*): ~ ***table*** Umrechnungstabelle *f*, b) *a. Computer*: 'Umwandlung *f*, c) *a. phls.* 'Umkehrung *f*; **4.** ⚙, *a.* ☿ 'Umstellung *f* (***to*** auf *e-e andere Produktion etc.*); **5.** ⚙, △ 'Umbau *m* (***into*** in *acc.*); **6.** ⚡ 'Umformung *f*; **7.** ⚗, *phys.* 'Umsetzung *f*; **8.** geistige Wandlung; Meinungsänderung *f*; **9.** 'Übertritt *m*, *bsd. eccl.* Bekehrung *f* (***to*** zu); **10.** ⚖ *a.* ~ ***to one's own use*** 'widerrechtliche Aneignung *od.* Verwendung, *a.* Veruntreuung *f*; **11.** *sport* Verwandlung *f* (*Torschuß*).

con·vert I *v/t.* [kən'vɜːt] **1.** *allg.* 'um-, verwandeln (*a.* ⚗), 'umformen (*a.* ⚡), 'umändern (***into*** in *acc.*); **2.** ⚙, △ 'umbauen (***into*** zu); **3.** ☿, ⚙ *Betrieb*, *Maschine*, *Produktion* 'umstellen (***to*** auf *acc.*); **4.** *metall.* frischen; **5.** ☿ a) *Geld* 'um-, einwechseln, *a.* 'umrechnen: ~ ***into cash*** zu Geld machen, flüssigmachen, b) *Wertpapiere*, *Schulden* konvertieren, 'umwandeln, c) *Aktien* zs.-legen, d) *Währung* 'umstellen (***to*** auf *acc.*); **6.** 𝔄 a) 'umrechnen (***into*** in *acc.*), b) *Gleichung* auflösen, c) *Proportionen* 'umkehren (*a. phls.*); **7.** *Computer*: 'umsetzen; **8.** *eccl.* bekehren (***to*** zu); **9.** (***to***) (zu *e-r anderen Ansicht*) bekehren, *a.* zum 'Übertritt (in *e-e andere Partei etc.*) veranlassen; **10.** ⚖ *a.* ~ ***to one's own use*** sich 'widerrechtlich aneignen, veruntreuen; **11.** *sport* (zum Tor) verwandeln; **II** *v/i.* **12.** 'umgewandelt (*etc.*) werden (→ I); **13.** sich verwandeln *od.* 'umwandeln (***into*** zu); **14.** sich verwandeln (*etc.*) lassen (***into*** in *acc.*); **III** *s.* ['kɒnvɜːt] **15.** *bsd. eccl.* Bekehrte(r *m*) *f*, Konver'tit(in): ***become a ~ to*** sich bekehren zu; **con'vert·ed** [-tɪd] *adj.* 'umge-, verwandelt *etc.*: ~ ***cruiser*** ⚓ Hilfskreuzer *m*; ~ ***flat*** in Teilwohnungen umgebaute große Wohnung; ~ ***steel*** Zementstahl *m*; **con'vert·er** [-tə] *s.* **1.** ⚙ 'Bessemerbirne *f*; **2.** ⚡ 'Umformer *m*; **3.** *TV* Wandler *m*; **4.** ⚙ Bleicher *m*, Appre'teur *m*; **5.** Bekehrer *m*; **con·vert·i·bil·i·ty** [kən͵vɜːtə'bɪlətɪ] *s.* **1.** 'Um-, Verwandelbarkeit *f*; **2.** ☿ Konvertierbar-, 'Umwandelbarkeit *f*; **con'vert·i·ble** [-təbl] **I** *adj.* □ **1.** 'um-, verwandelbar; **2.** ☿ konvertierbar, 'umwandelbar: ~ ***bond*** Wandelobligation *f*; **3.** auswechselbar, gleichbedeutend; **4.** bekehrbar; **5.** *mot.* mit Klappverdeck; **II** *s.* **6.** *mot.* Kabrio'lett *n.*

con·vex [kɒn'veks] *adj.* □ kon'vex, nach außen gewölbt; 𝔄 ausspringend (*Winkel*); **con·vex·i·ty** [kɒn'veksətɪ] *s.* kon'vexe Form.

con·vey [kən'veɪ] *v/t.* **1.** *Waren etc.* befördern, (ver)senden, (fort)schaffen, bringen; **2.** *bsd.* ⚙ (zu)führen, fördern; **3.** über'bringen, -'mitteln, bringen, geben: ~ ***greetings*** Grüße übermitteln; **4.** *phys. Schall* fortpflanzen, leiten, über'tragen; **5.** *Nachricht etc.* mitteilen, vermitteln; *Meinung*, *Sinn* ausdrücken; andeuten; (be)sagen: ~ ***an idea*** e-n Begriff geben; ***this word ~s nothing to me*** dieses Wort sagt mir nichts; **6.** über'tragen, abtreten (***to*** an *acc.*); **con'vey·ance** [-eɪəns] *s.* **1.** Beförderung *f*, Über'sendung *f*, Trans'port *m*, Spediti'on *f*: ***means of ~*** Transportmittel *n*; **2.** Über'bringung *f*, -'mittlung *f*, Vermittlung *f*, Mitteilung *f*; **3.** *phys.* Fortpflanzung *f*, Über'tragung *f*; **4.** ⚙ (Zu-) Leitung *f*, Zufuhr *f*; **5.** Beförderungs-, Trans'port-, Verkehrsmittel *n*; **6.** ⚖ a) Über'tragung *f*, Abtretung *f*, Auflassung *f*, b) Abtretungsurkunde *f*; **con'vey·anc·er** [-eɪənsə] *s.* ⚖ No'tar *m* für 'Eigentumsüber͵tragungen.

con·vey·er, **con·vey·or** [kən'veɪə] *s.* **1.** Beförderer *m*, (Über)'Bringer(in); **2.** ⚙ Fördergerät *n*, -band *n*, Förderer *m*; ~ ***band***, ~ ***belt*** *s.* laufendes Band, Förder-, Fließband *n*; ~ ***chain*** *s.* Becher-, Förderkette *f*; ~ ***spi·ral*** *s.* Förder-, Trans'portschnecke *f.*

con·vict I *v/t.* [kən'vɪkt] **1.** ⚖ über'führen, für schuldig erklären (***of*** *gen.*); **2.** verurteilen; **3.** über'zeugen (***of*** von *e-m Unrecht, Fehler etc.*); **II** *s.* ['kɒnvɪkt] **4.** ⚖ a) Verurteilte(r *m*) *f*, b) Strafgefangene(r *m*) *f*, Sträfling *m*: ~ ***colony*** Sträflingskolonie *f*; ~ ***labo(u)r*** Sträflingsarbeit *f*; **con'vic·tion** [-kʃn] *s.* **1.** ⚖ a) Über'führung *f*, Schuldspruch *m*, b) Verurteilung *f*: ***previous ~*** Vorstrafe *f*; **2.** Über'zeugung *f*: ***carry ~*** überzeugend wirken *od.* klingen; ***live up to one's ~s*** s-r Überzeugung gemäß leben; **3.** Anschauung *f*, Gesinnung *f*; **4.** (*Schuld- etc.*)Bewußtsein *n.*

con·vince [kən'vɪns] *v/t.* **1.** (*a. o.s.* sich) über'zeugen (***of*** von, ***that*** daß); **2.** ~ ***s.o. of s.th.*** j-m et. zum Bewußtsein bringen; **con'vinc·ing** [-sɪŋ] *adj.* □ über'zeugend: ~ ***proof*** schlagender Beweis; ***be ~*** überzeugen.

con·viv·i·al [kən'vɪvɪəl] *adj.* □ **1.** gastlich, festlich, Fest...; **2.** gesellig, gemütlich, lustig; **con·viv·i·al·i·ty** [kən͵vɪvɪ'ælətɪ] *s.* Geselligkeit *f*, Gemütlichkeit *f*, unbeschwerte Heiterkeit.

con·vo·ca·tion [͵kɒnvəʊ'keɪʃn] *s.* **1.** Ein-, Zs.-berufung *f*; **2.** *eccl. Brit.* Provinzi'alsy͵node *f*; Kirchenversammlung *f*; **3.** *univ.* a) *Brit.* gesetzgebende Versammlung (*Oxford etc.*); außerordentliche Se'natssitzung, b) *Am.* Promoti'ons- *od.* Eröffnungsfeier *f.*

con·voke [kən'vəʊk] *v/t.* (*bsd. amtlich*) ein-, zs.-berufen.

con·vo·lute ['kɒnvəluːt] *adj. bsd.* ⚘ zs.-gerollt, ringelförmig; '**con·vo·lut·ed** [-tɪd] *adj. bsd. zo.* zs.-gerollt, gebogen, gewunden, spi'ralig; **con·vo·lu·tion** [͵kɒnvə'luːʃn] *s.* Zs.-rollung *f*, -wicklung *f*, Windung *f.*

con·voy ['kɒnvɔɪ] **I** *s.* **1.** Geleit *n*, (Schutz)Begleitung *f*; **2.** ⚔ a) Es'korte *f*, Bedeckung *f*, b) (bewachter) Trans'port; **3.** ⚓ Geleitzug *m*; **4.** *a.* ⚔ 'Lastwagenko͵lonne *f*; **II** *v/t.* **5.** Geleitschutz geben (*dat.*), eskortieren.

con·vulse [kən'vʌls] *v/t.* **1.** erschüttern, in Zuckungen versetzen: ***be ~d with pain*** sich vor Schmerzen krümmen; ***be ~d*** (***with laughter***) e-n Lachkrampf bekommen; **2.** krampfhaft zs.-ziehen *od.* verzerren; **3.** *fig.* erschüttern, in Aufruhr versetzen; **con'vul·sion** [-lʃn] *s.* **1.** ⚕ Krampf *m*, Zuckung *f*: ***be seized***

with ~s Krämpfe bekommen; ***~s*** (***of laughter***) *fig.* Lachkrämpfe; **2.** *pol., fig.* Erschütterung *f* (*a. geol.*), Aufruhr *m*; **con'vul·sive** [-sɪv] *adj.* ☐ **1.** *a. fig.* krampfhaft, -artig, konvul'siv; **2.** *fig.* erschütternd.

co·ny ['kəʊnɪ] *s.* **1.** *zo.* Ka'ninchen *n*; **2.** Ka'ninchenfell *n*.

coo [ku:] **I** *v/i.* gurren (*a. fig.*); **II** *v/t. fig. et.* gurren; **III** *s.* Gurren *n*; **IV** *int. Brit. sl.* Mann!

cook [kʊk] **I** *s.* **1.** Koch *m*, Köchin *f*: ***too many ~s spoil the broth*** viele Köche verderben den Brei; **II** *v/t.* **2.** *Speisen* kochen, zubereiten, braten, backen: ***be ~ed alive*** F vor Hitze umkommen; **3.** *a.* ***~ up*** *fig.* a) zs.-brauen, erdichten, b) ‚frisieren', verfälschen: ***~ed account*** † F frisierte Abrechnung; ***~ up a story*** e-e Geschichte erfinden; ***he is ~ed*** *sl.* der ist ‚erledigt'; **III** *v/i.* **4.** kochen, sich kochen lassen: ***~ well***; **5.** ***what's ~ing*** F was tut sich?, was ist los?; **'~·book** *s. Am.* Kochbuch *n*.

cook·er ['kʊkə] *s.* **1.** Kocher *m*, Kochgerät *n*; Herd *m*; **2.** Kochgefäß *n*; **3.** *pl.* Kochobst *n*: ***these apples are good ~s*** das sind gute Kochäpfel.

cook·er·y ['kʊkərɪ] *s.* Kochen *n*; Kochkunst *f*; **~ book** *s. Brit.* Kochbuch *n*.

ˌcook|-'gen·er·al *s. Brit.* Mädchen *n* für alles; **'~-house** *s.* **1.** Küche(ngebäude *n*) *f* (*a.* ⚔); **2.** ⚓ Schiffsküche *f*.

cook·ie ['kʊkɪ] *s. Am.* **1.** (süßer) Keks, Plätzchen *n*; **2.** *sl.* a) Kerl *m*, b) ‚Puppe' *f*.

cook·ing ['kʊkɪŋ] **I** *s.* **1.** Kochen *n*, Kochkunst *f*; **2.** Küche *f*, Kochweise *f*; **II** *adj.* **3.** Koch...: ***~ apple***; **~ range** *s.* Kochherd *m*; **~ so·da** *s.* ⚗ 'Natron *n*.

'cook·out *s. Am.* Abkochen *n* (am Lagerfeuer).

cook·y ['kʊkɪ] → ***cookie***.

cool [ku:l] **I** *adj.* ☐ **1.** kühl, frisch; **2.** kühl, gelassen, kalt(blütig): ***as ~ as a cucumber*** ‚eiskalt', kaltblütig; ***keep ~!*** reg dich nicht auf!; ♪ ♫ ***Jazz*** ‚Cool Jazz' *m*; **3.** kühl, gleichgültig, lau; **4.** kühl, kalt, abweisend: ***a ~ reception*** ein kühler Empfang; **5.** unverfroren, frech: ***~ cheek*** Frechheit *f*; ***a ~ customer*** ein geriebener Kunde; **6.** *fig.* glatt, rund: ***a ~ thousand pounds*** glatte *od.* die Kleinigkeit von tausend Pfund; **7.** *sl.* ‚dufte', ‚Klasse', ‚toll': ***that's ~!***; **II** *s.* **8.** Kühle *f*, Frische *f* (*bsd. Luft*): ***the ~ of the evening*** die Abendkühle; **9.** *sl.* (Selbst)Beherrschung *f*: ***blow*** (*od.* ***lose***) ***one's ~*** hochgehen, die Beherrschung verlieren; ***keep one's ~*** ruhig bleiben, die Nerven behalten; **III** *v/t.* **10.** (ab)kühlen; → ***heel***[1] *Redew.*; **11.** *fig. Leidenschaften etc.* (ab)kühlen, beruhigen; *Zorn etc.* mäßigen; **IV** *v/i.* **12.** kühl werden, sich abkühlen; **13.** *a.* ***~ down*** *fig.* sich abkühlen, erkalten, nachlassen, sich beruhigen; **14.** ***~ down*** F ruhiger werden, sich abregen; **15.** ***~ it*** *sl.* ruhig bleiben, die Nerven behalten: ***~ it!*** immer mit der Ruhe!, reg dich ab!; **'cool·ant** [-lənt] *s.* ⚙ Kühlmittel *n*; **'cool·er** [-lə] *s.* **1.** (*Wein- etc.*)Kühler *m*; **2.** Kühlraum *m*; **3.** *sl.* ‚Kittchen' *n*, ‚Knast' *m*; **ˌcool-'head·ed** *adj.* **1.** besonnen, kaltblütig; **2.** leidenschaftslos.

coo·lie ['ku:lɪ] *s.* Kuli *m*.

cool·ing ['ku:lɪŋ] **I** *adj.* kühlend, erfrischend; Kühl...; **II** *s.* (Ab)Kühlung *f*; **~ coil** *s.* Kühlschlange *f*; **~ plant** *s.* Kühlanlage *f*.

cool·ness ['ku:lnɪs] *s.* **1.** Kühle *f* (*a. fig.*); **2.** Kaltblütigkeit *f*; **3.** Unfreundlichkeit *f*; **4.** Frechheit *f*.

coomb(e) [ku:m] *s.* Talmulde *f*.

coon [ku:n] *s.* **1.** *zo.* → ***raccoon***; **2.** *Am. sl.* a) Neger(in): ***~ song*** Negerlied *n*, b) ‚schlauer Hund'.

coop [ku:p] **I** *s.* **1.** Hühnerstall *m*; **2.** Fischkorb *m* (*zum Fangen*); **3.** F ‚Kabuff' *n*; **4.** F ‚Knast' *m*; **II** *v/t.* **5.** *oft* ***~ up***, ***~ in*** einsperren, einpferchen.

co-op ['kəʊɒp] *s.* F Co-op *m* (*Genossenschaft u. Laden*) (*abbr. für* ***cooperative***).

coop·er ['ku:pə] **I** *s.* **1.** Küfer *m*, Böttcher *m*; **2.** Mischbier *n*; **II** *v/t.* **3.** *Fässer* machen, ausbessern; **'coop·er·age** [-ərɪdʒ] *s.* Böttche'rei *f*.

co·op·er·ate [kəʊ'ɒpəreɪt] *v/t.* **1.** zs.-arbeiten (***with*** mit, ***to*** zu *e-m Zweck*, ***in*** an *dat.*); **2.** (***to***) mitwirken (an *dat.*), beitragen (zu), helfen (bei); **co·op·er·a·tion** [kəʊˌɒpə'reɪʃn] *s.* **1.** Zs.-arbeit *f*, Mitwirkung *f*; **2.** † a) Kooperati'on *f*, Zs.-arbeit *f*, b) Zs.-schluß *m*, Vereinigung *f* (zu e-r Genossenschaft); **co'op·er·a·tive** [-pərətɪv] **I** *adj.* ☐ **1.** zs.-arbeitend, mitwirkend; **2.** koopera'tiv, hilfsbereit; **3.** genossenschaftlich: ***~ movement*** Genossenschaftsbewegung *f*; ***~ society*** Konsumgenossenschaft *f*; ***~ store*** → 4; **II** *s.* **4.** Co-op *m*, Kon'sumladen *m*; **co'op·er·a·tive·ness** [-pərətɪvnɪs] *s.* Hilfsbereitschaft *f*; **co'op·er·a·tor** [-tə] *s.* **1.** Mitarbeiter(in), Mitwirkende(r *m*) *f*, Helfer(in); **2.** Mitglied *n* e-r Kon'sumgenossenschaft *f*.

co-opt [kəʊ'ɒpt] *v/t.* hin'zuwählen; **co-op·ta·tion** [ˌkəʊɒp'teɪʃn] *s.* Zuwahl *f*.

co·or·di·nate I *v/t.* [kəʊ'ɔ:dɪneɪt] **1.** koordinieren, bei-, gleichordnen, gleichschalten; zs.-fassen; **2.** in Einklang bringen, aufein'ander abstimmen; richtig anordnen, anpassen; **II** *adj.* [-dnət] **3.** koordiniert, bei-, gleichgeordnet; gleichrangig, -wertig, -artig: ***~ clause*** *ling.* beigeordneter Satz; **4.** ⩕ Koordinaten...; **III** *s.* [-dnət] **5.** Beigeordnetes *n*, Gleichwertiges *n*; **6.** ⩕ Koordi'nate *f*; **co·or·di·na·tion** [kəʊˌɔ:dɪ'neɪʃn] *s.* **1.** Koordinati'on *f* (*a. physiol. der Muskeln etc.*), Gleich-, Beiordnung *f*, Gleichstellung *f*, -schaltung *f*; richtige Anordnung; **2.** Zs.-fassung *f*; Zs.-arbeit *f*; **co'or·di·na·tor** [-tə] *s.* Koordi'nator *m*.

coot [ku:t] *s. orn.* Bläß-, Wasserhuhn *n*; → ***bald*** 1.

cop[1] [kɒp] *s.* Garnwickel *m*.

cop[2] [kɒp] *sl.* **I** *v/t.* **1.** erwischen (***at*** bei): ***~ it*** ‚sein Fett kriegen'; **2.** klauen; **II** *v/i.* **3.** ***~ out*** a) ‚aussteigen' (***of***, ***on*** aus), b) ‚sich drücken'; **III** *s.* **4.** ***it's a fair ~*** jetzt bin ich ‚dran'.

cop[3] [kɒp] *s. sl.* ‚Bulle' *m* (*Polizist*).

co·pal ['kəʊpəl] *s.* Ko'pal(harz *n*) *m*.

co·par·ce·nar·y [ˌkəʊ'pɑ:sənərɪ] *s.* ⚖ gemeinschaftliches (Grund)Eigentum (gesetzlicher Erben); **co·par·ce·ner** [ˌkəʊ'pɑ:sənə] *s.* ⚖ Miterbe *m*, -erbin *f*.

co·part·ner [ˌkəʊ'pɑ:tnə] *s.* Teilhaber *m*, Mitinhaber *m*; **ˌco'part·ner·ship** [-ʃɪp] *s.* † **1.** Teilhaberschaft *f*, **2.** a) Gewinnbeteiligung *f*, b) Mitbestimmungsrecht *n* (*der Arbeitnehmer*).

cope[1] [kəʊp] *v/i.* **1.** (***with***) gewachsen sein (*dat.*), fertig werden (mit), bewältigen (*acc.*), meistern (*acc.*); **2.** die Lage meistern, zu Rande kommen, ‚es schaffen'.

cope[2] [kəʊp] **I** *s.* **1.** *eccl.* Chorrock *m*; **2.** *fig.* Mantel *m*, Gewölbe *n*: ***~ of heaven*** Himmelszelt *n*; **3.** → ***coping***; **II** *v/t.* **4.** bedecken.

co·peck ['kəʊpek] *s.* Ko'peke *f* (*russische Münze*).

cop·er ['kəʊpə] *s.* Pferdehändler *m*.

Co·per·ni·can [kəʊ'pɜ:nɪkən] *adj.* koperni'kanisch.

'cope·stone → ***coping stone***.

cop·i·er ['kɒpɪə] *s.* **1.** → ***copyist***; **2.** ⚙ Kopiergerät *n*, Kopierer *m*.

co·pi·lot ['kəʊˌpaɪlət] *s.* ✈ 'Kopiˌlot *m*.

cop·ing ['kəʊpɪŋ] *s.* Mauerkappe *f*, -krönung *f*; **~ saw** *s.* Laubsäge *f*; **~ stone** *s.* **1.** Deck-, Kappenstein *m*; **2.** *fig.* Krönung *f*, Schlußstein *m*.

co·pi·ous ['kəʊpjəs] *adj.* ☐ **1.** reichlich, aus-, ergiebig, reich, um'fassend; **2.** produk'tiv, fruchtbar: ***~ writer***; **3.** wortreich; 'überschwenglich; **'co·pi·ous·ness** [-nɪs] *s.* **1.** Fülle *f*; 'Überfluß *m*; **2.** Wortreichtum *m*.

'cop-out *s. sl.* **1.** Vorwand *m*; **2.** ‚Rückzieher' *m*; **3.** a) ‚Aussteigen' *n*, b) *a.* ***~ artist*** ‚Aussteiger(in)'.

cop·per[1] ['kɒpə] **I** *s.* **1.** *min.* Kupfer *n*; **2.** Kupfermünze *f*: ***~s*** Kupfer-, Kleingeld *n*; **3.** Kupferbehälter *m*, -gefäß *n*, -kessel *m*; *bsd. Brit.* Waschkessel *m*; **II** *adj.* **4.** kupfern, Kupfer...; **5.** kupferrot; **III** *v/t.* **6.** verkupfern; **7.** mit Kupferblech beschlagen.

cop·per[2] ['kɒpə] → ***cop***[3].

cop·per·as ['kɒpərəs] *s.* ⚗ Vitri'ol *n*.

cop·per| beech *s.* ⚘ Blutbuche *f*; **ˌ~-'bot·tomed** *adj.* **1.** ⚓ a) mit Kupferbeschlag, b) seetüchtig; **2.** *fig.* kerngesund; **~ en·grav·ing** *s.* **1.** Kupferstich *m*; **2.** Kupferstechkunst *f*; **~ glance** *s. min.* Kupferglanz *m*; **'~·head** *s. zo.* Mokas'sinschlange *f*; **'~·plate** *s.* ⚙ **1.** Kupferstichplatte *f*; **2.** Kupferstich *m*; **3.** *fig.* gestochene Handschrift; **'~ˌplat·ed** *adj.* verkupfert; **'~·smith** *s.* Kupferschmied *m*.

cop·per·y ['kɒpərɪ] *adj.* kupferartig, -farbig, -haltig.

cop·pice ['kɒpɪs] *s.* **1.** 'Unterholz *n*, Gestrüpp *n*; Gebüsch *n*, Dickicht *n*; **2.** Gehölz *n*, niedriges Wäldchen.

cop·ra ['kɒprə] *s.* 'Kobra *f*.

copse [kɒps] → ***coppice***.

Copt [kɒpt] *s.* Kopte *m*, Koptin *f*.

'cop·ter ['kɒptə] F *für* ***helicopter***.

cop·u·la ['kɒpjʊlə] *s.* **1.** *ling. u. phls.* 'Kopula *f*; **2.** *anat.* Bindeglied *n*; **'cop·u·late** [-leɪt] *v/i.* kopulieren: a) koitieren, b) *zo.* sich paaren; **cop·u·la·tion** [ˌkɒpjʊ'leɪʃn] *s.* **1.** *ling. u. phls.* Verbindung *f*; **2.** Kopulati'on *f*: a) 'Koitus *m*, b) Paarung *f*; **'cop·u·la·tive** [-lətɪv] **I** *adj.* ☐ **1.** verbindend, Binde...; **2.** *ling.* kopula'tiv; **3.** *biol.* Kopulations...; **II** *s.* **4.** *ling.* 'Kopula *f*.

cop·y ['kɒpɪ] **I** *s.* **1.** Ko'pie *f*, Abschrift *f*: ***fair*** (*od.* ***clean***) ***~*** Reinschrift *f*; ***rough ~*** erster Entwurf, Konzept *n*, Kladde *f*; ***true ~*** (wort)getreue Abschrift; **2.** 'Durchschlag *m*, -schrift *f*; **3.** Abzug *m* (*a. phot.*), Abdruck *m*, Pause *f*; **4.** Nachahmung *f*, -bildung *f*, Reproduk'ti'on *f*, Ko'pie *f*, 'Wiedergabe *f*; **5.** Muster *n*, Mo'dell *n*, Vorlage *f*; Urschrift *f*; **6.** druckfertiges Manu'skript, lite'rarisches Materi'al; (*Zeitungs- etc.*)Stoff *m*, Text *m*; **7.** Ausfertigung *f*, Exem'plar *n*, Nummer *f* (*Zeitung etc.*); **8.** Urkunde *f*; **II** *v/t.* **9.** abschreiben, -drucken, -zeichnen, e-e Ko'pie anfertigen von; *Computer*: *Daten* über'tragen: **~ out** ins reine schreiben, abschreiben; **10.** *phot.* e-n Abzug machen von; **11.** nachbilden, reproduzieren, kopieren; **12.** nachahmen, -machen; **13.** 'wiedergeben, *Zeitungstext* wieder'holen; **III** *v/i.* **14.** kopieren, abschreiben; **15.** (vom Nachbarn) abschreiben (*Schule*); **16.** nachahmen; '**~·book I** *s.* **1.** (Schön-) Schreibheft *n*: ***blot one's ~*** F ,sich danebenbenehmen'; **2.** ☤ Kopierbuch *n*; **II** *adj.* **3.** alltäglich; **4.** nor'mal; '**~·cat** F **I** *s.* (sklavischer) Nachahmer; **II** *v/t.* (sklavisch) nachahmen; **~ desk** *s.* Redakti'onstisch *m*; **~ ed·i·tor** *s.* a) 'Zeitungsredakˌteur(in), b) 'Lektor *m*, Lek'torin *f*; '**~·hold** *s.* ⚖ *Brit.* Zinslehen *n*, -gut *n*; '**~·hold·er** *s.* **1.** ⚖ *Brit.* Zinslehenbesitzer *m*; **2.** *typ.* a) Manu'skripthalter *m*, b) Kor'rektorgehilfe *m*.

cop·y·ing| ink ['kɒpɪɪŋ] *s.* Kopiertinte *f*; **~ ma·chine** *s.* → ***copier*** 2; **~ pa·per** *s.* Ko'pierpaˌpier *n*; **~ pen·cil** *s.* Tintenstift *m*; **~ press** *s.* ⚙ Kopierpresse *f*; **~ test** *s.* Copy-test *m* (*werbepsychologischer Test*).

cop·y·ist ['kɒpɪɪst] *s.* **1.** Abschreiber *m*, Ko'pist *m*; **2.** Nachahmer *m*.

'**cop·y|ˌread·er** *Am.* → ***copy editor***; '**~·right** ⚖ **I** *s.* 'Copyright *n*, Urheberrecht *n* (***in*** an *dat.*): **~ *in designs*** Musterschutz *m*; **~ *reserved*** alle Rechte vorbehalten; **II** *v/t.* das Urheberrecht erwerben an (*dat.*); urheberrechtlich schützen; **III** *adj.* urheberrechtlich (geschützt); '**~ˌwrit·er** *s.* (*a.* Werbe)Texter *m*.

co·quet [kɒ'ket] **I** *v/i.* kokettieren, flirten; *fig.* liebäugeln (***with*** mit); **II** *adj.* → ***coquettish***; **co·quet·ry** ['kɒkɪtrɪ] *s.* Kokette'rie *f*; **co·quette** [kɒ'ket] *s.* ko'kette Frau; **co'quet·tish** [-tɪʃ] *adj.* □ ko'kett.

cor·al ['kɒrəl] **I** *s.* **1.** *zo.* Ko'ralle *f*; **2.** Ko'rallenstück *n*; **3.** Ko'rallenrot *n*; **4.** Beißring *m od.* Spielzeug *n* (für Babys) aus Ko'ralle; **II** *adj.* **5.** Korallen…; **6.** ko'rallenrot; **~ bead** *s.* **1.** Ko'rallenperle *f*; **2.** *pl.* Ko'rallenkette *f*; **~ is·land** *s.* Ko'ralleninsel *f*.

cor·al·lin ['kɒrəlɪn] *s.* ⚗ Koral'lin *n*; '**cor·al·line** [-laɪn] **I** *adj.* **1.** ko'rallenartig, -haltig; ko'rallenrot; **II** *s.* **2.** ♀ Ko'rallenalge *f*; **3.** → ***corrallin***; '**cor·al·lite** [-laɪt] *s.* **1.** Ko'rallenskeˌlett *n*; **2.** versteinerte Ko'ralle.

cor·al reef *s.* Ko'rallenriff *n*.

cor an·glais [ˌkɔːr'ɑ̃ːŋgleɪ] (*Fr.*) *s.* ♪ Englischhorn *n*.

cor·bel ['kɔːbəl] ⚠ **I** *s.* Kragstein *m*, Kon'sole *f*; **II** *v/t.* durch Kragsteine stützen.

cor·bie ['kɔːbɪ] *s. Scot.* Rabe *m*; '**~·steps** *s. pl.* ⚠ Giebelstufen *pl.*

cord [kɔːd] **I** *s.* **1.** Schnur *f*, Kordel *f*, Strick *m*, Strang *m*; **2.** *anat.* Band *n*, Schnur *f*, Strang *m*; → ***spinal cord*** *etc.*; **3.** ⚡ (Leitungs-, Anschluß)Schnur *f*; **4.** a) Rippe *f* (*e-s Stoffes*), b) gerippter Stoff, Rips *m*, *bsd.* → ***corduroy*** 1, *pl.* → ***corduroy*** 2; **5.** Klafter *m*, *n* (*Holz*); **II** *v/t.* **6.** (zu)schnüren, (fest)binden, befestigen; **7.** *Bücherrücken* rippen; '**cord·age** [-dɪdʒ] *s.* ⚓ Tauwerk *n*.

cor·date ['kɔːdeɪt] *adj.* ♀, *zo.* herzförmig (*Blatt*, *Muschel etc.*).

cord·ed ['kɔːdɪd] *adj.* **1.** ge-, verschnürt; **2.** gerippt (*Stoff*); **3.** Strick…; **4.** in Klaftern gestapelt (*Holz*).

cor·de·lier [ˌkɔːdɪ'lɪə] *s. eccl.* Franzis'kaner(mönch) *m*.

cor·dial ['kɔːdjəl] **I** *adj.* □ **1.** *fig.* herzlich, freundlich, warm, aufrichtig; **2.** ⚕ belebend, stärkend; **II** *s.* **3.** ⚕ belebendes Mittel, Stärkungsmittel *n*; **4.** Li'kör *m*; **cor·dial·i·ty** [ˌkɔːdɪ'ælətɪ] *s.* Herzlichkeit *f*, Wärme *f*.

cord·ite ['kɔːdaɪt] *s.* ⚔ Kor'dit *m*.

cor·don ['kɔːdn] **I** *s.* **1.** Kor'don *m*: a) ⚔ Postenkette *f*, b) Absperrkette *f*: **~ *of police***; **2.** Kette *f*, Spa'lier *n* (*Personen*); **3.** Spa'lier(obst)baum *m*; **4.** ⚠ Mauerkranz *m*, -sims *m*, *n*; **5.** Ordensband *n*; **II** *v/t.* **6.** *a.* **~ *off*** (mit Posten *etc.*) absperren, abriegeln; **~ bleu** [ˌkɔːdɔ̃ːm'blɜː] (*Fr.*) *s.* **1.** Cordon *m* bleu; **2.** hohe Per'sönlichkeit; **3.** *humor.* erstklassiger Koch.

cor·do·van ['kɔːdəvən] *s.* 'Korduan(leder) *n*.

cord| tire *Am.*, **~ tyre** *Brit. s. mot.* Kordreifen *m*.

cor·du·roy ['kɔːdərɔɪ] **I** *s.* **1.** Kord-, Ripssamt *m*; **2.** *pl.* Kordsamthose *f*; **II** *adj.* **3.** Kordsamt…; **~ road** *s. Am.* Knüppeldamm *m*.

cord·wain·er ['kɔːdˌweɪnə] *s.* Schuhmacher *m*: ***2s' Company*** Schuhmachergilde *f* (*London*).

'**cord·wood** *s. bsd. Am.* Klafterholz *n*.

core [kɔː] **I** *s.* **1.** ♀ Kerngehäuse *n*, Kern *m* (*Obst*); **2.** *fig.* Kern *m* (*a.* ⚙, ⚡), *das* Innerste, Herz *n*, Mark *n*; Seele *f* (*a. Kabel, Seil*): ***to the ~*** bis ins Mark *od.* Innerste, durch u. durch; **~ *memory*** *Computer*: Kernspeicher *m*; → ***hard core***; **3.** (Eiter)Pfropf *m* (*Geschwür*); **II** *v/t.* **4.** *Äpfel etc.* entkernen.

co·re·late *etc.* → ***correlate*** *etc.*

co·re·li·gion·ist [ˌkəʊrɪ'lɪdʒənɪst] *s.* Glaubensgenosse *m*, -genossin *f*.

cor·er ['kɔːrə] *s.* Fruchtentkerner *m*.

co·re·spond·ent, *Am.* **co·re·spond·ent** [ˌkəʊrɪ'spɒndənt] *s.* ⚖ Mitbeklagte(r *m*) *f* (*im Ehebruchsprozeß*).

core time *s.* Kernzeit *f* (*Ggs. Gleitzeit*).

cor·gi, **cor·gy** ['kɔːgɪ] → ***Welsh corgi***.

co·ri·a·ceous [ˌkɒrɪ'eɪʃəs] *adj.* **1.** ledern, Leder…; **2.** lederartig, zäh.

Co·rin·thi·an [kə'rɪnθɪən] **I** *adj.* **1.** ko'rinthisch: **~ *column*** korinthische Säule; **II** *s.* **2.** Ko'rinther(in); **3.** *pl. bibl.* (Brief *m* des Paulus an die) Ko'rinther *pl.*

cork [kɔːk] **I** *s.* **1.** ♀ Kork *m*, Korkrinde *f*, Korkeiche *f*; **2.** Kork(en) *m*, Stöpsel *m*, Pfropfen *m*; **3.** Angelkork *m*, Schwimmer *m*; **II** *adj.* **4.** Kork…; **III** *v/t.* **5.** ver-, zukorken; **6.** *Gesicht* mit gebranntem Kork schwärzen; '**cork·age** [-kɪdʒ] *s.* **1.** Verkorken *n*; **2.** Entkorken *n*; **3.** Korkengeld *n*; **corked** [-kt] *adj.* **1.** ver-, zugekorkt, verstöpselt; **2.** korkig, nach Kork schmeckend; **3.** mit Korkschwarz gefärbt; '**cork·er** [-kə] *s. sl.* **1.** *das* Entscheidende; **2.** entscheidendes Argu'ment; **3.** a) ,Knüller', ,tolles Ding', b) ,toller Kerl'; '**cork·ing** [-kɪŋ] *adj. sl.* ,toll', ,prima'.

cork| jack·et *s.* Kork-, Schwimmweste *f*; **~ oak** *s.* ♀ Korkeiche *f*; '**~·screw I** *s.* Korkenzieher *m*: **~ *curls*** Korkenzieherlocken; **II** *v/i.* sich schlängeln *od.* winden; **III** *v/t.* 'durchwinden, spi'ralig bewegen; F *fig.* mühsam her'ausziehen (***out of*** aus); **~ sole** *s.* Korkeinlegesohle *f*; **~ tree** → ***cork oak***; '**~·wood** *s.* **1.** ♀ Korkholzbaum *m*; **2.** Korkholz *n*.

cork·y ['kɔːkɪ] *adj.* **1.** korkartig, Kork…; **2.** → ***corked*** 2; **3.** F ,putzmunter'.

cor·mo·rant ['kɔːmərənt] *s.* **1.** *orn.* Kormo'ran *m*, Scharbe *f*, Seerabe *m*; **2.** *fig.* Vielfraß *m*.

corn¹ [kɔːn] **I** *s.* **1.** *coll.* Getreide *n*, Korn *n* (*Pflanze od. Frucht*); *engS.* a) *England*: Weizen *m*, b) *Scot.*, *Ir.* Hafer *m*, c) *Am.* Mais *m*, d) Hafer *m* (*Pferdefutter*): **~ *on the cob*** Mais *m* am Kolben (*als Gemüse*); **2.** Getreide- *od.* Samenkorn *n*; **3.** *Am.* → ***corn whisky***; **II** *v/t.* **4.** pökeln, einsalzen: ***~ed beef*** Corned beef *n*, Büchsenfleisch *n*.

corn² [kɔːn] *s.* ⚕ Hühnerauge *n*: ***tread on s.o.'s ~s*** *fig.* j-m auf die Hühneraugen treten.

corn| belt *s. Am.* Maisgürtel *m* (*im Mittleren Westen*); '**~·bind** *s.* ♀ Ackerwinde *f*; **~ bread** *s. Am.* Maisbrot *n*; **~ cake** *s. Am.* (Pfann)Kuchen *m* aus Maismehl; **~ chan·dler** *s. Brit.* Korn-, Saathändler *m*; '**~·cob** *s.* **1.** Maiskolben *m*; **2.** *a.* **~ *pipe*** Maiskolbenpfeife *f*; '**~ˌcock·le** *s.* ♀ Kornrade *f*.

cor·ne·a ['kɔːnɪə] *s. anat.* Hornhaut *f* (*des Auges*), 'Kornea *f*.

cor·nel ['kɔːnəl] *s.* ♀ Kor'nelkirsche *f*.

cor·ne·ous ['kɔːnɪəs] *adj.* hornig.

cor·ner ['kɔːnə] **I** *s.* **1.** (Straßen-, Häuser)Ecke *f*, *bsd. mot.* Kurve *f*: ***round the ~*** um die Ecke; ***blind ~*** unübersichtliche (Straßen)Biegung; ***cut ~s*** a) *mot.* die Kurven schneiden, b) *fig.* die Sache abkürzen; ***take a ~*** e-e Kurve nehmen (*Auto*); ***cut off a ~*** ein Stück (Weges) abschneiden; ***turn the ~*** um die (*Straßen*)Ecke biegen; ***he's turned the ~*** *fig.* er ist über den Berg; **2.** Winkel *m*, Ecke *f*: ***put a child in the ~*** ein Kind in die Ecke stellen; ***in a tight ~*** *fig.* in der Klemme, in Verlegenheit; ***drive s.o. into a ~*** j-n in die Enge treiben; ***look at s.o. from the ~ of one's eye*** j-n aus den Augenwinkeln ansehen; **3.** verborgener *od.* geheimer Winkel, entlegene Stelle; **4.** Gegend *f*, ,Ecke' *f*: ***from the four ~s of the earth*** aus allen Himmelsrichtungen, von überall her; **5.** ☤ a) spekula'tiver Aufkauf, b) (Aufkäufer)Ring *m*, Mono'pol(gruppe *f*) *n*: **~ *in wheat*** Weizen-Korner *m*; **6.** *sport* a) *Fußball etc.*: Eckball *m*, Ecke *f*, b) *Boxen*: (Ring)Ecke *f*; **II** *v/t.* **7.** in die Enge treiben; in Bedrängnis bringen; **8.** ☤ *Ware* (spekula'tiv) aufkaufen, *fig.* mit Beschlag belegen: **~ *the market*** den Markt *od.* alles aufkaufen; **III** *v/i.* **9.** *Am.* a) e-e Ecke *od.* e-n Winkel bilden, b) an e-r Ecke gelegen sein; **IV** *adj.* **10.** Eck…: **~ *house***; '**~ˌchis·el** *s.* ⚙ Winkelmeißel *m*.

cor·nered ['kɔ:nəd] *adj.* **1.** *in Zssgn:* ...eckig; **2.** in die Enge getrieben, in der Klemme.

cor·ner| kick *s. Fußball*: Eckstoß *m*; **~ seat** *s.* Eckplatz *m*; '**~·stone** *s.* ⚠ Eck- *od.* Grundstein *m*; *fig.* Eckpfeiler *m*, Grundstein *m*; '**~·ways**, '**~·wise** *adv.* **1.** mit der Ecke nach vorn; **2.** diago'nal.

cor·net ['kɔ:nɪt] *s.* **1.** ♪ a) (Pi'ston)Kor,nett *n* (*a. Orgelregister*), b) Kornet'tist *m*; **2.** spitze Tüte; **3.** a) *Brit.* Eistüte *f*, b) Cremerolle *f*; **4.** Schwesternhaube *f*; **5.** ⚔ *hist.* a) Fähnlein *n*, b) Kor'nett *m*, Fähnrich *m*; '**cor·net·(t)ist** [-tɪst] *s.* ♪ Kornet'tist *m*.

corn| ex·change *s.* Getreidebörse *f*; **~ field** *s.* Getreidefeld *n*; *Am.* Maisfeld *n*; '**~·flakes** *s. pl.* Corn-flakes *pl.*; **~ flour** *s.* Stärkemehl *n*; '**~,flow·er** *s.* Kornblume *f*.

cor·nice ['kɔ:nɪs] *s.* **1.** ⚠ Gesims *n*, Sims *m*, *n*; **2.** Kranz-, Randleiste *f*; **3.** Bilderleiste *f*; **4.** (Schnee)Wächte *f*.

Cor·nish ['kɔ:nɪʃ] **I** *adj.* aus Cornwall, kornisch; **II** *s.* kornische Sprache; '**~·man** [-mən] *s.* [*irr.*] Einwohner *m* von Cornwall.

'**corn|·loft** *s.* Getreidespeicher *m*; **~ pop·py**, **~ rose** *s.* ♀ Klatschmohn *m*, -rose *f*; '**~-stalk** *s.* **1.** Getreidehalm *m*; **2.** *Am.* Maisstengel *m*; **3.** F Bohnenstange *f* (*lange, dünne Person*); '**~·starch** *s. Am.* Stärkemehl *n*.

cor·nu·co·pi·a [,kɔ:njʊ'kəʊpjə] *s.* **1.** Füllhorn *n* (*a. fig.*); **2.** *fig.* (*of*) Fülle *f* (von), 'Überfluß *m* (an *dat.*).

corn whis·ky *s. Am.* Maiswhiskey.

corn·y ['kɔ:nɪ] *adj.* **1.** a) *Brit.* Korn..., b) *Am.* Mais...; **2.** getreidereich; **3.** körnig; **4.** *Am. sl.* a) schmalzig, sentimen'tal (*bsd.* ♪), b) kitschig, abgedroschen, c) ländlich.

co·rol·la [kə'rɒlə] *s.* Blumenkrone *f*.

cor·ol·lar·y [kə'rɒlərɪ] *s.* **1.** ⩓, *phls.* Folgesatz *m*; **2.** logische Folge *f* (*of*, *to* von *od. gen.*).

co·ro·na [kə'rəʊnə] *pl.* **-nae** [-ni:] *s.* **1.** *ast.* a) Krone *f* (*Sternbild*), b) Hof *m*, Ko'rona *f*, Strahlenkranz *m*; **2.** *a.* **~ discharge** ⚡ Glimmentladung *f*, Ko'rona *f*; **3.** ⚠ Kranzleiste *f*; **4.** *anat.* Zahnkrone *f*; **5.** ♀ Nebenkrone *f*; **6.** Kronleuchter *m*.

cor·o·nach ['kɒrənək] *s. Scot. u. Ir.* Totenklage *f*.

cor·o·nal ['kɒrənl] *s.* **1.** Stirnreif *m*, Dia'dem *n*; **2.** (Blumen)Kranz *m*.

cor·o·nar·y ['kɒrənərɪ] **I** *adj.* **1.** kronen-, kranzartig; **2.** ⚕ koro'nar, (Herz-) Kranz...: **~ artery** Kranzarterie *f*; **~ thrombosis** → **II** *s.* **3.** ⚕ Koro'narthrom,bose *f*.

cor·o·na·tion [,kɒrə'neɪʃn] *s.* **1.** Krönung *f*; **2.** Krönungsfeier *f*.

cor·o·ner ['kɒrənə] *s.* ⚖ Coroner *m* (*richterlicher Beamter zur Untersuchung der Todesursache in Fällen unnatürlichen Todes*); → **inquest** 1.

cor·o·net ['kɒrənɪt] *s.* **1.** kleine Krone; **2.** Adelskrone *f*; **3.** Dia'dem *n*; **4.** *zo.* Hufkrone *f* (*Pferd*); '**cor·o·net·ed** [-tɪd] *adj.* **1.** e-e Adelskrone *od.* ein Dia'dem tragend; **2.** adelig; **3.** mit Adelswappen (*Briefpapier*).

cor·po·ral¹ ['kɔ:pərəl] *s.* ⚔ 'Unteroffi,zier *m*.

cor·po·ral² ['kɔ:pərəl] *adj.* □ **1.** körperlich, leiblich: **~ punishment** körperliche Züchtigung; **2.** per'sönlich; **cor·po·ral·i·ty** [,kɔ:pə'rælətɪ] *s.* Körperlichkeit *f*.

cor·po·rate ['kɔ:pərət] *adj.* □ **1.** vereinigt, körperschaftlich, korpora'tiv, Körperschafts...; inkorporiert: **~ body** → **corporation** 1; **~ seal** a) *Brit.* Siegel *n* e-r juristischen Person, b) *Am.* Firmensiegel *n*; **~ stock** *Am.* (Gesellschafts)Aktien *pl.*; **~ tax** *Am.* Körperschaftssteuer *f*; **~ town** Stadt *f* mit eigenem Recht; **2.** gemeinsam, kollek'tiv;

cor·po·ra·tion [,kɔ:pə'reɪʃn] *s.* **1.** ⚖ ju'ristische Per'son: **~ tax** Körperschaftssteuer *f*; **2.** *Brit.* (rechtsfähige) Handelsgesellschaft; **3.** *a.* **stock ~** ✝ *Am.* 'Aktiengesellschaft *f*; **4.** Vereinigung *f*; Gilde *f*, Innung *f*, Zunft *f*; **5.** Stadtbehörde *f*; inkorporierte Stadtgemeinde; **6.** F Schmerbauch *m*; '**cor·po·ra·tive** [-tɪv] *adj.* **1.** korpora'tiv, körperschaftlich; *Am.* ✝ Gesellschafts...; **2.** *pol.* korpora'tiv (*Staat etc.*).

cor·po·re·al [kɔ:'pɔ:rɪəl] *adj.* □ **1.** körperlich, leiblich; **2.** materi'ell, dinglich, greifbar; **cor·po·re·al·i·ty** [kɔ:,pɔ:rɪ'ælətɪ] *s.* Körperlichkeit *f*.

cor·po·sant ['kɔ:pəzənt] *s.* ⚡ Elmsfeuer *n*.

corps [kɔ:] *pl.* **corps** [kɔ:z] *s.* **1.** ⚔ a) (Ar'mee)Korps *n*, b) Korps *n*, Truppe *f*: **volunteer ~** Freiwilligentruppe; **2.** Körperschaft *f*, Korps *n*; **3.** Korps *n*, Korporati'on *f*, (Stu'denten)Verbindung *f*; **~ de bal·let** [,kɔ:də'bæleɪ] (*Fr.*) *s.* Bal'lettgruppe *f*; **♀ Di·plo·ma·tique** ['kɔ:,dɪpləmæ'tɪk] (*Fr.*) *s.* Diplo'matisches Korps.

corpse [kɔ:ps] *s.* Leichnam *m*, Leiche *f*.

cor·pu·lence ['kɔ:pjʊləns], '**cor·pu·len·cy** [-sɪ] *s.* Korpu'lenz *f*, Beleibtheit *f*; '**cor·pu·lent** [-nt] *adj.* □ korpu'lent, beleibt.

cor·pus ['kɔ:pəs] *pl.* '**cor·po·ra** [-pərə] *s.* **1.** Korpus *n*, Sammlung *f* (*Werk, Gesetz etc.*); **2.** Groß-, Hauptteil *m*; **3.** ✝ ('Stamm)Kapi,tal *n* (*Ggs. Zinsen etc.*); **♀ Chris·ti** ['krɪstɪ] *s. eccl.* Fron'leichnam(sfest *n*) *m*.

cor·pus·cle ['kɔ:pʌsl] *s.* **1.** *biol.* (Blut-) Körperchen *n*; **2.** *phys.* Kor'puskel *n*, *f*, Elemen'tarteilchen *n*; **cor·pus·cu·lar** [kɔ:'pʌskjʊlə] *adj. phys.* Korpuskular...; **cor·pus·cule** [kɔ:'pʌskju:l] → **corpuscle**.

cor·pus| de·lic·ti [dɪ'lɪktaɪ] *s.* ⚖ 'Corpus *n* de'licti: a) ⚖ Tatbestand *m*, b) Beweisstück *n*, *bsd.* Leiche *f* (des Ermordeten); **~ ju·ris** ['dʒʊərɪs] *s.* ⚖ Corpus *n* juris, Gesetzessammlung *f*.

cor·ral [kɒ'rɑ:l] **I** *s.* **1.** Kor'ral *m*, (Vieh)Hof *m*, Pferch *m*, Einzäunung *f*; **2.** Wagenburg *f*; **II** *v/t.* **3.** *Wagen* zu e-r Wagenburg zs.-stellen; **4.** in e-n Pferch treiben; **5.** *fig.* einsperren; **6.** *Am.* F sich *et.* ‚schnappen'.

cor·rect [kə'rekt] **I** *v/t.* **1.** korrigieren, verbessern, berichtigen, richtigstellen; **2.** regulieren, regeln, ausgleichen; **3.** *Mängel* abstellen, beheben; **4.** zu'rechtweisen, tadeln: **I stand ~ed** ich gebe m-n Fehler zu; **5.** *j-n od. et.* bestrafen; **II** *adj.* □ **6.** richtig, fehlerfrei: **be ~** a) stimmen, b) recht haben; **7.** kor'rekt, schicklich, einwandfrei: **it is the ~ thing** es gehört sich; **~ behavio(u)r** korrektes Benehmen; **8.** genau, ordentlich; **cor'rec·tion** [-kʃn] *s.* **1.** Verbesserung *f*, Richtigstellung *f*, Berichtigen *n* (*a.* ⚙, *phys.*): **I speak under ~** ich kann mich natürlich (auch) irren; **2.** Korrek'tur *f* (*a.* ⚗, *phys.*, *typ. etc.*), (Fehler)Verbesserung *f*; **3.** Zu'rechtweisung *f*; **4.** Bestrafung *f*, ⚖ *a.* Besserung *f*: **house of ~** ⚖ Strafanstalt *f*; **5.** Bereinigung *f*, Abstellung *f*, Regulierung *f*; **cor'rec·tion·al** [-kʃənl] → **corrective**; **cor'rect·i·tude** [-tɪtju:d] *s.* Kor'rektheit *f* (*Benehmen*); **cor'rec·tive** [-tɪv] **I** *adj.* □ **1.** verbessernd, Verbesserungs..., Berichtigungs..., Korrektur...: **~ measure** Abhilfemaßnahme *f*; **2.** mildernd, lindernd; **3.** ⚖ Besserungs..., Straf...: **~ training** Besserungsmaßregel *f*; **II** *s.* **4.** Korrek'tiv *n*, Abhilfe *f*, Heil-, Gegenmittel *n*: **cor'rect·ness** [-nɪs] *s.* Richtigkeit *f*; Kor'rektheit *f*; **cor'rec·tor** [-tə] *s.* **1.** Verbesserer *m*; **2.** 'Kritiker(in); **3.** *mst* **~ of the press** *Brit. typ.* Kor'rektor *m*; **4.** Besserungsmittel *n*.

cor·re·late ['kɒrəleɪt] **I** *v/t.* in Wechselbeziehung bringen (**with** mit), aufein'ander beziehen; in Über'einstimmung bringen (**with** mit); **II** *v/i.* in Wechselbeziehung stehen (**with** mit), sich aufeinander beziehen; entsprechen (**with** *dat.*); **III** *s.* Korre'lat *n*, Gegenstück *n*; **cor·re·la·tion** [,kɒrə'leɪʃn] *s.* Wechselbeziehung *f*, gegenseitige Abhängigkeit, Entsprechung *f*; **cor·rel·a·tive** [kɒ'relətɪv] **I** *adj.* □ korrela'tiv, in Wechselbeziehung stehend, sich ergänzend; entsprechend; **II** *s.* Korre'lat *n*, Gegenstück *n*, Ergänzung *f*.

cor·re·spond [,kɒrɪ'spɒnd] *v/i.* **1.** (**with**, **to**) entsprechen (*dat.*), über'einstimmen, in Einklang stehen (mit); **2.** (**with**, **to**) passen (zu), sich eignen (für); **3.** (**to**) entsprechen (*dat.*), das Gegenstück sein (von), ana'log sein (zu); **4.** in Briefwechsel (✝ in Geschäftsverkehr) stehen (**with** mit).

cor·re·spond·ence [,kɒrɪ'spɒndəns] *s.* **1.** Über'einstimmung *f* (**with** mit, **between** zwischen *dat.*); **2.** Angemessenheit *f*, Entsprechung *f*; **3.** Korrespon'denz *f*: a) Briefwechsel *m*, b) Briefe *pl.*; **4.** *Zeitung*: Beiträge *pl.*; **~ clerk** *s.* ✝ Korrespon'dent(in); **~ col·umn** *s.* Leserbriefspalte *f*; **~ chess** *s.* Fernschach *n*; **~ course** *s.* Fernkurs *m*; **~ school** *s.* 'Fernlehrinsti,tut *n*.

cor·re·spond·ent [,kɒrɪ'spɒndənt] **I** *s.* Korrespon'dent(in): a) (Brief)Schreiber(in); Briefpartner(in), b) ✝ Geschäftsfreund *m*, c) *Zeitung*: Mitarbeiter(in); Einsender(in): **foreign ~** Auslandskorrespondent; **special ~** Sonderberichterstatter *m*; **II** *adj.* → ,**cor·re'spond·ing** [-dɪŋ] *adj.* □ **1.** entsprechend, gemäß (**to** *dat.*); **2.** in Briefwechsel stehend (**with** mit): **~ member** korrespondierendes Mitglied; ,**cor·re'spond·ing·ly** [-dɪŋlɪ] *adv.* entsprechend, demgemäß.

cor·ri·dor ['kɒrɪdɔ:] *s.* **1.** 'Korridor *m*, Gang *m*, Flur *m*; **2.** 🚂 'Korridor *m*, Seitengang *m*: **~ train** D-Zug *m*; **3.** *geogr.*, *pol.* 'Korridor *m* (*Landstreifen durch fremdes Gebiet*).

cor·ri·gen·dum [,kɒrɪ'dʒendəm] *pl.* **-da** [-də] *s.* **1.** zu verbessernder Druckfehler; **2.** *pl.* Druckfehlerverzeichnis *n*; **cor·ri·gi·ble** ['kɒrɪdʒəbl] *adj.* **1.** zu verbessern(d); **2.** lenksam, fügsam.

cor·rob·o·rate [kə'rɒbəreɪt] *v/t.* bekräftigen, bestätigen, erhärten; **cor·rob·o·ra·tion** [kəˌrɒbə'reɪʃn] *s.* Bekräftigung *f*, Bestätigung *f*, Erhärtung *f*; **cor'rob·o·ra·tive** [-bərətɪv], **cor'rob·o·ra·to·ry** [-bərətərɪ] *adj.* bestärkend, bestätigend.

cor·rode [kə'rəʊd] **I** *v/t.* **1.** ⚗, ⚙ zer-, anfressen, angreifen, korrodieren; wegätzen, -beizen; **2.** *fig.* zerfressen, zerstören, unter'graben, aushöhlen: ***corroding care*** nagende Sorge; **II** *v/i.* **3.** zerfressen werden, korrodieren; rosten; **4.** sich einfressen; **5.** verderben, verfallen; **cor'ro·dent** [-dənt] *Am.* **I** *adj.* ätzend; **II** *s.* Ätzmittel *n*; **cor'ro·sion** [-əʊʒn] *s.* **1.** ⚗, ⚙ Korrosi'on *f*, An-, Zerfressen *n*; Rostfraß *m*; Ätzen *n*, Beizen *n*; **2.** *fig.* Zerstörung *f*; **cor'ro·sive** [-əʊsɪv] **I** *adj.* ☐ **1.** ⚗, ⚙ zerfressend, ätzend, beizend, angreifend, Korrosions...; **2.** *fig.* nagend, quälend; **II** *s.* **3.** ⚗, ⚙ Ätz-, Beizmittel *n*; **cor'ro·sive·ness** [-əʊsɪvnɪs] *s.* ätzende Schärfe.

cor·ru·gate ['kɒrʊgeɪt] **I** *v/t.* wellen, riefen; runzeln, furchen; **II** *v/i.* sich wellen *od.* runzeln, runz(e)lig werden; **'cor·ru·gat·ed** [-tɪd] *adj.* runz(e)lig, gefurcht; gewellt, gerieft: **~ *iron*** (*od.* ***sheet***) Wellblech *n*; **~ *cardboard***, **~ *paper*** Wellpappe *f*; **cor·ru·ga·tion** [ˌkɒrʊ'geɪʃn] *s.* **1.** Runzeln *n*, Furchen *n*; Wellen *n*, Riefen *n*; **2.** Furche *f*, Falte *f* (*auf der Stirn*).

cor·rupt [kə'rʌpt] **I** *adj.* ☐ **1.** (*moralisch*) verdorben, schlecht, verworfen; **2.** unredlich, unlauter; **3.** kor'rupt, bestechlich, käuflich: **~ *practices*** Bestechungsmanöver *pl.*, Korruption *f*; **4.** faul, verdorben, schlecht; **5.** unrein, unecht, verfälscht, verderbt (*Text*); **II** *v/t.* **6.** verderben, zu'grunde richten: ***~ing influences*** verderbliche Einflüsse; **7.** verleiten, verführen; **8.** korrumpieren, bestechen; **9.** *Texte etc.* verderben, verfälschen, verunstalten; **10.** *fig.* anstecken, infizieren; **III** *v/i.* **11.** (*moralisch*) verderben, verkommen; **12.** schlecht werden, verderben; **cor'rupt·i·ble** [-təbl] *adj.* ☐ **1.** zum Schlechten neigend; **2.** bestechlich; **3.** verderblich; vergänglich; **cor'rup·tion** [-pʃn] *s.* **1.** Verdorbenheit *f*, Verworfenheit *f*; **2.** verderblicher Einfluß; **3.** Korrupti'on *f*: a) Kor'ruptheit *f*, Bestechlichkeit *f*, Käuflichkeit *f*, b) kor'rupte Me'thoden *pl.*, Bestechung *f*; **4.** Verfälschung *f*, Korrumpierung *f* (*Text etc.*); **5.** Fäulnis *f*; **cor'rup·tive** [-tɪv] *adj.* **1.** zersetzend, verderblich; **2.** *fig.* ansteckend; **cor'rupt·ness** [-nɪs] → ***corruption*** 1, 3a.

cor·sage [kɔː'sɑːʒ] *s.* **1.** Mieder *n*; **2.** 'Ansteckbuˌkett *n*.

cor·sair ['kɔːseə] *s.* **1.** *hist.* Kor'sar *m*, Seeräuber *m*; **2.** Kaperschiff *n*.

corse·let ['kɔːslɪt] *s.* **1.** *Am. mst* **cor·se·let** [ˌkɔːsə'let] Korse'lett *n*, Mieder *n*; **2.** *hist.* Harnisch *m*.

cor·set ['kɔːsɪt] *s. oft pl.* Kor'sett *n*; **'cor·set·ed** [-tɪd] *adj.* (ein)geschnürt; **'cor·set·ry** [-trɪ] *s.* Miederwaren *pl.*

Cor·si·can ['kɔːsɪkən] **I** *adj.* korsisch; **II** *s.* Korse *m*, Korsin *f*.

cor·tège [kɔː'teɪʒ] (*Fr.*) *s.* **1.** Gefolge *n* *e-s Fürsten etc.*; **2.** Zug *m*, Prozessi'on *f*: ***funeral*** **~** Leichenzug *m*.

cor·tex ['kɔːteks] *pl.* **-ti·ces** [-tɪsiːz] *s.* ♀, *zo.*, *anat.* Rinde *f*: ***cerebral*** **~** Großhirnrinde.

cor·ti·sone ['kɔːtɪzəʊn] *s.* ⚕ Korti'son *n*.

co·run·dum [kə'rʌndəm] *s. min.* Ko'rund *m*.

cor·us·cate ['kɒrəskeɪt] *v/i.* (auf)blitzen, funkeln, glänzen (*a. fig.*).

cor·vée ['kɔːveɪ] (*Fr.*) *s.* Fronarbeit *f*, -dienst *m* (*a. fig.*).

cor·vette [kɔː'vet] *s.* ⚓ Kor'vette *f*.

cor·vine ['kɔːvaɪn] *adj.* raben-, krähenartig.

Cor·y·don ['kɒrɪdən] *s.* **1.** *poet.* 'Korydon *m*, Schäfer *m*; **2.** schmachtender Liebhaber.

cor·ymb ['kɒrɪmb] *s.* ♀ Doldentraube *f*.

cor·y·phae·us [ˌkɒrɪ'fiːəs] *pl.* **-phae·i** [-'fiːaɪ] *s. antiq. u. fig.* Kory'phäe *f*; **co·ry·phée** ['kɒrɪfeɪ] *s.* Primaballe'rina *f*.

cos[1] [kɒs] *s.* ♀ Lattich *m*.

cos[2] [kəz] *cj.* F weil, da.

co·se·cant [ˌkəʊ'siːkənt] *s.* ⩓ 'Kosekans *m*.

cosh [kɒʃ] *Brit.* F **I** *s.* Totschläger *m*; **II** *v/t.* mit e-m Totschläger schlagen, *j-m* ‚eins über den Schädel hauen'.

cosh·er ['kɒʃə] *v/t.* verhätscheln.

co·sig·na·to·ry [ˌkəʊ'sɪgnətərɪ] *s.* 'Mitunterˌzeichner(in).

co·sine ['kəʊsaɪn] *s.* ⩓ 'Kosinus *m*.

co·si·ness ['kəʊzɪnɪs] *s.* Behaglichkeit *f*, Gemütlichkeit *f*.

cos·met·ic [kɒz'metɪk] **I** *adj.* (☐ ***~ally***) **1.** kos'metisch (*a. fig.*): **~ *treatment*** → 4; **~ (*plastic*) *surgery*** Schönheitschirurgie *f od.* -operation *f*; **2.** *fig.* kosmetisch, optisch; **II** *s.* **3.** kosmetisches Mittel, Schönheitsmittel *n*, *pl. a.* Kos'metika; **4.** *pl.* Kos'metik *f*, Schönheitspflege *f*; **cos·me·ti·cian** [ˌkɒzmə'tɪʃn] *s.*, **cos·me·tol·o·gist** [ˌkɒzmə'tɒlədʒɪst] Kos'metiker(in).

cos·mic, cos·mi·cal ['kɒzmɪk(l)] *adj.* ☐ kosmisch (*a. fig.*).

cos·mog·o·ny [kɒz'mɒgənɪ] *s.* Kosmogo'nie *f* (*Theorie über die Entstehung des Weltalls*); **cos'mog·ra·phy** [-grəfɪ] *s.* Kosmogra'phie *f*, Weltbeschreibung *f*; **cos'mol·o·gy** [-ɒlədʒɪ] *s.* Kosmolo'gie *f*.

cos·mo·naut ['kɒzmənɔːt] *s.* (Welt-) Raumfahrer *m*, Kosmo'naut *m*.

cos·mo·pol·i·tan [ˌkɒzmə'pɒlɪtən] **I** *adj.* kosmopo'litisch; *weitS.* weltoffen; **II** *s.* Kosmopo'lit *m*, Weltbürger(in); **ˌcos·mo'pol·i·tan·ism** [-tənɪzəm] *s.* Weltbürgertum *n*; *weitS.* Weltoffenheit *f*.

cos·mos ['kɒzmɒs] *s.* **1.** 'Kosmos *m*: a) Weltall *n*, b) Weltordnung *f*; **2.** Welt *f* für sich; **3.** ♀ 'Kosmos *m* (*Blume*).

Cos·sack ['kɒsæk] *s.* Ko'sak *m*.

cos·set ['kɒsɪt] *v/t.* verhätscheln.

cost [kɒst] **I** *s.* **1.** *stets sg.* Kosten *pl.*, Preis *m*, Aufwand *m*: **~ *of living*** Lebenshaltungskosten; **~ *of-living allowance*** Teuerungszulage *f*; ***~-of-living index*** Lebenshaltungsindex *m*; **2.** ✝ a) *a.* **~ *price*** (Selbst-, Gestehungs)Kosten *pl.*, Selbstkosten-, (Netto)Einkaufspreis *m*, b) (Un)Kosten *pl.*, Auslagen *pl.*, Spesen *pl.*: ***at*** **~** zum Selbstkostenpreis; **~ *accounting*** → ***costing***; **~ *accountant*** (Betriebs)Kalkulator *m*; **~-*covering*** kostendeckend; **~ *free*** kostenlos; **~ *plus*** Gestehungskosten plus Unternehmergewinn; **~ *of construction*** Baukosten; **3.** *fig.* Kosten *pl.*, Schaden *m*, Nachteil *m*: ***at my*** **~** auf m-e Kosten; ***at a heavy*** **~** unter schweren Opfern; ***at the*** **~** ***of his health*** auf Kosten s-r Gesundheit; ***to my*** **~** zu m-m Schaden; ***I know to my*** **~** ich weiß aus eigener (bitterer) Erfahrung; ***at all ~s***, ***at any*** **~** um jeden Preis; **4.** *pl.* ⚖ (Gerichts)Kosten *pl.*, Gebühren *pl.*; ***condemn s.o. in the ~s*** j-n zu den Kosten verurteilen; ***dismiss with ~s*** kostenpflichtig abweisen; ***allow ~s*** die Kosten bewilligen; **II** *v/t.* [*irr.*] **5.** kosten: ***it*** **~** ***me one pound*** es kostete mich ein Pfund; **6.** kosten, bringen um: ***it*** **~** ***him his life*** es kostete ihn das Leben; **7.** kosten, verursachen: ***it*** **~** ***me a lot of trouble*** es verursachte mir (*od.* kostete mich) große Mühe; **8.** [*pret. u. p.p.* **cost·ed**] ✝ kalkulieren, den Preis berechnen von: ***~ed at*** mit e-m Kostenanschlag von; **III** *v/i.* [*irr.*] **9.** ***it*** **~** ***him dearly fig.*** es kam ihm teuer zu stehen.

cos·tal ['kɒstl] *adj.* **1.** *anat.* Rippen..., kos'tal; **2.** ♀ (Blatt)Rippen...; **3.** *zo.* (Flügel)Ader...

co·star ['kəʊstɑː] *thea.*, *Film* **I** *s.* e-r der Hauptdarsteller; **II** *v/i.* e-e der Hauptrollen spielen: ***~ring*** in e-r der Hauptrollen.

cos·ter·mon·ger ['kɒstəˌmʌŋgə], *a.* **cos·ter** ['kɒstə] *s. Brit.* Straßenhändler(in) für Obst u. Gemüse *etc.*

cost·ing ['kɒstɪŋ] *s.* ✝ *Brit.* Kosten(be)rechnung *f*, Kalkulati'on *f*.

cos·tive ['kɒstɪv] *adj.* ☐ **1.** ⚕ verstopft, hartleibig; **2.** *fig.* geizig; **'cos·tive·ness** [-nɪs] *s.* **1.** ⚕ Verstopfung *f*; **2.** *fig.* Geiz *m*.

cost·li·ness ['kɒstlɪnɪs] *s.* **1.** Kostspieligkeit *f*; **2.** Pracht *f*; **cost·ly** ['kɒstlɪ] *adj.* **1.** kostspielig, teuer; **2.** kostbar, wertvoll; prächtig.

cost price → ***cost*** 2 a.

cos·tume ['kɒstjuːm] *s.* **1.** Ko'stüm *n*, Kleidung *f*, Tracht *f*: **~ *jewel(le)ry*** Modeschmuck *m*; **2.** *obs.* Ko'stüm(kleid) *n* (*für Damen*); **3.** ('Masken-, 'Bühnen-) Koˌstüm *n*: **~ *piece*** *thea.* Kostümstück *n*; **4.** Badeanzug *m*; **cos·tum·er** [kɒs'tjuːmə], **cos·tum·i·er** [kɒs'tjuːmɪə] *s.* **1.** Ko'stümverleiher(in); **2.** *thea.* Kostümi'er *m*.

co·sy ['kəʊzɪ] **I** *adj.* ☐ behaglich, gemütlich, traulich, heimelig; **II** *s.* Teehaube *f*, -wärmer *m*; Eierwärmer *m*.

cot[1] [kɒt] *s.* **1.** *Brit.* Kinderbettchen *n*: **~ *death*** ⚕ plötzlicher Kindstod; **2.** Feldbett *n*; **3.** leichte Bettstelle; **4.** ⚓ Schwingbett *n*, Koje *f*.

cot[2] [kɒt] *s.* **1.** (Schaf- *etc.*)Stall *m*; **2.** *obs.* Häus-chen *n*, Hütte *f*.

co·tan·gent [ˌkəʊ'tændʒənt] *s.* ⩓ 'Kotangens *m*.

cote [kəʊt] *s.* Stall *m*, Hütte *f*, Häuschen *n* (*für Kleinvieh etc.*).

co·te·rie ['kəʊtərɪ] *s.* **1.** *contp.* Kote'rie *f*, Klüngel *m*, 'Clique *f*; **2.** exklu'siver Zirkel.

co·thur·nus [kə'θɜːnəs] *pl.* **-ni** [-naɪ] *s.* **1.** *antiq.* Ko'thurn *m*; **2.** erhabener, pa'thetischer Stil.

co·tid·al lines [kəʊ'taɪdl] *s. pl.* ⚓ Isor-

ˈrhachien *pl.*
co·trus·tee, *Am.* **co·trus·tee** [ˌkəʊtrʌsˈtiː] *s.* Mitreuhänder *m.*
cot·tage [ˈkɒtɪdʒ] *s.* **1.** (kleines) Landhaus, Cottage *n*; **2.** *Am.* Ferienhaus *n*; **3.** *Am.* Wohngebäude *n* (*bsd. in e-m Heim*); *Hotel*: Depenˈdance *f*; **~ cheese** *s.* Hüttenkäse *m*; **~ hos·pi·tal** *s.* **1.** kleines Krankenhaus; **2.** *Am. aus Einzelgebäuden bestehendes Krankenhaus*; **~ in·dus·try** *s.* ˈHeimindustrie *f*; **~ pi·a·no** *s.* Piaˈnino *n*; **~ pud·ding** *s.* Kuchen *m* mit süßer Soße.
cot·tag·er [ˈkɒtɪdʒə] *s.* **1.** Cottagebewohner(in); **2.** *Am.* Urlauber(in) in e-m Ferienhaus.
cot·ter [ˈkɒtə] *s.* ⚙ a) (Schließ)Keil *m*, b) → **~ pin** *s.* Splint *m.*
cot·ton [ˈkɒtn] **I** *s.* **1.** Baumwolle *f*: ***absorbent ~*** Watte *f*; **2.** Baumwollpflanze *f*; **3.** Baumwollstoff *m*; **4.** *pl.* a) Baumwollwaren *pl.*, b) Baumwollkleidung *f*; **5.** (Näh-, Stick)Garn *n*; **II** *adj.* **6.** baumwollen, Baumwoll…; **III** *v/i.* **7.** *Am.* F (***with***) a) sich anfreunden (mit), b) gut auskommen (mit); **8. *~ on to*** F a) *et.* ‚kapieren', b) *Am.* → 7 a; **~ belt** *s. Am.* Baumwollzone *f*; **~ bud** *s.* Wattestäbchen *n*; **~ can·dy** *s. Am.* Zuckerwatte *f*; **~ gin** *s.* ⚙ Entˈkörnungsmaˌschine *f* (*für Baumwolle*); **~ grass** *s.* ⚘ Wollgras *n*; **~ mill** *s.* ˈBaumwollspinneˌrei *f*; **~ pick·er** *s.* Baumwollpflücker *m*; **~ press** *s.* Baumwollballenpresse *f*; **~ print** *s.* bedruckter Katˈtun; **ˈ~·seed** *s.* ⚘ Baumwollsamen *m*: ***~ oil*** Baumwollsamenöl *n*; **ˈ~·tail** *s. zo.* amer. ˈWildkaˌninchen *n*; **~ waste** *s.* **1.** Baumwollabfall *m*; **2.** ⚙ Putzwolle *f*; **ˈ~·wood** *s.* ⚘ *e-e* amer. Pappel; **~ wool** *s.* **1.** Rohbaumwolle *f*; **2.** (Verband-) Watte *f.*
cot·ton·y [ˈkɒtnɪ] *adj.* **1.** baumwollartig; **2.** flaumig, weich.
cot·y·le·don [ˌkɒtɪˈliːdən] *s.* ⚘ **1.** Keimblatt *n*; **2.** ♀ Nabelkraut *n.*
couch¹ [kaʊtʃ] **I** *s.* **1.** Couch *f* (*a. des Psychoanalytikers*), ˈLiege(ˌsofa *n*) *f*; **2.** Bett *n*; Lager *n* (*a. obs. hunt.*), Lagerstätte *f*; **3.** ⚙ Lage *f*, Schicht *f*, erster Anstrich; **II** *v/t.* **4.** *Gedanken etc.* in Worte fassen *od.* kleiden, ausdrücken; **5.** *Lanze* einlegen; **6.** ✱ *Star* stechen; **7. *be ~ed*** liegen; **III** *v/i.* **8.** liegen, lagern (*Tier*); **9.** (sich) kauern *od.* ducken.
couch² [kaʊtʃ] → ***couch grass.***
couch·ant [ˈkaʊtʃənt] *adj. her.* mit erhobenem Kopf liegend.
cou·chette [kuːˈʃet] *s.* 🚂 (Platz *m* in e-m) Liegewagen.
couch grass *s.* ⚘ Quecke *f.*
cou·gar [ˈkuːgə] *s. zo.* ˈPuma *m.*
cough [kɒf] **I** *s.* **1.** Husten *m*: ***give a ~*** (einmal) husten; **II** *v/i.* **2.** husten; **3.** *mot.* F ‚stottern', husten (*Motor*); **III** *v/t.* **4. *~ out*** *od.* ***up*** aushusten; **5. *~ up*** *sl.* herˈausrücken mit (*Geld, der Wahrheit etc.*); **~ drop** *s.* ˈHustenbonˌbon *m, n*; **~ mix·ture** *s.* Hustensaft *m.*
could [kʊd] *pret. von* ***can¹.***
cou·loir [ˈkuːlwɑː] (*Fr.*) *s.* **1.** Bergschlucht *f*; **2.** ⚙ ˈBaggermaˌschine *f.*
cou·lomb [ˈkuːlɒm] *s.* ⚡ Couˈlomb *n*, Amˈpere-Seˌkunde *f.*
coul·ter [ˈkəʊltə] *s.* ✓ Kolter *n*, Pflugmesser *n.*
coun·cil [ˈkaʊnsl] *s.* **1.** Rat *m*, Ratsversammlung *f*, beratende Versammlung; Beratung *f*: ***be in ~*** zu Rate sitzen; ***meet in ~*** e-e (Rats)Sitzung abhalten; ***Queen in*** ♀ *Brit.* Königin und Kronrat; ***~ of war*** Kriegsrat (*a. fig.*); **2.** Rat *m* (*Körperschaft*); *engS.* Gemeinderat *m*: ***municipal ~*** Stadtrat (*Behörde*); ***~ school*** Gemeindeschule *f*; **3.** Kirchenrat *m*, Synˈode *f*, Konˈzil *n*; **4.** Vorstand *m*, Komiˈtee *n*; **~ cham·ber** *s.* Ratszimmer *n*; **~ es·tate** *s. Brit.* städtische (soziˈale Wohn)Siedlung; **~ house** *s. Brit.* stadteigenes (Soziˈal)Wohnhaus.
coun·ci(l)·lor [ˈkaʊnsələ] *s.* Ratsmitglied *n*, -herr *m*, Stadtrat *m*, -rätin *f.*
coun·sel [ˈkaʊnsl] **I** *s.* **1.** Rat(schlag) *m*: ***take ~ of s.o.*** von j-m (e-n) Rat annehmen; **2.** Beratung *f*, Überˈlegung *f*: ***take*** (*od.* ***hold***) ***~ with*** a) sich beraten mit, b) sich Rat holen bei; ***take ~ together*** zusammen beratschlagen; **3.** Plan *m*, Absicht *f*; Meinung *f*, Ansicht *f*: ***divided ~s*** geteilte Meinungen; ***keep one's*** (***own***) ***~*** s-e Meinung *od.* Absicht für sich behalten; **4.** ⚖ (*ohne Artikel*) a) *Brit.* (Rechts)Anwalt *m*, b) *Am.* Rechtsberater *m*, -beistand *m*: ***~ for the defence*** Anwalt des Beklagten, *Strafprozeß*: Verteidiger *m*; ***~ for the prosecution*** Anklagevertreter *m*; **5.** ⚖ *coll.* juˈristische Berater *pl.*; **II** *v/t.* **6.** *j-m* raten *od.* e-n Rat geben; **7.** zu *et.* raten: ***~ delay*** Aufschub empfehlen;
ˈcoun·se(l)·lor [-lə] *s.* **1.** Berater(in), Ratgeber *m*; **2.** *a.* ***~-at-law*** *Am.* (Rechts)Anwalt *m*; **3.** (Studien-, Berufs)Berater *m.*
count¹ [kaʊnt] **I** *s.* **1.** Zählen *n*, (*a.* Volks- *etc.*)Zählung *f*, (Be)Rechnung *f*: ***keep ~ of s.th.*** et. genau zählen (können); ***lose ~*** a) die Übersicht verlieren (***of*** über), b) sich verzählen; ***by my ~*** nach m-r Schätzung; ***take the ~*** *Boxen*: ausgezählt werden; ***take a ~ of nine*** *Boxen*: bis neun angezählt werden; **2.** (End)Zahl *f*, Anzahl *f*, Ergebnis *n*; *sport* Punktzahl *f*; **3.** Berücksichtigung *f*: ***take*** (***no***) ***~ of*** (nicht) zählen *od.* (nicht) berücksichtigen (*acc.*); **4.** ⚖ (An)Klagepunkt *m*; **II** *v/t.* **5.** (ab-, auf-) zählen, (be)rechnen: ***~ the cost*** a) die Kosten berechnen, b) *fig.* die Folgen bedenken; **6.** (mit)zählen, einschließen, berücksichtigen: ***I ~ him among my friends*** ich zähle ihn zu m-n Freunden; ***~ing those present*** die Anwesenden eingeschlossen; ***not ~ing*** abgesehen von; **7.** erachten, schätzen, halten für: ***~ o.s. lucky*** sich glücklich schätzen; ***~ for*** (*od.* ***as***) ***lost*** als verloren ansehen; ***~ it a great hono(u)r*** es als große Ehre betrachten; **III** *v/i.* **8.** zählen, rechnen: ***he ~s among my friends*** er zählt zu m-n Freunden; ***~ing from today*** von heute an (gerechnet); ***I ~ on you*** ich rechne (*od.* verlasse mich) auf dich; **9.** mitzählen, gelten, von Wert sein: ***~ for nothing*** nichts wert sein, nicht von Belang sein; ***every little ~s*** auf jede Kleinigkeit kommt es an; ***he simply doesn't ~*** er zählt überhaupt nicht;
Zssgn mit adv.:
count| down *v/t.* **1.** *Geld* hinzählen; **2.** *a. v/i.* den Countdown ˈdurchführen (für), *a. weitS.* letzte (Start)Vorbereitungen treffen (für); **~ in** *v/t.* mitzählen, einschließen: ***count me in!*** ich bin dabei *od.* mache mit!; **~ off** *v/t. u. v/i.* abzählen; **~ out** *v/t.* **1.** (langsam) abzählen; **2.** ausschließen: ***count me out!*** ohne mich!; **3.** *Boxen u. Kinderspiel*: auszählen; **4.** *parl. Brit.* a) *Gesetzesvorlage* zu Fall bringen, b) *Unterhaussitzung* wegen Beschlußunfähigkeit vertagen; **~ o·ver** *v/t.* nachzählen; **~ up** *v/t.* zs.-zählen, ˈdurchrechnen.
count² [kaʊnt] *s.* (nichtbrit.) Graf *m*; → ***palatine¹*** 1.
count·down [ˈkaʊntdaʊn] *s.* ˈCountdown *m, n* (*a. fig.*).
coun·te·nance [ˈkaʊntənəns] **I** *s.* **1.** Gesichtsausdruck *m*, Miene *f*: ***his ~ fell*** er machte ein langes Gesicht; ***change one's ~*** s-n Gesichtsausdruck ändern, die Farbe wechseln; **2.** Fassung *f*, Haltung *f*, Gemütsruhe *f*: ***keep one's ~*** die Fassung bewahren; ***keep s.o. in ~*** j-n ermuntern, j-n unterstützen; ***put s.o. out of ~*** j-n aus der Fassung bringen; **3.** Ermunterung *f*, Unterˈstützung *f*: ***give*** (*od.* ***lend***) ***~ to*** *j-n* ermutigen, *j-n od. et.* unterstützen, Glaubwürdigkeit verleihen (*dat.*); **II** *v/t.* **4.** *j-n* ermuntern, (unter)ˈstützen; **5.** *et.* gutheißen.
count·er¹ [ˈkaʊntə] *s.* **1.** Ladentisch *m*, *a.* Theke *f* (*im Wirtshaus etc.*): ***under the ~*** unter dem Ladentisch (*verkaufen etc.*), unter der Hand, heimlich; **2.** Schalter *m* (*Bank etc.*); **3.** Spielmarke *f*; **4.** Zählperle *f*, -kugel *f* (*Kinder-Rechenmaschine*); **5.** ⚙ Zähler *m*, Zählgerät *n*, -werk *n.*
coun·ter² [ˈkaʊntə] **I** *adv.* **1.** entgegengesetzt; (***to***) entgegen, zuˈwider (*dat.*): ***run*** (*od.* ***go***) ***~ to*** zuwiderlaufen (*dat.*); ***~ to all rules*** entgegen allen *od.* wider alle Regeln; **II** *adj.* **2.** Gegen…, entgegengesetzt; **III** *s.* **3.** Abwehr *f*; *Boxen etc., a. fig.*: Konter(schlag) *m*; *fenc.* Paˈrade *f*; *Eislauf*: Gegenwende *f*; **4.** *zo.* Brustgrube *f* (*Pferd*); **IV** *v/t. u. v/i.* **5.** entgegenwirken, entgegnen; widerˈsprechen, zuˈwiderhandeln (*dat.*); **6.** *Boxen, Fußball etc., a. fig.*: kontern.
ˌcoun·ter|ˈact [-təˈræ-] *v/t.* **1.** entgegenwirken (*dat.*); bekämpfen, vereiteln; **2.** kompensieren, neutralisieren; **ˌ~ˈac·tion** [-təˈræ-] *s.* **1.** Gegenwirkung *f*, -maßnahme *f*; **2.** ˈWiderstand *m*, Oppositiˈon *f*; **3.** Durchˈkreuzung *f*; **ˌ~ˈac·tive** [-təˈræ-] *adj.* □ entgegenwirkend; **ˈ~·atˌtack** [-tərə-] **I** *s.* Gegenangriff *m* (*a. fig.*); **II** *v/i. u. v/t.* e-n Gegenangriff machen (gegen); **ˈ~·atˌtrac·tion** [-tərə-] *s.* **1.** *phys.* entgegengesetzte Anziehungskraft; **2.** *fig.* ˈGegenattraktiˌon *f*; **ˈ~ˌbal·ance I** *s.* Gegengewicht *n* (*a. fig.*); **II** *v/t.* [ˌkaʊntəˈbæləns] ein Gegengewicht bilden zu, ausgleichen, aufwiegen; die Waage halten (*dat.*); **ˈ~·blast** *s. fig.* Gegenschlag *m*, heftige Reaktiˈon; **ˈ~·blow** *s.* Gegenschlag *m* (*a. fig.*); **ˈ~·charge I** *s.* **1.** ⚖ Gegenklage *f*; **2.** ⚔ Gegenangriff *m*; **II** *v/t.* **3.** ⚖ e-e Gegenklage erheben gegen; **4.** ⚔ e-n Gegenangriff führen gegen; **ˈ~·check** *s.* **1.** a) Gegenwirkung *f*, b) Hindernis *n*; **2.** Gegen-, Nachprüfung *f*; **ˈ~·claim** ✝, ⚖ **I** *s.* Gegenforderung *f*; **II** *v/t.* als Gegenforderung verlangen; **ˌ~ˈclock·wise** → ***anticlockwise***; **ˌ~ˈcy·cli·cal** *adj.* □ ✝ konjunkˈtur-

dämpfend; ˌ~'**es·pi·o·nage** [-tər'e-] *s.* Spio'nageabwehr *f*, Abwehr(dienst *m*) *f*; '~·**feit** [-fɪt] **I** *adj.* **1.** nachgemacht, gefälscht, unecht, falsch: ~ ***coin*** Falschgeld *n*; **2.** vorgetäuscht, falsch; verstellt; **II** *s.* **3.** Fälschung *f*; **4.** Falschgeld *n*; **III** *v/t.* **5.** fälschen; **6.** heucheln, vorgeben, vortäuschen; '~ˌ**feit·er** [-ˌfɪtə] *s.* **1.** Fälscher *m*, Falschmünzer *m*; **2.** Heuchler(in); '~·**foil** *s.* **1.** (Kon'troll-)Abschnitt *m* (*Scheckbuch etc.*), Ku'pon *m*; **2.** a) Ku'pon *m*, Zins-, Divi'dendenschein *m*, b) Ta'lon *m* (*Erneuerungsschein*); '~·**inˌtel·li·gence** [-tərɪn-] Spio'nageabwehr(dienst *m*) *f*; '~ˌ**jump·er** *s.* F Ladenschwengel *m* (*Verkäufer*); '~·**man** [-mən] *s.* [*irr.*] Verkäufer *m*; ~·**mand** [ˌkaʊntə'mɑːnd] **I** *v/t.* **1.** wider'rufen, rückgängig machen, ✝ stornieren: ***until*** ~***ed*** bis auf Widerruf; **2.** absagen, abbestellen; **II** *s.* **3.** Gegenbefehl *m*; **4.** Wider'rufung *f*, Aufhebung; ✝ Stornierung *f*; '~·**march** *s.* **1.** ✕ Rückmarsch *m*; **2.** *fig.* völlige 'Umkehr; '~·**mark** *s.* Gegen-, Kon'trollzeichen *n* (*bsd. für die Echtheit*); '~ˌ**meas·ure** *s.* Gegenmaßnahme *f*; '~ˌ**mo·tion** *s.* **1.** Gegenbewegung *f*; **2.** *pol.* Gegenantrag *m*; '~·**move** *s.* Gegenzug *m*; '~ˌ**of·fer** [-tərˌɒ-] *s.* ✝ Gegenangebot *n*; '~ˌ**or·der** [-tərˌɔː-] **1.** ✝ Abbestellung *f*; **2.** ✕ Gegenbefehl *m*; '~·**pane** *s.* Tagesdecke *f*; '~·**part** *s.* **1.** Gegen-, Seitenstück *n*; **2.** genaue Ergänzung; **3.** Ebenbild *n*; **4.** Dupli'kat *n*; **5.** *fig.* ‚Gegen'über' *n*, Kol'lege *m*: ***his Soviet*** ~; '~·**plot** *s.* Gegenanschlag *m*; '~·**point** **I** *s.* ♪ 'Kontrapunkt *m*; **II** *v/t.* kontrapunktieren; '~·**poise** **I** *s.* **1.** Gegengewicht *n* (*a. fig.*); Gleichgewicht *n*; **II** *v/t.* **2.** als Gegengewicht wirken zu, ausgleichen; **3.** *fig.* im Gleichgewicht halten, ausgleichen, aufwiegen; ˌ~·**pro'duct·ive** *adj.* 'kontraproduktˌtiv, das Gegenteil bewirkend; '~·**ref·orˌma·tion** *s.* 'Gegenreformatiˌon *f*; '~·**rev·oˌlu·tion** *s.* 'Gegenrevolutiˌon *f*; '~·**shaft** *s.* ⚙ Vorlegewelle *f*: ~ ***gear*** Vorgelege *n*; '~·**sign** **I** *s.* **1.** ✕ Losungswort *n*; **2.** Gegenzeichen *n*; **II** *v/t.* **3.** gegenzeichnen; **4.** *fig.* bestätigen; ˌ~'**sig·na·ture** *s.* Gegenzeichnung *f*; '~·**sink** **I** *s.* **1.** Versenkbohrer *m*; **2.** Senkschraube *f*; **II** *v/t.* [*irr.* → ***sink***] ⚙ **3.** *Loch* ausfräsen; **4.** *Schraubenkopf* versenken; ˌ~'**ten·or** *s.* ♪ hoher Te'nor (*Stimme u. Sänger*); ~·**vail** ['kaʊntəveɪl] **I** *v/t.* aufwiegen, ausgleichen; **II** *v/i.* stark genug sein, ausreichen (***against*** gegen): ~***ing duty*** Ausgleichszoll *m*; '~·**weight** *s.* Gegengewicht *n* (*a. fig.* ***to*** gegen); '~·**word** *s.* Aller'weltswort *n*.

count·ess ['kaʊntɪs] *s.* **1.** Gräfin *f*; **2.** Kom'tesse *f*.

count·ing| glass ['kaʊntɪŋ] *s.* ⚙ Zählglas *n*, -lupe *f*; '~·**house** *s. bsd. Brit.* ✝ Bü'ro *n*; *engS.* Buchhaltung *f*; ~ **tube** *s.* Zählrohr *n*.

count·less ['kaʊntlɪs] *adj.* zahllos, unzählig.

'**count-out** *s. parl. Brit.* Vertagung *f* wegen Beschlußunfähigkeit.

coun·tri·fied ['kʌntrɪfaɪd] *adj.* **1.** ländlich, bäuerlich; **2.** *contp.* bäurisch, verbauert.

coun·try ['kʌntrɪ] **I** *s.* **1.** Land *n*, Staat *m*: ***in this*** ~ hierzulande; ~ ***of destination*** Bestimmungsland; ~ ***of origin*** Ursprungsland; ~ ***of adoption*** Wahlheimat *f*; **2.** Nati'on *f*, Volk *n*: ***appeal*** (*od.* ***go***) ***to the*** ~ *pol.* an das Volk appellieren, Neuwahlen ausschreiben; **3.** Vaterland *n*, Heimat(land *n*) *f*: ***the old*** ~ die alte Heimat; **4.** Gelände *n*, Landschaft *f*; Gebiet *n* (*a. fig.*): ***flat*** ~ Flachland *n*; ***wooded*** ~ waldige Gegend; ***unknown*** ~ unbekanntes Gebiet (*a. fig.*); ***new*** ~ *fig.* Neuland *n* (***to me*** für mich); ***go up*** ~ ins Innere reisen; **5.** Land *n* (*Ggs. Stadt*), Pro'vinz *f*: ***in the*** ~ auf dem Lande; ***go*** (***down***) ***into the*** ~ aufs Land *od.* in die Provinz gehen; **6.** *a.* ~-***and-western*** → ***country music***; **II** *adj.* **7.** Land…; Provinz…; ländlich: ~ ***life*** Landleben *n*; ~ **beam** *s. mot. Am.* Fernlicht *n*; '~-**bred** *adj.* auf dem Lande aufgewachsen; ~ **bump·kin** *s.* Bauerntölpel *m*; ~ **club** *s. Am.* Klub *m* auf dem Land (*für Städter*); ~ **cous·in** *s.* **1.** Vetter *m od.* Base *f* vom Lande; **2.** ‚Unschuld *f* vom Lande'; ~ **dance** *s.* englischer Volkstanz; '~·**folk** *s.* Landbevölkerung *f*; ~ **gen·tle·man** *s.* [*irr.*] **1.** Landedelmann *m*; **2.** Gutsbesitzer *m*; ~ **house** *s.* Landhaus *n*, Landsitz *m*; '~·**man** [-mən] *s.* [*irr.*] **1.** *a.* ***fellow*** ~ Landsmann *m*; **2.** Landmann *m*, Bauer *m*; ~ **mu·sic** *s.* Country-Music *f*; '~·**side** *s.* **1.** ländliche Gegend; Land(-schaft *f*) *n*; **2.** (Land)Bevölkerung *f*; '~-**wide** *adj.* landesweit, im ganzen Land; '~ˌ**wom·an** *s.* [*irr.*] **1.** *a.* ***fellow*** ~ Landsmännin *f*; **2.** a) Landbewohnerin *f*, b) Bäuerin *f*.

coun·ty ['kaʊntɪ] *s.* **1.** *Brit.* a) Grafschaft *f* (*Verwaltungsbezirk*); → ***county palatine***, b) ***the*** ~ die Bewohner *pl. od.* die Aristokra'tie e-r Grafschaft; **2.** *Am.* (Land)Kreis *m*, (Verwaltungs)Bezirk *m*; ~ **bor·ough** *s.*, ~ **cor·po·rate** *s. Brit.* Stadt *f*, die e-e eigene Grafschaft bildet; ~ **coun·cil** *s. Brit.* Grafschaftsrat *m* (*Behörde*); ~ **court** *s.* ⚖ **1.** *Brit.* Grafschaftsgericht *n* (*erstinstanzliches Zivilgericht*); **2.** *Am.* Kreisgericht *n*; ~ **fam·i·ly** *s. Brit.* vornehme Fa'milie mit Ahnensitz in e-r Grafschaft; ~ **hall** *s. Brit.* Rathaus *n* e-r Grafschaft; ~ **pal·a·tine** *s. Brit. hist.* Pfalzgrafschaft *f*; ~ **seat** *s.*, ~ **town** *s. Am.* Kreishauptstadt *f*.

coup [kuː] *s.* Coup *m*: a) Bra'vourstück *n*, Handstreich *m*, b) Staatsstreich *m*, Putsch *m*; ~ **de grâce** [ˌkuːdə'grɑːs] (*Fr.*) *s.* Gnadenstoß *m* (*a. fig.*); ~ **de main** [ˌkuːdə'mɛ̃ːŋ] (*Fr.*) *s. bsd.* ✕ Handstreich *m*; ~ **d'é·tat** [ˌkuːdeɪ'tɑː] (*Fr.*) → ***coup*** b.

cou·pé ['kuːpeɪ] *s.* **1.** Cou'pé *n*: a) *mst zweisitzige Limousine*, b) *geschlossene Kutsche für zwei Personen*; **2.** 🚂 *Brit.* Halbabteil *n*.

cou·ple ['kʌpl] **I** *s.* **1.** Paar *n*: ***in*** ~***s*** paarweise; ***a*** ~ ***of*** ein paar *Tage etc.*; **2.** (Braut-, Ehe-, Liebes)Paar *n*, Pärchen *n*; **3.** Koppel *f* (*Jagdhunde*): ***go*** (*od.* ***hunt***) ***in*** ~***s*** *fig.* stets gemeinsam handeln; **II** *v/t.* **4.** (zs.-, ver)koppeln, verbinden: ~***d with*** *fig.* gepaart (*od.* verbunden, gekoppelt) mit; **5.** ehelich verbinden; paaren; **6.** *in Gedanken* verbinden, zs.-bringen; **7.** ⚙ (an-, ein-, ver-)kuppeln; **8.** ⚡, ♪ koppeln; **III** *v/i.* **9.** heiraten; sich paaren; **cou·pler** ['kʌplə] *s.* **1.** ♪ Kopplung *f* (*Orgel*); **2.** *Radio*: Koppler *m*; **3.** ⚙ Kupplung *f*; **4.** a) Koppel(glied *n*) *f*, b) (Leitungs)Muffe *f*: ~ ***plug*** Gerätestecker *m*.

cou·ple skat·ing *s.* Paarlauf(en *n*) *m*.

cou·plet ['kʌplɪt] *s.* Reimpaar *n*.

cou·pling ['kʌplɪŋ] *s.* **1.** Verbindung *f*; **2.** Paarung *f*; **3.** ⚙ (*feste*) Kupplung; **4.** ⚡, *Radio*: Kopplung *f*; ~ **box** *s.* ⚙ Kupplungsmuffe *f*; ~ **chain** *s.* ⚙ Kupplungskette *f*; *pl.* 🚂 Kettenkupplung *f*; ~ **coil** *s.* ⚡, *Radio*: Kopplungsspule *f*.

cou·pon ['kuːpɒn] *s.* **1.** ✝ Cou'pon *m*, Ku'pon *m*, Zinsschein *m*: ***dividend*** ~ Dividendenschein; ~ ***bond*** *Am.* Inhaberschuldverschreibung *f* mit Zinsschein; ~ ***sheet*** Couponbogen *m*; **2.** a) Kassenzettel *m*, Gutschein *m*, Bon *m*, b) Berechtigungs-, Bezugsschein *m*; **3.** Abschnitt *m der Lebensmittelkarte etc.*, Marke *f*; **4.** Kon'trollabschnitt *m*; **5.** *Brit.* Tippzettel *m* (*Fußballtoto*).

cour·age ['kʌrɪdʒ] *s.* Mut *m*, Tapferkeit *f*: ***have the*** ~ ***of one's convictions*** stets s-r Überzeugung gemäß handeln, Zivilcourage haben; ***pluck up*** (*od.* ***take***) ~ Mut fassen; ***screw up*** (*od.* ***summon up***) ***one's*** ~, ***take one's*** ~ ***in both hands*** sein Herz in beide Hände nehmen; **cou·ra·geous** [kə'reɪdʒəs] *adj.* □ mutig, beherzt, tapfer.

cour·gette [ˌkʊə'ʒet] *s.* Zuc'chini *f*.

cour·i·er ['kʊrɪə] *s.* **1.** Eilbote *m*, (*a. diplomatischer etc.*) Ku'rier *m*; **2.** Reiseleiter(in); **3.** *Am.* Verbindungsmann *m* (*Agent*).

course [kɔːs] **I** *s.* **1.** Lauf *m*, Bahn *f*, Weg *m*, Gang *m*; Ab-, Verlauf *m*, Fortgang *m*: ***the*** ~ ***of life*** der Lauf des Lebens; ~ ***of events*** Gang der Ereignisse, Lauf der Dinge; ***the*** ~ ***of a disease*** der Verlauf e-r Krankheit; ***the*** ~ ***of nature*** der natürliche (Ver)Lauf; ***a matter of*** ~ e-e Selbstverständlichkeit; ***of*** ~ natürlich, gewiß, bekanntlich; ***in the*** ~ ***of*** im (Ver)Lauf (*gen.*), während (*gen.*); ***in*** ~ ***of construction*** im Bau (befindlich); ***in*** ~ ***of time*** im Laufe der Zeit; ***in due*** ~ zur gegebenen *od.* rechten Zeit; ***in the ordinary*** ~ ***of things*** normalerweise; ***let things take*** (*od.* ***run***) ***their*** ~ den Dingen ihren Lauf lassen; ***the disease took its*** ~ die Krankheit nahm ihren (natürlichen) Verlauf; **2.** (feste) Bahn, Strecke *f*, *sport* (Renn)Bahn *f*, (-)Strecke *f*, Piste *f*: ***golf*** ~ Golfbahn *f od.* -platz *m*; ***clear the*** ~ die Bahn frei machen; **3.** Fahrt *f*, Weg *m*; Richtung *f*; ⚓, ✈ Kurs *m* (*a. fig.*): ***on*** (***off***) ~ (nicht) auf Kurs; ***stand upon the*** ~ Kurs halten; ***steer a*** ~ e-n Kurs steuern (*a. fig.*); ***change one's*** ~ s-n Kurs ändern (*a. fig.*); ***keep to one's*** ~ *fig.* beharrlich s-n Weg verfolgen; ***take a new*** ~ e-n neuen Weg einschlagen; ~ ***computer*** Kursrechner *m*; ~ ***recorder*** Kursschreiber *m*; **4.** Lebensbahn *f*, -weise *f*: ***evil*** ~***s*** üble Gewohnheiten; **5.** Handlungsweise *f*, Verfahren *n*: ***a dangerous*** ~ ein gefährlicher Weg; → ***action*** 1; **6.** Gang *m*, Gericht *n* (*Speisen*); **7.** Reihe *f*, (Reihen)Folge *f*; 'Zyklus *m*: ~ ***of lectures*** Vortragsreihe; ~ ***of treatment*** ⚕ längere Behandlung, Kur *f*; **8.** *a.* ~ ***of instruction*** Kurs(us) *m*, Lehrgang *m*: ***a German*** ~ ein Deutschkursus, ein deutsches Lehrbuch; **9.** ⚠ Schicht *f*, Lage *f* (*Ziegel etc.*); **10.** ⚓ unteres großes Segel: ***main*** ~ Großsegel; **11.** (***monthly***) ~***s*** ⚘ Regel *f*, Periode *f*; **II** *v/t.* **12.** *bsd. Hasen* mit Hunden hetzen *od.* jagen; **III** *v/i.* **13.** rennen, eilen, jagen; **14.** an e-r Hetzjagd teilnehmen.

cours·er ['kɔːsə] *s. poet.* Renner *m*, schnelles Pferd; '**cours·ing** [-sɪŋ] *s.* (*bsd.* Hasen)Hetzjagd *f* mit Hunden.

court [kɔːt] **I** *s.* **1.** (Vor-, 'Hinter-, Innen)Hof *m*; **2.** 'Hintergäßchen *n*; Sackgasse *f*; kleiner Platz; **3.** *bsd. Brit.* stattliches Wohngebäude; **4.** (abgesteckter) Spielplatz: ***tennis*** ~ Tennisplatz; ***grass*** ~ Rasentennisplatz; **5.** Hof *m*, Resi'denz *f* (*Fürst etc.*): ***the*** ♀ ***of St. James*** der britische Königshof; ***be presented at*** ~ bei Hofe vorgestellt werden; **6.** a) fürstlicher Hof *od.* Haushalt, b) fürstliche Fa'milie, c) Hofstaat *m*; **7.** (Empfang *m* bei) Hof *m*: ***hold*** ~ Hof halten (*a. fig.*); **8.** fürstliche Regierung; **9.** ⚖ a) *a.* ~ ***of justice, law*** ~ Gericht(shof *m*) *n*, b) Gerichtshof *m*, *der od. die* Richter, c) Gerichtssitzung *f*, d) Gerichtssaal *m*: ***in*** ~ vor Gericht; ***out of*** ~ a) außergerichtlich, gütlich, b) nicht zur Sache gehörig, c) indiskutabel; ***bring into*** ~, ***take to*** ~ vor Gericht bringen; ***go to*** ~ klagen; ***laugh out of*** ~ *fig.* verlachen; → ***appeal*** 8, ***arbitration*** *etc.*; **10.** *fig.* Hof *m*, Cour *f*, Aufwartung *f*: ***pay*** (***one's***) ~ ***to*** a) *e-r Dame* den Hof machen, b) *j-m* s-e Aufwartung machen; **11.** Rat *m*, Versammlung *f*: ~ ***of directors*** Direktion *f*, Vorstand *m*; **II** *v/t.* **12.** den Hof machen, huldigen (*dat.*); **13.** um'werben (*a. fig.*), werben *od.* freien um; ‚poussieren' mit: ~***ing couple*** Liebespaar *n*; **14.** *fig.* werben *od.* buhlen *od.* sich bemühen um *et.*; suchen: ~ ***disaster*** das Schicksal herausfordern, mit dem Feuer spielen.

court| card *s. Kartenspiel*: Bildkarte *f*; ♀ **Cir·cu·lar** *s.* (*tägliche*) Hofnachrichten *pl.*; ~ **dress** *s.* Hoftracht *f*.

cour·te·ous ['kɜːtjəs] *adj.* □ höflich, liebenswürdig.

cour·te·san [ˌkɔːtɪ'zæn] *s.* Kurti'sane *f*.

cour·te·sy ['kɜːtɪsɪ] *s.* Höflichkeit *f*, Verbindlichkeit *f*, Liebenswürdigkeit *f* (*alle a. als Handlung*); Gefälligkeit *f*: ***by*** ~ aus Höflichkeit *od.* Gefälligkeit; ***by*** ~ ***of*** a) mit freundlicher Genehmigung von (*od. gen.*), b) durch, mittels; ~ ***light*** *mot.* Innenlampe *f*; ~ ***title*** Höflichkeits- *od.* Ehrentitel *m*; ~ ***call***, ~ ***visit*** Höflichkeits- *od.* Anstandsbesuch *m*.

cour·te·zan → ***courtesan***.

court| guide *s.* 'Hof-, 'Adelskaˌlender *m* (*Verzeichnis der hoffähigen Personen*); ~ **hand** *s.* gotische Kanz'leischrift; '~**·house** *s.* **1.** Gerichtsgebäude *n*; **2.** *Am.* Kreis(haupt)stadt *f*.

cour·ti·er ['kɔːtjə] *s.* Höfling *m*.

court·ly ['kɔːtlɪ] *adj.* **1.** vornehm, gepflegt, höflich; **2.** höfisch.

court| mar·tial *pl.* **courts mar·tial** *s.* Kriegsgericht *n*; ˌ~-'**mar·tial** *v/t.* vor ein Kriegsgericht stellen; ~ **mourn·ing** *s.* Hoftrauer *f*; ~ **or·der** *s.* ⚖ Gerichtsbeschluß *m*; ~ **plas·ter** *s. hist.* Heftpflaster *n*; ~ **room** *s.* Gerichtssaal *m*.

court·ship ['kɔːtʃɪp] *s.* **1.** Hofmachen *n*, Werben *n*, Freien *n*; **2.** *fig.* Werben *n* (***of*** um).

court| shoes *s. pl.* Pumps *pl.*; '~**·yard** *s.* Hof(raum) *m*.

cous·in ['kʌzn] *s.* **1.** a) Vetter *m*, Cou'sin *m*, b) Base *f*, Ku'sine *f*: ***first*** ~, ~ ***german*** leiblicher Vetter *od.* leibliche Base; ***second*** ~ Vetter *od.* Base zweiten Grades; **2.** *weitS.* Verwandte(r *m*) *f*.

cou·tu·rier [kuː'tjʊrɪeɪ] (*Fr.*) *s.* (Haute) Couturi'er *m*, Modeschöpfer *m*; **cou·tu'rière** [-ɪeə] (*Fr.*) *s.* Modeschöpferin *f*.

cove[1] [kəʊv] **I** *s.* **1.** kleine Bucht; **2.** *fig.* Schlupfwinkel *m*; **3.** ⚠ Wölbung *f*; **II** *v/t.* **4.** ⚠ (über)'wölben.

cove[2] [kəʊv] *s. sl.* Bursche *m*, Kerl *m*.

cov·en ['kʌvn] *s.* Hexensabbat *m*.

cov·e·nant ['kʌvənənt] **I** *s.* **1.** Vertrag *m*; feierliches Abkommen; **2.** ⚖ a) Vertrag *m*, b) Ver'tragsˌklausel *f*, c) bindendes Versprechen, Zusicherung *f*, d) Satzung *f*; **3.** *bibl.* a) Bund *m*; → ***ark*** 2, b) Verheißung *f*: ***the land of the*** ~ das Gelobte Land; **II** *v/i.* **4.** e-n Vertrag schließen, über'einkommen (***with*** mit, ***for*** über *acc.*); **5.** sich feierlich verpflichten, geloben; **III** *v/t.* **6.** vertraglich zusichern; '**cov·e·nant·ed** [-tɪd] *adj.* **1.** vertragsmäßig; **2.** vertraglich gebunden.

cov·en·trize ['kɒvəntraɪz] *v/t.* to'tal zerbomben, dem Erdboden gleichmachen; **Cov·en·try** ['kɒvəntrɪ] *npr. englische Stadt*: ***send s.o. to*** ~ *fig.* j-n gesellschaftlich ächten.

cov·er ['kʌvə] **I** *s.* **1.** Decke *f*; Deckel *m*; **2.** a) (Buch)Decke *f*, Einband *m*, b) 'Umschlag- *od.* Titelseite *f*: ~ ***design*** Titelbild *n*; ~ ***girl*** Covergirl *n*, Titelblattmädchen *n*; ***from*** ~ ***to*** ~ von Anfang bis Ende; **3.** a) 'Briefˌumschlag *m*, b) *Philatelie*: Ganzsache *f*: ***under*** (***the***) ***same*** ~ beiliegend; ***under separate*** ~ mit getrennter Post; ***under*** ~ ***of*** unter der (Deck)Adresse von; **4.** 'Schutzˌumschlag *m*, Hülle *f*, Futte'ral *n*; 'Überzug *m*, (Bett-, Möbel- *etc.*)Bezug *m*; ⚙ Schutzhaube *f*, -platte *f*, -mantel *m*; *mot.* (Reifen)Decke *f*, Mantel *m*; **5.** Gedeck *n* (*bei Tisch*): ~ ***charge*** (Kosten *pl.* für das) Gedeck; **6.** ⚔ a) Deckung *f*: ***take*** ~ Deckung nehmen, b) Feuerschutz *m*, c) (Luft)Sicherung *f*, Abschirmung *f*: ***air*** ~; **7.** *hunt.* Dickicht *n*, Lager *n*: ***break*** ~ ins Freie treten; **8.** Ob-, Schutzdach *n*: ***get under*** ~ sich unterstellen; **9.** *fig.* Schutz *m*: ***under*** ~ ***of night*** im Schutz der Nacht; **10.** *fig.* Deckmantel *m*, Tarnung *f*, Vorwand *m*: ***under*** ~ ***of friendship***; ~ ***address*** Deckadresse *f*; ~ ***name*** Deckname *m*; ***blow one's*** ~ ‚auffliegen'; **11.** ✝ Dekkung *f*, Sicherheit *f*; (Schadens-) Deckung *f*, Versicherungsschutz *m*; **II** *v/t.* **12.** be-, zudecken: ***remain*** ~***ed*** den Hut aufbehalten; ~ ***o.s. with glory*** *fig.* sich mit Ruhm bedecken; ~***ed with*** voll von, über u. über bedeckt mit; **13.** einhüllen, -wickeln (***with*** in *acc.*); **14.** be-, über'ziehen: ~***ed button*** bezogener Knopf; ~***ed wire*** umsponnener Draht; **15.** *fig.* decken, schützen, sichern (***from*** vor *dat.*, gegen): ~ ***o.s.*** sich absichern (***against*** gegen); **16.** ✝ decken: a) *Kosten* bestreiten, b) *Schulden, Verlust* abdecken, c) versichern; **17.** dekken, genügen für; **18.** enthalten, einschließen, um'fassen, be'inhalten; *a. statistisch, durch Werbung etc.* erfassen; *Thema* (erschöpfend) behandeln; → ***ground*** 2; **19.** *Presse, TV etc.*: berichten über (*acc.*); **20.** *Gebiet* bearbeiten, bereisen; **21.** sich über *e-e Fläche od. Zeitspanne* erstrecken; **22.** *e-e Strecke* zu'rücklegen; **23.** a) be-, verdecken, verhüllen, verbergen, b) *fig.* → ***cover up*** 2; **24.** ⚔ decken, schützen, sichern (***from*** vor *dat.* gegen); **25.** ⚔ a) *ein Gebiet* beherrschen, im Schußfeld haben, b) *Gelände* bestreichen, mit Feuer belegen; **26.** *mit e-r Waffe* zielen auf (*acc.*), *j-n* in Schach halten; **27.** *sport den Gegner* decken; **28.** *j-n* ‚beschatten'; **29.** *Hündin etc.* decken, *Stute a.* beschälen; ~ **in** *v/t.* **1.** decken, bedachen; **2.** füllen; ~ **o·ver** *v/t.* **1.** über'decken; **2.** ✝ *Emission* über'zeichnen; ~ **up I** *v/t.* **1.** zu-, verdecken; **2.** *fig.* vertuschen, verheimlichen, verbergen; **II** *v/i.* **3.** ~ ***for s.o.*** j-n decken; **4.** *Boxen*: sich decken.

cov·er·age ['kʌvərɪdʒ] *s.* **1.** Erfassung *f*, Einschluß *m*; erfaßtes Gebiet, erfaßte Menge; *Werbung*: erfaßter Per'sonenkreis; **2.** 'Umfang *m*; Reichweite *f*; Geltungsbereich *m*; **3.** ✝ a) → ***cover*** 11, b) Ver'sicherungsˌumfang *m*; **4.** *Zeitung etc.*: Berichterstattung *f* (***of*** über *acc.*); **5.** ⚔ → ***cover*** 6 c; '**cov·ered** [-əd] *adj.* be-, gedeckt: ~ ***court*** *Tennis*: Hallenplatz *m*; ~ ***market*** Markthalle *f*; ~ ***wag***(***g***)***on*** a) Planwagen *m*, b) geschlossener Güterwagen; → ***cover*** 14; '**cov·er·ing** [-ərɪŋ] **I** *s.* **1.** Bedeckung *f*; Be-, Ver-, Um'kleidung *f*; (*Fußboden-*) Belag *m*; → *a.* ***cover*** 4; **2.** *fig.* Schutz *m*, Deckung *f*; **3.** ⚔ → ***cover*** 6; **II** *adj.* **4.** deckend, Deck(ungs)...; ~ ***letter*** Begleitbrief *m*; ~ ***note*** → ***cover note***; **cov·er·let** ['kʌvəlɪt], *a.* '**cov·er·lid** [-lɪd] *s.* Tagesdecke *f*.

cov·er| note *s.* ✝ Deckungsbrief *m* (*Versicherung*); ~ **shot** *s. Film*: To'tale *f*; ~ **sto·ry** *s.* Titelgeschichte *f*.

cov·ert I *adj.* □ ['kʌvət] **1.** heimlich, versteckt, verborgen; verschleiert; **2.** → ***feme covert***; **II** *s.* ['kʌvə] **3.** Obdach *n*; Schutz *m*; **4.** Versteck *n*; **5.** *hunt.* Dickicht *n*; Lager *n*; ~ **coat** ['kʌvət] *s.* Covercoat *m* (*Sportmantel*).

cov·er·ture ['kʌvəˌtjʊə] *s.* ⚖ Ehestand *m der Frau*.

'**cov·er-up** *s. Am.* Tarnung *f*, Vertuschung *f* (***for*** *gen.*).

cov·et ['kʌvɪt] *v/t.* begehren, trachten nach; '**cov·et·a·ble** [-təbl] *adj.* begehrenswert; '**cov·et·ous** [-təs] *adj.* □ **1.** begehrlich, lüstern (***of*** nach); **2.** habsüchtig; '**cov·et·ous·ness** [-təsnɪs] *s.* **1.** Begehrlichkeit *f*; **2.** Habsucht *f*.

cov·ey ['kʌvɪ] *s.* **1.** *orn.* Brut *f*, Hecke *f*; **2.** *hunt.* Volk *n*, Kette *f*; **3.** Schar *f*, Schwarm *m*, Trupp *m*.

cov·ing ['kəʊvɪŋ] *s.* ⚠ **1.** Wölbung *f*; **2.** 'überhängendes Obergeschoß; **3.** schräge Seitenwände *pl.* (*Kamin*).

cow[1] [kaʊ] *s. zo.* **1.** Kuh *f*; **2.** Weibchen *n* (*bsd. Elefant, Wal etc.*).

cow[2] [kaʊ] *v/t.* einschüchtern: ~ ***s.o. into*** j-n zwingen zu.

cow·ard ['kaʊəd] **I** *s.* Feigling *m*; **II** *adj.* feig(e); '**cow·ard·ice** [-dɪs] *s.* Feigheit *f*; '**cow·ard·li·ness** [-lɪnɪs] *s.* **1.** Feigheit *f*; **2.** Gemeinheit *f*; '**cow·ard·ly**

[-lı] **I** *adj.* **1.** feig(e); **2.** gemein, ˈhinterhältig; **II** *adv.* **3.** feig(e).

ˈcow|·ber·ry [-bərı] *s.* ⚘ Preiselbeere *f*; **ˈ~·boy** *s.* **1.** *Am.* Cowboy *m*; **2.** Kuhjunge *m*; **ˈ~ˌcatch·er** *s.* 🚂 *Am.* Schienenräumer *m*.

cow·er [ˈkaʊə] *v/i.* **1.** kauern, hocken; **2.** sich ducken (*aus Angst etc.*).

cow| hand → ***cowboy*** 1; **ˈ~·herd** *s.* Kuhhirt *m*; **ˈ~·hide** *s.* **1.** Rindsleder *n*; **2.** Ochsenziemer *m*; **ˈ~·house** *s.* Kuhstall *m*.

cowl [kaʊl] *s.* **1.** Mönchskutte *f* (*mit Kapuze*); **2.** Kaˈpuze *f*; **3.** ⚙ Schornsteinkappe *f*; **4.** ⚙ a) *mot.* Haube *f*, b) Verkleidung *f*, c) → **ˈcowl·ing** [-lıŋ] *s.* ✈ ˈMotorhaube *f*.

ˈcow·man [-mən] *s.* [*irr.*] **1.** *Am.* Rinderzüchter *m*; **2.** Kuhknecht *m*.

ˈco-ˌwork·er *s.* Mitarbeiter(in).

cow| pars·nip *s.* ⚘ Bärenklau *f*, *m*; **ˈ~·pat** *s.* Kuhfladen *m*; **ˈ~·pox** *s.* ⚕ Kuhpocken *pl.*; **ˈ~ˌpunch·er** *s.* *Am.* F Cowboy *m*.

cow·rie, cow·ry [ˈkaʊrı] *s.* **1.** *zo.* ˈKaurischnecke *f*; **2.** ˈKauri(muschel *f*) *m*, *f*, Muschelgeld *n*.

ˈcow|·shed *s.* Kuhstall *m*; **ˈ~·slip** *s.* ⚘ **1.** *Brit.* Schlüsselblume *f*; **2.** *Am.* Sumpfdotterblume *f*.

cox [kɒks] F **I** *s.* → ***coxswain***; **II** *v/t.* *Rennboot* steuern: ***~ed four*** Vierer *m* mit (Steuermann).

cox·comb [ˈkɒkskəʊm] *s.* **1.** Geck *m*, Stutzer *m*; **2.** → ***cockscomb*** 1, 2.

cox·swain [ˈkɒksweın; ⚓ ˈkɒksn] **I** *s.* **1.** *Rudern*: Steuermann *m*; **2.** Bootsführer *m*; **II** *v/t.* **3.** → ***cox*** II.

coy [kɔı] *adj.* □ **1.** schüchtern, bescheiden, scheu; **2.** spröde, zimperlich (*Mädchen*); **ˈcoy·ness** [-nıs] *s.* Schüchternheit *f*; Sprödigkeit *f*.

coy·ote [ˈkɔıəʊt] *s.* *zo.* Koˈjote *m*, Präˈrie-, Steppenwolf *m*.

coz·en [ˈkʌzn] *v/t.* *u.* *v/i.* **1.** betrügen, prellen (***out of*** um); **2.** betören; verleiten (***into doing*** zu tun).

co·zi·ness *etc.* → ***cosiness*** *etc.*

crab¹ [kræb] **I** *s.* **1.** *zo.* a) Krabbe *f*, b) Taschenkrebs *m*: ***catch a ~*** *Rudern*: ‚e-n Krebs fangen', mit dem Ruder im Wasser steckenbleiben; **2.** ♋ *ast.* Krebs *m*; **3.** ⚙ Winde *f*, Hebezeug *n*, Laufkatze *f*; **4.** *pl.* *Würfeln*: niedrigster Wurf; **5.** → ***crab louse***; **II** *v/t.* **6.** ✈ schieben.

crab² [kræb] **I** *s.* **1.** a) Nörgler *m*, b) Nörgeˈlei *f*; **II** *v/t.* **2.** F (herˈum)nörgeln an (*dat.*); **3.** F verderben, -patzen; **III** *v/i.* **4.** nörgeln.

crab ap·ple *s.* ⚘ Holzapfel(baum) *m*.

crab·bed [ˈkræbıd] *adj.* □ **1.** a) mürrisch, b) boshaft, bitter, c) halsstarrig; **2.** verworren; kraus; **3.** kritzelig, unleserlich (*Schrift*); **crab·by** [ˈkræbı] → ***crabbed*** 1, 2.

crab louse *s.* [*irr.*] *zo.* Filzlaus *f*.

crack [kræk] **I** *s.* **1.** Krach *m*, Knall *m* (*Peitsche, Gewehr etc.*): ***the ~ of doom*** die Posaunen des Jüngsten Gerichts; ***~ of dawn*** Morgengrauen *n*; **2.** (heftiger) Schlag: ***in a ~*** im Nu; ***take a ~ at s.th.*** *sl.* es mit et. versuchen; **3.** Riß *m*, Sprung *m*; Spalt(e *f*) *m*, Schlitz *m*; **4.** F ‚Knacks' (*geistiger Defekt*); **5.** *sl.* a) Witz *m*, b) Sticheˈlei *f*; **6.** *sport* ‚Kaˈnone' *f*, ‚As' *n*; **7.** F Crack *n* (*Rauschgift*); **II** *adj.* **8.** F erstklassig, großartig: ***~ shot*** Meisterschütze *m*; ***~ regiment*** Eliteregiment *n*; **III** *int.* **9.** krach!; **IV** *v/i.* **10.** krachen, knallen, knacken, (auf)brechen; **11.** platzen, bersten, (auf-, zer)springen, Risse bekommen, (auf)reißen: ***get ~ing*** F loslegen (*anfangen*); ***~ing pace*** tolles Tempo; **12.** ˈüberschnappen (*Stimme*): ***his voice is ~ing*** er ist im Stimmbruch; **13.** *fig.* zs.-brechen; **V** *v/t.* **14.** knallen mit (*Peitsche*); knacken mit (*Fingern*): ***~ jokes*** Witze reißen; **15.** zerbrechen, (zer-)spalten, ein-, zerschlagen; **16.** *Nuß* (auf)knacken, *Ei* aufschlagen: ***~ a bottle*** e-r Flasche den Hals brechen; ***~ a code*** e-n Kode ‚knacken'; ***~ a crib*** *sl.* in ein Haus einbrechen; ***~ a safe*** e-n Geldschrank knacken; **17.** a) e-n Sprung machen in (*acc.*), b) sich *e-e Rippe etc.* anbrechen; **18.** *fig.* erschüttern, zerrütten, zerstören; **19.** ⚙ *Erdöl* kracken, spalten; ***~ down*** *v/i.* F (***on***) a) scharf vorgehen (gegen), ˈdurchgreifen (bei), b) ˈRazzia abhalten (bei); ***~ up*** **I** *v/i.* **1.** *fig.* (*körperlich od. seelisch*) zs.-brechen; **2.** ✈ abstürzen; **3.** sein Auto zu Schrott fahren; **4.** *Am.* F sich ‚kaˈputtlachen'; **II** *v/t.* **5.** *Fahrzeug* zu Schrott fahren; **6.** F ‚hochjubeln', (an-)preisen.

ˈcrack|-brained *adj.* verrückt; **ˈ~·down** *s.* F (***on***) scharfes Vorgehen (gegen), ˈDurchgreifen *n* (bei).

cracked [krækt] *adj.* **1.** zer-, gesprungen, geborsten, rissig: ***the cup is ~*** die Tasse hat e-n Sprung; **2.** F ‚angeknackst' (*Ruf etc.*); **3.** F verrückt.

crack·er [ˈkrækə] *s.* **1.** Cracker *m*, Kräcker *m*: a) (Knusper)Keks *m*, b) Schwärmer *m*, Frosch *m* (*Feuerwerk*), *a.* ˈKnallbonˌbon *m*, *n*; **2.** Nußknacker *m*; **ˈ~·jack** *Am.* F **I** *adj.* ˈprima, toll; **II** *s.* a) tolle Sache, b) toller Kerl; **ˈcrack·ers** *adj.* *Brit.* *sl.* verrückt, ˈübergeschnappt: ***go ~*** überschnappen.

ˈcrack·jaw F **I** *adj.* zungenbrecherisch; **II** *s.* Zungenbrecher *m*.

crack·le [ˈkrækl] **I** *v/i.* **1.** knistern, prasseln, knattern; **II** *v/t.* **2.** ⚙ *Glas od. Glasur* krakelieren; **III** *s.* **3.** Knistern *n*, Knattern *n*; **4.** ⚙ Krakelierung *f*, Krakeˈlee *f*, *n*: ***~ finish*** Eisblumenlackierung *f*; **5.** ⚙ Haarrißbildung *f*; **ˈcrackling** [-lıŋ] *s.* **1.** → ***crackle*** 3; **2.** a) knusprige Kruste des Schweinebratens, b) *mst pl.* *Am.* Schweinegrieben *pl.*

crack·nel [ˈkræknl] *s.* **1.** Knusperkeks *m*; **2.** → ***crackling*** 2 a.

ˈcrack·pot *sl.* **I** *s.* ‚Spinner' *m*, Verrückte(r *m*) *f*, **II** *adj.* verrückt.

cracks·man [ˈkræksmən] *s.* [*irr.*] *sl.* **1.** Einbrecher *m*; **2.** ‚Schränker' *m*, Geldschrankknacker *m*.

ˈcrack-up *s.* F *pol.*, ✝ (*a. körperlicher od. seelischer*) Zs.-bruch.

crack·y [ˈkrækı] → ***cracked*** 1, 3.

cra·dle [ˈkreıdl] **I** *s.* **1.** Wiege *f* (*a. fig.*): ***the ~ of civilization***; ***from the ~ to the grave*** von der Wiege bis zur Bahre; **2.** *fig.* Wiege *f*, Kindheit *f*, ˈAnfangsˌstadium *n*, Ursprung *m*: ***from the ~*** von Kindheit an; ***in the ~*** in den ersten Anfängen (steckend); **3.** *wiegenartiges Gerät, bsd.* ⚙ a) Hängegerüst *n* (*Bau*), b) Gründungseisen *n* (*Graveur*), c) Räderschlitten *m* (*für Arbeiten unter e-m Auto*), d) Schwingtrog *m* (*Goldwäscher*), e) (Teleˈfon)Gabel *f*, f) ⚔ Rohrwiege *f*; **4.** ⚓ Stapelschlitten *m*; **5.** ⚕ (Draht-)Schiene *f*, Schutzgestell *n*; **II** *v/t.* **6.** in die Wiege legen; **7.** in (den) Schlaf wiegen; **8.** auf-, großziehen; **9.** *den Kopf in den Armen etc.* bergen, betten.

craft [krɑːft] *s.* **1.** (Hand- *od.* Kunst-) Fertigkeit *f*, Kunst *f*, Geschicklichkeit *f*; → ***gentle*** 2; **2.** a) Gewerbe *n*, Handwerk *n*, b) Zunft *f*: ***film~*** Filmgewerbe; ***be one of the ~*** F vom ‚Bau' sein; **3.** ***the*** ♋ die Königliche Kunst (*Freimaurerei*); **4.** List *f*, Verschlagenheit *f*; **5.** ⚓ Fahrzeug *n*, Schiff *n*; *coll.* Fahrzeuge *pl.*, Schiffe *pl.*; **6.** a) ✈ Flugzeug *n*, *coll.* Flugzeuge *pl.*, b) Raumschiff *n*, -fahrzeug *n*; **ˈcraft·i·ness** [-tınıs] *s.* List *f*, Schlauheit *f*.

crafts·man [ˈkrɑːftsmən] *s.* [*irr.*] **1.** gelernter Handwerker; **2.** Kunsthandwerker *m*; **3.** *fig.* Könner *m*; **ˈcrafts·man·ship** [-ʃıp] *s.* Kunstfertigkeit *f*, handwerkliches Können *od.* Geschick.

craft·y [ˈkrɑːftı] *adj.* □ listig, schlau, verschlagen.

crag [kræg] *s.* Felsenspitze *f*, Klippe *f*; **ˈcrag·ged** [-gıd], **ˈcrag·gy** [-gı] *adj.* **1.** felsig, schroff; **2.** *fig.* knorrig (*Person*); **crags·man** [ˈkrægzmən] *s.* [*irr.*] geübter Bergsteiger, Kletterer *m*.

cram [kræm] **I** *v/t.* **1.** *a. fig.* ˈvollstopfen, -packen, -pfropfen, überˈfüllen (***with*** mit); **2.** überˈfüttern, ˈvollstopfen; **3.** *Geflügel* stopfen, mästen; **4.** (hinˈein-) stopfen, (-)zwängen (***into*** in *acc.*); **5.** F a) mit *j-m* ‚pauken', b) *et.* ‚pauken' *od.* ‚büffeln'; **II** *v/i.* **6.** sich (gierig) ˈvollessen, -stopfen; **7.** F ‚pauken', ‚büffeln': ***~ up on*** → 5 b; **III** *s.* **8.** F Gedränge *n*; **9.** F ‚Pauken' *n*: ***~ course*** Paukkurs *m*.

ˌcram-ˈfull *adj.* zum Bersten voll.

cram·mer [ˈkræmə] *s.* F **1.** ‚Einpauker' *m*; **2.** ‚Paukstudio' *n*; **3.** ‚Paukbuch' *n*.

cramp¹ [kræmp] **I** *s.* **1.** ⚙ Krampe *f*, Klammer *f*; Schraubzwinge *f*; **2.** *fig.* Zwang *m*, Fessel *f*; Einengung *f*; **II** *v/t.* **3.** ver-, anklammern, befestigen; **4.** *a.* ***~ up*** *fig.* einengen, einzwängen; hemmen: ***be ~ed for space*** (zu) wenig Platz haben; → ***style*** 1 b.

cramp² [kræmp] **I** *s.* ⚕ Krampf *m*; **II** *v/t.* Krämpfe auslösen in (*dat.*); **cramped** [-pt] *adj.* **1.** verkrampft; **2.** eng, beengt.

ˈcramp|·fish *s.* Zitterrochen *m*; **~ i·ron** *s.* **1.** (Stahl)Klammer *f*, Krampe *f*; **2.** △ Steinanker *m*.

cram·pon [ˈkræmpən], *Am.* *a.* **cram·poon** [kræmˈpuːn] *s.* *oft pl.* **1.** ⚙ Kanthaken *m*; **2.** *mount.* Steigeisen *n*.

cran·ber·ry [ˈkrænbərı] *s.* ⚘ Preisel-, Kranbeere *f*.

crane [kreın] **I** *s.* **1.** *orn.* *u.* ♋ *astr.* Kranich *m*; **2.** ⚙ Kran *m*: ***~ truck*** Kranwagen *m*; **II** *v/t.* **3.** mit e-m Kran heben; **4.** ***~ one's neck*** sich den Hals verrenken (***for*** nach); **~ fly** *s.* *zo.* (Erd)Schnake *f*.

cra·ni·a [ˈkreınjə] *pl.* *von* ***cranium***; **ˈcra·ni·al** [-jəl] *adj.* *anat.* Schädel…; **cra·ni·ol·o·gy** [ˌkreınıˈɒlədʒı] *s.* Schädellehre *f*; **ˈcra·ni·um** [-jəm] *pl.* **-ni·a** [-jə] *Am.* *a.* **-ni·ums** *s.* *anat.* Schädel *m*.

crank [kræŋk] **I** *s.* **1.** ⚙ Kurbel *f*, Schwengel *m*: ***~ case*** Kurbelgehäuse *n*, -kasten *m*; ***~ handle*** Kurbelgriff *m*; ***~ pin*** Kurbelzapfen *m*; ***~ shaft*** Kurbelwelle *f*; **2.** Wortspiel *n*; **3.** Maˈrotte *f*,

Grille *f*, fixe I'dee; **4.** ‚Spinner' *m*, (harmloser) Verrückter: ~ ***letter*** Brief *m* von e-m ‚Spinner'; **II** *v/t.* **5.** ⚙ kröpfen, krümmen; **6.** *oft* ~ ***up*** ankurbeln, *Motor* anlassen; *Maschine* 'durchdrehen; **III** *adj.* **7.** wack(e)lig, schwach; **8.** ⚓ rank; '**crank·i·ness** [-kɪnɪs] *s.* Wunderlichkeit *f*, Verschrobenheit *f*; '**crank·y** [-kɪ] *adj.* □ **1.** wunderlich, verschroben; **2.** → ***crank*** 7, 8.

cran·ny ['krænɪ] *s.* **1.** Ritze *f*, Spalte *f*, Riß *m*; **2.** Schlupfwinkel *m*.

crap¹ [kræp] *s. Am.* Fehlwurf *m beim* ***craps***.

crap² [kræp] V **I** *s.* a) Scheiße *f*: ***have a*** ~ → II, b) *fig.* ‚Mist' *m*, ‚Scheiß' *m*; **II** *v/i.* scheißen.

crape [kreɪp] *s.* **1.** Krepp *m*; **2.** Trauerflor *m*.

crap·py ['kræpɪ] *adj. sl.* ‚mistig', Scheiß...

craps [kræps] *s. pl. sg. konstr. Am. ein* Würfelspiel *n*: ***shoot*** ~ ***craps*** spielen.

crap·u·lence ['kræpjʊləns] *s.* Unmäßigkeit *f*, *bsd.* unmäßiger Alko'holgenuß.

crash¹ [kræʃ] **I** *v/i.* **1.** zs.-krachen, zerbrechen; **2.** (krachend) ab-, einstürzen; **3.** ✈ abstürzen, Bruch machen; *mot.* a) zs.-stoßen, b) verunglücken: ~ ***into*** krachen gegen; **4.** poltern, platzen, rasen, stürzen: ~ ***in*** hereinplatzen; ~ ***in on*** → 9; **5.** *fig. bsd.* ✝ zs.-brechen; **II** *v/t.* **6.** zertrümmern, zerschmettern; **7.** ✈ abstürzen *od.* e-e Bruchlandung machen mit; **8.** *mot.* zu Bruch fahren; **9.** *sl.* uneingeladen kommen zu *e-r Party*; **III** *s.* **10.** Krach(en *n*) *m*; **11.** Zs.-stoß *m*; Unfall *m*; **12.** ✈ Absturz *m*; **13.** ✝ (Börsen)Krach *m*, *allg.* Zs.-bruch; **IV** *adj.* **14.** *fig.* Schnell..., Sofort...

crash² [kræʃ] *s.* grober Leinendrell.

crash| bar·ri·er *s. Brit.* Leitplanke *f*; ~ **course** *s.* Schnell-, Inten'sivkurs *m*; ~ **di·et** *s.* radi'kale Abmagerungskur *f*; '~-**dive** *v/i.* ⚓ schnelltauchen (*U-Boot*); ~ **halt** *s.* 'Vollbremsung *f*; ~ **hel·met** *s.* Sturzhelm *m*; ~ **job** *s.* brandeilige Arbeit, Eilauftrag *m*; '~-**land** *v/i.* ✈ e-e Bruchlandung machen; ~ **land·ing** *s.* ✈ Bruchlandung *f*; ~ **test** *s. mot.* 'Crashtest *m*; ~ **truck** *s.* Rettungswagen *m*.

crass [kræs] *adj.* □ *fig.* kraß, grob; '**crass·ness** [-nɪs] *s.* **1.** Kraßheit *f*; **2.** krasse Dummheit.

crate [kreɪt] **I** *s.* **1.** Lattenkiste *f*, (Bier- *etc.*)Kasten *m*; **2.** großer Packkorb; **3.** *sl.* ‚Kiste' *f* (*Auto od. Flugzeug*); **II** *v/t.* **4.** in e-e Lattenkiste *etc.* verpacken.

cra·ter ['kreɪtə] *s.* **1.** *geol. etc. a.* ⚕ 'Krater *m*; **2.** (Bomben-, Gra'nat)Trichter *m*, -krater *m*.

cra·vat [krə'væt] *s.* Halstuch *n*; Kra'watte *f*.

crave [kreɪv] **I** *v/t.* **1.** flehen *od.* dringend bitten um; **II** *v/i.* **2.** sich (heftig) sehnen (***for*** nach); **3.** flehen, inständig bitten (***for*** um).

cra·ven ['kreɪvən] **I** *adj.* feige, zaghaft; **II** *s.* Feigling *m*, Memme *f*.

crav·ing ['kreɪvɪŋ] *s.* heftiges Verlangen, Sehnsucht *f*, (krankhafte) Begierde (***for*** nach).

craw [krɔː] *s. zo.* Kropf *m* (*Vogel*).

craw·fish ['krɔːfɪʃ] **I** *s. zo.* → ***crayfish***; **II** *v/i. Am.* F sich drücken, ‚kneifen'.

crawl [krɔːl] **I** *v/i.* **1.** kriechen: a) krabbeln, b) sich da'hinschleppen, schleichen (*a. Arbeit, Zeit*), c) im ‚Schneckentempo' gehen *od.* fahren; **2.** *fig.* (unter'würfig) kriechen (***to s.o.*** vor j-m); **3.** wimmeln (***with*** von); **4.** kribbeln, prickeln; **5.** *Schwimmen*: kraulen; **II** *s.* **6.** Kriechen *n*, Schleichen *n*: ***go at a*** ~ → 1 c; **7.** *Schwimmen*: Kraulstil *m*, Kraul(en) *n*; '**crawl·er** [-lə] *s.* **1.** Kriechtier *n*, Gewürm *n*; **2.** *fig.* Kriecher(in); **3.** F a) ‚Schnecke' *f*, b) Taxi *n* auf Fahrgastsuche; **4.** *pl.* Krabbelanzug *m für Kleinkinder*; **5.** *a.* ~ ***tractor*** ⚙ Raupen-, Gleiskettenfahrzeug *n*; **6.** *Schwimmen*: Krauler(in); '**crawl·y** [-lɪ] *adj.* F grus(e)lig.

cray·fish ['kreɪfɪʃ] *s. zo.* **1.** Flußkrebs *m*; **2.** Lan'guste *f*.

cray·on ['kreɪən] **I** *s.* **1.** Zeichen-, Bunt-, Pa'stellstift *m*: ***blue*** ~ Blaustift; **2.** Kreide-, Pa'stellzeichnung *f*; **II** *v/t.* **3.** mit Kreide *etc.* zeichnen; **4.** *fig.* skizzieren.

craze [kreɪz] **I** *v/t.* **1.** verrückt machen; **2.** *Töpferei*: krakelieren; **II** *s.* **3.** a) Ma'nie *f*, fixe I'dee, Verrücktheit *f*, b) ‚Fimmel' *m*: ***be the*** ~ die große Mode sein; ***the latest*** ~ der letzte Schrei; **crazed** [-zd] *adj.* **1.** wahnsinnig (***with*** vor *dat.*); **2.** (wild) begeistert, hingerissen (***about*** von); '**cra·zi·ness** [-zɪnɪs] *s.* Verrücktheit *f*.

cra·zy ['kreɪzɪ] *adj.* □ **1.** verrückt, wahnsinnig: ~ ***with pain***; **2.** F (***about***) begeistert (von); versessen (auf *acc.*); **3.** baufällig, wackelig; ⚓ seeuntüchtig; **4.** zs.-gestückelt; ~ **bone** *Am.* → ***funny bone***; ~ **pav·ing**, ~ **pave·ment** *s.* Mosa'ikpflaster *n*; ~ **quilt** *s.* Flickendecke *f*.

creak [kriːk] **I** *v/i.* knarren, kreischen, quietschen, knirschen: ~ ***along*** *fig.* sich dahinschleppen (*Handlung etc.*); **II** *s.* Knarren *n*, Knirschen *n*, Quietschen *n*; '**creak·y** [-kɪ] *adj.* □ knarrend, knirschend.

cream [kriːm] **I** *s.* **1.** Rahm *m*, Sahne *f*; **2.** Creme(speise) *f*; **3.** (*Haut-, Schuh- etc.*)Creme *f*; **4.** Cremesuppe *f*; **5.** *fig.* Creme *f*, Auslese *f*, E'lite *f*: ***the*** ~ ***of society***; **6.** Kern *m*, Po'inte *f* (*Witz*); **7.** Cremefarbe *f*; **II** *v/i.* **8.** Sahne bilden; **9.** schäumen; **III** *v/t.* **10.** absahnen, den Rahm abschöpfen von (*a. fig.*); **11.** Sahne bilden lassen; **12.** schaumig rühren; **13.** (*dem Tee od. Kaffee*) Sahne zugießen: ***do you*** ~ ***your tea?*** nehmen Sie Sahne?; **14.** *Am. sl. j-n* ‚fertigmachen'; **IV** *adj.* **15.** creme(farben); ~ **cake** *s.* Creme- *od.* Sahnetorte *f*; ~ **cheese** *s.* Rahm-, Vollfettkäse *m*; '~-ˌ**col·o(u)red** *adj.* creme(farben).

cream·er·y ['kriːmərɪ] *s.* **1.** Molke'rei *f*; **2.** Milchhandlung *f*.

cream| ice *s. Brit.* Sahneeis *n*, Speiseeis *n*; ~ **jug** *s.* Sahnekännchen *n*, -gießer *m*; ˌ~-'**laid** *adj.* cremefarben und gerippt (*Papier*); ~ **of tar·tar** *s.* ⚗ Weinstein *m*; ˌ~-'**wove** → ***cream-laid***.

cream·y ['kriːmɪ] *adj.* sahnig; *fig.* weich, samten.

crease [kriːs] **I** *s.* **1.** Falte *f*, Kniff *m*; **2.** Bügelfalte *f*; **3.** Eselsohr *n* (*Buch*); **4.** *Eishockey*: Torraum *m*; **II** *v/t.* **5.** falten, knicken, kniffen, 'umbiegen; **6.** zerknittern; **7.** *hunt. etc.* streifen, anschießen; **III** *v/i.* **8.** Falten bekommen *od.* werfen; knittern; **9.** sich falten lassen; **creased** [-st] *adj.* **1.** in Falten gelegt, gefaltet; **2.** mit Bügelfalte, gebügelt; **3.** zerknittert.

'**crease|-proof**, '~-**reˌsist·ant** *adj.* knitterfrei.

cre·ate [kriː'eɪt] *v/t.* **1.** (er)schaffen; **2.** schaffen, erzeugen: a) her'vorbringen, ins Leben rufen, b) her'vorrufen, verursachen; **3.** *thea., Mode*: kre'ieren, gestalten; **4.** gründen, ein-, errichten; **5.** ⚖ *Recht etc.* begründen; **6.** *j-n* ernennen zu: ~ ***s.o. a peer***; **cre'a·tion** [-'eɪʃn] *s.* **1.** (Er)Schaffung *f*; **2.** Erzeugung *f*, Schaffung *f*: a) Her'vorbringung *f*, b) Verursachung *f*, c) ***the*** ♀ *eccl.* die Schöpfung, die Erschaffung (der Welt): ***the whole*** ~ alle Geschöpfe, die ganze Welt; **3.** Geschöpf *n*, Krea'tur *f*; **4.** (Kunst-, Mode)Schöpfung *f*, Kreati'on *f*; Werk *n*; **5.** *thea.* Kre'ierung *f*, Gestaltung *f*; **6.** Gründung *f*, Errichtung *f*, Bildung *f*; **7.** Ernennung *f* (*zu e-m Rang*); **cre'a·tive** [-tɪv] *adj.* □ **1.** schöpferisch, (er)schaffend, *a.* krea'tiv; **2.** (***of s.th.***) *et.* verursachend; **cre'a·tive·ness** [-tɪvnɪs]; **cre·a·tiv·i·ty** [ˌkriːeɪ'tɪvətɪ] *s.* Kreativi'tät *f*, schöpferische Kraft; **cre'a·tor** [-tə] *s.* Schöpfer *m*, Erschaffer *m*, Erzeuger *m*, Urheber *m*: ***the*** ♀ der Schöpfer, Gott *m*.

crea·ture ['kriːtʃə] *s.* **1.** Geschöpf *n*, (Lebe)Wesen *n*, Krea'tur *f*: ***fellow*** ~ Mitmensch *m*; ***dumb*** ~ stumme Kreatur; ***lovely*** ~ süßes Geschöpf (*Frau*); ***silly*** ~ dummes Ding; ~ ***of habit*** Gewohnheitstier *n*; **2.** *fig. j-s* Krea'tur *f*, Werkzeug *n*; ~ **com·forts** *s. pl. die* leiblichen Genüsse, *das* leibliche Wohl.

crèche [kreɪʃ] (*Fr.*) *s.* **1.** Kinderhort *m*, -krippe *f*; **2.** *Am.* (Weihnachts)Krippe *f*.

cre·dence ['kriːdəns] *s.* **1.** Glaube *m*: ***give*** ~ ***to*** Glauben schenken (*dat.*); **2.** *a.* ~ ***table*** *eccl.* Kre'denz *f*.

cre·den·tials [krɪ'denʃlz] *s. pl.* **1.** Beglaubigungs- *od.* Empfehlungsschreiben *n*; **2.** (Leumunds)Zeugnis *n*; **3.** 'Ausweis(paˌpiere *pl.*) *m*.

cred·i·bil·i·ty [ˌkredɪ'bɪlətɪ] *s.* Glaubwürdigkeit *f*; **cred·i·ble** ['kredəbl] *adj.* □ glaubwürdig; zuverlässig: ***show credibly that*** ⚖ glaubhaft machen, daß.

cred·it ['kredɪt] **I** *s.* **1.** ✝ a) Kre'dit *m*, b) Ziel *n*: (***letter of***) ~ Akkredi'tiv *n*; ***on*** ~ auf Kredit; ***open a*** ~ e-n Kredit *od.* ein Akkreditiv eröffnen; ***30 days'*** ~ 30 Tage Ziel; **2.** ✝ a) Haben *n*, 'Kredit(seite *f*) *n*, b) Guthaben *n*, 'Kreditposten *m*, *pl. a.* Ansprüche: ***enter*** (***od. place***) ***it to my*** ~ schreiben Sie es mir gut; ~ ***advice*** Gutschriftsanzeige *f*; (***tax***) ~ *Am.* (Steuer)Freibetrag *m*; **3.** ✝ Kre'ditwürdigkeit *f*; **4.** Glaube(n) *m*, Ver-, Zutrauen *n*: ***give*** ~ ***to*** → 10; **5.** Glaubwürdigkeit *f*, Zuverlässigkeit *f*; **6.** Ansehen *n*, Achtung *f*, guter Ruf, Ehre *f*: ***be a*** ~ ***to s.o.***, ***reflect*** ~ ***on s.o.***, ***do s.o.*** ~, ***be to s.o.'s*** ~ j-m Ehre machen *od.* einbringen; ***he does me*** ~ mit ihm lege ich Ehre ein; ***to his*** ~ ***it must be said*** a) zu s-r Ehre muß man sagen, b) man muß es ihm hoch anrechnen; ***add to s.o.'s*** ~ j-s Ansehen erhöhen; ***with*** ~ ehrenvoll, mit Lob; **7.** Verdienst *n*, Anerkennung *f*, Lob *n*: ***get*** ~ ***for*** Anerkennung finden für; ***very much to his*** ~ sehr anerkennenswert von ihm; ***give***

s.o. (***the***) ~ ***for s.th.*** a) j-m et. hoch anrechnen, b) j-m et. zutrauen, c) j-m et. verdanken; ***take*** (***the***) ~ ***for*** sich *et.* als Verdienst anrechnen, den Ruhm *od.* alle Lorbeeren für *et.* in Anspruch nehmen; **8.** (***title and***) ~***s*** *pl. Film, TV*: Vor- *od.* Abspann *m*, Erwähnungen *pl.*; **9.** *ped. Am.* a) Anrechnungspunkt *m*, b) Abgangszeugnis *n*; **II** *v/t.* **10.** Glauben schenken (*dat.*), *j-m od. et.* glauben; *j-m* trauen; **11.** ~ ***s.o. with s.th.*** a) j-m et. zutrauen, b) j-m et. zuschreiben; **12.** † *Betrag* gutschreiben, kreditieren (***to s.o.*** j-m); *j-n* erkennen (***with*** für); **13.** *ped. Am.* (***s.o. with***) (j-m) Punkte anrechnen (für); **ˈcred·it·a·ble** [-təbl] *adj.* □ **1.** rühmlich, lobens-, anerkennenswert, ehrenvoll (***to*** für): ***be*** ~ ***to s.o.*** j-m Ehre machen; **2.** glaubwürdig.

cred·it| bal·ance *s.* † ˈKreditˌsaldo *m*, Guthaben *n*; ~ **card** *s.* † Kreˈditkarte *f*; ~ **in·ter·est** *s.* Habenzinsen *pl.*; ~ **note** *s.* † Gutschriftsanzeige *f*.

cred·i·tor [ˈkredɪtə] *s.* † **1.** Gläubiger (-in); **2.** a) *a.* ~ ***side*** Haben *n*, ˈKreditseite *f e-s Kontobuchs*, b) *pl. Bilanz*: Verbindlichkeiten *pl.*

cred·it| rat·ing *s. Am.* Kreˈditfähigkeit *f*; ~ **squeeze** *s.* † Kreˈditzange *f*; ~ **tit·les** *pl.* → ***credit*** 8; ˈ~ˌ**wor·thi·ness** *s.* † Kreˈditwürdigkeit *f*; ˈ~ˌ**wor·thy** *adj.* † kreˈditwürdig.

cre·do [ˈkriːdəʊ] *pl.* **-dos** *s.* **1.** *eccl.* ˈCredo *n*, Glaubensbekenntnis *n*; **2.** → ***creed*** 2.

cre·du·li·ty [krɪˈdjuːlətɪ] *s.* Leichtgläubigkeit *f*; **cred·u·lous** [ˈkredjʊləs] *adj.* □ leichtgläubig.

creed [kriːd] *s.* **1.** a) Glaubensbekenntnis *n*, b) Glaube *m*, Konfessiˈon *f*; **2.** *fig.* (*a. politische etc.*) Überˈzeugung, ˈKredo *n*.

creek [kriːk] *s.* **1.** Flüßchen *n*; kleiner Wasserlauf (*nur von der Flut gespeist*): ***up the*** ~ *fig.* in der Klemme (sitzend); **2.** kleine Bucht.

creel [kriːl] *s.* Fischkorb *m*.

creep [kriːp] **I** *v/i.* [*irr.*] **1.** *a. fig.* kriechen, (daˈhin)schleichen: ~ ***up on*** sich heranschleichen an (*acc.*); ~ ***into s.o.'s favo(u)r*** *fig.* sich bei j-m einschmeicheln; ~ ***in*** sich einschleichen (*Fehler*); ***old age is ~ing upon me*** das Alter naht heran; **2.** ⚘ kriechen, sich ranken; **3.** ⚙ kriechen; ϟ nacheilen; **4.** kribbeln: ***it made my flesh*** ~ dabei überlief es mich kalt, ich bekam eine Gänsehaut dabei; **II** *s.* **5.** → ***crawl*** 6; **6.** → ***creepage***; **7.** Schlupfloch *n*; **8.** *geol.* (Erd-) Rutsch *m*; **9.** *pl.* F Gruseln *n*, Gänsehaut *f*: ***the sight gave me the ~s*** bei dem Anblick überlief es mich kalt; **10.** *sl.* ‚Fiesling' *m*, ‚Scheißtyp' *m*; **ˈcreep·age** [-pɪdʒ] *s.* ⚙, ϟ Kriechen *n*; **ˈcreep·er** [-pə] *s.* **1.** *fig.* Kriecher(in); **2.** Kriechtier *n* (*Insekt, Wurm*); **3.** ⚘ Kriech- *od.* Kletterpflanze *f*; **4.** *orn.* Baumläufer *m*; **5.** *mount.* Steigeisen *n*; **6.** ⚓ Dragganker *m*; **7.** *pl. Am.* (einteiliger) Spielanzug; **8.** F weichsohliger Schuh; **ˈcreep·ing** [-pɪŋ] *adj.* □ **1.** kriechend, schleichend (*a. fig.*); **2.** ⚘ kriechend, kletternd; **3.** a) kribbelnd, b) grus(e)lig; **4.** → ***barrage***[1] 2; **ˈcreep·y** [-pɪ] *adj.* **1.** kriechend: a) krabbelnd, b) schleichend; **2.** grus(e)lig.

cre·mate [krɪˈmeɪt] *v/t. bsd. Leichen* verbrennen, einäschern; **creˈma·tion** [-eɪʃn] *s.* Feuerbestattung *f*, Einäscherung *f*; **cre·ma·to·ri·um** [ˌkreməˈtɔːrɪəm] *pl.* **-ri·ums, -ri·a** [-rɪə], **cre·ma·to·ry** [ˈkremətərɪ] *s.* Kremaˈtorium *n*.

crème [kreɪm] (*Fr.*) *s.* Creme *f*; ~ **de menthe** [ˌkreɪmdəˈmɑːnt] *s.* ˈPfefferminzliˌkör *m*; ~ **de la** ~ [-dlɑː-] *s. fig.* a) *das* Beste vom Besten; *die* Eˈlite (der Gesellschaft), Crème *f* de la Crème.

cre·nate [ˈkriːneɪt], **ˈcre·nat·ed** [-tɪd] *adj.* ⚘, ⚕ gekerbt, gefurcht; **cre·na·tion** [kriːˈneɪʃn] *s.* ⚘, ⚕ Kerbung *f*, Furchung *f*.

cren·el [ˈkrenl] *s.* Schießscharte *f*; **ˈcren·el(l)ate** [-nəleɪt] *v/t.* krenelieren, mit Zinnen *od.* zinnenartigem Ornaˈment versehen; **cren·el(l)a·tion** [ˌkrenəˈleɪʃn] *s.* Krenelierung.

Cre·ole [ˈkriːəʊl] **I** *s.* Kreˈole *m*, Kreˈolin *f*; **II** *adj.* kreˈolisch.

cre·o·sote [ˈkrɪəsəʊt] *s.* ⚗ Kreoˈsot *n*.

crêpe [kreɪp] *s.* **1.** Krepp *m*; **2.** → ~ ***rubber***; ~ **de Chine** [ˌkreɪpdəˈʃiːn] *s.* Crêpe *m* de Chine; ~ **pa·per** *s.* ˈKrepppaˌpier *n*; ~ **rub·ber** *s.* ˈKreppˌgummi *n, m*; ~ **su·zette** [suːˈzet] *s.* Crêpe *f* Suˈzette.

crep·i·tate [ˈkrepɪteɪt] *v/i.* knarren, knirschen, knacken, rasseln; **crep·i·ta·tion** [ˌkrepɪˈteɪʃn] *s.* Knarren *n*, Knirschen *n*, Knacken *n*, Rasseln *n*.

crept [krept] *pret. u. p.p.* von ***creep***.

cre·pus·cu·lar [krɪˈpʌskjʊlə] *adj.* **1.** Dämmerungs..., dämmerig; **2.** *zo.* im Zwielicht erscheinend.

cre·scen·do [krɪˈʃendəʊ] (*Ital.*) ♪ **I** *pl.* **-dos** *s.* Creˈscendo *n* (*a. fig.*); **II** *adv.* creˈscendo, stärker werdend.

cres·cent [ˈkresnt] **I** *s.* **1.** Halbmond *m*, Mondsichel *f*; **2.** *hist. pol.* Halbmond *m* (*Türkei od. Islam*); **3.** halbmondförmiger Gegenstand, Straßenzug *etc.*; **4.** ♪ Schellenbaum *m*; **5.** Hörnchen *n* (*Gebäck*); **II** *adj.* **6.** halbmondförmig; **7.** zunehmend.

cress [kres] *s.* ⚘ Kresse *f*.

crest [krest] **I** *s.* **1.** *zo.* Kamm *m* (*Hahn*); **2.** *zo.* a) (Feder-, Haar)Schopf *m*, Haube *f* (*Vögel*), b) Mähne *f*; **3.** Helmbusch *m*, -schmuck *m*; **4.** Helm *m*; **5.** Bergrücken *m*, Kamm *m*; **6.** Kamm *m* (*Welle*): ***he's riding*** (***along***) ***a*** ~ ***of the wave*** *fig.* er schwimmt momentan ganz oben; **7.** Gipfel *m*, Krone *f*, Scheitelpunkt *m*; **8.** Verzierung *f* über dem (Faˈmilien)Wappen: ***family*** ~ Familienwappen *n*; **9.** ⩓ Bekrönung *f*; **II** *v/t.* **10.** erklimmen; **III** *v/i.* **11.** hoch aufwogen; **ˈcrest·ed** [-tɪd] *adj.* mit e-m Kamm *od.* Schopf *od.* e-r Haube (versehen): ~ ***lark*** Haubenlerche *f*; **ˈcrestˌfall·en** *adj. fig.* geknickt, niedergeschlagen.

cre·ta·ceous [krɪˈteɪʃəs] *adj.* kreideartig, -haltig: ~ ***period*** Kreide(zeit) *f*.

Cre·tan [ˈkriːtn] **I** *adj.* kretisch, aus Kreta; **II** *s.* Kreter(in).

cre·tin [ˈkretɪn] *s.* ⚕ Kreˈtin *m* (*a. contp.*); **ˈcre·tin·ism** [-nɪzəm] *s.* Kretiˈnismus *m*; **ˈcre·tin·ous** [-nəs] *adj.* kreˈtinhaft.

cre·vasse [krɪˈvæs] *s.* **1.** tiefer Spalt *od.* Riß; **2.** Gletscherspalte *f*; **3.** *Am.* Bruch *m* im Deich.

crev·ice [ˈkrevɪs] *s.* Riß *m*, (Fels)Spalte *f*.

crew[1] [kruː] *pret. von* ***crow***[2].

crew[2] [kruː] *s.* **1.** ⚓, ✈ *etc.* Besatzung *f*, (*a. sport* Boots)Mannschaft *f*; **2.** (Arbeits)Gruppe *f*, (ˈArbeiter)Koˌlonne *f*; **3.** ⚙ (Bedienungs)Mannschaft *f*; **4.** (ˈDienst)Persoˌnal *n*; **5.** *Am.* Pfadfindergruppe *f*; **6.** *contp.* Bande *f*; ~ **cut** *s.* Bürste(nschnitt *m*) *f*.

crib [krɪb] **I** *s.* **1.** a) (Futter)Krippe *f*, b) Hürde *f*, Stall *m*; **2.** Kinderbettchen *n*; **3.** a) Hütte *f*, b) kleiner Raum; **4.** Weidenkorb *m* (*Fischfalle*); **5.** F a) kleiner Diebstahl, b) ‚Anleihe' *f*, Plagiˈat *n*; **6.** *ped.* F a) ‚Eselsbrücke' *f*, b) Spickzettel *m*; **7.** *Cribbage*: abgelegte Karten *pl.*; **II** *v/t.* **8.** ein-, zs.-pferchen; **9.** F ‚klauen' (*a. fig. plagiieren*), *ped.* abschreiben; **III** *v/i.* **10.** F abschreiben; **ˈcrib·bage** [-bɪdʒ] *s.* ˈCribbage *n* (*Kartenspiel*).

crick [krɪk] **I** *s.* Muskelkrampf *m*: ~ ***in one's back*** (***neck***) steifer Rücken (Hals); **II** *v/t.* ~ ***one's back*** (***neck***) sich e-n steifen Rücken (Hals) holen.

crick·et[1] [ˈkrɪkɪt] *s. zo.* Grille *f*, Heimchen *n*; → ***merry*** 1.

crick·et[2] [ˈkrɪkɪt] *s. sport* Kricket *n*: ~ ***bat*** Kricketschläger *m*; ~ ***field***, ~ ***ground*** Kricket(spiel)platz *m*; ~ ***pitch*** Feld *n* zwischen den beiden Dreistäben; ***not*** ~ F nicht fair *od.* anständig; **ˈcrick·et·er** [-tə] *s.* Kricketspieler *m*.

cri·er [ˈkraɪə] *s.* **1.** Schreier *m*; **2.** (öffentlicher) Ausrufer.

cri·key [ˈkraɪkɪ] *int. sl.* Mann!

crime [kraɪm] **I** *s.* **1.** ⚖ *u. fig.* a) Verbrechen *n*, b) → ***criminality*** 1: ~ ***novel*** Kriminalroman *m*; ~ ***rate*** Verbrechensquote *f*; ~ ***wave*** Welle *f* von Verbrechen; **2.** Frevel *m*, Übeltat *f*, Sünde *f*; **3.** *coll.* Krimiˈnalroˌmane *f*: ~***-writer*** ‚Krimi-Schreiber(in)'; **4.** F ‚Verbrechen' *n*, ‚Jammer' *m*, ‚Schande' *f*; **II** *v/t.* **5.** ⚔ beschuldigen.

Cri·me·an [kraɪˈmɪən] *adj.* die Krim betreffend: ~ ***War*** Krimkrieg *m*.

crim·i·nal [ˈkrɪmɪnl] **I** *adj.* **1.** verbrecherisch, krimiˈnell, strafbar: ~ ***act***; **2.** ⚖ strafrechtlich, Straf..., ... in Strafsachen: ~ ***jurisdiction***; ~ ***lawyer*** Strafrechtler *m*, Anwalt *m* für Strafsachen; **II** *s.* **3.** Verbrecher(in); ~ **ac·tion** *s.* ˈStrafproˌzeß *m*; ~ **code** *s.* Strafgesetzbuch *n*; ~ **con·ver·sa·tion** *s.* ⚖ *Brit. obs. u. Am.* Ehebruch *m* (*als Schadensersatzgrund*); ♀ **In·ves·ti·ga·tion De·part·ment** *s.* (*abbr.* ***CID***) *Brit.* oberste Krimiˈnalpoliˌzeibehörde *f*.

crim·i·nal·ist [ˈkrɪmɪnəlɪst] *s.* **1.** Krimiˈnaˈlist *m*, Strafrechtler *m*; **2.** Kriminoˈloge *m*; **crim·i·nal·i·ty** [ˌkrɪmɪˈnælətɪ] *s.* **1.** Kriminaliˈtät *f*, Verbrechertum *n*; **2.** Schuld *f*; Strafbarkeit *f*; **ˈcrim·i·nal·ize** *v/t.* **1.** *et.* unter Strafe stellen; **2.** *j-n, et.* kriminalisieren.

crim·i·nal| law *s.* Strafrecht *n*; ~ **neg·lect** *s.* grobe Fahrlässigkeit; ~ **of·fence**, *Am.* ~ **of·fense** *s.* strafbare Handlung; ~ **pro·ceed·ings** *s. pl.* Strafverfahren *n*.

crim·i·nate [ˈkrɪmɪneɪt] *v/t.* anklagen, (e-s Verbrechens) beschuldigen; **crim·i·na·tion** [ˌkrɪmɪˈneɪʃn] *s.* Anklage *f*, Beschuldigung *f*; **crim·i·nol·o·gist** [ˌkrɪmɪˈnɒlədʒɪst] *s.* Kriminoˈloge *m*; **crim·i·nol·o·gy** [ˌkrɪmɪˈnɒlədʒɪ] *s.* Kriminoloˈgie *f*.

crimp¹ [krɪmp] **I** *v/t.* **1.** kräuseln, knittern, fälteln, wellen; **2.** *Leder* zu'rechtbiegen; **3.** ⚙ bördeln; **4.** *Küche*: *Fisch, Fleisch* schlitzen; **5.** *Am. sl.* hindern, stören; **II** *s.* **6.** Kräuselung *f*, Welligkeit *f*; Krause *f*, Falte *f*; **7.** ⚙ Falz *m*; **8.** (Haar)Welle *f*, Locke *f*; **9.** *Am.* F Behinderung *f*.

crimp² [krɪmp] *v/t.* ⚓, ⚔ gewaltsam anwerben, pressen.

crim·son ['krɪmzn] **I** *s.* Karme'sin-, Hochrot *n*; **II** *adj.* karme'sin-, hochrot; *fig.* puterrot (***from*** vor *Zorn etc.*); **III** *v/t.* hochrot färben; **IV** *v/i.* puterrot werden; **~ ram·bler** *s.* ⚘ *blutrote Kletterrose*.

cringe [krɪndʒ] *v/i.* **1.** sich ducken, sich krümmen: **~ *at*** zurückschrecken vor (*dat.*); **2.** *fig.* kriechen, ‚katzbuckeln' (***to*** vor *dat.*); **'cring·ing** [-dʒɪŋ] *adj.* □ kriecherisch, unter'würfig.

crin·kle ['krɪŋkl] **I** *v/i.* **1.** sich kräuseln *od.* krümmen *od.* biegen; **2.** Falten werfen, knittern; **II** *v/t.* **3.** kräuseln, krümmen; **4.** faltig machen, zerknittern; **III** *s.* **5.** Fältchen *n*, Runzel *f*; **'crin·kly** [-lɪ] *adj.* **1.** kraus, faltig; **2.** zerknittert.

crin·o·line ['krɪnəliːn] *s. hist.* Krino'line *f*, Reifrock *m*.

crip·ple ['krɪpl] **I** *s.* **1.** Krüppel *m*; **II** *v/t.* **2.** a) zum Krüppel machen, b) lähmen; **3.** *fig.* lähmen, lahmlegen; **4.** ⚔ akti'ons- *od.* kampfunfähig machen; **'crip·pled** [-ld] *adj.* **1.** verkrüppelt; **2.** *fig.* lahmgelegt; **'crip·pling** [-lɪŋ] *adj. fig.* lähmend.

cri·sis ['kraɪsɪs] *pl.* **-ses** [-siːz] *s.* ⚕, *thea. u. fig.* 'Krise *f*, 'Krisis *f*: **~ *management*** Krisenmanagement *n*; **~ *staff*** Krisenstab *m*.

crisp [krɪsp] **I** *adj.* □ **1.** knusp(e)rig, mürbe: **~*bread*** Knäckebrot *n*; **2.** kraus, gekräuselt; **3.** frisch, fest (*Gemüse*); steif, unzerknittert (*Papier*); **4.** a) forsch, schneidig, b) flott, lebhaft; **5.** klar, knapp (*Stil etc.*); **6.** scharf, frisch (*Luft*); **II** *s.* **7.** *pl. bsd. Brit.* (Kar'toffel)Chips *pl.*; **III** *v/t.* **8.** knusp(e)rig machen; **9.** kräuseln; **IV** *v/i.* **10.** knusp(e)rig werden; **11.** sich kräuseln; **'crisp·ness** [-nɪs] *s.* **1.** Knusp(e)rigkeit *f*; **2.** Frische *f*, Schärfe *f*, Le'bendigkeit *f*; **'crisp·y** [-pɪ] → ***crisp*** 1, 2, 4.

criss·cross ['krɪskrɒs] **I** *adj.* **1.** gekreuzt, kreuz u. quer (laufend), Kreuz...; **II** *adv.* **2.** kreuzweise, kreuz u. quer, durchein'ander; **3.** *fig.* in die Quere, verkehrt; **III** *s.* **4.** Gewirr *n* von Linien; **5.** Kreuzzeichen *n* (*als Unterschrift*); **IV** *v/t.* **6.** (wieder'holt 'durch-) kreuzen, kreuz u. quer durch'ziehen; **V** *v/i.* **7.** sich kreuzen; kreuz u. quer verlaufen.

cri·te·ri·on [kraɪ'tɪərɪən] *pl.* **-ri·a** [-rɪə] *s.* **1.** Kri'terium *n*, Maßstab *m*, Prüfstein *m*: ***that is no ~*** das ist nicht maßgebend (***for*** für); **2.** (Unter'scheidungs)Merkmal *n*.

crit·ic ['krɪtɪk] *s.* **1.** Kritiker(in); **2.** (Kunst- *etc.*)Kritiker(in), Rezen'sent (-in); **3.** Krittler *m*, Tadler *m*; **'crit·i·cal** [-kl] *adj.* □ **1.** kritisch, tadelsüchtig (***of s.o.*** j-m gegen'über): ***be ~ of s.th.*** et. kritisieren *od.* beanstanden, Bedenken gegen et. haben; **2.** kritisch, kunstverständig; sorgfältig: **~ *edition*** kritische Ausgabe; **3.** kritisch, entscheidend: ***the ~ moment***; **4.** kritisch, bedenklich, gefährlich: **~ *situation***; **~ *supplies*** Mangelgüter; **5.** *phys.* kritisch: **~ *speed***; **~ *load*** Grenzbelastung *f*; **'crit·i·cism** [-ɪsɪzəm] *s.* Kri'tik *f*: a) kritische Beurteilung, b) (Buch- *etc.*)Besprechung *f*, Rezensi'on *f*, c) kritische Unter'suchung, d) Tadel *m*: ***textual ~*** Textkritik; ***open to ~*** anfechtbar; ***above ~*** über jede Kritik *od.* jeden Tadel erhaben; **'crit·i·cize** [-ɪsaɪz] *v/t.* kritisieren (*a. v/i.*): a) kritisch beurteilen, b) besprechen, rezensieren; c) Kri'tik üben an (*dat.*), tadeln, rügen; **cri·tique** [krɪ'tiːk] *s.* Kri'tik *f*, kritische Besprechung *od.* Abhandlung.

croak [krəʊk] **I** *v/i.* **1.** quaken (*Frosch*); krächzen (*Rabe*); **2.** unken (*Unglück prophezeien*); **3.** *sl.* ‚abkratzen' (*sterben*); **II** *v/t.* **4.** *et.* krächzen(d sagen); **5.** *sl.* abmurksen (*töten*); **III** *s.* **6.** Quaken *n*; Krächzen *n*; **7.** → ***croaker*** 1; **'croak·er** [-kə] *s.* **1.** Schwarzseher *m*, Miesmacher *m*; **2.** *Am. sl.* Quacksalber *m*; **'croak·y** [-kɪ] *adj.* □ krächzend.

Cro·at ['krəʊæt] *s.* Kro'ate *m*, Kro'atin *f*; **Cro·a·tian** [krəʊ'eɪʃjən] *adj.* kro'atisch.

cro·chet ['krəʊʃeɪ] **I** *s. a.* **~ *work*** Häkelarbeit *f*, Häke'lei *f*: **~ *hook*** Häkelnadel *f*; **II** *v/t. u. v/i. pret. u. p.p.* **'cro·cheted** [-ʃeɪd] häkeln.

crock¹ [krɒk] **I** *s.* **1.** Klepper *m*, alter Gaul; **2.** *sl.* a) ‚altes Wrack' (*Person od. Sache*), b) *Am.* ‚altes Ekel' *od.* ‚alter Säufer'; **II** *v/i.* **3.** *mst* **~ *up*** zs.-brechen, -krachen; **III** *v/t.* **4.** ka'puttmachen.

crock² [krɒk] *s.* **1.** irdener Topf *od.* Krug; **2.** Topfscherbe *f*; **'crock·er·y** [-kərɪ] *s.* (irdenes) Geschirr, Steingut *n*, Töpferware *f*.

croc·o·dile ['krɒkədaɪl] *s.* **1.** *zo.* Kroko'dil *n*; **2.** Kroko'dilleder *n*; **3.** *Brit.* F Zweierreihe *f* von Schulmädchen; **~ *tears*** *s. pl.* Kroko'dilstränen *pl.*

cro·cus ['krəʊkəs] *s.* ⚘ 'Krokus *m*.

Croe·sus ['kriːsəs] *s.* 'Krösus *m*.

croft [krɒft] *s. Brit.* **1.** kleines (Acker-) Feld (*beim Haus*); **2.** kleiner Bauernhof; **'croft·er** [-tə] *s. Brit.* Kleinbauer *m*.

crom·lech ['krɒmlek] *s.* 'Kromlech *m*, dru'idischer Steinkreis.

crone [krəʊn] *s.* altes Weib.

cro·ny ['krəʊnɪ] *s.* alter Freund, Kum'pan *m*: ***old ~*** Busenfreund, Intimus *m*, ‚Spezi' *m*.

crook [krʊk] **I** *s.* **1.** Hirtenstab *m*; **2.** *eccl.* Bischofs-, Krummstab *m*; **3.** Krümmung *f*, Biegung *f*; **4.** Haken *m*; **5.** (*Schirm*)Krücke *f*; **6.** F Gauner *m*, Betrüger *m*, *allg.* Ga'nove *m*: ***on the ~*** unehrlich, hintenherum; **II** *v/t. u. v/i.* **7.** (sich) krümmen, (sich) biegen; **'~·back** *s.* Buck(e)lige(r *m*) *f*; **'~·backed** *adj.* buck(e)lig.

crooked¹ [krʊkt] *adj.* mit e-r Krücke: **~ *stick*** Krückstock *m*.

crook·ed² ['krʊkɪd] *adj.* □ **1.** krumm, gekrümmt; gebeugt; **2.** buck(e)lig, verwachsen; **3.** *fig.* unehrlich, betrügerisch: **~ *ways*** ‚krumme' Wege.

croon [kruːn] *v/i. u. v/t.* leise *od.* schmachtend singen *od.* summen; **'croon·er** [-nə] *s.* Schlager-, Schnulzensänger *m*.

crop [krɒp] **I** *s.* **1.** Feldfrucht *f*, *bsd.* Getreide *n* auf dem Halm, Saat *f*: ***the ~s*** a) die Saaten, b) die Gesamternte; **~ *rotation*** Fruchtfolge *f*, -wechsel *m*; **2.** Bebauung *f*: ***in ~*** bebaut; **3.** Ernte *f*, Ertrag *m*: **~ *failure*** Mißernte *f*; **4.** *fig.* Ertrag *m*, Ausbeute *f* (***of*** an *dat.*); **5.** Menge *f*, Haufen *m* (*Sachen od. Personen*); **6.** *zo.* Kropf *m* (*Vögel*); **7.** a) Peitschenstock *m*, b) Reitpeitsche *f*; **8.** kurzer Haarschnitt, kurzgeschnittenes Haar; **II** *v/t.* **9.** abschneiden; *Haar* kurz scheren; *Ohren, Schwanz* stutzen; **10.** abbeißen, -fressen; **11.** ⚒ bepflanzen, bebauen; **III** *v/i.* **12.** (Ernte) tragen; **13.** *geol.* **~ *up***, **~ *out*** zutage treten; **14.** **~ *up*** *fig.* plötzlich auftauchen, -treten, sich zeigen; **'crop·eared** *adj.* mit gestutzten Ohren; **'crop·per** [-pə] *s.* **1.** ***a good ~*** e-e gut tragende Pflanze; **2.** F Fall *m*, Sturz *m*: ***come a ~*** ‚auf die Nase fallen' (*a. fig.*); **3.** *orn.* Kropftaube *f*.

cro·quet ['krəʊkeɪ] *sport* **I** *s.* 'Krocket *n*; **II** *v/t. u. v/i.* krockieren.

cro·quette [krɒ'ket] *s. Küche*: Kro'kette *f*.

cro·sier ['krəʊʒə] *s. R.C.* Bischofs-, Krummstab *m*.

cross [krɒs] **I** *s.* **1.** Kreuz *n* (*zur Kreuzigung*); **2.** ***the ~*** a) das Kreuz Christi, b) das Christentum, c) das Kruzi'fix *n*; **3.** Kreuz *n* (*Zeichen od. Gegenstand*): ***make the sign of the ~*** sich bekreuzigen; ***sign with a ~*** mit e-m Kreuz (*statt Unterschrift*) unterzeichnen; ***mark with a ~*** ankreuzen; **4.** (Ordens)Kreuz *n*; **5.** *fig.* Kreuz *n*, Leiden *n*, Not *f*: ***bear one's ~*** sein Kreuz tragen; **6.** Querstrich *m* (des Buchstabens t); **7.** Gaune'rei *f*, ‚krumme Tour': ***on the ~*** unehrlich; **8.** *biol.* Kreuzung *f*, Mischung *f*; *fig.* Mittelding *n*; **9.** Kreuzungspunkt *m*; **10.** *sport* Cross *m*: a) *Fußball etc.*: Schrägpaß *m*, b) *Tennis*: *diagonal geschlagener Ball*, c) *Boxen*: *Schlag über den Arm des Gegners*; **II** *v/t.* **11.** kreuzen, über Kreuz legen: **~ *one's legs*** die Beine kreuzen *od.* überschlagen; **~ *swords with s.o.*** die Klingen mit j-m kreuzen (*a. fig.*); **~ *s.o.'s hand*** (*od.* ***palm***) a) j-m (Trink)Geld geben, b) j-n ‚schmieren'; **12.** e-n Querstrich ziehen durch: **~ *one's t's*** sehr sorgfältig sein; **~ *a cheque*** e-n Scheck ‚kreuzen' (*als Verrechnungsscheck kennzeichnen*); → ***cheque***; **~ *off*** (*od.* ***out***) ausstreichen; **~ *off*** *fig. et.* ‚abschreiben'; **13.** durch-, über'queren, *Grenze* über'schreiten, *Zimmer* durch'schreiten, (hin'über)gehen, (-)fahren über (*acc.*): **~ *the ocean*** über den Ozean fahren; **~ *the street*** über die Straße gehen; ***it ~ed my mind*** es fiel mir ein, es kam mir in den Sinn; **~ *s.o.'s path*** j-m in die Quere kommen; **14.** sich kreuzen mit: ***your letter ~ed mine*** Ihr Brief kreuzte sich mit meinem; **~ *each other*** sich kreuzen, sich schneiden, sich treffen; **15.** *biol.* kreuzen; **16.** *fig. Plan* durch'kreuzen, vereiteln; entgegentreten (*dat.*): ***be ~ed in love*** Unglück in der Liebe haben; **17.** das Kreuzzeichen machen auf (*acc.*) *od.* über (*dat.*): **~ *o.s.*** sich bekreuzigen; **III** *v/i.* **18.** *a.* **~ *over*** hin'übergehen, -fahren; 'übersetzen; **19.** sich treffen; sich kreuzen (*Briefe*); **IV**

adj. □ **20.** quer (liegend, laufend), Quer…; schräg; sich (über)ˈschneidend; **21.** (***to***) entgegengesetzt (*dat.*), im ˈWiderspruch (zu), Gegen…; **22.** F ärgerlich, mürrisch, böse (***with*** mit): ***as ~ as two sticks*** bitterböse; **23.** *sl.* unehrlich.

cross| ac·tion *s.* ⚖ Gegen-, ˈWiderklage *f*; **~ ap·peal** *s.* ⚖ Anschlußberufung *f*; **ˈ~·bar** *s.* **1.** Querholz *n*, -riegel *m*, -stange *f*, -balken *m*; **2.** ⚙ Traˈverse *f*; **3.** a) *Fußball*: Querlatte *f*, b) *Hochsprung*: Latte *f*; **ˈ~·bench** *parl. Brit.* **I** *s.* Querbank *f* der Parˈteilosen (*im Oberhaus*); **II** *adj.* parˈteilos, unabhängig; **ˈ~·bones** *s. pl.* zwei gekreuzte Knochen unter e-m Totenkopf; **ˈ~·bow** [-bəʊ] *s.* Armbrust *f*; **ˈ~·bred** *adj. biol.* durch Kreuzung erzeugt, gekreuzt; **ˈ~·breed I** *s.* **1.** Mischrasse *f*; **2.** Kreuzung *f*, Mischling *m*; **II** *v/t.* [*irr.* → ***breed***] **3.** kreuzen; **ˌ~-ˈChan·nel** *adj.* den (ˈÄrmel)Kaˌnal überˈquerend: ***~ steamer*** Kanaldampfer *m*; **ˈ~·check I** *v/t.* **1.** (von verschiedenen Gesichtspunkten aus) überˈprüfen; **2.** *Eishokkey*: crosschecken; **II** *s.* **3.** mehrfache Überˈprüfung; **4.** *Eishockey*: ˈCrosscheck *m*; **ˌ~-ˈcoun·try I** *adj.* Querfeldein…; Gelände…, *mot. a.* geländegängig: ***~ skiing*** Skilanglauf *m*; ***~ race*** → **II** *s. sport* a) Querfeldˈein-, Crosslauf *m*, b) *Radsport*: Querfeldˈeinrennen *n*; **ˈ~ˌcur·rent** *s.* Gegenströmung *f* (*a. fig.*); **ˈ~·cut I** *adj.* **1.** a) quer schneidend, Quer…, b) quergeschnitten: ***~ file*** Doppelfeile *f*; ***~ saw*** Ablängsäge *f*; **II** *s.* **2.** Querweg *m*; **3.** ⚙ Kreuzhieb *m*.

crosse [krɒs] *s. sport* Laˈcrosse-Schläger *m*.

cross| en·try *s.* ✝ Gegenbuchung *f*; **ˈ~-exˌam·iˈna·tion** *s.* ⚖ Kreuzverhör *n*; **ˌ~-exˈam·ine** *v/t.* ⚖ ins Kreuzverhör nehmen; **ˈ~-eyed** *adj.* schielend; **ˈ~-fade** *v/t. Film etc.*: überˈblenden; **ˌ~-ˈfer·ti·lize** *v/i. biol.* sich kreuzweise (*fig.* gegenseitig) befruchten; **~ fire** *s.* ⚔ Kreuzfeuer *n* (*a. fig.*); **ˈ~-grained** *adj.* **1.** quergefasert; **2.** *fig.* ˈwiderspenstig, eigensinnig; kratzbürstig; **ˈ~ˌhatch·ing** *s.* Kreuzschraffierung *f*; **~ head, ~ head·ing** *s. Zeitung*: ˈZwischenˌüberschrift *f*.

cross·ing [ˈkrɒsɪŋ] *s.* **1.** Kreuzen *n*, Kreuzung *f* (*a. biol.*); **2.** Durch-, Überˈquerung *f*; **3.** ˈÜberfahrt *f*; (ˈStraßen *etc.*)ˌÜbergang *m*; **4.** (Straßen-, Eisenbahn)Kreuzung *f*: ***level*** (*Am.* ***grade***) ***~*** schienengleicher (*oft* unbeschrankter) Bahnübergang; **ˈ~ˌo·ver** *s. biol.* Crossing-ˈover *n*, Genaustausch *m* zwischen Chromoˈsomenpaaren.

ˈcross|-legged *adj.* mit ˈübergeschlagenen Beinen, *a.* im Schneidersitz; **ˈ~·light** *s.* schrägeinfallendes Licht.

cross·ness [ˈkrɒsnɪs] *s.* Verdrießlichkeit *f*, schlechte Laune.

ˈcross|ˌo·ver *s.* **1.** → ***crossing*** 2–4; **2.** *biol.* ausgetauschtes Gen; **3.** ⚡ a) Überˈkreuzung *f*, b) *opt.*, *TV* Bündelknoten *m*; **ˈ~·patch** *s.* F ‚Kratzbürste' *f*; **ˈ~·piece** *s.* ⚙ Querstück *n*, -balken *m*, -holz *n*; **ˈ~-pol·liˌna·tion** *s. bot.* Fremdbestäubung *f*; **ˌ~-ˈpur·pos·es** *s. pl.* **1.** ˈWiderspruch *m*: ***be at ~*** a) einander entgegenarbeiten, b) sich mißverstehen; ***talk at ~*** aneinander vorbeireden; **2.** *sg. konstr. ein* Frage- u. Antwort-Spiel *n*; **ˌ~-ˈques·tion I** *s.* ⚖ Frage *f* im Kreuzverhör; **II** *v/t.* → ***cross-examine***; **~ ref·er·ence** *s.* Kreuz-, Querverweis *m*; **ˈ~·road** *s.* **1.** Querstraße *f*; **2.** *pl. mst sg. konstr.* Straßenkreuzung *f*: ***at a ~s*** an e-r Kreuzung; ***at the ~s*** *fig.* am Scheidewege; **~ sec·tion** *s.* ⩓, ⚙ *u. fig.* Querschnitt *m* (***of*** durch); **ˈ~-stitch** *s.* Kreuzstich *m*; **~ sum** *s.* Quersumme *f*; **~ talk** *s.* **1.** *teleph. etc.* Nebensprechen *n*; **2.** Koˈpierefˌfekt *m* (*Tonband*); **3.** *Brit.* Wortgefecht *n*; **ˈ~·tie** *s.* Schienenschwelle *f*; **ˈ~·town** *adj. Am.* quer durch die Stadt (gehend *od.* fahrend *od.* reichend); **~ vot·ing** *s. Brit. pol.* Abstimmung *f* über Kreuz (*wobei einzelne Abgeordnete mit der Gegenpartei stimmen*); **ˈ~·walk** *s. Am.* ˈFußgängerˌüberweg *m*; **ˈ~·ways** → ***crosswise***; **~ wind** *s.* ✈, ⚓ Seitenwind *m*; **ˈ~·wise** *adv.* quer, kreuzweise; kreuzförmig; **ˈ~-word** (**puz·zle**) *s.* Kreuzworträtsel *n*.

crotch [krɒtʃ] *s.* **1.** Gabelung *f*; **2.** Schritt *m* (*der Hose od. des Körpers*).

crotch·et [ˈkrɒtʃɪt] *s.* **1.** ♪ Viertelnote *f*; **2.** Schrulle *f*, Maˈrotte *f*; **ˈcrotch·et·y** [-tɪ] *adj.* **1.** grillenhaft; **2.** F mürrisch, schrullenhaft, verschroben.

cro·ton [ˈkrəʊtən] *s.* ⚘ ˈKroton *m*; **♀ bug** *s. zo. Am.* Küchenschabe *f*.

crouch [kraʊtʃ] **I** *v/i.* **1.** hocken, sich (nieder)ducken, (sich zs.-)kauern; **2.** *fig.* kriechen, sich ducken (***to*** vor); **II** *s.* **3.** kauernde Stellung, geduckte Haltung; Hockstellung *f*.

croup¹ [kruːp] *s.* ⚕ Krupp *m*, Halsbräune *f*.

croup², **croupe** [kruːp] *s.* Kruppe *f des Pferdes*.

crou·pi·er [ˈkruːpɪə] *s.* Croupiˈer *m*.

crow¹ [krəʊ] *s.* **1.** *orn.* Krähe *f*: ***as the ~ flies*** a) schnurgerade, b) (in der) Luftlinie; ***eat ~*** *Am.* F zu Kreuze kriechen, ‚klein und häßlich' sein *od.* werden; ***have a ~ to pluck*** (*od.* ***pick***) ***with s.o.*** mit j-m ein Hühnchen zu rupfen haben; **2.** rabenähnlicher Vogel; **3.** *Am. contp.* Neger *m*.

crow² [krəʊ] **I** *v/i.* [*irr.*] **1.** krähen (*Hahn*, *a. Kind*); **2.** (vor Freude) quietschen; **3.** (***over***, ***about***) a) triumphieren (über *acc.*), b) protzen, prahlen (mit); **II** *s.* **4.** Krähen *n* (*Hahn*); **5.** (Freuden)Schrei(e *pl.*) *m*.

ˈcrow|·bar *s.* ⚙ Brech-, Stemmeisen *n*; **ˈ~·ber·ry** [-bərɪ] *s.* ⚘ Krähenbeere *f*.

crowd [kraʊd] **I** *s.* **1.** (Menschen)Menge *f*, Gedränge *n*: ***~s of people*** Menschenmassen; ***~ scene*** *Film*: Massenszene *f*; ***he would pass in a ~*** er ist nicht schlechter als andere; **2.** ***the ~*** das gemeine Volk; der Pöbel: ***follow the ~*** mit der Masse gehen; **3.** F ‚Verˈein' *m*, Bande *f* (*Gesellschaft*): ***a jolly ~***; **4.** Ansammlung *f*, Haufen *m*: ***a ~ of books***; **II** *v/i.* **5.** sich drängen, zs.-strömen; vorwärtsdrängen: ***~ in*** hinˈeinströmen, sich hinˈeindrängen; ***~ in upon s.o.*** auf j-n einstürmen (*Gedanken etc.*); **III** *v/t.* **6.** überˈfüllen, ˈvollstopfen (***with*** mit); → ***crowded*** 1; **7.** hinˈeinpressen, -stopfen (***into*** in *acc.*); **8.** (zs.-)drängen: ***~ (on) sail*** ⚓ alle Segel beisetzen; ***~ out*** verdrängen; ausschalten; (*wegen Platzmangels*) aussperren; **9.** *Am.* a) (vorwärts *etc.*)drängen, b) *Auto etc.* abdrängen, c) *j-m* im Nacken sitzen, d) *j-s Geduld, Glück etc.* strapazieren: ***~ing thirty*** an die Dreißig; ***~ up*** *Preise* in die Höhe treiben; **ˈcrowd·ed** [-dɪd] *adj.* **1.** (***with***) überˈfüllt, ˈvollgestopft (mit), voll, wimmelnd (von): ***~ to overflowing*** zum Bersten voll; ***~ profession*** überlaufener Beruf; **2.** gedrängt, zs.-gepfercht; **3.** bedrängt, beengt; **4.** voll ausgefüllt, arbeits-, ereignisreich: ***~ hours***.

ˈcrow·foot *pl.* **-foots** *s.* **1.** ⚘ Hahnenfuß *m*; **2.** → ***crow's-feet***.

crown [kraʊn] **I** *s.* **1.** Siegerkranz *m*, Ehrenkrone *f*; **2.** a) (Königs- *etc.*)Krone *f*, b) Herrschermacht *f*, Thron *m*: ***succeed to the ~*** den Thron besteigen, c) ***the ♀*** die Krone, der König *etc.*, *a.* der Staat *od.* Fiskus: ***~ cases*** *Brit.* Strafsachen; **3.** Krone *f* (*Abzeichen*); **4.** *fig.* Krone *f*, Palme *f*, *sport a.* (Meister)Titel *m*; **5.** Gipfel *m*: a) höchster Punkt, b) *fig.* Krönung *f*, Höhepunkt *m*; **6.** Krone *f* (*Währung*): a) *Brit. obs.* Fünfschillingstück *n*: ***half a ~*** 2 Schilling 6 Pence, b) *Währungseinheit von Dänemark, Norwegen, Schweden etc.*; **7.** a) Scheitel *m*, Wirbel *m* (*Kopf*), b) Kopf *m*, Schädel *m*; **8.** ⚘ (Baum)Krone *f*; **9.** a) *anat.* (Zahn)Krone *f*, b) (künstliche) Krone; **10.** a) Haarkrone *f*, b) Schopf *m*, Kamm *m* (*Vogel*); **11.** Kopf *m e-s Hutes*; **12.** ⩓ Krone *f*, Schlußstein *m* (*a. fig.*); **II** *v/t.* **13.** krönen: ***be ~ed king*** zum König gekrönt werden; ***~ed heads*** gekrönte Häupter; **14.** *fig.* krönen, ehren, belohnen; zieren, schmücken; **15.** *fig.* krönen, den Gipfel *od.* Höhepunkt bilden von: ***~ed with success*** von Erfolg gekrönt; **16.** *fig.* die Krone aufsetzen (*dat.*): ***~ all*** allem die Krone aufsetzen (*a. iro.*); ***to ~ all*** (*Redew.*) *iro.* zu allem Überfluß; **17.** *fig.* glücklich vollˈenden; **18.** ⚕ *Zahn* überˈkronen; **19.** *Damespiel*: zur Dame machen; **20.** *sl. j-m* ‚eins aufs Dach geben'; **~ cap** *s.* Kron(en)korken *m*; **♀ Col·o·ny** *s. Brit.* ˈKronkoloˌnie *f*; **~ glass** *s.* **1.** Mondglas *n*, Butzenscheibe *f*; **2.** Kronglas *n*.

crown·ing [ˈkraʊnɪŋ] *adj.* krönend, alles überˈbietend, höchst: ***~ achievement*** Glanzleistung *f*.

crown| jew·els *s. pl.* ˈKronjuˌwelen *pl.*, ˈReichskleinˌodien *pl.*; **~ land** *s.* Kron-, Staatsgut *n*; **♀ law** *s.* ⚖ *Brit.* Strafrecht *n*; **~ prince** *s.* Kronprinz *m*; **~ prin·cess** *s.* ˈKronprinˌzessin *f*; **~ wheel** *s.* ⚙ Kronrad *n* (*Uhr etc.*); *mot.* Antriebskegelrad *n*.

ˈcrow's|-feet [ˈkrəʊz-] *pl.* ‚Krähenfüße' *pl.*, Fältchen *pl.*; **~ nest** *s.* ⚓ Ausguck *m*, Krähennest *n*.

cru·cial [ˈkruːʃl] *adj.* **1.** ˈkritisch, entscheidend: ***~ moment***; ***~ point*** springender Punkt; ***~ test*** Feuerprobe *f*; **2.** schwierig; **3.** kreuzförmig, Kreuz…

cru·ci·ble [ˈkruːsɪbl] *s.* **1.** ⚙ (Schmelz-)Tiegel *m*: ***~ steel*** Tiegelgußstahl *m*; **2.** *fig.* Feuerprobe *f*.

cru·ci·fix [ˈkruːsɪfɪks] *s.* Kruziˈfix *n*; **cru·ci·fix·ion** [ˌkruːsɪˈfɪkʃn] *s.* Kreuzigung *f*; **ˈcru·ci·form** [-fɔːm] *adj.* kreuzförmig; **ˈcru·ci·fy** [-faɪ] *v/t.* **1.** kreuzigen (*a. fig.*); **2.** *fig.* a) martern, quälen, b) *Begierden* abtöten, c) *j-n* ‚fertigmachen'.

crud [krʌd] *s.* F Dreck *m*, ‚Mist' *m*.
crude [kruːd] *adj.* ☐ **1.** roh: a) ungekocht, b) unver-, unbearbeitet: **~ *oil*** Rohöl *n*; **2.** primi'tiv: a) plump, grob, b) simpel, c) bar'barisch; **3.** roh, grob, ungehobelt, unfein; **4.** roh, unfertig, unreif; 'undurchˌdacht: **~ *figures*** *Statistik*: rohe *od.* nicht aufgeschlüsselte Zahlen; **5.** grell, geschmacklos (*Farbe*); **6.** *fig.* ungeschminkt, nackt: **~ *facts***; **'crude·ness** [-nɪs] *s.* Roheit *f*, Grobheit *f*, Unfertigkeit *f*, Unreife *f* (*a. fig.*); **'cru·di·ty** [-dɪtɪ] *s.* **1.** → ***crudeness***; **2.** *et.* Unfertiges *od.* Unbearbeitetes; **3.** *et.* Geschmackloses.
cru·el ['krʊəl] **I** *adj.* ☐ **1.** grausam (***to*** gegen); **2.** hart, unbarmherzig, roh, gefühllos; **3.** schrecklich, mörderisch: **~ *heat***; **II** *adv.* **4.** F furchtbar, ‚grausam': **~ *hot***; **'cru·el·ty** [-tɪ] *s.* **1.** Grausamkeit *f* (***to*** gegen['über]); → ***mental cruelty***; **2.** Miß'handlung *f*, Quäle'rei *f*: **~ *to animals*** Tierquälerei; **3.** Schwere *f*, Härte *f*.
cru·et ['kruːɪt] *s.* **1.** Essig-, Ölfläschchen *n*; **2.** *R.C.* Meßkännchen *n*; **3.** *a.* **~ *stand*** Me'nage *f*, Gewürzständer *m*.
cruise [kruːz] **I** *v/i.* **1.** a) ⚓ kreuzen, e-e Kreuzfahrt *od.* Seereise machen, b) her'umfahren: ***cruising taxi*** Taxi *n* auf Fahrgastsuche; **2.** ✈, *mot.* mit Reisegeschwindigkeit fliegen *od.* fahren; **II** *s.* **3.** Seereise *f*, Kreuz-, Vergnügungsfahrt *f*; **~ con·trol** *s. mot.* Temporegler *m*; **~ mis·sile** *s.* ⚔ Marschflugkörper *m*.
cruis·er ['kruːzə] *s.* **1.** ⚓ a) Kreuzer *m*, b) Kreuzfahrtschiff *n*; **2.** *Am.* (Funk-)Streifenwagen *m*; **3.** *Boxen*: **~ *weight*** *Am.* Halbschwergewicht *n*; **'cruis·ing** [-zɪŋ] *adj.* ✈, *mot.* Reise…: **~ *speed***; **~ *gear*** *mot.* Schongang *m*; **~ *radius*** Aktionsradius *m*; **~ *level*** ✈ Reiseflughöhe *f*.
crumb [krʌm] **I** *s.* **1.** Krume *f*: a) Krümel *m*, Brösel *m*, Brosame *m*, b) *weicher Teil des Brotes*; **2.** *fig.* a) Brocken *m*, b) Krümchen *n*, *ein* bißchen; **3.** *sl.* ‚Blödmann' *m*; **II** *v/t.* **4.** *Küche*: panieren; **5.** zerkrümeln; **'crum·ble** [-mbl] **I** *v/t.* **1.** zerkrümeln, -bröckeln; **II** *v/i.* **2.** zerbröckeln, -fallen; **3.** *fig.* a) zerfallen, zu'grunde gehen, b) (langsam) zs.-brechen; **4.** ✝ abbröckeln (*Kurse*); **'crum·bling** [-mblɪŋ], **'crum·bly** [-mblɪ] *adj.* **1.** krüm(e)lig, bröck(e)lig; **2.** zerbröckelnd, -fallend; **crumb·y** ['krʌmɪ] *adj.* **1.** voller Krumen; **2.** weich, krüm(e)lig.
crum·pet ['krʌmpɪt] *s.* **1.** *Brit.* Sauerteigfladen *m*; **2.** *sl.* ‚Miezen' *pl.*: ***she's a nice piece of ~*** sie ist sehr sexy.
crum·ple ['krʌmpl] **I** *v/t.* **1.** *a.* **~ *up*** zerknittern, zer-, zs.-knüllen; **2.** *fig. j-n* 'umwerfen; **II** *v/i.* **3.** faltig *od.* zerdrückt werden, zs.-schrumpeln; **4.** *oft* **~ *up*** zs.-brechen (*a. fig.*), einstürzen.
crunch [krʌntʃ] **I** *v/t.* **1.** knirschend (zer)kauen; **2.** zermalmen; **II** *v/i.* **3.** knirschend kauen; **4.** knirschen; **III** *s.* **5.** Knirschen *n*; **6.** F *fig.* a) Druck(ausübung *f*) *m*, b) böse Situati'on, c) 'kritischer Mo'ment, 'Krise *f*; ***when it comes to the ~*** wenn es hart auf hart geht.
crup·per ['krʌpə] *s.* a) Schwanzriemen *m*, b) Kruppe *f* (*des Pferdes*).
cru·sade [kruː'seɪd] **I** *s. hist.* Kreuzzug *m* (*a. fig.*); **II** *v/i.* e-n Kreuzzug unter'nehmen; *fig.* zu Felde ziehen, kämpfen; **cru'sad·er** [-də] *s. hist.* Kreuzfahrer *m*; *fig.* Kämpfer *m*.
cruse [kruːz] *s. bibl.* irdener Krug.
crush [krʌʃ] **I** *s.* **1.** (zermalmender) Druck; **2.** Gedränge *n*, Gewühl *n*; **3.** große Gesellschaft *od.* Party; **4.** *sl.* Schwarm *m*: ***have a ~ on s.o.*** in j-n ‚verknallt' sein; **II** *v/t.* **5.** *a.* **~ *up*** *od.* ***down*** zerquetschen, -drücken, -malmen; **6.** zerstoßen, -kleinern, mahlen: **~*ed stone*** Schotter *m*; **7.** *a.* **~ *up*** zerknittern, -knüllen; **8.** drücken, drängen; **9.** *a.* **~ *out*** ausquetschen, -drükken; **10.** *a.* **~ *out*** *od.* ***down*** *fig.* er-, unter'drücken, über'wältigen, zerschmettern, zertreten, vernichten; **III** *v/i.* **11.** zerknittern, sich zerdrücken; **12.** zerbrechen; **13.** sich drängen; **'crush·a·ble** [-ʃəbl] *adj.* **1.** knitterfest; **2.** **~ *zone*** (*od.* ***bin***) *mot.* Knautschzone *f*; **crush bar·ri·er** *s. Brit.* Absperrung *f*; **'crush·er** [-ʃə] *s.* **1.** ⚙ a) Zer'kleinerungsmaˌschine *f*, Brechwerk *n*, b) Presse *f*, Quetsche *f*; **2.** F a) vernichtender Schlag, b) ‚tolles Ding'; **'crush·ing** [-ʃɪŋ] *adj.* ☐ *fig.* vernichtend, erdrükkend; **crush room** *s. thea.* Foy'er *n*.
crust [krʌst] **I** *s.* **1.** Kruste *f*, Rinde *f* (*Brot, Pastete*); **2.** Knust *m*, Stück *n* hartes Brot; **3.** *geol.* Erdkruste *f*; **4.** ⚕ Schorf *m*; **5.** ⚘, *zo.* Schale *f*; **6.** Niederschlag *m* (*in Weinflaschen*), Ablagerung *f*; **7.** *sl.* Frechheit *f*; **8.** Harsch *m*; **II** *v/t.* **9.** *a.* **~ *over*** mit e-r Kruste über'ziehen; **III** *v/i.* **10.** e-e Kruste bilden; verharschen (*Schnee*); → ***crusted***.
crus·ta·cea [krʌ'steɪʃjə] *s. pl. zo.* Krusten-, Krebstiere *pl.*; **crus'ta·cean** [-'steɪʃjən] **I** *adj.* zu den Krusten- *od.* Krebstieren gehörig, Krebs…; **II** *s.* Krusten-, Krebstier *n*; **crus'ta·ceous** [-'steɪʃjəs] → ***crustacean*** I.
crust·ed ['krʌstɪd] *adj.* **1.** mit e-r Kruste über'zogen: **~ *snow*** Harsch(schnee) *m*; **2.** abgelagert (*Wein*); **3.** *fig.* a) alt'hergebracht, b) eingefleischt, ‚verkrustet'; **'crust·y** [-tɪ] *adj.* ☐ **1.** krustig; **2.** mit e-r Kruste (versehen); **3.** *fig.* barsch.
crutch [krʌtʃ] *s.* **1.** Krücke *f*: ***go on ~es*** auf *od.* an Krücken gehen; **2.** *fig.* Krücke *f*, Stütze *f*.
crux [krʌks] *s.* **1.** springender Punkt; **2.** Schwierigkeit *f*: a) ‚Haken' *m*, b) harte Nuß, (schwieriges) Pro'blem; **3.** ♊ *ast.* Kreuz *n* des Südens.
cry [kraɪ] **I** *s.* **1.** Schrei *m* (*a. Tier*), Ruf *m* (***for*** nach): ***within ~*** (***of***) in Rufweite (von); ***a far ~ from*** *fig.* a) weit entfernt von, b) et. ganz anderes als; ***still a far ~*** *fig.* noch in weiter Ferne; **2.** Geschrei *n*: ***much ~ and little wool*** viel Geschrei u. wenig Wolle; ***the popular ~*** die Stimme des Volkes; **3.** Weinen *n*, Klagen *n*: ***have a good ~*** sich (ordentlich) ausweinen; **4.** Bitten *n*, Flehen *n*; **5.** (Schlacht)Ruf *m*; Schlag-, Losungswort *n*; **6.** *hunt.* Anschlagen *n*, Gebell *n* (*Meute*): ***in full ~*** *fig.* in voller Jagd *od.* Verfolgung; **7.** *hunt.* Meute *f*; *fig.* Herde *f*, Menge *f*: ***follow in the ~*** mit der Masse gehen; **II** *v/i.* **8.** schreien, laut (aus)rufen: **~ *for help*** um Hilfe rufen; **~ *for vengeance*** nach Rache schreien; **9.** weinen, heulen, jammern; **10.** *hunt.* anschlagen, bellen; **III** *v/t.* **11.** *et.* schreien, (aus)rufen; **12.** *Waren etc.* ausrufen; **13.** flehen um; **14.** weinen: **~ *one's eyes out*** sich die Augen ausweinen; **~ *o.s. to sleep*** sich in den Schlaf weinen; **~ *down*** *v/t.* her'untersetzen, -machen; **~ *off*** *v/t. u. v/i.* (plötzlich) absagen, zu'rücktreten (von); **~ *out*** **I** *v/t.* ausrufen; **II** *v/i.* aufschreien: **~ *against*** heftig protestieren gegen; ***for crying out loud!*** F verdammt noch mal!; **~ *up*** *v/t.* laut rühmen.
'cryˌba·by *s.* kleiner Schreihals; *fig. contp.* Heulsuse *f*.
cry·ing ['kraɪɪŋ] *adj. fig.* a) (himmel-)schreiend: **~ *shame***, b) dringend: **~ *need***.
cryo- [kraɪəʊ] *in Zssgn* Kälte…, Kryo…: ***cryogen*** Kältemittel *n*; ***cryogenic*** a) ⚙ kälteerzeugend, b) kryogenisch: **~-*computer***, ***cryosurgery*** ⚕ Kryo-, Kältechirurgie *f*.
crypt [krɪpt] *s.* ⚠ 'Krypta *f*, 'unterirdisches Gewölbe, Gruft *f*; **'cryp·tic** [-tɪk] *adj.* geheim, verborgen; rätselhaft, dunkel: **~ *colo(u)ring*** *zo.* Schutzfärbung *f*; **'cryp·ti·cal** [-tɪkl] *adj.* → ***cryptic***.
crypto- [krɪptəʊ] *in Zssgn* geheim, krypto…: **~-*communist*** verkappter Kommunist; **'cryp·to·gam** [-gæm] *s.* ⚘ Krypto'game *f*, Sporenpflanze *f*; **cryp·to·gam·ic** [ˌkrɪptəʊ'gæmɪk], **cryp·tog·a·mous** [krɪp'tɒgəməs] *adj.* ⚘ krypto'gamisch; **'cryp·to·gram** [-græm] *s.* Text *m* in Geheimschrift, verschlüsselter Text; **'cryp·to·graph** [-grɑːf] *s.* **1.** → ***cryptogram***; **2.** Geheimschriftgerät *n*; **cryp·tog·ra·phy** [krɪp'tɒgrəfɪ] *s.* Geheimschrift *f*; **cryp·tol·o·gist** [krɪp'tɒlədʒɪst] *s.* (Ver-, Ent)Schlüsseler *m*.
crys·tal ['krɪstl] **I** *s.* **1.** Kri'stall *m* (*a.* ⚒, *min., phys.*): ***as clear as ~*** *od.* **~ *clear*** a) kristallklar, b) *fig.* sonnenklar; **2.** *a.* **~ *glass*** a) Kri'stall(glas) *n*, b) *coll.* Kri'stall *n*, Glaswaren *pl.*; **3.** Uhrglas *n*; **4.** ⚡ a) (De'tektor)Kriˌstall *m*, b) (Kri'stall)Deˌtektor *m*, c) (Schwing)Quarz *m*: **~ *set*** Kristallempfänger *m*; **II** *adj.* Kristall…, kri'stallen; **5.** kri'stallklar; **~ *de·tec·tor*** → ***crystal*** 4 b; **~ *gaz·er*** *s.* Hellseher(in); **~ *gaz·ing*** *s.* Hellsehen *n*.
crys·tal·line ['krɪstəlaɪn] *adj. a.* ⚒, *min.* kristal'linisch, kri'stallen, kri'stallartig, Kristall…: **~ *lens*** *anat.* (Augen)Linse *f*; **'crys·tal·liz·a·ble** [-aɪzəbl] *adj.* kristallisierbar; **crys·tal·li·za·tion** [ˌkrɪstəlaɪ'zeɪʃn] *s.* Kristallisati'on *f*, Kristallisierung *f*, Kri'stallbildung *f*; **'crys·tal·lize** [-aɪz] **I** *v/t.* **1.** kristallisieren; **2.** *fig.* feste Form geben (*dat.*), klären; **3.** *Früchte* kandieren; **II** *v/i.* **4.** kristallisieren; **5.** *fig.* sich kristallisieren, kon'krete *od.* feste Form annehmen; **crys·tal·log·ra·phy** [ˌkrɪstə'lɒgrəfɪ] *s.* Kristallogra'phie *f*.
cub [kʌb] **I** *s.* **1.** *zo. das* Junge (*des Fuchses, Bären etc.*); **2.** *a.* ***unlicked ~*** grüner Junge; **3.** ‚Küken' *n*, Anfänger *m*: **~ *reporter*** (unerfahrener) junger Reporter; **4.** *a.* **~ *scout*** Wölfling *m*, Jungpfadfinder *m*; **II** *v/i.* **5.** Junge werfen (*Füchse etc.*).
cub·age ['kjuːbɪdʒ] → ***cubature***.
Cu·ban ['kjuːbən] **I** *adj.* ku'banisch; **II** *s.*

Ku'baner(in).

cu·ba·ture ['kju:bətʃə] *s.* ⩘ **1.** Raum(inhalts)berechnung *f*; **2.** Rauminhalt *m*.

cub·by(·hole) ['kʌbɪ(həʊl)] *s.* **1.** gemütliches Plätzchen; **2.** ‚Ka'buff' *n*, winziger Raum.

cube [kju:b] **I** *s.* **1.** ⩘ Würfel *m*, 'Kubus *m*; **2.** (*a.* Eis-, *phot.* Blitz)Würfel *m*: ~ **sugar** Würfelzucker *m*; **3.** ⩘ Ku'bikzahl *f*, dritte Po'tenz: ~ **root** Kubikwurzel *f*; **4.** Pflasterstein *m* (*in Würfelform*); **II** *v/t.* **5.** ⩘ kubieren: a) zur dritten Po'tenz erheben: **two ~d** zwei hoch drei (2^3), b) den Rauminhalt messen von (*od. gen.*); **6.** in Würfel schneiden *od.* pressen.

cu·bic ['kju:bɪk] *adj.* (□ **~ally**) **1.** Kubik…, Raum…: ~ **capacity** *mot.* Hubraum *m*; ~ **content** Rauminhalt *m*, Volumen *n*; ~ **metre**, *Am.* **meter** Kubik-, Raum-, Festmeter *m*; **2.** kubisch, würfelförmig, Würfel…; **3.** ⩘ kubisch: ~ **equation** kubische Gleichung, Gleichung dritten Grades.

cu·bi·cle ['kju:bɪkl] *s.* kleiner abgeteilter (Schlaf)Raum; Zelle *f*, Nische *f*, Ka'bine *f*; ⚡ Schallzelle *f*.

cub·ism ['kju:bɪzəm] *s.* Ku'bismus *m*; '**cub·ist** [-ɪst] **I** *s.* Ku'bist *m*; **II** *adj.* ku'bistisch.

cu·bit ['kju:bɪt] *s. hist.* Elle *f* (*Längenmaß*); '**cu·bi·tus** [-təs] *s. anat.* a) 'Unterarm *m*, b) Ell(en)bogen *m*.

cuck·old ['kʌkəʊld] **I** *s.* Hahnrei *m*; **II** *v/t.* zum Hahnrei machen, *j-m* Hörner aufsetzen.

cuck·oo ['kʊku:] **I** *s.* **1.** *orn.* Kuckuck *m*; **2.** Kuckucksruf *m*; **3.** *sl.* ‚Heini' *m*; **II** *v/i.* **4.** ‚kuckuck' rufen; **III** *adj.* **5.** *sl.* ‚bekloppt'; ~ **clock** *s.* Kuckucksuhr *f*; '**~,flow·er** *s.* ⚘ Wiesenschaumkraut *n*.

cu·cum·ber ['kju:kʌmbə] *s.* Gurke *f*; → **cool** 2; ~ **tree** *s. e-e* amer. Ma'gnolie.

cu·cur·bit [kju:'kɜ:bɪt] *s.* ⚘ Kürbisgewächs *n*.

cud [kʌd] *s.* Klumpen *m*, 'wiedergekäutes Futter: **chew the ~** a) wiederkäuen, b) *fig.* überlegen, nachdenken.

cud·dle ['kʌdl] **I** *v/t.* hätscheln, ‚knuddeln', *a.* schmusen mit; **II** *v/i.* ~ **up** a) sich kuscheln *od.* schmiegen (**to** an *acc.*), b) sich (wohlig) zs.-kuscheln: ~ **up together** sich aneinanderkuscheln; **III** *s.* enge Um'armung, Lieb'kosung *f*; '**cud·dle·some** [-səm], '**cud·dly** [-lɪ] *adj.* ‚knudd(e)lig'.

cudg·el ['kʌdʒəl] **I** *s.* Knüttel *m*, Keule *f*: **take up the ~s for s.o.** für j-n eintreten, für j-n e-e Lanze brechen; **II** *v/t.* prügeln: ~ **one's brains** *fig.* sich den Kopf zerbrechen (**for** wegen, **about** über *acc.*).

cue¹ [kju:] **I** *s.* **1.** *thea. etc., a. fig.* Stichwort *n*; ♪ Einsatz *m*: ~ **card** *TV* ‚Neger' *m*; (**dead**) **on ~** (genau) aufs Stichwort, *fig.* wie gerufen; **2.** Wink *m*, Fingerzeig *m*: **give s.o. his ~** j-m die Worte in den Mund legen; **take the ~ from s.o.** sich nach j-m richten; **II** *v/t.* **3.** *j-m* das Stichwort *od.* (♪) den Einsatz geben: ~ **s.o. in** *fig.* j-n ins Bild setzen.

cue² [kju:] *s.* **1.** Queue *n*, 'Billardstock *m*; **2.** → **queue** 2.

cuff¹ [kʌf] *s.* **1.** Man'schette *f* (*a.* ⚙), Stulpe *f*; Ärmel- (*Am. a.* Hosen)aufschlag *m*: ~ **link** Manschettenknopf *m*; **off the ~** *Am.* F aus dem Handgelenk *od.* Stegreif; **on the ~** *Am.* F a) auf Pump, b) gratis; **2.** *pl.* Handschellen *pl.*

cuff² [kʌf] **I** *v/t.* schlagen, *a.* ohrfeigen; **II** *s.* Schlag *m*, Klaps *m*.

cui·rass [kwɪ'ræs] *s.* **1.** *hist.* 'Küraß *m*, Brustharnisch *m*; **2.** ⚕ a) Gipsverband *m* um Rumpf u. Hals, b) *ein* 'Sauerstoffappa,rat *m*; **3.** *zo.* Panzer *m*; **cui·ras·sier** [,kwɪrə'sɪə] *s.* ⚔ Küras'sier *m*.

cui·sine [kwi:'zi:n] *s.* Küche *f* (*Kochkunst*): **French ~**.

cul-de-sac [,kʊldə'sæk, 'kʌldəsæk] *pl.* **-sacs** (*Fr.*) *s.* Sackgasse *f* (*a. fig.*).

cu·li·nar·y ['kʌlɪnərɪ] *adj.* Koch…, Küchen…: ~ **art** Kochkunst *f*; ~ **herbs** Küchenkräuter.

cull [kʌl] **I** *v/t.* **1.** pflücken; **2.** *fig.* auslesen, -suchen; **II** *s.* **3.** *et.* (als minderwertig) Aussortiertes.

culm¹ [kʌlm] *s.* **1.** Kohlenstaub *m*, Grus *m*; **2.** *geol.* Kulm *m*, *n*.

culm² [kʌlm] *s.* (Gras)Halm *m*.

cul·mi·nate ['kʌlmɪneɪt] *v/i.* **1.** *ast.* kulminieren; **2.** *fig.* den Höhepunkt erreichen; gipfeln (**in** in *dat.*); **cul·mi·na·tion** [,kʌlmɪ'neɪʃn] *s.* **1.** *ast.* Kulmina'ti'on *f*; **2.** *bsd. fig.* Gipfel *m*, Höhepunkt *m*, höchster Stand.

cu·lottes [kju:'lɒts] *s. pl.* Hosenrock *m*.

cul·pa·bil·i·ty [,kʌlpə'bɪlətɪ] *s.* Sträflichkeit *f*, Schuld *f*; **cul·pa·ble** ['kʌlpəbl] *adj.* □ sträflich, schuldhaft; strafbar: ~ **negligence** ⚖ grobe Fahrlässigkeit.

cul·prit ['kʌlprɪt] *s.* **1.** Schuldige(r *m*) *f*, *a. iro.* Missetäter(in); **2.** ⚖ a) Angeklagte(r *m*) *f*, b) Täter(in).

cult [kʌlt] *s.* **1.** *eccl.* Kult(us) *m*; **2.** *fig.* Kult *m* (*Verehrung*, *a. dumme Mode*): ~ **figure** a) Idol *n*, b) Kultbild *n*.

cul·ti·va·ble ['kʌltɪvəbl] *adj.* kultivierbar (*a. fig.*).

cul·ti·vate ['kʌltɪveɪt] *v/t.* **1.** ✓ a) *Boden* bebauen, bestellen, kultivieren, b) *Pflanzen* züchten, ziehen, (an)bauen; **2.** *fig.* entwickeln, verfeinern, fort-, ausbilden, *Kunst etc.* fördern; **3.** zivilisieren; **4.** *Kunst etc.* pflegen, betreiben, sich widmen (*dat.*); **5.** sich befleißigen (*gen.*), Wert legen auf (*acc.*); **6.** a) *e-e Freundschaft etc.* pflegen, b) freundschaftlichen Verkehr suchen *od.* pflegen mit, sich *j-n* ‚warmhalten'; '**cul·ti·vat·ed** [-tɪd] *adj.* **1.** bebaut, kultiviert (*Land*); **2.** ✓ gezüchtet, Kultur…; **3.** kultiviert, gebildet; **cul·ti·va·tion** [,kʌltɪ'veɪʃn] *s.* **1.** Bearbeitung *f*, Bestellung *f*, Bebauung *f*, Urbarmachung *f*: **under ~** bebaut; **2.** Anbau *m*, Ackerbau *m*; **3.** Züchtung *f*; **4.** *fig.* (Aus)Bildung *f*, Pflege *f*; **5.** Kul'tur *f*, Kultiviertheit *f*, Bildung *f*; '**cul·ti·va·tor** [-tə] *s.* **1.** Landwirt *m*; **2.** Züchter *m*; **3.** ✓ Kulti'vator *m* (*Gerät*).

cul·tur·al ['kʌltʃərəl] *adj.* □ **1.** Kultur…, kultu'rell; **2.** → **cultivated** 2;

cul·ture ['kʌltʃə] *s.* **1.** → **cultivation** 1, 2, 4; **2.** a) (*Obst- etc.*)Anbau *m*, (*Pflanzen*)Zucht *f*, b) (*Tier*)Zucht *f*, Züchtung *f* (*a. biol.*), c) (*Pflanzen-*, *a. Bakterien- etc.*)Kul'tur *f*: ~ **medium** künstlicher Nährboden; ~ **pearl** Zuchtperle *f*; **3.** Kul'tur *f*: a) (Geistes)Bildung *f*, b) Kultiviertheit *f*: ~ **vulture** F Kulturbeflissene(r *m*) *f*; **4.** Kul'tur *f*: a) Kul'turkreis *m*, b) Kul'turform *f od.* -stufe *f*: ~ **lag** partielle Kulturrückständigkeit; ~ **shock** Kulturschock *m*; '**cul·tured** [-tʃəd] *adj.* **1.** kultiviert, gepflegt, gebildet; **2.** gezüchtet: ~ **pearl** Zuchtperle *f*.

cul·ver ['kʌlvə] *s.* Ringeltaube *f*.

cul·vert ['kʌlvət] *s.* ⚙ (über'wölbter) 'Abzugska,nal; 'unterirdische (Wasser-) Leitung; ('Bach),Durchlaß *m*.

cum [kʌm] (*Lat.*) *prp.* **1.** mit, samt; **2.** *Brit.* F und gleichzeitig, … in 'einem: **garage-~-workshop**.

cum·ber·some ['kʌmbəsəm] *adj.* □ **1.** lästig, beschwerlich, hinderlich; **2.** schwerfällig, klobig.

Cum·bri·an ['kʌmbrɪən] **I** *adj.* Cumberland betreffend; **II** *s.* Bewohner(in) von Cumberland.

cum·brous ['kʌmbrəs] → **cumbersome**.

cum·in ['kʌmɪn] *s.* Kreuzkümmel *m*.

cum·mer·bund ['kʌməbʌnd] *s.* *Mode*: Kummerbund *m*.

cu·mu·la·tive ['kju:mjʊlətɪv] *adj.* □ **1.** *a.* ✝ kumula'tiv: ~ **dividend**; **2.** sich (an)häufend *od.* steigernd *od.* summierend; anwachsend; **3.** zusätzlich, verstärkend; ~ **ev·i·dence** *s.* ⚖ verstärkender Beweis; ~ **vot·ing** *s.* Kumulieren *n* (*bei Wahlen*).

cu·mu·lus ['kju:mjʊləs] *pl.* **-li** [-laɪ] *s.* 'Kumulus *m*, Haufenwolke *f*.

cu·ne·ate ['kju:nɪɪt] *adj. bsd.* ⚘ keilförmig; '**cu·ne·i·form** [-ɪɪfɔ:m] **I** *adj.* **1.** keilförmig; **2.** Keilschrift *f*: ~ **characters** → 3; **II** *s.* **3.** Keilschrift *f*; '**cu·ni·form** [-ɪfɔ:m] → **cuneiform**.

cun·ning ['kʌnɪŋ] **I** *adj.* □ **1.** listig, schlau; **2.** geschickt, klug; **3.** *Am.* F niedlich, ‚süß'; **II** *s.* **4.** Schlauheit *f*, Gerissenheit *f*; **5.** Geschicktheit *f*.

cunt [kʌnt] *s.* V Fotze *f*.

cup [kʌp] **I** *s.* **1.** Tasse *f*, Schale *f*: ~ **and saucer** Ober- und Untertasse; **that's not my ~ of tea** *Brit.* F das ist nicht mein Fall; **2.** Kelch *m* (*a. eccl.*), Becher *m*; **3.** *sport* Cup *m*, Po'kal *m*: ~ **final** Pokalendspiel *n*; ~ **tie** Pokalspiel *n*, -paarung *f*; **4.** Weinbecher *m*: **be fond of the ~** gern (einen) trinken; **be in one's ~s** zu tief ins Glas geschaut haben; **5.** Bowle *f*; **6.** *et.* Schalenförmiges, *z.B.* Büstenhalterschale *f od. sport* 'Unterleibs-, Tiefschutz *m*; **7.** *fig.* Kelch *m* (*der Freude*, *des Leidens*): **drink the ~ of joy** den Becher der Freude leeren; **drain the ~ of sorrow to the dregs** den Kelch des Leidens bis auf die Neige leeren; **his ~ is full** das Maß s-r Leiden (*od.* Freuden) ist voll; **8.** → **cupful** 2; **II** *v/t.* **9.** *Kinn* in die (hohle) Hand legen; *Hand* wölben über (*acc.*): **cupped hand** hohle Hand; **10.** ⚕ schröpfen; '**~,bear·er** *s.* Mundschenk *m*.

cup·board ['kʌbəd] *s.* (*bsd.* Speise-, Geschirr)Schrank *m*; ~ **bed** *s.* Schrankbett *n*; ~ **love** *s.* berechnende Liebe.

cu·pel [kju:pəl] *s.* ⚗, ⚙ Ku'pelle *f*.

cup·ful ['kʌpfʊl] *pl.* **-fuls** *s.* **1.** *e-e* Tasse (-voll); **2.** *Am. Küche*: ½ Pint *n* (*0,235 l*).

Cu·pid ['kju:pɪd] *s.* **1.** *antiq.* 'Kupido *m*, 'Amor *m* (*a. fig. Liebe*); **2.** ♀ Amo'rette *f*.

cu·pid·i·ty [kju:'pɪdətɪ] *s.* (Hab)Gier, Begierde *f*, Begehrlichkeit *f*.

cu·po·la ['kju:pələ] *s.* **1.** Kuppel(dach *n*) *f*; **2.** *a.* ~ **furnace** ⚙ Ku'polofen *m*; **3.** ⚔, ⚓ Panzerturm *m*.

cu·pre·ous ['kju:prɪəs] *adj.* kupfern; kupferartig, -haltig; '**cu·pric** [-ɪk] *adj.* ⚗ Kupfer...; ˌ**cu·pro'nick·el** [ˌkju:prəʊ-] *s.* Kupfernickel *n*; '**cu·prous** [-rəs] → ***cupric***.

cur [kɜ:] *s.* **1.** Köter *m*; **2.** *fig.* ‚Hund' *m*, ‚Schwein' *n*.

cur·a·bil·i·ty [ˌkjuərə'bɪlətɪ] *s.* Heilbarkeit *f*; **cur·a·ble** ['kjʊərəbl] *adj.* heilbar (*a.* ⚖ *Rechtsmangel*).

cu·ra·cy ['kjʊərəsɪ] *s. eccl.* Amt *n* e-s → '**cu·rate** [-rət] *s. eccl.* Hilfsgeistliche(r) *m*, Vi'kar *m*, Ku'rat *m*.

cur·a·tive ['kjuərətɪv] **I** *adj.* heilend, Heil...; **II** *s.* Heilmittel *n*.

cu·ra·tor [ˌkjʊə'reɪtə] *s.* **1.** Mu'seumsdiˌrektor *m*; **2.** *Brit. univ.* (*Oxford*) Mitglied *n* des Kura'toriums; **3.** ⚖ *Scot.* Vormund *m*; **4.** ⚖ Verwalter *m*, Pfleger *m*; ˌ**cu'ra·tor·ship** [-ʃɪp] *s.* Amt *n od.* Amtszeit *f* e-s ***curator***.

curb [kɜ:b] **I** *s.* **1.** a) Kan'dare *f*, b) Kinnkette *f*; **2.** *fig.* Zaum *m*, Zügel(ung *f*) *m*: ***put a ~ on s.th.*** e-r Sache Zügel anlegen, et. zügeln; **3.** *Am.* → ***kerb***; **4.** *vet.* Spat *m*, Hasenfuß *m*; **II** *v/t.* **5.** an die Kan'dare nehmen; **6.** *fig.* zügeln, im Zaum halten; drosseln, einschränken; **~ bit** *s.* Kan'darenstange *f*; **~ mar·ket** *Am.* → ***kerb*** 3; '**~·stone** *Am.* → ***kerbstone***.

curd [kɜ:d] *s. oft pl.* geronnene *od.* dicke Milch, Quark *m*: **~ *cheese*** Quark-, Weißkäse *m*; **cur·dle** ['kɜ:dl] **I** *v/t. Milch* gerinnen lassen: **~ *one's blood*** einem das Blut in den Adern erstarren lassen; **II** *v/i.* gerinnen, dick werden (*Milch*): ***it made my blood ~*** das Blut erstarrte mir in den Adern; '**curd·y** [-dɪ] *adj.* geronnen; dick, flockig.

cure [kjʊə] **I** *s.* **1.** ⚕ Heilmittel *n*; *fig.* Mittel *n* Re'zept *n* (***for*** gegen); **2.** ⚕ Kur *f*, Heilverfahren *n*, Behandlung *f*; **3.** ⚕ Heilung *f*: ***past ~*** a) unheilbar krank, b) unheilbar (*Krankheit*), c) *fig.* hoffnungslos; **4.** *eccl.* a) *a.* **~ *of souls*** Seelsorge *f*, b) Pfar'rei *f*; **II** *v/t.* **5.** ⚕ *j-n* (***of*** von) *od. Krankheit od. fig. Übel* heilen (*a.* ⚖ *Rechtsmangel etc.*), kurieren: **~ *s.o. of lying*** j-m das Lügen abgewöhnen; **6.** haltbar machen: a) räuchern, b) einpökeln, -salzen, c) trocknen, d) beizen; **7.** ⚙ a) vulkanisieren, b) aushärten (*Kunststoffe*); '**~·all** *s.* All'heilmittel *n*.

cu·ret·tage [kjʊə'retɪdʒ] *s.* ⚕ Ausschabung *f*.

cur·few ['kɜ:fju:] *s.* **1.** *hist.* a) Abendläuten *n*, b) Abendglocke *f*; **2.** Sperrstunde *f*; **3.** ⚔ a) Ausgehverbot *n*, b) Zapfenstreich *m*.

cu·ri·a ['kjʊərɪə] *s. R.C.* 'Kurie *f*.

cu·rie ['kjʊərɪ] *s. phys.* Cu'rie *n*.

cu·ri·o ['kjʊərɪəʊ] *pl.* **-os** *s.* → ***curiosity*** 2 a *u.* c.

cu·ri·os·i·ty [ˌkjʊərɪ'ɒsətɪ] *s.* **1.** Neugier *f*; Wißbegierde *f*; **2.** Kuriosi'tät *f*: a) Rari'tät *f*, *pl.* Antiqui'täten, b) Sehenswürdigkeit *f*, c) Kuri'osum *n* (*Sache od. Person*); **~ shop** *s.* Antiqui'täten-, Rari'tätenladen *m*.

cu·ri·ous ['kjʊərɪəs] *adj.* □ **1.** neugierig; wißbegierig: ***I am ~ to know if*** ich möchte gern wissen, ob; **2.** kuri'os, seltsam, merkwürdig: ***~ly enough*** merkwürdigerweise; **3.** F komisch, wunderlich.

curl [kɜ:l] **I** *v/t.* **1.** *Haar* locken *od.* kräuseln; **2.** *Wasser* kräuseln; *Lippen* (verächtlich) schürzen; **3.** **~ *up*** zs.-rollen: **~ *o.s. up*** → 6 a; **II** *v/i.* **4.** sich locken *od.* kräuseln (*Haar*); **5.** wogen, sich wellen *od.* winden; **6.** **~ *up*** a) sich hochringeln (*Rauch*), b) sich zs.-rollen: **~ *up on the sofa*** es sich auf dem Sofa gemütlich machen; **7.** *sport* Curling spielen; **III** *s.* **8.** Locke *f*: ***in ~s*** gelockt; **9.** (Rauch-) Ring *m*, Kringel *m*; **10.** Windung *f*; **11.** Kräuseln *n der Lippen*; **12.** ⚘ Kräuselkrankheit *f*; **curled** [-ld] → ***curly***; '**curl·er** [-lə] *s.* **1.** Lockenwickel *m*; **2.** *sport* Curlingspieler *m*.

cur·lew ['kɜ:lju:] *s.* Brachvogel *m*.

curl·i·cue ['kɜ:lɪkju:] *s.* Schnörkel *m*.

curl·ing ['kɜ:lɪŋ] *s.* **1.** Kräuseln *n*, Ringeln *n*; **2.** *sport* Curling *n*: **~ *stone*** Curlingstein *m*; **3.** ⚙ bördeln; **~ i·rons**, **~ tongs** *s. pl.* (Locken)Brennschere *f*.

'**curlˌpa·per** *s.* Pa'pierhaarwickel *m*.

curl·y ['kɜ:lɪ] *adj.* **1.** lockig, kraus, gekräuselt, **2.** wellig; gewunden; '**~-head**, '**~-pate** *s.* F Locken- *od.* Krauskopf *m* (*Person*).

cur·mudg·eon [kɜ:'mʌdʒən] *s.* Brummbär *m*.

cur·rant ['kʌrənt] *s.* **1.** Ko'rinthe *f*; **2.** ***red*** (***white***, ***black***) **~** rote (weiße, schwarze) Jo'hannisbeere.

cur·ren·cy ['kʌrənsɪ] *s.* **1.** 'Umlauf *m*, Zirkulati'on *f*: ***give ~ to*** *Gerücht etc.* in Umlauf setzen; **2.** a) (allgemeine) Geltung, (Allge'mein)Gültigkeit *f*, b) Gebräuchlichkeit *f*, Geläufigkeit *f*, c) Verbreitung *f*; **3.** ✝ a) Währung *f*, Va'luta *f*; → ***foreign*** 1, ***hard currency***, b) Zahlungsmittel *n od. pl.*, c) 'Geldˌumlauf *m*, d) 'umlaufendes Geld, e) Laufzeit *f* (*Wechsel*, *Vertrag*); **~ ac·count** *s.* ✝ 'Währungs-, De'visenˌkonto *n*; **~ bill** *s.* De'visenwechsel *m*; **~ bond** *s.* Fremdwährungsschuldverschreibung *f*; **~ re·form** *s.* 'WährungsreˌformJ *f*.

cur·rent ['kʌrənt] **I** *adj.* □ → ***currently***; **1.** laufend (*Jahr*, *Konto*, *Unkosten etc.*); **2.** gegenwärtig, jetzig, aktu'ell: **~ *events*** Tagesereignisse; **~ *price*** ✝ Tagespreis *m*; **3.** 'umlaufend, kursierend (*Geld*, *Gerücht etc.*); **4.** a) allgemein bekannt *od.* verbreitet, b) üblich, geläufig, gebräuchlich: ***not in ~ use*** nicht allgemein üblich, c) allgemein gültig *od.* anerkannt; **5.** ✝ a) (markt)gängig (*Ware*), b) gültig (*Geld*), c) verkehrsfähig, d) → 3; **II** *s.* **6.** Strömung *f*, Strom *m* (*beide a. fig.*): ***against the ~*** gegen den Strom; **~ *of air*** Luftstrom; **7.** *fig.* a) Trend *m*, Ten'denz *f*, b) (Ver)Lauf *m*, Gang *m*; **8.** ϟ Strom *m*; **~ ac·count** *s.* ✝ laufendes Konto, Girokonto *n*; **~ coin** *s.* gängige Münze (*a. fig.*); **~ ex·change** *s.* (***at the ~*** zum) Tageskurs *m*.

cur·rent·ly ['kʌrəntlɪ] *adv.* **1.** jetzt, zur Zeit, gegenwärtig; **2.** *fig.* fließend.

cur·rent me·ter *s.* ϟ Stromzähler *m*; **~ mon·ey** *s.* ✝ 'umlaufendes Geld.

cur·ric·u·lum [kə'rɪkjʊləm] *pl.* **-lums**, **-la** [-lə] *s.* Lehr-, Studienplan *m*; **~ vi·tae** ['vaɪti:] *s.* Lebenslauf *m*.

cur·ri·er ['kʌrɪə] *s.* Lederzurichter *m*.

cur·ry¹ ['kʌrɪ] **I** *s.* Curry(gericht *n*) *m*, *n*: **~ *powder*** Currypulver *n*; **II** *v/t.* mit Curry(soße) zubereiten: ***curried chicken*** Curryhuhn *n*.

cur·ry² ['kʌrɪ] *v/t.* **1.** *Pferd* striegeln; **2.** *Leder* zurichten; **3.** verprügeln; **4.** **~ *favo(u)r with s.o.*** sich bei j-m lieb Kind machen (wollen); '**~·comb** *s.* Striegel *m*.

curse [kɜ:s] **I** *s.* **1.** Fluch(wort *n*) *m*; Verwünschung *f*; **2.** *eccl.* Bann(fluch) *m*; Verdammnis *f*; **3.** Fluch *m*, Unglück *n* (***to*** für); **4.** ***the ~*** F die ‚Tage' (*der Frau*); **II** *v/t.* **5.** verfluchen, verwünschen, verdammen: **~ *him!*** der Teufel soll ihn holen!; **6.** fluchen auf (*acc.*), beschimpfen; **7.** *pass.* ***be ~d with s.th.*** mit et. gestraft *od.* geplagt sein; **III** *v/i.* **8.** fluchen, Flüche ausstoßen; '**curs·ed** [-sɪd] *adj.* □ *a.* F verflucht, verdammt, verwünscht.

cur·sive ['kɜ:sɪv] **I** *adj.* kur'siv: **~ *characters*** → **II** *s. typ.* Schreibschrift *f*.

cur·sor ['kɜ:rsə] *s.* ∡, ⚙ Schieber *m*, ⚙ *a.* Zeiger *m*; *Computer:* Positi'onsanzeiger *m*.

cur·so·ri·ness ['kɜ:sərɪnɪs] *s.* Flüchtigkeit *f*, Oberflächlichkeit *f*; **cur·so·ry** ['kɜ:sərɪ] *adj.* □ flüchtig, oberflächlich.

curst [kɜ:st] *obs. pret. u. p.p. von* ***curse***.

curt [kɜ:t] *adj.* □ **1.** kurz(gefaßt), knapp; **2.** (***with***) barsch, schroff (gegen), kurz angebunden (mit).

cur·tail [kɜ:'teɪl] *v/t.* **1.** (ab-, ver)kürzen; **2.** *Ausgaben etc.* kürzen, *a. Rechte* be-, einschränken, beschneiden; *Preise etc.* her'absetzen; **cur'tail·ment** [-mənt] *s.* **1.** (Ab-, Ver)Kürzung *f*; **2.** Kürzung *f*, Beschneidung *f*; Beschränkung *f*.

cur·tain ['kɜ:tn] **I** *s.* **1.** Vorhang *m* (*a. fig.*), Gar'dine *f*: ***draw the ~(s)*** den Vorhang (die Gardinen) zuziehen; ***draw the ~ over s.th.*** *fig.* et. begraben; ***lift the ~*** *fig.* den Schleier lüften; ***behind the ~*** hinter den Kulissen; **~ *of fire*** ⚔ Feuervorhang; **~ *of rain*** Regenwand *f*; **2.** *thea.* a) Vorhang *m*, b) Aktschluß *m*: ***the ~ rises*** der Vorhang geht auf; ***the ~ falls*** der Vorhang fällt (*a. fig.*); ***it's ~s for him*** F es ist aus mit ihm; ***now it's ~s!*** F jetzt ist der Ofen aus!, aus ist's!; **3.** *thea.* Her'vorruf *m*: ***take ten ~s*** zehn Vorhänge haben; **II** *v/t.* **4.** mit Vorhängen versehen; **~ call** → ***curtain*** 3; **~ fall** *s. thea.* Fallen *n* des Vorhanges; **~ lec·ture** *s.* Gar'dinenpredigt *f*; **~ rais·er** *s. thea.* **1.** kurzes Vorspiel; **2.** *fig.* Vorspiel *n*, Auftakt (***to*** zu); '**~-wall** *s.* △ **1.** Blendwand; **2.** Zwischenwand *f*.

curt·s(e)y ['kɜ:tsɪ] **I** *s.* Knicks *m*: ***drop a ~*** → **II** *v/i.* e-n Knicks machen, knicksen (***to*** vor *dat.*).

cur·va·ceous [kɜ:'veɪʃəs] *adj.* F ‚kurvenreich' (*Frau*); **cur·va·ture** ['kɜ:vətʃə] *s.* Krümmung *f* (*a.* ∡, *geol.*): **~ *of the spine*** ⚕ Rückgratverkrümmung *f*.

curve [kɜ:v] **I** *s.* **1.** Kurve *f* (*a.* ∡), Krümmung *f*, Biegung *f*, Bogen *m*; **2.** *pl.* F ‚Kurven' *pl.*, Rundungen *pl.*; **II** *v/t.* **3.** biegen, krümmen; **III** *v/i.* **4.** sich biegen *od.* wölben *od.* krümmen; **curved** [-vd] *adj.* gekrümmt, gebogen; krumm.

cur·vet [kɜ:'vet] **I** *s. Reitkunst:* Kur'bette *f*, Bogensprung *m*; **II** *v/i.* kurbettieren.

cur·vi·lin·e·ar [ˌkɜ:vɪ'lɪnɪə] *adj.* krummlinig (begrenzt).

cush·ion ['kʊʃn] **I** *s.* **1.** Kissen *n*, Polster

n (*a. fig.*); **2.** Wulst *m* (*für die Frisur*); **3.** Bande *f* (*Billard*); **4.** *vet.* Strahl *m* (*Pferdehuf*); **5.** ⚙ Puffer *m*, Dämpfer *m*; **6.** *phys.* ⚙ Luftkissen *n*; **II** *v/t.* **7.** durch Kissen schützen, polstern (*a. fig.*); **8.** *Stoß*, *Fall* dämpfen *od.* auffangen; **9.** weich betten; **10.** ⚙ abfedern; **'~·craft** *s.* Luftkissenfahrzeug(e *pl.*) *n*.

cush·ioned ['kʊʃənd] *adj.* **1.** gepolstert, Polster...; **2.** *fig.* bequem, behaglich; **3.** ⚙ stoßgedämpft.

cush·y ['kʊʃɪ] *adj. Brit. sl.* ‚gemütlich', bequem, angenehm: **~ *job***.

cusp [kʌsp] *s.* **1.** Spitze *f*; **2.** ⩓ Scheitelpunkt *m* (*Kurve*); **3.** *ast.* Horn *n* (*Halbmond*); **4.** ⚠ Nase *f* (*gotisches Maßwerk*); **cusped** [-pt], **'cus·pi·dal** [-pɪdl] *adj.* spitz (zulaufend).

cus·pi·dor ['kʌspɪdɔ:] *s. Am.* **1.** Spucknapf *m*; **2.** ✓ Speitüte *f*.

cuss [kʌs] *s.* F **1.** Fluch *m*: **~ *word*** Fluch *m*, Schimpfwort *n*; → ***tinker*** 1; **2.** Kerl *m*; **'cuss·ed** [-sɪd] *adj.* F **1.** verflucht, -flixt; **2.** boshaft, gemein; **'cuss·ed·ness** [-sɪdnɪs] *s.* F Bosheit *f*, Gemeinheit *f*, Tücke *f*.

cus·tard ['kʌstəd] *s.* Eiercreme *f*: (***running***) **~** Vanillesoße *f*; **'~-ap·ple** *s.* ⚘ Zimtapfel *m*; **~ pow·der** *s. ein* 'Pudding,pulver *n*; **~ pie** *s.* **1.** Sahnetorte *f*; **2.** *thea.* F Kla'mauk(komödie *f*) *m*.

cus·to·di·an [kʌ'stəʊdjən] *s.* **1.** Aufseher *m*, Wächter *m*, Hüter *m*; **2.** (⚖ Vermögens)Verwalter *m*, ⚖ *a.* Verwahrer *m*, *Am. a.* Vormund *m*; **cus·to·dy** ['kʌstədɪ] *s.* **1.** Aufsicht *f* (***of*** über *acc.*), (Ob)Hut *f*, Schutz *m*; **2.** Verwahrung *f*; Verwaltung *f*; **3.** ⚖ a) Gewahrsam *m*, Haft *f*: ***protective* ~** Schutzhaft *f*; ***take into* ~** verhaften, in Gewahrsam nehmen, b) Gewahrsam *m* (*tatsächlicher Besitz*), c) Sorgerecht *n*; **4.** ✝ *Am.* De'pot *n*.

cus·tom ['kʌstəm] **I** *s.* **1.** Brauch *m*, Gewohnheit *f*, Sitte *f*; *coll.* Sitten u. Gebräuche *pl.*, *pl.* Brauchtum *n*; **2.** ⚖ Gewohnheitsrecht *n*; **3.** ✝ Kundschaft *f*, Kunden(kreis *m*) *pl.*: ***draw*** (*od.* ***get***) ***a lot of* ~ *from*** viel Geschäft machen mit; ***take one's custom elsewhere*** anderswo Kunde werden; ***withdraw one's* ~ *from*** s-e Kundschaft entziehen (*dat.*); **4.** *pl.* a) Zoll *m*, b) Zoll(behörde *f*) *m*, Zollamt *n*; **II** *adj.* **5.** *Am.* a) auf Bestellung *od.* nach Maß arbeitend: **~ *tailor*** Maßschneider *m*, b) → ***custom-made***: **~*-built*** einzeln (*od.* nach Kundenangaben) angefertigt; **~ *shoes*** Maßschuhe; **'cus·tom·ar·i·ly** [-mərɪlɪ] *adv.* üblicherweise, herkömmlicherweise; **'cus·tom·ar·y** [-mərɪ] *adj.* □ **1.** gebräuchlich, herkömmlich, üblich, gewohnt, Gewohnheits...; **2.** ⚖ gewohnheitsrechtlich; **'cus·tom·er** [-mə] *s.* **1.** Kunde *m*, Kundin *f*; Abnehmer(in), Käufer(in): **~ *country*** Abnehmerland *n*; **~*'s check*** *Am.* Barscheck *m*; ***regular* ~** Stammkunde *m od.* -gast *m*; **2.** F Bursche *m*, ‚Kunde' *m*: ***queer* ~** komischer Kauz; ***ugly* ~** übler Kunde; **'cus·tom·ize** [-maɪz] *v/t.* **1.** ✝ auf den Kundenbedarf zuschneiden; **2.** *Auto etc.* individu'ell herrichten.

'cus·tom|·house *s.* Zollamt *n*; **'~-made** *adj.* nach Maß *od.* auf Bestellung *od.* spezi'ell angefertigt, Maß...

cus·toms| clear·ance *s.* Zollabfertigung *f*; **~ dec·la·ra·tion** *s.* 'Zolldeklarati,on *f*, -erklärung *f*; **~ ex·am·i·na·tion**, **~ in·spec·tion** *s.* 'Zollkon,trolle *f*; **~ of·fi·cer** *s.* Zollbeamte(r) *m*; **~ un·ion** *s.* 'Zollverein *m*, -uni,on *f*; **~ war·rant** *s.* Zollauslieferungsschein *m*; **~ ware·house** *s.* Zollager *n*.

cut [kʌt] **I** *s.* **1.** Schnitt *m*: ***a* ~ *above*** e-e Stufe besser als; → ***haircut***; **2.** Schnittwunde *f*; **3.** Hieb *m*, Schlag *m*: **~ *and thrust*** a) *Fechten*: Hieb u. Stoß *m* (*od.* Stich *m*), b) *fig.* (feindseliges) Hin u. Her, ‚Schlagabtausch' *m*; **4.** Schnitte *f*, Stück *n* (*bsd. Fleisch*); Ab-, Anschnitt *m*; Schur *f* (*Wolle*); Schlag *m* (*Holzfällen*); ✓ Mahd *f* (*Gras*); **5.** F (An)Teil *m*: ***my* ~ *is 10%***; **6.** (Zu)Schnitt *m*, Fas'son *f* (*bsd. Kleidung*); *fig.* Art *f*, Schlag *m*; **7.** *typ.* a) Druckstock *m*, b) Holzschnitt *m*, (Kupfer)Stich *m*, c) Kli'schee *n*; **8.** Schnitt *m*, Schliff *m* (*Edelstein*); **9.** Gesichtsschnitt *m*; **10.** Beschneidung *f*, Kürzung *f*, Streichung *f*, Abzug *m*, Abstrich *m* (*Preis*, *Lohn*, *a. Text etc.*): ***power* ~** ⚡ Stromsperre *f*; → ***short cut***; **11.** ⚙, 🚂 *etc.* Einschnitt *m*, Kerbe *f*, Graben *m*; **12.** a) Stich *m*, Bosheit *f*, b) Grußverweigerung *f*: ***give s.o. the* ~ *direct*** j-n ostentativ schneiden; **13.** *Kartenspiel*: Abheben *n*; **14.** *Tennis*: Schnitt *m*; **15.** *Film etc.*: Schnitt *m*, (scharfe) Über'blendung; **II** *adj.* **16.** ge-, beschnitten, behauen: **~ *flowers*** Schnittblumen; **~ *glass*** geschliffenes Glas, Kristall *n*; **~ *prices*** herabgesetzte Preise; ***well-~ features*** feingeschnittene Züge; **~ *and dried*** fix u. fertig, schablonenhaft; ***badly* ~ *about*** arg zugerichtet; **III** *v/t.* [*irr.*] **17.** (ab-, be-, 'durch-, zer)schneiden: **~ *one's finger*** sich in den Finger schneiden; **~ *one's nails*** sich die Nägel schneiden; **~ *a book*** ein Buch aufschneiden; **~ *a joint*** e-n Braten vorschneiden, zerlegen; **~ *to pieces*** zerstückeln; **18.** *Hecke* beschneiden, stutzen; **19.** *Gras*, *Korn* mähen; *Baum* fällen; **20.** schlagen; *Kohlen* hauen; *Weg* aushauen, -graben; *Holz* hacken; *Graben* stechen; *Tunnel* bohren: ***to* ~ *one's way*** sich e-n Weg bahnen (*a. fig.*); **21.** *Tier* verschneiden, kastrieren: **~ *horse*** Wallach *m*; **22.** *Kleid* zuschneiden; *et.* zu'rechtschneiden; *Stein* behauen; *Glas*, *Edelstein* schleifen: **~ *it fine*** *fig.* a) es (zu) knapp bemessen, b) es gerade noch schaffen; **23.** einschneiden, -ritzen, schnitzen; **24.** *Tennis*: *Ball* schneiden; **25.** *Text etc.*, *a. Betrag* beschneiden, kürzen, zs.-streichen; *sport Rekord* brechen; **26.** *Film*: a) schneiden, über'blenden: **~ *to*** hinüberblenden zu, b) abbrechen; **27.** verdünnen, verwässern; **28.** *fig. j-n* schneiden, nicht grüßen: **~ *s.o. dead*** j-n völlig ignorieren; **29.** *fig.* schneiden (*Wind*); verletzen, kränken (*Worte*); **30.** *Verbindung* abbrechen, aufgeben; fernbleiben von, *Vorlesung* ‚schwänzen'; **31.** *Zahn* bekommen; **32.** *Schlüssel* anfertigen; **33.** *Spielkarten* abheben; **IV** *v/i.* [*irr.*] **34.** schneiden (*a. fig.*), hauen: ***it* ~*s both ways*** es ist ein zweischneidiges Schwert; **~ *and come again*** greifen Sie tüchtig zu! (*beim Essen*); ***it* ~*s into his time*** es kostet ihn Zeit; **~ *into a conversation*** in e-e Unterhaltung eingreifen; **35.** sich schneiden lassen; **36.** F ‚abhauen': **~ *and run*** Reißaus nehmen; **37.** (*in der Schule etc.*) ‚schwänzen'; **38.** *Kartenspiel*: abheben; **39.** *sport* (den Ball) schneiden; **40.** **~ *across*** a) quer durch *et.* gehen, b) *fig.* hin'ausgehen über (*acc.*), c) *fig.* wider'sprechen, d) *fig. Am.* einbeziehen;

Zssgn mit adv.:

cut| a·long *v/i.* F sich auf die Beine machen; **~ back I** *v/t.* beschneiden, stutzen, *fig. a.* kürzen, zs.-streichen, verringern; **II** *v/i.* (zu)'rückblenden (***to*** auf *acc.*) (*Film*, *Roman etc.*); **~ down I** *v/t.* **1.** zerschneiden; **2.** *Baum* fällen, *j-n a.* niederschlagen; **3.** *fig.* a) → ***cut back*** I, b) drosseln; **II** *v/i.* **4.** **~ *on s.th.*** et. einschränken; **~ in I** *v/t.* **1.** ⚙ einschalten (*a. Filmszene*); **2.** *j-n* beteiligen (***on*** an *dat.*); **II** *v/i.* **3.** unter'brechen, sich einmengen *od.* einschalten (*a. teleph.*); **4.** einspringen; **5.** *mot.* einscheren; **6.** F (*beim Tanzen*) abklatschen; **~ loose I** *v/t.* **1.** trennen, losmachen; **2.** ***cut o.s. loose*** sich trennen *od.* lossagen; **II** *v/i.* **3.** sich gehenlassen; **4.** sich lossagen; **5.** *sl.* a) loslegen (***with*** mit), b) ‚auf den Putz hauen'; **~ off** *v/t.* **1.** abschneiden, -schlagen, -hauen: **~ *s.o.'s head*** j-n köpfen; **2.** unter'brechen, trennen; **3.** *Strom etc.* absperren, abdrehen; **4.** *Debatte* beenden; **5.** niederschlagen, da'hinraffen; vernichten; **6.** ***cut s.o. off with a shilling*** j-n enterben; **~ out I** *v/t.* **1.** aus-, zuschneiden: **~ *for a job*** wie geschaffen für e-n Posten; → ***work*** 1; **2.** *j-n* ausstechen; verdrängen; **3.** *Am. sl.* unter'lassen: ***cut it out!*** laß den Quatsch!; **4.** aufgeben; entfernen; *Am. Tier* von der Herde absondern; **5.** ⚙ ausschalten; **II** *v/i.* **6.** ⚙ sich ausschalten, aussetzen; **7.** ausscheren (*Fahrzeug*); **8.** *Kartenspiel*: ausscheiden; **~ short** *v/t.* **1.** unter'brechen; *j-m* ins Wort fallen; **2.** plötzlich beenden, kürzen; *es* kurz machen; **~ un·der** *v/t.* ✝ *j-n* unter'bieten; **~ up I** *v/t.* **1.** in Stücke schneiden, zerhauen; zerlegen; **2.** vernichten; **3.** F ‚verreißen', her'untermachen; **4.** tief betrüben, aufregen: ***be badly* ~** ganz ‚kaputt' sein; **II** *v/i.* **5.** *Brit.* F **~ *fat*** (*od.* ***rich***) reich sterben; **6.** F ‚den wilden Mann' spielen: **~ *rough*** ‚massiv' werden; **7.** *Am. sl.* a) ‚angeben', b) Unsinn treiben.

,cut-and-'dried *adj.* **1.** (fix und) fertig, fest(gelegt); **2.** scha'blonenhaft.

cu·ta·ne·ous [kju:'teɪnjəs] *adj.* ⚕ Haut...: **~ *eruption*** Hautausschlag *m*.

'cut·a·way I *s.* Cut(away) *m*; **II** *adj.* ⚙ Schnitt...(*-modell etc.*): **~ *view*** Ausschnitt(darstellung *f*) *m*.

'cut·back *s.* **1.** *Film*: Rückblende *f*; **2.** Kürzung *f*, Beschneidung *f*, Verringerung *f*.

cute [kju:t] *adj.* □ F **1.** schlau, clever; **2.** *Am.* niedlich, ‚süß'.

cu·ti·cle ['kju:tɪkl] *s.* ⚘, *anat.* Oberhaut *f*, Epi'dermis *f*; Nagelhaut *f*: **~ *scissors*** Hautschere *f*.

cu·tie ['kju:tɪ] *s. Am. sl.* ‚dufte Biene' (*Mädchen*).

'cut-in *s. Film*: a) Einschnitt(szene *f*) *m*, b) *a. Zeitung*: Zwischentitel *m*.

cu·tis ['kju:tɪs] *s. anat.* 'Kutis *f*, Lederhaut *f*.

cut·lass ['kʌtləs] *s.* **1.** ⚓ *hist.* Entermesser *n*; **2.** Ma'chete *f*.

cut·ler ['kʌtlə] *s.* Messerschmied *m*; '**cut·ler·y** [-ərɪ] *s.* **1.** Messerwaren *pl.*; **2.** *coll.* Eßbesteck(e *pl.*) *n*.

cut·let ['kʌtlɪt] *s.* Schnitzel *n*.

'**cut|·off** *s.* **1.** ⚙ (Ab)Sperrung *f*; **2.** ⚙, ϟ Ab-, Ausschaltung *f* (*a. Vorrichtung*); **3.** *Am.* Abkürzung(sweg *m*) *f*; '**~·out** *s.* **1.** Ausschnitt *m*; 'Ausschneidefi,gur *f*; **2.** ϟ a) Ausschalter *m*, Sicherung *f*; **3.** *mot.* Auspuffklappe *f*; '**~·purse** *s.* Taschendieb(in); '**~-rate** *adj.* ✝ ermäßigt, her'abgesetzt, billig (*a. fig.*).

cut·ter ['kʌtə] *s.* **1.** Schneidende(r) *m*; (Blech-, Holz)Schneider *m* (Stein)Hauer *m*; (Glas-, Dia'mant)Schleifer *m*; **2.** Zuschneider *m*; **3.** ⚙ Schneidewerkzeug *n*; **4.** *Film*: Cutter(in); **5.** *Küche*: Ausstechform *f*; **6.** ⚓ a) Kutter *m*, b) Beiboot *n*, c) *Am.* Küstenwachboot *n*.

'**cut·throat** **I** *s.* **1.** Mörder *m*; **2.** *fig.* Halsabschneider *m*; **II** *adj.* **3.** *fig.* mörderisch, halsabschneiderisch: **~ *competition***.

cut·ting ['kʌtɪŋ] **I** *s.* **1.** Schneiden *n*; Zuschneiden *n*; **2.** *bsd.* 🚂 Einschnitt *m*, 'Durchstich *m*; **3.** ⚙ a) Fräsen *n*, spanabhebende Bearbeitung, b) Kerbe *f*, Schlitz *m*, c) *pl.* Späne *pl.*, Schnitzel *pl.*; **4.** (Zeitungs)Ausschnitt *m*; **5.** *pl.* Schnitzel *pl.*, Abfälle *pl.*; **6.** ⚘ Ableger *m*, Steckling *m*; **7.** *Film*: Schnitt *m*; **II** *adj.* □ **8.** schneidend, Schneid(e)...; **9.** *fig.* schneidend (*Wind*), scharf (*Worte*), beißend (*Hohn*); **~ die** *s.* ⚙ Schneideisen *n*, 'Stanzscha,blone *f*; **~ edge** *s.* Schneide *f*; **~ nip·pers** *s. pl.* Kneifzange *f*; **~ torch** *s.* ⚙ Schneidbrenner *m*.

cut·tle ['kʌtl], '**~·fish** *s. zo.* (Gemeiner) Tintenfisch.

cy·a·nate ['saɪəneɪt] *s.* ⚗ Zya'nat *n*; **cy·an·ic** [saɪ'ænɪk] *adj.* Zyan...: **~ *acid*** Zyansäure *f*; '**cy·a·nide** [-naɪd] *s.* Zya'nid *n*: **~ *of potassium*** (*od.* ***potash***) Zyankali *n*; **cy·an·o·gen** [saɪ'ænədʒɪn] *s.* Zy'an *n*.

cy·ber·net·ics [,saɪbə'netɪks] *s. pl.* (*sg. konstr.*) Kyber'netik *f*; ,**cy·ber'net·ist** [-ɪst] *s.* Kyber'netiker *m*.

cyc·la·men ['sɪkləmən] *s.* ⚘ Alpenveilchen *n*.

cy·cle ['saɪkl] **I** *s.* **1.** 'Zyklus *m*, Kreis (-lauf) *m*, 'Umlauf *m*: ***lunar* ~** Mondzyklus; → ***business cycle***; ***come full* ~** a) e-n ganzen Kreislauf beschreiben, b) *fig.* zum Anfangspunkt zurückkehren; **2.** *a.* ϟ, *phys.* Peri'ode *f*: ***in* ~*s*** periodisch wiederkehrend; **~*s per second*** (*abbr.* ***cps***) Hertz; **3.** (Gedicht-, Sagen)Kreis *m*; **4.** Folge *f*, Reihe *f*, 'Serie *f*, 'Zyklus *m*; **5.** ⚙ 'Kreispro,zeß *m*; Arbeitsgang *m*; **6.** *mot.* Takt *m*: ***four-stroke* ~** Viertakt; ***four-~ engine*** Viertaktmotor *m*; **7.** a) Fahrrad *n*, b) Motorrad *n*, c) Dreirad *n*; **II** *v/i.* **8.** radfahren, radeln; **III** *v/t.* **9.** e-n Kreislauf 'durchmachen lassen; **10.** *a.* ⚙ peri'odisch wieder'holen; '**cy·clic**, '**cy·cli·cal** [-lɪk(l)] *adj.* □ **1.** zyklisch, peri'odisch, kreisläufig; **2.** ✝ konjunk'turbedingt, -po,litisch, Konjunktur...; '**cy·cling** [-lɪŋ] *s.* **1.** Radfahren *n*: **~ *tour*** Radtour *f*; **2.** Rad(renn)sport *m*; '**cy·clist** [-lɪst] *s.* Radfahrer(in).

cy·clo-cross [,saɪklə'krɒs] *s.* *Radsport*: Querfeld'einfahren *n*.

cy·clom·e·ter [saɪ'klɒmɪtə] *s.* **1.** ⚙ Wegmesser *m*; **2.** ⩚ Zyklo'meter *m*.

cy·cloid ['saɪklɔɪd] **I** *s.* ⩚ Zyklo'ide *f*; **II** *adj. allg.* zyklo'id.

cy·clone ['saɪkləʊn] *s.* **1.** *meteor.* a) Zy'klon *m*, Wirbelsturm *m*, b) Zy'klone *f*, Tief(druckgebiet) *n*; **2.** *fig.* Or'kan *m*.

cy·clo·p(a)e·di·a [,saɪkləʊ'pi:djə] → ***encyclop(a)edia***.

Cy·clo·pe·an [saɪ'kləʊpjən] *adj.* zy'klopisch, riesig; **Cy·clops** ['saɪklɒps] *pl.* **Cy·clo·pes** [saɪ'kləʊpi:z] *s.* Zy'klop *m*.

cy·clo·tron ['saɪklətrɒn] *s.* *Kernphysik*: 'Zyklotron *n*.

cy·der → ***cider***.

cyg·net ['sɪgnɪt] *s.* junger Schwan.

cyl·in·der ['sɪlɪndə] *s.* **1.** ⩚, ⚙, *typ.* Zy'linder *m*, Walze *f*: ***six-~ car*** Sechszylinderwagen *m*; **2.** ⚙ Trommel *f*, Rolle *f*; 'Meß-, 'Dampfzy,linder *m*; Gas-, Stahlflasche *f*; Stiefel *m* (*Pumpe*); **~ block** *s. mot.* Zy'linderblock *m*; **~ bore** *s.* Zy'linderbohrung *f*; **~ es·cape·ment** *s.* Zy'linderhemmung *f* (*Uhr*); **~ head** *s.* Zy'linderkopf *m*; **~ jack·et** *s.* Zy'lindermantel *m*; **~ print·ing** *s. typ.* Walzendruck *m*.

cy·lin·dri·cal [sɪ'lɪndrɪkl] *adj.* zy'lindrisch, Zylinder...

cym·bal ['sɪmbl] *s.* ♪ **1.** Becken *n*; **2.** 'Zimbel *f*; '**cym·bal·ist** [-bəlɪst] *s.* Bekkenschläger *m*; '**cym·ba·lo** [-bələʊ] *pl.* **-los** *s.* ♪ Hackbrett *n*.

Cym·ric ['kɪmrɪk] **I** *adj.* kymrisch, *bsd.* wa'lisisch; **II** *s. ling.* Kymrisch *n*.

cyn·ic ['sɪnɪk] *s.* **1.** Zyniker *m*, bissiger Spötter; **2.** ♎ *antiq. phls.* Kyniker *m*; '**cyn·i·cal** [-kl] *adj.* □ zynisch; '**cyn·i·cism** [-ɪsɪzəm] *s.* **1.** Zy'nismus *m*; **2.** zynische Bemerkung.

cy·no·sure ['sɪnəzjʊə] *s.* **1.** *fig.* Anziehungspunkt *m*, Gegenstand *m* der Bewunderung; **2.** *fig.* Leitstern *m*; **3.** ♎ *ast.* a) Kleiner Bär, b) Po'larstern *m*.

cy·pher → ***cipher***.

cy·press ['saɪprɪs] *s.* Zy'presse *f*.

Cyp·ri·ote ['sɪprɪəʊt], '**Cyp·ri·ot** [-ɪət] **I** *s.* Zypri'ot(in), Zyprer(in); **II** *adj.* zyprisch.

Cy·ril·lic [sɪ'rɪlɪk] *adj.* ky'rillisch.

cyst [sɪst] *s.* **1.** ⚕ Zyste *f*; **2.** Kapsel *f*, Hülle *f*; '**cyst·ic** [-tɪk] *adj.* **1.** ⚕ zystisch; **2.** *anat.* Blasen...; **cys·ti·tis** [sɪs'taɪtɪs] *s.* ⚕ Blasenentzündung *f*; '**cys·to·scope** [-təskəʊp] *s.* ⚕ Blasenspiegel *m*; **cys·tos·co·py** [sɪs'tɒskəpɪ] *s.* ⚕ Blasenspiegelung *f*.

cy·to·blast ['saɪtəʊblæst] *s. biol.* Zyto'blast *m*, Zellkern *m*.

cy·tol·o·gy [saɪ'tɒlədʒɪ] *s. biol.* Zytolo'gie *f*, Zellenlehre *f*.

czar [zɑ:] *s.* Zar *m*.

czar·das ['tʃɑ:dæʃ] *s.* 'Csárdás *m*.

czar·e·vitch ['zɑ:rəvɪtʃ] *s.* Za'rewitsch *m*; **cza·ri·na** [zɑ:'ri:nə] *s.* Zarin *f*; '**czar·ism** [-rɪzəm] *s.* Zarentum *n*; '**czar·ist** [-rɪst], **czar·is·tic** [zɑ:'rɪstɪk] *adj.* za'ristisch; **cza·rit·za** [zɑ:'rɪtsə] → ***czarina***.

Czech [tʃek] **I** *s.* **1.** Tscheche *m*, Tschechin *f*; **2.** *ling.* Tschechisch *n*; **II** *adj.* **3.** tschechisch.

Czech·o·slo·vak [,tʃekəʊ'sləʊvæk], *a.* ,**Czech·o·slo'vak·i·an** [-əʊsləʊ'vækɪən] **I** *s.* Tschechoslo'wake *m*, Tschechoslo'wakin *f*; **II** *adj.* tschechoslo'wakisch.

D

D, d [di:] *s.* **1.** D *n*, d *n* (*Buchstabe*); **2.** ♪ D *n*, d *n* (*Note*); **3.** *ped. Am.* Vier *f*, Ausreichend *n* (*Note*).

'd [-d] F *für* ***had, should, would: you'd.***

dab¹ [dæb] **I** *v/t.* **1.** leicht klopfen, antippen; **2.** be-, abtupfen; **3.** bestreichen; **4.** *typ.* abklatschen, klischieren; **5.** *a.* **~ *on*** *Farbe etc.* auftragen; **6.** *sl.* Fingerabdrücke machen von; **II** *v/i.* **7. ~ *at*** → 1, 2; **III** *s.* **8.** (leichter) Klaps, Tupfer *m*; **9.** Klecks *m*, Spritzer *m*; **10.** *Am. sl.* Fingerabdruck *m*.

dab² [dæb] *s.* F Könner *m*, ‚Künstler' *m*, Ex'perte *m*: ***be a ~ at s.th.*** et. aus dem Effeff können.

dab·ber ['dæbə] *s. typ.* a) Farbballen *m*, b) Klopfbürste *f*.

dab·ble ['dæbl] **I** *v/t.* **1.** bespritzen, besprengen; **II** *v/i.* **2.** planschen, plätschern; **3.** *fig.* **~ *in s.th.*** sich aus Liebhaberei *od.* oberflächlich *od.* dilet'tantisch mit et. befassen, ein bißchen *malen etc.*; **'dab·bler** [-lə] *s.* Ama'teur *m*, *contp.* Dilet'tant(in), Stümper(in).

dab·ster ['dæbstə] *s.* **1.** → ***dab²***; **2.** F *Am.* Stümper *m*.

dace [deɪs] *s. ichth.* Häsling *m*.

da·cha ['dætʃə] *s.* Datscha *f*.

dachs·hund ['dækshʊnd] *s. zo.* Dachshund *m*, Dackel *m*.

dac·tyl ['dæktɪl] *s.* Daktylus *m* (*Versfuß*); **dac·tyl·ic** [dæk'tɪlɪk] *adj. u. s.* dak'tylisch(er Vers).

dac·ty·lo·gram [dæk'tɪləʊgræm] *s.* Fingerabdruck *m*.

dad [dæd] *s.* F ‚Paps' *m*, Vati *m*.

Da·da·ism ['dɑ:dəɪzəm] *s.* Dada'ismus *m*; **'Da·da·ist** [-ɪst] **I** *s.* Dada'ist *m*; **II** *adj.* dada'istisch.

dad·dy ['dædɪ] → ***dad***; **~ long·legs** [ˌdædɪ'lɒŋlegz] *s. zo.* **1.** *Brit.* Schnake *f*; **2.** *Am.* Weberknecht *m*.

dae·mon → ***demon.***

daf·fo·dil ['dæfədɪl] *s.* ⚘ gelbe Nar'zisse, Osterblume *f*, -glocke *f*.

daft [dɑ:ft] *adj.* □ F verrückt, blöde, ‚doof', ‚bekloppt'.

dag·ger ['dægə] *s.* **1.** Dolch *m*: ***be at ~s drawn*** (***with***) *fig.* auf (dem) Kriegsfuß stehen (mit); ***look ~s at s.o.*** j-n mit Blicken durchbohren; **2.** *typ.* Kreuz (-zeichen) *n* (†).

da·go ['deɪgəʊ] *pl.* **-gos** *od.* **-goes** *s. sl. contp.* = *Spanier*, *Portugiese od. Italiener*; *weitS.* ‚Ka'nake' *m*, (verdammter) Ausländer.

da·guerre·o·type [də'gerəʊtaɪp] *s. phot.* a) Daguerreoty'pie *f*, b) Daguerreo'typ *n* (*Bild*).

dahl·ia ['deɪljə] *s.* ⚘ Dahlie *f*.

Dail Eir·eann [ˌdaɪl'eərən] *a.* **Dail** *s.* Abgeordnetenhaus *n von Eire.*

dai·ly ['deɪlɪ] **I** *adj.* **1.** täglich, Tage(s)…: ***our ~ bread*** unser täglich(es) Brot; **~ *wages*** Tagelohn *m*; **~ *newspaper*** → 5; **2.** alltäglich, häufig, ständig; **II** *adv.* **3.** täglich; **4.** immer, ständig; **III** *s.* **5.** Tageszeitung *f*; **6.** *Brit.* Zugeh-, Putzfrau *f*.

dain·ti·ness ['deɪntɪnɪs] *s.* **1.** Zierlichkeit *f*, Niedlichkeit *f*; **2.** wählerisches Wesen, Verwöhntheit *f*; **3.** Geziertheit *f*, Zimperlichkeit *f*; **4.** Schmackhaftigkeit *f*; **dain·ty** ['deɪntɪ] **I** *adj.* □ **1.** zierlich, niedlich, fein, reizend; **2.** köstlich, exqui'sit; **3.** wählerisch, verwöhnt (*bsd. im Essen*); **4.** geziert, zimperlich; **5.** lecker, schmackhaft; **II** *s.* **6.** *a. fig.* Lekkerbissen *m*, Delika'tesse *f*.

dair·y ['deərɪ] *s.* **1.** Molke'rei *f*; **2.** Milchwirtschaft *f*, Molke'rei(betrieb *m*) *f*; **3.** Milchhandlung *f*; **~ bar** *s. Am.* Milchbar *f*; **~ cat·tle** *s. pl.* Milchvieh *n*; **~ farm** *s.* auf Milchwirtschaft spezialisierter Bauernhof; **~ lunch** → ***dairy bar***; **'~·maid** *s.* **1.** Melkerin *f*; **2.** Molke'reiangestellte *f*; **'~·man** [-mən] *s.* [*irr.*] **1.** Milchmann *m*; **2.** Melker *m*, Schweizer *m*; **~ prod·uce** *s.* Molke'reipro,dukte *pl.*

da·is ['deɪɪs] *pl.* **-is·es** *s.* **1.** Podium *n*, E'strade *f*; **2.** *obs.* Baldachin *m*.

dai·sy ['deɪzɪ] **I** *s.* **1.** ⚘ Gänseblümchen *n*: (***double***) **~** Tausendschön(chen) *n*; ***be pushing up the daisies*** *sl.* ‚sich die Radies-chen von unten betrachten' (*tot sein*); → ***fresh*** 4; **2.** *sl.* a) 'Prachtexem,plar *n*, b) Prachtkerl *m*, ‚Perle' *f*; **II** *adj.* **3.** *sl.* erstklassig, prima; **'~·chain** *s.* **1.** Gänseblumenkränzchen *n*; **2.** *fig.* Reigen *m*, Kette *f*; **'~-ˌcut·ter** *s. sl.* **1.** Pferd *n* mit schleppendem Gang; **2.** *sport* Flachschuß *m*.

dale [deɪl] *s. poet.* Tal *n*; **dales·man** ['deɪlzmən] *s.* [*irr.*] Talbewohner *m* (*bsd. in Nordengland*).

dal·li·ance ['dælɪəns] *s.* **1.** Tröde'lei *f*, Bumme'lei *f*; **2.** Tände'lei *f*: a) Spiele'rei *f*, b) Schäke'rei *f*, Liebe'lei *f*; **dal·ly** ['dælɪ] **I** *v/i.* **1.** trödeln, Zeit vertändeln; **2.** tändeln, spielen, liebäugeln (***with*** mit); **3.** scherzen, schäkern; **II** *v/t.* **4. ~ *away*** *Zeit* vertrödeln; *Gelegenheit* verpassen.

Dal·ma·tian [dæl'meɪʃjən] **I** *adj.* **1.** dalma'tinisch; **II** *s.* **2.** Dalma'tiner(in); **3.** Dalma'tiner *m* (*Hund*).

dal·ton·ism ['dɔ:ltənɪzəm] *s.* ⚕ Farbenblindheit *f*.

dam¹ [dæm] **I** *s.* **1.** (Stau)Damm *m*, Wehr *n*, Talsperre *f*; **2.** Stausee *m*; **3.** *fig.* Damm *m*; **II** *v/t.* **4.** *a.* **~ *up*** a) stauen, (ab-, ein-, zu'rück)dämmen (*a. fig.*), b) (ab)sperren, hemmen (*a. fig.*).

dam² [dæm] *s. zo.* Mutter(tier *n*) *f*.

dam·age ['dæmɪdʒ] **I** *s.* **1.** (***to***) Schaden *m* (an *dat.*), (Be)Schädigung *f* (*gen.*): ***do ~*** Schaden anrichten; ***do ~ to*** → 6; **~ *by sea*** ⚓ Seeschaden *m*, Havarie *f*; **2.** Nachteil *m*, Verlust *m*; **3.** *pl.* ⚖ Schadensersatz *m*: ***for ~s*** auf Schadensersatz *klagen*; **4.** *sl.* Kosten *pl.*: ***what's the ~?*** was kostet es?; **II** *v/t.* **5.** beschädigen; **6.** *j-n*, *j-s Ruf etc.* schädigen, Schaden zufügen, *j-m* schaden; **'dam·age·a·ble** [-dʒəbl] *adj.* leicht zu beschädigen(d); **'dam·aged** [-dʒd] *adj.* **1.** beschädigt, schadhaft, de'fekt; **2.** verletzt, (körper)geschädigt; **3.** verdorben; **'dam·ag·ing** [-dʒɪŋ] *adj.* □ schädlich, nachteilig (***to*** für).

dam·a·scene(d) ['dæməsi:n(d)] *adj.* Damaszener…, damasziert.

dam·ask ['dæməsk] **I** *s.* **1.** Da'mast *m* (*Stoff*); **2.** *a.* **~ *steel*** Damas'zenerstahl *m*; **3.** *a.* **~ *rose*** ⚘ Damas'zenerrose *f*; **II** *adj.* **4.** Damast…; Damaszener…; **5.** rosarot; **III** *v/t.* **6.** *Stahl* damaszieren; **7.** da'mastartig weben; **8.** *fig.* verzieren.

dame [deɪm] *s.* **1.** *Brit.* a) Freifrau *f*, b) ♀ *der dem **knight** entsprechende Titel*: ♀ ***Diana X***; **2.** alte Dame: ♀ ***Nature*** Mutter *f* Natur; **3.** *ped.* Schul- *od.* Heimleiterin *f*; **4.** *Am. sl.* ‚Frau' *f*, Weibsbild *n*.

damn [dæm] **I** *v/t.* **1.** verdammen (*a. eccl.*); verwünschen, verfluchen: (***oh***) ***~!, ~ it*** (***all***)***!*** *sl.* verflucht!; **~ *you!*** *sl.* hol dich der Teufel!; ***well, I'll be ~ed!*** nicht zu glauben!, das ist die Höhe!; ***I'll be ~ed if*** a) ich freß 'nen Besen, wenn…, b) es fällt mir nicht im Traum ein (*das zu tun*); ***I'll be ~ed if I know!*** ich habe keinen blassen Dunst; **2.** verurteilen, verwerfen, ablehnen; **3.** vernichten, ruinieren; **II** *s.* **4.** Fluch *m*; **5.** ***I don't care a ~*** *sl.* das kümmert mich einen Dreck; ***not worth a ~*** keinen Pfifferling wert; **III** *adj. u. adv.* **6.** → ***damned*** 2, 3; **'dam·na·ble** [-nəbl] *adj.* □ **1.** verdammenswert; **2.** F ab'scheulich; **dam·na·tion** [dæm'neɪʃn] **I** *s.* **1.** Verdammung *f*; **2.** Ru'in *m*; **II** *int.* **3.** verflucht!; **damned** [dæmd] **I** *adj.* **1.** verdammt: ***the ~*** *eccl.* die Verdammten; **2.** *sl.* verflucht: **~ *fool*** Idiot *m*, ‚Blödmann' *m*; ***do one's ~est*** sein möglichstes tun; **3.** *a. adv. Bekräftigung*: *sl.* verdammt: ***a ~ sight better*** viel besser; ***every ~ one*** jeder einzelne; **~ *funny*** urkomisch; ***he ~ well ought to know*** das müßte er wahrhaftig wissen; **II** *int.* **4.** verdammt!; **damn·ing** ['dæmɪŋ] *adj. fig.* erdrükkend, vernichtend: **~ *evidence.***

Dam·o·cles ['dæməkli:z] *npr.* Damokles: ***sword of ~*** Damoklesschwert *n*.

damp [dæmp] **I** *adj.* □ **1.** feucht; dunstig: ***~ course*** △ Isolierschicht *f*; **II** *s.* **2.** Feuchtigkeit *f*; **3.** Dunst *m*; **4.** → ***fire-damp***; **5.** *fig.* Dämpfer *m*, Entmutigung *f*, Hemmnis *n*: ***cast a ~ over s.th.*** et. dämpfen *od.* lähmen, et. überschatten; **III** *v/t.* **6.** an-, befeuchten; **7.** *a.* ***~ down*** *fig. Eifer etc.* dämpfen (*a.* ♪, ϟ, *phys.*); (ab)schwächen, drosseln (*a.* ⚙); ersticken; ~ **course** *s.* △ Sperrbahn *f* (*gegen Nässe*).

damp·en ['dæmpən] **I** *v/t.* **1.** an-, befeuchten; **2.** *fig.* dämpfen, 'niederdrükken; entmutigen; **II** *v/i.* **3.** feucht werden; '**damp·er** [-pə] *s.* **1.** Dämpfer *m* (*bsd. fig.*): ***cast a ~ on*** dämpfen, lähmend wirken auf (*acc.*); **2.** ⚙ Ofen-, Zugklappe *f*, Schieber *m*; **3.** ♪ Dämpfer *m*; **4.** ϟ Dämpfung *f*; **5.** *Brit.* Stoßdämpfer *m*; '**damp·ish** [-pɪʃ] *adj.* etwas feucht, klamm; '**damp·ness** [-nɪs] *s.* Feuchtigkeit *f*; '**damp·proof** *adj.* feuchtigkeitsbeständig.

dam·sel ['dæmzl] *s. obs. od. iro.* Maid *f.*

dam·son ['dæmzən] *s.* ❦ Damas'zenerpflaume *f*; ~ **cheese** *s.* steifes Pflaumenmus.

dan [dæn] *s. Judo etc.*: Dan *m.*

dance [dɑːns] **I** *v/i.* **1.** tanzen: ***~ to s.o.'s pipe*** (*od.* ***tune***) *fig.* nach j-s Pfeife tanzen; **2.** tanzen: a) (her'um)hüpfen, b) flattern, schaukeln (*Blätter etc.*); **II** *v/t.* **3.** *e-n Tanz* tanzen: ***~ attendance on s.o.*** *fig.* um j-n scharwenzeln; **4.** *Tier* tanzen lassen; *Kind* schaukeln; **III** *s.* **5.** Tanz *m*: ***give a ~*** e-n Ball geben; ***lead s.o. a ~*** a) j-n zum Narren halten, b) j-m das Leben sauer machen; ***ℒ of Death*** Totentanz; ~ **hall** *s.* 'Tanzloˌkal *n.*

danc·er ['dɑːnsə] *s.* Tänzer(in).

danc·ing ['dɑːnsɪŋ] *s.* Tanzen *n*, Tanzkunst *f*; ~ **girl** *s.* (Tempel)Tänzerin *f* (*in Asien*); ~ **les·son** *s.* Tanzstunde *f*; ~ **mas·ter** *s.* Tanzlehrer *m.*

dan·de·li·on ['dændɪlaɪən] *s.* ❦ Löwenzahn *m.*

dan·der ['dændə] *s.*: ***get s.o.'s ~ up*** F j-n ‚auf die Palme' bringen.

dan·di·fied ['dændɪfaɪd] *adj.* stutzer-, geckenhaft, geschniegelt.

dan·dle ['dændl] *v/t.* **1.** *Kind* auf den Armen *od.* auf den Knien schaukeln; **2.** hätscheln; **3.** verhätscheln, verwöhnen.

dan·druff ['dændrəf] *a.* '**dan·driff** [-rɪf] *s.* (Kopf-, Haar)Schuppen *pl.*

dan·dy ['dændɪ] **I** *s.* **1.** Dandy *m*, Stutzer *m*; **2.** F *et.* Großartiges: ***the ~*** genau das Richtige; **3.** ⚓ Scha'luppe *f*; **4.** ⚓ a) Heckmaster *m*, b) Besansegel *n*; **II** *adj.* **5.** stutzerhaft; **6.** F erstklassig, prima, ‚bestens'; ~ **brush** *s.* Striegel *m.*

dan·dy·ish ['dændɪɪʃ] → ***dandy*** 5; '**dan·dy·ism** [-ɪzəm] stutzerhaftes Wesen.

Dane [deɪn] *s.* **1.** Däne *m*, Dänin *f*; **2.** → ***Great Dane.***

dan·ger ['deɪndʒə] **I** *s.* **1.** Gefahr *f* (***to*** für): ***in ~ of one's life*** in Lebensgefahr; ***be in ~ of falling*** Gefahr laufen zu fallen; ***the signal is at ~*** 🚂 das Signal steht auf Halt; **2.** Bedrohung *f*, Gefährdung *f* (***to*** *gen.*); **II** *adj.* Gefahren…: ***~ area*** Gefahrenzone *f*; Sperrgebiet *n*; ***be on*** (***off***) ***the ~ list*** in (außer) Lebensgefahr sein; ***~ money***, ***~ pay*** Gefahrenzulage *f*; ***~ point***, ***~ spot*** Gefahrenpunkt *m*; ***~ signal*** Not-, Warnsignal *n*; '**dan·ger·ous** [-dʒərəs] *adj.* □ **1.** gefährlich, gefahrvoll (***to*** für); **2.** bedenklich.

dan·gle ['dæŋgl] **I** *v/i.* **1.** baumeln, (her'ab)hängen; **2.** ***~ after s.o.*** sich an j-n anhängen, j-m nachlaufen: ***~ after girls***; **II** *v/t.* **3.** schlenkern, baumeln lassen: ***~ s.th. before s.o.*** *fig.* j-m et. verlockend in Aussicht stellen.

Dan·iel ['dænjəl] *s. bibl.* (das Buch) Daniel *m.*

Dan·ish ['deɪnɪʃ] **I** *adj.* **1.** dänisch; **II** *s.* **2.** ***the ~*** die Dänen; **3.** *ling.* Dänisch *n*, das Dänische; ~ **pas·try** *s. ein* Blätterteiggebäck *n.*

dank [dæŋk] *adj.* feucht, naßkalt, dumpfig.

Da·nu·bi·an [dæ'njuːbjən] *adj.* Donau…

daph·ne ['dæfnɪ] *s.* ❦ Seidelbast *m.*

dap·per ['dæpə] *adj.* **1.** a'drett, ele'gant, *iro.* geschniegelt; **2.** flink, gewandt.

dap·ple ['dæpl] *v/t.* tüpfeln, sprenkeln; '**dap·pled** [-ld] *adj.* **1.** gesprenkelt, gefleckt, scheckig; **2.** bunt.

ˌ**dap·ple-'grey** (**horse**) *s.* Apfelschimmel *m.*

dar·bies ['dɑːbɪz] *s. pl. sl.* Handschellen *pl.*

Dar·by and Joan ['dɑːbɪ ən(d) 'dʒəʊn] glückliches älteres Ehepaar: ***~ club*** Seniorenklub *m.*

dare [deə] **I** *v/i.* [*irr.*] **1.** es wagen, sich (ge)trauen; sich erdreisten, sich unter'stehen: ***he ~n't do it*** er wagt es nicht (zu tun); ***how ~ you say that?*** wie können Sie es wagen, das zu sagen?; ***don't*** (***you***) ***~ to touch me!*** untersteh dich nicht, mich anzurühren!; ***how ~ you!*** a) untersteh dich!, b) was fällt dir ein!; ***I ~ say*** a) ich glaube wohl, b) allerdings (*a. iro.*); **II** *v/t.* [*irr.*] **2.** *et.* wagen, riskieren; **3.** mutig begegnen (*dat.*), trotzen (*dat.*); **4.** *j-n* her'ausfordern: ***I ~ you!*** du traust dich ja nicht!; ***I ~ you to deny it*** wage nicht, es abzustreiten; '**~ˌdev·il I** *s.* Wag(e)hals *m*, Draufgänger *m*, Teufelskerl *m*; **II** *adj.* tollkühn, waghalsig; '**~ˌdev·il·(t)ry** *s.* Tollkühnheit *f.*

dar·ing ['deərɪŋ] **I** *adj.* □ **1.** wagemutig, kühn, verwegen; **2.** unverschämt, dreist; **3.** *fig.* gewagt, kühn; **II** *s.* **4.** Wagemut *m.*

dark [dɑːk] **I** *adj.* □ → ***darkly***; **1.** dunkel, finster: ***it is getting ~*** es wird dunkel; **2.** dunkel (*Farbe*): ***~ blue*** dunkelblau; ***~ hair*** braunes *od.* dunkles Haar; → ***horse*** 1; **3.** geheim(nisvoll), dunkel, verborgen, unklar: ***a ~ secret*** ein tiefes Geheimnis; ***keep s.th. ~*** et. geheimhalten; **4.** böse, finster, schwarz: ***~ thoughts***; **5.** düster, trübe, freudlos: ***a ~ future***; ***the ~ side of things*** die Schattenseite der Dinge; **6.** dunkel, unerforscht; kul'turlos; **II** *s.* **7.** Dunkel(heit *f*) *n*, Finsternis *f*: ***in the ~*** im Dunkel(n); ***at ~*** bei Einbruch der Dunkelheit; **8.** *pl. paint.* Schatten *m*; **9.** *fig.* Dunkel *n*, Ungewißheit *f*, *das* Geheime, Unwissenheit *f*: ***keep s.o. in the ~*** j-n im ungewissen lassen; ***I am in the ~*** ich tappe im dunkeln; ***a leap in the ~*** ein Sprung ins Ungewisse; ℒ **A·ges** *s. pl. das* frühe Mittelalter; ℒ **Con·ti·nent** *s. hist. der* dunkle Erdteil, Afrika *n.*

dark·en ['dɑːkən] **I** *v/t.* **1.** verdunkeln (*a. fig.*), verfinstern: ***don't ~ my door again!*** komm mir nie wieder ins Haus!; **2.** dunkel *od.* dunkler färben; **3.** *fig.* verdüstern, trüben; **II** *v/i.* **4.** dunkel werden, sich verdunkeln (*etc.* → I); '**dark·ish** [-kɪʃ] *adj.* **1.** etwas dunkel, schwärzlich; **2.** trübe; **3.** dämmerig.

dark lan·tern *s.* 'Blendlaˌterne *f.*

dark·ling ['dɑːklɪŋ] *adj.* sich verdunkelnd; '**dark·ly** [-lɪ] *adv. fig.* **1.** finster, böse; **2.** dunkel, geheimnisvoll; **3.** undeutlich; '**dark·ness** [-nɪs] *s.* **1.** *a. fig.* Dunkelheit *f*, Finsternis *f*; **2.** dunkle Färbung; **3.** *das* Böse: ***the powers of ~*** die Mächte der Finsternis; **4.** Unwissenheit *f*; **5.** Unklarheit *f*; **6.** Heimlichkeit *f.*

'**dark**|·**room** [-rʊm] *s. phot.* Dunkelkammer *f*; '**~-skinned** *adj.* dunkelhäutig; '**~-slide** *s. phot.* Kas'sette *f.*

dark·y ['dɑːkɪ] *s. contp.* Neger(in).

dar·ling ['dɑːlɪŋ] **I** *s.* **1.** Liebling *m*, Schatz *m*: ***~ of fortune*** Glückskind *n*; ***aren't you a ~*** du bist doch ein Engel; **II** *adj.* **2.** lieb, geliebt; Herzens…; **3.** reizend, ‚süß', entzückend.

darn[1] [dɑːn] **I** *v/t. Strümpfe etc.* stopfen, ausbessern; **II** *s. das* Gestopfte.

darn[2] [dɑːn] *v/t. sl. für* ***damn*** 1; **darned** [-nd] *adj. u. adv. sl. für* ***damned*** 2, 3.

darn·er ['dɑːnə] *s.* **1.** Stopfer(in); **2.** Stopf-ei *n*, -pilz *m.*

darn·ing ['dɑːnɪŋ] *s.* Stopfen *n*; ~ **egg** *s.* Stopf-ei *n*; ~ **nee·dle** *s.* Stopfnadel *f*; ~ **yarn** *s.* Stopfgarn *n.*

dart [dɑːt] **I** *s.* **1.** Wurfspeer *m*, -spieß *m*; **2.** (Wurf)Pfeil *m*; *fig.* Stachel *m des Spotts*; **3.** Satz *m*, Sprung *m*: ***make a ~ for*** losstürzen auf (*acc.*); **4.** *pl. sg. konstr.* Darts *n* (*Wurfpfeilspiel*): ***~-board*** Zielscheibe *f*; **5.** Abnäher *m* (*in Kleidern*); **II** *v/t.* **6.** schleudern, schießen; *Blicke* zuwerfen; **III** *v/i.* **7.** sausen, flitzen: ***~ at s.o.*** auf j-n losstürzen; ***~ off*** davonstürzen; **8.** sich blitzschnell bewegen, zucken, schnellen (*Schlange, Zunge*), huschen (*a. Auge*).

Dart·moor ['dɑːtˌmʊə] *a.* ~ **pris·on** *s. englische Strafanstalt.*

Dar·win·ism ['dɑːwɪnɪzəm] *s.* Darwi'nismus *m.*

dash [dæʃ] **I** *v/t.* **1.** schleudern, (heftig) stoßen *od.* schlagen, schmettern: ***~ to pieces*** zerschmettern; ***~ out s.o.'s brains*** j-m den Schädel einschlagen; **2.** (be)spritzen; (über)'schütten, über'gießen (*a. fig.*): ***~ off*** *od.* ***down*** *Schriftliches* hinwerfen, -hauen; **3.** *Hoffnung etc.* zunichte machen, vereiteln; **4.** *fig.* a) niederdrücken, deprimieren, b) aus der Fassung bringen, verwirren; **5.** (ver)mischen (*a. fig.*); **6.** F → ***damn*** 1: ***~ it*** (***all***)***!*** verflixt!; **II** *v/i.* **7.** sausen, flitzen, stürmen; *sport* spurten: ***~ off*** davonjagen, -stürzen; **8.** heftig (auf-) schlagen, prallen, klatschen; **III** *s.* **9.** Sprung *m*, (Vor)Stoß *m*; Anlauf *m*, Ansturm *m*: ***at a*** (*od.* ***one***) ***~*** mit 'einem Schlag; ***make a ~*** (***for***, ***at***) (los-) stürmen, sich stürzen (auf *acc.*); **10.** (Auf)Schlagen *n*, Prallen *n*, Klatschen *n*; **11.** Zusatz *m*; Schuß *m Rum etc.*; Prise *f Salz etc.*; Anflug *m*, Stich *m* (***of red*** ins Rote); Klecks *m* (*Farbe*): ***add a ~ of colo***(***u***)***r*** *fig.* e-n Farbtupfer aufsetzen; **12.** Federstrich *m*; *typ.* Gedankenstrich *m*; ♪, ℞, *tel.* Strich *m*; **13.** Schneid *m*, Schwung *m*, Schmiß *m*; Ele'ganz *f*: ***cut a ~*** Aufsehen erregen, e-e gute Figur abgeben; **14.** *sport* a) Kurzstreckenlauf *m*, b) Spurt *m*; **15.** ⚙ F → '**~board** *s.* ✈, *mot.* Arma'turen-, Instru'mentenbrett *n*.

dashed [dæʃt] *adj. u. adv.* F verflixt; '**dash·er** [-ʃə] *s.* **1.** Butterstößel *m*; **2.** F ele'gante Erscheinung, fescher Kerl; '**dash·ing** [-ʃɪŋ] *adj.* □ **1.** schneidig, forsch, kühn; **2.** ele'gant, flott, fesch.

das·tard ['dæstəd] *s.* (gemeiner) Feigling, Memme *f*; '**das·tard·li·ness** [-lɪnɪs] *s.* **1.** Feigheit *f*; **2.** Heimtücke *f*; '**das·tard·ly** [-lɪ] *adj.* **1.** feig(e); **2.** (heim)tückisch, gemein.

da·ta ['deɪtə] *s. pl. von* **datum** (*oft [fälschlich] sg. konstr.*) (*a. technische*) Daten *pl. od.* Angaben *pl. od.* Einzelheiten *pl. od.* 'Unterlagen *pl.*; Tatsachen *pl.*; ⚙ (Meß-, Versuchs)Werte *pl.*; *Computer*: Daten *pl.*: ***personal ~*** Personalangaben, Personalien; (***electronic***) ***~ processing*** (elektronische) Datenverarbeitung; ***~ bank*** Datenbank *f*; ***~ collection*** Datenerfassung *f*; ***~ display device*** Datensichtgerät *n*; ***~ exchange*** Datenaustausch *m*; ***~ input*** Dateneingabe *f*; ***~ output*** Datenausgabe *f*; ***~ printer*** Datendrucker *m* (*Gerät*); ***~ protection*** Datenschutz *m*; ***~ typist*** Datentypist(in).

date¹ [deɪt] *s.* ♀ **1.** Dattel *f*; **2.** *a.* ***~-tree*** Dattelpalme *f*.

date² [deɪt] **I** *s.* **1.** Datum *n*, Zeitangabe *f*, (Monats)Tag *m*: ***what's the ~ today?*** der Wievielte ist heute?; **2.** Datum *n*, Zeit(punkt *m*) *f*: ***at an early ~*** (recht) bald; ***of recent ~*** neu(eren Datums), modern; ***fix a ~*** e-n Termin festsetzen; **3.** Zeit(raum *m*) *f*, E'poche *f*: ***of Roman ~*** aus der Römerzeit; **4.** ✝ a) Ausstellungstag *m* (*Wechsel*), b) Frist *f*, Ziel *n*: ***~ of delivery*** Liefertermin *m*; ***~ of maturity*** Fälligkeitstag *m*; ***at long ~*** auf lange Sicht; **5.** heutiger Tag: ***of this*** (*od.* ***today's***) ***~*** heutig; ***four weeks after ~*** heute in vier Wochen; ***to ~*** bis heute; ***out of ~*** veraltet, überholt, unmodern; ***go out of ~*** veralten; ***up to ~*** zeitgemäß, modern, auf der Höhe (der Zeit), auf dem laufenden; ***bring up to ~*** auf den neuesten Stand bringen, modernisieren; → ***up-to-date***; **6.** F Verabredung *f*, Rendez'vous *n*: ***have a ~ with s.o.*** mit j-m verabredet sein; ***make a ~*** sich verabreden; **7.** F (Verabredungs)Partner(in): ***who is your ~?*** mit wem bist du verabredet?; **II** *v/t.* **8.** *Brief etc.* datieren: ***~ ahead*** voraus-, vordatieren; **9.** a) ein Datum *od.* e-e Zeit festsetzen *od.* angeben für, b) e-r bestimmten Zeit zuordnen; **10.** herleiten (***from*** aus); **11.** als über'holt *od.* veraltet kennzeichnen; **12.** *a.* ***~ up*** F a) sich verabreden mit, b) (*regelmäßig*) ‚gehen' mit: ***~ a girl***; **III** *v/i.* **13.** datieren, datiert sein (***from*** von); **14.** ***~ from*** (*od.* ***back to***) stammen *od.* sich herleiten aus, entstanden sein in (*dat.*); **15.** ***~ back to*** zu'rückreichen bis, zu'rückgehen auf (*e-e Zeit*); **16.** veralten, sich über'leben.

date block *s.* ('Abreiß)Kaˌlender *m*.

dat·ed ['deɪtɪd] *adj.* **1.** veraltet, über'holt; **2.** ***~ up*** F ‚ausgebucht' (*Person*), voll besetzt (*Tag*); '**date·less** [-lɪs] *adj.* **1.** undatiert; **2.** endlos; **3.** zeitlos (*Mode, Kunstwerk etc.*).

'**date**|**-line** *s.* **1.** Datumszeile *f* (*e-r Zeitung etc.*); **2.** *geogr.* Datumsgrenze *f*; **~ palm** → ***date¹*** 2; **~ stamp** *s.* Datums- *od.* Poststempel *m*.

da·ti·val [də'taɪvəl] *adj. ling.* Dativ...

da·tive ['deɪtɪv] **I** *s. a.* ***~ case*** *ling.* Dativ *m*, dritter Fall; **II** *adj.* da'tivisch, Dativ...

da·tum ['deɪtəm] *pl.* **-ta** [-tə] *s.* **1.** *et.* Gegebenes *od.* Bekanntes, Gegebenheit *f*; **2.** Vor'aussetzung *f*, Grundlage *f*; **3.** ⅌ gegebene Größe; **4.** → ***data***; **~ line** *s. surv.* Bezugslinie *f*; **~ point** *s.* **1.** ⅌, *phys.* Bezugspunkt *m*; **2.** *surv.* Nor'malfixpunkt *m*.

daub [dɔ:b] **I** *v/t.* **1.** be-, verschmieren, bestreichen; **2.** (***on***) schmieren, streichen (auf *acc.*); **3.** *Wand* bewerfen, verputzen; **4.** *fig.* besudeln; **II** *v/i.* **5.** *paint.* klecksen, schmieren; **III** *s.* **6.** (Lehm-) Bewurf *m*; **7.** *paint.* Schmiere'rei *f*, Farbenkleckse'rei *f*, schlechtes Gemälde; '**daub·(st)er** [-b(st)ə] *s.* Schmierer(in); Farbenkleckser(in).

daugh·ter ['dɔ:tə] *s.* **1.** Tochter *f* (*a. fig.*): ***~ language*** Tochtersprache *f*; → ***Eve¹***; **2.** → **~ com·pa·ny** *s.* ✝ Tochter (-gesellschaft) *f*; **~-in-law** ['dɔ:tərɪnlɔ:] *pl.* **~s-in-law** [-təz-] *s.* Schwiegertochter *f*; '**daugh·ter·ly** [-lɪ] *adj.* töchterlich.

daunt [dɔ:nt] *v/t.* einschüchtern, (er-) schrecken; entmutigen: ***nothing ~ed*** unverzagt; ***a ~ing task*** e-e beängstigende Aufgabe; '**daunt·less** [-lɪs] *adj.* □ unerschrocken.

dav·en·port ['dævnpɔ:t] *s.* **1.** kleiner Sekre'tär (*Schreibtisch*); **2.** *Am.* (*bsd.* Bett)Couch *f*.

Da·vy Jones's lock·er ['deɪvɪ'dʒəʊnzɪz] *s.* ⚓ Meeresgrund *m*, nasses Grab: ***go to ~*** ertrinken.

daw [dɔ:] *s. orn. obs.* Dohle *f*.

daw·dle ['dɔ:dl] **I** *v/i.* trödeln, bummeln; **II** *v/t. a.* ***~ away*** *Zeit* vertrödeln; '**daw·dler** [-lə] *s.* Trödler(in), Bummler(in).

dawn [dɔ:n] **I** *v/i.* **1.** tagen, dämmern, anbrechen (*Morgen, Tag*); **2.** *fig.* (her'auf)dämmern, erwachen, entstehen; **3.** ***~*** (***up***)***on*** *fig. j-m* dämmern, klarwerden, zum Bewußtsein kommen; **II** *s.* **4.** Morgendämmerung *f*, Tagesanbruch *m*: ***at ~*** beim Morgengrauen, bei Tagesanbruch; **5.** (An)Beginn *m*, Erwachen *n*, Anbruch *m*.

day [deɪ] *s.* **1.** Tag *m* (*Ggs. Nacht*): ***by ~*** bei Tage; ***before ~*** vor Tagesanbruch; ***~ and night*** Tag u. Nacht, immer; **2.** Tag *m* (*Zeitraum*): ***~'s work*** Tagesleistung *f*; ***three ~s from London*** drei Tage(reisen) von London; ***she is 30 if a ~*** sie ist mindestens 30 Jahre alt; **3.** *bestimmter* Tag: ***New Year's*** ♀ Neujahrstag; **4.** festgesetzter Tag: ***~ of payment*** ✝ Zahlungstermin *m*; **5.** *pl.* (Lebens)Zeit *f*, Zeit(en *pl.*) *f*, Tage *pl.*: ***in my young ~s*** in m-r Jugend; ***student ~s*** Studentenzeit; ***~ after ~*** Tag für Tag; ***the ~ after*** tags darauf; ***the ~ after tomorrow*** übermorgen; ***all ~ long*** den ganzen Tag, den lieben langen Tag; ***the ~ before yesterday*** vorgestern; ***~ by ~*** (tag)täglich, Tag für Tag; ***for ~s*** (***on end***) tagelang; ***call it a ~*** F (für heute) Schluß machen; ***have a nice ~!*** *Am.* mach's gut!; ***let's call it a ~!*** F Feierabend!, Schluß für heute!; ***carry*** (*od.* ***win***) ***the ~*** den Sieg davontragen; ***end one's ~s*** s-e Tage beschließen; ***every other ~*** alle zwei Tage, e-n Tag um den andern; ***fall on evil ~s*** ins Unglück geraten; ***he*** (*od.* ***it***) ***has had his*** (*od.* ***its***) ***~*** s-e beste Zeit ist vorüber; ***~ in, ~ out*** tagaus, tagein; ***in his ~*** zu s-r Zeit, einst; ***late in the ~*** reichlich spät; ***that's all in the ~'s work*** *fig.* das gehört alles mit dazu; ***that made my ~*** F damit war der Tag für mich gerettet; ***what's the time of ~?*** wieviel Uhr ist es?; ***know the time of ~*** *fig.* wissen, was die Glocke geschlagen hat; ***pass the time of ~ with s.o.*** j-n grüßen; ***one ~*** eines Tages, einmal; ***the other ~*** neulich; ***save the ~*** die Lage retten; ***some ~*** (***or other***) e-s Tages, nächstens einmal; (***in***) ***these ~s*** heutzutage; ***this ~*** heute; ***this ~ week*** heute in e-r Woche; ***this ~ last week*** heute vor e-r Woche; ***in those ~s*** damals; ***those were the ~s!*** das waren noch Zeiten!; ***to a ~*** auf den Tag genau; ***what ~ of the month is it?*** den Wievielten haben wir heute?; **~ bed** *s.* Bettcouch *f*; '**~·book** *s.* **1.** Tagebuch *n*; **2.** ✝ a) Jour'nal *n*, b) Verkaufsbuch *n*, c) Kassenbuch *n*; '**~·boy** *s. Brit.* Ex'terne(r) *m* (*e-s Internats*); '**~·break** *s.* (***at ~*** bei) Tagesanbruch *m*; ˌ**~-by-'day** *adj.* (tag)täglich; '**~-care cen·ter** *s. Am.* Kindertagesstätte *f*; '**~-care moth·er** *s. Am.* Tagesmutter *f*; **~ coach** *s.* 🚆 *Am.* Per'sonenwagen *m*; '**~·dream I** *s.* **1.** Wachtraum *m*, Träume'rei *f*; **2.** *fig.* Luftschloß *n*; **II** *v/i.* **3.** (mit offenen Augen) träumen; '**~ˌdream·er** *s.* Träumer(in); '**~·fly** *s. zo.* Eintagsfliege *f*; '**~·girl** *s. Brit.* Ex'terne *f* (*e-s Internats*); **~ la·bo(u)r·er** *s.* Tagelöhner *m*; **~ let·ter** *s. Am.* 'Briefteleˌgramm *n*.

'**day·light** *s.* **1.** Tageslicht *n*: ***by*** *od.* ***in ~*** bei Tag(eslicht); → ***broad*** 2; ***let ~ into s.th.*** *fig.* a) et. der Öffentlichkeit zugänglich machen, b) et. aufhellen; ***beat the ~s out of s.o.*** F j-n windelweich schlagen; ***he saw ~ at last*** *fig.* a) endlich ging ihm ein Licht auf, b) endlich sah er Land; **2.** (***at ~*** bei) Tagesanbruch *m*; **3.** (lichter) Zwischenraum; **~ sav·ing time** *s.* Sommerzeit *f*.

'**day**|**-long** *adj. u. adv.* den ganzen Tag (dauernd); **~ nurs·er·y** *s.* **1.** Kindertagesstätte *f*, -krippe *f*; **2.** Spielzimmer *n*; **~ re·lease** *s.* zur beruflichen Fortbildung freigegebene Zeit; '**~·room** *s.* Tagesraum *m*; **~ school** *s.* **1.** Exter'nat *n*, Schule *f* ohne Inter'nat; **2.** Tagesschule *f*; **~ shift** *s.* Tagschicht *f*: ***be on ~*** Tagschicht haben; **~ stu·dent** Ex'terne(r *m*) *f e-s Internats*; **~ tick·et** *s.* 🚆 Tagesrückfahrkarte *f*; '**~·time** *s.* **1.** Tageszeit *f*, (*heller*) Tag: ***in the ~*** bei Tage; **2.** ✝ Arbeitstag *m*; ˌ**~-to-'~** *adj.* (tag)'täglich: ***~ money*** ✝ Tagesgeld *n*.

daze [deɪz] **I** *v/t.* betäuben, lähmen (*a. fig.*); blenden; verwirren; **II** *s.* Betäubung *f*, Benommenheit *f*: ***in a ~*** benommen, betäubt; '**daz·ed·ly** [-zɪdlɪ] *adv.* betäubt *etc.* (→ **daze** I).

daz·zle ['dæzl] **I** *v/t.* **1.** blenden (*a. fig.*); **2.** *fig.* verwirren, verblüffen; **3.** ⚔ *durch Anstrich* tarnen; **II** *s.* **4.** Blenden *n*; Glanz *m*; **5.** *a.* ***~ paint*** ⚔ Tarnanstrich *m*; '**daz·zler** [-lə] *s.* F **1.** ‚Blender' *m*; **2.** ‚tolle Frau'; '**daz·zling** [-lɪŋ] *adj.* □ **1.** blendend, glänzend (*a. fig.*); *fig.* strahlend (schön); **2.** verwirrend.

D-Day ['di:deɪ] *s. Tag der alliierten Landung in der Normandie, 6. Juni 1944.*

dea·con ['di:kən] *s. eccl.* Dia'kon *m*; '**dea·con·ess** [-kənɪs] *s. eccl.* **1.** Dia'konin *f*; **2.** Diako'nisse *f*; '**dea·con·ry** [-rɪ] *s. eccl.* Diako'nat *n*.

de·ac·ti·vate [ˌdi:'æktɪveɪt] *v/t.* **1.** ⚔ a) *Einheit* auflösen, b) *Munition* entschärfen; **2.** außer Akti'on *od.* Betrieb setzen.

dead [ded] **I** *adj.* □ → ***deadly*** II; **1.** tot, gestorben, leblos: ***as ~ as a doornail*** (*od.* ***as mutton***) mausetot; ***~ body*** Leiche *f*, Leichnam *m*; ***he is a ~ man*** *fig.* er ist ein Kind des Todes; ***~ matter*** tote Materie (→ 11); ***~ and gone*** tot u. begraben (*a. fig.*); ***~ to the world*** F ‚total weg' (*bewußtlos, volltrunken*); ***I'm ~!*** F ich bin ‚total fertig'!; ***wait for a ~ man's shoes*** a) auf e-e Erbschaft warten, b) nur darauf warten, daß jemand stirbt (*um seine Position einzunehmen*); **2.** *fig. allg.* tot: a) ausgestorben: ***~ languages*** tote Sprachen, b) über'lebt, veraltet: ***~ customs***, c) matt, stumpf: ***~ colo(u)rs***; ***~ eyes***, d) nichtssagend, farb-, ausdruckslos, e) geistlos, f) leer, öde: ***~ streets***; ***~ land***, g) still, stehend: ***~ water***, h) *sport* nicht im Spiel: ***~ ball*** ‚toter Ball'; **3.** unzugänglich, unempfänglich (***to*** für), taub (***to*** gegen *Ratschläge etc.*); **4.** gefühllos, abgestorben: ***~ fingers***; **5.** *fig.* gefühllos, abgestumpft (***to*** gegen); **6.** erloschen: ***~ fire***; ***~ volcano***; ***~ passions***; **7.** ⚖ ungültig; **8.** *bsd.* ✝ still, ruhig, flau: ***~ season***; **9.** ✝ tot, umsatzlos: ***~ assets*** unproduktive (Kapital)Anlage; ***~ capital (stock)*** totes Kapital (Inventar); **10.** ⚙ a) tot, außer Betrieb, b) de'fekt: ***~ valve***; ***~ engine*** ausgefallener *od.* abgestorbener Motor, c) leer, erschöpft: ***~ battery***, d) tot, starr: ***~ axle***, e) ⚡ tot, strom-, spannungslos; **11.** *typ.* abgelegt: ***~ matter*** Ablegesatz *m*; **12.** *bsd.* ⚠ blind, Blend...: ***~ floor***; ***~ window*** totes Fenster; **13.** Sack... (*ohne Ausgang*): ***~ street*** Sackgasse *f*; **14.** schal, abgestanden: ***~ drinks***; **15.** verwelkt, dürr, abgestorben: ***~ flowers***; **16.** völlig, to'tal: ***~ calm*** Flaute *f*, (völlige) Windstille; ***~ certainty*** absolute Gewißheit; ***in ~ earnest*** in vollem Ernst; ***~ loss*** Totalverlust *m*, *fig.* totaler Ausfall (*Person*); ***~ silence*** Totenstille *f*; ***~ stop*** völliger Stillstand; ***come to a ~ stop*** schlagartig stehenbleiben *od.* aufhören; **17.** todsicher, unfehlbar: ***he is a ~ shot***; **18.** äußerst: ***a ~ strain***; ***a ~ push*** ein verzweifelter, aber vergeblicher Stoß; **II** *s.* **19.** stillste Zeit: ***at ~ of night*** mitten in der Nacht; ***the ~ of winter*** der tiefste Winter; **20.** ***the ~*** a) der (die, das) Tote, b) *coll.* die Toten: ***several ~*** mehrere Tote; ***rise from the ~*** von den Toten auferstehen; **III** *adv.* **21.** restlos, völlig, gänzlich, abso'lut, to'tal: ***~ asleep*** in tiefstem Schlaf; ***~ drunk*** sinnlos betrunken; ***~ slow!*** *mot.* Schritt fahren; ***~ straight*** schnurgerade; ***~ tired*** todmüde; ***the facts are ~ against him*** alles spricht gegen ihn; **22.** plötzlich, schlagartig, abrupt: ***stop ~***; **23.** genau: ***~ against*** genau gegenüber von (*od. dat.*); ***~ (set) against*** ganz u. gar *od.* entschieden gegen (*et.* eingestellt); ***~ set on*** scharf auf (*acc.*).

dead| ac·count *s.* ✝ 'umsatzloses Konto; ˌ**~-(and-)a'live** *adj. fig.* (tod)langweilig; '**~·beat** *s.* F **1.** Schnorrer *m*; **2.** Gammler *m*; ˌ**~-'beat** *adj.* F todmüde, völlig ka'putt; **~ cen·ter** *Am.*, **~ centre** *Brit. s.* ⚙ **1.** toter Punkt; **2.** genaue Mitte; **3.** tote Spitze (*der Drehbank*); **~ drop** *s. Spionage*: toter Briefkasten; **~ duck** *s.*: ***be a ~*** F keine Chance mehr haben, passé sein.

dead·en ['dedn] *v/t.* **1.** *Gefühl etc.* (ab-) töten, abstumpfen (***to*** gegen); betäuben; **2.** *Geräusch, Schlag etc.* dämpfen, (ab)schwächen; **3.** ⚙ mattieren.

dead| end *s.* **1.** Sackgasse *f* (*a. fig.*): ***come to a ~*** in e-e Sackgasse geraten; **2.** ⚙ blindes Ende; '**~-end** *adj.* **1.** ohne Ausgang, Sack...: ***~ street*** Sackgasse *f*; ***~ station*** Kopfbahnhof *m*; **2.** *fig.* ausweglos; **3.** ohne Aufstiegschancen: ***~ job***; **4.** verwahrlost, Slum...: ***~ kid*** verwahrlostes Kind; '**~·fall** *s.* Baumfalle *f*; **~ file** *s.* abgelegte Akte; **~ fire** *s.* Elmsfeuer *n*; **~ freight** *s.* ⚓ Fehlfracht *f*; **~ hand** → ***mortmain***; '**~·head** *s.* F a) Freikarteninhaber(in), b) Schwarzfahrer(in), c) *Am. contp.* ‚Blindgänger' *m*, ‚Niete' *f*, d) *Am.* Mitläufer *m*; **~ heat** *s. sport* totes Rennen; **~ let·ter** *s.* **1.** *fig.* toter Buchstabe (*unwirksames Gesetz*); **2.** unzustellbarer Brief; '**~·line** *s.* **1.** letzter *od.* äußerster Termin, Frist(ablauf *m*) *f*; *Zeitung*: Redakti'onsschluß *m*: ***~ pressure*** Termindruck *m*; ***meet the ~*** den Termin *od.* die Frist einhalten; **2.** Stichtag *m*; **3.** äußerste Grenze; **4.** *Am.* Todesstreifen *m* (*Strafanstalt*).

dead·li·ness ['dedlɪnɪs] *s. das* Tödliche; tödliche Wirkung.

dead| load *s.* ⚙ totes Gewicht, tote Last, Eigengewicht *n*; '**~·lock I** *s. fig.* toter Punkt, 'Patt(situatiˌon *f*) *n*: ***break the ~*** den toten Punkt überwinden; ***come to a ~*** → **II** *v/i.* sich festfahren, steckenbleiben, an e-m toten Punkt anlangen: ***~ed*** festgefahren.

dead·ly ['dedlɪ] **I** *adj.* **1.** tödlich, todbringend: ***~ poison***; ***~ precision*** tödliche Genauigkeit; ***~ sin*** Todsünde *f*; ***~ combat*** Kampf *m* auf Leben u. Tod; **2.** *fig.* unversöhnlich, grausam: ***~ enemy*** Todfeind *m*; ***~ fight*** mörderischer Kampf; **3.** totenähnlich: ***~ pallor*** Leichenblässe *f*; **4.** F schrecklich, groß, äußerst: ***~ haste***; **II** *adv.* **5.** totenähnlich: ***~ pale*** leichenblaß; **6.** F schrecklich, tod...: ***~ dull*** sterbenslangweilig.

dead| march *s.* ♪ Trauermarsch *m*; **~ ma·rine** *s. sl.* leere ‚Pulle'.

dead·ness ['dednɪs] *s.* **1.** Leblosigkeit *f*, Erstarrung *f*; *fig. a.* Leere *f*, Öde *f*; **2.** Gefühllosigkeit *f*, Gleichgültigkeit *f*, Kälte *f*; **3.** *bsd.* ✝ Flauheit *f*, Flaute *f*; **4.** Glanzlosigkeit *f*.

dead| net·tle *s.* ⚘ Taubnessel *f*; **~ pan** *s.* F ausdrucksloses Gesicht; '**~-pan** *adj.* **1.** ausdruckslos; **2.** mit ausdruckslosem Gesicht; **3.** *fig.* trocken (*Humor*); **~ point** *s.* ⚙ toter Punkt; **~ reck·on·ing** *s.* ⚓ gegißtes Besteck, Koppeln *n*; **~ set** *s.* **1.** *hunt.* Stehen *n des Hundes*; **2.** verbissene Feindschaft; **3.** hartnäckiges Bemühen *od.* Werben (***at*** um): ***make a ~ at*** sich hartnäckig bemühen um; **~ wa·ter** *s.* **1.** stehendes Wasser; **2.** ⚓ Kielwasser *n*, Sog *m*; **~ weight** *s.* **1.** a) ganze Last, volles Gewicht, b) totes Gewicht, Eigengewicht *n*; **2.** *fig.* schwere Last; '**~-weight ca·pac·i·ty** *s.* Tragfähigkeit *f*; '**~·wood** *s.* **1.** totes Holz, *weitS.* Reisig *n*; **2.** *fig.* Plunder *m*; ✝ Ladenhüter *m*; **3.** *fig. et.* Veraltetes *od.* Über'holtes; (nutzloser) 'Ballast.

de-aer·ate [di:'eɪəreɪt] *v/t.* entlüften.

deaf [def] *adj.* □ **1.** ⚕ taub: ***the ~*** die Tauben *pl.*; ***~ and dumb*** taubstumm; ***~-and-dumb language*** Taubstummensprache *f*; ***~ as a post*** stocktaub; → ***ear***[1] 1; **2.** schwerhörig; **3.** *fig.* (***to***) taub (gegen), unzugänglich (für); '**deaf-aid** *s.* Hörgerät *n*; '**deaf·en** [-fn] *v/t.* **1.** taub machen; betäuben; **2.** *Schall* dämpfen; **3.** *Wände* schalldicht machen; '**deaf·en·ing** [-fnɪŋ] *adj.* ohrenbetäubend; ˌ**deaf-'mute I** *adj.* taubstumm; **II** *s.* Taubstumme(r *m*) *f*; '**deaf·ness** [-nɪs] *s.* **1.** ⚕ Taubheit *f* (*a. fig.* ***to*** gegen); **2.** Schwerhörigkeit *f*.

deal[1] [di:l] **I** *v/i.* [*irr.*] **1.** (***with***) sich befassen *od.* beschäftigen *od.* abgeben (mit); **2.** (***with***) handeln (von), *et.* behandeln *od.* zum Thema haben; **3.** ***~ with*** sich mit *e-m Problem etc.* befassen *od.* ausein'andersetzen; *et.* in Angriff nehmen; **4.** ***~ with*** *et.* erledigen, mit *et. od. j-m* fertigwerden; **5.** ***~ with*** *od.* ***by*** behandeln (*acc.*), 'umgehen mit: ***~ fairly with s.o.*** j-n anständig behandeln, sich fair gegen j-n verhalten; **6.** ***~ with*** ✝ Geschäfte machen *od.* Handel treiben mit, in Geschäftsverkehr stehen mit; **7.** ✝ handeln, Handel treiben (***in*** mit): ***~ in paper***; **8.** dealen (*mit Rauschgift handeln*); **9.** *Kartenspiel*: geben; **II** *v/t.* [*irr.*] **10.** *oft* ***~ out*** *et.* ver-, austeilen: ***~ out rations***; ***~ s.o.*** (***s.th.***) ***a blow***, ***~ a blow at s.o.*** (***s.th.***) j-m (e-r Sache) e-n Schlag versetzen; **11.** *j-m et.* zuteilen; **12.** *Karten od. j-m e-e Karte* geben; **III** *s.* F **13.** Handlungsweise *f*, Verfahren *n*, Poli'tik *f*; → ***New Deal***; **14.** Behandlung *f*; → ***raw*** 10, ***square*** 37; **15.** Geschäft *n*, Handel *m*: ***it's a ~!*** abgemacht!; (***a***) ***good ~!*** gutes Geschäft!, nicht schlecht!; ***no ~!*** F da läuft nichts!; ***big ~!*** *Am. sl.* na und?, pah!; ***no big ~*** *Am. sl.* keine große Sache; **16.** Abkommen *n*, Über'einkunft *f*: ***make*** (*od.* ***do***) ***a ~*** ein Abkommen treffen, sich einigen; **17.** *Kartenspiel*: ***it is my ~*** ich muß geben.

deal[2] [di:l] *s.* **1.** Menge *f*, Teil *m*: ***a great ~ (of money)*** sehr viel (Geld); ***a good ~*** ziemlich viel, ein gut Teil; ***think a great ~ of s.o.*** sehr viel von j-m halten; **2.** e-e ganze Menge: ***a ~ worse*** F viel schlechter.

deal[3] [di:l] *s.* **1.** Diele *f*, Brett *n*, Planke *f* (*bsd. aus Kiefernholz*); **2.** Tannen- *od.* Kiefernholz *n*.

deal·er ['di:lə] *s.* **1.** ✝ Händler(in), Kaufmann *m*: ***~ in antiques*** Antiquitätenhändler; ***plain ~*** *fig.* ehrlicher Mensch; **2.** *Brit. Börse*: Dealer *m* (*der auf eigene Rechnung Geschäfte tätigt*); **3.** Dealer *m* (*Rauschgifthändler*); **4.** *Kartenspiel*: Geber(in); '**deal·ing** [-lɪŋ] *s.* **1.** *mst pl.* 'Umgang *m*, Verkehr *m*, Beziehungen *pl.*: ***have ~s with s.o.*** mit j-m zu tun haben; ***there is no ~ with***

her mit ihr ist nicht auszukommen; **2.** ♆ a) Handel *m*, Geschäft *n* (***in*** in *dat.*, mit), b) Geschäftsverkehr *m*, c) Geschäftsgebaren *n*; **3.** Verhalten *n*, Handlungsweise *f*; **4.** Austeilen *n*, Geben *n* (*von Karten*).
dealt [delt] *pret. u. p.p. von* ***deal***¹.
dean [diːn] *s.* **1.** *Brit. univ.* a) De'kan *m* (*Vorstand e-r Fakultät od. e-s College*), b) Fellow *m* mit besonderen Aufgaben (*Oxford, Cambridge*); **2.** *Am. univ.* a) Vorstand *m* e-r Fakul'tät, b) Hauptberater(in), Vorsteher(in) (*der Studenten*); **3.** *eccl.* De'kan *m*, De'chant *m*; **4.** Vorsitzende(r *m*) *f*, Präsi'dent(in): ***2 of the Diplomatic Corps*** Doyen *m* des Diplomatischen Korps; **'dean·er·y** [-nərɪ] *s.* Deka'nat *n*.
dear [dɪə] **I** *adj.* □ → ***dearly***; **1.** teuer, lieb (***to*** *dat.*): **~ *mother*** liebe Mutter; ***2 Sir,*** (*in Briefen*) Sehr geehrter Herr (*Name*)!; ***my ~est wish*** mein Herzenswunsch; ***for ~ life*** als ob es ums Leben ginge; ***hold ~*** (wert)schätzen; **2.** teuer, kostspielig; **II** *adv.* **3.** teuer: ***it cost him ~*** es kam ihm teuer zu stehen; → ***dearly*** 2; **III** *s.* **4.** Liebste(r *m*) *f*, Liebling *m*, Schatz *m*: ***isn't she a ~?*** ist sie nicht ein Engel?; ***there's a ~!*** sei (so) lieb!; **IV** *int.* **5. *oh ~!, ~, ~!, ~ me!*** du liebe Zeit!, ach je!; **dear·ie** ['dɪərɪ] → ***deary***; **'dear·ly** [-lɪ] *adv.* **1.** innig, herzlich; **2.** teuer; → ***buy*** 3; **'dear·ness** [-nɪs] *s.* **1.** Kostspieligkeit *f*, hoher Preis *od.* Wert (*a. fig.*); **2.** *das* Liebe(nswerte).
dearth [dɜːθ] *s.* **1.** Mangel *m* (***of*** an *dat.*); **2.** Hungersnot *f*.
dear·y ['dɪərɪ] *s.* F Liebling *m*, Schätzchen *n*.
death [deθ] *s.* **1.** Tod *m*: ***~s*** Todesfälle; ***to (the) ~*** zu Tode, bis zum äußersten; ***at 2's door*** an der Schwelle des Todes; ***bleed to ~*** (sich) verbluten; ***do to ~*** a) *j-n* umbringen, b) *fig. et.* ‚kaputtmachen' *od.* ‚zu Tode reiten'; ***done to ~*** F *Küche*: totgekocht; ***frozen to ~*** erfroren; ***sure as ~*** tod-, bombensicher; ***tired to ~*** todmüde; ***catch one's ~*** sich den Tod holen (*engS. durch Erkältung*); ***be in at the ~*** *fig.* das Ende miterleben; ***that will be his ~*** das wird ihm das Leben kosten; ***he'll be the ~ of me*** a) er bringt mich noch ins Grab, b) ich lach' mich noch tot über ihn; ***hold on like grim ~*** verbissen festhalten, sich festkrallen (***to*** an *dat.*); ***put to ~*** zu Tode bringen, *bsd.* hinrichten; **2.** Tod *m*, (Ab)Sterben *n*, Ende *n*, Vernichtung *f*: ***united in ~*** im Tode vereint; **~ ag·o·ny** *s.* Todeskampf *m*; **'~·bed** *s.* Sterbebett *n*: **~ *repentance*** Reue *f* auf dem Sterbebett; **~ ben·e·fit** *s.* **1.** Sterbegeld *n*; **2.** bei Todesfall fällige Versicherungsleistung; **'~·blow** *s.* Todesstreich *m*; *fig.* Todesstoß *m* (***to*** für); **~ cell** *s.* ⚖ Todeszelle *f*; **~ cer·tif·i·cate** *s.* Sterbeurkunde *f*, Totenschein *m*; **~ du·ty** *s. obs.* Erbschaftssteuer *f*; **~ grant** *s.* Sterbegeld *n*; **~ house** → ***~ row***; **~ in·stinct** *s. psych.* Todestrieb *m*; **~ knell** *s.* Totengeläut *n*, -glocke *f* (*a. fig.*).
death·less ['deθlɪs] *adj.* □ *bsd. fig.* unsterblich; **'death·like** *adj.*, **'death·ly** [-lɪ] *adj. u. adv.* totenähnlich, Todes..., Leichen..., toten...: **~ *pale*** leichenblaß.
death| mask *s.* Totenmaske *f*; **~ pen·al·ty** *s.* Todesstrafe *f*; **~ rate** *s.* Sterblichkeitsziffer *f*; **~ rat·tle** *s.* Todesröcheln *n*; **~ ray** *s.* Todesstrahl *m*; **~ roll** *s.* Zahl *f* der Todesopfer; ⚔ Gefallenen-, Verlustliste *f*; **~ row** *s. Am.* Todestrakt *m* (*e-r Strafanstalt*); **~'s head** *s.* **1.** Totenkopf *m* (*bsd. als Symbol*); **2.** *zo.* Totenkopf *m* (*Falter*); **~ throes** *s. pl.* Todeskampf *m*; **'~·trap** *s. fig.* ‚Mausefalle' *f*; **~ war·rant** *s.* **1.** ⚖ Hinrichtungsbefehl *m*; **2.** *fig.* Todesurteil *n*; **'~·watch** *s. Brit. a.* **~ *beetle*** zo. Klopfkäfer *m*; **~ wish** *s.* Todeswunsch *m*.
deb [deb] *s.* F *abbr. für* ***débutante***.
dé·bâ·cle [deɪ'bɑːkl] (*Fr.*) *s.* **1.** De'bakel *n*, Zs.-bruch *m*, Kata'strophe *f*; **2.** Massenflucht *f*, wildes Durchein'ander; **3.** *geol.* Eisgang *m*.
de·bar [dɪ'bɑː] *v/t.* **1.** (***from***) *j-n* ausschließen (von), hindern (an *dat. od.* zu *inf.*); **2. ~ *s.o. s.th.*** j-m et. versagen; **3.** *et.* verhindern.
de·bark [dɪ'bɑːk] → ***disembark***.
de·base [dɪ'beɪs] *v/t.* **1.** (cha'rakterlich) verderben, verschlechtern; **2.** (***o.s.*** sich) entwürdigen, erniedrigen; **3.** entwerten; im Wert mindern; *Wert* mindern; **4.** *Münzen* verschlechtern; **5.** verfälschen; **de'based** [-st] *adj.* **1.** verderbt (*etc.*); **2.** minderwertig (*Geld*); **3.** abgegriffen (*Wort*).
de·bat·a·ble [dɪ'beɪtəbl] *adj.* **1.** disku'tabel; **2.** strittig, fraglich, um'stritten; **3.** bestreitbar, anfechtbar; **de·bate** [dɪ'beɪt] **I** *v/i.* **1.** debattieren, diskutieren; **2. ~ *with o.s.*** hin u. her über'legen; **II** *v/t.* **3.** *et.* debattieren, erörtern, diskutieren; **4.** erwägen, sich *et.* über'legen; **III** *s.* **5.** De'batte *f* (*a. parl.*), Erörterung *f*: ***be under ~*** zur Debatte stehen; **~ *on request*** *parl.* aktuelle Stunde; **de'bat·er** [-tə] *s.* **1.** Debat'tierer *m*, Dispu'tant *m*; **2.** *parl.* Redner *m*; **de'bat·ing** [-tɪŋ] *adj.*: **~ *club*** *od.* ***society*** Debattierklub *m*.
de·bauch [dɪ'bɔːtʃ] **I** *v/t.* **1.** *sittlich* verderben; **2.** verführen, verleiten; **II** *s.* **3.** Ausschweifung *f*, Orgie *f*; **4.** Schwelge'rei *f*; **de'bauched** [-tʃt] *adj.* ausschweifend, liederlich, zügellos; **deb·au·chee** [ˌdebɔː'tʃiː] *s.* Wüstling *m*; **de'bauch·er** [-tʃə] *s.* Verführer *m*; **de'bauch·er·y** [-tʃərɪ] *s.* Ausschweifung (-en *pl.*) *f*, Orgie(n *pl.*) *f*; Schwelge'rei *f*.
de·ben·ture [dɪ'bentʃə] *s.* **1.** Schuldschein *m*; **2.** ♆ a) *a.* **~ *bond*, ~ *certificate*** Obligati'on *f*, Schuldverschreibung *f*, b) *Brit.* Pfandbrief *m*: **~ *holder*** Obligationsinhaber *m*; *Brit.* Pfandbriefinhaber(in); **~ *stock*** *Brit.* Obligationen *pl.*, Anleiheschuld *f*, *Am.* Vorzugsaktien erster Klasse; **3.** ♆ Rückzollschein *m*.
de·bil·i·tate [dɪ'bɪlɪteɪt] *v/t.* schwächen, entkräften; **de·bil·i·ta·tion** [dɪˌbɪlɪ'teɪʃn] *s.* Schwächung *f*, Entkräftung *f*; **de'bil·i·ty** [-lətɪ] *s.* Schwäche *f*, Kraftlosigkeit *f*, Erschöpfung(szustand *m*) *f*.
deb·it ['debɪt] **I** *s.* ♆ **1.** Debet *n*, Soll *n*, Schuldposten *m*: **~ *and credit*** Soll *n* u. Haben *n*; **2.** Belastung *f*: ***to the ~ of*** zu Lasten von; **3.** *a.* **~ *side*** Debetseite *f*: ***charge*** (*od.* ***carry***) ***a sum to s.o.'s ~*** j-s Konto mit e-r Summe belasten; **II** *v/t.* **4.** debitieren, belasten (***with*** mit); **III** *adj.* **5.** Debet..., Schuld...: **~ *account***; **~ *balance*** Debetsaldo *m*; ***your ~ balance*** Saldo *m* zu Ihren Lasten; **~ *entry*** Lastschrift *f*; **~ *note*** Lastschriftanzeige *f*.
de·block [ˌdiː'blɒk] *v/t.* ♆ *eingefrorene Konten* freigeben.
deb·o·nair(e) [ˌdebə'neə] *adj.* **1.** höflich, gefällig; **2.** heiter, fröhlich; **3.** 'lässig(-eleˌgant).
de·bouch [dɪ'baʊtʃ] *v/i.* **1.** ⚔ her'vorbrechen; **2.** einmünden, sich ergießen (*Fluß*).
De·brett [də'bret] *npr.*: ***~'s peerage*** *englisches Adelsregister*.
de·brief·ing [ˌdiː'briːfɪŋ] *s.* ⚔, ✈ Einsatzbesprechung *f* (*nach dem Flug*).
de·bris ['deɪbriː] *s.* Trümmer *pl.*, (Gesteins)Schutt *m* (*a. geol.*).
debt [det] *s.* Schuld *f* (*Geld od. fig.*); Verpflichtung *f*: ***~-collecting agency*** Inkassobüro *n*; **~ *collector*** Inkassobeauftragte(r) *m*; ***collection of ~s*** Inkasso *n*; ***bad ~s*** zweifelhafte Forderungen *od.* Außenstände; **~ *of gratitude*** Dankesschuld; **~ *of hono(u)r*** Ehrenschuld; ***pay one's ~ to nature*** der Natur s-n Tribut entrichten, sterben; ***run into ~*** in Schulden geraten; ***run up ~s*** Schulden machen; ***be in ~*** verschuldet sein, Schulden haben; ***be in s.o.'s ~*** *fig.* j-m verpflichtet sein, in j-s Schuld stehen; **'debt·or** [-tə] *s.* Schuldner(in), ♆ Debitor *m*: ***common ~*** Gemeinschuldner *m*.
de·bug [ˌdiː'bʌg] *v/t.* **1.** ⚙ F (die) ‚Mukken' *e-r Maschine* beseitigen; **2.** entwanzen (*a.* F *von Minispionen befreien*).
de·bunk [ˌdiː'bʌŋk] *v/t.* F entlarven.
de·bu·reauc·ra·tize [ˌdiːbjʊə'rɒkrətaɪz] *v/t.* entbürokratisieren.
de·bus [ˌdiː'bʌs] *v/i.* aus dem *od.* e-m Bus aussteigen.
dé·but, *Am.* **de·but** ['deɪbuː] (*Fr.*) *s.* De'büt *n*: a) erstes Auftreten (*thea. od. in der Gesellschaft*), b) Anfang *m*, Antritt *m* (*e-r Karriere etc.*): ***make one's ~*** sein Debüt geben; **déb·u·tant**, *Am.* **deb·u·tant** ['debjuːtɑ̃ːŋ] (*Fr.*) *s.* Debü'tant *m*; **déb·u·tante**, *Am.* **deb·u·tante** ['debjuːtɑːnt] (*Fr.*) *s.* Debü'tantin *f*.
deca- [dekə] *in Zssgn* zehn(mal).
dec·ade ['dekeɪd] *s.* **1.** De'kade *f*: a) Jahr'zehnt *n*, b) Zehnergruppe *f*; **2.** ϟ, ⚙ De'kade *f*.
dec·a·dence ['dekədəns] *s.* Deka'denz *f*, Entartung *f*, Verfall *m*, Niedergang *m*; **'dec·a·dent** [-nt] **I** *adj.* deka'dent, entartet, verfallend; Dekadenz...; **II** *s.* deka'denter Mensch.
de·caf·fein·ate [ˌdiː'kæfɪneɪt] *v/t. Kaffee* koffe'infrei machen.
dec·a·gon ['dekəgən] *s.* ⩓ Zehneck *n*;
dec·a·gram(me) ['dekəgræm] *s.* Deka'gramm *n*.
de·cal [dɪ'kæl] → ***decalcomania***.
de·cal·ci·fy [ˌdiː'kælsɪfaɪ] *v/t.* entkalken.
de·cal·co·ma·ni·a [dɪˌkælkəʊ'meɪnɪə] *s.* Abziehbild(verfahren) *n*.
dec·a|li·ter *Am.*, **~·li·tre** *Brit.* ['dekəˌliːtə] *s.* Deka'liter *m*, *n*; **2·log(ue)** ['dekəlɒg] *s. bibl.* Deka'log *m*, *die* Zehn Gebote *pl.*; **~·me·ter** *Am.*, **~·me·tre** *Brit.* ['dekəˌmiːtə] *s.* Deka'meter *m*, *n*.
de·camp [dɪ'kæmp] *v/i.* **1.** ⚔ das Lager

abbrechen; **2.** F sich aus dem Staube machen.

de·cant [dɪ'kænt] *v/t.* **1.** ab-, 'umfüllen; **2.** dekantieren, vorsichtig abgießen; **de'cant·er** [-tə] *s.* **1.** Ka'raffe *f*; **2.** Klärflasche *f*.

de·cap·i·tate [dɪ'kæpɪteɪt] *v/t.* **1.** enthaupten, köpfen; **2.** *Am.* F entlassen, ‚absägen'; **de·cap·i·ta·tion** [dɪˌkæpɪ'teɪʃn] *s.* **1.** Enthauptung *f*; **2.** *Am.* F ‚Rausschmiß' *m*.

de·car·bon·ate [ˌdiː'kɑːbəneɪt] *v/t.* Kohlensäure *od.* Kohlen'dioxyd entziehen (*dat.*); **de·car·bon·ize** [ˌdiː'kɑːbənaɪz] *v/t.* dekarbonisieren; **de·car·bu·rize** [ˌdiː'kɑːbjʊəraɪz] → ***decarbonize***.

de·car·tel·i·za·tion ['diːˌkɑːtəlaɪ'zeɪʃn] *s.* ✝ Entkartellisierung *f*, (Kon'zern-) Entflechtung *f*; **de·car·tel·ize** [ˌdiː'kɑːtəlaɪz] *v/t.* entflechten.

de·cath·lete [dɪ'kæθliːt] *s. sport* Zehnkämpfer *m*; **de·cath·lon** [dɪ'kæθlɒn] *s.* Zehnkampf *m*.

dec·a·tize ['dekətaɪz] *v/t. Seide* dekatieren.

de·cay [dɪ'keɪ] **I** *v/t.* **1.** verfallen, zerfallen (*a. phys.*), in Verfall geraten, zu'grunde gehen; **2.** verderben, verkümmern, verblühen; **3.** (ver)faulen (*a. Zahn*), (ver)modern, verwesen; **4.** schwinden, abnehmen, schwach werden, (her'ab)sinken: ***~ed with age*** altersschwach; **II** *s.* **5.** Verfall *m*, Zerfall *m* (*a. phys. von Radium etc.*): ***fall into ~*** → 1; **6.** Nieder-, Rückgang *m*, Verblühen *n*; Ru'in *m*; **7.** ⚕ Karies *f*, (Zahn)Fäule *f*; Schwund *m*; **8.** Fäulnis *f*, Vermodern *n*; **de'cayed** [-eɪd] *adj.* **1.** ver-, zerfallen; kraftlos; zerrüttet; **2.** her'untergekommen; **3.** verblüht; **4.** verfault, morsch; *geol.* verwittert; **5.** ⚕ kari'ös, schlecht (*Zahn*).

de·cease [dɪ'siːs] **I** *v/i.* sterben, verscheiden; **II** *s.* Tod *m*, Ableben *n*; **de'ceased** [-st] **I** *adj.* verstorben; **II** *s.* ***the ~*** a) der *od.* die Verstorbene, b) die Verstorbenen *pl.*

de·ce·dent [dɪ'siːdənt] *s.* ⚖ *Am.* **1.** → ***deceased*** II; **2.** Erb-lasser(in).

de·ceit [dɪ'siːt] *s.* **1.** Betrug *m*, (bewußte) Täuschung; Betrüge'rei *f*; **2.** Falschheit *f*, Tücke *f*; **de'ceit·ful** [-fʊl] *adj.* □ betrügerisch; falsch, 'hinterlistig; **de'ceit·ful·ness** [-fʊlnɪs] *s.* Falschheit *f*, 'Hinterlist *f*, Arglist *f*.

de·ceiv·a·ble [dɪ'siːvəbl] *adj.* leicht zu täuschen(d); **de·ceive** [dɪ'siːv] **I** *v/t.* **1.** täuschen (*Person od. Sache*), trügen (*Sache*): ***be ~d*** sich täuschen lassen, sich irren (***in*** in *dat.*); ***~ o.s.*** sich et. vormachen; **2.** *mst pass. Hoffnung etc.* enttäuschen; **II** *v/i.* **3.** trügen, täuschen (*Sache*); **de'ceiv·er** [-və] *s.* Betrüger (-in).

de·cel·er·ate [ˌdiː'seləreɪt] **I** *v/t.* verlangsamen; die Geschwindigkeit verringern von (*od. gen.*); **II** *v/i.* sich verlangsamen; s-e Geschwindigkeit verringern; **de·cel·er·a·tion** ['diːˌselə'reɪʃn] *s.* Verlangsamung *f*; Geschwindigkeitsabnahme *f*: ***~ lane*** *mot.* Verzögerungsspur *f*.

De·cem·ber [dɪ'sembə] *s.* De'zember *m*: ***in ~*** im Dezember.

de·cen·cy ['diːsnsɪ] *s.* **1.** Anstand *m*, Schicklichkeit *f*: ***for ~'s sake*** anstandshalber; ***sense of ~*** Anstandsgefühl *n*; **2.** Anständigkeit *f*; **3.** *pl.* Anstand *m*; **4.** *pl.* Annehmlichkeiten *pl. des Lebens*.

de·cen·ni·al [dɪ'senjəl] **I** *adj.* □ **1.** zehnjährig; **2.** alle zehn Jahre 'wiederkehrend; **II** *s.* **3.** *Am.* Zehn'jahrfeier *f*; **de'cen·ni·al·ly** [-lɪ] *adv.* alle zehn Jahre; **de'cen·ni·um** [-jəm] *pl.* **-ni·ums, -ni·a** [-jə] *s.* Jahr'zehnt *n*, De'zennium *n*.

de·cent ['diːsnt] *adj.* □ **1.** anständig: a) schicklich, b) sittsam, c) ehrbar; **2.** de'zent, unaufdringlich; **3.** F ‚anständig': a) annehmbar: ***a ~ meal***, b) nett: ***that was ~ of him***.

de·cen·tral·i·za·tion [diːˌsentrəlaɪ'zeɪʃn] *s.* Dezentralisierung *f*; **de·cen·tral·ize** [ˌdiː'sentrəlaɪz] *v/t.* dezentralisieren.

de·cep·tion [dɪ'sepʃn] *s.* **1.** Täuschung *f*, Irreführung *f*; **2.** Betrug *m*; **3.** Trugbild *n*; **de'cep·tive** [-ptɪv] *adj.* □ täuschend, irreführend, trügerisch: ***appearances are ~*** der Schein trügt.

deci- [desɪ] *in Zssgn* Dezi...

dec·i·bel ['desɪbel] *s. phys.* Dezi'bel *n*.

de·cide [dɪ'saɪd] **I** *v/t.* **1.** *et.* entscheiden; **2.** *j-n* bestimmen, veranlassen; *et.* bestimmen, festsetzen: ***~ the right moment***; ***that ~d me*** das gab für mich den Ausschlag, das bestärkte mich in m-m Entschluß; ***the weather ~d me against going*** aufgrund des Wetters entschloß ich mich, nicht zu gehen; **II** *v/i.* **3.** entscheiden, bestimmen, den Ausschlag geben; **4.** beschließen; sich entscheiden *od.* entschließen (***in favo[u]r of*** für; ***against doing*** nicht zu tun; ***to do*** zu tun); **5.** zu dem Schluß *od.* der Über'zeugung kommen: ***I ~d that it was worth trying***; **6.** feststellen, finden: ***we ~d that the weather was too bad***; **7.** ***~ (up)on*** sich entscheiden für *od.* über (*acc.*); festsetzen, -legen, bestimmen (*acc.*); **de'cid·ed** [-dɪd] *adj.* □ **1.** entschieden, unzweifelhaft, deutlich; **2.** entschieden, entschlossen, fest, bestimmt; **de'cid·ed·ly** [-dɪdlɪ] *adv.* entschieden, fraglos, bestimmt; **de'cid·er** [-də] *s.* **1.** *sport* Entscheidungskampf *m*, Stechen *n*; **2.** *das* Entscheidende, *die* Entscheidung.

de·cid·u·ous [dɪ'sɪdjʊəs] *adj.* **1.** ⚘ jedes Jahr abfallend: ***~ tree*** Laubbaum *m*; **2.** *zo.* abfallend (*Geweih etc.*).

dec·i|·gram(me) ['desɪgræm] *s.* Dezi'gramm *n*; **~·li·ter** *Am.*, **~·li·tre** *Brit.* ['desɪˌliːtə] *s.* Dezi'liter *m*, *n*.

dec·i·mal ['desɪml] ♈ **I** *adj.* □ → ***decimally***; dezi'mal, Dezimal...: ***~ fraction***; ***go ~*** das Dezimalsystem einführen; **II** *s.* a) Dezi'malzahl *f*, b) Dezi'male *f*, Dezi'malstelle *f*: ***circulating*** (***recurring***) ***~*** periodische (unendliche) Dezimalzahl; **'dec·i·mal·ize** [-məlaɪz] *v/t.* auf das Dezi'malsyˌstem 'umstellen; **'dec·i·mal·ly** [-məlɪ] *adv.* **1.** nach dem Dezi'malsyˌstem; **2.** in Dezi'malzahlen (ausgedrückt).

dec·i·mal| place *s.* Dezi'malstelle *f*; **~ point** *s.* Komma *n* (*im Englischen ein Punkt*) vor der ersten Dezi'malstelle: ***floating ~*** Fließkomma (*Taschenrechner etc.*); **~ sys·tem** *s.* Dezi'malsyˌstem *n*.

dec·i·mate ['desɪmeɪt] *v/t.* dezimieren, *fig. a.* stark schwächen *od.* vermindern; **dec·i·ma·tion** [desɪ'meɪʃn] *s.* Dezimierung *f*.

dec·i·me·ter *Am.*, **dec·i·me·tre** *Brit.* ['desɪˌmiːtə] *s.* Dezi'meter *m*, *n*.

de·ci·pher [dɪ'saɪfə] *v/t.* **1.** entziffern; **2.** dechiffrieren; **3.** *fig.* enträtseln; **de'ci·pher·a·ble** [-fərəbl] *adj.* entzifferbar; *fig.* enträtselbar; **de'ci·pher·ment** [-mənt] *s.* Entzifferung *f etc.*

de·ci·sion [dɪ'sɪʒn] *s.* **1.** Entscheidung *f* (*a.* ⚖); Entscheid *m*, Urteil *n*, Beschluß *m*: ***make*** (*od.* ***take***) ***a ~*** e-e Entscheidung treffen; **2.** Entschluß *m*: ***arrive at a ~***, ***come to a ~***, ***take a ~*** zu e-m Entschluß kommen; **3.** Entschlußkraft *f*, Entschlossenheit *f*: ***~ of character*** Charakterstärke *f*; **~-ˌmak·er** *s.* Entscheidungsträger *m*; **~-ˌmak·ing** *adj.* entscheidungstragend, entscheidend: ***~ board***.

de·ci·sive [dɪ'saɪsɪv] *adj.* □ **1.** entscheidend, ausschlag-, maßgebend; endgültig, schlüssig: ***be ~ in*** entscheidend beitragen zu; ***be ~ of*** entscheiden (*acc.*); ***~ battle*** Entscheidungsschlacht *f*; **2.** entschlossen, entschieden (*Person*); **de'ci·sive·ness** [-nɪs] *s.* **1.** entscheidende Kraft; **2.** Maßgeblichkeit *f*; **3.** Endgültigkeit *f*; **4.** Entschiedenheit *f*.

deck [dek] **I** *s.* **1.** ⚓ Deck *n*: ***on ~*** a) auf Deck, b) *Am.* F bereit, zur Hand; ***all hands on ~!*** alle Mann an Deck!; ***below ~*** unter Deck; ***clear the ~s*** (***for action***) a) das Schiff klar zum Gefecht machen, b) *fig.* sich bereitmachen; **2.** ✈ Tragdeck *n*, -fläche *f*; **3.** 🚃 (Wag'gon)Dach *n*; **4.** (Ober)Deck *n* (*Bus*); **5.** a) Laufwerk *n* (*e-s Plattenspielers*), b) → ***tape deck***; **6.** *sl.* ‚Briefchen' *n* (*Rauschgift*); Spiel *n*, Pack *m* (Spiel-) Karten; **II** *v/t.* **7.** *oft* ***~ out*** a) (aus-) schmücken, b) *j-n* her'ausputzen; **'~-chair** *s.* Liegestuhl *m*.

-deck·er [dekə] *s. in Zssgn* ...decker *m*; → ***three-decker***.

deck| game *s.* Bordspiel *n*; **~ hand** *s.* ⚓ Ma'trose *m*.

deck·le-edged [ˌdekl'edʒd] *adj.* **1.** mit Büttenrand; **2.** unbeschnitten: ***~ book***.

de·claim [dɪ'kleɪm] **I** *v/i.* **1.** reden, e-e Rede halten; **2.** ***~ against*** eifern *od.* wettern gegen; **3.** Phrasen dreschen; **II** *v/t.* **4.** deklamieren, (*contp.* bom'bastisch) vortragen.

dec·la·ma·tion [ˌdeklə'meɪʃn] *s.* **1.** Deklamati'on *f* (*a.* ♪); **2.** bom'bastische Rede; **3.** Ti'rade *f*; **4.** Vortragsübung *f*; **de·clam·a·to·ry** [dɪ'klæmətərɪ] *adj.* □ **1.** Rede..., Vortrags...; **2.** deklama'torisch; **3.** eifernd; **4.** bom'bastisch, thea'tralisch.

de·clar·a·ble [dɪ'kleərəbl] *adj.* zollpflichtig; **de'clar·ant** [-rənt] *s.* **1.** ⚖ Erschienene(r *m*) *f*; **2.** *Am.* Einbürgerungsanwärter(in).

dec·la·ra·tion [ˌdeklə'reɪʃn] *s.* **1.** Erklärung *f*, Aussage *f*: ***make a ~*** eine Erklärung abgeben; ***~ of intent*** Absichtserklärung; ***~ of war*** Kriegserklärung; **2.** Mani'fest *n*, Proklamati'on *f*; **3.** ⚖ a) *Am.* Klageschrift *f*, b) Beteuerung *f* (*an Eides Statt*); **4.** Anmeldung *f*, Angabe *f*: ***~ of bankruptcy*** ✝ Konkursanmeldung; ***customs ~*** Zolldeklaration *f*, -erklärung *f*; **5.** *Bridge*: Ansage *f*; **de·clar·a·tive** [dɪ'klærətɪv] *adj.*: ***~ sentence*** *ling.* Aussagesatz *m*; **de·clar·a·to·ry** [dɪ'klærətərɪ] *adj.* erklärend: ***be ~***

of erklären, darlegen, feststellen; ~ ***judgment*** ⚖ Feststellungsurteil *n*.
de·clare [dɪ'kleə] **I** *v/t.* **1.** erklären, aussagen, verkünden, bekanntmachen, proklamieren: ~ ***war*** (***on***) (*j-m*) den Krieg erklären, *fig.* (*j-m*) den Kampf ansagen; ***he was ~d winner*** er wurde zum Sieger erklärt; **2.** erklären, behaupten; **3.** angeben, anmelden; erklären, deklarieren (*Zoll*); † *Dividende* festsetzen; **4.** *Kartenspiel*: ansagen; **5.** ~ ***o.s.*** a) sich erklären (*a. durch Heiratsantrag*), sich offenbaren, s-e Meinung kundtun, b) sich im wahren Licht zeigen; ~ ***o.s. for s.th.*** sich zu e-r Sache bekennen; **II** *v/i.* **6.** erklären, bestätigen: ***well, I ~!*** ich muß schon sagen!, nanu!; **7.** sich erklären *od.* entscheiden (***for*** für; ***against*** gegen); **8.** ~ ***off*** a) absagen, b) sich lossagen (***from*** von); *Kricket*: ein Spiel vorzeitig abbrechen; **de'clared** [-eəd] *adj.* □ *fig.* erklärt (*Feind etc.*); **de'clar·ed·ly** [-eərɪdlɪ] *adv.* erklärtermaßen, ausgesprochen.
de·clas·si·fy [dɪ'klæsɪfaɪ] *v/t.* die Geheimhaltung (*gen.*) aufheben, *Dokumente etc.* freigeben.
de·clen·sion [dɪ'klenʃn] *s.* **1.** Abweichung *f*, Abfall *m* (***from*** von); **2.** Verfall *m*, Niedergang *m*; **3.** *ling.* Deklinati'on *f*; **de'clen·sion·al** [-ʃənl] *adj. ling.* Deklinations...
de·clin·a·ble [dɪ'klaɪnəbl] *adj. ling.* deklinierbar; **dec·li·na·tion** [ˌdeklɪ'neɪʃn] *s.* **1.** Neigung *f*, Abschüssigkeit *f*; **2.** Abweichung *f*; **3.** *ast., phys.* Deklinati'on *f*: ~ ***compass*** ⚓ Deklinationsbussole *f*; ***compass*** ~ Mißweisung *f*.
de·cline [dɪ'klaɪn] **I** *v/i.* **1.** sich neigen, sich senken; **2.** sich neigen, zur Neige *od.* zu Ende gehen: ***declining years*** Lebensabend *m*; **3.** abnehmen, nachlassen, zu'rückgehen; sich verschlechtern, schwächer werden; verfallen; **4.** sinken, fallen (*Preise*); **5.** (höflich) ablehnen; **II** *v/t.* **6.** neigen, senken; **7.** ablehnen, nicht annehmen, ausschlagen; es ablehnen (***doing*** *od.* ***to do*** zu tun); **8.** *ling.* deklinieren, beugen; **III** *s.* **9.** Neigung *f*, Senkung *f*, Abhang *m*; **10.** Neige *f*, Ende *n*: ~ ***of life*** Lebensabend *m*; **11.** Nieder-, Rückgang *m*, Abnahme *f*; Verschlechterung *f*: ***be on the*** ~ a) zur Neige gehen, b) im Niedergang begriffen sein, sinken; ~ ***of strength*** Kräfteverfall *m*; ~ ***of*** (*od.* ***in***) ***prices*** Preisrückgang; ~ ***in value*** Wertminderung *f*; **12.** ⚕ körperlicher *od.* geistiger Verfall, Siechtum *n*.
de·cliv·i·tous [dɪ'klɪvɪtəs] *adj.* abschüssig, steil; **de'cliv·i·ty** [-vətɪ] *s.* **1.** Abschüssigkeit *f*; **2.** Abhang *m*.
de·clutch [ˌdiː'klʌtʃ] *v/i. mot.* auskuppeln.
de·coct [dɪ'kɒkt] *v/t.* auskochen, absieden; **de'coc·tion** [-kʃn] *s.* **1.** Auskochen *n*, Absieden *n*; **2.** Absud *m*; *pharm.* De'kokt *n*.
de·code [ˌdiː'kəʊd] *v/t.* decodieren (*a. ling., Computer*), dechiffrieren, entschlüsseln, über'setzen; ˌ**de'cod·er** [-də] *s. a. Radio, Computer*: De'coder *m*.
dé·col·le·té [deɪ'kɒlteɪ] (*Fr.*) *adj.* **1.** (tief) ausgeschnitten (*Kleid*); **2.** dekolletiert (*Dame*).
de·col·o·nize [ˌdiː'kɒlənaɪz] *v/t.* dekolonisieren, in die Unabhängigkeit entlassen.
de·col·or·ant [diː'kʌlərənt] **I** *adj.* entfärbend, bleichend; **II** *s.* Bleichmittel *n*; **de'col·o(u)r·ize** [-raiz] *v/t.* entfärben, bleichen.
de·com·pose [ˌdiːkəm'pəʊz] **I** *v/t.* **1.** zerlegen, spalten; **2.** zersetzen; **3.** ⚗, *phys.* scheiden, abbauen; **II** *v/i.* **4.** sich auflösen, zerfallen; **5.** sich zersetzen, verwesen, verfaulen; ˌ**de·com'posed** [-zd] *adj.* verfault, verdorben; **de·com·po·si·tion** [ˌdiːkɒmpə'zɪʃn] *s.* **1.** ⚗, *phys.* Zerlegung *f*, Aufspaltung *f*, Scheidung *f*, Auflösung *f*, Abbau *m*; **2.** Zersetzung *f*, Zerfall *m*; **3.** Verwesung *f*, Fäulnis *f*.
de·com·press [ˌdiːkəm'pres] *v/t.* dekomprimieren, den Druck vermindern in (*dat.*); ˌ**de·com'pres·sion** [-eʃn] *s.* Dekompressi'on *f*, Druckverminderung *f*.
de·con·tam·i·nate [ˌdiːkən'tæmɪneɪt] *v/t.* entgiften, -seuchen, -strahlen; **de·con·tam·i·na·tion** ['diːkənˌtæmɪ'neɪʃn] *s.* Entgiftung *f*, -seuchung *f*, -gasung *f*.
de·con·trol [ˌdiːkən'trəʊl] **I** *v/t.* die Zwangsbewirtschaftung aufheben von *od.* für; *Waren, Handel* freigeben; **II** *s.* Aufhebung *f* der Zwangsbewirtschaftung, Freigabe *f*.
dé·cor ['deɪkɔː] (*Fr.*) *s.* ⚠, *thea. etc.* De'kor *m*, *n*, Ausstattung *f*.
dec·o·rate ['dekəreɪt] *v/t.* **1.** (aus-)schmücken, (ver)zieren, dekorieren; **2.** *Wohnung* a) (neu) tapezieren *od.* streichen, b) einrichten, ausstatten; **3.** *mit e-m Orden* dekorieren, auszeichnen; **dec·o·ra·tion** [ˌdekə'reɪʃn] *s.* **1.** Ausschmückung *f*, Verzierung *f*; **2.** Schmuck *m*, Zierat *m*, Dekorati'on *f*; **3.** Orden *m*, Ehrenzeichen *n*; **4.** *a.* ***interior*** ~ a) Innenausstattung *f*, b) 'Innenarchitekˌtur *f*.
Dec·o·ra·tion Day → ***Memorial Day***.
dec·o·ra·tive ['dekərətɪv] *adj.* □ dekora'tiv, schmückend, ornamen'tal, Zier..., Schmuck...: ~ ***plant*** Zierpflanze *f*; **dec·o·ra·tor** ['dekəreɪtə] *s.* **1.** Dekora'teur *m*; **2.** → ***interior*** 1; **3.** Maler *m* u. Tapezierer *m*.
dec·o·rous ['dekərəs] *adj.* □ schicklich, anständig.
de·cor·ti·cate [ˌdiː'kɔːtɪkeɪt] *v/t.* **1.** entrinden; schälen; **2.** enthülsen.
de·co·rum [dɪ'kɔːrəm] *s.* **1.** Anstand *m*, Schicklichkeit *f*, De'korum *n*; **2.** Eti'kette *f*, Anstandsformen *pl.*
de·coy I *s.* ['diːkɔɪ] **1.** Köder *m*, Lockspeise *f*; **2.** *a.* ~ ***duck*** Lockvogel *m* (*a. fig.*); **3.** *hunt.* Entenfang *m*, -falle *f*; **4.** ⚔ Scheinanlage *f*; **II** *v/t.* [dɪ'kɔɪ] **5.** ködern, locken; **6.** *fig.* (ver)locken, verleiten; ~ ***ship*** *s.* ⚓, ⚔ U-Boot-Falle *f*.
de·crease [diː'kriːs] **I** *v/i.* abnehmen, sich vermindern, kleiner werden: ~ ***in length*** kürzer werden; **II** *v/t.* vermindern, verringern, reduzieren, her'absetzen; **III** *s.* ['diːkriːs] Abnahme *f*, Verminderung *f*, Verringerung *f*; Rückgang *m*: ~ ***in prices*** Preisrückgang; ***be on the*** ~ → I; **de'creas·ing·ly** [-sɪŋlɪ] *adv.* immer weniger: ~ ***rare***.
de·cree [dɪ'kriː] **I** *s.* **1.** De'kret *n*, Erlaß *m*, Verfügung *f*, Verordnung *f*: ***issue a*** ~ e-e Verfügung erlassen; ***by*** ~ auf dem Verordnungsweg; **2.** ⚖ Entscheid *m*, Urteil *n*: ~ ***absolute*** rechtskräftiges (Scheidungs)Urteil; → ***nisi***; **3.** *fig.* Ratschluß *m Gottes*, Fügung *f des Schicksals*; **II** *v/t.* **4.** verfügen, an-, verordnen.
dec·re·ment ['dekrɪmənt] *s.* Abnahme *f*, Verminderung *f*.
de·crep·it [dɪ'krepɪt] *adj.* **1.** altersschwach, klapp(e)rig (*beide a. fig.*); **2.** verfallen, baufällig.
de·cres·cent [dɪ'kresnt] *adj.* abnehmend: ~ ***moon***.
de·cry [dɪ'kraɪ] *v/t.* schlecht-, her'untermachen, her'absetzen.
dec·u·ple ['dekjʊpl] **I** *adj.* zehnfach; **II** *s. das* Zehnfache; **III** *v/t.* verzehnfachen.
de·cus·sate [dɪ'kʌsət] *adj.* **1.** sich kreuzend *od.* schneidend; **2.** ⚘ kreuzgegenständig.
ded·i·cate ['dedɪkeɪt] *v/t.* (***to*** *dat.*) **1.** weihen, widmen; **2.** *s-e Zeit etc.* widmen; **3.** ~ ***o.s.*** sich widmen *od.* hingeben; sich zuwenden; **4.** *Buch etc.* widmen, zueignen; **5.** *Am.* feierlich eröffnen *od.* einweihen; **6.** a) der Öffentlichkeit zugänglich machen, b) dem öffentlichen Verkehr über'geben: ~ ***a road***; **7.** *dem Feuer, der Erde* über'antworten; **'ded·i·cat·ed** [-tɪd] *adj.* **1.** pflichtbewußt, hingebungsvoll; **2.** engagiert; **ded·i·ca·tion** [ˌdedɪ'keɪʃn] *s.* **1.** Weihung *f*, Widmung *f*; feierliche Einweihung; **2.** 'Hingabe *f* (***to*** an *acc.*), Engage'ment *n*; **3.** Widmung *f*, Zueignung *f*; **4.** *Am.* feierliche Einweihung *od.* Eröffnung; **5.** 'Übergabe *f* an den öffentlichen Verkehr; **'ded·i·ca·tor** [-tə] *s.* Widmende(r *m*) *f*; **'ded·i·ca·to·ry** [-kətərɪ] *adj.* (Ein)Weihungs..., Widmungs..., Zueignungs...
de·duce [dɪ'djuːs] *v/t.* **1.** folgern, schließen (***from*** aus); **2.** ab-, 'herleiten (***from*** von); **de'duc·i·ble** [-səbl] *adj.* **1.** zu folgern(d); **2.** ab-, 'herleitbar, 'herzuleiten(d).
de·duct [dɪ'dʌkt] *v/t. e-n Betrag* abziehen (***from*** von), einbehalten; (*von der Steuer*) absetzen: ***after ~ing*** nach Abzug von *od. gen.*; ***~ing expenses*** abzüglich (der) Unkosten; **de'duct·i·ble** [-təbl] *adj.* **1.** abzugsfähig; **2.** (*von der Steuer*) absetzbar; **de'duc·tion** [-kʃn] *s.* **1.** Abzug *m*, Abziehen *n*; **2.** † Abzug *m*, Ra'batt *m*, (Preis)Nachlaß *m*; **3.** (Schluß)Folgerung *f*, Schluß *m*; **4.** 'Herleitung *f*; **de'duc·tive** [-tɪv] *adj.* □ **1.** deduk'tiv, folgernd, schließend; **2.** → ***deducible***.
deed [diːd] **I** *s.* **1.** Tat *f*, Handlung *f*: ***in word and*** ~ in Wort u. Tat; **2.** Helden-, Großtat *f*; **3.** ⚖ (Vertrags-, *bsd.* Über'tragungs)Urkunde *f*, Doku'ment *n*: ~ ***of donation*** Schenkungsurkunde; **II** *v/t.* **4.** *Am.* urkundlich über'tragen (***to*** auf *j-n*); ~ ***poll*** *s.* ⚖ einseitige (gesiegelte) Erklärung (*e-r Vertragspartei*).
dee·jay ['diːdʒeɪ] *s.* F Diskjockey *m*.
deem [diːm] **I** *v/i.* denken, meinen; **II** *v/t.* halten für, erachten für, betrachten als: ***I ~ it advisable***.
de-e·mo·tion·al·ize [ˌdiːɪ'məʊʃnəlaɪz] *v/t.* versachlichen.
de-em·pha·size [ˌdiː'emfəsaɪz] *v/t.* bagatellisieren.
deem·ster ['diːmstə] *s.* Richter *m* (*auf der Insel Man*).
deep [diːp] **I** *adj.* □ → ***deeply***; **1.** tief

(*vertikal*): **~ *hole*; ~ *snow*; ~ *sea*** Tiefsee *f*; ***in ~ water*(*s*)** *fig.* in Schwierigkeiten; ***go off the ~ end*** a) *Brit.* in Rage kommen, b) *Am.* et. unüberlegt riskieren; **2.** tief (*horizontal*): **~ *cupboard*; ~ *forests*; ~ *border*** breiter Rand; ***they marched four ~*** sie marschierten in Viererreihen; ***three men ~*** drei Mann hoch (*zu dritt*); **3.** tief, vertieft, versunken (***in*** in *acc.*): **~ *in thought*; 4.** tief, gründlich, scharfsinnig: **~ *learning*** gründliches Wissen; **~ *intellect*** scharfer Verstand; ***a ~ thinker*** ein tiefer Denker; **5.** tief, heftig, stark, fest, schwer: **~ *sleep*** tiefer *od.* fester Schlaf; **~ *mourning*** tiefe Trauer; **~ *disappointment*** tiefe *od.* bittere Enttäuschung; **~ *interest*** großes Interesse; **~ *grief*** schweres Leid; **~ *in debt*** stark *od.* tief verschuldet; **6.** tief, innig, aufrichtig: **~ *love*; ~ *gratitude*; 7.** tief, dunkel; verborgen, geheim: **~ *night*** tiefe Nacht; **~ *silence*** tiefes *od.* völliges Schweigen; **~ *secret*** tiefes Geheimnis; **~ *designs*** dunkle Pläne; ***he is a ~ one*** *sl.* er hat es faustdick hinter den Ohren; **8.** schwierig: **~ *problem*; *that is too ~ for me*** das ist mir zu hoch; **9.** tief, dunkel (*Farbe, Klang*); **10.** *psych.* un(ter)bewußt; **11.** ⚕ subku'tan; **II** *adv.* **12.** tief (*a. fig.*): **~ *into the flesh*** tief ins Fleisch; ***still waters run ~*** stille Wasser sind tief; **~ *into the night*** (bis) tief in die Nacht (hinein); ***drink ~*** unmäßig trinken; **III** *s.* **13.** Tiefe *f* (*a. fig.*); Abgrund *m*: ***in the ~ of night*** in tiefster Nacht; **14. *the ~*** *poet.* das Meer.

'deep|-dish pie *s.* 'Napfpa͵stete *f*; **͵~-'draw** *v/t.* [*irr.*] ⚙ tiefziehen; **͵~-'drawn** *adj.* **1.** ⚙ tiefgezogen; **2. ~ *sigh*** tiefer Seufzer.

deep·en ['di:pən] **I** *v/t.* **1.** tiefer machen, vertiefen; verbreitern; **2.** *fig.* vertiefen (*a. Farben*), verstärken, steigern; **II** *v/i.* **3.** tiefer werden, sich vertiefen; **4.** *fig.* sich vertiefen *od.* steigern, stärker werden; **5.** dunkler werden.

'deep|-felt *adj.* tiefempfunden; **͵~-'freeze I** *s.* Tiefkühlgerät *n*, -truhe *f*, -schrank *m*; **II** *adj.* Tiefkühl…, Gefrier…; **III** *v/t.* [*irr.*] tiefkühlen, einfrieren; **͵~-'fro·zen** *adj.* tiefgefroren, Tiefkühl…; **'~-fry** *v/t.* fritieren, in schwimmendem Fett braten; **~ fry·er** *s.*, **'~-͵fry·ing pan** *s.* Fri'teuse *f*; **͵~-'laid** *adj.* schlau (*Plan*).

deep·ly ['di:plɪ] *adv.* tief (*a. fig.*): **~ *indebted*** äußerst dankbar; **~ *hurt*** tief *od.* schwer gekränkt; **~ *interested*** höchst interessiert; **~ *read*** sehr belesen; ***drink ~*** unmäßig trinken; ***go ~ into s.th.*** e-r Sache auf den Grund gehen.

deep·ness ['di:pnɪs] *s.* **1.** Tiefe *f* (*a. fig.*); **2.** Dunkelheit *f*; **3.** Gründlichkeit *f*; **4.** Scharfsinn *m*; **5.** Durch'triebenheit *f*.

͵deep|-'read *adj.* sehr belesen; **͵~-'rooted** *adj. bsd. fig.* tief eingewurzelt, fest verwurzelt; *fig. a.* eingefleischt; **͵~-'sea** *adj.* Tiefsee…, Hochsee…: **~ *fish*** Tiefseefisch *m*; **~ *fishing*** Hochseefischerei *f*; **͵~-'seat·ed** → ***deep-rooted***; **'~-set** *adj.* tiefliegend: **~ *eyes*; the ≈ South** *s. Am.* der tiefe Süden (*südlichste Staaten der USA*).

deer [dɪə] *pl.* **deer** *s.* **1.** *zo.* a) Hirsch *m*, b) Reh *n*: ***red ~*** Rot-, Edelhirsch; **2.** Hoch-, Rotwild *n*; **'~-͵for·est** *s.* Hochwildgehege *n*; **'~-hound** *s.* schottischer Jagdhund; **'~-lick** *s.* Salzlecke *f*; **'~-park** *s.* Wildpark *m*; **'~-shot** *s.* Rehposten *m* (*Schrot*); **'~-skin** *s.* Hirsch-, Rehleder *n*; **'~͵stalk·er** *s.* **1.** Pirscher *m*; **2.** Jagdmütze *f*; **'~͵stalk·ing** *s.* (Rotwild)Pirsch *f*.

de-es·ca·late [͵di:'eskəleɪt] **I** *v/t.* **1.** *Krieg etc.* deeskalieren; **2.** *fig.* her'unterschrauben; **II** *v/i.* **3.** deeskalieren; **de-es·ca·la·tion** [͵di:eskə'leɪʃn] *s. pol.* Deeskalati'on *f* (*a. fig.*).

de·face [dɪ'feɪs] *v/t.* **1.** entstellen, verunstalten, beschädigen; **2.** ausstreichen, unleserlich machen; **3.** *Briefmarken* entwerten; **de'face·ment** [-mənt] *s.* Entstellung *f* (*etc.*).

de fac·to [di:'fæktəʊ] (*Lat.*) **I** *adj.* De-facto-…; **II** *adv.* de 'facto, tatsächlich.

de·fal·ca·tion [͵di:fæl'keɪʃn] *s.* **1.** Veruntreuung *f*, Unter'schlagung *f*; **2.** unter'schlagenes Geld.

def·a·ma·tion [͵defə'meɪʃn] *s.* Verleumdung *f*, ⚖ *a.* (verleumderische) Beleidigung; **de·fam·a·to·ry** [dɪ'fæmətərɪ] *adj.* ☐ verleumderisch, Schmäh…: ***be ~ of s.o.*** j-n verleumden; **de·fame** [dɪ'feɪm] *v/t.* verleumden; **de·fam·er** [dɪ'feɪmə] *s.* Verleumder(in).

de·fat·ted [di:'fætɪd] *adj.* entfettet.

de·fault [dɪ'fɔ:lt] **I** *s.* **1.** (Pflicht)Versäumnis *n*, Unter'lassung *f*; **2.** *bsd.* ⚚ Nichterfüllung *f*, Verzug *m*, Versäumnis *n*, Säumnis *f*, Zahlungseinstellung *f*; *engS.* Zahlungsverzug *m*: ***be in ~*** im Verzug sein; **3.** ⚖ Nichterscheinen *n* vor Gericht: ***judg*(*e*)*ment by ~*** Versäumnisurteil *n*; **4.** *sport* Nichtantreten *n*; **5.** Fehlen *n*, Mangel *m*: ***in ~ of*** mangels, in Ermangelung (*gen.*); ***in ~ of which*** widrigenfalls; ***go by ~*** unterbleiben; **II** *v/i.* **6.** s-n Verpflichtungen nicht nachkommen: **~ *on s.th.*** et. vernachlässigen, mit et. im Rückstand sein; **7.** ⚚ s-n Verbindlichkeiten nicht nachkommen, im (Zahlungs)Verzug sein: **~ *on a debt*** s-e Schuld nicht bezahlen; **8.** ⚖ nicht vor Gericht erscheinen; **9.** *sport* nicht antreten; **III** *v/t.* **10.** *e-r Verpflichtung* nicht nachkommen, in Verzug geraten mit; **11.** ⚖ wegen Nichterscheinens (vor Gericht) verurteilen; **12.** *sport* nicht antreten (*zu e-m Kampf*); **de'fault·er** [-tə] *s.* **1.** Säumige(r *m*) *f*; **2.** ⚚ a) säumiger Zahler *od.* Schuldner, b) Zahlungsunfähige(r *m*) *f*; **3.** ⚖ vor Gericht nicht Erscheinende(r *m*) *f*; **4.** ⚔ *Brit.* Delin'quent *m*.

de·fea·sance [dɪ'fi:zns] *s.* ⚖ **1.** Aufhebung *f*, Annullierung *f*, Nichtigkeitserklärung *f*; **2.** Nichtigkeitsklausel *f*; **de'fea·si·ble** [-zəbl] *adj.* anfecht-, annullierbar.

de·feat [dɪ'fi:t] **I** *v/t.* **1.** besiegen, schlagen: ***it ~s me to inf.*** es geht über m-e Kraft zu *inf.*; **2.** *Angriff etc.* zu'rückschlagen, abwehren; **3.** *parl. Antrag* zu Fall bringen, ablehnen; **4.** vereiteln, zu'nichte machen: ***that ~s the purpose*** das verfehlt den Zweck; **II** *s.* **5.** Niederwerfung *f*, Besiegung *f*; **6.** Niederlage *f* (*a. fig.*): ***admit ~*** sich geschlagen geben; **7.** *parl.* Ablehnung *f*; **8.** Vereitelung *f*, Vernichtung *f*; **9.** 'Mißerfolg *m*, Fehlschlag *m*; **de'feat·ism** [-tɪzəm] *s.* Defä'tismus *m*, Miesmache'rei *f*; **de'feat·ist** [-tɪst] **I** *s.* Defä'tist *m*; **II** *adj.* defä'tistisch.

def·e·cate ['defɪkeɪt] **I** *v/t.* reinigen; *fig.* läutern; **II** *v/i.* ⚕ Stuhlgang haben; **def·e·ca·tion** [͵defɪ'keɪʃn] *s.* ⚕ Stuhlgang *m*.

de·fect I *s.* ['di:fekt] **1.** De'fekt *m*, Fehler *m* (***in*** an *dat.*, in *dat.*): **~ *in title*** ⚖ Fehler im Recht; **2.** Mangel *m*, Unvollkommenheit *f*, Schwäche *f*; **3.** (*geistiger od. psychischer*) De'fekt; ⚕ Gebrechen *n*: **~ *in character*** Charakterfehler *m*; **~ *of vision*** Sehfehler *m*; **II** *v/i.* [dɪ'fekt] **4.** abtrünnig werden; **5.** *zum Feind* 'übergehen; **de·fec·tion** [dɪ'fekʃn] *s.* **1.** Abfall *m*, Lossagung *f* (***from*** von); **2.** Treubruch *m*; **3.** 'Übertritt *m* (***to*** zu); **de·fec·tive** [dɪ'fektɪv] **I** *adj.* ☐ **1.** mangelhaft, unvollkommen: ***mentally ~*** schwachsinnig; ***he is ~ in*** es mangelt ihm an (*dat.*); **2.** schadhaft, de'fekt; **II** *s.* **3. *mental ~*** Schwachsinnige(r *m*) *f*; **de·fec·tive·ness** [dɪ'fektɪvnɪs] *s.* **1.** Mangelhaftigkeit *f*; **2.** Schadhaftigkeit *f*; **de·fec·tor** [dɪ'fektə] *s.* Abtrünnige(r *m*) *f*, 'Überläufer(in).

de·fence, *Am.* **de·fense** [dɪ'fens] *s.* **1.** Verteidigung *f*, Schutz *m*, Abwehr *f*: ***come to s.o.'s ~*** j-n verteidigen; **~ *mechanism*** *biol.*, *psych.* Abwehrmechanismus *m*; **2.** ⚖ *allg.* Verteidigung *f*, *a.* Einrede *f*: ***in his ~*** zu s-r Entlastung; ***conduct one's own ~*** sich selbst verteidigen; → ***counsel*** 4; ***witness*** 1; **3.** Verteidigung *f*, Rechtfertigung *f*: ***in his ~*** zu s-r Rechtfertigung; **4.** ⚔ Verteidigung *f*, *sport a.* Abwehr *f* (*Spieler od. deren Spielweise*); *pl.* Verteidigungsanlagen *pl.*: **~ *spending*** Verteidigungsausgaben *pl.*; **de'fence·less** [-lɪs] *adj.* ☐ **1.** schutz-, wehr-, hilflos; **2.** ⚔ unbefestigt; **de'fence·less·ness** [-lɪsnɪs] *s.* Schutz-, Wehrlosigkeit *f*.

de·fend [dɪ'fend] *v/t.* **1.** (***from, against***) verteidigen (gegen), schützen (vor *dat.*, gegen); **2.** *Meinung etc.* verteidigen, rechtfertigen; **3.** *Rechte* schützen, wahren; **4.** ⚖ a) *j-n* verteidigen, b) sich auf *e-e Klage* einlassen: **~ *the suit*** den Klageanspruch bestreiten; **de'fend·a·ble** [-dəbl] *adj.* zu verteidigen(d); **de'fend·ant** [-dənt] ⚖ **I** *s.* a) *Zivilrecht*: Beklagte(r *m*) *f*, b) *Strafrecht*: Angeklagte(r *m*) *f*; **II** *adj.* a) beklagt, b) angeklagt; **de'fend·er** [-də] *s.* **1.** Verteidiger *m*, *sport a.* Abwehrspieler *m*; **2.** Beschützer *m*.

de·fense *etc. Am.* → ***defence*** *etc.*

de·fen·si·ble [dɪ'fensəbl] *adj.* ☐ **1.** zu verteidigen(d), haltbar; **2.** zu rechtfertigen(d), vertretbar; **de'fen·sive** [-sɪv] **I** *adj.* ☐ **1.** defen'siv, verteidigend, schützend; abwehrend (*a. fig. Geste etc.*); **2.** Verteidigungs…; Schutz…, Abwehr… (*a. biol.*); **II** *s.* **3.** Defen'sive *f*, Verteidigung *f*: ***on the ~*** in der Defensive.

de·fer[1] [dɪ'fɜ:] *v/t.* **1.** auf-, verschieben; **2.** hin'ausschieben; zu'rückstellen (*Am. a.* ⚔).

de·fer[2] [dɪ'fɜ:] *v/i.* (***to***) sich fügen, nachgeben (*dat.*), sich beugen (vor *dat.*); sich *j-s* Wunsche fügen; **def·er·ence** ['defərəns] *s.* **1.** Ehrerbietung *f*, Achtung *f*: ***with all due ~ to*** bei aller Hochachtung vor (*dat.*); **2.** Nachgiebigkeit *f*,

Rücksicht(nahme) *f*: ***in ~ to your wishes*** wunschgemäß; **def·er·ent** [ˈdefərənt] *adj.*, **def·er·en·tial** [ˌdefəˈrenʃl] *adj.* □ **1.** ehrerbietig; **2.** rücksichtsvoll.

de·fer·ment [dɪˈfɜːmənt] *s.* **1.** Aufschub *m*; **2.** ⚔ *Am.* Zuˈrückstellung *f* (vom Wehrdienst); **deˈfer·ra·ble** [-ɜːrəbl] *adj.* **1.** aufschiebbar; **2.** ⚔ *Am.* zuˈrückstellbar.

de·ferred an·nu·i·ty [dɪˈfɜːd] *s.* hinˈausgeschobene Rente; **~ bond** *s. Am.* Obligatiˈon *f* mit aufgeschobener Zinszahlung; **~ pay·ment** *s.* **1.** Zahlungsaufschub *m*, **2.** Ratenzahlung *f*; **~ shares** *s. pl.* ✝ Nachzugsaktien *pl.*; **~ terms** *s. pl. Brit.* ˈAbzahlungssysˌstem *n*: ***on ~*** auf Abzahlung *od.* Raten.

de·fi·ance [dɪˈfaɪəns] *s.* **1.** a) Trotz *m*, ˈWiderstand *m*, b) Hohn *m*, offene Verachtung: ***in ~ of*** ungeachtet (*gen.*), trotz (*gen. od. dat.*), *e-m Gebot etc.* zuwider, *j-m* zum Trotz *od.* Hohn; ***bid ~, set at ~*** Trotz bieten, hohnsprechen (***to*** *dat.*); **2.** Herˈausforderung *f*; **deˈfi·ant** [-nt] *adj.* □ trotzig, herˈausfordernd.

de·fi·cien·cy [dɪˈfɪʃnsɪ] *s.* **1.** (***of***) Mangel *m* (an *dat.*), Fehlen *n* (von): ***~ disease*** ⚕ Mangelkrankheit *f*; **2.** Fehlbetrag *m*, Manko *n*, Ausfall *m*, Defizit *n*; **3.** Mangelhaftigkeit *f*, Schwäche *f*, Lücke *f*, Unzulänglichkeit *f*; **deˈfi·cient** [-nt] *adj.* □ **1.** unzureichend, mangelhaft, ungenügend: ***be ~ in*** ermangeln (*gen.*), es fehlen lassen an (*dat.*), arm sein an (*dat.*); ***he is ~ in courage*** ihm fehlt es an Mut; **2.** fehlend: ***~ amount*** Fehlbetrag *m*.

def·i·cit [ˈdefɪsɪt] *s.* **1.** ✝ Defizit *n*, Fehlbetrag *m*, ˈUnterbiˌlanz *f*; **2.** Mangel (***in*** an *dat.*); **~ spend·ing** *s.* ✝ Deficit-spending *n*, Defizitfinanzierung *f*.

de·file¹ I *s.* [ˈdiːfaɪl] **1.** Engpaß *m*, Hohlweg *m*; **2.** ⚔ Vorˈbeimarsch *m*; **II** *v/i.* [dɪˈfaɪl] **3.** defilieren, vorˈbeimarschieren.

de·file² [dɪˈfaɪl] *v/t.* **1.** beschmutzen, verunreinigen; **2.** *fig.* besudeln, beflecken, verunglimpfen; **3.** schänden; **4.** entweihen; **deˈfile·ment** [-mənt] *s.* Besudelung *f etc.*

de·fin·a·ble [dɪˈfaɪnəbl] *adj.* □ definier-, erklär-, bestimmbar; **de·fine** [dɪˈfaɪn] *v/t.* **1.** *Wort etc.* definieren, (genau) erklären; **2.** (genau) bezeichnen *od.* bestimmen; kennzeichnen, festlegen; klarmachen; **3.** scharf abzeichnen, (klar) umˈreißen, be-, umˈgrenzen.

def·i·nite [ˈdefɪnɪt] *adj.* □ **1.** bestimmt (*a. ling.*), präˈzis, klar, deutlich, eindeutig, genau; **2.** definiˈtiv, endgültig; **ˈdef·i·nite·ly** [-lɪ] *adv.* **1.** bestimmt (*etc.*); **2.** zweifellos, absoˈlut, entschieden; **ˈdef·i·nite·ness** [-nɪs] *s.* Bestimmtheit *f*; **def·i·ni·tion** [ˌdefɪˈnɪʃn] *s.* **1.** Definitiˈon *f*, (genaue) Erklärung; (Begriffs)Bestimmung *f*; **2.** Genauigkeit *f*, Exˈaktheit *f*; **3.** (*a.* Bild-, Ton-) Schärfe *f*, Präzisiˈon *f*; *TV* Auflösung *f*; **de·fin·i·tive** [dɪˈfɪnɪtɪv] **I** *adj.* □ **1.** definiˈtiv, endgültig; maßgeblich (*Buch*); **2.** → ***definite*** 1; **II** *s.* **3.** *ling.* Bestimmungswort *n*.

def·la·grate [ˈdefləgreɪt] *v/i.* (*u. v/t.*) ⚒ rasch abbrennen (lassen); **def·la·gra·tion** [ˌdefləˈgreɪʃn] *s.* ⚒ Verpuffung *f*.

de·flate [dɪˈfleɪt] *v/t.* **1.** (die) Luft ablassen aus, entleeren; **2.** ✝ *Geldumlauf etc.* deflationieren, herˈabsetzen; **3.** *fig.* a) *j-n* ‚klein u. häßlich machen', b) ernüchtern; **deˈfla·tion** [-eɪʃn] *s.* **1.** Ablassen *n* von Luft *od.* Gas; **2.** ✝ Deflatiˈon *f*; **deˈfla·tion·ar·y** [-eɪʃnərɪ] *adj.* ✝ deflatioˈnistisch, Deflations…

de·flect [dɪˈflekt] **I** *v/t.* ablenken, *sport a. Schuß* abfälschen; **II** *v/i.* abweichen (***from*** von); **deˈflec·tion**, *Brit. a.* **deˈflex·ion** [-ekʃn] *s.* **1.** Ablenkung *f* (*a. phys.*); **2.** Abweichung *f* (*a. fig.*); **3.** Ausschlag *m* (*Zeiger etc.*); **deˈflec·tor** [-tə] *s.* Deˈflektor *m*, Ablenkvorrichtung *f*: ***~ coil*** ϟ Ablenkspule *f*.

de·flo·rate [ˈdiːflɔːreɪt] → ***deflower***; **def·lo·ra·tion** [ˌdiːflɔːˈreɪʃn] *s.* Defloratiˈon *f*, Entjungferung *f*.

de·flow·er [ˌdiːˈflaʊə] *v/t.* **1.** deflorieren, entjungfern; **2.** *fig. e-r Sache* den Reiz nehmen.

de·fo·li·ant [ˌdiːˈfəʊlɪənt] *s.* ⚒, ⚔ Entlaubungsmittel *n*; **de·fo·li·ate** [ˌdiːˈfəʊlɪeɪt] *v/t.* entblättern, entlauben; **de·fo·li·a·tion** [ˌdiːfəʊlɪˈeɪʃn] *s.* Entblätterung *f*.

de·for·est·a·tion [diːˌfɒrɪˈsteɪʃn] *s.* Abforstung *f*, -holzung *f*; Entwaldung *f*.

de·form [dɪˈfɔːm] *v/t.* **1.** *a.* ⚙, *phys.* verformen; **2.** verunstalten, entstellen, deformieren; verzerren (*a. fig.*, ∧, *phys.*); **3.** *Charakter* verderben, ‚verbiegen'; **de·for·ma·tion** [ˌdiːfɔːˈmeɪʃn] *s.* **1.** *a.* ⚙, *phys.* Verformung *f*; **2.** Verunstaltung *f*, Entstellung *f*; ˈMißbildung *f*; **3.** ∧, *phys.* Verzerrung *f*; **deˈformed** [-md] *adj.* verformt (*etc.* → ***deform***); **deˈform·i·ty** [-mətɪ] *s.* **1.** Entstelltheit *f*, Häßlichkeit *f*; **2.** ˈMißbildung *f*, Auswuchs *m*; **3.** ˈmißgestaltete Perˈson *od.* Sache; **4.** Verderbtheit *f*, moˈralischer Deˈfekt.

de·fraud [dɪˈfrɔːd] *v/t.* betrügen (***of*** um): ***~ the revenue*** Steuern hinterziehen; ***with intent to ~*** in betrügerischer Absicht, arglistig; **de·frau·da·tion** [ˌdiːfrɔːˈdeɪʃn] *s.* Betrug *m*; Hinterˈziehung *f*, Unterˈschlagung *f*; **deˈfraud·er** [-də] *s.* ˈSteuerhinterˌzieher *m*.

de·fray [dɪˈfreɪ] *v/t. Kosten* tragen, bestreiten, bezahlen.

de·frock [ˌdiːˈfrɒk] → ***unfrock***.

de·frost [ˌdiːˈfrɒst] *v/t.* von Eis befreien, *Windschutzscheibe etc.* entfrosten, *Kühlschrank etc.* abtauen, *Tiefkühlkost etc.* auftauen: ***~ing rear window*** *mot.* heizbare Heckscheibe.

deft [deft] *adj.* □ geschickt, gewandt; **ˈdeft·ness** [-nɪs] *s.* Geschicktheit *f*, Gewandtheit *f*.

de·funct [dɪˈfʌŋkt] **I** *adj.* **1.** verstorben; **2.** erloschen, nicht mehr existierend, ehemalig; **II** *s.* **3.** ***the ~*** der *od.* die Verstorbene.

de·fuse [ˌdiːˈfjuːz] *v/t. Bombe etc.*, *fig. a. Lage etc.* entschärfen.

de·fy [dɪˈfaɪ] *v/t.* **1.** trotzen, Trotz *od.* die Stirn bieten (*dat.*); **2.** sich widerˈsetzen (*dat.*); **3.** sich hinˈwegsetzen über (*acc.*), verstoßen gegen; **4.** standhalten, Schwierigkeiten machen (*dat.*): ***~ description*** jeder Beschreibung spotten; ***~ translation*** (fast) unübersetzbar sein; **5.** herˈausfordern: ***I ~ anyone to do it*** den möchte ich sehen, der das fertigbringt; ***I ~ you to do it*** ich weiß genau, daß du es nicht (tun) kannst.

de·gauss [ˌdiːˈgaʊs] *v/t. Schiff* entmagnetisieren.

de·gen·er·a·cy [dɪˈdʒenərəsɪ] *s.* Degeneratiˈon *f*, Entartung *f*, Verderbtheit *f*; **de·gen·er·ate I** *v/i.* [dɪˈdʒenəreɪt] (***into***) entarten: a) *biol. etc.* degenerieren (zu), b) *allg.* ausarten (zu, in *acc.*), herˈabsinken (zu, auf die Stufe *gen.*), *a.* verflachen; **II** *adj.* [-rət] degeneriert, entartet; verderbt; **III** *s.* [-rət] degenerierter Mensch; **de·gen·er·a·tion** [dɪˌdʒenəˈreɪʃn] *s.* Degeneratiˈon *f*, Entartung *f*.

deg·ra·da·tion [ˌdegrəˈdeɪʃn] *s.* **1.** Degradierung *f* (*a.* ⚔), Ab-, Entsetzung *f*; **2.** Verminderung *f*, Schwächung *f*, Verschlechterung *f*; Entartung *f*, Degeneratiˈon *f* (*a. biol.*); **3.** Entwürdigung *f*, Erniedrigung *f*, Herˈabsetzung *f*; **4.** ⚒ Abbau *m*; **5.** *phys.* Degradatiˈon *f*; **6.** *geol.* Verwitterung *f*; **de·grade** [dɪˈgreɪd] **I** *v/t.* **1.** degradieren (*a.* ⚔), (her)ˈabsetzen; **2.** vermindern, herˈuntersetzen, verschlechtern; **3.** erniedrigen, entwürdigen; **4.** ⚒ abbauen; **II** *v/i.* **5.** (ab)sinken, herˈunterkommen; **6.** entarten; **de·grad·ing** [dɪˈgreɪdɪŋ] *adj.* erniedrigend, entwürdigend; herˈabsetzend.

de·gree [dɪˈgriː] *s.* **1.** Grad *m*, Stufe *f*, Maß *n*: ***by ~s*** allmählich; ***by slow ~s*** ganz allmählich; ***in some ~*** einigermaßen; ***in no ~*** keineswegs; ***in the highest ~*** im höchsten Maße *od.* Grad(e), aufs höchste; ***to what ~*** in welchem Maße, wie weit *od.* sehr; ***to a ~*** a) in hohem Maße, b) einigermaßen, c) → ***to a certain ~*** bis zu e-m gewissen Grade, ziemlich; **2.** ∧, *geogr.*, *phys.* Grad *m*: ***~ of latitude*** Breitengrad; ***32 ~s centigrade*** 32 Grad Celsius; ***~ of hardness*** Härtegrad; ***of high ~*** hochgradig; **3.** *univ.* Grad *m*, Würde *f*: ***doctor's ~*** Doktorwürde; ***take one's ~*** e-n akademischen Grad erwerben, (*zum Doktor*) promovieren; ***~ day*** Promotionstag *m*; **4.** (Verwandtschafts)Grad *m*; **5.** Rang *m*, Stand *m*: ***of high ~*** von hohem Rang; **6.** *ling. a.* ***~ of comparison*** Steigerungsstufe *f*; **7.** ♪ Tonstufe *f*, Interˈvall *n*.

de·gres·sion [dɪˈgreʃn] *s.* ✝ Degressiˈon *f*; **deˈgres·sive** [-esɪv] *adj.* ✝ degresˈsiv: ***~ depreciation*** degressive Abschreibung.

de·hu·man·ize [ˌdiːˈhjuːmənaɪz] *v/t.* entmenschlichen.

de·hy·drate [ˌdiːˈhaɪdreɪt] *v/t.* ⚒ dehyˈdrieren, das Wasser entziehen (*dat.*); dörren, trocknen: ***~d vegetables*** Trocken-, Dörrgemüse *n*; **de·hy·dra·tion** [ˌdiːhaɪˈdreɪʃn] *s.* Dehyˈdrierung *f*, Wasserentzug *m*; Dörren *n*, Trocknen *n*.

de-ice [ˌdiːˈaɪs] *v/t.* enteisen; **ˌde-ˈic·er** [-sə] *s.* Enteisungsmittel *n*, -anlage *f*, -gerät *n*.

de·i·de·ol·o·gize [ˈdiːˌaɪdɪˈɒlədʒaɪz] *v/t.* entideologisieren.

de·i·fi·ca·tion [ˌdiːɪfɪˈkeɪʃn] *s.* **1.** Apotheˈose *f*, Vergötterung *f*; **2.** *et.* Vergöttlichtes; **de·i·fy** [ˈdiːɪfaɪ] *v/t.* **1.** zum Gott erheben; **2.** als Gott verehren, anbeten (*a. fig.*).

deign [deɪn] **I** *v/i.* sich herˈablassen, geruhen, belieben (***to do*** zu tun); **II** *v/t.*

sich her'ablassen zu: ***he ~ed no answer.***

de·ism ['di:ɪzəm] *s.* De'ismus *m*; **de·ist** ['di:ɪst] *s.* De'ist(in); **de·is·tic**, **de·is·ti·cal** [di:'ɪstɪk(l)] *adj.* □ de'istisch; **de·i·ty** ['di:ɪtɪ] *s.* **1.** Gottheit *f*; **2. *the ℒ*** *eccl.* die Gottheit, Gott *m*.

de·ject·ed [dɪ'dʒektɪd] *adj.* □ niedergeschlagen, deprimiert; **de'jec·tion** [-kʃn] *s.* **1.** Niedergeschlagenheit *f*, Trübsinn *m*; **2.** ⚕ a) Stuhlgang *m*, b) Stuhl *m*, Kot *m*.

de ju·re [ˌdi:'dʒʊərɪ] (*Lat.*) **I** *adj.* De-jure-...; **II** *adv.* de 'jure, von Rechts wegen.

dek·ko ['dekəʊ] *s. sl.* (kurzer) Blick: ***have a ~*** mal schauen.

de·lac·ta·tion [ˌdi:læk'teɪʃn] *s.* ⚕ Abstillen *n*, Entwöhnung *f*.

de·lay [dɪ'leɪ] **I** *v/t.* **1.** ver-, auf-, hin'ausschieben, verzögern, verschleppen; **2.** auf-, hinhalten, hindern, hemmen; **II** *v/i.* **3.** zögern, zaudern; Zeit verlieren, sich aufhalten; **III** *s.* **4.** Aufschub *m*, Verzögerung *f*, Verzug *m*: ***without ~*** unverzüglich; ***~ of payment*** ✝ Zahlungsaufschub *m*; **de·layed** [dɪ'leɪd] *adj.* verzögert, verspätet, nachträglich, Spät...: ***~-action bomb*** Bombe *f* mit Verzögerungszünder; ***~ fuse*** Verzögerungszünder *m*; ***~ ignition*** ⚙ Spätzündung *f*; **de·lay·ing** [dɪ'leɪɪŋ] *adj.* aufschiebend, verzögernd; 'hinhaltend: ***~ action*** Verzögerung(saktion) *f*, Hinhaltung *f*; ⚔ hinhaltendes Gefecht; ***~ tactics*** Hinhaltetaktik *f*.

del cred·er·e [ˌdel'kredərɪ] *s.* ✝ Del'kredere *n*, Bürgschaft *f*.

de·le ['di:li:] (*Lat.*) *typ.* **I** *v/t.* tilgen, streichen; **II** *s.* Dele'atur(zeichen) *n*.

de·lec·ta·ble [dɪ'lektəbl] *adj.* □ köstlich; **de·lec·ta·tion** [ˌdi:lek'teɪʃn] *s.* Ergötzen *n*, Vergnügen *n*, Genuß *m*.

del·e·ga·cy ['delɪgəsɪ] *s.* Abordnung *f*, Delegati'on *f*; **'del·e·gate I** *s.* [-gət] **1.** Delegierte(r *m*) *f*, Vertreter(in), Abgeordnete(r *m*) *f*; **2.** *parl. Am.* Kon'greßabgeordnete(r *m*) *f* (*e-s Einzelstaats*); **II** *v/t.* [-geɪt] **3.** abordnen, delegieren; bevollmächtigen; **4.** (***to***) *Aufgabe*, *Vollmacht etc.* über'tragen, delegieren (an *acc.*); **del·e·ga·tion** [ˌdelɪ'geɪʃn] *s.* **1.** Abordnung *f*, Ernennung *f*; **2.** Über'tragung *f* (*Vollmacht etc.*), Delegieren *n*; Über'weisung *f*; **3.** Delegati'on *f*, Abordnung *f*; **4.** *pl. parl. Am. die* (Kon'greß)Abgeordneten *pl.* (*e-s Einzelstaats*).

de·lete [dɪ'li:t] *v/t.* tilgen, (aus)streichen, ausradieren.

del·e·te·ri·ous [ˌdelɪ'tɪərɪəs] *adj.* □ schädlich, verderblich, nachteilig.

de·le·tion [dɪ'li:ʃn] *s.* Streichung *f*: a) Tilgung *f*, b) *das* Ausgestrichene.

delft [delft] *a.* **delf** [delf] *s.* **1.** Delfter Fay'encen *pl.*; **2.** *allg.* glasiertes Steingut.

de·lib·er·ate I *adj.* □ [dɪ'lɪbərət] **1.** über'legt, wohlerwogen, bewußt, absichtlich, vorsätzlich: ***a ~ lie*** e-e bewußte Lüge; **2.** bedächtig: a) besonnen, vorsichtig, b) gemächlich, langsam; **II** *v/t.* [-bəreɪt] **3.** über'legen, erwägen; **III** *v/i.* [-bəreɪt] **4.** nachdenken, über'legen; **5.** beratschlagen, sich beraten (***on*** über *acc.*); **de'lib·er·ate·ness** [-nɪs] *s.* **1.** Vorsätzlichkeit *f*; **2.** Bedächtigkeit *f*;

de·lib·er·a·tion [dɪˌlɪbə'reɪʃn] *s.* **1.** Über'legung *f*; **2.** Beratung *f*; **3.** Bedachtsam-, Behutsamkeit *f*, Vorsicht *f*; **de'lib·er·a·tive** [-rətɪv] *adj.* beratend: ***~ assembly.***

del·i·ca·cy ['delɪkəsɪ] *s.* **1.** Zartheit *f*, Feinheit *f*; Zierlichkeit *f*; **2.** Zartheit *f*, Schwächlichkeit *f*; Empfindlichkeit *f*, Anfälligkeit *f*; **3.** Anstand *m*, Zartgefühl *n*, Takt *m*: ***~ of feeling*** Feinfühligkeit *f*; **4.** Feinheit *f*, Genauigkeit *f*; **5.** *fig.* Kitzligkeit *f*: ***negotiations of great ~*** sehr heikle Besprechungen; **6.** (*a. fig.*) Leckerbissen *m*, Delika'tesse *f*; **'del·i·cate** [-kət] *adj.* □ **1.** zart, fein, zierlich; **2.** zart (*a. Gesundheit*, *Farbe*), empfindlich, zerbrechlich, schwächlich: ***she was in a ~ condition*** sie war in anderen Umständen; **3.** fein, leicht, dünn; **4.** sanft, leise: ***~ hint*** zarter Wink; **5.** fein, genau; **6.** fein, anständig; **7.** vornehm; verwöhnt; **8.** heikel, kitzlig, schwierig; **9.** zartfühlend, feinfühlig, taktvoll; **10.** lecker, schmackhaft, deli'kat; **del·i·ca·tes·sen** [ˌdelɪkə'tesn] *s. pl.* **1.** Delika'tessen *pl.*, Feinkost *f*; **2.** *sg. konstr.* Feinkostgeschäft *n*.

de·li·cious [dɪ'lɪʃəs] *adj.* □ köstlich: a) wohlschmeckend, b) herrlich.

de·lict ['di:lɪkt] *s.* ⚖ De'likt *n*.

de·light [dɪ'laɪt] **I** *s.* Vergnügen *n*, Freude *f*, Wonne *f*, Entzücken *n*: ***to my ~*** zu m-r Freude; ***take ~ in*** → III; **II** *v/t.* erfreuen, entzücken; **III** *v/i.* ***~ in*** (große) Freude haben an (*dat.*), Vergnügen finden an (*dat.*); sich ein Vergnügen machen aus; **de'light·ed** [-tɪd] *adj.* □ entzückt, (hoch)erfreut (***with*** über *acc.*): ***I am*** (*od.* ***shall be***) ***~ to come*** ich komme mit dem größten Vergnügen; **de'light·ful** [-fʊl] *adj.* □ entzückend, reizend; herrlich, wunderbar.

de·lim·it [di:'lɪmɪt], **de·lim·i·tate** [dɪ'lɪmɪteɪt] *v/t.* abgrenzen, die Grenze(n) festsetzen von (*od. gen.*); **de·lim·i·ta·tion** [dɪˌlɪmɪ'teɪʃn] *s.* Abgrenzung *f*.

de·lin·e·ate [dɪ'lɪnɪeɪt] *v/t.* **1.** skizzieren, entwerfen, zeichnen; **2.** beschreiben, schildern, darstellen; **de·lin·e·a·tion** [dɪˌlɪnɪ'eɪʃn] *s.* **1.** Skizze *f*, Entwurf *m*, Zeichnung *f*; **2.** Beschreibung *f*, Schilderung *f*, Darstellung *f*.

de·lin·quen·cy [dɪ'lɪŋkwənsɪ] *s.* **1.** Vergehen *n*; **2.** Pflichtvergessenheit *f*; **3.** ⚖ Kriminali'tät *f*; → ***juvenile*** 1; **de'lin·quent** [-nt] **I** *adj.* **1.** straffällig, krimi'nell; **2.** pflichtvergessen: ***~ taxes*** *Am.* Steuerrückstände; **II** *s.* **3.** Delin'quent (-in), Straffällige(r *m*) *f*, (Straf)Täter (-in); → ***juvenile*** 1; **4.** Pflichtvergessene(r *m*) *f*.

del·i·quesce [ˌdelɪ'kwes] *v/i. bsd.* ⚗ zerfließen; wegschmelzen.

de·lir·i·ous [dɪ'lɪrɪəs] *adj.* □ **1.** ⚕ irreredend, phantasierend: ***be ~*** irrereden, phantasieren; **2.** *fig.* rasend, wahnsinnig (***with*** vor *dat.*): ***~*** (***with joy***) überglücklich.

de·lir·i·um [dɪ'lɪrɪəm] *s.* **1.** ⚕ De'lirium *n*, (Fieber)Wahn *m*; **2.** *fig.* Rase'rei *f*, Verzückung *f*; ***~ tre·mens*** ['tri:menz] *s.* De'lirium *n* 'tremens, Säuferwahnsinn *m*.

de·liv·er [dɪ'lɪvə] *v/t.* **1.** befreien, erlösen, retten (***from*** von, aus); **2.** *Frau* entbinden (***of*** von), *Kind* ‚holen' (*Arzt*): ***be ~ed of a child*** entbunden werden, entbinden; **3.** *Meinung* äußern; *Urteil* aussprechen; *Rede etc.* halten; **4. *~ o.s.*** äußern (***of*** *acc.*), sich äußern (***on*** über *acc.*); **5.** *Waren* liefern: ***~*** (***the goods***) F Wort halten, die Sache ‚schaukeln', ‚es schaffen'; **6.** ab-, ausliefern; über'geben, -'bringen, -'liefern; über'senden, (hin)befördern; **7.** *Briefe* zustellen; *Nachricht* bestellen; ⚖ zustellen; **8. *~ up*** abgeben, -treten, über'geben, -'liefern; ⚖ her'ausgeben: ***~ o.s. up*** sich ergeben *od.* stellen (***to*** *dat.*); **9.** *Schlag* versetzen; ⚔ (ab)feuern; **de'liv·er·a·ble** [-vərəbl] *adj.* ✝ lieferbar, zu liefern(d); **de'liv·er·ance** [-vərəns] *s.* **1.** Befreiung *f*, Erlösung *f*, (Er)Rettung *f* (***from*** aus, von); **2.** Äußerung *f*, Verkündung *f*; **de'liv·er·er** [-vərə] *s.* **1.** Befreier *m*, Erlöser *m*, (Er)Retter *m*; **2.** Über'bringer *m*.

de·liv·er·y [dɪ'lɪvərɪ] *s.* **1.** Lieferung *f*: ***on ~*** bei Lieferung, bei Empfang; ***take ~*** (***of***) abnehmen (*acc.*); **2.** ✉ Zustellung *f*; **3.** Ab-, Auslieferung *f*; Aushändigung *f*, 'Übergabe *f* (a. ⚖); **4.** Über'bringung *f*, -'sendung *f*, Beförderung *f*; **5.** ⚙ (Zu)Leitung *f*, Zuführung *f*; Förderung *f*; Leistung *f*; **6.** *rhet.* Vortragsweise *f*; **7.** *Baseball*, *Kricket*: 'Wurf (-ˌtechnik *f*) *m*; **8.** ⚔ Abfeuern *n*; **9.** ⚕ Entbindung *f*; ***~ charge*** *s.* ✉ Zustellgebühr *f*; ***~·man*** *s.* [*irr.*] Ausfahrer *m*; Verkaufsfahrer *m*; ***~ note*** *s.* ✝ Lieferschein *m*; ***~ or·der*** *s.* ✝ Auslieferungsschein *m*, Lieferschein *m*; ***~ pipe*** *s.* Leitungsröhre *f*; ***~ room*** *s.* ⚕ Entbindungssaal *m*, -zimmer *n*, Kreißsaal *m*; ***~ ser·vice*** *s.* ✉ Zustelldienst *m*; ***~ truck*** *s. mot. Am.*, ***~ van*** *s. Brit.* Lieferwagen *m*.

dell [del] *s.* kleines, enges Tal.

de·louse [ˌdi:'laʊs] *v/t.* entlausen.

Del·phic ['delfɪk] *adj.* delphisch, *fig. a.* dunkel, zweideutig.

del·phin·i·um [del'fɪnɪəm] *s.* ⚘ Rittersporn *m*.

del·ta ['deltə] *s. allg.* (*a.* Fluß)Delta *n*; ***~ con·nec·tion*** *s.* ϟ Dreieckschaltung *f*; ***~ rays*** *s. pl. phys.* Deltastrahlen *pl.*; ***~ wing*** *s.* ✈ Deltaflügel *m*.

del·toid ['deltɔɪd] **I** *adj.* deltaförmig; **II** *s. anat.* Deltamuskel *m*.

de·lude [dɪ'lu:d] *v/t.* **1.** täuschen, irreführen; (be)trügen: ***~ o.s.*** sich Illusionen hingeben, sich et. vormachen; **2.** verleiten (***into*** zu).

del·uge ['delju:dʒ] **I** *s.* **1.** (große) Über'schwemmung: ***the ℒ*** *bibl.* die Sintflut; **2.** *fig.* Flut *f*, (Un)Menge *f*; **II** *v/t.* **3.** *a. fig.* über'schwemmen, -'fluten, -'schütten.

de·lu·sion [dɪ'lu:ʒn] *s.* **1.** (Selbst)Täuschung *f*, Verblendung *f*, Wahn *m*, Irrglauben *m*; **2.** Trug *m*, Wahnvorstellung *f*: ***be*** (*od.* ***labo[u]r***) ***under the ~ that*** in dem Wahn leben, daß; → ***grandeur*** 3; **de'lu·sive** [-u:sɪv] *adj.* □ irreführend, trügerisch, Wahn...

de luxe [də'lʊks] *adj.* Luxus...

delve [delv] *v/i. fig.* (***into***) sich vertiefen (in *acc.*), erforschen, ergründen (*acc.*); graben (***for*** nach): ***~ among*** stöbern in (*dat.*).

de·mag·net·ize [ˌdi:'mægnɪtaɪz] *v/t.* entmagnetisieren.

dem·a·gog ['deməgɒg] *Am.* → ***dem-***

agogue; **dem·a·gog·ic**, **dem·a·gog·i·cal** [ˌdemə'gɒgɪk(l)] *adj.* □ dema'gogisch, aufwieglerisch; **'dem·a·gogue** [-gɒg] *s.* Dema'goge *m*; **'dem·a·gog·y** [-gɪ] *s.* Demago'gie *f*.
de·mand [dɪ'mɑːnd] **I** *v/t.* **1.** *Person*: *et.* verlangen, fordern, begehren (***of***, ***from*** von, *a.* ***that*** daß, ***to do*** zu tun): ***I ~ payment***; **2.** *Sache*: erfordern, verlangen (*acc.*, ***that*** daß), bedürfen (*gen.*): ***the matter ~s great care*** die Sache erfordert große Sorgfalt; **3.** *oft* ⚖ beanspruchen; **4.** wissen wollen, fragen nach: ***the police ~ed his name***; **II** *s.* **5.** Verlangen *n*, Forderung *f*, Ersuchen *n*: ***on ~*** a) auf Verlangen, b) ♰ bei Vorlage, bei Sicht; **6.** ♰ (***for***) Nachfrage *f* (nach), Bedarf *m* (an *dat.*) (*Ggs.* ***supply***): ***in ~*** *a. fig.* gefragt, begehrt, gesucht; **7.** (***on***) Anspruch *m*, Anforderung *f* (an *acc.*); Beanspruchung *f* (*gen.*): ***make great ~s on*** sehr in Anspruch nehmen (*acc.*), große Anforderungen stellen an (*acc.*); **8.** ⚖ (Rechts-) Anspruch *m*, Forderung *f*; **~ bill** *s.* ♰ *Am.* Sichtwechsel *m*; **~ de·pos·it** *s.* ♰ Sichteinlage *f*; **~ draft** → ***demand bill***.
de·mand·ing [dɪ'mɑːndɪŋ] *adj.* **1.** anspruchsvoll (*a. fig. Musik etc.*), schwierig; **2.** genau, streng; **3.** fordernd.
de·mand| man·age·ment *s.* Nachfragesteuerung *f*; **~ note** *s.* **1.** *Brit.* Zahlungsaufforderung *f*; **2.** Sichtwechsel *m*; **~ pull** *s.* 'Nachfrageinflatiˌon *f*.
de·mar·cate ['diːmɑːkeɪt] *v/t. a. fig.* abgrenzen (***from*** gegen, von); **de·mar·ca·tion** [ˌdiːmɑː'keɪʃn] *s.* Abgrenzung *f*, Grenzziehung *f*: ***line of ~*** a) Grenzlinie *f* (*a. fig.*), b) *pol.* Demarkationslinie *f*, c) *fig.* Trennungslinie *f*, -strich *m*.
dé·marche ['deɪmɑːʃ] (*Fr.*) *s.* De'marche *f*, diplo'matischer Schritt.
de·mean[1] [dɪ'miːn] *v/t.*: **~ *o.s.*** sich benehmen, sich verhalten.
de·mean[2] [dɪ'miːn] *v/t.*: **~ *o.s.*** sich erniedrigen; **de'mean·ing** [-nɪŋ] *adj.* erniedrigend.
de·mean·o(u)r [dɪ'miːnə] *s.* Benehmen *n*, Verhalten *n*, Haltung *f*.
de·ment·ed [dɪ'mentɪd] *adj.* □ wahnsinnig, verrückt (F *a. fig.*); **de'men·ti·a** [-nʃɪə] *s.* ⚕ **1.** Schwachsinn *m*; **2.** Wahn-, Irrsinn *m*.
de·mer·it [diː'merɪt] *s.* **1.** Schuld(haftigkeit) *f*, Fehler *m*, Mangel *m*; **2.** Unwürdigkeit *f*; **3.** Nachteil *m*, schlechte Seite; **4.** *mst* **~ *mark*** *ped. Am.* Tadel *m*, Minuspunkt *m*.
de·mesne [dɪ'meɪn] *s.* **1.** ⚖ Eigenbesitz *m*, freier Grundbesitz; Landgut *n*, Do'mäne *f*: ***Royal ~*** Krongut *n*; **2.** *fig.* Do'mäne *f*, Gebiet *n*.
'dem·i|·god ['demɪ-] *s.* Halbgott *m*; **'~·john** [-dʒɒn] *s.* Korbflasche *f*, 'Glasbalˌlon *m*.
de·mil·i·ta·rize [ˌdiː'mɪlɪtəraɪz] *v/t.* entmilitarisieren.
dem·i|-monde [ˌdemɪ'mɔ̃ːnd] *s.* Halbwelt *f*; **ˌ~-'pen·sion** *s.* 'Halbpensiˌon *f*; **~·rep** ['demɪrep] *s.* Frau *f* von zweifelhaftem Ruf.
de·mise [dɪ'maɪz] ⚖ **I** *s.* **1.** Be'sitzüberˌtragung *f od.* -verpachtung *f*: **~ *of the Crown*** Übergehen *n* der Krone *an den Nachfolger*; **2.** Ableben *n*, Tod *m*; **II** *v/t.* **3.** *allg. et.* über'tragen, *a.* verpachten *od.* vermachen.
dem·i·sem·i·qua·ver ['demɪsemɪˌkweɪvə] *s.* ♪ Zweiunddreißigstel(note *f*) *n*.
de·mis·sion [dɪ'mɪʃn] *s.* Rücktritt *m*, Abdankung *f*, Demissi'on *f*.
de·mo ['deməʊ] *s.* F **1.** ‚Demo' *f* (*Demonstration*); **2.** a) Vorführband *n*, b) Vorführwagen *m*.
de·mob [ˌdiː'mɒb] *v/t. Brit.* F → ***demobilize*** 1b.
de·mo·bi·li·za·tion ['diːˌməʊbɪlaɪ'zeɪʃn] *s.* Demobilisierung *f*: a) Abrüstung *f*, b) Entlassung *f* aus dem Wehrdienst; **de·mo·bi·lize** [diː'məʊbɪlaɪz] *v/t.* **1.** demobilisieren: a) abrüsten, b) *Truppen* entlassen, *Heer* auflösen; **2.** *Kriegsschiff* außer Dienst stellen.
de·moc·ra·cy [dɪ'mɒkrəsɪ] *s.* **1.** Demokra'tie *f*; **2.** ♀ *pol. Am.* die Demo'kratische Par'tei (*od.* deren Grundsätze); **dem·o·crat** ['deməkræt] *s.* **1.** Demo'krat(in); **2.** ♀ *Am. pol.* Demo'krat(in), Mitglied *n* der Demo'kratischen Par'tei; **dem·o·crat·ic** [ˌdemə'krætɪk] *adj.* (□ ***~ally***) **1.** demo'kratisch; **2.** ♀ *pol. Am.* demo'kratisch (*die Demokratische Partei betreffend*); **de·moc·ra·ti·za·tion** [dɪˌmɒkrətaɪ'zeɪʃn] *s.* Demokratisierung *f*; **de·moc·ra·tize** [dɪ'mɒkrətaɪz] *v/t.* demokratisieren.
dé·mo·dé [ˌdeɪməʊ'deɪ] (*Fr.*), **de·mod·ed** [diː'məʊdɪd] *adj.* altmodisch, außer Mode.
de·mog·ra·pher [diː'mɒgrəfə] *s.* Demo'graph *m*; **de'mog·ra·phy** [-fɪ] *s.* Demogra'phie *f*.
de·mol·ish [dɪ'mɒlɪʃ] *v/t.* **1.** ab-, niederreißen; **2.** *Festung* schleifen; **3.** ⚔ sprengen; **4.** *fig.* (*a. j-n*) vernichten, ka'puttmachen; **5.** *sport* F ‚über'fahren'; **dem·o·li·tion** [ˌdemə'lɪʃn] *s.* **1.** Abbruch *m*, Niederreißen *n*; **2.** Schleifen *n* (*Festung*); **3.** ⚔ Spreng...: **~ *bomb*** Sprengbombe *f*; **~ *squad*** Sprengkommando *n*; **4.** Vernichtung *f*.
de·mon (*myth. oft* ***daemon***) ['diːmən] **I** *s.* **1.** 'Dämon *m*, böser Geist, 'Satan *m* (*a. fig.*); **2.** *fig.* Teufelskerl *m*: **~ *for work*** ‚Wühler' *m*, unermüdlicher Arbeiter; **II** *adj.* **3.** dä'monisch, *fig a.* wild, besessen.
de·mon·e·ti·za·tion [diːˌmʌnɪtaɪ'zeɪʃn] *s.* Außer'kurssetzung *f*, Entwertung *f*; **de·mon·e·tize** [ˌdiː'mʌnɪtaɪz] *v/t.* außer Kurs setzen.
de·mo·ni·ac [dɪ'məʊnɪæk] **I** *adj.* **1.** dä'monisch, teuflisch; **2.** besessen, rasend, tobend; **II** *s.* **3.** Besessene(r *m*) *f*; **de·mo·ni·a·cal** [ˌdiːməʊ'naɪəkl] *adj.* □ → ***demoniac*** 1, 2; **de·mon·ic** [diː'mɒnɪk] *adj.* (□ ***~ally***) dä'monisch, teuflisch; **de·mon·ism** ['diːmənɪzəm] *s.* Dä'monenglaube *m*; **de·mon·ize** ['diːmənaɪz] *v/t.* dämonisieren, *fig. a.* verteufeln; **de·mon·ol·o·gy** [ˌdiːmə'nɒlədʒɪ] *s.* Dä'monenlehre *f*.
de·mon·stra·ble ['demənstrəbl] *adj.* □ beweisbar, nachweislich; **dem·on·strate** ['demənstreɪt] **I** *v/t.* **1.** demonstrieren: a) be-, nachweisen, b) veranschaulichen, darlegen; **2.** vorführen; **II** *v/i.* **3.** demonstrieren, e-e Demonstrati'on veranstalten; **dem·on·stra·tion** [ˌdemən'streɪʃn] *s.* **1.** Demon'strierung *f*, Veranschaulichung *f*, Darstellung *f*; **2.** a) Beweis *m* (***of*** für), b) Beweisführung *f*; **3.** Vorführung *f*, Demonstrati'on *f* (***to*** vor *j-m*): **~ *car*** Vorführwagen *m*; **4.** (Gefühls)Äußerung *f*, Bekundung *f*; **5.** Demonstrati'on *f* (*a. pol. u.* ⚔), Kundgebung *f*; **6.** ⚔ 'Täuschungsmaˌnöver *n*; **de·mon·stra·tive** [dɪ'mɒnstrətɪv] **I** *adj.* □ **1.** anschaulich (zeigend); über'zeugend, beweiskräftig: ***be ~ of*** → ***demonstrate*** 1; **2.** demonstra'tiv, ostenta'tiv, auffällig, betont; **3.** ausdrucks-, gefühlvoll; **4.** *ling.* Demonstrativ..., hinweisend: **~ *pronoun***; **II** *s.* **5.** *ling.* Demonstra'tivum *n*; **de·mon·stra·tive·ness** [dɪ'mɒnstrətɪvnɪs] *s.* das Demonstra'tive *od.* Ostenta'tive, Betontheit *f*; **'dem·on·stra·tor** [-reɪtə] *s.* **1.** Beweisführer *m*, Erklärer *m*; **2.** ♰ a) Vorführer(in), b) 'Vorführmoˌdell *n*; **3.** *pol.* Demon'strant(in); **4.** *univ.* a) Assi'stent *m*, b) ⚕ 'Prosektor *m*.
de·mor·al·i·za·tion [dɪˌmɒrəlaɪ'zeɪʃn] *s.* Demoralisati'on *f*: a) Sittenverfall *m*, Zuchtlosigkeit *f*, b) Entmutigung *f*, Demoralisierung *f*; **de·mor·al·ize** [dɪ'mɒrəlaɪz] *v/t.* demoralisieren: a) (sittlich) verderben, b) zersetzen, c) zermürben, entmutigen, d) die ('Kampf)Moˌral *od.* die Diszi'plin *der Truppe* unter'graben; **de·mor·al·iz·ing** [dɪ'mɒrəlaɪzɪŋ] *adj.* demoralisierend.
de·mote [ˌdiː'məʊt] *v/t.* **1.** degradieren; **2.** *ped. Am.* zu'rückversetzen.
de·moth(·ball) [ˌdiː'mɒθ(bɔːl)] *v/t.* ⚔ *Am. Flugzeuge etc.* ‚entmotten', wieder in Dienst stellen.
de·mo·tion [ˌdiː'məʊʃn] *s.* **1.** Degradierung *f*; **2.** *ped. Am.* Zu'rückversetzung *f*.
de·mo·ti·vate [ˌdiː'məʊtɪveɪt] *v/t.* demotivieren.
de·mount [ˌdiː'maʊnt] *v/t.* abmontieren, abnehmen; zerlegen; **de'mount·a·ble** [-təbl] *adj.* abmontierbar; zerlegbar.
de·mur [dɪ'mɜː] **I** *v/i.* **1.** Einwendungen machen, Bedenken äußern (***to*** gegen); zögern; **2.** ⚖ e-n Rechtseinwand erheben; **II** *s.* **3.** Einwand *m*, Bedenken *n*, Zögern *n*: ***without ~*** anstandslos, ohne Zögern.
de·mure [dɪ'mjʊə] *adj.* □ **1.** zimperlich, spröde; **2.** sittsam, prüde; **3.** zu'rückhaltend; **4.** gesetzt, ernst, nüchtern; **de'mure·ness** [-nɪs] *s.* **1.** Zimperlichkeit *f*; **2.** Zu'rückhaltung *f*; **3.** Gesetztheit *f*.
de·mur·rage [dɪ'mʌrɪdʒ] *s.* ♰ **1.** a) ⚓ 'Überliegezeit *f*, b) 🚃 zu langes Stehen (*bei der Entladung*); **2.** a) ⚓ ('Über-) Liegegeld *n*, b) 🚃 Wagenstandgeld *n*, c) Lagergeld *n*.
de·mur·rer [dɪ'mʌrə] *s.* ⚖ Rechtseinwand *m*.
de·my [dɪ'maɪ] *pl.* **-'mies** [-aɪz] *s.* **1.** Stipendi'at *m* (*Magdalen College, Oxford*); **2.** *ein Papierformat*.
den [den] *s.* **1.** Lager *n*, Bau *m*, Höhle *f wilder Tiere*: ***lion's ~*** Löwengrube *f*, *fig.* Höhle des Löwen; **2.** *fig.* Höhle *f*, Versteck *n*: ***robber's ~*** Räuberhöhle; **~ *of vice*** Lasterhöhle; **3.** a) (gemütliches) Zimmer, ‚Bude' *f*, b) Arbeitszimmer *n*, c) *contp.* ‚Loch' *n*, Höhle *f*.
de·na·tion·al·ize [ˌdiː'næʃnəlaɪz] *v/t.* **1.** entnationalisieren, den natio'nalen Cha'rakter nehmen (*dat.*); **2.** *j-m* die Staatsbürgerschaft aberkennen; **3.** ♰ entstaatlichen, reprivatisieren.
de·nat·u·ral·ize [ˌdiː'nætʃrəlaɪz] *v/t.* **1.**

s-r wahren Na'tur entfremden; **2.** *j-n* denaturalisieren, ausbürgern.

de·na·ture [ˌdiːˈneɪtʃə] *v/t.* ⚗ denaturieren.

de·na·zi·fi·ca·tion [diːˌnɑːtsɪfɪˈkeɪʃn] *s. pol.* Entnazifizierung *f.*

den·dri·form [ˈdendrɪfɔːm] *adj.* baumförmig; ˈ**den·droid** [-rɔɪd] *adj.* baumähnlich; ˈ**den·dro·lite** [-rəlaɪt] *s.* Pflanzenversteinerung *f*; **den·drol·o·gy** [denˈdrɒlədʒɪ] *s.* Dendroloˈgie *f*, Baumkunde *f.*

dene[1] [diːn] *s. Brit.* (Sand)Düne *f.*

dene[2] [diːn] *s.* kleines Tal.

de·ni·a·ble [dɪˈnaɪəbl] *adj.* abzuleugnen(d), zu verneinen(d); **de·ni·al** [dɪˈnaɪəl] *s.* **1.** Ablehnung *f*, Verweigerung *f*, -sagung *f*; Absage *f*, abschlägige Antwort: ***take no ~*** sich nicht abweisen lassen; **2.** Verneinung *f*, Leugnen *n*, Ab-, Verleugnung *f*: ***official ~*** Dementi *n.*

de·nic·o·tin·ize [ˌdiːnɪˈkɒtɪnaɪz] *v/t.* entnikotisieren: ***~d*** nikotinfrei, -arm.

de·ni·er[1] [dɪˈnaɪə] *s.* **1.** Leugner(in); **2.** Verweigerer *m.*

de·nier[2] [ˈdenɪə] *s.* ✝ Deniˈer *m* (*Einheit für die Fadenstärke bei Seidengarn etc.*).

de·nier[3] [dɪˈnɪə] *s. hist.* Deniˈer *m* (*Münze*).

den·i·grate [ˈdenɪgreɪt] *v/t.* anschwärzen, verunglimpfen; **den·i·gra·tion** [ˌdenɪˈgreɪʃn] *s.* Anschwärzung *f*, Verunglimpfung *f.*

den·im [ˈdenɪm] *s.* **1.** Köper *m*; **2.** *pl.* Overall *m od.* Jeans *pl.* aus Köper.

den·i·zen [ˈdenɪzn] *s.* **1.** Ein-, Bewohner *m* (*a. fig.*); **2.** *hist. Brit.* (teilweise) eingebürgerter Ausländer; **3.** *et.* Eingebürgertes (*Tier, Pflanze, Wort*); **4.** Stammgast *m.*

de·nom·i·nate [dɪˈnɒmɪneɪt] *v/t.* (be-)nennen, bezeichnen; **de·nom·i·na·tion** [dɪˌnɒmɪˈneɪʃn] *s.* **1.** Benennung *f*, Bezeichnung *f*; Name *m*; **2.** Gruppe *f*, Klasse *f*; **3.** (Maß- *etc.*)Einheit *f*; Nennwert *m* (*Banknoten*): ***shares in small ~s*** Aktien kleiner Stückelung; **4.** a) Konfessiˈon *f*, Bekenntnis *n*, b) Sekte *f*; **de·nom·i·na·tion·al** [dɪˌnɒmɪˈneɪʃənl] *adj.* konfessioˈnell, Konfessions…, Bekenntnis…: ***~ school***; **de·nom·i·na·tion·al·ism** [dɪˌnɒmɪˈneɪʃnəlɪzəm] *s.* Prinˈzip *n* des konfessioˈnellen ˈUnterrichts; **de·nom·i·na·tor** [dɪˈnɒmɪneɪtə] *s.* ♣ Nenner *m*: ***common ~*** gemeinsamer Nenner (*a. fig.*); → ***reduce*** 11.

de·no·ta·tion [ˌdiːnəʊˈteɪʃn] *s.* **1.** Bezeichnung *f*; **2.** Bedeutung *f*; **3.** Beˈgriffsˌumfang *m*; **de·note** [dɪˈnəʊt] *v/t.* **1.** be-, kennzeichnen, anzeigen, andeuten; **2.** bedeuten.

dé·noue·ment [deɪˈnuːmɑ̃ːŋ] (*Fr.*) *s.* **1.** Lösung *f* (des Knotens *im Drama etc.*); **2.** Ausgang *m.*

de·nounce [dɪˈnaʊns] *v/t.* **1.** öffentlich anprangern, brandmarken, verurteilen; **2.** anzeigen, *contp.* denunzieren (***to*** bei); **3.** *Vertrag* kündigen; **deˈnounce·ment** [-mənt] *s.* **1.** (öffentliche) Anprangerung *od.* Verurteilung; **2.** Anzeige *f*, *contp.* Denunziatiˈon *f*; **3.** Kündigung *f* (***of*** *gen.*), Rücktritt *m* (*vom Vertrag*).

dense [dens] *adj.* □ **1.** dicht (*a. phys.*), dick (*Nebel etc.*); **2.** gedrängt, eng; **3.** *fig.* beschränkt, schwer von Begriff; **4.** *phot.* dicht, kräftig (*Negativ*); ˈ**dense·ness** [-nɪs] *s.* **1.** Dichtheit *f*, Dichte *f*; **2.** *fig.* Beschränktheit *f*, Schwerfälligkeit *f*; ˈ**den·si·ty** [-sətɪ] *s.* **1.** Dichte *f* (*a.* ⚗, *phys.*), Dichtheit *f*: ***traffic ~*** Verkehrsdichte; **2.** Gedrängtheit *f*, Enge *f*; **3.** *fig.* Beschränktheit *f*, Dummheit *f*; **4.** *phot.* Dichte *f*, Schwärzung *f.*

dent [dent] **I** *s.* Beule *f*, Einbeulung *f*: ***make a ~ in*** F a) ein Loch reißen in (*Ersparnisse etc.*), b) *j-s Stolz etc.* ‚anknacksen'; **II** *v/t. u. v/i.* (sich) einbeulen: ***~ s.o.'s image*** *fig.* j-s Image schaden.

den·tal [ˈdentl] **I** *adj.* **1.** ⚕ Zahn…; zahnärztlich: ***~ floss*** Zahnseide *f*; ***~ plate*** Platte *f*, Zahnersatz *m*; ***~ surgeon*** Zahnarzt *m*; ***~ technician*** Zahntechniker(in); **2.** *ling.* Dental…, Zahn…: ***~ sound*** → 3; **II** *s.* **3.** *ling.* Denˈtal(laut) *m*; **den·tate** [ˈdenteɪt] *adj.* ♀, *zo.* gezähnt; **den·ta·tion** [denˈteɪʃn] *s.* ♀, *zo.* Zähnung *f*; **den·ti·cle** [ˈdentɪkl] *s.* Zähnchen *n*; **den·tic·u·lat·ed** [denˈtɪkjʊleɪtɪd] *adj.* **1.** gezähnt; **2.** gezackt; **den·ti·form** [ˈdentɪfɔːm] *adj.* zahnförmig; **den·ti·frice** [ˈdentɪfrɪs] *s.* Zahnputzmittel *n*; **den·tils** [ˈdentɪlz] *s. pl.* ⚠ Zahnschnitt *m*; **den·tine** [ˈdentiːn] *s.* ⚕ Denˈtin *n*, Zahnbein *n*; **den·tist** [ˈdentɪst] *s.* Zahnarzt *m*, -ärztin *f*; **den·tist·ry** [ˈdentɪstrɪ] *s.* Zahnheilkunde *f*; **den·ti·tion** [denˈtɪʃn] *s.* ⚕ **1.** Zahnen *n* (*der Kinder*); **2.** ˈZahnformel *f*, -syˌstem *n*; **den·ture** [ˈdentʃə] *s.* **1.** *anat.* Gebiß *n*; **2.** a) künstliches Gebiß, (ˈVoll)Proˌthese *f*, b) (ˈTeil)Proˌthese *f.*

de·nu·cle·ar·ize [ˌdiːˈnjuːklɪəraɪz] *v/t.* aˈtomwaffenfrei machen, e-e atomwaffenfreie Zone schaffen in (*dat.*).

den·u·da·tion [ˌdiːnjuːˈdeɪʃn] *s.* **1.** Entblößung *f*; **2.** *geol.* Abtragung *f*; **de·nude** [dɪˈnjuːd] *v/t.* **1.** (***of***) entblößen (von), berauben (*gen.*) (*a. fig.*); **2.** *geol.* bloßlegen.

de·nun·ci·a·tion [ˌdɪnʌnsɪˈeɪʃn] → ***denouncement***; **de·nun·ci·a·tor** [dɪˈnʌnsɪeɪtə] *s.* Denunziˈant(in); **de·nun·ci·a·to·ry** [dɪˈnʌnsɪətərɪ] *adj.* **1.** denunzierend; **2.** anprangernd, brandmarkend.

de·ny [dɪˈnaɪ] *v/t.* **1.** ab-, bestreiten, in Abrede stellen, dementieren, (ab)leugnen, verneinen: ***it cannot be denied that …, there is no ~ing (the fact) that …*** es läßt sich nicht *od.* es ist nicht zu leugnen *od.* bestreiten, daß; ***I ~ saying so*** ich bestreite, daß ich das gesagt habe; ***~ a charge*** e-e Beschuldigung zurückweisen; **2.** *Glauben*, *Freund* verleugnen; *Unterschrift* nicht anerkennen; **3.** *Bitte etc.* ablehnen; ⚖ *Antrag* abweisen; *j-m et.* abschlagen, verweigern, versagen: ***~ o.s. the pleasure*** sich das Vergnügen versagen; ***he was denied the privilege*** das Vorrecht wurde ihm versagt; ***he was hard to ~*** es war schwer, ihn abzuweisen; ***she denied herself to him*** sie versagte sich ihm; **4.** ***~ o.s. to s.o.*** sich vor j-m verleugnen lassen.

de·o·dor·ant [diːˈəʊdərənt] **I** *s.* De(s)odoˈrant *n*; **II** *adj.* de(s)odorierend; **de·o·dor·i·za·tion** [diːˌəʊdəraɪˈzeɪʃn] *s.* Desodorierung *f*; **de·o·dor·ize** [diːˈəʊdəraɪz] *v/t.* de(s)odorieren; **deˈo·dor·iz·er** [-raɪzə] → ***deodorant*** I.

de·ox·i·dize [diːˈɒksɪdaɪz] *v/t.* ⚗ den Sauerstoff entziehen (*dat.*).

de·part [dɪˈpɑːt] *v/i.* **1.** (***for*** nach) weg-, fortgehen, *bsd.* abreisen, abfahren; **2.** 🚂 *etc.* abgehen, abfahren, ✈ abfliegen; **3.** *a.* ***~ (from) this life*** ˈhinscheiden, entschlafen, sterben; **4.** (***from***) abweichen (von *e-r Regel*, *der Wahrheit etc.*), *Plan etc.* ändern, aufgeben: ***~ from one's word*** sein Wort brechen; **deˈpart·ed** [-tɪd] *adj.* **1.** vergangen; **2.** verstorben: ***the ~*** der *od.* die Verstorbene, *coll.* die Verstorbenen; **deˈpart·ment** [-mənt] *s.* **1.** Fach *n*, Gebiet *n*, Resˈsort *n*, Geschäftsbereich *m*: ***that's your ~!*** F das ist dein Ressort!; **2.** Abteilung *f*: ***~ of German*** *univ.* germanistische Abteilung; ***export ~*** ✝ Exportabteilung; ***~ store*** Waren-, Kaufhaus *n*; **3.** *pol.* Departeˈment *n* (*in Frankreich*); **4.** Dienst-, Geschäftsstelle *f*, Amt *n*: ***health ~*** Gesundheitsamt; **5.** *pol.* Miniˈsterium *n*: ***ℒ of Defense*** *Am.* Verteidigungsministerium; ***ℒ of the Interior*** *Am.* Innenministerium; **6.** ⚔ Bereich *m*, Zone *f*; **de·part·men·tal** [ˌdiːpɑːtˈmentl] *adj.* **1.** Abteilungs…; Bezirks…; Fach…; **2.** Ministerial…; **de·part·men·tal·ize** [ˌdiːpɑːtˈmentəlaɪz] *v/t.* in (viele) Abteilungen gliedern.

de·par·ture [dɪˈpɑːtʃə] *s.* **1.** Weggang *m*, *bsd.* ⚔ Abzug *m*: ***take one's ~*** sich verabschieden, weg-, fortgehen; **2.** a) Abreise *f*, b) 🚂 *etc.* Abfahrt *f*, ✈ Abflug *m*: (***time of***) ***~*** Abfahrts- *od.* Abflugzeit *f*; ***~ gate*** Flugsteig *m*; ***~ lounge*** Abflughalle *f*; ***~ platform*** Abfahrtsbahnsteig *m*; **3.** Abweichen *n*, Abweichung *f* (***from*** von *e-m Plan*, *e-r Regel etc.*); **4.** *fig.* Anfang *m*, Beginn *m*: ***a new ~*** a) ein neuer Anfang, b) ein neuer Weg, ein neues Verfahren; ***point of ~*** Ausgangspunkt *m*; **5.** ˈHinscheiden *n*, Tod *m.*

de·pend [dɪˈpend] *v/i.* **1.** (***on, upon***) abhängen (von), ankommen (auf *acc.*): ***it ~s on the weather, it ~s on you***; ***~ing on the quantity used*** je nach (der zu verwendenden) Menge; ***~ing on whether*** je nachdem, ob; ***that ~s*** F das kommt (ganz) darauf an, je nachdem; **2.** (***on, upon***) a) abhängig sein (von), b) angewiesen sein (auf *acc.*): ***he ~s on my help***; **3.** sich verlassen (***on, upon*** auf *acc.*): ***you may ~ on that man***; ***~ upon it!*** verlaß dich drauf!; **de·pend·a·bil·i·ty** [dɪˌpendəˈbɪlətɪ] *s.* Zuverlässigkeit *f*; **deˈpend·a·ble** [-dəbl] *adj.* □ verläßlich, zuverlässig; **de·pend·ance** [-dəns] *Am.* → ***dependence***; **de·pend·ant** [-dənt] **I** *s.* Abhängige(r *m*) *f*, *bsd.* (Faˈmilien)Angehörige(r *m*) *f*; **II** *adj. Am.* → ***dependent*** I; **deˈpend·ence** [-dəns] *s.* **1.** (***on, upon***) Abhängigkeit *f* (von), Angewiesensein *n* (auf *acc.*); Bedingtsein *n* (durch); **2.** Vertrauen *n*, Verlaß *m* (***on, upon*** auf *acc.*); **3.** ***in ~*** ⚖ in der Schwebe; **4.** Nebengebäude *n*, Depenˈdance *f*; **deˈpend·en·cy** [-dənsɪ] **1.** → ***dependence*** 1; **2.** *pol.* Schutzgebiet *n*, Koloˈnie *f*; **deˈpend·ent** [-dənt] **I** *adj.* **1.** (***on, upon***) abhängig (von): a) angewiesen (auf *acc.*), b) bedingt (durch); **2.** vertrauend, sich verlassend (***on, upon*** auf *acc.*); **3.** (***on***) ˈuntergeordnet (*dat.*), abhängig (von), unselbständig: ***~***

clause *ling.* Nebensatz *m*; **4.** her'abhängend (***from*** von); **II** *s.* **5.** *Am.* → ***dependant*** I.

de·peo·ple [ˌdiːˈpiːpl] *v/t.* entvölkern.

de·per·son·al·ize [ˌdiːˈpɜːsnəlaɪz] *v/t.* **1.** *psych.* entper'sönlichen; **2.** 'unperˌsönlich machen.

de·pict [dɪˈpɪkt] *v/t.* **1.** (ab)malen, zeichnen, darstellen; **2.** schildern, beschreiben, veranschaulichen.

dep·i·late [ˈdepɪleɪt] *v/t.* enthaaren, depilieren; **dep·i·la·tion** [ˌdepɪˈleɪʃn] *s.* Enthaarung *f*; **de·pil·a·to·ry** [dɪˈpɪlətərɪ] **I** *adj.* enthaarend; **II** *s.* Enthaarungsmittel *n*.

de·plane [ˌdiːˈpleɪn] *v/t. u. v/i.* aus dem Flugzeug ausladen (aussteigen).

de·plen·ish [dɪˈplenɪʃ] *v/t.* entleeren.

de·plete [dɪˈpliːt] *v/t.* **1.** (ent)leeren; **2.** Raubbau treiben mit; *Vorräte, Kräfte etc.* erschöpfen; *Bestand etc.* dezimieren: ~ ***a lake of fish*** e-n See abfischen; **de·ple·tion** [dɪˈpliːʃn] *s.* **1.** Entleerung *f*; **2.** Raubbau *m*; Erschöpfung *f*; ⚕ *a.* Erschöpfungszustand *m*; ✝ *a.* Sub'stanzverlust *m*.

de·plor·a·ble [dɪˈplɔːrəbl] *adj.* □ **1.** bedauerns-, beklagenswert; **2.** erbärmlich, kläglich; **de·plore** [dɪˈplɔː] *v/t.* beklagen: a) bedauern, b) miß'billigen, c) betrauern.

de·ploy [dɪˈplɔɪ] **I** *v/t.* **1.** ⚔ a) aufmarschieren lassen, entwickeln, entfalten, b) *a. allg.* verteilen, *Raketen etc.* aufstellen; **2.** *Arbeitskräfte etc.* einsetzen; **3.** *fig.* anwenden, einsetzen; **II** *v/i.* **4.** sich entwickeln, sich entfalten, ausschwärmen, Ge'fechtsformatiˌon annehmen; **III** *s.* **5.** → **de'ploy·ment** [-mənt] *s.* **1.** ⚔ Entfaltung *f*, -wicklung *f*, Aufmarsch *m*; Gliederung *f*; Aufstellung *f*; **2.** ✝ *etc.* Einsatz *m*, Verteilung *f*.

de·poi·son [ˌdiːˈpɔɪzn] *v/t.* entgiften.

de·po·lar·ize [ˌdiːˈpəʊləraɪz] *v/t.* **1.** ⚡, *phys.* depolarisieren; **2.** *fig. Überzeugung etc.* erschüttern.

de·po·lit·i·cize [ˌdiːpəˈlɪtɪsaɪz] *v/t.* entpolitisieren.

de·pone [dɪˈpəʊn] → ***depose*** II; **de'po·nent** [-nənt] **I** *adj.* **1.** ~ ***verb*** *ling.* → 2; **II** *s.* **2.** *ling.* De'ponens *n*; **3.** ⚖ vereidigter Zeuge; *in Urkunden: der (die)* Erschienene.

de·pop·u·late [ˌdiːˈpɒpjʊleɪt] *v/t.* (*v/i.* sich) entvölkern; **de·pop·u·la·tion** [diːˌpɒpjʊˈleɪʃn] *s.* Entvölkerung *f*.

de·port [dɪˈpɔːt] *v/t.* **1.** (zwangsweise) fortschaffen; **2.** *pol.* a) deportieren, b) ausweisen, *Ausländer* abschieben, c) *hist.* verbannen; **3.** ~ ***o.s.*** sich *gut etc.* betragen *od.* benehmen; **de·por·ta·tion** [ˌdiːpɔːˈteɪʃn] *s.* Deportati'on *f*, Zwangsverschickung *f*; Ausweisung *f*; *hist.* Verbannung *f*; **de·por·tee** [ˌdiːpɔːˈtiː] *s.* Deportierte(r *m*) *f*; **de'port·ment** [-mənt] *s.* **1.** Benehmen *n*, Betragen *n*, Verhalten *n*; **2.** (Körper)Haltung *f*.

de·pos·a·ble [dɪˈpəʊzəbl] *adj.* absetzbar; **de·pos·al** [dɪˈpəʊzl] *s.* Absetzung *f*; **de·pose** [dɪˈpəʊz] **I** *v/t.* **1.** absetzen, entheben (***from*** *gen.*); entthronen; **2.** ⚖ eidlich erklären, unter Eid zu Proto'koll geben; **II** *v/i.* (*bsd.* in Form e-r schriftlichen, beeideten Erklärung) aussagen *od.* bezeugen (***to s.th.*** et., ***that*** daß).

de·pos·it [dɪˈpɒzɪt] **I** *v/t.* **1.** ab-, niedersetzen, ab-, niederlegen; *Eier* (ab)legen; **2.** ⚗, ⚙, *geol.* ablagern, -setzen, anschwemmen; **3.** *Geld* a) einzahlen, *a. Sache* hinter'legen, deponieren; über'geben, b) anzahlen; **II** *v/i.* **4.** ⚗ sich absetzen *od.* ablagern *od.* niederschlagen; **III** *s.* **5.** ⚗, ⚙ Ablagerung *f*, (Boden)Satz *m*, Niederschlag *m*, Sedi'ment *n*; Schicht *f*, Belag *m*; **6.** ⚒, *geol.* Ablagerung *f*, Lager *n*, Flöz *n*; **7.** ✝ a) De'pot *n*: ***place on*** ~ einzahlen, hinterlegen, b) Einzahlung *f*, Einlage *f*, Guthaben *n*: ~***s*** Depositen; ~ ***account*** Termineinlagekonto *n*; **de'pos·i·tar·y** [-tərɪ] *s.* **1.** Deposi'tar *m*, Verwahrer(in); **2.** → ***depot*** 1.

dep·o·si·tion [ˌdepəˈzɪʃn] *s.* **1.** Amtsenthebung *f*; Absetzung *f* (***from*** von); **2.** ⚗, ⚙, *geol.* Ablagerung *f*, Niederschlag *m*; **3.** ⚖ (Proto'koll *n od.* Abgabe *f* e-r beeideten) Erklärung *od.* Aussage; **4.** (Bild *n* der) Kreuzabnahme *f Christi*; **de·pos·i·tor** [dɪˈpɒzɪtə] *s.* ✝ a) Hinter'leger(in), b) Einzahler(in), c) Kontoinhaber(in); **de·pos·i·to·ry** [dɪˈpɒzɪtərɪ] *s.* **1.** a) Aufbewahrungsort *m*, b) → ***depot*** 1; **2.** *fig.* Fundgrube *f*.

de·pot [ˈdepəʊ] *s.* **1.** De'pot *n*, Lagerhaus *n*, -platz *m*, Niederlage *f*; **2.** *Am.* Bahnhof *m*; **3.** ⚔ De'pot *n*: a) Gerätepark *m*, b) (Nachschub)Lager *n*, c) Sammelplatz *m*, d) Ersatztruppenteil *m*; **4.** ⚕ De'pot *n*.

dep·ra·va·tion [ˌdeprəˈveɪʃn] → ***depravity***; **de·prave** [dɪˈpreɪv] *v/t. moralisch* verderben; **de·praved** [dɪˈpreɪvd] *adj.* verderbt, verkommen, verworfen, schlecht; **de·prav·i·ty** [dɪˈprævətɪ] *s.* **1.** Verderbtheit *f*, Verworfenheit *f*; Schlechtigkeit *f*; **2.** böse Tat.

dep·re·cate [ˈdeprɪkeɪt] *v/t.* miß'billigen, verurteilen, verwerfen; **'dep·re·cat·ing** [-tɪŋ] *adj.* □ **1.** miß'billigend, ablehnend; **2.** entschuldigend; **3.** wegwerfend, (bescheiden) abwehrend; **dep·re·ca·tion** [ˌdeprɪˈkeɪʃn] *s.* 'Mißbilligung *f*; **'dep·re·ca·tor** [-tə] *s.* Gegner(in); **'dep·re·ca·to·ry** [-kətərɪ] → ***deprecating***.

de·pre·ci·ate [dɪˈpriːʃɪeɪt] **I** *v/t.* **1.** a) geringschätzen, b) her'absetzen, -würdigen; **2.** a) *im Preis od. Wert* her'absetzen, b) abschreiben; **3.** ✝ *Währung* abwerten; **II** *v/i.* **4.** im Preis *od.* Wert sinken; **de'pre·ci·at·ing** [-tɪŋ] → ***depreciatory***; **de·pre·ci·a·tion** [dɪˌpriːʃɪˈeɪʃn] *s.* **1.** a) Geringschätzung *f*, b) Her'absetzung *f*, -würdigung *f*; **2.** ✝ a) Wertminderung *f*, Kursverlust *m*, b) Abschreibung *f*, c) Abwertung *f*: ~ ***fund*** Abschreibungsfond *m*; **de'pre·ci·a·to·ry** [-ʃjətərɪ] *adj.* geringschätzig, verächtlich, abschätzig.

dep·re·da·tion [ˌdeprɪˈdeɪʃn] *s. oft pl.* **1.** Plünderung *f*, Verwüstung *f*; **2.** *fig.* Raubzug *m*; **dep·re·da·tor** [ˈdeprɪdeɪtə] *s.* Plünderer *m*.

de·press [dɪˈpres] *v/t.* **1.** a) *j-n* deprimieren, bedrücken, b) *Stimmung* drücken; **2.** *Tätigkeit, Handel* niederdrücken; *Preis, Wert* (her'ab)drücken, senken: ~ ***the market*** ✝ die Kurse drücken; **3.** *Leistung etc.* schwächen, her'absetzen; **4.** *Pedal, Taste etc.* (nieder)drücken; **de'pres·sant** [-snt] ⚕ **I** *adj.* dämpfend, beruhigend; **II** *s.* Depressi'onsmittel *n*.

de·pressed [dɪˈprest] *adj.* **1.** deprimiert, niedergeschlagen, bedrückt (*Person*), gedrückt (*Stimmung*, *a.* ✝ *Börse*); **2.** verringert, geschwächt (*Tätigkeit etc.*); **3.** ✝ flau (*Markt*), gedrückt (*Preis*), notleidend (*Industrie*); ~ **a·re·a** *s.* Notstandsgebiet *n*.

de·press·ing [dɪˈpresɪŋ] *adj.* □ **1.** deprimierend, bedrückend; **2.** kläglich; **de'pres·sion** [-eʃn] *s.* **1.** Depressi'on *f*, Niedergeschlagenheit *f*, Ge-, Bedrücktheit *f*; Melancho'lie *f*; **2.** Senkung *f*, Vertiefung *f*; *geol.* Landsenke *f*; **3.** ✝ Fallen *n* (*Preise*); Wirtschaftskrise *f*, Depressi'on *f*, Flaute *f*, Tiefstand *m*; **4.** *ast., surv.* Depressi'on *f*; **5.** *meteor.* Tief(druckgebiet) *n*; **6.** Abnahme *f*, Schwächung *f*; **7.** ⚕ Schwäche *f*, Entkräftung *f*; **de'pres·sive** [-sɪv] *adj.* deprimiert, *psych.* depres'siv.

dep·ri·va·tion [ˌdeprɪˈveɪʃn] *s.* **1.** Beraubung *f*, Entziehung *f*, Entzug *m*; **2.** (schmerzlicher) Verlust; **3.** Entbehrung *f*, Mangel *m*; **4.** *psych.* Deprivati'on *f*, (Liebes- *etc.*)Entzug *m*; **de·prive** [dɪˈpraɪv] *v/t.* **1.** (***of s.th.***) (*j-n od. et.* e-r Sache) berauben, (*j-m* et.) entziehen *od.* rauben *od.* nehmen: ***be ~d of s.th.*** et. entbehren (müssen); ***~d child*** *psych.* an Liebesentzug leidendes Kind; ***~d persons*** benachteiligte *od.* unterprivilegierte Personen; **2.** (***of s.th.***) *j-n* ausschließen (von et.), (*j-m* et.) vorenthalten; **3.** *eccl. j-n* absetzen.

depth [depθ] *s.* **1.** Tiefe *f*: ***eight feet in*** ~ acht Fuß tief; ***get out of one's*** ~ den (sicheren) Grund unter den Füßen verlieren (*a. fig.*); ***be out of one's*** ~ a) *im Wasser* nicht mehr stehen können, b) *fig.* ratlos *od.* unsicher sein, ‚schwimmen'; ***it is beyond my*** ~ es geht über m-n Horizont; **2.** Tiefe *f* (*als 3. Dimension*): ~ ***of a cupboard***; **3.** a) *a.* ~ ***of focus*** *od.* ***field*** Schärfentiefe *f*, b) *bsd. phot.* Tiefenschärfe *f*, c) Tiefe *f* (*von Farben, Tönen*); **4.** *oft pl.* Tiefe *f*, Mitte *f*, (*das*) Innerste (*a. fig.*): ***in the*** ~ ***of night*** mitten in der Nacht; ***in the*** ~ ***of winter*** mitten im Winter; ***from the*** ~ ***of misery*** aus tiefstem Elend; **5.** *fig.* a) Tiefe *f*: ~ ***of meaning***, b) tiefer Sinn, c) Tiefe *f*, Intensi'tät *f*: ~ ***of grief***; ***in*** ~ eingehend, tiefschürfend, d) (Gedanken)Tiefe *f*, Tiefgründigkeit *f*, e) Scharfsinn *m*, f) Dunkelheit *f*, Unklarheit *f*; **6.** ⚒ Teufe *f*; **7.** *psych.* 'Unterbewußtsein *n*: ~ ***analysis*** tiefenpsychologische Analyse; ~ ***interview*** Tiefeninterview *n*; ~ ***psychology*** Tiefenpsychologie *f*; ~ **bomb**, ~ **charge** *s.* ⚔ Wasserbombe *f*.

dep·u·rate [ˈdepjʊreɪt] *v/t.* ⚗, ⚕, ⚙ reinigen, läutern.

dep·u·ta·tion [ˌdepjʊˈteɪʃn] *s.* Deputati'on *f*, Abordnung *f*; **de·pute** [dɪˈpjuːt] *v/t.* **1.** abordnen, delegieren, deputieren; **2.** *Aufgabe etc.* über'tragen (***to*** *dat.*); **dep·u·tize** [ˈdepjʊtaɪz] **I** *v/t.* (als Vertreter) ernennen, abordnen; **II** *v/i.* ~ ***for s.o.*** j-n vertreten; **dep·u·ty** [ˈdepjʊtɪ] **I** *s.* **1.** (Stell)Vertreter(in), Beauftragte(r *m*) *f*; **2.** *pol.* Abgeordnete(r *m*) *f*; **II** *adj.* **3.** stellvertretend, Vize...: ~ ***chairman*** stellvertretende(r) Vorsitzende(r), Vizepräsident(in).

de·rac·i·nate [dɪˈræsɪneɪt] *v/t.* entwur-

zeln (*a. fig.*); ausrotten, vernichten.
de·rail [dɪ'reɪl] *v/i. u. v/t.* entgleisen (lassen); **de'rail·ment** [-mənt] *s.* Entgleisung *f*.
de·range [dɪ'reɪndʒ] *v/t.* **1.** in Unordnung bringen, durchein'anderbringen; **2.** stören; **3.** verrückt machen, (geistig) zerrütten; **de'ranged** [-dʒd] *adj.* **1.** in Unordnung, gestört: ***a ~ stomach*** e-e Magenverstimmung; **2.** ⚕ *a.* ***mentally ~*** geistesgestört; **de'range·ment** [-mənt] *s.* **1.** Unordnung *f*, Durchein'ander *n*; **2.** Störung *f*; **3.** ⚕ *a.* ***mental ~*** Geistesgestörtheit *f*.
de·ra·tion [ˌdiː'ræʃn] *v/t.* die Rationierung von … aufheben, *Ware* freigeben.
Der·by ['dɑːbɪ] *s.* **1.** *Rennsport:* a) (*das* englische) Derby (*in Epsom*), b) *allg.* Derby *n* (*Pferderennen*); **2.** ♀ *sport* (*bsd.* Lo'kal)Derby *n*; **3.** ♀ *Am.* ‚Me'lone' *f*.
der·e·lict ['derɪlɪkt] **I** *adj.* **1.** herrenlos, aufgegeben, verlassen; **2.** her'untergekommen, zerfallen, baufällig; **3.** nachlässig: ***~ in duty*** pflichtvergessen; **II** *s.* **4.** ⚖ herrenloses Gut; **5.** ⚓ a) aufgegebenes Schiff, b) treibendes Wrack; **6.** menschliches Wrack, *a.* Obdachlose(r *m*) *f*; **7.** Pflichtvergessene(r *m*) *f*; **der·e·lic·tion** [ˌderɪ'lɪkʃn] *s.* **1.** Aufgeben *n*, Preisgabe *f*; **2.** Verlassenheit *f*; **3.** Vernachlässigung *f*, Versäumnis *n*: ***~ of duty*** Pflichtversäumnis; **4.** Versagen *n*; **5.** Ver-, Zerfall *m*; **6.** ⚖ a) Besitzaufgabe *f*, b) Verlandung *f*, Landgewinn *m* in'folge Rückgangs des Wasserspiegels.
de·re·strict [ˌdiːrɪ'strɪkt] *v/t.* die Einschränkungsmaßnahmen aufheben für; **ˌde·re'stric·tion** [-kʃn] *s.* Aufhebung *f* der Einschränkungsmaßnahmen, *bsd.* der Geschwindigkeitsbegrenzung.
de·ride [dɪ'raɪd] *v/t.* verlachen, -höhnen, -spotten; **de'rid·er** [-də] *s.* Spötter *m*; **de'rid·ing·ly** [-dɪŋlɪ] *adv.* spöttisch.
de ri·gueur [dərɪ'gɜː] (*Fr.*) *pred. adj.* **1.** streng nach der Eti'kette; **2.** unerläßlich, ‚ein Muß'.
de·ri·sion [dɪ'rɪʒn] *s.* Hohn *m*, Spott *m*: ***hold in ~*** verspotten; ***bring into ~*** zum Gespött machen; ***be the ~ of s.o.*** j-s Gespött sein; **de·ri·sive** [dɪ'raɪsɪv], **de·ri·so·ry** [dɪ'raɪsərɪ] *adj.* □ höhnisch, spöttisch.
de·riv·a·ble [dɪ'raɪvəbl] *adj.* **1.** ab-, herleitbar (***from*** von); **2.** erreichbar, zu gewinnen(d) (***from*** aus); **der·i·va·tion** [ˌderɪ'veɪʃn] *s.* **1.** Ab-, Herleitung *f* (*a. ling.*); **2.** Ursprung *m*, Herkunft *f*, Abstammung *f*; **de·riv·a·tive** [dɪ'rɪvətɪv] **I** *adj.* **1.** abgeleitet; **2.** sekun'där; **II** *s.* **3.** *et.* Ab- *od.* Hergeleitetes; **4.** *ling.* Ableitung *f*, abgeleitete Form (*od.* ⚗ Funkti'on); **5.** ⚗ Deri'vat *n*, Abkömmling *m*; **de·rive** [dɪ'raɪv] **I** *v/t.* **1.** (***from***) herleiten (von), zu'rückführen (auf *acc.*), verdanken (*dat.*): ***be ~d from*** → 4; ***~d income*** ✝ abgeleitetes Einkommen; **2.** bekommen, erlangen, gewinnen: ***~d from coffee*** aus Kaffee gewonnen; ***~ profit from*** Nutzen ziehen aus; ***~ pleasure from*** Freude haben an (*dat.*); **3.** ⚗, ⚗, *ling.* ableiten; **II** *v/i.* **4.** ***~ from*** (ab)stammen *od.* herrühren *od.* abgeleitet sein *od.* sich ableiten von.
derm [dɜːm], **der·ma** ['dɜːmə] *s. anat.* Haut *f*; **der·mal** ['dɜːml] *adj. anat.* Haut…; **der·ma·ti·tis** [ˌdɜːmə'taɪtɪs] *s.* ⚕ Derma'titis *f*, Hautentzündung *f*; **der·ma·tol·o·gist** [ˌdɜːmə'tɒlədʒɪst] *s.* Dermato'loge *m*, Hautarzt *m*; **der·ma·tol·o·gy** [ˌdɜːmə'tɒlədʒɪ] *s.* ⚕ Dermatolo'gie *f*.
der·o·gate ['derəgeɪt] **I** *v/i.* (***from***) **1.** Abbruch tun, schaden (*dat.*), beeinträchtigen, schmälern (*acc.*); **2.** abweichen (von *e-r Norm etc.*); **II** *v/t.* **3.** her'absetzen; **der·o·ga·tion** [ˌderə'geɪʃn] *s.* **1.** Beeinträchtigung *f*, Schmälerung *f*, Nachteil *m*; **2.** Her'absetzung *f*; **de·rog·a·to·ry** [dɪ'rɒgətərɪ] *adj.* **1.** (***to***) nachteilig (für), abträglich (*dat.*), schädlich (*dat. od.* für): ***be ~*** schaden, beeinträchtigen; **2.** abfällig, geringschätzig (*Worte*).
der·rick ['derɪk] *s.* **1.** ⚙ a) Mastenkran *m*, b) Ausleger *m*; **2.** ⚙ Bohrturm *m*; **3.** ⚓ Ladebaum *m*.
der·ring-do [ˌderɪŋ'duː] *s.* Verwegenheit *f*, Tollkühnheit *f*.
der·vish ['dɜːvɪʃ] *s.* Derwisch *m*.
de·sal·i·nate [ˌdiː'sælɪneɪt] *v/t.* entsalzen.
des·cant I *s.* ['deskænt] **1.** *poet.* Lied *n*, Weise *f*; **2.** ♪ a) Dis'kant *m*, b) variierte Melo'die; **II** *v/i.* [dɪ'skænt] **3.** sich auslassen (***on*** über *acc.*); **4.** ♪ diskantieren.
de·scend [dɪ'send] **I** *v/i.* **1.** her'unter-, hin'untersteigen, -gehen, -kommen, -fahren, -fallen, -sinken; ab-, aussteigen; ⚒ einfahren; ✈ niedergehen, landen; **2.** sinken, fallen; sich senken (*Straße*), abfallen (*Gebirge*); **3.** *mst* ***be ~ed*** abstammen, herkommen (***from*** von, aus); **4.** (***to***) zufallen (*dat.*), 'übergehen, sich vererben (auf *acc.*); **5.** (***to***) sich hergeben, sich erniedrigen (zu); **6.** (***to***) 'übergehen (zu), eingehen (auf *ein Thema etc.*); **7.** (***on, upon***) sich stürzen (auf *acc.*), herfallen (über *acc.*), einfallen (in *acc.*); her'einbrechen (über *acc.*); *fig. j-n* ‚über'fallen' (*Besuch etc.*); **8.** ♪, *ast.* fallen, absteigen; **II** *v/t.* **9.** *Treppe etc.* her'unter-, hin'untersteigen, -gehen *etc.*; **de'scend·ant** [-dənt] *s.* **1.** Nachkomme *m*, Abkömmling *m*; **2.** *ast.* Deszen'dent *m*.
de·scent [dɪ'sent] *s.* **1.** Her'unter-, Hin'untersteigen *n*, Abstieg *m*; Talfahrt *f*; ⚒ Einfahrt *f*; ✈ Landung *f*; (*Fallschirm*)Absprung *m*; **2.** Abhang *m*, Abfall *m*, Senkung *f*, Gefälle *n*; **3.** *fig.* Abstieg *m*, Niedergang *m*, Fallen *n*, Sinken *n*; **4.** Abstammung *f*, Herkunft *f*, Geburt *f*; **5.** ⚖ Vererbung *f*, 'Übergang *m*, Über'tragung *f*; **6.** (***on, upon***) 'Überfall *m* (auf *acc.*), Einfall *m* (in *acc.*), Angriff *m* (auf *acc.*); **7.** *bibl.* Ausgießung *f* (*des Heiligen Geistes*); **8.** ***~ from the cross*** *paint.* Kreuzabnahme *f*.
de·scrib·a·ble [dɪ'skraɪbəbl] *adj.* zu beschreiben(d); **de·scribe** [dɪ'skraɪb] *v/t.* **1.** beschreiben, schildern; **2.** (***as***) bezeichnen (als), nennen (*acc.*); **3.** *bsd.* ⚗ *Kreis*, *Kurve* beschreiben; **de·scrip·tion** [dɪ'skrɪpʃn] *s.* **1.** Beschreibung *f* (*a.* ⚗ *etc.*), Darstellung *f*, Schilderung *f*: ***beautiful beyond ~*** unbeschreiblich *od.* unsagbar schön; **2.** Bezeichnung *f*; **3.** Art *f*, Sorte *f*: ***of the worst ~*** schlimmster Art; **de·scrip·tive** [dɪ'skrɪptɪv] *adj.* □ **1.** beschreibend, schildernd: ***~ geometry*** darstellende Geometrie; ***be ~ of*** beschreiben, bezeichnen; **2.** anschaulich (geschrieben *od.* schreibend).
de·scry [dɪ'skraɪ] *v/t.* gewahren, wahrnehmen, erspähen, entdecken.
des·e·crate ['desɪkreɪt] *v/t.* entweihen, -heiligen, schänden; **des·e·cra·tion** [ˌdesɪ'kreɪʃn] *s.* Entweihung *f*, -heiligung *f*, Schändung *f*.
de·seg·re·gate [ˌdiː'segrɪgeɪt] *v/t.* die Rassenschranken aufheben in (*dat.*); **de·seg·re·ga·tion** [ˌdiːsegrɪ'geɪʃn] *s.* Aufhebung *f* der Rassentrennung.
de·sen·si·tize [ˌdiː'sensɪtaɪz] *v/t.* **1.** ⚕ desensibilisieren, unempfindlich machen; **2.** *phot.* lichtunempfindlich machen.
de·sert¹ [dɪ'zɜːt] *s. oft pl.* **1.** Verdienst *n*; **2.** verdienter Lohn (*a. iro.*), Strafe *f*: ***get one's ~s*** s-n wohlverdienten Lohn empfangen.
des·ert² ['dezət] **I** *s.* **1.** Wüste *f*; **2.** Ödland *n*; **3.** *fig.* Öde *f*; Einöde *f*; **4.** *fig.* Öde *f*, Fadheit *f*; **II** *adj.* **5.** öde, wüst; verödet, verlassen; **6.** Wüsten…
de·sert³ [dɪ'zɜːt] **I** *v/t.* **1.** verlassen; im Stich lassen; ⚖ *Ehepartner* (böswillig) verlassen; **2.** untreu *od.* abtrünnig werden (*dat.*): ***~ the colo(u)rs*** ⚔ fahnenflüchtig werden; **II** *v/i.* **3.** ⚔ desertieren, fahnenflüchtig werden; 'überlaufen, -gehen (***to*** zu); **de'sert·ed** [-tɪd] *adj.* **1.** verlassen, ausgestorben, menschenleer; **2.** verlassen, einsam; **de'sert·er** [-tə] *s.* **1.** ⚔ a) Fahnenflüchtige(r) *m*, Deser'teur *m*, b) 'Überläufer *m*; **2.** *fig.* Abtrünnige(r *m*) *f*; **de'ser·tion** [-ɜːʃn] *s.* **1.** Verlassen *n*, Im'stichlassen *n*; **2.** Abtrünnigwerden *n*, Abfall *m* (***from*** von); **3.** ⚖ böswilliges Verlassen; **4.** ⚔ Fahnenflucht *f*.
de·serve [dɪ'zɜːv] **I** *v/t.* verdienen, verdient haben (*acc.*), würdig *od.* wert sein (*gen.*): ***~ praise*** Lob verdienen; **II** *v/i.* ***~ well of*** sich verdient gemacht haben um; ***~ ill of*** e-n schlechten Dienst erwiesen haben (*dat.*); **de'serv·ed·ly** [-vɪdlɪ] *adv.* verdientermaßen, mit Recht; **de'serv·ing** [-vɪŋ] *adj.* **1.** verdienstvoll, verdient (*Person*); **2.** verdienstlich, -voll (*Tat*); **3.** ***be ~ of*** → ***deserve*** I.
des·ha·bille ['dezæbiːl] → ***dishabille***.
des·ic·cate ['desɪkeɪt] *v/t. u. v/i.* (aus-)trocknen, ausdörren: ***~d milk*** Trockenmilch *f*; ***~d fruit*** Dörrobst *n*; **des·ic·ca·tion** [ˌdesɪ'keɪʃn] *s.* (Aus)Trocknung *f*, Trockenwerden *n*; **'des·ic·ca·tor** [-tə] *s.* ⚙ 'Trockenappaˌrat *m*.
de·sid·er·a·tum [dɪˌzɪdə'reɪtəm] *pl.* **-ta** [-tə] *s. et.* Erwünschtes, Erfordernis *n*, Bedürfnis *n*.
de·sign [dɪ'zaɪn] **I** *v/t.* **1.** entwerfen, (auf)zeichnen, skizzieren: ***~ a dress*** ein Kleid entwerfen; **2.** gestalten, ausführen, anlegen; **3.** *fig.* entwerfen, ausdenken, ersinnen: ***~ed to do s.th.*** dafür bestimmt *od.* darauf angelegt, et. zu tun (*Sache*); **4.** planen, beabsichtigen: ***~ doing*** (*od.* ***to do***) beabsichtigen zu tun; **5.** bestimmen: a) vorsehen (***for*** für, ***as*** als), b) ausersehen: ***~ed to be a priest*** zum Priester bestimmt; **II** *v/i.* **6.** Zeichner *od.* Konstruk'teur *od.* De'signer sein; **III** *s.* **7.** Entwurf *m*, Zeichnung *f*, Plan *m*, Skizze *f*; **8.** Muster *n*, Zeichnung *f*, Fi'gur *f*, Des'sin *n*: ***floral ~*** Blumenmuster; ***registered ~*** ⚖ Ge-

brauchsmuster; ***protection of ~s*** ⚖ Musterschutz *m*; **9.** a) Gestaltung *f*, Formgebung *f*, De'sign *n*, b) Bauart *f*, Konstrukti'on *f*, Ausführung *f*, Mo'dell *n*; → ***industrial design***; **10.** Anlage *f*, Anordnung *f*; **11.** Absicht *f*, Plan *m*; Zweck *m*, Ziel *n*: ***by ~*** mit Absicht; **12.** böse Absicht, Anschlag *m*: ***have ~s on*** (*od.* ***against***) et. im Schilde führen gegen, *a. iro.* e-n Anschlag vorhaben auf (*acc.*).

des·ig·nate ['dezɪgneɪt] **I** *v/t.* **1.** bezeichnen, (be)nennen; **2.** kennzeichnen; **3.** berufen, ausersehen, bestimmen, ernennen (***for*** zu); **II** *adj.* **4.** designiert, einstweilig ernannt: ***bishop ~***; **des·ig·na·tion** [ˌdezɪg'neɪʃn] *s.* **1.** Bezeichnung *f*, Name *m*; **2.** Kennzeichnung *f*; **3.** Bestimmung *f*; **4.** einstweilige Ernennung *od.* Berufung.

de·signed [dɪ'zaɪnd] *adj.* □ **1.** (***for***) bestimmt *etc.* (für); → ***design*** 3, 4, 5; **2.** vorsätzlich, absichtlich; **de'sign·ed·ly** [-nɪdlɪ] *adv.* → ***designed*** 2; **de'sign·er** [-nə] *s.* **1.** Entwerfer(in): a) (Muster-) Zeichner(in), b) De'signer(in), (Form-) Gestalter(in), Gebrauchsgraphiker(in), c) ⚙ Konstruk'teur *m*; **2.** Ränkeschmied *m*, Intri'gant(in); **de'sign·ing** [-nɪŋ] *adj.* □ ränkevoll, intri'gant.

de·sir·a·bil·i·ty [dɪˌzaɪərə'bɪlətɪ] *s.* Erwünschtheit *f*; **de·sir·a·ble** [dɪ'zaɪərəbl] *adj.* □ **1.** wünschenswert, erwünscht; **2.** begehrenswert, reizvoll; **de·sire** [dɪ'zaɪə] **I** *v/t.* **1.** wünschen, begehren, verlangen, wollen: ***if ~d*** auf Wunsch; ***leaves much to be ~d*** läßt viel zu wünschen übrig; **2.** *j-n* bitten, ersuchen; **II** *s.* **3.** Wunsch *m*, Verlangen *n*, Begehren *n* (***for*** nach); **4.** Wunsch *m*, Bitte *f*: ***at*** (*od.* ***by***) ***s.o.'s ~*** auf (j-s) Wunsch; **5.** Lust *f*, Begierde *f*; **6.** *das* Gewünschte; **de·sir·ous** [dɪ'zaɪərəs] *adj.* □ (***of***) begierig, verlangend (nach), wünschend (*acc.*): ***I am ~ to know*** ich möchte (sehr) gern wissen; ***the parties are ~ to ...*** (*in Verträgen*) die Parteien beabsichtigen, zu ...

de·sist [dɪ'zɪst] *v/i.* abstehen, ablassen, Abstand nehmen (***from*** von): ***~ from asking*** aufhören zu fragen.

desk [desk] **I** *s.* **1.** Schreibtisch *m*; **2.** (Lese-, Schreib-, Noten-, Kirchen-, ⚙ Schalt)Pult *n*; **3.** ✝ (Zahl)Kasse *f*: ***pay at the ~!*** zahlen Sie an der Kasse!; ***first ~*** ♪ erstes Pult (*Orchester*); **4.** *eccl. bsd. Am.* Kanzel *f*; **5.** *Am.* Redakti'on *f*: ***city ~*** Lokalredaktion; **6.** Auskunft (-sschalter *m*) *f*; **7.** Empfang *m*, Rezepti'on *f* (*im Hotel*): ***~ clerk*** *Am.* Empfangschef *m*; **II** *adj.* **8.** Schreibtisch..., Büro...: ***~ work***; ***~ calender*** Tischkalender *m*; ***~ sergeant*** diensthabender (Polizei)Wachtmeister; ***~ set*** Schreibzeug(garnitur *f*) *n*.

des·o·late I *adj.* □ ['desələt] **1.** wüst, unwirtlich, öde; verwüstet; **2.** verlassen, einsam; **3.** trostlos, *fig. a.* öde; **II** *v/t.* [-leɪt] **4.** verwüsten; **5.** einsam zu'rücklassen; **6.** betrüben, bekümmern; **'des·o·late·ness** [-nɪs] → ***desolation*** 2, 3; **des·o·la·tion** [ˌdesə'leɪʃn] *s.* **1.** Verwüstung *f*, -ödung *f*; **2.** Verlassenheit *f*, Einsamkeit *f*; **3.** Trostlosigkeit *f*, Elend *n*.

de·spair [dɪ'speə] **I** *v/i.* (***of***) verzweifeln (an *dat.*), ohne Hoffnung sein, alle Hoffnung aufgeben *od.* verlieren (auf *acc.*): ***the patient's life is ~ed of*** man bangt um das Leben des Kranken; **II** *s.* Verzweiflung *f* (***at*** über *acc.*), Hoffnungslosigkeit *f*: ***drive s.o. to ~, be s.o.'s ~*** j-n zur Verzweiflung bringen; **de'spair·ing** [-eərɪŋ] *adj.* □ verzweifelt.

des·patch *etc.* → ***dispatch*** *etc.*

des·per·a·do [ˌdespə'rɑːdəʊ] *pl.* **-does, -dos** *s.* Despe'rado *m*.

des·per·ate ['despərət] *adj.* □ **1.** verzweifelt: ***she was ~*** sie war (völlig) verzweifelt; ***a ~ deed*** e-e Verzweiflungstat; ***~ efforts*** verzweifelte *od.* krampfhafte Anstrengungen; ***~ remedy*** äußerstes Mittel; ***be ~ for s.th.*** *od.* ***to get s.th.*** et. verzweifelt *od.* ganz dringend brauchen, et. unbedingt haben wollen; **2.** verzweifelt, hoffnungs-, ausweglos: ***~ situation***; **3.** verzweifelt, despa'rat, zu allem fähig, zum Äußersten entschlossen (*Person*); **4.** F schrecklich: ***a ~ fool***; ***~ly in love*** wahnsinnig verliebt; ***not ~ly*** F a) nicht unbedingt, b) nicht übermäßig (*schön etc.*); **des·per·a·tion** [ˌdespə'reɪʃn] *s.* **1.** (höchste) Verzweiflung, Hoffnungslosigkeit *f*; **2.** Rase'rei *f*, Verzweiflung *f*: ***drive to ~*** rasend machen, zur Verzweiflung bringen.

des·pi·ca·ble ['despɪkəbl] *adj.* □ verächtlich, verachtenswert.

de·spise [dɪ'spaɪz] *v/t.* verachten, *Speise etc. a.* verschmähen: ***not to be ~d*** nicht zu verachten.

de·spite [dɪ'spaɪt] **I** *prp.* trotz (*gen.*), ungeachtet (*gen.*); **II** *s.* Bosheit *f*, Tücke *f*; Trotz *m*, Verachtung *f*: ***in ~ of*** → I.

de·spoil [dɪ'spɔɪl] *v/t.* plündern; berauben (***of*** *gen.*); **de'spoil·ment** [-mənt], **de·spo·li·a·tion** [dɪˌspəʊlɪ'eɪʃn] *s.* Plünderung *f*, Beraubung *f*.

de·spond [dɪ'spɒnd] **I** *v/i.* verzagen; verzweifeln (***of*** an *dat.*); **II** *s. obs.* Verzweiflung *f*; **de'spond·en·cy** [-dənsɪ] *s.* Verzagtheit *f*, Mutlosigkeit *f*; **de'spond·ent** [-dənt] *adj.* □, **de'spond·ing** [-dɪŋ] *adj.* □ verzagt, mutlos, kleinmütig.

des·pot ['despɒt] *s.* Des'pot *m*, Gewaltherrscher *m*; *fig.* Ty'rann *m*; **des·pot·ic, des·pot·i·cal** [de'spɒtɪk(l)] *adj.* □ des'potisch, herrisch, ty'rannisch; **'des·pot·ism** [-pətɪzəm] *s.* Despo'tismus *m*, Tyran'nei *f*, Gewaltherrschaft *f*.

des·qua·mate ['deskwəmeɪt] *v/i.* **1.** ⚕ sich abschuppen; **2.** sich häuten.

des·sert [dɪ'zɜːt] *s.* Des'sert *n*, Nachtisch *m*: ***~ spoon*** Dessertlöffel *m*.

des·ti·na·tion [ˌdestɪ'neɪʃn] *s.* **1.** Bestimmungsort *m*; Reiseziel *n*: ***country of ~*** ✝ Bestimmungsland *n*; **2.** Bestimmung *f*, Zweck *m*, Ziel *n*.

des·tine ['destɪn] *v/t.* bestimmen, vorsehen (***for*** für, ***to do*** zu tun); **'des·tined** [-nd] *adj.* bestimmt: ***~ for*** unterwegs nach (*Schiff etc.*); ***he was ~*** (***to*** *inf.*) es war ihm beschieden (zu *inf.*), er sollte (*inf.*); **'des·ti·ny** [-nɪ] *s.* **1.** Schicksal *n*, Geschick *n*, Los *n*: ***he met his ~*** sein Schicksal ereilte ihn; **2.** Vorsehung *f*; **3.** Verhängnis *n*, zwingende Notwendigkeit; **4.** ***the Destinies*** die Parzen (*Schicksalsgöttinnen*).

des·ti·tute ['destɪtjuːt] **I** *adj.* **1.** verarmt, mittellos, notleidend; **2.** (***of***) ermangelnd, entblößt (*gen.*), ohne (*acc.*), bar (*gen.*); **II** *s.* **3.** ***the ~*** die Armen; **des·ti·tu·tion** [ˌdestɪ'tjuːʃn] *s.* **1.** Armut *f*, (bittere) Not, Elend *n*; **2.** (völliger) Mangel (***of*** an *dat.*).

de·stroy [dɪ'strɔɪ] *v/t.* **1.** zerstören, vernichten; **2.** zertrümmern, *Gebäude etc.* niederreißen; **3.** *et.* ruinieren, unbrauchbar machen; **3.** *j-n, e-e Armee etc.* vernichten, *Insekten etc. a.* vertilgen; **4.** töten; **5.** *fig. j-n, j-s Ruf, Gesundheit etc.* ruinieren, zu'grunde richten, *Hoffnungen etc.* zu'nichte machen, zerstören; **6.** F *j-n* ka'putt- *od.* fertigmachen; **de'stroy·er** [-ɔɪə] *s. a.* ⚔, ⚓ Zerstörer *m*.

de·struct [dɪ'strʌkt] **I** *v/t.* **1.** ⚔ (aus Sicherheitsgründen) zerstören; **II** *v/i.* **2.** zerstört werden; **3.** sich selbst zerstören; **de'struct·i·ble** [-təbl] *adj.* zerstörbar; **de'struc·tion** [-kʃn] *s.* **1.** Zerstörung *f*, Vernichtung *f*; **2.** Abriß *m* (*e-s Gebäudes*); **3.** Tötung *f*; **de'struc·tive** [-tɪv] *adj.* □ **1.** zerstörend, vernichtend (*a. fig.*): ***be ~ of*** *et.* zerstören *od.* unter'graben; **2.** zerstörerisch, destruk'tiv, schädlich, verderblich: ***~ to health*** gesundheitsschädlich; **4.** rein negativ, destruk'tiv (*Kritik*); **de'struc·tive·ness** [-tɪvnɪs] *s.* **1.** zerstörende *od.* vernichtende Wirkung; **2.** *das* Destruk'tive, destruk'tive Eigenschaft; **de'struc·tor** [-tə] *s.* ⚙ (Müll)Verbrennungsofen *m*.

des·ue·tude [dɪ'sjuːɪtjuːd] *s.* Ungebräuchlichkeit *f*: ***fall into ~*** außer Gebrauch kommen.

de·sul·fu·rize [ˌdiː'sʌlfəraɪz] *v/t.* ⚗ entschwefeln.

des·ul·to·ri·ness ['desəltərɪnɪs] *s.* **1.** Zs.-hangs-, Plan-, Ziellosigkeit *f*; **2.** Flüchtigkeit *f*, Oberflächlichkeit *f*, Sprunghaftigkeit *f*; **des·ul·to·ry** ['desəltərɪ] *adj.* **1.** 'unzuˌsammenhängend, planlos, ziellos, oberflächlich; **2.** abschweifend, sprunghaft; **3.** unruhig; **4.** vereinzelt, spo'radisch.

de·tach [dɪ'tætʃ] **I** *v/t.* **1.** ab-, loslösen, losmachen, abtrennen, *a.* ⚙ abnehmen; **2.** absondern; befreien; **3.** ⚔ abkommandieren; **II** *v/i.* **4.** sich (los)lösen; **de'tach·a·ble** [-tʃəbl] *adj.* abnehmbar (*a.* ⚙); abtrennbar; lose; **de'tached** [-tʃt] *adj.*, **de'tached·ly** [-tʃtlɪ] *adv.* **1.** getrennt, gesondert; **2.** einzeln, frei-, al'leinstehend (*Haus*); **3.** *fig.* a) objek'tiv, unvoreingenommen, b) uninteressiert, c) distanziert; **4.** *fig.* losgelöst, entrückt; **de'tach·ment** [-mənt] *s.* **1.** Absonderung *f*, Abtrennung *f*, Loslösung *f*; **2.** *fig.* (innerer) Abstand, Di'stanz *f*, Losgelöstsein *n*, (innere) Freiheit; **3.** *fig.* Objektivi'tät *f*, Unvoreingenommenheit *f*; **4.** Gleichgültigkeit *f* (***from*** gegen); **5.** ⚔ → ***detail*** 5 a u. b.

de·tail ['diːteɪl] **I** *s.* **1.** De'tail *n*: a) Einzelheit *f*, b) *a. pl. coll.* (nähere) Einzelheiten *pl.*: ***in ~*** im einzelnen, ausführlich; ***go*** (*od.* ***enter***) ***into ~(s)*** ins einzelne gehen, es ausführlich behandeln; **2.** Einzelteil *n*; **3.** 'Nebensache *f*, -ˌumstand *m*, Kleinigkeit *f*; **4.** *Kunst etc.*: a) De'tail(darstellung *f*) *n*, b) Ausschnitt *m*; **5.** ⚔ a) Ab'teilung *f*, Trupp *m*, b) ('Sonder)Komˌmando *n*, c) 'Abkommanˌdierung *f*, d) Sonderauftrag *m*; **II** *v/t.* **6.** ausführlich berichten über (*acc.*), genau schildern; einzeln aufzählen *od.*

-führen; **7.** ⚔ abkommandieren; **ˈde·tailed** [-ld] *adj.* ausführlich, genau, eingehend.

de·tain [dɪˈteɪn] *v/t.* **1.** *j-n* auf-, abhalten, zuˈrück(be)halten, hindern; **2.** ⚖ *j-n* in (Unterˈsuchungs)Haft behalten; **3.** *et.* vorenthalten, einbehalten; **4.** *ped.* nachsitzen lassen; **de·tain·ee** [ˌdiːteɪˈniː] *s.* ⚖ Häftling *m*; **deˈtain·er** [-nə] *s.* ⚖ **1.** ˈwiderrechtliche Vorenthaltung; **2.** Anordnung *f* der Haftfortdauer.

de·tect [dɪˈtekt] *v/t.* **1.** entdecken; (herˈaus)finden, ermitteln; **2.** feststellen, wahrnehmen; **3.** aufdecken, enthüllen; **4.** ertappen (***in*** bei); **5.** *Radio*: gleichrichten; **deˈtect·a·ble** [-təbl] *adj.* feststellbar; **deˈtec·ta·phone** [-təfəʊn] *s. teleph.* Abhörgerät *n*; **deˈtec·tion** [-kʃn] *s.* **1.** Ent-, Aufdeckung *f*; Feststellung *f*; **2.** *Radio*: Gleichrichtung *f*; **3.** *coll.* Krimiˈnalroˌmane *pl.*; **deˈtec·tive** [-tɪv] **I** *adj.* Detektiv..., Kriminal...: **~ *force*** Kriminalpolizei *f*; **~ *story*** Kriminalroman *m*; ***do ~ work*** *bsd. fig.* Detektivarbeit leisten; **II** *s.* Detekˈtiv *m*, Krimiˈnalbeamte(r) *m*, Geˈheimpoliˌzist *m*; **deˈtec·tor** [-tə] *s.* **1.** Auf-, Entdecker *m*; **2.** ⚙ a) Sucher *m*, b) Anzeigevorrichtung *f*; **3.** ⚡ a) Deˈtektor *m*, b) Gleichrichter *m*.

de·tent [dɪˈtent] *s.* ⚙ Sperrhaken *m*, -klinke *f*, Sperre *f*; Auslösung *f*.

dé·tente [deɪˈtɑ̃ːnt] (*Fr.*) *s. bsd. pol.* Entspannung *f*.

de·ten·tion [dɪˈtenʃn] *s.* **1.** Festnahme *f*; **2.** (*a.* Unterˈsuchungs)Haft *f*, Gewahrsam *m*, Arˈrest *m*: **~ *barracks*** Militärgefängnis *n*; **~ *center*** *Am.*, **~ *home*** *Brit.* Jugendstrafanstalt *f*; **~ *colony*** Strafkolonie *f*; **3.** *ped.* Nachsitzen *n*, Arrest *m*; **4.** Ab-, Zuˈrückhaltung *f*; **5.** Einbehaltung *f*, Vorenthaltung *f*.

de·ter [dɪˈtɜː] *v/t.* abschrecken, abhalten (***from*** von).

de·ter·gent [dɪˈtɜːdʒənt] **I** *adj.* reinigend; **II** *s.* Reinigungs-, Wasch-, Geschirrspülmittel *n*.

de·te·ri·o·rate [dɪˈtɪərɪəreɪt] **I** *v/i.* **1.** sich verschlechtern *od.* verschlimmern, schlecht(er) werden, verderben; **2.** an Wert verlieren; **II** *v/t.* **3.** verschlechtern; **4.** beeinträchtigen; im Wert mindern; **de·te·ri·o·ra·tion** [dɪˌtɪərɪəˈreɪʃn] *s.* **1.** Verschlechterung *f*; Verfall *m*; **2.** Wertminderung *f*.

de·ter·ment [dɪˈtɜːmənt] *s.* **1.** Abschreckung *f*; **2.** → ***deterrent*** II.

de·ter·mi·na·ble [dɪˈtɜːmɪnəbl] *adj.* bestimmbar; **deˈter·mi·nant** [-nənt] **I** *adj.* **1.** bestimmend, entscheidend; **II** *s.* **2.** entscheidender Faktor; **3.** 𝔄, *biol.* Determiˈnante *f*; **deˈter·mi·nate** [-nət] *adj.* □ bestimmt, fest(gesetzt), entschieden; **de·ter·mi·na·tion** [dɪˌtɜːmɪˈneɪʃn] *s.* **1.** Ent-, Beschluß *m*; **2.** Entscheidung *f*; Bestimmung *f*, Festsetzung *f*; **3.** Bestimmung *f*, Ermittlung *f*, Feststellung *f*; **4.** Bestimmtheit *f*, Entschlossenheit *f*, Zielstrebigkeit *f*; feste Absicht; **5.** Ziel *n*, Begrenzung *f*; Ablauf *m*, Ende *n*; **6.** Richtung *f*, Neigung *f*, Drang *m*; **deˈter·mi·na·tive** [-nətɪv] **I** *adj.* □ **1.** (näher) bestimmend, einschränkend; **2.** entscheidend; **II** *s.* **3.** *et.* Entscheidendes *od.* Charakteˈristisches; **4.** *ling.* a) Determinaˈtiv *n*, b) Bestimmungswort *n*; **de·ter·mine** [dɪˈtɜːmɪn] **I** *v/t.* **1.** entscheiden; regeln; **2.** *et.* bestimmen, festsetzen; beschließen (*a.* ***to do*** zu tun, ***that*** daß); **3.** feststellen, ermitteln, herˈausfinden; **4.** *j-n* bestimmen, veranlassen (***to do*** zu tun); **5.** *bsd.* ⚖ beendigen, aufheben; **II** *v/i.* **6.** (***on***) sich entscheiden (für), sich entschließen (zu); beschließen (***on doing*** zu tun); **7.** *bsd.* ⚖ enden, ablaufen; **deˈter·mined** [-mɪnd] *adj.* □ (fest) entschlossen, fest, entschieden, bestimmt; **deˈter·min·er** [-mɪnə] *s. ling.* Bestimmungswort *n*; **deˈter·min·ism** [-mɪnɪzəm] *s. phls.* Determiˈnismus *m*.

de·ter·rence [dɪˈterəns] *s.* Abschreckung *f*; **deˈter·rent** [-nt] **I** *adj.* abschreckend; **II** *s.* Abschreckungsmittel *n*.

de·test [dɪˈtest] *v/t.* verabscheuen, hassen; **deˈtest·a·ble** [-təbl] *adj.* □ abˈscheulich, hassenswert; **de·tes·ta·tion** [ˌdiːteˈsteɪʃn] *s.* (***of***) Verabscheuung *f* (*gen.*), Abscheu *m* (vor *dat.*): ***hold in ~*** verabscheuen.

de·throne [dɪˈθrəʊn] *v/t.* entthronen (*a. fig.*); **deˈthrone·ment** [-mənt] *s.* Entthronung *f*.

det·o·nate [ˈdetəneɪt] **I** *v/t.* explodieren lassen, zur Exploſiˈon bringen; **II** *v/i.* explodieren; *mot.* klopfen; **ˈdet·o·nat·ing** [-tɪŋ] *adj.* ⚙ Spreng..., Zünd..., Knall...; **det·o·na·tion** [ˌdetəˈneɪʃn] *s.* Detonatiˈon *f*, Knall *m*; **ˈdet·o·na·tor** [-tə] *s.* ⚙ **1.** Briˈsanzsprengstoff *m*; **2.** Zünd-, Sprengkapsel *f*.

de·tour, dé·tour [ˈdiːˌtʊə] **I** *s.* **1.** ˈUmweg *m*; Abstecher *m*; **2.** a) ˈUmleitung *f*, b) Umˈgehungsstraße *f*; **3.** *fig.* ˈUmschweif *m*; **II** *v/i.* **4.** e-n ˈUmweg machen; **III** *v/t.* **5.** e-n ˈUmweg machen um; **6.** *Verkehr* ˈumleiten.

de·tract [dɪˈtrækt] **I** *v/t. Aufmerksamkeit etc.* ablenken; **II** *v/i.* (***from***) a) Abbruch tun (*dat.*), beeinträchtigen, schmälern (*acc.*), b) herˈabsetzen; **deˈtrac·tion** [-kʃn] *s.* **1.** a) Beeinträchtigung *f*, Schmälerung *f*, b) Herˈabsetzung *f*; **2.** Verunglimpfung *f*; **deˈtrac·tor** [-tə] *s.* **1.** Kritiker *m*, Herˈabsetzer *m*; **2.** Verunglimpfer *m*.

de·train [ˌdiːˈtreɪn] 🚂, ⚔ **I** *v/i.* aussteigen; **II** *v/t.* ausladen; **ˌdeˈtrain·ment** [-mənt] *s.* **1.** Aussteigen *n*; **2.** Ausladen *n*.

det·ri·ment [ˈdetrɪmənt] *s.* Schaden *m*, Nachteil *m*: ***to the ~ of*** zum Schaden *od.* Nachteil (*gen.*); ***without ~ to*** ohne Schaden für; ***be a ~ to health*** gesundheitsschädlich sein; **det·ri·men·tal** [ˌdetrɪˈmentl] *adj.* □ (***to***) schädlich, nachteilig (für), abträglich (*dat.*).

de·tri·tal [dɪˈtraɪtl] *adj. geol.* Geröll..., Schutt...; **deˈtrit·ed** [-tɪd] *adj.* **1.** abgenützt; abgegriffen (*Münze*); *fig.* abgedroschen; **2.** *geol.* verwittert; **de·tri·tion** [dɪˈtrɪʃn] *s. geol.* Ab-, Zerreibung *f*; **deˈtri·tus** [-təs] *s. geol.* Geröll *n*, Schutt *m*.

de trop [dəˈtrəʊ] (*Fr.*) *pred. adj.* ˈüberflüssig, zuˈviel (des Guten).

deuce [djuːs] *s.* **1.** *Würfeln, Kartenspiel*: Zwei *f*; **2.** *Tennis*: Einstand *m*; **3.** F Teufel *m*: ***who*** (***what***) ***the ~?*** wer (was) zum Teufel?; ***a ~ of a row*** ein Mordskrach (*Lärm od. Streit*); ***there's the ~ to pay*** F das dicke Ende kommt noch; ***play the ~ with*** Schindluder treiben mit *j-m*; **deuced** [-st] *adj.*, **ˈdeu·ced·ly** [-sɪdlɪ] *adv.* F verteufelt, verflixt.

deu·te·ri·um [djuːˈtɪərɪəm] *s.* Deuˈterium *n*, schwerer Wasserstoff.

Deu·ter·on·o·my [ˌdjuːtəˈrɒnəmɪ] *s. bibl.* Deuteroˈnomium *n*, Fünftes Buch Mose.

de·val·u·ate [ˌdiːˈvæljʊeɪt] ✝ abwerten; **de·val·u·a·tion** [ˌdiːvæljʊˈeɪʃn] *s.* ✝ Abwertung *f*; **de·val·ue** [ˌdiːˈvæljuː] → ***devaluate***.

dev·as·tate [ˈdevəsteɪt] *v/t.* verwüsten, vernichten (*beide a. fig.*); **ˈdev·as·tat·ing** [-tɪŋ] *adj.* □ **1.** verheerend, vernichtend (*a. Kritik etc.*); **2.** F eˈnorm, phanˈtastisch, ˈumwerfend; **dev·as·ta·tion** [ˌdevəˈsteɪʃn] *s.* Verwüstung *f*.

de·vel·op [dɪˈveləp] **I** *v/t.* **1.** *allg. Theorie, Kräfte, Tempo etc.* entwickeln (*a.* 𝔄, ♪, *phot.*), *Muskeln etc. a.* bilden, *Interesse etc. a.* zeigen, an den Tag legen, *Fähigkeiten etc. a.* entfalten, *Gedanken, Plan etc. a.* ausarbeiten, gestalten (***into*** zu); **2.** entwickeln, ausbauen: ***~ an industry***; **3.** *Bodenschätze, a. Bauland* erschließen, nutzbar machen; *Altstadt* sanieren; **4.** sich *e-e Krankheit* zuziehen, *Fieber etc.* bekommen; **II** *v/i.* **5.** sich entwickeln (***from*** aus); sich entfalten: **~ *into*** sich entwickeln zu, zu *et.* werden; **6.** zuˈtage treten, sich zeigen; **deˈvel·op·er** [-pə] *s.* **1.** *phot.* Entwickler *m*; **2.** ***late ~*** *psych.* Spätentwickler *m*; **3.** (Stadt)Planer *m*; **deˈvel·op·ing** [-pɪŋ] *adj.*: **~ *bath*** *phot.* Entwicklungsbad *n*; **~ *company*** Bauträger *m*; **~ *country*** *pol.* Entwicklungsland *n*; **deˈvel·op·ment** [-mənt] *s.* **1.** Entwicklung *f* (*a. phot.*); **2.** Entfaltung *f*, Entstehen *n*, Bildung *f*, Wachstum *n*; Schaffung *f*; **3.** Erschließung *f*, Nutzbarmachung *f*; Ausbau *m*, ˈUmgestaltung *f*: **~ *area*** Entwicklungs-, Notstandsgebiet *n*; ***ripe for ~*** baureif; **4.** ⚖ ✝ Entwicklung(sabteilung) *f*; **5.** Darlegung *f*, Ausarbeitung *f*; ˈDurchführung *f* (*a.* ♪); **de·vel·op·ment·al** [dɪˌveləpˈmentl] *adj.* Entwicklungs...

de·vi·ate [ˈdiːvɪeɪt] **I** *v/i.* abweichen, abgehen, abkommen (***from*** von); **II** *v/t.* ablenken.

de·vi·a·tion [ˌdiːvɪˈeɪʃn] *s.* **1.** Abweichung *f*, Abweichen *n* (***from*** von); **2.** *bsd. phys., opt.* Ablenkung *f*; **3.** ✈, ⚓ Abweichung *f*, Ablenkung *f*, Abtrieb *m*; **ˌde·viˈa·tion·ism** [-ʃənɪzəm] *s. pol.* Abweichlertum *n*; **ˌde·viˈa·tion·ist** [-ʃənɪst], **de·vi·a·tor** [ˈdiːvɪeɪtə] *s. pol.* Abweichler(in).

de·vice [dɪˈvaɪs] *s.* **1.** Plan *m*, Einfall *m*, Erfindung *f*: ***left to one's own ~s*** sich selbst überlassen; **2.** Anschlag *m*, böse Absicht, Kniff *m*; **3.** ⚙ Vor-, Einrichtung *f*, Gerät *n*; *fig.* Behelf *m*, Kunstgriff *m*; **4.** Wahlspruch *m*, Deˈvise *f*; **5.** *her.* Sinn-, Wappenbild *n*; **6.** Muster *n*, Zeichnung *f*.

dev·il [ˈdevl] **I** *s.* **1.** ***the ~***, *a.* ***the*** ⚖ der Teufel: ***between the ~ and the deep sea*** *fig.* zwischen zwei Feuern, in auswegloser Lage; ***like the ~*** F wie der Teufel, wie wahnsinnig; ***go to the ~*** *sl.* zum Teufel *od.* vor die Hunde gehen; ***go to the ~!*** scher dich zum Teufel!; ***play the ~ with*** F Schindluder treiben mit; ***the ~ take the hindmost*** den Letzten beißen die Hunde; ***there's the ~ to pay*** F das setzt was ab!; ***the ~!*** F a) (*verärgert*) zum Teufel!, zum Henker!, b) (*erstaunt*) Donnerwetter!; **2.** Teufel *m*, böser Geist, 'Satan *m* (*a. fig.*); → ***due*** 9; ***tattoo***[1] 2; **3.** *fig.* Laster *n*, Übel *n*; **4.** ***poor ~*** armer Teufel *od.* Schlukker; **5.** *a.* ***~ of a fellow*** Teufelskerl *m*, toller Bursche; **6.** ***a*** (*od.* ***the***) ***~*** F e-e verflixte Sache: ***~ of a job*** Heiden-, Mordsarbeit *f*; ***who*** (***what, how***) ***the ~ ...*** wer (was, wie) zum Teufel ...; ***~ a one*** kein einziger; **7.** Handlanger *m*, Laufbursche *m*; → ***printer*** 1; **8.** ⚖ As'sessor m (*bei e-m* ***barrister***); **9.** scharf gewürztes Gericht; **10.** ⚙ Reißwolf *m*; **II** *v/t.* **11.** F schikanieren, piesacken; **12.** scharf gewürzt braten: ***devil(l)ed eggs*** gefüllte Eier; **13.** ⚙ zerfasern, wolfen; **III** *v/i.* **14.** als As'sessor (*bei e-m* ***barrister***) arbeiten; **'~‚dodg·er** *s.* F Prediger *m*; **'~-fish** *s.* Seeteufel *m*.

dev·il·ish ['devlɪʃ] **I** *adj.* □ **1.** teuflisch; **2.** F fürchterlich, höllisch, verteufelt; **II** *adv.* **3.** → 2.

‚dev·il-may-'care *adj.* **1.** leichtsinnig; **2.** verwegen.

dev·il·ment ['devlmənt] *s.* **1.** Unfug *m*; **2.** Schurkenstreich *m*; **dev·il·ry** ['devlrɪ] *s.* **1.** Teufe'lei *f*, Untat *f*; **2.** 'Übermut *m*; **3.** Teufelsbande *f*; **4.** Teufelskunst *f*.

dev·il's| ad·vo·cate ['devlz] *s. R.C.* Advo'catus *m* Di'aboli; **'~-bones** *s. pl.* Würfel(spiel *n*) *pl.*; **~ book** *s.* (des Teufels) ‚Gebetbuch' *n* (*Spielkarten*); **~ darn·ing-nee·dle** *s. zo.* Li'belle *f*; **~ food cake** *s. Am.* schwere Schoko'ladentorte.

de·vi·ous ['di:vjəs] *adj.* □ **1.** abwegig, irrig; **2.** gewunden (*a. fig.*): ***~ path*** Ab-, Umweg *m*; **3.** verschlagen, unredlich: ***by ~ means*** auf krummen Wegen, ‚hintenherum'; ***~ step*** Fehltritt *m*; **'de·vi·ous·ness** [-nɪs] *s.* **1.** Abwegigkeit *f*; **2.** Gewundenheit *f*; **3.** Unaufrichtigkeit *f*, Verschlagenheit *f*.

de·vis·a·ble [dɪ'vaɪzəbl] *adj.* **1.** erdenkbar, -lich; **2.** ⚖ vermachbar; **de·vise** [dɪ'vaɪz] **I** *v/t.* **1.** ausdenken, ersinnen, erfinden, konstruieren; **2.** ⚖ *Grundbesitz* vermachen, hinter'lassen (***to*** *dat.*); **II** *s.* **3.** ⚖ Vermächtnis *n*; **dev·i·see** [‚devɪ'zi:] *s.* ⚖ Vermächtnisnehmer (-in); **de·vis·er** [dɪ'vaɪzə] *s.* Erfinder (-in); Planer(in); **de·vi·sor** [‚devɪ'zɔ:] *s.* ⚖ Erb-lasser(in).

de·vi·tal·ize [‚di:'vaɪtəlaɪz] *v/t.* der Lebenskraft berauben, schwächen.

de·void [dɪ'vɔɪd] *adj.*: ***~ of*** ohne (*acc.*), leer an (*dat.*), frei von, bar (*gen.*), ...los: ***~ of feeling*** gefühllos.

de·voir [de'vwɑ:] (*Fr.*) *s. obs.* **1.** Pflicht *f*; **2.** *pl.* Höflichkeitsbezeigungen *pl.*, Artigkeiten *pl.*

dev·o·lu·tion [‚di:və'lu:ʃn] *s.* **1.** Ab-, Verlauf *m*; **2.** *bsd.* ⚖ 'Übergang *m*, Über'tragung *f*; Heimfall *m*; *parl.* Über'weisung *f*; **3.** *pol.* ‚Dezentralisati'on *f*, Regionalisierung *f*; **4.** *biol.* Entartung *f*.

de·volve [dɪ'vɒlv] **I** *v/t.* **1.** (***upon***) über'tragen (*dat.*), abwälzen (auf *acc.*); **II** *v/i.* **2.** (***on, upon***) 'übergehen (auf *acc.*), zufallen (*dat.*); sich vererben auf (*acc.*); **3.** *j-m* obliegen.

De·vo·ni·an [de'vəʊnjən] **I** *adj.* **1.** Devonshire betreffend; **2.** *geol.* de'vonisch; **II** *s.* **3.** Bewohner(in) von Devonshire; **4.** *geol.* De'von *n*.

de·vote [dɪ'vəʊt] *v/t.* (***to*** *dat.*) **1.** widmen, opfern, weihen, 'hingeben; **2.** ***~ o.s.*** sich widmen *od.* 'hingeben; sich verschreiben; **de'vot·ed** [-tɪd] *adj.* □ **1.** 'hingebungsvoll: a) aufopfernd, treu, b) anhänglich, liebevoll, zärtlich, c) eifrig, begeistert; **2.** todgeweiht; **dev·o·tee** [‚devəʊ'ti:] *s.* **1.** begeisterter Anhänger; **2.** Verehrer *m*; Verfechter *m*; **3.** Frömmler *m*; **4.** Fa'natiker *m*, Eiferer *m*; **de'vo·tion** [-əʊʃn] *s.* **1.** Widmung *f*; **2.** 'Hingabe *f*: a) Ergebenheit *f*, Treue *f*, b) (Auf)Opferung *f*, c) Eifer *m*, 'Hingebung *f*, d) Liebe *f*, Verehrung *f*, innige Zuneigung; **3.** *eccl.* a) Andacht *f*, Frömmigkeit *f*, b) *pl.* Gebet(e *pl.*) *n*; **de'vo·tion·al** [-əʊʃənl] *adj.* **1.** andächtig, fromm; **2.** Andachts..., Erbauungs...

de·vour [dɪ'vaʊə] *v/t.* **1.** verschlingen, fressen; **2.** wegraffen; verzehren, vernichten; **3.** *fig. Buch* verschlingen; *mit Blicken* verschlingen *od.* verzehren; **4.** j-n verzehren (*Leidenschaft*): ***be ~ed by*** sich verzehren vor (*Gram etc.*); **de'vour·ing** [-ərɪŋ] *adj.* □ **1.** gierig; **2.** *fig.* verzehrend.

de·vout [dɪ'vaʊt] *adj.* □ **1.** fromm; **2.** *a. fig.* andächtig; **3.** innig, herzlich; **4.** sehnlich, eifrig; **de'vout·ness** [-nɪs] *s.* **1.** Frömmigkeit *f*; **2.** Andacht *f*, 'Hingabe *f*; **3.** Eifer *m*, Inbrunst *f*.

dew [dju:] *s.* **1.** Tau *m*; **2.** *fig.* Tau *m*: a) Frische *f*, b) Feuchtigkeit *f*, Tränen *pl.*; **'~·ber·ry** *s.* ♀ *e-e* Brombeere; **'~-drop** *s.* Tautropfen *m*.

dew·i·ness ['dju:mɪs] *s.* Tauigkeit *f*, (Tau)Feuchtigkeit *f*.

'dew|·lap *s.* **1.** *zo.* Wamme *f*; **2.** F (*altersbedingte*) Halsfalte; **~ point** *s. phys.* Taupunkt *m*; **~ worm** *s. Angeln*: Tauwurm *m*.

dew·y ['dju:ɪ] *adj.* □ **1.** taufeucht; *a. fig.* taufrisch; **2.** feucht; *poet.* um'flort (*Augen*); **3.** frisch, erfrischend; **'~-eyed** *adj. iro.* na'iv, ‚blauäugig'.

dex·ter ['dekstə] *adj.* **1.** recht, rechts (-seitig); **2.** *her.* rechts (*vom Beschauer aus links*); **dex·ter·i·ty** [dek'sterətɪ] *s.* **1.** Geschicklichkeit *f*; Gewandtheit *f*; **2.** Rechtshändigkeit *f*; **'dex·ter·ous** [-tərəs] *adj.* □ **1.** gewandt, geschickt, be'hend, flink; **2.** rechtshändig; **'dex·tral** [-trəl] *adj.* □ **1.** rechtsseitig; **2.** rechtshändig.

dextro- [dekstrəʊ] *in Zssgn* (nach) rechts.

dex·trose ['dekstrəʊs] *s.* ⚗ Dex'trose *f*, Traubenzucker *m*.

dex·trous ['dekstrəs] → ***dexterous***.

dhoo·ti ['du:tɪ], **dho·ti** ['dəʊtɪ] *pl.* **-tis** [-tɪz] *s.* (*Indien*) Lendentuch *n*.

di·a·be·tes [‚daɪə'bi:ti:z] *s.* ⚕ Dia'betes *m*, Zuckerkrankheit *f*; **di·a·bet·ic** [‚daɪə'betɪk] **I** *adj.* dia'betisch, zuckerkrank; **II** *s.* Dia'betiker(in), Zuckerkranke(r *m*) *f*.

di·a·ble·rie [dɪ'ɑ:bləri:] *s.* Zaube'rei *f*, Hexe'rei *f*, Teufe'lei *f*.

di·a·bol·ic, di·a·bol·i·cal [‚daɪə'bɒlɪk(l)] *adj.* □ dia'bolisch, teuflisch; **di·ab·o·lism** [daɪ'æbəlɪzəm] *s.* **1.** Teufe'lei *f*; **2.** Teufelskult *m*.

di·ac·id [daɪ'æsɪd] *adj.* zweisäurig.

di·ac·o·nate [daɪ'ækənɪt] *s. eccl.* Diako'nat *n*.

di·a·crit·ic [‚daɪə'krɪtɪk] **I** *adj.* dia'kritisch, unter'scheidend; **II** *s. ling.* dia'kritisches Zeichen.

di·ac·tin·ic [‚daɪæk'tɪnɪk] *adj. phys.* die ak'tinischen Strahlen 'durchlassend.

di·a·dem ['daɪədem] *s.* **1.** Dia'dem *n*, Stirnband *n*; **2.** Hoheit *f*, Herrscherwürde *f*, -gewalt *f*.

di·aer·e·sis [daɪ'ɪərɪsɪs] *s. ling.* a) Diä'rese *f*, b) Trema *n*.

di·ag·nose ['daɪəgnəʊz] *v/t.* ⚕ diagnostizieren, *fig. a.* bestimmen, feststellen; **di·ag·no·sis** [‚daɪəg'nəʊsɪs] *pl.* **-ses** [-si:z] *s.* ⚕ Dia'gnose *f*, Befund *m*, *fig. a.* Beurteilung *f*, Bestimmung *f*; **di·ag·nos·tic** [‚daɪəg'nɒstɪk] ⚕ **I** *adj.* (□ ***~ally***) dia'gnostisch: ***~ of*** *fig.* sympto'matisch für; **II** *s.* a) Sym'ptom *n*, b) *pl. sg. konstr.* Dia'gnostik *f*; **di·ag·nos·ti·cian** [‚daɪəgnɒs'tɪʃn] *s.* ⚕ Dia'gnostiker(in).

di·ag·o·nal [daɪ'ægənl] **I** *adj.* □ **1.** diago'nal; schräg(laufend), über Kreuz; **II** *s.* **2.** *a.* ***~ line*** ⩓ Diago'nale *f*; **3.** *a.* ***~ cloth*** Diago'nal *m*, schräggeripptes Gewebe.

di·a·gram ['daɪəgræm] *s.* Dia'gramm *n*, graphische Darstellung, Schaubild *n*, Plan *m*, Schema *n*: ***wiring ~*** ⚡ Schaltbild *n*, -plan *m*: ***you need a ~?*** *iro.* brauchst du e-e Zeichnung (dazu)?; **di·a·gram·mat·ic** [‚daɪəgrə'mætɪk] *adj.* (□ ***~ally***) diagram'matisch, graphisch, sche'matisch.

di·al ['daɪəl] **I** *s.* **1.** *a.* ***~ plate*** Zifferblatt *n* (*Uhr*); **2.** *a.* ***~ plate*** ⚙ Skala *f*, Skalen-, Ziffernscheibe *f*; **3.** *teleph.* Wähl-, Nummernscheibe *f*; **4.** *Radio*: Skalenscheibe *f*, Skala *f*: ***~ light*** Skalenbeleuchtung *f*; **5.** → ***sundial***; **6.** *sl.* Vi'sage *f* (*Gesicht*); **II** *v/t.* **7.** *teleph.* wählen: ***~ling code*** *Brit.* Vorwahl(nummer) *f*; ***~ tone*** *Am.*, ***~ling tone*** *Brit.* Amtszeichen *n*.

di·a·lect ['daɪəlekt] *s.* Dia'lekt *m*, Mundart *f*; **di·a·lec·tal** [‚daɪə'lektl] *adj.* □ dia'lektisch, mundartlich; **di·a·lec·tic** [‚daɪə'lektɪk] **I** *adj.* **1.** *phls.* dia'lektisch; **2.** spitzfindig; **3.** *ling.* → ***dialectal***; **II** *s.* **4.** *oft pl. phls.* Dia'lektik *f*; **5.** Spitzfindigkeit *f*; **di·a·lec·ti·cal** [‚daɪə'lektɪkl] *adj.* □ **1.** → ***dialectal***; **2.** → ***dialectic*** 1, 2; **di·a·lec·ti·cian** [‚daɪəlek'tɪʃn] *s. phls.* Dia'lektiker *m*.

di·a·logue, *Am. a.* **di·a·log** ['daɪəlɒg] *s.* Dia'log *m*, (Zwie)Gespräch *n*; **~ track** *s. Film*: Sprechband *n*.

di·al·y·sis [daɪ'ælɪsɪs] *s.* **1.** ⚗ Dia'lyse *f*; **2.** ⚕ Dia'lyse *f*, Blutwäsche *f*.

di·am·e·ter [daɪ'æmɪtə] *s.* **1.** ⩓ Dia'meter *m*, 'Durchmesser *m*; **2.** 'Durchmesser *m*, Dicke *f*, Stärke *f*: ***inner ~*** lichte Weite; **di·a·met·ri·cal** [‚daɪə'metrɪkl] *adj.* □ **1.** dia'metrisch; **2.** *fig.* diame'tral, genau entgegengesetzt.

di·a·mond ['daɪəmənd] **I** *s.* **1.** *min.* Dia'mant *m*: ***black ~*** a) schwarzer Diamant, b) *fig.* (Stein)Kohle *f*; ***rough ~*** a) ungeschliffener Diamant, b) *fig.* Mensch *m* mit gutem Kern u. rauher Schale; ***it was ~ cut ~*** es war Wurst wider Wurst, die beiden standen sich in nichts nach; **2.** ⚙ ('Glaser)Dia‚mant *m*; **3.** ⩓ a) Raute *f*, 'Rhombus *m*, b) spitzgestelltes Viereck; **4.** *Kartenspiel*: Karo *n*; **5.** *Baseball*: a) Spielfeld *n*, b) Innenfeld *n*; **6.** *typ.* Dia'mant *f* (*Schriftgrad*); **II** *adj.* **7.** dia'manten, Diamant...; **8.** rhombisch, rautenförmig; **~ cut·ter** *s.* Dia'mantschleifer *m*; **~ drill** *s.* ⚙ Dia'mantbohrer *m*; **~ field** *s.* Dia'mantenfeld *n*; **~ ju·bi·lee** *s.* dia'mantenes Jubi'läum; **~ mine** *s.* Dia'mantenmine *f*; **~ pane** *s.* rautenförmige Fensterscheibe; **'~-shaped** *adj.* rautenförmig; **~ wed·ding** *s.* dia'mantene Hochzeit.

di·an·thus [daɪ'ænθəs] *s.* ⚘ Nelke *f*.

di·a·per ['daɪəpə] **I** *s.* **1.** Di'aper *m*, Gänseaugenstoff *m*; **2.** *a.* **~ *pattern*** Rauten-, Karomuster *n*; **3.** *Am.* (Baby-) Windel *f*; **4.** Monatsbinde *f*; **II** *v/t.* **5.** mit Rautenmuster verzieren; **~ rash** *s.* ⚕ Wundsein *n beim Säugling*.

di·aph·a·nous [daɪ'æfənəs] *adj.* 'durchsichtig, -scheinend.

di·a·pho·ret·ic [ˌdaɪəfə'retɪk] *adj. u. s.* ⚕ schweißtreibend(es Mittel).

di·a·phragm ['daɪəfræm] *s.* **1.** *anat.* Scheidewand *f*, *bsd.* Zwerchfell *n*; **2.** ⚕ Dia'phragma *n* (*Verhütungsmittel*); **3.** *teleph. etc.* Mem'bran(e) *f*; **4.** *opt.*, *phot.* Blende *f*; **~ shut·ter** *s. phot.* Blendenverschluß *m*; **~ valve** *s.* Mem'branventil *n*.

di·a·rist ['daɪərɪst] *s.* Tagebuchschreiber(in); **'di·a·rize** [-raɪz] **I** *v/i.* Tagebuch führen; **II** *v/t.* ins Tagebuch eintragen.

di·ar·rh(o)e·a [ˌdaɪə'rɪə] *s.* ⚕ Diar'rhöe *f*, 'Durchfall *m*.

di·a·ry ['daɪərɪ] *s.* **1.** Tagebuch *n*: ***keep a ~*** ein Tagebuch führen; **2.** 'Taschenkaˌlender *m*, (Vor)Merkbuch *n*, Ter'min-, No'tizbuch *n*.

Di·as·po·ra [daɪ'æspərə] *s. allg.* Di'aspora *f*.

di·as·to·le [daɪ'æstəlɪ] *s.* ⚕ *u. Metrik*: Dia'stole *f*.

di·a·ther·my ['daɪəθɜːmɪ] *s.* ⚕ Diather'mie *f*.

di·ath·e·sis [daɪ'æθɪsɪs] *pl.* **-ses** [-siːz] *s.* ⚕ *u. fig.* Neigung *f*, Anlage *f*.

di·a·to·ma·ceous earth [ˌdaɪətə'meɪʃəs] *s. geol.* Kieselgur *f*.

di·a·ton·ic [ˌdaɪə'tɒnɪk] *adj.* ♪ dia'tonisch.

di·a·tribe ['daɪətraɪb] *s.* gehässiger Angriff, Hetze *f*, Hetzrede *f od.* -schrift *f*.

di·bas·ic [daɪ'beɪsɪk] *adj.* ⚗ zweibasisch.

dib·ber ['dɪbə] → ***dibble*** I.

dib·ble ['dɪbl] **I** *s.* Dibbelstock *m*, Pflanz-, Setzholz *n*; **II** *v/t. a.* **~ *in*** mit e-m Setzholz pflanzen; **III** *v/i.* mit e-m Setzholz Löcher machen, dibbeln.

dibs [dɪbz] *s.* **1.** *pl. sg. konstr. Brit. Kinderspiel mit Steinchen etc.*; **2.** F Recht *n* (***on*** auf *acc.*); **3.** *Am. sl.* (ein paar) ‚Kröten' *pl.* (*Geld*).

dice [daɪs] **I** *s. pl. von* ***die***² 1 Würfel *pl.*, Würfelspiel *n*: ***play*** (***at***) **~** → II; ***no ~!*** *Am. sl.* ‚da läuft nichts'!; → ***load*** 10; **II** *v/i.* würfeln, knobeln; **III** *v/t. Küche*: in Würfel schneiden.

dic·ey ['daɪsɪ] *adj.* F pre'kär, heikel.

di·chot·o·my [daɪ'kɒtəmɪ] *s.* Dichoto'mie *f*: a) *bsd. Logik*: Zweiteilung *f e-s Begriffs*, b) ⚘, *zo.* wieder'holte Gabelung.

di·chro·mat·ic [ˌdaɪkrəʊ'mætɪk] *adj.* **1.** dichro'matisch, zweifarbig; **2.** ⚕ dichro'mat.

dick [dɪk] *s.* **1.** *Brit. sl.* Kerl *m*; **2.** *Am. sl.* ‚Schnüffler' *m*: ***private ~*** Privatdetektiv *m*; **3.** V ‚Schwanz' *m*.

dick·ens ['dɪkɪnz] *s. sl.* Teufel *m*: ***what the ~!*** was zum Teufel!; ***a ~ of a mess*** ein böser Schlamassel.

dick·er¹ ['dɪkə] *v/i.* feilschen, schachern (***for*** um).

dick·er² ['dɪkə] *s.* ✝ zehn Stück.

dick·(e)y¹ ['dɪkɪ] *s.* F **1.** Hemdbrust *f*; **2.** Bluseneinsatz *m*; **3.** *a.* **~ *bow*** ‚Fliege' *f*, Schleife *f*; **4.** *a.* ***~-bird*** Vögelchen *n*, Piepmatz *m*; **5.** Rück-, Not-, Klappsitz *m*; **6.** *Brit.* F Esel *m*.

dick·(e)y² ['dɪkɪ] *adj.* F wack(e)lig, ‚mies': **~ *heart*** schwaches Herz.

di·cot·y·le·don [ˌdaɪkɒtɪ'liːdən] *s.* ⚘ Diko'tyle *f*, zweikeimblättrige Pflanze.

dic·ta ['dɪktə] *pl. von* ***dictum***.

dic·tate [dɪk'teɪt] **I** *v/t.* (***to*** *dat.*) **1.** *Brief etc.* diktieren; **2.** diktieren, vorschreiben, gebieten (*a. fig.*); **3.** auferlegen; **4.** eingeben; **II** *v/i.* **5.** diktieren, ein Dik'tat geben; **6.** diktieren, befehlen: ***he will not be ~d to*** er läßt sich keine Vorschriften machen; **III** *s.* ['dɪkteɪt] **7.** Gebot *n*, Befehl *m*, Dik'tat *n*: ***the ~s of reason*** das Gebot der Vernunft; **dic'ta·tion** [-eɪʃn] *s.* **1.** Dik'tat *n*: a) Diktieren *n*, b) Dik'tatschreiben *n*, c) diktierter Text; **2.** Befehl(e *pl.*) *m*, Geheiß *n*; **dic'ta·tor** [-tə] *s.* Dik'tator *m*, Gewalthaber *m*; **dic·ta·to·ri·al** [ˌdɪktə'tɔːrɪəl] *adj.* □ dikta'torisch; **dic'ta·tor·ship** [-təʃɪp] *s.* Dikta'tur *f*; **dic'ta·tress** [-trɪs] *s.* Dikta'torin *f*.

dic·tion ['dɪkʃn] *s.* **1.** Dikti'on *f*, Ausdrucksweise *f*, Stil *m*, Sprache *f*; **2.** (deutliche) Aussprache.

dic·tion·ar·y ['dɪkʃənrɪ] *s.* **1.** Wörterbuch *n*; **2.** (*bsd.* einsprachiges) enzyklo'pädisches Wörterbuch; **3.** Lexikon *n*, Enzyklopä'die *f*: ***a walking*** (*od.* ***living***) **~** *fig.* ein wandelndes Lexikon.

dic·to·graph ['dɪktəgrɑːf] *s.* Abhörgerät *n* (*beim Telefon*).

dic·tum ['dɪktəm] *pl.* **-ta** [-tə], **-tums** *s.* **1.** Machtspruch *m*; **2.** ⚖ richterliches Diktum, (Aus)Spruch *m*; **3.** Spruch *m*, geflügeltes Wort.

did [dɪd] *pret. von* ***do***¹.

di·dac·tic [dɪ'dæktɪk] *adj.* (□ ***~ally***) **1.** di'daktisch, lehrhaft, belehrend: **~ *play*** *thea.* Lehrstück *n*; **~ *poem*** Lehrgedicht *n*; **2.** schulmeisterlich.

did·dle¹ ['dɪdl] *v/t. sl.* beschwindeln, betrügen, übers Ohr hauen.

did·dle² ['dɪdl] *v/i.* F zappeln.

did·n't ['dɪdnt] F *für* ***did not***.

didst [dɪdst] *obs. 2. sg. pret. von* ***do***¹.

die¹ [daɪ] **I** *v/i. p.pr.* **dy·ing** ['daɪɪŋ] **1.** sterben (***of*** an): **~ *of hunger*** Hungers sterben, verhungern; **~ *from a wound*** an e-r Verwundung sterben; **~ *a violent death*** e-s gewaltsamen Todes sterben; **~ *of*** (*od.* ***with***) ***laughter*** *fig.* sich totlachen; **~ *of boredom*** vor Lange(r)weile fast umkommen; **~ *a beggar*** als Bettler sterben; **~ *hard*** a) zählebig sein (*a. Sache*), ‚nicht totzukriegen sein', b) nicht nachgeben (wollen); ***never say ~!*** nur nicht aufgeben!; → ***bed*** 1; ***boot***¹ 1; ***ditch*** 1; ***harness*** 1; **2.** eingehen (*Pflanze, Tier*), verenden (*Tier*); **3.** *fig.* ver-, 'untergehen, schwinden, aufhören, sich verlieren, verhallen, erlöschen, vergessen werden; **4.** *mst* ***be dying*** (***for***, ***to*** *inf.*) sich sehnen (nach; danach, zu *inf.*), brennen (auf *acc.*; darauf, zu *inf.*): ***I am dying to ...*** ich würde schrecklich gern; **II** *v/t.* **5.** e-s *natürlichen etc.* Todes sterben;

Zssgn mit adv.:

die| a·way *v/i.* **1.** schwächer werden, nachlassen, sich verlieren, schwinden; **2.** ohnmächtig werden; **~ down** *v/i.* **1.** → ***die away*** 1; **2.** ⚘ (von oben) absterben; **~ off** *v/i.* 'hin-, wegsterben; **~ out** *v/i.* aussterben (*a. fig.*).

die² [daɪ] *s.* **1.** *pl.* ***dice*** Würfel *m*: ***the ~ is cast*** die Würfel sind gefallen; ***straight as a ~*** a) pfeilgerade, b) *fig.* grundehrlich; → ***dice***; ***straight*** 4; **2.** Würfelspiel *n*; **3.** *bsd. Küche*: Würfel *m*; **4.** *pl.* ***dies*** ⚠ Würfel *m e-s Sockels*; **5.** *pl.* ***dies*** ⚙ a) (Preß-, Spritz)Form *f*, Gesenk *n*: ***lower ~*** Matrize *f*; ***upper ~*** Patrize *f*, b) (Münz)Prägestempel *m*, c) Schneideisen *n*, Stanze *f*, d) Gußform *f*.

'die|-a·way *adj.* schmachtend; **'~-cast** *v/t.* ⚙ spritzgießen, spritzen; **~ cast·ing** *s.* ⚙ Spritzguß *m*; **'~-hard I** *s.* **1.** unnachgiebiger Mensch, Dickschädel *m*; **2.** *pol.* hartnäckiger Reaktio'när; **3.** zählebige Sache; **II** *adj.* **4.** hartnäckig, zäh u. unnachgiebig; **5.** zählebig; **~ head** *s.* ⚙ Schneidkopf *m*.

di·e·lec·tric [ˌdaɪɪ'lektrɪk] ⚡ **I** *s.* Di'elektrikum *n*; **II** *adj.* (□ ***~ally***) die'lektrisch: **~ *strength*** Spannungs-, Durchschlagfestigkeit *f*.

die·en·ceph·a·lon [ˌdaɪɪn'sefələn] *s. anat.* Zwischenhirn *n*.

di·er·e·sis → ***diaeresis***.

Die·sel ['diːzl] **I** Diesel *m* (*Motor, Fahrzeug od. Kraftstoff*); **II** *adj.* Diesel...; **die·sel·ize** ['diːzəlaɪz] *v/t.* ⚙ auf Dieselbetrieb 'umstellen.

'dieˌsink·er *s.* ⚙ Werkzeugmacher *m*.

di·e·sis ['daɪɪsɪs] *pl.* **-ses** [-siːz] *s.* **1.** *typ.* Doppelkreuz *n*; **2.** ♪ Kreuz *n*.

di·es non [ˌdaɪiːz'nɒn] *s.* ⚖ gerichtsfreier Tag.

die stock *s.* ⚙ Schneidkluppe *f*.

di·et¹ ['daɪət] *s.* **1.** *parl.* a) 'Unterhaus *n* (*in Japan etc.*), b) *hist.* Reichstag *m*; **2.** ⚖ *Scot.* Ge'richtsterˌmin *m*.

di·et² ['daɪət] **I** *s.* **1.** Nahrung *f*, Ernährung *f*, (*a. fig. geistige*) Kost: ***vegetable ~*** vegetarische Kost; ***full*** (***low***) **~** reichliche (magere) Kost; **2.** ⚕ Di'ät *f*, Schon-, Krankenkost *f*: ***be*** (***put***) ***on a ~*** auf Diät gesetzt sein, diät leben (müssen); **II** *v/t.* **3.** *j-n* auf Di'ät setzen: **~ *o.s.*** → 4; **III** *v/i.* **4.** Di'ät halten; **'di·e·tar·y** [-tərɪ] ⚕ **I** *adj.* **1.** diä'tetisch, Diät...; **II** *s.* **2.** Di'ätvorschrift *f*; **3.** 'Speise(ratiˌon) *f*.

di·e·tet·ic [ˌdaɪə'tetɪk] *adj.* (□ ***~ally***) → ***dietary*** 1; **ˌdi·e'tet·ics** [-ks] *s. pl. sg. od. pl. konstr.* ⚕ Diä'tetik *f*, Di'ätkunde *f*; **ˌdi·e'ti·tian**, **ˌdi·e'ti·cian** [-'tɪʃn] *s.* Diä'tetiker(in).

dif·fer ['dɪfə] *v/i.* **1.** sich unter'scheiden, verschieden sein, abweichen (***from*** von); **2.** (*mst* ***with***, *a.* ***from***) nicht über'einstimmen (mit), anderer Meinung sein (als): ***I beg to ~*** ich bin (leider) anderer Meinung; **3.** uneinig sein (***on*** über *acc.*); → ***agree*** 2; **dif·fer·ence** ['dɪfrəns] *s.* **1.** 'Unterschied *m*, Verschiedenheit *f*: **~ *in price*** Preisunterschied; **~ *of opinion*** Meinungsverschiedenheit; ***that makes a (great) ~*** a) das macht et. (*od.* viel) aus, b) das ändert die Sache; ***it made all the ~*** das änderte die Sache vollkommen; ***it makes no ~ (to me)*** es ist (mir) gleich(gültig); ***what's the ~?*** was macht es schon aus?; **2.** 'Unterschied *m*, unter'scheidendes Merkmal: ***the ~ between him and his brother***; **3.** 'Unterschied *m* (*in Menge*), Diffe'renz *f* (*a.* †, A): ***split the ~*** a) sich in die Differenz teilen, b) e-n Kompromiß schließen; **4.** Besonderheit *f*: ***a film with a ~*** ein Film (von) ganz besonderer Art *od.* ‚mit Pfiff'; ***holidays with a ~*** Ferien ‚mal anders'; **5.** Meinungsverschiedenheit *f*, Diffe'renz *f*; **dif·fer·ent** ['dɪfrənt] *adj.* □ **1.** (***from***, *a.* ***to***) verschieden (von), abweichend (von); anders (*pred.* als), ander (*attr.* als): ***in two ~ countries*** in zwei verschiedenen Ländern; ***that's a ~ matter*** das ist etwas anderes; ***at ~ times*** verschiedentlich, mehrmals; **2.** außergewöhnlich, besonder.

dif·fer·en·tial [ˌdɪfə'renʃl] **I** *adj.* □ **1.** 'unterschiedlich, charakte'ristisch, Unterscheidungs...; **2.** ⚙, ⚡, A, *phys.* Differential...; **3.** † gestaffelt, Differential..., Staffel...: ***~ tariff***; **II** *s.* **4.** ⚙, *mot.* Differenti'al-, Ausgleichsgetriebe *n*; **5.** A Differenti'al *n*; **6.** ('Preis-, 'Lohn- *etc.*)Gefälle *n*, (-)Diffeˌrenz *f*; **~ cal·cu·lus** *s.* A Differenti'alrechnung *f*; **~ du·ty** *s.* † Differenti'alzoll *m*; **~ gear** *s.* ⚙ Differenti'al-, Ausgleichsgetriebe *n*; **~ rate** *s.* † 'Ausnahmetaˌrif *m*.

dif·fer·en·ti·ate [ˌdɪfə'renʃɪeɪt] **I** *v/t.* **1.** einen 'Unterschied machen zwischen (*dat.*), unter'scheiden; **2.** vonein'ander abgrenzen; unter'scheiden, trennen (***from*** von): ***be ~d*** → 4; **II** *v/i.* **3.** e-n 'Unterschied machen, unter'scheiden, differenzieren (***between*** zwischen *dat.*); **4.** sich unter'scheiden *od.* entfernen; sich verschieden entwickeln; **dif·fer·en·ti·a·tion** [ˌdɪfərenʃɪ'eɪʃn] *s.* Differenzierung *f*: a) Unter'scheidung *f*, b) (Auf)Teilung *f*, c) Spezialisierung *f*, d) A Ableitung *f*.

dif·fi·cult ['dɪfɪkəlt] *adj.* **1.** schwierig, schwer; **2.** beschwerlich, mühsam; **3.** schwierig, schwer zu behandeln(d); **'dif·fi·cul·ty** [-tɪ] *s.* **1.** Schwierigkeit *f*: a) Mühe *f*: ***with ~*** schwer, mühsam; ***have (od. find) ~ in doing s.th.*** et. schwierig (zu tun) finden, b) schwierige Sache, c) Hindernis *n*, 'Widerstand *m*: ***make difficulties*** Schwierigkeiten bereiten; **2.** *oft pl.* (*a.* Geld)Schwierigkeiten *pl.*, (-)Verlegenheit *f*.

dif·fi·dence ['dɪfɪdəns] *s.* Schüchternheit *f*, mangelndes Selbstvertrauen; **'dif·fi·dent** [-nt] *adj.* □ schüchtern, ohne Selbstvertrauen, scheu: ***be ~ about doing*** sich scheuen zu tun, *et.* nur zaghaft *od.* zögernd tun.

dif·fract [dɪ'frækt] *v/t. phys.* beugen; **dif'frac·tion** [-kʃn] *s. phys.* Beugung *f*, Diffrakti'on *f*.

dif·fuse [dɪ'fju:z] **I** *v/t.* **1.** ausgießen, -schütten; **2.** *bsd. fig.* verbreiten; **3.** ⚗, *phys., opt.* diffundieren: a) zerstreuen, b) vermischen, c) durch'dringen; **II** *v/i.* **4.** sich verbreiten; **5.** ⚗, *phys.* diffundieren: a) sich zerstreuen, b) sich vermischen, c) eindringen; **III** *adj.* [dɪ'fju:s] □ **6.** dif'fus: a) weitschweifig, langatmig, b) unklar (*Gedanken etc.*), c) ⚗, *phys.* zerstreut: ***~ light*** diffuses Licht; **7.** *fig.* verbreitet; **dif·fus·i·bil·i·ty** [dɪˌfju:zə'bɪlətɪ] *s. phys.* Diffusi'onsvermögen *n*; **dif'fus·i·ble** [-zəbl] *adj. phys.* diffusi'onsfähig; **dif·fu·sion** [dɪ'fju:ʒn] *s.* **1.** Ausgießen *n*; **2.** *fig.* Verbreitung *f*; **3.** Weitschweifigkeit *f*; **4.** ⚗, *phys., a. sociol.* Diffusi'on *f*; **dif·fu·sive** [dɪ'fju:sɪv] *adj.* □ **1.** *bsd. fig.* sich verbreitend; **2.** *fig.* weitschweifig; **3.** ⚗, *phys.* Diffusions...; **dif·fu·sive·ness** [dɪ'fju:sɪvnɪs] *s.* **1.** *phys.* Diffusi'onsfähigkeit *f*; **2.** *fig.* Weitschweifigkeit *f*.

dig [dɪg] **I** *s.* **1.** Grabung *f*; **2.** F (archäo'logische) Ausgrabung(sstätte); **3.** F Puff *m*, Stoß *m*: ***~ in the ribs*** Rippenstoß; **4.** F *fig.* (Seiten)Hieb *m* (***at*** auf *j-n*); **5.** *Am.* F ‚Büffler' *m*; **6.** *pl. Brit.* F ‚Bude' *f*, (*bsd. Studenten*)Zimmer *n*; **II** *v/t.* [*irr.*] **7.** *Loch etc.* graben; *Boden* 'umgraben; *Bodenfrüchte* ausgraben; **8.** *fig.* ‚ausgraben', ans Tageslicht bringen, her'ausfinden; **9.** F *j-m* e-n Stoß geben: ***~ spurs into a horse*** e-m Pferd die Sporen geben; **10.** F a) ‚kapieren', b) ‚stehen auf', ein ‚Fan' sein von, c) sich ansehen *od.* anhören; **III** *v/i.* [*irr.*] **11.** graben (***for*** nach); **12.** *fig.* a) forschen (***for*** nach), b) sich gründlich beschäftigen (***into*** mit); **13. ~ into** F a) ‚reinhauen' in *e-n Kuchen etc.*, b) sich einarbeiten in (*acc.*); **14.** *Am. sl.* ‚büffeln', ‚ochsen';

Zssgn mit adv.:

dig in I *v/t.* **1.** eingraben (*a. fig.*); **2.** ***dig o.s. in*** sich eingraben, *fig. a.* sich verschanzen; **II** *v/i.* **3.** ⚔ sich eingraben, sich verschanzen; **~ out** *v/t.* **1.** ausgraben; **2.** → ***dig*** 8; **~ up** *v/t.* **1.** 'um-, ausgraben; **2.** → ***dig*** 8.

di·gest [dɪ'dʒest] **I** *v/t.* **1.** *Speisen* verdauen; **2.** *fig.* verdauen: a) (innerlich) verarbeiten, über'denken, in sich aufnehmen, b) ertragen, verwinden; **3.** ordnen, einteilen; **4.** ⚗ digerieren, ausziehen, auflösen; **II** *v/i.* **5.** sich verdauen lassen: ***~ well*** leicht verdaulich sein; **6.** ⚗ sich auflösen; **III** *s.* ['daɪdʒest] **7.** (***of***) a) Auslese *f* (*a. Zeitschrift*), Auswahl *f* (aus), b) Abriß *m* (*gen.*), 'Überblick *m* (über *acc.*); **8.** ⚖ systematisierte Sammlung von Gerichtsentscheidungen; **di'gest·i·ble** [-təbl] *adj.* □ verdaulich, bekömmlich; **di'ges·tion** [-tʃən] *s.* **1.** Verdauung *f*: ***easy of ~*** leichtverdaulich; **2.** *fig.* (innerliche) Verarbeitung; **di'ges·tive** [-tɪv] **I** *adj.* □ **1.** verdauungsfördernd; **2.** bekömmlich; **3.** Verdauungs... (*-apparat, -trakt etc.*); **II** *s.* **4.** verdauungsförderndes Mittel.

dig·ger ['dɪgə] *s.* **1.** Gräber(in); **2.** → ***gold digger***; **3.** 'Grabgerät *n*, -maˌschine *f*; **4.** Erdarbeiter *m*; **5.** *a.* ***~ wasp*** Grabwespe *f*; **6.** *sl.* Au'stralier *m od.* Neu'seeländer *m*; **'dig·gings** [-gɪŋz] *s. pl.* **1.** *sg. od. pl. konstr.* Goldbergwerk *n*; **2.** Aushub *m* (*Erde*); **3.** → ***dig*** 6.

dig·it ['dɪdʒɪt] *s.* **1.** *anat., zo.* Finger *m od.* Zehe *f*; **2.** Fingerbreite *f* (*Maß*); **3.** *ast.* astro'nomischer Zoll ($^1/_{12}$ *des Sonnen- od. Monddurchmessers*); **4.** A a) eine der Ziffern von 0 bis 9, Einer *m*, b) Stelle *f*: ***three-~ number*** dreistellige Zahl; **'dig·it·al** [-tl] **I** *adj.* **1.** Finger...; **2.** Digital...: ***~ clock***; ***~ computer*** Digitalrechner *m*; **II** *s.* **3.** ♪ Taste *f*; **dig·i·tal·is** [ˌdɪdʒɪ'teɪlɪs] *s.* **1.** ⚘ Fingerhut *m*; **2.** ⚕ Digi'talis *n*; **'dig·i·tate, 'dig·i·tat·ed** [-teɪt(ɪd)] *adj.* **1.** ⚘ gefingert, handförmig; **2.** *zo.* gefingert.

dig·ni·fied ['dɪgnɪfaɪd] *adj.* würdevoll, würdig; **dig·ni·fy** ['dɪgnɪfaɪ] *v/t.* **1.** ehren, auszeichnen; Würde verleihen (*dat.*); **2.** zieren, schmücken; **3.** hochtrabend benennen.

dig·ni·tar·y ['dɪgnɪtərɪ] *s.* **1.** Würdenträger *m*; **2.** *eccl.* Prä'lat *m*; **dig·ni·ty** ['dɪgnɪtɪ] *s.* **1.** Würde *f*, würdevolles Auftreten; **2.** Würde *f*, (hoher) Rang, *a.* Ansehen *n*: ***beneath my ~*** unter m-r Würde; ***stand on one's ~*** sich nichts vergeben wollen; **3.** *fig.* Größe *f*: ***~ of soul*** Seelengröße, -adel *m*.

di·graph ['daɪgrɑ:f] *s. ling.* Di'graph *m* (*Verbindung von zwei Buchstaben zu einem Laut*).

di·gress [daɪ'gres] *v/i.* abschweifen; **di'gres·sion** [-eʃn] *s.* Abschweifung *f*; **di'gres·sive** [-sɪv] *adj.* □ **1.** abschweifend; **2.** abwegig.

digs [dɪgz] → ***dig*** 6.

di·he·dral [daɪ'hi:drəl] **I** *adj.* **1.** di'edrisch, zweiflächig: ***~ angle*** A Flächenwinkel *m*; **2.** ✈ V-förmig; **II** *s.* **3.** A Di'eder *m*, Zweiflächner *m*; **4.** ✈ V-Form *f*, V-Stellung *f*.

dike[1] [daɪk] **I** *s.* **1.** Deich *m*, Damm *m*; **2.** Erdwall *m*, erhöhter Fahrdamm; **3.** *a. fig.* Schutzwall *m*, *fig.* Bollwerk *n*; **4.** a) Graben *m*, b) Wasserlauf *m*; **5.** *a.* ***~ rock*** *geol.* Gangstock *m*; **II** *v/t.* **6.** eindämmen, -deichen.

dike[2] [daɪk] *v/t. a.* ***~ out*** *od.* ***up*** *Am.* F aufputzen.

dike[3] [daɪk] *s. sl.* ‚Lesbe' *f*.

dik·tat [dɪk'tɑ:t] *s.* (*Ger.*) *pol.* Dik'tat *n*.

di·lap·i·date [dɪ'læpɪdeɪt] **I** *v/t.* **1.** *Haus etc.* verfallen lassen; **2.** vergeuden; **II** *v/i.* **3.** verfallen, baufällig werden; **di'lap·i·dat·ed** [-tɪd] *adj.* **1.** verfallen, baufällig; **2.** klapp(e)rig (*Auto etc.*); **di·lap·i·da·tion** [dɪˌlæpɪ'deɪʃn] *s.* **1.** Verfall *m*, Baufälligkeit *f*; **2.** *geol.* Verwitterung *f*; **3.** *pl. Brit.* notwendige Repara'turen (*zu Lasten des Mieters*).

di·lat·a·bil·i·ty [daɪˌleɪtə'bɪlətɪ] *s. phys.* Dehnbarkeit *f*, (Aus)Dehnungsvermögen *n*; **di·lat·a·ble** [daɪ'leɪtəbl] *adj. phys.* (aus)dehnbar.

dil·a·ta·tion [ˌdaɪleɪ'teɪʃn] *s.* **1.** *phys.* Ausdehnung *f*; **2.** ⚕ Erweiterung *f*.

di·late [daɪ'leɪt] **I** *v/t.* **1.** (aus)dehnen, (aus)weiten, erweitern: ***with ~d eyes*** mit aufgerissenen Augen; **II** *v/i.* **2.** sich (aus)dehnen *od.* (aus)weiten *od.* erweitern; **3.** *fig.* sich (ausführlich) verbreiten *od.* auslassen (***[up]on*** über *acc.*); **di'la·tion** [-eɪʃn] → ***dilatation***; **di'la·tor** [-tə] *s.* Di'lator *m*: a) *anat.* Dehnmuskel *m*, b) ⚕ Dehnsonde *f*.

dil·a·to·ri·ness ['dɪlətərɪnɪs] *s.* Saumseligkeit *f*, Verschleppung *f*; **dil·a·to·ry** ['dɪlətərɪ] *adj.* □ **1.** aufschiebend (*a.* ⚖), verzögernd, 'hinhaltend, Verzögerungs..., Verschleppungs..., Hinhalte...: ***~ tactics***; **2.** langsam, saumselig.

dil·do ['dɪldəʊ] *s.* Godemi'ché *m* (*künstlicher Penis*).

di·lem·ma [dɪ'lemə] *s.* Di'lemma *n*, Zwangslage *f*, Klemme *f*: ***on the horns***

of a ~ in e-r Zwickmühle.
dil·et·tan·te [ˌdɪlɪˈtæntɪ] **I** *pl.* **-ti** [-tiː], **-tes** [-tɪz] *s.* **1.** Diletˈtant(in): a) Nichtfachmann *m*, Amaˈteur(in), b) *contp.* Stümper(in); **2.** Kunstliebhaber(in); **II** *adj.* **3.** → ˌ**dil·etˈtant·ish** [-tɪʃ] *adj.* □ diletˈtantisch; ˌ**dil·etˈtant·ism** [-tɪzəm] *s.* Dilettanˈtismus *m.*
dil·i·gence¹ [ˈdɪlɪʒɑ̃ːns] (*Fr.*) *s. hist.* Postkutsche *f.*
dil·i·gence² [ˈdɪlɪdʒəns] *s.* Fleiß *m*, Eifer *m*; *a.* ⚖ Sorgfalt *f*; ˈ**dil·i·gent** [-nt] *adj.* □ **1.** fleißig, emsig; **2.** sorgfältig, gewissenhaft.
dill [dɪl] *s.* ⚘ Dill *m*, Gurkenkraut *n.*
dil·ly-dal·ly [ˈdɪlɪdælɪ] *v/i.* F **1.** die Zeit vertrödeln, (herˈum)trödeln; **2.** zaudern, schwanken.
dil·u·ent [ˈdɪljʊənt] **I** *adj.* ⚕ verdünnend; **II** *s.* ⚗ Verdünnungsmittel *n.*
di·lute [daɪˈljuːt] **I** *v/t.* **1.** verdünnen, *bsd.* wässern; **2.** *Farben* dämpfen; **3.** *fig.* (ab)schwächen, verwässern: ***~ labo(u)r*** *Facharbeit in Arbeitsgänge zerlegen, deren Ausführung nur geringe Fachkenntnisse erfordert*; **II** *adj.* **4.** verdünnt; **5.** *fig.* (ab)geschwächt, verwässert; **diˈlut·ed** [-tɪd] *adj.* → ***dilute*** II; **dil·u·tee** [ˌdaɪljuːˈtiː] *s. zwischen dem angelernten u. dem Facharbeiter stehender Beschäftigter*; **di·lu·tion** [daɪˈluːʃn] *s.* **1.** Verdünnung *f*, Verwässerung *f*; **2.** verdünnte Lösung; **3.** *fig.* Abschwächung *f*, Verwässerung *f*: ***~ of labo(u)r*** *Zerlegung von Facharbeit in Arbeitsgänge, deren Ausführung nur geringe Fachkenntnisse erfordert.*
di·lu·vi·al [daɪˈluːvjəl], **diˈlu·vi·an** [-jən] *adj.* **1.** *geol.* diluviˈal, Eiszeit…; **2.** Überschwemmungs…; **3.** (Sint)Flut…; **diˈlu·vi·um** [-jəm] *s. geol.* Diˈluvium *n.*
dim [dɪm] **I** *adj.* □ **1.** (halb)dunkel, düster, trübe (*a. fig.*); **2.** undeutlich, verschwommen, schwach; **3.** blaß, matt (*Farbe*); **4.** F schwer von Begriff; **II** *v/t.* **5.** verdunkeln, verdüstern; trüben; **6.** *a.* ***~ out*** *Licht* abblenden, dämpfen; **7.** mattieren; **III** *v/i.* **8.** sich verdunkeln; **9.** matt *od.* trübe werden; **10.** undeutlich werden; verblassen (*a. fig.*).
dime [daɪm] *s. Am.* Zehnˈcentstück *n*; *fig.* Groschen *m*: ***~ novel*** Groschenroman *m*; ***~ store*** billiges Warenhaus; ***they are a ~ a dozen*** a) sie sind spottbillig, b) es gibt jede Menge davon.
di·men·sion [dɪˈmenʃn] **I** *s.* **1.** Dimensiˈon *f* (*a.* ⅌): a) Abmessung *f*, Maß *n*, Ausdehnung *f*, b) *pl. oft fig.* Ausmaß *n*, Größe *f*, ˈUmfang *m*: ***of vast ~s*** riesengroß; **II** *v/t.* **2.** bemessen, dimensionieren: ***amply ~ed***; **3.** mit Maßangaben versehen: ***~ed sketch*** Maßskizze *f*; **diˈmen·sion·al** [-ʃənl] *adj. mst in Zssgn* dimensioˈnal.
di·min·ish [dɪˈmɪnɪʃ] **I** *v/t.* **1.** vermindern (*a.* ♪), verringern; **2.** verkleinern (*a.* ⅌), herˈabsetzen (*a. fig.*); **3.** (ab-)schwächen; **4.** ⚠ verjüngen; **II** *v/i.* **5.** sich vermindern, abnehmen: ***~ in value*** an Wert verlieren.
dim·i·nu·tion [ˌdɪmɪˈnjuːʃn] *s.* **1.** Verminderung *f*, Verringerung *f*, Verkleinerung *f* (*a.* ♪); **2.** Abnahme *f*; **3.** ⚠ Verjüngung *f*; **di·min·u·ti·val** [dɪˌmɪnjʊˈtaɪvl] *adj.* □ → ***diminutive*** 2; **di·min·u·tive** [dɪˈmɪnjʊtɪv] **I** *adj.* □ **1.** klein, winzig; **2.** *ling.* Diminutiv…, Verkleinerungs…; **II** *s.* **3.** *ling.* Diminuˈtiv(um) *n*, Verkleinerungsform *f od.* -silbe *f.*
dim·i·ty [ˈdɪmɪtɪ] *s.* Dimity *m*, Barchentköper *m.*
dim·mer [ˈdɪmə] *s.* **1.** Dimmer *m* (*Helligkeitseinsteller*); **2.** *pl. mot.* a) Abblendlicht *n*, b) Standlicht *n*: ***~ switch*** Abblendschalter *m*; **dim·ness** [ˈdɪmnɪs] *s.* **1.** Dunkelheit *f*, Düsterkeit *f*; **2.** Mattheit *f*; **3.** Undeutlichkeit *f.*
di·mor·phic [daɪˈmɔːfɪk], **diˈmor·phous** [-fəs] *adj.* diˈmorph, zweigestaltig.
ˈ**dim-out** *s.* ⚔ Teilverdunkelung *f.*
dim·ple [ˈdɪmpl] **I** *s.* **1.** Grübchen *n* (*Wange*); **2.** Vertiefung *f*; **3.** Kräuselung *f* (*Wasser*); **II** *v/t.* **4.** Grübchen machen in (*acc.*); **5.** *Wasser* kräuseln; **III** *v/i.* **6.** Grübchen bekommen; **7.** sich kräuseln (*Wasser*); ˈ**dim·pled** [-ld], ˈ**dimp·ly** [-lɪ] *adj.* **1.** mit Grübchen; **2.** gekräuselt (*Wasser*).
ˌ**dimˈwit·ted** *adj. sl.* ‚dämlich'.
din [dɪn] **I** *s.* **1.** Lärm *m*, Getöse *n*; **2.** Geklirr *n* (*Waffen*), Gerassel *n*; **II** *v/t.* **3.** *durch Lärm* betäuben; **4.** *et.* dauernd (vor)predigen: ***~ s.th. into s.o.('s ears)*** j-m et. einhämmern; **III** *v/i.* **5.** lärmen; **6.** dröhnen (***with*** von).
dine [daɪn] **I** *v/i.* **1.** speisen, essen: ***~ in*** (***out***) zu Hause (auswärts) essen; ***~ off*** (*od.* ***on***) ***roast beef*** Rostbraten essen; **II** *v/t.* **2.** *j-n* bei sich zu Gast haben, bewirten; **3.** für … *Personen* Platz zum Essen haben, fassen (*Zimmer*, *Tisch*); ˈ**din·er** [-nə] *s.* **1.** Tischgast *m*; **2.** 🚂 Speisewagen *m*; **3.** *Am.* Imbißstube *f*, ˈEßloˌkal *n.*
di·nette [daɪˈnet] *s.* Eßecke *f.*
ding [dɪŋ] **I** *v/t.* **1.** läuten; **2.** → ***din*** 4; **II** *v/i.* **3.** läuten.
ding·dong [ˌdɪŋˈdɒŋ] **I** *s.* Bimbam *n*; **II** *adj.*: ***a ~ fight*** ein hin u. her wogender Kampf.
din·ghy [ˈdɪŋgɪ] *s.* **1.** ⚓ a) Dingi *n*, b) Beiboot *n*; **2.** Schlauchboot *n.*
din·gi·ness [ˈdɪndʒɪnɪs] *s.* **1.** trübe *od.* schmutzige Farbe; **2.** Schmuddeligkeit *f*; **3.** Schäbigkeit *f* (*a. fig.*); **4.** *fig.* Anrüchigkeit *f.*
din·gle [ˈdɪŋgl] *s.* Waldschlucht *f.*
din·go [ˈdɪŋgəʊ] *pl.* **-goes** *s. zo.* Dingo *m* (*Wildhund Australiens*).
ding·us [ˈdɪŋgəs] *s. Am. sl.* **1.** Dingsda *n*; **2.** ‚Ding' *n* (*Penis*).
din·gy [ˈdɪndʒɪ] *adj.* □ **1.** schmutzig, schmuddelig; **2.** schäbig (*a. fig.*); **3.** *fig.* anrüchig.
din·ing| car [ˈdaɪnɪŋ] *s.* 🚂 Speisewagen *m*; **~ hall** *s.* Speisesaal *m*; **~ room** *s.* Speise-, Eßzimmer *n*; **~ ta·ble** *s.* Eßtisch *m.*
din·kum [ˈdɪŋkəm] *adj. Austral.* F reˈell: ***~ oil*** die volle Wahrheit.
dink·y [ˈdɪŋkɪ] *adj.* F **1.** *Brit.* zierlich, niedlich, nett; **2.** *Am.* klein.
din·ner [ˈdɪnə] *s.* **1.** Hauptmahlzeit *f*, Mittag-, Abendessen *n*: ***after ~*** nach dem Essen, nach Tisch; ***be at ~*** bei Tisch sein; ***stay for*** (*od.* ***to***) ***~*** zum Essen bleiben; ***~ is ready*** es (*od.* das Essen) ist angerichtet; ***what are we having for ~?*** was gibt es zum Essen?; **2.** Diˈner *n*, Festessen *n*: ***at a ~*** bei *od.* auf e-m Diner; **~ coat** *s. bsd. Am.* Smoking *m*; **~ dance** *s.* Abendgesellschaft *f* mit Tanz; **~ jack·et** *s.* Smoking *m*; **~ pail** *s. Am.* Eßgefäß *n*; **~ par·ty** *s.* Tisch-, Abendgesellschaft *f*; **~ ser·vice**, **~ set** *s.* ˈSpeiseserˌvice *n*, Tafelgeschirr *n*; **~ ta·ble** *s.* Eßtisch *m*; **~ time** *s.* Tischzeit *f*; **~ wag·on** *s.* Servierwagen *m.*
di·no·saur [ˈdaɪnəʊsɔː] *s. zo.* Dinoˈsaurier *m.*
dint [dɪnt] **I** *s.* **1.** Beule *f*, Delle *f*; **2.** Strieme *f*; **3.** ***by ~ of*** kraft, vermöge, mittels (*alle gen.*); **II** *v/t.* **4.** einbeulen.
di·oc·e·san [daɪˈɒsɪsn] *eccl.* **I** *adj.* Diözesan…; **II** *s.* (Diözeˈsan)Bischof *m*; **di·o·cese** [ˈdaɪəsɪs] *s.* Diöˈzese *f.*
di·ode [ˈdaɪəʊd] *s.* ⚡ **1.** Diˈode *f*, Zweipolröhre *f*; **2.** Kriˈstalldiˌode *f.*
Di·o·nys·i·ac [ˌdaɪəˈnɪzɪæk], **Di·oˈnysian** [-zɪən] *adj.* dioˈnysisch.
di·op·ter *Am.*, *Brit.* **di·op·tre** [daɪˈɒptə] *s. phys.* Diopˈtrie *f*; **diˈop·tric** [-trɪk] *phys.* **I** *adj.* **1.** diˈoptrisch, lichtbrechend; **II** *s.* **2.** → ***diopter***; **3.** *pl. sg. konstr.* Diˈoptrik *f*, Brechungslehre *f.*
di·o·ra·ma [ˌdaɪəˈrɑːmə] *s.* Dioˈrama *n* (*plastisch wirkendes Schaubild*).
Di·os·cu·ri [ˌdaɪəʊˈskjʊəraɪ] *s. pl.* Diosˈkuren *pl.* (*Castor u. Pollux*).
di·ox·ide [daɪˈɒksaɪd] *s.* ˈDioˌxyd *n.*
dip [dɪp] **I** *v/t.* **1.** (ein)tauchen (***in***, ***into*** in *acc.*): ***~ one's hand into one's pocket*** in die Tasche greifen (*a. fig. Geld ausgeben*); **2.** färben; **3.** *Schafe etc.* dippen (*Desinfektionsbad*); **4.** *Kerzen* ziehen; **5.** ⚓ *Flagge* (zum Gruß) dippen, auf- u. niederholen; **6.** *a.* ***~ up*** schöpfen (***from***, ***out of*** aus); **7.** *mot. Scheinwerfer* abblenden; **II** *v/i.* **8.** ˈunter-, eintauchen; **9.** sich senken *od.* neigen (*Gelände*, *Waage*, *Magnetnadel*); **10.** ⚒ ab-, einfallen; **11.** nieder- u. wieder auffliegen; **12.** ✈ vor dem Steigen tiefer gehen; **13.** *fig.* hinˈeingreifen: ***~ into*** a) e-n Blick werfen in (*acc.*), sich flüchtig befassen mit, b) *Reserven* angreifen; ***~ into one's purse*** (*od.* ***pocket***) (tief) in die Tasche greifen; ***~ deep into the past*** die Vergangenheit erforschen; **III** *s.* **14.** Eintauchen *n*; **15.** kurzes Bad(en); **16.** ⚙ Farbbad *n*; Tauchbad *n*: ***~ brazing*** Tauchlöten *n*; **17.** Desinfektiˈonsbad *n* (*Schafe*); **18.** geschöpfte Flüssigkeit; **19.** *Am.* F Tunke *f*, Soße *f*; **20.** (gezogene) Kerze; **21.** Neigung *f*, Senkung *f*, Gefälle *n*; Neigungswinkel *m*; **22.** *geol.* Abdachung *f*; Einfallen *n*, Versinken *n*; **23.** schnelles Hinˈab(- u. Hinˈauf)Fliegen; **24.** ✈ plötzliches Tiefergehen vor dem Steigen; **25.** ⚓ Dippen *n* (*kurzes Niederholen der Flagge*); **26.** *fig.* flüchtiger Blick, ‚Ausflug' *m* (*in die Politik etc.*); **27.** Angreifen *n* (***into*** *e-s Vorrats etc.*); **28.** *sl.* Taschendieb *m.*
diph·the·ri·a [dɪfˈθɪərɪə] *s.* ⚕ Diphtheˈrie *f.*
diph·thong [ˈdɪfθɒŋ] *s. ling.* **1.** Diphˈthong *m*, ˈDoppelvoˌkal *m*; **2.** *die Ligatur* æ *od.* œ; **diph·thon·gal** [dɪfˈθɒŋgl] *adj. ling.* diphˈthongisch; **diph·thong·i·za·tion** [ˌdɪfθɒŋgaɪˈzeɪʃn] *s. ling.* Diphthongierung *f.*
di·ple·gi·a [daɪˈpliːdʒɪə] *s.* ⚕ Dipleˈgie *f*, doppelseitige Lähmung.
di·plo·ma [dɪˈpləʊmə] *s.* Diˈplom *n*, (*a.* Ehren-, Sieger)Urkunde *f*; **diˈplo·ma·cy** [-əsɪ] *s. pol.*, *a. fig.* Diplomaˈtie *f*; **diˈplo·maed** [-məd] *adj.* diplomiert, Diplom…; **dip·lo·mat** [ˈdɪpləmæt] *s.*

pol., *a. fig.* Diplo'mat *m*; **dip·lo·mat·ic** [ˌdɪplə'mætɪk] *adj.* (□ **~ally**) **1.** *pol.* diplo'matisch (*a. fig.*): **~ body** (*od.* **corps**) diplomatisches Korps; **~ service** diplomatischer Dienst; **2.** urkundlich; **dip·lo·mat·ics** [ˌdɪplə'mætɪks] *s. pl. sg. konstr.* Diplo'matik *f*, Urkundenlehre *f*; **di'plo·ma·tist** [-ətɪst] → **diplomat**; **di'plo·ma·tize** [-ətaɪz] *v/i.* diplo'matisch vorgehen.

di·po·lar [daɪ'pəʊlə] *adj.* ⚡ zweipolig; **di·pole** ['daɪpəʊl] *s.* Dipol *m*.

dip·per ['dɪpə] *s.* **1.** *orn.* Taucher *m*; **2.** Schöpflöffel *m*; **3.** ⚙ a) Baggereimer *m*, b) Bagger *m*; **4.** ⚙ Färber *m*, Beizer *m*; **5.** *ast.* ~, **Big ~** *Am.* Großer Bär; **Little ~** *Am.* Kleiner Bär; **6.** *s. eccl. obs.* 'Wiedertäufer *m*; **~ dredg·er** *s.* Löffelbagger *m*.

dip·ping ['dɪpɪŋ] *s.* **1.** ⚙ (Tauch)Bad *n*; **2.** *in Zssgn* Tauch…: **~ electrode**; **~ compass** Inklinationskompaß *m*; **~ rod** Wünschelrute *f*.

dip·so·ma·ni·a [ˌdɪpsəʊ'meɪnjə] *s.* ⚕ Dipsoma'nie *f* (*periodisch auftretende Trunksucht*); **ˌdip·so'ma·ni·ac** [-nɪæk] *s.* Dipso'mane *m*, Dipso'manin *f*.

'dip|·stick *s. mot.* (Öl- *etc.*)Meßstab *m*; **~ switch** *s. mot. Brit.* Abblendschalter *m*.

dip·ter·a ['dɪptərə] *s. pl. zo.* Zweiflügler *pl.*; **'dip·ter·al** [-rəl], **'dip·ter·ous** [-rəs] *adj.* zweiflügelig.

dip·tych ['dɪptɪk] *s.* Diptychon *n*.

dire ['daɪə] *adj.* **1.** gräßlich, entsetzlich, schrecklich; **2.** unheilvoll; **3.** äußerst, höchst: **be in ~ need of** *et.* ganz dringend brauchen.

di·rect [dɪ'rekt] **I** *v/t.* **1.** lenken, leiten, führen; beaufsichtigen; ♪ dirigieren; *Film*, *TV*: Re'gie führen bei: **~ed by** unter der Regie von; **2.** *Aufmerksamkeit*, *Blicke* richten, lenken (**to**, **towards** auf *acc.*): **be ~ed to doing s.th.** darauf abzielen, et. zu tun (*Verfahren etc.*); **3.** *Worte etc.* richten, *Brief* richten, adressieren (**to** an *acc.*); **4.** anweisen, beauftragen; (An)Weisung geben (*dat.*): **~ the jury as to the law** ⚖ den Geschworenen Rechtsbelehrung erteilen; **5.** anordnen, verfügen, bestimmen: **~ s.th. to be done** anordnen, daß et. geschieht; **as ~ed** nach Vorschrift, laut Anordnung; **6.** befehlen; **7.** (**to**) den Weg zeigen (nach, zu), verweisen (an *acc.*); **II** *v/i.* **8.** befehlen, bestimmen; **9.** ♪ dirigieren; *Film*, *TV*: Re'gie führen; **III** *adj.* □ → **directly**; **10.** di'rekt, gerade; **11.** di'rekt, unmittelbar (*a.* ⚙, ☤, *phys.*, *pol.*): **~ action** *pol.* direkte Aktion; **~ advertising** Werbung *f* beim Konsumenten; **~ costing** ☤ *Am.* Grenzkostenrechnung *f*; **~ current** ⚡ Gleichstrom *m*; **~ dial(l)ing** *teleph.* Durchwahl *f*; **~ distance dialing** *teleph. Am.* Selbstwählfernverkehr *m*; **~ evidence** ⚖ unmittelbarer Beweis; **~ hit** Volltreffer *m*; **~ line** direkte (Abstammungs)Linie; **~ method** direkte Methode (*Sprachunterricht*); **the ~ opposite** das genaue Gegenteil; **~ responsibility** persönliche Verantwortung; **~ selling** ☤ Direktverkauf *m*; **~ taxes** direkte Steuern; **~ train** durchgehender Zug; **12.** gerade, offen, deutlich: **~ answer**; **~ question**; **13.** *ling.* **~ method** direkte Methode; **~ object** direktes Objekt; **~ speech** direkte Rede; **14.** *ast.* rechtläufig; **IV** *adv.* **15.** di'rekt, unmittelbar (**to** zu, an *acc.*).

di·rec·tion [dɪ'rekʃn] *s.* **1.** Richtung *f* (*a.* ⚙, *phys.*, *fig.*): **sense of ~** Orts-, Orientierungssinn *m*; **in the ~ of** in (der) Richtung nach *od.* auf (*acc.*); **in all ~s** nach allen Richtungen *od.* Seiten; **in many ~s** in vieler Hinsicht; **2.** Leitung *f*, Führung *f*, Lenkung *f*: **under his ~** unter s-r Leitung; **3.** Leitung *f*, Direkti'on *f*, Direk'torium *n*; **4.** *Film*, *TV*: Re'gie *f*; **5.** *mst pl.* (An)Weisung *f*, Anleitung *f*, Belehrung *f*, Anordnung *f*, Vorschrift *f*, Richtlinie *f*: **by ~ of** auf Anordnung von; **give ~s** Anweisungen *od.* Vorschriften geben; **~s for use** Gebrauchsanweisung; **full ~s inside** genaue Anweisung(en) anbei; **6.** Anschrift *f*, A'dresse *f* (*Brief*).

di·rec·tion·al [dɪ'rekʃənl] *adj.* **1.** Richtungs…; **2.** ⚡ a) Richt…, b) Peil…; **~ aer·i·al**, *bsd. Am.* **~ an·ten·na** *s.* ⚡ 'Richtanˌtenne *f*, -strahler *m*; **~ beam** *s.* ⚡ Richtstrahl *m*; **~ ra·di·o** *s.* ⚡ **1.** Richtfunk *m*: **~ beacon** ⚓ Richtfunkfeuer *n*; **2.** Peilfunk *m*; **~ trans·mit·ter** *s.* ⚡ **1.** Richtfunksender *m*; **2.** Peilsender *m*.

di'rec·tion| find·er *s.* ⚡ (Funk)Peiler *m*, Peilempfänger *m*; **~ find·ing** *s.* a) (Funk)Peilung *f*, Richtungsbestimmung *f*, b) Peilwesen *n*: **~ set** Peilgerät *n*; **~ in·di·ca·tor** *s.* **1.** *mot.* (Fahrt)Richtungsanzeiger *m*, Blinker *m*; **2.** ✈ Kursweiser *m*.

di·rec·tive [dɪ'rektɪv] **I** *adj.* lenkend, leitend, richtungweisend; **II** *s.* Direk'tive *f*, (An)Weisung *f*, Vorschrift *f*; **di·rect·ly** [dɪ'rektlɪ] **I** *adv.* **1.** gerade, di'rekt; **2.** unmittelbar, di'rekt (*a.* ⚙): **~ proportional** direkt proportional; **~ opposed** genau entgegengesetzt; **3.** *bsd. Brit.* [F *a.* 'dreklɪ] so'fort, gleich, bald; **II** *cj.* **4.** *bsd. Brit.* [F *a.* 'dreklɪ] so'bald (als): **~ he entered** sobald er eintrat; **di'rect·ness** [-tnɪs] *s.* **1.** Di'rekt-, Geradheit *f*, gerade Richtung; **2.** Unmittelbarkeit *f*; **3.** Offenheit *f*; **4.** Deutlichkeit *f*.

di·rec·tor [dɪ'rektə] *s.* **1.** Di'rektor *m*, Leiter *m*, Vorsteher *m*; **2.** ☤ a) Di'rektor *m*: **~-general** Generaldirektor *m*, b) Mitglied *n* des Verwaltungsrats (*e-r AG*); → **board** 10; **3.** *Film etc.*: Regis'seur *m*; **4.** ♪ Diri'gent *m*; **5.** ⚔ Kom'mandogerät *n*; **di'rec·to·rate** [-tərət] *s.* **1.** → **directorship**; **2.** Direk'torium *n*, Leitung *f*; **3.** ☤ a) Direk'torium *n*, b) Verwaltungsrat *m*; **di'rec·tor·ship** [-ʃɪp] *s.* Direk'torenposten *m*, -stelle *f*.

di·rec·to·ry [dɪ'rektərɪ] *s.* **1.** a) A'dreßbuch *n*, b) Tele'fonbuch *n*, c) Branchenverzeichnis *n*: **~ enquiries**, *Am.* **~ assistance** Telefonauskunft *f*; **2.** *eccl.* Gottesdienstordnung *f*; **3.** Leitfaden *m*; **4.** Direk'torium *n*; **5.** ~ *hist.* Direk'torium *n* (*französische Revolution*).

di·rec·tress [dɪ'rektrɪs] *s.* Direk'torin *f*, Vorsteherin *f*, Leiterin *f*.

dire·ful ['daɪəfʊl] → **dire**.

dirge [dɜːdʒ] *s.* Klage-, Trauerlied *n*, Totenklage *f*.

dir·i·gi·ble ['dɪrɪdʒəbl] **I** *adj.* lenkbar; **II** *s.* lenkbares Luftschiff.

dirk [dɜːk] *s.* Dolch *m*.

dirn·dl ['dɜːndl] (*Ger.*) *s.* Dirndl(kleid) *n*.

dirt [dɜːt] *s.* **1.** Schmutz *m* (*a. fig.*), Kot *m*, Dreck *m*; **2.** Staub *m*, Boden *m*, (lockere) Erde; **3.** *fig.* Plunder *m*, Schund *m*; **4.** *fig.* unflätige Reden *pl.*; Gemeinheit(en *pl.*) *f*: **eat ~** sich widerspruchslos demütigen; **fling** (*od.* **throw**) **~ at s.o.** j-n in den Schmutz ziehen; **do s.o. ~** *sl.* j-n ganz gemein reinlegen; **treat s.o. like ~** j-n wie (den letzten) Dreck behandeln; **ˌ~-'cheap** *adj. u. adv.* spottbillig.

dirt·i·ness ['dɜːtɪnɪs] *s.* **1.** Schmutz *m*, Schmutzigkeit *f* (*a. fig.*); **2.** Gemeinheit *f*, Niedertracht *f*.

dirt| road *s. Am.* unbefestigte Straße; **~ track** *s. sport mot.* Aschenbahn *f*.

dirt·y ['dɜːtɪ] **I** *adj.* □ **1.** schmutzig, dreckig, Schmutz…: **~ brown** schmutzigbraun; **~ work** a) Schmutzarbeit *f*, b) *fig.* unsauberes Geschäft, Schurkerei *f*; **2.** *fig.* gemein, niederträchtig: **a ~ look** ein böser Blick; **a ~ lot** ein Lumpenpack; **~ trick** Gemeinheit *f*; **do the ~ on s.o.** *Brit. sl.* j-n gemein behandeln; **3.** *fig.* schmutzig, unflätig, unanständig: **a ~ mind** schmutzige Gedanken *od.* Phantasie; **4.** schlecht, *bsd.* ⚓ stürmisch (*Wetter*); **II** *v/t.* **5.** beschmutzen, besudeln (*a. fig.*); **III** *v/i.* **6.** schmutzig werden; schmutzen.

dis·a·bil·i·ty [ˌdɪsə'bɪlətɪ] *s.* **1.** Unvermögen *n*, Unfähigkeit *f*; **2.** ⚖ Rechtsunfähigkeit *f*; **3.** Körperbeschädigung *f*, -behinderung *f*; Gebrechen *n*; Arbeits-, Erwerbsunfähigkeit *f*; Invalidi'tät *f*; ⚔ → **disablement** 2; **4.** Unzulänglichkeit *f*; **5.** Benachteiligung *f*, Nachteil *m*; **~ ben·e·fit** *s.* Invalidi'tätsrente *f*; **~ in·sur·ance** *s.* Inva'lidenversicherung *f*; **~ pen·sion** *s.* (Kriegs)Versehrtenrente *f*.

dis·a·ble [dɪs'eɪbl] *v/t.* **1.** unfähig machen, außer'stand setzen (**from doing s.th.** et. zu tun); **2.** unbrauchbar *od.* untauglich machen (**for** für, zu); **3.** ⚔ a) dienstuntauglich machen, b) kampfunfähig machen; **4.** verkrüppeln; **5.** ⚖ geschäfts- *od.* rechtsunfähig machen; **dis'a·bled** [-ld] *adj.* **1.** ⚖ geschäfts- *od.* rechtsunfähig; **2.** arbeits-, erwerbsunfähig, inva'lide; **3.** ⚔ a) dienstuntauglich, b) kriegsversehrt: **a ~ ex-soldier** ein Kriegsversehrter, c) kampfunfähig; **4.** ⚔ manövrierunfähig, seeuntüchtig; **5.** *mot.* fahruntüchtig: **~ car**; **6.** unbrauchbar; **7.** (körperlich *od.* geistig) behindert; **dis'a·ble·ment** [-mənt] *s.* **1.** → **disability** 2, 3; **2.** ⚔ a) (Dienst-) Untauglichkeit *f*, b) Kampfunfähigkeit *f*.

dis·a·buse [ˌdɪsə'bjuːz] *v/t.* aus dem Irrtum befreien, e-s Besseren belehren, aufklären (**of s.th.** über *acc.*): **~ o.s.** (*od.* **one's mind**) **of s.th.** sich von et. (*Irrtümlichem*) befreien, sich et. aus dem Kopf schlagen.

dis·ac·cord [ˌdɪsə'kɔːd] **I** *v/i.* nicht über'einstimmen; **II** *s.* Uneinigkeit *f*; 'Widerspruch *m*.

dis·ac·cus·tom [ˌdɪsə'kʌstəm] *v/t.* abgewöhnen (**s.o. to s.th.** j-m et.).

dis·ad·van·tage [ˌdɪsəd'vɑːntɪdʒ] *s.* Nachteil *m*, Schaden *m*: **be at a ~**, **labo(u)r under a ~** im Nachteil sein; **to s.o.'s ~** zu j-s Nachteil *od.* Schaden; **put s.o. at a ~** j-n benachteiligen; **take s.o. at a ~** j-s ungünstige Lage ausnutzen; **sell to** (*od.* **at a**) **~** mit Verlust verkaufen; **dis·ad·van·ta·geous** [ˌdɪsædvɑːnˈteɪdʒəs] *adj.* □ nachteilig, ungünstig, unvorteilhaft, schädlich (**to** für).

dis·af·fect·ed [ˌdɪsəˈfektɪd] *adj.* □ **1.** (**to, towards**) unzufrieden (mit), abgeneigt (*dat.*); **2.** *pol.* unzuverlässig, untreu; **ˌdis·afˈfec·tion** [-kʃn] *s.* Unzufriedenheit *f* (**for** mit), (*a. pol.* Staats-) Verdrossenheit *f*.

dis·af·firm [ˌdɪsəˈfɜːm] *v/t.* **1.** (ab)leugnen; **2.** ⚖ aufheben, ˈumstoßen.

dis·af·for·est [ˌdɪsəˈfɒrɪst] *v/t.* **1.** ⚖ *e-m Wald* den Schutz durch das Forstrecht nehmen; **2.** abholzen.

dis·ag·i·o [dɪsˈædʒɪəʊ] *s.* ✝ Disˈagio *n*, Abschlag *m*.

dis·a·gree [ˌdɪsəˈgriː] *v/i.* **1.** (**with**) nicht überˈeinstimmen (mit), im ˈWiderspruch stehen (zu, mit); sich widerˈsprechen; **2.** (**with**) anderer Meinung sein (als), nicht zustimmen (*dat.*); **3.** (**with**) nicht einverstanden sein (mit), gegen *et.* sein, ablehnen (*acc.*); **4.** (sich) streiten (**on** über *acc.*); **5.** (**with** *j-m*) schlecht bekommen, nicht zuträglich sein (*Essen etc.*); **ˌdis·a-ˈgree·a·ble** [-ˈgrɪəbl] *adj.* □ **1.** unangenehm, widerlich, lästig; **2.** unliebenswürdig, eklig; **ˌdis·aˈgree·a·ble·ness** [-ˈgrɪəblnɪs] *s.* **1.** Widerwärtigkeit *f*; **2.** Lästigkeit *f*; **3.** Unliebenswürdigkeit *f*; **ˌdis·aˈgree·ment** [-mənt] *s.* **1.** Unstimmigkeit *f*, Verschiedenheit *f*, ˈWiderspruch *m*; **2.** Meinungsverschiedenheit *f*, ˈMißhelligkeit *f*, Streit *m*.

dis·al·low [ˌdɪsəˈlaʊ] *v/t.* **1.** nicht zulassen (*a.* ⚖) *od.* erlauben, verweigern; **2.** nicht anerkennen, nicht gelten lassen, *sport a.* annullieren, nicht geben; **ˌdis-alˈlow·ance** [-ˈlaʊəns] *s.* Nichtanerkennung *f*, *sport a.* Annullierung *f*.

dis·ap·pear [ˌdɪsəˈpɪə] *v/i.* **1.** verschwinden (**from** von, aus); **2.** verlorengehen, aufhören; **ˌdis·apˈpear·ance** [-ˈpɪərəns] *s.* **1.** Verschwinden *n*; **2.** ⚙ Schwund *m*; **ˌdis·apˈpear·ing** [-ˈpɪərɪŋ] *adj.* **1.** verschwindend; **2.** versenkbar.

dis·ap·point [ˌdɪsəˈpɔɪnt] *v/t.* **1.** enttäuschen: **be ~ed** enttäuscht sein (**at** *od.* **with** über *acc.*, **in** von *dat.*); **be ~ed of s.th.** um et. betrogen *od.* gebracht werden; **2.** *Hoffnung* (ent)täuschen, zuˈnichte machen; **ˌdis·apˈpoint·ed** [-tɪd] *adj.* □ enttäuscht; **ˌdis·apˈpoint·ing** [-tɪŋ] *adj.* □ enttäuschend; **ˌdis-apˈpoint·ment** [-mənt] *s.* **1.** Enttäuschung *f* (*a. von Hoffnungen etc.*): **to my ~** zu m-r Enttäuschung; **2.** Enttäuschung *f* (*enttäuschende Person od. Sache*).

dis·ap·pro·ba·tion [ˌdɪsæprəʊˈbeɪʃn] *s.* ˈMißbilligung *f*.

dis·ap·prov·al [ˌdɪsəˈpruːvl] *s.* (**of**) ˈMißbilligung *f* (*gen.*), ˈMißfallen *n* (über *acc.*); **dis·ap·prove** [ˌdɪsəˈpruːv] **I** *v/t.* mißˈbilligen, ablehnen; **II** *v/i.* daˈgegen sein: **~ of** → I; **ˌdis·apˈprov·ing·ly** [-vɪŋlɪ] *adv.* mißˈbilligend.

dis·arm [dɪsˈɑːm] **I** *v/t.* **1.** entwaffnen (*a. fig.*); **2.** unschädlich machen; *Bomben etc.* entschärfen; **3.** besänftigen; **II** *v/i.* **4.** *pol.*, ⚔ abrüsten; **disˈar·ma·ment** [-məmənt] *s.* **1.** Entwaffnung *f*; **2.** *pol.*, ⚔ Abrüstung *f*; **disˈarm·ing** [-mɪŋ] *adj.* □ *fig.* entwaffnend.

dis·ar·range [ˌdɪsəˈreɪndʒ] *v/t.* in Unordnung bringen; **ˌdis·arˈrange·ment** [-mənt] *s.* Verwirrung *f*, Unordnung *f*.

dis·ar·ray [ˌdɪsəˈreɪ] **I** *v/t.* in Unordnung bringen, durcheinˈanderbringen; **II** *s.* Unordnung *f*: **be in ~** a) in Unordnung sein, b) ⚔ in Auflösung begriffen sein; **throw into ~** → I.

dis·as·sem·ble [ˌdɪsəˈsembl] *v/t.* ⚙ auseinˈandernehmen, -montieren, zerlegen; **ˌdis·asˈsem·bly** [-blɪ] *s.* Zerlegung *f*, Abbau *m*.

dis·as·ter [dɪˈzɑːstə] *s.* Unglück *n* (**to** für), Unheil *n*, Kataˈstrophe *f*: **~ area** Katastrophengebiet *n*; **disˈas·trous** [-trəs] *adj.* □ unglückselig, unheil-, verhängnisvoll, katastroˈphal, verheerend.

dis·a·vow [ˌdɪsəˈvaʊ] *v/t.* **1.** nicht anerkennen, abrücken *od.* sich lossagen von; **2.** in Abrede stellen, ableugnen; **ˌdis·aˈvow·al** [-ˈvaʊəl] *s.* **1.** Nichtanerkennung *f*; **2.** Ableugnung *f*.

dis·band [dɪsˈbænd] **I** *v/t.* ⚔ *Truppen etc.* entlassen, auflösen; **II** *v/i. bsd.* ⚔ sich auflösen; **disˈband·ment** [-mənt] *s.* ⚔ Auflösung *f*.

dis·bar [dɪsˈbɑː] *v/t.* ⚖ aus der Anwaltschaft ausschließen.

dis·be·lief [ˌdɪsbɪˈliːf] *s.* Unglaube *m*, Zweifel *m* (**in** an *dat.*); **ˌdis·beˈlieve** [-iːv] **I** *v/t. et.* nicht glauben, bezweifeln; *j-m* nicht glauben; **II** *v/i.* nicht glauben (**in** an *acc.*); **ˌdis·beˈliev·er** [-iːvə] *s. a. eccl.* Ungläubige(r *m*) *f*, Zweifler(in).

dis·bur·den [dɪsˈbɜːdn] *v/t. mst fig.* von e-r Bürde befreien, entlasten (**of, from** von): **~ one's mind** sein Herz erleichtern.

dis·burse [dɪsˈbɜːs] *v/t.* **1.** be-, auszahlen; **2.** *Geld* auslegen; **disˈburse·ment** [-mənt] *s.* **1.** Auszahlung *f*; **2.** Auslage *f*, Verauslagung *f*.

disc [dɪsk] → **disk**.

dis·card [dɪˈskɑːd] **I** *v/t.* **1.** *Gewohnheit, Vorurteil etc.* ablegen, aufgeben, *Kleider etc.* ausscheiden, ausrangieren; **2.** *Freund* fallenlassen; **3.** *Karten* ablegen *od.* abwerfen; **II** *v/i.* **4.** *Kartenspiel*: Karten ablegen *od.* abwerfen; **III** *s.* [ˈdɪskɑːd] **5.** *Kartenspiel*: a) Ablegen *n*, b) abgeworfene Karte(n *pl.*); **6.** *et.* Abgelegtes, ausrangierte Sache: **go into the ~** *Am.* a) in Vergessenheit geraten, b) außer Gebrauch kommen.

dis·cern [dɪˈsɜːn] *v/t.* **1.** wahrnehmen, erkennen; **2.** feststellen; **3.** *obs.* unterˈscheiden (können); **disˈcern·i·ble** [-nəbl] *adj.* □ erkennbar, sichtbar; **dis-ˈcern·ing** [-nɪŋ] *adj.* scharf(sichtig), kritisch (urteilend), klug; **disˈcern-ment** [-mənt] *s.* **1.** Scharfblick *m*, Urteilskraft *f*; **2.** Einsicht *f* (**of** in *acc.*); **3.** Wahrnehmen *n*; **4.** Wahrnehmungsvermögen *n*.

dis·charge [dɪsˈtʃɑːdʒ] **I** *v/t.* **1.** *Waren, Wagen* ab-, ausladen; *Schiff* aus-, entladen; *Personen* ausladen, absetzen; *(Schiffs)Ladung* löschen; **2.** ⚡ entladen; **3.** ausströmen (lassen), aussenden, -stoßen, ergießen; absondern: **~ matter** ⚕ eitern; **4.** ⚔ *Geschütz etc.* abfeuern, abschießen; **5.** entlassen, verabschieden, fortschicken; **6.** *Gefangene* ent-, freilassen; *Patienten* entlassen; **7.** *s-n Gefühlen* Luft machen, *s-n Zorn* auslassen (**on** an *dat.*); *Flüche* ausstoßen; **8.** freisprechen, entlasten (**of** von); **9.** befreien, entbinden (**of, from** von); **10.** *Schulden* bezahlen, tilgen; *Wechsel* einlösen; *Verpflichtungen, Aufgabe* erfüllen; *s-n Verbindlichkeiten* nachkommen; *Schuldner* entlasten; *obs. Gläubiger* befriedigen; ⚖ *Urteil etc.* aufheben: **~ed bankrupt** entlasteter Gemeinschuldner; **11.** *Amt* ausüben, versehen; *Rolle* spielen; **12. ~ o.s.** sich ergießen, münden; **II** *v/i.* **13.** ⚡ sich entladen (*a. Gewehr*); **14.** sich ergießen, abfließen; **15.** ⚕ eitern; **III** *s.* **16.** Ent-, Ausladung *f*, Löschen *n* (*Schiff, Waren*); **17.** ⚡ Entladung *f*: **~ current** Entladestrom *m*; **18.** Ausfließen *n*, -strömen *n*, Abfluß *m*; Ausstoßen *n* (*Rauch*); **19.** Absonderung *f* (*Eiter*), Ausfluß *m*; **20.** Abfeuern *n* (*Geschütz etc.*); **21.** a) (Dienst)Entlassung *f*, b) (Entlassungs)Zeugnis *n*; **22.** Ent-, Freilassung *f*; **23.** ✝, ⚖ Befreiung *f*, Entlastung *f*; Rehabilitatiˈon *f*: **~ of a bankrupt** Aufhebung *f* des Konkursverfahrens; **24.** Erfüllung *f* (*Aufgabe*), Ausübung *f*, Ausführung *f*; **25.** Bezahlung *f*, Einlösung *f*; **26.** Quittung *f*: **~ in full** vollständige Quittung; **disˈcharg·er** [-dʒə] *s.* ⚡ Entlader *m*.

dis·ci·ple [dɪˈsaɪpl] *s.* Jünger *m* (*bsd. bibl.*; *a. fig.*), Schüler *m*; **disˈci·ple·ship** [-ʃɪp] *s.* Jünger-, Anhängerschaft *f*.

dis·ci·pli·nar·i·an [ˌdɪsɪplɪˈneərɪən] *s.* Zuchtmeister *m*, strenger Lehrer *od.* Vorgesetzter; **dis·ci·pli·nar·y** [ˈdɪsɪplɪnərɪ] *adj.* **1.** erzieherisch, Zucht...; **2.** disziplɪˈnarisch: **~ action** Disziplinarverfahren *n*; **~ punishment** Disziplinarstrafe *f*; **~ transfer** Strafversetzung *f*; **dis·ci·pline** [ˈdɪsɪplɪn] **I** *s.* **1.** Schulung *f*, Erziehung *f*; **2.** Disziˈplin *f* (*a. eccl.*), Zucht *f*; ˈSelbstdisziˌplin *f*; **3.** Bestrafung *f*, Züchtigung *f*; **4.** Disziˈplin *f*, Wissenszweig *m*; **II** *v/t.* **5.** schulen, erziehen; **6.** disziplinieren: a) an Disziˈplin gewöhnen, b) bestrafen: **well ~d** (wohl)diszipliniert; **badly ~d** disziplinlos, undiszipliniert.

dis·claim [dɪsˈkleɪm] *v/t.* **1.** abstreiten, in Abrede stellen; **2.** a) *et.* nicht anerkennen, b) *e-e Verantwortung* ablehnen, c) jede Verantwortung ablehnen für; **3.** widerˈrufen, dementieren; verzichten auf (*acc.*), keinen Anspruch erheben auf (*acc.*), ⚖ *a. Erbschaft* ausschlagen; **disˈclaim·er** [-mə] *s.* **1.** ⚖ Verzicht(leistung *f*) *m*, Ausschlagung *f* (*e-r Erbschaft*); **2.** ˈWiderruf *m*, Deˈmenti *n*.

dis·close [dɪsˈkləʊz] *v/t.* **1.** bekanntgeben, -machen; **2.** aufdecken, ans Licht bringen, enthüllen; **3.** zeigen, verraten, offenbaren; **disˈclo·sure** [-əʊʒə] *s.* **1.** Enthüllung *f*; **2.** Bekanntgabe *f*, Verlautbarung *f*; **3.** *Patentrecht*: Offenbarung *f*.

dis·co [ˈdɪskəʊ] *pl.* **-cos** *s.* F ‚Disko' *f* (*Diskothek*).

dis·cog·ra·phy [dɪsˈkɒgrəfɪ] *s.* Schallplattenverzeichnis *n*.

dis·col·o(u)r [dɪsˈkʌlə] **I** *v/t.* **1.** verfärben; entfärben; **2.** *fig.* entstellen; **II** *v/i.* **3.** sich verfärben; **4.** verschießen; **dis-col·o(u)r·a·tion** [dɪsˌkʌləˈreɪʃn] *s.* **1.** Verfärbung *f*; Entfärbung *f*; **2.** verschossene Stelle; **3.** Fleck *m*; **dis'col·o(u)red** [-əd] *adj.* verfärbt; verschossen.

dis·com·fit [dɪs'kʌmfɪt] *v/t.* **1.** aus der Fassung bringen, verwirren; **2.** *obs.* schlagen, besiegen; **3.** *j-s* Pläne durch'kreuzen; **dis'com·fi·ture** [-tʃə] *s.* **1.** *obs.* Niederlage *f*; **2.** Durch'kreuzung *f*; **3.** a) Verwirrung *f*, b) Verlegenheit *f*.

dis·com·fort [dɪs'kʌmfət] *s.* **1.** Unbehagen *n*; **2.** Verdruß *m*; **3.** *körperliche* Beschwerde.

dis·com·mode [ˌdɪskə'məʊd] *v/t.* belästigen, *j-m* zur Last fallen.

dis·com·pose [ˌdɪskəm'pəʊz] *v/t.* **1.** in Unordnung bringen; **2.** → ***disconcert*** 1; ˌ**dis·com'pos·ed·ly** [-zɪdlɪ] *adj.* verwirrt; ˌ**dis·com'po·sure** [-əʊʒə] *s.* Verwirrung *f*, Fassungslosigkeit *f*.

dis·con·cert [ˌdɪskən'sɜːt] *v/t.* **1.** aus der Fassung bringen, verwirren; **2.** beunruhigen; **3.** durchein'anderbringen; ˌ**dis·con'cert·ed** [-tɪd] *adj.* verwirrt; beunruhigt; ˌ**dis·con'cert·ing** [-tɪŋ] *adj.* beunruhigend, peinlich.

dis·con·nect [ˌdɪskə'nekt] *v/t.* **1.** trennen (***with***, ***from*** von); **2.** ⚙ auskuppeln, *Kupplung* ausrücken; **3.** ⚡ trennen; *Gerät* ausstecken; **4.** *Gas, Strom, Telefon* abstellen; *Telefongespräch* unter'brechen, *Teilnehmer* trennen; ˌ**dis·con'nect·ed** [-tɪd] *adj.* □ **1.** getrennt, losgelöst; **2.** zs.-hanglos; ˌ**dis·con·'nect·ing** [-tɪŋ] *adj.* ⚡ Trenn…, Ausschalt…; ˌ**dis·con'nec·tion** [-kʃn] *s.* **1.** Trennung *f* (*a.* ⚡); **2.** ⚙ Abstellung *f*; *teleph.* Unter'brechung *f*.

dis·con·so·late [dɪs'kɒnsələt] *adj.* □ untröstlich; trostlos (*a. fig.*).

dis·con·tent [ˌdɪskən'tent] *s.* **1.** Unzufriedenheit *f* (***at***, ***with*** mit); **2.** Unzufriedene(r *m*) *f*; ˌ**dis·con'tent·ed** [-tɪd] *adj.* □ unzufrieden (***with*** mit); ˌ**dis·con'tent·ment** [-mənt] → ***discontent*** 1.

dis·con·tin·u·ance [ˌdɪskən'tɪnjʊəns], ˌ**dis·con·tin·u'a·tion** [-njʊ'eɪʃn] *s.* **1.** Unter'brechung *f*; **2.** Einstellung *f* (*a.* ⚖ *des Verfahrens*); **3.** Aufgeben *n*; **dis·con·tin·ue** [ˌdɪskən'tɪnjuː] **I** *v/t.* **1.** unter'brechen, aussetzen; **2.** einstellen (*a.* ⚖), aufgeben; **3.** *Zeitung* abbestellen; **4.** aufhören (***doing*** zu tun); **II** *v/i.* **5.** aufhören; ˌ**dis·con·ti'nu·i·ty** [-tɪ'njuːətɪ] *s.* Diskontinui'tät *f*, Zs.-hanglosigkeit *f*; ˌ**dis·con'tin·u·ous** [-jʊəs] *adj.* □ **1.** diskontinuierlich, unter'brochen, 'unzuˌsammenhängend; **2.** sprunghaft.

dis·cord ['dɪskɔːd] *s.* **1.** Uneinigkeit *f*, Zwietracht *f*, Streit *m*; → ***apple***; **2.** ♪ Disso'nanz *f*, 'Mißklang *m*; **3.** Lärm *m*; **dis·cord·ance** [dɪ'skɔːdəns] *s.* **1.** Uneinigkeit *f*; **2.** 'Mißklang *m*, Disso'nanz *f*; **dis·cord·ant** [dɪ'skɔːdənt] *adj.* □ **1.** uneinig, sich wider'sprechend; **2.** 'unharˌmonisch; **3.** ♪ disso'nantisch, 'mißtönend.

dis·co·theque ['dɪskəʊtek] *s.* Disko'thek *f*.

dis·count ['dɪskaʊnt] **I** *s.* **1.** ✝ Preisnachlaß *m*, Abschlag *m*, Ra'batt *m*, Skonto *m*, *n*: ***allow a ~*** (e-n) Rabatt gewähren; **2.** ✝ a) Dis'kont *m*, Wechselzins *m*, b) → ***discount rate***; **3.** ✝ Abzug *m* (*vom Nominalwert*): ***at a ~*** a) unter Pari, b) *fig.* unbeliebt, nicht geschätzt *od.* gefragt; ***sell at a ~*** mit Verlust verkaufen; **4.** *fig.* Abzug *m*, Vorbehalt *m*, Abstriche *pl.*; **II** *v/t.* [*a.* dɪ'skaʊnt] **5.** ✝ e-n Abzug gewähren auf (*acc.*); **6.** *Wechsel* diskontieren; **7.** im Wert vermindern, beeinträchtigen; **8.** unberücksichtigt lassen; **9.** mit Vorsicht aufnehmen, nur teilweise glauben; **dis·count·a·ble** [dɪ'skaʊntəbl] *adj.* ✝ diskontierbar, dis'kontfähig.

dis·count| bank *s.* ✝ Dis'kontbank *f*; **~ bill** *s.* Dis'kontwechsel *m*; **~ bro·ker** *s.* ✝ Dis'kont-, Wechselmakler *m*.

dis·coun·te·nance [dɪ'skaʊntɪnəns] *v/t.* **1.** → ***discomfit*** 1; **2.** (offen) miß'billigen, ablehnen.

dis·count| house *s.* ✝ **1.** *Am.* Dis'count-, Dis'kontgeschäft *n*; **2.** *Brit.* Dis'kontbank *f*; **~ rate** *s.* ✝ Dis'kontsatz *m*; **~ shop**, **~ store** → ***discount house*** 1.

dis·cour·age [dɪ'skʌrɪdʒ] *v/t.* **1.** entmutigen; **2.** abschrecken, abhalten, *j-m* abraten (***from*** von; ***from doing*** *et.* zu tun); **3.** hemmen, beeinträchtigen; **4.** miß'billigen; **dis·cour·age·ment** [dɪ'skʌrɪdʒmənt] *s.* **1.** Entmutigung *f*; **2.** a) Abschreckung *f*, b) Abschreckungsmittel *n*; **3.** Hemmung *f*, Hindernis *n*, Schwierigkeit *f* (***to*** für); **dis·cour·ag·ing** [dɪ'skʌrɪdʒɪŋ] *adj.* □ entmutigend.

dis·course I *s.* ['dɪskɔːs] **1.** Unter'haltung *f*, Gespräch *n*; **2.** Abhandlung *f*, *bsd.* Vortrag *m*, Dis'kurs *m*, Predigt *f*; Abhandlung *f*; **II** *v/i.* [dɪ'skɔːs] **3.** e-n Vortrag halten (***on*** über *acc.*), *mst. fig.* predigen *od.* dozieren (***on*** über *acc.*); **4.** sich unter'halten (***on*** über *acc.*).

dis·cour·te·ous [dɪs'kɜːtjəs] *adj.* □ unhöflich; **dis'cour·te·sy** [-tɪsɪ] *s.* Unhöflichkeit *f*.

dis·cov·er [dɪ'skʌvə] *v/t.* **1.** *Land etc.* entdecken; **2.** entdecken, ausfindig machen, erspähen; **3.** entdecken, (her'aus)finden, (plötzlich) erkennen; **4.** aufdecken, enthüllen; **dis·cov·er·a·ble** [dɪ'skʌvərəbl] *adj.* **1.** zu entdekken(d); **2.** wahrnehmbar; **3.** feststellbar; **dis·cov·er·er** [dɪ'skʌvərə] *s.* Entdecker(in); **dis·cov·er·y** [dɪ'skʌvərɪ] *s.* **1.** Entdeckung *f* (*a. fig.*); **2.** Fund *m*; **3.** Feststellung *f*; **4.** Enthüllung *f*; **5.** ***~ of documents*** ⚖ Offenlegung *f* prozeßwichtiger Urkunden.

dis·cred·it [dɪs'kredɪt] **I** *v/t.* **1.** in Verruf *od.* 'Mißkreˌdit bringen (***with*** bei); ein schlechtes Licht werfen auf (*acc.*), diskreditieren; **2.** anzweifeln; keinen Glauben schenken (*dat.*); **II** *s.* **3.** schlechter Ruf, 'Mißkreˌdit *m*, Schande *f*: ***bring s.o. into ~***, ***bring ~ on s.o.*** → 1; **4.** Zweifel *m*: ***throw ~ on*** *et.* zweifelhaft erscheinen lassen; **dis'cred·it·a·ble** [-təbl] *adj.* □ schändlich; **dis·'cred·it·ed** [-tɪd] *adj.* **1.** verrufen, diskreditiert; **2.** unglaubwürdig.

dis·creet [dɪ'skriːt] *adj.* □ **1.** 'um-, vorsichtig, besonnen, verständig; **2.** dis'kret, taktvoll, verschwiegen.

dis·crep·an·cy [dɪ'skrepənsɪ] *s.* **1.** Diskre'panz *f*, Unstimmigkeit *f*, Verschiedenheit *f*; **2.** 'Widerspruch *m*, Zwiespalt *m*.

dis·crete [dɪ'skriːt] *adj.* □ **1.** getrennt, einzeln; **2.** unstet, unbeständig; **3.** 𝔄 unstetig, dis'kret.

dis·cre·tion [dɪ'skreʃn] *s.* **1.** 'Um-, Vorsicht *f*, Besonnenheit *f*, Klugheit *f*: ***act with ~*** vorsichtig handeln; **2.** Verfügungsfreiheit *f*, Machtbefugnis *f*: ***age*** (*od.* ***years***) ***of ~*** Alter *n* der freien Willensbestimmung, Strafmündigkeit *f* (*14 Jahre*); **3.** Gutdünken *n*, Belieben *n*; (⚖ freies) Ermessen: ***at*** (***your***) ***~*** nach (Ihrem) Belieben; ***it is within your ~*** es steht Ihnen frei; ***use your own ~*** handle nach eigenem Gutdünken *od.* Ermessen; ***surrender at ~*** bedingungslos kapitulieren; **4.** Diskreti'on *f*: a) Takt (-gefühl *n*) *m*, b) Zu'rückhaltung *f*, c) Verschwiegenheit *f*; **5.** Nachsicht *f*: ***ask for ~***; **dis·cre·tion·ar·y** [dɪ'skreʃnərɪ] *adj.* □ dem eigenen Gutdünken über'lassen, ins freie Ermessen gestellt, wahlfrei: ***~ clause*** ⚖ Kannvorschrift *f*; ***~ income*** frei verfügbares Einkommen; ***~ powers*** unumschränkte Vollmacht, Handlungsfreiheit *f*.

dis·crim·i·nate [dɪ'skrɪmɪneɪt] **I** *v/i.* (scharf) unter'scheiden, e-n 'Unterschied machen: ***~ between*** unterschiedlich behandeln (*acc.*); ***~ against s.o.*** j-n benachteiligen *od.* diskriminieren; ***~ in favo(u)r of s.o.*** j-n begünstigen *od.* bevorzugen; **II** *v/t.* (scharf) unter'scheiden; abheben, absondern (***from*** von); **dis·crim·i·nat·ing** [dɪ'skrɪmɪneɪtɪŋ] *adj.* □ **1.** unter'scheidend, charakte'ristisch; **2.** scharfsinnig, klug, urteilsfähig; anspruchsvoll; **3.** diskriminierend, benachteiligend; **4.** ✝ Differential…, Sonder…: ***~ duty*** Differentialzoll *m*; **5.** ⚡ Rückstrom…; Selektiv…; **dis·crim·i·na·tion** [dɪˌskrɪmɪ'neɪʃn] *s.* **1.** 'unterschiedliche Behandlung, Diskriminierung *f*: ***~ against*** (***in favo[u]r of***) ***s.o.*** Benachteiligung *f* (Begünstigung *f*) e-r Person; **2.** Scharfblick *m*, Urteilsfähigkeit *f*, Unter'scheidungsvermögen *n*; **dis·crim·i·na·tive** [dɪ'skrɪmɪnətɪv] *adj.* □, **dis·crim·i·na·to·ry** [dɪ'skrɪmɪnətərɪ] *adj.* **1.** charakte'ristisch, unter'scheidend; **2.** 'unterschiedlich (behandelnd); Sonder…, Ausnahme…

dis·cur·sive [dɪ'skɜːsɪv] *adj.* □ **1.** abschweifend, unbeständig; sprunghaft; **2.** weitschweifig, allgemein gehalten; **3.** *phls.* folgernd, diskur'siv.

dis·cus ['dɪskəs] *s. sport* Diskus *m*: ***~ throw*** Diskuswerfen *n*; ***~ thrower*** Diskuswerfer *m*.

dis·cuss [dɪ'skʌs] *v/t.* **1.** diskutieren, besprechen, erörtern; **2.** sprechen *od.* reden über (*acc.*); **3.** F sich *e-e Flasche Wein etc.* zu Gemüte führen; **dis·cus·sion** [dɪ'skʌʃn] *s.* **1.** Diskussi'on *f*, Erörterung *f*, Besprechung *f*: ***be under ~*** zur Debatte stehen, erörtert werden; ***matter for ~*** Diskussionsthema *n*; ***~ group*** Diskussionsgruppe *f*; **2.** Behandlung *f* (*e-s Themas*).

dis·dain [dɪs'deɪn] **I** *v/t.* **1.** verachten; *a. Essen etc.* verschmähen; **2.** es für unter s-r Würde halten (***doing***, ***to do*** zu tun); **II** *s.* **3.** Verachtung *f*, Geringschätzung *f*; **4.** Hochmut *m*; **dis'dain·ful** [-fʊl] *adj.* □ **1.** verachtungsvoll, geringschätzig: ***be ~ of s.th.*** *et.* verachten; **2.** hochmütig.

dis·ease [dɪ'ziːz] *s.* ⚕, *biol. u. fig.* Krankheit *f*, Leiden *n*; **dis·eased** [dɪ'ziːzd] *adj.* **1.** krank, erkrankt; **2.** krankhaft.

dis·em·bark [ˌdɪsɪmˈbɑːk] **I** *v/t.* ausschiffen; **II** *v/i.* sich ausschiffen, von Bord *od.* an Land gehen; **dis·em·bar·ka·tion** [ˌdɪsembɑːˈkeɪʃn] *s.* Ausschiffung *f.*

dis·em·bar·rass [ˌdɪsɪmˈbærəs] *v/t.* **1.** *j-m* aus e-r Verlegenheit helfen; **2.** (***o.s.*** sich) befreien (***of*** von).

dis·em·bod·i·ment [ˌdɪsɪmˈbɒdɪmənt] *s.* **1.** Entkörperlichung *f*; **2.** Befreiung *f* von der körperlichen Hülle; **dis·em·bod·y** [ˌdɪsɪmˈbɒdɪ] *v/t.* **1.** entkörperlichen: ***disembodied voice*** geisterhafte Stimme; **2.** *Seele* von der körperlichen Hülle befreien.

dis·em·bow·el [ˌdɪsɪmˈbaʊəl] *v/t.* **1.** ausnehmen, *erlegtes Wild a.* ausweiden; **2.** *j-m* den Bauch aufschlitzen.

dis·en·chant [ˌdɪsɪnˈtʃɑːnt] *v/t.* desillusionieren, ernüchtern: ***be ~ed with*** sich keinen Illusionen mehr hingeben über (*acc.*), enttäuscht sein von; **ˌdis·enˈchant·ment** [-mənt] *s.* Ernüchterung *f*, Enttäuschung *f.*

dis·en·cum·ber [ˌdɪsɪnˈkʌmbə] *v/t.* **1.** befreien (***of*** von *e-r Last etc.*) (*a. fig.*); **2.** ⚖ entschulden; *Grundstück etc.* hypoˈthekenfrei machen.

dis·en·fran·chise [ˌdɪsɪnˈfræntʃaɪz] → ***disfranchise.***

dis·en·gage [ˌdɪsɪnˈgeɪdʒ] **I** *v/t.* **1.** los-, freimachen, (los)lösen, befreien (***from*** von); **2.** befreien, entbinden (***from*** von); **3.** ⚙ loskuppeln, ausrücken, ausschalten: ***~ the clutch*** auskuppeln; **4.** ⚗ abscheiden, entbinden; **II** *v/i.* **5.** sich freimachen, loskommen (***from*** von); **6.** ⚔ sich absetzen (*vom Feind*); **ˌdis·enˈgaged** [-dʒd] *adj.* frei, nicht besetzt; abkömmlich; **ˌdis·enˈgage·ment** [-mənt] *s.* **1.** Befreiung *f*; Loslösung *f* (*a.* ⚔), Entbindung *f* (*a.* ⚗); **2.** ⚔ Absetzen *n*; *pol.* Disenˈgagement *n*; **ˌdis·enˈgag·ing** [-dʒɪŋ] *adj.*: ⚙ ***~ gear*** Ausrück-, Auskuppelungsvorrichtung *f*; ***~ lever*** Ausrückhebel *m.*

dis·en·tan·gle [ˌdɪsɪnˈtæŋgl] **I** *v/t.* entwirren (*a. fig.*), lösen; *fig.* befreien; **II** *v/i.* sich loslösen; *fig.* sich befreien; **ˌdis·enˈtan·gle·ment** [-mənt] *s.* Loslösung *f*; Entwirrung *f*; Befreiung *f.*

dis·en·ti·tle [ˌdɪsɪnˈtaɪtl] *v/t.* *j-m* e-n Rechtsanspruch nehmen: ***be ~d to*** keinen Anspruch haben auf (*acc.*).

dis·e·qui·lib·ri·um [ˌdɪsekwɪˈlɪbrɪəm] *s. bsd. fig.* gestörtes Gleichgewicht, Ungleichgewicht *n.*

dis·es·tab·lish [ˌdɪsɪˈstæblɪʃ] *v/t.* **1.** abschaffen; **2.** *Kirche* vom Staat trennen; **dis·es·tab·lish·ment** [ˌdɪsɪˈstæblɪʃmənt] *s.*: ***~ of the Church*** Trennung *f* von Kirche u. Staat.

dis·fa·vo(u)r [ˌdɪsˈfeɪvə] **I** *s.* ˈMißbilligung *f*, -fallen *n*; Ungnade *f*: ***regard with ~*** mit Mißfallen betrachten; ***be in*** (***fall into***) ***~*** in Ungnade gefallen sein (fallen); **II** *v/t.* ungnädig behandeln; ablehnen.

dis·fig·ure [dɪsˈfɪgə] *v/t.* **1.** entstellen, verunstalten; **2.** beeinträchtigen; Abbruch tun (*dat.*); **disˈfig·ure·ment** [-mənt] *s.* Entstellung *f*, Verunstaltung *f.*

dis·fran·chise [ˌdɪsˈfræntʃaɪz] *v/t.* *j-m* die Bürgerrechte *od.* das Wahlrecht entziehen; **ˌdisˈfran·chise·ment** [-tʃɪzmənt] *s.* Entziehung *f* der Bürgerrechte *etc.*

dis·gorge [dɪsˈgɔːdʒ] **I** *v/t.* **1.** ausspeien, -werfen, -stoßen, ergießen; **2.** *widerwillig* wieder herˈausgeben; **II** *v/i.* **3.** sich ergießen, sich entladen.

dis·grace [dɪsˈgreɪs] **I** *s.* **1.** Schande *f*, Schmach *f*: ***bring ~ on s.o.*** → 4; **2.** Schande *f*, Schandfleck *m* (***to*** für): ***he is a ~ to the party***; **3.** Ungnade *f*: ***be in ~ with*** in Ungnade gefallen sein bei; **II** *v/t.* **4.** Schande bringen über (*acc.*), *j-m* Schande bereiten; **5.** *j-m* s-e Gunst entziehen; mit Schimpf entlassen: ***be ~d*** in Ungnade fallen; **6.** ***~ o.s.*** a) sich blamieren, b) sich schändlich benehmen; **disˈgrace·ful** [-fʊl] *adj.* ☐ schändlich, schimpflich, schmachvoll.

dis·grun·tle [dɪsˈgrʌntl] *v/t. Am.* verärgern, verstimmen; **disˈgrun·tled** [-ld] *adj.* verärgert, verstimmt (***at*** über *acc.*), unwirsch.

dis·guise [dɪsˈgaɪz] **I** *v/t.* **1.** verkleiden, maskieren; tarnen; **2.** *Handschrift, Stimme* verstellen; **3.** *Gefühle, Wahrheit* verhüllen, verbergen, verhehlen; tarnen; **II** *s.* **4.** Verkleidung *f*, *a. fig.* Maske *f*, Tarnung *f*: ***in ~*** maskiert, verkleidet, *fig.* verkappt; → ***blessing***; **5.** Verstellung *f*; **6.** Vorwand *m*, Schein *m*; **disˈguised** [-zd] *adj.* verkleidet, maskiert *etc.*; *fig.* verkappt.

dis·gust [dɪsˈgʌst] **I** *s.* **1.** (***at***, ***for***) Ekel *m* (vor *dat.*), ˈWiderwille *m* (gegen): ***in ~*** mit Abscheu; **II** *v/t.* **2.** anekeln, anwidern; **3.** entrüsten, verärgern, empören; **disˈgust·ed** [-tɪd] *adj.* ☐ (***with***, ***at***) **1.** angeekelt, angewidert (von): ***~ with life*** lebensüberdrüssig; **2.** emˈpört, entrüstet (über *acc.*); **disˈgust·ing** [-tɪŋ] *adj.* ☐ **1.** ekelhaft, widerlich, abˈscheulich; **2.** F schrecklich.

dish [dɪʃ] **I** *s.* **1.** Schüssel *f*, Platte *f*, Teller *m*; **2.** Gericht *n*, Speise *f*: ***cold ~es*** kalte Speisen; **3.** *pl.* Geschirr *n*: ***~-cloth*** Spül-, *Brit.* Geschirrtuch *n*; → ***wash*** 16; **4.** F a) ‚dufte Puppe', b) ‚dufter Typ', c) ‚prima Sache'; **II** *v/t.* **5.** *mst* ***~ up*** *Speisen* anrichten, auftragen; **6.** ***~ up*** *fig.* auftischen; **7.** ***~ out*** a) austeilen, b) *sl.* auftischen, von sich geben; **8.** *sl.* ‚anschmieren', herˈeinlegen; **9.** *sl.* a) *j-n* ‚erledigen', ‚fertigmachen', b) *et.* restlos vermasseln; **10.** ⚙ *schüsselartig* wölben; vertiefen.

dis·ha·bille [ˌdɪsæˈbiːl] *s.* Negliˈgé *n*, Morgenrock *m*: ***in ~*** im Neglige.

dis·har·mo·ni·ous [ˌdɪshɑːˈməʊnjəs] *adj.* ☐ disharˈmonisch; **dis·har·mo·ny** [ˌdɪsˈhɑːmənɪ] *s.* Disharmoˈnie *f*, ˈMißklang *m.*

dis·heart·en [dɪsˈhɑːtn] *v/t.* entmutigen, deprimieren; **disˈheart·en·ing** [-nɪŋ] *adj.* ☐ entmutigend, bedrückend.

dished [dɪʃt] *adj.* **1.** konˈkav gewölbt; ⚙ gestürzt (*Räder*); **2.** F ‚erledigt', ‚kaˈputt'.

di·shev·el(l)ed [dɪˈʃevld] *adj.* **1.** zerzaust, wirr, aufgelöst (*Haar*); **2.** unordentlich, ungepflegt, schlampig.

dis·hon·est [dɪsˈɒnɪst] *adj.* ☐ unehrlich, unredlich; unlauter, betrügerisch; **disˈhon·es·ty** [-tɪ] *s.* Unehrlichkeit *f*, Unredlichkeit *f.*

dis·hon·o(u)r [dɪsˈɒnə] **I** *s.* **1.** Unehre *f*, Schmach *f*, Schande *f* (***to*** für); **2.** Beschimpfung *f*; **II** *v/t.* **3.** entehren (*a. Frau*); Schande bringen über (*acc.*); **4.** schimpflich behandeln; **5.** *sein Wort* nicht einlösen; **6.** ✝ *Scheck etc.* nicht honorieren, nicht einlösen; **disˈhon·o(u)r·a·ble** [-nərəbl] *adj.* ☐ **1.** schimpflich, unehrenhaft: ***~ discharge*** ⚔ unehrenhafte Entlassung; **2.** ehrlos; **disˈhon·o(u)r·a·ble·ness** [-nərəblnɪs] *s.* **1.** Schändlichkeit *f*, Gemeinheit *f*; **2.** Ehrlosigkeit *f.*

dish| rack *s.* Geschirrständer *m*; **~ tow·el** *s.* Geschirrtuch *n*; **ˈ~ˌwash·er** *s.* **1.** Tellerwäscher(in); **2.** Geˈschirrˌspülmaˌschine *f*; **ˈ~ˌwa·ter** *s.* Spülwasser *n.*

dish·y [ˈdɪʃɪ] *adj. sl.* schick, ‚toll': ***~ girl.***

dis·il·lu·sion [ˌdɪsɪˈluːʒn] **I** *s.* Ernüchterung *f*, Enttäuschung *f*; **II** *v/t.* ernüchtern, desillusionieren, von Illusiˈonen befreien; **ˌdis·ilˈlu·sion·ment** [-mənt] → ***disillusion*** I.

dis·in·cen·tive [ˌdɪsɪnˈsentɪv] **I** *s.* **1.** Abschreckungsmittel *n*: ***be a ~ to*** abschreckend wirken auf (*acc.*); **2.** ✝ leistungshemmender Faktor; **II** *adj.* **3.** abschreckend; **4.** ✝ leistungshemmend.

dis·in·cli·na·tion [ˌdɪsɪnklɪˈneɪʃn] *s.* Abneigung *f* (***for***, ***to*** gegen): ***~ to buy*** Kaufunlust *f*; **dis·in·cline** [ˌdɪsɪnˈklaɪn] *v/t.* abgeneigt machen; **ˌdis·inˈclined** [-ˈklaɪnd] *adj.* abgeneigt (***to*** *dat.*, ***to do*** zu tun).

dis·in·fect [ˌdɪsɪnˈfekt] *v/t.* desinfizieren, keimfrei machen; **ˌdis·inˈfect·ant** [-tənt] **I** *s.* Desinfektiˈonsmittel *n*; **II** *adj.* desinfizierend, keimtötend; **ˌdis·inˈfec·tion** [-kʃən] *s.* Desinfektiˈon *f*; **ˌdis·inˈfec·tor** [-tə] *s.* Desinfektiˈonsgerät *n.*

dis·in·fest [ˌdɪsɪnˈfest] *v/t.* von Ungeziefer *etc.* befreien, entwesen, entlausen.

dis·in·fla·tion [ˌdɪsɪnˈfleɪʃn] → ***deflation*** 2.

dis·in·gen·u·ous [ˌdɪsɪnˈdʒenjʊəs] *adj.* ☐ **1.** unaufrichtig; **2.** ˈhinterhältig, arglistig; **ˌdis·inˈgen·u·ous·ness** [-nɪs] *s.* **1.** Unredlichkeit *f*, Unaufrichtigkeit *f*; **2.** ˈHinterhältigkeit *f.*

dis·in·her·it [ˌdɪsɪnˈherɪt] *v/t.* enterben; **ˌdis·inˈher·it·ance** [-təns] *s.* Enterbung *f.*

dis·in·hi·bi·tion [ˌdɪsɪnhɪˈbɪʃn] *s. psych.* Enthemmung *f.*

dis·in·te·grate [dɪsˈɪntɪgreɪt] **I** *v/t.* **1.** (*a. phys.*) (in s-e Bestandteile) auflösen, aufspalten, zerkleinern; **2.** *fig.* auflösen, zersetzen, zerrütten; **II** *v/i.* **3.** sich (in s-e Bestandteile, *fig. a.* in nichts) auflösen, sich aufspalten, sich zersetzen; **4.** ver-, zerfallen (*a. fig.*); **dis·in·te·gra·tion** [dɪsˌɪntɪˈgreɪʃn] *s.* **1.** (*a. phys.*) Auflösung *f*, Aufspaltung *f*, Zerstückelung *f*, Zertrümmerung *f*, Zersetzung *f*; **2.** Zerfall *m* (*a. fig.*); **3.** *geol.* Verwitterung *f.*

dis·in·ter [ˌdɪsɪnˈtɜː] *v/t.* *Leiche* exhumieren, ausgraben (*a. fig.*).

dis·in·ter·est·ed [dɪsˈɪntrəstɪd] *adj.* ☐ **1.** uneigennützig, selbstlos; **2.** objekˈtiv, unvoreingenommen; **3.** unbeteiligt; **disˈin·ter·est·ed·ness** [-nɪs] *s.* **1.** Uneigennützigkeit *f*; **2.** Objektiviˈtät *f.*

dis·in·ter·ment [ˌdɪsɪnˈtɜːmənt] *s.* **1.** Exhumierung *f*; **2.** Ausgrabung *f* (*a. fig.*).

dis·joint [dɪsˈdʒɔɪnt] *v/t.* **1.** auseinˈandernehmen, zerlegen, zerstückeln; **2.** ⚕ ver-, ausrenken; **3.** (ab)trennen; **4.** *fig.* in Unordnung *od.* aus den Fugen bringen; **disˈjoint·ed** [-tɪd] *adj.* ☐ *fig.* zu-

'sammenhanglos, wirr.

dis·junc·tion [dɪs'dʒʌŋkʃn] *s.* Trennung *f*; **dis'junc·tive** [-ktɪv] *adj.* □ **1.** (ab-)trennend, ausschließend; **2.** *ling.*, *phls.* disjunk'tiv.

disk [dɪsk] *s.* **1.** *allg.* Scheibe *f*; **2.** ⚙ Scheibe *f*, La'melle *f*; Si'gnalscheibe *f*; **3.** ⚘, *anat.*, *zo.* Scheibe *f*, *anat. a.* Bandscheibe *f*: ***slipped ~*** Bandscheibenvorfall *m*; **4.** *teleph.* Wählscheibe *f*; **5.** *sport* a) Diskus *m*, b) *Eishockey*: Scheibe *f*, Puck *m*; **6.** (Schall)Platte *f*; **7.** *Computer*: Platte *f*; **~ brake** *s.* ⚙ Scheibenbremse *f*; **~ clutch** *s. mot.* Scheibenkupplung *f*; **~ jock·ey** *s.* Diskjockey *m*; **~ pack** *s. Computer*: Plattenstapel *m*; **~ valve** *s.* ⚙ 'Tellerven,til *n*.

dis·like [dɪs'laɪk] **I** *v/t.* nicht leiden können, nicht mögen; *et.* nicht gern *od.* (nur) ungern tun: ***make o.s. ~d*** sich unbeliebt machen; **II** *s.* Abneigung *f*, 'Widerwille *m* (***to***, ***of***, ***for*** gegen): ***take a ~ to*** e-e Abneigung fassen gegen.

dis·lo·cate ['dɪsləʊkeɪt] *v/t.* **1.** verrücken; *a. Industrie*, *Truppen etc.* verlagern; **2.** ⚕ ver-, ausrenken: ***~ one's arm*** sich den Arm verrenken; **3.** *fig.* erschüttern; **4.** *geol.* verwerfen; **dis·lo·ca·tion** [,dɪsləʊ'keɪʃn] *s.* **1.** Verrückung *f*; Verlagerung *f* (*a.* ⚔); **2.** ⚕ Verrenkung *f*; **3.** *fig.* Erschütterung *f*; **4.** *geol.* Verwerfung *f*.

dis·lodge [dɪs'lɒdʒ] *v/t.* **1.** entfernen, her'ausnehmen, losreißen; **2.** vertreiben, verjagen, verdrängen; **3.** ⚔ *Feind* aus der Stellung werfen; **4.** ausquartieren.

dis·loy·al [,dɪs'lɔɪəl] *adj.* □ untreu, treulos, verräterisch; ,**dis'loy·al·ty** [-tɪ] *s.* Untreue *f*, Treulosigkeit *f*.

dis·mal ['dɪzməl] **I** *adj.* □ **1.** düster, trübe, bedrückend, trostlos; **2.** furchtbar, gräßlich; **II** *s.* **3.** ***the ~s*** der Trübsinn: ***be in the ~s*** Trübsinn blasen; '**dis·mal·ly** [-məlɪ] *adv.* **1.** düster *etc.*; **2.** schmählich.

dis·man·tle [dɪs'mæntl] *v/t.* **1.** ab-, demontieren; *Bau* abbrechen, niederreißen; **2.** ausein'andernehmen, zerlegen; **3.** ⚓ a) abtakeln, b) abwracken; **4.** *Festung* schleifen; **5.** *Haus* (aus)räumen; **6.** unbrauchbar machen; **dis'man·tle·ment** [-mənt] *s.* **1.** Abbruch *m*, Demon'tage *f*; Zerlegung *f*; **2.** ⚓ Abtakelung *f*; **3.** ⚔ Schleifung *f*.

dis·may [dɪs'meɪ] **I** *v/t.* erschrecken, in Schrecken versetzen, bestürzen, entsetzen: ***not ~ed*** unbeirrt; **II** *s.* Schreck(en) *m*, Entsetzen *n*, Bestürzung *f*.

dis·mem·ber [dɪs'membə] *v/t.* zergliedern, zerstückeln, verstümmeln (*a. fig.*); **dis'mem·ber·ment** [-mənt] *s.* Zerstückelung *f etc.*

dis·miss [dɪs'mɪs] *v/t.* **1.** entlassen, gehen lassen, verabschieden: ***~!*** ⚔ weg(ge)treten!; **2.** entlassen (***from*** aus *dem Dienst*), absetzen, abbauen; wegschicken: ***be ~ed from the service*** ⚔ aus dem Heere *etc.* entlassen *od.* ausgestoßen werden; **3.** *Thema etc.* fallenlassen, aufgeben, hin'weggehen über (*acc.*), *Vorschlag* ab-, zu'rückweisen, *Gedanken* verbannen, von sich weisen; ⚖ *Klage* abweisen: ***~ from one's mind*** *et.* aus s-n Gedanken verbannen; ***~ as ... als ...*** abtun, kurzerhand als ... betrachten; **dis'miss·al** [-sl] *s.* **1.** Entlassung *f* (***from*** aus); **2.** Aufgabe *f*, Abtun *n*; **3.** ⚖ Abweisung *f*.

dis·mount [,dɪs'maʊnt] **I** *v/i.* **1.** absteigen, absitzen (***from*** von); **II** *v/t.* **2.** aus dem Sattel heben; abwerfen (*Pferd*); **3.** (ab)steigen von; **4.** abmontieren, ausbauen, ausein'andernehmen.

dis·o·be·di·ence [,dɪsə'bi:djəns] *s.* **1.** Ungehorsam *m* (***to*** gegen), Gehorsamsverweigerung *f*: ***civil ~*** *pol.* ziviler *od.* bürgerlicher Ungehorsam; **2.** Nichtbefolgung *f*; ,**dis·o'be·di·ent** [-nt] *adj.* □ ungehorsam (***to*** gegen); **dis·o·bey** [,dɪsə'beɪ] *v/t.* **1.** *j-m* nicht gehorchen, ungehorsam sein gegen *j-n*; **2.** *Gesetz etc.* nicht befolgen, miß'achten, *Befehl a.* verweigern: ***I will not be ~ed*** ich dulde keinen Ungehorsam.

dis·o·blige [,dɪsə'blaɪdʒ] *v/t.* **1.** ungefällig sein gegen *j-n*; **2.** *j-n* kränken; ,**dis·o'blig·ing** [-dʒɪŋ] *adj.* □ ungefällig, unfreundlich.

dis·or·der [dɪs'ɔ:də] **I** *s.* **1.** Unordnung *f*, Verwirrung *f*; **2.** (Ruhe)Störung *f*; Aufruhr *m*, Unruhe(n *pl.*) *f*; **3.** ungebührliches Betragen; **4.** ⚕ Störung *f*, Erkrankung *f*: ***mental ~*** Geistesstörung; **II** *v/t.* **5.** in Unordnung bringen, durchein'anderbringen, stören; **6.** *den Magen* verderben; **dis'or·dered** [-əd] *adj.* **1.** in Unordnung, durchein'ander (*beide a. fig.*); **2.** gestört, (*a.* geistes)krank: ***my stomach is ~*** ich habe mir den Magen verdorben; **dis'or·der·li·ness** [-lɪnɪs] *s.* **1.** Unordentlichkeit *f*; **2.** Schlampigkeit *f*; **3.** Unbotmäßigkeit *f*; **4.** Liederlichkeit *f*; **dis'or·der·ly** [-lɪ] *adj.* **1.** unordentlich, schlampig; **2.** ordnungs-, gesetzwidrig, aufrührerisch; **3.** Ärgernis erregend: ***~ conduct*** ⚖ ordnungswidriges Verhalten, grober Unfug; ***~ house*** *mst* Bordell *n*, *a.* Spielhölle *f*; ***~ person*** Ruhestörer *m*.

dis·or·gan·i·za·tion [dɪs,ɔ:gənaɪ'zeɪʃn] *s.* Desorganisati'on *f*, Auflösung *f*, Zerrüttung *f*, Unordnung *f*; **dis·or·gan·ize** [dɪs'ɔ:gənaɪz] *v/t.* auflösen, zerrütten, in Unordnung bringen, desorganisieren; **dis·or·gan·ized** [dɪs'ɔ:gənaɪzd] *adj.* in Unordnung, desorganisiert.

dis·o·ri·ent [dɪs'ɔ:rɪent] *v/t. a. psych.* desorientieren: ***~ed*** desorientiert, *psych. a.* ‚gestört', la'bil; **dis'o·ri·en·tate** [-teɪt] → ***disorient***.

dis·own [dɪs'əʊn] *v/t.* **1.** nicht (als sein eigen *od.* als gültig) anerkennen, nichts zu tun haben wollen mit; **2.** ableugnen; **3.** *Kind* verstoßen.

dis·par·age [dɪ'spærɪdʒ] *v/t.* **1.** in Verruf bringen; **2.** her'absetzen, verächtlich machen; **3.** verachten; **dis·par·age·ment** [dɪ'spærɪdʒmənt] *s.* Her'absetzung *f*, Verächtlichmachung *f*: ***no ~*** (***intended***) ohne Ihnen nahetreten zu wollen; **dis·par·ag·ing** [dɪ'spærɪdʒɪŋ] *adj.* □ gering-, abschätzig, verächtlich.

dis·pa·rate ['dɪspərət] **I** *adj.* □ ungleich(artig), (grund)verschieden, unvereinbar, dispa'rat; **II** *s. pl.* unvereinbare Dinge *pl.*; **dis·par·i·ty** [dɪ'spærətɪ] *s.* Verschiedenheit *f*: ***~ in age*** (*zu großer*) Altersunterschied *m*.

dis·pas·sion·ate [dɪ'spæʃnət] *adj.* □ leidenschaftslos, ruhig, gelassen, sachlich, nüchtern.

dis·patch [dɪ'spætʃ] **I** *v/t.* **1.** *j-n od. et.* (ab)senden, (ab)schicken, versenden, befördern, *Telegramm* aufgeben; **2.** abfertigen (*a.* 🚂); **3.** rasch *od.* prompt erledigen *od.* ausführen; **4.** ins Jenseits befördern, töten; **5.** F ‚wegputzen', rasch aufessen; **II** *s.* **6.** Absendung *f*, Versand *m*, Abfertigung *f*, Beförderung *f*; **7.** rasche Erledigung; **8.** Eile *f*, Schnelligkeit *f*: ***with ~*** eilends, prompt; **9.** (*oft* verschlüsselte) (Eil)Botschaft; **10.** Bericht *m* (*e-s Korrespondenten*); **11.** *pl.* Kriegsberichte *pl.*: ***mentioned in ~es*** ⚔ im Kriegsbericht rühmend erwähnt; **12.** Tötung *f*: ***happy ~*** Harakiri *n*; **~ boat** *s.* Ku'rierboot *n*; **~ box** *s.*, **~ case** *s.* **1.** Ku'riertasche *f*; **2.** *Brit.* Aktenkoffer *m*.

dis·patch·er [dɪ'spætʃə] *s.* **1.** 🚂 Fahrdienstleiter *m*; **2.** ☤ *Am.* Abteilungsleiter *m* für Produkti'onsplanung.

dis·patch| goods *s. pl.* Eilgut *n*; **~ note** *s.* Pa'ketkarte *f* für 'Auslandspa,ket; **~ rid·er** *s.* ⚔ Meldereiter *m*, -fahrer *m*.

dis·pel [dɪ'spel] *v/t.* *Menge etc.*, *a. fig.* *Befürchtungen etc.* zerstreuen, *Nebel* zerteilen.

dis·pen·sa·ble [dɪ'spensəbl] *adj.* □ entbehrlich, verzichtbar; erläßlich; **dis·pen·sa·ry** [dɪ'spensərɪ] *s.* **1.** 'Werks- *od.* 'Krankenhausapo,theke *f*; **2.** ⚔ a) Laza'rettapo,theke *f*, b) ('Kranken)Re,vier *n*; **dis·pen·sa·tion** [,dɪspen'seɪʃn] *s.* **1.** Aus-, Verteilung *f*; **2.** Gabe *f*; **3.** göttliche Fügung; Fügung *f* (*des Schicksals*), Walten *n* (*der Vorsehung*); **4.** religi'öses Sy'stem; **5.** Regelung *f*, Sy'stem *n*; **6.** ⚖, *eccl.* (***with***, ***from***) Dis'pens *m*, Befreiung *f* (von,) Erlaß *m* (*gen.*); **7.** Verzicht *m* (***with*** auf *acc.*); **dis·pense** [dɪ'spens] **I** *v/t.* **1.** aus-, verteilen; *Sakrament* spenden: ***~ justice*** Recht sprechen; **2.** *Arzneien* (nach Re'zept) zubereiten u. abgeben; **3.** dispensieren, entheben, befreien, entbinden (***from*** von); **II** *v/i.* **4.** Dis'pens erteilen; **5.** ***~ with*** a) verzichten auf (*acc.*), b) 'überflüssig machen, auskommen ohne: ***it can be ~d with*** man kann darauf verzichten, es ist entbehrlich; **dis·pens·er** [dɪ'spensə] *s.* **1.** Ver-, Austeiler *m*; **2.** ⚙ Spender *m* (*Gerät*); (*Briefmarken- etc.*)Auto'mat *m*; → **dis·pens·ing chem·ist** [dɪ'spensɪŋ] *s.* Apo'theker(in).

dis·per·sal [dɪ'spɜ:sl] *s.* **1.** (Zer)Streuung *f*; Verbreitung *f*; Zersplitterung *f*; **2.** ⚔, *a.* ☤ Auflockerung *f*; **~ a·pron** *s.* ✈ (ausein'andergezogener) Abstellplatz; **~ a·re·a** *s.* **1.** ✈ → ***dispersal apron***; **2.** ⚔ Auflockerungsgebiet *n*.

dis·perse [dɪ'spɜ:s] **I** *v/t.* **1.** verstreuen; **2.** → ***dispel***; **3.** *Nachrichten etc.* verbreiten; **4.** ⚗, *phys.* dispergieren, zerstreuen; **5.** ⚔ a) *Formation* auflockern, b) versprengen; **II** *v/i.* **6.** sich zerstreuen (*Menge*); **7.** sich auflösen; **8.** sich verteilen *od.* zersplittern; **dis·pers·ed·ly** [dɪ'spɜ:sɪdlɪ] *adv.* verstreut, vereinzelt; **dis·per·sion** [dɪ'spɜ:ʃn] *s.* **1.** Zerstreuung *f* (*a. fig.*); Verteilung *f* (*von Nebel*); **2.** a) Ⱥ, ⚔ Streuung *f*: ***~ pattern*** Trefferbild *n*, b) → ***dispersal*** 2; **3.** ⚗ Dispersi'on(sphase) *f*: ***~ agent*** Dispersionsmittel *n*; **4.** ℒ Zerstreuung *f*, Di'aspora *f der Juden*.

dis·pir·it [dɪ'spɪrɪt] *v/t.* entmutigen, niederdrücken, deprimieren; **dis'pir·it·ed** [-tɪd] *adj.* □ niedergeschlagen, mutlos, deprimiert.

dis·place [dɪs'pleɪs] *v/t.* **1.** versetzen, -rücken, -lagern, -schieben; **2.** verdrängen (*a.* ⚓); **3.** *j-n* ablösen, entlassen; **4.** ersetzen; **5.** verschleppen: **~d person** *hist.* Verschleppte(r *m*) *f*; **dis'place·ment** [-mənt] *s.* **1.** Verlagerung *f*, Verschiebung *f*; **2.** Verdrängung *f* (*a.* ⚓, *phys.*); ⚙ Kolbenverdrängung *f*; **3.** Ersetzung *f*, Ersatz *m*; **4.** *psych.* Af'fektverlagerung *f*: **~ activity** Übersprunghandlung *f*.

dis·play [dɪ'spleɪ] **I** *v/t.* **1.** entfalten: a) ausbreiten, b) *fig.* an den Tag legen, zeigen: **~ activity** (**strength** *etc.*); **2.** (*contp.* protzig) zur Schau stellen, zeigen; **3.** ✝ ausstellen, -legen; **4.** *typ.* her'vorheben; **II** *s.* **5.** Entfaltung *f* (*a. fig. von Tatkraft, Macht etc.*); **6.** (*a.* protzige) Zur'schaustellung; **7.** ✝ Ausstellung *f*, (Waren)Auslage *f*, Dis'play *n*: **be on ~** ausgestellt *od.* zu sehen sein; **8.** Aufwand *m*, Pomp *m*, Prunk *m*: **make a great ~** a) großen Prunk entfalten, b) **of s.th.** et. (protzig) zur Schau stellen; **9.** *Computer*: Dis'play *n*: a) Sichtanzeige *f*, b) Sichtbildgerät *n*; **10.** *typ.* Her'vorhebung *f*; **III** *adj.* **11.** ✝ Ausstellungs…, Schau…: **~ advertising** Displaywerbung *f*; **~ artist**, **~man** (Werbe)Dekorateur *m*; **~ box**, **~ pack** Schaupackung *f*; **~ case** Schaukasten *m*, Vitrine *f*; **~ window** Auslagefenster *n*; **12.** *Computer*: Display…, Sicht(bild)…: **~ unit** → 9 b; **~ be'havio(u)r** *s. zo.* Imponiergehabe *n*.

dis·please [dɪs'pli:z] *v/t.* **1.** *j-m* miß'fallen; **2.** *j-n* ärgern, verstimmen; **3.** *das Auge* beleidigen; **dis'pleased** [-zd] *adj.* (**at**, **with**) unzufrieden (mit), ungehalten (über *acc.*); **dis'pleas·ing** [-zɪŋ] *adj.* □ unangenehm; **dis·pleas·ure** [dɪs'pleʒə] *s.* 'Mißfallen *n* (**at** über *acc.*): **incur s.o.'s ~** j-s Unwillen erregen.

dis·port [dɪ'spɔ:t] *v/t.*: **~ o.s.** a) sich vergnügen *od.* amüsieren, b) her'umtollen, sich (ausgelassen) tummeln.

dis·pos·a·ble [dɪ'spəʊzəbl] **I** *adj.* **1.** (frei) verfügbar: **~ income**; **2.** ✝ Einweg…, Wegwerf…: **~ package**; **II** *s.* **3.** Einweg-, Wegwerfgegenstand *m*; **dis·pos·al** [dɪ'spəʊzl] *s.* **1.** Anordnung *f*, Aufstellung *f* (*a.* ⚔); Verwendung *f*; **2.** Erledigung *f*: a) (endgültige) Regelung *e-r Sache*, b) Vernichtung *f e-s Gegners etc.*; **3.** Verfügung(srecht *n*) *f* (**of** über *acc.*): **be at s.o.'s ~** j-m zur Verfügung stehen; **place s.th. at s.o.'s ~** j-m et. zur Verfügung stellen; **have the ~ of** verfügen (können) über (*acc.*); **4.** ✝, ⚖ a) 'Übergabe *f*, Über'tragung *f*, b) Veräußerung *f*, Verkauf *m*: **for ~** zum Verkauf; **5.** Beseitigung *f*, (Müll- *etc.*) Abfuhr *f*, (-)Entsorgung *f*; **dis·pose** [dɪ'spəʊz] **I** *v/t.* **1.** anordnen, aufstellen (*a.* ⚔); zu'rechtlegen, einrichten; ein-, verteilen; **2.** *j-n* bewegen, geneigt machen, veranlassen (**to** zu; **to do** zu tun); **II** *v/i.* **3.** verfügen, Verfügungen treffen; **4.** **~ of** a) (frei) verfügen *od.* disponieren über (*acc.*), b) entscheiden über (*acc.*), lenken, c) (endgültig) erledigen: **~ of an affair**, d) *j-n od. et.* abtun, abfertigen, e) loswerden, sich entledigen (*gen.*), f) wegschaffen, beseitigen: **~ of trash**, g) *e-n Gegner etc.* erledigen, unschädlich machen, vernichten, h) ⚔ *Bomben etc.* entschärfen, i) verzehren, trinken: **~ of a bottle**, j) über'geben, -'tragen: **~ of by will** testamentarisch vermachen, letztwillig verfügen über (*acc.*); **disposing mind** ⚖ Testierfähigkeit *f*, k) verkaufen, veräußern, ✝ *a.* absetzen, abstoßen, l) *s-e Tochter* verheiraten (**to** an *acc.*); **dis·posed** [dɪ'spəʊzd] *adj.* **1.** geneigt, bereit (**to** zu; **to do** zu tun); **2.** ⚕ anfällig (**to** für); **3.** gelaunt, gesinnt: **well-~** wohlgesinnt, **ill-~** übelgesinnt (**towards** *dat.*); **dis·po·si·tion** [ˌdɪspə'zɪʃn] *s.* **1.** a) Veranlagung *f*, Dispositi'on *f*, b) (Wesens)Art *f*; **2.** a) Neigung *f*, Hang *m* (**to** zu), b) ⚕ Anfälligkeit *f* (**to** für); **3.** Stimmung *f*; **4.** Anordnung *f*, Aufstellung *f* (*a.* ⚔); **5.** (**of**) a) Erledigung *f* (*gen.*), b) *bsd.* ⚖ Entscheidung *f* (über *acc.*); **6.** (*bsd.* göttliche) Lenkung; **7.** *pl.* Dispositi'onen *pl.*, Vorkehrungen *pl.*: **make** (**one's**) **~s** (s-e) Vorkehrungen treffen, disponieren; **8.** → **disposal** 3.

dis·pos·sess [ˌdɪspə'zes] *v/t.* **1.** enteignen, aus dem Besitz (**of** *gen.*) setzen; *Mieter* zur Räumung zwingen; **2.** berauben (**of** *gen.*); **3.** *sport j-m* den Ball abnehmen; ˌ**dis·pos'ses·sion** [-eʃn] *s.* Enteignung *f etc.*

dis·praise [dɪs'preɪz] *s.* Her'absetzung *f*: **in ~** geringschätzig.

dis·proof [ˌdɪs'pru:f] *s.* Wider'legung *f*.

dis·pro·por·tion [ˌdɪsprə'pɔ:ʃn] *s.* 'Mißverhältnis *n*; ˌ**dis·pro'por·tion·ate** [-ʃnət] *adj.* □ **1.** unverhältnismäßig (groß *od.* klein), in keinem Verhältnis stehend (**to** zu); **2.** über'trieben, unangemessen; **3.** unproportioniert.

dis·prove [ˌdɪs'pru:v] *v/t.* wider'legen.

dis·pu·ta·ble [dɪ'spju:təbl] *adj.* □ strittig; **dis·pu·tant** [dɪ'spju:tənt] *s.* Dispu'tant *m*, Gegner *m*.

dis·pu·ta·tion [ˌdɪspju:'teɪʃn] **1.** Dis'put *m*, Streitgespräch *n*, Wortwechsel *m*; **2.** Disputati'on *f*, wissenschaftliches Streitgespräch; ˌ**dis·pu'ta·tious** [-ʃəs] *adj.* □ streitsüchtig; **dis·pute** [dɪ'spju:t] **I** *v/i.* **1.** streiten, *Wissenschaftler*: *a.* disputieren (**on**, **about** über *acc.*); **2.** (sich) streiten, zanken; **II** *v/t.* **3.** streiten *od.* disputieren über (*acc.*); **4.** in Zweifel ziehen, anzweifeln; **5.** kämpfen um, *j-m et.* streitig machen; **III** *s.* **6.** Dis'put *m*, Kontro'verse *f*: **in** (*od.* **under**) **~** umstritten, strittig; **beyond** (*od.* **without**) **~** unzweifelhaft, fraglos; **7.** (heftiger) Streit.

dis·qual·i·fi·ca·tion [dɪsˌkwɒlɪfɪ'keɪʃn] *s.* **1.** Disqualifikati'on *f*, Disqualifizierung *f*; **2.** Untauglichkeit *f*, mangelnde Eignung *od.* Befähigung (**for** für); **3.** disqualifizierender 'Umstand; **4.** *sport* Disqualifikati'on *f*, Ausschluß *m*; **dis·qual·i·fy** [dɪs'kwɒlɪfaɪ] *v/t.* **1.** ungeeignet *od.* unfähig *od.* untauglich machen (**for** für): **be disqualified for** ungeeignet (*etc.*) sein für; **2.** für unfähig *od.* untauglich *od.* nicht berechtigt erklären (**for** zu): **~ s.o. from** (**holding**) **public office** j-m die Fähigkeit zur Ausübung e-s öffentlichen Amtes absprechen *od.* nehmen; **~ s.o. from driving** j-m die Fahrerlaubnis entziehen; **3.** *sport* disqualifizieren, ausschließen.

dis·qui·et [dɪs'kwaɪət] **I** *v/t.* beunruhigen; **II** *s.* Unruhe *f*, Besorgnis *f*; **dis'qui·et·ing** [-tɪŋ] *adj.* beunruhigend; **dis'qui·e·tude** [-aɪətju:d] → **disquiet** II.

dis·qui·si·tion [ˌdɪskwɪ'zɪʃn] *s.* ausführliche Abhandlung *od.* Rede.

dis·rate [dɪs'reɪt] *v/t.* ⚓ degradieren.

dis·re·gard [ˌdɪsrɪ'gɑ:d] **I** *v/t.* **1.** a) nicht beachten, ignorieren, außer acht lassen, b) absehen von, ausklammern; **2.** nicht befolgen, miß'achten; **II** *s.* **3.** Nichtbeachtung *f*, Ignorierung *f* (**of**, **for** *gen.*); **4.** 'Mißachtung *f* (**of**, **for** *gen.*); **5.** Gleichgültigkeit *f* (**of**, **for** gegen'über); ˌ**dis·re'gard·ful** [-fʊl] *adj.* □: **be ~ of** → **disregard** 1 a.

dis·rel·ish [ˌdɪs'relɪʃ] *s.* Abneigung *f*, 'Widerwille *m* (**for** gegen).

dis·re·mem·ber [ˌdɪsrɪ'membə] *v/t.* F *et.* vergessen (haben).

dis·re·pair [ˌdɪsrɪ'peə] *s.* Verfall *m*; Baufälligkeit *f*, schlechter (baulicher) Zustand: **in** (**a state of**) **~** baufällig; **fall into ~** baufällig werden.

dis·rep·u·ta·ble [dɪs'repjʊtəbl] *adj.* □ verrufen, anrüchig; **dis·re·pute** [ˌdɪsrɪ'pju:t] *s.* Verruf *m*, Verrufenheit *f*, schlechter Ruf: **bring into ~** in Verruf bringen.

dis·re·spect [ˌdɪsrɪ'spekt] **I** *s.* **1.** Re'spektlosigkeit *f* (**to**, **for** gegenüber); **2.** Unhöflichkeit *f* (**to** gegen); **II** *v/t.* **3.** sich re'spektlos benehmen gegen'über; **4.** unhöflich behandeln; ˌ**dis·re'spect·ful** [-fʊl] *adj.* □ **1.** re'spektlos (**to** gegen); **2.** unhöflich (**to** zu).

dis·robe [ˌdɪs'rəʊb] **I** *v/t.* entkleiden (*a. fig.*) (**of** *gen.*); **II** *v/i.* s-e Kleidung *od.* Amtstracht ablegen.

dis·root [ˌdɪs'ru:t] *v/t.* **1.** entwurzeln, ausreißen; **2.** vertreiben.

dis·rupt [dɪs'rʌpt] **I** *v/t.* **1.** zerbrechen, sprengen, zertrümmern; **2.** zerreißen, (zer)spalten; **3.** unter'brechen, stören; **4.** zerrütten; **5.** *Versammlung*, *Koalition etc.* sprengen; **II** *v/i.* **6.** zerreißen; **7.** ϟ 'durchschlagen; **dis'rup·tion** [-pʃn] *s.* **1.** Zerreißung *f*, Zerschlagung *f*; Unter'brechung *f*; **2.** Zerrissenheit *f*, Spaltung *f*; **3.** Bruch *m*; **4.** Zerrüttung *f*; **dis'rup·tive** [-tɪv] *adj.* **1.** zerbrechend, zertrümmernd, zerreißend; **2.** zerrüttend; **3.** ϟ Durchschlags…(-*festigkeit etc.*): **~ discharge** Durchschlag *m*.

dis·sat·is·fac·tion ['dɪsˌsætɪs'fækʃn] *s.* Unzufriedenheit *f* (**at**, **with** mit); '**disˌsat·is'fac·to·ry** [-ktərɪ] *adj.* unbefriedigend; **dis·sat·is·fied** [ˌdɪs'sætɪsfaɪd] *adj.* unzufrieden (**with**, **at** mit); **dis·sat·is·fy** [ˌdɪs'sætɪsfaɪ] *v/t.* nicht befriedigen, *j-n* verdrießen; *j-m* miß'fallen.

dis·sect [dɪ'sekt] *v/t.* **1.** zergliedern, zerlegen; **2.** a) ⚕ sezieren, b) ⚕, ⚘, *zo.* präparieren; **3.** *fig.* zergliedern, analysieren; **dis'sec·tion** [-kʃn] *s.* **1.** Zergliederung *f*, *fig. a.* a) Aufgliederung *f*, b) (genaue) Ana'lyse; **2.** ⚕ Sezieren *n*; **3.** ⚕, ⚘, *zo.* Präpa'rat *n*; **dis'sec·tor** [-tə] *s.* **1.** ⚕ Sezierer *m*; **2.** ⚕, ⚘, *zo.* Präpa'rator *m*.

dis·seise, **dis·seize** [ˌdɪ'si:z] *v/t.* ⚖ *j-m* 'widerrechtlich den Besitz entziehen; ˌ**dis'sei·sin**, ˌ**dis'sei·zin** [-zɪn] *s.* ⚖ 'widerrechtliche Besitzentziehung.

dis·sem·ble [dɪ'sembl] **I** *v/t.* **1.** verhehlen, verbergen, sich *et.* nicht anmerken lassen; **2.** vortäuschen, simulieren; **3.** *obs.* unbeachtet lassen; **II** *v/i.* **4.** sich verstellen, heucheln; **dis'sem·bler** [-lə] *s.* **1.** Heuchler(in); **2.** Simu'lant (-in).

dis·sem·i·nate [dɪ'semɪneɪt] *v/t.* **1.** *Saat* ausstreuen (*a. fig.*); **2.** *fig.* verbreiten: ~ **ideas**; ~**d sclerosis** ⚕ multiple Sklerose; **dis·sem·i·na·tion** [dɪˌsemɪ'neɪʃn] *s.* Ausstreuung *f*; *fig. a.* Verbreitung *f*.

dis·sen·sion [dɪ'senʃn] *s.* Meinungsverschiedenheit(en *pl.*) *f*, Diffe'renz(en *pl.*) *f*.

dis·sent [dɪ'sent] **I** *v/i.* **1.** (**from**) anderer Meinung sein (als), nicht über'einstimmen (mit); **2.** *eccl.* von der Staatskirche abweichen; **II** *s.* **3.** Meinungsverschiedenheit *f*, andere Meinung; **4.** *eccl.* Abweichen *n* von der Staatskirche; **dis'sent·er** [-tə] *s.* **1.** Andersdenkende(r *m*) *f*; **2.** *eccl.* a) Dissi'dent *m*, b) *oft* 2 Dis'senter *m*, Nonkonfor'mist (-in); **dis'sen·tient** [-nʃɪənt] **I** *adj.* andersdenkend, abweichend: **without a ~ vote** ohne Gegenstimme; **II** *s.* a) Andersdenkende(r *m*) *f*, b) Gegenstimme *f*: **with no ~** ohne Gegenstimme.

dis·ser·ta·tion [ˌdɪsə'teɪʃn] *s.* **1.** (wissenschaftliche) Abhandlung; **2.** Disserta'tion *f*.

dis·serv·ice [ˌdɪs'sɜːvɪs] *s.* (**to**) schlechter Dienst (an *dat.*): **do a ~** *j-m* e-n schlechten Dienst erweisen; **be of ~ to s.o.** j-m zum Nachteil gereichen.

dis·sev·er [dɪs'sevə] *v/t.* trennen, absondern, spalten.

dis·si·dence ['dɪsɪdəns] *s.* **1.** Meinungsverschiedenheit *f*; **2.** *pol.*, *eccl.* Dissi'dententum *n*; **'dis·si·dent** [-nt] **I** *adj.* **1.** andersdenkend, nicht über'einstimmend, abweichend; **II** *s.* **2.** Andersdenkende(r *m*) *f*; **3.** *eccl.* Dissi'dent(in), *pol. a.* Re'gimekritiker(in).

dis·sim·i·lar [ˌdɪ'sɪmɪlə] *adj.* □ (**to**) verschieden (von), unähnlich (*dat.*); **dis·sim·i·lar·i·ty** [ˌdɪsɪmɪ'lærətɪ] *s.* Verschiedenartigkeit *f*, Unähnlichkeit *f*; 'Unterschied *m*.

dis·sim·u·late [dɪ'sɪmjʊleɪt] **I** *v/t.* verbergen, verhehlen; **II** *v/i.* sich verstellen; heucheln; **dis·sim·u·la·tion** [dɪˌsɪmjʊ'leɪʃn] *s.* **1.** Verheimlichung *f*; **2.** Verstellung *f*, Heuche'lei *f*; **3.** ⚕ Dissimulati'on *f*.

dis·si·pate ['dɪsɪpeɪt] **I** *v/t.* **1.** zerstreuen (*a. fig. u. phys.*); *Nebel* zerteilen; **2.** a) verschwenden, vergeuden, verzetteln, b) *Geld* 'durchbringen, verprassen; **3.** *fig.* verscheuchen, vertreiben; **4.** *phys.* a) *Hitze* ableiten, b) in 'Wärmeenerˌgie 'umwandeln; **II** *v/i.* **5.** sich zerstreuen (*a. fig.*); sich zerteilen (*Nebel*); **6.** ein ausschweifendes Leben führen; **'dis·si·pat·ed** [-tɪd] *adj.* ausschweifend, zügellos; **dis·si·pa·tion** [ˌdɪsɪ'peɪʃn] *s.* **1.** Zerstreuung *f* (*a. fig. u. phys.*); **2.** Vergeudung *f*; **3.** Verprassen *n*, 'Durchbringen *n*; **4.** Ausschweifung(en *pl.*) *f*; zügelloses Leben; **5.** *phys.* a) Ableitung *f*, b) Dissipati'on *f*.

dis·so·ci·ate [dɪ'səʊʃɪeɪt] **I** *v/t.* **1.** trennen, loslösen, absondern (**from** von); **2.** ⚗ dissoziieren; **3. ~ o.s.** (**from**) sich lossagen *od.* distanzieren *od.* abrücken (von); **II** *v/i.* **4.** sich (ab)trennen *od.* loslösen; **5.** ⚗ dissoziieren; **dis·so·ci·a·tion** [dɪˌsəʊsɪ'eɪʃn] *s.* **1.** (Ab-)Trennung *f*, Loslösung *f*; **2.** Abrücken *n*; **3.** ⚗, *psych.* Dissoziati'on *f*.

dis·sol·u·bil·i·ty [dɪˌsɒljʊ'bɪlətɪ] *s.* **1.** Löslichkeit *f*; **2.** Auflösbarkeit *f*, Trennbarkeit *f*; **dis·sol·u·ble** [dɪ'sɒljʊbl] *adj.* **1.** löslich; **2.** ⚖ auflösbar, trennbar.

dis·so·lute ['dɪsəluːt] *adj.* □ ausschweifend, zügellos; **'dis·so·lute·ness** [-nɪs] *s.* Ausschweifung *f*, Zügellosigkeit *f*.

dis·so·lu·tion [ˌdɪsə'luːʃn] *s.* **1.** Auflösung *f* (*a. parl.*, ✝; *a. Ehe*); ⚖ *a.* Aufhebung *f*; **2.** Zersetzung *f*; **3.** Zerstörung *f*, Vernichtung *f*; **4.** ⚗ Lösung *f*.

dis·solv·a·ble [dɪ'zɒlvəbl] → **dissoluble**; **dis·solve** [dɪ'zɒlv] **I** *v/t.* **1.** auflösen (*a. fig.*, *Ehe*, *Parlament*, *Firma etc.*); *Ehe a.* scheiden; lösen (*a.* ⚗): ~**d in tears** in Tränen aufgelöst; **2.** ⚖ aufheben; **3.** auflösen, zersetzen; **4.** vernichten; **5.** *Geheimnis etc.* lösen; **6.** *Film*: über'blenden; **II** *v/i.* **7.** sich auflösen (*a. fig.*), zergehen, schmelzen; **8.** zerfallen; **9.** sich (in nichts) auflösen, verschwinden; **10.** *Film*: über'blenden, inein'ander 'übergehen; **III** *s.* **11.** *Film*: Über'blendung *f*; **dis'sol·vent** [-vənt] **I** *adj.* (auf)lösend; zersetzend; **II** *s.* ⚗ Lösungsmittel *n*.

dis·so·nance ['dɪsənəns] *s.* Disso'nanz *f*: a) ♪ 'Mißklang *m* (*a. fig.*), b) *fig.* Unstimmigkeit *f*; **'dis·so·nant** [-nt] *adj.* □ **1.** ♪ disso'nant (*a. fig.*); **2.** 'mißtönend; **3.** *fig.* unstimmig.

dis·suade [dɪ'sweɪd] *v/t.* **1.** *j-m* abraten (**from** von); **2.** *j-n* abbringen (**from** von); **dis'sua·sion** [-eɪʒn] *s.* **1.** Abraten *n*; **2.** Abbringen *n*; **dis'sua·sive** [-eɪsɪv] *adj.* □ abratend.

dis·syl·lab·ic, **dis·syl·la·ble** → **disyllabic**, **disyllable**.

dis·sym·met·ri·cal [ˌdɪsɪ'metrɪkl] *adj.* 'unsymˌmetrisch; **dis·sym·met·ry** [ˌdɪ'sɪmɪtrɪ] *s.* Asymme'trie *f*.

dis·taff ['dɪstɑːf] *s.* (Spinn)Rocken *m*; *fig. das* Reich der Frau: **~ side** weibliche Linie *e-r Familie*.

dis·tance ['dɪstəns] **I** *s.* **1.** a) Entfernung *f*, b) Ferne *f*: **at a ~** a) in einiger Entfernung, b) von weitem; **in the ~** in der Ferne; **from a ~** aus einiger Entfernung; **at an equal ~** gleich weit (entfernt); **a good ~ off** ziemlich weit entfernt; **braking ~** *mot.* Bremsweg *m*; **stopping ~** *mot.* Anhalteweg *m*; **within striking ~** handgreiflich nahe, in erreichbarer Nähe; → **hail** 7; **walking** II; **2.** Zwischenraum *m*, Abstand *m* (**between** zwischen); **3.** Entfernung *f*, Strecke *f*: **~ covered** zurückgelegte Strecke; **4.** *zeitlicher* Abstand, Zeitraum *m*; **5.** *fig.* Abstand *m*, Entfernung *f*, 'Unterschied *m*; **6.** *fig.* Di'stanz *f*, Abstand *m*, Re'serve *f*, Zu'rückhaltung *f*: **keep s.o. at a ~** j-m gegenüber reserviert sein, sich j-n vom Leib halten; **keep one's ~** den Abstand wahren, (die gebührende) Distanz halten; **7.** *paint. etc.* a) Perspek'tive *f*, b) *a. pl.* 'Hintergrund *m*, c) Ferne *f*; **8.** ♪ Inter'vall *n*; **9.** *sport* a) Di'stanz *f*, Strecke *f*, b) *fenc.*, *Boxen*: Di'stanz *f*, c) Langstrecke *f*: **~ race** Langstreckenlauf *m*; **~ runner** Langstreckenläufer(in); **II** *v/t.* **10.** über'holen, hinter sich lassen, *sport a.* distanzieren: ~**d** *fig.* distanziert; **11.** *fig.* über'flügeln; **'dis·tant** [-nt] *adj.* □ **1.** entfernt (*a. fig.*), weit (**from** von); fern (*Ort od. Zeit*): **~ relation** entfernte(r) *od.* weitläufige(r) Verwandte(r); **~ resemblance** entfernte *od.* schwache Ähnlichkeit; **~ dream** vager Traum, schwache Aussicht; **2.** weit vonein'ander entfernt; **3.** zu'rückhaltend, kühl, distanziert; **4.** ⚙ Fern...: **~ control** Fernsteuerung *f*; **~ reading instrument** Fernmeßgerät *n*.

dis·taste [ˌdɪs'teɪst] *s.* (**for**) 'Widerwille *m*, Abneigung *f* (gegen), Ekel *m*, Abscheu *m* (vor *dat.*); ˌ**dis'taste·ful** [-fʊl] *adj.* □ **1.** ekelerregend; **2.** *fig.* a) unangenehm, zu'wider (**to** *dat.*), b) ekelhaft, widerlich.

dis·tem·per[1] [dɪ'stempə] **I** *s.* **1.** Tempera- *od.* Leimfarbe *f*; **2.** 'Temperamaleˌrei *f* (*a. Bild*); **II** *v/t.* **3.** mit Temperafarbe(n) (an)malen.

dis·tem·per[2] [dɪ'stempə] *s.* **1.** *vet.* a) Staupe *f* (*bei Hunden*), b) Druse *f* (*bei Pferden*); **2.** *obs.* a) üble Laune, b) Unpäßlichkeit *f*, c) po'litische Unruhe(n *pl.*).

dis·tend [dɪ'stend] **I** *v/t.* (aus)dehnen, weiten; aufblähen; **II** *v/i.* sich (aus)dehnen *etc.*; **dis·ten·si·ble** [dɪ'stensəbl] *adj.* (aus)dehnbar; **dis·ten·sion** [dɪ'stenʃn] *s.* (Aus)Dehnung *f*; Aufblähung *f*.

dis·tich ['dɪstɪk] *s.* **1.** Distichon *n* (*Verspaar*); **2.** gereimtes Verspaar.

dis·til, *Am.* **dis·till** [dɪ'stɪl] **I** *v/t.* **1.** ⚗ a) ('um)destillieren, abziehen, b) abdestillieren (**from** aus), c) entgasen: ~**(l)ing flask** Destillierkolben *m*; **2.** *Branntwein* brennen (**from** aus); **3.** her'abtropfen lassen: **be ~led** sich niederschlagen; **4.** *fig. das Wesentliche* her'ausdestilˌlieren, -arbeiten (**from** aus); **II** *v/i.* **5.** ⚗ destillieren; **6.** (her'ab)tropfen; **7.** *fig.* sich her'auskristalliˌsieren; **dis·til·late** ['dɪstɪlət] *s.* ⚗ Destil'lat *n*; **dis·til·la·tion** [ˌdɪstɪ'leɪʃn] *s.* **1.** ⚗ Destillati'on *f*; **2.** Brennen *n* (*von Branntwein*); **3.** Ex'trakt *m*, Auszug *m*; **4.** *fig.* 'Quintesˌsenz *f*, Kern *m*; **dis·til·ler** [dɪ'stɪlə] *s.* Branntweinbrenner *m*; **dis·til·ler·y** [dɪ'stɪlərɪ] *s.* **1.** ⚗ Destil'lierappaˌrat *m*; **2.** Destilla'teur *m*, ('Branntwein)Brenneˌrei *f*.

dis·tinct [dɪ'stɪŋkt] *adj.* □ → **distinctly**; **1.** ver-, unter'schieden: **as ~ from** im Unterschied zu, zum Unterschied von; **2.** einzeln, getrennt, (ab)gesondert; **3.** eigen, selbständig; **4.** ausgeprägt, charakte'ristisch; **5.** klar, eindeutig, bestimmt, entschieden, ausgesprochen, deutlich; **dis·tinc·tion** [dɪ'stɪŋkʃn] *s.* **1.** Unter'scheidung *f*: **a ~ without a difference** e-e spitzfindige Unterscheidung; **2.** 'Unterschied *m*: **in ~ from** (*od.* **to**) im Unterschied zu, zum Unterschied von; **draw** (*od.* **make**) **a ~ between** e-n Unterschied machen zwischen (*dat.*); **3.** Unter'scheidungsmerkmal *n*, Kennzeichen *n*; **4.** her'vorragende Eigenschaft; **5.** Auszeichnung *f*, Ehrung *f*; **6.** (hoher) Rang; **7.** Würde *f*; Vornehmheit *f*; **8.** Ruf *m*, Berühmtheit *f*; **dis·tinc·tive** [dɪ'stɪŋktɪv] *adj.* □ **1.** unter'scheidend, Unterscheidungs...; **2.** kenn-, bezeichnend, charakte'ristisch (**of** für), besonder; **3.** deutlich, ausgesprochen; **dis·tinc·tive·ness** [dɪ'stɪŋktɪvnɪs] *s.* **1.** Besonderheit *f*; **2.** →

distinctness 1; **dis·tinct·ly** [dɪˈstɪŋ*k*tlɪ] *adv.* deutlich, *fig. a.* ausgesprochen; **dis·tinct·ness** [dɪˈstɪŋ*k*tnɪs] *s.* **1.** Deutlichkeit *f*, Klarheit *f*; **2.** Verschiedenheit *f*; **3.** Verschiedenartigkeit *f*.
dis·tin·gué [dɪˈstæŋgeɪ] (*Fr.*) *adj.* distinguˈiert, vornehm.
dis·tin·guish [dɪˈstɪŋgwɪʃ] **I** *v/t.* **1.** (***between***) unterˈscheiden (zwischen), (*zwei Dinge etc.*) auseinˈanderhalten: ***as ~ed from*** zum Unterschied von, im Unterschied zu; ***be ~ed by*** sich durch *et.* unterscheiden *od. weitS.* auszeichnen; **2.** wahrnehmen, erkennen; **3.** kennzeichnen, charakterisieren: ***~ing mark*** Merkmal *n*, Kennzeichen *n*; **4.** auszeichnen, rühmend herˈvorheben: ***~ o.s.*** sich auszeichnen (*a. iro.*); **II** *v/i.* **5.** unterˈscheiden, e-n ˈUnterschied machen; **dis·tin·guish·a·ble** [dɪˈstɪŋgwɪʃəbl] *adj.* □ **1.** unterˈscheidbar; **2.** wahrnehmbar, erkennbar; **3.** kenntlich (***by*** an *dat.*, durch); **dis·tin·guished** [dɪˈstɪŋgwɪʃt] *adj.* **1.** → ***distinguishable*** 1, 2; **2.** bemerkenswert, berühmt (***for*** wegen, ***by*** durch); **3.** vornehm; **4.** herˈvorragend, ausgezeichnet.
dis·tort [dɪˈstɔːt] *v/t.* **1.** verdrehen (*a. fig.*); *a. Gesicht* verzerren (*a.* ⚙, ϟ *u. fig.*); verrenken; ⚙ verformen: ***~ing mirror*** Vexier-, Zerrspiegel *m*; **2.** *fig. Tatsachen etc.* verdrehen, entstellen; **dis·tor·tion** [dɪˈstɔːʃn] *s.* **1.** Verdrehung *f* (*a. phys.*); Verrenkung *f*; Verzerrung *f* (*a.* ϟ, *phot.*); Verziehung *f*, Verwindung *f* (*a.* ⚙); **2.** *fig.* Entstellung *f*, Verzerrung *f*.
dis·tract [dɪˈstrækt] *v/t.* **1.** *Aufmerksamkeit*, *Person etc.* ablenken; **2.** *j-n* zerstreuen; **3.** erregen, aufwühlen; **4.** beunruhigen, stören, quälen; **5.** rasend machen; **dis·tract·ed** [dɪˈstræktɪd] *adj.* □ **1.** verwirrt; **2.** beunruhigt; **3.** außer sich, von Sinnen: ***~ with*** (*od.* ***by***) ***pain*** wahnsinnig vor Schmerzen; **dis·trac·tion** [dɪˈstrækʃn] *s.* **1.** Ablenkung *f*, *a.* Zerstreuung *f*; **2.** Zerstreutheit *f*; **3.** Verwirrung *f*; **4.** Wahnsinn *m*, Raseˈrei *f*: ***drive s.o. to ~*** j-n zur Raserei bringen; ***love to ~*** bis zum Wahnsinn lieben; **5.** *oft pl.* Ablenkung *f*, Zerstreuung *f*, Unterˈhaltung *f*.
dis·train [dɪˈstreɪn] ⚖ *v/i.*: ***~ (up)on*** a) *j-n* pfänden, b) *et.* mit Beschlag belegen; **dis·train·ee** [ˌdɪstreɪˈniː] *s.* Pfandschuldner(in); **dis·train·er** [dɪˈstreɪnə], **dis·train·or** [ˌdɪstreɪˈnɔː] *s.* Pfandgläubiger(in); **dis·traint** [dɪˈstreɪnt] *s.* Beschlagnahme *f*.
dis·traught [dɪˈstrɔːt] → ***distracted***.
dis·tress [dɪˈstres] **I** *s.* **1.** Qual *f*, Pein *f*, Schmerz *m*; **2.** Leid *n*, Kummer *m*, Sorge *f*; **3.** Elend *n*; Not(lage) *f*; **4.** ⚓ Seenot *f*: ***~ call*** Notruf *m*, SOS-Ruf *m*; ***~ rocket*** Notrakete *f*; ***~ signal*** Notsignal *n*; **5.** ⚖ a) Beschlagnahme *f*, b) mit Beschlag belegte Sache; **II** *v/t.* **6.** quälen, peinigen, bedrücken; beunruhigen; betrüben: ***~ o.s.*** sich sorgen (***about*** um); **7.** → ***distrain***; **dis·tressed** [dɪˈstrest] *adj.* **1.** (***about***) beunruhigt (über *acc.*, wegen), besorgt (um); **2.** bekümmert, betrübt; unglücklich; **3.** bedrängt, in Not, notleidend: ***~ area*** *Brit.* Notstandsgebiet *n*; ***~ ships*** Schiffe in Seenot; **4.** erschöpft; **dis·tress·ful** [dɪˈstresfʊl], **dis·tress·ing** [dɪˈstresɪŋ] *adj.* □ **1.** quälend; **2.** bedrückend.
dis·trib·ut·a·ble [dɪˈstrɪbjʊtəbl] *adj.* **1.** verteilbar; **2.** zu verteilen(d); **dis·trib·u·tar·y** [dɪˈstrɪbjʊtərɪ] *s. geogr.* abzweigender Flußarm, *bsd.* Deltaarm *m*; **dis·trib·ute** [dɪˈstrɪbjuːt] *v/t.* **1.** ver-, austeilen (***among*** unter *acc.*, ***to*** an *acc.*); **2.** zuteilen (***to*** *dat.*); **3.** ‡ a) *Waren* vertreiben, absetzen, b) *Filme* verleihen, c) *Dividende*, *Gewinne* ausschütten; **4.** *Post* zustellen; **5.** verbreiten; ausstreuen; *Farbe etc.* verteilen; **6.** auf-, einteilen; ⚔ gliedern; **7.** *typ.* a) *Satz* ablegen, b) *Farbe* auftragen; **dis·trib·u·tee** [dɪˌstrɪbjʊˈtiː] *s.* **1.** Empfänger(in); **2.** ⚖ Erbe *m*, Erbin *f*; **dis·trib·ut·er** → ***distributor***.
dis·trib·ut·ing| a·gent [dɪˈstrɪbjʊtɪŋ] *s.* ‡ (Großhandels)Vertreter *m*; **~ cen·ter** *Am.*, *Brit.* **~ cen·tre** *s.* ‡ ˈAbsatz-, Verˈteilungsˌzentrum *n*.
dis·tri·bu·tion [ˌdɪstrɪˈbjuːʃn] *s.* **1.** Ver-, Austeilung *f*; **2.** ⚙, ϟ a) Verteilung *f*, b) Verzweigung *f*; **3.** Ver-, Ausbreitung *f*; **4.** Einteilung *f*, *a.* ⚔ Gliederung *f*; **5.** a) Zuteilung *f*, b) Gabe *f*, Spende *f*; **6.** ‡ a) Vertrieb *m*, Absatz *m*, b) Verleih *m* (*von Filmen*), c) Ausschüttung *f* (*von Dividenden*, *Gewinnen*); **7.** Ausstreuen *n* (*von Samen*); **8.** Verteilen *n* (*von Farben etc.*); **9.** *typ.* a) Ablegen *n* (*des Satzes*), b) Auftragen *n* (*von Farbe*); **dis·trib·u·tive** [dɪˈstrɪbjʊtɪv] **I** *adj.* □ **1.** aus-, zu-, verteilend, Verteilungs…: ***~ share*** ⚖ gesetzlicher Erbteil; ***~ justice*** *fig.* ausgleichende Gerechtigkeit; **2.** jeden einzelnen betreffend; **3.** ⚗, *ling.* distribuˈtiv, Distributiv…; **II** *s.* **4.** *ling.* Distribuˈtivum *n*; **dis·trib·u·tor** [dɪˈstrɪbjʊtə] *s.* **1.** Verteiler *m* (*a.* ⚙, ϟ); **2.** ‡ a) Großhändler *m*, Geneˈralvertreter *m*, b) *pl.* (Film)Verleih *m*; **3.** ⚙ Verteilerdüse *f*.
dis·trict [ˈdɪstrɪkt] *s.* **1.** Diˈstrikt *m*, (Verwaltungs)Bezirk *m*, Kreis *m*; **2.** (Stadt)Bezirk *m*, (-)Viertel *n*; **3.** Gegend *f*, Gebiet *n*, Landstrich *m*; **~ at·tor·ney** *s. Am.* Staatsanwalt *m*; **ℒ Coun·cil** *s. Brit.* Bezirksamt *n*; **ℒ Court** *s.* ⚖ *Am.* (Bundes)Bezirksgericht *n*; **~ heat·ing** *s.* Fernheizung *f*; **~ judge** *s.* ⚖ *Am.* Richter *m* an e-m (Bundes)Bezirksgericht; **~ nurse** *s.* Gemeindeschwester *f*.
dis·trust [dɪsˈtrʌst] **I** *s.* ˈMißtrauen *n*, Argwohn *m* (***of*** gegen): ***have a ~ of s.o.*** j-m mißtrauen; **II** *v/t.* mißˈtrauen (*dat.*); **disˈtrust·ful** [-fʊl] *adj.* □ ˈmißtrauisch, argwöhnisch (***of*** gegen): ***~ of o.s.*** gehemmt, ohne Selbstvertrauen.
dis·turb [dɪˈstɜːb] **I** *v/t.* stören (*a.* ⚙, ϟ, ⚗, *meteor. etc.*): a) behindern, b) belästigen, c) beunruhigen, d) aufschrecken, -scheuchen, e) durcheinˈanderbringen, in Unordnung bringen: ***~ed at*** beunruhigt über (*acc.*); ***~ the peace*** ⚖ die öffentliche Sicherheit u. Ordnung stören; **II** *v/i.* stören; **dis·turb·ance** [dɪˈstɜːbəns] *s.* **1.** Störung *f* (*a.* ⚙, ϟ, ⚗, ⚡); **2.** Belästigung *f*; Beunruhigung *f*; Aufregung *f*; **3.** Unruhe *f*, Tuˈmult *m*, Aufruhr *m*: ***~ of the peace*** ⚖ öffentliche Ruhestörung; ***cause*** (*od.* ***create***) ***a ~*** ⚖ die öffentliche Sicherheit u. Ordnung stören; **4.** Verwirrung *f*; **5.** ***~ of possession*** ⚖ Besitzstörung *f*; **dis·turb·er** [dɪˈstɜːbə] *s.* Störenfried *m*, Unruhestifter(in); **dis·turb·ing** [dɪˈstɜːbɪŋ] *adj.* □ beunruhigend.
dis·un·ion [ˌdɪsˈjuːnjən] *s.* **1.** Trennung *f*, Spaltung *f*; **2.** Uneinigkeit *f*, Zwietracht *f*; **dis·u·nite** [ˌdɪsjuːˈnaɪt] *v/t. u. v/i.* (sich) trennen; *fig.* (sich) entzweien; **dis·u·nit·ed** [ˌdɪsjuːˈnaɪtɪd] *adj.* entzweit, verfeindet; **dis·u·ni·ty** [ˌdɪsˈjuːnətɪ] → ***disunion*** 2.
dis·use I *s.* [ˌdɪsˈjuːs] Nichtgebrauch *m*; Aufhören *n e-s Brauchs*: ***fall into ~*** außer Gebrauch kommen; **II** *v/t.* [ˌdɪsˈjuːz] nicht mehr gebrauchen; **dis·used** [ˌdɪsˈjuːzd] *adj.* **1.** ausgedient, nicht mehr benützt; **2.** stillgelegt (*Bergwerk etc.*), außer Betrieb.
dis·yl·lab·ic [ˌdɪsɪˈlæbɪk] *adj.* (□ ***~ally***) zweisilbig; **di·syl·la·ble** [dɪˈsɪləbl] *s.* zweisilbiges Wort.
ditch [dɪtʃ] **I** *s.* **1.** (Straßen)Graben *m*: ***last ~*** verzweifelter Kampf, Not(lage) *f*; ***die in the last ~*** bis zum letzten Atemzug kämpfen (*a. fig.*); **2.** Abzugsgraben *m*; **3.** Bewässerungs-, Wassergraben *m*; **4.** ✈ *sl.* ‚Bach' *m* (*Meer*, *Gewässer*); **II** *v/t.* **5.** mit e-m Graben versehen, Gräben ziehen durch; **6.** durch Abzugsgräben entwässern; **7.** F *Wagen* in den Straßengraben fahren: ***be ~ed*** im Straßengraben landen; **8.** *sl.* a) *Wagen etc.* stehenlassen, b) *j-m* entwischen, c) *j-m* den ‚Laufpaß' geben, *j-n* ‚sausen' lassen, d) *et.* ‚wegschmeißen', e) *Am. Schule* schwänzen; **9.** ✈ *sl. Maschine* im ‚Bach' landen; **III** *v/i.* **10.** Gräben ziehen *od.* ausbessern; **11.** ✈ *sl.* notlanden, notwassern; **ˈditch·er** [-tʃə] *s.* **1.** Grabenbauer *m*; **2.** Grabbagger *m*; **ˈditchˌwa·ter** *s.* abgestandenes, fauliges Wasser; → ***dull*** 4.
dith·er [ˈdɪðə] **I** *v/i.* **1.** bibbern, zittern; **2.** *fig.* schwanken (***between*** zwischen *dat.*); **3.** aufgeregt sein; **II** *s.* **4.** *fig.* Schwanken *n*; **5.** Aufregung *f*: ***be all of*** (*od.* ***in***) ***a ~*** F aufgeregt sein, ‚bibbern'.
dith·y·ramb [ˈdɪθɪræm*b*] *s.* **1.** Dithyˈrambus *m*; **2.** Lobeshymne *f*; **dith·y·ram·bic** [ˌdɪθɪˈræmbɪk] *adj.* dithyˈrambisch; enthusiˈastisch.
dit·to [ˈdɪtəʊ] (*abbr.* **do.**) **I** *adv.* dito, desˈgleichen: ***~ marks*** Ditozeichen *n*; ***say ~ to s.o.*** j-m beipflichten; **II** *s.* F Dupliˈkat *n*, Ebenbild *n*.
dit·ty [ˈdɪtɪ] *s.* Liedchen *n*.
di·u·ret·ic [ˌdaɪjʊəˈretɪk] **I** *adj.* diuˈretisch, harntreibend; **II** *s.* harntreibendes Mittel, Diuˈretikum *n*.
di·ur·nal [daɪˈɜːnl] *adj.* □ **1.** täglich (ˈwiederkehrend), Tag(es)…; **2.** *zo.* ˈtagakˌtiv, bei Tag auftretend.
di·va [ˈdiːvə] *s.* Diva *f*.
di·va·gate [ˈdaɪvəgeɪt] *v/i.* abschweifen; **di·va·ga·tion** [ˌdaɪvəˈgeɪʃn] *s.* Abschweifung *f*, Exˈkurs *m*.
di·va·lent [ˈdaɪˌveɪlənt] *adj.* ⚗ zweiwertig.
di·van [dɪˈvæn] *s.* **1.** a) Diwan *m*, (Liege)Sofa *n*, b) *a.* ***~ bed*** Bettcouch *f*; **2.** Diwan *m*: a) *orientalischer Staatsrat*, b) *Regierungskanzlei*, c) *Gerichtssaal*, d) *öffentliches Gebäude*; **3.** Diwan *m* (*orientalische Gedichtsammlung*).
di·var·i·cate [daɪˈværɪkeɪt] *v/i.* sich gabeln, sich spalten; abzweigen.
dive [daɪv] **I** *v/i.* **1.** tauchen (***for*** nach, ***into*** in *acc.*); **2.** ˈuntertauchen; **3.** e-n

Kopf- *od.* Hechtsprung (*a. Torwart*) machen; **4.** *Wasserspringen*: springen; **5.** ✈ e-n Sturzflug machen; **6.** (hastig) hin'eingreifen *od.* fahren (**into** in *acc.*); **7.** sich stürzen, verschwinden (**into** in *acc.*); **8.** (**into**) sich vertiefen (in *ein Buch etc.*); **9.** fallen (*Thermometer etc.*); **II** *s.* **10.** ('Unter)Tauchen *n*, ⚓ *a.* Tauchfahrt *f*; **11.** Kopfsprung *m*; Hechtsprung *m* (*a. des Torwarts*); ***make a ~*** → 3; ***take a ~*** *sport sl.* a) *Fußball*: ‚e-e Schwalbe bauen', b) ‚sich (einfach) hinlegen' (*Boxer*); **12.** *Wasserspringen*: Sprung *m*; **13.** ✈ Sturzflug *m*; **14.** F Spe'lunke *f*, Kneipe *f*; **'~·bomb** *v/t. u. v/i.* im Sturzflug mit Bomben angreifen; **~ bomb·er** *s.* Sturzkampfflugzeug *n*, Sturzbomber *m*, Stuka *m*.

div·er ['daɪvə] *s.* **1.** Taucher(in); *sport* Wasserspringer(in); **2.** *orn. ein* Tauchvogel *m*, *bsd.* Pinguin *m*.

di·verge [daɪ'vɜ:dʒ] *v/i.* **1.** divergieren (*a.* A, *phys.*), ausein'andergehen, -laufen, sich trennen; abweichen; **2.** abzweigen (**from** von); **3.** verschiedener Meinung sein; **di'ver·gence** [-dʒəns], **di'ver·gen·cy** [-dʒənsɪ] *s.* **1.** A, *phys. etc.* Diver'genz *f*; **2.** Ausein'anderlaufen *n*; **3.** Abzweigung *f*; **4.** Abweichung *f*; **5.** Meinungsverschiedenheit *f*; **di'ver·gent** [-dʒənt] *adj.* □ **1.** divergierend (*a.* A, *phys. etc.*); **2.** ausein'andergehend, -laufend; **3.** abweichend.

di·vers ['daɪvɜ:z] *adj. obs.* etliche.

di·verse [daɪ'vɜ:s] *adj.* □ **1.** verschieden, ungleich; **2.** mannigfaltig; **di·ver·si·fi·ca·tion** [daɪˌvɜ:sɪfɪ'keɪʃn] *s.* **1.** abwechslungsreiche Gestaltung; **2.** † Diversifizierung *f*, Streuung *f*: **~ (*of products*)** Verbreiterung *f* des Produktionsprogramms; ***~ of capital*** Anlagenstreuung *f*; **3.** Verschiedenartigkeit *f*; **di'ver·si·fied** [-sɪfaɪd] *adj.* **1.** verschieden(artig); **2.** † a) verteilt (*Risiko*), b) verteilt angelegt (*Kapital*), c) diversifiziert (*Produktion*); **di'ver·si·fy** [-sɪfaɪ] *v/t.* **1.** verschieden(artig) *od.* abwechslungsreich gestalten, variieren; **2.** † diversifizieren, streuen.

di·ver·sion [daɪ'vɜ:ʃn] *s.* **1.** Ablenkung *f*; **2.** ⚔ 'Ablenkungsmaˌnöver *n* (*a. fig.*); **3.** *Brit.* 'Umleitung *f* (*Verkehr*); **4.** *fig.* Zerstreuung *f*, Zeitvertreib *m*; **di'ver·sion·ar·y** [-ʃnərɪ] *adj.* ⚔ Ablenkungs...; **di'ver·sion·ist** *pol.* **I** *s.* Diversio'nist(in), Sabo'teur(in); **II** *adj.* diversio'nistisch.

di·ver·si·ty [daɪ'vɜ:sətɪ] *s.* **1.** Verschiedenheit *f*, Ungleichheit *f*; **2.** Mannigfaltigkeit *f*.

di·vert [daɪ'vɜ:t] *v/t.* **1.** ablenken, ableiten, abwenden (**from** von, **to** nach), lenken (**to** auf *acc.*); **2.** abbringen (**from** von); **3.** *Geld etc.* abzweigen (**to** für); **4.** *Brit. Verkehr* 'umleiten; **5.** zerstreuen, unter'halten; **di'vert·ing** [-tɪŋ] *adj.* □ unter'haltsam, amü'sant.

di·vest [daɪ'vest] *v/t.* **1.** entkleiden (**of** *gen.*); **2.** *fig.* entblößen, berauben (**of** *gen.*): **~ *s.o.* of** j-m *ein Recht etc.* entziehen *od.* nehmen; **~ *o.s.* of** *et.* ablegen, *et.* ab- *od.* aufgeben, sich *e-s Rechts etc.* entäußern; **di'vest·i·ture** [-tɪtʃə], **di'vest·ment** [-smənt] *s. fig.* Entblößung *f*, Beraubung *f*.

di·vide [dɪ'vaɪd] **I** *v/t.* **1.** (ein)teilen (**in**, **into** in *acc.*): **be ~d into** zerfallen in (*acc.*); **2.** A teilen, dividieren (**by** durch); **3.** verteilen (**between**, **among** unter *acc. od. dat.*): ***~ s.th. with s.o.*** et. mit j-m teilen; **4.** *a.* **~ up** zerteilen, zerlegen; zerstückeln, spalten; **5.** entzweien, ausein'anderbringen; **6.** trennen, absondern, scheiden (**from** von); *Haar* scheiteln; **7.** *Brit. parl.* (im Hammelsprung) abstimmen lassen; **II** *v/i.* **8.** sich teilen; zerfallen (**in**, **into** in *acc.*); **9.** A a) sich teilen lassen (**by** durch), b) aufgehen (**into** in *dat.*); **10.** sich trennen *od.* spalten; **11.** *parl.* im Hammelsprung abstimmen; **III** *s.* **12.** *Am.* Wasserscheide *f*; **13.** *fig.* Trennlinie *f*: ***the Great*** 2 der Tod; **di'vid·ed** [-dɪd] *adj.* geteilt (*a. fig.*): ***~ opinions*** geteilte Meinungen; ***~ counsel*** Uneinigkeit *f*; ***his mind was ~*** er war unentschlossen; ***~ against themselves*** unter sich uneins; ***~ highway*** *Am.* Schnellstraße *f*; ***~ skirt*** Hosenrock *m*.

div·i·dend ['dɪvɪdend] *s.* **1.** A Divi'dend *m*; **2.** † Divi'dende *f*, Gewinnanteil *m*: *Brit.* ***cum ~***, *Am.* ***~ on*** einschließlich Dividende; *Brit.* ***ex ~***, *Am.* ***~ off*** ausschließlich Dividende; ***pay ~s*** *fig.* sich bezahlt machen; **3.** ⚖ Rate *f*, (Kon'kurs)quote *f*; **~ cou·pon**, **~ war·rant** *s.* † Divi'dendenschein *m*.

di·vid·er [dɪ'vaɪdə] *s.* **1.** (Ver)Teiler(in); **2.** *pl.* Stechzirkel *m*; **3.** Trennwand *f*; **di'vid·ing** [-dɪŋ] *adj.* Trennungs..., Scheide...; ⚙ Teil...

div·i·na·tion [ˌdɪvɪ'neɪʃn] *s.* **1.** Weissagung *f*, Wahrsagung *f*; **2.** (Vor)Ahnung *f*.

di·vine [dɪ'vaɪn] **I** *adj.* □ **1.** Gottes..., göttlich, heilig: ***~ service*** Gottesdienst *m*; ***~ right of kings*** Königtum *n* von Gottes Gnaden, Gottesgnadentum *n*; **2.** *fig.* F göttlich, himmlisch; **II** *s.* **3.** Geistliche(r) *m*; **4.** Theo'loge *m*; **III** *v/t.* **5.** (vor'aus)ahnen; erraten; **6.** weissagen, prophe'zeien: ***divining rod*** Wünschelrute *f*; **di'vin·er** [-nə] *s.* **1.** Wahrsager *m*; **2.** (Wünschel)Rutengänger *m*.

div·ing ['daɪvɪŋ] *s.* **1.** Tauchen *n*; **2.** *sport* Wasserspringen *n*; **~ bell** *s.* Taucherglocke *f*; **~ board** *s.* Sprungbrett *n*; **~ duck** *s.* Tauchente *f*; **~ dress** → ***diving suit***; **~ hel·met** *s.* Taucherhelm *m*; **~ suit** *s.* Taucheranzug *m*; **~ tow·er** *s.* Sprungturm *m*.

di·vin·i·ty [dɪ'vɪnətɪ] *s.* **1.** Göttlichkeit *f*, göttliches Wesen; **2.** Gottheit *f*: ***the*** 2 die Gottheit, Gott; **3.** Theolo'gie *f*; **4.** *a.* ***~ fudge*** *Am. ein Schaumgebäck*; **div·i·nize** ['dɪvɪnaɪz] *v/t.* vergöttlichen.

di·vis·i·bil·i·ty [dɪˌvɪzɪ'bɪlətɪ] *s.* Teilbarkeit *f*; **di·vis·i·ble** [dɪ'vɪzəbl] *adj.* □ teilbar; **di·vi·sion** [dɪ'vɪʒn] *s.* **1.** (Auf-, Ein)Teilung *f* (**into** in *acc.*); Verteilung *f*, Gliederung *f*: ***~ of labo(u)r*** Arbeitsteilung; ***~ into shares*** † Stückelung *f*; **2.** Trennung *f*, Grenze *f*, Scheidelinie *f*, -wand *f*; **3.** Teil *m*, Ab'teilung *f* (*a. e-s Amtes etc.*), Abschnitt *m*; **4.** Gruppe *f*, Klasse *f*; **5.** ⚔ Divisi'on *f*; **6.** *sport* 'Liga *f*, (Spiel-, *Boxen etc.*: Gewichts)Klasse *f*; **7.** *pol.* Bezirk *m*; **8.** *parl.* (Abstimmung *f* durch) Hammelsprung *m*: ***go into ~*** zur Abstimmung schreiten; ***upon a ~*** nach Abstimmung; **9.** *fig.* Spaltung *f*, Kluft *f*; Uneinigkeit *f*, Diffe'renz *f*; **10.** A Divisi'on *f*, Dividieren *n*; **di·vi·sion·al** [dɪ'vɪʒənl] *adj.* □ **1.** Trenn..., Scheide...: ***~ line***; **2.** Abteilungs...; **3.** ⚔ Divisions...; **di·vi·sive** [dɪ'vaɪsɪv] *adj.* **1.** teilend; scheidend; **2.** entzweiend; trennend; **di·vi·sor** [dɪ'vaɪzə] *s.* A Di'visor *m*, Teiler *m*.

di·vorce [dɪ'vɔ:s] **I** *s.* **1.** ⚖ (Ehe)Scheidung *f*: ***~ action***, ***~ suit*** Scheidungsklage *f*, -prozeß *m*; ***obtain a ~*** geschieden werden; ***seek a ~*** auf Scheidung klagen; **2.** *fig.* (völlige) Trennung *f* (**from** von); **II** *v/t.* **3.** ⚖ *Ehegatten* scheiden; **4.** ***~ one's husband*** (***wife***) ⚖ sich von s-m Manne (s-r Frau) scheiden lassen; **5.** *fig.* (völlig) trennen, scheiden, (los-) lösen (**from** von); **di·vor·cee** [dɪˌvɔ:'si:] *s.* Geschiedene(r *m*) *f*.

div·ot ['dɪvət] *s.* **1.** *Scot.* Sode *f*, Rasenstück *n*; **2.** *Golf*: Divot *n*, Kote'lett *n*.

div·ul·ga·tion [ˌdaɪvʌl'geɪʃn] *s.* Enthüllung *f*, Preisgabe *f*.

di·vulge [daɪ'vʌldʒ] *v/t.* *Geheimnis etc.* enthüllen, preisgeben; **di'vulge·ment** [-mənt], **di'vul·gence** [-dʒəns] → ***divulgation***.

div·vy ['dɪvɪ] *v/t.* *oft* **~ up** *Am.* F aufteilen.

dix·ie[1] ['dɪksɪ] *s.* ⚔ *sl.* **1.** Kochgeschirr *n*; **2.** ‚'Gulaschkaˌnone' *f*.

Dix·ie[2] ['dɪksɪ] → ***Dixieland***; **'Dix·ie·crat** [-kræt] *s. Am. pol. Mitglied e-r Splittergruppe der Demokratischen Partei in den Südstaaten*; **'Dix·ie·land** *s.* **1.** *Bezeichnung für den Süden der USA*; **2.** ♪ Dixieland *m*, Dixie *m*.

diz·zi·ness ['dɪzɪnɪs] *s.* Schwindel(anfall) *m*; Benommenheit *f*; **diz·zy** ['dɪzɪ] **I** *adj.* □ **1.** schwindlig: ***~ spell*** Schwindelanfall *m*; **2.** schwindelnd, schwindelerregend: ***~ heights***; **3.** verwirrt, benommen; **4.** unbesonnen; **5.** F verrückt; **II** *v/t.* **6.** schwindlig machen; **7.** verwirren.

D-mark ['di:mɑ:k] *s.* Deutsche Mark.

do[1] [du:; dʊ] **I** *v/t.* [*irr.*] **1.** tun, machen: ***what can I ~ for you?*** womit kann ich dienen?; ***what does he ~ for a living?*** womit verdient er sein Brot?; ***~ right*** recht tun; → ***done*** 1; **2.** tun, ausführen, sich beschäftigen mit, verrichten, voll'bringen, erledigen: ***~ business*** Geschäfte machen; ***~ one's duty*** s-e Pflicht tun; ***~ French*** Französisch lernen; ***~ Shakespeare*** Shakespeare durchnehmen *od.* behandeln; ***~ it into German*** es ins Deutsche übersetzen; ***~ lecturing*** Vorlesungen halten; ***my work is done*** m-e Arbeit ist getan *od.* fertig; ***he had done working*** er war mit der Arbeit fertig; ***~ 60 miles per hour*** 60 Meilen die Stunde fahren; ***he did all the talking*** er führte das große Wort; ***it can't be done*** es geht nicht; ***~ one's best*** sein Bestes tun, sich alle Mühe geben; ***~ better*** a) (et.) Besseres tun *od.* leisten, b) sich verbessern; → ***done***; **3.** herstellen, anfertigen: ***~ a translation*** e-e Übersetzung machen; ***~ a portrait*** ein Porträt malen; **4.** *j-m et.* tun, zufügen, erweisen, gewähren: ***~ s.o. harm*** j-m schaden; ***~ s.o. an injustice*** j-m ein Unrecht zufügen, j-m unrecht tun; ***these pills ~ me (no) good*** diese Pillen helfen mir (nicht); **5.** bewirken, erreichen: ***I did it*** ich habe es geschafft; ***now you've done it!*** *b.s.* nun hast du es glücklich geschafft!; **6.**

herrichten, in Ordnung bringen, (zu'recht)machen, *Speisen* zubereiten: **~ a room** ein Zimmer aufräumen *od.* ‚machen'; **~ one's hair** sich das Haar machen, sich frisieren; **I'll ~ the flowers** ich werde die Blumen gießen; **7.** *Rolle etc.* spielen, ‚machen': **~ Hamlet** den Hamlet spielen; **~ the host** den Wirt spielen; **~ the polite** den höflichen Mann markieren; **8.** genügen, passen, recht sein (*dat.*): **will this glass ~ you?** genügt Ihnen dieses Glas?; **9.** F erschöpfen, ermüden: **he was pretty well done** er war ‚erledigt' (*am Ende s-r Kräfte*); **10.** F erledigen, abfertigen: **I'll ~ you next** ich nehme Sie als nächsten dran; **~ a town** e-e Stadt besichtigen *od.* ‚erledigen'; **that has done me** das hat mich ‚fertiggemacht' *od.* ruiniert; **~ 3 years in prison** *sl.* drei Jahre ‚abbrummen'; **11.** F ‚reinlegen', ‚übers Ohr hauen', ‚einseifen': **~ s.o. out of s.th.** j-n um et. betrügen *od.* bringen; **you have been done** (**brown**) du bist schön angeschmiert worden; **12.** F behandeln, versorgen, bewirten: **~ s.o. well** j-n gut versorgen; **~ o.s. well** es sich gutgehen lassen, sich gütlich tun; **II** *v/i.* [*irr.*] **13.** handeln, vorgehen, tun, sich verhalten: **he did well to come** er tat gut daran zu kommen; **nothing ~ing!** a) es ist nichts los, b) F nichts zu machen!, ausgeschlossen!; **it's ~ or die now!** jetzt geht's ums Ganze!; **have done!** hör auf!, genug davon!; → **Rome**; **14.** vor'ankommen, Leistungen voll'bringen: **~ well** a) es gut machen, Erfolg haben, b) gedeihen, gut verdienen (→ 15); **~ badly** schlecht daran sein, schlecht *mit et.* fahren; **he did brilliantly at his examination** er hat ein glänzendes Examen gemacht; **15.** sich befinden: **~ well** a) gesund sein, b) in guten Verhältnissen leben, c) sich gut erholen; **how ~ you ~?** a) guten Tag!, b) *obs.* wie geht es Ihnen?, c) es freut mich (, Sie kennenzulernen); **16.** genügen, ausreichen, passen, recht sein: **will this quality ~?** reicht diese Qualität aus?; **that will ~** a) das genügt, b) genug davon!; **it will ~ tomorrow** es hat Zeit bis morgen; **that won't ~** a) das genügt nicht, b) das geht nicht (an); **that won't ~ with me** das verfängt bei mir nicht; **it won't ~ to be rude** mit Grobheit kommt man nicht weit(er), man darf nicht unhöflich sein; **I'll make it ~** ich werde damit (schon) auskommen *od.* reichen; **III** *v/aux.* **17.** *Verstärkung*: **I ~ like it** es gefällt mir sehr; **~ be quiet!** sei doch still!; **he did come** er ist tatsächlich gekommen; **they did go, but** sie sind zwar *od.* wohl gegangen, aber; **18.** *Umschreibung*: a) *in Fragesätzen*: **~ you know him? No, I don't** kennst du ihn? Nein (, ich kenne ihn nicht), b) *in mit* **not** *verneinten Sätzen*: **he did not** (*od.* **didn't**) **come** er ist nicht gekommen; **19.** *bei Umstellung nach* **hardly**, **little** *etc.*: **rarely does one see such things** solche Dinge sieht man selten; **20.** *statt Wiederholung des Verbs*: **you know as well as I ~** Sie wissen so gut wie ich; **did you buy it? – I did!** hast du es gekauft? – jawohl!; **I take a bath – so ~ I** ich nehme ein Bad – ich auch; **21. you learn German, don't you?** du lernst Deutsch, nicht wahr?; **he doesn't work too hard, does he?** er arbeitet sich nicht tot, nicht wahr?;

Zssgn mit prp.:

do| by *v/i.* behandeln, handeln an (*dat.*): **do well by s.o.** j-n gut *od.* anständig behandeln; **do** (**[un]to others**) **as you would be done by** was du nicht willst, daß man dir tu', das füg auch keinem andern zu; **~ for** *v/i.* **1.** passen *od.* sich eignen für *od.* als; ausreichen für; **2.** F *j-m* den Haushalt führen; **3.** sorgen für; **4.** F zu'grunde richten, ruinieren: **he is done for** er ist ‚erledigt'; **~ to** → **do by**; **~ with** *v/t. u. v/i.* **1.** : **I can't do anything with him** (**it**) ich kann nichts mit ihm (damit) anfangen; **I have nothing to ~ it** ich habe nichts damit zu schaffen, es geht mich nichts an, es betrifft mich nicht; **I won't have anything to ~ you** ich will mit dir nichts zu schaffen haben; **2.** auskommen *od.* sich begnügen mit: **can you ~ bread and cheese for supper?** genügen dir Brot und Käse zum Abendessen?; **3.** er-, vertragen: **I can't ~ him and his cheek** ich kann ihn mit s-r Frechheit nicht ertragen; **4.** *mst* **could ~** (gut) gebrauchen können: **I could ~ the money**; **he could ~ a haircut** er müßte sich mal (wieder) die Haare schneiden lassen; **~ with·out** *v/i.* auskommen ohne, *et.* entbehren, verzichten auf (*acc.*): **we shall have to ~** wir müssen ohne (es) auskommen;

Zssgn mit adv.:

do| a·way with *v/i.* **1.** beseitigen, abschaffen, aufheben; **2.** *Geld* 'durchbringen; **3.** 'umbringen, töten; **~ down** *v/t.* F **1.** reinlegen, ‚übers Ohr hauen', ‚bescheißen'; **2.** ‚her'untermachen'; **~ in** *v/t. sl.* **1.** *j-n* 'umbringen; **2.** → **do down** 1; **3.** *j-n* ‚erledigen', ‚schaffen'; **~ out** *v/t.* F *Zimmer etc.* säubern; **~ up** *v/t.* **1.** a) zs.-schnüren, b) *Päckchen* verschnüren, zu'rechtmachen, c) einpakken, d) *Kleid etc.* zumachen; **2.** *das Haar* hochstecken; **3.** herrichten, in Ordnung bringen; **4.** → **do in** 3.

do² [du:] *pl.* **dos, do's** [-z] *s.* **1.** *sl.* Schwindel *m*, ‚Beschiß' *m*, fauler Zauber; **2.** *Brit.* F Fest *n*, ‚Festivi'tät' *f*, ‚große Sache'; **3. do's and don'ts** Gebote *pl. u.* Verbote *pl.*, Regeln *pl.*

do³ [dəʊ] *s.* ♪ do *n* (*Solmisationssilbe*).

do·a·ble ['du:əbl] *adj.* 'durchführ-, machbar; **'do-all** *s.* Fak'totum *n.*

doat [dəʊt] → **dote.**

doc [dɒk] F *abbr. für* **doctor.**

do·cent [dəʊ'sent] *s. Am.* Pri'vatdo,zent *m.*

doc·ile ['dəʊsaɪl] *adj.* □ **1.** fügsam, gefügig; **2.** gelehrig; **3.** fromm (*Pferd*); **do·cil·i·ty** [dəʊ'sɪlətɪ] *s.* **1.** Fügsamkeit *f*; **2.** Gelehrigkeit *f.*

dock¹ [dɒk] **I** *s.* **1.** Dock *n*: **dry ~, graving ~** Trockendock; **floating ~** Schwimmdock; **wet ~** Dockhafen *m*; **put in ~** → 6; **2.** Hafenbecken *n*, Anlegeplatz *m*: **~ authorities** Hafenbehörde *f*; **~ dues** → **dockage¹** 1; **~ strike** Dockarbeiterstreik *m*; **3.** *pl.* Docks *pl.*, Dock-, Hafenanlagen *pl.*; **4.** *Am.* Kai *m*; **5.** 🚂 *Am.* Laderampe *f*; **II** *v/t.* **6.** *Schiff* (ein)docken; **7.** *Raumschiffe* koppeln; **III** *v/i.* **8.** ins Dock gehen, docken; im Dock liegen; **9.** anlegen (*Schiff*); **10.** andocken (*Raumschiffe*).

dock² [dɒk] **I** *s.* **1.** Fleischteil *m* des Schwanzes; **2.** Schwanzstummel *m*; **3.** Schwanzriemen *m*; **4.** (Lohn- *etc.*)Kürzung *f*; **II** *v/t.* **5.** a) stutzen, b) den Schwanz stutzen *od.* kupieren (*dat.*); **6.** *fig.* beschneiden, kürzen.

dock³ [dɒk] *s.* ⚖ Anklagebank *f*: **be in the ~** auf der Anklagebank sitzen; **put in the ~** *fig.* anklagen.

dock⁴ [dɒk] *s.* ⚘ Ampfer *m.*

dock·age¹ ['dɒkɪdʒ] *s.* ⚓ **1.** Dock-, Hafengebühren *pl.*, Kaigebühr *f*; **2.** Docken *n*; **3.** → **dock¹** 3.

dock·age² ['dɒkɪdʒ] *s.* Kürzung *f.*

dock·er ['dɒkə] *s. Brit.* Dock-, Hafenarbeiter *m.*

dock·et ['dɒkɪt] **I** *s.* **1.** ⚖ a) Ge'richts-, Ter'minka,lender *m*, b) *Brit.* 'Urteilsre,gister *n*, c) *Am.* Pro'zeßliste *f*; **2.** Inhaltsangabe *f*, -vermerk *m*; **3.** *Am.* Tagesordnung *f*; **4.** ✝ a) A'dreßzettel *m*, Eti'kett *n*, b) *Brit.* Zollquittung *f*, c) *Brit.* Bestell-, Lieferschein *m*; **II** *v/t.* **5.** in e-e Liste eintragen (→ 1 b u. c); **6.** mit Inhaltsangabe *od.* Eti'kett versehen; **7.** *Am.* auf die Tagesordnung setzen.

dock·ing ['dɒkɪŋ] *s. Raumfahrt*: Andokken *n*, Kopp(e)lung *f.*

'dock|·land *s.* Hafenviertel *n*; **'~,mas·ter** *s.* 'Hafenkapi,tän *m*, Dockmeister *m*; **'~,war·rant** *s.* ✝ Docklagerschein *m*; **~ work·er** → **docker**; **'~·yard** *s.* ⚓ **1.** Werft *f*; **2.** *Brit.* Ma'rinewerft *f.*

doc·tor ['dɒktə] **I** *s.* **1.** Doktor *m*, Arzt *m*: **~'s stuff** F Medizin *f*; **that's just what the ~ ordered** das ist genau das richtige; **doll ~** F Puppendoktor; **2.** *univ.* Doktor *m*: **♀ of Divinity** (**Laws**) Doktor der Theologie (Rechte); **take one's ~'s degree** (zum Doktor) promovieren; **Dear ~** Sehr geehrter Herr Doktor!; **3. ♀ of the Church** Kirchenvater *m*; **4.** ⚓ *sl.* Smutje *m*, Schiffskoch *m*; **5.** ⚙ Schaber *m*, Abstreichmesser *n*; **6.** *Angeln*: künstliche Fliege; **II** *v/t.* **7.** ‚verarzten', ärztlich behandeln; **8.** F *Tier* kastrieren; **9.** ‚ausbessern', ‚zu'rechtflicken'; **10.** *a.* **~ up** a) *Wein etc.* (ver)panschen, b) *Abrechnungen etc.* ‚frisieren', (ver)fälschen; **III** *v/i.* **11.** F (als Arzt) praktizieren; **'doc·tor·al** [-tərəl] *adj.* Doktor(s)...: **~ candidate** Doktorand(in); **~ cap** Doktorhut *m*; **'doc·tor·ate** [-tərɪt] *s.* Dokto'rat *n*, Doktorwürde *f.*

doc·tri·naire [,dɒktrɪ'neə] **I** *s.* Doktri'när *m*, Prin'zipienreiter *m*; **II** *adj.* doktri'när.

doc·tri·nal [dɒk'traɪnl] *adj.* □ lehrmäßig, Lehr...; *weitS* dog'matisch: **~ proposition** Lehrsatz *m*; **~ theology** Dogmatik *f*; **doc·trine** ['dɒktrɪn] *s.* **1.** Dok'trin *f*, Lehre *f*, Lehrmeinung *f*; **2.** *bsd. pol.* Dok'trin *f*, Grundsatz *m*: **party ~** Parteiprogramm *n.*

doc·u·dra·ma ['dɒkjʊ,drɑ:mə] *s. Film, TV*: Dokumen'tarspiel *n.*

doc·u·ment ['dɒkjʊmənt] **I** *s.* **1.** Doku'ment *n*, Urkunde *f*, Schrift-, Aktenstück *n*, 'Unterlage *f*, *pl. a.* Akten *pl.*; **2.** Beweisstück *n*; **3.** (**shipping**) **~s** *pl.* ✝ Ver'lade-, 'Schiffspa,piere *pl.*: **~s against acceptance** (**payment**) Dokumente gegen Akzept (Bezahlung); **II**

v/t. [-ment] **4.** dokumentieren (*a. fig.*), (urkundlich) belegen; **5.** *Buch etc.* mit (genauen) Beleghinweisen versehen; **6.** ✝ mit den notwendigen Pa'pieren versehen; **doc·u·men·ta·ry** [ˌdɒkjʊ'mentərɪ] **I** *adj.* **1.** dokumen'tarisch, urkundlich: **~ *bill*** ✝ Dokumententratte *f*; **~ *evidence*** Urkundenbeweis *m*; **2.** *Film etc.*: Dokumentar..., Tatsachen...: **~ *film***; **~ *novel***; **II** *s.* Dokumen'tar-, Tatsachenfilm *m*; **doc·u·men·ta·tion** [ˌdɒkjʊmen'teɪʃn] *s.* Dokumentati'on *f*: a) Urkunden-, Quellenbenutzung *f*, b) dokumen'tarischer Nachweis *od.* Beleg.

dod·der¹ ['dɒdə] *s.* ♀ Teufelszwirn *m*, Flachsseide *f*.

dod·der² ['dɒdə] *v/i.* F **1.** zittern (*vor Schwäche*); **2.** wack(e)lig gehen, wakkeln; '**dod·dered** [-əd] *adj.* **1.** astlos (*Baum*); **2.** altersschwach, tatterig; '**dod·der·ing** [-ərɪŋ], '**dod·der·y** [-ərɪ] *adj.* F se'nil, tatterig, vertrottelt.

do·dec·a·gon [dəʊ'dekəgən] *s.* ⩓Zwölfeck *n*.

do·dec·a·he·dron [ˌdəʊdekə'hedrən] *pl.* **-drons, dra** [-drə] *s.* ⩓Dodeka'eder *n*, Zwölfflächner *m*; ˌ**do·dec·a'syl·la·ble** [-'sɪləbl] *s.* zwölfsilbiger Vers.

dodge [dɒdʒ] **I** *v/i.* **1.** (rasch) zur Seite springen, ausweichen; **2.** a) schlüpfen, b) sich verstecken, c) flitzen; **3.** Ausflüchte gebrauchen, Winkelzüge machen; **4.** sich drücken; **II** *v/t.* **5.** ausweichen (*dat.*); **6.** F sich drücken vor, um'gehen, aus dem Weg gehen (*dat.*), vermeiden; **III** *s.* **7.** Sprung *m* zur Seite, rasches Ausweichen; **8.** Kniff *m*, Trick *m*: ***be up to all the ~s*** mit allen Wassern gewaschen sein; **dodg·em (car)** ['dɒdʒəm] *s.* (Auto)Scooter *m*; '**dodg·er** [-dʒə] *s.* **1.** ‚Schlitzohr' *n*; **2.** Gauner *m*, Schwindler *m*; **3.** Drückeberger *m*; **4.** *Am.* Hand-, Re'klamezettel *m*; '**dodg·y** [-dʒɪ] *adj. Brit.* F **1.** vertrackt; **2.** ris'kant; **3.** nicht einwandfrei.

doe [dəʊ] *s. zo.* **1.** a) Damhirschkuh *f*, b) Rehgeiß *f*; **2.** *Weibchen der Hasen, Kaninchen etc.*

do·er ['du:ə] *s.* ‚Macher' *m*, Tatmensch *m*.

does [dʌz; dəz] *3. pres. sg. von* ***do¹***.

'**doe·skin** *s.* **1.** a) Rehfell *n*, b) Rehleder *n*; **2.** Doeskin *n* (*ein Wollstoff*).

doest [dʌst] *obs. od. poet. 2. pres. sg. von* ***do¹***: ***thou ~*** du tust.

doff [dɒf] *v/t.* **1.** *Kleider* ablegen, ausziehen; *Hut* lüften, ziehen; **2.** *fig. Gewohnheit* ablegen.

dog [dɒg] **I** *s.* **1.** *zo.* Hund *m*; **2.** *engS.* Rüde *m* (*männlicher Hund, Wolf* [*a.* ***dog-wolf***], *Fuchs* [*a.* ***dog-fox***] *etc.*); **3.** *oft* ***dirty ~*** (gemeiner) Hund *m*, Schuft *m*; **4.** F Bursche *m*, Kerl *m*: ***gay ~*** lustiger Vogel; ***lucky ~*** Glückspilz *m*; ***sly ~*** schlauer Fuchs; **5.** *ast.* a) ***Greater*** (***Lesser***) ♀ Großer (Kleiner) Hund, b) → ***Dog Star***; **6.** ***the ~s*** *Brit.* F das Windhundrennen; **7.** ⚙ a) Klaue *f*, Knagge *f*, b) Anschlag(bolzen) *m*, c) Bock *m*, Gestell *n*; **8.** ⚒ Hund *m*, Förderwagen *m*; **9.** → ***fire-dog***;

Besondere Redewendungen:

not a ~'s chance nicht die geringste Chance; ***~ in the manger*** Neidhammel *m*; ***~s of war*** Kriegsfurien; ***~'s dinner*** F Pfusch(arbeit *f*) *m*; ***~ does not eat ~*** eine Krähe hackt der anderen kein Auge aus; ***go to the ~s*** vor die Hunde gehen; ***every ~ has his day*** jeder hat einmal Glück im Leben; ***help a lame ~ over a stile*** j-m in der Not helfen; ***lead a ~'s life*** ein Hundeleben führen; ***lead s.o. a ~'s life*** j-m das Leben zur Hölle machen; ***let sleeping ~s lie*** a) schlafende Hunde soll man nicht wecken, laß die Finger davon, b) laß den Hund begraben sein, rühr nicht alte Geschichten auf; ***put on ~*** F‚angeben', vornehm tun; ***throw to the ~s*** wegwerfen, vergeuden, *fig.* den Wölfen (zum Fraß) vorwerfen, opfern;

II *v/t.* **10.** *j-m* auf dem Fuße folgen, *j-n* verfolgen, jagen, *j-m* nachspüren: ***~ s.o.'s steps*** j-m auf den Fersen bleiben; **11.** *fig.* verfolgen: ***~ged by bad luck***.

dog| bis·cuit *s.* Hundekuchen *m*; '**~·cart** *s.* Dogcart *m* (*Wagen*); ˌ**~-'cheap** *adj. u. adv.* F spottbillig; **~ col·lar** *s.* **1.** Hundehalsband *n*; **2.** F Kol'lar *n*, (steifer) Kragen *e-s Geistlichen*; **~ days** *s. pl.* Hundstage *pl.*

doge [dəʊdʒ] *s. hist.* Doge *m*.

'**dog|-ear** *s.* Eselsohr *n*; '**~-eared** *adj.* mit Eselsohren (*Buch*); **~ end** *s. Brit.* F (Ziga'retten)Kippe *f*; '**~·fight** *s.* Handgemenge *n*; ⚔Einzel-, Nahkampf *m*; ✈Kurven-, Luftkampf *m*; '**~·fish** *s.* kleiner Hai, *bsd.* Hundshai *m*.

dog·ged ['dɒgɪd] *adj.* □ verbissen, hartnäckig, zäh; '**dog·ged·ness** [-nɪs] *s.* Verbissenheit *f*, Zähigkeit *f*.

dog·ger ['dɒgə] *s.* ⚓ *Dogger m* (*zweimastiges Fischerboot*).

dog·ger·el ['dɒgərəl] **I** *s.* Knittelvers *m*; **II** *adj.* holperig (*Vers etc.*).

dog·gie ['dɒgɪ] → ***doggy*** 1; **~ bag** *s.* F Beutel *m* zum Mitnehmen von Essensresten (*im Restaurant*).

dog·gish ['dɒgɪʃ] *adj.* □ **1.** hundeartig, Hunde...; **2.** bissig, mürrisch.

dog·go ['dɒgəʊ] *adv.*: ***lie ~*** a) sich nicht mucksen, b) sich versteckt halten.

dog·gone ['dɒgɒn] *adj. u. int. Am.* F verdammt.

dog·gy ['dɒgɪ] **I** *s.* **1.** Hündchen *n*, Wauwau *m*; **II** *adj.* **2.** hundeartig; **3.** hundeliebend; **4.** *Am.* F todschick.

'**dog|·house** *s.* Hundehütte *f*: ***in the ~*** *Am.* F in Ungnade; **~ Lat·in** *s.* 'Küchenlaˌtein *n*; **~ lead** [li:d] *s.* Hundeleine *f*.

dog·ma ['dɒgmə] *pl.* **-mas, -ma·ta** [-mətə] *s.* **1.** *eccl.* Dogma *n*: a) Glaubenssatz *m*, b) 'Lehrsysˌtem *n*; **2.** Lehrsatz *m*; **3.** *fig.* Dogma *n*, Grundsatz *m*; **dog·mat·ic** [dɒg'mætɪk] **I** *adj.* (□ ***~ally***) *eccl. u. fig. contp.* dog'matisch; **II** *s. pl. sg. konstr.* Dog'matik *f*; '**dog·ma·tism** [-ətɪzəm] *s. contp.* Dogma'tismus *m*; '**dog·ma·tist** [-ətɪst] *s. eccl. u. fig.* Dog'matiker *m*; '**dog·ma·tize** [-ətaɪz] **I** *v/i. bsd. contp.* dogmatisieren, dog'matische Behauptungen aufstellen (***on*** über *acc.*); **II** *v/t.* dogmatisieren, zum Dogma erheben.

ˌ**do-'good·er** *s.* F Weltverbesserer *m*, Humani'tätsaˌpostel *m*.

'**dog|-ˌpad·dle** *v/i.* (wie ein Hund) paddeln; **~ rac·ing** *s.* Hunderennen *n*; '**~-rose** *s.* ♀ Heckenrose *f*.

'**dogsˌbod·y** ['dɒgz-] *s.* F ‚Kuli' *m* (*der die Dreckarbeit machen muß*).

'**dog's-ear** *etc.* → ***dog-ear*** *etc.*

'**dog|-show** *s.* Hundeausstellung *f*; '**~·skin** *s.* Hundsleder *n*; ♀ **Star** *s. ast.* Sirius *m*, Hundsstern *m*; **~ tag** *s.* **1.** Hundemarke *f*; **2.** ⚔ *Am. sl.* ‚Hundemarke' *f* (*Erkennungsmarke*); **~ tax** *s.* Hundesteuer *f*; ˌ**~-'tired** *adj.* F hundemüde; '**~-tooth** *s.* [*irr.*] ⚠ 'Zahnornaˌment *n*; '**~·trot** *s.* leichter Trab; '**~·watch** *s.* ⚓ ‚Plattfuß' *m* (*Wache*); '**~·wood** *s.* ♀ Hartriegel *m*.

doi·ly ['dɔɪlɪ] *s.* (Zier)Deckchen *n*.

do·ing ['du:ɪŋ] *s.* **1.** Tun *n*: ***that was your ~*** a) das hast du getan, b) es war deine Schuld; ***that will take some ~*** das will erst getan sein; **2.** *pl.* a) Taten *pl.*, Tätigkeit *f*, b) Vorfälle *pl.*, Begebenheiten *pl.*, c) Treiben *n*, Betragen *n*: ***fine ~s these!*** das sind mir schöne Geschichten!; **3.** *pl. sg. konstr. Brit.* F ‚Dingsbums' *n*.

doit [dɔɪt] *s.* Deut *m*: ***not worth a ~*** keinen Pfifferling wert.

ˌ**do-it-your'self** **I** *s.* Heimwerken *n*; **II** *adj.* Do-it-yourself..., Heimwerker...; ˌ**do-it-your'self·er** [-fə] *s.* F Heimwerker *m*.

dol·drums ['dɒldrəmz] *s. pl.* **1.** *geogr.* a) Kalmengürtel *m*, -zone *f*, b) Kalmen *pl.*, äquatori'ale Windstillen *pl.*; **2.** Niedergeschlagenheit *f*, Trübsinn *m*: ***in the ~*** a) deprimiert, Trübsal blasend, b) e-e Flaute durchmachend (*Geschäft etc.*).

dole [dəʊl] **I** *s.* **1.** milde Gabe, Almosen *n*; **2.** *bsd. Brit.* F ‚Stempelgeld' *n*: ***be*** (*od.* ***go***) ***on the ~*** stempeln gehen; **II** *v/t.* **3.** *mst* ***~ out*** sparsam aus-, verteilen.

dole·ful ['dəʊlfʊl] *adj.* □ traurig; trübselig; '**dole·ful·ness** [-nɪs] *s.* Trübseligkeit *f*.

dol·i·cho·ce·phal·ic [ˌdɒlɪkəʊse'fælɪk] *adj.* langköpfig, -schädelig.

'**do-ˌlit·tle** *s.* F Faulpelz *m*.

doll [dɒl] **I** *s.* **1.** Puppe *f*: ***~'s house*** Puppenstube *f*, -haus *n*; ***~'s pram*** *bsd. Brit.* Puppenwagen *m*; ***~'s face*** *fig.* Puppengesicht *n*; **2.** F ‚Puppe' *f* (*Mädchen*); *Am. sl. allg.* Frau *f*; **II** *v/t. u. v/i.* ***~ up*** F (sich) feinmachen: ***all ~ed up*** aufgedonnert.

dol·lar ['dɒlə] *s.* Dollar *m*: ***the almighty ~*** das Geld, der Mammon; ***~ diplomacy*** Dollardiplomatie *f*.

doll·ish ['dɒlɪʃ] *adj.* □ puppenhaft.

dol·lop ['dɒləp] *s.* F Klumpen *m*, ‚Klacks' *m*; *Am.* ‚Schuß' *m*: ***~ of brandy***.

doll·y ['dɒlɪ] **I** *s.* **1.** Püppchen *n*; **2.** ⚙ a) niedriger Trans'portkarren, b) *Film*: Kamerawagen *m*, c) 'Schmalspurlokomoˌtive *f* (*an Baustellen*); **3.** ⚙ Nietkolben *m*; **4.** Wäschestampfer *m*, -stößel *m*; **5.** *Am.* Anhängerbock *m* (*Sattelschlepper*); **6.** *a.* ***~ bird*** F ‚Püppchen' *n* (*Mädchen*); **II** *adj.* **7.** puppenhaft; **III** *v/t.* **8.** ***~ in*** (***out***) *Film*: *die Kamera* vorfahren (zu'rückfahren); **~ shot** *s. Film*: Fahraufnahme *f*.

dol·man ['dɒlmən] *pl.* **-mans** *s.* **1.** Damenmantel *m* mit capeartigen Ärmeln: ***~ sleeve*** capeartiger Ärmel; **2.** Dolman *m* (*Husarenjacke*).

dol·men ['dɒlmen] *s.* Dolmen *m* (*vorgeschichtliches Steingrabmal*).

dol·o·mite ['dɒləmaɪt] *s. min.* Dolo'mit *m*: ***the ♀s*** *geogr.* die Dolomiten.

do·lor *Am.* → ***dolour***; **dol·or·ous** [ˈdɒlərəs] *adj.* □ traurig, schmerzlich; **do·lour** [ˈdɒlə] *s.* Leid *n*, Pein *f*, Qual *f*, Schmerz *m*.

dol·phin [ˈdɒlfɪn] *s.* **1.** *zo.* a) Delˈphin *m*, b) Tümmler *m*; **2.** *ichth.* ˈGoldmaˌkrele *f*; **3.** ⚓ a) Ankerboje *f*, b) Dalbe *f*.

dolt [dəʊlt] *s.* Dummkopf *m*, Tölpel *m*; ˈ**dolt·ish** [-tɪʃ] *adj.* □ tölpelhaft, dumm.

do·main [dəʊˈmeɪn] *s.* **1.** Doˈmäne *f*, Staatsgut *n*; **2.** Landbesitz *m*; Herrengut *n*; **3.** (***power of***) ***eminent*** ~ *Am.* Enteignungsrecht *n des Staates*; **4.** *fig.* Doˈmäne *f*, Gebiet *n*, Bereich *m*, Sphäre *f*, Reich *n*.

dome [dəʊm] *s.* **1.** *allg.* Kuppel *f*; **2.** Wölbung *f*; **3.** *obs.* Dom *m*, *poet. a.* stolzer Bau; **4.** ⚙ Haube *f*, Deckel *m*; **5.** *Am.* ‚Birne' *f* (*Kopf*); **domed** [-md] *adj.* gewölbt; kuppelförmig.

Domes·day Book [ˈdu:mzdeɪ] *s. Reichsgrundbuch Englands* (*1086*).

ˈ**dome-shaped** → ***domed***.

do·mes·tic [dəʊˈmestɪk] **I** *adj.* (□ ~***ally***) **1.** häuslich, Haus…, Haushalts…, Familien…, Privat…: ~ ***affairs*** häusliche Angelegenheiten (→ 4); ~ ***court*** *Am.* Familiengericht *n*; ~ ***drama*** *thea.* bürgerliches Drama; ~ ***economy*** *od.* ***science*** Hauswirtschaft(slehre) *f*; ~ ***life*** Familienleben *n*; ~ ***relations law*** ⚖ *Am.* Familienrecht *n*; ~ ***servant*** → 6; **2.** häuslich (veranlagt): ***a*** ~ ***man***; **3.** inländisch, Inland(s)…, einheimisch, Landes…; Innen…, Binnen…: ~ ***bill*** ✝ Inlandswechsel *m*; ~ ***goods*** Inlandswaren; ~ ***mail*** *Am.* Inlandspost *f*; ~ ***trade*** Binnenhandel *m*; **4.** *pol.* inner, Innen…: ~ ***affairs*** innere *od.* innenpolitische Angelegenheiten (→ 1); ~ ***policy*** Innenpolitik *f*; **5.** zahm, Haus…: ~ ***animal*** Haustier *n*; **II** *s.* **6.** Hausangestellte(r *m*) *f*, Dienstbote *m*; **doˈmes·ti·cate** [-keɪt] *v/t.* **1.** domestizieren: a) zähmen, zu Haustieren machen, b) zu Kulturpflanzen machen; **2.** an häusliches Leben gewöhnen: ***not*** ~***d*** a) nichts vom Haushalt verstehend, b) nicht am Familienleben hängend, ‚nicht gezähmt'; **3.** *Wilde* zivilisieren; **do·mes·ti·ca·tion** [dəʊˌmestɪˈkeɪʃn] *s.* **1.** Domestizierung *f*: a) Zähmung *f*, b) ⚘ Kultivierung *f*; **2.** Gewöhnung *f* an häusliches Leben; **3.** Einbürgerung *f*; **do·mes·tic·i·ty** [ˌdəʊmeˈstɪsətɪ] *s.* **1.** (Neigung *f* zur) Häuslichkeit *f*; **2.** häusliches Leben; **3.** *pl.* häusliche Angelegenheiten *pl.*

dom·i·cile [ˈdɒmɪsaɪl], *Am. a.* ˈ**dom·i·cil** [-sɪl] **I** *s.* **1.** a) (ständiger *od.* bürgerlichrechtlicher) Wohnsitz, b) Wohnort *m*, c) Wohnung *f*; **2.** ✝ Sitz *m* e-r Gesellschaft; **3.** *a.* ***legal*** ~ ⚖ Gerichtsstand *m*; **II** *v/t.* **4.** ansässig *od.* wohnhaft machen, ansiedeln; **5.** ✝ *Wechsel* domizilieren; ˈ**dom·i·ciled** [-ld] *adj.* **1.** ansässig, wohnhaft; **2.** ~ ***bill*** ✝ Domizilwechsel *m*; **dom·i·cil·i·ar·y** [ˌdɒmɪˈsɪljərɪ] *adj.* Haus…, Wohnungs…: ~ ***arrest*** Hausarrest *m*; ~ ***visit*** Haussuchung *f*; **dom·i·cil·i·ate** [ˌdɒmɪˈsɪljeɪt] *v/t.* ✝ *Wechsel* domizilieren.

dom·i·nance [ˈdɒmɪnəns] *s.* **1.** (Vor-)Herrschaft *f*, (Vor)Herrschen *n*; **2.** Macht *f*; **3.** *biol.* Domiˈnanz *f*; ˈ**dom·i·nant** [-nt] **I** *adj.* □ **1.** dominierend, vorherrschend; **2.** beherrschend: a) bestimmend, entscheidend: ~ ***factor***, b) emˈporragend, weithin sichtbar; **3.** *biol.* domiˈnant, überlagernd; **4.** ♪ Dominant…; **II** *s.* **5.** *biol.* vorherrschendes Merkmal; ♪, *a.* ⚘ Domiˈnante *f*; ˈ**dom·i·nate** [-neɪt] **I** *v/t.* beherrschen (*a. fig.*): a) herrschen über (*acc.*), b) emˈporragen über (*acc.*); **II** *v/i.* dominieren, (vor)herrschen: ~ ***over*** herrschen über (*acc.*).

dom·i·na·tion [ˌdɒmɪˈneɪʃn] *s.* (Vor-)Herrschaft *f*; ˌ**dom·iˈneer** [-ˈnɪə] *v/i.* **1.** den Herrn spielen, anmaßend auftreten; **2.** (***over***) desˈpotisch herrschen (über *acc.*), tyrannisieren (*acc.*); ˌ**dom·iˈneer·ing** [-ˈnɪərɪŋ] *adj.* □ **1.** tyˈrannisch, herrisch, gebieterisch; **2.** anmaßend.

do·min·i·cal [dəˈmɪnɪkl] *adj. eccl.* des Herrn (Jesu): ~ ***day*** Tag *m* des Herrn (*Sonntag*); ~ ***prayer*** *das* Gebet des Herrn (*Vaterunser*); ~ ***year*** Jahr *n* des Herrn.

Do·min·i·can [dəˈmɪnɪkən] *eccl.* **I** *adj.* **1.** *eccl.* Dominikaner…, dominiˈkanisch; **2.** *pol.* dominikanisch; **II** *s.* **3.** *a.* ~ ***friar*** Dominiˈkaner(mönch) *m*; **4.** *pol.* Dominiˈkaner(in).

dom·i·nie [ˈdɒmɪnɪ] *s.* **1.** *Scot.* Schulmeister *m*; **2.** (Herr) Pastor *m*.

do·min·ion [dəˈmɪnjən] *s.* **1.** (Ober-)Herrschaft *f*, (Regierungs)Gewalt *f*; **2.** ⚖ a) Eigentumsrecht *n*, b) (tatsächliche) Gewalt (***over*** über *e-e Sache*); **3.** (Herrschafts)Gebiet *n*; **4.** a) *hist.* ⁓ Doˈminion *n* (*im Brit. Commonwealth*), b) ***the*** ⁓ *Am.* Kanada *n*.

dom·i·no [ˈdɒmɪnəʊ] *pl.* **-noes** *s.* **1.** a) *pl. sg. konstr.* Domino(spiel) *n*, b) Dominostein *m*; **2.** Domino *m* (*Maskenkostüm od. Person*); ~ **the·o·ry** *s. pol.* ˈDominotheoˌrie *f*.

don[1] [dɒn] *s.* **1.** ⁓ *span. Titel; weitS.* Spanier *m*; **2.** *Brit.* Universitätslehrer *m* (*Fellow od. Tutor*); **3.** Fachmann *m* (***at*** in *dat.*, für).

don[2] [dɒn] *v/t. et.* anziehen, *den Hut* aufsetzen.

do·nate [dəʊˈneɪt] *v/t.* schenken (*a.* ⚖), stiften, *a. Blut etc.* spenden (***to s.o.*** j-m); **doˈna·tion** [-eɪʃn] *s.* Schenkung *f* (*a.* ⚖), Stiftung *f*, Gabe *f*, Geschenk *n*, Spende *f*.

done [dʌn] **I** *p.p. von* **do**[1]; **II** *adj.* **1.** getan: ***well*** ~***!*** gut gemacht!, bravo!; ***it isn't*** ~ so et. tut man nicht, das gehört sich nicht; ***what is to be*** ~***?*** was ist zu tun?, was soll geschehen?; ~ ***at …*** *in Urkunden*: gegeben in *der Stadt New York etc.*; **2.** erledigt (*a. fig.*): ***get s.th.*** ~ et. erledigen (lassen); ***he gets things*** ~ er bringt et. zuwege; **3.** gar: ***is the meat*** ~ ***yet?***; ***well*** ~ durchgebraten; **4.** F fertig: ***have*** ~ ***with*** a) fertig sein mit (*a. fig.*), b) nicht mehr brauchen, c) nichts mehr zu tun haben wollen mit; **5.** *a.* ~ ***up***, ~ ***in*** erschöpft, ‚erledigt', ‚fertig'; **6.** ~***!*** abgemacht!

do·nee [dəʊˈni:] *s.* ⚖ Beschenkte(r *m*) *f*, Schenkungsempfänger(in).

dong [dɒŋ] *s. Am.* V ‚Pimmel' *m* (*Penis*).

don·jon [ˈdɒndʒən] *s.* **1.** Donˈjon *m*, Hauptturm *m*; **2.** Bergfried *m*, Burgturm *m*.

don·key [ˈdɒŋkɪ] **I** *s.* **1.** Esel *m* (*a. fig.*): ~***'s years*** *Brit.* F e-e ‚Ewigkeit'; **2.** → ***donkey engine***; **II** *adj.* **3.** ⚙ Hilfs…: ~ ***pump***; ~ **en·gine** *s.* ⚙ kleine (*transportable*) ˈHilfsmaˌschine; ˈ~**·work** *s.* F Dreckarbeit *f*.

don·nish [ˈdɒnɪʃ] *adj.* **1.** gelehrt; **2.** belehrend.

do·nor [ˈdəʊnə] *s.* Geber *m*; Schenker *m* (*a.* ⚖); Spender *m* (*a.* ⚕), Stifter *m*; ~ **card** *s.* Orˈganspenderausweis *m*.

ˈ**do-ˌnoth·ing** **I** *s.* Faulenzer(in); **II** *adj.* faul, nichtstuerisch.

Don Quix·ote [ˌdɒnˈkwɪksət] *s.* Don Quiˈchotte *m* (*weltfremder Idealist*).

don't [dəʊnt] **I** a) F *für* ***do not***, b) *sl. für* ***does not***; **II** *s.* F Verbot *n*; → ***do***[2] 3; ~ **know** *s.* a) Unentschiedene(r *m*) *f*, b) j-d, der (*bei e-r Umfrage*) keine Meinung hat.

doo·dle [ˈdu:dl] **I** *s.* gedankenlos hingezeichnete Fiˈgur(en *pl.*), Gekritzel *n*; **II** *v/i.* et. (gedankenlos) ˈhinkritzeln, ‚Männchen malen'.

doom [du:m] **I** *s.* **1.** Schicksal *n*; (*bsd.* böses) Geschick, Verhängnis *n*: ***he met his*** ~ das Schicksal ereilte ihn; **2.** Verderben *n*, ˈUntergang *m*, *a.* Tod *m*, *fig.* Todesurteil *n*; **3.** *obs.* Urteilsspruch *m*, Verdammung *f*; **4.** ***the day of*** ~ das Jüngste Gericht; → ***crack*** 1; **II** *v/t.* **5.** verurteilen, verdammen (***to*** zu): ~ ***to death***; **doomed** [-md] *adj.* a) verloren, dem ˈUntergang geweiht, b) *bsd. fig.* verdammt, verurteilt (***to*** zu, ***to do*** zu tun): ~ ***to failure*** zum Scheitern verurteilt; ***the*** ~ ***train*** der Unglückszug *m*; **dooms·day** [ˈdu:mzdeɪ] *s. das* Jüngste Gericht: ***till*** ~ bis zum Jüngsten Tag; **Dooms·day Book** → ***Domesday Book***; **doom·ster** [ˈdu:mstə] *s.* ˈWeltuntergangsproˌphet *m*.

door [dɔ:] *s.* **1.** Tür *f*: ***out of*** ~***s*** draußen, im Freien; ***within*** ~***s*** im Hause, drinnen; ***from*** ~ ***to*** ~ von Haus zu Haus; ***delivered to your*** ~ frei Haus (geliefert); ***two*** ~***s away*** (*od.* ***off***) zwei Häuser weiter; → ***next*** 1; **2.** Ein-, Zugang *m*, Tor *n*, Pforte *f* (*alle a. fig.*): ***at death's*** ~ am Rande des Grabes; ***lay s.th. at s.o.'s*** ~ j-m et. zur Last legen; ***lay the blame at s.o.'s*** ~ j-m die Schuld zuschieben; ***close*** (*od.* ***bang***, ***shut***) ***the*** ~ ***on*** a) *j-n* abweisen, b) *et.* unmöglich machen; ***open a*** ~ ***to s.th.*** et. ermöglichen, *b.s.* e-r Sache Tür u. Tor öffnen; ***see*** (*od.* ***show***) ***s.o. to the*** ~ j-n zur Tür begleiten; ***show s.o. the*** ~ j-m die Tür weisen; ***turn out of*** ~***s*** *j-n* hinauswerfen; → ***darken*** 1; ˈ~**·bell** *s.* Türklingel *f*; ~ **han·dle** *s.* Türgriff *m*, -klinke *f*; ˈ~ˌ**keep·er** *s.* Pförtner *m*; ˈ~**·key child** *s.* Schlüsselkind *n*; ˈ~**·knob** *s.* Türgriff *m*; ˈ~ˌ**knock·er** *s.* Türklopfer *m*; ˈ~**·man** [-mən] *s.* [*irr.*] (livrierter) Portiˈer; ˈ~**·mat** *s.* Fußmatte *f*, Fußabstreifer *m* (*a. fig. contp.*); ˈ~**·nail** *s.* Türnagel *m*; → ***dead*** 1; ˈ~**·plate** *s.* Türschild *n*; ˈ~**·post** *s.* Türpfosten *m*; ˈ~**·step** *s.* (Haus)Türstufe *f*: ***on s.o.'s*** ~ vor j-s Tür (*a. fig.*); ˌ~**-to-**ˈ~ *adj.* Haus-zu-Haus-…: ~ ***selling*** Verkauf *m* an der Haustür; ˈ~**·way** *s.* **1.** Torweg *m*; **2.** Türöffnung *f*; **3.** *fig.* Zugang *m*; ˈ~**·yard** *s. Am.* Vorgarten *m*.

dope [dəʊp] **I** *s.* **1.** Schmiere *f*, dicke Flüssigkeit; **2.** ✈ (Spann)Lack *m*, Firnis *m*; **3.** ⚙ Schmiermittel *n*; Zusatz (-stoff) *m*; Ben'zinzusatzmittel *n*; **4.** *sl.* ‚Stoff' *m*, Rauschgift *n*; **5.** *sl.* Reiz-, Aufputschmittel *n*; **6.** *oft* ***inside*** **~** *sl.* Geheimtip(s *pl.*) *m*, Informati'on (-en *pl.*) *f*; **7.** *sl.* Trottel *m*, Idi'ot *m*; **II** *v/t.* **8.** ✈ lackieren, firnissen; **9.** ⚙ *dem Benzin* ein Zusatzmittel beimischen; **10.** *sl. j-m* ‚Stoff' geben; **11.** *sl.* a) *sport* dopen: ***doping test*** Dopingkontrolle *f*, b) *e-m Pferd* ein leistungshemmendes Präpa'rat geben, c) *ein Getränk etc.* (mit e-m Betäubungsmittel) präparieren, d) *fig.* einschläfern, -lullen; **12.** *mst* **~** ***out*** *sl.* a) her'ausfinden, ausfindig machen, b) ausknobeln; **'~-fiend** *s. sl.* Rauschgiftsüchtige(r *m*) *f*.

dope·y ['dəʊpɪ] *adj. sl.* doof.

dor [dɔː], **dor·bee·tle** ['dɔːˌbiːtl] *s. zo.* **1.** Mist-, Roßkäfer *m*; **2.** Maikäfer *m*.

Do·ri·an ['dɔːrɪən] **I** *adj.* dorisch; **II** *s.* Dorier *m*; **Dor·ic** ['dɒrɪk] **I** *adj.* **1.** dorisch: **~** ***order*** ⌂ dorische (Säulen)Ordnung; **2.** breit, grob (*Mundart*); **II** *s.* **3.** Dorisch *n*, dorischer Dia'lekt; **4.** breiter *od.* grober Dia'lekt.

dorm [dɔːm] *s.* F *für* ***dormitory***.

dor·man·cy ['dɔːmənsɪ] *s.* Schlafzustand *m*, Ruhe(zustand *m*) *f* (*a.* ⚘); **'dor·mant** [-nt] *adj.* **1.** schlafend (*a. her.*), ruhend (*a.* ⚘), untätig (*a. Vulkan*); **2.** *zo.* Winterschlaf haltend; **3.** *fig.* a) schlummernd, la'tent, verborgen, b) unbenutzt, brachliegend: **~** ***talent***; **~** ***capital*** † totes Kapital: **~** ***partner*** † stiller Teilhaber; **~** ***title*** ⚖ ruhender *od.* nicht beanspruchter Titel; ***lie*** **~** ruhen, brachliegen.

dor·mer ['dɔːmə] *s.* ⌂ **1.** (Dach)Gaupe *f*; **2.** *a.* **~** ***window*** stehendes Dachfenster.

dor·mi·to·ry ['dɔːmɪtrɪ] *s.* **1.** Schlafsaal *m*; **2.** (*bsd.* Stu'denten)Wohnheim *n*; **~ sub·urb** *s.* Schlafstadt *f*.

dor·mouse ['dɔːmaʊs] *pl.* **-mice** [-maɪs] *s. zo.* Haselmaus *f*; → ***sleep*** 1.

dor·my ['dɔːmɪ] *adj. Golf*: dormy (*mit so viel Löchern führend, wie noch zu spielen sind*): ***be*** **~** ***two*** dormy 2 stehen.

dor·sal ['dɔːsl] *adj.* □ dor'sal (⚘, *zo., anat., ling.*), Rücken…

do·ry¹ ['dɔːrɪ] *s.* Dory *n* (*Boot*).

do·ry² ['dɔːrɪ] → ***John Dory***.

dos·age ['dəʊsɪdʒ] *s.* **1.** Dosierung *f*; **2.** → ***dose*** 1, 2; **dose** [dəʊs] **I** *s.* **1.** ⚕ Dosis *f*, (Arz'nei)Gabe *f*; **2.** *fig.* Dosis *f*, ‚Schuß' *m*, Porti'on *f*; **3.** *a.* **~** ***of clap*** V Tripper *m*; **II** *v/t.* **4.** *Arznei* dosieren; **5.** *j-m* Arz'nei geben; **6.** *Wein* zuckern.

doss [dɒs] *Brit. sl.* **I** *s.* ‚Falle' *f*, ‚Klappe' *f*, Schlafplatz *m*; **II** *v/i.* ‚pennen'.

dos·ser¹ ['dɒsə] *s.* Rücken(trag)korb *m*.

dos·ser² ['dɒsə] *s. sl.* **1.** ‚Pennbruder' *m*; **2.** → ***dosshouse***.

'doss·house *s. sl.* ‚Penne' *f* (*billige Pension*).

dos·si·er ['dɒsɪeɪ] *s.* Dossi'er *n*, Akten *pl.*, Akte *f*.

dost [dʌst; dəst] *obs. od. poet. 2. pres. sg. von* ***do¹***.

dot¹ [dɒt] *s.* ⚖ Mitgift *f*.

dot² [dɒt] **I** *s.* **1.** Punkt *m* (*a.* ♪), Tüpfelchen *n*: **~*s and dashes*** Punkte u. Striche, *tel.* Morsezeichen; ***come on the*** **~** F auf den Glockenschlag pünktlich kommen; ***since the year*** **~** F seit e-r Ewigkeit; **2.** Tupfen *m*, Fleck *m*; **3.** *et.* Winziges, Knirps *m*; **II** *v/t.* **4.** punktieren (*a.* ♪): **~*ted line***; ***sign on the*** **~*ted line*** (*fig.* ohne weiteres) unterschreiben; **5.** mit dem i-Punkt versehen: **~** ***the*** (*od.* ***one's***) ***i's*** [***and cross the*** (*od.* ***one's***) ***t's***] *fig.* peinlich genau *od.* penibel sein; **6.** tüpfeln; **7.** über'säen, sprenkeln: **~*ted with flowers***; **8.** *sl.* **~** ***s.o. one*** j-m eine ‚knallen'.

dot·age ['dəʊtɪdʒ] *s.* **1.** Senili'tät *f*: ***he is in his*** **~** er ist kindisch *od.* senil geworden; **2.** *fig.* Affenliebe *f*, Vernarrtheit *f*; **'do·tard** [-təd] *s.* se'niler Mensch; **dote** [dəʊt] *v/i.* **1.** kindisch *od.* senil sein; **2.** (***on***) vernarrt sein (in *acc.*), abgöttisch lieben (*acc.*).

doth [dʌθ; dəθ] *obs. od. poet. 3. pres. sg. von* ***do¹***.

dot·ing ['dəʊtɪŋ] *adj.* □ **1.** vernarrt (***on*** in *acc.*): ***he is a doting husband*** er liebt s-e Frau abgöttisch; **2.** se'nil, kindisch.

dot·ter·el, **dot·trel** ['dɒtrəl] *s. orn.* Mori'nell(regenpfeifer) *m*.

dot·ty ['dɒtɪ] *adj.* **1.** punktiert, getüpfelt; **2.** F wackelig; **3.** F ‚bekloppt'.

dou·ble ['dʌbl] **I** *adj.* □ **1.** doppelt, Doppel…, zweifach, gepaart: **~** ***the amount*** der doppelte *od.* zweifache Betrag; **~** ***bottom*** doppelter Boden (*Schiff, Koffer*); **~** ***doors*** Doppeltür *f*; **~** ***taxation*** Doppelbesteuerung *f*; **~** ***width*** doppelte Breite, doppelt breit; **~** ***pneumonia*** ⚕ doppelseitige Lungenentzündung; **~** ***standard of morals*** *fig.* doppelte *od.* doppelbödige Moral; **~** (***of***) ***what it was*** doppelt *od.* zweimal soviel wie vorher; **2.** Doppel…, verdoppelt, verstärkt: **~** ***ale*** Starkbier *n*; **3.** Doppel…, für zwei bestimmt: **~** ***bed*** Doppelbett *n*; **~** ***room*** Doppel-, Zweibettzimmer *n*; **4.** ⚘ gefüllt (*Blume*); **5.** ♪ eine Ok'tave tiefer, Kontra…; **6.** zwiespältig, zweideutig, doppelsinnig; **7.** unaufrichtig, falsch: **~** ***character***; **8.** gekrümmt, gebeugt; **II** *adv.* **9.** doppelt, noch einmal: **~** ***as long***; **10.** doppelt, zweifach: ***see*** **~** doppelt sehen; ***play*** (***at***) **~** ***or quit***(***s***) alles aufs Spiel setzen; **11.** paarweise, zu zweit: ***to sleep*** **~**; **III** *s.* **12.** *das* Doppelte *od.* Zweifache; **13.** Doppel *n*, Dupli'kat *n*: **14.** a) Gegenstück *n*, Ebenbild *n*, b) Double *n*, Doppelgänger *m*; **15.** Windung *f*, Falte *f*; **16.** Haken *m* (*bsd. Hase, a. Person*), plötzliche Kehrtwendung; **17.** ***at the*** **~** ⚔ im Schnellschritt; **18.** *mst pl. sg. konstr. sport* Doppel *n*: ***play a*** **~*s*** (***match***); ***men's*** **~*s*** Herrendoppel; **19.** *sport* a) Doppelsieg *m*, b) Doppelniederlage *f*; **20.** Doppelwette *f*; **21.** *Film*: Double *n*, *thea.* zweite Besetzung; **22.** *Bridge etc.*: Doppel *n*; **IV** *v/t.* **23.** verdoppeln (*a.* ♪); **24.** um das Doppelte über'treffen; **25.** *oft* **~** ***up*** ('um-, zs.-) falten, 'um-, zs.-legen, 'umschlagen; **26.** *Beine* 'überschlagen; *Faust* ballen; **27.** ⚓ um'segeln, -'schiffen; **28.** a) *Film, TV* als Double einspringen für, *j-n* doubeln, b) **~** ***the parts of A. and B.*** *thea. etc.* A. u. B. in e-r Doppelrolle spielen; **29.** *Spinnerei*: doublieren; **30.** *Karten*: *Gebot* doppeln; **V** *v/i.* **31.** sich verdoppeln; **32.** sich falten (lassen); **33.** a) plötzlich kehrtmachen, b) e-n Haken schlagen; **34.** *thea.* a) e-e Doppelrolle spielen, b) **~** ***for*** → 28a; **35.** ♪ zwei Instru'mente spielen; **36.** ⚔ a) im Schnellschritt marschieren, b) F Tempo vorlegen; **37.** a) den Einsatz verdoppeln, b) *Bridge*: doppeln.

Zssgn mit adv.:

dou·ble| back **I** *v/t.* → ***double*** 25; **II** *v/i.* kehrtmachen; **~ in** *v/t.* nach innen falten, einbiegen, -schlagen; **~ up** **I** *v/t.* **1.** → ***double*** 25; **2.** (zs.-)krümmen; **II** *v/i.* **3.** → ***double*** 32; **4.** sich krümmen *od.* biegen (*a. fig.* ***with*** vor *Schmerz, Lachen*); **5.** das Zimmer *etc.* gemeinsam benutzen: **~** ***on s.th.*** sich (in) et. teilen.

ˌdou·ble|-'act·ing, **ˌ~-'ac·tion** *adj.* ⚙ doppeltwirkend; **~ a·gent** *s. pol.* 'Doppelaˌgent *m*; **'~-ˌbar·rel(l)ed** *adj.* **1.** doppelläufig: **~** ***gun*** Doppelflinte *f*; **2.** zweideutig; **3.** zweifach: **~** ***name*** F Doppelname *m*; **~ bass** [beɪs] → ***contrabass***; **'~-ˌbed·ded** *adj.*: **~** ***room*** Zweibettzimmer *n*; **~ bend** *s.* S-Kurve *f*; **~ bill** *s.* Doppelveranstaltung *f*; **ˌ~-'breast·ed** *adj.* zweireihig (*Anzug*); **ˌ~-'check** *v/t.* genau nachprüfen; **~ chin** *s.* Doppelkinn *n*; **~ col·umn** *s.* Doppelspalte *f* (*Zeitung*): ***in*** **~*s*** zweispaltig; **ˌ~-'cross** *v/t.* ein doppeltes *od.* falsches Spiel treiben mit, *bsd. den Partner* ‚anschmieren'; **~ date** *s.* 'Doppelrendezˌvous *n* (*zweier Paare*); **ˌ~-'deal·er** *s.* falscher *od.* ‚linker' Kerl, Betrüger *m*; **ˌ~-'deal·ing** **I** *adj.* falsch, betrügerisch; **II** *s.* Betrug *m*, Gemeinheit *f*; **ˌ~-'deck·er** *s.* **1.** Doppeldecker *m* (*Schiff, Flugzeug, Omnibus*); **2.** a) zweistöckiges Haus *etc.*, b) E'tagenbett *n*, c) Ro'man *m* in zwei Bänden, d) *Am.* F Doppelsandwich *n*; **~ Dutch** *s.* F Kauderwelsch *n*; **ˌ~-'dyed** *adj.* **1.** zweimal gefärbt; **2.** *fig.* eingefleischt, Erz…: **~** ***villain*** Erzgauner *m*; **~ ea·gle** *s.* **1.** *her.* Doppeladler *m*; **2.** *Am. goldenes 20-Dollar-Stück*; **ˌ~-'edged** *adj.* zweischneidig (*a. fig.*): **~** ***sword***; **~ en·ten·dre** [ˌduːblɑ̃ːnˈtɑ̃ːndrə] (*Fr.*) *s. allg.* Zweideutigkeit *f*; **~ en·try** *s.* † **1.** doppelte Buchung; **2.** doppelte Buchführung; **~ ex·po·sure** *s. phot.* Doppelbelichtung *f*; **'~-faced** *adj.* heuchlerisch, scheinheilig, unaufrichtig; **~ fault** *s. Tennis*: Doppelfehler *m*; **~ fea·ture** *s. Film*: 'Doppelproˌgramm *n* (*zwei Spielfilme in jeder Vorstellung*); **~ first** *s. univ. Brit.* mit Auszeichnung erworbener ***honours degree*** in zwei Fächern; **'~ˌgang·er** [-ˌgæŋə] *s. psych.* Doppelgänger *m*; **~ har·ness** *s. fig.* Ehestand *m*, -joch *n*; **~ in·dem·ni·ty** *s. Am.* Verdoppelung *f* der Versicherungssumme (*bei Unfalltod*); **ˌ~-'joint·ed** *adj.* mit ‚Gummigelenken' (*Person*); **~ life** *s.* Doppelleben *n*; **~ mean·ing** *s.* Zweideutigkeit *f*; **ˌ~-'mind·ed** *adj.* **1.** wankelmütig, unentschlossen; **2.** unaufrichtig; **~ mur·der** *s.* Doppelmord *m*.

dou·ble·ness ['dʌblnɪs] *s.* **1.** *das* Doppelte; **2.** Doppelzüngigkeit *f*, Falschheit *f*.

ˌdou·ble|-'park *v/t. u. v/i. mot.* in zweiter Reihe parken; **ˌ~-'quick** ⚔ **I** *s.* → ***double time***; **II** *adv.* F im Eiltempo; **ˌ~-'spaced** *adj.* zweizeilig, mit doppeltem Zeilenabstand; **~ star** *s. ast.* Doppelstern *m*; **ˌ~-'stop** ♪ **I** *s.* Doppelgriff *m* (*Streichinstrument*); **II** *v/t.* Doppelgriffe

spielen auf (*dat.*).
dou·blet [ˈdʌblɪt] *s.* **1.** *hist.* Wams *n*; **2.** Paar *n* (*Dinge*); **3.** Duˈblette *f*: a) Dupliˈkat *n*, b) *typ.* Doppelsatz *m*; **4.** *pl.* Pasch *m* (*beim Würfeln*).
ˌ**dou·ble|-ˈtake** *s. sl.* ‚Spätzündung' *f* (*verzögerte Reaktion*): ***I did a ~ when*** ich stutzte zweimal, als; **~ talk** *s.* F doppeldeutiges Gerede, ‚Augenauswischeˈrei' *f*; **~ tax·a·tion** *s.* ⚕ Doppelbesteuerung *f*; ˈ**~-think** *s.* ‚Zwiedenken' *n*; **~ time** *s.* ⚔ a) Schnellschritt *m*, b) (langsamer) Laufschritt: ***in ~*** F im Eiltempo, fix; ˌ**~-ˈtongued** *adj.* doppelzüngig, falsch; ˌ**~-ˈtracked** *adj.* 🚂 zweigleisig.
dou·bling [ˈdʌblɪŋ] *s.* **1.** Verdoppelung *f*; **2.** Faltung *f*; **3.** Haken(schlagen *n*) *m*; **4.** Trick *m*; **dou·bly** [ˈdʌblɪ] *adv.* doppelt.
doubt [daʊt] **I** *v/i.* **1.** zweifeln; schwanken, Bedenken haben; **2.** zweifeln (***of, about*** an *e-r Sache*); (darˈan) zweifeln, (es) bezweifeln (***whether, if*** ob; ***that*** daß; *neg. u. interrog.* ***that, but that, but*** daß): ***I ~ whether he will come*** ich zweifle, ob er kommen wird; **II** *v/t.* **3.** *et.* bezweifeln: ***I ~ his honesty; I ~ it***; **4.** mißˈtrauen (*dat.*), keinen Glauben schenken (*dat.*): ***~ s.o.; ~ s.o's words***; **III** *s.* **5.** Zweifel *m* (***of*** an *dat.*, ***about*** hinsichtlich *gen.*; ***that*** daß): ***no ~, without ~, beyond ~*** zweifellos, fraglos, gewiß; ***I have no ~*** ich zweifle nicht (daran), ich bezweifle es nicht; ***be in ~ about*** Zweifel haben an (*dat.*); ***leave s.o. in no ~ about s.th.*** j-n nicht im ungewissen über et. lassen; → ***benefit*** 1; **6.** a) Bedenken *n*, Besorgnis *f*, (***about*** wegen), b) Argwohn *m*: ***raise ~s*** Zweifel aufkommen lassen; **7.** Ungewißheit *f*: ***be in ~*** unschlüssig sein; ˈ**doubt·er** [-tə] *s.* Zweifler(in); ˈ**doubt·ful** [-fʊl] *adj.* □ **1.** zweifelnd, im Zweifel, unschlüssig: ***be ~ of*** (*od.* ***about***) ***s.th.*** an e-r Sache zweifeln, im Zweifel über et. sein; **2.** zweifelhaft: a) unsicher, fraglich, unklar, b) fragwürdig, bedenklich, c) ungewiß, d) verdächtig, dubiˈos; ˈ**doubt·ful·ness** [-fʊlnɪs] *s.* **1.** Zweifelhaftigkeit *f*: a) Unsicherheit *f*, b) Fragwürdigkeit *f*, c) Ungewißheit *f*; **2.** Unschlüssigkeit *f*; ˈ**doubt·ing** [-tɪŋ] *adj.* □ zweifelnd: a) schwankend, unschlüssig, b) ˈmißtrauisch: ***℘ Thomas*** ungläubiger Thomas; ˈ**doubt·less** [-lɪs] *adv.* zweifellos, sicherlich.
dou·ceur [duˈsɜː] (*Fr.*) *s.* **1.** (Geld)Geschenk *n*, Trinkgeld *n*; **2.** Bestechungsgeld *n*.
douche [duːʃ] **I** *s.* **1.** Dusche *f*, Brause *f*: ***cold ~*** *a. fig.* kalte Dusche; **2.** ⚕ a) Spülung *f*, Dusche *f*, b) Irriˈgator *m*; **II** *v/t. u. v/i.* **3.** (sich) (ab)duschen; **4.** ⚕ (aus)spülen; **III** *v/i.* **5.** ⚕ e-e Spülung machen.
dough [dəʊ] *s.* **1.** Teig *m* (*a. weitS.*); **2.** *bsd. Am. sl.* ‚Zaster' *m* (*Geld*); ˈ**~·boy** *s.* **1.** Mehlkloß *m*; **2.** *a.* ˈ**~·foot** *Am. sl.* Landser *m* (*Infanterist*); ˈ**~·nut** *s.* Krapfen *m*, Berˈliner (Pfannkuchen) *m*.
dough·ty [ˈdaʊtɪ] *adj.* □ *obs. od. poet.* mannhaft, tapfer.
dough·y [ˈdəʊɪ] *adj.* **1.** teigig (*a. fig.*); **2.** klitschig, nicht ˈdurchgebacken.
dour [ˈdʊə] *adj.* □ **1.** mürrisch; **2.** streng, hart; **3.** halsstarrig, stur.
douse [daʊs] *v/t.* **1.** a) ins Wasser tauchen, b) begießen; **2.** F *Licht* auslöschen; **3.** ⚓ a) *Segel* laufen lassen, b) *Tau* loswerfen.
dove [dʌv] *s.* **1.** *orn.* Taube *f*: ***~ of peace*** Friedenstaube; **2.** Täubchen *n*, ‚Schatz' *m*; **3.** *eccl.* Taube *f* (*Symbol des Heiligen Geistes*); **4.** *pol.* ‚Taube' *f*: ***~s and hawks*** Tauben u. Falken; ˈ**~ˌcol·o(u)r** *s.* Taubengrau *n*; **~-cot(e)** [ˈdʌvkɒt] *s.* Taubenschlag *m*; ˈ**~-eyed** *adj.* sanftäugig; ˈ**~·like** *adj.* sanft.
ˈ**dove's-foot** [ˈdʌvz-] *s.* ⚘ Storchschnabel *m*.
ˈ**dove·tail I** *s.* **1.** ⚙ Schwalbenschwanz *m*, Zinke *f*; **II** *v/t.* **2.** verschwalben, verzinken; **3.** *fig.* fest zs.-fügen, (ineinˈander) verzahnen, verquicken; **4.** einfügen, -passen, -gliedern (***into*** in *acc.*); **5.** passend zs.-setzen; einpassen (***into*** in *acc.*); **III** *v/i.* **6.** genau passen (***into*** in *acc.*, zu; ***with*** mit); angepaßt sein (***with*** *dat.*); genau ineinˈandergreifen, -passen.
dow·a·ger [ˈdaʊədʒə] *s.* **1.** Witwe *f* (von Stande): ***queen ~*** Königinwitwe; ***~ duchess*** Herzoginwitwe; **2.** Maˈtrone *f*, würdevolle ältere Dame.
dow·di·ness [ˈdaʊdɪnɪs] *s.* Schäbigkeit *f*, Schlampigkeit *f*; **dow·dy** [ˈdaʊdɪ] **I** *adj.* □ **1.** schlechtgekleidet, ˈuneleˌgant, schäbig, schlampig; **II** *s.* **2.** nachlässig gekleidete Frau; **3.** *Am.* (*ein*) Apfelauflauf *m*.
dow·el [ˈdaʊəl] ⚙ **I** *s.* (Holz-, *a.* Wand-) Dübel *m*, Holzpflock *m*; **II** *v/t.* (ver)dübeln.
dow·er [ˈdaʊə] **I** *s.* **1.** ⚖ Wittum *n*; **2.** *obs.* Mitgift *f*; **3.** Begabung *f*; **II** *v/t.* **4.** ausstatten (*a. fig.*).
Dow-Jones av·er·age *od.* **in·dex** [ˌdaʊˈdʒəʊnz] *s.* ⚕ Dow-Jones-Index *m* (*Aktienindex der New Yorker Börse*).
down[1] [daʊn] *s.* **1.** a) Daunen *pl.*, flaumiges Gefieder, b) Daune *f*, Flaumfeder *f*: ***~ quilt*** Daunendecke *f*; **2.** Flaum *m* (*a.* ⚘), feine Härchen *pl.*
down[2] [daʊn] *s.* **1.** a) Hügel *m*, b) Düne *f*; **2.** *pl.* waldloses, *bsd.* grasbewachsenes Hügelland.
down[3] [daʊn] **I** *adv.* **1.** (*Richtung*) nach unten, her-, hinˈunter, her-, hinˈab, abwärts, zum Boden, nieder…: ***~ from*** von … herab, von … an, fort von; ***~ to*** bis (hinunter) zu; ***~ to the last man*** bis zum letzten Mann; ***~ to our times*** bis in unsere Zeit; ***burn ~*** niederbrennen; ***~!*** nieder!, *zum Hund*: leg dich!; ***~ with the capitalists!*** nieder mit den Kapitalisten!; **2.** *Brit.* a) nicht in London, b) nicht an der Universiˈtät: ***~ to the country*** aufs Land, in die Provinz; **3.** *Am.* ins Geschäftsviertel, in die Stadt (-mitte); **4.** südwärts; **5.** angesetzt: ***~ for Friday*** für Freitag angesetzt; ***~ for second reading*** *parl.* zur zweiten Lesung angesetzt; **6.** (in) bar, soˈfort: ***pay ~*** bar bezahlen; ***one pound ~*** ein Pfund sofort *od.* als Anzahlung; **7.** ***be ~ on s.o.*** F a) j-n ‚auf dem Kieker' haben, b) über j-n herfallen; **8.** (*Lage, Zustand*) unten; unten im Hause: ***~ below*** unten; ***~ there*** dort unten; ***~ under*** F in *od.* nach Australien *od.* Neuseeland; ***~ in the country*** auf dem Lande; ***~ south*** (unten) im Süden; ***he is not ~ yet*** er ist noch nicht unten *od.* (*morgens*) noch nicht aufgestanden; **9.** ˈuntergegangen (*Gestirne*); **10.** herˈabgelassen (*Haare, Vorhänge*); **11.** gefallen (*Preise, Temperatur etc.*); billiger (*Ware*); **12.** ***he was two points ~*** *sport* er lag zwei Punkte zurück; ***he is £10 ~*** *fig.* er hat 10 £ verloren; **13.** a) niedergestreckt, am Boden (liegend), b) *Boxen*: am Boden, ‚unten': ***~ and out*** k.o., *fig.* (*a. physisch u. psychisch*) ‚erledigt', ‚kaputt', ‚fix u. fertig'; ***~ with flu*** mit Grippe im Bett; **14.** niedergeschlagen, deprimiert; **15.** herˈuntergekommen, in elenden Verhältnissen lebend: ***~ at heels*** abgerissen; **II** *adj.* **16.** abwärts gerichtet, nach unten, Abwärts…: ***~ trend*** fallende Tendenz; **17.** *Brit.* von London abfahrend *od.* kommend: ***~ train***; ***~ platform*** Abfahrtsbahnsteig *m* (*in London*); **18.** *Am.* in Richtung Stadt(mitte), zum Geschäftsviertel (hin); **III** *prp.* **19.** her-, hinˈunter, her-, hinˈab, entlang: ***~ the hill*** den Hügel hinunter; ***~ the river*** flußabwärts; ***further ~ the river*** weiter unten am Fluß; ***~ the road*** die Straße entlang; ***~ the middle*** durch die Mitte; ***~ (the) wind*** ⚓ mit dem Wind; → ***downtown***; **20.** (*Zeit*) durch: ***~ the ages*** durch alle Zeiten; **IV** *s.* **21.** Nieder-, Rückgang *m*; Tiefstand *m*; **22.** Depressiˈon *f*, (seelischer) Tiefpunkt; **23.** F Groll *m*: ***have a ~ on s.o.*** j-n auf dem ‚Kieker' haben; **V** *v/t.* **24.** zu Fall bringen (*a. sport u. fig.*); niederschlagen; bezwingen; ruinieren; **25.** niederlegen: ***~ tools*** die Arbeit niederlegen, in den Streik treten; **26.** ✈ abschießen, ‚runterholen'; **27.** F *ein Getränk* ‚runterkippen'.
ˌ**down|-and-ˈout I** *adj.* völlig ‚erledigt', ‚restlos fertig'; ganz ‚auf den Hund' gekommen; **II** *s.* Pennbruder *m*; ˌ**~-at-(the-)ˈheels** *adj. allg.* heˈruntergekommen; ˈ**~·beat I** *s.* **1.** ♪ erster Schlag (*des Taktes*); **2.** ***on the ~*** *fig.* im Rückgang (begriffen); **II** *adj.* **3.** F pessiˈmistisch; ˈ**~·cast I** *adj.* **1.** niedergeschlagen (*a. Augen*), deprimiert; **2.** ⚙ einziehend (*Schacht*); **II** *s.* **3.** ⚙ Wetterschacht *m*.
down·er [ˈdaʊnə] *s. sl.* Beruhigungsmittel *n*.
ˈ**down|·fall** *s.* **1.** *fig.* Sturz *m*; **2.** starker Regen- *od.* Schneefall; **3.** *fig.* Nieder-, ˈUntergang *m*; ˈ**~·grade** *s.* **1.** Gefälle *n*; **2.** *fig.* Niedergang *m*: ***on the ~*** im Niedergang begriffen; **II** *v/t.* **3.** im Rang herˈabsetzen, degradieren; **4.** niedriger einstufen; **5.** ⚕ in der Qualiˈtät herabsetzen, verschlechtern; ˌ**~-ˈheart·ed** *adj.* niedergeschlagen, entmutigt; ˌ**~ˈhill I** *adv.* abwärts, bergˈab (*beide a. fig.*): ***he is going ~*** *fig.* es geht bergab mit ihm; **II** *adj.* abschüssig: ***~ race*** *Skisport*: Abfahrtslauf *m*; ˈ**~ˌhill·er** *s. Skisport*: Abfahrtsläufer(in).
Down·ing Street [ˈdaʊnɪŋ] *s.* Downing Street *f* (*Amtssitz des Premiers od. brit. Regierung*).
down| pay·ment *s.* **1.** Barzahlung *f*; **2.** Anzahlung *f*; ˈ**~·pipe** *s.* ⚙ Fallrohr *n*; ˈ**~·pour** *s.* Regenguß *m*, Platzregen *m*; ˈ**~·right I** *adj.* **1.** völlig, absoˈlut, toˈtal: ***a ~ lie*** e-e glatte Lüge; ***a ~ rogue*** ein Erzschurke; **2.** offen(herzig), gerade, ehrlich, unverblümt, unzweideutig; **II** *adv.* **3.** völlig, ganz u. gar, durch u.

durch, ausgesprochen, to'tal; **ˌ~'ri·ver** → ***downstream***; **ˌ~'stairs I** *adv.* **1.** (die Treppe) hin'unter *od.* her'unter, nach unten; **2.** a) unten (im Haus), b) e-e Treppe tiefer; **II** *adj.* **3.** im unteren Stockwerk (gelegen), unter; **III** *s.* **4.** *pl. a. sg. konstr.* unteres Stockwerk, 'Untergeschoß *n*; **ˌ~'state** *Am.* **I** *adv.* in der *od.* die Pro'vinz; **II** *s.* (*bsd.* südliche) Pro'vinz (*e-s Bundesstaates*); **ˌ~'stream I** *adv.* **1.** strom'abwärts; **2.** mit dem Strom; **II** *adj.* **3.** stromabwärts gelegen *od.* gerichtet; **'~·stroke** *s.* **1.** Grundstrich *m beim Schreiben*; **2.** ⚙ Abwärts-, Leerhub *m*; **'~·swing** *s.* Abwärtstrend *m*, Rückgang *m*; **ˌ~-to-'earth** *adj.* rein sachlich, nüchtern; **ˌ~'town** *Am.* **I** *adv.* **1.** im *od.* ins Geschäftsviertel, in der *od.* die Innenstadt; **II** *adj.* ['daʊntaʊn] **2.** zum Geschäftsviertel, im Geschäftsviertel (gelegen *od.* tätig): ~ ***Chicago*** die Innenstadt *od.* City von Chicago; **3.** ins *od.* durchs Geschäftsviertel (fahrend *etc.*); **III** *s.* ['daʊntaʊn] **4.** Geschäftsviertel *n*, Innenstadt *f*, City *f*; **'~ˌtrod·den** *adj.* unter'drückt; **'~·turn** → ***downswing***.

down·ward ['daʊnwəd] **I** *adv.* **1.** abwärts, hin'ab, hin'unter, nach unten; **2.** *fig.* abwärts, berg'ab; **3.** *zeitlich*: abwärts: ***from*** ... ~ ***to*** von... (herab) bis...; **II** *adj.* **4.** Abwärts... (*a.* ⚙, *phys. u. fig.*); *fig.* sinkend (*Preise etc.*); **'down·wards** [-wədz] → ***downward*** I.

down·y¹ ['daʊnɪ] *adj.* **1.** mit Daunen *od.* Flaum bedeckt; **2.** flaumig, weich; **3.** *sl.* gerieben, ausgekocht.

down·y² ['daʊnɪ] *adj.* sanft gewellt (u. mit Gras bewachsen).

dow·ry ['daʊərɪ] *s.* **1.** Mitgift *f*, Aussteuer *f*; **2.** Gabe *f*, Ta'lent *n*.

dowse¹ [daʊz] → ***douse***.

dowse² [daʊz] *v/i.* mit der Wünschelrute suchen; **'dows·er** [-zə] *s.* (Wünschel-)Rutengänger *m*; **'dows·ing-rod** [-zɪŋ] *s.* Wünschelrute *f*.

doy·en ['dɔɪən] *s.* (*Fr.*) **1.** Rangälteste(r) *m*; **2.** Doy'en *m eines diplomatischen Korps*; **3.** *fig.* Nestor *m*, Altmeister *m*.

doze [dəʊz] **I** *v/i.* dösen, (halb) schlummern: ~ ***off*** einnicken; **II** *s.* a) Dösen *n*, b) Nickerchen *n*.

doz·en ['dʌzn] *s.* **1.** *sg. u. pl.* (*vor Haupt- u. nach Zahlwörtern etc. außer nach* ***some***) Dutzend *n*: ***two*** ~ ***eggs*** 2 Dutzend Eier; **2.** Dutzend *n* (*a. weitS.*): ~***s of birds*** Dutzende von Vögeln; ***some*** ~***s of children*** einige Dutzend Kinder; ~***s of people*** F ein Haufen Leute; ~***s of times*** F x-mal, hundertmal; ***by the*** ~, ***in*** ~***s*** zu Dutzenden, dutzendweise; ***cheaper by the*** ~ im Dutzend billiger; ***do one's daily*** ~ Frühgymnastik machen; ***talk nineteen to the*** ~ *Brit.* reden wie ein Wasserfall; → ***baker*** 1.

doz·y ['dəʊzɪ] *adj.* □ schläfrig, verschlafen, dösig.

drab¹ [dræb] **I** *adj.* gelbgrau, graubraun; *fig.* grau, trüb(e); düster (*Farben etc.*); freudlos (*Dasein etc.*); langweilig; **II** *s.* Gelbgrau *n*, Graubraun *n*.

drab² [dræb] **1.** Schlampe *f*; **2.** Dirne *f*, Hure *f*.

drab·ble ['dræbl] → ***draggle*** I.

drachm [dræm] *s.* **1.** → ***drachma*** 1; **2.** → ***dram***.

drach·ma ['drækmə] *pl.* **-mas**, **-mae** [-miː] *s.* **1.** Drachme *f*; **2.** → ***dram***.

Dra·co ['dreɪkəʊ] *s. ast.* Drache *m*; **Dra·co·ni·an** [drə'kəʊnjən], **Dra·con·ic** [drə'kɒnɪk] *adj.* dra'konisch, hart, äußerst streng.

draff [dræf] *s.* **1.** Bodensatz *m*; *engS.* Trester *m*; **2.** Vieh-, Schweinetrank *m*.

draft [drɑːft] **I** *s.* **1.** Skizze *f*, Zeichnung *f*; **2.** Entwurf *m*: a) Skizze *f*, b) ⚙, ⚠ Riß *m*, c) Kon'zept *n*: ~ ***agreement*** Vertragsentwurf *m*; **3.** ⚔ a) ('Sonder-)Komˌmando *n*, Abteilung *f*, b) Ersatz (-truppe *f*) *m*, c) Aushebung *f*, Einberufung *f*, Einziehung *f*: ~ ***evader*** *Am.* Drückeberger *m*; ~***-exempt*** *Am.* vom Wehrdienst befreit; **4.** ✝ a) Zahlungsanweisung *f*, b) Tratte *f*, (trassierter) Wechsel, c) Scheck *m*, d) Ziehung *f*, Trassierung *f*: ~ (***payable***) ***at sight*** Sichttratte, -wechsel; **5.** ✝ Abhebung *f*, Entnahme *f*: ***to make a*** ~ ***on*** *Geld* abheben von; **6.** *fig.* (starke) Beanspruchung: ***make a*** ~ ***on*** in Anspruch nehmen (*acc.*); **7.** → ***draught***; *bsd. Am.* → ***draught*** 1, 7, 8; **II** *v/t.* **8.** skizzieren, entwerfen; **9.** *Schriftstück* aufsetzen, abfassen; **10.** ⚔ a) auswählen, abkommandieren, b) ⚔ einziehen, -berufen (***into*** zu); **draft·ee** [drɑːf'tiː] *s.* ⚔ *Am.* Einberufene(r) *m*, Eingezogene(r) *m*; **'draft·er** [-tə] *s.* **1.** Urheber *m*, Verfasser *m*, Planer *m*; **2.** → ***draftsman*** 2.

draft·ing| board ['drɑːftɪŋ] Zeichenbrett *n*; ~ **room** *s. Am.* ⚙ 'Zeichensaal, -büˌro *n*.

drafts·man ['drɑːftsmən] *s.* [*irr.*] **1.** (Konstrukti'ons-, Muster)Zeichner *m*; **2.** Entwerfer *m*, Verfasser *m*.

draft·y ['drɑːftɪ] *adj.* zugig.

drag [dræg] **I** *s.* **1.** ⚓ a) Schleppnetz *n*, b) Dregganker *m*; **2.** ✓ a) schwere Egge, b) Mistharke *f*; **3.** ⚙ Baggerschaufel *f*; **4.** ⚙ a) Rollwagen *m*, b) Lastschlitten *m*, Schleife *f*; **5.** vierspännige Kutsche; **6.** Hemmschuh *m* (*a. fig.* ***on*** für); **7.** *aer.*, *phys.* 'Luftˌwiderstand *m*; **8.** *hunt.* a) Fährte *f*, Witterung *f*, b) Schleppe *f* (*künstliche Fährte*), c) Schleppjagd *f*; **9.** *fig.* schleppendes Verfahren; **10.** F mühsame Sache, ‚Schlauch' *m*; **11.** F a) fade Sache, b) unangenehme *od.* ‚blöde' Sache: ***what a*** ~***!*** so ein Mist!, c) fader *od.* ‚mieser' Kerl; **12.** *Am.* F Einfluß *m*, Beziehungen *pl.*; **13.** F Zug *m* (***at***, ***on*** an *e-r Zigarette*); **14.** F (*bsd. von Transvestiten getragene*) Frauenkleidung: ~ ***queen*** Homosexuelle(r) *m* in Frauenkleidung; **15.** *Am.* F Straße *f*; **16.** F für ***drag race***; **II** *v/t.* **17.** schleppen, schleifen, zerren, ziehen: ~ ***one's feet*** schlurfen, *fig.* ‚langsam tun'; ~ ***the anchor*** ⚓ vor Anker treiben; **18.** mit e-m Schleppnetz absuchen (***for*** nach) *od.* fangen *od.* finden; **19.** ausbaggern; **20.** *fig.* hi'neinziehen, -bringen (***into*** in *acc.*); → ***drag in***; **III** *v/i.* **21.** geschleppt werden; **22.** schleppen, schleifen, zerren; schlurfen (*Füße*); **23.** *fig.* zerren, ziehen (***at*** an *dat.*); **24.** mit e-m Schleppnetz suchen, dreggen (***for*** nach); **25.** → ***drag on***; **26.** → ***drag behind***; **27.** ✝ schleppend gehen; **28.** ♪ schleppen; ~ **a·long I** *v/t.* (weg-)schleppen; **II** *v/i.* sich da'hinschleppen; ~ **a·way** *v/t.* wegschleppen, -zerren: ***drag o.s. away from*** *iro.* sich losreißen von; ~ **behind** *v/i. a. fig.* zu'rückbleiben, nachhinken; ~ **down** *v/t.* **1.** her'unterziehen; **2.** *fig.* *j-n* ‚fertigmachen', zermürben; ~ **in** *v/t.* **1.** hin'einziehen; **2.** *fig.* a) *j-n* (mit) hin'einziehen, b) *et.* (krampfhaft) aufs Tapet bringen, bei den Haaren her'beiziehen; ~ **on** *v/i. fig.* a) sich da'hinschleppen, b) sich in die Länge ziehen, sich hinziehen (*Rede etc.*); ~ **out** *v/t.* **1.** in die Länge ziehen, hin'ausziehen; **2.** *fig.* *et.* aus j-m her'ausholen; ~ **up** *v/t.* **1.** hochziehen; **2.** F *Skandal etc.* ausgraben; **3.** *fig.* *Kind* recht u. schlecht aufziehen.

drag| an·chor *s.* Treib-, Schleppanker *m*; ~ **chain** *s.* Hemmkette *f*.

drag·gle ['drægl] **I** *v/t.* **1.** beschmutzen; **II** *v/i.* **2.** nachschleifen; **3.** nachhinken; **'drag·gle·tail** *s.* Schlampe *f*.

'drag|·hound *s. hunt.* Jagdhund *m* für Schleppjagden; ~ **hunt** *s.* Schleppjagd *f*; **'~·lift** *s.* Schlepplift *m*; **'~·line** *s.* **1.** Schleppleine *f*, ✈ -seil *n*; **2.** Schürfkübelbagger *m*; **'~·net** *s.* **1.** a) ⚓ Schleppnetz *n*, b) *hunt.* Streichnetz *n*; **2.** *fig.* (Fahndungs)Netz *n* (*der Polizei*): ~ ***operation*** Großfahndung *f*.

drag·o·man ['drægəʊmən] *pl.* **-mans** *od.* **-men** *s. hist.* Dragoman *m*, Dolmetscher *m*.

drag·on ['drægən] *s.* **1.** Drache *m*, Lindwurm *m*, Schlange *f*: ***the old*** ♀ Satan *m*; **2.** F ‚Drache(n)' *m* (*zänkische Frau etc.*); **'~·fly** *s. zo.* Li'belle *f*; **~'s teeth** *s. pl.* **1.** ⚔ (Panzer)Höcker *pl.*; **2.** *fig.* Drachensaat *f*: ***sow*** ~ Zwietracht säen.

dra·goon [drə'guːn] **I** *s.* ⚔ Dra'goner *m*; **II** *v/t. fig.* zwingen (***into*** zu).

drag| race *s. mot.* Dragsterrennen *n*; **'~·rope** *s.* **1.** Schleppseil *n*; **2.** ✈ a) Leitseil *n*, b) Vertauungsleine *f*; ~ **show** *s.* F Transve'stitenshow *f*.

drag·ster ['drægstə] *s. mot.* Dragster *m* (*formelfreier Spezialrennwagen*).

drain [dreɪn] **I** *v/t.* **1.** *Land* entwässern, dränieren, trockenlegen; **2.** ⚕ a) *Wunde von Eiter* säubern, b) *Eiter* abziehen; **3.** *a.* ~ ***off***, ~ ***away*** (*Ab*)*Wasser etc.* ableiten, -führen, -ziehen; **4.** austrinken, leeren; → ***dreg*** 1; **5.** *Ort etc.* kanalisieren; **6.** *fig.* aufzehren, verschlukken; *Vorräte etc.* aufbrauchen, erschöpfen: ~***ed*** *fig.* erschöpft, *Person: a.* ausgelaugt; **7.** (***of***) berauben (*gen.*), arm machen (an *dat.*); **II** *v/i.* **8.** *a.* ~ ***off***, ~ ***away*** (langsam) abfließen, -tropfen; versickern; **9.** *a.* ~ ***away*** *fig.* da'hin-, verschwinden; **10.** (langsam) austrocknen; **11.** sich entwässern; **III** *s.* **12.** Ableitung *f*, Abfluß *m*, *fig. a.* Aderlaß *m*: ***foreign*** ~ ✝ Kapitalabwanderung *f*; → ***brain drain***; **13.** Abflußrohr *n*, 'Abzugskaˌnal *m*, Entwässerungsgraben *m*; Gosse *f*: ***down the*** ~ F ‚futsch', ‚im Eimer'; ***go down the*** ~ vor die Hunde gehen; ***pour down the*** ~ *Geld* zum Fenster hinauswerfen; **14.** *pl.* Kanalisati'on *f*; **15.** ⚕ Drän *m*, Ka'nüle *f*; **16.** *fig.* (***on***) Belastung *f*, Beanspruchung *f* (*gen.*): ***a great*** ~ ***on the purse*** e-e schwere finanzielle Belastung.

drain·age ['dreɪnɪdʒ] *s.* **1.** Ableitung *f*, Abfluß *m*; Entleerung *f*; **2.** Entwässerung *f*, Trockenlegung *f*, *a.* ⚕ Drai'nage *f*; **3.** Entwässerungsanlage *f*; **4.** Kanalisati'on *f*; **5.** Abwasser *n*; ~ **a·re·a**, ~

ba·sin *s.* Einzugsgebiet *n e-s Flusses*; **'~-tube** *s.* ⚕ 'Abflußka͵nüle *f.*
drain cock *s.* ⚙ Abflußhahn *m.*
drain·er ['dreɪnə] *s.* **1.** Abtropfgefäß *n*, Seiher *m*; **2.** → ***draining board.***
drain·ing board ['dreɪnɪŋ] *s.* Abtropfbrett *n.*
'drain-pipe *s.* **1.** Abflußrohr *n*; **2.** *pl. a.* **~ *trousers*** F Röhrenhose(n *pl.*) *f.*
drake [dreɪk] *s. orn.* Enterich *m.*
dram [dræm] *s.* **1.** Drachme *f* (*Gewicht*); **2.** ‚Schluck' *m* (*Whisky etc.*).
dra·ma ['drɑːmə] **I** *s.* **1.** Drama *n*: a) Schauspiel *n*, b) dra'matische Dichtung *od.* Litera'tur, Dra'matik *f*; **2.** Schauspielkunst *f*; **3.** *fig.* Drama *n*; **II** *adj.* **4.** Schauspiel...: **~ *school.***
dra·mat·ic [drə'mætɪk] *adj.* (□ **~*ally***) **1.** dra'matisch (*a.* ♪), Schauspiel..., Theater...: **~ *rights*** Aufführungsrechte; **~ *school*** Schauspielschule *f*; **~ *tenor*** ♪ Heldentenor *m*; **2.** *fig.* dramatisch, spannend, aufregend, erregend; **3.** *fig.* drastisch: **~ *changes*;** **dra'mat·ics** [-ks] *s. pl. sg. od. pl. konstr.* **1.** Dramatur'gie *f*; **2.** The'ater-, *bsd.* Liebhaberaufführungen *pl.*; **3.** *contp.* thea'tralisches Benehmen *od.* Getue.
dram·a·tis per·so·nae [͵drɑːmətɪs pɜː'səʊnaɪ] *s. pl.* **1.** Per'sonen *pl.* der Handlung; **2.** Rollenverzeichnis *n.*
dram·a·tist ['dræmətɪst] *s.* Dra'matiker *m*; **dram·a·ti·za·tion** [͵dræmətaɪ'zeɪʃn] *s.* Dramatisierung *f* (*a. fig.*), Bühnenbearbeitung *f*; **dram·a·tize** ['dræmətaɪz] **I** *v/t.* **1.** dramatisieren: a) für die Bühne bearbeiten, b) *fig.* aufbauschen: **~ *o.s.*** sich aufspielen; **II** *v/i.* **2.** sich für die Bühne *etc.* bearbeiten lassen; **3.** *fig.* über'treiben; **dram·a·tur·gic** [͵dræmə'tɜːdʒɪk] *adj.* drama'turgisch; **dram·a·tur·gist** ['dræmə͵tɜːdʒɪst] *s.* Drama'turg *m*; **dram·a·tur·gy** ['dræmə͵tɜːdʒɪ] *s.* Dramatur'gie *f.*
drank [dræŋk] *pret. von* ***drink.***
drape [dreɪp] **I** *v/t.* **1.** drapieren: a) (mit Stoff) behängen, b) in (schöne) Falten legen, c) *et.* hängen (***over*** über *acc.*), (ein)hüllen (***in*** in *acc.*); **II** *v/i.* **2.** schön fallen (*Stoff etc.*); **'drap·er** [-pə] *s.* Tuch-, Stoffhändler *m*: **~*'s* (*shop*)** Textilgeschäft *n*; **'dra·per·y** [-pərɪ] *s.* **1.** dekora'tiver Behang, Drapierung *f*; **2.** Faltenwurf *m*; **3.** *coll.* Tex'tilien *pl.*, Tex'til-, Webwaren *pl.*, Stoffe *pl.*; **4.** *Am.* Vorhangstoffe *pl.*, Vorhänge *pl.*
dras·tic ['dræstɪk] *adj.* (□ **~*ally***) drastisch (*a.* ⚕), 'durchgreifend, rigo'ros.
drat [dræt] *int.* F: **~ *it* (*you*)!** zum Teufel damit (mit dir)!; **'drat·ted** [-tɪd] *adj.* F verdammt.
draught [drɑːft] **I** *s.* **1.** Ziehen *n*, Zug *m*: **~ *animal*** Zugtier *n*; **2.** Fischzug *m* (*Fischen od. Fang*); **3.** Abziehen *n* (aus dem Faß): ***beer on* ~** Bier *n* vom Faß; **~ *beer*** *Brit.* Faßbier *n*; **4.** Zug *m*, Schluck *m*: ***a* ~ *of beer*** ein Schluck Bier; ***at a*** (*od.* ***one***) **~** auf 'einen Zug, mit 'einem Male; **5.** ⚕ Arz'neitrank *m*; **6.** ⚓ Tiefgang *m*; **7.** (Luft)Zug *m*, Zugluft *f*: ***there is a* ~** es zieht; **~ *excluder*** Dichtungsstreifen *m* (*für Türen etc.*); ***feel the* ~** F ‚den Wind im Gesicht spüren', in (finanzi'eller) Bedrängnis sein; **8.** ⚙ Zug *m* (*Schornstein etc.*); **9.** *pl. sg. konstr. Brit.* Damespiel *n*; **10.** → ***draft*** I; **II** *v/t.* **11.** → ***draft*** II; **'~-board** *s. Brit.* Dame- *od.* Schachbrett *n.*
draughts·man *s.* [*irr.*] **1.** ['drɑːftsmæn] *Brit.* Damestein *m*; **2.** [-mən] → ***draftsman.***
draught·y ['drɑːftɪ] *adj.* zugig.
draw [drɔː] **I** *s.* **1.** *a.* ⚙ Ziehen *n*, Zug *m*: ***quick on the* ~** F a) schnell (mit der Pistole), b) *fig.* ‚fix', schlagfertig; **2.** Ziehung *f*, Verlosung *f*; **3.** *fig.* Zugkraft *f*; **4.** a) Attrakti'on *f*, Glanznummer *f* (*Person od. Sache*), b) *thea.* Zugstück *n*, Schlager *m*; → ***box-office*** 2; **5.** *sport* Unentschieden *n*: ***end in a* ~** unentschieden ausgehen; **II** *v/t.* [*irr.*] **6.** *Wagen, Pistole, Schwert, Los, (Spiel)Karte, Zahn etc.* ziehen; *Gardine* zuziehen *od.* aufziehen; *Bier, Wein* abziehen, -zapfen; *Bogen(sehne)* spannen: **~ *s.o. into talk*** j-n ins Gespräch ziehen; → ***conclusion*** 3, ***bow***[2] 1, ***parallel*** 3; **7.** *fig.* anziehen, -locken, fesseln; her'vorrufen; *j-n zu et.* bewegen; *sich et.* zuziehen: ***feel* ~*n to s.o.*** sich zu j-m hingezogen fühlen; **~ *attention*** die Aufmerksamkeit lenken (***to*** auf *acc.*); **~ *an audience*** Zuhörer anlocken; **~ *ruin upon o.s.*** sich selbst sein Grab graben; **~ *tears from s.o.*** j-n zu Tränen rühren; **8.** *Gesicht* verziehen; → ***drawn*** 2; **9.** holen, sich verschaffen; entnehmen: **~ *water*** Wasser holen *od.* schöpfen; **~ (*a*) *breath*** Atem holen, *fig.* aufatmen; **~ *a sigh*** (auf)seufzen; **~ *consolation*** Trost schöpfen (***from*** aus); **~ *inspiration*** sich Anregung holen (***from*** von, bei, durch); **10.** *Mahlzeiten,* ⚔ *Rationen* in Empfang nehmen, *a. Gehalt, Lohn* beziehen; *Geld* holen, abheben, entnehmen; **11.** ziehen, auslosen: **~ *a prize*** e-n Preis gewinnen, *fig.* Erfolg haben; **~ *bonds*** ✝ Obligationen auslosen; **12.** *fig.* her'ausziehen, -bringen, her'aus-, entlocken: **~ *applause*** Beifall entlocken (***from*** *dat.*); **~ *information from s.o.*** j-n aushorchen; **~ *a reply from s.o.*** e-e Antwort aus j-m herausholen; **13.** ausfragen, -horchen (***s.o. on s.th*** j-n über et.); *j-n* aus s-r Reserve her'auslocken: ***he refused to be* ~*n*** er ließ sich nicht aushorchen; **14.** zeichnen: **~ *a portrait*; ~ *a line*** e-e Linie ziehen; **~ *it fine*** *fig.* es *zeitlich etc.* gerade noch schaffen; → ***line***[1] 12; **15.** gestalten, darstellen, schildern; **16.** *a.* **~ *up*** *Schriftstück* entwerfen, aufsetzen: **~ *a deed*** e-e Urkunde aufsetzen; **~ *a cheque*** (*Am.* ***check***) e-n Scheck ausstellen; **~ *a bill*** e-n Wechsel ziehen (***on*** auf *j-n*); **17.** ⚓ e-n Tiefgang von ... haben; **18.** *Tee* ziehen lassen; **19.** *geschlachtetes Tier* ausnehmen, *Wild a.* ausweiden; **20.** *hunt. Wald, Gelände* durch'stöbern, abpirschen; *Teich* ausfischen; **21.** ⚙ *Draht* ziehen; strecken, dehnen; **22.** **~ *the match*** *sport* unentschieden spielen; **III** *v/i.* [*irr.*] **23.** ziehen (*a. Tee, Schornstein*); **24.** das Schwert, die Pistole *etc.* ziehen, zur Waffe greifen; **25.** sich (*leicht etc.*) ziehen lassen; **26.** zeichnen, malen; **27.** Lose ziehen, losen (***for*** um); **28.** unentschieden spielen; **29.** sich (hin)begeben; sich nähern: **~ *close*** (***to s.o.*** j-m) näherrücken; **~ *round the table*** sich um den Tisch versammeln; **~ *into the station*** 🚂 in den Bahnhof einfahren; → ***draw near, level*** 11; **30.** ✝ (e-n Wechsel) ziehen (***on*** auf *acc.*); **31.** **~ *on*** in Anspruch nehmen (*acc.*), her'anziehen (*acc.*), Gebrauch machen von, zu'rückgreifen auf (*acc.*); *Kapital, Vorräte* angreifen: **~ *on one's imagination*** sich et. einfallen lassen;
Zssgn mit adv.:
draw| a·part I *v/i.* **1.** sich lösen, abrükken (***from*** von); **2.** sich ausein'anderleben; **II** *v/t.* **3.** → **~ *a·side*** *v/t. j-n* bei'seite nehmen, *a. et.* zur Seite ziehen; **~ *a·way* I** *v/t.* **1.** weg-, zu'rückziehen; **2.** ablenken; **3.** weglocken; **II** *v/i.* **4.** (***from***) sich entfernen (von); abrücken (von); **5.** (***from***) e-n Vorsprung gewinnen (vor *dat.*), sich lösen (von); **~ back I** *v/t.* **1.** *Truppen, Vorhang etc.* zu'rückziehen; **2.** ✝ *Zoll* zu'rückerhalten; **II** *v/i.* **3.** sich zu'rückziehen; **~ down** *v/t.* her'abziehen, *Jalousien* her'unterlassen; **~ in I** *v/t.* **1.** *a. Luft* einziehen; **2.** *fig. j-n* (mit) hin'einziehen; **3.** *Ausgaben etc.* einschränken; **II** *v/i.* **4.** einfahren (*Zug*); **5.** (an)halten (*Auto*); **6.** abnehmen, kürzer werden (*Tage*); **7.** sich einschränken; **~ near** *v/i.* sich nähern (***to*** *dat.*), her'anrücken; **~ off I** *v/t.* **1.** ab-, zu'rückziehen; **2.** ⚗ ausziehen; **3.** abzapfen; **4.** *Handschuhe etc.* ausziehen; **5.** *fig.* ablenken; **II** *v/i.* **6.** sich zurückziehen; **~ on I** *v/t.* **1.** anziehen: **~ *gloves*;** **2.** *fig.* a) anziehen, anlocken, b) verursachen; **II** *v/i.* **3.** sich nähern; **~ out I** *v/t.* **1.** her'ausziehen, -holen; **2.** *fig.* a) *Aussage* her'ausholen, -locken, b) *j-n* ausholen, -horchen; **3.** ⚔ *Truppen* a) abkommandieren, b) aufstellen; **4.** *fig.* ausdehnen, hin'ausziehen, in die Länge ziehen; **II** *v/i.* **5.** länger werden (*Tage*); **6.** ausfahren (*Zug*); **~ up I** *v/t.* **1.** her'aufziehen, aufrichten: ***draw o.s. up*** sich aufrichten; **2.** *Truppen etc.* aufstellen; **3.** a) → ***draw*** 16, b) ✝ *Bilanz* aufstellen, c) *Plan etc.* entwerfen; **4.** *j-n* innehalten lassen; **5.** *Pferd* zum Stehen bringen; **II** *v/i.* **6.** (an)halten; **7.** vorfahren (*Wagen*); **8.** aufmarschieren; **9.** (***with, to***) her'ankommen (an *acc.*), einholen (*acc.*).
'draw|·back *s.* **1.** Nachteil *m*, Hindernis *n*, ‚Haken' *m*; **2.** ✝ Zollrückvergütung *f*; **'~·bridge** *s.* Zugbrücke *f*; **'~·card** → ***drawing card.***
draw·ee [drɔː'iː] *s.* ✝ Bezogene(r) *m.*
draw·er ['drɔːə] *s.* **1.** Zeichner *m*; **2.** ✝ Aussteller *m e-s Wechsels*; **3.** [drɔː] a) Schublade *f*, -fach *n*, b) *pl.* Kom'mode *f*; **4.** *pl.* [drɔːz] *a.* ***pair of* ~*s*** a) 'Unterhose *f*, b) (Damen)Schlüpfer *m.*
draw·ing ['drɔːɪŋ] *s.* **1.** Ziehen *n*; **2.** Zeichnen *n*: ***out of* ~** verzeichnet; **3.** Zeichnung *f*, Skizze *f*; **4.** Ziehung *f*, Verlosung *f*; **5.** ✝ a) *pl.* Bezüge *pl.*, Einnahmen *pl.*, b) Abhebung *f*, c) Trassierung *f*, Ziehung *f* (*Wechsel*); **~ ac·count** *s.* ✝ **1.** Girokonto *n*; **2.** Spesenkonto *n*; **~ block** *s.* Zeichenblock *m*; **'~-board** *s.* Reiß-, Zeichenbrett *n*: ***back to the* ~!** F wir müssen noch einmal von vorn anfangen!; **~ card** *s. thea. Am.* Zugnummer *f* (*Stück od. Person*); **~ com·pass·es** *s. pl.* (Reiß-, Zeichen-) Zirkel *m*; **~ ink** *s.* (Auszieh)Tusche *f*; **~ pen** *s.* Reißfeder *f*; **~ pen·cil** *s.* Zeichenstift *m*; **~ pin** *s. Brit.* Reiß-, Heftzwecke *f*; **~ pow·er** *s. fig.* Zugkraft *f*; **~ room** *s.* **1.** Gesellschaftszimmer *n*, Sa-

ˈlon *m*: ***not fit for a*** **~** nicht ‚salonfähig'; **~** ***comedy*** Salonkomödie *f*; **2.** Empfang *m* (*Brit. bsd.* bei Hofe); **3.** 🚂 *Am.* Priˈvatabteil *n*: **~** ***car*** Salonwagen *m*; **~ set** *s.* Reißzeug *n*.
drawl [drɔːl] **I** *v/t. u. v/i.* gedehnt *od.* schleppend sprechen; **II** *s.* gedehntes Sprechen.
drawn [drɔːn] **I** *p.p. von* ***draw***; **II** *adj.* **1.** gezogen (*a.* ⚙ *Draht*); **2.** *fig.* a) abgespannt, b) verhärmt (*Gesicht*): **~** ***with pain*** schmerzverzerrt; **3.** *sport*: unentschieden: **~** ***match*** Unentschieden *n*; **~ but·ter (sauce)** *s.* Buttersoße *f*; **~ work** *s.* Hohlsaumarbeit *f*.
draw| po·ker *s. Kartenspiel*: Draw Poker *n*; **ˈ~·string** *s.* Zug- *od.* Vorhangschnur *f*; **~ well** *s.* Ziehbrunnen *m*.
dray [dreɪ] *a.* **~ cart** *s.* Rollwagen *m*; **~ horse** *s.* Zugpferd *n*; **ˈ~·man** [-mən] *s.* [*irr.*] Rollkutscher *m*.
dread [dred] **I** *v/t.* (sehr) fürchten, (große) Angst haben *od.* sich fürchten vor (*dat.*); **II** *s.* Furcht *f*, große Angst, Grauen *n* (***of*** vor *dat.*); **III** *adj. poet.* → ***dreadful*** 1; **ˈdread·ed** [-dɪd] *adj.* gefürchtet; **ˈdread·ful** [-fʊl] *adj.* □ **1.** furchtbar, schrecklich (*beide a. fig.* F); → ***penny dreadful***; **2.** F a) gräßlich, scheußlich, b) furchtbar groß *od.* lang, kolosˈsal; **ˈdread·nought** *s.* **1.** ⚔ Dreadnought *m*, Schlachtschiff *n*; **2.** dicker, wetterfester Stoff *od.* Mantel.
dream [driːm] **I** *s.* **1.** Traum *m*: ***pleasant ~s!*** F träume süß!; ***wet*** **~** ‚feuchter Traum' (*Pollution*); **2.** Traum(zustand) *m*, Träumeˈrei *f*; **3.** *fig.* (Wunsch-)Traum *m*, Sehnsucht *f*, Ideˈal *n*: **~** ***factory*** ‚Traumfabrik' *f*; **~** ***job*** Traumberuf *m*; **4.** *fig.* ‚Gedicht' *n*, Traum *m*: ***a ~ of a hat*** ein traumhaft schöner Hut; ***a perfect*** **~** traumhaft schön; **II** *v/i.* [*a. irr.*] **5.** träumen (***of*** von) (*a. fig.*); **6.** träumerisch *od.* verträumt sein; **7.** *mst neg.* ahnen: ***I shouldn't ~ of such a thing*** das würde mir nicht einmal im Traume einfallen; ***I shouldn't ~ of doing that*** ich würde nie daran denken, das zu tun; ***he little dreamt that*** er ahnte kaum, daß; **III** *v/t.* [*a. irr.*] **8.** träumen (*a. fig.*); **9.** **~** ***away*** verträumen; **10.** **~** ***up*** F sich *et.* einfallen lassen *od.* ausdenken; **ˈdream·boat** *s. sl.* a) ‚Schatz' *m*, b) ‚dufter Typ', c) Schwarm *m*, Ideˈal *n*; **ˈdream·er** [-mə] *s.* Träumer(in) (*a. fig.*); **ˈdream·i·ness** [-mɪnɪs] *s.* **1.** Verträumtheit *f*; **2.** Traumhaftigkeit *f*, Verschwommenheit *f*; **ˈdream·ing** [-mɪŋ] → ***dreamy*** 1.
ˈdream|·land *s.* Traumland *n*; **ˈ~·like** *adj.* traumhaft; **~ read·er** *s.* Traumdeuter(in).
dreamt [dremt] *pret. u. p.p. von* ***dream***.
dream world *s.* Traumwelt *f*.
dream·y [ˈdriːmɪ] *adj.* □ **1.** verträumt, träumerisch; **2.** traumhaft, verschwommen; **3.** F traumhaft (schön).
drear [drɪə] *adj. poet.* → ***dreary***; **drear·ie** [ˈdrɪərɪ] *s.* F fader *od.* ‚mieser' Typ; **drear·i·ness** [ˈdrɪərɪnɪs] *s.* **1.** Tristheit *f*, Trostlosigkeit *f*; **2.** Langweiligkeit *f*; **drear·y** [ˈdrɪərɪ] *adj.* □ **1.** *allg.* trist, trüb(selig); **2.** langweilig, fad(e); **3.** F ‚mies', ‚blöd'.
dredge¹ [dredʒ] **I** *s.* **1.** ⚙ Bagger *m*; **2.** Schleppnetz *n*; **II** *v/t.* **3.** ausbaggern; **4.** *oft* **~** ***up*** mit dem Schleppnetz fangen *od.* herˈaufholen; **5.** *fig.* a) **~** ***up*** *Tatsachen* ausgraben, b) durchˈforschen; **III** *v/i.* **6.** mit dem Schleppnetz fischen (***for*** nach); **7.** **~** ***for*** suchen nach.
dredge² [dredʒ] *v/t.* (mit Mehl *etc.*) bestreuen.
dredg·er¹ [ˈdredʒə] *s.* **1.** ⚙ Bagger *m*; **2.** Schwimmbagger *m*; **3.** Schleppnetzfischer *m*.
dredg·er² [ˈdredʒə] *s.* (Mehl- *etc.*)Streuer *m*.
dreg [dreg] *s.* **1.** *mst pl.* (Boden)Satz *m*, Hefe *f*: ***drain*** (*od.* ***drink***) ***to the ~s*** *Glas* bis zur Neige leeren; ***not a ~*** gar nichts; → ***cup*** 7; **2.** *mst pl. fig.* Abschaum *m* (*der Menschheit*), Hefe *f* (*des Volkes*): ***the ~s of mankind***.
drench [drentʃ] **I** *v/t.* **1.** durchˈnässen: ***~ed in blood*** blutgetränkt; ***~ed with rain*** vom Regen (völlig) durchnäßt; ***~ed in tears*** in Tränen gebadet; **2.** *vet. Tieren* Arzˈnei einflößen; **II** *s.* **3.** (Regen)Guß *m*; **4.** *vet.* Arzˈneitrank *m*; **ˈdrench·er** [-tʃə] *s.* **1.** Regenguß *m*; **2.** *vet.* Gerät *n* zum Einflößen von Arzˈneien.
Dres·den (chi·na) [ˈdrezdən] *s.* Meißner Porzelˈlan *n*.
dress [dres] **I** *s.* **1.** Kleidung *f*, Anzug *m* (*a.* ⚔); **2.** (Damen)Kleid *n*; **3.** Abend-, Gesellschaftskleidung *f*: ***full ~*** Gesellschaftsanzug *m*, Gala *f*; **4.** *fig.* Gewand *n*, Kleid *n*, Gestalt *f*; **II** *v/t.* **5.** be-, ankleiden, anziehen: **~** ***o.s.*** → 11; **6.** einkleiden; **7.** *thea.* mit Kosˈtümen ausstatten: **~** ***it*** Kostümprobe abhalten; **8.** schmücken, *Schaufenster etc.* dekorieren: **~** ***ship*** ⚓ über die Toppen flaggen; **9.** zuˈrechtmachen, herrichten, zubereiten, behandeln, bearbeiten; *Salat* anmachen; *Huhn etc.* koch- *od.* bratfertig machen; *Haare* frisieren; *Leder* zurichten; *Tuch* glätten, appretieren; *Erz etc.* aufbereiten; *Stein* behauen; *Flachs* hecheln; *Boden* düngen; ⚕ *Wunde* behandeln, verbinden; **10.** ⚔ (aus)richten; **III** *v/i.* **11.** sich ankleiden *od.* anziehen; **12.** Abend- *od.* Festkleidung anziehen, sich ‚in Gala werfen'; **13.** sich (*geschmackvoll etc.*) kleiden: **~** ***well*** (***badly***); **14.** ⚔ sich (aus)richten; **~ down** *v/t.* **1.** *Pferd* striegeln; **2.** F *j-m* ‚eins auf den Deckel geben'; **~ up I** *v/t.* **1.** fein anziehen, herausputzen; **II** *v/i.* **2.** sich feinmachen, sich auftakeln; **3.** sich kostümieren *od.* verkleiden.
dres·sage [ˈdresɑːʒ] **I** *s. sport* Dresˈsur(-reiten *n*) *f*; **II** *adj.* Dressur…
dress| cir·cle *s. thea.* erster Rang; **~ clothes** *s. pl.* Gesellschaftskleidung *f*; **~ coat** *s.* Frack *m*; **~ de·sign·er** *s.* Modezeichner(in).
dress·er¹ [ˈdresə] *s.* **1.** *thea.* a) Kostümiˈer *m*, b) Garderobiˈere *f*; **2.** j-d, der sich *sorgfältig etc.* kleidet; **3.** ⚕ Operatiˈonsassiˌstent *m*; **4.** ˈSchaufensterdekoraˌteur *m*; **5.** ⚙ a) Zurichter *m*, Aufbereiter *m*, b) Appretierer *m*.
dress·er² [ˈdresə] *s.* **1.** a) Küchen-, Geschirrschrank *m*, b) Anrichte *f*; **2.** → ***dressing table***.
dress·ing [ˈdresɪŋ] *s.* **1.** Ankleiden *n*; **2.** ⚙ a) (Nach)Bearbeitung *f*, Aufbereitung *f*, Zurichtung *f*; **3.** ⚙ Appreˈtur *f*; **4.** Zubereitung *f von Speisen*; **5.** a) Dressing *n* (*Salatsoße*), b) *Am.* Füllung *f*; **6.** ⚕ a) Verbinden *n* (*Wunde*), b) Verband *m*; **7.** 🌱 Dünger *m*; **~ case** *s.* Toiˈlettentasche *f*, ˈReiseneces͵saire *n*; **ˌ~-ˈdown** *s.* F Standpauke *f*, Rüffel *m*; **~ gown** *s.* Schlaf-, Morgenrock *m*; **~ room** *s.* **1.** Ankleidezimmer *n*; **2.** (ˈKünstler)Gardeˌrobe *f*; **3.** *sport* (ˈUmkleide)Kaˌbine *f*; **~ sta·tion** *s.* ⚔ (Feld)Verband(s)platz *m*; **~ ta·ble** *s.* Friˈsierkomˌmode *f*.
ˈdress|ˌmak·er *s.* (Damen)Schneider (-in); **ˈ~ˌmak·ing** *s.* Schneidern *n*; **~ pa·rade** *s.* **1.** Modevorführung *f*; **2.** Paˈrade *f* in ˈGalauniˌform; **~ pat·tern** *s.* Schnittmuster *n*; **~ re·hears·al** *s.* *thea.* Geneˈralprobe *f* (*a. fig.*), Koˈstümprobe *f*; **~ shield** *s.* Schweißblatt *n*; **~ shirt** *s.* Frackhemd *n*; **~ suit** *s.* Frackanzug *m*; **~ u·ni·form** *s.* ⚔ großer Dienstanzug *m*.
dress·y [ˈdresɪ] *adj.* **1.** eleˈgant (gekleidet), *weitS.* modebewußt; **2.** geschniegelt; **3.** F schick, fesch (*Kleid*).
drew [druː] *pret. von* ***draw***.
drib·ble [ˈdrɪbl] **I** *v/i.* **1.** tröpfeln (*a. fig.*); **2.** sabbern, geifern; **3.** *sport* dribbeln; **II** *v/t.* **4.** (herˈab)tröpfeln lassen, träufeln; **5.** *sport* **~** ***the ball*** (mit dem Ball) dribbeln.
drib·(b)let [ˈdrɪblɪt] kleine Menge; ***by ~s*** *fig.* in kleinen Mengen, kleckerweise.
dribs and drabs [ˌdrɪbzənˈdræbz] *s. pl.*: ***in ~*** F kleckerweise.
dried [draɪd] *adj.* getrocknet: **~** ***cod*** Stockfisch *m*; **~** ***fruit*** Dörrobst *n*; **~** ***milk*** Trockenmilch *f*.
dri·er¹ [ˈdraɪə] *s.* **1.** Trockenmittel *n*, Sikkaˈtiv *n*; **2.** ˈTrockenappaˌrat *m*, Trockner *m*: ***hair-~*** Fön *m*.
dri·er² [ˈdraɪə] *comp. von* ***dry***.
dri·est [ˈdraɪɪst] *sup. von* ***dry***.
drift [drɪft] **I** *s.* **1.** Treiben *n*; **2.** *fig.* Abwanderung *f*: **~** ***from the land*** Landflucht *f*; **3.** ⚓, ✈ Abtrift *f*, -trieb *m*; **4.** *Ballistik*: Seitenabweichung *f*; **5.** Drift(strömung) *f* (*im Meer*); (Strömungs)Richtung *f*; **6.** *fig.* a) Strömung *f*, Tenˈdenz *f*, Lauf *m*, Richtung *f*, b) Absicht *f*, c) Gedankengang *m*, d) Sinn *m*: ***the ~ of what he said*** was er meinte *od.* sagen wollte; **7.** a) Treibholz *n*, b) Treibeis *n*, c) Schneegestöber *n*; **8.** Treibgut *n*; **9.** (Schnee)Verwehung *f*, (Schnee-, Sand)Wehe *f*; **10.** *geol.* Geschiebe *n*; **11.** *fig.* Einfluß *m*, (treibende) Kraft; **12.** (Sich)ˈTreibenlassen *n*, Ziellosigkeit *f*: ***policy of ~***; **II** *v/i.* **13.** treiben (*a. fig.* ***into*** in *e-n Krieg etc.*), getrieben werden: ***let things ~*** den Dingen ihren Lauf lassen; **~** ***away*** a) abwandern, b) sich entfernen (***from*** von); **~** ***apart*** *fig.* sich auseinanderleben; **14.** sich (willenlos) treiben lassen; **15.** *auf et.* zutreiben; **16.** gezogen werden, geraten *od.* (hinein)schlittern (***into*** in *acc.*); **17.** sich häufen (*Sand, Schnee*); **III** *v/t.* **18.** (daˈhin)treiben, (fort)tragen; **19.** aufhäufen, zs.-tragen; **~ an·chor** *s.* ⚓ Treibanker *m*.
drift·er [ˈdrɪftə] *s.* **1.** zielloser Mensch, ‚Gammler' *m*; **2.** Treibnetzfischer(boot *n*) *m*.
drift| ice *s.* Treibeis *n*; **~ net** *s.* Treibnetz *n*; **ˈ~·wood** *s.* Treibholz *n*.
drill¹ [drɪl] **I** *s.* **1.** ⚙ ˈBohrgerät *n*, -ma-

ˌschine *f*, Bohrer *m*: **~ chuck** Bohrfutter *n*; **2.** Drill *m*: a) ⚔ Exerzieren *n*, b) (*Luftschutz- etc.*)Übung *f*, c) *fig.* strenge Schulung, d) ˈAusbildung(smeˌthode) *f*; **II** *v/t.* **3.** *Loch* bohren; **4.** ⚔ *u. fig.* drillen, einexerzieren: **~ him in Latin** ihm Lateinisch einpauken; **5.** *fig.* drillen, gründlich ausbilden; **III** *v/i.* **6.** (⚙ *engS.* ins Volle) bohren: **~ for oil** nach Öl bohren; **7.** ⚔ a) exerzieren (*a. fig.*), b) gedrillt *od.* ausgebildet werden.

drill² [drɪl] ↗ **I** *s.* **1.** (Saat)Rille *f*, Furche *f*; **2.** ˈDrill-, ˈSämaˌschine *f*; **II** *v/t.* **3.** *Saat* in Reihen säen; **4.** *Land* in Reihen besäen.

drill³ [drɪl] *s.* Drill(ich) *m*, Drell *m*.

drill| bit *s.* ⚙ **1.** Bohrspitze *f*; **2.** Einsatzbohrer *m*; **~ ground** *s.* ⚔ Exerzierplatz *m*.

drill·ing [ˈdrɪlɪŋ] *s.* **1.** Bohren *n*; **2.** Bohrung *f* (**for** nach *Öl etc.*); **3.** → **drill¹** 2; **~ rig** *s.* Bohrinsel *f*.

ˈ**drill|ˌmas·ter** *s.* **1.** ⚔ Ausbilder *m*; **2.** *fig.* ‚Einpauker' *m*; **~ ser·geant** *s.* ⚔ ˈAusbildungsˌunteroffiˌzier *m*.

dri·ly [ˈdraɪlɪ] *adv. von* **dry** (*mst fig.*).

drink [drɪŋk] **I** *s.* **1.** a) Getränk *n*, b) Drink *m*, alkoˈholisches Getränk, c) *coll.* Getränke *pl.*: **have a ~** et. trinken, e-n Drink nehmen; **have a ~ with s.o.** mit j-m ein Glas trinken; **a ~ of water** ein Schluck Wasser; **food and ~** Essen *n* u. Getränke *pl.*; **2.** das Trinken, der Alkohol: **take to ~** sich das Trinken angewöhnen; **3.** *sl. der* ‚große Teich' (*Meer*); **II** *v/t.* [*irr.*] **4.** *Tee etc.* trinken; *Suppe* essen: **~ s.o. under the table** j-n unter den Tisch trinken; **5.** trinken, saufen (*Tier*); **6.** trinken *od.* anstoßen auf (*acc.*); → **health** 3; **7.** (aus)trinken, leeren; → **cup** 7; **8.** *fig.* → **drink in**; **III** *v/i.* [*irr.*] **9.** trinken; **10.** saufen (*Tier*); **11.** trinken, *weitS. a.* ein Trinker sein; **12.** trinken *od.* anstoßen (**to** auf *acc.*): **~ to s.o.** *a.* j-m zuprosten; **~ a·way** *v/t.* **1.** *sein Geld etc.* vertrinken; **2.** *s-e Sorgen* im Alkohol ersäufen; **~ in** *v/t. fig.* **1.** *Luft etc.* einsaugen, (tief) einatmen; **2.** *fig.* (hingerissen) in sich aufnehmen, verschlingen: **~ s.o.'s words**; **~ off**, **~ up** *v/t.* austrinken.

drink·a·ble [ˈdrɪŋkəbl] *adj.* trinkbar, Trink...; **drink·er** [ˈdrɪŋkə] *s.* **1.** Trinkende(r *m*) *f*: **beer ~** Biertrinker *m*; **2.** Trinker(in): **a heavy ~**.

drink·ing [ˈdrɪŋkɪŋ] *s.* **1.** *allg.* Trinken *n*; **2.** → **~ bout** *s.* Trinkgelage *n*; **~ cup** *s.* Trinkbecher *m*; **~ foun·tain** *s.* Trinkbrunnen *m*; **~ song** *s.* Trinklied *n*; **~ straw** *s.* Trinkhalm *m*; **~ wa·ter** *s.* Trinkwasser *n*.

drip [drɪp] **I** *v/i.* **1.** (herˈab)tropfen, (-)tröpfeln; **2.** tropfen (*Wasserhahn*); **3.** triefen (**with** von, vor *dat.*) (*a. fig.*); **II** *v/t.* **4.** (herˈab)tröpfeln *od.* (herˈab-) tropfen lassen; **III** *s.* **5.** → **dripping** 1, 2; **6.** ⚠ Traufe *f*; **7.** ⚙ Tropfrohr *n*; **8.** ⚕ a) ˈTropfinfusiˌon *f*, b) Tropf *m*: **be on the ~** am Tropf hängen; **9.** F ‚Nulpe' *f*, ‚Blödmann' *m*; **~ cof·fee** *s. Am.* Filterkaffee *m*; ˌ**~-ˈdry I** *adj.* bügelfrei; **II** *v/t.* tropfnaß aufhängen; ˈ**~-feed** *v/t.* ⚕ parenteˈral *od.* künstlich ernähren.

drip·ping [ˈdrɪpɪŋ] **I** *s.* **1.** Tröpfeln *n*, Tropfen *n*; **2.** *a. pl.* herˈabtröpfelnde Flüssigkeit; **3.** (abtropfendes) Bratenfett: **~ pan** Fettpfanne *f*; **II** *adj.* **4.** *a. fig.* triefend (**with** von); **5.** *a.* **~ wet** triefend naß, tropfnaß.

ˈ**drip·proof** *adj.* ⚙ tropfwassergeschützt.

drive [draɪv] **I** *s.* **1.** Fahrt *f*, *bsd.* Aus-, Spaˈzierfahrt *f*: **take** (*od.* **go for**) **a ~** → **drive out** II; **an hour's ~ away** e-e Autostunde entfernt; **2.** a) Fahrweg *m*, -straße *f*, b) (priˈvate) Auf-, Einfahrt *f*, c) Zufahrtsstraße *f*; **3.** a) (Zs.-)Treiben *n* (*von Vieh etc.*), b) zs.-getriebene Tiere; **4.** Treibjagd *f*; **5.** ⚙ a) Antrieb *m*: **rear(-wheel) ~**, b) *mot. a.* Steuerung *f*: **left-hand ~**; **6.** ⚔ Vorstoß *m*; **7.** *sport* a) Schuß *m*, b) *Golf*, *Tennis*: Drive *m*, Treibschlag *m*; **8.** Tatkraft *f*, Schwung *m*, Eˈlan *m*, Dyˈnamik *f*; **9.** Trieb *m*, Drang *m*: **sexual ~** Geschlechtstrieb; **10.** (ˈSammel-, Verˈkaufs- *etc.*)Aktiˌon *f*, Kamˈpagne *f*, (*bes.* Werbe)Feldzug *m*; **II** *v/t.* [*irr.*] **11.** *Vieh*, *Wild*, *Keil*, *etc.* treiben; *Ball* treiben, (weit) schlagen, schießen; *Nagel* einschlagen, treiben (**into** in *acc.*); *Pfahl* einrammen; *Schwert etc.* stoßen; *Tunnel* bohren, treiben: **~ s.th. into s.o.** *fig.* j-m et. einbleuen; **~ all before one** *fig.* jeden Widerstand überwinden, unaufhaltsam sein; → **home** 13; **12.** vertreiben, -jagen; **13.** *hunt.* jagen, treiben; **14.** (zur Arbeit) antreiben, hetzen: **~ s.o. hard** a) j-n schinden, b) j-n in die Enge treiben; **~ o.s.** (**hard**) sich abschinden *od.* antreiben; **15.** *fig. j-n* dazu bringen *od.* treiben *od.* veranlassen *od.* zwingen (**to** zu; **to do** zu tun): **~ to despair** zur Verzweiflung treiben; **~ s.o. mad** j-n verrückt machen; **driven by hunger** vom Hunger getrieben; **16.** *Wagen* fahren, lenken, steuern; **17.** *j-n od. et.* (im Auto) fahren, befördern; **18.** ⚙ (an-, be)treiben (*mst pass.*): **driven by steam** mit Dampf betrieben, mit Dampfantrieb; **19.** zielbewußt ˈdurchführen: **~ a hard bargain** hart verhandeln; **he ~s a roaring trade** er treibt e-n schwunghaften Handel; **III** *v/i.* [*irr.*] **20.** (daˈhin)treiben, getrieben werden: **~ before the wind** ⚓ vor dem Winde treiben; **21.** eilen, stürmen, jagen; **22.** stoßen, schlagen; **23.** (e-n *od.* den Wagen) fahren: **can you ~?** können Sie Auto fahren?; **24.** **~ at** *fig.* (ab)zielen auf (*acc.*): **what is he driving at?** was will *od.* meint er eigentlich?, worauf will er hinaus?; **25.** schwer arbeiten (**at** an *dat.*);

Zssgn mit adv.:

drive| a·way I *v/t. a. fig.* vertreiben, verjagen; **II** *v/i.* wegfahren; **~ in I** *v/t.* **1.** *Pfahl* einrammen, *Nagel* einschlagen; **2.** *Vieh* eintreiben; **II** *v/i.* **3.** hinˈeinfahren; **~ on I** *v/t.* voˈrantreiben (*a. fig.*); **II** *v/i.* weiterfahren; **~ out I** *v/t.* aus-, vertreiben; **II** *v/i.* spazieren-, ausfahren; **~ up I** *v/t. Preise* in die Höhe treiben; **II** *v/i.* vorfahren (**to** vor *dat.*).

ˈ**drive-in I** *adj.* Auto..., Drive-in-...; **II** *s.* a) Auto-, Drive-in-Kino *n*, -rasthaus *n etc.*, b) Auto-, Drive-in-Schalter *m e-r Bank*.

driv·el [ˈdrɪvl] **I** *v/i.* **1.** sabbern, geifern; **2.** dummes Zeug schwatzen, faseln; **II** *s.* **3.** Geschwätz *n*, Gefasel *n*, Faseˈlei *f*; ˈ**driv·el·(l)er** [-lə] *s.* (blöder) Schwätzer.

driv·en [ˈdrɪvn] *p.p. von* **drive**.

driv·er [ˈdraɪvə] *s.* **1.** (An)Treiber *m*; **2.** Fahrer *m*, Lenker *m*, b) (*Kran- etc.*, *Brit. Lokomotiv*)Führer *m*, c) Kutscher *m*; **3.** (Vieh)Treiber *m*; **4.** F Antreiber *m*, (Leute)Schinder *m*; **5.** ⚙ a) Treibrad *n*, Ritzel *n*, b) Mitnehmer *m*, c) Ramme *f*; **6.** *Golf*: Driver *m* (*Holzschläger 1*); **~'s cab** *s.* ⚙ Führerhaus *n*; **~'s li·cense** *s. mot. Am.* Führerschein *m*; **~'s seat** *s.* Fahrer-, Führersitz *m*: **in the ~** *fig.* am Ruder.

drive| shaft → **driving shaft**; ˈ**~·way** *s.* → **drive** 2; ˈ**~-yourˌself** *adj. Am.* Selbstfahrer...: **~ car** Mietwagen *m*.

driv·ing [ˈdraɪvɪŋ] **I** *adj.* **1.** (an)treibend: **~ force** treibende Kraft; **~ rain** stürmischer Regen; **2.** a) ⚙ Antriebs..., Treib..., Trieb..., b) *TV* Treiber...(*-impulse etc.*); **3.** *mot.* Fahr...: **~ comfort**; **~ instructor** Fahrlehrer *m*; **~ lessons** Fahrstunden; **take ~ lessons** Fahrunterricht nehmen, den Führerschein machen; **~ licence** *Brit.* Führerschein *m*; **~ mirror** Rückspiegel *m*; **~ school** Fahrschule *f*; **~ test** Fahrprüfung *f*; **II** *s.* **4.** Treiben *n*; **5.** (Auto)Fahren *n*; **~ ax·le** *s.* Antriebsachse *f*; **~ belt** *s.* Treibriemen *m*; ˈ**~·gear** *s.* Triebwerk *n*, Getriebe *n*; **~ i·ron** *s. Golf*: Driving-Iron *m* (*Eisenschläger Nr. 1*); **~ pow·er** *s.* ⚙ Antriebskraft *f*, -leistung *f*; **~ shaft** *s.* ⚙ Antriebswelle *f*; **~ wheel** *s.* Triebrad *n*.

driz·zle [ˈdrɪzl] **I** *v/i.* nieseln; **II** *s.* Niesel-, Sprühregen *m*; ˈ**driz·zly** [-lɪ] *adj.* Niesel-, Sprüh...: **~ rain**; **it was a ~ day** es nieselte den ganzen Tag.

droll [drəʊl] *adj.* □ drollig, spaßig, komisch; **droll·er·y** [ˈdrəʊlərɪ] *s.* **1.** Posse *f*, Schwank *m*; **2.** Spaß *m*; **3.** Komik *f*, Spaßigkeit *f*.

drome [drəʊm] F *für* **aerodrome**, **airdrome**.

drom·e·dar·y [ˈdrɒmədərɪ] *s. zo.* Dromeˈdar *n*.

drone¹ [drəʊn] **I** *s.* **1.** *zo.* Drohne *f*; **2.** *fig.* Drohne *f*, Schmaˈrotzer *m*; **3.** ⚔ ferngesteuertes Flugzeug *n*; ˈFernlenkraˌkete *f*; **II** *v/i.* **4.** faulenzen; **III** *v/t.* **5.** **~ away** vertrödeln.

drone² [drəʊn] **I** *v/i.* **1.** brummen, summen, dröhnen; **2.** *fig.* leiern, eintönig reden; **II** *v/t.* **3.** herleiern; **III** *s.* **4.** ♪ a) Borˈdun *m*, b) Baßpfeife *f des Dudelsacks*; **5.** Brummen *n*, Summen *n*; **6.** *fig.* a) Geleier *n*, b) einschläfernder Redner.

droop [dru:p] **I** *v/i.* **1.** (schlaff) herˈabhängen *od.* -sinken; **2.** ermatten, erschlaffen; **3.** sinken, schwinden (*Mut etc.*), erlahmen (*Interesse etc.*); **4.** *fig.* den Kopf hängenlassen (*a. Blume*); **5.** † abbröckeln (*Preise*); **II** *v/t.* **6.** (schlaff) herˈabhängen lassen; **III** *s.* **7.** Herˈabhängen *n*, Senken *n*; **8.** Erschlaffen *n*; ˈ**droop·ing** [-pɪŋ] *adj.* □ **1.** (herˈunter)hängend, schlaff (*a. fig.*); **2.** matt; **3.** welk.

drop [drɒp] **I** *s.* **1.** Tropfen *m*: **in ~s** tropfenweise (*a. fig.*); **a ~ in the bucket** (*od.* **ocean**) *fig.* ein Tropfen auf e-n heißen Stein; **2.** ⚕ *mst pl.* Tropfen *pl.*; **3.** *fig.* a) Tropfen *m*, Tröpfchen *n*, b) Glas *n*, ‚Gläs-chen' *n*: **he has had a ~ too much** er hat ein Glas *od.* eins über den Durst getrunken; **4.** Bonˈbon *m*, *n*: **fruit ~s** Drops *pl.*; **5.** a) Fall *m*,

Fallen *n*: ***at the ~ of a hat*** F beim geringsten Anlaß; ***get*** *od.* ***have the ~ on s.o.*** F j-m (*beim Ziehen e-r Waffe*) zuvorkommen, *fig.* j-m gegenüber im Vorteil sein, b) Fall(tiefe *f*) *m*, 'Höhenˌunterschied *m*, c) steiler Abfall, Gefälle *n*; **6.** *fig.* Fall *m*, Sturz *m*, Rückgang *m*: ***~ in prices*** Preissturz, -rückgang; ***~ in the temperature*** Temperaturabfall, -sturz; ***~ in the voltage*** ↯ Spannungsabfall; **7.** → ***airdrop*** I; **8.** ⚙ a) (Fall-) Klappe *f*, -vorrichtung *f*, b) Falltür *f*, c) Vorrichtung *f* zum Her'ablassen von Lasten: (***letter***) ~ *Am.* (Brief)Einwurf *m*; **9.** *thea.* Vorhang *m*; **II** *v/i.* **10.** (her'ab)tropfen, (-)tröpfeln; **11.** (he'rab-, her'unter)fallen: ***let s.th. ~*** a) et. fallen lassen, b) → 26; **12.** (nieder-) sinken, fallen: ***~ into a chair***, ***~ dead*** tot umfallen; ***~ dead!*** *sl.* geh zum Teufel!; ***ready*** (*od.* ***fit***) ***to ~*** zum Umfallen müde; **13.** *fig.* aufhören, ‚einschlafen': ***our correspondence ~ped***; **14.** (ver-) fallen: ***~ into a habit*** in e-e Gewohnheit verfallen; ***~ asleep*** einschlafen; **15.** a) (ab)sinken, sich senken, b) sinken, fallen, her'untergehen (*Preise, Thermometer etc.*); **16.** sich senken (*Stimme*); **17.** sich legen (*Wind*); **18.** zufällig *od.* unerwartet kommen: ***~ into the room***; ***~ across s.o.*** (***s.th.***) zufällig auf j-n (et.) stoßen; **19.** *zo.* (Junge) werfen, *bsd.* a) lammen, b) kalben, c) fohlen; **III** *v/t.* **20.** (her'ab)tropfen *od.* (-)tröpfeln lassen; **21.** senken, her'ablassen; **22.** fallen lassen: ***~ a book***; **23.** (hin'ein)werfen (***into*** in *acc.*); **24.** *Bomben etc.* (ab)werfen; **25.** ⚓ *den Anker* auswerfen; **26.** *e-e Bemerkung* fallenlassen: ***~ a remark***; ***~ me a line!*** schreibe mir ein paar Zeilen!; **27.** *ein Thema, e-e Gewohnheit etc.* fallenlassen: ***~ a subject*** (***habit*** *etc.*); **28.** *e-e Tätigkeit* aufgeben, aufhören mit: ***~ the correspondence*** die Korrespondenz einstellen; ***~ it!*** hör auf damit!, laß das!; **29.** *j-n* fallenlassen, nichts mehr zu tun haben wollen mit; **30** *Am.* a) *j-n* entlassen, b) *sport Spieler* aus der Mannschaft nehmen; **31.** *zo. Junge, bsd. Lämmer* werfen; **32.** *e-e Last, a. Passagiere* absetzen; **33.** F *Geld* a) loswerden, b) verlieren; **34.** *Buchstaben etc.* auslassen: ***~ one's aitches*** a) das ‚h' nicht sprechen, b) *fig.* e-e vulgäre Aussprache haben; **35.** a) zu Fall bringen, zu Boden schlagen, b) F *j-n* ‚abknallen'; **36.** ab-, her'unterschießen: ***~ a bird***; **37.** *die Augen od. die Stimme* senken; **38.** *sport e-n Punkt, ein Spiel* abgeben (***to*** gegen);
Zssgn mit adv.:

drop| a·round *v/i.* F vor'beikommen, (kurz) ‚her'einschauen'; **~ a·way** *v/i.* **1.** abfallen; **2.** immer weniger werden; (e-r nach dem anderen) weggehen; **~ back**, **~ be·hind** *v/i.* **1.** zu'rückbleiben, -fallen; **2.** sich zu'rückfallen lassen; **~ down** *v/i.* **1.** her'abtröpfeln; **2.** her'unterfallen; **~ in** *v/i.* **1.** her'einkommen (*a. fig. Aufträge etc.*); **2.** (kurz) her'einschauen (***on*** bei), ‚her'einschneien'; **~ off I** *v/i.* **1.** abfallen (*a.* ↯); **2.** zu'rückgehen (*Umsatz etc.*), nachlassen (*Interesse etc.*); **3.** einschlafen, -nicken; **II** *v/t.* **4.** → ***drop*** 32; **~ out** *v/i.* **1.** her'ausfallen (***of*** aus); **2.** ‚aussteigen' (***of*** aus *der Politik, s-m Beruf etc.*), *a.* die Schule, das Studium abbrechen.

drop| ball *s. Fußball*: Schiedsrichterball *m*; **~ cur·tain** *s. thea.* Vorhang *m*; **'~-forge** *v/t.* ⚙ im Gesenk schmieden; **~ forg·ing** *s.* ⚙ **1.** Gesenkschmieden *n*; **2.** Gesenkschmiedestück *n*; **'~·head** *s.* **1.** ⚙ Versenkvorrichtung *f*; **2.** *mot. Brit. a.* ***~ coupé*** Kabrio'lett *n*; **~ kick** *s. sport* Dropkick *m*.

drop·let ['drɒplɪt] *s.* Tröpfchen *n*.

drop| let·ter *s.* **1.** *Am.* postlagernder Brief; **2.** Ortsbrief *m*; **'~·out** *s.* Dropout *m*: a) ‚Aussteiger' *m aus der Gesellschaft*, b) (Schul-, Studien)Abbrecher *m*, c) *Computer*: Sig'nalausfall *m*, d) *Tonband*: Schadstelle *f*.

drop·per ['drɒpə] *s.* Tropfglas *n*, Tropfenzähler *m*: ***eye ~*** Augentropfer *m*; **'drop·pings** [-pɪŋz] *s. pl.* **1.** Mist *m*, tierischer Kot; **2.** (Ab)Fallwolle *f*.

drop| scene *s.* **1.** *thea.* (Zwischen)Vorhang *m*; **2.** *fig.* Fi'nale *n*, Schlußszene *f*; **~ seat** *s.* Klappsitz *m*; **~ shot** *s. Tennis etc.*: Stoppball *m*; **~ shut·ter** *s. phot.* Fallverschluß *m*.

drop·si·cal ['drɒpsɪkl] *adj.* □ ⚕ **1.** wassersüchtig; **2.** ödema'tös.

'drop-stitch *s.* Fallmasche *f*.

drop·sy ['drɒpsɪ] *s.* ⚕ Wassersucht *f*.

dross [drɒs] *s.* **1.** ⚙ Schlacke *f*; **2.** Abfall *m*, Unrat *m*; *fig.* wertloses Zeug.

drought [draʊt] *s.* Dürre *f* (*a. fig. Mangel* ***of*** an *dat.*); (Zeit *f* der) Trockenheit *f*; **'drought·y** [-tɪ] *adj.* **1.** trocken, dürr; **2.** regenlos.

drove¹ [drəʊv] *pret. von* ***drive***.

drove² [drəʊv] *s.* **1.** (Vieh)Herde *f*; **2.** *fig.* Schar *f*: ***in ~s*** in hellen Scharen; **'dro·ver** [-və] *s.* Viehtreiber *m*.

drown [draʊn] **I** *v/i.* **1.** ertrinken; **II** *v/t.* **2.** ertränken, ersäufen: ***be ~ed*** → 1; ***~ one's sorrows*** s-e Sorgen (im Alkohol) ertränken; **3.** über'schwemmen (*a. fig.*): ***~ed in tears*** tränenüberströmt; **4.** *a.* ***~ out*** *fig.* übertönen.

drowse [draʊz] **I** *v/i.* **1.** dösen: ***~ off*** eindösen; **II** *v/t.* **2.** schläfrig machen; **3.** *mst* ***~ away*** *Zeit etc.* verdösen; **'drow·si·ness** [-zɪnɪs] *s.* Schläfrigkeit *f*; **'drow·sy** [-zɪ] *adj.* □ **1.** a) schläfrig, b) verschlafen (*a. fig.*); **2.** einschläfernd.

drub [drʌb] *v/t.* F **1.** (ver)prügeln: ***~ s.th. into s.o.*** j-m et. einbleuen; **2.** *sport* ‚über'fahren'; **'drub·bing** [-bɪŋ] *s.* F (Tracht *f*) Prügel *pl.*: ***take a ~*** *a. sport* Prügel beziehen, ‚über'fahren werden'.

drudge [drʌdʒ] **I** *s.* **1.** *fig.* F Packesel *m*, Arbeitstier *n*, Kuli *m*; **2.** → ***drudgery***; **II** *v/i.* **3.** sich (ab)placken, sich abschinden, schuften; **'drudg·er·y** [-dʒərɪ] *s.* Placke'rei *f*, Schinde'rei *f*; **'drudg·ing** [-dʒɪŋ] *adj.* □ **1.** mühsam; **2.** stumpfsinnig.

drug [drʌg] **I** *s.* **1.** Arz'nei(mittel *n*) *f*, Medika'ment *n*: ***be on a ~*** ein Medikament (ständig) nehmen; **2.** Rauschgift *n*, Droge *f* (*a. fig.*): ***be on ~s*** → 8; **3.** ***~ on*** (*Am. a.* ***in***) ***the market*** ✝ schwerverkäufliche Ware, *a.* Ladenhüter *m*; **II** *v/t.* **4.** *j-m* Medika'mente geben; **5.** *j-n* unter Drogen setzen; **6.** ein Betäubungsmittel beimischen (*dat.*); **7.** *j-n* betäuben (*a. fig.*): ***~ged with sleep*** schlaftrunken; **III** *v/i.* **8.** Drogen *od.* Rauschgift nehmen; **~ a·buse** *s.* **1.** 'Drogenˌmißbrauch *m*; **2.** Arz'neimittelˌmißbrauch *m*; **~ ad·dict** *s.* Drogen- *od.* Rauschgiftsüchtige(r *m*) *f*; **'~-adˌdict·ed** *adj.* **1.** drogen- *od.* rauschgiftsüchtig; **2.** arz'neimittelsüchtig; **~ ad·dic·tion** *s.* **1.** Drogen- *od.* Rauschgiftsucht *f*; **2.** Arz'neimittelsucht *f*; **~ de·pend·ence** *s.* Drogenabhängigkeit *f*.

drug·gist ['drʌgɪst] *s. Am.* **1.** Apo'theker *m*; **2.** Inhaber(in) e-s Drugstores.

drug| ped·dler, **'~ˌpush·er** *s.* Rauschgifthändler *m*, ‚Pusher' *m*; **~ scene** *s.* Drogenszene *f*.

drug·ster ['drʌgstə] → ***drug addict***.

'drug·store *s. Am.* **1.** Apo'theke *f*; **2.** Drugstore *m* (*Drogerie, Kaufladen u. Imbißstube*).

Dru·id ['dru:ɪd] *s.* Dru'ide *m*; **'Dru·id·ess** [-dɪs] *s.* Dru'idin *f*.

drum [drʌm] **I** *s.* **1.** ♪ Trommel *f*: ***beat the ~*** die Trommel schlagen *od.* (*a. fig.*) rühren, trommeln; **2.** *pl.* Schlagzeug *n*; **3.** Trommeln *n* (*a. fig. des Regens etc.*); **4.** ⚙ Trommel *f*, Walze *f*, Zy'linder *m*; **5.** ⚔ Trommel *f* (*am Maschinengewehr etc.*); **6.** Trommel *f*, trommelförmiger Behälter; **7.** *anat.* a) Mittelohr *n*, b) Trommelfell *n*; **8.** ⚠ Säulentrommel *f*; **II** *v/i.* **9.** *a. weitS.* trommeln (***on*** auf *acc.*, ***at*** an *acc.*); **10.** (rhythmisch) dröhnen; **11.** *fig. Am.* die Trommel rühren (***for*** für); **III** *v/t.* **12.** *Rhythmus* trommeln: ***~ s.th. into s.o.*** j-m et. einhämmern; **13.** trommeln auf (*acc.*); **~ out** *v/t. j-n* ausstoßen (***of*** aus); **~ up** *v/t.* a) zs.-trommeln, (an)werben, ‚auf die Beine stellen', b) *Am.* sich *et.* einfallen lassen.

drum| brake *s.* Trommelbremse *f*; **'~ˌfire** *s.* ⚔ Trommelfeuer *n* (*a. fig.*); **'~·head** *s.* **1.** ♪, *anat.* Trommelfell *n*; **2.** ***~ court martial*** ⚔ Standgericht *n*; **3.** ***~ service*** ⚔ Feldgottesdienst *m*; **~ ma·jor** *s.* ⚔ 'Tambourmaˌjor *m*; **~ ma·jor·ette** *s.* 'Tambourmaˌjorin *f*.

drum·mer ['drʌmə] *s.* **1.** ♪ a) Trommler *m*, b) Schlagzeuger *m*; **2.** ✝ *Am.* F Handlungsreisende(r) *m*.

'drum·stick *s.* **1.** Trommelstock *m*, -schlegel *m*; **2.** 'Unterschenkel *m* (*von zubereitetem Geflügel*).

drunk [drʌŋk] **I** *adj. mst pred.* **1.** betrunken (***on*** von): ***get ~*** sich betrinken; ***~ as a lord*** (*od.* ***a fish***) total blau; ***~ and incapable*** volltrunken; ***~ driving*** ⚖ Trunkenheit *f* am Steuer; **2.** *fig.* (be-) trunken, berauscht (***with*** vor, von): ***~ with joy*** freudetrunken; **II** *s.* **3.** *sl.* a) Betrunkene(r *m*) *f*, b) Säufer(in); **4.** a) Saufe'rei *f*, Besäufnis *n*, b) ‚Affe' *m*, Rausch *m*; **III** *p.p. von* ***drink***; **'drunk·ard** [-kəd] *s.* Säufer *m*, Trunkenbold *m*; **'drunk·en** [-kən] *adj.* □ betrunken; *fig.* → ***drunk*** 2: ***a ~ man*** ein Betrunkener; ***a ~ brawl*** ein im Rausch angefangener Streit; ***a ~ party*** ein Saufgelage *n*; **'drunk·en·ness** [-kənnɪs] *s.* Betrunkenheit *f*.

drupe [dru:p] *s.* ⚘ Steinfrucht *f*, -obst *n*.

dry [draɪ] **I** *adj.* □ **1.** trocken: ***not yet ~ behind the ears*** noch nicht trocken hinter den Ohren; ***~ cough*** trockener Husten; ***run ~*** austrocknen, versiegen; → ***dock¹*** 1; **2.** trocken, regenarm, niederschlagsarm: ***~ country***; ***~ summer***; **3.** dürr, ausgedörrt; **4.** ausgetrocknet; **5.** F durstig; **6.** durstig machend: ***~ work***; **7.** trockenstehend (*Kuh*); **8.** F 'trocken': a) mit Alkoholverbot: ***a ~ State***, b) ohne Alkohol: ***a ~ party***, c) weg vom Alkohol: ***he is now ~***; **9.** antialko'holisch: ***~ law*** Prohibitionsgesetz *n*; ***go ~*** das Alkoholverbot einführen; **10.** 'unproduk,tiv, ,ausgeschrieben': ***~ writer***; **11.** herb, trocken (*Wein etc.*); **12.** *fig.* trocken, langweilig; nüchtern: ***~ as dust*** strohtrocken, sterbenslangweilig; ***~ facts*** nüchterne *od.* nackte Tatsachen; **13.** *fig.* trocken: ***~ humo(u)r***; **II** *v/t.* **14.** (ab)trocknen: ***~ one's hands*** sich die Hände abtrocknen; **15.** *Obst* dörren; **16.** *a.* ***~ up*** austrocknen; trockenlegen; **III** *v/i.* **17.** trocknen, trocken werden; **18.** ***~ up*** a) ein-, ver-, austrocknen, b) F versiegen, aufhören, c) F die ,Klappe' halten: ***~ up!***; **IV** *s.* **19.** Trockenheit *f.*

dry·ad ['draɪəd] *s.* Dry'ade *f.*

dry-as-dust ['draɪəzdʌst] **I** *s.* Stubengelehrte(r) *m*; **II** *adj.* strohtrocken, sterbenslangweilig.

dry| bat·ter·y *s.* ⚡ 'Trockenbatte,rie *f*; **~ cell** *s.* ⚡ 'Trockenele,ment *n*; **,~-'clean** *v/t.* chemisch reinigen; **,~-'clean·er('s)** *s.* chemische Reinigung(sanstalt); **,~-'clean·ing** *s.* chemische Reinigung; **'~-cure** *v/t. Fleisch etc.* dörren *od.* einsalzen; **,~'dock** *v/t.* ⚓ ins Trockendock bringen.

dry·er ['draɪə] → ***drier***[1].

'dry|-farm *s.* Trockenfarm *f*; **'~-fly** *s.* *Angeln*: Trockenfliege *f*; **~ goods** *s. pl.* ✝ *Am.* Tex'tilien *pl.*; **~ ice** *s.* Trockeneis *n.*

dry·ing ['draɪɪŋ] *adj.* Trocken...

dry·ly → ***drily***.

dry meas·ure *s.* Trockenmaß *n.*

dry·ness ['draɪnɪs] *s.* Trockenheit *f*: a) trockener Zustand, b) Dürre *f*, c) Hu'morlosigkeit *f*, d) Langweiligkeit *f.*

'dry|-nurse I *s.* **1.** Säuglingsschwester *f*; **II** *v/t.* **2.** *Säuglinge* pflegen; **3.** F bemuttern (*a. fig.*); **'~-out farm** *s.* F Entziehungsheim *n*; **~ rot** *s.* **1.** Trockenfäule *f*; **2.** ⚘ Hausschwamm *m*; **3.** *fig.* Verfall *m*; **~ run** *s.* **1.** ⚔ *Am.* Übungsschießen *n* ohne scharfe Muniti'on; **2.** F Probe *f*, Test *m*; **'~-salt** *v/t.* dörren u. einsalzen; **,~-'shod** *adv.* trockenen Fußes.

du·al ['dju:əl] **I** *adj.* ☐ doppelt, Doppel..., Zwei..., ⚙ *a.* Zwillings...: ***~ carriageway*** *Brit.* Schnellstraße *f*; ***~-income family*** Doppelverdiener *pl.*; ***~ nationality*** doppelte Staatsangehörigkeit; ***~-purpose*** ⚙ Doppel..., Zwei..., Mehrzweck...; **II** *s. ling. a.* ***~ number*** 'Dual *m*, Du'alis *m*; **'du·al·ism** [-lɪzəm] *s.* Dua'lismus *m*; **du·al·i·ty** [dju:'ælətɪ] *s.* Duali'tät *f*, Zweiheit *f.*

dub [dʌb] *v/t.* **1.** ***~ s.o. a knight*** j-n zum Ritter schlagen; **2.** *fig. humor.* titulieren, nennen: ***they ~bed him Fatty***; **3.** ⚙ zurichten; **4.** *Leder* einfetten; **5.** a) *Film* synchronisieren, b) (nach)synchronisieren, c) ***~ in*** einsynchronisieren.

dub·bin ['dʌbɪn] *s.* Lederfett *n.*

dub·bing ['dʌbɪŋ] *s.* **1.** Ritterschlag *m*; **2.** *Film*: ('Nach)Synchronisati,on *f*; **3.** → ***dubbin***.

du·bi·ous ['dju:bjəs] *adj.* ☐ **1.** zweifelhaft: a) unklar, zweideutig, b) ungewiß, unbestimmt, c) fragwürdig, dubi'os, d) unzuverlässig; **2.** a) im Zweifel (***of, about*** über *acc.*), unsicher, b) unschlüssig; **'du·bi·ous·ness** [-nɪs] *s.* **1.** Zweifelhaftigkeit *f*; **2.** Ungewißheit *f*; **3.** Fragwürdigkeit *f.*

du·cal ['dju:kl] *adj.* herzoglich, Herzogs...

duc·at ['dʌkət] *s.* **1.** *hist.* Du'katen *m*; **2.** *pl. obs. sl.* ,Mo'neten' *pl.*

duch·ess ['dʌtʃɪs] *s.* Herzogin *f*; **duch·y** ['dʌtʃɪ] *s.* Herzogtum *n.*

duck[1] [dʌk] *s.* **1.** *pl.* **ducks**, *coll.* **duck** *orn.* (*engS.* weibliche) Ente: ***like a dying ~*** (***in a thunderstorm***) F völlig verdattert; ***take to s.th. like a ~ takes to water*** F sich in et. sofort in s-m Element fühlen; ***it ran off him like water off a ~'s back*** F es ließ ihn völlig kalt; ***play ~s and drakes*** a) Steine (über das Wasser) hüpfen lassen, b) (***with***) *fig.* aasen (mit); **2.** Ente *f*, Entenfleisch *n*: ***roast ~*** Entenbraten *m*; **3.** F ,(Gold-)Schatz' *m*, ,Süße(r' *m*) *f*; **4.** F a) ,Vogel' *m*, b) ,Tante' *f*: ***a funny old ~***; **5.** ⚔ Am'phibien-Lastkraftwagen *m*; **6.** *Kricket*: Null *f*, null Punkte *pl.*

duck[2] [dʌk] **I** *v/i.* **1.** (rasch) 'untertauchen; **2.** (*a. fig.*) sich ducken (***to*** vor *dat.*); **3.** *a.* ***~ out*** F ,verduften', verschwinden; ***~ out of*** → 5 c; **II** *v/t.* **4.** ('unter)tauchen; **5.** a) *den Kopf* ducken *od.* einziehen, b) *e-n Schlag* abducken, ausweichen (*dat.*), c) F sich ,drücken' vor (*dat.*), ausweichen (*dat.*).

duck[3] [dʌk] *s.* **1.** Segeltuch *n*; **2.** *pl.* Segeltuchhose *f.*

'duck|·bill *s.* **1.** *zo.* Schnabeltier *n*; **2.** ⚘ *Brit.* roter Weizen; **'~-billed plat·y·pus** → ***duckbill*** 1; **'~-board** *s.* Laufbrett *n.*

duck·ie ['dʌkɪ] → ***duck***[1] 3.

duck·ing ['dʌkɪŋ] *s.*: ***give s.o. a ~*** j-n untertauchen; ***get a ~*** völlig durchnäßt werden.

duck·ling ['dʌklɪŋ] *s.* Entchen *n.*

duck shot *s.* Entenschrot *m, n.*

duck·y ['dʌkɪ] F **I** *s.* → ***duck***[1] 3; **II** *adj.* ,goldig', ,süß'.

duct [dʌkt] *s.* **1.** ⚙ Röhre *f*, Leitung *f*; (*a.* ⚡ *Kabel- etc.*)Ka'nal *m*; **2.** ⚘, *anat.*, *zo.* Gang *m*, Ka'nal *m*; **'duc·tile** [-taɪl] *adj.* **1.** ⚙ dehn-, streck-, schmiedhämmerbar; **2.** biegsam, geschmeidig; **3.** fügsam; **duc·til·i·ty** [dʌk'tɪlətɪ] *s.* Dehnbarkeit *f etc.*; **'duct·less** [-lɪs] *adj.*: ***~ gland*** *anat.* endokrine Drüse, Hormondrüse *f.*

dud [dʌd] F **I** *s.* **1.** ⚔ Blindgänger *m* (*a. fig. Person*); **2.** ,Niete' *f*: a) Versager *m*, b) Reinfall *m*; **3.** *pl.* a) ,Kla'motten' *pl.* (*Kleider*), b) Krempel *m*; **4.** *a.* ***~ cheque*** (*Am.* ***check***) ungedeckter Scheck; **II** *adj.* **5.** ,mies', schlecht; **6.** gefälscht: ***~ note*** ,Blüte' *f.*

dude [dju:d] *s. Am.* a) Dandy *m*, b) Stadtmensch *m*, ,Stadtfrack' *m*: ***~ ranch*** Ferienranch *f.*

dudg·eon ['dʌdʒən] *s.*: ***in high ~*** sehr aufgebracht.

due [dju:] **I** *adj.* ☐ → ***duly***; **1.** ✝ fällig, so'fort zahlbar: ***fall*** (*od.* ***become***) ***~*** fällig werden; ***when ~*** bei Verfall *od.* Fälligkeit; ***~ date*** Fälligkeitstag *m*; ***the balance ~ to us from A.*** der uns von A. geschuldete Saldo; **2.** *zeitlich* fällig, erwartet: ***the train is ~ at ...*** der Zug ist um ... fällig *od.* soll um ... ankommen; ***he is ~ to return today*** er wird heute zurückerwartet; **3.** gebührend, angemessen, geziemend, gehörig: ***it is ~ to him*** (***to do, to say***) es steht ihm zu (zu tun, zu sagen) (→ *a.* 5); ***hono(u)r to whom hono(u)r is ~*** Ehre, wem Ehre gebührt; ***with all ~ respect to you*** bei aller dir schuldigen Achtung; ***after ~ consideration*** nach reiflicher Überlegung; ***in ~ time*** zur rechten *od.* gegebenen Zeit; → ***care*** 2, ***course*** 1, ***form*** 3; **4.** verpflichtet: ***be ~ to go*** gehen müssen *od.* sollen; **5.** ***~ to*** zuzuschreiben(d) (*dat.*), verursacht durch: ***~ to an accident*** auf einen Unfall *od.* Zufall zurückzuführen; ***death was ~ to cancer*** Krebs war die Todesursache; ***it is ~ to him*** es ist ihm zu verdanken; **6.** ***~ to*** (*inkorrekt statt* ***owing to***) wegen (*gen.*), auf Grund *od.* in'folge von (*od. gen.*): ***~ to his poverty***; **7.** *Am.* im Begriff *sein*; **II** *adv.* **8.** genau, gerade: ***~ east*** genau nach Osten; **III** *s.* **9.** *das* Gebührende, (An-)Recht *n*, Anspruch *m*: ***it is my ~*** es gebührt mir; ***to give you your ~*** um dir nicht unrecht zu tun; ***give the devil his ~*** *fig.* selbst dem Teufel *od.* s-m Feind Gerechtigkeit widerfahren lassen; ***give him his ~!*** das muß man ihm lassen!; **10.** *pl.* Gebühren *pl.*, Abgaben *pl.*, Beitrag *m.*

du·el ['dju:əl] **I** *s. a. fig.* Du'ell *n*, (Zwei)Kampf *m*: ***students' ~*** Mensur *f*; **II** *v/i.* sich duellieren; **'du·el·ist** [-lɪst] *s.* Duel'lant *m.*

du·en·na [dju:'enə] *s.* Anstandsdame *f.*

du·et [dju:'et] *s.* **1.** ♪ Du'ett *n*, Duo *n*: ***play a ~*** ein Duo *od.* (*am Klavier*) vierhändig spielen; **2.** *fig.* Duo *n*, Paar *n*, ,Pärchen' *n.*

duf·fel ['dʌfl] *s.* **1.** Düffel *m* (*Baumwollgewebe*): ***~ coat*** Dufflecoat *m*; **2.** *Am.* F Ausrüstung *f*: ***~ bag*** Matchbeutel *m.*

duff·er ['dʌfə] *s.* Trottel *m.*

duf·fle → ***duffel***.

dug[1] [dʌg] *pret. u. p.p. von **dig***.

dug[2] [dʌg] *s.* **1.** Zitze *f*; **2.** Euter *n.*

du·gong ['du:gɒŋ] *s. zo.* Seekuh *f.*

'dug-out *s.* **1.** ⚔ 'Unterstand *m*; **2.** Einbaum *m.*

duke [dju:k] *s.* Herzog *m*; **'duke·dom** [-dəm] *s.* **1.** Herzogswürde *f*; **2.** Herzogtum *n.*

dul·cet ['dʌlsɪt] *adj.* **1.** wohlklingend, einschmeichelnd: ***in ~ tone*** in süßem Ton; **'dul·ci·fy** [-sɪfaɪ] *v/t.* **1.** versüßen; **2.** *fig.* besänftigen; **'dul·ci·mer** [-sɪmə] *s.* ♪ **1.** Hackbrett *n*; **2.** Zimbal *n.*

dull [dʌl] **I** *adj.* ☐ **1.** dumm, schwer von Begriff; **2.** langsam, schwerfällig, träge; **3.** teilnahmslos, stumpf; **4.** langweilig, fade: ***a ~ evening***; ***~ as ditchwater*** F stinklangweilig; **5.** schwach (*Licht etc.*, *a. Sehkraft, Gehör*); **6.** matt, trübe (*Farbe, Augen*); dumpf (*Klang, Schmerz*); glanz-, leblos; **7.** stumpf (*Klinge*); **8.** trübe (*Wetter*); blind (*Spiegel*); **9.** ge-, betrübt; **10.** ⚓ windstill; ✝ flau, still; *Börse*: lustlos; **II** *v/t.* **11.** *Klinge* stumpf machen; **12.** mattieren, glanzlos machen; trüben; **13.** *fig.* a) abstumpfen, b) dämpfen, schwächen, mildern; *Schmerz* betäuben; **III** *v/i.* **14.** abstumpfen (*a. fig.*); **15.** sich trüben; **16.** abflauen; **'dull·ard** [-ləd] *s.* Dummkopf *m*; **'dull·ish** [-lɪʃ] *adj.* ziemlich dumm *etc.*; **'dul(l)·ness** [-nɪs] *s.* **1.** Dummheit *f*, Dumpfheit *f*; **2.** Langweiligkeit *f*; **3.** Trägheit *f*; **4.**

Schwäche *f*; **5.** Mattheit *f*; Trübheit *f*; Stumpfheit *f*; **6.** ✝ Flaute *f*.

du·ly ['dju:lı] *adv.* **1.** ordnungsgemäß, vorschriftsmäßig, wie es sich gehört, richtig; **2.** gebührend, gehörig; **3.** rechtzeitig, pünktlich.

dumb [dʌm] *adj.* □ **1.** *allg.* stumm (*a. fig.*); *~ animals* stumme Geschöpfe; *the ~ masses fig.* die stumme Masse; *strike s.o. ~* j-m die Sprache verschlagen; *struck ~ with horror* sprachlos vor Entsetzen; → *deaf* 1; **2.** *bsd. Am.* F doof, blöd; '**~-bell** *s.* **1.** *sport* Hantel *f*; **2.** *Am. sl.* Trottel *m*; **~'found** *v/t.* verblüffen; **~'found·ed** *adj.* verblüfft, sprachlos; **~ show** *s.* **1.** Gebärdenspiel *n*, stummes Spiel; **2.** Panto'mime *f*; **ˌ~-'wait·er** *s.* **1.** stummer Diener, Ser'viertisch *m*; **2.** Speisenaufzug *m*.

dum·dum ['dʌmdʌm], *a.* **~ bul·let** *s.* Dum'dum(geschoß) *n*.

dum·found *etc.* → *dumbfound etc.*

dum·my ['dʌmı] **I** *s.* **1.** *allg.* At'trappe *f*, ✝ *a.* Schau-, Leerpackung *f*; **2.** Kleider-, Schaufensterpuppe *f*; **3.** Puppe *f*, Fi'gur *f* (*als Zielscheibe od. für Crashtests*); **4.** ✝ *etc.* Strohmann *m*; **5.** (Karten-, *bsd.* Whistspiel *n* mit) Strohmann *m*; **6.** *Am.* F ,Blödmann' *m*; **7.** *Am.* vierseitige (Verkehrs)Ampel; **8.** *Brit.* (Baby)Schnuller *m*; **9.** *typ.* Blindband *m*; **II** *adj.* **10.** Schein...: *~ candidates*; *~ cartridge* ⚔ Exerzierpatrone *f*; *~ gun* Gewehr- *od.* Geschützattrappe *f*; *~ warhead* blinder Gefechtskopf.

dump [dʌmp] **I** *v/t.* **1.** ('hin)plumpsen *od.* ('hin)fallen lassen, 'hinwerfen; **2.** abladen, schütten, auskippen: *~ truck mot.* Kipper *m*; **3.** ⚔ lagern, stapeln; **4.** ✝ zu Dumpingpreisen verkaufen, verschleudern; **5.** a) *et.* wegwerfen, ,abladen', *Auto* loswerden, b) *j-n* abschieben, loswerden; **II** *s.* **6.** Plumps *m*, dumpfer Schlag; **7.** (Schutt-, Müll)Abladeplatz *m*, Müllhalde *f*; **8.** ⚒ Halde *f*; **9.** ⚔ (*Munitions- etc.*)De'pot *n*, Stapelplatz *m*, (Nachschub)Lager *n*; **10.** *sl.* a) Bruchbude *f* (*Haus*); ,Dreckloch' *n* (*Haus, Wohnung*), b) (elendes) Kaff; '**~·cart** *s.* Kippkarren *m*, -wagen *m*.

dump·er (truck) ['dʌmpə] *s. mot.* Kipper *m*.

dump·ing ['dʌmpıŋ] *s.* **1.** Schuttabladen *n*; **2.** ✝ Dumping *n*, Ausfuhr *f* zu Schleuderpreisen; *~* **ground** → *dump* 7.

dump·ling ['dʌmplıŋ] *s.* **1.** Kloß *m*, Knödel *m*; **2.** F ,Dickerchen' *n* (*Person*).

dumps [dʌmps] *s. pl.*: *be* (*down*) *in the ~* F ,down' *od.* deprimiert sein.

dump·y ['dʌmpı] *adj.* plump, unter'setzt.

dun¹ [dʌn] *v/t.* **1.** *Schuldner* mahnen, drängen: *~ning letter* Zahlungsaufforderung *f*; **2.** bedrängen, belästigen.

dun² [dʌn] **I** *adj.* grau-, schwärzlichbraun; dunkel (*a. fig.*); **II** *s.* Braune(r) *m* (*Pferd*).

dunce [dʌns] *s.* **1.** Dummkopf *m*; **2.** *ped.* schlechter Schüler.

dun·der·head ['dʌndəhed] *s.* Schwachkopf *m*; '**dun·derˌhead·ed** [-dıd] *adj.* schwachköpfig.

dune [dju:n] *s.* Düne *f*: *~ buggy mot.* Strandbuggy *m*.

dung [dʌŋ] **I** *s.* Mist *m*, Dung *m*, Dünger *m*; (Tier)Kot *m*: *~ beetle* Mistkäfer *m*; *~ fork* Mistgabel *f*; *~ heap*, *~ hill* Misthaufen *m*; *~ hill fowl* Hausgeflügel *n*; **II** *v/t.* düngen.

dun·ga·ree [ˌdʌŋgə'ri:] *s.* **1.** grober Baumwollstoff; **2.** *pl.* Arbeitsanzug *m*, -hose *f*.

dun·geon ['dʌndʒən] *s.* Burgverlies *n*; Kerker *m*.

dunk [dʌŋk] *v/i. u. v/t.* eintunken; *fig.* (ein)tauchen.

dun·no [də'nəʊ] F *für* (*I*) *don't know*.

du·o ['dju:əʊ] *pl.* **-os** → *duet*.

duo- [dju:əʊ] *in Zssgn* zwei.

du·o·dec·i·mal [ˌdju:əʊ'desıml] *adj.* ⅍ duodezi'mal; ˌ**du·o'dec·i·mo** [-məʊ] *pl.* **-mos** *s. typ.* **1.** Duo'dezforˌmat *n*; **2.** Duo'dezband *m*.

du·o·de·nal [ˌdju:əʊ'di:nl] *adj.*: *~ ulcer* ⚕ Zwölffingerdarmgeschwür *n*; ˌ**du·o'de·num** [-nəm] *s. anat.* Zwölf'fingerdarm *m*.

du·o·logue ['djʊəlɒg] *s.* **1.** Zwiegespräch *n*; **2.** Duo'drama *n*.

dupe [dju:p] **I** *s.* **1.** Betrogene(r *m*) *f*, ,Lackierte(r' *m*) *f*: *be the ~ of s.o.* auf j-n hereinfallen; **2.** Gimpel *m*, Leichtgläubige(r *m*) *f*; **II** *v/t.* **3.** *j-n* ,reinlegen', ,anschmieren', hinters Licht führen.

du·ple ['dju:pl] *adj.* zweifach: *~ ratio* ⅍ doppeltes Verhältnis; *~ time* ♪ Zweiertakt *m*; '**du·plex** [-leks] **I** *adj. mst* ⚙ doppelt, Doppel..., *a.* ⚡ Duplex...: *~ apartment* → II b; *~ burner* Doppelbrenner *m*; *~ house* → II a; *~ telegraphy* Gegensprech-, Duplextelegraphie *f*; **II** *s. Am.* a) 'Zweifaˌmilien-, Doppelhaus *n*, b) Maiso'nette *f*.

du·pli·cate ['dju:plıkət] **I** *adj.* **1.** doppelt, Doppel...: *~ proportion* ⅍ doppeltes Verhältnis; **2.** genau gleich *od.* entsprechend, Duplikat...: *~ key* Nachschlüssel *m*; *~ part* Ersatzteil *n*; *~ production* Reihen-, Serienfertigung *f*; **II** *s.* **3.** Dupli'kat *n*, Doppel *n*, Zweitschrift *f*; **4.** doppelte Ausfertigung: *in ~*; **5.** ✝ a) Se'kundawechsel *m*, b) Pfandschein *m*; **6.** Seitenstück *n*, Ko'pie *f*; **III** *v/t.* [-keıt] **7.** verdoppeln, im Dupli'kat herstellen; **8.** ein Dupli'kat anfertigen von; **9.** kopieren, abschreiben; **10.** ver'vielfältigen, 'umdrucken; **11.** *fig. et.* 'nachvollziehen; wieder'holen; **du·pli·ca·tion** [ˌdju:plı'keıʃn] *s.* **1.** Verdoppelung *f*; Ver'vielfältigung *f*; 'Umdruck *m*; **2.** Wieder'holung *f*; '**du·pli·ca·tor** [-keıtə] *s.* Ver'vielfältigungsappaˌrat *m*; **du·plic·i·ty** [dju:'plısətı] *s.* **1.** Doppelzüngigkeit *f*, Falschheit *f*; **2.** Duplizi'tät *f*.

du·ra·bil·i·ty [ˌdjʊərə'bılətı] *s.* **1.** Dauer (-haftigkeit) *f*; **2.** Haltbarkeit *f*; **du·ra·ble** ['djʊərəbl] **I** *adj.* □ **1.** dauerhaft; **2.** haltbar, ✝ *a.* langlebig: *~ goods* → **II** *s. pl.* ✝ Gebrauchsgüter *pl.*

du·ral·u·min [djʊə'ræljʊmın] *s.* Du'ral *n*, 'Duraluˌmin *n*.

du·ra·tion [djʊə'reıʃn] *s.* Dauer *f*: *for the ~* a) bis zum Ende, b) F für die Dauer des Krieges.

du·ress [djʊə'res] *s.* ⚖ **1.** Zwang *m* (*a. fig.*), Nötigung *f*: *act under ~* unter Zwang handeln; **2.** Freiheitsberaubung *f*.

dur·ing ['djʊərıŋ] *prp.* während: *~ the night* während (*od.* in *od.* im Laufe) der Nacht.

durst [dɜ:st] *pret. obs. von dare*.

dusk [dʌsk] **I** *s.* (Abend)Dämmerung *f*: *at ~* bei Einbruch der Dunkelheit; **II** *adj. poet.* düster; '**dusk·y** [-kı] *adj.* □ **1.** dunkel (*a. Hautfarbe*); **2.** dunkelhäutig.

dust [dʌst] **I** *s.* **1.** Staub *m*: *bite the ~ fig.* ins Gras beißen; *raise a ~* a) e-e Staubwolke aufwirbeln, b) *fig.* viel Staub aufwirbeln; *the ~ has settled fig.* die Aufregung hat sich gelegt; *shake the ~ off one's feet fig.* a) den Staub von seinen Füßen schütteln, b) entrüstet weggehen; *throw ~ in s.o.'s eyes fig.* j-m Sand in die Augen streuen; *in the ~ fig.* a) im Staube, gedemütigt, b) tot; *lick the ~ fig.* im Staube kriechen; → *dry* 12; **2.** Staub *m*, Asche *f*, sterbliche 'Überreste *pl.*: *turn to ~ and ashes* zu Staub u. Asche werden, zerfallen; **3.** *Brit.* a) Müll *m*, b) Kehricht *m*, *n*; **4.** ⚘ Blütenstaub *m*; **5.** (Gold- *etc.*)Staub *m*; **6.** Bestäubungsmittel *n*, Pulver *n*; **II** *v/t.* **7.** abstauben; **8.** *a. ~ down* ausbürsten, -klopfen: *~ s.o.'s jacket* F j-n vermöbeln; **9.** bestreuen, (ein)pudern; **10.** *Pulver etc.* stäuben, streuen; '**~·bin** [-*st*-] *s. Brit.* **1.** Mülleimer *m*; **2.** Mülltonne *f*; *~* **bowl** *s. Am. geogr.* Trockengebiet *n*; '**~-cart** [-*st*-] *s. Brit.* Müllwagen *m*; *~* **cloth** *s. Am.* Staubtuch *n*; '**~-coat** [-*st*-] *s.* Staubmantel *m*; *~* **cov·er** *s.* **1.** 'Schutzˌumschlag *m* (*um Bücher*); **2.** Schonbezug *m*.

dust·er ['dʌstə] *s.* **1.** Staubtuch *n*, -wedel *m*; **2.** Streudose *f*; **3.** Staubmantel *m*.

dust·ing ['dʌstıŋ] *s.* **1.** Abstauben *n*; **2.** (Ein)Pudern *n*: *~ powder* Körperpuder *m*; **3.** *sl.* Abreibung *f*, (Tracht *f*) Prügel *pl.*

dust| jack·et → *dust cover* 1; '**~·man** [-*t*mən] *s.* [*irr.*] *Brit.* Müllmann *m*; '**~·pan** [-*st*-] *s.* Kehrichtschaufel *f*; '**~·proof** *adj.* staubdicht; *~* **trap** *s.* ,Staubfänger' *m*; '**~·up** *s.* F **1.** ,Krach' *m*; **2.** (handgreifliche) Ausein'andersetzung.

dust·y ['dʌstı] *adj.* □ **1.** staubig; **2.** sandfarben; **3.** *fig.* verstaubt, fade: *not so ~* F gar nicht so übel; **4.** vage, unklar.

Dutch [dʌtʃ] **I** *adj.* **1.** holländisch, niederländisch: *talk to s.o. like a ~ uncle* j-m e-e Standpauke halten; **2.** *sl.* deutsch; **II** *adv.* **3.** *go ~* F getrennte Kasse machen; **III** *s.* **4.** *ling.* Holländisch *n*, das Holländische: *that's all ~ to me* das sind für mich böhmische Dörfer; **5.** *sl.* Deutsch *n*; **6.** *the ~ pl.* a) die Holländer *pl.*, b) *sl.* die Deutschen *pl.*: *that beats the ~!* F das ist ja die Höhe!; **7.** *be in ~ with s.o.* F bei j-m ,unten durch' sein; **8.** *my old ~ sl.* meine ,Alte' (*Ehefrau*); *~* **cour·age** *s.* F angetrunkener Mut.

'**Dutch|·man** [-mən] *s.* [*irr.*] **1.** Holländer *m*, Niederländer *m*: *I'm a ~ if* F ich lass' mich hängen, wenn; *... or I'm a ~* F ... oder ich will Hans heißen; **2.** *Am. sl.* Deutsche(r) *m*; *~* **tile** *s.* glasierte Ofenkachel *f*; *~* **treat** *s.* F Essen *n etc.*, bei dem jeder für sich bezahlt; '**~ˌwom·an** *s.* [*irr.*] Holländerin *f*, Niederländerin *f*.

du·te·ous ['dju:tjəs] → *dutiful*; '**du·ti·a·ble** [-jəbl] *adj.* zoll- *od.* steuerpflichtig; '**du·ti·ful** [-tıfʊl] *adj.* □ **1.** pflichtgetreu; **2.** gehorsam; **3.** pflichtgemäß.

du·ty ['dju:tɪ] *s.* **1.** Pflicht *f*, Schuldigkeit *f* (***to, towards*** gegen['über]): ***do one's ~*** s-e Pflicht tun (***by s.o.*** an j-m); (***as***) ***in ~ bound*** a) pflichtgemäß, b) *a.* ***~-bound*** verpflichtet (*et. zu tun*); ***~ call*** Pflichtbesuch *m*; **2.** Pflicht *f*, Aufgabe *f*, Amt *n*; **3.** (amtlicher) Dienst: ***on ~*** diensthabend, -tuend, im Dienst; ***be on ~*** Dienst haben, im Dienst sein; ***be off ~*** dienstfrei haben; ***~ chemist*** dienstbereite Apotheke; ***~ doctor*** ⚕ Bereitschaftsarzt *m*: ***~ officer*** ⚔ Offizier *m* vom Dienst; ***~ solicitor*** ⚖ *Brit.* Offizialverteidiger *m*; ***do ~ for*** a) *j-n* vertreten, b) *fig.* dienen *od.* benutzt werden als; **4.** Ehrerbietung *f*; **5.** ⚙ a) (Nutz-)Leistung *f*, b) Arbeitsweise *f*, c) Funkti'on *f*; **6.** ✝ a) Abgabe *f*, b) Gebühr *f*, c) Zoll *m*: ***~ on exports*** Ausfuhrzoll; ***~-free*** zollfrei; ***~-free shop*** Duty-free-Shop *m*; ***~-paid*** verzollt; ***pay ~ on*** *et.* verzollen *od.* versteuern.

du·um·vi·rate [dju:'ʌmvɪrət] *s.* Duumvi'rat *n*.

dwarf [dwɔ:f] **I** *pl. mst* **dwarv·es** [-vz] *s.* **1.** Zwerg(in) (*a. fig.*); **2.** ⚘, *zo.* Zwergpflanze *f od.* -tier *n*; **II** *adj.* **3.** *bsd.* ⚘, *zo.* Zwerg...; **III** *v/t.* **4.** verkümmern lassen, in der Entwicklung hindern *od.* hemmen (*beide a. fig.*); **5.** klein erscheinen lassen: ***be ~ed by*** verblassen neben (*dat.*); **6.** *fig.* in den Schatten stellen; **'dwarf·ish** [-fɪʃ] *adj.* □ zwergenhaft, winzig.

dwell [dwel] *v/i.* [*irr.*] **1.** wohnen, leben; **2.** *fig.* ***~ on*** verweilen bei, näher eingehen auf (*acc.*), Nachdruck legen auf (*acc.*); **3.** ***~ on*** ♪ *Ton* (aus)halten; **4.** ***~ in*** begründet sein in (*dat.*); **'dwell·er** [-lə] *s. mst in Zssgn* Bewohner(in); **'dwell·ing** [-lɪŋ] *s. a.* ***~ place*** Wohnung *f*, Wohnsitz *m*; Aufenthalt *m*: ***~ house*** Wohnhaus *n*; ***~ unit*** Wohneinheit *f*.

dwelt [dwelt] *pret. u. p.p.* von ***dwell***.

dwin·dle ['dwɪndl] *v/i.* abnehmen, schwinden, (zs.-)schrumpfen: ***~ away*** dahinschwinden.

dye [daɪ] **I** *s.* **1.** Farbstoff *m*, Farbe *f*; **2.** ⚙ Färbeflüssigkeit *f*; **3.** (Haar)Färbemittel *n*; **4.** Färbung *f* (*a. fig.*): ***of the deepest ~*** übelster Sorte; **II** *v/t.* **5.** färben: ***~d-in-the-wool*** in der Wolle gefärbt, *fig.* waschecht, *Politiker etc.* durch und durch; **III** *v/i.* **6.** sich färben (lassen); **'dye·house** *s.* Färbe'rei *f*.

dy·er ['daɪə] *s.* Färber *m*; ***~'s oak*** *s.* ⚘ Färbereiche *f*.

'dye|-stuff *s.* Farbstoff *m*; **'~-works** *s. pl. oft sg. konstr.* Färbe'rei *f*.

dy·ing ['daɪɪŋ] *adj.* **1.** sterbend: ***be ~*** im Sterben liegen; ***~ wish*** letzter Wunsch; ***~ words*** letzte Worte; ***to my ~ day*** bis an mein Lebensende; **2.** *a. fig.* aussterbend: ***~ tradition***; **3.** a) ersterbend (*Stimme*), b) verhallend; **4.** schmachtend (*Blick*).

dyke [daɪk] *s.* **1.** → ***dike***[1]; **2.** *sl.* ‚Lesbe' *f* (*Lesbierin*).

dy·nam·ic [daɪ'næmɪk] *adj.* (□ ***~ally***) dy'namisch (*a. allg. fig.*); **dy'nam·ics** [-ks] *s. pl. sg. konstr.* **1.** Dy'namik *f*: a) *phys. Bewegungslehre*, b) *fig.* Schwung *m*, Kraft *f*; **2.** *fig.* Triebkraft *f*, treibende Kraft; **dy·na·mism** ['daɪnəmɪzəm] *s.* **1.** *phls.* Dyna'mismus *m*; **2.** dy'namische Kraft, Dy'namik *f*.

dy·na·mite ['daɪnəmaɪt] **I** *s.* **1.** Dyna'mit *n*; **2.** F a) Zündstoff *m*, 'hochbri͵sante Sache, b) gefährliche Per'son *od.* Sache, c) ‚tolle' Person *od.* Sache, *e-e* ‚Wucht'; **II** *v/t.* **3.** (mit Dyna'mit) sprengen; **'dy·na·mit·er** [-tə] *s.* Sprengstoffattentäter *m*.

dy·na·mo ['daɪnəməʊ] *s.* **1.** ⚡ Dy'namo (-ma͵schine *f*) *m*, 'Gleichstrom-, 'Lichtma͵schine *f*; **2.** *fig.* ‚Ener'giebündel' *n*; **~-e·lec·tric** [͵daɪnəməʊɪ'lektrɪk] *adj.* (□ ***~ally***) *phys.* e'lektrody͵namisch; **͵dy·na'mom·e·ter** [-'mɒmɪtə] *s.* ⚙ Dynamo'meter *n*, Kraftmesser *m*.

dy·nas·tic [dɪ'næstɪk] *adj.* (□ ***~ally***) dy'nastisch; **dy·nas·ty** ['dɪnəstɪ] *s.* Dyna'stie *f*, Herrscherhaus *n*.

dyne [daɪn] *s. phys.* Dyn *n* (*Krafteinheit*).

dys·en·ter·y ['dɪsntrɪ] *s.* Dysente'rie *f*, Ruhr *f*.

dys·func·tion [dɪs'fʌŋkʃn] *s.* ⚕ Funkti'onsstörung *f*.

dys·lex·i·a [dɪs'leksɪə] *s.* ⚕ Dysle'xie *f*, Lesestörung *f*.

dys·pep·si·a [dɪs'pepsɪə] *s.* ⚕ Dyspe'p'sie *f*, Verdauungsstörung *f*; **dys'pep·tic** [-ptɪk] **I** *adj.* **1.** ⚕ dys'peptisch; **2.** *fig.* mißgestimmt; **II** *s.* **3.** Dys'peptiker (-in).

dys·tro·phy ['dɪstrəfɪ] *s.* ⚕ Dystro'phie *f*, Ernährungsstörung *f*.

E

E, e [iː] *s.* **1.** E *n*, e *n* (*Buchstabe*); **2.** ♪ E *n*, e *n* (*Note*); **3.** *ped. Am.* Fünf *f*, Mangelhaft *n* (*Note*).

each [iːtʃ] **I** *adj.* jeder, jede, jedes: **~ *man*** jeder (Mann); **~ *one*** jede(r) einzelne; **~ *and every one*** jeder einzelne, all u. jeder; **II** *pron.* (ein) jeder, (e-e) jede, (ein) jedes: **~ *of us*** jede(r) von uns; **~ *has a car*** jede(r) hat ein Auto; **~ *other*** einander, sich (gegenseitig); **III** *adv.* je, pro Per'son *od.* Stück: ***a penny* ~** je e-n Penny.

ea·ger ['iːgə] *adj.* ☐ **1.** eifrig: **~ *beaver*** F Übereifrige(r) *m*, ‚Arbeitspferd' *n*; **2.** (***for, after, to*** *inf.*) begierig (auf *acc.*, nach, zu *inf.*), erpicht (auf *acc.*); **3.** begierig, gespannt: ***an* ~ *look***; **4.** heftig (*Begierde etc.*); **'ea·ger·ness** [-nɪs] *s.* Eifer *m*; Begierde *f*; Ungeduld *f*.

ea·gle ['iːgl] *s.* **1.** *orn.* Adler *m*; **2.** *Am.* goldenes Zehn'dollarstück; **3.** *pl.* ⚔ Adler *m* (*Rangabzeichen e-s Obersten der US-Armee*); **4.** *Golf*: Eagle *n* (*zwei Schläge unter Par*); **,~-'eyed** *adj.* adleräugig, scharfsichtig; **~ owl** *s. orn.* Uhu *m*.

ea·glet ['iːglɪt] *s. orn.* junger Adler.

ea·gre ['eɪgə] *s.* Flutwelle *f*.

ear¹ [ɪə] *s.* **1.** *anat.* Ohr *n*: ***up to the* ~*s*** F bis über die Ohren; ***a word in your* ~** ein Wort im Vertrauen; ***be all* ~*s*** ganz Ohr sein; ***bring s.th. about one's* ~*s*** sich et. einbrocken *od.* auf den Hals laden; ***not to believe one's* ~*s*** s-n Ohren nicht trauen; ***his* ~*s were burning*** ihm klangen die Ohren; ***have one's* ~ *to the ground*** F die Ohren offenhalten; ***set by the* ~*s*** gegeneinander aufhetzen; ***fall on deaf* ~*s*** auf taube Ohren stoßen; ***turn a deaf* ~ *to*** taub sein gegen; ***it came to my* ~*s*** es kam mir zu Ohren; **2.** *fig.* Gehör *n*, Ohr *n*: ***by* ~** nach dem Gehör; ***play by* ~** nach dem Gehör spielen, improvisieren; ***play it by* ~** *fig.* (es) von Fall zu Fall entscheiden, es darauf ankommen lassen; ***have a good* ~** ein feines Gehör haben; ***an* ~ *for music*** musikalisches Gehör, *weitS.* Sinn *m* für Musik; **3.** *fig.* Gehör *n*, Aufmerksamkeit *f*: ***give*** (*od.* ***lend***) ***one's* ~ *to s.o.*** j-m Gehör schenken; ***have s.o.'s* ~** j-s Vertrauen genießen; **4.** Henkel *m*; Öse *f*, Öhr *n*.

ear² [ɪə] *s.* (Getreide)Ähre *f*, (Mais-)Kolben *m*.

ear|·ache ['ɪəreɪk] *s.* ✱ Ohrenschmerzen *pl.*; **'~-,catch·er** *s.* eingängige Melo'die; **'~·drops** *s. pl.* **1.** Ohrgehänge *n*; **2.** ✱ Ohrentropfen *pl.*; **'~·drum** *s. anat.* Trommelfell *n*; **'~·ful** [-fʊl] *s.*: ***get an* ~** F ‚et. zu hören bekommen'.

earl [ɜːl] *s.* (brit.) Graf *m*: ♀ ***Marshal*** Großzeremonienmeister *m*; **'earl·dom** [-dəm] *s.* **1.** Grafenwürde *f*; **2.** *hist.* Grafschaft *f*.

ear·li·er ['ɜːlɪə] *comp. von* ***early***; **I** *adv.* früher, 'vorher; **II** *adj.* früher, vergangen; **'ear·li·est** [-ɪɪst] *sup. von* ***early***; **I** *adv.* am frühesten, frühestens; **II** *adj.* frühest: ***at the* ~** frühestens; → ***convenience*** 1; **'ear·li·ness** [-ɪnɪs] *s.* **1.** Frühe *f*, Frühzeitigkeit *f*; **2.** Frühaufstehen *n*.

'ear·lobe *s.* Ohrläppchen *n*.

ear·ly ['ɜːlɪ] **I** *adv.* **1.** früh(zeitig): **~ *in the day*** früh am Tag; ***as* ~ *as May*** schon im Mai; **~ *on*** a) schon früh(zeitig), b) bald; **2.** bald: ***as* ~ *as possible*** so bald wie möglich; **3.** am Anfang; **4.** zu früh: ***he arrived five minutes* ~**; **5.** früher: ***he left five minutes* ~**; **II** *adj.* **6.** früh(zeitig): ***at an* ~ *hour*** zu früher Stunde; ***in his* ~ *days*** in s-r Jugend; ***it's* ~ *days yet*** *fig.* es ist noch früh am Tage; **~ *fruit*** Frühobst *n*; **~ *history*** Frühgeschichte *f*; **~ *riser*** Frühaufsteher(in); → ***bird*** 1; **7.** anfänglich, Früh...: ***the* ~ *Christians*** die ersten Christen; **8.** vorzeitig, zu früh: ***an* ~ *death***; ***you are* ~ *today*** du bist heute (et.) zu früh (dran); **9.** baldig, schnell: ***an* ~ *reply***; **~ morn·ing tea** *s. e-e* Tasse Tee(, die morgens ans Bett gebracht wird); **~ warn·ing sys·tem** *s.* ⚔ 'Frühwarnsys,tem *n*.

'ear|·mark **I** *s.* **1.** Ohrmarke *f* (*Vieh*); **2.** *fig.* Kennzeichen *n*, Merkmal *n*; **3.** Eselsohr *n*; **II** *v/t.* **4.** kenn-, bezeichnen; **5.** *Geld etc.* bestimmen, vorsehen, zu'rücklegen (***for*** für): **~*ed*** zweckgebunden (*Mittel etc.*); **'~·muff** *s.* Ohrenschützer *m*.

earn [ɜːn] *v/t.* **1.** *Geld etc.* verdienen (*a. fig.*): **~*ed income*** Arbeitseinkommen *n*; **~*ing capacity*** Ertragsfähigkeit *f*; **~*ing power*** a) Erwerbsfähigkeit *f*, b) Ertragsfähigkeit *f*; **~ *value*** Ertragswert *m*; ***a well-~ed rest*** e-e wohlverdiente Ruhepause; **2.** *fig.* (sich) *et.* verdienen, *Lob etc.* ernten.

ear·nest¹ ['ɜːnɪst] *s.* **1.** *a.* **~ *money*** Handgeld *n*, Anzahlung *f* (***of*** auf *acc.*): ***in* ~** als Anzahlung; **2.** *fig.* Zeichen *n* (*des guten Willens etc.*); **3.** *fig.* Vorgeschmack *m*.

ear·nest² ['ɜːnɪst] **I** *adj.* ☐ **1.** ernst; **2.** ernst-, gewissenhaft; **3.** ernstlich: a) ernst(gemeint), b) dringend, c) ehrlich, aufrichtig; **II** *s.* **4.** Ernst *m*: ***in good* ~** in vollem Ernst; ***are you in* ~?** ist das Ihr Ernst?; ***be in* ~ *about s.th.*** es ernst meinen mit et.; **'ear·nest·ness** [-nɪs] *s.* Ernst(haftigkeit *f*) *m*.

earn·ings ['ɜːnɪŋz] *s. pl.* Verdienst *m*: a) Einkommen *n*, Lohn *m*, Gehalt *n*, b) Einnahmen *pl.*, Gewinn *m*.

'ear|·phone *s.* **1.** a) Ohrhörer *m od.* -muschel *f*, b) Kopfhörer *m*; **2.** a) Haarschnecke *f*, b) *pl.* 'Schneckenfri,sur *f*; **'~·piece** *s.* **1.** Ohrenklappe *f*; **2.** a) *teleph.* Hörmuschel *f*, b) → ***earphone*** 1; **3.** (Brillen)Bügel *m*; **'~-,pierc·ing** *adj.* ohrenzerreißend; **'~·ring** *s.* Ohrring *m*; **'~·shot** *s.*: ***within*** (***out of***) **~** in (außer) Hörweite; **'~,split·ting** *adj.* ohrenzerreißend.

earth [ɜːθ] **I** *s.* **1.** Erde *f*, Erdball *m*, Welt *f*: ***on* ~** auf Erden, auf der Erde; ***why on* ~?** F warum in aller Welt?; ***cost the* ~** *fig.* ein Vermögen kosten; **2.** *das* (trockene) Land; Erde *f*, (Erd-)Boden *m*: ***down to* ~** *fig.* nüchtern, prosaisch, rea'listisch; ***come back to* ~** auf den Boden der Wirklichkeit zurückkehren; **3.** ☊ Erde *f*: ***rare* ~*s*** seltene Erden; **4.** (*Fuchs- etc.*)Bau *m*: ***run to* ~** a) *hunt. Fuchs etc.* bis in s-n Bau verfolgen (*Hund, Frettchen*), b) *fig.* aufstöbern, herausfinden, *a. j-n* zur Strecke bringen; ***gone to* ~** *fig.* untergetaucht; **5.** ⚡ *Brit.* a) Erdung *f*, Erde *f*, Masse *f*, b) Erdschluß *m*; **II** *v/t.* **6.** *mst* **~ *up*** ⚘ mit Erde bedecken, häufeln; **7.** ⚡ *Brit.* erden; **'~-born** *adj.* staubgeboren, irdisch, sterblich; **'~-bound** *adj.* erdgebunden.

earth·en ['ɜːθn] *adj.* irden, tönern, Ton...; **'~·ware I** *s.* Steingut(geschirr) *n*, Töpferware *f*; **II** *adj.* Steingut..., Ton...

earth·i·ness ['ɜːθɪnɪs] *fig.* Derbheit *f*, Urigkeit *f*.

earth·ling ['ɜːθlɪŋ] *s.* a) Erdenbürger (-in), b) *Science Fiction*: Erdbewohner (-in); **'earth·ly** [-lɪ] *adj.* **1.** irdisch, weltlich: **~ *joys***; **2.** F begreiflich: ***no* ~ *reason*** kein erfindlicher Grund; ***of no* ~ *use*** völlig unnütz; ***you haven't an* ~ (*chance*)** du hast nicht die geringste Chance.

earth| moth·er *s. fig.* Urweib *n*; **'~-,mov·ing** *adj.* ⚙ Erdbewegungs...: **~ *equipment***; **'~·quake** *s.* **1.** Erdbeben *n*; **2.** *fig.* 'Umwälzung *f*, Erschütterung *f*; **'~,shak·ing** *adj. fig.* welterschütternd; **~ trem·or** *s.* leichtes Erdbeben; **'~·ward(s)** [-wəd(z)] *adv.* erdwärts; **~ wave** *s.* **1.** Bodenwelle *f*; **2.** Erdbebenwelle *f*; **'~·worm** *s.* Regenwurm *m*.

earth·y ['ɜːθɪ] *adj.* **1.** erdig, Erd...; **2.** weltlich *od.* materi'ell (gesinnt); **3.** *fig.* a) grob, b) derb, ro'bust, urig (*Person, Humor etc.*).

ear| trum·pet *s.* ✱ Hörrohr *n*; **'~·wax** *s.* Ohrenschmalz *n*; **'~·wig** *s. zo.* Ohrwurm *m*; **,~'wit·ness** *s.* Ohrenzeuge *m*.

ease [iːz] **I** *s.* **1.** Bequemlichkeit *f*, Behagen *n*, Wohlgefühl *n*: ***at*** (***one's***) ~ a) ruhig, entspannt, gelöst, b) behaglich, c) gemächlich, d) ungeniert, ungezwungen, wie zu Hause; ***take one's*** ~ es sich bequem machen; ***be*** (*od.* ***feel***) ***at*** ~ sich wohl *od.* wie zu Hause fühlen; **2.** Gemächlichkeit *f*, *innere* Ruhe, Sorglosigkeit *f*, Entspannung *f*: ***ill at*** ~ unbehaglich, unruhig; ***put*** (*od.* ***set***) ***s.o. at*** ~ a) j-n beruhigen, b) j-m die Befangenheit nehmen; **3.** Ungezwungenheit *f*, Na'türlichkeit *f*, Zwanglosigkeit *f*, Freiheit *f*: ***live at*** ~ in guten Verhältnissen leben; ***at*** ~***!*** ⚔ rührt euch!; **4.** Linderung *f*, Erleichterung *f*; **5.** Spielraum *m*, Weite *f*; **6.** Leichtigkeit *f*: ***with*** ~ bequem, mühelos; **7.** ⚕ a) Nachgeben *n* (*Preise*), b) Flüssigkeit *f* (*Kapital*); **II** *v/t.* **8.** erleichtern, beruhigen: ~ ***one's mind*** sich erleichtern *od.* beruhigen; **9.** *Schmerzen* lindern; **10.** lockern, entspannen (*beide a. fig.*); **11.** sacht *od.* vorsichtig bewegen *od.* manövrieren: ~ ***one's foot into the shoe*** vorsichtig in den Schuh fahren; **12.** *mst* ~ ***down*** *die Fahrt etc.* verlangsamen, vermindern; **III** *v/i.* **13.** erleichtern; **14.** *mst* ~ ***off*** *od.* ***up*** a) nachlassen, sich abschwächen (*a.* ⚕ *Preise*), b) sich entspannen (*Lage*); c) (*bei der Arbeit*) kürzertreten, d) weniger streng sein (***on*** zu).

ea·sel ['i:zl] *s. paint.* Staffe'lei *f*.

ease·ment ['i:zmənt] *s.* ⚖ Grunddienstbarkeit *f*.

eas·i·ly ['i:zɪlɪ] *adv.* **1.** leicht, mühelos, bequem, glatt; **2.** a) sicher, durchaus, b) bei weitem; **'eas·i·ness** [-nɪs] *s.* **1.** Leichtigkeit *f*; **2.** Ungezwungenheit *f*, Zwanglosigkeit *f*; **3.** Leichtfertigkeit *f*; **4.** Bequemlichkeit *f*.

east [i:st] **I** *s.* **1.** Osten *m*: (***to the***) ~ ***of*** östlich von; ~ ***by north*** ⚓ Ost zu Nord; **2.** *a.* ☡ Osten *m*: ***the*** ☡ a) *Brit.* Ostengland *m*, b) *Am.* die Oststaaten *pl.*, c) *pol.* der Osten, d) der Orient, e) *hist.* das Oströmische Reich; **3.** *poet.* Ost (-wind) *m*; **II** *adj.* **4.** Ost…, östlich; **III** *adv.* **5.** nach Osten, ostwärts; **6.** ~ ***of*** östlich von (*od. gen.*); **'~·bound** *adj.* nach Osten fahrend *etc.*; ☡ **End** *s.* Eastend *n* (*Stadtteil Londons*); **,☡-'End·er** *s. Bewohner(in) des* ***East End***.

East·er ['i:stə] *s.* Ostern *n od. pl.*, Osterfest *n*: ***at*** ~ an *od.* zu Ostern; ~ ***Day*** Oster(sonn)tag *m*; ~ ***egg*** Osterei *n*.

east·er·ly ['i:stəlɪ] **I** *adj.* östlich, Ost…; **II** *adv.* von *od.* nach Osten.

east·ern ['i:stən] *adj.* **1.** östlich, Ost…; **2.** ostwärts, Ost…; ☡ **Church** *s. die* griechisch-ortho'doxe Kirche; ☡ **Empire** *s. hist. das* Oströmische Reich.

east·ern·er ['i:stənə] *s.* **1.** Bewohner (-in) des Ostens e-s Landes; **2.** ☡ *Am.* Oststaatler(in).

'East·er|·tide, ~ **time** *s.* Osterzeit *f*.

East In·di·a·man *s.* [*irr.*] *hist.* Ost'indienfahrer *m* (*Schiff*).

East Side *s. Am. Ostteil von Manhattan.*

east|·ward ['i:stwəd] *adj. u. adv.* ostwärts, nach Osten, östlich; **'~·wards** [-z] *adv.* → ***eastward***.

eas·y ['i:zɪ] **I** *adj.* □ → ***easily***; **1.** leicht, mühelos: ***an*** ~ ***victory***; ~ ***of access*** leicht zugänglich *od.* erreichbar; **2.** leicht, einfach: ***an*** ~ ***language***; ***an*** ~ ***task***; ~ ***money*** leichtverdientes Geld (→ 11 c); **3.** *a.* ~ ***in one's mind*** ruhig, unbesorgt (***about*** um), unbeschwert, sorglos: ***I'm*** ~ F ich bin mit allem einverstanden; **4.** bequem, leicht, angenehm: ***an*** ~ ***life***; ***live in*** ~ ***circumstances***, F ***be on*** ~ ***street*** in guten Verhältnissen leben; ***be*** ~ ***on the ear*** (***eye***) F hübsch anzuhören (anzusehen) sein; **5.** frei von Schmerzen *od.* Beschwerden: ***feel easier*** sich besser fühlen; **6.** gemächlich, gemütlich: ***an*** ~ ***walk***; **7.** nachsichtig (***on*** mit); **8.** leicht, mäßig, erträglich: ***an*** ~ ***penalty***; ***on*** ~ ***terms*** zu günstigen Bedingungen; ***be*** ~ ***on*** *et.* schonen *od.* nicht belasten; **9.** a) leichtfertig, b) lokker, frei (*Moral etc.*); **10.** ungezwungen, zwanglos, natürlich, frei: ~ ***manners***; ~ ***style*** leichter *od.* flüssiger Stil; **11.** ⚕ a) flau, lustlos (*Markt*), b) wenig gefragt (*Ware*), c) billig (*Geld*); **II** *adv.* **12.** leicht, bequem: ~ ***to clean*** leicht zu reinigen(d), pflegeleicht; ***go*** ~, ***take it*** ~ a) sich Zeit lassen, langsam tun, b) sich nicht aufregen; ***take it*** ~***!*** a) immer mit der Ruhe!, b) keine Bange!; ***go*** ~ ***on*** a) *j-n od. et.* sachte anfassen, b) schonend *od.* sparsam umgehen mit; ~***!***, F ~ ***does it!*** sachte!, langsam!; ***stand*** ~***!*** ⚔ rührt euch!; ***easier said than done*** (das ist) leichter gesagt als getan; ~ ***come***, ~ ***go*** wie gewonnen, so zerronnen; **'~-care** *adj.* pflegeleicht; ~ **chair** *s.* Sessel *m*; **'~,go·ing** *adj.* **1.** gelassen; **2.** unbeschwert; **3.** leichtlebig.

eat [i:t] **I** *s.* **1.** *pl.* F ‚Fres'salien' *pl.*, ‚Futter' *n*; **II** *v/t.* [*irr.*] **2.** essen (*Mensch*), fressen (*Tier*): ~ ***s.o. out of house and home*** j-n arm (fr)essen; ~ ***one's words*** alles(, was man gesagt hat,) zurücknehmen; ***don't*** ~ ***me*** F friß mich nur nicht (gleich) auf!; ***what's*** ~***ing him?*** F was (für e-e Laus) ist ihm über die Leber gelaufen?, was hat er denn?; (*siehe auch die Verbindungen mit anderen Substantiven*); **3.** zerfressen, -nagen, nagen an (*dat.*): ~***en by acid*** von Säure zerfressen; **4.** fressen, nagen: ~ ***holes into s.th.***; **5.** → ***eat up***; **III** *v/i.* **6.** essen: ~ ***well***; **7.** fressen (*Tier*); **8.** fressen, nagen (*a. fig.*): ~ ***into*** a) sich (hin)einfressen in (*acc.*), b) *Reserven etc.* angreifen, ein Loch reißen in (*acc.*): ~ ***through s.th.*** sich durch et. hindurchfressen; **9.** sich essen (lassen): ***it*** ~***s like beef***; *Zssgn mit adv.*:

eat| a·way I *v/t.* **1.** *geol.* a) erodieren, auswaschen, b) abtragen; **II** *v/i.* **2.** (tüchtig) zugreifen; **3.** ~ ***at*** → 1; ~ **out** *v/i.* auswärts essen, essen gehen; ~ **up** *v/t.* **1.** aufessen (*Mensch*), auffressen (*Tier*) (*beide a. v/i.*); **2.** *Reserven etc.* verschlingen, völlig aufbrauchen; **3.** *j-n* verzehren (*Gefühl*): ***be eaten up with envy*** vor Neid platzen; **4.** F a) ‚fressen', ‚schlucken' (*glauben*), b) *j-s Worte* verschlingen, c) *et.* mit den Augen verschlingen; **5.** F *Kilometer* ‚fressen' (*Auto*).

eat·a·ble ['i:təbl] **I** *adj.* eß-, genießbar; **II** *s. mst pl.* Eßwaren *pl.*; **eat·en** ['i:tn] *p.p. von* ***eat***; **eat·er** ['i:tə] *s.* Esser(in): ***be a poor*** ~ ein schwacher Esser sein.

eat·ing ['i:tɪŋ] **I** *s.* **1.** Essen *n*, Speise *f*; **II** *adj.* **2.** Eß…: ~ ***apple***; **3.** *fig.* nagend, zehrend; ~ **house** *s.* 'Eßlo,kal *n*.

eau de Co·logne [,əʊdəkə'ləʊn] (*Fr.*) *s.* Kölnischwasser *n*.

eaves [i:vz] *s. pl.* **1.** Dachgesims *n*, -vorsprung *m*; **2.** Traufe *f*; **'~·drop** *v/i.* (heimlich) lauschen *od.* horchen: ~ ***on*** *j-n, ein Gespräch* belauschen; **'~,drop·per** *s.* Horcher(in), Lauscher(in): ~***s hear what they deserve*** der Lauscher an der Wand hört s-e eigne Schand.

ebb [eb] **I** *s.* **1.** Ebbe *f*: ~ ***and flow*** Ebbe u. Flut, *fig. das* Hin u. Her *der Schlacht etc.*, *das* Auf u. Ab *der Wirtschaft etc.*; **2.** *fig.* Ebbe *f*, Tiefstand *m*: ***at a low*** ~ *fig.* auf e-m Tiefstand; **II** *v/i.* **3.** zu'rückgehen (*a. fig.*): ~ ***and flow*** steigen u. fallen, *fig. a.* kommen u. gehen; **4.** *a.* ~ ***away*** *fig.* verebben, abnehmen; ~ **tide** → ***ebb*** 1 u. 2.

eb·on ['ebən] *poet. für* ***ebony***; **'eb·on·ite** [-naɪt] *s.* Ebo'nit *n* (*Hartkautschuk*); **'eb·on·ize** [-naɪz] *v/t.* schwarz beizen; **'eb·on·y** [-nɪ] **I** *s.* Ebenholz(baum *m*) *n*; **II** *adj.* a) aus Ebenholz, b) (tief-) schwarz.

e·bul·li·ence [ɪ'bʌljəns], **e'bul·li·en·cy** [-sɪ] *s.* **1.** Aufwallen *n* (*a. fig.*); **2.** *fig.* 'Überschäumen *n*, -schwenglichkeit *f*; **e'bul·li·ent** [-nt] *adj.* □ *fig.* sprudelnd, 'überschäumend (***with*** von), 'überschwenglich; **eb·ul·li·tion** [,ebə'lɪʃən] → ***ebullience***.

ec·cen·tric [ɪk'sentrɪk] **I** *adj.* (□ ~***ally***) **1.** ⚙, ⚘ ex'zentrisch; **2.** *ast.* nicht rund; **3.** *fig.* ex'zentrisch: a) wunderlich, über'spannt, verschroben, b) ausgefallen; **II** *s.* **4.** Ex'zentriker(in); **5.** ⚙ Ex'zenter *m*: ~ ***wheel*** Exzenterscheibe *f*; **ec·cen·tric·i·ty** [,eksen'trɪsətɪ] *s.* ⚙, ⚘ *u. fig.* Exzentrizi'tät, *fig. a.* Über'spanntheit *f*, Verschrobenheit *f*.

Ec·cle·si·as·tes [ɪ,kli:zɪ'æsti:z] *s. bibl.* Ekklesi'astes *m*, der Prediger Salomo; **ec,cle·si'as·ti·cal** [-tɪkl] *adj.* □ kirchlich, geistlich: ~ ***law*** Kirchenrecht *n*; **ec,cle·si'as·ti·cism** [-tɪsɪzəm] *s.* Kirchentum *n*; Kirchlichkeit *f*.

ech·e·lon ['eʃəlɒn] **I** *s.* **1.** ⚔ a) Staffel (-ung) *f*, (Angriffs)Welle *f*: ***in*** ~ staffelförmig, b) ✈ 'Staffelflug *m*, -formati,on *f*, c) (Befehls)Ebene *f*; **2.** *fig.* Rang *m*, Stufe *f*: ***the upper*** ~***s*** die höheren Ränge; **II** *v/t.* **3.** staffeln, (staffelförmig) gliedern.

e·chi·no·derm [e'kaɪnədɜ:m] *s. zo.* Stachelhäuter *m*.

ech·o ['ekəʊ] **I** *pl.* **-oes** *s.* **1.** *a. fig.* Echo *n*, 'Widerhall *m*: (***sympathetic***) ~ Anklang *m*; ***find an*** ~ ein (…) Echo finden, Anklang finden; ***to the*** ~ laut, schallend; **2.** *fig.* Echo *n* (*Person*); **3.** ♪ Wieder'holung *f*; **4.** ⚡, *TV*: Echo *n*, *Radar*: *a.* Schattenbild *n*; **5.** (genaue) Nachahmung *f*; **II** *v/i.* **6.** 'widerhallen (***with*** von); **7.** hallen; **III** *v/t.* **8.** *Ton* zu'rückwerfen, 'widerhallen lassen; **9.** *fig.* 'Widerhall erwecken; **10.** *Worte* echoen; (*j-m*) *et.* nachbeten; **11.** echoen, nachahmen; ~ **sound·er** *s.* ⚓ Echolot *n*; ~ **sound·ing** *s.* ⚓ Echolotung *f*.

é·clair [eɪ'kleə] (*Fr.*) *s.* E'clair *n*.

é·clat ['eɪklɑ:] (*Fr.*) *s.* **1.** glänzender Erfolg, allgemeiner Beifall, öffentliches Aufsehen *n*; **2.** *fig.* Auszeichnung *f*, Geltung *f*.

ec·lec·tic [e'klektɪk] **I** *adj.* (□ ~***ally***) ek'lektisch; **II** *s.* Ek'lektiker *m*; **ec·lec·ti·cism** [e'klektɪsɪzəm] *s. phls.* Eklekti'zismus *m*.

e·clipse [ɪ'klɪps] **I** *s.* **1.** *ast.* Verfinsterung *f*, Finsternis *f*: **~ *of the moon*** Mondfinsternis; ***partial* ~** partielle Finsternis; **2.** Verdunkelung *f*; **3.** *fig.* Schwinden *n*, Niedergang *m*: ***in* ~** im Schwinden, *a.* in der Versenkung verschwunden; **II** *v/t.* **4.** *ast.* verfinstern; **5.** verdunkeln; **6.** *fig.* in den Schatten stellen, über'ragen.

ec·logue ['eklɒg] *s.* Ek'loge *f*, Hirtengedicht *n*.

eco- [i:kəʊ] *in Zssgn* öko'logisch, Umwelt..., Öko...; **ˌe·co·ca'tas·tro·phe** *s.* 'Umweltkataˌstrophe *f*; **e·co·cide** ['i:kəʊsaɪd] *s.* 'Umweltzerstörung *f*.

ec·o·log·i·cal [ˌi:kə'lɒdʒɪkl] *adj.* □ *biol.* öko'logisch, Umwelt...: **~ *system*** → ***ecosystem***; **ˌec·o'log·i·cal·ly** [-kəlɪ] *adv.*: **~ *harmful*** (*od.* ***noxious***) umweltfeindlich; **~ *beneficial*** umweltfreundlich; **e·col·o·gist** [i:'kɒlədʒɪst] *s. biol.* Öko'loge *m*; **e·col·o·gy** [i:'kɒlədʒɪ] *s. biol.* Ökolo'gie *f*.

e·co·no·met·rics [ɪˌkɒnə'metrɪks] *s. pl. sg. konstr.* ✝ Ökonome'trie *f*.

e·co·nom·ic [ˌi:kə'nɒmɪk] **I** *adj.* (□ **~*ally***) **1.** (natio'nal)ökoˌnomisch, (volks-) wirtschaftlich, Wirtschafts...: **~ *geography*** Wirtschaftsgeographie *f*; **~ *growth*** Wirtschaftswachstum *n*; **~ *miracle*** Wirtschaftswunder *n*; **~ *policy*** Wirtschaftspolitik *f*; **~ *science*** → 3; **2.** wirtschaftlich, ren'tabel; **II** *s. pl. sg. konstr.* **3.** a) Natio'nalökonoˌmie *f*, Volkswirtschaft(slehre) *f*, b) → ***economy*** 4; **ˌe·co'nom·i·cal** [-kl] *adj.* □ wirtschaftlich, sparsam, *Person a.* haushälterisch: ***be* ~ *with s.th.*** mit et. haushalten *od.* sparsam umgehen.

e·con·o·mist [ɪ'kɒnəmɪst] *s.* **1.** *a.* ***political* ~** Volkswirt(schaftler) *m*, Natio'nalökoˌnom *m*; **2.** sparsamer Wirtschafter, guter Haushälter; **e'con·o·mize** [-maɪz] **I** *v/t.* **1.** sparsam 'umgehen mit, haushalten mit, sparen; **2.** nutzbar machen; **II** *v/i.* **3.** sparen: a) sparsam wirtschaften, Einsparungen machen: **~ *on*** → 1, b) sich einschränken (***in*** in *dat.*); **e'con·o·miz·er** [-maɪzə] *s.* **1.** haushälterischer Mensch; **2.** ⚙ Sparanlage *f*, *bsd.* Wasser-, Luftvorwärmer *m*; **e·con·o·my** [ɪ'kɒnəmɪ] **I** *s.* **1.** Sparsamkeit *f*, Wirtschaftlichkeit *f*; **2.** *fig.* sparsame Anwendung, Sparsamkeit *f* in den (künstlerischen) Mitteln: **~ *of style*** knapper Stil; **3.** a) Sparmaßnahme *f*, b) Einsparung *f*, c) Ersparnis *f*; **4.** ✝ 'Wirtschaft(ssyˌstem *n od.* -lehre *f*) *f*: ***political* ~** → ***economic*** 3a; **5.** Sy'stem *n*, Aufbau *m*, Gefüge *n*; **II** *adj.* **6.** Spar...: **~ *bottle***; **~ *class*** ✈ Economyklasse *f*; **~ *drive*** Sparmaßnahmen *pl.*; **~-*priced*** preisgünstig, billig, Billig...

'e·co|ˌpol·i·cy *s.* 'Umweltpoliˌtik *f*; **'~ˌsys·tem** *s. biol.* 'Ökosyˌstem *n*; **'~·type** *s. biol.* Öko'typus *m*.

ec·ru ['eɪkru:] *adj.* e'krü, na'turfarben, ungebleicht (*Stoff*).

ec·sta·size ['ekstəsaɪz] *v/t.* (*u. v/i.*) in Ek'stase versetzen (geraten).

ec·sta·sy ['ekstəsɪ] *s.* **1.** Ek'stase *f*, Verzückung *f*, Rausch *m*, (Taumel *m* der) Begeisterung *f*: ***go into ecstasies over*** in Verzückung geraten über (*acc.*), hingerissen sein von; **2.** Aufregung *f*; **3.** ⚕ Ek'stase *f*, krankhafte Erregung; **ec·stat·ic** [ɪk'stætɪk] *adj.* (□ **~*ally***) **1.** ek'statisch, verzückt, begeistert, hingerissen; **2.** entzückend, hinreißend.

ec·to·blast ['ektəʊblɑ:st], **'ec·to·derm** [-dɜ:m] *s. biol.* Ekto'derm *n*, äußeres Keimblatt; **'ec·to·plasm** [-plæzəm] *s. biol. u. Spiritismus*: Ekto'plasma *n*.

ec·u·men·i·cal [ˌi:kju:'menɪkl] *adj. bsd. eccl.* öku'menisch: **~ *council*** a) *R.C.* ökumenisches Konzil, b) Weltkirchenrat *m*.

ec·ze·ma ['eksɪmə] *s.* ⚕ Ek'zem *n*.

E-Day ['i:deɪ] *s. pol. Tag des Beitritts Großbritanniens zur EWG.*

ed·dy ['edɪ] **I** *s.* (*Wasser-, Luft*)Wirbel *m*, Strudel *m* (*a. fig.*); **II** *v/i.* (um'her-) wirbeln.

e·del·weiss ['eɪdlvaɪs] *s.* Edelweiß *n*.

e·de·ma [i:'di:mə] → ***oedema***.

E·den ['i:dn] *s. bibl.* (der Garten) Eden *n*, das Para'dies (*a. fig.*).

edge [edʒ] **I** *s.* **1.** a) *a.* ***cutting* ~** Schneide *f*, b) Schärfe *f* (*der Klinge*): ***the knife has no* ~** das Messer schneidet nicht; ***put an* ~ *on s.th.*** et. schärfen *od.* schleifen; ***take the* ~ *off*** a) *Messer etc.* stumpf machen, b) *fig. e-r Sache* die Spitze abbrechen, die Schärfe nehmen; **2.** *fig.* Schärfe *f*, Spitze *f*, Heftigkeit *f*: ***give an* ~ *to s.th.*** et. verschärfen *od.* in Schwung bringen; ***not to put too fine an* ~ *on it*** kein Blatt vor den Mund nehmen; ***he is*** (*od.* ***his nerves are***) ***on* ~** er ist gereizt *od.* nervös; **3.** Ecke *f*, Zacke *f*, (scharfe) Kante; Grat *m*: **~ *of a chair*** Stuhlkante; ***set*** (***up***) ***on* ~** hochkant stellen; → ***tooth*** 1; **4.** Rand *m*, Saum *m*, Grenze *f*: ***the* ~ *of the lake*** der Rand *od.* das Ufer des Sees; **~ *of a page*** Rand e-r (Buch)Seite; ***on the* ~ *of*** a) am Rande (*der Verzweiflung etc.*), an der Schwelle (*gen.*), kurz vor (*dat.*), b) im Begriff (***of doing*** zu tun); **5.** Schnitt *m* (*Buch*); → ***gilt-edged*** 1; **6.** F Vorteil *m*: ***have the* ~ *on*** (*od.* ***over***) ***s.o.*** e-n Vorteil gegenüber j-m haben, j-m ‚voraus' *od.* ‚über' sein; **II** *v/t.* **7.** schärfen, schleifen; **8.** um'säumen, um'randen; begrenzen, einfassen; **9.** ⚙ beschneiden, abkanten; **10.** *langsam* schieben, rücken, drängen: **~ *o.s. into s.th.*** sich in et. (hinein)drängen; **III** *v/i.* **11.** sich *wohin* schieben *od.* drängen; *Zssgn mit adv.*:

edge| a·way *v/i.* **1.** (langsam) wegrükken; **2.** wegschleichen; **~ in I** *v/t.* einschieben; **II** *v/i.* sich hin'eindrängen *od.* -schieben; **~ off** → ***edge away***; **~ on** *v/t. j-n* antreiben; **~ out** *v/t.* (*v/i.* sich) hin'ausdrängen.

edged [edʒd] *adj.* **1.** schneidend, scharf; **2.** *in Zssgn* ...schneidig; **3.** eingefaßt, gesäumt; **4.** *in Zssgn* ...randig; **~ tool** *s.* **1.** → ***edge tool***; **2.** ***play with edge(d) tools*** *fig.* mit dem Feuer spielen.

edge| tool *s.* Schneidewerkzeug *n*; **'~·ways** [-weɪz], **'~·wise** [-waɪz] *adv.* a) seitlich, mit der Kante nach oben *od.* vorn, b) hochkant(ig): ***I couldn't get a word in* ~** *fig.* ich bin kaum zu Wort gekommen.

edg·ing ['edʒɪŋ] *s.* Rand *m*; Besatz *m*, Einfassung *f*, Borte *f*; **edg·y** ['edʒɪ] *adj.* **1.** kantig, scharf; **2.** *fig.* ner'vös, gereizt; **3.** *paint.* scharflinig.

ed·i·bil·i·ty [ˌedɪ'bɪlətɪ] *s.* Eß-, Genießbarkeit *f*; **ed·i·ble** ['edɪbl] **I** *adj.* eß-, genießbar: **~ *oil*** Speiseöl *n*; **II** *s. pl.* Eßwaren *pl.*

e·dict ['i:dɪkt] *s.* Erlaß *m*, *hist.* E'dikt *n*.

ed·i·fi·ca·tion [ˌedɪfɪ'keɪʃn] *s. fig.* Erbauung *f*.

ed·i·fice ['edɪfɪs] *s. a. fig.* Gebäude *n*, Bau *m*; **'ed·i·fy** [-faɪ] *v/t. fig.* erbauen, aufrichten; **'ed·i·fy·ing** [-faɪɪŋ] *adj.* □ erbaulich (*a. iro.*).

ed·it ['edɪt] *v/t.* **1.** *Texte etc.* a) her'ausgeben, edieren, b) redigieren, druckfertig machen; **2.** *Zeitung* als Her'ausgeber leiten; **3.** *Buch etc.* bearbeiten, zur Veröffentlichung fertigmachen; kürzen; *Film, Tonband* schneiden: **~ *out*** a) herausstreichen, b) herausschneiden; **~-*ing table*** *TV* Schneidetisch *m*; **4.** *Computer*: *Daten* aufbereiten; **5.** *fig.* zu'rechtstutzen; **e·di·tion** [ɪ'dɪʃn] *s.* **1.** Ausgabe *f*: ***pocket* ~** Taschen(buch)-ausgabe; ***morning* ~** Morgenausgabe (*Zeitung*); **2.** Auflage *f*: ***first* ~** erste Auflage, Erstdruck *m*, -ausgabe *f* (*Buch*); ***run into 20* ~*s*** 20 Auflagen erleben; **3.** *fig.* (*kleinere etc.*) Ausgabe *f*; **'ed·i·tor** [-tə] *s.* **1.** *a.* **~ *in chief*** Her'ausgeber(in) (*e-s Buchs etc.*); **2.** *Zeitung*: a) *a.* **~ *in chief*** 'Chefredakˌteur (-in), b) Redak'teur(in): ***the* ~*s*** die Redaktion; **3.** *Film, TV*: Cutter(in); **ed·i·to·ri·al** [ˌedɪ'tɔ:rɪəl] **I** *adj.* □ **1.** Herausgeber...; **2.** redaktio'nell, Redaktions...: **~ *staff*** Redaktion *f*; **II** *s.* **3.** 'Leitarˌtikel *m*; **ed·i·to·ri·al·ize** [ˌedɪ'tɔ:rɪəlaɪz] *v/i.* (e-n) 'Leitarˌtikel schreiben; **'ed·i·tor·ship** [-təʃɪp] *s.* Positi'on *f* e-s Her'ausgebers *od.* ('Chef)Redakˌteurs; **'ed·i·tress** [-trɪs] *s.* Her'ausgeberin *f etc.* (→ ***editor***).

ed·u·cate ['edju:keɪt] *v/t.* erziehen (*a. weitS.* ***to*** zu), unter'richten, (aus)bilden: ***he was* ~*d at ...*** er besuchte die (Hoch)Schule in ...; **'ed·u·cat·ed** [-tɪd] *adj.* **1.** gebildet; **2.** ***an* ~ *guess*** e-e fundierte Annahme.

ed·u·ca·tion [ˌedju:'keɪʃn] *s.* **1.** Erziehung *f* (*a. weitS.* ***to*** zu *demokratischem Denken etc.*), (Aus)Bildung *f*; **2.** (*erworbene*) Bildung, Bildungsstand *m*: ***general* ~** Allgemeinbildung *f*; **3.** Bildungs-, Schulwesen *n*; **4.** (Aus)Bildungsgang *m*; **5.** Päda'gogik *f*, Erziehungswissenschaft *f*; **ˌed·u'ca·tion·al** [-ʃənl] *adj.* □ **1.** erzieherisch, Erziehungs..., päda'gogisch, Unterrichts...: **~ *film*** Lehrfilm *m*; **~ *psychology*** Schulpsychologie *f*; **~ *television*** Schulfernsehen *n*; **~ *toys*** pädagogisch wertvolles Spielzeug; **2.** Bildungs...: **~ *leave*** Bildungsurlaub *m*; **~ *level*** Bildungsniveau *n*; **~ *misery*** Bildungsnotstand *m*; **ˌed·u'ca·tion·al·ist** [-ʃnəlɪst], *a.* **ˌed·u'ca·tion·ist** [-ʃnɪst] *s.* Päda'goge *m*, Päda'gogin *f*: a) Erzieher(in), b) Erziehungswissenschaftler(in); **ed·u·ca·tive** ['edju:kətɪv] *adj.* **1.** erzieherisch, Erziehungs...; **2.** bildend, Bildungs...; **'ed·u·ca·tor** ['edju:keɪtə] → ***educationalist***.

e·duce [i:'dju:s] *v/t.* **1.** her'ausholen, entwickeln; **2.** *Begriff* ableiten; **3.** ⚗ ausziehen, extrahieren.

ed·u·tain·ment [ˌedju:'teɪnmənt] *s.* bildende Unter'haltung (*pädagogisch wertvolle Spiele etc.*).

Ed·war·di·an [ed'wɔ:djən] *adj.* aus *od.* im Stil der Zeit König Eduards (*bsd.* Eduards VII.).

eel [iːl] *s.* Aal *m*; **~ buck**, **ˈ~·pot** *s.* Aalreuse *f*; **ˈ~·spear** *s.* Aalgabel *f*; **ˈ~·worm** *s. zo.* Älchen *n*, Fadenwurm *m*.

e'en [iːn] *poet.* → ***even***¹, ³.

e'er [eə] *poet.* → ***ever***.

ee·rie, **ee·ry** [ˈɪərɪ] *adj.* □ unheimlich, schaurig; **ˈee·ri·ness** [-nɪs] *s.* Unheimlichkeit *f*.

eff [ef] *v/i.*: **~ off** V ,abhauen'; → ***effing***.

ef·face [ɪˈfeɪs] *v/t.* **1.** wegwischen, -reiben, löschen; **2.** *bsd. fig.* auslöschen, tilgen; **3.** in den Schatten stellen: **~ *o.s.*** sich (bescheiden) zurückhalten, sich im Hintergrund halten; **efˈface·a·ble** [-səbl] *adj.* auslöschbar; **efˈface·ment** [-mənt] *s.* Auslöschung *f*, Tilgung *f*, Streichung *f*.

ef·fect [ɪˈfekt] **I** *s.* **1.** Wirkung *f* (***on*** auf *acc.*): ***take* ~** wirken (→ 4); **2.** (Ein-)Wirkung *f*, Einfluß *m*, Erfolg *m*, Folge *f*: ***of no* ~** nutzlos, vergeblich; **3.** (gesuchte) Wirkung, Eindruck *m*, Efˈfekt *m*: ***general* ~** Gesamteindruck; ***have an* ~ *on*** wirken auf (*acc.*); ***calculated*** *od.* ***meant for* ~** auf Effekt berechnet; ***straining after* ~** Effekthascherei *f*; **4.** Wirklichkeit *f*; ⚖ (Rechts)Wirksamkeit *f*, (-)Kraft *f*, Gültigkeit *f*: ***in* ~** a) tatsächlich, eigentlich, im wesentlichen, b) ⚖ *etc.* in Kraft, gültig; ***with* ~ *from*** mit Wirkung vom; ***come into*** (*od.* ***take***) **~** wirksam werden, in Kraft treten; ***carry into* ~** ausführen, verwirklichen; **5.** Inhalt *m*, Sinn *m*, Absicht *f*; Nutzen *m*: ***to the* ~ *that*** des Inhalts, daß; ***to this* ~** diesbezüglich, in diesem Sinn; ***words to this* ~** derartige Worte; **6.** ⚙ Leistung *f*, ˈNutzefˌfekt *m*; **7.** *pl.* ✝ a) Efˈfekten *pl.*, b) Vermögen(swerte *pl.*) *n*, Habe *f*, c) Barbestand *m*, d) (Bank)Guthaben *n*: ***no* ~*s*** ohne Deckung (*Scheck*); **II** *v/t.* **8.** be-, erwirken, verursachen; **9.** ausführen, erledigen, vollˈziehen, tätigen, bewerkstelligen: **~ *an insurance*** ✝ e-e Versicherung abschließen; **~ *payment*** Zahlung leisten; **efˈfec·tive** [-tɪv] **I** *adj.* □ **1.** wirksam, erfolgreich, wirkungsvoll, kräftig: **~ *range*** ⚔ wirksame Schußweite; **2.** eindrucks-, efˈfektvoll; **3.** (rechts)wirksam, rechtskräftig, gültig, in Kraft: **~ *from*** *od.* ***as of*** mit Wirkung vom; **~ *immediately*** mit sofortiger Wirkung; **~ *date*** Tag *m* des Inkrafttretens; ***become* ~** in Kraft treten; **4.** tatsächlich, effekˈtiv, wirklich; **5.** ⚔ dienstfähig, kampffähig, einsatzbereit: **~ *strength*** → 7b; **6.** ⚙ wirksam, nutzbar, Nutz...: **~ *capacity*** *od.* ***output*** Nutzleistung *f*; **II** *s. pl.* **7.** ⚔ a) einsatzfähige Solˈdaten *pl.*, b) Ist-Stärke *f*; **efˈfec·tive·ness** [-tɪvnɪs] *s.* Wirksamkeit *f*; **efˈfec·tu·al** [-tʃʊəl] *adj.* □ **1.** wirksam; **2.** → ***effective*** 3; **3.** wirklich, tatsächlich; **efˈfectu·ate** [-tjʊeɪt] → ***effect*** 8, 9.

ef·fem·i·na·cy [ɪˈfemɪnəsɪ] *s.* **1.** Weichlichkeit *f*, Verweichlichung *f*; **2.** unmännliches Wesen; **efˈfem·i·nate** [-nət] *adj.* □ **1.** weichlich, verweichlicht; **2.** unmännlich, weibisch.

ef·fer·vesce [ˌefəˈves] *v/i.* **1.** (auf)brausen, moussieren, sprudeln, schäumen; **2.** *fig.* (ˈüber)sprudeln, ˈüberschäumen; **ˌef·ferˈves·cence** [-sns] *s.* **1.** (Auf-)brausen *n*, Moussieren *n*; **2.** *fig.* (ˈÜber)Sprudeln *n*, ˈÜberschäumen *n*; **ˌef·ferˈves·cent** [-snt] *adj.* **1.** sprudelnd, schäumend; moussierend: **~ *powder*** Brausepulver *n*; **2.** *fig.* (ˈüber-)sprudelnd, ˈüberschäumend.

ef·fete [ɪˈfiːt] *adj.* erschöpft, entkräftet, kraftlos, verbraucht.

ef·fi·ca·cious [ˌefɪˈkeɪʃəs] *adj.* □ wirksam; **ef·fi·ca·cy** [ˈefɪkəsɪ] *s.* Wirksamkeit *f*.

ef·fi·cien·cy [ɪˈfɪʃənsɪ] *s. allg.* Effiziˈenz *f*: a) Tüchtigkeit *f*, Leistungsfähigkeit *f* (*a. e-s Betriebs etc.*), b) Wirksamkeit *f*, ⚙ (Nutz)Leistung *f*, Wirkungsgrad *m*, c) Tauglichkeit *f*, Brauchbarkeit *f*, d) ✝, ⚙ Wirtschaftlichkeit *f*: **~ *engineer***, **~ *expert*** ✝ Rationalisierungsfachmann *m*; **~ *wages*** leistungsbezogener Lohn; **~ *apartment*** *Am.* (Einzimmer)Appartement *n*; **efˈfi·cient** [-nt] *adj.* □ **1.** *allg.* effiziˈent: a) tüchtig, (*a.* ⚙ leistungs)fähig, b) wirksam, c) gründlich, d) zügig, rasch, e) ratioˈnell, wirtschaftlich, f) tauglich, gut funktionierend, ⚙ *a.* leistungsstark; **2.** **~ *cause*** *phls.* wirkende Ursache.

ef·fi·gy [ˈefɪdʒɪ] *s.* Bild(nis) *n*: ***burn s.o. in* ~** j-n in effigie *od.* symbolisch verbrennen.

ef·fing [ˈefɪŋ] *adj.* V verdammt, Scheiß...

ef·flo·resce [ˌeflɔːˈres] *v/i.* **1.** *bsd. fig.* aufblühen, sich entfalten; **2.** ⚗ ausblühen, -wittern; **ˌef·floˈres·cence** [-sns] *s.* **1.** *bsd. fig.* (Auf)Blühen *n*; **2.** Effloresˈzenz: a) ⚗ Ausblühen *n*, Beschlag *m*, b) ✻ Ausschlag *m*; **ˌef·floˈres·cent** [-snt] *adj.* **1.** *bsd. fig.* (auf)blühend; **2.** ⚗ ausblühend.

ef·flu·ence [ˈeflʊəns] *s.* Ausfließen *n*, -strömen *n*; Ausfluß *m*; **ˈef·flu·ent** [-nt] **I** *adj.* **1.** ausfließend, -strömend; **II** *s.* **2.** Ausfluß *m*; **3.** Abwasser *n*.

ef·flux [ˈeflʌks] *s.* **1.** Ausfluß *m*, Ausströmen *n*; **2.** *fig.* Ablauf *m* (*der Zeit*).

ef·fort [ˈefət] *s.* **1.** Anstrengung *f*: a) Bemühung *f*, Versuch *m*, b) Mühe *f*: ***make an* ~** sich bemühen, sich anstrengen; ***make every* ~** sich alle Mühe geben; ***put a lot of* ~ *into it*** sich gewaltig anstrengen bei der Sache; ***spare no* ~** keine Mühe scheuen; ***with an* ~** mühsam; **2.** F Leistung *f*: ***a good* ~**; **ˈef·fort·less** [-lɪs] *adj.* mühelos, leicht.

ef·fron·ter·y [ɪˈfrʌntərɪ] *s.* Frechheit *f*, Unverschämtheit *f*.

ef·ful·gence [ɪˈfʌldʒəns] *s.* Glanz *m*; **efˈful·gent** [-nt] *adj.* □ strahlend.

ef·fuse [ɪˈfjuːz] **I** *v/t.* **1.** ausgießen, ausströmen (lassen); **2.** *Licht etc.* verbreiten; **II** *v/i.* **3.** ausströmen; **III** *adj.* [-s] **4.** ♀ ausgebreitet; **ef·fu·sion** [ɪˈfjuːʒn] *s.* **1.** Ausströmen *n*; Ausgießung *f*; Erguß *m* (*a. fig.*): **~ *of blood*** ✻ Bluterguß; **2.** *phys.* Effusiˈon *f*; **3.** ˈÜberschwenglichkeit *f*; **efˈfu·sive** [-sɪv] *adj.* □ ˈüberschwenglich; **efˈfu·sive·ness** [-sɪvnɪs] → ***effusion*** 3.

e·gad [ɪˈɡæd] *int. obs.* F o Gott!

e·gal·i·tar·i·an [ɪˌɡælɪˈteərɪən] **I** *s.* Verfechter(in) des Egalitaˈrismus; **II** *adj.* egaliˈtär; **eˌgal·iˈtar·i·an·ism** [-nɪzəm] *s.* Egalitaˈrismus *m*.

egg¹ [eɡ] *s.* **1.** Ei *n*: ***in the* ~** *fig.* im Anfangsstadium; ***a bad* ~** *fig.* F ein übler Kerl; ***as sure as* ~*s is*** *od.* ***are* ~*s*** *sl.* todsicher; ***have*** (*od.* ***put***) ***all one's* ~*s in one basket*** alles auf ˈeine Karte setzen; ***lay an* ~** *thea. sl.* durchfallen; ***lay an* ~!** *sl.* ,leck mich'!; → ***grand mother***; **2.** *biol.* Eizelle *f*; **3.** ⚔ *sl.* ,Ei' *n*, ,Koffer' *m* (*Bombe etc.*).

egg² [eɡ] *v/t.* *mst* **~ *on*** anstacheln.

ˈegg|ˌbeat·er *s.* **1.** *Küche*: Schneebesen *m*; **2.** *Am.* F Hubschrauber *m*; **~ coal** *s.* Nußkohle *f*; **~ co·sy**, *Am.* **~ co·zy** *s.* Eierwärmer *m*; **ˈ~·cup** *s.* Eierbecher *m*; **~ flip** *s.* Eierflip *m*; **ˈ~·head** *s.* F ,Eierkopf' *m* (*Intellektueller*); **ˈ~·nog** → ***egg flip***; **ˈ~·plant** *s.* ♀ Eierfrucht *f*, Auberˈgine *f*; **~ roll** *s.* Frühlingsrolle *f*; **ˈ~-shaped** *adj.* eiförmig; **ˈ~·shell** **I** *s.* Eierschale *f*: **~ *china*** Eierschalenporzellan *n*; **II** *adj.* zerbrechlich; **ˈ~-spoon** *s.* Eierlöffel *m*; **ˈ~-ˌtim·er** *s.* Eieruhr *f*; **ˈ~-whisk** *s.* *Küche*: Schneebesen *m*.

e·go [ˈeɡəʊ] *pl.* **-os** *s.* **1.** *psych.* Ich *n*, Selbst *n*, Ego *n*; **2.** Selbstgefühl *n*, -bewußtsein *n*, *a.* Stolz *m*, F Selbstsucht *f*, Selbstgefälligkeit *f*: **~ *trip*** F ,Egotrip' *m* (*geistige Selbstbefriedigung*, *Angeberei etc.*); ***that will boost his* ~** das wird ihm Auftrieb geben *od.* ,guttun'; ***it feeds his* ~** das stärkt sein Selbstbewußtsein; ***his* ~ *was low*** s-e Moral war auf Null.

e·go·cen·tric [ˌeɡəʊˈsentrɪk] *adj.* egoˈzentrisch, ichbezogen; **e·go·ism** [ˈeɡəʊɪzəm] *s.* Egoˈismus *m* (*a. phls.*), Selbstsucht *f*; **e·go·ist** [ˈeɡəʊɪst] *s.* **1.** Egoˈist(in); **2.** → ***egotist*** 1; **e·go·is·tic**, **e·go·is·ti·cal** [ˌeɡəʊˈɪstɪk(l)] *adj.* □ egoˈistisch; **e·go·ma·ni·a** [ˌeɡəʊˈmeɪnjə] *s.* krankhafte Selbstsucht *od.* -gefälligkeit *f*; **e·go·tism** [ˈeɡəʊtɪzəm] *s.* **1.** Egoˈtismus *m*: a) ˈSelbstüberˌhebung *f*, b) Ichbezogenheit *f*, c) Geltungsbedürfnis *n*; **2.** → ***egoism***; **e·go·tist** [ˈeɡəʊtɪst] *s.* **1.** Egoˈtist(in), geltungsbedürftiger *od.* selbstgefälliger Mensch; **2.** → ***egoist*** 1; **e·go·tis·tic**, **e·go·tis·ti·cal** [ˌeɡəʊˈtɪstɪk(l)] *adj.* □ **1.** selbstgefällig, egoˈtistisch, geltungsbedürftig; **2.** → ***egoistic***.

e·gre·gious [ɪˈɡriːdʒəs] *adj.* □ unerhört, ungeheuer(lich), kraß, Erz...

e·gress [ˈiːɡres] *s.* **1.** Ausgang *m*; **2.** Ausgangsrecht *n*; **3.** *fig.* Ausweg *m*; **4.** *ast.* Austritt *m*; **e·gres·sion** [iːˈɡreʃn] *s.* Ausgang *m*, -tritt *m*.

e·gret [ˈiːɡret] *s.* **1.** *orn.* Silberreiher *m*; **2.** Reiherfeder *f*; **3.** ♀ Federkrone *f*.

E·gyp·tian [ɪˈdʒɪpʃn] **I** *adj.* **1.** äˈgyptisch: **~ *cotton*** Mako *f*, *m*, *n*; **II** *s.* **2.** Äˈgypter (-in); **3.** *ling.* Äˈgyptisch *n*.

E·gyp·to·log·i·cal [ɪˌdʒɪptəˈlɒdʒɪkl] *adj.* ägyptoˈlogisch; **E·gyp·tol·o·gist** [ˌiːdʒɪpˈtɒlədʒɪst] *s.* Ägyptoˈloge *m*; **E·gyp·tol·o·gy** [ˌiːdʒɪpˈtɒlədʒɪ] *s.* Ägyptoloˈgie *f*.

eh [eɪ] *int.* **1.** eh?: a) wie (bitte)?, b) nicht wahr?; **2.** ei!, sieh da!

ei·der [ˈaɪdə] *s. orn. a.* **~ *duck*** Eiderente *f*; **ˈ~·down** *s.* **1.** *coll.* Eiderdaunen *pl.*; **2.** Daunendecke *f*.

ei·det·ic [aɪˈdetɪk] *psych.* **I** Eiˈdetiker (-in); **II** *adj.* eiˈdetisch.

eight [eɪt] **I** *adj.* **1.** acht: **~*-hour day*** Achtstundentag *m*; **II** *s.* **2.** Acht *f* (*Zahl, Spielkarte etc.*): ***have one over the* ~** *sl.* e-n ,in der Krone' haben; **3.** *Rudern*: Achter *m* (*Boot od. Mannschaft*); **eight·een** [ˌeɪˈtiːn] **I** *adj.* achtzehn; **II** *s.* Achtzehn *f*; **eight·eenth** [ˌeɪˈtiːnθ] **I** *adj.* achtzehnt; **II** *s.* Achtzehntel *n*; **ˈeight·fold** *adj. u. adv.* achtfach; **eighth** [eɪtθ] **I** *adj.* □ acht(er, e, es); **II** *s.* Achtel *n* (*a.* ♪); **eighth·ly**

[ˈeɪtɪɪθ] *adv.* achtens; **ˈeight·i·eth** [-tɪɪθ] **I** *adj.* achtzigst; **II** *s.* Achtzigstel *n*; **ˈeight·y** [-tɪ] **I** *adj.* achtzig; **II** *s.* Achtzig *f*: ***the eighties*** die achtziger Jahre (*eines Jahrhunderts*); ***he is in his eighties*** er ist in den Achtzigern.

Ein·stein·i·an [aɪnˈstaɪnjən] *adj.* Einsteinsch(er, -e, -es).

ei·ther [ˈaɪðə] **I** *adj.* **1.** jeder, jede, jedes (*von zweien*), beide: ***on ~ side*** auf beiden Seiten; ***there is nothing in ~ bottle*** beide Flaschen sind leer; **2.** (irgend)ein (*von zweien*): ***~ way*** auf die e-e od. andere Art; ***~ half of the cake*** (irgend-) eine Hälfte des Kuchens; **II** *pron.* **3.** (irgend)ein (*von zweien*): ***~ of you can come*** (irgend)einer von euch (beiden) kann kommen; ***I didn't see ~*** ich sah keinen (von beiden); **4.** beides: ***~ is possible***; **III** *cj.* **5.** ***~ … or*** entweder … oder: ***~ be quiet or go!*** entweder sei still oder geh!; **6.** *neg.*: ***~ … or*** weder … noch: ***it isn't good ~ for parent or child*** es ist weder für Eltern noch Kinder gut; **IV** *adv.* **7.** *neg.*: ***nor … ~*** (und) auch nicht, noch: ***he could not hear nor speak ~*** er konnte weder hören noch sprechen; ***I shall not go ~*** ich werde auch nicht gehen; ***she sings, and not badly ~*** sie singt, und gar nicht schlecht; **8.** ***without ~ good or bad intentions*** ohne gute oder schlechte Absichten; **ˈ~-or** *s.* Entweder-Oder *n*.

e·jac·u·late [ɪˈdʒækjʊleɪt] **I** *v/t.* **1.** *physiol. Samen* ausstoßen; **2.** *Worte* ausstoßen; **II** *v/i.* **3.** *physiol.* ejakulieren; **4.** *fig.* aus-, herˈvorstoßen; **III** *s.* **5.** *physiol.* Ejakuˈlat *n*; **e·jac·u·la·tion** [ɪˌdʒækjʊˈleɪʃn] *s.* **1.** ⚕ Ejakulatiˈon *f*, Samenerguß *m*; **2.** a) Ausruf *m*, b) Stoßseufzer *m*, -gebet *n*; **eˈjac·u·la·to·ry** [-lətərɪ] *adj.* **1.** ⚕ Ejakulations…; **2.** hastig (ausgestoßen): ***~ prayer*** Stoßgebet *n*.

e·ject [ɪˈdʒekt] **I** *v/t.* **1.** (***from***) *j-n* hinˈauswerfen (aus), vertreiben (aus, von); entlassen (aus); **2.** ⚖ exmittieren, ausweisen (***from*** aus); **3.** ⚙ ausstoßen, -werfen; **II** *v/i.* **4.** ✈ den Schleudersitz betätigen; **eˈjec·tion** [-kʃn] *s.* **1.** (***from*** aus) Vertreibung *f*, Entfernung *f*; Entlassung *f*; **2.** ⚙ Ausstoßung *f*, Auswerfen *n*: ***~ seat*** ✈ Schleudersitz *m*; **eˈject·ment** [-mənt] *s.* **1.** → ***ejection*** 1; **2.** ⚖ a) Räumungsklage *f*, b) Herˈausgabeklage *f*; **eˈjec·tor** [-tə] *s.* **1.** Vertreiber *m*; **2.** ⚙ a)ˈAuswurfappaˌrat *m*, Strahlpumpe *f*, b) ⚔ (Paˈtronenhülsen)Auswerfer *m*: ***~ seat*** ✈ Schleudersitz *m*.

eke [iːk] *v/t.* ***~ out*** a) *Flüssigkeit, Vorrat etc.* strecken, b) *Einkommen* aufbessern, c) ***~ out a living*** sich (mühsam) durchschlagen.

el [el] *s.* **1.** L *n*, l *n* (*Buchstabe*); **2.** 🚂 F Hochbahn *f*.

e·lab·o·rate I *adj.* [ɪˈlæbərət] ☐ **1.** sorgfältig *od.* kunstvoll ausgeführt *od.* (aus)gearbeitet; **2.** (ˈwohl)durchˌdacht, (sorgfältig) ausgearbeitet: ***an ~ report***; **3.** a) kunstvoll, kompliziert, b) ˈumständlich; **II** *v/t.* [-bəreɪt] **4.** sorgfältig aus- *od.* herˈausarbeiten, verˈvollkommnen; **5.** *Theorie* entwickeln; **6.** genau darlegen; **III** *v/i.* **7.** ***~ (up)on*** ausführlich behandeln, sich verbreiten über (*acc.*); **eˈlab·o·rate·ness** [-nɪs] *s.* **1.** sorgfältige *od.* kunstvolle Ausführung; **2.** a) Sorgfalt *f*, b) Kompliziertheit *f*, c) ausführliche Behandlung; **e·lab·o·ra·tion** [ɪˌlæbəˈreɪʃn] *s.* **1.** → ***elaborateness*** 1; **2.** (Weiter)Entwicklung *f*.

é·lan [eɪˈlɑ̃ːŋ] (*Fr.*) *s.* Eˈlan *m*, Schwung *m*.

e·land [ˈiːlənd] *s.* ˈElenantiˌlope *f*.

e·lapse [ɪˈlæps] *v/i.* vergehen, verstreichen (*Zeit*), ablaufen (*Frist*).

e·las·tic [ɪˈlæstɪk] **I** *adj.* (☐ ***~ally***) **1.** eˈlastisch: a) federnd, spannkräftig (*alle a. fig.*), b) dehnbar, biegsam, geschmeidig (*a. fig.*): ***~ conscience*** weites Gewissen; ***an ~ word*** ein dehnbarer Begriff; **2.** *phys.* a) elastisch, b) expansiˈonsfähig (*Gas*), c) inkompresˈsibel (*Flüssigkeit*): ***~ force*** → ***elasticity***; **3.** Gummi…: ***~ band***; ***~ stocking*** Gummistrumpf *m*; **II** *s.* **4.** Gummiband *n*, -zug *m*; **5.** Gummigewebe *n*, -stoff *m*; **eˈlas·ti·cat·ed** [-keɪtɪd] *adj.* mit Gummizug; **e·las·tic·i·ty** [ˌelæˈstɪsətɪ] *s.* Elastiziˈtät *f*: a) Spannkraft *f* (*a. fig.*), b) Dehnbarkeit *f*, Biegsamkeit *f*, Geschmeidigkeit *f* (*a. fig.*).

e·late [ɪˈleɪt] *v/t.* **1.** mit Hochstimmung erfüllen, begeistern, freudig erregen; **2.** *j-m* Mut machen; **3.** *j-n* stolz machen; **eˈlat·ed** [-tɪd] *adj.* ☐ **1.** in Hochstimmung, freudig erregt (***at*** über *acc.*, ***with*** durch); **2.** stolz; **eˈla·tion** [-eɪʃn] *s.* **1.** Hochstimmung, freudige Erregung; **2.** Stolz *m*.

el·bow [ˈelbəʊ] **I** *s.* **1.** Ell(en)bogen *m*: ***at one's ~*** a) in Reichweite, bei der Hand, b) *fig.* an s-r Seite; ***out at ~s*** a) schäbig (*Kleidung*), b) schäbig gekleidet, heruntergekommen (*Person*); ***be up to the ~s in work*** bis über die Ohren in der Arbeit stecken; ***bend*** *od.* ***lift one's ~*** F ‚einen heben'; **2.** Biegung *f*, Krümmung *f*, Ecke *f*, Knie *n*; **3.** ⚙ Knie *n*; (Rohr)Krümmer *m*, Winkel (-stück *n*) *m*; **II** *v/t.* **4.** *mit dem Ellbogen* stoßen, drängen (*a. fig.*): ***~ s.o. out*** j-n hinausdrängen; ***~ o.s. through*** sich durchdrängeln; ***~ one's way*** → 5; **III** *v/i.* **5.** sich (mit den Ellbogen) e-n Weg bahnen (***through*** durch); **~ chair.** *s.* Arm-, Lehnstuhl *m*; **~ grease** *s. humor.* **1.** ‚Arm-, Knochenschmalz' *n* (*Kraft*); **2.** schwere Arbeit; **ˈ~·room** [-rʊm] *s.* Bewegungsfreiheit *f*, Spielraum *m* (*a. fig.*).

eld [eld] *s. obs.* **1.** (Greisen)Alter *n*; **2.** alte Zeiten *pl.*

eld·er¹ [ˈeldə] **I** *adj.* **1.** älter: ***my ~ brother*** mein älterer Bruder; **2.** rangälter: ***ℒ Statesman*** *pol. u. fig.* ‚großer alter Mann'; **II** *s.* **3.** (der, die) Ältere: ***he is my ~ by two years*** er ist zwei Jahre älter als ich; ***my ~s*** ältere Leute als ich; **4.** Reˈspektsperˌson *f*; **5.** *oft pl.* (Kirchen-, Gemeinde- *etc.*)Älteste(r) *m*.

el·der² [ˈeldə] *s.* Hoˈlunder *m*; **ˈel·derˌber·ry** *s.* Hoˈlunderbeere *f*.

eld·er·ly [ˈeldəlɪ] *adj.* ältlich: ***an ~ couple*** ein älteres Ehepaar; **eld·est** [ˈeldɪst] *adj.* ältest: ***my ~ brother*** mein ältester Bruder.

El Do·ra·do [ˌeldəˈrɑːdəʊ] *pl.* **-dos** *s.* (El)Doˈrado *n*.

e·lect [ɪˈlekt] **I** *v/t.* **1.** *j-n in ein Amt* wählen: ***~ s.o. to an office***; **2.** *et.* wählen, sich entscheiden für: ***~ to do s.th.*** sich (dazu) entschließen *od.* es vorziehen, et. zu tun; ***he was ~ed president*** er wurde zum Präsidenten gewählt; **3.** *eccl.* auserwählen; **II** *adj.* **4.** (*nachgestellt*) designiert, zukünftig: ***bride ~*** Zukünftige *f*, Braut *f*; ***the president ~*** *der* designierte Präsident; **5.** erlesen; **6.** *eccl.* (*von Gott*) auserwählt; **III** *s.* **7.** *eccl. u. fig.* ***the ~*** die Auserwählten *pl.*; **eˈlec·tion** [-kʃn] *s. mst pol.* Wahl *f*: ***~ campaign*** Wahlkampf *m*, -feldzug *m*; ***~ pledge*** Wahlversprechen *n*; ***~ returns*** Wahlergebnisse; **e·lec·tion·eer** [ɪˌlekʃəˈnɪə] *v/i. pol.* Wahlkampf betreiben: ***~ for s.o.*** für j-n Wahlpropaganda machen *od.* Stimmen werben; **e·lec·tion·eer·ing** [ɪˌlekʃəˈnɪərɪŋ] *s. pol.* ˈWahlpropaˌganda *f*, -kampf *m*, -feldzug *m*; **eˈlec·tive** [-tɪv] **I** *adj.* ☐ **1.** gewählt, durch Wahl, Wahl…; **2.** wahlberechtigt, wählend; **3.** *ped. Am.* wahlfrei, fakultaˈtiv: ***~ subject*** → 4; **II** *s.* **4.** *ped. Am.* Wahlfach *n*; **eˈlec·tor** [-tə] *s.* **1.** *pol.* a) Wähler(in), b) *Am.* Wahlmann *m*; **2.** ℒ *hist.* Kurfürst *m*; **eˈlec·tor·al** [-tərəl] *adj.* **1.** Wahl…, Wähler…: ***~ college*** *Am.* Wahlmänner *pl.* (*e-s Staates*); **2.** *hist.* Kurfürsten…; **eˈlec·tor·ate** [-tərət] *s.* **1.** *pol.* Wähler (-schaft *f*) *pl.*; **2.** *hist.* a) Kurwürde *f*, b) Kurfürstentum *n*; **eˈlec·tress** [-trɪs] *s.* **1.** Wählerin *f*; **2.** ℒ *hist.* Kurfürstin *f*.

e·lec·tric [ɪˈlektrɪk] *adj.* (☐ ***~ally***) **1.** a) eˈlektrisch: ***~ cable*** (***charge***, ***current***, ***light*** *etc.*), b) Elektro…: ***~ motor***, c) Elektrizitäts…: ***~ works***, d) eˌlektroˈtechnisch; **2.** *fig.* a) elektrisierend: ***an ~ effect***, b) spannungsgeladen: ***~ atmosphere***; **eˈlec·tri·cal** [-kl] → ***electric*** 1: ***~ engineer*** Elektroingenieur *m od.* -techniker *m*; ***~ engineering*** Elektrotechnik *f*.

e·lec·tric| arc *s.* Lichtbogen *m*; **~ art** *s.* Lichtkunst *f*; **~ blan·ket** *s.* Heizdecke *f*; **~ blue** *s.* Stahlblau *n*; **~ chair** *s.* ⚖ eˈlektrischer Stuhl; **~ cir·cuit** *s.* Stromkreis *m*; **~ cush·ion** *s.* Heizkissen *n*; **~ eel** *s. zo.* Zitteraal *m*; **~ eye** *s.* **1.** Fotozelle *f*; **2.** magisches Auge; **~ gui·tar** *s.* eˈlektrische Giˈtarre, ˈE-Giˌtarre *f*.

e·lec·tri·cian [ˌɪlekˈtrɪʃn] *s.* Eˈlektriker *m*, Eˌlektroˈtechniker *m*.

e·lec·tric·i·ty [ˌɪlekˈtrɪsətɪ] *s.* Elektriziˈtät *f*.

e·lec·tric| plant *s.* eˈlektrische Anlage; **~ ray** *s. zo.* Zitterrochen *m*; **~ shock** *s.* **1.** eˈlektrischer Schlag; **2.** ⚕ Eˈlektroschock *m*; **~ steel** *s.* ⚙ Eˈlektrostahl *m*; **~ storm** *s.* Gewittersturm *m*; **~ torch** *s.* (eˈlektrische) Taschenlampe.

e·lec·tri·fi·ca·tion [ɪˌlektrɪfɪˈkeɪʃn] *s.* **1.** Elektrisierung *f* (*a. fig.*); **2.** Elektrifizierung *f*; **e·lec·tri·fy** [ɪˈlektrɪfaɪ] *v/t.* **1.** elektrisieren (*a. fig.*), eˈlektrisch laden; **2.** elektrifizieren; **3.** *fig.* anfeuern, erregen, begeistern.

e·lec·tro [ɪˈlektrəʊ] *pl.* **-tros** *s. typ.* F Galˈvano *n*, Kliˈschee *n*.

electro- [ɪlektrəʊ] *in Zssgn* Elektro…, elektro…, eˈlektrisch.

eˌlec·tro|·aˈnal·y·sis [ɪˌlektrəʊ-] *s.* ⚗ Eˌlektroanaˈlyse *f*; **~ˈcar·di·o·gram** *s.* ⚕ Eˌlektrokardioˈgramm *n*, EKˈG *n*; **~ˈchem·is·try** *s.* Eˌlektrocheˈmie *f*.

e·lec·tro·cute [ɪˈlektrəkjuːt] *v/t.* **1.** auf dem eˈlektrischen Stuhl hinrichten; **2.** durch elektrischen Strom töten; **e·lec·tro·cu·tion** [ɪˌlektrəˈkjuːʃn] *s.* Hinrichtung *f od.* Tod *m* durch elektrischen Strom.

e·lec·trode [ɪ'lektrəʊd] *s.* ⚡ Elek'trode *f.*

e̦lec·tro|·dy'nam·ics *s. pl. sg. konstr.* E̦lektrody'namik *f*; **~·en·gi'neer·ing** *s.* E̦lektro'technik *f*; **~·ki'net·ics** *s. pl. sg. konstr.* E̦lektroki'netik *f.*

e·lec·trol·y·sis [ˌɪlek'trɒlɪsɪs] *s.* Elektro'lyse *f*; **e·lec·tro·lyte** [ɪ'lektrəʊlaɪt] *s.* Elektro'lyt *m.*

e̦lec·tro|'mag·net *s.* E̦lektroma'gnet *m*; **~·mag'net·ic** *adj.* (□ **~ally**) e̦lektroma'gnetisch; **~·me'chan·ics** *s. pl. sg. konstr.* E̦lektrome'chanik *f.*

e·lec·trom·e·ter [ˌɪlek'trɒmɪtə] *s.* E̦lektro'meter *n.*

e̦lec·tro|'mo·tive *adj.* e̦lektromo'torisch; **~'mo·tor** *s.* E̦lektro'motor *m.*

e·lec·tron [ɪ'lektrɒn] *phys.* **I** *s.* Elektron *n*; **II** *adj.* Elektronen...: **~ microscope**; **e·lec·tron·ic** [ˌɪlek'trɒnɪk] *adj.* (□ **~ally**) elek'tronisch, Elektronen...: **~ flash** *phot.* Elektronenblitz *m*; **~ music** elektronische Musik; **e·lec·tron·ics** [ˌɪlek'trɒnɪks] *s. pl. sg. konstr.* Elek'tronik *f* (*a. als Konstruktionsteil*).

e·lec·tro|·plate [ɪ'lektrəʊ-] **I** *v/t.* elektroplattieren, galvanisieren; **II** *s.* elektroplattierte Ware; **~·scope** [-əskəʊp] *s. phys.* E̦lektro'skop *n*; **~·scop·ic** [ɪˌlektrə'skɒpɪk] *adj.* (□ **~ally**) e̦lektro'skopisch; **~'ther·a·py** [ɪˌlektrəʊ-] *s.* ⚕ E̦lektrothera'pie *f*; **~·type I** *s.* **1.** Gal'vano *n*; **2.** ga̦lvano'plastischer Druck; **II** *v/t.* **3.** ga̦lvano'plastisch vervielfältigen.

el·e·gance ['elɪgəns] *s. allg.* Ele'ganz *f*; **'el·e·gant** [-nt] *adj.* □ **1.** ele'gant: a) fein, geschmackvoll, vornehm (u. schön), b) gewählt, gepflegt, c) anmutig, d) geschickt, gekonnt; **2.** F erstklassig, ‚prima'.

el·e·gi·ac [ˌelɪ'dʒaɪək] **I** *adj.* e'legisch (*a. fig. schwermütig*), Klage...; **II** *s.* elegischer Vers; *pl.* elegisches Gedicht; **el·e·gize** ['elɪdʒaɪz] *v/i.* e-e Ele'gie schreiben (**upon** auf *acc.*); **el·e·gy** ['elɪdʒɪ] *s.* Ele'gie *f*, Klagelied *n.*

el·e·ment ['elɪmənt] *s.* **1.** *allg.* Ele'ment *n*: a) *phls.* Urstoff *m*, b) Grundbestandteil *m*, c) ⚗ Grundstoff *m*, d) ⚙ Bauteil *n*, e) Grundlage *f*; **2.** Grundtatsache *f*, wesentlicher Faktor: **an ~ of risk** ein gewisses Risiko; **~ of surprise** Überraschungsmoment *n*; **~ of uncertainty** Unsicherheitsfaktor; **3.** ⚖ Tatbestandsmerkmal *n*; **4.** *pl.* Anfangsgründe *pl.*, Anfänge *pl.*, Grundlage(n *pl.*) *f*; **5.** *pl.* Na'turkräfte *pl.*, Ele'mente *pl.*; **6.** ('Lebens)Ele̦ment *n*, gewohnte Um'gebung: **be in** (**out of**) **one's ~** (nicht) in s-m Element sein; **7.** *fig.* Körnchen *n*, Fünkchen *n*, Hauch *m*: **an ~ of truth** ein Körnchen Wahrheit; **8.** a) ⚔ Truppenteil *m*, b) ✈ Rotte *f*; **9.** (Bevölkerungs-) Teil *m*, (*kriminelle etc.*) Ele'mente *pl.*; **el·e·men·tal** [ˌelɪ'mentl] *adj.* **1.** elemen'tar: a) ursprünglich, na'türlich, b) urgewaltig, c) wesentlich; **2.** Elementar..., Ur...

el·e·men·ta·ry [ˌelɪ'mentərɪ] *adj.* □ **1.** → **elemental** 1 *u.* 2; **2.** elemen'tar, Elementar..., Einführungs..., Anfangs..., grundlegend; **3.** elemen'tar, einfach; **4.** ⚗, ⩘, *phys.* elemen'tar, Elementar...: **~ particle** Elementarteilchen *n*; **5.** rudimen'tär, unentwickelt; **~ ed·u·ca·tion** *s.* **1.** Grundschul-, Volksschulbildung *f*; **2.** Volksschulwesen *n*; **~ school** *s.* Volks-, Grundschule *f.*

el·e·phant ['elɪfənt] *s.* **1.** *zo.* Ele'fant *m*: **~ seal** See-Elefant; **pink ~** F ‚weiße Mäuse' *pl.*, Halluzinationen *pl.*; **white ~** *fig.* lästiger *od.* kostspieliger Besitz; **2.** *ein Papierformat* (*711 × 584 mm*); **el·e·phan·ti·a·sis** [ˌelɪfən'taɪəsɪs] *s.* ⚕ Elefan'tiasis *f*; **el·e·phan·tine** [ˌelɪ'fæntaɪn] *adj.* **1.** ele'fantenartig, Elefanten...; **2.** *fig.* riesenhaft; **3.** plump, schwerfällig.

El·eu·sin·i·an [ˌelju:'sɪnɪən] *adj. antiq.* eleu'sinisch.

el·e·vate ['elɪveɪt] *v/t.* **1.** hoch-, em'porheben; aufrichten; erhöhen; **2.** *Blick* erheben; *Stimme* heben; **3.** (**to**) *j-n* erheben (in *den Adelsstand*), befördern (zu *e-m Posten*); **4.** *fig. j-n* (*seelisch*) erheben, erbauen; **5.** erheitern; **6.** *Niveau etc.* heben; **7.** ⚔ *Geschützrohr* erhöhen; **'el·e·vat·ed** [-tɪd] **I** *adj.* **1.** erhöht; Hoch...: **~ railway**, *Am.* **~ railroad** Hochbahn *f*; **2.** gehoben (*Position, Stil etc.*), erhaben (*Gedanken*); **3.** a) erheitert, b) F beschwipst; **II** *s.* **4.** *Am.* F Hochbahn *f*; **'el·e·vat·ing** [-tɪŋ] *adj.* **1.** *bsd.* ⚙ hebend, Hebe..., Höhen...; **2.** *fig.* a) erhebend, erbaulich, b) erheiternd; **el·e·va·tion** [ˌelɪ'veɪʃn] *s.* **1.** Hoch-, Em'porheben *n*; **2.** (Boden)Erhebung *f*, (An)Höhe *f*; **3.** Höhe *f* (*a. ast.*), (Grad *m* der) Erhöhung *f*; **4.** *geogr.* Meereshöhe *f*; **5.** ⚔ Richthöhe *f*; **6.** ⚙ Aufstellung *f*, Errichtung *f*; **7.** △ Aufriß *m*: **front ~** Vorderansicht *f*; **8.** a) (**to**) Erhebung *f* (in *den Adelsstand*), Beförderung *f* (zu *e-m Posten etc.*), b) gehobene Positi'on; **9.** *fig.* (*seelische*) Erhebung, Erbauung *f*; **10.** *fig.* Hebung *f* (*des Niveaus etc.*); **11.** *fig.* Erhabenheit *f*, Gehobenheit *f* (*des Stils etc.*); **'el·e·va·tor** [-tə] *s.* **1.** ⚙ a) Hebe-, Förderwerk *n*, b) Hebewerk *n*, c) *Am.* Fahrstuhl *m*, Aufzug *m*; **2.** Getreidesilo *m*; **3.** ✈ Höhensteuer *n*, -ruder *n*; **4.** *anat.* Hebemuskel *m.*

e·lev·en [ɪ'levn] **I** *adj.* **1.** elf; **II** *s.* **2.** Elf *f*; **3.** *sport* Elf *f*; **e̦lev·en-'plus** *s. ped. Brit. hist. im Alter von 11–12 Jahren abgelegte Prüfung, die über die schulische Weiterbildung entschied;* **e'lev·en·ses** [-zɪz] *s. pl. Brit.* F zweites Frühstück; **e'lev·enth** [-nθ] **I** *adj.* □ **1.** elft; → **hour** 2; **II** *s.* **2.** (*der, die, das*) Elfte; **3.** Elftel *n.*

elf [elf] *pl.* **elves** [elvz] *s.* **1.** Elf *m*, Elfe *f*; **2.** Kobold *m*; **3.** *fig.* a) Knirps *m*, b) (kleiner) Racker; **elf·in** ['elfɪn] **I** *adj.* Elfen..., Zwergen...; **II** *s.* → **elf**; **elf·ish** ['elfɪʃ] *adj.* **1.** elfenartig; **2.** schelmisch, koboldhaft.

'elf·lock *s.* Weichselzopf *m*, verfilztes Haar.

e·lic·it [ɪ'lɪsɪt] *v/t.* **1.** (**from** *j-m*, *e-m Instrument etc.*) *et.* entlocken; **2.** (**from** aus *j-m*) *e-e Aussage etc.* her'auslocken, -holen; **3.** *e-e Reaktion* auslösen, her'vorrufen; **4.** *et.* ans Licht bringen.

e·lide [ɪ'laɪd] *v/t. ling. Vokal od. Silbe* elidieren, auslassen.

el·i·gi·bil·i·ty [ˌelɪdʒə'bɪlətɪ] *s.* **1.** Eignung *f*, Befähigung *f*: **his eligibilities** s-e Vorzüge; **2.** Berechtigung *f*; **3.** Wählbarkeit *f*; **4.** Teilnahmeberechtigung *f*, *sport a.* Startberechtigung *f*; **el·i·gi·ble** ['elɪdʒəbl] **I** *adj.* □ **1.** (**for**) in Frage kommend (für): a) geeignet, akzep'tabel (für), b) berechtigt, befähigt (zu), qualifiziert (für): **~ for a pension** pensionsberechtigt, c) wählbar; **2.** wünschenswert, vorteilhaft; **3.** teilnahmeberechtigt, *sport a.* startberechtigt; **II** *s.* **4.** F in Frage kommende Per'son *od.* Sache.

e·lim·i·nate [ɪ'lɪmɪneɪt] *v/t.* **1.** beseitigen, entfernen, ausmerzen, *a.* ⩘ eliminieren (**from** aus); **2.** ausscheiden (*a.* ⚗, *physiol.*), ausschließen, *a. Gegner* ausschalten: **be ~d** *sport* ausscheiden; **3.** *fig. et.* ausklammern, ignorieren; **e·lim·i·na·tion** [ɪˌlɪmɪ'neɪʃn] *s.* **1.** Beseitigung *f*, Entfernung *f*, Ausmerzung *f*, Eliminierung *f*; **2.** ⩘ Eliminati'on *f*; **3.** ⚗, *physiol.*, *a. sport* Ausscheidung *f*: **~ contest** Ausscheidungs-, Qualifikationswettbewerb *m*; **4.** Ausschaltung *f* (*e-s Gegners*); **5.** *fig.* Ignorierung *f*; **e'lim·i·na·tor** [-tə] *s. Radio*: Sieb-, Sperrkreis *m.*

e·li·sion [ɪ'lɪʒn] *s. ling.* Elisi'on *f*, Auslassung *f* (*e-s Vokals od. e-r Silbe*).

e·lite [eɪ'li:t] (*Fr.*) *s.* E'lite *f*: a) Auslese *f*, (*das*) Beste, (*die*) Besten *pl.*, b) Führungs-, Oberschicht *f*, c) ⚔ E'lite-, Kerntruppe *f*; **e'lit·ism** [-tɪzəm] *s.* eli'täres Denken; **e'lit·ist** [-tɪst] *adj.* eli'tär.

e·lix·ir [ɪ'lɪksə] *s.* **1.** Eli'xier *n*, Zauber-, Heiltrank *m*: **~ of life** Lebenselixier; **2.** All'heilmittel *n.*

E·liz·a·be·than [ɪˌlɪzə'bi:θn] **I** *adj.* elisabe'thanisch; **II** *s.* Zeitgenosse *m* E'lisabeths I. von England.

elk [elk] *s. zo.* **1.** Elch *m*, Elen *m*, *n*; **2.** *Am.* Elk *m*, Wa'piti *m.*

ell [el] *s.* Elle *f*; → **inch** 2.

el·lipse [ɪ'lɪps] *s.* **1.** ⩘ El'lipse *f*; **2.** → **el'lip·sis** [-sɪs] *pl.* **-ses** [-si:z] *s. ling.* El'lipse *f*, Auslassung *f* (*a. typ.*); **el'lip·soid** [-sɔɪd] *s.* ⩘ Ellipso'id *n*; **el'lip·tic, el'lip·ti·cal** [-ptɪk(l)] *adj.* □ **1.** ⩘ el'liptisch; **2.** *ling.* elliptisch, unvollständig (*Satz*).

elm [elm] *s.* Ulme *f*, Rüster *f.*

el·o·cu·tion [ˌelə'kju:ʃn] *s.* **1.** Vortrag(sweise *f*) *m*, Dikti'on *f*; **2.** Vortragskunst *f*; **3.** Sprechtechnik *f*; **ˌel·o'cu·tion·ist** [-nɪst] *s.* **1.** Vortragskünstler(in); **2.** Sprecherzieher(in).

e·lon·gate ['i:lɒŋgeɪt] **I** *v/t.* **1.** verlängern; *bsd.* ⚙ strecken, dehnen; **II** *v/i.* **2.** sich verlängern; **3.** ⚘ spitz zulaufen; **III** *adj.* **4.** → **'e·lon·gat·ed** [-tɪd] *adj.* **1.** verlängert: **~ charge** ⚔ gestreckte Ladung; **2.** lang u. dünn; **e·lon·ga·tion** [ˌi:lɒŋ'geɪʃn] *s.* **1.** Verlängerung *f*; **2.** ⚙ Streckung *f*, Dehnung *f*; **2.** *ast.*, *phys.* Elongati'on *f.*

e·lope [ɪ'ləʊp] *v/i.* (mit s-m *od.* s-r Geliebten) ‚'durchbrennen': **~ with** *a. die Geliebte* entführen; **e'lope·ment** [-mənt] *s.* ‚'Durchbrennen' *n*; Flucht *f*; Entführung *f*; **e'lop·er** [-pə] *s.* Ausreißer(in).

el·o·quence ['eləkwəns] *s.* Beredsamkeit *f*, Redegewandtheit *f*, -kunst *f*; **'el·o·quent** [-nt] *adj.* □ **1.** beredt, redegewandt; **2.** *fig.* a) sprechend, ausdrucksvoll, b) beredt, vielsagend (*Blick etc.*).

else [els] *adv.* **1.** (*neg. u. interrog.*) sonst, weiter, außerdem: ***anything ~?***

sonst noch etwas?; ***what ~ can we do?***; was können wir sonst (noch) tun?; ***no one ~*** sonst *od.* weiter niemand; ***where ~?*** wo anders?, wo sonst (noch)?; **2.** anderer, andere, anderes: ***that's something ~*** das ist et. anderes; ***everybody ~*** alle anderen *od.* übrigen; ***somebody ~'s dog*** der Hund e-s anderen; **3.** *oft* ***or ~*** oder, sonst, wenn nicht: ***hurry,*** (***or***) ***~ you will be late*** beeile dich, oder du kommst zu spät *od.* sonst kommst du zu spät; ***or ~!*** (*drohend*) sonst passiert was!; **ˌ~ˈwhere** *adv.* **1.** sonst-, anderswo; **2.** ˈanderswoˈhin.

e·lu·ci·date [ɪˈluːsɪdeɪt] *v/t. Geheimnis etc.* aufhellen, aufklären; *Text, Gründe etc.* erklären; **e·lu·ci·da·tion** [ɪˌluːsɪˈdeɪʃn] *s.* Erklärung *f*; Aufhellung *f*, -klärung *f*; **eˈlu·ci·da·to·ry** [-tərɪ] *adj.* erklärend, aufhellend.

e·lude [ɪˈluːd] *v/t.* **1.** (geschickt) ausweichen, entgehen, sich entziehen (*dat.*); *Gesetz etc.* umˈgehen; **2.** *fig. j-m* entgehen, *j-s* Aufmerksamkeit entgehen; **3.** sich nicht (er)fassen lassen von, sich entziehen (*dat.*): ***it ~s definition*** es läßt sich nicht definieren; **4.** *j-m* nicht einfallen; **eˈlu·sion** [-uːʒn] *s.* **1.** (***of***) Ausweichen *n*, Entkommen *n* (vor *dat.*); Umˈgehung *f* (*gen.*); **2.** Ausflucht *f*, List *f*; **eˈlu·sive** [-uːsɪv] *adj.* □ **1.** ausweichend (***of*** *dat.*, vor *dat.*); **2.** schwer zu fassen(d) (*Dieb etc.*); **3.** schwerfaßbar, schwer zu definieren(d) *od.* zu übersetzen(d); **4.** umˈgehend; **5.** unzuverlässig; **eˈlu·sive·ness** [-uːsɪvnɪs] *s.* **1.** Ausweichen *n* (***of*** vor *dat.*), ausweichendes Verhalten; **2.** Unbestimmbarkeit *f*, Undefinierbarkeit *f*; **eˈlu·so·ry** [-uːsərɪ] *adj.* **1.** trügerisch; **2.** → ***elusive***.

e·lu·tri·ate [ɪˈluːtrɪeɪt] *v/t.* ⚒ (aus-)schlämmen.

el·ver [ˈelvə] *s. ichth.* junger Aal.

elves [elvz] *pl. von* ***elf***; **ˈelv·ish** [-vɪʃ] → ***elfish***.

E·ly·sian [ɪˈlɪzɪən] *adj.* eˈlysisch, *fig. a.* paraˈdiesisch; **Eˈly·si·um** [-əm] *s.* Eˈlysium *n*, *fig. a.* Paraˈdies *n*.

em [em] *s.* **1.** M *n*, m *n* (*Buchstabe*); **2.** *typ.* Geviert *n*.

'em [əm] F *für* ***them***: ***let 'em***.

e·ma·ci·ate [ɪˈmeɪʃɪeɪt] *v/t.* **1.** auszehren, ausmergeln; **2.** *Boden* auslaugen; **eˈma·ci·at·ed** [-tɪd] *adj.* **1.** abgemagert, ausgezehrt, ausgemergelt; **2.** ausgelaugt (*Boden*); **e·ma·ci·a·tion** [ɪˌmeɪsɪˈeɪʃn] *s.* **1.** Auszehrung *f*, Abmagerung *f*; **2.** Auslaugung *f*.

em·a·nate [ˈeməneɪt] *v/i.* **1.** ausströmen (*Gas etc.*), ausstrahlen (*Licht*) (***from*** von); **2.** *fig.* herrühren, ausgehen (***from*** von); **em·a·na·tion** [ˌeməˈneɪʃn] *s.* **1.** Ausströmen *n*; **2.** Ausströmung *f*, Ausstrahlung *f* (*beide a. fig.*); **3.** Auswirkung *f*; **4.** *phls., psych., eccl.* Emanatiˈon *f*.

e·man·ci·pate [ɪˈmænsɪpeɪt] *v/t.* **1.** (***o.s.*** sich) emanzipieren, unabhängig machen, befreien (***from*** von); **2.** *Sklaven* freilassen; **eˈman·ci·pat·ed** [-tɪd] *adj.* **1.** *allg.* emanzipiert: ***an ~ woman***; ***an ~ citizen*** ein mündiger Bürger; **2.** freigelassen (*Sklave*); **e·man·ci·pa·tion** [ɪˌmænsɪˈpeɪʃn] *s.* **1.** Emanzipatiˈon *f*; **2.** Freilassung *f*, Befreiung *f* (*a. fig.*) (***from*** von); **e·man·ci·pa·tion·ist** [ɪˌmænsɪˈpeɪʃnɪst] *s.* Befürworter(in) der Emanzipatiˈon *od.* der Sklavenbefreiung; **eˈman·ci·pa·to·ry** [-pətərɪ] *adj.* emanzipaˈtorisch.

e·mas·cu·late **I** *v/t.* [ɪˈmæskjʊleɪt] **1.** entmannen, kastrieren; **2.** *fig.* verweichlichen; **3.** entkräften, (ab)schwächen; verwässern; **4.** *Sprache* farb- *od.* kraftlos machen; **II** *adj.* [-lɪt] **5.** entmannt; **6.** verweichlicht; **7.** verwässert, kraftlos; **e·mas·cu·la·tion** [ɪˌmæskjʊˈleɪʃn] *s.* **1.** Entmannung *f*; **2.** Verweichlichung *f*; **3.** Schwächung *f*; **4.** *fig.* Verwässerung *f* (*Text etc.*).

em·balm [ɪmˈbɑːm] *v/t.* **1.** einbalsamieren; **2.** *fig. j-s Andenken* bewahren *od.* pflegen: ***be ~ed in*** fortleben in (*dat.*); **emˈbalm·ment** [-mənt] *s.* Einbalsamierung *f*.

em·bank [ɪmˈbæŋk] *v/t.* eindämmen, -deichen; **emˈbank·ment** [-mənt] *s.* **1.** Eindämmung *f*, -deichung *f*; **2.** (Erd-)Damm *m*; **3.** (Bahn-, Straßen)Damm *m*; **4.** gemauerte Uferstraße.

em·bar·go [emˈbɑːgəʊ] **I** *s.* **1.** ⚓ Emˈbargo *n*: a) (Schiffs)Beschlagnahme *f* (*durch den Staat*), b) Hafensperre *f*; **2.** ☤ a) Handelssperre *f*, b) *a. allg.* Sperre *f*, Verbot *n*: ***~ on imports*** Einfuhrsperre; **II** *v/t.* **3.** *Handel, Hafen* sperren, ein Emˈbargo verhängen über (*acc.*); **4.** beschlagnahmen.

em·bark [ɪmˈbɑːk] **I** *v/t.* **1.** ⚓, ✈ Passagiere an Bord nehmen, ⚓ *a.* einschiffen, *Waren a.* verladen (***for*** nach); **2.** *Geld* investieren (***in*** in *dat.*); **II** *v/i.* **3.** ⚓ sich einschiffen (***for*** nach), an Bord gehen; **4.** *fig.* (***on***) (*et.*) anfangen *od.* unterˈnehmen; **em·bar·ka·tion** [ˌembɑːˈkeɪʃn] *s.* ⚓ Einschiffung *f*, (*von Waren*) *a.* Verladung *f* (*a.* ✈); ✈ Einsteigen *n*.

em·bar·ras de rich·esse(s) [ɑ̃ːŋbɑˌrɑdəriːˈʃes] (*Fr.*) *s. die* Qual der Wahl.

em·bar·rass [ɪmˈbærəs] *v/t.* **1.** *j-n* in Verlegenheit bringen *od.* in e-e peinliche Lage versetzen, verwirren; **2.** *j-n* behindern, *j-m* lästig sein; **3.** in Geldverlegenheit bringen; **4.** *et.* behindern, erschweren, komplizieren; **emˈbar·rassed** [-st] *adj.* **1.** verlegen, peinlich berührt; **2.** ☤ in Geldverlegenheit; **emˈbar·rass·ing** [-sɪŋ] *adj.* □ unangenehm, peinlich (***to*** *dat.*); **emˈbar·rass·ment** [-mənt] *s.* **1.** Verlegenheit *f*; **2.** *bsd.* ⚕ Behinderung *f*, Störung *f*; **3.** Geldverlegenheit *f*.

em·bas·sy [ˈembəsɪ] *s.* **1.** Botschaft *f*: a) Botschaftsgebäude *n*, b) ˈBotschaftsperoˌnal *n*; **2.** diploˈmatische Missiˈon.

em·bat·tle [ɪmˈbætl] *v/t.* **1.** ⚔ in Schlachtordnung aufstellen: ***~d*** kampfbereit (*a. fig.*); **2.** △ mit Zinnen versehen.

em·bed [ɪmˈbed] *v/t.* **1.** (ein)betten, (ein)lagern, eingraben; **2.** *im Gedächtnis etc.* verankern.

em·bel·lish [ɪmˈbelɪʃ] *v/t.* **1.** verschöne(r)n, schmücken, verzieren; **2.** *fig. Erzählung etc.* ausschmücken; *die Wahrheit* beschönigen; **emˈbel·lish·ment** [-mənt] *s.* **1.** Verschönerung *f*, Schmuck *m*; **2.** *fig.* a) Ausschmückung *f*, b) Beschönigung *f*.

em·ber[1] [ˈembə] *s.* **1.** *mst pl.* glühende Kohle *od.* Asche; **2.** *pl. fig.* letzte Funken *pl.*

em·ber[2] [ˈembə] *adj.*: ***~ days*** *eccl.* Quatember(fasten *n*) *pl.*

em·ber[3] [ˈembə] *s. orn. a.* ***~goose*** Eistaucher *m*.

em·bez·zle [ɪmˈbezl] *v/t.* veruntreuen, unterˈschlagen; **emˈbez·zle·ment** [-mənt] *s.* Veruntreuung *f*, Unterˈschlagung *f*; **emˈbez·zler** [-lə] *s.* Veruntreuer(in).

em·bit·ter [ɪmˈbɪtə] *v/t.* **1.** *j-n* verbittern; **2.** *et.* (noch) verschlimmern; **emˈbit·ter·ment** [-mənt] *s.* **1.** Verbitterung *f*; **2.** Verschlimmerung *f*.

em·bla·zon [ɪmˈbleɪzn] *v/t.* **1.** heˈraldisch schmücken *od.* darstellen; **2.** schmükken; **3.** *fig.* feiern, verherrlichen, groß herˈausstellen; **4.** ˈauspoˌsaunen; **emˈbla·zon·ment** [-mənt] *s.* Wappenschmuck *m*; **emˈbla·zon·ry** [-rɪ] *s.* **1.** Wappenmaleˈrei *f*; **2.** Wappenschmuck *m*.

em·blem [ˈembləm] *s.* **1.** Emˈblem *n*, Symˈbol *n*: ***national ~*** Hoheitszeichen *n*; **2.** Kennzeichen *n*; **3.** *fig.* Verkörperung *f*; **em·blem·at·ic, em·blem·at·i·cal** [ˌemblɪˈmætɪk(l)] *adj.* □ symˈbolisch, sinnbildlich.

em·bod·i·ment [ɪmˈbɒdɪmənt] *s.* **1.** Verkörperung *f*; **2.** Darstellung *f*; **3.** ⚙ Anwendungsform *f*; **4.** Einverleibung *f*; **em·bod·y** [ɪmˈbɒdɪ] *v/t.* **1.** konˈkrete Form geben (*dat.*); **2.** verkörpern, darstellen; **3.** aufnehmen (***in*** in *acc.*); **4.** umˈfassen, in sich schließen.

em·bold·en [ɪmˈbəʊldən] *v/t.* ermutigen.

em·bo·lism [ˈembəlɪzəm] *s.* ⚕ Emboˈlie *f*.

em·bon·point [ˌɔ̃ːmbɔ̃ːmˈpwæ̃ːŋ] (*Fr.*) *s.* Embonˈpoint *m*, Beleibtheit *f*, ‚Bäuchlein' *n*.

em·bos·om [ɪmˈbʊzəm] *v/t.* **1.** ans Herz drücken; **2.** *fig.* ins Herz schließen; **3.** *fig.* umˈschließen.

em·boss [ɪmˈbɒs] *v/t.* ⚙ **1.** a) bosseln, erhaben *od.* in Reliˈef ausarbeiten, prägen, b) (mit dem Hammer) treiben; **2.** mit erhabener Arbeit schmücken; **3.** *Stoffe* gaufrieren; **emˈbossed** [-st] *adj.* ⚙ a) erhaben gearbeitet, Relief…, getrieben, b) geprägt, gepreßt, c) gaufriert; **emˈboss·ment** [-mənt] *s.* Reliˈefarbeit *f*.

em·bou·chure [ˌɒmbʊˈʃʊə] (*Fr.*) *s.* **1.** Mündung *f* (*Fluß*); **2.** ♪ a) Mundstück *n* (*Blasinstrument*), b) Ansatz *m*.

em·brace [ɪmˈbreɪs] **I** *v/t.* **1.** umˈarmen, in die Arme schließen; **2.** umˈschließen, umˈgeben, umˈklammern; *a. fig.* einschließen, umˈfassen; **3.** erfassen, (in sich) aufnehmen; **4.** *Religion, Angebot* annehmen; *Beruf, Gelegenheit* ergreifen; *Hoffnung* hegen; **II** *v/i.* **5.** sich umarmen; **III** *s.* **6.** Umˈarmung *f*.

em·bra·sure [ɪmˈbreɪʒə] *s.* **1.** △ Laibung *f*; **2.** ⚔ Schießscharte *f*.

em·bro·ca·tion [ˌembrəʊˈkeɪʃn] *s.* ⚕ **1.** Einreibemittel *n*; **2.** Einreibung *f*.

em·broi·der [ɪmˈbrɔɪdə] *v/t.* **1.** *Muster* sticken; **2.** *Stoff* besticken, mit Stickeˈrei verzieren; **3.** *fig. Bericht* ausschmücken, ‚garnieren'.

em·broi·der·y [ɪmˈbrɔɪdərɪ] *s.* **1.** Stickeˈrei *f*: ***do ~*** sticken; **2.** *fig.* Ausschmückung *f*; **~ cot·ton** *s.* Stickgarn *n*; **~ frame** *s.* Stickrahmen *m*.

em·broil [ɪmˈbrɔɪl] *v/t.* **1.** *j-n* verwickeln, hinˈeinziehen (***in*** in *acc.*); **2.** *j-n* in Konˈflikt bringen (***with*** mit); **3.** durchein-

'anderbringen, verwirren; **em'broil·ment** [-mənt] *s.* **1.** Verwicklung *f*; **2.** Verwirrung *f*.

em·bry·o ['embrɪəʊ] *pl.* **-os** *s. biol.* a) Embryo *m*, b) Fruchtkeim *m*: ***in ~*** *fig.* im Keim, im Entstehen, im Werden; **em·bry·on·ic** [ˌembrɪ'ɒnɪk] *adj.* **1.** Embryo..., embryo'nal; **2.** *fig.* (noch) unentwickelt, keimend, rudimen'tär.

em·bus [ɪm'bʌs] ⚔ **I** *v/t.* auf Kraftfahrzeuge verladen; **II** *v/i.* aufsitzen.

em·cee [em'siː] **I** *s.* Conférenci'er *m*; **II** *v/t.* (*u. v/i.*) als Conférencier leiten (fungieren).

e·mend [iː'mend] *v/t. Text* verbessern, korrigieren; **e·men·da·tion** [ˌiːmen'deɪʃn] *s.* Verbesserung *f*, Korrek'tur *f*; **e·men·da·tor** ['iːmendeɪtə] *s.* (Text-) Verbesserer *m*; **e'mend·a·to·ry** [-dətərɪ] *adj.* (text)verbessernd.

em·er·ald ['emərəld] **I** *s.* **1.** Sma'ragd *m*; **2.** Sma'ragdgrün *n*; **3.** *typ.* In'sertie *f* (*e-e 6½-Punkt-Schrift*); **II** *adj.* **4.** sma'ragdgrün; **5.** mit Sma'ragden besetzt; ≈ **Isle** *s. die* Grüne Insel (*Irland*).

e·merge [ɪ'mɜːdʒ] *v/i.* **1.** *allg.* auftauchen: a) an die (Wasser)Oberfläche kommen, b) *a. fig.* zum Vorschein kommen, sich zeigen, c) *fig.* sich erheben (*Frage*, *Problem*), d) *fig.* auftreten, in Erscheinung treten; **2.** her'vor-, her'auskommen (***from*** aus); **3.** sich her'ausstellen *od.* ergeben (*Tatsache*); **4.** (*als Sieger etc.*) her'vorgehen (***from*** aus); **5.** *fig.* aufstreben; **e'mer·gence** [-dʒəns] *s.* Auftauchen *n*, *fig. a.* Auftreten *n*, Entstehen *n*.

e·mer·gen·cy [ɪ'mɜːdʒənsɪ] **I** *s.* Not(lage *f*, -fall *m*) *f*, kritische Lage, Krise *f*, unvorhergesehenes Ereignis, dringender Fall: ***in an ~***, ***in case of ~*** im Notfall, notfalls; ***state of ~*** Notstand *m*, *pol. a.* Ausnahmezustand *m*; **II** *adj.* Not..., Behelfs..., (Aus)Hilfs...; *pol.* Notstands..., Soforthilfe..., **~ brake** *s.* Not-, *mot.* Handbremse *f*; **~ call** *s. teleph.* Notruf *m*; **~ de·cree** *s.* Notverordnung *f*; **~ door**, **~ ex·it** *s.* Notausgang *m*; **~ hos·pi·tal** *s.* A'kutkrankenhaus *n*; **~ land·ing** *s.* ✈ Notlandung *f*; **~ laws** *s. pl. pol.* Notstandsgesetze *pl.*; **~ meet·ing** *s.* Dringlichkeitssitzung *f*; **~ num·ber** *s.* Notruf(nummer *f*) *m*; **~ pow·ers** *s. pl. pol.* Vollmachten *pl.* auf Grund e-s Notstandsgesetzes; **~ ra·tion** *s.* ⚔ eiserne Rati'on; **~ ser·vice** *s.* Notdienst *m*; **~ ward** *s.* Notaufnahme *f*, 'Unfallstatiˌon *f*.

e·mer·gent [ɪ'mɜːdʒənt] *adj.* □ **1.** auftauchend (*a. fig.*); **2.** *fig.* (jung u.) aufstrebend (*Land*): **~ *country*** *a.* Schwellenland *n*.

e·mer·i·tus [iː'merɪtəs] *adj.* emeritiert: **~ *professor***.

em·er·y ['emərɪ] **I** *s. min.* Schmirgel *m*; **II** *v/t.* (ab)schmirgeln; **~ board** *s.* Sandblattnagelfeile *f*; **~ cloth** *s.* Schmirgelleinen *n*; **~ pa·per** *s.* 'Schmirgelpaˌpier *n*; **~ wheel** *s.* Schmirgelscheibe *f*.

e·met·ic [ɪ'metɪk] *pharm.* **I.** *adj.* e'metisch, Brechreiz erregend; **II** *s.* E'metikum *n*, Brechmittel *n* (*a. fig.*).

em·i·grant ['emɪgrənt] **I** *s.* Auswanderer *m*, Emi'grant(in); **II** *adj.* auswandernd, emigrierend, Auswanderungs...; **'em·i·grate** [-reɪt] *v/i.* emigrieren, auswandern; **em·i·gra·tion** [ˌemɪ'greɪʃn] *s.* Auswanderung *f*, Emigrati'on *f*.

em·i·nence ['emɪnəns] *s.* **1.** Erhöhung *f*, (An)Höhe *f*; **2.** hohe Stellung, (hoher) Rang, Würde *f*; **3.** Ansehen *n*, Berühmtheit *f*, Bedeutung *f*; **4.** bedeutende Per'sönlichkeit; **5.** ≈ *R.C.* Emi'nenz *f* (*Kardinal*).

é·mi·nence grise [ˌeɪmiːnɑ̃ːns'griːz] (*Fr.*) *s. pol.* graue Emi'nenz.

em·i·nent ['emɪnənt] *adj.* □ **1.** her'vorragend, ausgezeichnet, berühmt; **2.** emi'nent, bedeutend, außergewöhnlich; **3.** → ***domain*** 3; **'em·i·nent·ly** [-ntlɪ] *adv.* ganz besonders, in hohem Maße.

e·mir [e'mɪə] *s.* Emir *m*; **e'mir·ate** [-ɪərɪt] *s.* Emi'rat *n* (*Würde od. Land e-s Emirs*).

em·is·sar·y ['emɪsərɪ] *s.* **1.** Abgesandte(r) *m*, Emis'sär *m*; **2.** Ge'heimaˌgent *m*.

e·mis·sion [ɪ'mɪʃn] *s.* **1.** Ausstrahlung *f* (*von Licht etc.*), Ausstoß *m* (*von Rauch etc.*), Aus-, Verströmen *n*, *phys.* Emissi'on *f*; **2.** *physiol.* Ausfluß *m*, (*bsd.* Samen)Erguß *m*; **3.** ✝ Ausgabe *f* (*von Banknoten*), *von Wertpapieren*: *a.* Emissi'on *f*; **e'mis·sive** [-ɪsɪv] *adj.* ausstrahlend; **e·mit** [ɪ'mɪt] *v/t.* **1.** *Lava, Rauch* ausstoßen, *Licht etc.* ausstrahlen, *Gas etc.* aus-, verströmen, *phys. Elektronen etc.* emittieren; **2.** a) *e-n Ton, a. e-e Meinung* von sich geben, b) *e-n Schrei etc.* ausstoßen; **3.** ✝ *Banknoten* ausgeben, *Wertpapiere a.* emittieren.

Em·my ['emɪ] *pl.* **-mys**, **-mies** *s. Am.* Emmy *m* (*Fernsehpreis*).

e·mol·li·ent [ɪ'mɒlɪənt] **I** *adj.* erweichend (*a. fig.*); **II** *s. pharm.* erweichendes Mittel, Weichmacher *m*.

e·mol·u·ment [ɪ'mɒljʊmənt] *s. mst pl.* Einkünfte *pl.*

e·mote [ɪ'məʊt] *v/i.* emotio'nal reagieren, e-n Gefühlsausbruch erleiden *od.* (*thea.*) mimen.

e·mo·tion [ɪ'məʊʃn] *s.* **1.** Emoti'on *f*, Gemütsbewegung *f*, (Gefühls)Regung *f*, Gefühl *n*; **2.** Gefühlswallung *f*, Erregung *f*, Leidenschaft *f*; **3.** Rührung *f*, Ergriffenheit *f*; **e'mo·tion·al** [-ʃənl] *adj.* □ → ***emotionally***; **1.** emotio'nal, emotio'nell: a) gefühlsmäßig, -bedingt, b) Gefühls..., Gemüts..., seelisch, c) gefühlsbetont, empfindsam; **2.** gefühlvoll, rührselig; **3.** rührend, ergreifend; **e'mo·tion·al·ism** [-ʃnəlɪzəm] *s.* **1.** Gefühlsbetontheit *f*, Empfindsamkeit *f*; **2.** Gefühlsduse'lei; **3.** Gefühlsäußerung *f*; **e'mo·tion·al·ist** [-ʃnəlɪst] *s.* Gefühlsmensch *m*; **e·mo·tion·al·i·ty** [ɪˌməʊʃə'nælətɪ] *s.* Emotionali'tät *f*, emotio'nale Verhaltensweise; **e'mo·tion·al·ize** [-ʃnəlaɪz] **I** *v/t. j-n od. et.* emotionalisieren; **II** *v/i.* in Gefühlen schwelgen; **e'mo·tion·al·ly** [-ʃnəlɪ] *adv.* gefühlsmäßig, seelisch, emotio'nal, emotio'nell: **~ *disturbed*** seelisch gestört; **e'mo·tion·less** [-lɪs] *adj.* ungerührt, gefühllos, kühl; **e'mo·tive** [-əʊtɪv] *adj.* □ **1.** gefühlsbedingt, emo'tiv; **2.** gefühlvoll; **3.** gefühlsbetont: **~ *word*** Reizwort *n*.

em·pale → ***impale***.

em·pan·el [ɪm'pænl] *v/t.* in die Liste (*bsd.* der Geschworenen) eintragen: **~ *the jury*** *Am.* die Geschworenenliste aufstellen.

em·pa·thize ['empəθaɪz] *v/i.* Einfühlungsvermögen haben *od.* zeigen; sich einfühlen können (***with*** in *acc.*); **'em·pa·thy** [-θɪ] *s.* Einfühlung(svermögen *n*) *f*, Empa'thie *f*.

em·pen·nage [ɪm'penɪdʒ] *s.* ✈ Leitwerk *n*.

em·per·or ['empərə] *s.* Kaiser *m*; **~ moth** *s. zo.* kleines Nachtpfauenauge.

em·pha·sis ['emfəsɪs] *s.* **1.** *ling.* Betonung *f*, Ton *m*, Ak'zent *m*; **2.** *fig.* Betonung *f*, Gewicht *n*, Nachdruck *m*, Schwerpunkt *m*: ***lay ~ on s.th.*** Gewicht *od.* Wert auf e-e Sache legen, et. hervorheben *od.* betonen; ***give ~ to*** → **'em·pha·size** [-saɪz] *v/t.* (nachdrücklich) betonen (*a. ling.*), Nachdruck verleihen (*dat.*), her'vorheben, unter'streichen; **em·phat·ic** [ɪm'fætɪk] *adj.* (□ **~*ally***) nachdrücklich: a) betont, em'phatisch, ausdrücklich, deutlich, b) bestimmt, (ganz) entschieden.

em·phy·se·ma [ˌemfɪ'siːmə] *s.* ⚕ Emphy'sem *n*.

em·pire ['empaɪə] **I** *s.* **1.** (Kaiser)Reich *n*: ***the British ≈*** das Brit. Weltreich; ***≈ Day*** *obs. brit. Staatsfeiertag* (*am 24. Mai, dem Geburtstag Königin Victorias*); **~ *produce*** Erzeugnis *n* aus dem brit. Weltreich; **2.** ✝ *u. fig.* Im'perium *n*: ***tobacco ~***; **3.** Herrschaft *f* (***over*** über *acc.*); **II** *adj.* **4.** Reichs...: **~ *building*** a) Schaffung *f* e-s Weltreichs, b) *fig.* Schaffung e-s eigenen Imperiums *od.* e-r Hausmacht; **5.** Empire..., im Em'pirestil: **~ *furniture***.

em·pir·ic [em'pɪrɪk] **I** *s.* **1.** Em'piriker (-in), **2.** *obs.* Kurpfuscher *m*; **II** *adj.* **3.** → **em'pir·i·cal** [-kl] *adj.* □ em'pirisch, erfahrungsmäßig, Erfahrungs...; **em'pir·i·cism** [-ɪsɪzəm] *s.* **1.** Empi'rismus *m*; **2.** *obs.* Kurpfusche'rei *f*; **em'pir·i·cist** [-ɪsɪst] *s.* **1.** Em'piriker(in); **2.** *phls.* Empi'rist(in).

em·place [ɪm'pleɪs] *v/t.* ⚔ *Geschütz* in Stellung bringen; **em'place·ment** [-mənt] *s.* **1.** Aufstellung *f*; **2.** ⚔ a) In'stellungbringen *n*, b) Geschützstellung *f*, c) Bettung *f*.

em·plane [ɪm'pleɪn] ✈ **I** *v/t. Passagiere* an Bord nehmen, *Waren a.* verladen (***for*** nach); **II** *v/i.* an Bord gehen.

em·ploy [ɪm'plɔɪ] **I** *v/t.* **1.** *j-n* beschäftigen; an-, einstellen, einsetzen: ***be ~ed in doing s.th.*** damit beschäftigt sein, et. zu tun; **2.** an-, verwenden, gebrauchen; **II** *s.* **3.** a) → ***employment*** 1, b) Dienst(e *pl.*) *m*: ***be in s.o.'s ~*** in j-s Dienst(en) stehen, bei j-m angestellt *od.* beschäftigt sein; **em'ploy·a·ble** [-ɔɪəbl] *adj.* **1.** zu beschäftigen(d), anstellbar; **2.** arbeitsfähig; **3.** verwendbar; **em·ploy·é** [ɒm'plɔɪeɪ] *s.*, **em·ploy·ee** [ˌemplɔɪ'iː] *s.* Arbeitnehmer (-in), (*engS.* ***salaried ~***) Angestellte(r *m*) *f*: ***the ~s*** a) die Belegschaft *e-s Betriebs*, b) die Arbeitnehmer(schaft *f*) *pl*; **em'ploy·er** [-ɔɪə] *s.* **1.** Arbeitgeber(in), Unter'nehmer(in), Chef(in), Dienstherr(in): ***~'s contribution*** Arbeitgeberanteil *m*; ***~'s liability*** Unternehmerhaftpflicht *f*; ***~s' association*** Arbeitgeberverband *m*; **2.** ✝ Auftraggeber(in).

em·ploy·ment [ɪm'plɔɪmənt] *s.* **1.** Beschäftigung *f* (*a. allg.*), Arbeit *f*, (An-) Stellung *f*, Arbeitsverhältnis *n*: ***in ~*** beschäftigt; ***out of*** ~ stellen-, arbeitslos; ***full*** ~ Vollbeschäftigung; **2.** Ein-, Anstellung *f*; **3.** Beruf *m*, Tätigkeit *f*, Geschäft *n*; **4.** Gebrauch *m*, Ver-, Anwendung *f*, Einsatz *m*; ~ **a·gen·cy**, ~ **bu·reau** *s.* ˈStellenvermittlung(sbüˌro *n*) *f*; ~ **ex·change** *s. Brit. obs.* Arbeitsamt *n*; ~ **mar·ket** *s.* Stellen-, Arbeitsmarkt *m*; ~ **ser·vice a·gen·cy** *s. Brit.* Arbeitsamt *n*.

em·poi·son [ɪmˈpɔɪzn] *v/t.* **1.** *bsd. fig.* vergiften; **2.** verbittern.

em·po·ri·um [emˈpɔːrɪəm] *s.* **1.** a) Handelszentrum *n*, b) Markt *m* (*Stadt*); **2.** Warenhaus *n*.

em·pow·er [ɪmˈpaʊə] *v/t.* **1.** bevollmächtigen, ermächtigen (***to*** zu): ***be ~ed to*** befugt sein zu; **2.** befähigen (***to*** zu).

em·press [ˈemprɪs] *s.* Kaiserin *f*.

emp·ti·ness [ˈemptɪnɪs] *s.* **1.** Leerheit *f*, Leere *f*; **2.** *fig.* Hohlheit *f*, Leere *f*.

emp·ty [ˈemptɪ] **I** *adj.* **1.** leer: ~ ***of*** *fig.* bar (*gen.*), ohne; ~ ***of meaning*** nichtssagend; ***feel*** ~ F ‚Kohldampf haben'; ***on an ~ stomach*** auf nüchternen Magen; **2.** leer(stehend), unbewohnt; **3.** leer, unbeladen; **4.** *fig.* leer, hohl, nichtssagend; **II** *v/t.* **5.** (aus-, ent)leeren; **6.** *Glas etc.* leeren, austrinken; **7.** *Haus etc.* räumen; **8.** leeren, gießen, schütten (***into*** in *acc.*); **9.** berauben (***of*** *gen.*); **10.** ~ ***itself*** → 12; **III** *v/i.* **11.** sich leeren; **12.** sich ergießen, münden (***into the sea*** ins Meer); **IV** *s.* **13.** *pl.* ⚚ Leergut *n*; ˌ~-ˈ**hand·ed** *adj.* mit leeren Händen; ˌ~-ˈ**head·ed** *adj.* hohlköpfig.

e·mu [ˈiːmjuː] *s. orn.* Emu *m*.

em·u·late [ˈemjʊleɪt] *v/t.* wetteifern mit; nacheifern (*dat.*), es gleichtun wollen (*dat.*); **em·u·la·tion** [ˌemjʊˈleɪʃn] *s.* Wetteifer *m*; Nacheifern *n*.

e·mul·si·fy [ɪˈmʌlsɪfaɪ] *v/t.* emulgieren; **eˈmul·sion** [-lʃn] *s.* ⚗, ⚕, *phot.* Emulsiˈon *f*.

en [en] *s. typ.* Halbgeviert *n*.

en·a·ble [ɪˈneɪbl] *v/t.* **1.** *j-n* befähigen, in den Stand setzen, es *j-m* ermöglichen *od.* möglich machen (***to do*** zu tun); **2.** *j-n* berechtigen, ermächtigen: ***Enabling Act*** Ermächtigungsgesetz *n*; **3.** *et.* möglich machen, ermöglichen: ~ ***s.th. to be done*** es ermöglichen, daß et. geschieht; ***this ~s the housing to be detached*** dadurch kann das Gehäuse abgenommen werden.

en·act [ɪˈnækt] *v/t.* **1.** ⚖ a) *Gesetz* erlassen: ***~ing clause*** Einführungsklausel *f*, b) verfügen, verordnen, c) Gesetzeskraft verleihen (*dat.*); **2.** *thea.* a) *Stück* aufführen, inszenieren (*a. fig.*), b) *Person, Rolle* darstellen, spielen; **3.** ***be ~ed*** *fig.* stattfinden, über die Bühne *od.* vor sich gehen; **en·ac·tion** [ɪˈnækʃn], **en·act·ment** [ɪˈnæktmənt] *s.* **1.** ⚖ a) Erlassen *n* (*Gesetz*), b) Erhebung *f* zum Gesetz, c) Verfügung *f*, Verordnung *f*, Erlaß *m*; **2.** *thea.* a) Inszenierung *f* (*a. fig.*), b) Darstellung *f* (*e-r Rolle*).

en·am·el [ɪˈnæml] **I** *s.* **1.** Eˈmail(le *f*) *n*, Schmelzglas *n*; **2.** Glaˈsur *f* (*auf Töpferwaren*); **3.** *a.* ~ ***ware*** Eˈmailgeschirr *n*; **4.** Lack *m*; **5.** Nagellack *m*; **6.** Eˈmailmaleˌrei *f*; **7.** *anat.* Zahnschmelz *m*; **II** *v/t.* **8.** emaillieren: ***~(l)ing furnace*** Emaillierofen *m*; **9.** glasieren; **10.** lackieren; **11.** in Eˈmail malen; **en·am·el·(l)er** [ɪˈnæmlə] *s.* Emailˈleur *m*, Schmelzarbeiter *m*.

en·am·o(u)r [ɪˈnæmə] *v/t. mst pass.* verliebt machen: ***be ~ed of*** a) verliebt sein in (*acc.*), b) *fig.* sehr angetan sein von.

en bloc [ɑ̃ːŋˈblɒk] (*Fr.*) en bloc, im ganzen, als Ganzes.

en·cae·ni·a [enˈsiːnjə] *s.* Gründungs-, Stiftungsfest *n*.

en·cage [ɪnˈkeɪdʒ] *v/t.* (in e-n Käfig) einsperren, einschließen.

en·camp [ɪnˈkæmp] **I** *v/i.* sein Lager aufschlagen, *bsd.* ⚔ lagern; **II** *v/t. bsd.* ⚔ lagern lassen: ***be ~ed*** lagern; **enˈcamp·ment** [-mənt] *s.* ⚔ **1.** (Feld)Lager *n*; **2.** Lagern *n*.

en·cap·su·late [ɪnˈkæpsjʊleɪt] ein-, verkapseln; *fig.* kurz zs.-fassen.

en·case [ɪnˈkeɪs] *v/t.* **1.** einschließen; **2.** umˈschließen, umˈhüllen; **3.** ⚙ verkleiden, umˈmanteln.

en·cash [ɪnˈkæʃ] *v/t. Brit. Scheck etc.* einlösen; **enˈcash·ment** [-mənt] *s.* Einlösung *f*.

en·caus·tic [enˈkɔːstɪk] *paint.* **I** *adj.* enˈkaustisch, eingebrannt; **II** *s.* Enˈkaustik *f*; ~ **tile** *s.* buntglasierte Kachel.

en·ce·phal·ic [ˌenkeˈfælɪk] *adj.* ⚕ Gehirn…; ˌ**en·ceph·aˈli·tis** [-kefəˈlaɪtɪs] *s.* ⚕ Gehirnentzündung *f*, Enzephaˈlitis *f*.

en·chant [ɪnˈtʃɑːnt] *v/t.* **1.** verzaubern: ***~ed wood*** Zauberwald *m*; **2.** *fig.* bezaubern, entzücken; **enˈchant·er** [-tə] *s.* Zauberer *m*; **enˈchant·ing** [-tɪŋ] *adj.* ☐ bezaubernd, entzückend; **enˈchant·ment** [-mənt] *s.* **1.** Zauber *m*, Zaubeˈrei *f*; Verzauberung *f*; **2.** *fig.* a) Zauber *m*, b) Bezauberung *f*, c) Entzücken *n*; **enˈchant·ress** [-trɪs] *s.* **1.** Zauberin *f*; **2.** *fig.* bezaubernde Frau.

en·chase [ɪnˈtʃeɪs] *v/t.* **1.** *Edelstein* fassen; **2.** ziselieren: ***~d work*** getriebene Arbeit; **3.** (ein)gravieren.

en·ci·pher [ɪnˈsaɪfə] → ***encode***.

en·cir·cle [ɪnˈsɜːkl] *v/t.* **1.** umˈgeben, -ˈringen; **2.** umˈfassen, umˈschlingen; **3.** einkreisen (*a. pol.*), umˈzingeln, ⚔ *a.* einkesseln; **enˈcir·cle·ment** [-mənt] *s.* Einkreisung *f* (*a. pol.*), Umˈzingelung *f*, ⚔ *a.* Einkesselung *f*.

en·clasp [ɪnˈklɑːsp] → ***encircle*** 2.

en·clave **I** *s.* [ˈenkleɪv] Enˈklave *f*; **II** *v/t.* [enˈkleɪv] *Gebiet* einschließen, umˈgeben.

en·clit·ic [ɪnˈklɪtɪk] *ling.* **I** *adj.* (☐ ***~ally***) enˈklitisch; **II** *s.* enklitisches Wort, Enˈklitikon *n*.

en·close [ɪnˈkləʊz] *v/t.* **1.** (***in***) einschließen, ⚙ *a.* einkapseln (in *dat. od. acc.*), umˈgeben (mit); **2.** umˈringen; **3.** umˈfassen; **4.** *Land* einfried(ig)en, umˈzäunen; **5.** beilegen, -fügen (***in a letter*** e-m Brief); **enˈclosed** [-zd] *adj.* **1.** *a. adv.* anˈbei, beiliegend, in der Anlage: ~ ***please find*** in der Anlage erhalten Sie; **2.** ⚙ geschlossen, gekapselt: ~ ***motor***; **enˈclo·sure** [-əʊʒə] *s.* **1.** Einschließung *f*; **2.** Einfried(ig)ung *f*, Umˈzäunung *f*; **3.** eingehegtes Grundstück; **4.** Zaun *m*, Mauer *f*; **5.** Anlage *f* (*zu e-m Brief etc.*).

en·code [enˈkəʊd] *v/t. Text* verschlüsseln, chiffrieren, kodieren.

en·co·mi·um [enˈkəʊmjəm] *s.* Lobrede *f*, -lied *n*, Lobpreisung *f*.

en·com·pass [ɪnˈkʌmpəs] *v/t.* **1.** umˈgeben (***with*** mit); **2.** *fig.* umˈfassen, einschließen; **3.** *fig. j-s Ruin etc.* herˈbeiführen.

en·core [ɒŋˈkɔː] (*Fr.*) **I** *int.* **1.** da ˈcapo!, noch einmal!; **II** *s.* **2.** Daˈkapo(ruf *m*) *n*; **3.** a) Wiederˈholung *f*, b) Zugabe *f*: ***he got an*** ~ er mußte e-e Zugabe geben; **III** *v/t.* **4.** (durch Daˈkaporufe) nochmals verlangen: ~ ***a song***; **5.** *j-n* um e-e Zugabe bitten; **IV** *v/i.* da ˈcapo rufen.

en·coun·ter [ɪnˈkaʊntə] **I** *v/t.* **1.** *j-m od. e-r Sache* begegnen, *j-n od. et.* treffen, auf *j-n*, *a.* auf *Fehler*, *Widerstand*, *Schwierigkeiten etc.* stoßen; **2.** mit *j-m* (*feindlich*) zs.-stoßen *od.* aneinˈandergeraten; **3.** entgegentreten (*dat.*); **II** *v/i.* **4.** sich begegnen; **III** *s.* **5.** Begegnung *f*; **6.** Zs.-stoß *m* (*a. fig.*), Gefecht *n*; **7.** *psych.* Trainingsgruppensitzung *f*: ~ ***group*** Trainingsgruppe *f*.

en·cour·age [ɪnˈkʌrɪdʒ] *v/t.* **1.** *j-n* ermutigen, *j-m* Mut machen, *j-n* ermuntern (***to*** zu); **2.** *j-n* anfeuern; **3.** *j-m* zureden; **4.** *j-n* unterˈstützen, bestärken (***in*** in *dat.*); **5.** *et.* fördern, unterˈstützen, begünstigen; **enˈcour·age·ment** [-mənt] *s.* **1.** Ermutigung *f*, Ermunterung *f*, Ansporn *m* (***to*** für); **2.** Anfeuerung *f*; **3.** Unterstützung *f*, Bestärkung *f*; **4.** Förderung *f*, Begünstigung *f*; **enˈcour·ag·ing** [-dʒɪŋ] *adj.* ☐ **1.** ermutigend; **2.** hoffnungsvoll, vielversprechend.

en·croach [ɪnˈkrəʊtʃ] *v/i.* **1.** (***on, upon***) unbefugt eindringen *od.* -greifen (in *acc.*), sich ˈÜbergriffe leisten (in, auf *acc.*), (*j-s Recht*) verletzen; **2.** (***on, upon***) über Gebühr beanspruchen, mißbrauchen; zu weit gehen; **3.** (***on, upon***) *et.* beeinträchtigen, schmälern; **enˈcroach·ment** [-mənt] *s.* **1.** (***on, upon***) Eingriff *m* (in *acc.*), ˈÜbergriff *m* (in, auf *acc.*), Verletzung *f* (*gen.*); **2.** Beeinträchtigung *f*, Schmälerung *f* (***on, upon*** *gen.*); **3.** ˈÜbergreifen *n*, Vordringen *n*.

en·crust [ɪnˈkrʌst] **I** *v/t.* **1.** ver-, überˈkrusten; **2.** reich verzieren; **II** *v/i.* **3.** eine Kruste bilden; ˌ**en·crusˈta·tion** *s.* **1.** Krustenbildung *f*; **2.** reiche Verzierung.

en·cum·ber [ɪnˈkʌmbə] *v/t.* **1.** belasten (*a. Grundstück etc.*): ***~ed with mortgages*** hypothekarisch belastet; ***~ed with debts*** (völlig) verschuldet; **2.** (be)hindern; **3.** *Räume* vollstopfen, überˈladen; **enˈcum·brance** [-brəns] *s.* **1.** Last *f*, Belastung *f*; **2.** Hindernis *n*, Behinderung *f*; **3.** ⚚ (Grundstücks)Belastung *f*, Hypoˈtheken-, Schuldenlast *f*; **4.** (Faˈmilien)Anhang *m*, *bsd.* Kinder *pl.*: ***without ~(s)***; **enˈcum·branc·er** [-brənsə] *s.* ⚖ Hypoˈthekengläubiger (-in).

en·cy·clic, **en·cy·cli·cal** [enˈsɪklɪk(l)] **I** *adj.* ☐ enˈzyklisch; **II** *s. eccl.* (päpstliche) Enˈzyklika.

en·cy·clo·p(a)e·di·a [enˌsaɪkləʊˈpiːdjə] *s.* Enzyklopäˈdie *f*; **enˌcy·cloˈp(a)e·dic**, **enˌcy·cloˈp(a)e·di·cal** [-dɪk(l)] *adj.* enzykloˈpädisch, umˈfassend.

en·cyst [enˈsɪst] *v/t.* ⚕, *zo.* ein-, verkapseln; **enˈcyst·ment** [-mənt] *s.* ⚕, *zo.* Ein-, Verkapselung *f*.

end [end] **I** *s.* **1.** (*örtlich*) Ende *n*: ***begin at the wrong ~*** falsch herum anfangen; ***from one ~ to another***, ***from ~ to ~*** von Anfang bis (zum) Ende; ***at the ~ of the letter*** am Ende *od.* Schluß des

Briefes; ***no ~ of*** a) unendlich, unzählig, b) sehr viel(e); ***no ~ of trouble*** endlose Mühe *od.* Scherereien; ***no ~ of a fool*** F Vollidiot *m*; ***no ~ disappointed*** F maßlos enttäuscht; ***he thinks no ~ of himself*** er ist grenzenlos eingebildet; ***on ~*** a) ununterbrochen, b) aufrecht, hochkant; ***for hours on ~*** stundenlang; ***stand s.th. on ~*** et. hochkant stellen; ***my hair stood on ~*** mir standen die Haare zu Berge; ***at our*** (*od.* ***this***) ***~*** F bei uns, hier; ***be at an ~*** a) zu Ende sein, aussein, b) mit s-n Mitteln *od.* Kräften am Ende sein; ***at a loose ~*** a) müßig, b) ohne feste Bindung, c) verwirrt; ***there's an ~ of it!*** Schluß damit!, basta!; ***there's an ~ to everything*** alles hat mal ein Ende; ***come to an ~*** ein Ende nehmen, zu Ende gehen; ***come to a bad ~*** ein schlimmes Ende nehmen; ***go*** (***in***) ***off the deep ~*** F außer sich geraten, ‚hochgehen'; ***keep one's ~ up*** a) s-n Mann stehen, b) sich nicht unterkriegen lassen; ***make both ~s meet*** *finanziell* über die Runden kommen; ***make an ~ of*** (*od.* ***put an ~ to***) ***s.th.*** Schluß machen mit et., e-r Sache ein Ende setzen; ***put an ~ to o.s.*** s-m Leben ein Ende machen; ***he is the*** (***absolute***) ***~!*** F a) er ist das ‚Letzte'!, b) er ist ‚zum Brüllen'!; ***it's the ~*** F a) das ist das ‚Letzte', b) es ist ‚sagenhaft'; **2.** (äußerstes) Ende, *mst* entfernte Gegend: ***the other ~ of the street*** das andere Ende der Straße; ***the ~ of the road*** *fig.* das Ende; ***to the ~s of the earth*** bis ans Ende der Welt; **3.** ⚙ Spitze *f*, Kopf(ende *n*) *m*, Stirnseite *f*: ***~ to ~*** der Länge nach; ***~ on*** mit dem Ende *od.* der Spitze voran; **4.** (*zeitlich*) Ende *n*, Schluß *m*: ***in the ~*** am Ende, schließlich; ***at the ~ of May*** Ende Mai; ***to the bitter ~*** bis zum bitteren Ende; ***to the ~ of time*** bis in alle Ewigkeit; ***without ~*** unaufhörlich; ***no ~ in sight*** kein Ende abzusehen; **5.** Tod *m*, Ende *n*, 'Untergang *m*: ***near one's ~*** dem Tode nahe; ***the ~ of the world*** das Ende der Welt; ***you'll be the ~ of me!*** du bringst mich noch ins Grab!; **6.** Rest *m*, Endchen *n*, Stück(chen) *n*, Stummel *m*, Stumpf *m*: ***the ~ of a pencil***; **7.** ⚓ Kabel-, Tauende *n*; **8.** Folge *f*, Ergebnis *n*: ***the ~ of the matter was that*** die Folge (davon) war, daß; **9.** Ziel *n*, (End)Zweck *m*, Absicht *f*: ***to this ~*** zu diesem Zweck; ***to no ~*** vergebens; ***gain one's ~s*** s-n Zweck erreichen; ***for one's own ~*** zum eigenen Nutzen; ***private ~s*** Privatinteressen; ***the ~ justifies the means*** der Zweck heiligt die Mittel; **II** *v/t.* **10.** *a.* ***~ off*** beend(ig)en, zu Ende führen; *e-r Sache* ein Ende machen: ***~ it all*** F ‚Schluß machen' (*sich umbringen*); ***the dictionary to ~ all dictionaries*** das beste Wörterbuch aller Zeiten; **11.** a) *a.* ***~ up*** *et.* ab-, beschließen, b) *den Rest s-r Tage* verbringen, *s-e Tage* beschließen; **III** *v/i.* **12.** *a.* ***~ off*** enden, aufhören, schließen: ***all's well that ~s well*** Ende gut, alles gut; **13.** *a.* ***~ up*** enden, ausgehen (***by, in, with*** damit, daß): ***~ happily*** gut ausgehen; ***he ~ed by boring me*** schließlich langweilte er mich; ***~ in disaster*** mit e-m Fiasko enden; **14.** sterben; **15.** ***~ up*** a) enden, ‚landen' (***in prison*** im Gefängnis), b) enden (***as*** als): ***he ~ed up as an actor*** er wurde schließlich Schauspieler.

'end-all → ***be-all.***

en·dan·ger [ɪn'deɪndʒə] *v/t.* gefährden, in Gefahr bringen.

en·dear [ɪn'dɪə] *v/t.* beliebt machen (***to*** bei *j-m*): ***~ o.s. to s.o.*** a) j-s Zuneigung gewinnen, b) sich bei j-m lieb Kind machen; **en'dear·ing** [-ərɪŋ] *adj.* ☐ lieb, gewinnend; liebenswert; **en'dear·ment** [-mənt] *s.*: (***term of***) ***~*** Kosewort *n*, -name *m*; ***words of ~*** liebe *od.* zärtliche Worte.

en·deav·o(u)r [ɪn'devə] **I** *v/i.* (***after***) sich bemühen (um), streben (nach); **II** *v/t.* (ver)suchen, bemüht *od.* bestrebt sein (***to do s.th.*** et. zu tun); **III** *s.* Bemühung *f*, Bestreben *n*, Anstrengung *f*: ***to make every ~*** sich nach Kräften bemühen.

en·dem·ic [en'demɪk] **I** *adj.* (☐ ***~ally***) **1.** en'demisch: a) (ein)heimisch, b) ⚕ örtlich begrenzt (auftretend), c) *zo.*, ⚘ *in e-m bestimmten Gebiet verbreitet*; **II** *s.* **2.** ⚕ en'demische Krankheit; **3.** a) *zo.* en'demisches Tier, b) en'demische Pflanze.

end game *s.* **1.** Schlußphase *f* (*e-s Spiels*); **2.** *Schach*: Endspiel *n*.

end·ing ['endɪŋ] *s.* **1.** Ende *n*, (Ab-)Schluß *m*: ***happy ~*** glückliches Ende, Happy-End *n*; **2.** *ling.* Endung *f*; **3.** *fig.* Ende *n*, Tod *m*.

en·dive ['endɪv] *s.* ⚘ ('Winter)En,divie *f*.

end·less ['endlɪs] *adj.* ☐ **1.** endlos, ohne Ende, un'endlich; **2.** ewig, unauf'hörlich; **3.** unendlich lang; **4.** ⚙ endlos: ***~ belt*** endloses Band; ***~ chain*** endlose Kette, Raupenkette *f*, Paternosterwerk *n*; ***~ paper*** Endlos-, Rollenpapier *n*; ***~ screw*** Schraube *f* ohne Ende, Schnecke *f*; **'end·less·ness** [-nɪs] *s.* Un'endlichkeit *f*, Endlosigkeit *f*.

en·do·car·di·tis [ˌendəʊkɑː'daɪtɪs] *s.* ⚕ Herzinnenhautentzündung *f*, Endokar'ditis *f*; **en·do·car·di·um** [ˌendəʊ'kɑːdɪəm] *s. anat.* innere Herzhaut, Endo'kard *n*; **en·do·carp** ['endəʊkɑːp] *s.* ⚘ Endo'karp *n* (*innere Fruchthaut*); **en·do·crane** ['endəʊkreɪn] *s. anat.* Schädelinnenfläche *f*, Endo'kranium *n*; **en·do·crine** ['endəʊkraɪn] *adj.* endo'krin, mit innerer Sekreti'on: ***~ glands***; **en·dog·a·my** [en'dɒgəmɪ] *s. sociol.* Endoga'mie *f*; **en·dog·e·nous** [en'dɒdʒɪnəs] *adj. bsd.* ⚘ endo'gen; **en·do·par·a·site** [ˌendəʊ'pærəsaɪt] *s. zo.* Endopara'sit *m*; **en·do·plasm** ['endəʊplæzəm] *s. biol.* innere Proto'plasmaschicht, Endo'plasma *n*.

en·dorse [ɪn'dɔːs] *v/t.* **1.** a) *Dokument* auf der Rückseite beschreiben, b) e-n Vermerk *od.* Zusatz machen auf (*dat.*), c) *bsd. Brit.* e-e Strafe vermerken auf (*e-m Führerschein*); **2.** ♰ a) *Scheck etc.* indossieren, girieren, b) *a.* ***~ over*** über'tragen, -'weisen (***to*** *j-m*), c) *e-e Zahlung* auf der Rückseite des Schecks *etc.* bestätigen; **3.** a) *e-n Plan etc.* billigen, gutheißen, b) sich *e-r Ansicht etc.* anschließen: ***~ s.o.'s opinion*** j-m beipflichten; **en·dor·see** [ˌendɔː'siː] *s.* ♰ Indos'sat *m*, Indossa'tar *m*; Gi'rat *m*; **en'dorse·ment** [-mənt] *s.* **1.** Vermerk *m od.* Zusatz *m* (*auf der Rückseite von Dokumenten*); **2.** ♰ a) Indossa'ment *n*, Giro *n*, b) Über'tragung *f*: ***~ in blank*** Blankogiro; ***~ in full*** Vollgiro; **3.** *fig.* Billigung *f*, Unter'stützung *f*; **en'dors·er** [-sə] *s.* ♰ Indos'sant *m*, Gi'rant *m*: ***preceding ~*** Vormann *m*.

en·dow [ɪn'daʊ] *v/t.* **1.** dotieren, e-e Stiftung machen (*dat.*); **2.** *et.* stiften: ***~ s.o. with s.th.*** j-m et. stiften; **3.** *fig.* ausstatten (***with*** mit *e-m Talent etc.*); **en'dowed** [-aʊd] *adj.* **1.** gestiftet: ***well-~*** wohlhabend; ***~ school*** mit Stiftungsgeldern finanzierte Schule; **2.** ***~ with*** *fig.* ausgestattet mit: ***~ with many talents***; ***she is well ~*** *humor.* sie ist von der Natur reichlich ausgestattet; **en'dow·ment** [-mənt] *s.* **1.** a) Stiftung *f*, b) *pl.* Stiftungsgeld *n*: ***~ insurance*** (*Brit.* ***assurance***) ♰ Versicherung *f* auf den Todes- u. Erlebensfall; **2.** *fig.* Begabung *f*, Ta'lent *n*, *mst pl.* (körperliche *od.* geistige) Vorzüge *pl.*

end| pa·per *s.* Vorsatzblatt *n*; ***~ product*** *s.* ♰ *u. fig.* 'Endpro,dukt *n*; ***~ rhyme*** *s.* Endreim *m*.

en·dur·a·ble [ɪn'djʊərəbl] *adj.* ☐ erträglich, leidlich.

en·dur·ance [ɪn'djʊərəns] **I** *s.* **1.** Dauer *f*; **2.** Dauerhaftigkeit *f*; **3.** a) Ertragen *n*, Aushalten *n*, Erdulden *n*, b) Ausdauer *f*, Geduld *f*, Standhaftigkeit *f*: ***beyond*** (*od.* ***past***) ***~*** unerträglich, nicht auszuhalten(d); **4.** ⚙ Dauerleistung *f*; Lebensdauer *f*; **II** *adj.* **5.** Dauer...; ***~ flight*** *s.* ✈ Dauerflug *m*; ***~ limit*** *s.* ⚙ Belastungsgrenze *f*; ***~ run*** *s.* Dauerlauf *m*; ***~ test*** *s.* ⚙ Belastungs-, Ermüdungsprobe *f*.

en·dure [ɪn'djʊə] **I** *v/i.* **1.** an-, fortdauern; **2.** 'durchhalten; **II** *v/t.* **3.** aushalten, ertragen, erdulden, 'durchmachen: ***not to be ~d*** unerträglich; **4.** *fig.* (*nur neg.*) ausstehen, leiden: ***I cannot ~ him***; **en'dur·ing** [-ərɪŋ] *adj.* ☐ an-, fortdauernd, bleibend.

'end·ways [-weɪz], **'end·wise** [-waɪz] *adv.* **1.** mit dem Ende nach vorn *od.* oben; **2.** aufrecht; **3.** der Länge nach.

en·e·ma ['enɪmə] *s.* ⚕ **1.** Kli'stier *n*, Einlauf *m*; **2.** Kli'stierspritze *f*.

en·e·my ['ənəmɪ] **I** *s.* **1.** ⚔ Feind *m*; **2.** Gegner *m*, Feind *m*: ***the Old*** 2 *bibl.* der Teufel, der böse Feind; ***be one's own*** (***worst***) ***~*** sich selbst (am meisten) schaden *od.* im Wege stehen; ***make an ~ of s.o.*** sich j-n zum Feind machen; ***she made no enemies*** sie machte sich keine Feinde; **II** *adj.* **3.** feindlich, Feind...: ***~ action*** Feind-, Kriegseinwirkung *f*; ***~ alien*** feindlicher Ausländer; ***~ country*** Feindesland *n*; ***~ property*** ♰ Feindvermögen *n*.

en·er·get·ic [ˌenə'dʒetɪk] **I** *adj.* (☐ ***~ally***) **1.** e'nergisch: a) tatkräftig, b) nachdrücklich; **2.** (sehr) wirksam; **3.** *phys.* ener'getisch; **II** *s. pl. sg. konstr.* **4.** *phys.* Ener'getik *f*; **en·er·gize** ['enədʒaɪz] **I** *v/t.* **1.** *et.* kräftigen, Ener'gie verleihen (*dat.*); *j-n* anspornen; **2.** ⚡, ⚙, *phys.* erregen: ***~d*** ⚡ unter Spannung (stehend); **II** *v/i.* **3.** energisch handeln.

en·er·gu·men [ˌenɜː'gjuːmen] *s.* Enthusi'ast(in), Fa'natiker(in).

en·er·gy ['enədʒɪ] *s.* **1.** Ener'gie *f*: a) Kraft *f*, Nachdruck *m*, b) Tatkraft *f*; **2.** Wirksamkeit *f*, 'Durchschlagskraft *f*; **3.** ⚗, *phys.* Ener'gie *f*, Kraft *f*, Leistung *f*: ***~ crisis*** Energiekrise *f*; ***~-saving*** energiesparend.

en·er·vate ['enɜːveɪt] *v/t.* a) entnerven, b) entkräften, schwächen (*alle a. fig.*); **en·er·va·tion** [ˌenɜː'veɪʃn] *s.* **1.** Entnervung; **2.** Entkräftung *f*, Schwächung *f*; **3.** Schwäche *f*.

en·fee·ble [ɪn'fiːbl] *v/t.* schwächen.

en·feoff [ɪn'fef] *v/t. hist.* belehnen (***with*** mit); **en'feoff·ment** [-mənt] *s.* **1.** Belehnung *f*; **2.** Lehnsbrief *m*; **3.** Lehen *n*.

en·fi·lade [ˌenfɪ'leɪd] ⚔ **I** *s.* Flankenfeuer *n*; **II** *v/t.* (mit Flankenfeuer) bestreichen.

en·fold [ɪn'fəʊld] *v/t.* **1.** *a. fig.* einhüllen (***in*** in *acc.*), um'hüllen (***with*** mit); **2.** um'fassen, -'armen; **3.** falten.

en·force [ɪn'fɔːs] *v/t.* **1.** a) (mit Nachdruck) geltend machen: ~ ***an argument***, b) Geltung verschaffen (*dat.*), *Gesetz etc.* 'durchführen, c) ☤ *Forderungen* (gerichtlich) geltend machen, *Schuld* beitreiben, d) ⚖ Urteil voll'strecken: ~ ***a contract*** (s-e) Rechte aus e-m Vertrag geltend machen; **2.** (***on***, ***upon***) *et.* 'durchsetzen (bei *j-m*); *Gehorsam etc.* erzwingen (von *j-m*); **3.** (***on***, ***upon*** *dat.*) aufzwingen, auferlegen; **en'force·a·ble** [-səbl] *adj.* 'durchsetz-, erzwingbar; ⚖ voll'streckbar, beitreibbar; (ein)klagbar; **en'forced** [-st] *adj.* □ erzwungen, aufgezwungen: ~ ***sale*** Zwangsverkauf *m*; **en'forc·ed·ly** [-sɪdlɪ] *adv.* **1.** notgedrungen; **2.** zwangsweise, gezwungenermaßen; **en'force·ment** [-mənt] *s.* **1.** Erzwingung *f*, 'Durchsetzung *f*; **2.** a) ☤ (gerichtliche) Geltendmachung, b) ⚖ Voll'streckung *f*, Voll'zug *m*: ~ ***officer*** Vollzugsbeamte(r) *m*.

en·frame [ɪn'freɪm] *v/t.* einrahmen.

en·fran·chise [ɪn'fræntʃaɪz] *v/t.* **1.** *j-m* die Bürgerrechte *od.* das Wahlrecht verleihen: ***be ~d*** das Wahlrecht erhalten; **2.** *e-r Stadt* po'litische Rechte gewähren; **3.** *Brit. e-m Ort* Vertretung im 'Unterhaus verleihen; **4.** *Sklaven* freilassen; **5.** befreien (***from*** von); **en'fran·chise·ment** [-tʃɪzmənt] *s.* **1.** Verleihung *f* der Bürgerrechte *od.* des Wahlrechts; **2.** Gewährung *f* po'litischer Rechte; **3.** Freilassung *f*, Befreiung *f*.

en·gage [ɪn'geɪdʒ] **I** *v/t.* **1.** (***o.s.*** sich) (*vertraglich etc.*) verpflichten *od.* binden (***to do s.th.*** et. zu tun); **2.** ***become*** (*od.* ***get***) ***~d*** sich verloben (***to*** mit); **3.** *j-n* an-, einstellen, *Künstler etc.* engagieren; **4.** a) *et.* mieten, *Zimmer* belegen, nehmen, b) *Platz etc.* (vor)bestellen, belegen; **5.** *j-n*, *j-s Kräfte etc.* in Anspruch nehmen, *j-n* fesseln: ~ ***s.o. in conversation*** j-n ins Gespräch ziehen; ~ ***s.o.'s attention*** j-s Aufmerksamkeit auf sich lenken *od.* in Anspruch nehmen; **6.** ⚔ a) *Truppen* einsetzen, b) *Feind* angreifen, *Feindkräfte* binden; **7.** ⚙ einrasten lassen; *Kupplung etc.* einrücken, *e-n Gang* einlegen, -schalten; **II** *v/i.* **8.** sich verpflichten, es über'nehmen (***to do s.th.*** et. zu tun); **9.** Gewähr leisten, garantieren, sich verbürgen (***that*** daß); **10.** ⚔ angreifen, den Kampf beginnen; ~ ***in*** sich beschäftigen *od.* befassen *od.* abgeben mit; **11.** ~ ***in*** sich beteiligen an (*dat.*), sich einlassen in *od.* auf (*acc.*); **12.** ⚙ inein'andergreifen, einrasten; **en'gaged** [-dʒd] *adj.* **1.** verpflichtet; **2.** *a.* ~ ***to be married*** verlobt (***to*** mit); **3.** beschäftigt, nicht abkömmlich, ‚besetzt': ***are you ~?*** sind Sie frei?; ***be ~ in*** (*od.* ***on***) beschäftigt sein mit, arbeiten an (*dat.*); ***deeply ~ in conversation*** in ein Gespräch vertieft; ***my time is fully ~*** ich bin zeitlich völlig ausgelastet; **4.** *teleph. Brit.* besetzt: ~ ***tone*** *od.* ***signal*** Besetztzeichen *n*; **5.** ⚙ eingerückt, im Eingriff (stehend); **en'gage·ment** [-mənt] *s.* **1.** (*vertragliche etc.*) Verpflichtung *f*: ***without ~*** unverbindlich, ☤ *a.* freibleibend; ***be under an ~ to s.o.*** j-m (gegenüber) verpflichtet sein; ***~s*** ☤ Zahlungsverpflichtungen *pl.*; **2.** Verabredung *f*: ~ ***diary*** Terminkalender *m*; **3.** Verlobung *f* (***to*** mit): ~ ***ring*** Verlobungsring *m*; **4.** (An)Stellung *f*, Stelle *f*, Posten *m*; **5.** *thea.* Engage'ment *n*; **6.** Beschäftigung *f*, Tätigkeit *f*; **7.** ⚔ Kampf(handlung *f*) *m*, Gefecht *n*; **8.** ⚙ Eingriff *m*; **en'gag·ing** [-dʒɪŋ] *adj.* □ **1.** einnehmend, gewinnend; **2.** ⚙ Ein- u. Ausrück…: ~ ***gear***.

en·gen·der [ɪn'dʒendə] *v/t. fig.* erzeugen, her'vorbringen, -rufen.

en·gine ['endʒɪn] **I** *s.* **1.** a) *allg.* Ma'schine *f*, b) Motor *m*, c) 🚂 Lokomo'tive *f*; **2.** ⚙ Holländer *m*, Stoffmühle *f*; **3.** Feuerspritze *f*; **II** *v/t.* **4.** mit Ma'schinen *od.* Mo'toren *od.* e-m Motor versehen; ~ **block** *s.* Motorblock *m*; ~ **build·er** *s.* Ma'schinenbauer *m*; ~ **driv·er** *s.* Lokomo'tivführer *m*.

en·gi·neer [ˌendʒɪ'nɪə] **I** *s.* **1.** a) Ingeni'eur *m*, b) Techniker *m*, c) Me'chaniker *m*: ***~s*** *teleph.* Stördienst *m*; **2.** *a.* ***mechanical ~*** Ma'schinenbauer *m*, -ingeniˌeur *m*; **3.** *a.* ⚓ Maschi'nist *m*; **4.** *Am.* Lokomo'tivführer *m*; **5.** ⚔ Pio'nier *m*; **II** *v/t.* **6.** *Straßen*, *Brücken etc.* bauen, anlegen, konstruieren, errichten; **7.** *fig. geschickt* in die Wege leiten, ‚organisieren', ‚einfädeln', ‚deichseln'; **III** *v/i.* **8.** als Ingeni'eur tätig sein; **ˌen·gi'neer·ing** [-ɪərɪŋ] *s.* **1.** Technik *f*, *engS.* Ingeni'eurwesen *n*; (*a.* ***mechanical ~***) Ma'schinen- u. Gerätebau *m*: ~ ***department*** technische Abteilung, Konstruktionsbüro *n*; ~ ***sciences*** technische Wissenschaften; ~ ***standards committee*** Fachnormenausschuß *m*; ~ ***works*** Maschinenfabrik *f*; **2.** ***social ~*** angewandte Sozialwissenschaft; **3.** ⚔ Pio'nierwesen *n*.

en·gine| fit·ter *s.* Ma'schinenschlosser *m*, Mon'teur *m*; ~ **lathe** *s.* ⚙ Leitspindeldrehbank *f*; **'~·man** [-mən] *s.* [*irr.*] **1.** Maschi'nist *m*; **2.** Lokomo'tivführer *m*; ~ **room** *s.* Ma'schinenraum *m*.

en·gird [ɪn'gɜːd], **en'gir·dle** [-dl] *v/t.* um'gürten, -'geben, -'schließen.

Eng·land·er ['ɪŋgləndə] *s.* Engländer *m*: ***Little ~*** *pol. hist.* Gegner der imperialistischen Politik.

Eng·lish ['ɪŋglɪʃ] **I** *adj.* **1.** englisch: ~ ***disease***, ~ ***sickness*** ☤ ‚englische Krankheit'; ~ ***flute*** ♪ Blockflöte *f*; ~ ***studies*** *pl.* Anglistik *f*; **II** *s.* **2.** ***the ~*** die Engländer; **3.** *ling.* Englisch *n*, das Englische: ~ ~ britisches Englisch; ***in ~*** auf englisch, im Englischen; ***into ~*** ins Englische; ***from*** (***the***) ~ aus dem Englischen, ***the King's*** (*od.* ***Queen's***) ~ gutes, reines Englisch; ***in plain ~*** *fig.* ‚auf gut Deutsch', ‚im Klartext'; **4.** *typ.* Mittel *f* (*Schriftgrad*); **Eng·lish·ism** ['ɪŋlɪʃɪzəm] *s. bsd. Am.* **1.** *ling.* Briti'zismus *m*; **2.** englische Eigenart; **3.** Anglophi'lie *f*; **'Eng·lish·man** [-mən] *s.* [*irr.*] Engländer *m*; **'Eng·lishˌwom·an** *s.* [*irr.*] Engländerin *f*.

en·gorge [ɪn'gɔːdʒ] *v/t.* **1.** gierig verschlingen; **2.** ⚕ *Gefäß etc.* anschoppen: ***~d kidney*** Stauungsniere *f*.

en·graft [ɪn'grɑːft] *v/t.* **1.** (auf)pfropfen (***into*** in *acc.*, ***upon*** auf *acc.*); **2.** *fig.* a) einfügen, b) verankern (***into*** in *dat.*).

en·grained [ɪn'greɪnd] *adj. fig.* **1.** eingefleischt, unverbesserlich; **2.** eingewurzelt.

en·gram [ɪn'græm] *s. biol.*, *psych.* En'gramm *n*.

en·grave [ɪn'greɪv] *v/t.* **1.** (ein)gravieren, (ein)meißeln, *in Holz*: (ein)schnitzen, einschneiden (***on*** in, auf *acc.*); **2.** ***it is ~d*** (***up***)***on his memory*** (*od.* ***mind***) *fig.* es hat sich ihm tief eingeprägt; **en'grav·er** [-və] *s.* Gra'veur *m*, (Kunst-) Stecher *m*: ~ (***on copper***) Kupferstecher *m*; **en'grav·ing** [-vɪŋ] *s.* **1.** Gravieren *n*, Gravierkunst *f*; **2.** (Kupfer-, Stahl)Stich *m*; Holzschnitt *m*.

en·gross [ɪn'grəʊs] *v/t.* **1.** ⚖ a) *Urkunde* ausfertigen, b) e-e Reinschrift anfertigen von, c) in gesetzlicher *od.* rechtsgültiger Form ausdrücken, d) *parl. e-m Gesetzentwurf* die endgültige Fassung geben; **2.** ☤ a) *Ware* spekula'tiv aufkaufen, b) *den Markt* monopolisieren; **3.** *fig. j-s Aufmerksamkeit etc.* (ganz) in Anspruch nehmen; *et.* an sich reißen; **en'grossed** [-st] *adj.* vertieft, versunken (***in*** in *acc.*); **en'gross·ing** [-sɪŋ] *adj.* **1.** fesselnd, spannend; **2.** voll in Anspruch nehmend; **en'gross·ment** [-mənt] *s.* **1.** ⚖ Ausfertigung *f*, Reinschrift *f e-r Urkunde*; **2.** ☤ a) (spekula'tiver) Aufkauf, b) Monopolisierung *f*; **3.** Inanspruchnahme *f* (***of***, ***with*** durch).

en·gulf [ɪn'gʌlf] *v/t.* **1.** über'fluten; **2.** verschlingen (*a. fig.*).

en·hance [ɪn'hɑːns] *v/t.* **1.** erhöhen, vergrößern, steigern, heben; **2.** *et.* (vorteilhaft) zur Geltung bringen; **en'hance·ment** [-mənt] *s.* Steigerung *f*, Erhöhung *f*, Vergrößerung *f*.

e·nig·ma [ɪ'nɪgmə] *s.* Rätsel *n* (*a. fig.*); **e·nig·mat·ic**, **e·nig·mat·i·cal** [ˌenɪg'mætɪk(l)] *adj.* □ rätselhaft, dunkel; **e'nig·ma·tize** [-ətaɪz] **I** *v/i.* in Rätseln sprechen; **II** *v/t. et.* in Dunkel hüllen, verschleiern.

en·join [ɪn'dʒɔɪn] *v/t.* **1.** *et.* auferlegen, vorschreiben (***on s.o.*** j-m); **2.** *j-m* befehlen, einschärfen, *j-n* (eindringlich) mahnen (***to do*** zu tun); **3.** bestimmen, Anweisung(en) erteilen (***that*** daß); **4.** ⚖ unter'sagen (***s.th. on s.o.*** j-m et.; ***s.o. from doing s.th.*** j-m, et. zu tun).

en·joy [ɪn'dʒɔɪ] *v/t.* **1.** Vergnügen *od.* Gefallen finden *od.* Freude haben an (*dat.*), sich erfreuen an (*dat.*): ***I ~ dancing*** ich tanze gern, Tanzen macht mir Spaß; ***did you ~ the play?*** hat dir das (Theater)Stück gefallen?; ~ ***o.s.*** sich amüsieren *od.* gut unterhalten; ***did you ~ yourself in London?*** hat es dir in London gefallen?; ~ ***yourself!*** viel Spaß!; **2.** genießen, sich *et.* schmecken lassen: ***I ~ my food*** das Essen schmeckt mir; **3.** sich *e-s Besitzes* erfreuen, *et.* haben, besitzen, genießen; erleben: ~ ***good health*** sich e-r guten Gesundheit erfreuen; ~ ***a right*** ein Recht genießen *od.* haben; **en'joy·a·ble** [-ɔɪəbl] *adj.* □ **1.** brauch-, genießbar; **2.** angenehm, erfreulich, schön; **en'joy·ment** [-mənt] *s.* **1.** Genuß *m*, Vergnügen *n*, Gefallen *n*, Freude *f* (**of** an *dat.*); **2.** Genuß *m* (*e-s Besitzes od. Rechtes*), Besitz *m*: **quiet ~** ⚖ ruhiger Besitz; **3.** ⚖ Ausübung *f* (*e-s Rechts*).

en·kin·dle [ɪn'kɪndl] *v/t. fig.* entflammen, entzünden, entfachen.

en·lace [ɪn'leɪs] *v/t.* **1.** um'schlingen; **2.** verstricken.

en·large [ɪn'lɑːdʒ] **I** *v/t.* **1.** vergrößern (*a. phot.*), *Kenntnisse etc. a.* erweitern, *Einfluß etc. a.* ausdehnen: **~d and revised edition** erweiterte u. verbesserte Auflage; **~ the mind** den Gesichtskreis erweitern; **II** *v/i.* **2.** sich vergrößern *od.* ausdehnen *od.* erweitern, zunehmen; **3.** *phot.* sich vergrößern lassen; **4.** *fig.* sich verbreiten *od.* weitläufig auslassen (**upon** über *acc.*); **en'large·ment** [-mənt] *s.* **1.** Vergrößerung *f* (*a. phot.*), Erweiterung *f*, Ausdehnung *f*; ⚕ (Herz)Erweiterung *f*, (*Mandel- etc.*) Schwellung *f*; **2.** Erweiterungs-, Anbau *m*; **en'larg·er** [-dʒə] *s.* Vergrößerungsgerät *n*.

en·light·en [ɪn'laɪtn] *v/t. fig.* erleuchten, aufklären, belehren (**on, as to** über *acc.*); **en'light·ened** [-nd] *adj.* **1.** erleuchtet, aufgeklärt; **2.** verständig; **en'light·en·ing** [-nɪŋ] *adj.* aufschlußreich; **en'light·en·ment** [-mənt] *s.* Aufklärung *f*, Erleuchtung *f*: (**Age of**) ♀ *hist.* (Zeitalter *n* der) Aufklärung.

en·list [ɪn'lɪst] **I** *v/t.* **1.** *Soldaten* anwerben, *Rekruten* einstellen: **~ed men** *Am.* Unteroffiziere und Mannschaften; **2.** *fig. j-n* her'anziehen, gewinnen, engagieren (**in** für): **~ s.o.'s services** j-s Dienste in Anspruch nehmen; **II** *v/i.* **3.** ⚔ sich anwerben lassen, Sol'dat werden, sich (freiwillig) melden; **4.** (**in**) mitwirken (bei), sich beteiligen (an *dat.*); **en'list·ment** [-mənt] *s.* **1.** ⚔ (An)Werbung *f*, Einstellung *f*; **2.** ⚔ *Am.* a) Eintritt *m* in den Wehrdienst, b) (Dauer *m* der) (Wehr)Dienstverpflichtung; **3.** *fig.* Gewinnung *f* (*zur Mitarbeit*), Her'an-, Hin'zuziehung *f* (*von Helfern*).

en·liv·en [ɪn'laɪvn] *v/t.* beleben, in Schwung bringen, ‚ankurbeln'.

en masse [ɑ̃ːŋ'mæs] (*Fr.*) *adv.* **1.** in Massen; **2.** im großen; **3.** zu'sammen, als Ganzes.

en·mesh [ɪn'meʃ] *v/t.* **1.** in e-m Netz fangen; **2.** *fig.* verstricken.

en·mi·ty ['enmətɪ] *s.* Feindschaft *f*, -seligkeit *f*, Haß *m*: **at ~ with** verfeindet *od.* in Feindschaft mit; **bear no ~** nichts nachtragen.

en·no·ble [ɪ'nəʊbl] *v/t.* adeln (*a. fig.*), in den Adelsstand erheben; *fig.* veredeln, erhöhen; **en'no·ble·ment** [-mənt] *s.* **1.** Erhebung *f* in den Adelsstand; **2.** *fig.* Veredelung *f*.

en·nui [ɑ̃ː'nwiː] (*Fr.*) *s.* Langeweile *f*.

e·nor·mi·ty [ɪ'nɔːmətɪ] *s.* Ungeheuerlichkeit *f*: a) Enormi'tät *f*, b) Untat *f*, Greuel *m*, Frevel *m*; **e'nor·mous** [-məs] *adj.* □ e'norm, ungeheuer(lich), gewaltig, riesig; **e'nor·mous·ness** [-məsnɪs] *s.* Riesengröße *f*.

e·nough [ɪ'nʌf] **I** *adj.* genug, ausreichend: **~ bread, bread ~** genug Brot, Brot genug; **not ~ sense** nicht genug Verstand; **this is ~** (**for us**) das genügt (uns); **I was fool ~ to believe her** ich war so dumm u. glaubte ihr; **he was not man ~** (*od.* **~ of a man**) (**to** *inf.*) er war nicht Manns genug (zu *inf.*); **that's ~ to drive me mad** das macht mich (noch) wahnsinnig; **II** *s.* Genüge *f*, genügende Menge: **have** (**quite**) **~** (völlig) genug haben; **I've had ~, thank you** danke, ich bin satt; **I have ~ of it** ich bin (*od.* habe) es satt, ‚ich bin bedient'; **~ of that!, ~ said!** genug davon!, Schluß damit!; **~ and to spare** mehr als genug; **~ is as good as a feast** allzuviel ist ungesund; **III** *adv.* genug, genügend; ganz, recht, ziemlich: **it's a good ~ story** die Geschichte ist nicht übel; **he does not sleep ~** er schläft nicht genug; **be kind ~ to help me** sei so gut und hilf mir; **oddly ~** sonderbarerweise; **safe ~** durchaus sicher; **sure ~** tatsächlich, gewiß; **true ~** nur zu wahr; **well ~** recht *od.* ziemlich *od.* ganz gut; **he could do it well ~** (**but ...**) er könnte es (zwar) recht gut(, aber ...); **you know well ~** du weißt es (ganz) genau; **that's not good ~** das reicht nicht, das lasse ich nicht gelten.

en pas·sant [ɑ̃ːm'pæsɑ̃ːŋ] (*Fr.*) *adv.* en pas'sant: a) im Vor'beigehen, b) beiläufig, neben'her, -'bei.

en·plane [ɪn'pleɪn] → **emplane**.

en·quire *etc.* → **inquire** *etc.*

en·rage [ɪn'reɪdʒ] *v/t.* wütend machen; **en'raged** [-dʒd] *adj.* wütend, aufgebracht (**at, by** über *acc.*).

en·rapt [ɪn'ræpt] *adj.* hingerissen, entzückt; **en'rap·ture** [-tʃə] *v/t.* entzücken: **~d with** hingerissen von.

en·rich [ɪn'rɪtʃ] *v/t.* **1.** (*a.* **o.s.** sich) bereichern (*a. fig.*); wertvoll(er) machen; **2.** anreichern: a) ⚙, ⚗ veredeln, b) ↗ ertragreich(er) machen, c) den Nährwert erhöhen; **3.** ausschmücken, verzieren; **4.** *fig.* a) *Geist* bereichern, b) *Wert* steigern; **en'rich·ment** [-mənt] *s.* **1.** Bereicherung *f* (*a. fig.*); **2.** ⚙, ⚗ Anreicherung *f*; **3.** *fig.* Befruchtung *f*; **4.** Ausschmückung *f*.

en·rol(l) [ɪn'rəʊl] **I** *v/t.* **1.** *j-s Namen* eintragen, -schreiben (**in** in *acc.*); *univ. j-n* immatrikulieren: **~ o.s.** → 5; **2.** a) *mst* ⚔ (an)werben, b) ⚓ anmustern, anheuern, c) *Arbeiter* einstellen: **be enrolled** eingestellt werden, *in e-e Firma* eintreten; **3.** als Mitglied aufnehmen: **~ o.s. in a society** e-r Gesellschaft beitreten; **4.** ⚖ registrieren, protokollieren; **II** *v/i.* **5.** sich einschreiben (lassen), *univ.* sich immatrikulieren: **~ for a course** e-n Kurs belegen; **en'rol(l)·ment** [-mənt] *s.* **1.** Eintragung *f*, -schreibung *f*; *univ.* Immatrikulati'on *f*; **2.** *bsd.* ⚔ Anwerbung *f*, Einstellung *f*, Aufnahme *f*; **3.** Beitrittserklärung *f*; **4.** ⚖ Re'gister *n*.

en route [ɑ̃ːn'ruːt] (*Fr.*) *adv.* unterwegs (**for** nach); auf der Reise (**from ... to** von ... nach).

ens [enz] *pl.* **entia** ['enʃɪə] (*Lat.*) *s. phls.* Ens *n*, Sein *n*, Wesen *n*.

en·sconce [ɪn'skɒns] *v/t.* **1.** (*mst* **~ o.s.** sich) verstecken, verbergen; **2.** **~ o.s.** es sich bequem machen (*in e-m Sessel etc.*).

en·sem·ble [ɑ̃ːn'sɑ̃ːmbl] (*Fr.*) *s.* **1.** *das* Ganze, Gesamteindruck *m*; **2.** ♪, *thea.* En'semble *n*; **3.** *Mode*: En'semble *n*, Kom'plet *n*.

en·shrine [ɪn'ʃraɪn] *v/t.* **1.** *in e-n Schrein* einschließen; **2.** (als Heiligtum) bewahren; **3.** als Schrein dienen für.

en·shroud [ɪn'ʃraʊd] *v/t.* ein-, verhüllen (*a. fig.*).

en·sign ['ensaɪn; *bsd.* ⚔ *u.* ⚓ 'ensn] *s.* **1.** Fahne *f*, Stan'darte *f*, ⚓ (Schiffs-) Flagge, *bsd.* (Natio'nal)Flagge *f*: **white** (**red**) **~** Flagge der brit. Kriegs- (Handels)marine; **blue ~** Flagge der brit. Flottenreserve; **2.** ['ensaɪn] *hist. Brit.* Fähnrich *m*; **3.** ['ensn] ⚓ *Am.* Leutnant *m* zur See; **4.** (Rang)Abzeichen *n*.

en·si·lage ['ensɪlɪdʒ] ↗ **I** *s.* **1.** Silierung *f*; **2.** Silo-, Gärfutter *n*; **II** *v/t.* **3.** → **en·sile** [ɪn'saɪl] *v/t.* ↗ *Futterpflanzen* silieren.

en·slave [ɪn'sleɪv] *v/t.* versklaven, zum Sklaven machen (*a. fig.*): **be ~d by** *j-m od. e-r Sache* verfallen sein; **en'slave·ment** [-mənt] *s.* **1.** Versklavung *f*, Sklave'rei *f*; **2.** *fig.* (**to**) sklavische Abhängigkeit *f* (von) *od.* Bindung (an *acc.*), Hörigkeit *f*.

en·snare [ɪn'sneə] *v/t.* **1.** *in e-r Schlinge* fangen; **2.** *fig.* berücken, bestricken, um'garnen.

en·sue [ɪn'sjuː] *v/i.* **1.** 'darauf folgen, (nach)folgen; **2.** folgen, sich ergeben (**from** aus); **en'su·ing** [-ɪŋ] *adj.* (nach-) folgend.

en·sure [ɪn'ʃʊə] *v/t.* **1.** (**against, from**) (**o.s.** sich) sichern, sicherstellen (gegen), schützen (vor); **2.** Gewähr bieten für, garantieren (*et.*, **that** daß, **s.o. being** daß j-d ist); **3.** für *et.* sorgen: **~ that** dafür sorgen, daß.

en·tail [ɪn'teɪl] **I** *v/t.* **1.** ⚖ a) in ein Erbgut umwandeln, b) als Erbgut vererben (**on** auf *acc.*): **~ed estate** Erb-, Familiengut *n*; **~ed interest** beschränktes Eigentumsrecht; **2.** *fig.* a) mit sich bringen, zur Folge haben, nach sich ziehen, verursachen, b) erforderlich machen, erfordern; **II** *s.* **3.** ⚖ a) (Über'tragung *f* als) unveräußerliches Erbgut, b) (festgelegte) Erbfolge.

en·tan·gle [ɪn'tæŋgl] *v/t.* **1.** *Haare, Garn etc.* verwirren, ‚verfitzen'; **2.** (**o.s.** sich) verwickeln, -heddern (**in** in *acc.*); **3.** *fig.* verwickeln, verstricken: **~ o.s. in s.th., become ~d in s.th.** in e-e Sache verwickelt werden; **become ~d with s.o.** sich mit j-m einlassen; **en'tan·gle·ment** [-mənt] *s.* **1.** *a. fig.* Verwicklung *f*, Verwirrung *f*, Verstrickung *f*; **2.** *fig.* Kompliziertheit *f*; **3.** Liebschaft *f*, Liai'son *f*; **4.** ⚔ Drahtverhau *m*.

en·tente [ɑ̃ːn'tɑ̃ːnt] (*Fr.*) *s.* En'tente *f*, Bündnis *n*.

en·ter ['entə] **I** *v/t.* **1.** eintreten, -fahren, -steigen, (hin'ein)gehen, (-)kommen in (*acc.*), *Haus etc.* betreten; in *ein Land* einreisen; ⚔ einrücken in (*acc.*); ⚓, 🚂 einlaufen in (*acc.*): **~ the skull** in den Schädel eindringen (*Kugel etc.*); **the idea ~ed my head** (*od.* **mind**) mir kam der Gedanke, ich hatte die Idee; **2.** sich in *et.* begeben: **~ a hospital** ein Krankenhaus aufsuchen; **3.** eintreten in (*acc.*), beitreten (*dat.*), Mitglied werden (*gen.*): **~ s.o.'s service** in j-s Dienst treten; **~ a club** e-m Klub beitreten; **~ the university** sein Studium aufnehmen; ~ ***the army*** (***the Church***) Soldat (Geistlicher) werden; ~ ***a profession*** e-n Beruf ergreifen; **4.** eintragen, -schreiben; hin'einbringen; *j-n* aufnehmen, zulassen: ~ ***one's name*** sich einschreiben *od.* anmelden; ~ ***s.o. at a school*** j-n zur Schule anmelden; ***be ~ed*** *univ.* immatrikuliert werden; **5.** † (ver)buchen, eintragen: ~ ***to s.o.'s debit*** j-m *et.* in Rechnung stellen; → ***credit*** 2; ~ ***up*** *Posten* regelrecht verbuchen; **6.** *sport* melden, nennen (***for*** für); **7.** ⚓, † *Schiff* einklarieren; *Waren beim Zollamt* deklarieren; **8.** einreichen, -bringen, geltend machen: ~ ***an action*** ⚖ e-e Klage einreichen; ~ ***a motion*** *parl.* e-n Antrag einbringen; ~ ***a protest*** Protest erheben; **II** *v/i.* **9.** (ein)treten, her'ein-, hin'einkommen, -gehen; ⚔ einrücken; eindringen: ***I don't ~ in it*** *fig.* ich habe damit nichts zu tun; ~***!*** herein!; **10.** *sport* sich melden, nennen (***for*** für, zu); **11.** *thea.* auftreten: ≈ ***Hamlet*** Hamlet tritt auf; *Zssgn mit prp.*:

en·ter| in·to *v/i.* **1.** → ***enter*** 1, 2, 3; **2.** *Vertrag, Bündnis* eingehen, schließen: ~ ***an obligation*** e-e Verpflichtung eingehen; ~ ***a partnership*** sich assoziieren; **3.** *et.* beginnen, sich beteiligen an (*dat.*), eingehen auf (*acc.*), sich einlassen auf *od.* in (*acc.*): ~ ***correspondence*** in Briefwechsel treten; ~ ***a joke*** auf e-n Scherz eingehen; → ***detail*** 1; **4.** sich hin'einversetzen in (*acc.*): ~ ***s.o.'s feelings*** sich in j-n hineinversetzen, j-s Gefühle verstehen; ~ ***the spirit*** sich in den Geist *e-r Sache* einfühlen *od.* hineinversetzen; ~ ***the spirit of the game*** mitmachen; **5.** e-e Rolle spielen bei: ***this did not ~ our plans*** das war nicht eingeplant; ~ **on** *od.* **up·on** *v/i.* **1.** ⚖ Besitz ergreifen von: ~ ***an inheritance*** e-e Erbschaft antreten; **2.** a) *Thema* anschneiden, b) sich in *ein Gespräch* einlassen; **3.** a) beginnen, in *ein* (*neues*) *Stadium od. ein neues Lebensjahr* eintreten, b) *Amt* antreten, *Laufbahn* einschlagen; **4.** in *ein neues Stadium* treten.

en·ter·ic [en'terɪk] *adj.* **1.** *anat.* en'terisch, Darm…: ~ ***fever*** (Unterleibs)Typhus *m*; **2.** ⚕ darmlöslich: ~ ***pill***; **en·ter·i·tis** [ˌentə'raɪtɪs] *s.* ⚕ 'Darmkaˌtarrh *m*, Ente'ritis *f*; **en·ter·o·gas·tri·tis** [ˌentərəʊgæ'straɪtɪs] *s.* Magen-'Darm-Kaˌtarrh *m*; **en·ter·on** ['entərɒn] *pl.* **-ter·a** [-rə] *s.* Enteron *n*, (*bsd.* Dünn)Darm *m*.

en·ter·prise ['entəpraɪz] *s.* **1.** Unter'nehmen *n*, -'nehmung *f*; **2.** † Unter'nehmen *n*, Betrieb *m*: ***free ~*** freies Unternehmertum, freie (Markt)Wirtschaft; ***free ~ economist*** Marktwirtschaftler *m*; **3.** Initia'tive *f*, Unter'nehmungsgeist *m*, -lust *f*; **'en·ter·pris·ing** [-zɪŋ] *adj.* □ **1.** unter'nehmend, unter'nehmungslustig, mit Unter'nehmungsgeist; **2.** kühn, wagemutig.

en·ter·tain [ˌentə'teɪn] **I** *v/t.* **1.** (angenehm) unter'halten, amüsieren (*a. iro.*); **2.** *j-n* gastlich aufnehmen, bewirten, einladen; **3.** *Furcht, Hoffnung etc.* hegen; **4.** *Vorschlag etc.* in Erwägung ziehen, eingehen auf (*acc.*), nähertreten (*dat.*): ~ ***an idea*** sich mit e-m Gedanken tragen; **II** *v/i.* **5.** Gäste empfangen, ein gastliches Haus führen: ***they ~ a great deal*** sie haben oft Gäste; ˌ**en·ter'tain·er** [-nə] *s.* **1.** Gastgeber(in); **2.** Unter'halter(in), *engS.* Enter'tainer (-in), Unter'haltungskünstler(in); ˌ**en·ter'tain·ing** [-nɪŋ] *adj.* □ unter'haltend, -'haltsam, amü'sant; ˌ**en·ter'tain·ment** [-mənt] *s.* **1.** Unter'haltung *f*, Belustigung *f*: ***place of ~*** Vergnügungsstätte *f*; ~ ***tax*** Vergnügungssteuer *f*; ***much to his ~*** sehr zu s-r Belustigung; **2.** (*öffentliche*) Unterhaltung, *thea. etc. a.* Enter'tainment *n*: ~ ***electronics*** Unterhaltungselektronik *f*; ~ ***industry*** Unterhaltungsindustrie *f*; ~ ***value*** Unterhaltungswert *m*; **3.** Gastfreundschaft *f*, Bewirtung *f*: ~ ***allowance*** † Aufwandsentschädigung *f*; **4.** Fest *n*, Gesellschaft *f*.

en·thral(l) [ɪn'θrɔːl] *v/t.* **1.** *fig.* bezaubern, fesseln, in s-n Bann schlagen; **2.** *obs.* unter'jochen; **en'thrall·ing** [-lɪŋ] *adj.* fesselnd, bezaubernd; **en'thral(l)·ment** [-mənt] *s.* **1.** Bezauberung *f*; **2.** *obs.* Unter'jochung *f*.

en·throne [ɪn'θrəʊn] *v/t.* auf den Thron setzen, *a. eccl. Bischof* inthronisieren: ***be ~d*** *fig.* thronen; **en'throne·ment** [-mənt] *s.* Inthronisati'on *f*.

en·thuse [ɪn'θjuːz] F **I** *v/t.* begeistern; **II** *v/i.* (***about***) begeistert sein (von), schwärmen (für, von); **en'thu·si·asm** [-zɪæzəm] *s.* **1.** Enthusi'asmus *m*, Begeisterung *f* (***for*** für, ***about*** über *acc.*); **2.** Schwärme'rei *f*; **en'thu·si·ast** [-zɪæst] *s.* **1.** Enthusi'ast(in); **2.** Schwärmer(in); **en·thu·si·as·tic** [ɪnˌθjuːzɪ'æstɪk] *adj.* (□ ***~ally***) enthusi'astisch, begeistert (***about***, ***over*** über *acc.*): ***become*** (*od.* ***get***) ~ in Begeisterung geraten.

en·tice [ɪn'taɪs] *v/t.* **1.** locken: ~ ***s.o. away*** a) j-n weglocken (***from*** von), b) † j-n abwerben; ~ ***s.o.'s wife away*** j-m s-e Frau abspenstig machen; **2.** verlocken, -leiten, -führen (***into s.th.*** zu et., ***to do*** *od.* ***into doing*** zu tun); **en'tice·ment** [-mənt] *s.* **1.** (Ver-)Lockung *f*, (An)Reiz *m*; **2.** Verführung *f*, -leitung *f*; **en'tic·ing** [-sɪŋ] *adj.* □ verlockend, verführerisch.

en·tire [ɪn'taɪə] **I** *adj.* □ → ***entirely***; **1.** ganz, völlig, vollkommen, vollständig, vollzählig, kom'plett, Gesamt…; **2.** ganz, unversehrt, unbeschädigt; **3.** voll, ungeschmälert, uneingeschränkt: ***he enjoys my ~ confidence***; **4.** nicht kastriert: ~ ***horse*** Hengst *m*; **II** *s.* **5.** *das* Ganze; **6.** nicht kastriertes Pferd, Hengst *m*; **7.** ✉ Ganzsache *f*; **en'tire·ly** [-lɪ] *adv.* **1.** völlig, gänzlich, ganz u. gar; **2.** ausschließlich: ***it is ~ his fault***; **en'tire·ty** [-tɪ] *s. das* Ganze, Ganzheit *f*, Gesamtheit *f*: ***in its ~*** in s-r Gesamtheit, als Ganzes.

en·ti·tle [ɪn'taɪtl] *v/t.* **1.** *Buch etc.* betiteln: ***~d*** *Buch etc.* mit dem Titel …; **2.** *j-n* anreden, titulieren; **3.** (***to***) *j-n* berechtigen (zu), *j-m* ein Anrecht geben (auf *acc.*): ***be ~d to*** berechtigt sein zu, e-n (Rechts)Anspruch haben auf (*acc.*); ***~d to vote*** stimm-, wahlberechtigt; **en'ti·tle·ment** [-mənt] *s.* (berechtigter) Anspruch; zustehender Betrag.

en·ti·ty ['entətɪ] *s.* **1.** Dasein *n*; **2.** Wesen *n*, Ding *n*; **3.** ⚖ 'Rechtsperˌsönlichkeit *f*: ***legal ~*** juristische Person.

en·tomb [ɪn'tuːm] *v/t.* **1.** begraben, beerdigen; **2.** verschütten, lebendig begraben; **en'tomb·ment** [-mənt] *s.* Begräbnis *n*.

en·to·mo·log·i·cal [ˌentəmə'lɒdʒɪk(l)] *adj.* □ entomo'logisch, Insekten…; **en·to·mol·o·gist** [ˌentəʊ'mɒlədʒɪst] *s.* Entomo'loge *m*; **en·to·mol·o·gy** [ˌentəʊ'mɒlədʒɪ] *s.* Entomolo'gie *f*, In'sektenkunde *f*.

en·tou·rage [ˌɒntʊ'rɑːʒ] (*Fr.*) *s.* Entou'rage *f*: a) Um'gebung *f*, b) Gefolge *n*.

en·to·zo·on [ˌentəʊ'zəʊɒn] *pl.* **-zo·a** [-ə] *s. zo.* Ento'zoon *n* (*Parasit*).

entr'acte ['ɒntrækt] (*Fr.*) *s. thea.* Zwischenakt *m*, -spiel *n*.

en·trails ['entreɪlz] *s. pl.* **1.** *anat.* Eingeweide *pl.*; **2.** *fig. das* Innere.

en·train [ɪn'treɪn] 🚂 **I** *v/i.* einsteigen; **II** *v/t.* verladen.

en·trance[1] ['entrəns] *s.* **1.** a) Eintreten *n*, Eintritt *m*, b) 🚂, ⚓ Einlaufen *n*, Einfahrt *f*, c) ✈ Einflug *m*: ~ ***duty*** † Eingangszoll *m*; ***make one's ~*** eintreten, erscheinen (→ 4); **2.** Ein-, Zugang *m*; Zufahrt *f*, (*a.* Hafen)Einfahrt *f*: ~ ***hall*** (Eingangs-, Vor)Halle *f*, Hausflur *m*; **3.** Einlaß *m*, Ein-, Zutritt *m*: ~ ***fee*** a) Eintritt(sgeld *n*) *m*, b) Aufnahmegebühr *f*; ~ ***examination*** Aufnahmeprüfung *f*; ***no ~!*** Zutritt verboten!; **4.** *thea.* Auftritt *m*: ***make one's ~*** auftreten; **5.** (***on***, ***upon***) Antritt *m* (*e-s Amtes*, *e-r Erbschaft etc.*); **6.** *fig.* (***to***) Beginn *m* (*gen.*), Einstieg *m* (in *acc.*).

en·trance[2] [ɪn'trɑːns] *v/t.* in Verzückung versetzen, hinreißen: ***~d*** ver-, entzückt, hingerissen; ***~d with joy*** freudetrunken; **en'trance·ment** [-mənt] *s.* Verzückung *f*; **en'tranc·ing** [-sɪŋ] *adj.* hinreißend, bezaubernd.

en·trant ['entrənt] *s.* **1.** Eintretende(r *m*) *f*; **2.** neues Mitglied; **3.** Berufsanfänger(in) (***to*** in *dat.*); **4.** *bsd. sport* Teilnehmer(in), Konkur'rent(in), *a.* Bewerber(in).

en·trap [ɪn'træp] *v/t.* **1.** (in e-r Falle) fangen; **2.** verführen, verleiten (***into doing*** zu tun).

en·treat [ɪn'triːt] *v/t.* **1.** *j-n* dringend bitten *od.* ersuchen, anflehen; **2.** *et.* erflehen; **3.** *obs. od. bibl. j-n* behandeln; **en'treat·ing·ly** [-ɪŋlɪ] *adv.* flehentlich; **en'treat·y** [-tɪ] *s.* dringende Bitte, Flehen *n*.

en·trée ['ɒntreɪ] (*Fr.*) *s.* **1.** *bsd. fig.* Zutritt *m* (***into*** zu); **2.** *Küche*: a) En'tree *n*, Zwischengericht *n*, b) *Am.* Hauptgericht *n*; **3.** ♪ En'tree *n*.

en·tre·mets ['ɒntrəmeɪ; *pl.* 'ɒntrəmeɪz] (*Fr.*) *s.* a) Zwischengericht *n*, b) Süßspeise *f*.

en·trench [ɪn'trentʃ] *v/t.* ⚔ mit Schützengräben durch'ziehen, befestigen: ~ ***o.s.*** sich verschanzen *od.* festsetzen (*beide a. fig.*); ***~ed*** *fig.* eingewurzelt, verwurzelt; **en'trench·ment** [-mənt] *s.* ⚔ **1.** Verschanzung *f*; **2.** *pl.* Schützengräben *pl.*

en·tre·pôt ['ɒntrəpəʊ] (*Fr.*) *s.* † **1.** Lager-, Stapelplatz *m*; **2.** (Waren-, Zoll-) Niederlage *f*.

en·tre·pre·neur [ˌɒntrəprə'nɜː] (*Fr.*) *s.* **1.** † Unter'nehmer *m*; **2.** *Am.* Veranstalter *m*; ˌ**en·tre·pre'neur·i·al** [-ɜːrɪəl] *adj.* † unter'nehmerisch, Unternehmer…

en·tre·sol ['ɒntrəsɒl] *(Fr.)* *s.* ⚠ Zwischen-, Halbgeschoß *n.*
en·trust [ɪn'trʌst] *v/t.* **1.** anvertrauen (***to*** *dat.*); **2.** *j-n* betrauen (***with s.th.*** mit et.).
en·try ['entrɪ] *s.* **1.** Zugang *m*, Zutritt *m*, Einreise *f*: **~ *permit*** Einreisegenehmigung *f*; **~ *visa*** Einreisevisum *n*; ***no ~!*** Kein Zutritt!, *mot.* Keine Einfahrt!; **2.** Eintritt *m*, -gang *m*, -fahrt *f*, -zug *m*, -rücken *n*; **3.** Eingang(stür *f*) *m*, Einfahrt(stor *n*) *f*; (Eingangs)Halle *f*; **4.** *thea.* Auftritt *m*; **5.** (Amts-, Dienst)Antritt *m*: **~ *into office*** (***service***); **6.** ⚖ a) Besitzantritt *m*, -ergreifung *f* (***upon*** *gen.*), b) Eindringen *n*, -bruch *m*; **7.** *fig.* Beitritt *m* (***to, into*** zu); **8.** ✝, ⚓ Einklarierung *f*: **~ *inwards*** Einfuhrdeklaration *f*; **9.** Eintragung *f*, Vermerk *m*; **10.** ✝ a) Buchung *f*: ***credit*** **~** Gutschrift *f*; ***debit*** **~** Lastschrift *f*; ***make an ~*** (***of***) (*et.*) buchen, b) Posten *m*, c) Eingang *m* (*von Geldern*); **11.** Stichwort *n* (*Lexikon*); **12.** *bsd. sport* a) Meldung *f*, Nennung *f*, Teilnahme *f*: **~ *form*** (An)Meldeformular *n*; **~ *fee*** Nenngebühr *f*, Startgeld *n*, b) → ***entrant*** 4; '**~·phone** *s.* Sprechanlage *f*.
en·twine [ɪn'twaɪn] *v/t.* **1.** um'schlingen, um'winden, (ver)flechten (*a. fig.*); **~*d letters*** verschlungene Buchstaben; **2.** winden, schlingen (***about*** um).
en·twist [ɪn'twɪst] *v/t.* (ver)flechten, um'winden, verknüpfen.
e·nu·cle·ate [ɪ'nju:klɪeɪt] *v/t.* **1.** ⚕ *Tumor* ausschälen; **2.** *fig.* erläutern, deutlich machen.
e·nu·mer·ate [ɪ'nju:məreɪt] *v/t.* **1.** aufzählen; **2.** spezifizieren; **e·nu·mer·a·tion** [ɪˌnju:mə'reɪʃn] *s.* **1.** Aufzählung *f*; **2.** Liste *f*, Verzeichnis *n*; **e'nu·mer·a·tor** [-tə] *s.* Zähler *m* (*bei Volkszählungen*).
e·nun·ci·ate [ɪ'nʌnsɪeɪt] *v/t.* **1.** (deutlich) ausdrücken, -sprechen; **2.** behaupten, erklären, formulieren; *Grundsatz* aufstellen; **e·nun·ci·a·tion** [ɪˌnʌnsɪ'eɪʃn] *s.* **1.** Ausdruck *m*; Ausdrucks-, Vortragsweise *f*; **2.** Erklärung *f*, Verkündung *f*; Aufstellung *f* (*e-s Grundsatzes*); **e'nun·ci·a·tive** [-nʃɪətɪv] *adj.*: ***be ~ of s.th.*** et. ausdrücken.
en·ure → ***inure***.
en·vel·op [ɪn'veləp] **I** *v/t.* **1.** einwickeln, -schlagen, (ein)hüllen (***in*** in *acc.*); **2.** *oft fig.* um-, ver'hüllen, um'geben; **3.** ⚔ um'fassen, um'klammern; **II** *s.* **4.** *Am.* → **en·ve·lope** ['envələʊp] *s.* **1.** Decke *f*, Hülle *f* (*a. anat.*), 'Umschlag *m*; **2.** 'Briefˌumschlag *m*; **3.** ✈ (Bal'lon)Hülle *f*; **4.** ⚘ Kelch *m*; **en'vel·op·ment** [-mənt] *s.* **1.** Um'hüllung *f*, Hülle *f*; **2.** ⚔ Um'fassung(sangriff *m*) *f*, Um'klammerung *f*.
en·ven·om [ɪn'venəm] *v/t.* **1.** vergiften (*a. fig.*); **2.** *fig.* a) verschärfen, b) mit Haß erfüllen.
en·vi·a·ble ['envɪəbl] *adj.* ☐ beneidenswert, zu beneiden(d); '**en·vi·er** [-vɪə] *s.* Neider(in); '**en·vi·ous** [-vɪəs] *adj.* ☐ (***of***) neidisch (auf *acc.*), 'mißgünstig (gegen): ***be ~ of s.o. because of*** j-n beneiden um.
en·vi·ron [ɪn'vaɪərən] *v/t.* um'geben (*a. fig.*); **en'vi·ron·ment** [-mənt] *s.* **1.** *a.* **~*s*** *pl.* Um'gebung *f e-s Ortes*; **2.** *biol.*, *sociol.* Um'gebung *f*, 'Umwelt *f*, Mili'eu *n* (*a.* ⚗): **~ *policy*** Umweltpolitik *f*; **en·vi·ron·men·tal** [ɪnˌvaɪərən'mentl] *adj.* ☐ *biol.*, *psych.* Milieu..., Umwelt(s)...: **~ *pollution*** Umweltverschmutzung *f*; **~ *protection*** Umweltschutz *m*; **en·vi·ron·men·tal·ism** [ɪnˌvaɪərən'mentəlɪzəm] *s.* **1.** 'Umweltschutz(bewegung *f*) *m*; **2.** *sociol.* Environmenta'lismus *m*; **en·vi·ron·men·tal·ist** [ɪnˌvaɪərən'mentəlɪst] *s.* 'Umweltschützer(in); **en·vi·ron·men·tal·ly** [ɪnˌvaɪərən'mentəlɪ] *adv.* in bezug auf *od.* durch die Umwelt: **~ *beneficial*** (***harmful***) umweltfreundlich (-feindlich); **en·vi·rons** [ɪn'vaɪərənz] *s. pl.* Um'gebung *f*, 'Umgegend *f*.
en·vis·age [ɪn'vɪzɪdʒ] *v/t.* **1.** in Aussicht nehmen, ins Auge fassen, gedenken (***doing*** *et.* zu tun); **2.** sich *et.* vorstellen; **3.** *j-n, et.* begreifen (***as*** als).
en·vi·sion [ɪn'vɪʒn] *v/t.* sich *et.* vorstellen.
en·voy[1] ['envɔɪ] *s.* Zueignungs-, Schlußstrophe *f* (*e-s Gedichts*).
en·voy[2] ['envɔɪ] *s.* **1.** *pol.* Gesandte(r) *m*; **2.** Abgesandte(r) *m*, Be'vollmächtigte(r) *m*.
en·vy ['envɪ] **I** *s.* **1.** (***of***) Neid *m* (auf *acc.*), 'Mißgunst *f* (gegen): ***be eaten up with ~*** vor Neid platzen; → ***green*** 1; **2.** Gegenstand *m* des Neides: ***his car is the ~ of all*** alle beneiden ihn um sein Auto; **II** *v/t.* **3.** *j-n* (um *et.*) beneiden: ***I ~ (him) his car*** ich beneide ihn um sein Auto; **4.** *j-m et.* miß'gönnen.
en·wrap [ɪn'ræp] → ***wrap*** I.
en·zyme ['enzaɪm] *s.* ⚗ En'zym *n*, Fer'ment *n*.
e·o·cene ['i:əʊsi:n] *s. geol.* Eo'zän *n*; **e·o·lith·ic** [ˌi:əʊ'lɪθɪk] *adj. geol.* eo'lithisch.
e·on → ***aeon***.
ep·au·let(te) ['epəʊlet] *s.* ⚔ Epau'lette *f*, Achselschnur *f*, -stück *n*.
é·pée ['epeɪ] *(Fr.)* *s. fenc.* Degen *m*; **é·pee·ist** ['epeɪɪst] *s.* Degenfechter *m*.
ep·en·the·sis [e'penθɪsɪs] *s. ling.* Epen'these *f*, Lauteinfügung *f*.
e·pergne [ɪ'pɜ:n] *(Fr.)* *s.* Tafelaufsatz *m*.
e·phed·rin(e) [ɪ'fedrɪn; ⚗ 'efɪdri:n] *s.* ⚗ Ephe'drin *n*.
e·phem·er·a [ɪ'femərə] *s.* **1.** *zo. u. fig.* Eintagsfliege *f*; **2.** *pl. von* ***ephemeron***; **e'phem·er·al** [-rəl] *adj.* ephe'mer: a) eintägig, b) *fig.* flüchtig, kurzlebig; **e'phem·er·on** [-rɒn] *pl.* **-a** [-ə], **-ons** *s. zo. u. fig.* Eintagsfliege *f*.
E·phe·sian [ɪ'fi:ʒjən] *s.* **1.** 'Epheser(in); **2.** *pl. bibl.* (Brief *m* des Paulus an die) 'Epheser *pl.*
ep·ic ['epɪk] **I** *adj.* (☐ **~*ally***) **1.** episch: **~ *poem*** Epos *n*; **2.** *fig.* heldenhaft, he'roisch, Helden...: **~ *laughter*** homerisches Gelächter; **II** *s.* **3.** Epos *n*, Heldengedicht *n*; **4.** *allg.* episches Werk.
ep·i·cene ['epɪsi:n] *adj. ling. u. fig.* beiderlei Geschlechts.
ep·i·cen·ter *Am.*, **ep·i·cen·tre** ['epɪsentə] *Brit.*, **ep·i·cen·trum** [ˌepɪ'sentrəm] *s.* **1.** Epi'zentrum *n* (*Gebiet über dem Erdbebenherd*); **2.** *fig.* Mittelpunkt *m*.
ep·i·cure ['epɪˌkjʊə] *s.* Genießer *m*, Genußmensch *m*; Feinschmecker *m*; **ep·i·cu·re·an** [ˌepɪkjʊə'ri:ən] **I** *adj.* **1.** ♀ *phls.* epiku'reisch; **2.** a) genußsüchtig, schwelgerisch, b) feinschmeckerisch; **II** *s.* **3.** ♀ *phls.* Epiku'reer *m*; **4.** → ***epicure***; '**ep·i·cur·ism** [-kjʊərɪzəm] *s.* **1.** ♀ *phls.* Epikure'ismus *m*; **2.** Genußsucht *f*.
ep·i·cy·cle ['epɪsaɪkl] *s.* ⚩, *ast.* Epi'zykel *m*; **ep·i·cy·clic** [ˌepɪ'saɪklɪk] *adj.* epi'zyklisch: **~ *gear*** ⚙ Planetengetriebe *n*; **ep·i·cy·cloid** [ˌepɪ'saɪklɔɪd] *s.* ⚩ Epizyklo'ide *f*.
ep·i·dem·ic [ˌepɪ'demɪk] **I** *adj.* (☐ **~*ally***) ⚕ epi'demisch, seuchenartig, *fig. a.* grassierend; **II** *s.* ⚕ Epide'mie *f*, Seuche *f* (*beide a. fig.*); ˌ**ep·i'dem·i·cal** [-kl] → ***epidemic*** I; **ep·i·de·mi·ol·o·gy** [ˌepɪdi:mɪ'ɒlədʒɪ] *s.* ⚕ Epidemiolo'gie *f*.
ep·i·der·mis [ˌepɪ'dɜ:mɪs] *s. anat.* Epi'dermis *f*, Oberhaut *f*.
ep·i·gas·tri·um [ˌepɪ'gæstrɪəm] *s. anat.* Epi'gastrium *n*, Oberbauchgegend *f*, Magengrube *f*.
ep·i·glot·tis [ˌepɪ'glɒtɪs] *s. anat.* Epi'glottis *f*, Kehldeckel *m*.
ep·i·gone ['epɪgəʊn] *s.* Epi'gone *m*.
ep·i·gram ['epɪgræm] *s.* Epi'gramm *n*, Sinngedicht *n*, -spruch *m*; **ep·i·gram·mat·ic** [ˌepɪgrə'mætɪk] *adj.* (☐ **~*ally***) **1.** epigram'matisch; **2.** kurz u. treffend, scharf pointiert; **ep·i·gram·ma·tist** [ˌepɪ'græmətɪst] *s.* Epigram'matiker *m*; **ep·i·gram·ma·tize** [ˌepɪ'græmətaɪz] **I** *v/t.* **1.** kurz u. treffend formulieren; **2.** ein Epi'gramm verfassen über *od.* auf (*acc.*); **II** *v/i.* **3.** Epi'gramme verfassen.
ep·i·graph ['epɪgrɑ:f] *s.* **1.** Epi'graph *n*, Inschrift *f*; **2.** Sinnspruch *m*, Motto *n*; **ep·i·graph·ic** [ˌepɪ'græfɪk] *adj.* epi'graphisch; **e·pig·ra·phist** [e'pɪgrəfɪst] *s.* Epi'graphiker *m*, Inschriftenforscher *m*.
ep·i·lep·sy ['epɪlepsɪ] *s.* ⚕ Epilep'sie *f*; **ep·i·lep·tic** [ˌepɪ'leptɪk] **I** *adj.* epi'leptisch; **II** *s.* Epi'leptiker(in).
ep·i·logue, *Am. a.* **ep·i·log** ['epɪlɒg] *s.* **1.** Epi'log *m*: a) Nachwort *n*, b) *thea.* Schlußrede *f*, c) *fig.* Ausklang *m*, Nachspiel *n*, -lese *f*; **2.** *Radio*, *TV*: (Wort *n* zum) Tagesausklang *m*.
E·piph·a·ny [ɪ'pɪfənɪ] *s. eccl.* **1.** Epi'phanias *n*, Drei'königsfest *n*; **2.** ♀ Epipha'nie *f* (*göttliche Erscheinung*).
e·pis·co·pa·cy [ɪ'pɪskəpəsɪ] *s. eccl.* Episko'pat *m*, *n*: a) bischöfliche Verfassung, b) Gesamtheit *f* der Bischöfe, c) Amtstätigkeit *f* e-s Bischofs, d) Bischofsamt *n*, -würde *f*; **e'pis·co·pal** [-pl] *adj.* ☐ *eccl.* bischöflich, Bischofs...: ♀ ***Church*** Episkopalkirche *f*; **e·pis·co·pa·li·an** [ɪˌpɪskəʊ'peɪljən] **I** *adj.* **1.** bischöflich; **2.** zu e-r Episko'palkirche gehörig; **II** *s.* **3.** Mitglied *n* e-r Episko'palkirche; **e'pis·co·pate** [-kəʊpət] *s. eccl.* Episko'pat *m*, *n*: a) → ***episcopacy*** b *u.* d, b) Bistum *n*.
ep·i·sode ['epɪsəʊd] *s. allg.* Epi'sode *f*: a) Neben-, Zwischenhandlung *f* (*im Drama etc.*), eingeflochtene Erzählung, b) (Neben)Ereignis *n*, Vorfall *m*, Erlebnis *n*, c) ♪ Zwischenspiel *n*; **ep·i·sod·ic**, **ep·i·sod·i·cal** [ˌepɪ'sɒdɪk(l)] *adj.* ☐ epi'sodisch.
e·pis·te·mol·o·gy [eˌpɪsti:'mɒlədʒɪ] *s. phls.* Er'kenntnistheoˌrie *f*.
e·pis·tle [ɪ'pɪsl] *s.* **1.** E'pistel *f*, Sendschreiben *n*; **2.** ♀ a) *bibl.* (*Römer- etc.*) Brief *m*, b) *eccl.* E'pistel *f* (*Auszug aus* a); **3.** E'pistel *f*, (*bsd.* langer) Brief;

e'pis·to·lar·y [-stələrɪ] *adj.* Brief…

ep·i·style ['epɪstaɪl] *s.* △ Epi'styl *n*, Tragbalken *m*.

ep·i·taph ['epɪtɑːf] *s.* **1.** Epi'taph *n*, Grabschrift *f*; **2.** Totengedicht *n*.

ep·i·the·li·um [ˌepɪ'θiːljəm] *pl.* **-ums** *od.* **-a** [-ə] *s. anat.* Epi'thel *n*.

ep·i·thet ['epɪθet] *s.* **1.** E'pitheton *n*, Beiwort *n*, Attri'but *n*; **2.** Beiname *m*.

e·pit·o·me [ɪ'pɪtəmɪ] *s.* **1.** Auszug *m*, Abriß *m*, (kurze) Inhaltsangabe *od.* Darstellung: ***in ~*** a) auszugsweise, b) in gedrängter Form; **2.** *fig.* (***of***) a) kleines Gegenstück (zu), Minia'tur *f* (*gen.*), b) Verkörperung *f* (*gen.*); **e'pit·o·mize** [-maɪz] *v/t.* e-n Auszug machen aus, *et.* kurz darstellen *od.* ausdrücken.

ep·i·zo·on [ˌepɪ'zəʊɒn] *pl.* **-a** [-ə] *s. zo.* Epi'zoon *n*; **ep·i·zo·ot·ic** [ˌepɪzəʊ'ɒtɪk] *s. vet.* Epizoo'tie *f* (*Tierseuche*).

e·poch ['iːpɒk] *s.* **1.** E'poche *f* (*a. geol. u. ast.*), Zeitalter *n*, -abschnitt *m*: ***this marks an ~*** dies ist ein Markstein *od.* Wendepunkt (*in der Geschichte*); **ep·och·al** ['epɒkl] *adj.* epo'chal: a) Epochen…, b) → **'e·poch-ˌmak·ing** *adj.* e'pochemachend, bahnbrechend.

ep·o·nym ['epəʊnɪm] *s.* Epo'nym *n* (*Gattungsbezeichnung, die auf e-n Personennamen zurückgeht*).

ep·o·pee ['epəʊpiː] *s.* **1.** → ***epos***; **2.** epische Dichtung.

ep·os ['epɒs] *s.* **1.** Epos *n*, Heldengedicht *n*; **2.** (*mündlich überlieferte*) epische Dichtung.

Ep·som salt ['epsəm] *s., oft pl. sg. konstr.* Epsomer Bittersalz *n*.

eq·ua·bil·i·ty [ˌekwə'bɪlətɪ] *s.* **1.** Gleichmäßigkeit *f*; **2.** Gleichmut *m*; **eq·ua·ble** ['ekwəbl] *adj.* □ **1.** gleichförmig, -mäßig; **2.** ausgeglichen, gleichmütig, gelassen.

e·qual ['iːkwəl] **I** *adj.* □ → ***equally***; **1.** gleich: ***be ~ to*** gleich sein, gleichen (*dat.*) (→ *a.* 2); ***of ~ size***, ***~ in size*** gleich groß; ***with ~ courage*** mit demselben Mut; ***not ~ to*** geringer als; ***other things being ~*** unter sonst gleichen Umständen; **2.** entsprechend: ***~ to the demand***; ***be ~ to*** gleichkommen (*dat.*); → 1; ***~ to new*** wie neu; **3.** fähig, im'stande, gewachsen: ***~ to do*** fähig zu tun; ***~ to a task*** (***the occasion***) e-r Aufgabe (der Sache) gewachsen; **4.** aufgelegt, geneigt (***to*** *dat. od.* zu): ***~ to a cup of tea*** e-r Tasse Tee nicht abgeneigt; **5.** gleichmäßig; **6.** gleichberechtigt, -wertig, ebenbürtig: ***on ~ terms*** a) unter gleichen Bedingungen, b) auf gleicher Stufe stehend (***with*** mit); ***~ opportunities*** Chancengleichheit *f*; ***~ rights for women*** Gleichberechtigung *f* der Frau; **7.** gleichmütig, gelassen: ***~ mind*** Gleichmut *m*; **II** *s.* **8.** Gleichgestellte(r *m*) *f*, Ebenbürtige(r *m*) *f*: ***your ~s*** deinesgleichen; ***~s in age*** Altersgenossen; ***he has no ~***, ***he is without ~*** er hat nicht *od.* sucht seinesgleichen; ***be the ~ of s.o.*** j-m ebenbürtig sein; **III** *v/t.* **9.** gleichen (*dat.*), gleichkommen (***in*** an *dat.*): ***not to be ~(l)ed*** ohnegleichen (sein).

e·qual·i·tar·i·an [ɪˌkwɒlɪ'teərɪən] *etc.* → ***egalitarian*** *etc.*

e·qual·i·ty [iː'kwɒlətɪ] *s.* Gleichheit *f*: ***~ (of rights)*** Gleichberechtigung *f*; ***~ of opportunity*** Chancengleichheit *f*; ***~ of votes*** Stimmengleichheit *f*; ***be on an ~ with*** a) auf gleicher Stufe stehen mit (*j-m*), b) gleichbedeutend sein mit (*et.*); ***~ sign***, ***sign of ~*** ⟂ Gleichheitszeichen *n*; **e·qual·i·za·tion** [ˌiːkwəlaɪ'zeɪʃn] *s.* **1.** Gleichstellung *f*, -machung *f*; **2.** *bsd.* † Ausgleich(ung *f*) *m*: ***~ fund*** Ausgleichsfonds *m*; **3.** a) ⚙ Abgleich *m*, b) ϟ, *phot.* Entzerrung *f*.

e·qual·ize ['iːkwəlaɪz] **I** *v/t.* **1.** gleichmachen, -stellen, -setzen, angleichen; **2.** ausgleichen, kompensieren; **3.** a) ⚙ abgleichen, b) ϟ, *phot.* entzerren; **II** *v/i.* **4.** *sport* ausgleichen, den Ausgleich erzielen; **'e·qual·iz·er** [-zə] *s.* **1.** ⚙ Stabili'sator *m*; **2.** ϟ Entzerrer *m*; **3.** *sport* Ausgleichstreffer *m od.* -punkt *m*; **4.** *sl.* Schießeisen *n*; **'e·qual·ly** [-əlɪ] *adv.* ebenso, gleich(ermaßen), in gleicher Weise.

e·qua·nim·i·ty [ˌekwə'nɪmətɪ] *s.* Gleichmut *m*, Gelassenheit *f*.

e·quate [ɪ'kweɪt] **I** *v/t.* **1.** ausgleichen; **2.** *j-n, et.* gleichstellen, -setzen (***to***, ***with*** *dat.*); **3.** ⟂ in die Form e-r Gleichung bringen; **4.** als gleich(wertig) ansehen *od.* behandeln; **II** *v/i.* **5.** gleichen, entsprechen (***with*** *dat.*); **e'quat·ed** [-tɪd] *adj.* † Staffel…: ***~ calculation of interest*** Staffelzinsrechnung *f*; **e'qua·tion** [-eɪʃn] *s.* **1.** Ausgleich *m*; **2.** Gleichheit *f*; **3.** ⟂, ⚗, *ast.* Gleichung *f*: ***~ formula*** Gleichungsformel *f*; **4.** *sociol.* Ge'samtkomˌplex *m* der Fak'toren u. Mo'tive menschlichen Verhaltens; **e'qua·tor** [-tə] *s.* Ä'quator *m*; **e·qua·to·ri·al** [ˌekwə'tɔːrɪəl] *adj.* □ äquatori'al.

eq·uer·ry ['ekwərɪ; ɪ'kwerɪ] *s. Brit.* **1.** königlicher Stallmeister; **2.** per'sönlicher Diener (*e-s Mitglieds der königlichen Familie*).

e·ques·tri·an [ɪ'kwestrɪən] **I** *adj.* Reit(er)…: ***~ sports*** Reitsport *m*; ***~ statue*** Reiterstandbild *n*; **II** *s.* (Kunst)Reiter (-in).

equi- [iːkwɪ] *in Zssgn* gleich.

ˌe·quiˌ'an·gu·lar *adj.* ⟂ gleichwink(e)lig; **ˌ~'dis·tant** *adj.* □ gleich weit entfernt, in gleichem Abstand (***from*** von); **ˌ~'lat·er·al** *bsd.* ⟂ **I** *adj.* gleichseitig: ***~ triangle***; **II** *s.* gleichseitige Fi'gur.

e·qui·li·brate [ˌiːkwɪ'laɪbreɪt] *v/t.* **1.** ins Gleichgewicht bringen (*a. fig.*); **2.** ⚙ auswuchten; **3.** ϟ abgleichen; **e·qui·li·bra·tion** [ˌiːkwɪlaɪ'breɪʃn] *s.* **1.** Gleichgewicht *n*; **2.** Herstellung *f* des Gleichgewichts; **e·quil·i·brist** [iː'kwɪlɪbrɪst] *s.* Äquili'brist(in), *bsd.* Seiltänzer(in); **ˌe·qui'lib·ri·um** [-'lɪbrɪəm] *s. phys.* Gleichgewicht *n* (*a. fig.*), Ba'lance *f*.

e·quine ['iːkwaɪn] *adj.* Pferde…

e·qui·noc·tial [ˌiːkwɪ'nɒkʃl] **I** *adj.* **1.** Äquinoktial…, die Tagund'nachtgleiche betreffend: ***~ point*** → ***equinox*** 2; **II** *s.* **2.** *a.* ***~ circle*** *od.* ***line*** 'Himmelsäˌquator *m*; **3.** *pl.* → ***~ gale*** *s.* Äquinokti'alsturm *m*.

e·qui·nox ['iːkwɪnɒks] *s.* **1.** Äqui'noktium *n*, Tagund'nachtgleiche *f*: ***vernal ~*** Frühlingsäquinoktium; **2.** Äquinokti'alpunkt *m*.

e·quip [ɪ'kwɪp] *v/t.* **1.** ausrüsten, -statten (***with*** mit) (*a.* ⚙, ⚔, ⚓), *Klinik etc.* einrichten; **2.** *fig.* ausrüsten (***with*** mit), *j-m* das (geistige) Rüstzeug geben (***for*** für); **eq·ui·page** ['ekwɪpɪdʒ] *s.* **1.** Ausrüstung *f* (*a.* ⚔, ⚓); **2.** *obs.* Gebrauchsgegenstände *pl.*; **3.** Equi'page *f*, Kutsche *f*; **e'quip·ment** [-mənt] *s.* **1.** ⚔, ⚓ Ausrüstung *f*; **2.** a) *a.* ⚙ Ausrüstung *f*, -stattung *f*, b) *mst pl.* Ausrüstung(sgegenstände *pl.*) *f*, Materi'al *n*, c) ⚙ Einrichtung *f*, (Betriebs)Anlage(n *pl.*) *f*, Ma'schine(n *pl.*) *f*, Gerät *n*, Appara'tur *f*, d) 🚃 *Am.* rollendes Materi'al; **3.** *fig.* (geistiges) Rüstzeug.

e·qui·poise ['ekwɪpɔɪz] **I** *s.* **1.** Gleichgewicht *n* (*a. fig.*); **2.** *fig.* Gegengewicht *n* (***to*** zu); **II** *v/t.* **3.** im Gleichgewicht halten; **4.** ein Gegengewicht bilden zu.

eq·ui·ta·ble ['ekwɪtəbl] *adj.* □ **1.** gerecht, (recht u.) billig; **2.** 'unparˌteiisch; **3.** ⚖ a) auf dem Billigkeitsrecht beruhend, b) billigkeitsgerichtlich: ***~ mortgage*** † Hypothek *f* nach dem Billigkeitsrecht; **'eq·ui·ta·ble·ness** [-nɪs] → ***equity*** 1; **'eq·ui·ty** [-tɪ] *s.* **1.** Billigkeit *f*, Gerechtigkeit *f*, 'Unparˌteilichkeit *f*: ***in ~*** billiger-, gerechterweise; **2.** ⚖ a) (*ungeschriebenes*) Billigkeitsrecht: ***Court of ⁓*** Billigkeitsgericht *n*, b) Anspruch *m* nach dem Billigkeitsrecht; **3.** ⚖ Wert *m* nach Abzug aller Belastungen, reiner Wert (*e-s Hauses etc.*); **4.** † a) *a.* ***~ capital*** Eigenkapital *n* (*e-r Gesellschaft*), b) *a.* ***~ security*** Dividendenpapier *n*; **5.** ⁓ *Brit.* Gewerkschaft *f* der Schauspieler.

e·quiv·a·lence [ɪ'kwɪvələns] *s.* Gleichwertigkeit *f* (*a.* ⚗); **e'quiv·a·lent** [-nt] **I** *adj.* □ **1.** gleichwertig, -bedeutend, entsprechend: ***be ~ to*** gleichkommen, entsprechen (*dat.*), den gleichen Wert haben wie; **2.** ⚗, ⟂ gleichwertig, äquiva'lent; **II** *s.* **3.** Gegenwert *m* (***of*** von *od. gen.*); gleiche Menge; **4.** Gegen-, Seitenstück *n* (***of***, ***to*** zu); **5.** *genaue* Entsprechung, Äquiva'lent.

e·quiv·o·cal [ɪ'kwɪvəkl] *adj.* □ **1.** zweideutig, doppelsinnig; **2.** ungewiß, zweifelhaft; **3.** fragwürdig, verdächtig; **e'quiv·o·cal·ness** [-nɪs] *s.* Zweideutigkeit *f*; **e'quiv·o·cate** [-keɪt] *v/i.* zweideutig reden, Worte verdrehen; Ausflüchte machen; **e·quiv·o·ca·tion** [ɪˌkwɪvə'keɪʃn] *s.* Zweideutigkeit *f*; Ausflucht *f*; Wortverdrehung *f*; **e'quiv·o·ca·tor** [-keɪtə] *s.* Wortverdreher(in).

e·ra ['ɪərə] *s.* Ära *f*: a) Zeitrechnung *f*, b) E'poche *f*, Zeitalter *n*: ***mark an ~*** e-e Epoche einleiten.

e·rad·i·ca·ble [ɪ'rædɪkəbl] *adj.* ausrottbar, auszurotten(d); **e'rad·i·cate** [-keɪt] *v/t. mst fig.* ausrotten; **e·rad·i·ca·tion** [ɪˌrædɪ'keɪʃn] *s.* Ausrottung *f*.

e·rase [ɪ'reɪz] *v/t.* **1.** a) *Farbe etc.* ab-, auskratzen, b) *Schrift etc.* ausstreichen, -radieren, *a. Tonbandaufnahme* löschen: ***erasing head*** Löschkopf *m*; **2.** *fig.* auslöschen, (aus)tilgen (***from*** aus): ***~ from one's memory*** aus dem Gedächtnis löschen; **3.** a) vernichten, auslöschen, b) *Am. sl.* ‚kaltmachen' (*töten*); **e'ras·er** [-zə] *s.* **1.** Radiermesser *n*; **2.** Radiergummi *m*; **e·ra·sion** [ɪ'reɪʒn] *s.* **1.** → ***erasure***; **2.** ⚕ Auskratzung *f*; **e·ra·sure** [ɪ'reɪʒə] *s.* **1.** Ausradierung *f*, Tilgung *f*, Löschung *f*; **2.** ausradierte *od.* gelöschte Stelle.

ere [eə] *poet.* **I** *cj.* ehe, bevor; **II** *prp.* vor: ***~ long*** bald; ***~ this*** schon vorher; ***~ now*** vordem, bislang.

e·rect [ɪ'rekt] **I** *v/t.* **1.** aufrichten, -stellen; **2.** *Gebäude etc.* errichten, bauen; **3.** ⚙ aufstellen, montieren; **4.** *fig. Theorie* aufstellen; **5.** ⚖ einrichten, gründen; **6.** ∢ *das Lot, e-e Senkrechte* fällen, errichten; **II** *adj.* □ **7.** aufgerichtet, aufrecht: ***with head ~*** erhobenen Hauptes; ***stand ~(ly)*** geradestehen, *fig.* standhaft bleiben; **8.** *physiol.* erigiert (*Penis*); **9.** zu Berge stehend, sich sträubend (*Haare*); **e'rec·tile** [-taɪl] *adj.* **1.** aufrichtbar; **2.** aufgerichtet; **3.** *physiol.* erek'til, Schwell...: ***~ tissue***; **e'rect·ing** [-tɪŋ] *s.* **1.** ⚙ Aufbau *m*, Mon'tage *f*; **2.** *opt.* 'Bild,umkehrung *f*; **e'rec·tion** [-kʃn] *s.* **1.** Auf-, Errichtung *f*, Aufführung *f*; **2.** Bau *m*, Gebäude *n*; **3.** ⚙ Mon'tage *f*; **4.** *physiol.* Erekti'on *f*; **5.** ⚖ Gründung *f*; **e'rect·ness** [-nɪs] *s.* **1.** aufrechte Haltung (*a. fig.*); **2.** *a. fig.* Geradheit *f*; **e'rec·tor** [-tə] *s.* **1.** Erbauer *m*; **2.** *anat.* E'rektor *m*, Aufrichtmuskel *m*.

er·e·mite ['erɪmaɪt] *s.* Ere'mit *m*, Einsiedler *m*.

erg [ɜ:g], **er·gon** ['ɜ:gɒn] *s. phys.* Erg *n*, Ener'gieeinheit *f*.

er·go·nom·ics [,ɜ:gəʊ'nɒmɪks] *s. pl. sg. konstr. sociol.* Ergono'mie *f*, Ergo'nomik *f* (*Lehre von den Leistungsmöglichkeiten des Menschen*).

er·got ['ɜ:gət] *s.* ⚘ Mutterkorn *n*.

er·i·ca ['erɪkə] *s.* ⚘ Erika *f*.

Er·in ['ɪərɪn] *npr. poet.* Erin *n*, Irland *n*.

er·mine ['ɜ:mɪn] *s.* **1.** *zo.* Herme'lin *n* (*a. her.*); **2.** Herme'lin(pelz) *m*.

erne, *Am. a.* **ern** [ɜ:] *s. orn.* Seeadler *m*.

e·rode [ɪ'rəʊd] *v/t.* **1.** an-, zer-, wegfressen; **2.** *geol.* erodieren, auswaschen; **3.** ⚙ *u. fig.* verschleißen; **4.** *fig.* aushöhlen, unter'graben.

er·o·gen·ic [,erəʊ'dʒenɪk], **e·rog·e·nous** [ɪ'rɒdʒɪnəs] *adj. physiol.* ero'gen: ***~ zone***.

e·ro·sion [ɪ'rəʊʒn] *s.* **1.** Zerfressen *n*; **2.** *geol.* Erosi'on *f*, Auswaschung *f*; Verwitterung *f*; **3.** ⚙ Verschleiß *m*, Abnützung *f*, Schwund *m*; **4.** *fig.* Aushöhlung *f*; **e'ro·sive** [-əʊsɪv] *adj.* ätzend, zerfressend.

e·rot·ic [ɪ'rɒtɪk] **I** *adj.* (□ ***~ally***) e'rotisch; **II** *s.* E'rotiker(in); **e'rot·i·ca** [-kə] *pl.* E'rotika *pl.*; **e'rot·i·cism** [-ɪsɪzəm] *s.* E'rotik *f*.

err [ɜ:] *v/i.* **1.** (sich) irren: ***~ on the safe side, ~ on the side of caution*** übervorsichtig sein; ***to ~ is human*** Irren ist menschlich; **2.** falsch sein, fehlgehen (*Urteil*); **3.** (mo'ralisch) auf Abwege geraten.

er·rand ['erənd] *s.* Botengang *m*, Auftrag *m*: ***go on*** (*od.* ***run***) ***an ~*** e-n (Boten)Gang *od.* e-e Besorgung machen, e-n Auftrag ausführen; **'~-boy** *s.* Laufbursche *m*.

er·rant ['erənt] *adj.* **1.** um'herziehend, (-)wandernd, fahrend: ***~ knight***; **2.** *fig.* a) fehlgeleitet, auf Ab- *od.* Irrwegen, b) abtrünnig, fremdgehend (*Ehepartner*); **'er·rant·ry** [-trɪ] **1.** Um'herziehen *n*; **2.** *hist.* fahrendes Rittertum.

er·ra·ta [e'rɑ:tə] → ***erratum***.

er·rat·ic [ɪ'rætɪk] *adj.* (□ ***~ally***) **1.** (um'her)wandernd, (-)ziehend; **2.** *geol.*, ⚕ er'ratisch: ***~ block, ~ boulder*** erratischer Block, Findling *m*; **3.** ungleich-, unregelmäßig, regel-, ziellos; **4.** unstet, unberechenbar, sprunghaft.

er·ra·tum [e'rɑ:təm] *pl.* **-ta** [-tə] *s.* **1.** Druckfehler *m*; **2.** *pl.* Druckfehlerverzeichnis *n*, Er'rata *pl.*

err·ing ['ɜ:rɪŋ] *adj.* □ **1.** → ***erroneous***; **2.** a) irrend, sündig, b) → ***errant*** 2.

er·ro·ne·ous [ɪ'rəʊnjəs] *adj.* □ irrig, irrtümlich, unrichtig, falsch; **er'ro·ne·ous·ly** [-lɪ] *adv.* irrtümlicherweise, fälschlich, aus Versehen.

er·ror ['erə] *s.* **1.** Irrtum *m*, Fehler *m*, Versehen *n*: ***in ~*** irrtümlicherweise; ***be in ~*** sich irren; ***~s*** (***and omissions***) ***excepted*** ✝ Irrtümer (u. Auslassungen) vorbehalten; ***~ of omission*** Unterlassungssünde *f*; ***~ of judg(e)ment*** Trugschluß *m*, irrige Ansicht, falsche Beurteilung; **2.** ∢, *ast.* Fehler *m*, Abweichung *f*; ***~ rate*** Fehlerquote *f*; ***~ in range*** *a.* ⚔ Längenabweichung; **3.** ⚖ a) Tatsachen- *od.* Rechtsirrtum *m*: ***~ in law*** (***in fact***), b) Formfehler *m*, Verfahrensmangel *m*: ***writ of ~*** Revisionsbefehl *m*; **4.** Fehltritt *m*, Vergehen *n*.

er·satz ['eəzæts] (*Ger.*) **I** *s.* Ersatz(stoff) *m*; **II** *adj.* Ersatz...

Erse [ɛ:s] *ling.* **I** *adj.* **1.** gälisch; **2.** irisch; **II** *s.* **3.** Gälisch *n*; **4.** Irisch *n*.

erst·while ['ɜ:stwaɪl] **I** *adv.* ehedem, früher; **II** *adj.* ehemalig, früher.

e·ruc·tate [ɪ'rʌkteɪt] *v/i.* aufstoßen, rülpsen; **e·ruc·ta·tion** [,i:rʌk'teɪʃn] *s.* Aufstoßen *n*, Rülpsen *n*.

er·u·dite ['eru:daɪt] *adj.* □ gelehrt (*a. Abhandlung etc.*), belesen; **er·u·di·tion** [,eru:'dɪʃn] *s.* Gelehrsamkeit *f*, Belesenheit *f*.

e·rupt [ɪ'rʌpt] *v/i.* **1.** ausbrechen (*Vulkan, a. Ausschlag, Streit etc.*); **2.** *geol.* her'vorbrechen, eruptieren (*Lava etc.*); **3.** 'durchbrechen (*Zähne*); **4.** plötzlich auftauchen: ***~ into the room*** ins Zimmer platzen; **5.** *fig.* (zornig) losbrechen, ‚explodieren'; **e'rup·tion** [-pʃn] *s.* **1.** Ausbruch *m* (*e-s Vulkans, Streits etc.*); **2.** Her'vorbrechen *n*, *geol.* Erupti'on *f*; **3.** 'Durchbruch *m* (*der Zähne*); **4.** ⚕ Erupti'on *f*: a) Ausbruch *m e-s Ausschlags*, b) Ausschlag *m*; **5.** (Wut- *etc.*)Ausbruch *m*; **e'rup·tive** [-tɪv] *adj.* □ **1.** *geol.* erup'tiv: ***~ rock*** Eruptivgestein; **2.** ⚕ von Ausschlag begleitet.

er·y·sip·e·las [,erɪ'sɪpɪləs] *s.* ⚕ (Wund-) Rose *f*; **,er·y'sip·e·loid** [-lɔɪd] *s.* ⚕ (Schweine)Rotlauf *m*.

es·ca·lade [,eskə'leɪd] ⚔ *hist.* **I** *s.* Eska'lade *f*, Mauerersteigung *f* (*mit Leitern*), Erstürmung *f*; **II** *v/t.* mit Sturmleitern ersteigen.

es·ca·late ['eskəleɪt] **I** *v/t.* **1.** *Krieg etc.* eskalieren (*stufenweise verschärfen*); **2.** *Erwartungen, Preise etc.* höherschrauben; **II** *v/i.* **3.** eskalieren; **4.** steigen, in die Höhe gehen (*Preise etc.*); **es·ca·la·tion** [,eskə'leɪʃn] *s.* **1.** ⚔, *pol.* Eskalati'on *f*; **2.** ✝ *Am.* Anpassung *f* der Löhne *od.* Preise an gestiegene (Lebenshaltungs)Kosten; **'es·ca·la·tor** ['eskəleɪtə] *s.* **1.** Rolltreppe *f*; **2.** *a.* ***~ clause*** ✝ (Preis-, Lohn)Gleitklausel *f*.

es·ca·lope ['eskələʊp] *s.* (*bsd.* Wiener) Schnitzel *n*.

es·ca·pade [,eskə'peɪd] *s.* Eska'pade *f*: a) toller Streich, b) ‚Seitensprung' *m*.

es·cape [ɪ'skeɪp] **I** *v/t.* **1.** *j-m* entfliehen, -kommen, -rinnen; **2.** *e-r Sache* entgehen, -rinnen, *et.* vermeiden: ***he just ~d being killed*** er entging knapp dem Tode; ***I cannot ~ the impression*** ich kann mich des Eindrucks nicht erwehren; **3.** *fig. j-m* entgehen, über'sehen *od.* nicht verstanden werden von *j-m*: ***that fact ~d me*** diese Tatsache entging mir; ***the sense ~s me*** der Sinn leuchtet mir nicht ein; ***it ~d my notice*** ich bemerkte es nicht; **4.** (*dem Gedächtnis*) entfallen: ***his name ~s me*** sein Name ist mir entfallen; **5.** entfahren, -schlüpfen: ***an oath ~d him***; **II** *v/i.* **6.** (***from***) (ent)fliehen, entkommen, -rinnen, -laufen, -wischen, -weichen (aus, von), flüchten, ausbrechen (aus); **7.** (*oft* ***from***) sich retten (vor *dat.*), (ungestraft *od.* mit dem Leben) da'vonkommen; **8.** a) ausfließen, b) entweichen, ausströmen (*Gas etc.*); **III** *s.* **9.** Entrinnen *n*, -weichen *n*, -kommen *n*, Flucht *f* (***from*** aus, von): ***have a narrow ~*** mit knapper Not davon- *od.* entkommen; ***that was a narrow ~!*** das war knapp!, das hätte ins Auge gehen können!; ***make one's ~*** entkommen, sich aus dem Staub machen; **10.** Rettung *f* (***from*** vor *dat.*): (***way of***) ***~*** Ausweg *m*; **11.** Fluchtmittel *n*; → ***fire escape***; **12.** Ausströmen *n*, Entweichen *n*; **13.** *fig.* (Mittel *n* der) Entspannung *f od.* Zerstreuung *f*, Unter'haltung *f*: ***~ reading*** Unterhaltungslektüre *f*; ***~ art·ist*** *s.* **1.** Entfesselungskünstler *m*; **2.** Ausbrecherkönig *m*; ***~ car*** *s.* Fluchtwagen *m*; ***~ chute*** *s.* ✈ Notrutsche *f*; ***~ clause*** *s.* Befreiungsklausel *f*.

es·ca·pee [,eskeɪ'pi:] *s.* entwichener Strafgefangener, Ausbrecher *m*.

es·cape| hatch *s.* **1.** a) ⚓ Notluke *f*, b) ✈ Notausstieg *m*; **2.** *fig.* ‚Schlupfloch' *n*; ***~ mech·a·nism*** *s. psych.* 'Abwehrmecha,nismus *m*.

es·cape·ment [ɪ'skeɪpmənt] *s.* **1.** Hemmung *f* (*der Uhr*); **2.** Vorschub *m* (*der Schreibmaschine*); ***~ wheel*** *s.* **1.** Hemmungsrad *n* (*der Uhr*); **2.** Schaltrad *n* (*der Schreibmaschine*).

es·cape| pipe *s.* **1.** Abflußrohr *n*; **2.** Abzugsrohr *n* (*für Gase*); ***~-proof*** *adj.* ausbruchssicher; ***~ route*** *s.* Fluchtweg *m*; ***~ shaft*** *s.* Rettungsschacht *m*; ***~ valve*** *s.* 'Sicherheitsven,til *n*.

es·cap·ism [ɪs'keɪpɪzəm] *s. psych.* Eska'pismus *m*, Wirklichkeitsflucht *f*; **es·cap·ist** [ɪ'skeɪpɪst] **I** *s.* j-d, der vor der Reali'tät zu fliehen sucht; **II** *adj.* eska'pistisch, *weitS.* Zerstreuungs..., Unterhaltungs...: ***~ literature***.

es·ca·pol·o·gist [,eskeɪ'pɒlədʒɪst] *s.* **1.** → ***escape artist*** 1; **2.** *j-d, der sich immer wieder geschickt herauswindet*.

es·carp·ment [ɪ'skɑ:pmənt] *s.* **1.** ⚔ Böschung *f*; **2.** *geol.* Steilabbruch *m*.

es·cha·to·log·i·cal [,eskətə'lɒdʒɪkl] *adj. eccl.* eschato'logisch; **es·cha·tol·o·gy** [,eskə'tɒlədʒɪ] *s.* Eschatolo'gie *f*.

es·cheat [ɪs'tʃi:t] ⚖ **I** *s.* **1.** Heimfall *m* (*an den Staat*); **2.** Heimfallsgut *n*; **3.** Heimfallsrecht *n*; **II** *v/i.* **4.** an'heimfallen; **III** *v/t.* **5.** (als Heimfallsgut) einziehen.

es·chew [ɪs'tʃu:] *v/t. et.* (ver)meiden, scheuen, sich enthalten (*gen.*).

es·cort I *s.* ['eskɔ:t] **1.** ⚔ Es'korte *f*, Bedeckung *f*, Begleitmannschaft *f*; **2.** a) ✈, ⚓ Geleit(schutz *m*) *n*, b) *a.* ***~ vessel*** ⚓ Geleitschiff *n*: ***~ fighter*** ✈ Begleitjäger *m*; **3.** *fig.* a) Geleit *n*,

Schutz *m*, b) Begleitung *f*, Gefolge *n*, c) Begleiter(in): ~ ***agency*** Begleitagentur *f*; **II** *v/t*. [ɪ'skɔ:t] **4.** ⚔ eskortieren; **5.** ✈, ⚓ Geleit(schutz) geben (*dat.*); **6.** *fig*. a) geleiten, b) begleiten.

es·cri·toire [ˌeskri:'twɑ:] (*Fr.*) *s*. Schreibpult *n*.

es·crow [e'skrəʊ] *s*. ⚖ *bei e-m Dritten (als Treuhänder) hinterlegte Vertragsurkunde, die erst bei Erfüllung e-r Bedingung in Kraft tritt.*

es·cutch·eon [ɪ'skʌtʃən] *s*. **1.** Wappen (-schild *m*) *n*: ***a blot on his*** ~ *fig*. ein Fleck auf s-r (weißen) Weste; **2.** ⚙ a) (Deck)Schild *n* (*e-s Schlosses*), b) Abdeckung *f* (*e-s Schalters*); **3.** *zo*. Spiegel *m*, Schild *m*.

Es·ki·mo ['eskɪməʊ] *pl*. **-mos** *s*. **1.** Eskimo *m*; **2.** Eskimosprache *f*.

e·soph·a·gus [i:'sɒfəgəs] → ***oesophagus***.

es·o·ter·ic [ˌesəʊ'terɪk] *adj*. (□ ~***ally***) eso'terisch: a) *phls*. nur für Eingeweihte bestimmt, b) geheim, pri'vat.

es·pal·ier [ɪ'spæljə] *s*. **1.** Spa'lier *n*; **2.** Spa'lierbaum *m*.

es·pe·cial [ɪ'speʃl] *adj*. □ besonder: a) her'vorragend, b) Haupt…, hauptsächlich, spezi'ell; **es·pe·cial·ly** [ɪ'speʃəlɪ] *adv*. besonders, hauptsächlich: ***more*** ~ ganz besonders.

Es·pe·ran·tist [ˌespə'ræntɪst] *s*. *ling*. Esperan'tist(in); **Es·pe·ran·to** [ˌespə'ræntəʊ] *s*. Espe'ranto *n*.

es·pi·o·nage [ˌespɪə'nɑ:ʒ] *s*. Spio'nage *f*: ***industrial*** ~ Werkspionage.

es·pla·nade [ˌesplə'neɪd] *s*. **1.** Espla'nade *f* (*a*. ⚔ *hist*.), großer freier Platz; **2.** (*bsd*. 'Strand)Prome'nade *f*.

es·pous·al [ɪ'spaʊzl] *s*. **1.** (***of***) Eintreten *n*, Par'teinahme *f* (für); Annahme *f* (*gen*.); **2.** *pl*. *obs*. a) Vermählung *f*, b) Verlobung *f*; **es·pouse** [ɪ'spaʊz] *v/t*. **1.** Par'tei ergreifen für, eintreten für, sich *e-r Sache* verschreiben, *e-n Glauben* annehmen; **2.** *obs*. a) sich vermählen mit, zur Frau nehmen, b) (***to***) zur Frau geben (*dat*.), c) (***o.s.*** sich) verloben (***to*** mit).

es·pres·so [e'spresəʊ] (*Ital*.) *s*. **1.** Es'presso *m*; **2.** Es'pressomaˌschine *f*; ~ ***bar***, ~ ***ca·fé*** *s*. Es'presso(bar *f*) *n*.

es·prit ['espri:] (*Fr*.) *s*. Es'prit *m*, Geist *m*, Witz *m*; ~ ***de corps*** [ˌespri:də'kɔ:] (*Fr*.) *s*. Korpsgeist *m*.

es·py [ɪ'spaɪ] *v/t*. erspähen.

Es·qui·mau ['eskɪməʊ] *pl*. **-maux** [-məʊz] → ***Eskimo***.

es·quire [ɪ'skwaɪə] *s*. **1.** *Brit*. *obs*. → ***squire*** 1; **2.** *abbr*. ***Esq.*** (*ohne Mr., Dr. etc. auf Briefen dem Namen nachgestellt*): ***John Smith, Esq.*** Herrn John Smith.

ess [es] *s*. **1.** S *n*, s *n*; **2.** S-Form *f*.

es·say I *s*. ['eseɪ] **1.** Essay *m*, *n*, Abhandlung *f*, Aufsatz *m*; **2.** Versuch *m*; **II** *v/t*. *u*. *v/i*. [e'seɪ] **3.** versuchen; **'es·say·ist** [-ɪst] *s*. Essay'ist(in).

es·sence ['esns] *s*. **1.** *phls*. a) Es'senz *f*, Wesen *n*, b) Sub'stanz *f*, abso'lutes Sein; **2.** *fig*. Es'senz *f*, *das* Wesentliche, Kern *m*: ***of the*** ~ von entscheidender Bedeutung; **3.** Es'senz *f*, Ex'trakt *m*.

es·sen·tial [ɪ'senʃl] **I** *adj*. □ → ***essentially***; **1.** wesentlich; **2.** wichtig, unentbehrlich, erforderlich; lebenswichtig: ~ ***goods***; **3.** ⚗ ä'therisch: ~ ***oil***; **II** *s*. *mst pl*. **4.** *das* Wesentliche *od*. Wichtigste, Hauptsache *f*; wesentliche Punkte *pl*.; unentbehrliche Sache *od*. Per'son; **es·sen·ti·al·i·ty** [ɪˌsenʃɪ'ælətɪ] → ***essential*** 4; **es'sen·tial·ly** [-lɪ] *adv*. im wesentlichen, eigentlich, in der Hauptsache; in hohem Maße.

es·tab·lish [ɪ'stæblɪʃ] *v/t*. **1.** ein-, errichten, gründen; einführen; *Regierung* bilden; *Gesetz* erlassen; *Rekord*, *Theorie* aufstellen; ✝ *Konto* eröffnen; **2.** *j-n* einsetzen, 'unterbringen; ✝ etablieren: ~ ***o.s.*** sich niederlassen *od*. einrichten, ✝ *u*. *fig*. sich etablieren; **3.** *Kirche* verstaatlichen; **4.** feststellen, festsetzen; *s-e Identität etc*. nachweisen; **5.** Geltung verschaffen (*dat*.); *Forderung*, *Ansicht* 'durchsetzen; *Ordnung* schaffen; **6.** *Verbindung* herstellen; **7.** begründen: ~ ***one's reputation*** sich e-n Namen machen; **es·tab·lished** [ɪ'stæblɪʃt] *adj*. **1.** bestehend; **2.** feststehend, festbegründet, unzweifelhaft; **3.** planmäßig (*Beamter*): ***the*** ~ ***staff*** das Stammpersonal; **4.** ℒ ***Church*** Staatskirche *f*; **es·tab·lish·ment** [ɪ'stæblɪʃmənt] *s*. **1.** Er-, Einrichtung *f*; Einsetzung *f*; Gründung *f*, Einführung *f*, Schaffung *f*; **2.** Feststellung *f*, -setzung *f*; **3.** (*großer*) Haushalt; ✝ Unter'nehmen *n*, Firma *f*: ***keep a large*** ~ a) ein großes Haus führen, b) ein bedeutendes Unternehmen leiten; **4.** Anstalt *f*, Insti'tut *n*; **5.** organisierte Körperschaft: ***civil*** ~ Beamtenschaft *f*; ***military*** ~ stehendes Heer; ***naval*** ~ Flotte *f*; **6.** festes Perso'nal, Perso'nalod. ⚔ Mannschaftsbestand *m*; Sollstärke *f*: ***peace*** ~ Friedensstärke; ***war*** ~ Kriegsstärke; **7.** Staatskirche *f*; **8.** ***the*** ℒ das Establishment (*etablierte Macht*, *herrschende Schicht*, *konventionelle Gesellschaft*).

es·tate [ɪ'steɪt] *s*. **1.** Stand *m*, Klasse *f*, Rang *m*: ***the Three*** ℒ***s*** (***of the Realm***) *Brit*. die drei (*gesetzgebenden*) Stände; ***third*** ~ *Fr*. *hist*. dritter Stand, Bürgertum *n*; ***fourth*** ~ *humor*. Presse *f*; **2.** *obs*. (Zu)Stand *m*: ***man's*** ~ *bibl*. Mannesalter; **3.** ⚖ a) Besitz *m*, Vermögen *n*; → ***personal*** 1, ***real*** 3, b) (Kon'kursetc.)Masse *f*, Nachlaß *m*; **4.** ⚖ Besitzrecht *n*, Nutznießung *f*; **5.** Grundbesitz *m*, Besitzung *f*, Gut *n*: ***family*** ~ Familienbesitz *m*; **6.** (Wohn)Siedlung *f*; **7.** → ***estate car***; ~ ***a·gent*** *s*. *Brit*. **1.** Grundstücksmakler *m*; **2.** Grundstücksverwalter *m*; ~**-ˌbot·tled** *adj*. auf dem (Wein)Gut abgefüllt; *als Aufschrift*: Gutsabfüllung!; ~ ***car*** *s*. *Brit*. Kombiwagen *m*; ~ ***du·ty*** *s*. *Brit*. *obs*., ~ ***tax*** *s*. *Am*. Erbschaftssteuer *f*.

es·teem [ɪ'sti:m] **I** *v/t*. **1.** achten, (hoch-)schätzen; **2.** erachten *od*. ansehen als, halten für; **II** *s*. **3.** Wertschätzung *f*, Achtung *f*: ***to hold in*** (***high***) ~ achten.

es·ter ['estə] *s*. ⚗ Ester *m*.

Es·ther ['estə] *npr*. *u*. *s*. *bibl*. (das Buch) Esther *f*.

es·thete *etc*. → ***aesthete*** *etc*.

Es·tho·ni·an [e'stəʊnjən] **I** *s*. **1.** Este *m*, Estin *f*; **2.** *ling*. Estnisch *n*; **II** *adj*. **3.** estnisch, estländisch.

es·ti·ma·ble ['estɪməbl] *adj*. □ achtens-, schätzenswert; **es·ti·mate I** *v/t*. ['estɪmeɪt] **1.** (ab-, ein)schätzen, taxieren, veranschlagen (***at*** auf *acc*.): ***an*** ~***d 200 buyers*** schätzungsweise 200 Käufer; **2.** bewerten, beurteilen; **II** *s*. ['estɪmɪt] **3.** (Ab-, Ein)Schätzung *f*, Veranschlagung *f*, (Kosten)Anschlag *m*: ***rough*** ~ grober Überschlag; ***at a rough*** ~ grob geschätzt; **4.** ***the*** ℒ***s*** *pl*. *pol*. der (Staats-) Haushaltsplan; **5.** Bewertung *f*, Beurteilung *f*: ***form an*** ~ ***of*** *et*. beurteilen *od*. einschätzen; **es·ti·ma·tion** [ˌestɪ'meɪʃn] *s*. **1.** Urteil *n*, Meinung *f*: ***in my*** ~ nach m-r Ansicht; **2.** Bewertung *f*, Schätzung *f*; **3.** Achtung *f*: ***hold in*** (***high***) ~ hochschätzen.

es·ti·val → ***aestival***.

es·top [ɪ'stɒp] *v/t*. ⚖ rechtshemmenden Einwand erheben gegen, hindern (***from*** an *dat*., ***from doing*** zu tun); **es·top·pel** [ɪ'stɒpl] *s*. ⚖ Ausschluß *m* e-r Klage *od*. Einrede.

es·trange [ɪ'streɪndʒ] *v/t*. *j-n* entfremden (***from*** *dat*.): ***become*** ~***d*** a) sich entfremden (***from*** *dat*.), b) sich auseinanderleben; **es·tranged** [ɪ'streɪndʒd] *adj*. **1.** ***an*** ~ ***couple*** ein Paar, das sich auseinandergelebt hat; **2.** ⚖ getrennt lebend: ***his*** ~ ***wife*** s-e von ihm getrennt lebende Frau; ***she is*** ~ ***from her husband*** sie lebt von ihrem Mann getrennt; **es·trange·ment** [ɪ'streɪndʒmənt] *s*. Entfremdung *f* (***from*** von).

es·tro·gen ['estrədʒən] *s*. *biol*., ⚗ Östro'gen *n*.

es·tu·ar·y ['estjʊərɪ] *s*. **1.** (den Gezeiten ausgesetzte) Flußmündung; **2.** Meeresarm *m*, -bucht *f*.

et cet·er·a [ɪt'setərə] *abbr*. ***etc.***, ***&c.*** (*Lat*.) und so weiter; **et'cet·er·a** *s*. **1.** (*lange etc*.) Reihe; **2.** *pl*. allerlei Dinge.

etch [etʃ] *v/t*. *u*. *v/i*. **1.** ätzen; **2.** a) kupferstechen, b) radieren; **3.** schneiden, kratzen (***on*** in *acc*.): ***sharply*** ~***ed features*** *fig*. scharf geschnittene Gesichtszüge; ***the event was*** ~***ed on*** (*od*. ***in***) ***his memory*** das Ereignis hatte sich s-m Gedächtnis (tief) eingeprägt; **4.** *fig*. (klar *etc*.) zeichnen, (gut *etc*.) her'ausarbeiten; **etch·er** ['etʃə] *s*. **1.** Kupferstecher *m*; **2.** Radierer *m*; **etch·ing** ['etʃɪŋ] *s*. **1.** Ätzen *etc*. (→ ***etch*** 1, 2); **2.** a) Radierung *f*, b) Kupferstich *m*: ***come up and see my*** ~***s*** *humor*. wollen Sie sich m-e Briefmarkensammlung ansehen?

e·ter·nal [ɪ'tɜ:nl] **I** *adj*. □ **1.** ewig, immerwährend: ***the*** ℒ ***City*** die Ewige Stadt (*Rom*); **2.** unab'änderlich; **3.** F ewig, unaufhörlich; **II** *s*. **4.** ***the*** ℒ Gott *m*; **5.** *pl*. ewige Dinge *pl*.; **e'ter·nal·ize** [-nəlaɪz] *v/t*. verewigen; **e'ter·ni·ty** [-nətɪ] *s*. **1.** Ewigkeit *f* (*a*. F *fig*. *lange Zeit*): ***from here to*** ~, ***to all*** ~ bis in alle Ewigkeit; **2.** *eccl*. a) *das* Jenseits, b) *pl*. ewige Wahrheiten; **e'ter·nize** [-naɪz] → ***eternalize***.

eth·ane ['eθeɪn] *s*. ⚗ Ä'than *n*; **'eth·ene** ['eθi:n] *s*. Ä'then *n*, Äthy'len *n*; **eth·e·nol** ['eθənɒl] *s*. Vi'nylalkoˌhol *m*; **eth·e·nyl** ['eθənɪl] *s*. Äthyli'den *n*.

e·ther ['i:θə] *s*. **1.** ⚗, *phys*. Äther *m*; **2.** *poet*. Äther *m*, Himmel *m*; **e·the·re·al** [i:'θɪərɪəl] *adj*. □ **1.** ⚗ a) ätherartig, b) ä'therisch; **2.** ä'therisch, himmlisch; vergeistigt; **e·the·re·al·ize** [i:'θɪərɪəlaɪz] *v/t*. **1.** ⚗ ätherisieren; **2.** vergeistigen, verklären; **'e·ther·ize** [-əraɪz] *v/t*. □ **1.** ⚗ in Äther verwandeln; **2.** ⚕ mit Äther narkotisieren.

eth·ic ['eθɪk] **I** *adj*. **1.** → ***ethical***; **II** *s*. **2.**

pl. sg. konstr. Sittenlehre *f*, Ethik *f*; **3.** *pl.* Sittlichkeit *f*, Mo'ral *f*, Ethos *n*: ***professional ~s*** Standesehre *f*, Berufsethos; **'eth·i·cal** [-kl] *adj.* ☐ **1.** *phls.*, *a. ling.* ethisch; **2.** ethisch, mo'ralisch, sittlich; **3.** von ethischen Grundsätzen (geleitet); **4.** dem Berufsethos entsprechend; **5.** *pharm.* re'zeptpflichtig; **'eth·i·cist** [-ısıst] *s.* Ethiker *m*.

E·thi·o·pi·an [i:θı'əʊpjən] **I** *adj.* äthi'opisch; **II** *s.* Äthi'opier(in).

eth·nic ['eθnık] **I** *adj.* ☐ **1.** ethnisch, völkisch, Volks…: ***~ group*** Volksgruppe *f*; ***~ German*** Volksdeutsche(r *m*) *f*; ***~ joke*** Witz *m* auf Kosten e-r bestimmten Volksgruppe; **II** *s.* **2.** Angehörige(r *m*) *f* e-r (homo'genen) Volksgruppe; **3.** *pl.* sprachliche *od.* kultu'relle Zugehörigkeit; **'eth·ni·cal** [-kl] → ***ethnic*** I; **eth·nog·ra·pher** [eθ'nɒgrəfə] *s.* Ethno'graph *m*; **eth·no·graph·ic** [ˌeθnəʊ'græfık] *adj.* ☐ ethno'graphisch, völkerkundlich; **eth·nog·ra·phy** [eθ'nɒgrəfı] *s.* Ethnogra'phie *f*, (beschreibende) Völkerkunde; **eth·no·log·i·cal** [ˌeθnəʊ'lɒdʒıkl] *adj.* ☐ ethno'logisch; **eth·nol·o·gist** [eθ'nɒlədʒıst] *s.* Ethno'loge *m*, Völkerkundler *m*; **eth·nol·o·gy** [eθ'nɒlədʒı] *s.* Ethnolo'gie *f*, (vergleichende) Völkerkunde.

e·thol·o·gist [i:'θɒlədʒıst] *s.* Etho'loge *m*, (Tier)Verhaltensforscher *m*; **e'thol·o·gy** [-dʒı] *s.* Etholo'gie *f*, Verhaltensforschung *f*.

e·thos ['i:θɒs] *s.* **1.** Ethos *n*, Cha'rakter *m*, Wesensart *f*, Geist *m*, sittlicher Gehalt (*e-r Kultur*); **2.** ethischer Wert.

eth·yl ['eθıl; ⚗ 'i:θaıl] *s.* ⚗ Ä'thyl *n*: ***~ alcohol*** Äthylalkohol *m*; **eth·yl·ene** ['eθıli:n] *s.* Äthy'len *n*, Kohlenwasserstoffgas *n*.

et·i·quette ['etıket] *s.* Eti'kette *f*: a) Zeremoni'ell *n*, b) Anstandsregeln *pl.*, (gute) 'Umgangsformen *pl.*

E·ton| col·lar ['i:tn] *s.* breiter, steifer 'Umlegekragen; ***~ Col·lege*** *s. berühmte englische Public School*; ***~ crop*** *s.* Herrenschnitt *m* (*für Damen*).

E·to·ni·an [i:'təʊnjən] **I** *adj.* Eton…; **II** *s.* Schüler *m* des ***Eton College***.

E·ton jack·et *s.* schwarze, kurze Jacke *der Etonschüler*.

E·trus·can [ı'trʌskən] **I** *adj.* **1.** e'truskisch; **II** *s.* **2.** E'trusker(in); **3.** *ling.* E'truskisch *n*.

et·y·mo·log·ic, et·y·mo·log·i·cal [ˌetımə'lɒdʒık(l)] *adj.* ☐ etymo'logisch; **et·y·mol·o·gist** [ˌetı'mɒlədʒıst] *s.* Etymo'loge *m*; **et·y·mol·o·gy** [ˌetı'mɒlədʒı] *s. allg.* Etymolo'gie *f*; **et·y·mon** ['etımɒn] *s.* Etymon *n*, Stammwort *n*.

eu·ca·lyp·tus [ˌju:kə'lıptəs] *s.* ⚘ Euka'lyptus *m*.

Eu·cha·rist ['ju:kərıst] *s. eccl.* Euchari'stie *f*: a) *die Feier des heiligen Abendmahls*, b) *die eucharistische Gabe* (*Brot u. Wein*).

eu·chre ['ju:kə] *v/t. Am.* F prellen, betrügen.

Eu·clid ['ju:klıd] *s.* die (Eu'klidische) Geome'trie.

eu·gen·ic [ju:'dʒenık] **I** *adj.* (☐ ***~ally***) eu'genisch; **II** *s. pl. sg. konstr.* Eu'genik *f* (*Erbhygiene*); **eu·ge·nist** ['ju:dʒınıst] *s.* Eu'geniker *m*.

eu·lo·gist ['ju:lədʒıst] *s.* Lobredner(in); **eu·lo·gis·tic** [ˌju:lə'dʒıstık] *adj.* (☐ ***~ally***) preisend, lobend; **'eu·lo·gize** [-dʒaız] *v/t.* loben, preisen, rühmen; **'eu·lo·gy** [-dʒı] *s.* **1.** Lob(preisung *f*) *n*; **2.** Lobrede *f od.* -schrift *f*.

eu·nuch ['ju:nək] *s.* Eu'nuch *m*, *weitS. a.* Ka'strat *m*.

eu·pep·sia [ju:'pepsıə] *s.* ⚕ nor'male Verdauung; **eu'pep·tic** [-ptık] *adj.* **1.** ⚕ gut verdauend; **2.** *fig.* gutgelaunt.

eu·phe·mism ['ju:fımızəm] *s.* Euphe'mismus *m*, beschönigender Ausdruck, sprachliche Verhüllung; **eu·phe·mis·tic** [ˌju:fı'mıstık] *adj.* (☐ ***~ally***) euphe'mistisch, beschönigend, verhüllend.

eu·phon·ic [ju:'fɒnık] *adj.* (☐ ***~ally***) eu'phonisch, wohlklingend; **eu·pho·ny** ['ju:fənı] *s.* Eupho'nie *f*, Wohlklang *m*.

eu·phor·bi·a [ju:'fɔ:bjə] *s.* ⚘ Wolfsmilch *f*.

eu·pho·ri·a [ju:'fɔ:rıə] *s.* ⚕ *u. fig.* Eupho'rie *f*; **eu'phor·ic** [-'fɒrık] *adj.* (☐ ***~ally***) eu'phorisch; **eu·pho·ry** ['ju:fərı] → ***euphoria***.

eu·phu·ism ['ju:fju:ızəm] *s.* Euphu'ismus *m* (*schwülstiger Stil od. Ausdruck*); **eu·phu·is·tic** [ˌju:fju:'ıstık] *adj.* (☐ ***~ally***) euphu'istisch, schwülstig.

Eu·rail·pass ['jʊəreılpɑ:s] *s.* 🚂 Eu'railpaß *m*.

Eur·a·sian [jʊə'reıʒjən] **I** *s.* Eu'rasier (-in); **II** *adj.* eu'rasisch.

Euro- [jʊərəʊ] *in Zssgn* euro'päisch, Euro…

'Eu·ro|·cheque *s.* ☤ Eurocheque *m*, -scheck *m*: ***~ card*** Eurocheque-Karte *f*; **ˌ~'com·mun·ism** *s.* 'Eurokommuˌnismus *m*; **~·crat** ['jʊərəʊkræt] *s.* Euro'krat *m*; **'~ˌdol·lar** *s.* ☤ Eurodollar *m*.

Eu·ro·pe·an [ˌjʊərə'pi:ən] **I** *adj.* euro'päisch: ***~ (Economic) Community*** Europäische (Wirtschafts)Gemeinschaft; ***~ Parliament*** Europaparlament *n*; ***~ plan*** *Am.* Hotelzimmer-Vermietung *f* ohne Verpflegung; **II** *s.* Euro'päer(in); **ˌEu·ro'pe·an·ism** [-nızəm] *s.* Euro'päertum *n*; **ˌEu·ro'pe·an·ize** [-naız] *v/t.* europäisieren.

Eu·ro·vi·sion ['jʊərəʊˌvıʒn] *s. u. adj. TV* Eurovision(s…) *f*.

Eu·sta·chi·an tube [ju:'steıʃjən] *s. anat.* Eu'stachische Röhre, 'Ohrtromˌpete *f*.

eu·tha·na·si·a [ˌju:θə'neızjə] *s.* **1.** sanfter *od.* leichter Tod; **2.** Euthana'sie *f*: ***active (passive) ~*** ⚕ aktive (passive) Sterbehilfe.

e·vac·u·ant [ı'vækjʊənt] **I** *adj.* abführend; **II** *s.* Abführmittel *n*; **e·vac·u·ate** [ı'vækjʊeıt] *v/t.* **1.** ent-, ausleeren: ***~ the bowels*** a) den Darm entleeren, b) abführen; **2.** a) *Luft etc.* her'auspumpen, b) *Gefäß* luftleer pumpen; **3.** a) *Personen* evakuieren, b) ⚔ *Truppen* verlegen, *Verwundete etc.* abtransportieren, c) *Gebiet* evakuieren, *a. Haus* räumen; **e·vac·u·a·tion** [ıˌvækjʊ'eıʃn] *s.* **1.** Aus-, Entleerung *f*; **2.** ⚕ a) Stuhlgang *m*, b) Stuhl *m*, Kot *m*; **3.** a) Evakuierung *f*, b) ⚔ Verlegung *f* (*von Truppen*), 'Abtransˌport *m*, c) Räumung *f*; **e·vac·u·ee** [ıˌvækju:'i:] *s.* Evakuierte(r *m*) *f*.

e·vade [ı'veıd] *v/t.* **1.** ausweichen (*dat.*); **2.** *j-m* entkommen; **3.** sich *e-r Sache* entziehen, *e-r Sache* entgehen, ausweichen, *et.* um'gehen, vermeiden; sich *e-r Pflicht etc.* entziehen, ⚖ *Steuern* hinter'ziehen: ***~ a question*** e-r Frage ausweichen; ***~ definition*** sich nicht definieren lassen; **e'vad·er** [-də] *s. j-d, der sich e-r Sache entzieht*; → ***tax evader***.

e·val·u·ate [ı'væljʊeıt] *v/t.* **1.** auswerten; **2.** bewerten, beurteilen; **3.** abschätzen; **4.** berechnen; **e·val·u·a·tion** [ıˌvæljʊ'eıʃn] *s.* **1.** Auswertung *f*; **2.** Bewertung *f*, Beurteilung *f*; **3.** Schätzung *f*; **4.** Berechnung *f*.

ev·a·nesce [ˌi:və'nes] *v/i.* sich verflüchtigen; schwinden; **ˌev·a'nes·cence** [-sns] *s.* (Da'hin)Schwinden *n*, Verflüchtigung *f*; **ˌev·a'nes·cent** [-snt] *adj.* ☐ **1.** (ver-, da'hin)schwindend, flüchtig; **2.** vergänglich.

e·van·gel·ic [ˌi:væn'dʒelık] *adj.* (☐ ***~ally***) **1.** die Evan'gelien betreffend, Evangelien…; **2.** evan'gelisch; **ˌe·van'gel·i·cal** [-kl] *adj.* ☐ → ***evangelic***.

e·van·ge·lism [ı'vændʒəlızəm] *s.* Verkündigung *f* des Evan'geliums; **e'van·ge·list** [-lıst] *s.* **1.** Evange'list *m*; **2.** Evange'list *m*, Erweckungs-, Wanderprediger *m*; **3.** Patri'arch *m der Mormonen*; **e'van·ge·lize** [-laız] **I** *v/i.* das Evan'gelium verkünden; **II** *v/t.* (zum Christentum) bekehren.

e·vap·o·rate [ı'væpəreıt] **I** *v/i.* **1.** verdampfen, -dunsten, sich verflüchtigen; **2.** *fig.* verfliegen, sich verflüchtigen (*a.* F *abhauen*); **II** *v/t.* **3.** verdampfen *od.* verdunsten lassen; **4.** ⚙ ab-, eindampfen, evaporieren: ***~d milk*** Kondensmilch *f*; **e·vap·o·ra·tion** [ıˌvæpə'reıʃn] *s.* **1.** Verdampfung *f*, -dunstung *f*; **2.** *fig.* Verflüchtigung *f*, Verfliegen *n*; **e'vap·o·ra·tor** [-tə] *s.* ⚙ Abdampfvorrichtung *f*, Verdampfer *m*.

e·va·sion [ı'veıʒn] *s.* **1.** Entkommen *n*, -rinnen *n*; **2.** Ausweichen *n*, Um'gehung *f*, Vermeidung *f*; → ***tax evasion***; **3.** Ausflucht *f*, Ausrede *f*.

e·va·sive [ı'veısıv] *adj.* ☐ **1.** ausweichend: ***~ answer***; ***~ action*** Ausweichmanöver *n*; ***be ~*** *fig.* ausweichen; **2.** schwer faßbar *od.* feststellbar; **e'va·sive·ness** [-nıs] *s.* ausweichendes Verhalten.

Eve¹ [i:v] *npr. bibl.* Eva *f*: ***daughter of ~*** Evastochter *f* (*typische Frau*).

eve² [i:v] *s.* **1.** *poet.* Abend *m*; **2.** *mst* ♀ Vorabend *m*, -tag *m* (*e-s Festes*); **3.** *fig.* Vorabend *m*: ***on the ~ of*** am Vorabend von (*od. gen.*); ***be on the ~ of*** kurz vor (*dat.*) stehen.

e·ven¹ ['i:vn] *adv.* **1.** so'gar, selbst, auch: ***~ the king*** sogar der König; ***he ~ kissed her*** er küßte sie sogar; ***~ if, ~ though*** selbst wenn, wenn auch; ***~ now*** a) selbst jetzt, noch jetzt, b) eben *od.* gerade jetzt, c) schon jetzt; ***not ~ now*** selbst jetzt noch nicht, nicht einmal jetzt; ***or ~*** oder auch (nur), oder gar; ***without ~ looking*** ohne auch nur hinzusehen; **2.** *vor comp.* noch: ***~ better*** (sogar) noch besser; **3.** *nach neg.*: ***not ~*** nicht einmal; ***I never ~ saw it*** ich habe es nicht einmal gesehen; **4.** gerade, eben: ***~ as I expected*** gerade *od.* genau wie ich erwartete; ***~ as he spoke*** gerade als er sprach; ***~ so*** dennoch, trotzdem, immerhin, selbst dann.

e·ven² ['i:vn] **I** *adj.* ☐ **1.** eben, flach, gerade; **2.** waag(e)recht, horizon'tal; → ***keel*** 1; **3.** in gleicher Höhe (***with*** mit): ***~ with the ground*** dem Boden gleich;

4. gleich: **~ *chances*** gleiche Chancen; ***stand an ~ chance of winning*** e-e echte Siegeschance haben; ***~ money*** gleicher Einsatz (*Wette*); ***~ bet*** Wette *f* mit gleichem Einsatz; ***of ~ date*** ✝ gleichen Datums; **5.** ✝ a) ausgeglichen, schuldenfrei, b) ohne Gewinn od. Verlust: ***be ~ with s.o.*** mit j-m quitt sein; ***get ~ with s.o.*** mit j-m abrechnen *od.* quitt werden, *fig. a.* es j-m heimzahlen; → ***break even***; **6.** gleich-, regelmäßig; im Gleichgewicht (*a. fig.*); **7.** ausgeglichen, ruhig (*Gemüt etc.*): ***~ voice*** ruhige *od.* kühle Stimme; **8.** gerecht, ˈunparˌteiisch; **9.** a) gerade (*Zahl*), b) geradzahlig (*Schwingungen etc.*), c) rund, voll (*Summe*): ***~ page*** (Buch)Seite *f* mit gerader Zahl; **10.** genau, präˈzise: ***an ~ dozen*** genau ein Dutzend; **II** *v/t.* **11.** (ein)ebnen, glätten; **12.** *a.* ***~ out*** ausgleichen; **13.** ***~ up*** ✝ *Rechnung* aus-, begleichen, *Konten* abstimmen; **III** *v/i.* **14.** *mst.* ***~ out*** eben werden; **15.** *a.* ***~ out*** sich ausgleichen; **16.** ***~ up on*** mit *j-m* quitt werden.

e·ven³ [ˈi:vn] *s. poet.* Abend *m.*

ˌe·ven-ˈhand·ed *adj.* ˈunparˌteiisch, objekˈtiv.

eve·ning [ˈi:vnɪŋ] *s.* **1.** Abend *m*: ***in the ~*** abends, am Abend; ***on the ~ of*** am Abend (*gen.*); ***this*** (***tomorrow***) ***~*** heute (morgen) abend; **2.** ˈAbend(unterˌhaltung *f*) *m*, Gesellschaftsabend *m*; **3.** *fig.* Ende *n*, *bsd.* (*a.* ***~ of life***) Lebensabend *m*; **~ class·es** *s. pl. ped.* ˈAbendunterˌricht *m*; **~ dress** *s.* **1.** Abendkleid *n*; **2.** Gesellschaftsanzug *m*, *bsd.* a) Frack *m*, b) Smoking *m*; **~ pa·per** *s.* Abendzeitung *f*; **~ school** → ***night-school***; **~ shirt** *s.* Frackhemd *n*; **~ star** *s.* Abendstern *m.*

e·ven·ness [ˈi:vnnɪs] *s.* **1.** Ebenheit *f*, Geradheit *f*; **2.** Gleichmäßigkeit *f*; **3.** Gleichheit *f*; **4.** Gelassenheit *f*, Seelenruhe *f*, Ausgeglichenheit *f.*

ˈe·ven·song *s.* Abendandacht *f.*

e·vent [ɪˈvent] *s.* **1.** Ereignis *n*, Vorfall *m*, Begebenheit *f*: (***quite***) ***an ~*** ein großes Ereignis; ***after the ~*** hinterher, im nachhinein; ***before the ~*** vorher, im voraus; **2.** Ergebnis *n*, Ausgang *m*: ***in the ~*** schließlich; **3.** Fall *m*, ˈUmstand *m*: ***in either ~*** in jedem Fall; ***in any ~*** auf jeden Fall; ***at all ~s*** auf alle Fälle, jedenfalls; ***in the ~ of*** im Falle (*gen. od.* daß); **4.** *bsd. sport* a) Veranstaltung *f*, b) Disziˈplin *f* (*Sportart*), c) Wettbewerb *m*, -kampf *m.*

ˌe·ven-ˈtem·pered *adj.* ausgeglichen, gelassen, ruhig.

e·vent·ful [ɪˈventfʊl] *adj.* **1.** ereignisreich; **2.** denkwürdig, bedeutsam.

ˈe·ven·tide *s. poet.* (***at ~*** zur) Abendzeit *f.*

e·ven·tu·al [ɪˈventʃʊəl] *adj.* □ → ***eventually***; **1.** schließlich: ***this led to his ~ dismissal*** dies führte schließlich *od.* letzten Endes zu s-r Entlassung; **2.** *obs.* eventuˈell, etwaig; **e·ven·tu·al·i·ty** [ɪˌventʃʊˈælətɪ] *s.* Möglichkeit *f*, Eventualiˈtät *f*; **eˈven·tu·al·ly** [-lɪ] *adv.* schließlich, endlich; **eˈven·tu·ate** [-ʃʊeɪt] *v/i.* **1.** ausgehen, enden (***in*** in *dat.*); **2.** die Folge sein (***from*** *gen.*).

ev·er [ˈevə] *adv.* **1.** immer, ständig, unaufhörlich: ***for ~*** (***and ~***), ***for ~ and a day*** für immer (u. ewig); ***~ and again*** (*obs.* ***anon***) dann u. wann, hin und wieder; ***~ since***, ***~ after*** seit der Zeit, seitdem; ***yours ~ ...*** Viele Grüße, Dein(e) *od.* Ihr(e) ...; **2.** *vor comp.* immer: ***~ larger*** immer größer; ***~ increasing*** ständig zunehmend; **3.** *neg.*, *interrog.*, *konditional*: je(mals): ***do you ~ see him?*** siehst du ihn jemals?; ***if I ~ meet him*** falls ich ihn je treffe; ***did you ~?*** F hast du Töne?, na, so was!; ***the fastest ~*** F der (die, das) Schnellste aller Zeiten; **4.** nur, irgend, überˈhaupt: ***as soon as ~ I can*** sobald ich nur kann; ***what ~ do you mean?*** was (in aller Welt) meinst du denn (eigentlich)?; ***how ~ did he manage?*** wie hat er es nur fertiggebracht?; ***hardly ~***, ***seldom if ~*** fast niemals; **5.** ***~ so*** sehr, noch so: ***~ so simple*** ganz einfach; ***~ so long*** e-e Ewigkeit; ***~ so many*** sehr viele; ***thank you ~ so much!*** tausend Dank!; ***if I were ~ so rich*** wenn ich noch so reich wäre; ***~ such a nice man*** wirklich ein netter Mann.

ˈev·er|·glade *s. Am.* sumpfiges Flußgebiet; **ˈ~·green I** *adj.* **1.** immergrün; **2.** unverwüstlich, nie veraltend, immer wieder gern gehört: ***~ song*** → 4; **II** *s.* **3.** ⚘ a) immergrüne Pflanze, b) Immergrün *n*; **4.** Evergreen *m*, *n* (*Schlager*); **ˌ~ˈlast·ing I** *adj.* □ **1.** immerwährend, ewig (*a. Gott*, *Schnee*): ***~ flower*** → 5; **2.** *fig.* F unaufhörlich, endlos; **3.** dauerhaft, unbegrenzt haltbar, unverwüstlich; **II** *s.* **4.** Ewigkeit *f*; **5.** ⚘ Immorˈtelle *f*, Strohblume *f*; **ˌ~ˈmore** *adv.* **1.** immerfort: ***for ~*** in Ewigkeit; **2.** je(mals) wieder.

ev·er·y [ˈevrɪ] *adj.* **1.** jeder, jede, jedes, all: ***he has read ~ book on this subject***; ***~ other*** a) jeder andere, b) → ***other*** 6; ***~ day*** jeden Tag, alle Tage, täglich; ***~ four days*** alle vier Tage; ***~ fourth day*** jeden vierten Tag; ***~ now and then*** (*od.* ***again***), ***~ so often*** F gelegentlich, hin u. wieder; ***~ bit*** (***of it***) ganz, völlig: ***~ bit as good*** genauso gut; ***~ time*** a) jedesmal(, wenn), sooft, b) jederzeit, F *a.* allemal; **2.** jeder, jede, jedes (einzelne *od.* erdenkliche), all: ***her ~ wish*** jeder ihrer Wünsche, alle ihre Wünsche; ***have ~ reason*** allen Grund haben; ***their ~ liberty*** ihre ganze Freiheit; **ˈ~ˌbod·y** *pron.* jeder(mann); **ˈ~·day** *adj.* **1.** (all)täglich; **2.** Alltags...; **3.** (mittel)mäßig; **ˈ~·one, ~ one** *pron.* jeder(mann): ***in ~'s mouth*** in aller Munde; **ˈ☐·man** *s. bsd. thea.* Jedermann *m*; **ˈ~·thing** *pron.* **1.** alles: ***~ new*** alles Neue; **2.** F die Hauptsache, alles: ***speed is ~***; ***he*** (***it***) ***has ~*** F er (es) hat alles *od.* ist ‚phantastisch'; **ˈ~·where** *adv.* ˈüberall, allenthalben.

e·vict [ɪˈvɪkt] *v/t.* ⚖ **1.** *j-n* zur Räumung zwingen; *fig. j-n* gewaltsam vertreiben; **2.** wieder in Besitz nehmen; **eˈvic·tion** [-kʃn] *s.* ⚖ **1.** Zwangsräumung *f*, Herˈaussetzung *f*: ***~ order*** Räumungsbefehl *m*; **2.** Wiederinbeˈsitznahme *f.*

ev·i·dence [ˈevɪdəns] **I** *s.* **1.** ⚖ a) Beˈweis(mittel *n*, -stück *n*, -materiˌal *n*) *m*, Beweise *pl.*, Ergebnis *n* der Beweisaufnahme *f*, b) ˈUnterlage *f*, Beleg *m*, c) (Zeugen)Aussage *f*, Zeugnis *n*: ***a piece of ~*** ein Beweisstück; ***medical ~*** Aussage *f od.* Gutachten *n* des medizinischen Sachverständigen; ***for lack of ~*** mangels Beweises; ***in ~ of*** zum Beweis (*gen.*); ***offer in ~*** Beweisantritt *m*; ***on the ~*** auf Grund des Beweismaterials; ***admit in ~*** als Beweis zulassen; ***call s.o. in ~*** j-n als Zeugen benennen; ***give od. bear ~*** (***of***) (als Zeuge) aussagen (über *acc.*), *fig.* zeugen (von); ***hear ~*** Zeugen vernehmen; ***hearing od. taking of ~*** Beweisaufnahme *f*; ***turn King's*** (*od.* ***Queen's***, *Am.* ***State's***) ***~*** als Kronzeuge auftreten; **2.** Augenscheinlichkeit *f*, Klarheit *f*: ***in ~*** sichtbar, er-, offensichtlich; ***be much in ~*** stark in Erscheinung treten, deutlich feststellbar sein; stark vertreten sein; **3.** (An)Zeichen *n*, Spur *f*: ***there is no ~*** es ist nicht ersichtlich *od.* feststellbar, nichts deutet darauf hin; **II** *v/t.* **4.** dartun, be-, nachweisen, zeigen; **ˈev·i·dent** [-nt] *adj.* □ → ***evidently***; augenscheinlich, einleuchtend, offensichtlich, klar (ersichtlich); **ev·i·den·tial** [ˌevɪˈdenʃl] *adj.* □, **ev·i·den·tia·ry** [ˌevɪˈdenʃərɪ] *adj.* **1.** ⚖ beweiserheblich; Beweis...(*-kraft*, *-wert*); **2.** überˈzeugend: ***be ~ of*** *et.* (klar) beweisen; **ˈev·i·dent·ly** [-ntlɪ] *adv.* offensichtlich, zweifellos.

e·vil [ˈi:vl] **I** *adj.* □ **1.** übel, böse, schlimm: ***~ eye*** a) böser Blick, b) schlimmer Einfluß; ***the ☐ One*** der Teufel; ***~ repute*** schlechter Ruf; ***~ spirit*** böser Geist; **2.** gottlos, boshaft, schlecht: ***~ tongue*** Lästerzunge *f*; **3.** unglücklich: ***~ day*** Unglückstag *m*; ***fall on ~ days*** ins Unglück geraten; **II** *s.* **4.** Übel *n*, Unglück *n*: ***the lesser of two ~s, the lesser ~*** das geringere Übel; **5.** *das* Böse, Sünde *f*, Verderbtheit *f*: ***do ~*** Böses tun; ***the powers of ~*** die Mächte der Finsternis; ***the social ~*** die Prostitution; **ˌ~-disˈposed** → ***evil-minded***; **ˌ~-ˈdo·er** *s.* Übeltäter(in); **ˌ~-ˈmind·ed** *adj.* übelgesinnt, bösartig; **ˌ~-ˈspeak·ing** *adj.* verleumderisch.

e·vince [ɪˈvɪns] *v/t.* dartun, be-, erweisen, bekunden, zeigen.

e·vis·cer·ate [ɪˈvɪsəreɪt] *v/t.* **1.** *Tier* ausnehmen, *hunt. a.* ausweiden; **2.** *fig. et.* inhalts- *od.* bedeutungslos machen; **e·vis·cer·a·tion** [ɪˌvɪsəˈreɪʃn] *s.* Ausweidung *f.*

ev·o·ca·tion [ˌevəʊˈkeɪʃn] *s.* **1.** (Geister)Beschwörung *f*; **2.** *fig.* (***of***) a) Wachrufen *n* (*gen.*), b) Erinnerung *f* (an *acc.*); **3.** plastische Schilderung; **e·voc·a·tive** [ɪˈvɒkətɪv] *adj.* **1.** ***be ~ of*** erinnern an (*acc.*); **2.** sinnträchtig, beziehungsreich.

e·voke [ɪˈvəʊk] *v/t.* **1.** *Geister* herˈbeirufen, beschwören; **2.** *fig.* herˈvor-, wachrufen, wecken.

ev·o·lu·tion [ˌi:vəˈlu:ʃn] *s.* **1.** Entwicklung *f*, Entfaltung *f*, (Herˈaus)Bildung *f*; **2.** *biol.* Evolutiˈon *f*: ***theory of ~*** Evolutionstheorie *f*; **3.** Folge *f*, (Handlungs)Ablauf *m*; **4.** ⚔ Maˈnöver *n*, Bewegung *f*; **5.** *phys.* (*Gas- etc.*) Entwicklung *f*; **6.** Ꭿ Wurzelziehen *n*; **ˌev·oˈlu·tion·ar·y** [-nərɪ] *adj.* Entwicklungs..., *biol.* Evolutions...; **ˌev·oˈlu·tion·ist** [-ʃənɪst] **I** *s.* Anhänger(in) der (*biologischen*) Entwicklungslehre; **II** *adj.* die Entwicklungslehre betreffend.

e·volve [ɪˈvɒlv] **I** *v/t.* **1.** entwickeln, entfalten, herˈausarbeiten; **2.** *Gas*, *Wärme* aus-, verströmen; **II** *v/i.* **3.** sich entwikkeln *od.* entfalten (***into*** zu); **4.** entstehen (***from*** aus).

ewe [juː] *s. zo.* Mutterschaf *n*; ~ **lamb** *s. zo.* Schaflamm *n*.

ew·er [ˈjuːə] *s.* Wasserkrug *m*.

ex[1] [eks] *prp.* **1.** ✝ a) aus, ab, von: ~ ***factory*** ab Fabrik; ~ ***works*** ab Werk; → ***ex officio***, b) ohne, exkluˈsive: ~ ***all*** ausschließlich aller Rechte; ~ ***dividend*** ohne Dividende; **2.** → ***ex cathedra*** *etc.*

ex[2] [eks] *s.* X *n*, x *n* (*Buchstabe*).

ex- [eks] *in Zssgn* Ex…, ehemalig; Alt…

ex·ac·er·bate [ekˈsæsəbeɪt] *v/t.* **1.** *j-n* verärgern; **2.** *et.* verschlimmern; **ex·ac·er·ba·tion** [ekˌsæsəˈbeɪʃn] *s.* **1.** Verärgerung *f*; **2.** Verschlimmerung *f*.

ex·act [ɪgˈzækt] **I** *adj.* □ → ***exactly***; **1.** exˈakt, genau, (genau) richtig: ***the*** ~ ***time*** die genaue Zeit; ***the*** ~ ***sciences*** die exakten Wissenschaften; **2.** streng, genau: ~ ***rules***; **3.** meˈthodisch, gewissenhaft, sorgfältig (*Person*); **4.** genau, tatsächlich: ***his*** ~ ***words***; **II** *v/t.* **5.** *Gehorsam*, *Geld etc.* fordern, verlangen; **6.** *Zahlung* eintreiben, einfordern; **7.** *Geschick etc.* erfordern; **exˈact·ing** [-tɪŋ] *adj.* **1.** streng, genau; **2.** anspruchsvoll: ***an*** ~ ***customer***; ***be*** ~ hohe Anforderungen stellen; **3.** hart, aufreibend (*Aufgabe etc.*); **exˈac·tion** [-kʃn] *s.* **1.** Fordern *n*; **2.** Eintreiben *n*; **3.** (unmäßige) Forderung; **exˈact·i·tude** [-tɪtjuːd] → ***exactness***; **exˈact·ly** [-lɪ] *adv.* **1.** genau, exˈakt; **2.** sorgfältig; **3.** *als Antwort*: genau, ganz recht, du sagst (Sie sagen) es: ***not*** ~ a) nicht ganz, b) *iro.* nicht gerade *od.* eben *schön etc.*; **4.** *wo*, *wann etc.* eigentlich; **exˈact·ness** [-nɪs] *s.* **1.** Exˈaktheit *f*, Genauigkeit *f*, Richtigkeit *f*; **2.** Sorgfalt *f*.

ex·ag·ger·ate [ɪgˈzædʒəreɪt] **I** *v/t.* **1.** überˈtreiben; überˈtrieben darstellen; aufbauschen; **2.** ˈüberbewerten; **3.** ˈüberbetonen; **II** *v/i.* **4.** übertreiben; **exˈag·ger·at·ed** [-tɪd] *adj.* □ überˈtrieben, -ˈzogen; **ex·ag·ger·a·tion** [ɪgˌzædʒəˈreɪʃn] *s.* Überˈtreibung *f*.

ex·alt [ɪgˈzɔːlt] *v/t.* **1.** *im Rang* erheben, erhöhen (***to*** zu); **2.** (lob)preisen, verherrlichen: ~ ***to the skies*** in den Himmel heben; **3.** verstärken (*a. fig.*); **ex·al·ta·tion** [ˌegzɔːlˈteɪʃn] *s.* **1.** Erhebung *f*: ***♀ of the Cross*** *eccl.* Kreuzeserhöhung *f*; **2.** Begeisterung *f*, Ekˈstase *f*, Erregung *f*; **exˈalt·ed** [-tɪd] *adj.* **1.** gehoben: ~ ***style***; **2.** hoch: ~ ***rank***; ~ ***ideal***; **3.** begeistert; **4.** überˈtrieben hoch: ***have an*** ~ ***opinion of o.s.***

ex·am [ɪgˈzæm] F *für* ***examination*** 2.

ex·am·i·na·tion [ɪgˌzæmɪˈneɪʃn] *s.* **1.** Unterˈsuchung *f* (*a.* ⚕), Prüfung *f* (***of***, ***into*** *gen.*); Besichtigung *f*, ˈDurchsicht *f*: (***up***)***on*** ~ bei näherer Prüfung; ***be under*** ~ geprüft *od.* erwogen werden (→ *a.* 3); **2.** *ped.* Prüfung *f*, Exˈamen *n*: ~ ***paper*** Prüfungsarbeit *f*, -aufgabe(n *pl.*) *f*; ***take*** (*od.* ***go in for***) ***an*** ~ sich e-r Prüfung unterziehen; **3.** ⚖ a) *Zivilprozeß*: Vernehmung *f*, b) *Strafprozeß*: Verhör *n*: ***be under*** ~ vernommen werden (→ *a.* 1).

ex·am·ine [ɪgˈzæmɪn] **I** *v/t.* **1.** unterˈsuchen (*a.* ⚕), prüfen (*a. ped.*), examinieren, besichtigen, ˈdurchsehen, revidieren: ~ ***one's conscience*** sein Gewissen prüfen; **2.** ⚖ vernehmen, *Straftäter* verhören; **II** *v/i.* **3.** ~ ***into s.th.*** et. untersuchen; **ex·am·i·nee** [ɪgˌzæmɪˈniː] *s.* Prüfling *m*, (ˈPrüfungs)Kandiˌdat(in); **exˈam·in·er** [-nə] *s.* **1.** *allg.* Prüfer(in); **2.** ⚖ beauftragter Richter; **exˈam·in·ing bod·y** [-nɪŋ] *s.* Prüfungsausschuß *m*.

ex·am·ple [ɪgˈzɑːmpl] *s.* **1.** Beispiel *n* (***of*** für): ***for*** ~ zum Beispiel; ***without*** ~ beispiellos, ohnegleichen; **2.** Vorbild *n*, Beispiel *n*: ***hold up as an*** ~ als Beispiel hinstellen; ***set a good*** ~ ein gutes Beispiel geben; ***take an*** ~ ***by*** sich ein Beispiel nehmen an (*dat.*); **3.** warnendes Beispiel: ***let this be an*** ~ ***to you*** laß dir das e-e Warnung sein; ***make an*** ~ ***of s.o.*** an j-m ein Exempel statuieren.

ex·as·per·ate [ɪgˈzæspəreɪt] *v/t.* ärgern, wütend machen, aufbringen; **exˈas·per·at·ed** [-tɪd] *adj.* aufgebracht, erbost; **exˈas·per·at·ing** [-tɪŋ] *adj.* □ ärgerlich, zum Verzweifeln; **ex·as·per·a·tion** [ɪgˌzæspəˈreɪʃn] *s.* Wut *f*: ***in*** ~ wütend.

ex ca·the·dra [ˌekskəˈθiːdrə] **I** *adj.* maßgeblich, autoritaˈtiv; **II** *adv.* ex ˈcathedra; maßgeblich.

ex·ca·vate [ˈekskəveɪt] *v/t.* **1.** ausgraben (*a. fig.*), ausschachten, -höhlen; **2.** *Zahnmedizin*: exkavieren; **ex·ca·va·tion** [ˌekskəˈveɪʃn] *s.* **1.** Ausgrabung *f*; **2.** Ausschachtung *f*, Aushöhlung *f*; Aushub *m*; **3.** *geol.* Auskolkung *f*; **4.** *Zahnmedizin*: Exkavatiˈon *f*; **ˈex·ca·va·tor** [-tə] *s.* **1.** Ausgräber *m*; **2.** Erdarbeiter *m*; **3.** ⚙ (Trocken)Bagger *m*.

ex·ceed [ɪkˈsiːd] **I** *v/t.* **1.** überˈschreiten, -ˈsteigen (*a. fig.*); **2.** *fig.* a) hinˈausgehen über (*acc.*), b) *j-n*, *et.* überˈtreffen; **II** *v/i.* **3.** zu weit gehen, das Maß überˈschreiten; **4.** herˈausragen; **exˈceed·ing** [-dɪŋ] *adj.* □ → ***exceedingly***; **1.** außerˈordentlich, äußerst; **2.** mehr als, über: ***not*** ~ (von) höchstens; **exˈceed·ing·ly** [-dɪŋlɪ] *adv.* ˈüberaus, äußerst, aufs äußerste.

ex·cel [ɪkˈsel] **I** *v/t.* überˈtreffen (***o.s.*** sich selbst); **II** *v/i.* sich auszeichnen, herˈvorragen (***in*** *od.* ***at*** in *dat.*).

ex·cel·lence [ˈeksələns] *s.* **1.** Vorˈtrefflichkeit *f*; **2.** vorˈzügliche Leistung; **ˈEx·cel·len·cy** [-sɪ] *s.* Exzelˈlenz *f* (*Titel*): ***Your*** ~ Eure Exzellenz; **ˈex·cel·lent** [-nt] *adj.* □ vorˈzüglich, ausgezeichnet, herˈvorragend.

ex·cel·si·or [ekˈselsɪɔː] *s.* **1.** *Am.* Holzwolle *f*; **2.** *typ.* Brilˈlant *f* (*Schriftgrad*).

ex·cept [ɪkˈsept] **I** *v/t.* **1.** ausnehmen, -schließen (***from*** von, aus); **2.** sich *et.* vorbehalten; → ***error*** 1; **II** *v/i.* **3.** Einwendungen machen, Einspruch erheben (***against*** gegen); **III** *prp.* **4.** ausgenommen, außer, mit Ausnahme von (*od. gen.*): ~ ***for*** abgesehen von, bis auf (*acc.*); **IV** *cj.* **5.** es sei denn, daß; außer, wenn: ~ ***that*** außer, daß; **exˈcept·ing** [-tɪŋ] *prp.* (*nach* ***always*** *od. neg.*) ausgenommen, außer; **exˈcep·tion** [-pʃn] *s.* **1.** Ausnahme *f*: ***by way of*** ~ ausnahmsweise; ***with the*** ~ ***of*** mit Ausnahme von (*od. gen.*), außer, bis auf (*acc.*); ***without*** ~ ohne Ausnahme, ausnahmslos; ***make no*** ~(***s***) keine Ausnahme machen; ***an*** ~ ***to the rule*** e-e Ausnahme von der Regel; **2.** Einwendung *f*, Einwand *m*, Einspruch *m* (*a.* ⚖ *Rechtsmittelvorbehalt*): ***take*** ~ ***to*** a) Einwendungen machen *od.* protestieren gegen, b) Anstoß nehmen an (*dat.*); **exˈcep·tion·a·ble** [-pʃnəbl] *adj.* □ **1.** anfechtbar; **2.** anstößig; **exˈcep·tion·al** [-pʃənl] *adj.* □ → ***exceptionally***; **1.** außergewöhnlich, Ausnahme…, Sonder…: ~ ***case*** Ausnahmefall *m*; **2.** ungewöhnlich (gut); **exˈcep·tion·al·ly** [-pʃnəlɪ] *adv.* **1.** ausnahmsweise; **2.** außergewöhnlich.

ex·cerpt **I** *v/t.* [ekˈsɜːpt] **1.** *Textstelle* exzerpieren, ausziehen; **II** *s.* [ˈeksɜːpt] **2.** Exˈzerpt *n*, Auszug *m*; **3.** Sonder(ab)druck *m*.

ex·cess [ɪkˈses] *s.* **1.** ˈÜbermaß *n*, -fluß *m* (***of*** an *dat.*): ~ ***of …*** zuviel …; ***carry to*** ~ übertreiben, *et.* zu weit treiben; **2.** Exˈzeß *m*, Unmäßigkeit *f*, Ausschweifung *f*; *mst pl.* Ausschreitungen *pl.*: ***drink to*** ~ übermäßig trinken; **3.** ˈÜberschuß *m* (*a.* ✝, ⚙), Mehrsumme *f*: ***in*** ~ ***of*** mehr als, über …; ***be in*** ~ ***of*** überschreiten, -steigen; ~ ***of exports*** Ausfuhrüberschuß *m*; ~ **bag·gage** *s.* ✈ *Am.* ˈÜbergepäck *n*; ~ **cost** *s.* Mehrkosten *pl.*; ~ **cur·rent** *s.* ⚡ ˈÜberstrom *m*; ~ **fare** *s.* (Fahrpreis)Zuschlag *m*; ~ **freight** *s.* ˈÜberfracht *f*.

ex·ces·sive [ɪkˈsesɪv] *adj.* □ ˈübermäßig, überˈtrieben; unangemessen hoch (*Strafe etc.*).

ex·cess| lug·gage *s.* ✈ ˈÜbergepäck *n*; ~ **post·age** *s.* Nachporto *n*, -gebühr *f*; ~ **prof·its tax** *s. Am.* Mehrgewinnsteuer *f*; ~ **volt·age** *s.* ⚡ ˈÜberspannung *f*; ~ **weight** *s.* Mehrgewicht *n*.

ex·change [ɪksˈtʃeɪndʒ] **I** *v/t.* **1.** (***for***) aus-, ˈumtauschen (gegen), vertauschen (mit); **2.** *Geld* eintauschen, (ˈum)wechseln (***for*** gegen); **3.** (*gegenseitig*) *Blicke*, *Küsse*, *Plätze* tauschen; *Grüße*, *Gedanken*, *Gefangene etc.* austauschen; *Worte*, *Schüsse etc.* wechseln: ~ ***blows*** sich prügeln; **4.** ersetzen (***for*** durch); **5.** ⚙ auswechseln; **II** *v/i.* **6.** ~ ***for*** wert sein: ***2.50 D-marks*** ~ ***for one dollar***; **III** *s.* **7.** Tausch *m* (*a. Schach*), Aus-, ˈUmtausch *m*, Auswechselung *f*, Tauschhandel *m*: ***in*** ~ als Ersatz, dafür; ***in*** ~ ***for*** gegen, als Entgelt für; ~ ***of letters*** Schriftwechsel *m*; ~ ***of blows*** Schlagwechsel *m*, *Boxen*: *a.* Schlagabtausch *m*; ~ ***of shots*** Schußwechsel *m*; ~ ***of views*** Meinungsaustausch; **8.** ✝ a) (ˈUm)Wechseln *n*, Wechselverkehr *m*: ***money*** ~ Geldwechsel *m*, b) → ***bill***[2] 3, c) → ***rate***[1] 2, d) ***foreign*** ~ Devisen *pl.*, Valuta *f*, e) Wechselstube *f*; **9.** ✝ Börse *f*; **10.** (Fernsprech)Amt *n*, Vermittlung *f*; **exˈchange·a·ble** [-dʒəbl] *adj.* **1.** (aus)tausch-, auswechselbar (***for*** gegen); **2.** Tausch…

ex·change| bro·ker *s.* **1.** Wechselmakler *m*; **2.** Deˈvisenmakler *m*; ~ **con·trol** *s.* Deˈvisenbewirtschaftung *f*, -konˌtrolle *f*; ~ **list** *s.* ✝ Kurszettel *m*; ~ **of·fice** *s.* Wechselstube *f*; ~ **rate** *s.* ✝ ˈUmrechnungs-, Wechselkurs *m*; ~ **reg·u·la·tions** *s. pl.* ✝ Deˈvisenbestimmungen *pl.*; ~ **re·stric·tions** *s. pl.* ✝ Deˈvisenbeschränkungen *pl.*; ~ **stu·dent** *s.* ˈAustauschstuˌdent(in).

ex·cheq·uer [ɪksˈtʃekə] *s.* **1.** *Brit.* Schatzamt *n*, Staatskasse *f*, Fiskus *m*: ***the*** ♀ das Finanzministerium; ~ ***bill*** *obs.* Schatzwechsel *m*; ~ ***bond*** Schatzanweisung *f*; **2.** ✝ (Geschäfts)Kasse *f*.

ex·cis·a·ble [ekˈsaɪzəbl] *adj.* (verbrauchs)steuerpflichtig.

ex·cise¹ I *v/t.* [ekˈsaɪz] besteuern; II *s.* [ˈeksaɪz] *a.* ~ **duty** Verbrauchssteuer *f*: ~**man** Steuereinnehmer *m*.

ex·cise² [ekˈsaɪz] *v/t.* ⚕ herˈausschneiden, entfernen; **ex·ci·sion** [ekˈsɪʒn] *s.* **1.** ⚕ Exzisiˈon *f*, Ausschneidung *f*; **2.** Ausmerzung *f*.

ex·cit·a·bil·i·ty [ɪkˌsaɪtəˈbɪlətɪ] *s.* Reizbar-, Erregbarkeit *f*, Nervosiˈtät *f*; **ex·cit·a·ble** [ɪkˈsaɪtəbl] *adj.* reiz-, erregbar, nerˈvös; **ex·cit·ant** [ˈeksɪtənt] *s.* ⚕ Reizmittel *n*, ˈStimulans *n*; **ex·ci·ta·tion** [ˌeksɪˈteɪʃn] *s.* **1.** *a.* ⚡, ⚗ Erregung *f*; **2.** ⚕ Reiz *m*, ˈStimulus *m*.

ex·cite [ɪkˈsaɪt] *v/t.* **1.** *j-n* er-, aufregen: **get ~d** (**over**) sich aufregen (über *acc.*); **2.** *j-n* an-, aufreizen, aufstacheln; **3.** *j-n* (*sexuell*) erregen; **4.** *Interesse etc.* erregen, erwecken, herˈvorrufen; **5.** ⚕ *Nerv* reizen; **6.** ⚡ erregen; **7.** *phot.* lichtempfindlich machen; **exˈcit·ed** [-tɪd] *adj.* □ erregt; aufgeregt; **exˈcite·ment** [-mənt] *s.* **1.** Er-, Aufregung *f*; **2.** Reizung *f*; **exˈcit·er** [-tə] *s.* ⚡ Erreger *m*; **exˈcit·ing** [-tɪŋ] *adj.* **1.** erregend; aufregend; spannend, anregend, toll; **2.** ⚡ Erreger…

ex·claim [ɪkˈskleɪm] I *v/i.* **1.** ausrufen, (auf)schreien; **2.** eifern, wettern (**against** gegen); II *v/t.* **3.** ausrufen.

ex·cla·ma·tion [ˌekskləˈmeɪʃn] *s.* **1.** Ausruf *m*, (Auf)Schrei *m*; **2.** *a.* ~ **mark**, **note of ~**, *Am.* **point of ~** Ausrufe-, Ausrufungszeichen *n*; **3.** heftiger Proˈtest; **4.** *ling.* a) Ausrufesatz *m*, b) Interjektiˈon *f*; **ex·clam·a·to·ry** [ekˈsklæmətərɪ] *adj.* **1.** exklamaˈtorisch: ~ **style**; **2.** Ausrufe…: ~ **sentence**.

ex·clave [ˈekskleɪv] *s.* Exˈklave *f*.

ex·clude [ɪkˈsklu:d] *v/t.* ausschließen (**from** von): **not excluding myself** mich selbst nicht ausgenommen; **ex·ˈclu·sion** [-u:ʒən] *s.* **1.** Ausschließung *f*, Ausschluß *m* (**from** von): **to the ~ of** unter Ausschluß von; **2.** ⚙ Absperrung *f*.

ex·clu·sive [ɪkˈsklu:sɪv] I *adj.* □ → **exclusively**; **1.** ausschließend: ~ **of** ausschließlich (*gen.*), abgesehen von, ohne; **be ~ of** *et.* ausschließen; **2.** a) ausschließlich, alˈleinig, Allein…, Sonder…: ~ **agent** Alleinvertreter *m*; ~ **rights** ausschließliche Rechte; **be ~ to** beschränkt sein auf (*acc.*), b) Exklusiv…: ~ **contract** (**report** *etc.*); **3.** exkluˈsiv: a) vornehm, b) anspruchsvoll; **4.** unnahbar; II *s.* **5.** Exkluˈsivbericht *m*; **exˈclu·sive·ly** [-lɪ] *adv.* ausschließlich, nur; **exˈclu·sive·ness** [-nɪs] *s.* Exklusiviˈtät *f*.

ex·cog·i·tate [eksˈkɒdʒɪteɪt] *v/t.* (sich) *et.* ausdenken, ersinnen.

ex·com·mu·ni·cate [ˌekskəˈmju:nɪkeɪt] *v/t. R.C.* exkommunizieren; **ex·com·mu·ni·ca·tion** [ˈekskəˌmju:nɪˈkeɪʃn] *s.* Exkommunikatiˈon *f*.

ex·co·ri·ate [eksˈkɔ:rɪeɪt] *v/t.* **1.** die Haut abziehen von; *Baum* abrinden; **2.** *Haut* wund reiben, abschürfen; **3.** heftig angreifen, vernichtend kritisieren; **ex·co·ri·a·tion** [eksˌkɔ:rɪˈeɪʃn] *s.* **1.** (Haut)Abschürfung *f*; **2.** Wundreiben *n*.

ex·cre·ment [ˈekskrɪmənt] *s. oft pl.* Kot *m*, Exkreˈmente *pl*.

ex·cres·cence [ɪkˈskresns] *s.* **1.** Auswuchs *m* (*a. fig.*); **2.** ⚕ Wucherung *f*; **exˈcres·cent** [-nt] *adj.* **1.** auswachsend; wuchernd; **2.** *fig.* ˈüberflüssig; **3.** *ling.* eingeschoben.

ex·cre·ta [ekˈskri:tə] *s. pl.* Exˈkrete *pl.*; **ex·crete** [ekˈskri:t] *v/t.* absondern, ausscheiden; **exˈcre·tion** [-i:ʃn] *s.* **1.** Ausscheidung *f*; **2.** Exˈkret *n*.

ex·cru·ci·ate [ɪkˈskru:ʃɪeɪt] *v/t. fig.* quälen; **exˈcru·ci·at·ing** [-tɪŋ] *adj.* □ **1.** qualvoll, heftig; **2.** F schauderhaft, unerträglich.

ex·cul·pate [ˈekskʌlpeɪt] *v/t.* reinwaschen, rechtfertigen, freisprechen (**from** von); **ex·cul·pa·tion** [ˌekskʌlˈpeɪʃn] *s.* Entschuldigung *f*, Rechtfertigung *f*, Entlastung *f*.

ex·cur·sion [ɪkˈskɜ:ʃn] *s.* **1.** (*a.* wissenschaftliche) Exkursiˈon, Ausflug *m*, Abstecher *m*, Streifzug *m* (*alle a. fig.*): ~ **train** Sonder-, Ausflugszug *m*; **2.** Abschweifung *f*; **3.** Abweichung *f* (*a. ast.*); **exˈcur·sion·ist** [-ʃnɪst] *s.* Ausflügler (-in); **exˈcur·sive** [-ɜ:sɪv] *adj.* □ **1.** abschweifend; **2.** weitschweifig; **3.** sprunghaft; **exˈcur·sus** [-ɜ:səs] *pl.* **-sus·es** *s.* Exˈkurs *m* (*Erörterung od. Abschweifung*).

ex·cus·a·ble [ɪkˈskju:zəbl] *adj.* □ entschuldbar, verzeihlich.

ex·cuse I *v/t.* [ɪkˈskju:z] **1.** *j-n od. et.* entschuldigen, *j-m et.* verzeihen: ~ **me** a) entschuldigen Sie!, b) aber erlauben Sie mal!; ~ **me for being late**, ~ **my being late** verzeih, daß ich zu spät komme; **please ~ my mistake** bitte entschuldige m-n Irrtum; **2.** Nachsicht mit *j-m* haben; **3.** *et.* entschuldigen, überˈsehen; **4.** *et.* entschuldigen, e-e Entschuldigung für *et.* sein, rechtfertigen: **that does not ~ your conduct**; **5.** (**from**) *j-n* befreien (von), *j-m et.* erlassen: ~ **s.o. from attendance**; ~**d from duty** vom Dienst befreit; **he begs to be ~d** er läßt sich entschuldigen; **I must be ~d from doing this** ich muß es leider ablehnen, dies zu tun; **6.** *j-m et.* erlassen; II *s.* [-kju:s] **7.** Entschuldigung *f*: **offer** (*od.* **make**) **an ~** sich entschuldigen; **please make my ~s to her** bitte entschuldige mich bei ihr; **8.** Rechtfertigung *f*: **there is no ~ for his conduct** sein Benehmen ist nicht zu entschuldigen; **9.** Vorwand *m*, Ausrede *f*, Ausflucht *f*; **10.** dürftiger Ersatz: **a poor ~ for a car** e-e armselige ‚Kutsche'; **exˈcuse-me** *s.* Tanz *m* mit Abklatschen.

ˌex-diˈrec·to·ry *adj.*: ~ **number** *teleph.* Geheimnummer *f*.

ex·e·at [ˈeksɪæt] (*Lat.*) *s. Brit.* (kurzer) Urlaub (*für Studenten*).

ex·e·cra·ble [ˈeksɪkrəbl] *adj.* □ abˈscheulich, scheußlich; **ex·e·crate** [ˈeksɪkreɪt] I *v/t.* **1.** verfluchen, verwünschen; **2.** verabscheuen; II *v/i.* **3.** fluchen; **ex·e·cra·tion** [ˌeksɪˈkreɪʃn] *s.* **1.** Verwünschung *f*, Fluch *m*; **2.** Abscheu *m*: **hold in ~** verabscheuen.

ex·ec·u·tant [ɪgˈzekjʊtənt] *s.* Ausführende(r *m*) *f*, *bsd.* ♪ Vortragende(r *m*) *f*; **ex·e·cute** [ˈeksɪkju:t] *v/t.* **1.** aus-, ˈdurchführen, verrichten, tätigen; **2.** *Amt* ausüben; **3.** ♪, *thea.* vortragen, spielen; **4.** ⚖ a) *Urkunde* (rechtsgültig) ausfertigen, durch ˈUnterschrift, Siegel *etc.* vollˈziehen, b) *Urteil* vollˈstrecken, *bsd. j-n* hinrichten, c) *j-n* pfänden; **ex·e·cu·tion** [ˌeksɪˈkju:ʃn] *s.* **1.** Aus-, ˈDurchführung *f*, Verrichtung *f*: **carry into ~** ausführen; **2.** (*Art u. Weise der*) Ausführung: a) ♪ Vortrag *m*, Spiel *n*, Technik *f*, b) *Kunst*, *Literatur*: Darstellung *f*, Stil *m*; **3.** ⚖ a) Ausfertigung *f*, b) Errichtung *f* (*e-s Testaments*), c) Vollˈziehung *f*, (ˈUrteils-, *a.* ˈZwangs-) Vollˌstreckung *f*, Pfändung *f*, d) Hinrichtung *f*: **sale under ~** Zwangsversteigerung *f*; **levy ~ against a company** die Zwangsvollstreckung in das Vermögen e-r Gesellschaft betreiben; **ex·e·cu·tion·er** [ˌeksɪˈkju:ʃnə] *s.* **1.** Henker *m*, Scharfrichter *m*; **2.** *sport* Vollˈstrecker *m*; **exˈec·u·tive** [-tɪv] I *adj.* □ **1.** ausübend, vollˈziehend, *pol.* Exekutiv…: ~ **officer** Verwaltungsbeamte(r) *m*; ~ **power** → 3; **2.** ✝ geschäftsführend, leitend: ~ **board** Vorstand *m*; ~ **committee** Exekutivausschuß *m*; ~ **floor** Chefetage *f*; ~ **functions** Führungsaufgaben; ~ **post** leitende Stellung; ~ **staff** leitende Angestellte *pl.*; II *s.* **3.** Exekuˈtive *f*, vollˈziehende Gewalt (*im Staat*); **4.** *a.* **senior ~** ✝ leitender Angestellter; **5.** ⚔ *Am.* stellvertretender Kommanˈdeur; **exˈec·u·tor** [-tə] *s.* ⚖ Testaˈmentsvollˌstrecker *m*, Erbschaftsverwalter *m*: **literary ~** Nachlaßverwalter e-s Autors; **exˈec·u·to·ry** [-tərɪ] *adj.* **1.** ⚖ bedingt, erfüllungsbedürftig: ~ **contract**; **2.** Ausführungs…; **exˈec·u·trix** [-trɪks] *s.* ⚖ Testaˈmentsvollˌstreckerin *f*.

ex·e·ge·sis [ˌeksɪˈdʒi:sɪs] *s.* Exeˈgese *f*, (Bibel)Auslegung *f*; **ex·e·gete** [ˈeksɪdʒi:t] *s.* Exeˈget *m*; **ˌex·eˈget·ic** [-ˈdʒetɪk] I *adj.* □ exeˈgetisch, auslegend; II *s. pl. sg. konstr.* Exeˈgetik *f*.

ex·em·plar [ɪgˈzemplə] *s.* **1.** Muster(beispiel) *n*, Vorbild *n*; **2.** typisches Beispiel; **3.** *typ.* (Druck)Vorlage *f*; **exˈem·pla·ry** [-ərɪ] *adj.* □ **1.** exemˈplarisch: a) beispiel-, musterhaft, b) warnend, abschreckend, draˈkonisch (*Strafe etc.*); **2.** typisch, Muster…

ex·em·pli·fi·ca·tion [ɪgˌzemplɪfɪˈkeɪʃn] *s.* **1.** Erläuterung *f* durch Beispiele; Veranschaulichung *f*; **2.** Beleg *m*, Beispiel *n*, Muster *n*; **3.** ⚖ beglaubigte Abschrift, Ausfertigung *f*; **ex·em·pli·fy** [ɪgˈzemplɪfaɪ] *v/t.* **1.** veranschaulichen: a) durch Beispiele erläutern, b) als Beispiel dienen für; **2.** ⚖ e-e beglaubigte Abschrift machen von.

ex·empt [ɪgˈzempt] I *v/t.* **1.** *j-n* befreien, ausnehmen (**from** von *Steuern*, *Verpflichtungen etc.*): ~**ed amount** ✝ (Steuer)Freibetrag *m*; **2.** ⚔ (*vom Wehrdienst*) freistellen; II *adj.* befreit, ausgenommen, frei (**from** von): ~ **from taxes** steuerfrei; **exˈemp·tion** [-pʃn] *s.* **1.** Befreiung *f*, Freisein *n* (**from** von): ~ **from taxes** Steuerfreiheit *f*; ~ **from liability** ⚖ Haftungsausschluß *m*; **2.** ⚔ Freistellung *f* (*vom Wehrdienst*); **3.** *pl.* ⚖ unpfändbare Gegenstände *pl. od.* Beträge *pl.*; **4.** Sonderstellung *f*, Vorrechte *pl*.

ex·er·cise [ˈeksəsaɪz] I *s.* **1.** Ausübung *f* (*e-s Amtes*, *der Pflicht*, *e-r Kunst*, *e-s Rechts*, *der Macht etc.*), Gebrauch *m*, Anwendung *f*; **2.** *oft pl.* (*körperliche od. geistige*) Übung, (*körperliche*) Bewegung, *sport* (Turn)Übung *f*: **do**

one's ~s Gymnastik machen; **take ~** sich Bewegung machen; **~ therapy** Bewegungstherapie *f*; **physical ~** Leibesübungen *pl.*; (**military**) **~** a) Exerzieren *n*, b) Manöver *n*; (**religious**) **~** Gottesdienst *m*, Andacht *f*; **3.** Übungsarbeit *f*, Schulaufgabe *f*: **~-book** Schul-, Schreibheft *n*; **4.** ♪ Übung(sstück *n*) *f*; **5.** *pl. Am.* Feier(lichkeiten *pl.*) *f*; **II** *v/t.* **6.** *ein Amt, ein Recht, Macht, Einfluß* ausüben, *Einfluß, Recht, Macht* geltend machen, *et.* anwenden; *Geduld* üben; **7.** *Körper, Geist* üben, trainieren; **8.** *j-n* üben, ausbilden; **9.** *s-e Glieder, Tiere* bewegen; **10.** *j-n, j-s Geist* stark beschäftigen, plagen, beunruhigen: **be ~d** beunruhigt sein (**about** über *acc.*); **III** *v/i.* **11.** sich Bewegung machen; **12.** *sport* trainieren; **13.** ⚔ exerzieren.

ex·ert [ɪg'zɜːt] *v/t.* gebrauchen, anwenden; *Druck, Einfluß etc.* ausüben (**on** auf *acc.*); *Autorität* geltend machen: **~ o.s.** sich anstrengen; **ex'er·tion** [-ɜːʃn] *s.* **1.** Anwendung *f*, Ausübung *f*; **2.** Anstrengung *f*: a) Stra'paze *f*, b) Bemühung *f*.

ex·e·unt ['eksɪʌnt] (*Lat.*) *thea.* (sie gehen) ab: **~ omnes** alle ab.

ex·fo·li·ate [eks'fəʊlɪeɪt] *v/i. mst* ⚕ abblättern, sich abschälen; **ex·fo·li·a·tion** [eksˌfəʊlɪ'eɪʃn] *s.* Abblätterung *f*.

ex·ha·la·tion [ˌeksə'leɪʃn] *s.* **1.** Ausatmen *n*; **2.** Verströmen *n*; **3.** a) Gas *n*, b) Rauch *m*, c) Geruch *m*, Ausdünstung *f*; **ex·hale** [eks'heɪl] **I** *v/t.* **1.** ausatmen; **2.** *Gas, Geruch etc.* verströmen, *Rauch* ausstoßen; **II** *v/i.* **3.** ausströmen; **4.** ausatmen.

ex·haust [ɪg'zɔːst] **I** *v/t.* **1.** *mst* ⚙ a) (ent)leeren, b) luftleer pumpen, c) *Luft, Wasser etc.* her'auspumpen, *Gas* auspuffen, d) absaugen; **2.** *allg.* erschöpfen: a) *Boden* ausmergeln, b) *Bergwerk etc.* völlig abbauen, c) *Vorräte* ver-, aufbrauchen, d) *j-n* ermüden, entkräften, e) *j-s Kräfte* strapazieren; **3.** *Thema* erschöpfend behandeln; *alle Möglichkeiten* ausschöpfen; **II** *v/i.* **4.** ausströmen; **5.** sich entleeren; **III** *s.* **6.** ⚙ a) Dampfaustritt *m*, b) *a.* **~ gas** Abgas *n*, c) Auspuffgase *pl.*; **7.** *mot.* Auspuff *m*: **~ box** Auspufftopf *m*; **~ brake** Motorbremse *f*; **~ fumes** Abgase; **8.** → **exhauster**; **ex'haust·ed** [-tɪd] *adj.* **1.** aufgebraucht, zu Ende, erschöpft (*Vorräte*), vergriffen (*Auflage*), abgelaufen (*Frist, Versicherung*); **2.** *fig.* erschöpft, ermattet; **ex'haust·er** [-tə] *s.* ⚙ (Ent-)Lüfter *m*, Absaugevorrichtung *f*, Ex'haustor *m*; **ex'haust·ing** [-tɪŋ] *adj.* ermüdend, anstrengend, strapazi'ös; **ex'haus·tion** [-tʃn] *s.* **1.** ⚙ a) (Ent)Leerung *f*, b) Her'auspumpen *n*, c) Absaugung *f*; **2.** Ausströmen *n* (*von Dampf etc.*); **3.** Erschöpfung *f*, (völliger) Verbrauch; **4.** *fig.* Erschöpfung *f*, Ermüdung *f*, Entkräftung *f*; **5.** ⩚ Approximati'on *f*; **ex'haus·tive** [-tɪv] *adj.* □ **1.** *fig.* erschöpfend; **2.** → **exhausting**.

ex·haust| pipe *s.* ⚙ Auspuffrohr *n*; **~ pol·lu·tion** *s.* Luftverschmutzung *f* durch Abgase; **~ steam** *s.* ⚙ Abdampf *m*; **~ stroke** *s.* ⚙ Auspuffhub *m*; **~ valve** *s.* ⚙ 'Auslaßvenˌtil *n*.

ex·hib·it [ɪg'zɪbɪt] **I** *v/t.* **1.** ausstellen, zur Schau stellen: **~ goods**; **2.** *fig.* zeigen, an den Tag legen, entfalten; **3.** ⚖ vorlegen; **II** *v/i.* **4.** ausstellen; **III** *s.* **5.** Ausstellungstück *n*, Expo'nat *n*; **6.** ⚖ a) Eingabe *f*, b) Beweisstück *n*, Beleg *m*, c) Anlage *f zu e-m Schriftsatz*.

ex·hi·bi·tion [ˌeksɪ'bɪʃn] *s.* **1.** a) Ausstellung *f*, Schau *f*: **be on ~** ausgestellt sein, zu sehen sein, b) Vorführung *f*: **~ contest** *sport* Schaukampf *m*; **make an ~ of o.s.** sich lächerlich *od.* zum Gespött machen, ‚auffallen'; **2.** *fig.* Zur'schaustellung *f*, Bekundung *f*; **3.** ⚖ Vorlage *f*, Beibringung *f* (*von Beweisen etc.*); **4.** *Brit. univ.* Sti'pendium *n*; ˌ**ex·hi'bi·tion·er** [-ʃnə] *s. Brit. univ.* Stipendi'at *m*; ˌ**ex·hi'bi·tion·ism** [-ʃnɪzəm] *s. psych. u. fig.* Exhibitio'nismus *m*; ˌ**ex·hi'bi·tion·ist** [-ʃnɪst] *psych. u. fig.* **I** *s.* Exhibitio'nist *m*; **II** *adj.* exhibitio'nistisch; **ex·hib·i·tor** [ɪg'zɪbɪtə] *s.* **1.** Aussteller *m*; **2.** Kinobesitzer *m*.

ex·hil·a·rant [ɪg'zɪlərənt] → **exhilarating**; **ex·hil·a·rate** [ɪg'zɪləreɪt] *v/t.* **1.** erheitern; **2.** beleben, erfrischen; **ex'hil·a·rat·ed** [-tɪd] *adj.* erheitert, heiter, amüsiert; **ex'hil·a·rat·ing** [-tɪŋ] *adj.* □ erheiternd, erfrischend, amü'sant; **ex·hil·a·ra·tion** [ɪgˌzɪlə'reɪʃn] *s.* **1.** Erheiterung *f*; **2.** Heiterkeit *f*.

ex·hort [ɪg'zɔːt] *v/t.* ermahnen; **ex·hor·ta·tion** [ˌegzɔː'teɪʃn] *s.* Ermahnung *f*.

ex·hu·ma·tion [ˌekshjuː'meɪʃn] *s.* Exhumierung *f*; **ex·hume** [eks'hjuːm] *v/t.* **1.** *Leiche* exhumieren; **2.** *fig.* ausgraben.

ex·i·gence ['eksɪdʒəns], **ex·i·gen·cy** [-dʒənsɪ; ɪg'zɪ-] *s.* **1.** Dringlichkeit *f*; **2.** Not(lage) *f*; **3.** *mst pl.* (An)Forderung *f*; '**ex·i·gent** [-nt] *adj.* **1.** dringend, kritisch; **2.** anspruchsvoll.

ex·i·gu·i·ty [ˌeksɪ'gjuːətɪ] *s.* Dürftigkeit *f*; **ex·ig·u·ous** [eg'zɪgjʊəs] *adj.* dürftig.

ex·ile ['eksaɪl] **I** *s.* **1.** a) Ex'il *n*, b) Verbannung *f*: **government in ~** Exilregierung *f*; **the** ♀ *bibl.* die Babylonische Gefangenschaft; **2.** a) im Ex'il Lebende(r *m*) *f*, b) Verbannte(r *m*) *f*; **II** *v/t.* **3.** a) exilieren, b) verbannen (**from** aus), in die Verbannung schicken.

ex·ist [ɪg'zɪst] *v/i.* **1.** existieren, vor'handen sein, dasein: **do such things ~?** gibt es so etwas?; **right to ~** Existenzberechtigung *f*; **2.** sich finden, vorkommen (**in** in *dat.*); **3.** (**on**) existieren, leben (von); **ex'ist·ence** [-təns] *s.* **1.** Exi'stenz *f*, Vor'handensein *n*, Vorkommen *n*: **call into ~** ins Leben rufen; **be in ~** bestehen, existieren; **remain in ~** weiterbestehen; **2.** Exi'stenz *f*, Leben *n*, Dasein *n*: **a wretched ~** ein kümmerliches Dasein; **3.** Exi'stenz *f*, (Fort-)Bestand *m*; **ex'ist·ent** [-tənt] *adj.* **1.** existierend, bestehend, vor'handen, lebend; **2.** gegenwärtig.

ex·is·ten·tial [ˌegzɪ'stenʃl] *adj.* **1.** Existenz...; **2.** *phls.* Existential...; ˌ**ex·is'ten·tial·ism** [-ʃəlɪzəm] *s.* Existentia'lismus *m*, Exi'stenzphilosoˌphie *f*; ˌ**ex·is'ten·tial·ist** [-ʃəlɪst] *s.* Existentia'list (-in).

ex·ist·ing [ɪg'zɪstɪŋ] → **existent**.

ex·it ['eksɪt] **I** *s.* **1.** Abgang *m*: a) *thea.* Abtreten *n* (*von der Bühne*), b) *fig.* Tod *m*: **make one's ~** → 6a, 7; **2.** (*a.* Not)Ausgang *m*; **3.** ⚙ Abzug *m*, -fluß *m*, Austritt *m*; **4.** Ausreise *f*: **~ permit** Ausreisegenehmigung *f*; **~ visa** Ausreisevisum *n*; **5.** (Autobahn)Ausfahrt *f*; **II** *v/i.* **6.** *thea.* a) abgehen, abtreten, b) *Bühnenanweisung*: (*er, sie* geht) ab: ♀ **Romeo**; **7.** *fig.* sterben.

ex li·bris [eks'laɪbrɪs] (*Lat.*) *s.* Ex'libris *n*, Bücherzeichen *n*.

ˌ**ex·o·bi'ol·o·gy** [ˌeksəʊ-] *s.* Exo-, Ektobiolo'gie *f*.

ex·o·carp ['eksəʊkɑːp] *s.* ⚘ Exo'karp *n*, äußere Fruchthaut.

ex·o·crine ['eksəʊkraɪn] *physiol.* **I** *adj.* **1.** exo'krin; **II** *s.* **2.** äußere Sekreti'on; **3.** exo'krine Drüse.

ex·o·don·ti·a [ˌeksəʊ'dɒnʃɪə] *s.* ˌ**ex·o'don·tics** [-ntɪks] *s. pl. sg. konstr.* 'Zahnchirurˌgie *f*.

ex·o·dus ['eksədəs] *s.* **1.** a) *bibl. u. fig.* Auszug *m*, b) ♀ *bibl.* Exodus *m*, Zweites Buch Mose; **2.** *fig.* Ab-, Auswanderung *f*, Massenflucht *f*; Aufbruch *m*: **~ of capital** ✝ Kapitalabwanderung; **rural ~** Landflucht.

ex of·fi·ci·o [ˌeksə'fɪʃɪəʊ] (*Lat.*) **I** *adv.* von Amts wegen; **II** *adj.* Amts..., amtlich.

ex·on·er·ate [ɪg'zɒnəreɪt] *v/t.* **1.** *Angeklagten etc., a. Schuldner* entlasten (**from** von); **2.** *j-n* befreien, entbinden (**from** von); **ex·on·er·a·tion** [ɪgˌzɒnə'reɪʃn] *s.* **1.** Entlastung *f*; **2.** Befreiung *f*.

ex·or·bi·tance [ɪg'zɔːbɪtəns] *s.* Maßlosigkeit *f*; **ex'or·bi·tant** [-nt] *adj.* □ maßlos, über'trieben, unverschämt: **~ price** Wucherpreis *m*.

ex·or·cism ['eksɔːsɪzəm] *s.* Exor'zismus *m*, Teufelsaustreibung *f*, Geisterbeschwörung *f*; '**ex·or·cist** [-ɪst] *s.* Exor'zist *m*, Teufelsaustreiber *m*, Geisterbeschwörer *m*; '**ex·or·cize** [-saɪz] *v/t.* *Teufel* austreiben, *Geister* beschwören, bannen.

ex·or·di·um [ek'sɔːdjəm] *s.* Einleitung *f*, Anfang *m* (*e-r Rede*).

ex·o·ter·ic [ˌeksəʊ'terɪk] *adj.* (□ **~ally**) exo'terisch, für Außenstehende bestimmt, gemeinverständlich.

ex·ot·ic [ɪg'zɒtɪk] *adj.* (□ **~ally**) ex'otisch: a) aus-, fremdländisch, b) fremdartig, bi'zarr; **ex'ot·i·ca** [-kə] *s. pl.* E'xotika *pl.* (*fremdländische Kunstwerke*).

ex·pand [ɪk'spænd] **I** *v/t.* **1.** ausbreiten, -spannen, entfalten; **2.** ✝, *phys. u. fig.* ausdehnen, -weiten, erweitern: **~ed metal** Streckmetall *n*; **~ed plastics** Schaumkunststoffe; **~ed program(me)** erweitertes Programm; **3.** *Abkürzung* ausschreiben; **II** *v/i.* **4.** sich ausbreiten *od.* -dehnen; sich erweitern (*a. fig.*): **his heart ~ed with joy** sein Herz schwoll vor Freude; **5.** *fig.* sich entwickeln, aufblühen (**into** zu); größer werden; **6.** *fig.* a) *vor Stolz, Freude etc.* ‚aufblühen', b) aus sich her'ausgehen; **ex'pand·er** [-də] *s. sport* Ex'pander *m*; **ex'pand·ing** [-dɪŋ] *adj.* sich (aus)dehnend, dehnbar; **ex'panse** [-ns] *s.* weiter Raum, weite Fläche, Weite *f*, Ausdehnung *f*; *orn.* Spannweite *f*; **ex'pan·sion** [-nʃn] *s.* **1.** Ausbreitung *f*, Erweiterung *f*, Zunahme *f*; (✝ *Industrie-, Produktions-, a. Kredit*)Ausweitung *f*; *pol.* Expansi'on *f*: **ego ~** *psych.* gesteigertes Selbstgefühl; **2.** *a.* ⚙, *phys.* (Aus)Dehnung *f*, Expansi'on *f*: **~ engine** Expansionsmaschine *f*; **~ stroke** *mot.* Arbeitstakt *m*, Expansionshub *m*; **3.** 'Umfang *m*, Raum *m*, Weite *f*;

ex'pan·sion·ism [-nʃənɪzəm] *s.* Expansi'onspoliˌtik *f*; **ex'pan·sion·ist** [-nʃənɪst] **I** *s.* Anhänger(in) der Expansi'onspoliˌtik; **II** *adj.* Expansions…; **ex'pan·sive** [-nsɪv] *adj.* ☐ **1.** ausdehnungsfähig, ausdehnend, (Aus)Dehnungs…; **2.** ausgedehnt, weit, um'fassend; **3.** *fig.* mitteilsam, aufgeschlossen; **4.** *fig.* 'überschwenglich; **ex'pan·sive·ness** [-nsɪvnɪs] *s.* **1.** Ausdehnungsvermögen *n*; **2.** *fig.* a) Mitteilsamkeit *f*, Aufgeschlossenheit *f*, b) 'Überschwenglichkeit *f*.

ex par·te [ˌeks'pɑːtɪ] (*Lat.*) *adj. u. adv.* ⚖ einseitig (*Prozeßhandlung*).

ex·pa·ti·ate [ek'speɪʃɪeɪt] *v/i.* sich weitläufig auslassen *od.* verbreiten (***on*** über *acc.*); **ex·pa·ti·a·tion** [ekˌspeɪʃɪ'eɪʃn] *s.* weitläufige Erörterung, Erguß *m*, ‚Salm' *m*.

ex·pa·tri·ate I *v/t.* [eks'pætrɪeɪt] **1.** ausbürgern, expatriieren, *j-m* die Staatsangehörigkeit aberkennen: ~ ***o.s.*** auswandern, s-e Staatsangehörigkeit aufgeben; **II** *adj.* [-ɪət] **2.** verbannt, ausgebürgert; **3.** ständig im Ausland lebend; **III** *s.* [-ɪət] **4.** Ausgebürgerte(r *m*) *f*; **5.** (freiwillig) im Ex'il *od.* ständig im Ausland Lebende(r *m*) *f*; **ex·pa·tri·a·tion** [eksˌpætrɪ'eɪʃn] *s.* **1.** Ausbürgerung *f*, Aberkennung *f* der Staatsangehörigkeit; **2.** Auswanderung *f*; **3.** Aufgabe *f* s-r Staatsangehörigkeit.

ex·pect [ɪk'spekt] *v/t.* **1.** *j-n* erwarten: ***I ~ him to dinner*** ich erwarte ihn zum Essen; **2.** *et.* erwarten *od.* vor'hersehen; entgegensehen (*dat.*): ***I did not ~ that question*** auf diese Frage war ich nicht gefaßt *od.* vorbereitet; **3.** erwarten, hoffen, rechnen auf (*acc.*): ***I ~ you to come*** ich erwarte, daß du kommst; ***I ~ (that) he will come*** ich erwarte, daß er kommt; **4.** *et. von j-m* erwarten, verlangen: ***you ~ too much from him***; **5.** F annehmen, denken, vermuten: ***that is hardly to be ~ed*** das ist kaum anzunehmen; ***I ~ so*** ich denke ja (*od.* schon); **ex'pect·ance** [-təns], **ex'pect·an·cy** [-tənsɪ] *s.* (***of***) **1.** Erwartung *f* (*gen.*); Hoffnung *f*, Aussicht *f* (auf *acc.*); **2.** ✝, ⚖ Anwartschaft *f* (auf *acc.*); **ex'pect·ant** [-tənt] **I** *adj.* ☐ **1.** erwartend: ***be ~ of*** *et.* erwarten; ***~ heir*** a) ⚖ Erb(schafts)anwärter(in), b) Thronanwärter *m*; **2.** erwartungsvoll; **3.** zu erwarten(d); **4.** schwanger: ***~ mother*** werdende Mutter, Schwangere *f*; **II** *s.* **5.** ⚖ Anwärter(in) (***of*** auf *acc.*); **ex·pec·ta·tion** [ˌekspek'teɪʃn] *s.* **1.** Erwartung *f*, Erwarten *n*: ***beyond*** (***contrary to***) ~ über (wider) Erwarten; ***according to ~*** erwartungsgemäß; ***come up to ~*** den Erwartungen entsprechen; **2.** Gegenstand *m* der Erwartung; **3.** *oft pl.* Hoffnung *f*, Aussicht *f*: ***~ of life*** Lebenserwartung *f*; **ex'pect·ing** [-tɪŋ] *adj.*: ***she is ~*** F sie ist in anderen Umständen.

ex·pec·to·rant [ek'spektərənt] *adj. u. s. pharm.* schleimlösend(es Mittel); **ex·pec·to·rate** [ek'spektəreɪt] **I** *v/t.* ausspucken, -husten; **II** *v/i.* a) (aus-)spucken, b) Blut spucken; **ex·pec·to·ra·tion** [ekˌspektə'reɪʃn] *s.* **1.** Auswerfen *n*, Aushusten *n*, -spucken *n*; **2.** Auswurf *m*.

ex·pe·di·ence [ɪk'spiːdjəns], **ex'pe·di·en·cy** [-sɪ] *s.* **1.** Ratsamkeit *f*, Zweckmäßigkeit *f*; **2.** Nützlichkeit *f*, Zweckdienlichkeit *f*; **3.** Eigennutz *m*; **ex'pe·di·ent** [-nt] **I** *adj.* ☐ **1.** ratsam, angebracht; **2.** zweckmäßig, -dienlich, praktisch, nützlich, vorteilhaft; **3.** eigennützig; **II** *s.* **4.** (Hilfs)Mittel *n*, (Not)Behelf *m*.

ex·pe·dite ['ekspɪdaɪt] *v/t.* **1.** beschleunigen, fördern; **2.** schnell ausführen; **3.** befördern, expedieren.

ex·pe·di·tion [ˌekspɪ'dɪʃn] *s.* **1.** Eile *f*, Schnelligkeit *f*; **2.** (Forschungs)Reise *f*, Expediti'on *f*; **3.** ⚔ Feldzug *m*; **ˌex·pe'di·tion·ar·y** [-ʃnərɪ] *adj.* Expeditions…: ***~ force*** Expeditionskorps *n*; **ˌex·pe'di·tious** [-ʃəs] *adj.* ☐ schnell, rasch, prompt.

ex·pel [ɪk'spel] *v/t.* (***from***) **1.** vertreiben, wegjagen (aus, von); **2.** ausstoßen, -schließen, hi'nauswerfen (aus); **3.** aus-, verweisen, verbannen (aus); **4.** *Rauch etc.* ausstoßen (aus); **ex·pel·lee** [ˌekspe'liː] *s.* (Heimat)Vertriebene(r *m*) *f*.

ex·pend [ɪk'spend] *v/t.* **1.** *Geld* ausgeben; **2.** *Mühe, Zeit etc.* ver-, aufwenden (***on*** für); **3.** verbrauchen; **ex'pend·a·ble** [-dəbl] **I** *adj.* **1.** verbrauchbar, Verbrauchs…; **2.** entbehrlich; **3.** ⚔ (*im Notfall*) zu opfern(d); **II** *s.* **4.** *mst pl. et.* Entbehrliches; **5.** ⚔ verlorener Haufen; **ex'pend·i·ture** [-dɪtʃə] *s.* **1.** Aufwand *m*, Verbrauch *m* (***of*** an *dat.*); **2.** (Geld)Ausgabe(n *pl.*) *f*, (Kosten-)Aufwand *m*, Auslage(n *pl.*) *f*, Kosten *pl.*: ***cash ~*** ✝ Barauslagen.

ex·pense [ɪk'spens] *s.* **1.** → ***expenditure*** 2; **2.** *pl.* Unkosten *pl.*, Spesen *pl.*: ***~ account*** ✝ Spesenkonto *n*; ***~ allowance*** ✝ Aufwandsentschädigung *f*, Spesenvergütung *f*; ***travel(l)ing ~s*** Reisespesen; ***and all ~s paid*** und alle Unkosten *od.* Spesen (werden) vergütet; ***at an ~ of*** mit e-m Aufwand von; ***at great ~*** mit großen Kosten; ***at my ~*** auf m-e Kosten, für m-e Rechnung; ***they laughed at my ~*** *fig.* sie lachten auf m-e Kosten; ***at the ~ of his health*** auf Kosten s-r Gesundheit; ***go to great ~*** sich in (große) (Un)Kosten stürzen; ***put s.o. to great ~*** j-n in große (Un-)Kosten stürzen; ***spare no ~*** keine Kosten scheuen; **ex'pen·sive** [-sɪv] *adj.* ☐ teuer, kostspielig, aufwendig.

ex·pe·ri·ence [ɪk'spɪərɪəns] **I** *s.* **1.** a) Erfahrung *f*, (Lebens)Praxis *f*, b) Erfahrenheit *f*, (praktische) Erfahrung, Praxis *f*, praktische Kenntnisse *pl.*, Fach-, Sachkenntnis *f*: ***by*** (*od.* ***from***) ~ aus (eigener) Erfahrung; ***in my ~*** nach m-n Erfahrungen, m-s Wissens; ***~ in cooking*** Kochkenntnisse; ***business ~*** Geschäftserfahrung, -routine *f*; ***driving ~*** Fahrpraxis; ***previous ~*** Vorkenntnisse; **2.** Erlebnis *n*: ***I had a strange ~***; **3.** Vorkommnis *n*, Geschehnis *n*; **4.** *Am. eccl.* religi'öse Erweckung; **II** *v/t.* **5.** erfahren: a) kennenlernen, b) erleben, c) erleiden, *Schlimmes* 'durchmachen, *Vergnügen etc.* empfinden: ***~ kindness*** Freundlichkeit erfahren; ***~ difficulties*** auf Schwierigkeiten stoßen; **ex'pe·ri·enced** [-st] *adj.* erfahren, routiniert, bewandert, (fach-, sach)kundig.

ex·pe·ri·en·tial·ism [ɪkˌspɪərɪ'enʃəlɪzəm] *s. phls.* Empi'rismus *m*.

ex·per·i·ment I *s.* [ɪk'sperɪmənt] Versuch *m*, Experi'ment *n*; **II** *v/i.* [-ment] experimentieren, Versuche anstellen (***on, upon*** an *dat.*; ***with*** mit): ***~ with s.th.*** *a.* et. erproben.

ex·per·i·men·tal [ekˌsperɪ'mentl] *adj.* ☐ **1.** *phys.* Versuchs…, experimen'tell, Experimental…: ***~ animal*** Versuchstier *n*; ***~ physics*** Experimentalphysik *f*; ***~ station*** Versuchsanstalt *f*; **2.** experimentierfreudig; **3.** Erfahrungs…; **exˌper·i'men·tal·ist** [-təlɪst] *s.* Experimen'tator *m*; **exˌper·i'men·tal·ly** [-təlɪ] *adv.* experimen'tell, versuchsweise; **ex·per·i·men·ta·tion** [ekˌsperɪmen'teɪʃn] *s.* Experimentieren *n*.

ex·pert ['ekspɜːt] **I** *adj* [*pred. a.* ɪk'spɜːt] ☐ **1.** erfahren, kundig; **2.** geschickt, gewandt (***at, in*** in *dat.*); **3.** fachmännisch, fach-, sachkundig; Fach…(*-ingenieur, -wissen etc.*); **4.** Sachverständigen…: ***~ opinion*** (Sachverständigen-)Gutachten *n*; ***~ witness*** ⚖ Sachverständige(r *m*) *f*; **II** *s.* **5.** a) Fachmann *m*, Ex'perte *m*, b) Sachverständige(r *m*) *f*, Gutachter(in) (***at, in*** in *dat.*; ***on s.th.*** [auf dem Gebiet] e-r Sache); **ex·per·tise** [ˌekspɜː'tiːz] *s.* **1.** Exper'tise *f*, (Sachverständigen)Gutachten *n*; **2.** Sach-, Fachkenntnis *f*; **3.** (fachmännisches) Können; **'ex·pert·ness** [-nɪs] *s.* **1.** Erfahrenheit *f*; **2.** Geschicklichkeit *f*.

ex·pi·a·ble ['ekspɪəbl] *adj.* sühnbar; **'ex·pi·ate** [-ɪeɪt] *v/t.* sühnen, wieder'gutmachen, (ab)büßen; **ex·pi·a·tion** [ˌekspɪ'eɪʃn] *s.* Sühne *f*, Buße *f*: ***in ~ of s.th.*** um et. zu sühnen, als Sühne für et.; **'ex·pi·a·to·ry** [-ɪətərɪ] *adj.* sühnend, Sühn(e)…, Buß…: ***be ~ of*** *et.* sühnen.

ex·pi·ra·tion [ˌekspɪ'reɪʃn] *s.* **1.** Ausatmen *n*; **2.** *fig.* Ablauf *m* (*e-r Frist, e-s Vertrags*), Ende *n*; **3.** ✝ a) Fälligwerden *n*, b) Verfall *m* (*e-s Wechsels*): ***~ date*** Verfallsdatum *n*; **ex·pir·a·to·ry** [ɪk'spaɪərətərɪ] *adj.* Ausatmungs…

ex·pire [ɪk'spaɪə] *v/i.* **1.** ausatmen, -hauchen (*a. v/t.*); **2.** sein Leben aushauchen, verscheiden; **3.** ablaufen (*Frist, Vertrag etc.*), erlöschen (*Patent, Recht etc.*), enden, ungültig werden, verfallen; **4.** ✝ fällig werden; **ex'pired** [-əd] *adj.* ungültig, verfallen, erloschen; **ex'pi·ry** [-ərɪ] → ***expiration*** 2, 3.

ex·plain [ɪk'spleɪn] **I** *v/t.* **1.** erklären, erläutern, ausein'andersetzen (***s.th. to s.o.*** j-m et.): ***~ s.th. away*** a) sich aus et. herausreden, b) e-e einleuchtende Erklärung für et. finden; **2.** erklären, begründen, rechtfertigen: ***~ o.s.*** a) sich erklären, b) sich rechtfertigen; **II** *v/i.* **3.** es erklären: ***you have got a little ~ing to do*** da müßtest du (mir, uns) schon einiges erklären; **ex'plain·a·ble** [-nəbl] *adj.* → ***explicable***; **ex·pla·na·tion** [ˌeksplə'neɪʃn] *s.* **1.** Erklärung *f*, Erläuterung *f* (***for, of*** für): ***in ~ of*** als Erklärung für; ***make some ~*** e-e Erklärung abgeben; **2.** Er-, Aufklärung *f*; **3.** Verständigung *f*; **ex·plan·a·to·ry** [ɪk'splænətərɪ] *adj.* ☐ erklärend, erläuternd.

ex·ple·tive [ek'spliːtɪv] **I** *adj.* **1.** ausfüllend, (Aus)Füll…; **II** *s.* **2.** *ling.* Füllwort *n*; **3.** Füllsel *n*, Lückenbüßer *m*; **4.** a) Fluch *m*, b) Kraftausdruck *m*.

ex·pli·ca·ble [ɪk'splɪkəbl] *adj.* erklärbar, erklärlich; **ex·pli·cate** ['eksplɪkeɪt] *v/t.*

1. explizieren, erklären; **2.** *Theorie etc.* entwickeln; **ex·pli·ca·tion** [ˌeksplɪ-ˈkeɪʃn] *s.* **1.** Erklärung *f*, Erläuterung *f*; **2.** Entwicklung *f*.

ex·plic·it [ɪkˈsplɪsɪt] *adj.* □ **1.** deutlich, klar, ausdrücklich; **2.** offen, deutlich (*Person*) (***on*** in bezug auf *acc.*); **3.** ⩓ expliˈzit.

ex·plode [ɪkˈspləʊd] **I** *v/t.* **1.** a) zur Exploˈsion bringen, explodieren lassen, b) (in die Luft) sprengen; **2.** *fig.* a) *Plan etc.* über den Haufen werfen, zum Platzen bringen, zuˈnichte machen: ~ ***a myth*** e-e Illusion zerstören, b) *Theorie etc.* widerˈlegen, *e-m Gerücht etc.* den Boden entziehen; **II** *v/i.* **3.** a) explodieren, ⚔ *a.* krepieren (*Granate etc.*), b) in die Luft fliegen; **4.** *fig.* ausbrechen (***into***, ***with*** in *acc.*), ‚platzen' (***with*** vor *dat.*): ~ ***with fury*** vor Wut platzen, ‚explodieren'; ~ ***with laughter*** in schallendes Gelächter ausbrechen; **5.** *fig.* sprunghaft ansteigen, sich exploˈsionsartig vermehren; **exˈplod·ed view** [-dɪd] *s.* ⚙ Darstellung *f e-r Maschine etc.* in zerlegter Anordnung.

ex·ploit I *v/t.* [ɪkˈsplɔɪt] **1.** *et.* auswerten; *kommerziell* verwerten; ⚒ *etc.* ausbeuten, abbauen; **2.** *fig.* *b.s. et. od. j-n* ausbeuten, -nutzen; *et.* ausschlachten, Kapiˈtal schlagen aus; **II** *s.* [ˈeksplɔɪt] **3.** (Helden)Tat *f*; **4.** Großtat *f*, große Leistung; **ex·ploi·ta·tion** [ˌeksplɔɪˈteɪʃn] *s.* ☩ (*Patent- etc.*)Verwertung *f*; ⚙ Ausnutzung *f*, -beutung *f* (*beide a. fig. b.s.*); ⚒ Abbau *m*, Gewinnung *f*; **exˈploi·ter** [-tə] *s.* Ausbeuter *m* (*a. fig.*).

ex·plo·ra·tion [ˌekspləˈreɪʃn] *s.* **1.** Erforschung *f* (*e-s Landes*); **2.** Unterˈsuchung *f*.

ex·plor·a·tive [ekˈsplɒrətɪv], **exˈplor·a·to·ry** [-tərɪ] *adj.* **1.** (er)forschend, Forschungs...; **2.** Erkundungs..., untersuchend, sondierend; ⚙ *etc.* Versuchs..., Probe...: ~ ***drilling***; ~ ***talks*** Sondierungsgespräche; **ex·plore** [ɪkˈsplɔː] *v/t.* **1.** *Land* erforschen; **2.** erforschen, erkunden, unterˈsuchen (*a.* ⚕), sondieren; **ex·plor·er** [ɪkˈsplɔːrə] *s.* Forscher *m*, Forschungsreisende(r *m*) *f*.

ex·plo·sion [ɪkˈspləʊʒn] *s.* **1.** a) Exploˈsion *f* (*a. ling.*), Entladung *f*, b) Knall *m*, Detonatiˈon *f*; **2.** *fig.* Exploˈsion *f*: ***population*** ~; **3.** *fig.* Zerstörung *f*, Widerˈlegung *f*; **4.** *fig.* (*Wut- etc.*)Ausbruch *m*.

ex·plo·sive [ɪkˈspləʊsɪv] **I** *adj.* □ **1.** exploˈsiv, Knall..., Spreng..., Explosions...; **2.** *fig.* jähzornig, aufbrausend; **II** *s.* **3.** Exploˈsiv-, Sprengstoff *m*; **4.** *ling.* → ***plosive*** II; ~ **charge** *s.* Sprengladung *f*; ~ **cot·ton** *s.* Schießbaumwolle *f*; ~ **flame** *s.* Stichflamme *f*; ~ **force** *s.* Sprengkraft *f*.

ex·po·nent [ekˈspəʊnənt] *s.* **1.** ⩓ Expoˈnent *m*, Hochzahl *f*; **2.** *fig.* Expoˈnent (-in): a) Repräsenˈtant(in), Vertreter (-in), b) Verfechter(in); **3.** Interˈpret (-in); **ex·po·nen·tial** [ˌekspəʊˈnenʃl] ⩓ **I** *adj.* Exponential...; **II** *s.* Exponentiˈalgröße *f*.

ex·port I *v/t. u. v/i.* [ekˈspɔːt] **1.** exportieren, ausführen; **II** *s.* [ˈekspɔːt] **2.** Exˈport *m*, Ausfuhr(handel *m*) *f*; **3.** Exˈport-, ˈAusfuhrarˌtikel *m*; **4.** *pl.* a) (Geˈsamt)Exˌport *m*, (-)Ausfuhr *f*, b) Exˈportgüter *pl.*; **III** *adj.* [ˈekspɔːt] **5.** Ausfuhr..., Export...: ~ ***duty*** Ausfuhrzoll *m*; ~ ***license***, ~ ***permit*** Ausfuhrgenehmigung *f*; ~ ***trade*** Export-, Ausfuhr-, Außenhandel *f*; **exˈport·a·ble** [-təbl] *adj.* exˈportfähig, zur Ausfuhr geeignet; **ex·por·ta·tion** [ˌekspɔːˈteɪʃən] *s.* Ausfuhr *f*, Exˈport *m*; **exˈporter** [-tə] *s.* Exporˈteur *m*.

ex·pose [ɪkˈspəʊz] **I** *v/t.* **1.** *Kind* aussetzen; **2.** *Waren* ausstellen (***for sale*** zum Verkauf); **3.** *fig.* *e-r Gefahr*, *e-m Übel* aussetzen, preisgeben: ~ ***o.s.*** sich exponieren; ~ ***o.s. to ridicule*** sich lächerlich machen; **4.** *fig.* a) (***o.s.*** sich) bloßstellen, b) *j-n* entlarven, c) *et.* aufdecken, enthüllen; **5.** *et.* darlegen, auseinˈandersetzen; **6.** entblößen (*a.* ⚔), enthüllen, zeigen; **7.** *phot.* belichten; **II** *s.* **8.** *Am.* → ***exposé*** 2.

ex·po·sé [ekˈspəʊzeɪ] (*Fr.*) *s.* **1.** Expoˈsé *n*, Darlegung *f*; **2.** Enthüllung *f*, Entlarvung *f*.

ex·posed [ɪkˈspəʊzd] *adj.* **1.** *pred.* ausgesetzt (***to*** *dat.*); **2.** unverdeckt, offen (-liegend); **3.** ungeschützt, exponiert; **4.** *phot.* belichtet.

ex·po·si·tion [ˌekspəʊˈzɪʃn] *s.* **1.** Ausstellung *f*, Schau *f*; **2.** Darlegung(en *pl.*) *f*, Ausführung(en *pl.*) *f*; **3.** *thea. u.* ♪ Expositiˈon *f*; **ex·pos·i·tor** [ekˈspɒzɪtə] *s.* Erklärer *m*; **ex·pos·i·to·ry** [ekˈspɒzɪtərɪ] *adj.* erklärend.

ex·pos·tu·late [ɪkˈspɒstjʊleɪt] *v/i.* **1.** protestieren; **2.** ~ ***with*** *j-m* ernste Vorhaltungen machen, *j-n* zuˈrechtweisen; **ex·pos·tu·la·tion** [ɪkˌspɒstjʊˈleɪʃn] *s.* **1.** Proˈtest *m*; **2.** ernste Vorhaltung, Verweis *m*.

ex·po·sure [ɪkˈspəʊʒə] *s.* **1.** (Kindes-)Aussetzung *f*; **2.** Aussetzen *n*, Preisgabe *f*; **3.** Ausgesetztsein *n*, Preisgegebensein *n* (***to*** *dat.*): ***death from*** ~ Tod *m* durch Erfrieren *od.* vor Entkräftung *etc.*; **4.** Entblößung *f*: ***indecent*** ~ unsittliche (Selbst)Entblößung; **5.** *fig.* a) Bloßstellung *f*, b) Entlarvung *f*, c) Enthüllung *f*, Aufdeckung *f*; **6.** *phot.* Belichtung *f*: ~ ***meter*** Belichtungsmesser *m*; ***time*** ~ Zeitaufnahme *f*; ~ ***value*** Lichtwert *m* (*e-s Films*); **7.** Lage *f* (*e-s Gebäudes*): ***southern*** ~ Südlage.

ex·pound [ɪkˈspaʊnd] *v/t.* **1.** erklären, erläutern; *Theorie* entwickeln; **2.** auslegen.

ex·press [ɪkˈspres] **I** *v/t.* **1.** *obs.* *Saft* auspressen, ausdrücken; **2.** *fig.* ausdrücken, äußern, zum Ausdruck bringen: ~ ***o.s.*** sich äußern, sich erklären; ***be ~ed*** zum Ausdruck kommen; **3.** bezeichnen, bedeuten, darstellen; **4.** *Gefühle etc.* offenˈbaren, zeigen, bekunden; **5.** a) *Brit.* durch Eilboten *od.* als Eilgut schicken, b) *bsd. Am.* durch ein (ˈSchnell)TransˌportunterˌnehmenJ befördern lassen; **II** *adj.* □ → ***expressly***; **6.** ausdrücklich, bestimmt, deutlich, eindeutig; **7.** besonder: ***for the ~ purpose*** eigens zu dem Zweck; **8.** Expreß..., Schnell..., Eil...; **III** *adv.* **9.** → ***expressly***; **10.** *Brit.* durch Eilboten, per Exˈpreß, als Eilgut; **IV** *s.* **11.** *Brit.* a) Eilbote *m*, b) Eilbeförderung *f*, c) Eilbrief *m*, -gut *n*; **12.** 🚆 D-Zug *m*; **13.** *Am.* → ***express company***; **exˈpress·age** [-sɪdʒ] *s.* *Am.* **1.** Beförderung *f* durch ein (ˈSchnell)Transˌportunterˌnehmen; **2.** Eilfracht(gebühr) *f*.

ex·press| com·pa·ny *s.* *Am.* (ˈSchnell-)Transˌportunterˌnehmen *n*; ~ **de·liv·er·y** *s.* a) *Brit.* Eilzustellung *f*, b) → ***expressage*** 1; ~ **goods** *s. pl.* Eilfracht *f*, -gut *n*.

ex·pres·sion [ɪkˈspreʃn] *s.* **1.** Ausdruck *m*, Äußerung *f*: ***find ~ in*** sich äußern in (*dat.*); ***give ~ to*** Ausdruck verleihen (*dat.*); ***beyond ~*** unsagbar; **2.** Redensart *f*, Ausdruck *m*; **3.** Ausdrucksweise *f*, Diktiˈon *f*; **4.** Ausdruck(skraft *f*) *m*: ***with ~*** mit Gefühl, ausdrucksvoll; **5.** (Gesichts)Ausdruck *m*; **6.** ⩓ Ausdruck *m*, Formel *f*; **exˈpres·sion·ism** [-ʃnɪzəm] *s.* Expressioˈnismus *m*; **exˈpres·sion·ist** [-ʃnɪst] **I** *s.* Expressioˈnist(in); **II** *adj.* expressioˈnistisch; **exˈpres·sion·less** [-lɪs] *adj.* ausdruckslos.

ex·pres·sive [ɪkˈspresɪv] *adj.* □ **1.** ausdrückend (***of*** *acc.*): ***be ~ of*** *et.* ausdrükken; **2.** ausdrucksvoll; **3.** Ausdrucks...; **exˈpres·sive·ness** [-nɪs] *s.* **1.** Ausdruckskraft *f*; **2.** *das* Ausdrucksvolle; **exˈpress·ly** [-slɪ] *adv.* **1.** ausdrücklich; **2.** eigens, besonders.

exˈpress|·man [-mæn] *s.* [*irr.*] *Am.* Angestellte(r) *m* e-s (ˈSchnell)Transˌportunterˌnehmens; ~ **train** *s.* D-Zug *m*; **~·way** *s.* *bsd. Am.* Schnellstraße *f*.

ex·pro·pri·ate [eksˈprəʊprɪeɪt] *v/t.* ⚖ *j-n od. et.* enteignen; **ex·pro·pri·a·tion** [eksˌprəʊprɪˈeɪʃn] *s.* ⚖ Enteignung *f*.

ex·pul·sion [ɪkˈspʌlʃn] *s.* (***from***) **1.** Vertreibung *f* (aus); **2.** *pol.* Ausweisung *f*, Verbannung *f*, Abschiebung *f* (aus); **3.** Ausstoßung *f* (aus), Ausschließung (aus, von): ~ ***from school***; **4.** ⚕ Austreibung *f*; **exˈpul·sive** [-lsɪv] *adj.* aus-, vertreibend.

ex·punge [ekˈspʌndʒ] *v/t.* **1.** (aus)streichen; *a. fig.* löschen (***from*** aus); **2.** *fig.* ausmerzen, vernichten.

ex·pur·gate [ˈekspɜːgeɪt] *v/t.* *Buch etc.* (von anstößigen Stellen) reinigen: ***~d version*** gereinigte Version; **ex·pur·gation** [ˌekspɜːˈgeɪʃn] *s.* Reinigung *f*.

ex·qui·site [ˈekskwɪzɪt] *adj.* □ **1.** köstlich, (aus)erlesen, vorˈzüglich, ausgezeichnet, exquiˈsit; **2.** gepflegt, fein: ~ ***taste***; **3.** äußerst fein: ***an ~ ear***; **4.** äußerst, höchst; **5.** heftig: ~ ***pain***; ~ ***pleasure*** großes Vergnügen.

ex-serv·ice·man [ˌeksˈsɜːvɪsmən] *s.* [*irr.*] ehemaliger Solˈdat, Veteˈran *m*.

ex·tant [ekˈstænt] *adj.* (noch) vorˈhanden *od.* bestehend.

ex·tem·po·ra·ne·ous [ekˌstempəˈreɪnɪəs], **ex·tem·po·rar·y** [ɪkˈstempərərɪ] *adj.* □ improvisiert, extemporiert, unvorbereitet, aus dem Stegreif: ~ ***translation*** Stegreifübersetzung *f*; **ex·tem·po·re** [ekˈstempərɪ] **I** *adj. u. adv.* → ***extemporaneous***; **II** *s.* Improvisatiˈon *f*, Stegreifgedicht *n*, unvorbereitete Rede; **ex·tem·po·rize** [ɪkˈstempəraɪz] *v/t. u. v/i.* aus dem Stegreif *od.* unvorbereitet reden *od.* dichten *od.* spielen, improvisieren; **ex·tem·po·riz·er** [ɪkˈstempəraɪzə] *s.* Improviˈsator *m*, Stegreifdichter *m*.

ex·tend [ɪkˈstend] **I** *v/t.* **1.** (aus)dehnen, ausbreiten; **2.** verlängern; **3.** vergrößern, erweitern, ausbauen: ~ ***a factory***; **4.** *Seil etc.* spannen, ziehen; **5.** *Hand etc.* ausstrecken; **6.** *Nahrungsmittel* strecken; **7.** *fig.* *e-n Besuch*, *s-e Macht etc.* ausdehnen (***to*** auf *acc.*), *e-e*

Frist, s-n Paß, e-n Vertrag etc. verlängern, ✝ *a.* prolongieren; **8.** (***to, towards*** *dat.*) a) *Gunst, Hilfe etc.* gewähren, *Gutes* erweisen, b) *s-n Dank, Glückwunsch etc.* aussprechen, *e-e Einladung* schicken, c) *e-n* Gruß entbieten; **9.** ✈ *Fahrgestell* ausfahren; **10.** ⚔ ausschwärmen lassen; **11.** *Abkürzungen* voll ausschreiben; *Kurzschrift* in Normalschrift über'tragen; **12.** *sport* das Letzte her'ausholen aus (*e-m Pferd etc.*): ***~ o.s.*** sich völlig ausgeben; **II** *v/i.* **13.** sich ausdehnen *od.* erstrecken, reichen (***to*** bis zu); hin'ausgehen (***beyond*** über *acc.*); **14.** ⚔ ausschwärmen; **ex·'tend·ed** [-dɪd] *adj.* **1.** ausgedehnt (*a. Zeitraum*); **2.** ausgestreckt: ***~ hands***; **3.** verlängert; **4.** ausgebreitet; *typ.* breit: ***~ formation*** ⚔ auseinandergezogene Formation; ***~ order*** ⚔ geöffnete Ordnung; **5.** groß, um'fassend: ***~ family*** Großfamilie *f*.

ex·ten·si·bil·i·ty [ɪkˌstensə'bɪlətɪ] *s.* (Aus)Dehnbarkeit *f*; **ex·ten·si·ble** [ɪk'stensəbl] *adj.* (aus)dehnbar, (aus-)streckbar; ausziehbar (*Tisch*): ***~ table*** Ausziehtisch *m*.

ex·ten·sion [ɪk'stenʃn] *s.* **1.** Ausdehnung *f* (*a. fig.*; ***to*** auf *acc.*); Ausbreitung *f*; (*Frist- Kredit- etc.*)Verlängerung *f*, ✝ *a.* Prolongati'on *f*: ***~ of leave*** Nachurlaub *m*; **2.** ⚙ Dehnung *f*, Streckung *f* (*a.* ⚕); **3.** *fig.* Vergrößerung *f*, Erweiterung *f*, Ausbau *m*; **4.** Ausdehnung *f*, 'Umfang *m*; **5.** △ Anbau *m* (*Gebäude*); **6.** *teleph.* Nebenanschluß *m*, *a.* Appa'rat *m*; **7.** *phot.* (Kamera-)Auszug *m*; ***~*** **band·age** *s.* ⚕ Streckverband *m*; ***~*** **board** *s. teleph.* 'Hauszenˌtrale *f*; ***~*** **cord** *s.*, ***~*** **flex** *s.* ⚡ Verlängerungskabel *n*; ***~*** **lad·der** *s.* Ausziehleiter *f*; ***~*** **ta·ble** *s. Am.* Ausziehtisch *m*.

ex·ten·sive [ɪk'stensɪv] *adj.* □ ausgedehnt (*a.* ⩘ *u. fig.*), um'fassend; eingehend; exten'siv (*a.* ✓); **ex'ten·sive·ness** [-nɪs] *s.* Ausdehnung *f*, 'Umfang *m*; **ex'ten·sor** [-sə] *s. anat.* Streckmuskel *m*.

ex·tent [ɪk'stent] *s.* **1.** Ausdehnung *f*, Länge *f*, Weite *f*, Höhe *f*, Größe *f*; **2.** ⩘ *u. fig.* Bereich *m*; **3.** Raum *m*, Strecke *f*; **4.** *fig.* 'Umfang *m*, (Aus)Maß *n*, Grad *m*: ***to the ~ of*** bis zum Betrag *od.* zur Höhe von; ***to some*** (*od.* ***a certain***) ***~*** in gewissem Grade, einigermaßen; ***to the full ~*** in vollem Umfang, völlig.

ex·ten·u·ate [ek'stenjʊeɪt] *v/t.* **1.** abschwächen, mildern: ***extenuating circumstances*** ⚖ mildernde Umstände; **2.** beschönigen, bemänteln; **ex·ten·u·a·tion** [ekˌstenjʊ'eɪʃn] *s.* **1.** Abschwächung *f*, Milderung *f*; **2.** Beschönigung *f*.

ex·te·ri·or [ek'stɪərɪə] **I** *adj.* **1.** äußer, Außen...: ***~ angle*** Außenwinkel *m*; ***~ to*** abseits von, außerhalb (*gen.*); **2.** von außen (ein)wirkend *od.* kommend; **3.** *pol.* auswärtig: ***~ possessions***; ***~ policy***; **II.** *s.* **4.** *das* Äußere: a) Außenseite *f*, b) äußere Erscheinung *f* (*e-r Person*), c) *pol.* auswärtige Angelegenheiten *pl.*; **5.** *Film*: Außenaufnahme *f*.

ex·ter·mi·nant [ɪk'stɜːmɪnənt] *s.* Vertilgungsmittel *n*; **ex·ter·mi·nate** [ɪk'stɜːmɪneɪt] *v/t.* ausrotten (*a. fig.*), *Ungeziefer etc. a.* vertilgen; **ex·ter·mi·na·tion** [ɪkˌstɜːmɪ'neɪʃn] *s.* Ausrottung *f*, Vertilgung *f*: ***~ camp*** *hist.* Vernichtungslager *n*; **ex'ter·mi·na·tor** [-tə] *s.* **1.** Kammerjäger *m*; **2.** → ***exterminant***.

ex·tern [ek'stɜːn] *s.* **1.** Ex'terne(r *m*) *f* (*e-s Internats*); **2.** *Am.* ex'terner 'Krankenhausarzt *od.* -assiˌstent; **ex'ter·nal** [-nl] **I** *adj.* □ → ***externally***; **1.** äußer, äußerlich, Außen...: ***~ angle*** ⩘ Außenwinkel *m*; ***~ ear*** äußeres Ohr; ***for ~ use*** ⚕ zum äußerlichen Gebrauch, äußerlich; ***~ to*** außerhalb (*gen.*); ***~ world*** Außenwelt *f*; **2.** von außen (ein)wirkend *od.* kommend; **3.** (äußerlich) wahrnehmbar; **4.** ✝, *pol.* auswärtig, Außen..., Auslands...: ***~ affairs*** auswärtige Angelegenheiten; ***~ loan*** Auslandsanleihe *f*; ***~ trade*** Außenhandel *m*; **5.** ✝ außerbetrieblich, Fremd...; **II.** *s.* **6.** *mst pl. das* Äußere; **7.** *pl.* Äußerlichkeiten *pl.*, Nebensächlichkeiten *pl.*; **ex'ter·nal·ize** [-nəlaɪz] *v/t. psych.* **1.** objektivieren; **2.** *Konflikte* nach außen verlagern; **ex'ter·nal·ly** [-nəlɪ] *adv.* äußerlich, von außen.

ex·ter·ri·to·ri·al ['eksˌterɪ'tɔːrɪəl] *etc.* → ***extraterritorial*** *etc.*

ex·tinct [ɪk'stɪŋkt] *adj.* **1.** erloschen (*a. fig. Titel etc., geol. Vulkan*); **2.** ausgestorben (*Pflanze, Tier etc.*), 'untergegangen (*Rasse, Reich etc.*); nicht mehr existierend; **3.** abgeschafft, aufgehoben; **ex'tinc·tion** [-kʃn] *s.* **1.** Erlöschen *n*; **2.** Aussterben *n*, 'Untergang *m*; **3.** (Aus)Löschen *n*; **4.** Vernichtung *f*; **5.** Abschaffung *f*; **6.** Tilgung *f*; **7.** ⚡, *phys.* Löschung *f*.

ex·tin·guish [ɪk'stɪŋgwɪʃ] *v/t.* **1.** *Feuer, Lichter* (aus)löschen; **2.** *fig. Leben, Gefühl* auslöschen, ersticken, töten; **3.** vernichten; **4.** *fig.* in den Schatten stellen; **5.** *fig. j-n* zum Schweigen bringen; **6.** (*a.* ⚖) abschaffen, aufheben; **7.** *Schuld* tilgen; **ex'tin·guish·er** [-ʃə] *s.* **1.** Löschgerät *n*; **2.** Löschhütchen *n* (*für Kerzen*); **3.** Glut-, Ziga'rettentöter *m*.

ex·tir·pate ['ekstɜːpeɪt] *v/t.* **1.** (mit den Wurzeln) ausreißen; **2.** *fig.* ausmerzen, ausrotten; **3.** ⚕ exstirpieren, entfernen.

ex·tol, *Am. a.* **ex·toll** [ɪk'stəʊl] *v/t.* (lob)preisen, rühmen.

ex·tort [ɪk'stɔːt] *v/t.* (***from***) a) *et.* erpressen, erzwingen (von), b) *a. Bewunderung etc.* abringen, abnötigen (*dat.*).

ex·tor·tion [ɪk'stɔːʃn] *s.* **1.** Erpressung *f*; **2.** Wucher *m*; **ex'tor·tion·ate** [-nət] *adj.* **1.** erpresserisch; **2.** unmäßig, Wucher...; **ex'tor·tion·er** [-ʃnə], **ex'tor·tion·ist** [-nɪst] *s.* **1.** Erpresser *m*; **2.** Wucherer *m*.

ex·tra ['ekstrə] **I** *adj.* **1.** zusätzlich, Extra..., Sonder..., Neben...: ***~ charge*** Zuschlag *m*; ***~ charges*** Nebenkosten; ***~ dividend*** Extra-, Zusatzdividende *f*; ***~ pay*** Zulage *f*; ***~ time*** *sport* (Spiel-)Verlängerung *f*; ***if you pay an ~ two pounds*** wenn Sie noch zwei Pfund zulegen; **2.** besonder, außergewöhnlich; besonders gut: ***it is nothing ~*** es ist nichts Besonderes; **II** *adv.* **3.** extra, besonders: ***~ high***; ***~ late***; ***be charged for ~*** gesondert berechnet werden; **III** *s.* **4.** *et.* Außergewöhnliches, *bsd.* a) Sonderarbeit *f*, -leistung *f*, b) *bsd. mot.* Extra *n*, c) Sonderberechnung *f*, Zuschlag *m*: ***heating and light are ~s*** Heizung u. Licht werden gesondert berechnet; **5.** *pl.* Nebenkosten *pl.*; **6.** Extrablatt *n* (*Zeitung*); **7.** Aushilfskraft *f*; **8.** *thea., Film*: Sta'tist(in).

ex·tract **I** *v/t.* [ɪk'strækt] **1.** her'ausziehen, -holen (***from*** aus); **2.** extrahieren: a) ⚕ *Zahn*(*wurzel*) ziehen, b) ⚗ ausscheiden, -ziehen, c) *Metall etc.* gewinnen, d) ⩘ *Wurzel* ziehen; **3.** *Honig etc.* schleudern; **4.** *Beispiele etc.* ausziehen, exzerpieren (***from a text*** aus e-m Text); **5.** *fig.* (***from***) *et.* her'ausholen (aus), entlocken (*dat.*); **6.** *fig.* ab-, herleiten; **II** *s.* ['ekstrækt] **7.** *a.* ⚗ Auszug *m*, Ex'trakt *m*: ***~ of beef*** Fleischextrakt; ***~ of account*** Kontoauszug; **ex'trac·tion** [-kʃn] *s.* **1.** Her'ausziehen *n*; **2.** Extrakti'on *f*: a) ⚕ Ziehen *n* (*e-s Zahns*), b) ⚗ Ausziehen *n*, Ausscheidung *f*, Gewinnung *f*, c) ⩘ Ziehen *n* (*Wurzel*); **3.** *fig.* Entlockung *f*; **4.** Abstammung *f*, Herkunft *f*; **ex'trac·tive** [-tɪv] *adj.*: ***~ industry*** Industrie *f* zur Gewinnung von Naturprodukten; **ex'trac·tor** [-tə] *s.* **1.** ⚙, ⚔ Auszieher *m*, -werfer *m*; **2.** ⚕ (Geburts-, Zahn-, Wurzel)Zange *f*; **3.** Trockenschleuder *f*.

ex·tra·cur·ric·u·lar [ˌekstrəkə'rɪkjʊlə] *adj.* **1.** *ped., univ.* außerhalb des Stunden- *od.* Lehrplans; **2.** außerplanmäßig.

ex·tra·dit·a·ble ['ekstrədaɪtəbl] *adj.* **1.** auszuliefern(d): ***~ criminal***; **2.** auslieferungsfähig: ***~ offence***; **ex·tra·dite** ['ekstrədaɪt] *v/t.* ausliefern; **ex·tra·di·tion** [ˌekstrə'dɪʃn] *s.* Auslieferung *f*: ***request for ~*** Auslieferungsantrag *m*.

ˌex·tra|·ju'di·cial *adj.* ⚖ außergerichtlich; **ˌ~'mar·i·tal** *adj.* außerehelich; **ˌ~'mu·ral** *adj.* außerhalb der Mauern (*e-r Stadt od. Universität*): ***~ courses*** Hochschulkurse außerhalb der Universität; ***~ student*** Gasthörer(in).

ex·tra·ne·ous [ek'streɪnjəs] *adj.* □ **1.** fremd (***to*** *dat.*); **2.** unwesentlich; **3.** ***be ~ to*** nicht gehören zu.

ex·traor·di·nar·i·ly [ɪk'strɔːdnrəlɪ] *adv.*, **ex·traor·di·nar·y** [ɪk'strɔːdnrɪ] *adj.* **1.** außerordentlich: ***ambassador ~*** Sonderbotschafter *m*; **2.** ungewöhnlich, seltsam, merkwürdig.

ex·trap·o·late [ek'stræpəʊleɪt] *v/t.* extrapolieren.

ˌex·tra|'sen·so·ry *adj. psych.* außersinnlich: ***~ perception*** außersinnliche Wahrnehmung; **ˌ~·ter'res·trial** *adj.* außerirdisch; **'~ˌter·ri'to·ri·al** *adj.* ˌexterritori'al; **'~ˌter·ri·to·ri'al·i·ty** *s.* ˌExterritoriali'tät *f*; ***~*** **time** *s. sport* (Spiel)Verlängerung *f*.

ex·trav·a·gance [ɪk'strævəgəns] *s.* **1.** Verschwendung *f*; **2.** Ausschweifung *f*, Zügellosigkeit *f*; 'Übermut *m*; **3.** Extrava'ganz *f*, 'Übermaß *n*, Über'triebenheit *f*, Über'spanntheit *f*; **ex'trav·a·gant** [-nt] *adj.* □ **1.** verschwenderisch; **2.** ausschweifend, zügellos; **3.** extrava'gant, über'trieben, -'spannt; **ex·trav·a·gan·za** [ekˌstrævə'gænzə] *s.* **1.** phan'tastisches Werk (*Musik od. Literatur*); **2.** Ausstattungsstück *n*.

ex·treme [ɪk'striːm] **I** *adj.* □ → ***extremely***; **1.** äußerst, weitest, letzt: ***~ border*** äußerster Rand; ***~ value*** Extremwert *m*; → ***unction*** 3 c; **2.** äußerst, höchst; außergewöhnlich, über'trieben: ***~ case*** äußerster (Not)Fall; ***~ meas-***

ure drastische *od.* radikale Maßnahme; **~ *necessity*** zwingende Notwendigkeit; **~ *old age*** hohes Greisenalter; **~ *penalty*** höchste Strafe, *a.* Todesstrafe *f*; **3.** *pol.* ex'trem, radi'kal: **~ *Left*** äußerste Linke; **~ *views*; II** *s.* **4.** äußerstes Ende: ***at the other ~*** am entgegengesetzten Ende; **5.** *das* Äußerste, höchster Grad, Ex'trem *n*: ***awkward in the ~*** äußerst peinlich; ***go to ~s*** vor nichts zurückschrecken; ***go to the other ~*** ins andere Extrem fallen; **6.** 'Übermaß *n*, Über'triebenheit *f*: ***carry s.th. to an ~*** et. zu weit treiben; **7.** Gegensatz *m*: ***~s meet*** Extreme berühren sich; **8.** *pl. obs.* äußerste Not; **ex'treme·ly** [-lɪ] *adv.* äußerst, höchst; **ex'trem·ism** [-mɪzəm] *s.* Extre'mismus *m*, Radika'lismus *m*; **ex'trem·ist** [-mɪst] *s.* **I** Extre'mist(in), Radi'kale(r *m*) *f*; **II** *adj.* extre'mistisch; **ex'trem·i·ty** [-remətɪ] *s.* **1.** *das* Äußerste, äußerstes Ende, äußerste Grenze: ***to the last ~*** bis zum Äußersten; ***drive s.o. to extremities*** j-n zum Äußersten treiben; ***resort to extremities*** zu drastischen Mitteln greifen; **2.** *fig.* a) höchster Grad: ***~ of joy*** Übermaß der Freude, b) äußerste Not, verzweifelte Situation: ***reduced to extremities*** in größter Not, c) verzweifelter Gedanke; **3.** *pl.* Gliedmaßen *pl.*, Extremi'täten *pl.*

ex·tri·cate ['ekstrɪkeɪt] *v/t.* **1.** (***from***) her'auswinden, -ziehen (aus), befreien (aus, von): **~ *o.s.*** sich befreien; **2.** ⚗ *Gas* frei machen; **ex·tri·ca·tion** [ˌekstrɪ'keɪʃn] *s.* **1.** Befreiung *f*; **2.** ⚗ Freimachen *n*.

ex·trin·sic [ek'strɪnsɪk] *adj.* (□ ***~ally***) **1.** äußer; **2.** a) nicht zur Sache gehörig, b) unwesentlich: ***be ~ to s.th.*** nicht zu et. gehören.

ex·tro·ver·sion [ˌekstrəʊ'vɜːʃn] *s. psych.* Extro- *od.* Extraversi'on *f*; **ex·tro·vert** ['ekstrəʊvɜːt] *psych.* **I** *s.* Extro- *od.* Extraver'tierte(r *m*) *f*; **II** *adj.* extro- *od.* extraver'tiert.

ex·trude [ek'struːd] **I** *v/t.* **1.** ausstoßen, (her)'auspressen; **2.** ⚙ strangpressen; **II** *v/i.* **3.** vorstehen; **ex'tru·sion** [-uːʒn] *s.* **1.** Ausstoßung *f*; **2.** ⚙ a) Strangpressen *n*, b) Strangpreßling *m*.

ex·u·ber·ance [ɪg'zjuːbərəns] *s.* **1.** (***of***) ('Über)Fülle (von *od. gen.*), Reichtum *m* (an *dat.*); **2.** 'Überschwang *m*; Ausgelassenheit *f*; **3.** (Wort)Schwall *m*; **ex'u·ber·ant** [-nt] *adj.* □ **1.** üppig, ('über)reichlich; **2.** *fig.* a) 'überschwenglich, b) ('über)sprudelnd, ausgelassen; **3.** *fig.* (äußerst) fruchtbar.

ex·ude [ɪg'zjuːd] **I** *v/t.* **1.** ausschwitzen, absondern; **2.** *fig.* von sich geben, verströmen; **II** *v/i.* **3.** *a. fig.* ausströmen (***from*** aus, von).

ex·ult [ɪg'zʌlt] *v/i.* froh'locken, jubeln, triumphieren (***at***, ***over***, ***in*** über *acc.*); **ex'ult·ant** [-tənt] *adj.* □ froh'lockend, jubelnd, triumphierend; **ex·ul·ta·tion** [ˌegzʌl'teɪʃn] *s.* Jubel *m*, Froh'locken *n*.

ex·urb ['eksɜːb] *s. Am.* (vornehmes) Einzugsgebiet (*e-r Großstadt*); **ex·ur·ban·ite** [ɪg'zɜːbənaɪt] *s. Am.* Bewohner(in) e-s ***exurb***; **ex·ur·bia** [ɪg'zɜːbɪə] *s.* die (vornehmen) Außenbezirke *pl.*

eye [aɪ] **I** *s.* **1.** Auge *n*: ***an ~ for an ~*** *bibl.* Auge um Auge; ***under my ~s*** vor m-n Augen; ***up to the ~s in work*** bis über die Ohren in Arbeit; ***with one's ~s shut*** mit geschlossenen Augen (*a. fig.*); ***be all ~s*** ganz Auge sein; ***cry one's ~s out*** sich die Augen ausweinen; **2.** *fig.* Blick *m*, Gesichtssinn *m*, Auge(nmerk) *n*: ***with an ~ to*** a) im Hinblick auf (*acc.*), b) mit der Absicht zu (*inf.*); ***cast an ~ over*** e-n Blick werfen auf (*acc.*); ***catch*** (*od.* ***strike***) ***the ~*** ins Auge fallen; ***she caught his ~*** sie fiel ihm auf; ***catch the Speaker's ~*** *parl.* das Wort erhalten; ***do s.o. in the ~*** F j-n ‚reinlegen' *od.* ‚übers Ohr hauen'; ***give an ~ to s.th.*** et. anblicken, ein Auge auf et. haben; ***give s.o. the*** (***glad***) ***~*** j-m e-n einladenden Blick zuwerfen; ***have an ~ for*** e-n Sinn *od.* Blick *od.* ein (offenes) Auge haben für; ***he has an ~ for beauty*** er hat Sinn für Schönheit; ***have an ~ to s.th.*** a) ein Auge auf et. haben, b) auf et. achten; ***keep an ~ on*** ein (wachsames) Auge haben auf (*acc.*); ***make ~s at*** *j-m* verliebte Blicke zuwerfen; → ***meet*** 9; ***open s.o.'s ~s*** (***to s.th.***) j-m die Augen öffnen (für et.); ***that made him open his ~s*** das verschlug ihm die Sprache; ***you can see that with half an ~*** das sieht doch ein Blinder!; ***set*** (*od.* ***clap***) ***~s on*** zu Gesicht bekommen; ***close one's ~s to*** die Augen verschließen vor (*dat.*); ***my ~!*** F denkste!, von wegen!, Quatsch!; **3.** Ansicht *f*: ***in the ~s of*** nach Ansicht von; ***see ~ to ~ with s.o.*** mit j-m übereinstimmen; **4.** Öhr *n* (*Nadel*); Öse *f*; **5.** ⚘ Auge *n*, Knospe *f*; **6.** *zo.* Auge *n* (*Schmetterling*, *Pfauenschweif*); **7.** ⚠ rundes Fenster; **8.** Auge *n*, windstilles Zentrum *e-s Sturms*; **II** *v/t.* **9.** ansehen, betrachten, (scharf) beobachten, ins Auge fassen: ***~ s.o. from top to toe*** j-n von oben bis unten mustern.

'eye|-apˌpeal *s.* optische Wirkung, attrak'tive Gestaltung; **'~·ball** *s.* Augapfel *m*; **'~·black** *s.* Wimperntusche *f*; **'~·brow** *s.* Augenbraue *f*: **~ *pencil*** Augenbrauenstift *m*; ***raise one's ~s*** *fig.* die Stirn runzeln; ***cause raised ~s*** Aufsehen *od.* Mißfallen erregen; **'~-ˌcatch·er** *s.* Blickfang *m*; **'~-ˌcatch·ing** *adj.* ins Auge fallend, auffallend.

eyed [aɪd] *adj. in Zssgn* ...äugig; mit (...) Ösen.

'eye|·ful *s.* F **1.** ‚toller Anblick'; **2.** ‚tolle Frau'; **3. *get an ~ of this!*** sieh dir das mal an!; **'~·glass** *s.* **1.** Mon'okel *n*; **2.** *opt.* Oku'lar *n*; **3.** *pl. a.* ***pair of ~es*** *bsd. Am.* Brille *f*; **'~·hole** *s.* **1.** Augenhöhle *f*; **2.** Guckloch *n*; **'~·lash** *s. mst pl.* Augenwimper *f*; → ***bat***[3]; **~ lens** *s.* Oku'larlinse *f*.

eye·let ['aɪlɪt] *s.* **1.** Öse *f*; **2.** Loch *n*.

eye| lev·el *s.* (***on ~*** in) Augenhöhe *f*; **'~·lid** *s.* Augenlid *n*; → ***bat***[3]; **~ lin·er** *s.* Eyeliner *m*; **'~-ˌo·pen·er** *s.* **1.** *fig.* Über'raschung *f*, Entdeckung *f*: ***that was an ~ to me*** das hat mir die Augen geöffnet; **2.** *Am.* F (*bsd. alkoholischer*) ‚Muntermacher'; **'~·piece** *s. opt.* Oku'lar *n*; **~ rhyme** *s.* Augenreim *m*; **'~·shade** *s.* Sonnenschild *m*; **~ shad·ow** *s.* Lidschatten *m*; **'~·shot** *s.*: (***with***)***in*** (***beyond*** *od.* ***out of***) **~** in (außer) Sichtweite; **'~·sight** *s.* Augenlicht *n*, Sehkraft *f*: ***poor ~*** schwache Augen *pl.*; **~ sock·et** *s. anat.* Augenhöhle *f*; **'~ sore** *s. fig.* Schandfleck *m*, *et.* Häßliches; **'~·strain** *s.* Über'anstrengung *f* der Augen; **'~·tooth** *s.* [*irr.*] *anat.* Augen-, Eckzahn *m*: ***he'd give his eyeteeth for it*** er würde alles darum geben; **'~·wash** *s.* **1.** *pharm.* Augenwasser *n*; **2.** *fig.* a) ‚Quatsch' *m*, b) Augen(aus)wische'rei *f*; **ˌ~'wit·ness I** *s.* Augenzeuge *m*; **II** *v/t.* Augenzeuge sein *od.* werden von (*od. gen.*).

ey·rie ['aɪərɪ] *s. orn.* Horst *m*.

E·ze·ki·el, E·ze·chi·el [ɪ'ziːkjəl] *npr. u. s. bibl.* (das Buch) He'sekiel *m od.* E'zechiel *m*; **Ez·ra** ['ezrə] *npr. u. s. bibl.* (das Buch) Esra *m od.* Esdras *m*.

F

F, f [ef] *s.* **1.** F *n*, f *n* (*Buchstabe*); **2.** ♪ F *n*, f *n* (*Note*); **3.** ℒ *ped.* Sechs *f*, Ungenügend *n* (*Note*).

fab [fæb] *adj. sl.* → ***fabulous*** 2.

Fa·bi·an ['feɪbjən] **I** *adj.* **1.** Hinhalte…, Verzögerungs…: ~ ***tactics***; **2.** *pol.* die ***Fabian Society*** betreffend; **II** *s.* **3.** *pol.* Fabier(in); '**Fa·bi·an·ism** [-nɪzəm] *s.* Poli'tik *f* der → **Fa·bi·an So·ci·e·ty** *s.* (*sozialistische*) Gesellschaft der Fabier.

fa·ble ['feɪbl] *s.* **1.** Fabel *f* (*a. e-s Dramas*); Sage *f*, Märchen *n*; **2.** *coll.* a) Fabeln *pl.*, b) Sagen *pl.*; **3.** *fig.* ‚Märchen' *n*; '**fa·bled** [-ld] *adj.* **1.** legen'där; **2.** (frei) erfunden.

fab·ric ['fæbrɪk] *s.* **1.** Bau *m* (*a. fig*); Gebilde *n*; **2.** *fig.* a) Gefüge *n*, Struk'tur *f*, b) Sy'stem *n*; **3.** Stoff *m*, Gewebe *n*; ⚙ Leinwand *f*, Reifengewebe *n*: ~ ***gloves*** Stoffhandschuhe; '**fab·ri·cate** [-keɪt] *v/t.* **1.** fabrizieren, herstellen, (an)fertigen; **2.** *fig.* ‚fabrizieren': a) erfinden, b) fälschen; **fab·ri·ca·tion** [ˌfæbrɪ'keɪʃn] *s.* **1.** Herstellung *f*, Fabrikati'on *f*; **2.** *fig.* Erfindung *f*, ‚Märchen' *n*, Lüge *f*; **3.** Fälschung *f*; '**fab·ri·ca·tor** [-keɪtə] *s.* **1.** Hersteller *m*; **2.** *fig. b.s.* Erfinder *m*, Urheber *m e-r Lüge etc.*, Lügner *m*; **3.** Fälscher *m*.

fab·u·list ['fæbjʊlɪst] *s.* **1.** Fabeldichter (-in); **2.** Schwindler(in); '**fab·u·lous** [-ləs] *adj.* ☐ **1.** legen'där, Sagen…, Fabel…; **2.** *fig.* F fabel-, sagenhaft, ‚toll'.

fa·çade [fə'sɑːd] (*Fr.*) *s.* ⚠ Fas'sade *f* (*a. fig.*), Vorderseite *f*.

face [feɪs] **I** *s.* **1.** Gesicht *n*, Angesicht *n*, Antlitz *n* (*a. fig.*): ***for s.o.'s fair*** ~ *iro.* um j-s schönen Augen willen; ***in*** (***the***) ~ ***of*** a) angesichts (*gen.*), gegenüber (*dat.*), b) trotz (*gen. od. dat.*); ***in the*** ~ ***of danger*** angesichts der Gefahr; ***to s.o.'s*** ~ j-m ins Gesicht *sagen etc.*; ~ ***to*** ~ von Angesicht zu Angesicht; ~ ***to*** ~ ***with*** Auge in Auge mit, gegenüber, vor (*dat.*); ***fly in the*** ~ ***of*** a) *j-m* ins Gesicht fahren, b) *fig.* sich offen widersetzen (*dat.*), trotzen (*dat.*); ***I couldn't look him in the*** ~ ich konnte ihm (vor Scham) nicht in die Augen sehen; ***do*** (***up***) ***one's*** ~, F ***put one's*** ~ ***on*** sich ‚anmalen' (*schminken*); ***set one's*** ~ ***against s.th.*** sich e-r Sache widersetzen, sich gegen et. wenden; ***show one's*** ~ sich blicken lassen; ***shut the door in s.o.'s*** ~ j-m die Tür vor der Nase zuschlagen; **2.** (Gesichts)Ausdruck *m*, Aussehen *n*, Miene *f*: ***make*** (*od.* ***pull***) ***a*** ~ (*od.* ~***s***) ein Gesicht (*od.* e-e Grimasse) machen *od.* schneiden; ***make*** (*od.* ***pull***) ***a long*** ~ *fig.* ein langes Gesicht machen; ***put a bold*** ~ ***on*** a) *e-r Sache* gelassen entgegensehen, b) sich *et. Unangenehmes etc.* nicht anmerken lassen; ***put a good*** (*od.* ***brave***) ~ ***on the matter*** gute Miene zum bösen Spiel machen; **3.** *fig.* Stirn *f*, Unverfrorenheit *f*, Frechheit *f*: ***have the*** ~ ***to*** *inf.* die Stirn haben zu *inf.*; **4.** Ansehen *n*: ***save*** (***one's***) ~ das Gesicht wahren; ***lose*** ~ das Gesicht verlieren; ***loss of*** ~ Prestigeverlust *m*; **5.** *das* Äußere, Gestalt *f*, Erscheinung *f*, Anschein *m*: ***on the*** ~ ***of it*** auf den ersten Blick, oberflächlich betrachtet, vordergründig; ***put a new*** ~ ***on s.th.*** et. in neuem *od.* anderem Licht erscheinen lassen; **6.** Ober-, Außenfläche *f*, Fläche *f* (*a.* ⩓), Seite *f*; ⚙ Stirnfläche *f*; ⚙ (Amboß-, Hammer)Bahn *f*: ***the*** ~ ***of the earth*** die Erdoberfläche, die Welt; **7.** Oberseite *f*; rechte Seite (*Stoff etc.*): ***lying on its*** ~ nach unten gekehrt liegend; **8.** Fas'sade *f*, Vorderseite *f*; **9.** Bildseite *f* (*Spielkarte*); *typ.* Bild *n* (*Type*); Zifferblatt *n* (*Uhr*); **10.** Wand *f* (*Berg etc.*, ⚒ *Kohlenflöz*): ***at the*** ~ ⚒ am (Abbau)Stoß, vor Ort; **II** *v/t.* **11.** ansehen, *j-m* ins Gesicht sehen *od.* das Gesicht zuwenden; **12.** gegen'überstehen, -liegen, -sitzen, -treten (*dat.*); nach *Osten etc.* blicken *od.* liegen (*Raum*): ***the man facing me*** der Mann mir gegenüber; ***the house*** ~***s the sea*** das Haus liegt nach dem Meer zu; ***the window*** ~***s the street*** das Fenster geht auf die Straße; ***the room*** ~***s east*** das Zimmer liegt nach Osten; **13.** (mutig) entgegentreten *od.* begegnen (*dat.*), ins Auge sehen (*dat.*), die Stirn bieten (*dat.*): ~ ***the enemy***; ~ ***death*** dem Tod ins Auge blicken; ~ ***it out*** die Sache durchstehen; ~ ***s.o. off*** *Am.* es auf e-e Kraft- *od.* Machtprobe mit j-m ankommen lassen; → ***music*** 1; **14.** *oft* ***be*** ~***d with*** sich *e-r Gefahr etc.* gegen'übersehen, gegen'überstehen (*dat.*): ***he was*** ~***d with ruin*** er stand vor dem Nichts; **15.** *et.* hinnehmen, sich mit *et.* abfinden: ~ ***the facts***; ***let's*** ~ ***it, …!*** seien wir ehrlich, …!; **16.** 'umkehren, -wenden; *Spielkarten* aufdecken; **17.** *Schneiderei*: besetzen, einfassen, mit Aufschlägen versehen; **18.** ⚙ verkleiden, verblenden, über'ziehen; **19.** ⚙ *Stirnflächen* bearbeiten, (plan)schleifen, glätten; **III** *v/i.* **20.** *bsd.* ⚔ ~ ***about*** kehrtmachen (*a. fig.*): ***left*** ~***!*** *Am.* links um!; ***right about*** ~***!*** rechts um kehrt!; **21.** ~ ***off*** *Eishockey*: das Bully ausführen; **22.** ~ ***up to*** → 13, 15.

'**face**|**-a**ˌ**bout** → ***about-face***; ~ **brick** *s.* ⚠ Verblendstein *m*; ~ **card** *s. Kartenspiel*: Bild(karte *f*) *n*; '~**-cloth** *s.* Waschlappen *m*; ~ **cream** *s.* Gesichtscreme *f*.

-faced [feɪst] *adj. in Zssgn* mit e-m … Gesicht.

'**face**|**·down** *s. Am.* Kraft-, Machtprobe *f*; ~ **flan·nel** → ***facecloth***; ~ **grind·ing** *s.* ⚙ Planschleifen *n*; '~**-guard** *s.* Schutzmaske *f*; '~**-lathe** *s.* ⚙ Plandrehbank *f*.

face·less ['feɪslɪs] *adj.* gesichtslos, *fig. a.* ano'nym.

'**face**|**-lift I** *s.* → ***face-lifting***; **II** *v/t. fig.* verschönern; '~**-**ˌ**lift·ing** *s.* **1.** Gesichtsstraffung *f*, Facelifting *n*; **2.** *fig.* Verschönerung *f*, Renovierung *f*; '~**-off** *s.* **1.** *Eishockey*: Bully *n*: ~ ***circle*** Anspielkreis *m*; **2.** → ***facedown***; ~ **pack** *s.* Gesichtspackung *f*, -maske *f*.

fac·er ['feɪsə] *s.* **1.** Schlag *m* ins Gesicht (*a. fig.*); **2.** *fig.* Schlag *m* (ins Kon'tor); **3.** *Brit.* F ‚harte Nuß'.

'**face-**ˌ**sav·ing** *adj.*: ~ ***excuse*** Ausrede *f*, um das Gesicht zu wahren.

fac·et ['fæsɪt] **I** *s.* **1.** a) Fa'cette *f* (*a. fig.*), b) Schliff-, Kri'stallfläche *f*; **2.** *fig.* Seite *f*, A'spekt *m*; **II** *v/t.* **3.** facettieren: ~***ed eye*** *zo.* Facettenauge *n*.

fa·ce·tious [fə'siːʃəs] *adj.* ☐ scherzhaft, witzig, drollig, spaßig; **fa'ce·tious·ness** [-nɪs] *s.* Scherzhaftigkeit *f etc.*

ˌ**face**|**-to-'face** *adj.* **1.** per'sönlich; **2.** di'rekt; ~ **tow·el** *s.* (Gesichts)Handtuch *n*; ~ **val·ue** *s.* **1.** ✝ Nenn-, Nomi'nalwert *m*; **2.** scheinbarer Wert, *das* Äußere: ***take s.th. at its*** ~ et. für bare Münze nehmen *od.* unbesehen glauben.

fa·ci·a ['feɪʃə] *s. Brit.* **1.** Firmen-, Ladenschild *n*; **2.** *a.* ~ ***board***, ~ ***panel*** *mot.* Arma'turenbrett *n*.

fa·cial ['feɪʃl] **I** *adj.* ☐ a) Gesichts…: ~ ***pack*** Gesichtspackung *f*, b) des Gesichts, im Gesicht; **II** *s. Kosmetik*: Gesichtsbehandlung *f*.

-fa·cient [feɪʃənt] *in Zssgn* verursachend, machend.

fac·ile ['fæsaɪl] *adj.* ☐ **1.** leicht (zu tun *od.* zu meistern *etc.*); **2.** *fig.* oberflächlich; **3.** flüssig (*Stil*).

fa·cil·i·tate [fə'sɪlɪteɪt] *v/t.* erleichtern, fördern; **fa·cil·i·ta·tion** [fəsɪlɪ'teɪʃn] *s.* Erleichterung *f*, Förderung *f*; **fa'cil·i·ty** [-tɪ] *s.* **1.** Leichtigkeit *f* (*der Ausführung etc.*); **2.** Oberflächlichkeit *f*; **3.** Flüssigkeit *f* (*des Stils*); **4.** (günstige) Gelegenheit *f*, Möglichkeit *f* (***for*** für, zu); **5.** *mst pl.* Einrichtung(en *pl.*) *f*, Anlage(n *pl.*) *f*; **6.** *mst pl.* Erleichterung(en *pl.*) *f*, Vorteil(e *pl.*) *m*, Vergünstigung(en *pl.*) *f*, Annehmlichkeit(en *pl.*) *f*.

fac·ing ['feɪsɪŋ] *s.* **1.** ⚔ Wendung *f*, Schwenkung *f*: ***go through one's*** ~***s*** *fig.* zeigen (müssen), was man kann; ***put s.o. through his*** ~***s*** *fig.* j-n auf

Herz u. Nieren prüfen; **2.** Außen-, Oberschicht *f*, Belag *m*, 'Überzug *m*; **3.** ⚙ Plandrehen *n*: **~ lathe** Plandrehbank *f*; **4.** △ a) Verkleidung *f*, -blendung *f*, b) Bewurf *m*: **~ brick** Verblendstein *m*; **5.** *a.* **~ sand** ⚙ feingesiebter Formsand; **6.** *Schneiderei*: a) Aufschlag *m*, b) Besatz *m*, Einfassung *f*: **~s** ⚔ (Uniform-) Aufschläge.

fac·sim·i·le [fæk'sɪmɪlɪ] **I** *s.* **1.** Fak'simile *n*, Reprodukti'on *f*; **2.** *a.* **~ transmission** *od.* **broadcast(ing)** ϟ, *tel.* Bildfunk *m*: **~ apparatus** Bildfunkgerät *n*; **II** *v/t.* **3.** faksimilieren.

fact [fækt] *s.* **1.** Tatsache *f*, Wirklichkeit *f*, Wahrheit *f*: **~ and fancy** Dichtung u. Wahrheit; **~s and figures** genaue Daten; **naked** (*od.* **hard**) **~s** nackte Tatsachen; **in** (**point of**) **~** in der Tat, tatsächlich, genau gesagt; **it is a ~** es stimmt, es ist e-e Tatsache; **founded on ~** auf Tatsachen beruhend; **the ~** (**of the matter**) **is** Tatsache ist *od.* die Sache ist die (**that** daß); **know s.th. for a ~** et. (ganz) sicher wissen; **tell the ~s of life to a child** ein Kind (sexuell) aufklären; **2.** ⚖ a) Tatsache *f*: **in ~ and law** in tatsächlicher u. rechtlicher Hinsicht; **the ~s** (**of the case**) der Tatbestand *m*, die Tatumstände *pl.*, der Sachverhalt *m*, b) Tat *f*: **before** (**after**) **the ~** vor (nach) begangener Tat; → **accessory** 7; '**~,find·ing** *adj.* Untersuchungs…: **~ committee**; **~ tour** Informationsreise *f*.

fac·tion ['fækʃn] *s.* **1.** Fakti'on *f*, Splittergruppe *f*; **2.** Zwietracht *f*; '**fac·tion·al·ism** [-ʃnəlɪzəm] *s.* Par'teigeist *m*; '**fac·tion·ist** [-ʃənɪst] *s.* Par'teigänger *m*; '**fac·tious** [-ʃəs] *adj.* □ **1.** vom Par'teigeist beseelt, fakti'ös; **2.** aufrührerisch.

fac·ti·tious [fæk'tɪʃəs] *adj.* □ gekünstelt, künstlich.

fac·ti·tive ['fæktɪtɪv] *adj. ling.* fakti'tiv, bewirkend: **~ verb**.

fac·tor ['fæktə] *s.* **1.** *fig.* Faktor *m* (*a.* ♣, ⚕, *phys.*), (mitwirkender) 'Umstand, Mo'ment *n*, Ele'ment *n*: **safety ~** Sicherheitsfaktor; **2.** *biol.* Erbfaktor *m*; **3.** † a) (Handels)Vertreter *m*, Kommissio'när *m*, b) *Am.* Finan'zierungskommissio,när *m*; **4.** ⚖ *Scot.* (Guts-) Verwalter *m*; '**fac·tor·ing** [-tərɪŋ] *s.* † Factoring *n* (*Absatzfinanzierung u. Kreditrisikoabsicherung*); '**fac·to·ry** [-tərɪ] *s.* **1.** Fa'brik *f*: ♀ **Acts** Arbeiterschutzgesetze; **~ cost** Herstellungskosten *pl.*; **~ expenses** Gemeinkosten; **~ hand** Fabrikarbeiter *m*; **~ ship** Fabrikschiff *n*; **~-made** fabrikmäßig hergestellt, Fabrik… (*-ware etc.*); **2.** † Handelsniederlassung *f*, Fakto'rei *f*.

fac·to·tum [fæk'təʊtəm] *s.* Fak'totum *n*, ‚Mädchen *n* für alles'.

fac·tu·al ['fæktʃʊəl] *adj.* □ **1.** tatsächlich: **~ situation** Sachlage *f*, -verhalt *m*; **2.** Tatsachen…: **~ report**; **3.** sachlich.

fac·ul·ta·tive ['fækltətɪv] *adj.* fakulta'tiv, wahlfrei: **~ subject** *ped.* Wahlfach *n*; **fac·ul·ty** ['fæklti] *s.* **1.** Fähigkeit *f*, Vermögen *n*, Kraft *f*: **~ of hearing** Hörvermögen; **2.** Gabe *f*, Anlage *f*, Ta'lent *n*, Fähigkeit *f*: (**mental**) **faculties** Geisteskräfte; **3.** *univ.* a) Fakul'tät *f*, Abteilung *f*, b) (Mitglieder *pl.* e-r) Fakul'tät, Lehrkörper *m*, c) (Ver'waltungs)Perso,nal *n* (*a. e-r Schule*): **the medical ~** die medizinische Fakultät, *weitS.* die Mediziner *pl.*; **4.** ⚖ Ermächtigung *f*, Befugnis *f* (**for** zu, für).

fad [fæd] *s.* **1.** Mode(torheit) *f*; **2.** ‚Fimmel' *m*, Ma'rotte *f*; '**fad·dish** [-dɪʃ] **1.** Mode…, vor'übergehend; **2.** ex'zentrisch: **~ woman** Frau, die jede Mode (-torheit) mitmacht.

fade [feɪd] **I** *v/i.* **1.** (ver)welken; **2.** verschießen, -blassen, ver-, ausbleichen (*Farbe etc.*); **3.** *a.* **~ away** verklingen (*Lied, Stimme etc.*), abklingen (*Schmerzen etc.*), verblassen (*Erinnerung*), schwinden, zerrinnen (*Hoffnungen etc.*), verrauchen (*Zorn etc.*), sich auflösen (*Menge*), (in der Ferne *etc.*) verschwinden, immer weniger werden, ⚕ immer schwächer werden (*Person*); **4.** *Radio*: schwinden (*Ton, Sender*); **5.** ⚙ nachlassen (*Bremsen*); **6.** nachlassen, abbauen (*Sportler*); **7.** *bsd. Am.* F ‚verduften'; **8.** *Film, Radio*: über'blenden: **~ in** (*od.* **up**) auf- *od.* eingeblendet werden; **~** (**out**) aus- *od.* abgeblendet werden; **II** *v/t.* **9.** (ver)welken lassen; **10.** *Farbe etc.* ausbleichen; **11.** *a.* **~ out** *Ton, Bild* aus- *od.* abblenden: **~ in** (*od.* **up**) auf- *od.* einblenden; '**fad·ed** [-dɪd] *adj.* □ **1.** welk, verwelkt, -blüht (*alle a. fig. Schönheit etc.*); **2.** verblaßt, verblichen, -schossen; '**fade-in** *s. Film, Radio, TV*: Auf-, Einblendung *f*; '**fade·less** [-lɪs] *adj.* □ **1.** licht-, farbecht; **2.** *fig.* unvergänglich; '**fade-out** *s.* **1.** *Film, Radio, TV*: Aus-, Abblendung *f*: **do a ~** *sl.* ‚sich verziehen'; **2.** *phys.* Ausschwingen *n*; '**fad·er** [-də] *s. Radio, TV*: Auf- *od.* Abblendregler *m*; '**fad·ing** [-dɪŋ] **I** *adj.* **1.** (ver)welkend (*a. fig.*); **2.** ausbleichend (*Farbe*); **3.** matt, schwindend; **4.** *fig.* vergänglich; **II** *s.* **5.** (Ver)Welken *n*; **6.** Verblassen *n*, Ausbleichen *n*; **7.** *Radio*: Fading *n*, Schwund *m*: **~ control** Schwundregelung *f*; **8.** ⚙ Fading *n* (*Nachlassen der Bremswirkung*).

fae·cal ['fi:kl] *adj.* fä'kal, Kot…: **~ matter** Kot *m*; **fae·ces** ['fi:si:z] *s. pl.* Fä'kalien *pl.*, Kot *m*.

fa·er·ie, fa·er·y ['feərɪ] **I** *s. obs.* **1.** → **fairy** 1; **2.** Märchenland *n*; **II** *adj.* **3.** Feen…, Märchen…

fag[1] [fæg] *s. sl.* **1.** ‚Glimmstengel' *m*, Ziga'rette *f*; **2.** → **fag(g)ot** 5.

fag[2] [fæg] **I** *v/i.* **1.** *Brit.* sich (ab)schinden; **2.** **~ for s.o.** *Brit. ped.* e-m älteren Schüler Dienste leisten; **II** *v/t.* **3.** *a.* **~ out** F ermüden, erschöpfen; **4.** *Brit. ped.* sich von *e-m jüngeren Schüler* bedienen lassen; **III** *s.* **5.** Placke'rei *f*, Schinde'rei *f*; **6.** Erschöpfung *f*; **7.** *Brit. ped.* ‚Diener' *m* (→ 2).

fag[3] [fæg] → **fag(g)ot** 5.

,**fag-'end** *s.* **1.** Ende *n*, Schluß *m*; **2.** letzter *od.* schäbiger Rest; **3.** *Brit. sl.* (Ziga'retten)Kippe *f*.

fag·ging ['fægɪŋ] *s. a.* **~ system** *Brit. ped. die Sitte, daß jüngere Schüler den älteren Dienste leisten müssen.*

fag·(g)ot ['fægət] *s.* **1.** Reisigbündel *n*; **2.** Fa'schine *f*; **3.** ⚙ a) Bündel *n* Stahlstangen, b) 'Schweißpa,ket *n*; **4.** *Brit. Küche*: Frika'delle *f* aus Inne'reien; **5.** *sl.* ‚Homo' *m*, Schwule(r) *m*.

Fahr·en·heit ['færənhaɪt] *s.*: **10° ~** zehn Grad Fahrenheit, 10° F.

fa·ience [faɪ'ɑ̃:ns] (*Fr.*) *s.* Fay'ence *f*.

fail [feɪl] **I** *v/i.* **1.** versagen (*Stimme, Herz, Motor etc., a. fig. Person*); aufhören, zu Ende gehen, nicht (aus)reichen, versiegen (*Vorrat*); **2.** miß'raten (*Ernte*), nicht aufgehen (*Saat*); **3.** nachlassen, schwächer werden, schwinden, abnehmen: **his health ~ed** s-e Gesundheit ließ nach; **4.** unter'lassen, versäumen, verfehlen, vernachlässigen: **he ~ed to come** er kam nicht; **he never ~s to come** er kommt immer; **don't ~ to come!** komm ja (*od.* bestimmt)!; **he cannot ~ to win** er muß (einfach) gewinnen; **~ in one's duty** s-e Pflicht versäumen; **he ~s in perseverance** es fehlt ihm an Ausdauer; **5.** a) s-n Zweck verfehlen, miß'lingen, fehlschlagen, Schiffbruch erleiden, b) es nicht fertigbringen *od.* schaffen (zu *inf.*): **the plan ~ed** der Plan scheiterte; **if everything else ~s** wenn alle Stränge reißen; **I ~ to see why** ich sehe nicht ein, warum; **he ~ed in his attempt** der Versuch mißlang ihm; **it ~ed in its effect** die erhoffte Wirkung blieb aus; **a ~ed husband** als Ehemann ein Versager; **a ~ed artist** ein verkrachter Künstler; **6.** *ped.* 'durchfallen (**in** in *dat.*); **7.** † Bank'rott machen, in Kon'kurs geraten; **II** *v/t.* **8.** im Stich lassen, enttäuschen: **I will never ~ you**; **my courage ~ed me** mir sank der Mut; **words ~ me** mir fehlen die Worte; **9.** *j-m* fehlen; **10.** *ped.* a) *j-n* 'durchfallen lassen (*in der Prüfung*), b) 'durchfallen in (*der Prüfung*); **III** *s.* **11.** **he got a ~ in biology** *ped.* er ist in Biologie durchgefallen; **12.** **without ~** ganz bestimmt, unbedingt; '**fail·ing** [-lɪŋ] **I** *adj.*: **never ~** nie versagend, unfehlbar; **II** *prp.* in Ermangelung (*gen.*), ohne: **~ this** andernfalls; **~ which** widrigenfalls; **III** *s.* Mangel *m*, Schwäche *f*, Fehler *m*, De'fekt *m*.

'**fail|-safe**, '**~-proof** *adj.* pannensicher (*a. fig.*).

fail·ure ['feɪljə] *s.* **1.** Fehlen *n*; **2.** Ausbleiben *n*, Versagen *n*; **3.** Unter'lassung *f*, Versäumnis *n*: **~ to comply** Nichtbefolgung *f*; **~ to pay** Nichtzahlung *f*; **4.** Fehlschlag(en *n*) *m*, Scheitern *n*, Miß'lingen *n*, 'Mißerfolg *m*: **crop ~** Mißernte *f*; **5.** *fig.* Zs.-bruch *m*, Schiffbruch *m*; † Bank'rott *m*, Kon'kurs *m*: **meet with ~** → **fail** 5; **6.** ⚕, ⚙ (*Herz-, Nieren- etc.*)Versagen *n*, Störung *f*, De'fekt *m*, ⚙ *a.* Panne *f*; **7.** Abnahme *f*, Versiegen *n*; **8.** *ped.* 'Durchfallen *n* (*in der Prüfung*); **9.** a) Versager *m*, ‚Niete' *f* (*Person od. Sache*), b) ‚Reinfall' *m*, ‚Pleite' *f* (*Sache*).

faint [feɪnt] **I** *adj.* □ **1.** schwach, matt, kraftlos: **feel ~** sich matt *od.* e-r Ohnmacht nahe fühlen; **2.** schwach, matt (*Ton, Farbe, a. fig.*): **a ~ effort**; **I haven't got the ~est idea** ich habe nicht die leiseste Ahnung; **~ hope** schwache Hoffnung; **3.** furchtsam; **II** *s.* **4.** (**dead ~** tiefe) Ohnmacht; **III** *v/i.* **5.** schwach *od.* matt werden (**with** vor *dat.*); **6.** in Ohnmacht fallen (**with** vor *dat.*): **~ing fit** Ohnmachtsanfall *m*; '**~-heart** *s.* Feigling *m*; ,**~-'heart·ed** *adj.* □ feig(e), furchtsam.

faint·ness ['feɪntnɪs] *s.* **1.** Schwäche *f* (*a. fig.*), Mattigkeit *f*: **~ of heart** Feigheit *f*, Furchtsamkeit *f*; **2.** Ohnmachtsgefühl *n*.

fair¹ [feə] I *adj.* □ → ***fairly***; **1.** schön, hübsch, lieblich: ***the ~ sex*** das schöne Geschlecht; **2.** a) hell (*Haut, Haar*), blond (*Haar*), zart (*Teint, Haut*), b) hellhäutig; **3.** rein, sauber, tadel-, makellos, *fig. a.* unbescholten: ***~ name*** guter Ruf; **4.** *fig.* schön, gefällig: ***give s.o. ~ words*** j-n mit schönen Worten abspeisen; **5.** deutlich, leserlich: ***~ copy*** Reinschrift *f*; **6.** klar, heiter (*Himmel*), schön, trocken (*Wetter, Tag*): ***set ~*** beständig; **7.** frei, unbehindert: ***~ game*** jagdbares Wild, *bsd. fig.* Freiwild *n* (***to*** für); **8.** günstig (*Wind*), aussichtsreich, gut: ***~ chance*** reelle Chance; ***be in a ~ way to*** auf dem besten Wege sein zu; **9.** anständig: a) *bsd. sport* fair, b) ehrlich, offen, aufrichtig, c) ˈunparˌteiisch, d) fair: ***~ price*** angemessener Preis; ***~ and square*** offen u. ehrlich, anständig; ***~ play*** a) faires Spiel, b) *fig.* Anständigkeit *f*, Fairneß *f*; ***by ~ means or foul*** so oder so; ***~ is ~*** Gerechtigkeit muß sein!; ***~ enough!*** in Ordnung!; ***all's ~ in love and war*** im Krieg u. in der Liebe ist alles erlaubt; **10.** leidlich, ziemlich *od.* einigermaßen gut, nicht übel: ***be a ~ judge*** ein recht gutes Urteil haben (***of*** über *acc.*); ***~ to middling*** gut bis mittelmäßig, *iro.* ‚mittelprächtig'; ***~ average*** guter Durchschnitt; **11.** ansehnlich, beträchtlich, ganz schön: ***a ~ sum***; II *adv.* → *a.* ***fairly***; **12.** schön, gut, freundlich, höflich; **13.** rein, sauber, leserlich; **14.** günstig: ***bid*** (*od.* ***promise***) ***~*** a) sich gut anlassen, zu Hoffnungen berechtigen, b) Aussicht haben, versprechen (***to*** *inf.* zu *inf.*); **15.** anständig, fair: ***play ~*** fair spielen, *a. fig.* sich an die Spielregeln halten; **16.** genau: ***~ in the face*** mitten ins Gesicht; **17.** völlig; III *v/t.* **18.** ⚙ zurichten, glätten; **19.** *Flugzeug etc.* verkleiden.

fair² [feə] *s.* **1.** a) Jahrmarkt *m*, b) Volksfest *n*; **2.** Messe *f*, Ausstellung *f*: ***at the industrial ~*** auf der Industriemesse; **3.** Baˈsar *m*.

ˈ**fair|-faced** *adj.*: ***~ concrete*** ⚠ Sichtbeton *m*; ˈ**~·ground** *s.* **1.** Messegelände *n*; **2.** Rummelplatz *m*; ˌ**~-ˈhaired** *adj.* blond: ***~ boy*** *fig. iro.* Liebling *m* (*des Chefs etc.*).

fair·ing¹ [ˈfeərɪŋ] *s.* ✈ Verkleidung *f*.

fair·ing² [ˈfeərɪŋ] *s. obs.* Jahrmarktsgeschenk *n*.

fair·ly [ˈfeəlɪ] *adv.* **1.** ehrlich; **2.** anständig(erweise); **3.** gerecht(erweise); **4.** ziemlich; **5.** leidlich; **6.** völlig; **7.** geradezu; **8.** deutlich; **9.** genau.

ˌ**fair-ˈmind·ed** *adj.* aufrichtig, gerecht (denkend).

fair·ness [ˈfeənɪs] *s.* **1.** Schönheit *f*; **2.** a) Blondheit *f*, b) Hellhäutigkeit *f*; **3.** Klarheit *f* (*des Himmels*); **4.** Anständigkeit *f*: a) *bsd. sport* Fairneß *f*, b) Ehrlichkeit *f*, c) Gerechtigkeit *f*: ***in ~*** gerechterweise; ***in ~ to him*** um ihm Gerechtigkeit widerfahren zu lassen; **5.** ⚖, ✝ Lauterkeit *f* (*des Wettbewerbs etc.*).

ˌ**fair|-ˈspo·ken** *adj.* freundlich, höflich; ˈ**~·way** *s.* **1.** ⚓ Fahrwasser *n*, -rinne *f*; **2.** *Golf*: Fairway *n*; ˈ**~-ˌweath·er** *adj.* Schönwetter...: ***~ friends*** *fig.* Freunde nur in guten Zeiten.

fair·y [ˈfeərɪ] I *s.* **1.** Fee *f*, Elf(e *f*) *m*; **2.** *sl.* ‚Homo' *m*, Schwule(r) *m*; II *adj.* □ **3.** feenhaft (*a. fig.*): ***~ godmother*** *fig.* gute Fee; ˈ**~·land** *s.* Feen-, Märchenland *n*; **~ tale** *s.* Märchen *n* (*a. fig.*).

faith [feɪθ] *s.* **1.** (***in***) Glaube(n) *m* (an *acc.*), Vertrauen *n* (auf *acc.*, zu): ***have od. put ~ in*** a) Glauben schenken (*dat.*), b) Vertrauen haben zu; ***on the ~ of*** im Vertrauen auf (*acc.*); **2.** *eccl.* (*überzeugter*) Glaube(n), b) Glaube(nsbekenntnis *n*) *m*: ***the Christian ~***; **3.** Treue *f*, Redlichkeit *f*: ***breach of ~*** Treu-, Vertrauensbruch *m*; ***in good ~*** in gutem Glauben, gutgläubig (*a.* ⚖); ***in bad ~*** in böser Absicht, arglistig (*a.* ⚖), ⚖ bösgläubig; **4.** Versprechen *n*: ***keep one's ~*** (sein) Wort halten; ***~ cure*** → ***faith healing***.

faith·ful [ˈfeɪθfʊl] I *adj.* □ **1.** treu (***to*** *dat.*); **2.** (pflicht)getreu; **3.** ehrlich, aufrichtig; **4.** gewissenhaft; **5.** (wahrheits- *od.* wort)getreu, genau; **6.** glaubwürdig, zuverlässig; **7.** *eccl.* gläubig; II *s.* **8.** ***the ~*** *eccl.* die Gläubigen *pl.*; **9.** *pl.* treue Anhänger *pl.*; ˈ**faith·ful·ly** [-fʊlɪ] *adv.* **1.** treu, ergeben: ***Yours ~*** Mit freundlichen Grüßen (*Briefschluß*); **2.** → ***faithful*** 2–5; **3.** F nachdrücklich: ***promise ~*** fest versprechen; ˈ**faith·ful·ness** [-nɪs] *s.* **1.** (*a.* Pflicht)Treue *f*; **2.** Ehrlichkeit *f*; **3.** Gewissenhaftigkeit *f*; **4.** Genauigkeit *f*; **5.** Glaubwürdigkeit *f*.

faith| heal·er *s.* Gesundbeter(in); **~ heal·ing** *s.* Gesundbeten *n*.

faith·less [ˈfeɪθlɪs] *adj.* □ **1.** *eccl.* ungläubig; **2.** treulos; **3.** unehrlich.

fake [feɪk] F I *v/t.* **1.** nachmachen, fälschen; *Presse etc.*: *Foto etc.* ‚türken'; **2.** *Bilanz etc.* ‚frisieren'; **3.** vortäuschen; **4.** *sport* a) *Gegner* täuschen, b) *Schlag etc.* antäuschen; II *s.* **5.** Fälschung *f*, Nachahmung *f*; **6.** Schwindel *m*; **7.** Schwindler *m*, ‚Schauspieler' *m*, j-d, der nicht ‚echt' ist; III *adj.* **8.** nachgemacht, gefälscht; **9.** falsch; **10.** vorgetäuscht; ˈ**fak·er** *s.* **1.** Fälscher *m*; **2.** Simuˈlant(in); **3.** → ***fake*** 7.

fa·kir [ˈfeɪˌkɪə] *s.* **1.** Fakir *m*; **2.** *Am.* F → ***fake*** 7.

fal·con [ˈfɔːlkən] *s. orn.* Falke *m*; ˈ**fal·con·er** [-nə] *s. hunt.* Falkner *m*; ˈ**fal·con·ry** [-kənrɪ] *s.* **1.** Falkneˈrei *f*; **2.** Falkenbeize *f*, -jagd *f*.

fall [fɔːl] I *s.* **1.** Fall(en *n*) *m*, Sturz *m*: ***have a*** (***bad***) ***~*** (schwer) stürzen; ***ride for a ~*** a) verwegen reiten, b) *fig.* das Schicksal herausfordern; **2.** a) (Ab)Fallen *n* (*der Blätter etc.*), b) *Am.* Herbst *m*; **3.** Fallen *n* (*des Vorhangs*); **4.** Fall *m*, Faltenwurf *m* (*von Stoff*); **5.** *phys.* a) *a. **free ~*** freier Fall, b) Fallhöhe *f*, -strecke *f*; **6.** a) (*Regen-, Schnee*)Fall *m*, b) Regen-, Schneemenge *f*; **7.** Zs.-fallen *n*, Einsturz *m* (*e-s Hauses*); **8.** Fallen *n*, Sinken *n*, Abnehmen *n* (*Temperatur, Flut, Preis*): ***heavy ~ in prices*** Kurs-, Preissturz *m*; ***speculate on the ~*** auf Baisse spekulieren; **9.** Abfallen *n*, Gefälle *n*, Neigung *f* (*des Geländes*); **10.** Fall *m* (*a. e-r Festung etc.*), Sturz *m*, Nieder-, ˈUntergang *m*, Abstieg *m*, Verfall *m*, Ende *n*; **11.** Fall *m*, Fehltritt: ***the ℒ*** (***of man***) *bibl.* der (erste) Sündenfall *m*; **12.** *mst pl.* Wasserfall *m*; **13.** Wurf *m* (*Lämmer etc.*); **14.** *Ringen*: Niederwurf *m*: ***win by ~*** Schultersieg *m*; ***try a ~ with s.o.*** *fig.* sich mit j-m messen; II *v/i.* [*irr.*] **15.** fallen: ***the curtain ~s*** der Vorhang fällt; **16.** (ab)fallen (*Blätter etc.*); **17.** (heˈrunter)fallen, abstürzen: ***he fell to his death*** er stürzte tödlich ab; **18.** (ˈum-, hin-, nieder)fallen, zu Boden fallen, zu Fall kommen; **19.** ˈumfallen, -stürzen (*Baum etc.*); **20.** (*in Falten od. Locken*) herˈabfallen; **21.** *fig. allg.* fallen: a) (*im Kampf*) getötet werden, b) erobert werden (*Stadt etc.*), c) gestürzt werden (*Regierung*), d) e-n Fehltritt begehen (*Frau*); **22.** *fig.* fallen (*Preis, Temperatur, Flut*), abnehmen, sinken: ***his courage fell*** ihm sank der Mut; ***his face fell*** er machte ein langes Gesicht; **23.** abfallen, sich senken (*Gelände*); **24.** (*in Stücke*) zerfallen; **25.** (*zeitlich*) fallen: ***Easter ~s late this year***; **26.** herˈeinbrechen (*Nacht*); **27.** *fig.* fallen (*Worte etc.*); **28.** *krank, fällig etc.* werden: ***~ ill*** (***due***);

Zssgn mit prp.:

fall| a·mong *v/i.* unter ... (*acc.*) geraten *od.* fallen: ***~ the thieves*** *bibl. u. fig.* unter die Räuber fallen; **~ be·hind** *v/i.* zuˈrückbleiben hinter (*acc.*) (*a. fig.*); **~ for** *v/i.* F auf *et. od. j-n* reinfallen, *a.* sich in *j-n* ‚verknallen'; **~ from** *v/i.* abfallen von, abtrünnig *od.* untreu werden (*dat.*): ***~ grace*** a) sündigen, b) in Ungnade fallen; **~ in·to** *v/i.* **1.** kommen *od.* geraten *od.* verfallen in (*acc.*): ***~ disuse*** außer Gebrauch kommen; ***~ a habit*** in e-e Gewohnheit verfallen; → ***line¹*** 9; **2.** in *Teile* zerfallen: ***~ ruin*** zerfallen; **3.** münden in (*acc.*) (*Fluß*); **4.** fallen in (*ein Gebiet od. Fach*); **~ on** *v/i.* **1.** treffen, fallen auf (*acc.*) (*a. Blick etc.*); **2.** herfallen über (*acc.*), überˈfallen (*acc.*); **3.** in *et.* geraten: ***~ evil days*** e-e schlimme Zeit durchmachen müssen; **~ o·ver** *v/i.* fallen über (*acc.*): ***~ o.s. to do s.th.*** F sich ‚fast umbringen', et. zu tun; **~ to** *v/i.* **1.** mit *et.* beginnen: ***~ work***; **2.** fallen an (*acc.*), *j-m* zufallen *od.* obliegen (***to do*** zu tun); **~ un·der** *v/i. fig.* **1.** unter *ein Gesetz etc.* fallen, zu *et.* gehören; **2.** *der Kritik etc.* unterˈliegen; **~ with·in** → ***fall into*** 4.

Zssgn mit adv.:

fall| a·stern *v/i.* ⚓ zuˈrückbleiben; **~ a·way** *v/i.* **1.** → ***fall*** 23; **2.** → ***fall off*** 1; **~ back** *v/i.* **1.** zuˈrückweichen: ***~*** (***up***)***on*** *fig.* zurückgreifen auf (*acc.*); **2.** → **~ be·hind** *v/i. a. fig.* zuˈrückbleiben, -fallen: ***~ with*** in Rückstand *od.* Verzug geraten mit; **~ down** *v/i.* **1.** hin-, hinˈunterfallen; **2.** ˈumfallen, einstürzen; **3.** (*ehrfürchtig*) auf die Knie sinken, niederfallen; **4.** F (***on***) a) versagen (bei), b) Pech haben (mit); **~ in** *v/i.* **1.** einfallen, -stürzen; **2.** ⚔ antreten; **3.** *fig.* a) sich anschließen (*Person*), b) sich einfügen (*Sache*); **4.** ✝ ablaufen, fällig werden; **5.** ***~ with*** (zufällig) treffen (*acc.*), stoßen auf (*acc.*); **6.** ***~ with*** a) zustimmen (*dat.*), b) passen zu, entsprechen (*dat.*), c) sich anpassen (*dat.*); **~ off** *v/i. fig.* **1.** zuˈrückgehen, sinken, nachlassen, abnehmen; **2.** (***from***) abfallen (von), abtrünnig werden (*dat.*); **3.** ⚓ (vom Strich) abfallen; **4.** ✈ abrutschen; **~ out** *v/i.* **1.** herˈausfallen; **2.** *fig.* ausfallen, sich erweisen als; **3.** sich ereignen; **4.** ⚔ wegtreten; **5.** sich streiten *od.* entzweien; **~ o·ver** *v/i.* ˈumfallen, -kippen: ***~ backwards*** F sich ‚fast umbringen' (*et. zu tun*); ~ **through** *v/i.* **1.** 'durchfallen (*a. fig.*); **2.** *fig.* a) miß'lingen, b) ins Wasser fallen; ~ **to** *v/i.* **1.** zufallen (*Tür*); **2.** ‚reinhauen', (tüchtig) zugreifen (*beim Essen*); **3.** handgemein werden.

fal·la·cious [fə'leɪʃəs] *adj.* □ trügerisch: a) irreführend, b) irrig, falsch; **fal·la·cy** ['fæləsɪ] *s.* **1.** Trugschluß *m*, Irrtum *m*: ***popular*** ~ weitverbreiteter Irrtum; **2.** Unlogik *f*; **3.** Täuschung *f*.

fall·en ['fɔːlən] **I** *p.p. von* ***fall***; **II** *adj. allg.* gefallen: a) gestürzt (*a. fig.*), b) entehrt (*Frau*), c) (*im Kriege*) getötet, d) erobert (*Stadt etc.*): ~ ***angel*** gefallener Engel; **III** *s. coll.* ***the*** ~ die Gefallenen *pl.*; ~ **arch·es** *s. pl.* Senkfüße *pl.*

fall guy *s. Am.* F **1.** a) Opfer *n* (*e-s Betrügers*), b) ‚Gimpel' *m*; **2.** Sündenbock *m*.

fal·li·bil·i·ty [ˌfælə'bɪlətɪ] *s.* Fehlbarkeit *f*; **fal·li·ble** ['fæləbl] *adj.* □ fehlbar.

ˌ**fall·ing|-a'way**, ~ **off** ['fɔːlɪŋ] *s.* Rückgang *m*, Abnahme *f*, Sinken *n*; ~ **sick·ness** *s.* ⚕ Fallsucht *f*; ~ **star** *s.* Sternschnuppe *f*.

Fal·lo·pi·an tubes [fə'ləʊpɪən] *s. pl. anat.* Eileiter *pl.*

'**fall·out** *s.* **1.** *phys.* radioak'tiver Niederschlag, Fall'out *m*; **2.** *fig.* a) 'Nebenproˌdukt *n*, b) (böse) Auswirkung(en *pl.*).

fal·low[1] ['fæləʊ] **I** *adj.* brach(liegend): ***lie*** ~ brachliegen; **II** *s.* Brache *f*: a) Brachfeld *n*, b) Brachliegen *n*.

fal·low[2] ['fæləʊ] *adj.* falb, fahl, braungelb; '~**-deer** [-ləʊd-] *s. zo.* Damhirsch *m*, -wild *n*.

false [fɔːls] **I** *adj.* □ *allg.* falsch: a) unrichtig, fehlerhaft, irrig, b) unwahr, c) (***to***) treulos (gegen), untreu (*dat.*), d) irreführend, vorgetäuscht, trügerisch, 'hinterhältig, e) gefälscht, unecht, künstlich, f) Schein…, fälschlich (so genannt), g) 'widerrechtlich, rechtswidrig: ~ ***alarm*** blinder Alarm (*a. fig.*); ~ ***ceiling*** ⚠ Zwischendecke *f*; ~ ***coin*** Falschgeld *n*; ~ ***hair*** falsche Haare; ~ ***imprisonment*** ⚖ Freiheitsberaubung *f*; ~ ***key*** Nachschlüssel *m*; ~ ***pregnancy*** ⚕ Scheinschwangerschaft *f*; ~ ***shame*** falsche Scham; ~ ***start*** Fehlstart *m*; ~ ***step*** Fehltritt *m*; ~ ***tears*** Krokodilstränen; ~ ***teeth*** falsche Zähne; **II** *adv.* falsch, unaufrichtig: ***play s.o.*** ~ ein falsches Spiel mit j-m treiben; ˌ**false-'heart·ed** *adj.* falsch, treulos; '**false·hood** [-hʊd] *s.* **1.** Unwahrheit *f*, Lüge *f*; **2.** Falschheit *f*; '**false·ness** [-nɪs] *s. allg.* Falschheit *f*.

fal·set·to [fɔːl'setəʊ] *pl.* **-tos** *s.* Fistelstimme *f*, ♪ *a.* Fal'sett(stimme *f*) *n*.

fal·sies ['fɔːlsɪz] *s. pl.* F Schaumgummieinlagen *pl.* (*im Büstenhalter*).

fal·si·fi·ca·tion [ˌfɔːlsɪfɪ'keɪʃn] *s.* (Ver-) Fälschung *f*; **fal·si·fi·er** ['fɔːlsɪfaɪə] *s.* Fälscher(in); **fal·si·fy** ['fɔːlsɪfaɪ] *v/t.* **1.** fälschen; **2.** verfälschen, falsch *od.* irreführend darstellen; **3.** *Hoffnungen* enttäuschen; **fal·si·ty** ['fɔːlsətɪ] *s.* **1.** Irrtum *m*, Unrichtigkeit *f*; **2.** Lüge *f*, Unwahrheit *f*.

falt·boat ['fɔːltbəʊt] *s.* Faltboot *n*.

fal·ter ['fɔːltə] **I** *v/i.* schwanken: a) taumeln, b) zögern, zaudern, c) stocken (*a. Stimme*): ***his courage ~ed*** der Mut verließ ihn; **II** *v/t. et.* stammeln; '**fal·ter·ing** [-tərɪŋ] *adj.* □ *allg.* schwankend (→ ***falter*** I).

fame [feɪm] *s.* **1.** Ruhm *m*, (guter) Ruf, Berühmtheit *f*: ***of ill*** ~ berüchtigt; ***house of ill*** ~ Freudenhaus *n*; **2.** *obs.* Gerücht *n*; **famed** [-md] *adj.* berühmt, bekannt (***for*** wegen *gen.*, für).

fa·mil·iar [fə'mɪljə] **I** *adj.* □ **1.** vertraut: a) gewohnt: ***a*** ~ ***sight***, b) bekannt: ***a*** ~ ***face***, c) geläufig: ***a*** ~ ***expression***; ~ ***quotations*** geflügelte Worte; **2.** vertraut, bekannt (***with*** mit): ***be*** ~ ***with*** *a. et.* gut kennen; ***make o.s.*** ~ ***with*** a) sich mit *j-m* bekannt machen, b) sich mit *et.* vertraut machen; ***the name is*** ~ ***to me*** der Name ist mir vertraut; **3.** vertraut, in'tim, eng: ***a*** ~ ***friend***; ***be on*** ~ ***terms with s.o.*** mit j-m gut bekannt sein; (***too***) ~ *contp.* allzu familiär, plump-vertraulich; **4.** ungezwungen, famili'är; **II** *s.* **5.** Vertraute(r *m*) *f*; **6.** *a.* ~ ***spirit*** Schutzgeist *m*; **fa·mil·i·ar·i·ty** [fəˌmɪlɪ'ærətɪ] *s.* **1.** Vertrautheit *f*, Bekanntschaft *f* (***with*** mit); **2.** a) famili'äer Ton, Ungezwungenheit *f*, Vertraulichkeit *f*, b) *contp.* plumpe Vertraulichkeit; **fa·mil·iar·i·za·tion** [fəˌmɪljəraɪ'zeɪʃn] *s.* (***with***) Vertrautmachen *n od.* -werden *n* (mit), Gewöhnung *f* (an *acc.*); **fa'mil·iar·ize** [-əraɪz] *v/t.* (***with***) vertraut *od.* bekannt machen (mit), gewöhnen (an *acc.*).

fam·i·ly ['fæməlɪ] **I** *s.* **1.** Fa'milie *f* (*a. biol. u. fig.*): ~ ***of nations*** Völkerfamilie; ***she was living as one of the*** ~ sie gehörte zur Familie, sie hatte Familienanschluß; **2.** Fa'milie *f*: a) Geschlecht *n*, Sippe *f*, *a.* Verwandtschaft *f*, b) Ab-, Herkunft *f*: ***of*** (***good***) ~ aus gutem *od.* vornehmem Hause; **3.** *ling.* ('Sprach-) Faˌmilie *f*; **4.** ✈ Schar *f*; **II** *adj.* **5.** Familien…: ~ ***business*** (***tradition*** *etc.*); ~ ***doctor*** Hausarzt *m*; ~ ***environment*** häusliches Milieu; ~ ***warmth*** Nestwärme *f*; ***in a*** ~ ***way*** zwanglos; ***be in the*** ~ ***way*** F in anderen Umständen sein; ~ **al·low·ance** *s.* Kindergeld *n*; ~ **cir·cle** *s.* **1.** Fa'milienkreis *m*; **2.** *thea. Am.* oberer Rang; ~ **court** *s.* ⚖ Fa'miliengericht *n*; ~ **man** *s.* [*irr.*] **1.** Mann *m* mit Fa'milie, Fa'milienvater *m*; **2.** häuslicher Mensch; ~ **plan·ning** *s.* Fa'milienplanung *f*; ~ **skel·e·ton** *s.* streng gehütetes Fa'miliengeheimnis; ~ **tree** *s.* Stammbaum *m*.

fam·ine ['fæmɪn] *s.* **1.** Hungersnot *f*; **2.** Mangel *m*, Knappheit *f* (***of*** an *dat.*); **3.** Hunger *m* (*a. fig.*).

fam·ish ['fæmɪʃ] **I** *v/i.* **1.** *obs.* verhungern: ***be ~ing*** F am Verhungern sein; **2.** darben; **II** *v/t. obs.* verhungern lassen: ***he ate as if ~ed*** er aß, als ob er am Verhungern wäre.

fa·mous ['feɪməs] *adj.* □ **1.** berühmt (***for*** wegen *gen.*, für); **2.** F fa'mos, ausgezeichnet, prima.

fan[1] [fæn] **I** *s.* **1.** Fächer *m*: ~ ***dance***; ~ ***aerial*** ⚡ Fächerantenne *f*; **2.** ⚙ a) Venti'lator *m*, Lüfter *m*, b) *a.* ~ ***blower*** (Flügelrad)Gebläse *n*, c) ✓ (Worfel-) Schwinge *f*, d) ⚓ Flügel *m*, Schraubenblatt *n*; **II** *v/t.* **3.** *Luft* fächeln; **4.** um'fächeln, *j-m* Luft zufächeln; **5.** *Feuer* anfachen: ~ ***the flame*** *fig.* Öl ins Feuer gießen; **6.** *fig.* entfachen; (an)wedeln; **7.** ✓ worfeln, schwingen; **III** *v/i.* **8.** *oft* ~ ***out*** a) sich (fächerförmig) ausbreiten, b) ⚔ ausschwärmen.

fan[2] [fæn] *s.* F Fan *m*, begeisterter Anhänger: ~ ***club*** Fanclub *m*; ~ ***mail*** Verehrerpost *f*.

fa·nat·ic [fə'nætɪk] **I** *s.* Fa'natiker(in); **II** *adj.* → **fa'nat·i·cal** [-kl] *adj.* □ fa'natisch; **fa'nat·i·cism** [-ɪsɪzəm] *s.* Fana'tismus *m*.

fan·ci·er ['fænsɪə] *s.* (*Tier-, Blumen- etc.*)Liebhaber(in) *od.* Züchter(in); '**fan·ci·ful** [-ɪfʊl] *adj.* □ **1.** (allzu) phanta'siereich, schrullig, wunderlich (*Person*); **2.** bi'zarr, ausgefallen (*Sache*); **3.** eingebildet, unwirklich; **4.** phan'tastisch, wirklichkeitsfremd.

fan·cy ['fænsɪ] **I** *s.* **1.** Phanta'sie *f*: a) Einbildungskraft *f*, b) Phanta'sievorstellung *f*, c) (bloße) Einbildung; **2.** I'dee *f*, plötzlicher Einfall *m*: ***I have a*** ~ ***that*** ich habe so e-e Idee, daß; **3.** Laune *f*, Grille *f*; **4.** (individu'eller) Geschmack; **5.** (***for***) Neigung *f* (zu), Vorliebe *f* (für), Gefallen *n* (an *dat.*): ***have a*** ~ ***for*** gern haben (wollen) (*acc.*), Lust haben zu *od.* auf (*acc.*); ***take a*** ~ ***to*** Gefallen finden an (*dat.*), sympathisch finden (*acc.*); ***take*** (*od.* ***catch***) ***s.o.'s*** ~ j-m gefallen; ***just as the*** ~ ***takes you*** nach Lust u. Laune; **6.** *coll.* ***the*** ~ die (*Sport-, Tier- etc.*)Liebhaberwelt; **II** *adj.* **7.** Phantasie…, phan'tastisch: ~ ***name*** Phantasiename *m*; ~ ***price*** Phantasie-, Liebhaberpreis *m*; **8.** Mode…: ~ ***article***; **9.** (reich) verziert, bunt, kunstvoll, ausgefallen, extrafein: ~ ***cakes*** feines Gebäck; ~ ***car*** schicker Wagen; ~ ***dog*** Hund *m* aus e-r Liebhaberzucht; ~ ***foods*** Delikatessen; ~ ***words*** *contp.* geschwollene Ausdrücke; **III** *v/t.* **10.** sich *j-n od. et.* vorstellen: ~ (***that***)***!*** a) stell dir vor!, b) sieh mal einer an!, nanu!; ~ ***meeting you here!*** nanu, du hier?; **11.** glauben, denken, annehmen; **12.** ~ ***o.s.*** sich einbilden (***to be*** zu sein), sich halten für: ~ ***o.s.*** (***very important***) sich sehr wichtig vorkommen; **13.** gern haben *od.* mögen: ***I don't*** ~ ***this suit*** dieser Anzug gefällt mir nicht; **14.** Lust haben (auf *acc.*; ***doing*** zu tun): ***I could*** ~ ***an ice-cream*** ich hätte Lust auf ein Eis; **15.** ~ ***up*** *Am.* F aufputzen, ‚Pfiff geben' (*dat.*); ~ **ball** *s.* Ko'stümfest *n*, Maskenball *m*; ~ **dress** *s.* ('Masken)Koˌstüm *n*; ˌ~**-'dress** *adj.*: ~ ***ball*** → ***fancy ball***; ˌ~**-'free** *adj.* frei u. ungebunden; ~ **goods** *s. pl.* **1.** 'Modearˌtikel *pl.*; **2.** kleine Ge'schenkarˌtikel *pl.*, *a.* Nippes *pl.*; ~ **man** *s.* [*irr.*] *sl.* **1.** ‚Louis' *m*, Zuhälter *m*; **2.** Liebhaber *m*; ~ **pants** *s. Am. sl.* **1.** ‚feiner Pinkel'; **2.** ‚Waschlappen' *m*; ~ **wom·an** *s.* [*irr.*] **1.** Geliebte *f*; **2.** Prostituierte *f*; '~**-work** *s.* feine (Hand-) Arbeit.

fan·dan·gle [fæn'dæŋl] *s.* F ‚Firlefanz' *m*.

fane [feɪn] *s. poet.* Tempel *m*.

fan·fare ['fænfeə] *s.* ♪ Fan'fare *f*, Tusch *m*: ***with much*** ~ *fig.* mit großem Tamtam.

fang [fæŋ] *s.* **1.** *zo.* a) Fang(zahn) *m* (*Raubtier*), b) Hauer *m* (*Eber*), c) Giftzahn *m* (*Schlange*); **2.** *pl.* F Zähne *pl.*, ‚Beißer' *pl.*; **3.** *anat.* Zahnwurzel *f*; **4.** ⚙ Dorn *m*.

fan| heat·er *s.* Heizlüfter *m*; '~**·light** *s.* ⚠ (fächerförmiges) (Tür)Fenster,

Oberlicht *n*.
fan·ner ['fænə] *s.* ⚙ Gebläse *n*.
fan·ny ['fænɪ] *s.* **1.** *Am. sl.* ‚Arsch' *m*; **2.** *Brit.* V ‚Möse' *f*.
fan·ta·sia [fæn'teɪzjə] *s.* ♪ Fanta'sia *f*; **fan·ta·size** ['fæntəsaɪz] *v/i.* **1.** phantasieren (***about*** von); **2.** (mit offenen Augen) träumen; **fan'tas·tic** [-'tæstɪk] *adj.* (☐ ***~ally***) *allg.* phan'tastisch: a) unwirklich, b) verstiegen, über'spannt, c) ab'surd, aus der Luft gegriffen, d) F ‚toll'; **fan·ta·sy** ['fæntəsɪ] *s.* **1.** Phanta'sie *f*: a) Einbildungskraft *f*, b) Phanta'sievorstellung *f*, c) (Tag-, Wach)Traum *m*, d) Hirngespinst *n*; **2.** ♪ Fanta'sia *f*.
fan| trac·er·y *s.* △ Fächermaßwerk *n*; **~ vault·ing** *s.* △ Fächergewölbe *n*.
far [fɑː] **I** *adj.* **1.** fern, (weit) entfernt, weit; **2.** (*vom Sprecher aus*) entfernter: ***at the ~ end*** am anderen Ende; **3.** weit vorgerückt, fortgeschritten (***in*** in *dat.*); **II** *adv.* **4.** weit, fern: ***~ away***, ***~ off*** weit weg, weit entfernt; ***from ~*** von weit her; ***~ and near*** nah u. fern, überall; ***~ and wide*** weit und breit; ***~ and away the best*** a) bei weitem *od.* mit Abstand das Beste, b) bei weitem am besten; ***as ~ as*** a) soweit *od.* soviel (wie), insofern als, b) bis (nach); ***as ~ as that goes*** was das betrifft; ***as ~ back as 1907*** schon (im Jahre) 1907; ***in as*** (*od.* ***so***) ***~ as*** insofern als; ***so ~*** bisher, bis jetzt; ***so ~ so good*** so weit, so gut; ***~ from*** weit entfernt von, keineswegs; ***~ from completed*** noch lange *od.* längst nicht fertig; ***~ from rich*** alles andere als reich; ***~ from it!*** keineswegs!, ganz u. gar nicht!; ***I am ~ from believing it*** ich bin weit davon entfernt, es zu glauben; ***~ into*** bis weit *od.* hoch *od.* tief in (*acc.*); ***~ into the night*** bis spät *od.* tief in die Nacht; ***~ out*** a) weit draußen *od.* hinaus, b) F ‚toll'; ***be ~ out*** weit danebenliegen (*mit e-r Vermutung etc.*); ***~ up*** hoch oben; ***~ be it from me*** (***to*** *inf.*) es liegt mir fern (zu *inf.*); ***go ~*** a) weit *od.* lange (aus)reichen, b) es weit bringen; ***ten dollars don't go ~*** mit 10 Dollar kommt man nicht weit; ***go too ~*** *fig.* zu weit gehen; ***that went ~ to convince me*** das hat mich beinahe überzeugt; ***I will go so ~ as to say*** ich will sogar behaupten; **5.** *a.* ***by ~*** weit(aus), bei weitem, sehr viel, ganz: ***~ better*** viel besser; (***by***) ***~ the best*** a) weitaus der (die, das) beste, b) bei weitem am besten.
far·ad ['færəd] *s.* ⚡ Fa'rad *n*.
'far·a·way *adj.* **1.** → ***far*** 1; **2.** *fig.* verträumt, versonnen, (geistes)abwesend.
farce [fɑːs] *s.* **1.** *thea.* Posse *f*, Schwank *m*; **2.** *fig.* Farce *f*, ‚The'ater' *n*; **'far·ci·cal** [-sɪkl] *adj.* ☐ **1.** possenhaft, Possen…; **2.** *fig.* ab'surd.
fare [feə] **I** *s.* **1.** a) Fahrpreis *m*, -geld *n*, b) Flugpreis *m*: ***what's the ~?*** was kostet die Fahrt *od.* der Flug?; ***~ stage*** *Brit.* Fahrpreiszone *f*, Teilstrecke *f* (*Bus etc.*); ***any more ~s?*** noch jemand zugestiegen?; **2.** Fahrgast *m* (*bsd. e-s Taxis*); **3.** Kost *f* (*a. fig.*), Verpflegung *f*, Nahrung *f*: ***slender ~*** magere Kost; ***literary ~*** literarische Kost, geistiges ‚Menü'; **II** *v/i.* **4.** sich befinden; (er)gehen: ***how did you ~?*** wie ist es dir ergangen?; ***he ~d ill***, ***it ~d ill with him*** er war schlecht d(a)ran; ***we ~d no better*** uns ist es nicht besser ergangen; ***~ alike*** in der gleichen Lage sein; **5.** *poet.* reisen, sich aufmachen: ***~ thee well!*** leb wohl!
Far East *s.*: ***the ~*** der Ferne Osten.
ˌfare'well I *int.* lebe(n Sie) wohl!, lebt wohl!; **II** *s.* Lebe'wohl *n*, Abschiedsgruß *m*: ***bid s.o. ~*** j-m Lebewohl sagen; ***make one's ~s*** sich verabschieden; ***take one's ~ of*** Abschied nehmen von (*a. fig.*); ***~ to*** adieu …, nie wieder …; **III** *adj.* Abschieds…
ˌfar|-'famed *adj.* 'weithin berühmt; **ˌ~-'fetched** *adj. fig.* weithergeholt, an den Haaren her'beigezogen; **ˌ~-'flung** *adj.* **1.** weit(ausgedehnt); **2.** *fig.* weitgespannt; **3.** weitentfernt; **ˌ~-'go·ing** → ***far-reaching***.
fa·ri·na [fə'raɪnə] *s.* **1.** (feines) Mehl; **2.** ⚗ Stärke *f*; **3.** *Brit.* ♀ Blütenstaub *m*; **4.** *zo.* Staub *m*; **far·i·na·ceous** [ˌfærɪ'neɪʃəs] *adj.* Mehl…, Stärke…
farm [fɑːm] **I** *s.* **1.** (Bauern)Hof *m*, landwirtschaftlicher Betrieb, Gut(shof *m*) *n*, Farm *f*; **2.** (*Geflügel- etc.*)Farm *f*; **3.** *obs.* Bauernhaus *n*; **4.** *bsd. Am.* a) Sana'torium *n*, b) Entziehungsanstalt *f*; **II** *v/t.* **5.** *Land* bebauen, bewirtschaften; **6.** *Geflügel etc.* züchten; **7.** pachten; **8.** *oft* ***~ out*** verpachten, in Pacht geben (***to. s.o.*** j-m *od.* an j-n); **9.** *mst* ***~ out*** a) *Kinder* in Pflege geben, b) ✝ *Arbeit* vergeben (***to*** an *acc.*); **III** *v/i.* **10.** Landwirt sein; **'farm·er** [-mə] *s.* **1.** (Groß-)Bauer *m*, Landwirt *m*, Farmer *m*; **2.** Pächter *m*; **3.** (*Geflügel- etc.*)Züchter *m*.
farm| hand *s.* Landarbeiter(in); **'~-house** *s.* Bauern-, Gutshaus *n*: ***~ bread*** Landbrot *n*; ***~ butter*** Landbutter *f*.
farm·ing ['fɑːmɪŋ] *s.* **1.** Landwirtschaft; **2.** (*Geflügel- etc.*)Zucht *f*.
farm| la·bo(u)r·er → ***farm hand***; **~ land** *s.* Ackerland *n*; **'~·stead** *s.* Bauernhof *m*, Gehöft *n*; **~ work·er** → ***farm hand***; **'~·yard** *s.* Wirtschaftshof *m* (e-s Bauernhofs).
far·o ['feərəʊ] *s.* Phar(a)o *n* (*Kartenglücksspiel*).
far-off [ˌfɑːr'ɒf] → ***far*** 1, ***faraway*** 2.
far-out [ˌfɑːr'aʊt] *adj. sl.* **1.** ‚toll', ‚super'; **2.** ‚verrückt'.
far·ra·go [fə'rɑːgəʊ] *pl.* **-gos**, *Am.* **-goes** *s.* Kunterbunt *n* (***of*** aus, von).
ˌfar-'reach·ing *adj.* **1.** *bsd. fig.* weitreichend; **2.** *fig.* folgenschwer, tiefgreifend.
far·ri·er ['færɪə] *s.* Hufschmied *m*; ⚔ Beschlagmeister *m*.
far·row ['færəʊ] **I** *s.* Wurf *m* Ferkel: ***with ~*** trächtig (*Sau*); **II** *v/i.* ferkeln; **III** *v/t. Ferkel* werfen.
ˌfar|'see·ing *adj. fig.* weitblickend; **ˌ~-'sight·ed** *adj.* **1.** *fig.* → ***farseeing***; **2.** ⚕ weitsichtig; **ˌ~'sight·ed·ness** *s.* **1.** *fig.* Weitblick *m*, 'Umsicht *f*; **2.** ⚕ Weitsichtigkeit *f*.
fart [fɑːt] V **I** *s.* Furz *m*; **II** *v/i.* furzen: ***~ around*** *fig.* herumalbern, -blödeln.
far·ther ['fɑːðə] **I** *adj.* **1.** *comp. von* ***far***; **2.** → ***further*** 3, 4; **3.** entfernter (*vom Sprecher aus*): ***the ~ shore*** das gegenüberliegende Ufer; ***at the ~ end*** am anderen Ende; **II** *adv.* **4.** weiter: ***so far and no ~*** bis hierher u. nicht weiter; **5.** → ***further*** 1, 2; **'far·ther·most** → ***farthest*** 2; **'far·thest** [-ðɪst] **I** *adj.* **1.** *sup.* von ***far***; **2.** entferntest, weitest; **II** *adv.* **3.** am weitesten, am entferntesten.
far·thing ['fɑːðɪŋ] *s. Brit. hist.* Farthing *m* (¼ *Penny*): ***not worth a*** (***brass***) ***~*** *fig.* keinen (roten) Heller wert; ***it doesn't matter a ~*** das macht gar nichts.
Far West *s. Am. Gebiet der Rocky Mountains u. der pazifischen Küste.*
fas·ci·a ['feɪʃə] *pl.* **-ae** [-ʃiː] *s.* **1.** Binde *f*, (Quer)Band *n*; **2.** *zo.* Farbstreifen *m*; **3.** ['fæʃɪə] *anat.* Muskelhaut *f*; **4.** △ a) Gurtsims *m*, b) Bund *m* (*von Säulenschäften*); **5.** ⚕ (Bauch- *etc.*)Binde *f*; **6.** → ***facia***.
fas·ci·cle ['fæsɪkl] *s.* **1.** *a.* ♀ Bündel *n*, Büschel *n*; **2.** Fas'zikel *m*: a) (Teil)Lieferung *f*, Einzelheft *n* (*Buch*), b) Aktenbündel *n*; **fas·cic·u·lar** [fə'sɪkjʊlə], **fas·cic·u·late** [fə'sɪkjʊlət] *adj.* büschelförmig.
fas·ci·nate ['fæsɪneɪt] *v/t.* **1.** faszinieren: a) bezaubern, b) fesseln, packen, gefangennehmen: ***~d*** fasziniert, (wie) gebannt; **2.** hypnotisieren; **'fas·ci·nat·ing** [-tɪŋ] *adj.* ☐ faszinierend: a) hinreißend, b) fesselnd, spannend; **fas·ci·na·tion** [ˌfæsɪ'neɪʃn] *s.* **1.** Faszinati'on *f*, Bezauberung *f*; **2.** Zauber *m*, Reiz *m*.
Fas·cism ['fæʃɪzəm] *s. pol.* Fa'schismus *m*; **'Fas·cist** [-ɪst] **I** *s.* Fa'schist *m*; **II** *adj.* fa'schistisch.
fash·ion ['fæʃn] **I** *s.* **1.** Mode *f*: ***come into ~*** in Mode kommen; ***set the ~*** die Mode diktieren, *fig.* den Ton angeben; ***it is*** (***all***) ***the ~*** es ist (große) Mode; ***in the English ~*** nach englischer Mode (*od.* Art, → 2); ***out of ~*** aus der Mode, unmodern; ***~ designer*** Modedesigner(in); **2.** Sitte *f*, Brauch *m*, Art *f* (u. Weise *f*), Stil *m*, Ma'nier *f*: ***behave in a strange ~*** sich sonderbar benehmen; ***after their ~*** nach ihrer Weise; ***after*** (*od.* ***in***) ***a ~*** schlecht u. recht, ‚so lala'; ***an artist after a ~*** so etwas wie ein Künstler; **3.** (feine) Lebensart, gute Ma'nieren *pl.*: ***a man of ~***; **4.** Machart *f*, Form *f* (Zu)Schnitt *m*, Fas'son *f*; **II** *v/t.* **5.** herstellen, machen; **6.** bilden, formen, gestalten; **7.** anpassen; **III** *adv.* **8.** wie: ***horse-~*** nach Pferdeart, wie ein Pferd; **fash·ion·a·ble** ['fæʃnəbl] **I** *adj.* ☐ **1.** modisch, mo'dern; **2.** vornehm, ele'gant; **3.** in Mode, Mode…: ***~ complaint*** Modekrankheit *f*; **II** *s.* **4.** ***the ~s*** die elegante Welt, die Schickeria.
'fash·ion|ˌmon·ger *s.* Modenarr *m*; **~ pa·rade** *s.* Mode(n)schau *f*: **~ plate** *s.* **1.** Modebild *n*, -blatt *n*; **2.** F ‚'superele'gante' Per'son; **~ show** *s.* Mode(n)schau *f*.
fast¹ [fɑːst] **I** *adj.* **1.** schnell, geschwind, rasch: ***~ train*** Schnell-, D-Zug *m*; ***my watch is ~*** m-e Uhr geht vor: ***pull a ~ one on s.o.*** *sl.* j-n ‚reinlegen'; **2.** ‚schnell' (*hohe Geschwindigkeit gestattend*): ***~ road***; ***~ tennis-court***; ***~ lane*** *mot.* Überholspur *f*; **3.** *phot.* lichtstark; **4.** flott, leichtlebig; **II** *adv.* **5.** schnell: ***~ and furious*** Schlag auf Schlag; **6.** häufig, reichlich, stark; **7.** leichtsinnig: ***live ~*** ein flottes Leben führen.
fast² [fɑːst] **I** *adj.* **1.** fest(gemacht), befestigt, unbeweglich; fest zs.-haltend: ***make ~*** festmachen, befestigen, *Tür* (fest) verschließen; ***~ friend*** treuer Freund; **2.** beständig, haltbar: ***~ col-***

o(*u*)*r* (wasch)echte Farbe; ***~ to light*** lichtecht; **II** *adv.* **3.** fest, sicher: ***be ~ asleep*** fest schlafen; ***stuck ~*** festgefahren; ***play ~ and loose*** Schindluder treiben (***with*** mit).

fast³ [fɑːst] *bsd. eccl.* **I** *v/i.* **1.** fasten; **II** *s.* **2.** Fasten *n*: ***break one's ~*** das Fasten brechen, *a.* frühstücken; **3.** Fastenzeit *f.*

ˈfast|·back *s. mot.* (Wagen *m* mit) Fließheck *n*; **~ breed·er (re·ac·tor)** *s. phys.* schneller Brüter.

fas·ten [ˈfɑːsn] **I** *v/t.* **1.** befestigen, festmachen, -binden (***to, on*** an *dat.*); **2.** *a.* ***~ up*** (fest) zumachen, (ver-, ab)schließen, zuknöpfen, ver-, zuschnüren; zs.-fügen, verbinden: ***~ with nails*** zunageln; ***~ down*** a) befestigen, b) F *j-n* ‚festnageln' (***to*** auf *acc.*); **3.** *Augen* heften, *a. s-e Aufmerksamkeit* richten (***on*** auf *acc.*); **4.** ***~ (up)on*** *fig.* a) *j-m e-n Spitznamen* ‚anhängen', geben, b) *j-m et.* ‚anhängen' *od.* ‚in die Schuhe schieben'; **II** *v/i.* **5.** sich schließen *od.* festmachen lassen; **6.** ***~ (up)on*** a) sich heften *od.* klammern an (*acc.*), b) *fig.* sich stürzen auf (*acc.*), ‚einhaken' bei, aufs Korn nehmen (*acc.*); **ˈfas·ten·er** [-nə] *s.* Befestigung(smittel *n*, -vorrichtung *f*) *f*, Verschluß *m*, Halter *m*, Druckknopf *m*; **ˈfas·ten·ing** [-nɪŋ] *s.* **1.** → ***fastener***; **2.** Befestigung *f*, Sicherung *f*, Halterung *f.*

ˈfast-food res·tau·rant *s.* Schnellimbiß *m*, -gaststätte *f.*

fas·tid·i·ous [fæsˈtɪdɪəs] *adj.* □ anspruchsvoll, heikel, wählerisch; **fasˈtid·i·ous·ness** [-nɪs] *s.* anspruchsvolles Wesen.

fast·ing cure [ˈfɑːstɪŋ] *s.* Fasten-, Hungerkur *f.*

ˈfastˌmov·ing *adj.* **1.** schnell; **2.** *fig.* tempogeladen, spannend.

fast·ness¹ [ˈfɑːstnɪs] *s.* **1.** *obs.* Schnelligkeit *f*; **2.** *fig.* Leichtlebigkeit *f.*

fast·ness² [ˈfɑːstnɪs] *s.* **1.** Feste *f*, Festung *f*; **2.** Zufluchtsort *m*; **3.** ˈWiderstandsfähigkeit *f*, Beständigkeit *f* (***to*** gegen), Echtheit *f* (*von Farben*): ***~ to light*** Lichtechtheit *f.*

ˈfast-talk *v/t.* F *j-n* beschwatzen (***into doing s.th.*** et. zu tun).

fat [fæt] **I** *adj.* □ → ***fatly***; **1.** dick, beleibt, fett, feist: ***~ stock*** Mastvieh *n*; ***~ type*** *typ.* Fettdruck *m*; **2.** fett, fetthaltig, fettig, ölig: ***~ coal*** Fettkohle *f*; **3.** *fig.* ‚dick': ***~ bank account***; ***~ purse***; **4.** *fig.* fett, einträglich: ***a ~ job*** ein lukrativer Posten; ***~ soil*** fetter *od.* fruchtbarer Boden; ***a ~ lot it helps!*** *sl. iro.* das hilft mir (uns) herzlich wenig; ***a ~ chance*** *sl.* herzlich wenig Aussicht (-en); **II** *s.* **5.** *a.* ⚗, *biol.* Fett *n*: ***run to ~*** Fett ansetzen; ***the ~ is in the fire*** der Teufel ist los; **6.** ***the ~*** das Beste: ***live on*** (*od.* ***off***) ***the ~ of the land*** in Saus u. Braus leben; **III** *v/t.* **7.** *a.* ***~ up*** mästen: ***kill the ~ted calf*** a) *bibl.* das gemästete Kalb schlachten, b) ein Willkommensfest geben.

fa·tal [ˈfeɪtl] *adj.* □ **1.** tödlich, todbringend, mit tödlichem Ausgang: ***a ~ accident*** ein tödlicher Unfall; **2.** unheilvoll, verhängnisvoll (***to*** für): ***~ mistake***; **3.** schicksalhaft, entscheidend; **4.** Schicksals…: ***~ thread*** Lebensfaden *m*; **ˈfa·tal·ism** [-təlɪzəm] *s.* Fataˈlismus *m*; **ˈfa·tal·ist** [-təlɪst] *s.* Fataˈlist *m*; **fa·tal·is·tic** [ˌfeɪtəˈlɪstɪk] *adj.* (□ ***~ally***) fataˈlistisch.

fa·tal·i·ty [fəˈtælətɪ] *s.* **1.** Verhängnis *n*, Unglück *n*; **2.** Schicksalhaftigkeit *f*; **3.** tödlicher Ausgang *od.* Verlauf; **4.** Todesfall *m*, -opfer *n.*

fa·ta mor·ga·na [ˌfɑːtəmɔːˈgɑːnə] *s.* Fata Morˈgana *f.*

fate [feɪt] *s.* **1.** Schicksal *n*, Geschick *n*, Los *n*: ***he met his ~*** das Schicksal ereilte ihn; ***he met his ~ calmly*** er sah s-m Schicksal ruhig entgegen; ***seal s.o.'s ~*** j-s Schicksal besiegeln; **2.** Verhängnis *n*, Verderben *n*, ˈUntergang *m*: ***go to one's ~*** den Tod finden; **3.** Schicksalsgöttin *f*: ***the ☡s*** die Parzen; **ˈfat·ed** [-tɪd] *adj.* **1.** vom Schicksal (dazu) bestimmt: ***they were ~ to meet*** es war ihnen bestimmt, sich zu begegnen; **2.** dem ˈUntergang geweiht; **ˈfate·ful** [-fʊl] *adj.* □ **1.** schicksalhaft; **2.** verhängnisvoll; **3.** schicksalsschwer.

ˈfat|-head *s.* F ‚Blödmann' *m*; **ˈ~-ˌhead·ed** *adj.* dämlich, doof.

fa·ther [ˈfɑːðə] **I** *s.* **1.** Vater *m*: ***like ~ like son*** der Apfel fällt nicht weit vom Stamm; ***☡ Time*** Chronos *m*, die Zeit; **2.** ☡ (Gott)Vater *m*; **3.** *eccl.* a) Pastor *m*, b) *R.C.* Pater *m*, c) *R.C.* Vater *m* (*Bischof, Abt*): ***the Holy ☡*** der Heilige Vater; ***~ confessor*** Beichtvater; ***☡ of the Church*** Kirchenvater; **4.** *mst pl.* Ahn *m*, Vorfahr *m*: ***be gathered to one's ~s*** zu s-n Vätern versammelt werden; **5.** *fig.* Vater *m*, Urheber *m*: ***the ~ of chemistry***; ***☡ of the House*** *Brit.* dienstältestes Parlamentsmitglied; ***the wish was ~ to the thought*** der Wunsch war der Vater des Gedankens; **6.** *pl.* Stadt-, Landesväter *pl.*: ***the ☡s of the Constitution*** die Gründer der USA; **7.** väterlicher Freund (***to*** *gen.*); **II** *v/t.* **8.** *Kind* zeugen; **9.** *et.* ins Leben rufen, herˈvorbringen; **10.** wie ein Vater sein zu *j-m*; **11.** die Vaterschaft (*gen.*) anerkennen; **12.** *fig.* a) die Urheberschaft (*gen.*) anerkennen, b) die Urheberschaft (*gen.*) *od.* die Schuld für *et.* zuschreiben (***on, upon*** *dat.*); **☡ Christ·mas** *s. Brit.* Weihnachtsmann *m*; **~ fig·ure** *s. psych.* ˈVaterfiˌgur *f.*

fa·ther·hood [ˈfɑːðəhʊd] *s.* Vaterschaft *f*; **ˈfa·ther-in-law** [-ərɪn-] *s.* Schwiegervater *m*; **ˈfa·ther·land** *s.* Vaterland *n*: ***the ☡*** Deutschland *n*; **ˈfa·ther·less** [-lɪs] *adj.* vaterlos; **ˈfa·ther·li·ness** [-lɪnɪs] *s.* Väterlichkeit *f*; **ˈfa·ther·ly** [-lɪ] *adj. u. adv.* väterlich.

fath·om [ˈfæðəm] **I** *s.* **1.** a) ⚓ Faden *m* (*Tiefenmaß: 1,83 m*), b) *obs. u. fig.* Klafter *m, n*, c) ⚒ *Raummaß* (= *1,17 m³*); **II** *v/t.* **2.** ⚓ (aus)loten (*a. fig.*); **3.** *fig.* ergründen; **ˈfath·om·less** [-lɪs] *adj.* □ unergründlich (*a. fig.*); **fath·om line** *s.* ⚓ Lotleine *f.*

fa·tigue [fəˈtiːg] **I** *s.* **1.** Ermüdung *f* (*a.* ⚙), Erschöpfung *f* (*a.* ✓ *des Bodens*): ***~ strength*** ⚙ Dauerfestigkeit *f*; ***~ test*** ⚙ Ermüdungsprobe *f*; **2.** schwere Arbeit, Mühsal *f*, Straˈpaze *f*; **3.** ⚔ a) *a.* ***~ duty*** Arbeitsdienst *m*: ***~ detail, ~ party*** Arbeitskommando *n*, b) *pl. a.* ***~ clothes, ~ dress*** Arbeits-, Drillichanzug *m*; **II** *v/t. u. v/i.* **4.** ermüden (*a.* ⚙); **faˈti·guing** [-gɪŋ] *adj.* □ ermüdend, anstrengend.

fat·less [ˈfætlɪs] *adj.* ohne Fett, mager; **ˈfat·ling** [-lɪŋ] *s.* junges Masttier; **ˈfat·ly** [-lɪ] *adv. fig.* reichlich; **ˈfat·ness** [-nɪs] *s.* Fettheit *f*: a) Beleibtheit *f*, b) Fettigkeit *f*, Fetthaltigkeit *f*; **ˈfat·ten** [-tn] **I** *v/t.* **1.** fett *od.* dick machen: ***~ing*** dickmachend; **2.** *Tier*, F *a. Person* mästen; **3.** *Land* düngen; **II** *v/i.* **4.** fett *od.* dick werden; **5.** sich mästen (***on*** von); **ˈfat·tish** [-tɪʃ] *adj.* etwas fett, dicklich; **ˈfat·ty** [-tɪ] **I** *adj. a.* ⚗, ⚕ fetthaltig, fettig, Fett…: ***~ acid*** Fettsäure *f*; ***~ degeneration*** Verfettung *f*; ***~ heart*** Herzverfettung; ***~ tissue*** Fettgewebe *n*; **II** *s.* F Dickerchen *n.*

fa·tu·i·ty [fəˈtjuːətɪ] *s.* Albernheit *f*; **fat·u·ous** [ˈfætjʊəs] *adj.* □ albern, dumm.

fau·cal [ˈfɔːkl] *adj.* Kehl…, Rachen…; **fau·ces** [ˈfɔːsiːz] *s. pl. mst sg. konstr. anat.* Rachen *m.*

fau·cet [ˈfɔːsɪt] *s.* ⚙ *Am.* a) (Wasser-) Hahn *m*, b) (Faß)Zapfen *m.*

faugh [fɔː] *int.* pfui!

fault [fɔːlt] **I** *s.* **1.** Schuld *f*, Verschulden *n*: ***it is not his ~*** er hat *od.* trägt *od.* ihn trifft keine Schuld, es ist nicht s-e Schuld; ***be at ~*** schuld(ig) sein, die Schuld tragen (→ 4a); **2.** Fehler *m*, (⚖ *a.* Sach)Mangel *m*: ***find ~*** nörgeln, kritteln; ***find ~ with*** et. auszusetzen haben an (*dat.*), herumnörgeln an (*dat.*); ***to a ~*** allzu(sehr), ein bißchen zu *ordnungsliebend etc.*; **3.** (Chaˈrakter)Fehler *m*: ***inspite of all his ~s***; **4.** a) Fehler *m*, Irrtum *m*: ***be at ~*** sich irren, *hunt. u. fig. a.* auf der falschen Fährte sein, b) Vergehen *n*, Fehltritt *m*; **5.** ⚙ Deˈfekt *m*: a) Fehler *m*, Störung *f*, b) ⚡ Erd-, Leitungsfehler *m*; **6.** *Tennis etc.*: Fehler *m*; **7.** *geol.* Verwerfung *f*; **II** *v/t.* **8.** etwas auszusetzen haben an (*dat.*): ***he (it) can't be ~ed*** an ihm (daran) ist nichts auszusetzen; **9.** *et.* ‚verpatzen'; **III** *v/i.* **10.** e-n Fehler machen; **ˈ~ˌfind·er** *s.* Nörgler(in), Krittler(in); **ˈ~ˌfind·ing I** *s.* Kritteˈlei *f*, Nörgeˈlei *f*; **II** *adj.* nörglerisch, kritt(e)lig.

fault·i·ness [ˈfɔːltɪnɪs] *s.* Fehlerhaftigkeit *f*; **ˈfault·less** [-tlɪs] *adj.* □ einwand-, fehlerfrei, untadelig; **ˈfault·less·ness** [-tlɪsnɪs] *s.* Fehler-, Tadellosigkeit *f*; **ˈfault·y** [-tɪ] *adj.* □ fehlerhaft, schlecht, ⚙ *a.* deˈfekt: ***~ design*** Fehlkonstruktion *f.*

faun [fɔːn] *s. myth. u. fig.* Faun *m.*

fau·na [ˈfɔːnə] *s.* Fauna *f*, (*a.* Abhandlung *f* über e-e) Tierwelt *f.*

faux pas [ˌfəʊˈpɑː] *pl.* **pas** [pɑːz] *s.* Fauxˈpas *m.*

fa·vo(u)r [ˈfeɪvə] **I** *s.* **1.** Gunst *f*, Wohlwollen *n*: ***be*** (*od.* ***stand***) ***high in s.o.'s ~*** bei j-m in besonderer Gunst stehen *od.* gut angeschrieben sein; ***be in ~*** (***with***) beliebt sein (bei), begehrt sein (von); ***find ~*** Gefallen *od.* Anklang finden; ***find ~ with s.o.*** (*od.* ***in s.o.'s eyes***) Gnade vor j-s Augen finden, j-m gefallen; ***grant s.o. a ~*** j-m e-e Gunst gewähren; ***grant s.o. one's ~s*** j-m s-e Gunst gewähren (*Frau*); ***by ~ of*** a) mit gütiger Erlaubnis (*gen.*) *od.* von, b) überreicht von (*Brief*); ***in ~ of*** für, *a.* ✝ zugunsten von (*od. gen.*); ***who is in ~ (of it)?*** wer ist dafür?; ***out of ~*** a) in Ungnade (gefallen), b) nicht mehr gefragt *od.* beliebt; **2.** Gefallen *m*, Gefälligkeit *f*: ***as a ~*** aus Gefälligkeit; ***by ~***

of mit gütiger Erlaubnis von, durch gütige Vermittlung von; ***do me a ~*** tu mir e-n Gefallen; ***ask s.o. a ~*** j-n um e-n Gefallen bitten; ***we request the ~ of your company*** wir laden Sie höflich ein; **3.** Begünstigung *f*, Bevorzugung *f*: ***show ~ to s.o.*** j-n bevorzugen; ***under ~ of night*** im Schutze der Nacht; **4.** ✝ *obs.* Schreiben *n*; **5.** a) kleines (*auf e-r Party etc. verteiltes*) Geschenk, b) ˈScherzarˌtikel *m*; **6.** (Parˈtei- *etc.*)Abzeichen *n*; **II** *v/t.* **7.** günstig gesinnt sein (*dat.*), *j-m* wohlwollen *od.* gewogen sein; **8.** begünstigen: a) bevorzugen, vorziehen, *a. sport* favorisieren, b) günstig sein für, fördern, c) eintreten für, für *et.* sein; **9.** einverstanden sein (***with*** mit); **10.** *j-n* beehren *od.* erfreuen (***with*** mit); **11.** *j-m* ähnlich sein; **12.** schonen: ***~ one's leg***; **ˈfa·vo(u)r·a·ble** [-vərəbl] *adj.* □ **1.** wohlgesinnt, gewogen, geneigt (***to*** *dat.*); **2.** *allg.* günstig: a) vorteilhaft (***to***, ***for*** für), b) befriedigend, gut, c) positiv, zustimmend: ***~ answer***, d) vielversprechend; **ˈfa·vo(u)red** [-vəd] *adj.* begünstigt: ***the ~ few*** die Auserwählten; → ***most-favo(u)red-nation clause***; **ˈfa·vo(u)r·ite** [-vərɪt] **I** *s.* **1.** Liebling *m* (*a. fig. Schriftsteller, Schallplatte etc.*), *contp.* Günstling *m*: ***be s.o.'s*** (***great***) ***~*** bei j-m (sehr) beliebt sein; ***that book is a great ~ of mine*** dieses Buch liebe ich sehr; **2.** *sport* Favoˈrit(in); **II** *adj.* **3.** Lieblings…: ***~ dish*** Leibgericht *n*; **ˈfa·vo(u)r·it·ism** [-vərɪtɪzəm] *s.* Günstlings-, Vetternwirtschaft *f*.

fawn¹ [fɔːn] **I** *s.* **1.** *zo.* Damkitz *n*, Rehkalb *n*; **2.** Rehbraun *n*; **II** *adj.* **3.** *a.* ***~-colo(u)red*** rehbraun; **III** *v/t.* **4.** *ein Kitz* setzen.

fawn² [fɔːn] *v/i.* **1.** schwänzeln, wedeln; **2.** *fig.* (***upon***) scharˈwenzeln (um), katzbuckeln (vor *j-m*); **ˈfawn·ing** [-nɪŋ] *adj.* □ *fig.* kriecherisch, schmeichlerisch.

fay [feɪ] *s. poet.* Fee *f*.

faze [feɪz] *v/t.* F *j-n* durcheinˈanderbringen: ***not to ~ s.o.*** j-n kaltlassen.

fe·al·ty [ˈfiːəltɪ] *s.* **1.** *hist.* Lehenstreue *f*; **2.** *fig.* Treue *f*.

fear [fɪə] **I** *s.* **1.** Furcht *f*, Angst *f* (***of*** vor *dat.*, ***that*** *od.* ***lest*** daß …): ***be in ~ of*** → 6; ***in ~ of one's life*** in Todesangst; ***for ~ of*** a) aus Furcht vor (*dat.*) *od.* daß, b) um nicht, damit nicht; ***for ~ of losing it*** um es nicht zu verlieren; ***without ~ or favo(u)r*** ganz objektiv *od.* unparteiisch; ***no ~!*** keine Bange!; **2.** *pl.* Befürchtung *f*, Bedenken *n*; **3.** Sorge *f*, Besorgnis *f* (***for*** um); **4.** Gefahr *f*, Risiko *n*: ***there is not much ~ of that*** das ist kaum zu befürchten; **5.** Scheu *f*, Ehrfurcht *f* (***of*** vor): ***~ of God*** Gottesfurcht; ***put the ~ of God into s.o.*** j-m e-n heiligen Schrecken einjagen; **II** *v/t.* **6.** fürchten, sich fürchten vor (*dat.*), Angst haben vor (*dat.*); **7.** *et.* befürchten: ***~ the worst***; **8.** *Gott* fürchten; **III** *v/i.* **9.** sich fürchten, Angst haben; **10.** besorgt sein (***for*** um): ***never ~!*** sei unbesorgt!; **ˈfear·ful** [-fʊl] *adj.* □ **1.** furchtbar, fürchterlich, schrecklich (*alle a. fig.* F); **2.** furchtsam, angsterfüllt, bange (***of*** vor *dat.*); **3.** besorgt, in (großer) Sorge (***of*** um, ***that*** *od.* ***lest*** daß); **4.** ehrfürchtig; **ˈfear·less** [-lɪs] *adj.* □ furchtlos, unerschrocken; **ˈfear·less·ness** [-lɪsnɪs] *s.* Furchtlosigkeit *f*; **ˈfear·some** [-səm] *adj.* □ *mst humor.* furchterregend, schrecklich, gräßlich.

fea·si·bil·i·ty [ˌfiːzəˈbɪlətɪ] *s.* ˈDurchführbarkeit *f*, Machbarkeit *f*; **fea·si·ble** [ˈfiːzəbl] *adj.* □ aus-, ˈdurchführbar, machbar, möglich.

feast [fiːst] **I** *s.* **1.** *eccl.* Fest(tag *m*) *n*, Feiertag *m*; **2.** Festmahl *n*, -essen *n*; → ***enough*** II; **3.** (Hoch)Genuß *m*: ***a ~ for the eyes*** e-e Augenweide; **II** *v/t.* **4.** (festlich) bewirten; **5.** ergötzen: ***~ one's eyes on*** s-e Augen weiden an (*dat.*); **III** *v/i.* **6.** (***on***) schmausen (von), sich gütlich tun (an *dat.*); schwelgen (in *acc.*); **7.** (***on***) sich weiden (an *dat.*), schwelgen (in *dat.*).

feat [fiːt] *s.* **1.** Helden-, Großtat *f*: ***~ of arms*** Waffentat; **2.** (*technische etc.*) Großtat, große Leistung; **3.** a) Kunst-, Meisterstück *n*, b) Kraftakt *m*.

feath·er [ˈfeðə] **I** *s.* **1.** Feder *f*, *pl.* Gefieder *n*: ***in fine*** (*od.* ***full***) ***~*** F a) (bei) bester Laune, b) in Hochform; ***that is a ~ in his cap*** darauf kann er stolz sein; ***that will make the ~s fly*** da werden die Fetzen fliegen; ***you might have knocked me down with a ~*** ich war einfach ‚platt' (*erstaunt*); → ***bird*** 1, ***fur*** 3, ***white feather***; **2.** Pfeilfeder *f*; **3.** Schaumkrone *f* (*e-r Welle*); **II** *v/t.* **4.** mit Federn versehen *od.* schmücken; *Pfeil* fiedern; **5.** *Rudern*: *Riemen* flach drehen; **ˈ~-bed I** *s.* **1.** Maˈtratze *f* mit Federfüllung; **2.** *fig.* ‚gemütliche Sache'; **II** *v/t.* **3.** verhätscheln; **III** *v/i.* **4.** unnötige Arbeitskräfte einstellen; **ˈ~ˌbed·ding** *s.* (*gewerkschaftlich geforderte*) ˈÜberbesetzung mit Arbeitskräften; **ˈ~-brained** *adj.* **1.** schwachköpfig; **2.** leichtsinnig; **ˈ~-ˌdust·er** *s.* Staubwedel *m*.

feath·ered [ˈfeðəd] *adj.* gefiedert: ***~ tribe(s)*** Vogelwelt *f*.

feath·er·ing [ˈfeðərɪŋ] *s.* **1.** Gefieder *n*; **2.** Befiederung *f*; **3.** ✈ Segelstellung *f* (*Propeller*).

ˈfeath·er·weight I *s.* **1.** *sport* Federgewicht(ler *m*) *n*; **2.** ‚Leichtgewicht' *n* (*Person*); **3.** *fig. contp.* a) ‚Würstchen' *n* (*Person*), b) ‚kleine Fische' *pl.* (*et. Belangloses*); **II** *adj.* **4.** Federgewichts…

feath·er·y [ˈfeðərɪ] *adj.* feder(n)artig.

fea·ture [ˈfiːtʃə] **I** *s.* **1.** (Gesichts)Zug *m*; **2.** Merkmal *n*, Charakteˈristikum *n*, (Haupt)Eigenschaft *f*; Hauptpunkt *m*, -teil *m*, Besonderheit *f*; **3.** (Gesichts-)Punkt *m*, Seite *f*; **4.** (ˈHaupt)Attraktiˌon *f*, Darbietung *f*; **5.** *a.* ***~ film*** a) Spielfilm *m*, b) Hauptfilm *m*; **6.** *a.* ***~ program(me)*** *Radio*, *TV*: Feature *n*, (aktuˈeller) Dokumenˈtarbericht; **7.** *a.* ***~ article***, ***~ story*** Feature *n*, Speziˈalarˌtikel *m e-r Zeitung*; **II** *v/t.* **8.** kennzeichnen, bezeichnend sein für; **9.** (als Besonderheit) haben *od.* aufweisen, sich auszeichnen durch; **10.** (groß herˈaus-) bringen, herˈausstellen; (als Hauptschlager) zeigen *od.* bringen; *Film etc.*: in der Hauptrolle zeigen: ***a film featuring X*** ein Film mit X in der Hauptrolle; **ˈfea·ture-length** *adj.* mit Spielfilmlänge; **ˈfea·ture·less** [-lɪs] *adj.* nichtssagend.

feb·ri·fuge [ˈfebrɪfjuːdʒ] *s.* ⚕ Fiebermittel *n*; **fe·brile** [ˈfiːbraɪl] *adj.* fiebrig, Fieber…

Feb·ru·ar·y [ˈfebrʊərɪ] *s.* Februar *m*: ***in ~*** im Februar.

fe·cal *etc.* → ***faecal*** *etc.*

feck·less [ˈfeklɪs] *adj.* □ **1.** schwach, kraftlos; **2.** hilfslos; **3.** zwecklos.

fe·cund [ˈfiːkənd] *adj.* fruchtbar, produkˈtiv (*beide a fig.*); **ˈfe·cun·date** [-deɪt] *v/t.* fruchtbar machen; befruchten (*a. biol.*); **fe·cun·da·tion** [ˌfiːkənˈdeɪʃn] *s.* Befruchtung *f*; **fe·cun·di·ty** [fɪˈkʌndətɪ] *s.* Fruchtbarkeit *f*, Produktiviˈtät *f*.

fed¹ [fed] *pret. u. p.p. von **feed***.

fed² [fed] *s. Am.* F **1.** FBˈI-Aˌgent *m*; **2.** *mst.* ᘔ (*die*) ˈBundesreˌgierung.

fed·er·al [ˈfedərəl] **I** *adj.* □ *pol.* **1.** födeˈraˈtiv; **2.** *mst* ᘔ Bundes…: a) bundesstaatlich, den Bund *od.* die ˈBundesreˌgierung betreffend, b) *USA* Unions…: ***~ government*** Bundesregierung *f*; ***~ jurisdiction*** Bundesgerichtsbarkeit *f*; ***the ᘔ Republic*** (***of Germany***) die Bundesrepublik (Deutschland); ***ᘔ State*** *Am.* Bundesstaat *m*, (Einzel)Staat *m*; **3.** ᘔ *Am. hist.* födeˈraˈlistisch; **II** *s.* **4.** (*Am. hist.* ᘔ) Födeˈraˈlist *m*; ᘔ ***Bu·reau of In·ves·ti·ga·tion*** *s.* amer. Bundeskrimiˈnalamt *n od.* -poliˌzei *f* (*abbr.* ***FBI***).

fed·er·al·ism [ˈfedərəlɪzəm] *s. pol.* Födeˈraˈlismus *m*; **ˈfed·er·al·ist** [-ɪst] **I** *adj.* födeˈraˈlistisch; **II** *s.* Födeˈraˈlist *m*; **ˈfed·er·al·ize** [-laɪz] → ***federate*** I.

fed·er·ate [ˈfedəreɪt] **I** *v/t. u. v/i.* (sich) föderalisieren, (sich) zu e-m (Staaten-)Bund vereinigen; **II** *adj.* [-rət] föderiert, verbündet; **fed·er·a·tion** [ˌfedəˈreɪʃn] *s.* **1.** Föderatiˈon *f*: a) poˈlitischer Zs.-schluß, b) Staatenbund *m*; **2.** Bundesstaat *m*; **3.** ✝ (Zenˈtral-, Dach-)Verband *m*; **ˈfed·er·a·tive** [-rətɪv] *adj.* □ → ***federal*** 1.

fe·do·ra [fɪˈdɔːrə] *s. Am.* (weicher) Filzhut.

fee [fiː] **I** *s.* **1.** Gebühr: a) (ˈAnwalts- *etc.*)Honoˌrar *n*, Vergütung *f*, b) amtliche Gebühr, Taxe *f*, c) (Mitglieds)Beitrag *m*, d) (***admission*** *od.* ***entrance***) ***~*** Eintrittsgeld *n*, e) Trinkgeld *n*: ***doctor's ~*** Arztrechnung *f*; ***school ~(s)*** Schulgeld *n*; **2.** *Fußball*: Transˈfersumme *f*; **3.** *hist.* Lehn(s)gut *n*; **4.** ⚖ Eigentum(srecht) *n*: ***~ simple*** (unbeschränktes) Eigentumsrecht, Grundeigentum; ***~ tail*** erbrechtlich gebundenes Grundeigentum; ***hold land in ~*** Land zu eigen haben; **II** *v/t.* **5.** *j-m* e-e Gebühr *etc.* bezahlen.

fee·ble [ˈfiːbl] *adj.* □ *allg.* schwach, *fig. a.* lahm, kläglich (*Versuch*, *Ausrede etc.*), matt (*Lächeln*, *Stimme*); **ˌfee·ble-ˈmind·ed** *adj.* schwachsinnig; **ˈfee·ble·ness** [-nɪs] *s.* Schwäche *f*.

feed [fiːd] **I** *v/t.* [*irr.*] **1.** Nahrung zuführen (*dat.*), *Tier*, *Kind*, *Kranken* füttern (***on***, ***with*** mit), *e-m Menschen* zu essen geben, *e-m Tier* zu fressen geben, *Vieh* weiden lassen: ***~*** (***at the breast***) *Säugling* stillen; ***~ up*** a) *Vieh* mästen, b) *j-n* ‚hochpäppeln'; ***be fed up with*** F *et.* satt haben, ‚die Nase voll haben' von; ***I'm fed up to the teeth with him*** (***it***) F er (es) ‚steht mir bis hierher'; ***~ the fishes*** a) ‚die Fische füttern' (*bei Seekrankheit*), b) ertrinken; ***~ a cold*** bei Erkältung tüchtig essen; **2.** *Familie etc.* ernähren (**on** von), erhalten; **3.** versorgen (**with** mit); **4.** ⚙ a) *Maschine* speisen, beschicken, b) *Material* zuführen, *Werkstück* vorschieben, *Daten in e-n Computer* eingeben: **~ back** a) ϟ rückkoppeln, b) *fig.* zu'rückleiten (**to** an *acc.*); **5.** *Feuer* unter'halten; **6.** *fig.* a) *Gefühl, Hoffnung etc.* nähren, Nahrung geben (*dat.*), b) befriedigen: **~ one's vanity**; **~ one's eyes on** s-e Augen weiden an (*dat.*); **7.** *thea.* F *j-m* Stichworte liefern; **8.** *sport* F *j-n* ‚bedienen', mit Bällen ‚füttern'; **9.** *oft* **~ down**, **~ close** *Wiese* abweiden lassen; **II** *v/i.* [*irr.*] **10.** a) fressen (*Tier*), b) F ‚futtern' (*Mensch*); **11.** sich ernähren, leben (**on** von); **III** *s.* **12.** Fütterung *f*; F Mahlzeit *f*; **13.** Futter *n*, Nahrung *f*: **off one's ~** ohne Appetit; **out at ~** auf der Weide; **14.** ⚙ a) Speisung *f*, Beschickung *f*, (Materi'al)Zuführung *f*, b) (Werkzeug)Vorschub *m*; **15.** Zufuhr *f*, Ladung *f*; Beschickungsgut *n*; **'~·back** *s.* ϟ *u. fig.* Feedback *n*; **~ bag** *s. Am.* Futtersack *m*.

feed·er ['fi:də] *s.* **1. a heavy ~** ein starker Esser (*Mensch*) *od.* Fresser (*Tier*); **2.** ⚙ a) Beschickungsvorrichtung *f*, b) ϟ Speiseleitung *f*, Feeder *m*; **3.** *Verkehr*: Zubringerlinie *f*, -strecke *f*: **~ (road)** Zubringerstraße *f*; **4.** Bewässerungs-, Zuflußgraben *m*; Nebenfluß *m*; **5.** *Brit.* a) Lätzchen *n*, b) (Saug)Flasche *f*; **6.** *thea. Am.* F Stichwortgeber *m*; **~ line** *s.* **1.** *Verkehr*: Zubringerlinie *f*; **2.** → **feeder** 2 b.

feed hop·per *s.* Fülltrichter *m*.

feed·ing ['fi:dɪŋ] **I** *s.* **1.** Fütterung *f*; **2.** Ernährung *f*; **3.** ⚙ → **feed** 14 a; **II** *adj.* **4.** Zufuhr…; **~ bot·tle** *s.* (Saug)Flasche *f*; **~ cup** *s.* ⚕ Schnabeltasse *f*.

feed pipe *s.* Zuleitungsrohr *n*.

feel [fi:l] **I** *v/t.* [*irr.*] **1.** (an-, be)fühlen, betasten; **just ~ my hand** fühl mal m-e Hand (an); **~ one's way** sich vortasten (*a. fig.*), *fig.* vorsichtig vorgehen, sondieren; **~ s.o. up** *sl.* j-n ‚abgrapschen' *od.* ‚befummeln'; **2.** a) fühlen, (ver-) spüren, wahrnehmen, merken, b) empfinden: **~ the cold**; **~ pleasure** Freude *od.* Lust empfinden; **he felt the loss deeply** der Verlust traf ihn schwer; **~ s.o.'s wrath** j-s Zorn zu spüren bekommen; **make itself felt** spürbar werden, zu spüren sein; **a (long-)felt want** ein dringendes Bedürfnis, ein (längst) spürbarer Mangel; **3.** a) ahnen, spüren, b) glauben, c) halten für: **I ~ it (to be) my duty** ich halte es für m-e Pflicht; **4.** *a.* **~ out** *et.* sondieren, *j-m* ‚auf den Zahn fühlen'; **II** *v/i.* **5.** fühlen: a) empfinden, b) durch Tasten feststellen *od.* festzustellen suchen (**whether**, **if** ob; **how** wie); **6. ~ for** a) tasten nach, b) suchen nach, c) *et.* herauszufinden suchen; **7.** sich fühlen, sich befinden, sich vorkommen wie, sein: **~ cold** frieren; **I ~ cold** mir ist kalt; **~ ill** sich krank fühlen; **~ certain** sicher sein; **~ quite o.s. again** wieder ‚auf dem Posten' sein; **~ like (doing) s.th.** Lust haben zu et. (*od.* et. zu tun); **~ up to s.th.** a) sich e-r Sache gewachsen fühlen, b) sich in der Lage fühlen zu et., c) in (der) Stimmung sein zu et.; **8. ~ for** (*od.* **with**) **s.o.** Mitgefühl mit j-m haben; **we ~ with you** wir fühlen mit dir (*od.* euch); **9.** das Gefühl *od.* den Eindruck haben, finden, meinen, glauben (**that** daß): **I ~ that** ich finde, daß…; **how do you ~ about it?** was meinst du dazu: **it is felt in London** in London ist man der Ansicht; **~ strongly** a) entschiedene Ansichten haben, b) sich erregen (**about** über *acc.*); **10.** sich *weich etc.* anfühlen: **velvet ~s soft**; **11.** *impers.* **I know how it ~s to be hungry** ich weiß, was es heißt, hungrig zu sein; **III** *s.* **12.** Gefühl *n* (*wie sich et. anfühlt*): **a sticky ~**; **13.** (An-) Fühlen *n*: **soft to the ~** weich anzufühlen; **let me have a ~** laß mich mal fühlen; **14.** Gefühl *n*: a) Empfindung *f*, Eindruck *m*, b) Stimmung *f*, Atmo'sphäre *f*, c) feiner In'stinkt, ‚Riecher' *m* (**for** für): **clutch ~** *mot.* Gefühl für richtiges Kuppeln.

feel·er ['fi:lə] *s.* **1.** *zo.* Fühler *m* (*a. fig.*): **put** (*od.* **throw**) **out a ~** s-e Fühler ausstrecken, sondieren; **2.** ⚙ a) Dorn *m*, Fühler *m*, b) Taster *m*; **'feel·ing** [-lɪŋ] **I** *s.* **1.** Gefühl *n*, Gefühlssinn *m*; **2.** Gefühl(szustand *m*) *n*, Stimmung *f*: **bad** (*od.* **ill**) **~** Groll *m*, böses Blut, Feindseligkeit *f*; **good ~** a) gutes Gefühl, b) Wohlwollen *n*; **no hard ~s!** F a) nicht böse sein!, b) (das) macht nichts!; **3.** *pl.* Gefühle *pl.*, Empfindlichkeit *f*: **hurt s.o.'s ~s** j-s Gefühle *od.* j-n verletzen; **4.** Feingefühl, Empfindsamkeit: **have a ~ for** Gefühl haben für; **5.** (Gefühls)Eindruck *m*: **I have a ~ that** ich habe (so) das Gefühl, daß; **6.** Gefühl *n*, Gesinnung *f*, Ansicht *f*: **strong ~s** a) starke Überzeugung, b) Erregung *f*; **7.** Auf-, Erregung *f*, Rührung *f*: **with ~** a) mit Gefühl, gefühlvoll, b) mit Nachdruck, c) erbittert; **~s ran high** die Gemüter erhitzten sich; **8.** (Vor)Gefühl *n*, Ahnung *f*; **II** *adj.* □ **9.** fühlend, Gefühls…; **10.** gefühlvoll: a) mitfühlend, b) voll Gefühl, lebhaft.

feet [fi:t] *pl. von* **foot**.

feign [feɪn] **I** *v/t.* **1.** *et.* vortäuschen, *Krankheit a.* simulieren: **~ death** sich totstellen; **2.** *e-e Ausrede etc.* erfinden; **II** *v/i.* **3.** sich verstellen, so tun als ob, simulieren; **'feign·ed·ly** [-nɪdlɪ] *adv.* zum Schein.

feint^{1} [feɪnt] **I** *s.* **1.** *sport* Finte *f* (*a. fig.*); **2.** ⚔ Scheinangriff *m*, 'Täuschungsma,növer *n* (*a. fig.*); **II** *v/i.* **3.** *sport* fintieren: **~ at** (*od.* **upon**) *j-n* täuschen; **III** *v/t.* **4.** *sport Schlag etc.* antäuschen.

feint^{2} [feɪnt] *adj. typ.* schwach: **~ lines**.

feld·spar ['feldspɑ:] *s. min.* Feldspat *m*.

fe·lic·i·tate [fɪ'lɪsɪteɪt] *v/t.* (**on**) beglückwünschen, *j-m* gratulieren (zu); **fe·lic·i·ta·tion** [fɪ,lɪsɪ'teɪʃn] *s.* Glückwunsch *m*; **fe'lic·i·tous** [-təs] *adj.* □ glücklich (gewählt), treffend (*Ausdruck etc.*); **fe'lic·i·ty** [-tɪ] *s.* **1.** Glück(seligkeit *f*) *n*; **2.** a) glücklicher Einfall, b) glücklicher Griff, c) treffender Ausdruck.

fe·line ['fi:laɪn] **I** *adj.* **1.** Katzen…; **2.** katzenartig, -haft: **~ grace**; **3.** *fig.* falsch, tückisch; **II** *s.* **4.** Katze *f*.

fell^{1} [fel] *pret. von* **fall**.

fell^{2} [fel] *v/t. Baum* fällen, *Gegner a.* niederstrecken.

fell^{3} [fel] *adj. poet.* **1.** grausam, wild, mörderisch; **2.** tödlich.

fell^{4} [fel] *s.* **1.** Balg *m*, Tierfell *n*; Vlies *n*; **2.** struppiges Haar.

fell^{5} [fel] *s. Brit.* **1.** Hügel *m*, Berg *m*; **2.** Moorland *n*.

fel·lah ['felə] *pl.* **-lahs**, **fel·la·heen** [,felə'hi:n] (*Arab.*) *s.* Fel'lache *m*.

fell·er ['felə] F → **fellow** 4.

fel·loe ['feləʊ] *s.* (Rad)Felge *f*.

fel·low ['feləʊ] **I** *s.* **1.** Gefährte *m*, Gefährtin *f*, Genosse *m*, Genossin *f*, Kame'rad(in): **~s in misery** Leidensgenossen; **2.** Mitmensch *m*, Zeitgenosse *m*; **3.** Ebenbürtige(r *m*) *f*: **he will never have his ~** er wird nie seinesgleichen finden; **4.** F Kerl *m*, Bursche *m*, ‚Mensch' *m*, ‚Typ' *m*: **my dear ~** mein lieber Freund!; **good ~** guter Kerl; **old ~!** alter Knabe!; **a ~** man, einer; **5.** *der* (*die*, *das*) Da'zugehörige, *der* (*die*, *das*) andere *e-s Paares*: **where is the ~ of this shoe?**; **6.** Fellow *m*: a) Mitglied *n* e-s College (*Dozent, der im College wohnt*), b) Inhaber(in) e-s 'Forschungssti,pendiums, c) *Am.* Stu'dent(in) höheren Se'mesters, c) Mitglied *n* e-r gelehrten *etc.* Gesellschaft; **II** *adj.* **7.** Mit…: **~ being** Mitmensch *m*; **~ citizen** Mitbürger *m*; **~ countryman** Landsmann *m*; **~ feeling** a) Zs.-gehörigkeitsgefühl *n*, b) Mitgefühl *n*; **~ student** Studienkollege *m*, -kollegin *f*, Kommilitone *m*, Kommilitonin *f*; **~ travel(l)er** a) Mitreisende(r *m*) *f*, b) *pol.* Mitläufer(in), Sympathisant(in), *bsd.* Kommunistenfreund (-in).

fel·low·ship ['feləʊʃɪp] *s.* **1.** *oft* **good ~** a) Kame'radschaft(lichkeit) *f*, b) Geselligkeit *f*; **2.** (*geistige etc.*) Gemeinschaft, Verbundenheit *f*; **3.** Gemein-, Gesellschaft *f*, Gruppe *f*; **4.** *univ.* a) die Fellows *pl.*, b) *Brit.* Stellung *f* e-s Fellow, c) Sti'pendienfonds *m*, d) 'Forschungssti,pendium *n*.

fel·on^{1} ['felən] *s.* Nagelgeschwür *n*.

fel·on^{2} ['felən] *s.* (Schwer)Verbrecher *m*; **fe·lo·ni·ous** [fə'ləʊnjəs] *adj.* □ ⚖ verbrecherisch; **'fel·o·ny** [-nɪ] *s.* ⚖ *Am.* Verbrechen *n*, *Brit. obs.* Schwerverbrechen *n*.

fel·spar ['felspɑ:] → **feldspar**.

felt^{1} [felt] *pret. u. p.p. von* **feel**.

felt^{2} [felt] **I** *s.* Filz *m*; **II** *adj.* Filz…: **~-tip(ped) pen**, **~ tip** Filzschreiber *m*, -stift *m*; **III** *v/t. u. v/i.* (sich) verfilzen; **'felt·ing** [-tɪŋ] *s.* Filzstoff *m*.

fe·male ['fi:meɪl] **I** *adj.* **1.** weiblich (*a.* ⚘): **~ dog** Hündin *f*; **~ student** Studentin *f*; **2.** weiblich, Frauen…: **~ dress** Frauenkleidung *f*; **3.** ⚙ Hohl…, Steck…: **~ screw** Schraubenmutter *f*; **~ thread** Muttergewinde *n*; **II** *s.* **4.** a) Frau *f*, b) Mädchen *n*, c) *contp.* Weibsbild *n*, -stück *n*; **5.** *zo.* Weibchen *n*; **6.** ⚘ weibliche Pflanze.

feme| cov·ert [fi:m] *s.* ⚖ verheiratete Frau; **~ sole** *s.* ⚖ a) unverheiratete Frau, b) vermögensrechtlich selbständige Ehefrau: **~ trader** selbständige Geschäftsfrau.

fem·i·nine ['femɪnɪn] **I** *adj.* □ **1.** weiblich (*a. ling.*); **2.** weiblich, Frauen…: **~ voice**; **3.** fraulich, sanft, zart; **4.** weibisch, femi'nin; **II** *s.* **5.** *ling.* Femininum *n*.

fem·i·nin·i·ty [,femɪ'nɪnətɪ] *s.* **1.** Fraulich-, Weiblichkeit *f*; **2.** weibische *od.* femi'nine Art; **3.** *coll.* (*die*) (holde) Weiblichkeit; **fem·i·nism** ['femɪnɪzəm] *s.* Femi'nismus *m*; Frauenrechtsbewe-

gung *f*; **fem·i·nist** ['femɪnɪst] *s.* Frauenrechtler(in), Femi'nist(in).
fem·o·ral ['femərəl] *adj. anat.* Oberschenkel(knochen)...; **fe·mur** ['fi:mə] *pl.* **-murs** *od.* **fem·o·ra** ['femərə] *s.* Oberschenkel(knochen) *m.*
fen [fen] *s.* Fenn *n*: a) Marschland *n*, b) (Flach)Moor *n*: ***the ~s*** die Niederungen in ***East Anglia***.
fence [fens] **I** *s.* **1.** Zaun *m*, Einzäunung *f*, Gehege *n*: ***mend one's ~s*** *Am. pol.* s-e angeschlagene Position festigen; ***sit on the ~*** a) sich abwartend *od.* neutral verhalten, b) unschlüssig sein; **2.** *Reitsport*: Hindernis *n*; **3.** *sport das* Fechten; **4.** *sl.* a) Hehler *m*, b) Hehlernest *n*; **II** *v/t.* **5.** *a.* ***~ in*** einzäunen, einfriedigen: ***~ in*** (*od.* ***round***, ***off***) um'zäunen; ***~ off*** abzäunen; **6.** ***~ in*** einsperren; **7.** *fig.* schützen, sichern (***from*** vor *dat.*): ***~ off*** *Fragen etc.* abwehren, parieren; **8.** *sl. Diebesbeute* an e-n Hehler verkaufen; **III** *v/i.* **9.** fechten; **10.** *fig.* Ausflüchte machen, ausweichen; **11.** *sl.* Hehle'rei treiben; ***~ month*** *s. hunt. Brit.* Schonzeit *f.*
fenc·er ['fensə] *s. sport* **1.** Fechter(in); **2.** Springpferd *n.*
fence sea·son → ***fence month***.
fenc·ing ['fensɪŋ] *s.* **1.** *sport* Fechten *n*; **2.** *fig.* ausweichendes Verhalten, Ausflüchte *pl.*; **3.** a) Zaun *m*, b) Zäune *pl.*, c) 'Zaunmateri‚al *n.*
fend [fend] **I** *v/t.* **1.** ***~ off*** abwehren; **II** *v/i.* **2.** sich wehren; **3.** ***~ for*** sorgen für: ***~ for o.s.*** für sich selbst sorgen, sich ganz allein durchs Leben schlagen; '**fend·er** [-də] *s.* **1.** ⚙ Schutzvorrichtung *f*; **2.** *rail. etc.* Puffer *m*; **3.** *mot. Am.* Kotflügel *m*: ***~ bender*** F (Unfall *m* mit) Blechschaden *m*; **4.** Schutzblech *n am Fahrrad*; **5.** ⚓ Fender *m*; **6.** Ka'minvorsetzer *m*, -gitter *n.*
fen·es·tra·tion [‚fenɪ'streɪʃn] *s.* **1.** △ Fensteranordnung *f*; **2.** ⚕ 'Fensterung(soperati‚on) *f.*
fen fire *s.* Irrlicht *n.*
Fe·ni·an ['fi:njən] *hist.* **I.** *s.* Fenier *m*; **II** *adj.* fenisch; '**Fe·ni·an·ism** [-nɪzəm] *s.* Feniertum *n.*
fen·nel ['fenl] *s.* ⚘ Fenchel *m.*
feoff [fef] → ***fief***; **feoff·ee** [fe'fi:] *s.* ⚖ Belehnte(r) *m*: ***~ in*** (*od.* ***of***) ***trust*** Treuhänder(in); **feoff·er** ['fefə], **feof·for** [fe'fɔ:] *s.* ⚖ Lehnsherr *m.*
fe·ral ['fɪərəl] *adj.* **1.** wild(lebend); **2.** *fig.* wild, bar'barisch.
fer·e·to·ry ['ferɪtərɪ] *s.* Re'liquienschrein *m.*
fer·ment [fə'ment] **I** *v/t.* **1.** in Gärung bringen, *fig. a.* in Wallung bringen, erregen; **II** *v/i.* **2.** gären (*a. fig.*); **III** *s.* ['fɜ:ment] **3.** ⚗ Fer'ment *n*, Gärstoff *m*; **4.** ⚗ Gärung *f*, *fig. a.* (innere) Unruhe, Aufruhr *m*: ***the country was in a state of ~*** es gärte im Land; **fer·men·ta·tion** [‚fɜ:men'teɪʃn] *s.* **1.** ⚗ Fermentati'on *f*, Gärung *f* (*a. fig.*); **2.** *fig.* Aufruhr *m*, (innere) Unruhe.
fern [fɜ:n] *s.* ⚘ Farn(kraut *n*) *m*; '**fern·y** [-nɪ] *adj.* **1.** farnartig; **2.** voller Farnkraut.
fe·ro·cious [fə'rəʊʃəs] *adj.* □ **1.** wild, grausam, grimmig, heftig; **2.** *Am.* F a) ‚toll', b) *contp.* ‚grausam'; **fe·roc·i·ty** [fə'rɒsətɪ] *s.* Grausamkeit *f*, Wildheit *f.*
fer·re·ous ['ferɪəs] *adj.* eisenhaltig.
fer·ret ['ferɪt] **I** *s.* **1.** *zo.* Frettchen *n*; **2.** *fig.* ‚Spürhund' *m* (*Person*); **II** *v/i.* **3.** *hunt.* mit Frettchen jagen; **4.** ***~ about*** her'umsuchen (***for*** nach); **III** *v/t.* **5.** ***~ out*** *fig. et.* aufspüren, -stöbern, her'ausfinden.
fer·ric ['ferɪk] *adj.* ⚗ Eisen...; **fer·ri·cy·a·nide** [‚ferɪ'saɪənaɪd] *s.* Cy'aneisenverbindung *f*; **fer·rif·er·ous** [fe'rɪfərəs] *adj.* ⚗ eisenhaltig.
Fer·ris wheel ['ferɪs] *s.* Riesenrad *n.*
ferro- [ferəʊ] *in Zssgn* Eisen...; **‚~-'con·crete** *s.* 'Eisenbe‚ton *m*; '**~·type** *s. phot.* Ferroty'pie *f.*
fer·rous ['ferəs] *adj.* eisenhaltig, Eisen...
fer·rule ['feru:l] *s.* **1.** ⚙ Stockzwinge *f*; **2.** Muffe *f.*
fer·ry ['ferɪ] **I** *s.* **1.** Fähre *f*, Fährschiff *n*, -boot *n*; **2.** *a.* ***~ service*** Fährdienst *m*; **3.** ✈ Über'führungsdienst *m* (*von der Fabrik zum Flugplatz*); **4.** *Raumfahrt*: (Lande)Fähre *f*; **II** *v/t.* **5.** 'übersetzen; *bsd.* ✈ über'führen; befördern; **III** *v/i.* **6.** 'übersetzen; '**~·boat** → ***ferry*** 1; **~ bridge** *s.* **1.** Tra'jekt *m*, *n*, Eisenbahnfähre *f*; **2.** Landungsbrücke *f*; '**~·man** [-mən] *s.* [*irr.*] Fährmann *m.*
fer·tile ['fɜ:taɪl] *adj.* □ **1.** *a. fig.* fruchtbar, produk'tiv, reich (***in***, ***of*** an *dat.*); **2.** *fig.* schöpferisch; **fer·til·i·ty** [fə'tɪlətɪ] *s. a. fig.* Fruchtbarkeit *f*, Reichtum *m*; **fer·ti·li·za·tion** [‚fɜ:tɪlaɪ'zeɪʃn] *s.* **1.** Fruchtbarmachen *n*; **2.** *biol. u. fig.* Befruchtung *f*; **3.** ✓ Düngung *f*; '**fer·ti·lize** [-tɪlaɪz] *v/t.* **1.** fruchtbar machen; **2.** *biol. u. fig.* befruchten; **3.** ✓ düngen; '**fer·ti·liz·er** [-tɪlaɪzə] *s.* (Kunst)Dünger *m*, Düngemittel *n.*
fer·ule ['feru:l] **I** *s.* (flaches) Line'al (*zur Züchtigung*), (Zucht)Rute *f* (*a. fig.*); **II** *v/t.* züchtigen.
fer·ven·cy ['fɜ:vənsɪ] → ***fervo(u)r*** 1; '**fer·vent** [-nt] *adj.* □ **1.** *fig.* glühend, feurig, inbrünstig, leidenschaftlich; **2.** (glühend)heiß; '**fer·vid** [-vɪd] *adj.* □ → ***fervent*** 1; '**fer·vo(u)r** [-və] *s.* **1.** *fig.* Glut *f*, Feuer(eifer *m*) *n*, Leidenschaft *f*, Inbrunst *f*; **2.** Glut *f*, Hitze *f.*
fess(e) [fes] *s. her.* (Quer)Balken *m.*
fes·tal ['festl] *adj.* □ festlich, Fest...
fes·ter ['festə] **I** *v/i.* **1.** schwären, eitern: ***~ing sore*** Eiterbeule *f* (*a. fig.*); **2.** verwesen, verfaulen; **3.** *fig.* gären: ***~ in s.o.'s mind*** an j-m nagen *od.* fressen; **II** *s.* **4.** a) Schwäre *f*, eiternde Wunde, b) Geschwür *n.*
fes·ti·val ['festəvl] **I** *s.* **1.** Fest(tag *m*) *n*, Feier *f*; **2.** Festspiele *pl.*, 'Festival *n*; **II** *adj.* **3.** festlich, Fest...; **4.** Festspiel...; '**fes·tive** [-tɪv] *adj.* □ **1.** festlich, Fest...; **2.** fröhlich, gesellig; **fes·tiv·i·ty** [fe'stɪvətɪ] *s.* **1.** *oft pl.* Fest(lichkeit *f*) *n*; **2.** festliche Stimmung.
fes·toon [fe'stu:n] **I** *s.* Gir'lande *f*; **II** *v/t.* mit Gir'landen schmücken.
fe·tal ['fi:tl] *etc.* → ***foetal*** *etc.*
fetch [fetʃ] **I** *v/t.* **1.** (her'bei)holen, (her)bringen: ***~ a doctor*** e-n Arzt holen; ***~ s.o. round*** F j-n ‚rumkriegen'; **2.** *et. od. j-n* abholen; **3.** *Atem* holen: ***~ a sigh*** (auf)seufzen; ***~ tears*** (ein paar) Tränen hervorlocken; **4.** ***~ up*** *et.* erbrechen; **5.** apportieren (*Hund*); **6.** *Preis etc.* (ein)bringen, erzielen; **7.** *fig.* fesseln, anziehen, für sich einnehmen; **8.** *j-m e-n Schlag* versetzen: ***~ s.o. one*** j-m ‚eine langen' *od.* ‚runterhauen'; **9.** ⚓ erreichen; **II** *v/i.* **10.** ***~ and carry for s.o.*** j-s Handlanger sein, j-n bedienen; **11.** ***~ up*** F ‚landen' (***at***, ***in*** in *dat.*); '**fetch·ing** [-tʃɪŋ] *adj.* F reizend, bezaubernd.
fête [feɪt] **I** *s.* Fest(lichkeit *f*) *n*; **II** *v/t. j-n od. et.* feiern.
fet·id ['fetɪd] *adj.* □ stinkend.
fe·tish ['fi:tɪʃ] *s.* Fetisch *m*; '**fe·tish·ism** [-ʃɪzəm] *s.* Fetischkult *m*, *a. psych.* Feti'schismus *m*; '**fet·ish·ist** [-ʃɪst] *s.* Feti'schist *m.*
fet·lock ['fetlɒk] *s. zo.* **1.** Behang *m*; **2.** *a.* ***~ joint*** Fesselgelenk *n* (*des Pferdes*).
fet·ter ['fetə] **I** *s.* **1.** (Fuß)Fessel *f*; **2.** *pl. fig.* Fesseln *pl.*; **II** *v/t.* **3.** fesseln, *fig. a.* hemmen, behindern.
fet·tle ['fetl] *s.* Verfassung *f*, Zustand *m*: ***in good*** (*od.* ***fine***) ***~*** (gut) in Form.
fe·tus ['fi:təs] → ***foetus***.
feu [fju:] *s.* ⚖ *Scot.* Lehen *n.*
feud[1] [fju:d] **I** *s.* Fehde *f*: ***be at ~ with*** mit *j-m* in Fehde liegen; **II** *v/i.* sich befehden.
feud[2] [fju:d] *s.* ⚖ Lehen *n*, Lehn(s)gut *n*; '**feu·dal** [-dl] *adj.* ⚖ Feudal..., Lehns..., feu'dal; '**feu·dal·ism** [-dəlɪzəm] *s.* Feuda'lismus *m*; **feu·dal·i·ty** [fju:'dælətɪ] *s.* **1.** Lehenswesen *n*; **2.** Lehnbarkeit *f*; '**feu·da·to·ry** [-dətərɪ] **I** *s.* Lehnsmann *m*, Va'sall *m*; **II** *adj.* Lehns...
feuil·le·ton ['fɜ:ɪtɔ̃:ŋ] (*Fr.*) *s.* Feuille'ton *n*, kultu'reller Teil (*e-r Zeitung*).
fe·ver ['fi:və] **I** *s.* **1.** ⚕ Fieber *n*: ***~ heat*** a) Fieberhitze *f*, b) *fig.* → 2; **2.** *fig.* Fieber *n*, fieberhafte Aufregung, *a.* Sucht *f*, Rausch *m*: ***gold ~***; ***in a ~ of excitement*** in fieberhafter Aufregung; ***reach ~ pitch*** den Höhe- *od.* Siedepunkt erreichen; ***work at ~ pitch*** fieberhaft arbeiten; **II** *v/i.* **3.** fiebern (*a. fig.* ***for*** nach); '**fe·vered** [-əd] *adj.* **1.** fiebernd, fiebrig; **2.** *fig.* fieberhaft, aufgeregt; '**fe·ver·ish** [-vərɪʃ] *adj.* □ **1.** fieberkrank, fiebrig, Fieber...; **2.** *fig.* fieberhaft; '**fe·ver·ish·ness** [-vərɪʃnɪs] *s.* Fieberhaftigkeit *f* (*a. fig.*).
few [fju:] *adj. u. s.* (*pl.*) **1.** (*Ggs.* ***many***) wenige: ***~ persons***; ***some ~*** einige wenige; ***his friends are ~*** er hat (nur) wenige Freunde; ***no ~er than*** nicht weniger als; ***~ and far between*** (sehr) dünn gesät; ***the lucky ~*** die wenigen Glücklichen; **2.** ***a ~*** (*Ggs.* ***none***) einige, ein paar: ***a ~ days*** einige Tage; ***not a ~*** nicht wenige, viele; ***a good ~*** e-e ganze Menge; ***only a ~*** nur wenige; ***every ~ days*** alle paar Tage; ***have a ~*** F ein paar ‚kippen'; '**few·ness** [-nɪs] *s.* geringe Anzahl.
fey [feɪ] *adj. Scot.* **1.** todgeweiht; **2.** 'übermütig; **3.** 'übersinnlich.
fez [fez] *s.* Fes *m.*
fi·an·cé [fɪ'ɑ̃:ŋseɪ] (*Fr.*) *s.* Verlobte(r) *m*; **fi'an·cée** [-seɪ] (*Fr.*) *s.* Verlobte *f.*
fi·as·co [fɪ'æskəʊ] *pl.* **-cos** *s.* Fi'asko *n.*
fi·at ['faɪæt] *s.* **1.** ⚖ *Brit.* Gerichtsbeschluß *m*; **2.** Befehl *m*, Erlaß *m*; **3.** Ermächtigung *f*; ***~ mon·ey*** *s. Am.* Pa'piergeld *n* ohne Deckung.
fib [fɪb] **I** *s.* kleine Lüge, Schwinde'lei *f*, Flunke'rei *f*: ***tell a ~*** → **II** *v/i.* schwindeln, flunkern; '**fib·ber** [-bə] *s.* F Flunkerer *m*, Schwindler *m.*
fi·ber *Am.*, **fi·bre** ['faɪbə] *Brit. s.* **1.** ⚙,

biol. Faser *f*, Fiber *f*; **2.** Faserstoff *m*, -gefüge *n*, Tex'tur *f*; **3.** *fig.* a) Struk'tur *f*, b) Schlag *m*, Cha'rakter *m*: ***moral ~*** ‚Rückgrat *n*'; ***of coarse ~*** grobschlächtig; '**~board** *s.* ⚙ Holzfaserplatte *f*; '**~glass** *s.* ⚙ Fiberglas *n*.

fi·bril ['faɪbrɪl] *s.* **1.** Fäserchen *n*; **2.** ⚘ Wurzelfaser *f*; '**fi·brin** [-brɪn] *s.* **1.** Fi'brin *n*, Blutfaserstoff *m*; **2.** *a.* ***plant ~*** Pflanzenfaserstoff *m*; '**fi·broid** [-brɔɪd] **I** *adj.* faserartig, Faser...; **II** *s.* → **fi·bro·ma** [faɪ'brəʊmə] *pl.* **-ma·ta** [-mətə] *s.* ⚕ Fib'rom *n*; Fasergeschwulst *f*; **fi·bro·si·tis** [ˌfaɪbrəʊ'saɪtɪs] *s.* ⚕ Bindegewebsentzündung *f*; '**fi·brous** [-brəs] *adj.* □ **1.** faserig, Faser...; **2.** ⚙ sehnig (*Metall*).

fib·u·la ['fɪbjʊlə] *pl.* **-lae** [-liː] *s.* **1.** *anat.* Wadenbein *n*; **2.** *antiq.* Fibel *f*, Spange *f*.

fiche [fiːʃ] *s.* Fiche *n*, *m* (*Mikrodatenkarte*).

fick·le ['fɪkl] *adj.* unbeständig, launisch, *Person a.* wankelmütig; '**fick·le·ness** [-nɪs] *s.* Unbeständigkeit *f*, Wankelmut *m*.

fic·tile ['fɪktaɪl] *adj.* **1.** formbar; **2.** tönern, irden: ***~ art*** Töpferkunst *f*; ***~ ware*** Steingut *n*.

fic·tion ['fɪkʃn] *s.* **1.** (freie) Erfindung, Dichtung *f*; *contp.* ‚Märchen' *n*; **2.** a) Belle'tristik *f*, 'Prosa-, Ro'manliteraˌtur *f*: ***work of ~***, b) *coll.* Ro'mane *pl.*, Prosa *f* (*e-s Autors*); **3.** ⚖ Fikti'on *f*; '**fic·tion·al** [-ʃənl] *adj.* **1.** erdichtet; **2.** Roman...

fic·ti·tious [fɪk'tɪʃəs] *adj.* □ **1.** (frei) erfunden, fik'tiv; **2.** unwirklich, Phantasie..., Roman...; **3.** ⚖ *etc.* fik'tiv: a) angenommen: ***~ name***, b) fingiert, falsch, Schein...: ***~ bill*** ⚚ Kellerwechsel *m*; **fic'ti·tious·ness** [-nɪs] *s.* *das* Fik'tive; Unechtheit *f*.

fid·dle ['fɪdl] **I** *s.* **1.** ♪ Fiedel *f*, Geige *f*: ***play first*** (***second***) ***~*** *fig.* die erste (zweite) Geige spielen; → ***fit***[1] 5; **2.** *Brit.* F a) Schwindel *m*, Betrug *m*, Schiebung *f*, b) Manipulati'on *f*; **II** *v/i.* **3.** F fiedeln, geigen; **4.** *a.* ***~ about*** (*od.* ***around***) her'umtrödeln; **5.** (***with***) spielen (mit), her'umfingern (an *dat.*), *contp.* her'umpfuschen (an *dat.*); **III** *v/t.* **6.** F fiedeln; **7.** ***~ away*** F *Zeit* vertrödeln; **8.** *Brit.* F ‚frisieren', manipulieren; **IV** *int.* **9.** Quatsch!; ˌ**~-de-'dee** [-dɪ'diː] → ***fiddle*** 9; '**~-ˌfad·dle** [-ˌfædl] **I** *s.* **1.** Lap'palie *f*; **2.** Unsinn *m*; **II** *v/i.* **3.** dummes Zeug reden; **4.** die Zeit vertrödeln.

fid·dler ['fɪdlə] *s.* **1.** Geiger(in): ***pay the ~*** *Am.* F ‚blechen'; **2.** *Brit.* F Schwindler *m*.

'**fid·dle·stick I** *s.* Geigenbogen *m*; **II** *int.* ***~s!*** F Quatsch!

fid·dling ['fɪdlɪŋ] *adj.* F läppisch, geringfügig, ‚poplig'.

fi·del·i·ty [fɪ'delətɪ] *s.* **1.** (*a.* eheliche) Treue (***to*** gegenüber, zu); **2.** Genauigkeit *f*, genaue Über'einstimmung *od.* 'Wiedergabe: ***with ~*** wortgetreu; **3.** ϟ 'Wiedergabe(güte) *f*, Klangtreue *f*.

fidg·et ['fɪdʒɪt] **I** *s.* **1.** *oft pl.* ner'vöse Unruhe, Zappe'lei *f*; **2.** ‚Zappelphilipp' *m*, Zapp(e)ler *m*; **II** *v/t.* **3.** ner'vös *od.* zapp(e)lig machen; **III** *v/i.* **4.** (her'um)zappeln, zapp(e)lig sein; **5.** ***~ with*** (herum)spielen *od.* (-)fuchteln mit; '**fidg·et·i·ness** [-tɪnɪs] *s.* Zapp(e)ligkeit *f*, Nervosi'tät *f*; '**fidg·et·y** [-tɪ] *adj.* ner'vös, zappelig: ***~ Philipp*** → ***fidget*** 2.

fi·du·ci·ar·y [fɪ'djuːʃjərɪ] ⚖ **I** *s.* **1.** Treuhänder(in); **II** *adj.* **2.** treuhänderisch, Treuhand..., Treuhänder...; **3.** ⚚ ungedeckt (*Noten*).

fie [faɪ] *int. oft* ***~ upon you!*** pfui(, schäm dich)!

fief [fiːf] *s.* Lehen *n*, Lehn(s)gut *n*.

field [fiːld] **I** *s.* **1.** ✓ Feld *n*; **2.** ⚔ a) (*Gold-*, *Öl-* *etc.*)Feld *n*, b) (Gruben-) Feld *n*, (Kohlen)Flöz *n*: ***coal ~***; **3.** *fig.* Bereich *m*, (Sach-, Fach)Gebiet *n*: ***in the ~ of art*** auf dem Gebiet der Kunst; ***in his ~*** auf s-m Gebiet, in s-m Fach; ***~ of activity*** Tätigkeitsbereich; ***~ of application*** Anwendungsbereich; **4.** a) (weite) Fläche, b) ✈, ϟ, *phys.*, *a. her.* Feld *n*: ***~ of force*** Kraftfeld; ***~ of vision*** Blick-, Gesichtsfeld, *fig.* Gesichtskreis *m*, Horizont *m*; **5.** *sport* a) Spielfeld *n*, (Sport)Platz *m*: ***take the ~*** einlaufen, auf den Platz kommen (→ 6), b) Feld *n* (*geschlossene Gruppe*), c) Teilnehmer(feld *n*) *pl.*, Besetzung *f*, *fig.* Wettbewerbsteilnehmer *pl.*: ***fair ~ and no favo(u)r*** gleiche Bedingungen für alle; ***play the ~*** F sich keine Chance entgehen lassen (*in der Liebe*), d) *Baseball*, *Kricket*: 'Fängerparˌtei *f*; **6.** ⚔ a) *poet.* (Schlacht)Feld *n*, (Feld)Schlacht *f*, b) Feld *n*, Front *f*: ***in the ~*** an der Front, im Felde; ***hold*** (*od.* ***keep***) ***the ~*** sich behaupten; ***take the ~*** ins Feld rücken, den Kampf eröffnen; ***win the ~*** den Sieg davontragen; **7.** ⚔ Feld *n* (*im Geschützrohr*); **8.** ⚕ (Operati'ons)Feld *n*; **9.** *TV* Feld *n*, Rasterbild *n*; **10.** a) *bsd. psych.*, *sociol.* Praxis *f*, Wirklichkeit *f*, b) ⚚ Außendienst *m*, (praktischer) Einsatz; → ***field service***, ***field study***, ***fieldwork*** 2–4 *etc.*; **II** *v/t.* **11.** *sport Mannschaft*, *Spieler* aufs Feld schicken; **12.** *Baseball*, *Kricket*: a) *den Ball* auffangen u. zu'rückwerfen, b) *Spieler* im Feld aufstellen; **13.** *fig.* *e-e Frage etc.* kontern; **III** *v/i.* **14.** *Kricket etc.*: bei der 'Fängerparˌtei sein.

field| am·bu·lance *s.* ⚔ Sanka *m*, Sani'tätswagen *m*; **~ coil** *s.* ϟ Feldspule *f*; **~ day** *s.* **1.** ⚔ a) Felddienstübung *f*, b) 'Truppenpaˌrade *f*; **2.** *Am.* a) *ped.* Sportfest *n*, b) Exkursi'onstag *m*; **3.** ***have a ~*** *fig.* a) s-n großen Tag haben, b) e-n Mordsspaß haben (***with*** mit).

field·er ['fiːldə] *s.* *Kricket etc.*: a) Fänger *m*, b) Feldspieler *m*, c) *pl.* 'Fängerparˌtei *f*.

field| e·vent *s.* *sport* technische Diszi'plin, *pl. mst* 'Sprung- u. 'Wurfdisziˌplinen *pl.*; **~ glass**(**·es** *pl.*) *s.* Fernglas *n*, Feldstecher *m*; **~ goal** *s.* *Basketball*: Feldkorb *m*; **~ gun** *s.* ⚔ Feldgeschütz *n*; **~ hos·pi·tal** *s.* ⚔ 'Feldlazaˌrett *n*; **~ kitch·en** *s.* ⚔ Feldküche *f*; ♀ **Mar·shal** *s.* ⚔ Feldmarschall *m*; '**~-mouse** *s.* [*irr.*] Feldmaus *f*; **~ of·fi·cer** *s.* ⚔ 'Stabsoffiˌzier *m*; **~ pack** *s.* ⚔ Marschgepäck *n*, Tor'nister *m*; **~ re·search** *s.* ⚚ *etc.* Feldforschung *f*; **~ ser·vice** *s.* ⚚ Außendienst *m*.

fields·man ['fiːldzmən] *s.* [*irr.*] → ***fielder*** a, b.

field| sports *s. pl.* Sport *m* im Freien (*bsd. Jagen*, *Fischen*); **~ stud·y** *s.* Feldstudie *f*; **~ test** *s.* praktischer Versuch; **~ train·ing** *s.* ⚔ Geländeausbildung *f*; '**~·work** *s.* **1.** ⚔ Feldschanze *f*; **2.** praktische (wissenschaftliche) Arbeit, *a.* Arbeit *f* im Gelände; **3.** ⚚ Außendienst *m*, -einsatz *m*; **4.** *Markt-*, *Meinungsforschung*: Feldarbeit *f*; '**~ˌwork·er** *s.* **1.** ⚚ Außendienstmitarbeiter(in); **2.** Inter'viewer(in), Befrager(in).

fiend [fiːnd] *s.* **1.** a) *a. fig.* Satan *m*, Teufel *m*, b) Dämon *m*, *fig. a.* Unhold *m*; **2.** *bsd. in Zssgn*: a) Süchtige(r *m*) *f*: ***opium ~***, b) Fa'natiker(in), Narr *m*, Fex *m*: → ***fresh-air fiend***, c) *Am. sl.* ‚Ka'none' *f* (***at*** in *dat.*); '**fiend·ish** [-dɪʃ] *adj.* □ teuflisch, unmenschlich; *fig.* F verteufelt, ‚gemein'; '**fiend·ish·ness** [-dɪʃnɪs] *s.* teuflische Bosheit; *fig.* Gemeinheit *f*.

fierce [fɪəs] *adj.* □ **1.** wild, grimmig, wütend (*alle a. fig.*); **2.** heftig, scharf; **3.** grell; '**fierce·ness** [-nɪs] *s.* Wildheit *f*, Grimmigkeit *f*, Schärfe *f*, Heftigkeit *f*.

fi·er·y ['faɪərɪ] *adj.* □ **1.** brennend, glühend (*a. fig.*); **2.** *fig.* feurig, hitzig, heftig; **3.** feuerrot; **4.** feuergefährlich; **5.** Feuer...

fife [faɪf] ♪ **I** *s.* **1.** (Quer)Pfeife *f*; **2.** → ***fifer***; **II** *v/t. u. v/i.* **3.** (*auf der Querpfeife*) pfeifen; '**fif·er** [-fə] *s.* (Quer)Pfeifer *m*.

fif·teen [ˌfɪf'tiːn] **I** *adj.* **1.** fünfzehn; **II** *s.* **2.** Fünfzehn *f*; **3.** *Rugby*: Fünfzehn *f*; ˌ**fif'teenth** [-nθ] **I** *adj.* **1.** fünfzehnt; **II** *s.* **2.** *der* (*die*, *das*) Fünfzehnte; **3.** Fünfzehntel *n*.

fifth [fɪfθ] **I** *adj.* □ **1.** fünft; **II** *s.* **2.** *der* (*die*, *das*) Fünfte; **3.** Fünftel *n*; **4.** ♪ Quinte *f*; **~ col·umn** *s. pol.* Fünfte Ko'lonne.

fifth·ly ['fɪfθlɪ] *adv.* fünftens.

fifth wheel *s.* **1.** *mot.* a) Ersatzrad *n*, b) Drehschemel(ring) *m* (*Sattelschlepper*); **2.** *fig.* fünftes Rad am Wagen.

fif·ti·eth ['fɪftɪɪθ] **I** *adj.* **1.** fünfzigst; **II** *s.* **2.** *der* (*die*, *das*) Fünfzigste; **3.** Fünfzigstel *n*; **fif·ty** ['fɪftɪ] **I** *adj.* fünfzig; **II** *s.* Fünfzig *f*: ***in the fifties*** in den fünfziger Jahren (*e-s Jahrhunderts*); ***he is in his fifties*** er ist in den Fünfzigern; ˌ**fif·ty-'fif·ty** *adj. u. adv.* F fifty-fifty, ‚halbehalbe'.

fig[1] [fɪg] *s.* ⚘ **1.** Feige *f*: ***I don't care a ~*** (***for it***) F das ist mir schnuppe!; **2.** Feigenbaum *m*.

fig[2] [fɪg] **I** *s.* F **1.** Kleidung *f*, Gala *f*: ***in full ~*** in voller Gala; **2.** Zustand *m*: ***in good ~*** gut in Form; **II** *v/t.* **3.** ***~ out*** her'ausputzen.

fight [faɪt] **I** *s.* **1.** Kampf *m* (*a. fig.*), Gefecht *n*: ***make a ~ of it***, ***put up a ~*** kämpfen, sich wehren; ***put up a good ~*** sich tapfer schlagen; **2.** a) Schläge'rei *f*, Raufe'rei *f*, b) *sport* (Box)Kampf *m*: ***have a ~*** → 12; ***make a ~ for*** kämpfen um; **3.** Kampf(es)lust *f*, -fähigkeit *f*: ***show ~*** sich zur Wehr setzen; ***there is no ~ left in him*** er ist kampfmüde *od.* ‚fertig'; **4.** Streit *m*, Kon'flikt *m*; **II** *v/t.* [*irr.*] **5.** *j-n od. et.* bekämpfen, bekriegen, kämpfen mit *od.* gegen, sich schlagen mit, *sport a.* boxen gegen; *fig.* ankämpfen gegen (*e-e schlechte Gewohnheit etc.*): ***~ back*** (*od.* ***down***) *fig. Tränen*, *Enttäuschung* unterdrücken; ***~ off*** *j-n od. et.* abwehren, *a. e-e Erkältung etc.* bekämpfen; **6.** *e-n Krieg*, *e-n Pro-*

zeß führen, *e-e Schlacht* schlagen *od.* austragen, *e-e Sache* ausfechten: ~ ***a duel*** sich duellieren; ~ ***an election*** kandidieren; ~ ***it out*** es (untereinander) ausfechten; **7.** *et.* verfechten, sich einsetzen für; **8.** *et.* erkämpfen: ~ ***one's way*** sich durchschlagen; **9.** ⚔ *Truppen etc.* kommandieren, (im Kampf) führen; **II** *v/i.* [*irr.*] **10.** kämpfen (***with*** *od.* ***against*** mit *od.* gegen, ***for*** um): ~ ***against s.th.*** gegen et. ankämpfen; ~ ***back*** sich zur Wehr setzen; **11.** boxen; **12.** sich raufen *od.* prügeln *od.* schlagen.

fight·er ['faɪtə] *s.* **1.** Kämpfer *m*, Streiter *m*; **2.** Schläger *m*, Raufbold *m*; **3.** *sport* (*bsd.* Offen'siv)Boxer *m*; **4.** *a.* ~ ***plane*** ⚔, ✈ Jagdflugzeug *n*, Jäger *m*: ~-***bomber*** Jagdbomber *m*; ~ ***group*** *Brit.* Jagdgruppe *f*, *Am.* Jagdgeschwader *n*; ~-***interceptor*** Abfangjäger *m*; ~ ***pilot*** Jagdflieger *m*.

fight·ing ['faɪtɪŋ] **I** *s.* Kampf *m*, Kämpfe *pl*; **II** *adj.* Kampf…; streitlustig; ~ **chance** *s.* *e-e* re'elle Chance (*wenn man sich anstrengt*); ~ **cock** *s.* Kampfhahn *m* (*a. fig.*): ***live like a*** ~ in Saus u. Braus leben.

fig leaf *s.* Feigenblatt *n* (*a. fig.*).

fig·ment ['fɪgmənt] *s.* **1.** *oft* ~ ***of the imagination*** Phanta'siepro͵dukt *n*, reine Einbildung; **2.** ‚Märchen' *n*, (pure) Erfindung.

fig tree *s.* Feigenbaum *m*.

fig·ur·a·tive ['fɪgjʊrətɪv] *adj.* □ **1.** *ling.* bildlich, über'tragen, fi'gürlich, meta'phorisch; **2.** bilderreich (*Stil*); **3.** sym'bolisch.

fig·ure ['fɪgə] **I** *s.* **1.** Fi'gur *f*, Form *f*, Gestalt *f*, Aussehen *n*: ***keep one's*** ~ schlank bleiben; **2.** *fig.* Fi'gur *f*, Per'son *f*, Per'sönlichkeit *f*, (bemerkenswerte) Erscheinung: ***a public*** ~ e-e Persönlichkeit des öffentlichen Lebens; ~ ***of fun*** komische Figur; ***cut*** (*od.* ***make***) ***a poor*** ~ e-e traurige Figur abgeben; **3.** Darstellung *f* (*bsd. des menschlichen Körpers*), Bild *n*, Statue *f*; **4.** *a.* ⚙, ✎ Fi'gur *f*, *weitS. a.* Zeichnung *f*, Dia'gramm *n*; *a.* Abbildung *f*, Illustrati'on *f* (*in e-m Buch etc.*); **5.** *Tanz*, *Eiskunstlauf etc.*: Fi'gur *f*; **6.** (Stoff)Muster *n*; **7.** *a.* ~ ***of speech*** a) ('Rede-, 'Sprach)Fi͵gur *f*, b) Me'tapher *f*, Bild *n*; **8.** ♪ a) Fi'gur *f*, b) (Baß)Bezifferung *f*; **9.** Zahl(zeichen *n*) *f*, Ziffer *f*: ***run into three*** ~***s*** in die Hunderte gehen; ***be good at*** ~***s*** ein guter Rechner sein; **10.** Preis *m*, Summe *f*: ***at a low*** ~ billig; **II** *v/t.* **11.** gestalten, formen; **12.** bildlich darstellen, abbilden; **13.** *a.* ~ ***to o.s.*** sich *et.* vorstellen; **14.** verzieren (*a.* ♪); ⚙ mustern; **15.** ~ ***out*** F a) ausrechnen, b) ausknobeln, ‚rauskriegen', c) ‚kapieren': ***I can't*** ~ ***him out*** ich werde aus ihm nicht schlau; **III** *v/i.* **16.** ~ ***out at*** sich belaufen auf (*acc.*); **17.** ~ ***on*** *Am.* F a) rechnen mit, b) sich verlassen auf (*acc.*); **18.** erscheinen, vorkommen, e-e Rolle spielen: ~ ***large*** e-e große Rolle spielen; ~ ***on a list*** auf e-r Liste stehen; **19.** F (genau) passen: ***that*** ~***s!*** das ist klar!; ~ **dance** *s.* Fi'gurentanz *m*; '~-**head** *s.* ⚓ Gali'onsfi͵gur *f*, *fig. a.* ‚Aushängeschild' *n*; ~ **skat·er** *s.* *sport* (Eis)Kunstläufer(in); ~ **skat·ing** *s.* *sport* Eiskunstlauf *m*.

fig·u·rine ['fɪgjʊri:n] *s.* Statu'ette *f*, Figu'rine *f*.

fil·a·ment ['fɪləmənt] *s.* **1.** Faden *m* (*a. anat.*); Faser *f*; **2.** ♆ Staubfaden *m*; **3.** ⚡ (Glüh-, Heiz)Faden *m*: ~ ***battery*** Heizbatterie *f*.

fil·bert ['fɪlbət] *s.* ♆ **1.** Haselnußstrauch *m*; **2.** Haselnuß *f*.

filch [fɪltʃ] *v/t.* F ‚klauen' (*stehlen*).

file[1] [faɪl] **I** *s.* **1.** Aufreihdraht *m*, -faden *m*; **2.** (Akten-, Brief-, Doku'menten- *etc.*)Ordner *m*, Sammelmappe *f*, *a.* Kar'tei(kasten *m*) *f*; **3.** a) Akte(nstück *n*) *f*, *a.* Dossi'er *n* (*der Polizei etc.*): ~ ***number*** Aktenzeichen *n*, b) Akten (-bündel *n*, -stoß *m*) *pl.*, c) Ablage *f*, abgelegte Briefe *pl. od.* Pa'piere *pl.*: ***on*** ~ bei den Akten, d) *Computer*: Da'tei *f*, e) Liste *f*, Verzeichnis *n*; **4.** ⚔ Reihe *f*; **5.** Reihe *f* (*Personen od. Sachen hintereinander*); **II** *v/t.* **6.** *Briefe etc.* ablegen, einordnen, ab-, einheften, zu den Akten nehmen; **7.** *Antrag*, ⚖ *Klage* einreichen; **III** *v/i.* **8.** hinterein'ander *od.* ⚔ in Reihe (hi'nein-, hin'aus- *etc.*)marschieren.

file[2] [faɪl] **I** *s.* **1.** ⚙ Feile *f*; **II** *v/t.* **2.** ⚙ feilen; **3.** *Stil* feilen, glätten.

fi·let ['fɪlɪt] (*Fr.*) *s.* **1.** *Küche*: Fi'let *n*; **2.** *a.* ~ ***lace*** Fi'let *n*, Netz(sticke'rei *f*) *n*.

fil·i·al ['fɪljəl] *adj.* □ kindlich, Kindes…, Sohnes…, Tochter…; **fil·i·a·tion** [͵fɪlɪ'eɪʃn] *s.* **1.** Kindschaft(sverhältnis *n*) *f*: ~ ***proceeding*** ⚖ *Am.* Vaterschaftsprozeß *m*; **2.** Abstammung *f*; **3.** Herkunftsfeststellung *f*; **4.** Verzweigung *f*.

fil·i·bus·ter ['fɪlɪbʌstə] **I** *s.* **1.** *hist.* Freibeuter *m*; **2.** *parl. Am.* a) Obstrukti'on *f*, Verschleppungstaktik *f*, b) Obstrukti'onspo͵litiker *m*; **II** *v/i.* **3.** *parl. Am.* Obstrukti'on treiben; **III** *v/t.* **4.** *Antrag etc.* durch Obstrukti'on zu Fall bringen.

fil·i·gree ['fɪlɪgri:] *s.* Fili'gran(arbeit *f*) *n*.

fil·ing| **cab·i·net** ['faɪlɪŋ] *s.* Aktenschrank *m*; ~ **card** *s.* Kar'teikarte *f*.

fil·ings ['faɪlɪŋz] *s. pl.* Feilspäne *pl.*

Fil·i·pi·no [͵fɪlɪ'pi:nəʊ] **I** *pl.* **-nos** *s.* Fili'pino *m*; **II** *adj.* philip'pinisch.

fill [fɪl] **I** *s.* **1.** ***eat one's*** ~ sich satt essen; ***have one's*** ~ ***of s.th.*** genug von et. haben; ***weep one's*** ~ sich ausweinen; **2.** Füllung *f* (*Material od. Menge*): ***a*** ~ ***of petrol*** *mot.* e-e Tankfüllung; **II** *v/t.* **3.** (an-, aus-, 'voll)füllen: ~ ***s.o.'s glass*** j-m einschenken; ~ ***the sails*** die Segel (auf)blähen; **4.** ab-, einfüllen: ~ ***wine into bottles***; **5.** (*mit Nahrung*) sättigen; **6.** *Pfeife* stopfen; **7.** *Zahn* füllen, plombieren; **8.** *die Straßen, ein Stadion etc.* füllen; **9.** *a. fig.* erfüllen: ***smoke*** ~***ed the room***; ***grief*** ~***ed his heart***; ~***ed with fear*** angsterfüllt; **10.** *Amt*, *Posten* a) besetzen, b) ausfüllen, bekleiden: ~ ***s.o.'s place*** j-s Stelle einnehmen, j-n ersetzen; **11.** *Auftrag* ausführen: ~ ***an order***; → ***bill***[2] 4; **III** *v/i.* **12.** sich füllen, (*Segel*) sich (auf)blähen; ~ **in I** *v/t.* **1.** Loch *etc.* auf-, ausfüllen; **2.** *Brit. Formular* ausfüllen; **3.** a) *Namen etc.* einsetzen, b) *Fehlendes* ergänzen; **4.** ***fill s.o. in*** F (***on*** über *acc.*) j-n ins Bild setzen, j-n informieren; **II** *v/i.* **5.** einspringen (***for s.o.*** für j-n); ~ **out I** *v/t.* **1.** *bsd. Am. Formular* ausfüllen; **2.** *Bericht etc.* abrunden; **II** *v/i.* **3.** fülliger werden (*Figur*), (*Person a.*) zunehmen, (*Gesicht*) voller werden; ~ **up I** *v/t.* **1.** auf-, 'vollfüllen: ~ ***her up!*** F volltanken, bitte; **2.** → ***fill in*** 2; **II** *v/i.* **3.** sich füllen.

fill·er ['fɪlə] *s.* **1.** Füllvorrichtung *f*, *a.* 'Abfüllma͵schine *f*, Trichter *m*: ~ ***cap*** *mot.* Tankverschluß *m*; **2.** Füllstoff *m*, Zusatzmittel *n*; **3.** *paint.* Spachtel(masse *f*) *m*, Füller *m*; **4.** *fig.* Füllsel *n*, Füller *m*; **5.** *ling.* Füllwort *n*; **6.** Sprengladung *f*.

fil·let ['fɪlɪt] **I** *s.* **1.** Stirn-, Haarband *n*; **2.** Leiste *f*, Band *n*; **3.** Zierstreifen *m*, Fi'let *n* (*am Buch*); **4.** △ Leiste *f*, Rippe *f*; **5.** *Küche*: Fi'let *n*; **6.** ⚙ a) Hohlkehle *f*, b) Schweißnaht *f*; **II** *v/t.* **7.** mit e-m Haarband *od.* e-r Leiste *etc.* schmükken; **8.** *Küche*: a) filetieren, b) als Fi'let zubereiten.

fill·ing ['fɪlɪŋ] **I** *s.* **1.** Füllung *f*, Füllmasse *f*, Einlage *f*, Füllsel *n*; **2.** (Zahn)Plombe *f*, (-)Füllung *f*; **3.** *das* 'Voll-, Aus-, Auffüllen, Füllung *f*: ~ ***machine*** Abfüllmaschine *f*; ~ ***station*** *Am.* Tankstelle *f*; **II** *adj.* **4.** sättigend.

fil·lip ['fɪlɪp] **I** *s.* **1.** Schnalzer *m* (*mit Finger u. Daumen*); **2.** Klaps *m*; **3.** *fig.* Ansporn *m*, Auftrieb *m*: ***give a*** ~ ***to*** → 6; **II** *v/t.* **4.** schnippen, schnipsen; **5.** *j-m* e-n Klaps geben; **6.** *fig.* anspornen, in Schwung bringen.

fil·ly ['fɪlɪ] *s.* **1.** *zo.* Stutenfohlen *n*; **2.** *fig.* ‚wilde Hummel' (*Mädchen*).

film [fɪlm] **I** *s.* **1.** Mem'bran(e) *f*, Häutchen *n*, Film *m*; **2.** *phot.* Film *m*; **3.** Film *m*: ***the*** ~***s*** die Filmindustrie, der Film, das Kino; ***be in*** ~***s*** beim Film sein; ***shoot a*** ~ e-n Film drehen; **4.** (hauch)dünne Schicht, 'Überzug *m* (*Zellophan- etc.*)Haut *f*; **5.** (hauch)dünnes Gewebe, *a.* Faser *f*; **6.** Trübung *f* (*des Auges*), Schleier *f*; **II** *v/t.* **7.** (mit e-m Häutchen *etc.*) über'ziehen; **8.** a) *Szene etc.* filmen: ~***ed report*** Filmbericht *m*, b) *Roman etc.* verfilmen; **III** *v/i.* **9.** *a.* ~ ***over*** sich mit e-m Häutchen über'ziehen; **10.** a) sich (gut) verfilmen lassen, b) e-n Film drehen, filmen; ~ **li·brar·y** *s.* 'Filmar͵chiv *n*; ~ **mak·er** *s.* Filmemacher *m*; ~ **pack** *s.* *phot.* Filmpack *m*; ~ **reel** *s.* Filmspule *f*; '~-**set** *v/t.* [*irr.*] *typ.* im Foto- *od.* Filmsatz herstellen; ~ **star** *s.* Filmstar *m*; ~ **strip** *s.* **1.** Bildstreifen *m*; **2.** Bildband *n*; ~ **ver·sion** *s.* Verfilmung *f*.

film·y ['fɪlmɪ] *adj.* □ **1.** mit e-m Häutchen bedeckt; **2.** duftig, zart, hauchdünn; **3.** trübe, verschleiert (*Auge*).

fil·ter ['fɪltə] **I** *s.* **1.** Filter *m*, Seihtuch *n*, Seiher *m*; **2.** ⚗, ⚙, ⚡, *phot.*, *phys.*, *tel.* Filter *n*, *m*; **3.** *mot. Brit.* grüner Pfeil (*für Abbieger*); **II** *v/t.* **4.** filtern: a) ('durch)seihen, b) filtrieren: ~ ***off*** (***out***) ab- (heraus)filtern; **III** *v/i.* **5.** 'durchsikkern, (*Licht a.*) 'durchscheinen, -dringen; **6.** *fig.* ~ **out** *od.* **through** 'durchsickern (*Nachrichten etc.*); ~ ***into*** einsickern *od.* -dringen in (*acc.*); **7.** ~ ***out*** langsam *od.* grüppchenweise herauskommen (***of*** aus); **8.** *mot. Brit.* a) die Spur wechseln, b) sich einordnen (***to the left*** links), c) abbiegen (*bei grünem Pfeil*); ~ **bag** *s.* Filtertüte *f*; ~ **bed** *s.* **1.** Kläranlage *f*, -becken *n*; **2.** Filterschicht *f*; ~ **char·coal** *s.* ⚙ Filterkohle *f*; ~ **cir·cuit** *s.* ⚡ Siebkreis *m*; ~ **pa·per** *s.* 'Filterpa͵pier *n*; ~ **tip** *s.* **1.** Filter(mundstück *n*) *m*; **2.** 'Filterziga͵rette *f*; '~-**tipped** mit Filter, Filter…: ~ ***cigarette***.

filth [fɪlθ] *s.* **1.** Schmutz *m*, Dreck *m*; **2.** *fig.* Schmutz *m*, Schweine'rei(en *pl.*) *f*; **3.** a) unflätige Sprache, b) unflätige Ausdrücke *pl.*, Unflat *m*; **'filth·i·ness** [-θɪnɪs] *s.* Schmutzigkeit *f* (*a. fig.*); **'filth·y** [-θɪ] **I** *adj.* ☐ **1.** schmutzig, dreckig, *fig. a.* schweinisch; **2.** *fig.* unflätig; **3.** F ekelhaft, scheußlich: ~ ***mood***; ~ ***weather*** *a.* ‚Sauwetter' *n*; **II** *adv.* **4.** F ‚unheimlich', ‚furchtbar': ~ ***rich*** stinkreich.

fil·trate ['fɪltreɪt] **I** *v/t.* filtrieren; **II** *s.* Fil'trat *n*; **fil'tra·tion** [fɪl'treɪʃn] *s.* Filtrati'on *f*.

fin¹ [fɪn] *s.* **1.** *zo.* Flosse *f*, Finne *f*; **2.** ⚓ Kielflosse *f*; **3.** ✈ a) (Seiten)Flosse *f*, b) ⚔ Steuerschwanz *m* (*e-r Bombe*); **4.** ⚙ a) Grat *m*, (Guß)Naht *f*, b) (Kühl)Rippe *f*; **5.** Schwimmflosse *f*; **6.** *sl.* ‚Flosse' *f* (*Hand*).

fin² [fɪn] *s. Am. sl.* Fünf'dollarschein *m*.

fi·na·gle [fɪ'neɪgl] F **I** *v/t.* **1.** *et.* her'ausschinden; **2.** (sich) *et.* ergaunern; **3.** *j-n* betrügen, begaunern; **II** *v/i.* **4.** gaunern, mogeln.

fi·nal ['faɪnl] **I** *adj.* ☐ → ***finally*** **1.** letzt, schließlich; **2.** endgültig, End…, Schluß…: ~ ***assembly*** ⚙ Endmontage *f*; ~ ***date*** Schlußtermin *m*; ~ ***examination*** Abschlußprüfung *f*; ~ ***score*** *sport* Schlußstand *m*; ~ ***speech*** ⚖ Schlußplädoyer *n*; ~ ***storage*** Endlagerung *f* (*von Atommüll etc.*); ~ ***whistle*** *sport* Schlußpfiff *m*; **3.** endgültig: a) 'unwider͵ruflich, b) entscheidend, c) ⚖ rechtskräftig: ***after*** ~ ***judg(e)ment*** nach Rechtskraft des Urteils; **4.** per'fekt; **5.** *ling.* a) auslautend, End…; Schluß…, b) Absichts…, Final…: ~ ***clause***; **II** *s.* **6.** *a. pl.* Fi'nale *n*, Endkampf *m od.* -runde *f od.* -spiel *n od.* -lauf *m*; **7.** *mst pl. univ.* 'Schlußex͵amen *n*, -prüfung *f*; **8.** F Spätausgabe *f* (*e-r Zeitung*); **fi·na·le** [fɪ'nɑːlɪ] *s.* Fi'nale *n*: a) ♪ (*mst schneller*) Schlußsatz, b) *thea.* Schluß(szene *f*) *m* (*bsd. Oper*), c) *fig.* (dra'matisches) Ende; **'fi·nal·ist** [-nəlɪst] *s.* **1.** *sport* Fina'list(in), Endspiel-, Endkampf-, Endrundenteilnehmer(in); **2.** *univ.* Ex'amenskandi͵dat(in); **fi·nal·i·ty** [faɪ'nælətɪ] *s.* **1.** Endgültigkeit *f*; **2.** Entschiedenheit *f*; **'fi·nal·ize** [-nəlaɪz] *v/t.* **1.** be-, voll'enden, (endgültig) erledigen, abschließen; **2.** endgültige Form geben (*dat.*); **'fi·nal·ly** [-nəlɪ] *adv.* **1.** endlich, schließlich, zu'letzt; **2.** zum (Ab)Schluß; **3.** endgültig, defini'tiv.

fi·nance [faɪ'næns] **I** *s.* **1.** Fi'nanz *f*, Fi'nanzwesen *n*, -wirtschaft *f*, -wissenschaft *f*; **2.** *pl.* Fi'nanzen *pl.*, Einkünfte *pl.*, Vermögenslage *f*; **II** *v/t.* **3.** finanzieren; ~ ***act*** *s. pol.* Steuergesetz *n*; ~ ***bill*** *s.* **1.** *pol.* Fi'nanzvorlage *f*; **2.** ☤ Fi'nanzwechsel *m*; ~ ***com·pa·ny*** *s.* ☤ Finanzierungsgesellschaft *f*; ~ ***house*** *s.* ☤ *Brit.* 'Kundenkre͵ditbank *f*.

fi·nan·cial [faɪ'nænʃl] *adj.* ☐ finanzi'ell, Finanz…, Geld…, Fiskal…: ~ ***aid*** Finanzhilfe *f*; ~ ***backer*** Geldgeber *m*; ~ ***columns*** Handels-, Wirtschaftsteil *m*; ~ ***paper*** Börsen-, Handelsblatt *n*; ~ ***plan*** Finanzierungsplan *m*; ~ ***policy*** Finanzpolitik *f*; ~ ***situation*** (*od.* ***condition***) Vermögenslage *f*; ~ ***standing*** Kreditwürdigkeit *f*; ~ ***statement*** ☤ Bilanz *f*; ~ ***year*** a) ☤ Geschäftsjahr *n*, b) *parl.* Haushalts-, Rechnungsjahr *n*; **fi'nan·cier** [-nsɪə] **I** *s.* **1.** Finanzi'er *m*; **2.** Fi'nanz(fach)mann *m*; **II** *v/t.* **3.** finanzieren; **III** *v/i.* **4.** (*bsd.* skrupellose) Geldgeschäfte machen.

finch [fɪntʃ] *s. orn.* Fink *m*.

find [faɪnd] **I** *v/t.* [*irr.*] **1.** finden; **2.** finden, (an)treffen, stoßen auf (*acc.*): ***I found him in*** ich traf ihn zu Hause an; ~ ***a good reception*** e-e gute Aufnahme finden; **3.** entdecken, bemerken, sehen, feststellen, (her'aus)finden: ***he found that …*** er stellte fest *od.* fand, daß; ***I ~ it easy*** ich finde es leicht; ~ ***one's way*** den Weg finden (***to*** nach, zu), sich zurechtfinden (***in*** in *dat.*); ~ ***its way into*** *fig.* hineingeraten in (*acc.*) (*Sache*); ~ ***o.s.*** a) sich *wo od. wie* befinden, b) sich sehen: ~ ***o.s. surrounded***, c) sich finden, sich voll entfalten, s-e Fähigkeiten erkennen, d) zu sich selbst finden (→ 5); ***I found myself telling a lie*** ich ertappte mich bei e-r Lüge; **4.** finden: a) beschaffen, auftreiben, b) erlangen, sich verschaffen, c) *Zeit etc.* aufbringen; **5.** *j-n* versorgen, ausstatten (***in*** mit): ***be well found in clothes***; ***all found*** freie Station, freie Unterkunft u. Verpflegung; ~ ***o.s.*** sich selbst versorgen; **6.** ⚖ (be)finden für, erklären (für): ***he was found guilty***; **7.** ~ ***out*** a) *et.* herausfinden, -bekommen, b) *j-n* ertappen, entlarven, durch'schauen; **II** *v/i.* [*irr.*] **8.** ⚖ (be)finden, (für Recht) erkennen (***that*** daß): ~ ***for the defendant*** a) die Klage abweisen, b) *Strafprozeß*: den Angeklagten freisprechen; ~ ***against the defendant*** a) der Klage stattgeben, b) *Strafprozeß*: den Angeklagten verurteilen; **III** *s.* **9.** Fund *m*, Entdeckung *f*; **'find·er** [-də] *s.* **1.** Finder *m*, Entdecker *m*: ~***s keepers*** F wer etwas findet, darf es (auch) behalten; ~***'s reward*** Finderlohn *m*; **2.** *phot.* Sucher *m*; **'find·ing** [-dɪŋ] *s.* **1.** Fund *m*, Entdeckung *f*; **2.** *mst pl. phys. etc.* Befund *m* (*a.* ⚕), Feststellung(en *pl.*) *f*, Erkenntnis(se *pl.*) *f*; **3.** ⚖ Feststellung *f*, *der Geschworenen*: *a.* Spruch *m*: ~***s of fact*** Tatsachenfeststellungen; **4.** *pl.* Werkzeuge *pl. od.* Materi'al *n* (*von Handwerkern*).

fine¹ [faɪn] **I** *adj.* ☐ **1.** *allg.* fein: a) dünn, zart, zierlich: ~ ***china***, b) scharf: ***a ~ edge***, c) rein: ~ ***silver*** Feinsilber *n*; ***gold 24 carats*** ~ 24karätiges Gold, d) *aus kleinsten Teilchen bestehend*: ~ ***sand***, e) schön: ***a ~ ship***; ~ ***weather***, f) vornehm, edel: ***a ~ man***, g) geschmackvoll, gepflegt, ele'gant, h) angenehm, lieblich: ***a ~ scent***, i) feinsinnig: ***a ~ distinction*** ein feiner Unterschied; **2.** prächtig, großartig: ***a ~ view***; ***a ~ musician***; ***a ~ fellow*** ein feiner *od.* prächtiger Kerl (→ 3); **3.** F, *a. iro.* fein, schön: ***that's all very ~ but …*** das ist ja alles gut u. schön, aber …; ***a ~ fellow you are!*** *contp.* du bist mir ein schöner Genosse!; ***that's ~ with me!*** in Ordnung!; **4.** ⚙ fein, genau, Fein…; **II** *adv.* **5.** F fein: a) vornehm (*a. contp.*): ***talk ~***, b) sehr gut, ‚bestens': ***that will suit me ~*** das paßt mir ausgezeichnet; **6.** knapp: ***cut*** (*od.* ***run***) ***it ~*** ins Gedränge (*bsd.* in Zeitnot) kommen; **III** *v/t.* **7.** ~ ***away***, ~ ***down*** fein(er) machen, abschleifen, zuspitzen; **8.** *oft* ~ ***down*** *Wein etc.* läutern, klären; **9.** *metall.* frischen; **IV** *v/i.* **10.** ~ ***away***, ~ ***down***, ~ ***off*** fein(er) werden, abnehmen, sich abschleifen; **11.** sich klären.

fine² [faɪn] **I** *s.* **1.** ⚖ Geldstrafe *f*, Bußgeld *n*; **2.** ***in*** ~ a) schließlich, b) kurzum; **II** *v/t.* **3.** mit e-r Geldstrafe *od.* e-m Bußgeld belegen: ***he was ~d £2*** er mußte 2 Pfund (Strafe) bezahlen.

fine| ad·just·ment *s.* ⚙ Feineinstellung *f*; ~ ***arts*** *s. pl.* (*die*) schönen Künste *pl.*; **'~-bore** *v/t.* ⚙ präzisi'onsbohren; ~ ***cut*** *s.* Feinschnitt *m* (*Tabak*); **͵~-'draw** *v/t.* [*irr.* → ***draw***] **1.** fein zs.-nähen, kunststopfen; **2.** ⚙ *Draht* fein ausziehen; **͵~-'drawn** → ***fine-spun***.

fine·ness ['faɪnnɪs] *s. allg.* Feinheit *f*; **'fin·er·y** [-nərɪ] *s.* **1.** Putz *m*, Staat *m*; **2.** ⚙ a) Frischofen *m*, b) Frische'rei *f*; **fines** [faɪnz] *s. pl.* ⚙ Grus *m*, feingesiebtes Materi'al; **͵fine-'spun** *adj.* feingesponnen (*a. fig.*).

fi·nesse [fɪ'nes] **I** *s.* **1.** Fi'nesse *f*: a) Spitzfindigkeit *f*, b) (kleiner) Kunstgriff, Kniff *m*; **2.** Raffi'nesse *f*, Schlauheit *f*; **3.** *Kartenspiel*: Schneiden *n*; **II** *v/i.* **4.** *Kartenspiel*: schneiden; **5.** ‚tricksen', Kniffe anwenden.

͵fine|-'tooth(ed) *adj.* fein(gezahnt): ~ ***comb*** Staubkamm *m*; ***go over s.th. with a ~ comb*** a) et. genau durchsuchen, b) et. genau unter die Lupe nehmen; ~ ***tun·ing*** *s. Radio*: Feinabstimmung *f*.

fin·ger ['fɪŋgə] **I** *s.* **1.** Finger *m*: ***first***, ***second***, ***third*** ~ Zeige-, Mittel-, Ringfinger; ***fourth*** (*od.* ***little***) ~ kleiner Finger; ***get*** (*od.* ***pull***) ***one's ~ out*** *Brit.* F ‚Dampf dahintermachen'; ***have a*** (*od.* ***one's***) ~ ***in the pie*** die Hand im Spiel haben; ***keep one's ~s crossed for s.o.*** j-m den Dauem drücken *od.* halten; ***lay*** (*od.* ***put***) ***one's ~ on s.th.*** *fig.* den Finger auf et. legen; ***not to lay a ~ on s.o.*** j-m kein Härchen krümmen, j-n nicht anrühren; ***not to lift*** (*od.* ***raise***, ***stir***) ***a ~*** keinen Finger rühren; ***put the ~ on s.o.*** → 10; ***twist*** (*od.* ***wrap***, ***wind***) ***s.o.*** (***a***)***round one's little ~*** j-n um den (kleinen) Finger wickeln; ***work one's ~s to the bone*** (***for s.o.***) sich (für j-n) die Finger abarbeiten; → *a. Verbindungen mit anderen Verben u. Substantiven*; **2.** Finger(ling) *m* (*am Handschuh*); **3.** (Uhr)Zeiger *m*; **4.** Fingerbreit *m*; **5.** schmaler Streifen; schmales Stück; **6.** ⚙ Daumen *m*, Greifer *m*; **7.** *sl.* → ***finger man***; **II** *v/t.* **8.** a) betasten, befühlen, b) her'umfingern an (*dat.*), spielen mit; **9.** ♪ a) *et.* mit den Fingern spielen, b) *Noten* mit Fingersatz versehen; **10.** *Am.* F a) *j-n* verpfeifen, b) *j-n* beschatten, c) *Opfer* ausspähen; **III** *v/i.* **11.** her'umfingern (***at*** an *dat.*), spielen (***with*** mit); **'~·board** *s.* ♪ a) Griffbrett *n*, b) Klavia'tur *f*, c) Manu'al *n* (*der Orgel*); ~ ***bowl*** *s.* Fingerschale *f*; **'~·breadth** *s.* Fingerbreit *m*.

-fin·gered [fɪŋgəd] *adj. in Zssgn* mit … Fingern, …fing(e)rig.

fin·ger·ing ['fɪŋgərɪŋ] *s.* ♪ Fingersatz *m*.

fin·ger| man *s.* Spitzel *m* (*e-r Bande*); **'~·mark** *s.* Fingerabdruck *m* (*Schmutzfleck*); **'~·nail** *s.* Fingernagel *m*; ~ ***nut*** *s.* ⚙ Flügelmutter *f*; **'~-paint I** *s.* Fingerfarbe *f*; **II** *v/t. u. v/i.* mit Fingerfarben malen; ~ ***post*** *s.* **1.** Wegweiser *m*; **2.** *fig.* Fingerzeig *m*; **'~·print I** *s.* Fin-

gerabdruck *m*; **II** *v/t.* von *j-m* Fingerabdrücke machen; **'~·stall** *s.* Fingerling *m*; **'~·tip** *s. mst fig.* Fingerspitze *f*: ***have at one's ~s*** *Kenntnisse* parat haben; ***to one's ~s*** durch u. durch.
fin·i·cal ['fɪnɪkl] *adj.* □, **'fin·ick·ing** [-kɪŋ], **'fin·ick·y** [-kɪ] *adj.* **1.** über'trieben genau, pe'dantisch; **2.** heikel, ‚pingelig'; **3.** affek'tiert, geziert; **4.** knifflig.
fi·nis ['fɪnɪs] (*Lat.*) *s.* Ende *n*.
fin·ish ['fɪnɪʃ] **I** *s.* **1.** Ende *n*, Schluß *m*; **2.** *sport* a) Endspurt *m*, Finish *n*, b) Ziel *n*, c) Endkampf *m*, Entscheidung *f*: ***be in at the ~*** in die Endrunde kommen, *fig.* das Ende miterleben; **3.** Voll'endung *f*, letzter Schliff, Ele'ganz *f*; **4.** ⚙ a) (äußerliche) Ausführung, Bearbeitung(sgüte) *f*, Oberflächenbeschaffenheit *f*, b) ('Lack- *etc.*)ˌÜberzug *m*, c) Poli'tur *f*, d) Appre'tur *f*; **5.** gute Ausführung *od.* Verarbeitung; **6.** △ a) Ausbau *m*, b) Verputz *m*; **II** *v/t.* **7.** *a.* ***~ off*** voll'enden, beendigen, fertigstellen, erledigen, zu Ende führen: ***~ a task***; ***~ a book*** ein Buch auslesen *od.* zu Ende lesen; **8.** *a.* ***~ off*** (*od.* ***up***) a) *Vorräte* auf-, verbrauchen, b) aufessen *od.* austrinken; **9.** *a.* ***~ off*** a) *j-n* ‚erledigen', *j-m* den Rest geben' (*töten od. erschöpfen od. ruinieren*), b) *bsd. e-m Tier* den Gnadenschuß *od.* -stoß geben; **10.** a) *a.* ***~ off*** (*od.* ***~ up***) *et.* vervollkommnen, *e-r Sache* den letzten Schliff geben, b) *j-m* feine Lebensart beibringen; **11.** ⚙ nach-, fertigbearbeiten, *Papier* glätten, *Stoff* zurichten, appretieren, *Möbel etc.* polieren; **III** *v/i.* **12.** *a.* ***~ off*** (*od.* ***up***) enden, schließen, aufhören (***with*** mit): ***have you ~ed?*** bist du fertig?; ***he ~ed by saying*** abschließend *od.* zum Abschluß sagte er; **13.** *a.* ***~ up*** enden, *im Gefängnis etc.* ‚landen'; **14.** enden, zu Ende gehen; **15.** ***~ with*** mit *j-m od. et.* Schluß machen: ***I'm ~ed with him!*** mit ihm bin ich fertig!; ***have ~ed with s.o.*** (*od.* ***s.th.***) j-n (et.) nicht mehr brauchen; ***I haven't ~ed with you yet!*** ich bin noch nicht fertig mit dir!; **16.** *sport* einlaufen, durchs Ziel gehen: ***~ third*** *a.* Dritter werden, den dritten Platz belegen, *allg.* als dritter fertig sein.
fin·ished ['fɪnɪʃt] *adj.* **1.** beendet, fertig: ***half-~ products*** Halbfabrikate; ***~ goods*** Fertigwaren; ***~ part*** Fertigteil *n*; **2.** *fig.* F ‚erledigt' (*erschöpft od. ruiniert od. todgeweiht*): ***he is ~*** *a.* mit ihm ist es aus!; **3.** voll'endet, voll'kommen; **'fin·ish·er** [-ʃə] *s.* **1.** ⚙ a) Fertigbearbeiter *m*; Appretierer *m*, b) Ma'schine *f* zur Fertigbearbeitung, *z.B.* Fertigwalzwerk *n*; **2.** F vernichtender Schlag, ‚K.-'o.-Schlag' *m*; **3.** ***strong ~*** *sport* (starker) Spurtläufer.
fin·ish·ing ['fɪnɪʃɪŋ] **I** *s.* **1.** Voll'enden *n*, Fertigmachen *n*, -stellen *n*; **2.** ⚙ a) Fertigbearbeitung *f*, b) (abschließende) Oberflächenbehandlung *f*, *z.B.* Hochglanzpolieren *n*, c) Veredelung, d) Appre'tur *f* (*von Stoffen*); **3.** *sport* Abschluß *m*; **II** *adj.* **4.** abschließend; → ***touch*** 3; ***~ a·gent*** *s.* ⚙ Appre'turmittel *n*; ***~ in·dus·try*** *s.* Ver'edelungsindu,strie *f*, verarbeitende Indu'strie; ***~ lathe*** *s.* ⚙ Fertigdrehbank *f*; ***~ line*** *s.* *sport* Ziellinie *f*; ***~ mill*** *s.* ⚙ **1.** Feinwalzwerk *n*; **2.** Schlichtfräser *m*; ***~ post*** *s.* *sport* Zielpfosten *m*; ***~ school*** *s.* 'Mädchenpensioˌnat *n* (*zur Vorbereitung auf das gesellschaftliche Leben*).
fi·nite ['faɪnaɪt] *adj.* **1.** begrenzt, endlich (*a.* ⅍); **2.** *ling.* fi'nit: ***~ form*** *a.* Personalform *f*; ***~ verb*** Verbum *n* finitum.
fink [fɪŋk] *Am. sl.* **I** *s.* **1.** Streikbrecher *m*; **2.** Spitzel *m*; **3.** ‚Dreckskerl' *m*; **II** *v/i.* **4.** ***~ on*** *j-n* verpfeifen; **5.** ***~ out*** sich drücken, ‚aussteigen'.
Finn [fɪn] *s.* Finne *m*, Finnin *f*.
fin·nan had·dock ['fɪnən] *s.* geräucherter Schellfisch.
finned [fɪnd] *adj.* **1.** *ichth.* mit Flossen; **2.** ⚙ gerippt; **fin·ner** ['fɪnə] *s. zo.* Finnwal *m*.
Finn·ish ['fɪnɪʃ] **I** *adj.* finnisch; **II** *s. ling.* Finnisch *n*.
fin·ny ['fɪnɪ] *adj.* **1.** → ***finned*** 1; **2.** Flossen…, Fisch…
fiord [fɪ'ɔːd] *s. geogr.* Fjord *m*.
fir [fɜː] *s.* **1.** ♀ Tanne *f*, Fichte *f*; **2.** Tannen-, Fichtenholz *n*; ***~ cone*** *s.* Tannenzapfen *m*.
fire ['faɪə] **I** *s.* **1.** Feuer *n* (*a. Edelstein*): ***~ and brimstone*** a) *bibl.* Feuer u. Schwefel *m*, b) *eccl.* Hölle *f* u. Verdammnis *f*; ***be on ~*** brennen, in Flammen stehen, *fig.* Feuer u. Flamme sein; ***catch ~*** Feuer fangen, in Brand geraten, *fig.* in Hitze geraten; ***go through ~ and water for s.o.*** *fig.* für j-n durchs Feuer gehen; ***play with ~*** *fig.* mit dem Feuer spielen; ***pull s.th. out of the ~*** *fig.* et. aus dem Feuer reißen; ***set on ~***, ***set ~ to*** anzünden, in Brand stecken; **2.** Feuer *n* (*im Ofen etc.*): ***on a slow ~*** bei schwachem Feuer (*kochen*); **3.** Brand *m*, Feuer(sbrunst *f*) *n*: ***where's the ~?*** F wo brennt's?; **4.** *Brit.* Heizgerät *n*; **5.** *fig.* Feuer *n*, Glut *f*, Leidenschaft *f*, Begeisterung *f*; **6.** ⚔ Feuer *n*, Beschuß *m*: ***blank ~*** blindes Schießen; ***come under ~*** unter Beschuß geraten (*a. fig.*); ***come under ~ from s.o.*** *fig.* in j-s Schußlinie geraten; ***hang ~*** schwer losgehen (*Schußwaffe*), *fig.* auf sich warten lassen (*Sache*); ***hold one's ~*** *fig.* sich zurückhalten; ***miss ~*** versagen (*Schußwaffe*), *fig.* fehlschlagen; **II** *v/t.* **7.** anzünden, in Brand stecken; **8.** *Kessel* heizen, *Ofen* (be)feuern, beheizen: ***~ up inflation*** *fig.* die Inflation ‚anheizen'; **9.** *Ziegel* brennen; **10.** *Tee* feuern; **11.** *fig. j-n, j-s Gefühle* entflammen, *j-n* in Begeisterung versetzen, *j-s Phantasie* beflügeln; **12.** *a.* ***~ off*** a) *Schußwaffe* abfeuern, b) *Schuß* abfeuern, -geben, c) *Sprengladung*, *Rakete* zünden; **13.** *a.* ***~ off*** *fig.* a) *Fragen etc.* abschießen, b) *j-n mit Fragen* bombardieren; **14.** *Motor* anlassen; **15.** F *j-n* ‚feuern', ‚rausschmeißen'; **III** *v/i.* **16.** Feuer fangen, (an)brennen; **17.** ⚔ feuern, schießen (***at***, ***on*** auf *acc.*): ***~ away!*** F schieß los!; **18.** zünden (*Motor*); **19.** *a.* ***~ up*** ‚hochgehen', wütend werden.
fire| a·larm *s.* **1.** 'Feueraˌlarm *m*; **2.** Feuermelder *m*; **'~·arm** [-ərɑːm] *s.* Feuer-, Schußwaffe *f*: ***~ certificate*** *Brit.* Waffenschein *m*; **'~·ball** *s.* **1.** *hist.* ⚔ *u. ast.* Feuerkugel *f*; **2.** Feuerball *m* (*Sonne, Explosion etc.*); **3.** Kugelblitz *m*; ***~ bal·loon*** *s.* 'Heißluftbalˌlon *m*; **'~·brand** *s.* **1.** brennendes Holzscheit; **2.** *fig.* Unruhestifter *m*, Aufwiegler *m*; **'~·brick** *s.* feuerfester Ziegel, Scha'mottestein *m*; ***~ bri·gade*** *s. Brit.* Feuerwehr *f* (*a. fig. pol. etc.*); **'~·bug** *s. sl.* ‚Feuerteufel' *m*; ***~ clay*** *s.* feuerfester Ton, Scha'motte *f*; ***~ com·pa·ny*** *s.* **1.** *Am.* Feuerwehr *f*; **2.** → ***fire-office***; ***~ con·trol*** *s.* **1.** ⚔ Feuerleitung *f*; **2.** Brandbekämpfung *f*; **'~ˌcrack·er** *s.* Frosch *m* (*Knallkörper*); **'~·damp** *s.* ⚒ schlagende Wetter *pl.*, Grubengas *n*; ***~ de·part·ment*** *s. Am.* Feuerwehr *f*; **'~·dog** *s.* Ka'minbock *m*; **'~-ˌdrag·on** *s.* feuerspeiender Drache; ***~ drill*** *s.* **1.** 'Feueraˌlarmübung *f*; **2.** Feuerwehrübung *f*; **'~ˌeat·er** [-ərˌiː-] *s.* **1.** Feuerschlucker *m*; **2.** *fig.* ‚Eisenfresser' *m*; ***~ en·gine*** *s.* **1.** Feuerspritze *f*; **2.** Löschfahrzeug *n*; ***~ es·cape*** *s.* Feuerleiter *f*, -treppe *f*; ***~ ex·tin·guish·er*** *s.* Feuerlöscher *m*; ***~ fight·er*** *s.* Feuerwehrmann *m*; *pl.* Löschmannschaft *f*; **'~-ˌfight·ing** **I** *s.* Brandbekämpfung *f*; **II** *adj.* Lösch…, Feuerwehr…; **'~·fly** *s.* Glühwürmchen *n*; **'~·guard** *s.* **1.** Ka'mingitter *n*; **2.** Brandwache *f od.* -wart *m*; **'~·hose** *s.* Feuerwehrschlauch *m*; ***~ lane*** *f* Feuerschneise *f*; **'~·man** [-mən] *s.* [*irr.*] **1.** Feuerwehrmann *m*; *pl.* Löschmannschaft *f*; **2.** Heizer *m*; **'~-ˌof·fice** [-ərˌɒ-] *s. Brit.* Feuerversicherung(sanstalt) *f*; **'~·place** *s.* (offener) Ka'min; **'~·plug** *s.* ⚙ Hy'drant *m*; ***~ point*** *s.* Flammpunkt *m*; ***~ pol·i·cy*** *s. Brit.* 'Feuerversicherungspoˌlice *f*; ***~ pow·er*** *s.* ⚔ Feuerkraft *f*; **'~·proof** **I** *adj.* feuerfest, -sicher: ***~ curtain*** *thea.* eiserner Vorhang; **II** *v/t.* feuerfest machen; ***~ rais·er*** *s. Brit.* Brandstifter(in); ***~ ser·vice*** *s. Brit.* Feuerwehr *f*; ***~ ship*** *s.* ⚓ Brander *m*; **'~·side** *s.* **1.** (offener) Ka'min *m*: ***~ chat*** Plauderei *f* am Kamin; **2.** *fig.* häuslicher Herd, Da'heim *n*; ***~ sta·tion*** *s.* Feuerwehrwache *f*; **'~·storm** *s.* Feuersturm *m*; **'~·trap** *s.* ‚Mausefalle' *f* (*Gebäude ohne genügende Notausgänge*); ***~ wall*** *s.* Brandmauer *f*; **'~ˌward·en** *s. Am.* **1.** Brandmeister *m*; **2.** Brandwache *f*; **'~ˌwatch·er** *s. Brit.* Brandwache *f*, Luftschutzwart *m*; **'~ˌwa·ter** *s.* F ‚Feuerwasser' *n* (*Schnaps etc.*); **'~·wood** *s.* Brennholz *n*; **'~·works** *s. pl.* Feuerwerk *n* (*a. fig.*): ***a ~ of wit***; ***there were ~*** da flogen die Fetzen.
fir·ing ['faɪərɪŋ] *s.* **1.** ⚔ (Ab)Feuern *n*; **2.** ⚙ Zünden *n*; **3.** a) Heizen *n*, b) Feuerung *f*, c) 'Brennmateriˌal *n*; ***~ line*** *s.* ⚔ Feuerlinie *f*, -stellung *f*; Kampffront *f*: ***be in*** (*Am.* ***on***) ***the ~*** *fig.* in der Schußlinie stehen; ***~ or·der*** *s.* **1.** ⚔ Schießbefehl *m*; **2.** *mot.* Zündfolge *f*; ***~ par·ty***, ***~ squad*** *s.* ⚔ a) 'Ehrensaˌlutkomˌmando *n*, b) Exekuti'onskomˌmando *n*.
fir·kin ['fɜːkɪn] *s.* **1.** (Holz)Fäßchen *n*; **2.** Viertelfaß *n* (*Hohlmaß = etwa 40 l*).
firm¹ [fɜːm] **I** *adj.* □ **1.** fest, stark, hart; **2.** † fest: ***~ offer***, ***~ market***; **3.** fest, beständig; **4.** standhaft, fest, entschlossen, bestimmt: ***be ~ with s.o.*** j-m gegenüber hart sein; **II** *adv.* **5.** fest: ***stand ~*** *fig.* festbleiben; **III** *v/t.* **6.** *a.* ***~ up*** fest machen; **IV** *v/i.* **7.** *a.* ***~ up*** fest werden; **8.** *a.* ***~ up*** † anziehen (*Preise*), sich erholen (*Markt*).
firm² [fɜːm] *s.* Firma *f*: a) Firmenname *m*, b) Unter'nehmen *n*, Geschäft *n*, Betrieb *m*.
fir·ma·ment ['fɜːməmənt] *s.* Firma'ment

n, Himmelsgewölbe *n*.

firm·ness ['fɜːmnɪs] *s*. **1.** Festigkeit *f*, Entschlossenheit *f*, Beständigkeit *f*; **2.** ⚕ Festigkeit *f*, Stabili'tät *f*.

fir nee·dle *s*. Tannennadel *f*.

first [fɜːst] **I** *adj*. ☐ → ***firstly***; **1.** erst: ***at ~ hand*** aus erster Hand, direkt; ***in the ~ place*** zuerst, an erster Stelle; ***~ thing*** (***in the morning***) (morgens) als allererstes; ***~ things ~!*** das Wichtigste zuerst!; ***he doesn't know the ~ thing*** er hat keine (blasse) Ahnung; → ***cousin***; **2.** erst, best, bedeutendst, führend: ***~ officer*** ⚓ Erster Offizier; ***~ quality*** beste *od*. prima Qualität; **II** *adv*. **3.** zu'erst, voran: ***head ~*** (mit dem) Kopf voraus; **4.** zum erstenmal; **5.** eher, lieber; **6.** *a*. ***~ off*** F (zu)'erst (einmal): ***I must ~ do that***; **7.** zu'erst, als erst(er, -e, -es), an erster Stelle: ***~ come, ~ served*** wer zuerst kommt, mahlt zuerst; ***~ or last*** früher oder später; ***~ and last*** a) vor allen Dingen, b) im großen ganzen; ***~ of all*** zuallererst, vor allen Dingen; → 8; **III** *s*. **8.** (*der, die, das*) Erste *od*. (*fig*.) Beste: ***be ~ among equals*** Primus inter pares sein; ***at ~*** zuerst, anfangs, zunächst; ***from the ~*** von Anfang an; ***from ~ to last*** durchweg, von A bis Z; **9.** ♪ erste Stimme; **10.** *mot*. (*der*) erste Gang; **11.** *der* (Monats)Erste; **12.** 🚂 F erste Klasse; **13.** *univ*. *Brit*. *akademischer Grad erster Klasse*; **14.** *pl*. ⚕ Ware(n *pl*.) *f* erster Quali'tät, erste Wahl; **15.** ***~ of exchange*** ⚕ Primawechsel *m*; **~ aid** *s*. Erste Hilfe: ***render ~*** Erste Hilfe leisten; **ˌ~-'aid** *adj*. Erste-Hilfe-...: ***~ kit*** Verbandskasten *m*; ***~ post*** *od*. ***station*** Sanitätswache *f*, Unfallstation *f*; **~ bid** *s*. ⚕ Erstgebot *n*; **'~-born I** *adj*. erstgeboren; **II** *s*. (*der, die, das*) Erstgeborene; **~ cause** *s*. *phls*. Urgrund *m* aller Dinge, Gott *m*; **~ class** *s*. **1.** 🚂 *etc*. erste Klasse; **2.** *univ*. *Brit*. → ***first*** 13; **ˌ~-'class** *adj*. *u*. *adv*. **1.** erstklassig, ausgezeichnet; F prima; **2.** 🚂 *etc*. erster Klasse: ***~ mail*** a) *Am*. Briefpost *f*, b) *Brit*. bevorzugt beförderte Inlandspost; **~ cost** *s*. ⚕ Selbstkosten(preis *m*) *pl*., Gestehungskosten *pl*., Einkaufspreis *m*; **~ floor** *s*. **1.** *Brit*. erste(r) Stock, erste E'tage; **2.** *Am*. Erdgeschoß *n*; **~ fruits** *s*. *pl*. **1.** ⚘ Erstlinge *pl*.; **2.** *fig*. a) erste Erfolge *pl*., b) Erstlingswerk(e *pl*.) *n*; **ˌ~-gen·er'a·tion** *adj*. *Computer etc*. der ersten Generati'on; **ˌ~-'hand** *adj*. *u*. *adv*. aus erster Hand, di'rekt; **~ la·dy** *s*. First Lady *f*: a) *Gattin e-s Staatsoberhauptes*, b) *führende Persönlichkeit*: ***the ~ of jazz***; **~ lieu·ten·ant** *s*. ⚔ Oberleutnant *m*.

first·ling ['fɜːstlɪŋ] *s*. Erstling *m*; **first·ly** ['fɜːstlɪ] *adv*. erstens, zu'erst (einmal).

first| name *s*. Vorname *m*; **~ night** *s*. *thea*. Erst-, Uraufführung *f*, Premi'ere *f*; **ˌ~-'night·er** *s*. Premi'erenbesucher (-in); **~ pa·pers** *s*. *pl*. *Am*. (*erster*) *Antrag e-s Ausländers auf amer. Staatsangehörigkeit*; **~ per·son** *s*. **1.** *ling*. erste Per'son; **2.** Ich-Form *f* (*in Romanen etc*.); **~ prin·ci·ples** *s*. *pl*. 'Grundprinˌzipien *pl*.; **ˌ~-'rate** → ***first-class*** 1; **~ ser·geant** *s*. ⚔ *Am*. Hauptfeldwebel *m*; **~ strike** *s*. ⚔ (ato'marer) Erstschlag; **ˌ~-'time** *adj*.: ***~ voter*** Erstwähler(in).

firth [fɜːθ] *s*. Meeresarm *m*, Förde *f*.

fir tree *s*. Tanne(nbaum *m*) *f*.

fis·cal ['fɪskl] *adj*. ☐ fis'kalisch, steuerlich, Finanz...: ***~ policy*** Finanzpolitik *f*; ***~ stamp*** Banderole *f*; ***~ year*** a) *Am*. Geschäftsjahr *n*, b) *parl*. *Am*. Haushalts-, Rechnungsjahr *n*, c) *Brit*. Steuerjahr *n*.

fish [fɪʃ] **I** *pl*. **fish** *od*. (*Fischarten*) **fishes** *s*. **1.** Fisch *m*: ***fried ~*** Bratfisch; ***drink like a ~*** saufen wie ein Loch; ***like a ~ out of water*** wie ein Fisch auf dem Trockenen; ***I have other ~ to fry*** ich habe Wichtigeres zu tun; ***all is ~ that comes to his net*** er nimmt unbesehen alles (mit); ***a pretty kettle of ~*** F e-e schöne Bescherung; ***neither ~ nor flesh*** (***nor good red herring***), ***neither ~ nor fowl*** F weder Fisch noch Fleisch, nichts Halbes und nichts Ganzes; ***there are plenty more ~ in the sea*** F es gibt noch mehr davon auf der Welt; ***loose ~*** F lockerer Vogel; ***queer ~*** F komischer Kauz; → ***feed*** 1; **2.** *ast*. ***the*** 𝔖(***es*** *pl*.) die Fische *pl*.: ***be*** (***a***) 𝔖***es*** Fisch sein; **II** *v/t*. **3.** fischen, *Fische* fangen, angeln; **4.** a) fischen *od*. angeln in (*dat*.), b) *Fluß etc*. abfischen, absuchen: ***~ up*** *j-n* auffischen; **5.** *fig*. *a*. ***~ out*** her'vorkramen, -holen, -ziehen; **6.** ⚙ verlaschen; **III** *v/i*. **7.** (***for***) fischen, angeln (auf *acc*.); **8.** ***~ for*** *fig*. a) fischen nach: ***~ for compliments***, b) aussein auf (*acc*.): ***~ for information***; **9.** *a*. ***~ around*** kramen (***for*** nach).

fish| and chips *s*. *Brit*. Bratfisch *m* u. Pommes 'frites; **~ ball** *s*. 'Fischfrikaˌdelle *f*, -klops *m*; **~ bas·ket** *s*. (Fisch-) Reuse *f*; **'~·bone** *s*. Gräte *f*; **~ bowl** *s*. Goldfischglas *n*; **~ cake** → ***fish ball***; **~ eat·ers** *s*. *pl*. Fischbesteck *n*.

fish·er ['fɪʃə] *s*. **1.** Fischer *m*, Angler *m*; **2.** *zo*. Fischfänger *m*; **'fish·er·man** [-mən] *s*. [*irr*.] **1.** (*a*. Sport)Fischer *m*; **2.** Fischdampfer *m*; **'fish·er·y** [-ərɪ] *s*. **1.** Fische'rei *f*, Fischfang *m*; **2.** Fischzuchtanlage *f*; **3.** Fischgründe *pl*., Fanggebiet *n*.

'fish|-eye (**lens**) *s*. *phot*. 'Fischauge(n-objekˌtiv) *n*; **~ fin·gers** *s*. *pl*. *Küche*: Fischstäbchen *pl*.; **~ flour** *s*. Fischmehl *n*; **'~·glue** *s*. Fischleim *m*; **'~·hook** *s*. Angelhaken *m*.

fish·ing ['fɪʃɪŋ] *s*. **1.** Fischen *n*, Angeln *n*; **2.** → ***fishery*** 1, 3; **~ boat** *s*. Fischerboot *n*; **~ grounds** *s*. *pl*. → ***fishery*** 3; **~ in·dus·try** *s*. Fische'rei(gewerbe *n*) *f*; **'~·line** *s*. Angelschnur *f*; **'~·net** *s*. Fischnetz *n*; **~ pole** *s*., **~ rod** *s*. Angelrute *f*; **~ tack·le** *s*. Angel- *od*. Fische'reigeräte *pl*.; **~ vil·lage** *s*. Fischerdorf *n*.

fish| lad·der *s*. Fischleiter *f*, -treppe *f*; **~ meal** *s*. Fischmehl *n*; **'~ˌmon·ger** *s*. *Brit*. Fischhändler *m*; **'~·net** *adj*. Netz...: ***~ shirt***; ***~ stockings***; **~ oil** *s*. Fischtran *m*; **'~·plate** *s*. 🚂 Lasche *f*; **'~·pond** *s*. Fischteich *m*; **'~·pot** *s*. Fischreuse *f*; **~ slice** *s*. Fischheber *m*; **~ stor·y** *s*. *Am*. F ‚Seemannsgarn' *n*; **~ tank** *s*. A'quarium *n*; **'~·wife** *s*. [*irr*.] Fischhändlerin *f*: ***swear like a ~*** keifen wie ein Fischweib.

fish·y ['fɪʃɪ] *adj*. ☐ **1.** fischartig, Fisch...: ***~ eyes*** *fig*. Fischaugen; **2.** fischreich; **3.** F ‚faul', verdächtig: ***there's s.th. ~ about it*** daran ist irgend etwas faul.

fis·sile ['fɪsaɪl] *adj*. *bsd*. *phys*. spaltbar; **fis·sion** ['fɪʃn] *s*. **1.** *phys*. Spaltung *f* (*a*. *fig*.): ***~ bomb*** Atombombe *f*; **2.** *biol*. (Zell)Teilung *f*; **fis·sion·a·ble** ['fɪʃnəbl] → ***fissile***.

fis·sip·a·rous [fɪ'sɪpərəs] *adj*. *biol*. sich durch Teilung vermehrend, fissi'par.

fis·sure ['fɪʃə] *s*. Spalt(e *f*) *m*, Riß *m* (*a*. ⚕), Ritz(e *f*) *m*, Sprung *m*; **'fis·sured** [-əd] *adj*. gespalten, rissig (*a*. ⚙); ⚕ schrundig.

fist [fɪst] **I** *s*. **1.** Faust *f*: ***~ law*** Faustrecht *n*; **2.** *humor*. a) ‚Pfote' *f*, Hand *f*, b) ‚Klaue' *f*, Handschrift *f* (*a*. *fig*.); **3.** F Versuch *m* (***at*** mit); **II** *v/t*. **4.** mit der Faust schlagen; **5.** packen.

-fist·ed [fɪstɪd] *adj*. *in Zssgn* mit e-r ... Faust *od*. Hand, mit ... Fäusten.

'fist·ful [-fʊl] *s*. (*e-e*) Handvoll.

fist·ic, **fist·i·cal** ['fɪstɪk(l)] *adj*. *sport* Box...; **'fist·i·cuffs** [-kʌfs] *s*. *pl*. Faustschläge *pl*., Schläge'rei *f*.

fis·tu·la ['fɪstjʊlə] *s*. ⚕ Fistel *f*.

fit¹ [fɪt] **I** *adj*. ☐ **1.** a) passend, geeignet, b) fähig, tauglich: ***~ for service*** dienstfähig, (-)tauglich; ***~ to drink*** trinkbar; ***~ to drive*** fahrtüchtig; ***~ to eat*** eß-, genießbar; ***laugh ~ to burst*** F vor Lachen beinahe platzen; ***~ to kill*** F wie verrückt; ***he was ~ to be tied*** *Am*. F er hatte eine Stinkwut; ***he is not ~ for the job*** er ist für den Posten nicht geeignet; → ***drop*** 12; **2.** wert, würdig: ***not to be ~ to*** *inf*. es nicht verdienen zu *inf*.; ***not ~ to be seen*** nicht präsentabel *od*. vorzeigbar; **3.** angemessen, angebracht: ***more than ~*** über Gebühr; ***see*** (*od*. ***think***) ***~*** es für richtig *od*. angebracht halten (***to do*** zu tun); **4.** schicklich, geziemend: ***it is not ~ for us to do so*** es gehört sich *od*. ziemt sich nicht, daß wir das tun; **5.** a) gesund, b) fit, (gut) in Form: ***keep ~*** sich in Form *od*. fit halten; ***as ~ as a fiddle*** a) kerngesund, b) quietschvergnügt; **II** *s*. **6.** Paßform *f*, Sitz *m* (*Kleid*): ***it is a bad*** (***perfect***) ***~*** es sitzt schlecht (tadellos); ***it is a tight ~*** es sitzt stramm, *fig*. es ist sehr knapp bemessen; **7.** ⚙ Passung *f*; **III** *v/t*. **8.** passend *od*. geeignet machen (***for*** für), anpassen (***to*** an *acc*.); **9.** passen für *od*. auf (*j-n*), *e-r Sache* angemessen *od*. angepaßt sein: ***the key ~s the lock*** der Schlüssel paßt (ins Schloß); ***the description ~s him*** die Beschreibung trifft auf ihn zu; ***the name ~s him*** der Name paßt zu ihm; ***~ the facts*** (mit den Tatsachen überein)stimmen; ***to ~ the occasion*** (*Redew*.) dem Anlaß entsprechend; **10.** *j-m* passen (*Kleid etc*.); **11.** sich eignen für; **12.** *j-n* befähigen (***for*** für; ***to do*** zu tun); **13.** *j-n* vorbereiten, ausbilden (***for*** für); **14.** *a*. ⚙ ausrüsten, -statten, einrichten, versehen (***with*** mit); **15.** ⚙ a) einpassen, -bauen (***into*** in *acc*.), b) anbringen (***to*** an *dat*.), c) → ***fit up*** 2; **16.** a) an *j-m* Maß nehmen, b) *Kleid etc*. anprobieren; **IV** *v/i*. **17.** passen: a) sitzen (*Kleid*), b) angemessen sein, c) sich eignen; **18.** ***~ into*** passen in (*acc*.), sich einfügen in (*acc*.); **~ in I** *v/t*. einfügen, -passen, *a*. *fig*. *j-n od*. *et*. einschieben; **II** *v/i*. (***with***) passen (in *acc*.), über'einstimmen (mit); **~ on** *v/t*. **1.** *Kleid etc*. anprobieren; **2.** anbringen, (an)montieren (***to*** an *acc*.); **~ out** → ***fit¹*** 14; **~ up** *v/t*. **1.** → ***fit¹*** 14; **2.** ⚙ aufstellen, montieren.

fit² [fɪt] *s.* **1.** ⚕ *u. fig.* Anfall *m*, Ausbruch *m*: **~ of coughing** Hustenanfall; **~ of anger** Wutanfall; **~ of laughter** Lachkrampf *m*; **have a ~** F ,Zustände' *od.* e-n Lachkrampf kriegen; **give s.o. a ~** F a) j-m e-n Schrecken einjagen, b) j-n ,auf die Palme bringen'; **2.** (plötzliche) Anwandlung, Laune *f*: **~ of generosity** Anwandlung von Großzügigkeit, Spendierlaune; **by ~s (and starts)** a) stoß-, ruckweise, b) spo'radisch.

fitch [fɪtʃ], **fitch·ew** ['fɪtʃuː] *s. zo.* Iltis *m.*

fit·ful ['fɪtfʊl] *adj.* □ unstet, unbeständig, veränderlich; sprung-, launenhaft; **fit·ment** ['fɪtmənt] *s.* **1.** Einrichtungsgegenstand *m*; *pl.* Ausstattung *f*, Einrichtung *f*; **2.** *Am.* (Tropf- *etc.*)Vorrichtung *f*; **fit·ness** ['fɪtnɪs] *s.* **1.** Eignung *f*, Fähig-, Tauglichkeit *f*: **~ test** Eignungsprüfung *f* (→ 5); **2.** Zweckmäßigkeit *f*; **3.** Angemessenheit *f*; **4.** Schicklichkeit *f*; **5.** a) Gesundheit *f*, b) (gute) Form, Fitneß *f*: **~ room** Fitneßraum *m*; **~ test** *sport* Fitneßtest *m*; **~ trail** *Am.* Trimmpfad *m*; **fit·ted** ['fɪtɪd] *adj.* **1.** passend, geeignet; **2.** nach Maß (gearbeitet), zugeschnitten: **~ carpet** Teppichboden *m*; **~ coat** taillierter Mantel; **3.** Einbau...: **~ kitchen**; **fit·ter** ['fɪtə] *s.* **1.** Ausrüster *m*, Einrichter *m*; **2.** Schneider(in); **3.** ⚙ Mon'teur *m*, Me'chaniker *m*; Installa'teur *m*; (Ma'schinen)Schlosser *m*; **fit·ting** ['fɪtɪŋ] **I** *adj.* □ **1.** a) passend, geeignet, b) angemessen, c) schicklich; **II** *s.* **2.** Anprobe *f*; **3.** ⚙ Einpassen *n*, -bauen *n*; **4.** ⚙ Mon'tage *f*, Installieren *n*, Aufstellung *f*: **~ shop** Montagehalle *f*; **5.** *pl.* ⚙ Beschläge *pl.*, Zubehör *n*, Arma'turen *pl.*, Ausstattungsgegenstände *pl.*; **6.** ⚙ a) Paßarbeit *f*, b) Paßteil *n*, c) Bau-, Zubehörteil *n*, d) (Rohr)Verbindung *f*, e) Einrichtung *f*, Ausrüstung *f*, -stattung *f*; **'fit-up** *s. thea. Brit.* F **1.** provi'sorische Bühne; **2.** *a.* **~ company** (kleine) Wanderbühne.

five [faɪv] **I** *adj.* fünf; **~-and-ten** *Am.* billiges Kaufhaus; **~-day week** Fünftagewoche *f*; **~-finger exercise** ♪ Fünffingerübung *f*, *fig.* Kinderspiel *n*; **~-o'clock shadow** Anflug *m* von Bartstoppeln am Nachmittag; **~-year plan** Fünfjahresplan *m*; **II** *s.* Fünf *f*: **the ~ of hearts** die Herzfünf (*Spielkarte*); **'five-fold** *adj. u. adv.* fünffach; **'fiv·er** [-və] *s.* F *Brit.* Fünf'pfund-, *Am.* Fünf'dollarschein *m*; **fives** [-vz] *s. pl. sg. konstr. sport Brit. ein* Wandballspiel *n.*

fix [fɪks] **I** *v/t.* **1.** befestigen, festmachen, anheften, anbringen (**to** an *acc.*); → **bayonet** I; **2.** *fig.* verankern: **~ s.th. in s.o.'s mind** j-m et. einprägen; **3.** *fig. Termin, Preis etc.* festsetzen, -legen (**at** auf *acc.*), bestimmen, verabreden; **4.** *Blick, s-e Aufmerksamkeit etc.* richten, heften, *Hoffnung* setzen (**on** auf *acc.*); **5.** *j-s Aufmerksamkeit* fesseln; **6.** *j-n, et.* fixieren, anstarren; **7.** *die Schuld etc.* zuschreiben (**on** *dat.*); **8.** ✈, ⚓ die Positi'on bestimmen von (*od. gen.*); **9.** *phot.* fixieren; **10.** (zur mikro'skopischen Unter'suchung) präparieren; **11.** ⚙ *Werkstücke* feststellen; **12.** reparieren, instand setzen; **13.** *bsd. Am. et.* zu'rechtmachen, *Essen* zubereiten: **~ s.o. a drink** j-m e-n Drink mixen; **~ one's face** sich schminken; **~ one's hair** sich frisieren; **14.** *a.* **~ up** *et.* arrangieren, regeln, *a.* in Ordnung bringen, *Streit* beilegen; **15.** F a) *e-n Wahlkampf etc.* (vorher) ,arrangieren', manipulieren, b) *j-n* ,schmieren', bestechen; **16.** F es *j-m* ,besorgen' *od.* ,geben'; **17.** *mst* **~ up** a) *j-n* 'unterbringen, b) **with** *j-m et.* besorgen; **18.** *mst* **~ up** *Vertrag* (ab-)schließen; **II** *v/i.* **19.** ⚗ fest werden, erstarren; **20.** sich festsetzen; **21.** **~ (up)on** a) sich entscheiden *od.* entschließen für *od.* zu, *et.* wählen, b) → 3; **22.** *Am.* F vorhaben, planen: **it's ~ing to rain** es wird gleich regnen; **23.** *sl.* ,fixen' (*Drogensüchtiger*); **III** *s.* **24.** F üble Lage, ,Klemme' *f*, ,Patsche' *f*; **25.** F a) Schiebung *f*, b) Bestechung *f*; **26.** ✈, ⚓ a) Standort *m*, Positi'on *f*, b) Ortung *f*; **27.** *sl.* ,Fix' *m*, ,Schuß' *m* (*Drogeninjektion*): **give o.s. a ~** sich ,e-n Schuß setzen'; **fix·ate** ['fɪkseɪt] *v/t.* **1.** → **fix** 1; **2.** *Am. j-n, et.* fixieren; **3.** *fig.* erstarren *od.* stagnieren lassen; **4.** **be ~d on** *psych.* fixiert sein auf (*acc.*); **fix·a·tion** [fɪk'seɪʃn] *s.* **1.** Fi'xierung *f*, Befestigung *f*; **2.** Festlegung *f*; **3.** *psych.* a) → **fixed idea**, b) (*Mutter- etc.*)Bindung *f*, (-)Fi'xierung *f*; **'fix·a·tive** [-sətɪv] **I** *s.* Fixa'tiv *n*, Fi'xiermittel *n*; **II** *adj.* Fixier...

fixed [fɪkst] *adj.* □ → **fixedly**; **1.** fest (-angebracht), befestigt, (orts)fest, Fest...(*antenne etc.*); starr (*Geschütz, Kupplung etc.*): **of ~ purpose** *fig.* zielstrebig; **2.** ⚗ gebunden: **~ oil**; **3.** starr (*Blick*), unverwandt (*Aufmerksamkeit*); **4.** *bsd.* † fest(gelegt, -stehend): **~ assets** feste Anlagen, Anlagevermögen *n*; **~ capital** † Anlagekapital *n*; **~ cost** feste Kosten, Fixkosten *pl.*; **~ income** festes Einkommen; **~ price** fester Preis, Festpreis *m*, *a.* gebundener Preis; **5.** F abgekartet, manipuliert; **6.** F (*gut etc.*) versorgt *od.* versehen (**for** mit); **~ i·de·a** *s. psych.* fixe I'dee, Zwangsvorstellung *f*; **,~-'in·ter·est (-,bear·ing)** *adj.* † festverzinslich.

fix·ed·ly ['fɪksɪdlɪ] *adv.* starr, unverwandt.

fixed| point *s.* 𝔄 Fixpunkt *m*; **~ sight** *s.* ⚔ 'Standvi,sier *n*; **~ star** *s.* Fixstern *m*; **,~-'wing air·craft** *s.* ✈ Starrflügler *m.*

fix·er ['fɪksə] *s.* **1.** *phot.* Fi'xiermittel *n*; **2.** F ,Organi'sator' *m*, Manipu'lator *m*; **3.** *sl.* ,Dealer' *m*; **'fix·ing** [-ksɪŋ] *s.* **1.** Befestigen *n*, Anbringen *n*: **~ bolt** Haltebolzen *m*; **~ screw** Stellschraube *f*; **2.** Repara'tur *f*; **3.** *phot.* Fixieren *n*; **4.** *pl. bsd. Am.* a) Geräte *pl.*, b) Zubehör *n*, c) Zutaten *pl.*, *fig. a.* Drum u. Dran *n*; **'fix·i·ty** [-ksətɪ] *s.* Festigkeit *f*, Beständigkeit *f*: **~ of purpose** Zielstrebigkeit *f*; **'fix·ture** [-kstʃə] *s.* **1.** feste Anlage, Installati'onsteil *m*: **lighting ~** Beleuchtungskörper *m*; **2.** Inven'tarstück *n*, ⚖ festes Inven'tar *od.* Zubehör: **be a ~** *humor.* zum (lebenden) Inventar gehören; **~s and fittings** bewegliche u. unbewegliche Einrichtungsgegenstände; **3.** ⚙ Spannvorrichtung *f*, -futter *n*; **4.** *bsd. sport Brit.* (Ter'min *m* für e-e) Veranstaltung *f.*

fizz [fɪz] **I** *v/i.* **1.** zischen; **2.** moussieren, sprudeln; **3.** *fig.* sprühen (**with** vor *dat.*); **II** *s.* **4.** Zischen *n*; **5.** Sprudeln *n*; **6.** a) Sprudel *m*, b) Fizz *m* (*Mischgetränk*), c) F ,Schampus' *m* (*Sekt*); **'fiz·zle** [-zl] **I** *s.* **1.** → **fizz** 4; **2.** F ,Pleite' *f*, Mißerfolg *m*; **II** *v/i.* **3.** → **fizz** 1; **4.** *a.* **~ out** *fig.* verpuffen, im Sand verlaufen; **'fiz·zy** [-zɪ] *adj.* **1.** zischend; **2.** sprudelnd, moussierend.

fjord [fjɔːd] → **fiord.**

flab·ber·gast ['flæbəgɑːst] *v/t.* F verblüffen: **I was ~ed** ich war ,platt'.

flab·bi·ness ['flæbɪnɪs] *s.* **1.** Schlaffheit *f* (*a. fig.*); **2.** Schwammigkeit *f*; **flab·by** ['flæbɪ] *adj.* □ **1.** schlaff; **2.** schwammig; **3.** *fig.* ,schlapp', ,schlaff', schwach.

flac·cid ['flæksɪd] *adj.* → **flabby**; **flac·cid·i·ty** [flæk'sɪdətɪ] → **flabbiness.**

flack¹ [flæk] → **flak.**

flack² [flæk] *s. Am. sl.* 'Pressea,gent *m.*

flag¹ [flæg] **I** *s.* **1.** Fahne *f*, Flagge *f*: **~ of convenience** ⚓ Billigflagge *f*; **hoist** (*od.* **fly**) **one's ~** a) die Fahne aufziehen, b) das Kommando übernehmen (*Admiral*); **strike one's ~** a) die Flagge streichen, *fig. a.* kapitulieren, b) das Kommando abgeben (*Admiral*); **keep the ~ flying** *fig.* die Fahne hochhalten; **2.** → **flagship**; **3.** *sport* (Markierungs-)Fähnchen *n*; **4.** a) (Kar'tei)Reiter *m*, b) Lesezeichen *n*; **5.** *hunt.* Fahne *f* (*Schwanz*); **6.** *typ.* Im'pressum *n* (*e-r Zeitung*); **II** *v/t.* **7.** beflaggen; **8.** *sport Strecke* ausflaggen; **9.** *et.* signalisieren: **~ offside** *Fußball*: Abseits winken; **10.** **~ down** *Fahrzeug* anhalten, *Taxi* herbeiwinken, *sport Rennen, Fahrer* abwinken.

flag² [flæg] *s.* ⚘ gelbe *od.* blaue Schwertlilie.

flag³ [flæg] *v/i.* **1.** schlaff her'abhängen; **2.** *fig.* nachlassen, erlahmen, ermatten; **3.** langweilig werden.

flag⁴ [flæg] **I** *s.* (Stein)Platte *f*, Fliese *f*; **II** *v/t.* mit (Stein)Platten *od.* Fliesen belegen.

flag| cap·tain *s.* Komman'dant *m* des Flaggschiffs; **~ day** *s.* **1.** *Brit.* Opfertag *m* (*Straßensammlung*); **2.** 𝔖 *Am.* Jahrestag *m* der Natio'nalflagge (*14. Juni*).

flag·el·lant ['flædʒələnt] **I** *s. eccl.* Geißler *m*, Flagel'lant *m* (*a. psych.*); **II** *adj.* geißelnd (*a. fig.*); **'flag·el·late** [-leɪt] **I** *v/t.* geißeln (*a. fig.*); **II** *s. zo.* Geißeltierchen *n*; **flag·el·la·tion** [,flædʒə'leɪʃn] *s.* Geißelung *f* (*a. fig.*).

flag·eo·let [,flædʒəʊ'let] *s.* ♪ Flageo'lett *n.*

flag·ging¹ ['flægɪŋ] *adj.* erlahmend.

flag·ging² ['flægɪŋ] *s. collect.* a) (Stein-)Platten *pl.*, b) Fliesen *pl.*, c) gefliester Boden.

flag| lieu·ten·ant *s.* ⚓ *Brit.* Flaggleutnant *m*; **~ of·fi·cer** *s.* ⚓ 'Flaggoffi,zier *m.*

flag·on ['flægən] *s.* **1.** *bauchige* (Wein-)Flasche; **2.** (Deckel)Krug *m.*

fla·gran·cy ['fleɪgrənsɪ] *s.* **1.** Schamlosigkeit *f*, Ungeheuerlichkeit *f*; **2.** Kraßheit *f*; **'fla·grant** [-nt] *adj.* □ **1.** schamlos, schändlich, ungeheuerlich; **2.** kraß, ekla'tant, schreiend.

'flag|·ship *s.* ⚓ Flaggschiff *n* (*a. fig.*); *fig.* Aushängeschild *n*; **'~·staff**, **'~·stick** *s.* Fahnenstange *f*, -mast *m*, Flaggenmast, ⚓ Flaggenstock *m*; **~ sta·tion** *s.* 🚂 *Am.* Bedarfshaltestelle *f*; **'~·stone**

→ ***flag***[4] I; **~ stop** → ***flag station***; **'~-ˌwav·er** *s.* F Hur'rapatriˌot *m*; **'~-ˌwav·ing** I *s.* Hur'rapatrioˌtismus *m*; II *adj.* hur'rapatriˌotisch.
flail [fleɪl] I *s.* **1.** Dreschflegel *m*; II *v/t.* **2.** dreschen; **3.** wild einschlagen auf *j-n*; **4.** ***~ one's arms*** mit den Armen fuchteln.
flair [fleə] *s.* **1.** (besondere) Begabung, Ta'lent *n*; **2.** (feines) Gespür (***for*** für).
flak [flæk] (*Ger.*) *s.* **1.** ⚔ Flak *f*: a) 'Fliegerabwehr(kaˌnone *od.* -truppe) *f*, b) Flakfeuer *n*; **2.** *fig.* F (heftiger) ‚Beschuß', ‚Zunder' *m* (*Kritik etc.*).
flake [fleɪk] I *s.* **1.** (*Schnee-, Seifen-, Hafer- etc.*)Flocke *f*; **2.** dünne Schicht, Schuppe *f*, Blättchen *n*; **3.** Fetzen *m*, Splitter *m*; **4.** *Am. sl.* ‚Spinner' *m*; II *v/t.* **5.** abblättern; **6.** flockig machen; III *v/i.* **7.** in Flocken fallen; **8.** ***~ off*** abblättern, sich abschälen; **9.** ***~ out*** F a) ‚'umkippen' (*ohnmächtig werden*), b) ‚einpennen', c) ‚sich verziehen'; **flaked** [-kt] *adj.* flockig, Blättchen..., Flokken...; **'flak·y** [-kɪ] *adj.* **1.** flockig; **2.** blätterig: ***~ pastry*** Blätterteig *m*; **3.** *Am. sl.* verrückt.
flam·beau ['flæmbəʊ] *pl.* **-x** [-z] *od.* **-s** *s.* **1.** Fackel *f*; **2.** Leuchter *m*.
flam·boy·ance [flæm'bɔɪəns] *s.* **1.** Extrava'ganz *f*; **2.** über'ladener Schmuck; **3.** Grellheit *f*; **4.** *fig.* a) Bom'bast *m*, b) Großartigkeit *f*; **flam'boy·ant** [-nt] *adj.* □ **1.** extrava'gant; **2.** grell, leuchtend; **3.** farbenprächtig; **4.** *fig.* flammend; **5.** auffallend; **6.** über'laden (*a. Stil*); **7.** bom'bastisch, pom'pös; **8.** ⚠ wellig: ***~ style*** Flammenstil *m*.
flame [fleɪm] I *s.* **1.** Flamme *f*: ***be in ~s*** in Flammen stehen; **2.** *fig.* Feuer *n*, Flamme *f*, Glut *f*, Leidenschaft *f*, Heftigkeit *f*: ***fan the ~*** Öl ins Feuer gießen; **3.** Leuchten *n*, Glanz *m*; **4.** F ‚Flamme' *f*, ‚Angebetete' *f*: ***an old ~ of mine***; II *v/i.* **5.** lodern: ***~ up*** a) auflodern, b) in Flammen aufgehen, c) *fig.* aufbrausen; **6.** leuchten, (rot) glühen: ***her eyes ~d with anger*** ihre Augen flammten vor Wut; ***her cheeks ~d red*** ihr Gesicht flammte; **~ cut·ter** *s.* ⚙ Schneidbrenner *m*; **'~-proof** *adj. tech.* **1.** feuerfest; **2.** explosi'onsgeschützt; **'~-ˌthrow·er** *s.* ⚔ Flammenwerfer *m*.
flam·ing ['fleɪmɪŋ] *adj.* **1.** lodernd (*a. Farben etc.*), brennend; **2.** *fig.* glühend, leidenschaftlich; **3.** *Brit.* F a) verdammt: ***you ~ idiot!***, b) gewaltig, Mords...: ***a ~ row*** ein ‚Mordskrach'.
flam·ma·ble ['flæməbl] → ***inflammable***.
flan [flæn] *s.* Obst-, Käsekuchen *m*.
flange [flændʒ] ⚙ I *s.* **1.** Flansch *m*; **2.** Rad-, Spurkranz *m*; II *v/t.* **3.** (an)flanschen: ***~d motor*** Flanschmotor *m*; ***~d rim*** umbördelter Rand.
flank [flæŋk] I *s.* **1.** Flanke *f*, Weiche *f* (*der Tiere*); **2.** Seite *f*, Flanke *f* (*e-r Person*); **3.** Seite *f* (*e-s Gebäudes etc.*): ***~ clearance*** ⚙ Flankenspiel *n*; **4.** ⚔ Flanke *f*, Flügel *m* (*beide a. fig.*): ***turn the ~ (of)*** die Flanke (*gen.*) aufrollen; II *v/t.* **5.** flankieren, seitlich stehen von, säumen, um'geben; **6.** ⚔ flankieren, die Flanke (*gen.*) decken *od.* angreifen; **7.** flankieren, (seitwärts) um'gehen; III *v/i.* **8.** angrenzen, -stoßen; seitlich liegen; **'flank·ing** [-kɪŋ] *adj.* seitlich; angrenzend; ⚔ Flanken..., Flankierungs...: ***~ fire***; ***~ march*** Flankenmarsch *m*.
flan·nel ['flænl] I *s.* **1.** Fla'nell *m*: ***~-mouthed*** *Am. fig.* (aal)glatt; **2.** *pl.* Fla'nellkleidung *f*, *bsd.* Fla'nellhose *f*; **3.** *pl.* Fla'nellˌunterwäsche *f od.* -ˌunterhose *f*; **4.** *Brit.* Waschlappen *m*; **5.** *Brit.* F ‚Schmus' *m*; II *v/t.* **6.** mit Fla'nell bekleiden; **7.** mit Fla'nell abreiben; III *v/i.* **8.** *Brit.* F ‚Schmus' reden.
flan·nel·et(te) [ˌflænl'et] *s.* 'Baumwollflaˌnell *m*.
flap [flæp] I *s.* **1.** Schlag *m*, Klaps *m*; **2.** Flügelschlag *m*; **3.** (*Verschluß*)Klappe *f* (*Tasche, Briefkasten, Buchumschlag etc.*); **4.** (*Tisch-, Fliegen-,* ✈ *Lande-*) Klappe *f*; Falltür *f*; **5.** Lasche *f* (*Schuh, Karton*); **6.** weiche Krempe; **7.** ⚕ Hautlappen *m*; **8.** F Aufregung *f*: ***be (all) in a ~*** (ganz) aus dem Häuschen sein; ***don't get into a ~!*** reg dich nicht auf!; II *v/t.* **9.** e-n Klaps *od.* Schlag geben (*dat.*); **10.** auf u. ab (*od.* hin u. her) bewegen, mit *den Flügeln etc.* schlagen; III *v/i.* **11.** flattern; **12.** flattern, mit den Flügeln schlagen: ***~ off*** davonflattern; **13.** klatschen, schlagen (***against*** gegen); **14.** F sich aufregen; **15.** *Am.* F ‚quasseln'; **'~ˌdoo·dle** *s.* F Quatsch *m*; **'~-eared** *adj.* schlappohrig; **'~·jack** *s. bsd. Am.* Pfannkuchen *m*.
flap·per ['flæpə] *s.* **1.** Fliegenklappe *f*; **2.** Klappe *f*, her'abhängendes Stück; **3.** *zo.* (breite) Flosse; **4.** *sl.* ‚Flosse' *f* (*Hand*); **5.** *sl. hist.* ‚irre Type' (*Mädchen in den 20er Jahren*).
flare [fleə] I *s.* **1.** (auf)flackerndes Licht; Aufflackern *n*, -leuchten *n*, Lodern *n*; **2.** a) Leuchtfeuer *n*, b) 'Licht-, 'Feuersiˌgnal *n*, c) ⚔ Leuchtkugel *f od.* -bombe *f*; **3.** *fig.* → ***flare-up*** 2; **4.** *Mode*: Schlag *m*: ***with a ~*** ausgestellt (*Rock*), *Hose a.* mit Schlag; II *v/i.* **5.** flackern, lodern, leuchten: ***~ up*** a) aufflammen, -flackern, -lodern (*alle a. fig.*), b) *a.* ***~ out*** *fig.* aufbrausen; **6.** ausgestellt sein (*Rock etc.*); III *v/t.* **7.** flackern lassen; **8.** aufflammen lassen; **9.** mit Licht *od.* Feuer signalisieren; **10.** flattern lassen; **11.** *Mode*: ausstellen (*Rock etc.*), bauschen (→ *a.* 4); **~ pis·tol** *s.* ⚔ 'Leuchtpiˌstole *f*; **ˌ~-'up** [-ər'ʌp] *s.* **1.** Aufflakkern *n*, -lodern *n* (*a. fig.*); **2.** *fig.* a) Aufbrausen *n*, Wutausbruch *m*, b) ‚Krach' *m*, (plötzlicher) Streit.
flash [flæʃ] I *s.* **1.** Aufblitzen *n*, Blitz *m*, Strahl *m*: ***~ of fire*** Feuergarbe *f*; ***~ of hope*** *fig.* Hoffnungsstrahl; ***~ of wit*** Geistesblitz; ***like a ~*** *fig.* wie der Blitz; ***catch a ~ of*** *fig.* e-n Blick erhaschen von; ***give s.o. a ~*** *mot.* j-n anblinken; **2.** Stichflamme *f*: ***a ~ in the pan*** *fig.* a) e-e ‚Eintagsfliege' *f*, b) ein ‚Strohfeuer'; **3.** Augenblick *m*: ***in a ~*** im Nu, blitzartig, -schnell; ***for a ~*** e-n Augenblick lang; **4.** *Radio etc.*: 'Durchsage *f*, Kurzmeldung *f*; **5.** ⚔ *Brit.* (Uni'form-) Abzeichen *n*; **6.** *phot.* F Blitz(licht *n*) *m*; **7.** *bsd. Am.* F Taschenlampe *f*; **8.** *sl.* ‚Flash' *m* (*Drogenwirkung*); II *v/t.* **9.** *a.* ***~ on*** aufleuchten *od.* (auf)blitzen lassen: ***he ~ed a light in my face*** er leuchtete mir (plötzlich) ins Gesicht; ***~ one's lights*** *mot.* die Lichthupe betätigen; ***his eyes ~ed fire*** s-e Augen sprühten Feuer *od.* blitzten; ***~ s.o. a glance*** j-m e-n Blick zuwerfen; **10.** (*mit Licht*) signalisieren; **11.** F *et.* zükken *od.* kurz zeigen (***at s.o.*** j-m): ***~ a badge***; **12.** F zur Schau tragen, protzen mit; **13.** *Nachricht* (*per Funk etc.*) 'durchgeben; III *v/i.* **14.** aufflammen, (auf)blitzen; zucken (*Blitz, Lichtschein*); **15.** blinken; **16.** sich blitzartig bewegen, rasen, flitzen: ***~ by*** vorbeirasen, *fig.* wie im Flug(e) vergehen; ***it ~ed across*** (*od.* ***through***) ***his mind that*** plötzlich schoß es ihm durch den Kopf, daß; ***~ out*** *fig.* aufbrausen; **17.** ***~ back*** zurückblenden (*im Film etc.*) (***to*** auf *acc.*); IV *adj.* **18.** F → ***flashy***; **19.** F a) geschniegelt, ‚aufgedonnert' (*Person*), b) protzig; **20.** F falsch, gefälscht; **21.** *in Zssgn* Schnell...; **'~·back** *s.* **1.** Rückblende *f* (*Film, Roman etc.*); **2.** ⚙ (Flammen)Rückschlag *m*; **~ bomb** *s.* ⚔, *phot.* Blitzlichtbombe *f*; **~ bulb** *s. phot.* Blitzlicht(lampe *f*) *n*; **~ card** *s.* **1.** Illustrati'onstafel *f*; **2.** *sport* Wertungstafel *f*; **~ cube** *s. phot.* Blitzwürfel *m*.
flash·er ['flæʃə] *s.* **1.** *mot.* Lichthupe *f*; **2.** *Brit.* F Exhibitio'nist *m*.
flash| flood *s.* plötzliche Überschwemmung; **~ gun** *s. phot.* Blitzleuchte *f*, Elek'tronenblitzgerät *n*; **~ lamp** → ***flash bulb***; **'~·light** *s.* **1.** ⚓ Leuchtfeuer *n*; **2.** *phot.* Blitzlicht *n*; **3.** *Am.* Taschenlampe *f*; **4.** blinkendes Re'klamelicht; **'~ˌo·ver** *s.* ⚡ 'Überschlag *m*; **~ point** *s. phys.* Flammpunkt *m*; **~ weld·ing** *s.* ⚙ Abschmelzschweißen *n*.
flash·y ['flæʃɪ] *adj.* □ protzig, auffällig, grell, ‚knallig'.
flask [flɑːsk] *s.* **1.** (Taschen-, Reise-, Feld)Flasche *f*; **2.** ⚙ Kolben *m*, Flasche *f*; **3.** ⚙ Formkasten *m*.
flat[1] [flæt] I *s.* **1.** Fläche *f*, Ebene *f*; **2.** flache Seite: ***~ of the hand*** Handfläche *f*; **3.** Flachland *n*, Niederung *f*; **4.** Untiefe *f*, Flach *n*; **5.** ♪ B *n*; **6.** *thea.* Ku'lisse *f*; **7.** *mot.* ‚Plattfuß' *m*, Reifenpanne *f*; **8.** → ***flatcar***; **9.** ***the ~*** *Pferdesport*: die Flachrennen *pl.*; **10.** *pl.* flache Schuhe; II *adj.* **11.** flach, eben; platt (*a. Reifen*); ra'sant (*Flugbahn*): ***~ feet*** Plattfüße; ***the ~ hand*** die flache *od.* offene Hand; ***~ nose*** platte Nase; ***as ~ as a pancake*** F flach wie ein Brett (*Mädchen*); **12.** hingestreckt, flach am Boden liegend: ***knock ~*** umhauen; ***lay ~*** dem Erdboden gleichmachen; **13.** entschieden, glatt: ***a ~ refusal***; ***and that's ~*** und damit basta!; **14.** fade, schal (*Bier etc.*); **15.** *a.* ✝ lustlos, flau; **16.** a) langweilig, fad(e), ‚lahm', b) flach, oberflächlich; **17.** a) einheitlich: ***~ price*** (*od.* ***rate***) Einheitspreis *m*, b) pau'schal: ***~ fee*** Pauschalgebühr *f*; → ***flat price***, ***flat rate***; **18.** *paint.*, *phot.* a) matt, b) kon'trastlos; **19.** klanglos (*Stimme*); **20.** ♪ a) erniedrigt (*Note*), b) mit B-Vorzeichen (*Tonart*); **21.** leer (*Batterie*); III *adv.* **22.** flach: ***fall ~*** a) der Länge nach hinfallen, b) *fig.* F ‚danebengehen' (*mißglücken od. s-e Wirkung verfehlen*), *thea. etc.* ‚durchfallen'; **23.** genau: ***in 10 seconds ~***; ***in nothing ~*** blitzschnell; **24.** eindeutig; **25.** entschieden, kate'gorisch; **26.** ♪ a) um e-n halben Ton niedriger, b) zu tief: ***sing ~***; **27.** ohne Zinsen; **28.** F völlig: ***~ broke*** ‚total pleite'; **29.** ***~ out*** F auf

Hochtouren, ‚volle Pulle' (*fahren, arbeiten etc.*); **30.** ~ ***out*** F ‚to'tal erledigt'.

flat² [flæt] *s. Brit.* (E'tagen)Wohnung *f.*

'flat|-bed trail·er *s. mot.* Tiefladeanhänger *m*; **'~·boat** *s.* ⚓ Prahm *m*; **'~·car** *s.* 🚃 *Am.* Plattformwagen *m*; **~ cost** *s.* ✝ Selbstkosten(preis *m*) *pl.*; **'~·fish** *s.* Plattfisch *m*; **'~·foot** *s.* [*irr.*] **1.** ⚕ Platt-, Senkfuß *m*; **2.** *pl. a.* **~s** *sl.* ‚Bulle' *m* (*Polizist*); **,~-'foot·ed** *adj.* **1.** ⚕ plattfüßig: ***be*** ~ Plattfüße haben; **2.** ⚙ standfest; **3.** F ‚eisern', entschieden; **4.** *Brit.* F linkisch, unbeholfen; **'~-hunt** *v/i.*: ***go ~ing*** *Brit.* auf Wohnungssuche gehen; **'~i·ron** *s.* **1.** Bügeleisen *n*; **2.** ⚙ Flacheisen *n.*

flat·let ['flætlɪt] *s. Brit.* Kleinwohnung *f.*

flat·ly ['flætlɪ] *adv.* kate'gorisch, rundweg.

'flat·mate *s. Brit.* Mitbewohner(in).

flat·ness ['flætnɪs] *s.* **1.** Flachheit *f*; **2.** Plattheit *f*, Eintönigkeit *f*; **3.** Entschiedenheit *f*; **4.** ✝ Flauheit *f.*

'flat|-nosed pli·ers *s. pl.* ⚙ Flachzange *f*; **~ price** *s.* ✝ Pau'schalpreis *m*; **~ race** *s.* Flachrennen *n*; **~ rate** *s.* Einheits-, Pau'schalsatz *m*; **~ sea·son** *s.* 'Flachrennsai,son *f.*

flat·ten ['flætn] **I** *v/t.* **1.** flach *od.* eben *od.* glatt machen, (ein)ebnen, planieren: ~ ***o.s. against s.th.*** sich (platt) an et. drücken; **2.** ⚙ a) abflachen (*a.* ✈), b) ausbeulen, flach hämmern; **3.** dem Erdboden gleichmachen; **4.** F *Gegner* ‚flachlegen', *weitS.* ‚fertigmachen'; **5.** ♪ *Note* um e-n halben Ton erniedrigen; **6.** *paint. Farben* dämpfen, *a.* ⚙ grundieren; **II** *v/i.* **7.** flach *od.* eben werden; **~ out I** *v/t.* **1.** → ***flatten*** 2; **2.** ✈ *das Flugzeug* (*vor der Landung*) aufrichten; **II** *v/i.* **3.** → ***flatten*** 7; **4.** ✈ ausschweben.

flat·ter ['flætə] *v/t.* **1.** *j-m* schmeicheln: ***be ~ed*** sich geschmeichelt fühlen (***at, by*** durch); ~ ***s.o. into doing s.th.*** j-n so lange umschmeicheln, bis er et. tut; **2.** *fig. j-m* schmeicheln (*Bild etc.*): ***the picture ~s him*** das Bild ist geschmeichelt; **3.** *fig. dem Ohr, j-s Eitelkeit etc.* schmeicheln, wohltun; **4.** ~ ***o.s.*** a) sich schmeicheln *od.* einbilden (***that*** daß), b) sich beglückwünschen (***on*** zu); **'flat·ter·er** [-ərə] *s.* Schmeichler(in); **'flat·ter·ing** [-ərɪŋ] *adj.* □ schmeichelhaft: a) schmeichlerisch, b) geschmeichelt (*Bild etc.*); **'flat·ter·y** [-ərɪ] *s.* Schmeiche'lei *f.*

flat·tie ['flætɪ] → ***flatfoot*** 2.

'flat·top *s.* ⚓ *Am.* F Flugzeugträger *m.*

flat·u·lence ['flætjʊləns], **'flat·u·len·cy** [-sɪ] *s.* **1.** ⚕ Blähung(en *pl.*) *f*; **2.** *fig.* a) Hohlheit *f*, b) Schwülstigkeit *f*; **'flat·u·lent** [-nt] *adj.* □ **1.** blähend; **2.** *fig.* a) hohl, b) schwülstig.

'flat·ware *s. Am.* **1.** (Tisch-, Eß)Besteck *n*; **2.** flaches (Eß)Geschirr.

flaunt [flɔ:nt] **I** *v/t.* **1.** zur Schau stellen, protzen mit: ~ ***o.s.*** → 3; **2.** *Am. e-n Befehl etc.* miß'achten; **II** *v/i.* **3.** (her'um)stolzieren, paradieren; **4.** a) stolz wehen, b) prangen.

flau·tist ['flɔ:tɪst] *s.* ♪ Flötenspieler(in).

fla·vo(u)r ['fleɪvə] **I** *s.* **1.** (Wohl)Geschmack *m*, A'roma *n*, *a.* Geschmacksrichtung *f*: ~ ***enhancer*** Aromazusatz *m*; ***~-enhancing*** geschmacksverbessernd; **2.** Würze *f*, A'roma *n*, aro'matischer Geschmackstoff, ('Würz)Es,senz *f*; **3.** *fig.* Beigeschmack *m*, Anflug *m*; **II** *v/t.* **4.** würzen (*a. fig.*), Geschmack geben (*dat.*); **III** *v/i.* **5.** ~ ***of*** schmecken *od.* riechen nach (*a. fig. contp.*); **'fla·vo(u)red** [-əd] *adj.* würzig, schmackhaft; *in Zssgn* mit ... Geschmack; **'fla·vo(u)r·ing** [-vərɪŋ] *s.* → ***flavo(u)r*** 2; **'fla·vo(u)r·less** [-lɪs] *adj.* ohne Geschmack, fad(e), schal.

flaw [flɔ:] **I** *s.* **1.** Fehler *m*: a) Mangel *m*, Makel *m*, b) ⚙, ✝ fehlerhafte Stelle, De'fekt *m* (*a. fig.*), Fabrikati'onsfehler *m*; **2.** Sprung *m*, Riß *m*, Bruch *m*; **3.** Blase *f*, Wolke *f* (*im Edelstein*); **4.** ⚖ a) Formfehler *m*, b) Fehler *m* im Recht; **5.** *fig.* schwacher Punkt, Mangel *m*; **II** *v/t.* **6.** brüchig *od.* rissig machen; **7.** *fig.* Fehler aufzeigen in (*dat.*); **8.** verunstalten; **'flaw·less** [-lɪs] *adj.* □ fehler-, einwandfrei, tadellos; lupenrein (*Edelstein*).

flax [flæks] *s.* ⚘ **1.** Flachs *m*, Lein *m*; **2.** Flachs(faser *f*) *m*; **flax·en** ['flæksən] *adj.* **1.** Flachs...; **2.** flachsartig; **3.** flachsen, flachsfarben: ***~-haired*** flachsblond; **'flax·seed** *s.* ⚘ Leinsamen *m.*

flay [fleɪ] *v/t.* **1.** *Tier* abhäuten, *hunt.* abbalgen: ~ ***s.o. alive*** F a) kein gutes Haar an j-m lassen, b) j-n ‚zur Schnecke' machen; **2.** *et.* schälen; **3.** *j-n* auspeitschen; **4.** F *j-n* ausplündern *od.* ‚ausnehmen'.

flea [fli:] *s. zo.* Floh *m*: ***send s.o. away with a ~ in his ear*** j-m ‚heimleuchten'; **'~-bag** *s. sl.* **1.** a) ‚Flohkiste' *f* (*Bett*), b) Schlafsack *m*; **2.** ‚Schlampe' *f*; **'~·bite** *s.* **1.** Flohbiß *m*; **2.** Baga'telle *f*; **'~-,bit·ten** *adj.* **1.** von Flöhen zerbissen; **2.** rötlich gesprenkelt (*Pferd etc.*); **~ mar·ket** *s.* Flohmarkt *m.*

fleck [flek] **I** *s.* **1.** Licht-, Farbfleck *m*; **2.** a) (Haut)Fleck *m*, b) Sommersprosse *f*; **3.** (*Staub- etc.*)Teilchen *n*: ~ ***of dust***; ~ ***of mud*** Dreckspritzer *m*; ~ ***of snow*** Schneeflocke *f*; **II** *v/t.* **4.** → **'fleck·er** [-kə] *v/t.* sprenkeln.

flec·tion ['flekʃn] *etc. Am.* → ***flexion*** *etc.*

fled [fled] *pret. u. p.p. von* ***flee.***

fledge [fledʒ] **I** *v/t. Pfeil etc.* befiedern, mit Federn versehen; **II** *v/i. orn.* flügge werden: ***~d*** flügge; **'fledg(e)·ling** [-dʒlɪŋ] *s.* **1.** eben flügge gewordener Vogel; **2.** *fig.* Grünschnabel *m*, Anfänger *m.*

flee [fli:] **I** *v/i.* [*irr.*] **1.** fliehen, flüchten (***before, from*** vor *dat.*; ***from*** aus, von): ~ ***from justice*** sich der Strafverfolgung entziehen; **2.** eilen; **3.** ~ ***from*** → 5; **II** *v/t.* [*irr.*] **4.** fliehen aus: ~ ***the country***; **5.** aus dem Weg gehen (*dat.*), meiden.

fleece [fli:s] **I** *s.* **1.** Vlies *n*, Schaffell *n*; **2.** *a.* ~ ***wool*** Schur(wolle) *f*; **3.** *fig.* dikkes Gewebe, Flausch *m*; **4.** (Haar)Pelz *m*; **5.** Schnee- *od.* Wolkendecke *f*; **II** *v/t.* **6.** *fig.* schröpfen (***of*** um), ‚rupfen'; **7.** bedecken; **'flee·cy** [-sɪ] *adj.* wollig, weich: ~ ***cloud*** Schäfchenwolke *f.*

fleet¹ [fli:t] *s.* **1.** (*bsd.* Kriegs)Flotte *f*: ⚓ ***Admiral*** *Am.* Großadmiral *m*; ***merchant*** ~ Handelsflotte; **2.** ✈ Gruppe *f*, Geschwader *n*; **3.** ~ (***of cars***) Wagenpark *m.*

fleet² [fli:t] *adj.* □ **1.** schnell, flink: ~ ***of foot, ~-footed*** schnellfüßig; **2.** *poet.* → ***fleeting.***

fleet·ing ['fli:tɪŋ] *adj.* □ (schnell) da'hineilend, flüchtig, vergänglich: ~ ***time***; ~ ***glimpse*** flüchtiger (An)Blick *od.* Eindruck; **'fleet·ness** [-tnɪs] *s.* **1.** Schnelligkeit *f*; **2.** Flüchtigkeit *f.*

Fleet Street *s.* Fleet Street *f*: a) *das Londoner Presseviertel*, b) *fig. die* (*Londoner*) *Presse.*

Flem·ing ['flemɪŋ] *s.* Flame *m*, Flamin *f*, Flämin *f*; **'Flem·ish** [-mɪʃ] **I** *s.* **1.** ***the*** ~ die Flamen *pl.*; **2.** *ling.* Flämisch *n*; **II** *adj.* **3.** flämisch.

flench [flentʃ], **flense** [flenz] *v/t.* **1.** a) *den Wal* flensen, b) *den Walspeck* abziehen; **2.** *Seehund* häuten.

flesh [fleʃ] **I** *s.* **1.** Fleisch *n*: ***my own ~ and blood*** mein eigen Fleisch u. Blut; ***more than ~ and blood can bear*** einfach unerträglich; ***in ~*** *obs.* korpulent, dick; ***lose ~*** abmagern, abnehmen; ***put on ~*** Fett ansetzen, zunehmen; ***press*** (***the***) ~ *Am.* F Hände schütteln; (***bare***) ~ *iro.* (nacktes) Fleisch, ‚Fleischbeschau' *f*; → ***creep*** 4; **2.** Körper *m*, Leib *m*: ***in the ~*** leibhaftig, (höchst)persönlich, *weitS.* in natura; ***become one ~*** 'ein Leib u. 'eine Seele werden; **3.** a) *sündiges* Fleisch, b) Fleischeslust *f*: ***pleasures of the ~*** Freuden des Fleisches; **4.** Menschheit *f*: ***go the way of all ~*** den Weg allen Fleisches gehen; **5.** (Frucht)Fleisch *n*; **II** *v/t.* **6.** *Jagdhund* Fleisch kosten lassen; **7.** *Tierhaut* ausfleischen; **8.** *mst* ~ ***out*** *fig. Gesetz etc.* ‚mit Fleisch versehen', Sub'stanz verleihen (*dat.*); **'~-,col·o(u)r** *s.* Fleischfarbe *f*; **'~-,col·o(u)red** *adj.* fleischfarben.

flesh·ings ['fleʃɪŋz] *s. pl.* fleischfarbene Strumpfhose *f*; **flesh·ly** ['fleʃlɪ] *adj.* **1.** fleischlich: a) leiblich, b) sinnlich; **2.** irdisch, menschlich.

'flesh|-pot *s.*: ***the ~s of Egypt*** *fig.* die Fleischtöpfe Ägyptens; **~ tights** → ***fleshings***; **~ tints** *s. pl. paint.* Fleischtöne *pl.*; **~ wound** *s.* Fleischwunde *f.*

flesh·y ['fleʃɪ] *adj.* **1.** fleischig (*a. Früchte etc.*), dick; **2.** fleischartig.

fleur-de-lis [,flɜ:də'li:] *pl.* **fleurs-de-lis** [,flɜ:də'li:z] (*Fr.*) *s.* **1.** *her.* Lilie *f*; **2.** *königliches Wappen Frankreichs.*

flew [flu:] *pret. von* ***fly¹.***

flews [flu:z] *s. pl.* Lefzen *pl.*

flex [fleks] **I** *v/t. anat.* beugen, biegen: ~ ***one's knees***; ~ ***one's muscles*** die Muskeln anspannen, s-e Muskeln spielen lassen (*a. fig.*); **II** *s.* ⚡ *bsd. Brit.* (Anschluß-, Verlängerungs)Kabel *n*; **flex·i·bil·i·ty** [,fleksə'bɪlətɪ] *s.* **1.** Biegsamkeit *f*, Elastizi'tät *f*; **2.** *fig.* Flexibili'tät *f*, Wendigkeit *f*, Beweglichkeit *f*; **flex·i·ble** ['fleksəbl] *adj.* □ **1.** fle'xibel: a) biegsam, e'lastisch, b) *fig.* wendig, anpassungsfähig, geschmeidig: ~ ***car*** *mot.* wendiger Wagen; ~ ***drive shaft*** ⚙ Kardanwelle *f*; ~ ***gun*** schwenkbares Geschütz; ~ ***metal tube*** Metallschlauch *m*; ~ ***policy*** flexible Politik; ~ ***working hours*** gleitende Arbeitszeit; **2.** lenkbar, folg-, fügsam; **'flex·ile** [-ksɪl] → ***flexible***; **'flex·ion** [-kʃn] *s.* **1.** *bsd. anat.* Biegen *n*, Beugung *f*; **2.** *ling.* Flexi'on *f*, Beugung *f*; **'flex·ion·al** [-kʃənl] *adj. ling.* flektiert, Flexions..., Beugungs...; **'flex·or** [-ksə] *s. anat.* Beuger *m*, Beugemuskel *m*; **'Flex·time** (*Warenzeichen*) *s.* ✝ gleitende Arbeitszeit.

flib·ber·ti·gib·bet [,flɪbətɪ'dʒɪbɪt] *s.* a)

Klatschbase *f*, b) ‚verrückte Nudel'.

flick¹ [flɪk] **I** *s.* **1.** leichter, schneller Schlag, Klaps *m*; **2.** a) Schnipser *m*, (Finger)Schnalzen *n*, b) (Peitschen-) Schnalzen *n*, (-)Knall *m*: ***a ~ of the wrist*** schnelle Drehung des Handgelenks; **II** *v/t.* **3.** schnippen, schnipsen; e-n Klaps geben (*dat.*); *Schalter* an- *od.* ausknipsen; *Messer* (auf)schnappen lassen; **III** *v/i.* **4.** schnellen; **5.** ***~ through*** *Buch etc.* ˈdurchblättern.

flick² [flɪk] *s.* F a) Film *m*, b) *pl.* ‚Kintopp' *m*, Kino *n*.

flick·er [ˈflɪkə] **I** *s.* **1.** Flackern *n*: ***a ~ of hope*** ein Hoffnungsfunke; **2.** Zucken *n*; **3.** *TV* Flimmern *n*; **4.** Flattern *n*; **II** *v/i.* **5.** *a. fig.* (auf)flackern; **6.** zucken; **7.** *TV* flimmern; **8.** huschen (***over*** über *acc.*) (*Augen*).

flick knife *s.* [*irr.*] *Brit.* Schnappmesser *n*.

fli·er [ˈflaɪə] *s.* **1.** etwas, das fliegt (*Vogel, Insekt, etc.*); **2.** ✈ Flieger *m*: a) Piˈlot *m*, b) ‚Vogel' *m* (*Flugzeug*); **3.** Flieger *m* (*Trapezkünstler*); **4.** *Am.* a) Exˈpreß(zug) *m*, b) Schnell(auto)bus *m*; **5.** ⚙ Schwungrad *n*; **6.** ***take a ~*** F a) e-n Riesensatz machen, b) *Am.* sich auf e-e gewagte Sache einlassen; **7.** *Am.* Flugblatt *n*, Reˈklamezettel *m*; **8.** F *für* ***flying start.***

flight¹ [flaɪt] *s.* Flucht *f*: ***put to ~*** in die Flucht schlagen; ***take*** (***to***) ***~*** die Flucht ergreifen; ***~ of capital*** ⚚ Kapitalflucht; ***~ capital*** Fluchtkapital *n*.

flight² [flaɪt] *s.* **1.** Flug *m*, Fliegen *n*: ***in ~*** im Flug; **2.** ✈ a) Flug *m*, b) Flug(strecke *f*) *m*; **3.** Schwarm *m* (*Vögel od. Insekten*), Flug *m*, Schar *f* (*Vögel*): ***in the first ~*** *fig.* an der Spitze; **4.** ✈, ⚔ a) Schwarm *m* (*4 Flugzeuge*), b) Kette *f* (*3 Flugzeuge*); **5.** (*Geschoß-, Pfeil- etc.*) Hagel *m*; **6.** (*Gedanken- etc.*)Flug *m*, Schwung *m*; **7.** ***~ of stairs*** (*od.* ***steps***) Treppe *f*; **~ at·tend·ant** *s.* Flugbegleiter(in); **~ deck** *s.* **1.** ⚓ Flugdeck *n*; **2.** ✈ Cockpit *n*; **~ en·gi·neer** *s.* ˈBordingenieur *m*; **ˈ~-ˌfeath·er** *s. orn.* Schwungfeder *f*.

flight·i·ness [ˈflaɪtɪnɪs] *s.* **1.** Flatterhaftigkeit *f*; **2.** Leichtsinn *m*.

flight| in·struc·tor *s.* ✈ Fluglehrer *m*; **~ lane** *s.* ✈ Flugschneise *f*; **~ lieu·ten·ant** *s. Brit.* (Flieger)Hauptmann *m*; **~ me·chan·ic** *s.* ˈBordmeˌchaniker *m*; **~ path** *s.* **1.** ✈ Flugroute *f*; **2.** *Ballistik*: Flugbahn *f*; **~ re·cord·er** *s.* ✈ Flugschreiber *m*; **ˈ~-test** *v/t.* im Flug erproben: ***~ed*** flugerprobt; **~ tick·et** *s.* Flugticket *n*; **ˈ~-ˌworth·y** *adj.* flugtauglich (*Person*); fluggeeignet (*Maschine*).

flight·y [ˈflaɪtɪ] *adj.* □ **1.** flatterhaft, launisch, fahrig; **2.** leichtsinnig.

flim·flam [ˈflɪmflæm] **I** *s.* **1.** Quatsch *m*; **2.** ‚fauler Zauber', Trick(s *pl.*) *m*; **II** *v/t.* *j-n* ‚reinlegen'.

flim·si·ness [ˈflɪmzɪnɪs] *s.* **1.** Dünnheit *f*; **2.** *fig.* Fadenscheinigkeit *f*; **3.** Dürftigkeit *f*; **flim·sy** [ˈflɪmzɪ] **I** *adj.* □ **1.** (hauch)dünn, zart, leicht, schwach; **2.** *fig.* dürftig, ˈdurchsichtig, schwach, fadenscheinig: ***a ~ excuse***; **II** *s.* **3.** a) ˈDurchschlag-, ˈKohlepaˌpier *n*, b) ˈDurchschlag *m*; **4.** *pl.* F ‚Reizwäsche' *f*.

flinch¹ [flɪntʃ] *v/i.* **1.** zuˈrückschrecken (***from, at*** vor *dat.*); **2.** (zuˈrück)zucken, zs.-fahren (*vor Schmerz etc.*): ***without ~ing*** ohne mit der Wimper zu zucken.

flinch² [flɪntʃ] → ***flench.***

fling [flɪŋ] **I** *s.* **1.** Wurf *m*: (***at***) ***full ~*** mit voller Wucht; **2.** Ausschlagen *n* (*des Pferdes*); **3.** *fig.* F Versuch *m*: ***have a ~ at s.th.*** es mit et. probieren; ***have a ~ at s.o.*** über j-n herfallen, gegen j-n sticheln; **4.** ***have one's*** (*od.* ***a***) ***~*** sich austoben; **5.** *ein schottischer Tanz*; **II** *v/t.* [*irr.*] **6.** schleudern, werfen: ***~ open*** *Tür* aufreißen; ***~ s.th. in s.o.'s teeth*** *fig.* j-m et. ins Gesicht schleudern; ***~ o.s. at s.o.*** a) sich auf j-n stürzen, b) *fig.* sich j-m an den Hals werfen; ***~ o.s. into s.th.*** *fig.* sich in *od.* auf e-e Sache stürzen; **III** *v/i.* [*irr.*] **7.** eilen, stürzen (***out of the room*** aus dem Zimmer); **8.** ***~ out*** (***at***) ausschlagen (nach) (*Pferd*); *Zssgn mit adv.*:

fling| a·way *v/t.* **1.** wegwerfen; **2.** *fig.* *Zeit, Geld* vergeuden, verschwenden (***on*** für *et.*, an *j-n*); **~ back** *v/t.* *Kopf* zuˈrückwerfen; **~ down** *v/t.* zu Boden werfen; **~ off I** *v/t.* **1.** *Kleider, a. Joch, Skrupel* abwerfen; **2.** *Verfolger* abschütteln; **3.** *Gedicht etc.* ‚hinhauen'; **4.** *Bemerkung* fallenlassen; **II** *v/i.* **5.** daˈvonstürzen; **~ on** *v/t.* (sich) *Kleider* ˈüberwerfen; **~ out I** *v/t.* **1.** *j-n* hinˈauswerfen; **2.** *et.* wegwerfen; **3.** *Worte* herˈvorstoßen; **4.** *Arme* (plötzlich) ausstrecken; **II** *v/i.* **5.** → ***fling*** 7, 8.

flint [flɪnt] *s.* **1.** *min.* Flint *m*, Feuerstein *m* (*a. des Feuerzeugs*); **2.** → **~ glass** *s.* ⚙ Flintglas *n*; **ˈ~·lock** *s.* ⚔ *hist.* Steinschloß(gewehr) *n*.

flint·y [ˈflɪntɪ] *adj.* □ **1.** aus Feuerstein; **2.** kieselhart; **3.** *fig.* hart(herzig).

flip¹ [flɪp] **I** *v/t.* **1.** schnipsen, schnellen: ***~ off*** wegschnipsen; ***~*** (***over***) *Buchseiten, Schallplatte etc.* wenden, *a. Spion* ˈumdrehen; ***~ a coin*** e-e Münze hochwerfen (*zum Losen*); **2.** ***~ one's lid*** (*od.* ***top***) → 5; **II** *v/i.* **3.** schnipsen; **4.** ***~ through*** *Buch etc.* ˈdurchblättern; **5.** *a.* ***~ out*** *sl.* ‚ausflippen', ‚durchdrehen'; **III** *s.* **6.** Schnipser *m*; **7.** *sport* Salto *m*; **8.** ✈ *Brit.* F kurzer Rundflug; **IV** *adj.* **9.** F a) → ***flippant***, b) gut aufgelegt.

flip² [flɪp] *s.* Flip *m* (*alkoholisches Mischgetränk mit Ei*).

flip-flap [ˈflɪpflæp] → **ˈflip-flop** [-flɒp] *s.* **1.** Klappern *n*; **2.** *sport* Flic(k)flac(k) *m*, ˈHandstandˌüberschlag *m*; **3.** *a.* ***~ circuit*** ⚡ Flipflopschaltung *f*; **4.** ˈZehensanˌdale *f*; **II** *v/i.* **5.** klappern; **6.** *sport* e-n Flic(k)flac(k) machen.

flip·pan·cy [ˈflɪpənsɪ] *s.* **1.** ‚Schnoddrigkeit' *f*, vorlaute Art; **2.** Leichtfertigkeit *f*, Frivoliˈtät *f*; **ˈflip·pant** [-nt] *adj.* □ **1.** ‚schnodd(e)rig', vorlaut, frech; **2.** friˈvol, leichtfertig.

flip·per [ˈflɪpə] *s.* **1.** *zo.* (Schwimm)Flosse *f*; **2.** *sport* Schwimmflosse *f*; **3.** *sl.* ‚Flosse' *f* (*Hand*).

flirt [flɜːt] **I** *v/t.* **1.** schnipsen; **2.** wedeln mit: ***~ a fan***; **II** *v/i.* **3.** herˈumflattern; **4.** flirten (***with*** mit) (*a. fig. pol. etc.*): ***~ with death*** mit dem Leben spielen; **5.** *mit e-r Idee* spielen, liebäugeln; **III** *s.* **6.** a) koˈkette Frau, b) Schäker *m*; **7.** → **flir·ta·tion** [flɜːˈteɪʃn] *s.* **1.** Flirten *n*; **2.** Flirt *m*; **3.** Liebäugeln *n*; **flir·ta·tious** [flɜːˈteɪʃəs] *adj.* (gern) flirtend, koˈkett.

flit [flɪt] **I** *v/i.* **1.** flitzen, huschen, sausen; **2.** (umˈher)flattern; **3.** verfliegen (*Zeit*); **4.** *Brit.* F heimlich ausziehen; **II** *s.* **5.** *a.* ***moonlight ~*** *Brit.* F Auszug *m* bei Nacht u. Nebel.

flitch [flɪtʃ] *s.* **1.** *a.* ***~ of bacon*** gesalzene *od.* geräucherte Speckseite; **2.** Heilbuttschnitte *f*; **3.** Walspeckstück *n*.

fliv·ver [ˈflɪvə] *s. Am. sl.* **1.** kleine ‚Blechkiste' (*Auto, Flugzeug*); **2.** ‚Pleite' *f* (*Mißerfolg*).

float [fləʊt] **I** *v/i.* **1.** (im Wasser) treiben, schwimmen; **2.** ⚓ flott sein *od.* werden; **3.** schweben, treiben, gleiten; **4.** *a.* ⚚ ˈumlaufen, in ˈUmlauf sein; ⚚ gegründet werden; **5.** (ziellos) herˈumwandern; **6.** *Am.* häufig den Wohnsitz *od.* Arbeitsplatz wechseln; **II** *v/t.* **7.** schwimmen *od.* treiben lassen; *Baumstämme* flößen; **8.** ⚓ flottmachen; **9.** schwemmen, tragen (*Wasser*) (*a. fig.*); **10.** überˈschwemmen (*a. fig.*); **11.** *fig.* *Verhandlungen etc.* in Gang bringen, lancieren; *Gerücht etc.* in ˈUmlauf setzen; **12.** ⚚ a) *Gesellschaft* gründen, b) *Anleihe* auflegen, c) *Wertpapiere* in ˈUmlauf bringen; **13.** ⚚ floaten, den Wechselkurs (*gen.*) freigeben; **III** *s.* **14.** Floß *n*; **15.** schwimmende Landebrükke; **16.** *Angeln*: (Kork)Schwimmer *m*; **17.** *ichth.* Schwimmblase *f*; **18.** ⚙, ✈ Schwimmer *m*; **19.** *a.* ***~ board*** (Rad-)Schaufel *f*; **20.** a) niedriger Plattformwagen (*für Güter*), b) Festwagen *m* (*bei Umzügen etc.*); **21.** ⚙ a) Raspel *f*, b) Pflasterkelle *f*; **22.** *pl. thea.* Rampenlicht *n*; **23.** *Brit.* Notgroschen *m*; **ˈfloat·a·ble** [-təbl] *adj.* **1.** schwimmfähig; **2.** flößbar (*Fluß*); **ˈfloat·age, float·a·tion** → ***flotage, flotation.***

float bridge *s.* Floßbrücke *f*.

float·er [ˈfləʊtə] *s.* **1.** ⚚ Gründer *m e-r Firma*; **2.** ⚚ *Brit.* erstklassiges ˈWertpaˌpier; **3.** *Am.* F ‚Zugvogel' *m* (*j-d, der ständig Wohnsitz od. Arbeitsplatz wechselt*); **4.** Springer *m* (*im Betrieb*); **5.** *pol.* a) Wechselwähler *m*, b) *Wähler, der s-e Stimme illegal in mehreren Wahlbezirken abgibt*; **6.** *Am. sl.* Wasserleiche *f*.

float·ing [ˈfləʊtɪŋ] **I** *adj.* □ **1.** schwimmend, treibend, Schwimm…, Treib…; **2.** schwebend (*a. fig.*); **3.** lose, beweglich; **4.** schwankend; **5.** ohne festen Wohnsitz, wandernd; **6.** ⚚ a) ˈumlaufend (*Geld etc.*), b) schwebend (*Schuld*), c) flüssig (*Kapital*), d) fleˈxibel (*Wechselkurs*), e) frei konvertierbar (*Währung*); **II** *s.* **7.** ⚚ Floating *n*, Freigabe *f* des Wechselkurses; **~ an·chor** *s.* ⚓ Treibanker *m*; **~ as·sets** *s. pl.* ⚚ flüssige Akˈtiva *pl.*; **~ ax·le** *s.* ⚙ Schwingachse *f*; **~ bridge** *s.* Tonnen-, Floßbrücke *f*; **~ cap·i·tal** *s.* ⚚ ˈUmlaufvermögen *n*; **~ crane** *s.* ⚙ Schwimmkran *m*; **~ dec·i·mal point** → ***floating point***; **~ dock** *s.* ⚓ Schwimmdock *n*; **~ ice** *s.* Treibeis *n*; **~ kid·ney** *s.* ⚕ Wanderniere *f*; **~ light** *s.* ⚓ Leuchtboje *f od.* -schiff *n*; **~ mine** *s.* ⚔ Treibmine *f*; **~ point** *s. Computer etc.*: Fließkomma *n*; **~ pol·i·cy** *s.* ⚚ Pauˈschalpoˌlice *f*; **~ rib** *s. anat.* falsche Rippe; **~ trade** *s.* ⚚ Seefrachthandel *m*; **~ vote** (*od.* **vot·ers** *pl.*) *s. pol.* Wechselwähler *pl.*

ˈfloat|·plane *s.* ✈ Schwimmerflugzeug *n*; **~ switch** *s.* ⚡ Schwimmerschalter *m*; **~ valve** *s.* ⚙ ˈSchwimmervenˌtil *n*.

floc·cose [ˈflɒkəʊs], **ˈfloc·cu·lent** [-kjʊlənt] *adj.* flockig, wollig; **ˈfloc·cus** [-kəs] *pl.* **-ci** [-ksaɪ] *s.* **1.** Flocke *f*; **2.**

Büschel *n*; **3.** *orn.* Flaum *m*.

flock¹ [flɒk] **I** *s.* **1.** Herde *f* (*bsd. Schafe*); **2.** Schwarm *m*, *hunt.* Flug *m* (*Vögel*); **3.** Menge *f*, Schar *f* (*Personen*): ***come in ~s*** (in Scharen) herbeiströmen; **4.** *eccl.* Herde *f*, Gemeinde *f*; **II** *v/i.* **5.** *fig.* strömen: ***~ to a place*** zu e-m Ort (hin)strömen; ***~ to s.o.*** j-m zuströmen, in Scharen zu j-m kommen; ***~ together*** zs.-strömen.

flock² [flɒk] *s.* **1.** (Woll)Flocke *f*; **2.** *sg. od. pl.* a) Wollabfall *m*, b) Wollpulver *n* (*für Tapeten etc.*): ***~ (wall)paper*** Velourstapete *f*.

floe [fləʊ] *s.* Treibeis *n*, Eisscholle *f*.

flog [flɒg] *v/t.* **1.** prügeln, schlagen: ***~ a dead horse*** a) s-e Zeit verschwenden, b) offene Türen einrennen; ***~ s.th. to death*** *fig.* et. zu Tode reiten; **2.** auspeitschen; **3.** ***~ s.th. into s.o.*** j-m et. einbleuen; ***~ s.th. out of s.o.*** j-m et. austreiben; **4.** *Brit.* F *et.* ‚verscheuern', ‚verkloppen'; **'flog·ging** [-gɪŋ] *s.* **1.** Tracht *f* Prügel; **2.** Prügelstrafe *f*.

flood [flʌd] **I** *s.* **1.** Flut *f* (*a. Ggs. Ebbe*): ***on the ~*** mit der (*od.* bei) Flut; **2.** Über'schwemmung *f* (*a. fig.*), Hochwasser *n*: ***the* ♀ *bibl.*** die Sintflut; **3.** *fig.* Flut *f*, Strom *m*, Schwall *m* (*von Briefen, Worten etc.*): ***a ~ of tears*** ein Tränenstrom; **II** *v/t.* **4.** über'schwemmen, -'fluten (*a. fig.*): ***~ the market*** ✝ den Markt überschwemmen; **5.** unter Wasser setzen; **6.** ⚓ fluten; **7.** *mot. den Motor* ‚absaufen' lassen; **8.** *Fluß* anschwellen lassen; **9.** *fig.* strömen in (*acc.*), sich ergießen über (*acc.*); **III** *v/i.* **10.** *a. fig.* fluten, strömen, sich ergießen: ***~ in*** hereinströmen; **11.** a) anschwellen (*Fluß*), b) über die Ufer treten; **12.** 'überlaufen (*Bad etc.*); **13.** über'schwemmt werden; **~ con·trol** *s.* Hochwasserschutz *m*; **~ dis·as·ter** *s.* 'Hochwasserkata͵strophe *f*; **'~·gate** *s.* Schleusentor *n*, *fig.* Schleuse *f*: ***open the ~s to*** *fig.* Tür u. Tor öffnen (*dat.*).

flood·ing ['flʌdɪŋ] *s.* **1.** Über'schwemmung *f*; **2.** ⚕ Gebärmutterblutung *f*.

'flood|·light I *s.* **1.** Scheinwerfer-, Flutlicht *n*; **2.** *a.* ***~ projector*** Scheinwerfer *m*: ***under ~s*** bei Flutlicht; **II** *v/t.* [*irr.* → ***light¹***] (mit Scheinwerfern) beleuchten *od.* anstrahlen: ***floodlit*** in Flutlicht getaucht; ***floodlit match*** *sport* Flutlichtspiel *n*; **'~·mark** *s.* Hochwasserstandszeichen *n*; **'~-tide** *s.* Flut(zeit) *f*.

floor [flɔː] **I** *s.* **1.** (Fuß)Boden *m*: ***mop*** (*od.* ***wipe***) ***the ~ with s.o.*** j-n ‚fertigmachen', mit j-m ‚Schlitten fahren'; **2.** Tanzfläche *f*: ***take the ~*** auf die Tanzfläche gehen (→ 3); **3.** *parl.* Sitzungs-, Ple'narsaal *m*: ***cross the ~*** zur Gegenpartei übergehen; ***admit to the ~*** *j-m* das Wort erteilen; ***get*** (***have*** *od.* ***hold***) ***the ~*** das Wort erhalten (haben); ***take the ~*** das Wort ergreifen (→ 2); **4.** ✝ Börsensaal *m*; **5.** Stock(werk *n*) *m*, Geschoß *n*; → ***first floor*** *etc.*; **6.** (Meeres- *etc.*)Boden *m*, Grund *m*, (*Fluß-, Tal- etc.*, ⚒ *Strecken*)Sohle *f*; **7.** Minimum *n*: ***price ~***; ***cost ~*** Mindestkosten *pl.*; **II** *v/t.* **8.** e-n (Fuß)Boden legen in (*dat.*); **9.** zu Boden strecken, niederschlagen; **10.** F a) *j-n* ‚'umhauen': ***~ed*** sprachlos, ‚platt', b) *j-n* ‚schaffen'; **11.** *Am. das Gaspedal etc.* voll 'durchtreten; **'~·cloth** *s.* Scheuertuch *n*; **~ cov·er·ing** *s.* Fußbodenbelag *m*.

floor·er ['flɔːrə] *s.* F **1.** vernichtender Schlag, *fig. a.* ‚Schlag *m* ins Kon'tor'; **2.** ‚harte Nuß', knifflige Frage.

floor ex·er·cis·es *s. pl.* Bodenturnen *n*.

floor·ing ['flɔːrɪŋ] *s.* **1.** (Fuß)Boden *m*; **2.** Bodenbelag *m*.

floor| lamp *s.* Stehlampe *f*; **~ lead·er** *s. pol. Am.* Frakti'onsvorsitzende(r) *m*; **~ man·ag·er** *s.* **1.** ✝ Ab'teilungsleiter *m* (*in e-m Kaufhaus*); **2.** *pol. Am.* Geschäftsführer *m* (*e-r Partei*); **3.** *TV* Aufnahmeleiter *m*; **~ plan** *s.* **1.** Grundriß *m* (*e-s Stockwerks*); **2.** Raumverteilungsplan *m* (*auf e-r Messe etc.*); **~ show** *s.* Varie'tévorstellung *f* (*in e-m Nachtklub etc.*); **~ space** *s.* Bodenfläche *f*; **~ tile** *s.* Fußbodenfliese *f*; **'~͵walk·er** *s.* (aufsichtführender) Ab'teilungsleiter (*in e-m Kaufhaus*).

floo·zie ['fluːzɪ] *s. Am. sl.* ‚Flittchen' *n*.

flop [flɒp] **I** *v/i.* **1.** ('hin)plumpsen; **2.** (***into***) sich (in *e-n Sessel etc.*) plumpsen lassen; **3.** a) zappeln, b) flattern; **4.** F a) *ped.*, *thea. etc.* ‚'durchfallen', b) *allg.* e-e ‚Pleite' sein, ‚da'nebengehen'; **II** *v/t.* **5.** ('hin)plumpsen lassen; **III** *s.* **6.** Plumps *m*; **7.** F a) *thea. etc.* ‚'Durchfall' *m*, ‚Flop' *m*, b) ‚Pleite' *f*, ‚Reinfall' *m*, c) Versager *m*, ‚Niete' *f* (*Person*); **IV** *adv. u. int.* **8.** plumps; **'flop·house** *s. Am. sl.* ‚Penne' *f*, (billige) ‚Absteige'; **'flop·py** [-pɪ] *adj.* □ schlaff, schlotterig: ***~ ears*** Schlappohren; ***~ hat*** Schlapphut *m*; ***~ disk*** *Computer*: Diskette *f*.

flo·ra ['flɔːrə] *pl.* **-ras**, *a.* **-rae** [-riː] *s.* **1.** Flora *f*, (*a.* Abhandlung *f* über e-e) Pflanzenwelt *f*; **2.** *physiol.* (*Darm- etc.*) Flora *f*; **'flo·ral** [-rəl] *adj.* □ Blumen…, Blüten…, *a.* geblümt: ***~ design*** Blumenmuster *n*; ***~ emblem*** Wappenblume *f*.

Flor·en·tine ['flɒrəntaɪn] **I** *adj.* floren'tinisch, Florentiner…; **II** *s.* Floren'tiner(in).

flo·res·cence [flɔː'resns] *s.* ♀ Blüte (-zeit) *f* (*a. fig.*); **flo·ret** ['flɔːrɪt] *s.* Blümchen *n*.

flo·ri·cul·tur·e ['flɔːrɪkʌltʃə] *s.* Blumenzucht *f*.

flor·id ['flɒrɪd] *adj.* □ **1.** rot, gerötet: ***~ complexion***; **2.** blühend (*Gesundheit*); **3.** über'laden: a) blumig (*Stil*), b) 'übermäßig verziert; **4.** ♪ figuriert; **5.** ⚕ stark ausgeprägt (*Krankheit*).

Flo·rid·i·an [flɒ'rɪdɪən] **I** *adj.* Florida…; **II** *s.* Bewohner(in) von Florida.

flor·in ['flɒrɪn] *s.* **1.** *Brit. hist.* Zwei'schillingstück *n*; **2.** *obs.* (*bsd.* niederländischer) Gulden.

flo·rist ['flɒrɪst] *s.* Blumenhändler(in), -züchter(in).

floss¹ [flɒs] *s.* **1.** Ko'kon-, Seidenwolle *f*; **2.** Flo'rettgarn *n*; **3.** *a.* ***~ silk*** Schappe-, Flo'rettseide *f*; **4.** ♀ Seidenbaumwolle *f*; **5.** Flaum *m*, seidige Sub'stanz; **6.** *a.* ***dental ~*** Zahnseide *f*.

floss² [flɒs] *s.* ⚙ **1.** Glasschlacke *f*; **2.** *a.* ***~ hole*** Schlackenloch *n*.

floss·y ['flɒsɪ] *adj.* **1.** flo'rettseiden; **2.** seidig; **3.** *Am. sl.* ‚schick'.

flo·tage ['fləʊtɪdʒ] *s.* **1.** Schwimmen *n*; **2.** Schwimmfähigkeit *f*; **3.** *et.* Schwimmendes *od.* Treibendes, Treibgut *n*.

flo·ta·tion [fləʊ'teɪʃn] *s.* **1.** → ***flotage*** 1; **2.** Schweben *n*; **3.** ✝ a) Gründung *f* (*e-er Gesellschaft*), b) In'umlaufbringung *f* (*von Wertpapieren etc.*), c) Auflegung *f* (*e-r Anleihe*); **4.** ⚙ Flotati'on *f*.

flo·til·la [fləʊ'tɪlə] *s.* ⚓ Flot'tille *f*.

flot·sam ['flɒtsəm], *a.* **~ and jet·sam** *s.* **1.** ⚓ Strand-, Treibgut *n*; **2.** *fig.* Strandgut *n* des Lebens; **3.** *fig.* 'Überbleibsel *pl.*, Krimskrams *m*.

flounce¹ [flaʊns] *v/i.* **1.** erregt stürmen *od.* stürzen; **2.** stolzieren; **3.** sich her'umwerfen, zappeln.

flounce² [flaʊns] **I** *s.* Vo'lant *m*, Besatz *m*; Falbel *f*; **II** *v/t.* mit Vo'lants besetzen.

floun·der¹ ['flaʊndə] *v/i.* **1.** zappeln, strampeln, *fig. a.* sich (ab)quälen; **2.** taumeln, stolpern, um'hertappen; **3.** *fig.* sich verhaspeln, nicht weiterwissen, *a. sport* ins ‚Schwimmen' kommen.

floun·der² ['flaʊndə] *s. ichth.* Flunder *f*.

flour ['flaʊə] **I** *s.* **1.** Mehl *n*; **2.** feines Pulver, Mehl *n*; **II** *v/t.* **3.** *Am.* (zu Mehl) mahlen; **4.** mit Mehl bestreuen.

flour·ish ['flʌrɪʃ] **I** *v/i.* **1.** gedeihen, *fig. a.* blühen, florieren; **2.** auf der Höhe s-r Macht *od.* s-s Ruhmes stehen; **3.** wirken, erfolgreich sein (*Künstler etc.*); **4.** prahlen; **5.** sich geschraubt ausdrücken; **6.** sich auffällig benehmen; **7.** Schnörkel *od.* Floskeln machen; **8.** ♪ a) phantasieren, b) e-n Tusch spielen; **II** *v/t.* **9.** schwingen, schwenken; **10.** zur Schau stellen, protzen mit; **11.** (aus)schmücken; **III** *s.* **12.** Schwingen *n*, Schwenken *n*; **13.** Schwung *m*, schwungvolle Gebärde; **14.** Schnörkel *m*; **15.** Floskel *f*; **16.** ♪ a) bravou'röse Pas'sage, b) Tusch *m*: ***~ of trumpets*** Trompetenstoß *m*, Fanfare *f*, *fig.* (großes) Trara; **'flour·ish·ing** [-ʃɪŋ] *adj.* □ blühend, gedeihend, florierend: ***~ trade*** schwunghafter Handel.

flour·y ['flaʊərɪ] *adj.* mehlig.

flout [flaʊt] **I** *v/t.* **1.** verspotten, -höhnen; **2.** *Befehl, Ratschlag etc.* miß'achten, *Angebot etc.* ausschlagen; **II** *v/i.* **3.** spotten (***at*** über *acc.*), höhnen.

flow [fləʊ] **I** *v/i.* **1.** fließen, strömen, fluten, rinnen, laufen (*alle a. fig.*): ***~ freely*** in Strömen fließen (*Sekt etc.*); **2.** *fig.* da'hinfließen, gleiten; **3.** ⚓ steigen (*Flut*); **4.** wallen (*Haar, Kleid etc.*), lose he'rabhängen; **5.** *fig.* (***from***) herrühren (von), entspringen (*dat.*); **6.** *fig.* (***with***) reich sein (an *dat.*), 'überfließen (vor *dat.*), voll sein (von); **II** *v/t.* **7.** über'fluten, -'schwemmen; **III** *s.* **8.** Fließen *n*, Strömen *n* (*beide a. fig.*), Rinnen *n*: ***~ characteristics*** *phys.* Strömungsbild *n*; ***~ chart*** (*od.* ***sheet***) *Computer*, ✝ Flußdiagramm *n*; ***~ pattern*** *phys.* Stromlinienbild *n*; ***~ production***, ***~ system*** ✝ Fließbandfertigung *f*; **9.** Fluß *m*, Strom *m* (*beide a. fig.*): ***~ of traffic*** Verkehrsfluß, -strom; **10.** Zu- *od.* Abfluß *m*; **11.** Wallen *n*; **12.** *fig.* (*Wort- etc.*)Schwall *m*, Erguß *m* (*a. von Gefühlen*); **13.** *physiol.* F Peri'ode *f*.

flow·er ['flaʊə] **I** *s.* **1.** Blume *f*: ***say it with ~s!*** laßt Blumen sprechen!; **2.** ♀ a) Blüte *f*, b) Blütenpflanze *f*, c) Blüte (-zeit) *f* (*a. fig.*): ***be in ~*** in Blüte stehen, blühen; ***in the ~ of his life*** in der Blüte s-r Jahre; **3.** *fig. das* Beste *od.* Feinste, Auslese *f*, E'lite *f*; **4.** *fig.* Blüte *f*, Zierde *f*; **5.** ('Blumen)Orna͵ment *n*, (-)Verzierung *f*: ***~s of speech*** Flos-

keln; **6.** *typ.* Vi'gnette *f*; **7.** *pl.* ⚗ Blumen *pl.*: **~s of sulphur** Schwefelblumen *pl.*, -blüte *f*; **II** *v/i.* **8.** blühen, *fig. a.* in höchster Blüte stehen; **III** *v/t.* **9.** mit Blumen(mustern) verzieren, blüme(l)n; **~ bed** *s.* Blumenbeet *n*; **~ child** *s.* [*irr.*] ‚Blumenkind' *n* (*Hippie*).
flow·ered ['flaʊəd] *adj.* **1.** mit Blumen geschmückt; **2.** geblümt; **3.** *in Zssgn* ...blütig.
flow·er girl *s.* **1.** Blumenmädchen *n*; **2.** *Am.* blumenstreuendes Mädchen (*bei e-r Hochzeit*).
flow·er·ing ['flaʊərɪŋ] **I** *adj.* blühend, Blüten...: **~ plant** Blütenpflanze *f*; **II** *s.* Blüte(zeit) *f*.
flow·er| peop·le *s.* ‚Blumenkinder' *pl.* (*Hippies*); **~ piece** *s. paint.* Blumenstück *n*; **'~·pot** *s.* Blumentopf *m*; **~ show** *s.* Blumenausstellung *f*.
flow·er·y ['flaʊərɪ] *adj.* **1.** blumen-, blütenreich; **2.** geblümt; **3.** *fig.* blumig.
flow·ing ['fləʊɪŋ] *adj.* □ **1.** fließend, strömend; **2.** *fig.* flüssig (*Stil etc.*); **3.** wallend (*Bart, Kleid*); **4.** wehend, flatternd (*Haar etc.*).
'flow,me·ter *s.* ⚙ 'Durchflußmesser *m*.
flown [fləʊn] *p.p. von* **fly**[1].
flu [flu:] *s.* ⚕ F Grippe *f*.
flub [flʌb] *Am. sl.* **I** *s.* (grober) Schnitzer; **II** *v/i.* (e-n groben) Schnitzer machen, patzen.
flub·dub ['flʌbdʌb] *s. Am. sl.* Geschwafel *n*, ‚Quatsch' *m*.
fluc·tu·ate ['flʌktjʊeɪt] *v/i.* schwanken: a) fluktuieren (*a.* ✝), sich (ständig) verändern, b) *fig.* unschlüssig sein; **'fluc·tu·at·ing** [-tɪŋ] *adj.* schwankend: a) fluktuierend, b) unschlüssig; **fluc·tu·a·tion** [ˌflʌktjʊ'eɪʃn] *s.* **1.** Schwankung *f*, Fluktuati'on *f* (*beide a.* ✝, ⚡, *phys.*): **cyclical ~** ✝ Konjunkturschwankung; **2.** *fig.* Schwanken *n*.
flue[1] [flu:] *s.* **1.** ⚙ a) Rauchfang *m*, Esse *f*, b) Abzugsrohr *n*, (Feuerungs)Zug *m*: **~ gas** Rauch-, Abgas *n*, c) Heizröhre *f*, d) Flammrohr *n*, 'Feuerkaˌnal *m*; **2.** ♪ a) *a.* **~ pipe** Lippenpfeife *f*, b) Kernspalt *m der Orgelpfeife*.
flue[2] [flu:] *s.* Flusen *pl.*, Staubflocken *pl.*
flue[3] [flu:] *s.* ⚓ Schleppnetz *n*.
flu·en·cy ['flu:ənsɪ] *s.* Fluß *m* (*der Rede etc.*), Flüssigkeit *f* (*des Stils etc.*); Gewandtheit *f*; **'flu·ent** [-nt] *adj.* □ **1.** fließend, geläufig: **speak ~ German, be ~ in German** fließend deutsch sprechen; **2.** flüssig, ele'gant (*Stil etc.*), gewandt (*Redner etc.*).
fluff [flʌf] **I** *s.* **1.** Staubflocke *f*, Fussel(n *pl.*) *f*; **2.** Flaum *m* (*a. erster Bartwuchs*); **3.** F *sport, thea. etc.* ‚Patzer' *m*; **4.** *Am.* Schaumspeise *f*; **5.** *thea. Am.* F ‚leichte Kost'; **6.** *oft* **bit of ~** F ‚Betthäschen' *n*, ‚Mieze' *f*; **II** *v/t.* **7. ~ out, ~ up** a) *Federn* aufplustern, b) *Kissen etc.* aufschütteln; **8.** F *bsd. thea., sport* ‚verpatzen'; **III** *v/i.* **9.** F *thea., sport* ‚patzen'; **'fluf·fy** [-fɪ] *adj.* **1.** flaumig; **2.** *thea. Am.* F leicht, anspruchslos.
flu·id ['flu:ɪd] **I** *s.* **1.** Flüssigkeit *f*; **II** *adj.* **2.** flüssig; **3.** *fig.* → **fluent**; **4.** *fig.* fließend, veränderlich; **~ coupling, ~ clutch** *s.* ⚙ hy'draulische Kupplung; **~ drive** *s.* ⚙ Flüssigkeitsgetriebe *n*.
flu·id·i·ty [flu:'ɪdətɪ] *s.* **1.** *phys.* a) flüssiger Zustand, Flüssigkeit(sgrad *m*) *f*, b) Gasförmigkeit *f*; **2.** *fig.* Veränderlichkeit *f*; **3.** Flüssigkeit *f des Stils etc.*
flu·id| me·chan·ics *s. pl. sg. konstr. phys.* 'Strömungsmeˌchanik *f*; **~ ounce** *s. Hohlmaß*: a) *Brit.* = *28,4 ccm*, b) *Am.* = *29,6 ccm*; **~ pres·sure** *s.* ⚙, *phys.* hy'draulischer Druck.
fluke[1] [flu:k] *s.* **1.** ⚓ Ankerflügel *m*; **2.** ⚙ Bohrlöffel *m*; **3.** 'Widerhaken *m*; **4.** Schwanzflosse *f* (*des Wals*); **5.** *zo.* Leber-egel *m*.
fluke[2] [flu:k] *s.* **1.** ‚Dusel' *m*, ‚Schwein' *n*: **~ hit** Zufallstreffer *m*; **2.** *Billard*: glücklicher Stoß; **'fluk·(e)y** [-kɪ] *adj. sl.* **1.** Glücks..., Zufalls...; **2.** unsicher.
flume [flu:m] **I** *s.* **1.** Klamm *f*; **2.** künstlicher Wasserlauf, Ka'nal *m*; **II** *v/t.* **3.** durch e-n Kanal flößen.
flum·mer·y ['flʌmərɪ] *s.* **1.** *Küche*: a) (Hafer)Mehl *n*, b) Flammeri *m* (*Süßspeise*); **2.** F a) *fig.* leere Schmeiche'lei, b) ‚Quatsch' *m*.
flum·mox ['flʌməks] *v/t. sl.* verblüffen, aus der Fassung bringen.
flung [flʌŋ] *pret. u. p.p. von* **fling**.
flunk [flʌŋk] *ped. Am. sl.* **I** *v/t.* **1.** ‚'durchrauschen' *od.* ‚'durchrasseln' lassen; **2.** *oft* **~ out** von der Schule ‚werfen'; **3.** ‚'durchrasseln' in (*e-r Prüfung, e-m Fach*); **II** *v/i.* **4.** ‚'durchrasseln', ‚'durchrauschen'; **III** *s.* **5.** 'Durchfallen *n*.
flunk·(e)y ['flʌŋkɪ] *s.* **1.** *oft contp.* La'kai *m*; **2.** *contp.* Kriecher *m*, Speichellecker *m*; **3.** *Am.* Handlanger *m*; **'flunk·(e)y·ism** [-ɪɪzəm] *s.* Speichellecke'rei *f*.
flu·or ['flu:ɔ:] → **fluorspar**.
flu·o·resce [ˌflʊə'res] *v/i.* ⚗, *phys.* fluoreszieren; **ˌflu·o'res·cence** [-sns] *s.* ⚗, *phys.* Fluores'zenz *f*; **ˌflu·o'res·cent** [-snt] *adj.* fluoreszierend: **~ lamp** Leuchtstofflampe *f*; **~ screen** Leuchtschirm *m*; **~ tube** Leucht(stoff)röhre *f*.
flu·or·ic [flu:'ɒrɪk] *adj.* ⚗ Fluor...: **~ acid** Flußsäure *f*; **flu·o·ri·date** ['flʊərɪdeɪt] *v/t. Trinkwasser* fluorieren; **flu·o·ride** ['flʊəraɪd] *s.* ⚗ Fluo'rid *n*; **flu·o·rine** ['flʊəri:n] *s.* ⚗ Fluor *n*; **flu·o·rite** ['flʊəraɪt] *s.* → **fluorspar**; **flu·o·ro·scope** ['flʊərəskəʊp] *s.* ⚕ Fluoro'skop *n*, Röntgenbildschirm *m*; **fluo·ro·scop·ic** [ˌflʊərə'skɒpɪk] *adj.*: **~ screen** → **fluoroscope**; **'flu·or·spar** *s. min.* Flußspat *m*, Fluo'rit *n*.
flur·ry ['flʌrɪ] **I** *s.* **1.** a) Windstoß *m*, b) (Regen-, Schnee)Schauer *m*; **2.** *fig.* Hagel *m*, Wirbel *m von Schlägen etc.*; **3.** *fig.* Aufregung *f*, Unruhe *f*: **in a ~** aufgeregt; **4.** Hast *f*; **5.** ✝ kurze, plötzliche Belebung (*an der Börse*); **II** *v/t.* **6.** beunruhigen.
flush[1] [flʌʃ] **I** *v/i.* (aufgeregt) auffliegen; **II** *v/t. Vögel* aufscheuchen.
flush[2] [flʌʃ] **I** *s.* **1.** a) Erröten *n*, b) Röte *f*; **2.** (Wasser)Schwall *m*, Strom *m*; **3.** a) (Aus)Spülung *f*, b) (Wasser)Spülung *f* (*im WC*); **4.** (Gefühls)Aufwallung *f*, Hochgefühl *n*, Erregung *f*: **~ of anger** Wutanfall *m*; **~ of success** Triumphgefühl *n*; **~ of victory** Siegestaumel *m*; **5.** Glanz *m*, Blüte *f* (*der Jugend etc.*); **6.** ⚕ Wallung *f*, (Fieber)Hitze *f*; → **hot flushes**; **II** *v/t.* **7.** *j-n* erröten lassen; **8.** *a.* **~ out** (aus)spülen: **~ down** hinunterspülen; **~ the toilet** spülen; **9.** unter Wasser setzen; **10.** erregen, erhitzen: **~ed with anger** wutentbrannt; **~ed with joy** außer sich vor Freude; **III** *v/i.* **11.** erröten, rot werden (**with** vor *dat.*); **12.** strömen, schießen (*a. Blut*); **13.** spülen (*WC etc.*).
flush[3] [flʌʃ] **I** *adj.* **1.** eben, auf gleicher Höhe; **2.** ⚙ fluchtgerecht, glatt (anliegend), bündig (abschließend) (**with** mit) (*alle a. adv.*); **3.** a) ⚙ versenkt, Senk...: **~ screw**, b) ⚡ Unterputz...: **~ socket**; **4.** ('über)voll (**with** von); **5.** blühend, frisch; **6. ~** (**with money**) F gut bei Kasse; **~ with one's money** verschwenderisch; **II** *v/t.* **7.** ebnen, bündig machen; **8.** ⚙ *Fugen* ausstreichen.
flush[4] [flʌʃ] *Poker*: Flush *m*; → **royal** 1, **straight flush**.
flus·ter ['flʌstə] **I** *v/t.* durchein'anderbringen, aufregen, ner'vös machen; **II** *v/i.* a) ner'vös werden, durchein'anderkommen, b) sich aufregen; **III** *s.* → **flutter** 8.
flute [flu:t] **I** *s.* **1.** ♪ a) Flöte *f*, b) → **flutist**, c) *a.* **~ stop** 'Flötenreˌgister *n* (*Orgel*); **2.** ⚠, ⚙ Rille *f*, Riefe *f*, Hohlkehle *f*; **3.** ⚙ (Span-)Nut *f*; **4.** Rüsche *f*; **II** *v/i.* **5.** Flöte spielen, flöten (*a. fig.*); **III** *v/t.* **6.** *et.* auf der Flöte spielen, flöten (*a. fig.*); **7.** ⚠, ⚙ riefen, riffeln, auskehlen, kannelieren; *Stoff* kräuseln; **'flut·ed** [-tɪd] *adj.* **1.** flötenartig, sanft; **2.** gerieft, gerillt; **'flut·ing** [-tɪŋ] *s.* **1.** ⚠ Riffelung *f*; **2.** Falten *pl.*, Rüschen *pl.*; **3.** Flöten *n* (*a. fig.*); **'flut·ist** [-tɪst] *s.* Flö'tist(in).
flut·ter ['flʌtə] **I** *v/i.* **1.** flattern (*a.* ⚕ *Herz*), wehen; **2.** a) aufgeregt hin- und herrennen, b) aufgeregt sein; **3.** zittern; **4.** flackern; **II** *v/t.* **5.** schwenken, flattern lassen, wedeln mit, mit *den Flügeln* schlagen, mit *den Augendeckeln* ‚klimpern'; **6.** → **fluster** I; **III** *s.* **7.** Flattern *n* (*a.* ⚕ *Puls etc.*); **8.** Aufregung *f*, Tu'mult *m*: **all in a ~** ganz durcheinander; **9.** *Brit.* F kleine Spekulati'on *od.* Wette; **10.** *Schwimmen*: Kraulbeinschlag *m*.
flu·vi·al ['flu:vjəl] *adj.* fluvi'al, Fluß..., in Flüssen vorkommend.
flux [flʌks] *s.* **1.** Fließen *n*, Fluß *m* (*a.* ⚡, *phys.*); **2.** Ausfluß *m* (*a.* ⚕); **3.** Strom *m* (*a. fig.*), Flut *f* (*a. fig.*): **~ and reflux** Flut u. Ebbe (*a. fig.*); **~ of words** Wortschwall *m*; **4.** ständige Bewegung; Wandel *m*: **in** (**a state of**) **~** im Fluß; **5.** ⚙ Fluß-, Schmelzmittel *n*, Zuschlag *m*; **'flux·ion·al** [-kʃənl] *adj.* **1.** fließend, veränderlich; **2.** ⩲ Fluxions...
fly[1] [flaɪ] **I** *s.* **1.** Fliegen *n*, Flug *m* (*a.* ✈): **on the ~** im Fluge; **2.** *Brit. hist.* Einspänner *m*, Droschke *f*; **3.** a) Knopfleiste *f*, b) Hosenklappe *f*, -schlitz *m*; **4.** Zelttür *f*; **5.** ⚙ → **flywheel**; **6.** Unruh *f* (*Uhr*); **7.** *pl. thea.* Sof'fitten *pl.*; **II** *v/i.* [*irr.*] **8.** fliegen: **~ blind** (*od.* **on instruments**) ✈ blindfliegen; **~ high** (*od.* **at high game**) *fig.* hoch hinauswollen; → **let**[1] *Redew.*; **9.** flattern, wehen; **10.** verfliegen (*Zeit*), zerrinnen (*Geld*); **11.** stieben, fliegen (*Funken etc.*): **~ to pieces** zerspringen, bersten, reißen; **12.** stürmen, stürzen, sausen: **~ to arms** zu den Waffen eilen; **he flew into her arms** er flog in ihre Arme; **send s.o. ~ing** a) j-n fortjagen, b) j-n zu Boden schleudern; **send things ~ing** Sachen umherwerfen; **~ at s.o.** auf j-n losgehen; **I must ~!** F ich muß schleunigst weiter!; → **temper** 3; **13.** (*nur*

pres., inf. u. p.pr.) fliehen; **III** *v/t.* [*irr.*] **14.** fliegen lassen: **~ hawks** *hunt.* mit Falken jagen; → **kite** 1; **15.** ✈ a) *Flugzeug* fliegen, führen, b) *j-n, et.* (hin)fliegen, im Flugzeug befördern, c) *Strecke* fliegen, d) *Ozean etc.* über'fliegen; **16.** *Fahne, Flagge* a) führen, b) hissen, wehen lassen; **17.** *Zaun etc.* im Sprung nehmen; **18.** (*nur pres., inf. u. p.pr.*) a) fliehen aus, b) fliehen vor (*dat.*), meiden; **~ in** ✈ *v/t. u. v/i.* einfliegen; **~ off** *v/i.* **1.** fortfliegen; **2.** fortstürmen; **3.** abspringen (*Knopf*); **~ o·pen** *v/i.* auffliegen (*Tür etc.*); **~ out** *v/i.* **1.** ausfliegen; **2.** hin'ausstürzen; **3.** wütend werden: **~ at s.o.** auf j-n losgehen.

fly² [flaɪ] *s.* **1.** *zo.* Fliege *f*: ***a ~ in the ointment*** ein Haar in der Suppe; ***break a ~ on the wheel*** mit Kanonen nach Spatzen schießen; ***no flies on him*** (*od.* ***it***) F ,den legt man nicht so schnell aufs Kreuz'; ***they died*** (*od.* ***dropped***) ***like flies*** sie starben wie die Fliegen; ***he wouldn't hurt*** (*od.* ***harm***) ***a ~*** er tut keiner Fliege was zuleide; ***I would like to be a ~ on the wall*** da würde ich gern ,Mäuschen spielen'; **2.** *Angeln*: (künstliche) (Angel)Fliege: ***cast a ~*** e-e Angel auswerfen.

fly³ [flaɪ] *adj. sl.* gerissen, raffiniert.

fly·a·ble ['flaɪəbl] *adj.* ✈ **1.** flugtüchtig; **2. ~ *weather*** Flugwetter *n*.

fly| a·gar·ic *s.* ⚘ Fliegenpilz *m*; **'~·a·way** *adj.* **1.** flatternd; **2.** flatterhaft; **3.** *Am.* flugbereit; **'~·blow** *s.* Fliegenei *n*, -dreck *m*; **'~·blown** *adj.* **1.** von Fliegen beschmutzt; **2.** *fig.* besudelt; **'~·by** *s.* **1.** ✈ Vorbeiflug *m*; **2.** *Raumfahrt*: Flyby *n* (*Navigationstechnik*); **'~-by-night** F **I** *s.* **1.** *zo.* Nachtschwärmer *m*; **2.** a) Schuldner, der sich heimlich *od.* bei der Nacht aus dem Staub macht, b) † zweifelhafter Kunde; **II** *adj.* **3.** † zweifelhaft, anrüchig; **'~,catch·er** *s.* **1.** Fliegenfänger *m*; **2.** *orn.* Fliegenschnäpper *m*.

fly·er → ***flier***.

'fly-fish *v/i.* mit (künstlichen) Fliegen angeln.

fly·ing ['flaɪɪŋ] **I** *adj.* **1.** fliegend, Flug…; **2.** flatternd, fliegend, wehend; → ***colour*** 10; **3.** kurz, flüchtig: **~ *visit*** Stippvisite *f*; **4.** *sport* a) fliegend: → ***flying start***, b) mit Anlauf: **~ *jump***; **5.** schnell; **6.** fliehend, flüchtig; **II** *s.* **7.** a) Fliegen *n*, Flug *m*, b) Fliege'rei *f*, Flugwesen *n*; **~ boat** *s.* ✈ Flugboot *n*; **~ bomb** *s.* ⚔ fliegende Bombe, Ra'ketenbombe *f*; **~ bridge** *s.* **1.** Rollfähre *f*; **2.** ⚓ Laufbrücke *f*; **~ but·tress** *s.* ⚠ Strebebogen *m*; **~ cir·cus** *s.* ✈ **1.** ⚔ rotierende 'Staffelformati,on (*im Einsatz*); **2.** Schaufliegergruppe *f*; **~ col·umn** *s.* ⚔ fliegende *od.* schnelle Ko'lonne; **~ ex·hi·bi·tion** *s.* Wanderausstellung *f*; **~ field** *s.* (*kleiner*) Flugplatz; **~ fish** *s.* Fliegender Fisch; **~ fox** *s. zo.* Flughund *m*; **~ lane** *s.* ✈ (Ein-)Flugschneise *f*; ♀ **Of·fi·cer** *s.* ✈ *Brit.* Oberleutnant *m der* ***RAF***; **~ range** *s.* ✈ Akti'onsradius *m*; **~ sau·cer** *s.* fliegende 'Untertasse; **~ school** *s.* Fliegerschule *f*; **~ speed** *s.* Fluggeschwindigkeit *f*; **~ squad** *s. Brit.* 'Überfallkom,mando *n* (*Polizei*); **~ squad·ron** *s.* **1.** ✈ (Flieger)Staffel *f*; **2.** *Am.* a) fliegende Ko'lonne, b) 'Rollkom,mando *n*; **~ start** *s. sport* fliegender Start: ***get off to a ~*** glänzend wegkommen, *a. fig.* e-n glänzenden Start haben; **~ u·nit** *s.* ✈ fliegender Verband; **~ weight** *s.* ✈ Fluggewicht *n*; **~ wing** *s.* Nurflügelflugzeug *n*.

'fly|·leaf *s. typ.* Vorsatz-, Deckblatt *n*; **'~,o·ver** *s.* **1.** → ***fly-past***; **2.** *Brit.* ('Straßen-, 'Eisenbahn)Über,führung *f*; **'~,pa·per** *s.* Fliegenfänger *m*; **'~-past** *s.* ✈ 'Luftpa,rade *f*; **'~-rod** *s.* Angelrute *f* (*für künstliche Fliegen*); **~ sheet** *s.* **1.** Flug-, Re'klameblatt *n*; **2.** ('Zelt),Überdach *n*; **'fly,swat·ter** *s.* Fliegenklappe *f*, -klatsche *f*; **'~·weight** *sport* **I** *s.* Fliegengewicht(ler *m*) *n*; **II** *adj.* Fliegengewichts…; **'~·wheel** *s.* ⚙ Schwungrad *n*.

'f-,num·ber *s. phot.* **1.** Blende *f* (*Einstellung*); **2.** Lichtstärke *f* (*vom Objektiv*).

foal [fəʊl] *zo.* **I** *s.* Fohlen *n*, Füllen *n*: ***in*** (*od.* ***with***) **~** trächtig (*Stute*); **II** *v/t. Fohlen* werfen; **III** *v/i.* fohlen, werfen; **'~·foot** *pl.* **'~·foots** *s.* ⚘ Huflattich *m*.

foam [fəʊm] **I** *s.* Schaum *m*; **II** *v/i.* schäumen (***with rage*** *fig.* vor Wut): ***he ~ed at the mouth*** der Schaum stand ihm vor dem Mund, *fig. a.* er schäumte vor Wut; **III** *v/t.* schäumen: ***~ed concrete*** Schaumbeton *m*; ***~ed plastic*** Schaumstoff *m*; **~ ex·tin·guish·er** *s.* Schaum(feuer)löscher *m*; **~ rub·ber** *s.* Schaumgummi *n*, *m*.

foam·y ['fəʊmɪ] *adj.* schäumend.

fob¹ [fɒb] *s.* **1.** Uhrtasche *f* (*im Hosenbund*); **2.** *a.* **~ *chain*** Chate'laine *f* (*Uhrband, -kette*).

fob² [fɒb] *v/t.* **1. ~ *off s.th. on s.o.*** j-m et. ,andrehen' *od.* ,aufhängen'; **2. ~ *s.o. off*** j-n abspeisen, *j-n* abwimmeln (***with*** mit).

fob³, f.o.b, F.O.B. *abbr. für* ***free on board*** (→ ***free*** 13).

fo·cal ['fəʊkl] *adj.* **1.** ⩚, *phys., opt.* im Brennpunkt stehend (*a. fig.*), fo'kal, Brenn(punkt)…: **~ *distance*, ~ *length*** Brennweite *f*; **~ *plane*** Brennebene *f*; **~ *point*** Brennpunkt *m* (*a. fig.*); **2.** ⚕ fo'kal, Herd…; **'fo·cal·ize** [-kəlaɪz] → ***focus*** 4, 5.

fo'c's'le ['fəʊksl] → ***forecastle***.

fo·cus ['fəʊkəs] *pl.* **-cus·es, -ci** [-saɪ] **I** *s.* **1.** a) ⩚, ⚙, *phys.* Brennpunkt *m*, Fokus *m*, b) *TV* Lichtpunkt *m*, c) *phys.* Brennweite *f*, d) *opt.* Scharfeinstellung *f*: ***in ~*** scharf eingestellt, *fig.* klar und richtig; ***out of ~*** unscharf, verschwommen (*a. fig.*); ***bring into ~*** → 4, 5; **~ *control*** Scharfeinstellung *f* (*Vorrichtung*); **2.** *fig.* Brenn-, Mittelpunkt *m*: ***be the ~ of attention*** im Mittelpunkt des Interesses stehen; ***bring*** (***in***)***to ~*** in den Brennpunkt rücken; **3.** Herd *m* (*e-s Erdbebens, Aufruhrs etc.*), ⚕ *a.* Fokus *m*; **II** *v/t.* **4.** *opt., phot.* fokussieren, (*v/i.* sich) scharf einstellen; **5.** *phys.* (*v/i.* sich) im Brennpunkt vereinigen, (sich) sammeln; **6. ~ *on*** *fig.* (*v/i.* sich) konzentrieren *od.* richten auf (*acc.*).

fo·cus·(s)ing| lens ['fəʊkəsɪŋ] *s.* Sammellinse *f*; **~ scale** *s. phot.* Entfernungsskala *f*; **~ screen** *s. phot.* Mattscheibe *f*.

fod·der ['fɒdə] **I** *s.* (Trocken)Futter *n*; *humor.* ,Futter' *n*; **II** *v/t. Vieh* füttern.

foe [fəʊ] *s.* Feind *m* (*a. fig.*); *a. sport u. fig.* Gegner *m*, 'Widersacher *m* (***to*** *gen.*).

foe·tal ['fiːtl] *adj.* ⚕ fö'tal; **foe·tus** ['fiːtəs] *s.* ⚕ Fötus *m*.

fog [fɒg] **I** *s.* **1.** (dichter) Nebel; **2.** a) Dunst *m*, b) Dunkelheit *f*; **3.** *fig.* a) Nebel *m*, Verschwommenheit *f*, b) Verwirrung *f*: ***in a ~*** (völlig) ratlos; **4.** ⚙ (abgesprühter) Nebel; **5.** *phot.* Schleier *m*; **II** *v/t.* **6.** in Nebel hüllen, einnebeln; **7.** *fig.* verdunkeln, verwirren; **8.** *phot.* verschleiern; **III** *v/i.* **9.** neb(e)lig werden; (sich) beschlagen (*Scheibe etc.*); **'~-bank** *s.* Nebelbank *f*; **'~·bound** *adj.* **1.** in dichten Nebel eingehüllt; **2. *be ~*** ⚓, ✈ wegen Nebels festsitzen.

fo·gey → ***fogy***.

fog·gi·ness ['fɒgɪnɪs] *s.* **1.** Nebligkeit *f*; **2.** Verschwommenheit *f*, Unklarheit *f*; **'fog·gy** [-gɪ] *adj.* □ **1.** neb(e)lig; **2.** trüb, dunstig; **3.** *fig.* a) nebelhaft, verschwommen, unklar, b) benebelt (***with*** vor *dat.*): ***I haven't got the foggiest*** (***idea***) F ,ich habe keinen blassen Schimmer'; **4.** *phot.* verschleiert.

'fog|·horn *s.* Nebelhorn *n*; **'~·light** *s. mot.* Nebelscheinwerfer *m*.

fo·gy ['fəʊgɪ] *s. mst **old ~*** ,alter Knakker'; **'fo·gy·ish** [-ɪɪʃ] *adj.* verknöchert, verkalkt, altmodisch.

foi·ble ['fɔɪbl] *s. fig.* Faible *n*, (kleine) Schwäche *f*.

foil¹ [fɔɪl] *v/t.* **1.** a) vereiteln, durch'kreuzen, zu'nichte machen, b) *j-m* e-n Strich durch die Rechnung machen; **2.** *hunt. Spur* verwischen.

foil² [fɔɪl] **I** *s.* **1.** ⚙ (Me'tall- *od.* Kunststoff)Folie *f*, 'Blattme,tall *n*; **2.** ⚙ (Spiegel)Belag *m*; **3.** Folie *f*, 'Unterlage *f* (*für Edelsteine*); **4.** *fig.* Folie *f*, 'Hintergrund *m*: ***serve as a ~ to*** als Folie dienen (*dat.*); **5.** ⚠ Blattverzierung *f*; **II** *v/t.* **6.** ⚙ mit Me'tallfolie belegen; **7.** ⚠ mit Blätterwerk verzieren.

foil³ [fɔɪl] *s. fenc.* **1.** Flo'rett *n*; **2.** *pl.* Flo'rettfechten *n*.

foils·man ['fɔɪlzmən] *s.* [*irr.*] *fenc.* Flo'rettfechter *m*.

foist [fɔɪst] *v/t.* **1. ~ *s.th. on s.o.*** a) j-m et. ,andrehen', b) j-m et. aufhalsen; **2.** einschmuggeln.

fold¹ [fəʊld] **I** *v/t.* **1.** falten: **~ *cloth*** (***one's hands***); ***~ed mountains*** *geol.* Faltengebirge *n*; **~ *one's arms*** die Arme verschränken; **2.** *oft* **~ *up*** zs.-falten, -legen, -klappen; **3.** *a.* **~ *down*** a) 'umbiegen, kniffen, b) her'unterklappen: **~ *back*** *Bettdecke etc.* zurückschlagen, *Stuhllehne etc.* zurückklappen; **4.** ⚙ falzen; **5.** einhüllen, um'schließen: **~ *in one's arms*** in die Arme schließen; **6.** *Küche*: **~ *in*** *Ei etc.* einrühren, 'unterziehen; **II** *v/i.* **7.** sich falten *od.* zs.-legen *od.* zs.-klappen (lassen); **8.** *mst* **~ *up*** F a) zs.-brechen (*a. fig.*), b) † ,zumachen' (müssen), ,eingehen' (*Firma etc.*): **~ *up with laughter*** sich biegen vor Lachen; **III** *s.* **9.** Falte *f*, Windung *f*; 'Umschlag *m*; **10.** ⚙ Falz *m*, Kniff *m*; **11.** *typ.* Bogen *m*; **12.** *geol.* Bodenfalte *f*.

fold² [fəʊld] **I** *s.* **1.** (Schaf)Hürde *f*, Pferch *m*; **2.** Schafherde; **3.** *eccl.* a) (Schoß *m* der) Kirche, b) Herde *f*, Gemeinde *f*; **4.** *fig.* Schoß *m* der Fa'milie *od.* Par'tei: ***return to the ~***; **II** *v/t.* **5.** *Schafe* einpferchen.

-fold [-fəʊld] *in Zssgn* …fach, …fältig.

ˈfold|·a·way *adj.* zs.-klappbar, Klapp…: **~ *bed***; **ˈ~·boat** *s.* Faltboot *n.*
fold·er [ˈfəʊldə] *s.* **1.** ˈFaltproˌspekt *m*, -blatt *n*, Broˈschüre *f*, Heft *n*; **2.** Aktendeckel *m*, Mappe *f*, Schnellhefter *m*; **3.** ⚙ ˈFalzmaˌschine *f*, -bein *n*; **4.** Falzer *m* (*Person*).
fold·ing [ˈfəʊldɪŋ] *adj.* zs.-legbar, zs.-klappbar, aufklappbar, Falt…, Klapp…; **~ bed** *s.* Klappbett *n*; **~ bi·cy·cle** *s.* Klapp(fahr)rad *n*; **~ boat** *s.* Faltboot *n*; **~ cam·er·a** *s.* ˈKlappˌkamera *f*; **~ car·ton** *s.* Faltschachtel *f*; **~ chair** *s.* Klappstuhl *m*; **~ doors** *s. pl.* Flügeltür *f*; **~ gate** *s.* zweiflügeliges Tor; **~ hat** *s.* Klapphut *m*; **~ lad·der** *s.* Klappleiter *f*; **~ rule** *s.* zs.-legbarer Zollstock; **~ screen** *s.* spanische Wand; **~ ta·ble** *s.* Klapptisch *m*; **~ top** *s. mot.* Rolldach *n*.
fo·li·a·ceous [ˌfəʊlɪˈeɪʃəs] *adj.* blattartig; blätt(e)rig, Blätter…; **fo·li·age** [ˈfəʊlɪɪdʒ] *s.* **1.** Laub(werk) *n*, Blätter *pl.*: **~ *plant*** Blattpflanze *f*; **2.** ⚠ Blattverzierung *f*; **fo·li·aged** [ˈfəʊlɪɪdʒd] *adj.* **1.** *in Zssgn* …blätt(e)rig; **2.** ⚠ mit Blätterwerk verziert.
fo·li·ate [ˈfəʊlɪeɪt] **I** *v/t.* **1.** ⚠ mit Blätterwerk verzieren: **~*d capital*** Blätterkapitell *n*; **2.** ⚙ mit Folie belegen; **II** *v/i.* **3.** ⚘ Blätter treiben; **4.** sich in Blätter spalten; **III** *adj.* [-ɪət] **5.** belaubt; **6.** blattartig; **fo·li·a·tion** [ˌfəʊlɪˈeɪʃn] *s.* **1.** ⚘ Blattbildung *f*, -wuchs *m*, Belaubung *f*; **2.** ⚠ (Verzierung *f* mit) Blätterwerk *n*; **3.** ⚙ Foliierung *f*; Folie *f*; **4.** Paginierung *f* (*Buch*); **5.** *geol.* Schieferung *f*.
fo·li·o [ˈfəʊlɪəʊ] **I** *pl.* **-os** *s.* **1.** (Folio-)Blatt *n*; **2.** ˈFolio(forˌmat) *n*; **3.** *a.* **~ *volume*** Foliˈant *m*; **4.** nur vorderseitig numeriertes Blatt; **5.** Seitenzahl *f* (*Buch*); **6.** ✝ Kontobuchseite; **II** *v/t.* **7.** *Buch etc.* paginieren.
folk [fəʊk] **I** *pl.* **folk, folks** *s.* **1.** *pl.* (*die*) Leute *pl.*: ***poor ~***; **~*s say*** die Leute sagen; **2.** *pl.* (*nur* **~*s***) F *m-e etc.* ‚Leute' *pl.* (*Familie*); **3.** *obs.* Volk *n*, Natiˈon *f*; **4.** F ‚Folk' *m* (*Volksmusik*); **II** *adj.* **5.** Volks…: **~ *dance***.
folk·lore [ˈfəʊklɔː] *s.* Folkˈlore *f*: a) Volkskunde *f*, b) Volkstum *n* (*Bräuche etc.*); **ˈfolkˌlor·ism** [-ˌlɔːrɪzəm] → ***folklore*** a; **ˈfolkˌlor·ist** [-ˌlɔːrɪst] *s.* Folkloˈrist *m*, Volkskundler *m*; **ˌfolk·lorˈis·tic** [-lɔːˈrɪstɪk] *adj.* folkloˈristisch.
folk song *s.* **1.** Volkslied *n*; **2.** Folksong *m* (*bsd. sozialkritisches Lied*).
folk·sy [ˈfəʊksɪ] *adj.* **1.** F gesellig, ˈumgänglich; **2.** volkstümlich, *contp. a.* volkstümelnd.
fol·li·cle [ˈfɒlɪkl] *s.* **1.** ⚘ Fruchtbalg *m*; **2.** *anat.* a) Folˈlikel *n*, Drüsenbalg *m*, b) Haarbalg *m*.
fol·low [ˈfɒləʊ] **I** *s.* **1.** *Billard*: Nachläufer *m*; **II** *v/t.* **2.** *allg.* folgen (*dat.*): a) (*zeitlich u. räumlich*) nachfolgen (*dat.*), sich anschließen (*dat.*): **~ *s.o. close*** j-m auf dem Fuß folgen; ***a dinner ~ed by a dance*** ein Essen mit anschließendem Tanz, b) verfolgen (*acc.*), entlanggehen, -führen (*acc.*) (*Straße*), c) (*zeitlich*) folgen auf (*acc.*), nachfolgen (*dat.*): **~ *one's father as manager*** s-m Vater als Direktor (nach)folgen, d) nachgehen (*dat.*), verfolgen (*acc.*), sich widmen (*dat.*), betreiben (*acc.*), *Beruf* ausüben: **~ *one's pleasure*** s-m Vergnügen nachgehen; **~ *the sea*** (***the law***) Seemann (Jurist) sein, e) befolgen, beachten, *die Mode* mitmachen; sich richten nach (*Sache*): **~ *my advice***, f) *j-m als Führer od. Vorbild* folgen, sich bekennen zu, zustimmen (*dat.*): ***I cannot ~ your view*** Ihren Ansichten kann ich nicht zustimmen, g) folgen können (*dat.*), verstehen (*acc.*): ***do you ~ me?*** können Sie mir folgen?, h) (*mit dem Auge od. geistig*) verfolgen, beobachten (*acc.*): **~ *a tennis match***; **~ *events***; **3.** verfolgen (*acc.*), ⚔ *a.* nachstoßen (*dat.*): **~ *the enemy***; **III** *v/i.* **4.** (*räumlich od. zeitlich*) (nach)folgen, sich anschließen: **~ (*up*)*on*** folgen auf (*acc.*); ***I ~ed after him*** ich folgte ihm nach; ***as ~s*** wie folgt, folgendermaßen; ***letter to ~*** Brief folgt; **5.** *mst impers.* folgen, sich ergeben (***from*** aus): ***it ~s from this*** hieraus folgt; ***it does not ~ that*** dies besagt nicht, daß; ***so what ~s?*** und was folgt daraus?; ***it doesn't ~!*** das ist nicht unbedingt so!
Zssgn mit adv.:
fol·low| a·bout *v/t.* überall(ˈhin) folgen (*dat.*); **~ on** *v/i.* gleich weitermachen *od.* -gehen; **~ out** *v/t. Plan etc.* ˈdurchziehen; **~ through I** *v/t.* → ***follow out***; **II** *v/i. bsd. Golf*: ˈdurchschwingen; **~ up I** *v/t.* **1.** (eifrig *od.* eˈnergisch weiter-)verfolgen, *e-r Sache* nachgehen; *auf e-n Brief, Schlag etc. e-n anderen* folgen lassen, nachstoßen mit; **2.** *fig. e-n Vorteil* ausnutzen; **II** *v/i.* **3.** ⚔ nachstoßen (*a. fig.* ***with*** mit); **4.** ✝ nachfassen.
fol·low·er [ˈfɒləʊə] *s.* **1.** *obs.* Verfolger (-in); **2.** a) Anhänger *m* (*pol.*, *sport etc.*), Jünger *m*, Schüler *m*, b) *pl.* → ***following*** 1; **3.** *hist.* Gefolgsmann *m*; **4.** Begleiter *m*; **5.** *pol.* Mitläufer(in); **ˈfol·low·ing** [-əʊɪŋ] **I** *s.* **1.** a) Gefolge *n*, Anhang *m*, b) Gefolgschaft *f*, Anhänger *pl.*; **2. *the ~*** a) das Folgende, b) die Folgenden *pl.*; **II** *adj.* **3.** folgend; **III** *prp.* **4.** im Anschluß an (*acc.*).
ˌfol·low|-my-ˈlead·er [-əʊmɪ-] *s. Kinderspiel, bei dem jede Aktion des Anführers nachgemacht werden muß*; **ˌ~-ˈthrough** *s.* **1.** *bsd. Golf*: ˈDurchschwung *m*; **2.** *fig.* ˈDurchführung *f*; **ˈ~-up I** *s.* **1.** Weiterverfolgen *n e-r Sache*; **2.** Ausnutzung *f e-s Vorteils*; **3.** ⚔ Nachstoßen *n* (*a. fig.*); **4.** *bsd.* ✝ Nachfassen *n*; **5.** *Radio, TV etc.*: Fortsetzung *f* (***to*** *gen.*); **6.** ⚕ Nachbehandlung *f*; **II** *adj.* **7.** weiter, Nach…: **~ *advertising*** Nachfaßwerbung *f*; **~ *conference*** Nachfolgekonferenz *f*; **~ *file*** Wiedervorlagemappe *f*; **~ *letter*** Nachfaßschreiben *n*; **~ *order*** Anschlußauftrag *m*; **~ *question*** Zusatzfrage *f*.
fol·ly [ˈfɒlɪ] *s.* **1.** Narr-, Torheit *f*, Narreˈtei *f*; **2. *Follies*** *pl.* (*sg. konstr.*) *thea.* Reˈvue *f*.
fo·ment [fəʊˈment] *v/t.* **1.** ⚕ bähen, mit warmen ˈUmschlägen behandeln; **2.** *fig.* anfachen, schüren, aufhetzen (zu); **fo·men·ta·tion** [ˌfəʊmenˈteɪʃn] *s.* **1.** ⚕ Bähung *f*; heißer ˈUmschlag; **2.** *fig.* Aufhetzung *f*, -wiegelung *f*; **foˈment·er** [-tə] *s.* Aufwiegler(in), Schürer(in).
fond [fɒnd] *adj.* □ → ***fondly***; **1.** zärtlich, liebevoll; **2.** töricht, (allzu) kühn, überˈtrieben: **~ *hope***; ***it went beyond my ~est dreams*** es übertraf m-e kühnsten Träume; **3. *be ~ of*** *j-n od et.* lieben, mögen, gern haben: ***be ~ of smoking*** gern rauchen.
fon·dant [ˈfɒndənt] *s.* Fonˈdant *m*.
fon·dle [ˈfɒndl] *v/t.* (liebevoll) streicheln, hätscheln; **ˈfond·ly** [-lɪ] *adv.* **1.** → ***fond*** 1; **2. *I ~ hoped that …*** ich war so töricht zu hoffen, daß …; **ˈfond·ness** [-dnɪs] *s.* **1.** Zärtlichkeit *f*; **2.** Liebe *f*, Zuneigung (***of*** zu); **3.** Vorliebe (***for*** für).
font [fɒnt] *s.* **1.** *eccl.* Taufstein *m*, -becken *n*: **~ *name*** Taufname *m*; **2.** Ölbehälter *m* (*Lampe*); **3.** *poet.* Quelle *f*, Brunnen *m*.
fon·ta·nel(le) [ˌfɒntəˈnel] *s. anat.* Fontaˈnelle *f*.
food [fuːd] *s.* **1.** Essen *n*, Kost *f*, Nahrung *f*, Verpflegung *f*: **~ *and drink*** Essen u. Trinken; **~ *plant*** Nahrungspflanze *f*; **2.** Nahrungs-, Lebensmittel *pl.*: **~ *analyst*** Lebensmittelchemiker(in); **~ *poisoning*** Lebensmittelvergiftung *f*; **3.** Futter *n*; **4.** *fig.* Nahrung *f*, Stoff *m*: **~ *for thought*** Stoff zum Nachdenken; **ˈ~·stuff** → ***food*** 2.
fool¹ [fuːl] **I** *s.* **1.** Narr *m*, Närrin *f*, Dummkopf *m*, ‚Idiˈot(in)': ***he is no ~*** er ist nicht dumm; ***he is nobody's ~*** er läßt sich nichts vormachen; ***he is a ~ for*** F er ist ganz verrückt auf (*acc.*); ***I am a ~ to him*** ich bin ein Waisenknabe gegen ihn; ***make a ~ of*** → 4; ***make a ~ of o.s.*** sich lächerlich machen, sich blamieren; **2.** (Hof)Narr *m*, Hansˈwurst *m*: ***play the ~*** → 8; **II** *adj.* **3.** *Am.* F blöd, ‚doof': ***a ~ question***; **III** *v/t.* **4.** *j-n* zum Narren *od.* zum besten haben; **5.** betrügen (***out of*** um), täuschen; verleiten (***into doing*** zu tun); **6. ~ *away*** *Zeit etc.* vergeuden; **IV** *v/i.* **7.** Spaß machen, spaßen: ***he was only ~ing*** *Am.* er tat ja nur so (als ob); **8. ~ *about***, **~ *around*** herˈumalbern, Unsinn *od.* Faxen machen; **9.** (herˈum)spielen (***with*** mit, an *dat.*).
fool² [fuːl] *s. bsd. Brit. Süßspeise aus Obstpüree u. Sahne.*
fool·er·y [ˈfuːlərɪ] *s.* → ***folly*** 1.
ˈfool|ˌhar·di·ness *s.* Tollkühnheit *f*; **ˈ~ˌhar·dy** *adj.* tollkühn, verwegen.
fool·ing [ˈfuːlɪŋ] *s.* Dummheit(en *pl.*) *f*, Unfug *m*, Spieleˈrei *f*; **ˈfool·ish** [-lɪʃ] *adj.* □ dumm, töricht: a) albern, läppisch, b) unklug; **ˈfool·ish·ness** [-lɪʃnɪs] *s.* Dumm-, Tor-, Albernheit *f*; **ˈfool·proof** *adj.* **1.** kinderleicht, idiˈotensicher; **2.** ⚙ betriebssicher; **3.** todsicher.
fools·cap [ˈfuːlskæp] *s. Schreib- u. Druckpapierformat (34,2×43,1 cm).*
fool's| er·rand [fuːlz] *s.* ‚Metzgergang' *m*; **~ par·a·dise** *s.* Wolkenˈkuckucksheim *n*: ***live in a ~*** sich Illusionen hingeben.
foot [fʊt] **I** *pl.* **feet** [fiːt] *s.* **1.** Fuß *m*: ***on ~*** a) zu Fuß, b) *fig.* im Gange; ***on one's feet*** auf den Beinen (*a. fig.*); ***my ~*** (*od.* ***feet***)***!*** F von wegen!, Quatsch!; ***it is wet under ~*** der Boden ist naß; ***carry*** (*od.* ***sweep***) ***s.o. off his feet*** a) j-n begeistern, b) j-s Herz im Sturm erobern; ***fall on one's feet*** *fig.* immer auf die Füße fallen; ***get on*** (*od.* ***to***) ***one's feet*** aufstehen; ***find one's feet*** a) gehen lernen *od.* können, b) sich ‚finden', sich ‚freischwimmen', c) wissen, was man tun soll *od.* kann, d) festen Boden unter

den Füßen haben; ***have one ~ in the grave*** mit einem Fuß im Grabe stehen; ***put one's ~ down*** a) energisch werden, ein Machtwort sprechen, b) *mot.* Gas geben; ***put one's ~ in it***, *Am. a.* ***put one's ~ in one's mouth*** F ins Fettnäpfchen treten, sich danebenbenehmen; ***put one's best ~ forward*** a) sein Bestes geben, sich mächtig anstrengen, b) sich von der besten Seite zeigen; ***put s.o.*** (*od.* ***s.th.***) ***on his*** (***its***) ***feet*** *fig.* j-n (*od.* et.) wieder auf die Beine bringen; ***put*** *od.* ***set a*** (*od.* ***one's***) ***~ wrong*** et. Falsches tun *od.* sagen; ***set on ~*** *et.* in Gang bringen *od.* in die Wege leiten; ***set ~ on*** *od.* ***in*** betreten; ***tread under ~*** mit Füßen treten (*mst fig.*); → ***cold*** 3; **2.** Fuß *m* (*0,3048 m*): ***3 feet long*** 3 Fuß lang; **3.** *fig.* Fuß *m* (*Berg, Glas, Säule, Seite, Strumpf, Treppe*): ***at the ~ of the page*** unten auf *od.* am Fuß der Seite; **4.** Fußende *n* (*Bett, Tisch etc.*); **5.** ⚔ a) *hist.* Fußvolk *n*: ***500 ~*** 500 Fußsoldaten, b) Infante'rie *f*: ***the 4th ~*** Infanterieregiment Nr. 4; **6.** Versfuß *m*; **7.** Schritt *m*, Tritt *m*: ***a heavy ~***; **8.** *pl.* ***~s*** Bodensatz *m*; **II** *v/t.* **9.** ***~ it*** F a) ‚tippeln', zu Fuß gehen, b) tanzen; **10.** e-n Fuß anstricken an (*acc.*); **11.** bezahlen, begleichen; ***~ the bill***; **12.** *mst* ***~ up*** zs.-zählen, addieren.

foot·age ['fʊtɪdʒ] *s.* **1.** Gesamtlänge *f*, -maß *n* (*in Fuß*); **2.** Filmmeter *pl.*

ˌfoot|-and-'mouth dis·ease *s. vet.* Maul- u. Klauenseuche *f*; **'~·ball** *s. sport* a) Fußball(spiel *n*) *m*: b) *Am.* Football(spiel *n*) *m*: ***~ match*** (***team***) Fußballspiel *n* (-mannschaft *f*); ***~ pools*** *pl.* Fußballtoto *n*; **'~ˌball·er** *s.* Fußballspieler *m*, Fußballer *m*; **'~·bath** *s.* Fußbad *n*; **'~·boy** *s.* **1.** Laufbursche *m*; **2.** Page *m*; **~ brake** *s.* Fußbremse *f*; **'~·bridge** *s.* Fußgängerbrücke *f*, (Lauf-) Steg *m*; **~ can·dle** *s. phys.* Foot-candle *f* (*Lichteinheit*); **~ con·trol** *s.* ⚙ Fußsteuerung *f*, -schaltung *f*; **~ drop** *s.* ⚕ Spitzfuß *m*.

foot·ed ['fʊtɪd] *adj. mst in Zssgn* mit … Füßen, …füßig; **'foot·er** [-tə] *s.* **1.** *in Zssgn* … Fuß groß *od.* lang: ***a six-~*** ein sechs Fuß großer Mensch; **2.** *Brit. sl.* Fußball(spiel *n*) *m*.

'foot|·fall *s.* Schritt *m*, Tritt *m* (*Geräusch*); **~ fault** *s. Tennis*: Fußfehler *m*; **'~·gear** *s.* Schuhwerk *n*; **~ guard** *s.* Fußschutz *m*; **'~·hill** *s.* **1.** Vorberg *m*; **2.** *pl.* Ausläufer *pl.* e-s Gebirges; **'~·hold** *s.* Stand *m*, Raum *m* zum Stehen; *fig.* Halt *m*, Stütze *f*; ('Ausgangs)Basis *f*, (-)Positiˌon *f*: ***gain a ~*** (festen) Fuß fassen.

foot·ing ['fʊtɪŋ] *s.* **1.** → ***foothold***: ***lose*** (*od.* ***miss***) ***one's ~*** ausgleiten, den Halt verlieren; **2.** Aufsetzen *n* der Füße.

foo·tle ['fu:tl] F **I** *v/i.* **1.** *oft* ***~ around*** her'umtrödeln; **2.** a) her'umalbern, b) ‚Stuß' reden; **II** *v/t.* **3.** ***~ away*** *Zeit, Geld etc.* vergeuden, *Chance* vertun; **III** *s.* **4.** ‚Stuß' *m*.

'foot·lights *s. pl. thea.* **1.** Rampenlicht (-er *pl.*) *n*; **2.** Bühne *f* (*a. Schauspielerberuf*).

foo·tling ['fu:tlɪŋ] *adj. sl.* albern, läppisch.

'foot|·loose *adj.* (völlig) ungebunden *od.* frei; **'~·man** [-mən] *s.* [*irr.*] La'kai *m*, Diener *m*; **'~·mark** *s.* Fußspur *f*; **'~·note** *s.* Fußnote *f*; **ˌ~-'op·er·at·ed** *adj.* mit Fußantrieb, Tret…, Fuß…; **'~·pad** *s. obs.* Straßenräuber *m*; **~ pas·sen·ger** *s.* Fußgänger(in); **'~·path** *s.* **1.** (Fuß)Pfad *m*; **2.** Bürgersteig *m*; **'~·pound** *s.* Foot-pound *n* (*Arbeits- u. Energie-Einheit*); **'~-ˌpound·al** [-ˌpaʊndl] *n* Foot-poundal *n* (*1/32 Foot-pound*); **'~·print** *s.* Fußabdruck *m*, *pl. a.* Fußspur(en *pl.*) *f*; **'~·race** *s.* Wettlauf *m*; **'~·rest** *s.* Fußstütze *f*, -raste *f*; **~ rule** *s.* Zollstock *m*; **'~·sore** *adj.* fußkrank; **'~·step** *s.* **1.** Tritt *m*, Schritt *m*; **2.** Fuß(s)tapfe *f*: ***follow in s.o.'s ~s*** in j-s Fußstapfen treten, j-s Beispiel folgen; **'~·stool** *s.* Schemel *m*, Fußbank *f*; **~ switch** *s.* ⚙ Fußschalter *m*; **'~·way** *s.* Fußweg *m*; **'~·wear** → ***footgear***; **'~·work** *s. sport* Beinarbeit *f*.

foo·zle ['fu:zl] *sl.* **I** *v/t.* ‚verpatzen'; **II** *v/i.* ‚patzen', ‚Mist bauen'; **III** *s.* Murks *m*; ‚Patzer' *m*.

fop [fɒp] *s.* Stutzer *m*, Geck *m*, ‚Fatzke' *m*; **'fop·per·y** [-pərɪ] *s.* Affigkeit *f*; **'fop·pish** [-pɪʃ] *adj.* □ geckenhaft, affig.

for [fɔ:; fə] **I** *prp.* **1.** *allg.* für: ***a gift ~ him***; ***it is good ~ you***; ***I am ~ the plan***; ***an eye ~ beauty*** Sinn für das Schöne; ***it was very awkward ~ her*** es war sehr peinlich für sie, es war ihr sehr unangenehm; ***he spoilt their weekend ~ them*** er verdarb ihnen das ganze Wochenende; ***~ and against*** für u. wider; **2.** für, (mit der Absicht) zu, um (…willen): ***apply ~ the post*** sich um die Stellung bewerben; ***die ~ a cause*** für e-e Sache sterben; ***go ~ a walk*** spazierengehen; ***come ~ dinner*** zum Essen kommen; ***what ~?*** wozu?, wofür?; **3.** (*Wunsch, Ziel*) nach, auf (*acc.*): ***a claim ~ s.th.*** ein Anspruch auf e-e Sache; ***the desire ~ s.th.*** der Wunsch *od.* das Verlangen nach et.; ***call ~ s.o.*** nach j-m rufen; ***wait ~ s.th.*** auf etwas warten; ***oh, ~ a car!*** ach, hätte ich doch e-n Wagen!; **4.** a) (*passend od. geeignet*) für, b) (*bestimmt*) für *od.* zu: ***tools ~ cutting*** Werkzeuge zum Schneiden, Schneidewerkzeuge; ***the right man ~ the job*** der richtige Mann für diesen Posten; **5.** (*Mittel*) gegen: ***a remedy ~ influenza***; ***treat s.o. ~ cancer*** j-n gegen *od.* auf Krebs behandeln; ***there is nothing ~ it but to give in*** es bleibt nichts (anderes) übrig, als nachzugeben; **6.** (*als Belohnung*) für: ***a medal ~ bravery***; **7.** (*als Entgelt*) für, gegen, um: ***I sold it ~ £10*** ich verkaufte es für 10 Pfund; **8.** (*im Tausch*) für, gegen: ***I exchanged the knife ~ a pencil***; **9.** (*Betrag, Menge*) über (*acc.*): ***a postal order ~ £20***; **10.** (*Grund*) aus, vor (*dat.*), wegen (*gen. od. dat.*): ***~ this reason*** aus diesem Grund; ***~ fun*** aus *od.* zum Spaß; ***die ~ grief*** aus *od.* vor Gram sterben; ***weep ~ joy*** vor Freude weinen; ***I can't see ~ the fog*** ich kann nichts sehen wegen des Nebels *od.* vor lauter Nebel; **11.** (*als Strafe etc.*) für, wegen: ***punished ~ theft***; **12.** dank, wegen: ***were it not ~ his energy*** wenn er nicht so energisch wäre, dank s-r Energie; **13.** für, in Anbetracht (*gen.*), im Verhältnis zu: ***he is tall ~ his age*** er ist groß für sein Alter; ***it is rather cold ~ July*** es ist ziemlich kalt für Juli; ***~ a foreigner he speaks rather well*** für e-n Ausländer spricht er recht gut; **14.** (*zeitlich*) für, während (*gen.*), auf (*acc.*), für die Dauer von, seit: ***~ a week*** e-e Woche (lang); ***come ~ a week*** komme auf *od.* für e-e Woche; ***~ hours*** stundenlang; ***~ some time past*** seit längerer Zeit; ***the first picture ~ two months*** der erste Film in *od.* seit zwei Monaten; **15.** (*Strecke*) weit, lang: ***run ~ a mile*** e-e Meile (weit) laufen; **16.** nach, auf (*acc.*), in Richtung auf (*acc.*): ***the train ~ London*** der Zug nach London; ***the passengers ~ Rome*** die nach Rom reisenden Passagiere; ***start ~ Paris*** nach Paris abreisen; ***now ~ it! Brit.*** F jetzt (nichts wie) los *od.* drauf!, ran!; **17.** für, an Stelle von (*od. gen.*), (an)'statt: ***he appeared ~ his brother***; **18.** für, in Vertretung *od.* im Auftrage *od.* im Namen von (*od. gen.*): ***act ~ s.o.***; **19.** für, als: ***~ example*** als *od.* zum Beispiel; ***books ~ presents*** Bücher als Geschenk; ***take that ~ an answer*** nimm das als Antwort; **20.** trotz (*gen. od. dat.*): ***~ all that*** trotz alledem; ***~ all his wealth*** trotz s-s ganzen Reichtums, bei allem Reichtum; ***~ all you may say*** sage, was du willst; **21.** was … betrifft: ***as ~ me*** was mich betrifft *od.* an(be)langt; ***as ~ that matter*** was das betrifft; ***~ all I know*** soviel ich weiß; **22.** *nach adj. u. vor inf.*: ***it is too heavy ~ me to lift*** es ist so schwer, daß ich es nicht heben kann; es ist zu schwer für mich; ***he ran too fast ~ me to catch him*** er rannte zu schnell, als daß ich ihn hätte einholen können; ***it is impossible ~ me to come*** es ist mir unmöglich zu kommen, ich kann unmöglich kommen; ***it seemed useless ~ him to continue*** es erschien sinnlos, daß er noch weitermachen sollte; **23.** *mit s. od. pron. u. inf.*: ***it is time ~ you to go home*** es ist Zeit, daß du heimgehst; ***it is ~ you to decide*** die Entscheidung liegt bei Ihnen; ***he called ~ the girl to bring him tea*** er rief nach dem Mädchen, damit es ihm Tee bringe; ***don't wait ~ him to turn up yet*** wartet nicht darauf, daß er noch auftaucht; ***wait ~ the rain to stop!*** warte, bis der Regen aufhört!; ***there is no need ~ anyone to know*** es braucht niemand zu wissen; ***I should be sorry ~ you to think that*** es täte mir leid, wenn du das dächtest; ***he brought some papers ~ me to sign*** er brachte mir einige Papiere zur Unterschrift; **24.** (*ethischer Dativ*): ***that's a wine ~ you*** das ist vielleicht ein Weinchen, das nenne ich e-n Wein; ***that's gratitude ~ you!*** a) das ist (wahre) Dankbarkeit!, b) *iro.* von wegen Dankbarkeit!; **25.** *Am.* nach: ***he was named ~ his father***; **II** *cj.* **26.** a) denn, weil, b) nämlich; **III** *s.* **27.** Für *n*.

for·age ['fɒrɪdʒ] **I** *s.* **1.** (Vieh)Futter *n*; **2.** Nahrungssuche *f*; **3.** ⚔ 'Überfall *m*; **II** *v/i.* **4.** (nach) Nahrung *od.* Futter suchen; **5.** *fig.* her'umstöbern, -kramen (***for*** nach); **6.** ⚔ e-n 'Überfall machen; **III** *v/t.* **7.** mit Nahrung *od.* Futter versorgen; **8.** *obs.* (aus)plündern; **~ cap** *s.* ⚔ Feldmütze *f*.

for·ay ['fɒreɪ] **I** *s.* **1.** a) Beute-, Raubzug

m, b) ⚔ Ein-, ˈÜberfall *m*; **2.** *fig.* ‚Ausflug' *m* (***into*** in *acc.*); **II** *v/i.* **3.** plündern; **4.** einfallen (***into*** in *acc.*).

for·bade [fəˈbæd], *a.* **forˈbad** [-ˈbæd] *pret. von* ***forbid***.

for·bear¹ [ˈfɔːbeə] *s.* Vorfahr *m*.

for·bear² [fɔːˈbeə] **I** *v/t.* [*irr.*] **1.** unterˈlassen, Abstand nehmen von, sich enthalten (*gen.*): ***I cannot ~ laughing*** ich muß (einfach) lachen; **II** *v/i.* [*irr.*] **2.** Abstand nehmen (***from*** von); es unterlassen; **3.** nachsichtig sein (***with*** mit); **forˈbear·ance** [-eərəns] *s.* **1.** Unterˈlassung *f*; **2.** Geduld *f*, Nachsicht *f*; **forˈbear·ing** [-eərɪŋ] *adj.* ☐ nachsichtig, geduldig.

for·bid [fəˈbɪd] **I** *v/t.* [*irr.*] **1.** verbieten, unterˈsagen (*j-m et. od. zu tun*); **2.** unmöglich machen, ausschließen; **II** *v/i.* **3.** ***God ~!*** Gott behüte!; **forˈbid·den** [-dn] *p.p. von* ***forbid*** *u. adj.* verboten: ***~ fruit*** *fig.* verbotene Frucht; ***2 City*** *hist. die* Verbotene Stadt (*in Peking*); **forˈbid·ding** [-dɪŋ] *adj.* ☐ **1.** abschreckend, abstoßend, scheußlich; **2.** bedrohlich, gefährlich; **3.** ‚unmöglich', unerträglich.

for·bore [fɔːˈbɔː] *pret. von* ***forbear²***; **forˈborne** [-ɔːn] *p.p. von* ***forbear²***.

force [fɔːs] **I** *s.* **1.** (*a. fig. geistige, politische etc.*) Kraft (*a. phys.*), Stärke *f* (*a. Charakter*), Wucht *f*: ***join ~s*** a) sich zs.-tun, b) ⚔ s-e Streitkräfte vereinigen; **2.** Gewalt *f*, Macht *f*: ***by ~*** a) gewaltsam, b) zwangsweise; ***by ~ of arms*** mit Waffengewalt; **3.** Zwang *m* (*a.* ⚖), Druck *m*: ***~ of circumstances*** Zwang der Verhältnisse; **4.** Einfluß *m*, Wirkung *f*, Wert *m*; Nachdruck *m*, Überˈzeugungskraft *f*: ***by ~ of*** vermittels; ***~ of habit*** Macht *f* der Gewohnheit; ***lend ~ to*** Nachdruck verleihen (*dat.*); **5.** ⚖ (Rechts)Gültigkeit *f*, (-)Kraft *f*: ***in ~*** in Kraft, geltend; ***come*** (***put***) ***into ~*** in Kraft treten (setzen); **6.** *ling.* Bedeutung *f*, Gehalt *m*; **7.** ⚔ Streit-, Kriegsmacht *f*, Truppe(n *pl.*) *f*, Verband *m*: ***the*** (***armed***) ***~s*** die Streitkräfte; ***labo***(***u***)***r ~*** Arbeitskräfte *pl.*, Belegschaft *f*; ***a strong ~ of police*** ein starkes Polizeiaufgebot; **8.** ***the 2*** *Brit.* die Poliˈzei; **9.** F Menge *f*: ***in ~*** in großer Zahl *od.* Menge; ***the police came out in ~*** die Polizei rückte in voller Stärke aus; **II** *v/t.* **10.** zwingen, nötigen: ***~ s.o.'s hand*** j-n (zum Handeln) zwingen; ***~ one's way*** sich durchzwängen; ***~ s.th. from s.o.*** j-m et. entreißen; **11.** erzwingen, forcieren, ˈdurchsetzen: ***~ a smile*** gezwungen lächeln; **12.** treiben, drängen; *Preise* hochtreiben: ***~ s.th. on s.o.*** j-m et. aufdrängen *od.* -zwingen; **13.** 🌱 treiben, hochzüchten; **14.** forcieren, beschleunigen: ***~ the pace***; **15.** *j-m, a. e-r Frau, a. fig. dem Sinn etc.* Gewalt antun; *Ausdruck* zu Tode hetzen; **16.** *Tür etc.* aufbrechen, (-)sprengen; **17.** ⚔ erstürmen; überˈwältigen; **18.** ***~ down*** a) ✈ zur Landung zwingen, b) *Essen* hinˈunterwürgen.

forced [fɔːst] *adj.* ☐ **1.** erzwungen, forciert, Zwangs...: ***~ lubrication*** → ***force feed***; ***~ labo***(***u***)***r*** Zwangsarbeit *f*; ***~ landing*** ✈ Notlandung *f*; ***~ loan*** † Zwangsanleihe *f*; ***~ march*** ⚔ Eil-, Gewaltmarsch *m*; ***~ sale*** ⚖ Zwangsverkauf *m*, -versteigerung *f*; **2.** forciert, gekünstelt, gezwungen (*Lächeln etc.*); manieriert (*Stil etc.*); **ˈforc·ed·ly** [-sɪdlɪ] *adv.* → ***forced***.

force| feed *s.* ⚙ Druckschmierung *f*; **ˈ~-feed** *v/t.* [*irr.* → ***feed***] *j-n* zwangsernähren; **~ field** *s. phys.* Kräftefeld *n*.

force·ful [ˈfɔːsfʊl] *adj.* ☐ **1.** kräftig, wuchtig (*a. fig.*); **2.** eindringlich, -drucksvoll; zwingend, überˈzeugend (*Argumente etc.*); **ˈforce·ful·ness** [-nɪs] *s.* Eindringlichkeit *f*, Wucht *f*.

ˈforce-land **I** *v/t.* ✈ zur Notlandung zwingen; **II** *v/i.* notlanden.

force ma·jeure [ˌfɔːsmæˈʒɜː] (*Fr.*) *s.* ⚖ höhere Gewalt.

ˈforce-meat *s. Küche*: Farce *f*, (Fleisch-) Füllung *f*.

for·ceps [ˈfɔːseps] *s. sg. u. pl.* ⚕ a) Zange *f*, b) Pinˈzette *f*: ***~ delivery*** ⚕ Zangengeburt *f*.

force pump *s.* ⚙ Druckpumpe *f*.

for·ci·ble [ˈfɔːsəbl] *adj.* ☐ **1.** gewaltsam: ***~ feeding*** Zwangsernährung *f*; **2.** → ***forceful***.

forc·ing| bed [ˈfɔːsɪŋ], **~ frame** *s.* 🌱 Früh-, Mistbeet *n*; **~ house** *s.* Treibhaus *n*.

ford [fɔːd] **I** *s.* Furt *f*; **II** *v/i.* ˈdurchwaten; **III** *v/t.* durchˈwaten; **ˈford·a·ble** [-dəbl] *adj.* seicht.

fore [fɔː] **I** *adj.* vorder, Vorder..., Vor...; früher; **II** *s.* Vorderteil *m*, *n*, -seite *f*, Front *f*: ***to the ~*** a) bei der *od.* zur Hand, zur Stelle, b) am Leben, c) im Vordergrund: ***come to the ~*** a) hervortreten, in den Vordergrund treten, b) sich hervortun; **III** *int. Golf*: Achtung!

ˌfore-and-ˈaft [-ɔːrə-] *adj.* ⚓ längsschiffs: ***~ sail*** Stagsegel *n*.

fore·arm¹ [ˈfɔːrɑːm] *s.* ˈUnterarm *m*.

fore·arm² [fɔːrˈɑːm] *v/t.*: ***~ o.s.*** sich wappnen; → ***forewarn***.

ˈfore|·bear → ***forbear¹***; **~ˈbode** [-ˈbəʊd] *v/t.* **1.** vorˈhersagen, propheˈzeien; **2.** ahnen lassen, deuten auf (*acc.*); **3.** ein böses Omen sein für; **4.** *Schlimmes* ahnen, vorˈaussehen; **~ˈbod·ing** [-ˈbəʊdɪŋ] *s.* **1.** (böses) Vorzeichen *od.* Omen; **2.** (böse) Ahnung; **3.** Propheˈzeiung *f*; **ˈ~·cast** **I** *v/t.* [*irr.* → ***cast***] **1.** vorˈaussagen, vorˈhersehen; **2.** vorˈausberechnen, im vorˈaus schätzen *od.* planen; **3.** *Wetter etc.* vorˈhersagen; **II** *s.* **4.** Vorˈher-, Vorˈaussage *f*: ***weather ~*** Wetterbericht *m*, -vorhersage; **~·cas·tle** [ˈfəʊksl] *s.* ⚓ Back *f*, Vorderdeck *n*; **ˈ~ˌcheck·ing** *s. sport* Forechecking *n*, frühes Stören; **~ˈclose** *v/t.* **1.** ⚖ ausschließen (***of*** von *e-m Rechtsanspruch*); **2.** ***~ a mortgage*** a) e-e Hypothekenforderung geltend machen, b) e-e Hypothek (gerichtlich) für verfallen erklären, c) *Am.* aus e-r Hypothek die Zwangsvollstreckung betreiben; für verfallen erklären; **3.** (ver)hindern; **4.** *Frage etc.* vorˈwegnehmen; **~ˈclo·sure** *s.* ⚖ a) (gerichtliche) Verfallserklärung (*e-r Hypothek*), b) *Am.* Zwangsvollstreckung *f*: ***~ action*** Ausschlußklage *f*; ***~ sale*** *Am.* Zwangsversteigerung *f*; **ˈ~·deck** *s.* ⚓ Vorderdeck *n*; **~ˈdoom** *v/t.*: ***~ed*** (***to failure***) *fig.* von vornherein zum Scheitern verurteilt, totgeboren; **ˈ~ˌfa·ther** *s.* Ahn *m*, Vorfahr *m*; **ˈ~ˌfin·ger** *s.* Zeigefinger *m*; **ˈ~·foot** *s.* [*irr.*] **1.** *zo.* Vorderfuß *m*; **2.** ⚓ Stevenanlauf *m*; **ˈ~·front** *s.* vorderste Reihe (*a. fig.*): ***in the ~ of the battle*** ⚔ in vorderster Linie; ***be in the ~ of s.o.'s mind*** j-n (*geistig*) sehr beschäftigen; **~ˈgath·er** → ***forgather***; **~ˈgo** *v/t. u. v/i.* [*irr.* → ***go***] **1.** vorˈangehen (*dat.*), *zeitlich a.* vorˈhergehen (*dat.*): ***~ing*** vorhergehend, vorerwähnt, vorig; **2.** → ***forgo***; **ˈ~·gone** *adj.*: ***~ conclusion*** ausgemachte Sache, Selbstverständlichkeit *f*; ***his success was a ~ conclusion*** sein Erfolg stand von vornherein fest *od.* war ‚vorprogrammiert'; **ˈ~·ground** *s.* Vordergrund *m* (*a. fig.*); **ˈ~·hand** **I** *s.* **1.** Vorderhand *f* (*Pferd*); **2.** *sport* Vorhand(schlag *m*) *f*; **II** *adj.* **3.** *sport* Vorhand...

fore·head [ˈfɒrɪd] *s.* Stirn *f*.

ˈfore·hold *s.* ⚓ vorderer Laderaum.

for·eign [ˈfɒrən] *adj.* **1.** fremd, ausländisch, auswärtig, Auslands..., Außen...: ***~ affairs*** *pol.* auswärtige Angelegenheiten; ***~ aid*** Auslandshilfe *f*; ***~-born*** im Ausland geboren; ***~ bill*** (***of exchange***) † Auslandswechsel *m*; ***~ control*** Überfremdung *f*; ***~ country***, ***~ countries*** Ausland *n*; ***~ currency*** a) ausländische Währung, b) † Devisen *pl.*; ***~ department*** Auslandsabteilung *f*; ***~ language*** Fremdsprache *f*; ***~-language*** a) fremdsprachig, b) fremdsprachlich, Fremdsprachen...; ***2 Legion*** ⚔ Fremdenlegion *f*; ***~ minister*** *pol.* Außenminister *m*; ***2 Office*** *Brit.* Außenministerium *n*; ***~-owned*** in ausländischem Besitz (befindlich); ***~ policy*** Außenpolitik *f*; ***2 Secretary*** *Brit.* Außenminister *m*; ***~ trade*** † Außenhandel *m*; ***~ word*** a) Fremdwort *n*, b) Lehnwort *n*; ***~ worker*** Gastarbeiter(in); **2.** fremd (***to*** *dat.*): ***~ body*** (*od.* ***matter***) Fremdkörper *m*; ***that is ~ to his nature*** das ist ihm wesensfremd; **3.** ***~ to*** nicht gehörig *od.* passend zu.

for·eign·er [ˈfɒrənə] *s.* **1.** Ausländer (-in); **2.** *et.* Ausländisches (*z. B. Schiff, Produkt etc.*).

fore|ˈjudge *v/t.* im vorˈaus *od.* voreilig entscheiden *od.* beurteilen; **~ˈknow** *v/t.* [*irr.* → ***know***] vorˈherwissen, vorˈaussehen; **ˌ~ˈknowl·edge** *s.* Vorˈherwissen *n*, vorˈherige Kenntnis; **ˈ~ˌla·dy** *Am.* → ***forewoman***; **ˈ~·land** [-lənd] *s.* Vorland *n*, Vorgebirge *n*, Landspitze *f*; **ˈ~·leg** *s.* Vorderbein *n*; **ˈ~·lock** *s.* Stirnlocke *f*, -haar *n*: ***take time by the ~*** die Gelegenheit beim Schopfe fassen; **ˈ~·man** [-mən] *s.* [*irr.*] **1.** Werkmeister *m*, Vorarbeiter *m*, ⚒ Poˈlier *m*; Aufseher *m*; **2.** ⚖ Obmann *m der Geschworenen*; **ˈ~·mast** [-mɑːst; ⚓ -məst] *s.* ⚓ Fockmast *m*; **ˈ~·most** **I** *adj.* vorderst; erst, best, vornehmst; **II** *adv.* zuˈerst: ***first and ~*** zuallererst; ***feet ~*** mit den Füßen voran; **ˈ~·name** *s.* Vorname *m*; **ˈ~·noon** *s.* Vormittag *m*.

fo·ren·sic [fəˈrensɪk] *adj.* (☐ ***~ally***) foˈrensisch, Gerichts...: ***~ medicine***.

ˌfore|·orˈdain [-ɔːrɔː-] *v/t.* vorˈherbestimmen; **ˌ~·or·diˈna·tion** [-ɔːrɔː-] *s. eccl.* Vorˈherbestimmung *f*; **ˈ~·part** *s.* **1.** Vorderteil *m*; **2.** Anfang *m*; **ˈ~·play** *s.* (*sexuelles*) Vorspiel; **ˈ~ˌrun·ner** *s. fig.* **1.** Vorläufer *m*; **2.** Vorbote *m*, Anzeichen *n*; **ˈ~·sail** [-seɪl; ⚓ -sl] *s.* ⚓ Focksegel *n*; **~ˈsee** *v/t.* [*irr.* → ***see¹***] vorˈaussehen *od.* -wissen; **~ˈsee·a·ble** [-ˈsiːəbl] *adj.* vorˈauszusehen(d), absehbar: ***in***

the ~ future in absehbarer Zeit; **~'shad·ow** *v/t.* ahnen lassen, (drohend) ankündigen; **'~·sheet** *s.* ⚓ **1.** Fockschot *f*; **2.** *pl.* Vorderboot *n*; **'~·shore** *s.* Uferland *n*, (Küsten)Vorland *n*; **~'short·en** *v/t. Figuren* in Verkürzung *od.* perspek'tivisch zeichnen; **'~·sight** *s.* **1.** a) Weitblick *m*, b) (weise) Vor'aussicht; → ***hindsight*** 2; **2.** Blick *m* in die Zukunft; **3.** ⚔ (Vi'sier)Korn *n*; **'~·skin** *s. anat.* Vorhaut *f*.

for·est ['fɒrɪst] **I** *s.* Wald *m* (*a. fig. von Masten etc.*), Forst *m*: **~ *fire*** Waldbrand *m*; **II** *v/t.* aufforsten.

fore|'stall *v/t.* **1.** *j-m* zu'vorkommen; **2.** *e-r Sache* vorbeugen, *et.* vereiteln; **3.** *Einwand etc.* vor'wegnehmen; **4.** ✝ (spekula'tiv) aufkaufen; **'~·stay** *s.* ⚓ Fockstag *n*.

for·est·ed ['fɒrɪstɪd] *adj.* bewaldet; **'for·est·er** [-tə] *s.* **1.** Förster *m*; **2.** Waldbewohner *m* (*a. Tier*); **'for·est·ry** [-trɪ] *s.* **1.** Forstwirtschaft *f*, -wesen *n*; **2.** Wälder *pl.*

'fore|·taste *s.* Vorgeschmack *m*; **~'tell** *v/t.* [*irr.* → ***tell***] **1.** vor'her-, vor'aussagen; **2.** andeuten, ahnen lassen; **'~·thought** → ***foresight*** 1; **'~·top** [-tɒp; ⚓ -təp] *s.* ⚓ Fock-, Vormars *m*; **,~·top'gal·lant** *s.* ⚓ Vorbramsegel *n*: **~ *mast*** Vorbramstenge *f*; **'~·top·mast** *s.* ⚓ Fock-, Vormarsstenge *f*; **'~·top·sail** [-seɪl; ⚓ -sl] *s.* ⚓ Vormarssegel *n*.

for ev·er, for·ev·er [fə'revə] *adv.* **1.** *a.* **~ *and ever*** für *od.* auf immer, für alle Zeit; **2.** andauernd, ständig, unaufhörlich; **3.** F ,ewig' (lang); **for ev·er more, for'ev·er·more** *adv.* für immer u. ewig.

fore|'warn *v/t.* vorher warnen (***of*** vor *dat.*): ***~ed is forearmed*** gewarnt sein heißt gewappnet sein; **'~·wom·an** *s.* [*irr.*] **1.** Vorarbeiterin *f*, Aufseherin *f*; **2.** ⚖ Obmännin *f der Geschworenen*; **'~·word** *s.* Vorwort *n*; **'~·yard** *s.* ⚓ Fockrahe *f*.

for·feit ['fɔ:fɪt] **I** *s.* **1.** (Geld-, *a.* Vertrags)Strafe *f*, Buße *f*: ***pay the ~ of one's life*** mit s-m Leben bezahlen; **2.** Verlust *m*, Einbuße *f*; **3.** verwirktes Pfand: ***pay a ~*** ein Pfand geben; **4.** *pl.* Pfänderspiel *n*; **II** *v/t.* **5.** verwirken, verlieren, *fig.* einbüßen, verscherzen; **III** *adj.* **6.** verwirkt, verfallen; **'for·fei·ture** [-tʃə] *s.* Verlust *m*, Verwirkung *f*, Verfallen *n*, Einziehung *f*, Entzug *m*.

for·fend [fɔ:'fend] *v/t.* **1.** *obs.* verhüten: ***God ~!*** Gott behüte!; **2.** *Am.* schützen, sichern (***from*** vor *dat.*).

for·gath·er [fɔ:'gæðə] *v/i.* zs.-kommen, sich treffen; verkehren (***with*** mit).

for·gave [fə'geɪv] *pret. von* ***forgive***.

forge[1] [fɔ:dʒ] *v/i.*: **~ *ahead*** a) sich (mühsam) vor'ankämpfen, sich Bahn brechen, b) *fig.* (allmählich) Fortschritte machen, c) (sich) nach vorn drängen, *a. sport* sich an die Spitze setzen.

forge[2] [fɔ:dʒ] **I** *s.* **1.** Schmiede *f* (*a. fig.*); **2.** ⚙ a) Schmiedefeuer *n*, -esse *f*, b) Glühofen *m*, c) Hammerwerk *n*: **~ *lathe*** Schmiededrehbank *f*; **II** *v/t.* **3.** schmieden (*a. fig.*); **4.** *fig.* a) formen, schaffen, b) erfinden, sich ausdenken; **5.** fälschen: **~ *a document***; **'forge·a·ble** [-dʒəbl] *adj.* schmiedbar; **'forg·er** [-dʒə] *s.* **1.** Schmied *m*; **2.** Erfinder *m*, Erschaffer *m*; **3.** Fälscher *m*: **~** (***of coin***) Falschmünzer *m*; **'for·ger·y** [-dʒərɪ] *s.* **1.** Fälschen *n*: **~ *of a document*** ⚖ Urkundenfälschung *f*; **2.** Fälschung *f*, Falsifi'kat *n*.

for·get [fə'get] **I** *v/t.* [*irr.*] **1.** vergessen, nicht denken an (*acc.*), nicht bedenken, sich nicht erinnern an (*acc.*): ***I ~ his name*** sein Name ist mir entfallen; **2.** vergessen, verlernen: ***I have forgotten my French***; **3.** vergessen, unter'lassen: **~ *it!*** F a) vergiß es!, schon gut!, b) *iro.* das kannst du vergessen!; ***don't you ~ it*** merk dir das!; **4.** **~ *o.s.*** a) (nur) an andere denken, b) sich vergessen, ,aus der Rolle fallen'; **II** *v/i.* [*irr.*] **5.** vergessen: **~ *about it!*** denk nicht mehr daran!; ***I ~!*** das ist mir entfallen!; **for'get·ful** [-fʊl] *adj.* □ **1.** vergeßlich; **2.** achtlos, nachlässig (***of*** gegenüber): **~ *of one's duties*** pflichtvergessen; **for'get·ful·ness** [-fʊlnɪs] *s.* **1.** Vergeßlichkeit *f*; **2.** Achtlosigkeit *f*.

for'get-me-not *s.* ⚘ Ver'gißmeinnicht *n*.

for·giv·a·ble [fə'gɪvəbl] *adj.* verzeihlich, entschuldbar; **for·give** [fə'gɪv] *v/t.* [*irr.*] **1.** verzeihen, vergeben; **2.** *j-m e-e Schuld etc.* erlassen; **for'giv·en** [-vn] *p.p. von* ***forgive***; **for'give·ness** [-vnɪs] *s.* **1.** Verzeihung *f*, -gebung *f*; **2.** Versöhnlichkeit *f*; **for'giv·ing** [-vɪŋ] *adj.* □ **1.** versöhnlich, nachsichtig; **2.** verzeihend.

for·go [fɔ:'gəʊ] *v/t.* [*irr.* → ***go***] verzichten auf (*acc.*).

for·got [fə'gɒt] *pret.* [*u. p.p. obs.*] *von* ***forget***; **for'got·ten** [-tn] *p.p. von* ***forget***.

fork [fɔ:k] **I** *s.* **1.** (*Eß-, Heu-, Mist- etc.*) Gabel *f* (*a.* ⚙); **2.** ♪ (Stimm)Gabel *f*; **3.** Gabelung *f*, Abzweigung *f*; **4.** *Am.* a) Zs.-fluß *m*, b) *oft pl.* Gebiet *n* an e-r Flußgabelung; **II** *v/t.* **5.** gabelförmig machen, gabeln; **6.** mit e-r Gabel aufladen *od.* 'umgraben *od.* wenden; **7.** *Schach: zwei Figuren* gleichzeitig angreifen; **III** *v/i.* **8.** sich gabeln *od.* spalten; **~ *out***, **~ *over***, **~ *up*** *v/t. u. v/i.* ,blechen' (*zahlen*); **forked** [-kt] *adj.* gabelförmig, gegabelt, gespalten; zickzackförmig (*Blitz*); **'fork-lift** (**truck**) *s.* ⚙ Gabelstapler *m*.

for·lorn [fə'lɔ:n] *adj.* **1.** verlassen, einsam; **2.** verzweifelt, hilflos; unglücklich, elend; **~ *hope*** *s.* **1.** aussichtsloses Unter'nehmen; **2.** letzte (verzweifelte) Hoffnung; **3.** ⚔ a) verlorener Haufen *od.* Posten, b) 'Himmelfahrtskom,mando *n*.

form [fɔ:m] **I** *s.* **1.** Form *f*, Gestalt *f*, Fi'gur *f*; **2.** ⚙ Form *f*, Fas'son *f*, Mo'dell *n*, Scha'blone *f*; ⚠ Schalung *f*; **3.** Form *f*, Art *f*; Me'thode *f*, (An)Ordnung *f*, Schema *n*: ***in due ~*** vorschriftsmäßig; **4.** Form *f*, Fassung *f* (*Wort, Text, a. ling.*), Formel *f* (*Gebet etc.*); **5.** *phls.* Wesen *n*, Na'tur *f*; **6.** 'Umgangsform *f*, Ma'nieren *pl.*, Benehmen *n*: ***good*** (***bad***) **~** guter (schlechter) Ton; ***it is good*** (***bad***) **~** es gehört *od.* schickt sich (nicht); **7.** Formblatt *n*, Formu'lar *n*: ***printed ~*** Vordruck *m*; **~ *letter*** Schemabrief *m*; **8.** Formali'tät *f*, Äußerlichkeit *f*: ***matter of ~*** Formsache *f*; ***mere ~*** bloße Förmlichkeit; **9.** Form *f*, (körperliche *od.* geistige) Verfassung: ***in*** (*od.* ***on***) **~** (gut) in Form; ***off*** (*od.* ***out of***) **~** nicht in Form; **10.** *Brit.* a) (Schul-)Bank *f*, b) (Schul)Klasse *f*: **~ *master*** (***mistress***) Klassenlehrer(in); **11.** *typ.* → ***forme***; **II** *v/t.* **12.** formen, bilden (*a. ling.*); schaffen, gestalten (***into*** zu, ***after*** nach); *Regierung* bilden, *Gesellschaft etc.* gründen; **13.** *den Charakter etc.* formen, bilden; **14.** a) *e-n Teil etc.* bilden, ausmachen, b) dienen als; **15.** anordnen, zs.-stellen; **16.** ⚔ formieren, aufstellen; **17.** *e-n Plan* fassen, entwerfen; **18.** sich *e-e Meinung* bilden; **19.** *e-e Freundschaft etc.* schließen; **20.** *e-e Gewohnheit* annehmen; **21.** ⚙ formen; **III** *v/i.* **22.** sich formen *od.* bilden *od.* gestalten, Form annehmen, entstehen; **23.** *a.* **~ *up*** ⚔ sich formieren *od.* aufstellen, antreten.

-form [-fɔ:m] *in Zssgn* ...förmig.

for·mal ['fɔ:ml] **I** *adj.* □ → ***formally***; **1.** förmlich, for'mell: a) offizi'ell: **~ *call*** Höflichkeitsbesuch *m*, b) feierlich: **~ *event*** → 5; **~ *dress*** → 6, c) steif, 'unper,sönlich, d) (peinlich) genau, pe'dantisch (die Form wahrend), e) formgerecht, vorschriftsmäßig: **~ *contract*** förmlicher Vertrag; **2.** for'mal, for'mell: a) rein äußerlich, b) rein gewohnheitsmäßig, c) scheinbar, Schein...; **3.** for'mal: a) herkömmlich, konventio'nell: **~ *style***, b) schulmäßig, streng me'thodisch, c) Form...: **~ *defect*** ⚖ Formfehler *m*; **4.** regelmäßig: **~ *garden*** architektonischer Garten; **II** *s.* *Am.* **5.** Veranstaltung, für die Gesellschaftskleidung vorgeschrieben ist; **6.** Gesellschafts-, Abendanzug *m od.* -kleid *n*.

form·al·de·hyde [fɔ:'mældɪhaɪd] *s.* ⚗ Formalde'hyd *m*; **for·ma·lin** ['fɔ:məlɪn] *s.* ⚗ Forma'lin *n*.

for·mal·ism ['fɔ:məlɪzəm] *s. allg.* Forma'lismus *m*; **'for·mal·ist** [-lɪst] *s.* Forma'list *m*; **for·mal·is·tic** [,fɔ:mə'lɪstɪk] *adj.* forma'listisch; **for·mal·i·ty** [fɔ:'mælətɪ] *s.* **1.** Förmlichkeit: a) Herkömmlichkeit *f*, b) Zeremo'nie *f*, c) *das* Offizi'elle, d) Steifheit *f*, e) Umständlichkeit *f*: ***without ~*** ohne viel Umstände (zu machen); **2.** Formali'tät *f*: a) Formsache *f*, b) Formvorschrift *f*: ***for the sake of ~*** aus formellen Gründen; **3.** Äußerlichkeit *f*, leere Geste; **'for·mal·ize** [-laɪz] *v/t.* **1.** zur bloßen Formsache machen; **2.** formalisieren, feste Form geben (*dat.*); **'for·mal·ly** [-əlɪ] *adv.* **1.** for'mell, in aller Form; **2.** → ***formal***.

for·mat ['fɔ:mæt] **I** *s.* **1.** *typ.* a) Aufmachung *f*, b) For'mat *n*; **2.** Ein-, Ausrichtung *f*; **II** *v/t.* **3.** *Computer*: formatieren.

for·ma·tion [fɔ:'meɪʃn] *s.* **1.** Bildung *f*: a) Formung *f*, Gestaltung *f*, b) Entstehung *f*, Entwicklung *f*: **~ *of gas*** Gasbildung *f*, c) Gründung *f*: **~ *of a company***, d) Gebilde *n*: ***word ~s*** Wortbildungen; **2.** Anordnung *f*, Zs.-setzung *f*, Struk'tur *f*; **3.** ✈, ⚔, *sport* Formati'on *f*, Aufstellung *f*: **~ *flight*** Formations-, Verbandsflug *m*; **4.** *geol.* Formati'on *f*; **form·a·tive** ['fɔ:mətɪv] **I** *adj.* **1.** formend, gestaltend, bildend; **2.** prägend, Entwicklungs...: **~ *years of a person***; **3.** *ling.* formbildend: **~ *element*** → 5; **4.** ⚘, *zo.* morpho'gen; **II** *s.* **5.** *ling.* Forma'tiv *n*.

forme [fɔ:m] *s. typ.* (Druck)Form *f*.

form·er¹ [ˈfɔːmə] *s.* **1.** Former *m* (*a.* ⚙), Gestalter *m*; **2.** *ped. Brit. in Zssgn* Schüler(in) der … Klasse; **3.** ✈ Spant *m.*

for·mer² [ˈfɔːmə] *adj.* □ **1.** früher, vorig, ehe-, vormalig, vergangen: ***in ~ times*** vormals, einst; ***he is his ~ self again*** er ist wieder (ganz) der alte; ***the ~ Mrs. A.*** die frühere Frau A.; **2.** ***the ~*** *sg. u. pl.* ersterwähnt, -genannt, erster: ***the ~ …, the latter …*** der erstere…, der letztere; ˈ**for·mer·ly** [-lɪ] *adv.* früher, vor-, ehemals: ***Mrs. A., ~ B.*** a) Frau A., geborene B., b) Frau A., ehemalige Frau B.

ˈ**form**ˌ**fit·ting** *adj.* **1.** enganliegend: ***~ dress***; **2.** körpergerecht: ***~ chair***.

for·mic ac·id [ˈfɔːmɪk] *s.* ⚗ Ameisensäure *f.*

for·mi·da·ble [ˈfɔːmɪdəbl] *adj.* □ **1.** schrecklich, furchterregend; **2.** gewaltig, ungeheuer, eˈnorm; **3.** beachtlich, ernstzunehmend: ***~ opponent***; **4.** äußerst schwierig: ***~ problem***.

form·ing [ˈfɔːmɪŋ] *s.* **1.** Formen *n*; **2.** ⚙ (Ver)Formen *n*, Fassonieren *n*; **form·less** [ˈfɔːmlɪs] *adj.* □ formlos.

for·mu·la [ˈfɔːmjʊlə] *pl.* **-las**, **-lae** [-liː] *s.* **1.** ⚗, ℱ *etc.*, *a. mot.* Formel *f*, *pharm. u. fig. a.* Reˈzept *n*; **2.** Formel *f*, fester Wortlaut; **3.** *contp.* a) ‚Schema F', b) (leere) Phrase; ˈ**for·mu·lar·y** [-ərɪ] *s.* **1.** Formelsammlung *f*, -buch *n* (*bsd. eccl.*); **2.** *pharm.* Reˈzeptbuch *n*; ˈ**for·mu·late** [-leɪt] *v/t.* formulieren; **for·mu·la·tion** [ˌfɔːmjʊˈleɪʃn] *s.* Formulierung *f*, Fassung *f.*

ˈ**form·work** *s.* ⚠ (Ver)Schalung *f*, Schalungen *pl.*

for·ni·cate [ˈfɔːnɪkeɪt] *v/i.* unerlaubten außerehelichen Geschlechtsverkehr haben; *bibl. u. weitS.* Unzucht treiben, huren; **for·ni·ca·tion** [ˌfɔːnɪˈkeɪʃn] *s.* ⚖ unerlaubter außerehelicher Geschlechtsverkehr; *weitS.* Unzucht *f*, Hureˈrei *f*; ˈ**for·ni·ca·tor** [-tə] *s.* j-d, der unerlaubten außerehelichen Geschlechtsverkehr hat; *weitS.* Wüstling *m.*

for·rad·er [ˈfɒrədə] *adv.*: ***get no ~*** *Brit.* F nicht vom Fleck kommen.

for·sake [fəˈseɪk] *v/t.* [*irr.*] **1.** *j-n* verlassen, im Stich lassen; **2.** *et.* aufgeben; **forˈsak·en** [-kən] **I** *p.p. von* ***forsake***; **II** *adj.* (gott)verlassen, einsam; **forˈsook** [-ˈsʊk] *pret. von* ***forsake***.

for·sooth [fəˈsuːθ] *adv. iro.* wahrlich, fürˈwahr.

for·swear [fɔːˈsweə] *v/t.* [*irr.* → ***swear***] **1.** eidlich bestreiten; **2.** unter Proˈtest zuˈrückweisen; **3.** abschwören (*dat.*), feierlich entsagen (*dat.*); feierlich geloben (*es nie wieder zu tun etc.*); **4.** ***~ o.s.*** e-n Meineid leisten; **forˈsworn** [-ˈswɔːn] **I** *p.p. von* ***forswear***; **II** *adj.* meineidig.

for·syth·i·a [fɔːˈsaɪθjə] *s.* ⚘ Forˈsythie *f.*

fort [fɔːt] *s.* ⚔ Fort *n*, Feste *f*, Festungswerk *n*: ***hold the ~*** *fig.* ‚die Stellung halten'.

forte¹ [ˈfɔːteɪ] *s. fig. j-s* Stärke *f*, starke Seite.

for·te² [ˈfɔːtɪ] *adv.* ♪ forte, laut.

forth [fɔːθ] *adv.* **1.** herˈvor, vor, her; → ***bring forth*** *etc.*; **2.** herˈaus, hinaus; **3.** (dr)außen; **4.** voˈran, vorwärts; **5.** weiter: ***and so ~*** und so weiter; ***from that day ~*** von diesem Tag an; **6.** weg, fort; ˌ**~ˈcom·ing** *adj.* **1.** bevorstehend, kommend; **2.** erscheinend, unterˈwegs: ***be ~*** erfolgen, sich einstellen; **3.** in Kürze erscheinend (*Buch*) *od.* anlaufend (*Film*); **4.** bereitstehend, verfügbar; **5.** zuˈvor-, entgegenkommend (*Person*); **6.** mitteilsam; ˈ**~·right** *adj. u. adv.* offen (und ehrlich), gerade(herˈaus); ˌ**~ˈwith** [-ˈwɪθ] *adv.* soˈfort, (so)ˈgleich, unverzüglich.

for·ti·eth [ˈfɔːtɪɪθ] **I** *adj.* **1.** vierzigst; **II** *s.* **2.** Vierzigste(r *m*) *f*, *n*; **3.** Vierzigstel *n.*

for·ti·fi·a·ble [ˈfɔːtɪfaɪəbl] *adj.* zu befestigen(d); **for·ti·fi·ca·tion** [ˌfɔːtɪfɪˈkeɪʃn] *s.* **1.** ⚔ a) Befestigung *f*, b) Befestigung(sanlage) *f*, c) Festung *f*; **2.** (*a.* geistige *od.* moˈralische) Stärkung; **3.** a) Verstärkung *f* (*a.* ⚙), b) Anreicherung *f*; **4.** *fig.* Unterˈmauerung *f*; ˈ**for·ti·fi·er** [-faɪə] *s.* Stärkungsmittel *n*; **for·ti·fy** [ˈfɔːtɪfaɪ] *v/t.* **1.** (*a.* geistig *od.* moˈralisch) kräftigen, **2.** ⚙ verstärken; *Nahrungsmittel* anreichern; *Wein etc.* verstärken; **3.** ⚔ befestigen; **4.** bekräftigen, stützen, unterˈmauern; **5.** bestärken, ermutigen.

for·tis·si·mo [fɔːˈtɪsɪməʊ] *adv.* ♪ sehr stark *od.* laut, forˈtissimo.

for·ti·tude [ˈfɔːtɪtjuːd] *s.* (seelische) Kraft: ***bear s.th. with ~*** et. mit Fassung *od.* tapfer ertragen.

fort·night [ˈfɔːtnaɪt] *s. bsd. Brit.* vierzehn Tage: ***this day ~*** a) heute in 14 Tagen, b) heute vor 14 Tagen; ***a ~'s holiday*** ein vierzehntägiger Urlaub; ˈ**fort·night·ly** [-lɪ] *bsd. Brit.* **I** *adj.* vierzehntägig, halbmonatlich, Halbmonats…; **II** *adv.* alle 14 Tage; **III** *s.* Halbmonatsschrift *f.*

For·tran [ˈfɔːtræn] *s.* FORTRAN *n* (*Computersprache*).

for·tress [ˈfɔːtrɪs] *s.* ⚔ Festung *f*, *fig. a.* Bollwerk *n.*

for·tu·i·tous [fɔːˈtjuːɪtəs] *adj.* □ zufällig; **forˈtu·i·ty** [-tɪ] *s.* Zufall *m*, Zufälligkeit *f.*

for·tu·nate [ˈfɔːtʃnət] *adj.* □ **1.** glücklich: ***be ~*** a) Glück haben (*Person*), b) ein (wahres) Glück sein (*Sache*); ***how ~!*** welch ein Glück!, wie gut!; **2.** glückverheißend; günstig; vom Glück begünstigt (*Leben*); ˈ**for·tu·nate·ly** [-lɪ] *adv.* glücklicherweise, zum Glück.

for·tune [ˈfɔːtʃuːn] *s.* **1.** Glück(sfall *m*) *n*, (glücklicher) Zufall: ***good ~*** Gück; ***ill ~*** Unglück; ***try one's ~*** sein Glück versuchen; ***make one's ~*** sein Glück machen; **2.** *a.* ♀ *myth.* Forˈtuna *f*, Glücksgöttin *f*: ***~ favo(u)red him*** das Glück war ihm hold; **3.** Schicksal *n*, Geschick *n*, Los *n*: ***tell*** (*od.* ***read***) ***~s*** wahrsagen; ***read s.o.'s ~*** j-m die Karten legen *od.* aus der Hand lesen; ***have one's ~ told*** sich wahrsagen lassen; **4.** Vermögen *n*: ***make a ~*** ein Vermögen verdienen; ***come into a ~*** ein Vermögen erben; ***marry a ~*** e-e gute Partie machen; ***a small ~*** F ein kleines Vermögen (*viel Geld*); ˈ**~-**ˌ**hunt·er** [ˈfɔːtʃən-] *s.* Mitgiftjäger *m*; ˈ**~-**ˌ**tell·er** [ˈfɔːtʃən-] *s.* Wahrsager(in); ˈ**~-**ˌ**tell·ing** [ˈfɔːtʃən-] *s.* Wahrsageˈrei *f.*

for·ty [ˈfɔːtɪ] **I** *adj.* **1.** vierzig: ***the*** ♀ ***Thieves*** die 40 Räuber (*1001 Nacht*); → ***wink*** 4; **II** *s.* **2.** Vierzig: ***he is in his forties*** er ist in den Vierzigern; ***in the forties*** in den vierziger Jahren (*e-s Jahrhunderts*); **3.** ***the Forties*** die See zwischen Schottlands Nordˈost- u. Norwegens Südˈwestküste; **4.** ***the roaring forties*** stürmischer Teil des Ozeans (zwischen dem 39. u. 50. Breitengrad).

fo·rum [ˈfɔːrəm] *s.* **1.** *antiq. u. fig.* Forum *n*; **2.** Gericht *n*, Tribuˈnal *n* (*a. fig.*); *engS.* ⚖ Gerichtsort *m*, örtliche Zuständigkeit; **3.** Forum *n*, (öffentliche) Diskussiˈon(sveranstaltung).

for·ward [ˈfɔːwəd] **I** *adv.* **1.** vor, nach vorn, vorwärts, vorˈan, vorˈaus, weiter: ***from this day ~*** von heute an; ***freight ~*** ✝ Fracht gegen Nachnahme; ***buy ~*** ✝ auf Termin kaufen; ***go ~*** *fig.* Fortschritte machen, vorankommen; ***help ~*** weiterhelfen (*dat.*); → ***bring*** (***carry***, ***come***, *etc.*) ***forward***; **II** *adj.* □ **2.** vorwärts *od.* nach vorn gerichtet, Vorwärts…: ***a ~ motion***; ***~ defence*** ⚔ Vorwärtsverteidigung *f*; ***~ planning*** Vorausplanung *f*; ***~ speed*** *mot.* Vorwärtsgang *m*; ***~ strategy*** ⚔ Vorwärtsstrategie *f*; **3.** vorder; **4.** a) ⚘ frühreif (*a. fig. Kind*), b) zeitig (*Frühling etc.*); **5.** *zo.* a) hochträchtig, b) gutentwickelt; **6.** *fig.* a) fortgeschritten, b) fortschrittlich; **7.** *fig.* vorlaut, dreist; **8.** *fig.* a) vorschnell, -eilig, b) schnell bereit (***to do s.th.*** et. zu tun); **9.** ✝ auf Ziel *od.* Zeit, Termin…: ***~ business*** (***market***, ***sale***, *etc.*); ***~ rate*** Terminkurs *m*, Kurs *m* für Termingeschäfte; **III** *s.* **10.** *sport* Stürmer *m*: ***~ line*** Sturm(reihe *f*) *m*; **IV** *v/t.* **11.** a) fördern, begünstigen, b) beschleunigen; **12.** befördern, schikken, verladen; **13.** *Brief etc.* nachsenden, weiterbefördern.

for·ward·er [ˈfɔːwədə] *s.* Spediˈteur; ˈ**for·ward·ing** [-dɪŋ] **I** *s.* Versand *m*; **II** *adj.* Versand…: ***~ charges***; ***~ instructions***; ***~ agent*** Spediteur *m*; ***~ note*** Frachtbrief *m*; ***~ address*** Nachsendeadresse *f*; ˈ**for·ward-**ˌ**look·ing** *adj.* vorˈausschauend, fortschrittlich; ˈ**for·ward·ness** [-dnɪs] *s.* **1.** Frühzeitigkeit *f*, Frühreife *f* (*a.* ⚘); **2.** Dreistigkeit *f*, vorlaute Art; **3.** Voreiligkeit *f.*

for·wards [ˈfɔːwədz] → ***forward*** I.

fosse [fɒs] *s.* **1.** (Burg-, Wall)Graben *m*; **2.** *anat.* Grube *f.*

fos·sil [ˈfɒsl] **I** *s.* **1.** *geol.* Fosˈsil *n*; Versteinerung *f*; **2.** F ‚Fosˈsil' *n*: a) verkalkter *od.* verknöcherter Mensch, b) *et.* ‚Vorsintflutliches'; **II** *adj.* **3.** fosˈsil, versteinert: ***~ fuel*** fossiler Brennstoff; ***~ oil*** Erd-, Steinöl *n*; **4.** F a) verknöchert, verkalkt (*Person*), b) vorsintflutlich (*Sache*); **fos·sil·if·er·ous** [ˌfɒsɪˈlɪfərəs] *adj.* fosˈsilienhaltig; **fos·sil·i·za·tion** [ˌfɒsɪlaɪˈzeɪʃn] *s.* **1.** Versteinerung *f*; **2.** F Verknöcherung *f*; ˈ**fos·sil·ize** [-sɪlaɪz] **I** *v/t. geol.* versteinern; **II** *v/i.* versteinern; *fig.* verknöchern, verkalken.

fos·so·ri·al [fɒˈsɔːrɪəl] *adj. zo.* grabend, Grab…

fos·ter [ˈfɒstə] **I** *v/t.* **1.** *Kind etc.* a) aufziehen, b) in Pflege haben *od.* geben; **2.** *et.* fördern; begünstigen, protegieren; **3.** *Wunsch etc.* hegen, nähren; **II** *adj.* **4.** Pflege…: ***~ child*** (***father***, ***mother*** *etc.*).

fos·ter·ling [ˈfɒstəlɪŋ] *s.* Pflegekind *n.*

fought [fɔːt] *pret. u. p.p. von* ***fight***.

foul [faʊl] **I** *adj.* □ **1.** a) stinkend, widerlich, übelriechend (*a. Atem*), b) verpestet, schlecht (*Luft*), c) faul, verdorben (*Lebensmittel etc.*); **2.** schmutzig, verschmutzt; **3.** verstopft; **4.** voll Unkraut, überwachsen; **5.** schlecht, stürmisch (*Wetter etc.*), widrig (*Wind*); **6.** ⚓ a) unklar (*Taue etc.*), b) in Kollisi'on (geratend) (***of*** mit); **7.** *fig.* a) widerlich, ekelhaft, b) abscheulich, gemein: ~ ***deed*** ruchlose Tat, c) schädlich, gefährlich: ~ ***tongue*** böse Zunge, d) schmutzig, zotig, unflätig: ~ ***language***; **8.** F scheußlich; **9.** unehrlich, betrügerisch; **10.** *sport* unfair, regelwidrig; **11.** *typ.* a) unsauber (*Druck etc.*), b) voller Fehler *od.* Änderungen; **II** *adv.* **12.** auf gemeine Art, gemein (*etc.* → 7–10): ***play*** ~ *sport* foul spielen; ***play s.o.*** ~ j-m übel mitspielen; **13.** ***fall*** ~ ***of*** ⚓ zs.-stoßen mit (*a. fig.*); **III** *s.* **14.** ***through fair and*** ~ durch dick u. dünn; **15.** ⚓ Zs.-stoß *m*; **16.** *sport* a) Foul *n*, Regelverstoß *m*, b) → ***foul shot***; **IV** *v/t.* **17.** *a.* ~ ***up*** a) beschmutzen (*a. fig.*), verschmutzen, verunreinigen, b) verstopfen; **18.** *sport* foulen; **19.** ⚓ zs.-stoßen mit; **20.** *a.* ~ ***up*** sich verwickeln in (*dat.*) *od.* mit; **21.** ~ ***up*** F a) ‚vermasseln', ‚versauen', b) durchein'anderbringen; **V** *v/i.* **22.** schmutzig werden; **23.** ⚓ zs.-stoßen (***with*** mit); **24.** sich verwickeln; **25.** *sport* foulen, ein Foul begehen; **26.** ~ ***up*** F a), ‚Mist bauen', ‚patzen', b) durchein'anderkommen.

'foul|-mouthed *adj.* unflätig; ~ **play** *s.* **1.** *sport* unfaires Spiel, Unsportlichkeit *f*; **2.** (Gewalt)Verbrechen *n*, *bsd.* Mord *m*; ~ **shot** *s. Basketball*: Freiwurf *m*; '~-ˌ**spo·ken** → ***foul-mouthed***.

found¹ [faʊnd] *pret. u. p.p. von* ***find***.

found² [faʊnd] *v/t.* ⚙ schmelzen; gießen.

found³ [faʊnd] *fig.* **I** *v/t.* **1.** gründen, errichten; **2.** begründen, einrichten, ins Leben rufen, *Schule etc.* stiften: ***2ing Fathers*** *Am.* Staatsmänner aus der Zeit der Unabhängigkeitserklärung; **3.** *fig.* gründen, stützen (***on*** auf *acc.*): ***be ~ed on*** → 4; ***well-~ed*** wohlbegründet, fundiert; **II** *v/i.* **4.** (***on***) sich stützen (auf *acc.*), beruhen, sich gründen (auf *dat.*);

foun·da·tion [faʊn'deɪʃn] *s.* **1.** *oft pl.* △ Grundmauer *f*, Funda'ment *n* (*a. fig.*); 'Unterbau *m*, -lage *f*, Bettung *f* (*Straße etc.*); **2.** Grund(lage *f*) *m*, Basis *f*: ***without*** (***any***) ~ (völlig) unbegründet; ***shaken to the ~s*** in den Grundfesten erschüttert; ***lay the ~s of*** den Grund(stock) legen zu; **3.** Gründung *f*, Errichtung *f*; **4.** (gemeinnützige) Stiftung: ***be on the*** ~ Geld aus der Stiftung erhalten; **5.** Ursprung *m*, Beginn *m*; **6.** steifes (Zwischen)Futter: ~ ***muslin*** Steifleinen *n*; **7.** *a.* ~ ***garment*** a) Mieder *n*, b) Kor'sett *n*, c) *pl.* Mieder (-waren) *pl.*; **8.** *a.* ~ ***cream*** *Kosmetik*: Grundierung *f*; ~ **stone** *s.* Grundstein *m* (*a. fig.*); → ***lay¹*** 5.

found·er¹ ['faʊndə] *s.* Gründer *m*, Stifter *m*: ***~s' shares*** ✝ Gründeraktien.

found·er² ['faʊndə] *s.* ⚙ Gießer *m*.

found·er³ ['faʊndə] **I** *v/i.* **1.** ⚓ sinken, 'untergehen; **2.** einstürzen, -fallen; **3.** *fig.* scheitern; **4.** *vet.* a) lahmen, b) zs.-brechen (*Pferd*); **5.** steckenbleiben; **II** *v/t.* **6.** *Pferd* lahm reiten; **7.** *Schiff* zum Sinken bringen.

found·ling ['faʊndlɪŋ] *s.* Findling *m*, Findelkind *n*: ~ ***hospital*** Findelhaus *n*.

found·ress ['faʊndrɪs] *s.* Gründerin *f*, Stifterin *f*.

found·ry ['faʊndrɪ] *s.* ⚙ Gieße'rei *f*.

fount¹ [faʊnt] *s. typ.* (Setzkasten *m* mit) Schriftsatz *m*.

fount² [faʊnt] → ***fountain*** 2, 4a.

foun·tain ['faʊntɪn] *s.* **1.** Fon'täne *f*: a) Springbrunnen *m*, b) (Wasser)Strahl *m*; **2.** Quelle *f*, *fig. a.* Born *m*: ***2 of Youth*** Jungbrunnen *m*; **3.** a) (Trink-) Brunnen *m*, b) → ***soda fountain***; **4.** ⚙ a) (Öl-, Tinten- *etc.*)Behälter *m*, b) Reser'voir *n*; ˌ~-'**head** *s.* Quelle *f* (*a. fig.*); *fig.* Urquell *m*; '~-**pen** *s.* Füll(feder)halter *m*.

four [fɔː] **I** *adj.* **1.** vier; **II** *s.* **2.** Vier *f* (*Zahl, Spielkarte etc.*): ***the ~ of hearts*** die Herzvier; ***by ~s*** immer vier (auf einmal); ***on all ~s*** a) auf allen vieren, b) *fig.* stimmend, richtig; ***be on all ~s with*** übereinstimmen mit, genau entsprechen (*dat.*); **3.** *Rudern*: Vierer *m* (*Boot od. Mannschaft*); ˌ~-'**cor·nered** *adj.* viereckig, mit vier Ecken; '~-ˌ**cy·cle** *adj.*: ~ ***engine*** ⚙ Viertaktmotor *m*; '~-**eyes** *s. pl. sg. konstr.* F ‚Brillenschlange' *f*; ~ **flush** *s. Poker*: unvollständige Hand; '~-ˌ**flush·er** *s. Am.* Bluffer *m*, ‚falscher Fuffziger'; '~-**fold** *adj. u. adv.* vierfach; ˌ~-'**four** (**time**) *s.* ♪ Vier'vierteltakt *m*; ˌ~-'**hand·ed** *adj.* ♪, *zo.* vierhändig; 2 **Hun·dred** *s.*: ***the*** ~ *Am.* die Hautevolee (*e-r Gemeinde*); ˌ~-**in-'hand** [-ɔːrɪn-] *s.* **1.** Vierspänner *m*; **2.** Viergespann *n*; ˌ~-'**leaf**(**ed**) **clo·ver** *s.* ⚘ vierblätt(e)riges Kleeblatt; '~-**legged** *adj.* vierbeinig; ˌ~-'**let·ter word** *s.* unanständiges Wort; ˌ~-'**oar** [-ɔːr'ɔː] *s.* Vierer *m* (*Boot*); '~-**part** *adj.* ♪ vierstimmig (*Satz*); '~-**pence** [-pəns] *s. Brit. hist.* Vierpencestück *n*; ˌ~-'**post·er** *s.* **1.** Himmelbett *n*; **2.** ⚓ *sl.* Viermaster *m*; ˌ~'**score** *adj. obs.* achtzig; '~-ˌ**seat·er** *s. mot.* Viersitzer *m*; '~-**some** [-səm] *s. Golf*: Vierer *m*; *fig. humor.* ‚Quar'tett' *n*; ˌ~-'**speed gear** *s.* ⚙ Viergangetriebe *n*; ˌ~-'**square** *adj. u. adv.* **1.** qua'dratisch; **2.** *fig.* a) fest, unerschütterlich, b) grob, barsch; ˌ~-'**star** *adj.* Viersterne…: ~ ***general***; ~ ***hotel***; ˌ~-'**stroke** *adj.*: ~ ***engine*** ⚙ Viertaktmotor *m*.

four·teen [ˌfɔː'tiːn] **I** *adj.* vierzehn; **II** *s.* Vierzehn *f*; ˌ**four'teenth** [-nθ] **I** *adj.* vierzehnt; **II** *s.* a) (*der, die, das*) Vierzehnte, b) Vierzehntel *n*.

fourth [fɔːθ] **I** *adj.* □ **1.** viert; **2.** viertel; **II** *s.* **3.** (*der, die, das*) Vierte; **4.** Viertel *n*; **5.** ♪ Quarte *f*; **6.** ***the 2*** (***of July***) *Am.* der Vierte (Juli), der Unabhängigkeitstag; '**fourth·ly** [-lɪ] *adv.* viertens.

ˌ**four|-'way** *adj.*: ~ ***switch*** ⚡ Vierfach-, Vierwegeschalter *m*; ˌ~-'**wheel** *adj.* vierräd(e)rig; Vierrad…(*-antrieb, -bremse*).

fowl [faʊl] **I** *pl.* **fowls**, *coll. mst* **fowl** *s.* **1.** Haushuhn *n od.* -ente *f*, *a.* Truthahn *m*; *coll.* Geflügel *n* (*a. Fleisch*), Hühner *pl.*: ~ ***house*** Hühnerstall *m*; ~ ***pest*** Hühnerpest *f*; ~ ***pox*** Geflügelpocken *pl*; ~ ***run*** Hühnerhof *m*, Auslauf *m*; **2.** *selten* Vogel *m*, Vögel *pl.*: ***the ~(s) of the air*** *bibl.* die Vögel unter dem Himmel; **II** *v/i.* **3.** Vögel fangen *od.* schießen; '**fowl·er** [-lə] *s.* Vogelfänger *m*; '**fowl·ing** [-lɪŋ] *s.* Vogelfang *m*, -jagd *f*: ~-***piece*** Vogelflinte *f*; ~-***shot*** Hühnerschrot *n*.

fox [fɒks] **I** *s.* **1.** *zo.* Fuchs *m*: ***set the ~ to keep the geese*** den Bock zum Gärtner machen; ~ ***and geese*** Wolf u. Schafe (*ein Brettspiel*); **2.** (***sly old***) ~ *fig.* (schlauer) Fuchs; **3.** Fuchspelz(kragen) *m*; **II** *v/t.* **4.** *sl.* über'listen, ‚reinlegen'; **III** *v/i.* **5.** stockfleckig werden (*Papier*); ~ **brush** *s. hunt.* Lunte *f*, Fuchsschwanz *m*; '~-**glove** *s.* ⚘ Fingerhut *m*; '~-**hole** *s.* **1.** Fuchsbau *m*; **2.** ⚔ Schützenloch *n*; '~-**hunt**, '~-ˌ**hunt·ing** *s.* Fuchsjagd *f*; ~ **mark** *s.* Stockfleck *m*; '~-**tail** *s.* **1.** Fuchsschwanz *m*; **2.** ⚘ Fuchsschwanzgras *n*; ˌ~-'**ter·ri·er** *s. zo.* Foxterrier *m*; '~-**trot** *s. u. v/i.* Foxtrott *m* (tanzen).

fox·y ['fɒksɪ] *adj.* **1.** gerissen, listig; **2.** fuchsrot; **3.** stockfleckig (*Papier*).

foy·er ['fɔɪeɪ] (*Fr.*) *s. allg.* Fo'yer *n*.

fra·cas ['frækɑː] *pl.* ~ [-kɑːz] *s.* Aufruhr *m*, Spek'takel *m*.

frac·tion ['frækʃn] *s.* **1.** ⩚ Bruch *m*: ~ ***bar***, ~ ***line***, ~ ***stroke*** Bruchstrich *m*; **2.** Bruchteil *m*, Frag'ment *n*; Stückchen *n*, *ein* bißchen: ***not by a ~*** nicht im geringsten; ***by a ~ of an inch*** um ein Haar; ~ ***of a share*** ✝ Teilaktie *f*; **3.** 2 *eccl.* Brechen *n des Brotes*; '**frac·tion·al** [-ʃənl] *adj.* **1.** *a.* ⩚ Bruch…, gebrochen: ~ ***amount*** Teilbetrag *m*; ~ ***currency*** Scheidemünze *f*; ~ ***part*** Bruchteil *m*; **2.** *fig.* unbedeutend, mini'mal; **3.** ⚗ fraktioniert, teilweise; '**frac·tion·ar·y** [-ʃnərɪ] *adj.* Bruch(stück)…, Teil…; '**frac·tion·ate** [-ʃəneɪt] *v/t.* ⚗ fraktionieren.

frac·tious ['frækʃəs] *adj.* □ **1.** mürrisch, zänkisch, reizbar; **2.** störrisch; '**frac·tious·ness** [-nɪs] *s.* **1.** Reizbarkeit *f*; **2.** 'Widerspenstigkeit *f*.

frac·ture ['fræktʃə] **I** *s.* **1.** ⚕ Frak'tur *f*, Bruch *m* (*a. fig.*); **2.** *min.* Bruchfläche *f*; **3.** *ling.* Brechung *f*; **II** *v/t.* **4.** (zer)brechen: ~ ***one's arm*** sich den Arm brechen; ***~d skull*** Schädelbruch *m*; **III** *v/i.* **5.** (zer)brechen.

frag·ile ['frædʒaɪl] *adj.* **1.** zerbrechlich (*a. fig.*); **2.** ⚙ brüchig; **3.** *fig.* schwach, zart (*Gesundheit etc.*), gebrechlich (*Person*); **fra·gil·i·ty** [frə'dʒɪlətɪ] *s.* **1.** Zerbrechlichkeit *f*; **2.** Brüchigkeit *f*; **3.** *fig.* Ge-, Zerbrechlichkeit *f*, Zartheit *f*.

frag·ment ['frægmənt] *s.* **1.** Bruchstück *n* (*a.* ⚙), -teil *m*; **2.** Stück *n*, Brocken *m*, Splitter *m* (*a.* ⚔), Fetzen *m*; 'Überrest *m*; **3.** (lite'rarisches *etc.*) Frag'ment; **frag·men·tal** [fræg'mentl] *adj.* **1.** *geol.* Trümmer…; **2.** → '**frag·men·tar·y** [-tərɪ] *adj.* **1.** zerstückelt, aus Stücken bestehend; **2.** fragmen'tarisch, unvollständig, bruchstückhaft; **frag·men·ta·tion** [ˌfrægmen'teɪʃn] *s.* Zerstückelung *f*, -splitterung *f*: ~ ***bomb*** ⚔ Splitterbombe *f*.

fra·grance ['freɪgrəns] *s.* Wohlgeruch *m*, Duft *m*, A'roma *n*; '**fra·grant** [-nt] *adj.* □ **1.** wohlriechend, duftend: ***be ~ with*** duften nach; **2.** *fig.* angenehm, köstlich.

frail [freɪl] *adj.* □ **1.** zerbrechlich; **2.** a) zart, schwach, b) gebrechlich, c) (*charakterlich*) schwach, d) schwach, seicht (*Buch etc.*); '**frail·ty** [-tɪ] *s.* **1.** Zerbrechlichkeit *f*; **2.** a) Zartheit *f*, b) Gebrechlichkeit *f*; **3.** a) Schwachheit *f*, (mo'ralische) Schwäche, b) Fehltritt *m.*

fraise [freɪz] *s.* **1.** ⚔ Pali'sade *f*; **2.** ⚙ Bohrfräse *f.*

fram·b(o)e·si·a [fræm'bi:zɪə] *s.* ⚕ Frambö'sie *f* (*tropische Hautkrankheit*).

frame [freɪm] **I** *s.* **1.** (*Bilder-, Fenster- etc.*)Rahmen *m* (*a.* ⚙, *mot.*): **~ aerial** Rahmenantenne *f*; **2.** (*a. Brillen-, Schirm-, Wagen*)Gestell *n*, Gerüst *n*; **3.** Einfassung *f*; **4.** △ a) Balkenwerk *n*: **~ house** Holz- *od.* Fachwerkhaus *n*, b) Gerippe *n*, Ske'lett *n*: **steel ~**; **5.** *typ.* ('Setz)Re,gal *n*; **6.** ↯ Stator *m*; **7.** ✈, ⚓ a) Spant *n*, *m*, b) Gerippe *n*; **8.** *TV* a) Abtastfeld *n*, b) Raster(bild *n*) *m*; **9.** *Film*: Einzelbild *n*; **10.** *Comic strips*: Bild *n*; **11.** ⚘ verglaster Treibbeetkasten; **12.** *Weberei*: ('Spinn-, 'Web)Ma,schine *f*; **13.** a) Rahmen(erzählung *f*) *m*, b) 'Hintergrund *m*; **14.** Körper(bau) *m*, Fi'gur *f*: **the mortal ~** die sterbliche Hülle; **15.** *fig.* Rahmen *m*, Sy'stem *n*: **within the ~ of** im Rahmen (*gen.*); **16.** *bsd.* **~ of mind** (Gemüts)Verfassung *f*, (-)Zustand *m*, Stimmung *f*; **17.** → **frame-up**; **II** *v/t.* **18.** zs.-fügen, -setzen; **19.** a) *Bild etc.* (ein)rahmen, (-)fassen, b) *fig.* um'rahmen; **20.** *et.* ersinnen, entwerfen, *Plan* schmieden, *Gedicht etc.* machen, verfertigen, *Politik etc.* abstecken; **21.** *Worte, a. Entschuldigung etc.* formulieren; **22.** gestalten, formen, bilden; **23.** anpassen (**to** *dat.*); **24.** *a.* **~ up** *sl.* a) *et.* ‚drehen', ‚schaukeln', b) *j-m* et. ‚anhängen', *j-n* ‚reinhängen': **~ a match** ein Spiel (vorher) absprechen; **framed** [-md] *adj.* **1.** gerahmt; **2.** △ Fachwerk...; **3.** ⚓, ✈ in Spanten; **'fram·er** [-mə] *s.* **1.** (Bilder-)Rahmer *m*; **2.** *fig.* Gestalter *m*, Entwerfer *m.*

frame| saw *s.* ⚙ Spannsäge *f*; **~ sto·ry, ~ tale** *s.* Rahmenerzählung *f*; **~ tent** *s.* Steilwandzelt *n*; **'~-up** *s.* F **1.** Kom'plott *n*, In'trige *f*; Falle *f*; **2.** abgekartetes Spiel, Schwindel *m*; **'~·work** *s.* **1.** ⚙, *a.* ✈ *u. biol.* Gerüst *n*, Gerippe *n*; **2.** △ Fachwerk *n*, Gebälk *n*; **3.** 🚂 Gestell *n*; **4.** *fig.* Rahmen *m*, Gefüge *n*, Sy'stem *n*: **within the ~ of** im Rahmen (*gen.*).

franc [fræŋk] *s.* **1.** Franc *m* (*Währungseinheit Frankreichs etc.*); **2.** Franken *m* (*Währungseinheit der Schweiz*).

fran·chise ['fræntʃaɪz] *s.* **1.** *pol.* a) Wahl-, Stimmrecht *n*, b) Bürgerrecht(e *pl.*) *n*; **2.** *Am.* Privi'leg *n*; **3.** *hist.* Gerechtsame *f*; **4.** ☤ *bsd. Am.* a) *a. sport* Konzessi'on *f*, b) Al'leinverkaufsrecht *n*, c) 'Rechtsper,sönlichkeit *f*, d) Franchise *n*, Franchising *n* (*Vertriebsart*); **5.** *Versicherung*: Fran'chise *f.*

Fran·cis·can [fræn'sɪskən] **I** *s.* Franzis'kaner(mönch) *m*; **II** *adj.* Franziskaner...

Fran·co-Ger·man [,fræŋkəʊ'dʒɜ:mən] *adj.*: **the ~ War** der Deutsch-Französische Krieg (*1870/71*).

Fran·co·ni·an [fræŋ'kəʊnjən] *adj.* fränkisch.

Fran·co|·phile ['fræŋkəʊfaɪl], **'~·phil** [-fɪl] **I** *s.* Franko'phile *m*, Fran'zosenfreund *m*; **II** *adj.* franko'phil; **'~·phobe** [-fəʊb] **I** *s.* Fran'zosenhasser *m*, -feind *m*; **II** *adj.* fran'zosenfeindlich.

fran·gi·ble ['frændʒɪbl] *adj.* zerbrechlich.

fran·gi·pane ['frændʒɪpeɪn] *s. Art* Mandelcreme *f.*

Fran·glais ['frɑ̃:ŋgleɪ] (*Fr.*) *s. stark anglisiertes Französisch.*

Frank¹ [fræŋk] *s. hist.* Franke *m.*

frank² [fræŋk] **I** *adj.* □ → **frankly**; **1.** offen, aufrichtig, frei(mütig); **II** *s.* **2.** ✉ *hist.* a) Freivermerk *m*, b) Portofreiheit *f*; **III** *v/t.* **3.** *Brief* (*a.* mit der Ma'schine) frankieren: **~ing machine** Frankiermaschine *f*; **4.** *j-m* (freien) Zutritt verschaffen; **5.** *et.* amtlich freigeben.

frank³ [fræŋk] *Am.* F *für* **frank·furt·er** ['fræŋkfɜ:tə] *s.* Frankfurter (Würstchen *n*) *f.*

frank·in·cense ['fræŋkɪn,sens] *s.* Weihrauch *m.*

Frank·ish ['fræŋkɪʃ] *adj. hist.* fränkisch.

frank·lin ['fræŋklɪn] *s. hist.* **1.** Freisasse *m*; **2.** kleiner Landbesitzer.

frank·ly ['fræŋklɪ] *adv.* **1.** → **frank²** 1; **2.** frei her'aus, frank u. frei; **3.** *a.* **~ speaking** offen gestanden *od.* gesagt; **'frank·ness** [-nɪs] *s.* Offenheit *f*, Freimütigkeit *f.*

fran·tic ['fræntɪk] *adj.* □ (*mst* **~ally**) **1.** wild, außer sich, rasend (**with** vor *dat.*); wütend; **2.** verzweifelt: **~ efforts**; **3.** hektisch: **a ~ search.**

frap·pé ['fræpeɪ] (*Fr.*) **I** *adj.* eisgekühlt; **II** *s.* Frap'pé *m* (*Getränk*).

frat [fræt] *sl.* → **fraternity** 3.

fra·ter·nal [frə'tɜ:nl] **I** *adj.* □ **1.** brüderlich, Bruder...; **2.** *biol.* zweieiig: **~ twins**; **II** *s.* **3.** *a.* **~ association, ~ society** *Am.* Verein *m* zur Förderung gemeinsamer Interessen; **fra'ter·ni·ty** [-nətɪ] *s.* **1.** Brüderlichkeit *f*; **2.** Vereinigung *f*, Zunft *f*, Gilde *f*: **the angling ~** die Zunft der Angler; **the legal ~** die Juristen *pl.*; **3.** *Am.* Stu'dentenverbindung *f*; **frat·er·ni·za·tion** [,frætənaɪ'zeɪʃn] *s.* Verbrüderung *f*; **frat·er·nize** ['frætənaɪz] *v/i.* sich verbrüdern, *bsd.* ⚔ fraternisieren.

frat·ri·cid·al [,frætrɪ'saɪdl] *adj.* brudermörderisch: **~ war** Bruderkrieg *m*; **frat·ri·cide** ['frætrɪsaɪd] *s.* **1.** Bruder-, Geschwistermord *m*; **2.** Bruder-, Geschwistermörder *m.*

fraud [frɔ:d] *s.* **1.** ⚖ Betrug *m*, arglistige Täuschung: **by ~** arglistig; **obtain by ~** sich *et.* erschleichen; **~ department** Betrugsdezernat *n*; **2.** Schwindel *m*; **3.** F a) Schwindler *m*, ‚falscher Fuffziger', b) ‚Schauspieler' *m*, j-d, der nicht ‚echt' ist; **'fraud·u·lence** [-djʊləns] *s.* Betrüge'rei *f*; **'fraud·u·lent** [-djʊlənt] *adj.* □ betrügerisch, arglistig: **~ bankruptcy** betrügerischer Bankrott; **~ conversion** Unterschlagung *f*; **~ preference** Gläubigerbegünstigung *f*; **~ representation** Vorspiegelung *f* falscher Tatsachen.

fraught [frɔ:t] *adj.* **1.** *mst fig.* (**with**) voll (von), beladen (mit): **~ with danger** gefahrvoll; **~ with meaning** bedeutungsschwer, -schwanger; **~ with sorrow** kummerbeladen; **2.** F a) schlimm, b) ‚schwer im Druck'.

fray¹ [freɪ] *s.* **1.** (lauter) Streit; **2.** a) Schläge'rei *f*, b) ⚔ *u. fig.* Kampf *m*: **eager for the ~** kampflustig.

fray² [freɪ] **I** *v/t.* **1.** *a.* **~ out** *Stoff etc.* abtragen, 'durchscheuern, ausfransen, *a. fig.* abnutzen: **~ed nerves** strapazierte Nerven; **~ed at the edges** *fig.* sehr mitgenommen; **~ed temper** *fig.* gereizte Stimmung; **2.** *Geweih* fegen; **II** *v/i.* **3.** *a.* **~ out** sich abnutzen (*a. fig.*), sich ausfransen *od.* 'durchscheuern; **4.** *fig.* sich ereifern: **tempers began to ~** die Stimmung wurde gereizt.

fraz·zle ['fræzl] **I** *v/t.* **1.** ausfransen; **2.** *oft* **~ out** F *j-n* ‚fix u. fertig' machen; **II** *v/i.* **3.** sich ausfransen *od.* 'durchscheuern; **III** *s.* **4.** Franse *f*: **worn to a ~** F ‚fix u. fertig'; **work o.s. to a ~** F sich ‚kaputtmachen' (vor Arbeit); **burnt to a ~** total verkohlt.

freak [fri:k] **I** *s.* **1.** 'Mißbildung *f*, (*Mensch, Tier*) *a.* 'Mißgeburt *f*, Monstrosi'tät *f*: **~ of nature** Laune *f* der Natur, *contp.* Monstrum *n*; **~ show** Monstrositätenkabinett *n*; **2.** Grille *f*, Laune *f*; **3.** ‚verrückte' *od.* ‚irre' Sache; **4.** *sl.* ‚Freak' *m*: a) ‚irrer Typ', *contp.* ‚Ausgeflippte(r' *m*) *f*, ‚Spinner' *m*, b) (*Jazz-, Computer- etc.*)Narr *m*, c) Süchtige(r *m*) *f*: **pill ~**; **II** *adj.* **5.** → **freakish**; **III** *v/i.* **6.** **~ out** *sl.* ‚ausflippen' (*Süchtiger, a. allg. fig.*); **IV** *v/t.* **7.** *sl. j-n* ‚ausflippen' lassen; **'freak·ish** [-kɪʃ] *adj.* □ **1.** launisch, unberechenbar; **2.** ‚verrückt', ‚irr'; **'freak-out** *s. sl.* **1.** ‚Horrortrip' *m*; **2.** ‚Ausflippen' *n.*

freck·le ['frekl] **I** *s.* **1.** Sommersprosse *f*; **2.** Fleck(chen *n*) *m*; **II** *v/t.* **3.** tüpfeln, sprenkeln; **III** *v/i.* **4.** Sommersprossen bekommen; **'freck·led** [-ld] *adj.* sommersprossig.

free [fri:] **I** *adj.* □ (→ *a.* 18) **1.** frei: a) unabhängig, b) selbständig, c) ungebunden, d) ungehindert, e) uneingeschränkt, f) in Freiheit (befindlich): **a ~ man**; **the ♀ World**; **~ elections**; **you are ~ to go** es steht dir frei zu gehen; **2.** frei: a) *unbeschäftigt*: **I am ~ after 5 o'clock**, b) *ohne Verpflichtungen*: **a ~ evening**, c) nicht besetzt: **this room is ~**; **3.** frei: a) *nicht wörtlich*: **a ~ translation**, b) *nicht an Regeln gebunden*: **~ verse**; **~ skating** *sport* Kür(laufen *n*) *f*, c) frei gestaltet: **a ~ version**; **4.** (**from, of**) frei (von), ohne (*acc.*): **~ from error** fehlerfrei; **~ from infection** frei von ansteckenden Krankheiten; **~ from pain** schmerzfrei; **~ of debt** schuldenfrei; **~ and unencumbered** ⚖ unbelastet, hypothekenfrei; **~ of taxes** steuerfrei; **5.** ⚗ frei, nicht gebunden; **6.** frei, los(e); **7.** frei, unbefangen, ungezwungen: **~ manners**; **8.** a) offen(herzig), freimütig, b) unverblümt, c) unverschämt: **make ~ with** sich Freiheiten herausnehmen gegen *j-n*; **9.** allzu frei, unanständig: **~ talk**; **10.** freigebig, großzügig: **be ~ with s.th.**; **11.** leicht, flott, zügig; **12.** (kosten-, gebühren-) frei, kostenlos, unentgeltlich, gratis, zum Nulltarif: **~ copy** Freiexemplar *n*; **~ fares** Nulltarif *m*; **~ gift** ☤ Zugabe *f*, Gratisprobe *f*; **~ ticket** a) Freikarte *f*, b) Freifahrschein *m*; **13.** ☤ frei (*Klausel*): **~ on board** frei an Bord; **~ on rail** frei Waggon; **~ domicile** frei Haus; **14.** ☤ frei verfügbar: **~ assets**; **15.** öffentlich: **~ library** Volksbibliothek *f*; **be (made) ~ of s.th.** freien Zutritt zu et. haben; **16.** willig, bereit; **17.** *Turnen*: ohne Geräte: **~ gymnastics** Freiübungen; **II** *adv.* **18.** *allg.* frei (→ I): **go ~** frei ausgehen; **run ~** ⚙ leer laufen (*Maschine*); **III** *v/t.* **19.** *a. fig.* befreien (**from** von, aus); **20.** freilassen; **21.** entlasten (**from, of** von).

free| ar·e·a *s. fig.* Freiraum *m*; **~ back** *s. sport* Libero *m*; **'~·board** *s.* ⚓ Freibord *n*; **'~ˌboot·er** *s.* Freibeuter *m*; **♀ Church** *s.* Freikirche *f*; **'~-ˌcut·ting** *adj.*: **~ steel** ⚙ Automatenstahl *m*.

free·man ['fri:dmæn] *s.* [*irr.*] Freigelassene(r) *m*.

free·dom ['fri:dəm] *s.* **1.** a) Freiheit *f*, b) Unabhängigkeit *f*: **~ of the press** Pressefreiheit; **~ of the seas** Freiheit der Meere; **~ of the city** (*od.* **town**) Ehrenbürgerrecht; **~ from taxation** Steuerfreiheit; **~ fighter** Freiheitskämpfer (-in); **2.** freier Zutritt, freie Benutzung; **3.** Freimütigkeit *f*, Offenheit *f*; **4.** Zwanglosigkeit *f*; **5.** Aufdringlichkeit *f*, (plumpe) Vertraulichkeit; **6.** *phls.* Willensfreiheit *f*, Selbstbestimmung *f*.

free| en·er·gy *s. phys.* freie *od.* ungebundene Ener'gie; **~ en·ter·prise** *s.* freies Unter'nehmertum; **~ fall** *s.* ✈ *phys.* freier Fall; **~ fight** *s.* ('Massen-) Schlägeˌrei *f*; **'~-forˌall** [-ərˌɔ:l] F **1.** → **free fight**; **2.** wildes ‚Gerangel'; **~ hand** *s.*: **give s.o. a ~** j-m freie Hand lassen; **'~·hand** *adj.* **1.** Freihand…, freihändig: **~ drawing**; **2.** *fig.* a) frei, b) ausschweifend; **ˌ~'hand·ed** *adj.* **1.** freigebig, großzügig; **2.** → **freehand**; **ˌ~'heart·ed** *adj.* **1.** freimütig, offen (-herzig); **2.** → **freehanded** 1; **'~·hold** *s.* (volles) Eigentumsrecht an Grundbesitz: **~ flat** *Brit.* Eigentumswohnung *f*; **'~ˌhold·er** *s.* Grund- u. Hauseigentümer *m*; **~ kick** *s. Fußball*: Freistoß *m*: **(in)direct ~**; **~ la·bo(u)r** *s.* nichtorganisierte Arbeiter(schaft *f*) *pl.*; **'~·lance I** *s.* **1.** a) freier Schriftsteller *od.* Journa'list (*etc.*), Freiberufler *m*; freischaffender Künstler, b) freier Mitarbeiter; **2.** *pol.* Unabhängige(r) *m*, Par'teilose(r) *m*; **II** *adj.* **3.** freiberuflich (tätig), freischaffend; **III** *v/i.* **4.** freiberuflich tätig sein; **'~ˌlanc·er** → **freelance** 1; **~ list** *s.* **1.** Liste *f* zollfreier Ar'tikel; **2.** Liste *f* der Empfänger von 'Freikarten *od.* -exemˌplaren; **~ liv·er** *s.* Schlemmer *m*, Genießer *m*; **'~ˌload·er** *s. Am.* F ‚Schnorrer' *m*; **~ love** *s.* freie Liebe; **~ man** *s.* [*irr.*] *Fußball*: freier Mann, Libero *m*; **'~·man** *s.* [*irr.*] **1.** [-mæn] freier Mann; **2.** [-mən] (Ehren)Bürger *m* (*Stadt*); **~ mar·ket** *s.* ✝ **1.** freier Markt: **~ economy** freie Marktwirtschaft; **2.** *Börse*: Freiverkehr *m*; **'♀ma·son** *s.* Freimaurer *m*: **~s' lodge** Freimaurerloge *f*; **'♀ma·son·ry** *s.* **1.** Freimaure'rei *f*; **2.** *fig.* Zs.-gehörigkeitsgefühl *n*; **~ play** *s.* **1.** ⚙ Spiel *n*; **2.** *fig.* freie Hand; **~ port** *s.* Freihafen *m*; **'~-range** *adj.*: **~ hens** Freilandhühner; **~ rid·er** → **freeloader**; **~ share** *s.* ✝ Freiaktie *f*.

free·si·a ['fri:zjə] *s.* ⚘ Freesie *f*.

free| speech *s.* Redefreiheit *f*; **ˌ~-'spo·ken** *adj.* offen, freimütig; **ˌ~-'standing** *adj.*: **~ exercises** Freiübungen *pl.*; **~ sculpture** Freiplastik *f*; **~ state** *s.* Freistaat *m*; **ˌ~-'style** *sport* **I** *s.* Freistil (-schwimmen *n etc.*) *m*; **II** *adj.* Freistil…, Kür…: **~ skating** Kür(laufen *n*) *f*; **ˌ~'think·er** *s.* Freidenker *m*, Freigeist *m*; **ˌ~'think·ing** *s.*, **~ thought** *s.* Freidenke'rei *f*, -geiste'rei *f*; **~ throw** *s. Basketball*: Freiwurf *m*; **ˌ~'trade a·re·a** *s.* Freihandelszone *f*; **ˌ~'trad·er** *s.* Anhänger *m* des Freihandels; **~ vote** *s. parl.* Abstimmung *f* ohne Frakti'onszwang; **'~·way** *s. Am.* gebührenfreie Schnellstraße; **ˌ~'wheel** ⚙ **I** *s.* Freilauf *m*; **II** *v/i.* im Freilauf fahren; **ˌ~'wheel·ing** *adj.* F **1.** sorglos; **2.** frei u. ungebunden; **~ will** *s.* freier Wille, Willensfreiheit *f*.

freeze [fri:z] **I** *v/i.* [*irr.*] → **frozen**; **1.** frieren (*a. impers.*): **it is freezing hard** es friert stark; **I am freezing** mir ist eiskalt; **~ to death** erfrieren; **2.** gefrieren; **3.** *a.* **~ up** (*od.* **over**) ein-, zufrieren, vereisen; **4.** an-, festfrieren: **~ on to** *sl.* sich wie eine Klette an *j-n* heften; **5.** (*vor Kälte, fig. vor Schreck etc.*) erstarren, eisig werden (*Person, Gesicht*): **it made my blood ~** es ließ mir das Blut in den Adern erstarren; **~!** *sl.* keine Bewegung!; **II** *v/t.* [*irr.*] **6.** zum Gefrieren bringen: **I was frozen** mir war eiskalt; **7.** erfrieren lassen; **8.** *Fleisch etc.* einfrieren, tiefkühlen; ⚕ vereisen; **9.** *a. fig.* erstarren lassen, *fig. a.* lähmen: **~ out** *Am.* F *j-n* hinausekeln, kaltstellen; **10.** ✝ *Guthaben etc.* sperren, *a. Preise etc., pol. diplomatische Beziehungen* einfrieren: **~ prices** (**wages**) *a.* e-n Preis- (Lohn)stopp einführen; **III** *s.* **11.** Gefrieren *n*; **12.** Erstarrung *f*; **13.** 'Frost(periˌode *f*) *m*, Kälte(welle) *f*; **14.** ✝, *pol.* Einfrieren *n*, ✝ *a.* (Preis-, Lohn)Stopp *m*: **~ on wages**; **put a ~ on** → 10; **ˌ~-'dry** *v/t.* gefriertrocknen; **~ dry·er** *s.* Gefriertrockner *m*.

freez·er ['fri:zə] *s.* **1.** Ge'friermaˌschine *f od.* -kammer *f*; **2.** Tiefkühlgerät *n*; **3.** Gefrierfach *n* (*Kühlschrank*); **'freeze-up** *s.* starker Frost; **'freez·ing** [-zɪŋ] **I** *adj.* ☐ **1.** ⚙ Gefrier…, Kälte…: **~ compartment** → **freezer** 3; **below ~ point** unter dem Gefrierpunkt, unter Null; **2.** eisig; **3.** kalt, unnahbar; **II** *s.* **4.** Einfrieren *n* (*a.* ✝, *pol.*); **5.** *a.* ⚕ Vereisung *f*; **6.** Erstarrung *f*.

freight [freɪt] **I** *s.* **1.** Fracht *f*, Beförderung *f*; **2.** ⚓ (*Am. a.* ✈, 🚂, *mot.*) Fracht(gut *n*) *f*, Ladung *f*: **~ and carriage** *Brit.* See- und Landfracht; **3.** Fracht(gebühr) *f*: **~ forward** Fracht gegen Nachnahme; **4.** *Am.* → **freight train**; **II** *v/t.* **5.** *Schiff, Am. a. Güterwagen etc.* befrachten, beladen; **6.** *Güter* verfrachten; **'freight·age** [-tɪdʒ] *s.* **1.** Trans'port *m*; **2.** → **freight** 2, 3.

freight| bill *s.* ✝ *Am.* Frachtbrief *m*; **~ car** *s. Am.* Güterwagen *m*.

freight·er ['freɪtə] *s.* **1.** a) Frachtschiff *n*, Frachter *m*, b) Trans'portflugzeug *n*; **2.** a) Befrachter *m*, Reeder *m*, b) Ab-, Verlader *m*.

'freight|ˌlin·er *s. Brit.* Con'tainerzug *m*; **~ rate** *s.* ✝ Frachtsatz *m*; **~ sta·tion** *s. Am.* Güterbahnhof *m*; **~ train** *s. Am.* Güterzug *m*.

French [frentʃ] **I** *adj.* **1.** fran'zösisch: **~ master** Französischlehrer; **II** *s.* **2.** **the ~** die Franzosen *pl.*; **3.** *ling.* Fran'zösisch *n*: **in ~** a) auf französisch, b) im Französischen; **~ beans** *s. pl.* grüne Bohnen *pl.*; **~ Ca·na·di·an I** *s.* **1.** 'Frankokaˌnadier(in); **2.** *ling.* ka'nadisches Fran'zösisch; **II** *adj.* **3.** 'frankokaˌnadisch; **~ chalk** *s.* Schneiderkreide *f*; **~ doors** *Am.* → **French windows**; **~ dress·ing** *s.* French Dressing *n* (*Salatsoße aus Öl, Essig, Senf u. Gewürzen*); **~ fried po·ta·toes**, F **~ fries** [fraɪz] *s. pl. Am.* Pommes 'frites *pl.*; **~ horn** *s.* ♪ (Wald)Horn *n*; **~ kiss** *s.* Zungenkuß *m*; **~ leave** *s.*: **take ~** sich (auf) französisch empfehlen; **~ let·ter** *s.* F ‚Pa'riser' *m* (*Kondom*); **~ loaf** *s.* [*irr.*] Ba'guette *f*; **'~·man** [-mən] *s.* [*irr.*] Fran'zose *m*; **~ mar·i·gold** *s.* ⚘ Stu'dentenblume *f*; **~ pol·ish** *s.* 'Schellackpoliˌtur *f*; **~ roof** *s.* △ Man'sardendach *n*; **~ win·dows** *s. pl.* Ter'rassen-, Bal'kontür *f*; **'~ˌwom·an** *s.* [*irr.*] Fran'zösin *f*.

fre·net·ic [frə'netɪk] *adj.* (☐ **~ally**) → **frenzied**.

fren·zied ['frenzɪd] *adj.* **1.** fre'netisch (*Geschrei etc.*), rasend: **~ applause**; **2.** a) außer sich, rasend (**with** vor *dat.*), b) wild, hektisch; **fren·zy** ['frenzɪ] **I** *s.* **1.** Wahnsinn *m*, Rase'rei *f*: **in a ~ of hate** rasend vor Haß; **2.** wilde Aufregung; **3.** Verzückung *f*, Ek'stase *f*; **4.** Wirbel *m*, Hektik *f*; **II** *v/t.* **5.** rasend machen.

fre·quen·cy ['fri:kwənsɪ] *s.* **1.** Häufigkeit *f* (*a.* ⚕, *biol.*); **2.** *phys.* Fre'quenz *f*, Schwingungszahl *f*: **high ~** Hochfrequenz; **~ band** *s.* ⚡ Fre'quenzband *n*; **~ chang·er**, **~ con·vert·er** *s.* ⚡, *phys.* Fre'quenzwandler *m*; **~ curve** *s.* ⚕, *biol.* Häufigkeitskurve *f*; **~ mod·u·la·tion** *s. phys.* Fre'quenzmodulatiˌon *f*; **~ range** *s.* Fre'quenzbereich *m*.

fre·quent I *adj.* ['fri:kwənt] ☐ → **frequently**; **1.** häufig, (häufig) wieder'holt: **be ~** häufig vorkommen; **he is a ~ visitor** er kommt häufig zu Besuch; **2.** ⚕ beschleunigt (*Puls*); **II** *v/t.* [frɪ'kwent] **3.** häufig *od.* oft be-, aufsuchen, frequentieren; **fre·quen·ta·tive** [frɪ'kwentətɪv] *ling.* **I** *adj.* frequenta'tiv; **II** *s.* Frequenta'tiv(um) *n*; **fre·quent·er** [frɪ'kwentə] *s.* (fleißiger) Besucher, Stammgast *m*; **'fre·quent·ly** [-lɪ] *adv.* oft, häufig.

fres·co ['freskəʊ] **I** *pl.* **-cos**, **-coes** *s.* a) 'Freskomaleˌrei *f*, b) Fresko(gemälde) *n*; **II** *v/t.* in Fresko (be)malen.

fresh [freʃ] **I** *adj.* ☐ (→ *a.* 8); **1.** *allg.* frisch; **2.** neu: **~ evidence**; **~ news**; **~ arrival** Neuankömmling *m*; **make a ~ start** neu anfangen; **take a ~ look at** *et.* noch einmal *od.* von e-r anderen Seite betrachten; **3.** frisch: a) zusätzlich: **~ supplies**, b) *nicht alt*: **~ eggs**, c) *nicht eingemacht*: **~ vegetables** *a.* Frischgemüse *n*; **~ meat** Frischfleisch *n*; **~ herrings** grüne Heringe, d) sauber, rein: **~ shirt**; **4.** frisch: a) blühend, gesund: **~ complexion**, b) ausgeruht, erholt: (**as**) **~ as a daisy** quicklebendig; **5.** frisch: a) unverbraucht, b) erfrischend, c) kräftig: **~ wind**, d) kühl; **6.** *fig.* ‚grün', unerfahren; **7.** F frech, ‚pampig': **don't get ~ with me!** werd (mir) ja nicht frech!; **II** *adv.* **8.** frisch: **~ from** frisch *od.* direkt von *od.* aus; **III** *s.* **9.** Frische *f*, Kühle *f*: **~ of the day** der Tagesanfang; **10.** → **freshet**.

ˌfresh-'air fiend *s.* F 'Frischluftfaˌnatiker(in), -aˌpostel *m*.

fresh·en ['freʃn] **I** *v/t.* *a.* **~ up 1.** *j-n* erfrischen: **~ o.s. up** → 4; **2.** *fig. et.* auffrischen, ‚aufpolieren'; **II** *v/i. mst* **~ up 3.** frisch werden, aufleben; **4.** sich frisch machen; **5.** auffrischen (*Wind*); **'fresh·er** [-ʃə] *Brit.* F → **freshman**; **'fresh·et** [-ʃɪt] *s.* Hochwasser *n*, Flut *f* (*a. fig.*); **'fresh·man** [-mən] *s.* [*irr.*] Stu'dent *m* im ersten Se'mester; **'fresh·ness** [-ʃnɪs] *s.* Frische *f*; Neuheit *f*; Unerfahrenheit *f*.

fresh| wa·ter *s*. Süßwasser *n*; **'~ˌwa·ter** *adj*. **1.** Süßwasser…: ***~ fish***; **2.** *Am*. Provinz…: ***~ college***.

fret¹ [fret] *s*. ♪ Bund *m*, Griffleiste *f*.

fret² [fret] **I** *s*. △ *etc*. **1.** durch'brochene Verzierung; **2.** Gitterwerk *n*; **II** *v/t*. **3.** durch'brochen *od*. gitterförmig verzieren.

fret³ [fret] **I** *v/t*. **1.** ⚙, ⚗ an-, zerfressen, angreifen; **2.** abnutzen, -scheuern; **3.** *j-n* ärgern, reizen; **II** *v/i*. **4.** a) sich ärgern: ***~ and fume*** vor Wut schäumen, b) sich Sorgen machen; **III** *s*. **5.** Ärger *m*, Verärgerung *f*; **'fret·ful** [-fʊl] *adj*. □ ärgerlich, gereizt.

fret| saw *s*. ⚙ Laubsäge *f*; **'~·work** *s*. **1.** △ *etc*. Gitterwerk *n*; **2.** Laubsägearbeit *f*.

Freud·i·an ['frɔɪdjən] **I** *s*. Freudi'aner (-in); **II** *adj*. freudi'anisch, Freudsch: ***~ slip*** *psych*. Freudsche Fehlleistung.

fri·a·ble ['fraɪəbl] *adj*. bröck(e)lig, krümelig.

fri·ar ['fraɪə] *s*. *eccl*. (*bsd*. Bettel-) Mönch *m*: ***Black ♀*** Dominikaner *m*; ***Grey ♀*** Franziskaner *m*; ***White ♀*** Karmeliter *m*; **'fri·ar·y** [-ərɪ] *s*. Mönchskloster *n*.

fric·as·see ['frɪkəsiː] (*Fr.*) **I** *s*. Frikas'see *n*; **II** *v/t*. [ˌfrɪkə'siː] frikassieren.

fric·a·tive ['frɪkətɪv] *ling*. **I** *adj*. Reibe…; **II** *s*. Reibelaut *m*.

fric·tion ['frɪkʃn] **I** *s*. **1.** ⚙, *phys*. Reibung *f*, Frikti'on *f*; **2.** *bsd*. ⚕ Einreibung *f*; **3.** *fig*. Reibungen *pl*., Reibe'rei *f*, Spannung *f*, 'Mißhelligkeit *f*; **II** *adj*. **4.** ⚙, *phys*. Reibungs…: ***~ brake***; ***~ clutch***; ***~ drive*** Friktionsantrieb *m*; ***~ gear(ing)*** Friktionsgetriebe *n*; ***~ match*** Streichholz *n*; ***~ surface*** Lauffläche *f*; ***~ tape*** *Am*. Isolierband *n*; **'fric·tion·al** [-ʃənl] *adj*. **1.** Reibungs…, Friktions…; **2.** ***~ unemployment*** temporäre Arbeitslosigkeit; **'fric·tion·less** [-lɪs] *adj*. ⚙ reibungsfrei, -arm.

Fri·day ['fraɪdɪ] *s*. Freitag *m*: ***on ~*** am Freitag; ***on ~s*** freitags; → ***Good Friday***, ***girl Friday***.

fridge [frɪdʒ] *s*. *Brit*. F Kühlschrank *m*.

fried [fraɪd] *adj*. **1.** gebraten; → ***fry²*** 1; **2.** *Am*. *sl*. ‚blau', besoffen; **'~·cake** *s*. *Am*. Krapfen *m*.

friend [frend] *s*. **1.** Freund(in): ***~ at court*** ‚Vetter' (*einflußreicher Freund*); ***~ of the court*** ⚖ sachverständiger Beistand (des Gerichts); → ***next*** 1; ***be ~s with s.o.*** mit j-m befreundet sein; ***make ~s with*** mit *j-m* Freundschaft schließen; ***a ~ in need is a ~ indeed*** der wahre Freund zeigt sich erst in der Not; **2.** Bekannte(r *m*) *f*; **3.** Helfer(in), Förderer *m*; **4.** Hilfe *f*, Freund(in); **5.** *Brit*. a) ***my honourable ~*** *parl*. mein Herr Kollege *od*. Vorredner (*Anrede*), b) ***my learned ~*** ⚖ mein verehrter Herr Kollege; **6.** ***Society of ♀s*** Gesellschaft der Freunde, *die* Quäker; **'friend·less** [-lɪs] *adj*. ohne Freunde; **'friend·li·ness** [-lɪnɪs] *s*. Freund(schaft)lichkeit *f*; freundschaftliche Gesinnung; **'friend·ly** [-lɪ] **I** *adj*. **1.** freundlich; **2.** freundschaftlich, Freundschafts…: ***~ match*** *sport* Freundschaftsspiel *n*; ***a ~ nation*** e-e befreundete Nation; **3.** wohlwollend, -gesinnt: ***~ neutrality*** *pol*. wohlwollende Neutralität; ***♀ Society*** Versicherungsverein *m* auf Gegenseitigkeit; ***~ troops*** ⚔ eigene Truppen; **4.** günstig; **II** *s*. **5.** *sport* F Freundschaftsspiel *n*; **'friend·ship** [-ʃɪp] *s*. **1.** Freundschaft *f*; **2.** → ***friendliness***.

fri·er → ***fryer***.

Frie·sian ['friːzjən] → ***Frisian***.

frieze¹ [friːz] **I** *s*. **1.** △ Fries *m*; **2.** Zierstreifen *m* (*Tapete etc.*); **II** *v/t*. **3.** mit e-m Fries versehen.

frieze² [friːz] *s*. Fries *m* (*Wollzeug*).

frig [frɪg] V **I** *v/t*. ‚ficken'; **II** *v/i*. ‚wichsen'.

frig·ate ['frɪgɪt] *s*. ⚓ Fre'gatte *f*.

frige [frɪdʒ] → ***fridge***.

fright [fraɪt] **I** *s*. Scheck(en) *m*, Entsetzen *n*: ***get*** (*od*. ***have***) ***a ~*** erschrecken; ***give s.o. a ~*** j-n erschrecken; ***take ~*** a) erschrecken, b) scheuen (*Pferd*); ***get off with a ~*** mit dem Schrecken davonkommen; ***he looked a ~*** F er sah ‚verboten' aus; **II** *v/t*. *poet*. → ***frighten***; **'fright·en** [-tn] **I** *v/t*. **1.** a) *j-n* erschrecken (***s.o. to death*** j-n zu Tode), *j-m* e-n Schrecken einjagen, b) *j-m* Angst einjagen: ***~ s.o. into doing s.th.*** j-n so einschüchtern, daß er et. tut; ***I was ~ed*** ich erschrak *od*. bekam Angst (***of*** vor *dat*.); **2.** ***~ away*** vertreiben, -scheuchen; **II** *v/i*. **3.** ***he ~s easily*** a) er ist sehr schreckhaft, b) dem kann man leicht Angst einjagen; **'fright·ened** [-tnd] *adj*. erschreckt, erschrocken, verängstigt; **'fright·en·ing** [-tnɪŋ] *adj*. □ erschreckend; **'fright·ful** [-fʊl] *adj*. □ furchtbar, schrecklich, entsetzlich, gräßlich, scheußlich (*alle a*. F *fig*.); **'fright·ful·ly** [-flɪ] *adv*. furchtbar (*etc*.); **'fright·ful·ness** [-fʊlnɪs] *s*. **1.** Schrecklichkeit *f*; **2.** Schreckensherrschaft *f*, Terror *m*.

frig·id ['frɪdʒɪd] *adj*. □ **1.** kalt, frostig, eisig (*alle a. fig*.): ***~ zone*** *geogr*. kalte Zone; **2.** *fig*. kühl, steif; **3.** *psych*. fri'gid, gefühlskalt; **fri·gid·i·ty** [frɪ'dʒɪdətɪ] *s*. Kälte *f*, Frostigkeit *f* (*a. fig*.); *psych*. Frigidi'tät *f*.

frill [frɪl] **I** *s*. **1.** (Hals-, Hand)Krause *f*, Rüsche *f*; **2.** Pa'pierkrause *f*, Man'schette *f*; **3.** *zo*., *orn*. Kragen *m*; **4.** *mst pl*. *contp*. ‚Verzierungen' *pl*., Kinkerlitzchen *pl*., ‚Mätzchen' *pl*., ‚Firlefanz' *m*: ***put on ~s*** *fig*. ‚auf vornehm machen', sich aufplustern; ***without ~s*** ‚ohne Kinkerlitzchen', schlicht; **II** *v/t*. **5.** mit e-r Krause besetzen; **6.** kräuseln; **III** *v/i*. **7.** *phot*. sich kräuseln; **'frill·ies** [-lɪz] *s*. *pl*. *Brit*. F ‚Reizwäsche' *f*, 'Spitzenˌunterwäsche *f*.

fringe [frɪndʒ] **I** *s*. **1.** Franse *f*, Besatz *m*; **2.** Rand *m*, Einfassung *f*, Um'randung *f*; **3.** 'Ponyfriˌsur *f*; **4.** a) Randbezirk *m*, -gebiet *n* (*a. fig*.), b) *fig*. Rand(zone *f*) *m*, Grenze *f*: ***~s of civilization***, c) → ***fringe group***; → ***lunatic*** I; **II** *v/t*. **5.** mit Fransen besetzen; **6.** (um)'säumen; ***~ ben·e·fits*** *s*. *pl*. (Gehalts-, Lohn)Nebenleistungen *pl*.

fringed [frɪndʒd] *adj*. gefranst.

fringe group *s*. *sociol*. Randgruppe *f*.

frip·per·y ['frɪpərɪ] *s*. **1.** Putz *m*, Flitterkram *m*; **2.** Tand *m*, Plunder *m*; **3.** *fig*. → ***frill*** 4.

Fri·sian ['frɪzɪən] **I** *s*. **1.** Friese *m*, Friesin *f*; **2.** *ling*. Friesisch *n*; **II** *adj*. **3.** friesisch.

frisk [frɪsk] **I** *v/i*. **1.** her'umtollen, -hüpfen; **II** *v/t*. **2.** wedeln mit; **3.** *j-n* ‚filzen', *a. et*. durch'suchen; **III** *s*. **4.** a) Ausgelassenheit *f*, b) Freudensprung *m*; **5.** F ‚Filzen' *n*; **'frisk·i·ness** [-kɪnɪs] *s*. Lustigkeit *f*, Ausgelassenheit *f*; **'frisk·y** [-kɪ] *adj*. □ lebhaft, munter, ausgelassen.

fris·son ['frɪsɔ̃ːŋ] (*Fr.*) *s*. (leichter) Schauer.

frit [frɪt] *v/t*. ⚙ fritten, schmelzen.

frith [frɪθ] → ***firth***.

frit·ter¹ ['frɪtə] *s*. Bei'gnet *m* (*Gebäck*).

frit·ter² ['frɪtə] *v/t*. **1.** *mst* ***~ away*** verplempern, vergeuden; **2.** a) zerfetzen, b) in Streifen schneiden, *Küche*: schnetzeln.

fritz [frɪts] *s*. *Am*. *sl*.: ***on the ~*** kaputt, ‚im Eimer'.

friv·ol ['frɪvl] **I** *v/i*. (he'rum)tändeln; **II** *v/t*. ***~ away*** → ***fritter²*** 1; **fri·vol·i·ty** [frɪ'vɒlətɪ] *s*. Frivoli'tät *f*: a) Leichtsinn(igkeit *f*) *m*, Oberflächlichkeit *f*, b) Leichtfertigkeit *f* (*Rede od. Handlung*); **'friv·o·lous** [-vələs] *adj*. □ **1.** fri'vol, leichtsinnig, -fertig; **2.** nicht ernst zu nehmen(d); **3.** ⚖ schika'nös.

frizz¹ [frɪz] **I** *v/t*. *u*. *v/i*. (sich) kräuseln; **II** *s*. gekräuseltes Haar.

frizz² [frɪz] → ***frizzle¹*** I.

friz·zle¹ ['frɪzl] **I** *v/i*. brutzeln; **II** *v/t*. (braun) rösten.

friz·zle² ['frɪzl] → ***frizz¹***; **'friz·zly** [-lɪ], **'friz·zy** [-zɪ] *adj*. kraus, gekräuselt.

fro [frəʊ] *adv*.: ***to and ~*** hin u. her, auf u. ab.

frock [frɒk] **I** *s*. **1.** (Mönchs)Kutte *f*; **2.** (Damen)Kleid *n*; **3.** ⚓ Wolljacke *f*; **4.** Kinderkleid *n*, Kittel *m*; **5.** Gehrock *m*; **6.** (Arbeits)Kittel *m*; **II** *v/t*. **7.** mit e-m geistlichen Amt bekleiden; **8.** mit e-m Kittel bekleiden; ***~ coat*** *s*. Gehrock *m*.

frog [frɒg] *s*. **1.** *zo*. Frosch *m*: ***have a ~ in the throat*** e-n Frosch im Hals haben, heiser sein; **2.** Schnurbesatz *m*, -verschluß *m* (*Rock*); **3.** ⚔ Quaste *f*, Säbeltasche *f*; **4.** 🚂 Herz-, Kreuzungsstück *n*; **5.** ⚡ Oberleitungsweiche *f*; **6.** *zo*. Strahl *m* (*Pferdehuf*); **7.** *Am*. *sl*. Bizeps *m*; **8.** ♀ *sl*. *contp*. ‚'Scheißfranˌzose' *m*; ***~ kick*** *s*. *Schwimmen*: Grätschstoß *m*; **'~·man** [-mən] *s*. [*irr*.] Froschmann *m*, ⚔ *a*. Kampfschwimmer *m*; **'~·march** *v/t*. *j-n* (mit dem Gesicht nach unten) fortschleppen; ***~'s legs*** *s*. *pl*. Froschschenkel *pl*.; ***~ spawn*** *s*. **1.** *zo*. Froschlaich *m*; **2.** ⚘ Froschlaichalge *f*.

frol·ic ['frɒlɪk] **I** *s*. **1.** Her'umtollen *n*, Ausgelassenheit *f*; **2.** Jux *m*, Spaß *m*, Streich *m*; **II** *v/i*. *pret*. *u*. *p.p*. **'frol·icked** [-kt] **3.** her'umtollen, -toben; **'frol·ic·some** [-səm] *adj*. 'übermütig, ausgelassen.

from [frɒm; frəm] *prp*. von, von … her, aus, aus … her'aus: a) *Ort, Herkunft*: ***a gift ~ his son*** ein Geschenk von s-m Sohn; ***~ outside*** (*od*. ***without***) von (dr)außen; ***the train ~ X*** der Zug von *od*. aus X; ***he is ~ Kent*** er ist *od*. stammt aus Kent; *auf Sendungen*: ***~ …*** Absender …, b) *Zeit*: ***~ 2 to 4 o'clock*** von 2 bis 4 Uhr; ***~ now*** von jetzt an; ***~ a child*** von Kindheit an, c) *Entfernung*: ***6 miles ~ Rome*** 6 Meilen von Rom (entfernt); ***far ~ the truth*** weit von der Wahrheit entfernt, d) *Fortnehmen*:

stolen ~ the shop (***the table***) aus dem Laden (vom Tisch) gestohlen; ***take it ~ him!*** nimm es ihm weg!, e) *Anzahl*: ***~ six to eight boats*** sechs bis acht Boote, f) *Wandlung*: ***~ bad to worse*** immer schlimmer, g) *Unterscheidung*: ***he does not know black ~ white*** er kann Schwarz u. Weiß nicht unterscheiden, h) *Quelle*, *Grund*: ***~ my point of view*** von meinem Standpunkt (aus); ***~ what he said*** nach dem, was er sagte; ***painted ~ life*** nach dem Leben gemalt; ***he died ~ hunger*** er verhungerte; **~ a·bove** *adv*. von oben; **~ a·cross** *adv. u. prp.* von jenseits (*gen.*), von der anderen Seite (*gen.*); **~ a·mong** *prp.* aus ... her'aus; **~ be·fore** *prp.* aus der Zeit vor (*dat.*); **~ be·neath** *adv.* von unten; *prp.* unter (*dat.*) ... her'vor *od.* her'aus; **~ be·tween** *prp.* zwischen (*dat.*) ... her'vor; **~ be·yond** *adv. u. prp.* von jenseits (*gen.*); **~ in·side** *adv.* von innen; *prp.* aus ... her'aus: ***~ the house*** aus dem Inneren des Hauses (heraus); **~ out of** *prp.* aus ... her'aus; **~ un·der** → ***from beneath***.

frond [frɒnd] *s.* ⚘ (Farn)Wedel *m*.

front [frʌnt] **I** *s.* **1.** *allg.* Vorder-, Stirnseite *f*, Front *f*; **2.** ⚠ (Vorder)Front *f*, Fas'sade *f*; **3.** Vorderteil *n*; **4.** ⚔ a) Front *f*, Kampflinie *f*, -gebiet *n*, b) Frontbreite *f*: ***at the ~*** an der Front; ***on all ~s*** an allen Fronten (*a. fig.*); **5.** Vordergrund *f*, Spitze *f*: ***in ~*** an der *od.* die Spitze, vorn, davor; ***in ~ of*** vor (*dat.*); ***to the ~*** nach vorn; ***come to the ~*** *fig.* in den Vordergrund treten; ***up ~*** a) vorn, *fig. a.* an der Spitze, b) nach vorn, *fig. a.* an die Spitze; **6.** (Straßen-, Wasser)Front *f*: ***the ~*** *Brit.* die Strandpromenade; **7.** *fig.* Front *f*: a) (*bsd. politische*) Organisati'on, b) Sektor *m*: ***on the economic ~*** an der wirtschaftlichen Front; **8.** a) ‚Strohmann' *m*, b) ‚Aushängeschild' *n* (*e-r Interessengruppe od. Geheimorganisation etc.*); **9.** F ‚Fas'sade' *f*: ***put up a ~*** a) sich Allüren geben, b) ‚Theater spielen'; ***show a bold ~*** kühn auftreten; ***maintain a ~*** den Schein wahren; **10.** *poet.* a) Stirn *f*, b) Antlitz *n*; **11.** *fig.* Frechheit *f*: ***have the ~ to*** (*inf.*) die Stirn haben zu (*inf.*); **12.** Hemdbrust *f*; **13.** (falsche) Stirnlocken *pl.*; **14.** *meteor.* Front *f*: ***cold ~***; **II** *adj.* **15.** Front..., Vorder...: ***~ entrance***; ***~ row*** vorder(st)e Reihe; ***~ tooth*** Vorderzahn *m*; **16.** ***~ man*** ‚Strohmann' *m*; **17.** *ling.* Vorderzungen...; **III** *v/t.* **18.** gegen'überstehen, -liegen (*dat.*): ***the house ~s the sea*** das Haus liegt (nach) dem Meer zu; ***the windows ~ the street*** die Fenster gehen auf die Straße; **19.** *j-m* entgegen-, gegen'übertreten, *j-m* die Stirn bieten; **20.** mit e-r Front *od.* Vorderseite versehen; **21.** als Front *od.* Vorderseite dienen für; **22.** *ling.* palatalisieren; **23.** *TV Brit. Programm* moderieren; **IV** *v/i.* **24.** ***~ on*** (*od.* ***to***[***wards***]) → 18; **25.** ***~ for*** als ‚Strohmann' *od.* ‚Aushängeschild' fungieren für.

front·age ['frʌntɪdʒ] *s.* **1.** (Vorder)Front *f* (e-s Hauses): ***~ line*** Bau(flucht)linie *f*; ***~ road*** *Am. Parallelstraße zu e-r Schnellstraße* (*mit Wohnhäusern, Geschäften etc.*); ***have a ~ on*** → ***front*** 18; **2.** Land *n* an der Straßen- *od.* Wasserfront; **3.** Grundstück *n* zwischen der Vorderfront e-s Hauses u. der Straße; **4.** ⚔ Front- *od.* Angriffsbreite *f*.

fron·tal ['frʌntl] **I** *adj.* **1.** fron'tal, Vorder..., Front...: ***~ attack*** (***collision***) Frontalangriff *m* (-zs.-stoß *m*); ***~ axle*** ⚙ Vorderachse *f*; **2.** ⚙, *anat.* Stirn...; **II** *s.* **3.** *eccl.* Ante'pendium *n*; **4.** ⚠ Ziergiebel *m*; **~ bone** *s.* Stirnbein *n*; **~ sinus** *s.* Stirn(bein)höhle *f*.

front| bench *s. parl.* vordere Sitzreihe (*für Regierung u. Oppositionsführer*); **ˌ~-'bench·er** *s. parl.* führendes Frakti'onsmitglied; **~ door** *s.* Haus-, Vordertür *f*; **~ drive** *s. mot.* Frontantrieb *m*; **ˌ~-'end col·li·sion** *s. mot.* Auffahrunfall *m*; **~ en·gine** *s.* Frontmotor *m*.

fron·tier ['frʌnˌtɪə] **I** *s.* **1.** (Landes)Grenze *f*; **2.** *Am.* Grenzgebiet *n*, Grenze *f* (zum Wilden Westen): ***new ~s*** *fig.* neue Ziele; **3.** *fig. oft pl.* Grenze *f*, Grenzbereich *m*; Neuland *n*; **II** *adj.* **4.** Grenz...: ***~ town***; **ˌfron'tiers·man** [-ɪəzmən] *s.* [*irr.*] *Am. hist.* Grenzbewohner *m*.

fron·tis·piece ['frʌntɪspiːs] *s.* Fronti'spiz *n*: a) Titelbild *n* (*Buch*), b) ⚠ Giebelseite *f od.* -feld *n*.

front·let ['frʌntlɪt] *s.* **1.** *zo.* Stirn *f*; **2.** Stirnband *n*.

front| line *s.* ⚔ Kampffront *f*, Front(linie) *f*; **'~-line** *adj.*: ***~ officer*** Frontoffizier *m*; **~ page** *s.* Titelseite *f* (*Zeitung*); **'~-page** *adj.*: ***~ news*** wichtige *od.* aktuelle Nachricht(en); **~ pas·sen·ger** *s. mot.* Beifahrer(in); **ˌ~-'run·ner** *s.* **1.** *sport* a) Spitzenreiter *m* (*a. fig.*), b) Favo'rit(in); **2.** *pol.* 'Spitzenkandiˌdat(in); **3.** Tempoläufer *m*; **~ seat** *s.* Vordersitz *m*; **~ sight** *s.* ⚔ Korn *n*; **~ view** *s.* Vorderansicht *f*; **'~-wheel** *adj.*: ***~ drive*** ⚙ Vorderradantrieb *m*.

frosh [frɒʃ] *s. sg. u. pl. Am.* → ***freshman***.

frost [frɒst] **I** *s.* **1.** Frost *m*: ***10 degrees of ~*** *Brit.* 10 Grad Kälte; **2.** Eisblumen *pl.*, Reif *m*; **3.** *fig.* Kühle *f*, Kälte *f*, Frostigkeit *f*; **4.** *sl.* ‚Reinfall' *m*; ‚Pleite' *f*; **II** *v/t.* **5.** mit Reif *od.* Eis über'ziehen; **6.** ⚙ *Glas* mattieren; **7.** *Küche*: a) glasieren, mit Zuckerguß über'ziehen, b) mit (Puder)Zucker bestreuen; **8.** Frostschäden verursachen bei; **9.** *j-n* sehr kühl behandeln; **'~·bite** *s.* ⚕ Erfrierung *f*; **'~ˌbit·ten** *adj.* ⚕ erfroren.

frost·ed ['frɒstɪd] *adj.* **1.** bereift, über'froren; **2.** ⚙ mattiert: ***~ glass*** Matt-, Milchglas *n*; **3.** ⚕ erfroren; **4.** mit Zuckerguß, glasiert; **'frost·i·ness** [-tɪnɪs] *s.* Frost *m*, eisige Kälte (*a. fig.*); **'frost·ing** [-tɪŋ] *s.* **1.** Zuckerguß *m*, Gla'sur *f*; **2.** ⚙ Mattierung *f*; **'frost·work** *s.* Eisblumen *pl.*; **'frost·y** [-tɪ] *adj.* ☐ **1.** eisig, frostig (*a. fig.*); **2.** mit Reif *od.* Eis bedeckt; **3.** eisgrau: ***~ hair***.

froth [frɒθ] **I** *s.* **1.** Schaum *m*; **2.** ⚕ (Blasen)Schaum *m*; **3.** *fig.* ‚Firlefanz' *m*; **II** *v/t.* **4.** a) zum Schäumen bringen, b) zu Schaum schlagen; **III** *v/i.* **5.** schäumen (*a. fig. vor Wut*); **'froth·i·ness** [-θɪnɪs] *s.* **1.** Schäumen *n*, Schaum *m*; **2.** *fig.* Seicht-, Hohlheit *f*; **'froth·y** [-θɪ] *adj.* ☐ **1.** schaumig, schäumend; **2.** *fig.* seicht, hohl.

frou-frou ['fruːfruː] (*Fr.*) *s.* **1.** Knistern *n*, Rascheln *n* (*von Seide*); **2.** Flitter *m*.

fro·ward ['frəʊəd] *adj.* ☐ *obs.* eigensinnig.

frown [fraʊn] **I** *v/i.* a) die Stirn runzeln (***at*** über *acc.*; *a. fig.*), b) finster dreinschauen: ***~*** (***up***)***on*** stirnrunzelnd *od.* finster betrachten, *fig.* mißbilligen (*acc.*); **II** *v/t.* ***~ down*** *j-n* durch finstere Blicke einschüchtern; **III** *s.* Stirnrunzeln *n*; finsterer Blick; **'frown·ing** [-nɪŋ] *adj.* ☐ **1.** stirnrunzelnd; **2.** a) miß'billigend, b) finster (*Blick*); **3.** bedrohlich.

frowst [fraʊst] F **I** *s.* ‚Mief' *m*; **II** *v/i.* im ‚Mief' hocken; **'frowst·y** [-tɪ] *adj.* muffig, ‚miefig'.

frowz·i·ness ['fraʊzɪnɪs] *s.* **1.** Schlampigkeit *f*; Ungepflegtheit *f*; **2.** muffiger Geruch; **frowz·y** ['fraʊzɪ] *adj.* **1.** schlampig, ungepflegt; **2.** muffig.

froze [frəʊz] *pret. von* ***freeze***; **'fro·zen** [-zn] **I** *p.p. von* ***freeze***; **II** *adj.* **1.** (ein-, zu)gefroren; **2.** erfroren; **3.** gefroren, Gefrier...: ***~ food*** Tiefkühlkost *f*; ***~ meat*** Gefrierfleisch *n*; **4.** eisig, frostig (*a. fig.*); **5.** kalt, teilnahms-, gefühllos; **6.** ✝ eingefroren: a) festliegend: ***~ capital***, b) gestoppt: ***~ prices***; ***~ wages***; **7.** ***~ facts*** *Am.* unumstößliche Tatsachen.

fruc·ti·fi·ca·tion [ˌfrʌktɪfɪ'keɪʃn] *s.* ⚘ **1.** Fruchtbildung *f*; **2.** Befruchtung *f*.

fruc·ti·fy ['frʌktɪfaɪ] ⚘ **I** *v/i.* Früchte tragen (*a. fig.*); **II** *v/t.* befruchten (*a. fig.*); **fruc·tose** ['frʌktəʊs] *s.* Fruchtzucker *m*.

fru·gal ['fruːgl] *adj.* ☐ **1.** sparsam, haushälterisch (***of*** mit); **2.** genügsam, bescheiden; **3.** einfach, spärlich, fru'gal: ***a ~ meal***; **fru·gal·i·ty** [fruː'gælətɪ] *s.* Sparsamkeit *f*; Genügsamkeit *f*; Einfachheit *f*.

fru·giv·o·rous [fruː'dʒɪvərəs] *adj. zo.* fruchtfressend.

fruit [fruːt] **I** *s.* **1.** ⚘ a) Frucht *f*, b) Samenkapsel *f*; **2.** *coll.* a) Früchte *pl.*: ***bear ~*** Früchte tragen (*a. fig.*), b) Obst *n*; **3.** *bibl.* Nachkommen(schaft *f*) *pl.*: ***~ of the body*** Leibesfrucht *f*; **4.** *mst pl. fig.* Frucht *f*, Früchte *pl.*, Ergebnis *n*, Erfolg *m*, Gewinn *m*; **5.** *sl.* ‚Spinner' *m*; **6.** *Am. sl.* ‚Homo' *m*; **II** *v/i.* **7.** ⚘ (Früchte) tragen; **fruit·ar·i·an** [fruː'teərɪən] *s.* Obstesser(in), Rohköstler(in).

'fruit|·cake *s.* **1.** englischer Kuchen; **2.** *Brit. sl.* ‚Spinner' *m*; **~ cock·tail** *s.* Früchtecocktail *m*; **~ cup** *s.* Früchtebecher *m*.

fruit·er·er ['fruːtərə] *s.* Obsthändler *m*; **'fruit·ful** [-tfʊl] *adj.* ☐ **1.** fruchtbar (*a. fig.*); **2.** *fig.* erfolgreich; **'fruit·ful·ness** [-tfʊlnɪs] *s.* Fruchtbarkeit *f*.

fru·i·tion [fruː'ɪʃn] *s.* Erfüllung *f*, Verwirklichung *f*: ***come to ~*** sich verwirklichen, Früchte tragen.

fruit| jar *s.* Einweckglas *n*; **~ juice** *s.* Obstsaft *m*; **~ knife** *s.* [*irr.*] Obstmesser *n*.

fruit·less ['fruːtlɪs] *adj.* ☐ **1.** unfruchtbar; **2.** *fig.* frucht-, erfolglos, vergeblich.

fruit| ma·chine *s. Brit.* F 'Spielautoˌmat *m*; **~ pulp** *s.* Fruchtfleisch *n*; **~ sal·ad** *s.* **1.** 'Obstsaˌlat *m*; **2.** *fig. humor.* ‚La'metta' *n*, Ordenspracht *f*; **~ tree** *s.* Obstbaum *m*.

fruit·y ['fruːtɪ] *adj.* **1.** fruchtartig; **2.** fruchtig (*Wein*); **3.** so'nor (*Stimme*); **4.**

Brit. sl. ,saftig', ,gepfeffert' (*Witz*); **5.** *Am.* F ,schmalzig'.

fru·men·ta·ceous [ˌfru:mən'teɪʃəs] *adj.* getreideartig, Getreide...

frump [frʌmp] *s. a.* ***old ~*** ,alte Schachtel', ,Spi'natwachtel' *f*; **'frump·ish** [-pɪʃ], **'frump·y** [-pɪ] *adj.* **1.** altmodisch; **2.** schlampig, ungepflegt.

frus·trate [frʌ'streɪt] *v/t.* **1.** *et.* vereiteln, durch'kreuzen, zu'nichte machen; **2.** *j-n od. et.* hemmen, (be)hindern, *j-n* einengen, *j-n* am Fortkommen hindern; **3.** *j-m* die *od.* jede Hoffnung *od.* Aussicht nehmen, *j-n* zu'rückwerfen: ***I was ~d in my efforts*** meine Bemühungen wurden vereitelt; **4.** frustrieren: a) *j-n* entmutigen, b) *j-n* enttäuschen, c) mit Minderwertigkeitsgefühlen erfüllen; **frus'trat·ed** [-tɪd] *adj.* **1.** vereitelt, gescheitert: ***~ plans***; **2.** gescheitert (*Person*), ,verhindert' (*Maler etc.*); **3.** frustriert: a) entmutigt, b) enttäuscht, c) voller Minderwertigkeitsgefühle; **frus'trat·ing** [-tɪŋ] *adj.* frustrierend, enttäuschend, entmutigend; **frus'tra·tion** [-eɪʃn] *s.* **1.** Vereitelung *f*; **2.** Behinderung *f*, Hemmung *f*; **3.** Enttäuschung *f*, 'Mißerfolg *m*, Rückschlag *m*; **4.** *psych. u. allg.* Frustrati'on *f*: a) Enttäuschung *f*, b) *a.* ***sense of ~*** *das* Gefühl, ein Versager zu sein, Minderwertigkeitsgefühle *pl.*, Niedergeschlagenheit *f*; **5.** aussichtslose Sache (***to*** für).

frus·tum ['frʌstəm] *pl.* **-tums** *od.* **-ta** [-tə] *s.* ⩓ Stumpf *m*: ***~ of a cone*** Kegelstumpf.

fry¹ [fraɪ] *s. pl.* **1.** a) junge Fische *pl.*, b) Fischrogen *m*; **2.** ***small ~*** a) ,junges Gemüse', Kinder *pl.*, b) kleine (*unbedeutende*) Leute *pl.*, c) ,kleine Fische' *pl.*, Lappalien *pl.*

fry² [fraɪ] **I** *v/t.* **1.** braten: ***fried potatoes*** Bratkartoffeln; **2.** *Am. sl.* auf dem e'lektrischen Stuhl hinrichten; **II** *v/i.* **3.** braten, schmoren; **4.** *Am. sl.* auf dem e'lektrischen Stuhl hingerichtet werden; **III** *s.* **5.** Gebratenes *n*, *bsd.* gebratene Inne'reien *pl.*; **6.** *Am. bsd. in Zssgn*: Brat-, Grillfest *n*: ***fish ~***; **fry·er** ['fraɪə] *s.* **1.** j-d, der et. brät: ***he is a fish-~*** er hat ein Fischrestaurant; **2.** (*Fisch- etc.*)Bratpfanne *f*; **3.** *et.* zum Braten Geeignetes, *bsd.* Brathühnchen *n*; **fry·ing pan** ['fraɪɪŋ] *s.* Bratpfanne *f*: ***jump out of the ~ into the fire*** vom Regen in die Traufe kommen.

fuch·sia ['fju:ʃə] *s.* ⚘ Fuchsie *f*.

fuch·sine ['fu:ksi:n] *s.* ⚗ Fuch'sin *n*.

fuck [fʌk] V **I** *v/t.* **1.** ,ficken', ,vögeln': ***~ it!*** ,Scheiße'!; ***~ you!***, ***get ~ed!*** a) du Scheißkerl!, b) leck mich am Arsch!; **2.** ***~ up*** *et.* ,versauen' *od.* ,vermasseln': (***all***) ***~ed up*** (total) ,im Arsch'; **II** *v/i.* **3.** ,ficken', ,vögeln'; **4.** ***~ around*** *fig.* her'umgammeln; ***~ off!*** verpiß dich!; **III** *s.* **5.** ,Fick' *m*: ***I don't give a ~*** *fig.* das ist mir ,scheißegal'; ***~!*** ,Scheiße'!; **'fuck·er** [-kə] *s.* V **1.** ,Ficker' *m*; **2.** ,(Scheiß-)Kerl' *m*: ***poor ~*** armes Schwein; **'fuck·ing** [-kɪŋ] V **I** *adj.* verdammt, Scheiß... (*oft nur verstärkend*); **II** *adv.* verdammt: ***~ cold*** ,saukalt'; ***~ good*** ,unheimlich' gut, ,sagenhaft'.

fud·dle ['fʌdl] F **I** *v/t.* **1.** berauschen: ***~ o.s.*** → 3; **2.** verwirren; **II** *v/i.* **3.** saufen, sich ,vollaufen lassen'; **III** *s.* **4.** Verwirrung *f*: ***get in a ~*** durcheinanderkommen; **'fud·dled** [-ld] *adj.* F **1.** ,benebelt'; **2.** verwirrt.

fud·dy-dud·dy ['fʌdɪˌdʌdɪ] F **I** *s.* ,verkalkter Trottel'; **II** *adj.* ,verkalkt'.

fudge [fʌdʒ] F **I** *v/t.* **1.** *oft* ***~ up*** zu'rechtpfuschen, zs.-stoppeln; **2.** ,frisieren', fälschen; **II** *v/i.* **3.** ,blöd da'herreden'; **4.** ***~ on*** *e-m Problem etc.* ausweichen; **III** *s.* **5.** ,Quatsch' *m*, Blödsinn *m*; **6.** *Zeitung*: (Ma'schine *f od.* Spalte *f* für) letzte Meldungen *pl.*; **7.** *Küche*: (*Art*) Fon'dant *m*.

fu·el ['fjʊəl] **I** *s.* Brennstoff *m*: a) 'Brenn-, 'Heizmateriˌal *n*, b) Betriebs-, Treib-, Kraftstoff *m*: ***add ~ to the flames*** (*od.* ***fire***) *fig.* Öl ins Feuer gießen; ***add ~ to*** *fig. et.* schüren; **II** *v/i.* Brennstoff nehmen; *a.* ***~ up*** (auf)tanken, ⚓ bunkern; **III** *v/t.* mit Brennstoff versehen, ✈ *a.* betanken; ⚓ *Öl* bunkern: ***fuelled with*** be- *od.* getrieben mit; **ˌ~-'air mix·ture** *s. mot.* Kraftstoff-Luft-Gemisch *n*; **~ e·con·o·my** *s.* sparsamer Kraftstoffverbrauch; **~ feed** *s.* Brennstoffzuleitung *f*; **~ gas** *s.* Heizgas *n*; **~ ga(u)ge** *s. mot.* Kraftstoffmesser *m*, Ben'zinuhr *f*; **'~-ˌguzz·ling** *adj.* F ,ben'zinfressend' (*Motor etc.*); **~ in·jec·tion en·gine** *s.* Einspritzmotor *m*; **~ jet** *s.* Kraftstoffdüse *f*; **~ oil** *s.* Heizöl *n*; **~ pump** *s. mot.* Kraftstoff-, Ben'zinpumpe *f*; **~ rod** *s. Kernphysik*: Brennstab *m*.

fug [fʌg] *s.* F ,Mief' *m*.

fu·ga·cious [fju:'geɪʃəs] *adj.* kurzlebig (*a.* ⚘), flüchtig, vergänglich.

fug·gy ['fʌgɪ] *adj.* F ,miefig'.

fu·gi·tive ['fju:dʒɪtɪv] **I** *s.* a) Flüchtige(r *m*) *f*, b) *pol. etc.* Flüchtling *m*, c) Ausreißer *m*: ***~ from justice*** flüchtiger Rechtsbrecher; **II** *adj.* flüchtig, *fig. a.* vergänglich, kurzlebig.

fu·gle·man ['fju:glmæn] *s.* [*irr.*] (An-, Wort)Führer *m*.

fugue [fju:g] **I** *s.* **1.** ♪ Fuge *f*; **2.** *psych.* Fu'gue *f*; **II** *v/t. u. v/i.* **3.** ♪ fugieren.

ful·crum ['fʌlkrəm] *pl.* **-cra** [-krə] *s.* **1.** *phys.* Dreh-, Hebe-, Stützpunkt *m*; **2.** *fig.* Angelpunkt *m*.

ful·fil(l) [fʊl'fɪl] *v/t.* **1.** *allg.* erfüllen; **2.** voll'bringen, -'ziehen, ausführen; **ful'fil(l)·ment** [-mənt] *s.* Erfüllung *f*.

ful·gent ['fʌldʒənt] *adj.* □ *poet.* strahlend, glänzend; **ful·gu·rant** ['fʌlgjʊərənt] *adj.* (auf)blitzend.

full¹ [fʊl] **I** *adj.* □ → ***fully***; **1.** *allg.* voll: ***~ of*** voll von, voller *Fische etc.*, *fig. a.* a) reich an (*dat.*), b) (ganz) erfüllt von; ***~ of plans*** voller Pläne; ***~ of o.s.*** (ganz) von sich eingenommen; ***a ~ heart*** ein (über)volles Herz; **2.** voll, ganz: ***a ~ mile***; ***a ~ hour*** e-e volle *od.* ,geschlagene' Stunde; **3.** voll, rund, vollschlank; **4.** weit(geschnitten): ***a ~ skirt***; **5.** voll, kräftig: ***~ colo(u)r***, ***~ voice***; **6.** schwer, vollmundig: ***~ wine***; **7.** voll besetzt: ***~ up*** (voll) besetzt (*Bus etc.*); ***house ~!*** *thea.* ausverkauft!; **8.** ausführlich, genau, voll(ständig): ***~ details***; **9.** reichlich: ***a ~ meal***; **10.** a) voll, unbeschränkt: ***~ power*** Vollmacht *f*, b) voll (-berechtigt): ***~ member***; **11.** echt, rein: ***a ~ sister*** e-e leibliche Schwester; **12.** F ,voll': a) *a.* ***~ up*** satt, b) betrunken; **II** *adv.* **13.** völlig, gänzlich, ganz: ***know ~ well that*** ganz genau wissen, daß; **14.** gerade, genau, di'rekt: ***~ in the face***; **15.** ***~ out*** mit Vollgas *fahren*, auf Hochtouren *arbeiten*; **III** *s.* **16.** ***in ~*** voll(ständig); ***write in ~*** *et.* ausschreiben; ***to the ~*** vollständig, bis ins kleinste, total; ***at the ~*** auf dem Höhepunkt *od.* Höchststand.

full² [fʊl] *v/t.* ⚙ *Tuch* walken.

full| age *s.*: ***of ~*** ⚖ mündig, volljährig; **'~·back** *s.* a) *Fußball*, *Hockey*: Verteidiger *m*, b) *Rugby*: Schlußspieler *m*; **~ blood** *s. biol.* Vollblut *n*; **ˌ~-'blood·ed** *adj.* **1.** reinrassig, Vollblut...; **2.** *fig.* Vollblut...: ***~ socialist***; **ˌ~-'blown** *adj.* **1.** ⚘ ganz aufgeblüht; **2.** *fig.* a) voll entwickelt, ausgereift, b) F → ***fully fledged*** 2, 3; **~ board** *s.* 'Vollpensiˌon *f*; **ˌ~-'bod·ied** *adj.* **1.** schwer, üppig; **2.** schwer, vollmundig: ***~ wine***; **ˌ~-'bot·tomed** *adj.* **1.** breit, mit großem Boden: ***~ wig*** Allongeperücke *f*; **2.** ⚓ mit großem Laderaum; **'~-bound** *adj.* Ganzleder..., Ganzleinen...: ***~ book***; **~ dress** *s.* **1.** Gesellschaftsanzug *m*; **2.** ⚔ 'Galauniˌform *f*; **ˌ~-'dress** *adj.* **1.** Gala...: ***~ uniform***; **2.** ***~ rehearsal*** → ***dress rehearsal***; **3.** *fig.* groß angelegt, um'fassend.

ful·ler ['fʊlə] *s.* ⚙ **1.** (Tuch)Walker *m*; **2.** (halb)runder Setzhammer; **~'s earth** *s. min.* Fullererde *f*.

ˌfull|'face I *s.* **1.** En-'face-Bild *n*, Vorderansicht *f*; **2.** *typ.* (halb)fette Schrift; **II** *adj.* **3.** en face; **4.** *typ.* (halb)fett; **ˌ~-'faced** *adj.* **1.** mit vollem Gesicht, pausbäckig; **2.** *typ.* fett; **ˌ~-'fash·ioned** *Am.* → ***fully fashioned***; **ˌ~-'fledged** → ***fully fledged***; **~ gal·lop** *s.*: ***at ~*** in vollem *od.* gestrecktem Galopp; **ˌ~-'grown** *adj.* ausgewachsen; **~ hand** → ***full house*** 2; **ˌ~-'heart·ed** *adj.* rückhaltlos, voll; **~ house** *s.* **1.** *thea. etc.* volles Haus; **2.** *Poker*: Full house *n*; **ˌ~-'length** *adj.* **1.** in voller Größe, lebensgroß: ***~ portrait***; **2.** bodenlang (*Kleid*); **3.** abendfüllend (*Film*); **~ load** *s.* **1.** ⚙, ✈ Gesamtgewicht *n*; **2.** ⚡ Volllast *f*; **~ nel·son** *s. Ringen*: Doppelnelson *m*.

full·ness ['fʊlnɪs] *s.* **1.** Fülle *f*: ***in the ~ of time*** zur gegebenen Zeit; **2.** *fig.* ('Über)Fülle *f* (*des Herzens*); **3.** Körperfülle *f*; **4.** Sattheit *f* (*a. Farben*); **5.** ♪ Klangfülle *f*; **6.** Weite *f* (*Kleid*).

ˌfull|-'page *adj.* ganzseitig; **~ pro·fes·sor** *s. Am. univ.* Ordi'narius *m*; **ˌ~-'rigged** *adj.* **1.** ⚓ vollgetakelt; **2.** voll ausgerüstet; **~ scale** *s.* ⚙ na'türliche Größe; **ˌ~-'scale** *adj.* **1.** in na'türlicher Größe; **2.** *fig.* großangelegt, um'fassend: ***~ attack*** ⚔ Großangriff *m*; ***~ test*** Großversuch *m*; ***~ war*** regelrechter Krieg; **~ stop** *s.* **1.** (Schluß)Punkt *m*; **2.** *fig.* Schluß *m*, Ende *n*, Stillstand *m*; **ˌ~-'time I** *adj.* ✝ hauptberuflich (tätig): ***~ job*** Ganztagsstellung *f*, -beschäftigung *f*; **II** *adv.* ganztags; **'~-ˌtim·er** *s.* ganztägig Beschäftigte(r *m*) *f*; **ˌ~-'track** *adj.*: ***~ vehicle*** ⚙ Vollketten-, Raupenfahrzeug *n*; **ˌ~-'view** *adj.* ✈ Vollsicht...

ful·ly ['fʊlɪ] *adv.* voll, völlig, gänzlich; ausführlich: ***~ ten minutes*** volle zehn Minuten; ***~ automatic*** vollautomatisch; ***~ entitled*** vollberechtigt; **~ fash·ioned** *adj.* mit (voller) Paßform (*Strümpfe etc.*); **~ fledged** *adj.* **1.** flügge (*Vogel*); **2.** *fig.* richtig(gehend): ***a ~ pilot***; **3.** *fig.* ,ausgewachsen': ***a ~***

scandal.
ful·mar ['fʊlmə] *s. orn.* Fulmar *m*, Eissturmvogel *m*.
ful·mi·nant ['fʌlmɪnənt] *adj.* **1.** krachend; **2.** ⚕ plötzlich ausbrechend; **ful·mi·nate** ['fʌlmɪneɪt] **I** *v/i.* **1.** donnern, explodieren (*a. fig.*); **2.** *fig.* (los)donnern, wettern; **II** *v/t.* **3.** zur Explosi'on bringen; **4.** *fig. Befehle etc.* donnern; **III** *s.* **5.** ⚗ Fulmi'nat *n*: ~ ***of mercury*** Knallquecksilber *n*; '**ful·mi·nat·ing** [-neɪtɪŋ] *adj.* **1.** ⚗ explodierend, Knall…: ~ ***powder*** Knallpulver *n*; **2.** *fig.* donnernd, wetternd; **3.** → ***fulminant*** 2; **ful·mi·na·tion** [ˌfʌlmɪ'neɪʃn] *s.* **1.** Explosi'on *f*, Knall *m*; **2.** *fig.* Donnern *n*, Wettern *n*.
ful·ness *bsd. Am.* → ***fullness.***
ful·some ['fʊlsəm] *adj.* ☐ **1.** über'trieben: ~ ***flattery***; **2.** *obs.* widerlich.
ful·vous ['fʌlvəs] *adj.* rötlichgelb.
fum·ble ['fʌmbl] **I** *v/i.* **1.** *a.* ~ ***around*** a) um'hertappen, -tasten (***for*** nach): ~ ***for*** tappen *od.* suchen nach, b) (her'um-) fummeln (***at*** an *dat.*); **2.** (***with***) ungeschickt 'umgehen (mit), sich ungeschickt anstellen (bei); **3.** *sport* ‚patzen'; **II** *v/t.* **4.** ‚verpatzen'; **5.** ~ ***out*** *et.* mühsam (her'vor)stammeln; **III** *s.* **6.** (Her'um)Tappen *n*, (-)Fummeln *n*; **7.** *sport* ‚Patzer' *m*; '**fum·bler** [-lə] *s.* Stümper *m*, ‚Patzer' *m*; '**fum·bling** [-lɪŋ] *adj.* ☐ tappend; täppisch, ungeschickt.
fume [fju:m] **I** *s.* **1.** *oft pl.* a) (*unangenehmer*) Dampf, Rauch(gas *n*) *m*, Schwade *f*, b) Dunst *m*, Nebel *m*; **2.** *fig.* Koller *m*, Erregung *f*, Wut *f*; **3.** *fig.* Schall *m* u. Rauch *m*; **II** *v/t.* **4.** *Holz* räuchern, dunkler machen, beizen: ~***d oak*** dunkles Eichenholz; **III** *v/i.* **5.** rauchen, dunsten, dampfen; **6.** *fig.* wüten (***at*** gegen), (vor Wut) schäumen: ***fuming with anger*** kochend vor Wut.
fu·mi·gant ['fju:mɪgənt] *s.* Ausräucherungsmittel *n*; **fu·mi·gate** ['fju:mɪgeɪt] *v/t.* ausräuchern; **fu·mi·ga·tion** [ˌfju:mɪ'geɪʃn] *s.* Ausräucherung *f*; '**fu·mi·ga·tor** [-geɪtə] *s.* 'Ausräucherappaˌrat *m*.
fun [fʌn] **I** *s.* Scherz *m*, Spaß *m*, Ulk *m*: ***for*** (*od.* ***in***) ~ aus *od.* zum Spaß; ***for the ~ of it*** spaßeshalber, zum Spaß; ***it's not all ~ and games*** es ist gar nicht so rosig; ***it is*** ~ es macht Spaß; ***he*** (***it***) ***is great*** ~ F er (es) ist sehr amüsant *od.* lustig; ***have ~!*** viel Spaß!; ***make ~ of s.o.*** sich über j-n lustig machen; ***I don't see the ~ of it*** ich finde das (gar) nicht komisch; **II** *adj.* lustig, spaßig: ~ ***man*** → ***funster.***
func·tion ['fʌŋkʃn] **I** *s.* **1.** Funkti'on *f* (*a.* ⚖, ⚙, *biol.*, *ling.*, *phys.*): a) Aufgabe *f*, b) Zweck *m*, c) Tätigkeit *f*, d) Arbeits-, Wirkungsweise *f*, e) Amt *n*, f) (Amts-) Pflicht *f*, Obliegenheit *f*: ***out of*** ~ ⚙ außer Betrieb, kaputt; **2.** a) feierlicher *od.* festlicher Anlaß, Feier *f*, Zeremo'nie *f*, b) Veranstaltung *f*, (gesellschaftliches) Fest; **II** *v/i.* **3.** fungieren, tätig sein; **4.** ⚙ *etc.* funktionieren, arbeiten.
func·tion·al ['fʌŋkʃənl] *adj.* ☐ → ***functionally***; **1.** amtlich, dienstlich; **2.** a) ⚕, ⚖, ⚙ funktio'nell, Funktions…: ~ ***disorder*** ⚕ Funktionsstörung *f*, b) funkti'onsfähig, -tüchtig; **3.** sachlich, praktisch, zweckbetont, -mäßig: ~ ***building*** Zweckbau *m*; '**func·tion·al·ism** [-ʃnəlɪzəm] *s.* **1.** ⚠, *psych.* Funktiona'lismus *m*; **2.** Zweckmäßigkeit *f*; '**func·tion·al·ize** [-ʃnəlaɪz] *v/t.* funktionstüchtig machen, wirksam gestalten; '**func·tion·al·ly** [-ʃnəlɪ] *adv.* in funktioneller Hinsicht; '**func·tion·ar·y** [-ʃnərɪ] *s.* Funktio'när *m*.
fund [fʌnd] **I** *s.* **1.** a) Kapi'tal *n*, Geldsumme *f*, b) *zweckgebunden*: Fonds *m*: ***relief*** ~ Hilfsfonds; ***strike*** ~ Streikfonds; **2.** *pl.* (Bar-, Geld)Mittel *pl.*, Gelder *pl.*: ***be in ~s*** (gut) bei Kasse sein; ***no ~s*** ✝ kein Guthaben, keine Deckung; ***public ~s*** öffentliche Gelder; **3.** ***2s*** *pl.* a) *Brit.* fundierte 'Staatspaˌpiere *pl.*, Kon'sols *pl.*, b) *Am.* Ef'fekten *pl.*; **4.** *fig.* Vorrat *m*, Schatz *m*, Fülle *f*, Grundstock *m* (***of*** von, an *dat.*); **II** *v/t.* **5.** ✝ a) in 'Staatspaˌpieren anlegen, b) fundieren, konsolidieren: ~***ed debt*** fundierte Schuld; ~ **rais·er** *s. Veranstaltung zum Aufbringen von Geldmitteln, bsd.* Wohltätigkeitsveranstaltung *f*.
fun·da·ment ['fʌndəmənt] *s.* **1.** ⚠ *u. fig.* Funda'ment *n*; **2.** *humor. die* ‚vier Buchstaben' *pl.*, Gesäß *n*.
fun·da·men·tal [ˌfʌndə'mentl] **I** *adj.* ☐ → ***fundamentally***; **1.** fundamen'tal, grundlegend, wesentlich (***to*** für), Haupt…; **2.** grundsätzlich, Grund…, elemen'tar: ~ ***colo(u)r*** Grund-, Primärfarbe *f*; ~ ***particle*** *phys.* Elementarteilchen *n*; ~ ***research*** Grundlagenforschung *f*; ~ ***tone*** ♪ Grundton *m*; ~ ***truth(s)*** Grundwahrheit(en) *f*; **II** *s.* **3.** *oft pl.* 'Grundlage *f*, -prinˌzip *n*, -begriff *m*; **4.** ♪ Grundton *m*; ˌ**fun·da'men·tal·ism** [-təlɪzəm] *s. eccl.* Fundamenta'lismus *m*, streng wörtliche Bibelgläubigkeit; ˌ**fun·da'men·tal·ly** [-təlɪ] *adv.* im Grunde, im wesentlichen.
fu·ner·al ['fju:nərəl] **I** *s.* **1.** Begräbnis *n*, Beerdigung *f*, Bestattung *f*: ***that's your ~!*** *sl.* das ist deine Sache!; **2.** *a.* ~ ***procession*** Leichenzug *m*; **3.** *Am.* Trauerfeier *f*; **II** *adj.* **4.** Begräbnis…, Leichen…, Trauer…, Grab…: ~ ***director*** Bestattungsunternehmer *m*; ~ ***home*** (*od.* ***parlor***) *Am.* Leichenhalle *f*; ~ ***march*** ♪ Trauermarsch *m*; ~ ***pile***, ~ ***pyre*** Scheiterhaufen *m*; ~ ***service*** Trauergottesdienst *m*; ~ ***urn*** Totenurne *f*; '**fu·ner·ar·y** [-nərərɪ], **fu·ne·re·al** [fju:'nɪərɪəl] *adj.* ☐ **1.** Begräbnis…, Leichen… Trauer…; **2.** *fig.* düster, wie bei e-m Begräbnis.
'**fun·fair** *s. Brit.* Vergnügungspark *m*, Rummelplatz *m*.
fun·gal ['fʌŋgl] *adj.* Pilz…; **fun·gi** ['fʌŋgaɪ] *pl. von* ***fungus.***
fun·gi·ble ['fʌndʒɪbl] *adj.* ⚖ vertretbar (*Sache*): ~ ***goods*** Fungibilien.
fun·gi·cid·al [ˌfʌndʒɪ'saɪdl] *adj.* pilztötend; **fun·gi·cide** ['fʌndʒɪsaɪd] *s.* pilztötendes Mittel; **fun·goid** ['fʌŋgɔɪd] *adj.*, **fun·gous** ['fʌŋgəs] *adj.* pilz-, schwammartig, *a.* ⚕ schwammig; **fun·gus** ['fʌŋgəs] *pl.* **fun·gi** ['fʌŋgaɪ] *od.* **-gus·es** *s.* **1.** ⚘ Pilz *m*, Schwamm *m*; **2.** ⚕ Fungus *m*, schwammige Geschwulst; **3.** *humor.* Bart *m*.
fu·nic·u·lar [fju:'nɪkjʊlə] **I** *adj.* Seil…, Ketten…; **II** *s. a.* ~ ***railway*** (Draht-) Seilbahn *f*.
funk [fʌŋk] F **I** *s.* **1.** ‚Schiß' *m*, ‚Bammel' *m*, Angst *f*: ***be in a blue*** ~ a) ‚schwer Schiß haben' (***of*** vor *dat.*), b) völlig ‚down' sein; ~ ***hole*** ⚔ a) ‚Heldenkeller' *m*, Unterstand *m*, b) *fig.* Druckposten *m*; **2.** feiger Kerl; **3.** Drückeberger *m*; **II** *v/i.* **4.** ‚Schiß' haben *od.* bekommen; **5.** ‚kneifen', sich drücken; **III** *v/t.* **6.** ‚Schiß' haben vor (*dat.*); **7.** ‚kneifen' vor (*dat.*), sich drücken vor (*dat.*) *od.* um; '**funk·y** [-kɪ] *adj.* feig(e).
fun·nel ['fʌnl] **I** *s.* **1.** Trichter *m*; **2.** ⚓, 🚂 Schornstein *m*; **3.** ⚙ Luftschacht *m*; **4.** Vul'kanschlot *m*; **II** *v/t.* **5.** eintrichtern, -füllen; **6.** *fig.* schleusen.
fun·nies ['fʌnɪz] *s. pl.* F **1.** Comic strips *pl.*, Comics *pl.*; **2.** Witzseite *f*.
fun·ny ['fʌnɪ] *adj.* ☐ **1.** *a.* ~ ***haha*** komisch, drollig, lustig, ulkig; **2.** ‚komisch': a) *a.* ~ ***peculiar*** sonderbar, merkwürdig, b) F unwohl, c) F zweifelhaft, faul: ***the ~ thing is that*** das Merkwürdige ist, daß; ***funnily enough*** merkwürdigerweise; ~ ***business*** F ‚faule Sache', ‚krumme Tour'; ~ **bone** *s.* Musi'kantenknochen *m*; ~ **farm** *s. sl.* ‚Klapsmühle' *f*; '**~·man** [-mən] *s.* [*irr.*] Komiker *m*; ~ **pa·per** *s. Am.* Comic-Teil *m e-r Zeitung*.
fun·ster ['fʌnstə] *s.* F Spaßvogel *m*.
fur [fɜ:] **I** *s.* **1.** Pelz *m*, Fell *n*: ***make the ~ fly*** ‚Stunk' machen; **2.** a) Pelzbesatz *m*, b) *a.* ~ ***coat*** Pelzmantel *m*, c) *pl.* Pelzwerk *n*, -kleidung *f*, Rauchwaren *pl.*; **3.** *coll.* Pelztiere *pl.*: ~ ***and feather*** Haarwild u. Federwild *n*; **4.** ⚕ (Zungen)Belag *m*; **5.** ⚙ Kesselstein *m*; **II** *v/t.* **6.** mit Pelz besetzen *od.* füttern; **7.** ⚙ mit Kesselstein über'ziehen; **III** *v/i.* **8.** ⚙ Kesselstein ansetzen.
fur·be·low ['fɜ:bɪləʊ] *s.* **1.** Falbel *f*; Faltensaum *m*; **2.** *pl. contp.* ‚Firlefanz' *m*.
fur·bish ['fɜ:bɪʃ] *v/t.* **1.** polieren; **2.** *oft* ~ ***up*** herrichten, renovieren; **3.** *mst* ~ ***up*** *fig.* ‚aufpolieren', auffrischen.
fur·cate ['fɜ:keɪt] **I** *adj.* gabelförmig, gegabelt, gespalten; **II** *v/i.* sich gabeln *od.* teilen; **fur·ca·tion** [fɜ:'keɪʃn] *s.* Gabelung *f*.
fu·ri·ous ['fjʊərɪəs] *adj.* ☐ **1.** wütend; **2.** wild, aufbrausend: ~ ***temper***; **3.** wild, heftig, furi'os: ***a ~ attack.***
furl [fɜ:l] *v/t. Fahne, Segel* aufrollen, *Schirm* zs.-rollen.
fur·long ['fɜ:lɒŋ] *s.* Achtelmeile *f* (*201,17 m*).
fur·lough ['fɜ:ləʊ] *bsd.* ⚔ **I** *s.* (Heimat-) Urlaub *m*; **II** *v/t.* beurlauben.
fur·nace ['fɜ:nɪs] *s.* **1.** ⚙ (Schmelz-, Brenn-, Hoch)Ofen *m*: ***enamel(l)ing*** ~ Farbenschmelzofen; **2.** ⚙ (Heiz)Kessel *m*, Feuerung *f*; **3.** *fig.* ‚Backofen' *m*, glühendheißer Raum *od.* Ort; **4.** *fig.* Feuerprobe *f*, harte Prüfung: ***tried in the*** ~ gründlich erprobt.
fur·nish ['fɜ:nɪʃ] *v/t.* **1.** ausstatten, -rüsten, versehen, -sorgen (***with*** mit); **2.** *Wohnung* einrichten, ausstatten, möblieren: ~***ed room*** möbliertes Zimmer; **3.** *allg. a. Beweise etc.* liefern, beschaffen, er- *od.* beibringen; '**fur·nish·er** [-ʃə] *s.* **1.** Liefe'rant *m*; **2.** *Am.* Herrenausstatter *m*; '**fur·nish·ing** [-ʃɪŋ] *s.* **1.** Ausrüstung *f*, -stattung *f*; **2.** *pl.* Einrichtung *f*, Mobili'ar *n*: ***soft ~s*** Möbelstoffe; **3.** *pl. Am.* ('Herren)Beˌkleidungsarˌtikel *pl.*; **4.** ⚙ a) Zubehör *n*, *m*, b) Beschläge *pl.*

fur·ni·ture [ˈfɜːnɪtʃə] *s.* **1.** Möbel *pl.*, Einrichtung *f*, Mobiliˈar *n*: ***piece of ~*** Möbel(stück) *n*; ***~ remover*** Möbelspediteur *m od.* -packer *m*; ***~ van*** Möbelwagen *m*; **2.** Ausrüstung *f*, -stattung *f*; **3.** Inhalt *m*, Bestand *m*; **4.** *geistiges* Rüstzeug, Wissen *n*; **5.** ⚙ Zubehör *n*, *m*.

fu·ror [ˈfjuːrɔː] *s. Am.*, **fu·ro·re** [fjʊəˈrɔːrɪ] *s.* **1.** Ekˈstase *f*, Begeisterungstaumel *m*; **2.** Wut *f*; **3.** Fuˈrore *n*, Aufsehen: ***create a ~*** Furore machen.

furred [fɜːd] *adj.* **1.** mit Pelz besetzt *od.* bekleidet; **2.** ⚕ belegt (*Zunge*); **3.** ⚙ mit Kesselstein belegt.

fur·ri·er [ˈfʌrɪə] *s.* Kürschner *m*, Pelzhändler *m*; **ˈfur·ri·er·y** [-ərɪ] *s.* **1.** Pelzwerk *n*; **2.** Kürschneˈrei *f*.

fur·row [ˈfʌrəʊ] **I** *s.* **1.** ✓ Furche *f*; **2.** Bodenfalte *f*; **3.** ⚙ Rille *f*; **4.** Runzel *f*, Furche *f* (*a. anat.*); **II** *v/t.* **5.** pflügen; **6.** ⚙ riefen, auskehlen; **7.** *Wasser* durchˈfurchen; **8.** runzeln; **III** *v/i.* **9.** sich furchen (*Stirn etc.*).

fur·ry [ˈfɜːrɪ] *adj.* **1.** pelzartig, Pelz...; **2.** → ***furred*** 2.

fur seal *s. zo.* Bärenrobbe *f*.

fur·ther [ˈfɜːðə] **I** *adv.* **1.** *comp. von* ***far*** weiter, ferner, entfernter: ***no ~*** nicht weiter; ***I'll see you ~ first*** F ich werde dir was husten!; **2.** ferner, weiterhin, überˈdies, außerdem; **II** *adj.* **3.** weiter, ferner, entfernter: ***the ~ end*** das andere Ende; **4.** *fig.* weiter: ***~ education*** *Brit.* Fort-, Weiterbildung *f*; ***~ particulars*** weitere Einzelheiten, Näheres; ***until ~ notice*** bis auf weiteres; ***anything ~?*** (sonst) noch etwas?; **III** *v/t.* **5.** fördern, unterˈstützen; **ˈfur·ther·ance** [-ðərəns] *s.* Förderung *f*, Unterˈstützung *f*; **ˌfur·therˈmore** *adv.* ferner, überˈdies, außerdem; **ˈfur·ther·most** *adj.* **1.** fernst, weitest; **2.** äußerst; **fur·thest** [ˈfɜːðɪst] *adj. u. adv.* **1.** *sup. von* ***far***; **2.** *fig.* weitest, meist: ***at the ~*** höchstens; **II** *adv.* **3.** am weitesten.

fur·tive [ˈfɜːtɪv] *adj.* □ **1.** heimlich, verstohlen; **2.** heimlichtuerisch; **ˈfur·tive·ness** [-nɪs] *s.* Heimlichkeit *f*, Verstohlenheit *f*.

fu·run·cle [ˈfjʊərʌŋkl] *s.* ⚕ Fuˈrunkel *m*; **fu·run·cu·lo·sis** [fjʊˌrʌŋkjʊˈləʊsɪs] *s.* ⚕ Furunkuˈlose *f*.

fu·ry [ˈfjʊərɪ] *s.* **1.** (wilder) Zorn *m*, Wut *f*; **2.** Wildheit *f*, Heftigkeit *f*: ***like ~*** wie toll; **3.** ♀ *antiq.* Furie *f*; **4.** *fig.* Furie *f* (*böses Weib etc.*).

furze [fɜːz] *s.* ♀ Stechginster *m*.

fuse [fjuːz] **I** *s.* **1.** ⚔ Zünder *m*: ***~ cord*** Abreißschnur *f*; **2.** ⚡ (Schmelz)Sicherung *f*: ***~ box*** Sicherungsdose *f*, -kasten *m*; ***~ wire*** Sicherungsdraht *m*; ***he blew a ~*** ihm ist die Sicherung durchgebrannt (*a. fig.* F); ***he has a short ~*** *Am.* F bei ihm brennt leicht die Sicherung durch; **II** *v/t.* **3.** ⚔ Zünder anbringen an (*dat.*); **4.** ⚙ (ab)sichern; **5.** *phys.*, ⚙ (ver)schmelzen; **6.** *fig.* verschmelzen, vereinigen, ✝ *a.* fusionieren; **III** *v/i.* **7.** ⚡ ˈdurchbrennen; **8.** ⚙ schmelzen; **9.** *fig.* verschmelzen, ✝ *a.* fusionieren.

fu·se·lage [ˈfjuːzɪlɑːʒ] *s.* ✈ (Flugzeug-)Rumpf *m*.

fu·sel (oil) [ˈfjuːzl] *s.* Fuselöl *n*.

fu·si·ble [ˈfjuːzəbl] *adj.* schmelzbar, -flüssig: ***~ cut-out*** ⚡ Schmelzsicherung *f*.

fu·sil [ˈfjuːzɪl] *s.* ⚔ *hist.* Steinschloßflinte *f*, Musˈkete *f*; **fu·sil·ier**, *Am. a.* **fu·sil·eer** [ˌfjuːzɪˈlɪə] *s.* ⚔ Füsiˈlier *m*; **fu·sil·lade** [ˌfjuːzɪˈleɪd] **I** *s.* **1.** ⚔ Salve *f*; **2.** Exekutiˈonskomˌmando *n*; **3.** *fig.* Hagel *m*; **II** *v/t.* **4.** ⚔ unter Salvenfeuer nehmen; **5.** (standrechtlich) erschießen, füsilieren.

fus·ing [ˈfjuːzɪŋ] *s.* ⚙ Schmelzen *n*: ***~ burner*** Schneidbrenner *m*; ***~ point*** Schmelzpunkt *m*; **fu·sion** [ˈfjuːʒn] *s.* **1.** ⚙ Schmelzen *n*: ***~ welding*** Schmelzschweißen *n*; **2.** Schmelzmasse *f*; **3.** *biol.*, *opt.*, *Kernphysik*: Fusiˈon *f* (*Verschmelzung*): ***~ bomb*** Wasserstoffbombe *f*; ***~ reactor*** Fusionsreaktor *m*; **4.** *fig.* Verschmelzung *f*, Vereinigung *f*; Zs.-schluß *m*, Fusiˈon *f* (*a.* ✝, *pol.*).

fuss [fʌs] **I** *s.* **1.** a) (unnötige) Aufregung, b) Hektik *f*; **2.** ‚Wirbel' *m*, ‚Theˈater' *n*, Getue *n*: ***make a ~*** a) → 5, b) *a.* ***kick up a ~*** ‚Krach schlagen'; ***a lot of ~ about nothing*** viel Lärm um nichts; **3.** Ärger *m*, Unannehmlichkeiten *pl.*; **II** *v/i.* **4.** sich (unnötig) aufregen (***about*** über *acc.*): ***don't ~!*** nur keine Aufregung!, schon gut!; **5.** viel ‚Wirbel' *od.* ‚Wind' machen (***about***, ***of***, ***over*** um *j-n od. et.*); **6.** sich (viel) Umstände machen (***over*** mit *e-m Gast etc.*): ***~ over s.o.*** *a.* j-n bemuttern; ***~ about*** (*od.* ***around***) ‚herumfuhrwerken'; **7.** heikel sein; **III** *v/t.* **8.** *j-n* nerˈvös machen; **ˈfussˌbudg·et** *Am.* → ***fusspot***; **fuss·i·ness** [ˈfʌsɪnɪs] *s.* **1.** (unnötige) Aufregung; **2.** Hektik *f*; **3.** Kleinlichkeit *f*; **4.** heikle Art; **ˈfuss·pot** *s.* F Umstands-, Kleinigkeitskrämer *m*, ‚pingeliger' Kerl; **fuss·y** [ˈfʌsɪ] *adj.* □ **1.** a) aufgeregt, b) hektisch; **2.** kleinlich, ‚pingelig'; **3.** heikel, wählerisch, ‚eigen' (***about*** hinsichtlich *gen.*, mit).

fus·tian [ˈfʌstɪən] **I** *s.* **1.** Barchent *m*; **2.** *fig.* Schwulst *m*; **II** *adj.* **3.** Barchent...; **4.** *fig.* schwülstig.

fus·ti·ga·tion [ˌfʌstɪˈgeɪʃn] *s. humor.* Tracht *f* Prügel.

fust·i·ness [ˈfʌstɪnɪs] *s.* **1.** Moder(geruch) *m*; **2.** *fig.* Rückständigkeit *f*; **fust·y** [ˈfʌstɪ] *adj.* **1.** mod(e)rig, muffig; **2.** a) verstaubt, antiquiert, b) rückständig.

fu·tile [ˈfjuːtaɪl] *adj.* □ nutz-, sinn-, zweck-, aussichtslos, vergeblich; **fu·til·i·ty** [fjuːˈtɪlətɪ] *s.* Zweck-, Nutz-, Wert-, Sinnlosigkeit *f*.

fu·ture [ˈfjuːtʃə] **I** *s.* **1.** Zukunft *f*: ***in ~*** in Zukunft, künftig; ***in the near ~*** in der nahen Zukunft, bald; ***for the ~*** für die Zukunft, künftig; ***have no ~*** keine Zukunft haben; ***there is no ~ in that!*** das hat keine Zukunft!; **2.** *ling.* Fuˈtur(um) *n*, Zukunft *f*: ***~ perfect*** Futurum exactum, zweite Zukunft; **3.** *pl.* ✝ a) Terˈmingeschäfte *pl.*, b) Terˈminwaren *pl.*; **II** *adj.* **4.** (zu)künftig, Zukunfts...; **5.** *ling.* fuˈturisch: ***~ tense*** → 2; **6.** ✝ Termin...; ***~ life*** *s.* Leben *n* nach dem Tode.

fu·tur·ism [ˈfjuːtʃərɪzəm] *s. Kunst*: Fuˈrismus *m*; **ˈfu·tur·ist** [-ɪst] **I.** *adj.* **1.** futuˈristisch; **II.** *s.* **2.** Futuˈrist *m*; **3.** → ***futurologist***; **fu·tu·ri·ty** [fjuːˈtjʊərətɪ] *s.* **1.** Zukunft *f*; **2.** zukünftiges Ereignis; **3.** Zukünftigkeit *f*.

fu·tur·ol·o·gist [ˌfjuːtʃəˈrɒlədʒɪst] *s.* Futuroˈloge *m*, Zukunftsforscher *m*; **ˌfu·turˈol·o·gy** [-dʒɪ] *s.* Futuroloˈgie *f*, Zukunftsforschung *f*.

fuze *Am.* → ***fuse***.

fuzz [fʌz] **I** *s.* **1.** (feiner) Flaum *m*; **2.** Fusseln *pl.*, Fäserchen *pl.*; **3.** F a) Wuschelhaar(e *pl.*) *n*, b) ‚Zottelbart' *m*; **4.** *sl.* a) ‚Bulle' *m* (*Polizist*), b) ***the ~*** *coll.* die Bullen (*die Polizei*); **II** *v/t.* **5.** zerfasern; **6.** *fig.* ‚benebeln'; **III** *v/i.* **7.** zerfasern; **ˈfuzz·y** [-zɪ] *adj.* □ **1.** flaumig; **2.** faserig, fusselig; **3.** kraus, struppig (*Haar*); **4.** verschwommen; **5.** benommen.

fyl·fot [ˈfɪlfɒt] *s.* Hakenkreuz *n*.

G

G, g [dʒiː] *s.* **1.** G *n*, g *n* (*Buchstabe*); **2.** ♪ G *n*, g *n* (*Note*): ***G flat*** Ges *n*, ges *n*; ***G sharp*** Gis *n*, gis *n*; **3.** ***G*** *Am. sl.* ‚Riese' *m* (*1000 Dollar*).

gab [gæb] F **I** *s.* ‚Gequassel' *n*, Geschwätz *n*: ***stop your ~!*** halt den Mund!; ***the gift of the ~*** ein gutes Mundwerk; **II** *v/i.* ‚quasseln'.

gab·ar·dine [ˈgæbədiːn] *s.* Gabardine *m* (*feiner Wollstoff*).

gab·ble [ˈgæbl] **I** *v/i.* **1.** plappern; **2.** schnattern; **II** *v/t.* **3.** *et.* plappern; **4.** *et.* ‚herˈunterleiern'; **III** *s.* **5.** ‚Gebrabbel' *n*; **6.** Geschnatter *n*; **ˈgab·bler** [-lə] *s.* Schwätzer(in); **ˈgab·by** [-bɪ] *adj.* F geschwätzig.

gab·er·dine → ***gabardine***.

gab·fest [ˈgæbfest] *s. Am.* F ‚Quasseˈlei' *f*.

ga·bi·on [ˈgeɪbjən] *s.* ⚔ Schanzkorb *m*.

ga·ble [ˈgeɪbl] *s.* △ **1.** Giebel *m*; **2.** *a.* ***~ end*** Giebelwand *f*; **ˈga·bled** [-ld] *adj.* giebelig, Giebel…; **ˈga·blet** [-lɪt] *s.* giebelförmiger Aufsatz (*über Fenstern*), Ziergiebel *m*.

gad¹ [gæd] **I** *v/i.* *mst* ***~ about*** sich herˈumtreiben, ‚rumsausen'; **II** *s.* ***be on the ~*** → I.

gad² [gæd] *int.*: (***by***) ***~!*** *obs.* bei Gott!

ˈgad|·a·bout *s.* Herˈumtreiber(in); **ˈ~·fly** *s.* **1.** *zo.* Viehbremse *f*; **2.** *fig.* Störenfried *m*, lästiger Mensch.

gadg·et [ˈgædʒɪt] *s.* F **1.** a) Appaˈrat *m*, Gerät *n*, Vorrichtung *f*, b) *iro.* ‚Appaˈrätchen' *n*, ‚Kinkerlitzchen' *n*, technische Spieleˈrei; **2.** ‚Dingsbums' *n*; **3.** *fig.* ‚Dreh' *m*, Kniff *m*; **gad·ge·teer** [ˌgædʒɪˈtɪə] *s.* F Liebhaber *m* von technischen Spieleˈreien *od.* Neuerungen; **ˈgad·get·ry** [-trɪ] *s.* **1.** a) Appaˈrate *pl.*, b) *iro.* technische Spieleˈreien *pl.*; **2.** Beschäftigung *f* mit technischen Spieleˈreien; **ˈgad·get·y** [-tɪ] *adj.* F **1.** raffiniert (konstruiert); **2.** Apparate…; **3.** versessen auf technische Spieleˈreien.

Ga·dhel·ic [gæˈdelɪk] → ***Gaelic***.

gad·wall [ˈgædwɔːl] *s. orn.* Schnatterente *f*.

Gael [geɪl] *s.* Gäle *m*; **ˈGael·ic** [-lɪk] **I** *s. ling.* Gälisch *n*, das Gälische; **II** *adj.* gälisch.

gaff¹ [gæf] *s.* **1.** *Fischen*: Landungshaken *m*; **2.** ⚓ Gaffel *f*; **3.** Stahlsporn *m*; **4.** *Am. sl.* ‚Schlauch' *m*: ***stand the ~*** durchhalten; **5.** *Am. sl.* Schwindel *m*; **6.** *sl.* ‚Quatsch' *m*: ***blow the ~*** alles verraten, ‚plaudern'.

gaff² [gæf] *s. Brit. sl. a.* ***penny ~*** Varieˈté *n*, ‚Schmiere' *f*.

gaffe [gæf] *s.* Fauxˈpas *m*, (grobe) Taktlosigkeit.

gaf·fer [ˈgæfə] *s.* **1.** *humor.* ‚Opa' *m*; **2.** *Brit.* F a) Chef *m*, b) Vorarbeiter *m*.

gag [gæg] **I** *v/t.* **1.** knebeln, *fig. a.* mundtot machen; **2.** zum Würgen reizen; **3.** *a.* ***~ up*** *thea.* mit Gags spicken; **II** *v/i.* **4.** würgen (***on*** an *dat.*); **5.** *thea. etc.* F Gags anbringen, *allg.* witzeln; **III** *s.* **6.** Knebel *m*, *fig. a.* Knebelung *f*; **7.** ⚕ Mundsperrer *m*; **8.** *parl.* Schluß *m* der Deˈbatte; **9.** *thea. u. allg.* F Gag *m*: a) witziger Einfall, komische Poˈinte, ‚Knüller' *m*, b) Jux *m*, Ulk *m*, c) Trick *m*.

ga·ga [ˈgɑːgɑː] *adj. sl.* a) vertrottelt, b) ‚plemˈplem': ***go ~ over*** in Verzückung geraten über (*acc.*).

gag bit *s.* Zaumgebiß *n*.

gage¹ [geɪdʒ] **I** *s.* **1.** *hist. u. fig.* Fehdehandschuh *m*; **2.** (ˈUnter)Pfand *n*; **II** *v/t.* **3.** *obs.* zum Pfand geben.

gage² [geɪdʒ] → ***gauge***.

gage³ [geɪdʒ] → ***greengage***.

gag·gle [ˈgægl] **I** *v/i.* **1.** schnattern; **II** *s.* **2.** Geschnatter *n*; **3.** a) Gänseherde *f*, b) F schnatternde Schar: ***a ~ of girls***.

gag·man [ˈgægmən] *s.* [*irr.*] *thea. etc.* Gagman *m* (*Pointenerfinder etc.*).

gai·e·ty [ˈgeɪətɪ] *s.* **1.** Frohsinn *m*, Fröhlich-, Lustigkeit *f*; **2.** *oft pl.* Lustbarkeit *f*, Fest *n*; **3.** *fig.* (Farben)Pracht *f*.

gai·ly [ˈgeɪlɪ] *adv.* **1.** → ***gay*** 1, 2; **2.** unbekümmert, sorglos.

gain [geɪn] **I** *v/t.* **1.** *s-n Lebensunterhalt etc.* verdienen; **2.** gewinnen: ***~ time***; **3.** *das Ufer etc.* erreichen; **4.** *fig.* erreichen, erlangen, erringen: ***~ wealth*** Reichtümer erwerben; ***~ experience*** Erfahrung(en) sammeln; ***~ admission*** Einlaß finden; **5.** *j-m et.* einbringen, -tragen; **6.** zunehmen an (*dat.*): ***~ strength*** (***speed***) kräftiger (schneller) werden; ***he ~ed 10 pounds*** (***in weight***) er nahm 10 Pfund zu; **7.** ***~ over*** *j-n* für sich gewinnen; **8.** vorgehen um *2 Minuten etc.* (*Uhr*); **II** *v/i.* **9.** besser *od.* kräftiger werden; **10.** ✝ Gewinn *od.* Proˈfit machen; **11.** (an Wert) gewinnen, im Ansehen steigen, besser zur Geltung kommen; **12.** zunehmen (***in*** an *dat.*): ***~*** (***in weight***) (an Gewicht) zunehmen; **13.** (***on, upon***) a) näher herˈankommen (an *dat.*), (an) Boden gewinnen, aufholen (gegenˈüber), b) s-n Vorsprung vergrößern (vor *dat.*, gegenˈüber); **14.** (***on, upon***) ˈübergreifen (auf *acc.*); **15.** vorgehen (*Uhr*); **III** *s.* **16.** Gewinn *m*, Vorteil *m*, Nutzen *m* (***to*** für); **17.** Zunahme *f*, Steigerung *f*: ***~ in weight*** Gewichtszunahme; **18.** ✝ a) Gewinn *m*, Proˈfit *m*: ***for ~*** ⚖ gewerbsmäßig, in gewinnsüchtiger Absicht, b) Wertzuwachs *m*; **19.** ⚡, *phys.* Verstärkung *f*: ***~ control*** Lautstärkeregelung *f*;

ˈgain·er [-nə] *s.* **1.** Gewinner *m*; **2.** *sport* Auerbach(sprung) *m*: ***full ~*** Auerbachsalto *m*; ***half ~*** Auerbachkopfsprung *m*; **ˈgain·ful** [-fʊl] *adj.* □ einträglich, gewinnbringend: ***~ occupation*** Erwerbstätigkeit *f*; ***~ly employed*** erwerbstätig; **ˈgain·ings** [-nɪŋz] *s. pl.* Gewinn(e *pl.*) *m*, Einkünfte *pl.*, Proˈfit *m*; **ˈgain·less** [-lɪs] *adj.* **1.** unvorteilhaft, ohne Gewinn; **2.** nutzlos.

gain·say [ˌgeɪnˈseɪ] *v/t.* [*irr.* → ***say***] *obs.* **1.** *et.* bestreiten, leugnen: ***there is no ~ing that*** das läßt sich nicht leugnen; **2.** *j-m* widerˈsprechen.

gainst, ˈgainst [geɪnst] *poet. abbr. für* ***against***.

gait [geɪt] *s.* Gangart *f* (*a. fig. Tempo*), Gang *m*.

gai·ter [ˈgeɪtə] *s.* **1.** Gaˈmasche *f*; **2.** *Am.* Zugstiefel *m*.

gal¹ [gæl] *s.* F Mädchen *n*.

gal² [gæl] *s. phys.* Gal *n* (*Einheit der Beschleunigung*).

ga·la [ˈgɑːlə] **I** *adj.* **1.** festlich, Gala…; **II** *s.* **2.** *a.* ***~ occasion*** festlicher Anlaß, Fest *n*; **3.** Galaveranstaltung *f*; **4.** *sport Brit.* (*Schwimm- etc.*)Fest *n*.

ga·lac·tic [gəˈlæktɪk] *adj.* **1.** gaˈlaktisch, *ast.* Milchstraßen…; **2.** *physiol.* Milch…

Ga·la·tians [gəˈleɪʃjənz] *s. pl. bibl.* (Brief *m* des Paulus an die) Galater *pl.*

gal·ax·y [ˈgæləksɪ] *s.* **1.** *ast.* Milchstraße *f*, Galaˈxie *f*: ***the* ꝏ** die Milchstraße, die Galaxis; **2.** *fig.* Schar *f* (*prominenter etc. Personen*).

gale¹ [geɪl] *s.* Sturm *m*; steife Brise: ***~ force*** Sturmstärke *f*; ***~ of laughter*** Lachsalve *f*.

gale² [geɪl] *s.* ⚘ Heidemyrthe *f*.

ga·le·na [gəˈliːnə] *s. min.* Galeˈnit *m*, Bleiglanz *m*.

Ga·li·cian [gəˈlɪʃɪən] **I** *adj.* gaˈlizisch; **II** *s.* Gaˈlizier(in).

Gal·i·le·an¹ [ˌgælɪˈliːən] **I** *adj.* **1.** galiˈläisch; **II** *s.* **2.** Galiˈläer(in); **3.** ***the ~*** der Galiˈläer (*Christus*); **4.** Christ(in).

Gal·i·le·an² [ˌgælɪˈliːən] *adj.* galiˈleisch: ***~ telescope***.

gal·i·lee [ˈgælɪliː] *s.* △ Vorhalle *f*.

gal·i·pot [ˈgælɪpɒt] Galiˈpot-, Fichtenharz *n*.

gall¹ [gɔːl] *s.* **1.** *obs.* a) *anat.* Gallenblase *f*, b) *physiol.* Galle(nflüssigkeit) *f*; **2.** *fig.* Galle *f*: a) Bitterkeit *f*, Erbitterung *f*, b) Bosheit *f*; **3.** F Frechheit *f*.

gall² [gɔːl] **I** *s.* **1.** wund geriebene Stelle; **2.** *fig.* a) Ärger *m*, b) Ärgernis *n*; **II** *v/t.* **3.** wund reiben; **4.** (ver)ärgern; **III** *v/i.* **5.** reiben, scheuern; **6.** sich wund reiben; **7.** sich ärgern.

gall³ [gɔːl] *s.* ⚘ Galle *f*.

gal·lant ['gælənt] **I** *adj.* □ **1.** tapfer, heldenhaft; **2.** prächtig, stattlich; **3.** ga'lant: a) höflich, ritterlich, b) amou'rös, Liebes…; **II** *s.* **4.** Kava'lier *m*; **5.** Verehrer *m*; **6.** Geliebte(r) *m*; '**gal·lant·ry** [-trɪ] *s.* **1.** Tapferkeit *f*; **2.** Galante'rie *f*, Ritterlichkeit *f*; **3.** heldenhafte Tat; **4.** Liebe'lei *f*.

gall| blad·der *s. anat.* Gallenblase *f*; **~ duct** *s. anat.* Gallengang *m*.

gal·le·on ['gælɪən] *s.* ⚓ *hist.* Gale'one *f*.

gal·ler·y ['gælərɪ] *s.* **1.** △ a) Gale'rie *f*, b) Em'pore *f* (*in Kirchen*); **2.** *thea.* dritter Rang, *a. weitS.* Gale'rie *f*: ***play to the ~*** für die Galerie spielen, *fig. a.* nach Effekt haschen; **3.** ('Kunst-, Ge'mälde)Gale₁rie *f*; **4.** a) ⚓ Laufgang *m*, b) ⚙ Laufsteg *m*, c) ⚒ *u.* ⚔ Stollen *m*, d) → ***shooting-gallery***; **5.** *fig.* Gale'rie *f*, Schar *f* (*Personen*).

gal·ley ['gælɪ] *s.* **1.** ⚓ a) Ga'leere *f*, b) Langboot *n*; **2.** ⚓ Kom'büse *f*, Küche *f*; **3.** *typ.* Setzschiff *n*; **4.** *a.* **~ proof** *typ.* Fahne *f*; **~ slave** *s.* **1.** Ga'leerensklave *m*; **2.** *fig.* Sklave *m*, ‚Kuli' *m*; ₁**~-'west** *adv.*: ***knock ~*** *Am.* F a) *j-n* zs.-schlagen, b) *fig. j-n* ‚umhauen', c) *et.* (total) ‚kaputtmachen'.

'**gall·fly** *s. zo.* Gallwespe *f*.

gal·lic[1] ['gælɪk] *adj.*: **~ acid** ⚗ Gallussäure *f*.

Gal·lic[2] ['gælɪk] *adj.* **1.** gallisch; **2.** fran'zösisch; '**Gal·li·cism** [-ɪsɪzəm] *s. ling.* Galli'zismus *m*, französische Spracheigenheit; '**Gal·li·cize** [-ɪsaɪz] *v/t.* französi(si)sieren.

gal·li·na·ceous [₁gælɪ'neɪʃəs] *adj. orn.* hühnerartig.

gall·ing ['gɔːlɪŋ] *adj.* ärgerlich (*Sache*).

gal·li·pot[1] → ***galipot***.

gal·li·pot[2] ['gælɪpɒt] *s.* Salbentopf *m*, Medika'mentenbehälter *m*.

gal·li·vant [₁gælɪ'vænt] *v/i.* **1.** sich amüsieren; **2. ~ *around*** sich her'umtreiben.

'**gall·nut** *s.* ⚘ Gallapfel *m*.

gal·lon ['gælən] *s.* Gal'lone *f* (*Hohlmaß*; *Brit. 4,5459 l*, *Am. 3,7853 l*).

gal·loon [gə'luːn] *s.* Tresse *f*.

gal·lop ['gæləp] **I** *v/i.* **1.** galoppieren; **2.** F ‚sausen': **~ *through s.th.*** et. ‚im Ga'lopp' erledigen; **~ *through a book*** ein Buch durchfliegen; ***~ing consumption*** (***inflation***) galoppierende Schwindsucht (Inflation); **II** *v/t.* **3.** galoppieren lassen; **III** *s.* **4.** Ga'lopp *m* (*a. fig.*): ***at full ~*** in gestrecktem Galopp; **gal·lo·pade** [₁gælə'peɪd] → ***galop***.

Gal·lo·phile ['gæləʊfaɪl], '**Gal·lo·phil** [-fɪl] *s.* Fran'zosenfreund *m*; '**Gal·lo·phobe** [-fəʊb] *s.* Fran'zosenhasser *m*.

gal·lows ['gæləʊz] *s. pl. mst sg. konstr.* **1.** Galgen *m*; **2.** galgenähnliches Gestell, Galgen *m*; **~ bird** *s.* F Galgenvogel *m*; **~ hu·mo(u)r** *s.* 'Galgenhu₁mor *m*; **~ tree** → ***gallows*** 1.

'**gall·stone** *s.* ⚕ Gallenstein *m*.

Gal·lup poll ['gæləp] *s.* 'Meinungs₁umfrage *f*.

gal·lus·es ['gæləsɪz] *s. pl. Am.* F Hosenträger *pl*.

gal·op ['gæləp] **I** *s.* Ga'lopp *m* (*Tanz*); **II** *v/i.* e-n Ga'lopp tanzen.

ga·lore [gə'lɔː] *adv.* F ‚in rauhen Mengen': ***whisk(e)y ~*** *a.* jede Menge Whisky.

ga·losh [gə'lɒʃ] *s. mst pl.* 'Über-, Gummischuh *m*, Ga'losche *f*.

ga·lumph [gə'lʌmf] *v/i.* F stapfen, trapsen.

gal·van·ic [gæl'vænɪk] *adj.* (□ **~*ally***) ⚡, *phys.* gal'vanisch; *fig.* F elektrisierend; **gal·va·nism** ['gælvənɪzəm] *s.* **1.** *phys.* Galva'nismus *m*; **2.** ⚕ Galvanisati'on *f*; **gal·va·ni·za·tion** [₁gælvənaɪ'zeɪʃn] *s.* ⚕, ⚗ Galvanisierung *f*; **gal·va·nize** ['gælvənaɪz] *v/t.* **1.** ⚙ galvanisieren, (feuer)verzinken; **2.** ⚕ mit Gleichstrom behandeln; **3.** *fig.* F *j-n* elektrisieren: **~ *into action*** *j-n* schlagartig aktiv werden lassen; **gal·va·nom·e·ter** [₁gælvə'nɒmɪtə] *s. phys.* Galvano'meter *n*; **gal·va·no·plas·tic** [₁gælvənəʊ'plæstɪk] *adj.* ⚙ galvano'plastisch; **gal·va·no·plas·tics** [₁gælvənəʊ'plæstɪks] *s. pl. sg. konstr.*, **gal·va·no·plas·ty** [₁gælvənəʊ'plæstɪ] *s.* Galvano'plastik *f*, E₁lektroty'pie *f*; **gal·va·no·scope** ['gælvənəʊskəʊp] *s. phys.* Galvano'skop *n*.

gam·bit ['gæmbɪt] *s.* **1.** *Schach*: Gam'bit *n*, Eröffnung *f*; **2.** *fig.* a) erster Schritt, Einleitung *f*, b) (raffinierter) Trick.

gam·ble ['gæmbl] **I** *v/i.* **1.** (um Geld) spielen: **~ *with s.th.*** *fig.* et. aufs Spiel setzen; ***you can ~ on that*** darauf kannst du wetten; ***she ~d on his coming*** sie verließ sich darauf, daß er kommen würde; **2.** *Börse*: spekulieren; **II** *v/t.* **3. ~ *away*** verspielen (*a. fig.*); **4.** (als Einsatz) setzen (***on*** auf *acc.*), *fig.* aufs Spiel setzen; **III** *s.* **5.** Glücksspiel *n*, Ha'sardspiel *n* (*a. fig.*); **6.** *fig.* Wagnis *n*, Risiko *n*; '**gam·bler** [-lə] *s.* Spieler(in); *fig.* Hasar'deur *m*; '**gam·bling** [-blɪŋ] *s.* Spielen *n*: **~ *den*** Spielhölle *f*; **~ *debt*** Spielschuld *f*.

gam·boge [gæm'buːʒ] *s.* ⚗ Gummigutt *n*.

gam·bol ['gæmbl] **I** *v/i.* her'umtanzen, Luftsprünge machen; **II** *s.* Freuden-, Luftsprung *m*.

game[1] [geɪm] **I** *s.* **1.** Spiel *n*, Zeitvertreib *m*, Sport *m*: **2*s*** *pl.* (*Olympische etc.*) Spiele, *ped.* Sport; **~ *of golf*** Golfspiel; **~ *of skill*** Geschicklichkeitsspiel; ***play the ~*** *a. fig.* sich an die Spielregeln halten; ***play a good ~*** gut spielen; ***play ~s with s.o.*** *fig.* mit j-m sein Spiel treiben; ***play a losing ~*** auf der Verliererstraße sein; ***be on*** (***off***) ***one's ~*** gut (nicht) in Form sein; ***the ~ is yours*** du hast gewonnen; **2.** *sport* (einzelnes) Spiel, Par'tie *f* (*Schach etc.*); *Tennis*: Spiel *n* (*in e-m Satz*): ***~, set and match*** *Tennis*: Spiel, Satz u. Sieg; **3.** Scherz *m*, Ulk *m*: ***make ~ of*** sich lustig machen über (*acc.*); **4.** Spiel *n*, Unter'nehmen *n*, Plan *m*: ***the ~ is up*** das Spiel ist aus *od.* verloren; ***give the ~ away*** F sich *od.* alles verraten; ***play a double ~*** ein doppeltes Spiel treiben; ***play a waiting ~*** e-e abwartende Haltung einnehmen; ***I know his*** (***little***) ***~*** ich weiß, was er im Schilde führt; ***see through s.o.'s ~*** j-s Spiel *od.* j-n durchschauen; ***beat s.o. at his own ~*** j-n mit s-n eigenen Waffen schlagen; ***two can play at this ~!*** das kann ich auch!; **5.** *pl. fig.* Schliche *pl.*, Tricks *pl.*; **6.** Spiel *n* (*Geräte etc.*); **7.** F Branche *f*, Geschäft *n*: ***he is in the advertising ~*** er macht in Werbung; ***she's on the ~*** ‚sie geht auf den Strich'; **8.** *hunt.* Wild *n*: ***big ~*** Großwild; ***fly at higher ~*** höher hinaus wollen; **9.** Wildbret *n*: **~ *pie*** Wildpastete *f*; **II** *adj.* □ **10.** Jagd…, Wild…; **11.** schneidig, mutig; **12.** a) aufgelegt (***for*** zu), b) bereit (***for*** zu, ***to do*** zu tun): ***I am ~!*** ich bin dabei!, ich mache mit!; **III** *v/i.* **13.** (um Geld) spielen; **IV** *v/t.* **14. ~ *away*** verspielen.

game[2] [geɪm] *adj.* F lahm: ***a ~ leg***.

game| bag *s.* Jagdtasche *f*; **~ bird** *s.* Jagdvogel *m*; '**~·cock** *s.* Kampfhahn *m* (*a. fig.*); **~ fish** *s.* Sportfisch *m*; **~ fowl** *s.* **1.** Federwild *n*; **2.** Kampfhahn *m*; '**~₁keep·er** *s. Brit.* Wildhüter *m*; **~ li·cence** *s. Brit.* Jagdschein *m*.

game·ness ['geɪmnɪs] *s.* Mut *m*, Schneid *m*.

game| park *s.* Wildpark *m*; **~ plan** *s. Am. fig.* ‚Schlachtplan' *m*; **~ point** *s. sport* a) entscheidender Punkt, b) *Tennis*: Spielball *m*, c) *Tischtennis*: Satzball *m*; **~ pre·serve** *s.* Wildgehege *n*.

games·man·ship ['geɪmzmənʃɪp] *s. bsd. sport* die Kunst, mit allen (gerade noch erlaubten) Tricks zu gewinnen.

games| mas·ter [geɪmz] *s. ped. Brit.* Sportlehrer *m*; **~ mis·tress** *s. ped. Brit.* Sportlehrerin *f*.

game·some ['geɪmsəm] *adj.* □ lustig, ausgelassen.

game·ster ['geɪmstə] *s.* Spieler(in) (*um Geld*).

gam·ete [gæ'miːt] *s. biol.* Ga'met *m* (*Keimzelle*).

game ward·en *s.* Jagdaufseher *m*.

gam·in ['gæmɪn] *s.* Gassenjunge *m*.

gam·ing ['geɪmɪŋ] *s.* Spielen *n* (*um Geld*): **~ *laws*** Gesetze über Glücksspiele u. Wetten; **~ house** *s.* Spielhölle *f*, 'Spielka₁sino *n*; **~ ta·ble** *s.* Spieltisch *m*.

gam·ma ['gæmə] *s.* **1.** Gamma *n* (*griech. Buchstabe*): **~ *rays*** *phys.* Gammastrahlen; **2.** *phot.* Kon'trastgrad *m*; **3.** *ped. Brit.* Drei *f*, Befriedigend *n*.

gam·mer ['gæmə] *s. Brit.* F ‚Oma' *f*.

gam·mon[1] ['gæmən] *s.* **1.** (schwach)geräucherter Schinken; **2.** unteres Stück e-r Speckseite.

gam·mon[2] ['gæmən] *s.* ⚓ Bugsprietzurring *f*.

gam·mon[3] ['gæmən] F **I** *s.* **1.** Humbug *m*: a) Schwindel *m*, b) ‚Quatsch' *m*; **II** *v/i.* **2.** ‚quatschen', Unsinn reden; **3.** sich verstellen, so tun als ob; **III** *v/t.* **4.** *j-n* ‚reinlegen'.

gamp [gæmp] *s. Brit.* F (großer) Regenschirm, ‚Fa'miliendach' *n*.

gam·ut ['gæmət] *s.* **1.** ♪ Tonleiter *f*; **2.** *fig.* Skala *f*: ***run the whole ~ of emotion*** von e-m Gefühl ins andere taumeln.

gam·y ['geɪmɪ] *adj.* **1.** nach Wild riechend *od.* schmeckend: **~ *taste*** a) Wildgeschmack *m*, b) Hautgout *m*; **2.** F schneidig, mutig.

gan·der ['gændə] *s.* **1.** Gänserich *m*; → ***sauce*** 1; **2.** *fig.* F ‚Esel' *m*, Dussel *m*; **3.** *sl.* Blick *m*: ***take a ~ at*** sich (rasch) *et.* angucken.

gang [gæŋ] **I** *s.* **1.** ('Arbeiter)Ko₁lonne *f*, (-)Trupp *m*; **2.** Gang *f*, (Verbrecher-)Bande *f*; **3.** *contp.* Bande *f*, Horde *f*, Clique *f*; **4.** ⚙ Satz *m* (*Werkzeuge*): **~ *of tools***; **II** *v/i.* **5.** *mst* **~ *up*** sich zs.-tun, sich zs.-rotten (***on, against*** gegen).

'**gang|·bang** *s. sl.* a) *Geschlechtsverkehr mehrerer Männer nacheinander mit 'einer Frau*, b) *Vergewaltigung e-r Frau* *durch mehrere Männer nacheinander*; '~**·board** *s.* ⚓ Laufplanke *f*; ~ **boss** → ***ganger***; ~ **cut·ter** *s.* ⚙ Satz-, Mehrfachfräser *m.*

gang·er ['gæŋə] *s.* Vorarbeiter *m*, Kapo *m.*

'**gang·land** *s.* ‚'Unterwelt' *f.*

gan·gling ['gæŋglɪŋ] *adj.* schlaksig.

gan·gli·on ['gæŋglɪən] *pl.* **-a** [-ə] *s.* **1.** *anat.* Ganglion *n*, Nervenknoten *m*: ~ ***cell*** Ganglienzelle *f*; **2.** ⚕ 'Überbein *n*; **3.** *fig.* Knoten-, Mittelpunkt *m*, Zentrum *n.*

'**gang|·plank** → ***gangway*** 2b; ~ **rape** → ***gangbang*** b.

gan·grene ['gæŋgri:n] **I** *s.* **1.** ⚕ Brand *m*, Gan'grän *n*; **2.** *fig.* Fäulnis *f*, sittlicher Verfall; **II** *v/t. u. v/i.* **3.** ⚕ brandig machen (werden); '**gan·gre·nous** [-rɪnəs] *adj.* ⚕ brandig.

gang saw *s.* ⚙ Gattersäge *f.*

gang·ster ['gæŋstə] *s.* Gangster *m.*

'**gang·way I** *s.* **1.** 'Durchgang *m*, Pas'sage *f*; **2.** a) ⚓ Fallreep *n*, b) ⚓ Gangway *f*, Landungsbrücke *f*, c) ✈ Gangway *f*; **3.** *Brit. thea. etc.* (Zwischen)Gang *m*; **4.** ⚒ Strecke *f*; **5.** ⚙ a) Schräge *f*, Rutsche *f*, b) Laufbühne *f*; **II** *int.* **6.** Platz (machen) (, bitte)!

gan·net ['gænɪt] *s. orn.* Tölpel *m.*

gant·let ['gæntlɪt] → ***gauntlet***[1].

gan·try ['gæntrɪ] *s.* **1.** ⚙ Faßlager *n*; **2.** *a.* ~ ***bridge*** ⚙ Kranbrücke *f*: ~ ***crane*** Portalkran *m*; **3.** a) 🚂 Si'gnalbrücke *f*, b) *mot.* Schilderbrücke *f*; **4.** *a.* ~ ***scaffold*** *Raumfahrt*: Mon'tageturm *m.*

Gan·y·mede ['gænɪmi:d] *s.* **1.** *a.* ♕ Mundschenk *m*; **2.** *ast.* Gany'med *m.*

gaol [dʒeɪl] *bsd. Brit.* → ***jail*** *etc.*

gap [gæp] *s.* **1.** Lücke *f*, Spalt *m*, Öffnung *f*; **2.** ⚔ Bresche *f*, Gasse *f*; **3.** (Berg)Schlucht *f*; **4.** *fig.* a) Lücke *f*, b) Zwischenraum *m*, -zeit *f*, c) Unter'brechung *f*, d) Kluft *f*, 'Unterschied *m*: ***close the*** ~ die Lücke schließen; ***fill*** (*od.* ***stop***) ***a*** ~ e-e Lücke ausfüllen; ***leave a*** ~ e-e Lücke hinterlassen; ***dollar*** ~ 💲 Dollarlücke; ***rocket*** ~ Raketenlücke; ~ ***in one's education*** Bildungslücke; **5.** ⚡ Funkenstrecke *f.*

gape [geɪp] **I** *v/i.* **1.** den Mund aufreißen (*vor Staunen etc.*), staunen: ***stand gaping*** Maulaffen feilhalten; **2.** starren, glotzen, gaffen: ~ ***at s.o.*** j-n anstarren; **3.** gähnen; **4.** *fig.* klaffen, gähnen, sich öffnen *od.* auftun; **II** *s.* **5.** Gaffen *n*, Glotzen *n*; **6.** Staunen *n*; **7.** Gähnen *n*; **8.** ***the*** ~***s*** *pl. sg. konstr.* a) *vet.* Schnabelsperre *f*, b) *humor.* Gähnkrampf *m*; '**gap·ing** [-pɪŋ] *adj.* □ **1.** gaffend, glotzend; **2.** klaffend (*Wunde*), gähnend (*Abgrund*).

gap·py ['gæpɪ] *adj.* lückenhaft (*a. fig.*).

ga·rage ['gærɑ:dʒ] **I** *s.* **1.** Ga'rage *f*; **2.** Repara'turwerkstätte *f* u. Tankstelle *f*; **II** *v/t.* **3.** *Auto* a) in e-r Ga'rage ab- *od.* 'unterstellen, b) in die Ga'rage fahren.

garb [gɑ:b] **I** *s.* Tracht *f*, Gewand *n* (*a. fig.*); **II** *v/t.* kleiden.

gar·bage ['gɑ:bɪdʒ] *s.* **1.** *Am.* Abfall *m*, Müll *m*: ~ ***can*** Mülleimer *m*, -tonne *f*; ~ ***chute*** Müllschlucker *m*; **2.** *fig.* a) Schund *m*, b) ‚Abschaum' *m*; **3.** *Computer*: wertlose Daten *pl.*

gar·ble ['gɑ:bl] *v/t. Text etc.* a) durchein'anderbringen, b) verstümmeln, entstellen, ‚frisieren'.

gar·den ['gɑ:dn] **I** *s.* **1.** Garten *m*; **2.** *fig.* Garten *m*, fruchtbare Gegend: ***the*** ~ ***of England*** die Grafschaft Kent; **3.** *mst pl.* Gartenanlagen *pl.*, Park *m*: ***botanical*** ~(***s***) botanischer Garten; **II** *v/i.* **4.** gärtnern, im Garten arbeiten; **5.** Gartenbau treiben; **III** *adj.* **6.** Garten...: ~ ***plants***; ~ **cit·y** *s. Brit.* Gartenstadt *f*; ~ **cress** *s.* ⚘ Gartenkresse *f.*

gar·den·er ['gɑ:dnə] *s.* Gärtner(in).

gar·den| frame *s.* glasgedeckter Pflanzenkasten; ~ **gnome** *s.* Gartenzwerg *m.*

gar·de·ni·a [gɑ:'di:njə] *s.* ⚘ Gar'denie *f.*

gar·den·ing ['gɑ:dnɪŋ] *s.* **1.** Gartenbau *m*; **2.** Gartenarbeit *f.*

gar·den| mo(u)ld *s.* Blumen(topf)erde *f*; ~ **par·ty** *s.* Gartenfest *n*, -party *f*; ~ **path** *s.*: ***lead s.o. up the*** ~ *fig.* j-n hinters Licht führen; ♕ **State** *s. Am.* (*Beiname für*) New Jersey *n*; ~ **stuff** *s.* Gartenerzeugnisse *pl.*; ~ **sub·urb** *s. Brit.* Gartenvorstadt *f*; ~ **truck** *Am.* → ***garden stuff***; ~ **white** *s. zo.* Weißling *m.*

gar·gan·tu·an [gɑ:'gæntjʊən] *adj.* riesig, gewaltig, ungeheuer.

gar·gle ['gɑ:gl] **I** *v/t.* **1.** a) gurgeln mit: ~ ***salt water***, b) ~ ***one's throat*** → 3; **2.** *Worte* (her'vor)gurgeln; **II** *v/i.* **3.** gurgeln; **III** *s.* **4.** Gurgeln *n*; **5.** Gurgelmittel *n.*

gar·goyle ['gɑ:gɔɪl] *s.* **1.** △ Wasserspeier *m*; **2.** *fig.* Scheusal *n.*

gar·ish ['geərɪʃ] *adj.* □ grell, schreiend, aufdringlich, protzig.

gar·land ['gɑ:lənd] **I** *s.* **1.** Gir'lande *f* (*a.* △), Blumengewinde *n*, -gehänge *n*; (*a. fig.* Sieges)Kranz *m*; **2.** *fig.* (*bsd.* Gedicht)Sammlung *f*; **II** *v/t.* **3.** bekränzen.

gar·lic ['gɑ:lɪk] *s.* ⚘ Knoblauch *m*; '**garlick·y** [-kɪ] *adj.* **1.** knoblauchartig; **2.** nach Knoblauch schmeckend *od.* riechend.

gar·ment ['gɑ:mənt] *s.* **1.** Kleidungsstück *n*, *pl. a.* Kleider *pl.*; **2.** *fig.* Gewand *n*, Hülle *f.*

gar·ner ['gɑ:nə] **I** *s.* **1.** *obs.* Getreidespeicher *m*; **2.** *fig.* Speicher *m*, Vorrat *m* (***of*** *an dat.*); **II** *v/t.* **3.** a) speichern (*a. fig.*), b) aufbewahren, c) sammeln (*a. fig.*), d) erlangen, erwerben.

gar·net ['gɑ:nɪt] **I** *s. min.* Gra'nat *m*; **II** *adj.* gra'natrot.

gar·nish ['gɑ:nɪʃ] **I** *v/t.* **1.** schmücken, verzieren; **2.** *Küche*: garnieren (*a. fig. iro.*); **3.** ⚖ a) *Forderung beim Drittschuldner* pfänden, b) *dem Drittschuldner* ein Zahlungsverbot zustellen; **II** *s.* **4.** Orna'ment *n*, Verzierung *f*; **5.** *Küche*: Garnierung *f* (*a. fig. iro.*); **garnish·ee** [ˌgɑ:nɪ'ʃi:] ⚖ **I** *s.* Drittschuldner *m*; **II** *v/t.* → ***garnish*** 3; '**gar·nish·ment** [-mənt] *s.* **1.** → ***garnish*** 4; **2.** ⚖ a) (Forderungs)Pfändung *f*, b) Zahlungsverbot *n* an den Drittschuldner, c) *Brit.* Mitteilung *f* an den Pro'zeßgegner; '**gar·ni·ture** [-ɪtʃə] *s.* **1.** → ***garnish*** 4; **2.** Zubehör *n*, *m*, Ausstattung *f.*

ga·rotte → ***garrot(t)e***.

gar·ret ['gærət] *s.* a) Dachstube *f*, Man'sarde *f*, b) Dachgeschoß *n.*

gar·ri·son ['gærɪsn] ⚔ **I** *s.* **1.** Garni'son *f* (*Standort od. stationierte Truppen*); **II** *v/t.* **2.** *Ort* mit e-r Garni'son belegen; **3.** *Truppen* in Garni'son legen: ***be*** ~***ed*** in Garnison liegen; ~ **cap** *s.* Feldmütze *f*; ~ **com·mand·er** *s.* 'Standortkommanˌdant *m*; ~ **town** *s.* Garni'sonsstadt *f.*

gar·rot(t)e [gə'rɒt] **I** *s.* **1.** ('Hinrichtung *f* durch die) Ga(r)'rotte *f*; **2.** Erdrosselung *f*; **II** *v/t.* **3.** ga(r)rottieren; **4.** erdrosseln.

gar·ru·li·ty [gæ'ru:lətɪ] *s.* Geschwätzigkeit *f*; **gar·ru·lous** ['gærʊləs] *adj.* □ geschwätzig.

gar·ter ['gɑ:tə] **I** *s.* **1.** a) Strumpfband *n*, b) Sockenhalter *m*, c) *Am.* Strumpfhalter *m*, Straps *m*: ~ ***belt*** Hüfthalter *m*, -gürtel *m*; **2.** ***the*** ♕ a) *a.* ***the Order of the*** ♕ der Hosenbandorden (*der höchste brit. Orden*), b) der Hosenbandorden (*Abzeichen*), c) die Mitgliedschaft des Hosenbandordens; **II** *v/t.* **3.** mit e-m Strumpfband *etc.* befestigen *od.* versehen.

gas [gæs] **I** *s.* **1.** ⚗ Gas *n*; **2.** (Leucht-)Gas *n*; **3.** ⚒ Grubengas *n*; **4.** ⚕ Lachgas *n*; **5.** ⚔ (Gift)Gas *n*, (Gas)Kampfstoff *m*: ~ ***shell*** Gasgranate *f*; **6.** *mot.* F a) *Am.* Ben'zin *n*, ‚Sprit' *m*, b) 'Gas(peˌdal) *n*: ***step on the*** ~ Gas geben, ‚auf die Tube drücken' (*beide a. fig.*); **7.** *sl.* a) ‚Gequatsche' *n*, b) ‚Gaudi' *f*, Mordsspaß *m*: ***it's a*** (***real***) ~***!*** (das ist) zum Brüllen!, *weitS.* große Klasse!; **II** *v/t.* **8.** mit Gas versorgen *od.* füllen; **9.** ⚙ begasen; **10.** vergasen, mit Gas töten *od.* vernichten; **11.** ~ ***up*** *mot. Auto* volltanken; **III** *v/i.* **12.** *mst* ~ ***up*** *Am.* F (auf-)tanken; **13.** F ‚quatschen'; '~**·bag** *s.* **1.** ⚙ Gassack *m*, -zelle *f*; **2.** F ‚Quatscher' *m*; ~ **bomb** *s.* ⚔ Kampfstoffbombe *f*; ~ **bot·tle** *s.* ⚙ Gas-, Stahlflasche *f*; ~ **burn·er** *s.* Gasbrenner *m*; ~ **cham·ber** *s.* **1.** Gaskammer *f* (*zur Hinrichtung*); **2.** ⚔ Gasprüfraum *m*; ~ **coal** *s.* Gaskohle *f*; ~ **coke** *s.* (Gas)Koks *m*; ~ **cook·er** *s.* Gasherd *m*; ~ **cyl·in·der** *s.* Gasflasche *f*; ~ **en·gine** *s.* 'Gasmotor *m*, -maˌschine *f.*

gas·e·ous ['gæsjəs] *adj.* **1.** ⚗ a) gasartig, -förmig, b) Gas...; **2.** *fig.* leer.

gas| field *s.* (Erd)Gasfeld *n*; '~**-ˌfired** *adj.* mit Gasfeuerung, gasbeheizt; ~ **fit·ter** *s.* 'Gasinstallaˌteur *m*; ~ **fit·ting** *s.* **1.** 'Gasinstallatiˌon *f*; **2.** *pl.* 'Gasarmaˌturen *pl.*; ~ **gan·grene** *s.* ⚕ Gasbrand *m.*

gash [gæʃ] **I** *s.* **1.** klaffende Wunde, tiefer Schnitt *od.* Riß; **2.** Spalte *f*; **II** *v/t.* **3.** *j-m* e-e klaffende Wunde beibringen.

gas| heat·er *s.* Gasofen *m*; ~ **heat·ing** *s.* Gasheizung *f.*

gas·i·fi·ca·tion [ˌgæsɪfɪ'keɪʃn] *s.* ⚙ Vergasung *f*; **gas·i·fy** ['gæsɪfaɪ] **I** *v/t.* vergasen, in Gas verwandeln; **II** *v/i.* zu Gas werden.

gas jet *s.* Gasflamme *f*, -brenner *m.*

gas·ket ['gæskɪt] *s.* ⚙ 'Dichtung(smanˌschette *f*, -sring *m*) *f*: ***blow a*** ~ *fig.* F ‚durchdrehen'.

'**gas|·light** *s.* Gaslicht *n*, -lampe *f*; '~**ˌlight·er** *s.* **1.** Gasfeuerzeug *n*; **2.** Gasanzünder *m*; ~ **main** *s.* (Haupt-)Gasleitung *f*; '~**·man** [-mæn] *s.* [*irr.*] **1.** 'Gasinstallaˌteur *m*; **2.** Gasmann *m*, -ableser *m*; ~ **man·tle** *s.* (Gas)Glühstrumpf *m*; ~ **mask** *s.* ⚔ Gasmaske *f*; ~ **me·ter** *s.* ⚙ Gasuhr *f*, -zähler *m*; ~ **mo·tor** → ***gas engine***.

gas·o·lene, gas·o·line ['gæsəʊli:n] *s.* **1.** ⚗ Gaso'lin *n*, Gasäther *m*; **2.** *Am.* Ben'zin *n*: ~ ***ga(u)ge*** Kraftstoffmesser *m*, Benzinuhr *f*.

gas·om·e·ter [gæˈsɒmɪtə] *s*. Gasoˈmeter *m*, Gasbehälter *m*.

gas ov·en *s*. Gasherd *m*.

gasp [gɑːsp] **I** *v/i*. keuchen (*a. Maschine etc.*): **~ for breath** nach Luft schnappen; **it made me ~** mir stockte der Atem (*vor Erstaunen*); **~ for s.th.** *fig*. nach et. lechzen; **II** *v/t. a.* **~ out** Worte (herˈvor)keuchen: **~ one's life out** sein Leben aushauchen; **III** *s*. a) Keuchen *n*, b) Laut *m* des Erstaunens *od*. Erschreckens: **at one's last ~** in den letzten Zügen (liegend), *fig*. ‚am Eingehen'; **ˈgasp·er** [-pə] *s*. *Brit. sl.* ‚Stäbchen' *n* (*Zigarette*).

gas| pipe *s*. Gasrohr *n*; **ˈ~·proof** *adj*. gasdicht; **~ pump** *s*. *mot. Am.* Zapfsäule *f*; **~ range** *s*. *Am.* Gasherd *m*; **~ ring** *s*. Gasbrenner *m*, -kocher *m*.

gassed [gæst] *adj*. vergast, gaskrank, -vergiftet; **gas·ser** [ˈgæsə] *s*. **1.** Gas freigebende Ölquelle; **2.** F ‚Quatscher' *m*; **gas·sing** [ˈgæsɪŋ] *s*. **1.** ⚙ Behandlung *f* mit Gas; **2.** Vergasung *f*; **3.** F ‚Quatschen' *n*.

gas| sta·tion *s*. *Am.* Tankstelle *f*; **~ stove** *s*. Gasherd *m od.* -ofen *m*; **~ tank** *s*. Gas- *od. Am.* F Benˈzinbehälter *m*; **~ tar** *s*. Steinkohlenteer *m*.

gas·ter·o·pod [ˈgæstərəpɒd] → ***gastropod***.

ˈgas·tight *adj*. gasdicht.

gas·tric [ˈgæstrɪk] *adj*. ⚕ gastrisch, Magen...: **~ acid** Magensäure *f*; **~ flu** Darmgrippe *f*; **~ juice** Magensaft *m*; **~ ulcer** Magengeschwür *n*; **gas·tri·tis** [gæˈstraɪtɪs] *s*. ⚕ Gaˈstritis *f*, Magenschleimhautentzündung *f*; **gas·tro·en·ter·i·tis** [ˌgæstrəʊentəˈraɪtɪs] *s*. ⚕ Gastroenteˈritis *f*, ˈMagen-ˈDarm-Kaˌtarrh *m*; **gas·tro·in·tes·ti·nal** [ˌgæstrəʊɪnˈtestɪnl] ⚕ gastrointestiˈnal.

gas·trol·o·gist [gæˈstrɒlədʒɪst] *s*. **1.** ⚕ Facharzt *m* für Magenkrankheiten; **2.** *humor.* Kochkünstler *m*.

gas·tro·nome [ˈgæstrənəʊm], **gas·tron·o·mer** [gæˈstrɒnəmə] *s*. Feinschmecker *m*; **gas·tro·nom·ic**, **gas·tro·nom·i·cal** [ˌgæstrəˈnɒmɪk(l)] *adj*. ☐ feinschmeckerisch; **gas·tron·o·mist** [gæˈstrɒnəmɪst] → ***gastronome***; **gas·tron·o·my** [gæˈstrɒnəmɪ] *s*. **1.** Gastronoˈmie *f*, höhere Kochkunst; **2.** *fig*. Küche *f*: **the Italian ~**.

gas·tro·pod [ˈgæstrəpɒd] *s*. *zo*. Gastroˈpode *m*, Schnecke *f*.

gas·tro·scope [ˈgæstrəʊskəʊp] *s*. ⚕ Magenspiegel *m*.

gas| weld·ing *s*. ⚙ Gasschweißen *n*; **ˈ~·works** *s. pl. sg. konstr.* Gaswerk *n*.

gat [gæt] *s*. *Am. sl.* ‚Kaˈnone' *f*, ‚Ballermann' *m*, ‚Schießeisen' *n*.

gate [geɪt] **I** *s*. **1.** Tor *n*, Pforte *f*, *fig. a.* Zugang *m*, Weg *m* (**to** zu): **crash the ~** → ***gatecrash***; **2.** a) 🚂 Sperre *f*, Schranke *f*, b) ✈ Flugsteig *m*; **3.** (enger) Eingang, (schmale) ˈDurchfahrt; **4.** (Gebirgs)Paß *m*; **5.** ⚙ (Schleusen-)Tor *n*; **6.** *sport*: a) *Slalom*: Tor *n*, b) → ***starting gate***; **7.** *sport* a) Besucherzahl *f*, b) (Gesamt)Einnahmen *pl*., Kasse *f*; **8.** ⚙ Schieber *m*, Venˈtil *n*; **9.** *Gießerei*: (Einguß)Trichter *m*, Anschnitt *m*; **10.** *phot*. Bild-, Filmfenster *n*; **11.** ⚡ ˈTorimˌpuls *m*; **12.** *TV* Ausblendstufe *f*; **13.** *Am.* F a) ‚Rausschmiß' *m*, b) ‚Laufpaß' *m*: **get the ~** ‚gefeuert' werden; **give s.o. the ~** a) j-n ‚feuern', b) j-m den Laufpaß geben; **II** *v/t*. **14.** *ped., univ. Brit. j-m* den Ausgang sperren: **he was ~d** er erhielt Ausgangsverbot; **ˈ~·crash** *v/i*. (*u. v/t.*) F a) uneingeladen kommen *od*. gehen (zu *e-r Party etc.*), b) sich (ohne zu bezahlen) einschmuggeln (in *e-e Veranstaltung*); **ˈ~ˌcrash·er** *s*. F Eindringling *m*: a) uneingeladener Gast, b) *j-d, der sich in e-e Veranstaltung einschmuggelt*; **ˈ~ˌkeep·er** *s*. **1.** Pförtner *m*; **2.** 🚂 Bahn-, Schrankenwärter *m*; **ˈ~·leg(ged) ta·ble** *s*. Klapptisch *m*; **ˈ~-ˌmon·ey** → ***gate*** 7b; **ˈ~·post** *s*. Tor-, Türpfosten *m*: **between you and me and the ~** im Vertrauen *od*. unter uns (gesagt); **ˈ~·way** *s*. **1.** Torweg *m*, Einfahrt *f*; **2.** *fig*. Tor *n*, Zugang *m*.

gath·er [ˈgæðə] **I** *v/t*. **1.** *Personen* versammeln; → ***father*** 4; **2.** *Dinge* (an-)sammeln, anhäufen: **~ wealth**; **~ experience** Erfahrung(en) sammeln; **~ facts** Fakten zs.-tragen, Material sammeln; **~ strength** Kräfte sammeln; **3.** a) ernten, sammeln, b) *Blumen*, *Obst etc.* pflücken; **4.** *a.* **~ up** aufsammeln, -lesen, -heben: **~ together** zs.-raffen; **~ o.s. together** sich zs.-raffen; **~ s.o. in one's arms** j-n in s-e Arme schließen; **5.** erwerben, gewinnen, ansetzen: **~ dust** verstauben; **~ speed** Geschwindigkeit aufnehmen, schneller werden; **~ way** ⚓ in Fahrt kommen (*a. fig.*), *fig*. sich durchsetzen; **6.** *fig*. folgern (*a.* Ⱥ), schließen (**from** aus); **7.** *Näherei*: raffen, kräuseln, zs.-ziehen; → ***brow*** 1; **8.** **~ up** a) *Kleid etc.* aufnehmen, zs.-raffen, b) *die Beine* einziehen; **II** *v/i*. **9.** sich versammeln *od*. scharen (**round s.o.** um j-n); **10.** sich (an)sammeln, sich häufen; **11.** sich zs.-ziehen *od*. -ballen (*Wolken*, *Gewitter*); **12.** anwachsen, sich entwickeln, zunehmen; **13.** ⚕ a) reifen (*Abszeß*), b) eitern (*Wunde*); **ˈgath·er·er** [-ərə] *s*. **1.** Erntearbeiter(in), Schnitter(in), Winzer *m*; **2.** (Ein)Sammler *m*; Geldeinnehmer *m*; **ˈgath·er·ing** [-ðərɪŋ] *s*. **1.** Sammeln *n*; **2.** Sammlung *f*; **3.** a) (Menschen)Ansammlung *f*, b) Versammlung *f*, Zs.-kunft *f*; **4.** ⚕ a) Reifen *n*, b) Eitern *n*; **5.** Kräuseln *n*; **6.** *Buchbinderei*: Lage *f*.

gat·ing [ˈgeɪtɪŋ] *s*. **1.** ⚡ a) Austastung *f*, b) (Sigˈnal)Auswertung *f*; **2.** *ped., univ. Brit.* Ausgangsverbot *n*.

gauche [gəʊʃ] *adj*. **1.** linkisch; **2.** taktlos; **gau·che·rie** [ˈgəʊʃəriː] *s*. **1.** linkische Art; **2.** Taktlosigkeit *f*.

Gau·cho [ˈgaʊtʃəʊ] *pl*. **-chos** *s*. Gaucho *m*.

gaud [gɔːd] *s*. **1.** billiger Schmuck, Flitterkram *m*; **2.** *oft pl.* (überˈtriebener) Prunk; **ˈgaud·i·ness** [-dɪnɪs] *s*. **1.** → ***gaud***; **2.** Protzigkeit *f*, Geschmacklosigkeit *f*; **ˈgaud·y** [-dɪ] **I** *adj*. ☐ (farben-)prächtig, auffällig (bunt), *Farben*: grell, schreiend, *Einrichtung etc.*: protzig; **II** *s*. *ped., univ. Brit.* jährliches Festessen.

gauf·fer → ***goffer***.

gauge [geɪdʒ] **I** *s*. **1.** Norˈmal-, Eichmaß *n*; **2.** ⚙ Meßgerät *n*, Messer *m*, Anzeiger *m*: *bsd*. a) Pegel *m*, Wasserstandsanzeiger *m*, b) Manoˈmeter *n*, Druckmesser *m*, c) Lehre *f*, d) Maß-, Zollstab *m*, e) *typ*. Zeilenmaß *n*; **3.** ⚙ (Blech-, Draht)Stärke *f*; **4.** *Strumpfherstellung*: Gauge *n* (*Maschenzahl*); **5.** ⚔ Kaˈliber *n*; **6.** 🚂 Spur(weite) *f*; **7.** ⚓ *oft* ***gage*** Abstand *m*, Lage *f*: **have the lee** (**weather**) **~** zu Lee (Luv) liegen (*Schiff*); **8.** ˈUmfang *m*, Inhalt *m*: **take the ~ of** → 12; **9.** *fig*. Maßstab *m*, Norm *f*; **II** *v/t*. **10.** (ab)lehren, (ab-, aus)messen; **11.** eichen, justieren; **12.** *fig*. (ab)schätzen, beurteilen; **~ lathe** *s*. Präzisiˈonsdrehbank *f*.

gaug·er [ˈgeɪdʒə] *s*. Eichmeister *m*.

gaug·ing [ˈgeɪdʒɪŋ] *s*. ⚙ Eichung *f*, Messung *f*: **~ office** Eichamt *n*.

Gaul [gɔːl] *s*. **1.** Gallier *m*; **2.** Franˈzose *m*; **ˈGaul·ish** [-lɪʃ] **I** *adj*. gallisch; **II** *s*. *ling*. Gallisch *n*.

Gaull·ism [ˈgəʊlɪzəm] *s*. *pol*. Gaulˈlismus *m*.

gaunt [gɔːnt] *adj*. ☐ **1.** a) hager, mager, b) ausgemergelt; **2.** verlassen, öde; **3.** kahl.

gaunt·let[1] [ˈgɔːntlɪt] *s*. **1.** ⚔ *hist*. Panzerhandschuh *m*; **2.** *fig*. Fehdehandschuh *m*: **fling** (*od*. **throw**) **down the ~** (**to s.o.**) (j-m) den Fehdehandschuh hinwerfen, (j-n) herausfordern; **pick** (*od*. **take**) **up the ~** die Herausforderung annehmen; **3.** Schutzhandschuh *m*.

gaunt·let[2] [ˈgɔːntlɪt] *s*.: **run the ~** Spießruten laufen (*a. fig.*); **run the ~ of s.th.** et. durchstehen müssen.

gaun·try [ˈgɔːntrɪ] → ***gantry***.

gauss [gaʊs] *s*. *phys*. Gauß *n*.

gauze [gɔːz] *s*. **1.** Gaze *f*, ⚕ *a*. (Verbands)Mull *m*: **~ bandage** Mull-, Gazebinde *f*; **2.** *fig*. Dunst *m*, Schleier *m*; **ˈgauz·y** [-zɪ] *adj*. gazeartig, hauchdünn.

ga·vage [ˈgævɑːʒ] *s*. ⚕ künstliche Sonderernährung.

gave [geɪv] *pret. von* ***give***.

gav·el [ˈgævl] *s*. **1.** Hammer *m e-s Auktionators, Vorsitzenden etc.*; **2.** (Maurer)Schlegel *m*.

ga·vot(te) [gəˈvɒt] *s*. ♪ Gaˈvotte *f*.

gawk [gɔːk] **I** *s*. *contp*. (Bauern)Lackel *m*; **II** *v/i*. → ***gawp***; **ˈgawk·y** [-kɪ] *adj*. *contp*. ‚blöd(e)', trottelhaft.

gawp [gɔːp] *v/i*. glotzen: **~ at** anglotzen.

gay [geɪ] *adj*. ☐ → ***gaily***; **1.** lustig, fröhlich; **2.** a) bunt, (farben)prächtig: **~ with** belebt von, geschmückt mit, b) fröhlich, lebhaft (*Farben*); **3.** flott, *Person*: *a*. lebenslustig: **a ~ dog** ein ‚lockerer Vogel'; **4.** liederlich; **5.** *Am. sl.* ‚pampig', frech; **6.** F homosexuˈell, ‚schwul', Schwulen...: **2 Lib**(**eration**) *die* Schwulenbewegung.

gaze [geɪz] **I** *v/i*. starren: **~ at** anstarren; **~** (**up**)**on** ansichtig werden (*gen*.); **II** *s*. (starrer) Blick, Starren *n*.

ga·ze·bo [gəˈziːbəʊ] *s*. Gebäude *n* mit schönem Ausblick, Aussichtspunkt *m*.

ga·zelle [gəˈzel] *s*. *zo*. Gaˈzelle *f*.

gaz·er [ˈgeɪzə] *s*. Gaffer *m*.

ga·zette [gəˈzet] **I** *s*. **1.** Zeitung *f*; **2.** *Brit*. Amtsblatt *n*, Staatsanzeiger *m*; **II** *v/t*. **3.** *Brit*. im Amtsblatt bekanntgeben *od*. veröffentlichen; **gaz·et·teer** [ˌgæzəˈtɪə] *s*. alphaˈbetisches Ortsverzeichnis (mit Ortsbeschreibung).

gear [gɪə] **I** *s*. **1.** ⚙ a) Zahnrad *n*, b) *a. pl*. Getriebe *n*, Triebwerk *n*; **2.** ⚙ a) Überˈsetzung *f*, b) *mot. etc.* Gang *m*: **first** (**second**, *etc.*) **~**; **in high ~** in e-m hohen *od*. schnellen Gang; **get into** (**high**) **~** *fig*. in Fahrt *od*. Schwung kommen; ***in low*** (*od.* ***bottom***) ~ im ersten Gang; (***in***) ***top*** ~ im höchsten Gang; ***change*** (*Am.* ***shift***) ~(***s***) schalten; ***change into second*** ~ den zweiten Gang einlegen, c) *pl.* Gangschaltung *f* (*e-s Fahrrads*); **3.** ⚙ Eingriff *m*: ***in*** ~ a) eingerückt, eingeschaltet, b) *fig.* funktionierend, in Ordnung; ***in*** ~ ***with*** im Eingriff stehend mit; ***out of*** ~ a) ausgerückt, ausgeschaltet, b) *fig.* in Unordnung, nicht funktionierend; ***throw out of*** ~ ausrücken, -schalten, *fig.* durcheinanderbringen; **4.** ✈, ⚓ *etc. mst in Zssgn* Vorrichtung *f*, Gerät *n*; → ***landing gear*** *etc.*; **5.** Ausrüstung *f*, Gerät *n*, Werkzeug(e *pl.*) *n*, Zubehör *n*: ***fishing*** ~ Angelgerät *n*, -zeug *n*; **6.** F a) Hausrat *m*, b) Habseligkeiten *pl.*, Sachen *pl.*, c) Aufzug *m*, Kleidung *f*; **7.** (Pferde- *etc.*)Geschirr *n*; **II** *v/t.* **8.** ⚙ a) mit e-m Getriebe versehen, b) über'setzen, c) in Gang setzen (*a. fig.*): ~ ***up*** ins Schnelle übersetzen, *fig.* steigern, verstärken; **9.** *fig.* (***to***, ***for***) einstellen *od.* abstimmen (auf *acc.*), anpassen (*dat. od.* an *acc.*); **10.** ausrüsten; **11.** *a.* ~ ***up*** *Tiere* anschirren; **III** *v/i.* **12.** ⚙ a) eingreifen (***into***, ***with*** in *acc.*), b) inein'andergreifen; **13.** ~ ***up*** (***down***) *mot.* hin'auf- (her'unter)schalten; **14.** *fig.* (***with***) passen (zu), eingerichtet *od.* abgestimmt sein (auf *acc.*).

'gear|·box *s.* ⚙ Getriebe(gehäuse) *n*; ~ **change** *s. Brit. mot.* (Gang)Schaltung *f*; ~ **cut·ter** *s.* Zahnradfräser *m*; ~ **drive** → ***gearing*** 1.

gear·ed [gɪəd] *adj.* ⚙ verzahnt; Getriebe…; **gear·ing** ['gɪərɪŋ] *s.* ⚙ **1.** (Zahnrad)Getriebe *n*, Vorgelege *n*; **2.** Über'setzung *f* (*e-s Getriebes*); Transmissi'on *f*; **3.** Verzahnung *f*.

gear| le·ver *s.* Schalthebel *m*; ~ **ra·tio** *s.* Über'setzung(sverhältnis *n*) *f*; ~ **rim** *s.* Zahnkranz *m*; ~ **shaft** *s.* Getriebe-, Schaltwelle *f*; ~ **shift** *s. Am.* a) → ***gear change***, b) → ***gear lever***; '~**·wheel** *s.* Getriebe-, Zahnrad *n*.

geck·o ['gekəʊ] *pl.* **-os, -oes** *s. zo.* Gecko *m* (*Echse*).

gee[1] [dʒi:] *s.* G *n*, g *n* (*Buchstabe*).

gee[2] [dʒi:] **I** *s.* **1.** *Kindersprache*: ‚Hotte-'hü' *n* (*Pferd*); **II** *int.* **2.** *a.* ~ ***up!*** a) hott! (*nach rechts*), b) hü(h), hott! (*schneller*); **3.** *Am.* F na so was!, Mann!

geese [gi:s] *pl. von* ***goose***.

gee| whiz [ˌdʒi:'wɪz] → ***gee***[2] 3; '~**-whiz** *adj. Am.* F **1.** ‚toll', Super…; **2.** Sensations…

gee·zer ['gi:zə] *s.* F komischer (alter) Kauz, ‚Opa' *m*.

Gei·ger count·er ['gaɪgə] *s. phys.* Geigerzähler *m*.

gei·sha ['geɪʃə] *s.* Geisha *f*.

gel [dʒel] **I** *s.* **1.** Gel *n*; **II** *v/i.* **2.** gelieren; **3.** → ***jell*** 3.

gel·a·tin(e) [ˌdʒelə'ti:n] *s.* **1.** Gela'tine *f*; **2.** Gal'lerte *f*; **3.** *a.* ***blasting*** ~ 'Spreng-gelaˌtine *f*; **ge·lat·i·nize** [dʒə'lætɪnaɪz] *v/i. u. v/t.* gelatinieren (lassen); **ge·lat·i·nous** [dʒə'lætɪnəs] *adj.* gallertartig.

geld [geld] *v/t. Tier* kastrieren, verschneiden; **'geld·ing** [-dɪŋ] *s.* kastriertes Tier, *bsd.* Wallach *m*.

gel·id ['dʒelɪd] *adj.* □ eisig.

gel·ig·nite ['dʒelɪgnaɪt] *s.* ⚙ Gela'tine-dynaˌmit *n*.

gem [dʒem] **I** *s.* **1.** Edelstein *m*; **2.** Gemme *f*; **3.** *fig.* Perle *f*, Ju'wel *n*, Glanz-, Prachtstück *n*: ~ ***rôle*** *thea.* Glanzrolle *f*; **4.** *Am.* Brötchen *n*; **5.** *typ. e-e 3½-Punkt-Schrift*; **II** *v/t.* **6.** mit Edelsteinen schmücken.

gem·i·nate I *adj.* ['dʒemɪnət] paarweise, Doppel…; **II** *v/t. u. v/i.* [-neɪt] (sich) verdoppeln (*a. ling.*); **gem·i·na·tion** [ˌdʒemɪ'neɪʃn] *s.* Verdoppelung *f* (*a. ling.*).

Gem·i·ni ['dʒemɪnaɪ] *s. pl. ast.* Zwillinge *pl.*

gem·ma ['dʒemə] *pl.* **-mae** [-mi:] *s.* **1.** ♀ a) Gemme *f*, Brutkörper *m*, b) Blattknospe *f*; **2.** *biol.* Knospe *f*, Gemme *f*; **'gem·mate** [-meɪt] *adj. biol.* sich durch Knospung fortpflanzend; **gem·ma·tion** [dʒe'meɪʃn] *s.* **1.** ♀ Knospenbildung *f*; **2.** *biol.* Fortpflanzung *f* durch Knospen; **gem·mif·er·ous** [dʒe'mɪfərəs] *adj.* **1.** edelsteinhaltig; **2.** *biol.* → ***gemmate***.

gems·bok ['gemzbɒk] *s. zo.* 'Gemsan-tiˌlope *f*.

gen [dʒen] *Brit. sl.* **I** *s.* Informati'on(en *pl.*) *f*; **II** *v/t. u. v/i.*: ~ ***up*** (sich) informieren.

gen·der ['dʒendə] *s. ling.* Genus *n*, Geschlecht *n* (*a. humor. von Personen*).

gene [dʒi:n] *s. biol.* Gen *n*, Erbfaktor *m*: ~ ***pool*** Erbmasse *f*; ~ ***technology*** Gentechnologie *f*.

gen·e·a·log·i·cal [ˌdʒi:njə'lɒdʒɪkl] *adj.* □ genea'logisch: ~ ***tree*** Stammbaum *m*.

gen·e·al·o·gist [ˌdʒi:nɪ'ælədʒɪst] *s.* Genea'loge *m*, Ahnenforscher *m*; **ˌgen·e'al·o·gize** [-dʒaɪz] *v/i.* Stammbaumforschung treiben; **ˌgen·e'al·o·gy** [-dʒɪ] *s.* Genealo'gie *f*: a) Ahnenforschung *f*, b) Ahnentafel *f*, c) Abstammung *f*.

gen·er·a ['dʒenərə] *pl. von* ***genus***.

gen·er·al ['dʒenərəl] **I** *adj.* □ → ***generally***; **1.** allgemein, um'fassend: ~ ***knowledge*** (***medicine***) Allgemeinbildung *f* (-medizin *f*); ~ ***outlook*** allgemeine Aussichten; ***the*** ~ ***public*** die breite Öffentlichkeit; **2.** allgemein (*nicht spezifisch*): ~ ***dealer*** *Brit.* Gemischtwarenhändler *m*; ***the*** ~ ***reader*** der Durchschnittsleser; ~ ***store*** Gemischtwarenhandlung *f*; ~ ***term*** Allgemeinbegriff *m*; ***in*** ~ ***terms*** allgemein (ausgedrückt); **3.** allgemein (üblich), gängig, verbreitet: ~ ***practice***; ***as a*** ~ ***rule*** meistens; **4.** allgemein gehalten, ungefähr: ***a*** ~ ***idea*** e-e ungefähre Vorstellung; ~ ***resemblance*** vage Ähnlichkeit; ***in a*** ~ ***way*** in großen Zügen, in gewisser Weise; **5.** allgemein, General…, Haupt…: ~ ***agent*** ☿ Generalvertreter *m*; ~ ***manager*** ☿ Generaldirektor *m*; ~ ***meeting*** ☿ General-, Hauptversammlung *f*; **6.** (*Amtstiteln nachgestellt*) *mst* General…: ***consul*** ~ Generalkonsul *m*; **II** *s.* **7.** ⚔ a) Gene'ral *m*, b) Heerführer *m*, Feldherr *m*, Stra'tege *m*; **8.** ⚔ *Am.* a) (Vier-'Sterne-)Gene-ˌral *m* (*zweithöchster Offiziersrang*), b) ~ ***of the army*** Fünf-'Sterne-Geneˌral *m* (*höchster Offiziersrang*); **9.** *eccl.* ('Ordens)Geneˌral *m*; **10.** ***the*** ~ das Allgemeine: ♀ (*Überschrift*) Allgemeines; ***in*** ~ im allgemeinen.

gen·er·al| ac·cept·ance *s.* ☿ uneingeschränktes Ak'zept; ♀ **As·sem·bly** *s.* **1.** *pol.* Voll-, Gene'ralversammlung *f* (*der UNO*); **2.** *pol. Am.* Parla'ment *n* (*einiger Einzelstaaten*); **3.** *eccl.* oberstes Gericht der schottischen Kirche; ~ **car·go** *s.* ☿, ⚓ Stückgut(ladung *f*) *n*; ♀ **Cer·tif·i·cate of Ed·u·ca·tion** *s. ped. Brit.*: ~ ***O level*** *etwa*: mittlere Reife; ~ ***A level*** *etwa*: Abitur *n*; ~ **de·liv·er·y** *s.* ✉ *Am.* **1.** (Ausgabestelle *f* für) postlagernde Sendungen *pl.*; **2.** ‚postlagernd'; ~ **e·lec·tion** *s. pol.* allgemeine Wahlen *pl.*; ~ **head·quar·ters** *s. pl. mst sg. konstr.* ⚔ Großes Hauptquartier; ~ **hos·pi·tal** *s.* allgemeines Krankenhaus.

gen·er·al·is·si·mo [ˌdʒenərə'lɪsɪməʊ] *pl.* **-mos** *s.* ⚔ Genera'lissimus *m*, Oberbefehlshaber *m*.

gen·er·al·ist ['dʒenərəlɪst] *s.* Genera'list *m* (*Ggs. Spezialist*).

gen·er·al·i·ty [ˌdʒenə'rælətɪ] *s.* **1.** *pl.* allgemeine Redensarten *pl.*, Gemeinplätze *pl.*; **2.** Allgemeingültigkeit *f*; **3.** allgemeine Regel; **4.** Unbestimmtheit *f*; **5.** *obs.* Mehrzahl *f*, große Masse; **gen·er·al·i·za·tion** [ˌdʒenərəlaɪ'zeɪʃn] *s.* Verallgemeinerung *f*; **gen·er·al·ize** ['dʒenərəlaɪz] **I** *v/t.* **1.** verallgemeinern; **2.** auf e-e allgemeine Formel bringen; **3.** *paint.* in großen Zügen darstellen; **II** *v/i.* **4.** verallgemeinern; **gen·er·al·ly** ['dʒenərəlɪ] *adv.* **1.** *oft* ~ ***speaking*** allgemein, im allgemeinen, im großen u. ganzen; **2.** allgemein; **3.** gewöhnlich, meistens.

gen·er·al| med·i·cine *s.* Allge'meinme-diˌzin *f*; ~ **meet·ing** *s.* ☿ Gene'ral-, Hauptversammlung *f*; ~ **of·fi·cer** *s.* ⚔ Gene'ral *m*, Offi'zier *m* im Gene'ralsrang; ~ **par·don** *s.* (Gene'ral)Amne-ˌstie *f*; ♀ **Post Of·fice** *s.* Hauptpostamt *n*; ~ **prac·ti·tion·er** *s.* Arzt *m* für Allge'meinmediˌzin, praktischer Arzt; ˌ~-**'pur·pose** *adj.* ⚙ Mehrzweck…, Universal…

gen·er·al·ship ['dʒenərəlʃɪp] *s.* **1.** ⚔ Gene'ralsrang *m*; **2.** Strate'gie *f*: a) ⚔ Feldherrnkunst *f*, b) *a. allg.* geschickte Taktik.

gen·er·al| staff *s.* ⚔ Gene'ralstab *m*: ***chief of*** ~ Generalstabschef *m*; ~ **strike** *s.* ☿ Gene'ralstreik *m*.

gen·er·ate ['dʒenəreɪt] *v/t.* **1.** *bsd.* ⚗, *phys.* erzeugen (*a.* ⚗), *Gas, Rauch* entwickeln, *a.* ⚗ bilden; **2.** *biol.* zeugen; **3.** *fig.* erzeugen, her'vorrufen, bewirken, verursachen.

gen·er·at·ing sta·tion ['dʒenəreɪtɪŋ] *s.* ⚡ Kraftwerk *n*.

gen·er·a·tion [ˌdʒenə'reɪʃn] *s.* **1.** Generati'on *f*: ***the rising*** ~ die junge (*od.* heranwachsende) Generation; ~ ***gap*** Generationsunterschied *m*, Generationenkonflikt *m*; **2.** Generati'on *f*, Menschenalter *n* (*etwa 33 Jahre*): ~***s*** F e-e Ewigkeit; **3.** ⚙, ☿ Generati'on *f*: ***a new*** ~ ***of cars***; **4.** *biol.* Entwicklungsstufe *f*; **5.** Zeugung *f*, Fortpflanzung *f*; **6.** *bsd.* ⚗, ⚡, *phys.* Erzeugung *f* (*a.* ⚗), Entwicklung *f*; **7.** Entstehung *f*; **ˌgen·er'a·tion·al** [-ʃənl] *adj.* Generations…: ~ ***conflict***; **gen·er·a·tive** ['dʒenərətɪv] *adj.* **1.** *biol.* Zeugungs…, Fortpflanzungs…, Geschlechts…; **2.** *biol.* fruchtbar; **3.** *ling.* genera'tiv: ~ ***grammar***; **gen·er·a·tor** ['dʒenəreɪtə] *s.* **1.** ⚡ Gene'rator *m*, Stromerzeuger *m*, Dy'namomaˌschine *f*; **2.** ⚙ a) Gaserzeuger *m*:

~ gas Generatorgas *n*, b) Dampferzeuger *m*, -kessel *m*; **3.** ⚙ (Ab)Wälzfräser *m*; **4.** ⚗ Entwickler *m*; **5.** ♪ Grundton *m*.

ge·ner·ic [dʒɪ'nerɪk] *adj.* (□ **~ally**) **1.** allgemein, gene'rell; **2.** ge'nerisch, Gattungs…: **~ term** *od.* **name** Gattungsname *m*, Oberbegriff *m*.

gen·er·os·i·ty [ˌdʒenə'rɒsətɪ] *s.* **1.** Großzügigkeit *f*: a) Freigebigkeit *f*, b) Edelmut *m*, Hochherzigkeit *f*; **2.** edle Tat; **3.** Fülle *f*; **gen·er·ous** ['dʒenərəs] *adj.* □ **1.** großzügig: a) freigebig, b) edel, hochherzig; **2.** reichlich, üppig: **~ mouth** volle Lippen *pl.*; **3.** vollmundig, gehaltvoll (*Wein*); fruchtbar (*Boden*).

gen·e·sis ['dʒenɪsɪs] *s.* **1.** Genesis *f*, Ge'nese *f*, Entstehung *f*; **2.** ♀ *bibl.* Genesis *f*, Erstes Buch Mose; **3.** Ursprung *m*.

gen·et ['dʒenɪt] *s.* **1.** *zo.* Ge'nette *f*, Ginsterkatze *f*; **2.** Ge'nettepelz *m*.

ge·net·ic [dʒɪ'netɪk] **I** *adj.* (□ **~ally**) **1.** *bsd. biol.* ge'netisch: a) entwicklungsgeschichtlich, b) Vererbungs…, Erb…: **~ code** genetischer Kode; **~ engineering** Genmanipulation *f*; **II** *s. pl. biol.* **2.** *sg. konstr.* Ge'netik *f*, Vererbungslehre *f*; **3.** ge'netische Formen *pl.* u. Erscheinungen *pl.*; **ge'net·i·cist** [-ɪsɪst] *s. biol.* Ge'netiker *m*.

ge·nette [dʒɪ'net] → ***genet***.

ge·ne·va¹ [dʒɪ'ni:və] *s.* Ge'never *m*, Wa'cholderschnaps *m*.

Ge·ne·va² [dʒɪ'ni:və] **I** *npr.* Genf *n*; **II** *adj.* Genfer(…); **~ bands** *s. pl. eccl.* Beffchen *n*; **~ Con·ven·tion** *s. pol.*, ⚔ Genfer Konventi'on *f*; **~ cross** → ***red*** 1; **~ drive** *s.* ⚙ Mal'teserkreuzantrieb *m*; **~ gown** *s. eccl.* Ta'lar *m*.

ge·ni·al ['dʒi:njəl] *adj.* □ **1.** freundlich (*a. fig. Klima etc.*), herzlich: **in ~ company** in angenehmer Gesellschaft; **2.** belebend, anregend; **ge·ni·al·i·ty** [ˌdʒi:nɪ'ælətɪ] *s.* **1.** Freundlichkeit *f*, Herzlichkeit *f*; **2.** Milde *f* (*Klima*).

ge·nie ['dʒi:nɪ] *s.* dienstbarer Geist, Dschinn *m*.

ge·ni·i ['dʒi:nɪaɪ] *pl. von* ***genie*** *u.* ***genius*** 4.

gen·i·tal ['dʒenɪtl] *adj.* Zeugungs…, Geschlechts…, geni'tal: **~ gland** Keimdrüse *f*; **'gen·i·tals** [-lz] *s. pl.* Geni'talien *pl.*, Geschlechtsteile *pl.*

gen·i·ti·val [ˌdʒenɪ'taɪvl] *adj.* Genitiv…, genitivisch; **gen·i·tive** ['dʒenɪtɪv] *s. a.* **~ case** *ling.* Genitiv *m*, zweiter Fall.

gen·i·to-u·ri·nar·y [ˌdʒenɪtəʊ'jʊərɪnərɪ] *adj.* ⚕ urogeni'tal.

ge·ni·us ['dʒi:njəs] *pl.* **'ge·ni·us·es** *s.* **1.** Ge'nie *n*: a) geni'aler Mensch, b) (*ohne pl.*) Geniali'tät *f*, geni'ale Schöpferkraft; **2.** Begabung *f*, Gabe *f*; **3.** Genius *m*, Geist *m*, Seele *f*, *das* Eigentümliche (*e-r Nation etc.*): **~ of a period** Zeitgeist; **4.** *pl.* **'ge·ni·i** [-nɪaɪ] *antiq.* Genius *m*, Schutzgeist *m*: **good** (**evil**) **~** guter (böser) Geist (*a. fig.*); **~ lo·ci** ['ləʊsaɪ] (*Lat.*) *s.* a) Genius *m* loci, Schutzgeist *m* e-s Ortes, b) Atmo'sphäre *f* e-s Ortes.

gen·o·blast ['dʒenəʊblɑ:st] *s. biol.* reife Geschlechtszelle.

gen·o·cide ['dʒenəʊsaɪd] *s.* Geno'zid *m*, *n*, Völker-, Gruppenmord *m*.

Gen·o·ese [ˌdʒenəʊ'i:z] **I** *s.* Genu'eser (-in); **II** *adj.* genu'esisch, Genueser…

gen·o·type ['dʒenəʊtaɪp] *s. biol.* Geno'typ(us) *m*.

gen·re ['ʒɑ̃:ŋrə] (*Fr.*) *s.* **1.** Genre *n*, (*a.* Litera'tur)Gattung *f*: **~ painting** Genremalerei *f*; **2.** Form *f*, Stil *m*.

gent [dʒent] *s.* **1.** F *für* ***gentleman***; **2.** *pl. sg. konstr.* F ‚Herrenklo' *n*; **3.** *Am.* F ‚Knabe' *m*, Kerl *m*.

gen·teel [dʒen'ti:l] *adj.* □ **1.** *obs.* vornehm; **2.** vornehm tuend, geziert, affek'tiert; **3.** ele'gant, fein.

gen·tian ['dʒenʃɪən] *s.* ⚘ Enzian *m*; **~ bit·ter** *s. pharm.* 'Enziantinkˌtur *f*.

gen·tile ['dʒentaɪl] **I** *s.* **1.** Nichtjude *m*, -jüdin *f*, *bsd.* Christ(in); **2.** Heide *m*, Heidin *f*; **3.** 'Nichtmorˌmone *m*, -morˌmonin *f*; **II** *adj.* **4.** nichtjüdisch, *bsd.* christlich; **5.** heidnisch; **6.** 'nichtmorˌmonisch.

gen·til·i·ty [dʒen'tɪlətɪ] *s.* **1.** *obs.* vornehme Herkunft; **2.** Vornehmheit *f*; **3.** Vornehmtue'rei *f*.

gen·tle ['dʒentl] *adj.* □ **1.** freundlich, sanft, gütig, liebenswürdig: **~ reader** geneigter Leser; **2.** milde, ruhig, mäßig, leicht, sanft, zart: **~ blow** leichter Schlag; **~ craft** Angelsport *m*; **~ hint** zarter Wink; **~ rebuke** sanfter Tadel; **the ~ sex** das zarte Geschlecht; **~ slope** sanfter Abhang; **3.** zahm, fromm (*Tier*); **4.** edel, vornehm: **of ~ birth** von vornehmer Geburt; **'~·folk(s)** *s. pl.* vornehme Leute *pl.*

gen·tle·man ['dʒentlmən] *s.* [*irr.*] **1.** Gentleman *m*: a) Ehrenmann *m*, b) Mann *m* von Lebensart u. Cha'rakter: **~'s** (*od.* **gentlemen's**) **agreement** Gentleman's (*od.* Gentlemen's) Agreement *n*, † *etc.* Vereinbarung *f* auf Treu u. Glauben; **~'s ~** (Kammer)Diener *m*; **2.** Herr *m*: **gentlemen** a) (*Anrede*) m-e Herren!, b) *in Briefen*: Sehr geehrte Herren (*oft unübersetzt*); **~ farmer** Gutsbesitzer *m*; **~ friend** Freund *m e-r Dame*; **~ rider** Herrenreiter *m*; **Gentlemen('s)** Herren(toilette *f*) *pl.*; **3.** *Titel von Hofbeamten*: **~ in waiting** Kämmerer *m*; **~-at-arms** Leibgardist *m*; **4.** *obs.* Privati'er *m*; **5.** *hist.* a) Mann *m* von Stand, b) Edelmann *m*; **'~·like** → ***gentlemanly***; **'gen·tle·man·li·ness** [-lɪnɪs] *s.* **1.** vornehmes *od.* feines Wesen, Vornehmheit *f*; **2.** gebildetes *od.* feines Benehmen; **'gen·tle·man·ly** [-lɪ] *adj.* ‚gentlemanlike', vornehm, fein.

gen·tle·ness ['dʒentlnɪs] *s.* **1.** Freundlichkeit *f*, Güte *f*, Milde *f*, Sanftheit *f*; **2.** *obs.* Vornehmheit *f*.

'gen·tleˌwom·an *s.* [*irr.*] Dame *f* (von Lebensart u. Cha'rakter; von Stand *od.* Bildung); **'gen·tleˌwom·an·like**, **'gen·tleˌwom·an·ly** [-lɪ] *adj.* damenhaft, vornehm.

gen·tly ['dʒentlɪ] *adv. von* ***gentle***.

gen·try ['dʒentrɪ] *s.* **1.** Oberschicht *f*; **2.** *Brit.* Gentry *f*, niederer Adel; **3.** *a. pl. konstr.* F Leute *pl.*, Sippschaft *f*.

gen·u·flect ['dʒenju:flekt] *v/i.* (*bsd. eccl.*) knien, die Knie beugen, *contp.* e-n Kniefall machen (**before** vor *dat.*); **gen·u·flec·tion**, *Brit. a.* **gen·u·flex·ion** [ˌdʒenju:'flekʃn] *s.* Kniebeugung *f*; *fig.* Kniefall *m*.

gen·u·ine ['dʒenjʊɪn] *adj.* □ echt: a) au'thentisch, b) ernsthaft (*Angebot etc.*), c) aufrichtig (*Mitgefühl etc.*), d) ungekünstelt (*Lachen etc.*); **'gen·u·ine·ness** [-nɪs] *s.* Echtheit *f*.

ge·nus ['dʒi:nəs] *pl.* **gen·er·a** ['dʒenərə] *s.* **1.** ⚘, *zo.*, *phls.* Gattung *f*; **2.** *fig.* Art *f*, Klasse *f*.

ge·o·cen·tric [ˌdʒi:əʊ'sentrɪk] *adj. ast.* geo'zentrisch; **ˌge·o'chem·is·try** [-'kemɪstrɪ] *s.* Geoche'mie *f*; **ˌge·o'cy·clic** [-'saɪklɪk] *adj. ast.* geo'zyklisch.

ge·ode ['dʒi:əʊd] *s. min. allg.* Ge'ode *f*.

ge·o·des·ic, **ge·o·des·i·cal** [ˌdʒi:əʊ'desɪk(l)] *adj.* □ geo'dätisch; **ge·od·e·sist** [dʒi:'ɒdɪsɪst] *s.* Geo'dät *m*; **ge·od·e·sy** [dʒi:'ɒdɪsɪ] *s.* Geodä'sie *f* (*Erdvermessung*); **ˌge·o'det·ic**, **ˌge·o'det·i·cal** [-etɪk(l)] *adj.* geo'dätisch.

ge·og·ra·pher [dʒɪ'ɒgrəfə] *s.* Geo'graph (-in); **ge·o·graph·ic**, **ge·o·graph·i·cal** [dʒɪə'græfɪk(l)] *adj.* □ geo'graphisch: ***geographical mile***; **ge'og·ra·phy** [-fɪ] *s.* **1.** Geogra'phie *f*, Erdkunde *f*; **2.** geo'graphische Abhandlung; **3.** geo'graphische Beschaffenheit.

ge·o·log·ic, **ge·o·log·i·cal** [ˌdʒɪəʊ'lɒdʒɪk(l)] *adj.* □ geo'logisch; **ge·ol·o·gist** [dʒɪ'ɒlədʒɪst] *s.* Geo'loge *m*, Geo'login *f*; **ge·ol·o·gize** [dʒɪ'ɒlədʒaɪz] **I** *v/i.* geo'logische Studien betreiben; **II** *v/t.* geo'logisch unter'suchen; **ge·ol·o·gy** [dʒɪ'ɒlədʒɪ] *s.* **1.** Geolo'gie *f*; **2.** geo'logische Abhandlung; **3.** geo'logische Beschaffenheit.

ge·o·mag·net·ism [ˌdʒɪəʊ'mægnɪtɪzəm] *s. phys.* 'Erdmagneˌtismus *m*.

ge·o·man·cy ['dʒɪəʊmænsɪ] *s.* Geoman'tie *f*, Geo'mantik *f* (*Art Wahrsagerei*).

ge·om·e·ter [dʒɪ'ɒmɪtə] *s.* **1.** *obs.* Geo'meter *m*; **2.** Ex'perte *m* auf dem Gebiet der Geome'trie; **3.** *zo.* Spannerraupe *f*; **ge·o·met·ric**, **ge·o·met·ri·cal** [ˌdʒɪəʊ'metrɪk(l)] *adj.* □ geo'metrisch; **ge·om·e·tri·cian** [ˌdʒɪəʊme'trɪʃn] → ***geometer*** 1, 2; **ge'om·e·try** [-mətrɪ] *s.* **1.** Geome'trie *f*; **2.** geo'metrische Abhandlung.

ge·o·phys·i·cal [ˌdʒi:əʊ'fɪzɪkl] *adj.* geophysi'kalisch; **ˌge·o'phys·ics** [-ks] *s. pl., oft sg. konstr.* Geophy'sik *f*.

ge·o·pol·i·tics [ˌdʒi:əʊ'pɒlɪtɪks] *s. pl., oft sg. konstr.* Geopoli'tik *f*.

George [dʒɔ:dʒ] *s.*: **St ~** der heilige Georg (*Schutzpatron Englands*): **St ~'s Cross** Georgskreuz *n*; **~ Cross** *od.* **Medal** ⚔ *Brit.* Georgskreuz *n* (*Orden*); **by ~!** a) beim Zeus!, b) Mann!; **let ~ do it!** *Am. sl.* soll's machen, wer Lust hat!

geor·gette [dʒɔ:'dʒet] *Am.* ♀ *s.* Geor'gette *m* (*Seidenkrepp*).

Geor·gi·an ['dʒɔ:dʒjən] **I** *adj.* **1.** georgi'anisch: a) *aus der Zeit der Könige Georg I.–IV.* (*1714–1830*), b) *aus der Zeit der Könige Georg V. u. VI.* (*1910–52*); **2.** geor'ginisch (*den Staat Georgia, USA, betreffend*); **3.** ge'orgisch (*die Sowjetrepublik Georgien betreffend*); **II** *s.* **4.** Ge'orgier(in).

ge·o·sci·ence [ˌdʒi:əʊ'saɪəns] *s.* Geowissenschaft *f*.

ge·ra·ni·um [dʒɪ'reɪnjəm] *s.* ⚘ **1.** Storchschnabel *m*; **2.** Ge'ranie *f*.

ger·fal·con ['dʒɜ:ˌfɔ:lkən] *s. orn.* G(i)erfalke *m*.

ger·i·at·ric [ˌdʒerɪ'ætrɪk] **I** *adj.* ⚕ geri'atrisch; **II** *s. humor.* Greis *m*; **ger·i·a·tri·cian** [ˌdʒerɪə'trɪʃn] *s.* Geri'ater *m*, Facharzt *m* für Alterskrankheiten; **ˌger·i'at·rics** [-ks] *s. pl., oft sg. konstr.* Geria'trie *f*.

germ [dʒɜːm] **I** *s.* **1.** ⚘, *biol.* Keim *m* (*a. fig. Ansatz, Ursprung*); **2.** a) *biol.* Mi'krobe *f*, b) ⚕ Keim *m*, Ba'zillus *m*, Bak'terie *f*, Krankheitserreger *m*; **II** *v/i. u. v/t.* **3.** keimen (lassen).

ger·man¹ ['dʒɜːmən] *adj.* leiblich: ***brother*** ~ leiblicher Bruder.

Ger·man² ['dʒɜːmən] **I** *adj.* **1.** deutsch; **II** *s.* **2.** Deutsche(r *m*) *f*; **3.** *ling.* Deutsch *n*, das Deutsche: ***in*** ~ a) auf deutsch, b) im Deutschen; ***into*** ~ ins Deutsche; ***from*** (***the***) ~ aus dem Deutschen.

ˌ**Ger·man-A'mer·i·can** **I** *adj.* 'deutsch-ameriˌkanisch; **II** *s.* 'Deutschameriˌkaner(in).

ger·man·der [dʒɜː'mændə] *s.* ⚘ **1.** Ga'mander *m*; **2.** *a.* ~ ***speedwell*** Ga'manderehrenpreis *m*.

ger·mane [dʒɜː'meɪn] *adj.* (***to***) gehörig (zu), zs.-hängend (mit), betreffend (*acc.*), passend (zu).

Ger·man·ic¹ [dʒɜː'mænɪk] **I** *adj.* **1.** ger'manisch; **2.** deutsch; **II** *s.* **3.** *ling. das* Ger'manische.

ger·man·ic² [dʒɜː'mænɪk] *adj.* ⚗ Germanium...: ~ ***acid***.

Ger·man·ism ['dʒɜːmənɪzəm] *s.* **1.** *ling.* Germa'nismus *m*, deutsche Spracheigenheit; **2.** (typisch) deutsche Art; **3.** et. typisch Deutsches; **4.** Deutschfreundlichkeit *f*; '**Ger·man·ist** [-ɪst] *s.* Germa'nist(in); **Ger·man·i·ty** [dʒɜː'mænətɪ] → ***Germanism*** 2.

ger·ma·ni·um [dʒɜː'meɪnjəm] *s.* ⚗ Ger'manium *n*.

Ger·man·i·za·tion [ˌdʒɜːmənaɪ'zeɪʃn] *s.* Germanisierung *f*, Eindeutschung *f*; **Ger·man·ize** ['dʒɜːmənaɪz] **I** *v/t.* germanisieren, eindeutschen; **II** *v/i.* deutsch werden.

Ger·man mea·sles *s. pl. sg. konstr.* ⚕ Röteln *pl.*

Ger·man·o·phil [dʒɜː'mænəfɪl], **Ger'man·o·phile** [-faɪl] **I** *adj.* deutschfreundlich; **II** *s.* Deutschfreundliche(r *m*) *f*; **Ger'man·o·phobe** [-fəʊb] *s.* Deutschenhasser(in); **Ger·man·o·pho·bi·a** [dʒɜːˌmænə'fəʊbjə] *s.* Deutschfeindlichkeit *f*.

Ger·man| po·lice dog, ~ **shep·herd** (**dog**) *s. Am.* Deutscher Schäferhund; ~ **sil·ver** *s.* Neusilber *n*; ~ **steel** *s.* ⚙ Schmelzstahl *m*; ~ **text**, ~ **type** *s. typ.* Frak'tur(schrift) *f*.

germ| car·ri·er *s.* ⚕ Keim-, Ba'zillenträger *m*; ~ **cell** *s. biol.* Keimzelle *f*.

ger·men ['dʒɜːmɪn] *s.* ⚘ Fruchtknoten *m*.

ger·mi·cid·al [ˌdʒɜːmɪ'saɪdl] *adj.* keimtötend; **ger·mi·cide** ['dʒɜːmɪsaɪd] *adj. u. s.* keimtötend(es Mittel).

ger·mi·nal ['dʒɜːmɪnl] *adj.* □ **1.** *biol.* Keim(zellen)...; **2.** ⚕ Keim..., Bakterien...; **3.** *fig.* keimend, im Keim befindlich: ~ ***ideas***; '**ger·mi·nant** [-nənt] *adj.* keimend (*a. fig.*); '**ger·mi·nate** [-neɪt] ⚘ **I** *v/i.* keimen (*a. fig. sich entwickeln*); **II** *v/t.* zum Keimen bringen, keimen lassen (*a. fig.*); **ger·mi·na·tion** [ˌdʒɜːmɪ'neɪʃn] *s.* ⚘ Keimen *n* (*a. fig.*); '**ger·mi·na·tive** [-nətɪv] *adj.* ⚘ **1.** Keim...; **2.** (keim)entwicklungsfähig.

'**germ|·proof** *adj.* keimsicher, -frei; ~ **war·fare** *s.* ⚔ Bak'terienkrieg *m*, bio'logische Kriegführung.

ge·ron·toc·ra·cy [ˌdʒerɒn'tɒkrəsɪ] *s.* Gerontokra'tie *f*, Altenherrschaft *f*.

ger·on·tol·o·gist [ˌdʒerɒn'tɒlədʒɪst] Geronto'loge *m*; ˌ**ger·on'tol·o·gy** [-dʒɪ] → ***geriatrics***.

ger·ry·man·der ['dʒerɪmændə] **I** *v/t.* **1.** *pol.* die Wahlbezirksgrenzen in *e-m Gebiet* manipulieren; **2.** *Fakten* manipulieren, verfälschen; **II** *s.* **3.** *pol.* manipulierte Wahlbezirksabgrenzung.

ger·und ['dʒerənd] *s. ling.* Ge'rundium *n*; **ge·run·di·al** [dʒɪ'rʌndjəl] *adj. ling.* Gerundial...; **ger·un·di·val** [ˌdʒerən'daɪvl] *adj. ling.* Gerundiv..., gerun'divisch; **ge·run·dive** [dʒɪ'rʌndɪv] *s. ling.* Gerun'div *n*.

ges·ta·tion [dʒes'teɪʃn] *s.* **1.** a) Schwangerschaft *f*, b) *zo.* Trächtigkeit *f*; **2.** *fig.* Reifen *n*.

ges·ta·to·ri·al chair [ˌdʒestə'tɔːrɪəl] *s.* Tragsessel *m des Papstes*.

ges·tic·u·late [dʒe'stɪkjʊleɪt] *v/i.* gestikulieren, (her'um)fuchteln; **ges·tic·u·la·tion** [dʒeˌstɪkjʊ'leɪʃn] *s.* **1.** Gestikulati'on *f*, Gestik *f*, Gebärdenspiel *n*, Gesten *pl.*; **2.** lebhafte Geste; **ges·tic·u·la·to·ry** [-lətərɪ] *adj.* gestikulierend.

ges·ture ['dʒestʃə] **I** *s.* **1.** Gebärde *f*, Geste *f*: ~ ***of friendship*** *fig.* freundschaftliche Geste; **2.** Gebärdenspiel *n*; **II** *v/i.* **3.** → ***gesticulate***.

get [get] **I** *v/t.* [*irr.*] **1.** bekommen, erhalten, ‚kriegen': ~ ***it*** F ‚sein Fett kriegen', etwas ‚erleben'; ~ ***a*** (***radio***) ***station*** e-n Sender (rein)bekommen *od.* (-)kriegen; **2.** a) ~ ***s.th.*** (***for o.s.***), ***get o.s. s.th.*** sich et. verschaffen *od.* besorgen, et. erwerben *od.* kaufen *od.* finden: ~ (***o.s.***) ***a car***, b) ~ ***s.o. s.th.***, ~ ***s.th. for s.o.*** j-m et. besorgen *od.* verschaffen; **3.** *Ruhm etc.* erlangen, erringen, erwerben, *Sieg* erringen, erzielen, *Reichtum* erwerben, kommen zu, *Wissen, Erfahrung* erwerben, sich aneignen; **4.** *Kohle etc.* gewinnen, fördern; **5.** erwischen: a) (zu fassen) kriegen, packen, fangen, b) ertappen, c) treffen, d) *sl.* ‚kriegen', ‚erledigen' (*abschießen, töten*): (***I've***) ***got him!*** (ich) hab' ihn!; ***he'll*** ~ ***you yet!*** er kriegt dich doch (noch)!; ***he's got it bad***(***ly***) F *allg.* ‚ihn hat's bös erwischt'; ***you've got me there!*** F da bin ich überfragt!, da muß ich passen!; ***that ~s me!*** F a) das kapier' ich nicht!, b) das geht mir auf die Nerven!, c) das geht mir unter die Haut *od.* an die Nieren!; **6.** a) holen: ~ ***help*** (***a doctor***, *etc.*), b) bringen, holen: ~ ***me the book***, c) ('hin)bringen, *wohin* schaffen: ~ ***me to the hospital!***; **7.** (*a. telefonisch etc.*) erreichen; **8.** ***have got*** a) haben: ***I've got enough money***, b) (*mit inf.*) müssen: ***we have got to do it***; ***it's got to be wrong*** es muß falsch sein; **9.** machen, werden lassen: ~ ***o.s. dirty*** sich schmutzig machen; ~ ***one's feet wet*** nasse Füße bekommen; ~ ***s.o. nervous*** j-n nervös machen; **10.** (*mit p.p.*) lassen: ~ ***one's hair cut*** sich die Haare schneiden lassen; ~ ***the door shut*** die Tür zubekommen; ~ ***things done*** etwas zuwege bringen; **11.** (*mit inf. od. pres. p.*) dazu bringen *od.* bewegen: ~ ***s.o. to talk*** j-n zum Sprechen bringen; ~ ***the machine to work***, ~ ***the machine working*** die Maschine in Gang bringen; → ***go*** 21; **12.** a) machen, zubereiten: ~ ***dinner***, b) *Brit.* F essen, zu sich nehmen: ~ ***breakfast*** frühstücken; **13.** F ‚kapieren', verstehen (*a. hören*): ***I didn't ~ that!***; ***I don't ~ him*** ich versteh' nicht, was er will; ***don't ~ me wrong!*** versteh mich nicht falsch!; ***got it?*** kapiert?; ~ ***that!*** *iron.* a) was sagst du dazu?, b) sieh (*od.* hör) dir das (bloß mal) an!; **II** *v/i.* **14.** kommen, gelangen: ~ ***home*** nach Hause kommen, zu Hause ankommen; ~ ***into debt*** (***into a rage***) in Schulden (in Wut) geraten; ~ ***somewhere*** F weiterkommen, Erfolg haben; ***now we are ~ting somewhere!*** jetzt kommen wir der Sache schon näher!; ~ ***nowhere***, ***not to ~ anywhere*** nicht weiterkommen; ***that will ~ us nowhere!*** so kommen wir nicht weiter!; **15.** (*mit adj. od. p.p.*) werden: ~ ***old***; ~ ***better*** a) besser werden, sich (ver)bessern, b) sich erholen; ~ ***caught*** gefangen *od.* erwischt werden; ~ ***tired*** müde werden, ermüden; **16.** (*mit inf.*) dahin kommen: ~ ***to like it*** daran Gefallen finden, es allmählich mögen; ~ ***to know*** kennenlernen; ***how did you ~ to know that?*** wie hast du das erfahren?; ~ ***to be friends*** Freunde werden; **17.** (*mit pres. p.*) anfangen, beginnen: ***they got quarrel***(***l***)***ing***; ~ ***talking*** a) ins Gespräch kommen, b) zu reden anfangen; → ***go*** 21; **18.** *sl.* ‚abhauen': ~***!*** hau ab!;

Zssgn mit prp.:

get| a·round *v/i.* F **1.** *et.* um'gehen; **2.** a) *j-n* ‚her'umkriegen', b) *j-n* ‚reinlegen'; ~ **at** *v/i.* **1.** (her'an)kommen an (*acc.*), erreichen: ***I can't ~ my books***; **2.** an *j-n* ‚rankommen', *j-m* beikommen; **3.** *et.* ‚kriegen', ‚auftreiben'; **4.** *et.* her'ausbekommen, *e-r Sache* auf den Grund kommen; **5.** sagen wollen: ***what is he getting at?*** worauf will er hinaus?; **6.** *j-n* ‚schmieren', bestechen; ~ **be·hind** *v/i.* **1.** sich stellen hinter (*acc.*), *fig. a. j-n* unterstützen; **2.** zu'rückbleiben hinter (*dat.*); ~ **off** *v/i.* **1.** a) absteigen von, b) aussteigen aus; **2.** freikommen von; ~ **on** *v/i.* a) *Pferd, Wagen etc.* besteigen, b) einsteigen in (*acc.*): ~ ***to one's feet*** sich erheben; ~ **to** F hinter *et. od.* hinter *j-s* Schliche kommen; ~ **out of** *v/i.* **1.** her'aussteigen, -kommen, -gelangen aus; **2.** e-e Gewohnheit ablegen: ~ ***smoking*** sich das Rauchen abgewöhnen; **3.** *fig.* aus *e-r Sache* ‚aussteigen'; sich her'auswinden aus: ~ ***from under*** F sich rauswinden; **4.** sich drücken vor (*dat.*); **5.** *Geld etc.* aus *j-m* ‚her'ausholen'; **6.** *et.* bei *e-r Sache* ‚kriegen'; ~ **o·ver** *v/i.* **1.** (hin'über)kommen über (*acc.*); **2.** *fig.* hin'wegkommen über (*acc.*); **3.** *et.* über'stehen; ~ **round** → ***get around***; ~ **through** *v/i.* **1.** kommen durch (*e-e Prüfung, den Winter etc.*); **2.** *Geld* 'durchbringen; **3.** *et.* erledigen; ~ **to** *v/i.* **1.** kommen nach, erreichen; **2.** a) sich machen an (*acc.*), b) (*zufällig*) dazu kommen: ***we got to talking about it*** wir kamen darauf zu sprechen;

Zssgn mit adv.:

get| a·bout *v/i.* **1.** her'umgehen; **2.** he'rumkommen; **3.** (wieder) auf den Beinen sein (*nach Krankheit*); **4.** sich her'umsprechen *od.* verbreiten (*Gerücht*); ~ **a·cross I** *v/i.* **1.** *fig.* ‚ankommen': a) ‚einschlagen', Anklang finden:

the play got across, b) sich verständlich machen; **2.** (***to*** *j-m*) klarwerden; **II** *v/t.* **3.** *e-r Sache* Wirkung *od.* Erfolg verschaffen, *et.* an den Mann bringen: ***get an idea across***; **4.** *et.* klarmachen; **~ a·head** *v/i.* F vorankommen, Fortschritte machen: **~ *of s.o.*** j-n überholen *od.* überflügeln; **~ a·long** *v/i.* **1.** auskommen (***with*** mit *j-m*); **2.** zu'recht-, auskommen (***with*** mit *et.*); **3.** → ***get on*** 1; **4.** weitergehen: ***~!*** verschwinde!; **~ *with you!*** F a) verschwinde!, b) jetzt hör aber auf!; **5.** älter werden; **~ a·way** *v/i.* **1.** loskommen, sich losmachen: ***you can't ~ from that*** a) darüber kannst du dich nicht hinwegsetzen, b) das mußt du doch einsehen; ***you can't ~ from the fact that*** man kommt um die Tatsache nicht herum, daß; **2.** *bsd. sport* ,wegkommen': a) starten, b) sich lösen; **3.** → ***get along*** 4; **4.** entkommen, entwischen: ***he won't ~ with that*** damit kommt er nicht durch; ***he gets away with everything*** (*od.* ***with murder***) er kann sich alles erlauben; **~ back I** *v/t.* **1.** zu'rückbekommen: ***get one's own back*** F sich rächen; ***get one's own back on s.o.*** → 3; **II** *v/i.* **2.** zu'rückkommen; **3. ~ *at s.o.*** F sich an j-m rächen; **~ be·hind** *v/i.* zu'rückbleiben; in Rückstand kommen; **~ by** *v/i.* **1.** vor'bei-, 'durchkommen; **2.** aus-, zu'rechtkommen; ,es schaffen'; **~ down I** *v/i.* **1.** her'unterkommen, -steigen; **2.** aus-, absteigen; **3. ~ *to s.th.*** sich an et. (her'an-) machen; → ***business*** 5; **II** *v/t.* **4.** her'unterholen, -schaffen; **5.** aufschreiben; **6.** *Essen etc.* runterkriegen; **7.** *fig. j-n* ,fertigmachen'; **~ in I** *v/t.* **1.** hin'einbringen, -schaffen, -bekommen; **2.** *Ernte* einbringen; **3.** einfügen; **4.** *Bemerkung, Schlag etc.* anbringen; **5.** *Arzt etc.* (hin)'zuziehen; **II** *v/i.* **6.** hin'ein- *od.* her'eingelangen, -kommen: **7.** einsteigen; **8.** *pol.* (ins Parla'ment *etc.*) gewählt werden; **9. ~ *on*** F mitmachen bei; **10. ~ *with s.o.*** sich mit j-m anfreunden; **~ off I** *v/t.* **1.** *Kleid etc.* ausziehen; **2.** losbekommen, -kriegen; **3.** *Brief etc.* ,loslassen'; **II** *v/i.* **4.** abreisen; **5.** ✈ abheben; **6.** (***from***) absteigen (von), aussteigen (aus): ***tell s.o. where to ~*** F j-m ,Bescheid stoßen'; **7.** da'vonkommen: **~ *cheaply*** a) billig wegkommen, b) mit e-m blauen Auge davonkommen; **8.** entkommen; **9.** (*von der Arbeit*) wegkommen; **~ on I** *v/i.* **1.** vor'ankommen (*a. fig.*): **~ *in life*** a) es zu et. bringen, b) *a.* **~** (***in years***) älter werden; ***be getting on for sixty*** auf die Sechzig zugehen; **~ *without*** ohne *et.* auskommen; ***let's ~ with it!*** machen wir weiter!; ***it was getting on*** es wurde spät; **2.** → ***get along*** 1, 2; **3. ~ *to*** F a) *Brit.* sich in Verbindung setzen mit, *teleph. j-n* anrufen, b) *et.* ,spitzkriegen', c) *j-m* auf die Schliche kommen; **II** *v/t.* **4.** *et.* vor'antreiben; **~ out I** *v/t.* **1.** her'ausbekommen, -kriegen (*a. fig.*); **2.** a) her'ausholen, b) hin'ausschaffen; **3.** *Worte* her'ausbringen; **II** *v/i.* **4.** a) aussteigen, b) her'auskommen, c) hin'ausgehen: ***~!*** raus!; **~ *from under*** *Am.* F mit heiler Haut davonkommen; **5.** *fig.* F ,aussteigen'; **6.** → ***get out of*** (*Zssgn mit prp.*); **~ round** *v/i.* dazu kommen (***to doing s.th.*** et. zu tun); **~ through I** *v/t.* **1.** 'durchbringen, -bekommen (*a. fig.*); **2.** *et.* hinter sich bringen; **3.** (***to*** *j-m*) *et.* klarmachen; **II** *v/i.* **4.** *a. fig., a. ped., teleph.* 'durchkommen; **5.** (***with***) fertig werden mit, (*et.*) ,schaffen'; **6.** (***to*** *j-m*) klarwerden; **~ to·geth·er I** *v/t.* **1.** zs.-bringen; **2.** zs.-tragen; **3. *get it together*** F ,es bringen'; **II** *v/i.* **4.** zs.-kommen; **5.** sich einig werden; **~ up I** *v/t.* **1.** hin'aufbringen, -schaffen; **2.** ins Werk setzen; **3.** veranstalten, organisieren; **4.** (ein)richten, vorbereiten; **5.** konstruieren, zs.-basteln; **6.** (***o.s.*** sich) her'ausputzen; **7.** *Buch etc.* ausstatten; *Waren* (hübsch) aufmachen; **8.** *thea.* einstudieren; **9.** F ,büffeln'; **II** *v/i.* **10.** aufstehen.

get|-at-a·ble [get'ætəbl] *adj.* **1.** erreichbar (*Ort od. Sache*); **2.** zugänglich (*Ort od. Person*); **'~-a·way** *s.* **1.** F Flucht *f*, Entkommen *n*: **~ *car*** Fluchtwagen *m*; ***make one's ~*** entkommen, entwischen, sich aus dem Staub machen; **2.** ✈, *sport* Start *m*; **3.** *mot.* Anzugsvermögen *n*; **'~-off** *s.* ✈ Abheben *n*.

get·ter ['getə] *s.* ⚒ Hauer *m*.

'get|-to,geth·er *s.* Zs.-kunft *f*, zwangloses Bei'sammensein; **,~-'tough** *adj. Am.* F hart, aggres'siv: **~ *policy***; **'~-up** *s.* **1.** Aufbau *m*, Anordnung *f*; **2.** Aufmachung *f*: a) Ausstattung *f*, b) ,Aufzug' *m*, Kleidung *f*; **3.** *thea.* Inszenierung *f*.

gew·gaw ['gju:gɔ:] *s.* **1.** → ***gimcrack*** I; **2.** *fig.* Lap'palie *f*, Kleinigkeit *f*.

gey·ser *s.* **1.** ['gaɪzə] Geysir *m*, heiße Quelle; **2.** ['gi:zə] *Brit.* ('Gas-) ,Durchlauferhitzer *m*.

ghast·li·ness ['gɑ:stlɪnɪs] *s.* **1.** Grausigkeit *f*; schreckliches Aussehen; **2.** Totenblässe *f*; **ghast·ly** ['gɑ:stlɪ] **I** *adj.* **1.** gräßlich, greulich, entsetzlich (*alle a. fig.* F); **2.** gespenstisch; **3.** totenbleich; **4.** verzerrt (*Lächeln*); **II** *adv.* **5.** gräßlich *etc.*: **~ *pale*** totenblaß.

gher·kin ['gɜ:kɪn] *s.* Essig-, Gewürzgurke *f*.

ghet·to ['getəʊ] *pl.* **-tos** *s. hist. u. sociol.* G(h)etto *n*.

ghost [gəʊst] **I** *s.* **1.** Geist *m*, Gespenst *n*: ***lay a ~*** e-n Geist beschwören; ***lay the ~s of the past*** *fig.* Vergangenheitsbewältigung betreiben; ***the ~ walks*** *thea. sl.* es gibt Geld; **2.** Geist *m*, Seele *f* (*nur noch in*): ***give*** (*od.* ***yield***) ***up the ~*** den Geist aufgeben (*a. fig.* F); **3.** *fig.* Spur *f*, Schatten *m*: ***not the ~ of a chance*** F nicht die geringste Chance; ***the ~ of a smile*** der Anflug e-s Lächelns; **4.** → ***ghost writer***; **5.** *opt. TV* Doppelbild *n*; **II** *v/t.* **6.** *j-n* verfolgen (*Erinnerungen etc.*); **7.** *Buch etc.* als Ghostwriter schreiben; **III** *v/i.* **8.** Ghostwriter sein (***for*** für); **'~·like** → ***ghostly***.

ghost·li·ness ['gəʊstlɪnɪs] *s.* Geisterhaftigkeit *f*; **ghost·ly** ['gəʊstlɪ] *adj.* geisterhaft, gespenstisch.

ghost| sto·ry *s.* Geister-, Gespenstergeschichte *f*; **~ town** *s. Am.* Geisterstadt *f*, verödete Stadt; **~ train** *s.* Geisterbahn *f*; **~ word** *s.* Ghostword *n* (*falsche Wortbildung*); **'~-write** → ***ghost*** 7, 8; **~ writ·er** *s.* Ghostwriter *m*.

ghoul [gu:l] *s.* **1.** Ghul *m* (*leichenfressender Dämon*); **2.** *fig.* Unhold *m* (*Person mit makabren Gelüsten*), *z.B.* Grabschänder *m*; **'ghoul·ish** [-lɪʃ] *adj.* □ **1.** ghulenhaft; **2.** greulich, ma'kaber.

G.I. [,dʒi:'aɪ] (*von* ***Government Issue***) ⚔ *Am.* F **I** *s.* ,G'I' *m* (*US-Soldat*); **II** *adj.* GI-..., Kommiß...; *weitS.* vorschriftsmäßig.

gi·ant ['dʒaɪənt] **I** *s.* Riese *m*, *fig. a.* Gi'gant *m*, Ko'loß *m*; **II** *adj.* riesenhaft, riesig; *a.* ♀, *zo.* Riesen...: **~ *slalom*** Riesenslalom *m*; **~ *stride*** Riesenschritt *m*; **~(*'s*) *stride*** Rundlauf *m* (*Turngerät*); **~ *wheel*** Riesenrad *n*; **'gi·ant·ess** [-tes] *s.* Riesin *f*.

gib [gɪb] *s.* ⚙ **1.** Keil *m*, Bolzen *m*; **2.** 'Führungsline,al *n* (*e-r Werkzeugmaschine*); **3.** Ausleger *m* (*e-s Krans*).

gib·ber ['dʒɪbə] *v/i.* schnattern, quatschen; **'gib·ber·ish** [-ərɪʃ] *s.* Geschnatter *n*; Geschwätz, ,Geschwafel' *n*.

gib·bet ['dʒɪbɪt] **I** *s.* **1.** Galgen *m*; **2.** ⚙ Kran- *od.* Querbalken *m*; **II** *v/t.* **3.** *j-n* hängen; **4.** *fig.* anprangern, bloßstellen.

gib·bon ['gɪbən] *s. zo.* Gibbon *m*.

gib·bous ['gɪbəs] *adj.* **1.** gewölbt; **2.** buck(e)lig.

gibe [dʒaɪb] **I** *v/t.* verhöhnen, verspotten; **II** *v/i.* spotten (***at*** über *acc.*); **III** *s.* höhnische Bemerkung, Stiche'lei *f*, Seitenhieb *m*.

gib·lets ['dʒɪblɪts] *s. pl.* Inne'reien *pl.*, *bsd.* Hühner-, Gänseklein *n*.

gid·di·ness ['gɪdɪnɪs] *s.* **1.** Schwindel (-gefühl *n*) *m*; **2.** *fig.* a) Leichtsinn *m*, Flatterhaftigkeit *f*, b) Wankelmütigkeit *f*; **gid·dy** ['gɪdɪ] *adj.* □ **1.** schwind(e)lig: ***I am*** (*od.* ***feel***) **~** mir ist schwind(e)lig; **2.** *a. fig.* schwindelerregend, schwindelnd; **3.** *fig.* a) leichtsinnig, flatterhaft, b) ,verrückt', ,wild'.

gie [gi:] *Scot. für* ***give***.

gift [gɪft] **I** *s.* **1.** Geschenk *n*, Gabe *f*: ***make a ~ of*** *et.* schenken; ***I wouldn't have it as a ~*** das nähme ich nicht (mal) geschenkt; ***it's a ~!*** das ist ja geschenkt (*billig*)!; **2.** ⚖ Schenkung *f*; **3.** ⚖ Verleihungsrecht *n*: ***the office is in his ~*** er kann dieses Amt verleihen; **4.** *fig.* Begabung *f*, Gabe *f*, Ta'lent *n* (***for***, ***of*** für): **~ *for languages*** Sprachbegabung; ***of many ~s*** vielseitig begabt; → ***gab*** I; **II** *v/t.* **5.** (be)schenken; **'gift·ed** [-tɪd] *adj.* begabt, talen'tiert.

gift| horse *s.*: ***don't look a ~ in the mouth*** e-m geschenkten Gaul schaut man nicht ins Maul; **~ shop** *s.* Ge'schenkar,tikelladen *m*; **~ tax** Schenkungssteuer *f*; **~ to·ken**, **~ vouch·er** *s.* Geschenkgutschein *m*; **'~-wrap** *v/t.* geschenkmäßig verpacken; **'~-,wrap·ping** *s.* Ge'schenkpa,pier *n*.

gig¹ [gɪg] *s.* **1.** ⚓ Gig(boot *n*) *f*; **2.** Gig *f* (*Ruderboot*); **3.** Gig *n* (*zweirädriger, offener Einspänner*); **4.** Fischspeer *m*; **5.** ⚙ ('Tuch),Rauhma,schine *f*.

gig² [gɪg] *s.* ♪ F a) Engage'ment *n*, b) Auftritt *m*.

gi·gan·tic [dʒaɪ'gæntɪk] *adj.* (□ **~*ally***) gi'gantisch: a) riesenhaft, Riesen..., b) riesig, ungeheuer (groß).

gig·gle ['gɪgl] **I** *v/i. u. v/t.* kichern; **II** *s.* Gekicher *n*, Kichern *n*; **'gig·gly** [-lɪ] *adj.* ständig kichernd.

gig·o·lo ['ʒɪgələʊ] *pl.* **-los** *s.* Gigolo *m*.

Gil·ber·ti·an [gɪl'bɜ:tjən] *adj.* in der Art (*des Humors*) von W. S. Gilbert; *fig.* komisch, possenhaft.

gild¹ [gɪld] → ***guild***.

gild[2] [gɪld] *v/t.* [*irr.*] **1.** vergolden; **2.** *fig.* a) verschöne(r)n, (aus)schmücken, b) über'tünchen, verbrämen, c) versüßen: **~ *the pill*** die bittere Pille versüßen; **'gild·ed** [-dɪd] *adj.* vergoldet, golden (*a. fig.*): **~ *cage*** *fig.* goldener Käfig; **~ *youth*** Jeunesse dorée *f*; **'gild·er** [-də] *s.* Vergolder *m*; **'gild·ing** [-dɪŋ] *s.* **1.** Vergoldung *f*; **2.** *fig.* Verschönerung *f etc.* (→ **gild**[2] 2).

gill[1] [gɪl] *s.* **1.** *ichth.* Kieme *f*; **2.** *pl.* Doppelkinn *n*: ***rosy*** (***green***) ***about the ~s*** rosig, frischaussehend (grün im Gesicht); **3.** *orn.* Kehllappen *m*; **4.** ⚘ La'melle *f*: **~ *fungus*** Blätterpilz *m*; **5.** ⚙ (Heiz-, Kühl)Rippe *f*.

gill[2] [gɪl] *s. Scot.* **1.** waldige Schlucht; **2.** Gebirgsbach *m*.

gill[3] [dʒɪl] *s.* Viertelpinte *f* (*Brit. 0,14, Am. 0,12 Liter*).

Gill[4] [dʒɪl] *s. obs.* Liebste *f*.

gil·ly·flow·er ['dʒɪlɪˌflaʊə] *s.* ⚘ **1.** Gartennelke *f*; **2.** Lev'koje *f*; **3.** Goldlack *m*.

gilt [gɪlt] **I** *pret. u. p.p. von* **gild**[2]; **II** *adj.* **1.** → ***gilded***; **III** *s.* **2.** Vergoldung *f*; **3.** *fig.* Reiz *m*: ***take the ~ off the gingerbread*** der Sache den Reiz nehmen; **ˌ~-'edged** *adj.* **1.** mit Goldschnitt; **2.** **~ *securities*** ✝ mündelsichere (Wert)Papiere *pl*.

gim·bals ['dʒɪmbəlz] *s. pl.* ⚙ Kar'danringe *pl.*, -aufhängung *f*.

gim·crack ['dʒɪmkræk] **I** *s.* **1.** wertloser *od.* kitschiger Gegenstand *od.* Schmuck, (*a.* technische) Spiele'rei, ‚Mätzchen' *n*; **2.** *pl.* → ***gimcrackery***; **II** *adj.* **3.** wertlos, kitschig; **'gimˌcrack·er·y** [-kərɪ] *s.* Plunder *m*, ‚Kinkerlitzchen' *pl*.

gim·let ['gɪmlɪt] *s.* **1.** ⚙ Handbohrer *m*: **~ *eyes*** *fig.* stechende Augen; **2.** *Am. ein Cocktail.*

gim·mick ['gɪmɪk] *s.* F **1.** → ***gadget***; **2.** *fig.* ‚Dreh' *m*, (Re'klame- *etc.*)Masche *f*, ‚Aufhänger' *m*, ‚Knüller' *m*, *a.* Gimmick *m*, *n*; **'gim·mick·ry** [-krɪ] *s.* F (technische) Mätzchen *pl*.

gimp [gɪmp] *s. Schneiderei:* Gimpe *f*.

gin[1] [dʒɪn] *s.* Gin *m*, Wa'cholderschnaps *m*: **~ *and it*** Gin u. Wermut *m*; **~ *and tonic*** Gin Tonic *m*.

gin[2] [dʒɪn] **I** *s.* **1.** *a.* ***cotton ~*** Ent'körnungsmaˌschine *f*; **2.** ⚙ Hebezeug *n*, Winde *f*; ⚓ Spill *n*; **3.** ⚙ Göpel *m*, 'Förderma,schine *f*; **4.** *hunt.* Falle *f*, Schlinge *f*; **II** *v/t.* **5.** *Baumwolle* entkörnen; **6.** mit e-r Schlinge fangen.

gin·ger ['dʒɪndʒə] **I** *s.* **1.** ⚘ Ingwer *m*; **2.** Rötlich(gelb) *n*, Ingwerfarbe *f*; **3.** F a) ‚Mumm' *m*, Schneid *m* (*e-r Person*), b) Schwung *m*, ‚Schmiß' *m* (*a. e-r Sache*), c) ‚Pfeffer' *m*, ‚Pfiff' *m* (*e-r Geschichte etc.*); **II** *adj.* **4.** rötlich(gelb); **5.** F schwungvoll, ‚schmissig'; **III** *v/t.* **6.** mit Ingwer würzen; **7.** *a.* **~ *up*** *fig.* a) *et.* ‚ankurbeln', b) *j-n* aufmöbeln, c) *j-n* ‚scharfmachen', d) *e-m Film etc.* ‚Pfiff' geben; **~ ale**, **~ beer** *s.* Ginger-ale *n*, 'Ingwerlimoˌnade *f*; **'~·bread I** *s.* **1.** Ingwer-, Pfefferkuchen *m*; → **gilt** 3; **2.** *fig. contp.* über'ladene Verzierung, Kitsch *m*; **II** *adj.* **3.** kitschig, über'laden; **~ group** *s. pol. Brit.* Gruppe *f* von Scharfmachern.

gin·ger·ly ['dʒɪndʒəlɪ] *adv. u. adj.* sachte, behutsam; zimperlich.

'gin·ger|·nut *s.* Ingwerkeks *m*; **~ pop** *s.* F *für* ***ginger ale***; **'~·snap** *s.* Ingwerwaffel *f*; **~ wine** *s.* Ingwerwein *m*.

gin·ger·y ['dʒɪndʒərɪ] *adj.* **1.** Ingwer…; **2.** → ***ginger*** 4; **3.** *fig.* a) → ***ginger*** 5, b) beißend.

ging·ham ['gɪŋəm] *s.* Gingham *m*, Gingan *m* (*Baumwollstoff*).

gin·gi·vi·tis [ˌdʒɪndʒɪ'vaɪtɪs] *s.* ⚕ Zahnfleischentzündung *f*.

gink·go ['gɪŋkəʊ] *pl.* **-gos** *od.* **-goes** *s.* ⚘ Gingko *m* (*Baum*).

gin mill *s. Am.* F Kneipe *f*.

gin·ner·y ['dʒɪnərɪ] *s.* Entkörnungswerk *n* (*für Baumwolle*).

gin| pal·ace *s.* auffällig dekoriertes Wirtshaus; **~ rum·my** *s. Form des Rommés*; **~ sling** *s. Am.* Mischgetränk *n* mit Gin.

gip·sy ['dʒɪpsɪ] **I** *s.* **1.** Zi'geuner(in) (*a. fig.*); **2.** Zi'geunersprache *f*; **II** *adj.* **3.** zi'geunerhaft, Zigeuner…; **III** *v/i.* **4.** ein Zi'geunerleben führen; **'gip·sy·dom** [-dəm] *s.* **1.** Zi'geunertum *n*; **2.** *coll.* Zi'geuner *pl*.

gi·raffe [dʒɪ'rɑ:f] *s. zo.* Gi'raffe *f*.

gird [gɜ:d] *v/t.* [*irr.*] **1.** *obs. j-n* (um)'gürten; **2.** *Kleid etc.* gürten, mit e-m Gürtel halten; **3.** *oft* **~ *on*** *Schwert etc.* 'umgürten, an-, 'umlegen: **~ *s.th. on s.o.*** j-m et. umgürten; **4.** *j-m*, *sich* ein Schwert 'umgürten: **~ *o.s.*** (***up***), **~** (***up***) ***one's loins*** *fig.* sich rüsten *od.* wappnen; **5.** binden (***to*** an *acc.*); **6.** um'geben, -'schließen: ***sea-girt*** meerumschlungen; **7.** *fig.* ausstatten, -rüsten.

gird·er ['gɜ:də] *s.* ⚙ (Längs)Träger *m*: **~ *bridge*** Balken-, Trägerbrücke *f*.

gir·dle ['gɜ:dl] **I** *s.* **1.** Gürtel *m*, Gurt *m*; **2.** Hüfthalter *m*, -gürtel *m*; **3.** *anat. in Zssgn* (Knochen)Gürtel *m*; **4.** *fig.* Gürtel *m* (*Umkreis, Umgebung*); **II** *v/t.* **5.** um'gürten; **6.** um'geben, einschließen; **7.** *Baum* ringeln.

girl [gɜ:l] *s.* **1.** Mädchen *n*: ***a German ~*** e-e junge Deutsche; ***~'s name*** weiblicher Vorname; ***my eldest ~*** m-e älteste Tochter; ***the ~s*** F a) die Töchter *pl.* des Hauses, b) die Damen *pl.*; **2.** (Dienst-)Mädchen *n*; **3.** F ‚Mädchen' *n* (*e-s jungen Mannes*); **~ Fri·day** *s.* (unentbehrliche) Gehilfin, ‚rechte Hand' (*des Chefs, bsd. Sekretärin*); **'~·friend** *s.* Freundin *f*; **~ guide** *s. Brit.* Pfadfinderin *f*.

girl·hood ['gɜ:lhʊd] *s.* Mädchenzeit *f*, -jahre *pl.*, Jugend(zeit) *f*; **'girl·ie** [-lɪ] *s.* F Mädchen *n*: **~ *mag***(***azine***) ‚Titten u. Po'-Magazin *n*; **'girl·ish** [-lɪʃ] *adj.* □ mädchenhaft; **'girl·ish·ness** [-lɪʃnɪs] *s. das* Mädchenhafte; **girl scout** *s. Am.* Pfadfinderin *f*.

gi·ro ['dʒaɪrəʊ] *s.* (*der*) Postscheckdienst (*in England*): **~ *account*** Postscheckkonto *n*.

girt[1] [gɜ:t] *pret. u. p.p. von* **gird**.

girt[2] [gɜ:t] **I** *s.* 'Umfang *m*; **II** *v/t.* den 'Umfang messen von; **III** *v/i.* messen (*an Umfang*).

girth [gɜ:θ] **I** *s.* **1.** 'Umfang *m*; **2.** 'Körperˌumfang *m*; **3.** (Sattel-, Pack)Gurt *m*; **4.** ⚙ Tragriemen *m*, Gurt *m*; **II** *v/t.* **5.** *Pferd* gürten; **6.** an-, aufschnallen; **7.** a) → **gird** 6, b) → **girt**[2] II.

gis·mo → ***gizmo***.

gist [dʒɪst] *s.* **1.** *das* Wesentliche, Hauptpunkt *m*, -inhalt *m*, Kern *m der Sache*; **2.** ⚖ Grundlage *f*: **~ *of action*** Klagegrund *m*.

give [gɪv] **I** *s.* **1.** *fig.* a) Nachgiebigkeit *f*, b) Elastizi'tät *f*; → ***give and take***; **2.** Elastizi'tät *f* (*des Fußbodens etc.*); **II** *v/t.* [*irr.*] **3.** geben, (über)'reichen; schenken: ***he gave me a book***; **~ *a present*** ein Geschenk machen; **~ *s.o. a blow*** j-m e-n Schlag versetzen; **~ *it to him!*** F gib's ihm!, gib ihm Saures (*Strafe, Schelte*)!; **~ *me Mozart any time*** a) Mozart geht mir über alles, b) da lobe ich mir (doch) Mozart; **~ *as good as one gets*** (*od.* ***takes***) mit gleicher Münze zurückzahlen; **~ *or take*** plus/minus; **4.** geben, zahlen: ***how much did you ~ for that hat?***; **5.** (ab-, weiter)geben, über'tragen; (zu)erteilen, an-, zuweisen; verleihen: ***she gave me her bag to carry*** sie gab mir ihre Tasche zu tragen; **~ *s.o. a part in a play*** j-m e-e Rolle in e-m Stück geben; **~ *s.o. a title*** j-m e-n Titel verleihen; **6.** hingeben, widmen, schenken: **~ *one's attention to*** s-e Aufmerksamkeit widmen (*dat.*); **~ *one's mind to s.th.*** sich e-r Sache widmen; **~ *one's life*** sein Leben hingeben *od.* opfern (***for*** für); **7.** geben, (dar)bieten, reichen: ***he gave me his hand***; ***do ~ us a song*** singen Sie uns doch bitte ein Lied; **8.** gewähren, liefern, geben: ***cows ~ milk*** Kühe geben *od.* liefern Milch; **~ *no result*** kein Ergebnis zeitigen; ***it was not ~n him to*** *inf.* es war ihm nicht gegeben *od.* vergönnt, zu *inf.*; **9.** verursachen: **~ *pleasure*** Vergnügen bereiten *od.* machen; **~ *pain*** Schmerzen bereiten, weh tun; **10.** zugeben, -gestehen, erlauben: ***just ~ me 24 hours*** gib mir nur 24 Stunden (Zeit); ***I ~ you till tomorrow!*** ich gebe dir noch bis morgen Zeit!; ***I ~ you that point*** in diesem Punkt gebe ich dir recht; **11.** ausführen, äußern, vortragen: **~ *a cry*** e-n Schrei ausstoßen, aufschreien; **~ *a loud laugh*** laut auflachen; **~ *s.o. a look*** j-m e-n Blick zuwerfen, j-n anblicken; **~ *a party*** e-e Party geben; **~ *a play*** ein Stück geben *od.* aufführen; **~ *a lecture*** e-n Vortrag halten; **~ *one's name*** s-n Namen nennen *od.* angeben; **12.** beschreiben, mitteilen, geben: **~ *us the facts***; (***come on,***) ***~!*** *Am.* F sag schon!, raus mit der Sprache!; **III** *v/i.* [*irr.*] **13.** geben, schenken, spenden (***to*** *dat.*): **~ *generously***; **~ *and take*** *fig.* geben u. nehmen, einander entgegenkommen; **14.** nachgeben (*a.* ✝ *Preise*), -lassen, weichen, versagen: **~ *under pressure*** unter Druck nachgeben; ***his knees gave under him*** s-e Knie versagten; ***what ~s?*** *sl.* was ist los?; ***s.th.'s got to ~*** *sl.* es muß (doch) was passieren; **15.** a) nachgeben, (*Fußboden etc.*) *a.* federn, b) sich dehnen (*Schuhe etc.*): **~ *but not to break*** sich biegen, aber nicht brechen; ***the chair ~s comfortably*** der Stuhl federt angenehm; ***the foundations are giving*** das Fundament senkt sich; **16.** a) führen (***into*** in *acc.*; ***on*** auf *acc.*, nach) (*Straße etc.*), b) gehen (***on*** [***-to***] nach) (*Fenster etc.*);

Zssgn mit adv.:

give| a·way *v/t.* **1.** weg-, hergeben, verschenken (*a. fig. u. sport den Sieg etc.*); → ***bride***; **2.** *Preise* verteilen; **3.**

aufgeben, opfern, preisgeben; **4.** verraten: ***his accent gives him away***; ***give o.s. away*** sich verraten *od.* verplappern; → ***show*** 14; **~ back** *v/t.* **1.** zu'rückgeben; **2.** *Blick* erwidern; **~ forth** *v/t.* **1.** → ***give off***; **2.** *Ansicht etc.* äußern; **3.** veröffentlichen, bekanntgeben; **~ in I** *v/t.* **1.** *Gesuch etc.* einreichen, abgeben; **II** *v/i.* **2.** (***to*** *dat.*) a) nachgeben (*dat.*), b) sich anschließen (*dat.*); **3.** aufgeben, sich geschlagen geben; **~ off** *v/t. Dampf etc.* abgeben, *Gas, Wärme etc.* aus-, verströmen, *Rauch etc.* ausstoßen, *Geruch* verbreiten, ausströmen; **~ out I** *v/t.* **1.** ausgeben, aus-, verteilen; **2.** bekanntgeben: ***give it out that*** a) verkünden, daß, b) behaupten, daß; **3.** → ***give off***; **II** *v/i.* **4.** zu Ende gehen (*Kräfte, Vorrat*): ***his strength gave out*** die Kräfte verließen ihn; **5.** versagen (*Kräfte, Maschine etc.*); **~ o·ver I** *v/t.* **1.** über'geben (***to*** *dat.*); **2.** *et.* aufgeben: **~ *doing s.th.*** aufhören, et. zu tun; **3.** ***give o.s. over to*** sich *der Verzweiflung etc.* hingeben, verfallen (*dat.*): ***give o.s. over to drink***; **II** *v/i.* **4.** aufhören; **~ up I** *v/t.* **1.** aufgeben, aufhören mit, *et.* sein lassen: **~ *smoking*** das Rauchen aufgeben; **2.** (*als aussichtslos*) aufgeben: **~ *a plan***; ***he was given up by the doctors***; **3.** *j-n* ausliefern: ***give o.s. up*** sich (freiwillig) stellen (***to the police*** der Polizei); **4.** *et.* abgeben, abtreten (***to*** an *acc.*); **5.** ***give o.s. up to*** a) → ***give over*** 3, b) sich *e-r Sache* widmen; **II** *v/i.* **6.** (es) aufgeben, sich geschlagen geben, *weitS. a.* resignieren.

give| and take *s.* **1.** (*ein*) Geben u. Nehmen, beiderseitiges Nachgeben, Kompro'miß(bereitschaft *f*) *m*; **2.** Meinungsaustausch *m*; **ˌ~-and-'take** [-vənt-] *adj.* Kompromiß..., Ausgleichs...; **'~·a·way I** *s.* **1.** (ungewolltes) Verraten, Verplappern *n*; **2.** † a) Werbegeschenk *n*, b) kostenlos verteilte Zeitung; **3.** *a.* **~ *show*** *TV* Quiz(sendung *f*) *n*, Preisraten *n*; **II** *adj.* **4.** **~ *price*** Schleuderpreis *m*.

giv·en ['gɪvn] **I** *p.p. von* ***give***; **II** *adj.* **1.** gegeben, bestimmt: ***at a ~ time*** zur festgesetzten Zeit; ***under the ~ conditions*** unter den gegebenen Umständen; **2.** **~ *to*** a) ergeben, verfallen (*dat.*): **~ *to drinking***, b) neigend zu: **~ *to boasting***; **3.** ⚖, *phls.* gegeben, bekannt; **4.** vor'ausgesetzt: **~ *health*** Gesundheit vorausgesetzt; **5.** in Anbetracht (*gen.*): **~ *his temperament***; **6.** *auf Dokumenten*: gegeben, ausgefertigt (am): **~ *this 10th day of May***; **~ *name*** *s. Am.* Vorname *m*.

giv·er ['gɪvə] *s.* **1.** Geber(in), Spender(-in); **2.** † (*Wechsel*)Aussteller *m*.

giz·mo ['gɪzməʊ] *s. Am.* F ‚Dingsbums' *n*.

giz·zard ['gɪzəd] *s.* **1.** *ichth., orn.* Muskelmagen *m*; **2.** F Magen *m*: ***that sticks in my ~***.

gla·brous ['gleɪbrəs] *adj.* ⚘, *zo.* kahl.

gla·cé ['glæseɪ] (*Fr.*) *adj.* **1.** glasiert, mit Zuckerguß; **2.** kandiert; **3.** Glacé..., Glanz... (*Leder, Stoff*).

gla·cial ['gleɪsjəl] *adj.* **1.** *geol.* Eis..., Gletscher...: **~ *epoch*** *od.* ***period*** Eiszeit *f*; **~ *man*** Eiszeitmensch *m*; **2.** ⚗ Eis...: **~ *acetic acid*** Eisessig *m*; **3.** eisig (*a. fig.*); **gla·ci·a·tion** [ˌglæsɪ'eɪʃn] *s.* **1.** Vereisung *f*; **2.** Vergletscherung *f*.

gla·cier ['glæsjə] *s.* Gletscher *m*.

glac·i·ol·o·gy [ˌglæsɪ'ɒlədʒɪ] *s.* Glaziolo'gie *f*, Gletscherkunde *f*.

gla·cis ['glæsɪs; *pl.* -sɪz] *s.* **1.** Abdachung *f*; **2.** ⚔ Gla'cis *n*.

glad [glæd] *adj.* □ → ***gladly***; **1.** (*pred.*) froh, erfreut (***of***, ***at*** über *acc.*): ***I am ~ of it*** ich freue mich darüber, es freut mich; ***I am ~ to hear*** (***to say***) es freut mich zu hören (sagen zu können); ***I am ~ to come*** ich komme gern; ***I should be ~ to know*** ich möchte gern wissen; **2.** freudig, froh, fröhlich, erfreulich: ***give s.o. the ~ eye*** *sl.* j-m e-n einladenden Blick zuwerfen, j-m schöne Augen machen; ***give s.o. the ~ hand*** → ***gladhand***; **~ *rags*** F ‚Sonntagsstaat' *m*; **~ *news*** frohe Kunde; **'glad·den** [-dn] *v/t.* erfreuen.

glade [gleɪd] *s.* Lichtung *f*, Schneise *f*.

'glad-hand *v/t.* F *j-n* herzlich *od.* 'überschwenglich begrüßen.

glad·i·a·tor ['glædɪeɪtə] *s.* Gladi'ator *m*; *fig.* Streiter *m*, Kämpfer *m*; **glad·i·a·to·ri·al** [ˌglædɪə'tɔːrɪəl] *adj.* Gladiatoren...

glad·i·o·lus [ˌglædɪ'əʊləs] *pl.* **-li** [-laɪ] *od.* **-lus·es** *s.* ⚘ Gladi'ole *f*.

glad·ly ['glædlɪ] *adv.* mit Freuden, gern(e); **glad·ness** ['glædnɪs] *s.* Freude *f*, Fröhlichkeit *f*; **glad·some** ['glædsəm] *adj.* □ *obs.* **1.** erfreulich; **2.** freudig, fröhlich.

Glad·stone (**bag**) ['glædstən] *s.* zweiteilige leichte Reisetasche.

glair [gleə] **I** *s.* **1.** Eiweiß *n*; **2.** Eiweißleim *m*; **3.** eiweißartige Sub'stanz; **II** *v/t.* **4.** mit Eiweiß(leim) bestreichen.

glaive [gleɪv] *s. poet.* (Breit)Schwert *n*.

glam·or *Am.* → ***glamour***.

glam·or·ize ['glæməraɪz] *v/t.* **1.** (mit viel Re'klame *etc.*) verherrlichen; **2.** e-n besonderen Zauber verleihen (*dat.*); **'glam·or·ous** [-rəs] *adj.* bezaubernd (schön), zauberhaft; **glam·our** ['glæmə] **I** *s.* **1.** Zauber *m*, Glanz *m*, bezaubernde Schönheit: **~ *boy*** a) Schönling *m*, b) ‚toller Kerl'; **~ *girl*** Glamourgirl *n*, (Re'klame-, Film)Schönheit *f*; ***cast a ~ over*** bezaubern, *j-n* in s-n Bann schlagen; **2.** falscher Glanz; **II** *v/t.* **3.** bezaubern.

glance¹ [glɑːns] **I** *v/i.* **1.** e-n Blick werfen, (rasch *od.* flüchtig) blicken (***at*** auf *acc.*): **~ *over*** (*od.* ***through***) ***a letter*** e-n Brief überfliegen; **2.** (auf)blitzen, (auf-)leuchten; **3.** **~ *off*** abgleiten (von) (*Messer etc.*), abprallen (von) (*Kugel etc.*): ***hit*** (*od.* ***strike***) ***s.o. a glancing blow*** j-n (mit einem Schlag) streifen; **4.** (***at***) *Thema* flüchtig berühren *od.* streifen, *bsd.* anspielen (auf *acc.*); **II** *v/t.* **5.** **~ *one's eye over*** (*od.* ***through***) → 1; **III** *s.* **6.** flüchtiger Blick (***at*** auf *acc.*): ***at a ~*** mit 'einem Blick; ***at first ~*** auf den ersten Blick; ***take a ~ at*** → 1; **7.** (Auf-)Blitzen *n*, (Auf)Leuchten *n*; **8.** Abprallen *n*, Abgleiten *n*; **9.** (***at***) flüchtige Erwähnung (*gen.*), Anspielung *f* (auf *acc.*).

glance² [glɑːns] *s. min.* Blende *f*, Glanz *m*: ***lead ~*** Bleiglanz.

gland¹ [glænd] *s. biol.* Drüse *f*.

gland² [glænd] *s.* ⚙ **1.** Dichtungsstutzen *m*; **2.** Stopfbuchse *f*.

glan·dered ['glændəd] *adj. vet.* rotzkrank; **'glan·der·ous** [-dərəs] *adj.* **1.** Rotz...; **2.** rotzkrank; **glan·ders** ['glændəz] *s. pl. sg. konstr.* Rotz(krankheit *f*) *m* (*der Pferde*).

glan·du·lar ['glændjʊlə] *adj. biol.* drüsig, Drüsen...: **~ *fever*** (Pfeiffersches) Drüsenfieber; **'glan·du·lous** [-əs] → ***glandular***.

glans [glænz] *pl.* **'glan·des** [-diːz] *s. anat.* Eichel *f*.

glare¹ [gleə] **I** *v/i.* **1.** grell leuchten *od.* sein, *Farben*: *a.* schreiend sein; → ***glaring***; **2.** wütend starren: **~ *at s.o.*** j-n wütend anstarren; **II** *s.* **3.** blendendes Licht, greller Schein, grelles Leuchten: ***be in the full ~ of publicity*** im Scheinwerferlicht der Öffentlichkeit stehen; **4.** *fig. das* Grelle *od.* Schreiende; **5.** wütender Blick.

glare² [gleə] *Am.* **I** *s.* spiegelglatte Fläche: ***a ~ of ice***; **II** *adj.* spiegelglatt: **~ *ice*** Glatteis *n*.

glar·ing ['gleərɪŋ] *adj.* □ **1.** grell (*Sonne etc.*), *Farben*: *a.* schreiend; **2.** *fig.* kraß, ekla'tant (*Fehler etc.*), (himmel)schreiend (*Unrecht etc.*); **3.** wütend, funkelnd (*Blick*).

glass [glɑːs] **I** *s.* **1.** Glas *n*: ***broken ~*** Glasscherben *pl.*; **2.** → ***glassware***; **3.** a) (Trink)Glas *n*, b) Glas(gefäß) *n*; **4.** Glas(voll) *n*: ***a ~ too much*** ein Gläschen zuviel; **5.** Glas(scheibe *f*) *n*; **6.** Spiegel *m*; **7.** *opt.* a) Lupe *f*, Vergrößerungsglas *n*, b) *pl. a.* ***pair of ~es*** Brille *f*, c) Linse *f*, Augenglas *n*, d) (Fern- *od.* Opern)Glas *n*, e) Mikro'skop *n*; **8.** Uhrglas *n*; **9.** a) Thermo'meter *n*, b) Baro'meter *n*; **10.** Sanduhr *f*; **II** *v/t.* **11.** verglasen: **~ *in*** einglasen; **~ bead** Glasperle *f*; **~ block** *s.* ⚠ Glasziegel *m*; **~ blow·er** *s.* Glasbläser *m*; **~ blow·ing** *s.* Glasbläse'rei *f*; **~ brick** → ***glass block***; **~ case** *s.* Glasschrank *m*, Vi'trine *f*; **~ cloth** *s.* **1.** ⚙ Glas(faser)gewebe *n*; **2.** Gläsertuch *n*; **~ cul·ture** *s.* 'Treibhauskulˌtur *f*; **~ cut·ter** *s.* **1.** Glasschleifer *m*; **2.** ⚙ Glasschneider *m* (*Werkzeug*); **~ eye** *s.* Glasauge *n*; **~ fi·bre** *s.* Glasfaser *f*, -fiber *f*.

glass·ful ['glɑːsfʊl] *pl.* **-fuls** *s. ein* Glasvoll *n*.

'glass|·house *s.* **1.** → ***glasswork*** 2; **2.** Treibhaus *n*: ***people who live in ~s should not throw stones*** wer im Glashaus sitzt, soll nicht mit Steinen werfen; **3.** ⚔ *Brit. sl.* ‚Bau' *m* (*Gefängnis*); **~ jaw** *s. Boxen*: F ‚Glaskinn' *n*; **~ pa·per** *s.* 'Glaspaˌpier *n*; **'~·ware** *s.* Glas(waren *pl.*) *n*, Glasgeschirr *n*, -sachen *pl.*; **~ wool** *s.* ⚙ Glaswolle *f*; **'~·work** *s.* ⚙ **1.** Glas(waren)herstellung *f*; **2.** *pl. mst sg. konstr.* 'Glashütte *f*, -faˌbrik *f*.

glass·y ['glɑːsɪ] *adj.* □ **1.** gläsern, glasartig, glasig; **2.** glasig (*Auge*).

Glas·we·gian [glæs'wiːdʒjən] **I** *adj.* aus Glasgow; **II** *s.* Glasgower(in).

Glau·ber('s) salt ['glɔːbə(z)] *s.* Glaubersalz *n*.

glau·co·ma [glɔː'kəʊmə] *s.* ⚕ Glau'kom *n*, grüner Star; **glau·cous** ['glɔːkəs] *adj.* graugrün.

glaze [gleɪz] **I** *v/t.* **1.** verglasen, mit Glasscheiben versehen: **~ *in*** einglasen; **2.** polieren, glätten; **3.** ⚙, *a. Küche*: glasieren, mit Gla'sur über'ziehen; **4.** *paint.* lasieren; **5.** ⚙ *Papier* satinieren;

6. *Augen* glasig machen; **II** *v/i.* **7.** e-e Gla'sur *od.* Poli'tur annehmen, blank werden; **8.** glasig werden (*Augen*); **III** *s.* **9.** Poli'tur *f*, Glätte *f*, Glanz *m*; **10.** a) Gla'sur *f* (*a. auf Kuchen etc.*), b) Gla'surmasse *f*; **11.** La'sur *f*; **12.** ⚙ Satinierung *f*; **13.** Glasigkeit *f*; **14.** a) Eisschicht *f*, b) ✈ Vereisung *f*, c) *Am.* Glatteis *n*; **glazed** [-zd] *adj.* **1.** verglast, Glas...: **~ *veranda***; **2.** ⚙ glatt, blank, poliert, Glanz...: **~ *paper*** Glanzpapier *n*; **~ *tile*** Kachel *f*; **3.** glasiert; **4.** lasiert; **5.** satiniert; **6.** poliert; **7.** glasig (*Augen*); **8.** vereist: **~ *frost*** *Brit.* Glatteis *n*; **'glaz·er** [-zə] *s.* ⚙ **1.** Glasierer *m*; **2.** Polierer *m*; **3.** Satinierer *m*; **4.** Polier-, Schmirgelscheibe *f*; **'gla·zier** [-zjə] *s.* Glaser *m*; **'glaz·ing** [-zɪŋ] *s.* **1.** a) Verglasen *n*, b) Glaserarbeit *f*; **2.** Fenster(scheiben) *pl.*; **3.** ⚙ *u. Küche*: a) Gla'sur *f*, b) Glasieren *n*; **4.** a) Poli'tur *f*, b) Polieren *n*; **5.** Satinieren *n*; **6.** *paint.* a) La'sur *f*, b) Lasieren *n*; **'glaz·y** [-zɪ] *adj.* **1.** glasig, glasiert; **2.** glanzlos, glasig (*Auge*).

gleam [gli:m] **I** *s.* schwacher Schein, Schimmer *m* (*a. fig.*): **~ *of hope*** Hoffnungsschimmer; ***the ~ in his eye*** das Funkeln s-r Augen; **II** *v/i.* glänzen, leuchten, schimmern, *Augen a.* funkeln.

glean [gli:n] **I** *v/t.* **1.** *Ähren* (auf-, nach-) lesen, *Feld* sauber lesen; **2.** *fig.* sammeln, zs.-tragen, *a.* her'ausfinden: **~ *from*** schließen *od.* entnehmen aus; **II** *v/i.* **3.** Ähren lesen; **'glean·er** [-nə] *s.* Ährenleser *m*; *fig.* Sammler *m*; **'glean·ings** [-nɪŋz] *s. pl.* **1.** 🌾 Nachlese *f*; **2.** *fig. das* Gesammelte.

glebe [gli:b] *s.* **1.** ⚖, *eccl.* Pfarrland *n*; **2.** *poet.* (Erd)Scholle *f*, Feld *n*.

glede [gli:d] *s. orn.* Gabelweihe *f*.

glee [gli:] *s.* **1.** Fröhlichkeit *f*, Ausgelassenheit *f*; **2.** (*a.* Schaden)Freude *f*, Froh'locken *n*; **3.** ♪ *hist.* Glee *m* (*geselliges Lied*): **~ *club*** *bsd. Am.* Gesangverein *m*; **'glee·ful** [-fʊl] *adj.* □ **1.** ausgelassen, fröhlich; **2.** schadenfroh, froh'lockend; **'glee·man** [-mən] *s.* [*irr.*] *hist.* fahrender Sänger.

glen [glen] *s.* Bergschlucht *f*, Klamm *f*.

glen·gar·ry [glen'gærɪ] *s.* Mütze *f der Hochlandschotten.*

glib [glɪb] *adj.* □ **1.** a) zungen-, schlagfertig, b) gewandt, ‚fix‘: ***a ~ tongue*** e-e glatte Zunge; **2.** oberflächlich; **'glib·ness** [-nɪs] *s.* **1.** Zungen-, Schlagfertigkeit *f*; Gewandtheit *f*; **2.** Glätte *f*, Oberflächlichkeit *f*.

glide [glaɪd] **I** *v/i.* **1.** gleiten (*a. fig.*): **~ *along*** dahingleiten, -fliegen (*a. Zeit*); **~ *out*** hinausgleiten, -schweben (*Person*); **2.** ✈ a) gleiten, e-n Gleitflug machen, b) segeln; **II** *s.* **3.** (Da'hin)Gleiten *n*; **4.** ✈ a) Gleitflug *m*, b) Segelflug *m*: **~ *path*** Gleitweg *m*; **5.** → ***glissade*** 2; **6.** *ling.* Gleitlaut *m*; **'glid·er** [-də] *s.* **1.** ⚓ Gleitboot *n*; **2.** ✈ a) Segelflugzeug *n*, b) *a.* **~ *pilot*** Segelflieger(in); **3.** *Skisport*: Gleiter(in); **'glid·ing** [-dɪŋ] *s.* **1.** Gleiten *n*; **2.** ✈ a) → ***glide*** 3, b) *das* Segelfliegen.

glim·mer ['glɪmə] **I** *v/i.* **1.** glimmen, schimmern; **II** *s.* **2.** a) Glimmen *n*, b) *a. fig.* Schimmer *m*, (schwacher) Schein: ***a ~ of hope*** ein Hoffnungsschimmer; **3.** *min.* Glimmer *m*.

glimpse [glɪmps] **I** *s.* **1.** flüchtiger (An-) Blick: ***catch a ~ of*** → 4; **2.** (***of***) flüchtiger Eindruck (von), kurzer Einblick (in *acc.*); **3.** *fig.* Schimmer *m*, schwache Ahnung; **II** *v/t.* **4.** *j-n, et.* (nur) flüchtig zu sehen bekommen, e-n flüchtigen Blick erhaschen von; **III** *v/i.* **5.** flüchtig blicken (***at*** auf *acc.*).

glint [glɪnt] **I** *s.* Schimmer *m*, Schein *m*, Glitzern *n*; **II** *v/i.* schimmern, glitzern, blinken.

glis·sade [glɪ'sɑ:d] **I** *s.* **1.** *mount.* Abfahrt *f*; **2.** *Tanz*: Glis'sade *f*, Gleitschritt *m*; **II** *v/i.* **3.** *mount.* abfahren; **4.** *Tanz*: Gleitschritte machen.

glis·ten ['glɪsn] **I** *v/i.* glitzern, glänzen; **II** *s.* Glitzern *n*, Glanz *m*.

glit·ter ['glɪtə] **I** *v/i.* **1.** glitzern, funkeln, *a. fig.* strahlen, glänzen; → ***gold*** 1; **II** *s.* **2.** Glitzern *n* (*etc.*), Glanz *m*; **3.** *fig.* Pracht *f*, Prunk *m*, Glanz *m*; **'glit·ter·ing** [-tərɪŋ] *adj.* □ **1.** glitzernd (*etc.*); **2.** glanzvoll, prächtig.

gloat [gləʊt] *v/i.*: **~ *over*** sich weiden an (*dat.*): a) verzückt betrachten (*acc.*), b) sich hämisch *od.* diebisch freuen über (*acc.*); **'gloat·ing** [-tɪŋ] *adj.* □ schadenfroh, hämisch.

glob [glɒb] *s.* F ‚Klacks‘ *m*, ‚Klecks‘ *m*.

glob·al ['gləʊbl] *adj.* glo'bal: a) 'weltumˌfassend, Welt..., b) um'fassend, pau'schal, Gesamt...; **'glo·bate** [-beɪt] *adj.* kugelförmig.

globe [gləʊb] **I** *s.* **1.** Kugel *f*: **~ *of the eye*** Augapfel *m*; **2.** Pla'net *m*: ***the ~*** der Erdball, die Erdkugel, die Erde; **3.** *geogr.* Globus *m*; **4.** a) Lampenglocke *f*, b) Goldfischglas *n*; **5.** *hist.* Reichsapfel *m*; **II** *v/t. u. v/i.* **6.** kugelförmig machen (werden); **~ ar·ti·choke** *s.* ⚘ Arti'schocke *f*; **'~·fish** *s.* Kugelfisch *m*; **'~ˌtrot·ter** *s.* Weltenbummler(in), Globetrotter(in); **'~ˌtrot·ting I** *s.* Globetrotten *n*; **II** *adj.* Weltenbummler..., Globetrotter...

glo·bose ['gləʊbəʊs] → ***globular*** 1; **glo·bos·i·ty** [gləʊ'bɒsətɪ] *s.* Kugelform *f*, -gestalt *f*; **glob·u·lar** ['glɒbjʊlə] *adj.* □ **1.** kugelförmig: **~ *lightning*** Kugelblitz *m*; **2.** aus Kügelchen (bestehend); **glob·ule** ['glɒbju:l] *s.* Kügelchen *n*.

glom·er·ate ['glɒmərət] *adj.* (zs.-)geballt, knäuelförmig; **glom·er·a·tion** [ˌglɒmə'reɪʃn] *s.* Zs.-ballung *f*, Knäuel *m*, *n*.

gloom [glu:m] **I** *s.* **1.** *a. fig.* Dunkel *n*, Düsterkeit *f*; **2.** *fig.* düstere Stimmung, Schwermut *f*, Trübsinn *m*: ***cast a ~ over*** e-n Schatten werfen über (*acc.*); **II** *v/i.* **3.** traurig *od.* verdrießlich *od.* düster blicken *od.* aussehen; **4.** sich verdüstern; **'gloom·i·ness** [-mɪnɪs] *s.* **1.** → ***gloom*** 1, 2; **2.** *fig.* Hoffnungslosigkeit *f*; **'gloom·y** [-mɪ] *adj.* □ **1.** *a. fig.* düster, trübe; **2.** schwermütig, trübsinnig, düster, traurig; **3.** hoffnungslos.

glo·ri·fi·ca·tion [ˌglɔ:rɪfɪ'keɪʃn] *s.* **1.** Verherrlichung *f*; **2.** *eccl.* a) Verklärung *f*, b) Lobpreisung *f*; **3.** *Brit.* F lautes Fest; **glo·ri·fied** ['glɔ:rɪfaɪd] *adj.* F ‚besser‘: ***a ~ barn***; ***a ~ office boy***; **glo·ri·fy** ['glɔ:rɪfaɪ] *v/t.* **1.** verherrlichen; **2.** *eccl.* a) lobpreisen, b) verklären; **3.** erstrahlen lassen, e-e Zierde sein (*gen.*); **4.** F ‚aufmotzen‘, ‚hochjubeln‘; → ***glorified***.

glo·ri·ole ['glɔ:rɪəʊl] *s.* Glori'ole *f*, Heiligenschein *m*.

glo·ri·ous ['glɔ:rɪəs] *adj.* □ **1.** ruhmvoll, -reich, glorreich; **2.** herrlich, prächtig, wunderbar (*alle a.* F *fig.*): ***a ~ mess*** *iro.* ein schönes Chaos.

glo·ry ['glɔ:rɪ] **I** *s.* **1.** Ruhm *m*, Ehre *f*: ***covered in ~*** ruhmbedeckt; ***~ be!*** F a) juchhu!, b) Donnerwetter!; → ***Old Glory***; **2.** Stolz *m*, Zierde *f*, Glanz (-punkt) *m*; **3.** *eccl.* Verehrung *f*, Lobpreisung *f*; **4.** Herrlichkeit *f*, Glanz *m*, Pracht *f*, Glorie *f*; höchste Blüte; **5.** *eccl.* a) himmlische Herrlichkeit, b) Himmel *m*: ***gone to ~*** F in die ewigen Jagdgründe eingegangen (*tot*); ***send to ~*** F *j-n* ins Jenseits befördern; **6.** → ***gloriole***; **II** *v/i.* **7.** sich freuen, triumphieren, froh'locken (***in*** über *acc.*); **8.** (***in***) sich sonnen (in *dat.*), sich rühmen (*gen.*); **'~-hole** *s.* F a) Rumpelkammer *f od.* -kiste *f*; b) Kramschublade *f*.

gloss¹ [glɒs] **I** *s.* **1.** Glanz *m*: **~ *paint*** Glanzlack *m*; **2.** *fig.* äußerer Glanz; **II** *v/t.* **3.** glänzend machen; **4.** *mst* **~ *over*** *fig.* a) beschönigen, b) vertuschen.

gloss² [glɒs] **I** *s.* **1.** (Rand)Glosse *f*, Erläuterung *f*, Anmerkung *f*; **2.** Kommen'tar *m*, Auslegung *f*; **II** *v/t.* **3.** glossieren; **4.** *oft* **~ *over*** (absichtlich) irreführend deuten; **'glos·sa·ry** [-sərɪ] *s.* Glos'sar *n*.

gloss·eme [glɒ'si:m] *s. ling.* Glos'sem *n*.

gloss·i·ness ['glɒsɪnɪs] *s.* Glanz *m*; **gloss·y** ['glɒsɪ] **I** *adj.* □ **1.** glänzend: **~ *paper*** (Hoch)Glanzpapier *n*; **2.** auf ('Hoch)Glanzpaˌpier gedruckt, Hochglanz...: **~ *magazine***; **3.** *fig.* a) raffiniert, b) prächtig (aufgemacht); **II** *s.* **4.** 'Hochglanzmagaˌzin *n*.

glot·tal ['glɒtl] *adj.* **1.** *anat.* Stimmritzen...: **~ *chink*** → ***glottis***; **2.** *ling.* glot'tal: **~ *stop*** Knacklaut *m*; **glot·tis** ['glɒtɪs] *s. anat.* Stimmritze *f*.

glove [glʌv] **I** *s.* **1.** Handschuh *m*: ***fit (s.o.) like a ~*** a) (j-m) wie angegossen sitzen, b) *fig.* (auf j-n) haargenau passen; ***take the ~s off*** Ernst machen, ‚massiv werden‘; ***with the ~s off***, ***without ~s*** unsanft, rücksichts-, schonungslos; **2.** *sport* (Box-, Fecht-, Reit- *etc.*) Handschuh *m*; **3.** ***fling*** (*od.* ***throw***) ***down the ~*** (***to s.o.***) *fig.* (j-m) den Fehdehandschuh hinwerfen, (j-n) herausfordern; ***pick*** (*od.* ***take***) ***up the ~*** die Herausforderung annehmen; **II** *v/t.* **4.** mit Handschuhen bekleiden: **~*d*** behandschuht; **~ box**, **~ com·part·ment** *s. mot.* Handschuhfach *n*; **~ pup·pet** *s.* Handpuppe *f*.

glow [gləʊ] **I** *v/i.* **1.** glühen; **2.** *fig.* glühen: a) leuchten, strahlen, b) brennen (*Gesicht*); **3.** *fig.* (er)glühen, brennen (***with*** vor *dat.*): **~ *with anger*** vor Zorn glühen; **II** *s.* **4.** Glühen *n*, Glut *f*: ***in a ~*** glühend; **5.** *fig.* Glut *f*: a) Glühen *n*, Leuchten *n*, b) Hitze *f*, Röte *f* (*im Gesicht etc.*): ***in a ~***, ***all of a ~*** glühend, ganz gerötet, c) Feuer *n*, Leidenschaft *f*.

glow·er ['glaʊə] *v/i.* finster (drein)blikken: **~ *at*** finster anblicken.

glow·ing ['gləʊɪŋ] *adj.* □ **1.** glühend; **2.** *fig.* glühend: a) leuchtend, strahlend, b) brennend, c) 'überschwenglich, begeistert: ***a ~ account***; ***in ~ colo(u)rs*** in glühenden *od.* leuchtenden Farben

schildern etc.
glow| plug *s. mot.* Glühkerze *f*; **'~·worm** *s.* Glühwürmchen *n.*
gloze [gləʊz] → ***gloss*** 4.
glu·cose ['glu:kəʊs] *s.* ⚗ Glu'kose *f*, Glu'cose *f*, Traubenzucker *m.*
glue [glu:] **I** *s.* **1.** Leim *m*; **2.** Klebstoff *m*; **II** *v/t.* **3.** leimen, kleben (**on** auf *acc.*, **to** an *acc.*): **~ (together)** zs.-kleben; **4.** *fig.* (**to**) heften (auf *acc.*), drücken (an *acc.*, gegen): ***she remained ~d to her mother*** sie ‚klebte' an ihrer Mutter; ***~d to his TV set*** *er saß* wie angewachsen vor dem Bildschirm; **glue·y** ['glu:ɪ] *adj.* klebrig.
glum [glʌm] *adj.* □ **1.** verdrossen; **2.** bedrückt, niedergeschlagen.
glume [glu:m] *s.* ⚘ Spelze *f.*
glut [glʌt] **I** *v/t.* **1.** *den Hunger* stillen; **2.** über'sättigen (*a. fig.*): ***~ o.s. on*** (*od.* ***with***) sich überessen mit *od.* an (*dat.*); **3.** ⚕ *Markt* über'schwemmen; **4.** verstopfen; **II** *s.* **5.** Über'sättigung *f*; **6.** ⚕ 'Überangebot *n*, Schwemme *f*: ***~ of eggs***; ***a ~ in the market*** e-e Marktschwemme.
glu·tam·ic ac·id [glu:'tæmɪk] *s.* ⚗ Gluta'minsäure *f.*
glu·ten ['glu:tən] *s.* ⚗ Kleber *m*, Glu'ten *n*; **'glu·ti·nous** [-tɪnəs] *adj.* □ klebrig.
glut·ton ['glʌtn] *s.* **1.** Vielfraß *m* (*a. zo.*); **2.** *fig. ein* Unersättlicher: ***a ~ for books*** ein Bücherwurm, e-e Leseratte; ***a ~ for work*** ein Arbeitstier; **'glut·ton·ous** [-nəs] *adj.* □ gefräßig, unersättlich (*a. fig.*); **'glut·ton·y** [-nɪ] *s.* Gefräßigkeit *f*, Unersättlichkeit *f* (*a. fig.*).
glyc·er·in(e) ['glɪsəri:n], **'glyc·er·ol** [-rɒl] *s.* ⚗ Glyze'rin *n.*
glyph [glɪf] *s.* ⚠ Glypte *f*, Glyphe *f*: a) (verti'kale) Furche *od.* Rille, b) Skulp'tur *f.*
glyp·tic ['glɪptɪk] **I** *adj.* Steinschneide...; **II** *s. pl. sg. konstr.* Glyptik *f*, Steinschneidekunst *f*; **glyp·tog·ra·phy** [glɪp'tɒgrəfɪ] *s.* Glyptogra'phie *f*: a) Steinschneidekunst *f*, b) Gemmenkunde *f.*
G-man ['dʒi:mæn] *s.* [*irr.*] F G-Mann *m*, FB'I-A͵gent *m.*
gnarled [nɑ:ld] *adj.* **1.** knorrig (*Baum*, *a. Hand, Person etc.*); **2.** *fig.* mürrisch, ruppig.
gnash [næʃ] *v/t.* **1.** *et.* knirschend beißen; **2.** ***~ one's teeth*** mit den Zähnen knirschen (*vor Wut etc.*): ***wailing and ~ing of teeth*** Heulen u. Zähneklappern *n*; **'gnash·ers** [-ʃəz] *s. pl.* F ‚dritte Zähne' *pl.*
gnat [næt] *s. zo.* **1.** (Stech)Mücke *f*: ***strain at a ~*** *fig.* Haarspalterei betreiben; **2.** *Am.* Kriebelmücke *f.*
gnaw [nɔ:] **I** *v/t.* **1.** nagen an (*dat.*) (*a. fig.*), ab-, zernagen; **2.** zerfressen (*Säure etc.*); **3.** *fig.* quälen, zermürben; **II** *v/i.* **4.** nagen: ***~ at*** → 1; **5.** ***~ into*** sich einfressen in (*acc.*); **6.** *fig.* nagen, zermürben; **gnaw·er** ['nɔ:ə] *s. zo.* Nagetier *n*; **gnaw·ing** ['nɔ:ɪŋ] **I** *adj.* nagend (*a. fig.*); **II** *s.* Nagen *n* (*a. fig.*); *fig.* Qual *f.*
gneiss [naɪs] *s. geol.* Gneis *m.*
gnome¹ [nəʊm] *s.* **1.** Gnom *m*, *Zwerg m* (*beide a. contp. Person*), Kobold *m*; **2.** Gartenzwerg *m.*
gnome² ['nəʊmi:] *s.* Gnome *f*, Sinnspruch *m.*
gnom·ish ['nəʊmɪʃ] *adj.* gnomenhaft, zwergenhaft.
gno·sis ['nəʊsɪs] *s. phls.* Gnosis *f*; **Gnos·tic** ['nɒstɪk] **I** *adj.* gnostisch; **II** *s.* Gnostiker *m*; **Gnos·ti·cism** ['nɒstɪsɪzəm] *s.* Gnosti'zismus *m.*
gnu [nu:] *s. zo.* Gnu *n.*
go [gəʊ] **I** *pl.* **goes** [gəʊz] *s.* **1.** Gehen *n*: ***on the ~*** F ständig in Bewegung, immer ‚auf Achse'; ***from the word ~*** F von Anfang an; ***it's a ~!*** abgemacht!; **2.** F Schwung *m*, ‚Schmiß' *m*: ***he is full of ~*** er hat Schwung, er ist voller Leben *od.* sehr unternehmungslustig; **3.** F Mode *f*: ***be all the ~*** große Mode sein; **4.** F Erfolg *m*: ***make a ~ of it*** es zu e-m Erfolg machen, bei *od.* mit et. Erfolg haben; ***it's no ~!*** es geht nicht!, nichts zu machen!; **5.** F Versuch *m*: ***have a ~ at it!*** probier's doch mal!; ***at one ~*** auf 'einen Schlag, auf Anhieb; ***at the first ~*** gleich beim ersten Versuch; ***it's your ~!*** du bist an der Reihe *od.* dran!; **6.** F ‚Geschichte' *f*: ***what a ~!*** 'ne schöne Geschichte *od.* Bescherung!; ***it was a near ~!*** es ging gerade noch (mal) gut!; **7.** F a) Porti'on *f* (*e-r Speise*), b) Glas *n*: ***his third ~ of brandy*** sein dritter Kognak; **8.** Anfall *m* (*e-r Krankheit*): ***my second ~ of influenza*** m-e zweite Grippe; **II** *adj.* **9.** ⚙ F: ***you are ~ (for take-off)!*** alles klar (zum Start)!; **III** *v/i.* [*irr.*] **10.** gehen, fahren, reisen, sich begeben (**to** nach): ***~ on foot*** zu Fuß gehen; ***~ by train*** mit dem Zug fahren; ***~ by plane*** (*od.* ***air***) mit dem Flugzeug reisen, fliegen; ***~ to Paris*** nach Paris reisen *od.* gehen; ***there he goes!*** da ist er (ja)!; ***who goes there?*** ⚔ wer da?; **11.** verkehren, fahren (*Bus, Zug etc.*); **12.** (fort)gehen, abfahren, abreisen (**to** nach): ***don't ~ yet*** geh noch nicht (fort)!; ***let me ~!*** a) laß mich gehen!, b) laß mich los!; **13.** anfangen, loslegen: ***~!*** *sport* los!; ***~ to it!*** mach dich dran!, los!; ***here you ~ again!*** F jetzt fängst du schon wieder an!; ***here we ~ again*** F jetzt geht das schon wieder los!; ***just ~ and try it!*** versuch's doch mal!; ***here goes!*** also los!, jetzt geht's los!; **14.** gehen, führen: ***this road goes to York***; **15.** sich erstrecken, reichen, gehen (**to** bis): ***the belt doesn't ~ round her waist*** der Gürtel geht *od.* reicht nicht um ihre Taille; ***it goes a long way*** es reicht lange (aus); ***as far as it goes*** bis zu e-m gewissen Grade, soweit man das sagen kann; **16.** *fig.* gehen: ***~ as far as to say*** so weit gehen zu sagen; ***let it ~ at that!*** laß es dabei bewenden!; ***~ all out*** F sich ins Zeug legen (**for** für); *s. die Verbindungen mit anderen Stichwörtern*; **17.** ⅍ (**into**) gehen (in *acc.*), enthalten sein (in *dat.*): ***5 into 10 goes twice***; **18.** gehen, passen (**in**, **into** in *acc.*): ***it does not ~ into my pocket***; **19.** gehören (**in**, **into** in *acc.*, **on** auf *acc.*): ***the books ~ on this shelf*** die Bücher gehören *od.* kommen auf dieses Regal; **20.** ***~ to*** gehen an (*acc.*) (*Siegerpreis etc.*), zufallen (*dat.*) (*Erbe*); **21.** ⚙ *u. fig.* gehen, laufen, funktionieren: ***get ~ing*** ⚙ in Gang kommen, *fig. a.* in Schwung *od.* Fahrt kommen (*Person, Party etc.*), *Person*: *a.* loslegen; ***get s.th.*** (*od.* ***s.o.***) ***~ing*** et. (*Maschine, Projekt etc.*) in Gang bringen, et. (*Party etc.*) (*od.* j-n) in Schwung *od.* Fahrt bringen; ***keep ~ing*** ⚙ weiterlaufen, *fig.* weitermachen (*Person*); ***that hope kept her ~ing*** diese Hoffnung hielt sie aufrecht; ***this sum will keep you ~ing*** diese Summe wird dir (fürs erste) weiterhelfen; **22.** *kalt, schlecht, verrückt etc.* werden: ***~ blind*** erblinden; ***~ Conservative*** zu den Konservativen übergehen; ***~ decimal*** das Dezimalsystem einführen; **23.** (gewöhnlich) *in e-m Zustand* sein, sich befinden: ***~ armed*** bewaffnet sein; ***~ in rags*** (ständig) in Lumpen herumlaufen; ***~ hungry*** hungern; **24.** ***~ by*** (*od.* [***up***]***on***) sich halten an (*acc.*), gehen *od.* sich richten *od.* urteilen nach: ***have nothing to ~*** (***up***)***on*** keine Anhaltspunkte haben; ***~ing by her clothes*** ihrer Kleidung nach (zu urteilen); **25.** 'umgehen, im 'Umlauf sein, kursieren (*Gerüchte etc.*): ***the story goes*** es heißt, man erzählt sich; **26.** gelten (**for** für): ***what he says goes*** F was er sagt, gilt; ***that goes for you too!*** das gilt auch für dich!; ***it goes without saying*** das versteht sich von selbst; **27.** ***~ by the name of*** a) unter dem Namen ... laufen, b) auf den Namen ... hören (*Hund*); **28.** im allgemeinen sein: ***as men ~*** wie Männer eben *od.* (nun ein-) mal sind; **29.** vergehen, verstreichen: ***how time goes!***; ***one minute to ~*** noch e-e Minute; **30.** ⚕ (weg)gehen, verkauft werden: ***the coats went for £60***; **31.** (**on**, **in**) ausgegeben werden (für), aufgehen (in *dat.*) (*Geld*): ***all his money went in drink***; **32.** dazu beitragen, dienen (**to** zu): ***it goes to show*** dies zeigt, daran erkennt man; ***this only goes to show you the truth*** dies dient nur dazu, Ihnen die Wahrheit zu zeigen; **33.** (aus)gehen, verlaufen, sich entwickeln *od.* gestalten: ***it went well*** es ging gut (aus), es lief (alles) gut; ***things have gone badly with me*** es ist mir schlecht ergangen; ***the decision went against him*** die Entscheidung fiel zu s-n Ungunsten aus; ***~ big*** F ein Riesenerfolg sein; **34.** ***~ with*** gehen *od.* sich vertragen mit, passen zu: ***black goes well with yellow***; **35.** ertönen, läuten (*Glocke*), schlagen (*Uhr*): ***the door bell went*** es klingelte; ***bang went the gun*** die Kanone machte bumm; **36.** lauten (*Worte etc.*), gehen: ***this is how the tune goes*** so geht die Melodie; **37.** gehen, verschwinden, abgeschafft werden: ***my hat is gone!*** mein Hut ist weg!; ***he must ~*** er muß weg; ***these laws must ~*** diese Gesetze müssen weg; ***warmongering must ~!*** Schluß mit der Kriegshetze!; **38.** (da'hin)schwinden: ***his strength is ~ing***; ***my eyesight is ~ing*** m-e Augen werden immer schlechter; ***trade is ~ing*** der Handel kommt zum Erliegen; ***the shoes are ~ing*** die Schuhe gehen (langsam) kaputt; **39.** sterben: ***he is*** (***dead and***) ***gone*** er ist tot; **40.** (*pres. p. mit inf.*) *zum Ausdruck e-r Zukunft, e-r Absicht od. et. Unabänderlichem*: ***it is ~ing to rain*** es wird (gleich *od.* bald) regnen; ***he is ~ing to read it*** er wird *od.* will es (bald) lesen; ***she is ~ing to have a baby*** sie bekommt ein Kind; ***I was*** (***just***) ***~ing to do it*** ich wollte es

eben tun, ich war gerade dabei *od.* im Begriff, es zu tun; **41.** (*mit nachfolgendem Gerundium*) *mst* gehen: **~ swimming** schwimmen gehen; **he goes frightening people** er erschreckt immer die Leute; **42.** (da'ran)gehen, sich anschicken: **he went to find him** er ging ihn suchen; **he went and sold it** F er hat es doch tatsächlich verkauft; **43.** erlaubt sein: **everything goes here** hier ist alles erlaubt; **anything goes!** F alles ist ‚drin' (*möglich*); **44. pizzas to ~!** *Am.* Pizzas zum Mitnehmen!; **IV** *v/t.* [*irr.*] **45.** *e-n Betrag* wetten, setzen (**on** auf *acc.*); **46. ~ it** F a) (mächtig) rangehen, sich dahinterklemmen, b) es toll treiben, ‚auf den Putz hauen': **~ it alone** es ganz allein(e) machen; **~ it!** ran!, feste!, drauf!;

Zssgn mit prp.:

go| a·bout *v/i.* in Angriff nehmen, sich machen an (*acc.*), anpacken (*acc.*); **~ aft·er** *v/i.* **1.** nachlaufen (*dat.*); **2.** → **go for** 4; **~ a·gainst** *v/i.* wider'streben (*dat.*), *j-s Prinzipien* zu'widerlaufen; **~ at** *v/i.* **1.** losgehen auf (*acc.*); **2.** → **go about**; **~ be·hind** *v/i.* unter'suchen, auf den Grund gehen (*dat.*); **~ be·tween** *v/i.* vermitteln zwischen (*dat.*); **~ be·yond** *v/i. fig.* über'schreiten, *Erwartungen etc.* über'treffen; **~ by** *v/i.* **1.** sich richten nach, sich halten an (*acc.*), urteilen nach; **2.** auf *e-n Namen* hören; **~ for** *v/i.* **1.** holen (gehen); **2.** *e-n Spaziergang etc.* machen; **3.** gelten als *od.* für; **4.** streben nach, sich bemühen um; **5.** F losgehen auf (*acc.*), sich stürzen auf (*acc.*), *fig.* herziehen über (*acc.*); **6.** *sl.* ‚stehen' auf (*dat.*); **~ in·to** *v/i.* **1.** hin'eingehen in (*acc.*); **2.** eintreten in (*ein Geschäft etc.*): **~ business** Kaufmann werden; **3.** (genau) unter'suchen *od.* prüfen; eingehen auf (*acc.*); **4.** geraten in (*acc.*): **~ a faint** in Ohnmacht fallen; **~ off** *v/i.* **1.** abgehen von; **2.** *j-n, et.* nicht mehr mögen *od.* wollen; **~ on** *v/i.* **1.** sich stützen auf (*acc.*); **2.** sich richten nach, sich halten an (*acc.*), urteilen nach: **I have nothing to ~** ich habe keine Anhaltspunkte; **~ o·ver** → **go through** 1, 2, 3; **~ through** *v/i.* **1.** 'durchgehen, -nehmen, -sprechen; **2.** (gründlich) über'prüfen *od.* unter'suchen; **3.** 'durchsehen, -gehen, -lesen; **4.** durch'suchen; **5.** a) 'durchmachen, erleiden, b) erleben; **6.** *Vermögen* 'durchbringen; **~ with** *v/i.* **1.** begleiten; **2.** gehören zu; **3.** über'einstimmen mit; **4.** passen zu; **5.** mit *j-m* ‚gehen'; **~ without** *v/i.* **1.** auskommen ohne, sich behelfen ohne; **2.** verzichten auf (*acc.*);

Zssgn mit adv.:

go| a·bout *v/i.* **1.** um'hergehen, -fahren, -reisen; **2.** a) kursieren, im 'Umlauf sein (*Gerüchte etc.*), b) 'umgehen (*Grippe etc.*); **3.** ⚓ wenden; **~ a·head** *v/i.* **1.** vorwärts-, vor'angehen: **~!** *fig.* los!, nur zu!; **~ with** a) weitermachen mit, b) Ernst machen mit, durchführen; **2.** (*erfolgreich*) vor'ankommen; **3.** *bsd. sport* sich an die Spitze setzen; **~ a·long** *v/i.* **1.** weitergehen; **2.** *fig.* weitermachen; **3.** mitgehen, -kommen (**with** mit); **4. ~ with** einverstanden sein mit, mitmachen bei; **~ a·round** *v/i.* **1.** → **go about** 1, 2; **2.** → **go round**; **~ back** *v/i.* **1.** zu'rückgehen: **~ to** *fig.* zurückgehen auf (*acc.*), zurückreichen bis; **2. ~ on** *fig.* a) *j-n* im Stich lassen, b) *sein Wort etc.* nicht halten, c) *Entscheidung* rückgängig machen; **~ by** *v/i.* **1.** vor'beigehen (*a. Chance etc.*), -fahren; **2.** vergehen (*Zeit*): **in days gone by** in längst vergangenen Tagen; **~ down** *v/i.* **1.** hin'untergehen: **~ in history** *fig.* in die Geschichte eingehen; **2.** 'untergehen (*Schiff, Sonne etc.*); **3.** zu Boden gehen (*Boxer etc.*); **4.** *thea.* fallen (*Vorhang*); **5.** zu'rückgehen, sinken, fallen (*Fieber, Preise etc.*); **6.** a) sich im Niedergang befinden, b) zugrunde gehen; **7.** *sport* absteigen; **8.** ‚(runter)rutschen' (*Essen*); **9.** *fig.* (**with**) a) Anklang finden, ‚ankommen' (bei): **it went down well with him**, b) ‚geschluckt' werden: **that won't ~ with me** das nehme ich dir nicht ab; **10.** *Brit.* London verlassen; **11.** *univ. Brit.* a) die Universi'tät verlassen, b) in die Ferien gehen; **~ in** *v/i.* **1.** hin'eingehen: **~ and win!** auf in den Kampf!; **2. ~ for** a) sich befassen mit, betreiben, *Sport etc.* treiben, b) mitmachen bei, c) *ein Examen* machen, d) hinarbeiten auf (*acc.*), e) sich einsetzen für, f) sich begeistern für; **~ off** *v/i.* **1.** fort-, weggehen, -laufen; (*Zug etc.*) abfahren; *thea.* abgehen; **2.** losgehen (*Gewehr, Sprengladung etc.*); **3.** (**into**) los-, her'ausplatzen (mit), ausbrechen (in *Gelächter etc.*); **4.** nachlassen, sich verschlechtern; **5.** (*gut etc.*) von'statten gehen; **6.** a) einschlafen, b) ohnmächtig werden; **7.** verderben, schlecht werden (*Essen etc.*), sauer werden (*Milch*); **8.** ausgehen (*Licht etc.*); **~ on** *v/i.* **1.** weitergehen *od.* -fahren; **2.** weitermachen, fortfahren (**with** mit; **doing** zu tun): **~!** a) (mach) weiter!, b) *iro.* hör auf!, ach komm!; **~ reading** weiterlesen; **3.** fortdauern, weitergehen; **4.** vor sich gehen, vorgehen, passieren; **5.** sich ‚aufführen': **don't ~ like that!** hör schon auf damit!; **6.** F a) unaufhörlich reden (**about** über *acc.*, von), b) ständig her'umnörgeln (**at** an *dat.*); **7.** angehen (*Licht etc.*); **8. ~ for** gehen auf (*acc.*), bald sein: **it's going on for five o'clock**; **~ out** *v/i.* **1.** ausgehen: a) spazierengehen, b) zu Veranstaltungen *od.* Gesellschaften gehen, c) erlöschen (*Feuer, Licht*): **~ fishing** fischen (*od.* zum Fischen) gehen; **2.** in den Streik treten; **3.** aus der Mode kommen; **4.** *pol.* abgelöst werden; **5.** *sport* ausscheiden; **6.** zu'rückgehen (*Flut*); **7. ~ to** *j-m* entgegenschlagen (*Herz*), sich *j-m* zuwenden (*Sympathie*); **~ o·ver** *v/i.* **1.** hin'übergehen (**to** zu); **2.** 'übertreten, -gehen (**to** zu *e-r anderen Partei etc.*); **3.** vertagt werden; **4. ~ big** F ein Bombenerfolg sein; **~ round** *v/i.* **1.** her'umgehen (*a. fig. j-m im Kopf*); **2.** (für alle) (aus)reichen: **there is enough** (**of it**) **to ~**; **~ through** *v/i.* **1.** 'durchgehen, angenommen werden (*Antrag*); **2. ~ with** 'durchführen; **~ to·geth·er** *v/i.* **1.** zs.-passen (*Farben etc.*); **2.** F mitein'ander ‚gehen' (*Liebespaar*); **~ un·der** *v/i.* **1.** 'untergehen (*a. fig.*); **2.** *fig.* ‚eingehen' (*Firma etc.*), ‚ka'puttgehen'; **~ up** *v/i.* **1.** hin'aufgehen (*a. fig.*); **2.** *fig.* steigen (*Fieber, Preise etc.*); **3.** *thea.* hochgehen (*Vorhang*); **4.** gebaut werden; **5.** *Brit.* nach London fahren; **6.** *Brit.* (zum Se'mesteranfang) zur Universi'tät gehen; **7.** *sport* aufsteigen.

goad [gəʊd] **I** *s.* **1.** Stachelstock *m des Viehtreibers*; **2.** *fig.* Stachel *m*; Ansporn *m*; **II** *v/t.* **3.** antreiben; **4.** *mst* **~ on** *fig. j-n* an-, aufstacheln, (an)treiben (**into doing s.th.** dazu, et. zu tun).

'go-a·head I *adj.* **1.** voller Unter'nehmungsgeist *od.* Initia'tive, zielstrebig; **II** *s.* **2.** (Mensch *m* mit) Unter'nehmungsgeist *od.* Initia'tive; **3. get the ~** (**on**) ‚grünes Licht' bekommen (für); **give s.o. the ~** j-m ‚grünes Licht' geben.

goal [gəʊl] *s.* **1.** Ziel *n* (*a. fig.*); **2.** *sport* a) Ziel *n*, b) (*Fußball- etc.*)Tor *n*, c) Tor(erfolg *m*, -schuß *m*) *n*: **score a ~** ein Tor schießen; **~ a·re·a** *s. sport* Torraum *m*; **'~ˌget·ter** *s.* Torjäger *m*.

goal·ie ['gəʊlɪ] F → **goalkeeper**.

'goal|ˌkeep·er *s. sport* Tormann *m*, -wart *m*, -hüter(in); **~ kick** *s.* (Tor-)Abstoß *m*; **~ line** *s.* a) Torlinie *f*, b) Torauslinie *f*, c) *Rugby*: Mallinie *f*; **'~·mouth** *s.* Torraum *m*; **~ post** *s.* Torpfosten *m*.

ˌgo-as-you-'please *adj.* ungebunden.

goat [gəʊt] *s.* **1.** a) Ziege *f*, b) *a.* **he-~** Ziegenbock *m*: **play the** (**giddy**) **~** *fig.* herumkaspern; **get s.o.'s ~** *sl.* j-n ‚auf die Palme bringen'; **2.** *fig.* (geiler) Bock; **3.** F Sündenbock *m*; **4.** ♑ *ast.* → **Capricorn**; **goat·ee** [gəʊ'tiː] *s.* Spitzbart *m*; **'goat·herd** *s.* Ziegenhirt *m*; **'goat·ish** [-tɪʃ] *adj.* □ **1.** bockig; **2.** *fig.* geil.

'goat|'s-beard *s.* ⚘ Bocks- *od.* Geiß- *od.* Ziegenbart *m*; **'~·skin** *s.* Ziegenleder(flasche *f*) *n*; **'~·suck·er** *s. orn.* Ziegenmelker *m*.

gob¹ [gɒb] *s.* F **1.** (*a.* Schleim)Klumpen *m*; **2.** *oft pl.* ‚Haufen' *m*, Menge *f*.

gob² [gɒb] *s.* ⚓ *Am. sl.* ‚Blaujacke' *f*, Ma'trose *m* (*US-Kriegsmarine*).

gob·bet ['gɒbɪt] *s.* Brocken *m*.

gob·ble¹ ['gɒbl] **I** *v/t. mst* **~ up** verschlingen (*a. fig.*); **II** *v/i.* gierig essen.

gob·ble² ['gɒbl] **I** *v/i.* kollern (*Truthahn*); **II** *s.* Kollern *n*.

gob·ble·dy·gook ['gɒbldɪguːk] *s.* F **1.** ‚Be'amtenchiˌnesisch' *n*; **2.** (Be'rufs-) Jarˌgon *m*; **3.** ‚Geschwafel' *n*.

gob·bler¹ ['gɒblə] *s.* Fresser(in).

gob·bler² ['gɒblə] *s.* Truthahn *m*, Puter *m*.

Gob·e·lin ['gəʊbəlɪn] **I** *adj.* Gobelin…; **II** *s.* Gobe'lin *m*.

'go-beˌtween *s.* **1.** Mittelsmann *m*, Vermittler(in); **2.** Makler(in); **3.** Kuppler(in).

gob·let ['gɒblɪt] *s.* **1.** *obs.* Po'kal *m*; **2.** Kelchglas *n*.

gob·lin ['gɒblɪn] *s.* Kobold *m*.

go·by ['gəʊbɪ] *s. ichth.* Meergrundel *f*.

go-by ['gəʊbaɪ] *s.*: **give s.o. the ~** F j-n ‚schneiden' *od.* ignorieren; **give s.th. the ~** F die Finger von et. lassen.

'go-cart *s.* **1.** Laufstuhl *m* (*Gehhilfe für Kinder*); **2.** Sportwagen *m* (*für Kinder*); **3.** Handwagen *m*; **4.** → **go-kart**.

god [gɒd] *s.* **1.** Gott(heit *f*) *m*; Götze *m*, Abgott *m*: **~ of love** Liebesgott, Amor *m*; **ye ~s!** F heiliger Strohsack!; **a sight for the ~s** ein Bild für (die) Götter; **2.** ♀ Gott *m*: **♀'s acre** Gottesacker *m*; **house of ♀** Gotteshaus *n*; **play ~** den lieben Gott spielen; **♀ forbid!** Gott behüte!; ≈ ***help him*** Gott sei ihm gnädig; ***so help me*** ≈ so wahr mir Gott helfe; ≈ ***knows*** a) weiß Gott, b) wer weiß(, *ob etc.*); ≈ ***willing*** so Gott will; ***thank*** ≈ Gott sei Dank; ***for ≈'s sake*** a) um Gottes willen, b) verdammt noch mal!; ***the good*** ≈ der liebe Gott; ***good*** ≈***!***, ***my*** ≈***!***, ***(oh)*** ≈***!*** du lieber Gott!, lieber Himmel!; → ***act*** 1 *etc.*; **3.** *fig.* (Ab)Gott *m*; **4.** *pl. thea.* (Publikum *n* auf der) Gale'rie *f*, ‚O'lymp' *m*; **ˌ~-'aw·ful** *adj.* F scheußlich, ‚beschissen'; **'~·child** *s.* [*irr.*] Patenkind *n*; **'~·damn(ed)** *adj.*, *adv. u. int.* (gott)verdammt.

god·des ['gɒdɪs] *s.* Göttin *f* (*a. fig.*).

'god|ˌfa·ther I *s.* Pate *m* (*a. fig.*), Patenonkel *m*, Taufzeuge *m*: ***stand ~ to*** → **II** *v/t. a. fig.* Pate stehen bei, aus der Taufe heben; **'~ˌfear·ing** *adj.* gottesfürchtig; **'~·forˌsak·en** *adj. contp.* gottverlassen.

god·head ['gɒdhed] *s.* Gottheit *f*; **'god·less** [-lɪs] *adj.* ohne Gott; *fig.* gottlos; **'god·like** *adj.* **1.** gottähnlich, göttlich; **2.** göttergleich; **'god·li·ness** [-lɪnɪs] *s.* Frömmigkeit *f*; Gottesfurcht *f*; **'god·ly** [-lɪ] *adj.* fromm.

'god|ˌmoth·er *s.* Patin *f*, Patentante *f*; **'~ˌpar·ent** *s.* Pate *m*, Patin *f*; **'~·send** *s. fig.* Geschenk *n* des Himmels, Glücksfall *m*, Segen *m*; **'~·son** *s.* Patensohn *m*; **ˌ~'speed** *s.*: ***bid s.o.*** ~ j-m viel Glück *od.* glückliche Reise wünschen.

go·er ['gəʊə] *s.* **1.** ***be a good*** ~ gut laufen (*bsd. Pferd*); **2.** *in Zssgn mst* …besucher(in), …gänger(in).

gof·fer ['gəʊfə] **I** *v/t.* kräuseln, plissieren; **II** *s.* Plis'see *n*.

ˌgo-'get·ter *s.* F j-d, der weiß, was er will; Draufgänger *m*.

gog·gle ['gɒgl] **I** *v/i.* **1.** stieren, glotzen; **II** *s.* **2.** stierer Blick; **3.** *pl.* Schutzbrille *f*; **'~·box** *s. bsd. Brit.* F ‚Glotze' *f* (*Fernseher*).

go-go ['gəʊgəʊ] *adj.* **1.** ~ ***girl*** Go-go-Girl *n*; **2.** *fig.* a) schwungvoll, b) schick.

Goid·el·ic [gɔɪ'delɪk] → ***Gaelic.***

go-in ['gəʊɪn] *s.* Go-'in *n*.

go·ing ['gəʊɪŋ] **I** *s.* **1.** (Weg)Gehen *n*, Abreise *f*; **2.** Straßenzustand *m*, (*Pferdesport*) Geläuf *n*; **3.** Tempo *n*: ***good*** ~ ein flottes Tempo; ***rough*** (*od.* ***heavy***) ~ e-e Schinderei; ***while the*** ~ ***is good*** a) solange noch Zeit ist, b) solange es noch gut läuft; **II** *adj.* **4.** in Betrieb, arbeitend: ***a*** ~ ***concern*** ein gutgehendes Geschäft; **5.** vor'handen: ***still*** ~ noch zu haben; ***the best beer*** ~ das beste Bier, das es gibt; ***~, ~, gone!*** (*Auktion*) zum ersten, zum zweiten, zum dritten!; **ˌgo·ing-'o·ver** *s.* F **1.** Über'prüfung *f*; **2.** a) Tracht *f* Prügel, b) Standpauke *f*; **ˌgo·ings-'on** *s. pl.* F *mst b.s.* Vorgänge *pl.*, Treiben *n*: ***strange*** ~ merkwürdige Dinge.

goi·ter *Am.*, **goi·tre** *Brit* ['gɔɪtə] *s.* ⚕ Kropf *m*; **'goi·trous** [-trəs] *adj.* **1.** kropfartig; **2.** mit e-m Kropf (behaftet).

go-kart ['gəʊkɑːt] *s. mot.* Go-Kart *m*.

gold [gəʊld] **I** *s.* **1.** Gold *n*: ***all is not*** ~ ***that glitters*** es ist nicht alles Gold, was glänzt; ***a heart of*** ~ *fig.* ein goldenes Herz; ***worth one's weight in*** ~ unbezahlbar, nicht mit Gold aufzuwiegen; → ***good*** 8; **2.** Gold(münzen *pl.*) *n*; **3.** Geld *n*, Reichtum *m*; **4.** Goldfarbe *f*; **II** *adj.* **5.** aus Gold, golden, Gold…: ~ ***dollar*** Golddollar *m*; ~ ***watch*** goldene Uhr; **~ back·ing** *s.* † Golddeckung *f*; **~ bar** *s.* † Goldbarren *m*; **~ bloc** *s.* † Goldblock(länder *pl.*) *m*; **~ brick** *Am.* F **I** *s.* **1.** falscher Goldbarren; **2.** *fig.* a) wertlose Sache, b) Schwindel *m*, ‚Beschiß' *m*: ***sell s.o. a*** ~ → 4; **3.** Drückeberger *m*; **II** *v/t.* **4.** *j-n* ‚übers Ohr hauen'; **~ bul·lion** *s.* Gold *n* in Barren; **'~ˌdig·ger** *s.* **1.** Goldgräber *m*; **2.** *sl. Frau, die nur hinter dem Geld der Männer her ist*; **~ dust** *s.* Goldstaub *m*.

gold·en ['gəʊldən] *adj.* **1.** *mst fig.* golden: ~ ***days***; ~ ***disc*** goldene Schallplatte; ~ ***opportunity*** einmalige Gelegenheit; **2.** goldgelb, golden (*Haar etc.*); **~ age** *s. das* Goldene Zeitalter; **~ calf** *s. bibl. u. fig. das* Goldene Kalb; **~ ea·gle** *s. orn.* Gold-, Steinadler *m*; ≈ **Fleece** *s. myth. das* Goldene Vlies; **~ hand·shake** *s.* F **1.** Abfindung *f bei Entlassung*; **2.** ‚'Umschlag' *m* (*mit e-m Geldgeschenk der Firma*); **~ mean** *s. die* goldene Mitte, *der* goldene Mittelweg; **~ o·ri·ole** *s. orn.* Pi'rol *m*; **~ pheas·ant** *s. orn.* 'Goldfaˌsan *m*; **~ rule** *s.* **1.** *bibl.* goldene Sittenregel; **2.** *fig.* goldene Regel; **~ sec·tion** *s.* Goldener Schnitt; **~ wed·ding** *s.* goldene Hochzeit.

gold| fe·ver *s.* Goldfieber *n*, -rausch *m*; **'~·field** *s.* Goldfeld *n*; **'~·finch** *s. orn.* Stieglitz *m*, Distelfink *m*; **'~·fish** *s.* Goldfisch *m*; **'~·foil** *s.* Blattgold *n*; **'~ˌham·mer** *s. orn.* Goldammer *f*; **~ lace** *s.* Goldtresse *f*, -borte *f*; **~ leaf** *s.* Blattgold *n*; **~ med·al** *s.* 'Goldmeˌdaille *f*; **~ med·al·(l)ist** *s. sport* 'Goldmeˌdaillengewinner(in); **~ mine** *s.* Goldbergwerk *n*; Goldgrube *f* (*a. fig.*); **~ plate** *s.* goldenes Tafelgeschirr; **'~-ˌplat·ed** *adj.* vergoldet; **~ point** *s.* † Goldpunkt *m*; **~ rush** → ***gold fever***; **'~·smith** *s.* Goldschmied *m*; **~ stand·ard** *s.* Goldwährung *f*; ≈ **Stick** *s. Brit.* Oberst *m* der königlichen Leibgarde.

golf [gɒlf] *sport* **I** *s.* Golf(spiel) *n*; **II** *v/i.* Golf spielen; **~ ball** *s.* **1.** Golfball *m*; **2.** Kugelkopf *m* (*der Schreibmaschine*); **~ club** *s.* **1.** Golfschläger *m*; **2.** Golfklub *m*.

golf·er ['gɒlfə] *s.* Golfspieler(in).

golf links *s. pl.*, *a. sg. konstr.* Golfplatz *m*.

Go·li·ath [gəʊ'laɪəθ] *s. fig.* Goliath *m*, Riese *m*, Hüne *m*.

gol·li·wog(g) ['gɒlɪwɒg] *s.* **1.** gro'teske schwarze Puppe; **2.** *fig.* ‚Vogelscheuche' *f* (*Person*).

gol·ly ['gɒlɪ] *int. a.* ***by ~!*** F Menschenskind!, Mann!

go·losh [gə'lɒʃ] → ***galosh.***

Go·mor·rah, **Go·mor·rha** [gə'mɒrə] *s. fig.* Go'morr(h)a *n*, Sündenpfuhl *m*.

gon·ad ['gəʊnæd] *s.* ⚕ Keim-, Geschlechtsdrüse *f*.

gon·do·la ['gɒndələ] *s.* **1.** Gondel *f* (*a. e-s Ballons, e-r Seilbahn etc.*); **2.** *Am.* flaches Flußboot; **3.** *a.* ~ ***car*** 🚃 *Am.* offener Güterwagen; **gon·do·lier** [ˌgɒndə'lɪə] *s.* Gondoli'ere *m*.

gone [gɒn] **I** *p.p. von* ***go***; **II** *adj.* **1.** weg(gegangen), fort: ***he is ~***; ***be ~!*** fort mit dir!; ***I must be*** ~ ich muß weg; **2.** verloren, verschwunden, weg, da'hin; **3.** ‚hin', ‚futsch': a) weg, verbraucht, b) ka'putt, c) ruiniert, d) tot; ***a*** ~ ***case*** ein hoffnungsloser Fall; ***a*** ~ ***man*** → ***goner***; ***a*** ~ ***feeling*** ein Schwächegefühl; ***all his money is*** ~ sein ganzes Geld ist weg *od.* ‚futsch'; **4.** mehr als, älter als, über: ***he is ~ forty***; **5.** F (***on***) ganz ‚weg' (von): a) begeistert (von), b) ‚verknallt' (in *acc.*); **6.** *sl.* ‚high', ‚weg'; **7.** ***she's four months*** ~ F sie ist im 4. Monat;

gon·er ['gɒnə] *s.* 'Todeskandiˌdat *m*: ***he is a*** ~ F er ist ‚erledigt' (*a. weitS.*).

gon·fa·lon ['gɒnfələn] *s.* Banner *n*.

gong [gɒŋ] **I** *s.* **1.** Gong *m*; **2.** ⚔ *Brit. sl.* Orden *m*; **II** *v/t.* **3.** *Brit. Auto* durch 'Gongsiˌgnal stoppen (*Polizei*).

go·ni·om·e·ter [ˌgəʊnɪ'ɒmɪtə] *s.* ⚒ *u. Radio*: Winkelmesser *m*.

gon·o·coc·cus [ˌgɒnəʊ'kɒkəs] *pl.* **-coc·ci** [-'kɒkaɪ] *s.* ⚕ Gono'kokkus *m*.

gon·or·rhoe·a, *Am. mst* **gon·or·rhe·a** [ˌgɒnə'riːə] *s.* ⚕ Gonor'rhöe *f*, Tripper *m*.

goo [guː] *s. sl.* **1.** Schmiere *f*, klebriges Zeug; **2.** *fig.* sentimen'taler Kitsch, ‚Schmalz' *m*.

good [gʊd] **I** *adj.* **1.** gut, angenehm, erfreulich: ~ ***news***; ***it is ~ to be rich*** es ist angenehm, reich zu sein; ~ ***morning (evening)!*** guten Morgen (Abend)!; ~ ***afternoon!*** guten Tag! (*nachmittags*); ~ ***night!*** a) gute Nacht! (*a.* F *fig.*), b) guten Abend!; ***have a ~ time*** sich amüsieren; ***(it's a) ~ thing that*** es ist gut, daß; ***be ~ eating*** gut schmecken; **2.** gut, geeignet, nützlich, günstig, zuträglich: ***is this ~ to eat?*** kann man das essen?; ***milk is ~ for children*** Milch ist gut für Kinder; ~ ***for gout*** gut für *od.* gegen Gicht; ***that's ~ for you!*** *a. iro.* das tut dir gut!; ***get in ~ with s.o.*** sich mit j-m gut stellen; ***what is it ~ for?*** wofür ist es gut?, wozu dient es?; **3.** befriedigend, reichlich, beträchtlich: ***a ~ hour*** e-e gute Stunde; ***a ~ day's journey*** e-e gute Tagereise; ***a ~ many*** ziemlich viele; ***a ~ threshing*** e-e ordentliche Tracht Prügel; ~ ***money*** *sl.* hoher Lohn; **4.** (*vor adj.*) *verstärkend*: ***a ~ long time*** sehr lange (Zeit); ~ ***old age*** hohes Alter; ~ ***and angry*** F äußerst erbost; **5.** gut, tugendhaft: ***lead a ~ life*** ein rechtschaffenes Leben führen; ***a ~ deed*** e-e gute Tat; **6.** gut, gewissenhaft: ***a ~ father and husband*** ein guter Vater und Gatte; **7.** gut, gütig, lieb: ~ ***to the poor*** gut zu den Armen; ***it is ~ of you to help me*** es ist nett (von Ihnen), daß Sie mir helfen; ***be ~ enough*** (*od.* ***so ~ as***) ***to fetch it*** sei so gut und hole es; ***be ~ enough to hold your tongue!*** halt gefälligst deinen Mund!; ***my ~ man*** F mein Lieber!; **8.** artig, lieb, brav (*Kind*): ***be a ~ boy***; ***as ~ as gold*** a) kreuzbrav, b) goldrichtig; **9.** gut, geschickt, tüchtig (***at*** in *dat.*): ***a ~ rider*** ein guter Reiter; ***he is ~ at golf*** er spielt gut Golf; **10.** gut, geachtet: ***of ~ family*** aus guter Familie; **11.** gültig (*a.* †), echt: ***a ~ reason*** ein triftiger Grund; ***tell false money from ~*** falsches Geld von echtem unterscheiden; ***a ~ Republican*** ein guter *od.* überzeugter Republikaner; ***be as ~ as*** auf dasselbe hinauslaufen; ***as ~ as finished*** so gut wie fertig; ***he has as ~ as promised*** er hat es so gut wie versprochen; **12.** gut, genießbar, frisch: ***a ~ egg***; ***is this fish still ~?***; **13.** gut, gesund, kräftig: ***in ~ health*** bei guter Gesundheit, gesund; ***be ~ for*** ‚gut' sein für, fähig *od.* geeignet sein zu; ***I am ~ for another mile*** ich schaffe noch eine Meile; ***he is always ~ for a surprise*** er ist immer für e-e Überraschung gut; ***I am ~ for a walk*** ich habe Lust zu e-m Spaziergang; **14.** *bsd.* ⚚ gut, sicher, zuverlässig: ***a ~ firm*** e-e gute *od.* zahlungsfähige Firma; ***~ debts*** sichere Schulden; ***be ~ for any amount*** für jeden Betrag gut sein; **II** *s.* **15.** *das* Gute, Gutes *n*, Wohl *n*: ***the common ~*** das Gemeinwohl; ***do s.o. ~*** a) j-m Gutes tun, b) j-m gut-, wohltun; ***he is up to no ~*** er führt nichts Gutes im Schilde; ***it comes to no ~*** es führt zu nichts Gutem; **16.** Nutzen *m*, Vorteil *m*: ***for his ~*** zu s-m Nutzen; ***he is too nice for his own ~*** er ist viel zu nett; ***what is the ~ of it?, what ~ is it?*** was nützt es?, wozu soll das gut sein?; ***it's no ~*** a) es taugt nichts, b) es ist zwecklos; ***it is no ~ trying*** es hat keinen Wert *od.* Sinn, es zu versuchen; ***much ~ may it do you*** *iro.* wohl bekomm's!; ***for ~ (and all)*** für immer, endgültig, ein für allemal; ***to the ~*** obendrein, extra, ⚚ als Gewinn *od.* Kreditsaldo; ***it's all to the ~*** es ist nur zu s-m *etc.* Besten; **17.** ***the ~*** *pl.* die Guten *pl. od.* Rechtschaffenen *pl.*; **18.** *pl.* (bewegliche) Habe: ***~s and chattles*** Hab u. Gut *n*; F *j-s* ‚Siebensachen' *pl.*; **19.** *pl.* Güter *pl.*, Waren *pl.*, Gegenstände *pl.*: ***by ~s*** ⚚ *Brit.* als Frachtgut; → ***deliver*** 5.

Good| Book *s. die* Bibel; **ˌ~'by(e)** [-'baɪ] **I** *s.* **1.** Abschiedsgruß *m*: ***say ~ to*** *j-m* auf Wiedersehen sagen, sich von *j-m* verabschieden; ***you may say ~ to that!*** F das kannst du vergessen!; **2.** Abschied *m*; **II** *adj.* Abschieds...: ***~ kiss***; **III** *int.* [ˌgʊd'baɪ] **3.** auf Wiedersehen!, adi'eu!, a'de!: ***then ~ democracy!*** *fig. iron.* dann ade Demokratie!; **ˌ~'fel·low·ship** *s.* gute Kame'radschaft, Kame'radschaftlichkeit *f*; **~-for-noth·ing I** ['gʊdfəˌnʌθɪŋ] *adj.* nichtsnutzig; **II** [ˌgʊdfə'n-] *s.* Taugenichts *m*, Nichtsnutz *m*; ♁ **Fri·day** *s. eccl.* Kar'freitag *m*; **~ hu·mo(u)r** *s.* gute Laune; **ˌ~-'hu·mo(u)red** *adj.* □ **1.** bei guter Laune, gutaufgelegt; **2.** gutmütig.

good·ish ['gʊdɪʃ] *adj.* **1.** ziemlich gut; **2.** ziemlich (*Menge*); **good·li·ness** ['gʊdlɪnɪs] *s.* **1.** Güte *f*, Wert *m*; **2.** Anmut *f*; **3.** Schönheit *f*.

ˌgood|-'look·ing *adj.* gutaussehend, hübsch, schön; **~ looks** *s. pl.* gutes Aussehen, Schönheit *f*.

good·ly ['gʊdlɪ] *adj.* **1.** schön, anmutig; **2.** beträchtlich, ansehnlich; **3.** *oft iro.* glänzend, prächtig.

'good|·man [-mæn] *s.* [*irr.*] *obs.* Hausvater *m*, Ehemann *m*: ♁ ***Death*** Freund Hein *m*; **ˌ~-'na·tured** *adj.* □ gutmütig, gefällig; **ˌ~-'neigh·bo(u)r·li·ness** *s.* gutnachbarliches Verhältnis; ♁ **Neigh·bo(u)r pol·i·cy** *s.* Poli'tik *f* der guten Nachbarschaft.

good·ness ['gʊdnɪs] *s.* **1.** Tugend *f*, Frömmigkeit *f*; **2.** Güte *f*, Freundlichkeit *f*; **3.** Wert *m*, Güte *f*; *engS. das* Wertvolle *od.* Nahrhafte; **4.** ***~ gracious!, my ~!*** du meine Güte!, du lieber Gott!; ***~ knows*** weiß der Himmel; ***for ~' sake*** um Himmels willen; ***thank ~!*** Gott sei Dank!; ***I wish to ~*** wollte Gott.

goods| a·gent *s.* ⚚ ('Bahn)Spediˌteur *m*; **~ en·gine** *s. Brit.* 'Güterzuglokoˌmoˌtive *f*; **~ lift** *s. Brit.* Lastenaufzug *m*.

good speed *Am.* → ***godspeed***.

goods| sta·tion *s. Brit.* Güterbahnhof *m*; **~ train** *s. Brit.* Güterzug *m*; **~ van** *s. mot. Brit.* Lieferwagen *m*; **~ wag·on** *s. Brit.* Güterwagen *m*; **~ yard** *s. Brit.* Güter(bahn)hof *m*.

ˌgood|-'tem·pered *adj.* □ gutartig, -mütig, ausgeglichen; **ˌ~-'time Char·lie** ['tʃɑːlɪ] *s. Am.* F lebenslustiger *od.* vergnügungssüchtiger Mensch; **ˌ~'will** *s.* **1.** Wohlwollen *n*, guter Wille, Verständigungsbereitschaft *f*: ***~ tour*** *pol.* Goodwillreise *f*; ***~ visit*** Freundschaftsbesuch *m*; **2.** *mst* ***good will*** ⚚ a) Goodwill *m*, (ide'eller) Firmen- *od.* Geschäftswert (*guter Ruf*, *Kundenstamm etc.*).

good·y ['gʊdɪ] F **I** *s.* **1.** Bon'bon *m*, *n*, *pl.* Süßigkeiten *pl.*, gute Sachen; **2.** *fig.* ‚klasse Ding'; **3.** *Film etc.*: Gute(r *m*) *f* (*Ggs Schurke*); **4.** Tugendbold *m*, Mukker *m*; **II** *adj.* **5.** frömmelnd, ‚mora'linsauer'; **III** *int.* **6.** prima!, ‚Klasse'!; **'~-ˌgood·y** → ***goody*** 4, 5, 6.

goo·ey ['guːɪ] *adj. sl.* klebrig, schmierig.

goof [guːf] F **I** *s.* **1.** ‚Pfeife' *f*, Idi'ot *m*; **2.** ‚Schnitzer' *m*, ‚Patzer' *m*; **II** *v/t.* **3.** *oft* ***~ up*** ‚vermasseln'; **III** *v/i.* **4.** ‚Mist bauen'; **5.** *oft* ***~ around*** ‚her'umspinnen'.

'go-off *s.* Start *m*: ***at the first ~*** (gleich) beim ersten Mal, auf Anhieb.

'goof·y ['guːfɪ] *adj.* □ *sl.* ‚doof', ‚bekloppt'.

gook [gʊk] *s. Am. sl. contp.* ‚Schlitzauge' *n* (*Asiate*).

goon [guːn] *s. sl.* **1.** *Am.* angeheuerter Schläger; **2.** → ***goof*** 1.

goose [guːs] **I** *pl.* **geese** [giːs] *s.* **1.** *orn.* Gans *f*: ***cook s.o.'s ~*** F es j-m ‚besorgen', j-n ‚fertigmachen'; ***he's cooked his ~ with me*** F bei mir ist er ‚unten durch'; ***all his geese are swans*** bei ihm ist immer alles besser als bei andern; ***kill the ~ that lays the golden eggs*** das Huhn schlachten, das goldene Eier legt; → ***sauce*** 1; **2.** Gans *f*, Gänsebraten *m*; **3.** *fig.* a) Dummkopf *m*, b) (dumme) Gans; **4.** (*pl.* **goos·es**) Schneiderbügeleisen *n*; **II** *v/t.* **5.** F *j-n* (in den ‚Po') zwicken.

goose·ber·ry ['gʊzbərɪ] *s.* **1.** ⚘ Stachelbeere *f*: ***play ~*** F den Anstandswauwau spielen; **2.** *a.* ***~ wine*** Stachelbeerwein *m*; **~ fool** *s.* Stachelbeercreme *f* (*Speise*).

goose| bumps *s. pl.*, **~ flesh** *s. fig.* Gänsehaut *f*; **'~·neck** *s.* ⚙ Schwanenhals *m*; **~ pim·ples** *s. pl.* → ***goose bumps***; **'~-quill** *s.* Gänsekiel *m*; **'~-skin** → ***goose bumps***; **'~-step** *s.* ⚔ Pa'rade-, Stechschritt *m*.

goos·ey ['guːsɪ] *s. fig.* Gäns-chen *n*.

go·pher[1] ['gəʊfə] *s. Am. zo.* a) Taschenratte *f*, b) Ziesel *m*, c) Gopherschildkröte *f*, d) *a.* ***~ snake*** Schildkrötenschlange *f*.

go·pher[2] → ***goffer***.

go·pher[3] ['gəʊfə] *s. bibl. Baum, aus dessen Holz Noah die Arche baute*; **'~·wood** *s. Am.* ⚘ Gelbholz *n*.

Gor·di·an ['gɔːdjən] *adj.*: ***cut the ~ knot*** den gordischen Knoten durchhauen.

gore[1] [gɔː] *s.* (*bsd.* geronnenes) Blut.

gore[2] [gɔː] **I** *s.* **1.** Zwickel *m*, Keil(stück *n*) *m*; **II** *v/t.* **2.** keilförmig zuschneiden; **3.** e-n Zwickel einsetzen in (*acc.*).

gore[3] [gɔː] *v/t.* (*mit den Hörnern*) durch'bohren, aufspießen.

gorge [gɔːdʒ] **I** *s.* **1.** enge (Fels-) Schlucht; **2.** *rhet.* Kehle *f*, Schlund *m*: ***my ~ rises at it*** *fig.* mir wird übel davon *od.* dabei; **3.** Schlemme'rei *f*, Völle'rei *f*; **4.** △ Hohlkehle *f*; **II** *v/i.* **5.** schlemmen: ***~ on*** (*od.* ***with***) → 7; **III** *v/t.* **6.** gierig verschlingen; **7.** ***~ o.s. on*** (*od.* ***with***) sich vollfressen mit, *et.* in sich hineinschlingen.

gor·geous ['gɔːdʒəs] *adj.* □ **1.** prächtig, prachtvoll (*beide a. fig.* F); **2.** F großartig, wunderbar, ‚toll'.

Gor·gon ['gɔːgən] *s.* **1.** *myth.* Gorgo *f*; **2.** a) häßliches *od.* abstoßendes Weib, b) ‚Drachen' *m*; **gor·go·ni·an** [gɔː'gəʊnjən] *adj.* **1.** Gorgonen...; **2.** schauerlich.

go·ril·la [gə'rɪlə] *s.* **1.** *zo.* Go'rilla *m*; **2.** *Am. sl.* ‚Gorilla' *m*: a) Leibwächter *m e-s Gangsters etc.*, b) Scheusal *n*.

gor·mand·ize ['gɔːməndaɪz] **I** *v/t.* *et.* gierig verschlingen; **II** *v/i.* schlemmen; **'gor·mand·iz·er** [-zə] *s.* Schlemmer (-in).

gorse [gɔːs] *s.* ⚘ *Brit.* Stechginster *m*.

gor·y ['gɔːrɪ] *adj.* **1.** *poet.* a) blutbefleckt, voll Blut, b) blutig: ***~ battle***; **2.** *fig.* blutrünstig.

gosh [gɒʃ] *int.* F Mensch!, Mann!

gos·hawk ['gɒshɔːk] *s. orn.* Hühnerhabicht *m*.

gos·ling ['gɒzlɪŋ] *s.* **1.** junge Gans, Gäns-chen *n*; **2.** *fig.* Grünschnabel *m*.

ˌgo-'slow *s.* ⚚ *Brit.* Bummelstreik *m*.

gos·pel ['gɒspl] *s. eccl. a.* ♁ Evan'gelium *n* (*a. fig.*): ***take s.th. for ~*** et. für bare Münze nehmen; ***~ song*** Gospelsong *m*; ***~ truth*** *fig.* absolute Wahrheit; **'gos·pel·(l)er** [-pələ] *s.* Vorleser *m* des Evan'geliums: ***hot ~*** a) religiöser Eiferer, b) fa'natischer Befürworter.

gos·sa·mer ['gɒsəmə] **I** *s.* **1.** Alt'weibersommer *m*, Spinnfäden *pl.*; **2.** a) feine Gaze, b) hauchdünner Stoff; **3.** *et.* sehr Zartes u. Dünnes; **II** *adj.* **4.** leicht u. zart, hauchdünn.

gos·sip ['gɒsɪp] **I** *s.* **1.** Klatsch *m*, Tratsch *m*: ***~ column*** Klatschspalte *f*; ***~ columnist*** Klatschkolumnist(in); **2.** Plaude'rei *f*, Schwatz *m*, Plausch *m*; **3.** Klatschbase *f*; **II** *v/i.* **4.** klatschen, tratschen; **5.** plaudern; **'gos·sip·y** [-pɪ] *adj.* **1.** klatschhaft, -süchtig; **2.** schwatzhaft; **3.** im Plauderton (geschrieben).

got [gɒt] *pret. u. p.p. von* ***get***.

Goth [gɒθ] *s.* **1.** Gote *m*; **2.** *fig.* Bar'bar *m*.

Go·tham ['gəʊθəm, 'gɒ-] *s. Am.* (*Spitzname für*) New York; **'Go·tham·ite** *s.* [-maɪt] *humor.* New Yorker(in).

Goth·ic ['gɒθɪk] **I** *adj.* **1.** gotisch; **2.** *fig.* bar'barisch, roh; **3.** *typ.* a) *Brit.* gotisch, b) *Am.* Grotesk...; **4.** *Literatur*: a) ba'rock, ro'mantisch, b) Schauer...: ***~ novel***; **II** *s.* **5.** *ling.* Gotisch *n*; **6.** △ Gotik *f*, gotischer (Bau)Stil; **7.** *typ.* a) *Brit.* Frak'tur *f*, gotische Schrift, b) *Am.* Gro'tesk *f*; **Goth·i·cism** ['gɒθɪsɪzəm] *s.* **1.** Gotik *f*; **2.** *fig.* Barba'rei *f*, 'Unkulˌtur *f*.

ˌgo-to-'meet·ing *adj.* F Sonntags..., Ausgeh...: ***~ suit***.

got·ten ['gɒtn] *obs. od. Am. p.p. von* ***get.***

gou·ache [gʊ'ɑːʃ] *(Fr.) s. paint.* Gou'ache *f.*

gouge [gaʊdʒ] **I** *s.* **1.** ⚙ Hohlmeißel *m;* **2.** Rille *f*, Furche *f*; **3.** *Am.* F a) Gaune'rei *f*, b) Erpressung *f*; **II** *v/t.* **4.** *a.* ***~ out*** ⚙ ausmeißeln, -höhlen, -stechen; **5.** ***~ out s.o.'s eye*** a) j-m den Finger ins Auge stoßen, b) j-m ein Auge ausdrükken *od.* -stechen; **6.** *Am.* F a) *j-n* über'vorteilen, b) *e-e Summe* erpressen.

gou·lash ['guːlæʃ] *s.* Gulasch *n*: ***~ communism*** *pol. contp.* Gulaschkommunismus *m.*

gourd [gʊəd] *s.* **1.** ♀ Flaschenkürbis *m;* **2.** Kürbisflasche *f.*

gour·mand ['gʊəmənd] **I** *s.* **1.** Schlemmer *m*, Gour'mand *m*; **2.** → ***gourmet***; **II** *adj.* **3.** schlemmerisch.

gour·met ['gʊəmeɪ] *s.* Feinschmecker *m*, Gour'met *m.*

gout [gaʊt] *s.* **1.** ⚕ Gicht *f*; **2.** ♀ Gicht *f* (*Weizenkrankheit*): ***~-fly*** *zo.* gelbe Halmfliege; **'gout·y** [-tɪ] *adj.* □ ⚕ **1.** gichtkrank; **2.** zur Gicht neigend; **3.** gichtisch, Gicht...: ***~ concretion*** Gichtknoten *m.*

gov·ern ['gʌvn] **I** *v/t.* **1.** regieren (*a. ling.*); beherrschen (*a. fig.*); **2.** leiten, führen, verwalten, lenken; **3.** *fig.* regeln, bestimmen, maßgebend sein für, leiten: ***~ed by circumstances*** durch die Umstände bestimmt; ***I was ~ed by*** ich ließ mich leiten von ...; **4.** beherrschen, zügeln; **5.** ⚙ regeln, steuern; **II** *v/i.* **6.** regieren, herrschen (*a. fig.*); **'gov·ern·ance** [-nəns] *s.* **1.** Regierungsgewalt *f od.* -form *f*; **2.** *fig.* Herrschaft *f*, Gewalt *f*, Kon'trolle *f* (***of*** über *acc.*); **'gov·ern·ess** [-nɪs] **I** *s.* Erzieherin *f*, Gouver'nante *f*; **II** *v/i.* Erzieherin sein; **'gov·ern·ing** [-nɪŋ] *adj.* **1.** regierend, Regierungs...; **2.** leitend, Vorstands...: ***~ body*** Vorstand *m*, Leitung *f*; **3.** *fig.* leitend, Leit...: ***~ idea*** Leitgedanke *m*; **gov·ern·ment** ['gʌvnmənt] *s.* **1.** a) Regierung *f*, Herrschaft *f*, Kon'trolle *f* (***of, over*** über *acc.*), b) Regierungsgewalt *f*, c) Leitung *f*, Verwaltung *f*; **2.** Re'gierung(sform *f*, -ssy'stem *n*) *f*; **3.** (*e-s bestimmten Landes*) *mst* ♀ *die* Regierung: ***the British*** ♀; ***~ agency*** Regierungsstelle *f*, (-)Behörde *f*; ***~ bill*** *parl.* Regierungsvorlage *f*; ***~ spokesman*** Regierungssprecher *m*; **4.** Staat *m*: ***~ bonds, ~ securities*** a) Staatsanleihen, -papiere, b) *Am.* Bundesanleihen; ***~ employee*** Angestellte(r *m*) *f* des öffentlichen Dienstes; ***~ grant*** staatlicher Zuschuß; ***~ issue*** *Am. von der Regierung gestellte Ausrüstung*; ***~ monopoly*** Staatsmonopol *n*; **5.** *univ.* Politolo'gie *f*; **6.** *ling.* Rekti'on *f*; **gov·ern·men·tal** [ˌgʌvn'mentl] *adj.* □ Regierungs..., Staats..., staatlich; **gov·ern·men·tal·ize** [ˌgʌvn'mentəlaɪz] *v/t.* unter staatliche Kon'trolle bringen.

ˌgov·ern·ment|-in-'ex·ile *pl.* **ˌ~s-in-'ex·ile** *s. pol.* E'xilregierung *f*; **'~-owned** *adj.* staatseigen; **'~-run** *adj.* staatlich (*Rundfunk etc.*).

gov·er·nor ['gʌvənə] *s.* **1.** Gouver'neur *m* (*a. e-s Staates der USA*): ***~ general*** Generalgouverneur; **2.** ⚔ Komman'dant *m*; **3.** a) *allg.* Di'rektor *m*, Leiter *m*, Vorsitzende(r) *m*, b) Präsi'dent *m* (*e-r Bank*), c) *Brit.* Ge'fängnisdiˌrektor *m*, d) *pl.* Vorstand *m*, Direk'torium *n*; **4.** F *der* ,Alte': a) ,alter Herr' (*Vater*), b) Chef *m* (*a. als Anrede*); **5.** ⚙ Regler *m*: ***~ valve*** Reglerventil *n*; **'gov·er·nor·ship** [-ʃɪp] *s.* **1.** Gouver'neursamt *n*; **2.** Amtszeit *f* e-s Gouver'neurs.

gown [gaʊn] **I** *s.* **1.** Kleid *n*; **2.** *bsd.* ⚖ *u. univ.* Ta'lar *m*, Robe *f*; **3.** *coll.* Stu'denten(schaft *f*) *pl. u.* Hochschullehrer *pl.* (*e-r Universitätsstadt*): ***town and ~*** Stadt u. Universität; **II** *v/t.* **4.** mit e-m Ta'lar *etc.* bekleiden; **gowns·man** ['gaʊnzmən] *s.* [*irr.*] Robenträger *m* (*Anwalt, Richter, Geistlicher etc.*).

goy [gɔɪ] *s.* ,Goi' *m* (*jiddisch für Nichtjude*).

grab [græb] **I** *v/t.* **1.** (hastig *od.* gierig) ergreifen, an sich reißen, fassen, pakken, (sich) ,schnappen'; **2.** *fig.* a) sich ,schnappen', an sich reißen, b) *e-e Gelegenheit* beim Schopf ergreifen; **3.** F *Publikum* packen, fesseln; **II** *v/i.* **4.** ***~ at*** (hastig *od.* gierig) greifen *od.* ,schnappen' nach; **III** *s.* **5.** (hastiger *od.* gieriger) Griff (***for*** nach): ***make a ~ at*** → 1 u. 4; ***be up for ~s*** F für jeden zu haben *od.* zu gewinnen sein; **6.** *fig.* Griff (***for*** nach *der Macht etc.*); **7.** ⚙ (Bagger-, Kran)Greifer *m*: ***~ crane*** Greiferkran *m*; ***~ dredge(r)*** Greiferbagger *m*; ***~ handle*** Haltegriff *m*; ***~ bag*** *s. Am.* **1.** ,Grabbelsack' *m*; **2.** *fig.* Sammel'surium *n.*

grab·ber ['græbə] *s.* Habgierige(r *m*) *f*, ,Raffke' *m.*

grab·ble ['græbl] *v/i.* tasten, tappen, suchen (***for*** nach).

grab raid *s.* 'Raubˌüberfall *m.*

grace [greɪs] **I** *s.* **1.** Anmut *f*, Grazie *f*, Liebreiz *m*, Charme *m*: ***the three*** ♀***s*** *myth.* die drei Grazien; **2.** Anstand *m*, Takt *m*, Schicklichkeit *f*: ***have the ~ to do*** den Anstand haben zu tun; ***with ~*** mit Anstand *od.* Würde *od.* ,Grazie' (→ *a.* 3); **3.** Bereitwilligkeit *f*: ***with a good ~*** bereitwillig, gern; ***with a bad ~*** widerwillig, (nur) ungern; **4.** *mst pl.* gute Eigenschaft, schöner Zug: ***social ~s*** feine Lebensart; **5.** Gunst *f*, Wohlwollen *n*, Huld *f*, Gnade *f*: ***be in s.o.'s good ~s*** in j-s Gunst stehen, bei j-m gut angeschrieben sein; ***be in s.o.'s bad ~s*** bei j-m in Ungnade sein; ***fall from ~*** in Ungnade fallen; ***by way of ~*** ⚖ auf dem Gnadenwege; ***act of ~*** Gnadenakt *m*; **6.** ***by the ~ of God*** von Gottes Gnaden; ***in the year of ~*** im Jahre des Heils; **7.** *eccl.* a) *a.* ***state of ~*** Stand *m* der Gnade, b) Tugend *f*: ***~ of charity*** (Tugend der) Nächstenliebe *f*, c) ***say ~*** das Tischgebet sprechen; **8.** ✝, ⚖ Aufschub *m*, (Zahlungs-, Nach)Frist *f*: ***days of ~*** Respekttage *pl.*; ***grant s.o. a week's ~*** j-m e-e Woche Aufschub gewähren; **9.** ♀ (*Eure, Seine, Ihre*) Gnaden *pl.* (*Titel*): ***Your*** ♀ a) Eure Hoheit (*Herzogin*), b) Eure Exzellenz (*Erzbischof*); **10.** *a.* ***~ note*** ♪ Verzierung *f*; **II** *v/t.* **11.** zieren, schmücken; **12.** *fig.* a) zieren, b) (be)ehren, auszeichnen; **'grace·ful** [-fʊl] *adj.* □ **1.** anmutig, grazi'ös, reizend, ele'gant; **2.** geziemend, takt-, würdevoll: ***~ly*** *fig.* mit Anstand *od.* Würde *alt werden etc.*; **'grace·ful·ness** [-fʊlnɪs] *s.* Anmut *f*, Grazie *f*; **'grace·less** [-lɪs] *adj.* □ **1.** 'ungraziˌös, reizlos, 'uneleˌgant; **2.** *obs.* verworfen.

grac·ile ['græsaɪl] *adj.* zierlich, gra'zil, zart(gliedrig).

gra·cious ['greɪʃəs] **I** *adj.* □ **1.** gnädig, huldvoll, wohlwollend; **2.** *poet.* gütig, freundlich; **3.** *eccl.* gnädig, barmherzig (*Gott*); **4.** *obs.* für ***graceful*** 1; **5.** a) angenehm, b) geschmackvoll, schön: ***~ living*** elegantes Leben, kultivierter Luxus; **II** *int.* **6.** ***~ me!, ~ goodness!, good ~!*** du meine Güte!, lieber Himmel!; **'gra·cious·ness** [-nɪs] *s.* **1.** Gnade *f*, *eccl. a.* Barm'herzigkeit *f*; **2.** *poet.* Güte *f*, Freundlichkeit *f.*

grad [græd] *s.* F Stu'dent(in).

gra·date [grə'deɪt] **I** *v/t.* *Farben* abstufen, inein'ander 'übergehen lassen, abtönen; **II** *v/i.* stufenweise (inein'ander) 'übergehen; **gra·da·tion** [grə'deɪʃn] *s.* **1.** Abstufung *f*: a) Abtönung *f*, b) Staffelung *f*; **2.** Stufenleiter *f*, -folge *f*; **3.** *ling.* Ablaut *m.*

grade [greɪd] **I** *s.* **1.** Grad *m*, Stufe *f*, Klasse *f*; **2.** ⚔ *Am.* Dienstgrad *m*; **3.** (*höherer etc.*) (Be'amten)Dienst; **4.** Art *f*, Gattung *f*, Sorte *f*; Quali'tät *f*, Güte *f*, Klasse *f*: ♀ ***A*** ✝ (Güte)Klasse A (→ 6); **5.** Steigung *f*, Gefälle *n*, Neigung *f*, Ni'veau *n* (*a. fig.*): ***~ crossing*** (schienengleicher) Bahnübergang; ***at ~*** *Am.* auf gleicher Höhe; ***on the up ~*** aufwärts (-gehend), im Aufstieg; ***make the ~*** ,es schaffen'; **6.** *ped. Am.* a) (Schüler *pl.* e-r) Klasse *f*, b) Note *f*, Zen'sur *f*, c) *pl.* (Grund)Schule *f*: ***~ A*** (Note *f*) Sehr Gut *n* (→ 4); **II** *v/t.* **7.** sortieren, einteilen, -reihen, -stufen, staffeln; **8.** *ped.* benoten, zensieren; **9.** ***~ up*** verbessern, veredeln; ***~ (up)*** Vieh (auf)kreuzen; **10.** *Gelände* planieren; **11.** *ling.* ablauten; **12.** → ***gradate*** I; **'grad·er** [-də] *s.* **1.** a) Sortierer(in), b) Sor'tiermaˌschine *f*; **2.** ⚙ Pla'niermaˌschine *f*; **3.** *Am. ped. in Zssgn* ...kläßler *m*: ***fourth ~*** Viertkläßler.

grade school *s. Am.* Grundschule *f.*

gra·di·ent ['greɪdjənt] **I** *s.* **1.** Neigung *f*, Steigung *f*, Gefälle *n* (*des Geländes etc.*); **2.** ⚗ Gradi'ent *m* (*a. meteor.*), Gefälle *n*; **II** *adj.* **3.** gehend, schreitend; **4.** *zo.* Geh..., Lauf...

grad·u·al ['grædjʊəl] **I** *adj.* □ all'mählich, schritt-, stufenweise, langsam (fortschreitend), gradu'ell; **II** *s. eccl.* Gradu'ale *n*; **'grad·u·al·ly** [-əlɪ] *adv.* a) nach u. nach, b) → ***gradual*** I.

grad·u·ate ['grædʒʊət] **I** *s.* **1.** *univ.* a) 'Hochschulabsolˌvent(in), Aka'demiker (-in), b) Graduierte(r *m*) *f* (*bsd. Inhaber[in] des niedrigsten akademischen Grades*), c) *Am.* Stu'dent(in) an e-r ***graduate school***; **2.** *ped. Am.* ('Schul-)Absolˌvent(in): ***high-school ~*** *etwa* Abiturient(in); **3.** *fig. Am.* ,Pro'dukt' *n* (*e-r Anstalt etc.*); **4.** *Am.* Meßgefäß *n*; **II** *adj.* **5.** *univ.* a) Akademiker..., b) graduiert: ***~ student*** → 1, c) für Graduierte: ***~ course*** (Fach)Kurs *m* an e-r ***graduate school***; **6.** *Am.* staatlich geprüft, Diplom...: ***~ nurse***; **7.** → ***graduated*** 1; **III** *v/t.* [-djʊeɪt] **8.** ⚙ mit e-r Maßeinteilung versehen, in Grade einteilen, *a.* ⚗ gradieren; **9.** abstufen, staffeln; **10.** *univ.* graduieren, *j-m* e-n (*bsd. den niedrigsten*) aka'demischen Grad verleihen; **11.** *ped. Am.* a) *oft* ***be***

~d from die Abschlußprüfung bestehen an (*e-r Schule*), absolvieren, her'vorgehen aus, b) *j-n* (*in die nächste Klasse*) versetzen; **IV** *v/i.* [-djʊeɪt] **12.** *univ.* graduieren, e-n (*bsd. den niedrigsten*) aka'demischen Grad erwerben (*from* an *dat.*); **13.** *ped. Am.* die Abschlußprüfung bestehen: *~ from* → 11a; **14.** sich staffeln, sich abstufen: *~ into* a) sich entwickeln zu, b) allmählich übergehen in (*acc.*); **'grad·u·at·ed** [-jʊeɪtɪd] *adj.* **1.** abgestuft, gestaffelt; **2.** ⚙ graduiert, mit e-r Gradeinteilung: *~ dial* Skalenscheibe *f*; **grad·u·ate school** *s. univ. Am.* a) höhere 'Fachseˌmester *pl.* (*mit Studienziel ‚Magister'*), b) *Universität(seinrichtung) zur Erlangung höherer akademischer Grade*; **grad·u·a·tion** [ˌgrædjʊ'eɪʃn] *s.* **1.** Abstufung *f*, Staffelung *f*; **2.** ⚙ a) Gradeinteilung *f*, b) Grad-, Teilstrich(e *pl.*) *m*; **3.** ⚗ Gradierung *f*; **4.** *univ.* Graduierung *f*, Erteilung *f od.* Erlangung *f* e-s aka'demischen Grades; **5.** *ped. Am.* a) Absolvieren *n* (*from e-r Schule*), b) Schluß-, Verleihungsfeier *f*.

Graeco- [gri:kəʊ] *in Zssgn* griechisch, gräko...

graf·fi·to [grə'fi:təʊ] *pl.* **-ti** [-tɪ] *s.* **1.** (S)Graf'fito *m*, *n*, Kratzmale'rei *f*; **2.** *pl.* Wandkritze'leien *pl.*, Graf'fiti *pl.*

graft [grɑ:ft] **I** *s.* **1.** ♀ a) Pfropfreis *n*, b) veredelte Pflanze, c) Pfropfstelle *f*; **2.** ⚕ a) Transplan'tat *n*, b) Transplantati'on *f*; **3.** *bsd. Am.* F a) Korrupti'on *f*, b) Bestechungs-, Schmiergelder *pl.*; **II** *v/t.* **4.** ♀ a) *Zweig* pfropfen, b) *Pflanze* okulieren, veredeln; **5.** ⚕ *Gewebe* transplantieren, verpflanzen; **6.** *fig.* (*in*, [*up*]*on*) a) *et.* aufpfropfen (*dat.*), b) *Ideen etc.* einimpfen (*dat.*), c) über'tragen (auf *acc.*); **III** *v/i.* **7.** *bsd. Am.* F a) sich (durch 'Amtsˌmißbrauch) bereichern, b) Schmiergelder zahlen; **'graft·er** [-tə] *s.* **1.** ♀ a) Pfropfer *m*, b) Pfropfmesser *n*; **2.** *bsd. Am.* F kor'rupter Be'amter *od.* Po'litiker *etc.*

Grail [greɪl] *s. eccl.* Gral *m*.

grain [greɪn] **I** *s.* **1.** ♀ (Samen-, *bsd.* Getreide)Korn *n*; **2.** *coll.* Getreide *n*, Korn *n*; **3.** Körnchen *n*, (*Sand- etc.*) Korn *n*: *of fine ~* feinkörnig; → *salt* 1; **4.** *fig.* Spur *f*, *ein* bißchen: *a ~ of truth* ein Körnchen Wahrheit; *not a ~ of hope* kein Funke Hoffnung; **5.** ⚕ Gran *n* (*Gewicht*); **6.** a) Faser(ung) *f*, Maserung *f* (*Holz*), b) Narbe *f* (*Leder*), c) Korn *n*, Narbe *f* (*Papier*), d) *metall.* Korn *n*, Körnung *f*, e) Strich *m* (*Tuch*), f) *min.* Korn *n*, Gefüge *n*: *~ (side)* Narbenseite (*Leder*); *it goes against the ~ (with me) fig.* es geht mir gegen den Strich; **7.** *hist.* Coche'nille *f* (*Farbstoff*): *dyed in ~* a) im Rohzustand gefärbt, b) *a. fig.* waschecht; **8.** *phot.* a) Korn *n*, b) Körnigkeit *f* (*Film*); **II** *v/t.* **9.** körnen, granulieren; **10.** ⚙ *Leder*: a) enthaaren, b) körnen, narben; **11.** ⚙ *Holz etc.* (*künstlich*) masern, ädern; **12.** ⚙ a) *Papier* narben, b) in der Wolle färben; *~* **al·co·hol** *s.* ⚗ Ä'thylalkohol *m*; *~* **leath·er** *s.* genarbtes Leder.

gram[1] [græm] → *chickpea*.

gram[2] [græm] *Am.* → *gramme*.

gram·i·na·ceous [ˌgræmɪ'neɪʃəs], **gramin·e·ous** [grə'mɪnɪəs] *adj.* ♀ grasartig, Gras...; **gram·i·niv·o·rous** [ˌgræmɪ'nɪvərəs] *adj.* grasfressend.

gram·mar ['græmə] *s.* **1.** Gram'matik *f* (*a. Lehrbuch*): *bad ~* ungrammatisch; **2.** *fig.* Grundbegriffe *pl.*; **gram·mar·i·an** [grə'meərɪən] *s.* **1.** Gram'matiker (-in); **2.** Verfasser(in) e-r Gram'matik; **gram·mar school** *s.* **1.** *Brit.* höhere Schule, *etwa* Gym'nasium *n*; **2.** *Am. etwa* Grundschule *f*; **gram·mat·i·cal** [grə'mætɪkl] *adj.* ☐ gram'matisch, grammati'kalisch: *not ~* grammatisch falsch.

gramme [græm] *s.* Gramm *n*.

gram mol·e·cule *s. phys.* 'Grammmoleˌkül *n*.

Gram·my ['græmɪ] *s.* Grammy *m* (*amer. Schallplattenpreis*).

gram·o·phone ['græməfəʊn] *s.* a) Grammo'phon *n*, b) Plattenspieler *m*; *~* **rec·ord** *s.* Schallplatte *f*.

gram·pus ['græmpəs] *s. zo.* Schwertwal *m*: *blow like a ~ fig.* wie ein Nilpferd schnaufen.

gran·a·ry ['grænərɪ] *s.* Kornkammer *f* (*a. fig.*), Kornspeicher *m*.

grand [grænd] **I** *adj.* ☐ **1.** großartig, gewaltig, grandi'os, eindrucksvoll, prächtig: *in ~ style* großartig; **2.** (*geistig etc.*) groß, bedeutend, über'ragend; **3.** erhaben (*Stil etc.*); **4.** (*gesellschaftlich*) groß, hochstehend, vornehm, distinguiert: *~ air* Vornehmheit *f*, Würde *f*, *iro.* Gran'dezza *f*; *do the ~* den vornehmen Herrn spielen; *..., he said ~ly* ..., sagte er großartig; **5.** Haupt...: *~ question*; *~ staircase* Haupttreppe *f*; *~ total* Gesamtsumme *f*; **6.** F großartig, prächtig: *a ~ idea*; *have a ~ time* sich glänzend amüsieren; **II** *s.* **7.** ♪ Flügel *m*; **8.** *pl.* **grand** *Am. sl.* ‚Riese' *m* (*1000 Dollar*).

gran·dad → *granddad*.

gran·dam ['grændæm] *s.* **1.** Großmutter *f*; **2.** alte Dame.

'grand|·aunt *s.* Großtante *f*; **'~·child** [-ntʃ-] *s.* [*irr.*] Enkel(in); **'~·dad** [-ndæd] *s.* ‚Opa' *m* (*a. alter Mann*); **'~ˌdaugh·ter** [-nˌdɔ:-] *s.* Enkelin *f*; **ˌ~-'du·cal** [-ndʒd-] *adj.* großherzoglich; ~ **Duch·ess** [-ndd-] *s.* Großherzogin *f*; ~ **Duch·y** *s.* Großherzogtum *n*; ~ **Duke** *s.* **1.** Großherzog *m*; **2.** *hist.* (*russischer*) Großfürst.

gran·dee [græn'di:] *s.* Grande *m*.

gran·deur ['grændʒə] *s.* **1.** Großartigkeit *f* (*a. iro.*); **2.** Größe *f*, Erhabenheit *f*; **3.** Vornehmheit *f*, Hoheit *f*, Würde *f*: *delusions of ~* Größenwahnsinn *m*; **4.** Herrlichkeit *f*, Pracht *f*.

'grandˌfa·ther ['grændˌf-] *s.* Großvater *m*: *~('s) clock* Standuhr *f*; *~('s) chair* Ohrensessel *m*; **'grandˌfa·ther·ly** [-lɪ] *adj.* großväterlich (*a. fig.*).

gran·dil·o·quence [græn'dɪləkwəns] *s.* **1.** (Rede)Schwulst *m*, Bom'bast *m*; **2.** Großspreche'rei *f*; **gran'dil·o·quent** [-nt] *adj.* ☐ **1.** schwülstig, hochtrabend, ‚geschwollen'; **2.** großsprecherisch.

gran·di·ose ['grændɪəʊs] *adj.* ☐ **1.** großartig, grandi'os; **2.** pom'pös, prunkvoll; **3.** schwülstig, hochtrabend, bom'bastisch.

grand| ju·ry *s.* ⚖ *Am.* Anklagejury *f* (*Geschworene, die die Eröffnung des Hauptverfahrens beschließen od. ablehnen*); *~* **lar·ce·ny** *s.* ⚖ *Am.* schwerer Diebstahl; **~·ma** ['grænmɑ:], **~·mamma** ['grænməˌmɑ:] *s.* F 'Großmaˌma *f*, ‚Oma' *f*; *~* **mas·ter** *s.* **1.** *Schach*: Großmeister *m*; **2.** *Grand Master* Großmeister *m* (*der Freimaurer etc.*); **'~ˌmoth·er** [-nˌm-] *s.* Großmutter *f*: *teach your ~ to suck eggs!* das Ei will klüger sein als die Henne!; **'~ˌmoth·er·ly** [-lɪ] *adj.* großmütterlich (*a. fig.*); ~ **Na·tion·al** *s.* *Pferdesport*: Grand National *n* (*Hindernisrennen auf der Aintree-Rennbahn bei Liverpool*); **'~ˌneph·ew** [-nˌn-] *s.* Großneffe *m*.

grand·ness ['grændnɪs] → *grandeur*.

'grand|·niece [-nni:s] *s.* Großnichte *f*; *~* **old man** *s.* ‚großer alter Mann' (*e-r Berufsgruppe etc.*); ~ **Old Par·ty**, *abbr.* **GOP** *s. pol. Am. die* Republi'kanische Par'tei *der USA*; *~* **op·er·a** *s.* ♪ große Oper; **~·pa** ['grænpɑ:], **~·pa·pa** ['grænpəˌpɑ:] *s.* ‚Opa' *m*, 'Großpaˌpa *m*; **'~ˌpar·ent** [-nˌp-] *s.* **1.** Großvater *m od.* -mutter *f*; **2.** *pl.* Großeltern *pl.*; *~* **pi·an·o** *s.* ♪ (Kon'zert)Flügel *m*; **'~ˌsire** [-nˌs-] *s. obs.* **1.** alter Herr; **2.** Großvater *m*; **'~·son** [-ns-] *s.* Enkel *m*; *~* **slam** *s.* **1.** *Tennis*: Grand Slam *m*; **2.** → *slam*[2]; **'~·stand** [-ndʒ-] **I** *s. sport* 'Haupttriˌbüne *f*: *play to the ~* → III; **II** *adj.* Haupttribünen...: *~ seat*; *~ play* F Effekthascherei *f*; *~ finish* packendes Finish; **III** *v/i. Am.* F sich in Szene setzen, ‚e-e Schau abziehen'; *~* **tour** *s. hist.* Bildungs-, Kava'liersreise *f*; **'~ˌun·cle** *s.* Großonkel *m*.

grange [greɪndʒ] *s.* **1.** Farm *f*; **2.** kleiner Gutshof *od.* Landsitz.

gra·nif·er·ous [grə'nɪfərəs] *adj.* ♀ körnertragend.

gran·ite ['grænɪt] **I** *s. min.* Gra'nit *m* (*a. fig.*): *bite on ~ fig.* auf Granit beißen; **II** *adj.* Granit...; *fig.* hart, eisern, unbeugsam; **gra·nit·ic** [græ'nɪtɪk] → *granite* II.

gra·niv·o·rous [grə'nɪvərəs] *adj.* körnerfressend.

gran·nie, **gran·ny** ['grænɪ] *s.* F **1.** ‚Oma' *f*: *~ glasses* Nickelbrille *f*; **2.** *a. ~('s) knot* ⚓ Alt'weiberknoten *m*.

grant [grɑ:nt] **I** *v/t.* **1.** bewilligen, gewähren (*s.o. a credit etc.* j-m e-n Kredit *etc.*): *it was not ~ed to her* es war ihr nicht vergönnt; *God ~ that* gebe Gott, daß; **2.** *e-e Erlaubnis etc.* geben, erteilen; **3.** *e-e Bitte etc.* erfüllen, (*a.* ⚖ *e-m Antrag etc.*) stattgeben; **4.** ⚖ über'tragen, -'eignen, verleihen, *Patent* erteilen; **5.** zugeben, zugestehen, einräumen: *I ~ you that ...* ich gebe zu, daß ...; *~ed, but* zugegeben, aber; *~ed that ...* a) zugegeben, daß, b) angenommen, daß; *take for ~ed* a) *et.* als erwiesen annehmen, b) *et.* als selbstverständlich betrachten, c) gar nicht mehr wissen, was man an *j-m* hat; **II** *s.* **6.** a) Bewilligung *f*, Gewährung *f*, b) Zuschuß *m*, Unter'stützung *f*, Subventi'on *f*; **7.** (Ausbildungs-, Studien)Beihilfe *f*, Sti'pendium *n*; **8.** ⚖ a) Verleihung *f e-s Rechts*, Erteilung *f e-s Patents etc.*, b) (urkundliche) Über'tragung (*to* auf *acc.*); **9.** *Am.* zugewiesenes Amt;

gran·tee [grɑ:n'ti:] *s.* **1.** Begünstigte(r *m*) *f*; **2.** ⚖ a) Zessio'nar(in), Rechtsnachfolger(in), b) Privile'gierte(r *m*) *f*;

ˌgrant-in-'aid *pl.* **ˌgrants-in-'aid** *s.* a) *Brit.* Re'gierungszuschuß *m* an Kom'munen, b) *Am.* Bundeszuschuß *m* an

Einzelstaaten; **gran·tor** [grɑːnˈtɔː] *s.* ⚖ a) Zeˈdent(in), b) Liˈzenzgeber(in).
gran·u·lar [ˈgrænjʊlə] *adj.* **1.** gekörnt, körnig; **2.** granuliert; ˈ**gran·u·late** [-leɪt] **I** *v/t.* **1.** körnen, granulieren; **2.** *Leder* rauhen, narben; **II** *v/i.* körnig werden; ˈ**gran·u·lat·ed** [-leɪtɪd] *adj.* **1.** gekörnt, körnig, granuliert (*a.* ⚕): **~ *sugar*** Kristallzucker *m*; **2.** gerauht; **gran·u·la·tion** [ˌgrænjʊˈleɪʃn] *s.* **1.** ⚙ Körnen *n*, Granulieren *n*; **2.** Körnigkeit *f*; **3.** ⚕ Granulatiˈon *f*; ˈ**gran·ule** [-juːl] *s.* Körnchen *n*; ˈ**gran·u·lous** [-ləs] → ***granular***.
grape [greɪp] *s.* **1.** Weintraube *f*, -beere *f*: ***the*** (***juice of the***) **~** der Saft der Reben (*Wein*); ***but that's just sour ~s*** *fig.* aber ihm (*etc.*) hängen die Trauben zu hoch; → ***bunch*** 1; **2.** → ***grapevine*** 1; **3.** *pl. vet.* a) Mauke *f*, b) ˈRindertuberkuˌlose *f*; **~ *cure*** *s.* ⚕ Traubenkur *f*; ˈ**~·fruit** *s.* ⚘ Grapefruit *f*, Pampelmuse *f*; **~ *juice*** *s.* Traubensaft *m*; ˈ**~-louse** *s.* [*irr.*] *zo.* Reblaus *f*; ˈ**~·shot** *s.* ⚔ Karˈtätsche *f*; ˈ**~·stone** *s.* (Wein)Traubenkern *m*; **~ *sug·ar*** *s.* Traubenzucker *m*; ˈ**~·vine** *s.* **1.** ⚘ Weinstock *m*; **2.** F a) Gerücht *n*, b) *a.* **~ *telegraph*** ‚Buschtrommel' *f*, ˈNachrichtensyˌstem *n*: ***hear s.th. on the ~*** et. gerüchteweise hören.
graph [græf] *s.* **1.** Schaubild *n*, Diaˈgramm *n*, graphische Darstellung, Kurvenblatt *n*, -bild *n*; **2.** *bsd.* A Kurve *f*: **~ *paper*** Millimeterpapier *n*; **3.** *ling.* Graph *m*; ˈ**graph·ic** [-fɪk] **I** *adj.* (☐ **~*ally***) **1.** anschaulich, plastisch, lebendig (geschildert *od.* schildernd); **2.** graphisch, zeichnerisch: **~ *arts*** → 4; **~ *artist*** Graphiker(in); **3.** Schrift…, Schreib…; **II** *s. pl. sg. konstr.* **4.** Graphik, graphische Kunst; **5.** technisches Zeichnen; **6.** graphische Darstellung (*als Fach*); ˈ**graph·i·cal** [-fɪkl] *adj.* ☐ → ***graphic*** I.
graph·ite [ˈgræfaɪt] *s. min.* Graˈphit *m*, Reißblei *n*; **gra·phit·ic** [grəˈfɪtɪk] *adj.* Graphit…
graph·o·log·i·cal [ˌgræfəˈlɒdʒɪkl] *adj.* ☐ graphoˈlogisch; **graph·ol·o·gist** [græˈfɒlədʒɪst] *s.* Graphoˈloge *m*; **graph·ol·o·gy** [græˈfɒlədʒɪ] *s.* Grapholoˈgie *f*, Handschriftendeutung *f*.
grap·nel [ˈgræpnl] *s.* **1.** ⚓ a) Enterhaken *m*, b) Dregganker *m*, Dregge *f*; **2.** ⚙ a) Ankereisen *n*, b) (Greif)Haken *m*, Greifer *m*.
grap·ple [ˈgræpl] **I** *s.* **1.** → ***grapnel*** 1 a *u.* 2 b; **2.** a) Griff *m* (*a. beim Ringen etc.*), b) Handgemenge *n*, Kampf *m*; **II** *v/t.* **3.** ⚓ entern; **4.** ⚙ verankern, verklammern; **5.** packen, fassen; **III** *v/i.* **6.** e-n Enterhaken *od.* Greifer gebrauchen; **7.** ringen, kämpfen (*a. fig.*): **~ *with s.th.*** *fig.* sich mit et. herumschlagen.
grap·pling| hook, **~ i·ron** [ˈgræplɪŋ] → ***grapnel*** 1 a u. 2 b.
grasp [grɑːsp] **I** *v/t.* **1.** packen, fassen, (er)greifen; → ***nettle*** 1; **2.** an sich reißen; **3.** *fig.* verstehen, begreifen, (er-) fassen; **II** *v/i.* **4.** zugreifen, zupacken; **5.** **~ *at*** greifen nach; → ***shadow*** 2, ***straw*** 1; **6.** **~ *at*** *fig.* streben nach; **III** *s.* **7.** Griff *m*; **8.** a) Reichweite *f*, b) *fig.* Macht *f*, Gewalt *f*, Zugriff *m*: ***within one's ~*** in Reichweite, *fig. a.* greifbar nahe; ***within the ~ of*** in der Gewalt von (*od. gen.*); **9.** *fig.* Verständnis *n*, Auffassungsgabe *f*: ***it is within his ~*** das kann er begreifen; ***it is beyond his ~*** es geht über seinen Verstand; ***have a good ~ of s.th.*** et. gut beherrschen; ˈ**grasp·ing** [-pɪŋ] *adj.* ☐ habgierig.
grass [grɑːs] **I** *s.* **1.** ⚘ Gras *n*: ***hear the ~ grow*** *fig.* das Gras wachsen hören; ***not to let the ~ grow under one's feet*** nicht lange fackeln, keine Zeit verschwenden; **2.** Gras *n*, Rasen *m*: ***keep off the ~*** Betreten des Rasens verboten!; **3.** Grasland *n*, Weide *f*: ***be*** (***out***) ***at ~*** a) auf der Weide sein, b) F im Ruhestand sein; ***put*** (*od.* ***turn***) ***out to ~*** a) *Vieh* auf die Weide treiben, b) *bsd. e-m Rennpferd* das Gnadenbrot geben, c) F *j-n* in Rente schicken; **4.** *sl.* ‚Grass' *n*, Marihuˈana *n*; **II** *v/t.* **5.** a) *a.* **~ *down*** mit Gras besäen, b) *a.* **~ *over*** mit Rasen bedecken; **6.** *Vieh* weiden (lassen); **7.** *Wäsche* auf dem Rasen bleichen; **8.** *Vogel* abschießen; **9.** *sport Gegner* zu Fall bringen; **III** *v/i.* **10.** grasen, weiden; **11.** *Brit. sl.* ‚singen': **~ *on s.o.*** j-n ‚verpfeifen'; **~ *blade*** *s.* Grashalm *m*; **~ *court*** *s. Tennis*: Rasenplatz *m*; ˌ**~-ˈgreen** *adj.* grasgrün; ˈ**~-grown** *adj.* mit Gras bewachsen; ˈ**~ˌhop·per** *s.* **1.** *zo.* (Feld)Heuschrecke *f*, Grashüpfer *m*; **2.** ✈, ⚔ Leichtflugzeug *n*; ˈ**~·land** *s.* Weide(land *n*) *f*; ˈ**~·plot** *s.* Rasenplatz *m*; **~ *roots*** *s. pl.* **1.** *fig.* Wurzel *f*; **2.** *pol.* a) Basis *f* (*e-r Partei*), b) ländliche Bezirke *od.* Landbevölkerung *f*; ˈ**~·roots** *adj. pol.* a) (an) der Basis (*e-r Partei*), b) bodenständig: **~ *democracy***; **~ *snake*** *s. zo.* Ringelnatter *f*; **~ *wid·ow*** *s.* **1.** Strohwitwe *f*; **2.** *Am.* geschiedene *od.* getrennt lebende Frau; **~ *wid·ow·er*** *s.* **1.** Strohwitwer *m*; **2.** *Am.* geschiedener *od.* getrennt lebender Mann.
grass·y [ˈgrɑːsɪ] *adj.* grasbedeckt, grasig, Gras…
grate¹ [greɪt] **I** *v/t.* **1.** *Käse etc.* reiben, *Gemüse etc. a.* raspeln; **2.** a) knirschen mit: **~ *one's teeth***, b) kratzen mit, c) quietschen mit; **3.** *et.* krächzen(d sagen); **II** *v/i.* **4.** knirschen *od.* kratzen *od.* quietschen; **5.** weh tun ([***up***]***on s.o.*** j-m): **~ *on s.o.'s nerves*** an j-s Nerven zerren; **~ *on the ear*** dem Ohr weh tun; **~ *on s.o.'s ears*** j-m in den Ohren weh tun.
grate² [greɪt] *s.* **1.** Gitter *n*; **2.** (Feuer-, ⚙ Kessel)Rost *m*; **3.** Kaˈmin *m*; **4.** *Wasserbau*: Fangrechen *m*; ˈ**grat·ed** [-tɪd] *adj.* vergittert.
grate·ful [ˈgreɪtfʊl] *adj.* ☐ **1.** dankbar (***to s.o. for s.th.*** j-m für et.): ***a ~ letter*** ein Dank(es)brief; **2.** *fig.* dankbar (*Aufgabe etc.*); **3.** angenehm, wohltuend, willˈkommen (***to s.o.*** j-m); ˈ**grate·ful·ness** [-nɪs] *s.* Dankbarkeit *f*.
grat·er [ˈgreɪtə] *s.* Reibe *f*, Reibeisen *n*, Raspel *f*.
grat·i·cule [ˈgrætɪkjuːl] *s.* ⚙ **1.** a) (Grad)Netz *n*, Koordiˈnatensyˌstem *n*, b) mit e-m Netz versehene Zeichnung; **2.** Fadenkreuz *n*.
grat·i·fi·ca·tion [ˌgrætɪfɪˈkeɪʃn] *s.* **1.** Befriedigung *f*: a) Zuˈfriedenstellung *f*, b) Genugtuung *f* (***at*** über *acc.*); **2.** Freude *f*, Vergnügen *n*, Genuß *m*; **3.** *obs.* Gratifikatiˈon *f*; **grat·i·fy** [ˈgrætɪfaɪ] *v/t.* **1.** befriedigen: **~ *one's thirst for knowledge*** s-n Wissensdurst stillen; **2.** *j-m* gefällig sein; **3.** erfreuen: ***be gratified*** sich freuen; ***I am gratified to hear*** ich höre mit Genugtuung *od.* Befriedigung; **grat·i·fy·ing** [ˈgrætɪfaɪɪŋ] *adj.* ☐ erfreulich, befriedigend (***to*** für).
gra·tin [ˈgrætæ̃ŋ] (*Fr.*) *s.* **1.** Bratkruste *f*: ***au ~*** gratiniert, überbacken; **2.** Graˈtin *n*, gratinierte Speise.
grat·ing¹ [ˈgreɪtɪŋ] *adj.* ☐ **1.** kratzend, knirschend; **2.** krächzend, heiser; **3.** unangenehm.
grat·ing² [ˈgreɪtɪŋ] *s.* **1.** Gitter *n* (*a. phys.*), Gitterwerk *n*; **2.** ⚙ (Balken-, Lauf)Rost *m*; **3.** ⚓ Gräting *f*.
gra·tis [ˈgreɪtɪs] **I** *adv.* gratis, unentgeltlich, umˈsonst; **II** *adj.* unentgeltlich, frei, Gratis…
grat·i·tude [ˈgrætɪtjuːd] *s.* Dankbarkeit *f*: ***in ~ for*** aus Dankbarkeit für.
gra·tu·i·tous [grəˈtjuːɪtəs] *adj.* ☐ **1.** → ***gratis*** II; **2.** ⚖ ohne Gegenleistung; **3.** freiwillig, unverlangt; **4.** grundlos, unberechtigt, unverdient; **graˈtu·i·ty** [-tɪ] *s.* **1.** (Geld)Geschenk *n*, Gratifikatiˈon *f*, Sondervergütung *f*, Zuwendung *f*; **2.** Trinkgeld *n*.
gra·va·men [grəˈveɪmen] *s.* **1.** ⚖ a) (Haupt)Beschwerdegrund *m*, b) *das* Belastende *e-r Anklage*; **2.** *bsd. eccl.* Beschwerde *f*.
grave¹ [greɪv] *s.* **1.** Grab *n*: ***dig one's own ~*** sein eigenes Grab schaufeln; ***have one foot in the ~*** mit einem Bein im Grab stehen; ***rise from the ~*** (von den Toten) auferstehen; ***turn in one's ~*** sich im Grabe umdrehen; **2.** *fig.* Grab *n*, Tod *m*, Ende *n*.
grave² [greɪv] **I** *adj.* ☐ **1.** ernst: a) feierlich, b) bedenklich: **~ *illness*** (***voice***, *etc.*), c) gewichtig, schwerwiegend, d) gesetzt, würdevoll, e) schwer, tief: **~ *thoughts***; **2.** dunkel, gedämpft (*Farbe*); **3.** *ling.* fallend: **~ *accent*** → 5; **4.** tief (*Ton*); **II** *s.* **5.** *ling.* Gravis *m*, Acˈcent *m* grave.
grave³ [greɪv] *v/t.* [*irr.*] *obs.* **1.** *Figur* (ein)schnitzen, (-)meißeln; **2.** *fig.* eingraben, -prägen.
grave⁴ [greɪv] *v/t.* ⚓ *Schiffsboden* reinigen u. teeren.
ˈ**graveˌdig·ger** *s.* Totengräber *m* (*a. zo. u. fig.*).
grav·el [ˈgrævl] **I** *s.* **1.** Kies *m*: **~ *pit*** Kiesgrube *f*; **2.** Schotter *m*; **3.** *geol.* Geröll *n*; **4.** ⚕ Harngrieß *m*; **II** *v/t.* **5.** a) mit Kies bestreuen, b) beschottern; **6.** *fig.* verwirren, verblüffen.
grav·en [ˈgreɪvn] *p.p. von* ***grave³*** *u. adj.* geschnitzt: **~ *image*** Götzenbild *n*.
grav·er [ˈgreɪvə] → ***graving tool***.
Graves' dis·ease [greɪvz] *s.* ⚕ Basedowsche Krankheit.
ˈ**grave|·side** *s.*: ***at the ~*** am Grab; ˈ**~·stone** *s.* Grabstein *m*; ˈ**~·yard** *s.* Fried-, Kirchhof *m*.
grav·id [ˈgrævɪd] *adj.* a) schwanger, b) trächtig (*Tier*).
gra·vim·e·ter [grəˈvɪmɪtə] *s. phys.* Graviˈmeter *n*: a) Dichtemesser *m*, b) Schweremesser *m*.
grav·ing| dock [ˈgreɪvɪŋ] *s.* ⚓ Trockendock *n*; **~ *tool*** *s.* ⚙ Grabstichel *m*.
grav·i·tate [ˈgrævɪteɪt] *v/i.* **1.** sich (durch Schwerkraft) fortbewegen; **2.** *a. fig.* gravitieren, (hin)streben (***towards*** zu,

nach); **3.** *fig.* sich hingezogen fühlen, tendieren, (hin)neigen (***to, towards*** zu); **4.** sinken, fallen; **grav·i·ta·tion** [ˌgrævɪˈteɪʃn] *s.* **1.** *phys.* Gravitatiˈon *f*: a) Schwerkraft *f*, b) Gravitieren *n*; **2.** *fig.* Neigung *f*, Hang *m*, Tenˈdenz *f*; **grav·i·ta·tion·al** [ˌgrævɪˈteɪʃənl] *adj. phys.* Gravitations...: ***~ force*** Schwerkraft *f*; ***~ field*** Schwerefeld *n*; ***~ pull*** Anziehungskraft *f*.

grav·i·ty [ˈgrævətɪ] **I** *s.* **1.** Ernst *m*: a) Feierlichkeit *f*, b) Bedenklichkeit *f*, c) Gesetztheit *f*, d) Schwere *f*; **2.** ♪ Tiefe *f* (*Ton*); **3.** *phys.* a) *a.* ***force of ~*** Gravitatiˈon *f*, Schwerkraft *f*, b) (Erd)Schwere *f*, c) Erdbeschleunigung; → ***centre*** 1, ***specific*** 8; **II** *adj.* **4.** *phys.*, ⚙ Schwerkraft...: ***~ drive***; ***~ feed*** Gefällezuführung *f*; ***~ tank*** Falltank *m*.

gra·vure [grəˈvjʊə] *s.* Graˈvüre *f*.

gra·vy [ˈgreɪvɪ] *s.* **1.** Braten-, Fleischsaft *m*; **2.** (Fleisch-, Braten)Soße *f*; **3.** *sl.* a) lukraˈtive Sache, b) (unverhoffter) Gewinn: ***that's pure ~!*** das ist ja phantastisch!; ***~ beef*** *s.* Saftbraten *m*; ***~ boat*** *s.* Sauciˈere *f*, Soßenschüssel *f*; ***~ train*** *s.*: ***get on the ~*** *sl.* a) leicht ans große Geld kommen, b) ein Stück vom ‚Kuchen' abkriegen.

gray *etc. bsd. Am.* → ***grey*** *etc.*

graze¹ [greɪz] **I** *v/t.* **1.** *Vieh* weiden (lassen); **2.** abweiden, -grasen; **II** *v/i.* **3.** weiden, grasen (*Vieh*): ***grazing ground*** Weideland *n*.

graze² [greɪz] **I** *v/t.* **1.** streifen: a) leicht berühren, b) schrammen; **2.** ⚕ (ab-)schürfen, (auf)schrammen; **II** *v/i.* **3.** streifen; **III** *s.* **4.** Streifen *n*; **5.** ⚕ Abschürfung *f*, Schramme *f*; **6.** *a.* ***grazing shot*** Streifschuß *m*.

gra·zier [ˈgreɪzjə] *s.* Viehzüchter *m*.

grease I *s.* [gri:s] **1.** (*zerlassenes*) Fett, Schmalz *n*; **2.** ⚙ Schmierfett *n*, -mittel *n*, Schmiere *f*; **3.** a) Wollfett *n*, b) Schweißwolle *f*; **4.** *vet.* (Flechten)Mauke *f* (*Pferd*); **5.** *hunt.* Feist *n*: ***in ~ of pride*** (*od.* ***prime***) fett (*Wild*); **II** *v/t.* [gri:z] **6.** ⚙ (ein)fetten, (ab)schmieren; → ***lightning*** I; **7.** beschmieren; **8.** F *j-n* ‚schmieren', bestechen; ***~ cup*** *s.* ⚙ Staufferbüchse *f*; ***~ gun*** *s.* ⚙ (Ab-)Schmierpresse *f*; ***~ mon·key*** *s.* F ✈, *mot.* (*bsd.* ˈAuto-, ˈFlugzeug)Meˌchaniker *m*; ***~ paint*** *s. thea.* (Fett)Schminke *f*; ˈ**~·proof** *adj.* fettabstoßend.

greas·er [ˈgri:zə] *s.* **1.** Schmierer *m*, Öler *m*; **2.** ⚙ Schmiervorrichtung *f*; **3.** *Brit.* F ˈAutomeˌchaniker *m*; **4.** *Brit.* F *contp.* ‚Schleimscheißer' *m*; **5.** *Am. contp.* Mexiˈkaner *m*.

greas·i·ness [ˈgri:zɪnɪs] *s.* **1.** Fettig-, Öligkeit *f*; **2.** Schmierigkeit *f*; **3.** Schlüpfrigkeit *f*; **4.** *fig.* Aalglätte *f*; **greas·y** [ˈgri:zɪ] *adj.* □ **1.** fettig, schmierig, ölig; **2.** schmierig, beschmiert; **3.** glitschig, schlüpfrig; **4.** ungewaschen (*Wolle*); **5.** *fig.* a) aalglatt, b) ölig, c) schmierig.

great [greɪt] **I** *adj.* □ → ***greatly***; **1.** groß, beträchtlich: ***a ~ number*** e-e große Anzahl; ***a ~ many*** sehr viele; ***the ~ majority*** die große Mehrheit; ***live to a ~ age*** ein hohes Alter erreichen; **2.** groß, Haupt...: ***to a ~ extent*** in hohem Maße; ***~ friends*** dicke Freunde; **3.** groß, bedeutend, berühmt: ***a ~ poet***; ***a ~ city*** e-e bedeutende Stadt; ***~ issues*** wichtige Probleme; **4.** hochstehend, vornehm, berühmt: ***a ~ family***; ***the ~ world*** die gute Gesellschaft; **5.** großartig, vorˈzüglich, wertvoll: ***a ~ opportunity*** e-e vorzügliche Gelegenheit; ***it is a ~ thing to be healthy*** es ist viel wert, gesund zu sein; **6.** erhaben, hoch: ***~ thoughts***; **7.** eifrig: ***a ~ reader***; **8.** groß(geschrieben); **9.** *nur pred.* a) gut: ***he is ~ at golf*** er spielt (sehr) gut Golf, er ist ‚ganz groß' im Golfspielen, b) interessiert: ***he is ~ on dogs*** er ist ein großer Hundeliebhaber; **10.** F großartig, wunderbar, prima; ***we had a ~ time*** wir haben uns herrlich amüsiert, es war sagenhaft (schön); ***the ~ thing is that ...*** das Großartige (daran) ist, daß; **11.** *in Verwandtschaftsbezeichnungen*: a) Groß..., b) (*vor* ***grand...***) Ur...; **12.** *als Beiname*: ***the ℒ Elector*** der Große Kurfürst; ***Frederick the ℒ*** Friedrich der Große; **II** *s.* **13.** ***the ~*** *pl.* die Großen *pl.*, die Promiˈnenten *pl.*; **14.** *pl. Brit. univ.* ˈSchlußexˌamen *n* für den Grad des B.A. (*Oxford*).

ˌ**great|-ˈaunt** *s.* Großtante *f*; **ℒ Char·ter** → ***Magna C(h)arta***; ***~ cir·cle*** *s.* △ Großkreis *m* (*e-r Kugel*); ˈ**~·coat** *s.* (Herren)Mantel *m*; **ℒ Dane** *s. zo.* Dänische Dogge; ***~ di·vide*** *s.* **1.** *geogr.* Hauptwasserscheide *f*: ***the Great Divide*** die Rocky Mountains; ***cross the ~*** *fig.* die Schwelle des Todes überschreiten; **2.** *fig.* Krise *f*, entscheidende Phase.

Great·er Lon·don [ˈgreɪtə] *s.* Groß-London *n*.

ˌ**great|-ˈgrand·child** *s.* Urenkel(in); ˌ**~-ˈgrandˌdaugh·ter** *s.* Urenkelin *f*; ˌ**~-ˈgrandˌfa·ther** *s.* Urgroßvater *m*; ˌ**~-ˈgrandˌmoth·er** *s.* Urgroßmutter *f*; ˌ**~-ˈgrandˌpar·ents** *s. pl.* Urgroßeltern *pl.*; ˌ**~-ˈgrand·son** *s.* Urenkel *m*; ***~ gross*** *s.* zwölf Gros *pl.*; ˌ**~-ˈheart·ed** *adj.* **1.** beherzt; **2.** hochherzig; **ℒ Lakes** *s. pl. die* Großen Seen *pl.* (*USA*).

great·ly [ˈgreɪtlɪ] *adv.* sehr, höchst, außerordentlich, ˈüberaus.

Great| Mo·gul [ˈməʊgʌl] *s. hist.* Großmogul *m*; ˌ**ℒ-ˈneph·ew** *s.* Großneffe *m*.

great·ness [ˈgreɪtnɪs] *s.* **1.** Größe *f*, Erhabenheit *f*: ***~ of mind*** Geistesgröße; **2.** Größe *f*, Bedeutung *f*, Wichtigkeit *f*, Rang *m*; **3.** Ausmaß *n*.

ˌ**great|-ˈniece** *s.* Großnichte *f*; **ℒ Plains** *s. pl. Am. Präriegebiete im Westen der USA*; **ℒ Pow·ers** *s. pl. pol.* Großmächte *pl.*; **ℒ Seal** *s. Brit. hist.* Großsiegel *n*; ***~ tit*** *s. orn.* Kohlmeise *f*; ˌ**~-ˈun·cle** *s.* Großonkel *m*; **ℒ Wall (of Chi·na)** *s. die* Chiˈnesische Mauer; **ℒ War** *s.* (*bsd. der* Erste) Weltkrieg.

greave [gri:v] *s. hist.* Beinschiene *f*.

greaves [gri:vz] *s. pl.* Grieben *pl.*

grebe [gri:b] *s. orn.* (See)Taucher *m*.

Gre·cian [ˈgri:ʃn] **I** *adj.* **1.** (*bsd.* klassisch) griechisch; **II** *s.* **2.** Grieche *m*, Griechin *f*; **3.** Gräˈzist *m*.

greed [gri:d] *s.* Gier *f* (***for*** nach); Habgier *f*, -sucht *f*: ***~ for power*** Machtgier; ˈ**greed·i·ness** [-dɪnɪs] *s.* **1.** Gierigkeit *f*; **2.** Gefräßigkeit *f*; ˈ**greed·y** [-dɪ] *adj.* □ **1.** gierig (***for*** auf *acc.*, nach): ***~ for power*** machtgierig; **2.** habgierig; **3.** gefräßig, gierig.

Greek [gri:k] **I** *s.* **1.** Grieche *m*, Griechin *f*: ***when ~ meets ~*** *fig.* wenn zwei Ebenbürtige sich miteinander messen; **2.** *ling.* Griechisch *n*, das Griechische: ***that's ~ to me*** das sind für mich böhmische Dörfer; **II** *adj.* **3.** griechisch; ***~ Church*** *s.* ˌgriechisch-orthoˈdoxe *od.* -kaˈtholische Kirche; ***~ cross*** *s.* griechisches Kreuz; ***~ gift*** *s. fig.* Danaergeschenk *n*; ***~ Or·tho·dox Church*** → ***Greek Church***.

green [gri:n] **I** *adj.* □ **1.** *allg.* grün (*a. weitS. grünend, schneefrei, unreif*): ***~ apples*** (***fields***); ***~ food***, ***~ vegetables*** → 13; ***~ with envy*** grün *od.* gelb vor Neid; ***~ with fear*** schreckensbleich; **2.** grün, frisch: ***~ fish***; ***~ wine*** neuer Wein; **3.** roh, frisch, Frisch...: ***~ meat***; ***~ coffee*** Rohkaffee *m*; **4.** ⚙ nicht fertigverarbeitet: ***~ ceramics*** ungebrannte Töpferwaren; ***~ hide*** ungegerbtes Fell; ***~ ore*** Roherz *n*; **5.** ⚙ faˈbrikneu: ***~ assembly*** Erstmontage *f*; ***~ run*** Einfahren *n*, erster Lauf; **6.** *fig.* frisch: a) neu, b) lebendig: ***~ memories***; **7.** *fig.* grün, unerfahren, naˈiv: ***a ~ youth***; ***~ in years*** jung an Jahren; **8.** jugendlich: ***~ old age*** rüstiges Alter; **II** *s.* **9.** Grün *n*, grüne Farbe: ***the lights are at ~*** *mot.* die Ampel steht auf Grün; ***at ~*** bei Grün; **10.** Grünfläche *f*, Rasen(platz) *m*: ***village ~*** Dorfanger *m*, -wiese *f*; **11.** Golfplatz *m*; **12.** *pl.* Grün *n*, grünes Laub; **13.** *mst pl.* grünes Gemüse, Blattgemüse *n*; **14.** *fig.* Jugendfrische *f*; **15.** *sl.* ‚Kies' *m* (*Geld*); **III** *v/t.* **16.** grün machen *od.* färben; **IV** *v/i.* **17.** grün werden, grünen.

ˈ**green|·back** *s.* **1.** *Am.* F Dollarschein *m*; **2.** *zo.* Laubfrosch *m*; ***~ belt*** *s.* Grüngürtel *m* (*um e-e Stadt*); ***~ cheese*** *s.* **1.** unreifer Käse; **2.** Molkenkäse *m*; **3.** Kräuterkäse *m*; ***~ cloth*** *s. bsd. Am.* **1.** Spieltisch *m*; **2.** Billardtisch *m*; ***~ crop*** *s.* ⸙ Grünfutter *n*.

green·er·y [ˈgri:nərɪ] *s.* **1.** Grün *n*, Laub *n*; **2.** → ***greenhouse*** 1.

ˈ**green|-eyed** *adj. fig.* eifersüchtig, neidisch: ***the ~ monster*** die Eifersucht; ˈ**~·finch** *s. orn.* Grünfink *m*; ***~ fin·gers*** *s. pl.* F gärtnerische Begabung: ***he has ~*** bei ihm gedeihen alle Pflanzen, ‚er hat einen grünen Daumen'; ˈ**~·fly** *s. zo. Brit.* grüne Blattlaus; ˈ**~·gage** *s.* Reineˈclaude *f*; ˈ**~ˌgro·cer** *s.* Obst- u. Gemüsehändler *m*; ˈ**~ˌgro·cer·y** *s.* **1.** Obst- u. Gemüsehandlung *f*; **2.** *pl.* Obst *n* u. Gemüse *n*; ˈ**~·horn** *s.* F **1.** ‚Greenhorn' *n*, Grünschnabel *m*, (unerfahrener) Neuling; **2.** Gimpel *m*; ˈ**~·house** *s.* **1.** Treib-, Gewächshaus *n*; **2.** ✈ F Vollsichtkanzel *f*.

green·ish [ˈgri:nɪʃ] *adj.* grünlich.

Green·land·er [ˈgri:nləndə] *s.* Grönländer(in).

green| light *s.* grünes Licht (*bsd. der Verkehrsampel*; *a. fig. Genehmigung*): ***give s.o. the ~*** *fig.* j-m grünes Licht geben; ***~ lung*** *s. Brit.* ‚grüne Lunge', Grünflächen *pl.*; ˈ**~·man** [-mən] *s.* [*irr.*] Platzmeister *m* (*Golfplatz*).

green·ness [ˈgri:nnɪs] *s.* **1.** Grün *n*, *das* Grüne; **2.** *fig.* Frische *f*, Munterkeit *f*, Kraft *f*; **3.** *fig.* Unreife *f*, Unerfahrenheit *f*.

green| pound *s.* ☤ grünes Pfund (*EG-Verrechnungseinheit*); ˈ**~·room** [-rʊm] *s. thea.* ˈKünstlerzimmer *n*, -gardeˌrobe *f*; ˈ**~ˌsick·ness** *s.* ⚕ Bleichsucht *f*;

'~·stick (frac·ture) *s.* ⚕ Knickbruch *m*; **'~·stuff** *s.* **1.** Grünfutter *n*; **2.** grünes Gemüse; **'~·sward** *s.* Rasen *m*; **~ ta·ble** *s.* Konfe'renztisch *m*; **~ tea** *s.* grüner Tee; **~ thumb** *Am.* → ***green fingers***.

Green·wich (Mean) Time ['grɪnɪdʒ] *s.* Greenwicher Zeit.

greet [gri:t] *v/t.* **1.** grüßen; **2.** begrüßen, empfangen; **3.** *fig. dem Auge* begegnen, *ans Ohr* dringen, sich *j-m* bieten (*Anblick*); **4.** *e-e Nachricht etc. freudig etc.* aufnehmen; **'greet·ing** [-tɪŋ] *s.* **1.** Gruß *m*, Begrüßung *f*; **2.** *pl.* a) Grüße *pl.*, b) Glückwünsche *pl.*: ***~s card*** Glückwunschkarte *f*.

gre·gar·i·ous [grɪ'geərɪəs] *adj.* □ **1.** gesellig; **2.** *zo.* in Herden *od.* Scharen lebend, Herden...; **3.** ♀ traubenartig wachsend; **gre'gar·i·ous·ness** [-nɪs] *s.* **1.** Geselligkeit *f*; **2.** *zo.* Zs.-leben *n* in Herden.

Gre·go·ri·an [grɪ'gɔ:rɪən] *adj.* Gregori'anisch: ***~ calendar***; ***~ chant*** ♪ Gregorianischer Gesang.

greige [greɪʒ] *adj. u. s.* ⚙ na'turfarben(e Stoffe *pl.*).

grem·lin ['gremlɪn] *s. sl.* böser Geist, Kobold *m* (*der Maschinenschaden etc. anrichtet*).

gre·nade [grɪ'neɪd] *s.* **1.** ⚔ Ge'wehr-, 'Handgra,nate *f*; **2.** 'Tränengaspa,trone *f*; **gren·a·dier** [,grenə'dɪə] *s.* ⚔ Grena'dier *m*.

gres·so·ri·al [gre'sɔ:rɪəl] *adj. orn., zo.* Schreit..., Stelz...: ***~ birds***.

Gret·na Green mar·riage ['gretnə] *s.* Heirat *f* in Gretna Green (*Schottland*).

grew [gru:] *pret. von* ***grow***.

grey [greɪ] **I** *adj.* □ **1.** grau; **2.** grau (-haarig), ergraut: ***grow ~*** → 8; **3.** farblos, blaß; **4.** trübe, düster, grau: ***a ~ day***; ***~ prospects*** trübe Aussichten; **5.** ⚙ neu'tral, farblos, na'turfarben: ***~ cloth*** ungebleichter Baumwollstoff; **II** *s.* **6.** Grau *n*, graue Farbe: ***dressed in ~*** grau *od.* in Grau gekleidet; **7.** *zo.* Grauschimmel *m*; **III** *v/i.* **8.** grau werden, ergrauen: ***~ing*** angegraut (*Haare*); **~ a·re·a** *s.* **1.** *Statistik*: Grauzone *f*; **2.** *Brit.* Gebiet *n* mit hoher Arbeitslosigkeit; **'~·back** *s.* **1.** *zo.* Grauwal *m*; **2.** *Am.* F ‚Graurock' *m* (*Soldat der Südstaaten im Bürgerkrieg*); **~ crow** *s. orn.* Nebelkrähe *f*; **'~·fish** *s. ein* Hai(fisch) *m*; **~ goose** → ***greylag***; **,~-'head·ed** *adj.* **1.** grauköpfig; **2.** *fig.* alterfahren; **'~·hen** *s. orn.* Birk-, Haselhuhn *n*; **'~·hound** *s.* Windhund *m*; ***~-racing*** Windhundrennen *n*.

grey·ish ['greɪɪʃ] *adj.* gräulich, Grau...

grey·lag ['greɪlæg] *s. orn.* Grau-, Wildgans *f*.

grey| mar·ket *s.* ✝ grauer Markt; **~ mat·ter** *s.* **1.** ⚕ graue ('Hirnrinden-) Sub,stanz; **2.** F ‚Grips' *m*, ‚Grütze' *f* (*Verstand*); **~ mul·let** *s. ichth.* Meeräsche *f*.

grey·ness ['greɪnɪs] *s.* **1.** Grau *n*; **2.** *fig.* Trübheit *f*, Düsterkeit *f*.

grey squir·rel *s. zo.* Grauhörnchen *n*.

grid [grɪd] *s.* **1.** Gitter *n*, Rost *m*; **2.** ⚡ a) Bleiplatte *f*, b) Gitter *n* (*in Elektronenröhre*); **3.** ⚡ *etc.* Versorgungsnetz *n*; **4.** Gitternetz *n auf Landkarten*: ***~ded map*** Gitternetzkarte *f*; **5.** → ***gridiron*** 1, 4, 6; **~ bi·as** *s.* ⚡ Gittervorspannung *f*; **~ cir·cuit** *s.* ⚡ Gitterkreis *m*.

grid·dle ['grɪdl] *s.* **1.** Kuchen-, Backblech *n*: ***~ cake*** Pfannkuchen *m*; ***be on the ~*** F ‚in die Mangel genommen werden'; **2.** ⚙ Drahtsieb *n*.

'grid,i·ron *s.* **1.** Bratrost *m*; **2.** ⚙ Gitterrost *m*; **3.** Netz(werk) *n* (*Leitungen, Bahnlinien etc.*); **4.** ⚓ Balkenrost *m*; **5.** *thea.* Schnürboden *m*; **6.** *American Football*: F Spielfeld *n*.

grid| leak *s.* ⚡ 'Gitter(ableit),widerstand *m*; **~ line** *s.* Gitternetzlinie *f* (*auf Landkarten*); **~ plate** *s.* ⚡ Gitterplatte *f*; **~ square** *s.* 'Planqua,drat *n*.

grief [gri:f] *s.* Gram *m*, Kummer *m*, Leid *n*, Schmerz *m*: ***bring to ~*** zu Fall bringen, zugrunde richten; ***come to ~*** a) zu Schaden kommen, verunglücken, b) zugrunde gehen, c) fehlschlagen, scheitern: ***good ~!*** F meine Güte!; **'~-,strick·en** *adj.* kummervoll.

griev·ance ['gri:vns] *s.* **1.** Beschwerde (-grund *m*) *f*, (Grund *m* zur) Klage *f*: ***~ committee*** Schlichtungsausschuß *m*; **2.** Mißstand *m*; **3.** Groll *m*; **4.** Unzufriedenheit *f*; **grieve** [gri:v] **I** *v/t.* betrüben, bekümmern, *j-m* weh tun; **II** *v/i.* bekümmert sein, sich grämen (***at, about*** über *acc.*, wegen; ***for*** um); **'griev·ous** [-vəs] *adj.* □ **1.** schmerzlich, bitter, quälend; **2.** schwer, schlimm: ***~ error***, ***~ bodily harm*** ⚖ schwere Körperverletzung; **3.** bedauerlich; **'griev·ous·ness** [-vəsnɪs] *s. das* Schmerzliche *etc.*

grif·fin¹ ['grɪfɪn] *s.* **1.** *myth., her.* Greif *m*; **2.** → ***griffon¹***.

grif·fin² ['grɪfɪn] *s.* Neuankömmling *m* (*im Orient*).

grif·fon¹ ['grɪfən], *a.* **~ vul·ture** *s. orn.* Weißköpfiger Geier.

grif·fon² ['grɪfən] *s.* **1.** → ***griffin¹*** 1; **2.** Grif'fon *m* (*ein Vorstehhund*).

grift·er ['grɪftə] *s. Am. sl.* Gauner *m*.

grill¹ [grɪl] **I** *s.* **1.** Grill *m*, (Brat)Rost *m*; **2.** Grillen *n*; **3.** Gegrillte(s) *n*; **4.** → ***grillroom***; **II** *v/t.* **5.** *Fleisch etc.* grillen; **6.** ***~ o.s.*** sich (in der Sonne) grillen; **7.** *a.* ***give a ~ing*** F *j-n* ‚in die Mangel nehmen', ‚ausquetschen' (*bsd. Polizei*); **III** *v/i.* **8.** gegrillt werden.

grill² [grɪl] → ***grille***.

grille [grɪl] *s.* **1.** Tür-, Fenster-, Schaltergitter *n*; **2.** Gitterfenster *n*, Sprechgitter *n*; **3.** *mot.* (Kühler)Grill *m*; **grilled** [-ld] *adj.* vergittert.

grill·er ['grɪlə] → ***grill¹*** 1; **'grill·room** *s.* Grill(room) *m*.

grilse [grɪls] *s.*, *a. pl. ichth.* junger Lachs.

grim [grɪm] *adj.* □ **1.** grimmig: a) zornig, wütend, b) erbittert, verbissen: ***~ struggle***, c) hart, schlimm, grausam; **2.** schrecklich, grausig: ***~ accident***.

gri·mace [grɪ'meɪs] **I** *s.* Gri'masse *f*, Fratze *f*: ***make a ~***, ***make ~s*** → **II** *v/i.* e-e Gri'masse *od.* Gri'massen schneiden, das Gesicht verzerren *od.* verziehen.

gri·mal·kin [grɪ'mælkɪn] *s.* **1.** (alte) Katze; **2.** alte Hexe (*Frau*).

grime [graɪm] **I** *s.* (zäher) Schmutz *od.* Ruß; **II** *v/t.* beschmutzen; **'grim·i·ness** [-mɪnɪs] *s.* Schmutzigkeit *f*.

Grimm's law [grɪmz] *s. ling.* (Gesetz *n* der) Lautverschiebung *f*.

grim·ness ['grɪmnɪs] *s.* Grimmigkeit *f*, Schrecklichkeit *f*; Grausamkeit *f*, Härte *f*; Verbissenheit *f*.

grim·y ['graɪmɪ] *adj.* □ schmutzig, rußig.

grin [grɪn] **I** *v/i.* grinsen, feixen, *oft nur* (verschmitzt) lächeln: ***~ at s.o.*** j-n angrinsen *od.* anlächeln; ***~ to o.s.*** in sich hineingrinsen; ***~ and bear it*** a) gute Miene zum bösen Spiel machen, b) die Zähne zs.-beißen; **II** *v/t. et.* grinsend sagen; **III** *s.* Grinsen *n*, (verschmitztes) Lächeln.

grind [graɪnd] **I** *v/t.* [*irr.*] **1.** *Messer etc.* schleifen, wetzen, schärfen; *Glas* schleifen: ***~ in*** *Ventile* einschleifen; → ***ax*** 1; **2.** *a.* ***~ down*** (zer)mahlen, zerreiben, -kleinern, -stoßen, -stampfen, schroten; **3.** *Kaffee, Korn, Mehl etc.* mahlen; **4.** ⚙ schmirgeln, glätten, polieren; **5.** ***~ down*** abwetzen; → 2 *u.* 11; **6.** ***~ one's teeth*** mit den Zähnen knirschen; **7.** knirschend (*hinein*)bohren; **8.** *Leierkasten etc.* drehen; **9.** ***~ out*** a) *Zeitungsartikel etc.* her'unterschreiben, b) ♪ her'unterspielen; **10.** ***~ out*** *et.* mühsam her'vorbringen; **11.** *a.* ***~ down*** *fig.* (unter)'drücken, schinden, quälen: ***~ the faces of the poor*** die Armen (gnadenlos) ausbeuten; **12.** ***~ s.th. into s.o.*** F j-m et. ‚einpauken'; **II** *v/i.* [*irr.*] **13.** mahlen; **14.** knirschen; **15.** F sich plagen *od.* abschinden; **16.** *ped.* F ‚pauken', ‚ochsen', ‚büffeln'; **III** *s.* **17.** F Schinde'rei *f*: ***the daily ~***; **18.** *ped.* F a) ‚Pauken' *n*, ‚Büffeln' *n*, b) Streber(in), ‚Büffler(in)'; **19.** *Brit. sl.* ‚Nummer' *f* (*Koitus*); **'grind·er** [-də] *s.* **1.** (*Messer-, Scheren-, Glas*)Schleifer *m*; **2.** Schleifstein *m*; **3.** oberer Mühlstein; **4.** ⚙ a) 'Schleifma,schine *f*, b) Mahlwerk *n*, Mühle *f*, c) Quetschwerk *n*; **5.** a) (Kaffee)Mühle *f*, b) *a.* ***meat ~*** Fleischwolf *m*; **6.** *anat.* a) Backenzahn *m*, b) *pl. sl.* Zähne *pl.*; **'grind·ing** [-dɪŋ] **I** *s.* **1.** Mahlen *n*; **2.** Schleifen *n*; **3.** Knirschen *n*; **II** *adj.* **4.** mahlend (*etc.* → ***grind*** I *u.* II); **5.** Mahl..., Schleif...: ***~ mill*** a) Mahlwerk *n*, Mühle *f*, b) Schleif-, Reibmühle *f*; ***~ paste*** Schleifpaste *f*; **6.** ***~ work*** ‚Schinderei' *f*.

'grind·stone [-nds-] *s.* Schleifstein *m*: ***keep s.o.'s nose to the ~*** *fig.* j-n hart *od.* schwer arbeiten lassen; ***keep one's nose to the ~*** schwer arbeiten, sich ranhalten; ***get back to the ~*** sich wieder an die Arbeit machen.

grin·go ['grɪŋgəʊ] *pl.* **-gos** *s.* Gringo *m* (*lateinamer. Spottname für Ausländer, bsd. Angelsachsen*).

grip [grɪp] **I** *s.* **1.** Griff *m* (*a. die Art, et. zu packen*): ***come to ~s with*** a) aneinandergeraten mit, b) *fig.* sich auseinandersetzen mit, *et.* in Angriff nehmen; ***be at ~s with*** a) in e-n Kampf verwikkelt sein mit, b) *fig.* sich auseinandersetzen *od.* ernsthaft beschäftigen mit *e-r Sache*; **2.** *fig.* a) Griff *m*, Halt *m*, b) Herrschaft *f*, Gewalt *f*, Zugriff *m*, c) Verständnis *n*, ,'Durchblick' *m*: ***in the ~ of*** in den Klauen *od.* in der Gewalt (*gen.*); ***get a ~ on*** in s-e Gewalt *od.* (*geistig*) in den Griff bekommen; ***have a ~ on*** *et.* in der Gewalt haben, *fig. Zuhörer etc.* fesseln, gepackt halten; ***have a (good) ~ on*** *die Lage, e-e Materie etc.* (sicher) beherrschen, *die Situation etc.* (klar) erfassen; ***lose one's ~*** a) die Herrschaft verlieren (***of*** über *acc.*),

b) (*bsd. geistig*) nachlassen; **3.** (*bestimmter*) Händedruck *m* (*z.B. der Freimaurer*); **4.** (Hand)Griff *m* (*Koffer etc.*); **5.** Haarspange *f*; **6.** ⚙ Greifer *m*, Klemme *f*; **7.** ⚙ Griffigkeit *f* (*a. von Autoreifen*); **8.** *thea.* Ku'lissenschieber *m*; **9.** Reisetasche *f*; **II** *v/t.* **10.** packen, ergreifen; **11.** *fig. j-n* packen: a) ergreifen (*Furcht, Spannung*), b) *Leser, Zuhörer etc.* fesseln; **12.** *fig.* begreifen, verstehen; **13.** ⚙ festklemmen; **III** *v/i.* **14.** Halt finden; **15.** *fig.* packen, fesseln; ***~ brake*** *s.* ⚙ Handbremse *f.*

gripe [graɪp] **I** *v/t.* **1.** zwicken: ***be ~d*** Bauchschmerzen *od.* e-e Kolik haben; **2.** ⚓ *Boot etc.* sichern; **II** *v/i.* **3.** F nörgeln, ‚meckern'; **III** *s.* **4.** *pl.* ⚕ Bauchweh *n*, Kolik *f*; **5.** F (Grund *m* zur) ‚Mecke'rei' *f*; **6.** *pl.* ⚓ Seile *pl.* zum Festmachen.

grip·per ['grɪpə] *s.* ⚙ Greifer *m*, Halter *m*; **'grip·ping** [-pɪŋ] *adj.* **1.** *fig.* fesselnd, packend, spannend; **2.** ⚙ Greif…, Klemm…: ***~ lever*** Spannhebel *m*; ***~ tool*** Spannwerkzeug *n.*

'grip·sack *s. Am.* Reisetasche *f.*

gris·kin ['grɪskɪn] *s. Brit. Küche*: Rippenstück *n.*

gris·ly ['grɪzlɪ] *adj.* gräßlich.

grist [grɪst] *s.* **1.** Mahlgut *n*, -korn *n*: ***that's ~ to his mill*** das ist Wasser auf s-e Mühle; ***bring ~ to the mill*** Gewinn bringen; ***all is ~ to his mill*** er weiß aus allem Kapital zu schlagen; **2.** Malzschrot *m*, *n*; **3.** *Am.* ('Grundlagen)Materi͜al *n*; **4.** Stärke *f*, Dicke *f* (*Garn od. Tau*).

gris·tle ['grɪsl] *s.* Knorpel *m*; **'gris·tly** [-lɪ] *adj.* knorpelig.

grit [grɪt] **I** *s.* **1.** *geol.* a) grober Sand, Kies *m*, b) *a.* ***~ stone*** grober Sandstein; **2.** *fig.* Mut *m*, ‚Mumm' *m*; **3.** *pl.* Haferschrot *m*, *n*, -grütze *f*; **II** *v/i.* **4.** knirschen, mahlen; **III** *v/t.* **5.** ***~ one's teeth*** a) die Zähne zs.-beißen, b) mit den Zähnen knirschen; **'grit·ty** [-tɪ] *adj.* **1.** sandig, kiesig; **2.** *fig.* F mutig.

griz·zle¹ ['grɪzl] *v/i. Brit.* F **1.** quengeln; **2.** sich beklagen.

griz·zle² ['grɪzl] *s.* **1.** graue Farbe, Grau *n*; **2.** graues Haar; **'griz·zled** [-ld] *adj.* grau(haarig); **'griz·zly** [-lɪ] **I** *adj.* → ***grizzled***; **II** *s. a.* ***~ bear*** Grizzly(bär) *m*, Graubär *m.*

groan [grəʊn] **I** *v/i.* **1.** stöhnen, ächzen (***with*** vor; *a. fig. leiden* ***beneath, under*** unter *dat.*); **2.** ächzen, knarren (*Tür etc.*): ***a ~ing board*** (*od.* ***table***) ein überladener Tisch; **II** *v/t.* **3.** ächzen, unter Stöhnen äußern; **4.** ***~ down*** durch Laute des Unmuts zum Schweigen bringen; **III** *s.* **5.** Stöhnen *n*, Ächzen *n*: ***give a ~*** → 1; **6.** Laut *m* des Unmuts.

groats [grəʊts] *s. pl.* Hafergrütze *f.*

gro·cer ['grəʊsə] *s.* Lebensmittelhändler *m*; **'gro·cer·y** [-sərɪ] *s.* **1.** Lebensmittelgeschäft *n*; **2.** *mst pl.* Lebensmittel *pl.*; **3.** Lebensmittelhandel *m*; **gro·ce·te·ri·a** [ˌgrəʊsə'tɪərɪə] *s. Am.* Lebensmittelgeschäft *n* mit Selbstbedienung.

grog [grɒg] **I** *s.* Grog *m*; **II** *v/i.* Grog trinken.

grog·gi·ness ['grɒgɪnɪs] *s.* **1.** F Betrunkenheit *f*, ‚Schwips' *m*; **2.** Wack(e)ligkeit *f*; **3.** *a. Boxen*: Benommenheit *f*, (halbe) Betäubung; **'grog·gy** [-gɪ] *adj.* **1.** groggy: a) *Boxen*: angeschlagen, b) F erschöpft, ‚ka'putt', c) F wacklig (auf den Beinen); **2.** wacklig; **3.** morsch.

groin [grɔɪn] *s.* **1.** *anat.* Leiste *f*, Leistengegend *f*; **2.** ⚠ Grat(bogen) *m*, Rippe *f*; **3.** ⚙ Buhne *f*; **groined** [-nd] *adj.* gerippt: ***~ vault*** Kreuzgewölbe *n.*

grom·met ['grɒmɪt] → ***grummet***.

groom [gru:m] **I** *s.* **1.** Pferdepfleger *m*, Stallbursche *m*; **2.** Bräutigam *m*; **3.** *Brit.* Diener *m*, königlicher Be'amter; → ***bedchamber***; **II** *v/t.* **4.** *Pferd* striegeln, pflegen; **5.** *Person, Kleidung* pflegen: ***well-~ed*** gepflegt; **6.** *fig.* a) *j-n* aufbauen (***for presidency*** als zukünftigen Präsidenten), lancieren, b) *j-n als Nachfolger etc.* ‚her'anziehen'; **grooms·man** ['gru:mzmən] *s.* [*irr.*] *Am.* → ***best man***.

groove [gru:v] **I** *s.* **1.** Rinne *f*, Furche *f* (*a. anat.*): ***in the ~*** *sl. obs.* a) ‚groß in Form', b) *Am.* in Mode; **2.** ⚙ a) Rinne *f*, Furche *f*, b) Nut *f*, Hohlkehle *f*, Rille *f*, c) Kerbe *f*; **3.** Rille *f* (*e-r Schallplatte*); **4.** ⚙ Zug *m* (*in Gewehren etc.*); **5.** *fig.* a) gewohntes Geleise, b) altes Geleise, alter Trott, Scha'blone *f*, Rou'tine *f*: ***get into a ~*** in e-e Gewohnheit *od.* in e-n (immer gleichen) Trott verfallen; ***run*** (*od.* ***work***) ***in a ~*** sich in e-m ausgefahrenen Geleise bewegen, stagnieren; **6.** *sl.* ‚klasse Sache'; ***it's a ~!*** das ist klasse!; **II** *v/t.* **7.** ⚙ a) auskehlen, rillen, falzen, nuten, kerben, b) *Gewehrlauf etc.* ziehen; **III** *v/i. sl.* **8.** Spaß haben (***with*** bei *od.* mit); **9.** Spaß machen, ‚(große) Klasse sein'; **grooved** [-vd] *adj.* gerillt; genutet; **'groov·y** [-vɪ] *adj.* **1.** scha'blonenhaft; **2.** *sl.* ‚toll', ‚klasse'.

grope [grəʊp] **I** *v/i.* **1.** tasten (***for*** nach): ***~ about*** herumtasten, -tappen, -suchen; ***~ in the dark*** *bsd. fig.* im dunkeln tappen; ***~ for*** (*od.* ***after***) ***a solution*** nach e-r Lösung suchen; **II** *v/t.* **2.** tastend suchen: ***~ one's way*** sich vorwärtstasten; **3.** F *Mädchen* ‚befummeln'; **'grop·ing·ly** [-pɪŋlɪ] *adv.* tastend: a) tappend, b) *fig.* vorsichtig, unsicher.

gros·beak ['grəʊsbi:k] *s. orn.* Kernbeißer *m.*

gros·grain ['grəʊgreɪn] *adj. u. s.* grob gerippt(es Seidentuch).

gross [grəʊs] **I** *adj.* ☐ → ***grossly***; **1.** dick, feist, plump; **2.** grob(körnig); **3.** roh, grob, derb; **4.** schwer, grob (*Fehler, Pflichtverletzung etc.*): ***~ negligence*** ⚖ grobe Fahrlässigkeit; **5.** schwerfällig; **6.** dicht, stark, üppig: ***~ vegetation***; **7.** a) derb, grob, unfein, b) unanständig; **8.** brutto, Brutto…, Roh…, Gesamt…: ***~ amount*** Gesamtbetrag *m*; ***~ national product*** Bruttosozialprodukt *n*; ***~ profit*** Rohgewinn *m*; ***~ register(ed) ton*** Bruttoregistertonne *f*; ***~ tonnage*** Bruttotonnengehalt *m*; ***~ weight*** Bruttogewicht *n*; **II** *s.* **9.** *das* Ganze, *die* Masse: ***in*** (***the***) ***~*** im ganzen, in Bausch u. Bogen; **10.** *pl.* ***gross*** Gros *n* (*12 Dutzend*); **III** *v/t.* **11.** brutto verdienen *od.* einnehmen *od.* (*Film etc.*) einspielen; **'gross·ly** [-lɪ] *adv.* äußerst, maßlos, ungeheuerlich; ⚖ *etc.* grob: ***~ negligent***; **'gross·ness** [-nɪs] *s.* **1.** Schwere *f*, Ungeheuerlichkeit *f*; **2.** Roheit *f*, Derbheit *f*, Grobheit *f*; **3.** Anstößigkeit *f*, Unanständigkeit *f*; **4.** Dicke *f*; **5.** Plumpheit *f.*

gro·tesque [grəʊ'tesk] **I** *adj.* ☐ **1.** gro'tesk (*a. Kunst*); **II** *s.* **2.** *das* Gro'teske; **3.** *Kunst*: Gro'teske *f*, gro'teske Fi'gur; **gro'tesque·ness** [-nɪs] *s. das* Gro'teske.

grot·to ['grɒtəʊ] *pl.* **-toes** *od.* **-tos** *s.* Höhle *f*, Grotte *f.*

grot·ty ['grɒtɪ] *adj. Brit. sl.* **1.** ‚mies'; **2.** gräßlich, eklig.

grouch [graʊtʃ] F **I** *v/i.* **1.** nörgeln, ‚meckern', **II** *s.* **2.** a) ‚miese' Laune, b) ***have a ~*** → 1; **3.** a) ‚Meckerfritze' *m*, b) ‚Miesepeter' *m*; **'grouch·y** [-tʃɪ] *adj.* ☐ F a) ‚sauer', ‚grantig', b) nörglerisch.

ground¹ [graʊnd] **I** *s.* **1.** (Erd)Boden *m*, Erde *f*, Grund *m*: ***above ~*** a) oberirdisch, ⚒ über Tage, b) am Leben; ***below ~*** a) ⚒ unter Tage, b) unter der Erde, tot; ***down to the ~*** *fig.* völlig, total, restlos; ***from the ~ up*** *Am.* F von Grund auf; ***break new*** (*od.* ***fresh***) ***~*** Land urbar machen, *a. fig.* Neuland erschließen; ***cut the ~ from under s.o.'s feet*** j-m den Boden unter den Füßen wegziehen; ***fall to the ~*** zu Boden fallen, *fig.* sich zerschlagen, ins Wasser fallen; ***fall on stony ~*** *fig.* auf taube Ohren stoßen; ***get off the ~*** a) *v/t. fig. et.* in Gang bringen, *et.* verwirklichen, b) *v/i.* ✈ abheben, c) *v/i. fig.* in Gang kommen, verwirklicht werden; ***go to ~*** im Bau verschwinden (*Fuchs*), *fig.* ‚untertauchen' (*Verbrecher*); ***play s.o. into the ~*** *sport* F j-n in Grund u. Boden spielen; **2.** Boden *m*, Grund *m*, Gebiet *n* (*a. fig.*), Strecke *f*, Gelände *n*: ***on German ~*** auf deutschem Boden; ***be on safe ~*** sich auf sicherem Boden bewegen; ***be forbidden ~*** *fig.* tabu sein; ***cover much ~*** e-e große Strecke zurücklegen, *fig.* viel umfassen, weit reichen; ***cover the ~ well*** *fig.* nichts außer acht lassen, alles in Betracht ziehen; ***gain ~*** (an) Boden gewinnen, *fig. a.* um sich greifen, Fuß fassen; ***give*** (*od.* ***lose***) ***~*** (an) Boden verlieren (*a. fig.*); ***go over the ~*** *fig.* die Sache durchsprechen, alles gründlich prüfen; ***hold*** (*od.* ***stand***) ***one's ~*** standhalten, nicht weichen, sich *od.* s-n Standpunkt behaupten; ***shift one's ~*** seinen Standpunkt ändern, umschwenken; **3.** Grundbesitz *m*, Grund *m* u. Boden *m*, Lände'reien *pl.*; **4.** Gebiet *n*, Grund *m*, *bsd. sport* Platz *m*: ***cricket-~***; **5.** ***hunting-~*** Jagd(-gebiet *n*) *f*; **6.** *pl.* (Garten)Anlagen *pl.*: ***standing in its own ~s*** von Anlagen umgeben (*Haus*); **7.** Meeresboden *m*, (Meeres)Grund *m*: ***take ~*** auflaufen, stranden; **8.** *pl.* Bodensatz *m* (*Kaffee etc.*); **9.** Grundierung *f*, Grund(farbe *f*) *m*, Grund(fläche *f*) *m*; **10.** *a. pl.* Grundlage *f* (*a. fig.*); **11.** *fig.* (Beweg-)Grund *m*: ***~ for divorce*** Scheidungsgrund; ***on the ~(s) of*** auf Grund (*gen.*), wegen (*gen.*); ***on the ~(s) that*** mit der Begründung, daß; ***on medical ~s*** aus gesundheitlichen Gründen; ***have no ~(s) for*** keinen Grund haben für (*od.* zu *inf.*); **12.** ⚡ Erde *f*, Erdung *f*, Erdschluß *m*: ***~ cable*** Massekabel *n*; **13.** *thea.* Par'terre *n*; **II** *v/t.* **14.** niederlegen, -setzen; → ***arm²*** 1; **15.** ⚓ *Schiff* auf Grund setzen; **16.** ⚡ erden; **17.** ⚙, *paint.* grundieren; **18.** a) *e-m Flugzeug od. Piloten* Startverbot erteilen, b) *mot. Am. j-m* die Fahrerlaubnis entziehen:

be ~ed *a.* nicht (ab)fliegen *od.* starten können *od.* dürfen, (*Passagiere*) *a.* festsitzen; **19.** *fig.* (***on, in***) gründen, stützen (auf *acc.*), begründen (in *dat.*): ***~ed in fact*** auf Tatsachen beruhend; ***be ~ed in*** → 22; **20.** (***in***) j-n einführen (in *acc.*), *j-m* die Anfangsgründe beibringen (*gen.*): ***well ~ed in*** mit guten (Vor-) Kenntnissen in (*od. gen.*); **III** *v/i.* **21.** ⚓ stranden, auflaufen; **22.** (***on, upon***) beruhen (auf *dat.*), sich gründen (auf *acc.*).

ground² [graʊnd] **I** *pret. u. p.p. von* ***grind***; **II** *adj.* **1.** gemahlen: ***~ coffee***; **2.** matt(geschliffen); → ***ground glass***.

ground·age [ˈgraʊndɪdʒ] *s.* ⚓ *Brit.* Hafengebühr *f*, Ankergeld *n*.

ˌ**ground|-ˈair** *adj.* ✈ Boden-Bord-…; **~ a·lert** *s.* ✈, ⚔ Aˈlarm-, Startbereitschaft *f*; **~ an·gling** *s.* Grundangeln *n*; **~ at·tack** *s.* ✈ Angriff *m* auf Erdziele, Tiefangriff *m*; **~ bass** *s.* ♪ Grundbaß *m*; **~ box** *s.* ⚘ Zwergbuchsbaum *m*; **~ clear·ance** *s. mot.* Bodenfreiheit *f*; **~-col·o(u)r** *s.* Grundfarbe *f*; **~ con·nec·tion** → ***ground¹*** 12; ˈ**~-conˌtrolled ap·proach** *s.* ✈ GCˈA-Anflug *m* (*per Bodenradar*); **~ crew** *s.* ✈ ˈBodenpersoˌnal *n*; ˈ**~-fish** *s. ichth.* Grundfisch *m*; **~ fish·ing** *s.* Grundangeln *n*; **~ floor** *s. Brit.* Erdgeschoß *n*: ***get in on the ~*** F a) ✝ sich zu den Gründerbedingungen beteiligen, b) von Anfang an mit dabeisein, c) ganz unten anfangen (*in e-r Firma etc.*); **~ fog** *s.* Bodennebel *m*; **~ forc·es** *s. pl.* ⚔ Bodentruppen *pl.*, Landstreitkräfte *pl.*; **~ form** *s. ling.* a) Grundform *f*, b) Wurzel *f*, c) Stamm *m*; **~ frost** *s.* Bodenfrost *m*; **~ glass** *s.* **1.** Mattglas *n*; **2.** *phot.* Mattscheibe *f*; **~ game** *s. hunt. Brit.* Niederwild *n*; **~ hog** *s. zo.* Amer. Murmeltier *n*; **~ host·ess** *s.* ✈ Groundhostess *f*; **~ ice** *s. geol.* Grundeis *n*.

ground·ing [ˈgraʊndɪŋ] *s.* **1.** Fundaˈment *n*, ˈUnterbau *m*; **2.** a) Grundierung *f*, b) Grundfarbe *f*; **3.** ⚓ Stranden *n*; **4.** ⚡ Erdung *f*; **5.** a) ˈAnfangsˌunterricht *m*, Einführung *f*, b) (Vor)Kenntnisse *pl.*

ground·less [ˈgraʊndlɪs] *adj.* □ grundlos, unbegründet.

ground| lev·el *s. phys.* Bodennähe *f*; **~ line** *s.* ⚒ Grundlinie *f*; ˈ**~·man** [-ndmæn] *s.* [*irr.*] *sport* Platzwart *m*; **~ note** *s.* ♪ Grundton *m*; ˈ**~·nut** [-ndn-] *s.* Erdnuß *f*; **~ plan** *s.* **1.** ⚠ Grundriß *m*; **2.** *fig.* (erster) Entwurf, Konˈzept *n*; **~ plane** *s.* Horizonˈtalebene *f*; **~ plate** *s.* **1.** ⚠ Grundplatte *f*; **2.** ⚡ Erdplatte *f*; **~ rule** *s.* Grundregel *f*; **~ sea** *s.* ⚓ Grundsee *f*; **~ sheet** *s.* **1.** Zeltboden *m*; **2.** *sport* Regenplane *f* (*für das Spielfeld*); ˈ**~s·man** [-ndzmən] → ***groundman***; **~ speed** *s.* ✈ Geschwindigkeit *f* über Grund; **~ staff** → ***ground crew***; **~ sta·tion** *s.* ˈBodenstatiˌon *f*; **~ swell** *s.* **1.** (Grund)Dünung *f*; **2.** *fig.* Anschwellen *n*; ˌ**~-to-ˈair** *adj.* a) ✈ Boden-Bord-…: ***~ communication***, b) ⚔ Boden-Luft-…: ***~ weapon***; ˈ**~-ˌwa·ter lev·el** *s. geol.* Grundwasserspiegel *m*; **~ wave** *s.* ⚡, *phys.* Bodenwelle *f*; ˈ**~·work** *s.* **1.** ⚠ a) Erdarbeit *f*, b) ˈUnterbau *m*, Fundaˈment *n* (*a. fig.*); **2.** *fig.* Grundlage(n *pl.*) *f*; **3.** *paint. etc.* Grund *m*.

group [gruːp] **I** *s.* **1.** *allg.*, *a.* ⚗, ⚒, ♪, *biol., sociol. etc.* Gruppe *f*; **2.** *fig.* Gruppe *f*, Kreis *m*; **3.** *parl.* a) Gruppe *f* (*Partei mit zu wenig Abgeordneten für e-e Fraktion*, b) Fraktiˈon *f*; **4.** ✝ Gruppe *f*, Konˈzern *m*; **5.** ⚔ a) Gruppe *f*, b) Kampfgruppe *f* (*2 od. mehr Bataillone*); **6.** ✈ a) *Brit.* Geschwader *n*: ***~ captain*** Oberst *m* (*der* ***RAF***), b) *Am.* Gruppe *f*; **7.** ♪ a) Instruˈmenten- *od.* Stimmgruppe *f*, b) Notengruppe *f*; **II** *v/t.* **8.** gruppieren, anordnen; **9.** klassifizieren, einordnen; **III** *v/i.* **10.** sich gruppieren; **~ drive** *s.* ⚙ Gruppenantrieb *m*; **~ dy·nam·ics** *s. pl. sg. konstr. sociol., psych.* ˈGruppendyˌnamik *f*.

group·ie [ˈgruːpɪ] *s.* ‚Groupie' *n* (*weiblicher Fan*).

group| sex *s.* Gruppensex *m*; **~ ther·a·py** *s. psych.* ˈGruppentheraˌpie *f*; **~ work** *s. sociol.* Gruppenarbeit *f*.

grouse¹ [graʊs] *s. sg. u. pl. orn.* **1.** Waldhuhn *n*; **2.** Schottisches Moorhuhn.

grouse² [graʊs] **I** *v/i.* (***about***) meckern (über *acc.*), nörgeln (an *dat.*, über *acc.*); **II** *s.* Nörgeˈlei *f*, Gemecker *n*; ˈ**grous·er** [-sə] *s.* ‚Meckerfritze' *m*.

grout [graʊt] **I** *s.* **1.** ⚙ Vergußmörtel *m*; **2.** Schrotmehl *n*; **3.** *pl.* Hafergrütze *f*; **II** *v/t.* **4.** *Fugen* ausstreichen.

grove [grəʊv] *s.* Hain *m*, Gehölz *n*.

grov·el [ˈgrɒvl] *v/i.* **1.** am Boden kriechen; **2.** **~ *before*** (*od.* ***to***) ***s.o.*** *fig.* vor j-m kriechen, vor j-m zu Kreuze kriechen; **3.** **~ *in*** schwelgen in (*dat.*), frönen (*dat.*); ˈ**grov·el·(l)er** [-lə] *s. fig.* Kriecher *m*, Speichellecker *m*; ˈ**grov·el·(l)ing** [-lɪŋ] *adj.* □ *fig.* kriecherisch, unterˈwürfig.

grow [grəʊ] **I** *v/i.* [*irr.*] **1.** wachsen; **2.** ⚘ wachsen, vorkommen; **3.** wachsen: a) größer *od.* stärker werden, sich entwickeln, b) *fig.* anwachsen, zunehmen (***in*** an *dat.*); **4.** (allˈmählich) werden: **~ *rich***; **~ *less*** sich vermindern; **~ *light*** hell(er) werden, sich aufklären; **II** *v/t.* [*irr.*] **5.** (an)bauen, züchten, ziehen: **~ *apples***; **6.** (sich) wachsen lassen: **~ *one's hair long***; **~ *a beard*** sich e-n Bart stehen lassen;
Zssgn mit adv. u. prp.:
grow| a·way *v/i.*: **~ *from*** sich *j-m* entfremden; **~ *from*** → ***grow out of***; **~ in·to** *v/i.* **1.** hinˈeinwachsen in (*acc.*) (*a. fig.*); **2.** werden zu, sich entwickeln zu; **~ on** *v/i.* **1.** Einfluß *od.* Macht gewinnen über (*acc.*): ***the habit grows on one*** man gewöhnt sich immer mehr daran; **2.** *j-m* lieb werden *od.* ans Herz wachsen; **~ out of** *v/i.* **1.** herˈauswachsen aus: **~ *one's clothes***; **2.** *fig.* entwachsen (*dat.*), überˈwinden (*acc.*), ablegen: **~ *a habit***; **3.** erwachsen *od.* entstehen aus, e-e Folge sein (*gen.*); **~ up** *v/i.* **1.** auf-, herˈanwachsen: **~ (*into*) *a beauty*** sich zu e-r Schönheit entwickeln; **2.** erwachsen werden: ***~!*** sei kein Kindskopf!; **3.** sich einbürgern (*Brauch etc.*); **4.** sich entwickeln, entstehen; **~ up·on** → ***grow on***.

grow·er [ˈgrəʊə] *s.* **1.** (*schnell etc.*) wachsende Pflanze: ***a fast ~***; **2.** Züchter *m*, Pflanzer *m*, Erzeuger *m*, *in Zssgn* …bauer *m*; **grow·ing** [ˈgrəʊɪŋ] **I** *adj.* □ **1.** wachsend (*a. fig. zunehmend*); **II** *s.* **2.** Anbau *m*; **3.** Wachstum *n*: **~ *pains*** a) Wachstumsschmerzen, b) *fig.* Anfangsschwierigkeiten, ‚Kinderkrankheiten'.

growl [graʊl] **I** *v/i.* **1.** knurren (*Hund etc.*), brummen (*Bär*) (*beide a. fig. Person*): **~ *at*** *j-n* anknurren; **2.** (g)rollen (*Donner*); **II** *v/t.* **3.** *Worte* knurren; **III** *s.* **4.** Knurren *n*, Brummen *n*; **5.** (G)Rollen *n*; ˈ**growl·er** [-lə] *s.* **1.** knurriger Hund; **2.** *fig.* ‚Brummbär' *m*; **3.** *ichth.* Knurrfisch *m*; **4.** ⚡ Prüfspule *f*; **5.** kleiner Eisberg.

grown [grəʊn] **I** *p.p. von* ***grow***; **II** *adj.* **1.** gewachsen; → ***full-grown***; **2.** erwachsen: **~ *man*** Erwachsene(r) *m*; **3.** *a.* **~ *over*** be-, überˈwachsen; **~-up I** *adj.* [ˌgrəʊnˈʌp] **1.** erwachsen; **2.** a) für Erwachsene: **~ *books***, b) Erwachsenen…: **~ *clothes***; **II** *s.* [ˈgrəʊnʌp] **3.** Erwachsene(r *m*) *f*.

growth [grəʊθ] *s.* **1.** Wachsen *n*, Wachstum *n* (*a. fig. u.* ✝); **2.** Wuchs *m*, Größe *f*; **3.** Anwachsen *n*, Zunahme *f*, Zuwachs *m*; **4.** *fig.* Entwicklung *f*; **5.** a) Anbau *m*, b) Proˈdukt *n*, Erzeugnis *n*: ***of one's own ~*** selbstgezogen; **6.** ⚘ Schößling *m*, Trieb *m*; **7.** ⚕ Gewächs *n*, Wucherung *f*; **~ in·dus·try** *s.* ✝ ˈWachstumsinduˌstrie *f*; **~ rate** *s.* ✝ Wachstumsrate *f*.

groyne [grɔɪn] *s. Brit.* ⚙ Buhne *f*.

grub [grʌb] **I** *v/i.* **1.** a) graben, wühlen, b) jäten, c) roden; **2.** ‚wühlen', schwer arbeiten; **3.** *fig.* stöbern, wühlen, kramen; **4.** *sl.* ‚futtern', essen; **II** *v/t.* **5.** a) aufwühlen, b) ˈumgraben, c) roden; **6.** *oft* **~ *up*** a) ausjäten, b) (mit den Wurzeln) ausgraben, c) *fig.* ausgraben, aufstöbern; **III** *s.* **7.** *zo.* Made *f*, Larve *f*; **8.** *fig.* Arbeitstier *n*; **9.** *sl.* ‚Futter' *n* (*Essen*).

grub·ber [ˈgrʌbə] *s.* **1.** ⚒ a) Rodehacke *f*, -werkzeug *n*, b) Eggenpflug *m*; **2.** → ***grub*** 8; ˈ**grub·by** [-bɪ] *adj.* **1.** schmuddelig; **2.** madig.

ˈ**grub|·stake** *s. Am.* ⚒ *e-m Schürfer gegen Gewinnbeteiligung gegebene* Ausrüstung u. Verpflegung; ♀ **Street I** *s. fig.* armselige Liteˈraten *pl.*; **II** *adj.* (liteˈrarisch) minderwertig, ‚dritter Garniˈtur'.

grudge [grʌdʒ] **I** *v/t.* **1.** (***s.o. s.th.*** *od.* ***s.th. to s.o.***) (j-m et.) mißˈgönnen *od.* nicht gönnen, (j-n um et.) beneiden; **2.** **~ *doing s.th.*** et. nur widerwillig *od.* ungern tun; **II** *s.* **3.** Groll *m*: ***bear s.o. a ~, have a ~ against s.o.*** e-n Groll gegen j-n hegen; ˈ**grudg·er** [-dʒə] *s.* Neider *m*; ˈ**grudg·ing** [-dʒɪŋ] *adj.* □ **1.** neidisch, ˈmißgünstig; **2.** ˈwiderwillig, ungern (getan *od.* gegeben): ***she was very ~ in her thanks*** sie bedankte sich nur sehr widerwillig.

gru·el [ˈgrʊəl] *s.* Haferschleim *m*; Schleimsuppe *f*; ˈ**gru·el·(l)ing** [-lɪŋ] **I** *adj. fig.* mörderisch, aufreibend, zermürbend; **II** *s. Brit.* F a) harte Strafe *od.* Behandlung, b) Straˈpaze *f*, ‚Schlauch' *m*.

grue·some [ˈgruːsəm] *adj.* □ grausig, grauenhaft, schauerlich.

gruff [grʌf] *adj.* □ **1.** schroff, barsch, ruppig; **2.** rauh (*Stimme*); ˈ**gruff·ness** [-nɪs] *s.* **1.** Barsch-, Schroffheit *f*; **2.** Rauheit *f*.

grum·ble [ˈgrʌmbl] **I** *v/i.* **1.** a) murren, schimpfen (***at, about, over*** über *acc.*, wegen), b) knurren, brummen; **2.**

(g)rollen (*Donner*); **II** *s.* **3.** Murren *n*, Knurren *n*; **4.** (G)Rollen *n*; **'grum·bler** [-lə] *s.* Brummbär *m*, Nörgler *m*; **'grum·bling** [-lɪŋ] *adj.* □ **1.** brummig; **2.** murrend.

grume [gru:m] *s.* (*bsd.* Blut)Klümpchen *n*.

grum·met ['grʌmɪt] *s. Brit.* **1.** ⚓ Seilschlinge *f*; **2.** ⚙ (Me'tall)Öse *f*.

gru·mous ['gru:məs] *adj.* geronnen, dick, klumpig (*Blut etc.*).

grump [grʌmp] *s. Am.* F **1.** → ***grumbler***; **2.** *pl.* Mißmut *m*: ***have the ~s*** mißmutig sein; **grump·y** ['grʌmpɪ] *adj.* □ mürrisch, mißmutig.

Grun·dy ['grʌndɪ] *s.* engstirnige, sittenstrenge Per'son: ***Mrs. ~*** *a.* ,die Leute' *pl.* (*die gefürchtete öffentliche Meinung*): ***what will Mrs. ~ say?***

grunt [grʌnt] **I** *v/i. u. v/t.* **1.** grunzen; **2.** *fig.* murren, brummen; **3.** ächzen, stöhnen (***with*** vor *dat.*); **II** *s.* **4.** Grunzen *n*; **5.** → ***growler*** 3.

gryph·on ['grɪfən] → ***griffin***¹ 1.

'G-string *s.* **1.** ♪ G-Saite *f*; **2.** a) ,letzte Hülle' (*e-r Stripteasetänzerin*), b) Tanga *m* (*Mini-Bikini*).

gua·na ['gwɑ:nɑ:] → ***iguana***.

gua·no ['gwɑ:nəʊ] *s.* Gu'ano *m*.

guar·an·tee [ˌgærən'ti:] **I** *s.* **1.** Garan'tie *f*: a) Bürgschaft *f*, Sicherheit *f*, b) Gewähr *f*, Zusicherung *f*, c) Garan'tiefrist *f*: ~ (***card***) Garantieschein *m*; ***there is a one-year ~ on this camera*** die Kamera hat ein Jahr Garantie; **2.** Kauti'on *f*, Sicherheit(sleistung) *f*, Pfand(summe *f*) *n*; **3.** Bürge *m*, Bürgin *f*; **4.** Sicherheitsempfänger(in); **II** *v/t.* **5.** (sich ver-) bürgen für, Garan'tie leisten für; **6.** *et.* garantieren, gewährleisten, sicherstellen, verbürgen; **7.** schützen, sichern (***from***, ***against*** vor *dat.*, gegen); **ˌguar·an'tor** [-'tɔ:] *s. bsd.* ⚖ Bürge *m*, Bürgin *f*, Ga'rant(in); **guar·an·ty** ['gærəntɪ] → ***guarantee*** 1, 2, 3.

guard [gɑ:d] **I** *v/t.* **1.** (***against***, ***from***) (be)hüten, (be)schützen, bewahren (vor *dat.*), sichern (gegen): ***~ one's interests*** *fig.* s-e Interessen wahren; ***~ your tongue!*** hüte deine Zunge!; **2.** bewachen, beaufsichtigen; **3.** ⚙ (ab)sichern; **4.** *Schach*: *Figur* decken; **II** *v/i.* **5.** (***against***) auf der Hut sein, sich hüten *od.* schützen *od.* in acht nehmen (vor *dat.*), vorbeugen (*dat.*); **III** *s.* **6.** a) ⚔ *etc.* Wache *f*, (Wach)Posten *m*, b) Wächter *m*, c) Aufseher *m*, Wärter *m*; **7.** ⚔ a) Wachmannschaft *f*, Wache *f*, b) Garde *f*, Leibwache *f*: ***~ of hono(u)r*** Ehrenwache *f*, c) ***2s*** *pl. Brit.* 'Garde (-korps *n*, -regiˌment *n*) *f*; **8.** 🚂 a) *Brit.* Schaffner *m*, b) *Am.* Bahnwärter *m*; **9.** Bewachung *f*, Aufsicht *f*: ***keep under close ~*** scharf bewachen; ***be on ~*** auf Wache sein; ***stand*** (***mount***, ***relieve***, ***keep***) ***~*** Wache stehen (beziehen, ablösen, halten); **10.** *fenc.*, *Boxen etc.*, *a. Schach*: Deckung *f*: ***lower one's ~*** die Deckung herunternehmen, *fig.* sich e-e Blöße geben, nicht aufpassen; **11.** *fig.* Wachsamkeit *f*: ***on one's ~*** auf der Hut, vorsichtig; ***off one's ~*** nicht auf der Hut, unachtsam; ***put s.o. on his ~*** j-n warnen; ***throw s.o. off his ~*** j-n überrumpeln; **12.** ⚙ Schutzvorrichtung *f*, -gitter *n*, -blech *n*; **13.** a) Stichblatt *n* (*am Degen*), b) Bügel *m* (*am Gewehr*); **14.** *fig.* Vorsichtsmaßnahme *f*, Sicherung *f*; **~ boat** *s.* ⚓ Wachboot *n*; **~ book** *s.* **1.** *Brit.* Sammelalbum *n*; **2.** ⚔ Wachbuch *n*; **~ chain** *s.* Sicherheitskette *f*; **~ dog** *s.* Wachhund *m*; **~ du·ty** *s.* Wachdienst *m*: ***be on ~*** Wache haben.

guard·ed ['gɑ:dɪd] *adj.* □ *fig.* vorsichtig, zu'rückhaltend: ***~ hope*** gewisse Hoffnung; ***~ optimism*** gedämpfter Optimismus; **'guard·ed·ness** [-nɪs] *s.* Vorsicht *f*, Zu'rückhaltung *f*.

'guard·house *s.* ⚔ **1.** 'Wachloˌkal *n*, -haus *n*; **2.** Ar'restloˌkal *n*.

guard·i·an ['gɑ:djən] *s.* **1.** Hüter *m*, Wächter *m*: ***~ angel*** Schutzengel *m*; ***~ of the law*** Gesetzeshüter; **2.** ⚖ Vormund *m*: ***~ ad litem*** Prozeßvertreter *m* (*für Minderjährige od. Geschäftsunfähige*); **'guard·i·an·ship** [-ʃɪp] *s.* **1.** ⚖ Vormundschaft *f*: ***be*** (***place***) ***under ~*** unter Vormundschaft stehen (stellen); **2.** *fig.* Schutz *m*, Obhut *f*.

'guard|·rail *s.* **1.** Handlauf *m*; **2.** *mot.* Leitplanke *f*; **'~s·man** [-dzmən] *s.* [*irr.*] ⚔ **1.** → ***guard*** 6a; **2.** Gar'dist *m*; **3.** *Am.* Natio'nalgarˌdist *m*.

Gua·te·ma·lan [ˌgwætɪ'mɑ:lən] **I** *adj.* guatemal'tekisch; **II** *s.* Guatemal'teke *m*, -'tekin *f*.

gua·va ['gwɑ:və] *s.* ⚘ Gua'jave *f*.

gu·ber·na·to·ri·al [ˌgju:bənə'tɔ:rɪəl] *adj. bsd. Am.* Gouverneurs...

gudg·eon¹ ['gʌdʒən] *s.* **1.** *ichth.* Gründling *m*; **2.** *fig.* Gimpel *m*.

gudg·eon² ['gʌdʒən] *s.* **1.** ⚙ Zapfen *m*, Bolzen *m*: ***~ pin*** Kolbenbolzen; **2.** ⚓ Ruderöse *f*.

guel·der rose ['geldə] *s.* ⚘ Schneeball *m*.

Guelph, Guelf [gwelf] *s.* Welfe *m*, Welfin *f*; **'Guelph·ic**, **'Guelf·ic** [-fɪk] *adj.* welfisch.

guer·don ['gɜ:dən] *poet.* **I** *s.* Sold *m*, Lohn *m*; **II** *v/t.* belohnen.

gue·ril·la → ***guerrilla***.

Guern·sey ['gɜ:nzɪ] *s.* **1.** Guernsey (-rind) *n*; **2.** *a.* ♀ ⚓ 'Wollpulˌlover *m*.

guer·ril·la [gə'rɪlə] *s.* ⚔ **1.** Gue'rilla *m*, Parti'san *m*; **2.** *mst* ***~ war***(***fare***) Gue'rillakrieg *m*, *fig.* Kleinkrieg *m*.

guess [ges] **I** *v/t.* **1.** erraten: ***~ a riddle***; ***~ s.o.'s thoughts***; ***~ who!*** rate mal, wer!; **2.** (ab)schätzen (***at*** auf): ***~ s.o.'s age***; **3.** ahnen, vermuten; **4.** *bsd. Am.* F glauben, denken, meinen, ahnen; **II** *v/i.* **5.** schätzen (***at s.th.*** et.); **6.** a) raten, b) her'umraten (***at***, ***about*** an *dat.*): ***keep s.o. ~ing*** j-n im unklaren *od.* ungewissen lassen; ***~ing game*** Ratespiel *n*; **III** *s.* **7.** Schätzung *f*, Vermutung *f*, Annahme *f*: ***my ~ is that*** ich schätze *od.* vermute, daß; ***that's anybody's ~*** das weiß niemand; ***your ~ is as good as mine*** ich kann auch nur raten; ***a good ~!*** gut geraten *od.* geschätzt; ***at a ~*** bei bloßer Schätzung; ***at a rough ~*** grob geschätzt; ***by ~*** schätzungsweise; ***by ~ and by god*** F ,nach Gefühl u. Wellenschlag'; ***make*** (*od.* ***take***) ***a ~*** raten, schätzen; ***miss one's ~*** ,danebenhauen', falsch raten; **~ rope** → ***guest rope***; **~ stick** *s. Am. sl.* **1.** Rechenschieber *m*; **2.** Maßstab *m*.

guess·ti·mate F **I** *s.* ['gestɪmət] grobe Schätzung, bloße Rate'rei; **II** *v/t.* [-meɪt] ,über den Daumen peilen'.

'guess·work *s.* (bloße) Rate'rei, (reine) Vermutung(en *pl.*).

guest [gest] **I** *s.* **1.** Gast *m*: ***paying ~*** (Pensions)Gast; ***~ of hono(u)r*** Ehrengast; ***be my ~!*** aber bitte(, ja)!; **2.** ⚘, *zo.* Einmieter *m* (*Parasit*); **II** *v/i.* **3.** *bsd. Am. thea.* gastieren, als Gast mitwirken (***on*** bei); **~ book** *s.* Gästebuch *n*; **~ con·duc·tor** *s.* ♪ 'Gastdiriˌgent *m*; **'~·house** *s.* Pensi'on *f*; Gästehaus *n*; **~ room** [rʊm] *s.* Gästezimmer *n*; **~ rope**, **~ warp** ['ges-] *s.* ⚓ **1.** Schlepptrosse *f*; **2.** Bootstau *n*.

guf·faw [gʌ'fɔ:] **I** *s.* schallendes Gelächter; **II** *v/i.* laut lachen.

guid·a·ble ['gaɪdəbl] *adj.* lenkbar, lenksam; **'guid·ance** [-dns] *s.* **1.** Leitung *f*, Führung *f*; **2.** Anleitung *f*, Belehrung *f*, Unter'weisung *f*: ***for your ~*** zu Ihrer Orientierung; **3.** (*Berufs-*, *Ehe- etc.*)Beratung *f*, Führung *f*: ***~ counselor*** a) Berufs-, Studienberater *m*, b) Heilpädagoge *m*.

guide [gaɪd] **I** *v/t.* **1.** *j-n* führen, geleiten, *j-m* den Weg zeigen; **2.** ⚙ *u. fig.* lenken, leiten, führen, steuern; **3.** *et.*, *a. j-n* bestimmen: ***~ s.o.'s actions*** (***life***, *etc.*); ***be ~d by*** sich leiten lassen von, folgen (*dat.*), bestimmt sein von; **4.** anleiten, belehren, beraten(d zur Seite stehen *dat.*); **II** *s.* **5.** Führer(in), Leiter (-in); **6.** (Reise-, Fremden-, Berg- *etc.*) Führer *m*; **7.** (Reise- *etc.*)Führer *m* (***to*** durch, von) (*Buch*); **8.** (***to***) Leitfaden *m*, Handbuch *n* (*gen.*); **9.** Berater (-in); **10.** *fig.* Richtschnur *f*, Anhaltspunkt *m*: ***if that*** (***he***) ***is any ~*** wenn man sich danach (nach ihm) überhaupt richten kann; **11.** → ***girl guide***; **12.** a) Wegweiser *m*, b) 'Wegmarˌkierung(szeichen *n*) *f*; **13.** ⚙ Führung *f*; **~ bar** *s.* ⚙ Führungsschiene *f*; **~ beam** *s.* ✈ (Funk)Leitstrahl *m*; **~ blade** *s.* ⚙ Leitschaufel *f* (*Turbine*); **~ block** *s.* ⚙ Führungsschlitten *m*; **'~·book** → ***guide*** 7.

guid·ed ['gaɪdɪd] *adj.* **1.** (fern)gelenkt: ***~ missile*** ⚔ Fernlenkgeschoß *n*, Fernlenkkörper *m*; **2.** geführt: ***~ tour*** Führung *f*.

guide| dog *s.* Blindenhund *m*; **'~·line** *s.* **1.** ✈ Schleppseil *n*; **2.** (***on*** *gen.*) Richtlinie *f*, -schnur *f*; **'~·post** *s.* Wegweiser *m*; **~ pul·ley** *s.* ⚙ Leit-, 'Umlenkrolle *f*; **~ rail** *s.* → ***guide bar***; **~ rod** *s.* ⚙ Führungsstange *f*; **~ rope** *s.* ✈ Schlepptau *n*; **'~·way** *s.* ⚙ Führungsbahn *f*.

guid·ing ['gaɪdɪŋ] *adj.* führend, leitend, Lenk...: ***~ principle*** Leitprinzip *n*; **~ rule** *s.* Richtlinie *f*; **~ star** *s.* Leitstern *m*.

gui·don ['gaɪdən] *s.* **1.** Wimpel *m*, Fähnchen *n*, Stan'darte *f*; **2.** Stan'dartenträger *m*.

guild [gɪld] *s.* **1.** Gilde *f*, Zunft *f*, Innung *f*; **2.** Vereinigung *f*.

guil·der ['gɪldə] *s.* Gulden *m*.

ˌguild'hall *s.* **1.** *hist.* Gilden-, Zunfthaus *n*; **2.** Rathaus *n*: ***the*** ♀ *das Rathaus der City von London*.

guile [gaɪl] *s.* (Arg)List *f*, Tücke *f*; **'guile·ful** [-fʊl] *adj.* □ arglistig, tükkisch; **'guile·less** [-lɪs] *adj.* □ arglos, ohne Falsch, treuherzig, harmlos; **'guile·less·ness** [-lɪsnɪs] *s.* Harm-, Arglosigkeit *f*.

guil·lo·tine [ˌgɪlə'ti:n] **I** *s.* **1.** Guillo'tine *f*, Fallbeil *n*; **2.** ⚙ Pa'pierˌschneidema-

ˌschine *f*; **3.** *Brit. parl.* Befristung *f* der De'batte; **II** *v/t.* **4.** guillotinieren, durch die Guillo'tine hinrichten.

guilt [gɪlt] *s.* Schuld *f* (*a.* ⚖): ***joint ~*** Mitschuld; ***~ complex*** Schuldkomplex *m*; **'guilt·i·ness** [-tɪnɪs] *s.* **1.** Schuld *f*; **2.** Schuldbewußtsein *n*, -gefühl *n*; **'guilt·less** [-lɪs] *adj.* □ **1.** schuldlos, unschuldig (***of*** an *dat.*); **2.** *fig.* (***of***) a) unwissend, unerfahren (in *dat.*): ***be ~ of s.th.*** et. nicht kennen (*a. fig.*), b) frei *od.* unberührt (von), ohne (*acc.*); **'guilt·y** [-tɪ] *adj.* □ **1.** schuldig (***of*** *gen.*): ***find*** (***not***) ***~*** für (un)schuldig erklären (***on a charge*** e-r Anklage); **2.** schuldbewußt, -beladen: ***a ~ conscience*** ein schlechtes Gewissen.

guin·ea ['gɪnɪ] *s.* **1.** *Brit.* Gui'nee *f* (*£1.05*); **2.** → **~ fowl** *s.*, **~ hen** *s.* Perlhuhn *n*; **~ pig** *s.* **1.** Meerschweinchen *n*; **2.** *fig.* Ver'suchskaˌninchen *n*.

guise [gaɪz] *s.* **1.** Gestalt *f*, Erscheinung *f*, Aufmachung *f*: ***in the ~ of*** als ... (verkleidet); **2.** *fig.* Maske *f*, (Deck-)Mantel *m*: ***under the ~ of*** in der Maske (*gen.*), unter dem Deckmantel (*gen.*).

gui·tar [gɪ'tɑː] *s.* ♪ Gi'tarre *f*; **gui'tar·ist** [-rɪst] *s.* Gitar'rist(in), Gi'tarrenspieler(in).

gulch [gʌlʃ] *s. Am.* (Berg)Schlucht *f*.

gulf [gʌlf] **I** *s.* **1.** Golf *m*, Meerbusen *m*, Bucht *f*; **2.** *a. fig.* Abgrund *m*, Schlund *m*; **3.** *fig.* Kluft *f*; **4.** Strudel *m*; **II** *v/t.* **5.** *fig.* verschlingen.

gull¹ [gʌl] *s. orn.* Möwe *f*.

gull² [gʌl] **I** *v/t.* über'tölpeln; **II** *s.* Gimpel *m*, Trottel *m*.

gul·let ['gʌlɪt] *s.* **1.** *anat.* Schlund *m*, Speiseröhre *f*; **2.** Gurgel *f*, Kehle *f*; **3.** Wasserrinne *f*; **4.** ⚙ 'Förderkaˌnal *m*.

gul·li·bil·i·ty [ˌgʌlə'bɪlətɪ] *s.* Leichtgläubigkeit *f*, Einfalt *f*; **gul·li·ble** ['gʌləbl] *adj.* leichtgläubig, na'iv.

gul·ly ['gʌlɪ] *s.* **1.** (Wasser)Rinne *f*; **2.** ⚙ a) Gully *m*, Sinkkasten *m*, Senkloch *n*, b) *a.* ***~ drain*** 'Abzugskaˌnal *m*: ***~ hole*** Abflußloch *n*.

gulp [gʌlp] **I** *v/t. mst* ***~ down*** **1.** *Speise* hin'unterschlingen, *Getränk* hin'unterstürzen; **2.** *Tränen etc.* hin'unterschlukken, unter'drücken; **II** *v/i.* **3.** (*a. vor Rührung etc.*) schlucken; **4.** würgen; **III** *s.* **5.** (großer) Schluck: ***at one ~*** auf 'einen Zug.

gum¹ [gʌm] *s. mst pl. anat.* Zahnfleisch *n*.

gum² [gʌm] **I** *s.* **1.** ⚘, ⚙ a) Gummi *n*, *m*, b) Gummiharz *n*, c) Kautschuk *m*; **2.** Klebstoff *m*, *bsd.* Gummilösung *f*; **3.** → a) ***chewing gum***, b) ***gum arabic***, c) ***gum elastic***, d) ***gum tree***; **4.** ⚘ Gummifluß *m* (*Baumkrankheit*); **5.** 'Gummi(-bonˌbon) *m*, *n*; **6.** *pl. Am.* Gummischuhe *pl.*; **II** *v/t.* **7.** gummieren; **8.** (an-, ver)kleben; **9.** ***~ up*** a) verkleben, b) F *et.* ‚vermasseln'; **III** *v/i.* **10.** ⚘ Gummi absondern (*Baum*).

gum³ [gʌm], *a.* ♀ *s.*: ***my ~!, by ~!*** heiliger Strohsack!

gum| am·mo·ni·ac *s.* ⚗, ⚕ Ammoni'akgummi *n*, *m*; **~ ar·a·bic** *s.* Gummia'rabikum *n*; **'~·boil** *s.* ⚕ Zahngeschwür *n*; **'~·drop** → ***gum²*** 5; **~ e·las·tic** *s.* Gummie'lastikum *n*, Kautschuk *m*.

gum·my ['gʌmɪ] *adj.* **1.** gummiartig, klebrig; **2.** Gummi...; **3.** gummihaltig.

gump·tion ['gʌmpʃn] *s.* F **1.** ‚Köpfchen' *n*, ‚Grütze' *f*, ‚Grips' *m*; **2.** ‚Mumm' *m*, Schneid *m*.

gum| res·in *s.* ⚘ Schleim-, Gummiharz *n*; **'~·shield** *s. Boxen*: Zahnschutz *m*; **'~·shoe** *s. Am.* **1.** F a) 'Gummiˌüberschuh *m*, b) Tennis-, Turnschuh *m*; **2.** *sl.* ‚Schnüffler' *m* (*Detektiv*, *Polizist*); **~ tree** *s.* ⚘ **1.** Gummibaum *m*: ***be up a ~*** *sl.* in der Klemme sein *od.* sitzen; **2.** Euka'lyptus(baum) *m*; **3.** Tu'pelobaum *m*; **4.** Amberbaum *m*; **'~·wood** *s.* Holz *n* des Gummibaums (*etc.* → ***gum tree***).

gun [gʌn] **I** *s.* **1.** ⚔ Geschütz *n*, Ka'none *f* (*a. fig.*): ***bring up one's big ~s*** schweres Geschütz auffahren (*a. fig.*); ***go great ~s*** F ‚schwer in Fahrt sein'; ***stick to one's ~s*** *fig.* festbleiben, nicht weichen *od.* nachgeben; ***a big ~*** *sl.* ‚e-e große Kanone', ‚ein großes Tier'; **2.** (*engS.* Jagd)Gewehr *n*, Flinte *f*, Büchse *f*; **3.** ‚Ka'none' *f*, Pi'stole *f*, Re'volver *m*; **4.** *sport*: a) 'Startpisˌtole *f*, b) Startschuß *m*: ***jump the ~*** e-n Fehlstart verursachen, *fig.* voreilig handeln; **5.** Ka'nonen-, Sa'lutschuß *m*; **6.** Schütze *m*, Jäger *m*; **7.** ✈, ⚙ a) Drosselklappe *f*, b) Drosselhebel *m*: ***give the engine the ~*** Vollgas geben; **II** *v/i.* **8.** auf die Jagd gehen; schießen; **9.** ***~ for*** es abgesehen haben auf *j-n od. et.*; **III** *v/t.* **10.** a) schießen auf (*acc.*), b) erschießen, c) *mst* ***~ down*** niederschießen; **11.** *oft* ***~ up*** *mot.* F ‚auf Touren bringen': ***~ the car up*** (Voll)Gas geben.

gun| bar·rel *s.* ⚔ **1.** Geschützrohr *n*; **2.** Gewehrlauf *m*; **~ bat·tle** *s.* Feuergefecht *n*, Schieße'rei *f*; **'~·boat** *s.* Ka'nonenboot *n*: ***~ diplomacy***; **~ cam·er·a** *s.* ✈, ⚔ 'Foto-MˌG *n*; **~ car·riage** *s.* ⚔ La'fette *f*; **~ cot·ton** *s.* Schießbaumwolle *f*; **~ dog** *s.* Jagdhund *m*; **'~·fight** → ***gun battle***; **'~ˌfire** *s.* ⚔ Geschützfeuer *n*; **'~ˌhap·py** *adj.* schießwütig; **~ har·poon** *s.* ⚓ Ge'schützharˌpune *f*.

gunk [gʌŋk] *Am.* F **I** *s.* klebriges Zeug; **II** *v/t.* ***~ up*** verkleben.

gun| li·cence, *Am.* **~ li·cense** *s.* Waffenschein *m*; **'~·lock** *s.* Gewehrschloß *n*; **'~·man** [-mən] *s.* [*irr.*] Bewaffnete(r) *m*; Re'volverheld *m*; **'~ˌmet·al** *s.* Rotguß *m*; **~ moll** *s. Am. sl.* Gangsterbraut *f*; **~ mount** *s.* ⚔ La'fette *f*.

gun·ner ['gʌnə] *s.* **1.** ⚔ a) Kano'nier *m*, Artille'rist *m*, b) Richtschütze *m* (*Panzer etc.*), c) M'G-Schütze *m*, Gewehrführer *m*; **2.** ✈ Bordschütze *m*; **gun·ner·y** ['gʌnərɪ] *s.* ⚔ Schieß-, Geschützwesen *n*: ***~ officer*** Artillerieoffizier *m*.

gun·ny ['gʌnɪ] *s.* Juteleinwand *f*: ***~*** (***bag***) Jutesack *m*.

gun| pit *s.* ⚔ **1.** Geschützstand *m*; **2.** ✈ Kanzel *f*; **'~·play** → ***gun battle***; **'~·point** *s.*: ***at ~*** mit vorgehaltener (Schuß)Waffe; **'~ˌpow·der** *s.* Schießpulver *n*: ♀ ***Plot*** *hist.* Pulververschwörung *f* (*in London 1605*); **'~·room** [-rʊm] *s. Brit.* ⚓, ⚔ Ka'dettenmesse *f*; **'~ˌrun·ner** *s.* Waffenschmuggler *m*; **'~ˌrun·ning** *s.* Waffenschmuggel *m*.

gun·sel ['gʌnsl] *Am. sl.* **1.** → ***gunman***; **2.** ‚Fiesling' *m*; **3.** Trottel *m*.

'gun|·ship *s.* ✈, ⚔ Kampfhubschrauber *m*; **'~·shot** **1.** (Ka'nonen-, Gewehr-)Schuß *m*: ***~ wound*** Schußwunde *f*; **2.** ***within*** (***out of***) ***~*** in (außer) Schußweite (*a. fig.*); **'~-shy** *adj.* **1.** *hunt.* schußscheu (*Hund etc.*); **2.** *Am.* F 'mißtrauisch; **'~ˌsling·er** *s. Am.* F → ***gunman***; **'~·smith** *s.* Büchsenmacher *m*; **~ tur·ret** *s.* ⚔ **1.** Geschützturm *m*; **2.** ✈ Waffendrehstand *m*.

gun·wale ['gʌnl] *s.* **1.** ⚓ Schandeckel *m*; **2.** Dollbord *n* (*am Ruderboot*).

gur·gi·ta·tion [ˌgɜːdʒɪ'teɪʃn] *s.* (Auf-)Wallen *n*, Strudeln *n*.

gur·gle ['gɜːgl] *v/i.* gurgeln: a) gluckern (*Wasser*), b) glucksen (*Stimme*, *Person*, *Wasser etc.*).

Gur·kha ['gɜːkə] *s.* Gurkha *m*, *f* (*Mitglied e-s indischen Volksstamms*).

gu·ru ['gʊruː] *s.* Guru *m* (*a. fig.*).

gush [gʌʃ] **I** *v/i.* **1.** her'vorströmen, -schießen, sich ergießen (***from*** aus); **2.** 'überströmen (***with*** von); **3.** (***over***) *fig.* F schwärmen (von), sich 'überschwenglich *od.* verzückt äußern (über *acc.*); **II** *s.* **4.** Schwall *m*, Strom *m*, Erguß *m* (*alle a. fig.*); **5.** F Schwärme'rei *f*, 'Überschwenglichkeit *f*, (Gefühls)Erguß *m*; **'gush·er** [-ʃə] *s.* **1.** Springquelle *f* (*Erdöl*); **2.** F Schwärmer(in); **'gush·ing** [-ʃɪŋ] *adj.* □ **1.** ('über)strömend; **2.** → **'gush·y** [-ʃɪ] *adj.* überschwenglich, schwärmerisch.

gus·set ['gʌsɪt] **I** *s.* **1.** *Näherei etc.*: Zwickel *m*, Keil *m*; **2.** ⚙ Winkelstück *n*, Eckblech *n*; **II** *v/t.* **3.** e-n Zwickel *etc.* einsetzen in (*acc.*).

gust [gʌst] *s.* **1.** Windstoß *m*, Bö *f*; **2.** *fig.* (Gefühls)Ausbruch *m*, Sturm *m* (*der Leidenschaft etc.*).

gus·ta·tion [gʌ'steɪʃn] *s.* **1.** Geschmack *m*, Geschmackssinn *m*; **2.** Schmecken *n*; **gus·ta·to·ry** ['gʌstətərɪ] *adj.* Geschmacks...

gus·to ['gʌstəʊ] *s.* Begeisterung *f*, Genuß *m*, Gusto *m*.

gust·y ['gʌstɪ] *adj.* □ **1.** böig, stürmisch; **2.** *fig.* ungestüm.

gut [gʌt] **I** *s.* **1.** *pl.* Eingeweide *pl.*, Gedärme *pl.*: ***I hate his ~s*** F ich hasse ihn wie die Pest; **2.** *anat.* a) 'Darm(kaˌnal) *m*, b) (*bestimmter*) Darm; **3.** *a. pl.* F Bauch *m*; **4.** (*präparierter*) Darm; **5.** a) Engpaß *m*, b) enge 'Durchfahrt, Meerenge *f*; **6.** *pl.* F a) *das* Innere: ***the ~s of a machine***, b) Kern *m*, *das* Wesentliche, c) Gehalt *m*, Sub'stanz *f*: ***it has no ~s in it*** es steckt nichts dahinter; **7.** *pl.* ‚Mumm' *m*, Schneid *m*; **II** *v/t.* **8.** *Fisch etc.* ausnehmen, -weiden; **9.** *Haus etc.* a) ausrauben, b) ausbrennen: ***~ted by fire*** völlig ausgebrannt; **10.** *fig. Buch etc.* ‚ausschlachten'; **III** *adj.* **11.** F instink'tiv, von innen her'aus, *a.* leidenschaftlich: ***a ~ reaction***, **12.** von entscheidender Bedeutung: ***a ~ problem***; **'gut·less** [-lɪs] *adj.* ‚schlaff': a) ohne Schneid, b) ‚müde': ***a ~ enterprise***; **'gut·sy** [-tsɪ] *adj.* mutig, schneidig.

gut·ta-per·cha [ˌgʌtə'pɜːtʃə] *s.* **1.** ⚗ Gutta *n*; **2.** ⚘, ⚙ Gutta'percha *n*.

gut·ter ['gʌtə] **I** *s.* **1.** Dachrinne *f*; **2.** Gosse *f*, Rinnstein *m*; **3.** *fig. contp.* Gosse *f*: ***language of the ~***; ***take s.o. out of the ~*** j-n aus der Gosse auflesen; **4.** (Abfluß-, Wasser)Rinne *f*; **5.** ⚙ Rille *f*, Hohlkehlfuge *f*, Furche *f*; **6.** Kugelfangrinne *f* (*der Bowlingbahn*); **II** *v/t.* **7.** furchen, aushöhlen; **III** *v/i.* **8.** rinnen, strömen; **9.** tropfen (*Kerze*); **IV** *adj.* **10.** vul'gär, schmutzig, Schmutz...; **~ press** *s.* Skan'dal-, Sensati'onspresse

f; '**~·snipe** *s.* Gassenkind *n.*
gut·tur·al ['gʌtərəl] **I** *adj.* ☐ **1.** Kehl..., guttu'ral (*beide a. ling.*), kehlig; **2.** rauh, heiser; **II** *s.* **3.** *ling.* Kehllaut *m*, Guttu'ral *m.*
guv [gʌv], **guv·nor, guv'nor** ['gʌvnə] *sl.* → ***governor*** 4.
guy[1] [gaɪ] **I** *s.* **1.** F ‚Typ' *m*, Kerl *m*, ‚Bursche' *m*; **2.** ‚Vogelscheuche' *f*, ‚'Schießbudenfiˌgur' *f*; **3.** Zielscheibe *f* des Spotts; **4.** *Brit. Spottfigur des Guy Fawkes* (*die am **Guy Fawkes Day** verbrannt wird*); **II** *v/t.* **5.** F *j-n* lächerlich machen, verulken.
guy[2] [gaɪ] **I** *s.* **1.** *a.* ~ ***rope*** Halteseil *n*, -tau *n*; **2.** a) ⚙ (Ab)Spannseil *n* (*e-s Mastes*): ~ ***wire*** Spanndraht *m*, b) ⚓ Gei(tau *n*) *f*; **3.** Spannschnur *f* (*Zelt*); **II** *v/t.* **4.** mit e-m Tau *etc.* sichern, verspannen.
Guy Fawkes Day [ˌgaɪ'fɔːks] *s. Brit. der Jahrestag des **Gunpowder Plot*** (*5. November*).
guz·zle ['gʌzl] *v/t.* **1.** *a. v/i.* a) ‚saufen', b) ‚fressen'; **2.** *oft* ~ ***away*** *Geld* verprassen, *bsd.* ‚versaufen'.
gybe [dʒaɪb] *v/t. u. v/i.* ⚓ *Brit.* (sich) 'umlegen (*Segel beim Kreuzen*).
gym [dʒɪm] *s. sl. abbr. für **gymnasium*** *u. **gymnastics***: ~ ***shoe*** Turnschuh *m.*
gym·kha·na [dʒɪm'kɑːnə] *s.* Gym'khana *f* (*Geschicklichkeitswettbewerb für Reiter, a. Austragungsort*).
gym·na·si·um [dʒɪm'neɪzjəm] *pl.* **-si·ums, -si·a** [-zjə] *s.* **1.** Turnhalle *f*; **2.** *ped.* (*deutsches*) Gym'nasium; **gymnast** ['dʒɪmnæst] *s.* (Kunst)Turner(in); **gym'nas·tic** [-'næstɪk] **I** *adj.* **1.** (☐ ***~ally***) gym'nastisch, turnerisch, Turn..., Gymnastik...; **II** *s.* **2.** *pl. sg. konstr.* Turnen *n*, Gym'nastik *f*: ***mental ~s*** ‚Gehirnakrobatik' *f*; **3.** *mst pl.* Turn-, Gym'nastikübung *f.*
gyn·ae·co·log·ic, gyn·ae·co·log·i·cal [ˌgaɪnɪkə'lɒdʒɪk(l)] *adj.* ⚕ gynäko'logisch; **gyn·ae·col·o·gist** [ˌgaɪnɪ'kɒlədʒɪst] *s.* ⚕ Gynäko'loge *m*, -'login *f*, Frauenarzt *m*, Frauenärztin *f*; **gynae·col·o·gy** [ˌgaɪnɪ'kɒlədʒɪ] *s.* ⚕ Gynäkolo'gie *f.*
gyp [dʒɪp] *sl.* **I** *v/i. u. v/t.* **1.** ‚bescheißen', ‚neppen'; **II** *s.* **2.** a) ‚Beschiß' *m*, b) ‚Nepp' *m*; **3.** ***give s.o.*** ~ j-n ‚fertigmachen'; '**~-joint** *s. sl.* 'NepploˌKal *n.*
gyp·se·ous ['dʒɪpsɪəs] *adj. min.* gipsartig, Gips...; **gyp·sum** ['dʒɪpsəm] *s. min.* Gips *m.*
gyp·sy ['dʒɪpsɪ] *etc. bsd. Am.* → ***gipsy*** *etc.*
gy·rate **I** *v/i.* [ˌdʒaɪə'reɪt] kreisen, sich (im Kreis) drehen, wirbeln; **II** *adj.* ['dʒaɪərɪt] gewunden; ˌ**gy'ra·tion** [-eɪʃən] *s.* **1.** Kreisbewegung *f*, Drehung *f*; **2.** *anat., zo.* Windung *f*; **gy·ra·to·ry** ['dʒaɪərətərɪ] *adj.* kreisend, sich (im Kreis) drehend.
gyr·fal·con ['dʒɜːˌfɔːlkən] → ***gerfalcon.***
gy·ro·com·pass ['dʒaɪərəʊˌkʌmpəs] *s.* ⚓, *phys.* Kreiselkompaß *m*; '**gy·ro·graph** [-əʊgrɑːf] *s.* ⚙ Um'drehungszähler *m.*
gy·ro ho·ri·zon ['dʒaɪərəʊ] *s. ast.*, ✈ künstlicher Hori'zont.
gy·ro·pi·lot ['dʒaɪərəʊˌpaɪlət] *s.* ✈ Autopi'lot *m*; '**gy·ro·plane** [-rəpleɪn] *s.* ✈ Tragschrauber *m*; '**gy·ro·scope** [-rəskəʊp] *s.* **1.** *phys.* Gyro'skop *n*, Kreisel *m*; **2.** ⚓, ⚔ Ge'radlaufappaˌrat *m* (*Torpedo*); **gy·ro·scop·ic** [ˌdʒaɪərə'skɒpɪk] *adj.* (☐ ***~ally***) Kreisel..., gyro'skopisch; **gy·ro·sta·bi·liz·er** [ˌdʒaɪərəʊ'steɪbɪlaɪzə] *s.* ⚓, ✈ (Stabilisier-, Lage)Kreisel *m*; '**gy·ro·stat** [-rəʊstæt] *s.* Gyro'stat *m.*
gyve [dʒaɪv] *obs. od. poet.* **I** *s. mst pl.* (*bsd.* Fuß)Fessel *f*; **II** *v/t.* fesseln.

H

H, h [eɪtʃ] *s.* H *n*, h *n* (*Buchstabe*).

ha [hɑː] *int.* ha!, ah!

ha·be·as cor·pus [ˌheɪbjəsˈkɔːpəs] (*Lat.*) *s. a.* ***writ of ~*** ⚖ Vorführungsbefehl *m* zur Haftprüfung: ⚖ ***Act*** Habeas-Corpus-Akte *f* (*1679*).

hab·er·dash·er [ˈhæbədæʃə] *s.* **1.** Kurzwarenhändler(in); **2.** *Am.* Herrenausstatter *m*; **ˈhab·er·dash·er·y** [-ərɪ] *s.* **1.** a) Kurzwaren *pl.*, b) Kurzwarengeschäft *n*; **2.** *Am.* a) ˈHerrenbeˌkleidungsarˌtikel *pl.*, b) Herrenmodengeschäft *n*.

ha·bil·i·ments [həˈbɪlɪmənts] *s. pl.* (Amts)Kleidung *f*, Kleider *pl.*

hab·it [ˈhæbɪt] *s.* **1.** (An)Gewohnheit *f*: ***out of ~*** aus Gewohnheit; ***the force of ~*** die Macht der Gewohnheit; ***be in the ~ of doing s.th.*** pflegen *od.* die (An-)Gewohnheit haben, et. zu tun; ***get*** (*od.* ***fall***) ***into a ~*** sich et. angewöhnen; ***break o.s. of a ~*** sich et. abgewöhnen; ***make a ~ of s.th.*** et. zur Gewohnheit werden lassen; **2.** *oft* ***~ of mind*** Geistesverfassung *f*; **3.** *psych.* Habit *n*, *a. m*; **4.** ⚕ Sucht *f*; **5.** (Amts-, Berufs-) Kleidung *f*, Tracht *f*; **6.** ⚘ Habitus *m*, Wachstumsart *f*; **7.** *zo.* Lebensweise *f*.

hab·it·a·ble [ˈhæbɪtəbl] *adj.* □ bewohnbar; **hab·i·tant** *s.* **1.** [ˈhæbɪtənt] Einwohner(in); **2.** [ˈhæbɪtɔ̃ːŋ] a) ˈFrankokaˌnadier *m*, b) Einwohner *m* franˈzösischer Abkunft (*in Louisiana*); **hab·i·tat** [ˈhæbɪtæt] *s.* ⚘, *zo.* Habiˈtat *n*, Heimat *f*, Stand-, Fundort *m*; **hab·i·ta·tion** [ˌhæbɪˈteɪʃn] *s.* Wohnen *n*; Wohnung *f*, Behausung *f*, Aufenthalt *m*: ***unfit for human ~*** unbewohnbar.

ˈhab·it-ˌform·ing *adj.* **1.** zur Gewohnheit werdend; **2.** ⚕ suchterzeugend: ***~ drug*** Suchtmittel *n*.

ha·bit·u·al [həˈbɪtjʊəl] *adj.* □ **1.** gewohnt, üblich, ständig; **2.** gewohnheitsmäßig, Gewohnheits…, *contp. a.* noˈtorisch: ***~ criminal*** Gewohnheitsverbrecher *m*; ***~ drinker*** Gewohnheitstrinker (-in); **haˈbit·u·ate** [-jʊeɪt] *v/t.* **1.** (***o.s.*** sich) gewöhnen (***to*** an *acc.*; ***to doing s.th.*** daran, et. zu tun); **2.** *Am.* F frequentieren, häufig besuchen; **haˈbit·u·é** [-jʊeɪ] *s.* ständiger Besucher, Stammgast *m*.

ha·chures [hæˈʃjʊə] *s. pl.* Schraffierung *f*, Schrafˈfur *f*.

hack¹ [hæk] **I** *v/t.* **1.** (zer)hacken: ***~ off*** abhacken (von); ***~ out*** *fig.* grob darstellen, ‚hinhauen'; ***~ to pieces*** (*od.* ***bits***) in Stücke hacken, *fig.* ‚kaputtmachen'; **2.** (ein)kerben; **3.** ⚒ *Boden* (auf-, los-) hacken; **4.** ⚙ *Steine* behauen; **5.** *sport j-n* (gegen das Schienbein) treten; **II** *v/i.* **6.** hacken: ***~ at*** a) hacken nach, b) einhauen auf (*acc.*); **7.** trocken u. stoßweise husten: ***~ing cough*** → 12; **8.** *sport* treten, ‚holzen'; **III** *s.* **9.** Hieb *m*; **10.** Kerbe *f*; **11.** *sport* a) Tritt *m* (gegen das Schienbein), b) Trittwunde *f*; **12.** trokkener, stoßweiser Husten.

hack² [hæk] **I** *s.* **1.** a) Reit- *od.* Kutschpferd *n*, b) Mietpferd *n*, Gaul *m*, Klepper *m*; **2.** *Am.* a) (Miets)Droschke *f*, b) F Taxi *n*, c) → ***hackie***; **3.** a) Lohnschreiber *m*, Schriftsteller, der auf Bestellung arbeitet, b) Schreiberling *m*; **II** *adj.* **4.** ***~ writer*** → 3; **5.** einfallslos, mittelmäßig; **6.** → ***hackneyed***; **III** *v/i.* **7.** *Brit.* ausreiten; **8.** *Am.* F a) in e-m Taxi fahren, b) ein Taxi fahren; **9.** auf Bestellung arbeiten (*Schriftsteller*).

hack·er [ˈhækə] *s. Computer*: Hacker *m*.

hack·ie [ˈhækɪ] *s. Am.* F Taxifahrer *m*.

hack·le [ˈhækl] **I** *s.* **1.** ⚙ Hechel *f*; **2.** a) *orn.* (lange) Nackenfeder(n *pl.*), b) *pl.* (*aufstellbare*) Rücken- u. Halshaare *pl.* (*Hund*): ***have one's ~s up*** *fig.* wütend sein; ***this got his ~s up, his ~s rose*** (***at this***) das brachte ihn in Wut; **II** *v/t.* **3.** ⚙ hecheln.

hack·ney [ˈhæknɪ] *s.* **1.** → ***hack²*** 1; **2.** *a.* ***~ carriage*** Droschke *f*; **ˈhack·neyed** [-ɪd] *adj. fig.* abgenutzt, abgedroschen.

ˈhack·saw *s.* ⚙ Bügelsäge *f*.

had [hæd; həd] *pret. u. p.p. von* ***have***.

had·dock [ˈhædək] *s.* Schellfisch *m*.

Ha·des [ˈheɪdiːz] *s.* **1.** *antiq.* Hades *m*, ˈUnterwelt *f*; **2.** F Hölle *f*.

hae·mal [ˈhiːml] *adj. anat.* Blut(gefäß)…; **hae·mat·ic** [hiːˈmætɪk] **I** *adj.* a) blutgefüllt, b) Blut…, c) blutbildend; **II** *s.* ⚕ Häˈmatikum *n*, blutbildendes Mittel; **haem·a·tite** [ˈhemətaɪt] *s. min.* Hämaˈtit *m*; **hae·ma·tol·o·gy** [ˌheməˈtɒlədʒɪ] *s.* ⚕ Hämatoloˈgie *f*; **hae·mo·glo·bin** [ˌhiːməʊˈgləʊbɪn] *s.* Hämogloˈbin *n*, roter Blutfarbstoff; **hae·mo·phile** [ˈhiːməʊfaɪl] *s.* ⚕ Bluter *m*; **hae·mo·phil·i·a** [ˌhiːməʊˈfiːlɪə] *s.* ⚕ Bluterkrankheit *f*, Hämophiˈlie *f*; **hae·mo·phil·i·ac** [ˌhiːməʊˈfɪlɪæk] → ***haemophile***; **haem·or·rhage** [ˈhemərɪdʒ] *s.* (***cerebral ~*** Gehirn)Blutung *f*; **haem·or·rhoids** [ˈhemərɔɪdz] *s. pl.* ⚕ Hämorrhoˈiden *pl.*

haft [hɑːft] *s.* Griff *m*, Heft *n*, Stiel *m*.

hag [hæg] *s.* ‚alte Vettel', Hexe *f*.

hag·gard [ˈhægəd] **I** *adj.* □ **1.** wild, verstört: ***~ look***; **2.** a) abgehärmt, b) sorgenvoll, gequält, c) abgespannt, d) abgezehrt, hager; **3.** ***~ falcon*** → 4; **II** *s.* **4.** Falke, der ausgewachsen gefangen wurde.

hag·gle [ˈhægl] *v/i.* (***about, over***) schachern, feilschen, handeln (um); **ˈhag·gler** [-lə] *s.* Feilscher(in).

hag·i·og·ra·phy [ˌhægɪˈɒgrəfɪ] *s.* Hagiograˈphie *f* (*Erforschung u. Beschreibung von Heiligenleben*); **ˌhag·iˈol·a·try** [-ˈɒlətrɪ] *s.* Heiligenverehrung *f*.

ˈhagˌrid·den *adj.* **1.** gepeinigt, gequält; **2.** ***be ~*** *humor.* von Frauen schikaniert werden.

Hague| Con·ven·tions [heɪg] *s. pl. pol. die* Haager Abkommen *pl*; **~ Tri·bu·nal** *s. pol. der* Haager Schiedshof.

hail¹ [heɪl] **I** *s.* **1.** Hagel *m* (*a. fig. von Geschossen, Flüchen etc.*); **II** *v/i.* **2.** *impers.* hageln: ***it is ~ing*** es hagelt; **3.** *a.* ***~ down*** *fig.* (***on*** auf *acc.*) (nieder)hageln, (nieder)prasseln; **III** *v/t.* **4.** *a.* ***~ down*** *fig.* (nieder)hageln *od.* (-)prasseln lassen (***on*** auf *acc.*).

hail² [heɪl] **I** *v/t.* **1.** freudig *od.* mit Beifall begrüßen, zujubeln (*dat.*); **2.** *j-n, a. Taxi* herˈbeirufen *od.* -winken; **3.** *fig. et.* begrüßen, begeistert aufnehmen; **II** *v/i.* **4.** *bsd.* ⚓ rufen, sich melden; **5.** (her)stammen, (-)kommen (***from*** von *od.* aus); **III** *int.* **6.** heil!; **IV** *s.* **7.** Gruß *m*, Zuruf *m*: ***within ~*** (*od.* ***~ing distance***) in Ruf- *od.* Hörweite, *fig.* greifbar nahe; **ˈhail·er** *s. Am.* Megaˈphon *n*.

ˈhail|-ˌfel·low-ˌwell-ˈmet [-ləʊ-] **I** *s.* a) umgänglicher Mensch, b) *contp.* plump-vertraulicher Kerl; **II** *adj.* a) umgänglich, b) *contp.* plump-vertraulich, c) ***~ with*** (sehr) vertraut *od.* auf du u. du mit; **ˈ~·stone** *s.* Hagelkorn *n*, -schloße *f*; **ˈ~·storm** *s.* Hagelschauer *m*.

hair [heə] *s.* **1.** *ein* Haar *n*: ***by a ~*** *fig.* ganz knapp *gewinnen etc.*; ***to a ~*** haargenau; ***it turned on a ~*** es hing an e-m Faden; ***without turning a ~*** ohne mit der Wimper zu zucken, kaltblütig; ***split ~s*** Haarspalterei treiben; ***not to harm*** (*od.* ***hurt***) ***a ~ on s.o.'s head*** j-m kein Haar krümmen; **2.** *coll.* Haar *n*, Haare *pl.*: ***comb s.o.'s ~ for him*** (*od.* ***her***) F *fig.* j-m gehörig den Kopf waschen; ***do one's ~*** sich die Haare machen; ***get in s.o.'s ~*** F j-m auf die Nerven fallen; ***have s.o. by the short ~s*** F j-n in der Hand haben; ***have one's ~ cut*** sich die Haare schneiden lassen; ***have a ~ of the dog*** (***that bit you***) F e-n Schluck Alkohol trinken, um s-n ‚Kater' zu vertreiben; ***let one's ~ down*** a) sein Haar aufmachen, b) *fig.* sich ungeniert benehmen, c) aus sich herausgehen, d) sein Herz ausschütten; ***my ~ stood on end*** mir sträubten sich die Haare; ***keep s.o. out of one's ~*** F sich j-n vom Leib halten; ***keep your ~ on!*** F nur keine Aufregung; ***tear one's ~*** sich die Haare raufen; **3.** ⚘ Haar *n*; **4.** Härchen *n*, Fäserchen *n*; **ˈ~·breadth** *s.*: ***by a ~*** um Haaresbreite; ***escape by a ~*** mit knapper Not davonkommen; '~·brush *s.* **1.** Haarbürste *f*; **2.** Haarpinsel *m*; **~ clippers** *s. pl.* 'Haarschneidema,schine *f*; '~·cloth *s.* Haartuch *n*; '~-,com·pass·es *s. pl. a.* ***pair of ~*** Haar(strich)zirkel *m*; '~,curl·ing *adj.* F **1.** grausig; **2.** haarsträubend; '~·cut *s.* Haarschnitt *m*, *weitS.* Fri'sur *f*: ***have a ~*** sich die Haare schneiden lassen; '~·do *pl.* '~·dos *s.* F Fri'sur *f*; '~,dress·er *s.* Fri'seur *m*, Fri'seuse *f*; '~,dress·ing *s.* Frisieren *n*: ***~ salon*** Friseursalon *m*; '~,dri·er *s.* Haartrockner *m*: a) Fön *m*, b) Trockenhaube *f*.

haired [heəd] *adj.* **1.** behaart; **2.** *in Zssgn* ...haarig.

hair| fol·li·cle *s. anat.* Haarbalg *m*; '~·grip *s.* Haarklammer *f*.

hair·i·ness ['heərɪnɪs] *s.* Behaartheit *f*;

hair·less ['heəlɪs] *adj.* unbehaart, haarlos, kahl.

'hair|·line *s.* **1.** Haaransatz *m*; **2.** a) feiner Streifen (*Stoffmuster*), b) feingestreifter Stoff; **3.** Haarseil *n*; **4.** *a.* ***~ crack*** ⚙ Haarriß *m*; **5.** *opt.* Fadenkreuz *n*; **6.** → ***hair stroke***; **~ mat·tress** *s.* 'Roßhaarma,tratze *f*; **~ net** *s.* Haarnetz *n*; **~ oil** *s.* Haaröl *n*; '~·piece *s.* Haarteil *n*, *für Männer*: Tou'pet *n*; '~·pin *s.* **1.** Haarnadel *f*; **2.** *a.* ***~ bend*** Haarnadelkurve *f*; '~-,rais·er *s.* F *et.* Haarsträubendes, *z.B.* Horrorfilm *m*; '~-,rais·ing *adj.* F haarsträubend; **~ restor·er** *s.* Haarwuchsmittel *n*.

hair's breadth → ***hairbreadth***.

hair| shirt *s.* härenes Hemd; **~ sieve** *s.* Haarsieb *n*; **~ slide** *s.* Haarspange *f*; '~,split·ter *s. fig.* Haarspalter(in); '~,split·ting **I** *s.* Haarspalte'rei *f*; **II** *adj.* haarspalterisch; '~·spring *s.* ⚙ Haar-, Unruhfeder *f*; **~ stroke** *s.* Haarstrich *m* (*Schrift*); '~·style *s.* Fri'sur *f*; **~ styl·ist** *s.* Hair-Stylist *m*, 'Damenfri,seur *m*; '~-,trig·ger **I** *s.* **1.** Stecher *m* (*am Gewehr*); **II** *adj.* F **2.** äußerst reizbar (*Person*); **3.** la'bil; **4.** prompt.

hair·y ['heərɪ] *adj.* **1.** haarig, behaart; **2.** Haar...; **3.** F ‚haarig', schwierig.

hake [heɪk] *s. ichth.* Seehecht *m*.

ha·la·tion [hə'leɪʃn] *s. phot.* Halo-, Lichthofbildung *f*.

hal·berd ['hælbɜ:d] *s.* ⚔ *hist.* Helle'barde *f*; **hal·berd·ier** [,hælbə'dɪə] *s.* Hellebar'dier *m*.

hal·cy·on ['hælsɪən] **I** *s. orn.* Eisvogel *m*; **II** *adj.* halky'onisch, friedlich; **~ days** *s. pl.* **1.** halky'onische Tage *pl.*: a) Tage *pl.* der Ruhe (*auf dem Meer*), b) *fig.* Tage glücklicher Ruhe; **2.** *fig.* glückliche Zeit.

hale [heɪl] *adj.* gesund, kräftig: ***~ and hearty*** gesund u. munter.

half [hɑ:f] **I** *pl.* **halves** *s.* **1.** Hälfte *f*: ***an hour and a ~*** anderthalb Stunden; ***~ (of) the girls*** die Hälfte der Mädchen; ***~ the amount*** die halbe Menge *od.* Summe; ***cut in halves*** (*od.* ***~***) in zwei Hälften *od.* Teile schneiden, entzweischneiden, halbieren; ***do s.th. by halves*** et. nur halb tun; ***do things by halves*** halbe Sachen machen; ***not to do things by halves*** Nägel mit Köpfen machen; ***go halves with s.o.*** (gleichmäßig) mit j-m teilen, mit j-m (bei et.) halbpart machen; ***too clever by ~*** überschlau; ***a game and a ~*** F ein ‚Bombenspiel'; ***not good enough by ~*** lange nicht gut genug; ***torn in ~*** *fig.* hin- u. hergerissen; → ***better***[1] 1; **2.** *sport*: a) Halbzeit *f*, (Spiel)Hälfte *f*, b) (Spielfeld)Hälfte *f*, c) *Golf*: Gleichstand *m*, d) → ***halfback***; **3.** Fahrkarte *f* zum halben Preis; **4.** kleines Bier (*halbes Pint*); **II** *adj.* **5.** halb: ***a ~ mile***, *mst* ***~ a mile*** e-e halbe Meile; ***~ an hour***, ***a ~ hour*** e-e halbe Stunde; ***two pounds and a ~*** zweieinhalb Pfund; ***a ~ share*** ein halber Anteil, e-e Hälfte; ***~ knowledge*** Halbwissen *n*; ***at ~ the price*** zum halben Preis; ***that's ~ the battle*** damit ist es halb gewonnen; → ***mind*** 5, ***eye*** 2; **III** *adv.* **6.** halb, zur Hälfte: ***~ full***; ***my work is ~ done***; ***~ as much*** halb so viel; ***~ as much again*** anderthalbmal soviel; ***~ past ten*** halb elf (Uhr); **7.** halb(wegs), nahezu, fast: ***~ dead*** halbtot; ***not ~ bad*** F gar nicht übel; ***be ~ inclined*** beinahe geneigt sein; ***he ~ wished*** (***suspected***) er wünschte (vermutete) fast.

,half|-and-'half [-fənd'h-] **I** *s.* Halb-u.-halb-Mischung *f*; **II** *adj.* halb-u.-'halb; **III** *adv.* halb u. halb; '~·back *s.* **1.** *obs. Fußball etc.*: Läufer *m*; **2.** *Rugby*: Halbspieler *m*; ,~-'baked *adj. fig.* F **1.** ‚grün', unreif, unerfahren; **2.** unausgegoren, nicht durch'dacht (*Plan etc.*); **3.** blöd; **~ bind·ing** *s.* Halb(leder)band *m*; '~·blood *s.* **1.** Halbbürtigkeit *f*: ***brother of the ~*** Halbbruder *m*; **2.** → ***half-breed*** 1; ,~-'blood·ed → ***half-bred*** I; **~ board** *s. Hotel*: 'Halbpensi,on *f*; ,~-'bound *adj.* im Halbband (*Buch*); '~-bred **I** *adj.* halbblütig, Halbblut...; **II** *s.* Halbblut(tier) *n*; '~-breed **I** *s.* **1.** Mischling *m*, Halbblut *n* (*a. Tier*); **2.** *Am.* Me'stize *m*; **3.** ⚘ Kreuzung *f*; **II** *adj.* **4.** → ***half-bred***; '~-,broth·er *s.* Halbbruder *m*; '~-caste → ***half-breed*** 1 *u.* ***half-bred***; '~-cloth *adj.* in Halbleinen gebunden, Halbleinen...; **~ cock** *s.*: ***go off at ~*** F a) ‚hochgehen', wütend werden, b) ‚da'nebengehen'; **~ crown** *s. Brit. obs.* Halbkronenstück *n* (*Wert*: *2s.6d.*); **~ deck** *s.* ⚓ Halbdeck *n*; **~ face** *s. paint., phot.* Pro'fil *n*; ,~-'heart·ed *adj.* □ halbherzig; **~ hol·i·day** *s.* halber Feier- *od.* Urlaubstag; **~ hose** *s. coll., pl. konstr.* a) Halb-, Kniestrümpfe *pl.*, b) Socken *pl.*; ,~-'hour **I** *s.* halbe Stunde; **II** *adj.* a) halbstündig, b) halbstündlich; **III** *adv.* → ,~-'hour·ly *adv.* jede *od.* alle halbe Stunde, halbstündlich; ,~-'length *s. a.* ***~ portrait*** Brustbild *n*; '~-life (pe·ri·od) *s.* ⚗, *phys.* Halbwertzeit *f*; ,~-'mast *s.*: ***fly at ~*** auf halbmast *od.* ⚓ halbstock(s) setzen (*v/i.* wehen); **~ meas·ure** *s.* Halbheit *f*, halbe Sache; **~ moon** *s.* **1.** Halbmond *m*; **2.** (Nagel)Möndchen *n*; **~ mourning** *s.* Halbtrauer *f*; **~ nel·son** *s. Ringen*: Halbnelson *m*; ,~-'or·phan *s.* Halbwaise *f*; **~ pay** *s.* **1.** halbes Gehalt; **2.** ⚔ Halbsold *m*; Ruhegeld *n*: ***on ~*** außer Dienst; ~·pen·ny ['heɪpnɪ] *s.* **1.** *pl.* **half·pence** ['heɪpəns] halber Penny: ***three halfpence***, ***a penny ~*** eineinhalb Pennies; ***turn up again like a bad ~*** immer wieder auftauchen; **2.** *pl.* **half·pen·nies** ['heɪpnɪz] Halbpennystück *n*; '~-pint *s.* **1.** halbes Pint (*bsd. Bier*); **2.** F ‚halbe Porti'on'; ,~-seas-'o·ver *adj.* F ‚angesäuselt'; '~-,sis·ter *s.* Halbschwester *f*; ,~-'staff → ***half-mast***; **~ term** *s. univ. Brit. kurze Ferien in der Mitte e-s Trimesters*; ,~-'tide *s.* ⚓ Gezeitenmitte *f*; ,~-'tim·bered *adj.* ⚠ Fachwerk...; **~ time** *s.* **1.** halbe Arbeitszeit; **2.** *sport* Halbzeit *f*; ,~-'time **I** *adj.* **1.** Halbtags...: ***~ job***; **2.** *sport* Halbzeit...: ***~ score*** Halbzeitstand *m*; **II** *adv.* **3.** halbtags; ,~-'tim·er *s.* Halbtagsbeschäftigte(r *m*) *f*; **~ ti·tle** *s.* Schmutztitel *m*; '~·tone *s.* ♪, *paint., typ.* Halbton *m*: ***~ etching*** Autotypie *f*; ***~ process*** Halbtonverfahren *n*; '~-track **I** *s.* **1.** ⚙ Halbkettenantrieb *m*; **2.** Halbkettenfahrzeug *n*; **II** *adj.* **3.** Halbketten...; '~-truth *s.* Halbwahrheit *f*; ,~-'vol·ley *s. sport* Halbvolley *m*, Halbflugball *m*; ,~-'way **I** *adj.* **1.** auf halbem Weg *od.* in der Mitte (liegend): ***~ measures*** halbe Maßnahmen; **II** *adv.* **2.** auf halbem Weg, in der Mitte; → ***meet*** 4; **3.** teilweise, halb(wegs); ,~-'way house *s.* **1.** auf halbem Weg gelegenes Gasthaus; **2.** *fig.* a) 'Zwischenstufe *f*, -stati,on *f*, b) Kompro'miß *m*, *n*; **3.** Rehabilitati'onszentrum *n*; '~-wit *s.* Schwachkopf *m*, -sinnige(r *m*) *f*, Trottel *m*; ,~-'wit·ted *adj.* schwachsinnig, blöd; ,~-'year·ly *adv.* halbjährlich.

hal·i·but ['hælɪbət] *s.* Heilbutt *m*.

hal·ide ['hælaɪd] *s.* ⚗ Haloge'nid *n*.

hal·i·to·sis [,hælɪ'təʊsɪs] *s.* Hali'tose *f*, (übler) Mundgeruch.

hall [hɔ:l] *s.* **1.** Halle *f*, Saal *m*; **2.** a) Diele *f*, Flur *m*, b) (Empfangs-, Vor-) Halle *f*, Vesti'bül *n*; **3.** a) (Versammlungs)Halle *f*, b) großes (öffentliches) Gebäude: ***♀ of Fame*** Ruhmeshalle; **4.** *hist.* Gilden-, Zunfthaus *n*; **5.** *Brit.* Herrenhaus *n* (*e-s Landguts*); **6.** *univ.* a) *a.* ***~ of residence*** Stu'dentenheim *n*, b) *Brit.* (Essen *n* im) Speisesaal *m*, c) *Am.* Insti'tut *n*: ***Science ♀***; **7.** *hist.* a) Schloß *n*, Stammsitz *m*, b) Fürsten-, Königssaal *m*, c) Festsaal *m*; **~ clock** *s.* Standuhr *f*.

hal·le·lu·jah, **hal·le·lu·iah** [,hælɪ'lu:jə] **I** *s.* Halle'luja *n*; **II** *int.* halle'luja!

hal·liard ['hæljəd] → ***halyard***.

'hall·mark **I** *s.* **1.** Feingehaltsstempel *m* (*der Londoner Goldschmiedeinnung*); **2.** *fig.* (Güte)Stempel *m*, Gepräge *n*, (Kenn)Zeichen *n*; **II** *v/t.* **3.** *Gold od. Silber* stempeln; **4.** *fig.* kennzeichnen, stempeln.

hal·lo [hə'ləʊ] *bsd. Brit. für* **hello**.

hal·loo [hə'lu:] **I** *int.* hallo!, he!; **II** *s.* Hallo *n*; **III** *v/i.* (hallo) rufen *od.* schreien: ***don't ~ till you are out of the wood!*** freu dich nicht zu früh!

hal·low[1] ['hæləʊ] *v/t.* heiligen: a) weihen, b) als heilig verehren: ***~ed be Thy name*** geheiligt werde Dein Name.

hal·low[2] ['hæləʊ] → ***halloo***.

Hal·low·e'en [,hæləʊ'i:n] *s.* Abend *m* vor Aller'heiligen; **Hal·low·mas** ['hæləʊmæs] *s. obs.* Aller'heiligen(fest) *n*.

hall| por·ter *s. bsd. Brit.* Ho'tel-, Hausdiener *m*; '~·stand *s.* a) *Am. a.* ***~ tree*** Garde'robenständer *m*, b) 'Flurgarde,robe *f*.

hal·lu·ci·nate [hə'lu:sɪneɪt] *v/i.* halluzinieren; **hal·lu·ci·na·tion** [hə,lu:sɪ'neɪʃn] *s.* Halluzinati'on *f*; **hal·lu·ci·na·to·ry** [hə'lu:sɪnətərɪ] *adj.* halluzina'torisch; **hal·lu·ci·no·gen** [hə'lu:sɪnədʒen] *s.* ⚕ Halluzino'gen *n*.

'hall·way *s. Am.* **1.** (Eingangs)Halle *f*,

Diele *f*; **2.** Korridor *m*.

halm [hɑːm] → ***haulm***.

hal·ma [ˈhælmə] *s*. Halma(spiel) *n*.

ha·lo [ˈheɪləʊ] *pl*. **ha·loes, ha·los** *s*. **1.** Heiligen-, Glorienschein *m*, Nimbus *m* (*a. fig*.); **2.** *ast*. Halo *m*, Ring *m*, Hof *m*; **3.** *allg*. Ring *m*, (*phot*. Licht)Hof *m*; ˈ**ha·loed** [-əʊd] *adj*. mit e-m Heiligenschein *etc*. umˈgeben.

hal·o·gen [ˈhælədʒen] *s*. ⚗ Haloˈgen *n*, Salzbildner *m*: **~ *lamp*** Halogenlampe *f*, *mot*. -scheinwerfer *m*.

halt¹ [hɔːlt] **I** *s*. **1.** a) Halt *m*, Pause *f*, Rast *f*, Aufenthalt *m*, b) *a. fig*. Stillstand *m*: ***call a ~* (*to*)** (*fig*. Ein)Halt gebieten (*dat*.); ***bring to a ~*** → 3; ***come to a ~*** → 4; **2.** 🚌 *Brit*. (Bedarfs-) Haltestelle *f*, Haltepunkt *m*; **II** *v/t*. **3.** a) haltmachen lassen, anhalten (lassen), *a. fig*. zum Halten *od*. Stehen bringen; **III** *v/i*. **4.** a) anhalten, haltmachen, b) *a. fig*. zum Stehen *od*. Stillstand kommen: ***~!*** halt!

halt² [hɔːlt] *v/i*. **1.** *obs*. hinken; **2.** *fig*. ‚hinken' (*Vergleich etc*.), (*Vers etc*.) *a*. holpern; **3.** zögern, schwanken, stocken.

hal·ter [ˈhɔːltə] **I** *s*. **1.** Halfter *f*, *m*, *n*; **2.** Strick *m* (*zum Hängen*); **3.** rückenfreies Oberteil *od*. Kleid mit Nackenband; **II** *v/t*. **4.** *Pferd* (an)halftern; **5.** *j-n* hängen; ˈ**~·neck** → ***halter*** 3.

halt·ing [ˈhɔːltɪŋ] *adj*. ☐ **1.** *obs*. hinkend; **2.** *fig*. a) hinkend, b) holp(e)rig; **3.** stockend; **4.** zögernd, schwankend.

halve [hɑːv] *v/t*. **1.** halbieren: a) zu gleichen Hälften teilen, b) auf die Hälfte reduzieren; **2.** ⚙ verblatten.

halves [hɑːvz] *pl. von* ***half***.

hal·yard [ˈhæljəd] *s*. ⚓ Fall *n*.

ham [hæm] **I** *s*. **1.** Schinken *m*: ***~ and eggs*** Schinken mit (Spiegel)Ei; **2.** *anat*. (hinterer) Oberschenkel, Gesäßbacke *f*, *pl*. Gesäß *n*; **3.** F a) *a*. **~ *actor*** überˈtrieben *od*. miseˈrabel spielender Schauspieler, ˈSchmierenkomödiˌant (-in), b) *fig. contp*. ‚Schauspieler(in)', c) Stümper(in); **4.** F Amaˈteurfunker *m*; **II** *v/t*. **5.** F a) *e-e Rolle* überˈtrieben *od*. miseˈrabel spielen: ***~ it up*** → 6, b) *et*. verkitschen; **III** *v/i*. **6.** überˈtrieben *od*. miseˈrabel spielen, wie ein ˈSchmierenkomödiˌant auftreten.

ham·burg·er [ˈhæmbɜːgə] *s*. **1.** *Am*. Rinderhack *n*; **2.** a) *a*. ***⁀ steak*** Frikaˈdelle *f*, b) Hamburger *m*.

Ham·burg steak [ˈhæmbɜːg] → ***hamburger*** 2a.

hames [heɪmz] *s. pl*. Kummet *n*.

ˈ**ham|-ˌfist·ed**, ˈ**~-ˌhand·ed** *adj*. F ungeschickt, tolpatschig.

ha·mite¹ [ˈheɪmaɪt] *s. zo*. Ammoˈnit *m*.

Ham·ite² [ˈhæmaɪt] *s*. Haˈmit(in).

ham·let [ˈhæmlɪt] *s*. Weiler *m*, Flecken *m*, Dörfchen *n*.

ham·mer [ˈhæmə] **I** *s*. **1.** Hammer *m* (*a. anat*.): ***come* (*od*. *go*) *under the ~*** unter den Hammer kommen, versteigert werden; ***go at it ~ and tongs*** F a) ‚mächtig rangehen', b) (sich) streiten, daß die Fetzen fliegen; ***~ and divider*** *pol*. Hammer u. Zirkel (*Symbol der DDR*); ***~ and sickle*** *pol*. Hammer u. Sichel (*Symbol der UdSSR*); **2.** Hammer *m* (*Klavier etc*.); **3.** *sport* Hammer *m*; **4.** ⚙ a) Hammer(werk *n*) *m*, b) Hahn *m* (*e-r Feuerwaffe*); **II** *v/t*. **5.** (ein-)hämmern, (ein)schlagen: ***~ an idea into s.o.'s head*** *fig*. j-m e-e Idee einhämmern *od*. -bleuen; **6.** *a*. ***~ out*** a) *Metall* hämmern, bearbeiten, formen, b) *fig*. ausarbeiten, schmieden, c) *Differenzen* ‚ausbügeln'; **7.** *a*. ***~ together*** zs.-hämmern, -zimmern; **8.** F a) vernichtend schlagen, *sport a*. ‚überˈfahren', b) besiegen; **9.** *Börse*: *Brit*. für zahlungsunfähig erklären; **III** *v/i*. **10.** hämmern (*a. Puls etc*.): ***~ at*** einhämmern auf (*acc*.); ***~ away*** drauflos hämmern, -arbeiten; ***~ away* (*at*)** *fig*. sich abmühen (mit); **~ *blow*** *s*. Hammerschlag *m*; **~ *drill*** *s*. ⚙ Schlagbohrer *m*.

ham·mered [ˈhæməd] *adj*. ⚙ gehämmert, getrieben, Treib…

ham·mer| face *s*. ⚙ Hammerbahn *f*; **~ forg·ing** *s*. ⚙ Reckschmieden *n*; ˈ**~-ˌhard·en** *v/t*. ⚙ kalthämmern; ˈ**~·head** *s*. **1.** *ichth*. Hammerhai *m*; **2.** ⚙ (Hammer)Kopf *m*; **~·less** [ˈhæməlɪs] *adj*. mit verdecktem Schlaghammer (*Gewehr*); ˈ**~-lock** *s*. *Ringen*: Hammerlock *m* (*Griff*); **~ scale** *s*. ⚙ (Eisen)Hammerschlag *m*, Zunder *m*; ˈ**~·smith** *s*. ⚙ Hammerschmied *m*; **~ throw** *s*. *sport* Hammerwerfen *n*; **~ throw·er** *s*. *sport* Hammerwerfer *m*; ˈ**~·toe** *s*. ⚕ Hammerzehe *f*.

ham·mock [ˈhæmək] *s*. Hängematte *f*.

ham·per¹ [ˈhæmpə] *v/t*. **1.** (be)hindern, hemmen; **2.** stören.

ham·per² [ˈhæmpə] *s*. **1.** (Pack-, Trag-) Korb *m*; **2.** Geschenkkorb *m*, ‚Freßkorb' *m*.

ham·ster [ˈhæmstə] *s. zo*. Hamster *m*.

ˈ**ham·string** **I** *s*. **1.** *anat*. Kniesehne *f*; **2.** *zo*. Aˈchillessehne *f*; **II** *v/t*. [*irr*. → ***string***] **3.** (durch Zerschneiden der Kniesehnen) lähmen; **4.** *fig*. lähmen.

hand [hænd] **I** *s*. **1.** Hand *f* (*a. fig*.): ***~s off!*** Hände weg!; ***~s up!*** Hände hoch!; ***be in good ~s*** *fig*. in guten Händen sein; ***fall into s.o's ~s*** j-m in die Hände fallen; ***give* (*od*. *lend*) *a* (*helping*) *~*** (*j-m*) helfen; ***give s.o. a. ~ up*** j-m auf die Beine helfen; ***I am entirely in your ~s*** ich bin ganz in Ihrer Hand; ***I have his fate in my ~s*** sein Schicksal liegt in m-r Hand; ***he asked for her ~*** er hielt um ihre Hand an; ***get a big ~*** F starken Applaus bekommen; → *Bes. Redew*.; **2.** *zo*. a) Hand *f* (*Affe*), b) Vorderfuß *m* (*Pferd*), c) Schere *f* (*Krebs*); **3.** *pl*. Hände *pl*., Besitz *m*: ***change ~s*** → *Bes. Redew*.; **4.** (gute *od*. glückliche) Hand, Geschick *n*: ***he has a ~ for horses*** er versteht es, mit Pferden umzugehen; **5.** *oft in Zssgn* Arbeiter *m*, Mann (*a. pl*.), *pl*. Leute *pl*., ⚓ Maˈtrose: ***all ~s on deck!*** alle Mann an Deck!; **6.** Fachmann *m*, Routiniˈer *m*: ***an old ~*** *a*. ein alter ‚Hase' *od*. Praktikus; ***a good ~ at*** sehr geschickt in (*dat*.), ein guter *Golfspieler etc*.; **7.** Handschrift *f*: ***a legible ~***; **8.** Unterschrift *f*: ***set one's ~ to a document***; **9.** Handbreit *f* (*4 engl. Zoll*) (*nur für die Größe e-s Pferdes*); **10.** *Kartenspiel*: a) Spieler *m*, b) Blatt *n*, Karten *pl*.: ***show one's ~*** → *Bes. Redew*., c) Runde *f*, Spiel *n*; **11.** (Uhr-) Zeiger *m*; **12.** Seite *f* (*a. fig*.): ***on the right ~*** rechter Hand, rechts; ***on every ~*** überall, ringsum; ***on all ~s*** a) überall, b) von allen Seiten; ***on the one ~, on the other ~*** einerseits … andererseits; **13.** Büschel *m*, *n*, Bündel *n* (*Früchte*), Hand *f* (*Bananen*); **14.** *Fußball*: Handspiel *n*: ***~s!*** Hand!;

Besondere Redewendungen:

~ and foot a) an Händen u. Füßen (*fesseln*), b) *fig*. hinten u. vorn (*bedienen*); ***be ~ in glove* (*with*)** a) ein Herz u. ˈeine Seele sein (mit), b) *b.s*. unter ˈeiner Decke stecken (mit); ***~s down*** mühelos, spielend (*gewinnen etc*.); ***~ in ~*** Hand in Hand (*a. fig*.); ***~ over fist*** a) Hand über Hand (*klettern etc*.), b) schnell, spielend, c) zusehends; ***~ to ~*** Mann gegen Mann (*kämpfen*); ***at ~*** a) nahe, bei der Hand, b) nahe (bevorstehend), c) zur Hand, bereit, d) vorliegend; ***at first* (*second*) *~*** aus erster (zweiter) Hand *od*. Quelle; ***at the ~s of s.o.*** *schlechte Behandlung etc*. seitens j-s, durch j-n; ***by ~*** a) mit der Hand, b) durch Boten, c) mit der Flasche (*ein Kind ernähren*); ***made by ~*** handgefertigt, Handarbeit; ***take s.o. by the ~*** a) j-n bei der Hand nehmen, b) F j-n unter s-e Fittiche nehmen; ***from ~ to mouth*** von der Hand in den Mund (*leben*); ***in ~*** a) in der Hand, b) zur Verfügung, c) vorrätig, vorhanden, d) in Bearbeitung, e) *fig*. in der Hand *od*. Gewalt, f) im Gange; ***the matter in ~*** die vorliegende Sache; ***the stock in ~*** der Warenbestand; ***have the situation well in ~*** die Lage gut im Griff haben; ***take in ~*** a) *et*. in die Hand *od*. in Angriff nehmen, b) F *j-n* unter s-e Fittiche nehmen; ***on ~*** a) verfügbar, vorrätig, b) vorliegend, c) bevorstehend, d) *Am*. zur Stelle; ***have s.th. on one's ~s*** et. auf dem Hals haben; ***out of ~*** a) kurzerhand, ohne weiteres, b) außer Kontrolle, nicht mehr zu bändigen; ***get out of ~*** a) außer Rand u. Band geraten, *Party etc*.: *a*. ausarten, b) außer Kontrolle geraten (*Lage etc*.); ***to ~*** zur Hand; ***come to ~*** eingehen, eintreffen (*Brief etc*.); ***under ~*** a) unter Kontrolle, b) unter der Hand, heimlich; ***with a heavy ~*** mit harter Hand, streng; ***with a high ~*** selbstherrlich, willkürlich; ***change ~s*** in andere Hände übergehen, den Besitzer wechseln; ***force s.o.'s ~*** j-n zum Handeln zwingen; ***get s.th. off one's ~s*** et. loswerden; ***have a ~ in s.th.*** beteiligt sein an e-r Sache, *b.s. a*. die Hand im Spiel haben bei e-r Sache; ***have one's ~ in*** in Übung sein; ***hold ~s*** Händchen halten; ***hold* (*od*. *stay*) *one's ~*** sich zurückhalten; ***join ~s*** sich die Hände reichen, *fig. a*. sich verbünden *od*. zs.-tun; ***keep one's ~ in*** sich in Übung halten; ***keep a firm ~ on*** unter strenger Zucht halten; ***lay* (*one's*) *~s on*** a) anfassen, b) ergreifen, habhaft werden (*gen*.), erwischen, c) *gewaltsam* Hand an *j-n* legen, d) *eccl*. ordinieren; ***I can't lay my ~s on it*** ich kann es nicht finden; ***play into s.o.'s ~s*** j-m in die Hände arbeiten; ***put one's ~s on*** a) finden, b) sich erinnern an (*acc*.); ***shake ~s*** sich die Hände schütteln; ***shake ~s with s.o., shake s.o. by the ~*** j-m die Hand schütteln *od*. geben; ***show one's ~*** *fig*. s-e Karten aufdekken; ***take a ~ at a game*** bei e-m Spiel mitmachen; ***try one's ~ at s.th.*** et. versuchen, es mit et. probieren; ***wash one's ~s of it*** a) (in dieser Sache) s-e

Hände in Unschuld waschen, b) nichts mit der Sache zu tun haben wollen; ***I wash my ~s of him*** mit ihm will ich nichts mehr zu tun haben; → ***off hand***;
II *v/t.* **15.** ein-, aushändigen, (über)'geben, (-)'reichen (***s.o. s.th., s.th. to s.o.*** j-m et.): ***you have got to ~ it to him*** F das muß man ihm lassen (*anerkennend*); **16.** *j-m* helfen: ***~ s.o. into*** (***out of***) ***the car***;
Zssgn mit adv.:
hand| a·round *v/t.* her'umreichen; **~ back** *v/t.* zu'rückgeben; **~ down** *v/t.* **1.** *et.* her'unter- *od.* hin'unterreichen; **2.** *j-n* hin'untergeleiten; **3.** vererben, hinter'lassen (***to*** *dat.*); **4.** (***to***) *fig.* weitergeben (an *acc.*), über'liefern (*dat.*); **5.** ⚖ a) *Urteil etc.* verkünden, b) *Entscheidung e-s höheren Gerichts* e-m 'untergeordneten Gericht über'mitteln; **~ in** *v/t.* **1.** *et.* hin'ein- *od.* her'einreichen; **2.** abgeben, *Bericht*, *Gesuch etc.* einreichen; **~ on** *v/t.* **1.** weiterreichen, -geben; **2.** → ***hand down*** 3; **~ out** *v/t.* **1.** ausgeben, -teilen, verteilen (***to*** an *acc.*); **2.** *Ratschläge etc.* verteilen; **3.** verschenken; **~ o·ver** *v/t.* (***to*** *dat.*) **1.** über'geben; **2.** über'lassen; **3.** (her)geben, aushändigen; **4.** *j-n der Polizei etc.* über'geben; **~ up** *v/t.* hin'auf- *od.* her'aufreichen (***to*** *dat.*).
'hand|·bag [-ndb-] *s.* **1.** (Damen)Handtasche *f*; **2.** Handtasche *f*, -koffer *m*; **'~·ball** [-ndb-] *s. sport* Handball(spiel *n*) *m*; **'~-ˌbar·row** [-ndˌb-] *s.* **1.** → ***handcart***; **2.** Trage *f*; **'~·bell** [-ndb-] *s.* Tisch-, Handglocke *f*; **'~·bill** [-ndb-] *s.* Hand-, Re'klamezettel *m*, Flugblatt *n*; **'~·book** [-ndb-] *s.* **1.** Handbuch *n*; **2.** Reiseführer *m* (***of*** durch, von); **~ brake** *s.* ⚙ Handbremse *f*; **'~·breadth** [-ndb-] *s.* Handbreit *f*; **'~·cart** [-ndk-] *s.* Handkarre(n *m*) *f*; **'~·clasp** [-ndk-] *Am.* → ***handshake***; **'~·craft** [-ndk-] → ***handicraft***; **'~·cuff** [-ndk-] **I** *s. mst pl.* Handschellen *pl.*; **II** *v/t. j-m* Handschellen anlegen: ***~ed*** in Handschellen; **~ drill** *s.* ⚙ Handbohrer *m*.
-handed [hændɪd] *in Zssgn* ...händig, mit ... Händen.
'hand|·ful [-ndfʊl] *s.* **1.** Handvoll *f* (*a. fig. Personen*); **2.** F Plage *f* (*Person od. Sache*), ‚Nervensäge' *f*: ***he is a ~*** er macht einem ganz schön zu schaffen; **'~·glass** [-ndg-] *s.* **1.** Handspiegel *m*; **2.** (Lese)Lupe *f*; **~ gre·nade** *s.* ⚔ 'Handgraˌnate *f*; **'~·grip** [-ndg-] *s.* **1.** Händedruck *m*; **2.** *a.* ⚙ Griff *m*; **3. *come to ~s*** handgemein werden; **'~-held** *adj. Film*: tragbar (*Kamera*); **'~·hold** *s.* Halt *m*, Griff *m*.
hand·i·cap ['hændɪkæp] **I** *s.* Handikap *n*: a) *sport* Vorgabe *f*, b) Vorgaberennen *n od.* -spiel *n*, c) *fig.* Behinderung *f*, Hindernis *n*, Nachteil *m*, Erschwerung *f* (***to*** für); **II** *v/t. sport* (*a.* körperlich *od.* geistig) (be)hindern, benachteiligen, belasten: ***~ped*** behindert (*etc.*), gehandikapt.
hand·i·craft ['hændɪkrɑːft] *s.* **1.** Handfertigkeit *f*; **2.** (*bsd.* Kunst)Handwerk *n*.
hand·i·ness ['hændɪnɪs] *s.* **1.** Geschick(-lichkeit *f*) *n*; **2.** Handlichkeit *f*; **3.** Nützlichkeit *f*.
hand·i·work ['hændɪwɜːk] *s.* **1.** Handarbeit *f*; **2.** Werk *n*.
hand·ker·chief ['hæŋkətʃɪf] *s.* Taschentuch *n*.
'hand-ˌknit(·ted) *adj.* handgestrickt.
han·dle ['hændl] **I** *s.* **1.** Griff *m*, Stiel *m*; Henkel *m* (*Topf*); Klinke *f* (*Tür*); Schwengel *m* (*Pumpe*); ⚙ Kurbel *f*: ***a ~ to one's name*** F ein Titel; ***fly off the ~*** ‚hochgehen', wütend werden; **2.** *fig.* a) Handhabe *f*, b) Vorwand *m*; **II** *v/t.* **3.** anfassen, berühren; **4.** handhaben, hantieren mit, *Maschine* bedienen: ***~ with care! glass!*** Vorsicht, Glas!; **5.** a) *ein Thema etc.* behandeln, *e-e Sache a.* handhaben, b) *et.* erledigen, 'durchführen, abwickeln, c) mit *et. od. j-m* fertigwerden, *et.* deichseln: ***I can ~ it*** (***him***) damit (mit ihm) werde ich fertig; **6.** *j-n* behandeln, 'umgehen mit; **7.** a) *e-n Boxer* betreuen, trainieren, b) *Tier* dressieren (u. vorführen); **8.** sich beschäftigen mit; **9.** *Güter* befördern, weiterleiten; **10.** ☤ Handel treiben mit; **III** *v/i.* **11.** sich *leicht etc.* handhaben lassen; **12.** sich *weich etc.* anfühlen; **'~·bar** *s.* Lenkstange *f*.
hand·ler ['hændlə] *s.* **1.** Dres'seur *m*, Abrichter *m*; **2.** *Boxen*: a) Trainer *m*, b) Betreuer *m*, Sekun'dant *m*.
han·dling ['hændlɪŋ] *s.* **1.** Berühren *n*; **2.** Handhabung *f*; **3.** Führung *f*; **4.** *a. weitS.* Behandlung *f*; **5.** ☤ Beförderung *f*; **~ charg·es** *s. pl.* ☤ 'Umschlagspesen *pl.*
'hand|·loom *s.* Handwebstuhl *m*; **~ lug·gage** *s.* Handgepäck *n*; **ˌ~-'made** [-nd'm-] *adj.* von Hand gemacht, handgefertigt, Hand...; handgeschöpft (*Papier*): **~ *paper*** Büttenpapier *n*; **'~ˌmaid(·en)** [-ndˌm-] *s.* **1.** *obs. u. fig.* Dienerin *f*, Magd *f*; **2.** *fig.* Gehilfe *m*, Handlanger(in); **'~-me-ˌdown I** *adj.* **1.** fertig *od.* von der Stange (gekauft), Konfektions...; **2.** abgelegt, getragen; **II** *s.* **3.** Konfekti'onsanzug *m*, Kleid *n* von der Stange, *pl.* Konfekti'onskleidung *f*; **4.** abgelegtes Kleidungsstück; **ˌ~-'op·er·at·ed** *adj.* ⚙ mit Handantrieb, handbedient, Hand...; **~ or·gan** *s.* ♪ Drehorgel *f*; **'~·out** *s.* **1.** Almosen *n* (*a. fig.*), (milde) Gabe, *weitS.* (*Wahl- etc.*) Geschenk *n*; **2.** Pro'spekt *m*, Hand-, Werbezettel *m*; **3.** Handout *n* (*Informationsunterlage*); **'~-pick** *v/t.* **1.** mit der Hand pflücken *od.* auslesen: ***~ed*** handverlesen; **2.** F sorgsam auswählen; **'~·rail** *s.* Handlauf *m*; Handleiste *f*; **'~·saw** *s.* Handsäge *f*; **~'s breadth** *s.* Handbreit *f*.
hand·sel ['hænsl] *s. obs.* **1.** Neujahrs-, *od.* Einstandsgeschenk *n*; **2.** Morgengabe *f*; Hand-, Angeld *n*.
'hand|·set *s. teleph.* Hörer *m*; **'~·shake** *s.* Händedruck *m*; **'~-signed** *adj.* handsigniert.
hand·some ['hænsəm] *adj.* □ **1.** hübsch, schön, gutaussehend, stattlich; **2.** beträchtlich, ansehnlich, stattlich: ***a ~ sum***; **3.** großzügig, nobel, ‚anständig': ***~ is that ~ does*** edel ist, wer edel handelt; ***come down ~ly*** sich großzügig zeigen; **4.** *Am.* geschickt; **'hand·some·ness** [-nɪs] *s.* **1.** Schönheit *f*, Stattlichkeit *f*, gutes Aussehen; **2.** Beträchtlichkeit *f*; **3.** Großzügigkeit *f*.
'hand|·spike *s.* ⚓, ⚙ Handspake *f*, Hebestange *f*; **'~·spring** *s. sport* 'Handstandˌüberschlag *m*; **'~·stand** *s. sport* Handstand *m*; **ˌ~-to-'hand** *adj.* Mann gegen Mann: **~ *combat*** Nahkampf *m*; **ˌ~-to-'mouth** *adj.* kümmerlich: ***lead a ~ existence*** von der Hand in den Mund leben; **'~·wheel** *s.* ⚙ Hand-, Stellrad *n*; **'~ˌwrit·ing** *s.* **1.** (Hand-)Schrift *f*: **~ *expert*** ⚖ Schriftsachverständige(r *m*) *f*; **2.** *et.* Handgeschriebenes.
hand·y ['hændɪ] *adj.* □ **1.** zur Hand, bei der Hand, greifbar, leicht erreichbar; **2.** geschickt, gewandt; **3.** handlich, praktisch; **4.** nützlich: ***come in ~*** (sehr) gelegen kommen; **~ man** *s.* [*irr.*] Mädchen *n* für alles, Fak'totum *n*.
hang [hæŋ] **I** *s.* **1.** Hängen *n*, Fall *m*, Sitz *m* (*Kleid etc.*); **2.** F a) Sinn *m*, Bedeutung *f*, b) (richtige) Handhabung: ***get the ~ of s.th.*** et. ka'pieren, den ‚Dreh' rauskriegen; **3. *I don't care a ~*** F das ist mir völlig ‚schnuppe'; **II** *v/t. pret. u. p.p.* **hung** [hʌŋ] *nur 9 mst* **hanged**; **4.** (***on***) aufhängen (an *dat.*), hängen (an *acc.*): ***~ s.th. on a hook***; ***~ the head*** den Kopf hängen lassen *od.* senken; **5.** (*zum Trocknen etc.*) aufhängen: ***hung beef*** gedörrtes Rindfleisch; **6.** *Tür* einhängen; **7.** *Tapete* ankleben; **8.** behängen: ***hung with flags***; **9.** (auf-)hängen: ***~ o.s.*** sich erhängen; ***I'll be ~ed first*** F eher lasse ich mich hängen!; ***I'll be ~ed if*** F ‚ich will mich hängen lassen', wenn; ***~ it*** (***all***)***!*** F zum Henker damit!; **10.** → ***fire*** 6; **III** *v/i.* **11.** hängen, baumeln (***by***, ***on*** an *dat.*); → ***balance*** 2, ***thread*** 1; **12.** (her'ab)hängen, fallen (*Kleid etc.*); **13.** hängen, gehängt werden: ***he deserves to ~***; ***let s.th. go ~*** F sich den Teufel um et. scheren; ***let it go ~!*** F zum Henker damit!; **14.** (***on***) sich hängen (an *dat.*), sich klammern (an *acc.*): ***~ on s.o.'s lips*** (***words***) *fig.* an j-s Lippen (Worten) hängen; **15.** (***on***) hängen (an *dat.*), abhängen (von); **16.** sich senken *od.* neigen;
Zssgn mit prp.:
hang| a·bout, ~ a·round *v/i.* her'umlungern *od.* sich her'umtreiben in (*dat.*) *od.* bei; **~ on** → ***hang*** 14, 15; **~ o·ver** *v/i.* **1.** *fig.* hängen *od.* schweben über (*dat.*), drohen (*dat.*); **2.** sich neigen über (*acc.*); **3.** aufragen über (*acc.*);
Zssgn mit adv.:
hang| a·bout, ~ a·round *v/i.* **1.** her'umlungern, sich her'umtreiben; **2.** trödeln; **3.** warten; **~ back** *v/i.* **1.** zögern; **2.** → **~ be·hind** *v/i.* zu'rückbleiben, -hängen; **~ down** *v/i.* her'unterhängen; **~ on** *v/i.* **1.** (***to***) *a. fig.* sich klammern (an *acc.*), festhalten (*acc.*), nicht loslassen *od.* aufgeben; **2.** *teleph.* am Appa'rat bleiben; **3.** nicht nachlassen, ‚dranbleiben'; **4.** warten; **~ out I** *v/t.* **1.** (hin- *od.* her)'aushängen; **II** *v/i.* **2.** her'aushängen; **3.** ausgehängt sein; **4.** F a) hausen, sich aufhalten, b) sich her'umtreiben; **~ o·ver I** *v/i.* andauern; **II** *v/t.*: ***be hung over*** F e-n ‚Kater' haben; **~ to·geth·er** *v/i.* **1.** zs.-halten (*Personen*); **2.** zs.-hängen, verknüpft sein; **~ up I** *v/t.* **1.** aufhängen; **2.** aufschieben, hin'ausziehen: ***be hung up*** aufgehalten werden; **3. *be hung up on*** F a) e-n Komplex haben wegen, ‚es haben' mit, b) besessen sein von; **II** *v/i.* **4.** *teleph.* (den Hörer) auflegen, einhängen: ***she***

hung up on me! sie legte einfach auf!
hang·ar ['hæŋə] *s.* Hangar *m*, Flugzeughalle *f*, -schuppen *m*.
'hang·dog I *s.* **1.** Galgenvogel *m*, -strick *m*; **II** *adj.* **2.** gemein; **3.** jämmerlich: ***~ look*** Armesündermiene *f*.
hang·er ['hæŋə] *s.* **1.** a) (Auf)Hänger *m*, b) Ankleber *m*, c) Tapezierer *m*; **2.** a) Kleiderbügel *m*, b) Aufhänger *m* (*a.* ⚙), Schlaufe *f*; **3.** a) Hirschfänger *m*, b) kurzer Säbel.
ˌhang·er-'on [-ər'ɒn] *pl.* **ˌhang·ers-'on** *s. contp.* **1.** Anhänger *m*, *pl. a.* Anhang *m*; **2.** ‚Klette' *f*.
hang glid·er *s. sport* **1.** Hängegleiter *m*, (Flug)Drachen *m*; **2.** Drachenflieger(in).
hang·ing ['hæŋɪŋ] **I** *s.* **1.** (Auf)Hängen *n*; **2.** (Er)Hängen *n*: ***execution by ~*** Hinrichtung *f* durch den Strang; **3.** *mst pl.* Wandbehang *m*, Ta'pete *f*, Vorhang *m*; **II** *adj.* **4.** a) (her'ab)hängend, Hänge..., b) hängend, abschüssig, ter'rassenförmig: ***~ gardens***; **5.** ***a ~ matter*** e-e Sache, die e-n an den Galgen bringt; ***a ~ judge*** ein Richter, der mit der Todesstrafe rasch bei der Hand ist; **~ com·mit·tee** *s.* Hängeausschuß *m* (*bei Gemäldeausstellungen*).
'hang|·man [-mən] *s.* [*irr.*] Henker *m*; **'~·nail** *s.* ⚕ Niednagel *m*; **'~·out** *s.* F **1.** ‚Bude' *f*, Wohnung *f*; **2.** Treffpunkt *m*, 'Stammloˌkal *n*; **'~ˌo·ver** *s.* **1.** 'Überbleibsel *n*; **2.** F ‚Katzenjammer' *m* (*a. fig.*), ‚Kater' *m*; **'~·up** *s.* F **1.** a) Kom'plex *m*, b) Fimmel *m*: ***have a ~ about*** → ***hang up*** 3; **2.** Pro'blem *n*.
hank [hæŋk] *s.* **1.** Strang *m*, Docke *f* (*Garn etc.*); **2.** Hank *n* (*ein Garnmaß*); **3.** ⚓ Legel *m*.
han·ker ['hæŋkə] *v/i.* sich sehnen (***after***, ***for*** nach); **'han·ker·ing** [-ərɪŋ] *s.* Sehnsucht *f*, Verlangen *n* (***after***, ***for*** nach).
han·ky, *a.* **han·kie** ['hæŋkɪ] F → ***handkerchief***.
han·ky-pan·ky [ˌhæŋkɪ'pæŋkɪ] *s. sl.* **1.** Hokus'pokus *m*; **2.** ‚fauler Zauber', ‚Mätzchen' *n od. pl.*, Trick(s *pl.*) *m*; **3.** ‚Techtelmechtel' *n*.
Han·o·ve·ri·an [ˌhænəʊ'vɪərɪən] **I** *adj.* han'nover(i)sch; *pol. hist.* hannove'ranisch; **II** *s.* Hannove'raner(in).
Han·sard ['hænsəd] *s. parl. Brit.* Parla'mentsprotoˌkoll *n*.
hanse [hæns] *s. hist.* **1.** Kaufmannsgilde *f*; **2.** 2 Hanse *f*, Hansa *f*; **Han·se·at·ic** [ˌhænsɪ'ætɪk] *adj.* hanse'atisch, Hanse...: ***the ~ League*** die Hanse.
han·sel → ***handsel***.
han·som (cab) ['hænsəm] *s.* Hansom *m* (*zweirädrige Kutsche*).
hap [hæp] *obs.* **I** *s.* a) Zufall *m*, b) Glücksfall *m*; **II** *v/i.* → ***happen***; **ˌhap-'haz·ard** [-'hæzəd] **I** *adj. u. adv.* planwahllos, willkürlich; **II** *s.*: ***at ~*** aufs Geratewohl; **'hap·less** [-lɪs] *adj.* ☐ glücklos, unglücklich.
hap·pen ['hæpən] *v/i.* **1.** geschehen, sich ereignen, vorkommen, -fallen, passieren, stattfinden, vor sich gehen: ***what has ~ed?*** was ist geschehen *od.* passiert?; ***... and nothing ~ed*** ... u. nichts geschah; **2.** *impers.* zufällig geschehen, sich zufällig ergeben, sich (gerade) treffen: ***it ~ed that*** es traf *od.* ergab sich, daß; ***as it ~s*** a) wie es sich gerade trifft, b) wie es nun einmal so ist; **3.** ***~ to*** *inf.*: ***we ~ed to hear it*** wir hörten es zufällig; ***it ~ed to be hot*** zufällig war es heiß; **4.** ***~ to*** geschehen mit (*od. dat.*), passieren (*dat.*), zustoßen (*dat.*), werden aus: ***what is going to ~ to his plan?*** was wird aus s-m Plan?; ***if anything should ~ to me*** sollte mir et. zustoßen; **5.** ***~ (up)on*** a) zufällig begegnen (*dat.*) *od.* treffen (*acc.*), b) zufällig stoßen (auf *acc.*) *od.* finden (*acc.*); **6.** ***~ along*** F zufällig kommen; ***~ in*** F ‚hereinschneien'; **hap·pen·ing** ['hæpnɪŋ] *s.* **1.** a) Ereignis *n*, b) Eintreten *n e-s Ereignisses*; **2.** *thea. u. humor.* Happening *n*: ***~ artist*** Happenist *m*; **hap·pen·stance** ['hæpənstæns] *s. Am.* F Zufall *m*.
hap·pi·ly ['hæpɪlɪ] *adv.* **1.** glücklich; **2.** glücklicherweise, zum Glück; **'hap·pi·ness** [-nɪs] *s.* **1.** Glück *n* (*Gefühl*); **2.** glückliche Wahl (*e-s Ausdrucks etc.*), glückliche Formulierung; **hap·py** ['hæpɪ] *adj.* ☐ → ***happily***; **1.** *allg.* glücklich: a) glückselig, b) beglückt, erfreut (***at***, ***about*** über *acc.*): ***I am ~ to see you*** es freut mich, Sie zu sehen; ***I would be ~ to do that*** ich würde das sehr *od.* liebend gern tun; ***I am quite ~ (, thank you)!*** (danke,) ich bin wunschlos glücklich!, c) voller Glück: ***~ days***, d) erfreulich: ***~ event*** freudiges Ereignis, e) glückverheißend: ***~ news***, f) gut, trefflich: ***~ idea***, g) geglückt, treffend, passend: ***a ~ phrase***; **2.** *in Glückwünschen*: ***~ new year!*** gutes neues Jahr!; **3.** F beschwipst, ‚angesäuselt'; **4.** *in Zssgn* a) F wirr (im Kopf), benommen: → ***slaphappy***, b) begeistert, ‚verrückt', -freudig, -lustig: → ***trigger-happy***.
hap·py| dis·patch *s. euphem.* Hara'kiri *n*; **ˌ~-go-'luck·y** [-gəʊ-] *adj. u. adv.* unbekümmert, sorglos, leichtfertig, lässig.
hap·tic ['hæptɪk] *adj.* haptisch.
har·a·kir·i [ˌhærə'kɪrɪ] *s.* Hara'kiri *n* (*a. fig.*).
ha·rangue [hə'ræŋ] **I** *s.* **1.** Ansprache *f*, (flammende) Rede; **2.** Ti'rade *f*; **3.** Strafpredigt *f*; **II** *v/i.* **4.** e-e (bom'bastische *od.* flammende) Rede halten (*v/t.* vor *dat.*); **5.** e-e Strafpredigt halten (*v/t. j-m*).
har·ass ['hærəs] *v/t.* **1.** a) (ständig) belästigen, schikanieren, quälen, b) aufreiben, zermürben: ***~ed*** mitgenommen, (von Sorgen) gequält, (viel) geplagt; **2.** ⚔ stören: ***~ing fire*** Störfeuer *n*; **'har·ass·ment** [-mənt] *s.* **1.** Belästigung *f*; **2.** Schikanieren *n*, Schi'kane(n *pl.*) *f*; **3.** ⚔ 'Störmaˌnöver *pl.*
har·bin·ger ['hɑːbɪndʒə] **I** *s. fig.* a) Vorläufer *m*, b) Vorbote *m*: ***the ~ of spring***; **II** *v/t. fig.* ankündigen.
har·bo(u)r ['hɑːbə] **I** *s.* **1.** Hafen *m*; **2.** *fig.* Zufluchtsort *m*, 'Unterschlupf *m*; **II** *v/t.* **3.** beherbergen, Schutz *od.* Zuflucht gewähren (*dat.*); **4.** verbergen, verstecken: ***~ criminals***; **5.** *Gedanken, Groll etc.* hegen: ***~ thoughts of revenge***; **III** *v/i.* **6.** ⚓ (im Hafen) vor Anker gehen; **~ bar** *s.* Sandbank *f* vor dem Hafen; **~ dues** *s. pl.* Hafengebühren *pl.*; **~ mas·ter** *s.* Hafenmeister *m*; **~ seal** *s. zo.* Gemeiner Seehund.
hard [hɑːd] **I** *adj.* **1.** *allg.* hart (*a. Farbe, Stimme etc.*); **2.** fest: ***~ knot***; **3.** schwer, schwierig: a) mühsam, anstrengend, hart: ***~ work***, b) schwer zu bewältigen(d): ***~ problems*** schwierige Probleme; ***~ to believe*** kaum zu glauben; ***~ to imagine*** schwer vorstellbar; ***~ to please*** schwer zufriedenzustellen(d), ‚schwierig' (*Kunde etc.*); **4.** hart, zäh, 'widerstandsfähig: ***in ~ condition*** *sport* konditionsstark, fit; ***a ~ customer*** F ein schwieriger ‚Kunde', ein zäher Bursche; → ***nail*** *Bes. Redew.*; **5.** hart, angestrengt: ***~ studies***; **6.** hart arbeitend, fleißig: ***a ~ worker***; ***try one's ~est*** sich alle Mühe geben; **7.** heftig, stark: ***a ~ rain***; ***a ~ blow*** ein harter *od.* schwerer Schlag (*a. fig.* ***to*** für); ***be ~ on*** *Kleidung etc.* (sehr) strapazieren (→ 8); **8.** hart: a) streng, rauh: ***~ climate*** (***winter***), b) *fig.* hartherzig, gefühllos, streng, c) nüchtern, kühl (überlegend): ***a ~ businessman***, d) drückend: ***be ~ on s.o.*** j-n hart anfassen *od.* behandeln; ***it is ~ on him*** es ist hart für ihn; ***the ~ facts*** die harten *od.* nackten Tatsachen; ✝***~ sell(ing)*** aggressive Verkaufstaktik; ***~ times*** schwere Zeiten; ***have a ~ time*** Schlimmes durchmachen (müssen); ***he had a ~ time doing it*** es fiel ihm schwer, dies zu tun; ***give s.o. a ~ time*** j-m hart zusetzen, j-m das Leben sauer machen; **9.** a) sauer, herb (*Getränk*), b) hart (*Droge*), *Getränk*: *a.* stark, 'hochproˌzentig; **10.** *phys.* hart: ***~ water***, ***~ X rays***; ***~ wheat*** 🌾 Hartweizen *m*; **11.** ✝ hart (*Währung etc.*): ***~ dollars***; ***~ prices*** harte *od.* starre Preise; **12.** *Phonetik*: a) hart, stimmlos, b) nicht palatalisiert; **13.** ***~ up*** a) schlecht bei Kasse, in (Geld)Schwierigkeiten, b) in Verlegenheit (***for*** um); **II** *adv.* **14.** hart, fest; **15.** *fig.* hart, schwer: ***work ~***; ***brake ~*** scharf bremsen; ***drink ~*** ein starker Trinker sein; ***it will go ~ with him*** es wird unangenehm für ihn sein; ***hit s.o. ~*** a) j-m e-n harten Schlag versetzen, b) *fig.* ein harter Schlag für j-n sein; ***~ hit*** schwer betroffen; ***be ~ pressed***, ***be ~ put to it*** in schwerer Bedrängnis sein; ***look ~ at*** scharf ansehen; ***try ~*** sich alle Mühe geben; → ***die***[1] 1; **16.** nah(e), dicht: ***~ by*** ganz in der Nähe; ***~ on*** (*od.* ***after***) gleich nach; ***~ aport*** ⚓ hart Backbord; **III** *s.* **17.** ***get*** (***have***) ***a ~ on*** V e-n ‚Ständer' kriegen (haben).
ˌhard|-and-'fast *adj.* fest, bindend, 'unumstößlich: ***a ~ rule***; **'~·back** → ***hardcover*** II; **'~·ball** *s. Am.* Baseball(spiel *n*) *m*; **ˌ~-'bit·ten** *adj.* **1.** verbissen, hartnäckig; **2.** → ***hard-boiled*** 2a; **'~·board** *s.* Hartfaserplatte *f*; **ˌ~-'boiled** *adj.* **1.** hart(gekocht): ***a ~ egg***; **2.** F ‚knallhart': a) ‚abgebrüht', ‚hartgesotten', b) ‚ausgekocht', gerissen, c) von hartem Rea'lismus: ***~ fiction***; **~ case** *s.* **1.** Härtefall *m*; **2.** schwieriger Mensch; **3.** ‚schwerer Junge' (*Verbrecher*); **~ cash** *s.* ✝ **1.** a) Hartgeld *n*, b) Bargeld *n*: ***pay in ~*** (in) bar (be)zahlen; **2.** klingende Münze; **~ coal** *s.* Anthra'zit *m*, Steinkohle *f*; **~ core** *s.* **1.** *Brit.* Schotter *m*; **2.** *fig.* harter Kern (*e-r Bande etc.*); **ˌ~-'core** *adj. fig.* **1.** zum harten Kern gehörend; **2.** hart: ***~ pornography***; **~ court** *s. Tennis*: Hartplatz *m*; **'~ˌcov·er I** *adj.* gebunden: ***~ edition***; **II** *s.* Hard cover *n*, gebundene Ausgabe; **~ cur·ren·cy** *s.* ✝ harte Währung.
hard·en ['hɑːdn] **I** *v/t.* **1.** härten (*a.* ⚙),

hart *od.* härter machen; **2.** *fig.* hart *od.* gefühllos machen, verhärten: ***~ed*** verstockt, ‚abgebrüht'; ***a ~ed sinner*** ein verstockter Sünder; **3.** bestärken; **4.** abhärten (***to*** gegen); **II** *v/i.* **5.** hart werden, erhärten; **6.** *fig.* hart *od.* gefühllos werden, sich verhärten; **7.** *fig.* sich abhärten (***to*** gegen); **8.** a) ✝ *u. fig.* sich festigen, b) ✝ anziehen, steigen (*Preise*); **'hard·en·er** [-nə] *s.* Härtemittel *n*, Härter *m*; **'hard·en·ing** [-nɪŋ] **I** *s.* **1.** Härten *n*, Härtung *f* (*a.* ⚙): ***~ of the arteries*** Arterienverkalkung *f*; **2.** → ***hardener***; **II** *adj.* **3.** Härte…

ˌhard|-'fea·tured *adj.* mit harten *od.* groben Gesichtszügen; **~ fi·ber**, *Brit.* **~ fi·bre** *s.* ⚙ Hartfaser *f*; **~ goods** *s. pl.* ✝ *Am.* Gebrauchsgüter *pl.*; **~ hat** *s.* **1.** *Brit.* Me'lone *f* (*Hut*); **2.** a) Schutzhelm *m*, b) F Bauarbeiter *m*; **3.** *Brit.* 'Erzreaktioˌnär *m*; **ˌ~-'head·ed** *adj.* **1.** praktisch, nüchtern, rea'listisch; **2.** *Am.* starrköpfig, stur; **ˌ~-'heart·ed** *adj.* □ hart(herzig); **ˌ~-'hit·ting** *adj. fig.* hart, aggres'siv.

har·di·hood ['hɑːdɪhʊd], **'har·di·ness** [-ɪnɪs] *s.* **1.** Ausdauer *f*, Zähigkeit *f*; **2.** ✿ Winterfestigkeit *f*; **3.** Kühnheit *f*: a) Tapferkeit *f*, b) Verwegenheit *f*, c) Dreistigkeit *f*.

hard| la·bo(u)r *s.* ⚖ Zwangsarbeit *f*; **~ line** *s.* **1.** *bsd. pol.* harte Linie, harter Kurs: ***follow*** *od.* ***adopt a ~*** e-n harten Kurs einschlagen; **2.** *pl. Brit.* ‚Pech' *n* (***on*** für); **ˌ~-'line** *adj. bsd. pol.* hart, kompro'mißlos; **ˌ~-'lin·er** *s. bsd. pol.* j-d, der e-n harten Kurs einschlägt; **ˌ~-'luck sto·ry** *s. contp.*, ‚Jammergeschichte' *f*.

hard·ly ['hɑːdlɪ] *adv.* **1.** kaum, fast nicht: ***~ ever*** fast nie; ***I ~ know her*** ich kenne sie kaum; **2.** (wohl) kaum, schwerlich; **3.** mühsam, mit Mühe; **4.** hart, streng.

hard| mon·ey → ***hard cash***; **ˌ~-'mouthed** *adj.* **1.** hartmäulig (*Pferd*); **2.** *fig.* starrköpfig.

hard·ness ['hɑːdnɪs] *s.* **1.** Härte *f* (*a. fig.*); **2.** Schwierigkeit *f*; **3.** Hartherzigkeit *f*; **4.** 'Widerstandsfähigkeit *f*; **5.** Strenge *f*, Härte *f*.

ˌhard|-'nosed F → a) ***hard-boiled*** 2a, b) ***hard-headed*** 2; **~ pan** *s.* **1.** *geol.* Ortstein *m*; **2.** harter Boden; **3.** *fig.* a) Grund(lage *f*) *m*, b) Kern *m* (der Sache); **ˌ~-'press·ed** *adj.* (hart)bedrängt, unter Druck stehend; **~ rock** *s.* ♪ Hardrock *m*; **~ rub·ber** *s.* Hartgummi *m*; **~ sci·ence** *s.* (*e-e*) ex'akte Wissenschaft; **ˌ~-'set** *adj.* **1.** hartbedrängt; **2.** streng, starr; **3.** angebrütet (*Ei*); **'~-shell** *adj.* **1.** *zo.* hartschalig; **2.** *Am.* F ‚eisern'.

hard·ship ['hɑːdʃɪp] *s.* **1.** Not *f*, Elend *n*; **2.** *a.* ⚖ Härte *f*: ***work ~ on s.o.*** e-e Härte bedeuten für j-n; ***~ case*** Härtefall *m*.

hard| shoul·der *s. mot. Brit.* Standspur *f*; **~ sol·der** *s.* ⚙ Hartlot *n*; **'~-ˌsol·der** *v/t. u. v/i.* hartlöten; **~ tack** *s.* Schiffszwieback *m*; **'~·top** *s. mot.* Hardtop *n*, *m*: a) *festes, abnehmbares Autodach*, b) *Auto mit a*; **'~·ware** *s.* **1.** a) Me'tall-, Eisenwaren *pl.*, b) Haushaltswaren *pl.*; **2.** *Computer*, *a. Sprachlabor*: Hardware *f*; **3.** *a.* ***military ~*** Waffen *pl.* u. mili'tärische Ausrüstung; **4.** *Am. sl.* Schießeisen *n od. pl.*; **'~·wood** *s.* Hartholz *n*, *bsd.* Laubbaumholz *n*; **ˌ~-'work·ing** *adj.* fleißig, hart arbeitend.

har·dy ['hɑːdɪ] *adj.* □ **1.** a) zäh, ro'bust, b) abgehärtet; **2.** ✿ winterfest: ***~ annual*** a) winterfeste Pflanze, b) *humor.* Frage, die jedes Jahr wieder aktuell wird; **3.** kühn: a) tapfer, b) verwegen, c) dreist.

hare [heə] *s. zo.* Hase *m*: ***run with the ~ and hunt with the hounds*** *fig.* es mit beiden Seiten halten; ***start a ~*** *fig.* vom Thema ablenken; ***~ and hounds*** Schnitzeljagd *f*; **'~·bell** *s.* ✿ Glockenblume *f*; **'~·brained** *adj.* ‚verrückt'; **'~·foot** *s.* [*irr.*] ✿ **1.** Balsabaum *m*; **2.** Ackerklee *m*; **ˌ~'lip** *s.* ⚕ Hasenscharte *f*.

ha·rem ['hɑːriːm] *s.* Harem *m*.

'hare's-foot → ***harefoot***.

har·i·cot ['hærɪkəʊ] *s.* **1.** *a.* ***~ bean*** Gartenbohne *f*; **2.** 'Hammelraˌgout *n*.

hark [hɑːk] *v/i.* **1.** *obs. u. poet.* horchen: ***~ at him!*** *Brit.* F hör dir ihn (*od.* den) an!; **2.** ***~ back*** a) *hunt.* auf der Fährte zu'rückgehen (*Hund*), b) *fig.* zu'rückgreifen, -kommen, (*a. zeitlich*) zu'rückgehen (***to*** auf *acc.*); **hark·en** ['hɑːkən] → ***hearken***.

har·le·quin ['hɑːlɪkwɪn] **I** *s.* Harlekin *m*, Hans'wurst *m*; **II** *adj.* bunt, scheckig; **har·le·quin·ade** [ˌhɑːlɪkwɪ'neɪd] *s.* Harleki'nade *f*, Possenspiel *n*.

har·lot ['hɑːlət] *obs.* Hure *f*, Metze *f*; **'har·lot·ry** [-rɪ] *s.* Hure'rei *f*.

harm [hɑːm] **I** *s.* **1.** Schaden *m*: ***bodily ~*** körperlicher Schaden, ⚖ Körperverletzung *f*; ***come to ~*** zu Schaden kommen; ***do ~ to s.o.*** j-m schaden, j-m et. antun; (***there is***) ***no ~ done!*** es ist nichts (Schlimmes) passiert!; ***it does more ~ than good*** es schadet mehr, als daß es nützt; ***there is no ~ in doing*** (***s.th.***) es kann *od.* könnte nicht schaden, (et.) zu tun; ***mean no ~*** es nicht böse meinen; ***keep out of ~'s way*** die Gefahr meiden; ***out of ~'s way*** a) in Sicherheit, b) in sicherer Entfernung; **2.** Unrecht *n*, Übel *n*; **II** *v/t.* **3.** schaden (*dat.*), *j-n* verletzen (*a. fig.*); **'harm·ful** [-fʊl] *adj.* □ nachteilig, schädlich (***to*** für): ***~ publications*** ⚖ jugendgefährdende Schriften; **'harm·ful·ness** [-fʊlnɪs] *s.* Schädlichkeit *f*; **'harm·less** [-lɪs] *adj.* □ **1.** harmlos: a) unschädlich, ungefährlich, b) unschuldig, arglos, c) unverfänglich; **2.** ***keep*** (*od.* ***save***) ***s.o. ~*** ⚖ j-n schadlos halten; **'harm·less·ness** [-lɪsnɪs] *s.* Harmlosigkeit *f*.

har·mon·ic [hɑː'mɒnɪk] **I** *adj.* (□ ***~ally***) **1.** ♪, ⚕, *phys.* har'monisch (*a. fig.*); **II** *s.* **2.** ♪, *phys.* Har'monische *f*: a) Oberton *m*, b) Oberwelle *f*; **3.** *pl. oft sg. konstr.* ♪ Harmo'nielehre *f*; **har'mon·i·ca** [-kə] *s.* **1.** *hist.* 'Glasharˌmonika *f*; **2.** 'Mundharˌmonika *f*; **har'mo·ni·ous** [-'məʊnjəs] *adj.* □ har'monisch: a) ebenmäßig, b) wohlklingend, c) über'einstimmend, d) einträchtig; **har'mo·ni·ous·ness** [-'məʊnjəsnɪs] *s.* Harmo'nie *f*; **har'mo·ni·um** [-'məʊnjəm] *s.* ♪ Har'monium *n*; **har·mo·nize** ['hɑːmənaɪz] **I** *v/i.* **1.** harmonieren (*a.* ♪), zs.-passen, in Einklang sein (***with*** mit); **II** *v/t.* **2.** (***with***) harmonisieren, in Einklang bringen (mit); **3.** versöhnen; **4.** ♪ harmonisieren, mehrstimmig setzen; **har·mo·ny** ['hɑːmənɪ] *s.* **1.** Harmo'nie *f*: a) Wohlklang *m*, b) Eben-, Gleichmaß *n*, c) Einklang *m*, Eintracht *f*; **2.** ♪ Harmo'nie *f*.

har·ness ['hɑːnɪs] **I** *s.* **1.** (Pferde- *etc.*) Geschirr *n*: ***in ~*** *fig.* in der (täglichen) Tretmühle; ***die in ~*** in den Sielen sterben; ***~ horse*** *Am.* Traber(pferd *n*) *m*; ***~ race*** *Am.* Trabrennen *n*; **2.** a) *mot. etc.* (Sicherheits)Gurt *m* (*für Kinder*), b) (Fallschirm)Gurtwerk *n*; **3.** Laufgeschirr *n für Kinder*; **4.** *Am. sl.* (Arbeits-) Kluft *f*, Uni'form *f* (*e-s Polizisten etc.*); **5.** ✗ *hist.* Harnisch *m*; **II** *v/t.* **6.** *Pferd etc.* a) anschirren, b) anspannen (***to*** an *acc.*); **7.** *fig. Naturkräfte etc.* nutzbar machen.

harp [hɑːp] **I** *s.* **1.** ♪ Harfe *f*; **II** *v/i.* **2.** (die) Harfe spielen; **3.** *fig.* (***on, upon***) her'umreiten (auf *dat.*), dauernd reden (von); → ***string*** 5; **'harp·er** [-pə], **'harp·ist** [-pɪst] *s.* Harfe'nist(in).

har·poon [hɑː'puːn] **I** *s.* Har'pune *f*: ***~ gun*** Harpunengeschütz *n*; **II** *v/t.* harpunieren.

harp·si·chord ['hɑːpsɪkɔːd] *s.* ♪ Cembalo *n*.

har·py ['hɑːpɪ] *s.* **1.** *antiq.* Har'pyie *f*; **2.** *fig.* a) ‚Geier' *m*, Blutsauger *m*, b) Hexe *f* (*Frau*).

har·que·bus ['hɑːkwɪbəs] *s.* ✗ *hist.* Hakenbüchse *f*, Arke'buse *f*.

har·ri·dan ['hærɪdən] *s.* alte Vettel.

har·ri·er[1] ['hærɪə] *s.* **1.** Verwüster *m*; Plünderer *m*; **2.** *orn.* Weihe *f*.

har·ri·er[2] ['hærɪə] *s.* **1.** *hunt.* Hund *m* für die Hasenjagd; **2.** *sport* Querfeld'einläufer(in).

Har·ro·vi·an [hə'rəʊvjən] *s.* Schüler *m* (*der Public School*) von Harrow.

har·row ['hærəʊ] **I** *s.* **1.** ⚒ Egge *f*: ***under the ~*** *fig.* in großer Not; **II** *v/t.* **2.** ⚒ eggen; **3.** *fig.* quälen, peinigen; *Gefühl* verletzen; **'har·row·ing** [-əʊɪŋ] *adj.* □ quälend, qualvoll, schrecklich.

har·rumph [hə'rʌmpf] *v/i.* **1.** sich (gewichtig) räuspern; **2.** mißbilligend schnauben.

har·ry[1] ['hærɪ] *v/t.* **1.** verwüsten; **2.** plündern; **3.** quälen, peinigen.

Har·ry[2] ['hærɪ] *s.* ***old ~*** der Teufel; ***play old ~ with*** Schindluder treiben mit, ‚zur Sau' machen.

harsh [hɑːʃ] *adj.* □ **1.** *allg.* hart: a) rauh: ***~ cloth***, b) rauh, scharf: ***~ voice***; ***~ note***, c) grell: ***~ colo(u)r***, d) barsch, schroff: ***~ words***, e) streng: ***~ penalty***; **2.** herb, scharf, sauer: ***~ taste***; **'harsh·ness** [-nɪs] *s.* Härte *f*.

hart [hɑːt] *s.* Hirsch *m* (*nach dem 5. Jahr*): ***~ of ten*** Zehnender *m*.

har·te·beest ['hɑːtɪbiːst] *s. zo.* 'Kuhantiˌlope *f*.

'harts·horn *s.* ⚗ Hirschhorn *n*: ***salt of ~*** Hirschhornsalz *n*.

har·um-scar·um [ˌheərəm'skeərəm] **I** *adj.* F **1.** leichtsinnig, ‚verrückt'; **2.** flatterhaft; **II** *s.* **3.** leichtsinniger *etc.* Mensch.

har·vest ['hɑːvɪst] **I** *s.* **1.** Ernte *f*: a) Ernten *n*, b) Erntezeit *f*, c) (Ernte)Ertrag *m*; **2.** *fig.* Ertrag *m*, Früchte *pl.*; **II** *v/t.* **3.** ernten, *fig. a.* einheimsen; **4.** *Ernte* einbringen; **5.** *fig.* sammeln; **III** *v/i.* **6.** die Ernte einbringen; **'har·vest·er** [-tə] *s.* **1.** Erntearbeiter(in); **2.** a) 'Mäh-, 'Erntemaˌschine *f*, b) Mähbinder *m*: ***combined ~*** Mähdrescher *m*.

har·vest| fes·ti·val *s.* Ernte'dankfest *n*; **~ home** *s.* **1.** Ernte(zeit) *f*; **2.** Erntefest *n*; **3.** Erntelied *n*; **~ moon** *s.* Vollmond *m* (*im September*).

has [hæz; həz] *3. sg. pres. von* **have**; **'~-been** *s.* F **1.** *et.* Über'holtes; **2.** ‚ausrangierte' Per'son, j-d, der s-e Glanzzeit hinter sich hat.

hash¹ [hæʃ] **I** *v/t.* **1.** *Fleisch* (zer)hacken; **2.** *a.* **~ up** *fig. et.* ‚vermasseln', verpatzen; **II** *s.* **3.** *Küche*: Ha'schee *n*; **4.** *fig. et.* Aufgewärmtes, ‚Aufguß' *m*: **old ~** ‚ein alter Hut'; **5.** *fig.* Kuddelmuddel *n*: **make a ~ of** → 2; **settle s.o.'s ~** F es j-m ‚besorgen'.

hash² [hæʃ] *s.* F ‚Hasch' *n* (*Haschisch*).

hash·eesh, hash·ish ['hæʃiːʃ] *s.* Haschisch *n.*

has·n't ['hæznt] F *für* **has not**.

hasp [hɑːsp] **I** *s.* **1.** ⚙ a) Haspe *f*, Spange *f*, b) Schließband *n*; **2.** Haspel *f*, Spule *f* (*für Garn*); **II** *v/t.* **3.** mit e-r Haspe *etc.* verschließen, zuhaken.

has·sle ['hæsl] *s.* F **I** *s.* **1.** a) ‚Krach' *m*, b) Schläge'rei *f*; **2.** Mühe *f*, ‚Zirkus' *m*; **II** *v/i.* **3.** ‚Krach' haben *od.* sich prügeln; **III** *v/t.* **4.** *Am.* drangsalieren.

has·sock ['hæsək] *s.* **1.** Knie-, Betkissen *n*; **2.** Grasbüschel *n.*

hast [hæst] *obs. 2. sg. pres. von* **have**.

haste [heɪst] *s.* **1.** Eile *f*, Schnelligkeit *f*; **2.** Hast *f*, Eile *f*: **make ~** sich beeilen; **in ~** in Eile, hastig; **more ~, less speed** eile mit Weile; **~ makes waste** in der Eile geht alles schief; **'has·ten** [-sn] **I** *v/t.* a) *j-n* antreiben, b) *et.* beschleunigen; **II** *v/i.* sich beeilen, eilen, hasten: **I ~ to add that ...** ich muß gleich hinzufügen, daß; **'hast·i·ness** [-tɪnɪs] *s.* **1.** Eile *f*, Hastigkeit *f*, Über'eilung *f*, Voreiligkeit *f*; **2.** Heftigkeit *f*, Hitze *f*, ('Über-) Eifer *m*; **'hast·y** [-tɪ] *adj.* □ **1.** eilig, hastig, über'stürzt; **2.** voreilig, -schnell, über'eilt; **3.** heftig, hitzig.

hat [hæt] *s.* Hut *m*: **my ~!** *sl.* von wegen!, daß ich nicht lache; **a bad ~** *Brit.* F ein übler Kunde; **~ in hand** demütig, unterwürfig; **keep it under your ~!** behalte es für dich!, sprich nicht darüber!; **pass** (*od.* **send**) **the ~ round** den Hut herumgehen lassen, e-e Sammlung veranstalten; **take one's ~ off to s.o.** s-n Hut vor j-m ziehen (*a. fig.*); **~s off** (**to him**)**!** Hut ab (vor ihm)!; **I'll eat my ~ if** F ich fress' e-n Besen, wenn; **produce out of a ~** hervorzaubern; **talk through one's ~** F dummes Zeug reden; **throw** (*od.* **toss**) **one's ~ in the ring** F ‚s-n Hut in den Ring werfen' (*sich zum Kampf stellen od. kandidieren*); → **drop** 5.

hat·a·ble ['heɪtəbl] → **hateful**.

hatch¹ [hætʃ] *s.* **1.** ⚓, ✈ Luke *f*: **down the ~es!** *sl.* ‚runter damit'!, prost!; **2.** ⚓ Lukendeckel *m*; **3.** Bodenluke *f*, -tür *f*; **4.** Halbtür *f*; **5.** 'Durchreiche *f* (*für Speisen*).

hatch² [hætʃ] **I** *v/t.* **1.** *a.* **~ out** *Eier, Junge* ausbrüten: **the ~ed, matched and dispatched** → 7; **2.** *a.* **~ out** *fig.* aushecken, -brüten, -denken; **II** *v/i.* **3.** Junge ausbrüten; **4.** *a.* **~ out** *aus dem Ei* ausschlüpfen; **5.** *fig.* sich entwickeln; **III** *s.* **6.** Brut *f*; **7. ~es, matches, and dispatches** F Familienanzeigen *pl.*

hatch³ [hætʃ] **I** *v/t.* schraffieren; **II** *s.* Schraf'fur *f.*

'hatch·back *s. mot.* (Wagen *m* mit) Hecktür *f.*

'hat·check girl *s. Am.* Garde'robenfräulein *n.*

hatch·el ['hætʃl] **I** *s.* **1.** (Flachs- *etc.*)Hechel *f*; **II** *v/t.* **2.** hecheln; **3.** *fig.* quälen, piesacken.

hatch·er ['hætʃə] *s.* **1.** Bruthenne *f*; **2.** 'Brutappa,rat *m*; **3.** *fig.* Aushecker(in), Planer(in); **'hatch·er·y** [-ərɪ] *s.* Brutplatz *m.*

hatch·et ['hætʃɪt] *s.* (*a.* Kriegs)Beil *n*: **bury** (**take up**) **the ~** *fig.* das Kriegsbeil begraben (ausgraben); **'~-face** *s.* scharfgeschnittenes Gesicht; **~ job** *s.* F **1.** ‚Hinrichtung' *f*, ‚Abschuß' *m*; **2.** ‚Verriß' *m* (*Kritik*); **~ man** *s.* F **1.** ‚Henker' *m*, Killer *m*; **2.** ‚Zuchtmeister' *m.*

hatch·ing¹ ['hætʃɪŋ] *s.* **1.** Ausbrüten *n*; **2.** Ausschlüpfen *n*; **3.** Brut *f*; **4.** *fig.* Aushecken *n.*

hatch·ing² ['hætʃɪŋ] *s.* Schraffierung *f.*

'hatch·way → **hatch¹** 1–3.

hate [heɪt] **I** *v/t.* **1.** hassen (**like poison** wie die Pest): **~d** verhaßt; **2.** verabscheuen, hassen, nicht ausstehen können; **3.** nicht mögen *od.* wollen, sehr ungern tun: **I ~ to do it** ich tue es (nur) sehr ungern, es ist mir äußerst peinlich; **I ~ to think of it** bei dem (bloßen) Gedanken wird mir schlecht; **II** *s.* **4.** Haß *m* (**of, for** auf *acc.*, gegen): **full of ~, with ~** haßerfüllt; **~ object** Haßobjekt *n*; **~ tunes** *fig.* Haßgesänge *pl.*; **5.** *et.* Verhaßtes: **that's my pet ~** F das ist mir ein Greuel *od.* in tiefster Seele verhaßt; **6.** Abscheu *m* (**of, for** vor *dat.*, gegen); **'hate·a·ble** [-təbl], **'hate·ful** [-fʊl] *adj.* □ hassenswert, verhaßt, abscheulich; **'hat·er** [-tə] *s.* Hasser(in); **'hate,mong·er** *s.* (Auf)Hetzer *m.*

hath [hæθ; həθ] *obs. 3. sg. pres. von* **have**.

hat·less ['hætlɪs] *adj.* ohne Hut, barhäuptig.

'hat|·pin *s.* Hutnadel *f*; **'~·rack** *s.* Hutablage *f.*

ha·tred ['heɪtrɪd] *s.* (**of, for, against**) a) Haß *m* (gegen, auf *acc.*), b) Abscheu *m* (vor *dat.*).

hat stand *s.* Hutständer *m.*

hat·ter ['hætə] *s.* Hutmacher *m*, -händler *m*: **as mad as a ~** total verrückt.

hat| tree *s. Am.* Hutständer *m*; **~ trick** *s. sport* Hat-Trick *m*: **score a ~** e-n Hat-Trick erzielen.

haugh·ti·ness ['hɔːtɪnɪs] *s.* Hochmut *m*, Über'heblichkeit *f*, Arro'ganz *f*; **haugh·ty** ['hɔːtɪ] *adj.* □ hochmütig, -näsig, über'heblich, arro'gant.

haul [hɔːl] **I** *s.* **1.** Ziehen *n*, Zerren *n*, Schleppen *n*; **2.** kräftiger Zug, Ruck *m*; **3.** Fischzug *m*, *fig. a.* Fang *m*, Beute *f*: **make a big ~** e-n guten Fang *od.* reiche Beute machen; **4.** a) Beförderung *f*, Trans'port *m*, b) (Trans'port)Strecke *f*: **it was quite a ~ home** der Heimweg zog sich ganz schön hin; **in** (*od.* **over**) **the long ~** auf lange Sicht, c) Ladung *f*: **a ~ of coal**; **II** *v/t.* **5.** ziehen, zerren, schleppen; → **coal** 2; **6.** befördern, transportieren; **7.** ⚒ fördern; **8.** her'aufholen, (mit e-m Netz) fangen; **9.** ⚓ a) *Brassen* anholen, b) her'umholen, anluven: **~ the wind** an den Wind gehen, *fig.* sich zurückziehen; **III** *v/i.* **10.** ziehen, zerren (**on, at** an *dat.*); **11.** mit dem Schleppnetz fischen; **12.** 'umspringen (*Wind*); **13.** ⚓ a) abdrehen, b) an den Wind gehen, c) *fig.* s-e Meinung ändern; **~ down** *v/t.* **1.** *Flagge* ein- *od.* niederholen; **2.** *et.* her'unterschleppen *od.* -ziehen; **~ in** *v/t.* ⚓ *Tau* einholen; **~ off** *v/i.* **1.** ⚓ abdrehen; **2.** *Am.* F ausholen; **~ round** → **haul** 12; **~ up** *v/t.* **1.** → **haul** 9b; **2.** F sich *j-n* ‚vorknöpfen'; **3.** F a) *j-n* vor den ‚Kadi' schleppen, b) *j-n* ‚schleppen' (**before** vor *e-n Vorgesetzten etc.*).

haul·age ['hɔːlɪdʒ] *s.* **1.** Ziehen *n*, Schleppen *n*; **2.** a) Trans'port *m*, Beförderung *f*: **~ contractor** → **hauler** 2, b) Trans'portkosten *pl.*; **3.** ⚒ Förderung *f*; **'haul·er** [-lə], *Brit.* **'haul·ier** [-ljə] *s.* **1.** ⚒ Schlepper *m*; **2.** Trans'portunter,nehmer *m*, Spedi'teur *m.*

haulm [hɔːm] *s.* ♀ **1.** Halm *m*, Stengel *m*; **2.** *coll. Brit.* Halme *pl.*, Stengel *pl.*, (*Bohnen- etc.*)Stroh *n.*

haunch [hɔːntʃ] *s.* **1.** Hüfte *f*; **2.** *pl.* Gesäß *n*; **3.** *zo.* Keule *f*; **4.** *Küche*: Lendenstück *n*, Keule *f.*

haunt [hɔːnt] **I** *v/t.* **1.** 'umgehen *od.* spuken in (*dat.*): **this place is ~ed** hier spukt es; **2.** *fig.* a) verfolgen, quälen, b) *j-m* nicht mehr aus dem Kopf gehen; **3.** frequentieren, häufig besuchen; **II** *v/i.* **4.** ständig verkehren (**with** mit); **III** *s.* **5.** häufig besuchter Ort, *bsd.* Lieblingsplatz *m*: **holiday ~** beliebter Ferienort; **6.** a) Treffpunkt *m*, b) Schlupfwinkel *m*; **7.** *zo.* a) Lager *n*, b) Futterplatz *m*; **'haunt·ed** [-tɪd] *adj.*: **a ~ house** ein Haus, in dem es spukt; **he was a ~ man** er fand keine Ruhe mehr; **~ed eyes** gehetzter Blick; **'haunt·ing** [-tɪŋ] *adj.* □ **1.** quälend, beklemmend; **2.** unvergeßlich: **~ beauty** betörende Schönheit; **a ~ melody** e-e Melodie, die einen verfolgt.

haut·boy ['əʊbɔɪ] *obs.* → **oboe**.

hau·teur [əʊ'tɜː] *s.* Hochmut *m*, Arro'ganz *f.*

Ha·van·a [hə'vænə] *s.* Ha'vanna(zi,garre) *f.*

have [hæv; həv] **I** *v/t.* [*irr.*] **1.** *allg.* haben, besitzen: **he has a house** (**a friend, a good memory**); **you ~ my word for it** ich gebe Ihnen mein Wort darauf; **let me ~ a sample** gib *od.* schicke *od.* besorge mir ein Muster; **~ got** → **get** 8; **2.** haben, erleben: **we had a nice time** wir hatten es schön; **3.** a) *ein Kind* bekommen: **she had a baby in March**, b) *zo. Junge* werfen; **4.** *Gefühle, e-n Verdacht etc.* haben, hegen; **5.** behalten, haben: **may I ~ it?**; **6.** erhalten, bekommen: **we had no news from her**; (**not**) **to be had** (nicht) zu haben, (nicht) erhältlich; **7.** (erfahren) haben, wissen: **I ~ it from my friend**; **I ~ it from a reliable source** ich habe es aus verläßlicher Quelle (erfahren); **I ~ it!** ich hab's!; → **rumo(u)r** I; **8.** *Speisen etc.* zu sich nehmen, einnehmen, essen *od.* trinken: **what will you ~?** was nehmen Sie?; **I had a glass of wine** ich trank ein Glas Wein; **~ another sandwich!** nehmen Sie noch ein Sandwich!; **~ a cigar** e-e Zigarre rauchen; **~ a smoke?** wollen Sie (eine) rauchen?; → **breakfast** I, **dinner** 1, *etc.*; **9.** haben, ausführen, (mit)machen: **~ a discus-**

sion e-e Diskussion haben *od.* abhalten; ~ ***a walk*** e-n Spaziergang machen; **10.** können, beherrschen: ***she has no French*** sie kann kein Französisch; **11.** (be)sagen, behaupten: ***as Mr. B has it*** wie Herr B. sagt; ***he will ~ it that*** er behauptet steif und fest, daß; **12.** sagen, ausdrücken: ***as Byron has it*** wie Byron sagt, wie es bei Byron heißt; **13.** haben, dulden, zulassen: ***I won't ~ it!***, ***I am not having that!*** ich dulde es nicht!, ich will es nicht (haben); ***I won't ~ it mentioned*** ich will nicht, daß es erwähnt wird; ***he wasn't having any*** F er ließ sich auf nichts ein; **14.** haben, erleiden: ~ ***an accident***; **15.** *Brit.* F *j-n* ‚reinlegen', ‚übers Ohr hauen': ***you've been had!*** man hat dich reingelegt; **16.** (*vor inf.*) müssen: ***I ~ to go now***; ***he will ~ to do it***; ***we ~ to obey*** wir haben zu *od.* müssen gehorchen; ***it has to be done*** es muß getan werden; **17.** (*mit Objekt u. p.p.*) lassen: ***I had a suit made*** ich ließ mir e-n Anzug machen; ***they had him shot*** sie ließen ihn erschießen; **18.** (*mit Objekt u. p.p. zum Ausdruck des Passivs*): ***I had my arm broken*** ich brach mir den Arm; ***he had a son born to him*** ihm wurde ein Sohn geboren; ~ ***a tooth out*** sich e-n Zahn ziehen lassen; **19.** (*mit Objekt u. inf.*) (veran)lassen: ~ ***them come here at once!*** laß sie sofort hierherkommen!; ***I had him sit down*** ich ließ ihn Platz nehmen; **20.** (*mit Objekt u. inf.*) es erleben (müssen), daß: ***I had all my friends turn against me***; **21.** *in Wendungen wie*: ***he has had it*** F er ist ‚erledigt' (*a. tot*) *od.* ‚fertig'; ***the car has had it*** F das Auto ist ‚hin' *od.* ‚im Eimer'; ***he had me there*** da hatte er mich (an m-r schwachen Stelle *etc.*) erwischt; ***I would ~ you to know it*** ich möchte, daß Sie es wissen; ***let s.o. ~ it*** ‚es j-m besorgen *od.* geben', j-n ‚fertigmachen'; ~ ***it in for s.o.*** F j-n ‚auf dem Kieker haben'; ***I did'nt know he had it in him*** ich wußte gar nicht, daß er das Zeug dazu hat; ~ ***it off*** (***with s.o.***) *Brit. sl.* (mit j-m) ‚bumsen'; ***you are having me on!*** F du nimmst mich (doch) auf den Arm!; ~ ***it out with s.o.*** die Sache mit j-m endgültig bereinigen; ~ ***nothing on s.o.*** F a) j-m nichts anhaben können, nichts gegen j-n in der Hand haben, b) j-m in keiner Weise überlegen sein; ***I ~ nothing on tonight*** ich habe heute abend nichts vor; ~ ***it*** (***all***) ***over s.o.*** F j-m (haushoch) überlegen sein; ~ ***what it takes*** das Zeug dazu haben; **II** *v/i.* **22.** würde, täte (*mit* ***as well***, ***rather***, ***better***, ***best*** *etc.*): ***you had better go!*** es wäre besser, du gingest!; ***you had best go!*** du tätest am besten daran zu gehen; **III** *v/aux.* **23.** haben: ***I ~ seen*** ich habe gesehen; **24.** (*bei vielen v/i.*) sein: ***I ~ been*** ich bin gewesen; **IV** *s.* **25.** ***the ~s and the ~-nots*** die Begüterten u. die Habenichtse; **26.** *Brit.* F Trick *m.*

have·lock ['hævlɒk] *s. Am.* über den Nacken her'abhängender 'Mützenˌüberzug (*Sonnenschutz*).

ha·ven ['heɪvn] *s.* **1.** *mst fig.* (sicherer) Hafen; **2.** Zufluchtsort *m*, A'syl *n*, O'ase *f.*

'have-not → ***have*** 25.

hav·er·sack ['hævəsæk] *s. bsd.* ⚔ Pro-vi'anttasche *f.*

hav·ings ['hævɪŋz] *s. pl.* Habe *f.*

hav·oc ['hævək] *s.* Verwüstung *f*, Zerstörung *f*: ***cause ~*** große Zerstörungen anrichten *od.* (*a. fig.*) ein Chaos verursachen, schrecklich wüten; ***play ~ with***, ***make ~ of*** *et.* verwüsten *od.* zerstören, *fig.* verheerend wirken auf (*acc.*), übel zurichten.

haw[1] [hɔː] *s.* ♀ **1.** Mehlbeere *f* (*Weißdornfrucht*); **2.** → ***hawthorn***.

haw[2] [hɔː] **I** *int.* hm!, äh; **II** *v/i.* hm machen, sich räuspern; stockend sprechen.

Ha·wai·ian [hə'waɪən] **I** *adj.* ha'waiisch: ~ ***guitar*** Hawaiigitarre *f*; **II** *s.* Hawai'ianer(in).

'haw·finch *s. orn.* Kernbeißer *m.*

haw-haw I *int.* [ˌhɔː'hɔː] ha'ha!; **II** *s.* ['hɔːhɔː] (lautes) Ha'ha *n.*

hawk[1] [hɔːk] **I** *s.* **1.** *orn.* a) Falke *m*, b) Habicht *m*; **2.** *fig.* Halsabschneider *m*, Wucherer *m*; **3.** *pol.* ‚Falke' *m*: ***the ~s and the doves*** die Falken u. die Tauben; **II** *v/i.* **4.** (*mit Falken*) Jagd machen (***at*** auf *acc.*); **III** *v/t.* **5.** jagen.

hawk[2] [hɔːk] *v/t.* **1.** a) hausieren (gehen) mit (*a. fig.*), b) auf der Straße verkaufen; **2.** *a.* ~ ***about*** *Gerücht etc.* verbreiten.

hawk[3] [hɔːk] **I** *v/i.* sich räuspern; **II** *v/t. oft* ~ ***up*** aushusten; **III** *s.* Räuspern *n.*

hawk[4] [hɔːk] *s.* Mörtelbrett *n.*

hawk·er[1] ['hɔːkə] → ***falconer***.

hawk·er[2] ['hɔːkə] *s.* **1.** Hausierer(in); **2.** Straßenhändler(in).

'hawk-eyed *adj.* mit Falkenaugen, scharfsichtig.

hawk·ing ['hɔːkɪŋ] → ***falconry***.

hawk| moth *s. zo.* Schwärmer *m*; ~ **nose** *s.* Adlernase *f.*

hawse [hɔːz] *s.* ⚓ (Anker)Klüse *f*; **'haw·ser** [-zə] *s.* Trosse *f.*

'haw·thorn *s.* ♀ Weiß- *od.* Rot- *od.* Hagedorn *m.*

hay [heɪ] *s.* **1.** Heu *n*: ***make ~*** Heu machen; ***make ~ of s.th.*** *fig.* et. durcheinanderbringen *od.* zunichte machen; ***make ~ while the sun shines*** *fig.* das Eisen schmieden, solange es heiß ist; ***hit the ~*** *sl.* ‚sich in die Falle hauen'; **2.** *sl.* Marihu'ana *n*; **'~·cock** *s.* Heuschober *m*; ~ **fe·ver** *s.* ⚕ Heufieber *n*, -schnupfen *m*; ~ **field** *s.* Wiese *f* (*zum Mähen*); **'~·fork** *s.* Heugabel *f*; **~·loft** *s.* Heuboden *m*; **'~ˌmak·er** *s.* **1.** Heumacher *m*; **2.** ⚒, ⚙ Heuwender *m*; **3.** *sl. Boxen*: ‚Heumacher' *m*, wilder Schwinger; **'~·rick** *s.* Heumiete *f*; **'~·seed** *s.* **1.** Grassamen *m*; **2.** *Am.* F ‚Bauer' *m*; **'~·stack** → ***hayrick***; **'~ˌwire** *adj. sl.* a) ka'putt, b) (hoffnungslos) durchein'ander, c) verrückt (*Person*): ***go ~*** a) kaputtgehen (*Sache*), b) ‚schiefgehen', durcheinandergeraten (*Sache*), c) überschnappen.

haz·ard ['hæzəd] **I** *s.* **1.** Gefahr *f*, Wagnis *n*, Risiko *n* (*a. Versicherung*): ***health ~*** Gesundheitsrisiko; ~ ***bonus*** Gefahrenzulage *f*; ***at all ~s*** unter allen Umständen; ***at the ~ of one's life*** unter Lebensgefahr; **2.** Zufall *m*: ***by ~*** zufällig; **3.** (***game of***) ~ Glücks-, Ha'sardspiel *n*; **4.** *Golf*: Hindernis *n*; **5.** *Brit. Billard*: ***losing ~*** Verläufer *m*; ***winning ~*** Treffer *m*; **6.** *pl.* Launen *pl.* (*des Wetters*); **II** *v/t.* **7.** riskieren, wagen, aufs Spiel setzen; **8.** zu sagen wagen, riskieren: ~ ***a remark***; **9.** sich *e-r Gefahr etc.* aussetzen; **'haz·ard·ous** [-dəs] *adj.* □ gewagt, ris'kant, gefährlich, unsicher.

haze[1] [heɪz] *s.* **1.** Dunst(schleier) *m*, feiner Nebel; **2.** *fig.* Nebel *m*, Schleier *m*: ***his mind was in a ~*** a) er war wie betäubt, b) er ‚blickte nicht mehr durch'.

haze[2] [heɪz] *v/t. Am.* **1.** piesacken, schikanieren; **2.** beschimpfen.

ha·zel ['heɪzl] **I** *s.* **1.** ♀ Hasel(nuß)-strauch *m*; **2.** (Hasel)Nußbraun *n*; **II** *adj.* (hasel)nußbraun; **'~·nut** *s.* ♀ Haselnuß *f.*

ha·zi·ness ['heɪzɪnɪs] *s.* **1.** Dunstigkeit *f*; **2.** *fig.* Unklarheit *f*, Verschwommenheit *f*; **ha·zy** ['heɪzɪ] *adj.* □ **1.** dunstig, diesig, leicht nebelig; **2.** *fig.* verschwommen, nebelhaft: ***a ~ idea***; ***be ~ about*** nur e-e vage Vorstellung haben von; **3.** benommen.

H-bomb ['eɪtʃbɒm] *s.* ⚔ H-Bombe *f* (*Wasserstoffbombe*).

he [hiː; hɪ] **I** *pron.* **1.** er; **2.** ~ ***who*** wer; derjenige, welcher; **II** *s.* **3.** ‚Er' *m*: a) Junge *m od.* Mann *m*, b) *zo.* Männchen *n*; **III** *adj.* **4.** *in Zssgn* männlich, ...männchen: ***~-goat*** Ziegenbock *m.*

head [hed] **I** *v/t.* **1.** die Spitze bilden von (*od. gen.*), anführen, an der Spitze *od.* an erster Stelle stehen von (*od. gen.*): ~ ***a list***; **2.** vor'an-, vor'ausgehen (*dat.*); **3.** (an)führen, leiten: ***~ed by*** unter der Leitung von; **4.** lenken, steuern: ~ ***off*** a) 'um-, ablenken, b) abfangen, c) *fig.* abwenden, verhindern; **5.** betiteln; **6.** *bsd. Pflanzen* köpfen, *Bäume* kappen; **7.** *Fußball*: (~ ***in*** ein)köpfen; **II** *v/i.* **8.** a) gehen, fahren, b) (***for***) zu-, losgehen, -steuern (auf *acc.*): ***he is ~ing for trouble*** er wird noch Ärger kriegen; **9.** ⚓ Kurs halten, zusteuern (***for*** auf *acc.*); **10.** sich entwickeln: ~ (***up***) (e-n Kopf) ansetzen (*Kohl etc.*); **11.** entspringen (*Fluß*); **III** *s.* **12.** Kopf *m*: ***back of the ~*** Hinterkopf; ***have a ~*** F e-n ‚Brummschädel' haben; ***win by a ~*** um e-e Kopflänge *od.* (*a. fig.*) um e-e Nasenlänge gewinnen; → *Bes. Redew.*; **13.** *poet. u. fig.* Haupt *n*: ~ ***of the family*** Haupt der Familie, Familienoberhaupt; ***~s of state*** Staatsoberhäupter *pl.*; **14.** Kopf *m*, Verstand *m*, *a.* Begabung *f* (***for*** für): ***he has a*** (***good***) ~ ***for languages*** er ist (sehr) sprachbegabt; ***two ~s are better than one*** zwei Köpfe wissen mehr als einer; **15.** Spitze *f*, führende Stellung: ***at the ~ of*** an der Spitze (*gen.*); **16.** a) (An)Führer *m*, Leiter *m*, b) Chef *m*, c) Vorstand *m*, Vorsteher *m*, d) Di'rektor *m*, Direk'torin *f* (*e-r Schule*); **17.** Kopf(ende *n*) *m*, oberes Ende, oberer Teil *od.* Rand, Spitze *f*, *a.* oberer Absatz (*e-r Treppe*), Kopf *m* (*e-r Buchseite*, *e-s Briefes*, *e-r Münze*, *e-s Nagels*, *e-s Hammers etc.*): ***~s or tails?*** Kopf oder Wappen?; **18.** Kopf *m* (*e-r Brücke od. Mole*); oberes *od.* unteres Ende (*e-s Sees*); Boden *m* (*e-s Fasses*); **19.** Kopf *m*, Spitze *f*, vorderes Ende, Vorderteil *m*, *n*, ⚓ Bug *m*; **20.** Kopf *m*, (einzelne) Per'son: ***a pound a ~*** ein Pfund pro Person *od.* pro Kopf; **21.** a) (*pl.* ~) Stück *n* (*Vieh*):

50 ~ of cattle, b) *Brit.* Anzahl *f*, Herde *f*; **22.** (Haupt)Haar *n*: ***a fine ~ of hair*** schönes, volles Haar; **23.** ⚘ a) (*Salat- etc.*)Kopf *m*, b) (*Baum*)Krone *f*, Wipfel *m*; **24.** *anat.* Kopf *m* (*e-s Knochens etc.*); **25.** ⚕ ˈDurchbruchsstelle *f* (*e-s Geschwürs*); **26.** Vorgebirge *n*, Landspitze *f*, Kap *n*; **27.** *hunt.* Geweih *n*; **28.** Schaum(krone *f*) *m* (*vom Bier etc.*); **29.** *Brit.* Rahm *m*, Sahne *f*; **30.** Quelle *f* (*e-s Flusses*); **31.** a) ˈÜberschrift *f*, Titelkopf *m*, b) Abschnitt *m*, Kaˈpitel *n*, c) (Haupt)Punkt *m* (*e-r Rede etc.*), d) Ruˈbrik *f*, Kategoˈrie *f*, e) *typ.* (Titel-) Kopf *m*; **32.** *ling.* Oberbegriff *m*; **33.** ⚙ a) Stauwasser *n*, b) Staudamm *m*; **34.** *phys.*, ⚙ a) Gefälle *n*, b) Druckhöhe *f*, c) (Dampf- *etc.*)Druck *m*, d) Säule(nhöhe) *f*: ***~ of water*** Wassersäule; **35.** ⚙ a) Spindelkopf *m*, b) Spindelbank *f*, c) Supˈport *m* (*e-r Bohrbank*), d) (Gewinde)Schneidkopf *m*, e) Kopf-, Deckplatte *f*; **36.** (Wagen-, Kutschen-) Dach *n*; **37.** → ***heading***; **IV** *adj.* **38.** Kopf…; **39.** Spitzen…, Vorder…; **40.** Chef…, Haupt…, Ober…, Spitzen…, führend, oberst: ***~ cook*** Chefkoch *m*; *Besondere Redewendungen*: ***that is*** (*od.* ***goes***) ***above*** (*od.* ***over***) ***my ~*** das ist zu hoch für mich, das geht über m-n Horizont; ***talk above s.o.'s ~*** über j-s Kopf hinwegreden; ***by ~ and shoulders*** an den Haaren (*herbeiziehen*); (***by***) ***~ and shoulders*** um Haupteslänge (*größer etc.*), weitaus; ***~ and shoulders above s.o.*** j-m haushoch überlegen; ***from ~ to foot*** von Kopf bis Fuß; ***off*** (*od.* ***out of***) ***one's ~*** F ‚übergeschnappt'; ***I can do that*** (***standing***) ***on my ~*** F das kann ich im Schlaf, das mach' ich ‚mit links'; ***on this ~*** in diesem Punkt; ***out of one's own ~*** von sich aus; ***over s.o.'s ~*** *fig.* über j-s Kopf hinweg; ***~ over heels*** a) kopfüber (*stürzen*), b) bis über beide Ohren (*verliebt*), c) ***in debt*** bis über die Ohren in Schulden (*stecken*); ***~ first*** (*od.* ***foremost***) → ***headlong***; ***bite s.o.'s ~ off*** F j-m ‚den Kopf abreißen'; ***bring to a ~*** zum Ausbruch *od.* zur Entscheidung *od.* ‚zum Klappen' bringen; ***come to a ~*** a) ⚕ aufbrechen, eitern, b) sich zuspitzen, zur Entscheidung *od.* ‚zum Klappen' kommen; ***it entered my ~*** es fiel mir ein; ***gather ~*** überhandnehmen, immer stärker werden; ***give a horse his ~*** e-m Pferd die Zügel schießen lassen; ***give s.o. his ~*** j-m s-n Willen lassen, j-n gewähren *od.* machen lassen; ***give*** (***s.o.***) ***~*** *Am.* V (j-m e-n) ‚blasen'; ***go to the ~*** zu Kopfe steigen; ***have*** (*od.* ***be***) ***an old ~ on young shoulders*** für sein Alter (schon) sehr reif sein; ***keep one's ~*** kühlen Kopf bewahren; ***keep one's ~ above water*** sich über Wasser halten (*a. fig.*); ***knock s.th. on the ~*** F et. (*e-n Plan etc.*) ‚über den Haufen werfen'; ***laugh*** (***shout***) ***one's ~ off*** sich halb totlachen (sich die Lunge aus dem Hals schreien); ***lose one's ~*** *fig.* den Kopf verlieren; ***make ~*** gut vorankommen; ***make ~ against*** sich entgegenstemmen (*dat.*); ***I cannot make ~ or tail of it*** ich kann daraus nicht schlau werden; ***put s.th. into s.o.'s ~*** j-m et. in den Kopf setzen; ***put that out of your ~*** schlag dir das aus dem Kopf; ***they put their ~s together*** sie steckten ihre Köpfe zusammen; ***take s.th. into one's ~*** sich et. in den Kopf setzen; ***talk one's ~ off*** reden wie ein Wasserfall; ***talk s.o.'s ~ off*** ‚j-m ein Loch in den Bauch reden'; ***turn s.o.'s ~*** j-m den Kopf verdrehen.

ˈhead|·ache *s.* **1.** Kopfschmerzen *pl.*, -weh *n*; **2.** F *et., was Kopfzerbrechen od. Sorgen macht*, schwieriges Proˈblem, Sorge *f*; **ˈ~ˌach·y** *adj.* F **1.** an Kopfschmerzen leidend; **2.** Kopfschmerzen verursachend; **ˈ~·band** *s.* Stirnband *n*; **ˈ~·board** *s.* Kopfbrett *n* (*Bett*); **ˈ~·boy** *s. Brit. ped.* Schulsprecher *m*; **ˈ~·cheese** *s. Am.* Preßkopf *m* (*Sülzwurst*); **~ clerk** *s.* Büˈrochef *m*; **ˈ~·dress** *s.* **1.** Kopfschmuck *m*; **2.** Friˈsur *f*.

-headed [hedɪd] *in Zssgn* …köpfig.

head·ed [ˈhedɪd] *adj.* **1.** mit e-m Kopf *etc.* (versehen); **2.** mit e-r ˈÜberschrift (versehen), betitelt.

head·er [ˈhedə] *s.* **1.** △, ⚙ a) Schlußstein *m*, b) Binder *m*; **2.** ***take a ~*** a) *sport* e-n Kopfsprung machen, b) kopfüber *die Treppe etc. hinunter*-stürzen; **3.** *Fußball*: Kopfball *m*, -stoß *m*.

ˌhead|ˈfirst, **ˌ~ˈfore·most** → ***headlong***; **ˈ~·gear** *s.* **1.** Kopfbedeckung *f*; **2.** Kopfgestell *n*, Zaumzeug *n* (*vom Pferd*); **3.** ⚒ Fördergerüst *n*; **ˈ~ˌhunt·er** *s.* Kopfjäger *m*.

head·i·ness [ˈhedɪnɪs] *s.* **1.** Unbesonnenheit *f*, Ungestüm *n*; **2.** *das* Berauschende (*a. fig.*).

head·ing [ˈhedɪŋ] *s.* **1.** a) Kopfstück *n*, -ende *n*, b) Vorderende *n*, -teil *n*; **2.** ˈÜberschrift *f*, Titel(zeile *f*) *m*; **3.** Briefkopf *m*; **4.** (Rechnungs)Posten *m*; **5.** Thema *n*, Punkt *m*; **6.** ⚒ Stollen *m*; **7.** a) ✈ Steuerkurs *m*, b) ⚓ Kompaßkurs *m*; **8.** *Fußball*: Kopfballspiel *n*; **~ stone** *s.* △ Schlußstein *m*.

ˈhead|·lamp → ***headlight***; **ˈ~·land** *s.* **1.** ⚘ Rain *m*; **2.** [-lənd] Landspitze *f*, -zunge *f*.

head·less [ˈhedlɪs] *adj.* **1.** kopflos (*a. fig.*), ohne Kopf; **2.** *fig.* führerlos.

ˈhead|·light *s.* **1.** *mot. etc.* Scheinwerfer *m*: ***~ flasher*** Lichthupe *f*; **2.** ⚓ Mast-, Topplicht *n*; **ˈ~·line I** *s.* **1.** a) ˈÜberschrift *f*, b) *Zeitung*: Schlagzeile *f*, c) *pl. a.* ***~ news*** *Radio, TV*: (*das*) Wichtigste in Schlagzeilen: ***hit*** (*od.* ***make***) ***the ~s*** Schlagzeilen machen; **II** *v/t.* **2.** e-e Schlagzeile widmen (*dat.*); **3.** *fig.* groß herˈausstellen; **ˈ~ˌlin·er** *s. Am.* F **1.** *thea. etc.* Star *m*; **2.** promiˈnente Perˈsönlichkeit; **ˈ~·lock** *s. Ringen*: Kopfzange *f*; **ˈ~·long I** *adv.* **1.** kopfˈüber, mit dem Kopf vorˈan; **2.** *fig.* Hals über Kopf, blindlings; **II** *adj.* **3.** mit dem Kopf vorˈan: ***a ~ fall***; **4.** *fig.* überˈstürzt, unbesonnen, ungestüm; **~ louse** *s.* Kopflaus *f*; **~·man** *s.* [*irr.*] **1.** [ˈhedmæn] Führer *m*; **2.** Häuptling *m*; **3.** [ˌhedˈmæn] Vorarbeiter *m*; **ˌ~ˈmas·ter** *s.* Schulleiter *m*, Diˈrektor *m*; **ˌ~ˈmis·tress** *s.* Schulleiterin *f*, Direkˈtorin *f*; **~ mon·ey** *s.* Kopfgeld *n*; **~ of·fice** *s.* ˈHauptbüˌro *n*, -geschäftsstelle *f*, -sitz *m*, Zenˈtrale *f*; **ˌ~ˈon** *adj. u. adv.* **1.** fronˈtal: ***~ collision*** Frontalzusammenstoß *m*; **2.** diˈrekt; **ˈ~·phone** *s. mst pl.* Kopfhörer *m*; **ˈ~·piece** *s.* **1.** Kopfbedeckung *f*; **2.** Oberteil *n*, *bsd.* a) Türsturz *m*, b) Kopfbrett *n* (*Bett*); **3.** *typ.* ˈTitelviˌgnette *f*; **ˌ~ˈquar·ters** *s. pl. oft sg. konstr.* **1.** ⚔ a) ˈHauptquarˌtier *n*, b) Stab *m*, c) Komˈmandostelle *f*, d) ˈOberkomˌmando *n*; **2.** *allg.* (*Feuerwehr-, Partei- etc.*)Zenˈtrale *f*, (Poliˈzei-) Präˌsidium *n*; **3.** → ***head office***; **ˈ~·rest**, **~ re·straint** *s.* Kopfstütze *f*; **ˈ~·room** [-rʊm] *s.* lichte Höhe; **ˈ~·sail** *s.* ⚓ Fockmastsegel *n*; **ˈ~·set** *s.* Kopfhörer *m*.

head·ship [ˈhedʃɪp] *s.* (oberste) Leitung, Führung *f*.

head|·shrink·er [ˈhedˌʃrɪŋkə] *s.* F Psychoanaˈlytiker(in); **ˈ~·spring** *s.* **1.** Hauptquelle *f*; **2.** *fig.* Quelle *f*, Ursprung *m*; **3.** *sport* Kopfkippe *f*; **ˈ~·stall** → ***headgear*** 2; **ˈ~·stand** *s.* Kopfstand *m*; **~ start** *s.* **1.** *sport* a) Vorgabe *f*, b) Vorsprung *m* (*a. fig.*); **2.** *fig.* guter Start; **ˈ~·stock** *s.* ⚙ **1.** Spindelstock *m*; **2.** Triebwerkgestell *n*; **ˈ~·stone** *s.* **1.** △ a) Eck-, Grundstein *m* (*a. fig.*), b) Schlußstein *m*; **2.** Grabstein *m*; **ˈ~·strong** *adj.* eigensinnig, halsstarrig; **~ tax** *s.* Kopf-, *bsd.* Einwanderungssteuer *f* (*USA*); **ˌ~-to-ˈhead** *adj. Am.* **1.** Mann gegen Mann; **2.** Kopf-an-Kopf…: ***~ race***; **~ voice** *s.* Kopfstimme *f*; **ˈ~ˌwait·er** *s.* Oberkellner *m*; **ˈ~ˌwa·ter** *s. mst pl.* Oberlauf *m*, Quellgebiet *n* (*Fluß*); **ˈ~·way** *s.* **1.** ⚓ a) Fahrt *f* vorˈaus, b) Fahrt *f*, Geschwindigkeit *f*; **2.** *fig.* Fortschritt(e *pl.*) *m*: ***make ~*** vorankommen, Fortschritte machen; **3.** △ lichte Höhe; **4.** ⚒ *Brit.* Hauptstollen *m*; **5.** 🚆 Zugfolge *f*, -abstand *m*; **~ wind** *s.* Gegenwind *m*; **ˈ~·work** *s.* geistige Arbeit; **ˈ~ˌwork·er** *s.* Geistes-, Kopfarbeiter *m*.

head·y [ˈhedɪ] *adj.* □ **1.** unbesonnen, ungestüm; **2.** a) berauschend (*Getränk*; *a. fig.*), b) berauscht (***with*** von); **3.** *Am.* F schlau.

heal [hiːl] **I** *v/t.* **1.** *a. fig.* heilen, kurieren (***of*** von); **2.** *fig.* versöhnen, *Streit etc.* beilegen; **II** *v/i.* **3.** *oft* ***~ up***, ***~ over*** (zu)heilen; **ˈheal·er** [-lə] *s.* **1.** Hei-l(end)er *m*, *bsd.* Gesundbeter(in); **2.** Heilmittel *n*: ***time is a great ~*** die Zeit heilt alle Wunden; **ˈheal·ing** [-lɪŋ] **I** *s.* Heilung *f*; **II** *adj.* □ heilsam, heilend, Heil(ungs)…

health [helθ] *s.* **1.** Gesundheit *f*: ***~ care*** Gesundheitsfürsorge *f*; ***~ centre*** (*Am.* ***center***) Ärztezentrum *n*; ***~ certificate*** ärztliches Attest; ***~ club*** Fitneßclub *m*; ***~ food*** Reformkost *f*; ***~ food shop*** (*od.* ***store***) Reformhaus *n*; ***~ freak*** Gesundheitsfanatiker(in); ***~ insurance*** Krankenversicherung *f*; ***~ officer*** *Am.* a) Beamte(r) *m* des Gesundheitsamtes, b) ⚓ Hafen-, Quarantänearzt *m*; ***~ resort*** Kurort *m*; ***~ service*** Gesundheitsdienst *m*; ***~ visitor*** Gesundheitsfürsorger(in); **2.** *a.* ***state of ~*** Gesundheitszustand *m*: ***ill ~***; ***in good ~*** gesund, bei guter Gesundheit; **3.** Gesundheit *f*, Wohl *n*: ***drink*** (***to***) ***s.o.'s ~*** auf j-s Wohl trinken; ***your ~!*** auf Ihr Wohl!; ***here is to the ~ of the host*** ein Prosit dem Gastgeber!; **ˈhealth·ful** [-fʊl] *adj.* □ → ***healthy*** 1, 2; **ˈhealth·y** [-θɪ] *adj.* □ **1.** *allg.* gesund (*a. fig.*): ***~ body*** (***climate***, ***economy***, *etc.*); **2.** gesund(heitsfördernd), heilsam, bekömmlich; **3.** F gesund, kräftig: ***~ appetite***; **4.** ***not ~*** F ‚nicht gesund', schlecht, gefährlich.

heap [hi:p] **I** *s.* **1.** Haufe(n) *m*: ***in ~s*** haufenweise; ***be struck all of a ~*** F ‚platt' *od.* sprachlos sein; ***fall in a ~*** (in sich) zs.-sacken; **2.** F Haufen *m*, Menge *f*: ***~s of time*** e-e *od.* jede Menge Zeit; ***~s of times*** unzählige Male; ***~s better*** sehr viel besser; **3.** *sl.* ‚Schlitten' *m* (*Auto*); **II** *v/t.* **4.** häufen: ***a ~ed spoonful*** ein gehäufter Löffel(voll); ***~ up*** anhäufen, *fig. a.* aufhäufen; ***~ insults*** (***praises***) (***up***)***on s.o.*** j-n mit Beschimpfungen (Lob) überschütten; → ***coal*** 2; **5.** beladen, anfüllen.

hear [hɪə] [*irr.*] **I** *v/t.* **1.** hören: ***I ~ him laugh***(***ing***) ich höre ihn lachen; ***make o.s. ~d*** sich Gehör verschaffen; ***let's ~ it for him!*** *Am.* F Beifall für ihn!; **2.** (an)hören: ***~ a concert*** sich ein Konzert anhören; **3.** *j-m* zuhören, *j-n* anhören: ***~ s.o. out*** j-n ausreden lassen; **4.** hören *od.* achten auf (*acc.*), *j-s* Rat folgen: ***do you ~ me?*** hast du (mich) verstanden?; **5.** *Bitte etc.* erhören; **6.** *ped. Aufgabe od. Schüler* abhören; **7.** *et.* hören, erfahren (***about***, ***of*** über *acc.*); **8.** ⚖ a) verhören, vernehmen, b) *Sachverständige etc.* anhören, c) (über) *e-n Fall* verhandeln: ***~ and decide a case*** über e-n Fall befinden; → ***evidence*** 1; **II** *v/i.* **9.** hören: ***~! ~!*** *parl.* hört! hört! (*a. iro.*), bravo!, sehr richtig!; **10.** hören, erfahren, Nachricht erhalten (***from*** von; ***of***, ***about*** von, über [*acc.*]; ***that*** daß): ***you'll ~ of this!*** F das wirst du mir büßen!; ***I won't ~ of it*** ich erlaube *od.* dulde es nicht; ***he would not ~ of it*** er wollte davon nichts hören *od.* wissen; **heard** [hɜ:d] *pret. u. p.p. von* ***hear***; **'hear·er** [-ərə] *s.* (Zu)Hörer(in); **'hear·ing** [-ərɪŋ] *s.* **1.** Hören *n*: ***within*** (***out of***) ***~*** in (außer) Hörweite; ***in his ~*** in s-r Gegenwart, solange er noch in Hörweite ist; **2.** Gehör(sinn *m*) *n*: ***~ aid*** Hörhilfe *f*, -gerät *n*; ***~ spectacles*** *pl.* Hörbrille *f*; ***hard of ~*** schwerhörig; **3.** a) Anhören *n*, b) Gehör *n*, c) Audi'enz *f*: ***gain a ~*** sich Gehör verschaffen; ***give s.o. a ~*** j-n anhören; **4.** *thea. etc.* Hörprobe *f*; **5.** ⚖ a) Vernehmung *f*, b) *a.* ***preliminary ~*** 'Vorunter,suchung *f*, c) (mündliche) Verhandlung, Ter'min *m*; **6.** *bsd. pol.* Hearing *n*, Anhörung *f*.

heark·en ['hɑ:kən] *v/i. poet.* (***to***) a) horchen (auf *acc.*), b) Beachtung schenken (*dat.*).

'hear·say *s.* **1.** (***by ~*** vom) Hörensagen *n*; **2.** *a.* ***~ evidence*** ⚖ Beweis(e *pl.*) *m* vom Hörensagen, mittelbarer Beweis: ***~ rule*** *Regel über den grundsätzlichen Ausschluß aller Beweise vom Hörensagen.*

hearse [hɜ:s] *s.* Leichenwagen *m*.

heart [hɑ:t] *s.* **1.** *anat.* a) Herz *n*, b) Herzhälfte *f*; **2.** *fig.* Herz *n*: a) Seele *f*, Gemüt *n*, b) Liebe *f*, Zuneigung *f*, c) (Mit)Gefühl *n*, d) Mut *m*, e) Gewissen *n*: ***change of ~*** Gesinnungswandel *m*; ***affairs of the ~*** Herzensangelegenheiten; → *Bes. Redew.*; **3.** Herz *n*, (*das*) Innere, Kern *m*, Mitte *f*: ***in the ~ of*** inmitten (*gen.*), mitten in (*dat.*), im Herzen (*des Landes etc.*); **4.** Kern *m*, (*das*) Wesentliche: ***go to the ~ of s.th.*** zum Kern e-r Sache vorstoßen, e-r Sache auf den Grund gehen; ***the ~ of the matter*** der Kern der Sache, des Pudels Kern; **5.** Liebling *m*, Schatz *m*, *mein* Herz; **6.** *Kartenspiel*: a) Herz *n*, Cœur *n*, b) *pl.* Herz *n*, Cœur *n* (*Farbe*): ***king of ~s*** Herzkönig *m*; **7.** ⚘ Herz *n* (*Salat, Kohl*): ***~ of oak*** a) Kernholz *n* der Eiche, b) *fig.* Standhaftigkeit *f*;

Besondere Redewendungen:

~ and soul mit Leib u. Seele; ***~'s desire*** Herzenswunsch *m*; ***after my*** (***own***) ***~*** ganz nach m-m Herzen *od.* Geschmack *od.* Wunsch; ***at ~*** im Innersten, im Grunde (m-s *etc.* Herzens); (***have***, ***learn***) ***by ~*** auswendig (wissen, lernen); ***from one's ~*** von Herzen; ***in one's ~*** (***of ~s***) a) im Grunde s-s Herzens, b) insgeheim; ***in good ~*** ✓ in gutem Zustand (*Boden*), *fig. a.* in guter Verfassung, gesund, *a.* guten Mutes; ***to one's ~'s content*** nach Herzenslust; ***with all my ~*** von *od.* mit ganzem Herzen; ***with a heavy ~*** schweren Herzens; ***bless my ~!*** du meine Güte!; ***it breaks my ~*** es bricht mir das Herz; ***you are breaking my ~!*** *iro.* ich fang' gleich an zu weinen!; ***cross my ~!*** Hand aufs Herz!; ***eat one's ~ out*** sich vor Gram verzehren; ***not to have the ~ to do s.th.*** es nicht übers Herz bringen, et. zu tun; ***go to s.o.'s ~*** j-m zu Herzen gehen; ***my ~ goes out to*** ich empfinde tiefes Mitleid mit; ***have a ~!*** hab Erbarmen!; ***have no ~*** kein Herz *od.* Mitgefühl haben; ***I have your health at ~*** deine Gesundheit liegt mir am Herzen; ***I had my ~ in my mouth*** das Herz schlug mir bis zum Halse, ich war zu Tode erschrocken; ***have one's ~ in the right place*** das Herz auf dem rechten Fleck haben; ***his ~ is not in his work*** er ist nicht mit ganzem Herzen dabei; ***lose ~*** den Mut verlieren; ***lose one's ~ to s.o.*** sein Herz an j-n verlieren; ***open one's ~*** a) (***to s.o.*** j-m) sein Herz ausschütten, b) großmütig sein; ***clasp s.o. to one's ~*** j-n ans Herz *od.* an die Brust drücken; ***put one's ~ into s.th.*** mit Leib u. Seele bei et. sein; ***set one's ~ on*** sein Herz hängen an (*acc.*); ***my ~ sank into my boots*** das Herz rutschte mir in die Hose(n); ***take ~*** Mut fassen; ***I took ~ from that*** das machte mir Mut; ***take s.th. to ~*** sich et. zu Herzen nehmen; ***wear one's ~ on one's sleeve*** das Herz auf der Zunge tragen.

'heart|·ache *s.* Kummer *m*; ***~ ac·tion*** *s. physiol.* Herztätigkeit *f*; ***~ at·tack*** *s.* ✱ Herzanfall *m*; **'~·beat** *s.* **1.** *physiol.* Herzschlag *m* (*Pulsieren*); **2.** *fig. Am.* Herzstück *n*; **'~·break** *s.* (Herze)Leid *n*, Gram *m*; **'~,break·ing** *adj.* herzzerreißend; **'~,bro·ken** *adj.* (ganz) gebrochen, todunglücklich, untröstlich; **'~·burn** *s.* ✱ Sodbrennen *n*; ***~ con·di·tion***, ***~ dis·ease*** *s.* ✱ Herzleiden *n*.

-heart·ed [hɑ:tɪd] *in Zssgn* ...herzig, ...mütig.

heart·en ['hɑ:tn] *v/t.* ermutigen, aufmuntern; **'heart·en·ing** [-nɪŋ] *adj.* ermutigend.

heart| fail·ure *s.* ✱ a) Herzversagen *n*, b) 'Herzinsuffizi,enz *f*; **'~·felt** *adj.* tiefempfunden, herzlich, aufrichtig, innig.

hearth [hɑ:θ] *s.* **1.** Ka'min(platte *f*, -sohle *f*) *m*; **2.** Herd *m*, Feuerstelle *f*; **3.** ⚙ a) Schmiedeherd *m*, Esse *f*, b) Herd *m*, Hochofengestell *n*; **4.** *fig. a.* ***~ and home*** häuslicher Herd, Heim *n*; **'~·stone** *s.* **1.** → ***hearth*** 1 u. 4; **2.** Scheuerstein *m*.

heart·i·ly ['hɑ:tɪlɪ] *adv.* **1.** herzlich: a) von Herzen, innig, b) *iro.* äußerst, gründlich: ***dislike s.o. ~***; **2.** herzhaft, kräftig, tüchtig: ***eat ~***; **'heart·i·ness** [-nɪs] *s.* **1.** Herzlichkeit *f*: a) Innigkeit *f*, b) Aufrichtigkeit *f*; **2.** Herzhaftigkeit *f*, Kräftigkeit *f*.

'heart·land *s.* Herz-, Kernland *n*.

heart·less ['hɑ:tlɪs] *adj.* □ herzlos, grausam, gefühllos; **'heart·less·ness** [-nɪs] *s.* Herzlosigkeit *f*.

,heart|-'lung ma·chine *s.* ✱ 'Herz-'Lungen-Ma,schine *f*: ***put on the ~*** an die Herz-Lungen-Maschine anschließen; ***~ pace·mak·er*** *s.* ✱ Herzschrittmacher *m*; ***~ rate*** *s. physiol.* 'Herzfre,quenz *f*; **'~,rend·ing** *adj.* herzzerreißend; ***~ rot*** *s.* Kernfäule *f* (*Baum*); **'~'s-blood** *s.* Herzblut *n*; **'~,search·ing** *s.* Gewissenserforschung *f*; ***~ shake*** *s.* Kernriß *m* (*Baum*); **'~·shaped** *adj.* herzförmig; **'~·sick**, **'~·sore** *adj.* tiefbetrübt, todunglücklich; **'~·strings** *s. pl. fig.* Herz *n*, innerste Gefühle *pl.*: ***pull at s.o.'s ~*** j-m das Herz zerreißen, j-n tief rühren; ***play on s.o.'s ~*** mit j-s Gefühlen spielen; ***~ sur·ger·y*** *s.* ✱ 'Herzchirur,gie *f*; **'~·throb** *s.* **1.** *physiol.* Herzschlag *m*; **2.** F Schatz *m*, Schwarm *m*; **,~-to-'~** *adj.* offen, aufrichtig: ***~ talk***; ***~ trans·plant*** *s.* ✱ Herzverpflanzung *f*; **'~-,warm·ing** *adj.* **1.** herzerfrischend; **2.** bewegend; **'~-whole** *adj.* **1.** (noch) ungebunden, frei; **2.** aufrichtig, rückhaltlos.

heart·y ['hɑ:tɪ] **I** *adj.* □ → ***heartily***; **1.** herzlich: a) von Herzen kommend, warm, innig, b) aufrichtig, tiefempfunden, c) *iro.* ‚gründlich': ***~ dislike***; **2.** a) munter, b) e'nergisch, c) begeistert, d) herzlich, jovi'al; **3.** herzhaft, kräftig: ***~ appetite*** (***meal***, ***kick***); **4.** gesund, kräftig; **5.** fruchtbar (*Boden*); **II** *s.* **6.** *sport Brit.* F dy'namischer Spieler; **7.** F Ma'trose *m*: ***my hearties*** meine Jungs.

heat [hi:t] **I** *s.* **1.** Hitze *f*: a) große Wärme, b) heißes Wetter; **2.** Wärme *f* (*a. phys.*); **3.** a) Erhitztheit *f* (*des Körpers*), b) (*bsd.* Fieber)Hitze *f*; **4.** (Glüh-)Hitze *f*, Glut *f*; **5.** Schärfe *f* (*von Gewürzen etc.*); **6.** *fig.* a) Ungestüm *n*, b) Zorn *m*, Wut *f*, c) Leidenschaft(lichkeit) *f*, Erregtheit *f*, d) Eifer *m*: ***in the ~ of the moment*** im Eifer des Gefechts; ***in the ~ of passion*** ⚖ im Affekt; ***at one ~*** in 'einem Zug, auf 'einen Schlag; **7.** *sport* a) (Einzel)Lauf *m*, b) *a.* ***preliminary ~*** Vorlauf *m*, c) 'Durchgang *m*, Runde *f*; **8.** *zo.* Brunst *f*, *bsd.* a) Läufigkeit *f* (*e-r Hündin*), b) Rolligkeit *f* (*e-r Katze*), c) Rossen *n* (*e-r Stute*), d) Stieren *n* (*e-r Kuh*): ***in*** (*od.* ***on***) ***~*** brünstig; ***a bitch in ~*** e-e läufige Hündin; **9.** *metall.* a) Schmelzgang *m*, b) Charge *f*; **10.** F Druck *m*: ***turn on the ~*** Druck machen; ***turn*** (*od.* ***put***) ***the ~ on s.o.*** j-n unter Druck setzen; ***the ~ is on*** es herrscht ‚dicke Luft'; ***the ~ is off*** es hat sich wieder beruhigt; **11.** ***the ~*** *Am.* F die ‚Bullen' *pl.* (*Polizei*); **II** *v/t.* **12.** *a.* ***~ up*** erhitzen (*a. fig.*), heiß machen, *Speisen a.* aufwärmen; **13.** *Haus etc.* heizen; **14.** ***~ up*** *fig. Diskussion, Konjunktur etc.* anheizen; **III** *v/i.* **15.** sich erhitzen (*a. fig.*).

heat·a·ble ['hi:təbl] *adj.* **1.** erhitzbar; **2.** heizbar.

heat| ap·o·plex·y → ***heatstroke***; **~ bar·ri·er** *s.* ✈ Hitzemauer *f*, -schwelle *f*.

heat·ed ['hi:tɪd] *adj.* □ erhitzt: a) heiß geworden, b) *fig.* erhitzt *od.* erregt (***with*** von), hitzig: ***~ debate***.

heat·er ['hi:tə] *s.* **1.** Heizgerät *n*, -körper *m*, (Heiz)Ofen *m*; **2.** ⚡ Heizfaden *m*; **3.** (Plätt)Bolzen *m*; **4.** *sl.* ‚Ka'none' *f*, ‚Ballermann' *m* (*Pistole etc.*); **~ plug** *s. mot. Brit.* Glühkerze *f*.

heath [hi:θ] *s.* **1.** *bsd. Brit.* Heide(land *n*) *f*; **2.** ♀ a) Erika *f*, b) Heidekraut *n*; **'~-bell** *s.* ♀ Heide(blüte) *f*.

hea·then ['hi:ðn] **I** *s.* **1.** Heide *m*, Heidin *f*; **2.** *fig.* Bar'bar *m*; **II** *adj.* **3.** heidnisch, Heiden...; **4.** bar'barisch, unzivilisiert; **'hea·then·dom** [-dəm] *s.* **1.** Heidentum *n*; **2.** *die* Heiden *pl.*; **'hea·then·ish** [-ðənɪʃ] → ***heathen*** 3 u. 4; **'hea·then·ism** [-ðənɪzəm] *s.* **1.** Heidentum *n*; **2.** Barba'rei *f*.

heath·er ['heðə] → ***heath*** 2; **'~-bell** *s.* ♀ Glockenheide *f*; **'~-ˌmix·ture** *s.* gesprenkelter Wollstoff.

heat·ing ['hi:tɪŋ] **I** *s.* **1.** Heizung *f*; **2.** ⚙ a) Beheizung *f*, b) Heißwerden *n*, -laufen *n*; **3.** *phys.* Erwärmung *f*; **4.** Erhitzung *f* (*a. fig.*); **II** *adj.* **5.** heizend, *phys.* erwärmend; **6.** Heiz...: ***~ battery*** (***costs***, ***oil***, *etc.*); ***~ system*** Heizung *f*; **~ jack·et** *s.* ⚙ Heizmantel *m*; **~ pad** *s.* Heizkissen *n*; **~ sur·face** *s.* ⚙ Heizfläche *f*.

heat| in·su·la·tion *s.* ⚙ Wärmedämmung *f*; **'~·proof** *adj.* hitzebeständig; **~ pro·stra·tion** *s.* ⚕ Hitzschlag *m*; **~ pump** *s.* ⚙ Wärmepumpe *f*; **~ rash** *s.* ⚕ Hitzeausschlag *m*; **'~-reˌsist·ing** → ***heatproof***; **'~-seal** *v/t. Kunststoffe* heißsiegeln; **~ shield** *s. Raumfahrt*: Hitzeschild *m*; **~ spot** *s.* ⚕ Hitzebläschen *n*; **'~·stroke** *s.* ⚕ Hitzschlag *m*; **'~-treat** *v/t.* ⚙ wärmebehandeln (*a.* ⚕); **~ u·nit** *s. phys.* Wärmeeinheit *f*; **~ wave** *s.* Hitzewelle *f*.

heave [hi:v] **I** *v/t.* (⚓ [*irr.*] *pret. u. p.p.* **hove** [həʊv]) **1.** (hoch)heben, (-)wuchten, (-)stemmen, (-)hieven: ***~ coal*** Kohlen schleppen; ***~ s.o. into a post*** *fig.* j-n auf e-n Posten ‚hieven'; **2.** hochziehen, -winden; **3.** F schmeißen, schleudern; **4.** ⚓ hieven; *den Anker* lichten: ***~ the lead*** (***log***) loten (loggen); ***~ to*** beidrehen; **5.** ausstoßen: ***~ a sigh***; **6.** F ‚(aus)kotzen', erbrechen; **7.** aufschwellen, dehnen; **8.** heben u. senken; **II** *v/i.* (⚓ [*irr.*] *pret. u. p.p.* **hove** [həʊv]) **9.** sich heben u. senken, wogen (*a. Busen*): ***~ and set*** ⚓ stampfen (*Schiff*); **10.** keuchen; **11.** F a) ‚kotzen', sich über'geben, b) würgen, Brechreiz haben: ***his stomach ~d*** ihm hob sich der Magen; **12.** ⚓ a) hieven, ziehen (***at*** an *dat.*): ***~ ho!*** holt auf!, *allg.* hau ruck!, b) treiben: ***~ in***(***to***) ***sight*** in Sicht kommen, *fig. humor.* ‚aufkreuzen'; ***~ to*** beidrehen; **III** *s.* **13.** Heben *n*, Hub *m*, (mächtiger) Ruck; **14.** Hochziehen *n*, -winden *n*; **15.** Wurf *m*; **16.** *Ringen*: Hebegriff *m*; **17.** Wogen *n*: ***~ of the sea*** ⚓ Seegang *m*; **18.** *geol.* Verwerfung *f*; **19.** *pl. sg. konstr. vet.* Dämpfigkeit *f*; **ˌ~-'ho** [-'həʊ] *s.*: ***give s.o. the*** (***old***) ***~*** F a) j-n ‚rausschmeißen', b) j-m ‚den Laufpaß geben'.

heav·en ['hevn] *s.* **1.** Himmel(reich *n*) *m*: ***go to ~*** in den Himmel kommen; ***move ~ and earth*** *fig.* Himmel u. Hölle in Bewegung setzen; ***to ~***, ***to high ~s*** F zum Himmel *stinken etc.*; ***in the seventh ~*** (***of delight***) *fig.* im siebten Himmel; **2.** *fig.* Himmel *m*, Para'dies *n*: ***a ~ on earth***; ***it was ~*** es war himmlisch; **3.** ℒ Himmel *m*, Gott *m*, Vorsehung *f*: ***the ℒs*** die himmlischen Mächte; **4.** ***by ~!***, (***good***) ***~s!*** du lieber Himmel!; ***for ~'s sake*** um Himmels willen!; ***~ forbid!*** Gott behüte!; ***thank ~!*** Gott sei Dank!; ***~ knows what ...*** weiß der Himmel, was ...; **5.** *mst pl.* Himmel *m*, Firma'ment *n*: ***the northern ~s*** der nördliche (Sternen)Himmel; **6.** Himmel *m*, Klima *n*, Zone *f*.

heav·en·ly ['hevnlɪ] *adj.* himmlisch: a) Himmels...: ***~ body*** Himmelskörper *m*, b) göttlich, 'überirdisch: ***~ hosts*** himmlische Heerscharen, c) F himmlisch, wunderbar.

'heav·en|-sent *adj.* (wie) vom Himmel gesandt: ***it was a ~ opportunity*** es kam wie gerufen; **'~·ward** [-wəd] **I** *adv.* himmelwärts; **II** *adj.* gen Himmel gerichtet; **'~·wards** [-wədz] → ***heavenward*** I.

ˌheav·i·er-than-'air [ˌhevɪə-] *adj.* schwerer als Luft (*Flugzeug*).

heav·i·ly ['hevɪlɪ] *adv.* **1.** schwer (*etc.* → ***heavy***): ***suffer ~*** schwere (finanzielle) Verluste erleiden; **2.** mit schwerer Stimme; **'heav·i·ness** [-ɪnɪs] *s.* **1.** Schwere *f* (*a. fig.*); **2.** Gewicht *n*, Last *f*; **3.** Massigkeit *f*; **4.** Bedrückung *f*, Schwermut *f*; **5.** Schwerfälligkeit *f*; **6.** Schläfrigkeit *f*; **7.** Langweiligkeit *f*.

heav·y ['hevɪ] **I** *adj.* □ → ***heavily***; **1.** *allg.* schwer (*a.* ⚗, *phys.*): ***~ load***; ***~ steps***; ***~ benzene*** Schwerbenzin *n*; ***~ industry*** Schwerindustrie *f*; ***with a ~ heart*** schweren Herzens; **2.** ⚔ schwer: ***~ artillery*** (***bomber***, ***cruiser***); ***bring up one's*** (*od.* ***the***) ***~ guns*** *fig.* F schweres Geschütz auffahren; **3.** schwer: a) heftig, stark: ***~ fall*** schwerer Sturz; ***~ losses*** schwere Verluste; ***~ rain*** starker Regen; ***~ traffic*** starker Verkehr, *a.* schwere Fahrzeuge *pl.*, b) massig: ***~ body***, c) wuchtig: ***~ blow***, d) hart: ***~ fine*** hohe Geldstrafe; **4.** groß, beträchtlich: ***~ buyer*** Großabnehmer *m*; ***~ orders*** große Aufträge; **5.** schwer, stark, 'übermäßig: ***~ drinker*** (***eater***) starker Trinker (Esser); **6.** schwer: a) stark, 'hochproˌzentig: ***~ beer*** Starkbier *n*, b) stark, betäubend: ***~ perfume***, c) schwerverdaulich: ***~ food***; **7.** drückend, lastend: ***a ~ silence***; **8.** *meteor.* a) schwer: ***~ clouds***, b) finster, trüb: ***~ sky***, c) drückend: ***~ air***; **9.** schwer: a) schwierig, mühsam: ***a ~ task***, b) schwer verständlich: ***a ~ book***; **10.** (***with***) a) (schwer)beladen (mit), b) *fig.* über'laden (mit), voll (von); **11.** schwerfällig: ***~ style***; **12.** langweilig, stumpfsinnig; **13.** begriffsstutzig (*Person*); **14.** schläfrig, benommen (***with*** von): ***~ with sleep*** schlaftrunken; **15.** ernst, düster; **16.** *thea. etc.* würdevoll *od.* (ge)streng: ***a ~ husband***; **17.** ✝ flau, schleppend; **18.** unwegsam, lehmig: ***~ road***; **19.** grob: ***~ features***; **20.** a) *a.* ***~ with child*** (hoch)schwanger, b) *a.* ***~ with young*** *zo.* trächtig; **21.** *typ.* fett(gedruckt); **II** *adv.* **22.** schwer (*etc.*): ***hang ~*** dahinschleichen (*Zeit*); ***time was hanging ~ on my hands*** die Zeit wurde mir lang; ***lie ~ on s.o.*** schwer auf j-m lasten; **III** *s.* **23.** *thea. etc.* a) Schurke *m*, b) würdiger älterer Herr; **24.** *sport* F Schwergewichtler *m*; **25.** *pl. Am.* F warme 'Unterwäsche *f*; **26.** *Am.* F ‚schwerer Junge' (*Verbrecher*); **27.** ⚔ schwere Artille'rie; **ˌ~-'armed** *adj.* ⚔ schwerbewaffnet; **~ chem·i·cals** *s. pl.* 'Schwercheмiˌkalien *pl.*; **~ con·crete** *s.* 'Schwerbeˌton *m*; **~ cur·rent** *s.* ⚡ Starkstrom *m*; **ˌ~-'du·ty** *adj.* **1.** ⚙ Hochleistungs...; **2.** strapazierfähig; **ˌ~-'hand·ed** *adj.* **1.** *a. fig.* plump, unbeholfen; **2.** drückend; **ˌ~-'heart·ed** *adj.* niedergeschlagen, bedrückt; **~ hy·dro·gen** *s.* ⚗ schwerer Wasserstoff; **~ met·al** *s.* 'Schwermeˌtall *n*; **~ oil** *s.* ⚙ Schweröl *n*; **~ plate** *s.* Grobblech *n*; **~ spar** *s. min.* Schwerspat *m*; **~ type** *s. typ.* Fettdruck *m*; **~ wa·ter** *s.* ⚗ schweres Wasser; **'~·weight** **I** *s.* **1.** *sport* Schwergewicht (-ler *m*) *n*; **2.** ‚Schwergewicht' *n* (*Person od. Sache*); **3.** F Promi'nente(r) *m*, ‚großes Tier'; **II** *adj.* **4.** *sport* Schwergewichts...; **5.** schwer (*a. fig.*).

heb·dom·a·dal [heb'dɒmədl] *adj.* wöchentlich: ℒ ***Council*** *wöchentlich zs.-tretender Rat der Universität Oxford*.

He·bra·ic [hi:'breɪɪk] *adj.* (□ ***~ally***) he'bräisch; **He·bra·ism** ['hi:breɪɪzəm] *s.* **1.** *ling.* Hebra'ismus *m*; **2.** *das* Jüdische; **He·bra·ist** ['hi:breɪɪst] *s.* Hebra'ist(in).

He·brew ['hi:bru:] **I** *s.* **1.** He'bräer(in), Jude *m*, Jüdin *f*; **2.** *ling.* He'bräisch *n*; **3.** F Kauderwelsch *n*; **4.** *pl. sg. konstr. bibl.* (Brief *m* an die) He'bräer *pl.*; **II** *adj.* **5.** he'bräisch.

Heb·ri·de·an [ˌhebrɪ'di:ən] **I** *adj.* he'bridisch; **II** *s.* Bewohner(in) der He'briden.

hec·a·tomb ['hekətu:m] *s.* Heka'tombe *f* (*bsd. fig. gewaltige Menschenverluste*).

heck [hek] *s.* F Hölle *f*: ***a ~ of a row*** ein Höllenlärm; ***what the ~?*** was zum Teufel?; → *a.* ***hell*** 2.

heck·le ['hekl] *v/t.* **1.** *Flachs* hecheln; **2.** a) *j-n* ‚piesacken', b) *e-m Redner* durch Zwischenfragen zusetzen, ‚in die Zange nehmen'; **'heck·ler** [-lə] *s.* Zwischenrufer *m*.

hec·tare ['hektɑ:] *s.* Hektar *n*, *m*.

hec·tic ['hektɪk] *adj.* **1.** hektisch, schwindsüchtig: ***~ fever*** Schwindsucht *f*; ***~ flush*** hektische Röte; **2.** F fieberhaft, aufgeregt, hektisch: ***have a ~ time*** keinen Augenblick Ruhe haben.

hec·to·gram(me) ['hektəʊgræm] *s.* Hekto'gramm *n*; **'hec·to·graph** [-grɑ:f] **I** *s.* Hekto'graph *m*; **II** *v/t.* hektographieren; **'hec·toˌli·ter** *Am.*, **'hec·toˌli·tre** *Brit.* [-ˌli:tə] *s.* Hektoliter *m*, *n*.

hec·tor ['hektə] **I** *s.* Ty'rann *m*; **II** *v/t.* tyrannisieren, schikanieren: ***~ about*** (*od.* ***around***) *j-n* herumkommandieren; einhacken auf (*acc.*); **III** *v/i.* her'umkommandieren.

he'd [hi:d] F *für* a) ***he would***, b) ***he had***.

hedge [hedʒ] **I** *s.* **1.** Hecke *f*, *bsd.* Heckenzaun *m*; **2.** *fig.* Kette *f*, Absperrung *f*: ***a ~ of police***; **3.** *fig.* (Ab)Sicherung *f* (***against*** gegen); **4.** ✝ Hedge-, Deckungsgeschäft *n*; **II** *adj.* **5.** *fig.* drittrangig, schlecht; **III** *v/t.* **6.** *a.* **~ in** (*od.* **round**) a) mit e-r Hecke um'geben, einzäunen, b) *a.* **~ about** (*od.* **around**) *fig. et.* behindern, c) *fig. j-n* einengen: **~ off** *a. fig.* abgrenzen (**against** gegen); **7.** a) (ab)sichern (**against** gegen), b) sich gegen den Verlust *e-r Wette etc.* sichern: **~ a bet**; **~ one's bets** *fig.* auf Nummer Sicher gehen; **IV** *v/i.* **8.** *fig.* ausweichen, sich nicht festlegen (wollen), sich winden, ‚kneifen'; **9.** sich vorsichtig äußern; **10.** sich (ab)sichern (**against** gegen); **~ cut·ter** *s.* Heckenschere *f*; **~·hog** ['hedʒhɒg] *s.* **1.** *zo.* a) Igel *m*, b) *Am.* Stachelschwein *n*; **2.** ⚘ stachelige Samenkapsel; **3.** ⚔ a) Igelstellung *f*, b) Drahtigel *m*, c) ⚓ Wasserbombenwerfer *m*; '**~·hop** *v/i.* ✈ dicht über dem Boden fliegen; '**~ˌhop·per** *s.* ✈ *sl.* Tiefflieger *m*; **~ law·yer** *s.* 'Winkeladvoˌkat *m.*

hedg·er ['hedʒə] *s.* **1.** Heckengärtner *m*; **2.** *j-d, der sich nicht festlegen will.*

'**hedge|·row** *s.* Hecke *f*; **~ school** *s. Brit.* Klippschule *f*; **~ shears** *s. pl. a.* **pair of ~** Heckenschere *f*.

he·don·ic [hiː'dɒnɪk] *adj.* hedo'nistisch; **he·don·ism** ['hiːdəʊnɪzəm] *s. phls.* Hedo'nismus *m*; **he·don·ist** ['hiːdəʊnɪst] *s.* Hedo'nist *m*; **he·do·nis·tic** [ˌhiːdə'nɪstɪk] *adj.* hedo'nistisch.

hee·bie-jee·bies [ˌhiːbɪ'dʒiːbɪz] *s. pl.* F: **it gives me the ~, I get the ~** dabei wird's mir ganz ‚anders', da krieg' ich ‚Zustände'.

heed [hiːd] **I** *v/t.* beachten, achtgeben auf (*acc.*); **II** *v/i.* achtgeben; **III** *s.* Beachtung *f*: **give** (*od.* **pay**) **~ to, take ~ of** → I; **take ~** → II; '**heed·ful** [-fʊl] *adj.* □ achtsam: **be ~ of** → **heed** I; '**heed·less** [-lɪs] *adj.* □ achtlos, unachtsam: **be ~ of** keine Beachtung schenken (*dat.*); '**heed·less·ness** [-lɪsnɪs] *s.* Achtlosigkeit *f*, Unachtsamkeit *f*.

hee·haw [ˌhiː'hɔː] **I** *s.* **1.** 'I'ah *n* (*Eselsschrei*); **2.** *fig.* wieherndes Gelächter; **II** *v/i.* **3.** 'i'ahen; **4.** *fig.* wiehern(d lachen).

heel¹ [hiːl] **I** *v/t.* **1.** Absätze machen auf (*acc.*); **2.** Fersen anstricken an (*acc.*); **3.** *Fußball: den Ball* mit dem Absatz kicken; **II** *s.* **4.** Ferse *f*: **~ of the hand** *Am.* Handballen *m*; **5.** Absatz *m*, Hakken *m* (*vom Schuh*); **6.** Ferse *f* (*Strumpf, Golfschläger*); **7.** Fuß *m*, Ende *n*, Rest *m*, *bsd.* (Brot)Kanten *m*; **8.** vorspringender Teil, Sporn *m*; **9.** *Am. sl.* ‚Scheißkerl' *m*;

Besondere Redewendungen:

~ of Achilles Achillesferse *f*; **at** (*od.* **on**) **s.o.'s ~s** j-m auf den Fersen, dicht hinter j-m; **on the ~s of s.th.** *fig.* unmittelbar auf et. folgend, gleich nach et.; **down at ~** a) mit schiefen Absätzen, b) *a.* **out at ~s** *fig.* heruntergekommen (*Person, Hotel etc.*); abgerissen, schäbig; **under the ~ of** *fig.* unter *j-s* Knute; **bring to ~** *j-n* gefügig *od.* ‚kirre' machen; **come to ~** a) bei Fuß gehen (*Hund*), b) gefügig werden, ‚spuren'; **cool** (*od.* **kick**) **one's ~s** ungeduldig warten; **dig** (*od.* **stick**) **one's ~s in** F ‚sich auf die Hinterbeine stellen'; **drag one's ~s** *fig.* sich Zeit lassen; **kick up one's ~s** F ‚auf den Putz hauen'; **lay s.o. by the ~s** j-n zur Strecke bringen, j-n dingfest machen; **show a clean pair of ~s, take to one's ~s** Fersengeld geben, die Beine in die Hand nehmen; **tread on s.o.'s ~s** j-m auf die Hacken treten; **turn on one's ~s** (auf dem Absatz) kehrtmachen.

heel² [hiːl] *v/t. u. v/i. a.* **~ over** (sich) auf die Seite legen (*Schiff*), krängen.

ˌ**heel|-and-'toe walk·ing** *s. sport* Gehen *n*; '**~·ball** *s.* Polierwachs *n*; **~ bone** *s. anat.* Fersenbein *n*.

heeled [hiːld] *adj.* **1.** mit e-r Ferse *od.* e-m Absatz (versehen); **2.** → **well-heeled**; '**heel·er** [-lə] *s. pol. Am.* Handlanger *m*, ‚La'kai' *m*.

'**heel·tap** *s.* **1.** Absatzfleck *m*; **2.** letzter Rest, Neige *f* (*im Glas*): **no ~s!** ex!

heft [heft] *v/t.* **1.** hochheben; **2.** in der Hand wiegen; '**heft·y** [-tɪ] *adj.* F **1.** schwer; **2.** kräftig, stämmig; **3.** ‚mächtig', ‚saftig', gewaltig: **~ blow** (**prices**).

He·ge·li·an [heɪ'giːljən] *s. phls.* Hegeli'aner *m*.

he·gem·o·ny [hɪ'gemənɪ] *s. pol.* Hegemo'nie *f*.

heif·er ['hefə] *s.* Färse *f*, junge Kuh.

heigh [heɪ] *int.* hei!; he(da)!; ˌ**~-'ho** [-'həʊ] *int.* ach jeh!; oh!

height [haɪt] *s.* **1.** Höhe *f* (*a. ast.*): **10 feet in ~** 10 Fuß hoch; **~ of fall** Fallhöhe *f*; **2.** (Körper)Größe *f*: **what is your ~?** wie groß sind Sie?; **3.** Anhöhe *f*; Erhebung *f*; **4.** *fig.* Höhe(punkt *m*) *f*, Gipfel *m*: **at its ~** auf s-m (ihrem) *od.* dem Höhepunkt; **at the ~ of summer** (**of the season**) im Hochsommer (in der Hochsaison); **the ~ of folly** der Gipfel der Torheit; **dressed in the ~ of fashion** nach der neuesten Mode gekleidet; '**height·en** [-tn] **I** *v/t.* **1.** erhöhen (*a. fig.*); **2.** *fig.* vergrößern, -stärken, steigern, heben, vertiefen; **3.** her'vorheben; **II** *v/i.* **4.** wachsen, (an)steigen.

height| find·er, ~ ga(u)ge *s.* ✈ Höhenmesser *m*.

hei·nous ['heɪnəs] *adj.* □ ab'scheulich, gräßlich; '**hei·nous·ness** [-nɪs] *s.* Ab'scheulichkeit *f*.

heir [eə] *s.* **1.** ⚖ *u. fig.* Erbe *m* (**to** *od.* **of s.o.** j-s): **~ to the throne** Thronfolger *m*; **~-at-law, ~ general, ~ apparent** gesetzlicher Erbe; **~ presumptive** mutmaßlicher Erbe; **~ of the body** leiblicher Erbe; **heir·dom** ['eədəm] → **heirship**; **heir·ess** ['eərɪs] *s.* (*bsd.* reiche) Erbin; **heir·loom** ['eəluːm] *s.* (Fa'milien)Erbstück *n*; **heir·ship** ['eəʃɪp] *s.* **1.** Erbrecht *n*; **2.** Erbschaft *f*, Erbe *n*.

heist [haɪst] *Am. sl.* **I** *s.* a) ‚Ding' *n* (*Raubüberfall od. Diebstahl*), b) Beute *f*; **II** *v/t.* über'fallen; ‚klauen'; erbeuten.

held [held] *pret. u. p.p. von* **hold²**.

he·li·an·thus [ˌhiːlɪ'ænθəs] *s.* ⚘ Sonnenblume *f*.

hel·i·borne ['helɪbɔːn] *adj.* im Hubschrauber befördert.

hel·i·bus ['helɪbʌs] *s.* ✈ Hubschrauber *m* für Per'sonenbeförderung, Lufttaxi *n*.

hel·i·cal ['helɪkl] *adj.* □ spi'ralen-, schrauben-, schneckenförmig: **~ gear** ⚙ Schrägstirnrad *n*; **~ spring** Schraubenfeder *f*; **~ staircase** Wendeltreppe *f*.

hel·i·ces ['helɪsiːz] *pl. von* **helix**.

hel·i·cop·ter ['helɪkɒptə] ✈ **I** *s.* Hubschrauber *m*, Heli'kopter *m*: **~ gunship** Kampfhubschrauber; **II** *v/i. u. v/t.* mit dem Hubschrauber fliegen *od.* befördern.

helio- [hiːlɪəʊ-] *in Zssgn* Sonnen...

he·li·o·cen·tric [ˌhiːlɪəʊ'sentrɪk] *adj. ast.* helio'zentrisch; **he·li·o·chro·my** ['hiːlɪəʊˌkrəʊmɪ] *s.* 'Farbfotograˌfie *f*; **he·li·o·gram** ['hiːlɪəʊgræm] *s.* Helio'gramm *n*; **he·li·o·graph** ['hiːlɪəʊgrɑːf] **I** *s.* Helio'graph *m*; **II** *v/t.* heliographieren; **he·li·o·gra·vure** [ˌhiːlɪəʊgrə'vjʊə] *s. typ.* Heliogra'vüre *f*.

he·li·o·trope ['heljətrəʊp] *s.* ⚘, *min.* Helio'trop *n*.

he·li·o·type ['hiːlɪətaɪp] *s. typ.* Lichtdruck *m*.

hel·i·pad ['helɪpæd], '**hel·i·port** [-pɔːt] *s.* Heli'port *m*, Hubschrauberlandeplatz *m*.

he·li·um ['hiːljəm] *s.* ⚗ Helium *n*.

he·lix ['hiːlɪks] *pl.* **hel·i·ces** ['helɪsiːz] *s.* **1.** Spi'rale *f*; **2.** ⚒ Schneckenlinie *f*; **3.** *anat.* Helix *f*, Ohrleiste *f*; **4.** ⚠ Schnekke *f*; **5.** *zo.* Helix *f* (*Schnecke*); **6.** ⚗ Helix *f* (*Molekülstruktur*).

hell [hel] **I** *s.* **1.** Hölle *f* (*a. fig.*): **it was ~** es war die reinste Hölle; **catch** (*od.* **get**) **~** F ‚eins aufs Dach kriegen'; **come ~ or high water** F (ganz) egal, was passiert, unter allen Umständen; **give s.o. ~** F j-m ‚die Hölle heiß machen'; **~ for leather** F was das Zeug hält, wie verrückt; **there will be ~ to pay** F das werden wir schwer büßen müssen; **raise ~** F ‚e-n Mordskrach schlagen'; **suffer ~** (**on earth**) die Hölle auf Erden haben; **2.** F (*verstärkend*) Hölle *f*, Teufel *m*: **a ~ of a noise** ein Höllenlärm; **be in a ~ of a temper** e-e ‚Mordswut' *od.* e-e ‚Stinklaune' haben; **a** (*od.* **one**) **~ of a** (**good**) **car** ein ‚verdammt' guter Wagen; **a ~ of a guy** ein prima Kerl; **go to ~!** ‚scher dich zum Teufel'!, *a.* ‚du kannst mich mal!'; **get the ~ out of here!** mach, daß du rauskommst!; **like ~** wie verrückt (*arbeiten etc.*); **like** (*od.* **the**) **~ you did!** ‚e-n Dreck' hast du (getan)!; **what the ~ ...?** was zum Teufel ...?; **what the ~!** ach, was!; **~'s bells** → 6; **3.** F Spaß *m*: **for the ~ of it** aus Spaß an der Freud; **the ~ of it is that ...** das Komische *od.* Tolle daran ist, daß; **4.** Spielhölle *f*; **5.** *typ.* De'fektenkasten *m*; **II** *int.* **6.** F a) *Brit. sl. a.* **bloody ~!** verdammt!, b) (*überrascht*) Teufel, Teufel!, Mann!; **~, I didn't know** (**that**)**!** Mann, das hab' ich nicht gewußt!

he'll [hiːl] F *für* **he will**.

'**hell|ˌbend·er** *s.* **1.** *zo.* Schlammteufel *m*; **2.** *Am.* F ‚wilder Bursche'; ˌ**~'bent** *adj.* F **1. be ~ on** (**doing**) **s.th.** ganz versessen sein auf et. (darauf, et. zu tun); **2.** ‚verrückt', wild, leichtsinnig; '**~·broth** *s.* Hexen-, Zaubertrank *m*; '**~·cat** *s.* (wilde) Hexe, Xan'thippe *f*.

hel·le·bore ['helɪbɔː] *s.* ⚘ Nieswurz *f*.

Hel·lene ['heliːn] *s.* Hel'lene *m*, Grieche *m*; **Hel·len·ic** [he'liːnɪk] *adj.* hel'lenisch, griechisch; **Hel·len·ism** ['helɪnɪzəm] *s.* Helle'nismus *m*, Griechentum *n*; **Hel·len·ist** ['helɪnɪst] *s.* Helle'nist *m*; **Hel·len·is·tic** [ˌhelɪ'nɪstɪk] *adj.* helle'nistisch; **Hel·len·ize** ['helɪnaɪz] *v/t. u. v/i.* (sich) hellenisieren.

ˌ**hell|'fire** *s.* **1.** Höllenfeuer *n*; **2.** *fig.* Höllenqualen *pl.*; '**~·hound** *s.* **1.** Höllenhund *m*; **2.** *fig.* Teufel *m*.

hel·lion ['heljən] *s.* F Range *f*, *m*, Bengel

m.

hell·ish ['helɪʃ] *adj.* □ **1.** höllisch (*a. fig.* F); **2.** F ‚verteufelt', ‚scheußlich'.

hel·lo [hə'ləʊ] **I** *int.* **1.** hal'lo!, *überrascht*: *a.* na'nu!; **II** *pl.* **-los** *s.* **2.** Hal'lo *n*; **3.** Gruß *m*: ***say ~*** (***to s.o.***) (j-m) guten Tag sagen; **III** *v/i.* **4.** hal'lo rufen.

hell·uv·a ['heləvə] *adj. u. adv.* F ‚mordsmäßig', ‚toll': ***a ~ noise*** ein Höllenlärm; ***a ~ guy*** a) ein prima Kerl, b) ein toller Kerl.

helm¹ [helm] *s.* **1.** ⚓ a) Ruder *n*, Steuer *n*, b) Ruderpinne *f*: ***the ship answers the ~*** das Schiff gehorcht dem Ruder; **2.** *fig.* Ruder *n*, Führung *f*: ***~ of State*** Staatsruder; ***at the ~*** am Ruder *od.* an der Macht; ***take the ~*** das Ruder übernehmen.

helm² [helm] *s. obs.* Helm *m*; **helmed** [-md] *adj. obs.* behelmt.

hel·met ['helmɪt] *s.* **1.** ⚔ Helm *m*; **2.** (Schutz-, Sturz-, Tropen-, Taucher-) Helm *m*; **3.** ⚘ Kelch *m*; '**hel·met·ed** [-tɪd] *adj.* behelmt.

helms·man ['helmzmən] *s.* [*irr.*] ⚓ Steuermann *m* (*a. fig.*).

Hel·ot ['helət] *s. hist.* He'lot(e) *m*, *fig.* (*mst* ♀) *a.* Sklave *m*; '**hel·ot·ry** [-trɪ] *s.* **1.** He'lotentum *n*; **2.** *coll.* He'loten *pl.*

help [help] **I** *s.* **1.** Hilfe *f*, Beistand *m*, Mit-, Beihilfe *f*: ***by*** (*od.* ***with***) ***the ~ of*** mit Hilfe von; ***he came to my ~*** er kam mir zu Hilfe; ***it*** (***she***) ***is a great ~*** es (sie) ist e-e große Hilfe; ***can I be of any ~*** (***to you***)***?*** kann ich Ihnen (irgendwie) helfen *od.* behilflich sein?; **2.** Abhilfe *f*: ***there is no ~ for it*** da kann man nichts machen, es läßt sich nicht ändern; **3.** Hilfsmittel *n*; **4.** a) Gehilfe *m*, Gehilfin *f*, (*bsd.* Haus)Angestellte(r *m*) *f*, (*bsd.* Land)Arbeiter(in): ***domestic ~*** Hausgehilfin, b) *coll.* ('Dienst)Perso͵nal *n*, (Hilfs)Kräfte *pl.*; **II** *v/t.* **5.** *j-m* helfen *od.* beistehen *od.* behilflich sein, *j-n* unter'stützen (***in*** *od.* ***with s.th.*** bei et.): ***can I ~ you?*** a) kann ich Ihnen behilflich sein?, b) werden Sie schon bedient?; ***so ~ me*** (***I did***, *etc.*)***!*** Ehrenwort!; → ***god*** 2; **6.** fördern, beitragen zu; **7.** lindern, helfen *od.* Abhilfe schaffen bei; **8.** ***~ s.o. to s.th.*** a) j-m zu et. verhelfen, b) (*bsd. bei Tisch*) j-m et. reichen *od.* geben; ***~ o.s.*** sich bedienen, zugreifen; ***~ o.s. to*** a) sich bedienen mit, sich *et.* nehmen, b) sich *et.* aneignen *od.* nehmen (*a. iro. stehlen*); **9.** *mit* ***can***: abhelfen (*dat.*), *et.* verhindern, vermeiden, ändern: ***I can't ~ it*** a) ich kann's nicht ändern, b) ich kann nichts dafür; ***it can't be ~ed*** da kann man nichts machen, es läßt sich nicht ändern; (***not***) ***if I can ~ it*** (nicht,) wenn ich es vermeiden kann; ***how could I ~ it?*** a) was konnte ich dagegen tun?, b) was konnte ich dafür?; ***I can't ~ it*** a) ich kann es nicht ändern, b) ich kann nichts dafür; ***she can't ~ her freckles*** für ihre Sommersprossen kann sie nichts; ***don't be late if you can ~ it*** komme möglichst nicht zu spät!; ***I could not ~ laughing*** ich mußte einfach lachen; ***I can't ~ feeling*** ich werde das Gefühl nicht los; ***I can't ~ myself*** ich kann nicht anders; **III** *v/i.* **10.** helfen: ***every little ~s*** jede Kleinigkeit hilft; **11.** ***don't stay longer than you can ~!*** bleib nicht länger als nötig!;

Zssgn mit adv.:

help| down *v/t.* **1.** *j-m* her'unter-, hin'unterhelfen; **2.** *fig.* zum 'Untergang (*gen.*) beitragen; **~ in** *v/t.* *j-m* hin'einhelfen; **~ off** *v/t.* **1.** → ***help on*** 1; **2.** ***help s.o. off with his coat*** j-m aus dem Mantel helfen; **~ on** *v/t.* **1.** weiter-, forthelfen (*dat.*); **2.** ***help s.o. on with his coat*** j-m in den Mantel helfen; **~ out** **I** *v/t.* **1.** *j-m* her'aus-, hin'aushelfen (***of*** aus); **2.** *fig.* *j-m* aus der Not helfen; **3.** *fig.* *j-m* aushelfen, *j-n* unter'stützen; **II** *v/i.* **4.** aushelfen (***with*** bei, mit); **5.** helfen, nützlich sein; **~ through** *v/t.* *j-m* (hin)'durch-, hin'weghelfen; **~ up** *v/t.* *j-m* her'auf-, hin'aufhelfen.

help·er ['helpə] *s.* **1.** Helfer(in); **2.** Gehilfe *m*, Gehilfin *f*; → ***help*** 4; **help·ful** ['helpfʊl] *adj.* □ **1.** hilfsbereit, behilflich (***to*** *dat.*); **2.** hilfreich, nützlich (***to*** *dat.*); **help·ful·ness** ['helpfʊlnɪs] *s.* **1.** Hilfsbereitschaft *f*; **2.** Nützlichkeit *f*; **help·ing** ['helpɪŋ] **I** *adj.* helfend, hilfreich: ***lend*** (***s.o.***) ***a ~ hand*** (j-m) helfen *od.* behilflich sein; **II** *s.* Porti'on *f* (*e-r Speise*): ***have*** (*od.* ***take***) ***a second ~*** sich noch mal (davon) nehmen; **help·less** ['helplɪs] *adj.* □ *allg.* hilflos: ***be ~ with laughter*** sich totlachen; **help·less·ness** ['helplɪsnɪs] *s.* Hilflosigkeit *f.*

'**help·mate**, '**help·meet** *s. obs.* Gehilfe *m*, Gehilfin *f*; (Ehe)Gefährte *m*, (Ehe-) Gefährtin *f*, Gattin *f.*

hel·ter-skel·ter [͵heltə'skeltə] **I** *adv.* Hals über Kopf, in wilder Hast; **II** *adj.* hastig, über'stürzt; **III** *s.* Durchein'ander *n*, wilde Hast.

helve [helv] *s.* Griff *m*, Stiel *m*: ***throw the ~ after the hatchet*** *fig.* das Kind mit dem Bade ausschütten.

Hel·ve·tian [hel'vi:ʃjən] **I** *adj.* hel'vetisch, schweizerisch; **II** *s.* Hel'vetier (-in), Schweizer(in).

hem¹ [hem] **I** *s.* **1.** (Kleider-, Rock- *etc.*) Saum *m*; **2.** Rand *m*; **3.** Einfassung *f*; **II** *v/t.* **4.** *Kleid etc.* säumen; **5.** ***~ in***, ***~ about***, ***~ around*** um'randen, einfassen; **6.** ***~ in*** a) ⚔ einschließen, b) *fig.* einengen.

hem² [hm] **I** *int.* hm!, hem!; **II** *s.* H(e)m *n*, Räuspern *n*; **III** *v/i.* ‚hm' machen, sich räuspern; stocken (*im Reden*): ***~ and haw*** herumstottern, -drucksen.

he·mal *etc.* → ***haemal*** *etc.*

'**he-man** *s.* [*irr.*] F ‚He-man' *m*, ‚richtiger' Mann, sehr männlicher Typ.

he·mat·ic *etc.* → ***haematic*** *etc.*

hem·i·ple·gi·a [͵hemɪ'pli:dʒɪə] *s.* ⚕ einseitige Lähmung, Hemiple'gie *f.*

hem·i·sphere ['hemɪ͵sfɪə] *s. bsd. geogr.* Halbkugel *f*, Hemi'sphäre *f* (*a. anat. des Großhirns*); **hem·i·spher·i·cal** [͵hemɪ'sferɪkl], *a.* **hem·i·spher·ic** [͵hemɪ'sferɪk] *adj.* hemi'sphärisch, halbkugelig.

'**hem·line** *s.* (Kleider)Saum *m*: ***~s are going up again*** die Kleider werden wieder kürzer.

hem·lock ['hemlɒk] *s.* **1.** ⚘ Schierling *m*; **2.** *fig.* Schierlings-, Giftbecher *m*; **3.** *a.* ***~ fir***, ***~ spruce*** Hemlock-, Schierlingstanne *f.*

he·mo·glo·bin, **he·mo·phil·i·a**, **hem·or·rhage**, **hem·or·rhoids** *etc.* → ***haemo...***

hemp [hemp] *s.* **1.** ⚘ Hanf *m*; **2.** Hanf (-faser *f*) *m*; **3.** 'Hanfnar͵kotikum *n*, *bsd.* Haschisch *n*; '**hemp·en** [-pən] *adj.* hanfen, Hanf...

'**hem-stitch** **I** *s.* Hohlsaum(stich) *m*; **II** *v/t.* mit Hohlsaum nähen.

hen [hen] *s.* **1.** *orn.* Henne *f*, Huhn *n*: ***~'s egg*** Hühnerei *n*; **2.** Weibchen *n* (*von Vögeln*, *a. Krebs u. Hummer*); **3.** F a) (aufgeregte) ‚Wachtel', b) Klatschbase *f*; '**~·bane** *s.* ⚘, *pharm.* 'Bilsenkraut(ex͵trakt *m*) *n.*

hence [hens] *adv.* **1.** *a.* ***from ~*** (*räumlich*) von hier, von hinnen, fort: ***~ with it!*** weg damit!; ***go ~*** von hinnen gehen (*sterben*); **2.** *zeitlich*: von jetzt an, binnen: ***a week ~*** in *od.* nach einer Woche; **3.** folglich, daher, deshalb; **4.** hieraus, daraus: ***~ it follows that*** daraus folgt, daß; ͵**~'forth**, ͵**~'for·ward(s)** *adv.* von nun an, fort'an, künftig.

hench·man ['hentʃmən] *s.* [*irr.*] *bsd. pol.* a) Gefolgsmann *m*, b) *contp.* Handlanger *m*, *j-s* ‚Krea'tur' *f.*

'**hen|·coop** *s.* Hühnerstall *m*; **~ har·ri·er** *s. orn.* Kornweihe *f*; **~ hawk** *s. orn. Am.* Hühnerbussard *m*; ͵**~-'heart·ed** *adj.* feig(e).

hen·na ['henə] *s.* **1.** ⚘ Hennastrauch *m*; **2.** Henna *f* (*Färbemittel*); '**hen·naed** [-nəd] *adj.* mit Henna gefärbt.

'**hen|-͵par·ty** *s.* F Kaffeeklatsch *m*; '**~·pecked** [-pekt] *adj.* F unter dem Pan'toffel stehend: ***~ husband*** Pantoffelheld *m*; '**~·roost** *s.* Hühnerstange *f* *od.* -stall *m.*

hen·ry ['henrɪ] *pl.* **-rys**, **-ries** *s.* ϟ, *phys.* Henry *n* (*Induktionseinheit*).

hep [hep] → ***hip⁴***.

he·pat·ic [hɪ'pætɪk] *adj.* ⚕ he'patisch, Leber...; **hep·a·ti·tis** [͵hepə'taɪtɪs] *s.* ⚕ Leberentzündung *f*, Hepa'titis *f*; **hep·a·tol·o·gist** [͵hepə'tɒlədʒɪst] *s.* ⚕ Hepato'loge *m.*

'**hep·cat** *s. sl. obs.* Jazz-, *bsd.* Swingmusiker *m* *od.* -freund *m.*

hep·ta·gon ['heptəgən] *s.* Å Siebeneck *n*, Hepta'gon *n*; **hep·tag·o·nal** [hep'tægənl] *adj.* Å siebeneckig; **hep·ta·he·dron** [͵heptə'hedrən] *pl.* **-drons** *od.* **-dra** [-drə] *s.* Å Hepta'eder *n.*

hep·tath·lete [hep'tæθli:t] *s. sport* Siebenkämpferin *f*; **hep·tath·lon** [hep'tæθlɒn] *s.* Siebenkampf *m.*

her [hɜ:; hə] **I** *pron.* **1.** a) sie (*acc. von* ***she***), b) ihr (*dat. von* ***she***); **2.** F sie (*nom.*): ***it's ~*** sie ist es; **II** *poss. adj.* **3.** ihr, ihre; **III** *refl. pron.* **4.** sich: ***she looked about ~*** sie sah um sich.

her·ald ['herəld] **I** *s.* **1.** *hist.* a) Herold *m*, b) Wappenherold *m*; **2.** *fig.* Verkünder *m*; **3.** *fig.* (Vor)Bote *m*; **II** *v/t.* **4.** verkünden, ankündigen (*a. fig.*); **5.** *a.* ***~ in*** a) einführen, b) einleiten.

he·ral·dic [he'rældɪk] *adj.* he'raldisch, Wappen...; **her·ald·ry** ['herəldrɪ] *s.* **1.** He'raldik *f*, Wappenkunde *f*; **2.** a) Wappen *n*, b) he'raldische Sym'bole *pl.*

herb [hɜ:b] *s.* ⚘ a) Kraut *n*, b) Heilkraut *n*, c) Küchenkraut *n*: ***~ tea*** Kräutertee *m*; **her·ba·ceous** [hɜ:'beɪʃəs] *adj.* ⚘ krautartig, Kraut...: ***~ border*** (Stauden)Rabatte *f*; '**herb·age** [-bɪdʒ] *s.* **1.** *coll.* Kräuter *pl.*, Gras *n*; **2.** ⚖ *Brit.* Weiderecht *n*; '**herb·al** [-bl] **I** *adj.* Kräuter..., Pflanzen...; **II** *s.* Pflanzenbuch *n*; '**herb·al·ist** [-bəlɪst] *s.* **1.** Kräuter-, Pflanzenkenner(in); **2.** Kräutersammler(in), -händler(in); **3.** Herba'list(in), Kräuterheilkundige(r *m*) *f*; **her·bar·i·um** [hɜːˈbeərɪəm] *s*. Herˈbarium *n*.

her·bi·vore [ˈhɜːbɪvɔː] *s. zo.* Pflanzenfresser *m*; **her·biv·o·rous** [hɜːˈbɪvərəs] *adj.* pflanzenfressend.

Her·cu·le·an [ˌhɜːkjʊˈliːən] *adj.* herˈkulisch (*a. fig. riesenstark*), Herkules...: ***the ~ labo(u)rs*** die Arbeiten des Herkules; ***a ~ labo(u)r*** *fig.* e-e Herkulesarbeit; **Her·cu·les** [ˈhɜːkjʊliːz] *s. myth.*, *ast. u. fig.* Herkules *m*.

herd [hɜːd] **I** *s*. **1.** Herde *f*, (*wildlebender Tiere a.*) Rudel *n*; **2.** *contp.* Herde *f*, Masse *f* (*Menschen*): ***the common*** (*od.* ***vulgar***) **~** die Masse (Mensch), die große Masse; **3.** *in Zssgn* Hirt(in); **II** *v/t.* **4.** *Vieh* hüten; **5.** (***~ together*** zs.-)treiben; **III** *v/i.* **6.** *a.* ***~ together*** a) in Herden gehen *od.* leben, b) sich zs.-drängen; **7.** sich zs.-tun (***among***, ***with*** mit); **ˈ~·book** *s.* ⚘ Herdbuch *n*; **~ in·stinct** *s.* ˈHerdeninˌstinkt *m*, -trieb *m* (*a. fig.*); **ˈ~s·man** [-dzmən] *s.* [*irr.*] **1.** *Brit.* Hirt *m*; **2.** Herdenbesitzer *m*.

here [hɪə] **I** *adv.* **1.** hier: ***I am ~*** a) ich bin hier, b) ich bin da (*anwesend*); ***~ and there*** a) hier u. da, da u. dort, b) hierhin u. dorthin, c) hin u. wieder, hie u. da; ***~ and now*** hier u. jetzt *od.* heute; ***~, there and everywhere*** (all)überall; ***that's neither ~ nor there*** a) das gehört nicht zur Sache, b) das besagt nichts; ***we are leaving ~ today*** wir reisen heute von hier ab; ***~ goes*** F also los!; ***~'s to you!*** auf dein Wohl!; ***~ you are!*** hier (bitte)! (*da hast du es*); ***this ~ man*** *sl.* dieser Mann hier; **2.** (hier)her, hierhin: ***bring it ~!*** bring es hierher!; ***come ~!*** komm her!; ***this belongs ~*** das gehört hierher *od.* hierhin; **II** *s.* **3.** ***the ~ and now*** a) das Hier u. Heute, b) das Diesseits; **ˈ~·aˌbout(s)** [-ərə-] *adv.* hier herˈum, in dieser Gegend; **ˌ~ˈaft·er** [-ərˈɑː-] **I** *adv.* **1.** herˈnach, nachher; **2.** in Zukunft; **II** *s.* **3.** Zukunft *f*; **4.** (*das*) Jenseits; **ˌ~ˈby** *adv.* ˈhierdurch, hiermit.

he·red·i·ta·ble [hɪˈredɪtəbl] → ***heritable***; **her·e·dit·a·ment** [ˌherɪˈdɪtəmənt] *s.* ⚖ a) *Brit.* Grundstück *n* (als Bemessungsgrundlage für die Kommuˈnalabgaben), b) *Am.* vererblicher Vermögensgegenstand; **heˈred·i·tar·y** [-tərɪ] *adj.* ☐ **1.** erblich, er-, vererbt, Erb...: ***~ disease*** ⚕ Erbkrankheit *f*; ***~ portion*** ⚖ Pflichtteil *m*, *n*; ***~ succession*** *Am.* Erbfolge *f*; ***~ taint*** ⚕ erbliche Belastung; **2.** *fig.* Erb..., altˈhergebracht: ***~ enemy*** Erbfeind *m*; **heˈred·i·ty** [-tɪ] *s. biol.* **1.** Vererbbarkeit *f*, Erblichkeit *f*; **2.** ererbte Anlagen *pl.*, Erbmasse *f*.

ˌhere|ˈfrom *adv.* hieraus; **ˌ~ˈin** [-ərˈɪ-] *adv.* hierin; **ˌ~·in·aˈbove** *adv.* im vorstehenden, oben (*erwähnt*); **ˌ~·inˈaft·er** *adv.* nachstehend, im folgenden; **ˌ~ˈof** *adv.* hiervon, dessen.

her·e·sy [ˈherəsɪ] *s.* Ketzeˈrei *f*, Häreˈsie *f*; **ˈher·e·tic** [-ətɪk] **I** *s.* Ketzer(in); **II** *adj.* → **he·ret·i·cal** [hɪˈretɪkl] *adj.* ☐ ketzerisch.

ˌhere|ˈto [-ˈtuː] *adv.* **1.** hierzu; **2.** bisˈher; **ˌ~·toˈfore** [-tʊ-] *adv.* vordem, ehemals; **ˌ~ˈun·der** [-ərˈʌ-] **1.** → ***hereinafter***; **2.** ⚖ kraft dieses (*Vertrags etc.*); **ˌ~·unˈto** [-ərʌ-] → ***hereto***; **ˌ~·upˈon** [-ərə-] *adv.* hierauf, darauf(ˈhin); **ˌ~ˈwith** → ***hereby***.

her·it·a·ble [ˈherɪtəbl] *adj.* ☐ **1.** erblich, vererbbar; **2.** erbfähig; **ˈher·it·age** [-ɪtɪdʒ] *s.* **1.** Erbe *n*: a) Erbschaft *f*, Erbgut *n*, b) *ererbtes Recht etc.*; **2.** *bibl.* (*das*) Volk Israel; **ˈher·i·tor** [-ɪtə] *s.* ⚖ Erbe *m*.

her·maph·ro·dite [hɜːˈmæfrədaɪt] *s. biol.* Hermaphroˈdit *m*, Zwitter *m*; **herˈmaph·ro·dit·ism** [-daɪtɪzəm] *s. biol.* Hermaphrodiˈtismus *m*, Zwittertum *n od.* -bildung *f*.

her·met·ic [hɜːˈmetɪk] *adj.* (☐ **~ally**) herˈmetisch (*a. fig.*), luftdicht: ***~ seal*** luftdichter Verschluß.

her·mit [ˈhɜːmɪt] *s.* Einsiedler *m* (*a. fig.*), Ereˈmit *m*; **ˈher·mit·age** [-tɪdʒ] *s.* Einsiedeˈlei *f*, Klause *f*.

ˈher·mit-crab *s. zo.* Einsiedlerkrebs *m*.

her·ni·a [ˈhɜːnjə] *s.* ⚕ Bruch *m*, Hernie *f*; **ˈher·ni·al** [-jəl] *adj.*: ***~ truss*** ⚕ Bruchband *n*.

he·ro [ˈhɪərəʊ] *pl.* **-roes** *s.* **1.** Held *m*; **2.** *thea. etc.* Held *m*, ˈHauptperˌson *f*; **3.** *antiq.* Heros *m*, Halbgott *m*.

he·ro·ic [hɪˈrəʊɪk] **I** *adj.* (☐ **~ally**) **1.** heˈroisch (*a. paint. etc.*), heldenmütig, -haft, Helden...: ***~ age*** Heldenzeitalter *n*; ***~ couplet*** heroisches Reimpaar; ***~ poem*** → 4b; ***~ tenor*** ♪ Heldentenor *m*; ***~ verse*** → 4a; **2.** a) erhaben, b) hochtrabend (*Stil*); **3.** ⚕ drastisch, Radikal...; **II** *s.* **4.** a) heˈroisches Versmaß, b) heˈroisches Gedicht; **5.** *pl.* bomˈbastische Worte.

her·o·in [ˈherəʊɪn] *s.* Heroˈin *n*.

her·o·ine [ˈherəʊɪn] *s.* **1.** Heldin *f* (*a. thea. etc.*); **2.** *antiq.* Halbgöttin *f*; **ˈher·o·ism** [-ɪzəm] *s.* Heldentum *n*, Heroˈismus *m*; **he·ro·ize** [ˈhɪərəʊaɪz] **I** *v/t.* heroisieren, zum Helden machen; **II** *v/i.* den Helden spielen.

her·on [ˈherən] *s. orn.* Reiher *m*; **ˈher·on·ry** [-rɪ] *s.* Reiherhorst *m*.

he·ro| wor·ship *s.* **1.** Heldenverehrung *f*; **2.** Schwärmeˈrei *f*; **ˈ~-ˌwor·ship** *v/t.* **1.** als Helden verehren; **2.** schwärmen für.

her·pes [ˈhɜːpiːz] *s.* ⚕ Herpes *m*, Bläschenausschlag *m*.

her·pe·tol·o·gy [ˌhɜːpɪˈtɒlədʒɪ] *s.* Herpetoloˈgie *f*, Repˈtilienkunde *f*.

her·ring [ˈherɪŋ] *s. ichth.* Hering *m*; **ˈ~·bone I** *s.* **1.** *a.* ***~ design***, ***~ pattern*** Fischgrätenmuster *n*; **2.** fischgrätenartige Anordnung; **3.** *Stickerei*: ***~*** (***stitch***) Fischgrätenstich *m*; **4.** *Skilauf*: Grätenschritt *m*; **II** *v/t.* **5.** mit e-m Fischgrätenmuster nähen; **III** *v/i.* **6.** *Skilauf*: im Grätenschritt steigen; **~ pond** *s. humor. der* ,Große Teich' (*Atlantik*).

hers [hɜːz] *poss. pron.* ihrer (ihre, ihres), der (die, das) ihre *od.* ihrige: ***my mother and ~*** meine u. ihre Mutter; ***it is ~*** es gehört ihr; ***a friend of ~*** e-e Freundin von ihr.

her·self [hɜːˈself; hə-] *pron.* **1.** *refl.* sich: ***she hurt ~***; **2.** sich (selbst): ***she wants it for ~***; **3.** *verstärkend*: sie (*nom. od. acc.*) *od.* ihr (*dat.*) selbst: ***she ~ did it***, ***she did it ~*** sie selbst hat es getan, sie hat es selbst getan; ***by ~*** allein, ohne Hilfe, von selbst; **4.** ***she is not quite ~*** a) sie ist nicht ganz normal, b) sie ist nicht auf der Höhe; ***she is ~ again*** sie ist wieder die alte.

hertz [hɜːts] *s. phys.* Hertz *n*; **Hertz·i·an** [ˈhɜːtsɪən] *adj. phys.* Hertzsch: ***~ waves*** Hertzsche Wellen.

he's [hiːz; hɪz] F *für* a) ***he is***, b) ***he has***.

hes·i·tance [ˈhezɪtəns], **ˈhes·i·tan·cy** [-sɪ] *s.* Zögern *n*, Unschlüssigkeit *f*; **ˈhes·i·tant** [-nt] *adj.* **1.** zögernd, unschlüssig; **2.** *beim Sprechen*: stockend; **ˈhes·i·tate** [-teɪt] *v/i.* **1.** zögern, zaudern, unschlüssig sein, Bedenken haben (***to*** *inf.* zu *inf.*): ***not to ~ at*** nicht zurückschrecken vor (*dat.*); **2.** (*beim Sprechen*) stocken; **ˈhes·i·tat·ing·ly** [-teɪtɪŋlɪ] *adv.* zögernd; **hes·i·ta·tion** [ˌhezɪˈteɪʃən] *s.* **1.** Zögern *n*, Zaudern *n*, Unschlüssigkeit *f*: ***without any ~*** ohne (auch nur) zu zögern, bedenkenlos; **2.** Stocken *n*.

Hes·si·an [ˈhesɪən] **I** *adj.* **1.** hessisch; **II** *s.* **2.** Hesse *m*, Hessin *f*; **3.** ♀ Juteleinen *n* (*für Säcke etc.*); **~ boots** *s. pl.* Schaftstiefel *pl.*

het [het] *adj.*: ***~ up*** F ganz ,aus dem Häuschen'.

he·tae·ra [hɪˈtɪərə] *pl.* **-rae** [-riː], **heˈtai·ra** [-ˈtaɪərə] *pl.* **-rai** [-raɪ] *s. antiq.* Heˈtäre *f*.

hetero- [hetərəʊ] *in Zssgn* anders, verschieden, fremd.

het·er·o [ˈhetərəʊ] *pl.* **-os** *s.* F ,Hetero' *m* (*Heterosexuelle*[*r*]).

het·er·o·clite [ˈhetərəʊklaɪt] *ling.* **I** *adj.* heteroˈklitisch; **II** *s.* Heteˈrokliton *n*; **het·er·o·dox** [ˈhetərəʊdɒks] *adj.* **1.** *eccl.* heteroˈdox, anders-, irrgläubig; **2.** *fig.* ˈunkonventioˌnell; **het·er·o·dox·y** [ˈhetərəʊdɒksɪ] *s.* Andersgläubigkeit *f*, Irrglaube *m*; **ˈhet·er·o·dyne** [-əʊdaɪn] *adj. Radio*: ***~ receiver*** Überlagerungsempfänger *m*, Super(het) *m*; **het·er·o·ge·ne·i·ty** [ˌhetərəʊdʒɪˈniːətɪ] *s.* Verschiedenartigkeit *f*; **het·er·o·ge·ne·ous** [ˌhetərəʊˈdʒiːnjəs] *adj.* ☐ heteroˈgen, ungleichartig, verschiedenartig: ***~ number*** ⩓ gemischte Zahl; **het·er·on·o·mous** [ˌhetəˈrɒnɪməs] *adj.* heteroˈnom: a) unselbständig, b) *biol.* ungleichartig; **het·er·on·o·my** [ˌhetəˈrɒnɪmɪ] *s.* Heteronoˈmie *f*; **het·er·o·sex·u·al** [ˌhetərəʊˈseksjʊəl] **I** *adj.* heterosexuˈell; **II** *s.* Heterosexuˈelle(r *m*) *f*.

hew [hjuː] *v/t.* [*irr.*] hauen, hacken; *Steine* behauen; *Bäume* fällen; **~ down** *v/t.* ˈum-, niederhauen, fällen; **~ out** *v/t.* **1.** aushauen; **2.** *fig.* (mühsam) schaffen: ***~ a path for o.s.*** sich s-n Weg bahnen.

hew·er [ˈhjuːə] *s.* **1.** (Holz-, Stein)Hauer *m*: ***~s of wood and drawers of water*** a) *bibl.* Holzhauer u. Wasserträger, b) einfache Leute; **2.** ⚒ Hauer *m*; **hewn** [hjuːn] *p.p. von* ***hew***.

hex [heks] *Am.* F **I** *s.* **1.** Hexe *f*; **2.** Zauber *m*: ***put the ~ on*** → **II** *v/t.* **3.** *j-n* behexen; *et.* ,verhexen'.

hexa- [heksə] *in Zssgn* sechs; **hex·a·gon** [ˈheksəgən] *s.* ⩓ Hexaˈgon *n*, Sechseck *n*: ***~ voltage*** ϟ Sechsspannung *f*; **hex·ag·o·nal** [hekˈsægənl] *adj.* sechseckig; **ˈhex·a·gram** [-græm] *s.* Hexaˈgramm *n* (*Sechsstern*); **hex·a·he·dral** [ˌheksəˈhedrəl] *adj.* ⩓ sechsflächig; **hex·a·he·dron** [ˌheksəˈhedrən] *pl.* **-drons** *od.* **-dra** [-drə] *s.* ⩓ Hexaˈeder *n*; **hex·am·e·ter** [hekˈsæmɪtə] **I** *s.* Heˈxameter *m*; **II** *adj.* hexaˈmetrisch.

hey [heɪ] *int.* **1.** he!, heda!; **2.** *erstaunt*: he!, Mann!; **3.** hei; → ***presto*** I.

hey·day [ˈheɪdeɪ] *s.* Höhepunkt *m*, Blüte(zeit) *f*, Gipfel *m*: ***in the ~ of his power*** auf dem Gipfel s-r Macht.

H-hour ['eɪtʃˌaʊə] *s.* ⚔ die Stunde X (*Zeitpunkt für den Beginn e-r militärischen Aktion*).

hi [haɪ] *int.* **1.** he!, heda!; **2.** hal'lo!, F *als Begrüßung*: *a.* ‚Tag'!

hi·a·tus [haɪ'eɪtəs] *s.* **1.** Lücke *f*, Spalt *m*, Kluft *f*; **2.** *anat.*, *ling.* Hi'atus *m*.

hi·ber·nate ['haɪbəneɪt] *v/i.* über'wintern: a) *zo.* Winterschlaf halten, b) den Winter verbringen; **hi·ber·na·tion** [ˌhaɪbə'neɪʃn] *s.* Winterschlaf *m*, Über'winterung *f*.

Hi·ber·ni·an [haɪ'bɜːnjən] *poet.* **I** *adj.* irisch; **II** *s.* Irländer(in).

hi·bis·cus [hɪ'bɪskəs] *s.* ⚘ Eibisch *m*.

hic·cough, **hic·cup** ['hɪkʌp] **I** *s.* Schlukken *m*, Schluckauf *m*: ***have the ~s*** → **II** *v/i.* den Schluckauf haben.

hick [hɪk] *s. Am.* F ‚Bauer' *m*, 'Hinterwäldler *m*: ***~ girl*** Bauerntrampel *m*, *n*; ***~ town*** ‚(Provinz)Nest' *n*, Kaff *n*.

hick·o·ry ['hɪkərɪ] *s.* ⚘ **1.** Hickory(-baum) *m*; **2.** Hickoryholz *n od.* -stock *m*.

hid [hɪd] *pret. u. p.p. von* ***hide***[1]; **hid·den** [hɪdn] **I** *p.p. von* ***hide***[1]; **II** *adj.* □ verborgen, versteckt, geheim.

hide[1] [haɪd] **I** *v/t.* [*irr.*] (***from***) verbergen (*dat. od.* vor *dat.*): a) verstecken (vor *dat.*), b) verheimlichen (*dat. od.* vor *dat.*), c) verhüllen: ***~ from view*** den Blicken entziehen; **II** *v/i.* [*irr.*] *a.* ***~ out*** sich verstecken (*a. fig.* ***behind*** hinter *dat.*).

hide[2] [haɪd] **I** *s.* **1.** Haut *f*, Fell *n* (*beide a. fig.*): ***save one's ~*** die eigene Haut retten; ***tan s.o.'s ~*** F j-m das Fell gerben; ***I'll have his ~ for this!*** F das soll er mir bitter büßen!; **II** *v/t.* **2.** abhäuten; **3.** F *j-n* ‚verdreschen'.

hide[3] [haɪd] *s.* Hufe *f* (*altes engl. Feldmaß, 60–120 acres*).

ˌ**hide|-and-'seek** *s.* Versteckspiel *n*: ***play ~*** Versteck spielen (*a. fig.*); '**~·a·way** → ***hideout***; '**~·bound** *adj. fig.* engstirnig, beschränkt, borniert.

hid·e·ous ['hɪdɪəs] *adj.* □ ab'scheulich, scheußlich, schrecklich (*alle a.* F *fig.*); '**hid·e·ous·ness** [-nɪs] *s.* Scheußlichkeit *f etc.*

'**hide·out** *s.* **1.** Versteck *n*; **2.** Zufluchtsort *m*.

hid·ing[1] ['haɪdɪŋ] *s.* Versteck *n*: ***be in ~*** sich versteckt halten.

hid·ing[2] ['haɪdɪŋ] *s.* F Tracht *f* Prügel, ‚Dresche' *f*.

hie [haɪ] *v/i. obs. od. humor.* eilen.

hi·er·arch ['haɪərɑːk] *s. eccl.* Hier'arch *m*, Oberpriester *m*; **hi·er·ar·chic**, **hi·er·ar·chi·cal** [ˌhaɪə'rɑːkɪk(l)] *adj.* □ hier'archisch; '**hi·er·arch·y** [-kɪ] *s.* Hierar'chie *f*.

hi·er·o·glyph ['haɪərəʊglɪf] *s.* **1.** Hiero'glyphe *f*; **2.** *pl. mst sg. konstr.* Hiero'glyphenschrift *f*; **3.** *pl. humor.* Hiero'glyphen *pl.*, unleserliches Gekritzel; **hi·er·o·glyph·ic** [ˌhaɪərəʊ'glɪfɪk] **I** *adj.* (□ ***~ally***) **1.** hiero'glyphisch; **2.** rätselhaft; **3.** unleserlich; **II** *s.* **4.** → ***hieroglyph*** 1–3; **hi·er·o·glyph·i·cal** [ˌhaɪərəʊ'glɪfɪkl] *adj.* □ → ***hieroglyphic*** 1–3.

hi-fi [ˌhaɪ'faɪ] F **I** *s.* **1.** → ***high fidelity***; **2.** Hi-Fi-Anlage *f*; **II** *adj.* **3.** Hi-Fi-…

hig·gle ['hɪgl] → ***haggle***.

hig·gle·dy-pig·gle·dy [ˌhɪgldɪ'pɪgldɪ] F **I** *adv.* drunter u. drüber, (wie Kraut u. Rüben) durchein'ander; **II** *s.* Durchein'ander *n*, Tohuwa'bohu *n*.

high [haɪ] **I** *adj.* (□ → ***highly***) (→ ***higher***, ***highest***) **1.** hoch: ***ten feet ~***; ***a ~ tower***; **2.** hoch(gelegen): ***2 Asia*** Hochasien *n*; ***~ latitude*** *geogr.* hohe Breite; ***the ~est floor*** das oberste Stockwerk; **3.** hoch (*Grad*): ***~ prices*** (***temperature***); ***~ favo(u)r*** hohe Gunst; ***~ praise*** großes Lob; ***~ speed*** hohe Geschwindigkeit, ⚓ hohe Fahrt, äußerste Kraft; → ***gear*** 2a; **4.** stark, heftig: ***~ wind***; ***~ words*** heftige Worte; **5.** hoch (im Rang), Hoch…, Ober…, Haupt…: ***~ commissioner*** Hoher Kommissar; ***the Most 2*** der Allerhöchste (*Gott*); **6.** hoch, bedeutend, wichtig: ***~ aims*** hohe Ziele; ***~ politics*** hohe Politik; **7.** hoch (*Stellung*), vornehm, edel: ***of ~ birth***; ***~ society*** High-Society *f*, die vornehme Welt; ***~ and low*** hoch u. niedrig; **8.** hoch, erhaben, edel; **9.** hoch, gut, erstklassig: ***~ quality***; ***~ performance*** Hochleistung *f*; **10.** hoch, Hoch… (*auf dem Höhepunkt*): ***2 Middle Ages*** Hochmittelalter *n*; ***~ period*** Glanzzeit *f*; **11.** hoch, fortgeschritten (*Zeit*): ***~ summer*** Hochsommer *m*; ***~ antiquity*** fernes *od.* tiefes Altertum; ***it is ~ time*** es ist höchste Zeit; → ***noon***; **12.** *ling.* a) Hoch… (*Sprache*), b) hoch (*Laut*); **13.** a) hoch, b) schrill: ***~ voice***; **14.** hoch (*im Kurs*), teuer; **15.** → ***high and mighty***; **16.** ex'trem, eifrig: ***a ~ Tory***; **17.** lebhaft (*Farbe*): ***~ complexion*** a) rosiger Teint, b) gerötetes Gesicht; **18.** erregend, spannend: ***~ adventure***; **19.** a) heiter: ***in ~ spirits*** (in) gehobener Stimmung, b) F ‚blau' (*betrunken*), c) F ‚high' (*im Drogenrausch od. fig. in euphorischer Stimmung*); **20.** F ‚scharf', erpicht (***on*** auf *acc.*); **21.** *Küche*: angegangen, mit Haut'gout; **II** *adv.* **22.** hoch: ***aim ~*** *fig.* sich hohe Ziele setzen; ***run ~*** a) hochgehen (*Wellen*), b) toben (*Gefühle*); ***feelings ran ~*** die Gemüter erhitzten sich; ***play ~*** hoch *od.* mit hohem Einsatz spielen; ***pay ~*** teuer bezahlen; ***search ~ and low*** überall suchen; **23.** üppig: ***live ~***; **III** *s.* **24.** (An-)Höhe *f*: ***on ~*** a) hoch oben, droben, b) hoch (hinauf), c) im *od.* zum Himmel; ***from on ~*** a) von oben, b) vom Himmel; **25.** *meteor.* Hoch(druckgebiet) *n*; **26.** ⚙ a) höchster Gang, b) Geländegang *m*: ***shift into ~*** den höchsten Gang einlegen; **27.** *fig.* Höchststand *m*: ***reach a new ~***; **28.** F *für* ***high school***; **29.** ***he's still got his ~*** F er ist immer noch ‚high'.

high| al·tar *s. eccl.* 'Hochalˌtar *m*; ˌ**~-'al·ti·tude** *adj.* ✈ Höhen…: ***~ flight***; ***~ nausea*** Höhenkrankheit *f*; **~ and dry** *adj.* hoch u. trocken, auf dem trockenen: ***leave s.o. ~*** *fig.* j-n im Stich lassen; **~ and might·y** *adj.* F anmaßend, arro'gant; '**~·ball** *Am.* **I** *s.* **1.** Highball *m* (*Whisky-Cocktail*); **2.** 🚂 a) Freie-'Fahrt-Siˌgnal *n*, b) Schnellzug *m*; **II** *v/i. u. v/t.* **3.** F mit vollem Tempo fahren; **~ beam** *s. mot. Am.* Fernlicht *n*; '**~ˌbind·er** *s. Am.* F **1.** Gangster *m*; **2.** Gauner *m*; **3.** Rowdy *m*; '**~·blown** *adj. fig.* großspurig, aufgeblasen; '**~·born** *adj.* hochgeboren; '**~·boy** *s. Am.* Kom'mode *f* mit Aufsatz; '**~-bred** *adj.* vornehm, wohlerzogen; '**~·brow** *oft contp.* **I** *s.* Intellektu'elle(r *m*) *f*; **II** *adj. a.* '**~-browed** (betont) intellektu'ell, (geistig) anspruchsvoll, ‚hochgestochen'; **2 Church I** *s.* High-Church *f*, angli'kanische Hochkirche; **II** *adj.* hochkirchlich, der High-Church; ˌ**~-'class** *adj.* **1.** erstklassig; **2.** der High-Society; **~ command** *s.* ⚔ 'Oberkomˌmando *n*; **2 Court** (**of Jus·tice**) *s. Brit.* oberstes (*erstinstanzliches*) Zi'vilgericht; **~ day** *s.*: ***~s and holidays*** Fest- u. Feiertage; **~ div·ing** *s. sport* Turmspringen *n*; ˌ**~-'du·ty** *adj.* ⚙ Hochleistungs…

high·er ['haɪə] **I** *comp. von* ***high***; **II** *adj.* höher (*a. fig. Bildung, Rang etc.*), Ober…: ***the ~ mammals*** die höheren Säugetiere; ***~ mathematics*** höhere Mathematik; **III** *adv.* höher, mehr: ***bid ~***; '**~-up** [-ərʌ-] *s.* F ‚höheres Tier'.

high·est ['haɪɪst] **I** *sup. von* ***high***; **II** *adj.* höchst (*a. fig.*), Höchst…: ***~ bidder*** Meistbietende(r *m*) *f*; **III** *adv.* am höchsten: ***~ possible*** höchstmöglich; **IV** *s.* (*das*) Höchste: ***at its ~*** auf dem Höhepunkt.

high| ex·plo·sive *s.* 'hochexploˌsiver *od.* 'hochbriˌsanter Sprengstoff; ˌ**~-ex'plo·sive** *adj.* 'hochexploˌsiv: ***~ bomb*** Sprengbombe *f*; ˌ**~-fa'lu·tin** [-fə'luːtɪn], ˌ**~-fa'lu·ting** [-tɪŋ] *adj. u. s.* hochtrabend(es Geschwätz); **~ farm·ing** *s.* ⚒ inten'sive Bodenbewirtschaftung; **~ fi·del·i·ty** *s. Radio*: 'High-Fi'delity *f* (*hohe Wiedergabequalität*), Hi-Fi *n*; ˌ**~-fi'del·i·ty** *adj.* High-Fidelity-…, Hi-Fi-…; **~ fi·nance** *s.* 'Hochfiˌnanz *f*; ˌ**~'fli·er** → ***highflyer***; '**~-flown** *adj.* **1.** bom'bastisch, hochtrabend; **2.** hochgesteckt (*Ziele etc.*), hochfliegend (*Pläne*); ˌ**~'fly·er** *s.* **1.** Erfolgsmensch *m*; **2.** Ehrgeizling *m*, ‚Aufsteiger' *m*; ˌ**~-'fly·ing** *adj.* **1.** hochfliegend; **2.** → ***high-flown***; **~ fre·quen·cy** *s.* ⚡ 'Hochfreˌquenz *f*; ˌ**~-'fre·quen·cy** *adj.* Hochfrequenz…; **2 Ger·man** *s. ling.* Hochdeutsch *n*; ˌ**~-'grade** *adj.* erstklassig, hochwertig; **~ hand** *s.*: ***with a ~*** → ˌ**~-'hand·ed** *adj.* □ anmaßend, selbstherrlich, eigenmächtig; **~ hat** *s.* Zy'linder *m* (*Hut*); ˌ**~-'hat I** *s.* Snob *m*, hochnäsiger Mensch; **II** *adj.* hochnäsig; **III** *v/t. j-n* von oben her'ab behandeln; ˌ**~-'heeled** *adj.* hochhackig (*Schuhe*); **~ jump** *s. sport* Hochsprung *m*: ***be for the ~*** *Brit.* F ‚dran' sein; '**~·land** [-lənd] **I** *s.* Hoch-, Bergland *n*: ***the 2s of Scotland*** das schottische Hochland; **II** *adj.* hochländisch, Hochland…; '**2·land·er** [-ləndə] *s.* (*bsd. schottische*[*r*]) Hochländer(in); ˌ**~-'lev·el** *adj.* **1.** hoch: ***~ railway*** Hochbahn *f*; **2.** *fig.* auf hoher Ebene, Spitzen…: ***~ talks***; ***~ officials*** hohe Beamte; **~ life** *s.* Highlife *n* (*exklusives Leben der vornehmen Welt*); '**~·light I** *s.* **1.** *paint.*, *phot.* (Schlag)Licht *n*; **2.** *fig.* Höhe-, Glanzpunkt *m*; **3.** *pl.* (*Opern- etc.*)Querschnitt *m* (*Schallplatte etc.*); **II** *v/t.* **4.** *fig.* ein Schlaglicht werfen auf (*acc.*), her'vorheben, groß her'ausstellen; **5.** *fig.* den Höhepunkt (*gen.*) bilden.

high·ly ['haɪlɪ] *adv.* hoch, höchst, äußerst, sehr: ***~ gifted*** hochbegabt; ***~ placed*** *fig.* hochgestellt; ***~ strung*** → ***high-strung***; ***~ paid*** a) hochbezahlt, b) teuer bezahlt; ***think ~ of*** viel halten von.

High| Mass *s. eccl.* Hochamt *n*; ˌ♀-**'mind·ed** *adj.* hochgesinnt; ˌ♀-**'mind·ed·ness** *s.* hohe Gesinnung; ˌ♀-**'necked** *adj.* hochgeschlossen (*Kleid*).

high·ness ['haɪnɪs] *s.* **1.** *mst fig.* Höhe *f*; **2.** ♀ Hoheit *f* (*in Titeln*); **3.** Haut'gout *m* (*von Fleisch etc.*).

ˌ**high|-'pitched** *adj.* **1.** hoch (*Ton etc.*); **2.** △ steil; **3.** exaltiert: a) über'spannt, b) über'dreht, aufgeregt; **~ point** *s.* Höhepunkt *m*; ˌ**~-'pow·er(ed)** *adj.* **1.** ⚙ Hochleistungs…, Groß…, stark; **2.** *fig.* dy'namisch; ˌ**~-'pres·sure I** *adj.* **1.** ⚙ *u. meteor.* Hochdruck…: ***~ area*** Hoch (-druckgebiet) *n*; ***~ engine*** Hochdruckmaschine *f*; **2.** F a) aufdringlich, aggres'siv, b) dy'namisch: ***~ salesman***; **II** *v/t.* **3.** F *Kunden* ‚beknien', ‚bearbeiten'; ˌ**~-'priced** *adj.* teuer; **~ priest** *s.* Hohe'priester *m* (*a. fig.*); ˌ**~-'prin·ci·pled** *adj.* von hohen Grundsätzen; ˌ**~-'proof** *adj.* stark alko'holisch; '**~-ˌrank·ing** *adj.*: ***~ officer*** hoher Offizier; **~ re·lief** *s.* 'Hochreliˌef *n*; '**~·rise I** *adj.* Hoch (-haus)…: ***~ building*** → **II** *s.* Hochhaus *n*; '**~·road** *s.* Hauptstraße *f*: ***the ~ to success*** *fig.* der sicherste Weg zum Erfolg; **~ school** *s. Am.* High-School *f* (*weiterführende Schule*); ˌ**~-'sea** *adj.* Hochsee…; **~ sea·son** *s.* 'Hochsaiˌson *f*; **~ sign** *s. Am.* (*bsd.* warnendes) Zeichen; '**~-ˌsound·ing** *adj.* hochtönend, -trabend; ˌ**~-'speed** *adj.* **1.** ⚙ a) schnellaufend: ***~ motor***, b) Schnell…, Hochleistungs…: ***~ regulator***; ***~ steel*** Schnellarbeitsstahl *m*; **2.** *phot.* a) hochempfindlich: ***~ film***, b) lichtstark: ***~ lens***; ˌ**~-'spir·it·ed** *adj.* lebhaft, tempera'mentvoll; **~ spir·its** *s. pl.* fröhliche Laune, gehobene Stimmung; **~ spot** F → ***highlight*** 2; **~ street** *s.* Hauptstraße *f*; ˌ**~-'strung** *adj.* reizbar, (äußerst) ner'vös; **~ ta·ble** *s. Brit. univ.* erhöhte Speisetafel (*für Dozenten etc.*); '**~-tail** *v/i. a.* ***~ it*** *Am.* F (da'hin-, da'von)rasen, (-)flitzen; **~ tea** *s. bsd. Brit.* frühes Abendessen; **~ tech** [tek] → ***high technology***; ˌ**~-'tech** *adj.* 'hochtechnoˌlogisch; **~ tech·nol·o·gy** *s.* 'Hochtechnoloˌgie *f*; **~ ten·sion** *s.* ϟ Hochspannung *f*; ˌ**~-'ten·sion** *adj.* ϟ Hochspannungs…; **~ tide** *s.* **1.** Hochwasser *n* (*höchster Flutwasserstand*); **2.** *fig.* Höhepunkt *m*; ˌ**~-'toned** *adj.* **1.** *fig.* erhaben; **2.** vornehm; **~ trea·son** *s.* Hochverrat *m*; '**~-up** *s.* F ‚hohes Tier'; **~ volt·age** → ***high tension***; **~ wa·ter** → ***high tide*** 1; ˌ**~-'wa·ter mark** *s.* a) Hochwasserstandsmarke *f*, b) *fig.* Höchststand *m*; '**~·way** *s.* Haupt(verkehrs)straße *f*, Highway *m*: ***Federal ~*** *Am.* Bundesstraße *f*; ♀ ***Code*** *Brit.* Straßenverkehrsordnung *f*; ***~ robbery*** a) Straßenraub *m*, b) F *der* ‚reinste Nepp'; ***the ~ to success*** der sicherste Weg zum Erfolg; ***all the ~s and byways*** a) alle Wege, b) sämtliche Spielarten; '**~·way·man** [-mən] *s.* [*irr.*] Straßenräuber *m*.

hi·jack ['haɪdʒæk] **I** *v/t.* **1.** *Flugzeug* entführen; **2.** *Geldtransport etc.* über'fallen u. ausrauben; **II** *s.* **3.** Flugzeugentführung *f*; **4.** 'Überfall *m* (*auf Geldtransport etc.*); '**hiˌjack·er** [-kə] *s.* **1.** Flugzeugentführer *m*, 'Luftpiˌrat *m*; **2.** Räuber *m*; '**hiˌjack·ing** [-kɪŋ] → ***hijack*** II.

hike [haɪk] **I** *v/i.* **1.** wandern; **2.** marschieren; **3.** hochrutschen (*Kleidungsstück*); **II** *v/t.* **4.** *mst* ***~ up*** hochziehen; **5.** *Am. Preise etc.* (drastisch) erhöhen; **III** *s.* **6.** a) Wanderung *f*, b) ⚔ Geländemarsch *m*; **7.** *Am.* (drastische) Erhöhung: ***a ~ in prices***; '**hik·er** [-kə] *s.* Wanderer *m*.

hi·lar·i·ous [hɪ'leərɪəs] *adj.* □ vergnügt, 'übermütig, ausgelassen; **hi·lar·i·ty** [hɪ'lærətɪ] *s.* Ausgelassenheit *f*, 'Übermütigkeit *f*.

Hil·a·ry term ['hɪlərɪ] *s. Brit.* **1.** ⚖ *Gerichtstermine in der Zeit vom 11. Januar bis Mittwoch vor Ostern*; **2.** *univ.* 'Frühjahrsseˌmester *n*.

hill [hɪl] **I** *s.* **1.** Hügel *m*, Anhöhe *f*, kleiner Berg: ***up ~ and down dale*** bergauf u. bergab; ***be over the ~*** a) s-e besten Jahre hinter sich haben, b) *bsd.* ⚔ über den Berg sein; → ***old*** 3; **2.** (Erd- *etc.*)Haufen *m*; **II** *v/t.* **3.** *a.* ***~ up*** ⚒ *Pflanzen* häufeln; '**~ˌbil·ly** *s. Am.* F *contp.* Hinterwäldler *m*: ***~ music*** Hillbilly-Musik *f*; **~ climb** *s. mot.*, *Radsport*: Bergrennen *n*; '**~-ˌclimb·ing a·bil·i·ty** *s. mot.* Steigfähigkeit *f*.

hill·i·ness ['hɪlɪnɪs] *s.* Hügeligkeit *f*.

hill·ock ['hɪlək] *s.* kleiner Hügel.

ˌ**hill|'side** *s.* Hang *m*, (Berg)Abhang *m*; ˌ**~'top** *s.* Bergspitze *f*.

hill·y ['hɪlɪ] *adj.* hügelig.

hilt [hɪlt] *s.* Heft *n*, Griff *m* (*Schwert etc.*): ***up to the ~*** a) bis ans Heft, b) *fig.* total; ***armed to the ~*** bis an die Zähne bewaffnet; ***back s.o. up to the ~*** j-n voll (u. ganz) unterstützen; ***prove up to the ~*** unwiderleglich beweisen.

him [hɪm] *pron.* **1.** a) ihn (*acc.*), b) ihm (*dat.*); **2.** F er (*nom.*): ***it's ~*** er ist es; **3.** den(jenigen), wer: ***I saw ~ who did it***; **4.** *refl.* sich: ***he looked about ~*** er sah um sich.

Hi·ma·la·yan [ˌhɪmə'leɪən] *adj.* Himalaja…

him'self *pron.* **1.** *refl.* sich: ***he cut ~***; **2.** sich (selbst): ***he needs it for ~***; **3.** *verstärkend*: (er *od.* ihn *od.* ihm) selbst: ***he ~ said it, he said it ~*** er selbst sagte es, er sagte es selbst; ***by ~*** allein, ohne Hilfe, von selbst; **4.** ***he is not quite ~*** a) er ist nicht ganz normal, b) er ist nicht auf der Höhe; ***he is ~ again*** er ist wieder (ganz) der alte.

hind[1] [haɪnd] *s. zo.* Hindin *f*, Hirschkuh *f*.

hind[2] [haɪnd] *adj.* hinter, Hinter…: ***~ leg*** Hinterbein *n*; ***talk the ~ legs off a donkey*** F unaufhörlich reden; ***~ wheel*** Hinterrad *n*.

hind·er[1] ['haɪndə] *comp. von* ***hind***[2].

hin·der[2] ['hɪndə] **I** *v/t.* **1.** aufhalten; **2.** (***from***) hindern (an *dat.*), abhalten (von): ***~ed in one's work*** bei der Arbeit behindert *od.* gestört; **II** *v/i.* **3.** im Wege *od.* hinderlich sein, hindern.

Hin·di ['hɪndi:] *s. ling.* Hindi *n*.

'**hind·most** [-ndm-] *sup. von* ***hind***[2].

ˌ**hind'quar·ter** *s.* **1.** 'Hinterviertel *n* (*vom Schlachttier*); **2.** *pl.* a) 'Hinterteil *n*, Gesäß *n*, b) 'Hinterhand *f* (*vom Pferd*).

hin·drance ['hɪndrəns] *s.* **1.** Hinderung *f*; **2.** Hindernis *n* (***to*** für).

'**hind·sight** *s.* **1.** ⚔ Vi'sier *n*; **2.** *fig.* späte Einsicht: ***by ~, with the wisdom of ~*** ‚im nachhinein', hinterher; ***foresight is better than ~*** Vorsicht ist besser als Nachsicht; ***~ is easier than foresight*** hinterher ist man immer klüger (als vorher), *contp. a.* hinterher kann man leicht klüger sein (als vorher).

Hin·du [ˌhɪn'du:] **I** *s.* **1.** Hindu *m*; **2.** Inder *m*; **II** *adj.* **3.** Hindu…; **Hin·du·ism** ['hɪndu:ɪzəm] *s.* Hindu'ismus *m*; **Hin·du·sta·ni** [ˌhɪndʊ'stɑ:nɪ] **I** *s. ling.* Hindu'stani *n*; **II** *adj.* hindu'stanisch.

hinge [hɪndʒ] **I** *s.* **1.** ⚙ Schar'nier *n*, Gelenk *n*, (Tür)Angel *f*: ***off its ~s*** aus den Angeln, *fig. a.* aus den Fugen; **2.** *fig.* Angelpunkt *m*; **II** *v/t.* **3.** mit Scharnieren *etc.* versehen; **4.** *Tür etc.* einhängen; **III** *v/i.* **5.** *fig.*: ***~ on*** a) sich drehen um, b) abhängen von, ankommen auf (*acc.*); **hinged** [-dʒd] *adj.* (um ein Gelenk) drehbar, auf-, her'unter-, zs.-klappbar, Scharnier…; **hinge joint** *s.* **1.** → ***hinge*** 1; **2.** *anat.* Schar'niergelenk *n*.

hin·ny ['hɪnɪ] *s. zo.* Maulesel *m*.

hint [hɪnt] **I** *s.* **1.** Wink *m*: a) Andeutung *f*, b) Tip *m*, Hinweis *m*, Fingerzeig *m*: ***broad ~*** Wink mit dem Zaunpfahl; ***take a*** (*od.* ***the***) ***~*** den Wink verstehen; ***drop a ~*** e-e Andeutung machen; **2.** Anspielung *f* (***at*** auf *acc.*); **3.** Anflug *m*, Spur *f* (***of*** von); **II** *v/t.* **4.** andeuten, *et.* zu verstehen geben; **III** *v/i.* **5.** (***at***) e-e Andeutung machen (von), anspielen (auf *acc.*).

hin·ter·land ['hɪntəlænd] *s.* **1.** 'Hinterland *n*; **2.** Einzugsgebiet *n*.

hip[1] [hɪp] *s.* **1.** *anat.* Hüfte *f*: ***have s.o. on the ~*** *fig.* j-n in der Hand haben; **2.** → ***hip joint***; **3.** △ a) Walm *m*, b) Walmsparren *m*.

hip[2] [hɪp] *s.* ⚘ Hagebutte *f*.

hip[3] [hɪp] *int.*: ***~, ~, hurrah!*** hipp, hipp, hurra!

hip[4] [hɪp] *adj. sl.* **1.** ***be ~*** ‚voll dabei' sein (*in der Mode etc.*); **2.** ***be ~ to*** im Bilde *od.* auf dem laufenden sein über (*acc.*); ***get ~ to et.*** ‚spitzkriegen'.

'**hip|·bath** *s.* Sitzbad *n*; '**~·bone** *s. anat.* Hüftbein *n*; **~ flask** *s.* Taschenflasche *f*, ‚Flachmann' *m*; **~ joint** *s. anat.* Hüftgelenk *n*.

hipped[1] [hɪpt] *adj.* **1.** *in Zssgn* mit … Hüften; **2.** △ Walm…: ***~ roof.***

hipped[2] [hɪpt] *adj. Am. sl.* versessen, ‚scharf' (***on*** auf *acc.*).

hip·pie ['hɪpɪ] *s.* Hippie *m*.

hip·po ['hɪpəʊ] *pl.* **-pos** *s.* F *für* ***hippopotamus.***

hip·po·cam·pus [ˌhɪpəʊ'kæmpəs] *pl.* **-pi** [-paɪ] *s.* **1.** *myth.* Hippo'kamp *m*; **2.** *ichth.* Seepferdchen *n*; **3.** *anat.* Ammonshorn *n* (*des Gehirns*).

hip pock·et *s.* Gesäßtasche *f*.

Hip·po·crat·ic [ˌhɪpəʊ'krætɪk] *s.* hippo'kratisch: ***~ face***; ***~ oath.***

hip·po·drome ['hɪpədrəʊm] *s.* **1.** Hippo'drom *n*, Reitbahn *f*; **2.** a) Zirkus *m*, b) Varie'té(theˌater) *n*; **3.** *sport Am. sl.* ‚Schiebung' *f*.

hip·po·griff, hip·po·gryph ['hɪpəgrɪf] *s.* Hippo'gryph *m* (*Fabeltier*).

hip·po·pot·a·mus [ˌhɪpə'pɒtəməs] *pl.* **-mus·es, -mi** [-maɪ] *s. zo.* Fluß-, Nilpferd *n*.

hip·py ['hɪpɪ] → ***hippie.***

'**hip·shot** *adj.* **1.** mit verrenkter Hüfte;

2. *fig.* (lenden)lahm.

hip·ster ['hɪpstə] *s. sl.* **1.** ‚cooler Typ'; **2.** *pl. a.* ~ ***trousers*** *Brit.* Hüfthose *f.*

hir·a·ble ['haɪərəbl] *adj.* mietbar.

hire ['haɪə] **I** *v/t.* **1.** *et.* mieten, *Flugzeug* chartern: ~***d car*** Leih-, Mietwagen *m*; ~***d airplane*** Charterflugzeug *n*; **2.** *a.* ~ ***on*** a) *j-n* ein-, anstellen, b) *bsd.* ⚓ anheuern, c) *j-n* engagieren: ~***d killer*** bezahlter *od.* gekaufter Mörder, Killer *m*; **3.** *mst* ~ ***out*** vermieten; **4.** ~ ***o.s. out*** e-e Beschäftigung annehmen (***to*** bei); **II** *s.* **5.** Miete *f*: ***on*** (*od.* ***for***) ~ a) mietweise, b) zu vermieten(d); ***for*** ~ frei (*Taxi*); ***take*** (***let***) ***a car on*** ~ ein Auto (ver)mieten; ~ ***car*** Leih-, Mietwagen *m*; **6.** Entgelt *n*, Lohn *m*.

hire·ling ['haɪəlɪŋ] *mst contp.* **I** *s.* Mietling *m*; **II** *adj.* a) käuflich, b) *b.s.* angeheuert.

hire pur·chase *s. bsd. Brit.* ✝ Abzahlungs-, Teilzahlungs-, Ratenkauf *m*: ***buy on*** ~ auf Abzahlung kaufen; ˌ~-'**pur·chase** *adj.*: ~ ***agreement*** Abzahlungsvertrag *m*; ~ ***system*** Teilzahlungssystem *n*.

hir·er ['haɪərə] *s.* **1.** Mieter(in); **2.** Vermieter(in).

hir·sute ['hɜːsjuːt] *adj.* **1.** haarig, zottig, struppig; **2.** ⚘, *zo.* rauhhaarig, borstig.

his [hɪz] *poss. pron.* **1.** sein, seine: ~ ***family***; **2.** seiner (seine, seines), der (die, das) seine *od.* seinige: ***my father and*** ~ mein u. sein Vater; ***this hat is*** ~ das ist sein Hut, dieser Hut gehört ihm; ***a book of*** ~ eines seiner Bücher, ein Buch von ihm.

hiss [hɪs] **I** *v/i.* **1.** zischen; **II** *v/t.* **2.** auszischen, -pfeifen; **3.** zischeln; **III** *s.* **4.** Zischen *n*.

hist [sːt] *int.* sch!, pst!

his·tol·o·gist [hɪ'stɒlədʒɪst] *s.* ⚕ Histo'loge *m*; **his'tol·o·gy** [-dʒɪ] *s.* ⚕ Histolo'gie *f*, Gewebelehre *f*; **his'tol·y·sis** [-lɪsɪs] *s.* ⚕, *biol.* Histo'lyse *f*, Gewebszerfall *m*.

his·to·ri·an [hɪ'stɔːrɪən] *s.* Hi'storiker (-in), Geschichtsforscher(in); **his·tor·ic** [hɪ'stɒrɪk] *adj.* (□ ~***ally***) **1.** hi'storisch, geschichtlich (berühmt *od.* bedeutsam): ~ ***buildings***; ***a*** ~ ***speech***; **2.** → **his·tor·i·cal** [hɪ'stɒrɪkl] *adj.* □ **1.** hi'storisch: a) geschichtlich (belegt *od.* über'liefert): ***a***(***n***) ~ ***event***, b) Geschichts...: ~ ***science***, c) geschichtlich orientiert: ~ ***materialism*** historischer Materialismus, d) geschichtlich(en Inhalts): ~ ***novel*** historischer Roman; **2.** → ***historic*** 1; **3.** *ling.* hi'storisch: ~ ***present***; **his·to·ric·i·ty** [ˌhɪstə'rɪsətɪ] *s.* Geschichtlichkeit *f*; **his·to·ried** ['hɪstərɪd] → ***historic*** 1; **his·to·ri·og·ra·pher** [ˌhɪstɔːrɪ'ɒgrəfə] *s.* Historio'graph *m*, Geschichtsschreiber *m*; **his·to·ri·og·ra·phy** [ˌhɪstɔːrɪ'ɒgrəfɪ] *s.* Geschichtsschreibung *f*.

his·to·ry ['hɪstərɪ] *s.* **1.** Geschichte *f*: a) geschichtliche Vergangenheit *od.* Entwicklung, b) (*ohne art.*) Geschichtswissenschaft *f*: ~ ***book*** Geschichtsbuch *n*; ***ancient*** (***modern***) ~ alte (neuere) Geschichte; ~ ***of art*** Kunstgeschichte; ***go down in*** ~ ***as*** als ... in die Geschichte eingehen; ***make*** ~ Geschichte machen; → ***natural history***; **2.** Werdegang *m* (*a.* ⚙), Entwicklung *f*, (Entwicklungs-) Geschichte *f*; **3.** *allg.*, *a.* ⚕ Vorgeschichte *f*, Vergangenheit *f*: (***case***) ~ Krankengeschichte *f*, Anamnese *f*; ***have a*** ~; **4.** (*a.* Lebens)Beschreibung *f*, Darstellung *f*; **5.** *paint.* Hi'storienbild *n*; **6.** hi'storisches Drama.

his·tri·on·ic [ˌhɪstrɪ'ɒnɪk] **I** *adj.* (□ ~***ally***) **1.** Schauspiel(er)..., schauspielerisch; **2.** thea'tralisch; **II** *s.* **3.** *pl. a. sg. konstr.* a) Schauspielkunst *f*, b) *contp.* Schauspiele'rei *f*, thea'tralisches Getue.

hit [hɪt] **I** *s.* **1.** Schlag *m*, Hieb *m* (*a. fig.*); **2.** *a. sport u. fig.* Treffer *m*: ***make a*** ~ a) e-n Treffer erzielen, b) *fig.* gut ankommen (***with*** bei); **3.** Glücksfall *m*, Erfolg *m*; **4.** *thea.*, *Buch etc.*: Schlager *m*, ‚Knüller' *m*, Hit *m*: ***song*** ~ Schlager, Hit; ***he*** (***it***) ***was a great*** ~ (***with***) er (es) war ein großer Erfolg (bei); **5.** (Seiten)Hieb *m*, Spitze *f* (***at*** gegen); **6.** *bsd. Am. sl.* ‚Abschuß' *m*, Ermordung *f*; **II** *v/t.* [*irr.*] **7.** schlagen, stoßen; *Auto etc.* rammen: ~ ***one's head against s.th.*** mit dem Kopf gegen et. stoßen; **8.** treffen (*a. fig.*): ***be*** ~ ***by a bullet***; ***when it*** ~***s you*** *fig.* wenn es dich packt; ***you've*** ~ ***it*** *fig.* du hast es getroffen (*ganz recht*); **9.** (*seelisch*) treffen: ***be hard*** (*od.* ***badly***) ~ schwer getroffen sein (***by*** durch); **10.** stoßen *od.* kommen auf (*acc.*), treffen, finden: ~ ***the right road***; ~ ***a mine*** ⚓, ⚔ auf e-e Mine laufen; ~ ***the solution*** die Lösung finden; **11.** *fig.* geißeln, scharf kritisieren; **12.** erreichen, *et.* ‚schaffen': ***the car*** ~***s 100 mph***; ***prices*** ~ ***an all-time high*** die Preise erreichten e-e Rekordhöhe; ~ ***the town*** in der Stadt ankommen; **III** *v/i.* [*irr.*] **13.** treffen; **14.** schlagen (***at*** nach); **15.** stoßen, schlagen (***against*** gegen); **16.** ~ (***up***)***on*** → 10; ~ **back** *v/i.* zu'rückschlagen (*a. fig.*): ~ ***at s.o.*** j-m Kontra geben; ~ **off** *v/t.* **1.** treffend *od.* über'zeugend darstellen *od.* schildern; *die Ähnlichkeit* genau treffen; **2.** ***hit it off with s.o.*** sich bestens vertragen *od.* glänzend auskommen mit j-m; ~ **out** *v/i.* um sich schlagen: ~ ***at*** auf *j-n* einschlagen, *fig.* über *j-n od. et.* losziehen.

ˌ**hit**|**-and-'miss** *adj.* **1.** mit wechselndem Erfolg; **2.** → ***hit-or-miss***; ˌ~**-and-'run I** *adj.* **1.** ~ ***accident*** → 3; ~ ***driver*** (unfall)flüchtiger Fahrer; **2.** kurz(lebig); **II** *s.* **3.** Unfall *m* mit Fahrerflucht.

hitch [hɪtʃ] **I** *s.* **1.** Ruck *m*, Zug *m*; **2.** ⚓ Stich *m*, Knoten *m*; **3.** ‚Haken' *m*: ***there is a*** ~ (***somewhere***) die Sache hat (irgendwo) e-n Haken; ***without a*** ~ reibungslos, glatt; **II** *v/t.* **4.** (ruckartig) ziehen: ~ ***up one's trousers*** s-e Hosen hochziehen; **5.** befestigen, festhaken, ankoppeln, *Pferd* anspannen: ***get*** ~***ed*** → 8; **III** *v/i.* **6.** hinken; **7.** sich festhaken; **8.** *a.* ~ ***up*** F heiraten; **9.** → '~**·hike** *v/i.* F ‚per Anhalter' fahren, trampen; '~**hik·er** *s.* F Anhalter(in), Tramper (-in).

hi-tech [ˌhaɪ'tek] → ***high-tech***.

hith·er ['hɪðə] **I** *adv.* hierher: ~ ***and thither*** hierhin u. dorthin, hin und her; **II** *adj.* diesseitig: ***the*** ~ ***side*** die nähere Seite; ♀ ***India*** Vorderindien *n*; ˌ~'**to** [-'tuː] *adv.* bis'her, bis jetzt.

Hit·ler·ism ['hɪtlərɪzəm] *s.* Na'zismus *m*; '**Hit·ler·ite** [-raɪt] **I** *s.* Nazi *m*; **II** *adj.* na'zistisch.

hit| **list** *s. sl.* Abschußliste *f* (*a. fig.*); ~ **man** *s.* [*irr.*] *Am. sl.* Killer *m*; '~**-off** *s.* treffende Nachahmung, über'zeugende Darstellung; ~ **or miss** *adv.* aufs Gerate'wohl; ˌ~**-or-'miss** *adj.* **1.** sorglos, unbekümmert; **2.** aufs Gerate'wohl getan; ~ **pa·rade** *s.* 'Hitpaˌrade *f*.

Hit·tite ['hɪtaɪt] *s. hist.* He'thiter *m*.

hive [haɪv] **I** *s.* **1.** Bienenkorb *m*, -stock *m*; **2.** Bienenvolk *n*, -schwarm *m*; **3.** *fig.* a) *a.* ~ ***of activity*** *das* reinste Bienenhaus, b) Sammelpunkt *m*, c) Schwarm *m* (*von Menschen*); **II** *v/t.* **4.** *Bienen* in e-n Stock bringen; **5.** *Honig* im Bienenstock sammeln; **6.** *a.* ~ ***up*** *fig.* a) sammeln, b) auf die Seite legen; **7.** ~ ***off*** a) *Amt etc.* abtrennen (***from*** von), b) reprivatisieren; **III** *v/i.* **8.** in den Stock fliegen (*Bienen*): ~ ***off*** *fig.* a) abschwenken, b) sich selbständig machen; **9.** sich zs.-drängen.

hives [haɪvz] *s. pl. sg. od. pl. konstr.* ⚕ Nesselausschlag *m*.

ho [həʊ] *int.* **1.** halt!, holla!, heda!; **2.** na'nu!; **3.** *contp.* ha'ha!, pah!; **4.** ***westward*** ~***!*** auf nach Westen!; ***land*** ~***!*** ⚓ Land in Sicht!

hoar [hɔː] *adj. obs.* **1.** → ***hoary***; **2.** (*vom Frost*) bereift, weiß.

hoard [hɔːd] **I** *s.* a) Hort *m*, Schatz *m*, b) Vorrat *m* (***of*** an *dat.*); **II** *v/t. u. v/i. a.* ~ ***up*** horten, hamstern; '**hoard·er** [-də] *s.* Hamsterer *m*.

hoard·ing ['hɔːdɪŋ] *s.* **1.** Bau-, Bretterzaun *m*; **2.** *Brit.* Re'klamewand *f*.

ˌ**hoar'frost** *s.* (Rauh)Reif *m*.

hoarse [hɔːs] *adj.* □ heiser; '**hoarse·ness** [-nɪs] *s.* Heiserkeit *f*.

hoar·y ['hɔːrɪ] *adj.* □ **1.** weißlich; **2.** a) (alters)grau, ergraut, b) *fig.* altersgrau, (ur)alt, ehrwürdig.

hoax [həʊks] **I** *s.* **1.** Falschmeldung *f*, (Zeitungs)Ente *f*; **2.** Schabernack *m*, Streich *m*; **II** *v/t.* **3.** *j-n* zum besten haben, *j-m* e-n Bären aufbinden *od.* et. weismachen.

hob[1] [hɒb] **I** *s.* **1.** Ka'mineinsatz *m*, -vorsprung *m* (*für Kessel etc.*); **2.** → ***hobnail***; **3.** ⚙ a) (Ab)Wälzfräser *m*, b) Strehlbohrer *m*; **II** *v/t.* **4.** ⚙ abwälzen, verzahnen: ~***bing machine*** → 3a.

hob[2] [hɒb] *s.* Kobold *m*: ***play*** (*od.* ***raise***) ~ ***with*** Schindluder treiben mit.

hob·ble ['hɒbl] **I** *v/i.* **1.** humpeln, hoppeln, *a. fig.* hinken, holpern; **II** *v/t.* **2.** *e-m Pferd etc.* die Vorderbeine fesseln; **3.** hindern; **III** *s.* **4.** Humpeln *n*.

hob·ble·de·hoy [ˌhɒbldɪ'hɔɪ] *s.* F (junger) Tolpatsch *od.* Flegel.

hob·by ['hɒbɪ] *s. fig.* Steckenpferd *n*, Liebhabe'rei *f*, Hobby *n*; '~**·horse** *s.* **1.** Steckenpferd *n* (*a. fig.*); **2.** Schaukelpferd *n*; **3.** Karus'sellpferd *n*; '**hob·by·ist** [-ɪɪst] *s.* Hobby'ist *m*, *engS. a.* Bastler *m*, Heimwerker *m*.

hob·gob·lin ['hɒbgɒblɪn] *s.* **1.** Kobold *m*; **2.** *fig.* (Schreck)Gespenst *n*.

'**hob·nail** *s.* grober Schuhnagel; '**hob·nailed** *adj.* **1.** genagelt; **2.** *fig.* ungehobelt; '**hob·nail(ed) liv·er** *s.* ⚕ Säuferleber *f*.

'**hob·nob** *v/i.* **1.** in'tim *od.* ‚auf du u. du' sein, freundschaftlich verkehren (***with*** mit); **2.** plaudern (***with*** mit).

ho·bo ['həʊbəʊ] *pl.* **-bos, -boes** *s. Am.* **1.** Wanderarbeiter *m*; **2.** Landstreicher *m*, Tippelbruder *m*.

Hob·son's choice ['hɒbsnz] *s.*: ***it's*** ~

man hat keine andere Wahl.

hock¹ [hɒk] **I** *s.* **1.** *zo.* Sprung-, Fesselgelenk *n* (*der Huftiere*); **2.** Hachse *f* (*beim Schlachttier*); **II** *v/t.* **3.** → ***hamstring*** 3.

hock² [hɒk] *s.* **1.** weißer Rheinwein; **2.** trockener Weißwein.

hock³ [hɒk] F **I** *s.*: ***in ~*** a) verschuldet, b) versetzt, verpfändet, c) *Am.* im ‚Knast'; **II** *v/t.* versetzen, verpfänden.

hock·ey ['hɒkɪ] *s.* a) Hockey *n*, b) *bsd. Am.* Eishockey *n*: ***~ stick*** Hockeyschläger *m*.

'hock·shop *s. sl.* Pfandhaus *n*.

ho·cus ['həʊkəs] *v/t.* **1.** betrügen; **2.** *j-n* betäuben; **3.** *e-m Getränk* ein Betäubungsmittel beimischen; **ˌ~-'po·cus** [-'pəʊkəs] *s.* Hokus'pokus *m*: a) *Zauberformel*, b) Schwindel *m*, fauler Zauber.

hod [hɒd] *s.* **1.** ⚠ Mörteltrog *m*, Steinbrett *n* (*zum Tragen*): ***~ carrier*** → ***hodman*** 1; **2.** Kohleneimer *m*.

hodge·podge ['hɒdʒpɒdʒ] *bsd. Am.* → ***hotchpotch***.

'hod·man [-mən] *s.* [*irr.*] **1.** ⚠ Mörtel-, Ziegelträger *m*; **2.** Handlanger *m*.

ho·dom·e·ter [hɒ'dɒmɪtə] *s.* Hodo'meter *n*, Wegmesser *m*, Schrittzähler *m*.

hoe [həʊ] ⚒ **I** *s.* Hacke *f*; **II** *v/t.* *Boden* hacken; *Unkraut* aushacken: ***a long row to ~*** e-e schwere Aufgabe.

hog [hɒg] **I** *s.* **1.** (Haus-, Schlacht-) Schwein *n*, *Am. allg.* (*a.* Wild)Schwein *n*: ***go the whole ~*** F aufs Ganze gehen, ganze Arbeit leisten; **2.** F a) Vielfraß *m*, b) Flegel *m*, c) Schmutzfink *m*, Ferkel *n*; **3.** ⚓ Scheuerbesen *m*; **4.** ⚙ *Am.* (Reiß)Wolf *m*; **5.** → ***hogget***; **II** *v/t.* **6.** *den Rücken* krümmen; **7.** scheren, stutzen; **8.** (gierig) verschlingen, ‚fressen', *fig. a.* an sich reißen, mit Beschlag belegen: ***~ the road*** → 10; **III** *v/i.* **9.** den Rücken krümmen; **10.** F rücksichtslos in der (Fahrbahn)Mitte fahren; **'~-back** *s.* langer u. scharfer Gebirgskamm; **~ chol·er·a** *s. vet. Am.* Schweinepest *f*.

hog·get ['hɒgɪt] *s. Brit. noch ungeschorenes* einjähriges Schaf.

hog·gish ['hɒgɪʃ] *adj.* □ a) schweinisch, b) rücksichtslos, c) gierig, gefräßig.

hog·ma·nay ['hɒgməneɪ] *s. Scot.* Sil'vester *m*, *n*.

hog| mane *s.* gestutzte Pferdemähne; **'~'s-back** → ***hogback***.

hogs·head ['hɒgzhed] *s.* **1.** *Hohlmaß, etwa 240 l*; **2.** großes Faß.

'hog|·skin *s.* Schweinsleder *n*; **'~-tie** *v/t.* **1.** *e-m Tier* alle vier Füße zs.-binden; **2.** *fig.* lähmen, (be)hindern; **'~-wash** *s.* **1.** Schweinefutter *n*; **2.** *contp.* ‚Spülwasser' *n* (*Getränk*); **3.** Quatsch *m*, ‚Mist' *m*.

hoi(c)k [hɔɪk] *v/t.* ✈ hochreißen.

hoicks [hɔɪks] *int. hunt.* hussa! (*Hetzruf an Hunde*).

hoi pol·loi [ˌhɔɪ'pɒlɔɪ] (*Greek*) *s.* **1.** ***the ~*** die (breite) Masse, der Pöbel; **2.** *Am. sl.* ‚Tam'tam' *n* (***about*** um).

hoist¹ [hɔɪst] *obs. p.p.*: ***~ with one's own petard*** *fig.* in der eigenen Falle gefangen.

hoist² [hɔɪst] **I** *v/t.* **1.** hochziehen, -winden, hieven, heben; **2.** *Flagge*, *Segel* hissen; **3.** *Am. sl.* ‚klauen'; **4.** ***~ a few*** *Am. sl.* ein paar ‚heben'; **II** *s.* **5.** (Lasten)Aufzug *m*, Hebezeug *n*, Kran *m*, Winde *f*.

hoist·ing| cage ['hɔɪstɪŋ] *s.* ⚒ Förderkorb *m*; **~ crane** *s.* ⚙ Hebekran *m*; **~ en·gine** *s.* **1.** ⚙ Hebewerk *n*; **2.** ⚒ 'Förderma͵schine *f*.

hoi·ty-toi·ty [ˌhɔɪtɪ'tɔɪtɪ] **I** *adj.* **1.** hochnäsig; **2.** leichtsinnig; **II** *s.* **3.** Hochnäsigkeit *f*.

ho·k(e)y-po·k(e)y [ˌhəʊkɪ'pəʊkɪ] *s.* **1.** *sl.* → ***hocus-pocus***; **2.** Speiseeis *n*.

ho·kum ['həʊkəm] *s. sl.* **1.** *thea.* ‚Mätzchen' *pl.*, Kitsch *m*; **2.** ‚Krampf' *m*, Quatsch *m*.

hold¹ [həʊld] *s.* ⚓, ✈ Lade-, Frachtraum *m*.

hold² [həʊld] **I** *s.* **1.** Halt *m*, Griff *m*: ***catch*** (*od.* ***get, lay, seize, take***) ***~ of s.th.*** et. ergreifen *od.* in die Hand bekommen *od.* zu fassen bekommen *od.* erwischen; ***get ~ of s.o.*** j-n erwischen; ***get ~ of o.s.*** *fig.* sich in die Gewalt bekommen; ***keep ~ of*** festhalten; ***let go one's ~ of*** loslassen; ***miss one's ~*** danebengreifen; ***take ~*** *fig.* sich festsetzen, Wurzel fassen; **2.** Halt *m*, Stütze *f*: ***afford no ~*** keinen Halt bieten; **3.** *Ringen*: Griff *m*: (***with***) ***no ~s barred*** *fig.* mit harten Bandagen (*kämpfen*); **4.** (***on, over, of***) Gewalt *f*, Macht *f* (über *acc.*), Einfluß (auf *acc.*): ***get a ~ on s.o.*** j-n unter s-n Einfluß *od.* in s-e Macht bekommen; ***have a*** (***firm***) ***~ on s.o.*** j-n in s-r Gewalt haben, j-n beherrschen; **5.** *Am.* Einhalt *m*: ***put a ~ on s.th.*** et. stoppen; **6.** *Raumfahrt*: Unter'brechung *f* des Countdown; **II** *v/t.* [*irr.*] **7.** (fest)halten; **8.** sich *die Nase*, *die Ohren* zuhalten: ***~ one's nose*** (***ears***); **9.** *Gewicht*, *Last etc.* tragen, (aus)halten; **10.** *in e-m Zustand* halten: ***~ o.s. erect*** sich geradehalten; ***~*** (***o.s.***) ***ready*** (sich) bereithalten; **11.** (zu'rück-, ein-) behalten: ***~ the shipment*** die Sendung zurück(be)halten; ***~ everything!*** sofort aufhören!; **12.** zu'rück-, abhalten (***from*** von *et.*, ***from doing s.th.*** davon, et. zu tun); **13.** an-, aufhalten, im Zaume halten: ***there is no ~ing him*** er ist nicht zu halten *od.* zu bändigen; ***~ the enemy*** den Feind aufhalten; **14.** *Am.* a) *j-n* festnehmen: ***12 persons were held***, b) in Haft halten; **15.** *sport* sich erfolgreich verteidigen gegen *den Gegner*; **16.** *j-n* festlegen (***to*** auf *acc.*): ***~ s.o. to his word*** j-n beim Wort nehmen; **17.** a) *Versammlung*, *Wahl etc.* abhalten, b) *Fest etc.* veranstalten, c) *sport Meisterschaft etc.* austragen; **18.** (beibe)halten: ***~ the course***; **19.** *Alkohol* vertragen: ***~ one's liquor well*** e-e ganze Menge vertragen; **20.** ⚔ *u. fig.* *Stellung* halten, behaupten: ***~ one's own*** sich behaupten (***with*** gegen); ***~ the stage*** a) sich halten (*Theaterstück*), b) *fig.* die Szene beherrschen, im Mittelpunkt stehen; → ***fort***; **21.** innehaben: a) besitzen: ***~ land*** (***shares, etc.***), b) *Amt* bekleiden, c) *Titel* führen, d) *Platz etc.* einnehmen, e) *Rekord* halten; **22.** fassen: a) enthalten: ***the tank ~s 10 gallons***, b) Platz bieten für, 'unterbringen (können): ***the hotel ~s 500 guests***; ***the place ~s many memories*** der Ort ist voll von Erinnerungen; ***life ~s many surprises*** das Leben ist voller Überraschungen; ***what the future ~s*** was die Zukunft bringt; **23.** *Bewunderung etc.* hegen, *a. Vorurteile etc.* haben (***for*** für); **24.** behaupten, meinen: ***~*** (***the view***) ***that*** die Ansicht vertreten *od.* der Ansicht sein, daß; **25.** halten für: ***I ~ him to be a fool***; ***it is held to be true*** man hält es für wahr; **26.** ⚖ entscheiden (***that*** daß); **27.** *fig.* fesseln: ***~ the audience***; ***~ s.o.'s attention***; **28.** ***~ to*** *Am.* beschränken auf (*acc.*); **29.** ***~ against*** *j-m et.* vorwerfen *od.* verübeln; **30.** ♪ *Ton* (aus)halten; **III** *v/i.* [*irr.*] **31.** (stand)halten: ***will the bridge ~?***; **32.** (sich) festhalten (***by, to*** an *dat.*); **33.** sich verhalten: ***~ still*** stillhalten; **34.** *a.* ***~ good*** (weiterhin) gelten, gültig sein *od.* bleiben: ***the promise still ~s*** das Versprechen gilt noch; **35.** anhalten, andauern: ***the fine weather held***; ***my luck held*** das Glück blieb mir treu; **36.** einhalten: ***~!*** halt!; **37.** ***~ by*** (*od.* ***to***) *j-m od. e-r Sache* treu bleiben; **38.** ***~ with*** es halten mit *j-m*, für *j-n od. et.* sein;

Zssgn mit adv.:

hold| back I *v/t.* **1.** zu'rückhalten; **2.** → ***hold in***; **3.** zu'rückhalten mit, verschweigen; **II** *v/i.* **4.** sich zu'rückhalten (*a. fig.*); **5.** nicht mit der Sprache her'ausrücken; **~ down** *v/t.* **1.** niederhalten, *fig. a.* unter'drücken; **2.** F a) *e-n Posten* (inne)haben, b) sich *in e-r Stellung* halten; **~ forth I** *v/t.* **1.** (an)bieten; **2.** in Aussicht stellen; **II** *v/i.* **3.** sich auslassen *od.* verbreiten (***on*** über *acc.*); **4.** *Am.* stattfinden; **~ in I** *v/t.* im Zaum halten, zu'rückhalten: ***hold o.s. in*** a) → II, b) den Bauch einziehen; **II** *v/i.* sich zu'rückhalten; **~ off I** *v/t.* **1.** a) ab-, fernhalten, b) abwehren; **2.** *et.* aufschieben, *j-n* hinhalten; **II** *v/i.* **3.** sich fernhalten (***from*** von); **4.** a) zögern, b) warten; **5.** ausbleiben; **~ on** *v/i.* **1.** *a. fig.* (*a.* sich) festhalten (***to*** an *dat.*); **2.** aus-, 'durchhalten; **3.** andauern, -halten; **4.** *teleph.* am Appa'rat bleiben; **5.** ***~!*** immer langsam!, halt!; **6.** ***~ to*** *et.* behalten; **~ out I** *v/t.* **1.** *die Hand etc.* ausstrecken: ***hold s.th. out to s.o.*** j-m et. hinhalten; **2.** in Aussicht stellen: ***~ little hope*** wenig Hoffnung äußern *od.* haben; **3.** ***hold o.s. out as*** *Am.* sich ausgeben für *od.* als; **II** *v/i.* **4.** reichen (*Vorräte*); **5.** aus-, 'durchhalten; **6.** sich behaupten (***against*** gegen); **7.** ***~ on s.o.*** j-m et. vorenthalten *od.* verheimlichen; **8.** ***~ for*** F bestehen auf (*dat.*); **~ o·ver** *v/t.* **1.** *et.* vertagen, -schieben (***until*** auf *acc.*); **2.** ⚕ prolongieren; **3.** *Amt etc.* (weiter) behalten; **4.** *thea. etc.* *j-s* Engage'ment verlängern (***for*** um); **~ to·geth·er** *v/t. u. v/i.* zs.-halten (*a. fig.*); **~ up I** *v/t.* **1.** (hoch)heben; **2.** hochhalten: ***~ to view*** den Blicken darbieten; **3.** halten, stützen, tragen; **4.** aufrechterhalten; **5.** ***~ as*** als *Beispiel etc.* hinstellen; **6.** *j-n od. et.* aufhalten, *et.* verzögern; **7.** *j-n, e-e Bank etc.* über'fallen; **II** *v/i.* **8.** → ***hold out*** 5, 6; **9.** sich halten (*Preise, Wetter*); **10.** sich bewahrheiten.

'hold|·all *s.* Reisetasche *f*; **'~-back** *s.* Hindernis *n*.

hold·er ['həʊldə] *s.* **1.** *oft in Zssgn* Halter *m*, Behälter *m*; **2.** ⚙ a) Halter(ung *f*) *m*, b) Zwinge *f*; **3.** ⚡ (Lampen)Fassung *f*; **4.** Pächter *m*; **5.** ⚕ Inhaber(in) (*e-s Patents, Schecks etc.*), Besitzer(in):

previous ~ Vorbesitzer *m*; **6.** *sport* Inhaber(in) (*e-s Rekords, Titels etc.*).

'hold·fast *s.* **1.** ⚙ Klammer *f*, Zwinge *f*, Haken *m*, Kluppe *f*; **2.** ⚘ Haftscheibe *f*.

hold·ing ['həʊldɪŋ] *s.* **1.** (Fest)Halten *n*; **2.** ⚖ a) Pachtgut *n*, b) Pacht *f*, c) Grundbesitz *m*; **3.** *oft pl.* a) Besitz *m*, Bestand *m* (*an Effekten etc.*), b) (Aktien)Anteil *m*, (-)Beteiligung *f*: ***large steel ~s*** ☤ großer Besitz von Stahl(werks)aktien; **4.** ☤ a) Vorrat *m*, b) Guthaben *n*; **5.** ⚖ (gerichtliche) Entscheidung; **~ at·tack** *s.* ⚔ Fesselungsangriff *m*; **~ com·pa·ny** *s.* ☤ Dach-, Holdinggesellschaft *f*; **~ pat·tern** *s.* ✈ Warteschleife *f*.

'hold|ˌo·ver *s.* **1.** ,'Überbleibsel' *n* (*Amtsträger etc.*); **2.** *Film etc.*: a) Verlängerung *f*, b) *Künstler etc., dessen Engagement verlängert worden ist*; **'~-up** *s.* **1.** Verzögerung *f*, (*a.* Verkehrs)Stokkung *f*; **2.** (bewaffneter) ('Raub)ˌÜberfall.

hole [həʊl] **I** *s.* **1.** Loch *n*: ***be in a ~ fig.*** in der Klemme sitzen; ***make a ~ in fig.*** ein Loch reißen in (*Vorräte*); ***pick ~s in*** *fig.* a) an *e-r Sache* herumkritteln, b) *Argument etc.* zerpflücken, c) *j-m* am Zeug flicken; ***full of ~s*** *fig.* fehlerhaft, ,wack(e)lig' (*Theorie etc.*); ***like a ~ in the head*** F *unnötig* wie ein Kropf; **2.** Loch *n*, Grube *f*; **3.** Höhle *f*, Bau *m* (*Tier*); **4.** *fig.* ,Loch' *n*: a) (Bruch)Bude *f*, b) ,Kaff' *n*, c) Schlupfwinkel *m*; **5.** *Golf*: a) Hole *n*, Loch *n*, b) (Spiel)Bahn *f*: ***~ in one*** As *n*; **II** *v/t.* **6.** ein Loch machen in (*acc.*), durch'löchern; **7.** ⚒ schrämen; **8.** *Tier* in s-e Höhle treiben; **9.** *Golf*: *Ball* einlochen; **III** *v/i.* **10.** *mst* ***~ up*** a) sich in die Höhle verkriechen (*Tier*), b) *Am.* F sich verstecken *od.* -kriechen; **11.** *a.* ***~ out*** *Golf*: einlochen.

ˌhole-and-'cor·ner [-nd'k-] *adj.* **1.** heimlich, versteckt; **2.** anrüchig; **3.** armselig.

hol·i·day ['hɒlədɪ] **I** *s.* **1.** (***public ~*** gesetzlicher) Feiertag; **2.** freier Tag, Ruhetag *m*: ***have a ~*** e-n freien Tag haben (→ 3); ***have a ~ from*** sich von *et.* erholen können; **3.** *mst pl. bsd. Brit.* Ferien *pl.*, Urlaub *m*: ***the Easter ~s*** die Osterferien; ***be on ~*** im Urlaub sein; ***go on ~*** in Urlaub gehen; ***have a ~*** Urlaub haben (→ 2); ***take a ~*** Urlaub nehmen *od.* machen; ***~s with pay*** bezahlter Urlaub; **II** *adj.* **4.** Feiertags...: ***~ clothes*** Festtagskleidung *f*; **5.** *bsd. Brit.* Ferien..., Urlaubs...: ***~ camp*** Feriendorf *n*; ***~ course*** Ferienkurs *m*; **III** *v/i.* **6.** *bsd. Brit.* Ferien *od.* Urlaub machen; **'~ˌmak·er** *s. bsd. Brit.* Urlauber(in).

ˌho·li·er-than-'thou [ˌhəʊlɪə-] *Am.* F **I** *s.* ,Phari'säer' *m*; **II** *adj.* phari'säisch.

ho·li·ness ['həʊlɪnɪs] *s.* Heiligkeit *f*: ***His ᘔ*** Seine Heiligkeit (*Papst*).

ho·lism ['həʊlɪzəm] *s. phls.* Ho'lismus *m* (*Ganzheitstheorie*); **ho·lis·tic** [həʊ'lɪstɪk] *adj.* ho'listisch.

Hol·lands ['hɒləndz], *a.* **Hol·land gin** *s.* Ge'never *m*.

hol·ler ['hɒlə] *v/i. u. v/t.* F brüllen.

hol·low ['hɒləʊ] **I** *s.* **1.** Höhle *f*, (Aus-)Höhlung *f*, Hohlraum *m*: ***~ of the hand*** hohle Hand; ***~ of the knee*** Kniekehle *f*; ***have s.o. in the ~ of one's hand*** *fig.* j-n völlig in der Hand haben; **2.** Vertiefung *f*, Mulde *f*, Senke *f*; **3.** ⚙ a) Hohlkehle *f*, b) (Guß)Blase *f*; **II** *adj.* □ → *a.* III; **4.** hohl, Hohl...; **5.** hohl, dumpf (*Ton, Stimme*); **6.** *fig.* a) hohl, leer: ***feel ~*** Hunger haben, b) falsch: ***~ promises***; ***~ victory*** wertloser Sieg; **7.** hohl: a) eingefallen (*Wangen*), b) tiefliegend (*Augen*); **III** *adv.* **8.** hohl: ***ring ~*** hohl *od.* unglaubwürdig klingen; ***beat s.o. ~*** F j-n vernichtend schlagen; **IV** *v/t.* **9.** *oft* ***~ out*** aushöhlen, -kehlen; **~ bit** *s.* ⚙ Hohlmeißel *m*, -bohrer *m*; **~ charge** *s.* ⚔ Haft-Hohlladung *f*; **ˌ~-'cheeked** *adj.* hohlwangig; **'~-eyed** *adj.* hohläugig; **ˌ~-'ground** *adj.* ⚙ hohlgeschliffen.

hol·low·ness ['hɒləʊnɪs] *s.* **1.** Hohlheit *f*; **2.** Dumpfheit *f*; **3.** *fig.* a) Hohlheit *f*, Leere *f*, b) Falschheit *f*.

hol·low| square *s.* ⚔ Kar'ree *n*; **~ tile** *s.* ⚙ Hohlziegel *m*; **'~·ware** *s.* tiefes (Küchen)Geschirr (*Töpfe etc.*).

hol·ly ['hɒlɪ] *s.* **1.** ⚘ Stechpalme *f*; **2.** Stechpalmenzweige *pl.*

'hol·ly·hock *s.* ⚘ Stockrose *f*.

hol·o·caust ['hɒləkɔ:st] *s.* **1.** Massenvernichtung *f*, (*engS.* 'Brand)Kataˌstrophe *f*: ***the ᘔ*** *pol. hist.* der Holocaust; **2.** Brandopfer *n*.

hol·o|·cene ['hɒləʊsi:n] *s. geol.* Holo'zän *n*, Al'luvium *n*; **'~·gram** [-əʊgræm] *s. phys.* Holo'gramm *n*; **'~·graph** [-əʊgrɑ:f; -əʊgræf] *adj. u. s.* ⚖ eigenhändig geschrieben(e Urkunde).

hols [hɒlz] *s. pl. Brit.* F *für* ***holiday*** 3.

hol·ster ['həʊlstə] *s.* (Pi'stolen)Halfter *f*, *n*.

ho·ly ['həʊlɪ] **I** *adj.* □ **1.** heilig, (*Hostie etc.*) geweiht: ***~ cow*** (*od.* ***smoke***)**!** F ,heiliger Bimbam'!; **2.** fromm; **3.** gottgefällig; **II** *s.* **4.** ***the ~ of holies*** *bibl.* das Allerheiligste; **ᘔ Al·li·ance** *s. hist. die* Heilige Alli'anz; **~ bread** *s.* Abendmahlsbrot *n*, Hostie *f*; **ᘔ Cit·y** *s. die* Heilige Stadt; **~ day** *s.* kirchlicher Feiertag; **ᘔ Fa·ther** *s. der* Heilige Vater; **ᘔ Ghost** *s. der* Heilige Geist; **ᘔ Land** *s. das* Heilige Land; **ᘔ Of·fice** *s. R.C.* a) *hist. die* Inquisiti'on, b) *das* Heilige Of'fizium; **ᘔ Ro·man Em·pire** *s. hist. das* Heilige Römische Reich; **ᘔ Sat·ur·day** *s.* Kar'samstag *m*; **ᘔ Scrip·ture** *s. die* Heilige Schrift; **ᘔ See** *s. der* Heilige Stuhl; **ᘔ Spir·it** → ***Holy Ghost***; **~ ter·ror** *s.* F ,Nervensäge' *f*; **ᘔ Thurs·day** *s.* **1.** *R.C.* Grün'donnerstag *m*; **2.** (*anglikanische Kirche*) Himmelfahrtstag *m*; **ᘔ Trin·i·ty** *s. die* Heilige Drei'einigkeit *od.* Drei'faltigkeit; **~ wa·ter** *s. R.C.* Weihwasser *n*; **ᘔ Week** *s.* Karwoche *f*; **ᘔ Writ** → ***Holy Scripture***.

hom·age ['hɒmɪdʒ] *s.* **1.** *hist. u. fig.* Huldigung *f*: ***do*** (*od.* ***render***) ***~*** huldigen (***to*** *dat.*); **2.** *fig.* Reve'renz *f*: ***pay ~ to*** Anerkennung zollen (*dat.*), (s-e) Hochachtung bezeigen (*dat.*).

Hom·burg (hat) ['hɒmbɜ:g] *s.* Homburg *m* (*Herrenfilzhut*).

home [həʊm] **I** *s.* **1.** Heim *n*: a) Haus *n*, (*eigene*) Wohnung, b) Zu'hause *n*, Da'heim *n*, c) Elternhaus *n*: ***at ~*** zu Hause, daheim (*a. sport*) (→ 2); ***at ~ in*** (*od.* ***on, with***) *fig.* bewandert in (*dat.*), vertraut mit (*e-m Fachgebiet etc.*); ***not at ~*** (***to s.o.***) nicht zu sprechen (für j-n); ***feel at ~*** sich wie zu Hause fühlen; ***make o.s. at ~*** es sich bequem machen; tun, als ob man zu Hause wäre; ***make one's ~ at*** sich niederlassen in (*dat.*); ***away from ~*** abwesend, verreist, *bsd. sport* auswärts; **2.** Heimat *f* (*a.* ⚘, *zo. u. fig.*), Geburts-, Heimatland *n*: ***at ~*** a) im Lande, in der Heimat, b) im Inland, daheim; ***at ~ and abroad*** im In- u. Ausland; ***a letter from ~*** ein Brief von Zuhause; **3.** (ständiger *od.* jetziger) Wohnort, Heimatort *m*: ***last ~*** letzte Ruhestätte; **4.** Heim *n*, Anstalt *f*: ***~ for the aged*** Altenheim; ***~ for the blind*** Blindenheim, -anstalt; **5.** *sport* a) Ziel *n*, b) → ***home plate***, c) Heimspiel *n*, d) Heimsieg *m*; **II** *adj.* **6.** Heim...: a) häuslich, Familien..., b) zu Hause ausgeübt: ***~ life*** häusliches Leben, Familienleben *n*; ***~ remedy*** Hausmittel *n*; ***~baked*** selbstgebacken; **7.** Heimat...: ***~ address*** (***city, port*** *etc.*); ***~ fleet*** ⚓ Flotte *f* in Heimatgewässern; **8.** einheimisch, inländisch, Inland(s)..., Binnen...: ***~ affairs*** *pol.* innere Angelegenheiten; ***~ market*** Inlands-, Binnenhandel *m*; **9.** *sport* a) Heim...: ***~ advantage*** (***match, win, etc.***): ***~ strength*** Heimstärke *f*, b) Ziel...; **10.** a) (wohl)gezielt, wirkungsvoll (*Schlag etc.*), b) *fig.* treffend, beißend (*Bemerkung etc.*); → ***home thrust, home truth***; **III** *adv.* **11.** heim, nach Hause: ***the way ~*** der Heimweg; ***go ~*** nach Hause gehen (→ 13); → ***write*** 10; **12.** zu Hause, (wieder) da'heim; **13.** a) ins Ziel, b) im Ziel, c) bis zum Ausgangspunkt, d) ganz, soweit wie möglich: ***drive a nail ~*** e-n Nagel fest einschlagen; ***drive*** (*od.* ***bring***) ***s.th. ~ to s.o.*** j-m et. klarmachen *od.* beibringen *od.* vor Augen führen; ***drive a charge ~ to s.o.*** j-n überführen; ***go*** (*od.* ***get, strike***) ***~*** ,sitzen', s-e Wirkung tun; ***the thrust went ~*** der Hieb saß; **IV** *v/i.* **14.** zu'rückkehren; **15.** ✈ a) (*per Leitstrahl*) das Ziel anfliegen, b) *mst* ***~ in on*** *ein Ziel* auto'matisch ansteuern (*Rakete*); **V** *v/t.* **16.** *Flugzeug* (*per Radar*) einweisen, ,her'unterholen'.

ˌhome|-and-'home *adj. sport Am.* im Vor- u. Rückspiel ausgetragen: ***~ match***; **'~ˌbod·y** *s.* häuslicher Mensch, *contp.* Stubenhocker(in); **'~·bound** *adj.* ans Haus gefesselt: ***~ invalid***; **ˌ~'bred** *adj.* **1.** einheimisch; **2.** *obs.* hausbacken; **'~·brew** *s.* selbstgebrautes Getränk (*bsd.* Bier); **'~-ˌcom·ing** *s.* Heimkehr *f*; **~ con·tents** *s. pl.* Hausrat *m*; **ᘔ Coun·ties** *s. pl. die um London liegenden Grafschaften*; **~ e·co·nom·ics** *s. pl. sg. konstr.* Hauswirtschaft(slehre) *f*; **~ front** *s.* Heimatfront *f*; **~ ground** *s. sport* eigener Platz; *fig.* vertrautes Gelände; **ᘔ Guard** *s.* Bürgerwehr *f*; **'~-ˌkeep·ing** *adj.* häuslich, *contp.* stubenhockerisch; **'~·land** *s.* **1.** Heimat-, Vater-, Mutterland *n*; **2.** *pol.* Homeland *n*, Heimstatt *f* (*in Südafrika*).

home·less ['həʊmlɪs] *adj.* **1.** heimatlos; **2.** obdachlos; **'home·like** *adj.* wie zu Hause, gemütlich; **home·li·ness** ['həʊmlɪnɪs] *s.* **1.** Einfachheit *f*, Schlichtheit *f*; **2.** Gemütlichkeit *f*; **3.** *Am.* Reizlosigkeit *f*; **home·ly** ['həʊmlɪ] *adj.* **1.** → ***homelike***; **2.** freundlich; **3.** einfach, hausbacken; **4.** *Am.* reizlos: ***a ~ girl***.

ˌhome|'made *adj.* **1.** selbstgemacht, Hausmacher...; **2.** selbstgebastelt: ***~***

bomb; **3.** † a) einheimisch, im Inland hergestellt: **~ *goods***, b) hausgemacht: **~ *inflation***; **'~ˌmak·er** *s. Am.* **1.** Hausfrau *f*; **2.** Fa'milienpflegerin *f*; **'~ˌmak·ing** *s. Am.* Haushaltsführung *f*; **~ mar·ket** *s.* † Inlandsmarkt *m*; **~ me·chan·ic** *s.* Heimwerker *m*; **~ mov·ie** *s.* Heimkino *n.*

homeo- *etc.* → ***homoeo-*** *etc.*

home| of·fice *s.* **1.** ♔ *Brit.* 'Innenminiˌsterium *n*; **2.** *bsd.* † *Am.* Hauptsitz *m*; **~ perm** *s.* F Heim-Dauerwelle *f*; **~ plate** *s. Baseball*: Heimbase *n.*

hom·er ['həʊmə] *s.* F *für **home run**.*

Ho·mer·ic [həʊ'merɪk] *adj.* ho'merisch: **~ *laughter***.

home| rule *s. pol.* a) 'Selbstreˌgierung *f*, b) ♔ *hist.* Homerule *f* (*in Irland*); **~ run** *s. Baseball*: Homerun *m* (*Lauf über alle 4 Male*); ♔ **Sec·re·tar·y** *s. Brit.* 'Innenmiˌnister *m*; **'~·sick** *adj.*: ***be ~*** Heimweh haben; **'~ˌsick·ness** *s.* Heimweh *n*; **'~·spun I** *adj.* **1.** a) zu Hause gesponnen, b) Homespun…: **~ *clothing***; **2.** *fig.* schlicht, einfach; **II** *s.* **3.** Homespun *n* (*Streichgarn[gewebe]*); **'~·stead** *s.* **1.** Heimstätte *f*, Gehöft *n*; **2.** ⚖ *Am.* Heimstätte *f* (*Grundparzelle od. gegen Zugriff von Gläubigern geschützter Grundbesitz*); **~ straight**, **~ stretch** *s. sport* Zielgerade *f*: ***be on the ~*** *fig.* kurz vor dem Ziel stehen; **~ thrust** *s. fig.* wohlgezielter Hieb; **~ truth** *s.* harte Wahrheit, unbequeme Tatsache; **'~·ward** [-wəd] **I** *adv.* heimwärts, nach Hause; **II** *adj.* Heim…, Rück…; → ***bound***[2]; **'~·wards** [-wədz] → ***homeward*** I; **'~·work** *s.* **1.** *ped.* Hausaufgabe(n *pl.*) *f*, Schularbeiten *pl.*: ***do one's ~*** s-e Hausaufgaben machen (*a. fig. sich gründlich vorbereiten*); **2.** † Heimarbeit *f*; **'~ˌwork·er** *s.* † Heimarbeiter (-in); **'~ˌwreck·er** *s. j-d, der e-e Ehe zerstört.*

home·y *Am. für **homy**.*

hom·i·cid·al [ˌhɒmɪ'saɪdl] *adj.* **1.** mörderisch, mordlustig; **2.** Mord…, Totschlags…; **hom·i·cide** ['hɒmɪsaɪd] *s.* **1.** *allg.* Tötung *f*, *engS.* a) Mord *m*, b) Totschlag *m*: **~ *by misadventure*** *Am.* Unfall *m* mit Todesfolge; **~ (*squad*)** Mordkommission *f*; **2.** Mörder(in), Totschläger(in).

hom·i·ly ['hɒmɪlɪ] *s.* **1.** Homi'lie *f*, Predigt *f*; **2.** *fig.* Mo'ralpredigt *f.*

hom·ing ['həʊmɪŋ] **I** *adj.* **1.** heimkehrend: **~ *pigeon*** Brieftaube *f*; **~ *instinct*** *zo.* Heimkehrvermögen *n*; **2.** ⚔ zielansteuernd (*Rakete etc.*); **II** *s.* ✈ **3.** a) Zielflug *m*, b) Zielpeilung *f*, c) Rückflug *m*: **~ *beacon*** Zielflugfunkfeuer *n*; **~ *device*** Zielfluggerät *n.*

hom·i·nid ['hɒmɪnɪd] *zo.* **I** *adj.* menschenartig; **II** *s.* Homi'nide *m*, menschenartiges Wesen; **'hom·i·noid** [-nɔɪd] *adj. u. s.* menschenähnlich(es Tier).

hom·i·ny ['hɒmɪnɪ] *s. Am.* **1.** Maismehl *n*; **2.** Maisbrei *m.*

ho·mo ['həʊməʊ] *s.* F ‚Homo' *m.*

homo- [həʊməʊ; hɒməʊ], **homoeo-** [həʊmjəʊ] *in Zssgn* gleich(artig).

ho·moe·o·path ['həʊmjəʊpæθ] *s.* ⚕ Homöo'path(in); **ho·moe·o·path·ic** [ˌhəʊmjəʊ'pæθɪk] *adj.* (□ **~*ally***) ⚕ homöo'pathisch; **ho·moe·op·a·thist** [ˌhəʊmɪ'ɒpəθɪst] → ***homoeopath***; **ho·moe·op·a·thy** [ˌhəʊmɪ'ɒpəθɪ] *s.* ⚕ Homöopa'thie *f.*

ho·mo·e·rot·ic [ˌhəʊməʊɪ'rɒtɪk] *adj.* homoe'rotisch.

ho·mo·ge·ne·i·ty [ˌhɒməʊdʒe'niːətɪ] *s.* Homogeni'tät *f*, Gleichartigkeit *f*; **ho·mo·ge·ne·ous** [ˌhɒməʊ'dʒiːnjəs] *adj.* □ homo'gen: a) gleichartig, b) einheitlich; **ho·mo·gen·e·sis** [ˌhɒməʊ'dʒenɪsɪs] *s. biol.* Homoge'nese *f*; **ho·mog·e·nize** [hɒ'mɒdʒənaɪz] *v/t.* homogenisieren.

ho·mol·o·gate [hɒ'mɒləgeɪt] *v/t.* **1.** ⚖ a) genehmigen, b) beglaubigen, bestätigen; **2.** *Ski- u. Motorsport*: homologieren; **ho'mol·o·gous** [-gəs] *adj.* ⚗, ⩘, *biol.* homo'log.

hom·o·nym ['hɒməʊnɪm] *s. ling.* Homo'nym *n* (*a. biol.*), gleichlautendes Wort; **ho·mo·nym·ic** [ˌhɒməʊ'nɪmɪk], **ho·mon·y·mous** [hɒ'mɒnɪməs] *adj.* homo'nym.

ho·mo·phile ['hɒməʊfaɪl] **I** *s.* Homo'phile(r *m*) *f*; **II** *adj.* homo'phil.

hom·o·phone ['hɒməʊfəʊn] *s. ling.* Homo'phon *n*; **hom·o·phon·ic** [ˌhɒməʊ'fɒnɪk] *adj.* ♪, *ling.* homo'phon.

ho·mop·ter·a [həʊ'mɒptərə] *s. pl. zo.* Gleichflügler *pl.* (*Insekten*).

ho·mo·sex·u·al [ˌhɒməʊ'seksjʊəl] **I** *s.* Homosexu'elle(r *m*) *f*; **II** *adj.* homosexu'ell; **ho·mo·sex·u·al·i·ty** [ˌhɒməʊseksjʊ'ælətɪ] *s.* Homosexuali'tät *f.*

ho·mun·cu·lar [hɒ'mʌŋkjʊlə] *adj.* ho'munkulusähnlich; **ho'mun·cule** [-kjuːl], **ho'mun·cu·lus** [-kjʊləs] *pl.* **-li** [-laɪ] *s.* **1.** Ho'munkulus *m* (*künstlich erzeugter Mensch*); **2.** Menschlein *n*, Knirps *m.*

hom·y ['həʊmɪ] *adj.* F gemütlich.

hone [həʊn] **I** *s.* **1.** (feiner) Schleifstein; **II** *v/t.* **2.** honen, fein-, ziehschleifen; **3.** *fig.* a) schärfen, b) (aus)feilen.

hon·est ['ɒnɪst] *adj.* □ **1.** ehrlich: a) redlich, rechtschaffen, anständig, b) offen, aufrichtig; **2.** *humor.* wacker, bieder; **3.** ehrlich verdient; **4.** *obs.* ehrbar (*Frau*); **'hon·est·ly** [-lɪ] **I** *adv.* → ***honest***; **II** *int.* F a) offen gesagt, b) ehrlich!, c) *empört*: nein (*od.* also) wirklich!; **ˌhon·est-to-'God**, **ˌhon·est-to-'good·ness** *adj.* F echt, wirklich, ‚richtig'; **'hon·es·ty** [-tɪ] *s.* **1.** Ehrlichkeit *f*: a) Rechtschaffenheit *f*: **~ *is the best policy*** ehrlich währt am längsten, b) Aufrichtigkeit *f*; **2.** *obs.* Ehrbarkeit *f*; **3.** ⚘ 'Mondviˌole *f.*

hon·ey ['hʌnɪ] *s.* **1.** Honig *m* (*a. fig.*); **2.** ⚘ Nektar *m*; **3.** F *bsd. Am.* a) *Anrede*: ‚Schatz' *m*, Süße(r *m*) *f*, b) *Am.* ‚süßes' *od.* ‚schickes' Ding: ***a ~ of a car*** ein ‚klasse' Wagen; **'~·bag** *s. zo.* Honigmagen *m der Bienen*; **'~·bee** *s. zo.* Honigbiene *f*; **'~·bun(ch)** [-bʌn(tʃ)] → ***honey*** 3 a.

'hon·ey·comb [-kəʊm] **I** *s.* **1.** Honigwabe *f*; **2.** Waffelmuster *n* (*Gewebe*): **~ (*quilt*)** Waffeldecke *f*; **3.** ⚙ Lunker *m*, (Guß)Blase *f*; **4.** *in Zssgn* ⚙ Waben… (*-kühler, -spule etc.*): **~ *stomach*** *zo.* Netzmagen *m*; **II** *v/t.* **5.** (wabenartig) durch'löchern; **6.** *fig.* durch'setzen (***with*** mit); **'hon·ey·combed** [-kəʊmd] *adj.* **1.** durch'löchert, löcherig, zellig; **2.** ⚙ blasig; **3.** *fig.* (***with***) a) durch'setzt (mit), b) unter'graben (durch).

'hon·ey|·dew *s.* **1.** ⚘ Honigtau *m*, Blatthonig *m*: **~ *melon*** Honigmelone *f*; **2.** gesüßter Tabak; **'~-ˌeat·er** *s. orn.* Honigfresser *m.*

hon·eyed ['hʌnɪd] *adj.* **1.** voller Honig; **2.** *a. fig.* honigsüß.

hon·ey| ex·trac·tor *s.* Honigschleuder *f*; **~ flow** *s.* (Bienen)Tracht *f*; **'~·moon I** *s.* **1.** Flitterwochen *pl.*, Honigmond *m* (*a. iro. fig.*); **2.** Hochzeitsreise *f*; **II** *v/i.* **3.** a) die Flitterwochen verbringen, b) s-e Hochzeitsreise machen; **'~ˌmoon·er** *s.* a) ‚Flitterwöchner' *m*, b) Hochzeitsreisende(r *m*) *f*; **~ sac** *s. zo.* Honigmagen *m*; **'~ˌsuck·le** *s.* ⚘ Geißblatt *n.*

hon·ied ['hʌnɪd] → ***honeyed***.

honk [hɒŋk] **I** *s.* **1.** Schrei *m* (*der Wildgans*); **2.** 'Hupensiˌgnal *n*; **II** *v/i.* **3.** schreien; **4.** hupen.

honk·y-tonk ['hɒŋkɪtɒŋk] *s. Am. sl.* ‚Spe'lunke' *f.*

hon·or *etc. Am.* → ***honour*** *etc.*

hon·o·rar·i·um [ˌɒnə'reərɪəm] *pl.* **-rar·i·a** [-'reərɪə], **-rar·i·ums** *s.* (*freiwillig gezahltes*) Hono'rar; **hon·or·ar·y** ['ɒnərərɪ] *adj.* **1.** ehrend; **2.** Ehren…: **~ *doctor*** (***member***, *etc.*); **~ *debt*** Ehrenschuld *f*; **~ *degree*** ehrenhalber verliehener akademischer Grad; **3.** ehrenamtlich: **~ *secretary***; **hon·or·if·ic** [ˌɒnə'rɪfɪk] **I** *adj.* (□ **~*ally***) ehrend, Ehren…; **II** *s.* Ehrung *f*, Ehrentitel *m.*

hon·our ['ɒnə] **I** *s.* **1.** Ehre *f*: (***sense of***) **~** Ehrgefühl *n*; (***up***)***on my ~!***, *Brit.* F **~ *bright!*** Ehrenwort!; ***man of ~*** Ehrenmann *m*; ***point of ~*** Ehrensache *f*; ***do s.o. ~*** j-m zur Ehre gereichen, j-m Ehre machen; ***do s.o. the ~ of doing s.th.*** j-m die Ehre erweisen, et. zu tun; ***he is an ~ to his parents*** (***to his school***) er macht s-n Eltern Ehre (er ist e-e Zierde s-r Schule); ***put s.o. on his ~*** j-n bei s-r Ehre packen; (***in***) **~ *bound***, ***on one's ~*** moralisch verpflichtet; ***to his ~ it must be said*** zu s-r Ehre muß gesagt werden; (***there is***) **~ *among thieves*** (es gibt so etwas wie) Ganovenehre *f*; ***may I have the ~*** (***of the next dance***)***?*** darf ich (um den nächsten Tanz) bitten?; **2.** Ehrung *f*, Ehre(n *pl.*) *f*: a) Ehrerbietung *f*, Ehrenbezeigung *f*, b) Hochachtung *f*, c) Auszeichnung *f*, (Ehren)Titel *m*, Ehrenamt *n*, -zeichen *n*: ***in s.o.'s ~*** zu j-s *od.* j-m zu Ehren; ***hold*** (*od.* ***have***) ***in ~*** in Ehren halten; ***pay s.o. the last*** (*od.* ***funeral***) **~*s*** j-m die letzte Ehre erweisen; ***military ~s*** militärische Ehren; **~*s list*** *Brit.* Liste *f* der Titelverleihungen (*zum Geburtstag des Herrschers etc.*) (→ 3); → ***due*** 3; **3.** *pl. univ.* besondere Auszeichnung: **~*s degree*** *akademischer Grad mit Prüfung in e-m Spezialfach*; **~*s list*** *Liste der Studenten, die auf e-n **honours degree** hinarbeiten*; **~*s man*** *Brit.*, **~*s student*** *Am. Student, der e-n **honours degree** anstrebt od. innehat*; **4.** *pl.* Hon'neurs *pl.*: ***do the ~s*** die Honneurs machen, als Gastgeber(in) fungieren; **5.** *Kartenspiel*: Bild *n*; **6.** *Golf*: Ehre *f* (*Berechtigung zum 1. Schlag*): ***it is his ~*** er hat die Ehre; **7.** ***Your*** (***His***) **~** *obs.* Euer (Seine) Gnaden; **II** *v/t.* **8.** ehren; **9.** ehren, auszeichnen (***with*** mit); **10.** beehren (***with*** mit); **11.** *j-m zur Ehre gereichen od.* Ehre machen; **12.** *e-r Einladung etc.* Folge leisten; **13.** † a) *Scheck etc.* honorieren, einlösen, b) *Schuld* begleichen, c) *Vertrag* erfüllen; **hon·our·a·ble** ['ɒnərəbl] *adj.* □ **1.** achtbar, ehrenwert; **2.** rechtschaffen: ***an ~ man*** ein Ehrenmann; **3.** ehrenhaft, ehrlich (*Absicht etc.*); **4.** ehrenvoll, rühmlich; **5.** ♀ (*der od. die*) Ehrenwerte (*in Großbritannien: Adelstitel od. Titel der Ehrendamen des Hofes, der Mitglieder des Unterhauses, der Bürgermeister; in USA: Titel der Mitglieder des Kongresses, hoher Beamter, der Richter u. Bürgermeister*): ***Right*** ♀ (*der*) Sehr Ehrenwerte; → ***friend*** 5.

hooch [hu:tʃ] *s. Am.* F ‚Fusel' *m.*

hood [hʊd] **I** *s.* **1.** Ka'puze *f* (*a. univ. am Talar*); **2.** ⚘ Helm *m*; **3.** *orn.*, *zo.* Haube *f*, Schopf *m*; Brillenzeichnung *f* der Kobra; **4.** *mot.* a) *Brit.* Verdeck *n*, b) *Am.* (Motor)Haube *f*; **5.** ⚙ a) Kappe *f*, (Schutz)Haube *f*, b) Abzug(shaube *f*) *m* (*für Gas etc.*); **6.** → ***hoodlum***; **II** *v/t.* **7.** *j-m* e-e Ka'puze aufsetzen; **8.** be-, verdecken.

hood·ed ['hʊdɪd] *adj.* **1.** mit e-r Ka'puze bekleidet; **2.** ver-, bedeckt, verhüllt (*a. Augen*); **3.** *orn.* mit e-r Haube; **~ crow** *s. orn.* Nebelkrähe *f*; **~ seal** *s. zo.* Mützenrobbe *f*; **~ snake** *s. zo.* Kobra *f.*

hood·lum ['hu:dləm] *s.* F **1.** Rowdy *m*, ‚Schläger' *m*; **2.** Ga'nove *m*, Gangster *m.*

hoo·doo ['hu:du:] **I** *s. Am.* **1.** → ***voodoo*** I; **2.** a) Unglücksbringer *m*, b) Unglück *n*, Pech *n*; **II** *v/t.* **3.** a) verhexen, b) *j-m* Unglück bringen; **III** *adj.* **4.** Unglücks...

'**hood·wink** *v/t.* **1.** *obs.* die Augen verbinden (*dat.*); **2.** *fig.* hinters Licht führen, reinlegen.

hoo·ey ['hu:ɪ] *s. sl.* Quatsch *m*, Blödsinn *m.*

hoof [hu:f] *pl.* **hoofs**, **hooves** [hu:vz] **I** *s.* **1.** *zo.* a) Huf *m*, b) Fuß *m*: ***on the ~*** lebend (*Schlachtvieh*); **2.** *humor.* ‚Pe'dal' *n*, Fuß *m*; **3.** Huftier *n*; **II** *v/t.* **4.** F *Strecke* ‚tippeln': ***~ it*** → 6, 7; **5.** ***~ out*** *j-n* ‚rausschmeißen'; **III** *v/i.* **6.** F ‚tippeln', marschieren; **7.** F tanzen; ˌ**~-and-'mouth dis·ease** *s. vet.* Maul- u. Klauenseuche *f.*

hoofed [hu:ft] *adj.* gehuft, Huf...; '**hoof·er** [-fə] *s. Am. sl.* Berufstänzer (-in), *bsd.* Re'vuegirl *n.*

hoo-ha ['hu:hɑ:] *s.* F ‚Tam'tam' *n.*

hook [hʊk] **I** *s.* **1.** Haken *m* (*a.* ✂): ***~ and eye*** Haken u. Öse; ***~ and ladder*** *Am.* Gerätewagen *m* der Feuerwehr; ***by ~ or (by) crook*** mit allen Mitteln, so oder so; ***on one's own ~*** F auf eigene Faust; **2.** ⚙ a) (Klammer-, Dreh)Haken *m*, b) (Tür)Angel *f*, Haspe *f*; **3.** Angelhaken *m*: ***be off the ~*** F ‚aus dem Schneider' sein; ***get s.o. off the ~*** F j-m ‚aus der Patsche' helfen, j-n ‚herauspauken'; ***get o.s. off the ~*** sich aus der ‚Schlinge' ziehen; ***have s.o. on the ~*** F j-n ‚zappeln' lassen; ***that lets him off the ~*** damit ist er raus aus der Sache; ***fall for s.o. (s.th.) ~, line and sinker*** voll auf j-n (et.) ‚abfahren'; ***swallow s.th. ~, line and sinker*** et. voll u. ganz ‚schlucken'; **4.** ✓ Sichel *f*; **5.** a) scharfe Krümmung, b) gekrümmte Landspitze; **6.** *pl. sl.* ‚Griffel' *pl.* (*Finger*); **7.** ♪ Notenfähnchen *n*; **8.** *sport*: a) *Boxen*: Haken *m*: ***~ to the body*** Körperhaken, b) *Golf*: Hook *m* (*Kurvschlag*); **II** *v/t.* **9.** an-, ein-, fest-, zuhaken; **10.** fangen, (sich) angeln (*a. fig.* F): ***~ a husband*** sich e-n Mann angeln; ***he is ~ed*** F a) er zappelt im Netz, er ist ‚dran' od. ‚geliefert', b) → ***hooked*** 3; **11.** *sl.* ‚klauen', stehlen; **12.** krümmen; **13.** aufspießen; **14.** a) *Boxen*: *j-m* e-n Haken versetzen, b) *Golf*: *Ball* mit (e-m) Hook schlagen, c) (*Eis*)*Hockey*: *Gegner* haken; **15.** ***~ it*** F ‚verduften'; **III** *v/i.* **16.** sich zuhaken lassen; **17.** sich festhaken (***to*** an *dat.*); **~ on I** *v/t.* **1.** ein-, anhaken; **II** *v/i.* **2.** → ***hook*** 17; **3.** sich einhängen (***to s.o.*** bei j-m); **~ up** *v/t.* **1.** → ***hook on*** 1; **2.** zuhaken; **3.** ⚙ a) *Gerät* zs.-bauen, b) anschließen; **4.** *Radio, TV*: a) zs.-schalten, b) zuschalten (***with*** *dat.*).

hook·a(h) ['hʊkə] *s.* Huka *f* (*orientalische Wasserpfeife*).

hooked [hʊkt] *adj.* **1.** krumm, hakenförmig, Haken...; **2.** mit (e-m) Haken (versehen); **3.** F a) (***on***) süchtig (nach); *fig. a.* ‚scharf' (auf *acc.*), ‚verrückt' (nach): ***~ on heroin (television)*** heroin- (fernseh)süchtig, b) → ***hook*** 10.

hook·er ['hʊkə] *s.* **1.** ⚓ a) Huker *m*, Fischerboot *n*, b) *contp.* ‚alter Kahn'; **2.** *sl.* ‚Nutte' *f.*

hook·ey → ***hooky***.

'**hook|-nosed** *adj.* mit e-r Hakennase; '**~-up** *s.* **1.** *Radio, TV*: a) Zs.-, Konfe'renzschaltung *f*, b) Zuschaltung *f*; **2.** ϟ a) Schaltbild *n*, -schema *n*, b) Blockschaltung *f*; **3.** ⚙ Zs.-bau *m*; **4.** F a) Zs.-schluß *m*, Bündnis *n*, b) Absprache *f*; '**~-worm** *s. zo.* Hakenwurm *m.*

hook·y ['hʊkɪ] *s.*: ***play ~*** *Am.* F (*bsd.* die Schule) schwänzen.

hoo·li·gan ['hu:lɪgən] *s.* Rowdy *m*; '**hoo·li·gan·ism** [-nɪzəm] *s.* Rowdytum *n.*

hoop¹ [hu:p] **I** *s.* **1.** *allg.* Reif(en) *m* (*a. als Schmuck, bei Kinderspielen, im Zirkus etc.*): ***~ (skirt)*** Reifrock *m*; ***go through the ~(s)*** ‚durch die Mangel gedreht werden'; **2.** ⚙ a) (Faß)Reif(en) *m*, b) (Stahl)Band *n*, Ring *m*: ***~ iron*** Bandeisen *n*, c) Öse *f*, d) Bügel *m*; **3.** (Finger)Ring *m*; **4.** *Basketball*: Korbring *m*; **5.** *Krocket*: Tor *n*; **II** *v/t.* **6.** *Faß* binden; **7.** um'geben, -'fassen; **8.** *Basketball*: *Punkte* erzielen.

hoop² [hu:p] → ***whoop***.

hoop·er¹ ['hu:pə] *s.* Böttcher *m*, Küfer *m*, Faßbinder *m.*

hoop·er² ['hu:pə], **~ swan** *s. orn.* Singschwan *m.*

hoo·poe ['hu:pu:] *s. orn.* Wiedehopf *m.*

hoo·ray [hʊ'reɪ] → ***hurrah***.

hoos(e)·gow ['hu:sgaʊ] *s. Am. sl.* ‚Kittchen' *n*, ‚Knast' *m.*

hoot [hu:t] **I** *v/i.* **1.** (höhnisch) johlen: ***~ at s.o.*** j-n verhöhnen; **2.** schreien (*Eule*); **3.** *Brit.* a) hupen (*Auto*), b) pfeifen (*Zug etc.*), c) heulen (*Sirene etc.*); **II** *v/t.* **4.** *et.* johlen; **5.** *a.* ***~ down*** niederschreien, auspfeifen; **6.** ***~ out***, ***~ off*** durch Gejohle vertreiben; **III** *s.* **7.** (*johlender*) Schrei (*a. der Eule*), *pl.* Johlen *n*: ***it's not worth a ~*** F es ist keinen Pfifferling wert; ***I don't care two ~s*** F das ist mir völlig ‚piepe'; **8.** Hupen *n* (*Auto*); Heulen *n* (*Sirene*); '**hoot·er** [-tə] *s.* **1.** Johler(in); **2.** a) *mot.* Hupe *f*, b) Si'rene *f*, Pfeife *f.*

Hoo·ver ['hu:və] (*Fabrikmarke*) **I** *s.* Staubsauger *m*; **II** *v/t.* *mst* ♀ (ab)saugen; **III** *v/i.* (staub)saugen.

hooves [hu:vz] *pl. von* ***hoof***.

hop¹ [hɒp] **I** *v/i.* **1.** hüpfen, hopsen: ***~ on*** → 5; ***~ off*** F ‚abschwirren'; ***~ to it*** *Am.* F sich (*an die Arbeit*) ‚ranmachen'; **2.** F ‚schwofen', tanzen; **3.** F a) ‚flitzen', sausen, b) rasch *wohin* fahren *od.* fliegen; **II** *v/t.* **4.** hüpfen *od.* springen über (*acc.*): ***~ it*** ‚abschwirren'; **5.** F a) (auf-) springen auf (*acc.*), b) einsteigen in (*acc.*): ***~ a train***; **6.** ✈ über'fliegen, -'queren; **7.** *Am. Ball* hüpfen lassen; **8.** *Am.* F bedienen in (*dat.*); **III** *s.* **9.** Sprung *m*, Hops(er) *m*: ***~, step, and jump*** *sport* Dreisprung *m*; ***be on the ~*** F ‚auf Trab' sein; ***keep s.o. on the ~*** F j-n ‚in Trab halten'; ***catch s.o. on the ~*** F j-n erwischen *od.* überraschen; **10.** F ‚Schwof' *m*, Tanz *m*; **11.** *bsd.* ✈ F ‚Sprung' *m*, Abstecher *m*: ***only a short ~*** nur ein Katzensprung.

hop² [hɒp] **I** *s.* **1.** ⚘ a) Hopfen *m*, b) *pl.* Hopfen(blüten *pl.*) *m*: ***pick ~s*** → 4; **2.** *sl.* Rauschgift *n*, *engS.* Opium *n*; **II** *v/t.* **3.** *Bier* hopfen; **4.** ***~ up*** *sl.* a) (*durch e-e Droge*) ‚high' machen, b) aufputschen (*a. fig.*), c) *Am. Auto etc.* ‚frisieren'; **III** *v/i.* **5.** Hopfen zupfen; '**~-bind**, '**~-bine** *s.* Hopfenranke *f*; **~ dri·er** *s.* Hopfendarre *f.*

hope [həʊp] **I** *s.* **1.** Hoffnung *f* (***of*** auf *acc.*): ***live in ~(s)*** (immer noch) hoffen, die Hoffnung nicht aufgeben; ***in the ~ of*** *ger.* in der Hoffnung zu *inf.*; ***past ~*** hoffnungs-, aussichtslos; ***he is past all ~*** für ihn gibt es keine Hoffnung mehr; **2.** Hoffnung *f*: a) Zuversicht *f*, b) ***no ~ of success*** keine Aussicht auf Erfolg; ***not a ~*** F keine Chance; **3.** Hoffnung *f* (*Person od. Sache*): ***she is our only ~***; → ***white hope***; **4.** → ***forlorn hope***; **II** *v/i.* **5.** hoffen (***for*** auf *acc.*): ***~ against ~*** die Hoffnung nicht aufgeben, verzweifelt hoffen; ***~ for the best*** das Beste hoffen; ***I ~ so*** hoffentlich, ich hoffe (es); ***the ~d-for result*** das erhoffte Ergebnis; **III** *v/t.* **6.** *et.* hoffen; **~ chest** *s. Am.* F Aussteuertruhe *f.*

hope·ful ['həʊpfʊl] **I** *adj.* □ **1.** hoffnungs-, erwartungsvoll: ***be ~ of*** *et.* hoffen; ***be ~ about*** optimistisch sein hinsichtlich (*gen.*); **2.** (*a. iro.*) vielversprechend; **II** *s.* **3.** *a. iro.* a) hoffnungsvoller *od.* vielversprechender (junger) Mensch, b) ‚Opti'mist' *m*; '**hope·ful·ly** [-fʊlɪ] *adv.* **1.** → ***hopeful*** 1; **2.** hoffentlich; '**hope·ful·ness** [-nɪs] *s.* Opti'mismus *m.*

hope·less ['həʊplɪs] *adj.* □ hoffnungslos: a) verzweifelt, b) aussichtslos, c) unheilbar, d) mise'rabel, e) F unverbesserlich: ***a ~ drunkard***; '**hope·less·ly** [-lɪ] *adv.* **1.** → ***hopeless***; **2.** F heillos, to'tal; '**hope·less·ness** [-nɪs] *s.* Hoffnungslosigkeit *f.*

hop-o'-my-thumb [ˌhɒpəmɪ'θʌm] *s.* Knirps *m*, Zwerg *m.*

hop·per ['hɒpə] *s.* **1.** Hüpfende(r *m*) *f*; **2.** F Tänzer(in); **3.** *zo.* hüpfendes In'sekt, *bsd.* Käsemade *f*; **4.** ⚙ a) Fülltrichter *m*, b) (Schüttgut-, Vorrats)Behälter *m*, c) *a.* ***~(-bottom) car*** 🚂 Fallboden-, Selbstentladewagen *m*, d) Spülkasten *m*, e) *Computer*: Karteneingabefach *n.*

hop·ping mad ['hɒpɪŋ] *adj.*: ***be ~*** F e-e

,Stinkwut' (im Bauch) haben.
'hop|·scotch *s.* Himmel-und-Hölle-Spiel *n*; **'~·vine** → *hop-bind.*
Ho·rae ['hɔːriː] *s. pl. myth.* Horen *pl.*
Ho·ra·tian [hə'reɪʃjən] *adj.* ho'razisch: ~ *ode.*
horde [hɔːd] **I** *s.* Horde *f*, (wilder) Haufen; **II** *v/i.* e-e Horde bilden; in Horden zs.-leben.
ho·ri·zon [hə'raɪzn] *s.* (*a. fig. geistiger*) Hori'zont, Gesichtskreis *m*: ***apparent*** (*od.* ***sensible, visible***) ~ scheinbarer Horizont; ***celestial*** (*od.* ***rational, true***) ~ wahrer Horizont; ***on the*** ~ am Horizont (auftauchend *od.* sichtbar).
hor·i·zon·tal [ˌhɒrɪ'zɒntl] **I** *adj.* □ horizon'tal, waag(e)recht, ⚙ *a.* liegend (*Motor, Ventil etc.*), *a.* Seiten… (*bsd. Steuerung*); ~ ***line*** → **II** *s.* ✈ Horizon'tale *f*, Waag(e)rechte *f*; ~ **bar** *s. Turnen*: Reck *n*; ~ **com·bi·na·tion** *s.* ✝ Horizon'talverflechtung *f*, -konˌzern *m*; ~ **plane** *s.* ✈ Horizon'talebene *f*; ~ **pro·jec·tion** *s.* ✈ Horizon'talprojektiˌon *f*: ~ ***plane*** Grundrißebene *f*; ~ **rud·der** *s.* ⚓ Horizon'tal(steuer)ruder *n*, Tiefenruder *n*; ~ **sec·tion** *s.* ⚙ Horizon'talschnitt *m*.
hor·mo·nal [hɔː'məʊnl] *adj. biol.* hormo'nal, Hormon…; **hor·mone** ['hɔːməʊn] *s.* Hor'mon *n*.
horn [hɔːn] **I** *s.* **1.** *zo.* a) Horn *n*, b) *pl.* Geweih *n*; → ***dilemma***; **2.** *zo.* a) Horn *n* (*Nashorn*), b) Fühler *m* (*Insekt*), c) Fühlhorn *n* (*Schnecke*): ***draw*** (*od.* ***pull***) ***in one's ~s*** *fig.* die Hörner einziehen, ,zurückstecken'; **3.** *pl. fig.* Hörner *pl.* (*des betrogenen Ehemanns*): ***put ~s on s.o.*** j-m Hörner aufsetzen; **4.** (Pulver-, Trink)Horn *n*: ~ ***of plenty*** Füllhorn; **5.** ♪ a) Horn *n*, b) F'Blasinstruˌment *n*: ***blow one's own ~*** *fig.* ins eigene Horn stoßen; **6.** a) *mot.* Hupe *f*, b) ⚙ Si'gnalhorn *n*; **7.** a) (Schall)Trichter *m*, b) ⚡ Hornstrahler *m*; **8.** 'Horn(subˌstanz *f*) *n*: ~ ***handle*** Horngriff *m*; **9.** Horn *n* (*hornförmige Sache*), *bsd.* a) Bergspitze *f*, b) Spitze *f* (*der Mondsichel*), c) Schuhlöffel *m*: ***the*** ♀ (das) Kap Horn; **10.** Sattelknopf *m*; **11.** V ,Ständer' *m*: ~ ***pill*** Aphrodisiakum *n*; **II** *v/t.* **12.** a) mit den Hörnern stoßen, b) auf die Hörner nehmen; **III** *v/i.* **13.** ~ ***in*** *sl.* sich einmischen *od.* -drängen (***on*** in *acc.*); **'~·beam** *s.* ♀ Hain-, Weißbuche *f*; **'~·blende** *s. min.* Hornblende *f*.
horned [hɔːnd; *poet.* 'hɔːnɪd] *adj.* gehörnt, Horn…: ~ ***cattle*** Hornvieh *n*; ~ **owl** *s.* Ohreule *f*.
hor·net ['hɔːnɪt] *s. zo.* Hor'nisse *f*: ***bring a ~'s nest about one's ears, stir up a ~'s nest*** *fig.* in ein Wespennest stechen.
'horn|-fly *s. zo.* Hornfliege *f*; **'~·less** [-lɪs] *adj.* hornlos, ohne Hörner; **'~·pipe** *s.* ♪ Hornpipe *f* (*Blasinstrument od. alter Tanz*); **ˌ~-'rimmed** *adj.* mit Hornfassung: ~ ***spectacles*** Hornbrille *f*; **'~ˌswog·gle** [-ˌswɒgl] *v/t. sl. j-n* ,reinlegen'.
horn·y ['hɔːnɪ] *adj.* **1.** hornig, schwielig: ~***-handed*** mit schwieligen Händen; **2.** aus Horn, Horn…; **3.** V geil, ,scharf'.
hor·o·loge ['hɒrəlɒdʒ] *s.* Zeitmesser *m*, (Sonnen- *etc.*)Uhr *f*.
hor·o·scope ['hɒrəskəʊp] *s.* Horo'skop *n*: ***cast a ~*** ein Horoskop stellen; **'hor·o·scop·er** [-pə] *s.* Horo'skopsteller(in).
hor·ren·dous [hɒ'rendəs] □ → ***horrific.***
hor·ri·ble ['hɒrəbl] *adj.* □, **hor·rid** ['hɒrɪd] *adj.* □ schrecklich, fürchterlich, entsetzlich, gräßlich, scheußlich, ab'scheulich; **'hor·ri·ble·ness** [-nɪs] *s.*, **hor·rid·ness** ['hɒrɪdnɪs] *s.* Schrecklichkeit *etc.*
hor·rif·ic [hɒ'rɪfɪk] *adj.* (□ ~***ally***) **1.** schrecklich, entsetzlich; **2.** hor'rend; **hor·ri·fy** ['hɒrɪfaɪ] *v/t.* entsetzen.
hor·ror ['hɒrə] **I** *s.* **1.** Grau(s)en *n*, Entsetzen *n*: ***seized with*** ~ von Grauen gepackt; ***have the ~s*** F a) ,weiße Mäuse' sehen, b) ,am Boden zerstört' sein; **2.** (***of***) 'Widerwille *m* (gegen), Abscheu *m* (vor *dat.*): ***have a ~ of*** e-n Horror haben vor (*dat.*); **3.** a) Schrecken *m*, Greuel *m*, b) Greueltat *f*: ***the ~s of war*** die Schrecken des Krieges; ***scene of*** ~ Schreckensszene *f*; **4.** Entsetzlichkeit *f*, (*das*) Schauerliche; **5.** F Greuel *m* (*Person od. Sache*), Scheusal *n*, Ekel *n* (*Person*); **II** *adj.* **6.** Grusel…, Horror…: ~ ***film***; **'~-ˌstrick·en**, **'~-struck** *adj.* von Schrecken *od.* Grauen gepackt.
hors d'oeu·vre [ɔː'dɜːvrə] *pl.* **hors d'oeu·vres** [ɔː'dɜːvrəz] *s.* Hors'd'œuvre *n*, Vorspeise *f*.
horse [hɔːs] **I** *s.* **1.** *zo.* Pferd *n*, Roß *n*, Gaul *m*: ***to ~!*** ⚔ aufgesessen!; ***a dark ~*** *fig.* ein unbeschriebenes Blatt; ***that's a ~ of another colo(u)r*** *fig.* das ist etwas ganz anderes; ***straight from the ~'s mouth*** a) aus erster Hand, b) aus berufenem Mund; ***back the wrong ~*** aufs falsche Pferd setzen; ***wild ~s will not drag me there!*** keine zehn Pferde kriegen mich dorthin!; ***flog a dead ~*** a) offene Türen einrennen, b) sich unnötig mühen; ***give the ~ its head*** die Zügel schießen lassen; ***hold your ~s!*** F immer mit der Ruhe!; ***get on*** (*od.* ***mount***) ***one's high ~*** sich aufs hohe Roß setzen; ***ride*** (*od.* ***be on***) ***one's high ~*** auf dem *od.* s-m hohen Roß sitzen; ***spur a willing ~*** j-n unnötig antreiben; ***work like a ~*** wie ein Pferd arbeiten *od.* schuften; ***you can lead a ~ to the water but you can't make it drink*** man kann niemanden zu s-m Glück zwingen; **2.** a) Hengst *m*, b) Wallach *m*; **3.** *coll.* ⚔ Kavalle'rie *f*, Reite'rei *f*: ***1000 ~*** 1000 Reiter; ~ ***and foot*** Kavallerie u. Infanterie, die ganze Armee; **4.** ⚙ (Säge- *etc.*)Bock *m*, Ständer *m*, Gestell *n*; **5.** *Turnen*: Pferd *n*; **6.** *Schach*: F Pferd *n*, Springer *m*; **7.** *sl.* Hero'in *n*; **II** *v/t.* **8.** mit Pferden versehen: a) *Truppen* beritten machen, b) *Wagen* bespannen; **9.** auf ein Pferd setzen *od.* laden; **III** *v/i.* **10.** aufsitzen, aufs Pferd steigen; **11.** rossen (*Stute*); **12.** ~ ***around*** F Blödsinn treiben; **ˌ~-and-'bug·gy** *adj. Am.* ,vorsintflutlich'; ~ **ar·til·ler·y** *s.* ⚔ berittene Artille'rie; **'~·back** *s.*: ***on*** ~ zu Pferd(e); ***go on*** ~ reiten; ~ **bean** *s.* Saubohne *f*; ~ **chest·nut** *s.* ♀ 'Roßkaˌstanie *f*; ~ **cop·er** *s. Brit.* Pferdehändler *m*.
horsed [hɔːst] *adj.* **1.** beritten (*Person*); **2.** (mit Pferden) bespannt.
horse| deal·er *s.* Pferdehändler *m*; ~ **doc·tor** *s.* **1.** Tierarzt *m*; **2.** F ,Viehdoktor' *m* (*schlechter Arzt*); **'~-drawn** *adj.* von Pferden gezogen, Pferde…; **'~·flesh** *s.* **1.** Pferdefleisch *n*; **2.** *coll.* Pferde *pl.*; **'~·fly** *s. zo.* (Pferde)Bremse *f*; ♀ **Guards** *s. pl. Brit.* 'Gardekavalleˌriebriˌgade *f*; **'~·hair** *s.* Roß-, Pferdehaar *n*; ~ **lat·i·tudes** *s. pl. geogr.* Roßbreiten *pl.*; **'~·laugh** *s.* wieherndes Gelächter; ~ **mack·er·el** *s.* **1.** Thunfisch *m*; **2.** 'Roßmaˌkrele *f*; **'~·man** [-mən] *s.* [*irr.*] **1.** (geübter) Reiter; **2.** Pferdezüchter *m*; **'~·man·ship** [-mənʃɪp] *s.* Reitkunst *f*; ~ **op·er·a** *s.* F Western *m* (*Film*); **'~·play** *s.* ,Blödsinn' *m*, Unfug *m*; **'~·pond** *s.* Pferdeschwemme *f*; **'~ˌpow·er** *s. pl.* (*abbr.* ***h.p.***) *phys.* Pferdestärke *f* (= *1,01 PS*); ~ **race** *s.* Pferderennen *n*; **'~-ˌrac·ing** *s.* Pferderennen *n od. pl.*; **'~ˌrad·ish** *s.* ♀ Meerrettich *m*; ~ **sense** *s.* F gesunder Menschenverstand; **'~·shit** *s.* V ,Scheiß (-dreck)' *m*; **~·shoe** ['hɔːʃʃuː] **I** *s.* **1.** Hufeisen *n*; **2.** *pl. sg. konstr. Am.* Hufeisenwerfen *n*; **II** *adj.* **3.** Hufeisen…, hufeisenförmig: ~ ***bend*** (Straßen- *etc.*) Schleife *f*; ~ ***magnet*** Hufeisenmagnet *m*; ~ ***table*** in Hufeisenform aufgestellte Tische; ~ **show** *s.* Reit- u. Springturnier *n*; **'~·tail** *s.* **1.** Pferdeschwanz *m* (*a. fig. Mädchenfrisur*), Roßschweif *m* (*a. hist. als türkisches Rangabzeichen od. Feldzeichen*); **2.** ♀ Schachtelhalm *m*; ~ **trad·ing** *s.* **1.** Pferdehandel *m*; **2.** *pol.* F ,Kuhhandel' *m*; **'~·whip I** *s.* Reitpeitsche *f*; **II** *v/t.* (aus)peitschen; **'~ˌwom·an** *s.* [*irr.*] (geübte) Reiterin.
hors·y ['hɔːsɪ] *adj.* □ **1.** pferdenärrisch; **2.** Pferde…: ~ ***face***; ~ ***smell***; ~ ***talk*** Gespräch *n* über Pferde.
hor·ta·tive ['hɔːtətɪv], **'hor·ta·to·ry** [-tərɪ] *adj.* **1.** mahnend; **2.** anspornend.
hor·ti·cul·tur·al [ˌhɔːtɪ'kʌltʃərəl] *adj.* Gartenbau…: ~ ***show*** Gartenschau *f*; **hor·ti·cul·ture** ['hɔːtɪkʌltʃə] *s.* Gartenbau *m*; **ˌhor·ti'cul·tur·ist** [-ərɪst] *s.* 'Gartenbauexˌperte *m*.
ho·san·na [həʊ'zænə] **I** *int.* hosi'anna!; **II** *s.* Hosi'anna *n*.
hose [həʊz] **I** *s.* **1.** *coll., pl. konstr.* Strümpfe *pl.*; **2.** *hist.* (Knie)Hose *f*; **3.** *pl. a.* ***hoses*** Schlauch *m*: ***garden*** ~ Gartenschlauch; **4.** ⚙ Tülle *f*; **II** *v/t.* **5.** (mit e-m Schlauch) spritzen: ~ ***down*** abspritzen.
Ho·se·a [həʊ'zɪə] *npr. u. s. bibl.* (das Buch) Ho'sea *m od.* O'see *m*.
hose| pipe *s.* Schlauch(leitung *f*) *m*; **'~-proof** *adj.* ⚙ schwallwassergeschützt.
ho·sier ['həʊzɪə] *s.* Strumpfwarenhändler (-in); **'ho·sier·y** [-rɪ] *s. coll.* Strumpfwaren *pl.*
hos·pice ['hɒspɪs] *s.* **1.** *hist.* Hos'piz *n*, Herberge *f*; **2.** Sterbeklinik *f*.
hos·pi·ta·ble ['hɒspɪtəbl] *adj.* □ **1.** gastfreundlich, (*a. Haus etc.*) gastlich; **2.** *fig.* freundlich: ~ ***climate***; **3.** (***to***) empfänglich (für), aufgeschlossen (*dat.*).
hos·pi·tal ['hɒspɪtl] *s.* **1.** Krankenhaus *n*, Klinik *f*, Hospi'tal *n*: ~ ***fever*** klassisches Fleckfieber; ~ ***nurse*** Kranken(haus)schwester *f*; ~ ***social worker*** Krankenhausfürsorgerin *f*; ~ ***tent*** Sanitätszelt *n*; **2.** ⚔ Laza'rett *n*: ~ ***ship*** (***train***) Lazarettschiff *n* (-zug *m*); **3.** Tierklinik *f*; **4.** *hist.* Spi'tal *n*: a) Armenhaus *n*, b) Altersheim *n*, c) Erziehungsheim *n*; **5.** *hist.* Herberge *f*, Hos-

ˈpiz *n*; **6.** *humor.* Reparaˈturwerkstatt *f*: ***dolls' ~*** Puppenklinik *f*.

hos·pi·tal·i·ty [ˌhɒspɪˈtælətɪ] *s.* Gastfreundschaft *f*, Gastlichkeit *f*.

hos·pi·tal·i·za·tion [ˌhɒspɪtəlaɪˈzeɪʃn] *s.* **1.** Aufnahme *f od.* Einweisung *f* in ein Krankenhaus; **2.** Krankenhausaufenthalt *m*, -behandlung *f*; **hos·pi·tal·ize** [ˈhɒspɪtəlaɪz] *v/t.* **1.** ins Krankenhaus einliefern *od.* einweisen; **2.** im Krankenhaus behandeln.

Hos·pi·tal·(l)er [ˈhɒspɪtlə] *s.* **1.** *hist.* Hospitaˈliter *m*, Johanˈniter *m*; **2.** Barmˈherziger Bruder.

host¹ [həʊst] *s.* **1.** (Un)Menge *f*, Masse *f*: ***a ~ of questions*** e-e Unmenge Fragen; **2.** *poet.* (Kriegs)Heer *n*: ***the ~ of heaven*** a) die Gestirne, b) die himmlischen Heerscharen; ***the Lord of ~s*** *bibl.* der Herr der Heerscharen.

host² [həʊst] **I** *s.* **1.** Gastgeber *m*, Hausherr *m*: ***~ country*** Gastland *n*, *sport etc.* Gastgeberland *n*; **2.** (Gast)Wirt *m*: ***reckon without one's ~*** *fig.* die Rechnung ohne den Wirt machen; **3.** *TV etc.*: a) Talk-, Showmaster *m*, b) Modeˈrator *m*: ***your ~ was ...*** durch die Sendung führte (Sie) ...; **4.** *biol.* Wirt *m*, Wirtstier *n od.* -pflanze *f*; **II** *v/t.* **5.** a) *TV etc.*: Sendung moderieren, b) *Veranstaltung* ausrichten.

host³, *oft* ♀ [həʊst] *s. eccl.* Hostie *f*.

hos·tage [ˈhɒstɪdʒ] *s.* **1.** Geisel *f*: ***take (hold) s.o. ~*** j-n als Geisel nehmen (behalten); ***taking of ~s*** Geiselnahme *f*; **2.** *fig.* (ˈUnter)Pfand *n*.

hos·tel [ˈhɒstl] *s.* **1.** *mst* ***youth ~*** Jugendherberge *f*; **2.** (Studenten-, Arbeiter- *etc.*)Wohnheim *n*; **3.** → **ˈhos·tel·ry** [-rɪ] *s. obs.* Wirtshaus *n*.

host·ess [ˈhəʊstɪs] *s.* **1.** Gastgeberin *f*; **2.** (Gast)Wirtin *f*; **3.** ✈ Hoˈsteß *f*, Stewarˈdeß *f*; **4.** Hoˈsteß *f* (*Betreuerin, Führerin*); **5.** Animier-, Tischdame *f*.

hos·tile [ˈhɒstaɪl] *adj.* □ **1.** feindlich, Feind(es)...; **2.** (***to***) *fig.* a) feindselig (gegen), feindlich gesinnt (*dat.*), b) stark abgeneigt (*dat.*); **hos·til·i·ty** [hɒˈstɪlətɪ] *s.* **1.** Feindschaft *f*, Feindseligkeit *f* (***to*** gegen); **2.** Feindseligkeit *f* (*Handlung*); **3.** *pl.* ⚔ Feindseligkeiten *pl.*, Krieg(shandlungen *pl.*) *m*.

hos·tler [ˈɒslə] → ***ostler***.

hot [hɒt] **I** *adj.* □ **1.** heiß (*a. fig.*): ***~ climate***; ***~ tears***; ***I am ~*** mir ist heiß, ich bin erhitzt; ***get ~*** sich erhitzen (*a. fig. u.* ⚙); ***~ under the collar*** F wütend; ***I went ~ and cold*** es überlief mich heiß u. kalt; ***~ scent*** *hunt.* warme *od.* frische Fährte (*a. fig.*); **2.** warm, heiß: ***~ meal***; ***~ and ~*** ganz heiß, direkt vom Feuer; **3.** a) scharf (*Gewürz*), b) scharf (gewürzt): ***a ~ dish***; **4.** *fig.* heiß, hitzig, heftig: ***a ~ fight***; ***~ words*** heftige Worte; ***grow ~*** sich erhitzen (***over*** über *acc.*); **5.** leidenschaftlich, feurig: ***a ~ temper*** ein hitziges Temperament; ***be ~ for*** (*od.* ***on***) F ‚scharf' sein auf (*acc.*); **6.** wütend, erbost: ***all ~ and bothered*** ganz ‚aus dem Häuschen'; **7.** ‚heiß': a) *zo.* brünstig, b) F geil, ‚scharf' (*Person, Film etc.*); **8.** ‚heiß' (*im Suchspiel*): ***you are getting ~ter!*** a) (es wird) schon heißer!, b) *fig.* du kommst der Sache schon näher!; **9.** ganz neu *od.* frisch, ‚noch warm': ***~ from the press*** frisch aus der Presse (*Nachrichten*), soeben erschienen (*Buch*); **10.** F a) ‚toll' (*großartig*): ***he (it) is not so ~!*** er (es) ist nicht so toll!; ***~ stuff*** a) ‚dolles Ding', b) toller Kerl; ***be ~ at*** (*od.* ***on***) ‚ganz groß' sein in (*e-m Fach*); **11.** ‚heiß' (*vielversprechend*): ***a ~ tip***; ***~ favo(u)rite*** *bsd. sport* heißer *od.* hoher Favorit; **12.** ‚heiß' (*Jazz etc.*): ***~ music***; **13.** gefährlich: ***make it ~ for s.o.*** j-m die Hölle heiß machen, j-m ‚einheizen'; ***the place was getting too ~ for him*** ihm wurde der Boden zu heiß (unter den Füßen); ***be in ~ water*** in ‚Schwulitäten' sein; ***get into ~ water*** a) *j-n* in ‚Schwulitäten' bringen, b) in ‚Schwulitäten' geraten, ‚Ärger kriegen'; **14.** F a) ‚heiß' (*gestohlen, geschmuggelt etc.*): ***~ goods*** ‚heiße Ware', b) (von der Polizei) gesucht; **15.** a) ⚡ stromführend: → ***hot line***, ***hot wire***, b) *phys.* F ‚heiß' (*radioaktiv*); **16.** ⚙, ⚡ Heiß..., Warm..., Glüh...; **II** *adv.* **17.** heiß: ***the sun shines ~***; ***get it ~ (and strong)*** F ‚eins aufs Dach kriegen', sein ‚Fett' bekommen; ***give it s.o. ~ (and strong)*** F j-m die Hölle heiß machen, j-m ‚einheizen'; → ***blow¹*** 4; **III** *v/t.* **18.** *mst* ***~ up*** heiß machen; **19.** ***~ up*** F a) *Auto, Motor* ‚frisieren', ‚aufmotzen', b) ‚anheizen', c) Schwung bringen in (*acc.*), *et.* ‚aufmöbeln'; **IV** *v/i.* **20.** *mst* ***~ up*** heiß werden; **21.** ***~ up*** F a) sich verschärfen, b) schwungvoller werden.

hot| air *s.* **1.** ⚙ Heißluft *f*; **2.** *sl.* ‚heiße Luft', (leeres) Geschwätz; **ˌ~-ˈair** *adj.* ⚙ Heißluft...: ***~ artist*** F ‚Windmacher' *m*; **ˈ~·bed** *s.* **1.** ✓ Mist-, Frühbeet *n*; **2.** *fig.* Brutstätte *f*; **ˌ~-ˈblood·ed** *adj.* heißblütig; **~ cath·ode** *s.* ⚡ ˈGlühkaˌthode *f*.

hotch·pot [ˈhɒtʃpɒt] *s.* ⚖ Vereinigung *f* des Nachlasses zwecks gleicher Verteilung.

hotch·potch [ˈhɒtʃpɒtʃ] *s.* **1.** Eintopf (-gericht *n*) *m*, *bsd.* Gemüse(suppe *f*) *n* mit Hammelfleisch; **2.** *fig.* Mischmasch *m*.

hot dog *s.* Hot dog *n*, *a. m.*

ho·tel [həʊˈtel] *s.* Hoˈtel *n*: ***~ register*** Fremdenbuch *n*; **ho·tel·ier** [həʊˈtelɪeɪ], **hoˈtel-ˌkeep·er** *s.* Hoteliˈer *m*, Hoˈtelbesitzer(in) *od.* -diˌrektor *m*, -direkˌtorin *f*.

hot| flush·es *s. pl.* ⚕ fliegende Hitze; **ˈ~·foot** F **I** *adv.* schleunigst; **II** *v/i. a.* ***~ it*** rennen, flitzen; **ˈ~-ˌgal·va·nize** *v/t.* ⚙ feuerverzinken; **ˈ~-ˌgos·pel·(l)er** *s.* F Erweckungsprediger *m*; **ˈ~·head** *s.* Hitzkopf *m*; **ˌ~-ˈhead·ed** *adj.* hitzköpfig; **ˈ~·house** *s.* Treib-, Gewächshaus *n*; **~ line** *s. bsd. pol.* ‚heißer Draht'; **~ mon·ey** *s.* ✝ Hot money *n*, ‚heißes Geld'.

hot·ness [ˈhɒtnɪs] *s.* Hitze *f*.

ˈhot|·plate *s.* **1.** Koch-, Heizplatte *f*; **2.** Warmhalteplatte *f*; **~ pot** *s.* Eintopf *m*; **ˈ~-press** ⚙ **I** *s.* **1.** Heißpresse *f*; **2.** Dekatierpresse *f*; **II** *v/t.* **3.** heiß pressen; **4.** *Tuch* dekatieren; **5.** *Papier* satinieren; **~ rod** *s. Am. sl.* ‚frisierter' Wagen; **~ rod·der** [ˈrɒdə] *s. Am. sl.* **1.** Fahrer *m* e-s ***hot rod***; **2.** a) ‚Raser' *m*, b) Verkehrsrowdy *m*; **~ seat** *s. sl.* **1.** ✈ Schleudersitz *m* (*a. fig.*); **2.** *Am.* eˈlektrischer Stuhl; **ˈ~·shot I** *s. Am. sl.* **1.** ‚großes Tier'; **2.** *bsd. sport* ‚Kaˈnone' *f*, ‚As' *n*; **3.** ✈, *mot.* ‚Raˈkete' *f*; **II** *adj.* **4.** ‚groß', ‚toll'; **~ spot** *s.* **1.** *pol.* Krisenherd *m*; **2.** F ‚heißes Ding' (*Nachtklub etc.*); **~ spring** *s.* heiße Quelle, Therˈmalquelle *f*; **ˈ~·spur** *s.* Heißsporn *m*; **~ tube** *s.* ⚙ Heiz-, Glührohr *n*; **~ war** *s.* heißer Krieg; **ˌ~-ˈwa·ter** *adj.* Heißwasser...: ***~ heating***; ***~ bottle*** Wärmflasche *f*; **~ wire** *s.* **1.** ⚡ a) stromführender Draht, b) Hitzdraht *m*; **2.** *bsd. pol.* ‚heißer Draht'.

hound¹ [haʊnd] **I** *s.* **1.** Jagdhund *m*: ***ride to*** (*od.* ***follow the***) ***~s*** an e-r Parforcejagd (*bsd. Fuchsjagd*) teilnehmen; **2.** *sl.* ‚Hund' *m*, Schurke *m*; **3.** *Am. sl.* Faˈnatiker(in): ***movie ~*** Kinonarr *m*; **4.** Verfolger *m* (*Schnitzeljagd*); **II** *v/t.* **5.** *mst fig.* jagen, hetzen, drängen, verfolgen: ***~ down*** zur Strecke bringen; **6.** *a.* ***~ on*** (auf)hetzen, antreiben.

hound² [haʊnd] *s.* **1.** ⚓ Mastbacke *f*; **2.** *pl.* ⚙ Seiten-, Diagoˈnalstreben *pl.* (*an Fahrzeugen*).

hour [ˈaʊə] *s.* **1.** Stunde *f*: ***by the ~*** stundenweise; ***for ~s (and ~s)*** stundenlang; ***on the ~*** (jeweils) zur vollen Stunde; ***an ~'s work*** e-e Stunde Arbeit; ***10 minutes past the ~*** 10 Minuten nach voll; **2.** (Tages)Zeit *f*: ***at 14.20 ~s*** um 14 Uhr 20; ***at all ~s*** zu jeder Zeit; ***at an early ~*** früh, zu früher Stunde; ***at the eleventh ~*** *fig.* in letzter Minute, fünf Minuten vor zwölf; ***keep early ~s*** früh schlafen gehen (*u.* früh aufstehen); ***sleep till all ~s*** ‚bis in die Puppen' schlafen; ***the small ~s*** die frühen Morgenstunden; **3.** Zeitpunkt *m*, Stunde *f*: ***~ of death*** Todesstunde; ***his ~ has come*** a) s-e Stunde ist gekommen, b) *a.* ***his (last) ~ has struck*** s-e letzte Stunde *od.* sein letztes Stündlein ist gekommen *od.* hat geschlagen; ***question of the ~*** aktuelle Frage; **4.** *pl.* (Arbeits-) Zeit *f*, (Arbeits-, Geschäfts-, Dienst-) Stunden *pl.*: ***after ~s*** a) nach Geschäftsschluß, b) nach der Arbeit, c) *fig.* zu spät; **5.** *pl. eccl.* a) Stundenbuch *n*, b) *R.C.* Stundengebete *pl.*; **6.** ♀***s*** *pl. myth.* Horen *pl.*; **ˈ~-ˌcir·cle** *s. ast.* Stundenkreis *m*; **ˈ~·glass** *s.* Stundenglas *n*, *bsd.* Sanduhr *f*; **ˈ~-hand** *s.* Stundenzeiger *m*.

hou·ri [ˈhʊərɪ] *s.* **1.** Huri *f* (*mohammedanische Paradiesjungfrau*); **2.** *fig.* üppige Schönheit (*Frau*).

hour·ly [ˈaʊəlɪ] *adv. u. adj.* **1.** stündlich: ***~ wage*** Stundenlohn *m*; **2.** ständig, dauernd: ***in ~ fear***.

house [haʊs] **I** *pl.* **hous·es** [ˈhaʊzɪz] *s.* **1.** Haus *n* (*Gebäude u. Hausbewohner*): ***like a ~ on fire*** ganz ‚toll', ‚prima'; → ***safe*** 3; **2.** Wohnhaus *n*, Wohnung *f*, Heim *n*; Haushalt *m*: ***~ and home*** Haus u. Hof; ***keep ~*** a) das Haus hüten, b) (***for s.o.*** j-m) den Haushalt führen; ***put*** (*od.* ***set***) ***one's ~ in order*** s-e Angelegenheiten ordnen, sein Haus bestellen; → ***open*** 10; **3.** Faˈmilie *f*, Geschlecht *n*, (*bsd. Fürsten*)Haus *n*: ***the ♀ of Hanover***; **4.** *univ. Brit.* Haus *n*: a) Wohngebäude *n* (*e-s College, a. ped. e-s Internats*), b) College *n*; **5.** *thea.* a) (Schauspiel)Haus *n*: ***full ~*** volles Haus, b) Zuhörer *pl.*; → ***bring down*** 8, c) Vorstellung *f*: ***the second ~*** die zweite Vorstellung (*des Tages*); **6.** *mst* ♀ *parl.* Haus *n*, Kammer *f*, Parlaˈment *n*: ***the ♀*** a) → ***House of Com-***

mons (***Lords***, ***Representatives***), b) *coll.* das Haus (*die Abgeordneten*); ***enter the*** ℒ Parlamentsmitglied werden; ***there is a*** ℒ es ist Parlamentssitzung; ***no*** ℒ das Haus ist nicht beschlußfähig; **7.** ✝ Haus *n*, Firma *f*: ***the*** ℒ die Londoner Börse; ***on the ~*** auf Kosten des Hauses (*a. weitS. des Wirts od. Gastgebers*); **8.** *ast.* a) Haus *n*, b) Tierkreiszeichen *n*; **II** *v/t.* [haʊz] **9.** ˈunterbringen (*a.* ⚙); **10.** aufnehmen, beherbergen; **11.** Platz haben für; **III** *v/i.* [haʊz] **12.** hausen, wohnen.

house| a·gent *s. Brit.* Häusermakler *m*; **~ ar·rest** *s.* ˈHausarˌrest *m*; **ˈ~·boat** *s.* Hausboot *n*; **ˈ~ˌbod·y** → ***homebody***; **ˈ~·bound** *adj.* ans Haus gefesselt; **ˈ~·break** *v/t. Am.* **1.** *Hund etc.* stubenrein machen; **2.** F *fig.* a) *j-m* Manieren beibringen, b) *j-n* ‚kirre' machen; **ˈ~ˌbreak·er** *s.* **1.** ⚖ Einbrecher *m*; **2.** ˈAbbruchunterˌnehmer *m*; **ˈ~ˌbreak·ing** *s.* **1.** ⚖ Einbruch(sdiebstahl) *m*; **2.** Abbruch(arbeiten *pl.*) *m*; **ˈ~ˌbro·ken** *adj.* stubenrein (*Hund etc.*); **ˈ~·clean** *v/i.* **1.** Hausputz machen; **2.** (*a. v/t.*) *Am.* F gründlich aufräumen (in *dat.*); **ˈ~ˌclean·ing** *s.* **1.** Hausputz *m*; **2.** *Am.* F ˈSäuberungsaktiˌon *f*; **ˈ~·coat** *s.* Hauskleid *n*, Morgenrock *m*; **ˈ~·craft** *s. Brit.* Hauswirtschaftslehre *f*; **~ de·tec·tive** *s.* ˈHausdetekˌtiv *m* (*Hotel etc.*); **~ dog** *s.* Haushund *m*; **ˈ~·fly** *s. zo.* Stubenfliege *f*.

house·hold [ˈhaʊs*h*əʊld] **I** *s.* **1.** Haushalt *m*; **2.** ***the*** ℒ *Brit.* die königliche Hofhaltung: ℒ ***Brigade***, ℒ ***Troops*** Gardetruppen *pl.*; **II** *adj.* **3.** Haushalts…, häuslich: ***~ gods*** a) *antiq.* Hausgötter *pl.*, b) *fig.* heiliggehaltene Dinge *pl.*; ***~ remedy*** ⚕ Hausmittel *n*; ***~ soap*** Haushaltsseife *f*; **4.** allˈtäglich: ***a ~ word*** (*od.* ***name***) ein (fester *od.* geläufiger) Begriff; **ˈhouseˌhold·er** *s.* **1.** Haushaltsvorstand *m*; **2.** Haus- *od.* Wohnungsinhaber *m*.

ˈhouse|-ˌhunt·ing *s.* F Wohnungssuche *f*; **ˈ~ˌhus·band** *s.* Hausmann *m*; **ˈ~·keep** *v/i.* den Haushalt führen (***for s.o.*** j-m); **ˈ~ˌkeep·er** *s.* **1.** Haushälterin *f*, Wirtschafterin *f*; **2.** Hausmeister(in); **ˈ~ˌkeep·ing** *s.* Haushaltung *f*, -wirtschaft *f*: **~** (***money***) Wirtschaftsgeld *n*; **ˈ~·maid** *s.* Hausgehilfin *f*: ***~'s knee*** ⚕ Knieschleimbeutelentzündung *f*; **ˈ~ˌmas·ter** *s. ped. Brit.* Heimleiter *m* (*Lehrer, der für ein Wohngebäude e-s Internats zuständig ist*); **ˈ~·mate** *s.* Hausgenosse *m*, -genossin *f*; **ˈ~ˌmis·tress** *s. ped. Brit.* Heimleiterin *f* (*in e-m Internat*); ℒ **of Com·mons** *s. parl. Brit.* ˈUnterhaus *n*; ℒ **of Lords** *s. parl. Brit.* Oberhaus *n*; ℒ **of Rep·re·sent·a·tives** *s. parl. Am.* Repräsenˈtantenhaus *n* (*Unterhaus des US-Kongresses*); **~ or·gan** *s.* ✝ Hauszeitung *f*; **~ paint·er** *s.* Maler *m*, Anstreicher *m*; **~ par·ty** *s.* mehrtägige Party (*bsd. in e-m Landhaus*); **ˈ~·phone** *s. Am.* ˈHausteleˌfon *n*; **~ phy·si·cian** *s.* **1.** Hausarzt *m* (*im Hotel etc.*); **2.** *im Krankenhaus wohnender Arzt*; **~ plant** *s.* 🌿 Zimmerpflanze *f*; **ˈ~-proud** *adj.* überˈtrieben ordentlich, peˈnibel (*Hausfrau*); **ˈ~·room** [-rʊm] *s.*: ***give s.o. ~*** j-n (in sein Haus) aufnehmen; ***he wouldn't give it ~*** *fig.* er nähme es nicht einmal geschenkt; **~ search** *s.* ⚖ Haussuchung *f*; **ˌ~-toˈhouse** *adj.* von Haus zu Haus: ***~ collection*** Haussammlung *f*; ***~ selling*** Verkauf *m* an der Haustür; **ˈ~·top** *s.* Dach *n*: ***proclaim*** (*od.* ***shout***) ***from the ~s*** öffentlich verkünden, *et.* ‚an die große Glocke hängen'; **ˈ~·trained** *adj.* stubenrein (*Hund etc.*); **ˈ~ˌwarm·ing** (**par·ty**) *s.* Einzugsparty *f* (*im neuen Haus*).

ˈhouse·wife *s.* [*irr.*] **1.** Hausfrau *f*; **2.** [ˈhʌzɪf] *Brit.* ˈNäheˌtui *n*, Nähzeug *n*; **ˈhouseˌwife·ly** [-ˌwaɪflɪ] *adj.* hausfraulich; **ˈhouse·wif·er·y** [-wɪfərɪ] → ***housekeeping***; **ˈhouse·work** *s.* Haus(halts)arbeit *f*.

hous·ing¹ [ˈhaʊzɪŋ] *s.* **1.** ˈUnterbringung *f*; **2.** ˈUnterkunft *f*, Obdach *n*; **3.** Wohnung *f*, *coll.* Häuser *pl.*: ***~ development***, ***~ estate*** Wohnsiedlung *f*; ***~ development scheme*** Wohnungsbauprojekt *n*; ***~ shortage*** Wohnungsnot *f*; ***~ situation*** Lage *f* auf dem Wohnungsmarkt; ***~ unit*** Wohneinheit *f*; **4.** Wohnungsbau *m od.* -beschaffung *f*; **5.** ⚙ a) Gehäuse *n*, b) Gerüst *n*, c) Nut *f*.

hous·ing² [ˈhaʊzɪŋ] *s.* Satteldecke *f*.

hove [həʊv] *pret. u. p.p. von* ***heave***.

hov·el [ˈhɒvl] *s.* **1.** Schuppen *m*; **2.** *contp.* ‚Bruchbude' *f*, ‚Loch' *n*.

hov·el·(l)er [ˈhɒvlə] *s.* ⚓ **1.** Bergungsboot *n*; **2.** Berger *m*.

hov·er [ˈhɒvə] *v/i.* **1.** schweben (*a. fig.*); **2.** sich herˈumtreiben *od.* aufhalten (***about*** in der Nähe *gen.*); **3.** zögern, schwanken; **ˈ~·craft** *s. sg. u. pl.* Hovercraft *n*, Luftkissenfahrzeug *n*; **ˈ~·train** *s.* Hovertrain *m*, Schwebezug *m*.

how [haʊ] **I** *adv.* **1.** (*fragend*) wie: ***~ are you?*** wie geht es Ihnen?; ***~ do you do?*** (*bei der Vorstellung*) guten Tag!; ***~ about …?*** wie steht's mit …?; ***~ about a cup of tea?*** wie wäre es mit e-r Tasse Tee?; ***~ about it?*** (na,) wie wär's?; ***~ is it that …?*** wie kommt es, daß …?; ***~ now?*** was soll das bedeuten?; ***~ much?*** wieviel?; ***~ many?*** wie viele?, wieviel?; ***~ much is it?*** was kostet es?; ***~ do you know?*** woher wissen Sie das?; ***~ ever do you do it?*** wie machen Sie das nur?; **2.** (*ausrufend*) wie: ***~ absurd!***; ***and ~!*** F und wie!; ***here's ~!*** F auf Ihr Wohl!; **3.** (*relativ*) wie: ***I know ~ far it is*** ich weiß, wie weit es ist; ***he knows ~ to ride*** er kann reiten; ***I know ~ to do it*** ich weiß, wie man es macht; **II** *s.* **4.** Wie *n*: ***the ~ and the why*** das Wie u. Warum.

how·be·it [ˌhaʊˈbiːɪt] *obs.* **I** *adv.* nichtsdestoˈweniger; **II** *cj.* obˈgleich, obˈschon.

how·dah [ˈhaʊdə] *s.* (*mst gedeckter*) Sitz auf dem Rücken e-s Eleˈfanten.

how-do-you-do [ˌhaʊdjʊˈduː], **ˌhow-d'ye-ˈdo** [-djəˈduː] *s.* F: ***a nice ~*** e-e schöne ‚Bescherung'.

how·ev·er [haʊˈevə] **I** *adv.* **1.** wie auch (immer), wenn auch noch so: ***~ good***; ***~ it*** (***may***) ***be*** wie dem auch sei; ***~ you do it*** wie du es auch machst; **2.** F wie … bloß *od.* denn nur: ***~ did you do it?***; **II** *cj.* **3.** jeˈdoch, dennoch, doch, aber, inˈdes.

how·itz·er [ˈhaʊɪtsə] *s.* Hauˈbitze *f*.

howl [haʊl] **I** *v/i.* **1.** heulen (*Wölfe, Wind etc.*); **2.** brüllen, schreien (***with*** vor *dat.*); **3.** F ‚heulen', weinen; **4.** pfeifen (*Wind, Radio etc.*); **II** *v/t.* **5.** brüllen, schreien: ***~ down*** *j-n* niederschreien; **III** *s.* **6.** Heulen *n*, Geheul *n*; **7.** a) Schrei *m*: ***~s of laughter*** brüllendes Gelächter, b) Gebrüll *n*, Geschrei *n*: ***be a ~*** F ‚zum Brüllen' sein; **ˈhowl·er** [-lə] *s.* **1.** Heuler(in); **2.** *zo.* Brüllaffe *m*; **3.** F grober Schnitzer, ‚Heuler' *m*; **ˈhowl·ing** [-lɪŋ] *adj.* **1.** heulend, brüllend; **2.** F ‚toll', Mords…

how·so·ev·er [ˌhaʊsəʊˈevə] → ***however*** 1.

ˌhow-to-ˈdo-it book *s.* Bastelbuch *n*.

hoy¹ [hɔɪ] *s.* ⚓ Leichter *m*.

hoy² [hɔɪ] **I** *int.* **1.** he!, hoi!; **2.** ⚓ aˈhoi!; **II** *s.* **3.** He(ruf *m*) *n*.

hoy·den [ˈhɔɪdn] *s.* Range *f*, Wildfang *m* (*Mädchen*); **ˈhoy·den·ish** [-nɪʃ] *adj.* wild, ausgelassen.

hub [hʌb] *s.* **1.** (Rad)Nabe *f*: ***~cap*** *mot.* Radkappe *f*; **2.** *fig.* Mittel-, Angelpunkt *m*, Zentrum *n*: ***~ of the universe*** Mittelpunkt der Welt (*bsd. fig.*); **3.** ***the*** ℒ *Am.* (*Spitzname für*) Boston *n*.

hub·bub [ˈhʌbʌb] *s.* **1.** Stimmengewirr *n*; **2.** Lärm *m*, Tuˈmult *m*.

hub·by [ˈhʌbɪ] *s.* F ‚Männe' *m*, (Ehe-) Mann *m*.

hu·bris [ˈhjuːbrɪs] (*Greek*) *s.* Hybris *f*, freche ˈSelbstüberˌhebung.

huck·le [ˈhʌkl] *s.* **1.** *anat.* Hüfte *f*; **2.** Buckel *m*; **ˈ~·ber·ry** *s.* 🌿 Heidelbeere *f*; **ˈ~·bone** *s. anat.* **1.** Hüftknochen *m*; **2.** Fußknöchel *m*.

huck·ster [ˈhʌkstə] **I** *s.* **1.** → ***hawker²***; **2.** *contp.* Krämer(seele *f*) *m*, Feilscher *m*; **3.** *Am. sl.* ‚Reˈklamefritze' *m* (*Werbefachmann*); **II** *v/i.* **4.** hökern; hausieren; **5.** feilschen (***over*** um).

hud·dle [ˈhʌdl] **I** *v/t.* **1.** a) *mst* ***~ together*** (*od.* ***up***) zs.-werfen, auf e-n Haufen werfen, b) *wohin* stopfen; **2.** ***~ o.s.*** (***up***) → 6; ***~d up*** zs.-gekauert; **3.** *mst* ***~ together*** (*od.* ***up***) *Brit. Bericht etc.* a) ‚hinhauen', b) zs.-stoppeln; **4.** ***~ on*** sich *ein Kleid etc.* ˈüberwerfen, schlüpfen in (*acc.*); **5.** *fig.* vertuschen; **II** *v/i.* **6.** (***~ up*** sich zs.-)kauern; **7.** *a.* ***~ together*** (*od.* ***up***) sich zs.-drängen; **8.** **~** (***up***) ***against*** (*od.* ***to***) sich kuscheln *od.* schmiegen an (*acc.*); **III** *s.* **9.** a) (wirrer) Haufen, b) Wirrwarr *m*; **10.** ***go into a ~*** F a) die Köpfe zs.-stecken, ‚Kriegsrat halten', b) ***with o.s.*** ‚mal nachdenken', mit sich zu Rate gehen.

hue¹ [hjuː] *s.*: ***~ and cry*** *a. fig.* (Zeter-) Geschrei *n*, Gezeter *n*; ***raise a ~ and cry*** ein Zetergeschrei erheben, lautstark protestieren (***against*** gegen).

hue² [hjuː] *s.* Farbe *f*, (Farb)Ton *m*; Färbung *f* (*a. fig.*); **hued** [hjuːd] *adj. in Zssgn* …farbig, …farben.

huff [hʌf] **I** *v/t.* **1.** a) ärgern, verstimmen, b) kränken, c) ‚piesacken': ***~ s.o. into s.th.*** j-n zu et. zwingen; ***easily ~ed*** leicht ‚eingeschnappt', sehr übelnehmerisch; **2.** *Damespiel*: *Stein* wegnehmen; **II** *v/i.* **3.** a) sich ärgern, b) ‚einschnappen'; **4.** *a.* ***~ and puff*** a) schnaufen, pusten, b) (vor Wut) schnauben; **III** *s.* **5.** Ärger *m*, Verstimmung *f*: ***be in a ~*** verstimmt *od.* ‚eingeschnappt' sein; **huff·i·ness** [ˈhʌfɪnɪs] *s.* **1.** übelnehmerisches Wesen; **2.** Verärgerung *f*, Verstimmung *f*; **huff·ish** [ˈhʌfɪʃ], **huff·y** [ˈhʌfɪ] *adj.* □ **1.** übelnehmerisch; **2.** verärgert, ‚eingeschnappt'.

hug [hʌg] **I** *v/t.* **1.** umˈarmen, an sich

drücken: ~ ***o.s.*** sich beglückwünschen (***on***, ***over*** zu); **2.** *fig.* (zäh) festhalten an (*e-r Meinung etc.*); **3.** sich dicht halten an (*acc.*): ~ ***the coast*** (***the side of the road***) sich dicht an die Küste (an den Straßenrand) halten; ***the car ~s the road well*** *mot.* der Wagen hat e-e gute Straßenlage; **II** *v/i.* **4.** ein'ander *od.* sich um'armen; **III** *s.* **5.** Um'armung *f*: ***give s.o. a ~*** j-n umarmen.

huge [hjuːdʒ] *adj.* □ riesig, ungeheuer, e'norm, gewaltig, mächtig (*alle a. fig.*); **'huge·ly** [-lɪ] *adv.* gewaltig, ungeheuer, ungemein; **'huge·ness** [-nɪs] *s.* ungeheure Größe.

hug·ger·mug·ger ['hʌgəˌmʌgə] **I** *s.* **1.** ‚Kuddelmuddel' *m, n*; **2.** Heimlichtue'rei *f*; **II** *adj. u. adv.* **3.** unordentlich; **4.** heimlich, verstohlen; **III** *v/t.* **5.** vertuschen, verbergen.

Hu·gue·not ['hjuːgənɒt] *s.* Huge'notte *m*, Huge'nottin *f*.

huh [hʌ] *int.* **1.** wie?, was?; **2.** ha(ha)!

hu·la ['huːlə], ˌ**hu·la-'hu·la** *s.* Hula *f, m* (*Tanz der Eingeborenen auf Hawaii*).

hulk [hʌlk] *s.* **1.** ⚓ Hulk *f, m*; **2.** Ko'loß *m* (*Sache od. Person*): ***a ~ of a man*** *a.* ein Riesenkerl, ein ungeschlachter Kerl; **'hulk·ing** [-kɪŋ], **'hulk·y** *adj.* **1.** ungeschlacht; **2.** sperrig, klotzig.

hull[1] [hʌl] **I** *s.* ⚘ Schale *f*, Hülle *f* (*beide a. weitS.*), Hülse *f*; **II** *v/t.* schälen, enthülsen: ***~ed barley*** Graupen *pl.*

hull[2] [hʌl] **I** *s.* ⚓, ✈ Rumpf *m*: ~ ***down*** weit entfernt (*Schiff*); **II** *v/t.* ⚓ den Rumpf treffen *od.* durch'schießen.

hul·la·ba·loo [ˌhʌləbə'luː] *s.* Lärm *m*, Tu'mult *m*, Trubel *m*.

hul·lo [hə'ləʊ] → ***hello***.

hum [hʌm] **I** *v/i.* **1.** summen (*Bienen, Draht, Person etc.*); **2.** ⚡ brummen; **3.** ~ ***and ha***(***w***) a) ‚herumdrucksen', b) (hin u. her) schwanken; **4.** *a.* ~ ***with activity*** F voller Leben *od.* Aktivi'tät sein: ***make things*** ~ die Sache in Schwung bringen; **5.** ‚muffeln', stinken; **II** *v/t.* **6.** summen; **III** *s.* **7.** Summen *n*; **8.** ⚡ Brummen *n*; **9.** [*a.* mm] Hm *n*: ***~s and ha***(***w***)***s*** verlegenes Geräusper.

hu·man ['hjuːmən] **I** *adj.* □ → ***humanly***; **1.** menschlich (*a. weitS. Person, Charakter etc.*), Menschen..., Human... (*-medizin etc.*): ~ ***nature*** menschliche Natur; ~ ***engineering*** a) angewandte Betriebspsychologie, Arbeitsplatzgestaltung *f*, b) menschengerechte Gestaltung (*von Maschinen etc.*) zwecks optimaler Leistung; ~ ***interest*** *das* menschlich Ansprechende; ***~-interest story*** ergreifende *od.* ein menschliches Schicksal schildernde Geschichte; ~ ***relations*** zwischenmenschliche Beziehungen, (♆ innerbetriebliche) Kontaktpflege; ***the ~ race*** das Menschengeschlecht; ~ ***rights*** Menschenrechte; ~ ***touch*** menschliche Note; ***that's only ~*** das ist doch menschlich; ***I am only ~*** *iro.* ich bin auch nur ein Mensch; → ***err*** 1; **2.** → ***humane*** 1; **II** *s.* **3.** Mensch *m*;

hu·mane [hjuː'meɪn] *adj.* □ **1.** hu'man, menschlich: ***2 Society*** Gesellschaft *f* zur Verhinderung von Grausamkeiten an Tieren; **2.** → ***humanistic*** 1; **hu·mane·ness** [hjuː'meɪnnɪs] *s.* Humani'tät *f*, Menschlichkeit *f*.

hu·man·ism ['hjuːmənɪzəm] *s.* **1.** *oft* ***2*** Huma'nismus *m*; **2.** a) → ***humaneness***, b) → ***humanitarianism***; **'hu·man·ist** [-ɪst] **I** *s.* **1.** Huma'nist(in); **2.** → ***humanitarian*** II; **II** *adj.* → **hu·man·is·tic** [ˌhjuːmə'nɪstɪk] *adj.* (□ ***~ally***) **1.** huma'nistisch: ~ ***education***; **2.** a) → ***humane*** 1, b) → **hu·man·i·tar·i·an** [hjuːˌmænɪ'teərɪən] **I** *adj.* humani'tär, menschenfreundlich, Humanitäts...; **II** *s.* Menschenfreund *m*; **hu·man·i·tar·i·an·ism** [hjuːˌmænɪ'teərɪənɪzəm] *s.* Menschenfreundlichkeit *f*, humani'täre Gesinnung; **hu·man·i·ty** [hjuː'mænətɪ] *s.* **1.** die Menschheit; **2.** Menschsein *n*, menschliche Na'tur; **3.** Humani'tät *f*, Menschlichkeit *f*; **4.** *pl.* a) klassische Litera'tur, b) 'Altphiloloˌgie *f*, c) Geisteswissenschaften *pl.*

hu·man·i·za·tion [ˌhjuːmənaɪ'zeɪʃn] *s.* **1.** Humanisierung *f*; **2.** Vermenschlichung *f*, Personifizierung *f*; **hu·man·ize** ['hjuːmənaɪz] *v/t.* **1.** humanisieren, hu'maner gestalten; **2.** vermenschlichen, personifizieren.

ˌ**hu·man'kind** *s.* die Menschheit, das Menschengeschlecht; **'hu·man·ly** [-lɪ] *adv.* **1.** menschlich; **2.** nach menschlichen Begriffen: ~ ***possible*** menschenmöglich; ~ ***speaking*** menschlich gesehen; **3.** hu'man, menschlich.

hum·ble ['hʌmbl] **I** *adj.* □ bescheiden: a) demütig: ***in my ~ opinion*** nach m-r unmaßgeblichen Meinung; ***my ~ self*** meine Wenigkeit; ***Your ~ servant*** *obs.* Ihr ergebener Diener; ***eat ~ pie*** *fig.* klein beigeben, zu Kreuze kriechen, b) anspruchslos, einfach, c) niedrig, dürftig, ärmlich: ***of ~ birth*** von niedriger Geburt; **II** *v/t.* demütigen, erniedrigen; **'hum·ble·ness** [-nɪs] *s.* Demut *f*, Bescheidenheit *f*.

hum·bug ['hʌmbʌg] **I** *s.* **1.** ‚Humbug' *m*: a) Schwindel *m*, Betrug *m*, b) Unsinn *m*, ‚Mumpitz' *m*; **2.** Schwindler *m*, *bsd.* Hochstapler *m*, *a.* Scharlatan *m*; **3.** *a.* ***mint ~*** *Brit.* 'PfefferminzbonˌBon *m, n*; **II** *v/t.* **4.** betrügen, ‚reinlegen'.

hum·ding·er [hʌm'dɪŋgə] *s. sl.* **1.** ‚toller Bursche'; **2.** ‚tolles Ding'.

hum·drum ['hʌmdrʌm] **I** *adj.* **1.** eintönig, langweilig, fad; **II** *s.* **2.** Eintönigkeit *f*, Langweiligkeit *f*; **3.** langweilige Sache *od.* Per'son.

hu·mec·tant [hjuː'mektənt] *s.* ⚗ Feuchthaltemittel *n*.

hu·mer·al ['hjuːmərəl] *adj. anat.* **1.** Oberarmknochen...; **2.** Schulter...; **hu·mer·us** ['hjuːmərəs] *pl.* **-i** [-aɪ] *s.* Oberarm(knochen) *m*.

hu·mid ['hjuːmɪd] *adj.* feucht; **hu·mid·i·fi·er** [hjuː'mɪdɪfaɪə] *s.* Befeuchter *m*; **hu·mid·i·fy** [hjuː'mɪdɪfaɪ] *v/t.* befeuchten; **hu·mid·i·ty** [hjuː'mɪdətɪ] *s.* Feuchtigkeit(sgehalt *m*) *f*.

hu·mi·dor ['hjuːmɪdɔː] *s.* Feuchthaltebehälter *m*.

hu·mil·i·ate [hjuː'mɪlɪeɪt] *v/t.* erniedrigen, demütigen; **hu'mil·i·at·ing** [-tɪŋ] *adj.* demütigend, erniedrigend; **hu·mil·i·a·tion** [hjuːˌmɪlɪ'eɪʃn] *s.* Erniedrigung *f*, Demütigung *f*; **hu'mil·i·ty** [-ətɪ] → ***humbleness***.

hum·ming ['hʌmɪŋ] *adj.* **1.** summend; **2.** ⚡ brummend; **3.** F a) lebhaft, schwungvoll, b) geschäftig; **'~·bird** *s. orn.* Kolibri *m*; **'~-top** *s.* Brummkreisel *m*.

hum·mock ['hʌmək] *s.* **1.** Hügel *m*; **2.** Eishügel *m*.

hu·mor *etc. Am.* → ***humour*** *etc.*

hu·mor·esque [ˌhjuːmə'resk] *s.* ♪ Humo'reske *f*; **hu·mor·ist** ['hjuːmərɪst] *s.* **1.** Humo'rist(in); **2.** Spaßvogel *m*; ˌ**hu·mor'is·tic** [-'rɪstɪk] *adj.* (□ ***~ally***) humo'ristisch; **hu·mor·ous** ['hjuːmərəs] *adj.* □ hu'morvoll, hu'morig, lustig; **hu·mor·ous·ness** ['hjuːmərəsnɪs] *s.* hu'morvolle Art, (*das*) Hu'morvolle, Komik *f*.

hu·mour ['hjuːmə] **I** *s.* **1.** Gemütsart *f*, Tempera'ment *n*; **2.** Stimmung *f*, Laune *f*: ***in the ~ for*** aufgelegt zu; ***in a good*** (***bad***) ~ (bei) guter (schlechter) Laune; ***out of ~*** schlecht gelaunt; **3.** Hu'mor *m*, Spaß *m*; Komik *f*, *das* Komische (*e-r Situation etc.*); **4.** *a.* ***sense of ~*** (Sinn *m* für) Humor *m*; **5.** Spaß *m*; **6.** *physiol.* a) Körperflüssigkeit *f*, b) *obs.* Körpersaft *m*; **II** *v/t.* **7.** a) *j-m* s-n Willen tun *od.* lassen, b) *j-n od. et.* hinnehmen, mit Geduld ertragen; **'hu·mo(u)r·less** [-lɪs] *adj.* hu'morlos.

hump [hʌmp] **I** *s.* **1.** Buckel *m*, *bsd. des Kamels*: Höcker *m*; **2.** kleiner Hügel: ***be over the ~*** *fig.* über den Berg sein; **3.** *Brit.* F a) Trübsinn *m*, b) Stinklaune *f*: ***give s.o. the ~*** → 6; **II** *v/t.* **4.** *oft* ~ ***up*** (zu e-m Buckel) krümmen: ~ ***one's back*** e-n Buckel machen; **5.** a) sich *et.* aufladen, b) schleppen, tragen: ~ ***o.s.*** (*od.* ***it***) *Am. sl.* sich ‚ranhalten' (*anstrengen*); **6.** *Brit.* F a) *j-n* trübsinnig machen, b) *j-m* ‚auf den Wecker fallen'; **7.** V ‚bumsen' (*a. v/i.*); **'~·back** *s.* **1.** Buckel *m*; **2.** Bucklige(r *m*) *f*; **3.** *zo.* Buckelwal *m*; **'~·backed** *adj.* bucklig.

humped [hʌmpt] *adj.* **1.** bucklig, höckerig; **2.** holp(e)rig.

humph [mm; hʌmf] *int.* hm!, *contp.* pff!

hump·ty-dump·ty [ˌhʌmptɪ'dʌmptɪ] *s.* ‚Dickerchen' *n*.

hump·y ['hʌmpɪ] → ***humped***.

hu·mus ['hjuːməs] *s.* Humus *m*.

Hun [hʌn] *s.* **1.** Hunne *m*, Hunnin *f*; **2.** *fig.* Wan'dale *m*, Bar'bar *m*; **3.** F *contp.* Deutsche(r) *m*.

hunch [hʌntʃ] **I** *s.* **1.** → ***hump*** 1; **2.** Klumpen *m*; **3.** ***a ~*** F das *od.* so ein Gefühl, e-n *od.* den Verdacht (***that*** daß): ***play a ~*** e-r Intuition folgen; **II** *v/t.* **4.** *a.* ~ ***up*** → ***hump*** 4: ~ ***one's shoulders*** die Schultern hochziehen; **5.** *a.* ~ ***up*** (sich) kauern; **'~·back** → ***humpback*** 1 *u.* 2; **'~·backed** → ***humpbacked***.

hun·dred ['hʌndrəd] **I** *adj.* **1.** hundert: ***a*** (*od.* ***one***) ~ (ein)hundert; ***several ~ men*** mehrere hundert Mann; ***a ~ and one*** hundert(erlei), zahllose; **II** *s.* **2.** Hundert *n* (*a. Zahl*): ***by the ~*** hundertweise; ***several ~*** mehrere Hundert; ***~s of times*** hundertmal; ***~s of thousands*** Hunderttausende; ***~s and ~s*** Hunderte u. aber Hunderte; **3.** ⅍ Hunderter *m*; **4.** *hist. Brit.* Bezirk *m*, Hundertschaft *f*; **5.** ***~s and thousands*** Liebesperlen *pl.* (*auf Gebäck etc.*); **'~·fold I** *adj. u. adv.* hundertfach, -fältig; **II** *s. das* Hundertfache; **'~-perˌcent** *adj.* 'hundertproˌzentig; **'~-perˌcent·er** *s. pol. Am.* 'Hurrapatriˌot *m*.

hun·dredth ['hʌndrədθ] **I** *adj.* **1.** hundertst; **II** *s.* **2.** Hundertste(r *m*) *f*; **3.** Hundertstel *n*.

'hun·dred·weight *s.* a) *in England 112 lbs.*, b) *in USA 100 lbs.*, c) *a.* ***metric ~***

Zentner *m*.

hung [hʌŋ] *pret. u. p.p. von* **hang**.

Hun·gar·i·an [hʌŋ'geərɪən] **I** *adj.* **1.** ungarisch; **II** *s.* **2.** Ungar(in); **3.** *ling.* Ungarisch *n*.

hun·ger ['hʌŋgə] **I** *s.* **1.** Hunger *m*: **~ *is the best sauce*** Hunger ist der beste Koch; **2.** *fig.* Hunger *m*, Verlangen *n*, Durst *m* (***for, after*** nach); **II** *v/i.* **3.** hungern, Hunger haben; **4.** *fig.* hungern (***for, after*** nach); **III** *v/t.* **5.** aushungern; durch Hunger zwingen (***into*** zu); **~ march** *s.* Hungermarsch *m*; **~ strike** *s.* Hungerstreik *m*.

hun·gry ['hʌŋgrɪ] *adj.* □ **1.** hungrig: ***be*** (*od.* ***feel***) **~** hungrig sein, Hunger haben: ***go* ~** hungern; **~ *as a hunter*** (*od.* ***bear***) hungrig wie ein Wolf; **2.** *fig.* hungrig (***for*** nach): **~ *for knowledge*** wissensdurstig; **3.** ⚘ karg, mager (*Boden*).

hunk [hʌŋk] *s.* F großes Stück, (dicker) Brocken.

hunk·y-do·ry [ˌhʌŋkɪ'dɔːrɪ] *adj. Am. sl.* **1.** ,klasse', prima; **2.** bestens, ,in Butter'.

hunt [hʌnt] **I** *s.* **1.** Jagd *f*, Jagen *n*: ***the* ~ *is up*** die Jagd hat begonnen; **2.** 'Jagd(-reˌvier *n*) *f*; **3.** Jagd(gesellschaft) *f*; **4.** *fig.* Jagd *f*: a) Verfolgung *f*, b) Suche *f* (***for*** nach); **II** *v/t.* **5.** (*a. fig. j-n*) jagen, Jagd machen auf (*acc.*), hetzen: **~*ed look*** *fig.* gehetzter Blick; **~ *down*** erlegen, *a. fig.* zur Strecke bringen; **~ *out*** a) hinausjagen, b) *a.* **~ *up*** aufstöbern, -spüren, -treiben, *weitS.* forschen nach; **6.** *Revier* durch'jagen, -'stöbern, -'suchen (*a. fig.*) (***for*** nach); **7.** jagen mit (*Hunden, Pferden etc.*); **8.** *Radar, TV*: abtasten; **III** *v/i.* **9.** jagen: **~ *for*** Jagd machen auf (*acc.*) (*a. fig.*); **10.** **~ *after*** (*od.* ***for***) a) suchen nach, b) jagen, streben nach; **11.** ⚙ flattern; **'hunt·er** [-tə] *s.* **1.** Jäger *m* (*a. zo. u. fig.*): **~*-killer satellite*** ⚔ Killersatellit *m*; **2.** Jagdhund *m od.* -pferd *n*; **3.** Sprungdeckeluhr *f*.

hunt·ing ['hʌntɪŋ] **I** *s.* **1.** Jagd *f*, Jagen *n*; **2.** → ***hunt*** 4; **3.** *Radar, TV*: Abtastvorrichtung *f*; **II** *adj.* **4.** Jagd…; **~ box** → ***hunting lodge***; **~ cat** → ***cheetah***; **~ crop** *s.* Jagdpeitsche *f*; **~ ground** *s.* 'Jagdreˌvier *n*, -gebiet *n* (*a. fig.*): ***the happy* ~*s*** die ewigen Jagdgründe; **~ horn** *s.* Hift-, Jagdhorn *n*; **~ leop·ard** → ***cheetah***; **~ li·cence**, *Am.* **~ li·cense** *s.* Jagdschein *m*; **~ lodge** *s.* Jagdhütte *f*; **~ sea·son** *s.* Jagdzeit *f*.

hunt·ress ['hʌntrɪs] *s.* Jägerin *f*.

hunts·man ['hʌntsmən] *s.* [*irr.*] **1.** Jäger *m*, Weidmann *m*; **2.** Rüdemeister *m*; **'hunts·man·ship** [-ʃɪp] *s.* Jäge'rei *f*, Weidwerk *n*.

hur·dle ['hɜːdl] **I** *s.* **1.** *sport u. fig.* a) Hürde *f*, b) *Hindernislauf, Pferdesport*: Hindernis *n*: ***take*** (*od.* ***pass***) ***the* ~** *a. fig.* die Hürde nehmen; **2.** Hürde *f*, (Weiden-, Draht)Geflecht *n*; **3.** ⚙ Fa'schine *f*, Gitter *n*; **II** *v/t.* **4.** mit Hürden um'geben, um'zäunen; **5.** *ein Hindernis* über'springen; **6.** *fig. e-e Schwierigkeit* über'winden; **III** *v/i.* **7.** *sport*: e-n Hürden- *od.* Hindernislauf *od.* (*Pferdesport*) ein Hindernisrennen bestreiten; **'hur·dler** [-lə] *s. sport* a) Hürdenläufer (-in), b) Hindernisläufer *m*; **'hur·dle-race** *s. sport* a) Hürdenlauf *m*, b) Hindernislauf *m*, c) *Pferdesport*: Hindernisrennen *n*.

hur·dy-gur·dy ['hɜːdɪˌgɜːdɪ] *s.* ♪ a) Drehleier *f*, b) Leierkasten *m*.

hurl [hɜːl] **I** *v/t.* **1.** schleudern (*a. fig.*): **~ *abuse at s.o.*** j-m Beleidigungen ins Gesicht schleudern; **~ *o.s.*** sich stürzen (***on*** auf *acc.*); **II** *v/i.* **2.** *sport* Hurling spielen; **III** *s.* **3.** Schleudern *n*; **'hurl·er** [-lə] *s. sport* Hurlingspieler *m*; **'hurl·ey** [-lɪ] *s. sport* **1.** → ***hurling***; **2.** Hurlingstock *m*; **'hurl·ing** [-lɪŋ] *s. sport* Hurling (-spiel) *n* (*Art Hockey*).

hurl·y-burl·y ['hɜːlɪˌbɜːlɪ] **I** *s.* Tu'mult *m*, Aufruhr *m*; Wirrwarr *m*; **II** *adj.* turbu'lent.

hur·rah [hʊ'rɑː] **I** *int.* hur'ra!: **~ *for* …!** hoch *od.* es lebe …!; **II** *s.* Hur'ra(ruf *m*) *n*.

hur·ray [hʊ'reɪ] → ***hurrah***.

hur·ri·cane ['hʌrɪkən] *s.* a) Hurrikan *m*, Wirbelsturm *m*, b) Or'kan *m*, *fig. a.* Sturm *m*; **~ deck** *s.* ⚓ Sturmdeck *n*; **~ lamp** *s.* 'Sturmlaˌterne *f*.

hur·ried ['hʌrɪd] *adj.* □ eilig, hastig, schnell, über'eilt; **'hur·ri·er** [-ɪə] *s. Brit.* ⚒ Fördermann *m*.

hur·ry ['hʌrɪ] **I** *s.* **1.** Hast *f*, Eile *f*: ***in a* ~** eilig, hastig; ***be in a* ~** es eilig haben (***to do s.th.*** et. zu tun); ***there is no* ~** es eilt nicht, es hat keine Eile; ***in my* ~ *I forgot …*** vor lauter Eile vergaß ich …; ***you will not beat that in a* ~** F das machst du nicht so bald *od.* leicht nach; ***the* ~ *of daily life*** die Hetze des Alltags; ***in the* ~ *of business*** im Drang der Geschäfte; **II** *v/t.* **2.** schnell *od.* eilig befördern *od.* bringen: **~ *through*** *fig. Gesetzesvorlage etc.* durchpeitschen; **3.** *oft* **~ *up*** (*od.* ***on***) a) *j-n* antreiben, b) *et.* beschleunigen; **4.** *et.* über'eilen; **III** *v/i.* **5.** eilen, hasten: **~ *over s.th.*** et. hastig *od.* flüchtig erledigen; **6.** *oft* **~ *up*** sich beeilen: **~ *up!*** beeil dich!, (mach) schnell!; **ˌ~-'scur·ry** [-'skʌrɪ] → ***helter-skelter***; **'~-up** *adj. Am.* **1.** eilig, Eil…: **~ *job***; **2.** hastig: **~ *breakfast***.

hurst [hɜːst] *s.* **1.** (*obs. außer in Ortsnamen*) Forst *m*; **2.** *obs.* bewaldeter Hügel; **3.** *obs.* Sandbank *f*.

hurt [hɜːt] **I** *v/t.* [*irr.*] **1.** verletzen, verwunden (*beide a. fig.*): **~ *s.o.'s feelings***; ***feel* ~** gekränkt *od.* verletzt sein; → ***fly***[2] 1; **2.** schmerzen, weh tun (*dat.*) (*beide a. fig.*); drücken (*Schuh*); **3.** *j-m* schaden *od.* Schaden zufügen: ***it won't* ~ *you to inf.*** F du stirbst nicht gleich, wenn du; **4.** *et.* beschädigen; **II** *v/i.* [*irr.*] **5.** schmerzen, weh tun (*a. fig.*); **6.** schaden: ***that won't* ~** das schadet nichts; **7.** F Schmerzen haben, *a. fig.* leiden (***from*** an *dat.*); **III** *s.* **8.** Schmerz *m* (*a. fig.*); **9.** Verletzung *f*; **10.** Kränkung *f*; **11.** Schaden *m*, Nachteil *m*; **'hurt·ful** [-fʊl] *adj.* □ **1.** verletzend; **2.** schmerzlich; **3.** schädlich, nachteilig (***to*** für).

hur·tle ['hɜːtl] **I** *v/i.* **1.** *obs.* (***against***) zs.-prallen (mit), prallen, krachen (gegen); **2.** sausen, rasen; **3.** rasseln, poltern; **II** *v/t.* **4.** → ***hurl*** 1.

'hur·tle·ber·ry *s.* ⚘ Heidelbeere *f*.

hus·band ['hʌzbənd] **I** *s.* (Ehe)Mann *m*, Gatte *m*, Gemahl *m*; **II** *v/t.* haushälterisch *od.* sparsam 'umgehen mit, haushalten mit; **'hus·band·man** [-ndmən] *s.* [*irr.*] *obs.* Bauer *m*; **'hus·band·ry** [-rɪ] *s.* **1.** Landwirtschaft *f*; **2.** Haushalten *n*.

hush [hʌʃ] **I** *int.* **1.** still!, pst!; **II** *v/t.* **2.** zum Schweigen *od.* zur Ruhe bringen; **3.** *fig.* besänftigen, beruhigen; **4.** *mst* **~ *up*** vertuschen; **III** *v/i.* **5.** still werden; **IV** *s.* **6.** Stille *f*, Ruhe *f*; **'hush·a·by** [-ʃəbaɪ] *int.* eiapo'peia!; **hushed** [-ʃt] *adj.* lautlos, still.

ˌhush|-'hush *adj.* geheim(gehalten), Geheim…, heimlich; **'~-ˌmon·ey** *s.* Schweigegeld *n*.

husk [hʌsk] **I** *s.* **1.** ⚘ Hülse *f*, Schale *f*, Schote *f*, *Am. mst* Maishülse *f*; **2.** *fig.* (leere) Hülle, Schale *f*; **II** *v/t.* **3.** enthülsen, schälen; **'husk·er** [-kə] *s.* **1.** Enthülser(in); **2.** 'Schälmaˌschine *f*; **'husk·i·ly** [-kɪlɪ] *adv.* mit rauher *od.* heiserer Stimme; **'husk·i·ness** [-kɪnɪs] *s.* Heiserkeit *f*, Rauheit *f*; **'husk·ing** [-kɪŋ] *s.* **1.** Enthülsen *n*, Schälen *n*; **2.** *a.* **~ *bee*** *Am.* geselliges Maisschälen.

husk·y[1] ['hʌskɪ] **I** *adj.* □ **1.** hülsig; **2.** ausgedörrt; **3.** rauh, heiser; **4.** F stämmig, kräftig; **II** *s.* **5.** F stämmiger Kerl.

hus·ky[2] ['hʌskɪ] *s. zo.* Husky *m*, Eskimohund *m*.

hus·sar [hʊ'zɑː] *s.* ⚔ Hu'sar *m*.

Huss·ite ['hʌsaɪt] *s. hist.* Hus'sit *m*.

hus·sy ['hʌsɪ] *s.* **1.** Range *f*, ,Fratz' *m*; **2.** ,leichtes Mädchen', ,Flittchen' *n*.

hus·tings ['hʌstɪŋz] *s. pl. mst sg. konstr. pol.* a) Wahlkampf *m*, b) Wahl(en *pl.*) *f*.

hus·tle ['hʌsl] **I** *v/t.* **1.** a) stoßen, drängen, b) (an)rempeln; **2.** a) hetzen, (an-) treiben, b) drängen (***into doing s.th.*** dazu, et. zu tun); **3.** rasch *wohin* schaffen *od.* ,verfrachten'; **4.** sich beeilen mit; **5.** **~ *up*** *Am.* F ,herzaubern'; **6.** *Am.* F a) *et.* ergattern, b) sich *et.* ergaunern; **II** *v/i.* **7.** sich drängen, hasten, hetzen, sich beeilen; **8.** *Am.* F a) mit Hochdruck arbeiten, b) ,rangehen', Dampf da'hinter machen; **9.** *Am. sl.* a) ,klauen', b) Betrüge'reien begehen, c) betteln, d) auf Kundschaft ausgehen (*a. Prostituierte*), e) ,schwer hinterm Geld her sein'; **III** *s.* **10.** *mst* **~ *and bustle*** a) Gedränge *n*, b) Gehetze *n*, c) ,Betrieb' *m*; **11.** *Am.* F Gaune'rei *f*; **'hus·tler** [-lə] *s.* **1.** F rühriger Mensch, ,Wühler' *m*; **2.** *bsd. Am.* F a) ,Nutte' *f*, Prostitu'ierte *f*, b) (kleiner) Gauner.

hut [hʌt] **I** *s.* **1.** Hütte *f*; **2.** ⚔ Ba'racke *f*; **II** *v/t. u. v/i.* **3.** in Ba'racken *od.* Hütten 'unterbringen (wohnen): **~*ted camp*** Barackenlager *n*.

hutch [hʌtʃ] *s.* **1.** Kiste *f*, Kasten *m*; **2.** Trog *m*; **3.** (kleiner) Stall, Käfig *m*, Verschlag *m*; **4.** ⚒ Hund *m*; **5.** F Hütte *f*.

hut·ment ['hʌtmənt] *s.* ⚔ **1.** 'Unterbringung *f* in Ba'racken; **2.** Ba'rackenlager *n*.

huz·za [hʊ'zɑː] *obs.* → ***hurrah***.

hy·a·cinth ['haɪəsɪnθ] *s.* **1.** ⚘ Hya'zinthe *f*; **2.** *min.* Hya'zinth *m*.

hy·ae·na → ***hyena***.

hy·brid ['haɪbrɪd] **I** *s.* **1.** *biol.* Hy'bride *f*, *m*, Mischling *m*, Bastard *m*, Kreuzung *f*; **2.** *ling.* Mischwort *n*; **II** *adj.* **3.** hy'brid: a) *biol.* Misch…, Bastard…, Zwitter…, b) *fig.* ungleichartig, gemischt; **'hy·brid·ism** [-dɪzəm], **hy·brid·i·ty** [haɪ'brɪdətɪ] *s. biol.* Mischbildung *f*, Kreuzung *f*; **hy·brid·i·za·tion** [ˌhaɪbrɪdaɪ'zeɪʃn] *s.* Kreuzung *f*; **'hy-**

brid·ize [-daɪz] *v/t.* (*v/i.* sich) kreuzen.

Hy·dra [ˈhaɪdrə] *s.* **1.** Hydra *f*: a) *myth. vielköpfige Schlange*, b) *ast.* Wasserschlange *f*; **2.** ℒ *fig.* Hydra *f* (*kaum auszurottendes Übel*); **3.** ℒ *zo.* ˈSüßwasserpoˌlyp *m.*

hy·dran·ge·a [haɪˈdreɪndʒə] *s.* ⚘ Horˈtensie *f.*

hy·drant [ˈhaɪdrənt] *s.* Hyˈdrant *m.*

hy·drate [ˈhaɪdreɪt] ⚗ **I** *s.* Hyˈdrat *n*; **II** *v/t.* hydratisieren; ˈ**hy·drat·ed** [-tɪd] *adj.* ⚗, *min.* hyˈdrathaltig; **hy·dra·tion** [haɪˈdreɪʃn] *s.* ⚗ Hydra(ta)tiˈon *f.*

hy·drau·lic [haɪˈdrɔːlɪk] **I** *adj.* (□ **～ally**) ⚙, *phys.* hyˈdraulisch: a) (Druck-) Wasser…: **～ clutch** (**jack**, **press**) hydraulische Kupplung (Winde, Presse); **～ power** (**pressure**) Wasserkraft *f* (-druck *m*), b) unter Wasser erhärtend: **～ cement** hydraulischer Mörtel, Wassermörtel *m*; **II** *s. pl. sg. konstr. phys.* Hyˈdraulik *f* (*Wissenschaft*); **～ brake** *s. mot.* hyˈdraulische Bremse, Flüssigkeitsbremse *f*; **～ dock** *s.* ⚓ Schwimmdock *n*; **～ en·gi·neer** *s.* ˈWasserbauingeniˌeur *m*; **～ en·gi·neer·ing** *s.* Wasserbau *m.*

hy·dric [ˈhaɪdrɪk] *adj.* ⚗ Wasserstoff…: **～ oxide** Wasser *n*; ˈ**hy·dride** [-raɪd] *s.* ⚗ Hyˈdrid *n.*

hy·dro [ˈhaɪdrəʊ] *pl.* **-dros** *s.* F **1.** ✈ → **hydroplane** 1; **2.** ⚕ *Brit.* F Hoˈtel *n* mit hydroˈpathischen Einrichtungen.

hydro- [haɪdrəʊ] *in Zssgn* a) Wasser…, b) …wasserstoff *m.*

ˈ**hy·dro|·bomb** *s.* ⚔ ˈLufttorˌpedo *m*; ˌ**～ˈcar·bon** *s.* ⚗ Kohlenwasserstoff *m*; ˌ**～ˈcel·lu·lose** *s.* ⚗ ˈHydrozelluˌlose *f*; ˌ**～·ceˈphal·ic** [-əʊseˈfælɪk], ˌ**～ˈceph·a·lous** [-əʊˈsefələs] *adj.* ⚕ mit e-m Wasserkopf; ˌ**～ˈceph·a·lus** [-əʊˈsefələs] *s.* ⚕ Wasserkopf *m*; ˌ**～ˈchlo·ric** *adj.* ⚗ salzsauer: **～ acid** Salzsäure *f*, Chlorwasserstoff *m*; ˌ**～ˈchlo·ride** *s.* ⚗ ˈChlorhyˌdrat *n*; ˌ**～·cyˈan·ic ac·id** *s.* ⚗ Blausäure *f*, Zyˈanwasserstoffsäure *f*; ˌ**～·dyˈnam·ic** *adj. phys.* hydrodyˈnamisch; ˌ**～·dyˈnam·ics** *s. pl. mst sg. konstr. phys.* Hydrodyˈnamik *f*; ˌ**～·eˈlec·tric** *adj.* ⚙ hydroeˈlektrisch: **～ power station** (*od.* **plant**) Wasserkraftwerk *n*; ˌ**～·exˈtract** *v/t.* ⚙ zentrifugieren, entwässern; ˌ**～·fluˈor·ic ac·id** *s.* ⚗ Flußsäure *f*; ˈ**～·foil** *s.* ⚓ Tragflügel(boot *n*) *m.*

hy·dro·gen [ˈhaɪdrədʒən] *s.* ⚗ Wasserstoff *m*: **～ bomb**; **～ cylinder** Wasserstoffflasche *f*; **～ peroxide** Wasserstoffsuperoxyd *n*; **～ sulphide** Schwefelwasserstoff; ˈ**hy·dro·gen·ate** [-ədʒɪneɪt] *v/t.* ⚗ **1.** hydrieren; **2.** *Öl* härten; **hy·dro·gen·a·tion** [ˌhaɪdrədʒɪˈneɪʃn] *s.* ⚗ **1.** Hydrierung *f*; **2.** (Öl)Härtung *f*; ˈ**hy·dro·gen·ize** [-ədʒɪnaɪz] → **hydrogenate**; **hy·drog·e·nous** [haɪˈdrɒdʒɪnəs] *adj.* ⚗ wasserstoffhaltig, Wasserstoff…

hy·dro·graph·ic [ˌhaɪdrəʊˈgræfɪk] *adj.* (□ **～ally**) hydroˈgraphisch: **～ map** ⚓ Seekarte *f*; **～ office** (*od.* **department**) ⚓ Seewarte *f*; **hy·drog·ra·phy** [haɪˈdrɒgrəfɪ] *s.* **1.** Hydrograˈphie *f*, Gewässerkunde *f*; **2.** Gewässer *pl.* (*e-r Landkarte*).

hy·dro·log·ic, **hy·dro·log·i·cal** [ˌhaɪdrəʊˈlɒdʒɪk(l)] *adj.* □ hydroˈlogisch; **hy·drol·o·gy** [haɪˈdrɒlədʒɪ] *s.* Hydroloˈgie *f.*

hy·drol·y·sis [haɪˈdrɒlɪsɪs] *pl.* **-ses** [-siːz] *s.* ⚗ Hydroˈlyse *f*; **hy·dro·lyt·ic** [ˌhaɪdrəʊˈlɪtɪk] *adj.* hydroˈlytisch; **hy·dro·lyze** [ˈhaɪdrəlaɪz] *v/t.* hydrolysieren.

hy·drom·e·ter [haɪˈdrɒmɪtə] *s. phys.* Hydroˈmeter *n.*

hy·dro·path [ˈhaɪdrəʊpæθ] → **hydropathist**; **hy·dro·path·ic** [ˌhaɪdrəʊˈpæθɪk] ⚕ *adj.* hydroˈpathisch, Wasserkur…; **hy·drop·a·thist** [haɪˈdrɒpəθɪst] *s.* ⚕ Hydroˈpath *m*, Kneipparzt *m*; **hy·drop·a·thy** [haɪˈdrɒpəθɪ] *s.* ⚕ Hydrotheraˈpie *f.*

hy·dro|·pho·bi·a [ˌhaɪdrəʊˈfəʊbjə] *s.* ⚕ Hydrophoˈbie *f*: a) *a. psych.* Wasserscheu *f*, b) Tollwut *f*; **～·phyte** [ˈhaɪdrəʊfaɪt] *s.* ⚘ Wasserpflanze *f*; **～·plane** [ˈhaɪdrəʊpleɪn] **I** *s.* **1.** ✈ Wasserflugzeug *n*; **2.** ✈ Gleitfläche *f* (*e-s Wasserflugzeugs*); **3.** ⚓ Tragflügelboot *n*; **4.** ⚓ Tiefenruder *n* (*e-s U-Boots*); **II** *v/i.* **5.** *Am.* → **aquaplane** 3; ˌ**～ˈpon·ics** [-ˈpɒnɪks] *s. pl. sg. konstr.* ˈHydro-, ˈWasserkulˌtur *f*; ˌ**～·qui·none** [-kwɪˈnəʊn] *s. phot.* Hydrochiˈnon *n*; **～·scope** [ˈhaɪdrəskəʊp] *s.* ⚙ Unterˈwassersichtgerät *n*; **～·sphere** [ˈhaɪdrəsfɪə] *s.* Hydroˈsphäre *f* (*die Wasserhülle der Erde*); ˌ**～ˈstat·ic** [-ˈstætɪk] *adj.* hydroˈstatisch; ˌ**～ˈstat·ics** [-ˈstætɪks] *s. pl. sg. konstr.* Hydroˈstatik *f*; ˌ**～ˈther·a·py** [-ˈθerəpɪ] *s.* ⚕ Hydrotheraˈpie *f.*

hy·drous [ˈhaɪdrəs] *adj.* ⚗ wasserhaltig.

hy·drox·ide [haɪˈdrɒksaɪd] *s.* ⚗ Hydroˈxyd *n*: **～ of sodium** Ätznatron *n.*

hy·e·na [haɪˈiːnə] *s. zo.* Hyˈäne *f*: **laugh like a ～** F sich schieflachen.

hy·giene [ˈhaɪdʒiːn] *s.* **1.** Hygiˈene *f*, Gesundheitspflege *f*: **personal ～** Körperpflege; **dental** (**food**, **sex**) **～** Zahn- (Nahrungs-, Sexual)hygiene; **2.** → **hygienic** II; **hy·gi·en·ic** [haɪˈdʒiːnɪk] **I** *adj.* (□ **～ally**) hygiˈenisch; saniˈtär; **II** *s. pl. sg. konstr.* Hygiˈene *f*, Gesundheitslehre *f*; ˈ**hy·gi·en·ist** [-nɪst] *s.* Hygiˈeniker(in).

hy·gro·graph [ˈhaɪgrəgrɑːf] *s. meteor.* Hygroˈgraph *m*, selbstregistrierender Luftfeuchtigkeitsmesser; **hy·grom·e·ter** [haɪˈgrɒmɪtə] *s. meteor.* Hygroˈmeter *n*, Luftfeuchtigkeitsmesser *m*; **hy·gro·met·ric** [ˌhaɪgrəʊˈmetrɪk] *adj.* hygroˈmetrisch; **hy·grom·e·try** [haɪˈgrɒmɪtrɪ] *s.* Hygromeˈtrie *f*, Luftfeuchtigkeitsmessung *f*; ˈ**hy·gro·scope** [-əskəʊp] *s. meteor.* Hygroˈskop *n*, Feuchtigkeitsanzeiger *m*; **hy·gro·scop·ic** [ˌhaɪgrəʊˈskɒpɪk] *adj.* hygroˈskopisch, Feuchtigkeit anzeigend *od. a.* anziehend.

hy·ing [ˈhaɪɪŋ] *pres.p. von* **hie.**

hy·men [ˈhaɪmen] *s.* **1.** *anat.* Hymen *n*, Jungfernhäutchen *n*; **2.** *poet.* Ehe *f*, Hochzeit *f*; **3.** ℒ *myth.* Hymen *m*, Gott *m* der Ehe.

hy·me·nop·ter·a [ˌhaɪməˈnɒptərə] *s. pl. zo.* Hautflügler *pl.*

hymn [hɪm] **I** *s.* Hymne *f* (*a. fig. Loblied, -gesang*), Kirchenlied *n*, Choˈral *m*; **II** *v/t.* (lob)preisen; **III** *v/i.* Hymnen singen; **hym·nal** [ˈhɪmnəl] **I** *adj.* hymnisch, Hymnen…; **II** *s.* → ˈ**hymn-book** *s.* Gesangbuch *n*; **hym·nic** [ˈhɪmnɪk] *adj.* hymnenartig; ˈ**hym·no·dy** [-nəʊdɪ] *s.* **1.** Hymnensingen *n*; **2.** Hymnendichtung *f*; **3.** *coll.* Hymnen *pl.*

hy·oid (**bone**) [ˈhaɪɔɪd] *s. anat.* Zungenbein *n.*

hype¹ [haɪp] *sl.* **I** *s.* **1.** ‚Spritze' *f*, ‚Schuß' *m* (*Rauschgift*); **2.** ‚Fixer(in)'; **II** *v/i.* **3.** *mst* **～ up** ‚sich e-n Schuß setzen'; **III** *v/t.* **4.** **be ～d up** ‚high' sein (*a. fig.*).

hype² [haɪp] *sl.* **I** *s.* Trick *m*, ‚Beschiß' *m*; **II** *v/t. j-n* austricksen, ‚bescheißen'.

ˌ**hy·per·aˈcid·i·ty** [ˌhaɪpərə-] *s.* ⚕ Überˈsäuerung *f* (*des Magens*).

hy·per·bo·la [haɪˈpɜːbələ] *s.* 𝔄 Hyˈperbel *f* (*Kegelschnitt*); **hyˈper·bo·le** [-lɪ] *s. rhet.* Hyˈperbel *f*, Überˈtreibung *f*; **hy·per·bol·ic**, **hy·per·bol·i·cal** [ˌhaɪpəˈbɒlɪk(l)] *adj.* □ 𝔄, *rhet.* hyperˈbolisch.

hy·per·bo·re·an [ˌhaɪpəbɔːˈriːən] **I** *s. myth.* Hyperboˈreer *m*; **II** *adj.* hyperboˈreisch; ˌ**hy·per·corˈrect** [ˌhaɪpə-] *adj.* ˈhyperkorˌrekt (*a. ling.*); ˌ**hy·perˈcrit·i·cal** [ˌhaɪpə-] *adj.* □ hyperkritisch, allzu kritisch; ˈ**hy·perˌmar·ket** [ˈhaɪpə-] *s.* Groß-, Verbrauchermarkt *m*; **hy·per·me·tro·pi·a** [ˌhaɪpəmɪˈtrəʊpɪə], **hy·per·o·pi·a** [ˌhaɪpəˈrəʊpɪə] *s.* ⚕ ˈÜbersichtigkeit *f*; ˌ**hy·perˈsen·si·tive** [ˌhaɪpə-] *adj.* ˈüberempfindlich; ˌ**hy·perˈson·ic** [ˌhaɪpə-] *adj. phys.* hyperˈsonisch (*etwa über fünffache Schallgeschwindigkeit*); ˌ**hy·perˈten·sion** [ˌhaɪpə-] *s.* ⚕ Hypertoˈnie *f*, erhöhter Blutdruck.

hy·per·troph·ic [ˌhaɪpəˈtrɒfɪk], **hy·per·tro·phied** [haɪˈpɜːtrəʊfɪd] *adj.* ⚕, *biol. u. fig.* hyperˈtroph; **hy·per·tro·phy** [haɪˈpɜːtrəʊfɪ] ⚕, *biol. u. fig.* **I** *s.* Hypertroˈphie *f*; **II** *v/t.* (*v/i.* sich) ˈübermäßig vergrößern.

hy·phen [ˈhaɪfn] **I** *s.* **1.** Bindestrich *m*; **2.** Trennungszeichen *n*; **II** *v/t.* **3.** → ˈ**hy·phen·ate** [-fəneɪt] *v/t.* mit Bindestrich schreiben: **～d American** ‚Bindestrich-amerikaner' *m*; **hy·phen·a·tion** [ˌhaɪfəˈneɪʃn] *s.* a) Schreibung *f* mit Bindestrich, b) (Silben)Trennung *f.*

hyp·noid [ˈhɪpnɔɪd] *adj.* hypnoˈid, hypˈnose- *od.* schlafähnlich.

hyp·no·sis [hɪpˈnəʊsɪs] *pl.* **-ses** [-siːz] *s.* ⚕ Hypˈnose *f*; ˌ**hyp·noˈther·a·py** [ˌhɪpnəʊ-] *s. psych.* Hypnotheraˈpie *f*; **hypˈnot·ic** [-ˈnɒtɪk] **I** *adj.* (□ **～ally**) **1.** hypˈnotisch; **2.** einschläfernd; **3.** hypnotisierbar; **II** *s.* **4.** Hypˈnotikum *n*, Schlafmittel *n*; **5.** a) Hypnotisierte(r *m*) *f*, b) *j-d, der hypnotisierbar ist*; **hyp·no·tism** [ˈhɪpnətɪzəm] *s.* ⚕ **1.** Hypnoˈtismus *m*; **2.** a) Hypˈnose *f*, b) Hypnotisierung *f*; **hyp·no·tist** [ˈhɪpnətɪst] *s.* Hypnotiˈseur *m*; **hyp·no·ti·za·tion** [ˌhɪpnətaɪˈzeɪʃn] *s.* Hypnotisierung *f*; **hyp·no·tize** [ˈhɪpnətaɪz] *v/t.* ⚕ hypnotisieren (*a. fig.*).

hy·po¹ [ˈhaɪpəʊ] *s.* ⚗, *phot.* Fixiersalz *n*, ˈNatriumthiosulˌfat *n.*

hy·po² [ˈhaɪpəʊ] *pl.* **-pos** *s.* F → a) **hypodermic injection**, b) **hypodermic syringe.**

hy·po·chon·dri·a [ˌhaɪpəʊˈkɒndrɪə] *s.* ⚕ Hypochonˈdrie *f*; ˌ**hy·poˈchon·dri·ac** [-ɪæk] ⚕ **I** *adj.* (□ **～ally**) hypoˈchondrisch; **II** *s.* Hypoˈchonder *m.*

hy·poc·ri·sy [hɪˈpɒkrəsɪ] *s.* Heucheˈlei *f*, Scheinheiligkeit *f*; **hyp·o·crite** [ˈhɪpəkrɪt] *s.* Hypoˈkrit *m*, Heuchler(in), Scheinheilige(r *m*) *f*; **hyp·o·crit·i·cal** [ˌhɪpəʊˈkrɪtɪkl] *adj.* □ heuchlerisch, scheinheilig.

hy·po·der·mic [ˌhaɪpəʊˈdɜːmɪk] ⚕ **I** *adj.* (□ **～ally**) **1.** subkuˈtan, hypoderˈmal, unter der *od.* die Haut; **II** *s.* **2.** → ***hypodermic injection***; **3.** → ***hypodermic syringe***; **4.** subku'tan angewandtes Mittel; ~ **in·jec·tion** *s.* ⚕ subku'tane Injekti'on; ~ **nee·dle** *s.* ⚕ Nadel *f* für e-e subku'tane Spritze; ~ **syr·inge** *s.* ⚕ Spritze *f* zur subku'tanen Injekti'on.

hy·po|·phos·phate [ˌhaɪpəʊ'fɒsfeɪt] *s.* ⚗ 'Hypophosˌphat *n*; **~·phos·phor·ic ac·id** [ˌhaɪpəʊfɒs'fɒrɪk] *s.* ⚗ Hypo-, 'Unterphosphorsäure *f.*

hy·poph·y·sis [haɪ'pɒfɪsɪs] *pl.* **-ses** [-si:z] *s. anat.* Hirnanhangdrüse *f*, Hypo'physe *f.*

hy·pos·ta·sis [haɪ'pɒstəsɪs] *pl.* **-ses** [-si:z] *s.* **1.** *phls.* Hypo'stase *f*: a) Grundlage *f*, Sub'stanz *f*, b) Vergegenständlichung *f* (*e-s Begriffs*); **2.** ⚕, *biol.* Hypo'stase *f.*

hy·po|·sul·fite, *bsd. Brit.* **~·sul·phite** [ˌhaɪpəʊ'sʌlfaɪt] *s.* ⚗ **1.** Hyposul'fit *n*, 'unterschwefligsaures Salz; **2.** → ***hypo***¹; **~·sul·fu·rous**, *bsd. Brit.* **~·sul·phu·rous** [ˌhaɪpəʊ'sʌlfərəs] *adj.* ⚗ 'unterschweflig.

hy·po·tac·tic [ˌhaɪpəʊ'tæktɪk] *adj. ling.* hypo'taktisch, 'unterordnend.

hy·po·ten·sion [ˌhaɪpəʊ'tenʃn] *s.* ⚕ zu niedriger Blutdruck, Hypoto'nie *f.*

hy·pot·e·nuse [haɪ'pɒtənju:z] *s.* Å Hypote'nuse *f.*

hy·poth·ec ['haɪpəθɪk] *s.* ⚖ *Scot.* Hypo'thek *f*; **hy·poth·e·car·y** [haɪ'pɒθɪkərɪ] *adj.* ⚖ hypothe'karisch: ~ ***debts*** Hypothekenschulden; ~ ***value*** Beleihungswert *m*; **hy·poth·e·cate** [haɪ'pɒθɪkeɪt] *v/t.* **1.** ⚖ *Grundstück etc.* hypothe'karisch belasten; **2.** *Schiff* verbodmen; **3.** ⚚ *Effekten* lombardieren; **hy·poth·e·ca·tion** [haɪˌpɒθɪ'keɪʃn] *s.* **1.** ⚖ hypothe'karische Belastung (*Grundstück etc.*); **2.** Verbodmung *f* (*Schiff*); **3.** ⚚ Lombardierung *f* (*Effekten*).

hy·poth·e·sis [haɪ'pɒθɪsɪs] *pl.* **-ses** [-si:z] *s.* Hypo'these *f*: a) Annahme *f*, Vor'aussetzung *f*: ***working*** ~ Arbeitshypothese, b) (bloße) Vermutung; **hy·'poth·e·size** [-saɪz] **I** *v/i.* e-e Hypo'these aufstellen; **II** *v/t.* vor'aussetzen, annehmen, vermuten; **hy·po·thet·ic**, **hy·po·thet·i·cal** [ˌhaɪpəʊ'θetɪk(l)] *adj.* □ hypo'thetisch.

hyp·som·e·try [hɪp'sɒmɪtrɪ] *s. geogr.* Höhenmessung *f.*

hys·sop ['hɪsəp] *s.* **1.** ⚘ Ysop *m*; **2.** *R.C.* Weihwedel *m.*

hys·te·ri·a [hɪ'stɪərɪə] *s.* ⚕ *u. fig.* Hyste'rie *f*; **hys·ter·ic** [hɪ'sterɪk] ⚕ **I** *s.* **1.** Hy'steriker(in); **2.** *pl. mst sg. konstr.* Hyste'rie *f*, hy'sterischer Anfall: ***go*** (***off***) ***into*** **~*s*** a) e-n hysterischen Anfall bekommen, hysterisch werden, b) F e-n Lachkrampf bekommen; **II** *adj.* (□ **~*ally***) **3.** → **hys·ter·i·cal** [hɪ'sterɪkl] *adj.* □ ⚕ *u. fig.* hy'sterisch.

I

I¹, i [aɪ] *s.* I *n*, i *n* (*Buchstabe*).

I² [aɪ] **I** *pron.* ich; **II** *pl.* **I's** *s. das* Ich.

i·am·bic [aɪˈæmbɪk] **I** *adj.* jambisch; **II** *s.* a) Jambus *m* (*Versfuß*), b) jambischer Vers; **iˈam·bus** [-bəs] *pl.* **-bi** [-baɪ], **-bus·es** *s.* Jambus *m.*

ˈI-beam *s.* ⚙ Doppel-T-Träger *m*; I-Formstahl *m*: **~ *section*** I-Profil *n.*

I·be·ri·an [aɪˈbɪərɪən] **I** *s.* **1.** Iˈberer(in); **2.** *ling.* Iˈberisch *n*; **II** *adj.* **3.** iˈberisch; **4.** die iˈberische Halbinsel betreffend; **Ibero-** [-rəʊ] *in Zssgn* Ibero…; **~-*America*** Lateinamerika *n.*

i·bex [ˈaɪbeks] *s. zo.* Steinbock *m.*

i·bi·dem [ɪˈbaɪdem], *a.* **ib·id** [ˈɪbɪd] (*Lat.*) *adv.* ebenda (*bsd. für Textstelle etc.*).

i·bis [ˈaɪbɪs] *s. zo.* Ibis *m.*

ice [aɪs] **I** *s.* **1.** Eis *n*: ***broken* ~** Eisstücke *pl.*; ***dry* ~** Trockeneis (*feste Kohlensäure*); ***break the* ~** *fig.* das Eis brechen; ***skate on*** (*od.* ***over***) ***thin* ~** *fig.* a) ein gefährliches Spiel treiben, b) ein heikles Thema berühren; ***cut no* ~** F keinen Eindruck machen, ‚nicht ziehen'; ***that cuts no* ~ *with me*** F das zieht bei mir nicht; ***keep*** (*od.* ***put***) ***on* ~** F *et. od. j-n* ‚auf Eis legen'; **2.** a) *Am.* Gefrorenes *n* aus Fruchtsaft u. Zuckerwasser, b) *Brit.* (Speise)Eis *n*, c) → ***icing*** 2; **3.** *sl.* Diaˈmanten *pl.*, ‚Klunkern' *pl.*; **II** *v/t.* **4.** mit Eis bedecken; **5.** in Eis verwandeln, vereisen; **6.** mit *od.* in Eis kühlen; **7.** überˈzuckern, glasieren; **8.** *sl. j-n* ‚umlegen'; **III** *v/i.* **9.** gefrieren: **~ *up*** (*od.* ***over***) zufrieren, vereisen.

ice| age *s. geol.* Eiszeit *f*; **~ ax(e)** *s. mount.* Eispickel *m*; **~ bag** *s. Am.* Eisbeutel *m*; **ˈ~·berg** [-bɜːg] *s.* Eisberg *m* (*a. fig. sl. Person*): ***the tip of the* ~** die Spitze des Eisbergs (*a. fig.*); **ˈ~·blink** *s.* Eisblink *m*; **ˈ~·boat** *s.* **1.** Eissegler *m*, Segelschlitten *m*; **2.** Eisbrecher *m*; **ˈ~·bound** *adj.* eingefroren (*Schiff*); zugefroren (*Hafen*); vereist (*Straße*); **ˈ~·box** *s.* **1.** *bsd. Am.* Eis-, Kühlschrank *m*; **2.** *Brit.* Eisfach *n*; **3.** Eisbox *f*; **4.** F ‚Eiskeller' *m* (*Raum*); **ˈ~ˌbreak·er** *s.* ⚓ Eisbrecher *m* (*a. an Brücken*); **ˈ~·cap** *s.* (*bsd. arktische*) Eisdecke; **~ cream** *s.* (Speise)Eis *n*, Eiscreme *f*: ***vanilla* ~** Vanilleeis; **ˈ~-cream** *adj.* Eis…: **~ *bar*** *od.* ***parlo(u)r*** Eisdiele *f*; **~ *cone*** Eistüte *f*; **~ *soda*** Eis *n* in Sodawasser (*mit Sirup etc.*); **~ cube** *s.* Eiswürfel *m.*

iced [aɪst] *adj.* **1.** mit Eis bedeckt, vereist; **2.** eisgekühlt; **3.** gefroren; **4.** glasiert, mit ˈZuckerglaˌsur *od.* -guß.

ˈice|·fall *s.* gefrorener Wasserfall; **~ fern** *s.* Eisblume(n *pl.*) *f*; **~ floe** *s.* Eisscholle *f*; **~ foot** *s.* [*irr.*] (arktischer) Eisgürtel; **~ fox** *s. zo.* Poˈlarfuchs *m*; **ˈ~·free** *adj.* eis-, vereisungsfrei; **~ hock·ey** *s.* Eishockey *n*; **~ house** *s.* Kühlhaus *n.*

Ice·land·er [ˈaɪsləndə] *s.* Isländer(in); **Ice·lan·dic** [aɪsˈlændɪk] **I** *adj.* isländisch; **II** *s. ling.* Isländisch *n.*

ice| lol·ly *s. Brit.* Eis *n* am Stiel; **~ machine** *s.* ˈEis-, ˈKältemaˌschine *f*; **ˈ~·man** [-mæn] *s.* [*irr.*] *Am.* Eismann *m*, Eisverkäufer *m*; **~ pack** *s.* **1.** Packeis *n*; **2.** ⚕ ˈEisˌumschlag *m*, -beutel *m*; **3.** Kühlbeutel *m* (*in Kühltaschen etc.*); **~ pick** *s.* Eishacke *f*; **~ plant** *s.* ⚘ Eiskraut *n*; **~ rink** *s.* (Kunst)Eisbahn *f*; **~ run** *s.* Eis-, Rodelbahn *f*; **~ show** *s.* ˈEisreˌvue *f*; **ˈ~-skate I** *s.* Schlittschuh *m*; **II** *v/i.* Schlittschuh laufen; **~ wa·ter** *s.* **1.** Eiswasser *n*; **2.** Schmelzwasser *n*; **~ yacht** → ***iceboat*** 1.

ich·thy·o·log·i·cal [ˌɪkθɪəˈlɒdʒɪkl] *adj.* ichthyoˈlogisch; **ich·thy·ol·o·gy** [ˌɪkθɪˈɒlədʒɪ] *s.* Ichthyoloˈgie *f*, Fischkunde *f*; **ich·thy·oph·a·gous** [ˌɪkθɪˈɒfəgəs] *adj.* fisch(fr)essend; **ˌich·thy·oˈsau·rus** [-ˈsɔːrəs] *pl.* **-ri** [-raɪ] *s. zo.* Ichthyoˈsaurier *m.*

i·ci·cle [ˈaɪsɪkl] *s.* Eiszapfen *m.*

i·ci·ly [ˈaɪsɪlɪ] *adv.* eisig (*a. fig.*); **ˈi·ci·ness** [-nɪs] *s.* **1.** Eiseskälte *f* (*a. fig.*), eisige Kälte; **2.** Vereisung *f* (*Straße etc.*).

ic·ing [ˈaɪsɪŋ] *s.* **1.** Eisschicht *f*; Vereisung *f*; **2.** Zuckerguß *m*: **~ *sugar*** *Brit.* Puder-, Staubzucker *m*; **3.** *Eishockey*: unerlaubter Weitschuß.

i·con [ˈaɪkɒn] *s.* Iˈkone *f*, Heiligenbild *n*; **i·con·o·clasm** [aɪˈkɒnəʊklæzəm] *s.* Bilderstürmeˈrei *f* (*a. fig.*); **i·con·o·clast** [aɪˈkɒnəʊklæst] *s.* Bilderstürmer *m* (*a. fig.*); **i·con·o·clas·tic** [aɪˌkɒnəʊˈklæstɪk] *adj.* bilderstürmend; *fig.* bilderstürmerisch; **i·co·nog·ra·phy** [ˌaɪkɒˈnɒgrəfɪ] *s.* Ikonograˈphie *f*; **i·co·nol·a·try** [ˌaɪkɒˈnɒlətrɪ] *s.* Bilderverehrung *f*; **i·co·nol·o·gy** [ˌaɪkɒˈnɒlədʒɪ] *s.* Ikonoloˈgie *f*; **i·con·o·scope** [aɪˈkɒnəskəʊp] *s.* *TV* Ikonoˈskop *n*, Bildwandlerröhre *f.*

ic·tus [ˈɪktəs] *s.* ˈVersakˌzent *m.*

i·cy [ˈaɪsɪ] *adj.* ☐ **1.** eisig (*a. fig.*): **~ *cold*** eiskalt; **2.** vereist, eisig, gefroren.

id [ɪd] *s.* **1.** *psych.* Es *n*; **2.** *biol.* Id *n* (*Erbeinheit*).

I'd [aɪd] F *für* a) ***I would, I should***, b) ***I had.***

i·de·a [aɪˈdɪə] *s.* **1.** Iˈdee *f* (*a. phls.*, ♪): a) Vorstellung *f*, Begriff *m*, Ahnung *f*, b) Gedanke *m*: ***form an* ~ *of*** sich e-n Begriff machen von, sich *et.* vorstellen; ***I have an* ~ *that*** ich habe so das Gefühl, daß; (***I've***) ***no* ~!** (ich habe) keine Ahnung!; ***he hasn't the faintest* ~** er hat nicht die leiseste Ahnung; ***the very* ~!**, ***what an* ~!** *contp.* was für e-e Idee!, (na,) so was!, unmöglich!; ***the very* ~ *makes me sick!*** bei dem bloßen Gedanken (daran) wird mir schlecht!; ***you have no* ~ *how …*** du kannst dir nicht vorstellen, wie …; ***could you give me an* ~ *of where*** (*etc.*) ***…?*** können Sie mir ungefähr sagen, wo (*etc.*) …?; ***that's not my* ~ *of fun*** unter Spaß stell' ich mir was andres vor; ***it is my* ~ *that*** ich bin der Ansicht, daß; ***the* ~ *entered my mind*** mir kam der Gedanke; **2.** Iˈdee *f*: a) Einfall *m*, Gedanke *m*, b) Absicht *f*, Zweck *m*: ***not a bad* ~** keine schlechte Idee; ***the* ~ *is*** der Zweck der Sache ist …; ***that's the* ~!** genau (darum dreht sich's)!; ***what's the big* ~?** F was soll denn das?; ***whose bright* ~ *was that?*** wer hat sich denn das ausgedacht?; ***put* ~*s into s.o.'s head*** j-m e-n Floh ins Ohr setzen; ***have* ~*s*** F ‚Rosinen' im Kopf haben; ***don't get* ~*s about …*** mach dir keine Hoffnungen auf (*acc.*); **~*s man*** Ideenentwickler *m*; **iˈde·aed, iˈde·a'd** [-əd] *adj.* iˈdeenreich, voller Iˈdeen.

i·de·al [aɪˈdɪəl] **I** *adj.* ☐ → ***ideally***; **1.** ideˈal (*a. phls.*), vollˈendet, vollˈkommen, vorbildlich, Muster…; **2.** ideˈell: a) Ideen…, b) auf Ideˈalen beruhend, c) (nur) eingebildet; **3.** ♂ ideˈal, uneigentlich: **~ *number***; **II** *s.* **4.** Ideˈal *n*, Wunsch-, Vorbild *n*; **5.** *das* Ideˈelle (*Ggs. das Wirkliche*); **iˈde·al·ism** [-lɪzəm] *s.* Ideaˈlismus *m*; **iˈde·al·ist** [-lɪst] *s.* Ideaˈlist(in); **i·de·al·is·tic** [aɪˌdɪəˈlɪstɪk] *adj.* (☐ **~*ally***) ideaˈlistisch; **i·de·al·i·za·tion** [aɪˌdɪəlaɪˈzeɪʃn] *s.* Idealisierung *f*; **iˈde·al·ize** [-laɪz] *v/t. u. v/i.* idealisieren; **iˈde·al·ly** [-lɪ] *adv.* **1.** ideˈal(erweise), am besten; **2.** ideˈell, geistig; **3.** im Geiste.

i·dée fixe [ˌiːdeɪˈfiːks] (*Fr.*) *s.* fixe Iˈdee.

i·dem [ˈaɪdem] **I** *s.* derˈselbe (Verfasser), dasˈselbe (Buch *etc.*); **II** *adv.* beim selben Verfasser.

i·den·tic [aɪˈdentɪk] *adj.* → ***identical***; **~ *note pol.*** gleichlautende Note; **iˈden·ti·cal** [-kl] *adj.* ☐ (***with***) a) iˈdentisch (mit), (genau) gleich (*dat.*): **~ *twins*** eineiige Zwillinge, b) (der-, die-, das-) ˈselbe (wie), c) gleichbedeutend (mit), -lautend (wie).

i·den·ti·fi·a·ble [aɪˈdentɪfaɪəbl] *adj.* identifizier-, feststell-, erkennbar; **i·den·ti·fi·ca·tion** [aɪˌdentɪfɪˈkeɪʃn] *s.* **1.** Identifizierung *f*: a) Gleichsetzung *f* (***with*** mit), b) Feststellung *f* der Identiˈtät, Erkennung *f*: **~ *mark*** Kennzeichen *n*; **~ *papers***, **~ *card*** → ***identity card***; **~ *disk***, *Am.* **~ *tag*** ⚔ Erkennungsmarke *f*; **~ *parade*** ⚖ Gegenüberstellung *f* (zur Identifizierung e-s Verdächtigen); **2.** Legitimati'on *f*, Ausweis *m*; **3.** *Funk, Radar*: Kennung *f*; **i·den·ti·fy** [aɪ'dentɪfaɪ] **I** *v/t*. **1.** identifizieren, gleichsetzen, als i'dentisch betrachten (***with*** mit): **~ *o.s. with*** → 5; **2.** identifizieren, erkennen, die Identi'tät feststellen von (*od. gen.*); **3.** *biol.* die Art feststellen von (*od. gen.*); **4.** ausweisen, legitimieren; **II** *v/i*. **5. ~ *with*** *od.* ***to*** sich identifizieren mit.

i·den·ti·kit [aɪ'dentɪkɪt] *s*. ⚖ Phan'tombild(gerät) *n*.

i·den·ti·ty [aɪ'dentətɪ] *s*. Identi'tät *f*: a) Gleichheit *f*, b) Per'sönlichkeit *f*: ***loss of ~*** Identitätsverlust *m*; ***mistaken ~*** Personenverwechslung *f*; ***establish s.o.'s ~*** → ***identify*** 2; ***prove one's ~*** sich ausweisen; ***reveal one's ~*** sich zu erkennen geben; **~ card** *s*. (Perso'nal-) Ausweis *m*, Kenn-, Ausweiskarte *f*; **~ cri·sis** *s. psych*. Identi'tätskrise *f*.

id·e·o·gram ['ɪdɪəʊgræm], '**id·e·o·graph** [-grɑːf] *s*. Ideo'gramm *n*, Begriffszeichen *n*.

id·e·o·log·ic, **id·e·o·log·i·cal** [ˌaɪdɪə'lɒdʒɪk(l)] *adj*. ideo'logisch; **id·e·ol·o·gist** [ˌaɪdɪ'ɒlədʒɪst] *s*. **1.** Ideo'loge *m*; **2.** Theo'retiker *m*; **id·e·o·lo·gize** [ˌaɪdɪ'ɒlədʒaɪz] *v/t*. ideologisieren; **id·e·ol·o·gy** [ˌaɪdɪ'ɒlədʒɪ] *s*. **1.** Ideolo'gie *f*, Denkweise *f*; **2.** Begriffslehre *f*; **3.** reine Theo'rie.

ides [aɪdz] *s. pl. antiq*. Iden *pl*.

id·i·o·cy ['ɪdɪəsɪ] *s*. Idio'tie *f*: a) (⚕ hochgradiger) Schwachsinn, b) F Dummheit *f*, Blödsinn *m*.

id·i·om ['ɪdɪəm] *s. ling*. **1.** Idi'om *n*, Sondersprache *f*, Mundart *f*; **2.** Ausdrucksweise *f*, Sprache *f*; **3.** Sprachgebrauch *m*, -eigentümlichkeit *f*; **4.** idio'matische Wendung, Redewendung *f*; **id·i·o·mat·ic** [ˌɪdɪə'mætɪk] *adj*. (☐ **~*ally***) *ling*. **1.** idio'matisch, spracheigentümlich; **2.** sprachrichtig, -üblich.

id·i·o·plasm ['ɪdɪəplæzəm] *s. biol*. Idio'plasma *n*, Erbmasse *f*.

id·i·o·syn·cra·sy [ˌɪdɪə'sɪŋkrəsɪ] *s*. Idiosynkra'sie *f*: a) per'sönliche Eigenart *od.* Veranlagung *od.* Neigung, b) ⚕ krankhafte Abneigung.

id·i·ot ['ɪdɪət] *s*. Idi'ot *m*: a) ⚕ Schwachsinnige(r *m*) *f*, b) F Dummkopf *m*: **~ *card*** *TV* ‚Neger' *m*; **id·i·ot·ic** [ˌɪdɪ'ɒtɪk] *adj*. (☐ **~*ally***) idi'otisch: a) F dumm, blödsinnig, b) ⚕ geistesschwach, schwachsinnig.

i·dle ['aɪdl] **I** *adj*. (☐ ***idly***) **1.** untätig, müßig: ***the ~ rich*** die reichen Müßiggänger; **2.** unbeschäftigt, arbeitslos; **3.** ⚙ a) außer Betrieb, stillstehend, b) im Leerlauf, Leerlauf...: **~ *current*** a) Leerlaufstrom *m*, b) Blindstrom *m*; **~ *motion*** Leergang *m*; **~ *pulley*** → ***idler*** 2 b; **~ *wheel*** → ***idler*** 2 a; ***lie ~*** stilliegen; ***run ~*** → 9; **4.** † 'unproduk,tiv, brachliegend (*a.* ⚒), tot (*Kapital*); **5.** ruhig, still, ungenutzt: **~ *hours*** Mußestunden; **6.** faul, träge: **~ *fellow*** Faulenzer *m*; **7.** a) nutz-, zweck-, sinnlos, vergeblich, b) leer (*Worte etc.*), c) müßig (*Mutmaßungen etc.*): **~ *talk*** leeres *od.* müßiges Gerede; ***it would be ~ to*** *inf*. es wäre müßig *od.* sinnlos zu *inf*.; **II** *v/i*. **8.** faulenzen: **~ *about*** herumtrödeln; **9.** ⚙ leer laufen, im Leerlauf sein; **III** *v/t*. **10.** *mst* **~ *away*** vertrödeln, verbummeln, müßig zubringen; '**i·dled** [-ld] *adj*. → ***idle*** 2; '**i·dle·ness** [-nɪs] *s*. **1.** Untätigkeit *f*, Muße *f*; **2.** Faulheit *f*, Müßiggang *m*; **3.** a) Leere *f*, Hohlheit *f*, b) Müßigkeit *f*, Nutz-, Zwecklosigkeit *f*, Vergeblichkeit *f*; '**i·dler** [-lə] *s*. **1.** Faulenzer(in), Müßiggänger(in); **2.** a) Zwischenrad *n*, b) Leerlaufrolle *f*; '**i·dling** [-lɪŋ] *s*. **1.** Nichtstun *n*, Müßiggang *m*; **2.** ⚙ Leerlauf *m*; '**i·dly** [-lɪ] *adv*. → ***idle***.

i·dol ['aɪdl] *s*. I'dol *n*, Abgott *m* (*beide a. fig.*); Götze *m*, Götzenbild *n*: ***make an ~ of*** → ***idolize***.

i·dol·a·ter [aɪ'dɒlətə] *s*. **1.** Götzendiener *m*; **2.** *fig.* Anbeter *m*, Verehrer *m*; **i'dol·a·tress** [-trɪs] *s*. Götzendienerin *f*; **i'dol·a·trous** [-trəs] *adj*. ☐ **1.** *fig.* abgöttisch; **2.** Götzen...; **i'dol·a·try** [-trɪ] *s*. **1.** Abgötte'rei *f*, Götzendienst *m*; **2.** *fig.* Vergötterung *f*; **i·dol·i·za·tion** [ˌaɪdəlaɪ'zeɪʃn] *s*. **1.** Abgötte'rei *f*; **2.** *fig.* Vergötterung *f*; **i·dol·ize** ['aɪdəlaɪz] *v/t*. *fig.* abgöttisch verehren, vergöttern, anbeten.

i·dyl(l) ['ɪdɪl] *s*. **1.** I'dylle *f*, Hirtengedicht *n*; **2.** *fig.* I'dyll *n*; **i·dyl·lic** [aɪ'dɪlɪk] *adj*. (☐ **~*ally***) i'dyllisch.

if [ɪf] **I** *cj*. **1.** wenn, falls: **~ *I were you*** wenn ich Sie wäre, (ich) an Ihrer Stelle; **~ *and when*** *bsd*. ⚖ falls, im Falle (, daß); **~ *any*** wenn überhaupt einer (*od.* eine *od.* eines *od.* etwas), falls etwa *od.* je; **~ *anything*** a) wenn überhaupt etwas, b) wenn überhaupt (, *dann ist das Buch dicker etc.*); **~ *not*** wenn *od.* falls nicht; **~ *so*** wenn ja, *bsd. in Formularen*: *a.* zutreffendenfalls; **~ *only to prove*** und wäre es auch nur, um zu beweisen; **~ *I know Jim*** so wie ich Jim kenne; → ***as if***; **2.** wenn auch: ***he is nice ~ a bit silly***; **3.** ob: ***try ~ you can do it!***; ***I don't know ~ he will agree***; **4.** *ausrufend*: **~ *I had only known!*** hätte ich (das) nur gewußt!; **II** *s*. **5.** Wenn *n*: ***without ~s or buts*** ohne Wenn u. Aber.

ig·loo, *a.* **i·glu** ['ɪgluː] *s*. Iglu *m*.

ig·ne·ous ['ɪgnɪəs] *adj*. glühend: **~ *rock*** Erstarrungsgestein *n*, magmatisches Gestein.

ig·nis fat·u·us [ˌɪgnɪs'fætjʊəs] (*Lat.*) *s*. **1.** Irrlicht *n*; **2.** *fig.* Trugbild *n*.

ig·nite [ɪg'naɪt] **I** *v/t*. **1.** an-, entzünden; **2.** ⚡, *mot.* zünden; **II** *v/i*. **3.** sich entzünden, Feuer fangen; **4.** ⚡, *mot.* zünden; **ig'nit·er** [-tə] *s*. Zündvorrichtung *f*, Zünder *m*.

ig·ni·tion [ɪg'nɪʃn] *s*. **1.** An-, Entzünden *n*; **2.** ⚡, *mot.* Zündung *f*; **3.** ⚗ Erhitzung *f*; **~ charge** *s*. ⚙ Zündladung *f*; **~ coil** *s*. ⚡ Zündspule *f*; **~ de·lay** *s*. ⚙ Zündverzögerung *f*; **~ key** *s. mot*. Zündschlüssel *m*; **~ lock** *s*. ⚙ Zündschloß *n*; **~ point** *s*. Zünd-, Flammpunkt *m*; **~ spark** *s*. ⚡ Zündfunke *m*; **~ tim·ing** *s*. Zündeinstellung *f*; **~ tube** *s*. ⚗ Glührohr *n*.

ig·no·ble [ɪg'nəʊbl] *adj*. ☐ **1.** gemein, unedel, niedrig; **2.** schmachvoll, schändlich; **3.** von niedriger Geburt.

ig·no·min·i·ous [ˌɪgnəʊ'mɪnɪəs] *adj*. ☐ schändlich, schimpflich; **ig·no·min·y** ['ɪgnəmɪnɪ] *s*. **1.** Schmach *f*, Schande *f*; **2.** Schändlichkeit *f*.

ig·no·ra·mus [ˌɪgnə'reɪməs] *pl*. **-mus·es** *s*. Igno'rant(in), Nichtswisser(in).

ig·no·rance ['ɪgnərəns] *s*. Unwissenheit *f*: a) Unkenntnis *f* (***of*** *gen*.), b) *contp*. Igno'ranz *f*, Beschränktheit *f*: **~ *of the law is no excuse*** Unkenntnis schützt vor Strafe nicht; '**ig·no·rant** [-nt] *adj*. ☐ **1.** unkundig, nicht kennend *od.* wissend: ***be ~ of*** *et.* nicht wissen *od.* kennen, nichts wissen von; **2.** unwissend, ungebildet; '**ig·no·rant·ly** [-ntlɪ] *adv*. unwissentlich; **ig·nore** [ɪg'nɔː] *v/t*. **1.** ignorieren, nicht beachten *od.* berücksichtigen, keine No'tiz nehmen von; **2.** ⚖ *Am. Klage* verwerfen, abweisen.

i·gua·na [ɪ'gwɑːnə] *s. zo*. Legu'an *m*.

i·kon ['aɪkɒn] → ***icon***.

il·e·um ['ɪlɪəm] *s. anat*. Ileum *n*, Krummdarm *m*; '**il·e·us** [-əs] *s*. ⚕ Darmverschluß *m*.

i·lex ['aɪleks] *s*. ⚘ **1.** Stechpalme *f*; **2.** Stecheiche *f*.

il·i·ac ['ɪlɪæk] *adj*. Darmbein...

Il·i·ad ['ɪlɪəd] *s*. Ilias *f*, Ili'ade *f*: ***an ~ of woes*** *fig.* e-e endlose Leidensgeschichte.

il·i·um ['ɪlɪəm] *pl*. '**il·i·a** [-ə] *s. anat*. a) Darmbein *n*, b) Hüfte *f*.

ilk [ɪlk] *s*. **1.** ***of that ~*** *Scot.* gleichnamigen Ortes: ***Kinloch of that ~ = Kinloch of Kinloch***; **2.** Art *f*, Sorte *f*: ***people of that ~*** solche Leute.

ill [ɪl] **I** *adj*. **1.** (*nur pred.*) krank: ***be taken ~***, ***fall*** *od.* ***take ~*** erkranken (***with***, ***of*** an *dat*.); ***be ~ with a cold*** e-e Erkältung haben; **~ *with fear*** krank vor Angst; **2.** (*moralisch*) schlecht, böse, übel; → ***fame*** 1; **3.** böse, feindlich: **~ *blood*** böses Blut; ***with an ~ grace*** widerwillig, ungern; **~ *humo(u)r*** *od.* ***temper*** üble Laune; **~ *treatment*** schlechte Behandlung, Mißhandlung *f*; **~ *will*** Feindschaft *f*, Groll *m*; ***I bear him no ~ will*** ich trage ihm nichts nach; → ***feeling*** 2; **4.** nachteilig; ungünstig, schlecht, übel: **~ *effect*** üble Folge *od.* Wirkung; ***it's an ~ wind (that blows nobody good)*** et. Gutes ist an allem; → ***health*** 2, ***luck*** 1, ***omen*** I, ***weed*** 1; **5.** schlecht, unbefriedigend, fehlerhaft: **~ *breeding*** a) schlechte Erziehung, b) Ungezogenheit *f*; **~ *management*** Mißwirtschaft *f*; **~ *success*** Mißerfolg *m*, Fehlschlag *m*; **II** *adv*. **6.** schlecht, übel: **~ *at ease*** unruhig, unbehaglich, verlegen; **7.** böse, feindlich; ***take s.th. ~*** et. übelnehmen; ***speak (think) ~ of s.o.*** schlecht von j-m sprechen (denken); **8.** ungünstig: ***it went ~ with him*** es erging ihm schlecht; ***it ~ becomes you*** es steht dir schlecht an; **9.** ungenügend, schlecht: **~*-equipped***; **10.** schwerlich, kaum: ***I can ~ afford it*** ich kann es mir kaum leisten; **III** *s*. **11.** Übel *n*, 'Mißgeschick *n*, Ungemach *n*; **12.** *a. fig.* Leiden *n*, Krankheit *f*; **13.** *das* Böse, Übel *n*.

I'll [aɪl] F *für* ***I shall***, ***I will***.

ˌ**ill**|**-ad'vised** *adj*. ☐ **1.** schlechtberaten; **2.** unbesonnen, unklug; ˌ**~-af'fect·ed** → ***ill-disposed***; ˌ**~-as'sort·ed** *adj*. schlecht zs.-passend, zs.-gewürfelt; ˌ**~-'bred** *adj*. schlecht erzogen, ungezogen; ˌ**~-con'sid·ered** *adj*. unüberlegt, unbedacht, unklug; ˌ**~-dis'posed** *adj*. übelgesinnt (***towards*** *dat*.).

il·le·gal [ɪ'liːgl] *adj*. ☐ 'illeˌgal, ungesetzlich, gesetzwidrig, 'widerrechtlich, unerlaubt, verboten; **il·le·gal·i·ty** [ˌɪliː'gælətɪ] *s.* Gesetzwidrigkeit *f*: a) Ungesetzlichkeit *f*, Illegali'tät *f*, b) gesetzwidrige Handlung.

il·leg·i·bil·i·ty [ɪˌledʒɪ'bɪlətɪ] *s.* Unleserlichkeit *f*; **il·leg·i·ble** [ɪ'ledʒəbl] *adj.* □ unleserlich.

il·le·git·i·ma·cy [ˌɪlɪ'dʒɪtɪməsɪ] *s.* **1.** Unrechtmäßigkeit *f*; **2.** Unehelichkeit *f*, uneheliche Geburt(en *pl.*); ˌ**il·le'git·i·mate** [-mət] *adj.* □ **1.** unrechtmäßig, rechtswidrig; **2.** außer-, unehelich, illegi'tim; **3.** 'inkorˌrekt, falsch; **4.** unzulässig, illegi'tim; **5.** unlogisch.

ˌ**ill|-'fat·ed** *adj.* unselig: a) unglücklich, Unglücks…, b) verhängnisvoll, unglückselig; ˌ**~-'fa·vo(u)red** *adj.* □ unschön; ˌ**~-'found·ed** *adj.* unbegründet, fragwürdig; ˌ**~-'got·ten** *adj.* unrechtmäßig (erworben); ˌ**~-'hu·mo(u)red** *adj.* übelgelaunt.

il·lib·er·al [ɪ'lɪbərəl] *adj.* □ **1.** knauserig; **2.** engherzig, -stirnig; **3.** *pol.* 'illibeˌral; **il'lib·er·al·ism** [-rəlɪzəm] *s. pol.* 'illibeˌraler Standpunkt; **il·lib·er·al·i·ty** [ɪˌlɪbə'rælətɪ] *s.* **1.** Knause'rei *f*; **2.** Engherzigkeit *f*.

il·lic·it [ɪ'lɪsɪt] *adj.* □ → ***illegal***: **~ *trade*** Schleich-, Schwarzhandel *m*; **~ *work*** Schwarzarbeit *f*.

il·lit·er·a·cy [ɪ'lɪtərəsɪ] *s.* **1.** Unbildung *f*; **2.** Analpha'betentum *n*; **il'lit·er·ate** [-rət] **I** *adj.* **1.** ungebildet, unwissend; **2.** analpha'betisch, des Lesens u. Schreibens unkundig: ***he is* ~** er ist Analphabet; **3.** primi'tiv, unkultiviert: **~ *style***; **4.** fehlerhaft, voller Fehler; **II** *s.* **5.** Ungebildete(r *m*) *f*; **6.** Analpha'bet(in).

ˌ**ill|-'judged** *adj.* unbedacht, unklug; ˌ**~-'man·nered** *adj.* ungehobelt, ungezogen, mit schlechten 'Umgangsformen; ˌ**~-'matched** *adj.* schlecht zs.-passend; ˌ**~-'na·tured** *adj.* □ **1.** unfreundlich, boshaft; **2.** verärgert.

ill·ness ['ɪlnɪs] *s.* Krankheit *f*.

il·log·i·cal [ɪ'lɒdʒɪkl] *adj.* □ unlogisch; **il·log·i·cal·i·ty** [ˌɪlɒdʒɪ'kælətɪ] *s.* Unlogik *f*.

ˌ**ill|-'o·mened** → ***ill-fated***; ˌ**~-'starred** *adj.* unglücklich, unselig, vom Unglück verfolgt, unter e-m ungünstigen Stern (stehend); ˌ**~-'tem·pered** *adj.* schlechtgelaunt, übellaunig, mürrisch; ˌ**~-'timed** *adj.* ungelegen, unpassend, 'inopporˌtun; zeitlich schlecht gewählt; ˌ**~-'treat** *v/t.* miß'handeln; schlecht behandeln.

il·lu·mi·nant [ɪ'lju:mɪnənt] **I** *adj.* (er-)leuchtend, aufhellend; **II** *s.* Beleuchtungskörper *m*.

il·lu·mi·nate [ɪ'lju:mɪneɪt] **I** *v/t.* **1.** be-, erleuchten, erhellen; **2.** illuminieren, festlich beleuchten; **3.** *fig.* a) erläutern, erhellen, erklären, aufhellen, b) *j-n* erleuchten; **4.** *Bücher etc.* ausmalen, illuminieren; **5.** *fig.* Glanz verleihen (*dat.*); **II** *v/i.* **6.** sich erhellen; **il'lu·mi·nat·ed** [-tɪd] *adj.* beleuchtet, leuchtend, Leucht…, Licht…: **~ *advertising*** Leuchtreklame *f*; **il'lu·mi·nat·ing** [-tɪŋ] *adj.* **1.** leuchtend, Leucht…, Beleuchtungs…: **~ *gas*** Leuchtgas *n*; **~ *power*** Leuchtkraft *f*; **2.** *fig.* aufschlußreich, erhellend; **il·lu·mi·na·tion** [ɪˌlju:mɪ'neɪʃn] *s.* **1.** Be-, Erleuchtung *f*; **2.** *oft pl.* Illuminati'on *f*, Festbeleuchtung *f*; **3.** *fig.* a) Erläuterung *f*, Erhellung *f*, b) Erleuchtung *f*; **4.** *a. fig.* Licht *n* u. Glanz *m*; **5.** Illuminati'on *f*, Kolorierung *f*, Verzierung *f* (*von Büchern etc.*); **il'lu·mi·na·tive** [-nətɪv] → ***illuminating***.

il·lu·mine [ɪ'lju:mɪn] *v/t.* → ***illuminate*** 1–3.

ˌ**ill-'use** [-'ju:z] → ***ill-treat***.

il·lu·sion [ɪ'lu:ʒn] *s.* Illusi'on *f*: a) (Sinnes)Täuschung *f*; → ***optical***, b) Wahn *m*, Einbildung *f*, falsche Vorstellung, trügerische Hoffnung, c) Trugbild *n*, d) Blendwerk *n*: ***be under an* ~** e-r Täuschung unterliegen, sich Illusionen machen; ***be under the* ~ *that*** sich einbilden, daß; **il'lu·sion·ism** [-ʒənɪzəm] *s. bsd. phls.* Illusio'nismus *m*; **il'lu·sion·ist** [-ʒənɪst] *s.* Illusio'nist *m* (*a. phls.*): a) Schwärmer(in), Träumer(in), b) Zauberkünstler *m*.

il·lu·sive [ɪ'lu:sɪv] *adj.* □ illu'sorisch, trügerisch; **il'lu·sive·ness** [-nɪs] *s.* **1.** *das* Illu'sorische, Schein *m*; **2.** Täuschung *f*; **il'lu·so·ry** [-sərɪ] *adj.* □ → ***illusive***.

il·lus·trate ['ɪləstreɪt] *v/t.* **1.** erläutern, erklären, veranschaulichen; **2.** illustrieren, bebildern; **il·lus·tra·tion** [ˌɪlə'streɪʃn] *s.* Illustrati'on *f*: a) Erläuterung *f*, Erklärung *f*, Veranschaulichung *f*: ***in* ~ *of*** zur Veranschaulichung (*gen.*), b) Beispiel *n*, c) Bebildern *n*, Illustrieren *n*, d) Abbildung *f*, Bild *n*; **'il·lus·tra·tive** [-rətɪv] *adj.* □ erläuternd, veranschaulichend, Anschauungs…, Beispiel…: ***be* ~ *of*** → ***illustrate*** 1; **'il·lus·tra·tor** [-tə] *s. allg.* Illu'strator *m*.

il·lus·tri·ous [ɪ'lʌstrɪəs] *adj.* □ il'luster, berühmt, erhaben, erlaucht, glänzend.

I'm [aɪm] F *für* ***I am***.

im·age ['ɪmɪdʒ] *s.* **1.** Bild(nis) *n*; **2.** a) Standbild *n*, Bildsäule *f*, b) Heiligenbild *n*, c) Götzenbild *n*: **~*-worship*** Bilderanbetung *f*, *fig.* Götzendienst *m*; → ***graven***; **3.** ⚡, *opt., phys.* Bild *n*: **~ *converter tube*** *TV* Bildwandlerröhre *f*; **4.** Ab-, Ebenbild *n*: ***the (very)* ~ *of his father*** ganz der Vater; **5.** bildlicher Ausdruck, Vergleich *m*, Me'tapher *f*: ***speak in* ~*s*** in Bildern reden; **6.** a) Vorstellung *f*, I'dee *f*, (geistiges) Bild, b) Image *n* (*Persönlichkeitsbild*): ***the* ~ *of a politician***; **~ *building*** Imagepflege *f*; **7.** Verkörperung *f*; **'im·age·ry** [-dʒərɪ] *s.* **1.** Bilder *pl.*, Bildwerk(e *pl.*) *n*; **2.** Bilder(sprache *f*) *pl.*, Meta'phorik *f*; **3.** geistige Bilder *pl.*, Vorstellungen *pl.*

im·ag·i·na·ble [ɪ'mædʒɪnəbl] *adj.* □ vorstellbar, erdenklich, denkbar: ***the finest weather* ~** das denkbar schönste Wetter; **im'ag·i·nar·y** [-dʒɪnərɪ] *adj.* □ **1.** imagi'när (*a.* ⚡), nur in der Vorstellung vor'handen, eingebildet, (nur) gedacht, Schein…, Phantasie…; **2.** (frei) erfunden, imagi'när; **3.** ✝ fingiert.

im·ag·i·na·tion [ɪˌmædʒɪ'neɪʃn] *s.* **1.** Phanta'sie *f*, Vorstellungs-, Einbildungskraft *f*, Einfallsreichtum *m*: ***a man of* ~** ein phantasievoller *od.* ideenreicher Mann; ***he has no* ~** er ist phantasielos; ***use your* ~!** laß dir was einfallen!; **2.** Einfälle *pl.*, I'deenreichtum *m*; **3.** Vorstellung *f*, Einbildung *f*: ***in (my etc.)* ~** in der Vorstellung, im Geiste; ***pure* ~** reine Einbildung; **im·ag·i·na·tive** [ɪ'mædʒɪnətɪv] *adj.* □ **1.** phanta'siereich, erfinderisch, einfallsreich: **~ *faculty*** → ***imagination*** 1; **2.** phan'tastisch, phanta'sievoll: **~ *story***; **3.** *contp.* ‚erdichtet'; **im·ag·i·na·tive·ness** [ɪ'mædʒɪnətɪvnɪs] → ***imagination*** 1; **im·ag·ine** [ɪ'mædʒɪn] **I** *v/t.* **1.** sich *j-n od. et.* vorstellen *od.* denken: ***I* ~ *him as a tall man***; ***you can't* ~ *my joy***; ***you can't* ~ *how …*** du kannst dir nicht vorstellen *od.* du machst dir kein Bild, wie …; **2.** sich *et.* (*Unwirkliches*) einbilden: ***you are imagining things!*** du bildest dir das (alles) nur ein!; **3.** F glauben, denken, sich einbilden: ***don't* ~ *that I am satisfied***; **~ *to be*** halten für; **II** *v/i.* **4.** sich vorstellen *od.* denken: ***just* ~!** F stell dir vor!, denk (dir) nur!

i·ma·go [ɪ'meɪgəʊ] *pl.* **-goes** *od.* **i·mag·i·nes** [ɪ'meɪdʒɪni:z] *s.* **1.** *zo.* vollentwickeltes Insekt; **2.** *psych.* I'mago *n*.

im·bal·ance [ˌɪm'bæləns] *s.* **1.** Unausgewogenheit *f*, Unausgeglichenheit *f*; **2.** *bsd.* ⚕ gestörtes Gleichgewicht (*im Körperhaushalt etc.*); **3.** *bsd. pol.* Ungleichgewicht *n*.

im·be·cile ['ɪmbɪsi:l] **I** *adj.* □ **1.** ⚕ geistesschwach; **2.** *contp.* dumm, idi'otisch; **II** *s.* **3.** ⚕ Schwachsinnige(r *m*) *f*; **4.** *contp.* Idi'ot *m*, ‚Blödmann' *m*; **im·be·cil·i·ty** [ˌɪmbɪ'sɪlətɪ] *s.* **1.** ⚕ Schwachsinn *m*; **2.** *contp.* Idio'tie *f*, Blödheit *f*.

im·bibe [ɪm'baɪb] **I** *v/t.* **1.** *humor.* trinken; **2.** *fig. Ideen etc.* in sich aufnehmen, aufsaugen; **II** *v/i.* **3.** *humor.* trinken, bechern.

im·bro·glio [ɪm'brəʊlɪəʊ] *pl.* **-glios** *s.* **1.** Verwicklung *f*, Verwirrung *f*, Komplikati'on *f*, verzwickte Lage; **2.** a) ernstes 'Mißverständnis, b) heftige Ausein'andersetzung.

im·brue [ɪm'bru:] *v/t. mst fig.* (***with***, ***in***) baden (in *dat.*), tränken, *a.* beflecken (mit).

im·bue [ɪm'bju:] *v/t. fig.* erfüllen (***with*** mit): **~*d with*** erfüllt *od.* durchdrungen von.

im·i·ta·ble ['ɪmɪtəbl] *adj.* nachahmbar; **im·i·tate** ['ɪmɪteɪt] *v/t.* **1.** *j-n, j-s Stimme, Benehmen etc. od. et.* nachahmen, -machen, imitieren; **2.** *et.* imitieren, nachmachen, kopieren, *a.* fälschen; **3.** ähneln (*dat.*); **'im·i·tat·ed** [-teɪtɪd] *adj.* imitiert, unecht, künstlich; **im·i·ta·tion** [ˌɪmɪ'teɪʃn] **I** *s.* **1.** Nachahmung *f*, Imitati'on *f*: ***do an* ~ *of*** → ***imitate*** 1; **2.** Nachbildung *f*, -ahmung *f*, *das* Nachgeahmte, Imitati'on *f*, Ko'pie *f*; **3.** Fälschung *f*; **II** *adj.* **4.** unecht, künstlich, Kunst…, Imitations…: **~ *leather*** Kunstleder *n*; **'im·i·ta·tive** [-tətɪv] *adj.* □ **1.** nachahmend, -bildend; auf Nachahmung *fremder Vorbilder* beruhend: ***be* ~ *of*** → ***imitate*** 1; **2.** nachgemacht, -geahmt (***of*** *dat.*); **3.** *ling.* lautmalend: ***an* ~ *word***; **'im·i·ta·tor** [-teɪtə] *s.* Nachahmer *m*, Imi'tator *m*.

im·mac·u·late [ɪ'mækjʊlɪt] *adj.* □ **1.** *fig.* unbefleckt, makellos, rein: **2 *Conception*** *R.C.* Unbefleckte Empfängnis; **2.** untadelig, tadellos, einwandfrei; **3.** fleckenlos, sauber.

im·ma·nence ['ɪmənəns], **'im·ma·nen·cy** [-sɪ] *s. phls., eccl.* Imma'nenz *f*, Innewohnen *n*; **'im·ma·nent** [-nt] *adj.* imma'nent, innewohnend.

im·ma·te·ri·al [ˌɪmə'tɪərɪəl] *adj.* **1.** unkörperlich, unstofflich; **2.** unwesentlich, (*a.* ⚖) unerheblich, belanglos; ˌ**im·maˈte·ri·al·ism** [-lɪzəm] *s.* Immateriaˈlismus *m.*

im·ma·ture [ˌɪməˈtjʊə] *adj.* □ unreif, unentwickelt (*a. fig.*); ˌ**im·maˈtu·ri·ty** [-ˈtjʊərətɪ] *s.* Unreife *f.*

im·meas·ur·a·ble [ɪˈmeʒərəbl] *adj.* □ unermeßlich, grenzenlos, riesig.

im·me·di·a·cy [ɪˈmiːdjəsɪ] *s.* **1.** Unmittelbarkeit *f*, Diˈrektheit *f*; **2.** Unverzüglichkeit *f*; **im·me·di·ate** [ɪˈmiːdjət] *adj.* □ **1.** *Raum*: unmittelbar, nächst(gelegen): ~ **contact** unmittelbare Berührung; ~ **vicinity** nächste Umgebung; **2.** *Zeit*: unverzüglich, soˈfortig, ˈumgehend: ~ **answer**, ~ **steps** Sofortmaßnahmen; ~ **objective** Nahziel *n*; ~ **future** nächste Zukunft; **3.** augenblicklich, derzeitig: ~ **plans**; **4.** diˈrekt, unmittelbar; **5.** nächst (*Verwandtschaft*): **my ~ family** m-e nächsten Angehörigen; **imˈme·di·ate·ly** [-jətlɪ] **I** *adv.* **1.** unmittelbar, diˈrekt; **2.** soˈfort, ˈumgehend, unverzüglich, gleich, unmittelbar; **II** *cj.* **3.** *bsd. Brit.* soˈbald (als).

im·me·mo·ri·al [ˌɪmɪˈmɔːrɪəl] *adj.* □ un(vor)denklich, uralt: **from time ~** seit un(vor)denklichen Zeiten.

im·mense [ɪˈmens] *adj.* □ **1.** unermeßlich, ungeheuer, riesig, imˈmens; **2.** F gewaltig, eˈnorm, ‚riesig': **enjoy o.s. ~ly**; **imˈmen·si·ty** [-sətɪ] *s.* Unermeßlichkeit *f.*

im·merse [ɪˈmɜːs] *v/t.* **1.** (ein)tauchen (*a.* ⚙), versenken; **2.** *fig.* (**o.s.** sich) vertiefen *od.* versenken (**in** in *acc.*); **3.** *fig.* verwickeln, verstricken (**in** in *acc.*); **imˈmersed** [-st] *adj. fig.* (**in**) versunken, vertieft (in *acc.*); **im·mer·sion** [ɪˈmɜːʃn] *s.* **1.** Ein-, ˈUntertauchen *n*: ~ **heater** a) Tauchsieder *m*, b) Boiler *m*; **2.** *fig.* Versunkenheit *f*, Vertiefsein *n*; **3.** *eccl.* Immersiˈonstaufe *f*; **4.** *ast.* Immersiˈon *f.*

im·mi·grant [ˈɪmɪgrənt] **I** *s.* Einwanderer *m*, Einwanderin *f*, Immiˈgrant(in); **II** *adj.* a) einwandernd, b) ausländisch, Fremd…: ~ **workers**; **ˈim·mi·grate** [-greɪt] **I** *v/i.* einwandern, immiˈgrieren (**into**, **to** in *acc.*, nach); **II** *v/t.* ansiedeln (**into** in *dat.*); **im·mi·gra·tion** [ˌɪmɪˈgreɪʃn] *s.* Einwanderung *f*, Immigratiˈon *f*: ~ **officer** Beamte(r) *m* der Einwanderungsbehörde.

im·mi·nence [ˈɪmɪnəns] *s.* **1.** nahes Bevorstehen; **2.** drohende Gefahr, Drohen *n*; **ˈim·mi·nent** [-nt] *adj.* □ nahe bevorstehend, *a.* drohend.

im·mis·ci·ble [ɪˈmɪsəbl] *adj.* □ unvermischbar.

im·mo·bile [ɪˈməʊbaɪl] *adj.* unbeweglich: a) bewegungslos, b) starr, fest; **im·mo·bil·i·ty** [ˌɪməʊˈbɪlətɪ] *s.* Unbeweglichkeit *f*; **im·mo·bi·li·za·tion** [ɪˌməʊbɪlaɪˈzeɪʃn] *s.* **1.** Unbeweglichmachen *n*; ⚕ Ruhigstellung *f*, Immobilisierung *f*; **2.** ✝ a) Einziehung *f* (*von Münzen*), b) Festlegung *f* (*von Kapital*); **imˈmo·bi·lize** [-bɪlaɪz] *v/t.* **1.** unbeweglich machen; ⚕ ruhigstellen; ⚔ außer Gefecht setzen: **~d** bewegungsunfähig (*a. Auto etc.*); **2.** ✝ a) *Münzen* aus dem Verkehr ziehen, b) *Kapital* festlegen.

im·mod·er·ate [ɪˈmɒdərət] *adj.* □ unmäßig, maßlos, überˈtrieben, -ˈzogen.

im·mod·est [ɪˈmɒdɪst] *adj.* □ **1.** unbescheiden, anmaßend; **2.** schamlos, unanständig; **imˈmod·es·ty** [-tɪ] *s.* **1.** Unbescheidenheit *f*, Frechheit *f*; **2.** Unanständigkeit *f.*

im·mo·late [ˈɪməʊleɪt] *v/t.* **1.** opfern, zum Opfer bringen (*a. fig.*); **2.** schlachten (*a. fig.*); **im·mo·la·tion** [ˌɪməʊˈleɪʃn] *s. a. fig* Opferung *f*, Opfer *n.*

im·mor·al [ɪˈmɒrəl] *adj.* □ **1.** ˈunmoˌralisch, unsittlich; **2.** ⚖ sittenwidrig, unsittlich; **im·mo·ral·i·ty** [ˌɪməˈrælətɪ] *s.* ˈUnmoˌral *f*, Sittenlosigkeit *f*, Unsittlichkeit *f* (*a. Handlung*).

im·mor·tal [ɪˈmɔːtl] **I** *adj.* □ **1.** unsterblich (*a. fig.*); **2.** ewig, unvergänglich; **II** *s.* **3.** Unsterbliche(r *m*) *f* (*a. fig.*); **im·mor·tal·i·ty** [ˌɪmɔːˈtælətɪ] *s.* **1.** Unsterblichkeit *f* (*a. fig.*); **2.** Unvergänglichkeit *f*; **imˈmor·tal·ize** [-təlaɪz] *v/t.* unsterblich machen, verewigen.

im·mor·telle [ˌɪmɔːˈtel] *s.* ♀ Immorˈtelle *f*, Strohblume *f.*

im·mov·a·bil·i·ty [ɪˌmuːvəˈbɪlətɪ] *s.* **1.** Unbeweglichkeit *f*; **2.** *fig.* Unerschütterlichkeit *f*; **im·mov·a·ble** [ɪˈmuːvəbl] **I** *adj.* □ **1.** unbeweglich: a) ortsfest: ~ **property** → b) unbewegt, bewegungslos; **2.** *zeitlich* unveränderlich: ~ **feast** unbeweglicher Feiertag; **3.** *fig.* fest, unerschütterlich, unnachgiebig; **II** *s.* **4.** *pl.* ⚖ unbewegliches Eigentum, Immoˈbilien *pl.*, Liegenschaften *pl.*

im·mune [ɪˈmjuːn] **I** *adj.* **1.** ⚕ *u. fig.* (**from**, **against**, **to**) imˈmun (gegen), unempfänglich (für); **2.** (**from**, **against**, **to**) geschützt, gefeit (gegen), frei (von); **II** *s.* **3.** imˈmune Perˈson; **imˈmu·ni·ty** [-nətɪ] *s.* **1.** *allg.* Immuniˈtät *f*: a) ⚕ *u. fig.* Unempfänglichkeit *f*, b) ⚖ Freiheit *f*, Befreiung *f* (**from** von *Strafe*, *Steuer*); **2.** ⚖ Priviˈleg *n*, Sonderrecht *n*; **3.** Freisein *n* (**from** von); **im·mu·ni·za·tion** [ˌɪmjuːnaɪˈzeɪʃn] *s.* ⚕ Immunisierung *f*; **im·mu·nize** [ˈɪmjuːnaɪz] *v/t.* immunisieren; imˈmun machen (**against** gegen), schützen (vor *dat.*); **im·mu·no·gen** [ɪˈmjuːnəʊdʒen] *s.* ⚕ Antiˈgen *n*; **im·mu·nol·o·gy** [ˌɪmjuːˈnɒlədʒɪ] *s.* ⚕ Immuniˈtätsforschung *f*, -lehre *f.*

im·mure [ɪˈmjʊə] *v/t.* **1.** einsperren, -schließen, -kerkern: ~ **o.s.** sich abschließen; **2.** einmauern.

im·mu·ta·bil·i·ty [ɪˌmjuːtəˈbɪlətɪ] *s. a. biol.* Unveränderlichkeit *f*; **im·mu·ta·ble** [ɪˈmjuːtəbl] *adj.* □ unveränderlich, unwandelbar.

imp [ɪmp] *s.* **1.** Teufelchen *n*, Kobold *m*; **2.** *humor.* Schlingel *m*, Racker *m.*

im·pact I *s.* [ˈɪmpækt] **1.** An-, Zs.-prall *m*, Auftreffen *n*; **2.** *bsd.* ⚔ Auf-, Einschlag *m*: ~ **fuse** Aufschlagzünder *m*; **3.** ⚙, *phys.* a) Stoß *m*, Schlag *m*, b) Wucht *f*: ~ **extrusion** Schlagstrangpressen *n*; ~ **strength** ⚙ (Kerb)Schlagfestigkeit *f*; **4.** *fig.* a) (heftige) (Ein)Wirkung, Auswirkungen *pl.*, (starker) Einfluß (**on** auf *acc.*), b) (starker) Eindruck (**on** auf *acc.*), c) Wucht *f*, Gewalt *f*, d) (**on**) Belastung *f* (*gen.*), Druck *m* (auf *acc.*): **make an ~** (**on**) ‚einschlagen' *od.* e-n starken Eindruck hinterlassen (bei), sich mächtig auswirken (auf *acc.*); **II** *v/t.* [ɪmˈpækt] **5.** zs.-pressen; *a.* ⚕ einkeilen, -klemmen.

im·pair [ɪmˈpeə] *v/t.* **1.** verschlechtern; **2.** beeinträchtigen: a) nachteilig beeinflussen, schwächen, b) (ver)mindern, schmälern; **imˈpair·ment** [-mənt] *s.* Verschlechterung *f*; Beeinträchtigung *f*, Verminderung *f*, Schädigung *f*, Schmälerung *f.*

im·pale [ɪmˈpeɪl] *v/t.* **1.** *hist.* pfählen; **2.** aufspießen, durchˈbohren; **3.** *her. zwei Wappen* durch e-n senkrechten Pfahl verbinden.

im·pal·pa·ble [ɪmˈpælpəbl] *adj.* □ **1.** unfühlbar; **2.** äußerst fein; **3.** kaum (er)faßbar, nicht greifbar.

im·pan·el [ɪmˈpænl] → **empanel**.

im·par·i·syl·lab·ic [ˈɪmˌpærɪsɪˈlæbɪk] *adj. u. s. ling.* ungleichsilbig(es Wort).

im·par·i·ty [ɪmˈpærətɪ] *s.* Ungleichheit *f.*

im·part [ɪmˈpɑːt] *v/t.* **1.** (**to** *dat.*) geben: a) gewähren, zukommen lassen, b) *e-e Eigenschaft etc.* verleihen; **2.** mitteilen: a) kundtun (**to** *dat.*): ~ **news**, b) vermitteln (**to** *dat.*): ~ **knowledge**, c) *a. phys.* übertragen (**to** auf *acc.*): **~ a motion**.

im·par·tial [ɪmˈpɑːʃl] *adj.* □ ˈunparˌteiisch, unvoreingenommen, unbefangen; **im·par·ti·al·i·ty** [ˈɪmˌpɑːʃɪˈælətɪ] *s.* ˈUnparˌteilichkeit *f*, Unvoreingenommenheit *f.*

im·pass·a·ble [ɪmˈpɑːsəbl] *adj.* □ unpassierbar.

im·passe [æmˈpɑːs] (*Fr.*) *s.* Sackgasse *f*, *fig. a.* ausweglose Situatiˈon: **reach an ~** *fig.* in e-e Sackgasse geraten, e-n toten Punkt erreichen; **break the ~** aus der Sackgasse herauskommen.

im·pas·si·ble [ɪmˈpæsɪbl] *adj.* □ (**to**) gefühllos (gegen), unempfindlich (für).

im·pas·sioned [ɪmˈpæʃnd] *adj.* leidenschaftlich.

im·pas·sive [ɪmˈpæsɪv] *adj.* □ **1.** teilnahms-, leidenschaftslos, ungerührt; **2.** gelassen; **3.** unbewegt: ~ **face**.

im·paste [ɪmˈpeɪst] *v/t.* **1.** zu e-m Teig kneten; **2.** *paint. Farben* dick auftragen, paˈstos malen; **im·pas·to** [ɪmˈpæstəʊ] *s. paint.* Imˈpasto *n.*

im·pa·tience [ɪmˈpeɪʃns] *s.* **1.** Ungeduld *f*; **2.** (**of**) Unduldsamkeit *f*, Abneigung *f* (gegen[ˈüber]), Unwille *m* (über *acc.*); **imˈpa·tient** [-nt] *adj.* □ **1.** ungeduldig; **2.** (**of**) unduldsam (gegen), ungehalten (über *acc.*), unzufrieden (mit): **be ~ of** nicht (v)ertragen können (*acc.*), nichts übrig haben für; **3.** begierig (**for** nach, **to do** zu tun): **be ~ for** *et.* nicht erwarten können; **be ~ to do it** darauf brennen, es zu tun.

im·peach [ɪmˈpiːtʃ] *v/t.* **1.** *j-n* anklagen, beschuldigen (**of**, **with** *gen.*); **2.** ⚖ *Beamten etc.* (wegen e-s Amtsvergehens) anklagen; **3.** anzweifeln, anfechten, in Frage stellen: ~ **a witness** die Glaubwürdigkeit e-s Zeugen anzweifeln; **4.** angreifen, herˈabsetzen, tadeln, bemängeln; **imˈpeach·a·ble** [-tʃəbl] *adj.* anklag-, anfecht-, bestreitbar; **imˈpeach·ment** [-mənt] *s.* **1.** Anklage *f*, Beschuldigung *f*; **2.** (öffentliche) Anklage *e-s Ministers etc. wegen Amtsmißbrauchs, Hochverrats etc.*; **3.** Anfechtung *f*, Bestreitung *f* der Glaubwürdigkeit *od.* Gültigkeit; **4.** Inˈfragestellung *f*; **5.** Vorwurf *m*, Tadel *m.*

im·pec·ca·bil·i·ty [ɪmˌpekəˈbɪlətɪ] *s.* **1.** Sündlosigkeit *f*; **2.** Fehler-, Tadellosigkeit *f*; **im·pec·ca·ble** [ɪmˈpekəbl] *adj.* □ **1.** sünd(en)los, rein; **2.** tadellos, untadelig, einwandfrei.

im·pe·cu·ni·os·i·ty [ˌɪmpɪˌkjuːnɪˈɒsətɪ] *s.* Mittellosigkeit *f*, Armut *f*; **im·pe·cu·ni·ous** [ˌɪmpɪˈkjuːnjəs] *adj.* mittellos, arm.

im·ped·ance [ɪmˈpiːdəns] *s.* ⚡ Impeˈdanz *f*, ˈScheinˌwiderstand *m*.

im·pede [ɪmˈpiːd] *v/t.* **1.** *j-n* (be)hindern; **2.** *et.* erschweren, verhindern; **im·ped·i·ment** [ɪmˈpedɪmənt] *s.* **1.** Be-, Verhinderung *f*; **2.** Hindernis *n* (**to** für), ⚕ Behinderung *f*: **~ in one's speech** Sprachfehler *m*; **3.** ⚖ (*bsd.* Ehe)Hindernis *n*, Hinderungsgrund *m*; **im·ped·i·men·ta** [ɪmˌpedɪˈmentə] *s. pl.* **1.** ⚔ Gepäck *n*, Troß *m*; **2.** *fig.* Last *f*, (hinderliches) Gepäck, *j-s* ‚Siebensachen' *pl.*

im·pel [ɪmˈpel] *v/t.* **1.** (an-, vorwärts-) treiben, drängen; **2.** zwingen, nötigen: ***I felt ~led*** ich sah mich gezwungen *od.* veranlaßt, ich fühlte mich genötigt; **imˈpel·lent** [-lənt] **I** *adj.* (an)treibend, Trieb...; **II** *s.* Triebkraft *f*, Antrieb *m*; **imˈpel·ler** [-lə] *s.* ⚙ a) Flügel-, Laufrad *n*, b) Kreisel *m* (*e-r Pumpe*), c) ✈ Laderlaufrad *n*.

im·pend [ɪmˈpend] *v/i.* **1.** hängen, schweben (**over** über *dat.*); **2.** *fig.* a) unmittelbar bevorstehen, b) (**over**) drohend schweben (über *dat.*), drohen (*dat.*); **imˈpend·ing** [-dɪŋ] *adj.* nahe bevorstehend, drohend.

im·pen·e·tra·bil·i·ty [ɪmˌpenɪtrəˈbɪlətɪ] *s.* **1.** ˈUndurchˌdringlichkeit *f*; **2.** *fig.* Unerforschlichkeit *f*, Unergründlichkeit *f*; **im·pen·e·tra·ble** [ɪmˈpenɪtrəbl] *adj.* ☐ **1.** ˈundurchˌdringlich (**by** für); **2.** *fig.* unergründlich, unerforschlich; **3.** *fig.* (**to, by**) unempfänglich (für), unzugänglich (*dat.*).

im·pen·i·tence [ɪmˈpenɪtəns], **imˈpen·i·ten·cy** [-sɪ] *s.* Unbußfertigkeit *f*, Verstocktheit *f*; **imˈpen·i·tent** [-nt] *adj.* ☐ unbußfertig, verstockt, reuelos.

im·per·a·ti·val [ɪmˌperəˈtaɪvl] → ***imperative*** 3; **im·per·a·tive** [ɪmˈperətɪv] **I** *adj.* ☐ **1.** befehlend, gebieterisch, herrisch; **2.** ˈunumˌgänglich, zwingend, dringend (nötig), unbedingt erforderlich; **3.** *ling.* imperaˈtivisch, Imperativ..., Befehls...: **~ mood** → 5; **II** *s.* **4.** Befehl *m*, Gebot *n*; **5.** *ling.* Imperativ *m*, Befehlsform *f*.

im·per·cep·ti·bil·i·ty [ˈɪmpəˌseptəˈbɪlətɪ] *s.* Unwahrnehmbarkeit *f*; Unmerklichkeit *f*; **im·per·cep·ti·ble** [ˌɪmpəˈseptəbl] *adj.* ☐ **1.** nicht wahrnehmbar, unbemerkbar, unsichtbar, unhörbar; **2.** unmerklich; **3.** verschwindend klein.

im·per·fect [ɪmˈpɜːfɪkt] **I** *adj.* ☐ **1.** ˈunvollˌständig, ˈunvollˌendet; **2.** ˈunvollˌkommen (*a.* ♀, ♪): **~ rhyme** unreiner Reim; **3.** mangel-, fehlerhaft; **4.** *ling.* **~ tense** → 5; **II** *s.* **5.** *ling.* Imperfekt *n*, ˈunvollˌendete Vergangenheit; **im·per·fec·tion** [ˌɪmpəˈfekʃn] *s.* **1.** ˈUnvollˌkommenheit *f*, Mangelhaftigkeit *f*; **2.** Mangel *m*, Fehler *m*.

im·per·fo·rate [ɪmˈpɜːfərət] *adj.* **1.** *bsd. anat.* ohne Öffnung; **2.** nicht perforiert, ungezähnt (*Briefmarke*).

im·pe·ri·al [ɪmˈpɪərɪəl] **I** *adj.* ☐ **1.** kaiserlich, Kaiser...; **2.** Reichs...; **3.** das brit. Weltreich betreffend, Empire...: ♀ **Conference** Empire-Konferenz *f*; **4.** *Brit.* gesetzlich (*Maße u. Gewichte*): **~ gallon** (= *4,55 Liter*); **5.** großartig, herrlich; **II** *s.* **6.** Kaiserliche(r) *m* (*Soldat, Anhänger*); **7.** Knebelbart *m*; **8.** Imperiˈal(paˌpier) *n* (*Format: brit. 22×30 in., amer. 23×31 in.*); **imˈpe·ri·al·ism** [-lɪzəm] *s. pol.* Imperiaˈlismus *m*; **imˈpe·ri·al·ist** [-lɪst] **I** *s.* **1.** *pol.* Imperiaˈlist *m*; **2.** Kaiserliche(r) *m*; **II** *adj.* **3.** imperiaˈlistisch; **4.** kaiserlich, kaisertreu; **im·pe·ri·al·is·tic** [ɪmˌpɪərɪəˈlɪstɪk] *adj.* (☐ **~ally**) → ***imperialist*** 3, 4.

im·per·il [ɪmˈperɪl] *v/t.* gefährden.

im·pe·ri·ous [ɪmˈpɪərɪəs] *adj.* ☐ **1.** herrisch, anmaßend, gebieterisch; **2.** dringend, zwingend; **imˈpe·ri·ous·ness** [-nɪs] *s.* **1.** Herrschsucht *f*, Anmaßung *f*, herrisches Wesen; **2.** Dringlichkeit *f*.

im·per·ish·a·ble [ɪmˈperɪʃəbl] *adj.* ☐ unvergänglich, ewig.

im·per·ma·nence [ɪmˈpɜːmənəns], **imˈper·ma·nen·cy** [-sɪ] *s.* Unbeständigkeit *f*, Vergänglichkeit *f*; **imˈper·ma·nent** [-nt] *adj.* unbeständig, vorˈübergehend, nicht von Dauer.

im·per·me·a·bil·i·ty [ɪmˌpɜːmjəˈbɪlətɪ] *s.* ˈUnˌdurchlässigkeit *f*; **im·per·me·a·ble** [ɪmˈpɜːmjəbl] *adj.* ☐ ˈunˌdurchlässig (**to** für): **~ (to water)** wasserdicht.

im·per·mis·si·ble [ˌɪmpəˈmɪsəbl] *adj.* unzulässig, unerlaubt.

im·per·son·al [ɪmˈpɜːsnl] *adj. a. ling.* ˈunperˌsönlich: **~ account** ✝ Sachkonto *n*; **im·per·son·al·i·ty** [ɪmˌpɜːsəˈnælətɪ] *s.* ˈUnperˌsönlichkeit *f*.

im·per·son·ate [ɪmˈpɜːsəneɪt] *v/t.* **1.** personifizieren, verkörpern; **2.** imitieren, nachahmen; **3.** sich ausgeben als *od.* für; **im·per·son·a·tion** [ɪmˌpɜːsəˈneɪʃn] *s.* **1.** Personifikatiˈon *f*, Verkörperung *f*; **2.** Nachahmung *f*, Imitatiˈon *f*; **3.** (betrügerisches *od.* scherzhaftes) Auftreten (**of** als); **imˈper·son·a·tor** [-tə] *s.* **1.** *thea.* a) Imiˈtator *m*, b) Darsteller(in); **2.** Betrüger(in), Hochstapler(in).

im·per·ti·nence [ɪmˈpɜːtɪnəns] *s.* Unverschämtheit *f*, Frechheit *f*; **imˈper·ti·nent** [-nt] *adj.* ☐ **1.** unverschämt, frech; **2.** ⚖ nicht zur Sache gehörig, unerheblich; **3.** nebensächlich; **4.** unangebracht.

im·per·turb·a·bil·i·ty [ˈɪmpəˌtɜːbəˈbɪlətɪ] *s.* Unerschütterlichkeit *f*, Gelassenheit *f*, Gleichmut *m*; **im·per·turb·a·ble** [ˌɪmpəˈtɜːbəbl] *adj.* ☐ unerschütterlich, gelassen.

im·per·vi·ous [ɪmˈpɜːvjəs] *adj.* ☐ **1.** ˈundurchˌdringlich (**to** für), ˈunˌdurchlässig: **~ to rain** regendicht; **2.** *fig.* (**to**) unzugänglich (für *od. dat.*), unempfindlich (gegen); taub (gegen); **imˈper·vi·ous·ness** [-nɪs] *s.* **1.** ˈUndurchˌdringlichkeit *f*, -lässigkeit *f*; **2.** *fig.* Unzugänglichkeit *f*, Unempfindlichkeit *f*.

im·pe·tig·i·nous [ˌɪmpɪˈtɪdʒɪnəs] *adj.* ⚕ pustelartig; **ˌim·peˈti·go** [-ˈtaɪgəʊ] *s.* ⚕ Impeˈtigo *m*.

im·pet·u·os·i·ty [ɪmˌpetjʊˈɒsətɪ] *s.* **1.** Heftigkeit *f*, Ungestüm *n*; **2.** impulˈsive Handlung; **im·pet·u·ous** [ɪmˈpetjʊəs] *adj.* ☐ heftig, ungestüm; hitzig, überˈeilt, impulˈsiv; **im·pet·u·ous·ness** [ɪmˈpetjʊəsnɪs] → ***impetuosity***.

im·pe·tus [ˈɪmpɪtəs] *s.* **1.** *phys.* Stoß-, Triebkraft *f*, Schwung *m*; **2.** *fig.* Antrieb *m*, Anstoß *m*, Schwung *m*: ***give a fresh ~ to*** Auftrieb *od.* neuen Schwung verleihen (*dat.*).

im·pi·e·ty [ɪmˈpaɪətɪ] *s.* **1.** Gottlosigkeit *f*; **2.** Pieˈtätlosigkeit *f*.

im·pinge [ɪmˈpɪndʒ] *v/i.* **1.** (**on, upon**) stoßen (an *acc.*, gegen), zs.-stoßen (mit), auftreffen (auf *acc.*); **2.** fallen, einwirken (**on** auf *acc.*): **~ on the eye**; **~ on the ear** ans Ohr dringen; **3.** (**on**) sich auswirken (auf *acc.*), beeinflussen (*acc.*); **4.** (**on**) (ˈwiderrechtlich) eingreifen (in *acc.*), verstoßen (gegen *Rechte etc.*).

im·pi·ous [ˈɪmpɪəs] *adj.* ☐ **1.** gottlos, ruchlos; **2.** pieˈtätlos; **3.** reˈspektlos.

imp·ish [ˈɪmpɪʃ] *adj.* ☐ schelmisch, spitzbübisch, verschmitzt.

im·pla·ca·bil·i·ty [ɪmˌplækəˈbɪlətɪ] *s.* Unversöhnlichkeit *f*, Unerbittlichkeit *f*; **im·pla·ca·ble** [ɪmˈplækəbl] *adj.* ☐ unversöhnlich, unerbittlich.

im·plant [ɪmˈplɑːnt] *v/t. fig.* einimpfen, *a.* ⚕ einpflanzen (**in** *dat.*); **im·plan·ta·tion** [ˌɪmplɑːnˈteɪʃn] *s.* **1.** *fig.* Einimpfung *f*; **2.** *mst fig. od.* ⚕ Einpflanzung *f*.

im·plau·si·ble [ɪmˈplɔːzəbl] *adj.* nicht plauˈsibel, unwahrscheinlich, unglaubwürdig, -haft, wenig überˈzeugend.

im·ple·ment **I** *s.* [ˈɪmplɪmənt] **1.** Werkzeug *n* (*a. fig.*), Gerät *n*; **2.** ⚖ *Scot.* Erfüllung *f* (*e-s Vertrages*); **II** *v/t.* [-ment] **3.** aus-, ˈdurchführen; **4.** in Kraft setzen; **5.** ergänzen; **6.** ⚖ *Scot. Vertrag* erfüllen; **im·ple·men·tal** [ˌɪmplɪˈmentl], **im·ple·men·ta·ry** [ˌɪmplɪˈmentərɪ] *adj.* Ausführungs...: **~ orders** Ausführungsbestimmungen; **im·ple·men·ta·tion** [ˌɪmplɪmenˈteɪʃn] *s.* Erfüllung *f*, Aus-, ˈDurchführung *f*.

im·pli·cate [ˈɪmplɪkeɪt] *v/t.* **1.** *fig.* verwickeln, hinˈeinziehen (**in** in *acc.*), in Zs.-hang *od.* Verbindung bringen (**with** mit): **~d in** verwickelt in (*acc.*), betroffen von; **2.** *fig.* a) → ***imply*** 1, b) zur Folge haben; **im·pli·ca·tion** [ˌɪmplɪˈkeɪʃn] *s.* **1.** Verwicklung *f*, Verflechtung *f*, (enge) Verbindung, Zs.-hang *m*; **2.** (eigentliche) Bedeutung; Andeutung *f*; **3.** Konseˈquenz *f*, Folge *f*, Folgerung *f*, Auswirkung *f*: **by ~** a) als (natürliche) Folgerung *od.* Folge, b) implizite, durch sinngemäße Auslegung, ohne weiteres.

im·plic·it [ɪmˈplɪsɪt] *adj.* ☐ **1.** (mit *od.* stillschweigend) inbegriffen, stillschweigend, unausgesprochen; **2.** absoˈlut, vorbehalt-, bedingungslos: **~ faith (obedience)** blinder Glaube (Gehorsam); **imˈplic·it·ly** [-lɪ] *adv.* **1.** imˈplizite, stillschweigend, ohne weiteres; **2.** unbedingt; **imˈplic·it·ness** [-nɪs] *s.* **1.** Mitˈinbegriffensein *n*; Selbstverständlichkeit *f*; **2.** Unbedingtheit *f*.

im·plied [ɪmˈplaɪd] *adj.* (stillschweigend *od.* mit) inbegriffen, einbezogen, sinngemäß (darin) enthalten, impliziert: **~ condition**.

im·plode [ɪmˈpləʊd] *v/i. phys.* implodieren.

im·plore [ɪmˈplɔː] *v/t.* **1.** *j-n* anflehen, beschwören; **2.** *et.* erflehen, erbitten; **imˈplor·ing** [-ɔːrɪŋ] *adj.* ☐ flehentlich, inständig.

im·plo·sion [ɪmˈpləʊʒn] *s. phys.* Imploˈsiˈon *f*.

im·ply [ɪmˈplaɪ] *v/t.* **1.** einbeziehen, in sich schließen, (*stillschweigend*) beinhalten; **2.** mit sich bringen, darˈauf hinˈauslaufen: ***that implies*** daraus ergibt sich, das bedeutet; **3.** besagen, bedeuten, schließen lassen auf (*acc.*); **4.** andeuten, 'durchblicken lassen, implizieren.

im·po·lite [ɪmpəˈlaɪt] *adj.* □ unhöflich, grob.

im·pol·i·tic [ɪmˈpɒlətɪk] *adj.* □ 'undiplo-ˌmatisch, unklug.

im·pon·der·a·ble [ɪmˈpɒndərəbl] **I** *adj.* unwägbar (*a. phys.*), unberechenbar; **II** *s. pl.* Imponderaˈbilien *pl.*, Unwägbarkeiten *pl.*

im·port I *v/t.* [ɪmˈpɔːt] **1.** † importieren, einführen: ***~ing country*** Einfuhrland *n*; **2.** *fig.* einführen, hinˈeinbringen; **3.** bedeuten, besagen; **II** *s.* [ˈɪmpɔːt] **4.** † Einfuhr *f*, Imˈport *m*; *pl.* 'Einfuhrwaren *pl.*, -arˌtikel *pl.*; ***~ bounty*** Einfuhrprämie *f*; ***~ duty*** Einfuhrzoll *m*; ***~ licence*** (*Am.* ***license***), ***~ permit*** Einfuhrgenehmigung *f*; ***~ quota*** Einfuhrkontingent *n*; ***~ tariff*** Einfuhrzoll *m*; **5.** Bedeutung *f*, Sinn *m*; **6.** Wichtigkeit *f*, Bedeutung *f*, Tragweite *f*; **imˈport·a·ble** [-təbl] *adj.* † einführbar, importierbar.

im·por·tance [ɪmˈpɔːtns] *s.* **1.** Wichtigkeit *f*, Bedeutung *f*: ***attach ~ to*** Bedeutung beimessen (*dat.*); ***conscious*** (*od.* ***full***) ***of one's own ~*** → ***important*** 3; ***it is of no ~*** es ist unwichtig, es hat keine Bedeutung; **2.** Einfluß *m*, Ansehen *n*, Gewicht *n*: ***a person of ~*** e-e gewichtige Persönlichkeit; **imˈpor·tant** [-nt] *adj.* □ **1.** wichtig, wesentlich, bedeutend (***to*** für); **2.** herˈvorragend, bedeutend, angesehen, einflußreich; **3.** wichtigtuerisch, eingebildet, von s-r eigenen Wichtigkeit erfüllt.

im·por·ta·tion [ˌɪmpɔːˈteɪʃn] *s.* † **1.** Imˈport *m*, Einfuhr *f*; **2.** Einfuhrware(n *pl.*) *f*; **im·port·er** [ɪmˈpɔːtə] *s.* † Imporˈteur *m*.

im·por·tu·nate [ɪmˈpɔːtjʊnət] *adj.* □ lästig, zu-, aufdringlich; **im·por·tune** [ɪmpɔːˈtjuːn] *v/t.* dauernd (mit Bitten) belästigen, behelligen; **im·por·tu·ni·ty** [ˌɪmpɔːˈtjuːnətɪ] *s.* Aufdringlichkeit *f*, Hartnäckigkeit *f*.

im·pose [ɪmˈpəʊz] **I** *v/t.* **1.** *Pflicht, Steuer etc.* auferlegen, aufbürden (***on***, ***upon*** *dat.*): ***~ a tax on s.th.*** et. besteuern, et. mit e-r Steuer belegen; ***~ a penalty on s.o.*** e-e Strafe verhängen gegen j-n, j-n mit e-r Strafe belegen; ***~ law and order*** Recht u. Ordnung schaffen; **2.** ***~ s.th. on s.o.*** a) j-m et. aufdrängen, b) j-m et. ‚andrehen'; ***~ o.s. on s.o.*** → 7; **3.** *typ. Kolumnen* ausschießen; **4.** *eccl. die Hände* (segnend) auflegen; **II** *v/i.* **5.** (***upon***) beeindrucken (*acc.*), imponieren (*dat.*); **6.** ausnutzen, mißˈbrauchen (***on*** *acc.*): ***~ on s.o.'s kindness***; **7.** ***~ on s.o.*** sich j-m aufdrängen, j-m zur Last fallen; **8.** betrügen, hinterˈgehen (***on s.o.*** j-n); **imˈpos·ing** [-zɪŋ] *adj.* □ eindrucksvoll, imponierend, impoˈsant; **im·po·si·tion** [ˌɪmpəˈzɪʃn] *s.* **1.** Auferlegung *f*, Aufbürdung *f* (*von Steuern, Pflichten etc.*), Verhängung *f* (*e-r Strafe*): ***~ of taxes*** Besteuerung *f*; **2.** Last *f*, Belastung *f*; Auflage *f*, Pflicht *f*; **3.** Abgabe *f*, Steuer *f*; **4.** *ped. Brit.* Strafarbeit *f*; **5.** (schamlose) Ausnutzung (***on*** *gen.*), Zumutung *f*; **6.** Überˈvorteilung *f*, Schwindel *m*; **7.** *eccl.* (*Hand*)Auflegen *n*; **8.** *typ.* a) Ausschießen *n*, b) Forˈmatmachen *n*.

im·pos·si·bil·i·ty [ɪmˌpɒsəˈbɪlətɪ] *s.* Unmöglichkeit *f*; **im·pos·si·ble** [ɪmˈpɒsəbl] *adj.* □ **1.** *allg.* unmöglich: a) unausführbar, b) ausgeschlossen, c) unglaublich: ***it is ~ for me to do that*** ich kann das unmöglich tun; **2.** F ‚unmöglich': ***you are ~!***; **im·pos·si·bly** [ɪmˈpɒsəblɪ] *adv.* **1.** unmöglich; **2.** unglaublich: ***~ young***.

im·post [ˈɪmpəʊst] **I** *s.* **1.** † Auflage *f*, Abgabe *f*, Steuer *f*, *bsd.* Einfuhrzoll *m*; **2.** *sl. Pferderennen*: Handicap-Ausgleichsgewicht *n*; **II** *v/t.* **3.** *Am. Importwaren* zwecks Zollfestsetzung klassifizieren.

im·pos·tor [ɪmˈpɒstə] *s.* Betrüger(in), Schwindler(in), Hochstapler(in); **imˈpos·ture** [-tʃə] *s.* Betrug *m*, Schwindel *m*, Hochstapeˈlei *f*.

im·po·tence [ˈɪmpətəns], **ˈim·po·ten·cy** [-sɪ] *s.* **1.** a) Unvermögen *n*, Unfähigkeit *f*, b) Hilf-, Machtlosigkeit *f*, Ohnmacht *f*; **2.** Schwäche *f*, Kraftlosigkeit *f*; **3.** ⚕ Impotenz *f*; **ˈim·po·tent** [-nt] *adj.* □ **1.** a) unfähig, b) macht-, hilflos, ohnmächtig; **2.** schwach, kraftlos; **3.** ⚕ impotent.

im·pound [ɪmˈpaʊnd] *v/t.* **1.** *bsd. Vieh* einpferchen, einsperren; **2.** *Wasser* sammeln, stauen; **3.** ⚖ a) beschlagnahmen, b) sicherstellen, in (gerichtliche *od.* behördliche) Verwahrung nehmen.

im·pov·er·ish [ɪmˈpɒvərɪʃ] *v/t.* **1.** arm *od.* ärmer machen: ***be ~ed*** verarmen, verarmt sein; **2.** *Land etc.* auspowern, *Boden etc.* auslaugen; **3.** *fig.* a) ärmer machen, *kulturell etc.* verarmen lassen, b) *e-r Sache* den Reiz nehmen; **imˈpov·er·ish·ment** [-mənt] *s. a. fig.* Verarmung *f*; Auslaugung *f*.

im·prac·ti·ca·bil·i·ty [ɪmˌpræktɪkəˈbɪlətɪ] *s.* **1.** 'Undurchˌführbarkeit *f*, Unmöglichkeit *f*; **2.** Unbrauchbarkeit *f*; **3.** Unpassierbarkeit *f* (*e-r Straße etc.*); **im·prac·ti·ca·ble** [ɪmˈpræktɪkəbl] *adj.* □ **1.** 'undurchˌführbar, unmöglich; **2.** unbrauchbar; **3.** unpassierbar, unbefahrbar (*Straße*); **4.** unlenksam, störrisch (*Person*).

im·prac·ti·cal [ɪmˈpræktɪkl] *adj.* **1.** unpraktisch; **2.** (rein) theoˈretisch, sinnlos; **3.** → ***impracticable***.

im·pre·cate [ˈɪmprɪkeɪt] *v/t. Schlimmes* herˈabwünschen (***on***, ***upon*** auf *acc.*): ***~ curses on s.o.*** j-n verfluchen; **im·pre·ca·tion** [ˌɪmprɪˈkeɪʃn] *s.* Verwünschung *f*, Fluch *m*; **ˈim·pre·ca·to·ry** [-tərɪ] *adj.* Verwünschungs...

im·preg·na·bil·i·ty [ɪmˌpregnəˈbɪlətɪ] *s.* 'Unüberˌwindlichkeit *f etc.* (→ ***impregnable***); **im·preg·na·ble** [ɪmˈpregnəbl] *adj.* □ **1.** 'unüberˌwindlich, unbezwinglich, uneinnehmbar (*Festung*); **2.** unerschütterlich (***to*** gegenüber); **im·preg·nate I** *v/t.* [ˈɪmpregneɪt] **1.** *biol.* a) schwängern (*a. fig.*), b) befruchten (*a. fig.*); **2.** sättigen, durchˈdringen; ⚙ tränken, imprägnieren; **3.** *fig. et. od. j-n* durchˈdringen, erfüllen; **4.** *paint.* grundieren; **II** *adj.* [ɪmˈpregnɪt] **5.** *biol.* a) geschwängert, schwanger, b) befruchtet; **6.** *fig.* (***with***) voll (von), durchˈdrungen (von); **im·preg·na·tion** [ˌɪmpregˈneɪʃn] *s.* **1.** *biol.* a) Schwängerung *f*, b) Befruchtung *f*; **2.** Imprägnierung *f*, (Durch)ˈTränkung *f*, Sättigung *f*; **3.** *fig.* Befruchtung *f*, Durchˈdringung *f*, Erfüllung *f*.

im·pre·sa·ri·o [ˌɪmprɪˈsɑːrɪəʊ] *pl.* **-os** *s.* **1.** Impreˈsario *m*; **2.** (Theˈater- *etc.*)Diˌrektor *m*.

im·pre·scrip·ti·ble [ˌɪmprɪˈskrɪptəbl] *adj.* ⚖ a) unverjährbar, b) *a. fig.* unveräußerlich: ***~ rights***.

im·press¹ I *v/t.* [ɪmˈpres] **1.** beeindrucken, Eindruck machen auf (*acc.*), imponieren (*dat.*): ***be favo(u)rably ~ed by*** e-n guten Eindruck erhalten *od.* haben von; ***I am not ~ed*** das imponiert mir gar nicht; ***he is not easily ~ed*** er läßt sich nicht so leicht beeindrucken; **2.** *j-n* erfüllen, durchˈdringen (***with*** mit); **3.** einprägen, -schärfen, klarmachen (***on***, ***upon*** *dat.*); **4.** (auf)drücken (***on*** auf *acc.*), eindrücken; **5.** aufprägen, -drucken; **6.** *fig.* verleihen, erteilen (***upon*** *dat.*); **II** *v/i.* **7.** Eindruck machen, imponieren; **III** *s.* [ˈɪmpres] **8.** Prägung *f*; **9.** Abdruck *m*, Stempel *m*; **10.** *fig.* Gepräge *n*.

im·press² [ɪmˈpres] *v/t.* **1.** requirieren, beschlagnahmen; **2.** *bsd.* ⚓ (zum Dienst) pressen.

im·press·i·ble [ɪmˈpresəbl] → ***impressionable***.

im·pres·sion [ɪmˈpreʃn] *s.* **1.** Eindruck *m*: ***make a*** (***good***) ***~*** (***on s.o.***) (auf j-n) (e-n guten) Eindruck machen; ***give s.o. a wrong ~*** bei j-m e-n falschen Eindruck erwecken; ***leave s.o. with an ~*** bei j-m e-n Eindruck hinterlassen; ***first ~s are often wrong*** der erste Eindruck täuscht oft; **2.** Eindruck *m*, Vermutung *f*, Ahnung *f*: ***I have an ~*** (*od.* ***I am under the ~***) ***that*** ich habe den Eindruck, daß; **3.** Abdruck *m* (*a.* ⚕), Prägung *f*; **4.** Ab-, Aufdruck *m*; **5.** *typ.* a) Abzug *m*, b) (*bsd.* unveränderte) Auflage (*Buch*): ***new ~*** Neudruck *m*, -auflage *f*; **6.** *fig.* Nachahmung *f*: ***do*** (*od.* ***give***) ***an ~ of s.o.*** j-n imitieren; **imˈpres·sion·a·ble** [-ʃnəbl] **1.** für Eindrücke empfänglich; **2.** leicht zu beeindrucken(d), beeinflußbar, empfänglich; **imˈpres·sion·ism** [-ʃnɪzəm] *s.* Impressioˈnismus *m*; **imˈpres·sion·ist** [-ʃnɪst] **I** *s.* Impressioˈnist(in); **II** *adj.* → **im·pres·sion·is·tic** [ɪmˌpreʃəˈnɪstɪk] *adj.* (□ ***~ally***) impressioˈnistisch.

im·pres·sive [ɪmˈpresɪv] *adj.* □ eindrucksvoll, impoˈsant; **imˈpres·sive·ness** [-nɪs] *s. das* Eindrucksvolle *etc.*

im·pri·ma·tur [ˌɪmprɪˈmeɪtə] *s.* **1.** Impriˈmatur *n*, Druckerlaubnis *f*; **2.** *fig.* Zustimmung *f*, Billigung *f*.

im·print I *s.* [ˈɪmprɪnt] **1.** Ab-, Aufdruck *m*; **2.** Aufdruck *m*, Stempel *m*; **3.** *typ.* Imˈpressum *n*, Erscheinungs-, Druckvermerk *m*; **4.** *fig.* Stempel *m*, Gepräge *n*; *psych.* Prägung *f*; **II** *v/t.* [ɪmˈprɪnt] ([***up***]***on***) **5.** *typ.* aufdrucken (auf *acc.*); **6.** prägen (auf *acc.*); **7.** *fig.* einprägen (*dat.*); **8.** *Kuß* (auf)drücken (auf *acc.*).

im·pris·on [ɪmˈprɪzn] *v/t.* **1.** ins Gefängnis werfen, einsperren, inhaftieren; **2.** *fig.* a) einsperren, -schließen, gefangenhalten, b) beschränken; **imˈpris·on·ment** [-mənt] *s.* **1.** Einkerkerung *f*, Haft *f*, Gefangenschaft *f* (*a. fig.*); **2.** (***sentence of***) ***~*** ⚖ Freiheitsstrafe *f*; → ***false*** I.

im·prob·a·bil·i·ty [ɪmˌprɒbəˈbɪlətɪ] *s.* Unwahrscheinlichkeit *f*; **im·prob·a·ble**

[ɪmˈprɒbəbl] *adj.* □ **1.** unwahrscheinlich; **2.** unglaubwürdig.
im·pro·bi·ty [ɪmˈprəʊbətɪ] *s.* Unredlichkeit *f*, Unehrlichkeit *f*.
im·promp·tu [ɪmˈprɒmptjuː] **I** *s.* Impromp'tu *n* (*a.* ♪), Improvisati'on *f*; **II** *adj. u. adv.* improvisiert, aus dem Stegreif, Stegreif…
im·prop·er [ɪmˈprɒpə] *adj.* □ **1.** ungeeignet, unpassend, untauglich (***to*** für); **2.** unschicklich, ungehörig (*Benehmen*); **3.** a) unrichtig, falsch, b) unsachgemäß, c) unvorschriftsmäßig, d) 'mißbräuchlich: **~ *use*** Mißbrauch *m*; **4.** 𝔄 unecht: **~ *fraction***; **~ *integral*** uneigentliches Integral; **im·pro·pri·e·ty** [ˌɪmprəˈpraɪətɪ] *s.* **1.** Ungeeignetheit *f*, Untauglichkeit *f*; **2.** Unschicklichkeit *f*, Ungehörigkeit *f*; **3.** Unrichtigkeit *f*, *a. ling.* falscher Gebrauch.
im·prov·a·ble [ɪmˈpruːvəbl] *adj.* **1.** verbesserungsfähig; **2.** ✓ anbaufähig, kultivierbar; **im·prove** [ɪmˈpruːv] **I** *v/t.* **1.** *allg.*, *a.* ⚙ verbessern; **2.** verfeinern; **3.** verschönern; **4.** *Wert etc.* erhöhen, steigern; **5.** vor'anbringen, ausbauen; **6.** *Kenntnisse* erweitern: **~ *one's mind*** sich weiterbilden; **7.** *Gehalt* aufbessern; **8.** *Am. Land* a) erschließen, im Wert steigern, b) kultivieren, meliorieren; **9.** ausnützen; → ***occasion*** 3; **II** *v/i.* **10.** sich (ver)bessern, besser werden, Fortschritte machen, sich erholen (*gesundheitlich od.* ✝ *Preise*): **~ *in strength*** kräftiger werden; **~ *on acquaintance*** bei näherer Bekanntschaft gewinnen; ***the patient is improving*** dem Patienten geht es besser; **11.** **~ *on*** *od.* ***upon*** a) verbessern, b) über'treffen: ***not to be ~d upon*** nicht zu übertreffen(d); **im'prove·ment** [-mənt] *s.* **1.** (Ver-)Besserung *f*, Ver'vollkommnung *f*, Verschönerung *f*: **~ *in health*** Besserung der Gesundheit; **~ *of one's mind*** (Weiter)Bildung *f*; **~ *of one's knowledge*** Erweiterung *f* des Wissens; **2.** Verfeinerung *f*, Veredelung *f*: **~ *industry*** Veredelungsindustrie *f*; **3.** Erhöhung *f*, Steigerung *f*, ✝ *a.* Erholung *f*, Steigen *n*; **4.** Meliorati'on *f*: a) ✓ Bodenverbesserung *f*, b) Erschließung *f*, c) *Am.* Wertverbesserung *f* (*Grundstück etc.*); **5.** Verbesserung *f* (*a. Patent*), Fortschritt(e *pl.*) *m*, Neuerung *f*, Gewinn *m*: ***an ~ on*** *od.* ***upon*** e-e Verbesserung gegenüber; **im'prov·er** [-və] *s.* **1.** Verbesserer *m*; **2.** ⚙ Verbesserungsmittel *n*; **3.** ✝ Volon'tär *m*.
im·prov·i·dence [ɪmˈprɒvɪdəns] *s.* **1.** Unbedachtsamkeit *f*; **2.** Unvorsichtigkeit *f*, Leichtsinn *m*; **im'prov·i·dent** [-nt] *adj.* □ **1.** unbedacht; **2.** unvorsichtig, leichtsinnig (***of*** mit).
im·prov·ing [ɪmˈpruːvɪŋ] *adj.* □ **1.** (sich) bessernd; **2.** förderlich.
im·pro·vi·sa·tion [ˌɪmprəvaɪˈzeɪʃn] *s.* Improvisati'on *f* (*a.* ♪): a) unvorbereitete Veranstaltung, 'Stegreifrede *f*, -kompositi'on *f etc.*, b) Behelfsmaßnahme *f*, c) behelfsmäßige Vorrichtung; **im·prov·i·sa·tor** [ɪmˈprɒvɪzeɪtə] *s.* Improvi'sator *m*; **im·pro·vise** [ˈɪmprəvaɪz] *v/t. u. v/i. allg.* improvisieren: a) aus dem Stegreif *od.* unvorbereitet tun, b) rasch *od.* behelfsmäßig herstellen, aus dem Boden stampfen; **im·pro·vised** [ˈɪmprəvaɪzd] *adj.* improvisiert: a) unvorbereitet, Stegreif…, b) behelfsmäßig; **im·pro·vis·er** [ˈɪmprəvaɪzə] *s.* Improvi'sator *m*.
im·pru·dence [ɪmˈpruːdəns] *s.* Unklugheit *f*, Unvorsichtigkeit *f*; **im'pru·dent** [-nt] *adj.* □ unklug.
im·pu·dence [ˈɪmpjʊdəns] *s.* Unverschämtheit *f*, Frechheit *f*; **'im·pu·dent** [-nt] *adj.* □ unverschämt.
im·pugn [ɪmˈpjuːn] *v/t.* bestreiten, anfechten, angreifen; **im'pugn·a·ble** [-nəbl] *adj.* bestreit-, anfechtbar; **im'pugn·ment** [-mənt] *s.* Anfechtung *f*, Einwand *m*.
im·pulse [ˈɪmpʌls] *s.* **1.** Antrieb *m*, Stoß *m*, Triebkraft *f*; **2.** *fig.* Im'puls *m*: a) Anstoß *m*, Anreiz *m*, b) Anregung *f*, c) plötzliche Regung *od.* Eingebung: ***act on ~*** spontan *od.* impulsiv handeln; ***on the ~ of the moment*** e-r plötzlichen Regung folgend; **~ *buying*** ✝ Impulskauf *m*; **~ *goods*** ✝ Waren, die impulsiv gekauft werden; **3.** 𝔄, ⚕, ϟ, *phys.* Im'puls *m*: **~ *relais*** ϟ Stromstoßrelais *n*.
im·pul·sion [ɪmˈpʌlʃn] *s.* **1.** Stoß *m*, Antrieb *m*; Triebkraft *f*; **2.** *fig.* Im'puls *m*, Antrieb *m*; **im'pul·sive** [-lsɪv] *adj.* □ **1.** (an)treibend, Trieb…; **2.** *fig.* impul'siv, leidenschaftlich; **im'pul·sive·ness** [-lsɪvnɪs] *s.* impul'sive Art, Leidenschaftlichkeit *f*.
im·pu·ni·ty [ɪmˈpjuːnətɪ] *s.* Straflosigkeit *f*: ***with ~*** straflos, ungestraft.
im·pure [ɪmˈpjʊə] *adj.* □ **1.** unrein: a) schmutzig, unsauber, b) verfälscht, mit Beimischungen, c) *fig.* gemischt, nicht einheitlich (*Stil*), d) *fig.* fehlerhaft; **2.** *fig.* unrein (*a. eccl.*), schmutzig, unanständig; **im·pu·ri·ty** [ɪmˈpjʊərətɪ] *s.* **1.** Unreinheit *f*, Unsauberkeit *f*; **2.** Unanständigkeit *f*; **3.** ⚙ Verunreinigung *f*, Schmutz(teilchen *n*) *m*, Fremdkörper *m*.
im·put·a·ble [ɪmˈpjuːtəbl] *adj.* zuzuschreiben(d), beizumessen(d) (***to*** *dat.*); **im·pu·ta·tion** [ˌɪmpjuːˈteɪʃn] *s.* **1.** Zuschreibung *f*, Unter'stellung *f*; **2.** Be-, Anschuldigung *f*, Bezichtigung *f*; **3.** Makel *m*, (Schand)Fleck *m*; **im'put·a·tive** [-ətɪv] *adj.* □ **1.** zuschreibend; **2.** beschuldigend; **3.** unter'stellt; **impute** [ɪmˈpjuːt] *v/t.* (***to***) zuschreiben, zur Last legen, anlasten (*dat.*).
in [ɪn] **I** *prp.* **1.** *räumlich*: a) *auf die Frage wo?* in (*dat.*), an (*dat.*), auf (*dat.*): **~ *London*** in London; **~ *here*** hier drin (-nen); **~ *the*** (*od.* ***one's***) ***head*** im Kopf; **~ *the dark*** im Dunkeln; **~ *the sky*** am Himmel; **~ *the street*** auf der Straße; **~ *the country*** (***field***) auf dem Land (Feld), b) *auf die Frage wohin?* in (*acc.*): ***put it ~ your pocket!*** steck(e) es in deine Tasche!; **2.** *zeitlich*: in (*dat.*), an (*dat.*), unter (*dat.*), bei, während, zu: **~ *May*** im Mai; **~ *the evening*** am Abend; **~ *the beginning*** am *od.* im Anfang; **~ *a week*(*'s time*)** in *od.* binnen einer Woche; **~ *1960*** (im Jahre) 1960; **~ *his sleep*** während er schlief, im Schlaf; **~ *life*** zu Lebzeiten; ***not ~ years*** seit Jahren nicht (mehr); **~ *between meals*** zwischen den Mahlzeiten; **3.** *Zustand, Beschaffenheit, Art u. Weise*: in (*dat.*), auf (*acc.*), mit: **~ *a rage*** in Wut; **~ *trouble*** in Not; **~ *tears*** in Tränen (aufgelöst), unter Tränen; **~ *good health*** bei guter Gesundheit; **~ (*the*) *rain*** im *od.* bei Regen; **~ *German*** auf deutsch; **~ *a loud voice*** mit lauter Stimme; **~ *order*** der Reihe nach; **~ *a whisper*** flüsternd; **~ *a word*** mit 'einem Wort; **~ *this way*** in dieser *od.* auf diese Weise; **4.** *im Besitz, in der Macht*: in (*dat.*), bei, an (*dat.*): ***it is not ~ him*** es liegt ihm nicht; ***he has*** (***not***) ***got it ~ him*** er hat (nicht) das Zeug dazu; **5.** *Zahl, Maß*: in (*dat.*), aus, von, zu: **~ *twos*** zu zweien; **~ *dozens*** zu Dutzenden, dutzendweise; ***one ~ ten*** eine(r) *od.* ein(e)s von *od.* unter zehn, jede(r) *od.* jedes zehnte; **6.** *Beteiligung*: in (*dat.*), an (*dat.*), bei: **~ *the army*** beim Militär; **~ *society*** in der Gesellschaft; ***shares ~ a company*** Aktien e-r Gesellschaft; **~ *the university*** an der Universität; ***be ~ it*** beteiligt sein; ***he isn't ~ it*** er gehört nicht dazu; ***there is something*** (***nothing***) **~ *it*** a) es ist et. (nichts) d(a)ran, b) es lohnt sich (nicht); ***he is ~ there too*** er ist auch mit dabei, er ‚mischt auch mit'; **7.** *Richtung*: in (*acc.*), auf (*acc.*): ***trust ~ s.o.*** auf j-n vertrauen; **8.** *Zweck*: in (*dat.*), zu, als: **~ *my defence*** zu m-r Verteidigung; **~ *reply to*** in Beantwortung (*gen.*), als Antwort auf (*acc.*); **9.** *Grund*: in (*dat.*), aus, wegen, zu: **~ *despair*** in *od.* aus Verzweiflung; **~ *his hono*(*u*)*r*** ihm zu Ehren; **10.** *Tätigkeit*: in (*dat.*), bei, auf (*dat.*): **~ *reading*** beim Lesen; **~ *saying this*** indem ich dies sage; **~ *search of*** auf der Suche nach; **11.** *Material, Kleidung*: in (*dat.*), mit, aus, durch: **~ *bronze*** aus Bronze; ***written ~ pencil*** mit Bleistift geschrieben; **12.** *Hinsicht, Beziehung*: in (*dat.*), an (*dat.*), in bezug auf (*acc.*): **~ *size*** an Größe; ***a foot ~ length*** einen Fuß lang; **~ *that*** weil, insofern als; **13.** *Bücher etc.*: in (*dat.*), bei: **~ *Shakespeare*** bei Shakespeare; **14.** nach, gemäß: **~ *my opinion*** m-r Meinung nach; **II** *adv.* **15.** innen, drinnen: **~ *among*** mitten unter; **~ *between*** dazwischen, zwischendurch; ***be ~ for s.th.*** et. zu erwarten *od.* gewärtigen haben; ***he is ~ for a shock*** er wird nicht schlecht erschrecken; ***I am ~ for an examination*** mir steht e-e Prüfung bevor; ***now you're ~ for it*** jetzt bist du ‚dran', jetzt kannst du dich auf et. gefaßt machen; ***have it ~ for s.o.*** es auf j-n abgesehen haben, j-n auf dem ‚Kieker' haben; ***be well ~ with s.o.*** mit j-m gut stehen; ***breed ~ and*** Inzucht treiben; ***~-and-~ breeding*** Inzucht *f*; **~ *and out*** a) bald drinnen, bald draußen, b) hin u. her; **16.** hin'ein, her'ein, nach innen: ***walk ~*** hineingehen; ***come ~!*** herein!; ***the way ~*** der Eingang; **~ *with you!*** hinein mir dir!; **17.** da'zu, als Zugabe: ***throw ~*** zusätzlich geben; **III** *adj.* **18.** zu Hause; im Zimmer: ***Mr. B. is not ~*** Herr B. ist nicht zu Hause; **19.** da, angekommen: ***the post is ~***; ***the harvest is ~*** die Ernte ist eingebracht; **20.** a) drin, b) F ‚in', in Mode, c) *sport* am Spiel, ‚dran', d) *pol.* an der Macht, im Amt, am Ruder: **~ *party*** *pol.* Regierungspartei *f*; ***an ~ restaurant*** ein Restaurant, das gerade ‚in' ist; ***the ~ thing is to wear a wig*** es ist ‚in' *od.* gerade Mode, e-e Perücke zu tragen; **~ *side*** *Kricket*: Schlägerpartei *f*; ***be ~ on it*** F eingeweiht sein; **IV** *s.* **21.** *pl.* Re'gie-

rungspar,tei *f*; **22.** ***know the ~s and outs of s.th.*** genau Bescheid wissen bei e-r Sache.

in-[1] [ɪn] *in Zssgn* in…, innen, hinein…, Hin…, ein…

in-[2] [ɪn] *in Zssgn* un…, Un…, nicht.

in·a·bil·i·ty [ɪnəˈbɪlətɪ] *s.* Unfähigkeit *f*: ***~ to pay*** † Zahlungsunfähigkeit, Insolvenz *f*.

in·ac·ces·si·bil·i·ty [ˈɪnækˌsesəˈbɪlətɪ] *s.* Unzugänglichkeit *f etc.*; **in·ac·ces·si·ble** [ˌɪnækˈsesəbl] *adj.* □ unzugänglich: a) unerreichbar, b) unˈnahbar (***to*** für *od. dat.*) (*Person*).

in·ac·cu·ra·cy [ɪnˈækjʊrəsɪ] *s.* **1.** Ungenauigkeit *f*; **2.** Fehler *m*, Irrtum *m*; **inˈac·cu·rate** [-rət] *adj.* □ **1.** ungenau; **2.** irrig, falsch.

in·ac·tion [ɪnˈækʃn] *s.* **1.** Untätigkeit *f*, Passiviˈtät *f*; **2.** Trägheit *f*; **3.** Ruhe *f*; **inˈac·tive** [-ktɪv] *adj.* □ **1.** untätig; **2.** träge (*a. phys.*), müßig; **3.** † flau, lustlos: ***~ market***; ***~ account*** umsatzloses Konto; ***~ capital*** brachliegendes Kapital; **4.** ⚗ unwirksam, neuˈtral; **5.** ⚔ nicht akˈtiv, außer Dienst; **in·ac·tiv·i·ty** [ˌɪnækˈtɪvətɪ] *s.* **1.** Untätigkeit *f*; **2.** Trägheit *f* (*a. phys.*); **3.** † Unbelebtheit *f*, Lustlosigkeit *f*; **4.** ⚗ Unwirksamkeit *f*.

in·a·dapt·a·bil·i·ty [ˈɪnəˌdæptəˈbɪlətɪ] *s.* **1.** Mangel *m* an Anpassungsfähigkeit; **2.** Unanwendbarkeit *f* (***to*** auf *acc.*, für); **in·a·dapt·a·ble** [ˌɪnəˈdæptəbl] *adj.* **1.** nicht anpassungsfähig; **2.** (***to***) unanwendbar (auf *acc.*), untauglich (für).

in·ad·e·qua·cy [ɪnˈædɪkwəsɪ] *s.* Unzulänglichkeit *f etc.*; **inˈad·e·quate** [-kwət] *adj.* □ unzulänglich, mangelhaft; unangemessen.

in·ad·mis·si·bil·i·ty [ˈɪnədˌmɪsəˈbɪlətɪ] *s.* Unzulässigkeit *f*; **in·ad·mis·si·ble** [ˌɪnədˈmɪsəbl] *adj.* □ unzulässig, nicht statthaft.

in·ad·vert·ence [ˌɪnədˈvɜːtəns], **ˌin·adˈvert·en·cy** [-sɪ] *s.* **1.** Unachtsamkeit *f*; **2.** Unabsichtlichkeit *f*; Versehen *n*; **ˌin·adˈvert·ent** [-nt] *adj.* □ **1.** unachtsam; nachlässig; **2.** unabsichtlich, versehentlich.

in·ad·vis·a·bil·i·ty [ˈɪnədˌvaɪzəˈbɪlətɪ] *s.* Unratsamkeit *f*; **in·ad·vis·a·ble** [ˌɪnədˈvaɪzəbl] *adj.* nicht ratsam.

in·al·ien·a·ble [ɪnˈeɪljənəbl] *adj.* □ unveräußerlich: ***~ rights***.

in·al·ter·a·ble [ɪnˈɔːltərəbl] *adj.* □ unveränderlich, unabänderlich.

in·am·o·ra·ta [ɪnˌæməˈrɑːtə] *s.* Geliebte *f*; **inˌam·oˈra·to** [-təʊ] *pl.* **-tos** *s.* Geliebte(r) *m*.

ˌin|-and-ˈin → ***in*** 15; **ˌ~-and-ˈout** *adj.* wechselhaft, schwankend.

in·ane [ɪˈneɪn] *adj.* □ hohl, geistlos, albern.

in·an·i·mate [ɪnˈænɪmət] *adj.* □ **1.** leblos, unbelebt; **2.** unbeseelt; **3.** *fig.* langweilig, fad(e); **4.** † flau, matt; **in·an·i·ma·tion** [ɪnˌænɪˈmeɪʃn] *s.* Leblosigkeit *f*, Unbelebtheit *f*.

in·a·ni·tion [ˌɪnəˈnɪʃn] *s.* **1.** ⚕ Entkräftung *f*; **2.** (moˈralische) Schwäche, Leere *f*.

in·an·i·ty [ɪˈnænətɪ] *s.* Geistlosigkeit *f*, Albernheit *f*: a) geistige Leere, Hohl-, Seichtheit *f*, b) dumme Bemerkung, *pl.* dummes Geschwätz.

in·ap·pli·ca·bil·i·ty [ˈɪnˌæplɪkəˈbɪlətɪ] *s.* Unanwendbarkeit *f*; **in·ap·pli·ca·ble** [ɪnˈæplɪkəbl] *adj.* □ (***to***) unanwendbar, nicht anwendbar *od.* zutreffend (auf *acc.*); ungeeignet (für).

in·ap·po·site [ɪnˈæpəzɪt] *adj.* □ unangebracht, unpassend.

in·ap·pre·ci·a·ble [ˌɪnəˈpriːʃəbl] *adj.* □ unmerklich, unbedeutend.

in·ap·pro·pri·ate [ˌɪnəˈprəʊprɪət] *adj.* □ **1.** unpassend: a) ungeeignet (***to***, ***for*** für), b) unangebracht, ungehörig; **2.** unangemessen (***to*** *dat.*); **ˌin·apˈpro·pri·ate·ness** [-nɪs] *s.* **1.** Ungeeignetheit *f*; **2.** Ungehörigkeit *f*; **3.** Unangemessenheit *f*.

in·apt [ɪnˈæpt] *adj.* □ **1.** unpassend, ungeeignet; **2.** ungeschickt, untauglich; **3.** unfähig; **inˈapt·i·tude** [-tɪtjuːd], **inˈapt·ness** [-nɪs] *s.* **1.** Ungeeignetheit *f*; **2.** Ungeschicklichkeit *f*, Untauglichkeit *f*; **3.** Unfähigkeit *f*.

in·ar·tic·u·late [ˌɪnɑːˈtɪkjʊlət] *adj.* □ **1.** unartikuliert, undeutlich, unklar, schwer zu verstehen(d), unverständlich; **2.** undeutlich sprechend; **3.** unfähig, sich (deutlich) auszudrücken, wenig wortgewandt: ***he is ~*** a) er kann sich nicht ausdrücken, b) er ‚kriegt den Mund nicht auf'; ***~ with rage*** sprachlos vor Wut; **4.** *zo.* ungegliedert.

in·ar·tis·tic [ˌɪnɑːˈtɪstɪk] *adj.* (□ ***~ally***) unkünstlerisch.

in·as·much [ˌɪnəzˈmʌtʃ] *cj.*: ***~ as*** **1.** da (ja), weil; **2.** *obs.* inˈsofern als.

in·at·ten·tion [ˌɪnəˈtenʃn] *s.* **1.** Unaufmerksamkeit *f*, Unachtsamkeit *f* (***to*** gegenüber); **2.** Gleichgültigkeit *f* (***to*** gegen); **ˌin·atˈten·tive** [-ntɪv] *adj.* □ **1.** unaufmerksam (***to*** gegenüber); **2.** gleichgültig (***to*** gegen), nachlässig.

in·au·di·bil·i·ty [ɪnˌɔːdəˈbɪlətɪ] *s.* Unhörbarkeit *f*; **in·au·di·ble** [ɪnˈɔːdəbl] *adj.* □ unhörbar.

in·au·gu·ral [ɪˈnɔːgjʊrəl] **I** *adj.* Einführungs…, Einweihungs…, Antritts…, Eröffnungs…: ***~ speech*** → **II** *s.* Eröffnungs- *od.* Antrittsrede *f*; **in·au·gu·rate** [ɪˈnɔːgjʊreɪt] *v/t.* **1.** (feierlich) einführen *od.* einsetzen; **2.** einweihen, eröffnen; **3.** beginnen, einleiten: ***~ a new era***; **in·au·gu·ra·tion** [ɪˌnɔːgjʊˈreɪʃn] *s.* **1.** (feierliche) Amtseinsetzung, -einführung *f*: ***ℒ Day*** *Am.* Tag *m* des Amtsantritts des Präsidenten; **2.** Einweihung *f*, Eröffnung *f*; **3.** Beginn *m*.

in·aus·pi·cious [ˌɪnɔːˈspɪʃəs] *adj.* □ **1.** ungünstig, unheilvoll, -drohend; **2.** unglücklich; **ˌin·ausˈpi·cious·ness** [-nɪs] *s.* üble Vorbedeutung, Ungünstigkeit *f*.

ˌin-beˈtween I *s.* **1.** Mittel-, Zwischending; **2.** a) Mittelsmann *m*, b) † Zwischenhändler *m*; **II** *adj.* **3.** Zwischen…

in·board [ˈɪnbɔːd] ⚓ **I** *adj.* Innenbord…: ***~ engine*** → III; **II** *adv.* (b)innenbords; **III** *s.* Innenbordmotor *m*.

in·born [ˌɪnˈbɔːn] *adj.* angeboren.

in·bred [ˌɪnˈbred] *adj.* **1.** angeboren, ererbt; **2.** durch Inzucht erzeugt, Inzucht…

in·breed [ˌɪnˈbriːd] *v/t.* [*irr.* → ***breed***] durch Inzucht züchten; **ˌinˈbreed·ing** [-dɪŋ] *s.* Inzucht *f*.

in·cal·cu·la·bil·i·ty [ɪnˌkælkjʊləˈbɪlətɪ] *s.* Unberechenbarkeit *f*; **in·cal·cu·la·ble** [ɪnˈkælkjʊləbl] *adj.* □ **1.** unberechenbar (*a. fig. Person etc.*); **2.** unermeßlich.

in·can·des·cence [ˌɪnkænˈdesns] *s.* **1.** Weißglühen *n*, -glut *f*; **2.** Erglühen *n* (*a. fig.*); **ˌin·canˈdes·cent** [-nt] *adj.* **1.** weißglühend; **2.** ⚙ Glüh…: ***~ bulb*** ⚡ Glühbirne *f*; ***~ burner*** *phys.* Glühlichtbrenner *m*; ***~ filament*** ⚡ Glühfaden *m*; ***~ lamp*** ⚡ Glühlampe *f*; ***~ light*** *phys.* Glühlicht *n*; **3.** *fig.* leuchtend, strahlend.

in·can·ta·tion [ˌɪnkænˈteɪʃn] *s.* **1.** Beschwörung *f*; **2.** Zauber(spruch) *m*, Zauberformel *f*.

in·ca·pa·bil·i·ty [ɪnˌkeɪpəˈbɪlətɪ] *s.* Unfähigkeit *f*, Unvermögen *n*; **in·ca·pa·ble** [ɪnˈkeɪpəbl] *adj.* □ **1.** unfähig: a) untüchtig, b) unbegabt; **2.** nicht fähig (***of*** *gen.*, ***of doing*** zu tun), nicht imˈstande (***of doing*** zu tun): ***~ of a crime*** e-s Verbrechens nicht fähig; ***~ of working*** arbeitsunfähig; **3.** (*physisch*) hilflos: ***drunk and ~*** volltrunken; **4.** ungeeignet (***of*** für): ***~ of improvement*** nicht verbesserungsfähig; ***~ of solution*** unlösbar.

in·ca·pac·i·tate [ˌɪnkəˈpæsɪteɪt] *v/t.* **1.** unfähig *od.* untauglich machen (***for s.th.*** für et., ***from doing*** zu tun); *Gegner* außer Gefecht setzen; hindern (***from doing*** an *dat.*, zu tun); **2.** ⚖ für (geschäfts)unfähig erklären; **ˌin·caˈpac·i·tat·ed** [-tɪd] *adj.* **1.** erwerbs-, arbeitsunfähig; **2.** (körperlich *od.* geistig) behindert; **3.** (***legally***) ***~*** ⚖ geschäftsunfähig; **ˌin·caˈpac·i·ty** [-tɪ] *s.* **1.** Unfähigkeit *f*, Untauglichkeit *f* (***for*** für, zu; ***for doing*** zu tun): ***~*** (***for work***) Arbeits-, Erwerbs-, Berufsunfähigkeit; **2.** *a.* ***legal ~*** ⚖ Geschäftsunfähigkeit *f*: ***~ to sue*** *Am.* mangelnde Prozeßfähigkeit.

in·cap·su·late [ɪnˈkæpsjʊleɪt] → ***encapsulate***.

in·car·cer·ate [ɪnˈkɑːsəreɪt] *v/t.* **1.** einkerkern, einsperren (*a. fig.*); **2.** ⚕ *Bruch* einklemmen; **in·car·cer·a·tion** [ɪnˌkɑːsəˈreɪʃn] *s.* **1.** Einkerkerung *f*, Einsperrung *f* (*a. fig.*); **2.** ⚕ Einklemmung *f*.

in·car·nate I *v/t.* [ˈɪnkɑːneɪt] **1.** verkörpern; **2.** feste Form *od.* Gestalt geben (*dat.*); **II** *adj.* [ɪnˈkaːneɪt] **3.** *eccl.* fleischgeworden, in Menschengestalt; **4.** *fig.* leibˈhaftig: ***a devil ~*** ein Teufel in Menschengestalt; ***innocence ~*** die personifizierte Unschuld, die Unschuld in Person; **in·car·na·tion** [ˌɪnkɑːˈneɪʃn] *s.* Inkarnatiˈon *f*: a) ℒ *eccl.* Menschwerdung *f*, b) Inbegriff *m*, Verkörperung *f*.

in·case → ***encase***.

in·cau·tious [ɪnˈkɔːʃəs] *adj.* □ unvorsichtig, unbedacht.

in·cen·di·a·rism [ɪnˈsendjərɪzəm] *s.* **1.** Brandstiftung *f*; **2.** *fig.* Aufwiegelung *f*, Aufhetzung *f*; **in·cen·di·ar·y** [ɪnˈsendjərɪ] **I** *adj.* **1.** Feuer…, Brand…: ***~ bomb*** → 5 a; ***~ bullet*** → 5 b; **2.** ⚖ Brandstiftungs…: ***~ action*** Brandstiftung *f*; **3.** *fig.* aufwiegelnd, -hetzend: ***~ speech*** Hetzrede *f*; **II** *s.* **4.** Brandstifter(in); **5.** ⚔ a) Brandbombe *f*, b) Brandgeschoß *n*; **6.** *fig.* Unruhestifter *m*, Hetzer *m*.

in·cense[1] [ɪnˈsens] *v/t.* erzürnen: ***~d*** zornig, aufgebracht.

in·cense[2] [ˈɪnsens] **I** *s.* **1.** Weihrauch *m*:

~-burner *eccl.* Räucherfaß *n*, -vase *f*; **2.** Duft *m*; **3.** *fig.* ‚Weihrauch' *m*, Lobhude'lei *f*; **II** *v/t.* **4.** (mit Weihrauch) beräuchern; **5.** durch'duften; **6.** *fig. j-n* beweihräuchern.

in·cen·so·ry ['ɪnsensərɪ] *s. eccl.* Weihrauchfaß *n*.

in·cen·tive [ɪn'sentɪv] **I** *adj.* anspornend, antreibend, anreizend: **~ bonus** (**pay**) † Leistungsprämie *f* (-lohn *m*); **II** *s.* Ansporn *m*, († Leistungs)Anreiz *m*: **buying ~** Kaufanreiz.

in·cep·tion [ɪn'sepʃn] *s.* Beginn *m*, Anfang *m*; **in'cep·tive** [-ptɪv] *adj.* beginnend, anfangend, anfänglich, Anfangs...: **~ verb** *ling.* inchoatives Verb.

in·cer·ti·tude [ɪn'sɜːtɪtjuːd] *s.* Ungewißheit *f*, Unsicherheit *f*.

in·ces·sant [ɪn'sesnt] *adj.* □ unaufhörlich, unablässig, ständig.

in·cest ['ɪnsest] *s.* Blutschande *f*, In'zest *m*; **in·ces·tu·ous** [ɪn'sestjʊəs] *adj.* □ blutschänderisch, inzestu'ös.

inch [ɪntʃ] **I** *s.* Zoll *m* (= *2,54 cm*), *fig. a.* Zenti'meter *m od.* Milli'meter *m*: **every ~ a soldier** jeder Zoll ein Soldat; **~ by ~, by ~es** Zentimeter um Zentimeter, zentimeterweise, langsam; **not to yield an ~** nicht einen Zoll weichen *od.* nachgeben; **he came within an ~ of winning** er hätte um ein Haar gewonnen; **I came within an ~ of being killed** ich wurde um ein Haar getötet, ich bin dem Tod um Haaresbreite entgangen; **thrashed within an ~ of his life** fast zu Tode geprügelt; **give him an ~ and he'll take a yard** (*od.* **ell**) gibt man ihm den kleinen Finger, so nimmt er die ganze Hand; **II** *adj.* ...zöllig: **a two-~ rope**; **III** *v/t.* langsam *od.* zenti'meterweise schieben *od.* manövrieren; **IV** *v/i.* sich ganz langsam *od.* zentimeterweise (vorwärts- *etc.*)schieben; **inched** [ɪntʃt] *adj. in Zssgn* ...zöllig.

in·cho·ate ['ɪnkəʊeɪt] *adj.* **1.** angefangen, anfangend, Anfangs...; **2.** 'unvoll‚ständig, rudimen'tär; **'in·cho·a·tive** [-tɪv] **I** *adj.* **1.** → **inchoate** 1; **2.** *ling.* inchoa'tiv; **II** *s.* **3.** *ling.* inchoa'tives Verb.

in·ci·dence ['ɪnsɪdəns] *s.* **1.** Ein-, Auftreten *n*, Vorkommen *n*; **2.** Häufigkeit *f*, Verbreitung *f*: **~ of divorces** Scheidungsquote *f*, -rate *f*; **3.** a) Auftreffen *n* (**upon** auf *acc.*) (*a. phys.*), b) *phys.* Einfall(en *n*) *m* (*von Strahlen*); → **angle**[1] 1; **4.** † Anfall *m* (*e-r Steuer*): **~ of taxation** Verteilung *f* der Steuerlast, Steuerbelastung *f*; **'in·ci·dent** [-nt] **I** *adj.* **1.** (**to**) a) vorkommend (bei *od.* in *dat.*), b) → **incidental** 4; **2.** *bsd. phys.* ein-, auffallend, auftreffend (*Strahlen etc.*); **II** *s.* **3.** Vorfall *m*, Ereignis *n*, Vorkommnis *n*, *a. pol.* Zwischenfall *m*: **full of ~** ereignisreich; **4.** 'Neben‚umstand *m*, -sache *f*; **5.** Epi'sode *f*, Zwischenhandlung *f* (*im Drama etc.*); **6.** ⚖ a) (Neben)Folge *f* (**of** aus), b) 'Nebensache *f*, -‚umstand *m*.

in·ci·den·tal [‚ɪnsɪ'dentl] **I** *adj.* □ **1.** beiläufig, nebensächlich, Neben...: **~ earnings** Nebenverdienst *m*; **~ expenses** → 7; **~ music** Begleit-, Bühnen-, Filmmusik *f*, musikalischer Hintergrund; **2.** gelegentlich; **3.** zufällig; **4.** (**to**) gehörig (zu), verbunden *od.* zs.-hängend (mit): **be ~ to** gehören zu, verbunden sein mit; **the expenses ~ thereto** die dabei entstehenden *od.* damit verbundenen Unkosten; **5.** folgend (**upon** auf *acc.*), nachher auftretend: **~ images** *psych.* Nachbilder; **II** *s.* **6.** 'Neben‚umstand *m*, -sächlichkeit *f*; **7.** *pl.* † Nebenausgaben *pl.*, -spesen *pl.*; **‚in·ci'den·tal·ly** [-tlɪ] *adv.* **1.** beiläufig, neben'bei; **2.** zufällig; **3.** gelegentlich; **4.** neben'bei bemerkt, übrigens.

in·cin·er·ate [ɪn'sɪnəreɪt] *v/t.* verbrennen, *bsd. Leiche* einäschern; **in·cin·er·a·tion** [ɪn‚sɪnə'reɪʃn] *s.* Verbrennung *f*, Einäscherung *f*; **in'cin·er·a·tor** [-tə] *s.* Verbrennungsofen *m*, -anlage *f*.

in·cip·i·ence [ɪn'sɪpɪəns], **in'cip·i·en·cy** [-sɪ] *s.* Anfang *m*; Anfangsstadium *n*; **in'cip·i·ent** [-nt] *adj.* □ beginnend, einleitend, Anfangs...; **in'cip·i·ent·ly** [-ntlɪ] *adv.* anfänglich, anfangs.

in·cise [ɪn'saɪz] *v/t.* **1.** einschneiden in (*acc.*), aufschneiden (*a.* ⚕): **~d wound** Schnittwunde *f*; **2.** einritzen, -schnitzen, -kerben, -gravieren; **in·ci·sion** [ɪn'sɪʒn] *s.* (Ein)Schnitt *m* (*a.* ⚕), Kerbe *f*; **in'ci·sive** [-aɪsɪv] *adj.* □ *fig.* **1.** scharf: a) 'durchdringend: **~ intellect**, b) beißend: **~ irony**, c) prä'gnant: **~ style**; **2.** *anat.* Schneide(zahn)...; **in'ci·sive·ness** [-aɪsɪvnɪs] *s. fig.* Schärfe *f*, Prä'gnanz *f*; **in'ci·sor** [-zə] *s. anat.* Schneidezahn *m*.

in·ci·ta·tion [‚ɪnsaɪ'teɪʃn] *s.* **1.** Anregung *f*, Ansporn *m*, Antrieb *m*; **2.** → **incitement** 2; **in·cite** [ɪn'saɪt] *v/t.* **1.** anregen (*a.* ⚕), anspornen, anstacheln; **2.** aufhetzen, -wiegeln, ⚖ *a.* anstiften (**to** zu); **in·cite·ment** [ɪn'saɪtmənt] *s.* **1.** → **incitation** 1; **2.** Aufhetzung *f*, -wiegelung *f*, ⚖ *a.* Anstiftung *f* (**to commit a crime** zu e-m Verbrechen).

in·ci·vil·i·ty [‚ɪnsɪ'vɪlətɪ] *s.* Unhöflichkeit *f*, Grobheit *f*.

in·ci·vism ['ɪnsɪvɪzəm] *s.* Mangel *m* an staatsbürgerlicher Gesinnung.

'in-‚clear·ing *s.* † *Brit.* Gesamtbetrag *m* der auf e-e Bank laufenden Schecks, Abrechnungsbetrag *m*.

in·clem·en·cy [ɪn'klemənsɪ] *s.* Rauheit *f*, Unfreundlichkeit *f*: **~ of the weather** *a.* Unbilden *pl.* der Witterung; **in'clement** [-nt] *adj.* □ **1.** rauh, unfreundlich, streng (*Klima etc.*); **2.** hart, grausam.

in·clin·a·ble [ɪn'klaɪnəbl] *adj.* **1.** (hin-) neigend, tendierend (**to** zu); **2.** ⚙ schrägstellbar.

in·cli·na·tion [‚ɪnklɪ'neɪʃn] *s.* **1.** *fig.* Neigung *f*, Vorliebe *f*, Hang *m* (**to, for** zu): **~ to buy** † Kauflust *f*; **~ to stoutness** Neigung *od.* Anlage *f* zur Korpulenz; **2.** *fig.* Zuneigung *f* (**for** zu); **3.** ⚒, *phys.* a) Neigung *f*, Schrägstellung *f*, Senkung *f*, b) Abhang *m*, c) Neigungswinkel *m*, Gefälle *n*; **4.** *ast., phys.* Inklinati'on *f*; **in·cline** [ɪn'klaɪn] **I** *v/i.* **1.** sich neigen (**to, towards** nach), (schräg) abfallen; **2.** sich neigen (*Tag*); **3.** *fig.* neigen (**to, toward** zu): **~ to an opinion**; **~ to do s.th.** dazu neigen, et. zu tun; **4.** Anlage haben, neigen (**to** zu): **~ to corpulence**; **~ to red** ins Rötliche spielen; **5.** *fig.* (**to**) sich hingezogen fühlen (zu), gewogen sein (*dat.*); **II** *v/t.* **6.** *Kopf etc.* neigen: **~ one's ear to s.o.** *fig.* j-m sein Ohr leihen; **7.** *fig. j-n* bewegen, (dazu) veranlassen (**to** zu; **to do** zu tun): **this ~s me to doubt** dies läßt mich zweifeln; **this ~s me to go** im Hinblick darauf möchte ich lieber gehen; **III** *s.* **8.** Neigung *f*, Schräge *f*, Abhang *m*, Gefälle *n*; **in·clined** [ɪn'klaɪnd] *adj.* **1.** geneigt, aufgelegt (**to** zu): **be ~** dazu neigen, (dazu) aufgelegt sein (**to do** zu tun); **2.** (dazu) neigend *od.* veranlagt (**to** zu); **3.** geneigt, gewogen, wohlgesinnt (**to** *dat.*); **4.** geneigt, schräg, schief, abschüssig: **~ plane** *phys.* schiefe Ebene; **in·cli·nom·e·ter** [‚ɪnklɪ'nɒmɪtə] *s.* **1.** Inklinati'onskompaß *m*, -nadel *f*; **2.** ✈ Neigungsmesser *m*.

in·close [ɪn'kləʊz] → **enclose**.

in·clude [ɪn'kluːd] *v/t.* **1.** (in sich *od.* mit) einschließen, um'fassen, enthalten, be-inhalten: **all ~d** alles inbegriffen *od.* inklusive; **tax ~d** einschließlich *od.* inklusive Steuer; **2.** einschließen, betreffen, gelten für: **that ~s you, too!**; **~ me out!** *humor.* ohne mich!; **3.** einbeziehen, -schließen (**in** in *acc.*), rechnen (**among** unter *acc.*, zu); **4.** aufnehmen (**in** in *e-e Gruppe, Liste etc.*), erfassen; **5.** *j-n* (*in s-m Testament*) bedenken; **in'clud·ing** [-dɪŋ] *prp.* einschließlich (*gen.*), *bsd.* † inklu'sive (*Verpackung etc.*), *Gebühren etc.* (mit) inbegriffen, mit: **not ~** ausschließlich (*gen.*), *bsd.* † exklusive; **up to and ~** bis einschließlich; **in'clu·sion** [-uːʒn] *s.* **1.** Einbeziehung *f*, Einschluß *m* (*a. biol., min. etc.*) (**in** in *acc.*): **with the ~ of** → **including**; **2.** Aufnahme *f* (**in** in *acc.*); **in'clu·sive** [-uːsɪv] *adj.* □ **1.** einschließlich, inklu'sive (**of** *gen.*): **be ~ of** einschließen; (**to**) **Friday ~** (bis) einschließlich Freitag; **2.** alles einschließend *od.* enthaltend, † Inklusiv..., Pauschal...: **~ price**.

in·cog·ni·to [ɪn'kɒgnɪtəʊ] **I** *adv.* **1.** in'kognito, unter fremdem Namen: **travel ~**; **2.** ano'nym: **do good ~**; **II** *pl.* **-tos** *s.* **3.** In'kognito *n*; **4.** j-d, der in'kognito auftritt.

in·co·her·ence [‚ɪnkəʊ'hɪərəns] *s.* Zs.-hang(s)losigkeit *f*, Wirr-, Verwirrtheit *f*; **‚in·co'her·ent** [-nt] *adj.* □ zs.-hanglos, wirr (*a. Person*).

in·com·bus·ti·ble [‚ɪnkəm'bʌstəbl] *adj.* □ unverbrennbar.

in·come ['ɪŋkʌm] *s.* † Einkommen *n*, Einkünfte *pl.* (**from** aus): **~ bond** Schuldverschreibung *f* mit gewinnabhängiger Verzinsung *f*; **~ bracket** *od.* **group** Einkommensstufe *f*; **~ return** *Am.* Rendite *f*; **~ statement** *Am.* Gewinn- u. Verlustrechnung *f*; **~ tax** Einkommensteuer *f*; **~ tax return** Einkommensteuererklärung *f*; **live within** (**beyond**) **one's ~** s-n Verhältnissen entsprechend (über s-e Verhältnisse) leben.

in·com·er ['ɪn‚kʌmə] *s.* **1.** (Neu)Ankömmling *m*; **2.** † (Rechts)Nachfolger(in).

in·com·ing ['ɪn‚kʌmɪŋ] **I** *adj.* **1.** her'einkommend: **the ~ tide** die Flut; **2.** ankommend (*Telefongespräch, Zug etc.*); **3.** nachfolgend, neu (*Regierung, Präsident, Mieter etc.*); **4.** † eingehend (*Post etc.*): **~ goods** *od.* **stocks** Wareneingang *m*, -eingänge *pl.*; **~ orders** Auftragseingang *m*; **II** *s.* **5.** Ankommen *n*, Ankunft *f*; Eingang *m*; **6.** *pl.* † Eingänge *pl.*, Einkünfte *pl.*

in·com·men·su·ra·ble [‚ɪnkə'menʃərəbl] **I** *adj.* ☐ **1.** Ꭿ a) inkommensu'rabel, b) 'irratio,nal; **2.** nicht vergleichbar; **3.** völlig unverhältnismäßig, in keinem Verhältnis stehend (***with*** zu); **II** *s.* **4.** Ꭿ inkommensu'rable Größe; **in·com·men·su·rate** [ˌɪnkə'menʃərət] *adj.* ☐ **1.** (***to***) unangemessen (*dat.*), unvereinbar (mit); **2.** → ***incommensurable*** I.

in·com·mode [ˌɪnkə'məʊd] *v/t. j-m* lästig fallen, *j-n* belästigen, stören; ˌ**in·com'mo·di·ous** [-djəs] *adj.* ☐ unbequem: a) lästig (***to*** *dat. od.* für), b) beengt.

in·com·mu·ni·ca·ble [ˌɪnkə'mju:nɪkəbl] *adj.* ☐ nicht mitteilbar, nicht auszudrücken(d); **in·com·mu·ni·ca·do** [ˌɪnkəmju:nɪ'kɑ:dəʊ] *adj.* vom Verkehr mit der Außenwelt abgeschnitten, ⚖ *a.* in Einzel- *od.* Isolierhaft; ˌ**in·com'mu·ni·ca·tive** [-ətɪv] *adj.* ☐ nicht mitteilsam, zu'rückhaltend, reserviert.

in·com·pa·ra·ble [ɪn'kɒmpərəbl] *adj.* ☐ **1.** nicht zu vergleichen(d) (***with***, ***to*** mit); **2.** unvergleichlich, einzigartig; **in'com·pa·ra·bly** [-blɪ] *adv.* unvergleichlich.

in·com·pat·i·bil·i·ty ['ɪnkəmˌpætə'bɪlətɪ] *s.* Unverträglichkeit *f* (*a.* ⚕): a) Unvereinbarkeit *f*, 'Widersprüchlichkeit *f*, b) (*charakterliche*) Gegensätzlichkeit; **in·com·pat·i·ble** [ˌɪnkəm'pætəbl] *adj.* ☐ **1.** unver'einbar, 'widersprüchlich, ein'ander wider'sprechend; **2.** unverträglich: a) nicht zs.-passend (*a. Personen*), b) ⚕ inkompa'tibel (*Medikamente etc.*).

in·com·pe·tence [ɪn'kɒmpɪtəns], **in'com·pe·ten·cy** [-sɪ] *s.* **1.** Unfähigkeit *f*, Untüchtigkeit *f*; **2.** *bsd.* ⚖ a) Unzuständigkeit *f*, b) Unbefugtheit *f*, c) Unzulässigkeit *f* (*e-r Aussage etc.*), d) *Am.* Unzurechnungsfähigkeit *f*; **3.** Unzulänglichkeit *f*; **in'com·pe·tent** [-nt] *adj.* ☐ **1.** unfähig, untauglich, ungeeignet; **2.** ⚖ a) unbefugt, b) unzuständig, 'inkompeˌtent, c) *Am.* unzurechnungsfähig, geschäftsunfähig, d) unzulässig (*a. Beweis, Zeuge*); **3.** unzulänglich, mangelhaft.

in·com·plete [ˌɪnkəm'pli:t] *adj.* ☐ **1.** 'unvollˌständig, 'unvollˌendet; **2.** 'unvollˌkommen, lücken-, mangelhaft.

in·com·pre·hen·si·bil·i·ty [ɪnˌkɒmprɪhensə'bɪlətɪ] *s.* Unbegreiflichkeit *f*; **in·com·pre·hen·si·ble** [ɪnˌkɒmprɪ'hensəbl] *adj.* ☐ unbegreiflich.

in·con·ceiv·a·ble [ˌɪnkən'si:vəbl] *adj.* ☐ **1.** unbegreiflich, unfaßbar; **2.** undenkbar, unvorstellbar.

in·con·clu·sive [ˌɪnkən'klu:sɪv] *adj.* ☐ **1.** nicht über'zeugend *od.* schlüssig, ohne Beweiskraft; **2.** ergebnislos; ˌ**in·con'clu·sive·ness** [-nɪs] *s.* **1.** Mangel *m* an Beweiskraft; **2.** Ergebnislosigkeit *f*.

in·con·dite [ɪn'kɒndaɪt] *adj.* schlecht gemacht, mangelhaft; roh, grob.

in·con·gru·i·ty [ˌɪnkɒŋ'gru:ətɪ] *s.* **1.** Nichtüber'einstimmung *f*: a) 'Mißverhältnis *n*, b) Unver'einbarkeit *f*; **2.** 'Widersinnigkeit *f*; **3.** Unangemessenheit *f*; **4.** Ꭿ 'Inkongruˌenz *f*; **in·con·gru·ous** [ɪn'kɒŋgrʊəs] *adj.* ☐ **1.** nicht zuein'ander passend, nicht über'einstimmend, unver'einbar (***to***, ***with*** mit); **2.** 'widersinnig, ungereimt; **3.** unangemessen, ungehörig; **4.** Ꭿ 'inkongruˌent, nicht deckungsgleich.

in·con·se·quence [ɪn'kɒnsɪkwəns] *s.* **1.** 'Inkonseˌquenz *f*, Unlogik *f*, Folgewidrigkeit *f*; **2.** Belanglosigkeit *f*; **in'con·se·quent** [-nt] *adj.* ☐ **1.** 'inkonseˌquent, folgewidrig, unlogisch; **2.** nicht zur Sache gehörig, 'irreleˌvant; **3.** belanglos, unwichtig; **in·con·se·quen·tial** [ˌɪnkɒnsɪ'kwenʃl] → ***inconsequent***.

in·con·sid·er·a·ble [ˌɪnkən'sɪdərəbl] *adj.* ☐ unbedeutend, unerheblich, belanglos, gering(fügig).

in·con·sid·er·ate [ˌɪnkən'sɪdərət] *adj.* ☐ **1.** rücksichtslos, taktlos (***towards*** gegen); **2.** 'unüberˌlegt; ˌ**in·con'sid·er·ate·ness** [-nɪs] *s.* **1.** Rücksichtslosigkeit *f*; **2.** Unbesonnenheit *f*.

in·con·sist·en·cy [ˌɪnkən'sɪstənsɪ] *s.* **1.** (innerer) 'Widerspruch, Unver'einbarkeit *f*; **2.** 'Inkonseˌquenz *f*, Folgewidrigkeit *f*; **3.** Unbeständigkeit *f*, Wankelmut *m*; ˌ**in·con'sist·ent** [-nt] *adj.* ☐ **1.** unver'einbar, (ein'ander) wider'sprechend, gegensätzlich; **2.** 'inkonseˌquent, folgewidrig, ungereimt; **3.** unbeständig, *Person*: *a.* 'inkonseˌquent.

in·con·sol·a·ble [ˌɪnkən'səʊləbl] *adj.* ☐ untröstlich.

in·con·spic·u·ous [ˌɪnkən'spɪkjʊəs] *adj.* ☐ unauffällig: ***make o.s.*** ~ sich möglichst unauffällig verhalten.

in·con·stan·cy [ɪn'kɒnstənsɪ] *s.* **1.** Unbeständigkeit *f*, Veränderlichkeit *f*; **2.** Wankelmut *m*, Treulosigkeit *f*; **3.** Ungleichförmigkeit *f*; **in'con·stant** [-nt] *adj.* ☐ **1.** unbeständig, unstet; **2.** wankelmütig; **3.** ungleichförmig.

in·con·test·a·ble [ˌɪnkən'testəbl] *adj.* ☐ **1.** unbestreitbar, unanfechtbar; **2.** 'unumˌstößlich, 'unwiderˌleglich.

in·con·ti·nence [ɪn'kɒntɪnəns] *s.* **1.** (*bsd.* sexu'elle) Unmäßigkeit, Zügellosigkeit *f*, Unkeuschheit *f*; **2.** Nicht'haltenkönnen *n*, ⚕ *a.* 'Inkontiˌnenz *f*: ~ ***of speech*** Geschwätzigkeit *f*; ~ ***of urine*** ⚕ Harnfluß *m*; **in'con·ti·nent** [-nt] *adj.* ☐ **1.** ausschweifend, zügellos, unkeusch; **2.** unauf'hörlich; **3.** nicht im'stande *et.* zu'rückzuhalten *od.* bei sich zu behalten (*a.* ⚕).

in·con·tro·vert·i·ble [ˌɪnkɒntrə'vɜ:təbl] *adj.* ☐ unbestreitbar, unstrittig, unbestritten.

in·con·ven·ience [ˌɪnkən'vi:njəns] **I** *s.* Unbequemlichkeit *f*, Lästigkeit *f*, Unannehmlichkeit *f*, Schwierigkeit *f*: ***put s.o. to great*** ~ j-m große Ungelegenheiten bereiten; **II** *v/t.* belästigen, stören, *j-m* lästig sein, *j-m* Unannehmlichkeiten bereiten; ˌ**in·con'ven·ient** [-nt] *adj.* ☐ **1.** unbequem, lästig, störend, beschwerlich; **2.** *Zeit, Lage etc.*: ungünstig, ‚ungeschickt'.

in·con·vert·i·bil·i·ty ['ɪnkənˌvɜ:tə'bɪlətɪ] *s.* **1.** Unverwandelbarkeit *f*; **2.** † a) Nichtkonver'tierbarkeit *f*, Nicht'umwandelbarkeit *f* (*Guthaben*), b) Nicht'einlösbarkeit *f* (*Papiergeld*), c) Nicht'umsetzbarkeit *f* (*Waren*); **in·con·vert·i·ble** [ˌɪnkən'vɜ:təbl] *adj.* ☐ **1.** unverwandelbar; **2.** † a) nicht 'umwandelbar, nicht konvertierbar, b) nicht einlösbar, c) nicht 'umsetzbar.

in·cor·po·rate [ɪn'kɔ:pəreɪt] **I** *v/t.* **1.** vereinigen, verbinden, zs.-schließen; **2.** (***in***, ***into***) einverleiben (*dat.*), *Staatsgebiet a.* eingliedern; einbauen, integrieren (in *acc.*); **3.** *Stadt* eingemeinden; **4.** (***in***, ***into***) *als Mitglied* aufnehmen (in *acc.*); **5.** ⚖ als Körperschaft *od. Am.* als Aktiengesellschaft (amtlich) eintragen; 'Rechtsperˌsönlichkeit verleihen (*dat.*); gründen, inkorporieren lassen; **6.** aufnehmen, enthalten, einschließen; **7.** ⚙, ⚗ (ver)mischen; **II** *v/i.* **8.** sich verbinden *od.* vereinigen; **9.** ⚖ e-e Körperschaft *etc.* bilden; **10.** ⚙, ⚗ sich vermischen; **III** *adj.* [-pərət] **11.** → **in'cor·po·rat·ed** [-tɪd] *adj.* **1.** †, ⚖ a) (als Körperschaft) (amtlich) eingetragen, inkorporiert, b) *Am.* als Aktiengesellschaft eingetragen: ~ ***bank*** *Am.* Aktienbank *f*; ~ ***company*** *Brit.* rechtsfähige (Handels)Gesellschaft, *Am.* Aktiengesellschaft *f*; **2.** (***in***, ***into***) a) eng verbunden, zs.-geschlossen (mit), b) einverleibt (*dat.*); **3.** eingemeindet; **in·cor·po·ra·tion** [ɪnˌkɔ:pə'reɪʃn] *s.* **1.** Vereinigung *f*, Verbindung *f*; **2.** Einverleibung *f*, Eingliederung *f*, Aufnahme *f* (***into*** in *acc.*); **3.** Eingemeindung *f*; **4.** ⚖ a) Bildung *f od.* Gründung *f* e-r Körperschaft *od.* (*Am.*) e-r Aktiengesellschaft: ***articles of*** ~ *Am.* Satzung *f* (*e-r AG*); ***certificate of*** ~ Korporationsurkunde *f*, *Am.* Gründungsurkunde *f* (*e-r AG*), b) amtliche Eintragung; **in'cor·po·ra·tor** [-tə] *s. Am.* Gründungsmitglied *n*.

in·cor·po·re·al [ˌɪnkɔ:'pɔ:rɪəl] *adj.* ☐ **1.** unkörperlich, immateri'ell, geistig; **2.** ⚖ nicht greifbar: ~ ***hereditaments*** vererbliche Rechte; ~ ***rights*** Immaterialgüterrechte (*z. B. Patente*).

in·cor·rect [ˌɪnkə'rekt] *adj.* ☐ **1.** unrichtig, ungenau, irrig, falsch; **2.** 'inkorˌrekt, ungehörig (*Betragen*); ˌ**in·cor'rect·ness** [-nɪs] *s.* **1.** Unrichtigkeit *f*; **2.** Unschicklichkeit *f*.

in·cor·ri·gi·bil·i·ty [ɪnˌkɒrɪdʒə'bɪlətɪ] *s.* Unverbesserlichkeit *f*; **in·cor·ri·gi·ble** [ɪn'kɒrɪdʒəbl] *adj.* ☐ unverbesserlich.

in·cor·rupt·i·bil·i·ty ['ɪnkəˌrʌptə'bɪlətɪ] *s.* **1.** Unbestechlichkeit *f*; **2.** Unverderblichkeit *f*; **in·cor·rupt·i·ble** [ˌɪnkə'rʌptəbl] *adj.* ☐ **1.** unbestechlich, redlich; **2.** unverderblich, unvergänglich; **in·cor·rup·tion** ['ɪnkəˌrʌpʃn] *s.* **1.** Unbestechlichkeit *f*; **2.** Unverdorbenheit *f*; **3.** *bibl.* Unvergänglichkeit *f*.

in·crease [ɪn'kri:s] **I** *v/i.* **1.** zunehmen, sich vermehren, größer werden, (an-) wachsen: ~ ***in size*** an Größe zunehmen; ~***d demand*** Mehrbedarf *m*; **2.** steigen (*Preise*); sich steigern *od.* vergrößern *od.* verstärken *od.* erhöhen; **II** *v/t.* **3.** vergrößern, verstärken, vermehren, erhöhen, steigern: ~ ***tenfold*** verzehnfachen; **III** *s.* ['ɪnkri:s] **4.** Vergrößerung *f*, Vermehrung *f*, Verstärkung *f*, Erhöhung *f*, Zunahme *f*, (An)Wachsen *n*, Zuwachs *m*, Wachstum *n*, Steigen *n*, Steigerung *f*, Erhöhung *f*: ***be on the*** ~ zunehmen, wachsen; ~ ***in wages*** † Lohnerhöhung *f*, -steigerung *f*; ~ ***of trade*** Zunahme *od.* Aufschwung *m* des Handels; **5.** Ertrag *m*, Gewinn *m*; **in'creas·ing·ly** [-sɪŋlɪ] *adv.* immer mehr: ~ ***clear*** immer klarer.

in·cred·i·bil·i·ty [ɪnˌkredɪ'bɪlətɪ] *s.* **1.** Unglaubhaftigkeit *f*; **2.** Un'glaublichkeit *f*; **in·cred·i·ble** [ɪn'kredəbl] *adj.* ☐ **1.** unglaublich, unvor'stellbar (*a. fig.*

unerhört, äußerst); **2.** unglaubhaft.

in·cre·du·li·ty [ˌɪnkrɪˈdjuːlətɪ] *s.* Ungläubigkeit *f*; **in·cred·u·lous** [ɪnˈkredjʊləs] *adj.* ☐ ungläubig.

in·cre·ment [ˈɪnkrɪmənt] *s.* **1.** Zuwachs *m*, Zunahme *f*; **2.** ✝ (Gewinn-, Wert-) Zuwachs *m*, Mehrertrag *m*, -einnahme *f*; **3.** A̸ Zuwachs *m*, Inkreˈment *n*, *bsd.* positives Differentiˈal.

in·crim·i·nate [ɪnˈkrɪmɪneɪt] *v/t.* beschuldigen, belasten: **~ *o.s.*** sich (selbst) belasten; **inˈcrim·i·nat·ing** [-tɪŋ] *adj.* belastend; **in·crim·i·na·tion** [ɪnˌkrɪmɪˈneɪʃn] *s.* Beschuldigung *f*, Belastung *f*; **inˈcrim·i·na·to·ry** [-nətərɪ] → ***incriminating***.

in·crust [ɪnˈkrʌst] → ***encrust***.

in·crus·ta·tion [ˌɪnkrʌsˈteɪʃn] *s.* **1.** Verkrustung *f* (*a. fig.*); **2.** ⚙ a) Inkrustatiˈon *f*, Kruste *f*, b) Kesselstein(bildung *f*) *m*; **3.** Verkleidung *f*, Belag *m* (*Wand*); **4.** Einlegearbeit *f*.

in·cu·bate [ˈɪnkjʊbeɪt] **I** *v/t.* **1.** *Ei* ausbrüten (*a. künstlich*); **2.** *Bakterien* im Brutschrank züchten; **3.** *fig.* ausbrüten, aushecken; **II** *v/i.* **4.** brüten; **in·cu·ba·tion** [ˌɪnkjʊˈbeɪʃn] *s.* **1.** Ausbrütung *f*, Brüten *n*; **2.** ⚕ Inkubatiˈon *f*: **~ *period*** Inkubationszeit *f*; ˈ**in·cu·ba·tor** [-tə] *s.* a) ⚕ Brutkasten *m*, Inkuˈbator *m* (*für Babys*), b) Brutschrank *m* (*für Bakterien*), c) ˈBrutappaˌrat *m* (*für Küken, Eier*).

in·cu·bus [ˈɪŋkjʊbəs] *s.* **1.** ⚕ Alp(drücken *n*) *m*; **2.** *fig.* a) Alpdruck *m*, b) Schreckgespenst *n*.

in·cul·cate [ˈɪnkʌlkeɪt] *v/t.* einprägen, einschärfen, einimpfen (***on***, ***in s.o.*** j-m); **in·cul·ca·tion** [ˌɪnkʌlˈkeɪʃn] *s.* Einschärfung *f*.

in·cul·pate [ˈɪnkʌlpeɪt] *v/t.* **1.** an-, beschuldigen, anklagen; **2.** belasten; **in·cul·pa·tion** [ˌɪnkʌlˈpeɪʃn] *s.* **1.** An-, Beschuldigung *f*; **2.** Vorwurf *m*.

in·cult [ɪnˈkʌlt] *adj.* ˈunkultiˌviert, roh, grob.

in·cum·ben·cy [ɪnˈkʌmbənsɪ] *s.* **1.** a) Innehaben *n* e-s Amtes, b) Amtszeit *f*, c) Amt(sbereich *m*) *n*; **2.** *eccl. Brit.* (Besitz *m* e-r) Pfründe *f*; **3.** *fig.* Obliegenheit *f*; **inˈcum·bent** [-nt] **I** *adj.* ☐ **1.** obliegend: ***it is ~ upon him*** es ist s-e Pflicht; **2.** amtierend: ***the ~ mayor***; **II** *s.* **3.** Amtsinhaber(in); **4.** *eccl. Brit.* Pfründeninhaber *m*.

in·cu·nab·u·la [ˌɪnkjuːˈnæbjʊlə] *s. pl.* Inkuˈnabeln *pl.*, Wiegendrucke *pl.*

in·cur [ɪnˈkɜː] *v/t.* sich *et.* zuziehen; auf sich laden *od.* ziehen, geraten in (*acc.*): **~ *displeasure*** Mißfallen erregen; **~ *debts*** Schulden machen; **~ *losses*** Verluste erleiden; **~ *liabilities*** Verpflichtungen eingehen.

in·cur·a·bil·i·ty [ɪnˌkjʊərəˈbɪlətɪ] *s.* Unheilbarkeit *f*; **in·cur·a·ble** [ɪnˈkjʊərəbl] **I** *adj.* ☐ unheilbar; **II** *s.* unheilbar Kranke(r *m*) *f*.

in·cu·ri·ous [ɪnˈkjʊərɪəs] *adj.* ☐ **1.** nicht neugierig, gleichgültig, uninteressiert; **2.** ˈuninteresˌsant.

in·cur·sion [ɪnˈkɜːʃn] *s.* **1.** (feindlicher) Einfall, Raubzug *m*; **2.** Eindringen *n* (*a. fig.*); **3.** *fig.* Einbruch *m*, -griff *m*.

in·curve [ˌɪnˈkɜːv] *v/t.* (nach innen) krümmen, (ein)biegen.

in·debt·ed [ɪnˈdetɪd] *adj.* **1.** verschuldet; **2.** zu Dank verpflichtet: ***I am ~ to you for*** ich habe Ihnen zu danken für; **inˈdebt·ed·ness** [-nɪs] *s.* **1.** Verschuldung *f*, Schulden *pl.*; **2.** Dankesschuld *f*, Verpflichtung *f*.

in·de·cen·cy [ɪnˈdiːsnsɪ] *s.* **1.** Unanständigkeit *f*, Anstößigkeit *f*; **2.** Zote *f*; **inˈde·cent** [-nt] *adj.* ☐ **1.** unanständig, anstößig; *a.* ⚖ unsittlich, unzüchtig; **2.** ungebührlich: **~ *haste*** unziemliche Hast.

in·de·ci·pher·a·ble [ˌɪndɪˈsaɪfərəbl] *adj.* nicht zu entziffern(d).

in·de·ci·sion [ˌɪndɪˈsɪʒn] *s.* Unentschlossenheit *f*, Unschlüssigkeit *f*; ˌ**in·deˈci·sive** [-ˈsaɪsɪv] *adj.* ☐ **1.** nicht entscheidend: ***an ~ battle***; **2.** unentschlossen, unschlüssig, schwankend; **3.** unbestimmt.

in·de·clin·a·ble [ˌɪndɪˈklaɪnəbl] *adj. ling.* undeklinierbar.

in·dec·o·rous [ɪnˈdekərəs] *adj.* ☐ unschicklich, unanständig, ungehörig; **in·de·co·rum** [ˌɪndɪˈkɔːrəm] *s.* Unschicklichkeit *f*.

in·deed [ɪnˈdiːd] *adv.* **1.** in der Tat, tatsächlich, wirklich: ***it is very lovely ~*** es ist wirklich (sehr) hübsch; ***if ~*** wenn überhaupt; ***if ~ he were right*** falls er wirklich recht haben sollte; ***we think, ~ we know this is wrong*** wir glauben, ja wir wissen (sogar), daß dies falsch ist; **~ *I am quite sure*** ich bin (mir) sogar ganz sicher; ***yes, ~!*** ja tatsächlich! (→ 3); ***did you ~?*** tatsächlich?, ach wirklich?; ***you, ~!*** *iro.* ausgerechnet du!, Du? daß ich nicht lache!; ***what ~!*** *iro.* na, was wohl?; ***thank you very much ~!*** vielen herzlichen Dank!; ***this is ~ an exception*** das ist allerdings *od.* freilich e-e Ausnahme; **2.** zwar, wohl: ***it is ~ a good plan, but ...***; **3.** (*in Antworten*) *a.* ***yes ~*** a) allerdings(!), aber sicher(!), und ob(!), b) aber gern!, ja doch!, c) ach wirklich?, was Sie nicht sagen; **~ *you may not!*** aber ja nicht!, kommt nicht in Frage!

in·de·fat·i·ga·ble [ˌɪndɪˈfætɪgəbl] *adj.* ☐ unermüdlich.

in·de·fea·si·ble [ˌɪndɪˈfiːzəbl] *adj.* ☐ ⚖ unverletzlich, unantastbar.

in·de·fen·si·ble [ˌɪndɪˈfensəbl] *adj.* ☐ unhaltbar: a) ⚔ nicht zu verteidigen(d), b) *fig.* nicht zu rechtfertigen(d), unentschuldbar.

in·de·fin·a·ble [ˌɪndɪˈfaɪnəbl] *adj.* ☐ undefinierbar: a) unbestimmbar, b) unbestimmt.

in·def·i·nite [ɪnˈdefɪnət] *adj.* ☐ **1.** unbestimmt (*a. ling.*); **2.** unbegrenzt, unbeschränkt; **3.** unklar, undeutlich, ungenau; **inˈdef·i·nite·ly** [-lɪ] *adv.* **1.** auf unbestimmte Zeit; **2.** unbegrenzt; **inˈdef·i·nite·ness** [-nɪs] *s.* **1.** Unbestimmtheit *f*; **2.** Unbegrenztheit *f*.

in·del·i·ble [ɪnˈdeləbl] *adj.* ☐ unauslöschlich (*a. fig.*); untilgbar: **~ *ink*** Zeichen-, Kopiertinte *f*; **~ *pencil*** Tintenstift *m*.

in·del·i·ca·cy [ɪnˈdelɪkəsɪ] *s.* **1.** Unanständigkeit *f*, Unfeinheit *f*; **2.** Taktlosigkeit *f*; **inˈdel·i·cate** [-kət] *adj.* ☐ **1.** unanständig, unfein, derb; **2.** taktlos.

in·dem·ni·fi·ca·tion [ɪnˌdemnɪfɪˈkeɪʃn] *s.* **1.** ✝ a) → ***indemnity*** 1 a, b) Entschädigung *f*, Schadloshaltung *f*, Ersatzleistung *f*, c) → ***indemnity*** 1 c; **2.** ⚖ Sicherstellung *f* (*gegen Strafe*); **in·dem·ni·fy** [ɪnˈdemnɪfaɪ] *v/t.* **1.** entschädigen, schadlos halten (***for*** für); **2.** sicherstellen, sichern (***from***, ***against*** gegen); **3.** ⚖ *parl.* a) *j-m* Entlastung erteilen, b) *j-m* Straflosigkeit zusichern; **in·dem·ni·ty** [ɪnˈdemnətɪ] *s.* **1.** ✝ a) Sicherstellung *f* (*gegen Verlust od. Schaden*), Garanˈtie(versprechen *n*) *f*, b) → ***indemnification*** 1 b, c) Entschädigung(sbetrag *m*) *f*, Abfindung *f*: **~ *against liability*** Haftungsausschluß *m*; **~ *bond***, ***letter of ~*** Ausfallbürgschaft *f*; **~ *insurance*** Schadensversicherung *f*; → ***double indemnity***; **2.** ⚖, *parl.* Indemniˈtät *f*.

in·dent[1] [ɪnˈdent] **I** *v/t.* **1.** (ein-, aus-) kerben, auszacken: **~*ed coastline*** zerklüftete Küste; **2.** ⚙ (ver)zahnen; **3.** *typ. Zeile* einrücken; **4.** ⚖ *Vertrag* mit Doppel ausfertigen; **5.** ✝ *Waren* bestellen; **II** *v/i.* **6.** (***upon s.o. for s.th.***) (et. bei j-m) bestellen, (et. von j-m) anfordern; **III** *s.* [ˈɪndent] **7.** Kerbe *f*, Einschnitt *m*, Auszackung *f*; **8.** *typ.* Einzug *m*; **9.** ⚖ Vertragsurkunde *f*; **10.** ✝ (Auslands)Auftrag *m*; **11.** ⚔ *Brit.* Anforderung *f* (*von Vorräten*).

in·dent[2] **I** *v/t.* [ɪnˈdent] eindrücken, einprägen; **II** *s.* [ˈɪndent] Delle *f*, Vertiefung *f*.

in·den·ta·tion [ˌɪndenˈteɪʃn] *s.* **1.** Einschnitt *m*, Einkerbung *f*; Auszackung *f*, Zickzacklinie *f*; **2.** ⚙ Zahnung *f*; **3.** Einbuchtung *f*; Bucht *f*; **4.** *typ.* a) Einzug *m*, b) Absatz *m*; **5.** Vertiefung *f*, Delle *f*; **in·dent·ed** [ɪnˈdentɪd] *adj.* **1.** (aus)gezackt; **2.** ✝ vertraglich verpflichtet; **in·den·tion** [ɪnˈdenʃn] → ***indentation*** 1, 2, 4; **in·den·ture** [ɪnˈdentʃə] **I** *s.* **1.** Vertrag *m od.* Urkunde *f* (im Dupliˈkat); **2.** ✝, ⚖ Lehrvertrag *m*, -brief *m*: ***take up one's ~s*** ausgelernt haben; **3.** amtliche Liste; **4.** → ***indentation*** 1, 2; **II** *v/t.* **5.** ✝, ⚖ durch (*bsd.* Lehr)Vertrag binden, vertraglich verpflichten.

in·de·pend·ence [ˌɪndɪˈpendəns] *s.* **1.** Unabhängigkeit *f* (***on***, ***of*** von): ***Ⓢ Day*** *Am.* Unabhängigkeitstag *m* (*4. Juli*); **2.** Selbständigkeit *f*; **3.** hinreichendes Aus- *od.* Einkommen; ˌ**in·deˈpend·en·cy** [-sɪ] *s.* **1.** → ***independence***; **2.** unabhängiger Staat; **3.** Ⓢ → ***Congregationalism***; ˌ**in·deˈpend·ent** [-nt] **I** *adj.* ☐ **1.** unabhängig (***of*** von) (*a.* A̸, *ling.*), selbständig (*a. Person*): **~ *clause*** *ling.* Hauptsatz *m*; **2.** a) selbständig, -sicher, -bewußt, b) eigenmächtig, -ständig; **3.** *pol.* unabhängig (*Staat*), *Abgeordneter*: *a.* parˈteilos, *parl.* fraktiˈonslos; **4.** voneinˈander unabhängig: ***the various decisions were ~***; ***we arrived ~ly at the same results*** wir kamen unabhängig voneinander zu denselben Ergebnissen; **5.** finanziˈell unabhängig: **~ *gentleman***, ***man of ~ means*** Mann *m* mit Privateinkommen, Privatier *m*; **6.** eigen, Einzel...: **~ *axle*** ⚙ Schwingachse *f*; **~ *fire*** ⚔ Einzel-, Schützenfeuer *n*; **~ *suspension*** *mot.* Einzelaufhängung *f*; **II** *s.* **7.** Ⓢ *pol.* Unabhängige(r *m*) *f*, Parˈteilose(r *m*) *f*, *parl.* fraktiˈonsloser Abgeordneter; **8.** Ⓢ → ***Congregationalist***.

ˌ**in-ˈdepth** *adj.* tiefschürfend, eingehend: **~ *interview*** Tiefeninterview *n*, Intensivbefragung *f*.

in·de·scrib·a·ble [ˌɪndɪˈskraɪbəbl] *adj.* □ **1.** unbeschreiblich; **2.** unbestimmt, undefinierbar.

in·de·struct·i·bil·i·ty [ˈɪndɪˌstrʌktəˈbɪlətɪ] *s.* Unzerstörbarkeit *f*; **in·de·struct·i·ble** [ˌɪndɪˈstrʌktəbl] *adj.* □ unzerstörbar, (*a.* ✝) unverwüstlich.

in·de·ter·mi·na·ble [ˌɪndɪˈtɜːmɪnəbl] *adj.* □ unbestimmbar, nicht bestimmbar; ˌ**in·deˈter·mi·nate** [-nət] *adj.* □ **1.** unbestimmt (*a.* ⩘), unentschieden, ungewiß, nicht festgelegt; unklar, vage; **2.** → ***indeterminable***: ***of ~ sex***; ***~ sentence*** ⚖ (Freiheits)Strafe *f* von unbestimmter Dauer; **in·de·ter·mi·na·tion** [ˈɪndɪˌtɜːmɪˈneɪʃn] *s.* **1.** Unbestimmtheit *f*; **2.** Ungewißheit *f*; **3.** Unentschlossenheit *f*; ˌ**in·deˈter·min·ism** [-mɪnɪzəm] *s. phls.* Indetermiˈnismus *m*, Lehre *f* von der Willensfreiheit *f*.

in·dex [ˈɪndeks] **I** *pl.* ˈ**in·dex·es**, **in·di·ces** [ˈɪndɪsiːs] *s.* **1.** Inhalts-, Stichwortverzeichnis *n*, Taˈbelle *f*, (ˈSach)Reˌgister *n*, Index *m*; **2.** *a.* ***~ file*** Karˈtei *f*: ***~ card*** Karteikarte *f*; **3.** ⚙ a) (An)Zeiger *m*, b) (Einstell)Marke *f*, Strich *m*, c) Zunge *f* (*Waage*); **4.** *typ.* Hand(zeichen *n*) *f*; **5.** *fig.* a) (An)Zeichen *n* (***of*** für, von *od. gen.*), b) (***to***) Fingerzeig *m* (für), Hinweis *m* (auf *acc.*); **6.** *Statistik*: Indexziffer *f*, Vergleichs-, Meßzahl *f*, ✝ Index *m*: ***cost of living ~*** Lebenskosten-, Lebenshaltungsindex; ***share price ~*** Aktienindex; **7.** ⩘ a) Index *m*, Kennziffer *f*, b) Expoˈnent *m*: ***~ of refraction*** *phys.* Brechungsindex *od.* -exponent; **8.** *bsd. eccl.* Index *m* (*verbotener Bücher*); **9.** → ***index finger***; **II** *v/t.* **10.** mit e-m Inhaltsverzeichnis versehen; **11.** in ein Verzeichnis aufnehmen; **12.** *eccl.* auf den Index setzen; **13.** ⚙ a) *Revolverkopf etc.* schalten: ***~ing disc*** Schaltscheibe *f*, b) *in Maßeinheiten* einteilen; ***~ fin·ger*** *s.* Zeigefinger *m*; ˈ**~-linked** *adj.* indexgebunden: ***~ pension***; ***~ wage*** Indexlohn *m*; ***~ num·ber*** → ***index*** 6.

In·di·a| ink [ˈɪndjə] → ***Indian ink***; ˈ**~·man** [-mən] *s.* [*irr.*] (Ost)ˈIndienfahrer *m* (*Schiff*).

In·di·an [ˈɪndjən] **I** *adj.* **1.** (ost)ˈindisch; **2.** *bsd. Am.* indiˈanisch; **3.** *Am.* Mais…; **II** *s.* **4.** a) Inder(in), b) Ostˈindier(in); **5.** *bsd. Am.* Indiˈaner(in); ***~ club*** *s. sport* (Schwing)Keule *f*; ***~ corn*** *s.* Mais *m*; ***~ file*** *s.*: ***in ~*** im Gänsemarsch; ***~ giv·er*** *s. Am.* F *j-d, der s-e Geschenke zurückverlangt*; ***~ ink*** *s.* chiˈnesische Tusche; ***~ meal*** *s.* Maismehl *n*; ***~ pa·per*** → ***India paper***; ***~ summer*** *s.* Altˈweiber-, Spät-, Nachsommer *m*.

In·di·a| pa·per *s.* ˈDünndruckpaˌpier *n*; ˌ**~-ˈrub·ber** *s.* **1.** Kautschuk *m*, Gummi *n*, *m*: ***~ ball*** Gummiball *m*; ***~ tree***; **2.** Radiergummi *m*.

In·dic [ˈɪndɪk] *adj. ling.* indisch (*den indischen Zweig der indo-iranischen Sprachen betreffend*).

in·di·cate [ˈɪndɪkeɪt] *v/t.* **1.** anzeigen, angeben, bezeichnen, kennzeichnen; **2.** a) *Person*: andeuten, (an)zeigen, zu verstehen geben, b) *Sache*: hindeuten *od.* hinweisen auf (*acc.*), erkennen lassen (*acc.*), *a.* ⚙ anzeigen; **3.** ⚕ indizieren, erfordern: ***be ~d*** indiziert sein, *fig.* angezeigt *od.* angebracht sein; **in·di·ca·tion** [ˌɪndɪˈkeɪʃn] *s.* **1.** Anzeige *f*, Angabe *f*, Bezeichnung *f*; **2.** (***of***) a) (An-)Zeichen *n* (für), b) Hinweis *m* (auf *acc.*), c) (kurze) Andeutung: ***give ~ of*** *et.* anzeigen; ***there is every ~*** alles deutet darauf hin (***that*** daß); **3.** ⚕ a) Indikatiˈon *f*, b) Symˈptom *n* (*a. fig.*); **4.** ⚙ a) Anzeige *f*, b) Grad *m*, Stand *m*; **in·dic·a·tive** [ɪnˈdɪkətɪv] **I** *adj.* □ **1.** anzeigend, andeutend, hinweisend: ***be ~ of*** → ***indicate*** 2; **2.** *ling.* ˈindikaˌtivisch: ***~ mood*** → 3; **II** *s.* **3.** *ling.* Indikativ *m*, Wirklichkeitsform *f*; ˈ**in·di·ca·tor** [-tə] *s.* **1.** Anzeiger *m*; **2.** ⚙ a) Zeiger *m*, b) Anzeiger *m*, Anzeige- *od.* Ablesegerät *n*, Zähler *m*, (Leistungs)Messer *m*, c) Schauzeichen *n*, d) *mot.* Richtungsanzeiger *m*, e) *a.* ***~ telegraph*** ˈZeigerteleˌgraph *m*; **3.** ⚗ Indiˈkator *m*; **4.** *fig.* → ***index*** 5 *u.* 6; **in·dic·a·to·ry** [ɪnˈdɪkətərɪ] → ***indicative*** 1.

in·di·ces [ˈɪndɪsiːz] *pl. von* ***index***.

in·di·ci·um [ɪnˈdɪʃɪəm] *pl.* **-ci·a** [-ʃɪə] *s.* ✉ *Am.* aufgedruckter Freimachungsvermerk.

in·dict [ɪnˈdaɪt] *v/t.* ⚖ anklagen (***for*** wegen); **inˈdict·a·ble** [-təbl] *adj.* ⚖ strafrechtlich verfolgbar: ***~ offence*** schwurgerichtlich abzuurteilende Straftat, Verbrechen *n*; **inˈdict·ment** [-mənt] **1.** (forˈmelle) Anklage (*vor e-m Geschworenengericht*); **2.** a) Anklagebeschluß *m* (*der* ***grand jury***), b) (*Am. a.* ***bill of ~***) Anklageschrift *f*.

in·dif·fer·ence [ɪnˈdɪfrəns] *s.* **1.** (***to***) Gleichgültigkeit *f* (gegen), Interˈesselosigkeit *f* (gegenˈüber); **2.** Unwichtigkeit *f*: ***it is a matter of complete ~ to me*** das ist mir völlig gleichgültig; **3.** Mittelmäßigkeit *f*; **4.** Unwichtigkeit *f*; **inˈdif·fer·ent** [-nt] *adj.* □ **1.** (***to***) gleichgültig (gegen), interˈesselos (gegenˈüber); **2.** ˈunparˌteiisch; **3.** mittelmäßig, leidlich: ***~ quality***; **4.** mäßig, nicht besonders gut: ***a very ~ cook***; **5.** unwichtig; **6.** ⚕, ⚗, *phys.* neuˈtral, indiffeˈrent; **inˈdif·fer·ent·ism** [-ntɪzəm] *s.* (Neigung *f* zur) Gleichgültigkeit *f*.

in·di·gence [ˈɪndɪdʒəns] *s.* Armut *f*, Mittellosigkeit *f*.

in·di·gene [ˈɪndɪdʒiːn] *s.* **1.** Eingeborene(r *m*) *f*; **2.** a) einheimisches Tier, b) einheimische Pflanze; **in·dig·e·nize** [ɪnˈdɪdʒɪnaɪz] *v/t. Am.* **1.** *a. fig.* heimisch machen, einbürgern; **2.** (nur) mit einheimischem Persoˈnal besetzen; **in·dig·e·nous** [ɪnˈdɪdʒɪnəs] *adj.* □ **1.** *a.* ⚘, *zo.* einheimisch (***to*** in *dat.*); **2.** *fig.* angeboren (***to*** *dat.*).

in·di·gent [ˈɪndɪdʒənt] *adj.* □ arm, bedürftig, mittellos.

in·di·gest·ed [ˌɪndɪˈdʒestɪd] *adj. mst fig.* unverdaut; wirr; ˈundurchˌdacht; **in·di·gest·i·bil·i·ty** [ˈɪndɪˌdʒestəˈbɪlətɪ] *s.* Unverdaulichkeit *f*; ˌ**in·diˈgest·i·ble** [-təbl] *adj.* □ unverdaulich (*a. fig.*); ˌ**in·diˈges·tion** [-tʃn] *s.* ⚕ Magenverstimmung *f*, verdorbener Magen.

in·dig·nant [ɪnˈdɪgnənt] *adj.* □ (***at***, ***with***) entrüstet, ungehalten, empört (über *acc.*), peinlich berührt (von); **in·dig·na·tion** [ˌɪndɪgˈneɪʃn] *s.* Entrüstung *f*, Unwille *m*, Empörung *f* (***at*** über *acc.*): ***~ meeting*** Protestkundgebung *f*.

in·dig·ni·ty [ɪnˈdɪgnətɪ] *s.* Schmach *f*, Demütigung *f*, Kränkung *f*.

in·di·go [ˈɪndɪgəʊ] *pl.* **-gos** *s.* Indigo *m*: ***~-blue*** indigoblau; **in·di·got·ic** [ˌɪndɪˈgɒtɪk] *adj.* Indigo…

in·di·rect [ˌɪndɪˈrekt] *adj.* □ **1.** ˈindiˌrekt: ***~ lighting***; ***~ tax***; ***~ cost*** ✝ Gemeinkosten *pl.*; **2.** nicht diˈrekt *od.* gerade: ***~ route*** Umweg *m*; ***~ means*** Umwege, Umschweife; **3.** *fig.* krumm, unredlich; **4.** *ling.* ˈindiˌrekt, abhängig: ***~ object*** indirektes Objekt, Dativobjekt *n*; ***~ question*** indirekte Frage; ***~ speech*** indirekte Rede; **in·di·rec·tion** [ˌɪndɪˈrekʃn] *s.* **1.** ˈUmweg *m* (*a. fig. b.s. unlautere Methode*): ***by ~*** a) indirekt, auf Umwegen, b) *fig.* hinten herum, unehrlich; **2.** Unehrlichkeit *f*; **3.** Anspielung *f*; ˌ**in·diˈrect·ness** [-nɪs] *s.* **1.** ˈindiˌrekte Art u. Weise; **2.** → ***indirection***.

in·dis·cern·i·ble [ˌɪndɪˈsɜːnəbl] *adj.* nicht wahrnehmbar, unmerklich.

in·dis·ci·pline [ɪnˈdɪsɪplɪn] *s.* Disziˈplin-, Zuchtlosigkeit *f*.

in·dis·cov·er·a·ble [ˌɪndɪˈskʌvərəbl] *adj.* □ nicht zu entdecken(d).

in·dis·creet [ˌɪndɪˈskriːt] *adj.* □ **1.** ˈindisˌkret; **2.** taktlos; **3.** ˈunüberˌlegt.

in·dis·crete [ˌɪndɪˈskriːt] *adj.* homoˈgen, komˈpakt, zs.-hängend.

in·dis·cre·tion [ˌɪndɪˈskreʃn] *s.* **1.** Indiskretiˈon *f*; **2.** Taktlosigkeit *f*; **3.** ˈUnüberˌlegtheit *f*.

in·dis·crim·i·nate [ˌɪndɪˈskrɪmɪnət] *adj.* □ **1.** wahllos, blind, ˈunterschiedslos; **2.** kriˈtiklos, unkritisch; **3.** willkürlich; **in·dis·crim·i·na·tion** [ˈɪndɪˌskrɪmɪˈneɪʃn] *s.* **1.** Wahl-, Kriˈtiklosigkeit *f*, Mangel *m* an Urteilskraft; **2.** ˈUnterschiedslosigkeit *f*.

in·dis·pen·sa·bil·i·ty [ˈɪndɪˌspensəˈbɪlətɪ] *s.* Unerläßlichkeit *f*, Unentbehrlichkeit *f*; **in·dis·pen·sa·ble** [ˌɪndɪˈspensəbl] *adj.* □ **1.** unerläßlich, unentbehrlich (***for***, ***to*** für); **2.** ⚔ unabkömmlich; **3.** unbedingt einzuhalten(d) *od.* zu erfüllen(d) (*Pflicht etc.*).

in·dis·pose [ˌɪndɪˈspəʊz] *v/t.* **1.** untauglich machen (***for*** zu); **2.** unpäßlich machen, indisponieren; **3.** abgeneigt machen (***to do*** zu tun), einnehmen (***towards*** gegen); ˌ**in·disˈposed** [-zd] *adj.* **1.** indisponiert, unpäßlich; **2.** (***towards***, ***from***) a) nicht aufgelegt (zu), abgeneigt (*dat.*), b) eingenommen (gegen), abgeneigt (*dat.*); **in·dis·po·si·tion** [ˌɪndɪspəˈzɪʃn] *s.* **1.** Unpäßlichkeit *f*; **2.** Abneigung *f*, ˈWiderwille *m* (***to***, ***towards*** gegen).

in·dis·pu·ta·bil·i·ty [ˈɪndɪˌspjuːtəˈbɪlətɪ] *s.* Unbestreitbarkeit *f*, Unstrittigkeit *f*; **in·dis·pu·ta·ble** [ˌɪndɪˈspjuːtəbl] *adj.* □ **1.** unbestreitbar, unstrittig, nicht zu bestreiten(d); **2.** unbestritten.

in·dis·sol·u·bil·i·ty [ˈɪndɪˌsɒljʊˈbɪlətɪ] *s.* Unauflösbarkeit *f*; **in·dis·sol·u·ble** [ˌɪndɪˈsɒljʊbl] *adj.* □ **1.** unauflösbar, -lich; **2.** unzertrennlich; **3.** ⚗ unlöslich.

in·dis·tinct [ˌɪndɪˈstɪŋkt] *adj.* □ **1.** undeutlich; **2.** unklar, verworren, verschwommen; ˌ**in·disˈtinc·tive** [-tɪv] *adj.* □ ausdruckslos, nichtssagend; ˌ**in·disˈtinct·ness** [-nɪs] *s.* Undeutlichkeit *f etc.*

in·dis·tin·guish·a·ble [ˌɪndɪˈstɪŋgwɪʃəbl] *adj.* □ **1.** nicht zu unterˈscheiden(d) (***from*** von); **2.** nicht wahrnehmbar *od.* erkennbar; **3.** unmerklich.

in·dite [ɪnˈdaɪt] *v/t.* ver-, abfassen.

in·di·vid·u·al [ˌɪndɪˈvɪdjʊəl] **I** *adj.* □ → ***individually***; **1.** einzeln, Einzel…: ***each ~ word***; ***~ case*** Einzelfall *m*; ***~ consumer*** Einzelverbraucher *m*; ***~ drive*** ⚙ Einzelantrieb *m*; **2.** für ˈeine Perˈson bestimmt, eigen, perˈsönlich, einzel: ***~ credit*** Personalkredit *m*; ***~ property*** Privatvermögen *n*; ***~ psychology*** Individualpsychologie *f*; ***~ traffic*** Individualverkehr *m*; ***give ~ attention to*** individuell behandeln, s-e persönliche Aufmerksamkeit schenken (*dat.*); **3.** individuˈell, perˈsönlich, eigen(tümlich), charakteˈristisch: ***an ~ style***; **4.** verschieden: ***five ~ cups***; **II** *s.* **5.** ˈEinzelperˌson *f*, Indiˈviduum *n*, Einzelne(r) *m*; **6.** *mst contp.* Perˈson *f*, Indiˈviduum *n*; **7.** ⚖ naˈtürliche Perˈson *f*; ˌ**in·diˈvid·u·al·ism** [-lɪzəm] *s.* **1.** Individuaˈlismus *m*; **2.** Egoˈismus *m*; ˌ**in·diˈvid·u·al·ist** [-lɪst] **I** *s.* Individuaˈlist(in); **II** *adj.* → **in·di·vid·u·al·is·tic** [ˈɪndɪˌvɪdjʊəˈlɪstɪk] *adj.* (□ ***~ally***) individuaˈlistisch; **in·di·vid·u·al·i·ty** [ˈɪndɪˌvɪdjʊˈælətɪ] *s.* **1.** Individualiˈtät *f*, (perˈsönliche) Eigenart; **2.** *phls.* individuˈelle Exiˈstenz; **3.** → ***individual*** 5; **in·di·vid·u·al·i·za·tion** [ˈɪndɪˌvɪdjʊəlaɪˈzeɪʃn] *s.* **1.** Individualisierung *f*; **2.** Einzelbetrachtung *f*; ˌ**in·diˈvid·u·al·ize** [-laɪz] *v/t.* **1.** individualisieren, individuˈell gestalten *od.* behandeln, e-e individuˈelle *od.* eigene Note verleihen (*dat.*); **2.** einzeln betrachten; ˌ**in·diˈvid·u·al·ly** [-əlɪ] *adv.* **1.** einzeln, (jeder, jede, jedes) für sich; **2.** einzeln betrachtet, für sich genommen; **3.** perˈsönlich; ˌ**in·diˈvid·u·ate** [-jʊeɪt] *v/t.* **1.** → ***individualize*** 1; **2.** charakterisieren; **3.** unterˈscheiden (***from*** von).

in·di·vis·i·bil·i·ty [ˈɪndɪˌvɪzɪˈbɪlətɪ] *s.* Unteilbarkeit *f*; **in·di·vis·i·ble** [ˌɪndɪˈvɪzəbl] **I** *adj.* □ unteilbar; **II** *s.* ⩚ unteilbare Größe.

In·do-Chi·nese [ˌɪndəʊtʃaɪˈniːz] *adj.* indochiˈnesisch, ˈhinterindisch.

in·doc·ile [ɪnˈdəʊsaɪl] *adj.* **1.** ungelehrig; **2.** störrisch, unlenksam; **in·do·cil·i·ty** [ˌɪndəʊˈsɪlətɪ] *s.* **1.** Ungelehrigkeit *f*; **2.** Unlenksamkeit *f*.

in·doc·tri·nate [ɪnˈdɒktrɪneɪt] *v/t.* **1.** unterˈweisen, schulen (***in*** in *dat.*); *pol.* indoktrinieren; **2.** *j-m et.* einprägen, -bleuen, -impfen; **3.** durchˈdringen (***with*** mit); **in·doc·tri·na·tion** [ɪnˌdɒktrɪˈneɪʃn] *s.* Unterˈweisung *f*, Belehrung *f*, Schulung *f*; *pol.* Indoktrinatiˈon *f*, poˈlitische Schulung, ideoˈlogischer Drill; **inˈdoc·tri·na·tor** [-tə] *s.* Lehrer *m*, Instrukˈteur *m*.

ˈ**In·do|-ˌEu·roˈpe·an** [ˌɪndəʊ-] *ling.* **I** *adj.* **1.** ˈindogerˈmanisch; **II** *s.* **2.** *ling.* ˈIndogerˈmanisch *n*; **3.** ˈIndogerˈmane *m*, -gerˈmanin *f*; ˌ**~-Gerˈman·ic** → ***Indo-European*** 1 *u.* 2; ˌ**~-Iˈra·ni·an** *ling.* **I** *adj.* ˈindoiˈranisch, arisch; **II** *s.* ˈIndoiˈranisch *n*, Arisch *n*.

in·do·lence [ˈɪndələns] *s.* Indoˈlenz *f*: a) Trägheit *f*, b) Lässigkeit *f*, c) ⚕ Schmerzlosigkeit *f*; ˈ**in·do·lent** [-nt] *adj.* □ indoˈlent: a) träge, b) lässig, c) ⚕ schmerzlos.

in·dom·i·ta·ble [ɪnˈdɒmɪtəbl] *adj.* □ **1.** unbezähmbar, nicht ˈunterzukriegen(d); **2.** unbeugsam.

In·do·ne·sian [ˌɪndəʊˈniːzjən] **I** *adj.* indoˈnesisch; **II** *s.* Indoˈnesier(in).

in·door [ˈɪndɔː] *adj.* im *od.* zu Hause, Haus…, Zimmer…, Innen…, *sport* Hallen…: ***~ aerial*** ⚡ Zimmer-, Innenantenne *f*; ***~ dress*** Hauskleid(ung *f*) *n*; ***~ games*** a) Spiele fürs Haus, b) *sport* Hallenspiele; ***~ swimming pool*** Hallenbad *n*; **in·doors** [ˌɪnˈdɔːz] *adv.* **1.** im *od.* zu Hause, drin(nen); **2.** ins Haus.

in·dorse [ɪnˈdɔːs] *etc.* → ***endorse*** *etc.*

in·du·bi·ta·ble [ɪnˈdjuːbɪtəbl] *adj.* □ unzweifelhaft, zweifellos.

in·duce [ɪnˈdjuːs] *v/t.* **1.** *j-n* veranlassen, bewegen, (dazu) bringen, überˈreden (***to do*** zu tun); **2.** herˈbeiführen, verursachen, bewirken, herˈvorrufen, führen zu: ***~ a birth*** ⚕ e-e Geburt einleiten; ***~d sleep*** künstlicher Schlaf; **3.** ⚡ *Kernphysik, a. Logik*: induzieren: ***~ current*** Induktionsstrom *m*; **inˈduce·ment** [-mənt] *s.* **1.** a) Veranlassung *f*, Überˈredung *f*, b) Verleitung (***to*** zu); **2.** Anlaß *m*, Beweggrund *m*; **3.** *a.* ✝ Anreiz *m* (***to*** zu); **4.** Herˈbeiführung *f*.

in·duct [ɪnˈdʌkt] *v/t.* **1.** *in ein Amt etc.* einführen, -setzen; **2.** *j-n* einweihen (***to*** in *acc.*); **3.** ⚔ *Am. zum Militär* einberufen; **inˈduct·ance** [-təns] *s.* ⚡ **1.** Indukˈtanz *f*, indukˈtiver (ˈSchein)ˌWiderstand; **2.** ˈSelbstinduktiˌon *f*: ***~ coil*** Drosselspule *f*; **in·duc·tee** [ˌɪndʌkˈtiː] *s.* ⚔ *Am.* Einberufene(r) *m*, Reˈkrut *m*; **inˈduc·tion** [-kʃn] *s.* **1.** Einführung, -setzung *f* (*in ein Amt*); **2.** ⚙ Zuführung *f*, Einlaß *m*: ***~ pipe*** Einlaßrohr *n*; **3.** Herˈbeiführung *f*, Auslösung *f*; **4.** Einleitung *f*, Beginn *m*; **5.** ⚔ *Am.* Einberufung *f*: ***~ order*** Einberufungsbefehl *m*; **6.** Anführung *f* (*Beweise etc.*); **7.** ⚡ Induktiˈon *f*, sekunˈdäre Erregung: ***~ coil*** (***current***) Induktionsspule *f* (-strom *m*); ***~ motor*** Induktions-, Drehstrommotor *m*; **8.** ⩚, *phys.*, *phls.* Induktiˈon *f*: ***~ accelerator*** Elektronenbeschleuniger *m*; **inˈduc·tive** [-tɪv] *adj.* □ **1.** ⚡, *phys.*, *phls.* indukˈtiv, Induktions…; **2.** ⚕ e-e Reaktiˈon herˈvorrufend; **inˈduc·tor** [-tə] *s.* ⚡, *biol.* Inˈduktor *m*.

in·dulge [ɪnˈdʌldʒ] **I** *v/t.* **1.** *e-r Neigung etc.* nachgeben, frönen, sich hingeben, freien Lauf lassen; **2.** nachsichtig sein gegen: ***~ s.o. in s.th.*** j-m et. nachsehen; **3.** *j-m* nachgeben (***in*** in *dat.*): ***~ o.s. in*** → 7; **4.** *j-m* gefällig sein; **5.** *j-n* verwöhnen; **II** *v/i.* **6.** sich hingeben, frönen (***in*** *dat.*); **7.** ***~ in*** sich *et.* gönnen *od.* genehmigen *od.* leisten, *a.* sich gütlich tun an (*dat.*), *et.* essen *od.* trinken; **8.** F a) sich ‚einen genehmigen', b) sich e-e Zigarette *etc.* gönnen *od.* ‚genehmigen'; **inˈdul·gence** [-dʒəns] *s.* **1.** Nachsicht *f*, Milde *f* (***to***, ***of*** gegenüber); **2.** Nachgiebigkeit *f*; **3.** Gefälligkeit *f*; **4.** Verwöhnung *f*; **5.** Befriedigung *f* (*e-r Begierde etc.*); **6.** (***in***) Frönen *n* (*dat.*), Schwelgen *n* (in *dat.*), Genießen *n* (*gen.*): (***excessive***) ***~ in drink*** übermäßiger Alkoholgenuß; **7.** Wohlleben *n*, Genußsucht *f*; **8.** Schwäche *f*, Leidenschaft *f* (***of*** für); **9.** *R.C.* Ablaß *m*: ***sale of ~s*** Ablaßhandel *m*; **inˈdul·genced** [-dʒənst] *adj.*: ***~ prayer*** *R.C.* Ablaßgebet *n*; **inˈdul·gent** [-dʒənt] *adj.* □ (***to***) nachsichtig, mild (gegen); schonend, sanft (mit).

in·du·rate [ˈɪndjʊəreɪt] **I** *v/t.* **1.** (ver)härten, hart machen; **2.** *fig.* a) abstumpfen, b) abhärten (***against***, ***to*** gegen); **II** *v/i.* **3.** sich verhärten: a) hart werden, b) *fig.* gefühllos werden, abstumpfen; **4.** abgehärtet werden; **in·du·ra·tion** [ˌɪndjʊəˈreɪʃn] *s.* **1.** (Ver)Härtung *f*; **2.** *fig.* Abstumpfung *f*; **3.** Verstocktheit *f*.

in·dus·tri·al [ɪnˈdʌstrɪəl] **I** *adj.* □ **1.** industriˈell, gewerblich, Industrie…, Fabrik…, Gewerbe…, Wirtschafts…, Betriebs…, Werks…: ***~ accident*** Betriebsunfall *m*; ***~ waste*** Industrieabfälle *pl.*; **II** *s.* **2.** Industriˈelle(r) *m*; **3.** *pl.* Induˈstrieaktien *pl.*, -paˌpiere *pl.*; ***~ action*** *s.* Arbeitskampf(maßnahmen *pl.*) *m*; ***~ a·re·a*** *s.* Induˈstriegebiet *n*, -gelände *n*; ***~ de·sign*** *s.* Induˈstriedeˌsign *n*; ***~ de·sign·er*** *s.* Induˈstriedeˌsigner *m*; ***~ dis·pute*** *s.* Arbeitsstreitigkeit *f*; ***~ en·gi·neer·ing*** *s.* Inˈdustrial engiˈneering *n* (*Rationalisierung von Arbeitsprozessen*); ***~ es·pi·o·nage*** *s.* ˈWerk-, Induˈstriespioˌnage *f*; ***~ es·tate*** *s.* *Brit.* Induˈstriegebiet *n*; ***~ goods*** *s. pl.* Induˈstrieproˌdukte *pl.*, Investitiˈonsgüter *pl.*; ***~ in·ju·ry*** *s.* a) Berufsschaden *m*, b) Arbeitsunfall *m*.

in·dus·tri·al·ism [ɪnˈdʌstrɪəlɪzəm] *s.* Industriaˈlismus *m*; **inˈdus·tri·al·ist** [-ɪst] → ***industrial*** 2; **inˈdus·tri·al·i·za·tion** [ɪnˌdʌstrɪəlaɪˈzeɪʃn] *s.* Industrialisierung *f*; **inˈdus·tri·al·ize** [-aɪz] *v/t.* industrialisieren.

in·dus·tri·al| man·age·ment *s.* Betriebsführung *f*; ***~ med·i·cine*** *s.* Beˈtriebsmediˌzin *f*; ***~ na·tion*** *s.* Induˈstriestaat *m*; ***~ park*** *s. Am.* Induˈstriegebiet *n* (*e-r Stadt*); ***~ part·ner·ship*** *s.* ✝ *Am.* Gewinnbeteiligung *f* der Arbeitnehmer; ***~ prop·er·ty*** *s.* gewerbliches Eigentum; ***~ psy·chol·o·gy*** *s.* Beˈtriebspsychologˌgie *f*; ***~ re·la·tions*** *s. pl.* Beziehungen *pl.* zwischen Arbeitgeber u. Arbeitnehmern *od.* Gewerkschaften; ***~ re·la·tions court*** *s. Am.* Arbeitsgericht *n*; ***⁀ Rev·o·lu·tion*** *s.* *die* industriˈelle Revolutiˈon; ***~ school*** *s.* *Brit.* Gewerbeschule *f*; ***~ stocks*** *s. pl.* Induˈstriepaˌpiere *pl.*; ***~ town*** *s.* Induˈstriestadt *f*; ***~ tri·bu·nal*** *s.* Arbeitsgericht *n*.

in·dus·tri·ous [ɪnˈdʌstrɪəs] *adj.* □ fleißig, arbeitsam, emsig.

in·dus·try [ˈɪndəstrɪ] *s.* **1.** a) Induˈstrie *f* (*e-s Landes etc.*), b) Induˈstrie(zweig *m*) *f*, Gewerbe(zweig *m*) *n*, Branche *f*: ***the steel ~*** die Stahlindustrie; ***tourist ~*** Touˈristik *f*, Fremdenverkehrswesen *n*; **2.** Unterˈnehmer(schaft *f*) *pl.*, Arbeitgeber *pl.*; **3.** Fleiß *m*, Arbeitseifer *m*.

in·dwell [ˌɪnˈdwel] [*irr.* → ***dwell***] **I** *v/t.* **1.** bewohnen; **II** *v/i.* (***in***) **2.** wohnen (in *dat.*); **3.** *fig.* innewohnen (*dat.*); **in·dwell·er** [ˈɪnˌdwelə] *s. poet.* Bewohner(in).

in·e·bri·ate **I** *v/t.* [ɪˈniːbrɪeɪt] **1.** betrunken machen; **2.** *fig.* berauschen, trunken machen: ***~d by success*** vom Erfolg berauscht; **II** *s.* [-ɪət] **3.** Betrunkene(r) *m*; **4.** Alkoˈholiker(in); **III** *adj.* [-ɪət] **5.** betrunken; **6.** *fig.* berauscht; **in·e·bri·a·tion** [ɪˌniːbrɪˈeɪʃn], **in·e·bri·e·ty** [ˌɪniːˈbraɪətɪ] *s.* Trunkenheit *f* (*a. fig.*), betrunkener Zustand.

in·ed·i·bil·i·ty [ɪnˌedɪˈbɪlətɪ] *s.* Ungenießbarkeit *f*; **in·ed·i·ble** [ɪnˈedɪbl] *adj.* ungenießbar, nicht eßbar.

in·ed·it·ed [ɪnˈedɪtɪd] *adj.* **1.** unveröffentlicht; **2.** ohne Veränderungen her'ausgegeben, nicht redigiert.

in·ef·fa·ble [ɪn'efəbl] *adj.* □ **1.** unaussprechlich, unbeschreiblich; **2.** (unsagbar) erhaben.

in·ef·face·a·ble [ˌɪnɪ'feɪsəbl] *adj.* □ unauslöschlich.

in·ef·fec·tive [ˌɪnɪ'fektɪv] *adj.* □ **1.** unwirksam (*a.* ⚖), wirkungslos; **2.** frucht-, erfolglos; **3.** unfähig, untauglich; **4.** (*bsd. künstlerisch*) nicht wirkungsvoll; ˌ**in·ef'fec·tive·ness** [-nɪs] *s.* **1.** Wirkungslosigkeit *f*; **2.** Erfolglosigkeit *f.*

in·ef·fec·tu·al [ˌɪnɪ'fektjʊəl] *adj.* □ **1.** → ***ineffective*** 1 *u.* 2; **2.** kraftlos; ˌ**in·ef'fec·tu·al·ness** [-nɪs] *s.* **1.** → ***ineffectiveness***; **2.** Nutzlosigkeit *f*; **3.** Schwäche *f.*

in·ef·fi·ca·cious [ˌɪnefɪ'keɪʃəs] → ***ineffective*** 1, 2; **in·ef·fi·ca·cy** [ɪn'efɪkəsɪ] → ***ineffectiveness***.

in·ef·fi·cien·cy [ˌɪnɪ'fɪʃnsɪ] *s.* **1.** Wirkungslosigkeit *f*, 'Ineffiziˌenz *f*: ~ ***of a remedy***; **2.** Unfähigkeit *f*, Inkompe'tenz *f*, Leistungsschwäche *f* (*e-r Person*); **3.** 'unratioˌnelles Arbeiten *etc.*, Unwirtschaftlichkeit *f*, 'Unproduktiviˌtät *f*, 'Ineffiziˌenz *f*: ~ ***of a method***; ˌ**in·ef'fi·cient** [-nt] *adj.* □ **1.** unwirksam, wirkungslos, 'ineffiziˌent; **2.** unfähig, untauglich, untüchtig, 'inkompeˌtent; **3.** 'ineffiziˌent: a) leistungsschwach, b) 'unratioˌnell, 'unprodukˌtiv.

in·e·las·tic [ˌɪnɪ'læstɪk] *adj.* **1.** 'uneˌlastisch (*a. fig.*); **2.** *fig.* starr, nicht fle'xibel; **in·e·las·tic·i·ty** [ˌɪnɪlæs'tɪsətɪ] *s.* **1.** Mangel *m* an Elastizi'tät; **2.** *fig.* Starrheit *f*, Mangel *m* an Flexibili'tät.

in·el·e·gance [ɪn'elɪgəns] *s.* **1.** 'Uneleˌganz *f*, Mangel *m* an Ele'ganz (*a. fig.*); **2.** *fig.* a) Derbheit *f*, Geschmacklosigkeit *f*, b) Unbeholfenheit *f*; **in'el·e·gant** [-nt] *adj.* □ **1.** 'uneleˌgant, ohne Ele'ganz (*a. fig.*); **2.** *fig.* a) derb, geschmacklos, b) unbeholfen, plump.

in·el·i·gi·bil·i·ty [ɪnˌelɪdʒə'bɪlətɪ] *s.* **1.** Untauglichkeit *f*, mangelnde Eignung; **2.** Unwählbarkeit *f*, Unfähigkeit *f* (in ein Amt gewählt zu werden *etc.*); **3.** mangelnde Berechtigung; **in·el·i·gi·ble** [ɪn'elɪdʒəbl] **I** *adj.* □ **1.** ungeeignet, nicht in Frage kommend (***for*** für): ~ ***for military service*** (wehr)untauglich; **2.** unwählbar; **3.** ⚖ unfähig, nicht qualifiziert: ~ ***to hold an office***; **4.** (***for***) nicht berechtigt (zu), keinen Anspruch habend (auf *acc.*): ~ ***for a grant***; ~ ***to vote*** nicht wahlberechtigt; **5.** a) unerwünscht, b) unpassend; **II** *s.* **6.** ungeeignete *od.* nicht in Frage kommende Per'son.

in·e·luc·ta·ble [ˌɪnɪ'lʌktəbl] *adj.* unvermeidlich, unentrinnbar.

in·ept [ɪ'nept] *adj.* □ **1.** unpassend; **2.** ungeschickt; **3.** albern, dumm; **in'ept·i·tude** [-tɪtju:d], **in'ept·ness** [-nɪs] *s.* **1.** Ungeeignetheit *f*; **2.** Ungeschicktheit *f*; **3.** Albernheit *f*, Dummheit *f.*

in·e·qual·i·ty [ˌɪnɪ'kwɒlətɪ] *s.* **1.** Ungleichheit *f* (*a.* A, *sociol.*), Verschiedenheit *f*; **2.** Ungleichmäßigkeit *f*, Unregelmäßigkeit *f*; **3.** Unebenheit *f* (*a. fig.*); **4.** *ast.* Abweichung *f.*

in·eq·ui·ta·ble [ɪn'ekwɪtəbl] *adj.* □ ungerecht, unbillig; **in'eq·ui·ty** [-kwətɪ] *s.* Ungerechtigkeit *f*, Unbilligkeit *f.*

in·e·rad·i·ca·ble [ˌɪnɪ'rædɪkəbl] *adj.* □ *fig.* unausrottbar; tiefsitzend, tief eingewurzelt.

in·e·ras·a·ble [ˌɪnɪ'reɪzəbl] *adj.* □ unauslöschbar, unauslöschlich.

in·ert [ɪ'nɜ:t] *adj.* □ **1.** *phys.* träge: ~ ***mass***; **2.** ⚗ 'inakˌtiv: ~ ***gas*** Inert-, Edelgas *n*; **3.** unwirksam; **4.** *fig.* träge, untätig, schwerfällig, schlaff; **in·er·tia** [ɪ'nɜ:ʃjə] *s.* **1.** *phys.* (Massen)Trägheit *f*, Beharrungsvermögen *n*: ~ ***starter*** *mot.* Schwungkraftanlasser *m*; **2.** *fig.* Träg-, Faulheit *f*; **3.** ⚗ Iner'tie *f*, Reakti'onsträgheit *f*; **in·er·tial** [ɪ'nɜ:ʃjəl] *adj.* *phys.* Trägheits…; **in'ert·ness** [-nɪs] *s.* Trägheit *f.*

in·es·cap·a·ble [ˌɪnɪ'skeɪpəbl] *adj.* □ unvermeidlich: a) unentrinnbar, unabwendbar, b) unweigerlich.

in·es·sen·tial [ˌɪnɪ'senʃl] **I** *adj.* unwesentlich, nebensächlich; **II** *s. et.* Unwesentliches, Nebensache *f.*

in·es·ti·ma·ble [ɪn'estɪməbl] *adj.* □ unschätzbar, unbezahlbar.

in·ev·i·ta·bil·i·ty [ɪnˌevɪtə'bɪlətɪ] *s.* Unvermeidlichkeit *f*; **in·ev·i·ta·ble** [ɪn'evɪtəbl] **I** *adj.* □ unvermeidlich: a) unentrinnbar: ~ ***fate***, b) zwangsläufig, unweigerlich, c) *iro.* obli'gat; **II** *s.* ***the*** ~ das Unvermeidliche; **in·ev·i·ta·ble·ness** [ɪn'evɪtəblnɪs] → ***inevitability***.

in·ex·act [ˌɪnɪg'zækt] *adj.* □ ungenau; ˌ**in·ex'act·i·tude** [-tɪtju:d] *s.*, ˌ**in·ex'act·ness** [-nɪs] *s.* Ungenauigkeit *f.*

in·ex·cus·a·ble [ˌɪnɪk'skju:zəbl] *adj.* □ **1.** unverzeihlich; **2.** unverantwortlich; ˌ**in·ex'cus·a·bly** [-blɪ] *adv.* unverzeihlich(erweise).

in·ex·haust·i·bil·i·ty ['ɪnɪgˌzɔ:stə'bɪlətɪ] *s.* **1.** Unerschöpflichkeit *f*; **2.** Unermüdlichkeit *f*; **in·ex·haust·i·ble** [ˌɪnɪg'zɔ:stəbl] *adj.* □ **1.** unerschöpflich; **2.** unermüdlich.

in·ex·o·ra·bil·i·ty [ɪnˌeksərə'bɪlətɪ] *s.* Unerbittlichkeit *f*; **in·ex·o·ra·ble** [ɪn'eksərəbl] *adj.* □ unerbittlich.

in·ex·pe·di·en·cy [ˌɪnɪk'spi:djənsɪ] *s.* **1.** Unzweckmäßigkeit *f*; **2.** Unklugheit *f*; ˌ**in·ex'pe·di·ent** [-nt] *adj.* □ **1.** ungeeignet, unzweckmäßig, nicht ratsam; **2.** unklug.

in·ex·pen·sive [ˌɪnɪk'spensɪv] *adj.* nicht teuer, preiswert, billig.

in·ex·pe·ri·ence [ˌɪnɪk'spɪərɪəns] *s.* Unerfahrenheit *f*; ˌ**in·ex'pe·ri·enced** [-st] *adj.* unerfahren: ~ ***hand*** Nichtfachmann *m.*

in·ex·pert [ɪn'ekspɜ:t] *adj.* □ **1.** ungeübt, unerfahren (***in*** in *dat.*); **2.** ungeschickt; **3.** unsachgemäß.

in·ex·pi·a·ble [ɪn'ekspɪəbl] *adj.* □ **1.** unsühnbar; **2.** unversöhnlich.

in·ex·pli·ca·ble [ˌɪnɪk'splɪkəbl] *adj.* □ unerklärlich, unverständlich; ˌ**in·ex'pli·ca·bly** [-blɪ] *adv.* unerklärlich(erweise).

in·ex·plic·it [ˌɪnɪk'splɪsɪt] *adj.* □ nicht deutlich ausgedrückt, nur angedeutet; unklar.

in·ex·plo·sive [ˌɪnɪk'spləʊsɪv] *adj.* nicht explo'siv, explosi'onssicher.

in·ex·press·i·ble [ˌɪnɪk'spresəbl] *adj.* □ unaussprechlich, unsäglich.

in·ex·pres·sive [ˌɪnɪk'spresɪv] *adj.* □ **1.** ausdruckslos, nichtssagend; **2.** inhaltlos.

in ex·ten·so [ˌɪnɪk'stensəʊ] (*Lat.*) *adv.* vollständig, ungekürzt; ausführlich.

in·ex·tin·guish·a·ble [ˌɪnɪk'stɪŋgwɪʃəbl] *adj.* □ **1.** un(aus)löschbar; **2.** *fig.* unauslöschlich.

in·ex·tri·ca·ble [ɪn'ekstrɪkəbl] *adj.* □ **1.** unentwirrbar, un(auf)lösbar; **2.** gänzlich verworren.

in·fal·li·bil·i·ty [ɪnˌfælə'bɪlətɪ] *s.* Unfehlbarkeit *f* (*a. eccl.*); **in·fal·li·ble** [ɪn'fæləbl] *adj.* □ unfehlbar.

in·fa·mous ['ɪnfəməs] *adj.* □ **1.** verrufen, berüchtigt (***for*** wegen); **2.** schändlich, niederträchtig, gemein, in'fam; **3.** F mise'rabel, ‚saumäßig'; **4.** ehrlos: a) ⚖ der bürgerlichen Ehrenrechte verlustig, b) entehrend, ehrenrührig: ~ ***conduct***; '**in·fa·mous·ness** [-nɪs] → ***infamy*** 2; '**in·fa·my** [-mɪ] *s.* **1.** Ehrlosigkeit *f*, Schande *f*; **2.** Verrufenheit *f*; Schändlichkeit *f*, Niedertracht *f*; **3.** ⚖ Verlust *m* der bürgerlichen Ehrenrechte.

in·fan·cy ['ɪnfənsɪ] *s.* **1.** frühe Kindheit, Säuglingsalter *n*; **2.** ⚖ Minderjährigkeit *f*; **3.** *fig.* Anfangsstadium *n*: ***in its*** ~ in den Anfängen *od.* ‚Kinderschuhen' (steckend); '**in·fant** [-nt] **I** *s.* **1.** Säugling *m*, Baby *n*, kleines Kind; **2.** ⚖ Minderjährige(r *m*) *f*; **II** *adj.* **3.** Säuglings…, Kleinkinder…: ~ ***mortality*** Säuglingssterblichkeit *f*; ~ ***prodigy*** Wunderkind *n*; ~ ***school*** *Brit. etwa* Vorschule *f*; ~ ***welfare*** Säuglingsfürsorge *f*; ~ ***Jesus*** das Jesuskind; ***his*** ~ ***son*** sein kleiner Sohn; **4.** ⚖ minderjährig; **5.** *fig.* jung, in den Anfängen (befindlich).

in·fan·ta [ɪn'fæntə] *s.* In'fantin *f*; **in'fan·te** [-tɪ] *s.* In'fant *m.*

in·fan·ti·cide [ɪn'fæntɪsaɪd] *s.* **1.** Kindestötung *f*; **2.** Kindesmörder(in).

in·fan·tile ['ɪnfəntaɪl] *adj.* **1.** kindlich, Kinder…, Kindes…; **2.** jugendlich; **3.** infan'til, kindisch; ~ (**spi·nal**) **pa·ral·y·sis** *s.* ⚕ (spi'nale) Kinderlähmung.

in·fan·try ['ɪnfəntrɪ] *s.* ⚔ Infante'rie *f*, Fußtruppen *pl.*; '~·**man** [-mən] *s.* [*irr.*] ⚔ Infante'rist *m.*

in·farct [ɪn'fɑ:kt] *s.* ⚕ In'farkt *m*: ***cardiac*** ~ Herzinfarkt; **in'farc·tion** [-kʃn] *s.* In'farkt(bildung *f*) *m.*

in·fat·u·ate [ɪn'fætjʊeɪt] *v/t.* betören, verblenden (***with*** durch); **in'fat·u·at·ed** [-tɪd] *adj.* □ **1.** betört, verblendet (***with*** durch); **2.** vernarrt (***with*** in *acc.*); **in·fat·u·a·tion** [ɪnˌfætjʊ'eɪʃn] *s.* Verblendung *f*; Verliebt-, Vernarrtheit *f.*

in·fect [ɪn'fekt] *v/t.* **1.** ⚕ infizieren, anstecken (***with*** mit, ***by*** durch): ***become*** ~***ed*** sich anstecken; **2.** *Sitten* verderben; *Luft* verpesten; **3.** *fig. j-n* anstekken, beeinflussen; **4.** einflößen (***s.o. with s.th.*** j-m et.); **in'fec·tion** [-kʃn] *s.* **1.** ⚕ Infekti'on *f*, Ansteckung *f*: ***catch an*** ~ angesteckt werden, sich anstekken; **2.** ⚕ Ansteckungskeim *m*, Gift *n*; **3.** *fig.* Ansteckung *f*: a) Vergiftung *f*, b) (*a.* schlechter) Einfluß, Einwirkung *f*; **in'fec·tious** [-kʃəs] *adj.* □ ⚕ ansteckend (*a. fig. Lachen, Optimismus etc.*), infekti'ös, über'tragbar; **in'fec·tious·ness** [-kʃəsnɪs] *s.* ***das*** Ansteckende: a) ⚕ Über'tragbarkeit *f*, b) *fig.* Einfluß *m.*

in·fe·lic·i·tous [ˌɪnfɪ'lɪsɪtəs] *adj.* **1.** unglücklich; **2.** unglücklich (gewählt), ungeschickt (*Worte, Stil*); ˌ**in·fe'lic·i·ty** [-tɪ] *s.* **1.** Unglücklichkeit *f*; **2.** Unglück *n*, Elend *n*; **3.** unglücklicher *od.* ungeschickter Ausdruck *etc.*

in·fer [ɪnˈfɜː] *v/t.* **1.** schließen, folgern, ableiten (***from*** aus); **2.** schließen lassen auf (*acc.*), an-, bedeuten; **inˈfer·a·ble** [-ɜːrəbl] *adj.* zu schließen(d), zu folgern(d), ableitbar (***from*** aus); **in·fer·ence** [ˈɪnfərəns] *s.* (Schluß)Folgerung *f*, (Rück)Schluß *m*: ***make ~s*** Schlüsse ziehen; **in·fer·en·tial** [ˌɪnfəˈrenʃl] *adj.* □ **1.** zu folgern(d); **2.** folgernd; **3.** gefolgert; **in·fer·en·tial·ly** [ˌɪnfəˈrenʃəlɪ] *adv.* durch Schlußfolgerung.

in·fe·ri·or [ɪnˈfɪərɪə] **I** *adj.* **1.** (***to***) ˈuntergeordnet (*dat.*); niedriger, geringer, geringwertiger (als): ***be ~ to s.o.*** j-m nachstehen; ***he is ~ to none*** er nimmt es mit jedem auf; **2.** geringer, schwächer (***to*** als); **3.** ˈuntergeordnet, unter, nieder, zweitrangig: ***the ~ classes*** die unteren Klassen; ***~ court*** ⚖ niederer Gerichtshof; **4.** minderwertig, gering, (mittel)mäßig: ***~ quality***; **5.** unter, tiefer gelegen, Unter...; **6.** *typ.* tiefstehend (*z. B.* H_2); **7.** ***~ planet*** *ast.* unterer Planet (*zwischen Erde u. Sonne*); **II** *s.* **8.** ˈUntergeordnete(r *m*) *f*, Unterˈgebene(r *m*) *f*; **9.** Geringere(r *m*) *f*, Schwächere(r *m*) *f*.

in·fe·ri·or·i·ty [ɪnˌfɪərɪˈɒrətɪ] *s.* **1.** Minderwertigkeit *f*: ***~ complex*** (***feeling***) *psych.* Minderwertigkeitskomplex *m* (-gefühl *n*); **2.** (*a.* zahlen- *od.* mengenmäßige) Unterˈlegenheit; **3.** geringerer Stand *od.* Wert.

in·fer·nal [ɪnˈfɜːnl] *adj.* □ **1.** höllisch, Höllen...: ***~ machine*** Höllenmaschine *f*; ***~ regions*** Unterwelt *f*; **2.** *fig.* teuflisch; **3.** F gräßlich, höllisch; **inˈfer·no** [-nəʊ] *pl.* **-nos** *s.* Inˈferno *n*, Hölle *f*.

in·fer·tile [ɪnˈfɜːtaɪl] *adj.* unfruchtbar; **in·fer·til·i·ty** [ˌɪnfəˈtɪlətɪ] *s.* Unfruchtbarkeit *f*.

in·fest [ɪnˈfest] *v/t.* **1.** heimsuchen, *Ort* unsicher machen; **2.** plagen, verseuchen: ***~ed with*** geplagt von, verseucht durch; **3.** *fig.* überˈlaufen, -ˈschwemmen, -ˈfallen, sich festsetzen in (*dat.*): ***be ~ed with*** wimmeln von; **in·fes·ta·tion** [ˌɪnfeˈsteɪʃn] *s.* **1.** Heimsuchung *f*, (Land)Plage *f*; Belästigung *f*; **2.** *fig.* Überˈschwemmung *f*.

in·feu·da·tion [ˌɪnfjuːˈdeɪʃn] *s.* ⚖, *hist.* **1.** Belehnung *f*; **2.** ***~ of tithes*** Zehntverleihung *f* an Laien.

in·fi·del [ˈɪnfɪdəl] *eccl.* **I** *s.* Ungläubige(r *m*) *f*; **II** *adj.* ungläubig; **in·fi·del·i·ty** [ˌɪnfɪˈdelətɪ] *s.* **1.** Ungläubigkeit *f*; **2.** (*bsd.* eheliche) Untreue.

in·field [ˈɪnfiːld] *s.* **1.** ✓ a) dem Hof nahes Feld, b) Ackerland *n*; **2.** *Kricket*: a) inneres Spielfeld, b) die dort stehenden Fänger; **3.** *Baseball*: (Spieler *pl.* im) Innenfeld *n*.

in·fight·ing [ˈɪnˌfaɪtɪŋ] *s.* **1.** *Boxen*: Nahkampf *m*, Infight *m*; **2.** *fig.* Gerangel *n*, Hickhack *n*.

in·fil·trate [ˈɪnfɪltreɪt] **I** *v/t.* **1.** (*a.* ⚔) einsickern in (*acc.*), ˈdurchsickern durch; **2.** durchˈsetzen, -ˈtränken; **3.** eindringen lassen, einschmuggeln (***into*** in *acc.*); **4.** *pol.* a) unterˈwandern (*acc.*), b) *Agenten etc.* einschleusen (***into*** in *acc.*); **II** *v/i.* **5.** *a. fig.* einsickern, eindringen; **6.** *pol.* (***into***) sich einschleusen (in *acc.*), unterˈwandern (*acc.*); **in·fil·tra·tion** [ˌɪnfɪlˈtreɪʃn] *s.* **1.** Einsickern *n* (*a.* ⚔); Eindringen *n*; **2.** Durchˈtränkung *f*; **3.** *pol.* Unterˈwanderung *f*: ***~ of agents*** Einschleusen *n* von Agenten; **ˈin·fil·tra·tor** [-tə] *s. pol.* Unterˈwanderer *m*.

in·fi·nite [ˈɪnfɪnət] **I** *adj.* □ **1.** unˈendlich, endlos, unbegrenzt; **2.** ungeheuer, ˈallumˌfassend; **3.** *mit s. pl.* unzählige *pl.*; **4.** ***~ verb*** *ling.* Verbum *n* infinitum; **II** *s.* **5.** *das* Unˈendliche, unˈendlicher Raum; **6.** ***the*** ≈ Gott *m*; **ˈin·fi·nite·ly** [-lɪ] *adv.* **1.** unˈendlich; ungeheuer; **2.** ***~ variable*** ⚙ stufenlos (regelbar).

in·fin·i·tes·i·mal [ˌɪnfɪnɪˈtesɪml] **I** *adj.* □ winzig, unˈendlich klein; **II** *s.* unˈendlich kleine Menge; ***~ cal·cu·lus*** *s.* 𝔄 Infinitesiˈmalrechnung *f*.

in·fin·i·ti·val [ɪnˌfɪnɪˈtaɪvl] *adj. ling.* infinitivisch, Infinitiv...; **in·fin·i·tive** [ɪnˈfɪnətɪv] *ling.* **I** *s.* Infinitiv *m*, Nennform *f*; **II** *adj.* infinitivisch: ***~ mood*** Infinitiv *m*.

in·fin·i·tude [ɪnˈfɪnɪtjuːd] → ***infinity*** 1 *u.* 2; **inˈfin·i·ty** [-ətɪ] *s.* **1.** Unˈendlichkeit *f*, Unbegrenztheit *f*, Unermeßlichkeit *f*; **2.** unˈendliche Größe *od.* Zahl; **3.** 𝔄 unˈendliche Menge *od.* Größe, das Unˈendliche: ***to ~*** ad infinitum.

in·firm [ɪnˈfɜːm] *adj.* □ **1.** schwach, gebrechlich; **2.** *a.* ***~ of purpose*** wankelmütig, unentschlossen, willensschwach; **inˈfir·ma·ry** [-mərɪ] *s.* **1.** Krankenhaus *n*; **2.** Krankenzimmer *n* (*in Internaten etc.*); ⚔ (ˈKranken)ReˌVier *n*; **inˈfir·mi·ty** [-mətɪ] *s.* **1.** Gebrechlichkeit *f*, (Alters)Schwäche *f*; Krankheit *f*; **2.** *a.* ***~ of purpose*** Chaˈrakterschwäche *f*, Unentschlossenheit *f*.

in·fix I *v/t.* [ɪnˈfɪks] **1.** eintreiben, befestigen; **2.** *fig.* einprägen (***in*** *dat.*); **3.** *ling.* einfügen; **II** *s.* [ˈɪnfɪks] **4.** *ling.* Inˈfix *n*, Einfügung *f*.

in·flame [ɪnˈfleɪm] **I** *v/t.* **1.** *mst* ⚕ entzünden; **2.** *fig.* erregen, entflammen, reizen: ***~d with rage*** wutentbrannt; **II** *v/i.* **3.** sich entzünden (*a.* ⚕), Feuer fangen; **4.** *fig.* entbrennen (***with*** vor *dat.*, von); sich erhitzen, in Wut geraten; **inˈflamed** [-md] *adj.* entzündet; **in·flam·ma·bil·i·ty** [ɪnˌflæməˈbɪlətɪ] *s.* **1.** Brennbarkeit *f*, Entzündlichkeit *f*; **2.** *fig.* Erregbarkeit *f*, Jähzorn *m*; **in·flam·ma·ble** [ɪnˈflæməbl] **I** *adj.* **1.** brennbar, leicht entzündlich; **2.** feuergefährlich; **3.** *fig.* reizbar, jähzornig, hitzig; **II** *s.* **4.** *pl.* Zündstoffe *pl.*; **in·flam·ma·tion** [ˌɪnfləˈmeɪʃn] *s.* **1.** ⚕ Entzündung *f*; **2.** Aufflammen *n*; **3.** *fig.* Erregung *f*, Aufregung *f*; **in·flam·ma·to·ry** [ɪnˈflæmətərɪ] *adj.* **1.** ⚕ Entzündungs...; **2.** *fig.* aufrührerisch, Hetz...: ***~ speech***.

in·flat·a·ble [ɪnˈfleɪtəbl] *adj.* aufblasbar: ***~ boat*** Schlauchboot *n*; **in·flate** [ɪnˈfleɪt] *v/t.* **1.** aufblasen, aufblähen (*beide a. fig.*), mit Luft *etc.* füllen, *Reifen etc.* aufpumpen; **2.** ✝ *Preise* hochtreiben, ˈübermäßig steigern; **inˈflat·ed** [-tɪd] *adj.* **1.** aufgebläht, aufgeblasen (*beide a. fig. Person*): ***~ with pride*** stolzgeschwellt; **2.** *fig.* geschwollen (*Stil*); **3.** überˈhöht (*Preise*); **inˈfla·tion** [-eɪʃn] *s.* **1.** ✝ Inflatiˈon *f*: ***creeping*** (***galloping***) ***~*** schleichende (galoppierende) Inflation; ***rate of ~*** Inflationsrate *f*; **2.** *fig.* Dünkel *m*, Aufgeblasenheit *f*; **3.** *fig.* Schwülstigkeit *f*; **inˈfla·tion·ar·y** [-eɪʃnərɪ] *adj.* ✝ inflatioˈnär, inflatioˈnistisch, Inflations...: ***~ period*** Inflationszeit *f*; **inˈfla·tion·ism** [-eɪʃnɪzəm] *s.* ✝ Inflatioˈnismus *m*; **inˈfla·tion·ist** [-eɪʃnɪst] *s.* Anhänger *m* des Inflatioˈnismus.

in·flect [ɪnˈflekt] *v/t.* **1.** (nach innen) biegen; **2.** *ling.* flektieren, beugen, abwandeln; **inˈflec·tion** [-kʃn] *etc.* → ***inflexion*** *etc.*

in·flex·i·bil·i·ty [ɪnˌfleksəˈbɪlətɪ] *s.* **1.** Unbiegsamkeit *f*; **2.** Unbeugsamkeit *f*; **in·flex·i·ble** [ɪnˈfleksəbl] *adj.* □ **1.** ˈuneˌlastisch, unbiegsam; **2.** *fig.* a) unbeugsam, starr, b) unerbittlich.

in·flex·ion [ɪnˈflekʃn] n] *s.* **1.** Biegung *f*, Krümmung *f*; **2.** (meˈlodische) Modulatiˈon; **3.** (Ton)Veränderung *f der Stimme*, *weitS.* feine Nuˈance; **4.** *ling.* Flexiˈon *f*, Beugung *f*, Abwandlung *f*; **inˈflex·ion·al** [-ʃənl] *adj. ling.* flektierend, Flexions...

in·flict [ɪnˈflɪkt] *v/t.* **1.** *Leid etc.* zufügen; *Wunde*, *Niederlage* beibringen, *Schlag* versetzen, *Strafe* auferlegen, zudiktieren (***on***, ***upon*** *dat.*); **2.** aufbürden (***on***, ***upon*** *dat.*): ***~ o.s. on s.o.*** sich j-m aufdrängen; **inˈflic·tion** [-kʃn] *s.* **1.** Zufügung *f*, Auferlegung *f*; Verhängung *f* (*Strafe*); **2.** Last *f*, Plage *f*; **3.** Heimsuchung *f*, Strafe *f*.

in·flo·res·cence [ˌɪnflɔːˈresns] *s.* **1.** ⚘ a) Blütenstand *m*, b) *coll.* Blüten *pl.*; **2.** *a. fig.* Aufblühen *n*, Blüte *f*.

in·flow [ˈɪnfləʊ] → ***influx*** 1.

in·flu·ence [ˈɪnflʊəns] **I** *s.* **1.** Einfluß *m*, (Ein)Wirkung *f* (***on***, ***upon***, ***over*** auf *acc.*, ***with*** bei); ⚖ Beeinflussung *f*: ***be under s.o.'s ~*** unter j-s Einfluß stehen; ***under the ~ of drink*** unter Alkoholeinfluß; ***under the ~*** F ‚blau'; **2.** Einfluß *m*, Macht *f*: ***bring one's ~ to bear*** s-n Einfluß geltend machen; **II** *v/t.* **3.** beeinflussen, (ein)wirken *od.* Einfluß ausüben auf (*acc.*); **4.** bewegen, bestimmen; **in·flu·en·tial** [ˌɪnflʊˈenʃl] *adj.* □ **1.** einflußreich; maßgeblich; **2.** von (großem) Einfluß (***on*** auf *acc.*; ***in*** in *dat.*).

in·flu·en·za [ˌɪnflʊˈenzə] *s.* ⚕ Influˈenza *f*, Grippe *f*.

in·flux [ˈɪnflʌks] *s.* **1.** Einfließen *n*, Zustrom *m*, Zufluß *m*; **2.** ✝ (*Kapital- etc.*) Zufluß *m*, (Waren)Zufuhr *f*; **3.** Mündung *f* (*Fluß*); **4.** *fig.* Zustrom *m*: ***~ of visitors*** Besucherstrom *m*.

in·fo [ˈɪnfəʊ] *s.* F Informatiˈon *f*.

in·fold [ɪnˈfəʊld] → ***enfold***.

in·form [ɪnˈfɔːm] **I** *v/t.* (***of***) informieren (über *acc.*), verständigen, benachrichtigen, in Kenntnis setzen, unterˈrichten (von), *j-m* mitteilen (*acc.*): ***~ o.s. of s.th.*** sich über et. informieren; ***keep s.o. ~ed*** j-n auf dem laufenden halten; ***~ s.o. that*** j-n davon in Kenntnis setzen, daß; **II** *v/i.* ***~ against s.o.*** j-n anzeigen *od.* denunzieren.

in·for·mal [ɪnˈfɔːml] *adj.* □ **1.** zwanglos, ungezwungen, nicht forˈmell *od.* förmlich; **2.** ˈinoffiziˌell: ***~ visit*** (***talks***); **3.** *ling.* Umgangs...: ***~ speech***; **4.** ⚖ formlos: a) formfrei: ***~ contract***, b) formwidrig; **in·for·mal·i·ty** [ˌɪnfɔːˈmælətɪ] *s.* **1.** Zwanglosigkeit *f*, Ungezwungenheit *f*; **2.** ⚖ a) Formlosigkeit *f*, b) Formfehler *m*.

in·form·ant [ɪnˈfɔːmənt] *s.* **1.** Gewährsmann *m*, Inforˈmant(in), (Informa-

ti'ons)Quelle *f*; **2.** → ***informer***.
in·for·ma·tics [ˌɪnfəˈmætɪks] *s. pl. oft sg. konstr.* Infor'matik *f*.
in·for·ma·tion [ˌɪnfəˈmeɪʃn] *s.* **1.** Nachricht *f*, Mitteilung *f*, Meldung *f*, Informati'on *f* (*a. Computer*): ~ ***bureau***, ~ ***office*** Auskunftsstelle *f*, Auskunftei *f*; ~ ***desk*** Auskunft(sschalter *m*) *f*; ~ ***flow*** Informationsfluß *m*; ~ ***science*** Informatik *f*; **2.** Auskunft *f*, Bescheid *m*, Kenntnis *f*: ***give*** ~ Auskunft geben; ***we have no*** ~ wir sind nicht unterrichtet (***as to*** über *acc.*); **3.** Erkundigungen *pl.*: ***gather*** ~ sich erkundigen, Auskünfte einholen; **4.** Unter'weisung *f*: ***for your*** ~ zu Ihrer Kenntnisnahme; **5.** Einzelheiten *pl.*, Angaben *pl.*; **6.** ⚖ Anklage *f*, Anzeige *f*: ***lodge ~ against s.o.*** Anklage erheben gegen j-n, j-n anzeigen; ˌ**in·for'ma·tion·al** [-ʃənl] *adj.* informa'torisch, Informations…
in·form·a·tive [ɪnˈfɔːmətɪv] *adj.* **1.** informa'tiv, lehr-, aufschlußreich; **2.** mitteilsam; **in'form·a·to·ry** [-tərɪ] *adj.* → a) ***informational***, b) ***informative*** 1; **in'formed** [-md] *adj.* **1.** infor'miert, (gut) unter'richtet: ~ ***quarters*** unterrichtete Kreise; **2.** a) sachkundig, b) sachlich begründet *od.* einwandfrei, fun'diert; **3.** gebildet; **in'form·er** [-mə] *s.* **1.** Infor'mant(in), Denunzi'ant(in): (***common***) ~, (***police***) ~ Spitzel *m*; **2.** ⚖ Anzeigeerstatter(in).
in·fra [ˈɪnfrə] *adv.* unten: ***vide*** (*od.* ***see***) ~ siehe unten (*in Büchern*).
infra- [ɪnfrə] *in Zssgn* unter(halb).
in·frac·tion [ɪnˈfrækʃn] → ***infringement***.
in·fra dig [ˌɪnfrəˈdɪg] (*Lat. abbr.*) *adv. u. adj.* F unter m-r (*etc.*) Würde, unwürdig.
in·fran·gi·ble [ɪnˈfrændʒɪbl] *adj.* unzerbrechlich; *fig.* unverletzlich.
ˌ**in·fra**|ˈ**red** *adj. phys.* infrarot; ˌ**~'son·ic** *adj.* Infraschall…, unter der Schallgrenze liegend.
ˈ**in·fraˌstruc·ture** *s. allg.* 'Infrastrukˌtur *f*.
in·fre·quen·cy [ɪnˈfriːkwənsɪ] *s.* Seltenheit *f*; **in'fre·quent** [-nt] *adj.* □ **1.** selten; **2.** spärlich, dünn gesät.
in·fringe [ɪnˈfrɪndʒ] **I** *v/t. Gesetz, Eid etc.* brechen, verletzen, verstoßen gegen; **II** *v/i.* (***on, upon***) *Rechte etc.* verletzen, eingreifen (in *acc.*); **in'fringe·ment** [-mənt] *s.* (***on, upon***) (*Rechts- etc., a. Patent*)Verletzung *f*, (*Rechts-, Vertrags*)Bruch *m*, Über'tretung *f* (*gen.*); Verstoß *m* (gegen).
in·fu·ri·ate [ɪnˈfjʊərɪeɪt] *v/t.* wütend *od.* rasend machen; **in'fu·ri·at·ing** [-tɪŋ] *adj.* aufreizend, rasend machend.
in·fuse [ɪnˈfjuːz] *v/t.* **1.** aufgießen, -brühen, ziehen lassen: ~ ***tea*** Tee aufgießen; **2.** *fig.* einflößen (***into*** *dat.*); **3.** erfüllen (***with*** mit); **in'fus·er** [-zə] *s.*: (***tea***) ~ Tee-Ei *n*; **in'fu·si·ble** [-zəbl] *adj.* ⚗ unschmelzbar; **in'fu·sion** [-ʒn] *s.* **1.** Aufgießen *n*, -brühen *n*; **2.** Aufguß *m*, (Kräuter- *etc.*)Tee *m*; **3.** ⚕ Infusi'on *f*; **4.** *fig.* Einflößung *f*; **5.** *fig.* a) Beimischung *f*, b) Zufluß *m*.
in·fu·so·ri·a [ˌɪnfjuːˈzɔːrɪə] *s. pl. zo.* Infu'sorien *pl.*, Wimpertierchen *pl.*; ˌ**in·fu'so·ri·al** [-əl] *adj. zo.* Infusorien…: ~ ***earth*** *min.* Infusorienerde *f*, Kieselgur *f*; ˌ**in·fu'so·ri·an** [-ən] *zo.* **I** *s.* Wimpertierchen *n*, Infu'sorium *n*; **II** *adj.* → ***infusorial***.
in·gen·ious [ɪnˈdʒiːnjəs] *adj.* □ geni'al: a) erfinderisch, findig, b) geistreich, klug, c) sinn-, kunstvoll, raffiniert: ~ ***design***; **in'gen·ious·ness** [-nɪs] → ***ingenuity***.
in·gé·nue [ˈænʒeɪnjuː] *s.* **1.** na'ives Mädchen, ‚Unschuld' *f*; **2.** *thea.* Na'ive *f*.
in·ge·nu·i·ty [ˌɪndʒɪˈnjuːətɪ] *s.* **1.** Geniali'tät *f*, Erfindungsgabe *f*, Einfallsreichtum *m*, Findigkeit *f*, Geschicklichkeit *f*, Bril'lanz *f*; **2.** Raffi'nesse *f*, geni'ale Ausführung *etc.*
in·gen·u·ous [ɪnˈdʒenjʊəs] *adj.* □ **1.** offen(herzig), treuherzig, unbefangen, aufrichtig; **2.** na'iv, einfältig, unschuldig; **in'gen·u·ous·ness** [-nɪs] *s.* **1.** Offenheit *f*, Treuherzigkeit *f*; **2.** Naivi'tät *f*.
in·gest [ɪnˈdʒest] *v/t. Nahrung* aufnehmen; **in'ges·tion** [-tʃn] *s.* Nahrungsaufnahme *f*.
in·glo·ri·ous [ɪnˈglɔːrɪəs] *adj.* □ **1.** unrühmlich, schimpflich; **2.** *obs.* ruhmlos.
in·go·ing [ˈɪnˌgəʊɪŋ] *adj.* **1.** eintretend; **2.** neu (*Beamter, Mieter etc.*).
in·got [ˈɪŋgət] *s.* ⚙ Barren *m*, Stange *f*, Block *m*: ~ ***of gold*** Goldbarren *m*; ~ ***of steel*** Stahlblock *m*; ~ ***iron*** Flußstahl *m*, -eisen *n*.
in·graft [ɪnˈgrɑːft] → ***engraft***.
in·grain I *v/t.* [ˌɪnˈgreɪn] **1.** *obs.* in der Wolle *od.* Faser (*farbecht*) färben; **2.** *fig.* tief verwurzeln; **II** *adj.* [*attr.* ˈɪngreɪn; *pred.* ˌɪnˈgreɪn] **3.** → ˌ**in'grained** [-nd] *adj. fig.* **1.** tief verwurzelt: ~ ***prejudice***; **2.** eingefleischt: ~ ***habit***; **3.** unverbesserlich.
in·grate [ɪnˈgreɪt] *obs.* **I** *adj.* undankbar; **II** *s.* Undankbare(r *m*) *f*.
in·gra·ti·ate [ɪnˈgreɪʃɪeɪt] *v/t.*: ~ ***o.s. with s.o.*** sich bei j-m einschmeicheln; **in'gra·ti·at·ing** [-tɪŋ] *adj.* □ schmeichlerisch.
in·grat·i·tude [ɪnˈgrætɪtjuːd] *s.* Undank (-barkeit *f*) *m*.
in·gre·di·ent [ɪnˈgriːdjənt] *s.* ⚗, *Küche u. fig.*: Bestandteil *m*, Zutat *f*; *fig. a.* (*Charakter- etc.*)Merkmal *n*.
in·gress [ˈɪngres] *s.* **1.** Eintritt *m* (*a. ast.*), Eintreten *n* (***into*** in *acc.*); **2.** Zutritt *m*, Zugang (***into*** zu); **3.** Zustrom *m*: ~ ***of visitors***.
ˈ**in-group** *s. sociol.* Ingroup *f*.
in·grow·ing [ˈɪnˌgrəʊɪŋ] *adj.*, ˈ**in·grown** *adj.* ⚕ eingewachsen: ***an ~ nail***.
in·gui·nal [ˈɪŋgwɪnl] *adj.* ⚕ Leisten…
in·gur·gi·tate [ɪnˈgɜːdʒɪteɪt] *v/t. bsd. fig.* verschlingen, schlucken.
in·hab·it [ɪnˈhæbɪt] *v/t.* bewohnen, wohnen *od.* (*a. zo.*) leben in (*dat.*); **in'hab·it·a·ble** [-təbl] *adj.* bewohnbar; **in'hab·it·ant** [-tənt] *s.* **1.** Bewohner (-in) (*e-s Hauses etc.*), **2.** Einwohner (-in) (e-s *Orts, e-s Landes*).
in·ha·la·tion [ˌɪnhəˈleɪʃn] *s.* **1.** Einatmung *f*; **2.** ⚕ Inhalati'on *f*; **in·hale** [ɪnˈheɪl] **I** *v/t.* ⚕ einatmen, inhalieren; **II** *v/i.* inhalieren, *beim Rauchen*: *a.* Lungenzüge machen; **in·hal·er** [ɪnˈheɪlə] *s.* **1.** ⚕ Inhalati'onsappaˌrat *m*; **2.** j-d, der inhaliert.
in·har·mo·ni·ous [ˌɪnhɑːˈməʊnjəs] *adj.* □ 'unharˌmonisch: a) 'mißtönend, b) *fig.* uneinig.
in·here [ɪnˈhɪə] *v/i.* **1.** innewohnen: a) anhaften (***in s.o.*** j-m), b) eigen sein (***in s.th.*** e-r Sache); **2.** enthalten sein (***in*** in *dat.*); **in'her·ence** [-ərəns] *s.* Innewohnen *n*, Anhaften *n*; *phls.* Inhä'renz *f*; **in'her·ent** [-ərənt] *adj.* □ **1.** innewohnend, eigen, anhaftend (*alle*: ***in*** *dat.*): ~ ***defect*** (*od.* ***vice***) ⚖ innerer Fehler; **2.** eingewurzelt; **3.** *phls.* inhä'rent; **in'her·ent·ly** [-ərəntlɪ] *adv.* von Na'tur aus, schon an sich.
in·her·it [ɪnˈherɪt] **I** *v/t.* **1.** ⚖, *biol.*, *fig.* erben; **2.** *biol.*, *fig.* ererben; **II** *v/i.* **3.** ⚖ erben, Erbe sein; **in'her·it·a·ble** [-təbl] *adj.* **1.** ⚖, *biol.*, *fig.* vererbbar, erblich (*Sache*); **2.** erbfähig, -berechtigt (*Person*); **in'her·it·ance** [-təns] *s.* **1.** ⚖, *fig.* Erbe *n*, Erbschaft *f*, Erbteil *n*: ~ ***tax*** *Am.* Erbschaftssteuer *f*; **2.** ⚖, *biol.* Vererbung *f*: ***by*** ~ durch Vererbung, erblich; **in'her·it·ed** [-tɪd] *adj.* ererbt, Erb… (*a. ling.*); **in'her·i·tor** [-tə] *s.* Erbe *m* (*a. fig.*); **in'her·i·tress** [-trɪs], **in'her·i·trix** [-trɪks] *s.* Erbin *f*.
in·hib·it [ɪnˈhɪbɪt] *v/t.* **1.** *et.*, *psych.* *j-n* hemmen: **~*ed*** gehemmt; **2.** (***from***) *j-n* abhalten (von), hindern (an *dat.*): ~ ***s.o. from doing s.th.*** j-n daran hindern, et. zu tun; **in·hi·bi·tion** [ˌɪnhɪˈbɪʃn] *s.* **1.** Hemmung *f* (*a.* ⚕ *u. psych.*); **2.** Unter'sagung *f*, Verbot *n*; **3.** ⚖ Unter'sagungsbefehl *m* (*e-e Sache weiterzuverfolgen*); **in'hib·i·tor** [-tə] *s.* ⚗, ⚙ Hemmstoff *m*, (*Korrosions- etc.*) Schutzmittel *n*; **in'hib·i·to·ry** [-tərɪ] **1.** hemmend, Hemmungs… (*a.* ⚕ *u. psych.*), hindernd; **2.** unter'sagend, verbietend.
in·hos·pi·ta·ble [ɪnˈhɒspɪtəbl] *adj.* □ ungastlich: a) nicht gastfreundlich, b) unwirtlich: ~ ***climate***; **in·hos·pi·tal·i·ty** [ɪnˌhɒspɪˈtælətɪ] *s.* Ungastlichkeit *f*: a) mangelnde Gastfreundschaft *f*, b) Unwirtlichkeit *f*.
in·hu·man [ɪnˈhjuːmən] *adj.* □, **in·hu·mane** [ˌɪnhjuːˈmeɪn] *adj.* □ unmenschlich, 'inhuˌman; **in·hu·man·i·ty** [ˌɪnhjuːˈmænətɪ] *s.* Unmenschlichkeit *f*.
in·hume [ɪnˈhjuːm] *v/t.* beerdigen, bestatten.
in·im·i·cal [ɪˈnɪmɪkl] *adj.* □ (***to***) **1.** feindlich (gegen); **2.** schädlich, nachteilig (für).
in·im·i·ta·ble [ɪˈnɪmɪtəbl] *adj.* □ unnachahmlich, einzigartig.
in·iq·ui·tous [ɪˈnɪkwɪtəs] *adj.* □ **1.** ungerecht; **2.** frevelhaft; **3.** böse, lasterhaft, schlecht; **4.** gemein, niederträchtig; **in'iq·ui·ty** [-tɪ] *s.* **1.** Ungerechtigkeit *f*; **2.** Niederträchtigkeit *f*; **3.** Schandtat *f*, Frevel *m*; **4.** Sünde *f*, Laster *n*.
in·i·tial [ɪˈnɪʃl] **I** *adj.* □ **1.** anfänglich, Anfangs…, Ausgangs…, erst, ursprünglich: ~ ***advertising*** ⚚ Einführungswerbung *f*; ~ ***capital expenditure*** ⚚ Anlagekosten *pl.*; ~ ***material*** ⚚ Ausgangsmaterial *n*; ~ ***position*** ⚙, ⚔ *etc.* Ausgangsstellung *f*; ~ ***salary*** Anfangsgehalt *n*; ~ ***stages*** Anfangsstadium *n*; **2.** *ling.* anlautend; **II** *s.* **3.** (großer) Anfangsbuchstabe, Initi'ale *f*; **4.** *pl.* Mono'gramm *n*; **5.** *ling.* Anlaut *m*; **III** *v/t.* **6.** mit Initi'alen versehen *od.* unter'zeichnen, paraphieren; **7.** mit e-m Mono'gramm versehen; **in'i·tial·ly** [-ʃəlɪ] *adv.* am *od.* zu Anfang, anfänglich, zu'erst.
in·i·ti·ate I *v/t.* [ɪˈnɪʃɪeɪt] **1.** beginnen,

einleiten, -führen, ins Leben rufen; **2.** *j-n* einweihen, -arbeiten, -führen (***into, in*** in *acc.*); **3.** *j-n* einführen, aufnehmen (***into*** in *acc.*); **4.** *pol.* als erster beantragen; *Gesetzesvorlage* einbringen; **II** *adj.* [-ɪət] **5.** → ***initiated***; **III** *s.* [-ɪət] **6.** Eingeweihte(r *m*) *f*, Kenner(in); **7.** Eingeführte(r *m*) *f*; **8.** Neuling *m*, Anfänger (-in); **in'i·ti·at·ed** [-tɪd] *adj.* eingeführt, eingeweiht: ***the ~*** die Eingeweihten *pl.*;

in·i·ti·a·tion [ɪˌnɪʃɪ'eɪʃn] *s.* **1.** Einleitung *f*, Beginn *m*; **2.** (feierliche) Einführung, -setzung *f*, Aufnahme *f* (***into*** in *acc.*); **3.** Einweihung *f*, Weihe *f*.

in·i·ti·a·tive [ɪ'nɪʃɪətɪv] **I** *s.* **1.** Initia'tive *f*: a) erster Schritt *od.* Anstoß, Anregung *f*: ***take the ~*** die Initiative ergreifen, den ersten Schritt tun; ***on s.o.'s ~*** auf j-s Anregung hin; ***on one's own ~*** aus eigenem Antrieb, b) Unter'nehmungsgeist *m*; **2.** *pol.* (Ge'setzes)Initiaˌtive *f*; **II** *adj.* **3.** einleitend; **4.** beginnend.

in·i·ti·a·tor [ɪ'nɪʃɪeɪtə] *s.* **1.** Initi'ator *m*, Urheber *m*, Anreger *m*; **2.** ⚔ (Initi'al-) Zündladung *f*; **3.** ⚗ reakti'onsauslösende Sub'stanz; **in'i·ti·a·to·ry** [-ɪətərɪ] *adj.* **1.** einleitend; **2.** einweihend, Einweihungs...

in·ject [ɪn'dʒekt] *v/t.* **1.** ⚕ a) (*a.* ⚙) einspritzen, b) ausspritzen (***with*** mit), c) e-e Einspritzung machen in (*acc.*); **2.** *fig.* einflößen, einimpfen (***into*** *dat.*); **3.** *Bemerkung* einwerfen.

in·jec·tion [ɪn'dʒekʃn] *s.* ⚕ Injekti'on *f*: a) Einspritzung *f* (*a.* ⚙), Spritze *f*, b) *das Eingespritzte*, c) Einlauf *m*, d) Ausspritzung *f* (*e-r Wunde etc.*): ***~ of money*** *fig.* ‚Spritze' *f*, Geldzuschuß *m*; **~ cock** *s.* Einspritzhahn *m*; **~ die** *s.* ⚙ Spritzform *f*; **~ mo(u)ld·ing** *s.* Spritzguß(verfahren *n*) *m*; **~ noz·zle** *s.* Einspritzdüse *f*; **~ syr·inge** *s.* ⚕ Injekti'onsspritze *f*.

in·jec·tor [ɪn'dʒektə] *s.* ⚙ In'jektor *m*, Dampfstrahlpumpe *f*.

in·ju·di·cious [ˌɪndʒuː'dɪʃəs] *adj.* □ unklug, 'unüberˌlegt.

In·jun ['ɪndʒən] *s. Am. humor.* Indi'aner *m*: ***honest ~!*** Ehrenwort!

in·junc·tion [ɪn'dʒʌŋkʃn] *s.* **1.** ⚖ gerichtliche Verfügung, *bsd.* (gerichtlicher) Unter'lassungsbefehl: ***interim ~*** einstweilige Verfügung; **2.** ausdrücklicher Befehl.

in·jure ['ɪndʒə] *v/t.* **1.** verletzen, beschädigen, verwunden: ***~ one's leg*** sich am Bein verletzen; **2.** *fig. j-n, j-s Stolz etc.* kränken, verletzen; **3.** schaden (*dat.*), schädigen, beeinträchtigen; **'in·jured** [-əd] *adj.* **1.** verletzt: ***the ~*** die Verletzten; **2.** geschädigt: ***the ~ party*** der Geschädigte; **3.** gekränkt, verletzt: ***~ innocence*** gekränkte Unschuld; **in·ju·ri·ous** [ɪn'dʒʊərɪəs] *adj.* □ **1.** schädlich, nachteilig (***to*** für): ***be ~ (to)*** schaden (*dat.*); **2.** beleidigend, verletzend (*Worte*); **3.** un(ge)recht; **in·ju·ry** ['ɪndʒərɪ] *s.* **1.** Verletzung *f*, Wunde *f* (***to*** an *dat.*): ***~ to the head*** Kopfverletzung, -wunde; ***~ time*** *sport* Nachspielzeit *f*; **2.** (Be)Schädigung *f* (***to*** *gen.*), Schaden *m* (*a.* ⚖): ***~ to person (property)*** Personen-(Sach)schaden; **3.** *fig.* Verletzung *f*, Kränkung *f* (***to*** *gen.*); **4.** Unrecht *n*.

in·jus·tice [ɪn'dʒʌstɪs] *s.* Unrecht *n*, Ungerechtigkeit *f*: ***do s.o. an ~*** j-m ein Unrecht antun.

ink [ɪŋk] **I** *s.* **1.** Tinte *f*: ***copying ~*** Kopiertinte *f*; **2.** Tusche *f*: ***~ drawing*** Tuschzeichnung *f*; → ***Indian ink***; **3.** *typ.* (Druck)Farbe *f*; → ***printer*** 1; **4.** *zo.* Tinte *f*, Sepia *f*; **II** *v/t.* **5.** mit Tinte schwärzen *od.* beschmieren; **6.** *typ. Druckwalzen* einfärben; **7. *~ in*** *mit Tusche* ausziehen, tuschieren; **8. *~ out*** *mit Tinte* unleserlich machen, ausstreichen; **~ bag** → ***ink sac***; **~ blot** *s.* Tintenklecks *m*.

ink·er ['ɪŋkə] *s.* **1.** → ***inking-roller***; **2.** *typ.* Tuscher(in).

ink·ing ['ɪŋkɪŋ] *s. typ.* Einfärben *n*; **~ pad** *s.* Einschwärzballen *m*; **'~-ˌroll·er** *s.* Auftrag-, Farbwalze *f*.

ink·ling ['ɪŋklɪŋ] *s.* **1.** Andeutung *f*, Wink *m*; **2.** dunkle Ahnung: ***get an ~ of s.th.*** et. merken, ‚Wind von et. bekommen'; ***not the least ~*** nicht die leiseste Ahnung.

ink| pad *s.* Farb-, Stempelkissen *n*; **~ pot** *s.* Tintenfaß *n*; **~ sac** *s. zo.* Tintenbeutel *m*; **'~·stand** *s.* **1.** Tintenfaß *n*; **2.** Schreibzeug *n*; **'~·well** *s.* (eingelassenes) Tintenfaß.

ink·y ['ɪŋkɪ] *adj.* **1.** tiefschwarz; **2.** voll Tinte, tintig.

in·laid [ˌɪn'leɪd; *attr.* 'ɪnleɪd] *adj.* eingelegt, Einlege..., Mosaik...: ***~ floor*** Parkett(fußboden *m*) *n*; ***~ table*** Tisch *m* mit Einlegearbeit; ***~ work*** Einlegearbeit *f*.

in·land ['ɪnlənd] **I** *s.* **1.** In-, Binnenland *n*; **II** *adj.* **2.** binnenländisch, Binnen...: ***~ town*** Stadt im Binnenland; **3.** inländisch, einheimisch, Inland..., Landes...; **III** *adv.* [ɪn'lænd] **4.** im Innern des Landes; **5.** ins Innere des Landes, landeinwärts; **~ bill (of ex·change)** ['ɪnlənd] *s.* † Inlandwechsel *m*; **~ du·ty** *s.* † Binnenzoll *m*.

in·land·er ['ɪnləndə] *s.* Binnenländer(in).

'in·land| mail *s. Brit.* Inlandspost *f*; **~ nav·i·ga·tion** *s.* Binnenschiffahrt *f*; **~ prod·uce** *s.* † 'Landesproˌdukte *pl.*; **~ rev·e·nue** *s.* † *Brit.* a) Steueraufkommen *n*, b) 2 Steuerbehörde *f*; **~ trade** *s.* † Binnenhandel *m*; **~ wa·ters, ~ wa·ter·ways** *s. pl.* Binnengewässer *pl.*

in-laws ['ɪnlɔːz] *s. pl.* **1.** angeheiratete Verwandte *pl.*; **2.** Schwiegereltern *pl.*

in·lay I *v/t.* [*irr.* → ***lay***] [ˌɪn'leɪ] **1.** einlegen: ***~ with ivory***; **2.** furnieren; **3.** täfeln, parkettieren, auslegen; **II** *s.* ['ɪnleɪ] **4.** Einlegearbeit *f*, In'tarsia *f*; **5.** ⚕ (Zahn)Füllung *f*, Plombe *f*.

in·let ['ɪnlet] *s.* **1.** Meeresarm *m*, schmale Bucht; **2.** Eingang *m* (*a.* ⚕), Einlaß *m* (*a.* ⚙): ***~ valve*** ⚙ Einlaßventil *n*; **3.** Einsatz(stück *n*) *m*.

'in-line en·gine *s.* Reihenmotor *m*.

in·ly·ing ['ɪnˌlaɪɪŋ] *adj.* innen liegend, Innen..., inner.

in·mate ['ɪnmeɪt] *s.* **1.** Insasse *m*, Insassin *f* (*bsd. e-r Anstalt etc.*); **2.** *obs.* Hausgenosse *m*, -genossin *f*; **3.** Bewohner(in) (*a. fig.*).

in·most ['ɪnməʊst] *adj.* **1.** (*a. fig.*) innerst; **2.** *fig.* tiefst, geheimst.

inn [ɪn] *s.* **1.** Gasthaus *n*, -hof *m*; **2.** Wirtshaus *n*; **3. *Inns*** *pl.* ***of Court*** ⚖ *die* (Gebäude *pl.* der) vier Rechtsschulen in London.

in·nards ['ɪnədz] *s. pl.* F *das* Innere, *bsd.* a) *die* Eingeweide *pl.* (*a. fig.*), b) *Küche*: *die* Inne'reien *pl.*

in·nate [ˌɪ'neɪt] *adj.* □ angeboren, eigen (*in dat.*); **ˌin'nate·ly** [-lɪ] *adv.* von Na'tur (aus).

in·ner ['ɪnə] **I** *adj.* **1.** inner, inwendig, Innen...: ***~ door*** Innentür *f*; **2.** *fig.* inner, vertraut: ***the ~ circle*** der engere Kreis (*von Freunden etc.*); **3.** geistig, seelisch, inner(lich): ***~ life*** *das* Innen- *od.* Seelenleben; **4.** verborgen, geheim; **II** *s.* **5.** (Treffer *m* in das) Schwarze (*e-r Schießscheibe*); **~ man** *s.* [*irr.*] innerer Mensch: a) Seele *f*, Geist *m*, b) *humor. der* Magen *m*: ***refresh the ~*** sich stärken.

'in·ner·most → ***inmost***.

in·ner| span *s.* △ lichte Weite; **~ sur·face** *s.* Innenfläche *f*, -seite *f*; **~ tube** *s.* ⚙ (Luft)Schlauch *m e-s Reifens*.

in·ner·vate ['ɪnɜːveɪt] *v/t.* **1.** ⚕ innervieren, mit Nerven versorgen; **2.** anregen, beleben.

in·ning ['ɪnɪŋ] *s.* **1.** *Brit.* **~s** *pl. sg. konstr.*, *Am.* **~** *sg.*: ***have one's ~(s)*** a) *Kricket, Baseball*: dran *od.* am Spiel *od.* am Schlagen sein, b) *fig.* an der Reihe sein, *pol.* an der Macht *od.* am Ruder sein; **2.** *pl. Brit.* Gelegenheit *f*, Glück *n*, Chance *f*.

'innˌkeep·er *s.* Gastwirt(in).

in·no·cence ['ɪnəsəns] *s.* **1.** *allg.* Unschuld *f*: a) ⚖ *etc.* Schuldlosigkeit *f* (***of*** an *dat.*), b) Keuschheit *f*, c) Harmlosigkeit *f*, d) Arglosigkeit *f*, Naivi'tät *f*, Einfalt *f*; **2.** Unwissenheit *f*; **'in·no·cent** [-snt] **I** *adj.* □ **1.** unschuldig: a) schuldlos (***of*** an *dat.*): ***~ air*** Unschuldsmiene *f*, b) keusch, rein, c) harmlos, d) arglos, na'iv, einfältig; **2.** harmlos: ***an ~ sport***; **3.** unbeabsichtigt: ***an ~ deception***; **4.** unwissend: ***he is ~ of such things*** er hat noch nichts von solchen Dingen gehört; **5.** ⚖ a) → 1 a, b) gutgläubig, c) le'gal; **6.** (***of***) frei (von), bar (*gen.*), ohne (*acc.*): ***~ of conceit*** frei von (jedem) Dünkel; ***~ of reason*** bar aller Vernunft; ***he is ~ of Latin*** er kann kein Wort Latein; **II** *s.* **7.** Unschuldige(r *m*) *f*: ***the slaughter of the 2s*** a) *bibl.* der bethlehemitische Kindermord, b) *parl. sl.* das Über'bordwerfen von Vorlagen am Sessi'onsende; **8.** ‚Unschuld' *f*, na'iver Mensch, Einfaltspinsel *m*; **9.** Igno'rant(in), Nichtswisser(in).

in·noc·u·ous [ɪ'nɒkjʊəs] *adj.* □ unschädlich, harmlos.

in·no·vate ['ɪnəʊveɪt] *v/i.* Neuerungen einführen *od.* vornehmen; **in·no·va·tion** [ˌɪnəʊ'veɪʃn] *s.* Neuerung *f*, *a.* † Innovati'on *f*; **'in·no·va·tor** [-tə] *s.* Neuerer *m*.

in·nox·ious [ɪ'nɒkʃəs] *adj.* □ unschädlich.

in·nu·en·do [ˌɪnjuː'endəʊ] *pl.* **-does** *s.* **1.** (versteckte) Andeutung *od.* (boshafte) Anspielung, Anzüglichkeit *f*; **2.** Unter'stellung *f*.

in·nu·mer·a·ble [ɪ'njuːmərəbl] *adj.* □ unzählig, zahllos.

in·ob·serv·ance [ˌɪnəb'zɜːvəns] *s.* **1.** Unaufmerksamkeit *f*, Unachtsamkeit *f*; **2.** Nichteinhaltung *f*, -beachtung *f*.

in·oc·u·late [ɪ'nɒkjʊleɪt] *v/t.* **1.** ⚕ a) *Serum etc.* einimpfen (***on, into s.o.*** j-m), b) *j-n* impfen (***against*** gegen); **2. ~**

with *fig.* *j-m et.* einimpfen, *j-n* erfüllen mit; **3.** ⚘ okulieren; **in·oc·u·la·tion** [ɪˌnɒkjʊˈleɪʃn] *s.* **1.** ⚕ a) Impfung *f*: ~ ***gun*** Impfpistole *f*; ***preventive*** ~ Schutzimpfung, b) Einimpfung *f* (*a. fig.*); **2.** ⚘ Okulierung *f*.

in·o·dor·ous [ɪnˈəʊdərəs] *adj.* □ geruchlos.

in·of·fen·sive [ˌɪnəˈfensɪv] *adj.* □ harmlos.

in·of·fi·cious [ˌɪnəˈfɪʃəs] *adj.* ⚖ pflichtwidrig.

in·op·er·a·ble [ɪnˈɒpərəbl] *adj.* ⚕ inopeˈrabel, nicht operierbar.

in·op·er·a·tive [ɪnˈɒpərətɪv] *adj.* **1.** unwirksam: a) wirkungslos, b) ⚖ ungültig, nicht in Kraft; **2.** a) außer Betrieb, b) nicht einsatzfähig.

in·op·por·tune [ɪnˈɒpətjuːn] *adj.* □ ˈinopporˌtun, unangebracht, zur Unzeit (geschehen *etc.*), ungelegen.

in·or·di·nate [ɪˈnɔːdɪnət] *adj.* □ **1.** ˈübermäßig, überˈtrieben, maßlos; **2.** ungeordnet; **3.** unbeherrscht.

in·or·gan·ic [ˌɪnɔːˈgænɪk] *adj.* (□ ~***ally***) ˈun-, ⚗ ˈanorˌganisch.

in·os·cu·late [ɪˈnɒskjʊleɪt] *mst* ⚕ **I** *v/t.* vereinigen (***with*** mit), einmünden lassen (***into*** in *acc.*); **II** *v/i.* sich vereinigen; eng verbunden sein.

in·pa·tient [ˈɪnˌpeɪʃnt] *s.* ˈAnstaltspatiˌent(in), statioˈnärer Patiˈent: ~ ***treatment*** stationäre Behandlung.

in·pay·ment [ˈɪnˌpeɪmənt] *s.* ✝ Einzahlung *f*.

in·phase [ˈɪnfeɪz] *adj.* ϟ gleichphasig.

in-plant [ˈɪnplɑːnt] *adj.* ✝ innerbetrieblich, (beˈtriebs)inˌtern.

in·pour·ing [ˈɪnˌpɔːrɪŋ] **I** *adj.* (her-) ˈeinströmend; **II** *s.* (Her)ˈEinströmen *n*.

in·put [ˈɪnpʊt] *s.* Input *m*: a) ✝ eingesetzte Produktiˈonsmittel *pl.*: ~***-output analysis*** Input-Output-Analyse *f*, b) ⚙ eingespeiste Menge, c) ϟ zugeführte Spannung *od.* Leistung, (Leistungs-) Aufnahme *f*, ˈEingangsenerˌgie *f*: ~ ***amplifier*** *Radio*: Eingangsverstärker *m*; ~ ***circuit*** ϟ Eingangsstromkreis *m*; ~ ***impedance*** ϟ Eingangswiderstand *m*, d) *Computer*: (Daten-, Proˈgramm)Eingabe *f*.

in·quest [ˈɪnkwest] *s.* **1.** ⚖ a) gerichtliche Unterˈsuchung, b) *a.* ***coroner's*** ~ Gerichtsverhandlung *f* zur Feststellung der Todesursache (*bei ungeklärten Todesfällen*), c) Unterˈsuchungsergebnis *n*, Befund *m*; **2.** genaue Prüfung, Nachforschung *f*.

in·qui·e·tude [ɪnˈkwaɪətjuːd] *s.* Unruhe *f*, Besorgnis *f*.

in·quire [ɪnˈkwaɪə] **I** *v/t.* **1.** sich erkundigen nach, fragen nach, erfragen: ~ ***the price***; ~ ***one's way*** sich nach dem Weg erkundigen; **II** *v/i.* **2.** fragen, sich erkundigen (***of s.o.*** bei j-m; ***for*** nach; ***about*** über *acc.*, wegen): ~ ***after s.o.*** sich nach j-m *od.* nach j-s Befinden erkundigen; ~ ***within!*** Näheres im Hause (zu erfragen)!; **3.** ~ ***into*** unterˈsuchen, erforschen; **inˈquir·er** [-ərə] *s.* **1.** Fragesteller(in), Nachfragende(r *m*) *f*; **2.** Unterˈsuchende(r *m*) *f*; **inˈquir·ing** [-ərɪŋ] *adj.* □ forschend, fragend; neugierig.

in·quir·y [ɪnˈkwaɪərɪ] *s.* **1.** Erkundigung *f*, (An-, Nach)Frage *f*: ***on*** ~ auf Nachfrage *od.* Anfrage; ***make inquiries*** Erkundigungen einziehen (***of s.o.*** bei j-m; ***about*** über *acc.*, wegen); ***Inquiries*** *pl.* Auskunft(sstelle) *f*; **2.** Unterˈsuchung *f*, Prüfung *f* (***into*** *gen.*); (Nach)Forschung *f*: ***board of*** ~ Untersuchungsausschuß *m*; ~ **of·fice** *s.* ˈAuskunft(sbüˌro *n*) *f*.

in·qui·si·tion [ˌɪnkwɪˈzɪʃn] *s.* **1.** (gerichtliche *od.* amtliche) Unterˈsuchung; **2.** *R.C.* a) *hist.* Inquisitiˈon *f*, Ketzergericht *n*, b) Kongregatiˈon *f* des heiligen Ofˈfiziums; **3.** *fig.* strenges Verhör; ˌ**inquiˈsi·tion·al** [-ʃənl] *adj.* **1.** Untersuchungs...; **2.** *R.C.* Inquisitions...; **3.** → ***inquisitorial*** 3.

in·quis·i·tive [ɪnˈkwɪzətɪv] *adj.* □ **1.** wißbegierig; **2.** neugierig, naseweis; **inˈquis·i·tive·ness** [-nɪs] *s.* **1.** Wißbegierde *f*; **2.** Neugier(de) *f*; **inˈquis·i·tor** [-tə] *s.* *R.C.* Inquiˈsitor *m*: ***Grand*** ♀ Großinquisitor; **in·quis·i·to·ri·al** [ɪnˌkwɪzɪˈtɔːrɪəl] *adj.* □ **1.** ⚖ Untersuchungs...; **2.** *R.C.* Inquisitions...; **3.** inquisiˈtorisch, streng (verhörend); **4.** aufdringlich fragend, neugierig.

in re [ˌɪnˈreɪ] (*Lat.*) *prp.* ⚖ in Sachen, betrifft; ~ **rem** [ˌɪnˈrem] (*Lat.*) *adj.* ⚖ dinglich: ~ ***action***.

in·road [ˈɪnrəʊd] *s.* **1.** Angriff *m*, ˈÜberfall *m* (***on*** auf *acc.*), Einfall *m* (***in***, ***on*** in *acc.*); **2.** *fig.* (***on***, ***into***) Eingriff *m* (in *acc.*), ˈÜbergriff *m* (auf *acc.*), ˈübermäßige Inˈanspruchnahme (*gen.*); **3.** Eindringen *n*: ***make an*** ~ ***into*** *fig.* e-n Einbruch erzielen in (*dat.*).

in·rush [ˈɪnrʌʃ] *s.* (Her)ˈEinströmen *n*, Zustrom *m*.

in·sa·lu·bri·ous [ˌɪnsəˈluːbrɪəs] *adj.* ungesund; ˌ**in·saˈlu·bri·ty** [-ətɪ] *s.* Gesundheitsschädlichkeit *f*.

in·sane [ɪnˈseɪn] *adj.* □ wahn-, irrsinnig: a) ⚕ geisteskrank; → ***asylum*** 1, b) *fig.* verrückt, toll.

in·san·i·tar·y [ɪnˈsænɪtərɪ] *adj.* ˈunhygiˌenisch, gesundheitsschädlich.

in·san·i·ty [ɪnˈsænətɪ] *s.* Irr-, Wahnsinn *m*: a) ⚕ Geisteskrankheit *f*, b) *fig.* Verrücktheit *f*.

in·sa·ti·a·bil·i·ty [ɪnˌseɪʃjəˈbɪlətɪ] *s.* Unersättlichkeit *f*; **in·sa·ti·a·ble** [ɪnˈseɪʃjəbl], **in·sa·ti·ate** [ɪnˈseɪʃɪət] *adj.* unersättlich (*a. fig.*).

in·scribe [ɪnˈskraɪb] *v/t.* **1.** (ein-, auf-) schreiben; **2.** beschriften, mit e-r Inschrift versehen; **3.** *bsd.* ✝ eintragen: ~***d stock*** *Brit.* Namensaktien *pl.*; **4.** *Buch etc.* widmen (***to*** *dat.*); **5.** ⩓ einbeschreiben; **6.** *fig.* (fest) einprägen (***in*** *dat.*).

in·scrip·tion [ɪnˈskrɪpʃn] *s.* **1.** Beschriftung *f*; In-, Aufschrift *f*; **2.** Eintragung *f*, Registrierung *f* (*bsd. von Aktien*); **3.** Zueignung *f*, Widmung *f* (*Buch etc.*); **4.** ⩓ Einzeichnung *f*; **5.** ✝ *Brit.* (Ausgabe *f* von) Namensaktien *pl.*; **inˈscrip·tion·al** [-ʃənl], **inˈscrip·tive** [-ptɪv] *adj.* Inschriften...

in·scru·ta·bil·i·ty [ɪnˌskruːtəˈbɪlətɪ] *s.* Unergründlichkeit *f*; **in·scru·ta·ble** [ɪnˈskruːtəbl] *adj.* □ unergründlich: ~ ***face*** undurchdringliches Gesicht.

in·sect [ˈɪnsekt] *s.* **1.** *zo.* Inˈsekt *n*, Kerbtier *n*; **2.** *contp.* ‚Wurm' *m*, ‚Giftzwerg' *m* (*Person*); **in·sec·ti·cide** [ɪnˈsektɪsaɪd] *s.* Inˈsektengift *n*, Insektiˈzid *n*; **in·sec·ti·vore** [ɪnˈsektɪvɔː] *s.* *zo.* Inˈsektenfresser *m*; **in·sec·tiv·o·rous** [ˌɪnsekˈtɪvərəs] *adj.* *zo.* inˈsektenfressend.

in·sect pow·der *s.* Inˈsektenpulver *n*.

in·se·cure [ˌɪnsɪˈkjʊə] *adj.* □ **1.** unsicher: a) ungesichert, preˈkär, b) ungewiß, zweifelhaft; **2.** *psych.* unsicher, verunsichert: ***make s.o. feel*** ~ j-n verunsichern; ˌ**in·seˈcu·ri·ty** [-ʊərətɪ] *s.* **1.** Unsicherheit *f*; **2.** Ungewißheit *f*.

in·sem·i·nate [ɪnˈsemɪneɪt] *v/t.* **1.** (ein-, aus)säen; **2.** *biol.* (*bsd.* künstlich) befruchten; **3.** *fig.* einimpfen; **in·sem·i·na·tion** [ɪnˌsemɪˈneɪʃn] *s.* **1.** (Ein)Säen *n*; **2.** *biol.* Befruchtung *f*: ***artificial*** ~ künstliche Befruchtung.

in·sen·sate [ɪnˈsenseɪt] *adj.* □ **1.** leb-, empfindungs-, gefühllos; **2.** unsinnig, unvernünftig; **3.** → ***insensible*** 3.

in·sen·si·bil·i·ty [ɪnˌsensəˈbɪlətɪ] *s.* (***to***) **1.** (*a. fig.*) Gefühllosigkeit *f* (gegen), Unempfindlichkeit *f* (für); **2.** Bewußtlosigkeit *f*; **3.** Gleichgültigkeit *f* (gegen), Unempfänglichkeit *f* (für); Stumpfheit *f*; **in·sen·si·ble** [ɪnˈsensəbl] *adj.* □ **1.** unempfindlich, gefühllos (***to*** gegen): ~ ***from cold*** vor Kälte gefühllos; **2.** bewußtlos; **3.** (***of***, ***to***) unempfänglich (für), gleichgültig (gegen); **4.** ***be*** ~ ***of*** nicht (an)erkennen (*acc.*); **5.** unmerklich; **in·sen·si·bly** [ɪnˈsensəblɪ] *adv.* unmerklich.

in·sen·si·tive [ɪnˈsensətɪv] *adj.* (***to***) **1.** *a. phys.*, ⚙ unempfindlich (gegen); **2.** unempfänglich (für), gefühllos (gegen); **inˈsen·si·tive·ness** [-nɪs] *s.* Unempfindlichkeit *f*; Unempfänglichkeit *f*.

in·sen·ti·ent [ɪnˈsenʃnt] → ***insensible*** 1.

in·sep·a·ra·bil·i·ty [ɪnˌsepərəˈbɪlətɪ] *s.* **1.** Untrennbarkeit *f*; **2.** Unzertrennlichkeit *f*; **in·sep·a·ra·ble** [ɪnˈsepərəbl] **I** *adj.* □ **1.** untrennbar (*a. ling.*); **2.** unzertrennlich; **II** *s.* **3.** *pl. die* Unzertrennlichen *pl.*

in·sert I *v/t.* [ɪnˈsɜːt] **1.** einfügen, -setzen, -schieben, *Worte a.* einschalten, *Instrument etc.* einführen, *Schlüssel etc.* (hinˈein)stecken (***in***, ***into*** in *acc.*); **2.** ϟ ein-, zwischenschalten; **3.** *Münze* einwerfen; **4.** *Anzeige* (*in e-e Zeitung*) setzen, *ein Inserat* aufgeben; **II** *s.* [ˈɪnsɜːt] **5.** → ***insertion*** 2–4; **inˈser·tion** [-ɜːʃn] *s.* **1.** a) Einfügen *n* (*etc.* → ***insert***), b) Einfügung *f*, Ein-, Zusatz *m*, Einschaltung *f* (*a.* ϟ); Einwurf *m* (*Münze*); **2.** (Zeitungs)Beilage *f*; **3.** (Spitzen- *etc.*) Einsatz *m*; **4.** Inseˈrat *n*, Anzeige *f*.

ˈin-ˌser·vice *adj.* während der Dienstzeit: ~ ***training*** betriebliche Berufsförderung.

in·set I *s.* [ˈɪnset] **1.** → ***insertion*** 1 b, 2, 3; **2.** Eckeinsatz *m*, Nebenbild *n*, -karte *f*; **II** *v/t.* [*irr.* → ***set***] [ˌɪnˈset] *pret. u. p.p. Brit. a.* **in·set·ted** [ˌɪnˈsetɪd] **3.** einfügen, -setzen.

in·shore [ˌɪnˈʃɔː] **I** *adj.* **1.** an *od.* nahe der Küste: ~ ***fishing*** Küstenfischerei *f*; **II** *adv.* **2.** a) küstenwärts, b) nahe der Küste; **3.** ~ ***of*** näher der Küste als: ~ ***of a ship*** zwischen Schiff und Küste.

in·side [ˌɪnˈsaɪd] **I** *s.* **1.** Innenseite *f*, -fläche *f*, innere Seite: ***on the*** ~ innen; ***s.o. on the*** ~ *fig.* → ***insider*** 1; **2.** *das* Innere: ***from the*** ~ von innen; ~ ***out*** das Innere nach außen, umgestülpt, *Kleidung*: verkehrt herum, links; ***turn*** ~ ***out*** (völlig) umkrempeln, durcheinanderbringen, ‚auf den Kopf stellen'; ***know*** ~

out in- u. auswendig kennen; **3.** F ,Eingeweide' *pl.*: ***pain in one's ~*** Bauch- *od.* Leibschmerzen; **II** *adj.* **4.** inner, inwendig, Innen...: ***~ diameter*** lichter Durchmesser, lichte Weite; ***~ information*** interne Informationen *pl.*, Informationen *pl.* aus erster Quelle; ***~ job*** F Tat *f* e-s Eingeweihten *od.* Insiders; ***~ lane*** *sport* Innenbahn *f*; ***~ story*** Inside-Story *f* (*Bericht aus interner Sicht*); **III** *adv.* **5.** im Innern, innen, drin(nen); **6.** nach innen, hin'ein, her'ein: ***go ~***; ***put s.o. ~*** F j-n ,einlochen'; **7.** ***~ of*** a) innerhalb (*gen.*), binnen: ***~ of a week***, b) *Am.* → 8; **IV** *prp.* **8.** innerhalb (*gen.*), im Innern (*gen.*), in (*dat.*): ***be ~ the house***; **9.** in (*acc.*) ... (hin'ein *od.* her'ein): ***go ~ the house***; **in·sid·er** [ˌɪn'saɪdə] *s.* **1.** Eingeweihte(r *m*) *f*, Insider *m*; **2.** Zugehörige(r *m*) *f*, Mitglied *n*.

in·sid·i·ous [ɪn'sɪdɪəs] *adj.* □ **1.** heimtückisch, 'hinterhältig, tückisch; **2.** ⚕ tückisch, schleichend; **in'sid·i·ous·ness** [-nɪs] *s.* 'Hinterlist *f*, Tücke *f*.

in·sight ['ɪnsaɪt] *s.* (***into***) **1.** Einblick *m* (in *acc.*); **2.** Verständnis *n* (für), Kenntnis (*gen.*).

in·sig·ni·a [ɪn'sɪgnɪə] *s. pl.* In'signien *pl.*, Ab-, Ehrenzeichen *pl.*

in·sig·nif·i·cance [ˌɪnsɪg'nɪfɪkəns] *s.*, **ˌin·sig'nif·i·can·cy** [-sɪ] *s.* Bedeutungslosigkeit *f*, Unwichtigkeit *f*, Belanglosigkeit *f*, Geringfügigkeit *f*; **ˌin·sig'nif·i·cant** [-nt] *adj.* □ **1.** bedeutungs-, belanglos, unwichtig; geringfügig, unbedeutend; nichtssagend; **2.** verächtlich.

in·sin·cere [ˌɪnsɪn'sɪə] *adj.* □ unaufrichtig, falsch; **ˌin·sin'cer·i·ty** [-'serətɪ] *s.* Unaufrichtigkeit *f*.

in·sin·u·ate [ɪn'sɪnjʊeɪt] *v/t.* **1.** andeuten, anspielen auf (*acc.*): ***what are you insinuating?*** was wollen Sie damit sagen?; **2.** *j-m et.* zu verstehen geben, *et.* vorsichtig beibringen; **3.** ***~ o.s. into s.o.'s favo(u)r*** sich bei j-m einschmeicheln; **in'sin·u·at·ing** [-tɪŋ] *adj.* □ **1.** anzüglich; **2.** schmeichlerisch; **in·sin·u·a·tion** [ɪnˌsɪnjʊ'eɪʃn] *s.* **1.** Anspielung *f*, (versteckte) Andeutung; **2.** Schmeiche'leien *pl.*

in·sip·id [ɪn'sɪpɪd] *adj.* □ **1.** fade, geschmacklos, schal; **2.** *fig.* fade, abgeschmackt, geistlos; **in·si·pid·i·ty** [ˌɪnsɪ'pɪdətɪ] *s.* Geschmacklosigkeit *f*, Fadheit *f*, *fig. a.* Abgeschmacktheit *f*.

in·sist [ɪn'sɪst] *v/i.* **1.** (***on***) bestehen (auf *dat.*), dringen (auf *acc.*), verlangen (*acc.*), insis'tieren (auf *dat.*): ***I ~ on doing it*** ich bestehe darauf, es zu tun; ***if you ~!*** wenn Sie darauf bestehen!; **2.** (***on***) beharren (auf *dat.*, bei), bleiben (bei); **3.** beteuern (***on*** *acc.*); **4.** (***on***) her'vorheben, nachdrücklich betonen (*acc.*); **5.** es sich nicht nehmen lassen (***on doing*** zu tun); **6.** ***~ on*** *doing* immer wieder *umfallen etc.* (*Sache*); **in'sist·ence** [-təns], **in'sist·en·cy** [-tənsɪ] *s.* **1.** Bestehen *n*, Beharren *n* (***on, upon*** auf *dat.*); **2.** (***on***) Beteuerung *f* (*gen.*), Beharren (auf *dat.*); **3.** (***on, upon***) Betonung *f* (*gen.*); Nachdruck *m* (auf *dat.*); **4.** Beharrlichkeit *f*, Hartnäckigkeit *f*; **in'sist·ent** [-tənt] *adj.* □ **1.** beharrlich, dauernd, hartnäckig, drängend; **2.** ***be ~ on*** → ***insist*** 1–3; **3.** eindringlich, nachdrücklich, dringend; **4.** aufdringlich, grell (*Farbe, Ton*).

in·so·bri·e·ty [ˌɪnsəʊ'braɪətɪ] *s.* Unmäßigkeit *f* (*engS.* im Trinken).

ˌin·so'far → ***far*** 4.

in·so·la·tion [ˌɪnsəʊ'leɪʃn] *s.* Sonnenbestrahlung *f*; Sonnenbad *n*.

in·sole ['ɪnsəʊl] *s.* **1.** Brandsohle *f*; **2.** Einlegesohle *f*.

in·so·lence ['ɪnsələns] *s.* **1.** Über'heblichkeit *f*; **2.** Unverschämtheit *f*, Frechheit *f*; **'in·so·lent** [-nt] *adj.* □ **1.** anmaßend; **2.** unverschämt.

in·sol·u·bil·i·ty [ɪnˌsɒljʊ'bɪlətɪ] *s.* **1.** Un(auf)löslichkeit *f*; **2.** *fig.* Unlösbarkeit *f*; **in·sol·u·ble** [ɪn'sɒljʊbl] **I** *adj.* □ **1.** un(auf)löslich; **2.** unlösbar, unerklärlich; **II** *s.* **3.** ⚗ unlösliche Sub'stanz.

in·sol·ven·cy [ɪn'sɒlvənsɪ] *s.* ⚘ **1.** Zahlungsunfähigkeit *f*, Insol'venz *f*; **2.** Kon'kurs *m*; **in'sol·vent** [-nt] **I** *adj.* ⚘ **1.** zahlungsunfähig, insol'vent; **2.** *bsd. fig.* (*moralisch etc.*) bank'rott; **3.** Konkurs...: ***~ estate*** konkursreifer Nachlaß; **II** *s.* **4.** zahlungsunfähiger Schuldner.

in·som·ni·a [ɪn'sɒmnɪə] *s.* ⚕ Schlaflosigkeit *f*; **in'som·ni·ac** [-ɪæk] *s.* ⚕ an Schlaflosigkeit Leidende(r *m*) *f*.

in·so·much [ˌɪnsəʊ'mʌtʃ] *adv.* **1.** so (sehr), dermaßen (***that*** daß); **2.** → ***inasmuch***.

in·sou·ci·ance [ɪn'su:sjəns] *s.* Sorglosigkeit *f* (*etc.* →) **in'sou·ci·ant** [-nt] *adj.* sorglos, unbekümmert, gleichgültig, lässig.

in·spect [ɪn'spekt] *v/t.* **1.** unter'suchen, prüfen, nachsehen; **2.** besichtigen, sich (genau) ansehen, inspizieren; **3.** beaufsichtigen; **in'spec·tion** [-kʃn] *s.* **1.** Besichtigung *f*, An-, 'Durchsicht *f*, Einsicht(nahme) *f* (*von Akten etc.*): ***for your ~*** zur Ansicht; ***free ~*** Besichtigung ohne Kaufzwang; ***be*** (***laid***) ***open to ~*** zur Einsicht ausliegen; **2.** Unter'suchung *f*, Prüfung *f*, Kon'trolle *f*: ***~ hole*** ⚙ Schauloch *n*; ***~ lamp*** ⚙ Ableuchtlampe *f*; **3.** Besichtigung *f*, Inspekti'on *f*; **4.** Aufsicht *f*; **5.** ⚔ Ap'pell *m*; **in'spec·tor** [-tə] *s.* **1.** In'spektor *m*; Kontrol'leur *m* (*Bus etc.*), Aufseher *m*, Aufsichtsbeamte(r) *m*: ***customs ~*** Zollinspektor *m*; ***~ of schools*** Schulinspektor *m*; ***~ of weights and measures*** Eichmeister *m*; **2.** (Poli'zei)Inˌspektor *m*, (-)Kommisˌsar *m*; **3.** ⚔ Inspek'teur *m*; **in'spec·to·ral** [-tərəl] *adj.* Inspektor(en)...; Aufsichts...; **in'spec·tor·ate** [-tərət] *s.* Inspekto'rat *n*: a) Aufsichtsbezirk *m*, b) Aufsichtsbehörde *f*, c) Aufseheramt *n*; **in·spec·to·ri·al** [ˌɪnspek'tɔ:rɪəl] → ***inspectoral***; **in'spec·tor·ship** [-təʃɪp] **1.** In'spektoramt *n*; **2.** Aufsicht *f*.

in·spi·ra·tion [ˌɪnspə'reɪʃn] *s.* **1.** *eccl.* göttliche Eingebung, Erleuchtung *f*; **2.** Inspirati'on *f*, Eingebung *f*, (plötzlicher) Einfall; **3.** *et.* Inspirierendes; **4.** Anregung *f*: ***at the ~ of*** auf *j-s* Veranlassung; **5.** Begeisterung *f*; **in·spi·ra·tor** ['ɪnspəreɪtə] *s.* ⚕ Inha'lator *m*; **in·spir·a·to·ry** [ɪn'spaɪərətərɪ] *adj.* (Ein-) Atmungs...

in·spire [ɪn'spaɪə] *v/t.* **1.** begeistern, anfeuern; **2.** anregen, veranlassen; **3.** (***in s.o.***) *Gefühl etc.* einflößen, eingeben (j-m); erwecken, erregen (in j-m); **4.** *fig.* a) erleuchten, b) beseelen, erfüllen (***with*** mit), c) inspirieren; **5.** einatmen; **in'spired** [-əd] *adj.* **1.** *bsd. eccl.* erleuchtet; eingegeben; **2.** schöpferisch, einfallsreich; **3.** begeistert; **4.** a) glänzend, her'vorragend, b) schwungvoll; **5.** von ,oben' (*von der Regierung etc.*) veranlaßt; **in'spir·er** [-ərə] *s.* Anreger (-in); **in'spir·ing** [-ərɪŋ] *adj.* □ anregend, begeisternd, inspirierend.

in·spir·it [ɪn'spɪrɪt] *v/t.* beleben, beseelen, anfeuern, ermutigen.

in·sta·bil·i·ty [ˌɪnstə'bɪlətɪ] *s. mst fig.* **1.** Instabili'tät *f*, Unsicherheit *f*; **2.** Labili'tät *f*, Unbeständigkeit *f*.

in·stall [ɪn'stɔ:l] *v/t.* **1.** ⚙ a) installieren, montieren, aufstellen, einbauen, b) einrichten, (an)legen, anbringen; **2.** *j-n* bestallen; *in ein Amt* einsetzen, -führen; **3.** ***~ o.s.*** F sich niederlassen; **in·stal·la·tion** [ˌɪnstə'leɪʃn] *s.* **1.** ⚙ a) Installierung *f*, Einrichtung *f*, Einbau *m*, b) (*fertige*) Anlage *od.* Einrichtung; **2.** (Amts)Einsetzung *f*, Bestallung *f*.

in·stal(l)·ment[1] [ɪn'stɔ:lmənt] → ***installation***.

in·stal(l)·ment[2] [ɪn'stɔ:lmənt] *s.* **1.** ⚘ Rate *f*, Teil-, Ab-, Abschlags-, Ratenzahlung *f*: ***by ~s*** in Raten; ***first ~*** Anzahlung *f*; ***~ credit*** Teilzahlungskredit *m*; ***~ plan*** Teilzahlungssystem *n*; ***buy on the ~ plan*** auf Raten kaufen, ,abstottern'; **2.** (Teil)Lieferung *f* (*Buch etc.*); **3.** Fortsetzung *f* (*Roman etc.*), *Radio, TV*: *a.* (Sende)Folge *f*.

in·stance ['ɪnstəns] **I** *s.* **1.** (*einzelner*) Fall, Beispiel *n*: ***in this ~*** in diesem (*besonderen*) Fall; ***for ~*** zum Beispiel: ***as an ~ of s.th.*** als Beispiel für et.; **2.** Bitte *f*, Ersuchen *n*: ***at his ~*** auf sein Drängen *od.* Betreiben *od.* s-e Veranlassung; **3.** ⚖ In'stanz *f*: ***court of the first ~*** Gericht *n* erster Instanz; ***in the last ~*** in letzter Instanz, *fig.* letztlich; ***in the first ~*** *fig.* in erster Linie, zuerst; **II** *v/t.* **4.** als Beispiel anführen; **5.** mit Beispielen belegen; **'in·stan·cy** [-sɪ] *s.* Dringlichkeit *f*.

in·stant ['ɪnstənt] **I** *s.* **1.** Mo'ment *m*: a) (kurzer) Augenblick *m*, b) (genauer) Zeitpunkt; ***in an ~***, ***on the ~*** sofort, augenblicklich, im Nu; ***at this ~*** in diesem Augenblick; ***this ~*** sofort, augenblicklich; **II** *adj.* □ → ***instantly***; **2.** so'fortig, augenblicklich: ***~ camera*** *phot.* Instant-, Sofortbildkamera *f*; ***~ coffee*** Pulverkaffee *m*; ***~ meal*** Fertig-, Schnellgericht *n*; **3.** *abbr.* ***inst.***: ***the 10th ~*** der 10. dieses Monats; **4.** dringend.

in·stan·ta·ne·ous [ˌɪnstən'teɪnjəs] *adj.* □ **1.** so'fortig, unverzüglich, augenblicklich: ***death was ~*** der Tod trat auf der Stelle ein; **2.** gleichzeitig (*Ereignisse*); **3.** *phys.*, ⚙ momen'tan, Augenblicks...: ***~ photo*** Momentaufnahme *f*; ***~ shutter*** *phot.* Momentverschluß *m*; **ˌin·stan'ta·ne·ous·ly** [-lɪ] *adv.* so'fort, unverzüglich; auf der Stelle; **ˌin·stan'ta·ne·ous·ness** [-nɪs] *s.* Augenblicklichkeit *f*; Blitzesschnelle *f*.

in·stan·ter [ɪn'stæntə] *adv.* so'fort.

in·stant·ly ['ɪnstəntlɪ] *adv.* so'fort, unverzüglich, augenblicklich.

in·state [ɪn'steɪt] *v/t.* *in ein Amt* einsetzen.

in·stead [ɪn'sted] *adv.* **1.** ~ ***of*** (an)statt (*gen.*), an Stelle von: ~ ***of me*** statt meiner, an meiner Statt *od.* Stelle; ~ ***of going*** (an)statt zu gehen; ~ ***of at work*** statt bei der Arbeit; **2.** statt dessen: ***she sent the boy*** ~.

in·step ['ɪnstep] *s.* Rist *m*, Spann *m* (*Fuß*): ~ ***raiser*** Plattfußeinlage *f*; ***high in the*** ~ F hochnäsig.

in·sti·gate ['ɪnstɪgeɪt] *v/t.* **1.** an-, aufreizen, aufhetzen, anstiften (***to*** zu, ***to do*** zu tun); **2.** *et.* (*Böses*) anstiften, anfachen; **in·sti·ga·tion** [ˌɪnstɪ'geɪʃn] *s.* **1.** Anstiftung *f*, Aufhetzung *f*, -reizung *f*; **2.** Anregung *f*: ***at the*** ~ ***of*** auf Betreiben *od.* Veranlassung von (*od. gen.*); **'in·sti·ga·tor** [-tə] *s.* Anstifter(in), (Auf)Hetzer(in).

in·stil(l) [ɪn'stɪl] *v/t.* **1.** einträufeln, -tröpfeln; **2.** *fig.* (***into***) a) *j-m* einflößen, -impfen, beibringen, b) *et.* durch'dringen (mit), einfließen lassen (in *acc.*); **in·stil·la·tion** [ˌɪnstɪ'leɪʃn], **in'stil(l)·ment** [-mənt] *s.* **1.** Einträufelung *f*; **2.** *fig.* Einflößung *f*, Einimpfung *f*.

in·stinct I *s.* ['ɪnstɪŋkt] **1.** In'stinkt *m*, (Na'tur)Trieb *m*: ***by*** ~, ***on*** ~, ***from*** ~ instinktiv; **2.** a) instink'tives Gefühl, (sicherer) In'stinkt, b) Begabung *f* (***for*** für); II *adj.* [ɪn'stɪŋkt] **3.** belebt, durch'drungen, erfüllt (***with*** von); **in·stinc·tive** [ɪn'stɪŋktɪv] *adj.* □ instink'tiv: a) in'stinkt-, triebmäßig, Instinkt…, b) unwillkürlich, c) angeboren.

in·sti·tute ['ɪnstɪtjuːt] I *s.* **1.** Insti'tut *n*, Anstalt *f*; **2.** (gelehrte *etc.*) Gesellschaft; **3.** Insti'tut *n* (*Gebäude*); **4.** *pl. bsd.* ☤ Grundgesetze *pl.*, -lehren *pl.*; II *v/t.* **5.** ein-, errichten, gründen; einführen; **6.** einleiten, in Gang setzen: ~ ***an inquiry*** e-e Untersuchung einleiten; ~ ***legal proceedings*** Klage erheben, das Verfahren einleiten (***against*** gegen); **7.** *bsd. eccl. j-n* einsetzen, einführen.

in·sti·tu·tion [ˌɪnstɪ'tjuːʃn] *s.* **1.** Insti'tut *n*, Anstalt *f*, Einrichtung *f*, Stiftung *f*, Gesellschaft *f*; **2.** Insti'tut *n* (*Gebäude*); **3.** Instituti'on *f*, Einrichtung *f*, (über'kommene) Sitte, Brauch *m*; **4.** Ordnung *f*, Recht *n*, Satzung *f*; **5.** F a) alte Gewohnheit, b) vertraute Sache, feste Einrichtung, c) allbekannte Per'son; **6.** Ein-, Errichtung *f*, Gründung *f*; **7.** *eccl.* Einsetzung *f*; **ˌin·sti'tu·tion·al** [-ʃənl] *adj.* **1.** Institutions…, Instituts…, Anstalts…; **2.** ☤ *Am.* ~ ***advertising*** Repräsentationswerbung *f*; **ˌin·sti'tu·tion·al·ize** [-ʃənlaɪz] *v/t.* **1.** *et.* institutionalisieren; **2.** *j-n* in e-e Anstalt einweisen.

in·struct [ɪn'strʌkt] *v/t.* **1.** (be)lehren, unter'weisen, -'richten, schulen, ausbilden (***in*** in *dat.*); **2.** informieren, unter'richten; **3.** instruieren (*a.* ⚖), anweisen, beauftragen; **in'struc·tion** [-kʃn] *s.* **1.** Belehrung *f*, Schulung *f*, Ausbildung *f*, 'Unterricht *m*: ***private*** ~ Privatunterricht; ***course of*** ~ Lehrgang *m*, Kursus *m*; **2.** *pl.* Auftrag *m*, Vorschrift (-en *pl.*) *f*, (An)Weisung(en *pl.*) *f*, Verhaltungsmaßregeln *pl.*, Richtlinien *pl.*, (*a.* Betriebs)Anleitung *f*: ***according to*** ~***s*** auftrags-, weisungsgemäß, vorschriftsmäßig; ~***s for use*** Gebrauchsanweisung; **3.** *Am.* ⚖ *mst pl.* Rechtsbelehrung *f*; **4.** ⚔ *mst pl.* Dienstanweisung *f*, Instrukti'on *f*; **in'struc·tion·al** [-kʃənl] *adj.* Unterrichts…, Erziehungs…, Ausbildungs…, Lehr…: ~ ***film*** Lehrfilm *m*; ~ ***staff*** Lehrkörper *m*; **in'struc·tive** [-tɪv] *adj.* □ belehrend; lehr-, aufschlußreich; **in'struc·tive·ness** [-tɪvnɪs] *s.* *das* Belehrende; **in'struc·tor** [-tə] *s.* **1.** Lehrer *m*; **2.** Ausbilder *m* (*a.* ⚔); **3.** *univ. Am.* Do'zent *m*; **in'struc·tress** [-trɪs] *s.* Lehrerin *f*.

in·stru·ment ['ɪnstrʊmənt] I *s.* **1.** Instru'ment *n* (*a.* ♪): a) (feines) Werkzeug *n*, b) Appa'rat *m*, (*bsd.* Meß)Gerät *n*; **2.** *pl.* ⚕ Besteck *n*; **3.** ☤, ⚖ a) Doku'ment *n*, Urkunde *f*; 'Wertpaˌpier *n*: ~ ***of payment*** Zahlungsmittel *n*; ~ ***payable to bearer*** ☤ Inhaberpapier; ~ ***to order*** Orderpapier, b) *pl.* Instrumen'tarium *n*: ***the*** ~***s of credit policy***; **4.** *fig.* Werkzeug *n*: a) (Hilfs)Mittel *n*, b) Handlanger(in); II *v/t.* **5.** ♪ instrumentieren; III *adj.* **6.** ⚙ Instrumenten…: ~ ***board***, ~ ***panel*** a) Schalt-, Armaturenbrett *n*, b) ✈ Instrumentenbrett *n*; ~ ***maker*** Apparatebauer *m*, Feinmechaniker *m*; **7.** ✈ Blind…, Instrumenten…: ~ ***flying***; ~ ***landing***; **in·stru·men·tal** [ˌɪnstrʊ'mentl] *adj.* □ → ***instrumentally***; **1.** behilflich, dienlich, förderlich: ***be*** ~ ***in*** *ger.* behilflich sein *od.* wesentlich dazu beitragen, daß; e-e gewichtige Rolle spielen bei; **2.** ♪ Instrumental…; **3.** mit Instrumenten ausgeführt: ~ ***operation***; ~ ***error*** ⚙ Instrumentenfehler *m*; **4.** ~ ***case*** *ling.* Instrumental(is) *m*; **in·stru·men·tal·ist** [ˌɪnstrʊ'mentəlɪst] *s.* ♪ Instrumenta'list(in); **in·stru·men·tal·i·ty** [ˌɪnstrʊmen'tælətɪ] *s.* **1.** Mitwirkung *f*, Mithilfe *f*: ***through his*** ~; **2.** (Hilfs)Mittel *n*; Einrichtung *f*; **in·stru·men·tal·ly** [ˌɪnstrʊ'mentəlɪ] *adv.* durch Instrumente; **in·stru·men·ta·tion** [ˌɪnstrʊmen'teɪʃn] *s.* ♪ Instrumentati'on *f*.

in·sub·or·di·nate [ˌɪnsə'bɔːdnət] *adj.* unbotmäßig, wider'setzlich, aufsässig; **in·sub·or·di·na·tion** ['ɪnsəˌbɔːdɪ'neɪʃn] *s.* Unbotmäßigkeit *f etc.*; Gehorsamsverweigerung *f*, Auflehnung *f*.

in·sub·stan·tial [ˌɪnsəb'stænʃl] *adj.* **1.** sub'stanzlos, unkörperlich; **2.** unwirklich; **3.** wenig nahrhaft.

in·suf·fer·a·ble [ɪn'sʌfərəbl] *adj.* □ unerträglich, unausstehlich.

in·suf·fi·cien·cy [ˌɪnsə'fɪʃnsɪ] *s.* **1.** Unzulänglichkeit *f*, Mangel(haftigkeit *f*) *m*; Untauglichkeit *f*; **2.** ⚕ Insuffizi'enz *f*; **ˌin·suf'fi·cient** [-nt] *adj.* □ **1.** unzulänglich, unzureichend, ungenügend; **2.** untauglich, mangelhaft, unfähig.

in·suf·flate ['ɪnsʌfleɪt] *v/t.* **1.** *a.* ⚕, ⚙ (hin)'einblasen; **2.** *R.C.* anhauchen; **'in·suf·fla·tor** [-tə] *s.* ⚙, ⚕ 'Einblaseappaˌrat *m*.

in·su·lant ['ɪnsjʊlənt] *s.* ⚙ Iso'lierstoff *m*, -materiˌal *n*.

in·su·lar ['ɪnsjʊlə] *adj.* □ **1.** inselartig, insu'lar, Insel…; **2.** *fig.* isoliert, abgeschlossen; **3.** *fig.* engstirnig, beschränkt; **in·su·lar·i·ty** [ˌɪnsjʊ'lærətɪ] *s.* **1.** insu'lare Lage; **2.** *fig.* Abgeschlossenheit *f*; **3.** *fig.* Engstirnigkeit *f*, Beschränktheit *f*.

in·su·late ['ɪnsjʊleɪt] *v/t.* ⚡, ⚙ isolieren (*a. fig. absondern*); **'in·su·lat·ing** [-tɪŋ] *adj.* isolierend, Isolier…: ~ ***compound*** ⚡ Isoliermasse *f*; ~ ***joint*** ⚡ Isolierkupplung *f*; ~ ***switch*** Trennschalter *m*; ~ ***tape*** ⚡ Isolierband *n*; **in·su·la·tion** [ˌɪnsjʊ'leɪʃn] *s.* Isolierung *f*; **'in·su·la·tor** [-tə] *s.* **1.** ⚡ Iso'lator *m*; **2.** Isolierer *m* (*Arbeiter*).

in·su·lin ['ɪnsjʊlɪn] *s.* ⚕ Insu'lin *n*.

in·sult I *v/t.* [ɪn'sʌlt] beleidigen, beschimpfen; II *s.* ['ɪnsʌlt] (***to***) Beleidigung *f* (für) (*durch Wort od. Tat*), Beschimpfung *f* (*gen.*): ***offer an*** ~ ***to*** → I; **in'sult·ing** [-tɪŋ] *adj.* □ **1.** beleidigend, beschimpfend: ~ ***language*** Schimpfworte *pl.*; **2.** unverschämt, frech.

in·su·per·a·ble [ɪn'sjuːpərəbl] *adj.* □ 'unüberˌwindlich.

in·sup·port·a·ble [ˌɪnsə'pɔːtəbl] *adj.* □ unerträglich, unaus'stehlich.

in·sur·a·bil·i·ty [ɪnˌʃʊərə'bɪlətɪ] *s.* ☤ Versicherungsfähigkeit *f*; **in·sur·a·ble** [ɪn'ʃʊərəbl] *adj.* □ ☤ **1.** versicherungsfähig, versicherbar: ~ ***value*** Versicherungswert *m*; **2.** versicherungspflichtig.

in·sur·ance [ɪn'ʃʊərəns] I *s.* **1.** ☤ Versicherung *f*: ***buy*** ~ sich versichern (lassen); ***carry*** ~ versichert sein; ***effect*** (*od.* ***take out***) ***an*** ~ e-e Versicherung abschließen; **2.** ☤ a) Ver'sicherungspoˌlice *f*, b) Versicherungsprämie *f*; II *adj.* Versicherungs…: ~ ***agent*** (***broker***, ***company***, ***premium***, ***value***); ~ ***benefit*** Versicherungsleistung *f*; ~ ***certificate*** Versicherungsschein *m*; ~ ***claim*** Versicherungsanspruch *m*; ~ ***coverage*** Versicherungsschutz *m*; ~ ***fraud*** Versicherungsbetrug *m*; ~ ***office*** Versicherungsanstalt *f*; ~ ***policy*** Versicherungspolice *f*, -schein *m*; ***take out an*** ~ ***policy*** e-e Versicherung abschließen, sich versichern (lassen); **in'sur·ant** [-nt] → ***insured*** II.

in·sure [ɪn'ʃʊə] *v/t.* **1.** ☤ versichern (***against*** gegen; ***for*** mit *e-r Summe*): ~ ***oneself*** (***one's life***, ***one's house***); **2.** → ***ensure***; **in'sured** [-ʊəd] ☤ I *adj.*: ***the*** ~ ***party*** → II; II *s.* ***the*** ~ der *od.* die Versicherte, Versicherungsnehmer(in); **in'sur·er** [-ʊərə] *s.* ☤ Versicherer *m*, Versicherungsträger(in): ***the*** ~***s*** die Versicherungsgesellschaft *f*.

in·sur·gent [ɪn'sɜːdʒənt] I *adj.* aufrührerisch, aufständisch; re'bellisch (*a. fig.*); II *s.* Aufrührer *m*, Aufständische(r) *m*; Re'bell *m* (*a. pol. gegen die Partei*).

in·sur·mount·a·ble [ˌɪnsə'maʊntəbl] *adj.* □ 'unüberˌsteigbar; *fig.* 'unüberˌwindlich.

in·sur·rec·tion [ˌɪnsə'rekʃn] *s.* Aufruhr *m*, Aufstand *m*, Erhebung *f*, Empörung *f*; **ˌin·sur'rec·tion·al** [-ʃənl], **ˌin·sur'rec·tion·ar·y** [-ʃnərɪ] → ***insurgent*** I; **ˌin·sur'rec·tion·ist** [-ʃnɪst] → ***insurgent*** II.

in·sus·cep·ti·bil·i·ty ['ɪnsəˌseptə'bɪlətɪ] *s.* Unempfänglichkeit *f*, Unzugänglichkeit *f* (***to*** für); **in·sus·cep·ti·ble** [ˌɪnsə'septəbl] *adj.* **1.** (***of***) nicht fähig (zu), ungeeignet (für, zu); **2.** (***of***, ***to***) unempfänglich (für), unzugänglich (*dat.*).

in·tact [ɪn'tækt] *adj.* **1.** in'takt, heil, unversehrt; **2.** unberührt, unangetastet.

in·tagl·io [ɪn'tɑːlɪəʊ] *pl.* **-ios** *s.* **1.** In'taglio *n* (*Gemme mit eingeschnittenem Bild*); **2.** eingraviertes Bild; **3.** In'taglioverfahren *n*, -arbeit *f*; **4.** *typ. Am.* Tiefdruck *m*.

in·take ['ɪnteɪk] *s.* **1.** ⚙ a) Einlaß(öffnung *f*) *m*: ~ ***valve*** Einlaßventil *n*; ~ ***stroke*** *mot.* Saughub *m*, b) aufgenommene Ener'gie; **2.** Einnehmen *n*, Ein-, Ansaugen *n*; **3.** (Neu)Aufnahme *f*, Zustrom *m*, aufgenommene Menge: ~ ***of food*** Nahrungsaufnahme.

in·tan·gi·bil·i·ty [ɪnˌtændʒəˈbɪlətɪ] *s.* Nichtgreifbarkeit *f*, Unkörperlichkeit *f*; **in·tan·gi·ble** [ɪnˈtændʒəbl] **I** *adj.* □ **1.** nicht greifbar, immateri'ell (*a.* †), unkörperlich; **2.** *fig.* vage, unklar, unbestimmt; **3.** *fig.* unfaßbar; **II** *s.* **4.** *pl.* † immateri'elle Werte.

in·tar·si·a [ɪnˈtɑːsɪə] *s. Am.* In'tarsia *f*, Einlegearbeit *f*.

in·te·ger [ˈɪntɪdʒə] *s.* **1.** A ganze Zahl; **2.** → ***integral*** 5; **'in·te·gral** [-ɪgrəl] **I** *adj.* □ **1.** (*zur Vollständigkeit*) unerläßlich, integrierend, wesentlich, ⚙ (fest) eingebaut, e-e Einheit bildend (***with*** mit), integriert: ***an*** ~ ***part***; **2.** ganz, vollständig: ***an*** ~ ***whole*** → 5; **3.** → ***intact*** 2; **4.** A a) ganz(zahlig), b) Integral...: ~ ***calculus*** Integralrechnung *f*; **II** *s.* **5.** *ein* vollständiges *od.* einheitliches Ganzes; **6.** A Inte'gral *n*; **'in·te·grand** [-ɪgrænd] *s.* A Inte'grand *m*; **'in·te·grant** [-ɪgrənt] → ***integral*** 1.

in·te·grate [ˈɪntɪgreɪt] *v/t.* **1.** integrieren (*a.* A, ⚙), zu e-m Ganzen zs.-fassen, zs.-schließen, vereinigen, vereinheitlichen; **2.** vervollständigen; **3.** eingliedern, integrieren (***within*** in *acc.*); **4.** ϟ zählen (*Meßgerät*); **5.** *Am. Schule etc.* für Farbige zugänglich machen; **'in·te·grat·ed** [-tɪd] *adj.* **1.** einheitlich, geschlossen, zs.-gefaßt, integriert; † Verbund...: ~ ***economy***; **2.** zs.-hängend; **3.** ⚙ eingebaut, integriert (*Schaltung, Datenverarbeitung etc.*): ~ ***circuit*** ϟ integrierter Schaltkreis; **4.** *Am.* ohne Rassentrennung: ~ ***school***; **in·te·gra·tion** [ˌɪntɪˈgreɪʃn] *s.* **1.** Zs.-schluß *m*, Vereinigung *f*, Integrati'on *f*, Vereinheitlichung *f*; **2.** Vervollständigung *f*; **3.** Eingliederung *f*; **4.** A Integrati'on *f*; **5.** *Am.* Aufhebung *f* der Rassenschranken; **in·te·gra·tion·ist** [ˌɪntɪˈgreɪʃnɪst] *s. Am.* Verfechter(in) rassischer Gleichberechtigung.

in·teg·ri·ty [ɪnˈtegrətɪ] *s.* **1.** Rechtschaffenheit *f*, (cha'rakterliche) Sauberkeit, (mo'ralische) Integri'tät; **2.** Vollständigkeit *f*, Unversehrtheit *f*; **3.** Reinheit *f*; **4.** A Integri'tät *f*, Ganzzahligkeit *f*.

in·teg·u·ment [ɪnˈtegjʊmənt] *s. anat. biol.* Hülle *f*, Decke *f*, Haut *f*, Integu'ment *n*.

in·tel·lect [ˈɪntəlekt] *s.* **1.** Verstand *m*, Intel'lekt *m*, Denkvermögen *n*; **2.** kluger Kopf; *coll.* große Geister *pl.*, Intelli'genz *f*; **in·tel·lec·tu·al** [ˌɪntəˈlektjʊəl] **I** *adj.* □ → ***intellectually***; **1.** intellektu'ell: a) verstandesmäßig, Verstandes..., geistig, Geistes..., b) verstandesbetont, (geistig) anspruchsvoll: ~ ***power*** Geisteskraft *f*; **2.** intelli'gent; **II** *s.* **3.** Intellektu'elle(r *m*) *f*, Verstandesmensch *m*; **in·tel·lec·tu·al·ist** [ˌɪntəˈlektjʊəlɪst] → ***intellectual*** 3; **in·tel·lec·tu·al·i·ty** [ˈɪntəˌlektjʊˈælətɪ] *s.* Intellektuali'tät *f*, Verstandesmäßigkeit *f*; Geisteskraft *f*; **in·tel·lec·tu·al·ly** [ˌɪntəˈlektjʊəlɪ] *adv.* verstandesmäßig, mit dem Verstand.

in·tel·li·gence [ˌɪnˈtelɪdʒəns] *s.* **1.** Intelli'genz *f*: a) Klugheit *f*, Verstand *m*, b) scharfer Verstand, rasche Auffassungsgabe, c) → ***intellect*** 2: ~ ***quotient*** (***test***) Intelligenzquotient *m* (-test *m*); **2.** Einsicht *f*, Verständnis *n*; **3.** Nachricht *f*, Mitteilung *f*, Informati'on *f*, Auskunft *f*; ⚔ 'Nachrichtenmateriˌal *n*; **4.** *a.* ~ ***office***, ~ ***service***, ♀ ***Department*** ⚔ (geheimer) Nachrichtendienst: ~ ***officer*** Abwehr-, Nachrichtenoffizier *m*; **5.** ~ ***with the enemy*** (*verräterische*) Beziehungen *pl.* zum Feind; **in'tel·li·genc·er** [-sə] *s.* **1.** Berichterstatter (-in); **2.** A'gent(in), Spi'on(in); **in'tel·li·gent** [-nt] *adj.* □ **1.** intelli'gent, klug, gescheit; **2.** vernünftig: a) verständig, einsichtsvoll, b) vernunftbegabt; **in·tel·li·gent·si·a**, **in·tel·li·gent·zi·a** [ɪnˌtelɪˈdʒentsɪə] *s. pl. konstr. coll. die* Intelli'genz, *die* Intellektu'ellen *pl.*; **in·tel·li·gi·bil·i·ty** [ɪnˌtelɪdʒəˈbɪlətɪ] *s.* Verständlichkeit *f*; **in'tel·li·gi·ble** [-dʒəbl] □ verständlich, klar (***to*** für *od. dat.*).

in·tem·per·ance [ɪnˈtempərəns] *s.* Unmäßigkeit *f*, Zügellosigkeit *f*, *bsd.* Trunksucht *f*; **in'tem·per·ate** [-rət] *adj.* □ **1.** unmäßig, maßlos; **2.** ausschweifend, zügellos; unbeherrscht; **3.** trunksüchtig.

in·tend [ɪnˈtend] *v/t.* **1.** beabsichtigen, vorhaben, planen, im Sinne haben (***s.th.*** et.; ***to do*** *od.* ***doing*** zu tun); **2.** bestimmen (***for*** für, zu): ***our son is*** ~***ed for the navy*** unser Sohn soll (einmal) zur Marine gehen; ***what is it*** ~***ed for?*** was ist der Sinn (*od.* Zweck) der Sache?, was soll das?; **3.** sagen wollen, meinen: ***what do you*** ~ ***by this?***; **4.** bedeuten, sein sollen: ***it was*** ~***ed for a compliment*** es sollte ein Kompliment sein; **5.** wollen, wünschen; **in'tend·ant** [-dənt] *s.* Verwalter *m*; **in'tend·ed** [-dɪd] **I** *adj.* □ **1.** beabsichtigt, gewünscht; **2.** absichtlich; **3.** F zukünftig: ***my*** ~ ***wife***; **II** *s.* **4.** F Verlobte(r *m*) *f*: ***her*** ~ ihr Zukünftiger; **in'tend·ing** [-dɪŋ] *adj.* angehend, zukünftig; ...lustig, ...willig: ~ ***buyer*** † (Kauf)Interessent (-in), Kaufwillige(r).

in·tense [ɪnˈtens] *adj.* □ **1.** inten'siv: a) stark, heftig: ~ ***heat*** (***longing*** *etc.*), b) hell, grell: ~ ***light***, c) tief, satt: ~ ***colo(u)rs***, d) angespannt: ~ ***study***, e) (an-) gespannt, konzentriert: ~ ***look***, f) sehnlich, dringend, g) eindringlich: ~ ***style***; **2.** leidenschaftlich, stark gefühlsbetont; **in'tense·ly** [-lɪ] *adv.* **1.** äußerst, höchst; **2.** → ***intense***; **in'tense·ness** [-nɪs] *s.* Intensi'tät *f*: a) Stärke *f*, Heftigkeit *f*, b) Anspannung *f*, Angestrengtheit *f*, c) Feuereifer *m*, d) Leidenschaftlichkeit *f*, e) Eindringlichkeit *f*; **in·ten·si·fi·ca·tion** [ɪnˌtensɪfɪˈkeɪʃn] *s.* Verstärkung *f* (*a. phot.*); **in'ten·si·fi·er** [-sɪfaɪə] *s. a.* ⚙, *phot.* Verstärker *m*; **in'ten·si·fy** [-sɪfaɪ] **I** *v/t.* verstärken (*a. phot.*), steigern; **II** *v/i.* sich verstärken.

in·ten·sion [ɪnˈtenʃn] *s.* **1.** Verstärkung *f*; **2.** → ***intenseness*** a *u.* b; **3.** (Begriffs)Inhalt *m*.

in·ten·si·ty [ɪnˈtensətɪ] *s.* Intensi'tät *f*: a) (hoher) Grad, Stärke *f*, Heftigkeit *f*, b) ϟ, ⚙, *phys.* (*Laut-, Licht-, Strom- etc.*)Stärke *f*, Grad *m*, c) → ***intenseness***; **in'ten·sive** [-sɪv] **I** *adj.* □ **1.** inten'siv: a) stark, heftig, b) gründlich, erschöpfend: ~ ***study***; ~ ***course*** *ped.* Intensivkurs *m*; **2.** verstärkend (*a. ling.*); **3.** ⚕ a) stark wirkend, b) ~ ***care unit*** Intensivstation *f*; **4.** † inten'siv: a) ertragssteigernd, b) (*arbeits-, lohn-, kosten- etc.*)inten'siv; **II** *s.* **5.** *bsd. ling.* verstärkendes Ele'ment.

in·tent [ɪnˈtent] **I** *s.* **1.** Absicht *f*, Vorsatz *m*, Zweck *m*: ***criminal*** ~ ⚖ Vorsatz, (verbrecherische) Absicht; ***with*** ~ ***to defraud*** in betrügerischer Absicht; ***to all*** ~***s and purposes*** a) in jeder Hinsicht, durchaus, b) im Grunde, eigentlich, c) praktisch, sozusagen; ***declaration of*** ~ Absichtserklärung *f*; **II** *adj.* □ **2.** erpicht, versessen (***on*** auf *acc.*); **3.** (***on***) bedacht (auf *acc.*), eifrig beschäftigt (mit); **4.** aufmerksam, gespannt, eifrig.

in·ten·tion [ɪnˈtenʃn] *s.* **1.** Absicht *f*, Vorhaben *n*, Vorsatz *m*, Plan *m* (***to do*** *od.* ***of doing*** zu tun): ***with the best*** (***of***) ~***s*** in bester Absicht; **2.** *pl.* F (Heirats)Absichten *pl.*; **3.** Zweck *m* (*a. eccl.*), Ziel *n*; **4.** Sinn *m*, Bedeutung *f*; **in'ten·tion·al** [-ʃənl] *adj.* □ **1.** absichtlich, vorsätzlich; **2.** beabsichtigt; **in'ten·tioned** [-nd] *adj. in Zssgn* ...gesinnt: ***well-*****~** gutgesinnt, wohlmeinend.

in·tent·ness [ɪnˈtentnɪs] *s.* gespannte Aufmerksamkeit, Eifer *m*: ~ ***of purpose*** Zielstrebigkeit *f*.

in·ter [ɪnˈtɜː] *v/t.* beerdigen.

inter- [ɪntə] *in Zssgn* zwischen, Zwischen...; unter; gegen-, wechselseitig, ein'ander, Wechsel...

'in·ter·act[1] [-ərækt] *s. thea.* Zwischenakt *m*, -spiel *n*.

ˌin·terˈact[2] [-ərˈækt] *v/i.* aufein'ander wirken, sich gegenseitig beeinflussen; **ˌin·terˈac·tion** [-ərˈækʃn] *s.* Wechselwirkung *f*, Interakti'on *f*.

ˌin·terˈbreed *biol.* **I** *v/t.* [*irr.* → ***breed***] durch Kreuzung züchten, kreuzen; **II** *v/i.* [*irr.* → ***breed***] a) sich kreuzen, b) Inzucht betreiben.

in·ter·ca·lar·y [ɪnˈtɜːkələrɪ] *adj.* eingeschaltet, eingeschoben; Schalt...: ~ ***day*** Schalttag *m*; **in'ter·ca·late** [ɪnˈtɜːkəleɪt] *v/t.* einschieben, einschalten; **in·ter·ca·la·tion** [ɪnˌtɜːkəˈleɪʃn] *s.* **1.** Einschiebung *f*, Einschaltung *f*; **2.** Einlage *f*.

in·ter·cede [ˌɪntəˈsiːd] *v/i.* sich verwenden, sich ins Mittel legen, Fürsprache einlegen, intervenieren (***with*** bei, ***for*** für); bitten (***with*** bei *j-m*, ***for*** um *et.*); **ˌin·terˈced·er** [-də] *s.* Fürsprecher(in).

in·ter·cept I *v/t.* [ˌɪntəˈsept] **1.** *Brief, Meldung, Flugzeug, Boten etc.* abfangen; **2.** *Meldung* auffangen, mit-, abhören; **3.** unter'brechen, abschneiden; **4.** den Weg abschneiden (*dat.*); **5.** *Sicht* versperren; **6.** A a) abschneiden, b) einschließen; **II** *s.* [ˈɪntəsept] **7.** A Abschnitt *m*; **8.** aufgefangene Meldung; **ˌin·terˈcep·tion** [-pʃn] *s.* **1.** Ab-, Auffangen *n* (*Meldung etc.*); **2.** Ab-, Mithören *n* (*Meldung*): ~ ***service*** Abhör-, Horchdienst *m*; **3.** Abfangen *n* (*Flugzeug, Boten*): ~ ***flight*** Sperrflug *m*; ~ ***plane*** → ***interceptor*** 2; **4.** Unter'brechung *f*, Abschneiden *n*; **5.** Aufhalten *n*, Hinderung *f*; **ˌin·terˈcep·tor** [-tə] *s.* **1.** Auffänger *m*; **2.** *a.* ~ ***plane*** ✈ ⚔ Abfangjäger *m*.

in·ter·ces·sion [ˌɪntəˈseʃn] *s.* Fürbitte *f* (*a. eccl.*), Fürsprache *f*: ***make*** ~ ***to s.o. for*** bei j-m Fürsprache einlegen für, sich bei j-m verwenden für; (***service of***) ~ Bittgottesdienst *m*; ˌ**in·terˈces·sor** [-esə] *s.* Fürsprecher(in), Vermittler(in) (***with*** bei); ˌ**in·terˈces·so·ry** [-esərɪ] *adj.* fürsprechend.

in·ter·change [ˌɪntəˈtʃeɪndʒ] **I** *v/t.* **1.** untereinˈander austauschen, auswechseln; **2.** vertauschen, auswechseln (*a.* ⚙); einander abwechseln lassen; **II** *v/i.* **3.** abwechseln (***with*** mit), aufeinˈanderfolgen; **III** *s.* **4.** Austausch *m*; Aus-, Abwechslung *f*; Wechsel *m*, Aufeinˈanderfolge *f*; **5.** ✝ Tauschhandel *m*; **6.** *Am.* (Straßen)Kreuzung *f*; (Autobahn-) Kreuz *n*; **in·ter·change·a·bil·i·ty** [ˈɪntəˌtʃeɪndʒəˈbɪlətɪ] *s.* Auswechselbarkeit *f*; ˌ**in·terˈchange·a·ble** [-dʒəbl] *adj.* □ **1.** austauschbar, auswechselbar (*a.* ⚙, ✝); **2.** (miteinˈander) abwechselnd.

ˌ**in·ter·colˈle·gi·ate** *adj.* zwischen verschiedenen Colleges (bestehend).

in·ter·com [ˈɪntəkɒm] *s.* **1.** ✈, ⚓ Bordverständigung(sanlage) *f*; **2.** (Gegen-, Haus)Sprechanlage *f*, (Werk- *etc.*)Rufanlage *f*.

ˌ**in·ter·comˈmu·ni·cate** *v/i.* **1.** miteinˈander verkehren *od.* in Verbindung stehen; **2.** → ***communicate*** 4; ˈ**in·ter·comˌmu·niˈca·tion** *s.* gegenseitige Verbindung, gegenseitiger Verkehr: ~ ***system*** → ***intercom***.

ˌ**in·terˈcom·pa·ny** *adj.* zwischenbetrieblich.

ˌ**in·ter·conˈnect I** *v/t.* miteinˈander verbinden, ⚡ *a.* zs.-schalten; **II** *v/i.* miteinander verbunden werden *od.* sein, *fig. a.* in Zs.-hang (miteinander) stehen; ˌ**in·ter·conˈnec·tion 1.** (gegenseitige) Verbindung, *fig. a.* Zs.-hang *m*; **2.** ⚡ a) Zs.-Schaltung *f*, b) verkettete Schaltung.

ˈ**in·terˌcon·tiˈnen·tal** *adj.* interkontinenˈtal, Interkontinental...

ˈ**in·ter·course** *s.* **1.** ˈUmgang *m*, Verkehr *m* (***with*** mit); **2.** ✝ Geschäftsverkehr *m*; **3.** *a.* ***sexual*** ~ (Geschlechts-) Verkehr *m*.

ˌ**in·terˈcross I** *v/t.* **1.** einˈander kreuzen lassen; **2.** ⚘, *zo.* kreuzen; **II** *v/i.* **3.** sich kreuzen (*a.* ⚘, *zo.*).

ˈ**in·ter·cut** *s. Film etc.*: Einblendung *f*.

ˈ**in·ter·deˌnom·iˈna·tion·al** *adj.* interkonfessioˈnell.

ˌ**in·ter·deˈpend** *v/i.* voneinˈander abhängen; ˌ**in·ter·deˈpend·ence**, ˌ**in·ter·deˈpend·en·cy** *s.* gegenseitige Abhängigkeit; ˌ**in·ter·deˈpend·ent** *adj.* □ voneinˈander abhängig, eng zs.-hängend *od.* verflochten, ineinˈandergreifend.

in·ter·dict I *s.* [ˈɪntədɪkt] **1.** Verbot *n*; **2.** *eccl.* Interˈdikt *n*; **II** *v/t.* [ˌɪntəˈdɪkt] **3.** (amtlich) unterˈsagen, verbieten (***to s.o.*** j-m): ~ ***s.o. from s.th.*** j-n von et. ausschließen, j-m et. entziehen *od.* verbieten; **4.** *eccl.* mit dem Interˈdikt belegen; ˌ**in·terˈdic·tion** → ***interdict*** 1, 2.

in·ter·est [ˈɪntrɪst] **I** *s.* **1.** (***in***) Interˈesse *n* (an *dat.*, für), (An)Teilnahme *f* (an *dat.*): ***take an*** ~ ***in s.th.*** sich für et. interessieren; **2.** Reiz *m*, Interˈesse *n*: ***be of*** ~ (***to***) interessant *od.* reizvoll sein (für), interessieren (*acc.*); **3.** Wichtigkeit *f*, Bedeutung *f*: ***be of little*** ~ von geringer Bedeutung sein; ***of great*** ~ von großem Interesse; **4.** *bsd.* ✝ Beteiligung *f*, Anteil *m* (***in*** an *dat.*): ***have an*** ~ ***in s.th.*** an *od.* bei et. (*bsd.* finanziell) beteiligt sein; **5.** ✝ Interesˈsenten *pl.*, Kreise *pl.*: ***the banking*** ~ die Bankkreise *pl.*; ***the landed*** ~ die Grundbesitzer *pl.*; **6.** Interˈesse *n*, Vorteil *m*, Nutzen *m*, Gewinn *m*: ***be in*** (*od.* ***to***) ***the*** ~(***s***) ***of*** im Interesse von ... liegen; ***in your*** ~ zu Ihrem Vorteil; ***look after one's*** ~***s*** s-e Interessen wahren; ***study s.o.'s*** ~(***s***) j-s Vorteil im Auge haben; **7.** Einfluß *m*, Macht *f*: ***have*** ~ ***with*** Einfluß haben bei; **8.** (An)Recht *n*, Anspruch *m* (***in*** auf *acc.*); **9.** Gesichtspunkt *m*, Seite *f* (*in e-r Geschichte etc.*): → ***human*** I; **10.** (*nie pl.*) ✝ Zins(en *pl.*) *m*: ***and*** (*od.* ***plus***) ~ zuzüglich Zinsen; ***ex*** ~ ohne Zinsen; ***free of*** ~ zinslos; ***bear*** (*od.* ***yield***) ~ Zinsen tragen, sich verzinsen; ~ (***rate***) ✝ Zinsfuß *m*, -satz *m*; ~ ***account*** a) Zinsrechnung *f*, b) Zinsenkonto *n*; ~ ***certificate*** Zinsenvergütungsschein *m*; ~ ***pro and contra*** Soll- u. Habenzinsen *pl.*; ~ ***coupon*** (*od.* ***ticket***, ***warrant***) Zinscoupon *m*, -schein *m*; **11.** *fig.* Zinsen *pl.*: ***return a blow with*** ~ e-n Schlag mit Zins u. Zinseszinsen zurückgeben; **II** *v/t.* **12.** interessieren (***in*** für), *j-s* Interˈesse *od.* Teilnahme erwecken (***in s.th.*** an e-r Sache; ***for s.o.*** für j-n): ~ ***o.s. in*** sich interessieren für, Anteil nehmen an (*dat.*); **13.** interessieren, anziehen, reizen, fesseln; **14.** angehen, betreffen: ***everyone is*** ~***ed in this*** dies geht jeden an; **15.** *bsd.* ✝ beteiligen (***in*** an *dat.*); **16.** gewinnen (***in*** für).

in·ter·est·ed [ˈɪntrɪstɪd] *adj.* □ **1.** interessiert, Anteil nehmend (***in*** an *dat.*); aufmerksam: ***be*** ~ ***in*** sich interessieren für; ***I was*** ~ ***to know*** es interessierte mich zu wissen; **2.** *bsd.* ✝ beteiligt (***in*** an *dat.*, bei): ***the parties*** ~ die Beteiligten; **3.** voreingenommen, parˈteiisch; **4.** eigennützig: ~ ***motives***; ˈ**in·ter·est·ed·ly** [-lɪ] *adv.* mit Interˈesse, aufmerksam; ˈ**in·ter·est·ing** [-tɪŋ] *adj.* □ interesˈsant, fesselnd, anziehend: ***in an*** ~ ***condition*** *obs.* in anderen Umständen (*schwanger*); ˈ**in·ter·est·ing·ly** [-tɪŋlɪ] *adv.* interesˈsanterweise.

ˈ**in·ter·face** *s.* Zwischen-, Grenzfläche *f*; ⚡ Schnittstelle *f*.

in·ter·fere [ˌɪntəˈfɪə] *v/i.* **1.** sich einmischen, daˈzwischentreten, -kommen; dreinreden; sich Freiheiten herˈausnehmen; **2.** eingreifen, -schreiten: ***it is time to*** ~; **3.** *a.* ⚙ stören, hindern; **4.** zs.-stoßen (*a. fig.*), aufeinˈanderprallen; **5.** *phys.* aufeinˈandertreffen, sich kreuzen *od.* überˈlagern; ⚡ stören; **6.** ~ ***with*** a) *j-n* stören, unterˈbrechen, (be-) hindern, belästigen, b) *et.* stören, beeinträchtigen, sich einmischen in (*acc.*), störend einwirken auf (*acc.*); **7.** ~ ***in*** eingreifen in (*acc.*), sich befassen mit *od.* kümmern um; ˌ**in·terˈfer·ence** [-ɪərəns] *s.* **1.** Einmischung *f* (***in*** in *acc.*), Eingreifen *n* (***with*** in *acc.*); **2.** Störung *f*, Hinderung *f*, Beeinträchtigung *f* (***with*** *gen.*); **3.** Zs.-stoß(en *n*) *m* (*a. fig.*); **4.** *Am. sport* Abschirmen *n*: ***run*** ~ a) den balltragenden Stürmer abschirmen, b) (***for s.o.***) *fig.* (j-m) Schützenhilfe leisten; **5.** ⚡, *phys.* a) Interfeˈrenz *f*, Überˈlagerung *f*, b) Störung *f*: ***reception*** ~ Empfangsstörung *f*; ~ ***suppression*** Entstörung *f*; **in·ter·fe·ren·tial** [ˌɪntəfəˈrenʃl] *adj. phys.* Interferenz...; ˌ**in·terˈfer·ing** [-ɪərɪŋ] *adj.* □ **1.** störend, lästig: ***be always*** ~ F sich ständig einmischen; **2.** kollidierend, entgegenstehend: ~ ***claim***.

ˌ**in·terˈgla·cial** *adj. geol.* zwischeneiszeitlich, interglaziˈal.

in·ter·im [ˈɪntərɪm] **I** *s.* **1.** Zwischenzeit *f*: ***in the*** ~ in der Zwischenzeit, einstweilen, vorläufig; **2.** Interim *n*, einstweilige Regelung; **3.** ♀ *hist.* Interim *n*; **II** *adj.* **4.** einstweilig, vorläufig, Übergangs..., Interims..., Zwischen...: ~ ***report*** Zwischenbericht *m*; → ***injunction*** 1; ~ **aid** *s.* Überˈbrückungshilfe *f*; ~ **bal·ance** (**sheet**) *s.* ✝ ˈZwischenbiˌlanz *f*, -abschluß *m*; ~ **cer·tif·i·cate** *s.* ✝ Interimsschein *m*; ~ **cred·it** *s.* ✝ ˈZwischenkreˌdit *m*; ~ **div·i·dend** *s.* ✝ ˈInterimsdiviˌdende *f*.

in·te·ri·or [ɪnˈtɪərɪə] **I** *adj.* **1.** inner, innengelegen; Innen... (*a.* ⚠): ~ ***decoration***, ~ ***design*** a) Innenausstattung *f*, b) Innenarchitektur *f*; ~ ***decorator***, ~ ***designer*** a) Innenausstatter(in), b) Innenarchitekt(in); **2.** binnenländisch, Binnen...; **3.** inländisch, Inlands...; **4.** innerlich, geistig: ~ ***monologue*** *Literatur*: innerer Monolog; **II** *s.* **5.** *das* Innere (*a.* ⚠), Innenraum *m*; **6.** *das* Innere, Binnenland *n*; **7.** *phot.* Innenaufnahme *f*; **8.** *das* Innere, wahres Wesen; **9.** *pol.* innere Angelegenheiten *pl.*: ***Department of the*** ♀ *Am.* Innenministerium *n*.

in·ter·ject [ˌɪntəˈdʒekt] *v/t.* **1.** *Bemerkung* daˈzwischen-, einwerfen; daˈzwischenrufen; **2.** einschieben, einschalten; ˌ**in·terˈjec·tion** [-kʃn] *s.* **1.** Aus-, Zwischenruf *m*; **2.** *ling.* Interjektiˈon *f*; ˌ**in·terˈjec·tion·al** [-kʃənl] *adj.* □, ˌ**in·terˈjec·to·ry** [-tərɪ] *adj.* daˈzwischengeworfen, eingeschoben, Zwischen...

ˌ**in·terˈlace I** *v/t.* **1.** ineinˈander-, verflechten, verschlingen; **2.** durchˈflechten, verweben (*a. fig.*); **3.** (ver)mischen; **4.** *Computer*: verschachteln; **II** *v/i.* **5.** sich verflechten *od.* kreuzen: ***interlacing arches*** ⚠ verschränkte Bogen; **III** *s.* **6.** *TV* Zwischenzeile *f*.

ˈ**in·terˌlan·guage** *s.* Verkehrssprache *f*.

ˌ**in·terˈlard** *v/t. fig.* spicken, durchˈsetzen (***with*** mit).

ˈ**in·ter·leaf** *s.* [*irr.*] leeres Zwischenblatt; ˌ**in·terˈleave** *v/t.* **1.** *Bücher* durchˈschießen; **2.** *Computer*: verschachteln.

ˌ**in·terˈline** *v/t.* **1.** zwischen die Zeilen schreiben *od.* setzen, einfügen; **2.** *typ. Zeilen* durchˈschießen; **3.** *Kleidungsstück* mit e-m Zwischenfutter versehen; ˌ**in·terˈlin·e·ar** *adj.* **1.** daˈzwischengeschrieben, zwischenzeilig, Interlinear...; **2.** ~ ***space*** *typ.* Durchschuß *m*; ˈ**in·terˌlin·e·ˈa·tion** *s. das* Daˈzwischengeschriebene.

ˌ**in·terˈlink I** *v/t.* verketten (*a.* ⚡); **II** *s.* [ˈɪntəlɪŋk] Binde-, Zwischenglied *n*.

ˌ**in·terˈlock I** *v/i.* **1.** ineinˈandergreifen (*a. fig.*): ~***ing directorate*** ✝ Schachtelaufsichtsrat *m*; **2.** 🚂 verblockt sein: ~***ing signals*** Blocksignale; **II** *v/t.* **3.** zs.-schließen, ineinˈanderschachteln; **4.** ineinˈanderhaken, verzahnen; **5.** ⚙, 🚂 verblocken: ~***ing plant*** Stellwerk *n*.

in·ter·lo·cu·tion [ˌɪntələʊˈkjuːʃn] *s.* Gespräch *n*, Unterˈredung *f*; **in·ter·loc·u-**

tor [ˌɪntəˈlɒkjʊtə] *s.* Gesprächspartner (-in); **in·ter·loc·u·to·ry** [ˌɪntəˈlɒkjʊtərɪ] *adj.* **1.** in Gesprächsform; Gesprächs…; **2.** ⚖ vorläufig, Zwischen…: **~ *injunction*** einstweilige Verfügung.

in·ter·lop·er [ˈɪntələʊpə] *s.* **1.** Eindringling *m*; **2.** ✝ Schleichhändler *m*.

in·ter·lude [ˈɪntəluːd] *s.* **1.** Zwischenspiel *n* (*a.* ♪ *u. fig.*); **2.** Pause *f*; **3.** Zwischenzeit *f*; **4.** Epiˈsode *f*.

ˌin·terˈmar·riage *s.* **1.** Mischehe *f* (*zwischen verschiedenen Konfessionen*, *Rassen etc.*); **2.** Heirat *f* untereinˈander *od.* zwischen nahen Blutsverwandten; **ˌin·terˈmar·ry** *v/i.* **1.** untereinˈander heiraten (*Stämme etc.*), Mischehen eingehen; **2.** innerhalb der Faˈmilie heiraten.

ˌin·terˈmed·dle *v/i.* sich einmischen (***with***, ***in*** in *acc.*).

in·ter·me·di·ar·y [ˌɪntəˈmiːdjərɪ] **I** *adj.* **1.** → ***intermediate*** 1; **2.** vermittelnd; **II** *s.* **3.** Vermittler(in); **4.** ✝ Zwischenhändler *m*; **ˌin·terˈme·di·ate** [-jət] **I** *adj.* □ **1.** daˈzwischenliegend, Zwischen…, Mittel…: **~ *between*** liegend zwischen; **~ *colo*(*u*)*r*** (***credit***, ***product***, ***stage***, ***trade***) Zwischenfarbe *f* (-kredit *m*, -produkt *n*, -stadium *n*, -handel *m*); **~ *examination*** → 4; **II** *s.* **2.** Zwischenglied *n*, -form *f*, -stück *n*; **3.** ☤ ˈZwischenproˌdukt *n*; **4.** Zwischenprüfung *f*; **5.** Vermittler(in), Mittelsmann *m*.

in·ter·ment [ɪnˈtɜːmənt] *s.* Beerdigung *f*, Beisetzung *f*.

in·ter·mez·zo [ˌɪntəˈmetsəʊ] *pl.* **-mez·zi** [-tsiː] *od.* **-mez·zos** *s.* Interˈmezzo *n*, Zwischenspiel *n*.

in·ter·mi·na·ble [ɪnˈtɜːmɪnəbl] *adj.* □ **1.** grenzenlos, endlos; **2.** langwierig.

ˌin·terˈmin·gle → ***intermix***.

ˌin·terˈmis·sion *s.* Unterˈbrechung *f*, Aussetzen *n*; Pause *f*: ***without* ~** pausenlos, unaufhörlich, ständig.

in·ter·mit [ˌɪntəˈmɪt] **I** *v/t.* unterˈbrechen, aussetzen mit; **II** *v/i.* aussetzen, nachlassen; **ˌin·terˈmit·tence** [-təns] *s.* Aussetzen *n*, Unterˈbrechung *f*; **ˌin·terˈmit·tent** [-tənt] *adj.* □ mit Unterˈbrechungen, stoßweise; (zeitweilig) aussetzend, periˈodisch, intermittierend: ***be* ~** aussetzen; **~ *fever*** ⚕ Wechselfieber *n*; **~ *light*** ⚓ Blinkfeuer *n*.

ˌin·terˈmix **I** *v/t.* vermischen; **II** *v/i.* sich vermischen; **ˌin·terˈmix·ture** *s.* **1.** Mischung *f*; **2.** Beimischung *f*, Zusatz *m*.

in·tern¹ **I** *v/t.* [ɪnˈtɜːn] internieren; **II** *s.* [ˈɪntɜːn] *Am.* Internierte(r *m*) *f*.

in·tern² [ˈɪntɜːn] *Am.* **I** *s.* ⚕ Assiˈstenzarzt *m*, *a. ped.* Praktiˈkant(in); **II** *v/i.* als Assiˈstenzarzt (*in e-r Klinik*) tätig sein.

in·ter·nal [ɪnˈtɜːnl] **I** *adj.* □ **1.** inner, inwendig: **~ *organs*** *anat.* innere Organe; **~ *diameter*** Innendurchmesser *m*; **2.** ⚕ innerlich anzuwenden(d), einzunehmen(d): **~ *remedy***; **3.** inner(lich), geistig; **4.** einheimisch, in-, binnenländisch, Inlands…, Innen…, Binnen…: **~ *loan*** ✝ Inlandsanleihe *f*; **~ *trade*** Binnenhandel *m*; **5.** *pol.* inner, Innen…: **~ *affairs*** innere Angelegenheiten; **6.** *ped.* inˈtern, im College *etc.* wohnend; **7.** ✝ *etc.* (beˈtriebs)inˌtern, innerbetrieblich; **II** *s.* **8.** *pl. anat.* innere Orˈgane *pl.*; **9.** innere Naˈtur; **~-comˈbus·tion en·gine** *s.* ⚙ Verbrennungs-, Exploˈsionsmotor *m*.

in·ter·na·lize [ɪnˈtɜːnəlaɪz] *v/t. psych. et.* verinnerlichen, in sich aufnehmen.

in·ter·nal| med·i·cine *s.* ⚕ innere Meˈdizin; **~ rev·e·nue** *s. Am.* Steueraufkommen *n*: **2 *Office*** Finanzamt *n*; **~ rhyme** *s.* Binnenreim *m*; **~ spe·cial·ist** *s.* ⚕ Interˈnist *m*, Facharzt *m* für innere Krankheiten; **~ thread** *s.* ⚙ Innengewinde *n*.

ˌin·terˈna·tion·al **I** *adj.* □ **1.** internatioˈnal, zwischenstaatlich: **~ *candle*** *phys.* Internationale Kerze (*Lichtstärke*); **2.** Welt…, Völker…; **II** *s.* **3.** *sport* a) Internatioˈnale(r *m*) *f*, Natioˈnalspieler (-in), b) F internatioˈnaler Vergleichskampf; Länderspiel *n*; **4.** **2** *pol.* Internatioˈnale *f*; **5.** *pl.* ✝ internatioˈnal gehandelte ˈWertpaˌpiere *pl.*; **In·ter·na·tio·nale** [ˌɪntənæʃəˈnɑːl] *s.* Internatioˈnale *f* (*Kampflied*); **ˌin·terˈna·tion·al·ism** *s.* **1.** Internationaˈlismus *m*; **2.** internatioˈnale Zs.-arbeit; **ˌin·terˈna·tion·al·ist** *s.* **1.** Internationaˈlist *m*, Anhänger *m* des Internationaˈlismus; **2.** ⚖ Völkerrechtler *m*; **3.** → ***international*** 3a; **ˈin·terˌna·tionˈal·i·ty** *s.* internatioˈnaler Chaˈrakter; **ˌin·terˈna·tion·al·ize** *v/t.* **1.** internationalisieren; **2.** internatioˈnaler Konˈtrolle unterˈwerfen.

in·ter·na·tion·al| law *s.* Völkerrecht *n*; **2 Mon·e·tar·y Fund** *s.* Internatioˈnaler Währungsfonds; **~ mon·ey or·der** *s.* Auslandspostanweisung *f*; **~ re·ply cou·pon** *s.* internatioˈnaler Antwortschein.

in·terne [ˈɪntɜːn] → ***intern²*** I.

in·ter·ne·cine [ˌɪntəˈniːsaɪn] *adj.* **1.** gegenseitige Tötung bewirkend: **~ *duel***; **~ *war*** gegenseitiger Vernichtungskrieg; **2.** mörderisch, vernichtend.

in·tern·ee [ˌɪntɜːˈniː] *s.* Internierte(r *m*) *f*; **in·tern·ment** [ɪnˈtɜːnmənt] *s.* Internierung *f*: **~ *camp*** Internierungslager *n*.

ˈin·terˌo·ceˈan·ic [-ərˌəʊ-] *adj.* interozeˈanisch, zwischen (zwei) Weltmeeren liegend, (zwei) Weltmeere verbindend.

in·ter·pel·late [ɪnˈtɜːpeleɪt] *v/t. pol.* e-e Anfrage richten an (*acc.*); **in·ter·pel·la·tion** [ɪnˌtɜːpeˈleɪʃn] *s. pol.* Interpellatiˈon *f*.

ˌin·terˈpen·e·trate **I** *v/t.* völlig durchˈdringen; **II** *v/i.* sich gegenseitig durchˈdringen.

in·ter·phone [ˈɪntəfəʊn] → ***intercom***.

ˌin·terˈplan·e·tar·y *adj.* interplaneˈtarisch.

ˌin·terˈplay *s.* Wechselwirkung *f*, -spiel *n*.

In·ter·pol [ˈɪntəpɒl] *s.* Interpol *f* (*Internationale kriminalpolizeiliche Organisation*).

in·ter·po·late [ɪnˈtɜːpəʊleɪt] *v/t.* **1.** interpolieren; *et.* einschalten, -fügen; **2.** (durch Einschiebungen) ändern, *bsd.* verfälschen; **3.** 𝒜 interpolieren; **in·ter·po·la·tion** [ɪnˌtɜːpəʊˈleɪʃn] *s.* Interpolatiˈon *f* (*a.* 𝒜), Einschaltung *f*, Einschiebung *f* (*in e-n Text*).

ˌin·terˈpose **I** *v/t.* **1.** daˈzwischenstellen, -legen, -bringen; ⚙ zwischenschalten; **2.** *et.* in den Weg legen; **3.** *Bemerkung* einwerfen, einflechten; *Einwand etc.* vorbringen, *Veto* einlegen; **II** *v/i.* **4.** daˈzwischenkommen, -treten; **5.** vermitteln, intervenieren; **6.** (sich) unterˈbrechen (*im Reden*); **in·ter·po·si·tion** [ɪnˌtɜːpəˈzɪʃn] *s.* **1.** Eingreifen *n*; **2.** Vermittlung *f*, Einfügung *f*, Einschaltung *f* (*a.* ⚙).

in·ter·pret [ɪnˈtɜːprɪt] **I** *v/t.* **1.** interpretieren, auslegen, deuten; ansehen (***as*** als); *bsd.* ⚔ auswerten; **2.** dolmetschen; **3.** ♪, *thea. etc.* interpretieren, ˈwiedergeben, darstellen; **II** *v/i.* **4.** dolmetschen, als Dolmetscher fungieren; **in·ter·pre·ta·tion** [ɪnˌtɜːprɪˈteɪʃn] *s.* **1.** Erklärung *f*, Auslegung *f*, Deutung *f*; Auswertung *f*; **2.** (mündliche) ˈWiedergabe, Überˈsetzung *f*; **3.** ♪, *thea. etc.* Darstellung *f*, ˈWiedergabe *f*; Auffassung *f*, Interpretatiˈon *f e-r Rolle etc.*; **inˈter·pret·er** [-tə] *s.* **1.** Erklärer(in), Ausleger(in), Interˈpret(in); **2.** Dolmetscher(in); **3.** *Computer*: Interpreˈtierproˌgramm *n*; **inˈter·pret·er·ship** [-təʃɪp] *s.* Dolmetscherstellung *f*.

ˌin·terˈra·cial *adj.* **1.** verschiedenen Rassen gemeinsam, interˈrassisch; **2.** zwischenrassisch: **~ *tension*(*s*)** Rassenspannungen.

in·ter·reg·num [ˌɪntəˈregnəm] *pl.* **-na** [-nə], **-nums** *s.* **1.** Interˈregnum *n*: a) herrscherlose Zeit, b) Zwischenregierung *f*; **2.** Pause *f*, Unterˈbrechung *f*.

ˌin·ter·reˈlate **I** *v/t.* zueinˈander in Beziehung bringen; **II** *v/i.* zueinˈander in Beziehung stehen, zs.-hängen; **ˌin·ter·reˈlat·ed** *adj.* in Wechselbeziehung stehend, (untereinˈander) zs.-hängend; **ˌin·ter·reˈla·tion** *s.* Wechselbeziehung *f*.

in·ter·ro·gate [ɪnˈterəʊgeɪt] *v/t.* **1.** (be-) fragen; **2.** ausfragen, vernehmen, verhören; **in·ter·ro·ga·tion** [ɪnˌterəʊˈgeɪʃn] *s.* **1.** Frage *f* (*a. ling.*), Befragung *f*: **~ *mark***, ***point of* ~** *ling.* Fragezeichen *n*; **2.** Vernehmung *f*, Verhör *n*: **~ *officer*** Vernehmungsoffizier *m*, -beamter *m*; **in·ter·rog·a·tive** [ˌɪntəˈrɒgətɪv] **I** *adj.* □ fragend, Frage…: **~ *pronoun*** → II; **II** *s. ling.* Fragefürwort *n*; **inˈter·ro·ga·tor** [-tə] *s.* **1.** Fragesteller (-in); **2.** Vernehmungsbeamte(r) *m*; **3.** *pol.* Interpelˈlant *m*; **in·ter·rog·a·to·ry** [ˌɪntəˈrɒgətərɪ] **I** *adj.* **1.** fragend, Frage…; **II** *s.* **2.** Frage(stellung) *f*; **3.** ⚖ Beweisfrage *f* (*vor der Verhandlung*).

in·ter·rupt [ˌɪntəˈrʌpt] *v/t.* **1.** *allg.*, *a.* ⚡ unterˈbrechen, *a. j-m* ins Wort fallen; **2.** aufhalten, stören, hindern; **ˌin·terˈrupt·ed** [-tɪd] *adj.* □ unterˈbrochen (*a.* ⚡, ⚙, ⚘); **ˌin·terˈrupt·ed·ly** [-tɪdlɪ] *adv.* mit Unterˈbrechungen; **ˌin·terˈrupt·er** [-tə] *s.* **1.** Unterˈbrecher *m* (*a.* ⚡, ⚙); **2.** Zwischenrufer(in); Störer(in); **ˌin·terˈrup·tion** [-pʃn] *s.* **1.** Unterˈbrechung *f* (*a.* ⚡), Stockung *f*: ***without* ~** ununterbrochen; **2.** (⚙ Betriebs)Störung *f*.

in·ter·sect [ˌɪntəˈsekt] **I** *v/t.* (durch-) ˈschneiden; **II** *v/i.* sich schneiden *od.* kreuzen (*a.* 𝒜); **ˌin·terˈsec·tion** [-kʃn] *s.* **1.** Durchˈschneiden *n*; **2.** Schnitt-, Kreuzungspunkt *m*; **3.** 𝒜 a) Schnitt *m*, b) *a.* ***point of* ~** Schnittpunkt *m*, c) *a.* ***line of* ~** Schnittlinie *f*; **4.** *Am.* (Straßen- *etc.*)Kreuzung *f*; **5.** △ Vierung *f*.

ˈin·ter·sex *s. biol.* Interˈsex *n* (*geschlechtliche Zwischenform*); **ˌin·terˈsex·u·al** *adj.* zwischengeschlechtlich.

ˌin·terˈspace **I** *s.* Zwischenraum *m*, -zeit *f*; **II** *v/t.* Raum lassen zwischen (*dat.*); trennen.

in·ter·sperse [ˌɪntəˈspɜːs] *v/t.* **1.** einstreuen, hier und da einfügen (***among*** zwischen *acc.*); **2.** durch'setzen (***with*** mit).

'in·ter·state *adj. Am.* zwischenstaatlich, zwischen den US.-Bundesstaaten (bestehend *etc.*).

ˌin·terˈstel·lar *adj.* interstel'lar.

in·ter·stice [ɪn'tɜ:stɪs] *s.* **1.** Zwischenraum *m*; **2.** Lücke *f*, Spalte *f*; **in·ter·sti·tial** [ˌɪntə'stɪʃl] *adj.* in Zwischenräumen (gelegen), zwischenräumlich, Zwischen…

ˌin·terˈtrib·al *adj.* zwischen verschiedenen Stämmen (vorkommend).

ˌin·terˈtwine *v/t. u. v/i.* (sich) verflechten *od.* verschlingen.

ˌin·terˈur·ban [-ər'ɜ:-] *adj.* Überland…: ***~ bus***.

in·ter·val ['ɪntəvl] *s.* **1.** Zwischenraum *m*, -zeit *f*, Abstand *m*: ***at ~s*** dann und wann, periodisch; → ***lucid*** 1; **2.** Pause *f* (*a. thea. etc.*): ***~ signal*** *Radio*: Pausenzeichen *n*; **3.** ♪ Inter'vall *n*, Tonabstand *m*; ***~ train·ing*** *s. sport* Inter'valltraining *n*.

in·ter·vene [ˌɪntə'vi:n] *v/i.* **1.** (*zeitlich*) da'zwischenliegen, liegen zwischen (*dat.*); **2.** sich (in'zwischen) ereignen, (plötzlich) eintreten; **3.** (*unerwartet*) da'zwischenkommen: ***if nothing ~s***; **4.** sich einmischen (***in*** in *acc.*), einschreiten; **5.** (*helfend*) eingreifen, vermitteln; sich verwenden (***with s.o.*** bei j-m); **6.** *bsd.* ✝, ⚖ intervenieren; **ˌin·terˈven·tion** [-'venʃn] *s.* **1.** Da'zwischenliegen *n*, -kommen *n*; **2.** Vermittlung *f*; **3.** Eingreifen *n*, -schreiten *n*, -mischung *f*; **4.** ✝, *pol.* (⚖ 'Neben)Interventiˌon *f*; **5.** Einspruch *m*; **ˌin·terˈven·tion·ist** [-'venʃnɪst] *s. pol.* Befürworter *m* e-r Interventi'on, Interventio'nist *m*.

in·ter·view ['ɪntəvju:] **I** *s.* **1.** Inter'view *n*; **2.** Unter'redung *f*, (✝ *a.* Vorstellungs)Gespräch *n*: ***hours for ~s*** Sprechzeiten, -stunden *pl.*; **II** *v/t.* **3.** inter'viewen, ein Inter'view *od.* e-e Unter'redung haben mit, ein Gespräch führen mit; **in·ter·view·ee** [ˌɪntəvju:'i:] *s.* Inter'viewte(r *m*) *f*; *a.* Kandi'dat(in) (*für e-e Stelle*); **'in·ter·view·er** [-ju:ə] *s.* Inter'viewer(in); Leiter(in) e-s Vorstellungsgesprächs.

'in·ter·war *adj.*: ***the ~ period*** die Zeit zwischen den (Welt)Kriegen.

ˌin·terˈweave *v/t.* [*irr.* → ***weave***] **1.** verweben, verflechten (*a. fig.*); **2.** vermengen; **3.** durch'weben, -'flechten, -'wirken.

ˌin·terˈzon·al *adj.* Interzonen…

in·tes·ta·cy [ɪn'testəsɪ] *s.* ⚖ Fehlen *n* e-s Testa'ments; **in'tes·tate** [-teɪt] **I** *adj.* **1.** ohne Hinter'lassung e-s Testa'ments: ***die ~***; **2.** nicht testamen'tarisch geregelt: ***~ estate***; ***~ succession*** gesetzliche Erbfolge; **II** *s.* **3.** Erb-lasser(in), der (*od.* die) kein Testa'ment hinter'lassen hat.

in·tes·ti·nal [ɪn'testɪnl] *adj.* ⚕ Darm…: ***~ flora*** Darmflora *f*; **in·tes·tine** [ɪn'testɪn] **I** *s. anat.* Darm *m*; *pl.* Gedärme *pl.*, Eingeweide *pl.*: ***large ~*** Dickdarm; ***small ~*** Dünndarm; **II** *adj.* inner, einheimisch: ***~ war*** Bürgerkrieg *m*.

in·thral(l) [ɪn'θrɔ:l] *Am.* → ***enthral(l)***.

in·throne [ɪn'θrəʊn] *Am.* → ***enthrone***.

in·ti·ma·cy ['ɪntɪməsɪ] *s.* **1.** Intimi'tät *f*: a) Vertrautheit *f*, vertrauter 'Umgang, b) (*contp. plumpe*) Vertraulichkeit; **2.** in'time (*sexuelle*) Beziehungen *pl.*

in·ti·mate¹ ['ɪntɪmət] **I** *adj.* □ **1.** vertraut, innig, in'tim: ***on ~ terms*** auf vertrautem Fuß; **2.** eng, nah; **3.** per'sönlich; **4.** in'tim, in geschlechtlichen Beziehungen (stehend) (***with*** mit); **5.** gründlich: ***~ knowledge***; **6.** ⚙, ⚗ innig: ***~ contact***; ***~ mixture***; **II** *s.* **7.** Vertraute(r *m*) *f*, Intimus *m*.

in·ti·mate² ['ɪntɪmeɪt] *v/t.* **1.** andeuten, zu verstehen geben; **2.** nahelegen; **3.** ankündigen, mitteilen; **in·ti·ma·tion** [ˌɪntɪ'meɪʃn] *s.* **1.** Andeutung *f*, Wink *m*; **2.** Mitteilung *f*.

in·tim·i·date [ɪn'tɪmɪdeɪt] *v/t.* einschüchtern, abschrecken, bange machen; **in·tim·i·da·tion** [ɪnˌtɪmɪ'deɪʃn] *s.* Einschüchterung *f*; ⚖ Nötigung *f*.

in·ti·tle [ɪn'taɪtl] *Am.* → ***entitle***.

in·to ['ɪntʊ; 'ɪntə] *prp.* **1.** in (*acc.*), in (*acc.*) … hin'ein: ***go ~ the house***; ***get ~ debt*** in Schulden geraten; ***flog ~ obedience*** durch Prügel zum Gehorsam bringen; ***translate ~ English*** ins Englische übersetzen; ***far ~ the night*** tief in die Nacht; ***she is ~ her thirties*** sie ist Anfang dreißig; ***Socialist ~ Conservative*** die Verwandlung e-s Sozialisten in einen Konservativen; **2.** *Zustandsänderung*: zu: ***make water ~ ice*** Wasser zu Eis machen; ***turn ~ cash*** zu Geld machen; ***grow ~ a man*** ein Mann werden; **3.** 𝔄 in: ***divide ~ 10 parts*** in 10 Teile teilen; ***4 ~ 20 goes five times*** 4 geht in 20 fünfmal; **4.** ***be ~ s.th.*** F a) auf (*acc.*) et. ‚stehen', b) et. ‚am Wikkel' haben: ***he is ~ modern art now*** F er ‚hat es' jetzt (*beschäftigt sich*) mit moderner Kunst.

in·tol·er·a·ble [ɪn'tɒlərəbl] *adj.* □ unerträglich; **in'tol·er·a·ble·ness** [-nɪs] *s.* Unerträglichkeit *f*; **in'tol·er·ance** [-lərəns] *s.* **1.** 'Intoleˌranz *f*, Unduldsamkeit *f* (***of*** gegen); **2.** ⚕ 'Überempfindlichkeit *f* (***of*** gegen); **in'tol·er·ant** [-lərənt] *adj.* □ **1.** unduldsam, 'intoleˌrant (***of*** gegen); **2.** ***be ~ of*** nicht (v)ertragen können.

in·tomb [ɪn'tu:m] *Am.* → ***entomb***.

in·to·nate ['ɪntəʊneɪt] *v/t.* → ***intone***; **in·to·na·tion** [ˌɪntəʊ'neɪʃn] *s.* **1.** *ling.* Intonati'on *f*, Tonfall *m*; **2.** ♪ Intonati'on *f*: a) Anstimmen *n*, b) Psalmodieren *n*, c) Tonansatz *m*; **in·tone** [ɪn'təʊn] *v/t.* **1.** ♪ anstimmen, intonieren; **2.** ♪ psalmodieren; **3.** (mit *e-m bestimmten* Tonfall) (aus)sprechen.

in to·to [ɪn'təʊtəʊ] (*Lat.*) *adv.* **1.** im ganzen, insgesamt; **2.** vollständig.

in·tox·i·cant [ɪn'tɒksɪkənt] **I** *adj.* berauschend; **II** *s.* berauschendes Getränk, Rauschmittel *n*; **in'tox·i·cate** [-keɪt] *v/t.* (*a. fig.*) berauschen, (be)trunken machen: ***~d with*** berauscht *od.* trunken von *Wein*, *Liebe etc.*; **in·tox·i·ca·tion** [ɪnˌtɒksɪ'keɪʃn] *s. a. fig.* Rausch *m*, Trunkenheit *f*.

intra- [ɪntrə] *in Zssgn* innerhalb.

ˌin·traˈcar·di·ac *adj.* ⚕ im Herz'innern, intrakardi'al.

in·trac·ta·bil·i·ty [ɪnˌtræktə'bɪlətɪ] *s.* Unlenksamkeit *f*, 'Widerspenstigkeit *f*; **in·trac·ta·ble** [ɪn'træktəbl] *adj.* □ **1.** unlenksam, störrisch, halsstarrig; **2.** schwer zu bearbeiten(d) *od.* zu handhaben(d), ‚'widerspenstig'.

in·tra·dos [ɪn'treɪdɒs] *s.* ⚠ Laibung *f*.

in·tra·mu·ral [ˌɪntrə'mjʊərəl] *adj.* **1.** innerhalb der Mauern (*e-r Stadt*, *e-s Hauses etc.*) befindlich; **2.** innerhalb der Universi'tät.

ˌin·traˈmus·cu·lar *adj.* ⚕ intramusku'lär.

in·tran·si·gence [ɪn'trænsɪdʒəns] *s.* Unnachgiebigkeit *f*, Intransi'genz *f*; **in'tran·si·gent** [-nt] *adj. bsd. pol.* unnachgiebig, starr, intransi'gent.

in·tran·si·tive [ɪn'trænsɪtɪv] **I** *adj.* □ *ling.* intransitiv (*a.* 𝔄); **II** *s. ling.* Intransitiv *n*.

in·trant ['ɪntrənt] *s.* Neueintretende(r *m*) *f*, (*ein Amt*) Antretende(r *m*) *f*.

ˌin·traˈstate *adj.* innerstaatlich, *Am.* innerhalb e-s Bundesstaates.

ˌin·traˈve·nous *adj.* ⚕ intrave'nös.

in·trench [ɪn'trentʃ] → ***entrench***.

in·trep·id [ɪn'trepɪd] *adj.* □ unerschrokken; **in·tre·pid·i·ty** [ˌɪntrɪ'pɪdətɪ] *s.* Unerschrockenheit *f*.

in·tri·ca·cy ['ɪntrɪkəsɪ] *s.* **1.** Kompliziertheit *f*, Kniffligkeit *f*; **2.** Komplikati'on *f*, Schwierigkeit *f*; **'in·tri·cate** [-kət] *adj.* □ verwickelt, kompliziert, knifflig, schwierig.

in·trigue [ɪn'tri:g] **I** *v/i.* **1.** intrigieren, Ränke schmieden; **2.** ein Verhältnis haben (***with*** mit); **II** *v/t.* **3.** fesseln, faszinieren; **4.** neugierig machen; **5.** verblüffen; **III** *s.* **6.** In'trige *f*: a) Ränkespiel *n*, *pl.* Ränke *pl.*, Machenschaften *pl.*, b) Verwicklung *f* (*im Drama etc.*); **in'tri·guer** [-gə] *s.* Intri'gant(in); **in'tri·guing** [-gɪŋ] *adj.* □ **1.** fesselnd, faszinierend; **2.** verblüffend; **3.** intrigierend, ränkevoll.

in·trin·sic [ɪn'trɪnsɪk] *adj.* (□ ***~ally***) inner, wahr, eigentlich, wirklich, wesentlich, imma'nent: ***~ value*** innerer Wert; **in'trin·si·cal·ly** [-kəlɪ] *adv.* wirklich, eigentlich; an sich: ***~ safe*** ⚡ eigensicher.

in·tro·duce [ˌɪntrə'dju:s] *v/t.* **1.** einführen: ***~ a new method***; **2.** einleiten, eröffnen, anfangen; **3.** (***into*** in *acc.*) *et.* (her'ein)bringen; *Instrument etc.* einführen, -setzen; *Seuche* einschleppen; *parl. Gesetzesvorlage* einbringen; **4.** *Thema*, *Frage* anschneiden, aufwerfen; **5.** *j-n* (hin'ein)führen, (-)geleiten (***into*** in *acc.*); **6.** (***to***) *j-n* einführen (in *acc.*), bekannt machen (mit *et.*); **7.** (***to***) *j-n* bekannt machen (mit *j-m*), vorstellen (*dat.*); **ˌin·troˈduc·tion** [-'dʌkʃn] *s.* **1.** Einführung *f*; **2.** Einleitung *f*, Anbahnung *f*; **3.** Einleitung *f*, Vorrede *f*, -wort *n*; **4.** Leitfaden *m*, Anleitung *f*; **5.** Einführung *f* (*Instrument*); Einschleppung *f* (*Seuche*); *pol.* Einbringung *f* (*Gesetz*); **6.** Vorstellung *f*: ***letter of ~*** Empfehlungsbrief *m*; **ˌin·troˈduc·to·ry** [-'dʌktərɪ] *adj.* einleitend, Einleitungs…, Vor…

in·tro·mis·sion [ˌɪntrəʊ'mɪʃn] *s.* **1.** Einführung *f*; **2.** Zulassung *f*.

in·tro·spect [ˌɪntrəʊ'spekt] *v/t.* sich (innerlich) prüfen; **ˌin·troˈspec·tion** [-kʃn] *s.* Selbstbeobachtung *f*, Innenschau *f*, Introspekti'on *f*; **ˌin·troˈspec·tive** [-tɪv] *adj.* □ introspek'tiv, selbstprüfend, nach innen gewandt.

in·tro·ver·sion [ˌɪntrəʊ'vɜ:ʃn] *s.* **1.** Einwärtskehren *n*; **2.** *psych.* Introversi'on *f*, Introvertiertheit *f*; **in·tro·vert** **I** *s.*

['ɪntrəʊvɜːt] *psych.* introvertierter Mensch; **II** *v/t.* [ˌɪntrəʊ'vɜːt] nach innen richten, einwärtskehren; *psych.* introvertieren.

in·trude [ɪn'truːd] **I** *v/t.* **1.** *fig.* (unnötigerweise) hi'neinbringen: **~ one's own ideas into the argument**; **2. ~ s.th. upon s.o.** j-m et. aufdrängen; **~ o.s. upon s.o.** sich j-m aufdrängen; **II** *v/i.* **3.** sich eindrängen *od.* einmischen (**into** in *acc.*), sich aufdrängen (**upon** *dat.*); **4.** (**upon**) *j-n* stören, belästigen: **am I intruding?** störe ich?; **in'trud·er** [-də] *s.* **1.** Eindringling *m*; **2.** Zudringliche(r *m*) *f*, Störenfried *m*; **3.** ✈ Störflugzeug *n*; **in'tru·sion** [-uːʒn] *s.* **1.** Eindrängen *n*, Eindringen *n*; **2.** Einmischung *f*; **3.** Zu-, Aufdringlichkeit *f*; **4.** Belästigung *f* (**upon** *gen.*); **5.** ⚖ Besitzstörung *f*; **in'tru·sive** [-uːsɪv] *adj.* ☐ **1.** auf-, zudringlich, lästig; **2.** *geol.* eingedrungen; **3.** *ling.* 'unetymoˌlogisch (eingedrungen); **in'tru·sive·ness** [-uːsɪvnɪs] → **intrusion** 3.

in·tu·it [ɪn'tjuːɪt] *v/t. u. v/i.* intui'tiv erfassen *od.* wissen; **in·tu·i·tion** [ˌɪntjuː'ɪʃn] *s.* Intuiti'on *f*: a) unmittelbare Erkenntnis, b) Eingebung *f*, Ahnung *f*; **in·tu·i·tive** [ɪn'tjuːɪtɪv] *adj.* ☐ intui'tiv.

in·tu·mes·cence [ˌɪntjuː'mesns] *s.* **1.** Anschwellen *n*; **2.** ⚕ Anschwellung *f*, Geschwulst *f*; **ˌin·tu'mes·cent** [-nt] *adj.* (an)schwellend.

in·twine [ɪn'twaɪn] *Am.* → **entwine**.

in·un·date ['ɪnʌndeɪt] *v/t.* über'schwemmen (*a. fig.*); **in·un·da·tion** [ˌɪnʌn'deɪʃn] *s.* Über'schwemmung *f*, Flut *f* (*a. fig.*).

in·ure [ɪ'njʊə] **I** *v/t. mst pass.* (**to**) abhärten (gegen), gewöhnen (an *acc.*); **II** *v/i. bsd.* ⚖ wirksam *od.* gültig *od.* angewendet werden.

in·vade [ɪn'veɪd] *v/t.* **1.** einfallen *od.* eindringen *od.* einbrechen in (*acc.*); **2.** über'fallen, angreifen; **3.** *fig.* über'laufen, -'schwemmen, sich ausbreiten über (*acc.*); **4.** eindringen in (*acc.*), 'übergreifen auf (*acc.*); **5.** *fig.* erfüllen, ergreifen, befallen: **fear ~d all**; **6.** *fig.* verstoßen gegen, verletzen, antasten, eingreifen in (*acc.*); **in'vad·er** [-də] *s.* Eindringling *m*, Angreifer(in); *pl.* ⚔ Inva'soren *pl.*

in·va·lid¹ ['ɪnvəlɪd] **I** *adj.* **1.** a) krank, leidend, b) inva'lide, c) ⚔ dienstunfähig; **2.** Kranken...: **~ chair** Rollstuhl *m*; **~ diet** Krankenkost *f*; **II** *s.* **3.** Kranke(r *m*) *f*; **4.** Inva'lide *m*; **III** *v/t.* [ˌɪnvə'liːd] **5.** zum Inva'liden machen; **6.** *a.* **~ out** ⚔ dienstuntauglich erklären *od.* als dienstuntauglich entlassen: **be ~ed out** als Invalide (aus dem Heer) entlassen werden.

in·val·id² [ɪn'vælɪd] *adj.* ☐ **1.** (rechts)ungültig, null u. nichtig; **2.** nichtig, nicht stichhaltig (*Argumente*); **in'val·i·date** [-deɪt] *v/t.* **1.** außer Kraft setzen: a) (für) ungültig erklären, 'umstoßen, b) ungültig *od.* unwirksam machen; **2.** *Argument etc.* entkräften; **in·val·i·da·tion** [ɪnˌvælɪ'deɪʃn] *s.* **1.** Ungültigkeitserklärung *f*; **2.** Entkräftung *f*.

in·va·lid·ism ['ɪnvəlɪdɪzəm] *s.* ⚕ Invalidi'tät *f*.

in·va·lid·i·ty [ˌɪnvə'lɪdətɪ] *s.* **1.** *bsd.* ⚖ Ungültigkeit *f*, Nichtigkeit *f*; **2.** ⚕ *Am.* Invalidi'tät *f*.

in·val·u·a·ble [ɪn'væljʊəbl] *adj.* ☐ unschätzbar, unbezahlbar, von unschätzbarem Wert.

in·var·i·a·bil·i·ty [ɪnˌveərɪə'bɪlətɪ] *s.* Unveränderlichkeit *f*; **in·var·i·a·ble** [ɪn'veərɪəbl] **I** *adj.* ☐ unveränderlich, gleichbleibend; kon'stant (*a.* 𝔄); **II** *s.* 𝔄 Kon'stante *f*; **in·var·i·a·bly** [ɪn'veərɪəblɪ] *adv.* stets, ausnahmslos.

in·va·sion [ɪn'veɪʒn] *s.* **1.** (**of**) Invasi'on *f* (*gen.*): a) ⚔ *u. fig.* Einfall *m* (in *acc.*), 'Überfall *m* (auf *acc.*), b) Eindringen *n*, Einbruch *m* (in *acc.*); **2.** Andrang *m* (**of** zu); **3.** *fig.* (**of**) Eingriff *m* (in *acc.*), Verletzung *f* (*gen.*); **4.** ⚕ Anfall *m*; **in'va·sive** [-eɪsɪv] *adj.* **1.** ⚔ Invasions..., angreifend; **2.** (gewaltsam) eingreifend (**of** in *acc.*); **3.** zudringlich.

in·vec·tive [ɪn'vektɪv] *s.* Schmähung(en *pl.*) *f*, Beschimpfung *f*; *pl.* Schimpfworte *pl.*

in·veigh [ɪn'veɪ] *v/i.* (**against**) schimpfen (über, auf *acc.*), herziehen (über *acc.*).

in·vei·gle [ɪn'veɪgl] *v/t.* (**into**) **1.** verleiten, verführen (zu): **~ s.o. into doing s.th.** j-n dazu verleiten, *et.* zu tun; **2.** locken (in *acc.*); **in'vei·gle·ment** [-mənt] *s.* Verleitung *f etc.*

in·vent [ɪn'vent] *v/t.* **1.** erfinden, ersinnen; **2.** *fig.* erfinden, erdichten; **in'ven·tion** [-nʃn] *s.* **1.** Erfindung *f* (*a. fig.*); **2.** (Gegenstand *m etc.* der) Erfindung *f*; **3.** Erfindungsgabe *f*; **4.** *contp.* Märchen *n*; **in'ven·tive** [-tɪv] *adj.* ☐ **1.** erfinderisch (**of** in *dat.*); Erfindungs...; **2.** schöpferisch, einfallsreich, origi'nell; **in'ven·tive·ness** [-tɪvnɪs] → **invention** 3; **in'ven·tor** [-tə] *s.* Erfinder(in).

in·ven·to·ry ['ɪnvəntrɪ] *a.* ☿ **I** *s.* **1.** a) Inven'tar *n*, Bestandsverzeichnis, (-)Liste *f*, b) *Am.* Bestandsaufnahme *f*, Inven'tur *f*; **2.** Inven'tar *n*, Lagerbestand *m*, Vorräte *pl.*: **take ~** Inventur machen; **II** *v/t.* **3.** inventarisieren: a) e-e Bestandsaufnahme machen von, b) im Inven'tar verzeichnen.

in·verse [ɪn'vɜːs] **I** *adj.* ☐ 'umgekehrt, entgegengesetzt; 𝔄 in'vers, rezi'prok: **~ly proportional** umgekehrt proportional; **II** *s.* 'Umkehrung *f*, Gegenteil *n*; **in'ver·sion** [ɪn'vɜːʃn] *s.* **1.** 'Umkehrung *f* (*a.* ♪); **2.** ⚗, 𝔄, *ling.*, *meteor.* Inversi'on *f*, *psych. a.* Homosexuali'tät *f*.

in·vert **I** *v/t.* [ɪn'vɜːt] **1.** 'umkehren (*a.* ♪), 'umdrehen, 'umwenden (*a.* ⚡); **2.** *ling.* 'umstellen; **3.** ⚗ invertieren; **II** *s.* ['ɪnvɜːt] **4.** △ 'umgekehrter Bogen; **5.** ⚙ Sohle *f* (*Schleuse etc.*); **6.** *psych.* Invertierte(r *m*) *f*: a) Homosexu'elle(r) *m*, b) Lesbierin *f*, c) Transsexu'elle(r *m*) *f*.

in·ver·te·brate [ɪn'vɜːtɪbrət] **I** *adj.* **1.** *zo.* wirbellos; **2.** *fig.* rückgratlos; **II** *s.* **3.** *zo.* wirbelloses Tier: **the ~s** die Wirbellosen.

in·vert·ed [ɪn'vɜːtɪd] *adj.* **1.** 'umgekehrt; 'umgestellt; **2.** *psych.* invertiert, homosexu'ell; **3.** ⚙ hängend: **~ cylinders**; **~ engine** Hängemotor *m*; **~ com·mas** *s. pl.* Anführungszeichen *pl.*, ‚Gänsefüßchen' *pl.*; **~ flight** *s.* ✈ Rückenflug *m*; **~ im·age** *s. phys.* Kehrbild *n*.

in·vest [ɪn'vest] **I** *v/t.* **1.** ☿ investieren, anlegen (**in** in *dat.*); **2.** (**with**, **in** mit) bekleiden (*a. fig.*); bedecken, um'hüllen; **3.** (**with**) kleiden (in *acc.*), ausstatten (mit *Befugnissen etc.*); um'geben (mit); **4.** (in Amt u. Würden) einsetzen; **5.** ⚔ einschließen, belagern; **II** *v/i.* **6.** investieren (**in** in *dat.*); **7. ~ in** F ‚sein Geld investieren' in (*dat.*).

in·ves·ti·gate [ɪn'vestɪgeɪt] **I** *v/t.* unter'suchen, erforschen; ermitteln; **II** *v/i.* (**into**) nachforschen (nach), Ermittlungen anstellen (über *acc.*); **in·ves·ti·ga·tion** [ɪnˌvestɪ'geɪʃn] *s.* **1.** Unter'suchung *f*, Nachforschung *f*; *pl.* Ermittlung(en *pl.*) *f*, Re'cherchen *pl.*; **2.** *wissenschaftliche* (Er)Forschung; **in'ves·ti·ga·tive** [-tɪv] *adj.* recherchierend, Untersuchungs...: **~ journalism** Enthüllungsjournalismus *m*; **~ reporter** recherchierender Reporter; **in'ves·ti·ga·tor** [-tə] *s.* **1.** Unter'suchende(r) *m*, (Er-, Nach-) Forscher(in); **2.** Unter'suchungsbeamte(r) *m*; **3.** Prüfer(in).

in·ves·ti·ture [ɪn'vestɪtʃə] *s.* **1.** Investi'tur *f*, (feierliche) Amtseinsetzung *f*; **2.** Belehnung *f*; **3.** *fig.* Ausstattung *f*.

in·vest·ment [ɪn'vesmənt] *s.* **1.** ☿ a) Investierung *f*, b) Investiti'on(en *pl.*) *f*, (Kapi'tal-, Geld)Anlage *f*, Anlagewerte *pl.*: **that's a good ~** das ist e-e gute Geldanlage, *fig.* das lohnt sich *od.* macht sich bezahlt; **2.** ☿ Einlage *f*, Beteiligung *f* (*e-s Gesellschafters*); **3.** Ausstattung *f* (**with** mit); **4.** *biol.* (Außen-, Schutz)Haut *f*; **5.** ⚔ *obs.* Belagerung *f*; **6.** → **investiture** 1; **~ ad·vis·er** *s.* Anlageberater *m*; **~ bank** *s.* Investiti'ons-, In'vestmentbank *f*; **~ bank·ing** *s.* Ef'fektenbankgeschäft *n*; **~ bonds** *s. pl.* festverzinsliche 'Anlagepaˌpiere *pl.*; **~ com·pan·y** *s.* Kapi'talanlage-, In'vestmentgesellschaft *f*; **~ cred·it** *s.* Investiti'onskreˌdit *m*; **~ fund** *s.* **1.** Anlagefonds *m*; **2.** *pl.* Investiti'onsmittel *pl.*; **~ goods** *s. pl.* Investiti'onsgüter *pl.*; **~ shares** *s. pl.*, **~ stocks** *s. pl.* 'Anlagepaˌpiere *pl.*, -werte *pl.*; **~ trust** → **investment company**: **~ certificate** Anteilschein *m*, Investmentzertifikat *n*.

in·ves·tor [ɪn'vestə] *s.* ☿ In'vestor *m*, Geld-, Kapi'talanleger *m*.

in·vet·er·a·cy [ɪn'vetərəsɪ] *s.* Unausrottbarkeit *f*, *a.* ⚕ Hartnäckigkeit *f*; **in'vet·er·ate** [-rɪt] *adj.* ☐ **1.** eingewurzelt; **2.** ⚕ hartnäckig; **3.** eingefleischt, unverbesserlich.

in·vid·i·ous [ɪn'vɪdɪəs] *adj.* ☐ **1.** verhaßt, ärgerlich; **2.** gehässig, boshaft, gemein; **in'vid·i·ous·ness** [-nɪs] *s.* **1.** *das* Ärgerliche; **2.** Gehässigkeit *f*, Bosheit *f*, Gemeinheit *f*.

in·vig·i·la·tion [ɪnˌvɪdʒɪ'leɪʃn] *s. ped. Brit.* Aufsicht *f*.

in·vig·or·ate [ɪn'vɪgəreɪt] *v/t.* stärken, kräftigen, beleben, *bsd. fig.* erfrischen: **invigorating** stärkend *etc.*; **in·vig·or·a·tion** [ɪnˌvɪgə'reɪʃn] *s.* Kräftigung *f*, Belebung *f*.

in·vin·ci·bil·i·ty [ɪnˌvɪnsɪ'bɪlətɪ] *s.* Unbesiegbarkeit *f etc.*; **in·vin·ci·ble** [ɪn'vɪnsəbl] *adj.* ☐ unbesiegbar, 'unüberˌwindlich.

in·vi·o·la·bil·i·ty [ɪnˌvaɪələ'bɪlətɪ] *s.* Unverletzlichkeit *f*, Unantastbarkeit *f*; **in·vi·o·la·ble** [ɪn'vaɪələbl] *adj.* ☐ unverletzlich, unantastbar, heilig; **in·vi·o·late** [ɪn'vaɪələt] *adj.* ☐ **1.** unverletzt, unversehrt, nicht gebrochen (*Gesetz etc.*); **2.** unangetastet.

in·vis·i·bil·i·ty [ɪnˌvɪzəˈbɪlətɪ] *s.* Unsichtbarkeit *f*; **in·vis·i·ble** [ɪnˈvɪzəbl] *adj.* □ unsichtbar (***to*** für): ***~ ink***; ***~ exports***; ***~ mending*** Kunststopfen *n*; ***he was ~*** *fig.* er ließ sich nicht sehen.
in·vi·ta·tion [ˌɪnvɪˈteɪʃn] *s.* **1.** Einladung *f* (***to s.o.*** an j-n): ***~ to tea*** Einladung zum Tee; **2.** Aufforderung *f*, Ersuchen *n*; **3.** ***~ to bid*** ☤ Ausschreibung *f*; **in·vite** [ɪnˈvaɪt] *v/t.* **1.** einladen: ***~ s.o. in*** j-n hereinbitten; **2.** *j-n* auffordern, bitten (***to do*** zu tun); **3.** *et.* erbitten, ersuchen um, auffordern zu *et.*; ☤ ausschreiben; **4.** *Kritik, Gefahr etc.* herˈausfordern, sich aussetzen (*dat.*); **5.** a) einladen zu, ermutigen zu, b) (ver)locken (***to do*** zu tun); **in·vit·ing** [ɪnˈvaɪtɪŋ] *adj.* □ einladend, (ver)lockend.
in·vo·ca·tion [ˌɪnvəʊˈkeɪʃn] *s.* **1.** Anrufung *f*; **2.** *eccl.* Bittgebet *n*.
in·voice [ˈɪnvɔɪs] ☤ **I** *s.* Fakˈtura *f*, (Waren-, Begleit)Rechnung *f*: ***as per ~*** laut Rechnung; ***~ clerk*** Fakturist(in); **II** *v/t.* fakturieren, in Rechnung stellen.
in·voke [ɪnˈvəʊk] *v/t.* **1.** anrufen, anflehen, flehen zu; **2.** flehen um, erflehen; **3.** *fig.* zu Hilfe rufen, sich berufen auf (*acc.*), anführen, zitieren; **4.** *Geist* beschwören.
in·vol·un·tar·i·ness [ɪnˈvɒləntərɪnɪs] *s.* **1.** Unfreiwilligkeit *f*; **2.** ˈUnwillˌkürlichkeit *f*; **in·vol·un·tar·y** [ɪnˈvɒləntərɪ] *adj.* □ **1.** unfreiwillig; **2.** ˈunwillˌkürlich; **3.** unabsichtlich.
in·vo·lute [ˈɪnvəluːt] **I** *adj.* **1.** ⚘ eingerollt; **2.** *zo.* mit engen Windungen; **3.** *fig.* verwickelt; **II** *s.* **4.** ⩚ Evolˈvente *f*; **in·vo·lu·tion** [ˌɪnvəˈluːʃn] *s.* **1.** ⚘ Einrollung *f*; **2.** Involutiˈon *f*: a) *biol.* Rückbildung *f*, b) ⩚ Potenzierung *f*; **3.** Verwicklung *f*, Verwirrung *f*.
in·volve [ɪnˈvɒlv] (→ *a.* ***involved***) *v/t.* **1.** umˈfassen, einschließen, involvieren; **2.** nach sich ziehen, zur Folge haben, mit sich bringen, verbunden sein mit, bedeuten: ***~ great expense***; ***this would ~ (our) living abroad*** das würde bedeuten, daß wir im Ausland leben müßten; **3.** nötig machen, erfordern: ***~ hard work***; **4.** betreffen: a) angehen: ***the plan ~s all employees***, b) beteiligen (***in, with*** an *dat.*): ***the number of persons ~d***, c) sich handeln *od.* drehen um, gehen um, zum Gegenstand haben: ***the case ~d some grave offences***, d) in Mitleidenschaft ziehen: ***diseases that ~ the nervous system***; ***it wouldn't ~ you*** du hättest nichts damit zu tun; **5.** verwickeln, -stricken, hinˈeinziehen (***in*** in *acc.*): ***~d in a lawsuit*** in e-n Rechtsstreit verwickelt; ***~d in an accident*** in e-n Unfall verwikkelt, an e-m Unfall beteiligt; ***I am not getting ~d in this!*** ich lasse mich da nicht hineinziehen!; **6.** *j-n* (*seelisch, persönlich*) engagieren (***in*** in *dat.*): ***~ o.s. with s.o.*** sich mit j-m einlassen; ***be ~d with s.o.*** a) mit j-m zu tun haben, b) zu j-m e-e (enge) Beziehung haben, *erotisch*: *a.* mit j-m ein Verhältnis haben, es mit j-m ‚haben'; ***she was ~d with several men***; **7.** *j-n* in Schwierigkeiten bringen (***with*** mit); **8.** *et.* komplizieren, verwirren; **inˈvolved** [-vd] *adj.* (→ *a.* ***involve***) **1.** a) kompliziert, b) verworren: ***an ~ sentence***; **2.** betroffen, beteiligt: ***the persons ~***; **3.** ***be ~*** a) → ***involve*** 4 c, b) mitspielen (***in*** bei *e-r Sache*), c) auf dem Spiel stehen, gehen um: ***the national prestige was ~***; **4.** (***in***) verwickelt, verstrickt (in *acc.*), beteiligt (an *dat.*); **5.** einbegriffen; **6.** (***in, with***) a) stark beschäftigt (mit), versunken (in *acc.*), b) (stark) interessiert (an *dat.*); **7.** (*seelisch, innerlich*) engagiert: ***emotionally ~***; ***be deeply ~ with a girl*** e-e enge Beziehung zu e-m Mädchen haben, stark empfinden für ein Mädchen; **inˈvolve·ment** [-mənt] *s.* **1.** Verwicklung *f*, -strickung *f* (***in*** in *acc.*); **2.** Beteiligung *f* (***in*** an *dat.*); **3.** Betroffensein *n*; **4.** (*seelisches od. persönliches*) Engagement; **5.** (***with***) a) (*innere*) Beziehung (zu), b) (*sexuelles*) Verhältnis (mit), c) Umgang (mit); **6.** Kompliziertheit *f*; **7.** komplizierte Sache, Schwierigkeit *f*.
in·vul·ner·a·bil·i·ty [ɪnˌvʌlnərəˈbɪlətɪ] *s.* **1.** Unverwundbarkeit *f*; **2.** *fig.* Unanfechtbarkeit *f*; **in·vul·ner·a·ble** [ɪnˈvʌlnərəbl] *adj.* □ **1.** unverwundbar, ungefährdet, gefeit (***to*** gegen); **2.** *fig.* unanfechtbar.
in·ward [ˈɪnwəd] **I** *adj.* □ **1.** inner(lich), Innen…; nach innen gehend: ***~ parts*** *anat.* innere Organe; ***the ~ nature*** der Kern, das eigentliche Wesen; **2.** *fig.* seelisch, geistig, inner(lich); **3.** ***~ duty*** ☤ Eingangszoll *m*; ***~ journey*** ⚓ Heimfahrt *f*, -reise *f*; ***~ mail*** eingehende Post; **II** *s.* **4.** *das* Innere (*a. fig.*); **5.** *pl.* [ˈɪnədz] F a) innere Orˈgane *pl.*, Eingeweide *pl.*, b) *Küche*: Inneˈreien *pl.*; **III** *adv.* **6.** nach innen; **7.** im Innern (*a. fig.*); **ˈin·ward·ly** [-lɪ] *adv.* **1.** innerlich, im Innern (*a. fig.*); nach innen; **2.** im stillen, insgeheim, für sich, leise; **ˈin·ward·ness** [-nɪs] *s.* **1.** Innerlichkeit *f*; **2.** innere Naˈtur, wahre Bedeutung; **ˈin·wards** [-dz] → ***inward*** 6, 7.
in·weave [ˌɪnˈwiːv] *v/t.* [*irr.* → ***weave***] **1.** einweben (***into*** in *acc.*); **2.** *fig.* ein-, verflechten.
in·wrought [ˌɪnˈrɔːt] *adj.* **1.** eingewoben, eingearbeitet; **2.** verziert; **3.** *fig.* (eng) verflochten.
i·o·date [ˈaɪəʊdeɪt] *s.* ⚗ Joˈdat *n*; **i·od·ic** [aɪˈɒdɪk] *adj.* ⚗ jodhaltig, Jod…; **ˈi·o·dide** [-daɪd] *s.* ⚗ Joˈdid *n*; **ˈi·o·dine** [-diːn] *s.* Jod *n*: ***tincture of ~*** Jodtinktur *f*; **ˈi·o·dism** [-dɪzəm] *s.* Jodvergiftung *f*; **ˈi·o·dize** [-daɪz] *v/t.* jodieren, mit Jod behandeln.
i·on [ˈaɪən] *s. phys.* Iˈon *n*.
I·o·ni·an [aɪˈəʊnjən] **I** *adj.* iˈonisch; **II** *s.* Iˈonier(in).
I·on·ic[1] [aɪˈɒnɪk] *adj.* iˈonisch: ***~ order*** ionische Säulenordnung.
i·on·ic[2] [aɪˈɒnɪk] *adj. phys.* iˈonisch: ***~ centrifuge*** Ionenschleuder *f*; ***~ migration*** Ionenwanderung *f*.
i·o·ni·um [aɪˈəʊnɪəm] *s.* ⚗ Iˈonium *n*.
i·on·i·za·tion [ˌaɪənaɪˈzeɪʃn] *s. phys.* Ionisierung *f*; **i·on·ize** [ˈaɪənaɪz] *phys.* **I** *v/t.* ionisieren; **II** *v/i.* in Iˈonen zerfallen; **i·on·o·sphere** [aɪˈɒnəˌsfɪə] *s. phys.* Ionoˈsphäre *f*.
i·o·ta [aɪˈəʊtə] *s.* Jota *n* (*griech. Buchstabe*): ***not an ~*** *fig.* kein Jota *od.* bißchen.
IOU [ˌaɪəʊˈjuː] *s.* Schuldschein *m* (= ***I owe you***).
ip·so fac·to [ˌɪpsəʊˈfæktəʊ] (*Lat.*) gerade (*od.* alˈlein) durch diese Tatsache, eo ipso.
I·ra·ni·an [ɪˈreɪnjən] **I** *adj.* **1.** iˈranisch, persisch; **II** *s.* **2.** Iˈranier(in), Perser (-in); **3.** *ling.* Iˈranisch *n*, Persisch *n*.
I·ra·qi [ɪˈrɑːkɪ] **I** *s.* **1.** Iˈraker(in); **2.** *ling.* Iˈrakisch *n*; **II** *adj.* **3.** iˈrakisch.
i·ras·ci·bil·i·ty [ɪˌræsəˈbɪlətɪ] *s.* Jähzorn *m*, Reizbarkeit *f*; **i·ras·ci·ble** [ɪˈræsəbl] *adj.* □ jähzornig, reizbar.
i·rate [aɪˈreɪt] *adj.* zornig, wütend.
ire [ˈaɪə] *s. poet.* Zorn *m*, Wut *f*; **ˈire·ful** [-fʊl] *adj.* □ *poet.* zornig.
ir·i·des·cence [ˌɪrɪˈdesns] *s.* Schillern *n*; **ˌir·iˈdes·cent** [-nt] *adj.* schillernd, irisierend.
i·rid·i·um [aɪˈrɪdɪəm] *s.* ⚗ Iˈridium *n*.
i·ris [ˈaɪərɪs] *s.* **1.** *anat.* Regenbogenhaut *f*, Iris *f*; **2.** ⚘ Schwertlilie *f*.
I·rish [ˈaɪərɪʃ] **I** *adj.* **1.** irisch: ***the ~ Free State*** *obs.* der Irische Freistaat; → ***bull***[3]; **II** *s.* **2.** *ling.* Irisch *n*; **3.** ***the ~*** *pl.* die Iren *pl.*, die Irländer *pl.*; **ˈI·rish·ism** [-ʃɪzəm] *s.* irische (Sprach)Eigentümlichkeit.
ˈI·rish|·man [-mən] *s.* [*irr.*] Ire *m*, Irländer *m*; **~ stew** *s. Küche*: Irish Stew *n*; **~ ter·ri·er** *s.* Irischer Terrier; **ˈ~ˌwom·an** *s.* [*irr.*] Irin *f*, Irländerin *f*.
irk [ɜːk] *v/t.* ärgern, verdrießen; **ˈirk·some** [-səm] *adj.* □ **1.** ärgerlich, verdrießlich; **2.** lästig.
i·ron [ˈaɪən] **I** *s.* **1.** Eisen *n*: ***have (too) many ~s in the fire*** (zu) viele Eisen im Feuer haben; ***rule with a rod of ~*** *od.* ***with an ~ hand*** mit eiserner Faust regieren; ***strike while the ~ is hot*** das Eisen schmieden, solange es heiß ist; ***a man of ~*** ein harter Mann; ***he is made of ~*** er hat e-e eiserne Gesundheit; **2.** Brandeisen *n*, -stempel *m*; **3.** (Bügel-, Plätt)Eisen *n*; **4.** Steigbügel *m*; **5.** *Golf*: Eisen *n* (*Schläger*); **6.** ⚕ ˈEisen (-präpaˌrat) *n*: ***take ~*** Eisen einnehmen; **7.** *pl.* Hand-, Fußschellen *pl.*, Eisen *pl.*: ***put in ~s*** → 14; **8.** *pl.* ⚕ Beinschiene *f* (*Stützapparat*): ***put s.o.'s leg in ~s*** j-m das Bein schienen; **II** *adj.* **9.** eisern, Eisen…: ***~ bar*** Eisenstange *f*; **10.** *fig.* eisern: a) hart, kräftig: ***~ constitution*** eiserne Gesundheit; ***~ frame*** kräftiger Körper(bau), b) ehern, hart, grausam: ***~ fist*** *od.* ***hand*** eiserne Faust (→ 1); ***there was an ~ fist in a velvet glove*** bei all s-r Freundlichkeit war mit ihm doch nicht zu spaßen, c) unbeugsam, unerschütterlich: ***~ discipline*** eiserne Zucht; ***~ will*** eiserner Wille; **III** *v/t.* **11.** bügeln, plätten; **12.** ***~ out*** a) glätten, einebnen, glattwalzen, b) *fig.* ‚ausbügeln', in Ordnung bringen; **13.** ⚙ mit Eisen beschlagen; **14.** fesseln, in Eisen legen.
I·ron| Age *s.* Eisenzeit *f*; **~ Chan·cel·lor** *s.*: ***the ~*** der Eiserne Kanzler (*Bismarck*); **ˈ~·clad** **I** *adj.* **1.** gepanzert (*Schiff*), eisenverkleidet, -bewehrt, mit Eisenmantel; **2.** *fig.* eisern, starr, streng; **3.** *fig.* unangreifbar, absoˈlut stichhaltig: ***~ argument***; **II** *s.* **4.** *hist.* Panzerschiff *n*; **~ con·crete** *s.* ⚙ ˈEisenbeˌton *m*; **~ Cross** *s.* ⚔ Eisernes Kreuz (*Auszeichnung*); **~ Cur·tain** *s. pol.* ‚Eiserner Vorhang': ***~ countries*** *die* Länder *pl.* hinter dem Eisernen Vorhang; **~ Duke** *s.*: ***the ~*** der Eiserne Herzog (*Wellington*); **~ found·ry** *s.* Eisengießeˈrei *f*; **~ horse** *s.* F *obs.*

‚Dampfroß‘ *n* (*Lokomotive*).

i·ron·ic, i·ron·i·cal [aɪˈrɒnɪk(l)] *adj.* **1.** iˈronisch, spöttelnd, spöttisch; **2.** *Situation etc.*: seltsam, ‚komisch‘, paradox; **iˈron·i·cal·ly** [-ɪkəlɪ] *adv.* **1.** iˈronisch(erweise); **2.** komischerweise; **i·ro·nize** [ˈaɪərənaɪz] **I** *v/t. et.* ironisieren; **II** *v/i.* iˈronisch sein, spötteln.

i·ron·ing board [ˈaɪənɪŋ] *s.* Bügel-, Plättbrett *n*.

i·ron| lung *s.* ⚕ eiserne Lunge; **ˈ~ˌmas·ter** *s. Brit.* ˈEisenfabriˌkant *m*, *obs.* Eisenhüttenbesitzer *m*; **ˈ~ˌmon·ger** *s. bsd. Brit.* Eisenwaren-, Meˈtallwarenhändler(in); **ˈ~ˌmon·ger·y** *s. bsd. Brit.* **1.** Eisen-, Meˈtallwaren *pl.*; **2.** Eisenwaren-, Meˈtallwarenhandlung *f*; **~ ore** *s. metall.* Eisenerz *n*; **~ ox·ide** *s.* ⚗ ˈEisenoˌxyd *n*; **~ ra·tion** *s.* ⚔ eiserne Ratiˈon; **ˈ~·sides** *s.* **1.** *sg.* Mann *m* von großer Tapferkeit; **2.** *pl. hist.* Cromwells Reiteˈrei *f od.* Heer *n*; **3.** → ***ironclad*** 4; **ˈ~·ware** *s.* Eisen-, Meˈtallwaren *pl.*; **ˈ~·work** *s.* ⚙ ˈEisenbeschlag *m*, -konstruktiˌon *f*; **ˈ~·works** *s. pl. sg. konstr.* Eisenhütte *f*.

i·ron·y¹ [ˈaɪənɪ] *adj.* **1.** eisern; **2.** eisenhaltig (*Erde*); **3.** eisenartig.

i·ro·ny² [ˈaɪərənɪ] *s.* **1.** Iroˈnie *f*: ***~ of fate*** *fig.* Ironie des Schicksals; ***tragic ~*** tragische Ironie; ***the ~ of it!*** *fig.* welche Ironie (des Schicksals)!; **2.** iˈronische Bemerkung, Spötteˈlei *f*.

Ir·o·quois [ˈɪrəkwɔɪ] *pl.* **-quois** [-kwɔɪz] *s.* Iroˈkese *m*, Iroˈkesin *f*.

ir·ra·di·ance [ɪˈreɪdjəns] *s.* **1.** (An-, Aus-, Be)Strahlen *n*; **2.** Strahlenglanz *m*; **irˈra·di·ant** [-nt] *adj. a. fig.* strahlend (***with*** vor *dat.*); **irˈra·di·ate** [-dɪeɪt] *v/t.* **1.** bestrahlen (*a.* ⚕), erleuchten; **2.** ausstrahlen; **3.** *fig. Gesicht etc.* aufheitern, verklären; **4.** *fig. etc.* erhellen, Licht werfen auf (*acc.*); **ir·ra·di·a·tion** [ɪˌreɪdɪˈeɪʃn] *s.* **1.** (Aus)Strahlen *n*, Leuchten *n*; **2.** *phys.* a) ˈStrahlungsintensiˌtät *f*, b) speˈzifische ˈStrahlungsenerˌgie; **3.** Irradiatiˈon *f*: a) *phot.* Belichtung *f*, b) ⚕ Bestrahlung *f*, Durchˈleuchtung *f*; **4.** *fig.* Erhellung *f*.

ir·ra·tion·al [ɪˈræʃənl] **I** *adj.* ☐ **1.** unvernünftig: a) vernunftlos: ***~ animal***, b) ˈirratioˌnal (*a.* 𝔸, *phls.*), vernunftwidrig, unsinnig; **II** *s.* **2.** 𝔸 ˈIrratioˌnalzahl *f*; **3.** *the* ~ → **ir·ra·tion·al·i·ty** [ɪˌræʃəˈnælətɪ] *s.* Irrationaliˈtät *f* (*a.* 𝔸, *phls.*), *das* ˈIrratioˌnale, Unvernunft *f*, Unsinnigkeit *f*.

ir·re·but·ta·ble [ˌɪrɪˈbʌtəbl] *adj.* ˈunwiderˌlegbar.

ir·re·claim·a·ble [ˌɪrɪˈkleɪməbl] *adj.* ☐ **1.** unverbesserlich; **2.** ⛏ unbebaubar; **3.** ˈunwiederˌbringlich.

ir·rec·og·niz·a·ble [ɪˈrekəgnaɪzəbl] *adj.* ☐ nicht ˈwiederzuerˌkennen(d), unkenntlich.

ir·rec·on·cil·a·bil·i·ty [ɪˌrekənsaɪləˈbɪlətɪ] *s.* **1.** Unvereinbarkeit *f* (***to***, ***with*** mit); **2.** Unversöhnlichkeit *f*; **ir·rec·on·cil·a·ble** [ɪˈrekənsaɪləbl] **I** *adj.* ☐ **1.** unvereinbar (***to***, ***with*** mit); **2.** unversöhnlich; **II** *s.* **3.** *pol.* unversöhnlicher Gegner.

ir·re·cov·er·a·ble [ˌɪrɪˈkʌvərəbl] *adj.* ☐ **1.** unrettbar (verloren), ˈunwiederˌbringlich, unersetzlich: ***~ debt*** nicht beitreibbare (Schuld)Forderung; **2.** unheilbar, nicht wiederˈgutzumachen(d).

ir·re·deem·a·ble [ˌɪrɪˈdiːməbl] *adj.* ☐ **1.** nicht rückkaufbar; **2.** ☤ nicht (in Gold) einlösbar (*Papiergeld*); **3.** ☤ a) untilgbar; ***~ loan***, b) nicht ablösbar, unkündbar (*Schuldverschreibung etc.*); **4.** unrettbar (verloren), unverbesserlich, hoffnungslos.

ir·re·den·tism [ˌɪrɪˈdentɪzəm] *s. pol.* Irredenˈtismus *m*; **ˌir·reˈden·tist** [-ɪst] *pol.* **I** *s.* Irredenˈtist *m*; **II** *adj.* irredenˈtistisch.

ir·re·duc·i·ble [ˌɪrɪˈdjuːsəbl] *adj.* ☐ **1.** nicht zu vereinfachen(d); **2.** nicht reduzierbar, nicht zu vermindern(d): ***the ~ minimum*** das äußerste Mindestmaß.

ir·re·fran·gi·ble [ˌɪrɪˈfrændʒəbl] *adj.* **1.** unverletzlich, nicht zu überˈtreten(d); **2.** *opt.* unbrechbar.

ir·re·fu·ta·ble [ˌɪrɪˈfjuːtəbl] *adj.* ☐ ˈunwiderˌlegbar, nicht zu widerˈlegen(d).

ir·re·gard·less [ˌɪrɪˈgɑːdlɪs] *adj. Am.* F ***~ of*** ohne sich zu kümmern um.

ir·reg·u·lar [ɪˈregjʊlə] **I** *adj.* ☐ **1.** unregelmäßig (*a.* ✿, *ling*, *a. Zähne etc.*), ungleichmäßig, uneinheitlich; **2.** ungeordnet, unordentlich; **3.** ungehörig, ungebührlich; **4.** regel-, vorschriftswidrig; **5.** ungesetzlich, ungültig; **6.** uneben; ˈunsysteˌmatisch; **7.** ⚔ ˈirreguˌlär; **II** *s.* **8.** *pl.* Partiˈsanen *pl.*, Freischärler *pl.*; **ir·reg·u·lar·i·ty** [ɪˌregjʊˈlærətɪ] *s.* **1.** Unregelmäßigkeit *f* (*a. ling.*), Ungleichmäßigkeit *f*; **2.** Regelwidrigkeit *f*; ⚖ Formfehler *m*, Verfahrensmangel *m*; **3.** Ungehörigkeit *f*; **4.** Unebenheit *f*; **5.** Unordnung *f*; **6.** Vergehen *n*, Verstoß *m*; **7.** *pl.* ☤ *Am.* Ausschußware(n *pl.*) *f*.

ir·rel·e·vance [ɪˈreləvəns], **irˈrel·e·van·cy** [-sɪ] *s.* ˈIrreleˌvanz *f*, Unerheblichkeit *f*, Belanglosigkeit *f*, Unwesentlichkeit *f*; **irˈrel·e·vant** [-nt] *adj.* ☐ ˈirreleˌvant, belanglos, unerheblich (***to*** für) (*alle a.* ⚖), nicht zur Sache gehörig.

ir·re·li·gion [ˌɪrɪˈlɪdʒən] *s.* Religiˈonslosigkeit *f*, Unglaube *m*; Gottlosigkeit *f*; **ˌir·reˈli·gious** [-dʒəs] *adj.* ☐ **1.** ˈirreligiˌös, ungläubig, gottlos; **2.** religiˈonsfeindlich.

ir·re·me·di·a·ble [ˌɪrɪˈmiːdjəbl] *adj.* ☐ **1.** unheilbar; **2.** unabänderlich; **3.** → ***irreparable***.

ir·re·mis·si·ble [ˌɪrɪˈmɪsəbl] *adj.* ☐ **1.** unverzeihlich; **2.** unerläßlich.

ir·re·mov·a·ble [ˌɪrɪˈmuːvəbl] *adj.* ☐ **1.** nicht zu entfernen(d); unbeweglich (*a. fig.*); **2.** unabsetzbar.

ir·rep·a·ra·ble [ɪˈrepərəbl] *adj.* ☐ **1.** ˈirrepaˌrabel, nicht wiederˈgutzumachen(d); **2.** unersetzlich; **3.** unheilbar (*a.* ⚕).

ir·re·place·a·ble [ˌɪrɪˈpleɪsəbl] *adj.* unersetzlich, unersetzbar.

ir·re·press·i·ble [ˌɪrɪˈpresəbl] *adj.* ☐ **1.** unbezähmbar, unbändig; **2.** *Person*: a) nicht ˈunterzukriegen(d), unverwüstlich, b) temperaˈmentvoll.

ir·re·proach·a·ble [ˌɪrɪˈprəʊtʃəbl] *adj.* ☐ untadelig, einwandfrei, tadellos.

ir·re·sist·i·bil·i·ty [ˈɪrɪˌzɪstəˈbɪlətɪ] *s.* ˈUnwiderˌstehlichkeit *f*; **ir·re·sist·i·ble** [ˌɪrɪˈzɪstəbl] *adj.* ☐ **1.** ˈunwiderˌstehlich (*a. fig. Charme etc.*); **2.** unaufhaltsam.

ir·res·o·lute [ɪˈrezəluːt] *adj.* ☐ unentschlossen, schwankend; **irˈres·o·lute·ness** [-nɪs], **ir·res·o·lu·tion** [ˈɪˌrezəˈluːʃn] *s.* Unentschlossenheit *f*.

ir·re·spec·tive [ˌɪrɪˈspektɪv] *adj.* ☐: ***~ of*** ohne Rücksicht auf (*acc.*), ungeachtet (*gen.*), abgesehen von.

ir·re·spon·si·bil·i·ty [ˈɪrɪˌspɒnsəˈbɪlətɪ] *s.* **1.** Unverantwortlichkeit *f*; **2.** Verantwortungslosigkeit *f*; **ir·re·spon·si·ble** [ˌɪrɪˈspɒnsəbl] *adj.* ☐ **1.** unverantwortlich (*Handlung*); **2.** verantwortungslos (*Person*); **3.** ⚖ unzurechnungsfähig.

ir·re·spon·sive [ˌɪrɪˈspɒnsɪv] *adj.* **1.** teilnahms-, verständnislos, gleichgültig (***to*** gegenüber); **2.** unempfänglich (***to*** für); ***be ~ to a.*** nicht reagieren auf (*acc.*).

ir·re·triev·a·ble [ˌɪrɪˈtriːvəbl] *adj.* ☐ **1.** ˈunwiederˌbringlich, unrettbar (verloren): ***~ breakdown of marriage*** ⚖ unheilbare Zerrüttung der Ehe; **2.** unersetzlich; **3.** nicht wiederˈgutzumachen(d); **ˌir·reˈtriev·a·bly** [-əblɪ] *adv.*: ***~ broken down*** ⚖ unheilbar zerrüttet (*Ehe*).

ir·rev·er·ence [ɪˈrevərəns] *s.* **1.** Unehrerbietigkeit *f*, Reˈspekt-, Pieˈtätlosigkeit *f*; **2.** ˈMißachtung *f*; **irˈrev·er·ent** [-nt] *adj.* ☐ reˈspektlos, ehrfurchtslos, pieˈtätlos.

ir·re·vers·i·bil·i·ty [ˈɪrɪˌvɜːsəˈbɪlətɪ] *s.* **1.** Nichtˈumkehrbarkeit *f*; **2.** ˈUnwiderˌruflichkeit *f*; **ir·re·vers·i·ble** [ˌɪrɪˈvɜːsəbl] *adj.* ☐ **1.** nicht ˈumkehrbar; **2.** ⚙ nur in ˈeiner Richtung (laufend); **3.** ⚗, 𝔸, *phys.* irreverˈsibel; **4.** ˈunwiderˌruflich.

ir·rev·o·ca·bil·i·ty [ɪˌrevəkəˈbɪlətɪ] *s.* ˈUnwiderˌruflichkeit *f*; **ir·rev·o·ca·ble** [ɪˈrevəkəbl] *adj.* ☐ ˈunwiderˌruflich (*a.* ☤), endgültig.

ir·ri·ga·ble [ˈɪrɪgəbl] *adj.* ⛏ bewässerungsfähig; **ir·ri·gate** [ˈɪrɪgeɪt] *v/t.* **1.** ⛏ bewässern, berieseln; **2.** ⚕ spülen; **ir·ri·ga·tion** [ˌɪrɪˈgeɪʃn] *s.* **1.** ⛏ Bewässerung *f*, Berieselung *f*; **2.** ⚕ Spülung *f*.

ir·ri·ta·bil·i·ty [ˌɪrɪtəˈbɪlətɪ] *s.* Reizbarkeit *f* (*a.* ⚕); **ir·ri·ta·ble** [ˈɪrɪtəbl] *adj.* ☐ **1.** reizbar; **2.** gereizt, ⚕ *a.* empfindlich.

ir·ri·tant [ˈɪrɪtənt] **I** *adj.* Reiz erzeugend, Reiz...; **II** *s.* a) Reizmittel *n* (*a. fig.*), b) ⚔ Reiz(kampf)stoff *m*.

ir·ri·tate¹ [ˈɪrɪteɪt] *v/t.* reizen (*a.* ⚕), (ver)ärgern, irritieren: ***~d at*** (*od.* ***by*** *od.* ***with***) ärgerlich über (*acc.*).

ir·ri·tate² [ˈɪrɪteɪt] *v/t. Scot.* ⚖ für nichtig erklären.

ir·ri·tat·ing [ˈɪrɪteɪtɪŋ] *adj.* ☐ irritierend, aufreizend; ärgerlich, lästig; **ir·ri·ta·tion** [ˌɪrɪˈteɪʃn] *s.* **1.** Reizung *f*, Ärger *m*; **2.** ⚕ Reizung *f*, Reizzustand *m*.

ir·rupt [ɪˈrʌpt] *v/i.* eindringen, herˈeinbrechen; **irˈrup·tion** [-pʃn] *s.* Einbruch *m*: a) Eindringen *n*, (plötzliches) Herˈeinbrechen, b) (feindlicher) Einfall, ˈÜberfall *m*; **irˈrup·tive** [-tɪv] *adj.* herˈeinbrechend.

is [ɪz] *3. sg. pres. von* ***be***.

I·sa·iah [aɪˈzaɪə], *a.* **Iˈsa·ias** [-əs] *npr. u. s. bibl.* (das Buch) Jeˈsaja *m od.* Iˈsaias *m*.

is·chi·ad·ic [ˌɪskɪˈædɪk] *mst* **ˌis·chiˈat·ic** [-ˈætɪk] *adj.* **1.** *anat.* Hüft-, Sitzbein...; **2.** ⚕ ischiˈatisch.

i·sin·glass [ˈaɪzɪŋglɑːs] *s.* Hausenblase *f*, Fischleim *m*.

Is·lam [ˈɪzlɑːm] *s.* Isˈlam *m*; **Is·lam·ic** [ɪzˈlæmɪk] *adj.* isˈlamisch; **Is·lam·ize** [ˈɪzləmaɪz] *v/t.* islamisieren.

is·land [ˈaɪlənd] *s.* **1.** Insel *f* (*a. fig. u.*

⚕); **2.** Verkehrsinsel *f*; **ˈis·land·er** [-də] *s.* Inselbewohner(in), Insuˈlaner (-in).

isle [aɪl] *s. poet. u. in npr.* (kleine) Insel, *poet.* Eiland *n*.

ism [ˈɪzəm] *s.* Ismus *m* (*bloße Theorie*).

is·n't [ˈɪznt] F *für* ***is not***.

i·so·bar [ˈaɪsəʊbɑː] *s.* **1.** *meteor.* Isoˈbare *f*; **2.** *phys.* Isoˈbar *n*.

i·so·chro·mat·ic [ˌaɪsəʊkrəʊˈmætɪk] *adj. phys.* isochroˈmatisch, gleichfarbig.

i·so·late [ˈaɪsəleɪt] *v/t.* **1.** isolieren, absondern, abschließen (***from*** von); **2.** ⚗, ⚕, ⚡, *phys.* isolieren; **3.** *fig.* genau bestimmen; **ˈi·so·lat·ed** [-tɪd] *adj.* **1.** isoliert (*a.* ⚙), (ab)gesondert, alˈleinstehend, vereinzelt: **~ *case*** Einzelfall *m*; **2.** einsam, abgeschieden; **i·so·la·tion** [ˌaɪsəˈleɪʃn] *s.* ⚕, ⚙, *pol.*, *fig.* Isolierung *f*, Isolatiˈon *f*: **~ *ward*** Isolierstation *f*; ***in* ~** *fig.* einzeln, für sich (*betrachtet*); **i·so·la·tion·ism** [ˌaɪsəˈleɪʃnɪzəm] *s. pol.* Isolatioˈnismus *m*; **i·so·la·tion·ist** [ˌaɪsəˈleɪʃnɪst] *s. pol.* Isolatioˈnist *m*.

i·so·mer [ˈaɪsəʊmɜː] *s.* ⚗ Isoˈmer *n*; **i·so·mer·ic** [ˌaɪsəʊˈmerɪk] *adj.* ⚗ isoˈmer.

i·so·met·ric [ˌaɪsəʊˈmetrɪk] ⩘ **I** *adj.* isoˈmetrisch; **II** *s. pl. sg. konstr.* Isomeˈtrie *f* (*a. Muskeltraining*).

i·sos·ce·les [aɪˈsɒsɪliːz] *adj.* ⩘ gleichschenk(e)lig (*Dreieck*).

i·so·therm [ˈaɪsəʊθɜːm] *s.* Isoˈtherme *f*; **i·so·ther·mal** [ˌaɪsəʊˈθɜːml] *adj.* isoˈthermisch, gleich warm: **~ *line* → *isotherm***.

i·so·tope [ˈaɪsəʊtəʊp] *s.* ⚗, *phys.* Isoˈtop *n*.

Is·ra·el [ˈɪzreɪəl] *s. bibl.* (das Volk) Israel *n*; **Is·rae·li** [ɪzˈreɪlɪ] **I** *adj.* israˈelisch; **II** *s.* Israˈeli *m*; **Is·ra·el·ite** [ˈɪzˌrɪəlaɪt] **I** *s.* Israeˈlit(in); **II** *adj.* israeˈlitisch, jüdisch.

is·su·a·ble [ˈɪʃuːəbl] *adj.* **1.** auszugeben(d); **2.** ✝ emittierbar; **3.** ⚖ zu veröffentlichen(d); **ˈis·su·ance** [-əns] *s.* (Her)ˈAusgabe *f*; Ver-, Erteilung *f*.

is·sue [ˈɪʃuː] **I** *s.* **1.** Ausgabe *f*, Aus-, Erteilung *f*, Erlaß *m* (*Befehl*); **2.** Aus-, Herˈausgabe *f*; **3.** ✝ a) (Efˈfekten-)Emissiˌon *f*, (Aktien)Ausgabe *f*, Auflegen *n* (*Anleihe*); Ausstellung *f* (*Dokument*): ***date of* ~** Ausstellungsdatum *n*, Ausgabetag *m*; ***bank of* ~** Emissionsbank *f*, b) ˈWertpaˌpiere *pl.* derˈselben Emissiˈon; **4.** *bsd.* ⚔ Lieferung *f*, Ausgabe *f*, Zu-, Verteilung *f*; **5.** Ausgabe *f*: a) Veröffentlichung *f*, Auflage *f* (*Buch*), b) Nummer *f* (*Zeitung*); **6.** Streitfall *m*, (Streit)Frage *f*, Proˈblem *n*: ***at* ~** a) strittig, zur Debatte stehend, b) uneinig; ***point at* ~** strittige Frage; ***evade the* ~** ausweichen; ***join*** *od.* ***take* ~ *with s.o.*** sich mit j-m auf e-n Streit *od.* e-e Auseinandersetzung einlassen; **7.** (Kern)Punkt *m*, Fall *m*, Sachverhalt *m*: **~ *of fact*** (***law***) ⚖ Tatsachen-(Rechts)frage *f*; ***side* ~** Nebenpunkt *m*; ***the whole* ~** F das Ganze; ***raise an* ~** e-n Fall *od.* Sachverhalt anschneiden; **8.** Ergebnis *n*, Ausgang *m*, (Ab)Schluß *m*: ***in the* ~** schließlich; ***bring to an* ~** entscheiden; ***force an* ~** e-e Entscheidung erzwingen; **9.** Abkömmlinge *pl.*, leibliche Nachkommenschaft: ***die without* ~** ohne direkte Nachkommen sterben; **10.** *bsd.* ⚕ Ab-, Ausfluß *m*; **11.** Öffnung *f*, Mündung *f*; *fig.* Ausweg *m*; **II** *v/t.* **12.** *Befehle etc.* ausgeben, erteilen; **13.** ✝ *Banknoten* ausgeben, in ˈUmlauf setzen; *Anleihe* auflegen; *Dokumente* ausstellen: **~*d capital*** effektiv ausgegebenes (Aktien)Kapital; **14.** *Bücher* herˈausgeben, publizieren; **15.** ⚔ a) ausgeben, liefern, ver-, zuteilen, b) ausrüsten, beliefern (***with*** mit); **III** *v/i.* **16.** herˈauskommen, -strömen; herˈvorbrechen; **17.** (***from***) herrühren (von), entspringen (*dat.*); **18.** herˈauskommen, herˈausgegeben werden (*Schriften etc.*); **19.** ergehen, erteilt werden (*Befehl etc.*); **20.** enden (***in*** in *dat.*).

is·sue·less [ˈɪʃuːlɪs] *adj.* ohne Nachkommen.

is·su·er [ˈɪʃuːə] *s.* ✝ **1.** Aussteller(in); **2.** Ausgeber(in).

isth·mus [ˈɪsməs] *s.* **1.** *geogr.* Isthmus *m*, Landenge *f*; **2.** ⚕ Verengung *f*.

it¹ [ɪt] **I** *pron.* **1.** es (*nom. od. acc.*): ***do you believe it?*** glaubst du es?; **2.** *auf deutsches s. bezogen* (*nom., dat., acc.*) *m* er, ihm, ihn; *f* sie, ihr, sie; *n* es, ihm, es; *refl.* (*dat., acc.*) sich; **3.** *unpersönliches od. grammatisches Subjekt*: ***it rains*** es regnet; ***what time is it?*** wieviel Uhr ist es?; ***it is I*** (F ***me***) ich bin es; ***it was my parents*** es waren m-e Eltern; **4.** *unbestimmtes Objekt* (*oft unübersetzt*): ***foot it*** zu Fuß gehen; ***I take it that*** ich nehme an, daß; **5.** *verstärkend*: ***it is for this reason that*** gerade aus diesem Grunde …; **6.** *nach prp.*: ***at it*** daran; ***with it*** damit *etc.*; ***please see to it that*** bitte sorge dafür, daß; **II** *s.* **7.** F ‚das Nonplusˈultra', ‚ganz große Klasse': ***he thinks he's it***; **8.** F a) das gewisse Etwas, *bsd.* ˈSex-Apˌpeal *m*, b) Sex *m*, Geschlechtsverkehr *m*; **9.** F ***that's it!*** a) das ist es (ja)!, b) das wär's (gewesen)!; F ***this is it!*** gleich geht's los!

it² [ɪt], *a.* **I** *abbr. für* ***Italian***: ***gin and it*** Gin mit (italienischem) Wermut.

I·tal·ian [ɪˈtæljən] **I** *adj.* **1.** italiˈenisch: **~ *handwriting*** lateinische Schreibschrift; **II** *s.* **2.** Italiˈener(in); **3.** *ling.* Italiˈenisch *n*; **Iˈtal·ian·ate** [-neɪt] *adj.* italianisiert, nach italiˈenischer Art; **Iˈtal·ian·ism** [-nɪzəm] *s.* italiˈenische (Sprach- *etc.*)Eigenheit.

i·tal·ic [ɪˈtælɪk] **I** *adj.* **1.** *typ.* kurˈsiv; **2.** **I** *ling.* iˈtalisch; **II** *s. pl.* **3.** *typ.* Kurˈsivschrift *f*; **iˈtal·i·cize** [-ɪsaɪz] *typ. v/t.* **1.** in Kurˈsiv drucken; **2.** durch Kurˈsivschrift herˈvorheben.

itch [ɪtʃ] **I** *s.* **1.** Jucken *n*; **2.** ⚕ Krätze *f*; **3.** *fig.* brennendes Verlangen, Sucht *f* (***for*** nach): ***I have an* ~ *to do s.th.*** es ‚juckt' mich, et. zu tun; **II** *v/i.* **4.** jukken; **5.** *fig.* (***for***) brennen (auf *acc.*): ***I am* ~*ing to do s.th.*** es ‚juckt' mich, et. zu tun; ***my fingers* ~ *to do it*** es juckt mir (*od.* mich) in den Fingern, es zu tun; **itch·ing** [ˈɪtʃɪŋ] **I** *s.* **1.** → ***itch*** 1, 3; **II** *adj.* **2.** juckend; **3.** F a) ‚scharf', begierig, *a.* geil, b) nerˈvös; **itch·y** [ˈɪtʃɪ] *adj.* **1.** juckend; **2.** ⚕ krätzig; **3.** → ***itching*** 3.

i·tem [ˈaɪtəm] **I** *s.* **1.** Punkt *m* (*der Tagesordnung etc.*); Gegenstand *m*, Stück *n*; Einzelheit *f*, Deˈtail *n*; ✝ (Buchungs-, Rechnungs)Posten *m*; (ˈWaren)Arˌtikel *m*; **2.** (ˈPresse)Noˌtiz *f*, (kurzer) Arˈtikel; **II** *adv. obs.* **3.** desˈgleichen, ferner; **ˈi·tem·ize** [-maɪz] *v/t.* (einzeln) aufführen, spezifizieren.

it·er·ate [ˈɪtəreɪt] *v/t.* wiederˈholen; **it·er·a·tion** [ˌɪtəˈreɪʃn] *s.* Wiederˈholung *f*; **ˈit·er·a·tive** [-rətɪv] *adj.* (sich) wiederˈholend; *ling.* iteraˈtiv.

i·tin·er·a·cy [ɪˈtɪnərəsɪ], **iˈtin·er·an·cy** [-ənsɪ] *s.* Umˈherreisen *n*, -ziehen *n*; **iˈtin·er·ant** [-ənt] *adj.* □ (beruflich) reisend *od.* umˈherziehend, Reise…, Wander…: **~ *trade*** Wandergewerbe *n*; **iˈtin·er·ar·y** [aɪˈtɪnərərɪ] **I** *s.* **1.** Reiseroute *f*, -plan *m*; **2.** Reisebericht *m*; **3.** Reiseführer *m* (*Buch*); **4.** Straßenkarte *f*; **II** *adj.* **5.** Reise…; **iˈtin·er·ate** [ɪˈtɪnəreɪt] *v/i.* (umˈher)reisen.

its [ɪts] *pron.* sein, ihr, dessen, deren: ***the house and* ~ *roof*** das Haus u. sein (*od.* dessen) Dach.

it's [ɪts] F *für* a) ***it is***, b) ***it has***.

it·self [ɪtˈself] *pron.* **1.** *refl.* sich: ***the dog hides* ~**; **2.** sich (selbst): ***the kitten wants it for* ~**; **3.** *verstärkend*: selbst: ***like innocence* ~** wie die Unschuld selbst; ***by* ~** (für sich) allein, von selbst; ***in* ~** an sich (betrachtet); **4.** alˈlein (schon), schon: ***the garden* ~ *measures two acres***.

I've [aɪv] F *für* ***I have***.

i·vied [ˈaɪvɪd] *adj.* ˈefeuumˌrankt, mit Efeu bewachsen.

i·vo·ry [ˈaɪvərɪ] **I** *s.* **1.** Elfenbein *n*; **2.** Stoßzahn *m* (*des Elefanten*); **3.** ˈElfenbeinschnitzeˌrei *f*; **4.** *pl. sl.* a) *obs.* ‚Beißer' *pl.*, Gebiß *n*, b) (*Spiel*)Würfel *pl.*, c) Billardkugeln *pl.*, d) (Klaˈvier)Tasten *pl.*: ***tickle the ivories*** (auf dem Klavier) klimpern; **II** *adj.* **5.** elfenbeinern, Elfenbein…; **6.** elfenbeinfarben; **~ *nut*** *s.* ✿ Steinnuß *f*; **~ *tow·er*** *s. fig.* Elfenbeinturm *m*: ***live in an* ~** im Elfenbeinturm sitzen.

i·vy [ˈaɪvɪ] *s.* ✿ Efeu *m*; **I League** *s. die acht Eliteuniversitäten im Osten der U.S.A.*

iz·zard [ˈɪzəd] *s.*: ***from A to* ~** von A bis Z.

J

J, j [dʒeɪ] *s.* J *n*, j *n*, Jot *n* (*Buchstabe*).

jab [dʒæb] **I** *v/t.* **1.** (hin'ein)stechen, (-)stoßen; **II** *s.* **2.** Stich *m*, Stoß *m*; **3.** *Boxen*: Jab *m*, (kurze) Gerade; **4.** ⚕ F Spritze *f*.

jab·ber ['dʒæbə] **I** *v/t. u. v/i.* **1.** schnattern, quasseln, schwatzen; **2.** nuscheln, undeutlich sprechen; **II** *s.* **3.** Geplapper *n*, Geschnatter *n*.

jack [dʒæk] **I** *s.* **1.** Mann *m*, Bursche *m*: ***every man ~*** F jeder einzelne, alle (ohne Ausnahme); **2.** *Kartenspiel*: Bube *m*; **3.** ⚙ Hebevorrichtung *f*, Winde *f*: ***car ~*** Wagenheber *m*; **4.** *Brit. Bowls-Spiel*: Zielkugel *f*; **5.** *zo.* a) Männchen *n einiger Tiere*, b) → ***jackass*** 1; **6.** ⚓ Gösch *f*, Bugflagge *f*; **7.** ⚡ a) Klinke *f*, b) Steckdose *f*; **8.** *Am. sl.* ‚Zaster' *m* (*Geld*); **II** *v/t.* **9.** *mst* ***~ up*** hochheben, -winden; *Auto* aufbocken; *fig.* F *Preise* hochtreiben; **10.** ***~ in*** F *et.* ‚aufstecken', ‚hinschmeißen'; **III** *v/i.* **11.** ***~ off*** *Am.* V ‚wichsen'.

jack·al ['dʒækɔːl] *s.* **1.** *zo.* Scha'kal *m*; **2.** *contp.* Handlanger *m*.

jack·a·napes ['dʒækəneɪps] *s.* **1.** Geck *m*, Laffe *m*; **2.** Frechdachs *m*, (kleiner) Schlingel.

jack·ass ['dʒækæs] *s.* **1.** (männlicher) Esel; **2.** *fig. contp.* ‚Esel' *m*.

'jack|·boot *s.* Schaftstiefel *m*; **'~·daw** *s. orn.* Dohle *f*.

jack·et ['dʒækɪt] **I** *s.* **1.** Jacke *f*, Jac'kett *n*; → ***dust*** 8; **2.** ⚙ Mantel *m*, Um'mantelung *f*, Hülle *f*, Um'wicklung *f*; **3.** ⚔ (Geschoß-, *a.* Rohr)Mantel *m*; **4.** Buchhülle *f*, 'Schutzˌumschlag *m*; *Am. a.* (Schallplatten)Hülle *f*; **5.** Haut *f*, Schale *f*: ***potatoes (boiled) in their ~s***, *a.* ***~ potatoes*** Pellkartoffeln; **II** *v/t.* **6.** ⚙ um'manteln, verkleiden, verschalen; ***~ crown*** *s.* ⚕ Jacketkrone *f*.

Jack| Frost *s.* Väterchen *n* Frost; **'≈-ˌham·mer** *s.* Preßlufthammer *m*; **'≈-in-ˌof·fice** wichtigtuerischer Beamter; **'≈-in-the-box** *pl.* **'≈-in-the-ˌbox·es** *s.* Schachtelmännchen *n* (*Kinderspielzeug*): ***like a ~*** *fig.* wie ein Hampelmann; **~ Ketch** [ketʃ] *s. Brit. obs.* der Henker; **'≈·knife I** *s.* [*irr.*] **1.** Klappmesser *n*; **2.** *a.* ***~ dive*** *sport* Hechtbeuge *f* (*Kopfsprung*); **II** *v/t.* **3.** *a. v/i.* wie ein Taschenmesser zs.-klappen; **III** *v/i.* **4.** *sport* hechten; **5.** *mot.* sich querstellen (*Anhänger e-s Lastzugs*); **ˌ≈-of-'all-trades** *s.* Aller'weltskerl *m*, Hans'dampf *m* in allen Gassen; Fak'totum *n*; **ˌ≈-o'-'lan·tern** *pl.* **ˌ≈-o'-'lan·terns** [ˌdʒækəʊ-] **1.** Irrlicht *n* (*a. fig.*); **2.** 'Kürbislaˌterne *f*; **≈ plane** *s.* ⚙ Schrupphobel *m*; **'≈·pot** *s. Poker, Glücksspiel*: Jackpot *m*, *weitS. u. fig.* Haupttreffer *m*, *das* große Los, *fig. a.* ‚Schlager' *m*, Bombenerfolg *m*: ***hit the ~*** F *fig.* a) den Jackpot gewinnen, b) den Haupttreffer machen, c) großen Erfolg haben, den Vogel abschießen, d) ‚schwer absahnen'; **~ Ro·bin·son** *s.*: ***before you could say ~*** F im Nu, im Handumdrehen; **'≈·straw** *s.* a) Mi'kadostäbchen *n*, b) *pl.* Mi'kadospiel *n*; **≈ tar** *s.* ⚓ F Ma'trose *m*; **'≈-ˌtow·el** *s.* Rollhandtuch *n*.

Jac·o·be·an [ˌdʒækəʊ'biːən] *adj.* aus der Zeit Jakobs I.: ***~ furniture***.

Jac·o·bin ['dʒækəʊbɪn] *s.* **1.** *hist.* Jako'biner *m*, *fig. pol. a.* radi'kaler 'Umstürzler, Revolutio'när *m*; **2.** *orn.* Jako'binertaube *f*; **'Jac·o·bite** [-baɪt] *s. hist.* Jako'bit *m*.

Ja·cob's lad·der ['dʒeɪkəbz] *s.* **1.** *bibl.*, *a.* ⚘ Jakobs-, Himmelsleiter *f*; **2.** ⚓ Lotsentreppe *f*.

Ja·cuz·zi [dʒə'kuːziː] *s. Warenzeichen*: Whirlpool *m* (*Unterwassermassagebecken*).

jade¹ [dʒeɪd] *s.* **1.** *min.* Jade *m*; **2.** Jadegrün *n*.

jade² [dʒeɪd] *s.* **1.** Schindmähre *f*, Klepper *m*; **2.** Weibsstück *n*; **'jad·ed** [-dɪd] *adj.* **1.** erschöpft, abgespannt; **2.** über'sättigt, abgestumpft; **3.** schal (geworden): ***~ pleasures***.

jag [dʒæg] **I** *s.* **1.** Zacke *f*, Kerbe *f*; Zahn *m*; Auszackung *f*; Schlitz *m*, Riß *m*; **2.** *sl.* a) Schwips *m*, Rausch *m*: ***have a ~ on*** ‚e-n in der Krone haben', b) Sauftour *f*, Saufe'rei *f*, c) *bsd. fig.* Orgie *f*: ***go on a ~*** ‚einen draufmachen'; ***crying ~*** ‚heulendes Elend'; **II** *v/t.* **3.** auszakken, einkerben; **4.** zackig schneiden *od.* reißen; **'jag·ged** [-gɪd] *adj.* □ **1.** zakkig; schartig; **2.** schroff, zerklüftet; **3.** rauh, grob (*a. fig.*); **4.** *Am. sl.* ‚blau', besoffen.

jag·uar ['dʒægjʊə] *s. zo.* Jaguar *m*.

Jah [dʒɑː], **Jah·ve(h)** ['jɑːveɪ] *s.* Je'hova *m*.

jail [dʒeɪl] **I** *s.* **1.** Gefängnis *n*, Strafanstalt *f*; **2.** Gefängnis(haft *f*) *n*; **II** *v/t.* **3.** ins Gefängnis werfen, einsperren, inhaftieren; **'~·bird** *s.* F ‚Zuchthäusler' *m*, *engS.* ‚Knastbruder' *m*; **'~·break** *s.* Ausbruch *m* (aus dem Gefängnis); **'~ˌbreak·er** *s.* Ausbrecher *m*.

jail·er ['dʒeɪlə] *s.* (Gefängnis)Aufseher *m*, (-)Wärter *m*, *obs. u. fig.* Kerkermeister *m*.

jake [dʒeɪk] *Am.* F **I** *s.* **1.** Bauernlackel *m*, *weitS.* ‚Knülch' *m*; **2.** ‚Pinke' *f* (*Geld*); **II** *adj.* **3.** ‚bestens', in Ordnung: ***everything's ~***.

ja·lop·(p)y [dʒə'lɒpɪ] *s.* F ‚alte Kiste' (*Auto, Flugzeug*).

jal·ou·sie ['ʒæluziː] *s.* Jalou'sie *f*.

jam¹ [dʒæm] **I** *v/t.* **1.** *a.* ***~ in*** a) *et.* (hin'ein)zwängen, -stopfen, -quetschen, *Menschen a.* (-)pferchen, b) einklemmen, -keilen; **2.** (zs.-, zer)quetschen; *Finger etc.* einklemmen, sich *et.* quetschen; **3.** *et.* pressen, (heftig) drücken, *Knie etc.* rammen (***into*** in *acc.*): ***~ (one's foot) on the brakes*** heftig auf die Bremse treten; **4.** verstopfen, -sperren, blockieren: ***a road ~med with cars***; ***~med with people*** von Menschen verstopft, gedrängt voll; **5.** ⚙ verklemmen, blockieren; **6.** *Funk*: (*durch Störsender*) stören; **II** *v/i.* **7.** eingeklemmt sein, festsitzen; **8.** *a.* ***~ in*** sich (hin'ein)quetschen, (-)zwängen, (-)drängen; **9.** ⚙ (sich ver)klemmen; ⚔ Ladehemmung haben; **10.** *Jazz*: (frei) improvisieren; **III** *s.* **11.** Gedränge *n*, Gewühl *n*; **12.** Verstopfung *f*, Stauung *f*, (Verkehrs)Stockung *f*, (-)Stau *m*: ***traffic ~***; **13.** ⚙ Blockierung *f*, Klemmen *n*; ⚔ Ladehemmung *f*; **14.** F ‚Klemme' *f*: ***be in a ~*** in der Klemme *od.* Patsche sitzen; ***get s.o. out of a ~*** j-m aus der Klemme *od.* Patsche helfen.

jam² [dʒæm] *s.* **1.** Marme'lade *f*: ***~ jar*** Marmeladeglas *n*; **2.** *Brit.* F ‚schicke Sache': ***money for ~*** leichtverdientes Geld; ***~ tomorrow*** *iro.* schöne Versprechungen *od.* Aussichten; ***that's ~ for him*** das ist ein Kinderspiel für ihn.

Ja·mai·can [dʒə'meɪkən] **I** *adj.* jamai'kanisch; **II** *s.* Jamai'kaner(in); **Ja·mai·ca rum** [dʒə'meɪkə] *s.* Ja'maika-Rum *m*.

jamb [dʒæm] *s.* (Tür-, Fenster)Pfosten *m*.

jam·bo·ree [ˌdʒæmbə'riː] *s.* **1.** Pfadfindertreffen *n*; **2.** F ‚rauschendes Fest', ‚tolle Party'.

jam·mer ['dʒæmə] *s. Radio*: Störsender *m*; **'jam·ming** [-mɪŋ] *s.* **1.** ⚙ Klemmung *f*; Hemmung *f*; **2.** *Radio*: Störung *f*: ***~ station*** Störsender *m*; **'jam·my** [-mɪ] *adj. Brit. sl.* **1.** prima, ‚Klasse'; **2.** glücklich, Glücks…: ***~ fellow*** Glückspilz *m*.

ˌjam|-'packed *adj.* F vollgestopft, *Bus etc.* ‚knallvoll'; ***~ roll*** *s.* Bis'kuitrolle *f*; ***~ ses·sion*** *s.* Jam Session *f* (*Jazzimprovisation*).

Jane [dʒeɪn] **I** *npr.* Johanna *f*; **II** *s. a.* ≈ *sl.* ‚Weib' *n*.

jan·gle ['dʒæŋgl] **I** *v/i.* **1.** a) klirren, klimpern, b) bimmeln (*Glocken*); **2.** schimpfen; **II** *v/t.* **3.** a) klirren *od.* klimpern mit, b) bimmeln lassen; **4.** ***~ s.o.'s nerves*** j-m auf die Nerven gehen; **III** *s.* **5.** a) Klirren *n*, Klimpern *n*, b) Bimmeln *n*; **6.** Gekreisch *n*, laute Streite'rei.

jan·i·tor ['dʒænɪtə] *s.* **1.** Pförtner *m*; **2.** *bsd. Am.* Hausmeister *m.*

Jan·u·ar·y ['dʒænjʊərɪ] *s.* Januar *m*: ***in ~*** im Januar.

Ja·nus ['dʒeɪnəs] *s. myth.* Janus *m*; **'~-faced** *adj.* janusköpfig.

Jap [dʒæp] F *contp.* **I** *s.* ‚Japs' *m* (*Japaner*); **II** *adj.* ja'panisch.

ja·pan [dʒə'pæn] **I** *s.* **1.** Japanlack *m*; **2.** lackierte Arbeit (*in japanischer Art*); **II** *v/t.* **3.** mit Japanlack über'ziehen, lakkieren.

Jap·a·nese [ˌdʒæpə'niːz] **I** *adj.* **1.** ja'panisch; **II** *s.* **2.** Ja'paner(in); **3.** ***the ~*** *pl.* die Japaner; **4.** *ling.* Ja'panisch *n*, das Ja'panische.

jar[1] [dʒɑː] *s.* **1.** a) (*irdenes od. gläsernes*) Gefäß, Topf *m* (*ohne Henkel*), b) (Einmach)Glas *n*; **2.** *Brit.* F ‚Bierchen' *n.*

jar[2] [dʒɑː] **I** *v/i.* **1.** kreischen, quietschen, kratzen (*Metall etc.*), durch Mark u. Bein gehen; **2.** ♪ dissonieren; **3.** (***on, upon***) *das Ohr, ein Gefühl* beleidigen, verletzen, weh tun (*dat.*): ***~ on the ear, ~ on the nerves*** auf die Nerven gehen; **4.** sich ‚beißen', nicht harmonieren (*Farben etc.*); **5.** *fig.* sich nicht vertragen (*Ideen etc.*), im 'Widerspruch stehen (***with*** zu), sich wider'sprechen: ***~ring opinions*** widerstreitende Meinungen; **6.** schwirren, vibrieren; **II** *v/t.* **7.** kreischen *od.* quietschen lassen, ein unangenehmes Geräusch erzeugen mit; **8.** a) erschüttern, e-n Stoß versetzen (*dat.*), b) 'durchrütteln, c) sich *das Knie etc.* anstoßen *od.* stauchen; **9.** *fig.* a) erschüttern, e-n Schock versetzen (*dat.*), b) → 3; **III** *s.* **10.** Kreischen *n*, Quietschen *n*, unangenehmes Geräusch; **11.** Ruck *m*, Stoß *m*, Erschütterung *f* (*a. fig.*); *fig.* Schock *m*, Schlag *m*; **12.** ♪ *u. fig.* 'Mißton *m*; **13.** *fig.* 'Widerstreit *m.*

jar·di·nière [ˌʒɑːdɪ'njeə] (*Fr.*) *s.* **1.** Jardini'ere *f*: a) Blumenständer *m*, b) Blumenschale *f*; **2.** *Küche*: a) Gar'nierung *f*, b) (Fleisch)Gericht *n* à la jardinière.

jar·gon ['dʒɑːgən] *s. allg.* Jar'gon *m*: a) Kauderwelsch *n*, b) Fach-, Berufssprache *f*, c) Mischsprache *f*, d) ungepflegte Ausdrucksweise.

jar·ring ['dʒɑːrɪŋ] *adj.* □ **1.** 'mißtönend, kreischend, schrill, unangenehm, ‚nervtötend': ***a ~ note*** ein Mißton *od.* -klang (*a. fig.*); **2.** nicht harmonierend, *Farben*: *a.* sich beißend; → *a.* ***jar***[2] 5.

jas·min(e) ['dʒæsmɪn] *s.* ⚘ Jas'min *m.*

jas·per ['dʒæspə] *s. min.* Jaspis *m.*

jaun·dice ['dʒɔːndɪs] *s.* **1.** ⚕ Gelbsucht *f*; **2.** *fig.* a) Neid *m*, Eifersucht *f*, b) Feindseligkeit *f*; **'jaun·diced** [-st] *adj.* **1.** ⚕ gelbsüchtig; **2.** *fig.* voreingenommen, neidisch, eifersüchtig, scheel.

jaunt [dʒɔːnt] **I** *s.* Ausflug *m*, Spritztour *f*: ***go for*** (*od.* ***on***) ***a ~*** → **II** *v/i.* e-e Spritztour *od.* e-n Ausflug machen; **'jaun·ti·ness** [-tɪnɪs] *s.* Flottheit *f*, ‚Feschheit' *f*: a) Munterkeit *f*, ‚Spritzigkeit' *f*, Schwung *m*, b) flotte Ele'ganz; **'jaunt·ing-car** [-tɪŋ] *s. leichter, zweirädriger Wagen*; **'jaun·ty** [-tɪ] *adj.* □ fesch, flott: a) munter, ‚spritzig', b) keck, ele'gant: ***with one's hat at a ~ angle*** den Hut keck über dem Ohr.

Ja·va ['dʒɑːvə] *s. Am.* F Kaffee *m*; **Ja·va·nese** [ˌdʒɑːvə'niːz] **I** *adj.* **1.** ja'vanisch; **II** *s.* **2.** Ja'vaner(in): ***the ~*** die Javaner; **3.** *ling.* Ja'vanisch *n*, das Ja'vanische.

jave·lin ['dʒævlɪn] *s.* **1.** *a. sport* Speer *m*; **2.** ***the ~*** → ***~ throw(·ing)*** *s. sport* Speerwerfen *n*; ***~ throw·er*** *s.* Speerwerfer(in).

jaw [dʒɔː] **I** *s.* **1.** *anat., zo.* Kiefer *m*, Kinnbacken *m*, -lade *f*: ***lower ~*** Unterkiefer; ***upper ~*** Oberkiefer; **2.** *mst pl.* Mund *m*, Maul *n*: ***hold your ~!, none of your ~!*** F halt's Maul!; **3.** *mst pl.* Schlund *m*, Rachen *m* (*a. fig.*): ***~s of death*** *der* Rachen des Todes; **4.** ⚙ (Klemm)Backe *f*, Backen *m*; Klaue *f*: ***~ clutch*** Klauenkupplung *f*; **5.** *sl.* a) (freches) Geschwätz, Frechheit *f*, b) Schwatz *m*, ‚Tratsch' *m*, c) Mo'ralpredigt *f*; **II** *v/i.* **6.** *sl.* a) ‚quatschen', ‚tratschen', b) schimpfen; **III** *v/t.* **7.** ***~ out*** *sl.* *j-n* ‚anschnauzen'; **'~·bone** *s.* **1.** *anat., zo.* Kiefer(knochen) *m*, Kinnlade *f*; **2.** *Am. sl.* (***on ~*** auf) Kre'dit *m*; **'~ˌbreak·er** *s.* F Zungenbrecher *m* (*Wort*); **'~ˌbreak·ing** *adj.* F zungenbrecherisch; ***~ chuck*** *s.* ⚙ Backenfutter *n.*

jay [dʒeɪ] *s.* **1.** *orn.* Eichelhäher *m*; **2.** *fig.* ‚Trottel' *m*; **'~·walk** *v/i.* verkehrswidrig über die Straße gehen; **'~ˌwalk·er** *s.* unachtsamer Fußgänger.

jazz [dʒæz] **I** *s.* **1.** 'Jazz(muˌsik *f*) *m*: ***~ band*** Jazzkapelle *f*; **2.** *sl.* a) ‚Gequatsche' *n*, ‚blödes Zeug', b) ‚Quatsch' *m*, ‚Krampf' *m*: ***and all that ~*** und all der Mist; **II** *v/t.* **3.** *mst* ***~ up*** F a) verjazzen, b) *fig. et.* ‚aufmöbeln'; **III** *v/i.* **4.** jazzen; **5.** *Am. sl.* ‚vögeln'; **'jazz·er** [-zə] *s.* F Jazzmusiker *m*; **'jazz·y** [-zɪ] *adj.* F **1.** Jazz...; **2.** *fig.* a) ‚knallig', b) ‚toll', todschick.

jeal·ous ['dʒeləs] *adj.* □ **1.** eifersüchtig (***of*** auf *acc.*): ***a ~ wife***; **2.** (***of***) neidisch (auf *acc.*), 'mißgünstig (gegen): ***she is ~ of his fortune*** sie beneidet ihn um *od.* mißgönnt ihm s-n Reichtum; **3.** 'mißtrauisch (***of*** gegen); **4.** (***of***) besorgt (um), bedacht (auf *acc.*); **5.** *bibl.* eifernd (*Gott*); **'jeal·ous·y** [-sɪ] *s.* **1.** Eifersucht *f* (***of*** auf *acc.*); *pl.* Eifersüchte'leien; **2.** (***of***) Neid *m* (auf *acc.*), 'Mißgunst *f* (gegen); **3.** Achtsamkeit *f* (***of*** auf *acc.*).

jean *s.* **1.** [dʒeɪn] *Art* Baumwollköper *m*; **2.** *pl.* [dʒiːnz] Jeans *pl.*

jeep [dʒiːp] (*Fabrikmarke*) *s.* Jeep *m*: a) ⚔ *Art* Kübelwagen *m*, b) kleines geländegängiges Mehrzweckfahrzeug.

jeer [dʒɪə] **I** *v/i.* spotten, höhnen (***at*** über *acc.*); **II** *s.* Hohn *m*, Stiche'lei *f*; **'jeer·ing** [-ərɪŋ] **I** *s.* Verhöhnung *f*; **II** *adj.* □ höhnisch.

Je·ho·vah [dʒɪ'həʊvə] *s. bibl.* Je'hovah *m*; ***~'s Wit·ness·es*** *s. pl.* Zeugen *pl.* Jehovas.

je·june [dʒɪ'dʒuːn] *adj.* □ **1.** mager, ohne Nährwert: ***~ food***; **2.** trocken: a) dürr (*Boden*), b) *fig.* fade, nüchtern; **3.** *fig.* simpel, na'iv.

jell [dʒel] *Am.* F **I** *s.* **1.** → ***jelly*** 1–3; **II** *v/i.* **2.** → ***jelly*** II; **3.** *fig.* sich (her'aus-) kristallisieren, Gestalt annehmen; **4.** ‚zum Klappen kommen' (*Geschäft etc.*).

jel·lied ['dʒelɪd] *adj.* **1.** gallertartig, eingedickt; **2.** in Ge'lee *od.* As'pik: ***~ eel.***

jel·ly ['dʒelɪ] **I** *s.* **1.** Gallert *n*, Gal'lerte *f*, *Küche*: *a.* Ge'lee *n*, Sülze *f*, As'pik *n*; **2.** a) Ge'lee *n* (*Marmelade*), b) Götterspeise *f*, ‚Wackelpeter' *m*, c) (rote *etc.*) Grütze (*Süßspeise*); **3.** gallertartige *od.* ‚schwabbelige' Masse, Brei *m*: ***beat s.o. into a ~*** F j-n ‚zu Brei schlagen'; **4.** *Brit. sl.* Dyna'mit *n*; **II** *v/t.* **5.** zum Gelieren *od.* Erstarren bringen, eindikken; **6.** *Küche*: in Sülze *od.* As'pik *od.* Ge'lee (ein)legen; **III** *v/i.* **7.** gelieren, Ge'lee bilden; **8.** erstarren; ***~ ba·by*** *s.* Gummibärchen *n*; **'~·bean** *s.* 'Weingummi(bonˌbon) *n*; **'~·fish** *s.* **1.** Qualle *f*; **2.** *fig.* ‚Waschlappen' *m.*

jel·lo ['dʒeləʊ] *s. Am.* → ***jelly*** 2.

jem·my ['dʒemɪ] **I** *s.* Brecheisen *n*; **II** *v/t.* mit dem Brecheisen öffnen, aufstemmen.

jen·ny ['dʒenɪ] *s.* **1.** → ***spinning-jenny***; **2.** ⚙ Laufkran *m*; **3.** *zo.* Weibchen *n*; ***~ ass*** *s.* Eselin *f*; ***~ wren*** *s. orn.* (weiblicher) Zaunkönig.

jeop·ard·ize ['dʒepədaɪz] *v/t.* gefährden, aufs Spiel setzen; **'jeop·ard·y** [-dɪ] *s.* Gefahr *f*, Gefährdung *f*, Risiko *n*: ***put in ~*** → ***jeopardize***; ***no one shall be put twice in ~ for the same offence*** ⚖ niemand darf wegen derselben Straftat zweimal vor Gericht gestellt werden.

jer·e·mi·ad [ˌdʒerɪ'maɪəd] *s.* Jeremi'ade *f*, Klagelied *n*; **Jer·e·mi·ah** [ˌdʒerɪ'maɪə] *npr. u. s.* **1.** *bibl.* (das Buch) Jere'mia(s) *m*; **2.** *fig.* 'Unglücksproˌphet *m*, Schwarzseher *m*; **Jer·e'mi·as** [-əs] → ***Jeremiah*** 1.

jerk[1] [dʒɜːk] **I** *s.* **1.** a) Ruck *m*, plötzlicher Stoß *od.* Schlag *od.* Zug, b) Satz *m*, Sprung *m*, Auffahren *n*: ***by ~s*** ruck-, sprung-, stoßweise; ***with a ~*** plötzlich, mit e-m Ruck; ***give s.th. a ~*** → 5; ***put a ~ in it*** *sl.* tüchtig rangehen; **2.** ⚕ Zuckung *f*, Zucken *n*, (*bsd.* 'Knie-) Reˌflex *m*; **3.** *pl. Brit. mst* ***physical ~s*** *sl.* Freiübungen; Gym'nastik *f*; **4.** *Am. sl.* a) ‚Blödmann' *m*, ‚Knülch' *m*, b) → ***soda jerker***; **II** *v/t.* **5.** schnellen; ruckweise *od.* ruckartig *od.* plötzlich ziehen *od.* reißen *od.* stoßen *etc.*: ***~ o.s. free*** sich losreißen; **III** *v/i.* **6.** (zs.-)zucken; **7.** (hoch- *etc.*)schnellen; **8.** sich ruckweise bewegen: ***~ to a stop*** ruckartig anhalten; **9.** ***~ off*** *Am. sl.* ‚wichsen'.

jerk[2] [dʒɜːk] *v/t. Fleisch* in Streifen schneiden u. dörren.

jer·kin ['dʒɜːkɪn] *s.* **1.** ärmellose Jacke; **2.** *hist.* (Leder)Wams *n.*

'jerkˌwa·ter *Am.* F **I** *s.* **1.** *a.* ***~ town*** kleines ‚Kaff'; **2.** *a.* ***~ train*** Bummelzug *m*; **II** *adj.* **3.** unbedeutend, armselig.

jerk·y ['dʒɜːkɪ] *adj.* □ **1.** ruckartig, stoß-, ruckweise; krampfhaft; **2.** *Am.* F ‚blöd'.

jer·o·bo·am [ˌdʒerə'bəʊəm] *s. Brit.* Riesenweinflasche *f.*

jer·ry ['dʒerɪ] *s. Brit.* F **1.** Nachttopf *m*; **2.** ♀ a) Deutsche(r) *m*, deutscher Sol'dat, b) die Deutschen *pl.*; **'~-ˌbuild·er** *s.* F Bauschwindler *m*; **'~-built** *adj.* F unsolide gebaut: ***~ house*** ‚Bruchbude' *f*; ***~ can*** *s. Brit.* F Ben'zinkaˌnister *m.*

jer·sey ['dʒɜːzɪ] *s.* **1.** a) wollene Strickjacke, b) 'Unterjacke *f*; **2.** Jersey *m* (*Stoffart*); **3.** ♀ *zo.* Jerseyrind *n.*

jes·sa·mine ['dʒesəmɪn] → ***jasmin(e)***.

jest [dʒest] **I** *s.* **1.** Scherz *m*, Spaß *m*, Witz *m*: ***in ~*** im Spaß; ***make a ~ of***

witzeln über (*acc.*); **2.** Zielscheibe *f* des Witzes *od.* Spotts: ***standing ~*** Zielscheibe ständigen Gelächters; **II** *v/i.* **3.** scherzen, spaßen, ulken; **'jest·er** [-tə] *s.* **1.** Spaßmacher *m*, -vogel *m*; **2.** *hist.* (Hof)Narr *m*; **'jest·ing** [-tɪŋ] *adj.* □ scherzend, spaßhaft: ***no ~ matter*** nicht zum Spaßen; **'jest·ing·ly** [-tɪŋlɪ] *adv.* im *od.* zum Spaß.

Jes·u·it ['dʒezjʊɪt] *s. eccl.* Jesu'it *m*; **Jes·u·it·i·cal** [ˌdʒezjʊ'ɪtɪkl] *adj.* □ *eccl.* jesu'itisch, Jesuiten…; **'Jes·u·it·ry** [-rɪ] *s.* a) Jesui'tismus *m*, b) *contp.* Spitzfindigkeit *f*.

jet¹ [dʒet] **I** *s. min.* Ga'gat *m*, Pechkohle *f*, Jett *m*, *n*; **II** *adj. a.* ***~-black*** tief-, pech-, kohlschwarz.

jet² [dʒet] **I** *s.* **1.** (*Feuer-, Wasser- etc.*) Strahl *m*, Strom *m*: ***~ of flame*** Stichflamme *f*; **2.** ⚙ Strahlrohr *n*, Düse *f*; **3.** → a) ***jet engine***, b) ***jet plane***; **II** *v/t.* **4.** ausspritzen, -strahlen, her'vorstoßen; **III** *v/i.* **5.** her'vorschießen, ausströmen; **6.** mit Düsenflugzeug reisen, ‚jetten'; **~ age** *s.* Düsenzeitalter *n*; **~ bomb·er** *s.* ✈ Düsenbomber *m*; **~ en·gine** *s.* ⚙ Düsen-, Strahltriebwerk *n*; **~ fight·er** *s.* ✈ Düsenjäger *m*; **~ lag** *s.* (physische) Prob'leme *pl.* durch die Zeitumstellung (*nach langen Flugreisen*); **~ lin·er** *s.* ✈ Düsenverkehrsflugzeug *n*; **~ plane** *s.* ✈ Düsenflugzeug *n*, F ‚Düse' *f*, Jet *m*; **ˌ~-pro'pelled**, *abbr.* **ˌ~-'prop** *adj.* ✈ mit Düsenantrieb; **~ pro·pul·sion** *s.* ⚙, ✈ Düsen-, Rückstoß-, Strahlantrieb *m*.

jet·sam ['dʒetsəm] *s.* ⚓ **1.** Seewurfgut *n*, über Bord geworfene Ladung; **2.** Strandgut *n*; → ***flotsam***.

jet|set *s.* Jet-set *m*; **'~-ˌset·ter** *s.* Angehörige(r *m*) *f* des Jet-set.

jet·ti·son ['dʒetɪsn] **I** *s.* **1.** ⚓ Über'bordwerfen *n von Ladung*, Seewurf *m*; **2.** ✈ Notwurf *m*; **II** *v/t.* **3.** ⚓ über Bord werfen; **4.** ✈ im Notwurf abwerfen; **5.** *fig. Pläne etc.* über Bord werfen; *alte Kleider etc.* wegwerfen, *Personen* fallenlassen; **6.** *Raketenstufe* absprengen; **'jet·ti·son·a·ble** [-nəbl] *adj.* ✈ abwerfbar, Abwurf…(*-behälter etc.*): **~ *seat*** Schleudersitz *m*.

jet·ton ['dʒetn] *s.* Je'ton *m*.

jet tur·bine *s.* 'Strahlturˌbine *f*.

jet·ty ['dʒetɪ] *s.* ⚓ **1.** Landungsbrücke *f*, -steg *m*; **2.** Hafendamm *m*, Mole *f*; **3.** Strömungsbrecher *m* (*Brücke*).

Jew [dʒu:] *s.* Jude *m*, Jüdin *f*; **'~-ˌbait·er** *s.* Judenhetzer *m*; **'~-ˌbait·ing** *s.* Judenverfolgung *f*, -hetze *f*.

jew·el ['dʒu:əl] **I** *s.* **1.** Ju'wel *n*, Edelstein *m*, *weitS.* Schmuckstück *n*: ***~ box***, ***~ case*** Schmuckkästchen *n*; **2.** *fig.* Ju'wel *n*, Perle *f*; **3.** Stein *m* (*e-r Uhr*); **II** *v/t.* **4.** mit Ju'welen schmücken *od.* versehen, mit Edelsteinen besetzen; **5.** *Uhr* mit Steinen versehen; **'jew·el·(l)er** [-lə] *s.* Juwe'lier *m*; **'jew·el·ler·y**, *bsd. Am.* **'jew·el·ry** [-lrɪ] *s.* **1.** Ju'welen *pl.*; **2.** Schmuck(sachen *pl.*) *m*.

Jew·ess ['dʒu:ɪs] *s.* Jüdin *f*; **'Jew·ish** [-ɪʃ] *adj.* □ jüdisch, Juden…; **Jew·ry** ['dʒʊərɪ] *s.* **1.** *die Juden pl.*, (***world ~*** das Welt)Judentum; **2.** *hist.* Judenviertel *n*, G(h)etto *n*.

ˌJew's|-'ear *s.* ♀ Judasohr *n*; **ˌ~-'harp** *s.* ♪ Maultrommel *f*.

jib¹ [dʒɪb] *s.* **1.** ⚓ Klüver *m*: ***~ boom*** Klüverbaum *m*; ***the cut of his ~*** F s-e äußere Erscheinung *od.* sein Auftreten; **2.** ⚙ Ausleger *m* (*e-s Krans*).

jib² [dʒɪb] *v/i.* **1.** scheuen, bocken (***at*** vor *dat.*) (*Pferd*); **2.** *Brit. fig.* (***at***) a) scheuen, zu'rückweichen (vor *dat.*), b) sich sträuben (gegen), c) störrisch *od.* bokkig sein.

jibe¹ [dʒaɪb] *Am.* → ***gybe***.

jibe² [dʒaɪb] → ***gibe***.

jibe³ [dʒaɪb] *v/i. Am.* F über'einstimmen, sich entsprechen.

jif·fy [dʒɪfɪ], *a.* **jiff** [dʒɪf] *s.* F Augenblick *m*: ***in a ~*** im Nu; ***wait a ~!*** (einen) Moment!

jig¹ [dʒɪg] **I** *s.* **1.** ⚙ Spann-, Bohrvorrichtung *f*; **2.** ⚒ a) Kohlenwippe *f*, b) 'Setzmaˌschine *f*; **II** *v/t.* **3.** ⚙ mit e-r Einstellvorrichtung *od.* Schab'lone herstellen; **4.** ⚒ *Erze* setzen, scheiden.

jig² [dʒɪg] **I** *s.* **1.** ♪ Gigue *f* (*a. Tanz*); **2.** *Am. sl.* ‚Schwof' *m*, Tanzparty *f*: ***the ~ is up*** *fig.* das Spiel ist aus; **3.** *fig.* Freudentanz *m*; **II** *v/t.* **4.** schütteln; **III** *v/i.* **5.** e-e Gigue tanzen; **6.** hopsen, tanzen.

jig·ger ['dʒɪgə] *s.* **1.** Giguetänzer *m*; **2.** ⚓ a) Be'san(mast) *m*, b) Handtalje *f*; **3.** *Golf*: Jigger *m* (*Schläger*, *mst Nr. 4*); **4.** a) Schnapsglas *n*, b) ‚Schnäps-chen' *n*; **5.** *Am.* F Dings(bums) *n*, Appa'rat *m*; **6.** *a.* ***~ flea*** Sandfloh *m*; **jig·gered** ['dʒɪgəd] *adj.*: ***well, I'm ~*** (***if***) hol mich der Teufel(, wenn).

jig·ger·y-pok·er·y [ˌdʒɪgərɪ'pəʊkərɪ] *s. Brit.* F fauler Zauber, ‚Schmu' *m*.

jig·gle ['dʒɪgl] **I** *v/t.* (leicht) rütteln; **II** *v/i.* wippen, hüpfen, wackeln.

'jig·saw *s.* ⚙ **1.** Laubsäge *f*; **2.** 'Schweifsäge(maˌschine) *f*; **3.** → **~ puz·zle** *s.* Puzzle(spiel) *n*.

Jill [dʒɪl] → ***Gill⁴***.

jilt [dʒɪlt] *v/t.* a) *e-m Liebhaber* den Laufpaß geben, b) *ein Mädchen* sitzenlassen.

Jim Crow [ˌdʒɪm'krəʊ] *s. Am.* F **1.** *contp.* ‚Nigger' *m*; **2.** 'Rassendiskrimiˌnierung *f*: **~ *car*** 🚗 Wagen *m* für Farbige.

jim-jams ['dʒɪmdʒæmz] *s. pl. sl.* **1.** De'lirium *n* tremens; **2.** a) Nervenflattern *n*, b) Gänsehaut *f*.

jim·my ['dʒɪmɪ] → ***jemmy***.

jin·gle ['dʒɪŋgl] **I** *v/i.* **1.** klimpern, klirren, klingeln; **II** *v/t.* **2.** klingeln lassen, klimpern (mit), bimmeln (mit); **III** *s.* **3.** Geklingel *n*, Klimpern *n*; **4.** (eingängiges) Liedchen *od.* Vers-chen, *a.* Werbesong *m od.* -spruch *m*.

jin·go ['dʒɪŋgəʊ] **I** *pl.* **-goes** *s.* **1.** *pol.* Chauvi'nist(in); **2.** → ***jingoism***; **II** *int.* **3.** ***by ~!*** beim Zeus!; **'jin·go·ism** [-əʊɪzəm] *s. pol.* Chauvi'nismus *m*, Hur'rapatrioˌtismus *m*; **jin·go·is·tic** [ˌdʒɪŋgəʊ'ɪstɪk] *adj.* chauvi'nistisch.

jink [dʒɪŋk] **I** *s.* **1.** 'Ausweichmaˌnöver *n*; **2.** ***high ~s*** ‚Highlife' *n*, ‚tolle Party'; **II 3.** *v/i. u. v/t.* geschickt ausweichen.

jin·rik·i·sha, *a.* **jin·rick·sha** [dʒɪn'rɪkʃə] *s.* Rikscha *f*.

jinn [dʒɪn] *pl. von* **jin·nee** [dʒɪ'ni:] *s.* Dschin *m* (*islamischer Geist*).

jinx [dʒɪŋks] *sl.* **I** *s.* **1.** Unheilbringer *m*; *weitS.* Unglück *n*, Pech *n* (***for*** für): ***there is a ~ on it!*** das ist wie verhext!; ***put a ~ on*** → 3b; **2.** Unheil *n*; **II** *v/t.* **3.** a) Unglück bringen (*dat.*), b) *et.* ‚verhexen'.

jit·ter ['dʒɪtə] F **I** *v/i.* ner'vös sein, ‚Bammel' haben, ‚bibbern'; **II** *s.*: ***the ~s*** *pl.* a) ‚Bammel' *m* (*Angst*), b) ‚Zustände' *pl.*, ‚Tatterich' *m* (*Nervosität*); **'jit·ter·bug** [-bʌg] *s.* **1.** Jitterbug *m* (*Tanz*); **2.** *fig.* Nervenbündel *n*; **'jit·ter·y** [-ərɪ] *adj.* F nervös, ‚bibbernd'.

jiu·jit·su [dʒju:'dʒɪtsu:] → ***jujitsu***.

jive [dʒaɪv] **I** *s.* **1.** ♪ Jive *m*, (*Art*) 'Swingmuˌsik *f od.* -tanz *m*; **2.** *Am. sl.* Gequassel *n*; **II** *v/i.* **3.** Jive *od.* Swing tanzen *od.* spielen.

job¹ [dʒɒb] **I** *s.* **1.** *ein Stück* Arbeit *f*: ***a ~ of work*** e-e Arbeit; ***a good ~ of work*** e-e saubere Arbeit; ***be paid by the ~*** pro Auftrag bezahlt werden; ***odd ~s*** Gelegenheitsarbeiten; ***make a good ~ of it*** gute Arbeit leisten, s-e Sache gut machen; ***it was quite a ~*** es war (gar) nicht so einfach, es war e-e Mordsarbeit; ***I had a ~ to do it*** das war ganz schön schwer (für mich); ***on the ~*** a) an der Arbeit, ‚dran', b) in Aktion, c) ‚auf Draht'; **2.** Stück-, Ak'kordarbeit *f*: ***by the ~*** im Akkord; **3.** Stellung *f*, Tätigkeit *f*, Arbeit *f*, Job *m*: ***a ~ as a typist***; ***out of a ~*** stellungslos; ***know one's ~*** s-e Sache verstehen; ***on the ~ training*** Ausbildung *f* am Arbeitsplatz; ***create new ~s*** neue Arbeitsplätze schaffen; ***~s for the boys*** *pol.* F Vetternwirtschaft *f*; ***this is not everybody's ~*** dies liegt nicht jedem; **4.** Aufgabe *f*, Pflicht *f*, Sache *f*: ***it is your ~ to do it*** es ist deine Sache; **5.** F Sache *f*, Angelegenheit *f*, Lage *f*: ***a good ~*** (***too***)***!*** ein (wahres) Glück!; ***make the best of a bad ~*** a) retten, was zu retten ist, b) gute Miene zum bösen Spiel machen; ***I gave it up as a bad ~*** ich steckte es (*als aussichtslos*) auf; ***I gave him up as a bad ~*** ich ließ ihn fallen (*weil er nichts taugte etc.*); ***just the ~!*** genau das Richtige!; **6.** *sl.* a) Pro'fitgeschäft *n*, Schiebung *f*, ‚krumme Tour', b) ‚Ding' *n* (*Verbrechen*): ***pull a ~*** ein Ding drehen; ***do his ~ for him*** ihn ‚fertigmachen'; **7.** *bsd. Am.* F a) ‚Dings' *n*, ‚Appa'rat' *m* (*a. Auto etc.*), b) ‚Nummer' *f*, ‚Type' *f* (*Person*): ***he's a tough ~*** er ist ein unangenehmer Kerl; **II** *v/i.* **8.** Gelegenheitsarbeiten machen, ‚jobben'; **9.** im Ak'kord arbeiten; **10.** Zwischenhandel treiben; **11.** Maklergeschäfte treiben, mit Aktien handeln; **12.** ‚schieben', in die eigene Tasche arbeiten; **III** *v/t.* **13.** *a.* ***~ out*** † a) *Arbeit* im Ak'kord vergeben, b) *Auftrag* (weiter)vergeben; **14.** spekulieren mit; **15.** als Zwischenhändler verkaufen; **16.** veruntreuen; *Amt* miß'brauchen: ***~ s.o. into a post*** j-m e-n Posten zuschanzen.

Job² [dʒəʊb] *npr. bibl.* Hiob *m*, Job *m*: (***the Book of***) ***~*** (das Buch) Hiob *od.* Job; ***patience of ~*** *e-e* Engelsgeduld; ***that would try the patience of ~*** das würde selbst e-n Engel zur Verzweiflung treiben; ***~'s comforter*** schlechter Tröster (*der alles noch verschlimmert*); ***~'s news***, ***~'s post*** Hiobsbotschaft *f*.

job a·nal·y·sis *s.* 'Arbeitsplatzanaˌlyse *f*.

job·ber ['dʒɒbə] *s.* **1.** Gelegenheitsarbeiter *m*; **2.** Ak'kordarbeiter *m*: **3.** † Zwischen-, *Am.* Großhändler *m*; **4.** *Brit. Börse*: Jobber *m* (*der auf eigene Rechnung Geschäfte tätigt*); **5.** *Am.* 'Börsenspekuˌlant *m*; **6.** Geschäftemacher *m*, ‚Schieber' *m*, *a.* kor'rupter Beamter; **'job·ber·y** [-ərɪ] *s.* **1.** *b.s.* ‚Schiebung' *f*, Korrupti'on *f*; **2.** 'Amtsˌmißbrauch *m*; **'job·bing** [-bɪŋ] *s.* **1.** Gelegenheitsarbeit *f*; **2.** Ak'kordarbeit *f*; **3.** *Börse*: *Brit.* Ef'fektenhandel *m*, *a.* Spekulati'on(sgeschäfte *pl.*) *f*; **4.** Zwischen-, *Am.* Großhandel *m*; **5.** ‚Schiebung' *f*.

job| cre·a·tion *s.* Schaffung *f* von Arbeitsplätzen: **~ *scheme*** (*od.* ***program*[*me*]**) Arbeitsbeschaffungsprogramm *n*; **~ de·scrip·tion** *s.* Arbeits-(platz)-, Tätigkeitsbeschreibung *f*; **~ e·val·u·a·tion** *s.* Arbeits(platz)bewertung *f*; **~ hop·ping** *s.* häufiger Stellenwechsel (*zur Verbesserung des Einkommens*); **~ hunt·er** *s.* Stellungssuchende(r *m*) *f*; **~ kil·ler** *s.* Jobkiller *m* (*arbeitsplatzvernichtende Maschine etc.*); **'~·less** [-lɪs] **I** *adj.* arbeitslos; **II** *s.*: ***the ~ pl.*** die Arbeitslosen *pl.*; **~ line**, **~ lot** *s.* ✝ **1.** Gelegenheitskauf *m*; **2.** Ramsch-, Par'tieware(n *pl.*) *f*; **~ market** *s.* Arbeitsmarkt *m*; **~ print·ing** *s.* Akzi'denzdruck *m*; **~ ro·ta·tion** *s.* turnusmäßiger Arbeitsplatztausch; **~ secu·ri·ty** *s.* Sicherheit *f* des Arbeitsplatzes; **~ shar·ing** *s.* Jobsharing *n*, Arbeitsplatzteilung *f*; **~ work** *s.* **1.** Ak'kordarbeit *f*; **2.** → ***job printing***.

jock·ey ['dʒɒkɪ] **I** *s.* Jockey *m*, Jockei *m*; **II** *v/t.* a) manipulieren, b) betrügen (***out of*** um): **~ *into s.th.*** in et. hineinmanövrieren, zu et. verleiten; **~ *s.o. into a position*** j-m durch Protektion e-e Stellung verschaffen, ‚j-n lancieren'; **III** *v/i.* **~ *for*** ‚rangeln' um (*a. fig.*): **~ *for position*** *sport u. fig.* sich e-e gute (Ausgangs)Position zu schaffen suchen.

'jock·strap ['dʒɒk-] *s. bsd. sport* Suspen'sorium *n*.

jo·cose [dʒəʊ'kəʊs] *adj.* ☐ **1.** scherzhaft, komisch, drollig; **2.** heiter, ausgelassen.

joc·u·lar ['dʒɒkjʊlə] *adj.* ☐ **1.** scherzhaft, witzig; **2.** lustig, heiter; **joc·u·lar·i·ty** [ˌdʒɒkjʊ'lærətɪ] *s.* **1.** Scherzhaftigkeit *f*; **2.** Heiterkeit *f*.

joc·und ['dʒɒkənd] *adj.* ☐ lustig, fröhlich, heiter; **jo·cun·di·ty** [dʒəʊ'kʌndətɪ] *s.* Lustigkeit *f*.

jodh·purs ['dʒɒdpəz] *s. pl.* Reithose(n *pl.*) *f*.

jog [dʒɒg] **I** *v/t.* **1.** (an)stoßen, rütteln, ‚stupsen'; **2.** *fig.* aufrütteln: **~ *s.o.'s memory*** j-s Gedächtnis nachhelfen; **II** *v/i.* **3.** *a.* **~ *on***, **~ *along*** (da'hin)trotten, (-)zuckeln; **4.** sich auf den Weg machen, ‚loszuckeln'; **5.** *fig. a.* **~ *on*** a) weiterwursteln, b) s-n Lauf nehmen; **6.** *sport* ‚joggen', im Trimmtrab laufen; **III** *s.* **7.** (leichter) Stoß; **8.** Rütteln *n*; **9.** → ***jogtrot*** 1; **'jog·ging** [-gɪŋ] *s.* ‚Jogging' *n*, Trimmtrab *m*.

jog·gle ['dʒɒgl] **I** *v/t.* **1.** leicht schütteln *od.* rütteln; **2.** ⚙ verschränken, verzahnen; **II** *v/i.* **3.** sich schütteln, wackeln; **III** *s.* **4.** Stoß *m*, Rütteln *n*; **5.** ⚙ Verzahnung *f*, Nut *f u.* Feder *f*.

'jog·trot I *s.* **1.** gemächlicher Trab, Trott *m*; **2.** *fig.* Trott *m*: a) Schlendrian *m*, b) Eintönigkeit *f*; **II** *v/i.* **3.** → ***jog*** 3.

john¹ [dʒɒn] *s. Am. sl.* Klo *n*.

John² [dʒɒn] *npr. u. s. bibl.* Jo'hannes (-evanˌgelium *n*) *m*: **~ *the Baptist*** Johannes der Täufer; (***the Epistles of***) **~** die Johannesbriefe; **~ Bull** *s.* John Bull: a) *England*, b) *der* (*typische*) *Engländer*; **~ Doe** [dəʊ] *s.*: **~ *and Richard Roe*** ⚖ A. und B. (*fiktive Parteien*); **~ Do·ry** ['dɔːrɪ] *s. ichth.* Heringskönig *m*; **~ Han·cock** ['hænkɒk] *s. Am.* F *j-s* ‚Friedrich Wilhelm' *m* (*Unterschrift*).

john·ny ['dʒɒnɪ] *s. Brit.* F Bursche *m*, Typ *m*, ‚Knülch' *m*; **ˌ2-come-'late·ly** *s. Am.* F **1.** Neuankömmling *m*, Neuling *m*; **2.** *fig.* ‚Spätzünder' *m*; **2 on the spot** *s. Am.* F a) j-d, der ‚auf Draht' ist, b) Retter *m* in der Not.

John·so·ni·an [dʒɒn'səʊnjən] *adj.* **1.** Johnsonsch (*Samuel Johnson od. s-n Stil betreffend*); **2.** pom'pös, hochtrabend.

join [dʒɔɪn] **I** *v/t.* **1.** *et.* verbinden, -einigen, zs.-fügen (***to***, ***on to*** mit): **~ *hands*** a) die Hände falten, b) sich die Hand reichen (*a. fig.*), c) *fig.* sich zs.-tun; **2.** *Personen* vereinigen, zs.-bringen (***with***, ***to*** mit): **~ *in marriage*** verheiraten; **~ *in friendship*** freundschaftlich verbinden; **3.** *fig.* verbinden, -ein(ig)en: **~ *prayers*** gemeinsam beten; → ***battle*** 2, ***force*** 1, ***issue*** 6; **4.** sich anschließen (*dat. od.* an *acc.*), stoßen *od.* sich gesellen zu, sich einfinden bei: **~ *s.o. in*** (***doing***) ***s.th.*** et. zusammen mit j-m tun; **~ *s.o. in a walk*** (gemeinsam) mit j-m e-n Spaziergang machen, sich j-m auf e-m Spaziergang anschließen; **~ *one's regiment*** zu s-m Regiment stoßen; **~ *one's ship*** an Bord s-s Schiffes gehen; ***may I ~ you?*** a) darf ich mich Ihnen anschließen *od.* Ihnen Gesellschaft leisten, b) darf ich mitmachen?; ***I'll ~ you soon!*** ich komme bald (nach)!; ***will you ~ me in a drink?*** trinken Sie ein Glas mit mir?; → ***majority*** 1; **5.** *e-m Klub*, *e-r Partei etc.* beitreten, eintreten in (*acc.*): **~ *the army*** ins Heer eintreten, Soldat werden; **~ *a firm as a partner*** in e-e Firma als Teilhaber eintreten; **6.** a) teilnehmen *od.* sich beteiligen an (*dat.*), mitmachen bei, b) sich einlassen auf (*acc.*), *den Kampf* aufnehmen: **~ *an action*** *jur.* e-m Prozeß beitreten; **~ *a treaty*** e-m (Staats)Vertrag beitreten; **7.** sich vereinigen mit, zs.-kommen mit, (ein-)münden in (*acc.*) (*Fluß*, *Straße*); **8.** *math. Punkte* verbinden; **9.** (an)grenzen an (*acc.*); **II** *v/i.* **10.** sich vereinigen *od.* verbinden, zs.-kommen, sich treffen (***with*** mit); **11.** a) **~ *in*** (*s.th.*) → 6 a, b) **~ *with s.o. in s.th.*** sich j-m bei et. anschließen, et. gemeinsam tun mit j-m: **~ *in everybody!*** alle mitmachen!; **12.** anein'andergrenzen, sich berühren; **13.** **~ *up*** Sol'dat werden, zum Mili'tär gehen; **III** *s.* **14.** Verbindungsstelle *f*, -linie *f*, Naht *f*, Fuge *f*.

join·der ['dʒɔɪndə] *s.* **1.** Verbindung *f*; **2.** ⚖ a) *a.* **~ *of actions*** (objek'tive) Klagehäufung, b) *a.* **~ *of parties*** Streitgenossenschaft *f*, c) **~ *of issue*** Einlassung *f* (auf die Klage).

join·er ['dʒɔɪnə] *s.* Tischler *m*, Schreiner *m*: **~*'s bench*** Hobelbank *f*; **'join·er·y** [-ərɪ] *s.* **1.** Tischlerhandwerk *n*, Schreine'rei *f*; **2.** Tischlerarbeit *f*.

joint [dʒɔɪnt] **I** *s.* **1.** Verbindung(sstelle) *f*, *bsd.* a) *Tischlerei etc.*: Fuge *f*, Stoß *m*, b) (Löt)Naht *f*, Nahtstelle *f*, c) Falz *m* (*der Buchdecke*), d) *anat.*, *biol.*, ⚘, ⚙ Gelenk *n*: ***out of ~*** ausgerenkt, *bsd. fig.* aus den Fugen; → ***nose*** *Bes. Redew.*; **2.** Verbindungsstück *n*, Bindeglied *n*; **3.** Hauptstück *n* (*e-s Schlachttiers*), Braten(stück *n*) *m*; **4.** *sl.* ‚Bude' *f*, ‚Laden' *m*: a) Lo'kal *n*, ‚Schuppen' *m*, *contp.* ‚'Bumsloˌkal' *n*, Spe'lunke *f*, b) Gebäude; **5.** *sl.* Joint *m* (*Marihuanazigarette*); **II** *adj.* (☐ → ***jointly***) **6.** gemeinsam, gemeinschaftlich (*a.* ⚖): **~ *invention***; **~ *liability***; **~ *effort***; **~ *efforts*** vereinte Kräfte *od.* Anstrengungen; **~ *and several*** ⚖ gesamtschuldnerisch, solidarisch, zur gesamten Hand (→ ***jointly***); **~ *and several creditor*** (***debtor***) Gesamtgläubiger *m* (-schuldner *m*); ***take ~ action*** gemeinsam vorgehen, zs.-wirken; **7.** *bsd.* ⚖ Mit..., Neben...: **~ *heir*** Miterbe *m*; **~ *offender*** Mittäter *m*; **~ *plaintiff*** Mitkläger *m*; **8.** vereint, zs.-hängend; **III** *v/t.* **9.** verbinden, zs.-fügen; **10.** ⚙ a) fugen, stoßen, verbinden, -zapfen, b) *Fugen* verstreichen; **~ ac·count** *s.* ✝ Gemeinschaftskonto *n*: ***on*** (*od.* ***for***) **~** auf *od.* für gemeinsame Rechnung; **~ ad·ven·ture** → ***joint venture***; **~ cap·i·tal** *s.* ✝ Ge'sellschaftskapiˌtal *n*; **~ com·mit·tee** *s. pol.* gemischter Ausschuß; **~ cred·it** *s.* ✝ Konsorti'alkreˌdit *m*; **~ cred·i·tor** *s.* ⚖ Gesamthandgläubiger *m*; **~ debt** *s.* ⚖ gemeinsame Verbindlichkeit(en *pl.*) *f*, Gesamthandschuld *f*; **~ debt·or** *s.* ⚖ Mitschuldner *m*, Gesamthandschuldner *m*.

joint·ed ['dʒɔɪntɪd] *adj.* **1.** verbunden; **2.** gegliedert, mit Gelenken (versehen): **~ *doll*** Gliederpuppe *f*.

joint·ly ['dʒɔɪntlɪ] *adv.* gemeinschaftlich: **~ *and severally*** a) gemeinsam u. jeder für sich, b) solidarisch, zur gesamten Hand, gesamtschuldnerisch.

joint| own·er *s.* ✝ Miteigentümer(in), Mitinhaber(in); **~ own·er·ship** *s.* Miteigentum *n*; **~ res·o·lu·tion** *s. pol.* gemeinsame Resoluti'on; **~ stock** *s.* ✝ Ge'sellschafts-, 'Aktienkapiˌtal *n*; **ˌ~-'stock bank** *s.* Genossenschafts-, Aktienbank *f*; **ˌ~-'stock com·pa·ny** *s.* ✝ **1.** *Brit.* Aktiengesellschaft *f*; **2.** *Am.* offene Handelsgesellschaft auf Aktien; **ˌ~-'stock cor·po·ra·tion** *s. Am.* Aktiengesellschaft *f*; **~ ten·an·cy** *s.* ✝ Mitbesitz *m*, -pacht *f*; **~ un·der·tak·ing**, **~ ven·ture** *s.* ✝ **1.** Ge'meinschaftsunterˌnehmen *n*; **2.** Gelegenheitsgesellschaft *f*.

joist [dʒɔɪst] △ **I** *s.* (Quer)Balken *m*; (Quer-, Pro'fil)Träger *m*; **II** *v/t.* mit Pro'filträgern belegen.

joke [dʒəʊk] **I** *s.* **1.** Witz *m*: ***practical ~*** Schabernack *m*, Streich *m*; ***play a practical ~ on s.o.*** j-m einen Streich spielen; ***crack ~s*** Witze reißen; **2.** Scherz *m*, Spaß *m*: ***in ~*** zum Scherz; ***he cannot take*** (*od.* ***see***) ***a ~*** er versteht keinen Spaß; ***I don't see the ~!*** was soll daran so witzig sein?; ***it's no ~!*** a) (das ist) kein Witz!, b) das ist keine Kleinigkeit *od.* kein Spaß!; ***the ~ was on me*** der Spaß ging auf m-e Kosten; **II** *v/i.* **3.** Witze *od.* Spaß machen, scherzen, flachsen: ***I'm not joking!*** ich meine das ernst; ***you must be joking!*** soll das ein Witz sein?; **'jok·er** [-kə] *s.* **1.** Spaßvogel *m*, Witzbold *m*; **2.** *sl.* Kerl *m*, ‚Heini' *m*; **3.** Joker *m* (*Spielkarte*) (*a. fig.*); **4.** *Am. sl. mst pol.* ‚'Hintertürklausel' *f*;

'jok·ing [-kɪŋ] *s.* Scherzen *n*: **~ apart!** Scherz beiseite!
jol·li·fi·ca·tion [ˌdʒɒlɪfɪ'keɪʃn] *s.* F (feucht)fröhliches Fest, Festivi'tät *f*;
jol·li·ness ['dʒɒlɪnɪs], *mst* **jol·li·ty** ['dʒɒlətɪ] *s.* **1.** Fröhlichkeit *f*; **2.** Fest *n*.
jol·ly ['dʒɒlɪ] **I** *adj.* □ **1.** lustig, fi'del, vergnügt; **2.** F angeheitert, beschwipst; **3.** *Brit.* F a) nett, hübsch: **a ~ room**, b) *iro.* ‚schön', ‚furchtbar': **he must be a ~ fool** er muß (ja) ganz schön blöd sein; **II** *adv.* **4.** *Brit.* F ziemlich, ‚mächtig', ‚furchtbar': **~ late**; **~ nice** ‚unheimlich' nett; **~ good** *a. iro.* (ist ja) Klasse!; **a ~ good fellow** ein ‚prima' Kerl; **I ~ well told him** ich hab' es ihm (doch) ganz deutlich gesagt; **you'll ~ well** (**have to**) **do it!** du mußt (es tun), ob du willst oder nicht; **you ~ well know** du weißt das ganz genau; **III** *v/t.* F **5.** *mst* **~ along** *od.* **up** *j-n* bei Laune halten *od.* aufmuntern: **~ s.o. into doing s.th.** j-n zu e-r Sache ‚bequatschen'; **6.** *j-n* ‚veräppeln'.
jol·ly boat ['dʒɒlɪ] *s.* ⚓ Jolle *f*.
Jol·ly Rog·er ['rɒdʒə] *s.* Totenkopf-, Pi'ratenflagge *f*.
jolt [dʒəʊlt] **I** *v/t.* **1.** ('durch)rütteln, stoßen; **2.** *Am. Boxen*: (*Gegner*) erschüttern (*a. fig.*); **3.** *fig. j-m* e-n Schock versetzen; **4.** *j-n* aufrütteln; **II** *v/i.* **5.** rütteln, holpern (*Fahrzeug*); **III** *s.* **6.** Ruck *m*, Stoß *m*, Rütteln *n*; **7.** Schock *m*; **8.** (harter) Schlag; **9.** F a) Wirkung *f* (*e-r Droge etc.*), b) ‚Schuß' *m* (*Kognak, Droge*).
Jo·nah ['dʒəʊnə] *npr. u. s.* **1.** *bibl.* (das Buch) Jonas *m*; **2.** *fig.* Unheilbringer *m*; **'Jo·nas** [-əs] → **Jonah** 1.
josh [dʒɒʃ] *sl.* **I** *v/t.* ‚aufziehen', veräppeln; **II** *s.* Hänse'lei *f*.
Josh·u·a ['dʒɒʃwə] *npr. u. s. bibl.* (das Buch) Josua *m od.* Josue *m*.
joss| house [dʒɒs] *s.* chi'nesischer Tempel; **~ stick** *s.* Räucherstäbchen *n*.
jos·tle ['dʒɒsl] **I** *v/i.* drängeln: **~ against** → **II** *v/t.* anrempeln, schubsen; **III** *s.* a) Gedränge *n*, Dränge'lei *f*, b) Rempe'lei *f*.
Jos·u·e ['dʒɒzjʊiː] → **Joshua**.
jot [dʒɒt] **I** *s.*: **not a ~** nicht ein bißchen; **there's not a ~ of truth in it** da ist überhaupt nichts Wahres dran; **II** *v/t.* *mst* **~ down** schnell hinschreiben *od.* notieren *od.* hinwerfen; **'jot·ter** [-tə] *s.* No'tizbuch *n*; **'jot·ting** [-tɪŋ] *s.* (kurze) No'tiz.
joule [dʒuːl] *s. phys.* Joule *n*.
jounce [dʒaʊns] → **jolt** 1, 6, 7.
jour·nal ['dʒɜːnl] *s.* **1.** Jour'nal *n*, Zeitschrift *f*, Zeitung *f*; **2.** Tagebuch *n*; **3.** ✝ Jour'nal *n*, Memori'al *n*; **4.** **2s** *pl. parl. Brit.* Proto'kollbuch *n*; **5.** ⚓ Logbuch *n*; **6.** ⚙ (Achs-, Lager)Zapfen *m*: **~ bearing** *od.* **box** Achs-, Zapfenlager *n*; **jour·nal·ese** [ˌdʒɜːnə'liːz] *s. contp.* Zeitungsstil *m*; **'jour·nal·ism** [-nəlɪzəm] *s.* Journa'lismus *m*; **'jour·nal·ist** [-nəlɪst] *s.* Journa'list(in); **jour·nal·istic** [ˌdʒɜːnə'lɪstɪk] *adj.* journa'listisch.
jour·ney ['dʒɜːnɪ] **I** *s.* **1.** Reise *f*: **go on a ~** verreisen; **bus ~** Busfahrt *f*; **~'s end** Ende *n* der Reise, *fig.* ‚Endstation' *f*, *a.* Tod *m*; **2.** Reise *f*, Strecke *f*, Route *f*, Weg *m*, Fahrt *f*, Gang *m*: **it's a day's ~ from here** es ist e-e Tagereise von hier, man braucht e-n Tag, um von hier dorthin zu kommen; **II** *v/i.* **3.** reisen; wandern; **'~·man** [-mən] *s.* [*irr.*] (Handwerks)Geselle *m*: **~ baker** Bäckergeselle.
joust [dʒaʊst] *hist.* **I** *s.* Turnier *n*; **II** *v/i.* im Turnier kämpfen; *fig.* e-n Strauß ausfechten.
Jove [dʒəʊv] *npr.* Jupiter *m*: **by ~!** a) Donnerwetter!, b) beim Zeus!
jo·vi·al ['dʒəʊvjəl] *adj.* □ **1.** jovi'al (*a. contp.*), freundlich, aufgeräumt, gemütlich: **a ~ fellow**; **2.** freundlich, nett: **a ~ welcome**; **3.** heiter, vergnügt, lustig; **jo·vi·al·i·ty** [ˌdʒəʊvɪ'ælətɪ] *s.* Joviali'tät *f*, Freundlichkeit *f*, Fröhlichkeit *f*.
jowl [dʒaʊl] *s.* **1.** ('Unter)Kiefer *m*; **2.** (*mst* feiste *od.* Hänge)Backe *f*; → **cheek** 1; **3.** *zo.* Wamme *f*.
joy [dʒɔɪ] *s.* **1.** Freude *f* (**at** über *acc.*, **in**, **of** an *dat.*): **to my** (**great**) **~** zu m-r (großen) Freude; **leap for ~** vor Freude hüpfen; **tears of ~** Freudentränen; **it gives me great ~** es macht mir große Freude; **my children are a great ~ to me** m-e Kinder machen mir viel Freude; **wish s.o. ~** (**of**) j-m Glück wünschen (zu); **I wish you ~!** *iro.* (na, dann) viel Spaß!; **2.** *Brit.* F Erfolg *m*: **I didn't have any ~!** ich hatte keinen Erfolg!, es hat nicht geklappt!; **'joy·ful** [-fʊl] *adj.* □ **1.** freudig, erfreut, froh: **be ~** sich freuen; **2.** erfreulich, froh; **'joyful·ness** [-fʊlnɪs] *s.* Freude *f*, Fröhlichkeit *f*; **'joy·less** [-lɪs] *adj.* □ freudlos; **joy·ous** ['dʒɔɪəs] *adj.* □ → **joyful**.
joy| ride *s.* F Vergnügungsfahrt *f*, (wilde) Spritztour (*bsd.* in e-m gestohlenen Auto); **'~·stick** *s.* **1.** ✈ F Steuerknüppel *m*; **2.** *Computer*: Joystick *m*.
ju·bi·lant ['dʒuːbɪlənt] *adj.* □ jubelnd, froh'lockend, (glück)strahlend (*a. Gesicht*): **be ~** → **jubilate** 1; **ju·bi·late** **I** *v/i.* ['dʒuːbɪleɪt] **1.** jubeln, jubilieren, überglücklich sein, triumphieren; **II** **2** [ˌdʒuːbɪ'lɑːtɪ] (*Lat.*) *s. eccl.* **2.** (Sonntag *m*) Jubi'late *m* (*3. Sonntag nach Ostern*); **3.** Jubi'latepsalm *m*; **ju·bi·la·tion** [ˌdʒuːbɪ'leɪʃn] *s.* Jubel *m*.
ju·bi·lee ['dʒuːbɪliː] *s.* **1.** (*bsd.* fünfzigjähriges) Jubi'läum: **silver ~** fünfundzwanzigjähriges Jubiläum; **2.** *R.C.* Jubel-, Ablaßjahr *n*.
Ju·da·ic [dʒuː'deɪɪk] *adj.* ju'daisch, jüdisch; **Ju·da·ism** ['dʒuːdeɪɪzəm] *s.* **1.** Juda'ismus *m*; **2.** *das* Judentum; **Ju·da·ize** ['dʒuːdeɪaɪz] *v/t.* judaisieren, jüdisch machen.
Ju·das ['dʒuːdəs] **I** *npr. bibl.* Judas *m* (*a. fig. Verräter*): **~ kiss** Judaskuß *m*; **II** **2** *s.* Guckloch *n*, ‚Spi'on' *m*.
Jude [dʒuːd] *npr. u. s. bibl.* Judas *m*: (**the Epistle of**) **~** der Judasbrief.
jud·der ['dʒʌdə] *v/i.* **1.** rütteln, wackeln; **2.** vibrieren.
judge [dʒʌdʒ] **I** *s.* **1.** ⚖ Richter *m*; **2.** *mst* Preis-, *sport a.* Kampfrichter *m*; **3.** Kenner *m*: **a** (**good**) **~ of wine** ein Weinkenner; **I am no ~ of it** ich kann es nicht beurteilen; **I am no ~ of music, but** ich verstehe (zwar) nicht viel von Musik, aber; **I'll be the ~ of that** das müssen Sie mich schon selbst beurteilen lassen; **4.** *bibl.* a) Richter *m*, b) **2s** *pl. sg. konstr.* (*das* Buch der) Richter *pl.*; **II** *v/t.* **5.** ⚖ ein Urteil fällen *od.* Recht sprechen über (*acc.*), *e-n Fall* verhandeln; **6.** entscheiden (**s.th.** et.; **that** daß); **7.** beurteilen, bewerten, einschätzen (**by** nach); **8.** a) Preis-, *sport* Kampfrichter sein bei, b) *Leistungen etc.* (als Preisrichter *etc.*) bewerten; **9.** betrachten als, halten für; **III** *v/i.* **10.** ⚖ urteilen, Recht sprechen; **11.** *fig.* richten; **12.** urteilen (**by**, **from** nach; **of** über *acc.*): **~ for yourself!** urteilen Sie selbst!; **judging by his words** s-n Worten nach zu urteilen; **how can I ~?** wie soll 'ich das beurteilen?; **13.** schließen (**from**, **by** aus); **14.** Preis-, *sport* Kampfrichter sein; **15.** a) denken, vermuten, b) **~ of** sich *et.* vorstellen; **~ ad·vo·cate** *s.* ⚔ Kriegsgerichtsrat *m*; **'~-made law** *s.* auf richterlicher Entscheidung beruhendes Recht, geschöpftes Recht.
judg(e)·ment ['dʒʌdʒmənt] *s.* **1.** ⚖ (Gerichts)Urteil *n*, gerichtliche Entscheidung: **~ by default** Versäumnisurteil; **give** (*od.* **deliver**, **render**, **pronounce**) **~** ein Urteil erlassen *od.* verkünden (**on** über *acc.*); **pass ~** ein Urteil fällen (**on** über *acc.*); **sit in ~ on a case** Richter sein in e-m Fall; **sit in ~ on s.o.** über j-n zu Gericht sitzen; → **error** 1; **2.** Beurteilung *f*, Bewertung *f* (*a. sport etc.*), Urteil *n*; **3.** Urteilsvermögen *n*: **man of ~** urteilsfähiger Mann; **use your best ~!** handeln Sie nach Ihrem besten Ermessen; **4.** Urteil *n*, Ansicht *f*, Meinung *f*: **form a ~** sich ein Urteil bilden; **against my better ~** wider besseres Wissen; **give one's ~ on s.th.** sein Urteil über et. abgeben; **in my ~** meines Erachtens; **5.** Schätzung *f*: **~ of distance**; **6.** göttliches (Straf)Gericht, Strafe *f* (Gottes): **the Last 2**, **the Day of 2**, **2 Day** das Jüngste Gericht; **~ cred·i·tor** *s.* ⚖ Voll'streckungsgläubiger(in); **~ debt** *s.* ⚖ voll'streckbare Forderung, durch Urteil festgestellte Schuld; **~ debt·or** *s.* ⚖ Vollstreckungsschuldner(in); **'~-proof** *adj. Am.* ⚖ unpfändbar.
judge·ship ['dʒʌdʒʃɪp] *s.* Richteramt *n*.
ju·di·ca·ture ['dʒuːdɪkətʃə] *s.* ⚖ **1.** Rechtsprechung *f*, Rechtspflege *f*; **2.** Gerichtswesen *n*, Ju'stiz(verwaltung) *f*; → **supreme** 1; **3.** *coll.* Richter(stand *m*, -schaft *f*) *pl.*; **ju·di·cial** [dʒuː'dɪʃl] *adj.* □ **1.** ⚖ gerichtlich, Justiz..., Gerichts...: **~ error** Justizirrtum *m*; **~ murder** Justizmord *m*; **~ proceedings** Gerichtsverfahren *n*; **~ office** Richteramt *n*, richterliches Amt; **~ power** richterliche Gewalt; **~ separation** gerichtliche Trennung der Ehe; **~ system** Gerichtswesen *n*; **2.** ⚖ Richter..., richterlich; **3.** klar urteilend, kritisch; **ju·di·ci·ar·y** [dʒuː'dɪʃɪərɪ] ⚖ **I** *s.* **1.** → **judicature** 2, 3; **2.** *Am.* richterliche Gewalt; **II** *adj.* **3.** richterlich, rechtsprechend, gerichtlich: **2 Committee** *Am. parl.* Rechtsausschuß *m*.
ju·di·cious [dʒuː'dɪʃəs] *adj.* □ **1.** vernünftig, klug; **2.** 'wohlüberˌlegt, verständnisvoll; **ju'di·cious·ness** [-nɪs] *s.* Klugheit *f*, Einsicht *f*.
ju·do ['dʒuːdəʊ] *s. sport* Judo *n*; **'ju·doka** [-əʊkɑː] *s.* Ju'doka *m*.
Ju·dy ['dʒuːdɪ] → **Punch**[4].
jug[1] [dʒʌg] **I** *s.* **1.** Krug *m*, Kanne *f*, Kännchen *n*; **2.** *sl.* ‚Kittchen' *n*, ‚Knast' *m*; **II** *v/t.* **3.** schmoren *od.* dämpfen: **~ged hare** Hasenpfeffer *m*; **4.** *sl.* ‚einlochen'.
jug[2] [dʒʌg] **I** *v/i.* schlagen (*Nachtigall*); **II** *s.* Nachtigallenschlag *m*.

ˈ**jug·ful** [-fʊl] *pl.* **-fuls** *s. ein* Krug(voll) *m.*
jug·ger·naut [ˈdʒʌgənɔːt] *s.* **1.** Moloch *m*: ***the ~ of war***; **2.** *Brit.* schwerer ,Brummi', Schwerlastwagen *m*, Lastzug *m.*
jug·gins [ˈdʒʌgɪnz] *s. sl.* Trottel *m.*
jug·gle [ˈdʒʌgl] **I** *v/i.* **1.** jonglieren; **2.** ***~ with*** *fig.* (mit) *et.* jonglieren, *et.* manipulieren: ***~ with facts***; ***~ with one's accounts*** s-e Konten ,frisieren'; ***~ with words*** mit Worten spielen *od.* ,jonglieren', Worte verdrehen; **II** *v/t.* **3.** jonglieren mit; **4.** → 2; ˈ**jug·gler** [-lə] *s.* **1.** Jonˈgleur *m*; **2.** Schwindler *m*; ˈ**jug·gler·y** [-lərɪ] *s.* **1.** Jonglieren *n*; **2.** Taschenspieleˈrei *f*; **3.** Schwindel *m*, Hokusˈpokus *m.*
Ju·go·slav [ˌjuːgəʊˈslɑːv] **I** *s.* Jugoˈslawe *m*, Jugoˈslawin *f*; **II** *adj.* jugoˈslawisch.
jug·u·lar [ˈdʒʌgjʊlə] *anat.* **I** *adj.* Kehl…, Gurgel…; **II** *s. a.* ***~ vein*** Hals-, Drosselader *f*; ˈ**ju·gu·late** [-leɪt] *v/t. fig.* abwürgen.
juice [dʒuːs] *s.* **1.** Saft *m* (*a. fig.*): ***orange ~***; ***~ extractor*** Entsafter *m*; ***body ~s*** Körpersäfte; ***stew in one's own ~*** F im eigenen Saft schmoren; **2.** *sl.* a) ↯ ,Saft' *m*, Strom *m*, b) *mot.* Sprit *m*, c) *Am.* ,Zeug' *n*, Whisky *m*; **3.** *fig.* Kern *m*, Subˈstanz *f*, Esˈsenz *f*; ˈ**juic·i·ness** [-sɪnɪs] *s.* Saftigkeit *f*; ˈ**juic·y** [-sɪ] *adj.* **1.** saftig (*a. fig.*); **2.** F a) ,saftig', ,gepfeffert': ***~ scandal***, b) piˈkant, schlüpfrig: ***~ story***, c) interessant, ,mit Pfiff'; **3.** *Am.* F lukraˈtiv: ***~ contract***; **4.** *sl.* ,scharf', ,dufte': ***~ girl***.
ju·jit·su [dʒuːˈdʒɪtsuː] *s. sport* Jiu-Jitsu *n.*
ju·jube [ˈdʒuːdʒuːb] *s.* **1.** ⚘ Juˈjube *f*, Brustbeere *f*; **2.** *pharm.* ˈBrustbonˌbon *m, n.*
ju·jut·su [dʒuːˈdʒʊtsuː] → ***jujitsu***.
ˈ**juke|·box** [ˈdʒuːk-] *s.* Jukebox *f* (*Musikautomat*); ˈ**~-joint** *s. Am. sl.* ,ˈBumsloˌkal' *n*, ,Jukebox-Bude' *f.*
ju·lep [ˈdʒuːlep] *s.* **1.** süßliches (Arzˈnei-) Getränk; **2.** *Am.* Julep *m* (*alkoholisches Eisgetränk*).
Jul·ian [ˈdʒuːljən] *adj.* juliˈanisch: ***the ~ calendar*** der Julianische Kalender.
Ju·ly [dʒuːˈlaɪ] *s.* Juli *m*: ***in ~*** im Juli.
jum·ble [ˈdʒʌmbl] **I** *v/t.* **1.** *a.* ***~ together***, ***~ up*** zs.-werfen, in Unordnung bringen, (wahllos) vermischen, durcheinˈanderwürfeln; **II** *v/i.* **2.** *a.* ***~ together***, ***~ up*** durcheinˈandergeraten, -gerüttelt werden; **III** *s.* **3.** Durcheinˈander *n*, Wirrwarr *m*; **4.** Ramsch *m*: ***~ sale*** *Brit.* Wohltätigkeitsbasar *m*; ***~ shop*** Ramschladen *m.*
jum·bo [ˈdʒʌmbəʊ] *s.* **1.** Koˈloß *m*: ***~-sized*** riesig; **2.** → **jum·bo jet** *s.* ✈ Jumbo(-Jet) *m.*
jump [dʒʌmp] **I** *s.* **1.** Sprung *m* (*a. fig.*), Satz *m*: ***make*** (*od.* ***take***) ***a ~*** e-n Sprung machen; ***by ~s*** *fig.* sprungweise; (***always***) ***on the ~*** F (immer) auf den Beinen *od.* in Eile; ***keep s.o. on the ~*** j-n in Trab halten; ***get the ~ on s.o.*** F j-m zuvorkommen, j-m den Rang ablaufen; ***have the ~ on s.o.*** F j-m gegenüber im Vorteil sein; ***be*** (***stay***) ***one ~ ahead*** *fig.* (immer) e-n Schritt voraus sein (***of*** *dat.*); ***give a ~*** → 15; ***give s.o. a ~*** F j-n erschrecken; **2.** (Fallschirm)Absprung *m*: ***~ area*** Absprunggebiet *n*; **3.** *sport* (Hoch- *od.* Weit)Sprung *m*: ***high*** (***long*** *od. Am.* ***broad***) ***~***; **4.** *bsd. Reitsport*: Hindernis *n*: ***take the ~***; **5.** sprunghaftes Anwachsen, Emˈporschnellen *n* (***in prices*** der Preise *etc.*): ***~ in production*** rapider Produktionsanstieg; **6.** (plötzlicher) Ruck; **7.** *fig.* Sprung *m*: a) abrupter ˈÜbergang, b) Überˈspringen *n*, -ˈgehen *n*, Auslassen *n* (*von Buchseiten etc.*); **8.** a) *Film*: Sprung *m* (*Überblenden etc.*), b) *Computer*: (Proˈgramm)Sprung *m*; **9.** *Damespiel*: Schlagen *n*; **10.** a) Rückstoß *m* (*e-r Feuerwaffe*), b) ⚔ Abgangsfehler *m*; **11.** V ,Nummer' *f* (*Koitus*); **II** *v/i.* **12.** springen: ***~ at*** (*od.* ***to***) *fig.* sich stürzen auf (*acc.*), sofort zugreifen bei *e-m Angebot*, *Vorschlag etc.*, (sofort) aufgreifen, einhaken bei *e-r Frage etc.*; ***~ at the chance*** die Gelegenheit beim Schopf ergreifen, mit beiden Händen zugreifen; → ***conclusion*** 3; ***~ down s.o.'s throat*** F j-n ,anschnauzen'; ***~ off*** a) abspringen (von *s-m Fahrrad etc.*), b) *Am.* F loslegen; ***~ on s.o.*** F a) über j-n herfallen, b) j-m ,aufs Dach' steigen; ***~ out of one's skin*** aus der Haut fahren; ***~ to it*** F ,(d)rangehen', zupacken; ***~ to it!*** ran!, mach schon!; ***~ up*** aufspringen (***onto*** auf *acc.*); **13.** (*mit dem Fallschirm*) (ab-) springen; **14.** hopsen, hüpfen: ***~ up and down***; ***~ for joy*** e-n Freudensprung *od.* Freudensprünge machen; ***his heart ~ed for joy*** das Herz hüpfte ihm im Leibe; **15.** zs.-zucken, -fahren, aufschrecken, hochfahren (***at*** bei): ***the noise made him ~*** der Lärm schreckte ihn auf *od.* ließ ihn zs.-zucken; **16.** *fig.* abˈrupt ˈübergehen, -wechseln (***to*** zu): ***~ from one topic to another***; **17.** a) rütteln (*Wagen etc.*), b) gerüttelt werden, schaukeln, wackeln; **18.** *fig.* sprunghaft ansteigen, emˈporschnellen (*Preise etc.*); **19.** ⚙ springen (*Filmstreifen*, *Schreibmaschine etc.*); **20.** *Damespiel*: schlagen; **21.** *Bridge*: (unvermittelt) hoch reizen; **22.** pochen, pulsieren; **23.** F voller Leben sein: ***the place is ~ing*** dort ist ,schwer was los'; ***the party was ~ing*** die Party war ,schwer in Fahrt'; **III** *v/t.* **24.** (hinˈweg)springen über (*acc.*): ***~ the fence***; ***~ the rails*** entgleisen (*Zug*); **25.** *fig.* überˈspringen, auslassen: ***~ a few lines***; ***~ the lights*** F bei Rot über die Kreuzung fahren; ***~ the queue*** *Brit.* sich vordrängeln, aus der Reihe tanzen (*a. fig.*); → ***gun*** 4; **26.** springen lassen: ***he ~ed his horse over the ditch*** er setzte mit dem Pferd über den Graben; **27.** *Damespiel*: schlagen; **28.** *Bridge*: (zu) hoch reizen; **29.** *sl.* ,abhauen' von: ***~ ship*** (***town***); → ***bail***[1] 1; **30.** a) aufspringen auf (*acc.*), b) abspringen von (*e-m fahrenden Zug*); **31.** schaukeln: ***~ a baby on one's knee***; **32.** F *j-n* überfallen, über *j-n* herfallen; **33.** emˈporschnellen lassen, hochtreiben: ***~ prices***; **34.** *Am.* F *j-n* (plötzlich) *im Rang* befördern; **35.** V *Frau* ,bumsen'; **36.** → ***jump-start***.
jump ball *s. Basketball*: Sprungball *m.*
jumped-up [ˌdʒʌmptˈʌp] *adj.* F **1.** (parveˈnühaft) hochnäsig, ,hochgestochen'; **2.** improvisiert.
jump·er[1] [ˈdʒʌmpə] *s.* **1.** Springer(in): ***high ~*** *sport* Hochspringer(in); **2.** Springpferd *n*; **3.** ⚙ Steinbohrer *m*; Bohrmeißel *m*; **4.** ↯ Kurzschlußbrücke *f.*
jump·er[2] [ˈdʒʌmpə] *s.* **1.** (*Am.* ärmelloser) Pullover *m*; **2.** *bsd. Am.* Trägerkleid *n*, -rock *m*; **3.** (Kinder)Spielhose *f.*
jump·i·ness [ˈdʒʌmpɪnɪs] *s.* Nervosiˈtät *f.*
jump·ing [ˈdʒʌmpɪŋ] *s.* **1.** Springen *n*: ***~ pole*** Sprungstab *m*, -stange *f*; ***~ test*** *Reitsport*: (Jagd)Springen *n*; **2.** *Skisport*: Sprunglauf *m*, Springen *n*; ***~ bean*** *s.* ⚘ Springende Bohne; ***~ jack*** *s.* Hampelmann *m*; ˌ**~-ˈoff place** *s.* **1.** *fig.* Sprungbrett *n*, Ausgangspunkt *m*; **2.** *Am.* F Ende *n* der Welt.
jump| jet *s.* ✈ (Düsen)Senkrechtstarter *m*; ***~ leads*** *s. pl. mot.* Starthilfekabel *n*; ˈ**~-off** *s. Reitsport*: Stechen *n*; ***~ seat*** *s.* Not-, Klappsitz *m*; ˈ**~-start** *v/t. Auto* mittels Starthilfekabel anlassen; ***~ suit*** *s.* Overall *m*; ***~ turn*** *s. Skisport*: ˈUmsprung *m.*
jump·y [ˈdʒʌmpɪ] *adj.* nerˈvös.
junc·tion [ˈdʒʌŋkʃn] *s.* **1.** Verbindung(spunkt *m*) *f*, Vereinigung *f*, Zs.-treffen *n*; Treffpunkt *m*; Anschluß *m* (*a.* ⚙); (Straßen)Kreuzung *f*, (-)Einmündung *f*; **2.** 🚂 a) Knotenpunkt *m*, b) ˈAnschlußstatiˌon *f*; **3.** Berührung *f*; ***~ box*** *s.* ↯ Abzweig-, Anschlußdose *f*; ***~ line*** *s.* 🚂 Verbindungs-, Nebenbahn *f.*
junc·ture [ˈdʒʌŋktʃə] *s.* (kritischer) Augenblick *od.* Zeitpunkt: ***at this ~*** in diesem Augenblick, an dieser Stelle.
June [dʒuːn] Juni *m*: ***in ~*** im Juni.
jun·gle [ˈdʒʌŋgl] *s.* **1.** Dschungel *m*, *a. n* (*a. fig.*): ***~ fever*** Dschungelfieber *n*; ***law of the ~*** Faustrecht *n*; **2.** (undurchdringliches) Dickicht (*a. fig.*); *fig.* Gewirr *n*: ***~ gym*** Klettergerüst *n* (*für Kinder*); ˈ**jun·gled** [-ld] *adj.* mit Dschungel(n) bedeckt, verdschungelt.
jun·ior [ˈdʒuːnjə] **I** *adj.* **1.** junior (*mst nach Familiennamen u. abgekürzt zu Jr., jr., Jun., jun.*): ***George Smith jr.***; ***Smith ~*** Smith II (*von Schülern*); **2.** jünger (*im Amt*), ˈuntergeordnet, zweiter: ***~ clerk*** a) untere(r) Büroangestellte(r), b) zweiter Buchhalter, c) *jur. Brit.* Anwaltspraktikant *m*, d) kleiner Angestellter; ***~ counsel*** (*od.* ***barrister***) *jur. Brit.* → ***barrister*** (*als Vorstufe zum* ***King's Counsel***); ***~ partner*** jüngerer Teilhaber, *fig. der* kleinere Partner; ***~ staff*** untere Angestellte *pl.*; **3.** später, jünger, nachfolgend: ***~ forms*** *ped. Brit. die* Unterklassen, *die* Unterstufe; ***~ school*** *Brit.* Grundschule *f*; **4.** *jur.* rangjünger, (im Rang) nachstehend: ***~ mortgage***; **5.** *sport* Junioren…, Jugend…: ***~ championship***; **6.** *Am.* Kinder…, Jugend…: ***~ books***; **7.** jugendlich, jung: ***~ citizens*** Jungbürger *pl.*; ***~ skin***; **8.** *Am.* F kleiner(er, e, es): ***a ~ hurricane***; **II** *s.* **9.** Jüngere(r *m*) *f*: ***he is my ~ by 2 years***, ***he is 2 years my ~*** er ist (um) 2 Jahre jünger als ich; ***my ~s*** Leute, die jünger sind als ich; **10.** *univ. Am.* Stuˈdent *m* a) *im vorletzten Jahr vor s-r Graduierung*, b) *im 3. Jahr an e-m* ***senior college***, c) *im 1. Jahr an e-m* ***junior college***; **11.** *a.* ♀ (*ohne art*) a) Junior *m* (*Sohn mit dem Vornamen des Vaters*), b) *allg.* der Sohn, der Junge, c) *Am.* F Kleine(r) *m*; **12.** Jugendliche(r *m*) *f*, Herˈanwach-

sende(r *m*) *f*: ***~ miss*** *Am.* ‚junge Dame‘ (*Mädchen*); **13.** ˈUntergeordnete(r *m*) *f* (im Amt), jüngere(r) Angestellte(r): ***he is my ~ in this office*** a) er untersteht mir in diesem Amt, b) er ist in dieses Amt nach mir eingetreten; **14.** *Bridge*: Junior *m* (*Spieler, der rechts vom Alleinspieler sitzt*); **~ col·lege** *s. Am.* Juniˈorencollege *n* (*umfaßt die untersten Hochschuljahrgänge, etwa 16- bis 18jährige Studenten*); **~ high (school)** *s. Am.* (*Art*) Aufbauschule *f* (*für die **high school***) (*dritt- u. viertletzte Klasse der Grundschule u. erste Klasse der **high school***).

jun·ior·i·ty [ˌdʒuːnɪˈɒrətɪ] *s.* **1.** geringeres Alter *od.* Dienstalter; **2.** ˈuntergeordnete Stellung, niedrigerer Rang.

ju·ni·per [ˈdʒuːnɪpə] *s.* Waˈcholder *m.*

junk[1] [dʒʌŋk] **I** *s.* **1.** Trödel *m*, alter Kram, Plunder *m*: ***~ food*** *bsd. Am.* Nahrung *f* mit geringem Nährwert; ***~ market*** Trödel-, Flohmarkt *m*; ***~ dealer*** Trödler *m*, Altwarenhändler *m*; ***~ shop*** Trödelladen *m*; ***~ yard*** Schrottplatz *m*; **2.** *contp.* Schund *m*, ‚Mist‘ *m*, ‚Schrott‘ *m*; **3.** *sl.* ‚Stoff‘ *m* (*Rauschgift*); **II** *v/t.* **4.** *Am.* F a) wegwerfen, b) verschrotten, c) *fig.* zum alten Eisen *od.* über Bord werfen.

junk[2] [dʒʌŋk] *s.* Dschunke *f.*

jun·ket [ˈdʒʌŋkɪt] **I** *s.* **1.** a) Sahnequark *m*, b) Quarkspeise *f* mit Sahne; **2.** Festiviˈtät *f*, Fete *f*; **3.** *Am.* F sogenannte Dienstreise, Vergnügungsreise *f* auf öffentliche Kosten; **II** *v/i.* **4.** feiern, es sich wohl sein lassen.

junk·ie [ˈdʒʌŋkɪ] *s. sl.* ‚Fixer‘ *m*, Rauschgiftsüchtige(r *m*) *f.*

Ju·no·esque [ˌdʒuːnəʊˈesk] *adj.* juˈnonisch.

jun·ta [ˈdʒʌntə] (*Span.*) *s.* **1.** *pol.* (*bsd.* Miliˈtär)Junta *f*; **2.** → **ˈjun·to** [-təʊ] *pl.* **-tos** *s.* Clique *f.*

Ju·pi·ter [ˈdʒuːpɪtə] *s. myth. u. ast.* Jupiter *m.*

Ju·ras·sic [ˌdʒʊəˈræsɪk] *geol.* **I** *adj.* Jura…, juˈrassisch: ***~ period***; **II** *s.* ˈJuraformatiˌon *f.*

ju·rat [ˈdʒʊəræt] *s. Brit.* **1.** *hist.* Stadtrat *m* (*Person*) in den ***Cinque Ports***; **2.** Richter *m auf den Kanalinseln*; **3.** ⚖ Bekräftigungsformel *f* unter eidesstattlichen Erklärungen.

ju·rid·i·cal [ˌdʒʊəˈrɪdɪkl] *adj.* □ **1.** gerichtlich, Gerichts…; **2.** juˈristisch, Rechts…: ***~ person*** *Am.* juristische Person.

ju·ris·dic·tion [ˌdʒʊərɪsˈdɪkʃn] *s.* **1.** Rechtsprechung *f*; **2.** a) Gerichtsbarkeit *f*, b) (*örtliche u. sachliche*) Zuständigkeit (***of, over*** für): ***come under the ~ of*** unter die Zuständigkeit fallen (*gen.*); ***have ~ over*** zuständig sein für; **3.** a) Gerichtsbezirk *m*, b) Zuständigkeitsbereich *m*; **ju·risˈdic·tion·al** [-ʃənl] *adj.* Gerichtsbarkeits…, Zuständigkeits…; **ju·ris·pru·dence** [ˌdʒʊərɪsˈpruːdəns] *s.* Rechtswissenschaft *f*, Jurispruˈdenz *f*; **ju·rist** [ˈdʒʊərɪst] *s.* **1.** Juˈrist(in); **2.** *Brit.* Stuˈdent *m* der Rechte; **3.** *Am.* Rechtsanwalt *m*; **ju·ris·tic, ju·ris·ti·cal** [ˌdʒʊəˈrɪstɪk(l)] *adj.* □ juˈristisch, Rechts…

ju·ror [ˈdʒʊərə] *s.* **1.** ⚖ Geschworene(r *m*) *f*; **2.** Preisrichter(in).

ju·ry[1] [ˈdʒʊərɪ] *s.* **1.** ⚖ *die* Geschworenen *pl.*, Juˈry *f*: ***trial by ~, ~ trial*** Schwurgerichtsverfahren *n*; ***sit on the ~*** Geschworene(r) sein; **2.** Juˈry *f*, Preisrichterausschuß *m*, *sport a.* Kampfgericht *n*; **3.** Sachverständigenausschuß *m.*

ju·ry[2] [ˈdʒʊərɪ] *adj.* ⚓, ✈ Ersatz…, Hilfs…, Not…

ju·ry| box *s.* ⚖ Geschworenenbank *f*; **ˈ~·man** [-mən] *s.* [*irr.*] ⚖ Geschworene(r) *m*; **~ pan·el** *s.* ⚖ Geschworenenliste *f.*

jus [dʒʌs] *pl.* **ju·ra** [ˈdʒʊərə] (*Lat.*) *s.* Recht *n.*

jus·sive [ˈdʒʌsɪv] *adj. ling.* Befehls…, imperaˈtivisch.

just [dʒʌst] **I** *adj.* □ → II *u.* ***justly***; **1.** gerecht (***to*** gegen): ***be ~ to s.o.*** j-n gerecht behandeln; **2.** gerecht, richtig, angemessen, gehörig: ***it was only ~*** es war nur recht u. billig; ***~ reward*** gerechter *od.* (wohl)verdienter Lohn; **3.** rechtmäßig, wohlbegründet: ***a ~ claim***; **4.** berechtigt, gerechtfertigt, (wohl)begründet: ***~ indignation***; **5.** a) genau, korˈrekt, b) wahr, richtig; **6.** *bibl.* gerecht, rechtschaffen: ***the ~*** die Gerechten *pl.*; **7.** ♪ rein; **II** *adv.* **8.** *zeitlich*: a) gerade, (so)ˈeben: ***they have ~ left***; ***~ before I came*** kurz *od.* knapp bevor ich kam; ***~ after breakfast*** kurz *od.* gleich nach dem Frühstück; ***~ now*** eben erst, soeben (→ b), b) genau, gerade (*zu diesem Zeitpunkt*): ***~ as*** gerade als, genau in dem Augenblick als (→ 9); ***I was ~ going to say*** ich wollte gerade sagen; ***~ now*** a) gerade jetzt, b) jetzt gleich (→ a); ***~ then*** a) gerade damals, b) gerade in diesem Augenblick; ***~ five o'clock*** genau fünf Uhr; **9.** *örtlich u. fig.*: genau: ***~ there***; ***~ round the corner*** gleich um die Ecke; ***~ as*** ebenso wie; ***~ as good*** genausogut; ***~ about*** a) (so *od.* in) etwa, b) so ziemlich, c) so gerade, eben (noch); ***~ about here*** ungefähr hier, hier herum; ***~ so!*** ganz recht!; ***that's ~ it!*** das ist es ja gerade *od.* eben!; ***that's ~ like you!*** das sieht dir (ganz) ähnlich!; ***that's ~ what I thought!*** (genau) das hab' ich mir (doch) gedacht!; ***~ what do you mean (by that)?*** was (genau) wollen Sie damit sagen?; ***~ how many are they?*** wie viele sind es genau?; ***it's ~ as well*** (es ist) vielleicht besser *od.* ganz gut so; ***we might ~ as well go!*** da können wir genausogut auch gehen!; **10.** gerade (noch), ganz knapp, mit knapper Not: ***we ~ managed***; ***the bullet ~ missed him*** die Kugel ging ganz knapp an ihm vorbei; ***~ possible*** immerhin möglich, nicht unmöglich; ***~ too late*** gerade zu spät; **11.** nur, lediglich, bloß: ***~ in case*** nur für den Fall; ***~ the two of us*** nur wir beide; ***~ for the fun of it*** nur zum Spaß; ***~ a moment!*** (nur) e-n Augenblick!, *a. iro.* Moment (mal)!; ***~ give her a book*** schenk ihr doch einfach ein Buch; **12.** *vor imp.* a) doch, mal, b) nur: ***~ tell me*** sag (mir) mal, sag mir nur *od.* bloß; ***~ sit down, please!*** setzen Sie sich doch bitte; ***~ think!*** denk mal!; ***~ try!*** versuch's doch (mal)!; **13.** F einfach, wirklich: ***~ wonderful***.

jus·tice [ˈdʒʌstɪs] *s.* **1.** Gerechtigkeit *f* (***to*** gegen); **2.** Rechtmäßigkeit *f*, Berechtigung *f*, Recht *n*: ***with ~*** mit *od.* zu Recht; **3.** Gerechtigkeit *f*, gerechter Lohn: ***do ~ to*** a) *j-m od. e-r Sache* Gerechtigkeit widerfahren lassen, gerecht werden (*dat.*), b) *et.* (recht) zu würdigen wissen, *a. e-r Speise, dem Wein* tüchtig zusprechen; ***the picture did ~ to her beauty*** das Bild wurde ihrer Schönheit gerecht; ***do o.s. ~*** a) sein wahres Können zeigen, b) sich selbst gerecht werden; ***~ was done*** der Gerechtigkeit wurde Genüge getan; ***in ~ to him*** um ihm gerecht zu werden, fairerweise; **4.** ⚖ Gerechtigkeit *f*, Recht *n*, Juˈstiz *f*: ***administer ~*** Recht sprechen; ***flee from ~*** sich der verdienten Strafe (durch die Flucht) entziehen; ***bring to ~*** vor Gericht bringen; ***in ~*** von Rechts wegen; **5.** Richter *m*: ***Mr. ~ X.*** (*Anrede in England*); ***~ of the peace*** Friedensrichter (*Laienrichter*); **ˈjus·tice·ship** [-ʃɪp] *s.* Richteramt *n.*

jus·ti·ci·a·ble [dʒʌˈstɪʃɪəbl] *adj.* ⚖ justiˈabel, gerichtlicher Entscheidung unterˈworfen; **jusˈti·ci·ar·y** [-ɪərɪ] ⚖ **I** *s.* Richter *m*; **II** *adj.* Justiz…, gerichtlich.

jus·ti·fi·a·ble [ˈdʒʌstɪfaɪəbl] *adj.* □ zu rechtfertigen(d), berechtigt, vertretbar, entschuldbar; **ˈjus·ti·fi·a·bly** [-lɪ] *adv.* berechtigterweise.

jus·ti·fi·ca·tion [ˌdʒʌstɪfɪˈkeɪʃn] *s.* **1.** Rechtfertigung *f*: ***in ~ of*** zur Rechtfertigung von (*od. gen.*); **2.** Berechtigung *f*: ***with ~*** berechtigterweise, mit Recht; **3.** *typ.* Justierung *f*, Ausschluß *m*; **jus·ti·fi·ca·to·ry** [ˈdʒʌstɪfɪkeɪtərɪ] *adj.* rechtfertigend, Rechtfertigungs…; **jus·ti·fy** [ˈdʒʌstɪfaɪ] *v/t.* **1.** rechtfertigen (***before*** *od.* ***to s.o.*** vor j-m, j-m gegenüber); ***be justified in doing s.th.*** et. mit gutem Recht tun; ein Recht haben, et. zu tun; berechtigt sein, et. zu tun; **2.** a) gutheißen, b) entschuldigen, c) *j-m* recht geben; **3.** *eccl.* rechtfertigen, von Sündenschuld freisprechen; **4.** ⚙ richtigstellen, richten, justieren; **5.** *typ.* ausschließen.

just·ly [ˈdʒʌstlɪ] *adv.* **1.** richtig; **2.** mit *od.* zu Recht, gerechterweise; **3.** verdientermaßen; **ˈjust·ness** [-tnɪs] *s.* **1.** Gerechtigkeit *f*; **2.** Rechtmäßigkeit *f*; **3.** Richtigkeit *f*; **4.** Genauigkeit *f.*

jut [dʒʌt] **I** *v/i. a.* ***~ out*** vorspringen, herˈausragen: ***~ into s.th.*** in et. hineinragen; **II** *s.* Vorsprung *m.*

jute[1] [dʒuːt] ⚘ Jute *f.*

Jute[2] [dʒuːt] *s.* Jüte *m*; **Jut·land** [ˈdʒʌtlənd] *npr.* Jütland *n*: ***the Battle of ~*** *hist.* die Skagerrakschlacht.

ju·ve·nes·cence [ˌdʒuːvəˈnesns] *s.* **1.** Verjüngung *f*; **2.** Jugend *f.*

ju·ve·nile [ˈdʒuːvənaɪl] **I** *adj.* **1.** jugendlich, jung, Jugend…: ***~ book*** Jugendbuch *n*; ***~ court*** Jugendgericht *n*; ***~ delinquency*** Jugendkriminalität *f*; ***~ delinquent*** *od.* ***offender*** jugendlicher Täter; **II** *s.* **2.** Jugendliche(r *m*) *f*; **3.** *thea.* jugendlicher Liebhaber; **4.** Jugendbuch *n*; **ju·ve·nil·i·a** [ˌdʒuːvəˈnɪlɪə] *pl.* **1.** Jugendwerke *pl.* (*e-s Autors etc.*); **2.** Werke *pl.* für die Jugend; **ju·ve·nil·i·ty** [ˌdʒuːvəˈnɪlətɪ] *s.* **1.** Jugendlichkeit *f*; **2.** jugendlicher Leichtsinn; **3.** *pl.* Kindeˈreien *pl.*; **4.** *coll.* (*die*) Jugend.

jux·ta·pose [ˌdʒʌkstəˈpəʊz] *v/t.* nebeneinˈanderstellen: ***~d to*** angrenzend an (*acc.*); **jux·ta·po·si·tion** [ˌdʒʌkstəpəˈzɪʃn] *s.* Nebeneinˈanderstellung *f*, -liegen *n.*

K

K, k [keɪ] *s.* K *n*, k *n* (*Buchstabe*).
kab·(b)a·la [kəˈbɑːlə] → ***ca(b)bala***.
ka·di [ˈkɑːdɪ] → ***cadi***.
ka·ke·mo·no [ˌkækɪˈməʊnəʊ] *pl.* **-nos** *s.* Kakeˈmono *n* (*japanisches Rollbild*).
kale [keɪl] *s.* **1.** ⚘ Kohl *m*, *bsd.* Grün-, Blattkohl *m*: (***curly***) ~ Krauskohl *m*; **2.** Kohlsuppe *f*; **3.** *Am. sl.* ‚Zaster' *m*.
ka·lei·do·scope [kəˈlaɪdəskəʊp] *s.* Kaleidoˈskop *n* (*a. fig.*); **ka·lei·do·scop·ic, ka·lei·do·scop·i·cal** [kəˌlaɪdəˈskɒpɪk(l)] *adj.* □ kaleidoˈskopisch.
ˈkale·yard *s. Scot.* Gemüsegarten *m*; ~ **school** *s. schottische Heimatdichtung*.
Kan·a·ka [ˈkænəkə, kəˈnækə] *s.* Kaˈnake *m* (*Südseeinsulaner, a. contp.*).
kan·ga·roo [ˌkæŋgəˈruː] *pl.* **-roos** *s. zo.* Känguruh *n*; ~ **court** *s. Am. sl.* **1.** ˈilleˌgales Gericht (*z.B. unter Sträflingen*); **2.** korˈruptes Gericht.
Kant·i·an [ˈkæntɪən] *phls.* **I** *adj.* kantisch; **II** *s.* Kantiˈaner(in).
ka·o·lin(e) [ˈkeɪəlɪn] *s. min.* Kaoˈlin *n*.
ka·ra·te [kəˈrɑːtɪ] *s.* Kaˈrate *n*; ~ **chop** *s.* Kaˈrateschlag *m*.
kar·ma [ˈkɑːmə] *s.* **1.** *Buddhismus etc.*: Karma *n*; **2.** *allg.* Schicksal *n*.
kat·a·bat·ic wind [ˌkætæˈbætɪk] *s.* Fallwind *m*, kataˈbatischer Wind.
kay·ak [ˈkaɪæk] *s.* Kajak *m, n*: ***two-seater*** ~ *sport* Kajakzweier *m*.
kay·o [ˌkeɪˈəʊ] F *für* ***knock out*** *od.* ***knockout***.
ke·bab [kəˈbæb] *s.* Keˈbab *n* (*orientalisches Fleischspießgericht*).
keck [kek] *v/i.* würgen, (sich) erbrechen (müssen).
kedge [kedʒ] ⚓ **I** *v/t.* warpen, verholen; **II** *s. a.* ~ ***anchor*** Wurf-, Warpanker *m*.
kedg·er·ee [ˌkedʒəˈriː] *s. Brit. Ind.* Kedgeˈree *n* (*Reisgericht mit Fisch, Eiern, Zwiebeln etc.*).
keel [kiːl] **I** *s.* **1.** ⚓ Kiel *m*: ***on an even*** ~ im Gleichgewicht, *fig. a.* gleichmäßig, ruhig: ***be on an even ~ again*** *fig.* wieder im Lot sein; **2.** *poet.* Schiff *n*; **3.** Kiel *m*: a) ✈ Längsträger *m*, b) ⚘ Längsrippe *f*; **II** *v/t.* **4.** ~ ***over*** a) (ˈum-)kippen, kentern lassen, b) kielˈoben legen; **III** *v/i.* **5.** ~ ***over*** ˈumschlagen, -kippen (*a. fig.*), kentern; kielˈoben liegen; **6.** F ‚umkippen' (*Person etc.*); **ˈkeel·age** [-lɪdʒ] *s.* ⚓ Kielgeld *n*, Hafengebühren *pl.*; **ˈkeel·haul** *v/t.* **1.** *j-n* kielholen; **2.** *fig.* *j-n* ‚zs.-stauchen'; **keel·son** [ˈkelsn] → ***kelson***.
keen[1] [kiːn] *adj.* □ → ***keenly***; **1.** scharf (geschliffen): ~ ***edge*** scharfe Schneide; **2.** scharf (*Wind*), schneidend (*Kälte*); **3.** beißend (*Spott*); **4.** scharf, ˈdurchdringend: ~ ***glance*** (***smell***); **5.** grell (*Licht*), schrill (*Ton*); **6.** heftig, stark (*Schmerzen*); **7.** scharf (*Augen*), fein (*Sinne*): ***be ~-eyed*** (***~-eared***) scharfe Augen (ein feines Gehör) haben; **8.** fein, ausgeprägt (*Gefühl*; ***of*** für): ***a ~ sense of literature***; **9.** heftig, stark, groß (*Freude etc.*): ~ ***desire*** heftiges Verlangen, heißer Wunsch; ~ ***interest*** starkes *od.* lebhaftes Interesse; ~ ***competition*** scharfe Konkurrenz; **10.** *a.* ***~-witted*** scharfsinnig; ***a ~ mind*** ein scharfer Verstand; **11.** eifrig, begeistert, leidenschaftlich: ***a ~ swimmer***; ~ ***on*** begeistert von, sehr interessiert an (*dat.*); ***he is ~ on dancing*** er ist ein begeisterter Tänzer; ***he is very ~*** F er ist ‚schwer auf Draht'; ***you shouldn't be too ~!*** du solltest dich etwas zurückhalten!; (→ *a.* 13); **12.** (stark) interessiert (*Bewerber etc.*); **13.** F erpicht, versessen, ‚scharf' (***on, about*** auf *acc.*): ***he is ~ on doing*** (*od.* ***to do***) ***it*** er ist sehr darauf erpicht *od.* scharf darauf, es zu tun, es liegt ihm (sehr) viel daran, es zu tun; ***I am not ~ on it*** ich habe wenig Lust dazu, ich mache mir nichts daraus, es liegt mir nichts daran, ich lege keinen (gesteigerten) Wert darauf; ***I am not ~ on sweets*** ich mag keine Süßigkeiten; ***I am not ~ on that idea*** ich bin nicht gerade begeistert von dieser Idee; ***as ~ as mustard*** (***on***) F ganz versessen (auf *acc.*), Feuer u. Flamme (für); **14.** *Brit.* F niedrig, gut: ~ ***prices***; **15.** *Am.* F ‚prima', ‚prächtig'.
keen[2] [kiːn] *Ir.* **I** *s.* Totenklage *f*; **II** *v/i.* wehklagen; **III** *v/t.* beklagen.
ˌkeen-ˈedged *adj.* **1.** → ***keen***[1] 1; **2.** *fig.* messerscharf.
keen·ly [ˈkiːnlɪ] *adv.* **1.** scharf (*etc.* → ***keen***[1]); **2.** ungemein, äußerst, sehr; **ˈkeen·ness** [-nnɪs] *s.* **1.** Schärfe *f* (*a. fig.*); **2.** Heftigkeit *f*; **3.** Eifer *m*, starkes Interˈesse, Begeisterung *f*; **4.** Scharfsinn *m*; **5.** Feinheit *f*; **6.** *fig.* Bitterkeit *f*.
keep [kiːp] **I** *s.* **1.** a) Burgverlies *n*, b) Bergfried *m*; **2.** a) (ˈLebens)ˌUnterhalt *m*, b) ˈUnterkunft *f* u. Verpflegung *f*: ***earn one's ~*** s-n Lebensunterhalt verdienen; **3.** ˈUnterhaltskosten *pl.*: ***the ~ of a horse***; **4.** Obhut *f*, Verwahrung *f*; **5.** ***for ~s*** F auf *od.* für immer, endgültig; **II** *v/t.* [*irr.*] **6.** (be)halten, haben: ~ ***the ticket in your hand*** behalte die Karte in der Hand!; ***he kept his hands in his pockets*** er hatte die Hände in den Taschen; **7.** *j-n od. et.* lassen, (*in e-m gewissen Zustand*) (er)halten: ~ ***apart*** getrennt halten, auseinanderhalten; ~ ***a door closed*** e-e Tür geschlossen halten; ~ ***s.th. dry*** et. trocken halten *od.* vor Nässe schützen; ~ ***s.o. from doing s.th.*** j-n davon abhalten, et. zu tun; ~ ***s.th. to o.s.*** et. für sich behalten; ~ ***s.o. informed*** j-n auf dem laufenden halten; ~ ***s.o. waiting*** j-n warten lassen; ~ ***s.th. going*** et. in Gang halten; ~ ***s.o. going*** a) j-n finanziell unterstützen, b) j-n am Leben erhalten; ~ ***s.th. a secret*** et. geheimhalten (***from s.o.*** vor j-m); **8.** *fig.* (er)halten, (be)wahren: ~ ***one's balance*** das *od.* sein Gleichgewicht (be)halten *od.* wahren; ~ ***one's distance*** Abstand halten *od.* bewahren; **9.** (*im Besitz*) behalten: ***you may ~ the book***; ~ ***the change!*** behalten Sie den Rest (*des Geldes*)!; ~ ***your seat!*** bleiben Sie (doch) sitzen!; **10.** *fig.* halten, sich halten *od.* behaupten in *od.* auf (*dat.*): ~ ***the stage*** sich auf der Bühne behaupten; **11.** *j-n* auf-, ˈhinhalten: ***don't let me ~ you!*** laß dich nicht aufhalten!; **12.** (fest)halten, bewachen: ~ ***s.o.*** (***a***) ***prisoner*** (*od.* ***in prison***) j-n gefangenhalten; ~ ***s.o. for lunch*** j-n zum Mittagessen dabehalten; ***she ~s him here*** sie hält ihn hier fest, er bleibt ihretwegen hier; ~ (***the***) ***goal*** *sport* das Tor hüten, im Tor stehen; **13.** aufheben, (auf)bewahren: ***I ~ all my old letters***; ~ ***a secret*** ein Geheimnis bewahren; ~ ***for a later date*** für später *od.* für e-n späteren Zeitpunkt aufheben; **14.** (aufrechter)halten, unterˈhalten: ~ ***an eye on s.o.*** j-n im Auge behalten; ~ ***good relations with s.o.*** zu j-m gute Beziehungen unterhalten; **15.** pflegen, (er)halten: ~ ***in*** (***good***) ***repair*** in gutem Zustand erhalten; ***a well-kept garden*** ein gutgepflegter Garten; **16.** *e-e Ware* führen, auf Lager haben: ***we don't ~ this article***; **17.** *Schriftstücke* führen, halten: ~ ***a diary***; ~ (***the***) ***books*** Buch führen; ~ ***a record of s.th.*** über (*acc.*) et. Buch führen *od.* Aufzeichnungen machen; **18.** *ein Geschäft etc.* führen, verwalten, vorstehen (*dat.*): ~ ***a shop*** ein (Laden)Geschäft führen *od.* betreiben; **19.** *ein Amt etc.* innehaben: ~ ***a post***; **20.** *Am. e-e Versammlung etc.* (ab)halten: ~ ***an assembly***; **21.** *ein Versprechen etc.* (ein)halten, einlösen: ~ ***a promise***; ~ ***an appointment*** e-e Verabredung einhalten; **22.** *das Bett, Haus, Zimmer* hüten, bleiben in (*dat.*): ~ ***one's bed*** (***house, room***); **23.** *Vorschriften etc.* be(ob)achten, (ein)halten, befolgen: ~ ***the rules***; **24.** *ein Fest* begehen, feiern: ~ ***Christmas***; **25.** ernähren, er-, unterˈhalten, sorgen für: ***have a family to ~***; **26.** (*bei sich*) haben, halten, beherbergen: ~ ***boarders***; **27.** sich halten *od.* zulegen: ~ ***a maid*** ein Hausmädchen haben *od.* (sich) halten;

a kept woman e-e Mätresse; ***~ a car*** sich e-n Wagen halten, ein Auto haben; **28.** (be)schützen: ***God ~ you!***; **III** *v/i.* [*irr.*] **29.** bleiben: ***~ in bed***; ***~ at home***; ***~ in sight*** in Sicht(weite) bleiben; ***~ out of danger*** sich außer Gefahr halten; ***~*** (***to the***) ***left*** sich links halten, links fahren *od.* gehen; ***~ straight on*** (immer) geradeaus gehen; → ***clear*** 6; **30.** sich halten, (*in e-m gewissen Zustand*) bleiben: ***~ cool*** kühl bleiben (*a. fig.*); ***~ quiet!*** sei still!; ***~ to o.s.*** für sich bleiben, sich zurückhalten; ***~ friends*** (weiterhin) Freunde bleiben: ***~ in good health*** gesund bleiben; ***the milk*** (***weather***) ***will ~*** die Milch (das Wetter) wird sich halten; ***the weather ~s fine*** das Wetter bleibt schön; ***that*** (***matter***) ***will ~*** F diese Sache hat Zeit *od.* eilt nicht; ***how are you ~ing?*** wie geht es dir?; **31.** *mit ger.* weiter…: ***~ going*** a) weitergehen, b) weitermachen; ***~*** (***on***) ***laughing*** weiterlachen, nicht aufhören zu lachen, dauernd *od.* unaufhörlich lachen; ***~ smiling!*** immer nur lächeln!, Kopf hoch!

Zssgn mit prp. u. adv.:

keep| a·head *v/i.* an der Spitze *od.* vorn(e) bleiben: ***~ of j-m*** vorausbleiben; **~ at** *v/i.* **1.** weitermachen mit: ***~ it!*** bleib dran!, weiter so!; **2.** ***~ s.o.*** j-n nicht in Ruhe lassen, j-m ständig zusetzen, j-n dauernd ‚bearbeiten'; **~ a·way I** *v/i.* wegbleiben, sich fernhalten (***from*** von); im Hintergrund bleiben; **II** *v/t.* fernhalten (***from*** von); **~ back I** *v/t.* **1.** *allg.* zurückhalten: a) fernhalten, b) *fig. Geld etc.* einbehalten, c) *et.* verschweigen (***from s.o.*** j-m); **2.** *j-n, et.* aufhalten; *et.* verzögern; *Schüler* dabehalten; **II** *v/i.* **3.** im Hintergrund bleiben; **~ down I** *v/t.* **1.** unten halten, *Kopf a.* ducken; **2.** *fig. Preise etc.* niedrig halten, be-, einschränken; **3.** *fig.* nicht auf- *od.* hochkommen lassen, unter'drükken; **4.** *Essen etc.* bei sich behalten; **5.** *Schüler* (eine Klasse) wiederholen lassen; **II** *v/i.* **6.** unten bleiben; **7.** sich geduckt halten; **~ from I** *v/t.* **1.** ab-, zu'rück-, fernhalten von, hindern an (*dat.*), bewahren vor (*dat.*): ***he kept me from work*** er hielt mich von m-r Arbeit ab; ***he kept me from danger*** er bewahrte mich vor Gefahr; ***I kept him from knowing too much*** ich verhinderte, daß er zuviel erfuhr; **2.** vorenthalten, verschweigen: ***you are keeping s.th. from me*** du verschweigst mir et.; **II** *v/i.* **3.** sich fernhalten von, sich enthalten (*gen.*), *et.* unterlassen *od.* nicht tun: ***I couldn't ~ laughing*** ich mußte einfach lachen; **~ in I** *v/t.* **1.** nicht außer Haus lassen, *bsd. Schüler* nachsitzen lassen; **2.** *Gefühle etc.* im Zaume halten; **3.** *Feuer* nicht ausgehen lassen; **4.** *Bauch* einziehen; **II** *v/i.* **5.** (dr)innen bleiben; **6.** anbleiben (*Feuer*); **7.** ***~ with*** gut Freund bleiben mit, sich gut stellen mit; **~ off I** *v/t.* fernhalten (von); *die Hände* weglassen (von); **II** *v/i.* sich fernhalten (von), *a. Getränk etc.* meiden: ***if the rain keeps off*** wenn es nicht regnet; ***~ the grass!*** Betreten des Rasens verboten; **~ on I** *v/t.* **1.** *Kleider* anbehalten; *Hut* aufbehalten; **2.** *Angestellte etc.* behalten, weiterbeschäftigen; **II** *v/i.* **3.** *mit ger.* weiter…: ***~ doing s.th.*** a) *et.* weiter tun, b) *et.* immer wieder tun, c) *et.* dauernd tun; → ***keep*** 31; **4.** ***~ at s.o.*** an j-m her'umnörgeln, auf j-n ‚einhacken'; **5.** weitergehen *od.* -fahren: ***keep straight on!*** immer geradeaus!; **~ out I** *v/t.* **1.** nicht her'einlassen, abhalten: ***~ s.o.*** (***the light*** *etc.*); **2.** schützen *od.* bewahren vor (*dat.*), *j-n a.* her'aushalten aus (*e-r Sache*); **II** *v/i.* **3.** draußen bleiben, nicht her'einkommen, *Zimmer etc.* nicht betreten: ***~!*** a) bleib draußen!, b) „Zutritt verboten"; **4.** ***~ of*** sich her'aushalten aus, *et.* meiden: ***~ of debt*** keine Schulden machen; ***~ of sight*** sich nicht sehen lassen; ***~ of mischief!*** mach keine Dummheiten!; ***you ~ of this!*** halten Sie sich da raus!; **~ to I** *v/t.* **1.** ***keep s.o. to his promise*** j-n auf sein Versprechen festnageln; ***keep s.th. to a minimum*** et. auf ein Minimum beschränken; **2.** ***keep o.s. to o.s.*** für sich bleiben, Gesellschaft meiden; **II** *v/i.* **3.** festhalten an (*dat.*), bleiben bei: ***~ one's word***; ***~ the rules*** an den Regeln festhalten, die Vorschriften einhalten; ***~ the subject*** (*od.* ***point***) bleiben Sie beim Thema!; **4.** bleiben in (*dat.*) *od.* auf (*acc.*) *etc.*: ***~ one's bed*** (*od.* ***room***) im Bett (in s-m Zimmer) bleiben; ***~ the left!*** halten Sie sich links!; ***~ o.s.*** → 2; **~ to·geth·er I** *v/t.* zu'sammenhalten; **II** *v/i.* a) zu'sammenbleiben, b) zu'sammenhalten (*Freunde etc.*); **~ un·der** *v/t.* **1.** *j-n* unter'drükken, unten halten: ***you won't keep him under*** den kriegst du nicht klein; **2.** *j-n* unter Nar'kose halten; **3.** *Gefühle* unter'drücken, zügeln; **4.** *Feuer* unter Kon'trolle halten; **~ up I** *v/t.* **1.** aufrecht (*a.* über Wasser) halten, hochhalten; **2.** *fig. Freundschaft, Moral etc.* aufrechterhalten, *Preise etc. a.* hoch halten, *et.* beibehalten, *Sitte etc.* weiterpflegen, *Tempo etc.* halten: ***~ a correspondence*** in Briefwechsel bleiben; ***~ it up!*** (nur) weiter so!; **3.** *Haus etc.* unter'halten, in'stand halten; **4.** *j-n* am Schlafen (-gehen) hindern; **II** *v/i.* **5.** andauern, -halten, nicht nachlassen; **6.** *lange etc.* aufbleiben: ***we ~ late***; **7.** ***~ with*** a) mit *j-m od. et.* Schritt halten, *fig. a.* mithalten (können), b) *j-m, e-r Sache* folgen können, c) sich auf dem laufenden halten über (*acc.*), d) in Kon'takt bleiben mit *j-m*: ***~ with the times*** mit der Zeit gehen; ***~ with the Joneses*** den Nachbarn nicht nachstehen wollen.

keep·er ['ki:pə] *s.* **1.** Wächter *m*, Aufseher *m*, (Gefangenen-, Irren-, Tier-, Park-, Leuchtturm)Wärter *m*, Betreuer (-in): ***am I my brother's ~?*** *bibl.* soll ich m-s Bruders Hüter sein?; **2.** Verwahrer *m*, Verwalter *m*: ***Lord ♀ of the Great Seal*** Großsiegelbewahrer *m*; **3.** *mst in Zssgn*: a) Inhaber(in), Besitzer (-in): → ***innkeeper*** *etc.*, b) Halter(in), Züchter(in): → ***beekeeper***, c) j-d, der et. besorgt, betreut *od.* verteidigt: (***goal***) ***~*** *sport* Torwart *m*; **4.** ⚙ a) Schutzring *m*, b) Verschluß *m*, Schieber *m*, c) ϟ Ma'gnetanker *m*; **5.** ***be a good ~*** sich gut halten (*Obst, Fisch etc.*); **6.** *sport abbr. für* ***wicket-~***.

ˌkeep-'fresh bag *s.* Frischhaltebeutel *m*.

keep·ing ['ki:pɪŋ] **I** *s.* **1.** Verwahrung *f*, Aufsicht *f*, Pflege *f*, (Ob)Hut *f*: ***in safe ~*** in guter Obhut, sicher verwahrt; ***have in one's ~*** in Verwahrung *od.* unter s-r Obhut haben; ***put s.th. in s.o.'s ~*** j-m et. zur Aufbewahrung geben; **2.** 'Unterhalt *m*; **3.** ***be in*** (***out of***) ***~ with*** mit et. (nicht) in Einklang stehen *od.* (nicht) übereinstimmen, *e-r Sache* (nicht) entsprechen; ***in ~ with the times*** zeitgemäß; **4.** Gewahrsam *m*, Haft *f*; **II** *adj.* **5.** haltbar: ***~ apples*** Winteräpfel.

keep·sake ['ki:pseɪk] *s.* Andenken *n* (*Geschenk etc.*): ***as*** (*od.* ***for***) ***a ~*** zum Andenken.

kef·ir ['kefɪə] *s.* Kefir *m* (*Getränk aus gegorener Milch*).

keg [keg] *s.* **1.** kleines Faß, Fäßchen *n*; **2.** *Brit.* (Alu'minium)Behälter *m* für Bier: ***~*** (***beer***) Bier *n* vom Faß; **3.** *Am. Gewichtseinheit für Nägel = 45,3 kg.*

kelp [kelp] *s.* ⚘ **1.** *ein* Seetang *m*; **2.** Kelp *n*, Seetangasche *f*.

kel·pie ['kelpɪ] *s. Scot.* Nix *m*, Wassergeist *m* in Pferdegestalt.

kel·son ['kelsn] *s.* ⚓ Kielschwein *n*.

kel·vin ['kelvɪn] *s. phys.* Kelvin *n*: ***~ temperature*** Kelvintemperatur *f*, thermody'namische Temperatur.

Kelt·ic ['keltɪk] → ***Celtic***.

ken [ken] **I** *s.* **1.** Gesichtskreis *m*, *fig. a.* Hori'zont *m*: ***that is beyond*** (*od.* ***outside***) ***my ~*** das entzieht sich m-r Kenntnis; **2.** (Wissens)Gebiet *n*; **II** *v/t.* **3.** *bsd. Scot.* kennen, verstehen, wissen.

ken·nel ['kenl] **I** *s.* **1.** Hundehütte *f*; **2.** *pl. mst sg. konstr.* a) Hundezwinger *m*, b) Hunde-, Tierheim *n*; **3.** *a. fig.* Meute *f*, Pack *n* (*Hunde*); **4.** *fig.* ‚Loch' *n*, armselige Behausung; **II** *v/t.* **5.** in e-r Hundehütte *od.* in e-m (Hunde)Zwinger halten.

Ken·tuck·y Der·by [ken'tʌkɪ] *s. sport das wichtigste amer. Pferderennen* (*für Dreijährige*).

kep·i ['keɪpi:] *s.* ⚔ Käppi *n*.

kept [kept] **I** *pret. u. p.p. von* ***keep***; **II** *adj.*: ***~ woman*** Mä'tresse *f*; ***she is a ~ woman*** *a.* sie läßt sich aushalten.

kerb [kɜ:b] *s.* **1.** Bord-, Randstein *m*, Bord-, Straßenkante *f*: ***~ drill*** Verkehrserziehung *f* für Fußgänger; **2.** ***on the ~*** † im Freiverkehr; ***~ mar·ket*** † Freiverkehrsmarkt *m*, Nachbörse *f*: ***~ price*** Freiverkehrskurs *m*; **'~-stone** → ***kerb*** 1: ***~ broker*** Freiverkehrsmakler *m*.

ker·chief ['kɜ:tʃɪf] *s.* Hals-, Kopftuch *n*.

ker·fuf·fle [kə'fʌfl] *s. Brit.* F **1.** Lärm *m*, Krach *m*; **2.** *a.* ***fuss and ~*** ‚The'ater' *n*, ‚Gedöns' *n*.

ker·mess ['kɜ:mɪs], **'ker·mis** [-mɪs] *s.* **1.** Kirmes *f*, Kirchweih *f*; **2.** *Am.* 'Wohltätigkeitsbaˌsar *m*.

ker·nel ['kɜ:nl] *s.* **1.** (Nuß- *etc.*)Kern *m*; **2.** (Hafer-, Mais- *etc.*)Korn *n*; **3.** *fig.* Kern *m*, *das* Innerste, Wesen *n*; **4.** ⚙ (*Guß- etc.*)Kern *m*.

ker·o·sene, **ker·o·sine** ['kerəsi:n] *s.* ⚗ Kero'sin *n*.

kes·trel ['kestrəl] *s.* Turmfalke *m*.

ketch [ketʃ] *s.* ⚓ Ketsch *f* (*zweimastiger Segler*).

ketch·up ['ketʃəp] *s.* Ketchup *m, n*.

ket·tle ['ketl] *s.* (*Koch*)Kessel *m*: ***put the ~ on*** (Tee- *etc.*)Wasser aufstellen; ***a pretty*** (*od.* ***nice***) ***~ of fish*** F e-e schöne Bescherung; **'~·drum** *s.* ♪ (Kessel)Pauke *f*; ˈ**~ˌdrum·mer** *s.* ♪ (Kessel)Pauker *m.*

key [kiː] **I** *s.* **1.** Schlüssel *m*: ***false ~*** Nachschlüssel *m*, Dietrich *m*; ***power of the ~s*** *R.C.* Schlüsselgewalt *f*; ***turn the ~*** abschließen; **2.** *fig.* Schlüssel *m*, Lösung *f* (***to*** zu): ***the ~ to a problem*** (***riddle*** *etc.*); ***the ~ to success*** der Schlüssel zum Erfolg; **3.** *fig.* Schlüssel *m*: a) *Buch mit Lösungen*, b) Zeichenerklärung *f* (*auf e-r Landkarte etc.*), c) Übersetzung(sschlüssel *m*) *f*, d) Code (-schlüssel) *m*; **4.** Kennwort *n*, Chiffre *f* (*in Inseraten etc.*); **5.** ♪ a) Taste *f*, b) Klappe *f* (*an Blasinstrumenten*), c) Tonart *f*: ***major*** (***minor***) ***~*** Dur *n* (Moll *n*); ***in the ~ of C minor*** in c-Moll; ***sing off ~*** falsch singen; ***in ~ with*** *fig.* in Einklang mit, d) → ***key signature***; **6.** *fig.* Ton(art *f*) *m*: ***in a high*** (***low***) ***~*** laut (leise); ***all in the same ~*** alles im selben Ton(fall), monoton; ***in a low ~*** a) *paint. phot.* matt (getönt), in matten Farben (gehalten), b) *fig.* ‚lahm', ‚müde'; **7.** ⚙ a) Keil *m*, Splint *m*, Bolzen *m*, b) Schraubenschlüssel *m*, c) Taste *f* (*der Schreibmaschine etc.*); **8.** ⚡ a) Taste *f*, Druckknopf *m*, b) Taster *m*, ˈTastkonˌtakt *m*; **9.** *tel.* Taster *m*, Geber *m*; **10.** *typ.* Setz-, Schließkeil *m*; **11.** △ Keil *m*, Schlußstein *m*; **12.** ⚔ Schlüsselstellung *f*, Macht *f* (***to*** über *acc.*); **II** *adj.* **13.** *fig.* Schlüssel…: ***~ position*** Schlüsselstellung *f*, -position *f*; ***~ official*** Beamter in e-r Schlüsselstellung; **III** *v/t.* **14.** *a.* ***~ in***, ***~ on*** ver-, festkeilen; **15.** a) *tel.* tasten, geben, b) *Computer etc.*: tasten: ***~ in*** eintasten, -geben; **16.** ♪ stimmen: ***~ the strings***; **17.** (***to***, ***for***) anpassen (an *acc.*), abstimmen (auf *acc.*); **18.** *fig.*: ***~ up*** a) *j-n* in nervöse Spannung versetzen, b) *allg. et.* steigern: ***~ed up*** (an)gespannt, überreizt, ‚überdreht'; **19.** mit e-m Kennwort versehen; ˈ**~·board I** *s.* **1.** ♪ a) Klaviaˈtur *f*, Tastaˈtur *f* (*Klavier*), b) Manuˈal *n* (*Orgel*): ***~ instruments***, ***~s*** *pl.* Tasteninstrumente; **2.** Tasten *pl.*, Tastaˈtur *f* (*Schreibmaschine etc.*); **II** *v/t.* **3.** *Computer etc.*: eintasten, -geben; **~ bu·gle** *s.* ♪ Klappenhorn *n*; **~ date** *s.* Stichtag *m*; **~ fos·sil** *s. geol.* ˈLeitfosˌsil *n*; ˈ**~·hole** *s.* **1.** Schlüsselloch *n*: ***~ report*** *fig.* Bericht *m* mit intimen Einzelheiten; **2.** *Am.* F *Basketball*: Freiwurfraum *m*; **~ in·dus·try** *s.* ˈSchlüsselinduˌstrie *f*; **~ man**, *a.* ˈ**~·man** [-mæn] *s.* [*irr.*] ˈSchlüsselfiˌgur *f*, Mann *m* in e-r ˈSchlüsselposiˌtiˌon; **~ map** *s.* ˈÜbersichtskarte *f*; **~ mon·ey** *s.* Abstandssumme *f*, (ˈMiet-)Kautiˌon *f*; ˈ**~·move** *s. Schach*: Schlüsselzug *m*; ˈ**~·note I** *s.* **1.** ♪ Grundton *m*; **2.** *fig.* Grundton *m*, -gedanke *m*, Leitgedanke *m*, Hauptthema *n*; **3.** *pol. Am.* Parˈteilinie *f*, -proˌgramm *n*: ***~ address*** programmatische Rede; ***~ speaker*** → ***keynoter***; **II** *v/t.* **4.** *pol. Am.* a) e-e programˈmatische Rede halten auf (*e-m Parteitag etc.*), b) programˈmatisch verkünden, c) als Grundgedanken enthalten; **5.** kennzeichnen; ˈ**~ˌnot·er** *s. pol. Am.* Hauptsprecher *m*, poˈlitischer Proˈgrammredner *m*; **~ punch** *s.* ⚙ (Karten-, Tastaˈtur)Locher *m*; ˈ**~-punch op·er·a·tor** *s.* Locher(in); **~ ring** *s.* Schlüsselring *m*; **~ sig·na·ture** *s.* ♪ Vorzeichen *n od. pl.*; ˈ**~·stone** *s.* **1.** △ Schlußstein *m*; **2.** *fig.* Grundpfeiler *m*, Fundaˈment *n*; **~ stroke** *s.* Anschlag *m*; ˈ**~·way** *s.* ⚙ Keilnut *f*; **~ wit·ness** *s.* ⚖ Hauptzeuge *m*; **~ word** *s.* Schlüssel-, Stichwort *n*.

kha·ki [ˈkɑːkɪ] **I** *s.* **1.** Khaki *n*; **2.** a) Khakistoff *m*, b) ˈKhakiuniˌform *f*; **II** *adj.* **3.** khaki, staubfarben.

khan¹ [kɑːn] → ***caravansary***.

khan² [kɑːn] *s.* Khan *m* (*orientalischer Fürstentitel*); ˈ**khan·ate** [-neɪt] *s.* Khaˈnat *n* (*Land e-s Khans*).

khe·dive [kɪˈdiːv] *s.* Kheˈdive *m*.

kib·butz [kiːˈbuːts] *pl.* **kibˈbutz·im** [-tsɪm] *s.* Kibˈbuz *m*.

khi [kaɪ] *s.* Chi *n* (*griech. Buchstabe*).

kibe [kaɪb] *s.* ⚕ offene Frostbeule.

kib·itz [ˈkɪbɪts] *v/i.* ‚kiebitzen'; ˈ**kib·itz·er** [-tsə] *s.* F **1.** Kiebitz *m* (*Zuschauer*, *bsd. beim Kartenspiel*); **2.** *fig.* Besserwisser *m*.

ki·bosh [ˈkaɪbɒʃ] *s.*: ***put the ~ on*** *sl. et.* ‚kaˈputtmachen' *od.* ‚vermasseln'.

kick [kɪk] **I** *s.* **1.** (Fuß)Tritt *m* (*a. fig.*), Stoß *m*: ***give*** *s.o. od. s.th.* ***a ~*** → 9; ***get the ~*** ‚(raus)fliegen' (*entlassen werden*); ***what he needs is a ~ in the pants*** er braucht mal e-n kräftigen Tritt in den Hintern; **2.** Rückstoß *m* (*Schußwaffe*); **3.** *Fußball*: Schuß *m*; **4.** *Schwimmen*: Beinschlag *m*; **5.** F (Stoß)Kraft *f*, Enerˈgie *f*, Eˈlan *m*: ***give a ~ to*** *et.* in Schwung bringen, *e-r Sache* ‚Pfiff' verleihen; ***he has no ~ left*** er hat keinen Schwung mehr; ***a novel with a ~*** ein Roman mit ‚Pfiff'; **6.** F (Nerven)Kitzel *m*: ***get a ~ out of s.th.*** an et. mächtig Spaß haben; ***just for ~s*** nur zum Spaß; **7.** (*berauschende*) Wirkung: ***this cocktail has got a ~*** der Cocktail ‚hat es aber in sich'; **8.** *Am.* F a) Groll *m*, b) (Grund *m* zur) Beschwerde *f*; **II** *v/t.* **9.** (mit dem Fuß) stoßen *od.* treten, e-n Fußtritt versetzen (*dat.*): ***~ s.o.'s behind*** j-m in den Hintern treten; ***~ s.o. downstairs*** j-n die Treppe hinunterwerfen; ***~ upstairs*** *fig. j-n* durch Beförderung kaltstellen; ***I felt like ~ing myself*** ich hätte mich ohrfeigen können; **10.** *sport* a) *Ball* treten, kicken, b) *Tor*, *Freistoß etc.* schießen: ***~ a goal***; **11.** *sl.* ‚runterkommen' von (*e-m Rauschgift*, *e-r Gewohnheit*); **III** *v/i.* **12.** (mit dem Fuß) stoßen *od.* treten: ***~ at*** treten nach; **13.** um sich treten; **14.** strampeln (*bsd. Baby*); **15.** das Bein hochwerfen (*Tänzer*); **16.** ausschlagen (*Pferd*); **17.** zuˈrückstoßen, -prallen (*Schußwaffe*); **18.** *mot.* ‚stottern'; **19.** F a) ‚meutern', sich mit Händen u. Füßen wehren, (***against***, ***at*** gegen), b) ‚meckern', nörgeln (***about*** über *acc.*); **20.** → ***kick off*** 3; ***~ a·bout*** *od.* ***~ a·round*** **I** *v/t.* **1.** *Ball* heˈrumkicken; **2.** F *j-n* heˈrumstoßen, schikanieren; **3.** F a) *Idee etc.* ‚beschwatzen', diskutieren, b) ‚spielen' *od.* sich befassen mit; **II** *v/i.* **4.** F herˈumreisen; **5.** F ‚rumliegen' (*Sache*); ***~ in*** **I** *v/t.* **1.** *Tür etc.* eintreten; **2.** *sl.* beisteuern; **II** *v/i.* **3.** *sl.* beisteuern; ***~ off*** **I** *v/i.* **1.** *Fußball*: anstoßen, den Anstoß ausführen; **2.** F loslegen (***with*** mit); **3.** *Am. sl.* ‚abkratzen' (*sterben*); **II** *v/t.* **4.** wegschleudern; **5.** F *et.* starten, in Gang setzen; ***~ out*** *v/t.* **1.** *Fußball*: ins Aus schießen; **2.** *sl.* ‚rausschmeißen'; ***~ up*** *v/t.* hochschleudern; *Staub* aufwirbeln; → ***heel¹*** *Redew.*, ***row³*** I.

ˈ**kick·back** *s.* **1.** F heftige Reaktiˈon; **2.** *Am. sl.* a) *allg.* Provisiˈon *f*, Anteil *m*, b) (geheime) Rückvergütung *f*, c) Schmiergeld *n*.

ˈ**kick·down** *s. mot.* Kickdown *m* (*Durchtreten des Gaspedals*).

kick·er [ˈkɪkə] *s.* **1.** (Aus)Schläger *m* (*Pferd*); **2.** *Brit.* a) Kicker *m*, Fußballspieler *m*, b) *Rugby*: Kicker *m* (*Spezialist für Frei- und Strafstöße*); **3.** ‚Meckerer' *m*, Queruˈlant(in).

ˈ**kick|·off** *s.* **1.** *Fußball*: Anstoß *m*; **2.** F Start *m*, Anfang *m*; ˈ**~-start** *v/t. mot.* anlassen; ˈ**~-ˌstart·er** *s. mot.* Kickstarter *m*, Tretanlasser *m*; **~ turn** *s. Skisport*: Spitzkehre *f*.

kid¹ [kɪd] **I** *s.* **1.** *zo.* Zicklein *n*, Kitz(e *f*) *n*; **2.** *a.* ***~ leather*** Ziegen-, Glaˈcéleder *n*; → ***kid glove***; **3.** F ‚Kleine(r' *m*) *f*, Kind *n*, Junge *m*, Mädchen *n*: ***my ~ brother*** mein kleiner Bruder; ***that's ~ stuff!*** das ist was für (kleine) Kinder!; **II** *v/i.* **4.** zickeln.

kid² [kɪd] F **I** *v/t. j-n* a) ‚verkohlen', b) ‚aufziehen', ‚auf den Arm nehmen': ***don't ~ me*** erzähl mir doch keine Märchen; ***don't ~ yourself*** mach dir doch nichts vor; **II** *v/i.* a) albern, Jux machen, b) schwindeln: ***he was only ~ding*** er hat (ja) nur Spaß gemacht; ***no ~ding!*** im Ernst!, ehrlich!; ***you are ~ding!*** das sagst du doch nur so!

kid·dy [ˈkɪdɪ] → ***kid¹*** 3.

kid| glove *s.* Glaˈcéhandschuh *m* (*a. fig.*): ***handle with ~s*** *fig.* mit Samt- *od.* Glacéhandschuhen anfassen; ˈ**~-glove** *adj. fig.* **1.** anspruchsvoll, wählerisch; **2.** sanft, diploˈmatisch.

kid·nap [ˈkɪdnæp] *v/t.* kidnappen, entführen; ˈ**kid·nap·(p)er** [-pə] *s.* Kidnapper(in), Entführer(in); ˈ**kid·nap·(p)ing** [-pɪŋ] *s.* Kidnapping *n*, Entführung *f*, Menschenraub *m*.

kid·ney [ˈkɪdnɪ] *s.* **1.** *anat.* Niere *f* (*a. als Speise*); **2.** *fig.* Art *f*, Schlag *m*, Sorte *f*: ***a man of the same ~*** ein Mann vom gleichen Schlag; **~ bean** *s.* ⚘ Weiße Bohne; **~ ma·chine** *s.* ⚕ künstliche Niere; ˈ**~-shaped** *adj.* nierenförmig; **~ stone** *s.* ⚕ Nierenstein *m*.

kill [kɪl] **I** *v/t.* **1.** (***o.s.*** sich) töten, ˈumbringen: ***~ off*** abschlachten, ausrotten, vertilgen, beseitigen, ‚abmurksen'; ***~ two birds with one stone*** *fig.* zwei Fliegen mit e-r Klappe schlagen; ***be ~ed*** getötet werden, ums Leben kommen, umkommen, sterben; ***be ~ed in action*** ⚔ (im Krieg *od.* im Kampf) fallen; **2.** *Tiere* schlachten; **3.** *hunt.* erlegen, schießen; **4.** ⚔ abschießen, zerstören, vernichten, *Schiff* versenken; **5.** töten, *j-s* Tod verursachen: ***his reckless driving will ~ him one day*** sein leichtsinniges Fahren wird ihn noch das Leben kosten; ***the job*** (*etc.*) ***is ~ing me*** die Arbeit (*etc.*) bringt mich (noch) um; ***the sight nearly ~ed me*** der Anblick war zum Totlachen; **6.** a) zuˈgrunde richten, ruinieren, kaˈputtmachen, b) *Knospen etc.* vernichten, zerstören; **7.** *fig.* widerˈrufen, ungültig machen, streichen; **8.** *fig. Gefühle* (ab)töten, ersticken; **9.** *Schmerzen* stillen; **10.** unwirksam machen, *Wirkung etc.* aufheben, *Farben* übertönen, ‚erschlagen'; **11.**

Geräusche schlucken; **12.** *fig. ein Gesetz etc.* zu Fall bringen, *e-n Plan* durch'kreuzen; **13.** durch Kri'tik vernichten; **14.** *sport den Ball* töten; **15.** *Zeit* totschlagen: **~ time**; **16.** a) *e-e Maschine etc.* abstellen, abschalten, *den Motor a.* ‚abwürgen', b) *Lichter* ausschalten; **17.** F a) *e-e Flasche etc.* austrinken, b) *e-e Zigarette* ausdrücken; **II** *v/i.* **18.** töten: a) den Tod verursachen *od.* her'beiführen, b) morden; **19.** F unwider'stehlich *od.* hinreißend sein, e-n tollen Eindruck machen: **dressed to ~** todschick gekleidet, *contp.* aufgedonnert; **III** *s.* **20.** *bsd. hunt.* a) Tötung *f* (*des Wildes*), Abschuß *m*, b) erlegtes Wild, Strecke *f*: **be in at the ~** *fig.* am Schluß dabei sein; **21.** a) ⚔ Zerstörung *f*, b) ✈ Abschuß *m*, c) ⚓ Versenkung *f*.

kill·er ['kɪlə] *s.* **1.** Mörder *m*, Killer *m*; **2.** *a. fig.* Schlächter *m*; **3.** tödliche Krankheit *etc.*; et., das e-n umbringt; **4.** *bsd. in Zssgn* Vertilgungsmittel *n*; **5.** *Am.* F a) schicke *od.* ‚tolle' Frau, b) ‚toller' Bursche, c) ‚tolle' Sache, d) mörderischer Schlag; **~ in·stinct** *s.* 'Killerin,stinkt *m*; **~ whale** *s. zo.* Schwertwal *m*.

kill·ing ['kɪlɪŋ] **I** *s.* **1.** a) Tötung *f*, Morden *n*, b) Mord(fall) *m*: **three more ~s in London**; **2.** Schlachten *n*; **3.** *hunt.* Erlegen *n*; **4. make a ~** e-n Riesengewinn machen; **II** *adj.* ☐ **5.** tödlich, vernichtend, mörderisch (*a. fig.*): **a ~ glance** ein vernichtender Blick; **a ~ pace** ein mörderisches Tempo; **6.** *a.* **~ly funny** F urkomisch, zum Brüllen.

'**kill|·joy** *s.* Spielverderber(in), Störenfried *m*, Miesmacher(in); '**~-time** *adj.* zum Zeitvertreib getan *etc.*

kiln [kɪln] *s.* Brenn-, Trocken-, Röst-, Darrofen *m*, Darre *f*; '**~-dry** *v/t.* (*im Ofen*) dörren, darren, brennen, rösten.

ki·lo ['kiːləʊ] *s.* Kilo *n*.

kil·o|·gram(me) ['kɪləʊgræm] *s.* Kilo'gramm *n*, Kilo *n*; **~·gram·me·ter** *Am.*, **~·gram·me·tre** *Brit.* [ˌkɪləʊgræm'miːtə] *s.* 'Meterkilo,gramm *n*; **~·hertz** ['kɪləʊhɜːts] *s.* ϟ, *phys.* Kilo'hertz *n*; **~·li·ter** *Am.*, **~·li·tre** *Brit.* ['kɪləʊˌliːtə] *s.* Kilo'liter *m*, *n*; **~·me·ter** *Am.*, **~·me·tre** *Brit.* ['kɪləʊˌmiːtə] *s.* Kilo'meter *m*; **~·met·ric**, **~·met·ri·cal** [ˌkɪləʊ'metrɪk(l)] *adj.* kilo'metrisch; **~·ton** ['kɪləʊtʌn] *s.* **1.** 1000 Tonnen *pl.*; **2.** *phys. Sprengkraft, die 1000 Tonnen TNT entspricht*; **~·volt** ['kɪləʊvəʊlt] *s.* ϟ Kilo'volt *n*; **~·watt** ['kɪləʊwɒt] *s.* ϟ Kilo'watt *n*: **~ hour** Kilowattstunde *f*.

kilt [kɪlt] **I** *s.* **1.** Kilt *m*, Schottenrock *m*; **II** *v/t.* **2.** aufschürzen; **3.** fälteln, plissieren; '**kilt·ed** [-tɪd] *adj.* mit e-m Kilt (bekleidet).

ki·mo·no [kɪ'məʊnəʊ] *pl.* **-nos** *s.* Kimono *m*.

kin [kɪn] **I** *s.* **1.** Fa'milie *f*, Sippe *f*; **2.** *coll. pl. konstr.* (Bluts)Verwandtschaft *f*, Verwandte *pl.*; → **kith**, **next** 1; **II** *adj.* **3.** (**to**) verwandt (mit), ähnlich (*dat.*).

kind[1] [kaɪnd] *s.* **1.** Art *f*: a) Typ *m*, Gattung *f*, b) Sorte *f*, c) Beschaffenheit *f*: **all ~s of** alle möglichen, alle Arten von; **all of a ~** (**with**) von der gleichen Art (wie); **the only one of its ~** das einzige s-r Art; **two of a ~** zwei von derselben Sorte; **what ~ of ...?** was für ein ...?; **nothing of the ~** a) keineswegs, b) nichts dergleichen; **you'll do nothing of the ~** *a.* das wirst du schön bleibenlassen; **these ~** (**of people**) F diese Art Menschen; **he is not that ~ of person** F er ist nicht so (einer); **your ~** Leute wie Sie; **I know your ~** Ihre Sorte *od.* Ihren Typ kenne ich; **s.th. of the ~** etwas Derartiges, so etwas; **that ~ of** (**a**) **book** so ein Buch; **I haven't got that ~ of money** F soviel Geld hab' ich nicht; **he felt a ~ of compunction** er empfand so etwas wie Reue; **I ~ of expected it** F ich hatte es halb *od.* irgendwie erwartet; **I ~ of promised it** F ich habe es so halb u. halb versprochen; **he is ~ of funny** F er ist etwas *od.* ein bißchen komisch; **I was ~ of disappointed** F ich war schon ein bißchen enttäuscht; **I had ~ of thought that ...** F ich hatte eigentlich *od.* fast gedacht, daß; **that's not my ~ of film** F solche Filme sind nicht mein Fall; **2.** Natu'ralien *pl.*, Waren *pl.*: **pay in ~**; **I shall pay him in ~!** *fig.* dem werd' ich es in gleicher Münze zurückzahlen; **3.** *eccl.* Gestalt *f* (*von Brot u. Wein beim Abendmahl*).

kind[2] [kaɪnd] *adj.* ☐ → **kindly** II; **1.** gütig, freundlich, liebenswürdig, nett, lieb, gut (**to s.o.** zu j-m): **be so ~ as to** (*inf.*) seien Sie bitte so gut *od.* freundlich, zu (*inf.*); **would you be ~ enough to** wären Sie (vielleicht) so nett *od.* gut, zu *inf.*; **that was very ~ of you** das war wirklich nett *od.* lieb von dir; **2.** gutartig, fromm (*Pferd*).

kin·der·gar·ten ['kɪndəˌgɑːtn] *s.* a) Kindergarten *m*, b) Vorschule *f*.

kind·heart·ed [ˌkaɪnd'hɑːtɪd] *adj.* gütig, gutherzig; ˌ**kind'heart·ed·ness** [-nɪs] *s.* (Herzens)Güte *f*.

kin·dle ['kɪndl] **I** *v/t.* **1.** an-, entzünden; **2.** *fig.* entflammen, -zünden, -fachen, *Interesse etc.* wecken; **3.** erleuchten; **II** *v/i.* **4.** *a. fig.* Feuer fangen, aufflammen; **5.** *fig.* (**at**) a) sich erregen (über *acc.*), b) sich begeistern (für).

kind·li·ness ['kaɪndlɪnɪs] → **kindness**.

kin·dling ['kɪndlɪŋ] *s.* Anmach-, Anzündholz *n*.

kind·ly ['kaɪndlɪ] **I** *adj.* **1.** → **kind**[2]; **II** *adv.* **2.** gütig, freundlich; **3.** F freundlicherweise, liebenswürdig(erweise), gütig(st), freundlich(st): **~ tell me** sagen Sie mir bitte; **take ~ to** sich befreunden mit, sich hingezogen fühlen zu, liebgewinnen; **he didn't take ~ to that** das hat ihm gar nicht gefallen, das paßte ihm gar nicht; **will you ~ shut up!** *iro.* willst du gefälligst den Mund halten!; '**kind·ness** [-dnɪs] *s.* **1.** Güte *f*, Freundlichkeit *f*, Liebenswürdigkeit *f*: **out of the ~ of one's heart** aus reiner (Herzens)Güte; **please, have the ~ to** bitte, seien Sie so freundlich, zu *inf.*; **2.** Gefälligkeit *f*: **do s.o. a ~** j-m e-n Gefallen tun.

kin·dred ['kɪndrɪd] **I** *s.* **1.** (Bluts)Verwandtschaft *f*; **2.** *coll. pl. konstr.* Verwandte *pl.*, Verwandtschaft *f*, Fa'milie *f*; **II** *adj.* **3.** (bluts)verwandt; **4.** *fig.* verwandt, ähnlich, gleichartig: **~ languages**; **~ spirit** Gleichgesinnte(r *m*) *f*; **he and I are ~ spirits** er u. ich sind geistesverwandt *od.* verwandte Seelen.

kin·e·mat·ic, **kin·e·mat·i·cal** [ˌkɪnɪ'mætɪk(l)] *adj. phys.* kine'matisch; ˌ**kin·e'mat·ics** [-ks] *s. pl. sg. konstr. phys.* Kine'matik *f*, Bewegungslehre *f*.

ki·net·ic [kaɪ'netɪk] *adj. phys.* ki'netisch: **~ energy**; **ki'net·ics** [-ks] *s. pl. sg. konstr. phys.* Ki'netik *f*, Bewegungslehre *f*.

king [kɪŋ] **I** *s.* **1.** König *m*: **~ of beasts** König der Tiere (*Löwe*); → **King's Counsel** *etc.*; **2.** a) ℒ **of** ℒ**s** *eccl. der* König der Könige (*Gott, Christus*), b) (**Book of**) ℒ**s** *bibl.* (*das* Buch der) Könige *pl.*; **3.** a) *Kartenspiel, Schach*: König *m*, b) *Damespiel*: Dame *f*; **4.** *fig.* König *m*, Ma'gnat *m*: **oil ~**; **II** *v/i.* **5. ~ it** König sein, den König spielen, herrschen (**over** über *acc.*).

king·dom ['kɪŋdəm] *s.* **1.** Königreich *n*; **2.** *a.* ℒ **of heaven** Himmelreich *n*, *das* Reich Gottes; **send s.o. to ~ come** F j-n ins Jenseits befördern; **till ~ come** F bis in alle Ewigkeit; **3.** *fig.* (Na'tur-)Reich *n*: **animal** (**vegetable**, **mineral**) **~** Tier- (Pflanzen-, Mineral)reich *n*.

'**king|·fish·er** *s. orn.* Eisvogel *m*; ℒ **James Bi·ble** *od.* **Ver·sion** *s. autorisierte englische Bibelübersetzung*.

king·let ['kɪŋlɪt] *s.* unbedeutender König, Duo'dezfürst *m*.

'**king·ly** [-lɪ] *adj. u. adv.* königlich, maje'stätisch.

'**king|·mak·er** *s. bsd. fig.* Königsmacher *m*; '**~·pin** *s.* **1.** ⚙ Achsschenkelbolzen *m*; **2.** *Kegelspiel*: König *m*; **3.** F a) *der* ‚Hauptmacher', der wichtigste Mann, b) *die* Hauptsache, *der* Dreh- u. Angelpunkt; ℒ**'s Bench** (**Di·vi·sion**) *s.* ⚖ *Brit. Abteilung des* **High Court of Justice**, *zuständig für* a) *Zivilsachen* (*Obligations- und Deliktsrecht, Handels-, Steuer- u. Seesachen*), b) *Strafsachen* (*als oberste Instanz für* **summary offences**); ℒ**'s Coun·sel** *s.* ⚖ *Brit.* Anwalt *m* der Krone; ℒ**'s Eng·lish** → **English** 3; **~'s ev·i·dence** → **evidence** 1.

king·ship ['kɪŋʃɪp] *s.* Königtum *n*.

'**king-size(d)** *adj.* 'über,durchschnittlich groß, Riesen..., *fig.* F *a.* Mords...: **~ cigarettes** King-size-Zigaretten.

King's Speech *s. Brit.* Thronrede *f*.

kink [kɪŋk] **I** *s.* **1.** *bsd.* ⚓ Kink *f*, Knick *m*, Schleife *f* (*Draht, Tau*); **2.** (Muskel-)Zerrung *f od.* (-)Krampf *m*; **3.** *fig.* a) Schrulle *f*, Tick *m*, b) ‚Macke' *f*, De'fekt *m*; **4.** *Brit.* F Abartigkeit *f*; **II** *v/i.* **5.** e-e Kink *etc.* haben (→ 1); **III** *v/t.* **6.** knicken, knoten, verknäueln; '**kink·y** [-kɪ] *adj.* **1.** voller Kinken, verdreht (*Tau etc.*); **2.** wirr, kraus (*Haar*); **3.** F a) spleenig, ‚irre', ausgefallen, ‚verrückt', b) *Brit.* per'vers, abartig.

kins·folk ['kɪnzfəʊk] *s. pl.* Verwandtschaft *f*, (Bluts)Verwandte *pl.*

kin·ship ['kɪnʃɪp] *s.* **1.** (Bluts)Verwandtschaft *f*; **2.** *fig.* Verwandtschaft *f*.

kins|·man ['kɪnzmən] *s.* [*irr.*] (Bluts-)Verwandte(r) *m*, Angehörige(r) *m*; **~·wom·an** ['kɪnzˌwʊmən] *s.* [*irr.*] (Bluts)Verwandte *f*, Angehörige *f*.

ki·osk ['kiːɒsk] *s.* **1.** Kiosk *m*, Verkaufsstand *m*; **2.** *Brit.* Tele'fonzelle *f*.

kip [kɪp] *sl.* **I** *s.* **1.** Schläfchen *n*; **2.** ‚Falle' *f*, ‚Klappe' *f* (*Bett*); **II** *v/i.* **3.** a) ‚pennen' (*schlafen*), b) *mst* **~ down** sich ‚hinhauen'.

kip·per ['kɪpə] **I** *s.* **1.** Räucherhering *m*, Bückling *m*; **2.** Lachs *m* (*während der*

Laichzeit); **II** *v/t.* **3.** *Heringe* einsalzen u. räuchern: ***~ed herring*** → 1.
Kir·ghiz ['kɜ:gɪz] *s.* Kir'gise *m.*
kirk [kɜ:k] *s. Scot.* Kirche *f.*
Kirsch [kɪəʃ] *s.* Kirsch(wasser *n*) *m.*
kiss [kɪs] **I** *s.* **1.** Kuß *m*: ***~ of death*** *fig.* Todesstoß *m*; ***~ of life*** Mund-zu-Mund-Beatmung *f*; ***blow*** (*od.* ***throw***) ***a ~ to s.o.*** j-m e-e Kußhand zuwerfen; **2.** leichte Berührung (*zweier Billardbälle etc.*); **3.** *Am.* Bai'ser *n* (*Zuckergebäck*); **4.** Zuckerplätzchen *n*; **II** *v/t.* **5.** küssen: ***~ away*** *Tränen* fortküssen; ***~ s.o. good night*** j-m e-n Gutenachtkuß geben: ***~ s.o. goodbye*** j-m e-n Abschiedskuß geben; ***you can ~ your money goodbye!*** F dein Geld hast du gesehen!; ***~ one's hand to s.o.*** j-m e-e Kußhand zuwerfen; ***~ s.o.'s hand*** j-m die Hand küssen; → ***book*** 1, ***rod*** 2; **6.** *fig.* leicht berühren; **III** *v/i.* **7.** sich küssen: ***~ and make up*** sich mit e-m Kuß versöhnen; **8.** *fig.* sich leicht berühren; **'kiss·a·ble** *adj.* küssenswert; **kiss curl** *s. Brit.* Schmachtlocke *f*; **'kiss·er** [-sə] *s. sl.* ‚Fresse' *f* (*Mund od. Gesicht*).
kiss·ing gate ['kɪsɪŋ] *s.* kleines Schwingtor (*das immer nur eine Person durchläßt*).
'kiss|-off *s. Am. sl.* **1.** Ende *n* (*a. Tod*); **2.** ‚Rausschmiß' *m*; **'~-proof** *adj.* kußecht, -fest.
kit [kɪt] **I** *s.* **1.** (*Angel-, Reit- etc.*)Ausrüstung *f*: ***gym ~*** Sportsachen *pl.*, -zeug *n*; **2.** ⚔ a) Mon'tur *f*, b) Gepäck *n*; **3.** a) Arbeitsgerät *n*, Werkzeug(e *pl.*) *n*, b) Werkzeugkasten *m*, -tasche *f*, Flickzeug *n*, c) Baukasten *m*, d) Bastelsatz *m*, e) *allg.* Behälter *m*: ***first-aid ~*** Verbandskasten *m*; **4.** *Zeitungswesen*: Pressemappe *f*; **5.** F a) Kram *m*, Zeug *n*, ‚Sachen' *pl.*, b) Sippe *f*, ‚Blase' *f*: ***the whole ~*** (***and caboodle***) der ganze Kram *od.* der ganze ‚Verein'; **II** *v/t.* **6.** ***~ out*** *od.* ***up*** ausstatten (***with*** mit); **'~·bag** *s.* **1.** Reisetasche *f*; **2.** ⚔ Kleider-, Seesack *m.*
kitch·en ['kɪtʃɪn] **I** *s.* Küche *f*; **II** *adj.* Küchen…, Haushalts…; **kitch·en·et(te)** [ˌkɪtʃɪ'net] *s.* Kleinküche *f*, Kochnische *f.*
kitch·en| foil *s.* Haushalts- *od.* Alufolie *f*; **~ gar·den** *s.* Gemüsegarten *m*; **'~·maid** *s.* Küchenmädchen *n*; **~ mid·den** *s.* vorgeschichtlicher (Küchen-)Abfallhaufen; **~ po·lice** *s.* ⚔ *Am.* Küchendienst *m*; **~ range** *s.* Küchen-, Kochherd *m*; **~ scales** *s. pl.* Küchenwaage *f*; **~ sink** *s.* Ausguß *m*, Spülstein *m*, ‚Spüle' *f*: ***everything but the ~*** *humor.* alles, der ganze Krempel; ***~ drama*** *thea.* realistisches Sozialdrama; **'~·ware** *s.* Küchengeschirr *n od.* -geräte *pl.*
kite [kaɪt] *s.* **1.** (Pa'pier-, Stoff)Drachen *m*: ***fly a ~*** a) e-n Drachen steigen lassen, b) *fig.* e-n Versuchsballon loslassen, c) → 3; **2.** *orn.* Gabelweihe *f*; **3.** ⚚ F Gefälligkeits-, Kellerwechsel *m*: ***fly a ~*** Wechselreiterei betreiben; → 1; **4.** ✈ *sl.* ‚Kiste' *f*, ‚Mühle' *f* (*Flugzeug*); **5.** ***2 mark*** *Brit.* (amtliches) Gütezeichen; **~ bal·loon** *s.* ⚔ 'Fessel-, 'Drachenbalˌlon *m*; **'~-ˌfly·ing** *s.* **1.** Steigenlassen *n* e-s Drachens; **2.** *fig.* Loslassen *n* e-s Ver'suchsbalˌlons, Sondieren *n*; **3.** ⚚ F Wechselreite'rei *f.*
kith [kɪθ] *s.*: ***~ and kin*** (Bekannte u.) Verwandte *pl.*; ***with ~ and kin*** mit Kind u. Kegel.
kitsch [kɪtʃ] *s.* Kitsch *m.*
kit·ten ['kɪtn] **I** *s.* Kätzchen *n*, junge Katze: ***have ~s*** F ‚Zustände' kriegen; **II** *v/i.* Junge werfen (*Katze*); **'kit·ten·ish** [-nɪʃ] *adj.* **1.** wie ein Kätzchen (geartet); **2.** (kindlich) verspielt *od.* ausgelassen.
kit·ty¹ ['kɪtɪ] *s.* Mieze *f*, Kätzchen *n.*
kit·ty² ['kɪtɪ] *s.* **1.** *Kartenspiel*: (Spiel-)Kasse *f*; **2.** (gemeinsame) Kasse.
ki·wi ['ki:wi:] *s.* **1.** *orn.* Kiwi *m*; **2.** ⚘ Kiwi *f.*
klax·on ['klæksn] *s.* (Auto)Hupe *f.*
klep·to·ma·ni·a [ˌkleptəʊ'meɪnjə] *s. psych.* Kleptoma'nie *f*; **ˌklep·to'ma·ni·ac** [-nɪæk] **I** *s.* Klepto'mane *m*, Klepto'manin *f*; **II** *adj.* klepto'manisch.
klieg light [kli:g] *s. Film*: Jupiterlampe *f.*
klutz [klʌts] *s. Am. sl.* ‚Trottel' *m.*
knack [næk] *s.* **1.** Trick *m*, Kniff *m*, ‚Dreh' *m*; **2.** Geschick(lichkeit *f*) *n*, Kunst *f*, Ta'lent *n*: ***the ~ of writing*** die Kunst des Schreibens; ***have the ~ of s.th.*** den Dreh von et. heraushaben, wissen, wie man et. macht; ***I've lost the ~*** ich krieg' es nicht mehr hin.
knack·er ['nækə] *s.* **1.** *Brit.* Abdecker *m*, Schinder *m*; **2.** 'Abbruchunterˌnehmer *m*; **'knack·ered** *adj. Brit. sl.* (ganz) ‚ka'putt', ‚to'tal geschafft'.
knag [næg] *s.* Knorren *m*, Ast *m* (*im Holz*).
knap·sack ['næpsæk] *s.* **1.** ⚔ Tor'nister *m*; **2.** Rucksack *m*, Ranzen *m.*
knave [neɪv] *s.* **1.** *obs.* Schurke *m*, Schuft *m*, Spitzbube *m*; **2.** *Kartenspiel*: Bube *m*, Unter *m*; **'knav·er·y** [-vərɪ] *s. obs.* **1.** Schurke'rei *f*; **2.** Gaune'rei *f*; **'knav·ish** [-vɪʃ] *adj.* □ *obs.* schurkisch.
knead [ni:d] *v/t.* **1.** kneten; **2.** ('durch-)kneten, massieren; **3.** *fig.* formen (***into*** zu); **'knead·ing-trough** [-dɪŋ] *s.* Backtrog *m.*
knee [ni:] **I** *s.* **1.** Knie *n*: ***on one's*** (***bended***) ***~s*** auf Knien, kniefällig; ***bend*** (*od.* ***bow***) ***the ~ to*** niederknien vor (*dat.*); ***bring s.o. to his ~s*** j-n auf *od.* in die Knie zwingen; ***give a ~ to s.o.*** j-n unterstützen; ***go on one's ~s to*** a) niederknien vor (*dat.*), b) *fig. j-n* kniefällig bitten; **2.** ⚙ a) Knie(stück) *n*, Winkel *m*, b) Knie(rohr) *n*, (Rohr-)Krümmer *m*; **II** *v/t.* **3.** mit dem Knie stoßen; **4.** F *Hose an den Knien* ausbeulen; **~ bend(·ing)** *s.* Kniebeuge *f*; **~ breech·es** *s. pl.* Kniehose(n *pl.*) *f*; **'~·cap** *s.* **1.** *anat.* Kniescheibe *f*; **2.** Knieleder *n*, -schützer *m*; **ˌ~-'deep** *adj.* knietief, bis an die Knie (reichend); **ˌ~-'high** **1.** → ***knee-deep***; **2.** kniehoch; **'~-hole desk** *s.* Schreibtisch *m* mit Öffnung für die Knie; **~ jerk** *s.* ⚕ 'Knie(sehnen)reˌflex *m*; **'~-joint** *s. anat.*, ⚙ Kniegelenk *n.*
kneel [ni:l] *v/i.* [*irr.*] *a.* ***~ down*** (nieder)knien (***to*** vor *dat.*).
'knee|-length *adj.* knielang: ***~ skirt*** kniefreier Rock; **~ pad** *s.* Knieschützer *m*; **'~-pan** → ***kneecap*** 1; **~ pipe** *s.* ⚙ Knierohr *n*; **~ shot** *s. Film*: 'Halbtoˌtale *f.*
knell [nel] **I** *s.* **1.** Totenglocke *f*, Grabgeläute *n* (*a. fig.*): ***sound the ~*** → 3; **2.** *fig.* Vorbote *m*, Ankündigung *f*; **II** *v/i.* **3.** läuten; **III** *v/t.* **4.** (*bsd. durch Läuten*) a) bekanntgeben, b) zs.-rufen.
knelt [nelt] *pret. u. p.p. von* ***kneel***.
knew [nju:] *pret von* ***know***.
Knick·er·bock·er ['nɪkəbɒkə] *s.* **1.** (*Spitzname für den*) New Yorker; **2.** ***2s*** *pl.* Knickerbocker *pl.* (*Hose*).
knick·ers ['nɪkəz] *s. pl. Brit.* (Damen-)Schlüpfer *m*: ***get one's ~ in a twist*** *humor.* sich ‚ins Hemd machen'; ***~!*** Quatsch!, ‚Mist'!
knick-knack ['nɪknæk] *s.* **1.** a) Nippsache *f*, b) billiger Schmuck; **2.** Spiele'rei *f*, Schnickschnack *m.*
knife [naɪf] **I** *pl.* **knives** [naɪvz] *s.* **1.** Messer *n* (*a.* ⚙, ⚕): ***play a good ~ and fork*** ein starker Esser sein; ***before you can say "~"*** ehe man sich's versieht; ***have*** (***got***) ***one's ~ into s.o.*** j-n ‚gefressen' haben, es auf j-n abgesehen haben; ***war to the ~*** Krieg bis aufs Messer; ***be*** (***go***) ***under the ~*** F unterm Messer (*des Chirurgen*) sein (unters Messer kommen); ***turn the ~*** (***in the wound***) *fig.* Salz in die Wunde streuen; ***watch s.o. like a ~*** F j-n scharf beobachten; **II** *v/t.* **2.** mit e-m Messer bearbeiten; **3.** a) einstechen auf (*acc.*), mit e-m Messer stechen, b) erstechen, erdolchen; **4.** *Am. sl. bsd. pol. j-m* in den Rücken fallen, *j-n* ‚abschießen'; **'~-edge** *s.* **1.** (Messer)Schneide *f*: ***on a ~*** *fig.* sehr aufgeregt (***about*** wegen); ***be balanced on a ~*** *fig.* auf des Messers Schneide stehen; **2.** ⚙ Waageschneide *f*; **'~-edged** *adj.* messerscharf; **~ grind·er** *s.* **1.** Scheren-, Messerschleifer *m*; **2.** Schleifrad *n*, -stein *m*; **~ rest** *s.* Messerbänkchen *n.*
knif·ing ['naɪfɪŋ] *s.* Messersteche'rei *f.*
knight [naɪt] **I** *s.* **1.** *hist.* Ritter *m*, Edelmann *m*; **2.** *Brit.* Ritter *m* (*niederster, nicht erblicher Adelstitel*; *Anrede*: ***Sir*** *u. Vorname*); **3.** Ritter *m* e-s Ordens: ***2 of the Bath*** Ritter des Bath-Ordens; ***2 of the Garter*** Ritter des Hosenbandordens; ***~ of the pen*** *humor.* Ritter der Feder (*Schriftsteller*); → ***Hospital(l)er*** 1; **4.** *fig.* Ritter *m*, Kava'lier *m*; **5.** *Schach*: Springer *m*, Pferd *n*; **II** *v/t.* **6.** a) zum Ritter schlagen, b) adeln, in den Ritterstand erheben; **'knight·age** [-tɪdʒ] *s.* **1.** *coll.* Ritterschaft *f*; **2.** Ritterstand *m*; **3.** Ritterliste *f.*
knight| bach·e·lor *pl.* **~s bach·e·lor** *s.* Ritter *m* (*Mitglied des niedersten englischen Ritterordens*); **~ er·rant** *pl.* **~s er·rant** *s.* **1.** fahrender Ritter; **2.** *fig.* ‚Don Qui'xote' *m*; **ˌ~-'er·rant·ry** *s.* **1.** fahrendes Rittertum; **2.** *fig.* a) Abenteuerlust *f*, unstetes Leben, b) Donquichotte'rie *f.*
knight·hood ['naɪthʊd] *s.* **1.** Rittertum *n*, -würde *f*, -stand *m*: ***receive a ~*** in den Ritterstand erhoben werden; **2.** *coll.* Ritterschaft *f.*
knight·ly ['naɪtlɪ] *adj. u. adv.* ritterlich.
Knight Tem·plar → ***Templar*** 1 *u.* 2.
knit [nɪt] **I** *v/t.* [*irr.*] **1.** a) stricken, b) ⚙ wirken: ***~ two, purl two*** zwei rechts, zwei links (stricken); **2.** *a.* ***~ together*** zs.-fügen, verbinden, verknüpfen, vereinigen (*alle a. fig.*); → ***close-knit***, ***well-knit***; **3.** ***~ up*** a) fest verbinden, b) ab-, beschließen; **4.** *Stirn* runzeln, *Augenbrauen* zs.-ziehen; **II** *v/i.* [*irr.*] **5.** a)

stricken, b) ⚙ wirken; **6.** *a.* **~ *up*** sich (eng) verbinden *od.* zs.-fügen (*a. fig.*), zs.-wachsen (*Knochen etc.*); **III** *s.* **7.** Strickart *f*; ˈ**knit·ted** [-tɪd] *adj.* gestrickt, Strick…, Wirk…; ˈ**knit·ter** [-tə] *s.* **1.** Stricker(in); **2.** ⚙ ˈStrick-, ˈWirkmaˌschine *f.*

knit·ting [ˈnɪtɪŋ] *s.* **1.** a) Stricken *n*, b) ⚙ Wirken *n*; **2.** Strickzeug *n*, -arbeit *f*; **~ ma·chine** *s.* ˈStrickmaˌschine *f*; **~ nee·dle** *s.* Stricknadel *f.*

ˈ**knit·wear** *s.* Strick-, Wirkwaren *pl.*

knives [naɪvz] *pl. von* ***knife.***

knob [nɒb] *s.* **1.** (runder) Griff, Knopf *m*, Knauf *m*: ***with ~s on*** *sl.* (na) und ob!, und wie!; ***and the same to you with*** (***brass***) ***~s on!*** *sl.* das kann man erst recht von dir behaupten!; **2.** Knorren *m*, Ast *m* (*im Holz*); **3.** Buckel *m*, Beule *f*, Höcker *m*; **4.** Stück(chen) *n* (*Zucker etc.*); **5.** ⚠ Knauf *m*; **6.** *Am. sl.* ‚Birne' *f* (*Kopf*); **7.** *Brit.* V ‚Schwanz' *m* (*Penis*); ˈ**knob·bly** [-blɪ] *adj.* ‚knubbelig': **~ *knees*** ‚Knubbelknie' *pl.*; ˈ**knob·by** [-bɪ] *adj.* **1.** knorrig; **2.** knoten-, knopf-, knaufartig.

knock [nɒk] **I** *s.* **1.** Schlag *m*, Stoß *m*: ***he has had*** (*od.* ***taken***) ***a few ~s*** *fig.* F er hat ein paar Nackenschläge eingesteckt; ***take the ~*** *sl.* ‚schwer bluten müssen'; ***the table has had a few ~s*** F der Tisch hat ein paar Schrammen abgekriegt; **2.** Klopfen *n*, Pochen *n*: ***there is a ~*** (***at the door***) es klopft; ***I'll give you a ~ at six*** *Brit.* F ich klopfe um sechs (an Ihre Tür) (*zum Wecken*); **II** *v/t.* **3.** schlagen, stoßen: **~ *s.o. cold*** → ***knock out*** 2; **~ *the bottom out of s.th.***, **~ *s.th. on the head*** *fig.* F et. zunichte machen, *Pläne* über den Haufen werfen; **~ *s.o. sideways*** (*od.* ***for a loop***) F j-n ‚glatt umhauen'; **~ *one's head against*** a) mit dem Kopf stoßen gegen, b) die Stirn bieten (*dat.*); **~ *s.th. into s.o.*** j-m et. einhämmern *od.* einbleuen; **~ *spots off s.o.*** (***s.th.***) F j-m (e-r Sache) haushoch überlegen sein; **4.** klopfen, schlagen; **5.** F herˈuntermachen, herziehen über (*acc.*), kritisieren: ***don't ~ him*** (***so hard***)***!*** mach ihn nicht (allzu) schlecht!; **6.** F *j-n* ‚ˈumhauen', ˈumwerfen, sprachlos machen; **III** *v/i.* **7.** schlagen, klopfen, pochen (***at the door*** an die Tür): **~ *before entering!*** bitte anklopfen!; **8.** stoßen, schlagen, prallen (***against***, ***into*** gegen *od.* auf *acc.*); **9.** ⚙ a) rattern, rütteln (*Maschine*), b) klopfen (*Motor, Brennstoff*); *Zssgn mit adv.*:

knock| a·bout, *bsd. Am.* **~ a·round I** *v/t.* **1.** herˈumstoßen (*a. fig. schikanieren*); **2.** verprügeln; **3.** übel zurichten; **II** *v/i.* **4.** F sich herˈumtreiben (***with*** mit); **5.** herˈumziehen; **6.** ‚rumliegen' (*Sache*); **~ back** *v/t. Brit.* F **1.** *Whisky etc.* ‚hinter die Binde gießen', ‚kippen'; **2.** *j-n et.* kosten: ***that has ~ed me back a few pounds***; **3.** *fig. j-n* ‚ˈumhauen', ˈumwerfen; **~ down** *v/t.* **1.** niederschlagen, zu Boden schlagen (*a. fig.*); **2.** → ***knock over*** 2; **3.** *Haus* abreißen; **4.** ⚙ zerlegen, auseinˈandernehmen; **5.** ✝ a) *bei Auktionen*: (***to s.o.*** j-m) *et.* zuschlagen, b) F mit *dem Preis* ‚runtergehen', c) F *j-n* herˈunterhandeln (***to*** auf *acc.*); **~ off I** *v/t.* **1.** herˈunter-, abschlagen, weghauen; **2.** F aufhören mit: **~ *work*** → 7; ***knock it off!*** *sl.* hör doch auf damit!; **3.** F a) *et.* rasch erledigen, b) *et.* ‚ˈhinhauen', aus dem Ärmel schütteln; **4.** ✝ *vom Preis* abziehen: ***he knocked £10 off the bill*** er hat £10 (von der Rechnung) nachgelassen; **5.** F a) *Brit.* ‚klauen', stehlen, b) *Bank etc.* ausrauben, c) *j-n* ‚umlegen' (*töten*); **6.** V *Mädchen* ‚bumsen'; **II** *v/i.* **7.** F Feierabend machen; **~ out** *v/t.* **1.** (her)ˈausschlagen, -klopfen; **2.** *sport* a) *Boxen*: k.o. schlagen, niederschlagen, b) *Gegner* ausschalten; **3.** F *j-n* ‚umhauen': a) verblüffen, b) erschöpfen, c) ‚ins Land der Träume schicken' (*Droge etc.*); **4.** ⚔ abschießen; **5.** F *Melodie* ‚runterspielen, -hacken'; **~ o·ver** *v/t.* **1.** ˈumwerfen (*a. fig.*), ˈumstoßen; **2.** überˈfahren; **~ to·geth·er** *v/t.* **1.** schnell zs.-bauen *od.* -basteln, *Essen etc.* rasch zuˈrechtmachen; **2.** aneinˈanderstoßen: ***knock people's heads together*** *fig.* die Leute zur Vernunft bringen; **~ up I** *v/t.* **1.** (*durch Klopfen*) wecken; **2.** F *Essen etc.* rasch ‚auf die Beine stellen' *od.* zuˈrechtmachen; **3.** F *Haus etc.* rasch ‚ˈhinstellen'; **4.** *Brit.* F *Geld* ‚machen' (*verdienen*); **5.** *j-n* ‚fertigmachen' *od.* ‚schaffen' (*erschöpfen*); **6.** V *Am.* *e-r Frau* ein Kind machen, *e-e Frau* ‚anbumsen'; **II** *v/i.* **7.** *Tennis etc.*: sich warm- *od.* einspielen.

ˈ**knock|·aˌbout I** *adj.* **1.** *thea.* F Radau…, Klamauk…; **2.** Alltags…, strapaˈzierfähig: **~ *clothes***; **~ *car*** Gebrauchswagen *m*; ˌ**~ˈdown I** *adj.* **1.** niederschmetternd (*a. fig.*): **~ *blow*** a) Schlag *m*, der j-n umwirft, b) *Boxen*: Niederschlag *m*, c) *fig.* Nackenschlag *m*, schwerer Schlag; **2.** ⚙ zerlegbar, zs.-legbar; **3.** ✝ äußerst, niedrigst: **~ *price*** Schleuderpreis *m*; **II** *s.* **4.** ✝ F Preissenkung *f*; **5.** F zerlegbares Möbelstück *od.* Gerät; **6.** ***give s.o. a ~ to s.o.*** *Am.* F j-n j-m vorstellen.

knock·er [ˈnɒkə] *s.* **1.** (Tür)Klopfer *m*; **2.** *sl.* Nörgler *m*, Krittler *m*; **3.** *pl.* V ‚Titten' *pl.*; ˈ**knock·ing** [ˈnɒkɪŋ] *s.* **1.** Klopfen *n* (*a. mot.*); **2.** F Kriˈtik *f* (***of*** an *dat.*): ***he has taken a bad ~*** er wurde schwer in die Pfanne gehauen.

ˌ**knock|-ˈkneed** *adj.* X-beinig; ˈ**~-knees** *s. pl.* X-Beine *pl.*; ˈ**~·out I** *s.* **1.** *Boxen*: Knockout *m*, K. ˈo. *m*, Niederschlag *m*; **2.** *fig.* vernichtende Niederlage, tödlicher Schlag, *das* ‚Aus' (***for*** für *j-n*); **3.** F großartige *od.* ‚tolle' Sache *od.* Perˈson: ***she's a real ~*** sie sieht toll aus; **II** *adj.* **4.** *Boxen*: K.-o.-…: **~ *blow*** K.-o.-Schlag *m*; **~ *system*** K.-o.-System *n*; **~ *match*** Ausscheidungsspiel *n*; **5.** *fig.* vernichtend; **6.** *Am. sl.* Betäubungs…: **~ *pill***; ˈ**~-proof** *adj. mot.* klopffest; **~ rat·ing** *s. mot.* Okˈtanzahl *f*; ˌ**~ˈup** *s. sport* Einspielen *n.*

knoll [nəʊl] *s.* Hügel *m*, Kuppe *f.*

knot [nɒt] **I** *s.* **1.** Knoten *m*: ***tie s.o.*** (***up***) ***into ~s*** *fig.* F j-n ‚fertigmachen'; ***his stomach was in a ~*** sein Magen krampfte sich zusammen; **2.** Schleife *f*, Schlinge *f*, ⚔ *a.* Achselstück *n*; **3.** Knorren *m*, Ast *m* (*im Holz*); **4.** ⚘ Knoten *m*, Knospe *f*, Auge *n*; **5.** ⚓ Knoten *m*: a) Stich *m* (*im Tau*), b) Seemeile *f* (*1,853 km/h*); **6.** *fig.* Knoten *m*, Schwierigkeit *f*, Proˈblem *n*: ***cut the ~*** den Knoten ˈdurchhauen; **7.** *fig.* Band *n* *der Ehe etc.*: ***tie the ~*** den Bund fürs Leben schließen; **8.** Knäuel *m*, *n*, Haufen *m* (*Menschen etc.*); **9.** ⚕ (*Gicht- etc.*)Knoten *m*; **II** *v/t.* **10.** (ver)knoten, (ver)knüpfen; **11.** *fig.* verwickeln, verwirren; **III** *v/i.* **12.** (e-n) Knoten bilden; **13.** *fig.* sich verwickeln; ˈ**~·hole** *s.* Astloch *n.*

knot·ted [ˈnɒtɪd] *adj.* **1.** ver-, geknotet; **2.** → ˈ**knot·ty** [-tɪ] *adj.* **1.** knorrig (*Holz*); **2.** knotig, *fig.* verzwickt, schwierig, kompliziert.

knout [naʊt] *s.* Knute *f.*

know [nəʊ] **I** *v/t.* [*irr.*] **1.** *allg.* wissen: ***come to ~*** erfahren, hören; ***he ~s what to do*** er weiß, was zu tun ist; **~ *what's what***, **~ *all about it*** genau Bescheid wissen; (***and***) ***don't I ~ it!*** und ob ich das weiß!, ***he wouldn't ~*** (***that***) er kann das nicht *od.* kaum wissen; ***I wouldn't ~!*** das kann ich leider nicht sagen!; *iro.* weiß ich doch nicht!; ***for all I ~*** a) soviel ich weiß, b) was weiß ich?; ***I would have you ~ that*** ich möchte betonen *od.* Ihnen klarmachen, daß; ***I have never ~n him to lie*** m-s Wissens hat er nie gelogen; ***what do you ~!*** F na, so was!; **2.** (es) können *od.* verstehen (***how to do*** zu tun): ***do you ~ how to do it?*** wissen Sie, wie man das macht?, können Sie das?; ***he ~s how to treat children*** er versteht mit Kindern umzugehen; ***do you ~ how to drive a car?*** können Sie Auto fahren?; ***he ~s*** (***some***) ***German*** er kann (etwas) Deutsch; **3.** kennen, vertraut sein mit: ***I have ~n him for years*** ich kenne ihn (schon) seit Jahren; ***he ~s a thing or two*** F ‚er ist nicht von gestern', er weiß (ganz gut) Bescheid; ***get to ~*** a) *j-n, et.* kennenlernen, b) *et.* erfahren, herausfinden; ***after I first knew him*** nachdem ich s-e Bekanntschaft gemacht hatte; **4.** erfahren, erleben: ***he has ~n better days*** er hat bessere Tage gesehen; ***I have ~n it to happen*** ich habe das schon erlebt; → ***known*** II, ***mind*** 4; **5.** (ˈwieder)erkennen, unterˈscheiden: ***I should ~ him anywhere*** ich würde ihn überall erkennen; **~ *one from the other*** e-n vom anderen unterscheiden (können), die beiden auseinanderhalten können; ***before you ~ where you are*** im Handumdrehen; ***I don't ~ whether I shall ~ him again*** ich weiß nicht, ob ich ihn wiedererkennen werde; **6.** *Bibl.* (*geschlechtlich*) erkennen; **II** *v/i.* [*irr.*] **7.** wissen (***of*** von, um), im Bilde sein *od.* Bescheid wissen (***about*** über *acc.*), sich auskennen (***about*** in *dat.*), et. verstehen (***about*** von); ***I ~ of s.o. who*** ich weiß *od.* kenne j-n, der; ***let me ~*** (***about it***) laß es mich wissen, sag mir Bescheid (darüber); ***I ~ better!*** so dumm bin ich nicht!; ***I ~ better than to say that*** ich werde mich hüten, das zu sagen; ***you ought to ~ better*** (***than that***) das sollten Sie besser wissen, so dumm werden Sie doch nicht sein; ***he ought to ~ better than to go swimming after a big meal*** er sollte so viel Verstand haben zu wissen, daß man nach e-m reichlichen Mahl nicht baden geht; ***they don't ~ any better*** sie kennen's nicht anders; ***not that I ~ of*** F nicht daß ich wüßte; ***do*** (*od.* ***don't***) ***you ~?*** F nicht wahr?; ***you ~*** (*oft un-*

übersetzt) a) weißt du, wissen Sie, b) nämlich, c) schon, na ja; **III** *s.* **8.** ***be in the ~*** Bescheid wissen, im Bilde *od.* eingeweiht sein.

know·a·ble [ˈnəʊəbl] *adj.* was man wissen kann.

ˈ**know|-(it-)all** *s.* Besserwisser *m*, ‚Klugscheißer' *m*; ˈ**~-how** *s.* Know-ˈhow *n*: a) Sachkenntnis *f*, Fachwissen *n*, (praktische, *bsd.* technische) Erfahrung, b) ⚙ Herstellungsverfahren *pl.*

know·ing [ˈnəʊɪŋ] **I** *adj.* □ **1.** intelliˈgent, geschickt; **2.** verständnisvoll, wissend: ***~ smile***; ***with a ~ hand*** mit kundiger Hand; **3.** schlau, raffiniert: ***a ~ one*** ein Schlauberger; **II** *s.* **4.** Wissen *n*: ***there is no ~*** man kann nie wissen; ˈ**know·ing·ly** [-lɪ] *adv.* **1.** schlau, klug; **2.** verständnisvoll, wissend; **3.** wissentlich, bewußt, absichtlich.

knowl·edge [ˈnɒlɪdʒ] *s. nur sg.* **1.** Kenntnis *f*, Wissen *n*: ***have ~ of*** Kenntnis haben von, wissen (*acc.*); ***have no ~ of*** nichts wissen von *od.* über (*acc.*); ***without my ~*** ohne mein Wissen; ***the ~ of the victory*** die Kunde *od.* Nachricht vom Siege; ***it has come to my ~*** es ist mir zu Ohren gekommen, ich habe erfahren; ***to*** (***the best of***) ***my ~*** m-s Wissens, soviel ich weiß; ***to the best of my ~ and belief*** nach bestem Wissen u. Gewissen; ***not to my ~*** nicht daß ich wüßte; ***~ of life*** Lebenserfahrung *f*; → ***carnal***; **2.** Wissen *n*, Kenntnisse *pl.*: ***a good ~ of German*** gute Deutschkenntnisse; ***my ~ of Dickens*** was ich von Dickens kenne; ˈ**knowl·edge·a·ble** [-dʒəbl] *adj.* kenntnisreich, (gut) unterˈrichtet: ***he is very ~ about wines*** er weiß gut Bescheid über Weine, er ist ein Weinkenner.

known [nəʊn] **I** *p.p. von* ***know***; **II** *adj.* bekannt: ***~ quantity*** ⩓ bekannte Größe; ***make ~*** bekanntmachen; ***make o.s. ~ to s.o.*** F sich j-m vorstellen; ***~ to all*** allbekannt; ***the ~ facts*** die anerkannten Tatsachen.

knuck·le [ˈnʌkl] **I** *s.* **1.** Fingergelenk *n*, -knöchel *m*: ***a rap over the ~s*** *fig.* ein Verweis, e-e Rüge; **2.** (Kalbs- *od.* Schweins)Haxe (*od.* Hachse) *f*: ***near the ~*** *fig.* F reichlich ‚gewagt' (*Witz etc.*); **II** *v/i.* **3.** ***~ down***, ***~ under*** sich beugen, sich unterˈwerfen (***to*** *dat.*), klein beigeben; **4.** ***~ down to s.th.*** sich an et. ‚ranmachen', sich hinter et. ‚klemmen': ***~ down to work*** sich an die Arbeit machen; ˈ**~·bone** *s. anat., zo.* Knöchelbein *n*; ˈ**~ˌdust·er** *s.* Schlagring *m*; **~ joint** *s.* **1.** *anat.* Knöchel-, Fingergelenk *n*; **2.** ⚙ Karˈdan-, Kreuzgelenk *n.*

knurl [nɜːl] **I** *s.* **1.** Knoten *m*, Ast *m*, Buckel *m*; **2.** ⚙ Rändelrad *n*; **II** *v/t.* **3.** rändeln, kordeln: ***~ed screw*** Rändelschraube *f.*

KO [ˌkeɪˈəʊ] → ***knockout*** 1 *u.* ***knock out.***

ko·a·la [kəʊˈɑːlə] *s. zo.* Koˈala(bär) *m.*

kohl·ra·bi [ˌkəʊlˈrɑːbɪ] *s.* ⚘ Kohlˈrabi *m.*

kol·khoz, **kol·khos** [kɒlˈhɔːz] *s.* Kolchos *m, n*, Kolˈchose *f.*

kook [kʊk] *s. Am.* F ‚komischer Typ', ‚Spinner' *m*; **kook·y** [ˈkʊkɪ] *adj. Am.* F ‚irr', verrückt.

ko·pe(c)k [ˈkəʊpek] → ***copeck.***

Ko·ran [kɒˈrɑːn] *s.* Koˈran *m.*

Ko·re·an [kəˈrɪən] **I** *s.* Koreˈaner(in); **II** *adj.* koreˈanisch.

ko·sher [ˈkəʊʃə] *adj.* koscher: ***~ food***; ***~ restaurant***; ***not quite ~*** *fig.* F nicht ganz koscher.

ko·tow [ˌkəʊˈtaʊ], **kow·tow** [ˌkaʊˈtaʊ] **I** *s.* Koˈtau *m*, unterˈwürfige Ehrenbezeigung; **II** *v/i. a. fig.* e-n Koˈtau machen: ***~ to s.o.*** e-n Kotau machen (*fig. a.* kriechen) vor j-m.

kraal [krɑːl; *in Südafrika mst* krɔːl] *s. S.Afr.* Kral *m.*

kraft [krɑːft], *a.* **~ pa·per** *s. Am.* braunes ˈPackpaˌpier.

kraut [kraʊt] *sl. contp.* **I** *s.* Deutsche(r *m*) *f*; **II** *adj.* deutsch.

Krem·lin [ˈkremlɪn] *npr.* Kreml *m*; **Krem·lin·ol·o·gist** [ˌkremlɪˈnɒlədʒɪst] *s.* Sowjetoˈloge *m*, Kremlforscher(in).

ku·dos [ˈkjuːdɒs] *s.* F Ruhm *m*, Ehre *f.*

Ku-Klux-Klan [ˌkjuːklʌksˈklæn] *s. Am. pol.* ˈKu-Klux-ˈKlan *m* (*rassistischer amer. Geheimbund*).

ku·lak [ˈkuːlæk] (*Russ.*) *s.* Kuˈlak *m*, Großbauer *m.*

kum·quat [ˈkʌmkwɒt] *s.* ⚘ Kumquat *f.*

kung fu [ˌkʌŋˈfuː; ˌkʊŋ-] *s.* Kungˈfu *n* (*chines. Kampfsport*).

Kurd [kɜːd] *s.* Kurde *m*, Kurdin *f*; ˈ**Kurd·ish** [-ɪʃ] *adj.* kurdisch.

kur·saal [ˈkʊəzɑːl] *s.* (*Ger.*) Kursaal *m*, -haus *n.*

Kyr·i·e [ˈkɪəriːeɪ], **~ e·le·i·son** [əˈleɪsɒn] *s. eccl.* Kyrie (eˈleison) *n.*

L

L, l [el] *s.* L *n*, l *n* (*Buchstabe*).
laa·ger [ˈlɑːgə] *s. S.Afr.* Lager *n*, *bsd.* Wagenburg *f*.
lab [læb] *s.* F La'bor *n*.
la·bel [ˈleɪbl] **I** *s.* **1.** Eti'kett *n* (*a. fig.*), (Klebe-, Anhänge)Zettel *m od.* (-) Schild(chen) *n*, Anhänger *m*, Aufkleber *m*; **2.** *fig.* a) Bezeichnung *f*, b) (Kenn)Zeichen *n*, Signa'tur *f*; **3.** Aufschrift *f*, Beschriftung *f*; **4.** Label *n*, 'Schallplatteneti,kett *n od.* F -firma *f*; **5.** *Computer*: Label *n* (*Markierung in e-m Programm*); **6.** △ Kranzleiste *f*; **II** *v/t.* **7.** etikettieren, mit e-m Zettel *od.* Schild(chen) versehen; **8.** beschriften, mit e-r Aufschrift versehen: ***~(l)ed "poison"*** mit der Aufschrift „Gift"; **9.** *a.* ***~ as*** *fig.* als ... bezeichnen, zu ... stempeln, abstempeln als; **'la·bel·(l)er** [-lə] *s.* Etiket'tierma,schine *f*.
la·bi·a [ˈleɪbɪə] *pl. von* ***labium***.
la·bi·al [ˈleɪbjəl] **I** *adj. anat.*, *ling.* Lippen..., labi'al; **II** *s.* Lippenlaut *m*, Labi'al *m*.
la·bile [ˈleɪbaɪl] *adj. allg.* la'bil.
la·bi·o·den·tal [ˌleɪbɪəʊˈdentl] *ling.* **I** *adj.* labioden'tal; **II** *s.* Labioden'tal *m*, Lippenzahnlaut *m*.
la·bi·um [ˈleɪbɪəm] *pl.* **-bi·a** [-bɪə] *s. anat.* Labium *n*, (*bsd.* Scham)Lippe *f*.
la·bor *etc. Am.* → ***labour*** *etc.*
lab·o·ra·to·ry [*Brit.* ləˈbɒrətərɪ; *Am.* ˈlæbrəˌtɔːrɪ] *s.* **1.** Labora'torium *n*: ***~ assistant*** Laborant(in); ***~ technician*** Chemotechniker(in); ***~ stage*** Versuchsstadium *n*; **2.** *fig.* Werkstätte *f*.
la·bo·ri·ous [ləˈbɔːrɪəs] *adj.* □ mühsam: a) anstrengend, schwierig, b) 'umständlich, schwerfällig (*Stil etc.*).
la·bor un·ion *s. Am.* Gewerkschaft *f*.
la·bour [ˈleɪbə] *Brit.* **I** *s.* **1.** a) (*bsd.* schwere) Arbeit, b) Anstrengung *f*, Mühe *f*: ***~ of Hercules*** Herkulesarbeit *f*; ***~ of love*** Liebesdienst *m*, gern *od.* unentgeltlich getane Arbeit; → ***hard labo(u)r***; **2.** a) Arbeiterschaft *f*, Arbeiter(klasse *f*) *pl.*, b) Arbeiter *pl.*, Arbeitskräfte *pl.*: ***cheap ~***; ***shortage of ~*** Arbeitskräftemangel *m*; → ***skilled*** 2; **3.** ♀ (*ohne Artikel*) → ***Labour Party***; **4.** ⚕ Wehen *pl.*: ***be in ~*** in den Wehen liegen; **II** *v/i.* **5.** arbeiten (***at*** an *dat.*); **6.** sich anstrengen (***to*** *inf.* zu *inf.*), sich abmühen (***at***, ***with*** mit; ***for*** um *acc.*); **7.** *a.* ***~ along*** sich mühsam fortbewegen *od.* da'hinschleppen, sich (da'hin)quälen; **8.** stampfen, schlingern (*Schiff*); **9.** (***under***) zu leiden haben (unter *dat.*), zu kämpfen haben (mit *Schwierigkeiten etc.*), kranken (an *dat.*); → ***delusion*** 2; **10.** ⚕ in den Wehen liegen; **III** *v/t.* **11.** ausführlich eingehen auf (*acc.*), eingehend behandeln, *iro.* ‚breittreten', her'umreiten auf (*dat.*): ***I need not ~ the point***; ***~ camp*** *s.* Arbeitslager *n*; ♀ **Day** *s.* Tag *m* der Arbeit; ***~ dis·pute*** *s.* ✝ Arbeitskampf *m*.
la·bo(u)red [ˈleɪbəd] *adj.* **1.** → ***laborious***; **2.** → ***labo(u)ring*** 2; **'la·bo(u)r·er** [-ərə] *s.* (*bsd. ungelernter*) Arbeiter.
La·bour Ex·change *s. Brit. obs.* Arbeitsamt *n*.
la·bo(u)r force *s.* Arbeitskräfte *pl.*, Belegschaft *f* (*e-s Betriebs*).
la·bo(u)r·ing [ˈleɪbərɪŋ] *adj.* **1.** arbeitend, werktätig: ***the ~ classes***; **2.** mühsam, schwer (*Atem*).
'la·bo(u)r-in,ten·sive *adj.* ✝ 'arbeitsinten,siv.
la·bour·ite [ˈleɪbəraɪt] *s. Brit.* Anhänger (-in) *od.* Mitglied *n* der ***Labour Party***.
la·bo(u)r| lead·er *s.* Arbeiterführer *m*; **~ mar·ket** *s.* Arbeitsmarkt *m*; **~ pains** *s. pl.* ⚕ Wehen *pl.*
La·bour Par·ty *s. Brit. pol. die* Labour Party.
la·bo(u)r| re·la·tions *s. pl.* Beziehungen *pl.* zwischen Arbeitgeber(n) u. Arbeitnehmern; **'~-,sav·ing** *adj.* arbeitssparend.
Lab·ra·dor (dog) [ˈlæbrədɔː] *s. zo.* Neu'fundländer *m* (*Hund*).
la·bur·num [ləˈbɜːnəm] *s.* ♆ Goldregen *m*.
lab·y·rinth [ˈlæbərɪnθ] *s.* **1.** Laby'rinth *n*, Irrgarten *m* (*beide a. fig.*); **2.** *fig.* Wirrwarr *m*, Durchein'ander *n*; **3.** *anat.* Laby'rinth *n*, inneres Ohr; **lab·y·rin·thine** [ˌlæbəˈrɪnθaɪn] *adj.* laby'rinthisch (*a. fig.*).
lac¹ [læk] *s.* Gummilack *m*, Lackharz *n*.
lac² [læk] *s. Brit. Ind.* Lak *n* (*100 000*, *mst Rupien*).
lace [leɪs] **I** *s.* **1.** Spitze *f* (*Stoff*); **2.** Litze *f*, Borte *f*, Tresse *f*, Schnur *f*: ***gold ~***; **3.** Schnürband *n*, -senkel *m*; → ***laced*** 1; **4.** Schnur *f*, Band *n*; **II** *v/t.* **5.** *a.* ***~ up*** (zu-, zs.-)schnüren; **6.** *j-n*, *j-s Taille* schnüren; **7.** ***~ s.o.*** F → 14; **8.** *Finger etc.* ineinanderschlingen; **9.** mit Spitzen *od.* Litzen besetzen; Schnürsenkel einziehen in; **10.** mit Streifenmuster verzieren; **11.** *fig.* durch'setzen (***with*** mit): ***a story ~d with jokes***; **12.** e-n Schuß Alkohol zugeben (*dat.*); **III** *v/i.* **13.** *a.* ***~ up*** sich schnüren (lassen); **14.** ***~ into*** F a) auf *j-n* einprügeln, b) *j-n* anbrüllen; **laced** [-st] *adj.* **1.** geschnürt, Schnür...: ***~ boot*** Schnürstiefel *m*; **2.** mit e-m Schuß Alkohol, ‚mit Schuß': ***~ coffee***.
lace| pa·per *s.* Pa'pierspitzen *pl.*; **~ pil·low** *s.* Klöppelkissen *n*.
lac·er·ate [ˈlæsəreɪt] *v/t.* **1.** a) aufreißen, -schlitzen, zerfetzen, -kratzen, b) zerfleischen, zerreißen; **2.** *fig.* *j-n*, *j-s Gefühle* zutiefst verletzen; **lac·er·a·tion** [ˌlæsəˈreɪʃn] *s.* **1.** Zerreißung *f*, Zerfleischung *f* (*a. fig.*); **2.** ⚕ Schnitt-, Riß-, Fleischwunde *f*, Riß *m*.
'lace|-up (shoe) *s.* Schnürschuh *m*; **'~·work** *s.* **1.** Spitzenarbeit *f*, -muster *n*; **2.** *weitS.* Fili'gran(muster) *n*.
lach·ry·mal [ˈlækrɪml] **I** *adj.* **1.** Tränen...: ***~ gland***; **II** *s.* **2.** *pl. anat.* 'Tränenappa,rat *m*; **3.** *hist.* Tränenkrug *m*; **'lach·ry·mose** [-məʊs] *adj.* □ **1.** weinerlich; **2.** *fig.* rührselig: ***~ story***.
lac·ing [ˈleɪsɪŋ] *s.* **1.** Litzen *pl.*, Tressen *pl.*; **2.** → ***lace*** 3; **3.** ‚Schuß' *m* (Alkohol); **4.** Tracht *f* Prügel.
lack [læk] **I** *s.* (***of***) Mangel *m* (an *dat.*), Fehlen *n* (von): ***for ~ of time*** aus Zeitmangel; ***there was no ~ of*** es fehlte nicht *od.* da war kein Mangel an (*dat.*); **II** *v/t.* Mangel haben an (*dat.*), *et.* nicht haben *od.* besitzen: ***he ~s time*** ihm fehlt es an (der nötigen) Zeit, er hat keine Zeit; **III** *v/i.*: ***be ~ing*** fehlen, nicht vorhanden sein; ***wine was not ~ing*** an Wein fehlte es nicht; ***he ~ed for nothing*** es fehlte ihm an nichts; ***be ~ing in*** → II.
lack·a·dai·si·cal [ˌlækəˈdeɪzɪkəl] *adj.* □ **1.** lustlos, gelangweilt, gleichgültig; **2.** schlaff, lasch.
lack·ey [ˈlækɪ] *s. bsd. fig. contp.* La'kai *m*.
'lack|,lus·ter *Am.*, **'~,lus·tre** *Brit. adj.* glanzlos, matt, *fig. a.* farblos.
la·con·ic [ləˈkɒnɪk] *adj.* (□ ***~ally***) **1.** la'konisch, kurz u. treffend; **2.** wortkarg; **lac·o·nism** [ˈlækənɪzəm] *s.* Lako'nismus *m*: a) La'konik *f*, la'konische Kürze, b) la'konischer Ausspruch.
lac·quer [ˈlækə] **I** *s.* **1.** (Farb)Lack *m*, (Lack)Firnis *m*; **2.** a) (Nagel)Lack *m*, b) Haarspray *m*; **3.** *a.* ***~ ware*** Lackarbeit *f*, -waren *pl.*; **II** *v/t.* **4.** lackieren.
la·crosse [ləˈkrɒs] *s.* La'crosse *n* (*Ballspiel*): ***~ stick*** La'crosseschläger *m*.
lac·tate [ˈlækteɪt] **I** *v/t. physiol. Milch* absondern; **II** *s.* ⚗ Lak'tat *n*; **lac·ta·tion** [lækˈteɪʃn] *s.* Laktati'on *f*: a) Milchabsonderung *f*, b) Stillen *n*, c) Stillzeit *f*; **'lac·te·al** [-tɪəl] **I** *adj.* Milch..., milchähnlich; **II** *s. pl.* Milch-, Lymphgefäße *pl.*; **'lac·tic** [-tɪk] *adj.* Milch...: ***~ acid*** Milchsäure *f*; **lac·tif·er·ous** [lækˈtɪfərəs] *adj.* milchführend: ***~ duct*** Milchgang *m*; **lac·tom·e·ter** [lækˈtɒmɪtə] *s.* Lakto'meter *n*, Milchwaage *f*; **'lac·tose** [-təʊs] *s.* Lak'tose *f*, Milchzucker *m*.
la·cu·na [ləˈkjuːnə] *pl.* **-nae** [-niː] *od.* **-nas** *s.* Lücke *f*, La'kune *f*: a) *anat.* Spalt *m*, Hohlraum *m*, b) (Text- *etc.*)

Lücke *f*; **la'cu·nar** [-nə] *s.* ⚠ Kas'settendecke *f*.

la·cus·trine [lə'kʌstraɪn] *adj.* See…: **~ dwellings** Pfahlbauten.

lac·y ['leɪsɪ] *adj.* spitzenartig, Spitzen…

lad [læd] *s.* **1.** (junger) Kerl *od.* Bursche, Junge *m*: ***he's just a ~!*** er ist (doch) noch ein Junge!; ***come on, ~s!*** los, Jungs!; ***he's a bit of a ~*** F *Brit.* er ist ein ziemlicher Draufgänger *od.* Schwerenöter; **2.** *Brit.* Stallbursche *m*.

lad·der ['lædə] **I** *s.* **1.** Leiter *f* (*a. fig.*): ***the social ~*** *fig.* die gesellschaftliche Stufenleiter; ***the ~ of fame*** die (Stufen-)Leiter des Ruhms; ***kick down the ~*** die Leute loswerden wollen, die e-m beim Aufstieg geholfen haben; **2.** *Brit.* Laufmasche *f*; **3.** *Tischtennis etc.*: Ta'belle *f*; **II** *v/i.* **4.** *Brit.* Laufmaschen bekommen (*Strumpf*); **III** *v/t.* **5.** *Brit.* zerreißen: ***~ one's stockings*** sich e-e Laufmasche holen; **'~·proof** *adj. Brit.* (lauf)maschenfest (*Strumpf*).

lad·die ['lædɪ] *s. bsd. Scot.* F Bürschchen *n*.

lade [leɪd] *p.p. a.* **'lad·en** [-dn] *v/t.* **1.** (be)laden, befrachten; **2.** *Waren* ver-, aufladen; **'lad·en** [-dn] **I** *p.p. von* ***lade***; **II** *adj.* (***with***) *a. fig.* beladen *od.* befrachtet (mit), voll (von), voller: ***~ with fruit*** (schwer) beladen mit Obst.

la-di-da(h) [ˌlɑːdɪ'dɑː] *adj. Brit.* F affektiert, vornehmtuerisch, ‚affig'.

la·dies'| choice *s.* Damenwahl *f* (*beim Tanz*); **~ man** *s.* [*irr.*] Frauenheld *m*, Char'meur *m*; **~ room** → ***lady*** 6.

lad·ing ['leɪdɪŋ] *s.* **1.** (Ver)Laden *n*; **2.** Ladung *f*; → ***bill***[2] 3.

la·dle ['leɪdl] **I** *s.* **1.** Schöpflöffel *m*, (Schöpf-, Suppen)Kelle *f*; **2.** ⚙ Gießkelle *f*, -löffel *m*; **3.** Schaufel *f* (*am Wasserrad*); **II** *v/t.* **4.** *a.* **~ out** (aus)schöpfen, *a.* F *fig. Lob etc.* austeilen.

la·dy ['leɪdɪ] **I** *s.* **1.** Dame *f*: ***she is no*** (*od.* ***not a***) **~** sie ist keine Dame; ***an English ~*** e-e Engländerin; ***young ~*** junge Dame, junges Mädchen; ***young ~!*** *iro.* (mein) liebes Fräulein!; ***his young ~*** F s-e (kleine) Freundin; ***my*** (***dear***) **~** (verehrte) gnädige Frau; ***ladies and gentlemen*** m-e (sehr verehrten) Damen u. Herren; **2.** Lady *f* (*Titel*): ***my ~!*** Mylady!, gnädige Frau; **3.** *obs. od.* F (*außer wenn auf e-e* ***Lady*** *angewandt*) Gattin *f*, Gemahlin *f*: ***the old ~*** F a) die alte Dame (*Mutter*), b) m-e *etc.* ‚Alte' (*Frau*); **4.** Herrin *f*, Gebieterin *f*: ***~ of the house*** Hausherrin, Dame *f* des Hauses; ***our sovereign ~*** *Brit.* die Königin; **5.** ***Our*** ***ℒ*** Unsere Liebe Frau, die Mutter Gottes: ***Church of Our ℒ*** Marien-, (Lieb)Frauenkirche *f*; **6.** ***Ladies*** *pl. sg. konstr.* 'Damentoiˌlette *f*, ‚Damen' *n*; **II** *adj.* **7.** weiblich: ***~ doctor*** Ärztin *f*; ***~ friend*** Freundin *f*; ***~ mayoress*** Frau *f* (Ober)Bürgermeister; ***~ dog*** *humor.* ‚Hundedame' *f*.

'la·dy|·bird *s. zo.* Ma'rienkäfer(chen *n*) *m*; **ℒ Boun·ti·ful** *s. fig.* gute Fee; **'~·bug** *Am.* → ***ladybird***; **ℒ Day** *s. eccl.* Ma'riä Verkündigung *f*; **'~ˌfin·ger** *s.* Löffelbiskuit *n*; **ˌ~-in-'wait·ing** *s.* Hofdame *f*; **'~ˌkill·er** *s.* F Herzensbrecher *m*, Ladykiller *m*; **'~·like** *adj.* damenhaft, vornehm; **'~·love** *s. obs.* Geliebte *f*; **ℒ of the Bed·cham·ber** *s. Brit.* königliche Kammerfrau, Hofdame *f*.

la·dy·ship ['leɪdɪʃɪp] *s.* Ladyschaft *f* (*Stand u. Anrede*): ***her*** (***your***) **~** ihre (Eure) Ladyschaft.

la·dy's| maid *s.* Kammerzofe *f*; **'~-ˌslip·per** *s.* ♀ Frauenschuh *m*.

lag[1] [læg] **I** *v/i.* **1.** *mst* **~ *behind*** *a. fig.* zu'rückbleiben, nicht mitkommen, nach-, hinter'herhinken; **2.** *mst* **~ *behind*** a) sich verzögern, b) zögern, c) ⚡ nacheilen; **II** *s.* **3.** Zu'rückbleiben *n*, Rückstand *m*, Verzögerung *f* (*a.* ⚙, *phys.*): ***cultural ~*** kultureller Rückstand; **4.** 'Zeitabstand *m*, -ˌunterschied *m*; **5.** ⚡ negative Phasenverschiebung, (Phasen)Nacheilung *f*.

lag[2] [læg] *s. Brit. sl.* **1.** ‚Knastschieber' *m*, ‚Knacki' *m*; **2.** ***do a ~*** ‚(im Knast) sitzen'.

lag[3] [læg] **I** *s.* **1.** (Faß)Daube *f*; **2.** ⚙ Verschalungsbrett *n*; **II** *v/t.* **3.** mit Dauben versehen; **4.** ⚙ *Rohre etc.* isolieren, um'wickeln.

lag·an ['lægən] *s.* ⚖, ⚓ versenktes (Wrack)Gut.

la·ger (**beer**) ['lɑːgə] *s.* Lagerbier *n* (*ein helles Bier*).

lag·gard ['lægəd] **I** *adj.* ☐ **1.** langsam, bummelig, faul; **II** *s.* **2.** ‚Trödler(in)', Bummler(in); **3.** Nachzügler(in).

lag·ging ['lægɪŋ] *s.* ⚙ **1.** Verkleidung *f*, Verschalung *f*; **2.** a) Isolierung *f*, b) Iso'liermateriˌal *n*.

la·goon [lə'guːn] *s.* La'gune *f*.

la·ic, la·i·cal ['leɪɪk(l)] *adj.* weltlich, Laien…; **'la·i·cize** [-ɪsaɪz] *v/t.* säkularisieren.

laid [leɪd] *pret. u. p.p. von* ***lay***[1]: ***~ up*** → ***lay up*** 4; **'~·back** *adj. Am.* **1.** entspannend; **2.** entspannt, ruhig.

lain [leɪn] *p.p. von* ***lie***[2].

lair [leə] *s.* **1.** *zo.* a) Lager *n*, b) Höhle *f*, Bau *m* (*des Wildes*); **2.** *allg.* Lager(statt *f*) *n*; **3.** F *fig.* a) Versteck *n*, b) Zuflucht(sort *m*) *f*.

laird [leəd] *s. Scot.* Gutsherr *m*.

lais·sez-faire [ˌleɪseɪ'feə] (*Fr.*) *s.* Laissez-'faire *n* (*Gewährenlassen, Nichteinmischung*).

la·i·ty ['leɪətɪ] *s.* **1.** Laienstand *m*, Laien *pl.* (*Ggs. Geistlichkeit*); **2.** Laien *pl.*, Nichtfachleute *pl.*

lake[1] [leɪk] *s.* **1.** (*bsd.* rote) Pig'mentfarbe, Farblack *m*; **2.** Beizenfarbstoff *m*.

lake[2] [leɪk] *s.* (Binnen)See *m*: ***the Great ℒ*** der große Teich (*der Atlantische Ozean*); ***the Great ℒs*** die Großen Seen (*an der Grenze zwischen USA u. Kanada*); ***the ~s*** → **ℒ Dis·trict** *s. das* Seengebiet (*im Nordwesten Englands*); **~ dwell·er** *s.* Pfahlbauer *m*; **~ dwell·ing** *s.* Pfahlbau *m*; **'ℒ·land** → ***Lake District***; **ℒ po·et** *s.* Seendichter *m* (*e-r der 3 Dichter der* ***Lake school***); **ℒ school** *s.* Seeschule *f* (*die Dichter Southey, Coleridge u. Wordsworth*).

lam[1] [læm] *sl.* **I** *v/t.* verdreschen, ‚vermöbeln'; **II** *v/i.*: **~ *into*** a) → I, b) *fig.* auf *j-n* ‚einhauen'.

lam[2] [læm] *Am. sl.* **I** *s.*: ***on the ~*** im ‚Abhauen' (begriffen), auf der Flucht (*vor der Polizei*); ***take it on the ~*** → **II** *v/i.* ‚türmen', ‚Leine ziehen'.

la·ma ['lɑːmə] *s. eccl.* Lama *m*; **'la·ma·ism** [-əɪzəm] *s. eccl.* Lama'ismus *m*; **'la·ma·ser·y** [-əsərɪ] *s.* Lamakloster *n*.

lamb [læm] **I** *s.* **1.** Lamm *n*: ***in*** (*od.* ***with***) **~** trächtig (*Schaf*); ***like a ~*** *fig.* wie ein Lamm, lammfromm; ***like a ~ to the slaughter*** *fig.* wie ein Lamm zur Schlachtbank; **2.** Lamm(fleisch) *n*; **3.** ***the ℒ*** (***of God***) *eccl.* das Lamm (Gottes); **4.** F Schätzchen *n*; **II** *v/i.* **5.** lammen: ***~ing time*** Lammzeit *f*.

lam·baste [læm'beɪst] *v/t. sl.* **1.** ‚vermöbeln' (*verprügeln*); **2.** *fig.* ‚her'unterputzen', ‚zs.-stauchen'.

lam·ben·cy ['læmbənsɪ] *s.* **1.** Züngeln *n* (*e-r Flamme*); **2.** *fig.* (*geistreiches*) Funkeln, Sprühen *n*; **'lam·bent** [-nt] *adj.* ☐ **1.** züngelnd, flackernd; **2.** sanft strahlend; **3.** *fig.* sprühend, funkelnd (*Witz*).

lamb·kin ['læmkɪn] *s.* **1.** Lämmchen *n*; **2.** *fig.* ‚Schätzchen' *n*.

'lamb·skin *s.* **1.** Lammfell *n*; **2.** Schafleder *n*.

lamb's| tails *s. pl.* ♀ **1.** *Brit.* Haselkätzchen *pl.*; **2.** *Am.* Weiden-, Palmkätzchen *pl.*; **~ wool** *s.* Lammwolle *f*.

lame [leɪm] **I** *adj.* ☐ **1.** lahm, hinkend: **~ *in*** (*od.* ***of***) ***one leg*** auf 'einem Bein lahm; **2.** *fig.* ‚lahm', ‚müde': ***~ efforts***; ***~ story***; ***~ excuse*** faule Ausrede; ***~ verses*** holprige *od.* hinkende Verse; **II** *v/t.* **3.** lahm machen, lähmen (*a. fig.*); **~ duck** *s.* F **1.** Körperbehinderte(r *m*) *f*; **2.** ‚Versager' *m*, ‚Niete' *f*; **3.** ✝ ruinierter ('Börsen)Spekuˌlant; **4.** *Am. pol. nicht wiedergewählter Amtsinhaber, bsd. Kongreßmitglied od. Präsident, bis zum Ende s-r Amtsperiode.*

la·mel·la [lə'melə] *pl.* **-lae** [-liː] *s. allg.* La'melle *f*, Plättchen *n*; **la'mel·lar** [-lə], **lam·el·late** ['læməleɪt] *adj.* la'mellenartig, Lamellen…

lame·ness ['leɪmnɪs] *s.* **1.** Lahmheit *f* (*a. fig., contp.*); **2.** *fig.* Schwäche *f*; **3.** Hinken *n* (*von Versen*).

la·ment [lə'ment] **I** *v/i.* **1.** jammern, (weh)klagen, lamentieren (***for*** *od.* ***over*** um); **2.** trauern (***for*** *od.* ***over*** um); **II** *v/t.* **3.** bejammern, beklagen, bedauern, betrauern; **III** *s.* **4.** Jammer *m*, Wehklage *f*, Klage(lied *n*) *f*; **lam·en·ta·ble** ['læməntəbl] *adj.* ☐ **1.** beklagenswert, bedauerlich; **2.** *contp.* erbärmlich, kläglich, jämmerlich (schlecht); **lam·en·ta·tion** [ˌlæmen'teɪʃn] *s.* **1.** Jammern *n*, Lamentieren *n*, (Weh)Klage *f*, *iro. a.* La'mento *n*; **2.** ***ℒs*** (***of Jeremiah***) *pl. mst sg. konstr. bibl.* Klagelieder *pl.* Jere'miae.

lam·i·na ['læmɪnə] *pl.* **-nae** [-niː] *s.* **1.** Plättchen *n*, Blättchen *n*; **2.** (dünne) Schicht; **3.** ♀ Blattspreite *f*; **'lam·i·nal** [-nl], **'lam·i·nar** [-nə] *adj.* **1.** blätterig; **2.** (blättchenartig) geschichtet; **3.** *phys.* lami'nar: **~ *flow*** Laminarströmung *f*; **'lam·i·nate** [-neɪt] **I** *v/t.* **1.** ⚙ a) auswalzen, strecken, b) in Blättchen aufspalten, c) schichten; **2.** mit Plättchen belegen, mit Folie über'ziehen; **II** *v/i.* **3.** sich in Plättchen *od.* Schichten spalten; **III** *s.* **4.** ⚙ (Plastik-, Verbund)Folie *f*; **IV** *adj.* **5.** → ***laminar***.

lam·i·nat·ed ['læmɪneɪtɪd] *adj.* la'mellenartig, Lamellen…; ⚙ *a.* blättrig *od.* geschichtet: ***~ glass*** Verbundglas *n*; ***~ material*** Schichtstoff *m*; ***~ paper*** Hartpapier *n*; ***~ sheet*** Schichtplatte *f*; ***~ spring*** Blattfeder *f*; ***~ wood*** Sperr-, Preßholz *n*; **lam·i·na·tion** [ˌlæmɪ'neɪʃn] *s.* **1.** ⚙ a) Lamellierung *f*, b) Streckung *f*, c) Schichtung *f*; **2.** 'Blätterstrukˌtur *f*.

lam·mer·gei·er, lam·mer·gey·er ['læməgaɪə] *s. orn.* Lämmergeier *m.*

lamp [læmp] *s.* **1.** Lampe *f*; (*Straßen- etc.*)La'terne *f*: ***smell of the ~*** nach ‚saurem Schweiß riechen', mehr Fleiß als Talent verraten; **2.** ϟ Lampe *f*: a) Glühbirne *f*, b) Leuchte *f*; **3.** *fig.* Leuchte *f*, Licht *n*; **'~·black** *s.* Lampenruß *m*, -schwarz *n*; **~ chim·ney** *s.* 'Lampenzyˌlinder *m*; **'~·light** *s.* (***by ~*** bei) Lampenlicht *n.*

lam·poon [læm'pu:n] **I** *s.* Spott- *od.* Schmähschrift *f*, Pam'phlet *n*, Sa'tire *f*; **II** *v/t.* (*schriftlich*) verspotten, -höhnen; **lam'poon·er** [-nə], **lam'poon·ist** [-nɪst] *s.* Pamphle'tist(in).

'lamp·post *s.* La'ternenpfahl *m*: ***between you and me and the ~*** F (ganz) unter uns (gesagt).

lam·prey ['læmprɪ] *s. ichth.* Lam'prete *f*, Neunauge *n.*

'lamp·shade *s.* Lampenschirm *m.*

Lan·cas·tri·an [læŋ'kæstrɪən] *Brit.* **I** *s.* **1.** Bewohner(in) der Stadt *od.* Grafschaft Lancaster; **2.** *hist.* Angehörige(r *m*) *f od.* Anhänger(in) des Hauses Lancaster; **II** *adj.* **3.** Lancaster…

lance [lɑ:ns] **I** *s.* **1.** Lanze *f*, Speer *m*: ***break a ~ for*** (*od.* ***on behalf of***) ***s.o.*** e-e Lanze für j-n brechen; **2.** → ***lancer*** 1; **3.** → ***lancet*** 1; **II** *v/t.* **4.** mit e-r Lanze durch'bohren; **5.** ⚕ mit e-r Lan'zette öffnen: ***~ a boil*** ein Geschwür (*fig.* e-e Eiterbeule) aufstechen; **~ cor·po·ral** *s.* ⚔ *Brit.* Ober-, Hauptgefreite(r) *m.*

lanc·er ['lɑ:nsə] *s.* **1.** ⚔ *hist.* U'lan *m*; **2.** *pl. sg. konstr.* Lanci'er *m* (*Tanz*).

lan·cet ['lɑ:nsɪt] *s.* **1.** ⚕ Lan'zette *f*; **2.** △ a) *a.* ***~ arch*** Spitzbogen *m*, b) *a.* ***~ window*** Spitzbogenfenster *n.*

land [lænd] **I** *s.* **1.** Land *n* (*Ggs. Meer, Wasser*): ***by ~*** auf dem Landweg; ***by ~ and by sea*** zu Wasser u. zu Lande; ***make ~*** ⚓ Land sichten; ***see how the ~ lies*** sehen, wie der Hase läuft, die Lage ‚peilen'; **2.** Land *n*, Boden *m*: ***live off the ~*** a) von den Früchten des Landes leben, b) sich aus der Natur ernähren (*Soldaten etc.*); **3.** Land *n*, Grund *m* u. Boden *m*, Grundbesitz *m*, Lände'reien *pl.*; **4.** Land *n* (*Staat, Region*): ***far-off ~s*** ferne Länder; **5.** *fig.* Land *n*, Reich *n*: ***~ of the living*** Diesseits *n*; ***~ of dreams*** Reich der Träume; **II** *v/i.* **6.** ⚓, ✈ landen; ⚓ anlegen; **7.** landen, an Land gehen, aussteigen; **8.** landen, (an-)kommen: ***he ~ed in a ditch*** er landete in e-m Graben; ***~ on one's feet*** auf die Füße fallen (*a. fig.*); ***~ (up) in prison*** im Gefängnis landen; **9.** *sport* durchs Ziel gehen; **III** *v/t.* **10.** *Personen, Waren, Flugzeug* landen; *Schiffsgüter* landen, löschen, ausladen; *Fisch(fang)* an Land bringen; **11.** *bsd. Fahrgäste* absetzen; **12.** *j-n in Schwierigkeiten etc.* bringen, verwickeln: ***~ s.o. in difficulties***; ***~ s.o. with s.th.*** j-m et. aufhalsen *od.* einbrocken; ***~ o.s.*** (*od.* ***be ~ed***) ***in*** (hinein)geraten in (*acc.*); **13.** F a) *e-n Schlag od. Treffer* landen: ***I ~ed him one*** ich hab' ihm eine geknallt *od.* ‚verpaßt'; **14.** F *j-n od. et.* ‚erwischen', (sich) ‚schnappen', ‚kriegen': ***~ a prize*** sich e-n Preis ‚holen'; ***~ a good contract*** e-n guten Vertrag ‚an Land ziehen'.

land a·gent *s.* **1.** Grundstücksmakler *m*; **2.** *Brit.* Gutsverwalter *m.*

lan·dau ['lændɔ:] *s.* Landauer *m* (*Kutsche*).

land| bank *s.* 'Bodenkreˌdit-, Hypo'thekenbank *f*; **~ car·riage** *s.* 'Landtransˌport *m*, -fracht *f*; **~ crab** *s. zo.* Landkrabbe *f.*

land·ed ['lændɪd] *adj.* Land…, Grund…: ***~ estate***, ***~ property*** Grundbesitz *m*, -eigentum *n*; ***~ gentry*** Landadel *m*; ***~ proprietor*** Grundbesitzer (-in); ***the ~ interest*** *coll.* die Grundbesitzer.

'land|·fall *s.* ⚓ Landkennung *f*, Sichten *n* von Land; **~ forc·es** *s. pl.* ⚔ Landstreitkräfte *pl.*; **'~·grave** [-ndg-] *s. hist.* (deutscher) Landgraf; **'~ˌhold·er** *s.* Grundbesitzer *m od.* -pächter *m.*

land·ing ['lændɪŋ] *s.* **1.** ⚓ Landen *n*, Landung *f*: a) Anlegen *n* (*e-s Schiffs*), b) Ausschiffung *f* (*von Personen*), c) Ausladen *n*, Löschen *n* (*der Fracht*); **2.** ⚓ Lande-, Anlegeplatz *m*; **3.** ✈ Landung *f*; **4.** △ Treppenabsatz *m*; **~ beam** *s.* ✈ Landeleitstrahl *m*; **~ card** *s.* Einreisekarte *f*; **~ craft** *s.* ⚓, ⚔ Landungsboot *n*; **~ field** *s.* ✈ Landeplatz *m*, -bahn *f*; **~ flap** *s.* ✈ Landeklappe *f*; **~ gear** *s.* ✈ Fahrgestell *n*, -werk *n*; **~ net** *s.* Hamen *m*, Kescher *m*; **~ par·ty** *s.* ⚔ 'Landungstrupp *m*, -komˌmando *n*; **~ place** → ***landing*** 2; **~ stage** *s.* ⚓ Landungsbrücke *f*, -steg *m*; **~ strip**, **~ track** → ***air strip.***

'landˌla·dy ['lænˌl-] *s.* (Haus-, Gast-, Pensi'ons)Wirtin *f.*

land·less ['lændlɪs] *adj.* ohne Grundbesitz.

'land|·locked *adj.* 'landumˌschlossen, ohne Zugang zum Meer: ***~ country*** Binnenstaat *m*; **'~ˌlop·er** [-ˌləʊpə] *s.* Landstreicher *m*; **'~·lord** ['lænl-] *s.* **1.** Grundbesitzer *m*; **2.** Hauseigentümer *m*; **3.** Hauswirt *m*, ⚖ *a.* Hauswirtin *f*; **4.** (Gast)Wirt *m*; **'~ˌlub·ber** *s.* ⚓ ‚Landratte' *f*; **'~·mark** [-ndm-] *s.* **1.** Grenzstein *m*; **2.** ⚓ Seezeichen *n*; **3.** ⚔ Gelände-, Orientierungspunkt *m*; **4.** Wahrzeichen *n* (*e-r Stadt etc.*); **5.** *fig.* Meilen-, Markstein *m*, Wendepunkt *m*: ***a ~ in history***; **'~·mine** [-ndm-] *s.* ⚔ Landmine *f*; **~ of·fice** *s. Am.* Grundbuchamt *n*; **'~ˌof·fice busi·ness** *s. Am.* F ‚Bombengeschäft' *n*; **'~ˌown·er** *s.* Land-, Grundbesitzer(in); **~ re·form** *s.* 'Bodenreˌform *f*; **~ reg·is·ter** *s.* Grundbuch *n.*

land·scape ['lænskeɪp] **I** *s.* **1.** Landschaft *f* (*a. paint.*); **2.** Landschaftsmale'rei *f*; **II** *v/i.* **3.** landschaftlich *od.* gärtnerisch gestalten, anlegen; **~ ar·chi·tect** *s.* **1.** 'Landschaftsarchiˌtekt(in); **2.** → **~ gar·den·er** *s.* Landschaftsgärtner (-in), 'Gartenarchiˌtekt(in); **~ gar·den·ing** *s.* Landschaftsgärtne'rei *f*; **~ paint·er** → **land·scap·ist** ['lænˌskeɪpɪst] *s.* Landschaftsmaler(in).

'land|·slide [-nds-] *s.* **1.** Erdrutsch *m*; **2.** *a.* ***~ victory*** *pol. fig.* ‚Erdrutsch' *m*, über'wältigender (Wahl)Sieg; **'~·slip** [-nds-] *Brit.* → ***landslide*** 1; **~ sur·vey·or** *s.* Geo'meter *m*, Land(ver)messer *m*; **~ swell** [-nds-] *s.* ⚓ einlaufende Dünung; **~ tax** *s. obs.* Grundsteuer *f*; **~ tor·toise** *s. zo.* Landschildkröte *f*; **'~ˌwait·er** *s. Brit.* 'Zollinˌspektor *m.*

land·ward ['lændwəd] **I** *adj.* land('ein)wärts (gelegen); **II** *adv. a.* **'land·wards** [-dz] land(ein)wärts.

lane [leɪn] *s.* **1.** (Feld)Weg *m*, (Hecken-) Pfad *m*; **2.** Gasse *f*: a) Gäßchen *n*, Sträßchen *n*, b) 'Durchgang *m*: ***form a ~*** Spalier stehen, e-e Gasse bilden; **3.** Schneise *f*; **4.** ⚓ Fahrrinne *f*, (Fahrt-) Route *f*; **5.** ✈ (Flug)Schneise *f*; **6.** *mot.* (Fahr)Spur *f*: ***get in ~!*** bitte einordnen!; **7.** *sport* (*einzelne*) Bahn (*e-s Läufers, Schwimmers etc.*).

lang·syne [ˌlæŋ'saɪn] *Scot.* **I** *adv.* vor langer Zeit; **II** *s.* längst vergangene Zeit; → ***auld lang syne.***

lan·guage ['læŋgwɪdʒ] *s.* **1.** Sprache *f*: ***foreign ~s*** Fremdsprachen; ***~ of flowers*** *fig.* Blumensprache; ***talk the same ~*** *a. fig.* dieselbe Sprache sprechen; **2.** Sprache *f*, Ausdrucks-, Redeweise *f*, Worte *pl.*: ***bad ~*** ordinäre Ausdrücke, Schimpfworte; ***strong ~*** a) Kraftausdrücke, b) harte Worte *od.* Sprache; **3.** Sprache *f*, Stil *m*; **4.** (Fach)Sprache *f*: ***medical ~***; **5.** *sl.* ordi'näre Sprache: ***~, Sir!*** ich verbitte mir solche (gemeinen) Ausdrücke!; **~ bar·ri·er** *s.* Sprachschranke *f*; **~ lab·o·ra·to·ry** *s. ped.* 'Sprachlaˌbor *n.*

lan·guid ['læŋgwɪd] *adj.* □ **1.** schwach, matt, schlaff; **2.** schleppend, träge; **3.** gelangweilt, lustlos, lau; **4.** lässig, träge; **5.** ✝ flau, lustlos (*Markt*).

lan·guish ['læŋgwɪʃ] *v/i.* **1.** ermatten, erschlaffen, erlahmen (*a. fig. Interesse, Konversation*); **2.** (ver)schmachten, da'hinsiechen, -welken: ***~ in prison*** im Gefängnis schmachten; **3.** da'niederliegen (*Handel, Industrie etc.*); **4.** schmachtend blicken; **5.** schmachten (***for*** nach); **6.** Sehnsucht haben, sich härmen (***for*** nach); **'lan·guish·ing** [-ʃɪŋ] *adj.* □ **1.** ermattend, erlahmend (*a. fig.*); **2.** (ver)schmachtend, (da'hin-) siechend, leidend; **3.** sehnsuchtsvoll, schmachtend (*Blick*); **4.** lustlos, träge (*a.* ✝), langsam; **5.** langsam (*Tod*), schleichend (*Krankheit*).

lan·guor ['læŋgə] *s.* **1.** Mattigkeit *f*, Schlaffheit *f*; **2.** Trägheit *f*, Schläfrigkeit *f*; **3.** Stumpfheit *f*, Gleichgültigkeit *f*, Lauheit *f*; **4.** Stille *f*, Schwüle *f*; **'lan·guor·ous** [-ərəs] *adj.* □ **1.** matt; **2.** schlaff, träge; **3.** stumpf, gleichgültig; **4.** schläfrig, wohlig; **5.** schmelzend (*Musik etc.*); **6.** (*a. sinnlich*) schwül.

lank [læŋk] *adj.* □ **1.** lang u. dünn, schlank, mager; **2.** glatt, strähnig (*Haar*); **'lank·i·ness** [-kɪnɪs] *s.* Schlaksigkeit *f*; **'lank·y** [-kɪ] *adj.* hoch aufgeschossen, schlaksig.

lan·o·lin(e) ['lænəʊlɪn (-li:n)] *s.* ⚗ Lano'lin *n*, Wollfett *n.*

lan·tern ['læntən] *s.* **1.** La'terne *f*; **2.** Leuchtkammer *f* (*e-s Leuchtturms*); **3.** △ La'terne *f* (*durchbrochener Dachaufsatz*); **'~-jawed** *adj.* hohlwangig; **~ jaws** *s. pl.* eingefallene Wangen *pl.*; **~ slide** *s. obs.* Dia(posi'tiv) *n*, Lichtbild *n*: ***~ lecture*** Lichtbildervortrag *m.*

lan·yard ['lænjəd] *s.* **1.** ⚓ Taljereep *n*; **2.** ⚔ a) *obs.* Abzugsleine *f* (*Kanone*), b) Traggurt *m* (*Pistole*), c) (Achsel-) Schnur *f*; **3.** Schleife *f.*

lap[1] [læp] *s.* **1.** Schoß *m* (*e-s Kleides od. des Körpers*; *a. fig.*): ***sit on s.o.'s ~***; ***in the ~ of the church***; ***drop into s.o.'s ~*** j-m in den Schoß fallen; ***in Fortune's ~***

im Schoß des Glücks; ***it is in the ~ of the gods*** es liegt im Schoß der Götter; ***live in the ~ of luxury*** ein Luxusleben führen; **2.** (Kleider- *etc.*)Zipfel *m.*

lap² [læp] **I** *v/t.* **1.** falten, wickeln (***round, about*** um); **2.** einwickeln, -schlagen, -hüllen; **3.** *a. fig.* um'hüllen, (ein)betten, (-)hüllen: ***~ped in luxury*** von Luxus umgeben; **4.** überein'anderlegen, über'lappt anordnen; **5.** *sport* a) *Gegner* über'runden, b) *e-e Strecke* zu'rücklegen (*in 1 Minute etc.*); **II** *v/i.* **6.** sich winden *od.* legen (***round*** um); **7.** hin'ausragen, -gehen (*a. fig.*; ***over*** über *acc.*); **8.** über'lappen; **9.** *sport* die *od.* s-e Runde drehen *od.* laufen (***at*** in e-r Zeit von); **III** *s.* **10.** ⚙ Wickelung *f*, Windung *f*, Lage *f*; **11.** Über'lappung *f*, 'Überstand *m*; **12.** 'überstehender Teil, Vorstoß *m*; **13.** *Buchbinderei*: Falz *m*; **14.** *sport* Runde *f*; **15.** E'tappe *f* (*e-r Reise*, *a. fig.*).

lap³ [læp] **I** *v/t.* **1.** *a.* ***~ up*** auflecken; **2.** ***~ up*** a) *Suppe etc.* gierig (hin'unter-)schlürfen, b) F *et.* ‚fressen' (*glauben*), c) F *et.* gierig (in sich) aufnehmen, *et.* liebend gern hören *etc.*: ***they ~ped it up*** es ging ihnen ‚runter wie Öl'; **3.** plätschern gegen; **II** *v/i.* **4.** lecken, schlecken, schlürfen; **5.** plätschern; **III** *s.* **6.** Lecken *n*; **7.** Plätschern *n.*

'lap-dog *s.* Schoßhund *m.*

la·pel [lə'pel] *s.* (Rock)Aufschlag *m*, Re'vers *n*, *m.*

lap·i·dar·y ['læpɪdərɪ] **I** *s.* **1.** Edelsteinschneider *m*; **II** *adj.* **2.** Stein…; **3.** Steinschleiferei…; **4.** (Stein)Inschriften…; **5.** in Stein gehauen; **6.** *fig.* wuchtig, lapi'dar.

lap·is laz·u·li [ˌlæpɪs'læzjʊlaɪ] *s. min.* Lapis'lazuli *m.*

Lap·land·er ['læplændə] → ***Lapp*** I.

Lapp [læp] **I** *s.* Lappe *m*, Lappin *f*, Lappländer(in); **II** *adj.* lappisch.

lap·pet ['læpɪt] *s.* **1.** Zipfel *m*; **2.** *anat.*, *zo.* Hautlappen *m.*

Lap·pish ['læpɪʃ] → ***Lapp*** II.

lapse [læps] **I** *s.* **1.** Lapsus *m*, Fehler *m*, Versehen *n*: ***~ of the pen*** Schreibfehler *m*; ***~ of justice*** Justizirrtum *m*; ***~ of taste*** Geschmacksverirrung *f*; **2.** Fehltritt *m*, Vergehen *n*, Entgleisung *f*: ***~ from duty*** Pflichtversäumnis *n*; ***~ from faith*** Abfall *m* vom Glauben; **3.** Absinken *n*, Abgleiten *n*, Verfall(en *n*) *m* (***into*** in *acc.*); **4.** a) Ablauf *m*, Vergehen *n* (*e-r Zeit*), b) ⚖ (Frist)Ablauf *m*, c) Zeitspanne *f*; **5.** ⚖ a) Verfall *m*, Erlöschen *n e-s Anspruchs etc.*, b) Heimfall *m* (*von Erbteilen etc.*); **6.** Aufhören, Verschwinden *n*, Aussterben *n*; **II** *v/i.* **7.** a) verstreichen (*Zeit*), b) ablaufen (*Frist*); **8.** verfallen (***into*** in *acc.*): ***~ into silence***; **9.** absinken, abgleiten, verfallen (***into*** in *Barbarei etc.*); **10.** e-n Fehltritt tun, (mo'ralisch) entgleisen, sündigen; **11.** abfallen (***from faith*** vom Glauben); ***~ from duty*** s-e Pflicht versäumen; **12.** ‚einschlafen', aufhören (*Beziehung*, *Unterhaltung etc.*); **13.** ⚖ a) verfallen, erlöschen (*Recht etc.*), b) heimfallen (***to*** an *acc.*).

lap·wing ['læpwɪŋ] *s. orn.* Kiebitz *m.*

lar·board ['lɑːbəd] ⚓ *obs.* **I** *s.* Backbord *n*; **II** *adj.* Backbord…

lar·ce·ner ['lɑːsənə], **'lar·ce·nist** [-nɪst] *s.* ⚖ Dieb *m*; **'lar·ce·ny** [-nɪ] *s.* ⚖ Diebstahl *m.*

larch [lɑːtʃ] *s.* ⚘ Lärche *f.*

lard [lɑːd] **I** *s.* **1.** Schweinefett *n*, -schmalz *n*; **II** *v/t.* **2.** *Fleisch* spicken: ***~ing needle*** (*od. pin*) Spicknadel *f*; **3.** *fig.* spicken (***with*** mit); **'lard·er** [-də] *s.* Speisekammer *f*, -schrank *m.*

large [lɑːdʒ] **I** *adj.* □ → ***largely***; **1.** groß: ***a ~ room*** (***horse, rock***, *etc.*); (***as***) ***~ as life*** in (voller) Lebensgröße (*a. humor.*); ***~r than life*** überlebensgroß; **2.** groß (*beträchtlich*): ***a ~ business*** (***family, sum***, *etc.*); ***a ~ meal*** e-e reichliche Mahlzeit; ***~ farmer*** Großbauer *m*; ***~ producer*** Großerzeuger *m*; **3.** um'fassend, ausgedehnt, weit(gehend): ***~ powers*** umfassende Vollmachten; **4.** *obs.* großzügig; → *a.* ***large-minded***; **II** *adv.* **5.** groß: ***write ~***; ***it was written ~ all over his face*** *fig.* es stand ihm (deutlich) im Gesicht geschrieben; **6.** großspurig: ***talk ~*** ‚große Töne spucken'; **III** *s.* **7.** ***at ~*** a) auf freiem Fuß, in Freiheit: ***set s.o. at ~*** j-n auf freien Fuß setzen, b) (sehr) ausführlich: ***discuss s.th. at ~***, c) ganz allgemein, d) in der Gesamtheit: ***the nation at ~***; ***talk at ~*** ins Blaue hineinreden; **8.** ***in*** (***the***) ***~*** a) im großen, in großem Maßstab, b) im ganzen; **ˌ~-'hand·ed** *adj. fig.* freigebig; **ˌ~-'heart·ed** *adj. fig.* großherzig.

large·ly ['lɑːdʒlɪ] *adv.* **1.** in hohem Maße, großen-, größtenteils; **2.** weitgehend, im wesentlichen; **3.** reichlich; **4.** allgemein.

ˌlarge-'mind·ed *adj.* vorurteilslos, tole'rant, aufgeschlossen.

large·ness ['lɑːdʒnɪs] *s.* **1.** Größe *f*; **2.** Größe *f*, Weite *f*, 'Umfang *m*; **3.** Großzügigkeit *f*, Freigebigkeit *f*; **4.** Großmütigkeit *f.*

'large-scale *adj.* groß(angelegt), 'umfangreich, ausgedehnt, Groß…: ***~ attack*** ⚔ Großangriff *m*; ***~ experiment*** Großversuch *m*; ***~ manufacture*** Serienherstellung *f*; ***a ~ map*** e-e Karte in großem Maßstab.

lar·gess(e) [lɑː'dʒes] *s.* **1.** Freigebigkeit *f*; **2.** a) Gabe *f*, reiches Geschenk, b) reiche Geschenke *pl.*

larg·ish ['lɑːdʒɪʃ] *adj.* ziemlich groß.

lar·i·at ['lærɪət] *s.* Lasso *m*, *n.*

lark¹ [lɑːk] *s. orn.* Lerche *f*: ***rise with the ~*** mit den Hühnern aufstehen.

lark² [lɑːk] F **I** *s.* **1.** Jux *m*, Ulk *m*, Spaß *m*: ***for a ~*** zum Spaß, aus Jux; ***have a ~*** s-n Spaß haben *od.* treiben; ***what a ~!*** ist ja lustig *od.* ‚zum Brüllen'!; **2.** a) ‚Ding' *n*, Sache *f*, b) Quatsch *m*; **II** *v/i.* **3.** *a.* ***~ about*** *od.* ***around*** her'umalbern, -blödeln.

lark·spur ['lɑːkspɜː] *s.* ⚘ Rittersporn *m.*

lar·ri·kin ['lærɪkɪn] *s. bsd. Austral.* (jugendlicher) Rowdy.

lar·va ['lɑːvə] *pl.* **-vae** [-viː] *s. zo.* Larve *f*; **'lar·val** [-vl] *adj. zo.* Larven…; **'lar·vi·cide** [-vɪsaɪd] *s.* Raupenvertilgungsmittel *n.*

la·ryn·ge·al [ˌlærɪn'dʒiːəl] *adj.* Kehlkopf…; **ˌlar·yn'gi·tis** [-'dʒaɪtɪs] *s.* ⚕ Kehlkopfentzündung *f.*

la·ryn·go·scope [lə'rɪŋgəskəʊp] *s.* ⚕ Kehlkopfspiegel *m.*

lar·ynx ['lærɪŋks] *s. anat.* Kehlkopf *m.*

las·civ·i·ous [lə'sɪvɪəs] *adj.* □ las'ziv: a) geil, lüstern, b) schlüpfrig: ***~ story***.

la·ser ['leɪzə] *s. phys.* Laser *m*; ***~ beam*** *s. phys.* Laserstrahl *m.*

lash¹ [læʃ] **I** *s.* **1.** a) Peitschenschnur *f*, b) Peitsche(nende *n*) *f*; **2.** Peitschen-, Rutenhieb *m*: ***the ~ of her tongue*** *fig.* ihre scharfe Zunge; **3.** Peitschen *n* (*a. fig. des Regens*, *des Sturms etc.*); **4.** *fig.* (Peitschen)Hieb *m*; **5.** (Augen)Wimper *f*; **II** *v/t.* **6.** *j-n* peitschen, schlagen, auspeitschen: ***~ the tail*** mit dem Schwanz um sich schlagen; ***~ the sea*** das Meer peitschen (*Sturm*); **7.** peitschen *od.* schlagen an (*acc.*) *od.* gegen (*Regen etc.*); **8.** *fig.* geißeln, abkanzeln; **9.** heftig (an)treiben: ***~ the audience into a fury*** das Publikum aufpeitschen; ***~ o.s. into a fury*** sich in e-e Wut hineinsteigern; **III** *v/i.* **10.** *a. fig.* peitschen, schlagen: ***~ about*** (wild) um sich schlagen; ***~ into s.o.*** a) auf j-n einschlagen, b) *fig.* j-n wild attackieren; **11.** *fig.* peitschen, (*Regen*) *a.* prasseln: ***~ down*** niederprasseln; **12.** ***~ out*** a) (wild) um sich schlagen, b) ausschlagen (*Pferd*), c) (***at***) vom Leder ziehen (gegen), ‚einhauen' (auf *j-n*); **13.** ***~ out on*** F a) (*mit Geld*) ‚auf den Putz hauen' bei *et.*, b) sich *j-m* gegenüber spendabel zeigen.

lash² [læʃ] *v/t. a.* ***~ down*** festbinden, -zurren (***to, on*** an *dat.*).

lash·ing¹ ['læʃɪŋ] *s.* **1.** a) Auspeitschung *f*, b) Prügel *pl.*; **2.** *pl. Brit.* F Masse(n *pl.*) *f* (*Speise etc.*).

lash·ing² ['læʃɪŋ] *s.* **1.** Anbinden *n*; **2.** ⚓ Laschung *f*, Tau(werk) *n.*

lass [læs] *s. bsd. Brit.* **1.** Mädchen *n*; **2.** ‚Schatz' *m*; **las·sie** ['læsɪ] → ***lass***.

las·si·tude ['læsɪtjuːd] *s.* Mattigkeit *f.*

las·so [læ'suː] **I** *pl.* **-so(e)s** *s.* Lasso *m*, *n*; **II** *v/t.* mit e-m Lasso fangen.

last¹ [lɑːst] **I** *adj.* □ → ***lastly***; **1.** letzt: ***~ but one*** vorletzt; ***~ but two*** drittletzt; ***for the ~ time*** zum letzten Male; ***to the ~ man*** bis auf den letzten Mann; **2.** letzt, vorig: ***~ Monday, Monday ~*** (am) letzten *od.* vorigen Montag; ***~ night*** a) gestern abend, b) in der vergangenen Nacht; ***~ week*** in der letzten *od.* vorigen Woche; ***the week before ~*** (die) vorletzte Woche; ***this day ~ week*** heute vor e-r Woche; ***on May 6th ~*** am vergangenen 6. Mai; **3.** neuest, letzt: ***the ~ news***; ***the ~ thing in jazz*** das Neueste im Jazz; **4.** letzt, al'lein übrigbleibend: ***the ~ hope*** die letzte (verbleibende) Hoffnung; ***my ~ pound*** mein letztes Pfund; **5.** letzt, endgültig, entscheidend; → ***word*** 1; **6.** äußerst: ***of the ~ importance*** von höchster Bedeutung; ***this is my ~ price*** dies ist mein äußerster *od.* niedrigster Preis; **7.** letzt, am wenigsten erwartet *od.* geeignet, unwahrscheinlich: ***the ~ man I would choose*** der letzte, den ich wählen würde; ***he is the ~ person I expected to see*** mit ihm hatte ich am wenigsten gerechnet; ***this is the ~ thing to happen*** das ist völlig unwahrscheinlich; **8.** *contp.* ‚letzt', mise'rabelst; **II** *adv.* **9.** zu'letzt, als letzter, -e, -es, an letzter Stelle: ***~ of all*** ganz zuletzt, zu allerletzt; ***~ but not least*** nicht zuletzt, nicht zu vergessen; **10.** zu'letzt, das letztemal, zum letzten Male: ***I ~ met him in Berlin***; **11.** zu guter Letzt; **12.** *in Zssgn*: ***~-mentioned*** letzterwähnt, -genannt; **III** *s.* **13.** ***at ~*** a) endlich, b) schließlich, zuletzt; ***at long ~*** schließlich (doch noch); **14.** *der* (*die*, *das*) Letzte: ***the ~ of the Mohicans*** der letzte Mohikaner; ***he was the ~ to arrive*** er traf als letzter ein; ***he would be the ~ to do that*** er wäre der letzte, der so etwas täte; **15.** *der* (*die*, *das*) Letztgenannte *od.* Letzte; **16.** F a) letzte Erwähnung, b) letzter (An)Blick, c) letztes Mal: ***breathe one's ~*** s-n letzten Atemzug tun; ***hear the ~ of*** zum letzten Male (*od.* nichts mehr) hören von *et. od. j-m*; ***we shall never hear the ~ of this*** das werden wir noch lang zu hören kriegen; ***look one's ~ on s.th.*** e-n (aller)letzten Blick auf et. werfen; ***we shall never see the ~ of that man*** den (Mann) werden wir nie mehr los; **17.** Ende *n*: ***to the ~*** a) bis zum äußersten, b) bis zum Ende (*od.* Tod).

last² [lɑːst] **I** *v/i.* **1.** (an-, fort)dauern, währen: ***too good to ~*** zu schön, um lange zu währen *od.* um wahr zu sein; ***it won't ~*** es wird nicht lange anhalten *od.* so bleiben; **2.** bestehen: ***as long as the world ~s***; **3.** ˈdurch-, aushalten: ***he won't ~ much longer*** er wird's nicht mehr lange machen; **4.** (sich) halten: ***the paint will ~***; ***~ well*** haltbar sein; **5.** (aus)reichen, genügen: ***while the money ~s*** solange das Geld reicht; ***I must make my money ~*** ich muß mit m-m Gelde auskommen; **II** *v/t.* **6.** *a.* ***~ out*** *j-m* reichen: ***it will ~ us a week***; **7.** *mst* ***~ out*** a) überˈdauern, b) ˈdurchhalten, c) (es mindestens) ebenso lange aushalten wie.

last³ [lɑːst] *s.* Leisten *m*: ***put on the ~*** über den Leisten schlagen; ***stick to your ~!*** *fig.* (Schuster,) bleib bei deinem Leisten!

ˌlast-ˈditch *adj.*: ***~ stand*** *ein* letzter (verzweifelter) Widerstand *od.* Versuch.

last·ing [ˈlɑːstɪŋ] **I** *adj.* □ dauerhaft, dauernd, anhaltend, *Material etc. a.* haltbar: ***~ impression*** nachhaltiger Eindruck; **II** *s.* Lasting *n* (*fester Kammgarnstoff*); **ˈlast·ing·ness** [-nɪs] *s.* Dauer(haftigkeit) *f*, Haltbarkeit *f*.

last·ly [ˈlɑːstlɪ] *adv.* zuˈletzt, schließlich, am Ende, zum Schluß.

latch [lætʃ] **I** *s.* **1.** Klinke *f*, (Schnapp-)Riegel *m*: ***on the ~*** nur eingeklinkt (*Tür*); **2.** Schnappschloß *n*; **II** *v/t.* **3.** ein-, zuklinken; **III** *v/i.* **4.** sich einklinken, einschnappen; **5.** ***~ on to*** F a) sich (wie e-e Klette) an *j-n* hängen, b) *e-e Idee* (gierig) aufgreifen, c) *et.* kapieren *od.* ‚spitzkriegen'.

ˈlatch·key *s.* **1.** Drücker *m*, Schlüssel *m* (*für ein Schnappschloß*); **2.** Haus- *od.* Wohnungsschlüssel *m*: ***~ child*** Schlüsselkind *n*.

late [leɪt] **I** *adj.* □ → ***lately***; **1.** spät: ***at a ~ hour*** zu später Stunde, spät (*beide a. fig.*); ***on Monday at the ~st*** spätestens am Montag; ***it is*** (***getting***) ***~*** es ist (schon) spät; ***at a ~r time*** später, zu e-m späteren Zeitpunkt; → ***latest*** I; **2.** vorgerückt, spät, Spät…: ***~ edition*** (***programme***, ***summer***) Spätausgabe *f* (-programm *n*, -sommer *m*); ⁓ ***Latin*** Spätlatein *n*; ***the ~ 18th century*** das späte 18. Jahrhundert; ***in the ~ eighties*** gegen Ende der achtziger Jahre; ***a man in his ~ eighties*** ein Endachtziger; ***in ~ May*** Ende Mai; **3.** verspätet, zu spät: ***be ~*** zu spät kommen (***for s.th.*** zu et.), sich verspäten, spät dran sein, 🚂 *etc.* Verspätung haben: ***be ~ for dinner*** zu spät zum Essen kommen; ***he was ~ with the rent*** er bezahlte s-e Miete mit Verspätung *od.* zu spät; **4.** letzt, jüngst, neu: ***the ~ war*** der letzte Krieg; ***of ~ years*** in den letzten Jahren; **5.** a) letzt, früher, ehemalig, b) verstorben: ***the ~ headmaster*** der letzte *od.* der verstorbene Schuldirektor; ***the ~ government*** die letzte *od.* vorige Regierung; ***my ~ residence*** m-e frühere Wohnung; ***~ of Oxford*** früher in Oxford (wohnhaft); **II** *adv.* **6.** spät: ***of ~*** in letzter Zeit, neuerdings; ***as ~ as last year*** erst *od.* noch letztes Jahr; ***until as ~ as 1984*** noch bis 1984; ***better ~ than never*** lieber spät als gar nicht; ***~ into the night*** bis spät in die Nacht; ***sit*** (*od.* ***stay***) ***up ~*** bis spät in die Nacht *od.* lange aufbleiben; ***it's a bit ~*** F es ist schon ein bißchen spät dafür; (***even***) ***~ in life*** (auch noch) in hohem Alter; ***not ~r than*** spätestens, nicht später als; ***~r on*** später, nachher; ***see you ~r!*** bis später!, bis bald!; ***~ in the day*** F reichlich spät, ‚ein bißchen' spät; **7.** zu spät: ***come ~***; ***the train arrived 20 minutes ~*** der Zug hatte 20 Minuten Verspätung; **ˈ~-ˌcom·er** *s.* Zuˈspätgekommene(r *m*) *f*, Nachzügler(in), *fig. a. e-e* Neuerscheinung, *et.* Neues: ***he is a ~ in this field*** *fig.* er ist neu in diesem (Fach)Gebiet.

late·ly [ˈleɪtlɪ] *adv.* **1.** vor kurzem, kürzlich; **2.** in letzter Zeit, seit einiger Zeit, neuerdings.

la·ten·cy [ˈleɪtənsɪ] *s.* Laˈtenz *f*, Verborgenheit *f*.

late·ness [ˈleɪtnɪs] *s.* **1.** späte Zeit, spätes Stadium: ***the ~ of the hour*** die vorgerückte Stunde; **2.** Verspätung *f*, Zuˈspätkommen *n*.

la·tent [ˈleɪtənt] *adj.* □ laˈtent (*a.* ⚕, *phys.*, *psych.*), verborgen: ***~ abilities***; ***~ buds*** unentwickelte Knospen; ***~ heat*** *phys.* latente *od.* gebundene Wärme; ***~ period*** Latenzstadium *n od.* -zeit *f*.

lat·er [ˈleɪtə] *comp. von* ***late***.

lat·er·al [ˈlætərəl] **I** *adj.* □ **1.** seitlich, Seiten…, Neben…, Quer…: ***~ angle*** (***view***, ***wind***) Seitenwinkel *m* (-ansicht *f*, -wind *m*); ***~ branch*** Seitenlinie *f* (*e-s Stammbaums*); ***~ thinking*** unorthodoxe Denkmethode(n *pl.*) *f*; **2.** *anat.*, *ling.* lateˈral; **II** *s.* **3.** Seitenteil *n*, -stück *n*; **4.** *ling.* Lateˈral *m*; **ˈlat·er·al·ly** [-rəlɪ] *adv.* seitlich, seitwärts; von der Seite.

Lat·er·an [ˈlætərən] *s.* Lateˈran *m*.

lat·est [ˈleɪtɪst] **I** *sup. von* ***late***; **II** *adj.* **1.** spätest; **2.** neuest: ***the ~ fashion*** (***news***, *etc.*); **3.** letzt: ***he was the ~ to come*** er kam als letzter; **III** *adv.* **4.** am spätesten: ***he came ~*** er kam als letzter; **IV** *s.* **5.** (*der*, *die*, *das*) Neueste; **6.** ***at the ~*** spätestens.

la·tex [ˈleɪteks] *s.* ⚘ Milchsaft *m*, Latex *m*.

lath [lɑːθ] *s.* **1.** Latte *f*, Leiste *f*: → ***thin*** 2; **2.** *coll.* Latten(werk *n*) *pl.*

lathe [leɪð] *s.* ⚙ **1.** Drehbank *f*: ***~ tool*** Drehstahl *m*; ***~ tooling*** Bearbeitung *f* auf der Drehbank; **2.** Töpferscheibe *f*.

lath·er [ˈlɑːðə] **I** *s.* **1.** (Seifen)Schaum *m*; **2.** Schweiß *m* (*bsd. e-s Pferdes*): ***in a ~*** schweißgebadet; ***be in a ~ about s.th.*** F sich über et. aufregen; **II** *v/t.* **3.** einseifen; **III** *v/i.* **4.** schäumen.

Lat·in [ˈlætɪn] **I** *s.* **1.** *ling.* La'tein(isch) *n*, das Lateinische; **2.** *antiq.* a) Laˈtiner *m*, b) Römer *m*; **3.** Roˈmane *m*, Roˈmanin *f*, Südländer(in); **II** *adj.* **4.** *ling.* laˈteinisch, Latein…; **5.** a) roˈmanisch: ***the ~ peoples***, b) südländisch: ***~ temperament***; **6.** *eccl.* römisch-kaˈtholisch: ***~ Church***; **7.** laˈtinisch; **ˌ~-Aˈmer·i·can I** *adj.* laˈteinameriˌkanisch; **II** *s.* Laˈteinameriˌkaner(in).

Lat·in·ism [ˈlætɪnɪzəm] *s.* Latiˈnismus *m*; **ˈLat·in·ist** [-nɪst] *s.* Latiˈnist(in), ‚Laˈteiner' *m*; **Lat·in·i·za·tion** [ˌlætɪnaɪˈzeɪʃn] *s.* Latinisierung *f*; **ˈLat·in·ize** [-naɪz] *v/t.* latinisieren; **La·ti·no** [ləˈtiːnəʊ] *pl.* **-nos** *s. Am.* F (*US-*)*Einwohner* (*-in*) *lateinamerikanischer Abkunft*.

lat·ish [ˈleɪtɪʃ] *adj.* etwas spät.

lat·i·tude [ˈlætɪtjuːd] *s.* **1.** *ast.*, *geogr.* Breite *f*: ***degree of ~*** Breitengrad *m*; ***in ~ 40° N.*** auf dem 40. Grad nördlicher Breite; **2.** *pl. geogr.* Breiten *pl.*, Gegenden *pl.*: ***low ~s*** niedere Breiten; ***cold ~s*** kalte Gegenden; **3.** *fig.* a) Spielraum *m*, Freiheit *f*: ***allow s.o. great ~*** j-m große Freiheit gewähren, b) großzügige Auslegung (*e-s Begriffs etc.*); **4.** *phot.* Belichtungsspielraum *m*; **lat·i·tu·di·nal** [ˌlætɪˈtjuːdɪnl] *adj. geogr.* Breiten…

lat·i·tu·di·nar·i·an [ˌlætɪtjuːdɪˈneərɪən] **I** *adj.* libeˈral, toleˈrant, *eccl. a.* freisinnig; **II** *s. bsd. eccl.* Freigeist *m*; **ˌlat·i·tu·diˈnar·i·an·ism** [-nɪzəm] *s. eccl.* Liberaliˈtät *f*, Toleˈranz *f*.

la·trine [ləˈtriːn] *s.* Laˈtrine *f*.

lat·ter [ˈlætə] **I** *adj.* □ → ***latterly***; **1.** *von zweien*: letzter: ***the ~ name*** der letztere *od.* letztgenannte Name; **2.** neuer, jünger: ***in these ~ days*** in der jüngsten Zeit; **3.** letzt, später: ***the ~ years of one's life***; ***the ~ half of June*** die zweite Junihälfte; ***the ~ part of the book*** die zweite Hälfte des Buches; **II** *s.* **4.** ***the ~*** a) der (die, das) letztere, b) die letzteren *pl.*; **ˈ~·day** *adj.* aus neuester Zeit, moˈdern; **ˈ~-day saints** *s. pl. eccl. die* Heiligen *pl.* der letzten Tage (*Mormonen*).

lat·ter·ly [ˈlætəlɪ] *adv.* **1.** in letzter Zeit, neuerdings; **2.** am Ende.

lat·tice [ˈlætɪs] **I** *s.* **1.** Gitter(werk) *n*; **2.** Gitterfenster *n od.* -tür *f*; **3.** Gitter(muster) *n*; **II** *v/t.* **4.** vergittern; ***~ bridge*** *s.* ⚙ Gitterbrücke *f*; ***~ frame***, ***~ gird·er*** *s.* ⚙ Gitter-, Fachwerkträger *m*; ***~ win·dow*** *s.* Gitter-, Rautenfenster *n*; **ˈ~·work** → ***lattice*** 1.

Lat·vi·an [ˈlætvɪən] **I** *adj.* **1.** lettisch; **II** *s.* **2.** Lette *m*, Lettin *f*; **3.** *ling.* Lettisch *n*.

laud [lɔːd] **I** *s.* Lobgesang *m*; **II** *v/t.* loben, preisen, rühmen; **ˈlaud·a·ble** [-dəbl] *adj.* □ löblich, lobenswert.

lau·da·num [ˈlɒdnəm] *s. pharm.* Lauˈdanum *n*, ˈOpiumtinkˌtur *f*.

lau·da·tion [lɔːˈdeɪʃn] *s.* Lob *n*; **laud·a·to·ry** [ˈlɔːdətərɪ] *adj.* lobend, Belobigungs…, Lob…

laugh [lɑːf] **I** *s.* **1.** Lachen *n*, Gelächter *n*, *thea. etc. a.* ‚Lacher' *m*, *contp.* (*böse etc.*) Lache: ***with a ~*** lachend; ***have a good ~ at s.th.*** herzlich über e-e Sache lachen; ***have the ~ of s.o.*** über j-n (am Ende) triumphieren; ***have the ~ on***

one's side die Lacher auf s-r Seite haben; ***the ~ was on me*** der Scherz ging auf m-e Kosten; ***raise a ~*** Gelächter erregen, e-n Lacherfolg erzielen; ***what a ~!*** (das) ist ja zum Brüllen!; ***he*** (***it***) ***is a ~*** F er (es) ist doch zum Lachen; ***just for ~s*** nur zum Spaß; **II** *v/i.* **2.** lachen (*a. fig.*): ***to make s.o. ~*** j-n zum Lachen bringen; ***don't make me ~!*** *iro.* daß ich nicht lache!; ***he ~s best who ~s last*** wer zuletzt lacht, lacht am besten; → ***wrong*** 2; **3.** *fig.* lachen, strahlen (*Himmel etc.*); **III** *v/t.* **4.** lachend äußern: ***~ a bitter ~*** bitter lachen; → ***court*** 9;
Zssgn mit adv. u. prp.:
~ at *v/i.* lachen *od.* sich lustig machen über *j-n od. e-e Sache, j-n* auslachen; **~ a·way I** *v/t.* **1.** → ***laugh off***; **2.** *Sorgen etc.* durch Lachen verscheuchen; **3.** *Zeit* mit Scherzen verbringen; **II** *v/i.* **4.** drauf'loslachen, lachen u. lachen; **~ down** *v/t. j-n* durch Gelächter zum Schweigen bringen *od.* mit Lachen über'tönen, auslachen; **~ off** *v/t. et.* lachend *od.* mit e-m Scherz abtun.

laugh·a·ble ['lɑːfəbl] *adj.* □ lachhaft, lächerlich, komisch.

laugh·ing ['lɑːfɪŋ] **I** *s.* **1.** Lachen *n*, Gelächter *n*; **II** *adj.* □ **2.** lachend; **3.** lustig: ***it is no ~ matter*** das ist nicht zum Lachen; **4.** *fig.* lachend, strahlend: ***a ~ sky***; **~ gas** *s.* ⚗ Lachgas *n*; **~ gull** *s. orn.* Lachmöwe *f*; **~ hy·e·na** *s. zo.* 'Flekkenhyˌäne *f*; **~ jack·ass** *s. orn.* Rieseneisvogel *m*; '**~-stock** *s.* Gegenstand *m* des Gelächters, Zielscheibe *f* des Spottes: ***make a ~ of o.s.*** sich lächerlich machen.

laugh·ter ['lɑːftə] *s.* Lachen *n*, Gelächter *n*.

launch [lɔːntʃ] **I** *v/t.* **1.** *Boot* aussetzen, ins Wasser lassen; **2.** *Schiff* a) vom Stapel lassen, b) taufen: ***be ~ed*** vom Stapel laufen *od.* getauft werden; **3.** ✈ katapultieren, abschießen; **4.** *Torpedo, Geschoß* abschießen, *Rakete a.* starten; **5.** *et.* schleudern, werfen: ***~ o.s into*** → 12; **6.** *Rede, Kritik, Protest etc., a. e-n Schlag* vom Stapel lassen, loslassen; **7.** *et.* in Gang bringen, einleiten, starten, lancieren; **8.** *et.* lancieren: a) *Produkt, Buch, Film etc.* her'ausbringen, b) *Anleihe* auflegen, *Aktien* ausgeben; **9.** *j-n* lancieren, (gut) einführen, *j-m* ‚Starthilfe' geben; **10.** ⚔ *Truppen* einsetzen, *an e-e Front etc.* schicken *od.* werfen; **II** *v/i.* **11.** *mst* ***~ out***, ***~ forth*** losfahren, starten: ***~ out on a journey*** sich auf e-e Reise begeben; **12.** ***~ out*** (***into***) *fig.* a) sich (in *die Arbeit, e-e Debatte etc.*) stürzen, b) loslegen (mit *e-r Rede, e-r Tätigkeit etc.*), c) (*et.*) anpacken, (*e-e Karriere, ein Projekt etc.*) starten: ***~ out into*** → *a.* 6; **13.** ***~ out*** a) e-n Wortschwall von sich geben, b) F viel Geld springen lassen; **III** *s.* **14.** ⚓ Bar'kasse *f*; **15.** → ***launching***; '**launch·er** [-tʃə] *s.* **1.** ⚔ a) (Ra'keten)Werfer *m*, b) Abschußvorrichtung *f* (*Fernlenkgeschosse*); **2.** ✈ Kata'pult *m, n*, Startschleuder *f*.

launch·ing ['lɔːntʃɪŋ] *s.* **1.** ⚓ a) Stapellauf *m*, b) Aussetzen *n* (*von Booten*); **2.** Abschuß *m*, *e-r Rakete*: *a.* Start *m*; **3.** ⚔ Kata'pultstart *m*; **4.** *fig.* a) Starten *n*, In-'Gang-Setzen *n*, b) Start *m*, c) Einsatz *m*; **5.** Lancierung *f*, Einführung *f* (*e-s Produkts etc.*), Herausgabe *f* (*e-s Buches etc.*); **~ pad**, **~ plat·form** *s.* Abschußrampe *f* (*e-r Rakete*); **~ rope** *s.* ✈ Startseil *n*; **~ site** *s.* ⚔ (Ra'keten-)ˌAbschußˌbasis *f*; **~ ve·hi·cle** *s.* 'StartraˌKete *f*.

laun·der ['lɔːndə] **I** *v/t.* *Wäsche* waschen (u. bügeln); F *fig. illegal erworbenes Geld* ‚waschen'; **II** *v/i.* sich (*leicht etc.*) waschen lassen; **laun·der·ette** [ˌlɔːndə'ret] *s.* 'WaschsaˌIon *m*; '**laun·dress** [-drɪs] *s.* Wäscherin *f*.

laun·dry ['lɔːndrɪ] *s.* **1.** Wäsche'rei *f*; **2.** F (schmutzige *od.* frisch gereinigte) Wäsche; **~ list 1.** Wäschezettel *m*; **2.** *Am.* F lange Liste.

lau·re·ate ['lɔːrɪət] **I** *adj.* **1.** lorbeergekrönt, -geschmückt; -bekränzt; **II** *s.* **2.** *mst* ***poet ~*** Hofdichter *m*; **3.** Preisträger *m*.

lau·rel ['lɒrəl] *s.* **1.** ⚘ Lorbeer(baum) *m*; **2.** *mst pl. fig.* Lorbeeren *pl.*, Ehren *pl.*, Ruhm *m*: ***look to one's ~s*** sich behaupten wollen; ***reap*** (*od.* ***win*** *od.* ***gain***) ***~s*** Lorbeeren ernten; ***rest on one's ~s*** sich auf s-n Lorbeeren ausruhen; '**lau·rel(l)ed** [-ld] *adj.* **1.** lorbeergekrönt; **2.** preisgekrönt.

lav [læv] *s. Brit.* F ‚Klo' *n*.

la·va ['lɑːvə] *s. geol.* Lava *f*.

lav·a·to·ry ['lævətərɪ] *s.* Toi'lette *f*: ***public ~*** *a.* (öffentliche) Bedürfnisanstalt.

lav·en·der ['lævəndə] **I** *s.* **1.** ⚘ La'vendel *m* (*a. Farbe*); **2.** La'vendel(wasser) *n*; **II** *adj.* **3.** la'vendelfarben.

lav·ish ['lævɪʃ] **I** *adj.* □ a) großzügig, reich, fürstlich, üppig (*Geschenke etc.*), b) reich, 'überschwenglich (*Lob etc.*), c) großzügig, verschwenderisch (***of*** mit, ***in*** in *dat.*) (*Person*): ***be ~ of*** (*od.* ***with***) um sich werfen mit, nicht geizen mit, verschwenderisch umgehen mit; **II** *v/t.* verschwenden, verschwenderisch (aus-) geben: ***~ s.th. on s.o.*** j-n mit et. überhäufen; '**lav·ish·ness** [-nɪs] *s.* Großzügigkeit *f* (*etc.*); Verschwendung(ssucht) *f*.

law [lɔː] *s.* **1.** (*objektives*) Recht, (*das*) Gesetz *od.* (*die*) Gesetze *pl.*: ***by*** (*od.* ***in***, ***under the***) ***~*** nach dem Gesetz, von Rechts wegen, gesetzlich; ***under German ~*** nach deutschem Recht; ***contrary to ~*** gesetz-, rechtswidrig; ***~ and order*** Recht (*od.* Ruhe) u. Ordnung, *contp.* ‚Law and order'; ***become*** (*od.* ***pass into***) ***~*** Gesetz *od.* rechtskräftig werden; ***lay down the ~*** (alles) bestimmen, das Sagen haben; ***take the ~ into one's own hands*** zur Selbsthilfe greifen; ***his word is the ~*** was er sagt, gilt; **2.** Recht *n*: a) 'RechtssyˌStem *n*: ***the English ~***, b) (*einzelnes*) Rechtsgebiet: ***~ of nations*** Völkerrecht; **3.** (*einzelnes*) Gesetz: ***Election ℒ***; ***he is a ~ unto himself*** er tut, was er will; ***is there a ~ against it?*** *iro.* ist das (etwa) verboten?; **4.** Rechtswissenschaft *f*, Jura *pl.*: ***read*** (*od.* ***study***, ***take***) ***~*** Jura studieren; ***be in the ~*** Jurist sein; ***practise ~*** e-e Anwaltspraxis ausüben; **5.** Gericht *n*, Rechtsweg *m*: ***go to ~*** vor Gericht gehen, den Rechtsweg beschreiten, prozessieren; ***go to ~ with s.o.*** j-n verklagen, gegen j-n prozessieren; **6.** ***the ~*** F die Polizei: ***call in the ~***; **7.** (*künstlerisches etc.*) Gesetz: ***the ~s of poetry***; **8.** (Spiel)Regel *f*: ***the ~s of the game***; **9.** a) (Na'tur)Gesetz *n*, b) (wissenschaftliches) Gesetz: ***the ~ of gravity***, c) (Lehr)Satz *m*: ***~ of sines*** Sinussatz; **10.** *eccl.* a) (göttliches) Gesetz, *coll. die* Gebote (Gottes), b) ***the ℒ*** (***of Moses***) das Gesetz (des Moses), c) ***the ℒ*** das Alte Testament; **11.** *hunt.*, *sport* Vorgabe *f*; '**~-aˌbid·ing** *adj.* gesetzestreu, ordnungsliebend: ***~ citizen***; '**~ˌbreak·er** *s.* Ge'setzesüberˌtreter(in); **~ court** *s.* Gericht(shof *m*) *n*.

law·ful ['lɔːfʊl] *adj.* □ **1.** gesetzlich, le'gal; **2.** rechtmäßig, legi'tim: ***~ son*** ehelicher *od.* legitimer Sohn; **3.** rechtsgültig, gesetzlich anerkannt: ***~ marriage*** gültige Ehe; '**law·ful·ness** [-nɪs] *s.* Gesetzlichkeit *f*, Legali'tät *f*; Rechtsgültigkeit *f*.

'**lawˌgiv·er** *s.* Gesetzgeber *m*.

law·less ['lɔːlɪs] *adj.* □ **1.** gesetzlos (*Land*, *Person*); **2.** gesetzwidrig, unrechtmäßig; '**law·less·ness** [-nɪs] *s.* **1.** Gesetzlosigkeit *f*; **2.** Gesetzwidrigkeit *f*.

Law Lord *s.* Mitglied *n* des brit. Oberhauses mit richterlicher Funkti'on.

lawn[1] [lɔːn] *s.* Rasen *m*.

lawn[2] [lɔːn] *s.* Li'non *m*, Ba'tist *m*.

lawn| mow·er *s.* Rasenmäher *m*; **~ sprin·kler** *s.* Rasensprenger *m*; **~ tennis** *s.* Rasentennis *n*.

law| of·fice *s.* 'Anwaltskanzˌlei *f*, -praxis *f*; **~ of·fi·cer** *s.* ⚖ **1.** Ju'stizbeamte(r) *m*; **2.** *Brit. für* a) ***Attorney General***, b) ***Solicitor General***; **~ re·ports** *s. pl.* Urteilssammlung *f*, Sammlung *f* von richterlichen Entscheidungen; **~ school** *s.* **1.** 'Rechtsakadeˌmie *f*; **2.** *univ. Am.* ju'ristische Fakul'tät; **~ student** *s.* 'JurastuˌDent(in); '**~-suit** *s.* ⚖ a) Pro'zeß *m*, Verfahren *n*, b) Klage *f*: ***bring a ~*** e-n Prozeß anstrengen, Klage einreichen (***against*** gegen).

law·yer ['lɔːjə] *s.* **1.** (Rechts)Anwalt *m*, (-)Anwältin *f*; **2.** Rechtsberater(in); **3.** Ju'rist(in).

lax [læks] *adj.* □ **1.** lax, locker, (nach-) lässig (***about*** hinsichtlich *gen.*, mit): ***~ morals*** lockere Sitten; **2.** lose, schlaff, locker; **3.** unklar, verschwommen; **4.** *Phonetik*: schlaff artikuliert; **5.** ***~ bowels*** a) offener Leib, b) 'Durchfall *m*; **lax·a·tive** ['læksətɪv] ⚕ **I** *s.* Abführmittel *n*; **II** *adj.* abführend; **lax·i·ty** ['læksətɪ], '**lax·ness** [-nɪs] *s.* **1.** Laxheit *f*, Lässigkeit *f*; **2.** Schlaffheit *f*, Lockerheit *f* (*a. fig.*); **3.** Verschwommenheit *f*.

lay[1] [leɪ] **I** *s.* **1.** *bsd. geogr.* Lage *f*: ***the ~ of the land*** *fig.* die Lage; **2.** Schicht *f*, Lage *f*; **3.** Schlag *m* (*Tauwerk*); **4.** V a) ‚Nummer' *f* (*Koitus*), b) ***she is an easy ~*** die ist gleich ‚dabei'; ***she is a good ~*** sie ‚bumst' gut; **II** *v/t.* [*irr.*] **5.** *allg.* legen: ***~ it on the table***; ***~ a cable*** ein Kabel (ver)legen; ***~ a bridge*** e-e Brükke schlagen; ***~ eggs*** Eier legen; ***~ the foundation(s) of*** *fig.* den Grund(stock) legen zu; ***~ the foundation-stone*** den Grundstein legen; → *die Verbindungen mit den entsprechenden Substantiven etc.*; **6.** *fig.* legen, setzen: ***~ stress on*** Nachdruck legen auf (*acc.*), betonen; ***~ an ambush*** e-n Hinterhalt legen; ***~ the ax(e) to a tree*** die Axt an e-n Baum legen; ***the scene is laid in Rome*** der Schauplatz *od.* Ort der Handlung ist Rom, *thea.* das Stück *etc.* spielt in Rom; **7.** anordnen, herrichten: **~ *the table*** (*od.* ***the cloth***) den Tisch decken; **~ *the fire*** das Feuer (*im Kamin*) anlegen; **8.** belegen, bedecken: **~ *the floor with a carpet***; **9.** (***before***) vorlegen (*dat.*), bringen (vor *acc.*): **~ *one's case before a commission***; **10.** geltend machen, erheben: **~ *an information against s.o.*** Klage erheben *od.* (Straf)Anzeige erstatten gegen; **11.** a) *Strafe etc.* verhängen, b) *Steuern* auferlegen; **12.** *Schuld etc.* zuschreiben, zur Last legen: **~ *a mistake to s.o.('s charge)*** j-m e-n Fehler zur Last legen; **13.** *Schaden* festsetzen (***at*** auf *acc.*); **14.** a) *et.* wetten, b) setzen auf (*acc.*); **15.** *e-n Plan* schmieden; **16.** 'umlegen, niederwerfen: **~ *s.o. low*** (*od.* ***in the dust***) j-n zu Boden strecken; **17.** *Getreide etc.* zu Boden drücken; **18.** *Wind, Wogen etc.* beruhigen, besänftigen: ***the wind is laid*** der Wind hat sich gelegt; **19.** *Staub* löschen; **20.** *Geist* bannen, beschwören; → ***ghost*** 1; **21.** ⚓ *Kurs* nehmen auf (*acc.*), ansteuern; **22.** ⚔ *Geschütz* richten; **23.** V ‚umlegen', ‚bumsen'; **III** *v/i.* [*irr.*] **24.** (Eier) legen; **25.** wetten; **26.** zuschlagen: **~ *about one*** um sich schlagen; **~ *into s.o.*** *sl.* auf j-n einschlagen; **~ *to*** (mächtig) ‚rangehen' an *e-e Sache*; **27.** (*fälschlich für* ***lie***[2] II) liegen;

Zssgn mit adv.:

lay| a·bout *v/i.* (heftig) um sich schlagen; **~ a·side**, **~ by** *v/t.* **1.** bei'seite legen; **2.** *fig.* a) aufgeben, b) ‚ausklammern'; **3.** *Geld etc.* beiseite *od.* auf die ‚hohe Kante' legen, zu'rücklegen; **~ down I** *v/t.* **1.** hinlegen; **2.** *Amt, Waffen etc.* niederlegen; **3.** *sein Leben* hingeben, opfern; **4.** *Geld* hinter'legen; **5.** *Grundsatz, Regeln etc.* aufstellen, festlegen, -setzen, vorschreiben, *Bedingung in e-m Vertrag* niederlegen, verankern; → ***law*** 1; **6.** a) die Grundlagen legen für, b) planen, entwerfen; **7.** ✓ besäen *od.* bepflanzen (***in, to, under, with*** mit); **8.** *Wein etc.* (ein)lagern; **II** *v/i.* **9.** *fälschlich für* ***lie down*** 1; **~ in** *v/t.* sich eindecken mit, einlagern; *Vorrat* anlegen; **~ off I** *v/t.* **1.** *Arbeiter* (vor'übergehend) entlassen; **2.** *die Arbeit* einstellen; **3.** *das Rauchen etc.* aufgeben: **~ *smoking***; **4.** in Ruhe lassen: **~ (*it*)!** hör auf (damit)!; **II** *v/i.* **5.** aufhören; **~ on I** *v/t.* **1.** *Steuer etc.* auferlegen; **2.** *Peitsche* gebrauchen; **3.** *Farbe etc.* auftragen: ***lay it on*** a) (***thick***) *fig.* ‚dick auftragen', übertreiben, b) e-e ‚saftige' Rechnung stellen, c) draufschlagen; **4.** a) *Gas etc.* installieren, b) *Haus* ans (*Gas- etc.*)Netz anschließen; **5.** F a) auftischen, b) bieten, sorgen für, c) veranstalten, arrangieren; **II** *v/i.* **6.** zuschlagen, angreifen; **~ o·pen** *v/t.* **1.** bloßlegen; **2.** *fig.* a) aufdecken, b) offenlegen; **~ out** *v/t.* **1.** ausbreiten; **2.** *Toten* aufbahren; **3.** *Geld* ausgeben; **4.** *allg.* gestalten, *Garten etc.* anlegen, *et.* entwerfen, planen, anordnen, *typ.* aufmachen, das Layout *e-r Zeitschrift etc.* machen; **5.** *sl.* a) *j-n* zs.-schlagen, b) *j-n* ‚'umlegen', ‚kaltmachen'; **6. ~ *o.s. out*** F sich ‚mächtig ranhalten'; **~ o·ver** *Am.* **I** *v/t. et.* zu'rückstellen; **II** *v/i.* Aufenthalt haben, 'Zwischenstati,on machen; **~ to** *v/i.* ⚓ beidrehen; **~ up** *v/t.* **1.** → ***lay in***; **2.** ansammeln, anhäufen; **3.** a) ⚓ *Schiff* auflegen, außer Dienst stellen, b) *mot.* stillegen; **4. *be laid up*** (***with***) bettlägerig sein (wegen), im Bett liegen (mit *Grippe etc.*).

lay[2] [leɪ] *pret. von* ***lie***[2].

lay[3] [leɪ] *adj.* Laien...: a) *eccl.* weltlich; b) laienhaft, nicht fachmännisch: ***to the ~ mind*** für den Laien(verstand).

lay[4] [leɪ] *s. obs.* **1.** Bal'lade *f*; **2.** Lied *n*.

'lay|·a·bout *s. bsd. Brit.* F Faulenzer *m*; **~ broth·er** *s. eccl.* Laienbruder *m*; **'~-by** *s. mot. Brit.* a) Rastplatz *m*, Parkplatz *m*, b) Parkbucht *f* (*Landstraße*); **~ days** *s. pl.* ⚓ Liegetage *pl.*, -zeit *f*; **'~-down** → ***lie-down***.

lay·er I *s.* ['leɪə] **1.** Schicht *f*, Lage *f*: ***in ~s*** schicht-, lagenweise; **2.** Leger *m*, *in Zssgn* ...leger *m*; **3.** Leg(e)henne *f*: ***this hen is a good ~*** diese Henne legt gut; **4.** ✓ Ableger *m*; **5.** ⚔ 'Höhenrichtkano,nier *m*; **II** *v/t.* **6.** ✓ durch Ableger vermehren; **7.** über'lagern, schichtweise legen; **'~-cake** *s.* Schichttorte *f*.

lay·ette [leɪ'et] *s.* Babyausstattung *f*.

lay fig·ure *s.* **1.** Gliederpuppe *f* (*als Modell*); **2.** *fig.* Mario'nette *f*, Null *f*.

lay·ing ['leɪɪŋ] *s.* **1.** Legen *n* (*etc.* → ***lay***[1] II u. III): **~ *on of hands*** Handauflegen *n*; **2.** Gelege *n* (*Eier*); **3.** △ Bewurf *m*, Putz *m*.

lay| judge *s.* Laienrichter(in); **'~·man** [-mən] *s.* [*irr.*] **1.** Laie *m* (*Ggs. Geistlicher*); **2.** Laie *m*, Nichtfachmann *m*; **'~-off** *s.* **1.** (vor'übergehende) Entlassung; **2.** Feierschicht *f*; **'~·out** *s.* **1.** Planung *f*, Anordnung *f*, Anlage *f*; **2.** Plan *m*, Entwurf *m*; **3.** *typ.*, *a. Elektronik*: Layout *n*: **~ *man*** Layouter *m*; **4.** Aufmachung *f* (*e-r Zeitschrift etc.*); **~ sis·ter** *s.* Laienschwester *f*; **'~,wom·an** *s.* [*irr.*] Laiin *f*.

laze [leɪz] **I** *v/i. a.* **~ *around*** faulenzen, bummeln, auf der faulen Haut liegen; **II** *v/t.* **~ *away*** *Zeit* verbummeln; **III** *s.*: ***have a ~*** → I; **la·zi·ness** ['leɪzɪnɪs] *s.* Faulheit *f*, Trägheit *f*.

la·zy ['leɪzɪ] *adj.* □ träg(e): a) faul, b) langsam, sich langsam bewegend; **'~·bones** *s.* F Faulpelz *m*.

'ld [d] F *für* ***would*** *od.* ***should***.

lea [liː] *s. poet.* Flur *f*, Aue *f*.

leach [liːtʃ] **I** *v/t.* **1.** 'durchsickern lassen; **2.** (aus)laugen; **II** *v/i.* **3.** 'durchsickern.

lead[1] [liːd] **I** *s.* **1.** Führung *f*, Leitung *f*: ***under s.o.'s ~***; **2.** Führung *f*, Spitze *f*: ***be in the ~, have the ~*** an der Spitze stehen, führen(d sein), *sport etc.* in Führung *od.* vorn liegen; ***take the ~*** a) *a. sport* die Führung übernehmen, sich an die Spitze setzen, b) die Initiative ergreifen, c) vorangehen, neue Wege weisen; **3.** *bsd. sport* a) Führung *f*: ***have a two-goal ~*** mit zwei Toren führen, b) Vorsprung *m*: ***one minute's ~*** 'eine Minute Vorsprung (***over s.o.*** vor j-m); **4.** Vorbild *n*, Beispiel *n*: ***give s.o. a ~*** j-m mit gutem Beispiel vorangehen; ***follow s.o.'s ~*** j-s Beispiel folgen; **5.** Hinweis *m*, Fingerzeig *m*, Anhaltspunkt *m*, Spur *f*: ***the police have several ~s***; **6.** *Kartenspiel*: a) Vorhand *f*: ***your ~!*** Sie spielen aus!, b) zu'erst ausgespielte Karte; **7.** *thea.* a) Hauptrolle *f*, b) Hauptdarsteller(in); **8.** ♪ a) Eröffnung *f*, Auftakt *m*, b) *Jazz etc.*: Lead *n*, Führungsstimme *f* (*Trompete etc.*); **9.** *Zeitung*: a) → ***lead story***, b) (zs.-fassende) Einleitung; **10.** (Hunde)Leine *f*; **11.** ⚡ a) Leiter *m*, b) (Zu)Leitung *f*, c) *a.* ***phase ~*** Voreilung *f*; **12.** ⚙ Steigung *f* (*e-s Gewindes*); **13.** ⚔ Vorhalt *m*; **II** *v/t.* [*irr.*] **14.** führen: **~ *the way*** vorangehen; ***this is ~ing us nowhere*** das bringt uns nicht weiter; → ***nose*** *Redew.*; **15.** *j-n* führen, bringen (***to*** nach, zu) (*a. Straße etc.*); → ***temptation***; **16.** (an)führen, an der Spitze stehen von, *a. Orchester etc.* leiten, *Armee* führen *od.* befehligen: **~ *the field*** *sport* das Feld anführen, vorn liegen; **17.** *j-n* dazu bringen, bewegen, verleiten (***to do s.th.*** et. zu tun): ***this led me to believe*** das machte mich glauben(, *daß*); **18.** a) *ein behagliches etc. Leben* führen, b) *j-m ein elendes etc. Leben* bereiten: **~ *s.o. a dog's life*** j-m das Leben zur Hölle machen; **19.** *Karte, Farbe etc.* aus-, anspielen; **20.** *Kabel etc.* führen, legen; **III** *v/i.* [*irr.*] **21.** führen: a) vor'angehen, den Weg weisen (*a. fig.*), b) die erste Stelle einnehmen, c) *sport* in Führung liegen (***by*** mit *7 Metern etc.*): **~ *by points*** nach Punkten führen; **22. ~ *to*** a) führen *od.* gehen zu *od.* nach (*Straße etc.*), b) *fig.* führen zu: ***this is ~ing nowhere*** das führt zu nichts; **23.** *Kartenspiel*: ausspielen (***with s.th.*** et.): ***who ~s?***; **24.** *Boxen*: angreifen (mit der Linken *od.* Rechten): ***he ~s with his right*** *a.* s-e Führungshand ist die Rechte, er ist Rechtsausleger; **~ *with one's chin*** *fig.* das Schicksal herausfordern;

Zssgn mit adv.:

lead| a·stray *v/t.* in die Irre führen, *fig. a.* irre-, verführen; **~ a·way I** *v/t.* **1.** a) *j-n* wegführen, b) → ***lead off*** 1; **2.** *fig. j-n* abbringen (***from*** von *e-m Thema etc.*); **3. *be led away*** sich verleiten lassen; **II** *v/i.* **4. ~ *from*** von *e-m Thema etc.* wegführen; **~ off I** *v/t.* **1.** *j-n* abführen; **2.** *fig.* einleiten, eröffnen; **II** *v/i.* **3.** den Anfang machen; **~ on I** *v/i.* vor'angehen; **II** *v/t. fig.* a) *j-n* hinters Licht führen, b) *j-n* auf den Arm nehmen, c) *j-n* an der Nase herumführen; **~ up I** *v/t.* (***to***) a) (hin'auf)führen (auf *acc.*), b) (hin'über)führen (zu); **II** *v/i.* **~ *to*** *fig.* a) (all'mählich) führen zu, 'überleiten zu, *et.* einleiten: ***what is he leading up to?*** worauf will er hinaus?

lead[2] [led] **I** *s.* **1.** ⚒ Blei *n*; **2.** ⚓ Senkblei *n*, Lot *n*: ***cast*** (*od.* ***heave***) ***the ~*** loten; **3.** Blei *n*, Kugeln *pl.* (*Geschosse*); **4.** Gra'phit *m*, Reißblei *n*; **5.** (Bleistift)Mine *f*; **6.** *typ.* 'Durchschuß *m*; **7.** Bleifassung *f* (*Fenster*); **8.** *pl. Brit.* a) bleierne Dachplatten *pl.*, b) Bleidach *n*; **II** *v/t.* **9.** verbleien; **10.** mit Blei beschweren; **11.** *typ.* durch'schießen; **~ con·tent** *s.* ⚒ Bleigehalt *m* (*im Benzin*).

lead·en ['ledn] *adj.* bleiern (*a. fig. Glieder, Schlaf etc.*; *a. bleigrau*), Blei...

lead·er ['liːdə] *s.* **1.** Führer(in), Erste(r *m*) *f*, *sport a.* Ta'bellenführer *m*; **2.** (An)Führer(in), (*pol. Partei-, Fraktions-, Oppositions-*, ⚔ *bsd. Zug-, Gruppen*)Führer *m*: ***♀ of the House*** *parl.* Vorsitzende(r) *m* des Unterhauses; **3.** ♪ a) Kon'zertmeister *m*, erster Violi'nist, b) Führungsstimme *f* (*erster Sopran od. Bläser etc.*), c) *Am.* (Or-

ˈchester-, Chor)Leiter *m*, Diriˈgent *m*; **4.** Leiter(in) (*e-s Projekts etc.*); **5.** Leitpferd *n od.* -hund *m*; **6.** ⚖ *Brit.* erster Anwalt (*mst Kronanwalt*): **~ *for the defence*** Hauptverteidiger *m*; **7.** *bsd. Brit.* ˈLeitarˌtikel *m* (*Zeitung*): **~ *writer*** Leitartikler *m*; **8.** *allg. fig.* ‚Spitzenreiter' *m*, *pl. a.* Spitzengruppe *f*; **9.** ✝ a) ˈLockarˌtikel *m*, b) ˈSpitzenarˌtikel *m*, führendes Proˈdukt, c) *pl. Börse*: führende Werte *pl.*, d) *Statistik*: Index *m*; **10.** ⚘ Leit-, Haupttrieb *m*; **11.** *anat.* Sehne *f*; **12.** Startband *n* (*e-s Films etc.*); **13.** *typ.* Leit-, Taˈbellenpunkt *m*.

lead·er·ship [ˈli:dəʃɪp] *s.* **1.** Führung *f*, Leitung *f*; **2.** ˈFührungsqualiˌtäten *pl.*

ˌ**lead-ˈin** [ˌli:d-] **I** *adj.* **1.** ⚡ Zuleitungs…, *a. fig.* Einführungs…; **II** *s.* **2.** (Anˈtennen- *etc.*)Zuleitung *f*; **3.** *fig.* Einleitung *f*.

lead·ing [ˈli:dɪŋ] führend: a) erst, vorderst: ***the ~ car***, b) *fig.* Haupt…: **~ *part*** *thea.* Hauptrolle *f*; **~ *product*** Spitzenprodukt *n*, c) tonangebend, maßgeblich: **~ *citizen*** prominenter Bürger; **~ ar·ti·cle** → ***leader*** 7, 9 a, b; **~ case** *s.* ⚖ Präzeˈdenzfall *m*; **~ la·dy** *s.* Hauptdarstellerin *f*; **~ light** *s.* F *fig.* ‚Leuchte' *f* (*Person*); **~ man** *s.* [*irr.*] Hauptdarsteller *m*; **~ note** *s.* ♪ Leitton *m*; **~ ques·tion** *s.* ⚖ Suggeˈstivfrage *f*; **~ reins**, *Am.* **~ strings** *s. pl.* **1.** Leitzügel *m*; **2.** Gängelband *n* (*a. fig.*): ***in ~*** *fig.* a) in den Kinderschuhen (stekkend), b) am Gängelband.

lead| pen·cil [led] *s.* Bleistift *m*; **~ poi·son·ing** *s.* ⚕ Bleivergiftung *f*.

lead sto·ry [li:d] *s. Zeitung*: ˈHauptarˌtikel *m*, ‚Aufmacher' *m*.

leaf [li:f] **I** *pl.* **leaves** [li:vz] *s.* **1.** ⚘ (*a.* Blumen)Blatt *n*, *pl. a.* Laub *n*: ***in ~*** belaubt, grün; ***come into ~*** ausschlagen, grün werden; **2.** *coll.* a) Teeblätter *pl.*, b) Tabakblätter *pl.*; **3.** Blatt *n* (*im Buch*): ***take a ~ out of s.o.'s book*** *fig.* sich an j-m ein Beispiel nehmen; ***turn over a new ~*** *fig.* ein neues Leben beginnen; **4.** ⚙ a) Flügel *m* (*Tür*, *Fenster etc.*), b) Klappe *od.* Ausziehplatte *f* (*Tisch*), c) ⚔ (*Visier*)Klappe *f*; **5.** ⚙ Blatt *n*, (dünne) Folie: ***gold ~*** Blattgold *n*; **6.** ⚙ Blatt *n* (*Feder*); **II** *v/t. u. v/i.* **7.** **~ *through*** ˈdurchblättern.

leaf·age [ˈli:fɪdʒ] *s.* Laub(werk) *n*.

leaf| bud *s.* Blattknospe *f*; **~ green** *s.* ⚘ Blattgrün *n* (*a. Farbe*).

leaf·less [ˈli:flɪs] *adj.* blätterlos, entblättert, kahl.

leaf·let [ˈli:flɪt] *s.* **1.** ⚘ Blättchen *n*; **2.** a) Flugblatt *n*, b) Hand-, Reˈklamezettel *m*, c) Merkblatt *n*, d) Proˈspekt *m*, e) Broˈschüre *f*.

leaf spring *s.* ⚙ Blattfeder *f*.

leaf·y [ˈli:fɪ] *adj.* **1.** belaubt, grün; **2.** Laub…; **3.** blattartig, Blatt…

league¹ [li:g] *s.* **1.** Liga *f*, Bund *m*: ***2 of Nations*** *hist.* Völkerbund; **2.** Bündnis *n*, Bund *m*: ***be in ~ with*** im Bunde sein mit, unter ˈeiner Decke stecken mit; ***be in ~ against s.o.*** sich gegen j-n verbündet haben; **3.** *sport* Liga *f*: ***he is not in the same ~*** (***with me***) *fig.* da (an mich) kommt er nicht ran.

league² [li:g] *s. obs.* Wegstunde *f*, Meile *f* (*etwa 4 km*).

leak [li:k] **I** *s.* **1.** a) ⚓ Leck *n*, b) undichte Stelle, Loch *n*: ***spring a ~*** ein Leck *etc.* bekommen; ***take a ~*** *sl.* ‚pinkeln' (gehen), c) → ***leakage*** 1; **2.** *fig.* a) ‚undichte Stelle' (*in e-m Amt etc.*), b) ˈDurchsickern *n* (*von Informationen*), c) gezielte Indiskretiˈon: ***a ~ to the press*** *a.* e-e der Presse zugespielte Information *etc.*; **3.** ⚡ a) Streuung(sverluste *pl.*) *f*, b) Fehlerstelle *f*; **II** *v/i.* **4.** lecken (*a.* ⚡ streuen), leck *od.* undicht sein, *Eimer etc. a.* (aus)laufen, tropfen; **5.** *a.* **~ *out*** a) ausströmen, entweichen (*Gas*), b) auslaufen, sickern, tropfen (*Flüssigkeit*), c) ˈdurchsickern (*a. fig. Nachricht etc.*); **III** *v/t. a.* **~ *out*** **6.** ˈdurchlassen: ***the container ~ed*** (***out***) ***oil*** aus dem Behälter lief Öl aus; **7.** *fig. Nachricht etc.* ˈdurchsickern lassen: **~ *s.th.*** (***out***) ***to*** *j-m* et. zuspielen.

leak·age [ˈli:kɪdʒ] *s.* **1.** a) Lecken *n*, Auslaufen *n*, -strömen *n*, -treten *n*, b) → ***leak*** 1 a *u.* 2; **2.** *a. fig.* Schwund *m*, Verlust *m*; **3.** ✝ Lecˈkage *f*; **~ cur·rent** *s.* ⚡ Leck-, Ableitstrom *m*.

leak·y [ˈli:kɪ] *adj.* leck, undicht.

lean¹ [li:n] *adj.* **1.** a) mager (*a. fig. Ernte*, *Fleisch*, *Jahre*, *Lohn etc.*), schmal, hager, b) schlank; **2.** ⚙ Mager… (*-kohle etc.*), Spar… (*-beton*, *-gemisch etc.*).

lean² [li:n] **I** *v/i.* [*irr.*] **1.** sich neigen (***to*** nach), *Person a.* sich beugen (***over*** über *acc.*), (sich) lehnen (***against*** gegen, an *acc.*), sich stützen (***on*** auf *acc.*): **~ *back*** sich zurücklehnen; **~ *over*** sich (vor)neigen *od.* (vor)beugen; **~ *over backward*(*s*)** F sich ‚fast umbringen' (*et. zu tun*); **~ *to*(*ward*) *s.th.*** *fig.* zu et. (hin)neigen *od.* tendieren; **2.** **~ *on*** *fig.* a) sich auf *j-n* verlassen, b) F *j-n* unter Druck setzen; **II** *v/t.* [*irr.*] **3.** neigen, beugen; **4.** lehnen (***against*** gegen, an *acc.*), (auf)stützen (***on***, ***upon*** auf *acc.*); **III** *s.* **5.** Hang *m*, Neigung *f* (***to*** nach); ˈ**lean·ing** [-nɪŋ] **I** *adj.* sich neigend, geneigt, schief: **~ *tower*** schiefer Turm; **II** *s.* Neigung *f*, Tenˈdenz *f* (*a. fig.* ***towards*** zu).

lean·ness [ˈli:nnɪs] *s.* Magerkeit *f* (*a. fig. der Ernte*, *Jahre etc.*).

leant [lent] *bsd. Brit. pret. u. p.p. von* ***lean²***.

ˈ**lean-to** [-tu:] **I** *pl.* **-tos** *s.* Anbau *m od.* Schuppen (*mit Pultdach*); **II** *adj.* angebaut, Anbau…, sich anlehnend.

leap [li:p] **I** *v/i.* [*irr.*] **1.** springen: ***look before you ~*** erst wägen, dann wagen; ***ready to ~ and strike*** sprungbereit; **~ *for joy*** vor Freude hüpfen (*a. Herz*); **2.** *fig.* a) springen, b) sich stürzen, c) *a.* **~ *up*** (auf)lodern (*Flammen*), d) *a.* **~ *up*** hochschnellen (*Preise etc.*): **~ *into view*** plötzlich sichtbar werden *od.* auftauchen; **~ *at*** sich (förmlich) auf *e-e Gelegenheit etc.* stürzen; **~ *into fame*** mit ˈeinem Schlag berühmt werden; **~ *to a conclusion*** voreilig e-n Schluß ziehen; **~ *to the eye***, **~ *out*** ins Auge springen; **II** *v/t.* [*irr.*] **3.** überˈspringen (*a. fig.*), springen über (*acc.*); **4.** *Pferd etc.* springen lassen (***over*** über *acc.*); **III** *s.* **5.** Sprung *m* (*a. fig.*): ***a ~ in the dark*** *fig.* ein Sprung ins Ungewisse; ***a great ~ forward*** *fig.* ein großer Sprung *od.* Schritt nach vorn; ***by ~s*** (***and bounds***) *fig.* sprunghaft; ˈ**~-frog** **I** *s.* Bockspringen *n*; **II** *v/i.* bockspringen; **III** *v/t.* bockspringen über (*acc.*), e-n Bocksprung machen über (*acc.*).

leapt [lept] *pret. u. p.p. von* ***leap***.

leap year *s.* Schaltjahr *n*.

learn [lɜ:n] **I** *v/t.* [*irr.*] **1.** (er)lernen; **2.** (***from***) a) erfahren, hören (von), b) ersehen, entnehmen (aus *e-m Brief etc.*); **3.** *sl.* ‚lernen' (*lehren*); **II** *v/i.* [*irr.*] **4.** lernen: ***he will never ~!*** er lernt es nie!; **5.** erfahren, hören (***of***, ***about*** von); ˈ**learn·ed** [-nɪd] *adj.* ☐ gelehrt, *Buch etc.*: *a.* wissenschaftlich, *Beruf etc.*: *a.* akaˈdemisch; ˈ**learn·er** [-nə] *s.* **1.** Anfänger(in); **2.** (*a. mot.* Fahr)Schüler (-in), Lernende(r *m*) *f*: ***slow ~*** Lernschwache(r *m*) *f*; ˈ**learn·ing** [-nɪŋ] *s.* **1.** Gelehrsamkeit *f*, Gelehrtheit *f*, Wissen *n*: ***man of ~*** Gelehrte(r) *m*; **2.** (Er)Lernen *n*; **learnt** [-nt] *pret. u. p.p. von* ***learn***.

lease [li:s] **I** *s.* **1.** Pacht-, Mietvertrag *m*; **2.** a) Verpachtung *f* (***to*** an *acc.*), b) Pacht *f*, Miete *f*, c) → ***leasing***: ***a new ~ of life*** *fig.* ein neues Leben, noch e-e (Lebens)Frist (*nach Krankheit etc.*); ***put out to*** (*od.* ***to let out on***) **~** → 5; ***take s.th. on ~***, ***take a ~ of s.th.*** → 6; ***by*** (*od.* ***on***) **~** auf Pacht; **3.** Pachtbesitz *m*, -grundstück *n*; **4.** Pacht- *od.* Mietzeit *f od.* -verhältnis *n*; **II** *v/t.* **5.** **~ *out*** verpachten *od.* vermieten (***to*** an *acc.*); **6.** pachten *od.* mieten, *Investitionsgüter a.* leasen.

ˈ**lease|·hold** [-*ʃ*əʊ-] **I** *s.* **1.** Pacht- *od.* Mietbesitz *m*, Pacht- *od.* Mietgrundstück *n*, Pachtland *n*; **II** *adj.* **2.** gepachtet, Pacht…; ˈ**~ˌhold·er** *s.* Pächter(in), Mieter(in).

leas·er [ˈli:sə] *s.* Pächter(in), Mieter(in), *von Investitionsgütern etc.*: *a.* Leasingnehmer(in).

leash [li:ʃ] **I** *s.* **1.** (Koppel-, Hunde)Leine *f*: ***hold in ~*** a) → 4, b) *fig.* im Zaum halten; ***strain at the ~*** a) an der Leine zerren, b) *fig.* vor Ungeduld platzen; **2.** *hunt.* Koppel *f* (*drei Hunde*, *Füchse etc.*); **II** *v/t.* **3.** (zs.-)koppeln; **4.** an der Leine halten.

leas·ing [ˈli:sɪŋ] *s.* **1.** Pachten *n*, Mieten *n*; **2.** Verpachten *n od.* Vermieten *n*, *von Investitionsgütern etc.*: *a.* Leasing *n*.

least [li:st] **I** *adj.* (*sup. von* ***little***) geringst: a) kleinst, wenigst, mindest, b) unbedeutendst; **II** *s. das* Mindeste, *das* Wenigste: ***at*** (***the***) **~** mindestens, wenigstens, zum mindesten; ***at the very ~*** allermindestens; ***not in the ~*** nicht im geringsten *od.* mindesten; ***say the ~*** (***of it***) gelinde gesagt; **~ *said soonest mended*** je weniger Worte (darüber) desto besser; ***that's the ~ of my worries*** das ist m-e geringste Sorge; **III** *adv.* am wenigsten: **~ *of all*** am allerwenigsten; ***not ~*** nicht zuletzt; ***the ~ complicated solution*** die unkomplizierteste Lösung; ***with the ~ possible effort*** mit möglichst geringer Anstrengung.

leath·er [ˈleðə] **I** *s.* **1.** Leder *n* (*a. fig. humor. Haut*; *sport sl. Ball*): **~ *goods*** Lederwaren *pl.*; **2.** Lederball *m*, -lappen *m*, -riemen *m etc.*; **3.** *pl.* a) Lederhose(n *pl.*) *f*, b) ˈLedergaˌmaschen *pl.*; **II** *v/t.* **4.** mit Leder überˈziehen; **5.** F ‚versohlen'; ˈ**~·neck** *s.* ⚔ *Am.* F ‚Ledernacken' *m*, Maˈrineinfanteˌrist *m* (*des U.S. Marine Corps*).

leath·er·y [ˈleðərɪ] *adj.* ledern, zäh.

leave¹ [li:v] **I** *v/t.* [*irr.*] **1.** *allg.* verlassen:

a) von *j-m od. e-m Ort* weggehen, b) abreisen *od.* abfahren *od.* abfliegen von (***for*** nach), c) von *der Schule* abgehen, d) *j-n od. et.* im Stich lassen, *et.* aufgeben; **2.** lassen: ***~ open*** offenlassen; ***it ~s me cold*** F es läßt mich kalt; ***~ it at that*** F es dabei belassen *od.* (bewenden) lassen; ***~ things as they are*** die Dinge so lassen, wie sie sind; → ***leave alone***; **3.** (übrig)lassen: ***6 from 8 ~s 2*** 8 minus 6 ist 2; ***be left*** übrig sein, (übrig-) bleiben; ***there's nothing left for us but to go*** uns bleibt nichts übrig, als zu gehen; ***to be left till called for*** postlagernd; **4.** *Narbe etc.* zu'rücklassen, *Eindruck, Nachricht, Spur etc.* hinter'lassen: ***~ s.o. wondering whether*** j-n im Zweifel darüber lassen, ob; ***~ s.o. to himself*** j-n sich selbst überlassen; **5.** *s-n Schirm etc.* stehen- *od.* liegenlassen, vergessen; **6.** über'lassen, an'heimstellen (***to*** *dat.*): ***I ~ it to you*** (***to decide***); ***~ it to me!*** überlaß das mir!, laß mich das *od.* nur machen; ***~ nothing to accident*** nichts dem Zufall überlassen; **7.** (*nach dem Tode*) hinter'lassen, zu'rücklassen: ***he ~s a wife and five children***; **8.** vermachen, vererben (***to s.o.*** j-m); **9.** (*auf der Fahrt*) *links od. rechts* liegen lassen: ***~ the mill on the left***; **10.** aufhören mit, (unter)'lassen, *Arbeit etc.* einstellen; **II** *v/i.* [*irr.*] **11.** (fort-, weg-) gehen, (ab)reisen *od.* (ab)fahren *od.* (ab)fliegen (***for*** nach); **12.** gehen, die Stellung aufgeben;
Zssgn mit adv.:
leave| a·bout *v/t.* her'umliegen lassen; **~ a·lone** *v/t.* **1.** al'lein lassen; **2.** *j-n od. et.* in Ruhe lassen; *et.* auf sich beruhen lassen: ***leave well alone*** die Finger davon lassen; **~ a·side** *v/t.* bei'seite lassen; **~ be·hind** *v/t.* **1.** da-, zu'rücklassen; **2.** → ***leave***[1] 4, 5; **3.** *Gegner etc.* hinter sich lassen; **~ off I** *v/t.* **1.** weglassen; **2.** *Kleid etc.* a) nicht anziehen, b) ablegen, nicht mehr tragen; **3.** aufhören mit, *die Arbeit* einstellen; **4.** *Gewohnheit etc.* aufgeben; **II** *v/i.* **5.** aufhören; **~ on** *v/t. Kleid etc.* anbehalten, *a. Licht etc.* anlassen; **~ out** *v/t.* **1.** aus-, weglassen; **2.** draußen lassen; **3.** *j-n* ausschließen (***of*** von): ***leave her out of this!*** laß sie aus dem Spiel!; **~ o·ver** *v/t.* (*als Rest*) übriglassen: ***be left over*** übrig(geblieben) sein.

leave[2] [li:v] *s.* **1.** Erlaubnis *f*, Genehmigung *f*: ***ask ~ of s.o.*** j-n um Erlaubnis bitten; ***take ~ to say*** sich zu sagen erlauben; ***by your ~!*** mit Verlaub!; ***without so much as a by your ~*** *iro.* mir nichts, dir nichts; **2.** *a.* ***~ of absence*** Urlaub *m*: (***go on***) ***~*** auf Urlaub (gehen); ***a man on ~*** ein Urlauber; **3.** Abschied *m*: ***take*** (***one's***) ***~*** sich verabschieden, Abschied nehmen (***of s.o.*** von j-m); ***have taken ~ of one's senses*** nicht (mehr) ganz bei Trost sein.

leav·en ['levn] **I** *s.* **1.** a) Sauerteig *m* (*a. fig.*), b) Hefe *f*, c) → ***leavening***; **II** *v/t.* **2.** *Teig* a) säuern, b) (auf)gehen lassen; **3.** *fig.* durch'setzen, -'dringen; **'leav·en·ing** [-nɪŋ] *s.* Treibmittel *n*, Gär(ungs)stoff *m*.

leaves [li:vz] *pl. von* ***leaf***.

'leave-ˌtak·ing *s.* Abschied(nehmen *n*) *m*.

leav·ing cer·tif·i·cate ['li:vɪŋ] *s.* Abgangszeugnis *n*.

leav·ings ['li:vɪŋz] *s. pl.* **1.** 'Überbleibsel *pl.*, Reste *pl.*; **2.** Abfall *m*.

Leb·a·nese [ˌlebə'ni:z] **I** *adj.* liba'nesisch; **II** *s.* a) Liba'nese *m*, Liba'nesin *f*, b) *pl.* Liba'nesen *pl.*

lech·er ['letʃə] *s.* Wüstling *m*, *humor.* ‚Lustmolch' *m*; **lech·er·ous** ['letʃərəs] *adj.* □ lüstern, geil; **'lech·er·y** [-ərɪ] *s.* Lüsternheit *f*, Geilheit *f*.

lec·tern ['lektɜ:n] *s. eccl.* (Lese- *od.* Chor)Pult *n*.

lec·ture ['lektʃə] **I** *s.* **1.** Vortrag *m*; *univ.* Vorlesung *f*, Kol'leg *n* (***on*** über *acc.*, ***to*** vor *dat.*): ***~ room*** Vortrags-, *univ.* Hörsaal *m*; ***~ tour*** Vortragsreise *f*; **2.** Strafpredigt *f*: ***give*** (*od.* ***read***) ***s.o. a ~*** → 5; **II** *v/i.* **3.** e-n Vortrag *od.* Vorträge halten (***to s.o. on s.th.*** vor j-m über e-e Sache); **4.** *univ.* e-e Vorlesung *od.* Vorlesungen halten, lesen (***on*** über *acc.*); **III** *v/t.* **5.** *j-m* e-e Strafpredigt *od.* Standpauke halten; **'lec·tur·er** [-tʃərə] *s.* **1.** Vortragende(r *m*) *f*; **2.** *univ.* Do'zent(in), Hochschullehrer(in); **3.** *Church of England*: Hilfsprediger *m*; **'lec·ture·ship** [-ʃɪp] *s. univ.* Dozen'tur *f*, Lehrauftrag *m*.

led [led] *pret. u. p.p. von* ***lead***[1].

ledge [ledʒ] *s.* **1.** Leiste *f*, Kante *f*; **2.** a) (Fenster)Sims *m od. n*, b) (Fenster-) Brett *n*; **3.** (Fels)Gesims *n*, (-)Vorsprung *m*; **4.** Felsbank *f*, Riff *n*.

ledg·er ['ledʒə] *s.* **1.** ✝ Hauptbuch *n*; **2.** ⚠ Querbalken *m*, Sturz *m* (*e-s Gerüsts*); **3.** große Steinplatte; **~ line** *s.* **1.** Angelleine *f* mit festliegendem Köder; **2.** ♪ Hilfslinie *f*.

lee [li:] *s.* **1.** (wind)geschützte Stelle; **2.** Windschattenseite *f*; **3.** ⚓ Lee(seite) *f*.

leech [li:tʃ] *s.* **1.** *zo.* Blutegel *m*: ***stick like a ~ to s.o.*** *fig.* wie e-e Klette an j-m hängen; **2.** *fig.* Blutsauger *m*, Schma'rotzer *m*.

leek [li:k] *s.* ⚘ (Breit)Lauch *m*, Porree *m*.

leer [lɪə] **I** *s.* (lüsterner *od.* gehässiger *od.* boshafter) (Seiten)Blick, anzügliches Grinsen; **II** *v/i.* (lüstern *etc.*) schielen (***at*** nach); anzüglich grinsen; **leer·y** ['lɪərɪ] *adj. sl.* **1.** schlau; **2.** argwöhnisch (***of*** gegenüber).

lees [li:z] *s. pl.* Bodensatz *m*, Hefe *f* (*a. fig.*): ***drink*** (*od.* ***drain***) ***to the ~*** *bsd. fig.* bis zur Neige leeren.

lee| shore *s.* ⚓ Leeküste *f*; **~ side** *s.* ⚓ Leeseite *f*.

lee·ward ['li:wəd; ⚓ 'lu:əd] **I** *adj.* Lee...; **II** *s.* Lee(seite) *f*: ***to ~*** → **III** *adv.* leewärts.

'lee·way *s.* **1.** ⚓, *a.* ✈ Abtrift *f*: ***make ~*** abtreiben; **2.** *fig.* Rückstand *m*: ***make up ~*** (den Rückstand) aufholen, (das Versäumte) nachholen; **3.** *fig.* Spielraum *m*.

left[1] [left] *pret. u. p.p. von* ***leave***[1].

left[2] [left] **I** *adj.* **1.** link (*a. pol.*); **II** *adv.* **2.** links: ***move ~*** nach links rücken; ***turn ~*** links abbiegen; ***~ turn!*** ⚔ links um!; **III** *s.* **3.** Linke *f* (*a. pol.*), linke Seite: ***on*** (*od.* ***to***) ***the ~*** (***of***) links (von), linker Hand (von); ***on our ~*** zu unserer Linken, links von uns; ***to the ~*** nach links; ***keep to the ~*** sich links halten, links fahren; ***the ~ of the party*** *pol.* der linke Flügel der Partei; **4.** *Boxen*: a) Linke *f* (*Faust*), b) Linke(r *m*) *f* (*Schlag*); **'~-hand** *adj.* **1.** link; **2.** → ***left-handed*** 1–4; **ˌ~-'hand·ed** *adj.* □ **1.** linkshändig: ***a ~ person*** → ***left-hander*** 1; **2.** linkshändig, link (*Schlag etc.*); **3.** link, linksseitig; **4.** ⚙ linksgängig, -läufig, Links...: ***~ drive*** Linkssteuerung *f*; ***~ screw*** linksgängige Schraube; **5.** zweifelhaft, fragwürdig: ***~ compliments***; **6.** linkisch, ungeschickt; **7.** *hist.* morga'natisch, zur linken Hand (*Ehe*); **ˌ~-'hand·er** *s.* **1.** Linkshänder(in); **2.** *Boxen*: Linke *f*.

left·ist ['leftɪst] *pol.* **I** *s.* Linke(r *m*) *f*, 'Linkspoˌlitiker(in), -stehende(r *m*) *f*; **II** *adj.* linksgerichtet, -stehend, Links...

ˌleft|-'lug·gage lock·er *s. Brit.* (Gepäck)Schließfach *n*; **ˌ~-'lug·gage** (**of·fice**) *s. Brit.* Gepäckaufbewahrung(sstelle) *f*; **'~ˌo·ver I** *adj.* übrig(geblieben); **II** *s.* 'Überbleibsel *n*, (*bsd.* Speise)Rest *m*.

'left|-wing *adj. pol.* dem linken Flügel angehörend, Links..., *Person*: *a.* linksgerichtet, -stehend; **ˌ~-'wing·er** *s.* **1.** → ***leftist*** I; **2.** *sport* Linksaußen *m*.

leg [leg] **I** *s.* **1.** a) Bein *n*, b) 'Unterschenkel *m*; → *Bes. Redew.*; **2.** (*Hammel- etc.*)Keule *f*: ***~ of mutton***; **3.** a) Bein *n* (*Hose, Strumpf*), b) Schaft *m* (*Stiefel*); **4.** a) Bein *n* (*Tisch etc.*), b) Stütze *f*, c) Schenkel *m* (*Zirkel etc., a.* ⚖ *Dreieck*); **5.** E'tappe *f*, Abschnitt *m*, Teilstrecke *f*; **6.** *sport* a) E'tappe *f*, Teilstrecke *f*, b) Runde *f*, c) 'Durchgang *m*, Lauf *m*; **II** *v/i.* **7.** *mst* ***~ it*** F a) tippeln, marschieren, b) rennen;
Besondere Redewendungen:
on one's ~s a) stehend (*bsd. um e-e Rede zu halten*), b) auf den Beinen (*Ggs. bettlägerig*); ***be on one's last ~s*** es nicht mehr lange machen, ‚am Eingehen' sein, auf dem letzten Loch pfeifen; ***find one's ~s*** s-e Beine gebrauchen lernen, *fig.* sich finden; ***give s.o. a ~ up*** j-m (hin)aufhelfen, *fig.* j-m unter die Arme greifen; ***have not a ~ to stand on*** *fig.* keinerlei Beweise *od.* keine Chance haben; ***pull s.o.'s ~*** F j-n ‚auf den Arm nehmen' *od.* aufziehen; ***shake a ~*** a) F das Tanzbein schwingen, b) *sl.* ‚Tempo machen'; ***stand on one's own ~s*** auf eigenen Füßen stehen; ***stretch one's ~s*** sich die Beine vertreten.

leg·a·cy ['legəsɪ] *s.* ⚖ Le'gat *n*, Vermächtnis *n* (*a. fig.*), *fig. a.* Erbe *n*, *contp.* Hinter'lassenschaft *f*.

le·gal ['li:gl] *adj.* □ **1.** gesetzlich, rechtlich: ***~ holiday*** gesetzlicher Feiertag; ***~ reserves*** ✝ gesetzliche Rücklagen; **2.** le'gal: a) (rechtlich *od.* gesetzlich) zulässig, gesetzmäßig, b) rechtsgültig: ***~ claim***; ***not ~*** gesetzlich verboten *od.* nicht zulässig; ***make ~*** legalisieren; **3.** Rechts..., ju'ristisch: ***~ adviser*** Rechtsberater(in); ***~ aid*** Prozeßkostenhilfe *f*; ***~ capacity*** Geschäftsfähigkeit *f*; ***~ entity*** juristische Person; ***~ force*** Rechtskraft *f*; ***~ position*** Rechtslage *f*; ***~ remedy*** Rechtsmittel *n*; **4.** gerichtlich: ***a ~ decision***; ***take ~ action*** (*od.* ***steps***) ***against s.o.*** gegen j-n gerichtlich vorgehen; **le·gal·ese** [ˌli:gə'li:z] *s.* Ju'ristensprache *f*, -jarˌgon *m*; **le·gal·i·ty** [li:'gælətɪ] *s.* Legali'tät *f*, Gesetzlichkeit *f*, Rechtmäßigkeit *f*, Zulässigkeit *f*.

le·gal·i·za·tion [ˌli:gəlaɪ'zeɪʃn] *s.* Legali-

sierung *f*; **le·gal·ize** ['li:gəlaɪz] *v/t.* legalisieren, rechtskräftig machen, *a.* amtlich beglaubigen, beurkunden.
leg·ate¹ ['legɪt] *s.* (päpstlicher) Le'gat.
le·gate² [lɪ'geɪt] *v/t.* (testamen'tarisch) vermachen.
leg·a·tee [ˌlegə'ti:] *s.* ⚖ Lega'tar(in), Vermächtnisnehmer(in).
le·ga·tion [lɪ'geɪʃn] *s. pol.* Gesandtschaft *f*, Vertretung *f*.
leg·a·tor [ˌlegə'tɔ:; *Am.* lɪ'geɪtə] *s.* ⚖ Vermächtnisgeber(in), Erb-lasser(in).
leg·end ['ledʒənd] *s.* **1.** Sage *f*, (*a.* 'Heiligen)Leˌgende *f*; **2.** Le'gende *f*: a) erläuternder Text, Beschriftung *f*, 'Bildˌunterschrift *f*, b) Zeichenerklärung *f* (*auf Karten etc.*), c) Inschrift *f*; **3.** *fig.* legen'däre Gestalt *od.* Sache, Mythus *m*; '**leg·end·ar·y** [-dərɪ] *adj.* legen'där: a) sagenhaft, Sagen…, b) berühmt.
leg·er·de·main [ˌledʒədə'meɪn] *s.* Taschenspiele'rei *f*, *a. fig.* (Taschenspieler)Trick *m*.
-legged [legd] *adj. bsd. in Zssgn* mit (…) Beinen, …beinig; **leg·gings** ['legɪŋz] *s. pl.* **1.** (hohe) Ga'maschen *pl.*; **2.** 'Überhose *f*; **leg·gy** ['legɪ] *adj.* langbeinig.
leg·i·bil·i·ty [ˌledʒɪ'bɪlətɪ] *s.* Leserlichkeit *f*; **leg·i·ble** ['ledʒəbl] *adj.* □ (gut) leserlich.
le·gion ['li:dʒən] *s.* **1.** *antiq.* ⚔ Legi'on *f* (*a. fig. Unzahl*): ***their name is ~*** *fig.* ihre Zahl ist Legion; **2.** Legi'on *f*, (*bsd.* Frontkämpfer)Verband *m*: ***the American*** (***British***) ***2***; ***2 of Hono***(***u***)***r*** *französische* Ehrenlegion; ***the*** (***Foreign***) ***2*** die (französische) Fremdenlegion; '**legion·ar·y** [-dʒənərɪ] **I** *adj.* Legions…; **II** *s.* Legio'När *m*; **le·gion·naire** [ˌli:dʒə'neə] *s.* ('Fremden- *etc.*)Legioˌnär *m*.
leg·is·late ['ledʒɪsleɪt] **I** *v/i.* Gesetze erlassen; **II** *v/t.* durch Gesetze bewirken *od.* schaffen: ***~ away*** durch Gesetze abschaffen; **leg·is·la·tion** [ˌledʒɪs'leɪʃn] *s.* Gesetzgebung *f* (*a. weitS.* [erlassene] Gesetze *pl.*); '**leg·is·la·tive** [-lətɪv] **I** *adj.* □ **1.** gesetzgebend, legisla'tiv; **2.** Legislatur…, Gesetzgebungs…; **II** *s.* **3.** → ***legislature***; '**leg·is·la·tor** [-leɪtə] *s.* Gesetzgeber *m*; '**leg·is·la·ture** [-leɪtʃə] *s.* Legisla'tive *f*, gesetzgebende Körperschaft.
le·git [lɪ'dʒɪt] *sl. für* ***legitimate*** I, ***legitimate drama***.
le·git·i·ma·cy [lɪ'dʒɪtɪməsɪ] *s.* **1.** Legitimi'tät *f*: a) Rechtmäßigkeit *f*, b) Ehelichkeit *f*: ***~ of birth***, c) Berechtigung *f*, Gültigkeit *f*; **2.** (Folge)Richtigkeit *f*.
le·git·i·mate [lɪ'dʒɪtɪmət] **I** *adj.* □ **1.** legi'tim: a) gesetzmäßig, gesetzlich, b) rechtmäßig, berechtigt (*Forderung etc.*), c) ehelich: ***~ birth***; ***~ son***; **2.** (folge)richtig, begründet, einwandfrei; **II** *v/t.* [-meɪt] **3.** legitimieren: a) für gesetzmäßig erklären, b) ehelich machen; **4.** als (rechts)gültig anerkennen; **5.** rechtfertigen; ***~* dra·ma** *s.* **1.** lite'rarisch wertvolles Drama; **2.** echtes Drama (*Ggs. Film etc.*).
le·git·i·ma·tion [lɪˌdʒɪtɪ'meɪʃn] *s.* Legitimati'on *f*: a) Legitimierung *f*, *a.* Ehelichkeitserklärung *f*, b) 'Ausweis(paˌpiere *pl.*) *m*; **le·git·i·ma·tize** [lɪ'dʒɪtɪmətaɪz], **le·git·i·mize** [lɪ'dʒɪtɪmaɪz] → ***legitimate*** 3, 4, 5.
leg·less ['leglɪs] *adj.* ohne Beine, beinlos.
'**leg|·man** *s.* [*irr.*] *bsd. Am.* **1.** Re'porter *m* (im Außendienst); **2.** ‚Laufbursche' *m*; '**~-pull** *s.* F Veräppelung *f*, Scherz *m*; '**~-room** [-rʊm] *s. mot.* Beinfreiheit *f*; '**~-show** *s.* F ‚Beinchenschau' *f*, Re'vue *f*.
leg·ume ['legju:m] *s.* **1.** ♀ a) Hülsenfrucht *f*, b) Hülse *f* (*Frucht*); **2.** *mst pl.* a) Hülsenfrüchte *pl.* (*als Gemüse*), b) Gemüse *n*; **le·gu·mi·nous** [le'gju:mɪnəs] *adj.* Hülsen…; hülsentragend.
'**leg·work** *s.* F Laufe'rei *f*.
lei·sure ['leʒə] **I** *s.* **1.** Muße *f*, Freizeit *f*: ***at ~*** → ***leisurely***; ***be at ~*** Zeit *od.* Muße haben; ***at your ~*** wenn es Ihnen (gerade) paßt; **2.** → ***leisureliness***; **II** *adj.* Muße…, frei: ***~ hours***; ***~ activities*** Freizeitbeschäftigungen *pl.*, -gestaltung *f*; ***~ industry*** Freizeitindustrie *f*; ***~ time*** Freizeit *f*; ***~ wear*** Freizeit(be)kleidung *f*; '**lei·sured** [-əd] *adj.* frei, unbeschäftigt, müßig: ***the ~ classes*** die begüterten Klassen; '**lei·sure·li·ness** [-lɪnɪs] *s.* Gemächlichkeit *f*, Gemütlichkeit *f*; '**lei·sure·ly** [-lɪ] *adj. u. adv.* gemächlich, gemütlich.
leit·mo·tiv, *a.* **leit·mo·tif** ['laɪtməʊˌti:f] *s. bsd.* ♪ 'Leitmoˌtiv *n*.
lem·ming ['lemɪŋ] *s. zo.* Lemming *m*.
lem·on ['lemən] **I** *s.* **1.** Zi'trone *f*; **2.** Zi'tronenbaum *m*; **3.** Zi'tronengelb *n*; **4.** *sl.* ‚Niete' *f*: a) ‚Flasche' *f* (*Person*), b) ‚Gurke' *f* (*Sache*): ***hand s.o. a ~*** ‚j-n schwer drankriegen'; **II** *adj.* **5.** zi'tronengelb; **lem·on·ade** [ˌlemə'neɪd] *s.* Zi'tronenlimoˌnade *f*.
lem·on| dab *s. ichth.* Rotzunge *f*; ***~* sole** *s. ichth.* Seezunge *f*; ***~* squash** *s. Brit.* Zi'tronenlimoˌnade *f*; ***~* squeez·er** *s.* Zi'tronenpresse *f*.
le·mur ['li:mə] *s. zo.* Le'mur(e) *m*, Maki *m*.
lem·u·res ['lemjʊri:z] *s. pl. myth.* Le'muren *pl.* (*Gespenster*).
lend [lend] *v/t.* [*irr.*] **1.** (aus-, ver)leihen: ***~ s.o. money*** (*od.* ***money to s.o.***) j-m Geld leihen, an j-n Geld verleihen; **2.** *fig. Würde etc.* verleihen (***to*** *dat.*); **3.** *Hilfe etc.* leisten, gewähren: ***~ itself to*** sich eignen zu *od.* für (*Sache*); → ***ear¹*** 3, ***hand*** 1; **4.** *s-n Namen* hergeben (***to*** zu): ***~ o.s. to*** sich hergeben zu; **lend·er** ['lendə] *s.* Aus-, Verleiher(in), Geld-, Kre'ditgeber(in); **lend·ing li·brar·y** ['lendɪŋ] *s.* 'Leihbücheˌrei *f*.
ˌ**Lend-'Lease Act** *s. hist.* Leih-Pacht-Gesetz *n* (*1941*).
length [leŋθ] *s.* **1.** *allg.* Länge *f*: a) *als Maß*, *a.* Stück *n* (*Stoff etc.*): ***two feet in ~*** 2 Fuß lang, b) (*a.* lange) Strecke, c) 'Umfang *m* (*Buch, Liste etc.*), d) (*a.* lange) Dauer (*a. Phonetik*); **2.** *sport* Länge *f* (Vorsprung): ***win by a ~*** mit e-r Länge (Vorsprung) siegen;
Besondere Redewendungen:
at ~ a) lang, ausführlich, b) endlich, schließlich; ***at full ~*** a) in allen Einzelheiten, ganz ausführlich, b) der Länge nach (*hinfallen*); ***at great*** (***some***) ***~*** sehr (ziemlich) ausführlich; ***for any ~ of time*** für längere Zeit; (***over all***) ***the ~ and breadth of France*** in ganz Frankreich (herum); ***go*** (***to***) ***great ~s*** a) sehr weit gehen, b) sich sehr bemühen; ***he went*** (***to***) ***the ~ of asserting*** er ging so weit zu behaupten; ***go*** (***to***) ***all ~s*** aufs Ganze gehen, vor nichts zurückschrecken; ***go any ~*** alles (Erdenkliche) tun.
length·en ['leŋθən] **I** *v/t.* **1.** verlängern, länger machen; **2.** ausdehnen; **3.** *Wein etc.* strecken; **II** *v/i.* **4.** sich verlängern, länger werden; **5.** ***~ out*** sich in die Länge ziehen; '**length·en·ing** [-θənɪŋ] *s.* Verlängerung *f*.
length·i·ness ['leŋθɪnɪs] *s.* Langatmigkeit *f*, Weitschweifigkeit *f*.
'**length·ways** [-weɪz], *Am.* '**length·wise** *adv.* der Länge nach, längs.
length·y ['leŋθɪ] *adj.* □ **1.** (sehr) lang; **2.** *fig.* ermüdend *od.* 'übermäßig lang, langatmig.
le·ni·en·cy ['li:njənsɪ], *a.* **le·ni·ence** ['li:njəns] *s.* Milde *f*, Nachsicht *f*; '**le·ni·ent** [-nt] *adj.* □ mild(e), nachsichtig (***to***[***wards***] gegen'über).
lens [lenz] *s.* **1.** *anat.* Linse *f* (*a. phys.*, ⚙); **2.** *opt.* a) Linse *f*, b) Lupe *f*, (Vergrößerungs)Glas *n*; **3.** *phot.* Objek'tiv *n*, ‚Linse' *f*: ***~ aperture*** Blende *f*; ***~ screen*** Gegenlichtblende *f*.
lent¹ [lent] *pret. u. p.p. von* ***lend***.
Lent² [lent] *s.* Fasten(zeit *f*) *pl.*
len·tic·u·lar [len'tɪkjʊlə] *adj.* □ **1.** linsenförmig, *bsd. anat.* Linsen…; **2.** *phys.* bikon'vex.
len·til ['lentɪl] *s.* ♀ Linse *f*.
Lent| lil·y *s.* ♀ Nar'zisse *f*; ***~* term** *s. Brit.* 'Frühjahrstriˌmester *n*.
Le·o ['li:əʊ] *s. ast.* Löwe *m*.
le·o·nine ['li:əʊnaɪn] *adj.* Löwen…
leop·ard ['lepəd] *s. zo.* Leo'pard *m*: ***black ~*** Schwarzer Panther; ***the ~ can't change its spots*** *fig.* die Katze läßt das Mausen nicht; ***~ cat*** *s. zo.* Ben'galkatze *f*.
le·o·tard ['li:əʊtɑ:d] *s.* Tri'kot(anzug *m*) *n*, *sport* Gym'nastikanzug *m*.
lep·er ['lepə] *s.* **1.** Leprakranke(r *m*) *f*; **2.** *fig.* Aussätzige(r *m*) *f*.
lep·i·dop·ter·ous [ˌlepɪ'dɒptərəs] *adj.* Schmetterlings…
lep·re·chaun ['leprəkɔ:n] *s. Ir.* Kobold *m*.
lep·ro·sy ['leprəsɪ] *s.* ⚕ Lepra *f*; '**leprous** [-əs] *adj.* a) leprakrank, b) le'prös, Lepra…
les·bi·an ['lezbɪən] **I** *adj.* lesbisch; **II** *s.* Lesbierin *f*; '**les·bi·an·ism** [-nɪzəm] *s.* lesbische Liebe, Lesbia'nismus *m*.
lese-maj·es·ty [ˌli:z'mædʒɪstɪ] *s.* **1.** *a. fig.* Maje'stätsbeleidigung *f*; **2.** Hochverrat *m*.
le·sion ['li:ʒn] *s.* **1.** Verletzung *f*, Wunde *f*; **2.** krankhafte Veränderung (*e-s Organs*).
less [les] **I** *adv.* (*comp. von* ***little***) weniger (***than*** als): ***a ~ known*** (*od.* ***~-known***) ***author*** ein weniger bekannter Autor; ***~ and ~*** immer weniger *od.* seltener; ***still*** (*od.* ***much***) ***~*** noch viel weniger, geschweige denn; ***the ~ so as*** (dies) um so weniger, als; **II** *adj.* (*comp. von* ***little***) geringer, kleiner, weniger: ***in ~ time*** in kürzerer Zeit; ***of ~ importance*** (***value***) von geringerer Bedeutung (von geringerem Wert); ***no ~ a person than Churchill***; *a.* ***Churchill, no ~*** kein Geringerer als Churchill; **III** *s.* weniger, e-e kleinere Menge *od.* Zahl, ein geringeres (Aus)Maß: ***for ~*** billiger; ***do with ~*** mit weniger auskommen; ***little ~ than robbery*** so gut

wie *od.* schon fast Raub; ***nothing ~ than*** zumindest; ***nothing ~ than a disaster*** e-e echte Katastrophe; ***~ of that!*** hör auf damit!; **IV** *prp.* weniger, minus, ✝ abzüglich.

les·see [leˈsiː] *s.* Pächter(in) *od.* Mieter (-in), *von Investitionsgütern etc.*: *a.* Leasingnehmer(in).

less·en [ˈlesn] **I** *v/i.* sich vermindern *od.* verringern, abnehmen, geringer werden, nachlassen; **II** *v/t.* vermindern, -ringern, -kleinern; *fig.* herˈabsetzen, schmälern; ˈ**less·en·ing** [-nɪŋ] *s.* Nachlassen *n*, Abnahme *f*, Verringerung *f*, -minderung *f*.

less·er [ˈlesə] *adj.* (*nur attr.*) kleiner, geringer; unbedeutender.

les·son [ˈlesn] *s.* **1.** Lektiˈon *f* (*a. fig. Denkzettel, Strafe*), Übungsstück *n*, (*a.* Haus)Aufgabe *f*; **2.** (Lehr-, ˈUnterrichts)Stunde *f*; *pl.* ˈUnterricht *m*, Stunden *pl.*: ***give ~s*** Unterricht erteilen; ***take ~s from s.o.*** Stunden *od.* Unterricht bei j-m nehmen; **3.** *fig.* Lehre *f*: ***this was a ~ to me*** das war mir e-e Lehre; ***let this be a ~ to you*** laß dir das zur Lehre *od.* Warnung dienen; ***he has learnt his ~*** er hat s-e Lektion gelernt; **4.** *eccl.* Lesung *f*.

les·sor [leˈsɔː] *s.* Verpächter(in) *od.* Vermieter(in), *von Investitionsgütern etc.*: *a.* Leasinggeber(in).

lest [lest] *cj.* **1.** (*mst mit folgendem* ***should*** *konstr.*) daß *od.* daˈmit nicht; aus Furcht, daß; **2.** (*nach Ausdrücken des Befürchtens*) daß: ***fear ~***.

let[1] [let] **I** *s.* **1.** *Brit.* F a) Vermietung *f*, b) Mietwohnung *f*, Mietshaus *n*: ***get a ~ for*** e-n Mieter finden für; **II** *v/t.* [*irr.*] **2.** lassen, *j-m* erlauben: ***~ him talk!*** laß ihn reden!; ***~ me help you*** lassen Sie mich Ihnen helfen; ***~ s.o. know*** j-n wissen lassen *od.* Bescheid sagen; ***~ into*** a) (her)einlassen in (*acc.*), b) *j-n* einweihen in *ein Geheimnis*, c) *Stück Stoff etc.* einsetzen in (*acc.*); ***~ s.o. off a penalty*** j-m e-e Strafe erlassen; ***~ s.o. off a promise*** j-n von e-m Versprechen entbinden; **3.** vermieten (***to*** an *acc.*, ***for*** auf *ein Jahr etc.*): ***"to ~"*** „zu vermieten"; **4.** *Arbeit etc.* vergeben (***to*** an *j-n*); **III** *v/aux.* [*irr.*] **5.** lassen, mögen, sollen (*zur Umschreibung des Imperativs der 1. u. 2. Person*): ***~ us go! Yes, ~'s!*** gehen wir! Ja, gehen wir! (*od.* Ja, einverstanden!); ***~ him go there at once!*** er soll sofort hingehen!; ***~'s not*** (F ***don't let's***) ***quarrel!*** wir wollen doch nicht streiten!; (***just***) ***~ them try*** das sollen sie nur versuchen; ***~ me see!*** Moment mal!; ***~ A be equal to B*** nehmen wir an, A ist gleich B; ***~ it be known that*** man soll *od.* alle sollen wissen, daß; **IV** *v/i.* [*irr.*] **6.** sich vermieten (lassen) (***at, for*** für);

Besondere Redewendungen:

~ alone a) geschweige denn, ganz zu schweigen von, b) → ***let alone***; ***~ loose*** loslassen; ***~ be*** a) *et.* sein lassen, die Finger lassen von, b) *et. od. j-n* in Ruhe lassen; ***~ fall*** a) (*a. fig. Bemerkung*) fallen lassen, b) ⩘ *Senkrechte* fällen (***on, upon*** auf *acc.*); ***~ fly*** a) *et.* abschießen, *fig. et.* vom Stapel lassen, b) (*v/i.*) schießen (***at*** auf *acc.*), c) *fig.* vom Leder ziehen, grob werden; ***~ go*** a) loslassen, fahren lassen, b) es sausen lassen, c) draufˈlos rasen *od.* schießen *etc.*, d) loslegen; ***~ o.s. go*** a) sich gehenlassen, b) aus sich herausgehen; ***~ go of s.th.*** et. loslassen; ***~ it go at that*** laß es dabei bewenden;

Zssgn mit adv.:

let| a·lone *v/t.* **1.** alˈlein lassen, verlassen; **2.** *j-n od. et.* in Ruhe lassen; *et.* sein lassen; die Finger von *et.* lassen (*a. fig.*): ***let well alone*** lieber die Finger davon lassen; ***~ down*** *v/t.* **1.** hinˈunter- *od.* herˈunterlassen: ***let s.o. down gently*** mit j-m glimpflich verfahren; **2.** a) *j-n* im Stich lassen (***on*** bei), b) *j-n* enttäuschen, c) *j-n* blamieren; **3.** die Luft aus *e-m Reifen* lassen; ***~ in*** *v/t.* **1.** (her)ˈeinlassen; **2.** *Stück etc.* einlassen, -setzen; **3.** einweihen (***on*** in *acc.*); **4.** ***let s.o. in for*** j-m *et.* aufhalsen *od.* einbrocken; ***let o.s. in for*** sich *et.* einbrokken *od.* einhandeln, sich auf *et.* einlassen; ***~ off*** *v/t.* **1.** *Sprengladung etc.* loslassen, *Gewehr etc.* abfeuern; *Gas etc.* ablassen; → ***steam*** 1; **2.** *Witz etc.* vom Stapel lassen; **3.** *j-n* laufen *od.* gehen lassen, *mit e-r Geldstrafe etc.* daˈvonkommen lassen; ***~ on*** F **I** *v/i.* **1.** ‚plaudern' (*Geheimnis verraten*); **2.** vorgeben, so tun als ob; **II** *v/t.* **3.** ‚ausplaudern', verraten; **4.** sich *et.* anmerken lassen; ***~ out*** *v/t.* **1.** hinˈaus- *od.* herˈauslassen; **2.** *Kleid* auslassen; **3.** *Geheimnis* ausplaudern; **4.** → ***let***[1] 3, 4; ***~ up*** *v/i.* F **1.** a) nachlassen, b) aufhören; **2.** ***~ on*** ablassen von, *j-n* in Ruhe lassen.

let[2] [let] *s.* **1.** *Tennis*: Netzaufschlag *m*, Netz(ball *m*) *n*; **2.** ***without ~ or hindrance*** völlig unbehindert.

ˈ**let·down** *s.* **1.** Nachlassen *n*; **2.** F Enttäuschung *f*; **3.** ✈ Herˈuntergehen *n*.

le·thal [ˈliːθl] *adj.* **1.** tödlich, todbringend; **2.** Todes…

le·thar·gic, le·thar·gi·cal [lɪˈθɑːdʒɪk(l)] *adj.* ☐ leˈthargisch: a) ⚕ schlafsüchtig, b) teilnahmslos, stumpf, träg(e); **leth·ar·gy** [ˈleθədʒɪ] *s.* Letharˈgie *f*: a) Teilnahmslosigkeit *f*, Stumpfheit *f*, b) ⚕ Schlafsucht *f*.

Le·the [ˈliːθiː] *s.* **1.** Lethe *f* (*Fluß des Vergessens im Hades*); **2.** *poet.* Vergessen(heit *f*) *n*.

Lett [let] → ***Latvian***.

let·ter [ˈletə] **I** *s.* **1.** Buchstabe *m* (*a. fig. buchstäblicher Sinn*): ***to the ~*** *fig.* buchstabengetreu, (ganz) exakt; ***the ~ of the law*** der Buchstabe des Gesetzes; ***in ~ and in spirit*** dem Buchstaben u. dem Sinne nach; **2.** Brief *m*, Schreiben *n* (***to*** an *acc.*): ***by ~*** brieflich, schriftlich; ***~ of application*** Bewerbungsschreiben; ***~ of attorney*** ⚖ Vollmacht *f*; ***~ of credit*** ✝ Akkreditiv *n*; **3.** *pl.* Urkunde *f*: ***~s of administration*** ✝ Nachlaßverwalter-Zeugnis *n*; ***~s testamentary*** Testamentsvollstrecker-Zeugnis *n*; ***~s*** (*od.* ***~***) ***of credence***, ***~s credential*** *pol.* Beglaubigungsschreiben *n*; ***~s patent*** ✝ (*sg. od. pl. konstr.*) Patent(urkunde *f*) *n*; **4.** *typ.* a) Letter *f*, Type *f*, b) *coll.* Lettern *pl.*, Typen *pl.*, c) Schrift(art) *f*; **5.** *pl.* a) (schöne) Literaˈtur, b) Bildung *f*, c) Wissenschaft *f*: ***man of ~s*** a) Literat *m*, b) Gelehrter *m*; **II** *v/t.* **6.** beschriften; mit Buchstaben bezeichnen; *Buch* betiteln.

let·ter| bomb *s.* Briefbombe *f*; ˈ**~·box** *s.* *bsd. Brit.* Briefkasten *m*; **~ card** *s.* Briefkarte *f*.

let·tered [ˈletəd] *adj.* **1.** a) (liteˈrarisch) gebildet, b) gelehrt; **2.** beschriftet, bedruckt.

let·ter| file *s.* Briefordner *m*; ˈ**~-ˌfound·er** *s. typ.* Schriftgießer *m*.

ˈ**let·ter·head** *s.* **1.** (gedruckter) Briefkopf; **2.** ˈKopfpaˌpier *n*.

let·ter·ing [ˈletərɪŋ] *s.* Aufdruck *m*, Beschriftung *f*.

ˌ**let·ter-ˈper·fect** *adj.* **1.** *thea.* rollensicher; **2.** *allg.* buchstabengetreu.

ˈ**let·ter|·press** *s. typ.* **1.** (Druck)Text *m*; **2.** Hoch-, Buchdruck *m*; **~ scales** *s. pl.* Briefwaage *f*; ˈ**~·weight** *s.* Briefbeschwerer *m*.

Let·tish [ˈletɪʃ] → ***Latvian***.

let·tuce [ˈletɪs] *s.* ⚘ (*bsd.* ˈKopf)SaˌIat *m*.

ˈ**let-up** *s.* F Nachlassen *n*, Aufhören *n*, Unterˈbrechung *f*: ***without ~*** unaufhörlich.

leu·co·cyte [ˈljuːkəʊsaɪt] *s.* *physiol.* Leukoˈzyte *f*, weißes Blutkörperchen.

leu·co·ma [ljuːˈkəʊmə] *s.* ⚕ Leuˈkom *n* (*Hornhauttrübung*).

leu·k(a)e·mi·a [ljuːˈkiːmɪə] *s.* ⚕ Leukäˈmie *f*.

Le·van·tine [ˈlevəntaɪn] **I** *s.* Levanˈtiner (-in); **II** *adj.* levanˈtinisch.

lev·ee[1] [ˈlevɪ] *s.* (Ufer-, Schutz)Damm *m*, (Fluß)Deich *m*.

lev·ee[2] [ˈlevɪ] *s.* **1.** *hist.* Leˈver *n*, Morgenempfang *m* (*e-s Fürsten*); **2.** *Brit.* Nachmittagsempfang *m*; **3.** *allg.* Empfang *m*.

lev·el [ˈlevl] **I** *s.* **1.** Ebene *f* (*a. geogr.*), ebene Fläche; **2.** Horizonˈtale *f*, Waagrechte *f*; **3.** Höhe *f* (*a. geogr.*), (*Meeres-, Wasser-, physiol. Alkohol-, Blutzucker- etc.*)Spiegel *m*, (*Geräusch-, Wasser*)Pegel *m*: ***on a ~*** (***with***) auf gleicher Höhe (mit); ***he's on the ~*** F a) er ist ‚in Ordnung', b) er meint es ehrlich; **4.** *fig.* (*a. geistiges*) Niˈveau, Stand *m*, Grad *m*, Stufe *f*: ***high ~ of education***; ***the ~ of prices*** das Preisniveau; ***low production ~*** niedriger Produktionsstand; ***come down to the ~ of others*** sich auf das Niveau anderer begeben; ***sink to the ~ of cut-throat practices*** auf das Niveau von Halsabschneidern absinken; ***find one's ~*** *fig.* den Platz einnehmen, der e-m zukommt; **5.** (*politische etc.*) Ebene: ***a conference at*** (*od.* ***on***) ***the highest ~*** e-e Konferenz auf höchster Ebene; **6.** ⚙ a) Liˈbelle *f*, b) Wasserwaage *f*; **7.** ⚙, *surv.* Nivelˈlierinstruˌment *n*; **8.** ⚒ a) Sohle *f*, b) Sohlenstrecke *f*; **II** *adj.* **9.** eben: ***a ~ road***; **10.** horizonˈtal, waag(e)recht; **11.** gleich (*a. fig.*): ***~ crossing*** schienengleicher Übergang; ***a ~ teaspoon(ful)*** ein gestrichener Teelöffel (voll); ***~*** (***with***) a) auf gleicher Höhe (mit), b) gleich hoch (wie); ***draw ~ with*** *j-n* einholen, *fig. a.* mit *j-m* gleichziehen; ***~ with the ground*** a) zu ebener Erde, b) in Bodenhöhe; ***make ~ with the ground*** dem Erdboden gleichmachen; **12.** ausgeglichen: ***~ race*** *a.* Kopf-an-Kopf-Rennen *n*; ***~ stress*** *ling.* schwebende Betonung; ***~ temperature*** gleichbleibende Temperatur; **13.** a) vernünftig, b) ausgeglichen (*Person*), c) kühl, ruhig (*a. Stimme*), d) ausgewogen (*Urteil*); **14.** F ‚anständig', ehrlich, fair; **III** *v/t.*

15. (ein)ebnen, planieren: ~ (***with the ground***) dem Erdboden gleichmachen; **16.** *j-n* zu Boden schlagen; **17.** *fig.* a) gleichmachen, nivellieren, ‚einebnen', b) *Unterschiede* aufheben, c) ausgleichen; **18.** in horizon'tale Lage bringen; **19.** (***at, against***) a) *Waffe, Blick, a. Kritik etc.* richten (auf *acc.*), b) *Anklage* erheben (gegen); **IV** *v/i.* **20.** zielen (***at*** auf *acc.*); **21.** ~ ***with s.o.*** F j-m gegenüber ehrlich sein; ~ **down** *v/t.* **1.** *Löhne, Preise etc.* nach unten angleichen; **2.** auf ein tieferes Ni'veau her'abdrücken; ~ **off** *od.* **out I** *v/t.* (*v/i.* das Flugzeug) abfangen *od.* aufrichten; **II** *v/i. fig.* sich einpendeln (***at*** bei); ~ **up** *v/t.* **1.** (nach oben) angleichen; **2.** auf ein höheres Ni'veau heben.

ˌ**lev·el-'head·ed** *adj.* vernünftig, nüchtern, klar.

lev·el·(l)er ['levlə] *s. sociol.* ‚Gleichmacher' *m* (*Faktor*).

le·ver ['li:və] **I** *s.* **1.** ⚙, *phys.* a) Hebel *m*, b) Brechstange *f*; **2.** ⚙ Anker *m* (*der Uhr*): ~ ***escapement*** Ankerhemmung *f*; ~ ***watch*** Ankeruhr *f*; **3.** *fig.* Druckmittel *n*; **II** *v/t.* **4.** hebeln, mit e-m Hebel bewegen, (hoch- *etc.*)stemmen: ~ ***up***; '**le·ver·age** [-vərɪdʒ] *s.* **1.** ⚙ Hebelkraft *f*, -wirkung *f*; **2.** *fig.* a) Einfluß *m*, b) Druckmittel *n*: ***put*** ~ ***on s.o.*** j-n unter Druck setzen.

lev·er·et ['levərɪt] *s.* Junghase *m*, Häschen *n*.

le·vi·a·than [lɪ'vaɪəθn] *s. bibl.* Levi'athan *m*, (See)Ungeheuer *n*; *fig.* Ungetüm *n*, Gi'gant *m*.

lev·i·tate ['levɪteɪt] *v/i. u. v/t.* (frei) schweben (lassen); **lev·i·ta·tion** [ˌlevɪ'teɪʃn] *s.* Levitati'on *f*, (freies) Schweben.

lev·i·ty ['levətɪ] *s.* Leichtfertigkeit *f*, Frivoli'tät *f*.

lev·y ['levɪ] **I** *s.* **1.** ✝ a) Erhebung *f* (*von Steuern etc.*), b) Abgabe *f*: ***capital*** ~ Kapitalabgabe, c) Beitrag *m*, 'Umlage *f*; **2.** ⚖ Voll'streckungsvollˌzug *m*; **3.** ⚔ a) Aushebung *f*, b) *a. pl.* ausgehobene Truppen *pl.*, Aufgebot *n*; **II** *v/t.* **4.** *Steuern etc.* erheben, *a. Geldstrafe* auferlegen (***on*** *dat.*); **5.** a) beschlagnahmen, b) *Beschlagnahme* 'durchführen; **6.** ⚔ a) *Truppen* ausheben, b) *Krieg* anfangen *od.* führen ([***up***]***on*** gegen).

lewd [lu:d] *adj.* □ **1.** lüstern, geil; **2.** unanständig, schmutzig; '**lewd·ness** [-nɪs] *s.* **1.** Lüsternheit *f*; **2.** Unanständigkeit *f*.

lex·i·cal ['leksɪkl] *adj.* □ lexi'kalisch; **lex·i·cog·ra·pher** [ˌleksɪ'kɒgrəfə] *s.* Lexiko'graph(in), Wörterbuchverfasser (-in); **lex·i·co·graph·ic**, **lex·i·co·graph·i·cal** [ˌleksɪkəʊ'græfɪk(l)] *adj.* □ lexiko'graphisch; **lex·i·cog·ra·phy** [ˌleksɪ'kɒgrəfɪ] *s.* Lexikogra'phie *f*; **lex·i·col·o·gy** [ˌleksɪ'kɒlədʒɪ] *s.* Lexikolo'gie *f*; '**lex·i·con** [-kən] *s.* Lexikon *n*.

li·a·bil·i·ty [ˌlaɪə'bɪlətɪ] *s.* **1.** ✝, ⚖ a) Verpflichtung *f*, Verbindlichkeit *f*, Schuld *f*, *Bilanz*: Passivposten *m*, *pl.* Pas'siva *pl.*, b) Haftung *f*, Haftpflicht *f*, Haftbarkeit *f*: ~ ***insurance*** Haftpflichtversicherung *f*; → ***limited*** I, c) (*Beitrags-, Schadensersatz- etc.*)Pflicht *f*: ~ ***for damages***; **2.** Verantwortlichkeit *f*: ***criminal*** ~ strafrechtliche Verantwortung; **3.** Ausgesetztsein *n*, Unter'worfensein *n* (***to s.th.*** e-r Sache): ~ ***to penalty*** Strafbarkeit *f*; **4.** (***to***) Hang *m* (zu), Anfälligkeit *f* (für).

li·a·ble ['laɪəbl] *adj.* **1.** ✝, ⚖ verantwortlich, haftbar, -pflichtig (***for*** für): ***be*** ~ ***for*** haften für; ***hold s.o.*** ~ j-n haftbar machen; **2.** verpflichtet (***for*** zu); (*steuer- etc.*)pflichtig: ~ ***to*** (*od.* ***for***) ***military service*** wehrpflichtig; **3.** (***to***) neigend (zu), ausgesetzt (*dat.*), unter'worfen (*dat.*): ***be*** ~ ***to*** a) *e-r Sache* ausgesetzt sein *od.* unterliegen, b) (*mit inf.*) leicht *et. tun* (können), in Gefahr sein *vergessen etc.* zu *werden*, c) (*mit inf.*) *et.* wahrscheinlich *tun*: ***be*** ~ ***to a fine*** e-r Geldstrafe unterliegen; ~ ***to prosecution*** strafbar.

li·aise [lɪ'eɪz] *v/i.* (***with***) als Verbindungsmann fungieren (zu), die Verbindung aufrechterhalten (mit).

li·ai·son [li:'eɪzɔ̃:ŋ, ⚔ -zən] (*Fr.*) *s.* **1.** Zs.-arbeit *f*, Verbindung *f*: ~ ***officer*** a) ⚔ Verbindungsoffizier *m*, b) Verbindungsmann *m*; **2.** Liai'son *f*: a) (Liebes-) Verhältnis *n*, b) *ling.* Bindung *f*.

li·a·na [lɪ'ɑ:nə] *s.* ♀ Li'ane *f*.

li·ar ['laɪə] *s.* Lügner(in).

Li·as ['laɪəs] *s. geol.* Lias *m*, *f*, schwarzer Jura.

li·ba·tion [laɪ'beɪʃn] *s.* **1.** Trankopfer *n*; **2.** *humor.* Zeche'rei *f*.

li·bel ['laɪbl] **I** *s.* **1.** ⚖ a) Verleumdung *f*, üble Nachrede, Beleidigung *f* (*durch e-e Veröffentlichung*) (***of, on*** *gen.*), b) Klageschrift *f*; **2.** *allg.* (***on***) Verleumdung *f* (*gen.*), Beleidigung *f* (*gen.*), Hohn *m* (auf *acc.*); **II** *v/t.* **3.** ⚖ (schriftlich *etc.*) verleumden; **4.** *allg.* verunglimpfen; '**li·bel·(l)ant** [-lənt] *s.* ⚖ Kläger(in); **li·bel·(l)ee** [ˌlaɪbə'li:] *s.* ⚖ Beklagte(r *m*) *f*; '**li·bel·(l)ous** [-bləs] *adj.* □ verleumderisch.

lib·er·al ['lɪbərəl] **I** *adj.* □ **1.** libe'ral, frei(sinnig), vorurteilsfrei, aufgeschlossen; **2.** großzügig: a) freigebig (***of*** mit), b) reichlich (bemessen): ***a*** ~ ***gift*** ein großzügiges Geschenk; ***a*** ~ ***quantity*** e-e reichliche Menge, c) frei, weitherzig: ~ ***interpretation***, d) allgemein(bildend): ~ ***education*** allgemeinbildende Erziehung *od.* (gute) Allgemeinbildung; ~ ***profession*** freier Beruf; **3.** *mst* ~ *pol.* libe'ral: ~ ***Party***; **II** *s.* **4.** *oft* ~ *pol.* Libe'rale(r *m*) *f*; ~ **arts** *s. pl.* Geisteswissenschaften *pl.* (*Philosophie, Literatur, Sprachen, Soziologie etc.*).

lib·er·al·ism ['lɪbərəlɪzəm] *s.* **1.** → ***liberality*** b; **2.** ~ *pol.* Libera'lismus *m*; **lib·er·al·i·ty** [ˌlɪbə'rælətɪ] *s.* Großzügigkeit *f*: a) Freigebigkeit *f*, b) libe'rale Einstellung, Liberali'tät *f*; **lib·er·al·i·za·tion** [ˌlɪbərəlaɪ'zeɪʃn] *s.* ✝, *pol.* Liberalisierung *f*; '**lib·er·al·ize** [-laɪz] *v/t.* ✝, *pol.* liberalisieren.

lib·er·ate ['lɪbəreɪt] *v/t.* **1.** befreien (***from*** von) (*a. fig.*); **2.** ⚗ freisetzen; **lib·er·a·tion** [ˌlɪbə'reɪʃn] *s.* **1.** Befreiung *f*; **2.** ⚗ Freisetzen *n od.* -werden *n*; '**lib·er·a·tor** [-tə] *s.* Befreier *m*.

Li·be·ri·an [laɪ'bɪərɪən] **I** *s.* Li'berier(in); **II** *adj.* li'berisch.

lib·er·tin·age ['lɪbətɪnɪdʒ] → ***libertinism***; '**lib·er·tine** [-ti:n] *s.* Wüstling *m*; '**lib·er·tin·ism** [-tɪnɪzəm] *s.* Sittenlosigkeit *f*, Liberti'nismus *m*.

lib·er·ty ['lɪbətɪ] *s.* **1.** Freiheit *f*: a) persönliche *etc.* Freiheit: ***religious*** ~ Religionsfreiheit, b) freie Wahl, Erlaubnis *f*: ***large*** ~ ***of action*** weitgehende Handlungsfreiheit, c) *mst pl.* Privi'leg *n*, (Vor)Recht *n*, d) *b.s.* Ungehörigkeit *f*, Frechheit *f*; **2.** *hist. Brit.* Freibezirk *m* (*e-r Stadt*);

Besondere Redewendungen:

at ~ a) in Freiheit, frei, b) berechtigt, c) unbenützt; ***be at*** ~ ***to do s.th.*** et. tun dürfen; ***you are at*** ~ ***to go*** es steht Ihnen frei zu gehen, Sie können gehen; ***set at*** ~ in Freiheit setzen, freilassen; ***take the*** ~ ***to do*** (*od.* ***of doing***) ***s.th.*** sich die Freiheit nehmen, et. zu tun; ***take liberties with*** a) sich Freiheiten gegen *j-n* herausnehmen, b) willkürlich mit *et.* umgehen.

li·bid·i·nous [lɪ'bɪdɪnəs] *adj.* □ lüstern, triebhaft, *psych.* libidi'nös, wollüstig; **li·bi·do** [lɪ'bi:dəʊ] *s. psych.* Li'bido *f*.

Li·bra ['laɪbrə] *s. ast.* Waage *f*; '**Li·bran** [-rən] *s.* Waage(mensch *m*) *f*.

li·brar·i·an [laɪ'breərɪən] *s.* Bibliothe'kar (-in); **li'brar·i·an·ship** [-ʃɪp] *s.* **1.** Bibliothe'karsstelle *f*; **2.** Biblio'thekswissenschaft *f*.

li·brar·y ['laɪbrərɪ] *s.* **1.** Biblio'thek *f*: a) *öffentliche* Büche'rei, b) *private* Büchersammlung, c) Studierzimmer *n*, d) Buchreihe *f*; **2.** Schallplattensammlung *f*; ~ **sci·ence** → ***librarianship*** 2.

li·bret·to [lɪ'bretəʊ] *s.* ♪ Li'bretto *n*, Text(buch *n*) *m*.

Lib·y·an ['lɪbɪən] **I** *adj.* libysch; **II** *s.* Libyer(in).

lice [laɪs] *pl. von* ***louse***.

li·cence ['laɪsəns] **I** *s.* **1.** Erlaubnis *f*, Genehmigung *f*; **2.** (*a.* ✝ *Export-, Herstellungs-, Patent-, Verkaufs*)Li'zenz *f*, Konzessi'on *f*, behördliche Genehmigung, *z.B.* Schankerlaubnis *f*; amtlicher Zulassungsschein, Zulassung *f*, (*Führer-, Jagd-, Waffen- etc.*)Schein *m*: ~ ***fee*** Lizenz- *od.* Konzessionsgebühr *f*; ~ ***holder*** Führerscheininhaber *m*; ~ ***number*** *mot.* Kraftfahrzeug- *od.* Kfz-Nummer *f*; ~ ***plate*** *mot.* amtliches *od.* polizeiliches Kennzeichen, Nummernschild *n*; ~ ***to practise medicine*** (ärztliche) Approbation; **3.** Heiratserlaubnis *f*; **4.** (*künstlerische, dichterische*) Freiheit; **5.** Zügellosigkeit *f*; **II** *v/t.* **6.** → ***license*** I; '**li·cense** [-ns] **I** *v/t.* **1.** *j-m* e-e (behördliche) Genehmigung *od.* e-e Li'zenz *od.* e-e Konzessi'on erteilen; **2.** *et.* lizenzieren, konzessionieren, (amtlich) genehmigen *od.* zulassen; **3.** *Buch* zur Veröffentlichung *od. Theaterstück* zur Aufführung freigeben; **4.** *j-n* ermächtigen; **II** *s.* **5.** *Am.* → ***licence*** I; '**li·censed** [-st] *adj.* **1.** konzessioniert, lizenziert, amtlich zugelassen: ~ ***house*** (*od.* ***premises***) Lokal *n* mit Schankkonzession; **2.** Lizenz...: ~ ***construction*** Lizenzbau *m*; **3.** privilegiert; **li·cen·see** [ˌlaɪsən'si:] *s.* **1.** Li'zenznehmer(in); **2.** Konzessi'onsinhaber(in); '**li·cens·er** [-sə] *s.* Li'zenzgeber *m*, Konzessi'onserteiler *m*; **li·cen·ti·ate** [laɪ'senʃɪət] *s. univ.* **1.** Lizenti'at *m*; **2.** (*Grad*) Lizenti'at *n*.

li·cen·tious [laɪ'senʃəs] *adj.* □ unzüchtig, ausschweifend, lasterhaft.

li·chen ['laɪkən] *s.* ♀, ⚕ Flechte *f*.

lich gate [lɪtʃ] *s. überdachtes* Friedhofstor.

lick [lɪk] **I** *v/t.* **1.** (be-, ab)lecken, lecken

an (*dat.*): ~ ***off*** ablecken; ~ ***up*** auflekken; ~ ***one's lips*** sich die Lippen lekken; ~ ***s.o.'s boots*** *fig.* vor j-m kriechen; ~ ***into shape*** *fig.* in die richtige Form bringen, zurechtbiegen, -stutzen; → ***dust*** 1; **2.** F a) *j-n* ‚verdreschen', b) schlagen, besiegen, c) über'treffen, ‚schlagen': ***this ~s everything!***, d) *et.* ‚schaffen', fertigwerden mit *e-m Problem*: ***we have got it ~ed!***; **II** *v/i.* **3.** lecken (***at*** an *dat.*), *fig. a.* a) plätschern (*Welle*), b) züngeln (*Flamme*); **III** *s.* **4.** Lecken *n*: ***give s.th. a ~*** an et. lecken; ***a ~ and a promise*** e-e flüchtige Arbeit *etc.*, *bsd.* e-e ‚Katzenwäsche'; **5.** (*ein*) bißchen: ***a ~ of paint***; ***he didn't do a ~ of work*** *Am.* F er hat keinen Strich getan; **6.** F a) Schlag *m*, b) ‚Tempo' *n*: (***at***) ***full ~*** mit größter Geschwindigkeit; **7.** Salzlecke *f*.

ˌlick·e·ty-'split [ˌlɪkətɪ-] *adv. Am.* F wie der Blitz.

lick·ing ['lɪkɪŋ] *s.* **1.** Lecken *n*; **2.** F (Tracht *f*) Prügel *pl.*, Abreibung *f* (*a. fig. Niederlage*).

'lickˌspit·tle *s.* Speichellecker *m*.

lic·o·rice ['lɪkərɪs] → ***liquorice***.

lid [lɪd] *s.* **1.** Deckel *m* (*a.* F *Hut*): ***put the ~ on s.th.*** *Brit.* F a) e-r Sache die Krone aufsetzen, b) et. endgültig ‚erledigen'; ***clamp*** (*od.* ***put***) ***the ~ on s.th.*** *Am.* a) et. verbieten, b) scharf vorgehen gegen et., c) et. (*Nachricht etc.*) sperren; **2.** (Augen)Lid *n*.

li·do ['li:dəʊ] *s. Brit.* Frei- *od.* Strandbad *n*.

lie¹ [laɪ] **I** *s.* Lüge *f*, Schwindel *m*: ***tell a ~*** (*od.* ***lies***) lügen; → ***white lie***; ***give s.o. the ~*** j-n der Lüge bezichtigen; ***give the ~ to*** *et. od. j-n* Lügen strafen; ***he lived a ~*** sein Leben war e-e einzige Lüge; **II** *v/i.* lügen: ~ ***to s.o.*** a) j-n belügen, j-n anlügen, b) j-m vorlügen (***that*** daß).

lie² [laɪ] **I** *s.* **1.** Lage *f* (*a. fig.*): ***the ~ of the land*** *Brit. fig.* die Lage (der Dinge); **II** *v/i.* [*irr.*] **2.** *allg.* liegen: a) *im Bett, im Hinterhalt, in Trümmern etc.* liegen, b) *ausgebreitet, tot etc.* daliegen, c) begraben sein, ruhen, d) gelegen sein, sich befinden, e) lasten (***on*** auf *der Seele*, im *Magen etc.*), f) begründet liegen, bestehen (***in*** in *dat.*): ~ ***dying*** im Sterben liegen; ~ ***behind*** *fig.* a) hinter *j-m* liegen (*Erlebnis etc.*), b) dahinterstecken (*Motiv etc.*); ~ ***in s.o.'s way*** j-m zur Hand *od.* möglich sein, *a.* in j-s Fach schlagen; ***his talents do not ~ that way*** dazu hat er kein Talent; ~ ***on s.o.*** ⚖ j-m obliegen; ~ ***under a suspicion*** unter e-m Verdacht stehen; ~ ***under a sentence of death*** zum Tode verurteilt sein; ~ ***with s.o.*** *obs. od. bibl.* j-m beischlafen, mit j-m schlafen; ***as far as ~s with me*** soweit es in m-n Kräften steht; ***it ~s with you to do it*** es liegt an dir, es zu tun; **3.** sich (hin)legen: ~ ***on your back!*** leg dich auf den Rücken!; **4.** führen, verlaufen (*Straße etc.*); **5.** ⚖ zulässig sein (*Klage etc.*): ***appeal ~s to the Supreme Court*** Rechtsmittel können beim Obersten Gericht eingelegt werden;

Zssgn mit adv.:

lie| back *v/i.* sich zu'rücklegen; *fig.* die Hände in den Schoß legen; ~ **down** *v/i.* **1.** sich hinlegen; **2.** ~ ***under***, ***take lying down*** *Beleidigung etc.* widerspruchslos hinnehmen, sich *et.* gefallen lassen: ***we won't take that lying down!*** das lassen wir uns nicht (so einfach) bieten!; ~ **in** *v/i.* **1.** im Bett bleiben; **2.** im Wochenbett liegen; ~ **off** *v/i.* **1.** ⚓ vom Land *etc.* abhalten; **2.** *fig.* pausieren; ~ **low** *v/i.* sich versteckt halten; ~ **o·ver** *v/i.* liegenbleiben, aufgeschoben werden; ~ **to** *v/i.* ⚓ beiliegen; ~ **up** *v/i.* **1.** ruhen (*a. fig.*); **2.** das Bett *od.* das Zimmer hüten (müssen); **3.** außer Betrieb sein.

lied [li:d] *pl.* **lie·der** ['li:də] (*Ger.*) *s.* ♪ (*deutsches* Kunst)Lied.

lie de·tec·tor *s.* 'Lügendeˌtektor *m*.

'lie-down *s.* F Schläfchen *n*.

lief [li:f] *adv. obs.* gern: ***~er than*** lieber als; ***I had*** (*od.* ***would***) ***as ~*** ... ich würde eher *sterben etc.*, ich *ginge etc.* ebensogern.

liege [li:dʒ] **I** *s.* **1.** *a.* ~ ***lord*** Leh(e)nsherr *m*; **2.** *a.* ***~man*** Leh(e)nsmann *m*; **II** *adj.* **3.** Leh(e)ns...

lien [lɪən] *s.* ⚖ (***on***) Pfandrecht *n* (***an*** *dat.*), Zu'rückbehaltungsrecht *n* (auf *acc.*).

lieu [lju:] *s.*: ***in ~ of*** an Stelle von (*od. gen.*), anstatt (*gen.*); ***in ~*** (***of that***) statt dessen.

lieu·ten·an·cy [*Brit.* lef'tenənsɪ; ⚓ le't-; *Am.* lu:'t-] *s.* ⚔, ⚓ Leutnantsrang *m*.

lieu·ten·ant [*Brit.* lef'tenənt; ⚓ le't-; *Am.* lu:'t-] *s.* **1.** ⚔, ⚓ a) *allg.* Leutnant *m*, b) *Brit.* (*Am.* ***first ~***) Oberleutnant *m*, c) ⚓ (*Am. a.* ~ ***senior grade***) Kapi'tänleutnant *m*: ~ ***junior grade*** *Am.* Oberleutnant zur See; **2.** Statthalter *m*; **3.** *fig.* rechte Hand, ‚Adju'tant'; ~ **colo·nel** *s.* ⚔ Oberst'leutnant *m*; ~ **com·mand·er** *s.* ⚓ Kor'vettenkapiˌtän *m*; ~ **gen·er·al** *s.* ⚔ Gene'ralleutnant *m*; ~ **gov·er·nor** *s.* 'Vizegouverˌneur *m* (*im brit. Commonwealth od. e-s amer. Bundesstaates*).

life [laɪf] *pl.* **lives** [laɪvz] *s.* **1.** (*organisches*) Leben; → ***large*** 1; **2.** Leben *n*: a) Lebenserscheinungen *pl.*, b) Lebewesen *pl.*: ***there is no ~ on the moon***; ***plant ~*** Pflanzen(welt *f*) *pl.*; **3.** (Menschen)Leben *n*: ***they lost their lives*** sie kamen ums Leben; ***three lives were lost*** drei Menschenleben sind zu beklagen; ~ ***and limb*** Leib u. Leben; **4.** Leben *n* (*e-s Einzelwesens*): ***it is a matter of ~ and death*** es geht um Leben oder Tod; ***early in ~*** in jungen Jahren, (schon) früh; **5.** Leben *n*, Lebenszeit *f*, *a.* ⚙ Lebensdauer *f*: ***all his ~*** sein ganzes Leben (lang); **6.** Leben(skraft *f*) *n*: ***there is still ~ in the old dog yet!*** *humor.* so alt u. klapprig bin ich (*od.* ist er) noch gar nicht!; **7.** a) Bestehen *n*, b) ⚖, ⚕ Gültigkeitsdauer *f*, Laufzeit *f*: ***the ~ of a contract*** (***an insurance***, ***patent***, *etc.*), c) *parl.* Legisla'turperiˌode *f*; **8.** Lebensweise *f*, -führung *f*, -wandel *m*; Leben *n*: ***lead an honest ~*** ein ehrbares Leben führen; ***lead the ~ of Riley*** F leben wie Gott in Frankreich; **9.** Leben *n*, Welt *f* (*menschliches Tun u. Treiben*): ~ ***in Canada*** das Leben in Kanada; ***see ~*** das Leben kennenlernen *od.* genießen, die Welt sehen; **10.** Leben *n*, Lebhaftigkeit *f*, Lebendigkeit *f*: ***put ~ into s.th.*** e-e Sache beleben, Leben in et. bringen; ***he was the ~ and soul of*** er war die Seele *des Unternehmens etc.*, er brachte Leben in *die Party etc.*; **11.** Leben(sbeschreibung *f*) *n*, Biogra'phie *f*: ***the ≈ of Churchill***; **12.** *Versicherungswesen*: Lebensversicherung(en *pl.*) *f*;

Besondere Redewendungen:

for ~ a) fürs (ganze) Leben, b) *bsd.* ⚖ *u. pol.* lebenslänglich, auf Lebenszeit, c) *a.* ***for one's ~***, ***for dear ~*** ums (liebe) Leben *rennen etc.*; ***not for the ~ of me*** F nicht um alles in der Welt; ***not on your ~!*** nie(mals)!; ***never in my ~*** meiner Lebtag (noch) nicht; ***to the ~*** lebensecht, naturgetreu; ***bring to ~*** *fig.* lebendig werden lassen; ***bring s.o. back to ~*** j-n wiederbeleben *od.* ins Leben zurückrufen; ***come to ~*** *fig.* lebendig werden, *Person*: *a.* munter werden; ***seek s.o.'s ~*** j-m nach dem Leben trachten; ***save s.o.'s ~*** j-m das Leben retten, *fig. humor.* j-n ‚retten'; ***sell one's ~ dearly*** *fig.* sein Leben teuer verkaufen; ***such is ~*** so ist das Leben; ***take s.o.'s*** (***one's own***) ~ j-m (sich [selbst]) das Leben nehmen; ***this is the ~!*** F Mann, ist das ein Leben!

ˌlife|-and-'death [-fən'd-] *adj. Kampf etc.* auf Leben u. Tod; ~ **an·nu·i·ty** *s.* Leibrente *f*; ~ **as·sur·ance** *s. Brit.* Lebensversicherung *f*; **'~·belt** *s.* Rettungsgürtel *m*; **'~·blood** *s.* Herzblut *n* (*a. fig.*); **'~·boat** *s.* ⚓ Rettungsboot *n*; ~ **buoy** *s.* Rettungsboje *f*; ~ **cy·cle** *s.* **1.** Lebenszyklus *m*; **2.** Lebensphase *f*; ~ **ex·pect·an·cy** *s.* Lebenserwartung *f*; ~ **force** *s.* Lebenskraft *f*, lebenspendende Kraft; **'~ˌgiv·ing** *adj.* lebenspendend, belebend; **'~·guard** *s.* **1.** ⚔ Leibgarde *f*; **2.** Rettungsschwimmer *m*, Bademeister *m*; **≈ Guards** *s. pl.* ⚔ Leibgarde *f* (zu Pferde), 'Gardekavalleˌrie *f*; ~ **in·sur·ance** *s.* Lebensversicherung *f*; ~ **in·ter·est** *s.* ⚖ lebenslänglicher Nießbrauch; ~ **jack·et** *s.* Schwimmweste *f*.

life·less ['laɪflɪs] *adj.* □ leblos: a) tot, b) unbelebt, c) *fig.* matt, schwunglos, ‚lahm', ⚕ lustlos (*Börse*).

'life|·like *adj.* lebenswahr, -echt, na'turgetreu; **'~·line** *s.* **1.** ⚓ Rettungsleine *f*; **2.** Si'gnalleine *f* (*für Taucher*); **3.** *fig.* a) Lebensader *f* (*Versorgungsweg*), b) lebenswichtige Sache, ‚Rettungsanker' *m*; **4.** Lebenslinie *f* (*in der Hand*); **'~·long** *adj.* lebenslänglich; ~ **mem·ber** *s.* Mitglied *n* auf Lebenszeit; ~ **of·fice** *s. Brit.* Lebensversicherungsgesellschaft *f*; ~ **pre·serv·er** *s.* **1.** *Am.* ⚓ Schwimmweste *f*, Rettungsgürtel *m*; **2.** Totschläger *m* (*Waffe*).

lif·er ['laɪfə] *s. sl.* **1.** Lebenslängliche(r *m*) *f* (*Strafgefangene*[*r*]); **2.** → ***life sentence***; **3.** *Am.* Be'rufssolˌdat *m*.

life| raft *s.* Rettungsfloß *n*; **'~ˌsav·er** *s.* **1.** Lebensretter(in); **2.** → ***lifeguard*** 2; **3.** *fig.* a) ‚rettender Engel', b) *die* ‚Rettung' (*Sache*); ~ **sen·tence** *s.* ⚖ lebenslängliche Freiheitsstrafe; **'~-size(d)** *adj.* lebensgroß, in Lebensgröße; ~ **span** *s.* Leben(sspanne *f*, -zeit *f*) *n*; ~ **style** *s.* Lebensstil *m*; **'~-supˌport sy·stem** *n* ✈, ⚙ 'Lebenserhaltungssyˌstem *n*; ~ **ta·ble** *s.* 'Sterblichkeitstaˌbelle *f*; **'~·time I** *s.* Lebenszeit *f*, Leben *n*, *a.* ⚙ Lebensdauer *f*: ***the chance of a ~*** e-e einmalige Chance; **II** *adj.* lebenslänglich, Lebens...; ~ **vest** *s.* Rettungs-, Schwimmweste *f*; ˌ**~-ˈwork** *s.* Lebenswerk *n*.

lift [lɪft] **I** *s.* **1.** (Auf-, Hoch)Heben *n*; **2.** stolze *etc.* Kopfhaltung; **3.** ⚙ a) Hub (-höhe *f*) *m*, b) Hubkraft *f*; **4.** ✈ a) Auftrieb *m*, b) Luftbrücke *f*; **5.** *fig.* a) Hilfe *f*, b) (innerer) Auftrieb *m*: ***give s.o. a ~*** a) j-m helfen, b) j-m Auftrieb geben, j-n aufmuntern, c) j-n (im Auto) mitnehmen; **6.** a) *Brit.* Lift *m*, Aufzug *m*, Fahrstuhl *m*, b) (Ski-, Sessel)Lift *m*; **II** *v/t.* **7.** *a.* ***~ up*** (auf-, emˈpor-, hoch-) heben; *Augen*, *Stimme etc.* erheben: ***~ s.th. down*** et. herunterheben; ***not to ~ a finger*** keinen Finger rühren; **8.** *fig.* a) (*geistig od. sittlich*) heben, b) *aus der Armut etc.* emˈporheben, c) *a.* ***~ up*** (*innerlich*) erheben, aufmuntern; **9.** *Preise* erhöhen; **10.** *Kartoffeln* ausgraben, ernten; **11.** ‚mitgehen lassen', ‚klauen', stehlen (*a. fig. plagiieren*); **12.** *Gesicht etc.* liften, straffen: ***have one's face ~ed*** sich das Gesicht liften lassen; **13.** *Blockade*, *Verbot*, *Zensur etc.* aufheben; **III** *v/i.* **14.** sich heben (*a. Nebel*); sich (hoch)heben lassen: ***~ off*** ✈ abheben, starten; ˈ**lift·er** [-tə] *s.* **1.** (*sport* Gewicht)Heber *m*; **2.** ⚙ a) Hebegerät *n*, b) Nocken *m*, c) Stößel *m*; **3.** ‚Langfinger' *m* (*Dieb*).

lift·ing [ˈlɪftɪŋ] *adj.* Hebe…, Hub…; **~ jack** *s.* ⚙ Hebewinde *f*, *mot.* Wagenheber *m*.

ˈ**lift-off** *s.* **1.** Start *m* (*Rakete*); **2.** Abheben *n* (*Flugzeug*).

lig·a·ment [ˈlɪgəmənt] *s. anat.* Ligaˈment *n*, Band *n*.

lig·a·ture [ˈlɪgəˌtʃʊə] **I** *s.* **1.** Binde *f*, Band *n*; **2.** *typ. u.* ♪ Ligaˈtur *f*; **3.** ⚕ Abbindungsschnur *f*, Bindung *f*; **II** *v/t.* **4.** ver-, ⚕ abbinden.

light¹ [laɪt] **I** *s.* **1.** *allg.* Licht *n* (*Helligkeit*, *Schein*, *Beleuchtung*, *Lichtquelle*, *Lampe*, *Tageslicht*, *fig. Aspekt*, *Erleuchtung*): ***by the ~ of a candle*** beim Schein e-r Kerze, bei Kerzenlicht; ***bring*** (***come***) ***to ~*** *fig.* ans Licht *od.* an den Tag bringen (kommen); ***cast*** (*od.* ***shed***, ***throw***) ***a ~ on s.th.*** *fig.* Licht auf et. werfen; ***place*** (*od.* ***put***) ***in a favo***(***u***)***rable ~*** *fig.* in ein günstiges Licht stellen *od.* rücken; ***see the ~*** *eccl.* erleuchtet werden; ***see the ~*** (***of day***) *fig.* bekannt *od.* veröffentlicht werden; ***I see the ~!*** mir geht ein Licht auf!; (***seen***) ***in the ~ of these facts*** im Lichte *od.* angesichts dieser Tatsachen; ***show s.th. in a different ~*** et. in e-m anderen Licht erscheinen lassen; ***hide one's ~ under a bushel*** *fig.* sein Licht unter den Scheffel stellen; ***let there be ~!*** *Bibl.* es werde Licht; ***he went out like a ~*** F er war sofort ‚weg' (*eingeschlafen*); **2.** Licht *n*: a) Lampe *f*, *a. pl.* Beleuchtung *f* (*beide a. mot. etc.*): ***~s out*** ⚔ Zapfenstreich *m*; ***~s out!*** Lichter aus!, b) (Verkehrs)Ampel *f*; → ***green light***, ***red*** 1; **3.** ⚓ a) Leuchtfeuer *n*, b) Leuchtturm *m*; **4.** Feuer *n* (*zum Anzünden*), *a.* Streichholz *n*: ***put a ~ to s.th.*** et. anzünden; ***strike a ~*** ein Streichholz anzünden; ***will you give me a ~?*** darf ich Sie um Feuer bitten?; **5.** *fig.* Leuchte *f* (*Person*): ***a shining ~*** e-e Leuchte, ein großes Licht; **6.** Lichtöffnung *f*, *bsd.* Fenster *n*, Oberlicht *n*; **7.** *paint.* a) Licht *n*, heller Teil (*e-s Gemäldes*); **8.** *fig.* Verstand *m*, geistige Fähigkeiten *pl.*: ***according to his ~s*** so gut er es eben versteht; **9.** *pl. sl.* Augen *pl.*; **II** *adj.* **10.** hell: ***~-red*** hellrot; **III** *v/t.* [*irr.*] **11.** *a.* ***~ up*** anzünden; **12.** *oft* ***~ up*** beleuchten, erhellen (*a. das Gesicht*); ***~ up*** *Augen etc.* aufleuchten lassen; **13.** *j-m* leuchten; **IV** *v/i.* [*irr.*] **14.** *a.* ***~ up*** sich entzünden, angehen (*Feuer*, *Licht*); **15.** *mst* ***~ up*** *fig.* sich erhellen, strahlen (*Gesicht*), aufleuchten (*Augen etc.*); **16.** ***~ up*** a) die Pfeife *etc.* anzünden, sich e-e Zigarette anstecken, b) Licht machen.

light² [laɪt] **I** *adj.* □ → ***lightly***; **1.** *allg.* leicht (*z. B. Last*; *Kleidung*; *Mahlzeit*, *Wein*, *Zigarre*; ⚔ *Infanterie*, ⚓ *Kreuzer etc.*; *Hand*, *Schritt*, *Schlaf*; *Regen*, *Wind*; *Arbeit*, *Fehler*, *Strafe*; *Charakter*; *Musik*, *Roman*): ***~ of foot*** leichtfüßig; ***a ~ girl*** ein ‚leichtes' Mädchen; ***~ current*** ⚡ Schwachstrom *m*; ***~ metal*** Leichtmetall *n*; ***~ literature*** (*od.* ***reading***) Unterhaltungsliteratur *f*; ***~ railway*** Kleinbahn *f*; ***~ in the head*** benommen; ***~ on one's feet*** leichtfüßig; ***with a ~ heart*** leichten Herzens; ***no ~ matter*** keine Kleinigkeit; ***make ~ of*** a) *et.* auf die leichte Schulter nehmen, b) bagatellisieren; **2.** zu leicht: ***~ weights*** Untergewichte; **3.** locker (*Brot*, *Erde*, *Schnee*); **4.** sorglos, unbeschwert, heiter; **5.** a) leicht beladen, b) unbeladen; **II** *adv.* **6.** leicht: ***travel ~*** mit leichtem Gepäck reisen.

light³ [laɪt] *v/i.* [*irr.*] **1.** fallen (***on*** auf *acc.*); **2.** sich niederlassen (***on*** auf *dat.*) (*Vogel etc.*); **3.** ***~*** (***up***)***on*** *fig.* (zufällig) stoßen auf (*acc.*); **4.** ***~ out*** *sl.* ‚verduften'; **5.** ***~ into*** F herfallen über *j-n*.

light bar·ri·er *s.* ⚡ Lichtschranke *f*.

light·en¹ [ˈlaɪtn] **I** *v/i.* **1.** hell werden, sich erhellen; **2.** blitzen; **II** *v/t.* **3.** erhellen.

light·en² [ˈlaɪtn] **I** *v/t.* **1.** leichter machen, erleichtern (*beide a. fig.*); **2.** *Schiff* (ab)leichtern; **3.** aufheitern; **II** *v/i.* **4.** leichter werden (*a. fig. Herz etc.*).

light·er¹ [ˈlaɪtə] *s.* Anzünder *m* (*a. Gerät*); (Taschen)Feuerzeug *n*.

light·er² [ˈlaɪtə] *s.* ⚓ Leichter(schiff *n*) *m*, Prahm *m*; ˈ**light·er·age** [-ərɪdʒ] *s.* Leichtergeld *n*.

ˌ**light·er-than-ˈair** *adj.*: ***~ craft*** Luftfahrzeug *n* leichter als Luft.

ˈ**light**|-ˌ**fin·gered** *adj.* **1.** geschickt; **2.** langfingerig, diebisch; ˈ**~-ˌfoot·ed** *adj.* leicht-, schnellfüßig; ˌ**~-ˈhead·ed** *adj.* **1.** leichtsinnig, -fertig; **2.** ˈübermütig, ausgelassen; **3.** a) wirr, leicht verrückt, b) schwind(e)lig; ˌ**~-ˈheart·ed** *adj.* □ fröhlich, heiter, unbeschwert; ***~ heavy-weight*** *s. sport* Halbschwergewicht (-ler *m*) *n*; ˈ**~·house** *s.* Leuchtturm *m*.

light·ing [ˈlaɪtɪŋ] *s.* **1.** Beleuchtung *f*; ***~ effects*** Lichteffekte; ***~ point*** ⚡ Brennstelle *f*; **2.** Anzünden *n*; ˌ**~-ˈup time** *s.* Zeit *f* des Einschaltens der Straßenbeleuchtung *od.* (*mot.*) der Scheinwerfer.

light·ly [ˈlaɪtlɪ] *adv.* **1.** *allg.* leicht: ***~ come ~ go*** wie gewonnen, so zerronnen; **2.** gelassen, leicht; **3.** leichtfertig; **4.** leichthin; **5.** geringschätzig.

light·ness [ˈlaɪtnɪs] *s.* **1.** Leichtheit *f*, Leichtigkeit *f* (*a. fig.*); **2.** Leichtverdaulichkeit *f*; **3.** Milde *f*; **4.** Behendigkeit *f*; **5.** Heiterkeit *f*; **6.** Leichtfertigkeit *f*, Leichtsinn *m*, Oberflächlichkeit *f*.

light·ning [ˈlaɪtnɪŋ] **I** *s.* Blitz *m*: ***struck by ~*** vom Blitz getroffen; ***like*** (***greased***) ***~*** *fig.* wie der *od.* ein geölter Blitz; **II** *adj.* blitzschnell, Schnell…: ***~ artist*** Schnellzeichner *m*; ***with ~ speed*** mit Blitzesschnelle; **~ ar·rest·er** *s.* ⚡ Blitzschutzsicherung *f*; **~ bug** *s. Am.* Leuchtkäfer *m*; **~ con·duc·tor**, **~ rod** *s.* Blitzableiter *m*; **~ strike** *s.* Blitzstreik *m*.

light| **oil** *s.* ⚙ Leichtöl *n*; **~ pen** *s. Computer*: Lichtgriffel *m*.

lights [laɪts] *s. pl.* (Tier)Lunge *f*.

ˈ**light**|**·ship** *s.* ⚓ Feuer-, Leuchtschiff *n*; **~ source** *s.* ⚡, *phys.* Lichtquelle *f*; ˈ**~·weight I** *adj.* leicht; **II** *s. sport* Leichtgewicht(ler *m*) *n*; F *fig.* a) ‚kein großes Licht', b) unbedeutender Mensch; ˈ**~-year** *s. ast.* Lichtjahr *n*.

lig·ne·ous [ˈlɪgnɪəs] *adj.* holzig, holzartig, Holz…; ˈ**lig·ni·fy** [-nɪfaɪ] **I** *v/t.* in Holz verwandeln; **II** *v/i.* verholzen; ˈ**lig·nin** [-nɪn] *s.* ⚗ Liˈgnin *n*, Holzstoff *m*; ˈ**lig·nite** [-naɪt] *s.* Braunkohle *f*, *bsd.* Liˈgnit *m*.

lik·a·ble [ˈlaɪkəbl] *adj.* liebenswert, symˈpathisch, nett.

like¹ [laɪk] **I** *adj. u. prp.* **1.** gleich (*dat.*), wie (*a. adv.*): ***a man ~ you*** ein Mann wie du; ***~ a man*** wie ein Mann; ***what is he ~?*** a) wie sieht er aus?, b) wie ist er?; ***he is ~ that*** er ist nun mal so; ***he is just ~ his brother*** er ist genau (so) wie sein Bruder; ***that's just ~ him!*** das sieht ihm ähnlich!; ***that's just ~ a woman!*** typisch Frau!; ***what does it look ~?*** wie sieht es aus?; ***it looks ~ rain*** es sieht nach Regen aus; ***feel ~*** (***doing***) ***s.th.*** zu et. aufgelegt sein, Lust haben, et. zu tun, et. gern tun wollen; ***a fool ~ that*** ein derartiger *od.* so ein Dummkopf; ***a thing ~ that*** so etwas; ***I saw one ~ it*** ich sah ein ähnliches (*Auto etc.*); ***there is nothing ~*** es geht nichts über (*acc.*); ***it is nothing ~ as bad as that*** es ist bei weitem nicht so schlimm; ***something ~ 100 tons*** so etwa 100 Tonnen; ***this is something ~!*** F das läßt sich hören!; ***that's more ~ it!*** das läßt sich (schon) eher hören!; ***~ master, ~ man*** wie der Herr, so's Gescherr; **2.** gleich: ***a ~ amount*** ein gleicher Betrag; ***in ~ manner*** a) auf gleiche Weise, b) gleichermaßen; **3.** ähnlich: ***the portrait is not ~*** das Porträt ist nicht ähnlich; ***as ~ as two eggs*** ähnlich wie ein Ei dem anderen; **4.** ähnlich, gleich-, derartig: ***… and other ~ problems*** … und andere derartige Probleme; **5.** F *od. obs.* (*a. adv.*) wahrˈscheinlich: ***he is ~ to pass his exam*** er wird sein Examen wahrscheinlich bestehen; ***~ enough***, ***as ~ as not*** höchstwahrscheinlich; **6.** *sl.* ‚oder so': ***let's go to the cinema ~***; **II** *cj.* **7.** *sl.* (*fälschlich für* ***as***) wie: ***~ I said***; ***~ who?*** wie wer, zum Beispiel?; **8.** *dial.* als ob; **III** *s.* **9.** *der* (*die*, *das*) Gleiche: ***his ~*** seinesgleichen; ***the ~*** der-, desgleichen; ***and the ~*** und dergleichen; ***the ~***(***s***) ***of*** so etwas wie, solche wie; ***the ~***(***s***) ***of that*** so etwas, etwas derartiges; ***the ~s of you*** F Leute wie Sie.

like² [laɪk] **I** *v/t.* (gern) mögen: a) gern

haben, (gut) leiden können, lieben, b) gern essen, trinken *etc.*: **~ doing** (*od.* **to do**) gern tun; **much ~d** sehr beliebt; **I ~ it** es gefällt mir; **I ~ him** ich hab' ihn gern, ich mag ihn (gern), ich kann ihn gut leiden; **I ~ fast cars** mir gefallen *od.* ich habe Spaß an schnellen Autos; **how do you ~ it?** wie gefällt es dir?, wie findest du es?; **we ~ it here** es gefällt uns hier; **I ~ that!** *iro.* so was hab' ich gern!; **what do you ~ better?** was hast du lieber?, was gefällt dir besser?; **I should ~ to know** ich möchte gerne wissen; **I should ~ you to be here** ich hätte gern, daß du hier wär(e)st; **~ it or not** ob du willst oder nicht; **~ it or lump it!** F wenn du nicht willst, dann laß es eben bleiben!; **I ~ steak, but it doesn't ~ me** *humor.* ich esse Beefsteak gern, aber es bekommt mir nicht; **II** *v/i.* wollen: (**just**) **as you ~** (ganz) wie du willst; **if you ~** wenn du willst; **III** *s.* Neigung *f*, Vorliebe *f*: **~s and dislikes** Neigungen u. Abneigungen.

-like [laɪk] *in Zssgn* wie, ...artig, ...ähnlich, ...mäßig.

like·a·ble → **likable**.

like·li·hood ['laɪklɪhʊd] *s.* Wahr'scheinlichkeit *f*: **in all ~** aller Wahrscheinlichkeit nach; **there is a strong ~ of his succeeding** es ist sehr wahrscheinlich, daß es ihm gelingt; **like·ly** ['laɪklɪ] **I** *adj.* **1.** wahr'scheinlich, vor'aussichtlich: **not ~** schwerlich, kaum; **it is not ~** (**that**) **he will come**, **he is not ~ to come** es ist nicht wahrscheinlich, daß er kommen wird; **which is his most ~ route?** welchen Weg wird er voraussichtlich *od.* am ehesten einschlagen?; **this is not ~ to happen** das wird wahrscheinlich nicht *od.* wohl kaum geschehen; **not ~!** *iro.* wohl kaum!; **2.** glaubhaft: **a ~ story!** *iro.* wer's glaubt, wird selig!; **3.** a) möglich, b) geeignet, in Frage kommend, c) aussichtsreich, d) vielversprechend: **a ~ candidate**; **a ~ explanation** e-e mögliche Erklärung; **a ~ place** ein möglicher Ort (*wo sich et. befindet etc.*); **II** *adv.* **4.** wahr'scheinlich: **as ~ as not**, **very ~** höchstwahrscheinlich.

ˌlike-'mind·ed *adj.* gleichgesinnt: **be ~ with s.o.** mit j-m übereinstimmen.

lik·en ['laɪkən] *v/t.* vergleichen (**to** mit).

like·ness ['laɪknɪs] *s.* **1.** Ähnlichkeit *f* (**to** mit); **2.** Gleichheit *f*; **3.** Gestalt *f*, Form *f*; **4.** Bild *n*, Por'trät *n*: **to have one's ~ taken** sich malen *od.* fotografieren lassen; **5.** Abbild *n* (**of** *gen.*).

'like·wise *adv. u. cj.* eben-, gleichfalls, des'gleichen, ebenso.

lik·ing ['laɪkɪŋ] *s.* **1.** Zuneigung *f*: **have** (**take**) **a ~ for** (*od.* **to**) **s.o.** zu j-m eine Zuneigung haben (fassen), an j-m Gefallen haben (finden); **2.** (**for**) Gefallen *n* (an *dat.*), Neigung *f* (zu), Geschmack *m* (an *dat.*): **be greatly to s.o.'s ~** j-m sehr zusagen; **this is not to my ~** das ist nicht nach meinem Geschmack; **it's too big for my ~** es ist mir (einfach) zu groß.

li·lac ['laɪlək] **I** *s.* **1.** ⚘ Spanischer Flieder; **2.** Lila *n* (*Farbe*); **II** *adj.* **3.** lila (-farben).

Lil·li·pu·tian [ˌlɪlɪ'pju:ʃjən] **I** *adj.* **1.** a) winzig, zwergenhaft, b) Liliput..., Klein(st)...; **II** *s.* **2.** Lilipu'taner(in); **3.** Zwerg *m*.

lilt [lɪlt] **I** *s.* **1.** fröhliches Lied; **2.** rhythmischer Schwung; **3.** a) singender Tonfall, b) fröhlicher Klang: **a ~ in her voice**; **II** *v/t. u. v/i.* **4.** trällern.

lil·y ['lɪlɪ] *s.* ⚘ Lilie *f*: **~ of the valley** Maiglöckchen *n*; **paint the ~** *fig.* schönfärben; **ˌ~-'liv·ered** *adj.* feig(e).

limb [lɪm] *s.* **1.** *anat.* Glied *n*, *pl.* Glieder *pl.*, Gliedmaßen *pl.*; **2.** Ast *m*: **out on a ~** F in e-r gefährlichen Lage; **3.** *fig.* a) Glied *n*, Teil *m*, b) Arm *m*, c) *ling.* (Satz)Glied *n*, d) ⚖ Absatz *m*; **4.** F ,Satansbraten' *m*.

lim·ber¹ ['lɪmbə] **I** *adj.* geschmeidig (*a. fig.*), gelenkig; **II** *v/t. u. v/i.* **~ up** (sich) geschmeidig machen, (sich) lockern, *v/i. a.* Lockerungsübungen machen, sich warm machen *od.* spielen.

lim·ber² [lɪmbə] **I** *s.* ⚔ Protze *f*; **II** *v/t. u. v/i. mst* **~ up** ⚔ aufprotzen.

lim·bo ['lɪmbəʊ] *s.* **1.** *eccl.* Vorhölle *f*; **2.** Gefängnis *n*; **3.** *fig.* a) ,Rumpelkammer' *f*, b) Vergessenheit *f*, c) Schwebe (-zustand *m*) *f*: **be in a ~** ,in der Luft hängen' (*Person od. Sache*).

lime¹ [laɪm] **I** *s.* **1.** ⚗ Kalk *m*; **2.** ↗ Kalkdünger *m*; **3.** Vogelleim *m*; **II** *v/t.* **4.** kalken, mit Kalk düngen.

lime² [laɪm] *s.* ⚘ Linde *f*.

lime³ [laɪm] *s.* ⚘ Li'mone *f*, Limo'nelle *f*.

'lime|·kiln *s.* Kalkofen *m*; **'~·light** *s.* **1.** ⚙ Kalklicht *n*; **2.** *fig.* (**be in the ~** im) Rampenlicht *n od.* (im) Licht *n* der Öffentlichkeit *od.* (im) Mittelpunkt *m* des (öffentlichen) Inter'esses (stehen).

li·men ['laɪmen] *s. psych.* (Bewußtseins- *od.* Reiz)Schwelle *f*.

lime pit *s.* **1.** Kalkbruch *m*; **2.** Kalkgrube *f*; **3.** *Gerberei*: Äscher *m*.

Lim·er·ick ['lɪmərɪk] *s.* Limerick *m* (*5-zeiliger Nonsensvers*).

'lime|·stone *s. min.* Kalkstein *m*; **~ tree** *s.* ⚘ Linde(nbaum *m*) *f*.

lim·ey ['laɪmɪ] *s. Am. sl.* ,Tommy' *m* (*Brite*).

lim·it ['lɪmɪt] **I** *s.* **1.** *bsd. fig.* a) Grenze *f*, Schranke *f*, b) Begrenzung *f*, Beschränkung *f* (**on** *gen.*): **within ~s** in Grenzen, bis zu e-m gewissen Grade; **without ~** ohne Grenzen, grenzen-, schrankenlos; **there is a ~ to everything** alles hat seine Grenzen; **there is no ~ to his ambition** sein Ehrgeiz kennt keine Grenzen; **off ~s** *Am.* Zutritt verboten (**to** für); **that's my ~!** a) mehr schaffe ich nicht!, b) höher kann ich nicht gehen!; **that's the ~!** F das ist (doch) die Höhe!; **he is the ~!** F er ist unglaublich *od.* unmöglich!; **go to the ~** F bis zum Äußersten gehen, *sport* über die Runden kommen; → **speed limit**; **2.** ℞, ⚙ Grenze *f*, Grenzwert *m*; **3.** zeitliche Begrenzung, Frist *f*: **extreme ~** ✝ äußerster Termin; **4.** ✝ a) Höchstbetrag *m*, b) Limit *n*, Preisgrenze *f*: **lowest ~** äußerster *od.* letzter Preis; **II** *v/t.* **5.** begrenzen, beschränken, einschränken (**to** auf *acc.*); *Preise* limitieren: **~ o.s. to** sich beschränken auf (*acc.*); **lim·i·ta·tion** [ˌlɪmɪ'teɪʃn] *s.* **1.** *fig.* Grenze *f*: **know one's ~s** s-e Grenzen kennen; **2.** Begrenzung *f*, Ein-, Beschränkung *f*; **3.** (**statutory period of**) **~** ⚖ Verjährung(sfrist) *f*: **be barred by the statute of ~** verjähren *od.* verjährt sein; **'lim·it·ed** [-tɪd] **I** *adj.* beschränkt, begrenzt (**to** auf *acc.*): **~** (**express**) **train** → II; **~ in time** zeitlich begrenzt; **~** (**liability**) **company** ✝ *Brit.* Aktiengesellschaft *f*; **~ monarchy** konstitutionelle Monarchie; **~ partner** ✝ Kommanditist(in); **~ partnership** ✝ Kommanditgesellschaft; **II** *s.* Schnellzug *m od.* Bus *m* mit Platzkarten; **'lim·it·less** [-lɪs] *adj.* grenzenlos.

lim·net·ic [lɪm'netɪk] *adj.* Süßwasser...

lim·ou·sine ['lɪmu:zi:n] *s. mot.* **1.** *Brit.* Wagen *m* mit Glastrennscheibe; **2.** *Am.* Kleinbus *m*.

limp¹ [lɪmp] *adj.* □ **1.** schlaff, schlapp (*a. fig. kraftlos, schwach*): **go ~** erschlaffen, *Person*: *a.* ,abschlaffen'; **2.** biegsam, weich: **~ book cover**.

limp² [lɪmp] **I** *v/i.* **1.** hinken (*a. fig. Vers etc.*), humpeln; **2.** sich schleppen (*a. Schiff etc.*); **II** *s.* **3.** Hinken *n*: **walk with a ~** → 1.

lim·pet ['lɪmpɪt] *zo.* Napfschnecke *f*: **like a ~** *fig.* wie e-e Klette; **~ mine** *s.* ⚔ Haftmine *f*.

lim·pid ['lɪmpɪd] *adj.* □ 'durchsichtig, klar (*a. fig. Stil etc.*), hell, rein; **lim·pid·i·ty** [lɪm'pɪdətɪ], **'lim·pid·ness** [-nɪs] *s.* 'Durchsichtigkeit *f*, Klarheit *f*.

limp·ness ['lɪmpnɪs] *s.* Schlaff-, Schlappheit *f*.

lim·y ['laɪmɪ] *adj.* **1.** Kalk..., kalkig: a) kalkhaltig, b) kalkartig; **2.** gekalkt.

lin·age ['laɪnɪdʒ] *s.* **1.** → **alignment**; **2.** a) Zeilenzahl *f*, b) 'Zeilenhonoˌrar *n*.

linch·pin ['lɪntʃpɪn] *s.* ⚙ Lünse *f*, Vorstecker *m*, Achsnagel *m*.

lin·den ['lɪndən] *s.* ⚘ Linde *f*.

line¹ [laɪn] **I** *s.* **1.** Linie *f*, Strich *m*; **2.** a) (*Hand- etc.*)Linie *f*: **~ of fate** Schicksalslinie, b) Falte *f*, Runzel *f*, c) Zug *m* (*im Gesicht*); **3.** Zeile *f*: **drop s.o. a ~** j-m ein paar Zeilen schreiben; **read between the ~s** zwischen den Zeilen lesen; **4.** *TV* (Bild)Zeile *f*; **5.** a) Vers *m*, b) *pl. Brit. ped.* Strafarbeit *f*, c) *thea. etc.* Rolle *f*, Text *m*; **6.** *pl.* F Trauschein *m*; **7.** F a) Informati'on *f*, Hinweis *m*: **get a ~ on** e-e Information erhalten über (*acc.*); **8.** *Am.* F a) ,Platte' *f* (*Geschwätz*), b) ,Tour' *f*, ,Masche' *f* (*Trick*); **9.** Linie *f*, Richtung *f*: **~ of attack** Angriffsrichtung, *fig.* Taktik *f*; **~ of fire** ⚔ Schußlinie *f*; **~ of sight** a) Blickrichtung *f*, b) *a.* **~ of vision** Gesichtslinie, -achse *f*; **he said s.th. along these ~s** er sagte etwas in dieser Richtung; → **resistance** 1; **10.** *pl. fig.* Grundsätze *pl.*, Richtlinie(n *pl.*) *f*, Grundzüge *pl.*: **along these ~s** a) nach diesen Grundsätzen, b) folgendermaßen; **along general ~s** ganz allgemein, in großen Zügen; **11.** Art *f* (u. Weise), Me'thode *f*: **~ of approach** Art, et. anzupacken, Methode *f*; **~ of argument** (Art der) Argumentation *f*; **~ of reasoning** Denkmethode *f*, -weise *f*; **take a strong ~** energisch auftreten *od.* werden (**with s.o.** j-m gegenüber); **take the ~ that** den Standpunkt vertreten, daß; **don't take that ~ with me!** komm mir ja nicht so! → **hard line** 1; **12.** Grenze *f*, Grenzlinie *f*: **draw the ~** (**at**) *fig.* die Grenze ziehen (bei); **I draw the ~ at that!** da hört es bei mir auf; **lay** (*od.* **put**) **on the ~** *fig. sein Leben, s-n Ruf etc.* aufs Spiel setzen; **be on the ~** auf dem Spiel stehen; **I'll lay it**

on the ~ for you! F das kann ich Ihnen genau sagen!; **13.** *pl.* a) Linien(führung *f*) *pl.*, Kon'turen *pl.*, Form *f*, b) Riß *m*, Entwurf *m*; **14.** a) Reihe *f*, Kette *f*, b) *bsd. Am.* (Menschen-, *a.* Auto)Schlange *f*: ***stand in ~*** (***for***) anstehen *od.* Schlange stehen (nach); ***drive in ~*** *mot.* Kolonne fahren; ***be in ~ for*** *fig.* Aussichten haben auf (*acc.*) *od.* Anwärter sein für; **15.** Übereinstimmung *f*: ***be in*** (***out of***) ***~*** (nicht) übereinstimmen *od.* im Einklang sein (***with*** mit); ***bring*** (*od.* ***get***) ***into ~*** a) in Einklang bringen (***with*** mit), b) *j-n* ‚auf Vordermann' bringen, c) *pol.* gleichschalten; ***fall into ~*** sich einordnen, *fig.* sich anschließen (***with*** *j-m*); ***toe the ~*** ‚spuren', sich der (*Partei- etc.*)Disziplin beugen; ***in ~ of duty*** *bsd.* ⚔ in Ausübung des Dienstes; **16.** a) (Abstammungs)Linie *f*, b) Fa'milie *f*, Geschlecht *n*: ***the male ~*** die männliche Linie; ***in the direct ~*** in direkter Linie; **17.** *pl.* Los *n*, Geschick *n*: ***hard ~s*** F Pech *n*; **18.** Fach *n*, Gebiet *n*, Sparte *f*: ***~*** (***of business***) Branche *f*, Geschäftszweig *m*; ***that's not in my ~*** das schlägt nicht in mein Fach, das liegt mir nicht; ***that's more in my ~*** das liegt mir schon eher; **19.** (*Verkehrs-, Eisenbahn- etc.*)Linie *f*, Strecke *f*, Route *f*, *engS.* Gleis *n*: ***ship of the ~*** Linienschiff *n*; ***~s of communications*** ⚔ rückwärtige Verbindungen; ***he was at the end of the ~*** *fig.* er war am Ende; ***that's the end of the ~!*** *fig.* Endstation!; **20.** (*Eisenbahn-, Luftverkehrs-, Autobus*)Gesellschaft *f*; **21.** a) ϟ, ⚙ Leitung *f*, *bsd.* Tele'fon- *od.* Tele'grafenleitung *f*: ***the ~ is engaged*** (*Am.* ***busy***) die Leitung ist besetzt; ***hold the ~!*** bleiben Sie am Apparat!; ***three ~s*** 3 Anschlüsse; → ***hot line***; **22.** ⚙ (Fertigungs)Straße *f*; **23.** ♆ a) Sorte *f*, Warengattung *f*, b) Posten *m*, Par'tie *f*, c) Ar'tikel(ˌserie *f*) *m od. pl.*; **24.** ⚔ a) Linie *f*: ***behind the enemy's ~s*** hinter den feindlichen Linien; ***~ of battle*** vorderste Linie, Kampflinie, b) Front *f*: ***go up the ~*** an die Front gehen; ***all along the ~***, (***all***) ***down the ~*** *fig.* auf der ganzen Linie, voll (u. ganz); ***go down the ~ for*** *Am.* F sich voll einsetzen für, c) Linie *f* (*Formation beim Antreten*), d) Fronttruppe *f*: ***the ~s*** die Linienregimenter; **25.** *geogr.* Längen- *od.* Breitenkreis *m*: ***the*** ≈ der Äquator; **26.** ⚓ Linie *f*: ***~ abreast*** Dwarslinie; ***~ ahead*** Kiellinie; **27.** (Wäsche)Leine *f*, (starke) Schnur, Seil *n*, Tau *n*; **28.** *teleph.* a) Draht *m*, b) Kabel *n*; **29.** Angelschnur *f*; **II** *v/i.* **30.** → ***line up*** 1, 2; **III** *v/t.* **31.** linieren; **32.** zeichnen, skizzieren; **33.** *Gesicht* (durch)'furchen; **34.** *Straße etc.* säumen: ***soldiers ~d the street*** Soldaten bildeten an der Straße Spalier; ***~ in*** *v/t.* einzeichnen; ***~ off*** *v/t.* abgrenzen; ***~ through*** *v/t.* 'durchstreichen; ***~ up*** **I** *v/i.* **1.** sich in e-r Linie *od.* Reihe aufstellen; **2.** Schlange stehen; **3.** *fig.* sich zs.-schließen; **II** *v/t.* **4.** in Linie *od.* in e-r Reihe aufstellen; **5.** aufstellen; **6.** *fig.* F *et.* ‚auf die Beine stellen', organisieren, arrangieren.

line² [laɪn] *v/t.* **1.** *Kleid etc.* füttern; **2.** ⚙ ausfüttern, -gießen, -kleiden, -schlagen, (innen) über'ziehen: ***~ one's*** (***own***) ***pockets*** in die eigene Tasche arbeiten, sich bereichern.

lin·e·age ['lɪnɪɪdʒ] *s.* **1.** (geradlinige) Abstammung; **2.** Stammbaum *m*; **3.** Geschlecht *n*, Fa'milie *f*.

lin·e·al ['lɪnɪəl] *adj.* □ geradlinig, in di'rekter Linie, di'rekt (*Abstammung, Nachkomme*).

lin·e·a·ment ['lɪnɪəmənt] *s.* (Gesichts-, *fig.* Cha'rakter)Zug *m*.

lin·e·ar ['lɪnɪə] *adj.* □ **1.** Linien…, geradlinig, *bsd.* ⩘, ⚙, *phys.* line'ar (*Gleichung, Elektrode, Perspektive etc.*), Linear…; **2.** Längen…(*-ausdehnung, -maß etc.*); **3.** Linien…, Strich…, strichförmig.

line| block *s.* → ***line etching***; **~ draw·ing** *s.* Strichzeichnung *f*; **~ etch·ing** *s.* *Kunst*: Strichätzung *f*; **'~·man** [-mən] *s.* [*irr.*] *Am.* **1.** 🚂 Streckenarbeiter *m*; **2.** → ***linesman*** 1.

lin·en ['lɪnɪn] **I** *s.* **1.** Leinen *n*, Leinwand *f*, Linnen *n*; **2.** (Bett-, 'Unter- *etc.*)Wäsche *f*: ***wash one's dirty ~ in public*** *fig.* s-e schmutzige Wäsche vor allen Leuten waschen; **II** *adj.* **3.** leinen, Leinen…: ***~ closet*** (*od.* ***cupboard***) Wäscheschrank *m*.

lin·er¹ ['laɪnə] *s.* **1.** ⚙ Futter *n*, Buchse *f*; **2.** Einsatz(stück *n*) *m*.

lin·er² ['laɪnə] *s.* **1.** ⚓ Linienschiff *n*; **2.** → ***air liner***.

lines·man ['laɪnzmən] *s.* [*irr.*] **1.** ϟ (Fernmelde)Techniker *m*, *engS.* Störungssucher *m*; **2.** 🚂 Streckenwärter *m*; **3.** *sport* Linienrichter *m*.

'line-up *s.* **1.** *sport* (Mannschafts)Aufstellung *f*, Aufgebot *n*; **2.** Gruppierung *f*; **3.** *Am.* ‚Schlange' *f*.

lin·ger ['lɪŋgə] *v/i.* **1.** (*a. fig.*) (noch) verweilen, (zu'rück)bleiben (*beide a. Gefühl, Geschmack, Erinnerung etc.*), sich aufhalten; *fig. a.* nachklingen (*Töne, Gefühl etc.*): ***~ on*** *fig.* (noch) fortleben *od.* -bestehen (*Brauch etc.*); ***~ on a subject*** bei e-m Thema verweilen; **2.** a) zögern, b) trödeln; **3.** da'hinsiechen (*Kranker*); **4.** sich hinziehen *od.* -schleppen.

lin·ge·rie ['læ̃:nʒəri:] (*Fr.*) *s.* ('Damen-)ˌUnterwäsche *f*.

lin·ger·ing ['lɪŋgərɪŋ] *adj.* □ **1.** a) verweilend, b) langsam, zögernd; **2.** (zu'rück)bleibend, nachklingend (*Ton, Gefühl etc.*); **3.** schleppend; **4.** schleichend (*Krankheit*); **5.** lang: a) sehnsüchtig, b) innig, c) prüfend: ***a ~ look***.

lin·go ['lɪŋgəʊ] *pl.* **-goes** [-gəʊz] *s.* Kauderwelsch *n*, *engS. a.* ('Fach)Jarˌgon *m*.

lin·gua fran·ca [ˌlɪŋgwə'fræŋkə] *s.* Verkehrssprache *f*.

lin·gual ['lɪŋgwəl] **I** *adj.* Zungen…; **II** *s.* Zungenlaut *m*.

lin·guist ['lɪŋgwɪst] *s.* **1.** Sprachforscher (-in), Lingu'ist(in); **2.** Fremdsprachler (-in), Sprachkundige(r *m*) *f*: ***he is a good ~*** er ist sehr sprachbegabt; **lin·guis·tic** [lɪŋ'gwɪstɪk] *adj.* (□ ***~ally***) **1.** sprachwissenschaftlich, lingu'istisch; **2.** Sprach(en)…; **lin·guis·tics** [lɪŋ'gwɪstɪks] *s. pl.* (*mst sg. konstr.*) Sprachwissenschaft *f*, Lingu'istik *f*.

lin·i·ment ['lɪnɪmənt] *s.* ⚕ Einreibemittel *n*.

lin·ing ['laɪnɪŋ] *s.* **1.** Futter(stoff *m*) *n*, (Aus)Fütterung *f* (*von Kleidern etc.*); **2.** ⚙ Futter *n*, Ver-, Auskleidung *f*; Ausmauerung *f*; (*Brems- etc.*)Belag *m*; → ***silver lining***.

link [lɪŋk] **I** *s.* **1.** (Ketten)Glied *n*; **2.** *fig.* a) Glied *n* (*in e-r Kette von Ereignissen etc.*), b) Bindeglied *n*; → ***missing*** 1; **3.** *freundschaftliche etc.* Bande *pl.*; **4.** Verbindung *f*, -knüpfung *f*, Zs.-hang *m* (***between*** zwischen); **5.** Man'schettenknopf *m*; **6.** ⚙ Glied *n* (*a.* ϟ), Verbindungsstück *n*, Gelenk *n*; **7.** *tel.* a) Streckenabschnitt *m*, b) Über'tragungsweg *m*; **8.** *TV* a) Verbindungsstrecke *f*, b) → ***linkup*** 3; **9.** *surv.* Meßkettenglied *n*; **10.** → ***links***; **II** *v/t.* **11.** *a.* ***~ up*** *od.* ***together*** (***with***) a) verbinden, -knüpfen (mit): ***~ arms*** (***with***) sich einhaken (bei *j-m*), b) mitein'ander in Verbindung *od.* Zs.-hang bringen, c) anein'anderkoppeln: ***be ~ed*** (***with***) zs.-hängen *od.* in Zs.-hang stehen (mit); ***~ed*** ⚗ gekoppelt (*a. biol. Gene*); **III** *v/i.* **12.** (***with***) a) sich verbinden (lassen) (mit), b) verknüpft sein (mit).

link·age ['lɪŋkɪdʒ] *s.* **1.** Verkettung *f*, *Computer*: *a.* Pro'grammverbindung *f*; **2.** ⚙ Gestänge *n*, Gelenkviereck *n*; **3.** ⚗, *biol.* Koppelung *f*, (*a. phys. Atom- etc.*)Bindung *f*.

links [lɪŋks] *s. pl.* **1.** *bsd. Scot.* Dünen *pl.*; **2.** (*a. sg. konstr.*) Golfplatz *m*.

'link·up *s.* **1.** → ***link*** 4; **2.** (Anein'ander-)Koppeln *n*; **3.** *Radio, TV*: Zs.-schaltung *f*.

linn [lɪn] *s. bsd. Scot.* **1.** Teich *m*; **2.** Wasserfall *m*.

lin·net ['lɪnɪt] *s. orn.* Hänfling *m*.

li·no ['laɪnəʊ] *abbr. für* ***linoleum***; **li·no·cut** ['laɪnəʊkʌt] *s.* Lin'olschnitt *m*.

li·no·le·um [lɪ'nəʊljəm] *s.* Lin'oleum *n*.

lin·o·type ['laɪnəʊtaɪp] *s.* *typ.* **1.** *a.* ≈ Linotype *f* (*Markenname für e-e Zeilensetz- u. -gießmaschine*); **2.** ('Setzmaˌschinen)Zeile *f*.

lin·seed ['lɪnsi:d] *s.* ⚘ Leinsamen *m*; **~ cake** *s.* Leinkuchen *m*; **~ oil** *s.* Leinöl *n*.

lint [lɪnt] **I** *s.* **1.** ⚕ Schar'pie *f*, Zupflinnen *n*; **2.** *Am.* Fussel *f*; **II** *v/i.* **3.** *Am.* Fusseln bilden, fusseln.

lin·tel ['lɪntl] *s.* ⚠ (Tür-, Fenster)Sturz *m*.

li·on ['laɪən] *s.* **1.** *zo.* Löwe *m* (*a. fig. Held*; *a. ast.* ≈): ***the ~'s share*** *fig.* der Löwenanteil; ***go into the ~'s den*** *fig.* sich in die Höhle des Löwen wagen; **2.** ‚Größe' *f*, Berühmtheit *f* (*Person*); **3.** *pl.* Sehenswürdigkeiten *pl.* (*e-s Ortes*); **'li·on·ess** [-nes] *s.* Löwin *f*; **'li·onˌheart·ed** *adj.* furchtlos, mutig; **li·on·ize** ['laɪənaɪz] *v/t.* *j-n* feiern, zum Helden des Tages machen.

lip [lɪp] *s.* **1.** Lippe *f*: ***hang on s.o.'s ~s*** an j-s Lippen hängen; ***keep a stiff upper ~*** Haltung bewahren; ***lick*** (*od.* ***smack***) ***one's ~s*** sich die Lippen lekken; → ***bite*** 7; **2.** F Unverschämtheit *f*: ***none of your ~!*** keine Frechheiten!; **3.** Rand *m* (*Wunde, Schale, Krater etc.*); **4.** Tülle *f*, Schnauze *f* (*Krug etc.*).

'lip|-read *v/t. u. v/i.* [*irr.* → ***read***] von den Lippen ablesen; **'~-ˌread·ing** *s.* Lippenlesen *n*; **~ ser·vice** *s.* Lippendienst *m*: ***pay ~ to*** ein Lippenbekenntnis ablegen zu *e-r Idee etc.*; **'~·stick** *s.* Lippenstift *m*.

li·quate ['laɪkweɪt] *v/t.* *metall.* (aus)seigern.

liq·ue·fa·cient [ˌlɪkwɪ'feɪʃnt] **I** *s.* Verflüssigungsmittel *n*; II *adj.* verflüssigend; **ˌliq·ueˈfac·tion** [-ˈfækʃn] *s.* Verflüssigung *f*; **liq·ue·fi·a·ble** [ˈlɪkwɪfaɪəbl] *adj.* schmelzbar; **liq·ue·fy** [ˈlɪkwɪfaɪ] *v/t. u. v/i.* (sich) verflüssigen; schmelzen; **li·ques·cent** [lɪˈkwesnt] *adj.* sich (leicht) verflüssigend, schmelzend.

li·queur [lɪˈkjʊə] *s.* Liˈkör *m*.

liq·uid [ˈlɪkwɪd] I *adj.* □ **1.** flüssig; Flüssigkeits…: ***~ measure*** Flüssigkeitsmaß *n*; ***~ crystal*** Flüssigkristall *m*; ***~ crystal display*** Flüssigkristallanzeige *f*; **2.** a) klar, hell u. glänzend, b) feucht (schimmernd): ***~ eyes***; ***~ sky***; **3.** perlend, wohltönend; **4.** *ling.* liˈquid, fließend: ***~ sound*** → 7; **5.** † liˈquid, flüssig: ***~ assets***; II *s.* **6.** Flüssigkeit *f*; **7.** *Phonetik*: Liquida *f*, Fließlaut *m*.

liq·ui·date [ˈlɪkwɪdeɪt] *v/t.* **1.** a) *Schulden etc.* tilgen, b) *Schuldbetrag* feststellen; **2.** *Konten* abrechnen, saldieren; **3.** † *Unternehmen* liquidieren; **4.** † *Wertpapier* flüssigmachen, realisieren; **5.** *j-n* liquidieren (*umbringen*); **liq·ui·da·tion** [ˌlɪkwɪˈdeɪʃn] *s.* **1.** † a) Liquidatiˈon *f*, Abwicklung *f* (*Unternehmen*): ***go into ~*** in Liquidation treten, b) Tilgung *f* (*von Schulden*), c) Abrechnung *f*, d) Realisierung *f*; **2.** *fig.* Liquidierung *f*, Beseitigung *f*; **ˈliq·ui·da·tor** [-tə] *s.* † Liquiˈdator *m*, Abwickler *m*.

li·quid·i·ty [lɪˈkwɪdətɪ] *s.* **1.** flüssiger Zustand; **2.** † Liquidiˈtät *f*, (Geld)Flüssigkeit *f*.

liq·uor [ˈlɪkə] I *s.* **1.** alkoˈholisches Getränk, *coll.* Spirituˈosen *pl.*, Alkohol *m* (*bsd. Branntwein u. Whisky*): ***in ~, the worse for ~*** betrunken; **2.** Flüssigkeit *f*; *pharm.* Arzˈneilösung *f*; **3.** ⚙ a) Lauge *f*, b) Flotte *f* (*Färbebad*); II *v/i.* **4.** *mst* ***~ up*** *sl.* ‚einen heben'; III *v/t.* **5.** ***get ~ed up*** sich ‚vollaufen' lassen; **~ cab·i·net** *s.* Hausbar *f*.

liq·uo·rice [ˈlɪkərɪs] *s.* Laˈkritze *f*.

lisp [lɪsp] I *v/i.* **1.** (*a. v/t. et.*) lispeln, mit der Zunge anstoßen; **2.** stammeln; II *s.* **3.** Lispeln *n*, Anstoßen *n* (mit der Zunge).

lis·some, *a.* **lis·som** [ˈlɪsəm] *adj.* **1.** geschmeidig; **2.** wendig, aˈgil.

list[1] [lɪst] I *s.* Liste *f*, Verzeichnis *n*: ***on the ~*** auf der Liste; ***~ price*** † Listenpreis *m*; II *v/t.* a) verzeichnen, aufführen, erfassen, katalogisieren; in e-e Liste eintragen, b) aufzählen: ***~ed*** *Am.* † amtlich notiert, börsenfähig (*Wertpapier*).

list[2] [lɪst] *s.* **1.** Saum *m*, Rand *m*; **2.** *Weberei*: Salband *n*, Webekante *f*; **3.** (Sal)Leiste *f*; **4.** *pl. hist.* a) Schranken *pl.* (*e-s Turnierplatzes*), b) Kampfplatz *m* (*a. fig.*): ***enter the ~s*** *fig.* in die Schranken treten, zum Kampf antreten.

list[3] [lɪst] ⚓ I *s.* Schlagseite *f*; II *v/i.* Schlagseite haben.

lis·ten [ˈlɪsn] *v/i.* **1.** horchen, hören, lauschen (***to*** auf *acc.*): ***~ to*** a) *j-m* zuhören, *j-n* anhören, b) auf *j-n od. j-s Rat* hören, *j-m* Gehör schenken, c) *e-m Rat etc.* folgen: ***~!*** hör mal (zu)!; ***~ for*** auf *et. od. j-n* horchen (*warten*); → ***reason*** 1; **2.** ***~ in*** a) Radio hören, b) (*am Telefon etc.*) mithören *od.* mit anhören (***on s.th.*** et.): ***~ in to*** *et.* im Radio hören; **ˈlis·ten·er** [-nə] *s.* **1.** Horcher(in), Lauscher(in); **2.** Zuhörer(in); **3.** *Radio*: Hörer(in).

lis·ten·ing post [ˈlɪsnɪŋ] *s.* ⚔ **1.** Horchposten *m* (*a. fig.*); **2.** Abhörstelle *f*.

list·less [ˈlɪstlɪs] *adj.* □ lustlos, teilnahmslos, matt, aˈpathisch.

lists [lɪsts] → ***list***[2] 4.

lit [lɪt] I *pret. u. p.p.* von ***light***[1] *u.* ***light***[3]; II *adj. mst* ***~ up*** *sl.* ‚blau' (*betrunken*).

lit·a·ny [ˈlɪtənɪ] *s. eccl. u. fig.* Litaˈnei *f*.

li·ter [ˈliːtə] *Am.* → ***litre***.

lit·er·a·cy [ˈlɪtərəsɪ] *s.* **1.** Fähigkeit *f* zu lesen u. zu schreiben; **2.** (liteˈrarische) Bildung, Belesenheit *f*; **ˈlit·er·al** [-rəl] I *adj.* □ **1.** wörtlich, wortgetreu: ***~ translation***; **2.** wörtlich, buchstäblich, eigentlich: ***~ sense***; **3.** nüchtern, wahrheitsgetreu: ***~ account***; ***the ~ truth*** die reine Wahrheit; **4.** *fig.* buchstäblich: ***~ annihilation***; ***a ~ disaster*** e-e wahre *od.* echte Katastrophe; **5.** peˈdantisch, proˈsaisch (*Person*); **6.** Buchstaben…, Schreib…: ***~ error*** → 7; II *s.* **7.** Schreib- *od.* Druckfehler *m*; **ˈlit·er·al·ism** [-əlɪzəm], **ˈlit·er·al·ness** [-rəlnɪs] *s.* **1.** Festhalten *n* am Buchstaben, *bsd.* strenge *od.* allzu wörtliche Überˈsetzung *od.* Auslegung, Buchstabenglaube *m*; **2.** *Kunst*: Reaˈlismus *m*.

lit·er·ar·y [ˈlɪtərərɪ] *adj.* □ **1.** liteˈrarisch, Literatur…: ***~ historian*** Literaturhistoriker(in); ***~ history*** Literaturgeschichte *f*; ***~ language*** Schriftsprache *f*; **2.** schriftstellerisch: ***a ~ man*** ein Literat; ***~ property*** geistiges Eigentum; **3.** liteˈrarisch gebildet; **4.** gewählt: ***a ~ expression***; **lit·er·ate** [ˈlɪtərət] I *adj.* **1.** des Lesens u. Schreibens kundig; **2.** (liteˈrarisch) gebildet; **3.** liteˈrarisch; II *s.* **4.** j-d, der Lesen u. Schreiben kann; **5.** Gebildete(r *m*) *f*; **lit·e·ra·ti** [ˌlɪtəˈrɑːtiː] *s. pl.* **1.** Liteˈraten *pl.*; **2.** *die* Gelehrten *pl.*; **lit·e·ra·tim** [ˌlɪtəˈrɑːtɪm] (*Lat.*) *adv.* buchstäblich, (wort)wörtlich; **lit·er·a·ture** [ˈlɪtərətʃə] *s.* **1.** Literaˈtur *f*, Schrifttum *n*; **2.** Schriftstelleˈrei *f*; **3.** Druckschriften *pl.*, *bsd.* Proˈspekte *pl.*, ˈUnterlagen *pl.*

lithe [laɪð] *adj.* □ geschmeidig; **ˈlithe·ness** [-nɪs] *s.* Geschmeidigkeit *f*.

lith·o·chro·mat·ic [ˌlɪθəʊkrəʊˈmætɪk] *adj.* Farben-, Buntdruck…

lith·o·graph [ˈlɪθəʊgrɑːf] I *s.* Lithograˈphie *f*, Steindruck *m* (*Erzeugnis*); II *v/t. u. v/i.* lithographieren; **li·thog·ra·pher** [lɪˈθɒgrəfə] *s.* Lithoˈgraph *m*; **lith·o·graph·ic** [ˌlɪθəʊˈgræfɪk] *adj.* (□ ***~ally***) lithoˈgraphisch, Steindruck…; **li·thog·ra·phy** [lɪˈθɒgrəfɪ] *s.* Lithograˈphie *f*, Steindruck *m*.

Lith·u·a·ni·an [ˌlɪθjuːˈeɪnjən] I *s.* **1.** Litauer(in); **2.** *ling.* Litauisch *n*; II *adj.* **3.** litauisch.

lit·i·gant [ˈlɪtɪgənt] ⚖ I *s.* Proˈzeßführende(r *m*) *f*, (streitende) Parˈtei; II *adj.* streitend, proˈzeßführend; **lit·i·gate** [ˈlɪtɪgeɪt] *v/i.* (*u. v/t.*) prozessieren (um), streiten (um); **lit·i·ga·tion** [ˌlɪtɪˈgeɪʃn] *s.* Rechtsstreit *m*, Proˈzeß *m*; **li·ti·gious** [lɪˈtɪdʒəs] *adj.* □ **1.** ⚖ a) Prozeß…, b) strittig, streitig; **2.** proˈzeß-, streitsüchtig.

lit·mus [ˈlɪtməs] *s.* ⚗ Lackmus *n*; **ˈ~-ˌpa·per** *s.* ˈLackmuspaˌpier *n*.

li·tre [ˈliːtə] *s. Brit.* Liter *m*, *n*.

lit·ter [ˈlɪtə] I *s.* **1.** Sänfte *f*; **2.** Trage *f*; **3.** Streu *f*; **4.** herˈumliegende Sachen *pl.*, *bsd.* (herˈumliegendes) Paˈpier u. Abfälle *pl.*; **5.** Wust *m*, Unordnung *f*; **6.** *zo.* Wurf *m Ferkel etc.*; II *v/t.* **7.** *mst* ***~ down*** a) Streu legen für *Tiere*, b) *Stall, Boden* einstreuen, c) *Pflanzen* abdekken; **8.** a) verunreinigen, b) unordentlich verstreuen, herˈumliegen lassen, c) *Zimmer* in Unordnung bringen, d) *oft* ***~ up*** (unordentlich) herˈumliegen in (*dat.*) *od.* auf (*dat.*): ***be ~ed with*** übersät sein mit (*a. fig.*); **9.** *zo. Junge* werfen; III *v/i.* **10.** (Junge) werfen.

lit·tle [ˈlɪtl] I *adj.* **1.** klein: ***a ~ house*** ein kleines Haus, ein Häuschen; ***a ~ one*** ein Kleines (*Kind*); ***our ~ ones*** unsere Kleinen; ***the ~ people*** die Elfen; ***~ things*** Kleinigkeiten *pl.*; **2.** kurz (*Strecke od. Zeit*); **3.** wenig: ***~ hope***; ***a ~ honey*** ein wenig *od.* ein bißchen *od.* etwas Honig; **4.** klein, gering(fügig), unbedeutend: ***of ~ interest*** von geringem Interesse; **5.** klein(lich), beschränkt, engstirnig: ***~ minds*** Kleingeister *pl.*; **6.** gemein, erbärmlich; **7.** *iro.* klein: ***her poor ~ efforts***; ***his ~ ways*** s-e kleinen Eigenarten *od.* Schliche; II *adv.* **8.** wenig, kaum, nicht sehr: ***he ~ knows*** er ahnt ja nicht (***that*** daß); ***we see ~ of her*** wir sehen sie nur sehr selten; ***make ~ of*** *et.* bagatellisieren; ***think ~ of*** wenig halten von; III *s.* **9.** Kleinigkeit *f*, *das* Wenige, *ein* bißchen: ***a ~*** ein wenig, ein bißchen; ***not a ~*** nicht wenig; ***after a ~*** nach e-m Weilchen; ***for a ~*** für ein Weilchen; ***a ~ rash*** ein bißchen voreilig; ***~ by ~*** nach und nach; ***~ or nothing*** so gut wie nichts; ***what ~ I have seen*** das wenige, das ich gesehen habe; ***every ~ helps*** auch der kleinste Beitrag hilft; **ˈlit·tle·ness** [-nɪs] *s.* **1.** Kleinheit *f*; **2.** Geringfügigkeit *f*, Bedeutungslosigkeit *f*; **3.** Kleinlichkeit *f*; **4.** Beschränktheit *f*.

lit·to·ral [ˈlɪtərəl] I *adj.* a) Küsten…, b) Ufer…; II *s.* Küstenland *n*, -strich *m*.

li·tur·gic, **li·tur·gi·cal** [lɪˈtɜːdʒɪk(l)] *adj.* □ liˈturgisch; **lit·ur·gy** [ˈlɪtədʒɪ] *s. eccl.* Liturˈgie *f*.

liv·a·ble [ˈlɪvəbl] *adj.* **1.** *a.* ***~-in*** wohnlich; **2.** *mst* ***~-with*** ˈumgänglich (*Person*); **3.** erträglich.

live[1] [lɪv] I *v/i.* **1.** *allg.* leben: ***~ to a great age*** ein hohes Alter erreichen; ***~ to be eighty*** achtzig Jahre alt werden; ***~ to see*** *et.* erreichen; ***~ off*** leben von, sich ernähren von; *b.s.* auf *j-s* Kosten leben; ***~ on*** a) weiter-, fortleben, b) *a.* ***~ by*** leben *od.* sich ernähren von; ***~ through s.th.*** et. mit- *od.* durchmachen, et. miterleben; ***~ with*** a) *a. iro.* mit *der Atombombe etc.* leben, b) *bsd. sport* F mit *e-m Gegner etc.* mithalten; ***we ~ and learn!*** man lernt nie aus!; ***~ and let ~*** leben u. leben lassen; ***he will ~ to regret it!*** das wird er noch bereuen!; **2.** (über)ˈleben, am Leben bleiben: ***the patient will ~!***; **3.** leben, wohnen: ***~ in a town***; **4.** leben, ein *ehrliches etc.* Leben führen: ***~ well*** gut leben; ***~ to o.s.*** (ganz) für sich leben; **5.** leben, das Leben genießen: ***she wanted to ~*** sie wollte (et. er)leben; (***then***) ***you haven't ~d!*** *humor.* du weißt ja gar nicht, was du versäumt hast!; II *v/t.* **6.** *ein anständiges etc. Leben* führen *od.* leben: ***~ one's own life*** sein eigenes Leben leben; **7.** (vor)leben, im Leben verwirklichen: ***he ~d a lie*** sein Leben war

e-e einzige Lüge;
Zssgn mit adv.:
live| down *v/t. et.* (durch tadellosen Lebenswandel) vergessen machen, sich reinwaschen *od.* rehabilitieren von: ***I will never live it down*** das wird man mir nie vergessen; **~ in** *v/i.* im Haus *od.* Heim *etc.* wohnen, nicht außerhalb wohnen; **~ out** *v/i.* außerhalb wohnen; **~ to·geth·er** *v/i.* zu'sammen leben *od.* wohnen; **~ up I** *v/i.*: ***~ to*** *den Anforderungen, Erwartungen etc.* entsprechen, *a. s-m Ruf* gerecht werden; *sein Versprechen* halten; **II** *v/t.*: ***live it up*** ‚auf den Putz hauen', ‚toll leben'.
live² [laɪv] **I** *adj.* (*nur attr.*) **1.** le'bendig: a) lebend: ***~ animals***, b) *fig.* lebhaft (*a. Debatte etc.*); rührig, tätig, e'nergisch (*Person*); **2.** aktu'ell: ***a ~ question***; **3.** glühend (*Kohle etc.*) (*a. fig.*); ⚔ scharf (*Munition*); ungebraucht (*Streichholz*); ϟ stromführend, geladen: ***~ wire*** *fig.* ‚Energiebündel' *n*; ***~ load*** ⚙ Nutzlast *f*; ***~ steam*** ⚙ Frischdampf *m*; **4.** *Radio, TV*: di'rekt, live, Direkt…, Original…, Live-…: ***~ broadcast*** Live-Sendung *f*, Direktübertragung *f*; **5.** ⚙ a) Trieb…, b) angetrieben; **II** *adv.* **6.** *Radio, TV*: di'rekt, live: ***the game will be broadcast ~.***
-lived [lɪvd] *in Zssgn* …lebig.
live·li·hood ['laɪvlɪhʊd] *s.* 'Lebensˌunterhalt *m*, Auskommen *n*: ***earn*** (*od.* ***make***) ***a*** (*od.* ***one's***) **~** sein Brot *od.* s-n Lebensunterhalt verdienen.
live·li·ness ['laɪvlɪnɪs] *s.* **1.** Lebhaftigkeit *f*; **2.** Le'bendigkeit *f*.
live·long ['lɪvlɒŋ] *adj. poet.*: ***all the ~ day*** den lieben langen Tag.
live·ly ['laɪvlɪ] *adj.* □ **1.** *allg.* lebhaft, le'bendig (*Person, Geist, Gespräch, Rhythmus, Gefühl, Erinnerung, Farbe, Beschreibung etc.*): ***~ hope*** starke Hoffnung; **2.** kräftig, vi'tal; **3.** lebhaft, aufregend (*Zeit*): ***make it*** (*od.* ***things***) ***~ for*** *j-m* (tüchtig) einheizen; ***we had a ~ time*** es war ‚schwer was los'; **4.** flott (*Tempo*).
liv·en ['laɪvn] *mst* **~ up I** *v/t.* beleben, Leben *od.* Schwung bringen in (*acc.*); **II** *v/i.* sich beleben, in Schwung kommen.
liv·er¹ ['lɪvə] *s. anat.* Leber *f*.
liv·er² ['lɪvə] *s.*: ***be a fast ~*** ein flottes Leben führen; ***be a good ~*** ‚gut leben'.
liv·er·ied ['lɪvərɪd] *adj.* livriert.
liv·er·ish ['lɪvərɪʃ] *adj.* F **1.** ***be ~*** es an der Leber haben; **2.** reizbar, mürrisch.
Liv·er·pud·li·an [ˌlɪvə'pʌdlɪən] **I** *adj.* aus *od.* von Liverpool; **II** *s.* Liverpooler(in).
'liv·er·wort *s.* ⚘ Leberblümchen *n*.
liv·er·y ['lɪvərɪ] *s.* **1.** Li'vree *f*; **2.** (*bsd.* Amts- *od.* Gilden)Tracht *f*; *fig.* (*a. zo. Winter- etc.*)Kleid *n*; **3.** → ***livery company***; **4.** Pflege *f* u. 'Unterbringung *f* (*von Pferden*) gegen Bezahlung: ***at ~*** in Futter *stehen etc.*; **5.** *Am.* → ***livery stable***; **6.** a) 'Übergabe *f*, Über'tragung *f*, b) *Brit.* 'Übergabe *f* von vom Vormundschaftsgericht freigegebenem Eigentum; **~ com·pa·ny** *s.* (Handels-)Zunft *f* der ***City of London***; **'~·man** [-mən] *s.* [*irr.*] Zunftmitglied *n*; **~ serv·ant** *s.* livrierter Diener; **~ sta·ble** *s.* Mietstall *m*.
lives [laɪvz] *pl. von* ***life***.
'live·stock ['laɪv-] *s.* Vieh(bestand *m*) *n*, lebendes Inven'tar.
liv·id ['lɪvɪd] *adj.* □ **1.** bläulich; bleifarben, graublau; **2.** fahl, aschgrau, blaß (***with*** vor *dat.*); **3.** *Brit.* F ‚fuchsteufelswild'; **li·vid·i·ty** [lɪ'vɪdətɪ], **'liv·id·ness** [-nɪs] *s.* Fahlheit *f*, Blässe *f*.
liv·ing ['lɪvɪŋ] **I** *adj.* □ **1.** lebend (*a. Sprachen*), le'bendig (*a. fig. Glaube, Gott etc.*): ***no man ~*** kein Sterblicher; ***not a ~ soul*** keine Menschenseele; ***while ~*** zu Lebzeiten; ***the greatest of ~ statesmen*** der größte lebende Staatsmann; ***~ death*** trostloses Dasein; ***within ~ memory*** seit Menschengedenken; **2.** glühend (*Kohle*); **3.** gewachsen (*Fels*); **4.** Lebens…: ***~ conditions***; **II** *s.* **5.** ***the ~*** die Lebenden; **6.** (das) Leben; **7.** Leben *n*, Lebensweise *f*, -führung *f*: ***good ~*** üppiges Leben; **8.** 'Lebensˌunterhalt *m*: ***make a ~*** s-n Lebensunterhalt verdienen (***as*** als, ***out of*** durch); **9.** Leben *n*, Wohnen *n*; **10.** *eccl. Brit.* Pfründe *f*; **~ room** [rʊm] *s.* Wohnzimmer *n*; **~ space** *s.* **1.** Wohnraum *m*, -fläche *f*; **2.** *pol.* Lebensraum *m*; **~ wage** *s.* ausreichender Lohn.
lix·iv·i·ate [lɪk'sɪvɪeɪt] *v/t.* auslaugen.
liz·ard ['lɪzəd] *s.* **1.** *zo.* a) Eidechse *f*, b) Echse *f*; **2.** Eidechsenleder *n*.
'll [l; əl] F *für* ***will*** 1, 2, 4 *od.* ***shall***.
lla·ma ['lɑːmə] *s. zo.* Lama(wolle *f*) *n*.
lo [ləʊ] *int. obs.* siehe!, seht!: ***~ and behold!*** *oft humor.* sieh(e) da!
loach [ləʊtʃ] *s. ichth.* Schmerle *f*.
load [ləʊd] **I** *s.* **1.** Last *f* (*a. phys.*); **2.** *fig.* Last *f*, Bürde *f*: ***take a ~ off s.o.'s mind*** j-m e-e Last von der Seele nehmen; ***that takes a ~ off my mind!*** da fällt mir ein Stein vom Herzen!; **3.** Ladung *f* (*a. e-r Schußwaffe*; *a. Am. sl. Menge Alkohol*), Fracht *f*, Fuhre *f*: ***a bus~ of tourists*** ein Bus voll(er) Touristen; ***have a ~ on*** *Am. sl.* ‚schwer geladen' haben; ***get a ~ of this!*** F hör mal gut zu!; ***~s of*** F e-e Unmasse *od.* massenhaft *od.* jede Menge *Geld, Fehler etc.*; **4.** *fig.* Belastung *f*: (***work***) **~** (Arbeits)Pensum *n*; **5.** ⚙, ϟ a) Last *f*, (Arbeits)Belastung *f*, b) Leistung *f*: ***~ capacity*** a) Ladefähigkeit *f*, b) Tragfähigkeit *f*, c) ϟ Belastbarkeit *f*; **II** *v/t.* **6.** beladen; **7.** *Güter, Schußwaffe etc.* laden; aufladen: ***~ the camera*** *phot.* e-n Film einlegen; **8.** *fig. j-n* über'häufen (***with*** mit *Arbeit, Geschenken, Vorwürfen etc.*): ***he's ~ed*** *sl.* a) er hat Geld wie Heu, b) er hat ‚schwer geladen' *od.* ist ‚blau'; **9.** *den Magen* über'laden; **10.** beschweren: ***~ dice*** Würfel präparieren: ***~ the dice*** *fig.* die Karten zinken; ***the dice are ~ed against him*** *fig.* er hat kaum e-e Chance; ***~ed question*** Fangfrage *f*; **11.** *Wein* verfälschen; **III** *v/i.* **12.** *a.* **~ up** (auf-, ein)laden.
load·er ['ləʊdə] *s.* **1.** (Ver)Lader *m*; **2.** Verladevorrichtung *f*; **3.** *hunt.* Lader *m*; **4.** ⚔ Ladeschütze *m*.
load·ing ['ləʊdɪŋ] *s.* **1.** (Be-, Auf)Laden *n*; **2.** a) Laden *n* (*e-r Schußwaffe*), b) Einlegen *n* e-s Films (*in die Kamera*); **3.** Ladung *f*, Fracht *f*; **4.** ⚙, ϟ, ✈ Belastung *f*; **5.** *Versicherung*: Verwaltungskostenanteil *m* (*der Prämie*); **~ bridge** *s.* Verlade-, ✈ Fluggastbrücke *f*; **~ coil** *s.* ϟ Belastungsspule *f*.
load| line *s.* ⚓ Lade(wasser)linie *f*; **'~·star** → ***lodestar***; **'~·stone** → ***lodestone***.
loaf¹ [ləʊf] *pl.* **loaves** [ləʊvz] *s.* **1.** Laib *m* (*Brot*), *weitS.* Brot *n*: ***half a ~ is better than no bread*** (etwas ist) besser als gar nichts; **2.** Zuckerhut *m*: ***~ sugar*** Hutzucker *m*; **3.** *a.* ***meat ~*** Hackbraten *m*; **4.** *Brit. sl.* ‚Birne' *f*: ***use your ~*** denk mal ein bißchen (nach)!
loaf² [ləʊf] **I** *v/i. a.* ***~ about*** (*od.* ***around***) her'umlungern, bummeln; faulenzen; **II** *v/t.* ***~ away*** *Zeit* verbummeln; **'loaf·er** [-fə] *s.* **1.** Faulenzer *m*, Nichtstuer *m*; Her'umtreiber(in); **2.** *Am.* Mokas'sin *m* (*Schuh*).
loam [ləʊm] *s.* Lehm(boden) *m*; **'loam·y** [-mɪ] *adj.* lehmig, Lehm…
loan [ləʊn] **I** *s.* **1.** (Ver)Leihen *n*, Ausleihung *f*: ***as a ~***, ***on ~*** leihweise; ***it's on ~***, ***it's a ~*** es ist geliehen; ***ask for the ~ of s.th.*** et. leihweise erbitten; ***put out to ~*** verleihen; **2.** Anleihe *f* (*a. fig.*): ***take up a ~ on*** e-e Anleihe aufnehmen auf *e-e Sache*; ***government ~*** Staatsanleihe; **3.** Darlehen *n*, Kre'dit *m*: ***~ on securities*** Lombarddarlehen; ***bankrate for ~s*** Lombardsatz *m*; **4.** Leihgabe *f* (*für e-e Ausstellung*); **II** *v/t. u. v/i.* **5.** (ver-, aus)leihen (***to*** *dat.*); **~ bank** *s.* Darlehensbank *f*; **~ of·fice** *s.* Darlehenskasse *f*; **~ shark** *s.* F ‚Kre'dithai' *m*; **~ trans·la·tion** *s. ling.* 'Lehnüberˌsetzung *f*; **~ word** *s. ling.* Lehnwort *n*.
loath [ləʊθ] *adj.* (*nur pred.*) abgeneigt, nicht willens: ***be ~ to do s.th.*** et. nur sehr ungern tun; ***nothing ~*** durchaus nicht abgeneigt.
loathe [ləʊð] *v/t. et. od. j-n* verabscheuen, hassen, nicht ausstehen können; **'loath·ing** [-ðɪŋ] *s.* Abscheu *m*, Ekel *m*; **'loath·ing·ly** [-ðɪŋlɪ] *adv.* mit Abscheu *od.* Ekel; **'loath·some** [-səm] *adj.* □ widerlich, ab'scheulich, verhaßt; ekelhaft, eklig.
loaves [ləʊvz] *pl. von* ***loaf¹***.
lob [lɒb] **I** *s.* **1.** *Tennis*: Lob *m*; **II** *v/t.* **2.** *den Ball* lobben; **3.** (*engS. et.* von unten her) werfen.
lob·by ['lɒbɪ] **I** *s.* **1.** a) Vor-, Eingangshalle *f*, Vesti'bül *n*, *bsd. thea., Hotel*: Foy'er *n*, b) Wandelgang *m*, -halle *f*, Korridor *m*, *parl. a.* Lobby *f*; **2.** *pol.* Lobby *f*, (Vertreter *pl.* e-r) Inter'essengruppe *f*; **II** *v/t. u. v/i.* **3.** (auf Abgeordnete) Einfluß nehmen: ***~ for*** (mit Hilfe e-r Lobby) für die Annahme *e-s Antrags etc.* arbeiten; **~ (*through*)** *Gesetzesantrag* mit Hilfe e-r Lobby durchbringen; **'lob·by·ist** [-ɪɪst] *s. pol.* Lobby'ist(in).
lobe [ləʊb] *s.* ⚘, *anat.* Lappen *m*: ***~ of the ear*** Ohrläppchen *n*; **lobed** [-bd] *adj.* gelappt, lappig.
lob·ster ['lɒbstə] *s. zo.* **1.** Hummer *m*: ***as red as a ~*** *fig.* krebsrot; **2.** (***spiny***) **~** Languste *f*.
lob·ule ['lɒbjuːl] *s.* ⚘, *anat.* Läppchen *n*.
lo·cal ['ləʊkl] **I** *adj.* □ **1.** lo'kal, örtlich, Lokal…, Orts…: ***~ authorities*** *pl.*, ***~ government*** Gemeinde-, Stadt-, Kommunalverwaltung *f*; ***~ call*** *teleph.* Ortsgespräch *n*; ***~ news*** Lokalnachrichten *pl.*; ***~ politics*** Lokalpolitik *f*; ***~ time*** Ortszeit *f*; ***~ traffic*** Lokal-, Orts-, Nahverkehr *m*; ***~ train*** → 5; **2.** Orts…, ortsansässig: a) hiesig, b) dortig: ***the ~***

doctor; **3.** lo'kal, örtlich, Lokal…: ~ ***an(a)esthesia*** → 10; ~ ***colo(u)r*** *fig.* Lokalkolorit *n*; ***a ~ custom*** ein ortsüblicher Brauch; ~ ***expression*** ortsgebundener Ausdruck; **4.** *Brit.* (*als Postvermerk*) Ortsdienst!; **II** *s.* **5.** Vororts-, Nahverkehrszug *m*; **6.** *Am. Zeitung*: Lo'kalnachricht *f*; **7.** *Am.* Ortsgruppe *f* (*e-r Gewerkschaft etc.*); **8.** *pl.* Ortsansässige *pl.*; **9.** *Brit.* F Ortsgasthaus *n*, *a.* Stammkneipe *f*; **10.** ⚕ Lo'kalanästhe,sie *f*, örtliche Betäubung.

lo·cale [ləʊ'kɑːl] *s.* Schauplatz *m*, Ort *m* (*e-s Ereignisses etc.*).

lo·cal·ism ['ləʊkəlɪzəm] *s.* Provinzia'lismus *m*: a) *ling.* örtliche (Sprach)Eigentümlichkeit, b) provinzi'elle Borniertheit, c) Lo'kalpatrio,tismus *m*.

lo·cal·i·ty [ləʊ'kælətɪ] *s.* **1.** a) Ort *m*: ***sense of ~*** Ortssinn *m*, b) Gegend *f*; **2.** (örtliche) Lage.

lo·cal·i·za·tion [,ləʊkəlaɪ'zeɪʃn] *s.* Lokalisierung *f*, örtliche Bestimmung *od.* Festlegung *od.* Begrenzung; **lo·cal·ize** ['ləʊkəlaɪz] *v/t.* **1.** lokalisieren: a) örtlich festlegen *od.* fixieren, b) (örtlich) begrenzen (***to*** auf *acc.*); **2.** Lo'kalkolo,rit geben (*dat.*).

lo·cate [ləʊ'keɪt] **I** *v/t.* **1.** ausfindig machen, die örtliche Lage *od.* den Aufenthalt ermitteln von (*od. gen.*); **2.** a) ⚓ *etc.* orten, b) ⚔ *Ziel etc.* ausmachen; **3.** *Büro etc.* errichten, einrichten; **4.** a) (*an e-m bestimmten Ort*) an- *od.* 'unterbringen, b) *an e-n Ort* verlegen: ***be ~d*** gelegen sein, *wo* liegen *od.* sich befinden; **II** *v/i.* **5.** *Am.* F sich niederlassen; **lo'ca·tion** [-eɪʃn] *s.* **1.** Lage *f*: a) Platz *m*, Stelle *f*, b) Standort *m*, Ort *m*, Örtlichkeit *f*; **2.** Ausfindigmachen *n*, Lokalisierung *f*, ⚓ *etc.* Ortung *f*; **3.** *Am.* a) Grundstück *n*, b) angewiesenes Land; **4.** *Film*: Gelände *n* für Außenaufnahmen, Drehort *m*: ***on ~*** auf Außenaufnahme; ~ ***shots*** Außenaufnahmen *pl.*; **5.** Niederlassung *f*, Siedlung *f*: **6.** *Computer*: 'Speicherstelle *f*, -a,dresse *f*.

loc·a·tive ['lɒkətɪv] *ling.* **I** *adj.* Lokativ…: ~ ***case*** → **II** *s.* Lokativ *m*, Ortsfall *m*.

loch [lɒk; lɒx] *s. Scot.* **1.** See *m*; **2.** Bucht *f*.

lo·ci ['ləʊsaɪ] *pl. u. gen. von* ***locus***.

lock¹ [lɒk] **I** *s.* **1.** (*Tür- etc.*)Schloß *n*: ***under ~ and key*** a) hinter Schloß u. Riegel (*Person*), b) unter Verschluß (*Sache*); **2.** Verschluß *m*, Schließe *f*; **3.** Sperrvorrichtung *f*; **4.** (*Gewehr- etc.*) Schloß *n*: ***~, stock, and barrel*** a) ganz u. gar, voll und ganz, mit Stumpf u. Stiel, b) mit allem Drum u. Dran, c) mit Sack u. Pack; **5.** a) Schleuse(nkammer) *f*, b) Luft-, Druckschleuse *f*; **6.** Knäuel *m*, *n*, Stau *m* (*von Fahrzeugen*); **7.** *mot. bsd. Brit.* Einschlag *m* (*der Vorderräder*); **8.** *Ringen*: Fessel(griff *m*) *f*; **II** *v/t.* **9.** (ab-, zu-, ver)schließen, zusperren, verriegeln; **10.** *a.* ~ ***up*** a) *j-n* einschließen, (ein)sperren, (***in, into*** in *acc.*), b) → ***lock up*** 2; **11.** (*in die Arme*) schließen, *a. Ringen*: um'fassen, -'klammern: ***~ed*** a) eng umschlungen, b) festgekeilt, *fig.* festsitzend, c) ineinander verkrallt: ***~ed in conflict***; **12.** inein'anderschlingen, *die Arme* verschränken; → ***horn***; **13.** ⚙ sperren, sichern, arretieren, festklemmen; **14.** *mot. Räder* blockieren; **15.** *Schiff* ('durch)schleusen; **16.** *Kanal* mit Schleusen versehen; **17.** ✝ *Geld* festlegen, fest anlegen; **III** *v/i.* **18.** (ab-) schließen; **19.** sich schließen lassen; **20.** ⚙ inein'andergreifen, einrasten; **21.** *mot.* a) sich einschlagen lassen, b) blockieren (*Räder*); **22.** geschleust werden (*Schiff*);

Zssgn mit adv.:

lock| a·way *v/t.* weg-, einschließen; ~ **down** *v/t. Schiff* hin'abschleusen; ~ **in** *v/t.* einschließen, -sperren; ~ **on** *v/i.* (***to***) **1.** *Radar*: (*Ziel*) erfassen u. verfolgen; **2.** *Raumfahrt*: (an)koppeln (an *acc.*); **3.** *fig.* a) einhaken (bei), b) sich ,verbeißen' (in *acc.*); ~ **out** *v/t.* (*a. Arbeiter*) aussperren; ~ **up** *v/t.* **1.** → ***lock¹*** 9, 10; **2.** ver-, ein-, wegschließen; **3.** *Kapital* festlegen, fest anlegen; **4.** *Schiff* hin'aufschleusen.

lock² [lɒk] *s.* **1.** Locke *f*; *pl. poet.* Haar *n*; **2.** (Woll)Flocke *f*; **3.** Strähne *f*, Büschel *n*.

lock·age ['lɒkɪdʒ] *s.* **1.** Schleusen(anlage *f*) *pl.*; **2.** Schleusengeld *n*; **3.** ('Durch)Schleusen *n*.

lock·er ['lɒkə] *s.* **1.** (verschließbarer) Kasten *od.* Schrank, Spind *m*, *n*: ~ ***room*** Umkleideraum *m*, *sport* (Umkleide)Kabine *f*; → ***shot²*** 4; **2.** Schließfach *n*.

lock·et ['lɒkɪt] *s.* Medail'lon *n*.

lock| gate *s.* Schleusentor *n*; '**~·jaw** *s.* ⚕ Kaumuskelkrampf *m*; '**~·nut** *s.* ⚙ Gegenmutter *f*; '**~·out** *s.* Aussperrung *f* (*von Arbeitern*); '**~·smith** *s.* Schlosser *m*; ~ **stitch** *s.* Kettenstich *m*; '**~-up** *s.* **1.** a) Gefängnis *n*, b) (Haft)Zelle(n *pl.*) *f*; **2.** *Brit.* (kleiner) Laden; **3.** *mot.* 'Einzelga,rage *f*; **4.** Schließen *n*, (Tor-) Schluß *m*; **5.** feste Anlage (*von Kapital*).

lo·co¹ ['ləʊkəʊ] *adj. Am. sl.* ,bekloppt', verrückt.

lo·co² ['ləʊkəʊ] *s.* Lok *f* (*Lokomotive*).

lo·co·mo·tion [,ləʊkə'məʊʃn] *s.* **1.** Fortbewegung *f*; **2.** Fortbewegungsfähigkeit *f*; '**lo·co,mo·tive** [-əʊtɪv] **I** *adj.* sich fortbewegend, fortbewegungsfähig, Fortbewegungs…: ~ ***engine*** → **II** *s.* Lokomo'tive *f*.

lo·cum ['ləʊkəm] F *für* ~ **te·nens** [,ləʊkəm'tiːnenz] *pl.* ~ **te·nen·tes** [-tɪ'nentiːz] *s.* Vertreter(in) (*z. B. e-s Arztes*).

lo·cus ['ləʊkəs] *pl. u. gen.* **lo·ci** ['ləʊsaɪ] *s.* (⩕ geo'metrischer) Ort.

lo·cust ['ləʊkəst] *s.* **1.** *zo.* Heuschrecke *f*; **2.** *a.* ~ ***tree*** ⚘ a) Ro'binie *f*, b) Jo'hannisbrotbaum *m*; **3.** ⚘ Jo'hannisbrot *n*, Ka'rube *f*.

lo·cu·tion [ləʊ'kjuːʃn] *s.* **1.** Ausdrucksweise *f*, Redestil *m*; **2.** Redewendung *f*, Ausdruck *m*.

lode [ləʊd] *s.* ⚒ (Erz)Gang *m*, Ader *f*; '**~·star** *s.* Leitstern *m* (*a. fig.*), *bsd.* Po'larstern *m*; '**~·stone** *s.* **1.** Ma'gneteisen(stein *m*) *n*; **2.** *fig.* Ma'gnet *m*.

lodge [lɒdʒ] **I** *s.* **1.** *allg.* Häus-chen *n*: a) (Jagd-, Ski- *etc.*)Hütte *f*, b) Pförtnerhaus *n*, c) Parkwächter-, Forsthaus *n*; **2.** Pförtner-, Porti'erloge *f*; **3.** *Am.* Zen'tralgebäude *n* (*in e-m Park etc.*); **4.** (*bsd.* Freimaurer)Loge *f*; **5.** (*Indianer-*) Wigwam *m*; **II** *v/i.* **6.** (***with***) a) logieren, (*bsd.* in 'Untermiete) wohnen (bei), b) über'nachten (bei); **7.** stecken (-bleiben) (*Kugel etc.*); **III** *v/t.* **8.** *j-n* a) 'unterbringen, aufnehmen, b) in 'Untermiete nehmen; **9.** *Geld* deponieren, hinter'legen; **10.** ✝ *Kredit* eröffnen; **11.** *Antrag, Beschwerde etc.* einreichen, *Anzeige* erstatten, *Berufung, Protest* einlegen (***with*** bei); **12.** *Kugel, Messer etc.* (hin'ein)jagen, *Schlag* landen; '**lodge·ment** [-mənt] → ***lodgment***; '**lodg·er** [-dʒə] *s.* ('Unter)Mieter(in).

lodg·ing ['lɒdʒɪŋ] *s.* **1.** 'Unterkunft *f*, ('Nacht)Quar,tier *n*; **2.** *pl.* a) (*bsd.* möbliertes) Zimmer, b) (möblierte) Zimmer *pl.*, c) Mietwohnung *f*; '**~-house** *s.* Fremdenheim *n*, Pensi'on *f*.

lodg·ment ['lɒdʒmənt] *s.* **1.** ⚖ Einreichung *f* (*Klage, Antrag etc.*); Erhebung *f* (*Beschwerde, Protest etc.*); Einlegung *f* (*Berufung*); **2.** Hinter'legung *f*, Deponierung *f*.

lo·ess ['ləʊɪs] *s. geol.* Löß *m*.

loft [lɒft] **I** *s.* **1.** (Dach-, *a.* ✓ Heu)Boden *m*, Speicher *m*; **2.** ⚠ Em'pore *f* (*für Kirchenchor, Orgel*); **3.** Taubenschlag *m*; **II** *v/t. u. v/i. Golf*: (den Ball) hochschlagen; '**loft·er** [-tə] *s. Golf*: Schläger *m* für Hochbälle.

loft·i·ness ['lɒftɪnɪs] *s.* **1.** Höhe *f*; **2.** Erhabenheit *f* (*a. fig.*); **3.** Hochmut *m*; **loft·y** ['lɒftɪ] *adj.* ☐ **1.** hoch(ragend); **2.** *fig.* a) erhaben, b) hochfliegend, c) *contp.* hochtrabend; **3.** stolz, hochmütig.

log¹ [lɒg] **I** *s.* **1.** a) (Holz)Klotz *m*, (-)Block *m*, b) (*Feuer*)Scheit *n*, c) (*gefällter*) (Baum)Stamm: ***in the ~*** unbehauen; ***roll a ~ for s.o.*** *Am.* j-m e-n Dienst erweisen, *bsd.* j-m et. zuschanzen; ***sleep like a ~*** schlafen wie ein Klotz *od.* Bär; **2.** ⚓ Log *n*; **3.** ⚓ *etc.* → ***logbook***: ***keep a ~ (of)*** Buch führen (über *acc.*); **II** *v/t.* **4.** ⚓ loggen: a) *Entfernung* zu'rücklegen, b) *Geschwindigkeit etc.* in das Logbuch eintragen.

log² [lɒg] → ***logarithm***.

lo·gan·ber·ry ['ləʊgənbərɪ] *s.* ⚘ Loganbeere *f* (*Kreuzung zwischen Bärenbrombeere u. Himbeere*).

log·a·rithm ['lɒgərɪðəm] *s.* ⩕ Loga'rithmus *m*; **log·a·rith·mic, log·a·rith·mi·cal** [,lɒgə'rɪðmɪk(l)] *adj.* ☐ loga'rithmisch.

'**log|·book** *s.* **1.** ⚓ Log-, ✈ Bord-, *mot.* Fahrtenbuch *n*; **2.** *mot. Brit.* Kraftfahrzeugbrief *m*; **3.** Reisetagebuch *n*; ~ **cab·in** *s.* Blockhaus *n*.

log·ger·head ['lɒgəhed] *s.*: ***be at ~s (with s.o.)*** sich (mit j-m) in den Haaren liegen.

log·gia ['ləʊdʒə] *s.* ⚠ Loggia *f*.

log·ic ['lɒdʒɪk] *s. phls. u. fig.* Logik *f*; '**log·i·cal** [-kl] *adj.* ☐ **1.** logisch (*a. fig. folgerichtig od. natürlich*); **2.** *Computer*: logisch, Logik…; **lo·gi·cian** [ləʊ'dʒɪʃn] *s.* Logiker *m*; **lo·gis·tic** [ləʊ'dʒɪstɪk] **I** *adj.* **1.** *phls. u.* ⚔ lo'gistisch; **II** *s.* **2.** *phls.* Lo'gistik *f*; **3.** *pl. mst sg. konstr. bsd.* ⚔ Lo'gistik *f*.

log·o ['lɒgəʊ] → ***logotype***.

log·o·gram ['lɒgəʊgræm] *s.* Logo'gramm *n*, Wortzeichen *n*.

log·o·type ['lɒgəʊtaɪp] *s.* ✝ Firmen- *od.* Markenzeichen *n*.

'**log|·roll** *pol. Am.* **I** *v/t. Gesetz* durch gegenseitige ,Schützenhilfe' 'durchbringen; **II** *v/i.* sich gegenseitig in die Hände arbeiten; **'~ₗroll·ing** *s. pol.* ‚Kuhhandel' *m*, gegenseitige Unter'stützung (*zur Durchsetzung von Gruppeninteressen etc.*).

loin [lɔɪn] *s.* **1.** (*mst pl.*) *anat.* Lende *f*: ***gird up one's ~s*** *fig.* s-e Lenden gürten, sich rüsten; **2.** *pl. bibl. u. poet.* a) Lenden *pl.* (*Fortpflanzungsorgane*), b) Schoß *m* (*der Frau*); **3.** *Küche*: Lende(nstück *n*) *f*; **'~·cloth** *s.* Lendentuch *n*.

loi·ter ['lɔɪtə] **I** *v/i.* **1.** bummeln, trödeln; **2.** her'umlungern, -stehen, sich her'umtreiben; **II** *v/t.* **3.** ***~ away*** *Zeit* vertrödeln; **'loi·ter·er** [-ərə] *s.* **1.** Bummler (-in), Faulenzer(in); **2.** Her'umtreiber(in).

loll [lɒl] **I** *v/i.* **1.** sich rekeln *od.* (her'um-) lümmeln; **2.** sich lässig lehnen (***against*** gegen); **3.** ***~ out*** her'aushängen, baumeln (*Zunge*); **II** *v/t.* **4.** *a.* ***~ out*** *die Zunge* her'aushängen lassen.

lol·li·pop ['lɒlɪpɒp] *s.* **1.** Lutscher *m* (*Stielbonbon*); **2.** *Brit.* Eis *n* am Stiel.

lol·lop ['lɒləp] *v/i.* F a) ‚latschen', b) hoppeln.

lol·ly ['lɒlɪ] *s.* **1.** F für ***lollipop***; **2.** *Brit. sl.* ‚Kies' *m* (*Geld*).

Lon·don·er ['lʌndənə] *s.* Londoner(in).

lone [ləʊn] *adj.* einsam: ***play a ~ hand*** *fig.* e-n Alleingang machen; → ***wolf*** 1; **'lone·li·ness** [-lɪnɪs] *s.* Einsamkeit *f*; **'lone·ly** [-lɪ] *adj. allg.* einsam: ***be ~ for*** *Am.* F Sehnsucht haben nach *j-m*; **lon·er** ['ləʊnə] *s.* F Einzelgänger(in); **'lone·some** [-səm] *adj.* □ → ***lonely***.

long¹ [lɒŋ] **I** *adj.* **1.** *allg.* lang (*a. fig. langwierig, a. ling.*): ***two miles*** (***weeks***) ***~***; ***~ journey*** (***list***, ***syllable***); ***~ years of misery***; ***~ measure*** Längenmaß *n*; ***~ wave*** ⚡ Langwelle *f*; ***~er*** *comp.* länger; ***a ~ chance***, ***~ odds*** *fig.* geringe Aussichten; ***a ~ dozen*** 13 Stück; ***~ drink*** Longdrink *m*; ***a ~ guess*** e-e vage Schätzung; **2.** lang, hoch(gewachsen): ***a ~ fellow***; **3.** groß, zahlreich: ***a ~ family***; ***a ~ figure*** eine vielstellige Zahl; ***a ~ price*** ein hoher Preis; **4.** weitreichend: ***a ~ memory***; ***take a ~ view*** weit vorausblicken; **5.** ☤ langfristig, mit langer Laufzeit, auf lange Sicht; **6.** a) ☤ eingedeckt (***of*** mit), b) ***~ on*** F reichlich versehen mit, *fig. a.* voller *Ideen etc.*; **II** *adv.* **7.** lang, lange: ***~ dead*** schon lange tot; ***as*** (*od.* ***so***) ***~ as*** a) solange (wie), b) sofern; vorausgesetzt, daß; ***~ after*** lange (da)nach; ***~ ago*** vor langer Zeit; ***not ~ ago*** vor kurzem; ***as ~ ago as 1900*** schon 1900; ***all day ~*** den ganzen Tag (lang); ***be ~*** a) lange dauern (*Sache*), b) lange brauchen ([***in***] ***doing s.th.*** et. zu tun); ***don't be*** (***too***) ***~!*** mach nicht so lang!, beeil dich!; ***I shan't be ~!*** (ich) bin gleich wieder da!; ***not ~ before*** kurz bevor; ***it was not ~ before*** es dauerte nicht lange, bis *er kam etc.*; ***so ~!*** tschüs!, bis später (dann)!; ***no*** (*od.* ***not any***) ***~er*** nicht (mehr) länger, nicht mehr; ***for how much ~er?*** wie lange noch?; ***~est*** *sup.* am längsten; **III** *s.* **8.** (e-e) lange Zeit: ***at the ~est*** längstens, höchstens; ***before ~*** bald, binnen kurzem; ***for ~*** lange (Zeit); ***it is ~ since*** es ist lange her, daß; **9.** ***take ~*** lange brauchen; ***the ~ and the short of it*** a) die ganze Geschichte, b) mit 'einem Wort, kurz'um; **10.** Länge *f*: a) *Phonetik*: langer Laut, b) *Metrik*: lange Silbe; **11.** *pl.* a) lange Hose, b) 'Übergrößen *pl.*

long² [lɒŋ] *v/i.* sich sehnen (***for*** nach): ***~ for*** *a. j-n od. et.* herbeisehnen; ***I ~ed to see him*** ich sehnte mich danach, ihn zu sehen; ***the*** (***much***) ***~ed-for rest*** die (heiß)ersehnte Ruhe.

'long|·boat *s.* ⚓ Großboot *n*, großes Beiboot (*e-s Segelschiffs*); **'~·bow** [-bəʊ] *s. hist.* Langbogen *m*: ***draw the ~*** F übertreiben, dick auftragen; **'~·case clock** *s.* Standuhr *f*; **ₗ~-'dat·ed** *adj.* langfristig; **ₗ~-'dis·tance I** *adj.* **1.** *teleph. etc.* Fern…(*-gespräch*, *-empfang*, *-leitung etc.*; *a. -fahrt*, *-lastzug*, *-verkehr etc.*); **2.** ✈, *sport* Langstrecken… (*-bomber*, *-flug*, *-lauf etc.*); **II** *adv.* **3.** ***call ~*** ein Ferngespräch führen; **III** *s.* **4.** *teleph. Am.* a) Fernamt *n*, b) Ferngespräch *n*; **ₗ~-drawn-'out** *adj. fig.* langatmig, in die Länge gezogen.

longe [lʌndʒ] → ***lunge²***.

lon·ge·ron ['lɒndʒərən] *s.* ✈ Rumpf(längs)holm *m*.

lon·gev·i·ty [lɒn'dʒevətɪ] *s.* Langlebigkeit *f*, langes Leben.

ₗlong|-'haired *adj.* **1.** langhaarig (*a. contp.*), *zo.* Langhaar…; **2.** (betont) intellektu'ell; **'~·hand** *s.* Langschrift *f*, (gewöhnliche) Schreibschrift; **ₗ~'head·ed** *adj.* **1.** langköpfig; **2.** gescheit, klug; **'~·horn** *s.* **1.** langhörniges Tier; **2.** langhörniges Rind, *Am.* Longhorn *n*.

long·ing ['lɒŋɪŋ] **I** *adj.* □ sehnsüchtig, verlangend; **II** *s.* Sehnsucht *f*, Verlangen *n* (***for*** nach).

long·ish ['lɒŋɪʃ] *adj.* ziemlich lang.

lon·gi·tude ['lɒndʒɪtju:d] *s. geogr.* Länge *f*; **lon·gi·tu·di·nal** [ₗlɒndʒɪ'tju:dɪnl] *adj.* □ **1.** *geogr.* Längen…; **2.** Längs…; **lon·gi·tu·di·nal·ly** [ₗlɒndʒɪ'tju:dɪnəlɪ] *adv.* längs, der Länge nach.

long| johns *s. pl.* F lange 'Unterhose; **~ jump** *s. sport* Weitsprung *m*; **'~-legged** *adj.* langbeinig; **ₗ~-'lived** *adj.* langlebig; **'~-ₗplay·ing rec·ord** *s.* Langspielplatte *f*; **~ prim·er** *s. typ.* Korpus *f* (*Schriftgrad*); **ₗ~-'range** *adj.* **1.** ⚔ weittragend, Fernkampf…, Fern…; ✈ Langstrecken…: ***~ bomber***; **2.** auf lange Sicht (geplant), langfristig; **'~·shore·man** [-mən] *s.* [*irr.*] Hafenarbeiter *m*; **~ shot** *s.* **1.** *Film*: To'tale *f*; **2.** *sport etc.* (krasser) Außenseiter; **3.** a) ris'kante Wette, b) (ziemlich) aussichtslose Sache, c) wilde Vermutung: ***not by a ~*** nicht entfernt, längst nicht (*so gut etc.*); **ₗ~-'sight·ed** *adj.* **1.** ⚕ weitsichtig; **2.** *fig.* weitblickend, 'umsichtig; **ₗ~-'stand·ing** *adj.* seit langer Zeit bestehend, langjährig, alt; **ₗ~-'suf·fer·ing I** *s.* Langmut *f*; **II** *adj.* langmütig; **'~-term** *adj.*, **'~·time** *adj.* langfristig, Langzeit…

lon·gueur [lɒŋ'gɜ:] (*Fr.*) *s.* Länge *f* (*in e-m Roman etc.*).

ₗlong-'wind·ed [-'wɪndɪd] *adj. fig.* langatmig.

loo [lu:] *Brit.* F **I** *s.* Klo *n*; **II** *v/i.* aufs Klo gehen.

loo·fa(h) ['lu:fə] → ***luffa***.

look [lʊk] **I** *s.* **1.** Blick *m* (***at*** auf *acc.*, nach): ***have a ~ at s.th.*** (sich) et. ansehen; ***take a good ~ (at it)!*** sieh es dir genau an!; ***have a ~ round*** sich (mal) umsehen; **2.** Miene *f*, Ausdruck *m*; **3.** *oft pl.* Aussehen *n*: (***good***) ***~s*** gutes Aussehen; ***I do not like the ~ of it*** die Sache gefällt mir (gar) nicht; **II** *v/i.* **4.** schauen, blicken, (hin)sehen (***at***, ***on*** auf *acc.*, nach): ***don't ~!*** nicht hersehen!; ***don't ~ like that!*** schau nicht so (drein)!; ***~ here!*** schau mal (her)!, hör mal (zu)!; → ***leap*** 1; **5.** (nach)schauen, nachsehen: ***~ who is here!*** schau, wer da kommt!, *humor.* ei, wer kommt denn da!; ***~ and see!*** überzeugen Sie sich (selbst)!; **6.** *krank etc.* aussehen (*a. fig.*): ***things ~ bad for him*** es sieht schlimm für ihn aus; ***it ~s as if*** es sieht (so) aus, als ob; ***~ like*** aussehen wie; ***it ~s like snow*** es sieht nach Schnee aus; ***he ~s like winning*** es sieht so aus, als ob er gewinnen sollte; ***it ~s all right to me*** es scheint (mir) in Ordnung zu sein; ***it ~s well on you*** es steht dir gut; **7.** aufpassen; → *Zssgn mit prp.* ***look to***; **8.** *nach e-r Richtung* liegen, gehen (***toward***, ***to*** nach) (*Zimmer etc.*); **III** *v/t.* **9.** *j-m in die Augen etc.* sehen *od.* schauen *od.* blicken: ***~ s.o. in the eyes***; **10.** aussehen wie: ***he ~s an idiot***; ***he doesn't ~ his age*** man sieht ihm sein Alter nicht an; ***he ~s it!*** so sieht er auch aus!; **11.** durch Blicke ausdrücken: ***~ compassion*** mitleidig dreinschauen; → ***dagger*** 1;

Zssgn mit prp.:

look| a·bout *v/i.*: ***~ one*** sich 'umsehen, um sich blicken; **~ aft·er** *v/i.* **1.** *j-m* nachblicken; **2.** sehen nach, aufpassen auf (*acc.*), sich kümmern um, sorgen für: ***~ o.s.*** a) für sich selbst sorgen, b) auf sich aufpassen; **~ at** *v/i.* (*a.* sich *j-n*, *et.*) ansehen, -schauen, betrachten, blicken auf (*acc.*), *fig. a. et.* prüfen: ***to ~ him*** wenn man ihn (so) ansieht; ***he wouldn't ~ it*** er wollte nichts davon wissen; ***he*** (***it***) ***isn't much to ~*** er (es) sieht nicht ‚berühmt' aus; **~ for** *v/i.* **1.** suchen (nach), sich 'umsehen nach; **2.** erwarten; **~ in·to** *v/i.* **1.** blicken in (*acc.*); **2.** *fig. et.* unter'suchen, prüfen; **~ on** *v/i.* betrachten, ansehen (***as*** als); **~ through** *v/i.* **1.** blicken durch; **2.** 'durchsehen, -lesen; **3.** *fig. j-n od. et.* durch'schauen; **~ to** *v/i.* **1.** achten *od.* achtgeben auf (*acc.*): ***~ it that*** achte darauf, daß; sieh zu, daß; **2.** zählen auf (*acc.*), von *j-m* erwarten, *daß er* …: ***I ~ you to help me*** (*od.* ***for help***) ich erwarte Hilfe von dir; **3.** sich wenden *od.* halten an (*acc.*); **~ up·on** → ***look on***;

Zssgn mit adv.:

look| a·bout *v/i.* sich 'umsehen (***for*** nach); **~ a·head** *v/i.* **1.** nach vorn blikken *od.* schauen; **2.** *fig.* a) vor'ausschauen, b) Weitblick haben; **~ a·round** → ***look about***; **~ back** *v/i.* **1.** sich 'umsehen; *a. fig.* zu'rückblicken (***upon*** auf *acc.*, ***to*** nach, zu); **2.** *fig.* schwankend werden; **~ down** *v/i.* **1.** her'ab-, her'untersehen (*a. fig.* [***up***]***on s.o.*** auf j-n); **2.** *bsd.* ☤ sich verschlechtern; **~ for·ward** *v/i.*: ***~ to*** sich freuen auf (*acc.*): ***I am looking forward to seeing him*** ich freue mich darauf, ihn zu sehen; **~ in** *v/i. als Besucher* her'ein- *od.* hin'einschauen (***on*** bei); **~ on** *v/i.* zusehen, -schauen (***at*** bei); **~ out I** *v/i.* **1.** her'aus- *od.* hin'aussehen, -schauen (***of the window*** zum *od.* aus dem Fenster); **2.** Ausschau halten (***for*** nach); **3.** (***for***) gefaßt sein (auf *acc.*), auf der Hut sein (vor *dat.*), aufpassen (auf *acc.*): ***~!*** paß auf!, Vorsicht!; **4.** Ausblick gewähren, (hin'aus)gehen (***on*** auf *acc.*) (*Fenster etc.*); **II** *v/t.* **5.** (her'aus)suchen; **~ o·ver** *v/t.* **1.** 'durchsehen, (über)'prüfen; **2.** sich *et. od. j-n* ansehen, *j-n* mustern; **~ round** *v/i.* sich 'umsehen; **~ through** *v/t.* → ***look over*** 1; **~ up I** *v/i.* **1.** hin'aufblicken (***at*** auf *acc.*); aufblikken (*fig.* ***to s.o.*** zu j-m); **2.** F *a.* ↑ sich bessern; steigen (*Preise*): ***things are looking up*** es geht bergauf; **II** *v/t.* **3.** *Wort* nachschlagen; **4.** *j-n* be- *od.* aufsuchen; **5.** ***look s.o. up and down*** j-n von oben bis unten mustern.

'look-a,like *s.* F Doppelgänger(in).

look·er ['lʊkə] *s.* F: ***be a*** (***good***) **~** gut *od.* ‚toll' aussehen; ***she is not much of a ~*** sie sieht nicht besonders gut aus; **,~-'on** [-ər'ɒn] *pl.* **,look·ers-'on** *s.* Zuschauer(in) (***at*** bei).

'look-in *s.* **1.** F kurzer Besuch; **2.** *sl.* Chance *f.*

'look·ing-glass ['lʊkɪŋ-] *s.* Spiegel *m.*

'look-out *s.* **1.** Ausschau *f*: ***be on the ~ for*** nach *et.* Ausschau halten; ***keep a good ~*** (***for***) auf der Hut sein (vor *dat.*); **2.** *a.* ⚓ Ausguck *m*; **3.** Wache *f*, Beobachtungsposten *m*; **4.** *fig.* Aussicht(en *pl.*) *f*; **5.** ***that's his ~*** F das ist s-e Sache *od.* sein Problem.

'look-see *s.*: ***have a ~*** *sl.* a) (kurz) mal nachgucken, b) sich mal umsehen.

loom¹ [lu:m] *s.* Webstuhl *m.*

loom² [lu:m] *v/i.* *oft* **~ up 1.** (drohend) aufragen: **~ *large*** *fig.* a) sich auftürmen, b) von großer Bedeutung sein *od.* scheinen; **2.** undeutlich *od.* bedrohlich auftauchen; **3.** *fig.* a) sich abzeichnen, b) bedrohlich näherrücken, c) sich zs.-brauen.

loon¹ [lu:n] *s. orn.* Seetaucher *m.*

loon² [lu:n] *s.* F ‚Blödmann' *m.*

loon·y ['lu:nɪ] *sl.* **I** *adj.* ‚bekloppt', verrückt; **II** *s.* Verrückte(r *m*) *f*; **~ bin** *s. sl.* ‚Klapsmühle' *f.*

loop [lu:p] **I** *s.* **1.** Schlinge *f*, Schleife *f*; **2.** ⚡, 🚂, *Computer, Eislauf, Fingerabdruck, Fluß etc.*: Schleife *f*; **3.** a) Schlaufe *f*, b) Öse *f*; **4.** ✈ *etc.* Looping *m, n*; **5.** ⚕ Spi'rale *f* (*Verhütungsmittel*); **6.** → ***loop aerial***; **II** *v/t.* **7.** in e-e Schleife *od.* in Schleifen legen, schlingen; **8.** ***~ the ~*** ✈ e-n Looping drehen; **9.** ⚡ zur Schleife schalten; **III** *v/i.* **10.** e-e Schleife machen, sich schlingen *od.* winden; **~ aer·i·al** *s.*, **~ an·ten·na** *s.* ⚡ 'Rahmenan,tenne *f*, Peilrahmen *m*; **'~-hole** *s.* **1.** (Guck)Loch *n*; **2.** ⚔ a) Sehschlitz *m*, b) Schießscharte *f*; **3.** *fig.* Schlupfloch *n*, 'Hintertürchen *n*: ***a ~ in the law*** eine Lücke im Gesetz; **,~-the-'loop** *s. Am.* Achterbahn *f.*

loose [lu:s] **I** *adj.* □ **1.** los(e): ***come*** (*od.* ***get, work***) **~** a) abgehen (*Knöpfe*), b) sich ablösen (*Farbe etc.*), c) sich lockern, d) loskommen; ***let ~*** a) loslassen, b) *s-m Ärger etc.* Luft machen; **2.** frei, befreit (***of, from*** von): ***break ~*** a) sich losreißen, b) sich lösen (***from*** von), *fig. a.* sich freimachen (***from*** von); **3.** lose (hängend) (*Haar etc.*): **~ *ends*** *fig.* (noch zu erledigende) Kleinigkeiten; ***be at a ~ end*** a) nicht wissen, was man mit sich anfangen soll, b) ohne geregelte Tätigkeit sein; **4.** a) locker (*Boden, Glieder, Gürtel, Husten, Schraube, Zahn etc.*), b) offen, lose, unverpackt (*Ware*): ***buy s.th. ~*** et. offen kaufen; **~ *bowels*** offener Leib, *a.* Durchfall *m*; **~ *change*** Kleingeld *n*; **~ *connection*** ⚡ Wackelkontakt *m*; *fig.* lose Beziehung; **~ *dress*** weites *od.* lose sitzendes Kleid; **~ *leaves*** lose Blätter; **5.** *fig.* einzeln, verstreut, zs.-hanglos; **6.** ungenau: **~ *translation*** freie Übersetzung; **7.** *fig.* locker, lose (*unmoralisch*): **~ *girl*** (***life, morals***); **~ *tongue*** loses Mundwerk; **II** *adv.* **8.** lose, locker; **III** *v/t.* **9.** → ***loosen*** 1; **10.** befreien, lösen (***from*** von); **11.** lockern: **~ *one's hold of*** *et.* loslassen; **12.** *mst* **~ *off*** *Waffe, Schuß* abfeuern; **IV** *v/i.* **13.** *mst* **~ *off*** schießen, feuern (***at*** auf *acc.*): **~ *off at s.o.*** *fig.* loswettern gegen j-n; **V** *s.* **14.** ***be on the ~*** a) frei herumlaufen, b) die Gegend ‚unsicher machen', c) ‚einen draufmachen'; **,~-'joint·ed** *adj.* **1.** (außerordentlich) gelenkig; **2.** schlaksig; **,~'leaf** *adj.* Loseblatt...: **~ *binder*** (*od.* ***book***) Loseblatt-, Ringbuch *n*, Schnellhefter *m.*

loos·en ['lu:sn] **I** *v/t.* **1.** *Knoten etc., a.* ⚕ *Husten, fig. Zunge* lösen; ⚕ *Leib* öffnen; **2.** *Griff, Gürtel, Schraube etc., a. Disziplin etc.* lockern; ⚒ *Boden* auflokkern; **II** *v/i.* **3.** sich lockern (*a. fig.*), sich lösen; **~ up I** *v/t.* *Muskeln etc.* lockern; *fig. j-n* auflockern; **II** *v/i.* *bsd. sport* sich (auf)lockern, *fig. a.* auftauen (*Person*).

loose·ness ['lu:snɪs] *s.* **1.** Lockerheit *f*; **2.** Schlaffheit *f*; **3.** Ungenauigkeit *f*, Unklarheit *f*; **4.** Freiheit *f der Übersetzung*; **5.** ⚕ 'Durchfall *m*; **6.** lose Art, Liederlichkeit *f.*

loot [lu:t] **I** *s.* **1.** (Kriegs-, Diebes)Beute *f*; **2.** *fig.* Beute *f*; **3.** F ‚Kies' *m* (*Geld*); **II** *v/t.* **4.** erbeuten; **5.** plündern; **III** *v/i.* **6.** plündern; **'loot·er** [-tə] *s.* Plünderer *m*; **'loot·ing** [-tɪŋ] *s.* Plünderung *f.*

lop¹ [lɒp] *v/t.* **1.** *Baum etc.* beschneiden, stutzen; **2.** *oft* **~ *off*** *Äste, a. Kopf etc.* abhauen, -hacken.

lop² [lɒp] *v/i. u. v/t.* schlaff (her'unter-) hängen (lassen).

lope [ləʊp] **I** *v/i.* (da'her)springen *od.* (-)trotten; **II** *s.*: ***at a ~*** im Galopp, in großen Sprüngen.

'lop|-eared *adj.* mit Hängeohren; **'~-ears** *s. pl.* Hängeohren *pl.*; **,~-'sid·ed** *adj.* **1.** schief (*a. fig.*), nach einer Seite hängend; **2.** einseitig (*a. fig.*).

lo·qua·cious [ləʊ'kweɪʃəs] *adj.* □ redselig, geschwätzig; **lo'qua·cious·ness** [-nɪs], **lo'quac·i·ty** [-'kwæsətɪ] *s.* Redseligkeit *f.*

lord [lɔ:d] **I** *s.* **1.** Herr *m*, Gebieter *m* (***of*** über *acc.*): ***her ~ and master*** *bsd. humor.* ihr Herr u. Gebieter; ***the ~s of creation*** *a. humor.* die Herren der Schöpfung; **2.** *fig.* Ma'gnat *m*; **3.** Lehensherr *m*; → ***manor***; **4.** ***the ℒ*** a) *a.* ***ℒ God*** (Gott) der Herr, b) *a.* ***our ℒ*** (Christus) der Herr; ***the ℒ's day*** der Tag des Herrn; ***the ℒ's Prayer*** das Vaterunser; ***the ℒ's Supper*** das (heilige) Abendmahl; ***the ℒ's table*** der Tisch des Herrn (*a. Abendmahl*), der Altar; ***in the year of our ℒ*** im Jahre des Herrn; (***good***) ***ℒ!*** (du) lieber Gott *od.* Himmel!; **5.** ***ℒ*** Lord *m* (*Adliger od. Würdenträger, z.B. Bischof, hoher Richter*): ***the ℒs*** *Brit. parl.* das Oberhaus; ***live like a ~*** leben wie ein Fürst; **6.** ***my ℒ*** [mɪ'lɔ:d; ⚖ *Brit. oft* mɪ'lʌd] My'lord, Euer Lordschaft, ⚖ Euer Ehren (*Anrede*); **II** *v/i.* **7.** *oft* **~ *it*** den Herren spielen: ***to ~ it over*** a) sich *j-m* gegenüber als Herr aufspielen, b) herrschen über (*acc.*).

Lord| Cham·ber·lain (of the House·hold) *s.* Haushofmeister *m*; **~ Chan·cel·lor** *s.* Lordkanzler *m* (*Präsident des Oberhauses, Präsident der* ***Chancery Division*** *des* ***Supreme Court of Judicature*** *sowie des* ***Court of Appeal***, *Kabinettsmitglied, Bewahrer des Großsiegels*); **~ Chief Jus·tice of Eng·land** *s.* ⚖ Lord'oberrichter *m* (*Vorsitzender der* ***King's Bench Division*** *des* ***High Court of Justice***); **ℒ in wait·ing** *s.* königlicher Kammerherr (*wenn e-e Königin regiert*); **~ Jus·tice** *pl.* **Lords Jus·tic·es** *s. Brit.* Lordrichter *m* (*Richter des* ***Court of Appeal***); **ℒ lieu·ten·ant** *pl.* **lords lieu·ten·ant** *s.* **1.** *hist. Vertreter der Krone in den englischen Grafschaften*; *jetzt oberster Exekutivbeamter*; **2.** ***Lord Lieutenant*** a) *hist.* Vizekönig *m* von Irland (*bis 1922*), b) *Vertreter der Krone in e-r Grafschaft.*

lord·li·ness ['lɔ:dlɪnɪs] *s.* **1.** Großzügigkeit *f*; **2.** Würde *f*; **3.** Pracht *f*, Glanz *m*; **4.** Arro'ganz *f.*

lord·ling ['lɔ:dlɪŋ] *s. contp.* Herrchen *n*, kleiner Lord.

lord·ly ['lɔ:dlɪ] *adj. u. adv.* **1.** großzügig; **2.** vornehm, edel, Herren...; **3.** herrisch; **4.** stolz; **5.** arro'gant; **6.** prächtig.

Lord| May·or *pl.* **Lord May·ors** *s. Brit.* Oberbürgermeister *m*: ***~'s Day*** *Tag des Amtsantritts des Oberbürgermeisters von London (9. November)*; ***~'s Show*** *Festzug des Oberbürgermeisters von London am 9. November*; **~ Priv·y Seal** *s.* Lord'siegelbewahrer *m*; **~ Prov·ost** *pl.* **Lord Prov·osts** *s.* Oberbürgermeister *m* (*der vier größten schottischen Städte*).

lord·ship ['lɔ:dʃɪp] *s.* **1.** Lordschaft *f*: ***your*** (***his***) **~** Euer (Seine) Lordschaft; **2.** *hist.* Herrschaftsgebiet *n* e-s Lords; **3.** *fig.* Herrschaft *f.*

lord| spir·it·u·al *pl.* **lords spir·it·u·al** *s.* *geistliches Mitglied des brit. Oberhauses*; **~ tem·po·ral** *pl.* **lords tem·po·ral** *s. weltliches Mitglied des brit. Oberhauses.*

lore [lɔ:] *s.* **1.** (*Tier- etc.*)Kunde *f*, (über'liefertes) Wissen; **2.** Sagen- u. Märchengut *n*, Über'lieferungen *pl.*

lorn [lɔ:n] *adj. obs. od. poet.* verlassen, einsam.

lor·ry ['lɒrɪ] *s.* **1.** *Brit.* Last(kraft)wagen *m*, Lastauto *n*; **2.** 🚂, ⚒ Lore *f*, Lori *f.*

lose [lu:z] **I** *v/t.* [*irr.*] **1.** *allg. Sache, j-n, Gesundheit, das Leben, Verstand, a. Weg, Zeit etc.* verlieren: **~ *o.s.*** a) sich verlieren (*a. fig.*), b) sich verirren; **~ *interest*** a) das Interesse verlieren, b) uninteressant werden (*Sache*); ***she lost the baby*** sie verlor das Baby (*durch Fehlgeburt*); → ***lost***; *s. a. Verbindungen mit verschiedenen Substantiven*; **2.** *Vermögen, Stellung* verlieren, einbüßen, kommen um; **3.** *Vorrecht etc.* verlieren, verlustig gehen (*gen.*); **4.** a) *Schlacht, Spiel etc.* verlieren, b) *Preis etc.* nicht erringen *od.* bekommen, c) *Gesetzesan-*

trag nicht ˈdurchbringen; **5.** *Zug etc., a. Gelegenheit* versäumen, verpassen; **6.** a) *Worte etc.* ‚nicht mitbekommen', b) ***he lost his listeners*** F s-e Zuhörer kamen nicht mit; **7.** aus den Augen verlieren; → ***sight*** 3; **8.** vergessen, verlernen: ***I have lost my French***; **9.** nachgehen, zuˈrückbleiben (*Uhr*); **10.** *Krankheit etc.* loswerden, *Verfolger a.* abschütteln; **11.** *j-n s-e Stellung etc.* kosten, bringen um: ***this will ~ you your position***; **12.** ***~ it*** *mot. sl.* die Kontrolle über den Wagen verlieren; **II** *v/i.* [*irr.*] **13.** verlieren, Verluste erleiden (***on*** bei, ***by*** durch); **14.** *fig.* verlieren: ***the poem ~s in translation*** das Gedicht verliert (sehr) in der Übersetzung; **15.** (***to***) verlieren (gegen), unterˈliegen (*dat.*); **16.** ***~ out*** F a) verlieren, b) ‚in den Mond gucken' (***on*** bei): ***~ on*** *a. et.* nicht kriegen; **ˈlos·er** [-zə] *s.* **1.** Verlierer(in): ***a good*** (***bad***) ***~***; ***be a ~ by*** Schaden *od.* e-n Verlust erleiden durch; ***come off a ~*** den kürzeren ziehen; **2.** F ‚Verlierer' *m*, Versager *m*; **ˈlos·ing** [-zɪŋ] *adj.* **1.** verlierend; **2.** verlustbringend, Verlust...: ***~ bargain*** † Verlustgeschäft *n*; **3.** verloren, aussichtslos (*Schlacht, Spiel*).

loss [lɒs] *s.* **1.** Verlust *m*: a) Einbuße *f*, Ausfall *m* (***in*** an *dat.*, von *od. gen.*): ***~ of blood*** (***time***) Blut- (Zeit)verlust; ***~ of pay*** Lohnausfall; ***a dead ~*** totaler Verlust, *fig.* ‚Pleite' *f*, totaler Reinfall (*Sache*), ‚totaler Ausfall', ‚Niete' *f* (*Person*), b) Nachteil *m*, Schaden *m*: ***it's your ~!*** das ist dein Problem!, c) *verlorene Sache od. Person*: ***he is a great ~ to his firm***, d) Verschwinden *n*, Verlieren *n*, e) *verlorene Schlacht, Wette etc., a.* Niederlage *f*, f) Abnahme *f*, Schwund *m*: ***~ in weight*** Gewichtsverlust, -abnahme; **2.** *mst pl.* ⚔ Verluste *pl.*, Ausfälle *pl.*; **3.** *Versicherungswesen*: Schadensfall *m*; **4.** ***at a ~*** a) † mit Verlust (*arbeiten, verkaufen etc.*), b) in Verlegenheit (***for*** um): ***be at a ~*** *a.* nicht mehr ein u. aus wissen; ***be at a ~ for words*** (*od.* ***what to say***) keine Worte finden (können), nicht wissen, was man (dazu) sagen soll; ***he is never at a ~ for an excuse*** er ist nie um e-e Ausrede verlegen; ***~ lead·er*** *s.* † ˈLockarˌtikel *m*; **ˈ~-ˌmak·er** *s.* † *Brit.* **1.** mit Verlust arbeitender Betrieb; **2.** Verlustgeschäft *n*.

lost [lɒst] **I** *pret. u. p.p. von* ***lose***; **II** *adj.* **1.** verloren: ***~ articles*** (***battle, friend, time*** *etc.*); ***a ~ chance*** e-e verpaßte Gelegenheit; ***~ property office*** Fundbüro *n*; **2.** verloren(gegangen), vernichtet, (da)ˈhin: ***be ~*** a) verlorengehen (***to*** an *acc.*), b) zugrunde gehen, untergehen, c) umkommen, den Tod finden, d) verschwinden, e) verschwunden *od.* verschollen sein, f) vergessen sein, g) versunken *od.* vertieft sein (***in*** in *acc.*); ***~ in thought***; ***I am ~ without my car!*** ohne mein Auto bin ich verloren *od.* ‚aufgeschmissen'!; **3.** verirrt: ***be ~*** sich verirrt *od.* verlaufen haben, sich nicht mehr zurechtfinden (*a. fig.*); ***get ~*** sich verirren; ***get ~!*** F verschwinde!; ***I'm ~!*** F da komm' ich nicht mehr mit!; **4.** *fig.* verschwendet, vergeudet (***on s.o.*** an j-n): ***that's ~ on him*** *a.* a) das läßt ihn kalt, b) dafür hat er keinen Sinn, c) das versteht er nicht.

lot [lɒt] **I** *s.* **1.** Los *n*: ***cast*** (*od.* ***draw***) ***~s*** losen, Lose ziehen (***for*** um); ***throw in one's ~ with s.o.*** das Los mit j-m teilen, sich (auf Gedeih u. Verderb) mit j-m zs.-tun; ***by ~*** durch (das) Los; **2.** Anteil *m*; **3.** Los *n*, Schicksal *n*: ***it falls to my ~*** es ist mein Los, es fällt mir zu (*et. zu tun*); **4.** *bsd. Am.* a) Stück *n* Land, Grundstück *n*, *bsd.* Parˈzelle *f*, b) Bauplatz *m*, c) (Park- *etc.*)Platz *m*; **5.** *Am.* Filmgelände *n*, *bsd.* Studio *n*; **6.** † a) Arˈtikel *m*, b) Parˈtie *f*, Posten *m* (*von Waren*): ***in ~s*** partienweise; **7.** Gruppe *f*, Gesellschaft *f*, ‚Verein' *m*: ***the whole ~*** a) die ganze Gesellschaft, der ganze ‚Laden', b) → 8; **8.** ***the ~*** alles, das Ganze: ***take the ~!***; ***that's the ~*** das ist alles; **9.** (Un)Menge *f*: ***a ~ of***, ***~s of*** viel, e-e Menge, ein Haufen *Geld etc.*; ***~s and ~s of people*** e-e Unmasse Menschen; ***~s!*** *in Antworten*: jede Menge!; **10.** F Kerl *m*: ***a bad ~*** ein übler Bursche; **II** *adv.* **11.** ***a ~***, F ***~s*** a) (sehr) viel: ***a ~ better***, ***I read a ~***, b) (sehr) oft: ***I see her a ~***.

loth [ləʊθ] → ***loath***.

Lo·thar·i·o [ləʊˈθɑːrɪəʊ] *s.* Schwerenöter *m*.

lo·tion [ˈləʊʃn] *s.* (*Augen-, Haut-, Rasier- etc.*)Wasser *n*, Lotiˈon *f*.

lot·ter·y [ˈlɒtərɪ] *s.* **1.** Lotteˈrie *f*: ***~ ticket*** Lotterielos *n*; **2.** *fig.* Glückssache *f*, Lotteˈriespiel *n*.

lo·tus [ˈləʊtəs] *s.* **1.** *Sage*: Lotos *m* (*Frucht*); **2.** ⚘ a) Lotos(blume *f*) *m*, b) Honigklee *m*; **ˈ~-ˌeat·er** *s.* **1.** (*in der Odyssee*) Lotosesser *m*; **2.** Träumer *m*, Müßiggänger *m*, tatenloser Genußmensch.

loud [laʊd] *adj.* □ **1.** (*a. adv.*) laut (*a. fig.*): ***~ admiration***; **2.** schreiend, auffallend, grell: ***~ colo(u)rs***; **ˌ~-ˈhail·er** *s. Brit.* Megaˈphon *n*; **ˈ~·mouth** *s.* F **1.** Großmaul *n*; **2.** ‚dummer Quatscher'; **ˈ~·mouthed** *adj.* großmäulig.

loud·ness [ˈlaʊdnɪs] *s.* **1.** Lautheit *f*, *a. phys.* Lautstärke *f*; **2.** Lärm *m*; **3.** *das* Auffallende, Grellheit *f*.

ˌloudˈspeak·er *s.* ⚡ Lautsprecher *m*.

lounge [laʊndʒ] **I** *s.* **1.** a) Halle *f*, Diele *f*, Gesellschaftsraum *m* (*Hotel*), b) *thea.* Foyˈer *n*, c) Abflug-, Wartehalle (*Flughafen*), d) *a.* ***~ bar*** ✈, ⚓, 🚃 Saˈlon *m*; **2.** Wohndiele *f*, -zimmer *n*; **3.** Sofa *n*, Liege *f*; **II** *v/i.* **4.** sich rekeln; **5.** faulenzen; **6.** ***~ about*** (*od.* ***around***) heˈrumliegen *od.* -sitzen *od.* -stehen *od.* -schlendern; **7.** schlendern; **III** *v/t.* **8.** ***~ away*** *Zeit* verbummeln; ***~ bar*** Saˈlon *m* (*e-s Restaurants*); ***~ chair*** *s.* Klubsessel *m*; ***~ liz·ard*** *s.* F Saˈlonlöwe *m*; ***~ suit*** *s. Brit.* Straßenanzug *m*.

lour, lour·ing → ***lower***[1], ***lowering***.

louse [laʊs] **I** *pl.* **lice** [laɪs] *s.* **1.** *zo.* Laus *f*; **2.** *sl.* ‚Fiesling' *m*, Scheißkerl *m*; **II** *v/t.* [laʊz] **3.** (ent)lausen; **4.** ***~ up*** *sl.* versauen, -masseln; **ˈlous·y** [-zɪ] *adj.* **1.** verlaust; **2.** *sl.* a) ‚fies', (hunds)gemein, b) miseˈrabel, ‚beschissen': ***the film was ~***; ***I feel ~***, c) ‚lausig': ***for ~ two dollars***; **3.** ***~ with*** *sl.* wimmelnd von; ***~ with people***; ***~ with money*** stinkreich.

lout [laʊt] *s.* Flegel *m*, Rüpel *m*; **ˈlout·ish** [-tɪʃ] *adj.* □ flegel-, rüpelhaft.

lou·ver, *Brit. a.* **lou·vre** [ˈluːvə] *s.* **1.** △ *hist.* Dachtürmchen *n*; **2.** Jalouˈsie *f* (*a.* ⚙ *Luft-, Kühlschlitze*).

lov·a·ble [ˈlʌvəbl] *adj.* □ liebenswert, reizend, ‚süß'.

lov·age [ˈlʌvɪdʒ] *s.* ⚘ Liebstöckel *n, m*.

love [lʌv] **I** *s.* **1.** (*sinnliche od. geistige*) Liebe (***of, for, to***[***wards***] zu): ***~ of music*** Liebe zur Musik, Freude *f* an der Musik; ***~ of adventure*** Abenteuerlust *f*; ***the ~ of God*** a) die Liebe Gottes, b) die Liebe zu Gott; ***for the ~ of God*** um Gottes willen; ***be in ~*** (***with s.o.***) verliebt sein (in j-n); ***fall in ~*** (***with s.o.***) sich verlieben (in j-n); ***make ~*** sich (*sexuell*) lieben; ***make ~ to s.o.*** a) j-n (*körperlich*) lieben, b) *obs.* j-n umˈwerben, j-m gegenüber zärtlich werden; ***send one's ~ to s.o.*** j-n grüßen lassen; ***give her my ~!*** grüße sie herzlich von mir!; ***~*** *als Briefschluß*: herzliche Grüße; ***for ~*** a) umsonst, gratis, b) *a.* ***for the ~ of it*** (nur) zum Spaß; ***play for ~*** um nichts spielen; ***not for ~ or money*** nicht für Geld u. gute Worte; ***there is no ~ lost between them*** sie haben nichts füreinander übrig; **2.** ♀ die Liebe, (Gott *m*) Amor *m*; **3.** *pl. Kunst*: Amoˈretten *pl.*; **4.** Liebling *m*, Schatz *m*; **5.** F a) mein Lieber, b) m-e Liebe; **6.** Liebe *f*, Liebschaft *f*; **7.** F lieber *od.* goldiger Kerl: ***he*** (***she***) ***is a ~***; **8.** F reizende *od.* goldige *od.* ‚süße' Sache *od.* Perˈson: ***a ~ of a child*** (***hat***); **9.** *bsd. Tennis*: null: ***~ all*** null beide; ***~ fifteen*** null fünfzehn; **II** *v/t.* **10.** *j-n* lieben; **11.** *et.* lieben, sehr mögen: ***~ to do*** (*od.* ***doing***) ***s.th.*** etwas (schrecklich) gern tun; ***we ~d having you with us*** wir haben uns sehr über deinen Besuch gefreut; ***~ af·fair*** *s.* ˈLiebesafˌfäre *f*; **ˈ~·bird** *s.* **1.** *orn.* Unzertrennliche(r) *m*; **2.** *pl.* F ‚Turteltauben' *pl.*; ***~ child*** *s.* Kind *n* der Liebe; ***~ game*** *s. Tennis*: Zu-ˈNull-Spiel *n*; **ˌ~-ˈhate re·la·tion·ship** *s.* Haßliebe *f*.

love·less [ˈlʌvlɪs] *adj.* □ **1.** ohne Liebe; **2.** lieblos.

love| let·ter *s.* Liebesbrief *m*; ***~ life*** *s.* Liebesleben *n*.

love·li·ness [ˈlʌvlɪnɪs] *s.* Lieblichkeit *f*, Schönheit *f*.

ˈlove|·lock *s.* Schmachtlocke *f*; **ˈ~·lorn** [-lɔːn] *adj.* liebeskrank, vor Liebeskummer *od.* Liebe vergehend.

love·ly [ˈlʌvlɪ] *adj.* □ **1.** a) lieblich, schön, hübsch, b) *allg., a.* F *u. iro.* schön, wunderbar, reizend, entzükkend, c) lieb, nett (***of you*** von dir); **2.** F ‚süß', niedlich.

ˈlove|-ˌmak·ing *s.* (*körperliche*) Liebe; Liebesspiele *pl.*, -kunst *f*; ***~ match*** *s.* Liebesheirat *f*; ***~ nest*** *s.* ‚Liebesnest' *n*; ***~ po·tion*** *s.* Liebestrank *m*.

lov·er [ˈlʌvə] *s.* **1.** a) Liebhaber *m*, Geliebte(r) *m*, b) Geliebte *f*; **2.** *pl.* Liebende *pl.*, Liebespaar *n*: ***~s' lane*** *humor.* ‚Seufzergäßchen' *n*; ***they were ~s*** sie liebten sich *od.* hatten ein Verhältnis miteinander; **3.** Liebhaber(in), (*Musik- etc.*)Freund(in); **ˈ~·boy** *s.* F Casaˈnova *m*.

love| seat *s.* Plaudersofa *n*; ***~ set*** *s. Tennis*: Zu-ˈNull-Satz *m*; **ˈ~·sick** *adj.* liebeskrank: ***be ~*** *a.* Liebeskummer haben; ***~ song*** *s.* Liebeslied *n*; ***~ sto·ry*** *s.* Liebesgeschichte *f*.

lov·ing [ˈlʌvɪŋ] *adj.* □ liebend, liebevoll, Liebes...: ***~ words***; ***your ~ father*** (*als*

Briefschluß) Dein Dich liebender Vater; ~ **cup** *s.* Po'kal *m*; ˌ~-'**kind·ness** *s.* **1.** (göttliche) Gnade *od.* Barm'herzigkeit; **2.** Herzensgüte *f.*

low¹ [ləʊ] **I** *adj. u. adv.* **1.** nieder, niedrig (*a. Preis, Temperatur, Zahl etc.*): ***of ~ birth*** von niedriger Abkunft; ***~ pressure*** Tiefdruck *m*; ***~ speed*** niedrige *od.* geringe Geschwindigkeit; ***~ water*** ⚓ tiefster Gezeitenstand; ***at the ~est*** wenigstens, mindestens; ***be at its ~est*** auf dem Tiefpunkt angelangt sein; → ***lower³***, ***opinion*** 2; **2.** tief (*a. fig.*): ***~ bow***; ***~ flying*** Tiefflug *m*; ***the sun is ~*** die Sonne steht tief; → ***low-necked***; **3.** knapp (*Vorrat etc.*): ***run ~*** knapp werden, zur Neige gehen; ***I am ~ in funds*** ich bin nicht gut bei Kasse; **4.** schwach: ***~ light***; ***~ pulse***; **5.** einfach, fru'gal (*Kost*); **6.** be-, gedrückt: ***~ spirits*** gedrückte Stimmung; ***feel ~*** a) in gedrückter Stimmung *od.* niedergeschlagen sein, b) sich elend fühlen; **7.** minderwertig, schlecht: ***~ quality***; **8.** a) niedrig (*denkend od. gesinnt*): ***~ thinking*** niedrige Denkungsart, b) ordi'när, vul'gär: ***a ~ expression***; ***a ~ fellow***, c) gemein, niederträchtig: ***a ~ trick***; **9.** nieder, primi'tiv: ***~ forms of life*** niedere Lebensformen; ***~ race*** primitive Rasse; **10.** a) tief (*Ton etc.*), b) leise (*Ton, Stimme etc.*): ***in a ~ voice*** leise; **11.** *Phonetik*: offen (*Vokal*); **12.** ⚙, *mot.* erst, niedrigst (*Gang*): ***in ~ gear***; **II** *adv.* **13.** niedrig (*zielen etc.*); **14.** tief: ***bow*** (***hit****, etc.*) ***~***; ***sunk thus ~*** *fig.* so tief gesunken; ***bring s.o. ~*** *fig.* j-n zu Fall bringen *od.* ruinieren *od.* demütigen; ***lay s.o. ~*** a) j-n niederstrecken, b) *fig.* j-n zur Strecke bringen; ***be laid ~*** (***with***) darniederliegen (mit *e-r Krankheit*); **15.** a) leise, b) tief: ***sing ~***; **16.** kärglich: ***live ~***; **17.** billig: ***buy*** (***sell***) ***~***; **18.** niedrig, mit geringem Einsatz: ***play ~***; **III** *s.* **19.** *meteor.* Tief(druckgebiet) *n*; **20.** *fig.* Tiefstand *m*: ***reach a new ~*** e-n neuen Tiefstand erreichen; **21.** *mot.* erster Gang.

low² [ləʊ] **I** *v/i. u. v/t.* brüllen, muhen (*Rind*); **II** *s.* Brüllen *n*, Muhen *n*.

ˌ**low**|-'**born** *adj.* von niedriger Geburt; '**~·boy** *s. Am.* niedrige Kom'mode; '**~·brow** F **I** *s.* Ungebildete(r *m*) *f*, ‚Unbedarfte(r' *m*) *f*; **II** *adj.* geistig anspruchslos, *Person*: *a.* ungebildet, ‚unbedarft'; ˌ**~-'cal·o·rie** *adj.* kalo'rienarm; **2 Church** *s. eccl.* Low Church *f* (*protestantisch-pietistische Sektion der anglikanischen Kirche*); **~ com·e·dy** *s.* Schwank *m*, ‚Klamotte' *f*; '**~-cost** *adj.* billig, preisgünstig; **2 Coun·tries** *s. pl. die Niederlande, Belgien u. Luxemburg*; '**~-down** F **I** *adj.* fies, gemein; **II** *s.* (volle) Informati'onen *pl.*, *die* Wahrheit, genaue Tatsachen *pl.*, 'Hintergründe *pl.* (***on*** über *acc.*).

low·er¹ ['laʊə] *v/i.* **1.** finster *od.* drohend blicken: ***~ at*** *j-n* finster anblicken; **2.** *fig.* bedrohlich aussehen (*Himmel, Wolken etc.*); **3.** *fig.* drohen (*Ereignisse*).

low·er² ['ləʊə] **I** *v/t.* **1.** niedriger machen; **2.** *Augen, Gewehrlauf etc., a. Stimme, Preis, Kosten, Niveau, Temperatur, Ton etc.* senken; *fig. Moral* senken, *a. Widerstand etc.* schwächen; **3.** her'unter- *od.* hin'unterlassen, niederlassen; *Fahne, Segel* niederholen, *Rettungsboote* aussetzen; **4.** *fig.* erniedrigen: ***~ o.s.*** sich herablassen (*et. zu tun*); **II** *v/i.* **5.** sinken, fallen, sich senken.

low·er³ ['ləʊə] **I** *adj.* (*comp. von* ***low¹*** I) **1.** tiefer, niedriger; **2.** unter, Unter…: **2 *Chamber*** (*od.* ***House***) *parl.* Unter-, Abgeordnetenhaus *n*; ***the ~ class*** *sociol.* die untere Klasse *od.* Schicht; ***~ deck*** Unterdeck *n*; ***~ jaw*** Unterkiefer *m*; ***~ region*** Unterwelt *f* (*Hölle*); ***~ school*** Unter- u. Mittelstufe *f*; **3.** *geogr.* Unter…, Nieder…: **2 *Austria*** Niederösterreich *n*; **II** *adv.* **4.** tiefer: ***~ down the river*** (***list***) weiter unten am Fluß (auf der Liste).

low·er·ing ['laʊərɪŋ] *adj.* □ finster, düster, drohend.

low·er·most ['ləʊəməʊst] → ***lowest***.

low·est ['ləʊɪst] **I** *adj.* tiefst, niedrigst, unterst (*etc.*, → ***low¹*** I): ***~ bid*** ✝ Mindestgebot *n*; **II** *adv.* am tiefsten (*etc.*).

'**low**|-ˌ**fly·ing** *adj.* tieffliegend: ***~ plane*** Tiefflieger *m*; **~ fre·quen·cy** *s.* ϟ 'Niederfreˌquenz *f*; **2 Ger·man** *s. ling.* Niederdeutsch *n*, Plattdeutsch *n*; ˌ**~-'key**(**ed**) *adj.* gedämpft (*Farbe, Ton, Stimmung etc.*), *fig. a.* a) (sehr) zurückhaltend, b) bedrückt, c) unaufdringlich; '**~·land** [-lənd] **I** *s. oft pl.* Flach-, Tiefland *n*: ***the 2s*** das schottische Tiefland; **II** *adj.* Tiefland(s)…; '**~·land·er** [-ləndə] *s.* **1.** Tieflandbewohner(in); **2.** 2 (schottischer) Tieflände r; **2 Lat·in** *s. ling.* nichtklassisches La'tein; ˌ**~-'lev·el** *adj.* niedrig (*a. fig.*): ***~ officials***; ***~ talks*** *pol.* Gespräche *pl.* auf unterer Ebene; ***~ attack*** ✈ Tief(flieger)angriff *m*.

low·li·ness ['ləʊlɪnɪs] *s.* **1.** Niedrigkeit *f*; **2.** Bescheidenheit *f*.

low·ly ['ləʊlɪ] *adj. u. adv.* **1.** niedrig, gering, bescheiden; **2.** tief(stehend), primi'tiv, niedrig; **3.** demütig, bescheiden.

Low| **Mass** *s. R.C.* Stille Messe; ˌ**2-'mind·ed** *adj.* niedrig (gesinnt), gemein; ˌ**2-'necked** *adj.* tief ausgeschnitten (*Kleid*).

low·ness ['ləʊnɪs] *s.* **1.** Niedrigkeit *f* (*a. fig., contp.*); **2.** Tiefe *f* (*e-r Verbeugung, e-s Tons etc.*); **3.** ***~ of spirits*** Niedergeschlagenheit *f*; **4.** a) Gemeinheit *f*, b) ordi'näre Art.

ˌ**low**|-'**noise** *adj.* rauscharm (*Tonband*); ˌ**~-'pitched** *adj.* **1.** ♪ tief; **2.** mit geringer Steigung (*Dach*); **~ pres·sure** *s.* **1.** ⚙ Nieder-, 'Unterdruck *m*; **2.** *meteor.* Tiefdruck *m*; ˌ**~-'pres·sure** *adj.* a) Niederdruck…, b) *meteor.* Tiefdruck…; ˌ**~-'priced** *adj.* ✝ billig; ˌ**~-'spir·it·ed** *adj.* niedergeschlagen, gedrückt; **2 Sun·day** *s.* Weißer Sonntag (*erster Sonntag nach Ostern*); **~ ten·sion** *s.* ϟ Niederspannung *f*; ˌ**~-'ten·sion** *adj.* ϟ Niederspannungs…; **~ tide** *s.* ⚓ Niedrigwasser *n*; ˌ**~-'volt·age** *adj.* ϟ **1.** Niederspannungs…; **2.** Schwachstrom…; **~ wa·ter** *s.* ⚓ Ebbe *f*, Niedrigwasser *n*: ***be in ~*** *fig.* auf dem trockenen sitzen; ˌ**~-'wa·ter mark** *s.* **1.** ⚓ Niedrigwassermarke *f*; **2.** *fig.* Tiefpunkt *m*, -stand *m*.

loy·al ['lɔɪəl] *adj.* □ **1.** (***to***) loy'al (gegenüber), treu (ergeben) (*dat.*); **2.** (ge)treu (***to*** *dat.*); **3.** aufrecht, redlich; **loy·al·ist** ['lɔɪəlɪst] **I** *s.* Loya'list(in): a) *allg.* Treugesinnte(r *m*) *f*, b) *hist.* Königstreue(r *m*) *f*; **II** *adj.* loya'listisch; '**loy·al·ty** [-tɪ] *s.* Loyali'tät *f*, Treue *f* (***to*** zu, gegen).

loz·enge ['lɒzɪndʒ] *s.* **1.** *her.*, ✠ Raute *f*, Rhombus *m*; **2.** *pharm.* (*bsd.* 'Husten-) Paˌstille *f*.

lub·ber ['lʌbə] *s.* **1.** a) Flegel *m*, b) Trottel *m*; **2.** ⚓ Landratte *f*.

lu·bri·cant ['lu:brɪkənt] *s.* Gleit-, ⚙ Schmiermittel *n*; **lu·bri·cate** ['lu:brɪkeɪt] *v/t.* ⚙ *u. fig.* schmieren, ölen; **lu·bri·ca·tion** [ˌlu:brɪ'keɪʃn] *s.* ⚙ *u. fig.* Schmieren *n*, Schmierung *f*, Ölen *n*: ***~ chart*** Schmierplan *m*; ***~ point*** Schmierstelle *f*, -nippel *m*; '**lu·bri·ca·tor** [-keɪtə] *s.* ⚙ Öler *m*, Schmiervorrichtung *f*; **lu·bric·i·ty** [lu:'brɪsətɪ] *s.* **1.** Gleitfähigkeit *f*, Schlüpfrigkeit *f* (*a. fig.*); **2.** ⚙ Schmierfähigkeit *f*.

luce [lu:s] *s. ichth.* (ausgewachsener) Hecht.

lu·cent ['lu:snt] *adj.* **1.** glänzend, strahlend; **2.** 'durchsichtig, klar.

lu·cern(e) [lu:'sɜ:n] *s.* ⚘ Lu'zerne *f*.

lu·cid ['lu:sɪd] *adj.* □ **1.** *fig.* klar: ***~ interval*** *psych.* lichter Augenblick; **2.** → ***lucent***; **lu·cid·i·ty** [lu:'sɪdətɪ], '**lu·cid·ness** [-nɪs] *s. fig.* Klarheit *f*.

Lu·ci·fer ['lu:sɪfə] *s. bibl.* Luzifer *m* (*a. ast. Venus als Morgenstern*).

luck [lʌk] *s.* **1.** Schicksal *n*, Geschick *n*, Zufall *m*: ***as ~ would have it*** wie es der Zufall wollte, (un)glücklicherweise; ***bad*** (*od.* ***hard, ill***) ***~*** a) Unglück *n*, Pech *n*, b) *als Einschaltung*: Pech gehabt!; ***good ~*** Glück *n*; ***good ~!*** viel Glück!; Hals- u. Beinbruch!; ***worse ~*** unglücklicherweise, leider; ***be down on one's ~*** e-e Pechsträhne haben; ***just my ~!*** so geht es mir immer; **2.** Glück *n*: ***for ~*** als Glücksbringer; ***be in*** (***out of***) ***~*** (kein) Glück haben; ***try one's ~*** sein Glück versuchen; ***with ~*** mit ein bißchen Glück; ***here's ~!*** F Prost!; **luck·i·ly** ['lʌkɪlɪ] *adv.* zum Glück, glücklicherweise; **luck·i·ness** ['lʌkɪnɪs] *s.* Glück *n*; '**luck·less** [-lɪs] *adj.* □ glücklos.

luck·y ['lʌkɪ] *adj.* □ → ***luckily***; **1.** Glücks…, glücklich: ***a ~ day*** ein Glückstag; ***~ hit*** Glückstreffer *m*; ***be ~*** Glück haben; ***you ~ thing!*** F du Glückliche(r *m*) *f*!; ***you are ~ to be alive!*** du kannst von Glück sagen, daß du noch lebst!; ***it was ~ that*** ein Glück, daß …, zum Glück …; **2.** glückbringend, Glücks…: ***~ bag***, ***~ dip*** Glücksbeutel *m*, -topf *m*; ***~ star*** Glücksstern *m*.

lu·cra·tive ['lu:krətɪv] *adj.* □ einträglich, lukra'tiv.

lu·cre ['lu:kə] *s.* Gewinn(sucht *f*) *m*, Geld(gier *f*) *n*: ***filthy ~*** schnöder Mammon, gemeine Profitgier.

lu·di·crous ['lu:dɪkrəs] *adj.* □ **1.** lächerlich, ab'surd; **2.** spaßig, drollig.

lu·do ['lu:dəʊ] *s.* Mensch, ärgere dich nicht *n* (*Würfelspiel*).

lu·es ['lu:i:z] *s.* ⚕ Lues *f*, Syphilis *f*.

luff [lʌf] ⚓ **I** *s.* **1.** Luven *n*; **2.** Luv(seite) *f*, Windseite *f*; **II** *v/t. u. v/i.* **3.** *a.* ***~ up*** anluven.

luf·fa ['lʌfə] *s.* ⚘ *u.* ✝ Luffa *f*.

lug¹ [lʌg] *v/t.* zerren, schleppen: ***~ in*** *fig.* an den Haaren herbeiziehen, *Thema* (mit Gewalt) hineinbringen.

lug² [lʌg] *s.* **1.** (Leder)Schlaufe *f*; **2.** ⚙ a) Henkel *m*, Öhr *n*, b) Knagge *f*, Zinke *f*, c) Ansatz *m*; **3.** *Scot. od. Brit.* F Ohr *n*; **4.** *sl.* Trottel *m*.

luge [lu:ʒ] **I** *s.* Renn-, Rodelschlitten *m*; **II** *v/i.* rodeln.

lug·gage ['lʌgɪdʒ] *s. Brit.* Gepäck *n*; **~ boot** *s. mot.* Kofferraum *m*; **~ car·ri·er** *s.* Gepäckträger *m* (*am Fahrrad*); **~ in·sur·ance** *s.* (Reise)Gepäckversicherung *f*; **~ lock·er** *s.* (Gepäck)Schließfach *n*; **~ rack** *s.* **1.** Gepäcknetz *n*; **2.** *mot.* Gepäckträger *m*; **'~-van** *s.* Packwagen *m*.
lug·ger ['lʌgə] *s.* ⚓ Logger *m* (*Schiff*).
lu·gu·bri·ous [lu:'gu:brɪəs] *adj.* □ schwermütig, kummervoll.
Luke [lu:k] *npr. u. s. bibl.* 'Lukas(evanˌgelium *n*) *m*.
luke·warm ['lu:kwɔ:m] *adj.* □ lau (-warm); *fig.* lau; **'luke·warm·ness** [-nɪs] *s.* Lauheit *f* (*a. fig.*).
lull [lʌl] **I** *v/t.* **1.** *mst* **~ to sleep** einlullen (*a. fig.*); **2.** *fig.* beruhigen, *a. j-s Befürchtungen etc.* beschwichtigen: **~ into** (**a false sense of**) **security** in Sicherheit wiegen; **II** *s.* **3.** Pause *f*; **4.** (Wind-)Stille *f*, Flaute *f* (*a.* ✝), *fig. a.* Stille *f* (*vor dem Sturm*): **a ~ in conversation** e-e Gesprächspause.
lull·a·by ['lʌləbaɪ] *s.* Wiegenlied *n*.
lu·lu ['lu:lu:] *s. Am. sl.* ‚dolles Ding', schicke Sache.
lum·ba·go [lʌm'beɪgəʊ] *s.* ⚕ Hexenschuß *m*, Lum'bago *f*.
lum·bar ['lʌmbə] *adj. anat.* Lenden…, lum'bal.
lum·ber[1] ['lʌmbə] **I** *s.* **1.** *bsd. Am.* Bau-, Nutzholz *n*; **2.** Gerümpel *n*, Plunder *m*; **II** *v/t.* **3.** *bsd. Am. Holz* aufbereiten; **4.** *a.* **~ up** vollstopfen, -pfropfen.
lum·ber[2] ['lʌmbə] *v/i.* **1.** trampeln, trappen; **2.** (da'hin)rumpeln (*Fahrzeug*).
lum·ber·ing ['lʌmbərɪŋ] *adj.* □ schwerfällig.
'lum·ber|·jack *s. bsd. Am.* Holzfäller *m*; **'~jack·et** *s.* Lumberjack *m*; **~ mill** *s.* Sägewerk *n*; **~ room** *s.* Rumpelkammer *f*; **~ trade** *s.* (Bau)Holzhandel *m*; **~ yard** *s.* Holzplatz *m*.
lu·men ['lu:mən] *s. phys.* Lumen *n*.
lu·mi·nar·y ['lu:mɪnərɪ] *s.* Leuchtkörper *m*, *bsd. ast.* Himmelskörper *m*; *fig.* Leuchte *f* (*Person*); **lu·mi·nes·cence** [ˌlu:mɪ'nesns] *s.* Lumines'zenz *f*; **lu·mi·nes·cent** [ˌlu:mɪ'nesnt] *adj.* lumineszierend, leuchtend; **lu·mi·nos·i·ty** [ˌlu:mɪ'nɒsətɪ] *s.* **1.** Leuchten *n*, Glanz *m*; **2.** *ast.*, *phys.* Lichtstärke *f*, Helligkeit *f*; **'lu·mi·nous** [-nəs] *adj.* □ **1.** leuchtend, Leucht…(*-farbe*, *-kraft*, *-uhr*, *-zifferblatt etc.*), *bsd. phys.* Licht…(*-energie etc.*); **2.** *fig.* a) klar, b) lichtvoll, bril'lant.
lum·mox ['lʌməks] *s. Am.* F Trottel *m*.
lump [lʌmp] **I** *s.* **1.** Klumpen *m*: **have a ~ in one's throat** *fig.* e-n Kloß im Hals haben; **2.** a) Schwellung *f*, Beule *f*, b) Geschwulst *f*; **3.** Stück *n Zucker etc.*; **4.** *metall.* Luppe *f*; **5.** *fig.* Masse *f*: **all of** (*od.* **in**) **a ~** alles auf einmal; **in the ~** a) pauschal, in Bausch u. Bogen, b) im großen; **6.** F ‚Klotz' *m* (*langweiliger od. stämmiger Kerl*); **7. the ~** *Brit.* die Selbständigen *pl.* im Baugewerbe; **II** *adj.* **8.** Stück…: **~ coal**; **~ sugar** Würfelzucker *m*; **9.** Pauschal…(*-fracht*, *-summe etc.*); **III** *v/t.* **10.** *oft* **~ together** a) zs.-tun, -legen, b) *fig. a.* in 'einen Topf werfen, über 'einen Kamm scheren, c) *fig.* zs.-fassen; **11. if you don't like it you can ~ it** a) wenn es dir nicht paßt, kannst du's ja bleiben lassen, b) du wirst dich eben damit abfinden müssen; **IV** *v/i.* **12.** Klumpen bilden; **'lump·ish** [-pɪʃ] *adj.* □ **1.** schwerfällig, klobig, plump; **2.** dumm; **'lump·y** [-pɪ] *adj.* □ **1.** klumpig; **2.** → **lumpish** 1; **3.** ⚓ unruhig (*See*).
lu·na·cy ['lu:nəsɪ] *s.* ⚕ Wahn-, Irrsinn *m* (*a. fig.* F).
lu·nar ['lu:nə] *adj.* Mond…, Lunar…: **~ landing** Mondlandung *f*; **~ landing vehicle** Mondlandefahrzeug *n*; **~ module** Mondfähre *f*; **~ rock** Mondgestein *n*; **~ rover** Mondfahrzeug *n*; **~ year** Mondjahr *n*.
lu·na·tic ['lu:nətɪk] **I** *adj.* wahn-, irrsinnig, geisteskrank: **~ fringe** F *pol.* extremistische Randgruppe; **II** *s.* Wahnsinnige(r *m*) *f*, Irre(r *m*) *f*: **~ asylum** Irrenanstalt *f*.
lunch [lʌntʃ] **I** *s.* Mittagessen *n*, Lunch *m*: **~ break** Mittagspause *f*; **~ counter** Imbißbar *f*; **~ hour**, **~ time** Mittagszeit *f*, -pause *f*; **II** *v/i.* das Mittagessen einnehmen; **III** *v/t. j-n* zum Mittagessen einladen, beköstigen.
lunch·eon ['lʌntʃən] → **lunch**: **~ meat** Frühstücksfleisch *n*; **~ voucher** Essen(s)marke *f*; **lunch·eon·ette** [ˌlʌntʃə'net] *s. Am.* Imbißstube *f*.
lu·nette [lu:'net] *s.* **1.** Lü'nette *f*: a) ⚠ Halbkreis-, Bogenfeld *n*, b) ⚔ Brillschanze *f*, c) Scheuklappe *f* (*Pferd*); **2.** flaches Uhrglas.
lung [lʌŋ] *s. anat.* Lunge(nflügel *m*) *f*: **the ~s** die Lunge (*als Organ*); **~ power** Stimmkraft *f*.
lunge[1] [lʌndʒ] **I** *s.* **1.** *fenc.* Ausfall *m*, Stoß *m*; **2.** Satz *m od.* Sprung *m* vorwärts; **II** *v/i.* **3.** *fenc.* ausfallen (**at** gegen); **4.** sich stürzen (**at** auf *acc.*); **III** *v/t.* **5.** *Waffe etc.* stoßen.
lunge[2] [lʌndʒ] **I** *s.* Longe *f*, Laufleine *f* (*für Pferde*); **II** *v/t.* longieren.
lu·pin(e)[1] ['lu:pɪn] *s.* ⚘ Lu'pine *f*.
lu·pine[2] ['lu:paɪn] *adj.* Wolfs…, wölfisch.
lurch[1] [lɜ:tʃ] **I** *s.* **1.** Taumeln *n*, Torkeln *n*; **2.** ⚓ Schlingern *n*, Rollen *n*; **3.** Ruck *m*; **II** *v/i.* **4.** ⚓ schlingern; **5.** taumeln, torkeln.
lurch[2] [lɜ:tʃ] *s.*: **leave in the ~** *fig.* im Stich lassen.
lure [ljʊə] **I** *s.* **1.** Köder *m* (*a. fig.*); **2.** *fig.* Lockung *f*, Verlockungen *pl.*, Reiz *m*; **II** *v/t.* **3.** (an)locken, ködern: **~ away** fortlocken; **4.** verlocken (**into** zu).
lu·rid ['ljʊərɪd] *adj.* □ **1.** grell; **2.** fahl, gespenstisch (*Beleuchtung etc.*); **3.** *fig.* a) düster, finster, unheimlich, b) grausig, gräßlich.
lurk [lɜ:k] **I** *v/i.* **1.** lauern (*a. fig.*); **2.** *fig.* a) verborgen liegen, b) (heimlich) drohen; **3.** *a.* **~ about** *od.* **around** her'umschleichen; **II** *s.* **4. on the ~** auf der Lauer; **'lurk·ing** [-kɪŋ] *adj. fig.* versteckt, lauernd, heimlich.
lus·cious ['lʌʃəs] *adj.* □ **1.** köstlich, lekker, *a.* saftig; **2.** üppig; **3.** *Mädchen, Figur etc.*: prächtig, ‚knackig'.
lush[1] [lʌʃ] *adj.* □ ⚘ saftig, üppig (*a. fig.*).
lush[2] [lʌʃ] *s. Am. sl.* **1.** ‚Stoff' *m* (*Whisky etc.*); **2.** Säufer(in).
lust [lʌst] **I** *s.* **1.** a) (sinnliche) Begierde, b) (Sinnes)Lust *f*, Wollust *f*; **2.** Gier *f*, Gelüste *n*, Sucht *f* (**of**, **for** nach): **~ of power** Machtgier *f*; **~ for life** Lebensgier *f*; **II** *v/i.* **3.** gieren (**for**, **after** nach): **they ~ for power** es gelüstet sie nach Macht.
lus·ter ['lʌstə] *Am.* → **lustre**.
lust·ful ['lʌstfʊl] *adj.* □ wollüstig, geil, lüstern.
lust·i·ly ['lʌstɪlɪ] *adv.* kräftig, mächtig, mit Macht *od.* Schwung, *a.* aus voller Kehle *singen*.
lus·tre ['lʌstə] *s.* **1.** Glanz *m* (*a. min. u. fig.*); **2.** Lüster *m*: a) Kronleuchter *m*, b) *Halbwollgewebe*, c) *Glanzüberzug auf Porzellan etc.*; **'lus·tre·less** [-lɪs] *adj.* glanzlos, stumpf; **lus·trous** ['lʌstrəs] *adj.* □ glänzend.
lust·y ['lʌstɪ] *adj.* (□ → **lustily**) **1.** kräftig, gesund u. munter; **2.** lebhaft, voller Leben, schwungvoll; **3.** kräftig, kraftvoll.
lu·ta·nist ['lu:tənɪst] *s.* Lautenspieler (-in), Laute'nist(in).
lute[1] [lu:t] *s.* ♪ Laute *f*.
lute[2] [lu:t] **I** *s.* **1.** ⚙ Kitt *m*, Dichtungsmasse *f*; **2.** Gummiring *m*; **II** *v/t.* **3.** (ver)kitten.
lu·te·nist ['lu:tənɪst] → **lutanist**.
Lu·ther·an ['lu:θərən] **I** *s. eccl.* Luthe'raner(in); **II** *adj.* lutherisch; **'Lu·ther·an·ism** [-rənɪzəm] *s.* Luthertum *n*.
lu·tist ['lu:tɪst] → **lutanist**.
lux [lʌks] *pl.* **lux**, **'lux·es** *s. phys.* Lux *n* (*Einheit der Beleuchtungsstärke*).
lux·ate ['lʌkseɪt] *v/t.* ⚕ aus-, verrenken; **lux·a·tion** [lʌk'seɪʃn] *s.* Verrenkung *f*, Luxati'on *f*.
luxe [lʊks] *s.* Luxus *m*; → **de luxe**.
lux·u·ri·ance [lʌg'zjʊərɪəns], **lux'u·ri·an·cy** [-sɪ] *s.* **1.** Üppigkeit *f*; **2.** Fülle *f* (**of** an *dat.*), Pracht *f*; **lux'u·ri·ant** [-nt] *adj.* □ üppig (*Vegetation etc.*, *a. fig.*); **lux·u·ri·ate** [lʌg'zjʊərɪeɪt] *v/i.* **1.** schwelgen (*a. fig.*) (**in** in *dat.*); **2.** üppig wachsen *od.* gedeihen; **lux'u·ri·ous** [-rɪəs] *adj.* □ **1.** Luxus…, luxuri'ös, üppig; **2.** schwelgerisch, verschwenderisch (*Person*); **3.** genüßlich, wohlig; **lux·ury** ['lʌkʃərɪ] *s.* **1.** Luxus *m*: a) Wohlleben *n*: **live in ~** im Überfluß leben, b) (Hoch)Genuß *m*: **permit o.s. the ~ of doing** sich den Luxus gestatten, *et.* zu tun, c) Aufwand *m*, Pracht *f*; **2.** a) 'Luxusarˌtikel *m*, b) Genußmittel *n*.
lych gate [lɪtʃ] → **lich gate**.
lye [laɪ] *s.* ⚗ Lauge *f*.
ly·ing[1] ['laɪɪŋ] **I** *pres.p. von* **lie**[1]; **II** *adj.* lügnerisch, verlogen; **III** *s.* Lügen *n od. pl.*
ly·ing[2] ['laɪɪŋ] **I** *pres.p. von* **lie**[2]; **II** *adj.* liegend; **ˌ~-'in** *s.* a) Entbindung *f*, b) Wochenbett *n*: **~ hospital** Entbindungsanstalt *f*, -heim *n*.
lymph [lɪmf] *s.* **1.** Lymphe *f*: a) *physiol.* Gewebeflüssigkeit *f*, b) ⚕ Impfstoff *m*; **2.** *poet.* Quellwasser *n*; **lym·phat·ic** [lɪm'fætɪk] ⚕ **I** *adj.* lym'phatisch, Lymph…: **~ gland**; **II** *s.* Lymphgefäß *n*.
lynch [lɪntʃ] *v/t.* lynchen; **~ law** *s.* 'Lynchjuˌstiz *f*.
lynx [lɪŋks] *s. zo.* Luchs *m*; **'~-eyed** *adj. fig.* luchsäugig.
lyre ['laɪə] *s.* ♪, *ast.* Leier *f*, Lyra *f*.
lyr·ic ['lɪrɪk] **I** *adj.* (□ **~ally**) **1.** lyrisch (*a. fig.*); **2.** Musik…: **~ drama**; **II** *s.* **3.** a) lyrisches Gedicht, b) *pl.* Lyrik *f*; **4.**

pl. (Lied)Text *m*; ˈ**lyr·i·cal** [-kl] *adj.* □ → ***lyric*** I; ˈ**lyr·i·cism** [-ɪsɪzəm] *s.* **1.** Lyrik *f*, lyrischer Chaˈrakter *od.* Stil; **2.** Schwärmeˈrei *f*; ˈ**lyr·ist** [-ɪst] *s.* Lyriker(in).

M

M, m [em] *s.* M *n*, m *n* (*Buchstabe*).
ma [mɑː] *s.* F Ma'ma *f*.
ma'am [mæm] *s.* (*Anrede*) **1.** F *für* ***madam***; **2.** [mɑːm; mæm] *Brit.* a) Maje'stät (*Königin*), b) Hoheit (*Prinzessin*).
mac¹ [mæk] *s. Brit.* F → ***mackintosh***.
Mac² [mæk] *s. Am.* F ‚Chef' *m*.
ma·ca·bre [mə'kɑːbrə], *Am. a.* **ma'ca·ber** [-bə] *adj.* ma'kaber: a) grausig, b) Toten…
ma·ca·co [mə'keɪkəʊ] *s. zo.* Maki *m*.
mac·ad·am [mə'kædəm] **I** *s.* **1.** Maka'dam-, Schotterdecke *f*; **2.** Schotterstraße *f*; **3.** a) Maka'dam *m*, b) Schotter *m*; **II** *adj.* **4.** beschottert, Schotter…: ***~ road***; **mac'ad·am·ize** [-maɪz] *v/t.* makadamisieren.
mac·a·ro·ni [ˌmækə'rəʊnɪ] *s. sg. u. pl.* Makka'roni *pl*.
mac·a·roon [ˌmækə'ruːn] *s.* Ma'krone *f*.
ma·caw [mə'kɔː] *s. orn.* Ara *m*.
mac·ca·ro·ni → ***macaroni***.
mace¹ [meɪs] *s.* Mus'katblüte *f*.
mace² [meɪs] *s.* **1.** ⚔ *hist.* Streitkolben *m*; **2.** Amtsstab *m*; **3.** *a.* ***~-bearer*** Träger *m* des Amtsstabes; **4.** (***Chemical***) ⚘ (*TM*) chemische Keule (*Reizgas*).
mac·er·ate ['mæsəreɪt] *v/t.* **1.** (*a. v/i.*) (aufquellen u.) aufweichen; **2.** *biol. Nahrungsmittel* aufschließen; **3.** ausmergeln; **4.** ka'steien.
Mach [mɑːk] *s.* ⚔ *phys.* Mach *n*: ***at ~ two*** (mit) Mach 2 *fliegen*.
Mach·i·a·vel·li·an [ˌmækɪə'velɪən] *adj.* machiavel'listisch, skrupellos.
mach·i·nate ['mækɪneɪt] *v/i.* Ränke schmieden, intrigieren; **mach·i·na·tion** [ˌmækɪ'neɪʃn] *s.* Anschlag *m*, In'trige *f*, Machenschaft *f*, *pl. a.* Ränke; **'mach·i·na·tor** [-tə] *s.* Ränkeschmied *m*, Intri'gant(in).
ma·chine [mə'ʃiːn] **I** *s.* **1.** ⚙ Ma'schine *f* (F *a. Auto, Motorrad, Flugzeug etc.*); **2.** Appa'rat *m*, Vorrichtung *f*, (*thea.* 'Bühnen)Mechaˌnismus *m*: ***the god from the ~*** Deus *m* ex machina (*e-e plötzliche Lösung*); **3.** *fig.* ‚Ma'schine' *f*, ‚Roboter' *m* (*Mensch*); **4.** *pol.* (Par'tei)Maˌschine *f*, (Re'gierungs)Appaˌrat *m*; **II** *v/t.* **5.** ⚙ maschi'nell herstellen; maschi'nell drucken; (maschi'nell) bearbeiten; *engS. Metall* zerspanen; **~ age** *s.* Ma'schinenzeitalter *n*; **~ fit·ter** *s.* ⚙ Ma'schinenschlosser *m*; **~-gun** ⚔ **I** *s.* Ma'schinengewehr *n*; **II** *v/t.* mit Ma'schinengewehrfeuer belegen; **~ lan·guage** *s. Computer*: Ma'schinensprache *f*; **~-made** *adj.* **1.** maschi'nell (hergestellt), Fabrik…: ***~ paper*** Maschinenpapier *n*; **2.** *fig.* stereo'typ; **~ pis·tol** *s.* Ma'schinenpisˌtole *f*.
ma·chin·er·y [mə'ʃiːnərɪ] *s.* **1.** Maschine'rie *f*, Ma'schinen(park *m*) *pl.*; **2.** Mecha'nismus *m*, (Trieb)Werk *n*; **3.** *fig.* Maschine'rie *f*, Räderwerk *n*, (*Regierungs*)Ma'schine *f*; **4.** dra'matische Kunstmittel *pl*.
ma·chine| shop *s.* ⚙ Ma'schinenhalle *f*, -saal *m*; **~ tool** *s.* ⚙ 'Werkzeugmaˌschine *f*; **~-ˌwash·a·ble** *adj.* 'waschmaˌschinenfest (*Stoff etc.*).
ma·chin·ist [mə'ʃiːnɪst] *s.* **1.** ⚙ a) Ma'schineningeniˌeur *m*, b) Ma'schinenschlosser *m*, c) Maschi'nist *m* (*a. thea.*); **2.** Ma'schinennäherin *f*.
ma·chis·mo [mæ'tʃɪzməʊ] *s.* Ma'chismo *m*, Männlichkeitswahn *m*.
Mach num·ber [mɑːk] *s. phys.* Machzahl *f*.
ma·cho ['mætʃəʊ] **I** *s.* ‚Macho' *m*, ‚Kraft- *od.* Sexprotz' *m*; **II** *adj.* ‚macho', (betont) männlich.
mac·in·tosh → ***mackintosh***.
mack·er·el ['mækrəl] *pl.* **-el** *s. ichth.* Ma'krele *f*; **~ sky** *s. meteor.* (Himmel *m* mit) Schäfchenwolken *pl*.
Mack·i·naw ['mækɪnɔː] *s. a.* ***~ coat*** *Am.* Stutzer *m*, kurzer Plaidmantel.
mack·in·tosh ['mækɪntɒʃ] *s.* Regen-, Gummimantel *m*.
mack·le ['mækl] **I** *s.* **1.** dunkler Fleck; **2.** *typ.* Schmitz *m*, verwischter Druck; **II** *v/t. u. v/i.* **3.** *typ.* schmitzen.
ma·cle ['mækl] *s. min.* **1.** 'Zwillingskriˌstall *m*; **2.** dunkler Fleck.
macro- [mækrəʊ] *in Zssgn* Makro…, (sehr) groß: ***~climate*** Großklima *n*.
mac·ro·bi·ot·ic [ˌmækrəʊbaɪ'ɒtɪk] *adj.* makrobi'otisch; **ˌmac·ro·bi'ot·ics** [-ks] *s. pl. sg. konstr.* Makrobi'otik *f*.
mac·ro·cosm ['mækrəʊkɒzəm] *s.* Makro'kosmos *m*.
ma·cron ['mækrɒn] *s.* Längestrich *m* (*über Vokalen*).
mad [mæd] *adj.* □ → ***madly***; **1.** wahnsinnig, verrückt, toll (*alle a. fig.*): ***go ~*** verrückt werden; ***it's enough to drive one ~*** es ist zum Verrücktwerden; ***like ~*** wie toll *od.* wie verrückt (*arbeiten etc.*); ***a ~ plan*** ein verrücktes Vorhaben; → ***hatter***, ***drive*** 15; **2.** (***after***, ***about***, ***for***, ***on***) versessen (auf *acc.*), verrückt (nach), vernarrt (in *acc.*): ***she is ~ about music***; **3.** F außer sich, verrückt (***with*** vor *Freude*, *Schmerzen*, *Wut etc.*); **4.** *bsd. Am.* F wütend, böse (***at***, ***about*** über *acc.*, auf *acc.*); **5.** toll, wild, 'übermütig: ***they are having a ~ time*** bei denen geht's toll zu, sie amüsieren sich toll; **6.** wild (geworden): ***a ~ bull***; **7.** tollwütig (*Hund*).
Mad·a·gas·can [ˌmædə'gæskən] **I** *s.* Made'gasse *m*, Made'gassin *f*; **II** *adj.* made'gassisch.
mad·am ['mædəm] *s.* **1.** gnädige Frau *od.* gnädiges Fräulein (*Anrede*); **2.** Bor'dellwirtin *f*, Puffmutter *f*.
'mad·cap I *s.* ‚verrückter Kerl'; **II** *adj.* ‚verrückt', wild, verwegen.
mad·den ['mædn] **I** *v/t.* verrückt *od.* toll *od.* rasend machen (*a. fig. wütend machen*); **II** *v/i.* verrückt *etc.* werden; **'mad·den·ing** [-nɪŋ] *adj.* □ verrückt *etc.* machend: ***it is ~*** es ist zum Verrücktwerden.
mad·der¹ ['mædə] *comp. von* ***mad***.
mad·der² ['mædə] *s.* ⚘, ⚙ Krapp *m*.
mad·dest ['mædɪst] *sup. von* ***mad***.
mad·ding ['mædɪŋ] *adj. poet.* **1.** rasend, tobend: ***the ~ crowd***; **2.** → ***maddening***.
'mad-ˌdoc·tor *s.* Irrenarzt *m*.
made [meɪd] **I** *pret. u. p.p. von* ***make***; **II** *adj.* **1.** (künstlich) hergestellt: ***~ dish*** aus mehreren Zutaten zs.-gestelltes Gericht; ***~ gravy*** künstliche Bratensoße; ***~ road*** befestigte Straße; ***~ of wood*** aus Holz, Holz…; ***English-~*** ✝ *Artikel* englischer Fabrikation; **2.** gemacht, arriviert: ***a ~ man***; ***he had got it ~*** F er hatte es geschafft; **3.** *körperlich* gebaut: ***a well-~ man***.
ˌmade|-to-'meas·ure, **ˌ~-to-'or·der** *adj.* ✝ nach Maß angefertigt, Maß…, *a. fig.* maßgeschneidert, nach Maß; **ˌ~-'up** *adj.* **1.** (frei) erfunden: ***a ~ story***; **2.** geschminkt; **3.** ✝ Fertig…, Fabrik…: ***~ clothes*** Konfektionskleidung *f*.
'mad·house *s.* Irren-, *fig. a.* Tollhaus *n*.
mad·ly ['mædlɪ] *adv.* **1.** wie verrückt, wie wild: ***they worked ~ all night***; **2.** F schrecklich, wahnsinnig: ***~ in love***; **3.** verrückt(erweise).
'mad·man [-mən] *s.* [*irr.*] Verrückte(r) *m*, Irre(r) *m*.
mad·ness ['mædnɪs] *s.* **1.** Wahnsinn *m*, Tollheit *f* (*a. fig.*); **2.** *bsd. Am.* Wut *f* (***at*** über *acc.*).
mad·re·pore [ˌmædrɪ'pɔː] *s. zo.* Madre'pore *f*, 'Löcherkoˌralle *f*.
mad·ri·gal ['mædrɪgl] *s.* ♪ Madri'gal *n*.
'madˌwom·an *s.* [*irr.*] Wahnsinnige *f*, Irre *f*.
mael·strom ['meɪlstrɒm] *s.* Mahlstrom *m*, Strudel *m* (*a. fig.*): ***~ of traffic*** Verkehrsgewühl *n*.
Mae West [ˌmeɪ'west] *s. sl.* **1.** ⚓ aufblasbare Schwimmweste; **2.** ⚔ *Am.* Panzer *m* mit Zwillingsturm.
Maf·fi·a ['mæfɪə] → ***Mafia***.
maf·fick ['mæfɪk] *v/i. Brit. obs.* ausgelassen feiern.
Ma·fia ['mæfɪə] *s.* Mafia *f*; **ma·fi·o·so** [ˌmæfɪ'əʊsəʊ] *pl.* **-sos** *od.* **-si** [-sɪ] *s.* Mafi'oso *m*.
mag¹ [mæg] F *für* ***magazine*** 4.

mag² [mæg] ⚙ *sl. für* ***magneto***: **~-*generator*** Magnetodynamo *m*.

mag·a·zine [ˌmægəˈziːn] *s*. **1.** ⚔ a) (ˈPulver)Magaˌzin *n*, Munitiˈonslager *n*, b) Versorgungslager *n*, c) Magaˈzin *n* (*in Mehrladewaffen*): **~ *gun***, **~ *rifle*** Mehrladegewehr *n*; **2.** ⚙ Magaˈzin *n* (*a. Computer*), Vorratsbehälter *m*; **3.** ✝ Magaˈzin *n*, Speicher *m*, Lagerhaus *n*; *fig*. Vorrats-, Kornkammer *f* (*fruchtbares Gebiet*); **4.** Magaˈzin *n*, (*oft* illustrierte) Zeitschrift.

mag·da·len [ˈmægdəlɪn] *s*. *fig*. Magdaˈlena *f*, reuige Sünderin.

ma·gen·ta [məˈdʒentə] **I** *s*. ⚗ Maˈgenta (-rot) *n*, Fuchˈsin *n*; **II** *adj*. maˈgentarot.

mag·got [ˈmægət] *s*. **1.** *zo*. Made *f*, Larve *f*; **2.** *fig*. Grille *f*; ˈ**mag·got·y** [-tɪ] *adj*. **1.** madig; **2.** *fig*. schrullig.

Ma·gi [ˈmeɪdʒaɪ] *s*. *pl*.: ***the*** (***three***) **~** die (drei) Weisen aus dem Morgenland, die Heiligen Drei Könige.

mag·ic [ˈmædʒɪk] **I** *s*. **1.** Maˈgie *f*, Zaubeˈrei *f*; **2.** Zauber(kraft *f*) *m* (*a. fig*.): ***it works like* ~** es ist die reinste Hexerei; **II** *adj*. (□ **~*ally***) **3.** magisch, Wunder…, Zauber…: **~ *carpet*** fliegender Teppich; **~ *eye*** ⚡ magisches Auge; **~ *lamp*** Wunderlampe *f*; **~ *lantern*** Laterna *f* magica; **~ *square*** magisches Quadrat; **4.** zauberhaft: **~ *beauty***; ˈ**mag·i·cal** [-kl] → ***magic*** II.

ma·gi·cian [məˈdʒɪʃn] *s*. **1.** Magier *m*, Zauberer *m*; **2.** Zauberkünstler *m*.

mag·is·te·ri·al [ˌmædʒɪˈstɪərɪəl] *adj*. □ **1.** obrigkeitlich, behördlich; **2.** maßgeblich; **3.** herrisch.

mag·is·tra·cy [ˈmædʒɪstrəsɪ] *s*. **1.** ⚖, *pol*. *Amt e-s* ***magistrate***; **2.** Richterschaft *f*; **3.** *pol*. Verwaltung *f*; **mag·is·tral** [məˈdʒɪstrəl] *adj*. *pharm*. magiˈstral (*nach ärztlicher Vorschrift*); ˈ**mag·is·trate** [-reɪt] *s*. **1.** a) ⚖ Richter *m* (an e-m ***magistrates' court***), b) (***police***) **~** *Am*. Poliˈzeirichter *m*; **2.** (Verˈwaltungs)Beˌamte(r) *m*: ***chief* ~** *Am*. a) Präsiˈdent *m*, b) Gouverˈneur *m*, c) Bürgermeister *m*; **mag·is·trates' court** *s*. ⚖ *erstinstanzliches Gericht für einfache Fälle*.

Mag·na C(**h**)**ar·ta** [ˌmægnəˈkɑːtə] *s*. **1.** *hist*. Magna Charta *f* (*der große Freibrief des englischen Adels* [*1215*]); **2.** Grundgesetz *n*.

mag·na·nim·i·ty [ˌmægnəˈnɪmətɪ] *s*. Edelmut *m*, Großmut *f*; **mag·nan·i·mous** [mægˈnænɪməs] *adj*. □ großmütig, hochherzig.

mag·nate [ˈmægneɪt] *s*. **1.** Maˈgnat *m*: a) ˈGroßindustriˌelle(r) *m*, b) Großgrundbesitzer *m*; **2.** Größe *f*, einflußreiche Perˈsönlichkeit.

mag·ne·sia [mægˈniːʃə] *s*. ⚗ Maˈgnesia *f*, Maˈgnesiumoˌxyd *n*; **magˈne·sian** [-ʃn] *adj*. **1.** Magnesia…; **2.** Magnesium…; **magˈne·si·um** [-iːzjəm] *s*. ⚗ Maˈgnesium *n*.

mag·net [ˈmægnɪt] *s*. Maˈgnet *m* (*a. fig*.); **mag·net·ic** [mægˈnetɪk] *adj*. (□ **~*ally***) **1.** maˈgnetisch, Magnet…(*-feld, -kompaß, -nadel, -pol etc*.): **~ *attraction*** magnetische Anziehung(skraft) (*a. fig*.); **~ *declination*** Mißweisung *f*; **~ *tape recorder*** Magnettongerät *n*; **2.** *fig*. faszinierend, fesselnd, maˈgnetisch; **mag·net·ics** [mægˈnetɪks] *s*. *pl*. (*mst sg. konstr*.) Wissenschaft *f* vom Magneˈtismus; ˈ**mag·net·ism** [-tɪzəm] *s*. **1.** *phys*. Magneˈtismus *m*; **2.** *fig*. (maˈgnetische) Anziehungskraft; **mag·net·i·za·tion** [ˌmægnɪtaɪˈzeɪʃn] *s*. Magnetisierung *f*; ˈ**mag·net·ize** [-taɪz] *v/t*. **1.** magnetisieren; **2.** *fig*. (wie ein Maˈgnet) anziehen, fesseln; ˈ**mag·net·iz·er** [-taɪzə] *s*. ⚕ Magnetiˈseur *m*.

mag·ne·to [mægˈniːtəʊ] *pl*. **-tos** *s*. ⚡ Maˈgnetzünder *m*.

magneto- [mægniːtəʊ] *in Zssgn* Magneto…; **mag·ne·to-e·lec·tric** [mægˌniːtəʊɪˈlektrɪk] *adj*. maˈgneto-eˌlektrisch.

mag·ni·fi·ca·tion [ˌmægnɪfɪˈkeɪʃn] *s*. **1.** Vergrößern *n*; **2.** Vergrößerung *f*; **3.** *phys*. Vergrößerungsstärke *f*; **4.** ⚡ Verstärkung *f*.

mag·nif·i·cence [mægˈnɪfɪsns] *s*. Großartigkeit *f*, Herrlichkeit *f*; **magˈnif·i·cent** [-nt] *adj*. □ großartig, prächtig, herrlich (*alle a*. F *fig*.).

mag·ni·fi·er [ˈmægnɪfaɪə] *s*. **1.** Vergrößerungsglas *n*, Lupe *f*; **2.** ⚡ Verstärker *m*; **3.** Verherrlicher *m*; **mag·ni·fy** [ˈmægnɪfaɪ] *v/t*. *opt. u. fig*. **1.** vergrößern: **~*ing glass*** → ***magnifier*** 1; **2.** *fig*. aufbauschen; **3.** ⚡ verstärken.

mag·nil·o·quence [mægˈnɪləʊkwəns] *s*. **1.** Großsprecheˈrei *f*; **2.** Schwulst *m*, Bomˈbast *m*; **magˈnil·o·quent** [-nt] *adj*. □ **1.** großsprecherisch; **2.** hochtrabend, bomˈbastisch.

mag·ni·tude [ˈmægnɪtjuːd] *s*. Größe *f*, Größenordnung *f* (*a. ast*., ⚹), *fig. a*. Ausmaß *n*, Schwere *f*: ***a star of the first* ~** ein Stern erster Größe; ***of the first* ~** von äußerster Wichtigkeit.

mag·no·li·a [mægˈnəʊljə] *s*. ✿ Maˈgnolie *f*.

mag·num [ˈmægnəm] *s*. Zweiˈquartflasche *f* (*etwa 2 l enthaltend*); ˌ**~ ˈo·pus** [-ˈəʊpəs] *s*. Meister-, Hauptwerk *n*.

mag·pie [ˈmægpaɪ] *s*. **1.** *zo*. Elster *f*; **2.** *fig*. Schwätzer(in); **3.** *fig*. sammelwütiger Mensch; **4.** *Scheibenschießen*: zweiter Ring von außen.

ma·gus [ˈmeɪgəs] *pl*. **-gi** [-dʒaɪ] *s*. **1.** ♀ *antiq. persischer* Priester; **2.** Zauberer *m*; **3.** *a*. ♀ *sg. von* ***Magi***.

ma·ha·ra·ja(**h**) [ˌmɑːhəˈrɑːdʒə] *s*. Mahaˈradscha *m*; ˌ**ma·haˈra·nee** [-ɑːniː] *s*. Mahaˈrani *f*.

mahl·stick [ˈmɔːlstɪk] → ***maulstick***.

ma·hog·a·ny [məˈhɒgənɪ] **I** *s*. **1.** ✿ Mahaˈgonibaum *m*; **2.** Mahaˈgoni(holz) *n*; **3.** Mahaˈgoni(farbe *f*) *n*; **4.** ***have*** (*od*. ***put***) ***one's feet under s.o.'s* ~** F j-s Gastfreundschaft genießen; **II** *adj*. **5.** Mahagoni…; **6.** mahaˈgonifarben.

ma·hout [məˈhaʊt] *s*. *Brit. Ind*. Eleˈfantentreiber *m*.

maid [meɪd] *s*. **1.** (junges) Mädchen, *poet. u. iro*. Maid *f*: **~ *of hono*(*u*)*r*** a) Ehren-, Hofdame *f*, b) *Am*. *erste* Brautjungfer; ***old* ~** alte Jungfer; **2.** (Dienst-) Mädchen *n*, Magd *f*: **~-*of-all-work*** *bsd. fig*. Mädchen für alles; **3.** *poet*. Jungfrau *f*: ***the* ♀ (*of Orleans*)**.

maid·en [ˈmeɪdn] **I** *adj*. **1.** mädchenhaft, Mädchen…: **~ *name*** Mädchenname *e-r Frau*; **2.** jungfräulich, unberührt (*a. fig*.): **~ *soil***; **3.** unverheiratet: **~ *aunt***; **4.** Jungfern…, Antritts…: **~ *flight*** ✈ Jungfernflug *m*; **~ *speech*** *parl*. Jungfernrede *f*; **~ *voyage*** ⚓ Jungfernfahrt *f*; **II** *s*. **5.** → ***maid*** 1; **6.** *Scot. hist*. Guilloˈtine *f*; **7.** *Rennsport*: a) Maiden *n* (*Pferd, das noch nie gesiegt hat*), b) Rennen *n* für Maidens; ˈ**~·hair** (**fern**) *s*. ✿ Frauenhaar(farn *m*) *n*; ˈ**~·head** *s*. **1.** → ***maidenhood***; **2.** *anat*. Jungfernhäutchen *n*; ˈ**~·hood** [-hʊd] *s*. **1.** Jungfräulichkeit *f*, Jungfernschaft *f*; **2.** Jungˈmädchenzeit *f*.

maid·en·like [ˈmeɪdnlaɪk], ˈ**maid·en·ly** [-lɪ] *adj*. **1.** → ***maiden*** 1; **2.** jungfräulich, züchtig.

ˈ**maidˌserv·ant** → ***maid*** 2.

mail¹ [meɪl] **I** *s*. **1.** Post(sendung) *f*, *bsd*. Brief- *od*. Paˈketpost *f*: ***by* ~** *Am*. mit der Post; ***by return* ~** *Am*. postwendend, umgehend; ***incoming* ~** Posteingang *m*; ***outgoing* ~** Postausgang *m*; **2.** Briefbeutel *m*, Postsack *m*; **3.** Post (-dienst *m*) *f*: ***the Federal* ♀*s*** *Am*. die Bundespost; **4.** Postversand *m*; **5.** Postauto *n*, -boot *n*, -bote *m*, -flugzeug *n*, -zug *m*; **II** *adj*. **6.** Post…: **~-*boat*** Post-, Paketboot *n*; **III** *v/t*. **7.** *bsd. Am*. (ab-) schicken, aufgeben; zuschicken (***to*** *dat*.): **~*ing list*** ✝ Adressenliste *f*, -kartei *f*.

mail² [meɪl] **I** *s*. **1.** Kettenpanzer *m*: ***coat of* ~** Panzerhemd *n*; **2.** (Ritter-) Rüstung *f*; **3.** *zo*. Panzer *m*; **II** *v/t*. **4.** panzern.

mail·a·ble [ˈmeɪləbl] *adj*. *Am*. postversandfähig.

ˈ**mail**|**·bag** *s*. Postbeutel *m*; ˈ**~·box** *s*. *Am*. Briefkasten *m*; ˈ**~·car** *s*. *Am*. Postwagen *m*; ˈ**~ˌcar·ri·er** *s*. → ***mailman***; ˈ**~-clad** *adj*. gepanzert; ˈ**~·coach** *s*. *Brit*. **1.** Postwagen *m*; **2.** *hist*. Postkutsche *f*.

mailed [meɪld] *adj*. gepanzert (*a. zo*.): ***the* ~ *fist*** *fig*. die eiserne Faust.

ˈ**mail**|**·man** [-mən] *s*. [*irr*.] *Am*. Briefträger *m*; **~ or·der** *s*. ✝ Bestellung *f* (*von Waren*) durch die Post; ˈ**~-ˌor·der** *adj*. Postversand…: **~ *business*** Versandhandel *m*; **~ *catalog*(*ue*)** Versandhauskatalog *m*; **~ *house*** (Post)Versandgeschäft *n*.

maim [meɪm] *v/t*. verstümmeln (*a. fig. Text*); zum Krüppel machen; lähmen (*a. fig*.).

main [meɪn] **I** *adj*. □ → ***mainly***; **1.** Haupt…, größt, wichtigst, vorwiegend, hauptsächlich: **~ *clause*** *ling*. Hauptsatz *m*; **~ *deck*** ⚓ Hauptdeck *n*; **~ *girder*** ⚠ Längsträger *m*; **~ *office*** Hauptbüro *n*; **~ *road*** Hauptverkehrsstraße *f*; ***the* ~ *sea*** die offene *od*. hohe See; **~ *station*** a) *teleph*. Hauptanschluß *m*, b) Hauptbahnhof *m*; ***the* ~ *thing*** die Hauptsache; ***by* ~ *force*** mit äußerster Kraft, mit (aller) Gewalt; **2.** ⚓ groß, Groß…: **~ *brace*** Großbrasse *f*; **II** *s*. **3.** *mst pl*. a) Haupt(gas- *etc*.)leitung *f*: (***gas***) **~*s***; (***water***) **~*s***, b) ⚡ Haupt-, Stromleitung *f*, c) (Strom)Netz *n*: ***operating on the* ~*s***, **~*s-operated*** mit Netzanschluß *od*. -betrieb; **~*s adapter*** Netzteil *n*; **~*s failure*** Stromausfall *m*; **~*s voltage*** Netzspannung *f*; **4.** a) Hauptrohr *n*, b) Hauptkabel *n*; **5.** 🚂 *Am*. Hauptlinie *f*; **6.** Hauptsache *f*, Kern *m*: ***in*** (*Am. a*. ***for***) ***the* ~** hauptsächlich, in der Hauptsache; **7.** *poet*. *die* hohe See; **8.** → ***might***¹ 2; **~ chance** *s*.: ***have an eye to the* ~** s-n eigenen Vorteil im Auge haben; ˈ**~·frame** *s*. *Computer*: Großrechner *m*; **~ fuse** *s*. ⚡ Hauptsicherung *f*; ˈ**~·land** [-lənd] *s*.

Festland *n*; **~ line** *s.* **1.** 🚂 *etc.*, *a.* ⚔ Hauptlinie *f*: **~ *of resistance*** Hauptkampflinie *f*; **2.** *Am.* Hauptverkehrsstraße *f*; **3.** *sl.* a) Hauptvene *f*, b) ‚Schuß' *m* (*Heroin etc.*); **'~·line** *v/i. sl.* ‚fixen'; **'~ˌlin·er** *s. sl.* ‚Fixer(in)'.

main·ly ['meɪnlɪ] *adv.* hauptsächlich, vorwiegend.

main|·mast ['meɪnmɑːst; ⚓ -məst] *s.* ⚓ Großmast *m*; **~·sail** ['meɪnseɪl; ⚓ -sl] *s.* ⚓ Großsegel *n*; **'~·spring** *s.* **1.** Hauptfeder *f* (*Uhr etc.*); **2.** *fig.* (Haupt)Triebfeder *f*, treibende Kraft; **'~·stay** *s.* **1.** ⚓ Großstag *n*; **2.** *fig.* Hauptstütze *f*; **'~·stream** *s. fig.* Hauptströmung *f*; ♀ **Street** *adj. Am.* provinzi'ell-materia'listisch.

main·tain [meɪn'teɪn] *v/t.* **1.** *Zustand*, *gute Beziehungen etc.* (aufrecht)erhalten, *e-e Haltung etc.* beibehalten, *Ruhe u. Ordnung etc.* (be)wahren: **~ *a price*** † e-n Preis halten; **2.** in'stand halten, pflegen, ⚙ *a.* warten; **3.** *Briefwechsel etc.* unter'halten, (weiter)führen; **4.** (*in e-m bestimmten Zustand*) lassen, bewahren: **~ *s.th. in (an) excellent condition***; **5.** *Familie etc.* unter'halten, versorgen; **6.** behaupten (***that*** daß, ***to*** zu); **7.** *Meinung*, *Recht etc.* verfechten; auf *e-r Forderung* bestehen: **~ *an action*** ⚖ e-e Klage anhängig machen; **8.** *j-n* unter'stützen, *j-m* beipflichten; ⚖ *e-e Prozeßpartei* 'widerrechtlich unterstützen; **9.** nicht aufgeben, behaupten: **~ *one's ground*** *bsd. fig.* sich behaupten; **main'tain·a·ble** [-nəbl] *adj.* verfechtbar, haltbar; **main'tain·er** [-nə] *s.* Unter'stützer *m*: a) Verfechter *m* (*Meinung etc.*), b) Versorger *m*; **main'tain·or** [-nə] *s.* ⚖ außenstehender Pro'zeßtreiber; **main·te·nance** ['meɪntənəns] *s.* **1.** In'standhaltung *f*, Erhaltung *f*; **2.** ⚙ Wartung *f*: **~ *man*** Wartungsmonteur *m*; **~-*free*** wartungsfrei; **3.** 'Unterhalt(smittel *pl.*) *m*: **~ *grant*** Unterhaltszuschuß *m*; **~ *order*** ⚖ Anordnung *f* von Unterhaltszahlungen; **4.** Aufrechterhaltung *f*, Beibehalten *n*; **5.** Behauptung *f*, Verfechtung *f*; **6.** ⚖ 'illeˌgale Unter'stützung e-r pro'zeßführenden Par'tei.

'main|·top *s.* ⚓ Großmars *m*; **~ yard** *s.* ⚓ Großrah(e) *f*.

mai·son·(n)ette [ˌmeɪzə'net] *s.* **1.** Maiso'nette *f*; **2.** Einliegerwohnung *f*.

maize [meɪz] *s. Brit.* ♀ Mais *m*.

ma·jes·tic [mə'dʒestɪk] *adj.* (□ **~ally**) maje'stätisch; **maj·es·ty** ['mædʒəstɪ] *s.* **1.** Maje'stät *f*: ***His (Her)*** ♀ Seine (Ihre) Majestät; ***Your*** ♀ Eure Majestät; **2.** *fig.* Maje'stät *f*, Erhabenheit *f*, Hoheit *f*.

ma·jol·i·ca [mə'jɒlɪkə] *s.* Ma'jolika *f*.

ma·jor ['meɪdʒə] **I** *s.* **1.** Ma'jor *m*; **2.** ⚖ Volljährige(r *m*) *f*, Mündige(r *m*) *f*; **3.** *hinter Eigennamen*: der Ältere; **4.** ♪ a) Dur *n*, b) 'Durakˌkord *m*, c) Durtonart *f*; **5.** *phls.* a) *a.* **~ *term*** Oberbegriff *m*, b) *a.* **~ *premise*** Obersatz *m*; **6.** *univ. Am.* Hauptfach *n*; **II** *adj.* **7.** größer (*a. fig.*); *fig.* bedeutend: **~ *attack*** Großangriff *m*; **~ *event*** *bsd. sport* Großveranstaltung *f*, *weitS.* ‚große Sache'; **~ *repair*** größere Reparatur; **~ *shareholder*** Großaktionär(in); → ***operation*** 9; **8.** ⚖ volljährig, mündig; **9.** ♪ a) groß (*Terz etc.*), b) Dur...: **~ *key*** Durtonart *f*; ***C* ~** C-Dur *n*; **III** *v/t.* **10.** (*v/i.* **~ *in***) *Am.* als Hauptfach studieren; **ˌ~-'gen·er·al** *s.* ⚔ Gene'ralmaˌjor *m*.

ma·jor·i·ty [mə'dʒɒrətɪ] *s.* **1.** Mehrheit *f*: **~ *of votes*** (Stimmen)Mehrheit, Majori'tät *f*; **~ *decision*** Mehrheitsbeschluß *m*; **~ *leader*** *Am.* Fraktionsführer *m* der Mehrheitspartei; **~ *rule*** Mehrheitsregierung *f*; ***in the ~ of cases*** in der Mehrzahl der Fälle; ***join the ~*** a) sich der Mehrheit anschließen, b) zu den Vätern versammelt werden (*sterben*); ***win by a large ~*** mit großer Mehrheit gewinnen; **2.** ⚖ Voll-, Großjährigkeit *f*; **3.** ⚔ Ma'jorsrang *m*, -stelle *f*.

ma·jor| league *s. sport Am.* oberste Spielklasse; **~ mode** *s.* ♪ Dur(tonart *f*) *n*; **~ scale** *s.* Durtonleiter *f*.

ma·jus·cule ['mædʒəskjuːl] *s.* Ma'juskel *f*, großer Anfangsbuchstabe.

make [meɪk] **I** *s.* **1.** a) Mach-, Bauart *f*, Form *f*, b) Erzeugnis *n*, Fabri'kat *n*: ***our own ~*** (unser) eigenes Fabrikat; ***of best English ~*** beste englische Quali'tät; **2.** *Mode*: Schnitt *m*, Fas'son *f*; **3.** † a) (Fa'brik)Marke *f*, b) ⚙ Typ *m*, Bau (-art *f*) *m*; **4.** (*Körper*)Bau *m*; **5.** Anfertigung *f*, Herstellung *f*; **6.** ⚡ Schließen *n* (*Stromkreis*): ***be at ~*** geschlossen sein; **7.** ***be on the ~*** *sl.* a) auf Geld (*od.* e-n Vorteil) aussein, ‚schwer dahinterher' sein, b) auf ein (sexuelles) Abenteuer aussein; **II** *v/t.* [*irr.*] **8.** *allg. z. B. Einkäufe*, *Einwände*, *Feuer*, *Reise*, *Versuch* machen; *Frieden* schließen; *e-e Rede* halten; → ***face*** 2, ***war*** 1 *etc.*; **9.** machen: a) anfertigen, herstellen, erzeugen (***from***, ***of***, ***out of*** von, aus), b) verarbeiten, bilden, formen (***to***, ***into*** in *acc.*, zu), c) *Tee etc.* (zu)bereiten, d) *Gedicht etc.* verfassen; **10.** errichten, bauen, *Garten*, *Weg etc.* anlegen; **11.** (er)schaffen: ***God made man*** Gott schuf den Menschen; ***you are made for this job*** du bist für diese Arbeit wie geschaffen; **12.** *fig.* machen zu: ***he made her his wife***; ***to ~ enemies of*** sich zu Feinden machen; **13.** ergeben, bilden, entstehen lassen: ***many brooks ~ a river***; ***oxygen and hydrogen ~ water*** Wasserstoff u. Sauerstoff bilden Wasser; **14.** verursachen: a) *ein Geräusch*, *Lärm*, *Mühe*, *Schwierigkeiten* machen, b) bewirken, (mit sich) bringen: ***prosperity ~s contentment***; **15.** (er)geben, den Stoff abgeben zu, dienen als (*Sache*): ***this ~s a good article*** das gibt e-n guten Artikel; ***this book ~s good reading*** dieses Buch liest sich gut; **16.** sich erweisen als (*Person*): ***he would ~ a good salesman*** er würde e-n guten Verkäufer abgeben; ***she made him a good wife*** sie war ihm e-e gute Frau; **17.** bilden, (aus)machen: ***this ~s the tenth time*** das ist das zehnte Mal; → ***difference*** 1, ***one*** 6, ***party*** 2; **18.** (*mit adj., p.p. etc.*) machen: **~ *angry*** zornig machen, erzürnen; **~ *known*** bekanntmachen, -geben; → ***make good***; **19.** (*mit folgendem s.*) machen zu, ernennen zu: ***they made him a general, he was made a general*** er wurde zum General ernannt; ***he made himself a martyr*** er wurde zum Märtyrer; **20.** *mit inf.* (*act. ohne* ***to***, *pass. mit* ***to***) *j-n* veranlassen, lassen, bringen, zwingen *od.* nötigen zu: **~ *s.o. wait*** j-n warten lassen; ***we made him talk*** wir brachten ihn zum Sprechen; ***they made him repeat it*** man ließ es ihn wiederholen; **~ *s.th. do***, **~ *do with s.th.*** mit et. auskommen, sich mit et. behelfen; **21.** *fig.* machen: **~ *much of*** a) viel Wesens um *et. od. j-n* machen, b) sich viel aus *et.* machen, viel von *et.* halten; → ***best*** 7, ***most*** 3, ***nothing*** *Redew.*; **22.** sich e-e Vorstellung von *et.* machen, *et.* halten für: ***what do you ~ of it?*** was halten Sie davon?; **23.** F *j-n* halten für: ***I ~ him a greenhorn***; **24.** schätzen auf (*acc.*): ***I ~ the distance three miles***; **25.** feststellen: ***I ~ it a quarter to five*** nach m-r Uhr ist es viertel vor fünf; **26.** erfolgreich 'durchführen: → ***escape*** 9; **27.** *j-m* zum Erfolg verhelfen, *j-s* Glück machen: ***I can ~ and break you*** ich kann aus Ihnen et. machen oder Sie auch fertigmachen; **28.** sich *ein Vermögen etc.* erwerben, verdienen, *Geld*, *Profit* machen, *Gewinn* erzielen; → ***name*** *Redew.*; **29.** ‚schaffen': a) *Strecke* zu'rücklegen: ***can we ~ it in 3 hours?***, b) *Geschwindigkeit* erreichen: **~ *60 mph.***; **30.** F *et.* erreichen, ‚schaffen', *akademischen Grad* erlangen, *sport etc. Punkte*, *a. Schulnote* erzielen, *Zug* erwischen: **~ *it*** es schaffen; **~ *the team*** in die Mannschaft aufgenommen werden; **31.** *sl. Frau* ‚'umlegen' (*verführen*); **32.** ankommen in (*dat.*), erreichen: **~ *port*** ⚓ in den Hafen einlaufen; **33.** ⚓ sichten, ausmachen: **~ *land***; **34.** *Brit. Mahlzeit* einnehmen; **35.** *Fest etc.* veranstalten; **36.** *Preis* festsetzen, machen; **37.** *Kartenspiel*: a) *Karten* mischen, b) *Stich* machen; **38.** ⚡ *Stromkreis* schließen; **39.** *ling. Plural etc.* bilden, werden zu; **40.** sich belaufen auf (*acc.*), ergeben, machen: ***two and two ~ four*** 2 u. 2 macht *od.* ist 4; **III** *v/i.* [*irr.*] **41.** sich anschicken, den Versuch machen (***to do*** zu tun): ***he made to go*** er wollte gehen; **42.** (***to*** nach) a) sich begeben *od.* wenden, b) führen, gehen (*Weg etc.*), sich erstrecken, c) fließen; **43.** einsetzen (*Ebbe*, *Flut*), (an)steigen (*Flut etc.*); **44.** **~ *as if*** (*od.* ***as though***) so tun als ob *od.* als wenn: **~ *believe*** (***that*** *od.* ***to do***) vorgeben (daß *od.* zu tun); **45.** **~ *like*** *Am. sl.* sich verhalten wie: **~ *like a father***;

Zssgn mit prp.:

make| aft·er *v/i. obs. j-m* nachsetzen, *j-n* verfolgen; **~ a·gainst** *v/i.* **1.** ungünstig sein für, schaden (*dat.*); **2.** sprechen gegen (*a. fig.*); **~ for** *v/i.* **1.** a) zugehen auf (*acc.*), sich aufmachen nach, zustreben (*dat.*), b) ⚓ lossteuern (*a. fig.*) *od.* Kurs haben auf (*acc.*), c) sich stürzen auf (*acc.*); **2.** beitragen zu, förderlich sein *od.* dienen (*dat.*): ***it makes for his advantage*** es wirkt sich für ihn günstig aus; ***the aerial makes for better reception*** die Antenne verbessert den Empfang; **~ to·ward(s)** *v/i.* zugehen auf (*acc.*), sich bewegen nach, sich nähern (*dat.*); **~ with** *v/i. Am. sl.* loslegen mit: **~ *the feet!*** nun lauf schon!

Zssgn mit adv.:

make| a·way *v/i.* sich da'vonmachen: **~ *with*** a) sich davonmachen mit (*Geld etc.*), b) *et. od. j-n* beseitigen, aus dem Weg(e) räumen, c) *Geld etc.* durchbringen, d) sich entledigen (*gen.*); ~ **good I** *v/t.* **1.** a) (wieder)'gutmachen, b) ersetzen, vergüten: ~ ***a deficit*** ein Defizit decken; **2.** begründen, rechtfertigen, nachweisen; **3.** *Versprechen, sein Wort* halten; **4.** *den Erwartungen* entsprechen; **5.** *Flucht etc.* glücklich bewerkstelligen; **6.** (*berufliche etc.*) *Stellung* ausbauen; **II** *v/i.* **7.** sich 'durchsetzen, sein Ziel erreichen; **8.** sich bewähren, den Erwartungen entsprechen; ~ **off** *v/i.* sich da'vonmachen, ausreißen (***with*** mit *Geld etc.*); ~ **out I** *v/t.* **1.** *Scheck etc.* ausstellen; *Urkunde* ausfertigen; *Liste etc.* aufstellen; **2.** ausmachen, erkennen; **3.** *Sachverhalt etc.* feststellen, her'ausbekommen; **4.** a) *j-n* ausfindig machen, b) aus *j-m od. et.* klug werden; **5.** entziffern; **6.** a) behaupten, b) beweisen, c) *j-n als Lügner etc.* hinstellen; **7.** *Am.* *mühsam* zustande bringen; **8.** *Summe* voll machen; **9.** halten für; **II** *v/i.* **10.** *bsd. Am.* F Erfolg haben: ***how did you ~?*** wie haben Sie abgeschnitten?; **11.** *bsd. Am.* (*mit j-m*) auskommen; **12.** vorgeben, (so) tun (als ob); ~ **o·ver** *v/t.* **1.** *Eigentum* über'tragen, -'eignen, vermachen; **2.** 'umbauen; *Anzug etc.* 'umarbeiten, ~ **up I** *v/t.* **1.** bilden, zs.-setzen: ***be made up of*** bestehen *od.* sich zs.-setzen aus; **2.** *Arznei, Bericht etc.* zs.-stellen; *Schriftstück* aufsetzen, *Liste etc.* aufstellen; *Paket* (ver-) packen, verschnüren; **3.** *a. thea.* zu'rechtmachen, schminken, pudern; **4.** *Geschichte etc.* sich ausdenken, *a. b.s.* erfinden: ***a made-up story***; **5.** a) *Versäumtes* nachholen; → ***leeway*** 2, b) 'wiedergewinnen: ~ ***lost ground***; **6.** ersetzen, vergüten; **7.** *Rechnung, Konten* ausgleichen; *Bilanz* ziehen; → ***account*** 5; **8.** *Streit etc.* beilegen; **9.** ver'vollständigen, *Fehlendes* ergänzen, *Betrag, Gesellschaft etc.* voll machen; **10.** ***make it up*** a) es wieder'gutmachen, b) → 17; **11.** *typ.* um'brechen; **II** *v/i.* **12.** sich zu'rechtmachen, *bsd.* sich pudern *od.* schminken; **13.** (***for***) Ersatz leisten, als Ersatz dienen (für), vergüten (*acc.*); **14.** aufholen, wieder'gutmachen, wettmachen (***for*** *acc.*): ~ ***for lost time*** die verlorene Zeit wieder wettzumachen suchen; **15.** *Am.* sich nähern (***to*** *dat.*); **16.** (***to***) F (*j-m*) schöntun, sich anbiedern (bei *j-m*), sich her'anmachen (an *j-n*); **17.** sich versöhnen *od.* wieder vertragen (***with*** mit).

make| and break *s.* ⚡ Unter'brecher *m*; **ˌ~-and-'break** *adj.* ⚡ zeitweilig unter'brochen: ~ ***contact*** Unterbrecherkontakt *m*; **'~-beˌlieve I** *s.* **1.** a) Verstellung *f*, b) Heuche'lei *f*; **2.** Vorwand *m*; **3.** Schein *m*, Spiegelfechte'rei *f*; **II** *adj.* **4.** vorgeblich, scheinbar, falsch: ~ ***world*** Scheinwelt *f*.

mak·er ['meɪkə] *s.* **1.** a) Macher *m*, Verfertiger *m*; Aussteller(in) *e-r Urkunde*, b) ✝ Hersteller *m*, Erzeuger *m*; **2. *the* ♀** der Schöpfer (*Gott*): ***meet one's ~*** das Zeitliche segnen.

'make|-ˌread·y *s. typ.* Zurichtung *f*; **'~·shift I** *s.* Notbehelf *m*; **II** *adj.* behelfsmäßig, Behelfs…, Not…

'make-up *s.* **1.** Aufmachung *f*: a) *Film etc.*: Ausstattung *f*, Kostümierung *f*, Maske *f*: ~ ***man*** Maskenbildner *m*, b) Verpackung *f*, ✝ Ausstattung *f*: ~ ***charge*** *Schneiderei*: Macherlohn *m*; **2.** Schminke *f*, Puder *m*; **3.** Make-up *n*: a) Schminken *n*, b) Pudern *n*; **4.** *fig. humor.* Aufmachung *f*, (Ver)Kleidung *f*; **5.** Zs.-setzung *f*; *sport* (*Mannschafts-*) Aufstellung *f*; **6.** Körperbau *m*; **7.** Veranlagung *f*, Na'tur *f*; **8.** *fig. humor. Am.* erfundene Geschichte; **9.** *typ.* 'Umbruch *m*.

'make·weight *s.* **1.** (Gewichts)Zugabe *f*, Zusatz *m*; **2.** Gegengewicht *n* (*a. fig.*); **3.** *fig.* a) Lückenbüßer *m* (*Person*), b) Notbehelf *m*.

mak·ing ['meɪkɪŋ] *s.* **1.** Machen *n*: ***this is of my own ~*** das habe ich selbst gemacht; **2.** Erzeugung *f*, Herstellung *f*, Fabrikati'on *f*: ***be in the ~*** *a. fig.* im Werden *od.* im Kommen *od.* in der Entwicklung sein; **3.** a) Zs.-setzung *f*, b) Verfassung *f*, c) Bau(art *f*) *m*, Aufbau *m*, d) Aufmachung *f*; **4.** Glück *n*, Chance *f*: ***this will be the ~ of him*** damit ist er ein gemachter Mann; **5.** *pl.* ('Roh)Materiˌal *n* (*a. fig.*): ***he has the ~s of*** er hat das Zeug *od.* die Anlagen zu; **6.** *pl.* Pro'fit *m*, Verdienst *m*; **7.** *pl.* F *die* (nötigen) Zutaten *pl.*

mal- [mæl] *in Zssgn* a) schlecht, b) mangelhaft, c) übel, d) Miß…, un…

Mal·a·chi ['mæləkaɪ], *a.* **Mal·a·chi·as** [ˌmælə'kaɪəs] *npr. u. s. bibl.* (das Buch) Male'achi *m od.* Mala'chias *m*.

mal·a·chite ['mæləkaɪt] *s. min.* Mala'chit *m*, Kupferspat *m*.

mal·ad·just·ed [ˌmælə'dʒʌstɪd] *adj. psych.* nicht angepaßt, mi'lieugestört; **ˌmal·ad'just·ment** [-smənt] *s.* **1.** mangelnde Anpassung, Mi'lieustörung *f*; **2.** ⚙ Falscheinstellung *f*; **3.** 'Mißverhältnis *n*.

'mal·adˌmin·is'tra·tion *s.* **1.** schlechte Verwaltung; **2.** *pol.* 'Mißwirtschaft *f*.

ˌmal·a'droit *adj.* □ **1.** ungeschickt; **2.** taktlos.

mal·a·dy ['mælədɪ] *s.* Krankheit *f*, Gebrechen *n*, Übel *n* (*a. fig.*).

ma·la fi·de [ˌmeɪlə'faɪdɪ] (*Lat.*) *adj. u. adv.* arglistig, ⚖ *a.* bösgläubig.

ma·laise [mæ'leɪz] *s.* **1.** Unpäßlichkeit *f*; **2.** *fig.* Unbehagen *n*.

mal·a·prop·ism ['mæləprɒpɪzəm] *s.* (lächerliche) Wortverwechslung, 'Mißgriff *m*; **mal·ap·ro·pos** [ˌmæl'æprəpəʊ] **I** *adj.* **1.** unangebracht; **2.** unschicklich; **II** *adv.* **3.** a) zur Unzeit, b) im falschen Augenblick; **III** *s.* **4.** *et.* Unangebrachtes.

ma·lar ['meɪlə] *anat.* **I** *adj.* Backen…; **II** *s.* Backenknochen *m*.

ma·lar·i·a [mə'leərɪə] *s.* ⚕ Ma'laria *f*; **ma'lar·i·al** [-əl], **ma'lar·i·an** [-ən], **ma'lar·i·ous** [-ɪəs] *adj.* Malaria…, ma'lariaverseucht.

ma·lar·k(e)y [mə'lɑːkɪ] *s. Am. sl.* ‚Quatsch' *m*, ‚Käse' *m*.

Ma·lay [mə'leɪ] **I** *s.* **1.** Ma'laie *m*, Ma'laiin *f*; **2.** Ma'laiisch *n*; **II** *adj.* **3.** ma'laiisch; **Ma'lay·an** [-eɪən] *adj.* ma'laiisch.

'mal·conˌtent I *adj.* unzufrieden (*a. pol.*); **II** *s.* Unzufriedene(r *m*) *f*.

male [meɪl] **I** *adj.* **1.** männlich (*a. biol. u.* ⚙): ~ ***child*** Knabe *m*; ~ ***choir*** Männerchor *m*; ~ ***cousin*** Vetter *m*; ~ ***nurse*** Krankenpfleger *m*; ~ ***plug*** ⚙ Stecker *m*; ~ ***rhyme*** männlicher Reim; ~ ***screw*** Schraube(nspindel) *f*; **2.** *weitS.* männlich, mannhaft; **II** *s.* **3.** a) Mann *m*, b) Knabe *m*: ~ ***model*** Dressman *m*; **4.** *zo.* Männchen *n*; **5.** ⚘ männliche Pflanze.

mal·e·dic·tion [ˌmælɪ'dɪkʃn] *s.* Fluch *m*, Verwünschung *f*; **ˌmal·e'dic·to·ry** [-ktərɪ] *adj.* verwünschend, Verwünschungs…, Fluch…

mal·e·fac·tor ['mælɪfæktə] *s.* Misse-, Übeltäter *m*; **'mal·e·fac·tress** [-trɪs] *s.* Misse-, Übeltäterin *f*.

ma·lef·ic [mə'lefɪk] *adj.* (□ ***~ally***) ruchlos, bösartig; **ma'lef·i·cent** [-ɪsnt] *adj.* **1.** bösartig; **2.** schädlich (***to*** für *od. dat.*); **3.** verbrecherisch.

ma·lev·o·lence [mə'levələns] *s.* 'Mißgunst *f*, Feindseligkeit *f* (***to*** gegen), Böswilligkeit *f*; **ma'lev·o·lent** [-nt] *adj.* □ **1.** 'mißgünstig, widrig (*Umstände etc.*); **2.** feindselig, böswillig, übelwollend.

mal·fea·sance [mæl'fiːzəns] *s.* ⚖ strafbare Handlung.

ˌmal·for'ma·tion *s. bsd.* ⚕ 'Mißbildung *f*.

ˌmal'func·tion I *s.* **1.** ⚕ Funkti'onsstörung *f*; **2.** ⚙ schlechtes Funktionieren, Versagen *n*, De'fekt *m*; **II** *v/i.* **3.** schlecht funktionieren, de'fekt sein, versagen.

mal·ice ['mælɪs] *s.* **1.** Böswilligkeit *f*, Bosheit *f*; Arglist *f*, Tücke *f*; **2.** Groll *m*: ***bear s.o.*** ~ j-m grollen, e-n Groll gegen j-n hegen; **3.** ⚖ (böse) Absicht, Vorsatz *m*: ***with ~ aforethought*** (*od.* ***prepense***) vorsätzlich; **4.** (schelmische) Bosheit: ***with ~*** boshaft, maliziös;

ma·li·cious [mə'lɪʃəs] *adj.* □ **1.** böswillig, boshaft; **2.** arglistig, (heim)tückisch; **3.** gehässig; **4.** hämisch; **5.** ⚖ böswillig, vorsätzlich; **6.** malizi'ös, boshaft; **ma·li·cious·ness** [mə'lɪʃəsnɪs] → ***malice*** 1, 2.

ma·lign [mə'laɪn] **I** *adj.* □ **1.** verderblich, schädlich; **2.** unheilvoll; **3.** böswillig; **4.** ⚕ bösartig; **II** *v/t.* **5.** verleumden, beschimpfen.

ma·lig·nan·cy [mə'lɪgnənsɪ] *s.* Böswilligkeit *f*; Bösartigkeit *f* (*a.* ⚕); Bosheit *f*; Arglist *f*; Schadenfreude *f*; **ma'lig·nant** [-nt] **I** *adj.* □ **1.** böswillig; bösartig (*a.* ⚕); **2.** arglistig, (heim)tückisch; **3.** schadenfroh; **4.** gehässig; **II** *s.* **5.** *hist. Brit.* Roya'list *m*; **6.** Übelgesinnte(r *m*) *f*; **ma'lig·ni·ty** [-nətɪ] → ***malignancy***.

ma·lin·ger [mə'lɪŋgə] *v/i.* sich krank stellen, simulieren, ‚sich drücken'; **ma'lin·ger·er** [-ərə] *s.* Simu'lant *m*, Drückeberger *m*.

mall[1] [mɔːl] *s.* **1.** Prome'nade(nweg *m*) *f*; **2.** Mittelstreifen *m e-r Autobahn*; **3.** *Am.* Einkaufszentrum, Fußgängerzone *f*.

mall[2] [mɔːl] *s. orn.* Sturmmöwe *f*.

mal·lard ['mæləd] *pl.* **-lards**, *coll.* **-lard** *s. orn.* Stockente *f*.

mal·le·a·ble ['mælɪəbl] *adj.* **1.** ⚙ a) (kalt-) hämmerbar, b) dehn-, streckbar, c) verformbar; **2.** *fig.* gefügig, geschmeidig; ~ **cast i·ron** *s.* ⚙ **1.** Tempereisen *n*; **2.** Temperguß *m*; ~ **i·ron** *s.* ⚙ **1.** a) Schmiedeeisen *n*, b) schmiedbarer Guß; **2.** → ***malleable cast iron***.

mal·le·o·lar [mə'liːələ] *adj. anat.* Knöchel…

mal·let ['mælɪt] *s.* **1.** Holzhammer *m*, Schlegel *m*; **2.** ⚙, ⚒ Fäustel *m*: ~ ***toe*** ⚕

Hammerzehe *f*; **3.** *sport* Schlagholz *n*, Schläger *m*.
mal·low ['mæləʊ] *s.* ⚘ Malve *f*.
malm [mɑːm] *s. geol.* Malm *m*.
ˌ**mal·nu'tri·tion** *s.* 'Unterernährung *f*, schlechte Ernährung.
mal·o·dor·ous [mæl'əʊdərəs] *adj.* übelriechend.
ˌ**mal'prac·tice** *s.* **1.** Übeltat *f*; **2.** ⚖ a) Vernachlässigung *f* der beruflichen Sorgfalt, b) Kunstfehler *m*, Fahrlässigkeit *f des Arztes*, c) Untreue *f im Amt etc.*
malt [mɔːlt] **I** *s.* **1.** Malz *n*: ~ **kiln** Malzdarre *f*; ~ **liquor** gegorener Malztrank, *bsd.* Bier *n*; **II** *v/t.* **2.** mälzen, malzen: ~**ed milk** Malzmilch *f*; **3.** unter Zusatz von Malz herstellen; **III** *v/i.* **4.** zu Malz werden.
Mal·tese [ˌmɔːl'tiːz] **I** *s. sg. u. pl.* **1.** a) Mal'teser(in), b) Malteser *pl.*; **2.** *ling.* Mal'tesisch *n*; **II** *adj.* **3.** mal'tesisch, Malteser...; ~ **cross** *s.* **1.** Mal'teserkreuz *n*; **2.** ⚘ Brennende Liebe.
'**malt-house** *s.* Mälze'rei *f*.
malt·ose ['mɔːltəʊs] *s.* ⚗ Malzzucker *m*.
ˌ**mal'treat** *v/t.* **1.** schlecht behandeln, malträtieren; **2.** miß'handeln; ˌ**mal'treat·ment** *s.* **1.** schlechte Behandlung; **2.** Miß'handlung *f*.
mal·ver·sa·tion [ˌmælvɜː'seɪʃn] *s.* ⚖ **1.** Amtsvergehen *n*; **2.** Veruntreuung *f*, 'Unterschleif *m*.
ma·mil·la [mæ'mɪlə] *pl.* **-lae** [-liː] *s.* **1.** *anat.* Brustwarze *f*; **2.** *zo.* Zitze *f*; **mam·il·lar·y** ['mæmɪlərɪ] *adj.* **1.** *anat.* Brustwarzen...; **2.** brustwarzenförmig.
mam·ma¹ [mə'mɑː] *s.* Mutti *f*.
mam·ma² ['mæmə] *pl.* **-mae** [-miː] *s.* **1.** *anat.* (weibliche) Brust, Brustdrüse *f*; **2.** *zo.* Zitze *f*, Euter *n*.
mam·mal ['mæml] *s. zo.* Säugetier *n*; **mam·ma·li·an** [mæ'meɪljən] *zo.* **I** *s.* Säugetier *n*; **II** *adj.* Säugetier...
mam·ma·ry ['mæmərɪ] *adj.* **1.** *anat.* Brust(warzen)..., Milch...: ~ **gland** Milchdrüse *f*; **2.** *zo.* Euter...
mam·mil·la *etc. Am.* → **mamilla** *etc.*
mam·mo·gram ['mæməʊgræm] *s.* ⚕ Mammo'gramm *n*; **mam·mo·gra·phy** [mæ'mɒgrəfɪ] *s.* Mammogra'phie *f*.
mam·mon ['mæmən] *s.* Mammon *m*; '**mam·mon·ism** [-nɪzəm] *s.* Mammonsdienst *m*, Geldgier *f*.
mam·moth ['mæməθ] **I** *s. zo.* Mammut *n*; **II** *adj.* Mammut...(*-baum, -unternehmen etc.*), riesig, Riesen...
mam·my ['mæmɪ] *s.* **1.** F Mami *f*; **2.** *Am. obs.* (schwarzes) Kindermädchen.
man [mæn] **I** *pl.* **men** [men] *s.* **1.** Mensch *m*; **2.** *oft* 2 *coll.* (*mst ohne* **the**) der Mensch, die Menschen *pl.*, die Menschheit: **rights of** ~ Menschenrechte; → **measure** 5; **3.** Mann *m*: ~ **about town** Lebemann; **the** ~ **in the street** der Mann auf der Straße, der Durchschnittsmensch; ~ **of God** Diener *m* Gottes; ~ **of letters** a) Literat *m*, Schriftsteller *m*, b) Gelehrter *m*; ~ **of all work** a) Faktotum *n*, b) Allerweltskerl *m*; ~ **of straw** Strohmann; ~ **of the world** Weltmann; ~ **of few** (**many**) **words** Schweiger *m* (Schwätzer *m*); **Oxford** ~ Oxforder (Akademiker) *m*; **I have known him** ~ **and boy** ich kenne ihn von Jugend auf; **be one's own** ~ a) sein eigener Herr sein, b) im Vollbesitz s-r Kräfte sein; **the** ~ **Smith** (besagter) Smith; **my good** ~! *herablassend*: mein lieber Herr!; → **honour** 1; **4.** *weitS.* a) Mann *m*, Per'son *f*, b) jemand, c) man: **a** ~ jemand; **any** ~ irgend jemand, jedermann; **no** ~ niemand; **few men** wenige (Leute); **every** ~ **jack** F jeder einzelne; ~ **by** ~ Mann für Mann, einer nach dem andern; **as one** ~ wie 'ein Mann, geschlossen; **to a** ~ bis auf den letzten Mann; **give a** ~ **a chance** einem e-e Chance geben; **what can a** ~ **do in such a case?** was kann man da schon machen?; **5.** F Mensch *m*, Menschenskind *n*: ~ **alive!** Menschenskind!; **hurry up,** ~! Mensch, beeil dich!; **6.** (Ehe)Mann *m*: ~ **and wife** Mann u. Frau; **7.** a) Diener *m*, b) Angestellte(r) *m*, c) Arbeiter *m*: **men working** Baustelle (*Hinweis auf Verkehrsschildern*), d) *hist.* Lehnsmann *m*; **8.** ⚔, ⚓ Mann *m*: a) Sol'dat *m*, b) ⚓ Ma'trose *m*, c) *pl.* Mannschaft *f*: ~ **on leave** Urlauber *m*; **20 men** zwanzig Mann; **9.** *der* Richtige: **be the** ~ **for s.th.** der Richtige für et. (*e-e Aufgabe*) sein; **I am your** ~! ich bin Ihr Mann!; **10.** *Brettspiel*: Stein *m*, ('Schach)Fiˌgur *f*; **II** *v/t.* **11.** ⚔, ⚓ bemannen; *a. e-n Arbeitsplatz* besetzen; **12.** *fig. j-n* stärken: ~ **o.s.** sich ermannen; **III** *adj.* **13.** männlich: ~ **cook** Koch *m*.
man·a·cle ['mænəkl] **I** *s. mst pl.* (Hand-)Fessel *f*, -schelle *f* (*a. fig.*); **II** *v/t. j-m* Handfesseln *od.* -schellen anlegen, *j-n* fesseln (*a. fig.*).
man·age ['mænɪdʒ] **I** *v/t.* **1.** *Geschäft etc.* führen, verwalten; *Betrieb etc.* leiten; *Gut etc.* bewirtschaften; **2.** *Künstler etc.* managen; **3.** zu'stande bringen, bewerkstelligen, es fertigbringen (**to do** zu tun) (*a. iro.*): **he** ~**d to** (*inf.*) es gelang ihm zu (*inf.*); **4.** ‚deichseln', ‚managen': ~ **matters** ‚die Sache managen'; **5.** F *Arbeit, Essen* bewältigen, ‚schaffen'; **6.** 'umgehen (können) mit: a) *Werkzeug etc.* handhaben, bedienen, b) *j-n* zu behandeln *od.* zu ‚nehmen' wissen, c) *j-n* bändigen, mit *j-m etc.* fertigwerden: **I can** ~ **him** ich werde (schon) mit ihm fertig; **7.** lenken (*a. fig.*); **II** *v/i.* **8.** das Geschäft *od.* den Betrieb *etc.* führen; die Aufsicht haben; **9.** auskommen, sich behelfen (**with** mit); **10.** F a) ‚es schaffen', 'durchkommen, zu Rande kommen, b) ermöglichen: *can you come?* **I'm afraid, I can't** ~ (**it**) es geht leider nicht *od.* es ist mir leider nicht möglich; '**man·age·a·ble** [-dʒəbl] *adj.* ☐ **1.** lenksam, fügsam; **2.** handlich, leicht zu handhaben(d); '**man·age·a·ble·ness** [-dʒəblnɪs] *s.* **1.** Lenk-, Fügsamkeit *f*; **2.** Handlichkeit *f*; '**man·age·ment** [-mənt] *s.* **1.** (Haus-*etc.*)Verwaltung *f*; **2.** ☤ Management *n*, Unter'nehmensführung *f*: ~ **consultant** Unternehmensberater *m*; → **industrial management**; **3.** ☤ Geschäftsleitung *f*, Direkti'on *f*: **under new** ~ unter neuer Leitung; **labo(u)r and** ~ Arbeitnehmer *pl.* u. Arbeitgeber *pl.*; **4.** ⚘ Bewirtschaftung *f* (*Gut etc.*); **5.** Geschicklichkeit *f*, (kluge) Taktik; **6.** Kunstgriff *m*, Trick *m*; **7.** Handhabung *f*, Behandlung *f*; '**man·ag·er** [-dʒə] *s.* **1.** (Haus-*etc.*)Verwalter *m*; **2.** ☤ a) Manager *m*, b) Führungskraft *f*, c) Geschäftsführer *m*, Leiter *m*, Di'rektor *m*: **board of** ~**s** Direktorium *n*; **3.** *thea.* a) Inten'dant *m*, b) Regis'seur *m*, c) Manager *m* (*a. sport*), Impre'sario *m*; **4. be a good** ~ gut *od.* sparsam wirtschaften können; **man·ag·er·ess** [ˌmænɪdʒə'res] *s.* **1.** (Haus- *etc.*)Verwalterin *f*; **2.** ☤ a) Managerin *f*, b) Geschäftsführerin *f*, Leiterin *f*, Direk'torin *f*; **3.** Haushälterin *f*; **man·a·ge·ri·al** [ˌmænə'dʒɪərɪəl] *adj.* geschäftsführend, Direktions..., leitend: ~ **functions**; **in** ~ **capacity** in leitender Stellung; ~ **qualities** Führungsqualitäten; ~ **staff** leitende Angestellte *pl.*
man·ag·ing ['mænɪdʒɪŋ] *adj.* geschäftsführend, leitend, Betriebs...; ~ **board** *s.* ☤ Direk'torium *n*; ~ **clerk** *s.* ☤ **1.** Geschäftsführer *m*; **2.** Bü'rovorsteher *m*; ~ **com·mit·tee** *s.* ☤ Vorstand *m*; ~ **di·rec·tor** *s.* ☤ Gene'raldiˌrektor *m*, Hauptgeschäftsführer *m*.
Man·chu [ˌmæn'tʃuː] **I** *s.* **1.** Mandschu *m* (*Eingeborener der Mandschurei*); **2.** *ling.* Mandschu *n*; **II** *adj.* **3.** man'dschurisch; **Man·chu·ri·an** [mæn'tʃʊərɪən] → **Manchu** 1, 3.
man·da·mus [mæn'deɪməs] *s.* ⚖ *hist.* (*heute*: **order of** ~) Befehl *m e-s höheren Gerichts an ein untergeordnetes.*
man·da·rin¹ ['mændərɪn] *s.* **1.** *hist.* Manda'rin *m* (*chinesischer Titel*); **2.** F ‚hohes Tier' (*hoher Beamter*); **3.** 2 *ling.* Manda'rin *n*.
man·da·rin² ['mændərɪn] *s.* ⚘ Manda'rine *f*.
man·da·tar·y ['mændətərɪ] *s.* ⚖ Manda'tar *m*: a) (Pro'zeß)Beˌvollmächtigte(r) *m*, Sachwalter *m*, b) Manda'tarstaat *m*.
man·date ['mændeɪt] **I** *s.* **1.** ⚖ a) Man'dat *n* (*a. parl.*), (Pro'zeß)ˌVollmacht *f*, b) Geschäftsbesorgungsauftrag *m*, c) Befehl *m e-s übergeordneten Gerichts*; **2.** *pol.* a) Man'dat *n* (*Schutzherrschaftsauftrag*), b) Man'dat(sgebiet) *n*; **3.** *R.C.* päpstlicher Entscheid; **II** *v/t.* **4.** *pol.* e-m Man'dat unter'stellen: ~**d territory** Mandatsgebiet *n*; **man·da·tor** [mæn'deɪtə] *s.* ⚖ Man'dant *m*, Vollmachtgeber *m*; '**man·da·to·ry** [-dətərɪ] **I** *adj.* **1.** ⚖ vorschreibend, Muß...: ~ **regulation** Mußvorschrift *f*; **to make s.th.** ~ **upon s.o.** j-m et. vorschreiben; **2.** obliga'torisch, verbindlich, zwangsweise; **II** *s.* **3.** → **mandatary**.
man·di·ble ['mændɪbl] *s. anat.* **1.** Kinnbacken *m*, -lade *f*; **2.** 'Unterkieferknochen *m*.
man·do·lin(e) ['mændəlɪn] *s.* ♪ Mando'line *f*.
man·drake ['mændreɪk] *s.* ⚘ Al'raun(e *f*) *m*; Al'raunwurzel *f*.
man·drel, *a.* **man·dril** ['mændrəl] *s.* ⚙ (Spann)Dorn *m*; (Drehbank)Spindel *f*; *für Holz*: Docke(nspindel) *f*.
mane [meɪn] *s.* Mähne *f* (*a. weitS.*).
'**man-ˌeat·er** *s.* **1.** Menschenfresser *m*; **2.** menschenfressendes Tier; **3.** F ‚männermordendes Wesen' (*Frau*).
maned [meɪnd] *adj.* mit Mähne; Mähnen...: ~ **wolf**.
ma·nège, *a.* **ma·nege** [mæ'neɪʒ] *s.* **1.** Ma'nege *f*: a) Reitschule *f*, b) Reitbahn *f*, c) Reitkunst *f*; **2.** Gang *m*, Schule *f*; **3.** Zureiten *n*.
ma·nes ['mɑːneɪz] *s. pl.* Manen *pl.*

ma·neu·ver [mə'nu:və] *etc. Am.* → ***ma-nœuvre** etc.*

man·ful ['mænfʊl] *adj.* □ mannhaft, beherzt; '**man·ful·ness** [-nɪs] *s.* Mannhaftigkeit *f*; Beherztheit *f*.

man·ga·nate ['mæŋgəneɪt] *s.* ⚗ man'gansaures Salz; **man·ga·nese** ['mæŋgəni:z] *s.* ⚗ Man'gan *n*; **man·gan·ic** [mæŋ'gænɪk] *adj.* man'ganhaltig, Mangan…

mange [meɪndʒ] *s. vet.* Räude *f*.

man·gel-wur·zel ['mæŋgl,wɜ:zl] *s.* ⚘ Mangold *m*.

man·ger ['meɪndʒə] *s.* Krippe *f* (*a. ast.* ♋); Futtertrog *m*; → ***dog** Redew.*

man·gle¹ ['mæŋgl] *v/t.* **1.** zerfleischen, -fetzen, -stückeln; **2.** *fig. Text* verstümmeln.

man·gle² ['mæŋgl] **I** *s.* (Wäsche)Mangel *f*; **II** *v/t.* mangeln.

man·gler ['mæŋglə] *s.* Fleischwolf *m*.

man·go ['mæŋgəʊ] *pl.* **-goes** [-z] *s.* Mango *f* (*Frucht*); Mangobaum *m*.

man·grove ['mæŋgrəʊv] *s.* ⚘ Man'grove(nbaum *m*) *f*.

man·gy ['meɪndʒɪ] *adj.* □ **1.** *vet.* krätzig, räudig; **2.** *fig.* a) eklig, b) schäbig.

'**man,han·dle** *v/t.* **1.** F miß'handeln; **2.** mit Menschenkraft bewegen *od.* befördern *od.* meistern.

'**man·hole** *s.* ⚙ Mann-, Einsteigloch *n*; (Straßen)Schacht *m*.

man·hood ['mænhʊd] *s.* **1.** Menschentum *n*; **2.** Mannesalter *n*; **3.** Männlichkeit *f*; **4.** Mannhaftigkeit *f*; **5.** *coll.* die Männer *pl*.

'**man|-,hour** *s.* Arbeitsstunde *f*; '**~·hunt** *s.* Großfahndung *f*.

ma·ni·a ['meɪnjə] *s.* **1.** ⚕ Ma'nie *f*, Wahn(sinn) *m*, Besessensein *n*: ***religious ~*** religiöses Irresein; **2.** *fig.* (***for***) Sucht *f* (nach), Leidenschaft *f* (für), Ma'nie *f*, ‚Fimmel' *m*: ***collector's ~*** Sammlerwut *f*; ***sport ~*** ‚Sportfimmel'; **ma·ni·ac** ['meɪnɪæk] **I** *s.* Wahnsinnige(r *m*) *f*, Verrückte(r *m*) *f*; **II** *adj.* wahnsinnig, verrückt, irr(e); **ma·ni·a·cal** [mə'naɪəkl] *adj.* □ → ***maniac*** II.

ma·nic ['mænɪk] *psych.* **I** *adj.* manisch: ***~-depressive*** manisch-depressiv(e Person); **II** *s.* manische Per'son.

man·i·cure ['mænɪ,kjʊə] **I** *s.* Mani'küre *f*: a) Hand-, Nagelpflege *f*, b) Hand-, Nagelpflegerin *f*; **II** *v/t. u. v/i.* mani'küren; '**man·i,cur·ist** [-ərɪst] *s.* Mani'küre *f* (*Person*).

man·i·fest ['mænɪfest] **I** *adj.* □ **1.** offenbar-, -kundig, augenscheinlich, mani'fest (*a.* ⚕); **II** *v/t.* **2.** offen'baren, bekunden, kundtun, manifestieren; **3.** be-, erweisen; **III** *v/i.* **4.** *pol.* Kundgebungen veranstalten; **5.** erscheinen (*Geister*); **IV** *s.* **6.** ⚓ Ladungsverzeichnis *n*; **7.** ✝ ('Schiffs)Mani,fest *n*, *bsd. Am.* ✈ Passa'gierliste *f*; **man·i·fes·ta·tion** [,mænɪfe'steɪʃn] *s.* **1.** Offen'barung *f*, Äußerung *f*, Manifestati'on *f*; **2.** (deutliches) Anzeichen, Sym'ptom *n*: ***~ of life*** Lebensäußerung *f*; **3.** *pol.* Demonstrati'on *f*; **4.** Erscheinen *n e-s Geistes*; **man·i·fes·to** [,mænɪ'festəʊ] *s.* Mani'fest *n*: a) öffentliche Erklärung, b) *pol.* Grundsatzerklärung *f*, (Par'tei-, 'Wahl)Pro,gramm *n*.

man·i·fold ['mænɪfəʊld] **I** *adj.* □ **1.** mannigfaltig, vielfach, -fältig; **2.** ⚙ Mehr(fach)…, Mehrzweck…; **II** *s.* **3.** ⚙ a) Sammelleitung *f*, b) Rohrverzweigung *f*: ***intake ~*** *mot.* Einlaßkrümmer *m*; **4.** Ko'pie *f*, Abzug *m*; **III** *v/t.* **5.** *Text* vervielfältigen, hektographieren; ***~ paper*** *s.* 'Manifold-Pa,pier *n* (*festes Durchschlagpapier*); ***~ plug*** *s.* ⚡ Vielfachstecker *m*; ***~ writ·er*** *s.* Ver'vielfältigungsappa,rat *m*.

man·i·kin ['mænɪkɪn] *s.* **1.** Männchen *n*, Knirps *m*; **2.** Glieder-, Schaufensterpuppe *f*, ('Anpro,bier)Mo,dell *n*; **3.** ⚕ ana'tomisches Mo'dell, Phan'tom *n*; **4.** → ***mannequin*** 1.

Ma·nil·(l)a [mə'nɪlə] *s. abbr. für* a) ***~ cheroot***, b) ***~ hemp***, c) ***~ paper***; ***~ che·root*** *s.* Ma'nilazi,garre *f*; ***~ hemp*** *s.* Ma'nilahanf *m*; ***~ pa·per*** *s.* Ma'nilapa,pier *n*.

ma·nip·u·late [mə'nɪpjʊleɪt] **I** *v/t.* **1.** manipulieren, (künstlich) beeinflussen: ***~ prices***; **2.** (geschickt) handhaben; ⚙ bedienen; **3.** *j-n od. et.* manipulieren *od.* geschickt behandeln; **4.** *et.* ‚deichseln', ‚schaukeln'; **5.** *Konten etc.* ‚frisieren'; **II** *v/i.* **6.** manipulieren; **ma·nip·u·la·tion** [mə,nɪpjʊ'leɪʃn] *s.* **1.** Manipulati'on *f*: ***~ of currency***; **2.** (Kunst)Griff *m*, Verfahren *n*; **3.** *b.s.* Machenschaft *f*, Manipulati'on *f*; **ma'nip·u·la·tive** [-lətɪv] → ***manipulatory***; **ma'nip·u·la·tor** [-tə] *s.* **1.** (geschickter) Handhaber; **2.** Drahtzieher *m*, Manipulierer *m*; **ma'nip·u·la·to·ry** [-lətərɪ] *adj.* **1.** durch Manipulati'on her'beigeführt; **2.** manipulierend; **3.** Handhabungs…

man·kind [mæn'kaɪnd] *s.* **1.** die Menschheit; **2.** *coll.* die Menschen *pl.*, der Mensch; **3.** ['mænkaɪnd] *coll.* die Männer *pl*.

'**man·like** *adj.* **1.** menschenähnlich; **2.** wie ein Mann, männlich; **3.** → ***mannish***.

man·li·ness ['mænlɪnɪs] *s.* **1.** Männlichkeit *f*; **2.** Mannhaftigkeit *f*; **man·ly** ['mænlɪ] *adj.* **1.** männlich; **2.** mannhaft; **3.** Mannes…: ***~ sports*** Männersport *m*.

'**man-made** *adj.* Kunst…, künstlich: ***~ satellite***; ***~ fibre*** (*Am.* ***fiber***) ⚙ Kunstfaser *f*.

man·na ['mænə] *s. bibl.* Manna *n*, *f* (*a.* ⚘ *u. fig.*).

man·ne·quin ['mænɪkɪn] *s.* **1.** Mannequin *n*: ***~ parade*** Mode(n)schau *f*; **2.** → ***manikin*** 2.

man·ner ['mænə] *s.* **1.** Art *f* (und Weise *f*) (*et. zu tun*): ***after*** (*od.* ***in***) ***this ~*** auf diese Art *od.* Weise, so: ***in such a ~*** (***that***) so *od.* derart (, daß); ***in what ~?*** wie?; ***adverb of ~*** *ling.* Umstandswort der Art u. Weise, Modaladverb *n*; ***in a ~*** auf e-e Art, gewissermaßen; ***in a ~ of speaking*** sozusagen; ***all ~ of things*** alles mögliche; ***no ~ of doubt*** gar kein Zweifel; ***by no ~ of means*** in keiner Weise; **2.** Art *f*, Betragen *n*, Auftreten *n*, Verhalten *n* (***to*** zu): ***I don't like his ~*** ich mag s-e Art nicht; ***to the ~ born*** hineingeboren (*in bestimmte Verhältnisse*), von Kind auf damit vertraut; ***as to the ~ born*** wie selbstverständlich, als ob er *etc.* es immer so getan hätte; **3.** *pl.* Benehmen *n*, 'Umgangsformen *pl.*, Ma'nieren *pl.*: ***bad*** (***good***) ***~s***; ***we shall teach them ~s*** ‚wir werden sie Mores lehren'; ***it is bad ~s*** es gehört sich nicht; **4.** *pl.* Sitten *pl.* (u. Gebräuche *pl.*); **5.** *paint. etc.* Stil(art *f*) *m*, Ma'nier *f*; '**man·nered** [-əd] *adj.* **1.** *mst in Zssgn* gesittet, geartet: ***ill-~*** von schlechtem Benehmen, ungezogen; **2.** gekünstelt, manie'riert; '**man·ner·ism** [-ərɪzəm] *s.* **1.** *Kunst etc.*: Manie'rismus *m*, Künste'lei *f*; **2.** Manie'riertheit *f*, Gehabe *n*; **3.** eigenartige Wendung (*in der Rede etc.*); '**man·ner·li·ness** [-əlɪnɪs] *s.* gutes Benehmen, Ma'nierlichkeit *f*; '**man·ner·ly** [-əlɪ] *adj.* ma'nierlich, gesittet.

man·ni·kin → ***manikin***.

man·nish ['mænɪʃ] *adj.* masku'lin, unweiblich.

ma·nœu·vra·ble [mə'nu:vrəbl] *adj.* **1.** ⚔ manövrierfähig; **2.** ⚙ lenk-, steuerbar; *weitS.* (*a. fig.*) wendig, beweglich; **ma·nœu·vre** [mə'nu:və] **I** *s.* **1.** ⚔, ⚓ Ma'növer *n*: a) taktische Bewegung, b) Truppen-, ⚓ Flottenübung *f*, ✈ 'Luftma,növer *n*; **2.** *fig.* Ma'növer *n*, Schachzug *m*, List *f*; **II** *v/t. u. v/i.* **3.** manövrieren (*a. fig.*): ***~ s.o. into s.th.*** j-n in et. hineinmanövrieren; **ma'nœu·vrer** [-vərə] *s. fig.* **1.** (schlauer) Taktiker; **2.** Intri'gant *m*.

man-of-war [,mænəv'wɔ:], *pl.* **,men-of-'war** [,men-] *s.* ⚓ Kriegsschiff *n*.

ma·nom·e·ter [mə'nɒmɪtə] *s.* ⚙ Mano'meter *n*, Druckmesser *m*.

man·or ['mænə] *s.* **1.** Ritter-, Landgut *n*: ***lord*** (***lady***) ***of the ~*** Gutsherr(in); **2.** *a.* ***~ house*** Herrenhaus *n*; **ma·no·ri·al** [mə'nɔ:rɪəl] *adj.* herrschaftlich, (Ritter-)Guts…, Herrschafts…

man·qué(**e** *f*) *m* ['mɑ̃:ŋkeɪ] (*Fr.*) *adj.* verhindert, ‚verkracht': ***a poet manqué***.

'**man,pow·er** *s.* **1.** menschliche Arbeitskraft *od.* -leistung; **2.** 'Menschenpoten-ti,al *n*: *bsd.* a) Kriegsstärke *f* (*e-s Volkes*), b) (verfügbare) Arbeitskräfte *pl*.

man·sard ['mænsɑ:d] *s.* **1.** *a.* ***~ roof*** Man'sardendach *n*; **2.** Man'sarde *f*.

'**man,serv·ant** *pl.* '**men,serv·ants** *s.* Diener *m*.

man·sion ['mænʃn] *s.* **1.** (herrschaftliches) Wohnhaus, Villa *f*; **2.** *bsd. pl. Brit.* (großes) Mietshaus; ***~ house*** *s. Brit.* **1.** Herrenhaus *n*, -sitz *m*; **2.** ***the*** ♋ *Amtssitz des **Lord Mayor** von London.*

'**man,slaugh·ter** *s.* ⚖ Totschlag *m*, Körperverletzung *f* mit Todesfolge: ***involuntary ~*** fahrlässige Tötung; ***voluntary ~*** Totschlag im Affekt.

man·tel ['mæntl] *abbr. für* a) ***mantelpiece***, b) ***mantelshelf***; '**~·piece** *s.* **1.** Ka'mineinfassung *f*, -mantel *m*; **2.** → '**~·shelf** *s.* Ka'minsims *m*, *n*.

man·tis ['mæntɪs] *pl.* **-tis·es** *s. zo.* Gottesanbeterin *f* (*Heuschrecke*).

man·tle ['mæntl] **I** *s.* **1.** Mantel *m* (*a. zo.*), (ärmelloser) 'Umhang; **2.** *fig.* (Schutz-, Deck)Mantel *m*, Hülle *f*; **3.** ⚙ Mantel *m*; (Glüh)Strumpf *m*; **4.** *Gußtechnik*: Formmantel *m*; **II** *v/i.* **5.** sich über'ziehen (***with*** mit); sich röten (*Gesicht*); **III** *v/t.* **6.** über'ziehen; **7.** verhüllen (*a. fig. bemänteln*).

,man-to-'man *adj.* von Mann zu Mann: ***a ~ talk***.

'**man·trap** *s.* **1.** Fußangel *f*; **2.** *fig.* Falle *f*.

man·u·al ['mænjʊəl] **I** *adj.* □ **1.** mit der Hand, Hand…, manu'ell: ***~ alphabet*** Fingeralphabet *n*; ***~ exercises*** ⚔ Griffeüben *n*; ~ ***labo(u)r*** Handarbeit *f*; ~ ***training*** *ped.* Werkunterricht *m*; ~***ly operated*** ⚙ mit Handbetrieb, handgesteuert; **2.** handschriftlich: ~ ***bookkeeping***; **II** *s.* **3.** a) Handbuch *n*, Leitfaden *m*: (***instruction***) ~ Bedienungsanleitung(en *pl.*) *f*, b) ⚔ Dienstvorschrift *f*; **4.** ♪ Manu'al *n* (*Orgel etc.*).

man·u·fac·to·ry [ˌmænjʊ'fæktərɪ] *s. obs.* Fa'brik *f.*

man·u·fac·ture [ˌmænjʊ'fæktʃə] **I** *s.* **1.** Fertigung *f*, Erzeugung *f*, Herstellung *f*, Fabrikati'on *f*: ***year of*** ~ Herstellungs-, Baujahr *n*; **2.** Erzeugnis *n*, Fabri'kat *n*; **3.** Indu'strie(zweig *m*) *f*; **II** *v/t.* **4.** verfertigen, erzeugen, herstellen, fabrizieren (*a. fig. Beweismittel etc.*): ~***d goods*** Fabrik-, Fertig-, Manufakturwaren; **5.** verarbeiten (***into*** zu); ˌ**man·u'fac·tur·er** [-tʃərə] *s.* **1.** Hersteller *m*, Erzeuger *m*; **2.** Fabri'kant *m*; ˌ**man·u'fac·tur·ing** [-tʃərɪŋ] *adj.* **1.** Herstellungs…, Produktions…: ~ ***cost*** Herstellungskosten *pl.*; ~ ***efficiency*** Produktionsleistung *f*; ~ ***industries*** Fertigungsindustrien; ~ ***plant*** Fabrikationsbetrieb *m*; ~ ***process*** Herstellungsverfahren *n*; **2.** Industrie…, Fabrik…, Gewerbe…

ma·nure [mə'njʊə] **I** *s.* **1.** Dünger *m*; **2.** Dung *m*: ***liquid*** ~ (Dung)Jauche *f*; **II** *v/t.* **3.** düngen.

man·u·script ['mænjʊskrɪpt] **I** *s.* Manu'skript *n*: a) Handschrift *f* (*alte Urkunde etc.*), b) Urschrift *f* (*e-s Autors*), c) *typ.* Satzvorlage *f*; **II** *adj.* Manuskript…, handschriftlich.

man·y ['menɪ] **I** *adj.* **1.** viele, viel: ~ ***times*** oft; ***as*** ~ ebensoviel(e); ***as*** ~ ***again*** doppelt soviel(e); ***as*** ~ ***as forty*** (nicht weniger als) vierzig; ***one too*** ~ einer zuviel; ***be one too*** ~ ***for*** F *j-m* ‚über' sein; ***they behaved like so*** ~ ***children*** sie benahmen sich wie (die) Kinder; **2.** ~ ***a*** manch, manch ein: ~ ***a man*** manch einer; ~ ***a time*** des öfteren; **II** *s.* **3.** viele: ***the*** ~ *pl. konstr.* die (große) Masse; ~ ***of us*** viele von uns; ***a good*** ~ ziemlich viel(e); ***a great*** ~ sehr viele; ~-**sid·ed** [ˌmenɪ'saɪdɪd] *adj.* vielseitig (*a. fig.*); *fig.* vielschichtig (*Problem etc.*); ~-**sid·ed·ness** [ˌmenɪ'saɪdɪdnɪs] *s.* **1.** Vielseitigkeit *f* (*a. fig.*); **2.** *fig.* Vielschichtigkeit *f.*

Mao·ism ['maʊɪzəm] *s.* Mao'ismus *m*; '**Mao·ist** [-ɪst] **I** *s.* Mao'ist(in); **II** *adj.* mao'istisch.

map [mæp] **I** *s.* **1.** (Land- *etc.*, *a.* Himmels)Karte *f*: ~ ***of the city*** Stadtplan *m*; ***by*** ~ nach der Karte; ***off the*** ~ F a) abgelegen, ‚hinter dem Mond' (gelegen), b) bedeutungslos; ***on the*** ~ F a) (noch) da *od.* vorhanden, b) beachtenswert; ***put on the*** ~ *fig. Stadt etc.* bekannt machen, Geltung verschaffen (*dat.*); **2.** *sl.* ‚Vi'sage' *f*, ‚Fresse' *f* (*Gesicht*); **II** *v/t.* **3.** e-e Karte machen von, karto'graphisch darstellen; **4.** *Gebiet* karto'graphisch erfassen; **5.** auf e-r Karte eintragen; **6.** ~ ***out*** *fig.* (vor'aus-) planen, ausarbeiten, *s-e Zeit* einteilen; ~ **case** *s.* Kartentasche *f*; ~ **ex·er·cise** *s.* ⚔ Planspiel *n.*

ma·ple ['meɪpl] **I** *s.* **1.** ⚘ Ahorn *m*; **2.** Ahornholz *n*; **II** *adj.* **3.** aus Ahorn (-holz), Ahorn…; ~ **sug·ar** *s.* Ahornzucker *m.*

map·per ['mæpə] *s.* Karto'graph *m.*

ma·quis ['mæki:] *pl.* **-quis** [-ki:] *s.* **1.** ⚘ Macchia *f*; **2.** a) Ma'quis *m*, fran'zösische 'Widerstandsbewegung (*im 2. Weltkrieg*), b) Maqui'sard *m*, (fran'zösischer) 'Widerstandskämpfer.

mar [mɑ:] *v/t.* **1.** (be)schädigen: ~-***resistant*** ⚙ kratzfest; **2.** ruinieren; **3.** *fig. Pläne etc.* stören, beeinträchtigen; *Schönheit, Spaß* verderben.

mar·a·bou ['mærəbu:] *s. orn.* Marabu *m.*

mar·a·schi·no [ˌmærə'ski:nəʊ] *s.* Mara'schino(liˌkör) *m.*

mar·a·thon ['mærəθn] **I** *s. sport* **1.** *a.* ~ ***race*** Marathonlauf *m*; **2.** *fig.* Dauerwettkampf *m*; **II** *adj.* **3.** *sport* Marathon…: ~ ***runner***; **4.** *fig.* Marathon…, Dauer…: ~ ***session.***

ma·raud [mə'rɔ:d] ⚔ **I** *v/i.* plündern; **II** *v/t.* verheeren, (aus)plündern; **ma'raud·er** [-də] *s.* Plünderer *m.*

mar·ble ['mɑ:bl] **I** *s.* **1.** *min.* Marmor *m*: ***artificial*** ~ Gipsmarmor, Stuck *m*; **2.** Marmorstatue *f*, -bildwerk *n*; **3.** a) Murmel(kugel) *f*, b) *pl. sg. konstr.* Murmelspiel *n*: ***play*** ~***s*** (mit) Murmeln spielen; ***he's lost his*** ~***s*** *Brit. sl.* ‚er hat nicht mehr alle'; **4.** marmorierter Buchschnitt; **II** *adj.* **5.** marmorn, aus Marmor; **6.** marmoriert, gesprenkelt; **7.** *fig.* steinern, gefühllos; **III** *v/t.* **8.** marmorieren, sprenkeln: ~***d meat*** durchwachsenes Fleisch.

mar·cel [mɑ:'sel] **I** *v/t. Haar* ondulieren; **II** *s. a.* ~ ***wave*** Ondulati'on(swelle) *f.*

march¹ [mɑ:tʃ] **I** *v/i.* **1.** ⚔ *etc.* marschieren, ziehen: ~ ***off*** abrücken; ~ ***past*** (***s.o.***) (an j-m) vorbeiziehen *od.* -marschieren; ~ ***up*** anrücken; **2.** *fig.* fortschreiten; Fortschritte machen; **II** *v/t.* **3.** *Strecke* marschieren, zu'rücklegen; **4.** marschieren lassen: ~ ***off prisoners*** Gefangene abführen; **III** *s.* **5.** ⚔ Marsch *m* (*a.* ♪): ***slow*** ~ langsamer Parademarsch; ~ ***order*** *Am.* Marschbefehl *m*; **6.** Marsch(strecke *f*) *m*: ***a day's*** ~ ein Tagemarsch; **7.** ⚔ Vormarsch *m* (***on*** auf *acc.*); **8.** *fig.* (Ab-) Lauf *m*, (Fort)Gang *m*: ***the*** ~ ***of events***; **9.** *fig.* Fortschritt *m*: ***the*** ~ ***of progress*** die fortschrittliche Entwicklung; **10.** ***steal a*** ~ (***up***)***on s.o.*** j-m ein Schnippchen schlagen, j-m zuvorkommen.

march² [mɑ:tʃ] **I** *s.* **1.** *hist.* Mark *f*; **2.** a) *mst pl.* Grenzgebiet *n*, -land *n*, b) Grenze *f*; **II** *v/i.* **3.** grenzen (***upon*** an *acc.*); **4.** e-e gemeinsame Grenze haben (***with*** mit).

March³ [mɑ:tʃ] *s.* März *m*: ***in*** ~ im März; ***as mad as a*** ~ ***hare*** F total übergeschnappt.

march·ing ['mɑ:tʃɪŋ] *adj.* ⚔ Marsch…, marschierend: ~ ***order*** a) Marschausrüstung *f*, b) Marschordnung *f*; ***in heavy*** ~ ***order*** feldmarschmäßig; ~ ***orders*** *Brit.* Marschbefehl *m*; ***he got his*** ~ ***orders*** F er bekam den ‚Laufpaß'.

mar·chion·ess ['mɑ:ʃənɪs] *s.* Mar'quise *f*, Markgräfin *f.*

march·pane ['mɑ:tʃpeɪn] *s. obs.* Marzi'pan *n.*

Mar·di Gras [ˌmɑ:dɪ'grɑ:] (*Fr.*) *s.* Fastnacht(sdienstag *m*) *f.*

mare [meə] *s.* Stute *f*: ***the grey*** ~ ***is the better horse*** *fig.* die Frau ist der Herr im Hause; ~***'s nest*** *fig.* a) ‚Windei' *n*, *a.* (Zeitungs)Ente *f*, b) ‚Saustall' *m.*

mar·ga·rine [ˌmɑ:dʒə'ri:n] *s.* Marga'rine *f.*

marge [mɑ:dʒ] *s. Brit.* F Marga'rine *f.*

mar·gin ['mɑ:dʒɪn] **I** *s.* **1.** Rand *m* (*a. fig.*); **2.** *a. pl.* (Seiten)Rand *m* (*bei Büchern etc.*): ***as per*** ~ ☤ wie nebenstehend; **3.** Grenze *f* (*a. fig.*): ~ ***of income*** Einkommensgrenze; **4.** Spielraum *m*: ***leave a*** ~ Spielraum lassen; **5.** *fig.* 'Überschuß *m*, (*ein*) Mehr *n* (*an Zeit, Geld etc.*): ***safety*** ~ Sicherheitsfaktor *m*; ***by a narrow*** ~ mit knapper Not; **6.** *mst* ***profit*** ~ ☤ (Gewinn-, Verdienst-) Spanne *f*, Marge *f*, Handelsspanne *f*: ***interest*** ~ Zinsgefälle *n*; **7.** ☤, *Börse*: Hinter'legungssumme *f*, Deckung *f* (*von Kursschwankungen*), Marge *f*: ~ ***business*** *Am.* Effektendifferenzgeschäft *n*; **8.** ☤ Rentabili'tätsgrenze *f*; **9.** *sport* (***by a*** ~ ***of four seconds*** mit vier Sekunden) Abstand *m od.* Vorsprung *m*; **II** *v/t.* **10.** mit Rand(bemerkungen) versehen; **11.** an den Rand schreiben; **12.** ☤ *durch Hinterlegung* decken; '**mar·gin·al** [-nl] *adj.* □ **1.** am *od.* auf dem Rand, Rand…: ~ ***note*** Randbemerkung *f*; ~ ***release*** a) Randauslösung *f*, b) Randlöser *m* (*der Schreibmaschine*); **2.** am Rande, Grenz… (*a. fig.*); **3.** *fig.* Mindest…: ~ ***capacity***; **4.** ☤ a) zum Selbstkostenpreis, b) knapp über der Rentabili'tätsgrenze (liegend), Grenz…: ~ ***cost*** Grenz-, Mindestkosten *pl.*; ~ ***sales*** Verkäufe zum Selbstkostenpreis; **mar·gi·na·li·a** [ˌmɑ:dʒɪ'neɪljə] *s. pl.* Margi'nalien *pl.*, Randbemerkungen *pl.*; '**mar·gin·al·ly** [-nəlɪ] *adv. fig.* **1.** geringfügig; **2.** (nur) am Rande.

mar·grave ['mɑ:greɪv] *s. hist.* Markgraf *m*; **mar·gra·vi·ate** [mɑ:'greɪvɪət] *s.* Markgrafschaft *f*; '**mar·gra·vine** [-grəvi:n] *s.* Markgräfin *f.*

mar·gue·rite [ˌmɑ:gə'ri:t] *s.* ⚘ **1.** Marge'rite *f*; **2.** Gänseblümchen *n.*

mar·i·gold ['mærɪgəʊld] *s.* ⚘ Ringelblume *f*; Stu'dentenblume *f.*

mar·i·jua·na, *a.* **mar·i·hua·na** [ˌmærɪ'hwɑ:nə] *s.* **1.** ⚘ Marihu'anahanf *m*; **2.** Marihu'ana *n* (*Droge*).

mar·i·nade [ˌmærɪ'neɪd] *s.* **1.** Mari'nade *f*; **2.** marinierter Fisch; **mar·i·nate** ['mærɪneɪt] *v/t. Fisch* marinieren.

ma·rine [mə'ri:n] **I** *adj.* **1.** See…: ~ ***warfare***; ~ ***court*** *Am.* ⚖ Seegericht *n*; ~ ***insurance*** See(transport)versicherung *f*; **2.** Meeres…: ~ ***plants***; **3.** Schiffs…; **4.** Marine…: 2 ***Corps*** *Am.* ⚔ Marineinfanteriekorps *n*; **II** *s.* **5.** Ma'rine *f*: ***mercantile*** ~ Handelsmarine; **6.** ⚔ Ma'rineinfanteˌrist *m*: ***tell that to the*** ~***s!*** F das kannst du deiner Großmutter erzählen!; **7.** *paint.* Seestück *n.*

mar·i·ner ['mærɪnə] *s. poet. od.* ⚖ Seemann *m*, Ma'trose *m*: ***master*** ~ Kapitän *m* e-s Handelsschiffs.

Mar·i·ol·a·try [ˌmeərɪ'ɒlətrɪ] *s.* Ma'rienkult *m*, -verehrung *f.*

mar·i·o·nette [ˌmærɪə'net] *s.* Mario'nette *f* (*a. fig.*).

mar·i·tal ['mærɪtl] *adj.* □ ehelich, Ehe…, Gatten…: ~ ***partners*** Ehegatten; ~ ***relations*** eheliche Beziehungen; ~ ***status*** ⚖ Familienstand *m*; ***disruption of*** ~ ***relations*** Zerrüttung *f* der

Ehe.

mar·i·time ['mærɪtaɪm] *adj.* **1.** See…, Schiffahrts…: ~ **court** Seeamt *n*; ~ **insurance** Seeversicherung *f*; ~ **law** Seerecht *n*; **2.** a) seefahrend, Seemanns…, b) Seehandel (be)treibend; **3.** an der See liegend *od.* lebend, Küsten…; **4.** *zo.* an der Küste lebend, Strand…; ♀ **Com·mis·sion** *s. Am. Oberste Handelsschiffahrtsbehörde der USA*; ~ **ter·ri·to·ry** *s.* ⚖ Seehoheitsgebiet *n*.

mar·jo·ram ['mɑːdʒərəm] *s.* ⚘ Majoran *m*.

mark¹ [mɑːk] **I** *s.* **1.** Markierung *f*, Marke *f*, Mal *n*; *engS.* Fleck *m*: **adjusting** ~ ⚙ Einstellmarke; **2.** *fig.* Zeichen *n*: ~ **of confidence** Vertrauensbeweis *m*; ~ **of respect** Zeichen der Hochachtung; **3.** (Kenn)Zeichen *n*, (Merk)Mal *n*; *zo.* Kennung *f*: **distinctive** ~ Kennzeichen; **4.** (Schrift-, Satz)Zeichen *n*: **question** ~ Fragezeichen; **5.** (An)Zeichen *n*: **a** ~ **of great carelessness**; **6.** (Eigentums)Zeichen *n*, Brandmal *n*; **7.** Strieme *f*, Schwiele *f*; **8.** Narbe *f* (*a.* ⚙); **9.** Kerbe *f*, Einschnitt *m*; **10.** Kreuz *n als Unterschrift*; **11.** Ziel(scheibe *f*; *a. fig.*) *n*: **wide of** (*od.* **beside**) **the** ~ *fig.* a) fehl am Platz, nicht zur Sache gehörig, b) ‚fehlgeschossen'; **you are quite off** (*od.* **wide of**) **the** ~ *fig.* Sie irren sich gewaltig; **hit the** ~ (ins Schwarze) treffen; **miss the** ~ a) fehl-, vorbeischießen, b) sein Ziel *od.* s-n Zweck verfehlen, ‚danebenhauen'; **12.** *fig.* Norm *f*: **below the** ~ unterdurchschnittlich, nicht auf der Höhe; **up to the** ~ a) der Sache gewachsen, b) den Erwartungen entsprechend, c) *gesundheitlich etc.* auf der Höhe; **within the** ~ innerhalb der erlaubten Grenzen, berechtigt (**in doing** zu tun); **overshoot the** ~ über das Ziel hinausschießen, zu weit gehen; **13.** (aufgeprägter) Stempel, Gepräge *n*; **14.** Spur *f* (*a. fig.*): **leave one's** ~ **upon** a) s-n Stempel aufdrücken (*dat.*), b) bei *j-m* s-e Spuren hinterlassen; **make one's** ~ sich e-n Namen machen (**in** in *dat.*, **upon** bei), Vorzügliches leisten; **15.** *fig.* Bedeutung *f*, Rang *m*: **a man of** ~ e-e markante Persönlichkeit; **16.** † a) (Waren)Zeichen *n*, Fa'brik-, Schutzmarke *f*, (Handels)Marke *f*, b) Preisangabe *f*; **17.** ⚔ *Brit.* Mo'dell *n*, Type *f* (*Panzerwagen etc.*); **18.** (Schul-) Note *f*, Zen'sur *f*: **obtain full** ~**s** in allen Punkten voll bestehen; **give s.o. full** ~**s** (**for**) *fig.* j-m höchstes Lob spenden (für); **bad** ~ Note für schlechtes Benehmen; **bad** ~**s** (ein) schlechtes Zeugnis; **19.** *sport* a) *Fußball etc.*: (Strafstoß-) Marke *f*, b) *Laufsport*: Startlinie *f*, c) *Boxen*: *sl.* Magengrube *f*: **on your** ~**s!** auf die Plätze!; **get off the** ~ starten; **20. not my** ~ *sl.* nicht mein Geschmack, nicht das Richtige für mich; **21.** *sl.* ‚Gimpel' *m*, leichtes Opfer: **be an easy** ~ leicht ‚reinzulegen' sein; **22.** *hist.* a) Mark *f* (*Grenzgebiet*), b) All'mende *f*; **II** *v/t.* **23.** markieren (*a.* ⚔), (*a. fig. j-n, et., ein Zeitalter*) kennzeichnen; bezeichnen; *Wäsche* zeichnen; † *Waren* auszeichnen, *Preis* festsetzen; *Temperatur etc.* anzeigen; *fig.* ein Zeichen sein für: **to** ~ **the occasion** aus diesem Anlaß, zur Feier des Tages; **the day was** ~**ed by heavy fighting** der Tag stand im Zeichen schwerer Kämpfe; → **time** 18; **24.** brandmarken; **25.** Spuren hinter'lassen auf (*dat.*); **26.** zeigen, zum Ausdruck bringen; **27.** be-, vermerken, achtgeben auf (*acc.*), sich merken; **28.** *ped. Arbeiten* zensieren; **29.** bestimmen (**for** für); **30.** *sport* a) *Gegenspieler* decken, markieren, b) *Punkte etc.* notieren; **III** *v/i.* **31.** achtgeben, aufpassen: ~**!** Achtung!; ~ **you** wohlgemerkt; ~ **down** *v/t.* **1.** † (*im Preis*) her'absetzen; **2.** bestimmen, vormerken (**for** für, zu); ~ **off** *v/t.* **1.** abgrenzen, -stecken; **2.** *auf e-r Liste* abhaken; **3.** *fig.* (ab)trennen; **4.** ⚑ *Strecke* ab-, auftragen; ~ **out** *v/t.* **1.** bestimmen, ausersehen (**for** für, zu); **2.** abgrenzen, (*durch Striche etc.*) bezeichnen, markieren; ~ **up** *v/t.* † **1.** (*im Preis etc.*) hin'auf-, her'aufsetzen; **2.** *Diskontsatz etc.* erhöhen.

mark² [mɑːk] *s.* † **1.** (deutsche) Mark: **blocked** ~ Sperrmark; **2.** *hist.* Mark *f* (*Münze, Goldgewicht*).

Mark³ [mɑːk] *npr. u. s. bibl.* 'Markus (-evan,gelium *n*) *m*.

'mark·down *s.* † niedrigere Auszeichnung (*e-r Ware*), Preissenkung *f*.

marked [mɑːkt] *adj.* □ **1.** markiert, gekennzeichnet; mit e-r Aufschrift versehen; **2.** † bestätigt (*Am.* gekennzeichnet) (*Scheck*); **3.** mar'kant, ausgeprägt; **4.** deutlich, merklich: ~ **progress**; **5.** auffällig, ostenta'tiv: ~ **indifference**; **6.** gezeichnet: **a face** ~ **with smallpox** ein pockennarbiges Gesicht; **a** ~ **man** *fig.* ein Gezeichneter; **'mark·ed·ly** [-kɪdlɪ] *adv.* deutlich, ausgesprochen.

mark·er ['mɑːkə] *s.* **1.** Anschreiber *m*; *Billard*: Mar'kör *m*; **2.** ⚔ a) Anzeiger *m* (*beim Schießstand*), b) Flügelmann *m*; **3.** a) Kennzeichen *n*, b) (Weg- *etc.*) Markierung *f*; **4.** Lesezeichen *n*; **5.** *Am.* a) Straßenschild *n*, b) Gedenktafel *f*; **6.** ✈ a) Sichtzeichen *n*: ~ **panel** Fliegertuch *n*, b) Leuchtbombe *f*.

mar·ket ['mɑːkɪt] † **I** *s.* **1.** Markt *m* (*Handel*): **be in the** ~ **for** Bedarf haben an (*a. fig.*); **come into the** ~ (zum Verkauf) angeboten werden, auf den Markt kommen; **place** (*od.* **put**) **on the** ~ → 11; **sale in the open** ~ freihändiger Verkauf; **2.** *Börse*: Markt *m*: **railway** ~ Markt für Eisenbahnwerte; **3.** (*a.* Geld)Markt *m*, Börse *f*, Handelsverkehr *m*: **active** (**dull**) ~ lebhafter (lustloser) Markt; **play the** ~ an der Börse spekulieren; **4.** a) Marktpreis *m*, b) Marktpreise *pl.*: **the** ~ **is low** (**rising**); **at the** ~ zum Marktpreis, *Börse*: zum ‚Bestens'-Preis; **5.** Markt(platz) *m*, Handelsplatz *m*: **in the** ~ auf dem Markt; (**covered**) ~ Markthalle *f*; **6.** *Am.* (Lebensmittel)Geschäft *n*: **meat** ~; **7.** (Wochen- *od.* Jahr)Markt *m*; **8.** Markt *m* (*Absatzgebiet*): **hold the** ~ a) den Markt beherrschen, b) (durch Kauf *od.* Verkauf) die Preise halten; **9.** Absatz *m*, Verkauf *m*, Markt *m*: **find a** ~ Absatz finden (*Ware*); **find a** ~ **for** *et.* an den Mann bringen; **meet with a ready** ~ schnellen Absatz finden; **10.** (**for**) Nachfrage *f* (nach), Bedarf *m* (an *dat.*); **II** *v/t.* **11.** auf den Markt bringen; vertreiben; **III** *v/i.* **12.** einkaufen; auf dem Markt handeln; Märkte besuchen; **IV** *adj.* **13.** Markt…: ~ **day**; **14.** Börsen…; **15.** Kurs…: ~ **profit**; **'mar·ket·a·ble** [-təbl] *adj.* marktfähig, -gängig; börsenfähig.

mar·ket| a·nal·y·sis *s.* † 'Marktana,lyse *f*; ~ **con·di·tion** *s.* † Marktlage *f*, Konjunk'tur *f*; ~ **e·con·o·my** *s.* † (**free** ~, **social** ~ freie, sozi'ale) Marktwirtschaft; ~ **fluc·tu·a·tion** *s.* † **1.** Konjunk'turbewegung *f*; **2.** *pl.* Konjunk'turschwankungen *pl.*; ~ **gar·den** *s. Brit.* Handelsgärtne'rei *f*.

mar·ket·ing ['mɑːkɪtɪŋ] **I** *s.* **1.** † Marketing *n*, Marktversorgung *f*, 'Absatzpoli,tik *f*, -förderung *f*; **2.** Marktbesuch *m*; **II** *adj.* **3.** Markt…: ~ **association** Marktverband *m*; ~ **company** Vertriebsgesellschaft *f*; ~ **organization** Absatzorganisation *f*; ~ **research** Absatzforschung *f*.

mar·ket| in·ves·ti·ga·tion *s.* 'Marktunter,suchung *f*; ~ **lead·ers** *s. pl.* führende Börsenwerte *pl.*; ~ **let·ter** *s. Am.* Markt-, Börsenbericht *m*; ~ **niche** *s.* Marktnische *f*, -lücke *f*; **'~-,o·ri·ent·ed** *adj.* † marktorientiert; **'~-place** *s.* Marktplatz *m*; ~ **price** *s.* **1.** Marktpreis *m*; **2.** *Börse*: Kurs(wert) *m*; ~ **quo·ta·tion** *s.* Börsennotierung *f*, Marktkurs *m*: **list of** ~**s** Markt-, Börsenzettel *m*; ~ **rate** → **market price**; ~ **re·search** *s.* † Marktforschung *f*; ~ **re·search·er** *s.* † Marktforscher *m*; ~ **rig·ging** *s.* Kurstreibe'rei *f*, 'Börsenma,növer *n*; ~ **share** *s.* Marktanteil *m*; ~ **stud·y** *s.* † 'Marktunter,suchung *f*; ~ **swing** *s. Am.* Konjunk'turperi,ode *f*; **'~-town** *s.* Markt(flecken) *m*; ~ **val·ue** *s.* Kurs-, Verkehrswert *m*.

mark·ing ['mɑːkɪŋ] **I** *s.* **1.** Kennzeichnung *f*, Markierung *f*; Bezeichnung *f* (*a.* ♪); *ped.* Zensieren *n*; ✈ Hoheitsabzeichen *n*; **2.** *zo.* (Haut-, Feder)Musterung *f*, Zeichnung *f*; **II** *adj.* **3.** ⚙ markierend: ~ **awl** Reißahle *f*; ~ **ink** Zeichen-, Wäschetinte *f*.

marks·man ['mɑːksmən] *s.* [*irr.*] guter Schütze, Meisterschütze *m*, *bsd.* ⚔ *u. Polizei*: Scharfschütze *m*; **'marks·man·ship** [-ʃɪp] *s.* **1.** Schießkunst *f*; **2.** Treffsicherheit *f*.

'mark·up *s.* † **1.** a) höhere Auszeichnung (*e-r Ware*), b) Preiserhöhung *f*; **2.** Kalkulati'onsaufschlag *m*; **3.** *Am.* im Preis erhöhter Ar'tikel.

marl [mɑːl] **I** *s. geol.* Mergel *m*; **II** *v/t.* ✓ mergeln.

mar·ma·lade ['mɑːməleɪd] *s.* (*bsd.* O'rangen)Marme,lade *f*.

mar·mo·set ['mɑːməʊzet] *s. zo.* Krallenaffe *m*.

mar·mot ['mɑːmət] *s. zo.* **1.** Murmeltier *n*; **2.** Prä'riehund *m*.

mar·o·cain ['mærəkeɪn] *s.* Maro'cain *n* (*ein Kreppgewebe*).

ma·roon¹ [mə'ruːn] **I** *v/t.* **1.** (*auf e-r einsamen Insel etc.*) aussetzen; **2.** *fig.* a) im Stich lassen, b) von der Außenwelt abschneiden; **II** *v/i.* **3.** *Brit.* her'umlungern; **4.** *Am.* einsam zelten; **III** *s.* **5.** Busch-, Ma'ronneger *m* (*Westindien u. Guayana*); **6.** Ausgesetzte(r *m*) *f*.

ma·roon² [mə'ruːn] **I** *s.* **1.** Ka'stanienbraun *n*; **2.** Ka'nonenschlag *m* (*Feuerwerk*); **II** *adj.* **3.** ka'stanienbraun.

mar·plot ['mɑːplɒt] *s.* **1.** Quertreiber *m*; **2.** Spielverderber *m*, Störenfried *m*.

marque [mɑːk] *s.* ⚓ *hist.*: **letter**(**s**) **of** ~

(***and reprisal***) Kaperbrief *m*.
mar·quee [mɑːˈkiː] *s*. **1.** großes Zelt; **2.** *Am.* Marˈkise *f*, Schirmdach *n* (*über e-m Hoteleingang etc.*); **3.** Vordach *n* (*über Haustür*).
mar·quess [ˈmɑːkwɪs] *s*. → ***marquis***.
mar·que·try, *a*. **mar·que·te·rie** [ˈmɑːkɪtrɪ] *s*. Inˈtarsia *f*, Marketeˈrie *f*, Holzeinlegearbeit *f*.
mar·quis [ˈmɑːkwɪs] *s*. Marˈquis *m* (*englischer Adelstitel*).
mar·riage [ˈmærɪdʒ] *s*. **1.** Heirat *f*, Vermählung *f*, Hochzeit *f* (***to*** mit); → ***civil*** 4; **2.** Ehe(stand *m*) *f*: ***~ of convenience*** Vernunftehe, Geldheirat *f*; ***by ~*** angeheiratet; ***of his*** (***her***) ***first ~*** aus erster Ehe; ***related by ~*** verschwägert; ***contract a ~*** die Ehe eingehen; ***give s.o. in ~*** j-n verheiraten; ***take s.o. in ~*** j-n heiraten; **3.** *fig.* Vermählung *f*, innige Verbindung; **ˈmar·riage·a·ble** [-dʒəbl] *adj*. heiratsfähig: ***~ age*** Ehemündigkeit *f*.
mar·riage| ar·ti·cles *s. pl.* ⚖ Ehevertrag *m*; **~ bro·ker** *s*. Heiratsvermittler *m*; **~ bu·reau** *s*. ˈHeiratsinstiˌtut *n*; **~ cer·e·mo·ny** *s*. Trauung *f*; **~ cer·tif·i·cate** *s*. Trauschein *m*; **~ con·tract** *s*. ⚖ Ehevertrag *m*; **~ flight** *s*. *Bienenzucht*: Hochzeitsflug *m*; **~ guid·ance** *s*. Eheberatung *f*: ***~ counsel(l)or*** Eheberater(in); **~ li·cence**, *Am.* **~ li·cense** *s*. ⚖ (kirchliche, *Am.* amtliche) Eheerlaubnis; **~ lines** *s. pl. Brit.* F Trauschein *m*; **~ por·tion** *s*. ⚖ Mitgift *f*; **~ set·tle·ment** *s*. ⚖ Ehevertrag *m*.
mar·ried [ˈmærɪd] *adj*. **1.** verheiratet, Ehe…, ehelich: ***~ life*** Eheleben *n*; ***~ man*** Ehemann *m*; ***~ state*** Ehestand *m*; **2.** *fig.* eng *od.* innig (miteinˈander) verbunden.
mar·ron [ˈmærən] *s*. ⚘ Maˈrone *f*.
mar·row¹ [ˈmærəʊ] *s*. **1.** *anat.* (Knochen)Mark *n*; **2.** *fig.* Mark *n*, Kern *m*, *das* Innerste *od.* Wesentlichste; Lebenskraft *f*: ***to the ~*** (***of one's bones***) bis aufs Mark, bis ins Innerste; → ***pith*** 2.
mar·row² [ˈmærəʊ] *s*. *Am.* *mst* ***~ squash***, *Brit.* *a.* ***vegetable ~*** ⚘ Eier-, Markkürbis *m*.
ˈmar·row·bone *s*. **1.** Markknochen *m*; **2.** *pl. humor.* Knie *pl.*; **3.** *pl.* → ***crossbones***.
mar·row·less [ˈmærəʊlɪs] *adj*. *fig.* mark-, kraftlos.
mar·row·y [ˈmærəʊɪ] *adj*. *a. fig.* markig, kernig, kräftig.
mar·ry¹ [ˈmærɪ] **I** *v/t*. **1.** heiraten, sich vermählen *od.* verheiraten mit: ***be married to*** verheiratet sein mit; ***get married to*** sich verheiraten mit; **2.** *a.* ***~ off*** *Sohn, Tochter* verheiraten (***to*** an *acc.*, mit); **3.** *ein Paar* trauen (*Geistlicher*); **4.** *fig.* eng verbinden *od.* verknüpfen (***to*** mit); **II** *v/i*. **5.** (sich ver-) heiraten: ***~ing man*** F Heiratslustige(r) *m*, Ehekandidat *m*; ***~ in haste and repent at leisure*** schnell gefreit, lang bereut.
mar·ry¹ [ˈmærɪ] *int. obs.* fürˈwahr!
Mars [mɑːz] *npr. u. s.* Mars *m* (*Kriegsgott od. Planet*).
marsh [mɑːʃ] *s*. **1.** Sumpf(land *n*) *m*, Marsch *f*; **2.** Moˈrast *m*.
mar·shal [ˈmɑːʃl] **I** *s*. **1.** ⚔ Marschall *m*; **2.** ⚖ *Brit.* Gerichtsbeamte(r) *m*; **3.** ⚖ *Am.* a) ***US ~*** (ˈBundes)Vollˌzugsbeamte(r) *m*, b) Beˈzirkspoliˌzeichef *m*, c) *a.* ***city ~*** Poliˈzeidiˌrektor *m*, d) *a.* ***fire ~*** ˈBranddiˌrektor *m*; **4.** *hist.* ˈHofmarˌschall *m*; **5.** Zereˈmonienmeister *m*; Festordner *m*; *mot.* Rennwart *m*; **II** *v/t*. **6.** aufstellen (*a.* ⚔); (an)ordnen, arrangieren: ***~ wag(g)ons into trains*** Züge zs.-stellen; ***~ one's thoughts*** *fig.* s-e Gedanken ordnen; **7.** (*bsd. feierlich*) (hinˈein)geleiten (***into*** in *acc.*); **8.** ✈ einwinken; **ˈmar·shal·(l)ing yard** [-ʃlɪŋ] *s*. 🚂 Rangier-, Verschiebebahnhof *m*.
ˈmarsh|-ˌfe·ver *s*. ⚕ Sumpffieber *n*; **~ gas** *s*. Sumpfgas *n*; **ˈ~·land** *s*. Sumpf-, Marschland *n*; **ˌ~ˈmal·low** *s*. **1.** ⚘ Echter Eibisch, Alˈthee *f*; **2.** Marshˈmallow *n* (*Süßigkeit*); **~ mar·i·gold** *s*. ⚘ Sumpfdotterblume *f*.
marsh·y [ˈmɑːʃɪ] *adj*. sumpfig, moˈrastig, Sumpf…
mar·su·pi·al [mɑːˈsjuːpjəl] *zo.* **I** *adj*. **1.** Beuteltier…; **2.** Beutel…; **II** *s*. **3.** Beuteltier *n*.
mart [mɑːt] *s*. **1.** Markt *m*, Handelszentrum *n*; **2.** Auktiˈonsraum *m*; **3.** *obs. od. poet.* Markt(platz) *m*, (Jahr)Markt *m*.
mar·ten [ˈmɑːtɪn] *s*. *zo.* Marder *m*.
mar·tial [ˈmɑːʃl] *adj*. □ **1.** kriegerisch, streitbar; **2.** miliˈtärisch, solˈdatisch: ***~ music*** Militärmusik *f*; **3.** Kriegs…, Militär…: ***~ law*** Kriegs-, Standrecht *n*; ***state of ~ law*** Ausnahmezustand *m*; ***~ arts*** asiatische Kampfsportarten.
Mar·ti·an [ˈmɑːʃjən] **I** *s*. **1.** Marsmensch *m*; **II** *adj*. **2.** Mars…, kriegerisch; **3.** *ast.* Mars…
mar·tin [ˈmɑːtɪn] *s*. *orn.* Mauerschwalbe *f*.
mar·ti·net [ˌmɑːtɪˈnet] *s*. Leuteschinder *m*, Zuchtmeister *m*.
mar·tyr [ˈmɑːtə] **I** *s*. **1.** Märtyrer(in), Blutzeuge *m*; **2.** *fig.* Märtyrer(in), Opfer *n*: ***make a ~ of o.s.*** sich für et. aufopfern, *iro.* den Märtyrer spielen: ***die a ~ to*** (*od.* ***in the cause of***) ***science*** sein Leben im Dienst der Wissenschaft opfern; **3.** F Dulder *m*, armer Kerl: ***be a ~ to gout*** ständig von Gicht geplagt werden; **II** *v/t*. **4.** zum Märtyrer machen; **5.** zu Tode martern; **6.** martern, peinigen; **ˈmar·tyr·dom** [-dəm] *s*. **1.** Marˈtyrium *n* (*a. fig.*), Märtyrertod *m*; **2.** Marterqualen *pl.* (*a. fig.*); **ˈmar·tyr·ize** [-əraɪz] *v/t*. **1.** (***o.s.*** sich) zum Märtyrer machen (*a. fig.*); **2.** → ***martyr*** 6.
mar·vel [ˈmɑːvl] **I** *s*. **1.** Wunder(ding) *n*: ***engineering ~s*** Wunder der Technik; ***be a ~ at s.th.*** et. fabelhaft können; **2.** Muster *n* (***of*** an *dat.*): ***he is a ~ of patience*** er ist die Geduld selber; ***he is a perfect ~*** F er ist phantastisch *od.* ein Phänomen; **II** *v/i*. **3.** sich (ver)wundern, staunen (***at*** über *acc.*); **4.** sich verwundert fragen, sich wundern (***that*** daß, ***how*** wie, ***why*** warum).
mar·vel·(l)ous [ˈmɑːvələs] *adj*. □ **1.** erstaunlich, wunderbar; **2.** unˈglaublich; **3.** F fabelhaft, phanˈtastisch.
Marx·i·an [ˈmɑːksjən] → ***Marxist***; **ˈMarx·ism** [-sɪzəm] *s*. Marˈxismus *m*; **ˈMarx·ist** [-sɪst] **I** *s*. Marˈxist(in); **II** *adj*. marˈxistisch.
mar·zi·pan [ˌmɑːzɪˈpæn] *s*. Marziˈpan *n*.
mas·car·a [mæˈskɑːrə] *s*. Wimperntusche *f*.
mas·cot [ˈmæskət] *s*. Masˈkottchen *n*, Talisman *m*; Glücksbringer(in): ***radiator ~*** *mot.* Kühlerfigur *f*.
mas·cu·line [ˈmæskjʊlɪn] **I** *adj*. **1.** männlich, maskuˈlin (*a. ling.*); Männer…; **2.** unweiblich, maskuˈlin; **II** *s*. **3.** *ling.* Maskuˈlinum *n*; **mas·cu·lin·i·ty** [ˌmæskjʊˈlɪnətɪ] *s*. **1.** Männlichkeit *f*; **2.** Mannhaftigkeit *f*.
mash¹ [mæʃ] **I** *s*. **1.** *Brauerei etc.*: Maische *f*; **2.** ✓ Mengfutter *n*; **3.** Brei *m*, Mansch *m*; **4.** *Brit.* Karˈtoffelbrei *m*; **5.** *fig.* Mischmasch *m*; **II** *v/t*. **6.** (ein)maischen; **7.** zerdrücken, -quetschen: ***~ed potatoes*** Kartoffelbrei *m*.
mash² [mæʃ] *obs. sl.* **I** *v/t*. **1.** *j-m* den Kopf verdrehen; **2.** flirten mit; **II** *v/i*. **3.** flirten, schäkern.
mash·er¹ [ˈmæʃə] *s*. **1.** Stampfer *m* (*Küchengerät*); **2.** *Brauerei*: ˈMaischappaˌrat *m*.
mash·er² [ˈmæʃə] *s*. *obs. sl.* Schwerenöter *m*, ‚Schäker' *m*.
mask [mɑːsk] **I** *s*. **1.** Maske *f* (*a.* △), Larve *f*: ***death-~*** Totenmaske; **2.** (Schutz-, Gesichts)Maske *f*: ***fencing ~*** Fechtmaske; ***oxygen ~*** ⚕ Sauerstoffmaske; **3.** Gasmaske *f*; **4.** Maske *f*: a) Maskierte(r *m*) *f*, b) ˈMaskenkoˌstüm *n*, Maskierung *f*, c) *fig.* Verkappung *f*: ***throw off the ~*** *fig.* die Maske fallen lassen; ***under the ~ of*** unter dem Deckmantel (*gen.*); **5.** maskenhaftes Gesicht; **6.** *Kosmetik*: (Gesichts)Maske *f*; **7.** → ***masque***; **8.** ⚔ Tarnung *f*, Blende *f*; **9.** *phot.* Vorsatzscheibe *f*; **II** *v/t*. **10.** *j-n* maskieren, verkleiden, vermummen; *fig.* verschleiern, -hüllen; **11.** ⚔ tarnen; **12.** *a.* ***~ out*** ⚙ korrigieren, retuschieren; *Licht* abblenden; **masked** [-kt] *adj*. **1.** maskiert (*a.* ⚘); Masken…: ***~ ball*** Maskenball *m*; **2.** ⚔, ✝ getarnt: ***~ advertising*** Schleichwerbung *f*; **ˈmask·er** [-kə] *s*. Maske *f*, Maskenspieler *m*.
mas·och·ism [ˈmæsəʊkɪzəm] *s*. ⚕, *psych.* Masoˈchismus *m*; **ˈmas·och·ist** [-ɪst] *s*. Masoˈchist *m*.
ma·son [ˈmeɪsn] **I** *s*. **1.** Steinmetz *m*; **2.** Maurer *m*; **3.** *oft* ♀ Freimaurer *m*; **II** *v/t*. **4.** mauern; **Ma·son·ic** [məˈsɒnɪk] *adj*. freimaurerisch, Freimaurer…; **ˈma·son·ry** [-rɪ] *s*. **1.** Steinmetz-, Maurerarbeit *f od.* -handwerk *n*; **2.** Mauerwerk *n*; **3.** *mst.* ♀ Freimaureˈrei *f*.
masque [mɑːsk] *s*. *thea. hist.* Maskenspiel *n*.
mas·quer·ade [ˌmæskəˈreɪd] **I** *s*. **1.** Maskeˈrade *f*: a) Maskenball *m*, b) Maskierung *f*, c) *fig.* Theˈater *n*, Verstellung *f*, d) *fig.* Maske *f*, Verkleidung *f*; **II** *v/i*. **2.** an e-r Maskerade teilnehmen; **3.** sich maskieren *od.* verkleiden (*a. fig.*); **4.** *fig.* sich ausgeben (***as*** als).
mass¹ [mæs] **I** *s*. **1.** *allg.* Masse *f* (*a.* ⚙ *u. phys.*): ***a ~ of blood*** ein Klumpen Blut; ***a ~ of troops*** e-e Truppenansammlung; ***in the ~*** im großen u. ganzen; **2.** Mehrzahl *f*: ***the*** (***great***) ***~ of imports*** der überwiegende Teil der Einfuhr; **3.** ***the ~*** die Masse, die Allgeˈmeinheit: ***the ~es*** die ‚breite' Masse; **II** *v/t*. **4.** (*v/i.* sich) (an)sammeln *od.* (an)häufen, (*v/i.* sich) zs.-ballen; ⚔ (*v/i.* sich) massieren *od.* konzentrieren; **III** *adj*. **5.**

Massen…: ~ ***acceleration*** *phys.* Massenbeschleunigung *f*; ~ ***communication*** Massenkommunikation *f*; ~ ***meeting*** Massenversammlung *f*; ~ ***murder*** Massenmord *m*; ~ ***society*** Massengesellschaft *f*.

Mass² [mæs] *s. eccl.* (*a.* ♪) Messe *f*; → ***High*** (***Low***) ***Mass***; ~ ***was said*** die Messe wurde gelesen; ***to attend*** (***the***) (*od.* ***go to***) ~ zur Messe gehen; ~ ***for the dead*** Toten-, Seelenmesse.

mas·sa·cre [ˈmæsəkə] **I** *s.* Gemetzel *n*, Masˈsaker *n*, Blutbad *n*; **II** *v/t.* niedermetzeln, massakrieren.

mas·sage [ˈmæsɑːʒ] **I** *s.* Masˈsage *f*: ~ ***parlo*(*u*)*r*** Massagesalon *m*; **II** *v/t.* massieren.

mas·seur [mæˈsɜː] (*Fr.*) *s.* Masˈseur *m*; **mas·seuse** [mæˈsɜːz] (*Fr.*) *s.* Masˈseurin *f*, Masˈseuse *f*.

mas·sif [ˈmæsiːf] *s. geol.* Geˈbirgsmasˌsiv *n*, -stock *m*.

mas·sive [ˈmæsɪv] *adj.* ☐ **1.** masˈsiv (*a. geol.*, *a. Gold etc.*), schwer, massig; **2.** *fig.* masˈsiv, gewaltig, wuchtig, ‚klotzig'; ˈ**mas·sive·ness** [-nɪs] *s.* **1.** Masˈsive(s) *n*, Schwere(s) *n*; **2.** Gediegenheit *f* (*Gold etc.*); **3.** *fig.* Wucht *f*.

mass| me·di·a *s. pl.* Massenmedien *pl.*; ˈ**~-proˌduce** *v/t.* serienmäßig herstellen: ***~d articles*** Massen-, Serienartikel; ~ **pro·duc·tion** *s.* ✝ ˈMassen-, ˈSerienproduktiˌon *f*: ***standardized*** ~ Fließarbeit *f*.

mass·y [ˈmæsɪ] → ***massive***.

mast¹ [mɑːst] **I** *s.* **1.** ⚓ (Schiffs)Mast *m*: ***sail before the*** ~ (als Matrose) zur See fahren; **2.** (Gitter-, Leitungs-, Anˈtennen-, ✈ Anker)Mast *m*; **II** *v/t.* **3.** ⚓ bemasten: ***three-~ed*** dreimastig.

mast² [mɑːst] *s.* ✓ Mast(futter *n*) *f*.

mas·tec·to·my [mæˈstektəmɪ] *s.* ⚕ ˈBrustamputatiˌon *f*.

mas·ter [ˈmɑːstə] **I** *s.* **1.** Meister *m* (*a. Kunst u. fig.*), Herr *m*, Gebieter *m*: ***the*** ***ℒ*** *eccl.* der Herr (*Christus*); ***be ~ of s.th.*** et. (*a. e-e Sprache*) beherrschen; ***be ~ of o.s.*** sich in der Gewalt haben; ***be ~ of the situation*** Herr der Lage sein; ***be one's own ~*** sein eigener Herr sein; ***be ~ of one's time*** über s-e Zeit (nach Belieben) verfügen können; **2.** Besitzer *m*, Eigentümer *m*, Herr *m*: ***make o.s. ~ of s.th.*** et. in s-n Besitz bringen; **3.** Hausherr *m*; **4.** Meister *m*, Sieger *m*; **5.** a) Lehrherr *m*, Meister *m*, b) *a.* ⚖ Dienstherr *m*, Arbeitgeber *m*, c) (Handwerks)Meister *m*: ~ ***tailor*** Schneidermeister; ***like ~ like man*** wie der Heer, so's Gescherr; **6.** Vorsteher *m*, Leiter *m e-r Innung etc.*; **7.** ⚓ (ˈHandels)Kapiˌtän *m*: ***~'s certificate*** Kapitänspatent *n*; **8.** *bsd. Brit.* Lehrer *m*: ~ ***in English*** Englischlehrer; **9.** *Brit. univ.* Rektor *m* (*Titel der Leiter einiger Colleges*); **10.** *univ.* Maˈgister *m* (*Grad*): ***ℒ of Arts*** Magister Artium; ***ℒ of Science*** Magister der Naturwissenschaften; **11.** junger Herr (*a. als Anrede für Knaben bis zu 16 Jahren*); **12.** *Brit.* (*in Titeln*): Leiter *m*, Aufseher *m* (*am königlichen Hof etc.*): ***ℒ of Ceremonies*** a) Zeremonienmeister *m*, b) Conférencier *m*; ***ℒ of the Horse*** Oberstallmeister *m*; **13.** ⚖ protoˈkollführender Gerichtsbeamter: ***ℒ of the Rolls*** Oberarchivar *m*; **14.** → ***master copy*** 1; **II** *v/t.* **15.** Herr sein *od.* werden über (*acc.*) (*a. fig.*), *a. Sprache etc.* beherrschen; *Aufgabe*, *Schwierigkeit* meistern; **16.** *Tier* zähmen; *a. Leidenschaften etc.* bändigen; **III** *adj.* **17.** Meister…, meisterhaft, -lich; **18.** Meister…, Herren…; **19.** Haupt…, hauptsächlich: ~ ***file*** Hauptkartei *f*; ~ ***switch*** ⚡ Hauptschalter *m*; **20.** leitend, führend.

ˌ**mas·ter|-at-ˈarms** [-ərətˈɑː-] *pl.* ˌ**mas·ters-at-ˈarms** [-əzətˈɑː-] *s.* ⚓ ˈSchiffsproˌfos *m* (*Polizeioffizier*); ~ **build·er** *s.* Baumeister *m*; ~ **car·pen·ter** *s.* Zimmermeister *m*; ~ **chord** *s.* ♪ Domiˈnantdreiklang *m*; ~ **clock** *s.* Zenˈtraluhr *f* (*e-r Uhrenanlage*); ~ **cop·y** *s.* **1.** Origiˈnalkoˌpie *f* (*a. Film etc.*); **2.** ˈHandexemˌplar *n* (*e-s literarischen etc. Werks*).

mas·ter·ful [ˈmɑːstəfʊl] *adj.* ☐ **1.** herrisch, gebieterisch; **2.** → ***masterly***.

mas·ter| fuse *s.* ⚡ Hauptsicherung *f*; ~ **ga**(**u**)**ge** *s.* ⚙ Urlehre *f*; ˈ**~·key** *s.* **1.** Hauptschlüssel *m*; **2.** *fig.* Schlüssel *m*.

mas·ter·less [ˈmɑːstəlɪs] *adj.* herrenlos; ˈ**mas·ter·li·ness** [-lɪnɪs] *s.* meisterhafte Ausführung, Meisterschaft *f*; ˈ**mas·ter·ly** [-lɪ] *adj. u. adv.* meisterhaft, -lich, Meister…

ˈ**mas·ter|·mind I** *s.* **1.** überˈragender Geist, Geˈnie *n*; **2.** (führender) Kopf; **II** *v/t.* **3.** der Kopf (*gen.*) sein, leiten; ˈ**~·piece** *s.* Meisterstück *n*, -werk *n*; ~ **plan** *s.* Gesamtplan *m*; ~ **ser·geant** *s.* ⚔ *Am.* (Ober)Stabsfeldwebel *m*.

mas·ter·ship [ˈmɑːstəʃɪp] *s.* **1.** meisterhafte Beherrschung (***of*** *gen.*), Meisterschaft *f*; **2.** Herrschaft *f*, Gewalt *f* (***over*** über *acc.*); **3.** Vorsteheramt *n*; **4.** Lehramt *n*.

ˈ**mas·ter|-stroke** *s.* Meisterstreich *m*, -stück *n*, Glanzstück *n*; ~ **tooth** *s.* [*irr.*] Eck-, Fangzahn *m*; ~ **touch** *s.* **1.** Meisterhaftigkeit *f*, -schaft *f*; **2.** Meisterzug *m*; **3.** ⚙ *u. fig.* letzter Schliff; ˈ**~·work** → ***masterpiece***.

mas·ter·y [ˈmɑːstərɪ] *s.* **1.** Herrschaft *f*, Gewalt *f* (***of***, ***over*** über *acc.*); **2.** Überˈlegenheit *f*, Oberhand *f*: ***gain the ~ over s.o.*** über j-n die Oberhand gewinnen; **3.** Beherrschung *f* (*e-r Sprache etc.*); **4.** → ***master touch*** 1.

ˈ**mast-head** *s.* **1.** ⚓ Masttop *m*, Mars *m*: ~ ***light*** Topplicht *n*; **2.** *typ.* Imˈpressum *n e-r Zeitung*.

mas·tic [ˈmæstɪk] *s.* **1.** Mastix(harz *n*) *m*; **2.** ⚘ Mastixstrauch *m*; **3.** Mastik *m*, ˈMastixzeˌment *m*.

mas·ti·cate [ˈmæstɪkeɪt] *v/t.* (zer-)kauen; **mas·ti·ca·tion** [ˌmæstɪˈkeɪʃn] *s.* Kauen *n*; ˈ**mas·ti·ca·tor** [-tə] *s.* **1.** Kauende(r *m*) *f*; **2.** Fleischwolf *m*; **3.** ⚙ ˈMahlmaˌschine *f*; ˈ**mas·ti·ca·to·ry** [-kətərɪ] *adj.* Kau…, Freß…

mas·tiff [ˈmæstɪf] *s.* Mastiff *m*, Bulldogge *f*, englische Dogge.

mas·ti·tis [mæˈstaɪtɪs] *s.* ⚕ Brust(drüsen)entzündung *f*; **mas·toid** [ˈmæstɔɪd] *adj. anat.* mastoˈid, brust(warzen)förmig; **mas·tot·o·my** [mæˈstɒtəmɪ] *s.* ⚕ ˈBrustoperatiˌon *f*.

mas·tur·bate [ˈmæstəbeɪt] *v/i.* masturbieren; **mas·tur·ba·tion** [ˌmæstəˈbeɪʃn] *s.* Masturbatiˈon *f*.

mat¹ [mæt] **I** *s.* **1.** Matte *f* (*a. Ringen, Turnen*): ~ ***position*** *Ringen*: Bank *f*; ***be on the ~*** a) am Boden sein, b) *sl. fig.* ‚dran' sein, in der Tinte sitzen, *a.* e-e Zigarre verpaßt kriegen; **2.** ˈUntersetzer *m*, -satz *m*: ***beer ~*** Bierdeckel *m*; **3.** Vorleger *m*, Abtreter *m*; **4.** grober Sack; **5.** verfilzte Masse (*Haar etc.*), Gewirr *n*; **6.** (*glasloser*) Wechselrahmen; **II** *v/t.* **7.** mit Matten belegen; **8.** (*v/i.* sich) verflechten; **9.** (*v/i.* sich) verfilzen (*Haar*).

mat² [mæt] **I** *adj.* matt (*a. phot.*), glanzlos, mattiert; **II** *v/t.* mattieren.

match¹ [mætʃ] **I** *s.* **1.** *der od. die od. das gleiche od.* Ebenbürtige: ***his ~*** a) seinesgleichen, b) sein Ebenbild *n*, c) j-d, der es mit ihm aufnehmen kann; ***meet one's ~*** s-n Meister finden; ***be a ~ for s.o.*** j-m gewachsen sein; ***be more than a ~ for s.o.*** j-m überlegen sein; **2.** Gegenstück *n*, Passende(s) *n*; **3.** (zs.-passendes) Paar, Gespann *n* (*a. fig.*): ***they are an excellent ~*** sie passen ausgezeichnet zueinander; **4.** ✝ Arˈtikel *m* gleicher Qualiˈtät: ***exact ~*** genaue Bemusterung; **5.** (Wett)Kampf *m*, Wettspiel *n*, Parˈtie *f*, Treffen *n*: ***boxing ~*** Boxkampf; ***singing ~*** Wettsingen *n*; **6.** a) Heirat *f*, b) *gute etc.* Parˈtie (*Person*): ***make a ~*** (***of it***) e-e Ehe stiften *od.* zustande bringen; **II** *v/t.* **7.** *j-n* passend verheiraten (***to***, ***with*** mit); **8.** *j-n od. et.* vergleichen (***with*** mit); **9.** *j-n* ausspielen (***against*** gegen); **10.** passend machen, anpassen (***to***, ***with*** an *acc.*); *a. ehelich* verbinden, zs.-fügen; ⚡ angleichen: ***~ing circuit*** Anpassungskreis *m*; **11.** entsprechen (*dat.*), *a. farblich etc.* passen zu: ***well-~ed*** gut zs.-passend; **12.** et. gleiches *od.* Passendes auswählen *od.* finden zu: ***can you ~ this velvet for me?*** haben Sie et. Passendes zu diesem Samtstoff?; **13.** *nur pass.*: ***be ~ed*** *j-m* ebenbürtig *od.* gewachsen sein, *e-r Sache* gleichkommen; ***not to be ~ed*** unerreichbar; **III** *v/i.* **14.** zs.-passen, überˈeinstimmen (***with*** mit), entsprechen (***to*** *dat.*): ***a brown coat and gloves to ~*** ein brauner Mantel u. dazu passende Handschuhe.

match² [mætʃ] *s.* **1.** Zünd-, Streichholz *n*; **2.** Zündschnur *f*; **3.** *hist.* Lunte *f*; ˈ**~·box** *s.* Streichholzschachtel *f*.

match·less [ˈmætʃlɪs] *adj.* ☐ unvergleichlich, einzigartig.

ˈ**matchˌmak·er** *s.* **1.** Ehestifter(in), *b.s.* Kuppler(in); **2.** Heiratsvermittler(in).

match| point *s. sport* (für den Sieg) entscheidender Punkt; *Tennis etc.*: Matchball *m*; ˈ**~·wood** *s.* (Holz)Späne *pl.*, Splitter *pl.*: ***make ~ of s.th.*** aus et. Kleinholz machen, et. kurz u. klein schlagen.

mate¹ [meɪt] **I** *s.* **1.** a) (ˈArbeits)Kameˌrad *m*, Genosse *m*, Gefährte *m*, b) *als Anrede*: Kameˈrad *m*, ‚Kumpel' *m*, c) Gehilfe *m*, Handlanger *m*; **2.** a) (Lebens)Gefährte *m*, Gatte *m*, Gattin *f*, b) *bsd. orn.* Männchen *n od.* Weibchen *n*, c) Gegenstück *n* (*von Schuhen etc.*); **3.** *Handelsmarine*: ˈSchiffsoffiˌzier *m*; **4.** ⚓ Maat *m*: ***cook's ~*** Kochsmaat; **II** *v/t.* **5.** (*paarweise*) verbinden, *bsd.* vermählen, -heiraten; *Tiere* paaren; **6.** *fig.* einˈander anpassen: ~ ***words with deeds*** auf Worte entsprechende Taten folgen lassen; **III** *v/i.* **7.** sich vermählen, (*a. weitS.*) sich verbinden; *zo.* sich paaren;

8. ⚙ eingreifen (*Zahnräder*); aufein'ander arbeiten (*Flächen*): ***mating surfaces*** Arbeitsflächen.

mate² [meɪt] → ***checkmate***.

ma·te·ri·al [mə'tɪərɪəl] **I** *adj.* □ **1.** materi'ell, physisch, körperlich; **2.** stofflich, Material...: ***~ damage*** Sachschaden *m*; ***~ defect*** Materialfehler *m*; ***~ fatigue*** ⚙ Materialermüdung *f*; ***~ goods*** Sachgüter; **3.** materia'listisch (*Anschauung etc.*); **4.** materi'ell, leiblich: ***~ well-being***; **5.** a) sachlich wichtig, gewichtig, von Belang, b) wesentlich, ausschlaggebend (***to*** für); ⚖ erheblich: ***~ facts***; ***a ~ witness*** ein unentbehrlicher Zeuge; **6.** *Logik*: sachlich (*Folgerung etc.*); **7.** ⩚ materi'ell (*Punkt etc.*); **II** *s.* **8.** Materi'al *n*, Stoff *m* (*beide a. fig.*; ***for*** zu *e-m Buch etc.*); ⚙ Werkstoff *m*; (Kleider-)Stoff *m*; **9.** *coll. od. pl.* Materi'al(ien *pl.*) *n*, Ausrüstung *f*: ***building ~s*** Baustoffe; ***cleaning ~s*** Putzzeug *n*; ***war ~*** Kriegsmaterial; ***writing ~s*** Schreibmaterial(ien); **10.** *oft pl. fig.* 'Unterlagen *pl.*, *urkundliches etc.* Materi'al; **ma'te·ri·al·ism** [-lɪzəm] *s.* Materia'lismus *m*; **ma'te·ri·al·ist** [-lɪst] **I** *s.* Materia'list(in); **II** *adj. a.* **ma·te·ri·al·is·tic** [məˌtɪərɪə'lɪstɪk] *adj.* (□ ***~ally***) materia'listisch; **ma·te·ri·al·i·za·tion** [məˌtɪərɪəlaɪ'zeɪʃn] *s.* **1.** Verkörperung *f*; **2.** *Spiritismus*: Materialisati'on *f*; **ma'te·ri·al·ize** [-laɪz] **I** *v/t.* **1.** *e-r Sache* stoffliche Form geben, *et.* verkörperlichen; **2.** *et.* verwirklichen; **3.** *bsd. Am.* materia'listisch machen: ***~ thought***; **4.** *Geister* erscheinen lassen; **II** *v/i.* **5.** (feste) Gestalt annehmen, sich verkörpern (***in*** in *dat.*); **6.** sich verwirklichen, Tatsache werden, zu'stande kommen; **7.** sich materialisieren, erscheinen (*Geister*).

ma·té·ri·el [məˌtɪərɪ'el] *s.* Ausrüstung *f*, (⚔ 'Kriegs)Materiˌal *n*.

ma·ter·nal [mə'tɜːnl] *adj.* □ a) mütterlich, Mutter...: ***~ instinct*** (***love***), b) *Verwandte(r) etc.* mütterlicherseits, c) Mütter...: ***~ mortality*** Müttersterblichkeit *f*.

ma·ter·ni·ty [mə'tɜːnətɪ] **I** *s.* Mutterschaft *f*; **II** *adj.* Wöchnerinnen..., Schwangerschafts..., Umstands...(*-kleidung*): ***~ allowance*** (*od.* ***benefit***) Mutterschaftsbeihilfe *f*; ***~ dress*** Umstandskleid *n*; ***~ home***, ***~ hospital*** Entbindungsklinik *f*; ***~ leave*** Mutterschaftsurlaub *m*; ***~ ward*** Entbindungsstation *f*.

mat·ey ['meɪtɪ] **I** *adj.* kame'radschaftlich, vertraulich, famili'är; **II** *s. Brit.* F ‚Kumpel' *m* (*Anrede*).

math [mæθ] *s. Am. für* ***maths***.

math·e·mat·i·cal [ˌmæθə'mætɪkl] *adj.* □ **1.** mathe'matisch; **2.** *fig.* (mathe'matisch) ex'akt; **math·e·ma·ti·cian** [ˌmæθəmə'tɪʃn] *s.* Mathe'matiker(in); **ˌmath·e'mat·ics** [-ks] *s. pl. mst sg. konstr.* Mathema'tik *f*: ***higher*** (***new***) ***~*** höhere (neue) Mathematik.

maths [mæθs] *s. Brit.* F ‚Mathe' *f* (*Mathematik*).

mat·ins ['mætɪnz] *s. pl. oft* ♀ a) *R.C.* (Früh)Mette *f*, b) *Church of England*: 'Morgenliturˌgie *f*.

mat·i·nee, **mat·i·née** ['mætɪneɪ] *s. thea.* Mati'nee *f*, *bsd.* Nachmittagsvorstellung *f*.

mat·ing ['meɪtɪŋ] *s. bsd. orn.* Paarung *f*: ***~ season*** Paarungszeit *f*.

ma·tri·ar·chal [ˌmeɪtrɪ'ɑːkl] *adj.* matriar'chalisch; **ma·tri·arch·y** ['meɪtrɪɑːkɪ] *s.* Mutterherrschaft *f*, Matriar'chat *n*; **ˌma·tri'cid·al** [-ɪ'saɪdl] *adj.* muttermörderisch; **ma·tri·cide** ['meɪtrɪsaɪd] *s.* **1.** Muttermord *m*; **2.** Muttermörder(in).

ma·tric·u·late [mə'trɪkjʊleɪt] **I** *v/t.* immatrikulieren (*an e-r Universität*); **II** *v/i.* sich immatrikulieren (lassen); **III** *s.* Immatrikulierte(r *m*) *f*; **ma·tric·u·la·tion** [məˌtrɪkjʊ'leɪʃn] *s.* Immatrikulati'on *f*.

mat·ri·mo·ni·al [ˌmætrɪ'məʊnjəl] *adj.* □ ehelich, Ehe...: ***~ agency*** Heiratsinstitut *n*; ***~ cases*** ⚖ Ehesachen; ***~ law*** Eherecht *n*; **mat·ri·mo·ny** ['mætrɪmənɪ] *s.* Ehe(stand *m*) *f*.

ma·trix ['meɪtrɪks] *pl.* **-tri·ces** [-trɪsiːz] *s.* **1.** Mutter-, Nährboden *m* (*beide a. fig.*), 'Grundsubˌstanz *f*; **2.** *physiol.* Matrix *f*: a) Mutterboden *m*, b) Gewebeschicht *f*, c) Gebärmutter *f*; **3.** *min.* a) Grundmasse *f*, b) Ganggestein *n*; **4.** ⚙, *typ.* Ma'trize *f* (*a. Schallplattenherstellung*); **5.** ⩚ Matrix *f*: ***~ algebra*** Matrizenrechnung *f*.

ma·tron ['meɪtrən] *s.* **1.** würdige Dame, Ma'trone *f*; **2.** Hausmutter *f* (*e-s Internats etc.*), Wirtschafterin *f*; **3.** a) Vorsteherin *f*, b) Oberschwester *f*, Oberin *f im Krankenhaus*, c) Aufseherin *f im Gefängnis etc.*; **'ma·tron·ly** [-lɪ] *adj.* ma'tronenhaft (*a. adv.*), gesetzt: ***~ duties*** hausmütterliche Pflichten.

mat·ted¹ ['mætɪd] *adj.* mattiert.

mat·ted² ['mætɪd] *adj.* **1.** mit Matten bedeckt: ***a ~ floor***; **2.** verflochten: ***~ hair*** verfilztes Haar.

mat·ter ['mætə] **I** *s.* **1.** Ma'terie *f* (*a. phys., phls.*), Materi'al *n*, Stoff *m*; *biol.* Sub'stanz *f*: → ***foreign*** 2, ***grey matter***; **2.** Sache *f* (*a.* ⚖), Angelegenheit *f*: ***this is a serious ~***; ***the ~ in hand*** die vorliegende Angelegenheit; ***a ~ of fact*** e-e Tatsache; ***as a ~ of fact*** tatsächlich, eigentlich; ***a ~ of course*** e-e Selbstverständlichkeit; ***as a ~ of course*** selbstverständlich; ***a ~ of form*** e-e Formsache; ***~ (in issue)*** ⚖ Streitgegenstand *m*; ***a ~ of taste*** (e-e) Geschmackssache; ***a ~ of time*** e-e Frage der Zeit; ***it is a ~ of life and death*** es geht um Leben u. Tod; ***it's no laughing ~*** es ist nichts zum Lachen; ***for that ~*** was das (an)betrifft, schließlich; ***in the ~ of*** a) hinsichtlich (*gen.*), b) ⚖ in Sachen *A. gegen B.*; **3.** *pl.* (*ohne Artikel*) die 'Umstände *pl.*, die Dinge *pl.*: ***to make ~s worse*** was die Sache noch schlimmer macht; ***as ~s stand*** wie die Dinge liegen; **4.** ***the ~*** die Schwierigkeit: ***what's the ~?*** was ist los?, wo fehlt's?; ***what's the ~ with him*** (***it***)***?*** was ist los mit ihm (damit)?; ***no ~!*** es hat nichts zu sagen!; ***it's no ~ whether*** es spielt keine Rolle, ob; ***no ~ what he says*** was er auch sagt; ***no ~ who*** gleichgültig wer; **5.** ***a ~ of*** (*mit verblaßter Bedeutung*) Sache *f*, etwas: ***it's a ~ of £5*** es kostet 5 Pfund; ***a ~ of three weeks*** ungefähr 3 Wochen; ***it was a ~ of five minutes*** es dauerte nur 5 Minuten; ***it's a ~ of common knowledge*** es ist allgemein bekannt; **6.** *fig.* Stoff *m* (*Dichtung*), Thema *n*, Gegenstand *m*, Inhalt *m* (*Buch*), innerer Gehalt; **7.** *mst postal* ***~*** Postsache *f*: ***printed ~*** Drucksache *f*; **8.** *typ.* a) Manu'skript *n*, b) (Schrift)Satz *m*: ***live ~***, ***standing ~*** Stehsatz *m*; **9.** ⚕ Eiter *m*; **II** *v/i.* **10.** von Bedeutung sein (***to*** für), dar'auf ankommen (***to s.o.*** j-m): ***it doesn't ~*** (es) macht nichts; ***it ~s little*** es ist ziemlich einerlei, es spielt kaum e-e Rolle; **11.** ⚕ eitern.

ˌmat·ter|-of-'course [-tərəv'k-] *adj.* selbstverständlich; **ˌ~-of-'fact** [-tərəv'f-] *adj.* sachlich, nüchtern; pro'saisch.

Mat·thew ['mæθjuː] *npr. u. s. bibl.* Mat'thäus(evanˌgelium *n*) *m*.

mat·ting ['mætɪŋ] *s.* ⚙ **1.** Mattenstoff *m*; **2.** Matten(belag *m*) *pl.*

mat·tock ['mætək] *s.* (Breit)Hacke *f*, ⛏ Karst *m*.

mat·tress ['mætrɪs] *s.* Ma'tratze *f*.

mat·u·ra·tion [ˌmætjʊ'reɪʃn] *s.* **1.** ⚕ (Aus)Reifung *f*, Eiterung *f* (*Geschwür*); **2.** *biol., a. fig.* Reifen *n*.

ma·ture [mə'tjʊə] **I** *adj.* □ **1.** *allg.* reif (*a. Käse, Wein*; *a.* ⚕ *Geschwür*); **2.** reif (*Person*): a) voll entwickelt, b) *fig.* gereift, mündig; **3.** *fig.* reiflich erwogen, ('wohl)durchˌdacht: ***upon ~ reflection*** nach reiflicher Überlegung; ***~ plans*** ausgereifte Pläne; **4.** ✝ fällig, zahlbar (*Wechsel*); **II** *v/t.* **5.** reifen (lassen), zur Reife bringen; *fig. Pläne* reifen lassen; **III** *v/i.* **6.** reif werden, (her'an-, aus)reifen; ✝ fällig werden; **ma'tured** [-əd] *adj.* **1.** (aus)gereift; **2.** abgelagert; **3.** ✝ fällig; **ma'tu·ri·ty** [-ərətɪ] *s.* **1.** Reife *f* (*a.* ⚕ *u. fig.*): ***bring*** (***come***) ***to ~*** zur Reife bringen (kommen); ***~ of judg(e)ment*** Reife des Urteils; **2.** ✝ Fälligkeit *f*, Verfall(zeit *f*) *m*: ***at*** (*od.* ***on***) ***~*** bei Fälligkeit; ***~ date*** Fälligkeitstag *m*; **3.** *fig. pol.* Mündigkeit *f* (*des Bürgers*).

ma·tu·ti·nal [ˌmætjuː'taɪnl] *adj.* morgendlich, Morgen..., früh.

mat·y ['meɪtɪ] *Brit.* → ***matey***.

maud·lin ['mɔːdlɪn] **I** *s.* weinerliche Gefühlsduse'lei; **II** *adj.* weinerlich sentimen'tal, rührselig.

maul [mɔːl] **I** *s.* **1.** ⚙ Schlegel *m*, schwerer Holzhammer; **II** *v/t.* **2.** *j-n, et.* übel zurichten, *j-n* 'durchprügeln, miß'handeln: ***~ about*** roh umgehen mit; **3.** ‚her'unterreißen' (*Kritiker*).

maul·stick ['mɔːlstɪk] *s. paint.* Malerstock *m*.

maun·der ['mɔːndə] *v/i.* **1.** schwafeln, faseln; **2.** ziellos um'herschlendern *od.* handeln.

Maun·dy Thurs·day ['mɔːndɪ] *s. eccl.* Grün'donnerstag *m*.

mau·so·le·um [ˌmɔːsə'lɪəm] *s.* Mauso'leum *n*, Grabmal *n*.

mauve [məʊv] **I** *s.* Malvenfarbe *f*; **II** *adj.* malvenfarbig, mauve.

mav·er·ick ['mævərɪk] *s. Am.* **1.** herrenloses Vieh ohne Brandzeichen; **2.** mutterloses Kalb; **3.** F *pol.* Einzelgänger *m*, *allg.* Außenseiter *m*.

maw [mɔː] *s.* **1.** (Tier)Magen *m*, *bsd.* Labmagen *m* (*der Wiederkäuer*); **2.** *fig.* Rachen *m des Todes etc.*

mawk·ish ['mɔːkɪʃ] *adj.* □ **1.** süßlich, abgestanden (*Geschmack*); **2.** *fig.* rührselig, süßlich, kitschig.

'maw·seed *s.* Mohnsame(n) *m*.

'maw·worm *s. zo.* Spulwurm *m*.

max·i ['mæksɪ] **I** *s.* Maximode *f*: ***wear ~*** maxi tragen; **II** *adj.* Maxi...: ***~ dress***.

max·il·la [mæk'sɪlə] *pl.* **-lae** [-liː] *s.* **1.**

anat. (Ober)Kiefer *m*; **2.** *zo.* Fußkiefer *m*, Zange *f*; **max'il·lar·y** [-ərı] **I** *adj. anat.* (Ober)Kiefer..., maxil'lar; **II** *s.* Oberkieferknochen *m*.

max·im ['mæksım] *s.* Ma'xime *f*.

max·i·mal ['mæksıml] *adj.* maxi'mal, Maximal..., Höchst...; **'max·i·mize** [-maız] *v/t.* ✝, ⚙ maximieren; **max·i·mum** ['mæksıməm] **I** *pl.* **-ma** [-mə], **-mums** *s.* **1.** Maximum *n*, Höchstgrenze *f*, -maß *n*, -stand *m*, -wert *m* (*a.* 𝔄): ***smoke a ~ of 20 cigarettes a day*** maximal 20 Zigaretten am Tag rauchen; **2.** ✝ Höchstpreis *m*, -angebot *n*, -betrag *m*; **II** *adj.* **3.** höchst, größt, Höchst..., Maximal...: ***~ load*** ⚙, ⚡ Höchstbelastung *f*; ***~ safety load*** (*od.* ***stress***) zulässige Beanspruchung; ***~ performance*** Höchst-, Spitzenleistung *f*; ***~ permissible speed*** zulässige Höchstgeschwindigkeit; ***~ wages*** Höchst-, Spitzenlohn *m*.

'max·i,sin·gle *s.* Maxisingle *f* (*Schallplatte*).

may¹ [meı] *v/aux.* [*irr.*] **1.** (*Möglichkeit, Gelegenheit*) *sg.* kann, mag, *pl.* können, mögen: ***it ~ happen any time*** es kann jederzeit geschehen; ***it might happen*** es könnte geschehen; ***you ~ be right*** du magst recht haben; ***he ~ not come*** vielleicht kommt er nicht; ***he might lose his way*** er könnte sich verirren; **2.** (*Erlaubnis*) *sg.* darf, kann (*a.* ⚖), *pl.* dürfen können: ***you ~ go***; ***~ I ask?*** darf ich fragen?; ***we might as well go*** da können wir ebensogut auch gehen; **3.** *ungewisse Frage*: ***how old ~ she be?*** wie alt mag sie wohl sein?; ***I wondered what he might be doing*** ich fragte mich, was er wohl tue; **4.** *Wunschgedanke, Segenswunsch*: ***~ you be happy!*** sei glücklich!; ***~ it please your Majesty*** Eure Majestät mögen geruhen; **5.** *familiäre od. vorwurfsvolle Aufforderung*: ***you might help me*** du könntest mir (eigentlich) helfen; ***you might at least write me*** du könntest mir wenigstens schreiben; **6.** ***~*** *od.* ***might*** *als Konjunktivumschreibung*: ***I shall write to him so that he ~ know our plans***; ***whatever it ~ cost***; ***difficult as it ~ be*** so schwierig es auch sein mag; ***we feared they might attack*** wir fürchteten, sie könnten *od.* würden angreifen.

May² [meı] *s.* **1.** Mai *m*, *poet.* (*fig. a.* ♀) Lenz *m*: ***in ~*** im Mai; **2.** ♀ ⚘ Weißdornblüte *f*.

may·be ['meıbi:] *adv.* viel'leicht.

May| bug *s. zo.* Maikäfer *m*; ***~ Day*** *s.* der 1. Mai; **'♀·day** *s. internationales Funknotsignal*; **'~,flow·er** *s.* **1.** ⚘ a) Maiblume *f*, b) *Am.* Primelstrauch *m*; **2.** ♀ *hist. Name des Auswandererschiffs der* ***Pilgrim Fathers***; **'~·fly** *s. zo.* Eintagsfliege *f*.

may·hap ['meıhæp] *adv. obs. od. dial.* viel'leicht.

may·hem ['meıhem] *s.* **1.** *bsd. Am.* ⚖ schwere Körperverletzung; **2.** *fig.* a) ‚Gemetzel' *n*, b) Chaos *n*, Verwüstung *f*.

may·on·naise [,meıə'neız] *s.* Mayon'naise(gericht *n*) *f*: ***~ of lobster*** Hummermayonnaise *f*.

may·or [meə] *s.* Bürgermeister *m*; **'may·or·al** [-ərəl] *adj.* bürgermeisterlich; **'may·or·ess** [-rıs] *s.* **1.** Gattin *f* des Bürgermeisters; **2.** *Am.* Bürgermeisterin *f*.

'May|·pole, ♀ *s.* Maibaum *m*; ***~ queen*** *s.* Mai(en)königin *f*; **'~·thorn** *s.* ⚘ Weißdorn *m*.

maz·a·rine [,mæzə'ri:n] *adj.* maza'rin-, dunkelblau.

maze [meız] *s.* **1.** Irrgarten *m*, Laby'rinth *n*, *fig. a.* Gewirr *n*; **2.** *fig.* Verwirrung *f*: ***in a ~*** → **mazed** [-zd] *adj.* verdutzt, verblüfft.

Mc·Coy [mə'kɔı] *s. Am. sl.*: ***the real ~*** der wahre Jakob, der (die, das) Richtige.

'M-day *s.* Mo'bilmachungstag *m*.

me [mi:; mı] **I** *pron.* **1.** (*dat.*) mir: ***he gave ~ money***; ***he gave it*** (***to***) ***~***; **2.** (*acc.*) mich: ***he took ~ away*** er führte mich weg; **3.** F ich: ***it's ~*** ich bin's; **II** ♀ *s.* **4.** *psych.* Ich *n*.

mead¹ [mi:d] *s.* Met *m*.

mead² [mi:d] *poet. für* ***meadow***.

mead·ow ['medəʊ] *s.* Wiese *f*; ***~ grass*** *s.* ⚘ Rispengras *n*; ***~ saf·fron*** *s.* ⚘ (*bsd.* Herbst)Zeitlose *f*; **'~·sweet** *s.* ⚘ **1.** Mädesüß *n*; **2.** *Am.* Spierstrauch *m*.

mead·ow·y ['medəʊı] *adj.* wiesenartig, -reich, Wiesen...

mea·ger *Am.*, **mea·gre** *Brit.* ['mi:gə] *adj.* ☐ **1.** mager, dürr; **2.** *fig.* dürftig, kärglich; **'mea·ger·ness** *Am.*, **'mea·gre·ness** *Brit.* [-nıs] *s.* **1.** Magerkeit *f*; **2.** Dürftigkeit *f*.

meal¹ [mi:l] *s.* **1.** Schrotmehl *n*; **2.** Mehl *n*, Pulver *n* (*aus Nüssen, Mineralen etc.*).

meal² [mi:l] *s.* Mahl(zeit *f*) *n*, Essen *n*: ***have a ~*** e-e Mahlzeit einnehmen; ***make a ~ of s.th.*** et. verzehren; ***~s on wheels*** Essen *n* auf Rädern.

meal·ies ['mi:lız] (*S.Afr.*) *s. pl.* Mais *m*.

meal| tick·et *s. Am.* **1.** Essensbon(s *pl.*) *m*; **2.** *sl.* a) *b.s.* ‚Ernährer' *m*, b) Einnahmequelle *f*, ‚Goldesel' *m*, c) Kapi'tal *n*: ***his voice is his ~***; **'~·time** *s.* Essenszeit *f*.

meal·y ['mi:lı] *adj.* **1.** mehlig: ***~ potatoes***; **2.** mehlhaltig; **3.** (wie) mit Mehl bestäubt; **4.** blaß (*Gesicht*); **'~-mouthed** *adj.* **1.** heuchlerisch, glattzüngig; **2.** leisetreterisch: ***be ~ about it*** um den (heißen) Brei herumreden.

mean¹ [mi:n] **I** *v/t.* [*irr.*] **1.** *et.* beabsichtigen, vorhaben, im Sinn haben: ***I ~ it*** es ist mir Ernst damit; ***~ to do s.th.*** et. zu tun gedenken, et. tun wollen; ***he ~s no harm*** er meint es nicht böse; ***I didn't ~ to disturb you*** ich wollte dich nicht stören; ***without ~ing it*** ohne es zu wollen; → ***business*** 4; **2.** bestimmen (***for*** zu): ***he was meant to be a barrister*** er war zum Anwalt bestimmt; ***the cake is meant to be eaten*** der Kuchen ist zum Essen da; ***that remark was meant for you*** das war auf dich abgezielt; **3.** meinen, sagen wollen: ***by 'liberal' I ~*** unter ‚liberal' verstehe ich; ***I ~ his father*** ich meine s-n Vater; ***I ~ to say*** ich will sagen; **4.** bedeuten: ***that ~s a lot of work***; ***he ~s all the world to me*** er bedeutet mir alles; ***that ~s war*** das bedeutet Krieg; ***what does 'fair' ~?*** was bedeutet *od.* heißt (das Wort) ‚fair'?; **II** *v/i.* [*irr.*] **5.** ***~ well*** (***ill***) ***by*** (*od.* ***to***) ***s.o.*** j-m wohlgesinnt (übel gesinnt) sein.

mean² [mi:n] *adj.* ☐ **1.** gering, niedrig: ***~ birth*** niedrige Herkunft; **2.** ärmlich, schäbig: ***~ streets***; **3.** unbedeutend, gering: ***no ~ artist*** ein recht bedeutender Künstler; ***no ~ foe*** ein nicht zu unterschätzender Gegner; **4.** schäbig, gemein; ***feel ~*** sich schäbig vorkommen; **5.** geizig, schäbig, ‚filzig'; **6.** *Am.* F a) bösartig, ‚ekelhaft', b) ‚bös', scheußlich (*Sache*), c) ‚toll', ‚wüst': ***a ~ fighter***, d) *Am.* unpäßlich: ***feel ~*** sich elend fühlen.

mean³ [mi:n] **I** *adj.* **1.** mittel, mittler, Mittel...; 'durchschnittlich, Durchschnitts...: ***~ life*** a) mittlere Lebensdauer, b) *phys.* Halbwertzeit *f*; ***~ sea level*** *das* Normalnull; ***~ value*** Mittelwert *m*; **II** *s.* **2.** Mitte *f*, *das* Mittlere, Mittel *n*, 'Durchschnitt(szahl *f*) *m*; 𝔄 Mittel(wert *m*) *n*: ***hit the happy ~*** die goldene Mitte treffen; ***arithmetical ~*** arithmetisches Mittel; → ***golden mean***; **3.** *pl. sg. od. pl. konstr.* (Hilfs)Mittel *n od. pl.*, Werkzeug *n*, Weg *m*: ***by all ~s*** auf alle Fälle, unbedingt; ***by any ~s*** etwa, vielleicht, möglicherweise; ***by no ~s*** durchaus nicht, keineswegs, auf keinen Fall; ***by some ~s or other*** auf die eine oder andere Weise, irgendwie; ***by ~s of*** mittels, durch; ***by this*** (*od.* ***these***) ***~s*** hierdurch; ***~ of production*** Produktionsmittel; ***~s of transport***(***ation***) Beförderungsmittel; ***find the ~s*** Mittel und Wege finden; → ***end*** 9, ***way***¹ 1; **4.** *pl.* (Geld)Mittel *pl.*, Vermögen *n*, Einkommen *n*: ***live within*** (***beyond***) ***one's ~s*** s-n Verhältnissen entsprechend (über s-e Verhältnisse) leben; ***a man of ~s*** ein bemittelter Mann; ***~s test*** *Brit.* (behördliche) Einkommens- *od.* Bedürftigkeitsermittlung.

me·an·der [mı'ændə] **I** *s. bsd. pl.* Windung *f*, verschlungener Pfad, Schlängelweg *m*; ⚠ Mä'ander(linien *pl.*) *m*, Schlangenlinie *f*; **II** *v/i.* sich winden, (sich) schlängeln.

mean·ing ['mi:nıŋ] **I** *s.* **1.** Absicht *f*, Zweck *m*, Ziel *n*; **2.** Sinn *m*, Bedeutung *f*: ***full of ~*** bedeutungsvoll, bedeutsam; ***what's the ~ of this?*** was soll das bedeuten?; ***words with the same ~*** Wörter mit gleicher Bedeutung; ***full of ~*** → 3; ***if you take my ~*** wenn Sie verstehen, was ich meine; **II** *adj.* ☐ **3.** bedeutungsvoll, bedeutsam (*Blick etc.*); **4.** *in Zssgn* in ... Absicht: ***well-~*** wohlmeinend, -wollend; **'mean·ing·ful** [-fʊl] *adj.* bedeutungsvoll; **'mean·ing·less** [-lıs] *adj.* **1.** sinn-, bedeutungslos; **2.** ausdruckslos (*Gesicht*).

mean·ness ['mi:nnıs] *s.* **1.** Niedrigkeit *f*, niedriger Stand; **2.** Wertlosigkeit *f*, Ärmlichkeit *f*; **3.** Schäbigkeit *f*: a) Gemeinheit *f*, Niederträchtigkeit *f*, b) Geiz *m*; **4.** *Am.* F Bösartigkeit *f*.

meant [ment] *pret. u. p.p. von* ***mean***¹.

,mean|'time I *adv.* in'zwischen, mittler'weile, unter'dessen; **II** *s.* Zwischenzeit *f*: ***in the ~*** → I; ***~ time*** *s. ast.* mittlere (Sonnen)Zeit; **,~'while** → ***meantime*** I.

mea·sles ['mi:zlz] *s. pl. sg. konstr.* **1.** ⚕ Masern *pl.*: ***false ~***, ***German ~*** Röteln *pl.*; **2.** *vet.* Finnen *pl.* (*der Schweine*); **'mea·sly** [-lı] *adj.* **1.** ⚕ masernkrank; **2.** *vet.* finnig; **3.** *sl.* elend, schäbig, lumpig.

meas·ur·a·ble ['meʒərəbl] *adj.* ☐ meßbar: ***within ~ distance of*** *fig.* nahe (*dat.*); **'meas·ur·a·ble·ness** [-nɪs] *s.* Meßbarkeit *f.*

meas·ure ['meʒə] **I** *s.* **1.** Maß(einheit *f*) *n*: ***long ~*** Längenmaß; ***~ of capacity*** Hohlmaß; **2.** *fig.* richtiges Maß, Ausmaß *n*: ***beyond*** (*od.* ***out of***) ***all ~*** über alle Maßen, grenzenlos; ***in a great ~*** in großem Maße, großenteils, überaus; ***in some ~, in a*** (***certain***) ***~*** gewissermaßen, bis zu e-m gewissen Grade; ***for good ~*** obendrein; **3.** Messen *n*, Maß *n*: ***take the ~ of s.th.*** et. abmessen; ***take s.o.'s ~*** a) j-m (*zu e-m Anzug*) Maß nehmen, b) *fig.* j-n taxieren *od.* einschätzen; → ***made-to-measure***; **4.** Maß *n*, Meßgerät *n*; ***weigh with two ~s*** *fig.* mit zweierlei Maß messen; → ***tape-measure***; **5.** Maßstab *m* (***of*** für): ***be a ~ of s.th.*** e-r Sache als Maßstab dienen; ***man is the ~ of all things*** der Mensch ist das Maß aller Dinge; **6.** Anteil *m*, Porti'on *f*, gewisse Menge; **7.** a) ✗ Maß(einheit *f*) *n*, Teiler *m*, Faktor *m*, b) ⚗, *phys.* Maßeinheit *f*: ***~ of variation*** Schwankungsmaß; ***common ~*** gemeinsamer Teiler; **8.** (abgemessener) Teil, Grenze *f*: ***set a ~ to s.th.*** et. begrenzen; **9.** *Metrik*: a) Silbenmaß *n*, b) Versglied *n*, c) Versmaß *n*; **10.** ♪ Metrum *n*, Takt *m*, Rhythmus *m*: ***tread a ~*** tanzen; **11.** *poet.* Weise *f*, Melo'die *f*; **12.** *pl.* *geol.* Lager *n*, Flöz *n*; **13.** *typ.* Zeilen-, Satz-, Ko'lumnenbreite *f*; **14.** *fig.* Maßnahme *f*, -regel *f*, Schritt *m*: ***take ~s*** Maßnahmen ergreifen; ***take legal ~s*** den Rechtsweg beschreiten; **15.** ⚖ gesetzliche Maßnahme, Verfügung *f*: ***coercive ~*** Zwangsmaßnahme; **II** *v/t.* **16.** (ver)messen, ab-, aus-, zumessen: ***~ one's length*** *fig.* längelang hinfallen; ***~ swords*** a) die Klingen messen, b) (***with***) die Klingen kreuzen (mit) (*a. fig.*); ***~ s.o. for a suit of clothes*** j-m Maß nehmen zu e-m Anzug; **17.** ***~ out*** ausmessen, die Ausmaße bestimmen; **18.** *fig.* ermessen; **19.** (ab)messen, abschätzen (***by*** an *dat.*): ***~d by*** gemessen an; **20.** beurteilen (***by*** nach); **21.** vergleichen, messen (***with*** mit): ***~ one's strength with s.o.*** s-e Kräfte mit j-m messen; **III** *v/i.* **22.** Messungen vornehmen; **23.** messen, groß sein: ***it ~s 7 inches*** es mißt 7 Zoll, es ist 7 Zoll lang; **24.** ***~ up*** (***to***) die Ansprüche (*gen.*) erfüllen, her'anreichen (an *acc.*); **'meas·ured** [-əd] *adj.* **1.** (ab)gemessen: ***~ in the clear*** (*od.* ***day***) ⚙ im Lichten gemessen; ***~ value*** Meßwert *m*; **2.** richtig proportioniert; **3.** (ab)gemessen, gleich-, regelmäßig: ***~ tread*** gemessener Schritt; **4.** 'wohlüber,legt, abgewogen, gemessen: ***to speak in ~ terms*** sich maßvoll ausdrücken; **5.** im Versmaß, metrisch; **'meas·ure·less** [-lɪs] *adj.* unermeßlich, unbeschränkt; **'meas·ure·ment** [-mənt] *s.* **1.** (Ver-)Messung *f*, (Ab)Messen *n*; **2.** Maß *n*; *pl.* Abmessungen *pl.*, Größe *f*, Ausmaße *pl.*; **3.** ⚓ Tonnengehalt *m*.

meas·ur·ing ['meʒərɪŋ] *s.* **1.** Messen *n*, (Ver)Messung *f*; **2.** *in Zssgn*: Meß...; ***~ bridge*** *s.* ⚡ Meßbrücke *f*; ***~ di·al*** *s.* Rundmaßskala *f*; ***~ glass*** *s.* Meßglas *n*; ***~ in·stru·ment*** *s.* Meßgerät *n*; ***~ range*** *s.* Meßbereich *m*; ***~ tape*** *s.* Maß-, Meßband *n*, Bandmaß *n*.

meat [miːt] *s.* **1.** Fleisch *n* (*als Nahrung*; *Am. a. von Früchten etc.*): ***~s*** a) Fleischwaren, b) Fleichgerichte; ***fresh ~*** Frischfleisch; ***butcher's ~*** Schlachtfleisch; ***~ and drink*** Speise *f* u. Trank *m*; ***this is ~ and drink to me*** es ist mir e-e Wonne; ***one man's ~ is another man's poison*** des einen Freud ist des andern Leid; **2.** Fleischspeise *f*: ***cold ~*** kalte Platte; ***~ tea*** kaltes Abendbrot mit Tee; **3.** *fig.* Sub'stanz *f*, Gehalt *m*, Inhalt *m*: ***full of ~*** gehaltvoll; ***~ ax(e)*** *s.* Schlachtbeil *n*; **'~·ball** *s.* **1.** Fleischklößchen *n*; **2.** *Am. sl.* ‚Heini' *m*; ***~ broth*** *s.* Fleischbrühe *f*; **'~,chop·per** *s.* **1.** Hackmesser *n*; **2.** → ***~ grind·er*** *s.* Fleischwolf *m*; ***~ ex·tract*** *s.* 'Fleischex,trakt *m*; ***~ fly*** *s.* *zo.* Schmeißfliege *f*; ***~ in·spec·tion*** *s.* Fleischbeschau *f*.

meat·less ['miːtlɪs] *adj.* fleischlos.

meat| loaf *s.* Hackbraten *m*; **'~·man** [-mæn] *s.* [*irr.*] *Am.* Fleischer *m*; ***~ meal*** *s.* Fleischmehl *n*; ***~ pie*** *s.* 'Fleischpa,stete *f*; ***~ pud·ding*** *s.* Fleischpudding *m*; ***~ safe*** *s.* Fliegenschrank *m*.

meat·y ['miːtɪ] *adj.* **1.** fleischig; **2.** fleischartig; **3.** *fig.* gehaltvoll, handfest, so'lid.

Mec·can·o [mɪ'kɑːnəʊ] (*TM*) *s.* Sta'bilbaukasten *m* (*Spielzeug*).

me·chan·ic [mɪ'kænɪk] **I** *adj.* **1.** → ***mechanical***; **II** *s.* **2.** a) Me'chaniker *m*, Maschi'nist *m*, Mon'teur *m*, (Auto-)Schlosser *m*, b) Handwerker *m*; **3.** *pl. sg. konstr. phys.* a) Me'chanik *f*, Bewegungslehre *f*: ***~s of fluids*** Strömungslehre *f*, b) *a.* ***practical ~s*** Ma'schinenlehre *f*; **4.** *pl. sg. konstr.* ⚙ Konstrukti'on *f* von Ma'schinen *etc.*: ***precision ~s*** Feinmechanik *f*; **5.** *pl. sg. konstr.* Mecha'nismus *m* (*a. fig.*); **6.** *pl. sg. konstr. fig.* Technik *f*: ***the ~s of playwriting***; **me'chan·i·cal** [-kl] *adj.* ☐ **1.** ⚙ me'chanisch (*a. phys.*); maschi'nell, Maschinen...; auto'matisch: ***~ drawing*** maschinelles Zeichnen; ***~ force*** *phys.* mechanische Kraft; ***~ engineer*** Maschinenbauingenieur *m*; ***~ engineering*** Maschinenbau(kunde *f*) *m*; ***~ woodpulp*** Holzschliff *m*; **2.** *fig.* me'chanisch, auto'matisch; **me'chan·i·cal·ness** [-klnɪs] *s.* *das* Me'chanische; **mech·a·ni·cian** [,mekə'nɪʃn] → ***mechanic*** 2.

mech·a·nism ['mekənɪzəm] *s.* **1.** Mecha'nismus *m*: ***~ of government*** *fig.* Regierungs-, Verwaltungsapparat *m*; **2.** *biol, physiol., phls., psych.* Mecha'nismus *m*; **3.** *paint. etc.* Technik *f*; **mech·a·nis·tic** [,mekə'nɪstɪk] *adj.* (☐ ***~ally***) *phls.* mecha'nistisch; **mech·a·ni·za·tion** [,mekənaɪ'zeɪʃn] *s.* Mechanisierung *f*; **'mech·a·nize** [-naɪz] *v/t.* mechanisieren, ✕ *a.* motorisieren: ***~d division*** ✕ Panzergrenadierdivision *f*.

me·co·ni·um [mɪ'kəʊnjəm] *s.* *physiol.* Kindspech *n*.

med·al ['medl] *s.* Me'daille *f*: a) Denk-, Schaumünze *f*; → ***reverse*** 4, b) Orden *m*, Ehrenzeichen *n*, Auszeichnung *f*: ***℞ of Honor*** *Am.* ✕ Tapferkeitsmedaille; ***~ ribbon*** Ordensband *n*.

med·aled, **med·al·ist** *Am.* → ***medalled, medallist.***

med·alled ['medld] *adj.* ordengeschmückt.

me·dal·lion [mɪ'dæljən] *s.* **1.** große Denk- *od.* Schaumünze, Me'daille *f*; **2.** Medail'lon *n*; **med·al·list** ['medlɪst] *s.* **1.** Me'daillenschneider *m*; **2.** *bsd. sport* (*Gold- etc.*)Medaillengewinner(in).

med·dle ['medl] *v/i.* **1.** sich (ein-)mischen (***with, in*** in *acc.*); **2.** sich (unaufgefordert) befassen, sich abgeben, sich einlassen (***with*** mit); **3.** her'umhantieren, -spielen (***with*** mit); **'med·dler** [-lə] *s.* j-d, der sich (ständig) in fremde Angelegenheiten mischt, aufdringlicher Mensch; **'med·dle·some** [-səm] *adj.* aufdringlich.

me·di·a[1] ['medɪə] *pl.* **-di·ae** [-dɪiː] *s. ling.* Media *f*, stimmhafter Verschlußlaut.

me·di·a[2] ['miːdjə] **1.** *pl. von* ***medium***; **2.** Medien *pl.*: ***~ research*** Medienforschung *f*; ***mixed ~*** a) Multimedia *pl.*, b) *Kunst*: Mischtechnik *f*.

me·di·ae·val *etc.* → ***medieval*** *etc.*

me·di·al ['miːdjəl] **I** *adj.* ☐ **1.** mittler, Mittel...: ***~ line*** Mittellinie *f*; **2.** *ling.* medi'al, inlautend: ***~ sound*** Inlaut *m*; **3.** Durchschnitts...; **II** *s.* **4.** → ***media***[1].

me·di·an ['miːdjən] **I** *adj.* die Mitte bildend, mittler, Mittel...: ***~ salaries*** ✝ mittlere Gehälter; ***~ strip*** *Am. mot.* Mittelstreifen *m*; **II** *s.* Mittellinie *f*, -wert *m*; ***~ line*** *s.* ✗ a) Mittellinie *f* (*a. anat.*), b) Halbierungslinie *f*; ***~ point*** *s.* ✗ Mittelpunkt *m*, Schnittpunkt *m* der Winkelhalbierenden.

me·di·ant ['miːdjənt] *s.* ♪ Medi'ante *f*.

me·di·ate ['miːdɪeɪt] **I** *v/i.* **1.** vermitteln (*a. v/t.*), den Vermittler spielen (***between*** zwischen *dat.*); **2.** da'zwischen liegen, ein Bindeglied bilden; **II** *adj.* [-dɪət] ☐ **3.** mittelbar, 'indi,rekt; **4.** → ***median*** I; **me·di·a·tion** [,miːdɪ'eɪʃn] *s.* Vermittlung *f*, Fürsprache *f*; *eccl.* Fürbitte *f*: ***through his ~***; **'me·di·a·tor** [-tə] *s.* Vermittler *m*; Fürsprecher *m*; *eccl.* Mittler *m*; **me·di·a·to·ri·al** [,miːdɪə'tɔːrɪəl] *adj.* ☐ vermittelnd, (Ver)Mittler...; **'me·di·a·tor·ship** [-təʃɪp] *s.* (Ver)Mittleramt *n*, Vermittlung *f*; **'me·di·a·to·ry** [-dɪətərɪ] → ***mediatorial***; **me·di·a·trix** [,miːdɪ'eɪtrɪks] *s.* Vermittlerin *f*.

med·ic ['medɪk] **I** *adj.* → ***medical*** 1; **II** *s.* F Medi'ziner *m* (*Arzt od. Student*), ✕ Sani'täter *m*.

Med·i·caid ['medɪkeɪd] *s. Am. Gesundheitsfürsorge(programm) für Bedürftige.*

med·i·cal ['medɪkl] **I** *adj.* ☐ **1.** medi'zinisch, ärztlich, Kranken..., *a.* inter'nistisch: ***~ attendance*** ärztliche Behandlung; ***~ board*** Gesundheitsbehörde *f*; ***~ certificate*** ärztliches Attest; ***℞ Corps*** ✕ Sanitätstruppe *f*; ***℞ Department*** ✕ Sanitätswesen *n*; ***~ examiner*** a) Amtsarzt *m*, -ärztin *f*, b) Vertrauensarzt *m*, -ärztin *f* (*Krankenkasse*), c) *Am.* Leichenbeschauer(in); ***~ history*** Krankengeschichte *f*; ***~ jurisprudence*** Gerichtsmedizin *f*; ***~ man*** → 3 a; ***~ officer*** Amtsarzt *m*, -ärztin *f*; ***~ practitioner*** praktischer Arzt, praktische Ärztin; ***~ retirement*** vorzeitige Pensionierung aus gesundheitlichen Gründen; ***~ science*** medizinische Wissenschaft, Medizin *f*; ***~ specialist*** Facharzt *m*, -ärztin *f*; ***~ student*** Mediziner(in), Medizinstudent(in); ***℞ Superintendent***

Chefarzt *m*, -ärztin *f*; **~ *ward*** innere Abteilung (*e-r Klinik*); **on ~ *grounds*** aus gesundheitlichen Gründen; **2.** Heil..., heilend; **II** *s.* **3.** F a) ‚Doktor' *m* (*Arzt*), b) ärztliche Unter'suchung; **me·dic·a·ment** [me'dɪkəmənt] *s.* Medika'ment *n*, Heil-, Arz'neimittel *n*.

Med·i·care ['medɪkeə] *s. Am.* Gesundheitsfürsorge *f* (*bsd. für Senioren*).

med·i·cate ['medɪkeɪt] *v/t.* **1.** medi'zinisch behandeln; **2.** mit Arz'neistoff versetzen *od.* imprägnieren: **~*d cotton*** medizinische Watte; **~*d bath*** (***wine***) Medizinalbad *n* (-wein *m*); **med·i·ca·tion** [ˌmedɪ'keɪʃn] *s.* **1.** Beimischung *f* von Arz'neistoffen; **2.** Verordnung *f*, medi'zinische *od.* medikamen'töse Behandlung; **'med·i·ca·tive** [-keɪtɪv] *adj.*, **me·dic·i·nal** [me'dɪsɪnl] *adj.* □ Medizinal..., medi'zinisch, heilkräftig, -sam, Heil...: **~ *herbs*** Heilkräuter; **~ *spring*** Heilquelle *f*.

med·i·cine ['medsɪn] *s.* **1.** Medi'zin *f*, Arz'nei *f* (*a. fig.*): ***take one's ~*** a) s-e Medizin (ein)nehmen, b) *fig.* ‚die Pille schlucken'; **2.** a) Heilkunde *f*, ärztliche Wissenschaft, b) innere Medi'zin (*Ggs. Chirurgie*); **3.** Zauber *m*, Medi'zin *f* (*bei Indianern etc.*): ***he is bad ~*** *Am. sl.* er ist ein gefährlicher Bursche; **~ ball** *s. sport* Medi'zinball *m*; **~ chest** *s.* Arz'neischrank *m*, 'Hausapoˌtheke *f*; **'~-man** [-mæn] *s.* [*irr.*] Medi'zinmann *m*.

med·i·co ['medɪkəʊ] *pl.* **-cos** *s.* → ***medic*** II.

medico- [medɪkəʊ] *in Zssgn* medi'zinisch, Mediko...: **~*legal*** gerichtsmedizinisch.

me·di·e·val [ˌmedɪ'iːvl] *adj.* □ mittelalterlich (*a.* F *fig. altmodisch, vorsintflutlich*); **ˌme·di'e·val·ism** [-vəlɪzəm] *s.* **1.** Eigentümlichkeit *f od.* Geist *m* des Mittelalters; **2.** Vorliebe *f* für das Mittelalter; **3.** Mittelalterlichkeit *f*; **ˌme·di'e·val·ist** [-vəlɪst] *s.* Mediä'vist(in), Erforscher(in) *od.* Kenner(in) des Mittelalters.

me·di·o·cre [ˌmiːdɪ'əʊkə] *adj.* mittelmäßig, zweitklassig; **me·di·oc·ri·ty** [ˌmiːdɪ'ɒkrətɪ] *s.* **1.** Mittelmäßigkeit *f*, mäßige Begabung; **2.** unbedeutender Mensch, kleiner Geist.

med·i·tate ['medɪteɪt] **I** *v/i.* nachsinnen, -denken, grübeln, meditieren (***on, upon*** über *acc.*); **II** *v/t.* erwägen, planen, sinnen auf (*acc.*); **med·i·ta·tion** [ˌmedɪ'teɪʃn] *s.* **1.** Meditati'on *f*, tiefes Nachdenken, Sinnen *n*; **2.** (*bsd.* fromme) Betrachtung, Andacht *f*: ***book of ~s*** Andachts-, Erbauungsbuch *n*; **'med·i·ta·tive** [-tətɪv] *adj.* □ **1.** nachdenklich; **2.** besinnlich (*a. Buch etc.*).

med·i·ter·ra·ne·an [ˌmedɪtə'reɪnjən] **I** *adj.* **1.** von Land um'geben; binnenländisch; **2.** ♀ mittelmeerisch, mediter'ran, Mittelmeer...: ♀ ***Sea*** → 3; **II** *s.* **3.** ♀ Mittelmeer *n*, Mittelländisches Meer; **4.** ♀ Angehörige(r *m*) *f* der mediter'ranen Rasse.

me·di·um ['miːdjəm] **I** *pl.* **-di·a** [-djə], **-di·ums** *s.* **1.** *fig.* Mitte *f*, Mittel *n*, Mittelweg *m*: ***the happy ~*** die goldene Mitte, der goldene Mittelweg; **2.** *phys.* Mittel *n*, Medium *n*; **3.** ✝, *biol.* Medium *n*, Träger *m*, Mittel *n*: ***circulating ~, currency ~*** ✝ Umlaufs-, Zahlungsmittel; ***dispersion ~*** ⚗ Dispersionsmittel; **4.** 'Lebenseleˌment *n*, -bedingungen *pl.*; **5.** *fig.* Um'gebung *f*, Mili'eu *n*; **6.** (*a. künstlerisches, a. Kommunikations-*) Medium *n*, (Hilfs-, Werbe- *etc.*)Mittel *n*; Werkzeug *n*, Vermittlung *f*: ***by*** (*od.* ***through***) ***the ~ of*** durch, vermittels; → ***media***[2]; **7.** *paint.* Bindemittel *n*; **8.** *Spiritismus etc.*: Medium *n*; **9.** *typ.* Medi'anpaˌpier *n*; **II** *adj.* **10.** mittler, Mittel..., Durchschnitts..., *a.* mittelmäßig: **~ *quality*** mittlere Qualität; **~ *price*** Durchschnittspreis *m*; **~*-price car*** *mot.* Wagen *m* der mittleren Preisklasse; **~ brown** *s.* Mittelbraun *n*; **'~-ˌdat·ed** *adj.* ✝ mittelfristig; **'~-faced** *adj. typ.* halbfett.

me·di·um·is·tic [ˌmiːdjə'mɪstɪk] *adj. Spiritismus*: medi'al (begabt).

me·di·um| size *s.* Mittelgröße *f*; **'~-size(d)** *adj.* mittelgroß: **~ *car*** Mittelklassewagen *m*; **'~-term** *adj.* mittelfristig; **~ wave** *s. Radio*: Mittelwelle *f*.

med·lar ['medlə] *s.* ⚘ **1.** Mispelstrauch *m*; **2.** Mispel *f* (*Frucht*).

med·ley ['medlɪ] **I** *s.* **1.** Gemisch *n*; *contp.* Mischmasch *m*, Durchein'ander *n*; **2.** ♪ Potpourri *n*, Medley *n*; **II** *adj.* **3.** gemischt, wirr; bunt; **4.** *sport* Lagen...: **~ *swimming***; **~ *relay*** a) *Schwimmen*: Lagenstaffel *f*, b) *Laufsport*: Schwellstaffel *f*.

me·dul·la [me'dʌlə] *s.* **1.** *anat.* (Knochen)Mark *n*: **~ *spinalis*** Rückenmark; **2.** ⚘ Mark *n*; **me'dul·lar·y** [-ərɪ] *adj.* medul'lär, Mark...

meed [miːd] *s. poet.* Lohn *m*.

meek [miːk] *adj.* □ **1.** mild, sanft(mütig); **2.** demütig, 'unterwürfig; **3.** fromm (*Tier*): ***as ~ as a lamb*** *fig.* lammfromm; **'meek·ness** [-nɪs] *s.* **1.** Sanftmut *f*, Milde *f*; **2.** Demut *f*, 'Unterwürfigkeit *f*.

meer·schaum ['mɪəʃəm] *s.* Meerschaum(pfeife *f*) *m*.

meet [miːt] **I** *v/t.* [*irr.*] **1.** begegnen (*dat.*), treffen, zs.-treffen mit, treffen auf (*acc.*), antreffen: **~ *s.o. in the street***; ***well met!*** schön, daß wir uns treffen!; **2.** abholen; **~ *s.o. at the station*** j-n von der Bahn abholen; ***be met*** abgeholt *od.* empfangen werden; ***come*** (***go***) ***to ~ s.o.*** j-m entgegenkommen (-gehen); **3.** *j-n* kennenlernen: ***when I first met him*** als ich s-e Bekanntschaft machte; ***pleased to ~ you*** F sehr erfreut, Sie kennenzulernen; **~ *Mr. Brown!*** *bsd. Am.* darf ich Sie mit Herrn B. bekannt machen?; **4.** *fig. j-m* entgegenkommen (***half-way*** auf halbem Wege); **5.** (*feindlich*) zs.-treffen *od.* -stoßen mit, begegnen (*dat.*), stoßen auf (*acc.*); *sport* antreten gegen (*Konkurrenten*); **6.** *a. fig. j-m* gegen'übertreten; → ***fate*** 1; **7.** *fig.* entgegentreten (*dat.*): a) *e-r Sache* abhelfen, *der Not* steuern, *Schwierigkeiten* über'winden, *e-m Übel* begegnen, *der Konkurrenz* Herr werden, b) *Einwände* wider'legen, entgegnen auf (*acc.*); **8.** *parl.* sich vorstellen (*dat.*): **~ (*the*) *parliament***; **9.** berühren, münden in (*acc.*) (*Straßen*), stoßen *od.* treffen auf (*acc.*), schneiden (*a.* ⩗): **~ *s.o.'s eye*** a) j-m ins Auge fallen, b) j-s Blick erwidern; **~ *the eye*** auffallen; ***there is more in it than ~s the eye*** da steckt mehr dahinter; **10.** *Anforderungen etc.* entsprechen, gerecht werden (*dat.*), über'einstimmen mit: ***the supply ~s the demand*** das Angebot entspricht der Nachfrage; ***be well met*** gut zs.-passen; ***that won't ~ my case*** das löst mein Problem nicht; **11.** *j-s Wünschen* entgegenkommen *od.* entsprechen, *Forderungen* erfüllen, *Verpflichtungen* nachkommen, *Unkosten* bestreiten (***out of*** aus), *Nachfrage* befriedigen, *Rechnungen* begleichen, *j-s Auslagen* decken, *Wechsel* honorieren *od.* decken: **~ *the claims of one's creditors*** s-e Gläubiger befriedigen; **II** *v/i.* [*irr.*] **12.** zs.-kommen, -treffen, -treten; **13.** sich begegnen, sich treffen, sich finden: **~ *again*** sich wiedersehen; **14.** (*feindlich od. im Spiel*) zs.-stoßen, anein'andergeraten, sich messen; *sport* aufein'andertreffen (*Gegner*); **15.** sich kennenlernen, zs.-treffen; **16.** sich vereinigen (*Straßen etc.*), sich berühren; **17.** genau zs.-treffen *od.* -stimmen *od.* -passen, sich decken; zugehen (*Kleidungsstück*); → ***end*** 1; **18.** **~ *with*** a) zs.-treffen mit, sich vereinigen mit, b) (an)treffen, finden, (zufällig) stoßen auf (*acc.*), c) erleben, erleiden, erfahren, betroffen werden von, erhalten, *Billigung* finden, *Erfolg* haben: **~ *with an accident*** e-n Unfall erleiden, verunglücken; **~ *with a kind reception*** freundlich aufgenommen werden; **III** *s.* **19.** *Am.* a) Treffen *n* (*von Zügen etc.*), b) → ***meeting*** 3 b; **20.** *Brit. hunt.* a) Jagdtreffen *n* (*zur Fuchsjagd*), b) Jagdgesellschaft *f*.

meet·ing ['miːtɪŋ] *s.* **1.** Begegnung *f*, Zs.-treffen *n*, -kunft *f*; **2.** (***at a ~*** auf e-r) Versammlung *od.* Konfe'renz *od.* Sitzung *od.* Tagung: **~ *of creditors*** (***members***) Gläubiger- (Mitglieder-) versammlung; **3.** a) Zweikampf *m*, Du'ell *n*, b) *sport* Treffen *n*, Wettkampf *m*, Veranstaltung *f*; **4.** Zs.-treffen *n* (*zweier Linien etc.*), Zs.-fluß *m* (*zweier Flüsse*); **'~-place** *s.* Treffpunkt *m* (*a. weitS.*), Tagungs-, Versammlungsort *m*.

meg(a)- [meg(ə)] *in Zssgn* a) (riesen-) groß, b) Milli'on.

meg·a·cy·cle ['megəˌsaɪkl] *s.* ϟ Megahertz *n*; **'meg·a·death** [-deθ] *s.* Tod *m* von e-r Milli'on Menschen (*bsd. in e-m Atomkrieg*); **'meg·a·fog** [-fɒg] *s.* ⚓ 'Nebelsiˌgnal(anlage *f*) *n*; **'meg·a·lith** [-lɪθ] *s.* Mega'lith *m*, großer Steinblock.

megalo- [megələʊ] *in Zssgn* groß.

meg·a·lo·car·di·a [ˌmegələʊ'kɑːdɪə] *s.* ⚕ Herzerweiterung *f*; **meg·a·lo·ma·ni·a** [ˌmegələʊ'meɪnjə] *s. psych.* Größenwahn *m*; **meg·a·lop·o·lis** [ˌmegə'lɒpəlɪs] *s.* **1.** Riesenstadt *f*; **2.** Ballungsgebiet *n*.

meg·a·phone ['megəfəʊn] **I** *s.* Mega'phon *n*; **II** *v/t. u. v/i.* durch ein Mega'phon sprechen; **'meg·a·ton** [-tʌn] *s.* Megatonne *f* (*1 Million Tonnen*); **'meg·a·watt** [-wɒt] *s.* ϟ Megawatt *n*.

meg·ger ['megə] *s.* ϟ Megohm'meter *n*.

me·gilp [mə'gɪlp] **I** *s.* Leinöl-, Retuschierfirnis *m*; **II** *v/t.* firnissen.

meg·ohm ['megəʊm] *s.* ϟ Meg'ohm *n*.

me·grim ['miːgrɪm] *s.* **1.** ⚕ *obs.* Mi'gräne *f*; **2.** *obs.* Grille *f*, Schrulle *f*; **3.** *pl. obs.* Schwermut *f*, Melancho'lie *f*; **4.** *pl. vet.* Koller *m* (*der Pferde*).

mel·an·cho·li·a [ˌmelən'kəʊljə] *s.* ⚕

Melancho'lie *f*, Schwermut *f*; ˌ**mel·an·'cho·li·ac** [-lıæk], ˌ**mel·an'chol·ic** [-'kɒlık] **I** *adj.* melan'cholisch, schwermütig, traurig, schmerzlich; **II** *s.* Melan'choliker(in), Schwermütige(r *m*) *f*; **mel·an·chol·y** ['melənkəlı] **I** *s.* Melancho'lie *f*: a) ⚕ Depressi'on *f*, b) Schwermut *f*, Trübsinn *m*; **II** *adj.* melan'cholisch: a) schwermütig, trübsinnig, b) *fig.* traurig, düster, trübe.

mé·lange [meı'lɑ̃:nʒ] (*Fr.*) *s.* Mischung *f*, Gemisch *n*.

me·las·sic [mı'læsık] *adj.* ⚗ Melassin...(*-säure etc.*).

Mel·ba toast ['melbə] *s.* dünne, hartgeröstete Brotscheiben *pl.*

me·lee *Am.*, **mê·lée** ['meleı] (*Fr.*) *s.* Handgemenge *n*; *fig.* Tu'mult *m*; Gewühl *n*.

mel·io·rate ['mi:ljəreıt] **I** *v/t.* **1.** (ver-)bessern; **2.** ✓ meliorieren; **II** *v/i.* sich (ver)bessern; **mel·io·ra·tion** [ˌmi:ljə'reıʃn] *s.* (Ver)Besserung *f*; ✓ Meliorati'on *f*.

me·lis·sa [mı'lısə] *s.* ⚘, ⚕ (Zi'tronen-)Meˌlisse *f*.

mel·lif·er·ous [me'lıfərəs] *adj.* **1.** ⚘ honigerzeugend; **2.** *zo.* Honig tragend *od.* bereitend; **mel'lif·lu·ence** [-flʊəns] *s.* **1.** Honigfluß *m*; **2.** *fig.* Süßigkeit *f*; **mel'lif·lu·ent** [-flʊənt] *adj.* □ (wie Honig) süß *od.* glatt da'hinfließend; **mel'lif·lu·ous** [-flʊəs] *adj.* □ *fig.* honigsüß.

mel·low ['meləʊ] **I** *adj.* □ **1.** reif, saftig, mürbe, weich (*Obst*); **2.** ✓ a) leicht zu bearbeiten(d), locker, b) reich (*Boden*); **3.** ausgereift, mild (*Wein*); **4.** sanft, mild, zart, weich (*Farbe, Licht, Ton etc.*); **5.** *fig.* gereift u. gemildert, mild, freundlich, heiter (*Person*): ***of ~ age*** von gereiftem Alter; **6.** angeheitert, beschwipst; **II** *v/t.* **7.** weich *od.* mürbe machen, *Boden* auflockern; **8.** *fig.* sänftigen, mildern; **9.** (aus)reifen, reifen lassen (*a. fig.*); **III** *v/i.* **10.** weich *od.* mürbe *od.* mild *od.* reif werden (*Wein etc.*); **11.** *fig.* sich abklären *od.* mildern; '**mel·low·ness** [-nıs] *s.* **1.** Weichheit *f* (*a. fig.*), Mürbheit *f*; **2.** ✓ Gare *f*; **3.** Gereiftheit *f*; **4.** Milde *f*, Sanftheit *f*.

me·lo·de·on [mı'ləʊdjən] *s.* ♪ **1.** Me'lodium(orgel *f*) *n* (*ein amer. Harmonium*); **2.** *Art* Ak'kordeon *n*; **3.** *obs. Am.* Varie'té(theˌater) *n*.

me·lod·ic [mı'lɒdık] *adj.* me'lodisch; **me'lod·ics** [-ks] *s. pl. sg. konstr.* ♪ Melo'dielehre *f*, Me'lodik *f*; **me·lo·di·ous** [mı'ləʊdjəs] *adj.* □ melo'dienreich, wohlklingend; **mel·o·dist** ['melədıst] *s.* **1.** 'Liedersänger(in), -kompoˌnist(in); **2.** Me'lodiker *m*; **mel·o·dize** ['melədaız] **I** *v/t.* **1.** me'lodisch machen; **2.** *Lieder* vertonen; **II** *v/i.* **3.** Melo'dien singen *od.* komponieren; **mel·o·dra·ma** ['meləʊˌdrɑ:mə] *s.* Melo'dram(a) *n* (*a. fig.*); **mel·o·dra·mat·ic** [ˌmeləʊdrə'mætık] *adj.* (□ ***~ally***) melodra'matisch.

mel·o·dy ['melədı] *s.* **1.** ♪ (*a. ling. u. fig.*) Melo'die *f*, Weise *f*; **2.** Wohllaut *m*, -klang *m*.

mel·on ['melən] *s.* **1.** ⚘ Me'lone *f*: ***water-~*** Wassermelone; **2.** ***cut a ~*** ☤ *sl.* e-e Sonderdividende ausschütten.

melt [melt] **I** *v/i.* **1.** (zer)schmelzen, flüssig werden; sich auflösen, auf-, zergehen (***into*** in *acc.*): ***~ down*** zerfließen; → ***butter*** 1; **2.** sich auflösen; **3.** aufgehen (***into*** in *acc.*), sich verflüchtigen; **4.** zs.-schrumpfen; **5.** *fig.* zerschmelzen, zerfließen (***with*** vor *dat.*): ***~ into tears*** in Tränen zerfließen; **6.** *fig.* auftauen, weich werden, schmelzen; **7.** verschmelzen, *ineinander* 'übergehen (*Ränder, Farben etc.*): ***outlines ~ing into each other***; **8.** (ver)schwinden, zur Neige gehen (*Geld etc.*): ***~ away*** dahinschwinden, -schmelzen; **9.** *humor.* vor Hitze vergehen, zerfließen; **II** *v/t.* **10.** schmelzen, lösen; **11.** (zer-)schmelzen *od.* (zer)fließen lassen (***into*** in *acc.*); *Butter* zerlassen; ⚙ schmelzen: ***~ down*** einschmelzen; **12.** *fig.* rühren, erweichen: ***~ s.o.'s heart***; **13.** *Farben etc.* verschmelzen lassen; **III** *s.* **14.** Schmelzen *n* (*Metall*); **15.** a) Schmelze *f*, geschmolzene Masse, b) → ***melting charge***.

melt·ing ['meltıŋ] *adj.* □ **1.** schmelzend, Schmelz...: ***~ heat*** schwüle Hitze; **2.** *fig.* a) weich, zart, b) schmelzend, schmachtend, rührend (*Worte etc.*); ***~ charge*** *s. metall.* Schmelzgut *n*, Einsatz *m*; ***~ fur·nace*** *s.* ⚙ Schmelzofen *m*; ***~ point*** *s. phys.* Schmelzpunkt *m*; ***~ pot*** *s.* Schmelztiegel *m* (*a. fig. Land etc.*): ***put into the ~*** *fig.* von Grund auf ändern; ***~ stock*** *s. metall.* Charge *f*, Beschickungsgut *n* (*Hochofen*).

mem·ber ['membə] *s.* **1.** Mitglied *n*, Angehörige(r *m*) *f* (*e-s Klubs, e-r Familie, Partei etc.*): ♀ ***of Parliament*** *Brit.* Abgeordnete(r *m*) *f* des Unterhauses; ♀ ***of Congress*** *Am.* Kongreßmitglied *n*; **2.** *anat.* a) Glied(maße *f*) *n*, b) (männliches) Glied, Penis *m*; **3.** ⚙ (Bau)Teil *n*; **4.** *ling.* Satzteil *m*, -glied *n*; **5.** Ᵽ a) Glied *n* (*Reihe etc.*), b) Seite *f* (*Gleichung*); '**mem·bered** [-əd] *adj.* **1.** gegliedert; **2.** *in Zssgn* ...gliedrig: ***four-~*** viergliedrig; '**mem·ber·ship** [-ʃıp] *s.* **1.** Mitgliedschaft *f*, Zugehörigkeit *f*: ***~ card*** Mitgliedsausweis *m*; ***~ fee*** Mitgliedsbeitrag *m*; **2.** Mitgliederzahl *f*; *coll. die* Mitglieder *pl.*

mem·brane ['membreın] *s.* **1.** *anat.* Mem'bran(e) *f*, Häutchen *n*: ***drum ~*** Trommelfell *n*; ***~ of connective tissue*** Bindegewebshaut *f*; **2.** *phys.*, ⚙ Mem'bran(e) *f*; **mem·bra·ne·ous** [mem'breınjəs], **mem·bra·nous** [mem'breınəs] *adj. anat.*, ⚙ häutig, Membran...: ***~ cartilage*** Hautknorpel *m*.

me·men·to [mı'mentəʊ] *pl.* **-tos** [-z] *s.* Me'mento *n*, Mahnzeichen *n*; Erinnerung *f* (***of*** an *acc.*).

mem·o ['meməʊ] *s.* F Memo *n*, No'tiz *f*.

mem·oir ['memwɑ:] *s.* **1.** Denkschrift *f*, Abhandlung *f*, Bericht *m*; **2.** *pl.* Memo'iren *pl.*, Lebenserinnerungen *pl.*

mem·o·ra·bil·i·a [ˌmemərə'bılıə] (*Lat.*) *s. pl.* Denkwürdigkeiten *pl.*; **mem·o·ra·ble** ['memərəbl] *adj.* □ denkwürdig.

mem·o·ran·dum [ˌmemə'rændəm] *pl.* **-da** [-də], **-dums** *s.* **1.** Vermerk *m* (*a.* 'Akten)Noˌtiz *f*: ***make a ~ of et.*** notieren; ***urgent ~*** Dringlichkeitsvermerk; **2.** ⚖ Schriftsatz *m*; Vereinbarung *f*, Vertragsurkunde *f*: ***~ of association*** Gründungsurkunde (*e-r Gesellschaft*); **3.** ☤ a) Kommissi'onsnota *f*: ***send on a ~*** in Kommission senden, b) Rechnung *f*, Nota *f*; **4.** *pol.* diplo'matische Note, Denkschrift *f*, Memo'randum *n*; **5.** Merkblatt *n*; ***~ book*** *s.* No'tizbuch *n*, Kladde *f*.

me·mo·ri·al [mı'mɔ:rıəl] **I** *adj.* **1.** Gedächtnis...: ***~ service*** Gedenkgottesdienst *m*; **II** *s.* **2.** Denkmal *n*, Ehrenmal *n*; Gedenkfeier *f*; **3.** Andenken *n* (***for*** an *acc.*); **4.** ⚖ Auszug *m* (*aus e-r Urkunde etc.*); **5.** Denkschrift *f*, Eingabe *f*, Gesuch *n*; **6.** *pl.* → ***memoir*** 2; ♀ ***Day*** *s. Am.* Volkstrauertag *m* (*30. Mai*); **me'mo·ri·al·ize** [-laız] *v/t.* **1.** e-e Denk- *od.* Bittschrift einreichen bei: ***~ Congress***; **2.** erinnern an (*acc.*), e-e Gedenkfeier abhalten für.

mem·o·rize ['meməraız] *v/t.* **1.** sich einprägen, auswendig lernen, memorieren; **2.** niederschreiben, festhalten, verewigen; '**mem·o·ry** [-rı] *s.* **1.** Gedächtnis *n*, Erinnerung(svermögen *n*) *f*: ***from ~, by ~*** aus dem Gedächtnis, auswendig; ***call to ~*** sich *et.* ins Gedächtnis zurückrufen; ***escape s.o.'s ~*** j-s Gedächtnis *od.* j-m entfallen; ***if my ~ serves me*** (***right***) wenn ich mich recht erinnere; → ***commit*** 1; **2.** Erinnerung(szeit) *f* (***of*** an *acc.*): ***within living ~*** seit Menschengedenken; ***before ~, beyond ~*** in unvordenklichen Zeiten; **3.** Andenken *n*, Erinnerung *f*: ***in ~ of*** zum Andenken an (*acc.*); → ***blessed*** 1; **4.** Reminis'zenz *f*, Erinnerung *f* (*an Vergangenes*); **5.** *Computer*: Speicher *m*: ***~ bank*** Speicherbank *f*.

mem·sa·hib ['memˌsɑ:hıb] *s. Brit. Ind.* euro'päische Frau.

men [men] *pl. von* ***man***.

men·ace ['menəs] **I** *v/t.* **1.** bedrohen, gefährden; **2.** *et.* androhen; **II** *v/i.* **3.** drohen, Drohungen ausstoßen; **III** *s.* **4.** (Be)Drohung *f* (***to*** *gen.*), *fig. a.* drohende Gefahr (***to*** für); **5.** F ‚Scheusal' *n*, Nervensäge *f*; '**men·ac·ing** [-sıŋ] *adj.* □ drohend.

mé·nage, me·nage [me'nɑ:ʒ] (*Fr.*) *s.* Haushalt(ung *f*) *m*.

me·nag·er·ie [mı'nædʒərı] *s.* Menage'rie *f*, Tierschau *f*.

mend [mend] **I** *v/t.* **1.** ausbessern, flikken, reparieren: ***~ stockings*** Strümpfe stopfen; ***~ a friendship*** *fig.* e-e Freundschaft ‚kitten'; **2.** *fig.* (ver)bessern: ***~ one's efforts*** s-e Anstrengungen verdoppeln; ***~ one's pace*** den Schritt beschleunigen; ***~ one's ways*** sich (*sittlich*) bessern; ***least said soonest ~ed*** je weniger geredet wird, desto rascher wird alles wieder gut; **II** *v/i.* **3.** sich bessern; **4.** genesen: ***be ~ing*** auf dem Wege der Besserung sein; **III** *s.* **5.** ☤ *u. allg.* Besserung *f*: ***be on the ~*** → 4; **6.** ausgebesserte Stelle, Stopfstelle *f*, Flikken *m*; '**mend·a·ble** [-dəbl] *adj.* (aus-)besserungsfähig.

men·da·cious [men'deıʃəs] *adj.* □ lügnerisch, verlogen, lügenhaft; **men'dac·i·ty** [-'dæsətı] *s.* **1.** Lügenhaftigkeit *f*, Verlogenheit *f*; **2.** Lüge *f*, Unwahrheit *f*.

Men·de·li·an [men'di:ljən] *adj. biol.* Mendelsch, Mendel...; '**Men·de·lize** ['mendəlaız] *v/i.* mendeln.

men·di·can·cy ['mendıkənsı] *s.* Bette'lei *f*, Betteln *n*; '**men·di·cant** [-nt] **I** *adj.* **1.** bettelnd, Bettel...: ***~ friar*** → 3; **II** *s.* **2.** Bettler(in); **3.** Bettelmönch *m*.

men·dic·i·ty [men'dısətı] *s.* **1.** Bette'lei

f; **2.** Bettelstand *m*: ***reduce to ~*** *fig.* an den Bettelstab bringen.

mend·ing ['mendɪŋ] *s.* **1.** (Aus)Bessern *n*, Flicken *n*: ***his boots need ~*** seine Stiefel müssen repariert werden; ***invisible ~*** Kunststopfen *n*; **2.** *pl.* Stopfgarn *n*.

'men·folk(s) *s. pl.* Mannsvolk *n*, -leute *pl*.

me·ni·al ['mi:njəl] **I** *adj.* ☐ **1.** *contp.* knechtisch, niedrig (*Arbeit*): ***~ offices*** niedrige Dienste; **2.** knechtisch, unter'würfig; **II** *s.* **3.** Diener(in), Knecht *m*, La'kai *m* (*a. fig.*): ***~s*** Gesinde *n*.

me·nin·ge·al [mɪ'nɪndʒɪəl] *adj. anat.* Hirnhaut…; **men·in·gi·tis** [ˌmenɪn'dʒaɪtɪs] *s.* ⚕ Menin'gitis *f*, (Ge)Hirnhautentzündung *f*.

me·nis·cus [mɪ'nɪskəs] *pl.* **-nis·ci** [-'nɪsaɪ] *s.* **1.** Me'niskus *m*: a) halbmondförmiger Körper, b) *anat.* Gelenkscheibe *f*; **2.** *opt.* Me'niskenglas *n*.

men·o·pause ['menəʊpɔ:z] *s. physiol.* Wechseljahre *pl.*, Klimak'terium *n*.

men·ses ['mensi:z] *s. pl. physiol.* Menses *pl.*, Regel *f* (*der Frau*).

men·stru·al ['menstrʊəl] *adj.* **1.** *ast.* Monats…: ***~ equation*** Monatsgleichung *f*; **2.** *physiol.* Menstruations…: ***~ flow*** Regelblutung *f*; **'men·stru·ate** [-ʊeɪt] *v/i.* menstruieren, die Regel haben; **men·stru·a·tion** [ˌmenstrʊ'eɪʃn] *s.* Menstruati'on *f*, (monatliche) Regel, Peri'ode *f*.

men·sur·a·bil·i·ty [ˌmenʃʊrə'bɪlətɪ] *s.* Meßbarkeit *f*; **men·sur·a·ble** ['menʃʊrəbl] *adj.* **1.** meßbar; **2.** ♪ Mensural…: ***~ music***.

men·tal ['mentl] **I** *adj.* ☐ **1.** geistig, innerlich, intellektu'ell, Geistes…(*-kraft, -zustand etc.*): ***~ arithmetic*** Kopfrechnen *n*; ***~ reservation*** geheimer Vorbehalt, Mentalreservation *f*; → ***note*** 2; **2.** (geistig-)seelisch; **3.** ⚕ geisteskrank, -gestört, F verrückt: ***~ disease*** Geisteskrankheit *f*; ***~ home***, ***~ hospital*** Nervenheilanstalt *f*; ***~ patient***, ***~ case*** Geisteskranke(r *m*) *f*; ***~ly handicapped*** geistig behindert; **II** *s.* **4.** F Verrückte(r *m*) *f*; **~ age** *s. psych.* geistiges Alter; **~ cru·el·ty** *s.* ⚖ seelische Grausamkeit; **~ de·fi·cien·cy** *s.* ⚕ Geistesbehinderung *f*; **~ de·range·ment** *s.* **1.** ⚖ krankhafte Störung der Geistestätigkeit; **2.** ⚕ Geistesstörung *f*, Irrsinn *m*; **~ hy·giene** *s.* ⚕ 'Psychohygiˌene *f*.

men·tal·i·ty [men'tælətɪ] *s.* Mentali'tät *f*, Denkungsart *f*, Gesinnung *f*; Wesen *n*, Na'tur *f*.

men·thol ['menθɒl] *s.* ⚗ Men'thol *n*; **'men·tho·lat·ed** [-θəleɪtɪd] *adj.* Men'thol enthaltend, Menthol…

men·tion ['menʃn] **I** *s.* **1.** Erwähnung *f*: ***to make (no) ~ of s.th.*** et. (nicht) erwähnen; ***hono(u)rable ~*** ehrenvolle Erwähnung; **2.** lobende Erwähnung; **II** *v/t.* **3.** erwähnen, anführen: ***(please) don't ~ it!*** bitte!, gern geschehen!, (es ist) nicht der Rede wert!; ***not to ~*** ganz zu schweigen von; ***not worth ~ing*** nicht der Rede wert; **'men·tion·a·ble** [-ʃnəbl] *adj.* erwähnenswert.

men·tor ['mentɔ:] *s.* Mentor *m*, treuer Ratgeber.

men·u ['menju:] (*Fr.*) *s.* **1.** Speise(n)karte *f*; **2.** Speisenfolge *f*.

me·ow [mɪ'aʊ] **I** *v/i.* mi'auen (*Katze*); **II** *s.* Mi'auen *n*.

me·phit·ic [me'fɪtɪk] *adj.* verpestet, giftig (*Luft, Geruch etc.*).

mer·can·tile ['mɜ:kəntaɪl] *adj.* **1.** kaufmännisch, handeltreibend, Handels…: ***~ agency*** a) Handelsauskunftei *f*, b) Handelsvertretung *f*; ***~ law*** Handelsrecht *n*; ***~ marine*** Handelsmarine *f*; ***~ paper*** ⚚ Warenpapier *n*; **2.** ⚚ Merkantil…: ***~ system*** *hist.* Merkantilismus *m*; **'mer·can·til·ism** [-tɪlɪzəm] *s.* **1.** Handels-, Krämergeist *m*; **2.** kaufmännischer Unter'nehmergeist; **3.** ⚚ *hist.* Merkanti'lismus *m*.

mer·ce·nar·y ['mɜ:sɪnərɪ] **I** *adj.* ☐ **1.** gedungen, Lohn…: ***~ troops*** Söldnertruppen; **2.** *fig.* feil, käuflich; **3.** *fig.* gewinnsüchtig: ***~ marriage*** Geldheirat *f*; **II** *s.* **4.** ⚔ Söldner *m*; *contp.* Mietling *m*.

mer·cer ['mɜ:sə] *s. Brit.* Seiden- u. Tex'tilienhändler *m*; **'mer·cer·ize** [-əraɪz] *v/t.* *Baumwollfasern* merzerisieren; **'mer·cer·y** [-ərɪ] *s.* ⚚ *Brit.* **1.** Seiden-, Schnittwaren *pl.*; **2.** Seiden-, Schnittwarenhandlung *f*.

mer·chan·dise ['mɜ:tʃəndaɪz] **I** *s.* **1.** *coll.* Ware(n *pl.*) *f*, Handelsgüter *pl.*: ***an article of ~*** eine Ware; **II** *v/i.* **2.** Handel treiben, Waren vertreiben; **III** *v/t.* **3.** *Waren* vertreiben; **4.** Werbung machen für *e-e Ware*, den Absatz *e-r Ware* steigern; **'mer·chan·dis·ing** [-zɪŋ] ⚚ **I** *s.* **1.** Merchandising *n*, Ver'kaufspoliˌtik *f* u. -förderung *f* (*durch Marktforschung, wirksame Gütergestaltung, Werbung etc.*); **2.** Handel(sgeschäfte *pl.*) *m*; **II** *adj.* **3.** Handels…

mer·chant ['mɜ:tʃənt] ⚚ **I** *s.* **1.** (Groß-)Kaufmann *m*, Handelsherr *m*, Großhändler *m*: ***the ~s*** die Kaufmannschaft, Handelskreise *pl.*; **2.** *bsd. Am.* Ladenbesitzer *m*, Krämer *m*; **3.** ***~ of doom*** *Brit. sl.* ‚Unke' *f*, Schwarzseher(in); **4.** ⚓ *obs.* Handelsschiff *n*; **II** *adj.* **5.** Handels…, Kaufmanns…; **'mer·chant·a·ble** [-təbl] *adj.* marktgängig.

mer·chant| bank *s.* Handelsbank *f*; **~ fleet** *s.* ⚓ Handelsflotte *f*; **'~·man** [-mən] *s.* [*irr.*] ⚓ Kauffahr'tei-, Handelsschiff *n*; **~ na·vy** *s.* 'Handelsmaˌrine *f*; **~ prince** *s.* ⚚ reicher Kaufherr, Handelsfürst *m*; **~ ship** *s.* Handelsschiff *n*.

mer·ci·ful ['mɜ:sɪfʊl] *adj.* ☐ (***to***) barm'herzig, mitleidvoll (gegen), gütig (gegen, zu); gnädig (*dat.*); **'mer·ci·ful·ly** [-fʊlɪ] *adv.* **1.** → ***merciful***; **2.** glücklicherweise; **'mer·ci·ful·ness** [-nɪs] *s.* Barm'herzigkeit *f*, Erbarmen *n*, Gnade *f* (*Gottes*); **'mer·ci·less** [-lɪs] *adj.* ☐ unbarmherzig, erbarmungslos, mitleidlos; **'mer·ci·less·ness** [-lɪsnɪs] *s.* Erbarmungslosigkeit *f*.

mer·cu·ri·al [mɜ:'kjʊərɪəl] *adj.* ☐ **1.** ⚗ Quecksilber…; **2.** *fig.* lebhaft, quecksilb(e)rig; **3.** *myth.* Merkur…: ***2 wand*** Merkurstab *m*; **mer'cu·ri·al·ism** [-lɪzəm] *s.* ⚕ Quecksilbervergiftung *f*; **mer'cu·ri·al·ize** [-laɪz] *v/t.* ⚕, *phot.* mit Quecksilber behandeln; **mer'cu·ric** [-rɪk] *adj.* ⚗ Quecksilber…

mer·cu·ry ['mɜ:kjʊrɪ] *s.* **1.** 2 *myth. ast.* Mer'kur *m*; *fig.* Bote *m*; **2.** ⚗, ⚕ Quecksilber *n*: ***~ column*** → 3; ***~ poisoning*** Quecksilbervergiftung *f*; **3.** Quecksilber(säule *f*) *n*: ***the ~ is rising*** das Barometer steigt (*a. fig.*); **4.** ⚘ Bingelkraut *n*; **~ pres·sure ga(u)ge** *s. phys.* 'Quecksilbermanoˌmeter *n*.

mer·cy ['mɜ:sɪ] *s.* **1.** Barm'herzigkeit *f*, Mitleid *n*, Erbarmen *n*; Gnade *f*: ***be at the ~ of s.o.*** in j-s Gewalt sein, j-m auf Gnade u. Ungnade ausgeliefert sein; ***at the ~ of the waves*** den Wellen preisgegeben; ***throw o.s. on s.o.'s ~*** sich j-m auf Gnade u. Ungnade ergeben; ***be left to the tender mercies of*** *iro.* der rauhen Behandlung von … ausgesetzt sein; ***Sister of 2*** Barmherzige Schwester; **2.** Glück *n*, Segen *m*, (wahre) Wohltat: ***it is a ~ that he left***; **~ kill·ing** *s.* Sterbehilfe *f*.

mere [mɪə] *adj.* ☐ bloß, nichts als, rein, völlig: ***~(st) nonsense*** purer Unsinn; ***~ words*** bloße Worte; ***he is no ~ craftsman*** er ist kein bloßer Handwerker; ***the ~st accident*** der reinste Zufall; **'mere·ly** [-lɪ] *adv.* bloß, rein, nur, lediglich.

mer·e·tri·cious [ˌmerɪ'trɪʃəs] *adj.* ☐ **1.** *obs.* dirnenhaft; **2.** *fig.* a) falsch, verlogen, b) protzig.

merge [mɜ:dʒ] **I** *v/t.* **1.** (***in***) verschmelzen (mit), aufgehen lassen (in *dat.*), einverleiben (*dat.*): ***be ~d in*** in *et.* aufgehen; **2.** ⚖ tilgen, aufheben; **3.** ⚚ a) fusionieren, b) *Aktien* zs.-legen; **II** *v/i.* **4.** ***~ in*** sich verschmelzen mit, aufgehen in (*dat.*); **5.** a) *mot.* sich (in den Verkehr) einfädeln, b) zs.-laufen (*Straßen*); **'mer·gence** [-dʒəns] *s.* Aufgehen *n* (***in*** in *dat.*), Verschmelzung *f* (***into*** mit); **'merg·er** [-dʒə] *s.* **1.** ⚚ Fusi'on *f*, Fusionierung *f von Gesellschaften*; Zs.-legung *f von Aktien*; **2.** ⚖ a) Verschmelzung(svertrag *m*) *f*, Aufgehen *n* (*e-s Besitzes od. Vertrages in e-m anderen etc.*), b) Konsumpti'on *f* (*e-r Straftat durch e-e schwerere*).

me·rid·i·an [mə'rɪdɪən] **I** *adj.* **1.** mittägig, Mittags…; **2.** *ast.* Kulminations…, Meridian…: ***~ circle*** Meridiankreis *m*; **3.** *fig.* höchst; **II** *s.* **4.** *geogr.* Meridi'an *m*, Längenkreis *m*: ***prime ~*** Nullmeridian; **5.** *poet.* Mittag(szeit *f*) *m*; **6.** *ast.* Kulminati'onspunkt *m*; **7.** *fig.* Höhepunkt *m*, Gipfel *m*; *fig.* Blüte(zeit) *f*; **me'rid·i·o·nal** [-dɪənl] **I** *adj.* ☐ **1.** *ast.* meridio'nal, Meridian…, Mittags…; **2.** südlich, südländisch; **II** *s.* **3.** Südländer (-in), *bsd.* 'Südfranˌzose *m*, -franˌzösin *f*.

me·ringue [mə'ræŋ] *s.* Me'ringe *f*, Schaumgebäck *n*, Bai'ser *n*.

me·ri·no [mə'ri:nəʊ] *pl.* **-nos** [-z] *s.* **1.** *a.* ***~ sheep*** *zo.* Me'rinoschaf *n*; **2.** ⚚ a) Me'rinowolle *f*, b) Me'rino *m* (*Kammgarnstoff*).

mer·it ['merɪt] **I** *s.* **1.** Verdienst(lichkeit *f*) *n*: ***according to one's ~*** nach Verdienst *belohnen etc.*; ***a man of ~*** e-e verdiente Persönlichkeit; ***Order of 2*** Verdienstorden *m*; ***~ pay*** ⚚ leistungsbezogene Bezahlung; ***~ rating*** Leistungsbeurteilung *f*; **2.** Wert *m*, Vorzug *m*: ***of architectural ~*** von architektonischem Wert, erhaltungswürdig; **3.** ***the ~s*** *pl.* ⚖ *u. fig.* die Hauptpunkte, der sachliche Gehalt, die wesentlichen (⚖ *a.* materiell-rechtlichen) Gesichtspunkte: ***on its (own) ~s*** dem wesentlichen Inhalt nach, an (u. für) sich betrachtet; ***on the ~s*** ⚖ in der Sache selbst, nach materiellem Recht; ***decision on the ~s***

Sachentscheidung *f*; ***inquire into the ~s of a case*** e-r Sache auf den Grund gehen; **II** *v/t.* **4.** *Lohn, Strafe etc.* verdienen; **'mer·it·ed** [-tɪd] *adj.* ☐ verdient; **'mer·it·ed·ly** [-tɪdlɪ] *adv.* verdientermaßen.

me·ri·toc·ra·cy [ˌmerɪ'tɒkrəsɪ] *s. sociol.* **1.** (herrschende) E'lite; **2.** Leistungsgesellschaft *f*.

mer·i·to·ri·ous [ˌmerɪ'tɔːrɪəs] *adj.* ☐ verdienstvoll.

mer·lin ['mɜːlɪn] *s. orn.* Merlin-, Zwergfalke *m*.

mer·maid ['mɜːmeɪd] *s.* Meerweib *n*, Seejungfrau *f*, Nixe *f*; **'mer·man** [-mæn] *s.* [*irr.*] Wassergeist *m*, Triton *m*, Nix *m*.

mer·ri·ly ['merəlɪ] *adv. von* ***merry***; **'mer·ri·ment** [-ɪmənt] *s.* **1.** Fröhlichkeit *f*, Lustigkeit *f*; **2.** Belustigung *f*, Lustbarkeit *f*, Spaß *m*.

mer·ry ['merɪ] *adj.* ☐ **1.** lustig, fröhlich: ***as ~ as a lark*** (*od.* ***cricket***) kreuzfidel; ***make ~*** lustig sein, feiern, scherzen; **2.** scherzhaft, spaßhaft, lustig: ***make ~ over*** sich lustig machen über (*acc.*); **3.** beschwipst, angeheitert; **~ an·drew** ['ændruː] *s.* Hans'wurst *m*, Spaßmacher *m*; **'~-go-ˌround** [-gəʊˌr-] *s.* Karus'sell *n*; *fig.* Wirbel *m*; **'~-ˌmak·ing** *s.* Belustigung *f*, Lustbarkeit *f*, Fest *n*; **'~·thought** → ***wishbone*** 1.

me·sa ['meɪsə] *s. geogr. Am.* Tafelland *n*; **~ oak** *s. Am.* Tischeiche *f*.

mes·en·ter·y ['mesəntərɪ] *s. anat., zo.* Gekröse *n*.

mesh [meʃ] **I** *s.* **1.** Masche *f*: **~ *stocking*** Netzstrumpf *m*; **2.** ⚙ Maschenweite *f*; **3.** *mst pl. fig.* Netz *n*, Schlingen *pl.*: ***be caught in the ~es of the law*** sich in den Schlingen des Gesetzes verfangen (haben); **4.** ⚙ Inein'andergreifen *n*, Eingriff *m* (*von Zahnrädern*): ***be in ~*** im Eingriff sein; **5.** → ***mesh connection***; **II** *v/t.* **6.** in e-m Netz fangen, verwickeln; **7.** ⚙ in Eingriff bringen, einrücken; **8.** *fig.* (mitein'ander) verzahnen; **III** *v/i.* **9.** ⚙ ein-, inein'andergreifen (*Zahnräder*); **~ con·nec·tion** *s.* ⚡ Vieleck-, *bsd.* Deltaschaltung *f*.

meshed [meʃt] *adj.* netzartig; ...maschig: ***close-~*** engmaschig.

'mesh·work *s.* Maschen *pl.*, Netzwerk *n*; Gespinst *n*.

mes·mer·ic, mes·mer·i·cal [mez'merɪk(l)] *adj.* **1.** mesmerisch, 'heilmaˌgnetisch; **2.** *fig.* hyp'notisch, ma'gnetisch, faszinierend.

mes·mer·ism ['mezmərɪzəm] *s.* Mesme'rismus *m*, tierischer Magne'tismus; **'mes·mer·ist** [-ɪst] *s.* 'Heilmagnetiˌseur *m*; **'mes·mer·ize** [-raɪz] *v/t.* mesmerisieren; *fig.* faszinieren, bannen.

mesne [miːn] *adj.* ⚖ Zwischen..., Mittel...: **~ *lord*** Afterlehnsherr *m*; **~ in·ter·est** *s.* ⚖ Zwischenzins *m*.

meso- [mesəʊ] *in Zssgn* Zwischen..., Mittel...; **ˌmes·o'lith·ic** [-'lɪθɪk] *adj.* meso'lithisch, mittelsteinzeitlich.

mes·on ['miːzɒn] *s. phys.* Meson *n*.

Mes·o·zo·ic [ˌmesəʊ'zəʊɪk] *geol.* **I** *adj.* meso'zoisch; **II** *s.* Meso'zoikum *n*.

mess [mes] **I** *s.* **1.** *obs.* Gericht *n*, Speise *f*: **~ *of pottage*** *bibl.* Linsengericht; **2.** Viehfutter *n*; **3.** ⚔ Ka'sino *n*, Speiseraum *m*; ⚓ Messe *f*, Back *f*: ***officers' ~*** Offiziersmesse; **4.** *fig.* Mischmasch *m*, Mansche'rei *f*; **5.** *fig.* a) Durchein'ander *n*, Unordnung *f*, b) Schmutz *m*, ‚Schweine'rei' *f*, c) ‚Schla'massel' *m*, ‚Patsche' *f*, Klemme *f*: ***in a ~*** beschmutzt, in Unordnung, *fig.* in der Klemme; ***get into a ~*** in die Klemme kommen; ***make a ~*** Schmutz machen; ***make a ~ of*** → 6 c; ***make a ~ of it*** alles vermasseln *od.* versauen, Mist bauen; ***you made a nice ~ of it*** da hast du was Schönes angerichtet; ***he was a ~*** er sah gräßlich aus, *fig.* er war völlig verwahrlost; → ***pretty*** 2; **II** *v/t.* **6.** *a.* **~ *up*** a) beschmutzen, b) in Unordnung *od.* Verwirrung bringen, c) *fig.* verpfuschen, vermasseln, verhunzen; **III** *v/i.* **7.** (*an e-m gemeinsamen Tisch*) essen (***with*** mit): **~ *together*** ⚓ zu 'einer Back gehören; **8.** manschen, panschen (***in*** in *dat.*); **9.** **~ *with*** sich einmischen; **10.** **~ *about***, **~ *around*** her'ummurksen, (-)pfuschen, F *fig.* sich her'umtreiben.

mes·sage ['mesɪdʒ] *s.* **1.** Botschaft *f* (*a. bibl.*), Sendung *f*: ***can I take a ~?*** kann ich et. ausrichten?; **2.** Mitteilung *f*, Bescheid *m*, Nachricht *f*: ***get the ~*** F (es) kapieren; ***radio ~*** Funkmeldung *f*, -spruch *m*; **3.** *fig.* Botschaft *f*, Anliegen *n e-s Dichters etc.*; **'~-ˌtak·ing ser·vice** *s. teleph.* (Fernsprech)Auftragsdienst *m*.

mes·sen·ger ['mesɪndʒə] *s.* **1.** (Post- *etc.*)Bote *m*: (***express*** *od.* ***special***) **~** Eilbote; ***by ~*** durch Boten; **2.** Ku'rier *m*; ⚔ *a.* Melder *m*; **3.** *fig.* (Vor)Bote *m*, Verkünder *m*; **4.** ⚓ a) Anholtau *n*, b) Ankerkette *f*; **~ air·plane** *s.* ⚔ Ku'rierflugzeug *n*; **~ boy** *s.* Laufbursche *m*, Botenjunge *m*; **~ dog** *s.* Meldehund *m*; **~ pi·geon** *s.* Brieftaube *f*.

mess hall *s.* ⚔, ⚓ Messe *f*, Ka'sino (-raum *m*) *n*, Speisesaal *m*.

Mes·si·ah [mɪ'saɪə] *s. bibl.* Mes'sias *m*, Erlöser *m*; **Mes·si·an·ic** [ˌmesɪ'ænɪk] *adj.* messi'anisch.

mess｜jack·et *s.* ⚓ kurze Uni'formjacke; **~ kit** *s.* ⚔ Kochgeschirr *n*, Eßgerät *n*; **'~·mate** *s.* ⚔, ⚓ Meßgenosse *m*, 'Tischkameˌrad *m*; **~ ser·geant** *s.* ⚔ 'Küchenˌunteroffiˌzier *m*; **'~·tin** *s.* ⚔, ⚓ *bsd. Brit.* Eßgeschirr *n*.

mes·suage ['meswɪdʒ] *s.* ⚖ Wohnhaus *n* (*mst mit Ländereien*), Anwesen *n*.

'mess-up *s.* F **1.** Durchein'ander *n*; **2.** Mißverständnis *n*.

mess·y ['mesɪ] *adj.* ☐ **1.** unordentlich, schlampig; **2.** unsauber, schmutzig.

mes·ti·zo [me'stiːzəʊ] *pl.* **-zos** [-z] *s.* Me'stize *m*; Mischling *m*.

met [met] *pret. u. p.p. von* ***meet***.

met·a·bol·ic [ˌmetə'bɒlɪk] *adj.* **1.** *physiol.* meta'bolisch, Stoffwechsel...; **2.** sich (ver)wandelnd; **me·tab·o·lism** [me'tæbəlɪzəm] *s.* **1.** *biol.* Metabo'lismus *m*, Formveränderung *f*; **2.** *physiol., a.* ⚘ Stoffwechsel *m*: ***general ~***, ***total ~*** Gesamtstoffwechsel; → ***basal*** 2; **3.** ⚗ Metabo'lismus *m*; **me·tab·o·lize** [me'tæbəlaɪz] *v/t.* 'umwandeln.

met·a·car·pal [ˌmetə'kɑːpl] *anat.* **I** *adj.* Mittelhand...; **II** *s.* Mittelhandknochen *m*; **ˌmet·a'car·pus** [-pəs] *pl.* **-pi** [-paɪ] *s.* **1.** Mittelhand *f*; **2.** Vordermittelfuß *m*.

met·age ['miːtɪdʒ] *s.* **1.** amtliches Messen (*des Inhalts od. Gewichts bsd. von Kohlen*); **2.** Meßgeld *n*.

met·al ['metl] **I** *s.* **1.** ⚗, *min.* Me'tall *n*; **2.** ⚙ a) 'Nichteisenmeˌtall *n*, b) Me'talllegierung *f*, *bsd.* 'Typen-, Ge'schützmeˌtall *n*, c) 'Gußmeˌtall *n*: ***brittle ~***, ***red ~*** Rotguß *m*; ***fine ~*** Weiß-, Feinmetall; ***grey ~*** graues Gußeisen; **3.** *min.* a) Regulus *m*, Korn *n*, b) (Kupfer)Stein *m*; **4.** ⚒ Schieferton *m*; **5.** ⚙ (flüssige) Glasmasse; **6.** *pl. Brit.* Eisenbahnschienen *pl.*: ***run off the ~s*** entgleisen; **7.** *her.* Me'tall *n* (*Gold- u. Silberfarbe*); **8.** *Straßenbau*: Beschotterung *f*, Schotter *m*; **9.** *fig.* Mut *m*; **II** *v/t.* **10.** mit Me'tall bedecken *od.* versehen; **11.** 🛤, *Straßenbau*: beschottern; **III** *adj.* **12.** Metall..., me'tallen; **~ age** *s.* Bronze- u. Eisenzeitalter *n*; **'~-clad** *adj.* ⚙ me'tallgekapselt; **'~-coat** *v/t.* mit Me'tall über'ziehen; **~ cut·ting** *s.* ⚙ spanabhebende Bearbeitung; **~ found·er** *s.* Me'tallgießer *m*; **~ ga(u)ge** *s.* Blechlehre *f*.

met·al·ize *Am.* → ***metallize***.

me·tal·lic [mɪ'tælɪk] *adj.* (☐ **~*ally***) **1.** me'tallen, Metall...: **~ *cover*** a) ⚙ Metallüberzug *m*, b) ✈ Metalldeckung *f*; **~ *currency*** Metallwährung *f*, Hartgeld *n*; **2.** me'tallisch (glänzend *od.* klingend): **~ *voice***; **~ *beetle*** Prachtkäfer *m*; **met·al·lif·er·ous** [ˌmetə'lɪfərəs] *adj.* me'tallführend, -reich; **met·al·line** ['metəlaɪn] *adj.* **1.** me'tallisch; **2.** me'tallhaltig; **met·al·lize** ['metəlaɪz] *v/t.* metallisieren.

met·al·loid ['metəlɔɪd] **I** *adj.* metallo'idisch; **II** *s.* ⚗ Metallo'id *n*.

met·al·lur·gic, met·al·lur·gi·cal [ˌmetə'lɜːdʒɪk(l)] *adj.* metall'urgisch; **met·al·lur·gist** [me'tælədʒɪst] *s.* Metall'urg(e) *m*; **met·al·lur·gy** [me'tælədʒɪ] *s.* Metallur'gie *f*, Hüttenkunde *f*, -wesen *n*.

met·al｜plat·ing *s.* ⚙ Plattierung *f*; **'~-ˌpro·ces·sing**, **'~ˌwork·ing** **I** *s.* Me'tallbearbeitung *f*; **II** *adj.* me'tallverarbeitend.

met·a·mor·phic [ˌmetə'mɔːfɪk] *adj.* **1.** *geol.* meta'morph; **2.** *biol.* gestaltverändernd; **ˌmet·a'mor·phose** [-fəʊz] **I** *v/t.* **1.** (***to, into***) 'umgestalten (zu), verwandeln (in *acc.*); **2.** verzaubern, -wandeln (***to, into*** in *acc.*); **II** *v/i.* **3.** *zo.* sich verwandeln; **ˌmet·a'mor·pho·sis** [-fəsɪs] *pl.* **-ses** [-siːz] *s.* Metamor'phose *f* (*a. biol., physiol.*), Verwandlung *f*.

met·a·phor ['metəfə] *s.* Me'tapher *f*, bildlicher Ausdruck.

met·a·phor·i·cal [ˌmetə'fɒrɪkl] *adj.* ☐ meta'phorisch, bildlich.

met·a·phrase ['metəfreɪz] **I** *s.* Meta'phrase *f*, wörtliche Über'setzung; **II** *v/t.* a) wörtlich über'tragen, b) um'schreiben.

met·a·phys·i·cal [ˌmetə'fɪzɪkl] *adj.* ☐ **1.** *phls.* meta'physisch; **2.** 'übersinnlich; ab'strakt; **met·a·phy·si·cian** [ˌmetəfɪ'zɪʃn] *s. phls.* Meta'physiker *m*; **ˌmet·a'phys·ics** [-ks] *s. pl. sg. konstr. phls.* Metaphy'sik *f*.

met·a·plasm ['metəplæzəm] *s.* **1.** *ling.* Meta'plasmus *m*, Wortveränderung *f*; **2.** *biol.* Meta'plasma *n*.

me·tas·ta·sis [mɪ'tæstəsɪs] *pl.* **-ses** [-siːz] *s.* **1.** ⚕ Meta'stase *f*, Tochtergeschwulst *f*; **2.** *biol.* Stoffwechsel *m*.

met·a·tar·sal [ˌmetə'tɑːsl] *anat.* **I** *adj.* Mittelfuß...; **II** *s.* Mittelfußknochen *m*;

ˌmet·a'tar·sus [-səs] *pl.* **-si** [-saɪ] *s. anat., zo.* Mittelfuß *m.*

mete [mi:t] **I** *v/t.* **1.** *poet.* (ab-, aus)messen, durch'messen; **2.** *mst* ~ ***out*** (*a. Strafe*) zumessen (***to*** *dat.*); **3.** *fig.* ermessen; **II** *s. mst pl.* **4.** Grenze *f*: ***know one's ~s and bounds*** *fig.* Maß u. Ziel kennen.

me·tem·psy·cho·sis [ˌmetempsɪ'kəʊsɪs] *pl.* **-ses** [-si:z] *s.* Seelenwanderung *f*, Metempsy'chose *f.*

me·te·or ['mi:tjə] *s. ast.* a) Mete'or *m* (*a. fig.*), b) Sternschnuppe *f*; **me·te·or·ic** [ˌmi:tɪ'ɒrɪk] *adj.* **1.** *ast.* mete'orisch, Meteor…: ~ ***shower*** Sternschnuppenschwarm *m*; **2.** *fig.* mete'orhaft: a) glänzend: ~ ***fame***, b) ko'metenhaft, rasch: ***his ~ rise to power***; **'me·te·or·ite** [-jəraɪt] *s. ast.* Meteo'rit *m*, Mete'orstein *m*; **me·te·or·o·log·ic, me·te·or·o·log·i·cal** [ˌmi:tjərə'lɒdʒɪk(l)] *adj.* □ *phys.* meteoro'logisch, Wetter…, Luft…: ~ ***conditions*** Witterungsverhältnisse; ~ ***office*** Wetteramt *n*; ~ ***satellite*** Wettersatellit *m*; **me·te·or·ol·o·gist** [ˌmi:tjə'rɒlədʒɪst] *s. phys.* Meteoro'loge *m*, Meteoro'login *f*; **me·te·or·ol·o·gy** [ˌmi:tjə'rɒlədʒɪ] *s. phys.* **1.** Meteorolo'gie *f*; **2.** meteoro'logische Verhältnisse *pl.* (*e-r Gegend*).

me·ter¹ ['mi:tə] *Am.* → ***metre***.

me·ter² ['mi:tə] **I** *s.* ⚙ Messer *m*, Meßgerät *n*, Zähler *m*: ***electricity ~*** elektrischer Strommesser *od.* Zähler; **II** *v/t.* (*mit e-m Meßinstrument*) messen: ~ ***out*** *et.* abgeben, dosieren; **'~·maid** *s.* F Poli'tesse *f.*

meth·ane ['mi:θeɪn] *s.* ⚗ Me'than *n.*

me·thinks [mɪ'θɪŋks] *v/impers. obs. od. poet.* mich dünkt, mir scheint.

meth·od ['meθəd] *s.* **1.** Me'thode *f*; *bsd.* ⚙ Verfahren *n*: ~ ***of doing s.th.*** Art u. Weise *f*, et. zu tun; ***by a ~*** nach e-r Methode; **2.** 'Lehrmeˌthode *f*; **3.** Sy'stem *n*; **4.** *phls.* (logische) 'Denkmeˌthode; **5.** Ordnung *f*, Me'thode *f*, Planmäßigkeit *f*: ***work with ~*** methodisch arbeiten; ***there is ~ in his madness*** sein Wahnsinn hat Methode; ***there is ~ in this*** da ist System drin; **me·thod·ic, me·thod·i·cal** [mɪ'θɒdɪk(l)] *adj.* □ **1.** me'thodisch, syste'matisch; **2.** über'legt.

Meth·od·ism ['meθədɪzəm] *s. eccl.* Metho'dismus *m*; **'Meth·od·ist** [-ɪst] **I** *s.* **1.** *eccl.* Metho'dist(in); **2.** 2 *fig. contp.* Frömmler *m*, Mucker *m*; **II** *adj.* **3.** *eccl.* metho'distisch.

meth·od·ize ['meθədaɪz] *v/t.* me'thodisch ordnen; **'meth·od·less** [-dlɪs] *adj.* □ plan-, sy'stemlos.

meth·od·ol·o·gy [ˌmeθə'dɒlədʒɪ] *s.* **1.** Methodolo'gie *f*; **2.** Me'thodik *f.*

Me·thu·se·lah [mɪ'θju:zələ] *npr. bibl.* Me'thusalem *m*: ***as old as ~*** (so) alt wie Methusalem.

meth·yl ['meθɪl; ⚗ 'mi:θaɪl] *s.* ⚗ Me'thyl *n*: ~ ***alcohol*** Methylalkohol *m*; **meth·yl·ate** ['meθɪleɪt] ⚗ **I** *v/t.* **1.** methylieren; **2.** denaturieren: ***~d spirits*** denaturierter Spiritus, Brennspiritus *m*; **II** *s.* **3.** Methy'lat *n*; **meth·yl·ene** ['meθɪli:n] *s.* ⚗ Methy'len *n*; **me·thyl·ic** [mɪ'θɪlɪk] *adj.* ⚗ Methyl…

me·tic·u·los·i·ty [mɪˌtɪkjʊ'lɒsətɪ] *s.* peinliche Genauigkeit, Akri'bie *f*; **me·tic·u·lous** [mɪ'tɪkjʊləs] *adj.* □ peinlich genau, a'kribisch.

mé·tier ['meɪtɪeɪ] *s.* **1.** Gewerbe *n*; **2.** *fig.* (Spezi'al)Gebiet *n*, Meti'er *n.*

me·ton·y·my [mɪ'tɒnɪmɪ] *s.* Metony'mie *f*, Begriffsvertauschung *f.*

me·tre ['mi:tə] *s. Brit.* **1.** Versmaß *n*, Metrum *n*; **2.** Meter *m, n.*

met·ric ['metrɪk] **I** *adj.* (□ ***~ally***) **1.** metrisch: ~ ***system***; ~ ***method of analysis*** ⚗ Maßanalyse *f*; **2.** → ***metrical*** 2; **II** *s. pl. sg. konstr.* **3.** Metrik *f*, Verslehre *f*; ♪ Rhythmik *f*, Taktlehre *f*; **'met·ri·cal** [-kl] *adj.* □ **1.** → ***metric*** 1; **2.** a) metrisch, Vers…, b) rhythmisch; **'met·ri·cate** [-keɪt] *v/t. u. v/i. Brit.* (sich) auf das metrische Sy'stem 'umstellen.

met·ro·nome ['metrənəʊm] *s.* ♪ Metro'nom *n*, Taktmesser *m.*

me·trop·o·lis [mɪ'trɒpəlɪs] *s.* **1.** Metro'pole *f*, Haupt-, Großstadt *f*: ***the 2*** *Brit.* London; **2.** Hauptzentrum *n*; **3.** *eccl.* Sitz *m* e-s Metropo'liten *od.* Erzbischofs; **met·ro·pol·i·tan** [ˌmetrə'pɒlɪtən] **I** *adj.* **1.** hauptstädtisch, Stadt…; **2.** *eccl.* erzbischöflich; **II** *s.* **3.** a) Metropo'lit *m* (*Ostkirche*), Erzbischof *m*; **4.** Bewohner(in) der Hauptstadt; Großstädter(in).

met·tle ['metl] *s.* **1.** Veranlagung *f*; **2.** Eifer *m*, Mut *m*, Feuer *n*: ***be on one's ~*** vor Eifer brennen; ***put s.o. on his ~*** j-n zur Aufbietung aller s-r Kräfte anspornen; ***try s.o.'s ~*** j-n auf die Probe stellen; ***horse of ~*** feuriges Pferd; **'met·tled** [-ld], **'met·tle·some** [-səm] *adj.* feurig, mutig.

mew¹ [mju:] *s. orn.* Seemöwe *f.*

mew² [mju:] *v/i.* mi'auen (*Katze*).

mew³ [mju:] *s.* **1.** Mauserkäfig *m*; **2.** *pl. sg. konstr.* a) Stall *m*: ***the Royal 2s*** der Königliche Marstall, b) *Brit. zu Wohnungen umgebaute ehemalige Stallungen.*

mewl [mju:l] *v/i.* **1.** quäken, wimmern (*Baby*); **2.** mi'auen.

Mex·i·can ['meksɪkən] **I** *adj.* mexi'kanisch; **II** *s.* Mexi'kaner(in).

mez·za·nine ['metsəni:n] *s.* △ **1.** Mezza'nin *n*, Zwischengeschoß *n*; **2.** *thea.* Raum *m* unter der Bühne.

mez·zo ['medzəʊ] (*Ital.*) **I** *adj.* **1.** ♪ mezzo, mittel, halb: ~ ***forte*** halblaut; **II** *s.* **2.** → ***mezzo-soprano***; **3.** → ***mezzotint***; **ˌ~-so'pra·no** *s.* ♪ 'Mezzosoˌpran *m*; **'~·tint I** *s.* **1.** *Kupferstecherei*: Mezzo'tinto *n*, Schabkunst *f*; **2.** Schabkunstblatt *n*: ~ ***engraving*** Stechkunst *f* in Mezzotintomanier; **II** *v/t.* **3.** in Mezzo'tinto gravieren.

mi·aow [mi:'aʊ] → ***meow***.

mi·asm ['maɪæzəm], **mi·as·ma** [mɪ'æzmə] *pl.* **-ma·ta** [-mətə] *s.* ⚕ Mi'asma *n*, Krankheitsstoff *m*; **mi·as·mal** [mɪ'æzml], **mi·as·mat·ic, mi·as·mat·i·cal** [ˌmɪəz'mætɪk(l)] *adj.* ansteckend.

mi·aul [mi:'aʊl; mɪ'ɔ:l] *v/i.* mi'auen.

mi·ca ['maɪkə] *min.* **I** *s.* Glimmer(erde *f*) *m*; **II** *adj.* Glimmer…: ~ ***capacitor*** ⚡ Glimmerkondensator *m*; **mi·ca·ceous** [maɪ'keɪʃəs] *adj.* Glimmer…

Mi·cah ['maɪkə] *npr. u. s. bibl.* (das Buch) Micha *m od.* Mi'chäas *m.*

mice [maɪs] *pl. von* ***mouse***.

Mich·ael·mas ['mɪklməs] *s.* Micha'elis *n*, Michaelstag *m* (*29. September*); ~ **Day** *s.* **1.** Michaelstag *m* (*29. September*); **2.** *e-r der 4 brit. Quartalstage*; ~ **term** *s. Brit. univ.* 'Herbstseˌmester *n.*

Mick [mɪk] → ***Mike¹***.

Mick·ey ['mɪkɪ] *s.* **1.** *Am. sl.* ✈ Bordradar *n*; **2.** ***take the 2 out of s.o.*** j-n ‚veräppeln'; **3.** → ~ **Finn** [fɪn] *s. sl.* a) präparierter Drink, b) Betäubungsmittel *n.*

micro- [maɪkrəʊ] *in Zssgn*: a) Mikro…, (sehr) klein, b) ein milli'onstel, c) mikro'skopisch.

mi·crobe ['maɪkrəʊb] *s. biol.* Mi'krobe *f*; **mi·cro·bi·al** [maɪ'krəʊbjəl], **mi·cro·bic** [maɪ'krəʊbɪk] *adj.* mi'krobisch, Mikroben…; **mi·cro·bi·o·sis** [ˌmaɪkrəʊbaɪ'əʊsɪs] *s.* ⚕ Mi'krobeninfektiˌon *f.*

ˌmi·cro'chem·is·try *s.* Mikroche'mie *f.*

'mi·cro·chip *s. Computer*: Mikrochip *m.*

'mi·croˌcir·cuit *s.* Mikroschaltung *f.*

mi·cro·cosm ['maɪkrəʊkɒzəm] *s.* Mikro'kosmos *m* (*a. phls. u. fig.*); **mi·cro·cos·mic** [ˌmaɪkrəʊ'kɒzmɪk] *adj.* mikro'kosmisch.

'mi·croˌe·lec'tron·ics *s. pl. sg. konstr. phys.* Mikroelek'tronik *f.*

mi·cro·fiche ['maɪkrəʊfi:ʃ] *s.* Mikrofiche *m.*

'mi·cro·film *phot.* **I** *s.* Mikrofilm *m*; **II** *v/t.* auf Mikrofilm aufnehmen.

'mi·cro·gram *Am.*, **'mi·cro·gramme** *Brit. s. phys.* Mikro'gramm *n* (*ein millionstel Gramm*).

'mi·cro·groove *s.* **1.** Mikrorille *f*; **2.** Schallplatte *f* mit Mikrorillen.

'mi·cro·inch *s.* ein milli'onstel Zoll.

mi·crom·e·ter [maɪ'krɒmɪtə] *s.* **1.** *phys.* Mikro'meter *n* (*ein millionstel Meter*): ~ ***adjustment*** ⚙ Feinsteinstellung *f*; ~ (***caliper***) Feinmeßschraube *f*; **2.** *opt.* Oku'lar-Mikroˌmeter *n* (*an Fernrohren etc.*).

mi·cron ['maɪkrɒn] *pl.* **-crons, -cra** [-krə] *s.* ⚗, *phys.* Mikron *n* (*ein tausendstel Millimeter*).

ˌmi·cro'or·gan·ism *s.* Mikroorga'nismus *m.*

mi·cro·phone ['maɪkrəfəʊn] *s.* ⚡ **1.** (***at the ~*** am) Mikro'phon *n*; **2.** *teleph.* Sprechmuschel *f*; **3.** F Radio *n*: ***through the ~*** durch den Rundfunk.

ˌmi·cro'pho·to·graph *s.* **1.** Mikrofoto (-gra'fie *f*) *n*; **2.** → **ˌmi·cro·pho'tog·ra·phy** *s.* Mikrofotogra'fie *f.*

ˌmi·cro'proc·es·sor *s. Computer*: Mikropro'zessor *m.*

mi·cro·scope ['maɪkrəskəʊp] **I** *s.* Mikro'skop *n*: ***reflecting ~*** Spiegelmikroskop; ~ ***stage*** Objektivtisch *m*; **II** *v/t.* mikro'skopisch unter'suchen; **mi·cro·scop·ic, mi·cro·scop·i·cal** [ˌmaɪkrə'skɒpɪk(l)] *adj.* □ **1.** mikro'skopisch: ~ ***examination***; ~ ***slide*** Objektträger *m*; **2.** (peinlich) genau; **3.** mikro'skopisch klein, verschwindend klein.

'mi·croˌsec·ond *s.* Mikrose'kunde *f* (*eine millionstel Sekunde*).

ˌmi·cro'sur·ger·y *s.* ⚕ Mikrochirur'gie *f.*

'mi·cro·volt *s. phys.* Mikrovolt *n.*

'mi·cro·wave *s.* ⚡ Mikrowelle *f*, Dezi'meterwelle *f*: ~ ***engineering*** Höchstfrequenztechnik *f*; ~ ***oven*** Mikrowellenherd *m.*

mic·tu·ri·tion [ˌmɪktjʊə'rɪʃn] *s.* ⚕ **1.** U'rindrang *m*; **2.** Harnen *n.*

mid¹ [mɪd] *adj. attr. od. in Zssgn* mittler, Mittel…: ***in ~air*** mitten in der Luft, frei schwebend; ***in the ~ 16th century*** in der Mitte des 16. Jhs.; ***in ~-April*** Mitte April; ***in ~ ocean*** auf offener See.

mid² [mɪd] *prp. poet.* in'mitten von (*od. gen.*).

Mi·das ['maɪdæs] **I** *npr. antiq.* Midas *m* (*König von Phrygien*): ***he has the ~ touch*** *fig.* er macht aus allem Geld; **II** *s.* ♀ *zo.* Midasfliege *f.*

'mid·day I *s.* Mittag *m*; **II** *adj.* mittägig, Mittags…

mid·dle ['mɪdl] **I** *adj.* **1.** mittler, Mittel… (*a. ling.*): ***~ finger*** Mittelfinger *m*; ***~ quality*** ✝ Mittelqualität *f*; ***~ management*** mittleres Management; **II** *s.* **2.** Mitte *f*: ***in the ~*** in der Mitte; ***in the ~ of speaking*** mitten in der Rede; ***in the ~ of July*** Mitte Juli; **3.** Mittelweg *m*; **4.** Mittelstück *n* (*a. e-s Schlachttieres*); **5.** Mitte *f* (*des Leibes*), Taille *f*; **6.** Medium *n* (*griechische Verbalform*); **7.** *Logik*: Mittelglied *n* (*e-s Schlusses*); **8.** *Fußball*: Flankenball *m*; **9.** *a.* ***~ article*** *Brit.* Feuille'ton *n*; **10.** *pl.* ✝ Mittelsorte *f*; **11.** Mittelsmann *m*; **III** *v/t.* **12.** in die Mitte plazieren; *Fußball*: zur Mitte flanken.

mid·dle| age *s.* mittleres Alter; **ˌ♀-'Age** *adj.* mittelalterlich; **ˌ~-'aged** *adj.* mittleren Alters; **♀ Ag·es** *s. pl. das* Mittelalter; **~ A·mer·i·ca** *s. Am.* die (konserva'tive) ameri'kanische Mittelschicht; **'~·brow** F **I** *s.* geistiger ‚Nor'malverbraucher'; **II** *adj.* von 'durchschnittlichen geistigen Inter'essen; **ˌ~-'class** *adj.* zum Mittelstand gehörig, Mittelstands…; **~ class·es** *s. pl.* Mittelstand *m*; **~ course** *s. fig.* Mittelweg *m*; **~ dis·tance** *s.* **1.** *paint., phot.* Mittelgrund *m*; **2.** *sport* Mittelstrecke *f*; **ˌ~-'dis·tance** *adj. sport* Mittelstrecken…: ***~ runner*** Mittelstreckler(in); **~ ear** *s. anat.* Mittelohr *n*; **♀ East** *s. geogr.* **1.** *der* Mittlere Osten; **2.** *Brit. der* Nahe Osten; **♀ Eng·lish** *s. ling.* Mittelenglisch *n*; **♀ High Ger·man** *s. ling.* Mittelhochdeutsch *n*; **ˌ~-'in·come** *adj.* mit mittlerem Einkommen; **~ in·i·tial** *s. Am.* Anfangsbuchstabe *m* des zweiten Vornamens; **~ life** *s.* die mittleren Lebensjahre *pl.*; **'~·man** [-mæn] *s.* [*irr.*] **1.** Mittelsmann *m*; **2.** ✝ Zwischenhändler *m*; **'~·most** *adj.* ganz in der Mitte (liegend); **~ name** *s.* **1.** zweiter Vorname; **2.** *fig.* her'vorstechende Eigenschaft; **ˌ~-of-the-'road** *adj. bsd. pol.* gemäßigt; neu'tral; **~ rhyme** *s.* Binnenreim *m*; **'~-sized** *adj.* von mittlerer Größe; **~ watch** *s.* ⚓ Mittelwache *f* (*zwischen Mitternacht u. 4 Uhr morgens*); **'~-weight** *s. sport* Mittelgewicht(ler *m*) *n*; **♀ West** *s. Am.* (*u. Kanada*) Mittelwesten *m*, *der* mittlere Westen.

mid·dling ['mɪdlɪŋ] **I** *adj.* □ → *a.* II; **1.** von mittlerer Güte *od.* Sorte, mittelmäßig, Mittel…: ***fair to ~*** ‚so lala', ‚mittelprächtig'; ***~ quality*** ✝ Mittelqualität *f*; **2.** F leidlich (*Gesundheit*); **3.** F ziemlich groß; **II** *adv.* F **4.** (*a.* ***~ly***) leidlich, ziemlich; **5.** ziemlich gut; **III** *s.* **6.** *mst pl.* ✝ Mittelsorte *f*; **7.** *pl.* Mittelmehl *n*; **8.** *pl. metall.* 'Zwischenproˌdukt *n.*

mid·dy ['mɪdɪ] *s.* **1.** F *für* ***midshipman***; **2.** → **~ blouse** *s.* Ma'trosenbluse *f.*

'mid·field *s. sport* Mittelfeld *n* (*a. Spieler*): ***~ man, ~ player*** Mittelfeldspieler *m.*

midge [mɪdʒ] *s.* **1.** *zo.* kleine Mücke; **2.** → ***midget*** 1.

midg·et ['mɪdʒɪt] **I** *s.* **1.** Zwerg *m*, Knirps *m*; **2.** *et.* Winziges; **II** *adj.* **3.** Zwerg…, Miniatur…, Kleinst…: ***~ car*** *mot.* Klein(st)wagen *m*; ***~ railroad*** Liliputbahn *f.*

mid·i ['mɪdɪ] **I** *s.* Midimode *f*: ***wear ~*** midi tragen; **II** *adj.* Midi…: ***~ skirt*** → **'mid·i·skirt** *s.* Midirock *m.*

'mid·land [-lənd] **I** *s.* **1.** *mst pl.* Mittelland *n*; **2.** ***the ♀s*** *pl.* Mittelengland *n*; **II** *adj.* **3.** binnenländisch; **4.** ♀ *geogr.* mittelenglisch.

'mid·life cri·sis *s. psych.* Midlife-crisis *f*, Krise *f* in der Lebensmitte.

'mid·most [-məʊst] **I** *adj.* ganz in der Mitte (liegend); innerst; **II** *adv.* (ganz) im Innern *od.* in der Mitte.

'mid·night I *s.* (***at ~*** um) Mitternacht *f*; **II** *adj.* mitternächtlich, Mitternachts…: ***burn the ~ oil*** bis spät in die Nacht arbeiten *od.* aufbleiben; **~ blue** *s.* Mitternachtsblau *n* (*Farbe*); **~ sun** *s.* **1.** Mitternachtssonne *f*; **2.** ⚓ Nordersonne *f.*

'mid|·noon *s.* Mittag *m*; **ˌ~-'off** (**ˌ~-'on**) *s. Kricket*: **1.** links (rechts) vom Werfer po'stierter Spieler; **2.** links (rechts) vom Werfer liegende Seite des Spielfelds; **'~·riff** *s.* **1.** *anat.* Zwerchfell *n*; **2.** *Am.* a) Mittelteil *m e-s Damenkleids*, b) zweiteilige Kleidung, c) Obertaille *f*, d) Magengrube *f*; **'~·ship** ⚓ **I** *s.* Mitte *f* des Schiffs; **II** *adj.* Mittschiffs…: ***~ section*** Hauptspant *n*; **'~·ship·man** [-mən] *s.* [*irr.*] ⚓ **1.** *Brit.* Leutnant *m* zur See; **2.** *Am.* 'Seeoffiˌziersanwärter *m*; **'~·ships** *adv.* ⚓ mittschiffs.

midst [mɪdst] *s.*: ***in the ~ of*** inmitten (*gen.*), mitten unter (*dat.*); ***in their*** (***our***) ***~*** mitten unter ihnen (uns); ***from our ~*** aus unserer Mitte.

'mid·stream *s.* Strommitte *f*: ***in ~*** *fig.* mittendrin.

'midˌsum·mer I *s.* **1.** Mitte *f* des Sommers, Hochsommer *m*; **2.** *ast.* Sommersonnenwende *f*; **II** *adj.* **3.** hochsommerlich, Hochsommer…; **♀ Day** *s.* **1.** Jo'hannistag *m* (*24. Juni*); **2.** *e-r der 4 brit. Quartalstage.*

ˌmid|'way I *s.* **1.** Hälfte *f* des Weges, halber Weg; **2.** *Am.* Haupt-, Mittelstraße *f* (*auf Ausstellungen etc.*); **II** *adj.* **3.** mittler; **III** *adv.* **4.** auf halbem Wege; **ˌ~'week I** *s.* Mitte *f* der Woche; **II** *adj.* (in der) Mitte der Woche stattfindend.

mid·wife ['mɪdwaɪf] *s.* [*irr.*] Hebamme *f*, Geburtshelferin *f* (*a. fig.*); **'mid·wife·ry** [-wɪfərɪ] *s.* Geburtshilfe *f*, *fig. a.* Mithilfe *f.*

ˌmid|'win·ter *s.* **1.** Mitte *f* des Winters; **2.** *ast.* Wintersonnenwende *f*; **ˌ~'year I** *adj.* **1.** in der Mitte des Jahres vorkommend, in der Jahresmitte; **II** *s.* **2.** Jahresmitte *f*; **3.** *Am.* F a) um die Jahresmitte stattfindende Prüfung, b) *pl.* Prüfungszeit *f* (*um die Jahresmitte*).

mien [mi:n] *s.* Miene *f*, Gesichtsausdruck *m*; Gebaren *n*: ***noble ~*** vornehme Haltung.

miff [mɪf] *s.* F Verstimmung *f.*

might¹ [maɪt] *s.* **1.** Macht *f*, Gewalt *f*: ***~ is*** (***above***) ***right*** Gewalt geht vor Recht; **2.** Stärke *f*, Kraft *f*: ***with ~ and main, with all one's ~*** aus Leibeskräften, mit aller Gewalt.

might² [maɪt] *pret. von* ***may¹***.

'might-have-ˌbeen *s.* **1.** et., was hätte sein können; **2.** Per'son, die es zu et. hätte bringen können.

might·i·ly ['maɪtɪlɪ] *adv.* **1.** mit Macht, heftig, kräftig; **2.** F e'norm, mächtig, sehr; **'might·i·ness** [-ɪnɪs] *s.* Macht *f*, Gewalt *f*; **might·y** ['maɪtɪ] **I** *adj.* □ → ***mightily*** *u.* II; **1.** mächtig, gewaltig, heftig, groß, stark; → ***high and mighty***; **2.** *fig.* gewaltig, riesig, mächtig; **II** *adv.* **3.** F mächtig, riesig, ungeheuer: ***~ easy*** kinderleicht; ***~ fine*** prima.

mi·graine ['mi:greɪn] (*Fr.*) *s.* ⚕ Mi'gräne *f*; **'mi·grain·ous** [-nəs] *adj.* durch Migräne verursacht, Migräne…

mi·grant ['maɪgrənt] **I** *adj.* **1.** Wander…, Zug…; → *a.* ***migratory***; **II** *s.* **2.** Wandernde(r *m*) *f*; 'Umsiedler(in); **3.** *zo.* Zugvogel *m*; Wandertier *n*; **mi·grate** [maɪ'greɪt] *v/i.* (aus-, ab)wandern, (*a. orn.* fort)ziehen; **mi·gra·tion** [maɪ'greɪʃn] *s.* Wanderung *f* (*a.* ⚗, *zo., geol.*); Zug *m* (*Menschen od. Wandertiere*); *orn.* (Vogel)Zug *m*: ***~ of*** (***the***) ***peoples*** Völkerwanderung; ***intramolecular ~*** ⚗ intramolekulare Wanderung; → ***ionic²***; **mi·gra·tion·al** [maɪ'greɪʃənl] *adj.* Wander…, Zug…; **'mi·gra·to·ry** [-rətərɪ] *adj.* **1.** (aus)wandernd; **2.** Zug…, Wander…: ***~ bird*** Zugvogel *m*; ***~ instinct*** Wandertrieb *m*; **3.** um'herziehend, no'madisch: ***~ life*** Wanderleben *n*; ***~ worker*** Wanderarbeiter(in).

Mike¹ [maɪk] **I** *npr.* (*Kosename für*) Michael; **II** *s.* ♀ *sl.* a) Ire *m*, b) Katho'lik *m.*

mike² [maɪk] *v/i. sl.* her'umlungern.

mike³ [maɪk] *s.* F ‚Mikro' *n* (*Mikrophon*).

mil [mɪl] *s.* **1.** Tausend *n*: ***per ~*** per Mille; **2.** ⚙ 1/1000 Zoll *m* (*Drahtmaß*); **3.** ⚔ (Teil)Strich *m.*

mil·age ['maɪlɪdʒ] → ***mileage***.

Mil·a·nese [ˌmɪlə'ni:z] **I** *adj.* mailändisch; **II** *s. sg. u. pl.* Mailänder(in), Mailänder *pl.*

milch [mɪltʃ] *adj.* milchgebend, Milch…; **'milch·er** [-tʃə] → ***milker*** 3.

mild [maɪld] *adj.* □ mild (*a. Strafe, Wein, Wetter etc.*); gelind, sanft; leicht (*Droge, Krankheit, Zigarre etc.*), schwach: ***~ attempt*** schüchterner Versuch; ***~ steel*** ⚙ Flußstahl *m*; ***to put it ~(ly)*** a) sich gelinde ausdrücken, b) gelinde gesagt; ***draw it ~*** mach's mal halblang!

mil·dew ['mɪldju:] **I** *s.* **1.** ⚘ Mehltau (-pilz) *m*, Brand *m* (*am Getreide*); **2.** Schimmel *m*, Moder *m*: ***spot of ~*** Moder- *od.* Stockfleck *m* (*in Papier etc.*); **II** *v/t.* **3.** mit Mehltau *od.* Schimmel- *od.* Moderflecken über'ziehen: ***be ~ed*** verschimmelt sein (*a. fig.*); **III** *v/i.* **4.** brandig *od.* schimm(e)lig *od.* mod(e)rig werden (*a. fig.*); **'mil·dewed** [-dju:d], **'mil·dew·y** [-dju:ɪ] *adj.* **1.** brandig, mod(e)rig, schimm(e)lig; **2.** ⚘ von Mehltau befallen; mehltauartig.

mild·ness ['maɪldnɪs] *s.* Milde *f*; Sanftheit *f*; Sanftmut *f.*

mile [maɪl] *s.* Meile *f* (*zu Land = 1,609 km*): ***Admiralty ~*** *Brit.* englische Seemeile (*= 1,8532 km*); ***air ~*** Luftmeile (*= 1,852 km*); ***nautical ~, sea ~*** Seemeile (*= 1,852 km*); ***~ after ~ of fields,***

~s and ~s of fields meilenweite Felder; ***~s apart*** meilenweit auseinander, *fig.* himmelweit entfernt; ***miss s.th. by a ~*** *fig.* et. (meilen)weit verfehlen.
mile·age [ˈmaɪlɪdʒ] *s.* **1.** Meilenlänge *f*, -zahl *f*; **2.** zuˈrückgelegte Meilenzahl *od.* Fahrstrecke, Meilenstand *m*: ***~ indicator, ~ recorder*** *mot.* Meilenzähler *m*; **3.** *a.* ***~ allowance*** Meilengeld *n* (*Vergütung*); **4.** Fahrpreis *m* per Meile; **5.** *a.* ***~ book*** 🚂 *Am.* Fahrscheinheft *n*; **6.** F ***get a lot of ~ out of it*** jede Menge (dabei) rausholen; ***there's no ~ in it*** das bringt nichts (ein).
mile·om·e·ter [maɪˈlɒmɪtə] *s. mot.* Meilenzähler *m*.
ˈ**mile·stone** *s.* Meilenstein *m* (*a. fig.*).
mil·foil [ˈmɪlfɔɪl] *s.* ⚘ Schafgarbe *f*.
mil·i·ar·i·a [ˌmɪlɪˈeərɪə] *s.* ⚕ Frieselfieber *n*; **mil·i·ar·y** [ˈmɪlɪərɪ] *adj.* ⚕ miliˈar, hirsekornartig: ***~ fever*** → ***miliaria***; ***~ gland*** Hirsedrüse *f*.
mil·i·tan·cy [ˈmɪlɪtənsɪ] *s.* **1.** Kriegszustand *m*, Kampf *m*; **2.** Kampfgeist *m*; ˈ**mil·i·tant** [-tənt] **I** *adj.* ☐ miliˈtant: a) streitend, kämpfend, b) streitbar, kriegerisch; **II** *s.* Kämpfer *m*, Streiter *m*; ˈ**mil·i·ta·rist** [-tərɪst] *s.* **1.** *pol.* Militaˈrist *m*; **2.** Wehr- *od.* Miliˈtärexperte *m*; **mil·i·ta·ris·tic** [ˌmɪlɪtəˈrɪstɪk] *adj.* militaˈristisch; ˈ**mil·i·ta·rize** [-təraɪz] *v/t.* militarisieren.
mil·i·tar·y [ˈmɪlɪtərɪ] **I** *adj.* ☐ **1.** miliˈtärisch, Militär…: ***of ~ age*** in wehrpflichtigem Alter; **2.** Heeres…, Kriegs…; **II** *s. pl. konstr.* **3.** Miliˈtär *n*, Solˈdaten *pl.*, Truppen *pl.*; **~ a·cad·e·my** *s.* **1.** Miliˈtärakadeˌmie *f*; **2.** *Am.* (*zivile*) Schule mit miliˈtärischer Ausbildung; **~ col·lege** *s. Am.* Miliˈtärcollege *n*; **~ gov·ern·ment** *s.* Miliˈtärreˌgierung *f*; **~ jun·ta** *s.* Miliˈtärjunta *f*; **~ law** *s.* Wehr(straf)recht *n*; **~ map** *s.* Geneˈralstabskarte *f*; **~ po·lice** *s.* Miliˈtärpoliˌzei *f*; **~ ser·vice** *s.* Miliˈtär-, Wehrdienst *m*; **~ ser·vice book** *s.* Wehrpaß *m*; **~ stores** *s. pl.* Miliˈtärbedarf *m*, ˈKriegsmateriˌal *n* (*Munition, Proviant etc.*); **~ tes·ta·ment** *s.* ⚖ ˈNottestaˌment *n* (*von Militärpersonen im Krieg*); **~ tri·bu·nal** *s.* Miliˈtärgericht *n*.
mil·i·tate [ˈmɪlɪteɪt] *v/i.* (***against***) sprechen (gegen), widerˈstreiten (*dat.*), *e-r Sache* entgegenwirken; ***~ for*** eintreten *od.* kämpfen für.
mi·li·tia [mɪˈlɪʃə] *s.* ⚔ Miˈliz *f*, Bürgerwehr *f*.
milk [mɪlk] **I** *s.* **1.** Milch *f*: ***~ and water*** *fig.* kraftloses Zeug, seichtes Gewäsch; ***~ of human kindness*** *fig.* Milch der frommen Denkungsart; ***~ of sulphur*** ⚗ Schwefelmilch; ***it is no use crying over spilt ~*** geschehen ist geschehen, hin ist hin; → ***coconut*** 1; **2.** ⚘ (Pflanzen)Milch *f*; **II** *v/t.* **3.** melken; **4.** *fig. j-n* schröpfen, ‚ausnehmen'; **5.** ⚡ *Leitung* ‚anzapfen', abhören; **III** *v/i.* **6.** Milch geben; ˌ**~-and-ˈwa·ter** *adj.* saft- u. kraftlos, seicht; **~ bar** *s.* Milchbar *f*; **~ crust** *s.* ⚕ Milchschorf *m*; **~ duct** *s. anat.* Milchdrüsengang *m*.
milk·er [ˈmɪlkə] *s.* **1.** Melker(in); **2.** ⚙ ˈMelkmaˌschine *f*; **3.** Milchkuh *f od.* -schaf *n od.* -ziege *f*.
milk| **float** *s. Brit.* Milchwagen *m*; ˈ**~·man** [-mən] *s.* [*irr.*] Milchmann *m*; **~ run** *s.* ✈ *sl.* **1.** Rouˈtineeinsatz *m*; **2.** ‚gemütliche Sache', gefahrloser Einsatz; **~ shake** *s.* Milchshake *m*; ˈ**~·sop** *s. fig. contp.* Muttersöhnchen *n*; **~ sug·ar** *s.* ⚗ Milchzucker *m*, Lakˈtose *f*; **~ tooth** *s.* [*irr.*] Milchzahn *m*; ˈ**~·weed** *s.* ⚘ **1.** Schwalbenwurzgewächs *n*; **2.** Wolfsmilch *f*.
milk·y [ˈmɪlkɪ] *adj.* **1.** ☐ milchig, Milch…; milchweiß; **2.** *min.* milchig, wolkig (*bsd. Edelsteine*); **3.** *fig.* a) sanft, b) weichlich, ängstlich; ♀ **Way** *s. ast.* Milchstraße *f*.
mill[1] [mɪl] **I** *s.* **1.** (Mehl-, Mahl)Mühle *f*; → ***grist*** 1; **2.** ⚙ (*Kaffee-, Öl-, Säge- etc.*)Mühle *f*, Zerkleinerungsvorrichtung *f*: ***go through the ~*** *fig.* e-e harte Schule durchmachen; ***put s.o. through the ~*** j-n hart rannehmen; ***have been through the ~*** viel durchgemacht haben; **3.** *metall.* Hütten-, Hammer-, Walzwerk *n*; **4.** *a.* ***spinning-~*** ⚙ Spinneˈrei *f*; **5.** ⚙ a) *Münzerei*: Prägwerk *n*, b) *Glasherstellung*: Schleifkasten *m*; **6.** Faˈbrik *f*, Werk *n*; **7.** F Prügeˈlei *f*; **II** *v/t.* **8.** *Korn etc.* mahlen; **9.** ⚙ *allg.* bearbeiten, *z. B. Holz, Metall* fräsen, *Papier, Metall* walzen, *Tuch, Leder* walken, *Münzen* rändeln, *Eier, Schokolade* quirlen, schlagen, *Seide* moulinieren; **10.** F ‚ˈdurchwalken'; **III** *v/i.* **11.** F sich prügeln; **12.** ***~ about*** *od.* ***around*** (ˈrund)herˈumlaufen, herˈumirren: ***~ing crowd*** Gewühl *n*, wogende Menge.
mill[2] [mɪl] *s. Am.* Tausendstel *n* (*bsd.* 1/1000 *Dollar*).
mill| **bar** *s.* ⚙ Plaˈtine *f*; ˈ**~·board** *s.* starke Pappe, Pappdeckel *m*; ˈ**~·course** *s.* **1.** Mühlengerinne *n*; **2.** Mahlgang *m*.
mil·le·nar·i·an [ˌmɪlɪˈneərɪən] **I** *adj.* **1.** tausendjährig; **2.** *eccl.* das Tausendjährige Reich (Christi) betreffend; **II** *s.* **3.** *eccl.* Chiliˈast *m*; **mil·le·nar·y** [mɪˈlenərɪ] **I** *adj.* **1.** aus tausend (Jahren) bestehend, von tausend Jahren; **II** *s.* **2.** (Jahr)ˈTausend *n*; **3.** Jahrˈtausendfeier *f*; **mil·len·ni·al** [mɪˈlenɪəl] *adj.* **1.** *eccl.* das Tausendjährige Reich betreffend; **2.** e-e Jahrˈtausendfeier betreffend; **3.** tausendjährig; **mil·len·ni·um** [mɪˈlenɪəm] *pl.* **-ni·ums** *od.* **-ni·a** [-nɪə] *s.* **1.** Jahrˈtausend *n*; **2.** Jahrˈtausendfeier *f*; **3.** *eccl.* Tausendjähriges Reich (Christi); **4.** *fig.* Paraˈdies *n* auf Erden.
mil·le·pede [ˈmɪlɪpiːd] *s. zo.* Tausendfüß(l)er *m*.
mill·er [ˈmɪlə] *s.* **1.** Müller *m*; **2.** ⚙ ˈFräsmaˌschine *f*.
mil·les·i·mal [mɪˈlesɪml] **I** *adj.* ☐ **1.** tausendst; **2.** aus Tausendsteln bestehend; **II** *s.* **3.** Tausendstel *n*.
mil·let [ˈmɪlɪt] *s.* ⚘ (Rispen)Hirse *f*.
ˈ**mill-hand** *s.* Mühlen-, Faˈbrik-, Spinneˈreiarbeiter *m*.
milli- [mɪlɪ] *in Zssgn* Tausendstel.
ˌ**mil·liˈam·me·ter** *s.* ⚡ ˈMilliamˌpereˌmeter *n*.
mil·li·ard [ˈmɪljɑːd] *s. Brit.* Milliˈarde *f*.
mil·li·bar [ˈmɪlɪbɑː] *s. meteor.* Milliˈbar *n*.
ˈ**mil·li·gram(me)** *s.* Milliˈgramm *n*; ˈ**mil·li·me·ter** *Am.*, ˈ**mil·li·me·tre** *Brit. s.* Milliˈmeter *m, n*.
mil·li·ner [ˈmɪlɪnə] *s.* Hut-, Putzmacherin *f*, Moˈdistin *f*; ˈ**mil·li·ner·y** [-nərɪ] *s.* **1.** Putz-, Modewaren *pl.*; **2.** Hutmacherhandwerk *n*; **3.** ˈHutsaˌlon *m*.
mill·ing [ˈmɪlɪŋ] *s.* **1.** Mahlen *n*; **2.** ⚙ a) Walken *n*, b) Rändeln *n*, c) Fräsen *n*, d) Walzen *n*; **3.** *sl.* Tracht *f* Prügel; **~ cut·ter** *s.* ⚙ Fräser *m*; **~ ma·chine** *s.* **1.** ˈFräsmaˌschine *f*; **2.** Rändelwerk *n*; **~ prod·uct** *s.* ˈMühlen- *od.* ⚙ ˈWalzproˌdukt *n*.
mil·lion [ˈmɪljən] *s.* **1.** Milliˈon *f*: ***a ~ times*** millionenmal; ***two ~ men*** 2 Millionen Mann; ***by the ~*** nach Millionen; ***~s of people*** *fig.* e-e Unmasse Menschen; **2.** ***the ~*** die große Masse, das Volk; **mil·lion·aire**, *bsd. Am.* **mil·lion·naire** [ˌmɪljəˈneə] *s.* Millioˈnär *m*; **mil·lion·air·ess** [ˌmɪljəˈneərɪs] *s.* Millioˈnärin *f*; ˈ**mil·lion·fold** *adj. u. adv.* milliˈonenfach; ˈ**mil·lionth** [-nθ] **I** *adj.* milliˈonst; **II** *s.* Milliˈonstel *n*.
mil·li·pede [ˈmɪlɪpiːd], *a.* ˈ**mil·li·ped** [-ped] → ***millepede***.
ˈ**mil·liˌsec·ond** *s.* ˈMilliseˌkunde *f*.
ˈ**mill**|**·pond** *s.* Mühlteich *m*; ˈ**~·race** *s.* Mühlgerinne *n*.
Mills bomb [mɪlz], **Mills gre·nade** *s.* ⚔ ˈEierˌhandgraˌnate *f*.
ˈ**mill**|**·stone** *s.* Mühlstein *m* (*a. fig. Last*): ***be a ~ round s.o.'s neck*** *fig.* j-m ein Klotz am Bein sein; ***see through a ~*** *fig.* das Gras wachsen hören; ˈ**~·wheel** *s.* Mühlrad *n*.
mi·lom·e·ter → ***mileometer***.
milt[1] [mɪlt] *s. anat.* Milz *f*.
milt[2] [mɪlt] *ichth.* **I** *s.* Milch *f* (*der männlichen Fische*); **II** *v/t. den Rogen* mit Milch befruchten; ˈ**milt·er** [-tə] *s. ichth.* Milchner *m*.
mime [maɪm] **I** *s.* **1.** *antiq.* Mimus *m*, Possenspiel *n*; **2.** Mime *m*; **3.** Possenreißer *m*; **II** *v/t.* **4.** mimen, nachahmen.
mim·e·o·graph [ˈmɪmɪəgrɑːf] **I** *s.* Mimeoˈgraph *m* (*Vervielfältigungsapparat*); **II** *v/t.* vervielfältigen; **mim·e·o·graph·ic** [ˌmɪmɪəˈgræfɪk] *adj.* (☐ ***~ally***) mimeoˈgraphisch, vervielfältigt.
mi·met·ic [mɪˈmetɪk] *adj.* (☐ ***~ally***) **1.** nachahmend (*a. ling. lautmalend*); *b.s.* nachäffend, Schein…; **2.** *biol.* fremde Formen nachbildend.
mim·ic [ˈmɪmɪk] **I** *adj.* **1.** mimisch, (durch Gebärden) nachahmend; **2.** Schauspiel…: ***~ art*** Schauspielkunst *f*; **3.** nachgeahmt, Schein…; **II** *s.* **4.** Nachahmer *m*, Imiˈtator *m*; **III** *v/t. pret. u. p.p.* ˈ**mim·icked** [-kt], *pres. p.* ˈ**mim·ick·ing** [-kɪŋ] **5.** nachahmen, -äffen; **6.** ⚘, *zo.* sich *in der Farbe etc.* angleichen (*dat.*); ˈ**mim·ic·ry** [-krɪ] *s.* **1.** Nachahmen *n*, -äffung *f*; **2.** *zo.* Mimikry *f*, Angleichung *f*.
mi·mo·sa [mɪˈməʊzə] *s.* ⚘ Miˈmose *f*.
min·a·ret [ˈmɪnəret] *s.* ⛪ Minaˈrett *n*.
min·a·to·ry [ˈmɪnətərɪ] *adj.* drohend, bedrohlich.
mince [mɪns] **I** *v/t.* **1.** zerhacken, in kleine Stücke zerschneiden; ˈdurchdrehen: ***~ meat*** Hackfleisch machen; **2.** *fig.* mildern, bemänteln: ***~ one's words*** affektiert sprechen; ***not to ~ matters*** (*od.* ***one's words***) kein Blatt vor den Mund nehmen; **3.** geziert tun: ***~ one's steps*** → 5 b; **II** *v/i.* **4.** Fleisch (*a.* Fett, Gemüse) kleinschneiden *od.* zerkleinern, Hackfleisch machen; **5.** a) sich geziert benehmen, b) geziert gehen, trippeln; **III** *s.* **6.** *bsd. Brit.* → ***mincemeat*** 2; ˈ**~·meat** *s.* **1.** Paˈstetenfüllung *f* (*aus Korinthen, Äpfeln, Rosinen, Rum*

etc. mit od. ohne Fleisch); **2.** Hackfleisch *n*, Gehacktes *n*: ***make ~ of*** *fig.* a) ‚aus *j-m* Hackfleisch machen', b) *Argument etc.* ‚(in der Luft) zerreißen'; **~ pie** *s. mit* ***mincemeat*** *gefüllte Pastete.*

minc·er ['mɪnsə] → ***mincing machine.***

minc·ing ['mɪnsɪŋ] *adj.* □ *fig.* geziert, affektiert; **~ ma·chine** *s.* 'Fleischhackmaˌschine *f*, Fleischwolf *m*.

mind [maɪnd] **I** *s.* **1.** Sinn *m*, Gemüt *n*, Herz *n*: ***have s.th. on one's ~*** et. auf dem Herzen haben; **2.** Seele *f*, Verstand *m*, Geist *m*: ***presence of ~*** Geistesgegenwart *f*; (***the triumph of***) ***~ over matter*** *oft iro.* der Sieg des Geistes über die Materie; ***before one's ~'s eye*** vor s-m geistigen Auge; ***be of sound ~, be in one's right ~*** bei (vollem) Verstand sein; ***of sound ~ and memory*** ⚖ im Vollbesitz s-r geistigen Kräfte; ***be out of one's ~*** nicht (recht) bei Sinnen sein, verrückt sein; ***lose one's ~*** den Verstand verlieren; ***close one's ~ to s.th.*** sich gegen et. verschließen; ***have an open ~*** unvoreingenommen sein; ***cast back one's ~*** sich zurückversetzen (***to*** nach, in *acc.*); ***enter s.o.'s ~*** j-m in den Sinn kommen; ***put*** (*od.* ***give***) ***one's ~ to s.th.*** sich mit e-r Sache befassen; ***put s.th. out of one's ~*** sich et. aus dem Kopf schlagen; ***read s.o.'s ~*** j-s Gedanken lesen; ***that blows your ~!*** F da ist man (einfach) ‚fertig'!; **3.** Geist *m* (*a. phls.*): ***the human ~; things of the ~*** geistige Dinge; ***history of the ~*** Geistesgeschichte *f*; ***his is a fine ~*** er hat e-n feinen Verstand, er ist ein kluger Kopf; ***one of the greatest ~s of his time*** *fig.* e-r der größten Geister *od.* Köpfe s-r Zeit; **4.** Meinung *f*, Ansicht *f*: ***in*** (*od.* ***to***) ***my ~*** m-r Ansicht nach, m-s Erachtens; ***be of s.o.'s ~*** j-s Meinung sein; ***change one's ~*** sich anders besinnen; ***speak one's ~*** (***freely***) s-e Meinung frei äußern; ***give s.o. a piece of one's ~*** j-m gründlich die Meinung sagen; ***know one's own ~*** wissen, was man will; ***be in two ~s about s.th.*** mit sich selbst über et. nicht einig sein; ***there can be no two ~s about it*** darüber kann es keine geteilte Meinung geben; **5.** Neigung *f*, Lust *f*; Absicht *f*: ***have*** (***half***) ***a ~ to do s.th.*** (beinahe) Lust haben, et. zu tun; ***have s.th. in ~*** et. im Sinne haben; ***I have you in ~*** ich denke (dabei) an dich; ***have it in ~ to do s.th.*** beabsichtigen, et. zu tun; ***make up one's ~*** a) sich entschließen, e-n Entschluß fassen, b) zur Überzeugung kommen (***that*** daß), sich klarwerden (***about*** über *acc.*); ***I can't make up your ~*** *iro.* ich kann mir nicht deinen Kopf zerbrechen; **6.** Erinnerung *f*, Gedächtnis *n*: ***bear*** (*od.* ***keep***) ***in ~*** (immer) an *et.* denken, *et.* nicht vergessen, bedenken; ***call to ~*** sich *et.* ins Gedächtnis zurückrufen, sich an *et.* erinnern; ***put s.o. in ~ of s.th.*** j-n an et. erinnern; ***nothing comes to ~*** nichts fällt einem dabei ein; ***time out of ~*** seit (*od.* vor) undenklichen Zeiten; **II** *v/t.* **7.** merken, (be)achten, achtgeben, hören auf (*acc.*): ***~ one's P's and Q's*** F sich ganz gehörig in acht nehmen; ***~ you write*** F denk daran (*od.* vergiß nicht) zu schreiben; **8.** sich in acht nehmen, sich hüten vor (*dat.*): ***~ the step!*** Achtung, Stufe!; **9.** sorgen für, sehen nach: ***~ the children*** sich um die Kinder kümmern, die Kinder hüten; ***~ your own business!*** kümmere dich um deine eigenen Dinge!; ***don't ~ me!*** laß dich durch mich nicht stören!; ***never ~ him!*** kümmere dich nicht um ihn!; **10.** et. haben gegen, es nicht gern sehen *od.* mögen, sich stoßen an (*dat.*): ***do you ~ my smoking?*** haben Sie et. dagegen, wenn ich rauche?; ***would you ~ coming?*** würden Sie so freundlich sein zu kommen?; ***I don't ~*** (***it***) ich habe nichts dagegen, meinetwegen; ***I wouldn't ~ a drink*** ich hätte nichts gegen einen Drink; **III** *v/i.* **11.** achthaben, aufpassen, bedenken: ***~*** (***you***)***!*** wohlgemerkt; ***never ~!*** laß es gut sein!, es hat nichts zu sagen!, es macht nichts! (→ *a.* 12); **12.** et. da'gegen haben: ***I don't ~*** ich habe nichts dagegen, meinetwegen; ***I don't ~ if I do*** F ja, ganz gern *od.* ich möchte schon; ***he ~s a great deal*** er ist allerdings dagegen, es macht ihm sehr viel aus; ***never ~!*** mach dir nichts draus!

'mind|ˌbend·ing, '~ˌblow·ing, '~ˌbog·gling *adj. sl.* ‚irr(e)', ‚toll'.

mind·ed ['maɪndɪd] *adj.* **1.** geneigt, gesonnen: ***if you are so ~*** wenn das deine Absicht ist; **2.** *in Zssgn* a) gesinnt: ***evil-~*** böse gesinnt; ***small-~*** kleinlich, b) *religiös, technisch etc.* veranlagt: ***religious-~***, c) interes'siert an (*dat.*): ***air-~*** flugbegeistert.

'mind-exˌpand·ing *adj.* bewußtseinserweiternd, psyche'delisch.

mind·ful ['maɪndfʊl] *adj.* □ (***of***) aufmerksam, achtsam (auf *acc.*), eingedenk (*gen.*): ***be ~ of*** achten auf; **'mind·less** ['maɪndlɪs] *adj.* □ **1.** (***of***) unbekümmert (um), ohne Rücksicht (auf *acc.*), uneingedenk (*gen.*); **2.** hirn-, gedankenlos, ‚blind'; **3.** geistlos, unbeseelt.

'mind|-ˌread·er *s.* Gedankenleser(in); **'~-ˌread·ing** *s.* Gedankenlesen *n*.

mine[1] [maɪn] **I** *poss. pron.* der (die, das) mein(ig)e: ***what is ~*** was mir gehört, das Meinige; ***a friend of ~*** ein Freund von mir; ***me and ~*** ich u. die Mein(ig)en *od.* meine Familie; **II** *poss. adj. poet. od. obs.* mein: ***~ eyes*** meine Augen; ***~ host*** (der) Herr Wirt.

mine[2] [maɪn] **I** *v/i.* **1.** minieren; **2.** schürfen, graben (***for*** nach); **3.** sich eingraben (*Tiere*); **II** *v/t.* **4.** *Erz, Kohlen* abbauen, gewinnen; **5.** ⚓, ⚔ a) verminen, b) minieren; **6.** *fig.* unter'graben, -mi'nieren; **III** *s.* **7.** *oft pl.* ⚒ Mine *f*, Bergwerk *n*, Zeche *f*, Grube *f*; **8.** ⚓, ⚔ (*Luft-, See*)Mine *f*: ***spring a ~*** e-e Mine springen lassen (*a. fig.*); **9.** *fig.* Fundgrube *f* (***of*** an *dat.*): ***a ~ of information***; **~ bar·ri·er** *s.* ⚔ Minensperre *f*; **~ de·tec·tor** *s.* ⚔ Minensuchgerät *n*; **'~·field** *s.* ⚔ Minenfeld *n*; **~ fore·man** *s.* [*irr.*] ⚒ Obersteiger *m*; **~ gas** *s.* **1.** Me'than *n*; **2.** ⚒ Grubengas *n*, schlagende Wetter *pl.*; **'~ˌlay·er** [-ˌleɪə] *s.* ⚓, ⚔ Minenleger *m*.

min·er ['maɪnə] *s.* **1.** ⚒ Bergarbeiter *m*, -mann *m*, Grubenarbeiter *m*, Kumpel *m*: ***~s' association*** Knappschaft *f*; ***~'s lamp*** Grubenlampe *f*; ***~'s lung*** ⚕ (Kohlen)Staublunge *f*; **2.** ⚓, ⚔ Minenleger *m*.

min·er·al ['mɪnərəl] **I** *s.* **1.** Mine'ral *n*; **2.** *bsd. pl.* Mine'ralwasser *n*; **II** *adj.* **3.** mine'ralisch, Mineral...; **4.** ⚗ 'anorˌganisch; **~ car·bon** *s.* Gra'phit *m*; **~ coal** *s.* Steinkohle *f*; **~ de·pos·it** *s.* Erzlagerstätte *f*.

min·er·al·ize ['mɪnərəlaɪz] *v/t. geol.* **1.** vererzen; **2.** mineralisieren, versteinern; **3.** mit 'anorˌganischem Stoff durch'setzen; **min·er·al·og·i·cal** [ˌmɪnərə'lɒdʒɪkl] *adj.* □ *min.* minera'logisch; **min·er·al·o·gy** [ˌmɪnə'rælədʒɪ] *s.* Mineralo'gie *f*.

min·er·al| oil *s.* Erdöl *n*, Pe'troleum *n*, Mine'ralöl *n*; **~ spring** *s.* Mine'ralquelle *f*, Heilbrunnen *m*; **~ wa·ter** *s.* Mine'ralwasser *n*.

'mineˌsweep·er *s.* ⚓, ⚔ Minenräum-, Minensuchboot *n*.

min·e·ver ['mɪnɪvə] → ***miniver.***

min·gle ['mɪŋgl] **I** *v/i.* **1.** verschmelzen, sich vermischen, sich verbinden (***with*** mit): ***with ~d feelings*** *fig.* mit gemischten Gefühlen; **2.** *fig.* sich (ein)mischen (***in*** in *acc.*), sich mischen (***among, with*** unter *acc.*); **II** *v/t.* **3.** vermischen, -mengen.

min·i ['mɪnɪ] **I** *s.* **1.** Minimode *f*: ***wear ~*** mini tragen; **2.** Minikleid *n*, -rock *m etc.*; **II** *adj.* **3.** Mini...

min·i·a·ture ['mɪnətʃə] **I** *s.* **1.** Minia'tur (-gemälde *n*) *f*; **2.** *fig.* Minia'turausgabe *f*: ***in ~*** im kleinen, en miniature, Miniatur...; **3.** ⚔ kleine Ordensschnalle; **II** *adj.* **4.** Miniatur..., Klein..., im kleinen; **~ cam·er·a** *s. phot.* Kleinbildkamera *f*; **~ cur·rent** *s.* ⚡ Mini'mal-, 'Unterstrom *m*; **~ grand** *s.* ♪ Stutzflügel *m*; **~ ri·fle shoot·ing** *s.* 'Kleinkaˌliberschießen *n*.

min·i·a·tur·ist ['mɪnəˌtjʊərɪst] *s.* Minia'turmaler(in); **min·i·a·tur·ize** ['mɪnətʃəraɪz] *v/t. bsd. elektronische Elemente* miniaturisieren.

'min·i|·bus *s. mot.* Mini-, Kleinbus *m*; **'~·cab** *s. mot.* Minicar *m* (*Kleintaxi*); **'~·car** *s. mot.* Kleinwagen *m*; **'~·dress** *s.* Minikleid *n*.

min·i·kin ['mɪnɪkɪn] **I** *adj.* **1.** affektiert, geziert; **2.** winzig, zierlich; **II** *s.* **3.** kleine Stecknadel; **4.** *fig.* Knirps *m*.

min·im ['mɪnɪm] *s.* **1.** ♪ halbe Note; **2.** *et.* Winziges; Zwerg *m*; **3.** *pharm.* 1/60 Drachme *f* (*Apothekermaß*); **4.** Grundstrich *m* (*Kalligraphie*); **'min·i·mal** [-ml] *adj.* kleinst, mini'mal, Mindest...; **'min·i·mize** [-maɪz] *v/t.* **1.** auf das Mindestmaß zu'rückführen, möglichst gering halten; **2.** als geringfügig darstellen, bagatellisieren; **'min·i·mum** [-məm] **I** *pl.* **-ma** [-mə] *s.* Minimum *n* (*a.* ⚗), Mindestmaß *n*, -betrag *m*, -stand *m*: ***with a ~ of effort*** mit e-m Minimum an *od.* von Anstrengung; **II** *adj.* mini'mal, mindest, Mindest..., kleinst: ***~ output*** Leistungsminimum *n*; ***~ price*** Mindestpreis *m*; ***~ wage*** Mindestlohn *m*.

min·ing ['maɪnɪŋ] **I** *s.* Bergbau *m*, Bergwerk(s)betrieb *m*; **II** *adj.* Bergwerks..., Berg(bau)..., Gruben..., Montan...: ***~ academy*** Bergakademie *f*; ***~ law*** Bergrecht *n*; **~ dis·as·ter** *s.* Grubenunglück *n*; **~ en·gi·neer** *s.* 'Berg(bau)ingeniˌeur *m*; **~ in·dus·try** *s.* 'Bergbau-, Mon'tanindusˌtrie *f*; **~ share** *s.* Kux *m*.

min·ion ['mɪnjən] *s.* **1.** Günstling *m*; **2.** *contp.* Speichellecker *m*: **~ of the law** *oft humor.* Gesetzeshüter *m*; **3.** *typ.* Kolo'nel *f* (*Schriftgrad*).
'**min·i·skirt** *s.* Minirock *m*.
'**min·i-state** *s. pol.* Zwergstaat *m*.
min·is·ter ['mɪnɪstə] **I** *s.* **1.** *eccl.* Geistliche(r) *m*, Pfarrer *m* (*bsd. e-r Dissenterkirche*); **2.** *pol. Brit.* Mi'nister(in), *a.* Premi'ermiˌnister(in): **2 of the Crown** (Kabinetts)Minister(in); **2 of Labour** Arbeitsminister(in); **3.** *pol.* Gesandte(r *m*) *f*: **~ plenipotentiary** bevollmächtigter Gesandter; **4.** *fig.* Diener *m*, Werkzeug *n*; **II** *v/t.* **5.** darreichen; *eccl. die Sakramente* spenden; **III** *v/i.* **6.** (**to**) behilflich *od.* dienlich sein (*dat.*) (*a. fig. fördern*): **~ to the wants of others** für die Bedürfnisse anderer sorgen; **7.** *eccl.* Gottesdienst halten; **min·is·te·ri·al** [ˌmɪnɪ'stɪərɪəl] *adj.* □ **1.** amtlich, Verwaltungs..., 'untergeordnet: **~ officer** Verwaltungs-, Exekutivbeamte(r) *m*; **2.** *eccl.* geistlich; **3.** *pol.* a) Ministerial..., Minister..., b) Regierungs...: **~ bill** Regierungsvorlage *f*; **4.** Hilfs..., dienlich (**to** *dat.*); '**min·is·trant** [-trənt] **I** *adj.* **1.** (**to**) dienend (zu), dienstbar (*dat.*); **II** *s.* **2.** Diener(in); **3.** *eccl.* Mini'strant *m*; **min·is·tra·tion** [ˌmɪnɪ'streɪʃn] *s.* Dienst *m* (**to** an *dat.*); *bsd. kirchliches* Amt; '**min·is·try** [-trɪ] *s.* **1.** *eccl.* geistliches Amt; **2.** *pol. Brit.* a) Mini'sterium *n* (*a. Amtsdauer u. Gebäude*), b) Mi'nisterposten *m*, -amt *n*, c) Kabi'nett *n*, Regierung *f*; **3.** *pol. Brit.* Amt *n* e-s Gesandten; **4.** *eccl. coll.* Geistlichkeit *f*.
min·i·um ['mɪnɪəm] *s.* **1.** → **vermilion** 1; **2.** ⚗ Mennige *f*.
min·i·ver ['mɪnɪvə] *s.* Grauwerk *n*, Feh *n* (*Pelz*).
mink [mɪŋk] *s.* **1.** *zo.* Nerz *m*; **2.** Nerz (-fell *n*) *m*.
min·now ['mɪnəʊ] *s.* **1.** *ichth.* Elritze *f*; **2.** *fig. contp.* (*eine*) ‚Null', (*ein*) Niemand *m*.
mi·nor ['maɪnə] **I** *adj.* **1.** a) kleiner, geringer, b) klein, unbedeutend, geringfügig; 'untergeordnet (*a. phls.*): **~ casualty** ⚔ Leichtverwundete(r) *m*; **~ offence** (*Am.* **-se**) ⚖ (leichtes) Vergehen; **the 2 Prophets** *bibl.* die kleinen Propheten; **of ~ importance** von zweitrangiger Bedeutung, c) Neben..., Hilfs..., Unter...: **a ~ group** eine Untergruppe; **~ premise** → 7; **~ subject** *Am. univ.* Nebenfach *n*; **2.** minderjährig; **3.** *Brit.* jünger (*in Schulen*): **Smith ~** Smith der Jüngere; **4.** ♪ a) klein (*Terz etc.*), b) Moll...: **C ~** c-Moll *n*; **~ key** Molltonart *f*; **in ~ key** *fig.* (etwas) gedämpft; **~ mode** Mollgeschlecht *n*; **II** *s.* **5.** Minderjährige(r *m*) *f*; **6.** ♪ a) Moll *n*, b) 'Mollakˌkord *m*, c) Molltonart *f*; **7.** *phls.* 'Untersatz *m*; **8.** *Am. univ.* Nebenfach *n*; **III** *v/i.* **9.** **~ in** *Am. univ.* als Nebenfach studieren; **mi·nor·i·ty** [maɪ'nɒrətɪ] *s.* **1.** Minderjährigkeit *f*, Unmündigkeit *f*; **2.** Minori'tät *f*, Minderheit *f*, -zahl *f*: **~ government** (**party**) Minderheitsregierung (-partei) *f*; **be in the ~** in der Minderheit *od.* -zahl sein.
min·ster ['mɪnstə] *s. eccl.* **1.** Münster *n*; **2.** Klosterkirche *f*.
min·strel ['mɪnstrəl] *s.* **1.** *hist.* Spielmann *m*; Minnesänger *m*; **2.** *poet.* Sänger *m*, Dichter *m*; '**min·strel·sy** [-sɪ] *s.* **1.** Musi'kantentum *n*; **2.** a) Minnesang *m*, -dichtung *f*, b) *poet.* Dichtkunst *f*, Dichtung *f*; **3.** *coll.* Spielleute *pl.*
mint[1] [mɪnt] *s.* **1.** ⚘ Minze *f*: **~ sauce** (saure) Minzsoße; **2.** 'Pfefferminz(liˌkör) *m*.
mint[2] [mɪnt] **I** *s.* **1.** Münze *f*: a) Münzstätte *f*, -anstalt *f*, b) Münzamt *n*: **a ~ of money** F ein Haufen Geld; **2.** *fig.* (reiche) Fundgrube, Quelle *f*; **II** *adj.* **3.** (wie) neu, tadellos erhalten, (*Buch etc.*): **in ~ condition**; **4.** postfrisch (*Briefmarke*); **III** *v/t.* **5.** *Geld* münzen, schlagen, prägen; **6.** *fig. Wort etc.* prägen; '**mint·age** [-tɪdʒ] *s.* **1.** Münzen *n*, Prägung *f* (*a. fig.*); **2.** *das* Geprägte, Geld *n*; **3.** Prägegebühr *f*.
min·u·end ['mɪnjʊend] *s.* ⩘ Minu'end *m*.
min·u·et [ˌmɪnjʊ'et] *s.* ♪ Menu'ett *n*.
mi·nus ['maɪnəs] **I** *prp.* **1.** ⩘ minus, weniger; **2.** F ohne: **~ his hat**; **II** *adv.* **3.** minus, unter Null (*Temperatur*); **III** *adj.* **4.** Minus..., negativ: **~ amount** Fehlbetrag *m*; **~ quantity** → 6; **~ sign** → 5; **IV** *s.* **5.** Minuszeichen *n*; **6.** Minus *n*, negative Größe; **7.** Mangel *m* (**of** an *dat.*).
mi·nus·cule ['mɪnəskju:l] *s.* Mi'nuskel *f*, kleiner (Anfangs)Buchstabe.
min·ute[1] ['mɪnɪt] **I** *s.* **1.** Mi'nute *f* (*a. ast.*, ⩘, ⚠): **for a ~** e-e Minute (lang); **~ hand** Minutenzeiger *m* (*Uhr*); **to the ~** auf die Minute genau; (**up**) **to the ~** hypermodern; **2.** Augenblick *m*: **in a ~** sofort; **just a ~!** Moment mal!; **the ~ that** sobald; **3.** ✝ a) Kon'zept *n*, kurzer Entwurf, b) No'tiz *f*, Memo'randum *n*: **~ book** Protokollbuch *n*; **4.** *pl.* ⚖, *pol.* ('Sitzungs)Protoˌkoll *n*, Niederschrift *f*: (**the**) **~s of the proceedings** Verhandlungsprotokoll *n*; **keep the ~s** das Protokoll führen; **II** *v/t.* **5.** a) entwerfen, aufsetzen, b) notieren, protokollieren.
mi·nute[2] [maɪ'nju:t] *adj.* □ **1.** sehr klein, winzig: **in the ~st details** in den kleinsten Einzelheiten; **2.** *fig.* unbedeutend, geringfügig; **3.** peinlich genau, minuzi'ös.
min·ute·ly[1] ['mɪnɪtlɪ] **I** *adj.* jede Mi'nute geschehend, Minuten...; **II** *adv.* jede Mi'nute, von Minute zu Minute.
mi·nute·ly[2] [maɪ'nju:tlɪ] *adv. von* **minute**[2]; **mi·nute·ness** [maɪ'nju:tnɪs] *s.* **1.** Kleinheit *f*, Winzigkeit *f*; **2.** minuzi'öse Genauigkeit.
mi·nu·ti·a [maɪ'nju:ʃɪə] *pl.* **-ti·ae** [-ʃɪi:] (*Lat.*) *s.* Einzelheit *f*, De'tail *n*.
minx [mɪŋks] *s.* Range *f*, ‚kleines Biest'.
mir·a·cle ['mɪrəkl] *s.* Wunder *n* (*a. fig.* **of** an *dat.*); Wundertat *f*, -kraft *f*: **to a ~** phantastisch (gut); **work ~s** Wunder tun *od.* vollbringen; **~ drug** Wunderdroge *f*; **~ play** *hist. eccl.* Mirakelspiel *n*; **mi·rac·u·lous** [mɪ'rækjʊləs] **I** *adj.* □ 'überna̩türlich, wunderbar (*a. fig.*); Wunder...: **~ cure** Wunderkur *f*; **II** *s. das* Wunderbare; **mi·rac·u·lous·ly** [mɪ'rækjʊləslɪ] *adv.* (wie) durch ein Wunder, wunderbar(erweise).
mi·rage ['mɪrɑ:ʒ] *s.* **1.** *phys.* Luftspiegelung *f*, Fata Mor'gana *f*; **2.** *fig.* Trugbild *n*.
mire ['maɪə] **I** *s.* **1.** Schlamm *m*, Sumpf *m*, Kot *m* (*alle a. fig.*): **drag s.o. through the ~** *fig.* j-n in den Schmutz ziehen; **be deep in the ~** ‚tief in der Klemme sitzen'; **II** *v/t.* **2.** in den Schlamm fahren *od.* setzen: **be ~d** im Sumpf *etc.* stecken(bleiben); **3.** beschmutzen, besudeln; **III** *v/i.* **4.** im Sumpf versinken.
mir·ror ['mɪrə] **I** *s.* **1.** Spiegel *m* (*a. zo.*): **hold up the ~ to s.o.** *fig.* j-m den Spiegel vorhalten; **2.** *fig.* Spiegel(bild *n*) *m*; **II** *v/t.* **3.** 'widerspiegeln: **be ~ed** sich (wider)spiegeln (**in** in *dat.*); **4.** mit Spiegel(n) versehen: **~ed room** Spiegelzimmer *n*; **~ fin·ish** *s.* ⚙ Hochglanz *m*; '**~-inˌvert·ed** *adj.* seitenverkehrt; **~ sym·me·try** *s.* ⩘, *phys.* 'Spiegelsymmeˌtrie *f*; '**~-ˌwrit·ing** *s.* Spiegelschrift *f*.
mirth [mɜ:θ] *s.* Fröhlichkeit *f*, Heiterkeit *f*, Freude *f*; '**mirth·ful** [-fʊl] *adj.* □ fröhlich, heiter, lustig; '**mirth·ful·ness** [-fʊlnɪs] *s.* → **mirth**; '**mirth·less** [-lɪs] *adj.* freudlos, trüb(e).
mir·y ['maɪərɪ] *adj.* **1.** sumpfig, schlammig, kotig; **2.** *fig.* schmutzig, gemein.
mis- [mɪs] *in Zssgn* falsch, Falsch..., miß..., Miß...; schlecht; Fehl...
ˌ**mis·ad'ven·ture** *s.* Unfall *m*, Unglück *n*; 'Mißgeschick *n*; ˌ**mis·a'lign·ment** *s.* ⚙ Flucht(ungs)fehler *m*; *Radio*, *TV*: schlechte Ausrichtung; ˌ**mis·al'li·ance** *s.* Mesalli'ance *f*, 'Mißheirat *f*.
mis·an·thrope ['mɪzənθrəʊp] *s.* Menschenfeind *m*, Misan'throp *m*; **mis·an·throp·ic**, **mis·an·throp·i·cal** [ˌmɪzən'θrɒpɪk(l)] *adj.* □ menschenfeindlich, misan'thropisch; **mis·an·thro·pist** [mɪ'zænθrəpɪst] → **misanthrope**; **mis·an·thro·py** [mɪ'zænθrəpɪ] *s.* Menschenhaß *m*, Misanthro'pie *f*.
'**misˌap·pli'ca·tion** *s.* falsche Verwendung; *b.s.* 'Mißbrauch *m*; ˌ**mis·ap'ply** *v/t.* **1.** falsch anbringen *od.* anwenden; **2.** → **misappropriate** 1.
'**misˌap·pre'hend** *v/t.* 'mißverstehen; '**misˌap·pre'hen·sion** *s.* 'Mißverständnis *n*, falsche Auffassung: **be** *od.* **labo(u)r under a ~** sich in e-m Irrtum befinden.
ˌ**mis·ap'pro·pri·ate** *v/t.* **1.** sich 'widerrechtlich aneignen, unter'schlagen; **2.** falsch anwenden: **~d capital** ✝ fehlgeleitetes Kapital; '**mis·apˌpro·pri'a·tion** *s.* ⚖ 'widerrechtliche Aneignung *od.* Verwendung, Unter'schlagung *f*, Veruntreuung *f*.
ˌ**mis·be'come** *v/t.* [*irr.* → **become**] *j-m* schlecht stehen, sich nicht schicken *od.* ziemen für; ˌ**mis·be'com·ing** *adj.* → **unbecoming**.
'**mis·beˌgot·ten** *adj.* **1.** unehelich (gezeugt); **2.** → **misgotten**; **3.** mise'rabel, verkorkst.
ˌ**mis·be'have** *v/i. od. v/refl.* **1.** sich schlecht benehmen *od.* aufführen, sich da'nebenbenehmen; ungezogen sein (*Kind*); **2.** **~ with** sich einlassen *od.* in'tim werden mit; ˌ**mis·be'hav·io(u)r** *s.* **1.** schlechtes Betragen, Ungezogenheit *f*; **2.** **~ before the enemy** ⚔ *Am.* Feigheit *f* vor dem Feind.
ˌ**mis·be'lief** *s.* Irrglaube *m*; irrige Ansicht; ˌ**mis·be'lieve** *v/i.* irrgläubig sein.
ˌ**mis'cal·cu·late** **I** *v/t.* falsch berechnen *od.* (ab)schätzen; **II** *v/i.* sich verrechnen, sich verkalkulieren; '**misˌcal·cu'la·tion** *s.* Rechen-, Kalkulati'onsfehler *m*.
ˌ**mis'call** *v/t.* falsch *od.* zu Unrecht (be-)

nennen.

ˌ**mis'car·riage** *s.* **1.** Fehlschlag(en *n*) *m*, Miß'lingen *n*: **~ *of justice*** ⚖ Fehlspruch *m*, -urteil *n*, Justizirrtum *m*; **2.** ✝ Versandfehler *m*; **3.** Fehlleitung *f* (*Brief*); **4.** ⚕ Fehlgeburt *f*; ˌ**mis'car·ry** *v/i.* **1.** miß'lingen, -'glücken, fehlschlagen, scheitern; **2.** verlorengehen (*Brief*); **3.** ⚕ e-e Fehlgeburt haben.

ˌ**mis'cast** *v/t.* [*irr.* → ***cast***] *thea. etc. Rolle* fehlbesetzen: ***be*** **~** a) e-e Fehlbesetzung sein (*Schauspieler*), b) *fig.* s-n Beruf verfehlt haben.

mis·ce·ge·na·tion [ˌmɪsɪdʒɪ'neɪʃn] *s.* Rassenmischung *f*.

mis·cel·la·ne·ous [ˌmɪsɪ'leɪnjəs] *adj.* □ **1.** ge-, vermischt, di'vers; **2.** mannigfaltig, verschiedenartig; ˌ**mis·cel'la·ne·ous·ness** [-nɪs] *s.* **1.** Gemischtheit *f*; **2.** Vielseitigkeit *f*; Mannigfaltigkeit *f*; **mis·cel·la·ny** [mɪ'selənɪ] *s.* **1.** Gemisch *n*, Sammlung *f*, Sammelband *m*; **2.** *pl.*, vermischte Schriften *pl.*, Mis'zellen *pl.*

ˌ**mis'chance** *s.* 'Mißgeschick *n*: ***by*** **~** durch e-n unglücklichen Zufall, unglücklicherweise.

mis·chief ['mɪstʃɪf] *s.* **1.** Unheil *n*, Unglück *n*, Schaden *m*: ***do*** **~** Unheil anrichten; ***mean*** **~** Böses im Schilde führen; ***make*** **~** Zwietracht säen, böses Blut machen; ***run into*** **~** in Gefahr kommen; **2.** Ursache *f* des Unheils, Übelstand *m*, Unrecht *n*, Störenfried *m*; **3.** Unfug *m*, Possen *m*: ***get into*** **~** et. ‚anstellen'; ***keep out of*** **~** keine Dummheiten machen, brav sein; ***that will keep you out of*** **~*!*** damit du auf keine dummen Gedanken kommst!; **4.** Racker *m* (*Kind*); **5.** 'Übermut *m*, Ausgelassenheit *f*: ***be full of*** **~** immer Unfug im Kopf haben; **6.** *euphem. der* Teufel: ***what*** (***why***) ***the*** **~** ***...?*** was (warum) zum Teufel ...?; '**~-ˌmak·er** *s.* → ***troublemaker***.

mis·chie·vous ['mɪstʃɪvəs] *adj.* □ **1.** nachteilig, schädlich, verderblich; **2.** boshaft, mutwillig, schadenfroh, schelmisch; '**mis·chie·vous·ness** [-nɪs] *s.* **1.** Schädlichkeit *f*; **2.** Bosheit *f*; **3.** Schalkhaftigkeit *f*, Ausgelassenheit *f*.

mis·ci·ble ['mɪsəbl] *adj.* mischbar.

ˌ**mis·con'ceive** *v/t.* falsch auffassen *od.* verstehen, sich e-n falschen Begriff machen von; ˌ**mis·con'cep·tion** *s.* 'Mißverständnis *n*, falsche Auffassung.

mis·con·duct I *v/t.* [ˌmɪskən'dʌkt] **1.** schlecht führen *od.* verwalten; **2. ~ *o.s.*** sich schlecht betragen *od.* benehmen, e-n Fehltritt begehen; **II** *s.* [ˌmɪs'kɒndʌkt] **3.** Ungebühr *f*, schlechtes Betragen *od.* Benehmen; **4.** Verfehlung *f*, *bsd.* Ehebruch *m*, Fehltritt *m*; ⚔ schlechte Führung: **~ *in office*** ⚖ Amtsvergehen *n*.

ˌ**mis·con'struc·tion** *s.* 'Mißdeutung *f*, falsche Auslegung; ˌ**mis·con'strue** *v/t.* falsch auslegen, miß'deuten, 'mißverstehen.

mis·cre·ant ['mɪskrɪənt] **I** *adj.* gemein, ab'scheulich; **II** *s.* Schurke *m*.

ˌ**mis'date I** *v/t.* falsch datieren; **II** *s.* falsches Datum.

ˌ**mis'deal** *v/t. u. v/i.* [*irr.* → ***deal***] **~** (***the cards***) sich vergeben.

ˌ**mis'deed** *s.* Missetat *f*.

mis·de·mean [ˌmɪsdɪ'miːn] *v/i. u. v/refl.* sich schlecht betragen, sich vergehen; ˌ**mis·de'mean·o(u)r** [-nə] *s.* ⚖ Vergehen *n*, minderes De'likt.

ˌ**mis·di'rect** *v/t.* **1.** *j-n od. et.* fehl-, irreleiten: **~*ed charity*** falsch angebrachte Wohltätigkeit; **2.** ⚖ *die Geschworenen* falsch belehren; **3.** *Brief* falsch adressieren.

mise en scène [ˌmiːzɑ̃ːn'seɪn] (*Fr.*) *s. thea. u. fig.* Inszenierung *f*.

ˌ**mis·em'ploy** *v/t.* **1.** schlecht anwenden; **2.** miß'brauchen.

mi·ser ['maɪzə] *s.* Geizhals *m*.

mis·er·a·ble ['mɪzərəbl] *adj.* □ **1.** elend, jämmerlich, erbärmlich, armselig, kläglich (*alle a. contp.*); **2.** traurig, unglücklich: ***make s.o.*** **~**; **3.** *contp. allg.* mise'rabel.

mi·ser·li·ness ['maɪzəlɪnɪs] *s.* Geiz *m*; **mi·ser·ly** ['maɪzəlɪ] *adj.* geizig.

mis·er·y ['mɪzərɪ] *s.* Elend *n*, Not *f*; Trübsal *f*, Jammer *m*; ***put s.o. out of his*** **~** *mst iro.* j-n von s-m Leiden erlösen.

mis·fea·sance [mɪs'fiːzəns] *s.* ⚖ **1.** pflichtwidrige Handlung; **2.** 'Mißbrauch *m* (*der Amtsgewalt*).

ˌ**mis'fire I** *v/i.* **1.** versagen (*Waffe*); **2.** *mot.* fehlzünden, aussetzen; **3.** *fig.* ‚da'nebengehen'; **II** *s.* **4.** Versager *m*; **5.** *mot.* Fehlzündung *f*.

'**mis·fit** *s.* **1.** schlechtsitzendes Kleidungsstück; **2.** nicht passendes Stück; **3.** F *fig.* Außenseiter(in), Eigenbrötler(in).

mis'for·tune *s.* 'Mißgeschick *n*.

mis'give *v/t.* [*irr.* → ***give***] *Böses* ahnen lassen: ***my heart*** **~*s me*** mir schwant (***that*** daß, ***about s.th.*** et.); **mis'giv·ing** *s.* Befürchtung *f*, böse Ahnung, Zweifel *m*.

mis'got·ten *adj.* unrechtmäßig erworben.

ˌ**mis'gov·ern** *v/t.* schlecht regieren; ˌ**mis'gov·ern·ment** *s.* 'Mißregierung *f*, schlechte Regierung.

ˌ**mis'guide** *v/t.* fehlleiten, verleiten, irreführen; ˌ**mis'guid·ed** *adj.* fehl-, irregeleitet; irrig, unangebracht.

ˌ**mis'han·dle** *v/t.* miß'handeln; *weitS.* falsch behandeln, schlecht handhaben; verpatzen.

mis·hap ['mɪshæp] *s.* Unglück *n*, Unfall *m*; *mot.* (*a. humor. fig.*) Panne *f*.

ˌ**mis'hear** *v/t. u. v/i.* [*irr.* → ***hear***] falsch hören, sich verhören (bei).

mish·mash ['mɪʃmæʃ] *s.* Mischmasch *m*.

ˌ**mis·in'form I** *v/t.* *j-m* falsch berichten, *j-n* falsch unter'richten; **II** *v/i.* falsch aussagen (***against*** gegen); ˌ**mis·in·for'ma·tion** *s.* falscher Bericht, falsche Auskunft.

ˌ**mis·in'ter·pret** *v/t.* miß'deuten, falsch auffassen *od.* auslegen; '**mis·inˌter·pre'ta·tion** *s.* 'Mißdeutung *f*, falsche Auslegung.

ˌ**mis'join·der** *s.* ⚖ unzulässige Klagehäufung; unzulässige Zuziehung (*e-s Streitgenossen*).

ˌ**mis'judge** *v/i. u. v/t.* **1.** falsch (be)urteilen, verkennen; **2.** falsch schätzen: ***I*** **~*d the distance***; ˌ**mis'judge·ment** *s.* irriges Urteil; falsche Beurteilung.

ˌ**mis'lay** *v/t.* [*irr.* → ***lay***] *et.* verlegen.

ˌ**mis'lead** *v/t.* [*irr.* → ***lead***] irreführen; *fig. a.* verführen, verleiten (***into doing*** zu tun): ***be misled*** sich verleiten lassen; ˌ**mis'lead·ing** *adj.* irreführend.

ˌ**mis'man·age I** *v/t.* schlecht verwalten, unrichtig handhaben; **II** *v/i.* schlecht wirtschaften; ˌ**mis'man·age·ment** *s.* schlechte Verwaltung, 'Mißwirtschaft *f*.

ˌ**mis'matched** *adj.* nicht zs.-passend, ungleich (*Paar*).

ˌ**mis'name** *v/t.* falsch benennen.

mis·no·mer [ˌmɪs'nəʊmə] *s.* **1.** ⚖ Namensirrtum *m* (*in e-r Urkunde*); **2.** falsche Benennung *od.* Bezeichnung.

mi·sog·a·mist [mɪ'sɒgəmɪst] *s.* Ehefeind *m*.

mi·sog·y·nist [mɪ'sɒdʒɪnɪst] *s.* Frauenfeind *m*; **mi'sog·y·ny** [-nɪ] *s.* Frauenhaß *m*, Mysogy'nie *f*.

ˌ**mis'place** *v/t.* **1.** *et.* verlegen; **2.** an e-e falsche Stelle legen *od.* setzen; **3.** *fig.* falsch *od.* übel anbringen: **~*d*** unangebracht, deplaziert.

mis·print I *v/t.* [ˌmɪs'prɪnt] verdrucken, fehldrucken; **II** *s.* ['mɪsprɪnt] Druckfehler *m*.

ˌ**mis·pro'nounce** *v/t.* falsch aussprechen; '**mis·proˌnun·ci'a·tion** *s.* falsche Aussprache.

ˌ**mis·quo'ta·tion** *s.* falsches Zi'tat; ˌ**mis'quote** *v/t. u. v/i.* falsch anführen *od.* zitieren.

ˌ**mis'read** *v/t.* [*irr.* → ***read***] **1.** falsch lesen; **2.** miß'deuten.

'**misˌrep·re'sent** *v/t.* **1.** falsch *od.* ungenau darstellen; **2.** entstellen, verdrehen; '**misˌrep·re·sen'ta·tion** *s.* falsche Darstellung *od.* Angabe (*a.* ⚖), Verdrehung *f*.

ˌ**mis'rule I** *v/t.* **1.** schlecht regieren; **II** *s.* **2.** schlechte Re'gierung, 'Mißregierung *f*; **3.** Unordnung *f*.

miss¹ [mɪs] *s.* **1.** 2 *in der Anrede*: Fräulein *n*: ***2 Smith***; ***2 America*** Miß Amerika (*die Schönheitskönigin von Amerika*); **2.** *humor.* (junges) ‚Ding', Dämchen *n*; **3.** F (*ohne folgenden Namen*) Fräulein *n*.

miss² [mɪs] **I** *v/t.* **1.** *Chance, Zug etc.* verpassen, versäumen; *Beruf, Person, Schlag, Weg, Ziel* verfehlen: **~ *the point*** (***of an argument***) das Wesentliche (e-s Arguments) nicht begreifen; ***he didn't*** **~ *much*** a) er versäumte nicht viel, b) ihm entging fast nichts; **~*ed approach*** ✈ Fehlanflug *m*; → ***boat*** 1, ***bus*** 1, ***fire*** 6 *etc.*; **2.** *a.* **~ *out*** auslassen, über'gehen, -'springen; **3.** nicht haben, nicht bekommen; **4.** nicht hören können, über'hören; **5.** vermissen; **6.** (ver-)missen, entbehren: ***we*** **~ *her very much*** sie fehlt uns sehr; **7.** vermeiden: ***he just*** **~*ed being hurt*** er ist gerade (noch) e-r Verletzung entgangen; ***I just*** **~*ed running him over*** ich hätte ihn beinahe überfahren; **II** *v/i.* **8.** fehlen, nicht treffen: a) da'nebenschießen, -werfen, -schlagen *etc.*, b) da'nebengehen (*Schuß etc.*); **9.** miß'glücken, -'lingen, fehlschlagen, ‚da'nebengehen'; **10.** **~ *out on*** a) über'sehen, auslassen, b) sich entgehen lassen, c) *et.* nicht kriegen; **III** *s.* **11.** Fehlschuß *m*, -wurf *m*, -stoß *m*: ***every shot a*** **~** jeder Schuß (ging) daneben; **12.** Verpassen *n*, Versäumen *n*, Verfehlen *n*, Entrinnen *n*: ***a*** **~ *is as good as a mile*** a) knapp daneben ist auch daneben, b) mit knapper Not entrinnen ist immerhin entrinnen; ***give s.th. a*** **~** a) et. vermeiden, et.

nicht nehmen, et. nicht tun *etc.*, die Finger lassen von et., b) → 10 a; **13.** Verlust *m*.

mis·sal ['mɪsl] *s. eccl.* Meßbuch *n*.

mis·shap·en [ˌmɪs'ʃeɪpən] *adj.* 'mißgestaltet, ungestalt, unförmig.

mis·sile ['mɪsaɪl; *Am.* -səl] **I** *s.* **1.** (Wurf-) Geschoß *n*, Projek'til *n*; **2.** *a.* ***ballistic ~, guided ~*** ⚔ Flugkörper *m*, Fernlenkwaffe *f*, Ra'kete(ngeschoß *n*) *f*; **II** *adj.* **3.** Wurf…; Raketen…: ***~ site*** Raketenstellung *f*.

miss·ing ['mɪsɪŋ] *adj.* **1.** fehlend, weg, nicht da, verschwunden: ***~ link*** *biol.* fehlendes Glied, Zwischenstufe *f* (*zwischen Mensch u. Affe*); **2.** vermißt (⚔ *a.* ***~ in action***), verschollen: ***be ~*** vermißt sein *od.* werden; ***the ~*** die Vermißten, die Verschollenen.

mis·sion ['mɪʃn] *s.* **1.** *pol.* Gesandtschaft *f*; Ge'sandtschaftsperso͵nal *n*; **2.** *pol.*, ⚔ Missi'on *f im Ausland*; **3.** (⚔ Kampf)Auftrag *m*; ✈ Einsatz *m*, Feindflug *m*: ***on (a) special ~*** mit besonderem Auftrag; ***~ accomplished!*** Auftrag ausgeführt!; **4.** *eccl.* a) Missi'on *f*, Sendung *f*, b) Missio'narstätigkeit *f*: ***foreign (home) ~*** äußere (innere) Mission, c) Missi'on(sgesellschaft) *f*, d) Missi'onsstati͵on *f*; **5.** Missi'on *f*, Sendung *f*, (innere) Berufung, Lebenszweck *m*: ***~ in life*** Lebensaufgabe *f*; **mis·sion·ar·y** ['mɪʃnərɪ] **I** *adj.* missio'narisch, Missions…: ***~ work***; **II** *s.* Missio'nar(in).

mis·sis ['mɪsɪz] *s.* **1.** *sl.* gnä' Frau (*Hausfrau*); **2.** F ‚Alte' *f*, ‚bessere Hälfte' (*Ehefrau*).

mis·sive ['mɪsɪv] *s.* Sendschreiben *n*.

ˌ**mis'spell** *v/t.* [*a. irr.* → ***spell***] falsch buchstabieren *od.* schreiben; ˌ**mis'spell·ing** *s.* **1.** falsches Buchstabieren; **2.** Rechtschreibfehler *m*.

ˌ**mis'spend** *v/t.* [*irr.* → ***spend***] falsch verwenden, *a. s-e Jugend etc.* vergeuden.

ˌ**mis'state** *v/t.* falsch angeben, unrichtig darstellen; ˌ**mis'state·ment** *s.* falsche Angabe *od.* Darstellung.

mis·sus ['mɪsəs] → ***missis***.

miss·y ['mɪsɪ] *s.* F kleines Fräulein.

mist [mɪst] **I** *s.* **1.** (feiner) Nebel, feuchter Dunst, *Am. a.* Sprühregen *m*; **2.** *fig.* Nebel *m*, Schleier *m*: ***be in a ~*** ganz irre *od.* verdutzt sein; **3.** F Beschlag *m*, Hauch *m* (*auf e-m Glas*); **II** *v/i.* **4.** *a.* ***~ over*** nebeln, neblig sein (*a. fig.*); sich trüben (*Augen*); (sich) beschlagen (*Glas*); **III** *v/t.* **5.** um'nebeln.

mis·tak·a·ble [mɪ'steɪkəbl] *adj.* verkennbar, (leicht) zu verwechseln(d), 'mißzuverstehen(d); **mis·take** [mɪ'steɪk] **I** *v/t.* [*irr.* → ***take***] **1.** (***for***) verwechseln (mit), (fälschlich) halten (für), verfehlen, nicht erkennen, verkennen, sich irren in (*dat.*): ***~ s.o.'s character*** sich in j-s Charakter irren; **2.** falsch verstehen, 'mißverstehen; **II** *v/i.* [*irr.* → ***take***] **3.** sich irren, sich versehen; **III** *s.* **4.** 'Mißverständnis *n*; **5.** Irrtum *m* (*a.* ⚖), Fehler *m*, Versehen *n*, 'Mißgriff *m*: ***by ~*** irrtümlich, aus Versehen; ***make a ~*** e-n Fehler machen, sich irren; ***and no ~*** F bestimmt, worauf du dich verlassen kannst; **6.** (Schreib-, Sprach-, Rechen-) Fehler *m*; **mis'tak·en** [-kn] *adj.* □ **1.** im Irrtum: ***be ~*** sich irren; ***unless I am very much ~*** wenn ich mich nicht sehr irre; ***we were quite ~ in him*** wir haben uns in ihm ziemlich getäuscht; **2.** irrtümlich, falsch, verfehlt (*Politik etc.*): (***case of***) ***~ identity*** Personenverwechslung *f*; ***~ kindness*** unangebrachte Freundlichkeit.

mis·ter ['mɪstə] *s.* **1.** ♂ Herr *m* (*abbr.* ***Mr*** *od.* ***Mr.***): ***Mr President*** Herr Präsident; **2.** F *als bloße Anrede*: (mein) Herr!, ‚Meister'!, ‚Chef'!

ˌ**mis'time** *v/t.* zur unpassenden Zeit sagen *od.* tun; e-n falschen Zeitpunkt wählen für, *bsd. sport* schlecht timen.

ˌ**mis'timed** *adj.* unpassend, unangebracht, zur Unzeit, *bsd. sport* schlecht getimed.

mist·i·ness ['mɪstɪnɪs] *s.* **1.** Nebligkeit *f*, Dunstigkeit *f*; **2.** Unklarheit *f*, Verschwommenheit *f* (*a. fig.*).

mis·tle·toe ['mɪsltəʊ] *s.* ♀ **1.** Mistel *f*; **2.** Mistelzweig *m*.

ˌ**mis·trans'late** *v/t. u. v/i.* falsch über'setzen.

mis·tress ['mɪstrɪs] *s.* **1.** Herrin *f* (*a. fig.*), Gebieterin *f*, Besitzerin *f*: ***she is ~ of herself*** sie weiß sich zu beherrschen; **2.** Frau *f* des Hauses, Hausfrau *f*; **3.** *bsd. Brit.* Lehrerin *f*: ***chemistry ~*** Chemielehrerin; **4.** Kennerin *f*, Meisterin *f in e-r Kunst etc.*; **5.** Mä'tresse *f*, Geliebte *f*; **6.** → ***Mrs.***

ˌ**mis'tri·al** *s.* ⚖ fehlerhaft geführter (*Am. a.* ergebnisloser) Pro'zeß.

ˌ**mis'trust I** *s.* **1.** 'Mißtrauen *n*, Argwohn *m* (***of*** gegen); **II** *v/t.* **2.** *j-m* miß'trauen, nicht trauen; **3.** zweifeln an (*dat.*); **mis'trust·ful** *adj.* □ 'mißtrauisch, argwöhnisch (***of*** gegen).

mist·y ['mɪstɪ] *adj.* □ **1.** (leicht) neb(e)lig, dunstig; **2.** *fig.* nebelhaft, verschwommen, unklar.

ˌ**mis·un·der'stand** *v/t. u. v/i.* [*irr.* → ***understand***] 'mißverstehen; ˌ**mis·un·der'stand·ing** *s.* **1.** 'Mißverständnis *n*; **2.** 'Mißhelligkeit *f*, Diffe'renz *f*; ˌ**mis·un·der'stood** *adj.* **1.** 'mißverstanden; **2.** verkannt, nicht richtig gewürdigt.

ˌ**mis'us·age** → ***misuse*** 1.

mis·use I *s.* [ˌmɪs'juːs] **1.** 'Mißbrauch *m*, falscher Gebrauch, falsche Anwendung; **2.** Miß'handlung *f*; **II** *v/t.* [ˌmɪs'juːz] **3.** miß'brauchen, falsch *od.* zu unrechten Zwecken gebrauchen; falsch anwenden; **4.** miß'handeln.

mite¹ [maɪt] *s. zo.* Milbe *f*.

mite² [maɪt] *s.* **1.** Heller *m*; *weitS.* kleine Geldsumme: ***contribute one's ~ to*** sein Scherflein beitragen zu; ***not a ~*** kein bißchen; **2.** F kleines Ding, Dingelchen *n*: ***a ~ of a child*** ein Würmchen.

mi·ter ['maɪtə] *Am.* → ***mitre***.

mit·i·gate ['mɪtɪgeɪt] *v/t.* *Schmerz etc.* lindern; *Strafe etc.* mildern; *Zorn* besänftigen, mäßigen: ***mitigating circumstances*** ⚖ (straf)mildernde Umstände; **mit·i·ga·tion** [ˌmɪtɪ'geɪʃn] *s.* **1.** Linderung *f*, Milderung *f*; **2.** Milderung *f*, Abschwächung *f*: ***plead in ~*** ⚖ a) für Strafmilderung plädieren, b) strafmildernde Umstände geltend machen; **3.** Besänftigung *f*, Mäßigung *f*.

mi·to·sis [maɪ'təʊsɪs] *pl.* **-ses** [-siːz] *s. biol.* Mi'tose *f*, 'indi͵rekte *od.* chromoso'male (Zell)Kernteilung.

mi·tre ['maɪtə] **I** *s.* **1.** a) Mitra *f*, Bischofsmütze *f*, b) *fig.* Bischofsamt *n*, -würde *f*; **2.** ⚙ a) → ***mitre joint, mitre square***, b) Gehrungsfläche *f*; **II** *v/t.* **3.** mit der Mitra schmücken, zum Bischof machen; **4.** ⚙ a) auf Gehrung verbinden, b) gehren, auf Gehrung zurichten; **III** *v/i.* **5.** ⚙ sich in 'einem Winkel treffen; ***~ box*** *s.* ⚙ Gehrlade *f*; ***~ gear*** *s.* Kegelrad *n*, Winkelgetriebe *n*; ***~ joint*** *s.* Gehrfuge *f*; ***~ square*** *s.* Gehrdreieck *n*; ***~ valve*** *s.* 'Kegelven͵til *n*; ***~ wheel*** *s.* Kegelrad *n*.

mitt [mɪt] *s.* **1.** Halbhandschuh *m*; **2.** *Baseball*: Fanghandschuh *m*; **3.** → ***mitten*** 1 *u.* 3; **4.** *Am. sl.* ‚Flosse' *f* (*Hand*).

mit·ten ['mɪtn] *s.* **1.** Fausthandschuh *m*, Fäustling *m*: ***get the ~*** F a) e-n Korb bekommen, abgewiesen werden, b) ‚(hinaus)fliegen', entlassen werden; **2.** → ***mitt*** 1; **3.** *sl.* Boxhandschuh *m*.

mit·ti·mus ['mɪtɪməs] (*Lat.*) *s.* **1.** ⚖ a) *richterlicher Befehl an die Gefängnisbehörde zur Aufnahme e-s Häftlings*, b) *Befehl zur Übersendung der Akten an ein anderes Gericht*; **2.** F ‚blauer Brief', Entlassung *f*.

mix [mɪks] **I** *v/t.* **1.** (ver)mischen, vermengen (***with*** mit); *Cocktail etc.* mixen, mischen; *Teig* anrühren, mischen: ***~ into*** mischen in (*acc.*); ***~ up*** zs.-, durcheinandermischen, *fig.* völlig durcheinanderbringen, verwechseln (***with*** mit); ***be ~ed up*** *fig.* a) verwickelt sein *od.* werden (***in, with*** in *acc.*), b) (*geistig*) ganz durcheinander sein; **2.** *biol.* kreuzen; **3.** *Stoffe* melieren; **4.** *fig.* verbinden: ***~ business with pleasure*** das Angenehme mit dem Nützlichen verbinden; **II** *v/i.* **5.** sich (ver)mischen; **6.** sich mischen lassen; **7.** *gut etc.* auskommen (***with*** mit); **8.** verkehren (***with*** mit, ***in*** in *dat.*): ***~ in the best society***; **III** *s.* **9.** (*Am. a.* koch- *od.* back-, gebrauchsfertige) Mischung: ***cake ~*** Backmischung; **10.** F Durchein'ander *n*, Mischmasch *m*; **11.** *sl.* Keile'rei *f*.

mixed [mɪkst] *adj.* **1.** gemischt (*a. fig. Gefühl, Gesellschaft, Metapher*); **2.** vermischt, Misch…; **3.** F verwirrt, kon'fus; ***~ bag*** *s.* F bunte Mischung; ***~ blood*** *s.* **1.** gemischtes Blut; **2.** Mischling *m*; ***~ car·go*** *s.* ⚓ Stückgutladung *f*; ***~ con·struc·tion*** *s.* Gemischtbauweise *f*; ***~ dou·bles*** *s. pl. sg. konstr. sport* gemischtes Doppel: ***play a ~***; ***~ e·con·o·my*** *s.* ⚓ gemischte Wirtschaftsform; ˌ**~-e'con·o·my** *adj.* ⚓ gemischtwirtschaftlich; ***~ for·est*** *s.* Mischwald *m*; ***~ frac·tion*** *s.* ⅍ gemischter Bruch; ***~ mar·riage*** *s.* Mischehe *f*; ***~ me·di·a*** *s. pl.* **1.** Multi'media *pl.*; **2.** *Kunst*: Mischtechnik *f*; ***~ pick·les*** *s. pl.* Mixed Pickles *pl.* (*Essiggemüse*).

mix·er ['mɪksə] *s.* **1.** Mischer *m*; **2.** Mixer *m* (*von Cocktails etc.*) (*a. Küchengerät*); **3.** ⚙ Mischer *m*, 'Mischma͵schine *f*; **4.** ⚡ *Fernsehen etc.*: Mischpult *n*; **5.** ***be a good (bad) ~*** F kontaktfreudig (kontaktarm) sein; **mix·ture** ['mɪkstʃə] *s.* **1.** Mischung *f* (*a. von Tee, Tabak etc.*), Gemisch *n* (*a.* ⚗); **2.** *mot.* Gas-Luft-Gemisch *n*; **3.** *pharm.* Mix'tur *f*; **4.** *biol.* Kreuzung *f*; **5.** Beimengung *f*; **'mix-up** *s.* F **1.** Durchein'ander *n*; **2.** Verwechslung *f*; **3.** Handgemenge *n*.

miz·(z)en ['mɪzn] *s.* ⚓ **1.** Be'san(segel *n*) *m*; **2.** → **'~-mast** [-mɑːst; ⚓ -məst] *s.* Be'san-, Kreuzmast *m*; **'~-sail** → ***miz(z)en*** 1; **'~-ˌtop'gal·lant** *s.* Kreuzbramsegel *n*.

miz·zle ['mɪzl] *dial.* **I** *v/i.* nieseln; **II** *s.* Nieseln *n*, Sprühregen *m*.

mne·mon·ic [niː'mɒnɪk] **I** *adj.* **1.** mnemo'technisch; **2.** mne'monisch, Gedächtnis…; **II** *s.* **3.** Gedächtnishilfe *f*; **4.** → ***mnemonics*** 1; **mne'mon·ics** [-ks] *s. pl.* **1.** *a. sg. konstr.* Mnemo'technik *f*, Gedächtniskunst *f*; **2.** mne'monische Zeichen *pl.*; **mne·mo·tech·nics** [ˌniːməʊ'teknɪks] *s. pl. a. sg. konstr.* → ***mnemonics*** 1.

mo [məʊ] *s.* F Mo'ment *m*: ***wait half a ~!*** (eine) Sekunde!

moan [məʊn] **I** *s.* **1.** Stöhnen *n*, Ächzen *n* (*a. fig. des Windes etc.*); **II** *v/i.* **2.** stöhnen, ächzen; **3.** (weh)klagen, jammern; **'moan·ful** [-fʊl] *adj.* □ (weh-)klagend.

moat [məʊt] ⚔ *hist.* **I** *s.* (Wall-, Burg-, Stadt)Graben *m*; **II** *v/t.* mit e-m Graben um'geben.

mob [mɒb] **I** *s.* **1.** Mob *m*, zs.-gerotteter Pöbel(haufen): ***~ law*** Lynchjustiz *f*; ***~ psychology*** Massenpsychologie *f*; **2.** Pöbel *m*, Gesindel *n*; **3.** *sl.* a) (Verbrecher)Bande *f*, b) *allg.* Bande *f*, Sippschaft *f*; **II** *v/t.* **4.** lärmend herfallen über (*acc.*); anpöbeln; angreifen, attakkieren; *Geschäfte etc.* stürmen.

mo·bile ['məʊbaɪl] **I** *adj.* **1.** beweglich, wendig (*a. Geist etc.*); schnell (beweglich); **2.** unstet, veränderlich; lebhaft (*Gesichtszüge*); **3.** leichtflüssig; **4.** ⚙, ⚔ fahrbar, beweglich, mo'bil, ⚔ *a.* motorisiert: ***~ crane*** Autokran *m*; ***~ home*** *mot.* Wohnwagen *m*; ***~ warfare*** Bewegungskrieg *m*; ***~ workshop*** Werkstattwagen *m*; **5.** ⚚ flüssig: ***~ funds***; **II** 2 *s* **6.** *Kunst*: Mobile *n*; **mo·bil·i·ty** [məʊ'bɪlətɪ] *s.* **1.** Beweglichkeit *f*, Wendigkeit *f*; **2.** Mobili'tät *f*, Freizügigkeit *f* (*der Arbeitnehmer etc.*).

mo·bi·li·za·tion [ˌməʊbɪlaɪ'zeɪʃn] *s.* Mobilisierung *f*: a) ⚔ Mo'bilmachung *f*, b) *bsd. fig.* Aktivierung *f*, Aufgebot *n* (*der Kräfte etc.*), c) ⚚ Flüssigmachung *f*; **mo·bi·lize** ['məʊbɪlaɪz] *v/t.* mobilisieren: a) ⚔ mo'bilmachen, *a.* dienstverpflichten, b) *fig. Kräfte etc.* aufbieten, einsetzen, c) ⚚ *Kapital* flüssigmachen.

mob·oc·ra·cy [mɒ'bɒkrəsɪ] *s.* **1.** Pöbelherrschaft *f*; **2.** (herrschender) Pöbel.

mobs·man ['mɒbzmən] *s.* [*irr.*] **1.** Gangster *m*; **2.** *Brit. sl.* (ele'ganter) Taschendieb.

mob·ster ['mɒbstə] *Am. sl. für* ***mobsman*** 1.

moc·ca·sin ['mɒkəsɪn] *s.* **1.** Mokas'sin *m* (*a. Damenschuh*); **2.** *zo.* Mokas'sinschlange *f*.

mo·cha[1] ['mɒkə] **I** *s.* **1.** *a.* ***~ coffee*** 'Mokka(kafˌfee) *m*; **2.** Mochaleder *n*; **II** *adj.* **3.** Mokka…

mo·cha[2] ['məʊkə], 2 **stone** *s. min.* Mochastein *m*.

mock [mɒk] **I** *v/t.* **1.** verspotten, -höhnen, lächerlich machen; **2.** (*zum Spott*) nachäffen; **3.** *poet.* nachahmen; **4.** täuschen, narren; **5.** spotten (*gen.*), trotzen (*dat.*), nicht achten (*acc.*); **II** *v/i.* **6.** sich lustig machen, spotten (***at*** über *acc.*); **III** *s.* **7.** → ***mockery*** 1–3; **8.** Nachahmung *f*, Fälschung *f*; **IV** *adj.* **9.** nachgemacht, Schein…, Pseudo…: ***~ attack*** ⚔ Scheinangriff *m*; ***~ battle*** ⚔ Scheingefecht *n*; ***~ king*** Schattenkönig *m*; **mock·er** ['mɒkə] *s.* **1.** Spötter(in); **2.** Nachäffer(in); **mock·er·y** ['mɒkərɪ] *s.* **1.** Spott *m*, Hohn *m*, Spötte'rei *f*; **2.** Gegenstand *m* des Spottes, Gespött *n*: ***make a ~ of*** zum Gespött (der Leute) machen; **3.** Nachäffung *f*; **4.** *fig.* Possenspiel *n*, Farce *f*.

ˌmock-he'ro·ic *adj.* (□ ***~ally***) 'komischhe'roisch (*Gedicht etc.*).

mock·ing ['mɒkɪŋ] **I** *s.* Spott *m*, Gespött *n*; **II** *adj.* □ spöttisch; **'~·bird** *s. orn.* Spottdrossel *f*.

mock| moon *s. ast.* Nebenmond *m*; ***~ tri·al*** *s.* ⚖ 'ScheinproˌzeB *m*; ***~ tur·tle*** *s. Küche*: Kalbskopf *m* en tor'tue; ***~ tur·tle soup*** *s.* falsche Schildkrötensuppe; **'~-up** *s.* Mo'dell *n* (in na'türlicher Größe), At'trappe *f*.

mod·al ['məʊdl] *adj.* □ **1.** mo'dal (*a. phls., ling.*, ♪): ***~ proposition*** *Logik*: Modalsatz *m*; ***~ verb*** modales Hilfsverb; **2.** *Statistik*: typisch; **mo·dal·i·ty** [məʊ'dælətɪ] *s.* Modali'tät *f* (*a.* ⚚, *pol.*, *phls.*), Art *f* u. Weise *f*, Ausführungsart *f*.

mode[1] [məʊd] *s.* **1.** (Art *f* u.) Weise *f*, Me'thode *f*: ***~ of action*** ⚙ Wirkungsweise; ***~ of life*** Lebensweise; ***~ of operation*** Verfahrensweise; ***~ of payment*** ⚚ Zahlungsweise; **2.** (Erscheinungs-)Form *f*, Art *f*: ***heat is a ~ of motion*** Wärme ist e-e Form der Bewegung; **3.** *Logik*: a) Modali'tät *f*, b) Modus *m* (*e-r Schlußfigur*); **4.** ♪ Modus *m*, Tonart *f*, -geschlecht *n*; **5.** *ling.* Modus *m*, Aussageweise *f*; **6.** *Statistik*: Modus *m*, häufigster Wert.

mode[2] [məʊd] *s.* Mode *f*, Brauch *m*.

mod·el ['mɒdl] **I** *s.* **1.** Muster *n*, Vorbild *n* (***for*** für): ***after*** (*od.* ***on***) ***the ~ of*** nach dem Muster von (*od. gen.*); ***he is a ~ of self-control*** er ist ein Muster an Selbstbeherrschung; **2.** (*fig.* 'Denk)MoˌdeIl *n*, Nachbildung *f*: ***working ~*** Arbeitsmodell; **3.** Muster *n*, Vorlage *f*; **4.** *paint. etc.* Mo'dell *n*: ***act as a ~ to a painter*** e-m Maler Modell stehen *od.* sitzen; **5.** *Mode*: a) Mannequin *n*, Vorführdame *f*: ***male ~*** Dressman *m*, b) Mo'dellkleid *n*; **6.** ⚙ a) Bau(weise *f*) *m*, b) (Bau)Muster *n*, Mo'dell *n*, Typ(e *f*) *m*; **II** *adj.* **7.** vorbildlich, musterhaft, Muster…: ***~ farm*** landwirtschaftlicher Musterbetrieb; ***~ husband*** Mustergatte *m*; ***~ plant*** ⚚ Musterbetrieb *m*; ***~ school*** Musterschule *f*; **8.** Modell…: ***~ airplane***; ***~ builder*** ⚙ Modellbauer *m*; ***~ dress*** → 5 b; **III** *v/t.* **9.** nach Mo'dell formen *od.* herstellen; **10.** modellieren, nachbilden; abformen; **11.** *fig.* formen, gestalten (***after***, ***on***, ***upon*** nach [dem Vorbild *gen.*]): ***~ o.s. on*** sich *j-n* zum Vorbild nehmen; **IV** *v/i.* **12.** *Kunst*: modellieren; **13.** Mo'dell stehen *od.* sitzen; **14.** Kleider vorführen, als Mannequin *od.* Dressman arbeiten; **'mod·el·(l)er** [-lə] *s.* **1.** Modellierer *m*; **2.** Mo'dell-, Musterbauer *m*; **'mod·el·(l)ing** [-lɪŋ] **I** *s.* **1.** Modellieren *n*; **2.** Formgebung *f*, Formung *f*; **3.** Mo'dellstehen *od.* -sitzen *n*; **II** *adj.* **4.** Modellier…: ***~ clay***.

mo·dem ['məʊdem] *s. Computer, teleph.* Modem *m* (*Datenübertragungsgerät*).

mod·er·ate ['mɒdərət] **I** *adj.* □ **1.** gemäßigt (*a. Sprache etc.*; *a. pol.*), mäßig; **2.** mäßig *im Trinken etc.*; fru'gal (*Lebensweise*); **3.** mild (*Winter*, *Strafe etc.*); **4.** vernünftig, maßvoll (*Forderung etc.*); angemessen, niedrig (*Preis*); **5.** mittelmäßig; **II** *s.* **6.** (*pol. mst* 2) Gemäßigte(r *m*) *f*; **III** *v/t.* [-dəreɪt] **7.** mäßigen, mildern; beruhigen; **8.** einschränken; **9.** ⚙, *phys.* dämpfen, abbremsen; **IV** *v/i.* [-dəreɪt] **10.** sich mäßigen; **11.** nachlassen (*Wind etc.*); **'mod·er·ate·ness** [-nɪs] *s.* Mäßigkeit *f etc.*; **mod·er·a·tion** [ˌmɒdə'reɪʃn] *s.* **1.** Mäßigung *f*, Maß(halten) *n*: ***in ~*** mit Maß; **2.** Mäßigkeit *f*; **3.** *pl. univ.* erste öffentliche Prüfung *in Oxford*; **4.** Milderung *f*; **'mod·er·a·tor** [-dəreɪtə] *s.* **1.** Mäßiger *m*, Beruhiger *m*; Vermittler *m*; **2.** Vorsitzende(r) *m*; Diskussi'onsleiter *m*; *univ.* Exami'nator *m* (*Oxford*); **3.** a) Mode'rator *m* (*Vorsitzender e-s Kollegiums reformierter Kirchen*), b) *TV*: Mode'rator *m*, Modera'torin *f*, Pro'grammleiter(in); **4.** ⚙, *phys.* Mode'rator *m*.

mod·ern ['mɒdən] **I** *adj.* **1.** mo'dern, neuzeitlich: ***~ times*** die Neuzeit; ***the ~ school*** (*od.* ***side***) *ped. Brit.* die Realabteilung; **2.** mo'dern, (neu)modisch; **3.** *mst* 2 *ling.* a) mo'dern, Neu…, b) neuer: 2 ***Greek*** Neugriechisch *n*; ***~ languages*** neuere Sprachen; 2 ***Languages*** (*als Fach*) Neuphilologie *f*; **II** *s.* **4.** mo'derner Mensch, Fortschrittliche(r *m*) *f*; **5.** Mensch *m* der Neuzeit; **6.** *typ.* neuzeitliche An'tiqua; **'mod·ern·ism** [-dənɪzəm] *s.* **1.** Moder'nismus *m*: a) mo'derne Einstellung, b) mo'dernes Wort, mo'derne Redewendung(en *pl.*); **2.** *eccl.* Moder'nismus *m*; **mo·der·ni·ty** [mɒ'dɜːnətɪ] *s.* **1.** Moderni'tät *f*, (*das*) Mo'derne; **2.** *et.* Mo'dernes; **mod·ern·i·za·tion** [ˌmɒdənaɪ'zeɪʃn] *s.* Modernisierung *f*; **'mod·ern·ize** [-dənaɪz] *v/t. u. v/i.* (sich) modernisieren.

mod·est ['mɒdɪst] *adj.* □ **1.** bescheiden, anspruchslos (*Person od. Sache*): ***~ income*** bescheidenes Einkommen; **2.** anständig, sittsam; **3.** maßvoll, vernünftig; **'mod·es·ty** [-tɪ] *s.* **1.** Bescheidenheit *f* (*Person*, *Einkommen etc.*): ***in all ~*** bei aller Bescheidenheit; **2.** Anspruchslosigkeit *f*, Einfachheit *f*; **3.** Schamgefühl *n*; Sittsamkeit *f*.

mod·i·cum ['mɒdɪkəm] *s.* kleine Menge, *ein* bißchen: ***a ~ of truth*** ein Körnchen Wahrheit.

mod·i·fi·a·ble ['mɒdɪfaɪəbl] *adj.* modifizierbar, (ab)änderungsfähig; **mod·i·fi·ca·tion** [ˌmɒdɪfɪ'keɪʃn] *s.* **1.** Modifikati'on *f*: a) Abänderung *f*: ***make a ~ to*** → ***modify*** 1 a, b) Abart *f*, modifizierte Form, c) Einschränkung *f*, nähere Bestimmung, d) *biol.* nichterbliche Abänderung, e) *ling.* nähere Bestimmung, f) *ling.* lautliche Veränderung, 'Umlautung *f*; **2.** Mäßigung *f*; **mod·i·fy** ['mɒdɪfaɪ] *v/t.* **1.** modifizieren: a) abändern, teilweise 'umwandeln, b) einschränken, näher bestimmen; **2.** mildern, mäßigen; abschwächen; **3.** *ling.* *Vokal* 'umlauten.

mod·ish ['məʊdɪʃ] *adj.* □ **1.** modisch, mo'dern; **2.** Mode…

mods [mɒdz] *s. pl. Brit.* Halbstarke *pl.* von betont dandyhaftem Äußeren (*in den 60er Jahren*) (*Ggs.* ***rockers***).

mod·u·lar [ˈmɒdjʊlə] *adj.* ⩓, ⚙ Modul…: ~ ***design*** Modulbauweise *f.*

mod·u·late [ˈmɒdjʊleɪt] **I** *v/t.* **1.** abstimmen, regulieren; **2.** anpassen (***to*** an *acc.*); **3.** dämpfen; **4.** *Stimme, Ton etc., a. Funk* modulieren: ***~d reception*** ⚡ Tonempfang *m*; **II** *v/i.* **5.** ♪ modulieren (***from*** von, ***to*** nach), die Tonart wechseln; **6.** allˈmählich ˈübergehen (***into*** in *acc.*); **mod·u·la·tion** [ˌmɒdjʊˈleɪʃn] *s.* **1.** Abstimmung *f*, Regulierung *f*; **2.** Anpassung *f*; **3.** Dämpfung *f*; **4.** ♪, *Funk, a. Stimme*: Modulatiˈon *f*; **5.** Intonatiˈon *f*, Tonfall *m*; ˈ**mod·u·la·tor** [-tə] *s.* **1.** Regler *m*; ⚡ Moduˈlator *m*: ~ ***of tonality*** *Film*: Tonblende *f*; **2.** ♪ die Tonverwandtschaft (*nach der Tonic-Solfa-Methode*) darstellende Skala; ˈ**mod·ule** [-djuːl] *s.* **1.** Modul *m*, Model *m*, Maßeinheit *f*, Einheits-, Verhältniszahl *f*; **2.** ⚙ Moˈdul *n* (*austauschbare Funktionseinheit*), ⚡ *a.* Baustein *m*; **3.** ⚙ Baueinheit *f*: ~ ***construction*** Baukastensystem *n*; **4.** *Raumfahrt*: (*Kommando- etc.*)Kapsel *f*; ˈ**mod·u·lus** [-ləs] *pl.* **-li** [-laɪ] *s.* ⩓, *phys.* Modul *m*: ~ ***of elasticity*** Elastizitätsmodul.

Mo·gul [ˈməʊgʌl] *s.* **1.** Mogul *m*: ***the*** (***Great*** *od.* ***Grand***) ~ der Großmogul; **2.** ♀ *Am. humor.* ‚großes Tier', ‚Bonze' *m*, Maˈgnat *m*.

mo·hair [ˈməʊheə] *s.* **1.** Moˈhair *m* (*Angorahaar*); **2.** Moˈhairstoff *m*, -kleidungsstück *n*.

Mo·ham·med·an [məʊˈhæmɪdən] **I** *adj.* mohammeˈdanisch; **II** *s.* Mohammeˈdaner(in).

moi·e·ty [ˈmɔɪətɪ] *s.* **1.** Hälfte *f*; **2.** Teil *m*.

moire [mwɑː] *s.* **1.** Moiˈré *m, n*, Wasserglanz *m auf Stoffen*; **2.** moirierter Stoff; **moi·ré** [ˈmwɑːreɪ] **I** *adj.* moiriert, gewässert, geflammt, mit Wellenmuster; **II** *s.* → ***moire*** 1.

moist [mɔɪst] *adj.* □ feucht, naß; ˈ**moisten** [-sn] **I** *v/t.* an-, befeuchten, benetzen; **II** *v/i.* feucht werden; nässen; ˈ**moist·ness** [-nɪs] *s.* Feuchte *f*; ˈ**moisture** [-tʃə] *s.* Feuchtigkeit *f*: ***~-proof*** feuchtigkeitsfest; ˈ**mois·tur·iz·er** [-tʃəraɪzə] *s.* **1.** Feuchtigkeitscreme *f*; **2.** Luftbefeuchter *m*.

moke [məʊk] *s. Brit. sl.* Esel *m* (*a. fig.*).

mo·lar[1] [ˈməʊlə] *anat.* **I** *s.* Backenzahn *m*, Moˈlar *m*; **II** *adj.* Mahl…, Backen…: ~ ***tooth*** → I.

mo·lar[2] [ˈməʊlə] *adj.* **1.** *phys.* Massen…: ~ ***motion*** Massenbewegung *f*; **2.** ⚗ moˈlar, Mol…: ~ ***weight*** Mol-, Molargewicht *n*.

mo·lar[3] [ˈməʊlə] *adj.* ⚕ Molen…

mo·las·ses [məʊˈlæsɪz] *s. sg. u. pl.* **1.** Meˈlasse *f*; **2.** (Zucker)Sirup *m*.

mold [məʊld] *etc. Am.* → ***mould*** *etc.*

mole[1] [məʊl] *s. zo.* Maulwurf *m* (*a.* F *fig. eingeschleuster Agent*).

mole[2] [məʊl] *s.* (kleines) Muttermal, *bsd.* Leberfleck *m*.

mole[3] [məʊl] *s.* Mole *f*, Hafendamm *m*.

mole[4] [məʊl] *s.* ⚗ Mol *n*, ˈGrammoleˌkül *n*.

mole[5] [məʊl] *s.* ⚕ Mole *f*, Mondkalb *n*.

ˈ**mole-ˌcrick·et** *s. zo.* Maulwurfsgrille *f*.

mo·lec·u·lar [məʊˈlekjʊlə] *adj.* ⚗, *phys.* molekuˈlar, Molekular…: ~ ***biology***; ~ ***weight***; **mo·lec·u·lar·i·ty** [məʊˌlekjʊˈlærətɪ] *s.* ⚗, *phys.* Molekuˈlarzustand *m*; **mol·e·cule** [ˈmɒlɪkjuːl] *s.* **1.** ⚗, *phys.* Moleˈkül *n*; **2.** *fig.* winziges Teilchen.

ˈ**mole**|-**hill** *s.* Maulwurfshügel *m*, -haufen *m*; → ***mountain*** I; ˈ**~·skin** *s.* **1.** Maulwurfsfell *n*; **2.** ✝ Moleskin *m, n*, Englischleder *n* (*Baumwollgewebe*); **3.** *pl.* Hose *f* aus Moleskin.

mo·lest [məʊˈlest] *v/t.* belästigen; **moles·ta·tion** [ˌməʊleˈsteɪʃn] *s.* Belästigung *f*.

Moll, *a.* ♀ [mɒl] *s. sl.* **1.** ‚Nutte' *f* (*Prostituierte*); **2.** Gangsterbraut *f*.

mol·li·fi·ca·tion [ˌmɒlɪfɪˈkeɪʃn] *s.* **1.** Besänftigung *f*; **2.** Erweichung *f*; **mol·li·fy** [ˈmɒlɪfaɪ] *v/t.* **1.** besänftigen, beruhigen, beschwichtigen; **2.** weich machen, erweichen.

mol·lusc [ˈmɒləsk] → ***mollusk***.

mol·lus·can [mɒˈlʌskən] **I** *adj.* Weichtier…; **II** *s.* → **mol·lusk** [ˈmɒləsk] *s. zo.* Molˈluske *f*, Weichtier *n*.

mol·ly·cod·dle [ˈmɒlɪˌkɒdl] **I** *s.* Weichling *m*, Muttersöhnchen *n*; **II** *v/t.* verhätscheln.

molt [məʊlt] *Am.* → ***moult***.

mol·ten [ˈməʊltən] *adj.* **1.** geschmolzen, (schmelz)flüssig: ~ ***metal*** flüssiges Metall; **2.** gegossen, Guß…

mo·lyb·date [mɒˈlɪbdeɪt] *s.* ⚗ Molybˈdat *n*, molybˈdänsaures Salz; **moˈlyb·de·nite** [-dɪnaɪt] *s. min.* Molybdäˈnit *m*.

mom [mɒm] *s.* F *bsd. Am.* **1.** Mami *f*; **2.** ‚Oma' *f* (*alte Frau*); ˌ**~-and-ˈpop store** *s. Am.* F Tante-Emma-Laden *m*.

mo·ment [ˈməʊmənt] *s.* **1.** Moˈment *m*, Augenblick *m*: ***one*** (*od.* ***just a***) ~***!*** (nur) e-n Augenblick!; ***in a*** ~ in e-m Augenblick, sofort; **2.** Zeitpunkt *m*, Augenblick *m*: ~ ***of truth*** Stunde *f* der Wahrheit; ***the very ~ I saw him*** in dem Augenblick, in dem ich ihn sah; ***at the*** ~ im Augenblick, gerade (jetzt *od.* damals); ***at the last*** ~ im letzten Augenblick; ***not for the*** ~ im Augenblick nicht; ***to the*** ~ auf die Sekunde genau, pünktlich; **3.** Bedeutung *f*, Tragweite *f*, Belang *m* (***to*** für); **4.** *phys.* Moˈment *n*: ~ ***of inertia*** Trägheitsmoment; **momen·tal** [məʊˈmentl] *adj. phys.* Momenten…; ˈ**mo·men·tar·y** [-tərɪ] *adj.* □ **1.** momenˈtan, augenblicklich; **2.** vorˈübergehend, flüchtig; **3.** jeden Augenblick geschehend *od.* möglich; ˈ**moment·ly** [-lɪ] *adv.* **1.** augenblicklich, in e-m Augenblick; **2.** von Seˈkunde zu Seˈkunde: ***increasing*** ~; **3.** e-n Augenblick lang; **mo·men·tous** [məʊˈmentəs] *adj.* □ bedeutsam, folgenschwer, von großer Tragweite; **mo·men·tousness** [məʊˈmentəsnɪs] *s.* Bedeutsam-, Wichtigkeit *f*, Tragweite *f*.

mo·men·tum [məʊˈmentəm] *pl.* **-ta** [-tə] *s.* **1.** *phys.* Imˈpuls *m*, Moˈment *n e-r Kraft*: ~ ***theorem*** Momentensatz *m*; **2.** ⚙ Triebkraft *f*; **3.** *allg.* Wucht *f*, Schwung *m*, Fahrt *f*: ***gather*** (*od.* ***gain***) ~ in Fahrt kommen, Stoßkraft gewinnen; ***lose*** ~ (an) Schwung verlieren.

mon·ad [ˈmɒnæd] *s.* **1.** *phls.* Moˈnade *f*; **2.** *biol.* Einzeller *m*; **3.** ⚗ einwertiges Eleˈment *od.* Aˈtom; **mo·nad·ic** [mɒˈnædɪk] *adj.* **1.** moˈnadisch, Monaden…; **2.** ⩓ eingliedrig, -stellig.

mon·arch [ˈmɒnək] *s.* Monˈarch(in), Herrscher(in); **mo·nar·chal** [mɒˈnɑːkl] *adj.* □ monˈarchisch; **mo·nar·chic** *adj.*, **mo·nar·chi·cal** [mɒˈnɑːkɪk(l)] *adj.* □ **1.** monˈarchisch; **2.** monarˈchistisch; **3.** königlich (*a. fig.*); ˈ**monarch·ism** [-kɪzəm] *s.* Monarˈchismus *m*; ˈ**mon·arch·ist** [-kɪst] **I** *s.* Monarˈchist(in); **II** *adj.* monarˈchistisch; ˈ**monarch·y** [-kɪ] *s.* Monarˈchie *f*.

mon·as·ter·y [ˈmɒnəstərɪ] *s.* (Mönchs-) Kloster *n*; **mo·nas·tic** [məˈnæstɪk] *adj.* (□ ***~ally***) **1.** klösterlich, Kloster…; **2.** mönchisch (*a. fig.*), Mönchs…: ~ ***vows*** Mönchsgelübde *n*; **mo·nas·ti·cism** [məˈnæstɪsɪzəm] *s.* **1.** Mönch(s)tum *n*; **2.** mönchisches Leben, Asˈkese *f*.

mon·a·tom·ic [ˌmɒnəˈtɒmɪk] *adj.* ⚗ ˈeinaˌtomig.

Mon·day [ˈmʌndɪ] *s.* Montag *m*: ***on*** ~ am Montag; ***on ~s*** montags.

mon·e·tar·y [ˈmʌnɪtərɪ] *adj.* ✝ **1.** Geld…, geldlich, finanziˈell; **2.** Währungs…(*-einheit, -reform etc.*); **3.** Münz…: ~ ***standard*** Münzfuß *m*; ˈ**mone·tize** [-taɪz] *v/t.* **1.** zu Münzen prägen; **2.** zum gesetzlichen Zahlungsmittel machen; **3.** den Münzfuß (*gen.*) festsetzen.

mon·ey [ˈmʌnɪ] *s.* ✝ **1.** Geld *n*; Geldbetrag *m*, -summe *f*: ~ ***on*** (*od.* ***at***) ***call*** Tagesgeld; ***be out of*** ~ kein Geld haben; ***short of*** ~ knapp an Geld, ‚schlecht bei Kasse'; ~ ***due*** ausstehendes Geld; ~ ***on account*** Guthaben *n*; ~ ***on hand*** verfügbares Geld; ***get one's ~'s worth*** et. (*Vollwertiges*) für sein Geld bekommen; **2.** Geld *n*, Vermögen *n*: ***make*** ~ Geld machen, gut verdienen (***by*** bei); ***marry*** ~ sich reich verheiraten; ***have ~ to burn*** Geld wie Heu haben; **3.** Geldsorte *f*; **4.** Zahlungsmittel *n*; **5.** ***monies*** *pl.* ⚖ Gelder *pl.*, (Geld-) Beträge *pl.*; ˈ**~-bag** *s.* **1.** Geldbeutel *m*; ⚔ Brustbeutel *m*; **2.** *pl.* F a) Geldsäcke *pl.*, Reichtum *m*, b) *sg. konstr.* ‚Geldsack' *m* (*reiche Person*); ~ **bill** *s. parl.* Fiˈnanzvorlage *f*; ˈ**~-box** *s.* Sparbüchse *f*; ~ **bro·ker** *s.* Fiˈnanzmakler *m*; ˈ**~ˌchang·er** *s.* **1.** Geldwechsler *m*; **2.** ˈWechselautoˌmat *m*.

mon·eyed [ˈmʌnɪd] *adj.* **1.** reich, vermögend; **2.** Geld…: ~ ***corporation*** ✝ *Am.* Geldinstitut *n*; ~ ***interest*** Finanzwelt *f*.

ˈ**mon·ey**|ˌ**grub·ber** [-ˌgrʌbə] *s.* Geldraffer *m*; ˈ**~ˌgrub·bing** [-ˌgrʌbɪŋ] *adj.* geldraffend, -gierig; ˈ**~ˌlend·er** *s.* ✝ Geldverleiher *m*; ~ **let·ter** *s.* Geld-, Wertbrief *m*; ˈ**~ˌmak·er** *s.* **1.** guter Geschäftsmann; **2.** Bombengeschäft *n*, ‚Renner' *m*, ‚Goldgrube' *f*; ˈ**~-ˌmak·ing** **I** *adj.* gewinnbringend, einträglich; **II** *s.* Geldverdienen *n*; ~ **mar·ket** *s.* ✝ Geldmarkt *m*; ~ **mat·ters** *s. pl.* Geldangelegenheiten *pl.*; ~ **or·der** *s.* **1.** Postanweisung *f*; **2.** Zahlungsanweisung *f*; ˈ**~ˌspin·ner** *s.* → ***moneymaker*** 2.

mon·ger [ˈmʌŋgə] *s.* (*mst in Zssgn*) **1.** Händler *m*, Krämer *m*: ***fish~*** Fischhändler; **2.** *fig. contp.* Verbreiter(in) *von Gerüchten etc.*; → ***scaremonger***, ***warmonger*** *etc.*

Mon·gol [ˈmɒŋgɒl] **I** *s.* **1.** Monˈgole *m*, Monˈgolin *f*; **2.** *ling.* Monˈgolisch *n*; **II** *adj.* **3.** → ***Mongolian*** I; **Mon·go·li·an** [mɒŋˈgəʊljən] **I** *adj.* **1.** monˈgolisch; **2.**

mongoˈlid, gelb (*Rasse*); **3.** → ***Mongoloid*** I; **II** *s.* **4.** → ***Mongol*** 1; **5.** → ***Mongoloid*** II; ˈ**Mon·gol·oid** [-lɔɪd] *bsd.* ⚕ **I** *adj.* mongoloˈid; **II** *s.* Mongoloˈide(r *m*) *f.*
mon·goose [ˈmɒŋguːs] *s. zo.* Mungo *m.*
mon·grel [ˈmʌŋgrəl] **I** *s.* **1.** *biol.* Bastard *m*; **2.** Köter *m*, Promeˈnadenmischung *f*; **3.** Mischling *m* (*Mensch*); **4.** Zwischending *n*; **II** *adj.* **5.** Bastard…, Misch…: **~ *race*** Mischrasse *f.*
'mongst [mʌŋst] *abbr. für* ***among(st)***.
mon·ick·er [ˈmɒnɪkə] → ***moniker***.
mon·ies [ˈmʌnɪz] *s. pl.* → ***money*** 5.
mon·i·ker [ˈmɒnɪkə] *s. sl.* (Spitz)Name *m.*
mon·ism [ˈmɒnɪzəm] *s. phls.* Moˈnismus *m.*
mo·ni·tion [məʊˈnɪʃn] *s.* **1.** (Er)Mahnung *f*; **2.** Warnung *f.*
mon·i·tor [ˈmɒnɪtə] **I** *s.* **1.** (Er)Mahner *m*; **2.** Warner *m*; **3.** *ped.* Klassenordner *m*; **4.** ⚓ *Art* Panzerschiff *n*; **5.** ⚡, *tel.* a) Abhörer(in), b) Abhorchgerät *n*; **6.** ⚡ *etc.* Monitor *m*, Konˈtrollgerät *n*, -schirm *m*; **II** *v/t.* **7.** *tel.* ab-, mithören, überˈwachen (*a. fig.*); **8.** ⚡ *Akustik etc.* durch Abhören kontrollieren; **9.** auf Radioaktiviˈtät überˈprüfen; ˈ**mon·i·tor·ing** [-tərɪŋ] *adj.* ⚡, *tel.* Mithör…, Prüf…, Überwachungs…: **~ *desk*** Misch-, Reglerpult *n*; ˈ**mon·i·to·ry** [-tərɪ] *adj.* **1.** (er)mahnend, Mahn…; **2.** warnend, Warnungs…
monk [mʌŋk] *s.* **1.** *eccl.* Mönch *m*; **2.** *zo.* Mönchsaffe *m*; **3.** *typ.* Schmierstelle *f.*
mon·key [ˈmʌŋkɪ] **I** *s.* **1.** *zo.* a) Affe *m* (*a. fig. humor.*), b) *engS.* kleinerer (langschwänziger) Affe (*Ggs.* ***ape***); **2.** ⚙ a) Ramme *f*, b) Fallhammer *m*; **3.** *Brit. sl.* Wut *f*: ***get*** (*od.* ***put***) ***s.o.'s ~ up*** j-n auf die Palme bringen; ***get one's ~ up*** ‚hochgehen', in Wut geraten; **4.** *sl.* 500 Dollar *od.* brit. Pfund; **II** *v/i.* **5.** Possen treiben; **6.** F (***with***) spielen (mit), herˈumpfuschen (an *dat.*): **~** (***about***) (herum)albern; **III** *v/t.* **7.** nachäffen; ˈ**~-bread** *s.* ⚘ Affenbrotbaum-Frucht *f*; **~ busi·ness** *s. sl.* **1.** ‚krumme Tour', ‚fauler Zauber'; **2.** ‚Blödsinn' *m*, Unfug *m*; **~ en·gine** *s.* ⚙ (Pfahl)Ramme *f*; ˈ**~-jack·et** *s.* ⚔ Affenjäckchen *n*; ˈ**~-shine** *s. Am. sl.* (dummer *od.* ˈübermütiger) Streich, ‚Blödsinn' *m*; ˈ**~-wrench** *s.* ⚙ ‚Engländer' *m*, Univerˈsal(schrauben)schlüssel *m*: ***throw a ~ into s.th.*** *Am.* F et. behindern *od.* beeinträchtigen.
monk·ish [ˈmʌŋkɪʃ] *adj.* **1.** Mönchs…; **2.** *mst contp.* mönchisch, Pfaffen…
mon·o [ˈmɒnəʊ] F **I** *s. Radio etc*: Mono *n*; **II** *adj.* mono (abspielbar), Mono…
mono- [mɒnəʊ] *in Zssgn* ein…, einfach…; **mon·o·ac·id** [ˌmɒnəʊˈæsɪd] ⚗ **I** *adj.* einsäurig; **II** *s.* einbasige Säure; **mon·o·car·pous** [ˌmɒnəʊˈkɑːpəs] *adj.* ⚘ **1.** einfrüchtig (*Blüte*); **2.** nur einmal fruchtend.
mon·o·chro·mat·ic [ˌmɒnəʊkrəʊˈmætɪk] *adj.* (□ **~*ally***) monochroˈmatisch, einfarbig; **mon·o·chrome** [ˈmɒnəkrəʊm] **I** *s.* **1.** einfarbiges Gemälde; **2.** Schwarzˈweißaufnahme *f*; **II** *adj.* **3.** monoˈchrom.
mon·o·cle [ˈmɒnəkl] *s.* Monˈokel *n.*
mo·no·coque [ˈmɒnəkɒk] (*Fr.*) *s.* ✈ **1.** Schalenrumpf *m*; **2.** Flugzeug *n* mit Schalenrumpf: **~ *construction*** ⚙ Schalenbau(weise *f*) *m.*
mo·noc·u·lar [mɒˈnɒkjʊlə] *adj.* monokuˈlar, für ˈein Auge.
mon·o·cul·ture [ˈmɒnəʊˌkʌltʃə] *s.* ⚒ ˈMonokulˌtur *f*; **mo·nog·a·mous** [mɒˈnɒgəməs] *adj.* monoˈgam(isch); **mo·nog·a·my** [mɒˈnɒgəmɪ] *s.* Monogaˈmie *f*, Einehe *f*; **mon·o·gram** [ˈmɒnəgræm] *s.* Monoˈgramm *n*; **mon·o·graph** [ˈmɒnəgrɑːf] *s.* Monograˈphie *f*; **mon·o·hy·dric** [ˌmɒnəʊˈhaɪdrɪk] *adj.* ⚗ einwertig: **~ *alcohol***; **mon·o·lith** [ˈmɒnəʊlɪθ] *s.* Monoˈlith *m*; **mon·o·lith·ic** [ˌmɒnəʊˈlɪθɪk] *adj.* monoˈlithisch; *fig.* giˈgantisch; **mo·nol·o·gize** [mɒˈnɒlədʒaɪz] *v/i.* monologisieren, ein Selbstgespräch führen; **mon·o·logue** [ˈmɒnəlɒg] *s.* Monoˈlog *m*, Selbstgespräch *n*; **mon·o·ma·ni·a** [ˌmɒnəʊˈmeɪnjə] *s.* Monomaˈnie *f*, fixe Iˈdee.
mo·no·mi·al [mɒˈnəʊmjəl] *s.* ∆ eingliedrige Zahlengröße.
mon·o·phase [ˈmɒnəʊfeɪz] *adj.* ⚡ einphasig; **mon·o·pho·bi·a** [ˌmɒnəʊˈfəʊbjə] *s.* Monophoˈbie *f*; **mon·o·phtong** [ˈmɒnəfθɒŋ] Monoˈphtong *m*, einfacher Selbstlaut; **mon·o·plane** [ˈmɒnəʊpleɪn] *s.* ✈ Eindecker *m.*
mo·nop·o·list [məˈnɒpəlɪst] *s.* ☤ Monopoˈlist *m*; Monoˈpolbesitzer(in); **mo·ˈnop·o·lize** [-laɪz] *v/t.* monopolisieren: a) ☤ ein Monoˈpol erringen *od.* haben für, b) *fig.* an sich reißen: **~ *the conversation*** die Unterhaltung ganz allein bestreiten, c) *fig.* *j-n od. et.* mit Beschlag belegen; **moˈnop·o·ly** [-lɪ] *s.* ☤ **1.** Monoˈpol(stellung *f*) *n*; **2.** (***of***) Monoˈpol *n* (auf *acc.*); Alˈleinverkaufs-, Alˈleinbetriebs-, Alˈleinherstellungsrecht *n* (für): ***market*** **~** Marktbeherrschung *f*; **3.** *fig.* Monoˈpol *n*, alˈleiniger Besitz, alˈleinige Beherrschung: **~ *of learning*** Bildungsmonopol.
mon·o·rail [ˈmɒnəʊreɪl] *s.* 🚂 **1.** Einschiene *f*; **2.** Einwegbahn *f.*
mon·o·syl·lab·ic [ˌmɒnəʊsɪˈlæbɪk] *adj.* (□ **~*ally***) *ling. u. fig.* einsilbig; **mon·o·syl·la·ble** [ˈmɒnəˌsɪləbl] *s.* einsilbiges Wort: ***speak in ~s*** einsilbige Antworten geben.
mon·o·the·ism [ˈmɒnəʊθiːˌɪzəm] *s. eccl.* Monotheˈismus *m*; ˈ**mon·o·theˌist** [-ˌɪst] **I** *s.* Monotheˈist *m*; **II** *adj.* → **mon·o·the·is·tic, mon·o·the·is·ti·cal** [ˌmɒnəʊθiːˈɪstɪk(l)] *adj.* monotheˈistisch.
mon·o·tone [ˈmɒnətəʊn] *s.* **1.** monoˈtones Geräusch, gleichbleibender Ton; eintönige Wiederˈholung; **2.** → ***monotony***; **mo·not·o·nous** [məˈnɒtnəs] *adj.* □ monoˈton, eintönig (*a. fig.*); **mo·not·o·ny** [məˈnɒtnɪ] *s.* Monotoˈnie *f*, Eintönigkeit *f*, *fig. a.* Einförmigkeit *f*, (ewiges) Einerlei.
mon·o·type [ˈmɒnəʊtaɪp] (*Fabrikmarke*) *s. typ.* **1.** ⚲ Monotype *f*; **2.** mit der Monotype hergestellte Letter.
mon·o·va·lent [ˈmɒnəʊˌveɪlənt] *adj.* ⚗ einwertig; **mon·ox·ide** [mɒˈnɒksaɪd] *s.* ⚗ ˈMonoˌxyd *n.*
mon·soon [mɒnˈsuːn] *s.* Monˈsun *m.*
mon·ster [ˈmɒnstə] **I** *s.* **1.** *a. fig.* Monster *n*, Ungeheuer *n*, Scheusal *n*; **2.** Monstrum *n*: a) ˈMißgeburt *f*, -bildung *f*, b) *fig.* Ungeheuer *n*, Koˈloß *m*; **II** *adj.* **3.** ungeheuer(lich), Riesen…, Monster…: **~ *film*** Monsterfilm *m*; **~ *meeting*** Massenversammlung *f.*
mon·strance [ˈmɒnstrəns] *s. eccl.* Monˈstranz *f.*
mon·stros·i·ty [mɒnˈstrɒsətɪ] *s.* **1.** Ungeheuerlichkeit *f*; **2.** → ***monster*** 2.
mon·strous [ˈmɒnstrəs] *adj.* □ **1.** monˈströs: a) ungeheuer, riesig, b) ungeˈheuerlich, gräßlich, scheußlich, c) ˈmißgestaltet, unförmig, ungestalt; **2.** un-, ˈwidernaˌtürlich; **3.** abˈsurd, lächerlich; ˈ**mon·strous·ness** [-nɪs] *s.* **1.** Ungeˈheuerlichkeit *f*; **2.** Riesenhaftigkeit *f*; **3.** ˈWidernaˌtürlichkeit *f.*
mon·tage [mɒnˈtɑːʒ] *s.* **1.** (ˈBild-, ˈFoto-) Monˌtage *f*; **2.** *Film, Radio etc.*: Monˈtage *f.*
month [mʌnθ] *s.* **1.** Monat *m*: ***this day ~*** heute in *od.* vor e-m Monat; ***by the ~*** (all)monatlich; ***a ~ of Sundays*** e-e ewig lange Zeit; **2.** F vier Wochen *od.* 30 Tage; **month·ly** [ˈmʌnθlɪ] **I** *s.* **1.** Monatsschrift *f*; **2.** *pl.* → ***menses***; **II** *adj.* **3.** einen Monat dauernd; **4.** monatlich, Monats…: **~ *salary*** Monatsgehalt *n*; **III** *adv.* **5.** monatlich, einmal im Monat, jeden Monat.
mon·ti·cule [ˈmɒntɪkjuːl] *s.* **1.** (kleiner) Hügel; **2.** Höckerchen *n.*
mon·u·ment [ˈmɒnjʊmənt] *s.* Monuˈment *n*, (*a.* Grab-, Naˈtur- *etc.*)Denkmal *n* (***to*** für, ***of*** *gen.*): ***a ~ of literature*** *fig.* ein Literaturdenkmal; **mon·u·men·tal** [ˌmɒnjʊˈmentl] *adj.* □ **1.** monumenˈtal, gewaltig, impoˈsant; **2.** F kolosˈsal, ungeheuer: **~ *stupidity***; **3.** Denkmal(s)…, Gedenk…; Grabmal(s)…
moo [muː] **I** *v/i.* muhen; **II** *s.* Muhen *n.*
mooch [muːtʃ] *sl.* **I** *v/i.* **1.** *a.* **~ *about*** herˈumlungern, -strolchen: **~ *along*** dahinlatschen; **II** *v/t.* **2.** ‚klauen', stehlen; **3.** schnorren, erbetteln.
mood[1] [muːd] *s.* **1.** *ling.* Modus *m*, Aussageweise *f*; **2.** ♪ Tonart *f.*
mood[2] [muːd] *s.* **1.** Stimmung *f* (*a. paint.*, ♪ *etc.*), Laune *f*: ***be in the ~ to work*** zur Arbeit aufgelegt sein; ***be in no ~ for a walk*** nicht zu e-m Spaziergang aufgelegt sein, keine Lust haben spazierenzugehen; ***change of ~*** Stimmungsumschwung *m*; **~ *music*** stimmungsvolle Musik; **2.** *paint.*, *phot.* Stimmungsbild *n*; **mood·i·ness** [ˈmuːdɪnɪs] *s.* **1.** Launenhaftigkeit *f*; **2.** Übellaunigkeit *f*; **3.** Trübsinn(igkeit *f*) *m*; **mood·y** [ˈmuːdɪ] *adj.* **1.** □ launisch, launenhaft; **2.** übellaunig, verstimmt; **3.** trübsinnig.
moon [muːn] **I** *s.* **1.** Mond *m*: ***full ~*** Vollmond; ***new ~*** Neumond; ***once in a blue ~*** F alle Jubeljahre einmal, höchst selten; ***be over the ~*** F ganz selig sein; ***cry for the ~*** nach etwas Unmöglichem verlangen; ***promise s.o. the ~*** j-m das Blaue vom Himmel (herunter) versprechen; ***reach for the ~*** nach den Sternen greifen; ***shoot the ~*** F bei Nacht u. Nebel ausziehen (*Mieter*); **2.** *ast.* Traˈbant *m*, Satelˈlit *m*: ***man-made*** (*od.* ***baby***) **~** (Erd)Satellit, ‚Sputnik' *m*; **3.** *poet.* Mond *m*, Monat *m*; **II** *v/i.* **4.** *mst* **~ *about*** umˈherlungern, -geistern; **III** *v/t.* **5.** **~ *away*** *Zeit* vertrödeln, verträumen; ˈ**~-beam** *s.* Mondstrahl *m*: ˈ**~-calf** *s.* [*irr.*] **1.** ‚Mondkalb' *n*, Trottel *m*; **2.**

Träumer *m*; **'~·faced** *adj.* vollmondgesichtig; **'~·light I** *s.* Mondlicht *n*, -schein *m*: ♀ ***Sonata*** ♪ Mondscheinsonate *f*; **II** *adj.* mondhell, Mondlicht...: ***~ flit(ting)*** *sl.* heimliches Ausziehen bei Nacht (*wegen Mietschulden*); **'~ˌlight·er** *s.* Schwarzarbeiter *m*; **'~·lit** *adj.* mondhell; **~ rak·er** *s.* ⚓ Mondsegel *n*; **'~·rise** *s.* Mondaufgang *m*; **'~·set** *s.* 'Mondˌuntergang *m*; **'~·shine** *s.* **1.** Mondschein *m*; **2.** *fig.* a) Schwindel *m*, fauler Zauber, b) Unsinn *m*, Geschwafel *n*; **3.** *sl.* geschmuggelter *od.* schwarzgebrannter Alkohol; **'~ˌshin·er** *s. Am. sl.* Alkoholschmuggler *m*; Schwarzbrenner *m*; **'~·stone** *s. min.* Mondstein *m*; **'~·struck** *adj.* **1.** mondsüchtig; **2.** verrückt.

moon·y ['mu:nɪ] *adj.* **1.** (halb)mondförmig; **2.** Mond...; **3.** mondhell, Mondlicht...; **4.** F a) verträumt, dösig, b) beschwipst, c) verrückt.

moor[1] [mʊə] *s.* **1.** Ödland *n*, *bsd.* Heideland *n*; **2.** Hochmoor *n*; Bergheide *f*.

moor[2] [mʊə] **I** *v/t.* **1.** ⚓ vertäuen, festmachen; *fig.* verankern, sichern; **II** *v/i.* ⚓ **2.** festmachen, ein Schiff vertäuen; **3.** sich festmachen; **4.** festgemacht *od.* vertäut liegen.

Moor[3] [mʊə] *s.* Maure *m*; Mohr *m*.

moor·age ['mʊərɪdʒ] → ***mooring***.

'moor|·fowl, **~ game** *s.* (schottisches) Moorhuhn; **'~·hen** *s.* **1.** weibliches Moorhuhn; **2.** Gemeines Teichhuhn.

moor·ing ['mʊərɪŋ] *s.* ⚓ **1.** Festmachen *n*; **2.** *mst pl.* Vertäuung *f* (*Schiff*); **3.** *pl.* Liegeplatz *m*; **4.** Anlegegebühr *f*; **~ buoy** *s.* ⚓ Festmacheboje *f*; **~ rope** *s.* Halteleine *f*.

Moor·ish ['mʊərɪʃ] *adj.* maurisch.

'moor·land [-lənd] *s.* Heidemoor *n*.

moose [mu:s] *pl.* **moose** *s. zo.* Elch *m*.

moot [mu:t] **I** *s.* **1.** *hist.* (beratende) Volksversammlung; **2.** ⚖, *univ.* Diskussi'on *f* fik'tiver (Rechts)Fälle; **II** *v/t.* **3.** *Frage* aufwerfen, anschneiden; **4.** erörtern, diskutieren; **III** *adj.* **5.** a) strittig: ***~ point***, b) (rein) aka'demisch: ***~ question***.

mop[1] [mɒp] **I** *s.* **1.** Mop *m* (*Fransenbesen*); Schrubber *m*; Wischlappen *m*; **2.** (Haar)Wust *m*; **3.** ⚓ Dweil *m*; **4.** ⚙ Schwabbelscheibe *f*; **II** *v/t.* **5.** auf-, abwischen: ***~ one's face*** sich das Gesicht (ab)wischen; → ***floor*** 1; **6.** ***~ up*** a) (mit dem Mop) aufwischen, b) ⚔ *sl.* (*vom Feinde*) säubern, *Wald* durch'kämmen, c) *sl. Profit etc.* ‚schlucken', d) *sl.* aufräumen mit.

mop[2] [mɒp] **I** *v/i. mst* ***~ and mow*** Gesichter schneiden; **II** *s.* Gri'masse *f*: ***~s and mows*** Grimassen.

mope [məʊp] **I** *v/i.* **1.** den Kopf hängen lassen, Trübsal blasen; **II** *v/t.* **2.** (*nur pass.*) ***be ~d*** niedergeschlagen sein; ‚sich mopsen' (*langweilen*); **III** *s.* **3.** Trübsalbläser(in); **4.** *pl.* Trübsinn *m*.

mo·ped ['məʊped] *s. mot. Brit.* Moped *n*.

'mop·head *s.* F a) Wuschelkopf *m*, b) Struwwelpeter *m*.

mop·ing ['məʊpɪŋ] *adj.* □; **'mop·ish** [-ɪʃ] *adj.* □ trübselig, a'pathisch, kopfhängerisch; **'mop·ish·ness** [-ɪʃnɪs] *s.* Lustlosigkeit *f*, Griesgrämigkeit *f*, Trübsinn *m*.

mop·pet ['mɒpɪt] *s.* F Püppchen *n* (*a. fig. Kind, Mädchen*).

'mop·ping-up ['mɒpɪŋ-] *s.* ⚔ *sl.* **1.** Aufräumungsarbeit *f*; **2.** Säuberung *f* (*vom Feinde*): ***~ operation*** Säuberungsaktion *f*.

mo·raine [mɒ'reɪn] *s. geol.* Mo'räne *f*.

mor·al ['mɒrəl] **I** *adj.* □ **1.** *allg.* mo'ralisch: a) sittlich: ***~ force***; ***~ sense*** sittliches Empfinden, b) geistig: ***~ obligation*** moralische Verpflichtung; ***~ support*** moralische Unterstützung; ***~ victory*** moralischer Sieg, c) vernunftgemäß: ***~ certainty*** moralische Gewißheit, d) Moral..., Sitten...: ***~ law*** Sittengesetz *n*; ***~ theology*** Moraltheologie *f*, e) sittenstreng, tugendhaft: ***a ~ life***; **2.** (sittlich) gut: ***a ~ act***; **3.** cha'rakterlich: ***~ly firm*** innerlich gefestigt; **II** *s.* **4.** Mo'ral *f*, Nutzanwendung *f* (*e-r Geschichte etc.*): ***draw the ~ from*** die Lehre ziehen aus; **5.** mo'ralischer Grundsatz: ***point the ~*** den sittlichen Standpunkt betonen; **6.** *pl.* Mo'ral *f*, sittliches Verhalten, Sitten *pl.*: ***code of ~s*** Sittenkodex *m*; **7.** *pl. sg. konstr.* Sittenlehre *f*, Ethik *f*.

mo·rale [mɒ'rɑ:l] *s.* Mo'ral *f*, Haltung *f*, Stimmung *f*, (Arbeits-, Kampf)Geist *m*: ***the ~ of the army*** die Kampfmoral *od.* Stimmung der Armee; ***raise*** (***lower***) ***the ~*** die Moral heben (senken).

mor·al| fac·ul·ty *s.* Sittlichkeitsgefühl *n*; **~ haz·ard** *s. Versicherungswesen*: subjek'tives Risiko, Risiko *n* falscher Angaben des Versicherten; **~ in·san·i·ty** *s. psych.* mo'ralischer De'fekt.

mor·al·ist ['mɒrəlɪst] *s.* **1.** Mora'list *m*, Sittenlehrer *m*; **2.** Ethiker *m*.

mo·ral·i·ty [mə'rælətɪ] *s.* **1.** Mo'ral *f*, Sittlichkeit *f*, Tugend(haftigkeit) *f*; **2.** Morali'tät *f*, sittliche Gesinnung; **3.** Ethik *f*, Sittenlehre *f*; **4.** *pl.* mo'ralische Grundsätze *pl.*, Ethik *f* (*e-r Person*); **5.** *contp.* Mo'ralpredigt *f*; **6.** → **~ play** *s. hist. thea.* Morali'tät *f*.

mor·al·ize ['mɒrəlaɪz] **I** *v/i.* **1.** moralisieren (***on*** über *acc.*); **II** *v/t.* **2.** mo'ralisch auslegen; **3.** versittlichen, die Mo'ral (*gen.*) heben; **'mor·al·iz·er** [-zə] *s.* Sittenprediger(in).

mor·al| phi·los·o·phy, **~ sci·ence** *s.* Mo'ralphilosoˌphie *f*, Ethik *f*.

mo·rass [mə'ræs] *s.* **1.** Mo'rast *m*, Sumpf (-land *n*) *m*; **2.** *fig.* a) Wirrnis *f*, b) Klemme *f*, schwierige Lage.

mor·a·to·ri·um [ˌmɒrə'tɔ:rɪəm] *pl.* **-ri·ums** *s.* ✝ Mora'torium *n*, Zahlungsaufschub *m*, Stillhalteabkommen *n*, Stundung *f*; **mor·a·to·ry** ['mɒrətərɪ] *adj.* Moratoriums..., Stundungs...

Mo·ra·vi·an [mə'reɪvjən] **I** *s.* **1.** Mähre *m*, Mährin *f*; **2.** *ling.* Mährisch *n*; **II** *adj.* **3.** mährisch: ***~ Brethren*** *eccl. die* Herrnhuter Brüdergemein(d)e.

mor·bid ['mɔ:bɪd] *adj.* □ mor'bid, krankhaft, patho'logisch: ***~ anatomy*** ⚕ pathologische Anatomie; **mor·bid·i·ty** [mɔ:'bɪdətɪ] *s.* **1.** Krankhaftigkeit *f*; **2.** Erkrankungsziffer *f*.

mor·dan·cy ['mɔ:dənsɪ] *s.* Bissigkeit *f*, beißende Schärfe; **'mor·dant** [-dənt] **I** *adj.* □ **1.** beißend: a) brennend (*Schmerz*), b) *fig.* scharf, sar'kastisch (*Worte etc.*); **2.** ⚙ a) beizend, ätzend, b) *Farben* fixierend; **II** *s.* **3.** ⚙ a) Ätzwasser *n*, b) (*bsd. Färberei*) Beize *f*.

more [mɔ:] **I** *adj.* **1.** mehr: (***no***) ***~ than*** (nicht) mehr als; ***they are ~ than we*** sie sind zahlreicher als wir; **2.** mehr, noch (mehr), weiter: ***some ~ tea*** noch etwas Tee; ***one ~ day*** noch ein(en) Tag; ***so much the ~ courage*** um so mehr Mut; ***he is no ~*** er ist nicht mehr (*ist tot*); **3.** größer (*obs. außer in*): ***the ~ fool*** der größere Tor; ***the ~ part*** der größere Teil; **II** *adv.* **4.** mehr: ***~ dead than alive*** mehr *od.* eher tot als lebendig; ***~ and ~*** immer mehr; ***~ and ~ difficult*** immer schwieriger; ***~ or less*** mehr oder weniger, ungefähr; ***the ~*** um so mehr; ***the ~ so because*** um so mehr, da; ***all the ~ so*** nur um so mehr; ***no*** (*od.* ***not any***) ***~ than*** ebensowenig wie; ***neither*** (*od.* ***no***) ***~ nor less than stupid*** nicht mehr u. nicht weniger als dumm; **5.** (*zur Bildung des comp.*): ***~ important*** wichtiger; ***~ often*** öfter; **6.** noch: ***once ~*** noch einmal; ***two hours ~*** noch zwei Stunden; **7.** noch mehr, ja so'gar: ***it is wrong and, ~, it is foolish***; **III** *s.* **8.** Mehr *n* (***of*** an *dat.*); **9.** mehr: ***~ than one person has seen it*** mehr als einer hat es gesehen; ***we shall see ~ of him*** wir werden ihn noch öfter sehen; ***and what is ~*** und was noch wichtiger ist; ***no ~*** nicht(s) mehr.

mo·rel [mɒ'rel] *s.* ♀ **1.** Morchel *f*; **2.** Nachtschatten *m*; **3.** → **mo·rel·lo** [mə'reləʊ] *pl.* **-los** *s.* ♀ Mo'relle *f*, Schwarze Sauerweichsel.

more·o·ver [mɔ:'rəʊvə] *adv.* außerdem, über'dies, ferner, weiter.

mo·res ['mɔ:ri:z] *s. pl.* Sitten *pl.*

mor·ga·nat·ic [ˌmɔ:gə'nætɪk] *adj.* (□ ***~ally***) morga'natisch.

morgue [mɔ:g] *s.* **1.** Leichenschauhaus *n*; **2.** F Ar'chiv *n* (*e-s Zeitungsverlages etc.*).

mor·i·bund ['mɒrɪbʌnd] *adj.* **1.** sterbend, dem Tode geweiht; **2.** *fig.* zum Aussterben *od.* Scheitern verurteilt.

Mor·mon ['mɔ:mən] *eccl.* **I** *s.* Mor'mone *m*, Mor'monin *f*; **II** *adj.* mor'monisch: ***~ Church*** mormonische Kirche, Kirche Jesu Christi der Heiligen der letzten Tage; ***~ State*** *Beiname für* Utah *n* (*USA*).

morn [mɔ:n] *s. poet.* Morgen *m*.

morn·ing ['mɔ:nɪŋ] **I** *s.* **1.** a) Morgen *m*, b) Vormittag *m*: ***in the ~*** morgens, am Morgen, vormittags; ***early in the ~*** frühmorgens, früh am Morgen; ***on the ~ of May 5*** am Morgen des 5. Mai; ***one*** (***fine***) ***~*** eines (schönen) Morgens; ***this ~*** heute früh; ***the ~ after*** am Morgen darauf, am darauffolgenden Morgen; ***good ~!*** guten Morgen!; ***~!*** F ('n) Morgen!; **2.** *fig.* Morgen *m*, Beginn *m*; **3.** *poet.* a) Morgendämmerung *f*, b) ♀ Au'rora *f*; **II** *adj.* **4.** a) Morgen..., Vormittags..., b) Früh...; **~ call** *s.* Weckdienst *m* (*im Hotel etc.*); **~ coat** *s.* Cut(away) *m*; **~ dress** *s.* **1.** Hauskleid *n*; **2.** Besuchs-, Konfe'renzanzug *m*, ‚Stresemann' *m* (*schwarzer Rock mit gestreifter Hose*); **~ gift** *s.* ⚖ *hist.* Morgengabe *f*; **~ glo·ry** *s.* ♀ Winde *f*; **~ gown** *s.* Morgenrock *m*; Hauskleid *n* (*der Frau*); **~ per·form·ance** *s. thea.* Frühvorstellung *f*, Mati'nee *f*; **~ prayer** *s. eccl.* **1.** Morgengebet *n*; **2.** Frühgottesdienst *m*; **~ sick·ness** *s.* ⚕ morgendliches Erbrechen (*bei Schwangeren*); **~ star** *s.* **1.** *ast.*, *a.* ⚔ *hist.* Morgenstern *m*; **2.** ⚘ Men'tzelie *f*.

Mo·roc·can [mə'rɒkən] **I** *adj.* marok'kanisch; **II** *s.* Marok'kaner(in).

mo·roc·co [mə'rɒkəʊ] *pl.* **-cos** [-z] *s. a.* ~ ***leather*** Saffian(leder *n*) *m*.

mo·ron ['mɔːrɒn] *s.* **1.** Schwachsinnige(r *m*) *f*; **2.** F Trottel *m*, Idi'ot *m*; **mo·ron·ic** [mə'rɒnɪk] *adj.* schwachsinnig.

mo·rose [mə'rəʊs] *adj.* □ mürrisch, grämlich, verdrießlich; **mo'rose·ness** [-nɪs] *s.* Verdrießlichkeit *f*.

mor·pheme ['mɔːfiːm] *s. ling.* Mor'phem *n*.

mor·phi·a ['mɔːfjə], **'mor·phine** [-fiːn] *s.* ⚗ Morphium *n*; **'mor·phin·ism** [-fɪnɪzəm] *s.* **1.** Morphi'nismus *m*, Morphiumsucht *f*; **2.** Morphiumvergiftung *f*; **'mor·phin·ist** [-fɪnɪst] *s.* Morphi'nist(in).

morpho- [mɔːfəʊ] *in Zssgn* Form…, Gestalt…, Morpho…

mor·pho·log·ic, **mor·pho·log·i·cal** [ˌmɔːfə'lɒdʒɪk(l)] *adj.* □ morpho'logisch, Form…: ~ ***element*** Formelement *n*; **mor·phol·o·gy** [mɔː'fɒlədʒɪ] *s.* Morpholo'gie *f*.

mor·ris ['mɒrɪs] *s. a.* ~ ***dance*** Mo'riskentanz *m*; ~ **tube** *s.* Einstecklauf *m* (*für Gewehre*).

mor·row ['mɒrəʊ] *s. mst poet.* morgiger *od.* folgender Tag: ***the ~ of*** a) der Tag nach, b) *fig.* die Zeit unmittelbar nach.

Morse[1] [mɔːs] **I** *adj.* Morse…: ~ ***code*** Morsealphabet *n*; **II** *v/t. u. v/i.* ♀ morsen.

morse[2] [mɔːs] → ***walrus***.

mor·sel ['mɔːsl] **I** *s.* **1.** Bissen *m*, Happen *m*; **2.** Stückchen *n*, *das* bißchen; **3.** Leckerbissen *m*; **II** *v/t.* **4.** in kleine Stückchen teilen, in kleinen Porti'onen austeilen.

mort[1] [mɔːt] *s. hunt.* ('Hirsch)ˌTotsiˌgnal *n*.

mort[2] [mɔːt] *s. ichth.* dreijähriger Lachs.

mor·tal ['mɔːtl] **I** *adj.* □ **1.** sterblich; **2.** tödlich: a) verderblich, todbringend (***to*** für): ~ ***wound***, b) erbittert: ~ ***battle***; ~ ***hatred*** tödlicher Haß; **3.** Tod(es)…: ~ ***agony*** Todeskampf *m*; ~ ***enemies*** Todfeinde; ~ ***fear*** Todesangst *f*; ~ ***hour*** Todesstunde *f*; ~ ***sin*** Todsünde *f*; **4.** menschlich, irdisch, Menschen…: ~ ***life*** irdisches Leben, Vergänglichkeit *f*; ***by no ~ means*** F auf keine menschenmögliche Art; ***of no ~ use*** F absolut zwecklos; ***every ~ thing*** F alles menschenmögliche; **5.** F Mords…, ‚mordsmäßig': ***I'm in a ~ hurry*** ich hab's furchtbar eilig; **6.** ewig, sterbenslangweilig: ***three ~ hours*** drei endlose Stunden; **II** *s.* **7.** Sterbliche(r *m*) *f*; **mor·tal·i·ty** [mɔː'tælətɪ] *s.* **1.** Sterblichkeit *f*; **2.** die (sterbliche) Menschheit; **3.** *a.* ~ ***rate*** a) Sterblichkeit(sziffer) *f*, b) ⚙ Verschleiß(quote *f*) *m*.

mor·tar[1] ['mɔːtə] **I** *s.* **1.** ⚗ Mörser *m*; **2.** *metall.* Pochladen *m*; **3.** ⚔ a) Mörser *m* (*Geschütz*), b) Gra'natwerfer *m*: ~ ***shell*** Wurfgranate *f*; **4.** (Feuerwerks-)Böller *m*; **II** *v/t.* **5.** ⚔ mit Mörsern beschießen, mit Gra'natwerferfeuer belegen.

mor·tar[2] ['mɔːtə] *s.* ⚠ Mörtel *m*.

'mor·tar·board *s.* **1.** ⚠ Mörtelbrett *n*; **2.** *univ.* qua'dratisches Ba'rett.

mort·gage ['mɔːgɪdʒ] ⚖ **I** *s.* **1.** Verpfändung *f*; Pfandgut *n*: ***give in ~*** verpfänden; **2.** Pfandbrief *m*; **3.** Hypo'thek *f*: ***by ~*** hypothekarisch; ***lend on ~*** auf Hypothek (ver)leihen; ***raise a ~*** e-e Hypothek aufnehmen (***on*** auf *acc.*); **4.** Hypo'thekenbrief *m*; **II** *v/t.* **5.** (*a. fig.*) verpfänden (***to*** an *acc.*); **6.** hypothe'karisch belasten, e-e Hypo'thek aufnehmen auf (*acc.*); ~ **bond** *s.* Hypo'thekenpfandbrief *m*; ~ **deed** *s.* **1.** Pfandbrief *m*; **2.** Hypo'thekenbrief *m*.

mort·ga·gee [ˌmɔːgə'dʒiː] *s.* ⚖ Hypothe'kar *m*, Pfand- *od.* Hypo'thekengläubiger *m*; ˌ**mort·ga'gor** [-'dʒɔː] *s.* Pfand- *od.* Hypo'thekenschuldner *m*.

mor·ti·cian [mɔː'tɪʃən] *s. Am.* Leichenbestatter *m*.

mor·ti·fi·ca·tion [ˌmɔːtɪfɪ'keɪʃn] *s.* **1.** Demütigung *f*, Kränkung *f*; **2.** Ärger *m*, Verdruß *m*; **3.** Ka'steiung *f*; Abtötung *f* (*Leidenschaften*); **4.** ⚕ (kalter) Brand, Ne'krose *f*; **mor·ti·fy** ['mɔːtɪfaɪ] **I** *v/t.* **1.** demütigen, kränken; **2.** *Gefühle* verletzen; **3.** *Körper*, *Fleisch* ka'steien; *Leidenschaften* abtöten; **4.** ⚕ brandig machen, absterben lassen; **II** *v/i.* **5.** ⚕ brandig werden, absterben.

mor·tise ['mɔːtɪs] ⚙ **I** *s.* a) Zapfenloch *n*, b) Stemmloch *n*, c) (Keil)Nut *f*, d) Falz *m*, Fuge *f*; **II** *v/t.* a) verzapfen, b) einstemmen, c) einzapfen (***into*** in *acc.*); ~ **chis·el** *s.* Lochbeitel *m*; ~ **ga(u)ge** *s.* Zapfenstreichmaß *n*; ~ **joint** *s.* Verzapfung *f*; ~ **lock** *s.* (Ein-)Steckschloß *n*.

mort·main ['mɔːtmeɪn] *s.* ⚖ unveräußerlicher Besitz, Besitz *m* der Toten Hand: ***in ~*** unveräußerlich.

mor·tu·ar·y ['mɔːtjʊərɪ] **I** *s.* Leichenhalle *f*; **II** *adj.* Leichen…, Begräbnis…

mo·sa·ic[1] [məʊ'zeɪɪk] **I** *s.* **1.** Mosa'ik *n* (*a. fig.*); **2.** ('Luftbild)Mosaˌik *n*, Reihenbild *n*; **II** *adj.* **3.** Mosaik…; mosa'ikartig.

Mo·sa·ic[2] *adj.*, **Mo·sa·i·cal** [məʊ'zeɪɪk(l)] *adj.* mo'saisch.

Mo·selle [məʊ'zel] *s.* Mosel(wein) *m*.

mo·sey ['məʊzɪ] *v/i. Am. sl.* **1.** *a.* ~ ***along*** da'hinlatschen; **2.** ‚abhauen'.

Mos·lem ['mɒzlem] **I** *s.* Moslem *m*; **II** *adj.* mos'lemisch, mohamme'danisch.

mosque [mɒsk] *s.* Mo'schee *f*.

mos·qui·to [mə'skiːtəʊ] *s.* **1.** *pl.* **-toes** *zo.* Stechmücke *f*, *bsd.* Mos'kito *m*; **2.** *pl.* **-toes** *od.* **-tos** ✈ Mos'kito *m* (*brit. Bomber*); ~ **boat**, ~ **craft** *s.* Schnellboot *n*; ~ **net** *s.* Mos'kitonetz *n*; ♀ **State** *s. Am.* (*Beiname für*) New Jersey *n* (*USA*).

moss [mɒs] *s.* **1.** ⚘ Moos *n*; **2.** (Torf-)Moor *n*; **'~-grown** *adj.* **1.** moosbewachsen, bemoost; **2.** *fig.* altmodisch, über'holt.

moss·i·ness ['mɒsɪnɪs] *s.* **1.** 'Moosˌüberzug *m*; **2.** Moosartigkeit *f*, Weichheit *f*; **moss·y** ['mɒsɪ] *adj.* **1.** moosig, bemoost; **2.** moosartig; **3.** Moos…: ~ ***green*** Moosgrün *n*.

most [məʊst] **I** *adj.* □ → ***mostly***; **1.** meist, größt; höchst, äußerst; ***the ~ fear*** die meiste *od.* größte Angst; ***for the ~ part*** größten-, meistenteils; **2.** (*vor e-m Substantiv im pl.*) die meisten: ~ ***people*** die meisten Leute; **II** *s.* **3.** *das* meiste, *das* Höchste, *das* Äußerste: ***at (the) ~*** höchstens, bestenfalls; ***make the ~ of*** *et.* nach Kräften ausnützen, (noch) das Beste aus *et.* herausholen; **4.** das meiste, der größte Teil: ***he spent ~ of his time there*** er verbrachte die meiste Zeit dort; **5.** die meisten: ***better than ~*** besser als die meisten; ***~ of my friends*** die meisten m-r Freunde; **III** *adv.* **6.** am meisten: ***~ of all*** am allermeisten; **7.** *zur Bildung des Superlativs*: ***the ~ important point*** der wichtigste Punkt; **8.** *vor adj.* höchst, äußerst, 'überaus: ***it's ~ kind of you***.

-most [məʊst] *in Zssgn Bezeichnung des sup.*: ***in~***, ***top~*** *etc.*

'most-ˌfa·vo(u)red-'na·tion clause *s. pol.* Meistbegünstigungsklausel *f*.

most·ly ['məʊstlɪ] *adv.* **1.** größtenteils, im wesentlichen, in der Hauptsache; **2.** hauptsächlich.

mote [məʊt] *s.* (Sonnen)Stäubchen *n*: ***the ~ in another's eye*** *bibl.* der Splitter im Auge des anderen.

mo·tel [məʊ'tel] *s.* Mo'tel *n*.

mo·tet [məʊ'tet] *s.* ♪ Mo'tette *f*.

moth [mɒθ] *s.* **1.** *pl.* **moths** *zo.* Nachtfalter *m*; **2.** *pl.* **moths** *od. coll.* **moth** (Kleider)Motte *f*; **'~·ball I** *s.* Mottenkugel *f*: ***put in ~s*** → **II** *v/t. Kleidung*, *a. Maschinen etc.* einmotten; *fig. Plan etc.* ‚auf Eis legen'; **'~-ˌeat·en** *adj.* **1.** von Motten zerfressen; **2.** *fig.* veraltet, anti'quiert.

moth·er[1] ['mʌðə] **I** *s.* **1.** Mutter *f* (*a. fig.*); **II** *adj.* **2.** Mutter…: ♀***'s Day*** Muttertag *m*; **III** *v/t.* **3.** (*mst fig.*) gebären, her'vorbringen; **4.** bemuttern; **5.** ~ ***a novel on s.o.*** j-m e-n Roman zuschreiben.

moth·er[2] ['mʌðə] **I** *s.* Essigmutter *f*; **II** *v/i.* Essigmutter ansetzen.

Moth·er Car·ey's chick·en ['keərɪz] *s. orn.* Sturmschwalbe *f*.

moth·er| cell *s. biol.* Mutterzelle *f*; ~ **church** *s.* **1.** Mutterkirche *f*; **2.** Hauptkirche *f*; ~ **coun·try** *s.* **1.** Mutterland *n*; **2.** Vater-, Heimatland *n*; ~ **earth** *s.* Mutter *f* Erde; ~ **fix·a·tion** *s. psych.* Mutterfixierung *f*, -bindung *f*; **'~ˌfuck·er** *s. fig.* V ‚Scheißkerl' *m*.

moth·er·hood ['mʌðəhʊd] *s.* **1.** Mutterschaft *f*; **2.** *coll. die* Mütter *pl.*

'moth·er-in-law [-ðərɪn-] *pl.* **'moth·ers-in-law** [-ðəzɪn-] *s.* Schwiegermutter *f*.

'moth·er·land → ***mother country***.

moth·er·less ['mʌðəlɪs] *adj.* mutterlos.

'moth·er·li·ness ['mʌðəlɪnɪs] *s.* Mütterlichkeit *f*.

moth·er| liq·uor *s.* ⚗ Mutterlauge *f*; ~ **lode** *s.* ⚒ Hauptader *f*.

moth·er·ly ['mʌðəlɪ] *adj. u. adv.* mütterlich.

moth·er| of pearl *s.* Perl'mutter *f*, Perl'mutt *n*; ˌ**~-of-'pearl** [-ðərəv'p-] *adj.* perl'muttern, Perlmutt…

moth·er| ship *s.* ⚓ *Brit.* Mutterschiff *n*; ~ **su·pe·ri·or** *s. eccl.* Oberin *f*, Äb'tissin *f*; **'~-tie** *s. psych.* Mutterbindung *f*; ~ **tongue** *s.* Muttersprache *f*; ~ **wit** *s.* Mutterwitz *m*.

moth·er·y ['mʌðərɪ] *adj.* hefig, trübe.

moth·y ['mɒθɪ] *adj.* **1.** voller Motten; **2.** mottenzerfressen.

mo·tif [məʊ'tiːf] *s.* **1.** ♪ ('Leit)Moˌtiv *n*; **2.** *paint. etc.*, *Literatur*: Mo'tiv *n*, Vorwurf *m*; **3.** *fig.* Leitgedanke *m*.

mo·tile ['məʊtaɪl] *adj. biol.* freibeweglich; **mo·til·i·ty** [məʊ'tɪlətɪ] *s.* selbständiges Bewegungsvermögen.

mo·tion ['məʊʃn] **I** *s.* **1.** Bewegung *f* (*a.*

phys., ⚗, ♪): ***go through the ~s of doing s.th.*** *fig.* et. mechanisch *od.* pro forma tun; **2.** Gang *m* (*a.* ⚙): ***set in ~*** in Gang bringen, in Bewegung setzen; → ***idle*** 3; **3.** (Körper-, Hand)Bewegung *f*, Wink *m*: ***~ of the head*** Zeichen *n* mit dem Kopf; **4.** Antrieb *m*: ***of one's own ~*** aus eigenem Antrieb, *a.* freiwillig; **5.** *pl.* Schritte *pl.*, Handlungen *pl.*: ***watch s.o.'s ~s***; **6.** ⚖, *parl. etc.* Antrag *m*: ***carry a ~*** e-n Antrag durchbringen; ***~ of no confidence*** Mißtrauensantrag *m*; **7.** *physiol.* Stuhlgang *m*; **II** *v/i.* **8.** winken (***with*** mit, ***to*** *dat.*); **III** *v/t.* **9.** *j-m* (zu)winken, *j-n* durch e-n Wink auffordern (***to do*** zu tun), *j-n wohin* winken; ˈ**mo·tion·less** [-lɪs] *adj.* bewegungslos, regungslos, unbeweglich.

mo·tion| pic·ture *s.* Film *m*; ˈ**~-ˌpic·ture** *adj.* Film…: ***~ camera***; ***~ projector*** Filmprojektor *m*; **~ stud·y** *s.* Bewegungs-, Rationalisierungsstudie *f*; **~ ther·a·py** *s.* ⚕ Beˈwegungstheraˌpie *f*.

mo·ti·vate [ˈməʊtɪveɪt] *v/t.* **1.** motivieren: a) *et.* begründen, b *j-n* anregen, anspornen; **2.** *et.* anregen, herˈvorrufen; **mo·ti·va·tion** [ˌməʊtɪˈveɪʃn] *s.* **1.** Motivierung *f*: a) Begründung *f*, b) Motivatiˈon *f*, Ansporn *m*, Antrieb *m*: ***~ research*** Motivforschung *f*; **2.** Anregung *f*.

mo·tive [ˈməʊtɪv] **I** *s.* **1.** Moˈtiv *n*, Beweggrund *m*, Antrieb *m* (***for*** zu); **2.** → ***motif*** 1 *u.* 2; **II** *adj.* **3.** bewegend, treibend (*a. fig.*): ***~ power*** Triebkraft *f*; **III** *v/t.* **4.** *mst pass.* der Beweggrund sein von, veranlassen: ***an act ~d by hatred*** e-e vom Haß diktierte Tat.

mo·tiv·i·ty [məʊˈtɪvətɪ] *s.* Bewegungsfähigkeit *f*, -kraft *f*.

mot·ley [ˈmɒtlɪ] **I** *adj.* **1.** bunt (*a. fig. Menge etc.*), scheckig; **II** *s.* **2.** *hist.* Narrenkleid *n*; **3.** Kunterbunt *n*.

mo·tor [ˈməʊtə] **I** *s.* **1.** ⚙ (*bsd.* Eˈlektro-, Verbrennungs)Motor *m*; **2.** *fig.* treibende Kraft; **3.** *bsd. Brit.* a) Kraftwagen *m*, Auto *n*, b) Motorfahrzeug *n*; **4.** *anat.* a) Muskel *m*, b) moˈtorischer Nerv; **II** *adj.* **5.** bewegend, (an)treibend; **6.** Motor…; **7.** Auto…; **8.** *anat.* moˈtorisch; **III** *v/i.* **9.** *mot.* fahren; **IV** *v/t.* **10.** in e-m Kraftfahrzeug befördern; **~ ac·ci·dent** *s.* Autounfall *m*; **~ am·bu·lance** *s.* Krankenwagen *m*, Ambuˈlanz *f*; ˈ**~-asˌsist·ed** *adj.*: ***~ bicycle*** a) Fahrrad *n* mit Hilfsmotor, b) Mofa *n*; **~ bi·cy·cle** → ***motorcycle***; ˈ**~·bike** F *für* ***motorcycle***; ˈ**~·boat** *s.* Motorboot *n*; ˈ**~·bus** *s.* Autobus *m*; ˈ**~·cade** [-keɪd] *s.* ˈAutokoˌlonne *f*; ˈ**~·car** *s.* **1.** Kraftwagen *m*, Auto(moˈbil) *n*: ***~ industry*** Automobilindustrie *f*; **2.** 🚃 Triebwagen *m*; **~ car·a·van** *s.* *Brit.* ˈWohnmoˌbil *n*; **~ coach** → ***coach*** 3; **~ court** → ***motel***; ˈ**~ˌcy·cle I** *s.* Motorrad *n*; **II** *v/i.* a) Motorrad fahren, b) mit dem Motorrad fahren; ˈ**~ˌcy·clist** *s.* Motorradfahrer(in); ˈ**~-ˌdriv·en** *adj.* mit Motorantrieb, Motor…; ˈ**~·drome** [-drəʊm] *s.* Motoˈdrom *n*.

mo·tored [ˈməʊtəd] *adj.* ⚙ **1.** motorisiert, mit e-m Motor *od.* mit Moˈtoren (versehen); **2.** …motorig.

mo·tor| en·gine *s.* ˈKraftmaˌschine *f*; **~ fit·ter** *s.* Autoschlosser *m*; **~ home** ˈWohnmoˌbil *n*.

mo·tor·ing [ˈməʊtərɪŋ] *s.* Autofahren *n*; Motorsport *m*: ***school of ~*** Fahrschule *f*; ˈ**mo·tor·ist** [-ɪst] *s.* Kraft-, Autofahrer(in).

mo·tor·i·za·tion [ˌməʊtəraɪˈzeɪʃn] *s.* Motorisierung *f*; **mo·tor·ize** [ˈməʊtəraɪz] *v/t.* ⚙ *u.* ⚔ motorisieren: ***~d unit*** ⚔ (voll)motorisierte Einheit.

mo·tor launch *s.* ˈMotorbarˌkasse *f*.

mo·tor·less [ˈməʊtəlɪs] *adj.* motorlos: ***~ flight*** Segelflug *m*.

mo·tor| lor·ry *s. Brit.* Lastkraftwagen *m*; ˈ**~·man** [-mən] *s.* [*irr.*] Wagenführer *m*; **~ me·chan·ic** *s.* ˈAutomeˌchaniker *m*; **~ nerve** *s. anat.* moˈtorischer Nerv, Bewegungsnerv *m*; **~ oil** *s.* Motoröl *n*; **~ pool** *s.* Fahrbereitschaft *f*; **~ road** *s.* Autostraße *f*; **~ scoot·er** *s.* Motorroller *m*; **~ ship** *s.* Motorschiff *n*; **~ show** *s.* Automoˈbilausstellung *f*; **~ start·er** *s.* (Motor)Anlasser *m*; **~ tor·pe·do boat** *s.* ⚓, ⚔ Schnellboot *n*; **~ trac·tor** *s.* Traktor *m*, Schlepper *m*, ˈZugmaˌschine *f*; **~ truck** *s.* **1.** *bsd. Am.* Lastkraftwagen *m*; **2.** ⚡ Eˈlektrokarren *m*; **~ van** *s. Brit.* Lieferwagen *m*; **~ ve·hi·cle** *s.* Kraftfahrzeug *n*; ˈ**~·way** *s. Brit.* Autobahn *f*.

mot·tle [ˈmɒtl] *v/t.* sprenkeln, marmorieren; ˈ**mot·tled** [-ld] *adj.* gesprenkelt, gefleckt, bunt.

mot·to [ˈmɒtəʊ] *pl.* **-toes**, **-tos** *s.* Motto *n*, Wahl-, Sinnspruch *m*.

mou·jik [ˈmuːʒɪk] → ***muzhik***.

mould[1] [məʊld] **I** *s.* **1.** ⚙ (Gieß-, Guß-) Form *f*: ***cast in the same ~*** *fig.* aus demselben Holz geschnitzt; **2.** (Körper-) Bau *m*, Gestalt *f*, (*äußere*) Form; **3.** Art *f*, Naˈtur *f*, Chaˈrakter *m*; **4.** ⚙ a) Hohlform *f*, b) Preßform *f*, c) Koˈkille *f*, Hartgußform *f*, d) Maˈtrize *f*, e) (ˈForm)Moˌdell *n*, f) Gesenk *n*; **5.** ⚙ a) ˈGußmateriˌal *n*, b) Guß(stück *n*) *m*; **6.** *Schiffbau*: Mall *n*; **7.** ⚠ a) Sims *m*, *n*, b) Leiste *f*, c) Hohlkehle *f*; **8.** *Küche*: Form *f* (*für Speisen*): ***jelly ~*** Puddingform; **9.** *geol.* Abdruck *m* (*Versteinerung*); **II** *v/t.* **10.** ⚙ gießen; (ab)formen, modellieren; pressen; *Holz* profilieren; ⚓ abmallen; **11.** formen (*a. fig. Charakter*), bilden, gestalten (***on*** nach dem Muster von); **III** *v/i.* **12.** Gestalt annehmen, sich formen.

mould[2] [məʊld] **I** *s.* **1.** Schimmel *m*, Moder *m*; **2.** ⚘ Schimmelpilz *m*; **II** *v/i.* **3.** schimm(e)lig werden, (ver)schimmeln.

mould[3] [məʊld] *s.* **1.** lockere Erde, Gartenerde *f*; **2.** Humus(boden) *m*.

mould·a·ble [ˈməʊldəbl] *adj.* (ver-) formbar, bildsam: ***~ material*** ⚙ Preßmasse *f*.

mould·er[1] [ˈməʊldə] *s.* **1.** ⚙ Former *m*, Gießer *m*; **2.** *fig.* Gestalter(in).

mould·er[2] [ˈməʊldə] *v/i. a.* ***~ away*** vermodern, (*zu Staub*) zerfallen.

mould·i·ness [ˈməʊldɪnɪs] *s.* Moder *m*, Schimm(e)ligkeit *f*; (*a. fig.*) Schalheit *f*; *fig. sl.* Fadheit *f*.

mould·ing [ˈməʊldɪŋ] *s.* **1.** Formen *n*, Formgebung *f*; **2.** Formgießeˈrei *f*, -arbeit *f*; Modellieren *n*; **3.** Formstück *n*; Preßteil *n*; **4.** → ***mould***[1] 7; **~ board** *s.* **1.** Formbrett *n*; **2.** *Küche*: Kuchen-, Nudelbrett *n*; **~ clay** *s.* ⚙ Formerde *f*, -ton *m*; **~ ma·chine** *s.* **1.** *Holzbearbeitung*: ˈKehl(hobel)maˌschine *f*; **2.** *metall.* ˈFormmaˌschine *f*; **3.** ˈSpritzmaˌschine *f* (*für Spritzguß etc.*); **~ press** *s.* Formpresse *f*; **~ sand** *s.* Formsand *m*.

mould·y [ˈməʊldɪ] *adj.* **1.** schimm(e)lig; **2.** Schimmel…, schimmelartig: ***~ fungi*** Schimmelpilze; **3.** muffig, schal (*a. fig.*), *sl.* fad.

moult [məʊlt] *zo.* **I** *v/i.* (sich) mausern (*a. fig.*); sich häuten; **II** *v/t.* *Federn, Haut* abwerfen, verlieren; **III** *s.* Mauser(ung) *f*; Häutung *f*.

mound[1] [maʊnd] *s.* **1.** Erdwall *m*, -hügel *m*; **2.** Damm *m*; **3.** *Baseball*: Abwurfstelle *f*.

mound[2] [maʊnd] *s. hist.* Reichsapfel *m*.

mount[1] [maʊnt] **I** *v/t.* **1.** *Berg, Pferd, Barrikaden etc., fig. den Thron* besteigen; *Treppen* hinˈaufgehen, ersteigen; *Fluß* hinˈauffahren; **2.** beritten machen: ***~ troops***; ***~ed police*** berittene Polizei; **3.** errichten; *a. Maschine* aufstellen, montieren (*a. phot., TV*); anbringen, einbauen, befestigen; *Papier, Bild* aufkleben, -ziehen; *Edelstein* fassen; *Messer etc.* mit e-m Griff versehen, stielen; ⚕ *Versuchsobjekt* präparieren; *Präparat im Mikroskop* fixieren; **4.** zs.-bauen, -stellen, arrangieren; *thea. Stück* inszenieren, *fig. a.* aufziehen; **5.** ⚔ a) *Geschütz* in Stellung bringen, b) *Posten* aufstellen; → ***guard*** 9; **6.** ⚓ bewaffnet sein mit, *Geschütz* führen; **II** *v/i.* **7.** (auf-, emˈpor-, hoch)steigen; **8.** *fig.* (an)wachsen, steigen, sich auftürmen (*bsd. Schulden, Schwierigkeiten etc.*): ***~ing suspense*** (***debts***) wachsende Spannung (Schulden); **9.** *oft* ***~ up*** sich belaufen (***to*** auf *acc.*); **III** *s.* **10.** Gestell *n*; ⚙ Ständer *m*, Halterung *f*, ˈUntersatz *m*; Fassung *f*; (Wechsel)Rahmen *m*, Passeparˈtout *n*; ˈAufziehkarˌton *m*; ⚔ (Geˈschütz)Laˌfette *f*; Obˈjektträger *m* (*Mikroskop*); **11.** Pferd *n*, Reittier *n*.

mount[2] [maʊnt] *s.* **1.** *poet.* a) Berg *m*, b) Hügel *m*; **2.** ♀ (*in Eigennamen*) Berg *m*: ***♀ Sinai***; ***♀ of Venus*** *Handlesekunst f*: Venusberg *m*.

moun·tain [ˈmaʊntɪn] **I** *s.* Berg *m* (*a. fig. von Arbeit etc.*); *pl.* Gebirge *n*: ***make a ~ out of a molehill*** aus e-r Mücke e-n Elefanten machen; **II** *adj.* Berg…, Gebirgs…: ***~ artillery*** Gebirgsartillerie *f*; **~ ash** *s. e-e* Eberesche *f*; **~ bike** *s.* Mountain bike *n*, Geländefahrrad *n*; **~ chain** *s.* Berg-, Gebirgskette *f*; **~ crys·tal** *s.* ˈBergkriˌstall *m*; **~ cock** *s.* Auerhahn *m*.

moun·tained [ˈmaʊntɪnd] *adj.* bergig, gebirgig.

moun·tain·eer [ˌmaʊntɪˈnɪə] **I** *s.* **1.** Bergbewohner(in); **2.** Bergsteiger(in); **II** *v/i.* **3.** bergsteigen; ˌ**moun·tainˈeer·ing** [-ˈnɪərɪŋ] **I** *s.* Bergsteigen *n*; **II** *adj.* bergsteigerisch; **moun·tain·ous** [ˈmaʊntɪnəs] *adj.* **1.** bergig, gebirgig; **2.** Berg…, Gebirgs…; **3.** *fig.* riesig, gewaltig.

moun·tain| rail·way *s.* Bergbahn *f*; **~ range** *s.* Gebirgszug *m*, -kette *f*; **~ sick·ness** *s.* ⚕ Berg-, Höhenkrankheit *f*; ˈ**~·side** *s.* Berg(ab)hang *m*; **~ slide** *s.* Bergrutsch *m*; **♀ State** *s. Am.* (*Beiname für*) a) Monˈtana *n*, b) West Virˈginia *n* (*USA*); **~ troops** *s. pl.* Gebirgstruppen *pl.*; **~ wood** *s.* ˈHolzasˌbest *m*.

moun·te·bank [ˈmaʊntɪbæŋk] *s.* **1.** Quacksalber *m*; Marktschreier *m*; **2.** Scharlatan *m*.

mount·ing ['maʊntɪŋ] *s.* **1.** ⚙ a) Einbau *m*, Aufstellung *f*, Mon'tage *f* (*a. phot., TV etc.*), b) Gestell *n*, Rahmen *m*, c) Befestigung *f*, Aufhängung *f*, d) (Auf-) Lagerung *f*, e) Arma'tur *f*, f) (Ein)Fassung *f* (*Edelstein*), g) Ausstattung *f*, h) *pl.* Fenster-, Türbeschläge *pl.*, i) *pl.* Gewirre *n* (*an Türschlössern*), j) (*Weberei*) Geschirr *n*, Zeug *n*; **2.** ϟ (Ver-) Schaltung *f*, Installati'on *f*; **~ brack·et** *s.* Befestigungsschelle *f*.

mourn [mɔ:n] **I** *v/i.* **1.** trauern, klagen (***at, over*** über *acc.*; ***for, over*** um); **2.** Trauer(kleidung) tragen, trauern; **II** *v/t.* **3.** *j-n* betrauern, *a. et.* beklagen, trauern um *j-n*; '**mourn·er** [-nə] *s.* Trauernde(r *m*) *f*, Leidtragende(r *m*) *f*; '**mourn·ful** [-fʊl] *adj.* □ trauervoll, traurig, düster, Trauer…

mourn·ing ['mɔ:nɪŋ] **I** *s.* **1.** Trauer(n *n*) *f*; ***national ~*** Staatstrauer; **2.** Trauer (-kleidung) *f*: ***in ~*** in Trauer; ***go into*** (***out of***) ***~*** Trauer anlegen (die Trauer ablegen); **II** *adj.* □ **3.** trauernd; **4.** Trauer…: **~ *band*** Trauerband *n*, -flor *m*; **~ bor·der**, **~ edge** *s.* Trauerrand *m*; **~ pa·per** *s.* Pa'pier *n* mit Trauerrand.

mouse [maʊs] **I** *pl.* **mice** [maɪs] *s.* **1.** *zo.*, *a. Computer*: Maus *f*: ***~trap*** Mausefalle *f* (*a. fig.*); **2.** ⚙ Zugleine *f* mit Gewicht; **3.** F Feigling *m*; **4.** *sl.* ‚blaues Auge', ‚Veilchen' *n*; **II** *v/i.* [maʊz] **5.** mausen, Mäuse fangen; '**~-ˌcol·o(u)red** *adj.* mausfarbig, -grau.

mousse [mu:s] *s.* Schaumspeise *f*.

mous·tache [mə'stɑ:ʃ] *s.* Schnurrbart *m* (*a. zo.*).

mous·y ['maʊsɪ] *adj.* **1.** von Mäusen heimgesucht; **2.** mausartig; mausgrau; **3.** *fig.* grau, trüb; **4.** *fig.* leise; furchtsam; farblos; unscheinbar.

mouth [maʊθ] **I** *pl.* **mouths** [maʊðz] *s.* **1.** Mund *m*: ***give ~*** Laut geben, anschlagen (*Hund*); ***by word*** (*od.* ***way***) ***of ~*** mündlich; ***keep one's ~ shut*** F den Mund halten; ***shut s.o.'s ~*** j-m den Mund stopfen; ***stop s.o.'s ~*** j-m (durch Bestechung) den Mund stopfen; ***down in the ~*** F niedergeschlagen, bedrückt; → ***wrong*** 2; **2.** Maul *n*, Schnauze *f*, Rachen *m* (*Tier*); **3.** Mündung *f* (*Fluß, Kanone etc.*); Öffnung *f* (*Flasche, Sack*); Ein-, Ausgang *m* (*Höhle, Röhre etc.*); Ein-, Ausfahrt *f* (*Hafen etc.*); ♪ → ***mouthpiece*** 1; **4.** ⚙ a) Mundloch *n*, b) Schnauze *f*, c) Öffnung *f*, d) Gichtöffnung *f* (*Hochofen*), e) Abstichloch *n* (*Hoch-, Schmelzofen*); **II** *v/t.* [maʊð] **5.** (*bsd.* affek'tiert *od.* gespreizt) (aus-) sprechen; **6.** *Worte* (*unhörbar*) mit den Lippen formen; **7.** in den Mund *od.* ins Maul nehmen; '**mouth·ful** [-fʊl] *pl.* **-fuls** *s.* **1.** *ein* Mundvoll *m*, Brocken *m* (*a. fig. ellenlanges Wort*); **2.** kleine Menge; **3.** *sl.* großes Wort.

'**mouth|-ˌor·gan** *s.* ♪ **1.** 'Mundharˌmonika *f*; **2.** Panflöte *f*; '**~·piece** *s.* **1.** ♪ Mundstück *n*, Ansatz *m*; **2.** ⚙ a) Schalltrichter *m*, Sprechmuschel *f*, b) Mundstück *n* (*a. e-r Tabakspfeife od. Gasmaske*), Tülle *f*; **3.** *fig.* Sprachrohr *n* (*a. Person*); ⚖ *sl.* (Straf)Verteidiger *m*; **4.** Gebiß *n* (*Pferdezaum*); **5.** *Boxen*: Zahnschutz *m*; **ˌ~-to-'~ res·pi·ra·tion** *s.* ⚕ Mund-zu-Mund-Beatmung *f*; '**~·wash** *s.* Mundwasser *n*; '**~-ˌwa·ter·ing** *adj.* lecker.

mov·a·bil·i·ty [ˌmu:və'bɪlətɪ] *s.* Beweglichkeit *f*, Bewegbarkeit *f*.

mov·a·ble ['mu:vəbl] **I** *adj.* □ **1.** beweglich (*a.* ⚙; *a.* ⚖ *Eigentum, Feiertag*), bewegbar: **~ *goods*** → 5; **2.** a) verschiebbar, verstellbar, b) fahrbar; **3.** ⚒ ortsveränderlich; **II** *s.* **4.** *pl.* Möbel *pl.*; **5.** *pl.* ⚖ Mo'bilien *pl.*, bewegliche Habe; **~ kid·ney** *s.* ⚕ Wanderniere *f*.

move [mu:v] **I** *v/t.* **1.** fortbewegen, -rükken, von der Stelle bewegen, verschieben; ⚔ *Einheit* verlegen: **~ *up*** a) *Truppen* heranbringen, b) *ped. Brit. Schüler* versetzen; F **~ *it*** Tempo!; **2.** entfernen, fortbringen, -schaffen; **3.** bewegen (*a. fig.*), in Bewegung setzen *od.* halten, (an)treiben: **~ *on*** vorwärtstreiben; **4.** *fig.* bewegen, rühren, ergreifen: ***be ~d to tears*** zu Tränen gerührt sein; **5.** *j-n* veranlassen, bewegen, hinreißen (***to*** zu): **~ *to anger*** erzürnen; **6.** *Schach etc.*: e-n Zug machen mit, ziehen; **7.** *et.* beantragen, Antrag stellen auf (*acc.*), vorschlagen: **~ *an amendment*** *parl.* e-n Abänderungsantrag stellen; **8.** *Antrag* stellen, einbringen; **II** *v/i.* **9.** sich bewegen, sich rühren, sich regen; ⚙ laufen, in Gang sein (*Maschine etc.*); **10.** sich fortbewegen, gehen, fahren: **~ *on*** weitergehen: **~ *with the times*** *fig.* mit der Zeit gehen; **11.** sich entfernen, abziehen, abmarschieren; *wegen Wohnungswechsels* ('um)ziehen (***to*** nach): **~ *in*** einziehen; ***if ~d*** falls verzogen; **12.** fortschreiten, weitergehen (*Vorgang*); **13.** verkehren, sich bewegen: **~ *in good society***; **14.** a) vorgehen, Schritte unter'nehmen (***in s.th.*** in e-r Sache, ***against*** gegen), b) *a.* **~ *in*** handeln, zupacken, losschlagen: ***he ~d quickly***; **15.** **~ *for*** beantragen, (e-n) Antrag'stellen auf (*acc.*); **~ *that*** beantragen, daß; **16.** *Schach etc.*: e-n Zug machen, ziehen; **17.** ⚕ sich entleeren (*Darm*); **18.** **~ *up*** ⚚ anziehen, steigen (*Preise*); **III** *s.* **19.** (Fort)Bewegung *f*, Aufbruch *m*: ***on the ~*** in Bewegung, auf den Beinen; ***get a ~ on!*** *sl.* Tempo!, mach(t) schon!; ***make a ~*** a) aufbrechen, sich (von der Stelle) rühren, b) → 14 b; **20.** 'Umzug *m*; **21.** *Schach etc.*: Zug *m*; *fig.* Schritt *m*, Maßnahme *f*: ***a clever ~*** ein kluger Schachzug (*od.* Schritt); ***make the first ~*** den ersten Schritt tun; '**move·ment** [-mənt] *s.* **1.** Bewegung *f* (*a. fig., pol., eccl., paint. etc.*); ⚔, ⚓ (Truppen- *od.* Flotten)Bewegung *f*: **~ *by air*** Lufttransport *m*; **2.** *mst pl.* Handeln *n*, Schritte *pl.*, Maßnahmen *pl.*; **3.** (rasche) Entwicklung, Fortschreiten *n* (*von Ereignissen, e-r Handlung*); **4.** Bestrebung *f*, Ten'denz *f*, (mo'derne) Richtung; **5.** ♪ a) Satz *m*: ***a ~ of a sonata***, b) Tempo *n*; **6.** ⚙ a) Bewegung *f*, b) Lauf *m* (*Maschine*), c) Gang-, Gehwerk *n* (*der Uhr*), 'Antriebsmechaˌnismus *m*; **7.** *a.* **~ *of the bowels*** ⚕ Stuhlgang *m*; **8.** ⚚ (Kurs-, Preis)Bewegung *f*; 'Umsatz *m* (*Börse, Markt*): ***downward ~*** Senkung *f*, Fallen *n*; ***retrograde ~*** rückläufige Bewegung; ***upward ~*** Steigen *n*, Aufwärtsbewegung *f* (*der Preise*); '**mov·er** [-və] *s.* **1.** *fig.* treibende Kraft, Triebkraft *f*, Antrieb *m* (*a. Person*); **2.** ⚙ Triebwerk *n*, Motor *m*; → ***prime mover***; **3.** Antragsteller(in); **4.** *Am.* a) Spedi'teur *m*, b) (Möbel)Packer *m*.

mov·ie ['mu:vɪ] *Am.* F **I** *s.* **1.** Film(streifen) *m*; **2.** *pl.* a) Filmwesen *n*, b) Kino *n*, c) Kinovorstellung *f*: ***go to the ~s*** ins Kino gehen; **II** *adj.* **3.** Film…, Kino…, Lichtspiel…: **~ *camera*** Filmkamera *f*; **~ *projector*** Filmprojektor *m*; **~ *star*** Filmstar *m*; '**~-ˌgo·er** *s. Am.* F Kinobesucher(in).

mov·ing ['mu:vɪŋ] *adj.* □ **1.** beweglich, sich bewegend; **2.** bewegend, treibend: **~ *power*** treibende Kraft; **3.** a) rührend, bewegend, b) eindringlich, packend; **~ coil** *s.* ϟ Drehspule *f*; **~ magnet** *s.* 'Drehmaˌgnet *m*; **~ pic·ture** F → ***motion picture***; **~ stair·case** *s.* Rolltreppe *f*; **~ van** *s.* Möbelwagen *m*.

mow[1] [məʊ] **I** *v/t.* [*a. irr.*] (ab)mähen, schneiden: **~ *down*** niedermähen (*a. fig.*); **II** *v/i.* [*a. irr.*] mähen.

mow[2] [maʊ] *s.* **1.** Getreidegarbe *f*, Heuhaufen *m*; **2.** Heu-, Getreideboden *m*.

mow·er ['məʊə] *s.* **1.** Mäher(in), Schnitter(in); **2.** a) Rasenmäher *m*, b) → '**mow·ing-maˌchine** ['məʊɪŋ-] *s.* 'MähmaˌSchine *f*.

mown [məʊn] *p.p. von* **mow**[1].

Mr, **Mr.** → ***mister*** 1.

Mrs, **Mrs.** ['mɪsɪz] *s.* Frau *f* (*Anrede für verheiratete Frauen*): ***Mrs Smith***.

Ms, **Ms.** [mɪz] *Anrede für Frauen ohne Berücksichtigung des Familienstandes*.

mu [mju:] *s.* My *n* (*griechischer Buchstabe*).

much [mʌtʃ] **I** *s.* **1.** Menge *f*, große Sache, Besondere(s) *n*: ***nothing ~*** nichts Besonderes; ***it did not come to ~*** es kam nicht viel dabei heraus; ***think ~ of s.o.*** viel von j-m halten; ***he is not ~ of a dancer*** er ist kein großer Tänzer; → ***make*** 21; **II** *adj.* **2.** viel: ***too ~*** zu viel; **III** *adv.* **3.** sehr: **~ *to my regret*** sehr zu m-m Bedauern; **4.** (*in Zssgn*) viel…: **~-*admired***; **5.** (*vor comp.*) viel, weit: **~ *stronger***; **6.** (*vor sup.*) bei weitem, weitaus: **~ *the oldest***; **7.** fast: ***he did it in ~ the same way*** er tat es auf ungefähr die gleiche Weise; ***it is ~ the same thing*** es ist ziemlich dasselbe;

Besondere Redewendungen:

~ *as I would like* so gern ich (auch) möchte; ***as ~ as*** so viel wie; ***he did not as ~ as write*** er schrieb nicht einmal; ***as ~ again*** noch einmal soviel; ***he said as ~*** das war (ungefähr) der Sinn s-r Worte; ***this is as ~ as to say*** das heißt mit anderen Worten; ***as ~ as to say*** als wenn er (*etc.*) sagen wollte; ***I thought as ~*** das habe ich mir gedacht; ***so ~*** a) so sehr, b) so viel, c) lauter, nichts als; ***so ~ the better*** um so besser; ***so ~ for our plans*** soviel (wäre also) zu unseren Plänen (zu sagen); ***not so ~ as*** nicht einmal; ***without so ~ as to move*** ohne sich auch nur zu bewegen; ***so ~ so*** (und zwar) so sehr; **~ *less*** a) viel weniger, b) geschweige denn; **~ *like a child*** ganz wie ein Kind.

much·ly ['mʌtʃlɪ] *adv. obs. od. humor.* sehr, viel, besonders; '**much·ness** [-tʃnɪs] *s.* große Menge: ***much of a ~*** F ziemlich *od.* praktisch dasselbe.

mu·ci·lage ['mju:sɪlɪdʒ] *s.* **1.** ⚘ (Pflanzen)Schleim *m*; **2.** *bsd. Am.* Klebstoff *m*, Gummilösung *f*; **mu·ci·lag·i·nous** [ˌmju:sɪ'lædʒɪnəs] *adj.* **1.** schleimig; **2.** klebrig.

muck [mʌk] **I** *s.* **1.** Mist *m*, Dung *m*; **2.**

Kot *m*, Dreck *m*, Unrat *m*, Schmutz *m* (*a. fig.*); **3.** *Brit.* F Blödsinn *m*, ‚Mist' *m*: ***make a ~ of*** → 6; **II** *v/t.* **4.** düngen; *a.* ***~ out*** ausmisten; **5.** *oft* ***~ up*** F beschmutzen; **6.** *sl.* verpfuschen, verhunzen, ‚vermasseln'; **III** *v/i.* **7.** *mst* ***~ about*** *sl.* a) her'umlungern, b) her'umpfuschen (***with*** an *dat.*), c) her'umalbern; **8.** ***~ in*** F mit anpacken; **'muck·er** [-kə] *s.* **1.** *sl.* a) ‚Blödmann' *m*, b) ‚Kumpel' *m*; **2.** ⚒ Lader *m*: ***~'s car*** Minenhund *m*; **3.** *sl.* a) schwerer Sturz, b) *fig.* ‚Reinfall' *m*: ***come a ~*** auf die ‚Schnauze' fallen, *fig. a.* ‚reinfallen'.

'muck|-hill *s.* Mist-, Dreckhaufen *m*; **'~-rake** *v/i. fig.* im Schmutz her'umwühlen; *Am. sl.* Skan'dale aufdecken; **'~,rak·er** *s. Am.* Skan'dalmacher *m*.

muck·y ['mʌkɪ] *adj.* schmutzig, dreckig (*a. fig.*).

mu·cous ['mju:kəs] *adj.* schleimig, Schleim...: ***~ membrane*** Schleimhaut *f*; **'mu·cus** [-kəs] *s. biol.* Schleim *m*.

mud [mʌd] *s.* **1.** Schlamm *m*, Matsch *m*: ***~ and snow tyres*** (*Am.* ***tires***) *mot.* Matsch-u.-Schnee-Reifen; **2.** Mo'rast *m*, Kot *m*, Schmutz *m* (*alle a. fig.*): ***drag in the ~*** *fig.* in den Schmutz ziehen; ***stick in the ~*** im Schlamm steckenbleiben, *fig.* aus dem Dreck nicht mehr herauskommen; ***sling*** (*od.* ***throw***) ***~ at s.o.*** *fig.* j-n mit Schmutz bewerfen; ***his name is ~ with me*** er ist für mich erledigt; ***~ in your eye!*** F prost!; → ***clear*** 1; **'~-bath** *s.* ⚕ Moor-, Schlammbad *n*.

mud·di·ness ['mʌdɪnɪs] *s.* **1.** Schlammigkeit *f*, Trübheit *f* (*a. des Lichts*); **2.** Schmutzigkeit *f*.

mud·dle ['mʌdl] **I** *s.* **1.** Durchein'ander *n*, Unordnung *f*, Wirrwarr *m*: ***make a ~ of s.th.*** et. durcheinanderbringen *od.* ‚vermasseln'; ***get into a ~*** in Schwierigkeiten geraten; **2.** Verworrenheit *f*, Unklarheit *f*: ***be in a ~*** in Verwirrung *od.* verwirrt sein; **II** *v/t.* **3.** *Gedanken etc.* verwirren: ***~ up*** verwechseln, durcheinanderwerfen; **4.** in Unordnung bringen, durchein'anderbringen; **5.** ‚benebeln' (*bsd. durch Alkohol*): ***~ one's brains*** sich benebeln; **6.** verpfuschen, verderben; **III** *v/i.* **7.** pfuschen, stümpern, ‚wursteln': ***~ about*** herumwursteln (***with*** an *dat.*); ***~ on*** weiterwursteln; ***~ through*** sich durchwursteln; **'mud·dle·dom** [-dəm] *s. humor.* Durchein'ander *n*; **'mud·dle-,head·ed** *adj.* wirr (-köpfig), kon'fus; **'mud·dler** [-lə] *s.* **1.** j-d, der sich 'durchwurstelt; Wirrkopf *m*; Pfuscher *m*; **2.** *Am.* ('Um)Rührlöffel *m*.

mud·dy ['mʌdɪ] **I** *adj.* ☐ **1.** schlammig, trüb(e) (*a. Licht*); Schlamm...: ***~ soil***; **2.** schmutzig; **3.** *fig.* unklar, verworren, kon'fus; **4.** verschwommen (*Farbe*); **II** *v/t.* **5.** trüben; **6.** beschmutzen.

'mud|·guard *s.* **1.** a) *mot.* Kotflügel *m*, b) Schutzblech *n* (*Fahrrad*); **2.** ⚙ Schmutzfänger *m*; **'~-hole** *s.* **1.** Schlammloch *n*; **2.** ⚙ Schlammablaß *m*; **'~-lark** *s.* Gassenjunge *m*, Dreckspatz *m*; ***~ pack*** *s.* ⚕ Fangopackung *f*; **'~,sling·er** [-,slɪŋə] *s.* F Verleumder (-in); **'~,sling·ing** [-,slɪŋɪŋ] F **I** *s.* Beschmutzung *f*, Verleumdung *f*; **II** *adj.* verleumderisch.

muff [mʌf] **I** *s.* **1.** Muff *m*; **2.** F *sport. u. fig.* ‚Patzer' *m*; **3.** F ‚Flasche' *f*, Stümper *m*; **4.** ⚙ a) Stutzen *m*, b) Muffe *f*; **II** *v/t.* **5.** F *sport u. fig.* ‚verpatzen'; **III** *v/i.* **6.** F ‚patzen'.

muf·fin ['mʌfɪn] *s.* Muffin *n*: a) *Brit.* Hefeteigsemmel *f*, b) *Am. kleine süße Semmel*.

muf·fle ['mʌfl] **I** *v/t.* **1.** *oft* ***~ up*** einhüllen, einwickeln; *Ruder* um'wickeln; **2.** *Ton etc.* dämpfen (*a. fig.*); **II** *s.* **3.** *metall.* Muffel *f*: ***~ furnace*** Muffelofen *m*; **4.** ⚙ Flaschenzug *m*; **'muf·fler** [-lə] *s.* **1.** (dicker) Schal *m*, Halstuch *n*; **2.** ⚙ Schalldämpfer *m*; *mot.* Auspufftopf *m*; ♪ Dämpfer *m*.

muf·ti ['mʌftɪ] *s.* **1.** Mufti *m*; **2.** ⚔ Zi'vilkleidung *f*: ***in ~*** in Zivil.

mug [mʌg] **I** *s.* **1.** Krug *m*; **2.** Becher *m*; **3.** *sl.* a) Vi'sage *f*, Gesicht *n*: ***~ shot*** Kopfbild *n* (*bsd. für das Verbrecheralbum*), *Film etc.*: Großaufnahme *f*, b) ‚Fresse' *f*, Mund *m*, c) Gri'masse *f*; **4.** *Brit. sl.* a) Trottel *m*, b) Büffler *m*, Streber *m*; **5.** *Am. sl.* a) Boxer *m*, b) Ga'nove *m*; **II** *v/t.* **6.** *sl. bsd. Verbrecher* fotografieren; **7.** *sl.* über'fallen, niederschlagen u. ausrauben; **8.** *a.* ***~ up*** *Brit. sl.* ‚büffeln', ‚ochsen'; **III** *v/i.* **9.** *sl.* Gri'massen schneiden; **10.** *Am. sl.* ‚schmusen'; **'mug·ger** [-gə] *s. sl.* Straßenräuber *m*.

mug·gi·ness ['mʌgɪnɪs] *s.* **1.** Schwüle *f*; **2.** Muffigkeit *f*; **'mug·ging** [-gɪŋ] *s. sl.* 'Raub,überfall *m* (auf der Straße); **mug·gy** ['mʌgɪ] *adj.* **1.** schwül (*Wetter*); **2.** dumpfig, muffig.

'mug·wort *s.* ⚘ Beifuß *m*.

mug·wump ['mʌgwʌmp] *s. Am.* **1.** F ‚hohes Tier'; **2.** *pol. sl.* a) Unabhängige(r *m*) *f*, Einzelgänger(in), b) ‚Re'bell(in)', Abtrünnige(r *m*) *f*.

mu·lat·to [mju:'lætəʊ] **I** *pl.* **-toes** *s.* Mu'latte *m*, Mu'lattin *f*; **II** *adj.* Mulatten...

mul·ber·ry ['mʌlbərɪ] *s.* **1.** Maulbeerbaum *m*; **2.** Maulbeere *f*.

mulch [mʌltʃ] ⚘ **I** *s.* Mulch *m*; **II** *v/t.* mulchen.

mulct [mʌlkt] **I** *s.* **1.** Geldstrafe *f*; **II** *v/t.* **2.** mit e-r Geldstrafe belegen; **3.** a) *j-n* betrügen (***of*** um), b) *Geld etc.* ‚abknöpfen' (***from s.o.*** j-m).

mule [mju:l] *s.* **1.** *zo.* a) Maultier *n*, b) Maulesel *m*; **2.** *biol.* Bastard *m*, Hy'bride *f*; **3.** *fig.* sturer Kerl, Dickkopf *m*; **4.** ⚙ a) (Motor)Schlepper *m*, Traktor *m*, b) 'Förderlokomo,tive *f*, c) 'Mule-(spinn)ma,schine *f* (*Spinnerei*); **5.** Pan'toffel *m*; **'mule-,jen·ny** → ***mule*** 4 c; **mule skin·ner**, *Am.* F **mu·le·teer** [,mju:lɪ'tɪə] *s.* Maultiertreiber *m*; **mule track** *s.* Saumpfad *m*.

mul·ish ['mju:lɪʃ] *adj.* ☐ störrisch, stur.

mull¹ [mʌl] **I** *v/t.* F verpatzen, verpfuschen; **II** *v/i.* ***~ over*** F *Am.* nachdenken, -grübeln über (*acc.*).

mull² [mʌl] *v/t. Getränk* heiß machen u. (süß) würzen: ***~ed wine*** Glühwein *m*.

mull³ [mʌl] *s.* (⚕ Verband)Mull *m*.

mull⁴ [mʌl] *s. Scot.* Vorgebirge *n*.

mul·la(h) ['mʌlə] *s. eccl.* Mulla *m*.

mul·le(i)n ['mʌlɪn] *s.* ⚘ Königskerze *f*, Wollkraut *n*.

mull·er ['mʌlə] *s.* ⚙ Reibstein *m*.

mul·let ['mʌlɪt] *s. ichth.* **1.** *a.* ***grey ~*** Meeräsche *f*; **2.** *a.* ***red ~*** Seebarbe *f*.

mul·li·gan ['mʌlɪgən] *s. Am.* F Eintopfgericht *n*.

mul·li·ga·taw·ny [,mʌlɪgə'tɔ:nɪ] *s.* Currysuppe *f*.

mul·li·grubs ['mʌlɪgrʌbz] *s. pl.* F **1.** Bauchweh *n*; **2.** miese Laune.

mul·lion ['mʌlɪən] *s.* △ Mittelpfosten *m* (*Fenster etc.*).

mul·tan·gu·lar [mʌl'tæŋgjʊlə] *adj.* vielwink(e)lig, -eckig.

mul·te·i·ty [mʌl'ti:ətɪ] *s.* Vielheit *f*.

multi- [mʌltɪ] *in Zssgn*: viel..., mehr..., ...reich, Mehrfach..., Multi...

mul·ti ['mʌltɪ] *s.* ☨ F ‚Multi' *m*.

'mul·ti,ax·le drive *s. mot.* Mehrachsenantrieb *m*; **'mul·ti,col·o(u)r**, **'mul·ti-,col·o(u)red** *adj.* mehrfarbig, Mehrfarben...; **,mul·ti'en·gine(d)** *adj.* 'mehrmo,torig.

mul·ti·far·i·ous [,mʌltɪ'feərɪəs] *adj.* ☐ mannigfaltig.

'mul·ti·form *adj.* vielförmig, -gestaltig; **'mul·ti·graph** *typ.* **I** *s.* Ver'vielfältigungsma,schine *f*; **II** *v/t. u. v/i.* vervielfältigen; **'mul·ti·grid tube** *s.* ϟ Mehrgitterröhre *f*; **,mul·ti'lat·er·al** *adj.* **1.** vielseitig (*a. fig.*); **2.** *pol.* mehrseitig, multilate'ral; **,mul·ti'lin·gual** *adj.* mehrsprachig; **,mul·ti'me·di·a** *s. pl.* Medienverbund *m*, Multi'media *pl.*; **,mul·ti·mil·lion'aire** *s.* 'Multimillio,när *m*; **,mul·ti'na·tion·al** **I** *adj. bsd.* ☨ multinatio'nal; **II** *s.* multinatio'naler Kon'zern, ‚Multi' *m*; **mul·tip·a·rous** [mʌl'tɪpərəs] *adj.* mehrgebärend; **,mul·ti'par·tite** *adj.* **1.** vielteilig; **2.** → ***multilateral*** 2.

mul·ti·ple ['mʌltɪpl] **I** *adj.* ☐ **1.** viel-, mehrfach; **2.** mannigfaltig; **3.** *biol.*, ⚕, 𝒜 mul'tipel; **4.** ⚙, ϟ a) Mehr(fach)..., Vielfach...: ***~ switch***, b) Parallel...; **5.** *ling.* zs.-gesetzt (*Satz*); **II** *s.* **6.** Vielfache(s) *n* (*a.* 𝒜); **7.** *a.* ***~ connection*** ϟ Paral'lelschaltung *f*: ***in ~*** parallel (geschaltet); ***~ birth*** *s.* ⚕ Mehrlingsgeburt *f*; **'~-disk clutch** *s. mot.* La'mellenkupplung *f*; ***~ fac·tors*** *s. pl. biol.* poly'mere Gene *pl.*; **,~-'par·ty** *adj. pol.* Mehrparteien...: ***~ system***; ***~ plug*** *s.* ϟ Mehrfachstecker *m*; ***~ pro·duc·tion*** *s.* ☨ Serienherstellung *f*; ***~ root*** *s.* 𝒜 mehrwertige Wurzel; ***~ scle·ro·sis*** *s.* ⚕ mul'tiple Skle'rose; ***~ shop*** *s.*, ***~ store*** *s.* ☨ Ketten-, Fili'algeschäft *n*; ***~ thread*** *s.* ⚙ mehrgängiges Gewinde.

mul·ti·plex ['mʌltɪpleks] **I** *adj.* **1.** mehr-, vielfach; **2.** ϟ, *tel.* Mehrfach...(*-betrieb*, *-telegrafie etc.*); **II** *v/t.* **3.** ϟ, *tel.* a) in Mehrfachschaltung betreiben, b) gleichzeitig senden; **'mul·ti·pli·a·ble** [-plaɪəbl] *adj.* multiplizierbar; **mul·ti·pli·cand** [,mʌltɪplɪ'kænd] *s.* 𝒜 Multipli'kand *m*; **'mul·ti·pli·cate** [-plɪkeɪt] *adj.* mehr-, vielfach; **mul·ti·pli·ca·tion** [,mʌltɪplɪ'keɪʃn] *s.* **1.** Vermehrung *f* (*a.* ⚘); **2.** 𝒜 a) Multiplikati'on *f*: ***~ sign*** Mal-, Multiplikationszeichen *n*; ***~ table*** *das* Einmaleins, b) Vervielfachung *f*; **3.** ⚙ (Ge'triebe)Über,setzung *f*; **mul·ti·plic·i·ty** [,mʌltɪ'plɪsətɪ] *s.* **1.** Vielfalt *f*; **2.** Menge *f*, Vielzahl *f*, -heit *f*; **3.** 𝒜 a) Mehr-, Vielwertigkeit *f*, b) Mehrfachheit *f*; **'mul·ti·pli·er** [-plaɪə] *s.* **1.** Vermehrer *m*; **2.** 𝒜 a) Multipli'kator *m*, b) Multipli'zierma,schine *f*; **3.** *phys.* a) Verstärker *m*, b) Vergrößerungslinse *f*, Lupe *f*; **4.** ϟ 'Vor- *od.* 'Neben,widerstand *m*; **5.** ⚙ Über'setzung *f*; **'mul·ti·ply** [-plaɪ] **I** *v/t.* **1.** vermehren (*a. biol.*), vervielfältigen: *~ing glass opt.* Vergrößerungsglas *n*, -linse *f*; **2.** ✗ multiplizieren (***by*** mit); **3.** ⚡ vielfachschalten; **II** *v/i.* **4.** multiplizieren; **5.** sich vermehren *od.* vervielfachen.

ˌmul·ti|ˈpo·lar *adj.* ⚡ viel-, mehrpolig; **ˌ~-ˈpur·pose** *adj.* Mehrzweck...: ***~ aircraft***; **ˌ~ˈra·cial** *adj.* gemischtrassig, Vielvölker...: ***~ state***; **ˈ~ˌseat·er** *s.* ✈ Mehrsitzer *m*; **ˈ~·speed** *adj.* ⚙ Mehrgang...; **ˈ~·stage** *adj.* ⚙, ⚡ mehrstufig, Mehrstufen...: ***~ rocket***; **ˌ~-ˈsto·r(e)y** *adj.* vielstöckig: ***~ building*** Hochhaus *n*; ***~ parking garage***, ***~ car park*** Park(hoch)haus *n*.

mul·ti·tude [ˈmʌltɪtjuːd] *s.* **1.** große Zahl, Menge *f*; **2.** Vielheit *f*; **3.** Menschenmenge *f*: ***the ~*** der große Haufen, die Masse; **mul·ti·tu·di·nous** [ˌmʌltɪˈtjuːdɪnəs] *adj.* □ **1.** (sehr) zahlreich; **2.** mannigfaltig, vielfältig.

ˌmul·ti|ˈva·lent *adj.* ⚗ mehr-, vielwertig; **ˈ~·way** *adj.* ⚡ mehrwegig: ***~ plug*** Vielfachstecker *m*.

mum¹ [mʌm] F **I** *int.* pst!, still!; ***~'s the word!*** (aber) Mund halten!; **II** *adj.* still, stumm.

mum² [mʌm] *v/i.* **1.** sich vermummen; **2.** Mummenschanz treiben.

mum³ [mʌm] *s.* F Mami *f*.

mum·ble [ˈmʌmbl] **I** *v/t. u. v/i.* **1.** murmeln; **2.** mummeln, knabbern; **II** *s.* **3.** Gemurmel *n*.

Mum·bo Jum·bo [ˌmʌmbəʊ ˈdʒʌmbəʊ] *s.* **1.** Popanz *m*; **2.** ♀ a) Hokusˈpokus *m*, fauler Zauber, b) Kauderwelsch *n*.

mum·mer [ˈmʌmə] *s.* **1.** Vermummte(r *m*) *f*, Maske *f* (*Person*); **2.** *contp.* Komödiˈant *m*; **ˈmum·mer·y** [-ərɪ] *s.* **1.** *contp.* Mummenschanz *m*, Maskeˈrade *f*; **2.** Hokusˈpokus *m*.

mum·mi·fi·ca·tion [ˌmʌmɪfɪˈkeɪʃn] *s.* **1.** Mumifizierung *f*; **2.** ⚕ trockener Brand; **mum·mi·fy** [ˈmʌmɪfaɪ] **I** *v/t.* mumifizieren; **II** *v/i. a. fig.* vertrocknen, -dorren.

mum·my¹ [ˈmʌmɪ] *s.* **1.** Mumie *f* (*a. fig.*); **2.** Brei *m*, breiige Masse.

mum·my² [ˈmʌmɪ] *s.* F Mutti *f*.

mump [mʌmp] *v/i.* **1.** schmollen, schlecht gelaunt sein; **2.** F schnorren, betteln; **ˈmump·ish** [-pɪʃ] *adj.* □ mürrisch.

mumps [mʌmps] *s. pl.* **1.** *sg. konstr.* ⚕ Mumps *m*; **2.** miese Laune.

munch [mʌntʃ] *v/t. u. v/i.* schmatzend kauen, ‚mampfen'.

Mun·chau·sen·ism [mʌnˈtʃɔːznɪzəm] Münchhausiˈade *f*, phanˈtastische Geschichte.

mun·dane [ˈmʌndeɪn] *adj.* □ **1.** weltlich, Welt...; **2.** irdisch, weltlich: ***~ poetry*** weltliche Dichtung; **3.** proˈsaisch, nüchtern.

mu·nic·i·pal [mjuːˈnɪsɪpl] *adj.* □ **1.** städtisch, Stadt...; kommuˈnal, Gemeinde...: ***~ elections*** Kommunalwahlen; **2.** Selbstverwaltungs...: ***~ town*** → ***municipality*** 1; **3.** Land(es)...: ***~ law*** Landesrecht *n*; **~ bank** *s.* † Kommuˈnalbank *f*; **~ bonds** *s. pl.* † Kommuˈnalobligatiˌonen *pl.*, Stadtanleihen *pl.*; **~ cor·po·ra·tion** *s.* **1.** Gemeindebehörde *f*; **2.** Körperschaft *f* des öffentlichen Rechts.

mu·nic·i·pal·i·ty [mjuːˌnɪsɪˈpælətɪ] *s.* **1.** Stadt *f* mit Selbstverwaltung; Stadtbezirk *m*; **2.** Stadtbehörde *f*, -verwaltung *f*; **mu·nic·i·pal·ize** [mjuːˈnɪsɪpəlaɪz] *v/t.* **1.** *Stadt* mit Obrigkeitsgewalt ausstatten; **2.** *Betrieb etc.* kommunalisieren.

mu·nic·i·pal| loan *s.* Kommuˈnalanleihe *f*; **~ rates**, **~ tax·es** *s. pl.* Gemeindesteuern *pl.*, -abgaben *pl.*

mu·nif·i·cence [mjuːˈnɪfɪsns] *s.* Freigebigkeit *f*, Großzügigkeit *f*; **muˈnif·i·cent** [-nt] *adj.* □ freigebig, großzügig.

mu·ni·ment [ˈmjuːnɪmənt] *s.* **1.** *pl.* ⚖ Rechtsurkunde *f*; **2.** Urkundensammlung *f*, Arˈchiv *n*.

mu·ni·tion [mjuːˈnɪʃn] **I** *s. mst pl.* ˈKriegsmateriˌal *n*, -vorräte *pl.*, *bsd.* Munitiˈon *f*: ***~ plant*** Rüstungsfabrik *f*; ***~ worker*** Munitionsarbeiter(in); **II** *v/t.* mit Materiˈal *od.* Munitiˈon versehen, ausrüsten.

mu·ral [ˈmjʊərəl] **I** *adj.* Mauer..., Wand...; **II** *s. a.* ***~ painting*** Wandgemälde *n*.

mur·der [ˈmɜːdə] **I** *s.* **1.** (***of***) Mord *m* (an *dat.*), Ermordung *f* (*gen.*): ***~ will out*** *fig.* die Sonne bringt es an den Tag; ***the ~ is out*** *fig.* das Geheimnis ist gelüftet; ***cry blue ~*** F zetermordio schreien; ***get away with ~*** F sich alles erlauben können; ***it was ~!*** F es war fürchterlich!; **II** *v/t.* **2.** (er)morden; **3.** *fig.* (*a. Sprache*) verschandeln, verhunzen; **4.** *sport* F ‚ausein'andernehmen'; **ˈmur·der·er** [-ərə] *s.* Mörder *m*; **ˈmur·der·ess** [-ərɪs] *s.* Mörderin *f*; **ˈmur·der·ous** [-dərəs] *adj.* □ **1.** mörderisch (*a. fig. Hitze, Tempo etc.*); **2.** Mord...: ***~ intent***; **3.** tödlich, todbringend; **4.** blutdürstig; **mur·der squad** *s. Brit.* ˈMordkommissiˌon *f*.

mure [mjʊə] *v/t.* **1.** einmauern; **2.** *mst* ***~ up*** einsperren.

mu·ri·ate [ˈmjʊərɪət] *s.* ⚗ **1.** Muriˈat *n*, Hydrochloˈrid *n*; **2.** ˈKaliumchloˌrid *n*; **mu·ri·at·ic** [ˌmjʊərɪˈætɪk] *adj.* salzsauer: ***~ acid*** Salzsäure *f*.

murk·y [ˈmɜːkɪ] *adj.* □ dunkel, düster, trüb (*alle a. fig.*).

mur·mur [ˈmɜːmə] **I** *s.* **1.** Murmeln *n*, (leises) Rauschen (*Wasser, Wind etc.*); **2.** Gemurmel *n*; **3.** Murren *n*: ***without a ~*** ohne zu murren; **4.** ⚕ Geräusch *n*; **II** *v/i.* **5.** murmeln (*a. Wasser etc.*); **6.** murren (***at***, ***against*** gegen); **III** *v/t.* **7.** murmeln; **ˈmur·mur·ous** [-mərəs] *adj.* □ **1.** murmelnd; **2.** murrend.

mur·rain [ˈmʌrɪn] *s.* Viehseuche *f*.

mus·ca·dine [ˈmʌskədɪn], **ˈmus·cat** [-kət], **mus·ca·tel** [ˌmʌskəˈtel] *s.* Muskaˈteller(wein) *m*, -traube *f*.

mus·cle [ˈmʌsl] **I** *s.* **1.** *anat.* Muskel *m*, Muskelfleisch *n*: ***not to move a ~*** *fig.* sich nicht rühren, nicht mit der Wimper zucken; **2.** *fig. a.* ***~ power*** Muskelkraft *f*; **3.** *Am. sl.* Muskelprotz *m*, ‚Schläger' *m*; **4.** *fig.* F Macht *f*, Einfluß *m*, ‚Muskeln' *pl.*; **II** *v/i.* **5.** ***~ in*** *bsd. Am.* F sich rücksichtslos eindrängen; **ˈ~-bound** *adj.*: ***be ~*** eine überentwickelte Muskulatur haben; **~ man** [mæn] *s.* **1.** ˈMuskelpaˌket *n*, -mann *m*; **2.** ‚Schläger' *m*.

Mus·co·vite [ˈmʌskəʊvaɪt] **I** *s.* **1.** a) Moskoˈwiter(in), b) Russe *m*, Russin *f*; **2.** ♀ *min.* Muskoˈwit *m*, Kaliglimmer *m*; **II** *adj.* **3.** a) moskoˈwitisch, b) russisch.

mus·cu·lar [ˈmʌskjʊlə] *adj.* □ **1.** Muskel...: ***~ atrophy*** Muskelschwund *m*; **2.** muskuˈlös; **mus·cu·lar·i·ty** [ˌmʌskjʊˈlærətɪ] *s.* Muskelkraft *f*, muskuˈlöser Körperbau; **ˈmus·cu·la·ture** [-lətʃə] *s. anat.* Muskulaˈtur *f*.

Muse¹ [mjuːz] *s. myth.* Muse *f* (*fig. a.* ♀).

muse² [mjuːz] *v/i.* **1.** (nach)sinnen, (-)denken, (-)grübeln (***on***, ***upon*** über *acc.*); **2.** in Gedanken versunken sein, träumen; **ˈmus·er** [-zə] *s.* Träumer(in), Sinnende(r *m*) *f*.

mu·se·um [mjuːˈzɪəm] *s.* Muˈseum *n*: ***~ piece*** Museumsstück *n* (*a. fig.*).

mush¹ [mʌʃ] *s.* **1.** Brei *m*, Mus *n*; **2.** *Am.* (Mais)Brei *m*; **3.** F a) Gefühlsduseˈlei *f*, b) sentimenˈtales Zeug; **4.** *Radio*: Knistergeräusch *n*: ***~ area*** Störgebiet *n*.

mush² [mʌʃ] *v/i. Am.* **1.** durch den Schnee stapfen; **2.** mit Hundeschlitten fahren.

mush·room [ˈmʌʃrʊm] **I** *s.* **1.** ♣ a) Ständerpilz *m*, b) *allg.* eßbarer Pilz, *bsd.* Champignon *m*: ***grow like ~s*** → 6 a; **2.** *fig.* Emˈporkömmling *m*; **II** *adj.* **3.** Pilz...; pilzförmig: ***~ bulb*** ⚡ Pilzbirne *f*; ***~ cloud*** Atompilz *m*; **4.** plötzlich entstanden; Eintags...: ***~ fame***; **III** *v/i.* **5.** Pilze sammeln; **6.** *fig.* a) wie Pilze aus dem Boden schießen, b) sich ausbreiten (*Flammen*); **IV** *v/t.* **7.** F *Zigarette* ausdrücken.

mush·y [ˈmʌʃɪ] *adj.* □ **1.** breiig, weich; **2.** *fig.* a) weichlich, b) F gefühlsduselig.

mu·sic [ˈmjuːzɪk] *s.* **1.** Muˈsik *f*, Tonkunst *f*; *konkr.* Kompositiˈon(en *pl. coll.*) *f*: ***face the ~*** F ‚die Suppe auslöffeln'; ***set to ~*** vertonen; **2.** Noten(blatt *n*) *pl.*: ***play from ~*** vom Blatt spielen; **3.** *coll.* Musiˈkalien *pl.*: ***~ shop*** → ***music house***; **4.** *fig.* Muˈsik *f*, Wohllaut *m*, Gesang *m*; **5.** (Muˈsik)Kaˌpelle *f*.

mu·si·cal [ˈmjuːzɪkl] **I** *adj.* □ **1.** Musik...: ***~ history***; ***~ instrument***; **2.** meˈlodisch; **3.** musiˈkalisch (*Person, Komödie etc.*); **II** *s.* **4.** Musical *n*; **5.** F *für* ***musical film***; **~ art** *s.* (Kunst *f* der) Muˈsik *f*, Tonkunst *f*; **~ box** *s. Brit.* Spieldose *f*; **~ chairs** *s. pl.* ‚Reise *f* nach Jeˈrusalem' (*Gesellschaftsspiel*); **~ clock** *s.* Spieluhr *f*; **~ film** *s.* Muˈsikfilm *m*; **~ glass·es** *s. pl.* ♪ ˈGlasharˌmonika *f*.

mu·si·cal·i·ty [ˌmjuːzɪˈkælətɪ], **mu·si·cal·ness** [ˈmjuːzɪklnɪs] *s.* **1.** Musikaliˈtät *f*; **2.** Wohlklang *m*.

ˈmu·sic|-apˌpre·ciˈa·tion rec·ord *s.* Schallplatte *f* mit muˈsikkundlichem Kommenˈtar; **~ book** *s.* Notenheft *n*, -buch *n*; **~ box** *s.* **1.** Spieldose *f*; **2.** → ***jukebox***; **~ hall** *s. Brit.* Varieˈté(theˌater) *n*; **~ house** *s.* Musiˈkalienhandlung *f*.

mu·si·cian [mjuːˈzɪʃn] *s.* **1.** (*bsd.* Berufs)Musiker(in): ***be a good ~*** a) gut spielen *od.* singen, b) sehr musikalisch sein; **2.** Musiˈkant *m*.

mu·si·col·o·gy [ˌmjuːzɪˈkɒlədʒɪ] *s.* Muˈsikwissenschaft *f*.

mu·sic| pa·per *s.* ˈNotenpaˌpier *n*; **~ rack**, **~ stand** *s.* Notenständer *m*; **~ stool** *s.* Klaˈvierstuhl *m*.

mus·ing [ˈmjuːzɪŋ] **I** *s.* **1.** Sinnen *n*, Grübeln *n*, Nachdenken *n*; **2.** *pl.* Träumeˈreien *pl.*; **II** *adj.* □ **3.** nachdenklich, sinnend, in Gedanken (versunken).

musk [mʌsk] *s.* **1.** *zo.* Moschus *m* (*a. Geruch*), Bisam *m*; **2.** → ***musk deer***;

3. Moschuspflanze *f*; **~ bag** *s. zo.* Moschusbeutel *m*; **~ deer** *s. zo.* Moschustier *n*.
mus·ket ['mʌskɪt] *s.* ⚔ *hist.* Mus'kete *f*, Flinte *f*; **mus·ket·eer** [ˌmʌskɪ'tɪə] *s. hist.* Muske'tier *m*; '**mus·ket·ry** [-trɪ] *s.* **1.** *hist. coll.* a) Mus'keten *pl.*, b) Muske'tiere *pl.*; **2.** *hist.* Mus'ketenschießen *n*; **3.** ⚔ 'Schießˌunterricht *m*: **~ *manual*** Schießvorschrift *f*.
musk| ox *s. zo.* Moschusochse *m*; '**~-rat** *s. zo.* Bisamratte *f*; **~ rose** *s.* ✿ Moschusrose *f*.
musk·y ['mʌskɪ] *adj.* □ **1.** nach Moschus riechend; **2.** Moschus…
Mus·lim ['mʊslɪm] → ***Moslem***.
mus·lin ['mʌzlɪn] *s.* Musse'lin *m*.
mus·quash ['mʌskwɒʃ] → ***muskrat***.
muss [mʌs] *bsd. Am.* F **I** *s.* Durchein'ander *n*, Unordnung *f*; **II** *v/t. oft* **~ *up*** durchein'anderbringen, in Unordnung bringen, *Haar* verwuscheln.
mus·sel ['mʌsl] *s.* Muschel *f*.
Mus·sul·man ['mʌslmən] **I** *pl.* **-mans**, *a.* **-men** [-mən] *s.* Muselman(n) *m*; **II** *adj.* muselmanisch.
muss·y ['mʌsɪ] *adj. Am.* F unordentlich; verknittert; schmutzig.
must[1] [mʌst] **I** *v/aux.* **1.** *pres.* muß, mußt, müssen, müßt: ***I ~ go now*** ich muß jetzt gehen; ***he ~ be over eighty*** er muß über achtzig (Jahre alt) sein; **2.** *neg.* darf, darfst, dürfen, dürft: ***you ~ not smoke here*** du darfst hier nicht rauchen; **3.** *pret.* a) mußte, mußtest, mußten, mußtet: ***it was too late now, he ~ go on***; ***just as I was busiest, he ~ come*** gerade als ich am meisten zu tun hatte, mußte er kommen, b) *neg.* durfte, durftest, durften, durftet; **II** *adj.* **4.** unerläßlich, abso'lut notwendig: ***a ~ book*** ein Buch, das man (unbedingt) gelesen haben muß; **III** *s.* **5.** Muß *n*: ***it is a ~*** es ist unerläßlich *od.* unbedingt erforderlich (→ *a.* 4).
must[2] [mʌst] *s.* Most *m*.
must[3] [mʌst] *s.* **1.** Moder *m*, Schimmel *m*; **2.** Modrigkeit *f*.
mus·tache [mə'stɑːʃ; *Am.* 'mʌstæʃ] *Am.* → ***moustache***.
mus·tang ['mʌstæŋ] *s.* **1.** *zo.* Mustang *m* (*halbwildes Präriepferd*); **2.** ⚔ ✈ Mustang *m* (*amer. Jagdflugzeug im 2. Weltkrieg*).
mus·tard ['mʌstəd] *s.* **1.** Senf *m*, Mostrich *m*; → ***keen***[1] 13; **2.** ✿ Senf *m*; **3.** *Am. sl.* a) ‚Mordskerl' *m*, b) ‚tolle' Sache, c) ‚Pfeffer' *m*, Schwung *m*; **~ gas** *s.* ⚔ Senfgas *n*, Gelbkreuz *n*; **~ plas·ter** *s.* ⚕ Senfpflaster *n*; **~ poul·tice** *s.* ⚕ Senfpackung *f*; **~ seed** *s.* **1.** ✿ Senfsame *m*: ***grain of ~*** *bibl.* Senfkorn *n*; **2.** *hunt.* Vogelschrot *m, n*.
mus·ter ['mʌstə] **I** *v/t.* **1.** ⚔ a) (zum Ap'pell) antreten lassen, mustern, b) aufbieten: **~ *in*** (***out***) *Am.* einziehen (entlassen, ausmustern); **2.** zs.-bringen, auftreiben; **3.** *a.* **~ *up*** *fig.* aufbieten, *s-e Kraft* zs.-nehmen, *Mut* fassen; **II** *v/i.* **4.** sich versammeln, ⚔ *a.* antreten; **III** *s.* **5.** ⚔ Ap'pell *m*, Pa'rade *f*; Musterung *f*: ***pass ~*** *fig.* durchgehen, Billigung finden (***with*** bei); **6.** ⚔ → ***muster roll*** 2; **7.** Versammlung *f*; **8.** Aufgebot *n*; **~ book** *s.* ⚔ Stammrollenbuch *n*; **~ roll** *s.* **1.** ⚓ Musterrolle *f*; **2.** ⚔ Stammrolle *f*.
mus·ti·ness ['mʌstɪnɪs] *s.* **1.** Muffigkeit *f*, Modrigkeit *f*; **2.** *fig.* Verstaubtheit *f*;
mus·ty ['mʌstɪ] *adj.* □ **1.** muffig; **2.** mod(e)rig; **3.** schal (*a. fig.*); **4.** *fig.* verstaubt.
mu·ta·bil·i·ty [ˌmjuːtə'bɪlətɪ] *s.* **1.** Veränderlichkeit *f*; **2.** *fig.* Unbeständigkeit *f*; **3.** *biol.* Mutati'onsfähigkeit *f*; **mu·ta·ble** ['mjuːtəbl] *adj.* □ **1.** veränderlich; **2.** *fig.* unbeständig; **3.** *biol.* mutati'onsfähig; **mu·tant** ['mjuːtənt] *biol.* **I** *adj.* **1.** mutierend; **2.** mutati'onsbedingt; **II** *s.* **3.** Vari'ante *f*, Mu'tant *m*; **mu·tate** [mjuː'teɪt] **I** *v/t.* **1.** verändern; **2.** *ling.* 'umlauten: **~*d vowel*** Umlaut *m*; **II** *v/i.* **3.** sich ändern; **4.** *ling.* 'umlauten; **5.** *biol.* mutieren; **mu·ta·tion** [mjuː'teɪʃn] *s.* **1.** (Ver)Änderung *f*; **2.** 'Umwandlung *f*: **~ *of energy*** *phys.* Energieumformung *f*; **3.** *biol.* a) Mutati'on *f* (*a.* ♪), b) Mutati'onsproˌdukt *n*; **4.** *ling.* 'Umlaut *m*.
mute [mjuːt] **I** *adj.* □ **1.** stumm (*a. ling.*), *weitS. a.* still, schweigend: **~ *sound*** *ling.* Verschlußlaut *m*; **II** *s.* **2.** Stumme(r *m*) *f*; **3.** *thea.* Sta'tist(in); **4.** ♪ Dämpfer *m*; **5.** *ling.* a) stummer Buchstabe, b) Verschlußlaut *m*; **III** *v/t.* **6.** ♪ *Instrument* dämpfen.
mu·ti·late ['mjuːtɪleɪt] *v/t.* verstümmeln (*a. fig.*); **mu·ti·la·tion** [ˌmjuːtɪ'leɪʃn] *s.* Verstümmelung *f*.
mu·ti·neer [ˌmjuːtɪ'nɪə] **I** *s.* Meuterer *m*; **II** *v/i.* meutern; **mu·ti·nous** ['mjuːtɪnəs] *adj.* □ **1.** meuterisch; **2.** aufrührerisch, re'bellisch (*a. fig.*); **mu·ti·ny** ['mjuːtɪnɪ] **I** *s.* **1.** Meute'rei *f*; **2.** Auflehnung *f*, Rebelli'on *f*; **II** *v/i.* **3.** meutern.
mut·ism ['mjuːtɪzəm] *s.* (Taub)Stummheit *f*.
mutt [mʌt] *s. Am. sl.* **1.** Trottel *m*, Schafskopf *m*; **2.** Köter *m*, Hund *m*.
mut·ter ['mʌtə] **I** *v/i.* **1.** (*a. v/t. et.*) murmeln: **~ *to o.s.*** vor sich hinmurmeln; **2.** murren (***at*** über *acc.*; ***against*** gegen); **II** *s.* **3.** Gemurmel *n*; **4.** Murren *n*.
mut·ton ['mʌtn] *s.* Hammelfleisch *n*: ***leg of ~*** Hammelkeule *f*; → ***dead*** 1; **~ chop** *s.* **1.** 'Hammelkoteˌlett *n*; **2.** *pl.* Kote'letten *pl.* (*Backenbart*); '**~head** *s.* F ‚Schafskopf' *m*.
mu·tu·al ['mjuːtʃʊəl] *adj.* □ **1.** gegen-, wechselseitig: **~ *aid*** gegenseitige Hilfe; **~ *building association*** Baugenossenschaft *f*; ***by ~ consent*** in gegenseitigem Einvernehmen; **~ *contributory negligence*** ⚖ beiderseitiges Verschulden; **~ *improvement society*** Fortbildungsverein *m*; **~ *insurance*** † Versicherung *f* auf Gegenseitigkeit; **~ *investment trust***, **~ *fund*** *Am.* Investmentfonds *m*; **~ *will*** ⚖ gegenseitiges Testament; ***it's ~*** *iro.* es beruht auf Gegenseitigkeit; **2.** gemeinsam: ***our ~ friends***; **mu·tu·al·i·ty** [ˌmjuːtjʊ'ælətɪ] *s.* Gegenseitigkeit *f*.
mu·zhik, mu·zjik ['muːʒɪk] *s.* Muschik *m*, russischer Bauer.
muz·zle ['mʌzl] **I** *s.* **1.** Maul *n*, Schnauze *f* (*Tier*); **2.** Maulkorb *m*; **3.** Mündung *f e-r Feuerwaffe*; **4.** ⚙ Mündung *f*; Tülle *f*; **II** *v/t.* **5.** e-n Maulkorb anlegen (*dat.*); *fig. a. Presse etc.* knebeln, mundtot machen, den Mund stopfen (*dat.*); **~ brake** *s.* ⚔ Mündungsbremse *f*; **~ burst** *s.* ⚔ Mündungskrepierer *m*; '**~-ˌload·er** *s.* ⚔ *hist.* Vorderlader *m*; **~ ve·loc·i·ty** *s. Ballistik*: Mündungs-, Anfangsgeschwindigkeit *f*.
muz·zy ['mʌzɪ] *adj.* □ F **1.** zerstreut, verwirrt; **2.** dus(e)lig; **3.** stumpfsinnig.
my [maɪ] *poss. pron.* mein(e): ***I must wash ~ face*** ich muß mir das Gesicht waschen; (***oh***) **~!** F (du) meine Güte!
my·al·gi·a [maɪ'ældʒɪə] *s.* ⚕ 'Muskelrheuma(ˌtismus *m*) *n*.
my·col·o·gy [maɪ'kɒlədʒɪ] *s.* ✿ **1.** Pilzkunde *f*, Mykolo'gie *f*; **2.** Pilzflora *f*, Pilze *pl.* (*e-s Gebiets*).
my·cose ['maɪkəʊs] *s.* ⚗ My'kose *f*.
my·co·sis [maɪ'kəʊsɪs] *s.* ⚕ Pilzkrankheit *f*, My'kose *f*.
my·e·li·tis [ˌmaɪə'laɪtɪs] *s.* Mye'litis *f*: a) Rückenmarksentzündung *f*, b) Knochenmarksentzündung *f*; **my·e·lon** ['maɪəlɒn] *s.* Rückenmark *n*.
my·o·car·di·o·gram [ˌmaɪəʊ'kɑːdɪəʊgræm] *s.* ⚕ Eˌlektrokardio'gramm *n*; ˌ**my·o'car·di·o·graph** [-grɑːf] *s.* ⚕ Eˌlektrokardio'graph *m*, EK'G-Appaˌrat *m*; **my·o·car·di·tis** [ˌmaɪəʊkɑː'daɪtɪs] *s.* Herzmuskelentzündung *f*.
my·ol·o·gy [maɪ'ɒlədʒɪ] *s.* Myolo'gie *f*, Muskelkunde *f*, -lehre *f*.
my·o·ma [maɪ'əʊmə] *s.* ⚕ My'om *n*.
my·ope ['maɪəʊp] *s.* ⚕ Kurzsichtige(r *m*) *f*; **my·o·pi·a** [maɪ'əʊpjə] *s.* ⚕ Kurzsichtigkeit *f* (*a. fig.*); **my·op·ic** [maɪ'ɒpɪc] *adj.* kurzsichtig; **my·o·py** ['maɪəpɪ] → ***myopia***.
myr·i·ad ['mɪrɪəd] **I** *s.* Myri'ade *f*; *fig. a.* Unzahl *f*; **II** *adj.* unzählig.
myr·mi·don ['mɜːmɪdən] *s.* Scherge *m*, Häscher *m*; Helfershelfer *m*: **~ *of law*** Hüter *m* des Gesetzes.
myrrh [mɜː] *s.* ✿ Myrrhe *f*.
myr·tle ['mɜːtl] *s.* ✿ **1.** Myrthe *f*; **2.** *Am.* Immergrün *n*.
my·self [maɪ'self] *pron.* **1.** (*verstärkend*) (ich *od.* mir *od.* mich) selbst: ***I did it ~*** ich selbst habe es getan; ***I ~ wouldn't do it*** ich (persönlich) würde es sein lassen; ***it is for ~*** es ist für mich (selbst); **2.** *refl.* mir (*dat.*), mich (*acc.*): ***I cut ~*** ich habe mich geschnitten.
mys·te·ri·ous [mɪ'stɪərɪəs] *adj.* □ mysteri'ös: a) geheimnisvoll, b) rätsel-, schleierhaft, unerklärlich; **mys'te·ri·ous·ness** [-nɪs] *s.* Rätselhaftigkeit *f*, Unerklärlichkeit *f*, *das* Geheimnisvolle *od.* Mysteri'öse.
mys·ter·y ['mɪstərɪ] *s.* **1.** Geheimnis *n*, Rätsel *n* (***to*** für *od. dat.*): ***make a ~ of*** *et.* geheimhalten; ***wrapped in ~*** in geheimnisvolles Dunkel gehüllt; ***it's a complete ~ to me*** es ist mir völlig schleierhaft; **2.** Rätselhaftigkeit *f*, Unerklärlichkeit *f*; **3.** *eccl.* My'sterium *n*; **4.** *pl.* Geheimlehre *f*, -kunst *f*; My'sterien *pl.*; **5.** → ***mystery play*** 1; **6.** *Am.* → **~ nov·el** *s.* Krimi'nalroˌman *m*; **~ play** *s.* **1.** *hist.* My'sterienspiel *n*; **2.** *thea.* Krimi'nalstück *n*; **~ ship** *s.* ⚓ U-Boot-Falle *f*; **~ tour** *s.* Fahrt *f* ins Blaue.
mys·tic ['mɪstɪk] **I** *adj.* (□ **~*ally***) **1.** mystisch; **2.** *fig.* rätselhaft, mysteri'ös, geheimnisvoll; **3.** geheim, Zauber…; **II** *s.* **4.** Mystiker(in); Schwärmer(in); '**mys·ti·cal** [-kl] *adj.* □ **1.** sym'bolisch; **2.** → ***mystic*** 1, 2; '**mys·ti·cism** [-ɪsɪzəm] *s. phls., eccl.* a) Mysti'zismus *m*, Glaubensschwärme'rei *f*, b) Mystik *f*.
mys·ti·fi·ca·tion [ˌmɪstɪfɪ'keɪʃn] *s.* **1.** Täuschung *f*, Irreführung *f*; **2.** Foppe-

ˈrei *f*; **3.** Verwirrung *f*, Verblüffung *f*;
mys·ti·fy [ˈmɪstɪfaɪ] *v/t.* **1.** täuschen, hinters Licht führen, foppen; **2.** verwirren, verblüffen; **3.** in Dunkel hüllen.
myth [mɪθ] *s.* **1.** (Götter-, Helden)Sage *f*, Mythos *m* (*a. pol.*), Mythus *m*, Mythe *f*; **2.** Märchen *n*, erfundene Geschichte; **3.** *fig.* Mythus *m* (*legendär gewordene Person od. Sache*).
myth·ic, **myth·i·cal** [ˈmɪθɪk(l)] *adj.* □ **1.** mythisch, sagenhaft; Sagen…; **2.** *fig.* erdichtet, fikˈtiv.
myth·o·log·ic, **myth·o·log·i·cal** [ˌmɪθəˈlɒdʒɪk(l)] *adj.* □ mythoˈlogisch; **my·thol·o·gist** [mɪˈθɒlədʒɪst] *s.* Mythoˈloge *m*; **my·thol·o·gize** [mɪˈθɒlədʒaɪz] *v/t.* mythologisieren; **my·thol·o·gy** [mɪˈθɒlədʒɪ] *s.* **1.** Mytholoˈgie *f*, Götter- u. Heldensagen *pl.*; **2.** Sagenforschung *f*, -kunde *f*.

N

N, n [en] *s.* **1.** N *n*, n *n* (*Buchstabe*); **2.** ⚗ N *n* (*Stickstoff*); **3.** 𝔄 N *n*, n *n* (*unbestimmte Konstante*).
nab [næb] *v/t.* F **1.** schnappen, erwischen; **2.** sich *et.* schnappen.
na·bob [ˈneɪbɒb] *s.* Nabob *m* (*a. fig. Krösus*).
na·celle [næˈsel] *s.* ✈ **1.** (Flugzeug-)Rumpf *m*; **2.** (Motor-, Luftschiff)Gondel *f*; **3.** Balˈlonkorb *m*.
na·cre [ˈneɪkə] *s.* Perlmutt(er *f*) *n*; **ˈna·cre·ous** [-krɪəs], **ˈna·crous** [-krəs] *adj.* **1.** perlmutterartig; **2.** Perlmutt(er)…
na·dir [ˈneɪˌdɪə] *s.* **1.** *ast.*, *geogr.* Naˈdir *m*, Fußpunkt *m*; **2.** *fig.* Tief-, Nullpunkt *m*.
nag¹ [næg] *s.* **1.** kleines Reitpferd, Pony *n*; **2.** F *contp.* Gaul *m*.
nag² [næg] **I** *v/t.* **1.** herˈumnörgeln an (*dat.*); *j-m* zusetzen; **II** *v/i.* **2.** nörgeln, keifen: **~ at** → 1; **3.** *fig.* nagen, bohren; **III** *s.* **4.** → **ˈnag·ger** [-gə] *s.* Nörgler (-in); **ˈnag·ging** [-gɪŋ] **I** *s.* Nörgeˈlei *f*, Gekeife *n*; **II** *adj.* nörgelnd, keifend, *fig.* nagend.
nai·ad [ˈnaɪæd] *s.* **1.** *myth.* Naˈjade *f*, Wassernymphe *f*; **2.** *fig.* (Bade)Nixe *f*.
nail [neɪl] **I** *s.* **1.** (Finger-, Zehen)Nagel *m*; **2.** ⚙ Nagel *m*; Stift *m*; **3.** *zo.* a) Nagel *m*, b) Klaue *f*, Kralle *f*;
Besondere Redewendungen:
a ~ in s.o.'s coffin ein Nagel zu j-s Sarg; **on the ~** auf der Stelle, sofort, bar *bezahlen*; **to the ~** bis ins letzte, vollendet; **hit the (right) ~ on the head** *fig.* den Nagel auf den Kopf treffen; **hard as ~s** eisern: a) fit, in guter Kondition, b) unbarmherzig; **right as ~s** ganz richtig;
II *v/t.* **4.** (an)nageln (**on** auf *acc.*, **to** an *acc.*): **~ed to the spot** wie an- *od.* festgenagelt; **~ to the barndoor** *fig. Lüge etc.* festnageln; → **colour** 10; **5.** benageln, mit Nägeln beschlagen; **6.** *a.* **~ up** vernageln; **7.** *fig. Augen etc.* heften, *Aufmerksamkeit* richten (**to** auf *acc.*); **8.** → **nail down** 2; **9.** F a) schnappen, erwischen, b) sich *et.* schnappen, c) ‚klauen', d) *et.* ‚spitzkriegen' (*entdekken*); **~ down** *v/t.* **1.** zunageln; **2.** *fig.* *j-n* festnageln (**to** auf *acc.*); **3.** *fig. et.* endgültig beweisen; **~ up** *v/t.* **1.** zs.-nageln; **2.** zu-, vernageln; **3.** *fig.* zs.-basteln: **a nailed-up drama**.
ˈnail|-bed *s. anat.* Nagelbett *n*; **ˈ~-brush** *s.* Nagelbürste *f*; **~ en·am·el** *s.* Nagellack *m*; **~ file** *s.* Nagelfeile *f*; **ˈ~-head** *s.* ⚙ Nagelkopf *m*; **~ pol·ish** *s.* Nagellack *m*; **ˈ~-ˌpull·er** *s.* ⚙ Nagelzieher *m*; **~ scis·sors** *s. pl.* Nagelschere *f*; **~ var·nish** *s. Brit.* Nagellack *m*.
na·ïve [nɑːˈiːv], *a.* **na·ive** [neɪv] *adj.* □ *allg.* naˈiv (*a. Kunst*); **na·ïve·té** [nɑːˈiːvteɪ], *a.* **na·ive·ty** [ˈneɪvtɪ] *s.* Naiviˈtät *f*.
na·ked [ˈneɪkɪd] *adj.* □ **1.** nackt, bloß, unbedeckt: ♀ **Lady** ⚘ Herbstzeitlose *f*; **2.** bloß, unbewaffnet (*Auge*); **3.** bloß, blank (*Schwert*; ⚙ *Draht*); **4.** nackt, kahl (*Feld*, *Raum*, *Wand etc.*); **5.** entblößt (**of** von): **~ of all provisions** bar aller Vorräte; **6.** a) schutz-, wehrlos, b) preisgegeben (**to** *dat.*); **7.** nackt, unverhüllt: **~ facts**; **~ truth**; **8.** ⚖ bloß, unbestätigt: **~ confession**; **~ possession** tatsächlicher Besitz (*ohne Rechtsanspruch*); **ˈna·ked·ness** [-nɪs] *s.* **1.** Nacktheit *f*, Blöße *f*; **2.** Kahlheit *f*; **3.** Schutz-, Wehrlosigkeit *f*; **4.** Mangel *m* (**of** an *dat.*); **5.** *fig.* Unverhülltheit *f*.
nam·a·ble [ˈneɪməbl] *adj.* **1.** benennbar; **2.** nennenswert.
nam·by-pam·by [ˌnæmbɪˈpæmbɪ] **I** *adj.* **1.** seicht, abgeschmackt; **2.** affektiert, ‚etepeˈtete'; **3.** sentimenˈtal; **II** *s.* **4.** sentimentales Zeug; **5.** sentimentaler Mensch; **6.** Mutterkindchen *n*.
name [neɪm] **I** *v/t.* **1.** nennen; erwähnen, anführen; **2.** (be)nennen (**after**, **from** nach), e-n Namen geben (*dat.*): **~d** genannt, namens; **3.** beim (richtigen) Namen nennen; **4.** a) ernennen (zu), b) nomiˈnieren, vorschlagen (**for** für); **5.** *Datum etc.* bestimmen; **6.** *parl. Brit.* mit Namen zur Ordnung rufen: **~!** a) zur Ordnung rufen!, b) *allg.* Namen nennen!; **II** *s.* **7.** Name *m*: **what is your ~?** wie heißen Sie?; **in ~ only** nur dem Namen nach; **8.** Name *m*, Bezeichnung *f*, Benennung *f*; **9.** Schimpfname *m*: **call s.o. ~s** j-n beschimpfen; **10.** Name *m*, Ruf *m*: **a bad ~**; → *Bes. Redew.*; **11.** (berühmter) Name, (guter) Ruf: **a man of ~** ein Mann von Ruf; **12.** Name *m*, Berühmtheit *f* (*Person*): **the great ~s of our century**; **13.** Geschlecht *n*, Faˈmilie *f*;
Besondere Redewendungen:
by ~ a) mit Namen, namentlich, b) namens, c) dem Namen nach; **a man by** (*od.* **of**) **the ~ of A.** ein Mann namens A.; **in the ~ of** a) um (*gen.*) willen, b) im Namen *des Gesetzes etc.*, c) auf *j-s* Namen *bestellen etc.*; **I haven't a penny to my ~** ich besitze keinen Pfennig; **give one's ~** s-n Namen nennen; **give it a ~!** F heraus damit!, sagen Sie, was Sie (haben) wollen!; **give s.o.** (**s.th.**) **a bad ~** j-n (et.) in Verruf bringen; **give a dog a bad ~ and hang him** j-n wegen s-s schlechten Rufs *od.* auf Grund von Gerüchten verurteilen; **have a ~ for being** dafür bekannt sein, *et.* zu sein; **make one's ~**, **make** (*od.* **win**) **a ~ for o.s.** sich e-n Namen machen (**as** als, **by** durch); **put one's ~ down for** a) kandidieren für, b) sich anmelden für, c) sich vormerken lassen für; **send in one's ~** sich (an)melden (lassen); **what's in a ~?** was bedeutet schon ein Name?; **that's the ~ of the game!** darum dreht es sich!
ˈname|-ˌcall·ing *s.* Beschimpfung(en *pl.*) *f*; **ˈ~-child** *s.*: **my ~** das nach mir benannte Kind.
named [neɪmd] *adj.* **1.** genannt, namens; **2.** genannt, erwähnt: **~ above** oben genannt.
ˈname|-day *s.* **1.** Namenstag *m*; **2.** ✝ Abrechnungstag *m*; **ˈ~-ˌdrop·per** *s.* j-d, der ständig mit promiˈnenten Bekannten angibt; **ˈ~-ˌdrop·ping** *s.* Wichtigtueˈrei *f* durch Erwähnung von Promiˈnenten, die man angeblich kennt.
name·less [ˈneɪmlɪs] *adj.* □ **1.** namenlos, unbekannt, obˈskur; **2.** ungenannt, unerwähnt; anoˈnym; **3.** unehelich (*Kind*); **4.** *fig.* namenlos, unbeschreiblich (*Furcht etc.*); **5.** unaussprechlich, abˈscheulich; **ˈname·ly** [-lɪ] *adv.* nämlich.
name| part *s. thea.* Titelrolle *f*; **~ plate** *s.* **1.** Tür-, Firmen-, Namens-, Straßenschild *n*; **2.** ⚙ Typenschild *n*; **ˈ~·sake** *s.* Namensvetter *m*, -schwester *f*.
nam·ing [ˈneɪmɪŋ] *s.* Namengebung *f*.
nan·cy [ˈnænsɪ] *s. sl.* **1.** Muttersöhnchen *n*; **2.** ‚Homo' *m*.
nan·ny [ˈnænɪ] *s.* **1.** Kindermädchen *n*; **2.** Oma *f*; **3.** → **~ goat** *s.* Ziege *f*.
nap¹ [næp] **I** *v/i.* **1.** ein Schläfchen *od.* ein Nickerchen machen; **2.** *fig.* ‚schlafen': **catch s.o. ~ping** j-n überrumpeln; **II** *s.* **3.** Schläfchen *n*, ‚Nickerchen' *n*: **take a ~** → 1.
nap² [næp] **I** *s.* **1.** Haar(seite *f*) *n e-s Gewebes*; **2.** a) *Spinnerei*: Noppe *f*, b) *Weberei*: (Gewebe)Flor *m*; **II** *v/t. u. v/i.* **3.** noppen, rauhen.
nap³ [næp] *s.* **1.** Naˈpoleon *n* (*Kartenspiel*): **a ~ hand** *fig.* gute Chancen; **go ~** a) die höchste Zahl von Stichen ansagen, b) *fig.* alles auf eine Karte setzen; **2.** Setzen *n* auf eine einzige Gewinnchance.
na·palm [ˈneɪpɑːm] *s.* ⚔ Napalm *n*.
nape [neɪp] *s. mst* **~ of the neck** Genick *n*, Nacken *m*.
naph·tha [ˈnæfθə] *s.* ⚗ **1.** Naphtha *n*, ˈLeuchtpeˌtroleum *n*; **2.** (ˈSchwer)Benˌzin *n*: **cleaner's ~** Waschbenzin; **painter's ~** Testbenzin; **ˈnaph·tha·lene** [-liːn] *s.* Naphthaˈlin *n*; **naph·tha·len·ic** [ˌnæfθəˈlenɪk] *adj.* naphthaˈlinsauer: **~ acid** Naphthalinsäure *f*; **naph·thal·ic** [næfˈθælɪk] *adj.* naphˈthalsauer:

~ *acid* Naphthalsäure *f*; **ˈnaph·tha·line** [-liːn] → ***naphthalene***.

nap·kin [ˈnæpkɪn] *s.* **1.** *a.* ***table*** ~ Servi'ette *f*; **2.** Wischtuch *n*; **3.** *bsd. Brit.* Windel *f*; **4.** *a.* ***sanitary*** ~ *Am.* Monatsbinde *f*.

napped [næpt] *adj.* genoppt, gerauht (*Tuch*); **nap·ping** [ˈnæpɪŋ] *s.* **1.** Ausnoppen *n* (*der Wolle*); **2.** Rauhen *n*: ~ ***comb*** Aufstreichkamm *m*.

nap·py [ˈnæpɪ] *s. bsd. Brit.* F Windel *f*.

nar·cis·sism [nɑːˈsɪsɪzəm] *s. psych.* Narˈzißmus *m*; **narˈcis·sist** [-ɪst] *s.* Narˈzißt (-in).

nar·cis·sus [nɑːˈsɪsəs] *pl.* **-sus·es** [-sɪz] *s.* ⚘ Narˈzisse *f*.

nar·co·sis [nɑːˈkəʊsɪs] *s.* Narˈkose *f*.

nar·cot·ic [nɑːˈkɒtɪk] **I** *adj.* (□ ~***ally***) **1.** narˈkotisch (*a. fig. einschläfernd*); **2.** Rauschgift…; **II** *s.* **3.** Narˈkotikum *n*, Betäubungsmittel *n* (*a. fig.*); **4.** Rauschgift *n*: ~***s squad*** Rauschgiftdezernat *n*; **nar·co·tism** [ˈnɑːkətɪzəm] *s.* **1.** Narkoˈtismus *m* (*Sucht*); **2.** narˈkotischer Zustand *od.* Rausch; **nar·co·tize** [ˈnɑːkətaɪz] *v/t.* narkotisieren.

nard [nɑːd] *s.* **1.** ⚘ Narde *f*; **2.** *pharm.* Nardensalbe *f*.

nark [nɑːk] *sl.* **I** *s.* **1.** Poliˈzeispitzel *m*; **II** *v/t.* **2.** bespitzeln; **3.** ärgern.

nar·rate [nəˈreɪt] *v/t. u. v/i.* erzählen; **narˈra·tion** [-eɪʃn] *s.* Erzählung *f*; **nar·ra·tive** [ˈnærətɪv] **I** *s.* **1.** Erzählung *f*, Geschichte *f*; **2.** Bericht *m*, Schilderung *f*; **II** *adj.* □ **3.** erzählend: ~ ***poem***; **4.** Erzählungs…: ~ ***skill*** Erzählergabe *f*; **narˈra·tor** [-tə] *s.* Erzähler(in).

nar·row [ˈnærəʊ] **I** *adj.* □ **1.** eng, schmal: ***the*** ~ ***seas*** der Ärmelkanal u. die Irische See; **2.** eng (*a. fig.*), (*räumlich*) beschränkt, knapp: ***within*** ~ ***bounds*** in engen Grenzen; ***in the*** ~***est sense*** im engsten Sinne; **3.** *fig.* eingeschränkt, beschränkt; **4.** → ***narrow-minded***; **5.** knapp, beschränkt (*Mittel, Verhältnisse*); **6.** knapp (*Entkommen, Mehrheit etc.*); **7.** gründlich, eingehend; genau: ~ ***investigations***; **II** *v/i.* **8.** enger *od.* schmäler werden, sich verengen (***into*** zu); **9.** knapper werden; **III** *v/t.* **10.** enger *od.* schmäler machen, verenge(r)n; **11.** einengen, beengen; **12.** *a.* ~ ***down*** (***to*** auf *acc.*) be-, einschränken, begrenzen, eingrenzen; **13.** *Maschen* abnehmen; **14.** engstirnig machen; **IV** *s.* **15.** Enge *f*, enge *od.* schmale Stelle; *pl.* a) (Meer)Enge *f*, b) *bsd. Am.* Engpaß *m*.

nar·row| ga(u)ge *s.* 🚂 Schmalspur *f*; **ˈ~-ga(u)ge** [-rəʊg-], *a.* **ˌ~-ˈga(u)ged** [-rəʊˈg-] *adj.* Schmalspur…; **ˌ~-ˈmind·ed** [-rəʊˈmaɪndɪd] *adj.* engherzig, -stirnig, borniert, kleinlich; **ˌ~-ˈmind·ed·ness** [-rəʊˈmaɪndɪdnɪs] *s.* Engstirnigkeit *f*, Borniertheit *f*.

nar·row·ness [ˈnærəʊnɪs] *s.* **1.** Enge *f*, Schmalheit *f*; **2.** Knappheit *f*; **3.** → ***narrow-mindedness***; **4.** Gründlichkeit *f*.

na·sal [ˈneɪzl] **I** *adj.* □ → ***nasally***; **1.** Nasen…: ~ ***bone***; ~ ***cavity***; ~ ***organ*** *humor.* Riechorgan *n*; ~ ***septum*** Nasenscheidewand *f*; **2.** *ling.* naˈsal, Nasal…: ~ ***twang*** Näseln *n*; **II** *s.* **3.** *ling.* Naˈsal(laut) *m*; **na·sal·i·ty** [neɪˈzælətɪ] *s.* Nasaliˈtät *f*; **na·sal·i·za·tion** [ˌneɪzəlaɪˈzeɪʃn] *s.* Nasalierung *f*, nasale Aussprache; **ˈna·sal·ize** [-zəlaɪz] **I** *v/t.* nasalieren; **II** *v/i.* näseln, durch die Nase sprechen; **ˈna·sal·ly** [-zəlɪ] *adv.* **1.** nasal, durch die Nase; **2.** näselnd.

nas·cent [ˈnæsnt] *adj.* **1.** werdend, entstehend: ~ ***state*** Entwicklungszustand *m*; **2.** ⚗ freiwerdend.

nas·ti·ness [ˈnɑːstɪnɪs] *s.* **1.** Schmutzigkeit *f*; **2.** Ekligkeit *f*; **3.** Unflätigkeit *f*; **4.** Gefährlichkeit *f*; **5.** a) Bosheit *f*, b) Gemeinheit *f*, c) Übelgelauntheit *f*.

nas·tur·tium [nəˈstɜːʃəm] *s.* ⚘ Kapuˈziner- *od.* Brunnenkresse *f*.

nas·ty [ˈnɑːstɪ] **I** *adj.* □ **1.** schmutzig; **2.** ekelhaft, eklig, widerlich (*alle a. fig.*): ~ ***taste***; ~ ***fellow***; **3.** *fig.* schmutzig, zotig; **4.** *fig.* böse, schlimm, gefährlich: ~ ***accident***; **5.** *fig.* a) bös, gehässig, garstig (***to*** zu, gegen), b) fies, niederträchtig, c) übelgelaunt, ‚eklig'; **II** *s.* **6.** *mst pl. Video*: ‚ˈSchmutz- u. ˈHorror-Kasˌsette' *f*.

na·tal [ˈneɪtl] *adj.* Geburts…: ~ ***day***; **na·tal·i·ty** [nəˈtælətɪ] *s. bsd. Am.* Geburtenziffer *f*.

na·ta·tion [nəˈteɪʃn] *s.* Schwimmen *n*; **na·ta·to·ri·al** [ˌneɪtəˈtɔːrɪəl] *adj.* Schwimm…: ~ ***bird***; **na·ta·to·ry** [ˈneɪtətərɪ] *adj.* Schwimm…

na·tion [ˈneɪʃn] *s.* **1.** Natiˈon *f*: a) Volk *n*, b) Staat *m*; **2.** (Indiˈaner)Stamm *m*.

na·tion·al [ˈnæʃənl] **I** *adj.* □ **1.** natioˈnal, National…, Landes…, Volks…: ~ ***language*** Landessprache *f*; **2.** staatlich, öffentlich, Staats…: ~ ***debt*** Staatsschuld *f*, öffentliche Schuld; **3.** (ein)heimisch; **4.** landesweit (*Streik etc.*), ˈüberregioˌnal (*Zeitung etc.*); **II** *s.* **5.** Staatsangehörige(r *m*) *f*; ~ **an·them** *s.* Natioˈnalhymne *f*; ~ **as·sem·bly** *s. pol.* Natioˈnalversammlung *f*; ~ **bank** *s.* ✝ Landes-, Natioˈnalbank *f*; ~ **cham·pi·on** *s.* Landesmeister(in); ~ **con·ven·tion** *s. pol. Am.* Parˈteikonvent *m* (*zur Nominierung des Präsidentschaftskandidaten etc.*); ~ **e·con·o·my** *s.* ✝ Volkswirtschaft *f*; ꝰ **Gi·ro** *s.* ✉ *Brit.* Postscheck-, Postgirodienst *m*; ꝰ **Guard** *s. Am.* Natioˈnalgarde *f* (*Art Miliz*); ꝰ **Health Ser·vice** *s. Brit.* Staatlicher Gesundheitsdienst; ~ **in·come** *s.* ✝ Soziˈalproˌdukt *n*; ꝰ **In·sur·ance** *s. Brit.* Soziˈalversicherung *f*.

na·tion·al·ism [ˈnæʃnəlɪzəm] *s.* **1.** Natioˈnalgefühl *n*, Nationaˈlismus *m*; **2.** ✝ *Am.* Verˈstaatlichungspoliˌtik *f*; **ˈna·tion·al·ist** [-ɪst] **I** *s. pol.* Nationaˈlist (-in); **II** *adj.* nationaˈlistisch; **na·tion·al·i·ty** [næʃəˈnælətɪ] *s.* **1.** Nationaliˈtät *f*, Staatsangehörigkeit *f*; **2.** Natiˈon *f*; **na·tion·al·i·za·tion** [ˌnæʃnəlaɪˈzeɪʃn] *s.* **1.** *bsd. Am.* Einbürgerung *f*, Naturalisierung *f*; **2.** ✝ Verstaatlichung *f*; **3.** Verwandlung *f* in e-e (*einheitliche, unabhängige etc.*) Nation; **ˈna·tion·al·ize** [-laɪz] *v/t.* **1.** einbürgern, naturalisieren; **2.** ✝ verstaatlichen; **3.** zu e-r Nation machen; **4.** *Problem etc.* zur Sache der Nation machen.

na·tion·al| park *s.* Natioˈnalpark *m* (*Naturschutzgebiet*); ~ **prod·uct** *s.* ✝ Soziˈalproˌdukt *n*; ~ **ser·vice** *s.* ⚔ Wehrdienst *m*; ꝰ **So·cial·ism** *s. pol. hist.* Natioˈnalsoziaˌlismus *m*.

ˈna·tion|·hood [-hʊd] *s.* (natioˈnale) Souveräniˈtät; **ˈ~-state** *s.* Natioˈnalstaat *m*; **ˌ~-ˈwide** *adj.* allgemein, das ganze Land umˈfassend.

na·tive [ˈneɪtɪv] **I** *adj.* □ **1.** angeboren (***to s.o.*** j-m), naˈtürlich (*Recht etc.*); **2.** eingeboren, Eingeborenen…: ~ ***quarter***; ***go*** ~ unter den *od.* wie die Eingeborenen leben, *fig.* verwahrlosen; **3.** (ein)heimisch, inländisch, Landes…: ~ ***plant*** ⚘ einheimische Pflanze; ~ ***product***; **4.** heimatlich, Heimat…: ~ ***country*** Heimat *f*, Vaterland *n*; ~ ***language*** Muttersprache *f*; ~ ***speaker*** *ling.* Muttersprachler(in); ~ ***town*** Heimat-, Vaterstadt *f*; **5.** ursprünglich, urwüchsig, naˈturhaft: ~ ***beauty***; **6.** ursprünglich, eigentlich: ***the*** ~ ***sense of a word***; **7.** gediegen (*Metall etc.*); **8.** *min.* a) roh, Jungfern…, b) naˈtürlich vorkommend; **II** *s.* **9.** Eingeborene(r *m*) *f*; **10.** Einheimische(r *m*) *f*, Landeskind *n*: ***a*** ~ ***of Berlin*** ein gebürtiger Berliner; **11.** ⚘ einheimisches Gewächs; **12.** *zo.* einheimisches Tier; **13.** Naˈtive *f*, (künstlich) gezüchtete Auster; **ˈ~-born** *adj.* gebürtig: ***a*** ~ ***American***.

na·tiv·i·ty [nəˈtɪvətɪ] *s.* **1.** Geburt *f* (*a. fig.*): ***the*** ꝰ *eccl.* a) die Geburt Christi (*a. paint. etc.*), b) Weihnachten *n*, c) Maˈriä Geburt (*8. September*); ꝰ ***play*** Krippenspiel *n*; **2.** *ast.* Nativiˈtät *f*, (Geˈburts)Horoˌskop *n*.

na·tron [ˈneɪtrən] *s. min.* kohlensaures Natron.

nat·ter [ˈnætə] *Brit.* F **I** *v/i.* plauschen, plaudern; **II** *s.* Plausch *m*, Schwatz *m*.

nat·ty [ˈnætɪ] *adj.* □ F schick, piekfein (angezogen), eleˈgant (*a. fig.*).

nat·u·ral [ˈnætʃrəl] **I** *adj.* □ → ***naturally***; **1.** naˈtürlich, Natur…: ~ ***disaster*** Naturkatastrophe *f*; ~ ***law*** Naturgesetz *n*; ***die a*** ~ ***death*** e-s natürlichen Todes sterben; → ***person*** 1; **2.** naˈturgemäß, -bedingt; **3.** angeboren, naˈtürlich, eigen (***to*** *dat.*): ~ ***talent***; **4.** → ***natural-born***; **5.** reˈal, wirklich, physisch; **6.** selbstverständlich, naˈtürlich: ***it comes quite*** ~ ***to him*** es ist ihm ganz selbstverständlich; **7.** naˈtürlich, ungekünstelt (*Benehmen etc.*); **8.** naˈturgetreu, naˈtürlich (wirkend) (*Nachahmung, Bild etc.*); **9.** unbearbeitet, Natur…, Roh…: ~ ***steel*** Rohstahl *m*; **10.** naˈturhaft, urwüchsig; **11.** naˈtürlich, unehelich (*Kind, Vater etc.*); **12.** ⅌ naˈtürlich: ~ ***number*** natürliche Zahl; **13.** ♪ a) ohne Vorzeichen: ~ ***key*** C-Dur-Tonart *f*, b) mit e-m Auflösungszeichen (versehen) (*Note*), c) Vokal…: ~ ***music***; **II** *s.* **14.** *obs.* Idiˈot(in); **15.** ♪ a) Auflösungszeichen *n*, b) mit e-m Auflösungszeichen versehene Note, c) Stammton *m*, d) weiße Taste (*Klaviatur*); **16.** F a) Naˈturtaˌlent *n* (*Person*), b) (sicherer) Erfolg (*a. Person*); *e-e* ‚klare Sache' (***for s.o.*** für j-n); **ˈ~-born** *adj.* von Geburt, geboren: ~ ***genius***; ~ **fre·quen·cy** *s. phys.* ˈEigenfreˌquenz *f*; ~ **gas** *s. geol.* Erdgas *n*; ~ **his·to·ry** *s.* Naˈturgeschichte *f*.

nat·u·ral·ism [ˈnætʃrəlɪzəm] *s. phls., paint. etc.* Naturaˈlismus *m*; **ˈnat·u·ral·ist** [-ɪst] **I** *s.* **1.** *phls., paint. etc.* Naturaˈlist *m*; **2.** Naˈturwissenschaftler(in), -forscher(in), *bsd.* Zooˈloge *m*, Zooˈlogin *f od.* Boˈtaniker(in); **3.** *Brit.* a) Tierhändler *m*, b) (ˈTier)Präpaˌrator *m*; **II** *adj.* **4.** naturaˈlistisch; **nat·u·ral·is·tic** [ˌnætʃrəˈlɪstɪc] *adj.* (□ ~***ally***) **1.** *phls., paint. etc.* naturalistisch; **2.** naˈturkundlich, -geschichtlich.

nat·u·ral·i·za·tion [ˌnætʃrəlaɪˈzeɪʃn] *s.* Naturalisierung *f*, Einbürgerung *f*; **nat·u·ral·ize** [ˈnætʃrəlaɪz] *v/t.* **1.** naturalisieren, einbürgern; **2.** einbürgern (*a. ling. u. fig.*), ⚘, *zo.* heimisch machen; **3.** akklimatisieren (*a. fig.*).

nat·u·ral·ly [ˈnætʃrəlɪ] *adv.* **1.** von Naˈtur (aus); **2.** instinkˈtiv, sponˈtan; **3.** auf naˈtürlichem Wege, naˈtürlich; **4.** *a. int.* naˈtürlich, selbstverständlich; ˈ**nat·u·ral·ness** [-rəlnɪs] *s. allg.* Naˈtürlichkeit *f*.

nat·u·ral| phi·los·o·phy *s.* **1.** Naˈturphilosoˌphie *f*, -kunde *f*; **2.** Phyˈsik *f*; **~ re·li·gion** *s.* Naˈturreligiˌon *f*; **~ rights** *s. pl.* ⚖, *pol.* Naˈturrechte *pl. des Menschen*; **~ scale** *s.* **1.** ♪ Stammtonleiter *f*; **2.** 𝔄 Achse *f* der naˈtürlichen Zahlen; **~ sci·ence** *s.* Naˈturwissenschaft *f*; **~ se·lec·tion** *s. biol.* naˈtürliche Auslese; **~ sign** *s.* ♪ Auflösungszeichen *n*; **~ state** *s.* Naˈturzustand *m*.

na·ture [ˈneɪtʃə] *s.* **1.** Naˈtur *f*, Schöpfung *f*; **2.** (*a.* ♀; *ohne art.*) Naˈtur(kräfte *pl.*) *f*: ***law of ~*** Naturgesetz *n*; ***from ~*** nach der Natur *malen etc.*; ***back to ~*** zurück zur Natur; ***in the state of ~*** in natürlichem Zustand, nackt; → ***debt, true*** 4; **3.** Naˈtur *f*, Veranlagung *f*, Chaˈrakter *m*, (Eigen-, Gemüts)Art *f*, Natuˈrell *n*: ***animal ~*** das Tierische *im Menschen*; ***by ~*** von Natur (aus); ***human ~*** die menschliche Natur; ***of good ~*** gutherzig, -mütig; ***it is in her ~*** es liegt in ihrem Wesen; → ***second*** 1; **4.** Art *f*, Sorte *f*: ***of*** (*od.* ***in***) ***the ~ of a trial*** nach Art (*od.* in Form) e-s Verhörs; ***~ of the business*** Gegenstand *m* der Firma; **5.** (naˈtürliche) Beschaffenheit; **6.** Naˈtur *f*, naˈtürliche Landschaft: ***~ conservation*** Naturschutz *m*; ***♀ Conservancy*** *Brit.* Naturschutzbehörde *f*; ***~ reserve*** Naturschutzgebiet *n*; ***~ trail*** Naturlehrpfad *m*; **7. *ease*** (*od.* ***relieve***) **~** sich erleichtern (*urinieren etc.*).

-natured [neɪtʃəd] *in Zssgn* geartet, …artig, …mütig: ***good-~*** gutartig.

na·tur·ism [ˈneɪtʃərɪzəm] *s.* ˈFreikörperkulˌtur *f*; ˈ**na·tur·ist** [-ɪst] *s.* FKˈK-Anhänger(in).

na·tur·o·path [ˈneɪtʃərəʊpæθ] *s.* ⚕ **1.** Heilpraktiker(in); **2.** Naˈturheilkundige(r *m*) *f*.

naught [nɔːt] **I** *s.* Null *f*: ***bring*** (***come***) ***to ~*** zunichte machen (werden); ***set at ~*** *Mahnung etc.* in den Wind schlagen; **II** *adj. obs.* keineswegs.

naugh·ti·ness [ˈnɔːtɪnɪs] *s.* Ungezogenheit *f*, Unartigkeit *f*; **naugh·ty** [ˈnɔːtɪ] *adj.* ☐ **1.** ungezogen, unartig; **2.** ungehörig (*Handlung*); **3.** unanständig, schlimm (*Wort etc.*): **~, ~!** F aber, aber!

nau·se·a [ˈnɔːsjə] *s.* **1.** Übelkeit *f*, Brechreiz *m*; **2.** Seekrankheit *f*; **3.** *fig.* Ekel *m*; ˈ**nau·se·ate** [-sɪeɪt] **I** *v/i.* **1.** (e-n) Brechreiz empfinden, sich ekeln (***at*** vor *dat.*); **II** *v/t.* **2.** sich ekeln vor (*dat.*); **3.** anekeln, *j-m* Übelkeit erregen: ***be ~d*** (***at***) → 1; ˈ**nau·se·at·ing** [-sɪeɪtɪŋ], ˈ**nau·seous** [-sjəs] *adj.* ☐ ekelerregend, widerlich.

nau·tic [ˈnɔːtɪk] → ***nautical.***

nau·ti·cal [ˈnɔːtɪkl] *adj.* ☐ ⚓ nautisch, Schiffs…, See(fahrts)…; **~ al·ma·nac** *s.* nautisches Jahrbuch; **~ chart** *s.* Seekarte *f*; **~ mile** *s.* ⚓ Seemeile *f* (*1,852 km*).

na·val [ˈneɪvl] *adj.* ⚓ **1.** Flotten…, (Kriegs)Marine…; **2.** See…, Schiffs…; **~ a·cad·e·my** *s.* ⚓ **1.** Maˈrine-Akadeˌmie *f*; **2.** Navigatiˈonsschule *f*; **~ air·plane** *s.* Maˈrineflugzeug *n*; **~ ar·chi·tect** *s.* ˈSchiffbauingeniˌeur *m*; **~ base** *s.* ˈFlottenstützpunkt *m*, -ˌbasis *f*; **~ bat·tle** *s.* Seeschlacht *f*; **~ ca·det** *s.* ˈSeekaˌdett *m*; **~ forc·es** *s. pl.* Seestreitkräfte *pl.*; **~ of·fi·cer** *s.* **1.** Maˈrineoffiˌzier *m*; **2.** *Am.* (höherer) Hafenzollbeamter; **~ pow·er** *s. pol.* Seemacht *f*.

nave¹ [neɪv] *s.* ⚠ Mittel-, Hauptschiff *n*: ***~ of a cathedral.***

nave² [neɪv] *s.* ⚙ (Rad)Nabe *f*.

na·vel [ˈneɪvl] *s.* **1.** *anat.* Nabel *m*, *fig. a.* Mitte(lpunkt *m*) *f*; **2.** → **~ or·ange** *s.* ˈNaveloˌrange *f*; ˈ**~-string** *s. anat.* Nabelschnur *f*.

nav·i·cert [ˈnævɪsɜːt] *s.* ✝, ⚓ Naviˈcert *n* (*Geleitschein*).

na·vic·u·lar [nəˈvɪkjʊlə] *adj.* nachen-, kahnförmig: **~** (***bone***) *anat.* Kahnbein *n*.

nav·i·ga·bil·i·ty [ˌnævɪgəˈbɪlətɪ] *s.* **1.** ⚓ a) Schiffbarkeit *f* (*e-s Gewässers*), b) Fahrtüchtigkeit *f*; **2.** ✈ Lenkbarkeit *f*; **nav·i·ga·ble** [ˈnævɪgəbl] *adj.* **1.** ⚓ a) schiffbar, (be)fahrbar, b) fahrtüchtig; **2.** ✈ lenkbar (*Luftschiff*); **nav·i·gate** [ˈnævɪgeɪt] **I** *v/i.* **1.** schiffen, (zu Schiff) fahren; **2.** *bsd.* ⚓, ✈ steuern, orten (***to*** nach); **II** *v/t.* **3.** *Gewässer* a) befahren, b) durchˈfahren; **4.** ✈ durchˈfliegen; **5.** steuern, lenken; **nav·i·ga·tion** [ˌnævɪˈgeɪʃn] *s.* **1.** ⚓ Nautik *f*, Navigatiˈon *f*, Schiffsführung *f*, Schiffahrtskunde *f*; **2.** ✈ Navigatiˈonskunde *f*; **3.** ⚓ Schiffahrt *f*, Seefahrt *f*; **4.** ✈, ⚓ a) Navigatiˈon *f*, b) Ortung *f*; **nav·i·ga·tion·al** [ˌnævɪˈgeɪʃnl] *adj.* Navigations…

nav·i·ga·tion| chan·nel *s.* Fahrwasser *n*; **~ chart** *s.* Navigatiˈonskarte *f*; **~ guide** *s.* Bake *f*; **~ light** *s.* Positiˈonslicht *n*; **~ of·fi·cer** *s.* ⚓, ✈ Navigatiˈonsoffiˌzier *m*.

nav·i·ga·tor [ˈnævɪgeɪtə] *s.* **1.** ⚓ a) Seefahrer *m*, b) Nautiker *m*, c) Steuermann *m*, d) *Am.* Navigatiˈonsoffiˌzier *m*; **2.** ✈ a) (Aero)ˈNautiker *m*, b) Beobachter *m*.

nav·vy [ˈnævɪ] *s.* **1.** *Brit.* Kaˈnal-, Erd-, Streckenarbeiter *m*; **2.** ⚙ Exkaˈvator *m*, Löffelbagger *m*.

na·vy [ˈneɪvɪ] *s.* ⚓ **1.** *mst* ♀ ˈKriegsmaˌrine *f*; **2.** (Kriegs)Flotte *f*; **~ blue** *s.* Maˈrineblau *n*; ˌ**~-ˈblue** *adj.* maˈrineblau; ♀ **Board** *s. Brit.* Admiraliˈtät *f*; **~ league** *s.* Flottenverein *m*; ♀ **List** *s.* Maˈrineˌrangliste *f*; **~ yard** *s.* Maˈrinewerft *f*.

nay [neɪ] **I** *adv.* **1.** *obs.* nein; **2.** *obs.* ja soˈgar; **II** *s.* **3.** *parl. etc.* Nein(stimme *f*) *n*: ***the ~s have it!*** der Antrag ist abgelehnt!

Naz·a·rene [ˌnæzəˈriːn] *s.* Nazaˈrener *m* (*a. Christus*).

naze [neɪz] *s.* Landspitze *f*.

Na·zi [ˈnɑːtsɪ] *pol. contp.* **I** *s.* Nazi *m*; **II** *adj.* Nazi…; ˈ**Na·zism** [-ɪzəm] *s.* Naˈzismus *m*.

neap [niːp] **I** *adj.* niedrig, abnehmend (*Flut*); **II** *s. a.* **~ tide** Nippflut *f*; **III** *v/i.* zuˈrückgehen (*Flut*).

near [nɪə] **I** *adv.* **1.** nahe, (ganz) in der Nähe; **2.** nahe (bevorstehend) (*Ereignis etc.*): ***~ upon five o'clock*** ziemlich genau um 5 Uhr; **3.** F annähernd, nahezu, fast: ***not ~ so bad*** bei weitem nicht so schlecht;

Besondere Redewendungen:

~ at hand a) nahe, in der Nähe, dicht dabei, b) *fig.* nahe bevorstehend, vor der Tür; ***~ by*** → ***nearby*** I; ***come*** (*od.* ***go***) ***~ to*** a) sich ungefähr belaufen auf (*acc.*), b) *e-r Sache* sehr nahekommen, fast *et.* sein; ***come ~ to doing s.th.*** et. beinahe tun; ***draw ~*** heranrücken (*a. Zeitpunkt*); ***live ~*** sparsam *od.* kärglich leben; ***sail ~ to the wind*** ⚓ hart am Wind segeln;

II *adj.* ☐ → **I** *u.* ***nearly***; **4.** nahe(gelegen), in der Nähe: ***the ~est place*** der nächste Ort; ***~ miss*** a) ⚔ Nahkrepierer *m*, b) ✈ Beinahzusammenstoß *m*, c) *fig.* fast ein Erfolg; **5.** kurz, nahe (*Weg*): ***the ~est way*** der kürzeste Weg; **6.** nahe (*Zeit, Ereignis*): ***the ~ future***; **7.** nahe (verwandt): ***the ~est relations*** die nächsten Verwandten; **8.** eng (befreundet), inˈtim: ***a ~ friend***; **9.** aˈkut, brennend (*Frage, Problem etc.*); **10.** knapp (*Entkommen, Rennen etc.*): ***that was a ~ thing*** F ‚das hätte ins Auge gehen können'; **11.** genau, (wort)getreu (*Übersetzung etc.*); **12.** sparsam, geizig; **13.** link (*vom Fahrer aus; Pferd, Fahrbahnseite etc.*): ***~ horse*** Handpferd *n*; **14.** Imitations…: ***~ leather***; ***~ beer*** Dünnbier *n*; ***~ silk*** Halbseide *f*; **III** *prp.* **15.** nahe, in der Nähe von (*od. gen.*), nahe an (*dat.*) *od.* bei, unweit (*gen.*): ***~ s.o.*** j-m nahe; ***~ doing s.th.*** nahe daran, et. zu tun; **16.** (*zeitlich*) nahe, nicht weit von; **IV** *v/t. u. v/i.* **17.** sich nähern, näherkommen (*dat.*): ***be ~ing completion*** der Vollendung entgegengehen.

near·by I [ˌnɪəˈbaɪ] *adv. bsd. Am.* in der Nähe, nahe; **II** [ˈnɪəbaɪ] *adj.* nahe(gelegen).

Near East *s. geogr., pol.* **1.** *Brit. obs. die* Balkanstaaten *pl.*; **2.** *der* Nahe Osten.

near·ly [ˈnɪəlɪ] *adv.* **1.** beinahe, fast; **2.** annähernd: ***not ~*** bei weitem nicht, nicht annähernd; **3.** genau, gründlich; **near·ness** [ˈnɪənɪs] *s.* **1.** Nähe *f*; **2.** Innigkeit *f*, Vertrautheit *f*; **3.** große Ähnlichkeit; **4.** Knauserigkeit *f*.

near| point *s. opt.* Nahpunkt *m*; ˈ**~side** *s. mot.* Beifahrerseite *f*; ˌ**~-ˈsight·ed** *adj.* kurzsichtig; ˌ**~-ˈsight·ed·ness** *s.* Kurzsichtigkeit *f*.

neat¹ [niːt] *adj.* ☐ **1.** sauber: a) ordentlich, reinlich, b) hübsch, nett (*a. fig.*), aˈdrett, geschmackvoll, c) klar, ˈübersichtlich, d) geschickt; **2.** treffend (*Antwort etc.*); **3.** a) rein: ***~ silk***, b) pur: ***~ whisky***; **4.** *sl.* prima.

neat² [niːt] **I** *s. pl.* **1.** *coll.* Rind-, Hornvieh *n*, Rinder *pl.*; **2.** Ochse *m*, Rind *n*; **II** *adj.* **3.** Rind(er)…

'neath, neath [niːθ] *prp. poet. od. dial.* unter (*dat.*), ˈunterhalb (*gen.*).

neat·ness [ˈniːtnɪs] *s.* **1.** Ordentlichkeit *f*, Sauberkeit *f*; **2.** Gefälligkeit *f*, Nettigkeit *f*; Zierlichkeit *f*; **3.** schlichte Eleˈganz, Klarheit *f* (*Stil etc.*); **4.** Geschicklichkeit *f*; **5.** Unvermischtheit *f* (*Getränke etc.*).

ˈ**neat's|-foot oil** *s.* Klauenfett *n*; ˈ**~-leath·er** *s.* Rindsleder *n*.

neb·u·la ['nebjʊlə] *pl.* **-lae** [-li:] *s.* **1.** *ast.* Nebel(fleck) *m*; **2.** ⚕ a) Trübheit *f* (*des Urins*), b) Hornhauttrübung *f*; **'neb·u·lar** [-lə] *adj. ast.* **1.** Nebel(fleck)..., Nebular...; **2.** nebelartig; **neb·u·los·i·ty** [ˌnebjʊ'lɒsətɪ] *s.* **1.** Neb(e)ligkeit *f*; **2.** Trübheit *f*; **3.** *fig.* Verschwommenheit *f*; **4.** → ***nebula*** 1; **'neb·u·lous** [-ləs] *adj.* □ **1.** neb(e)lig, wolkig (*a. Flüssigkeit*); *ast.* Nebel...; **2.** *fig.* verschwommen, nebelhaft.

nec·es·sar·i·ly ['nesəsərəlɪ] *adv.* **1.** notwendigerweise; **2.** unbedingt: ***you need not ~ do it***; **nec·es·sar·y** ['nesəsərɪ] **I** *adj.* □ **1.** notwendig, nötig, erforderlich (***to*** für): ***it is ~ for me to do it*** es ist nötig, daß ich es tue; ***a ~ evil*** ein notwendiges Übel; ***if ~*** nötigenfalls; **2.** unvermeidlich, zwangsläufig, notwendig: ***a ~ consequence***; **3.** notgedrungen; **II** *s.* **4.** Erfordernis *n*, Bedürfnis *n*: ***necessaries of life*** Notbedarf *m*, Lebensbedürfnisse; ***strict necessaries*** unentbehrliche Unterhaltsmittel; **5.** ⚖ Be'darfsarˌtikel *m*.

ne·ces·si·tar·i·an [nɪˌsesɪ'teərɪən] *phls.* **I** *s.* Determi'nist *m*; **II** *adj.* determi'nistisch.

ne·ces·si·tate [nɪ'sesɪteɪt] *v/t.* **1.** notwendig *od.* nötig machen, erfordern, verlangen; **2.** *j-n* zwingen, nötigen; **ne·ces·si·ta·tion** [nɪˌsesɪ'teɪʃn] *s.* Nötigung *f*, Zwang *m*; **ne'ces·si·tous** [-təs] *adj.* □ **1.** bedürftig, notleidend; **2.** dürftig, ärmlich (*Umstände*); **3.** notgedrungen (*Handlung*); **ne'ces·si·ty** [-tɪ] *s.* **1.** Notwendigkeit *f*: a) Erforderlichkeit *f*, b) 'Unumˌgänglichkeit *f*, Unvermeidlichkeit *f*, c) Zwang *m*: ***as a ~, of ~*** notwendigerweise; ***be under the ~ of doing*** gezwungen sein zu tun; **2.** (dringendes) Bedürfnis: (***the bare***) ***necessities of life*** (die dringendsten) Lebensbedürfnisse; **3.** Not *f*, Zwangslage *f*, *a.* ⚖ Notstand *m*: ***~ is the mother of invention*** Not macht erfinderisch; ***~ knows no law*** Not kennt kein Gebot; ***in case of ~*** im Notfall; → ***virtue*** 3; **4.** Not(lage) *f*, Bedürftigkeit *f*.

neck [nek] **I** *s.* **1.** Hals *m* (*a. Flasche, Gewehr, Saiteninstrument*); **2.** Nacken *m*, Genick *n*: ***break one's ~*** sich das Genick brechen; ***crane one's ~*** sich den Hals ausrenken (***at*** nach); ***get it in the ~*** *sl.* ‚eins aufs Dach bekommen'; ***risk one's ~*** Kopf u. Kragen riskieren; ***stick one's ~ out*** F viel riskieren, den Kopf hinhalten; ***be up to one's ~ in s.th.*** bis über die Ohren in et. stecken; ***win by a ~*** *sport* um e-e Kopflänge gewinnen (*Pferd*); ***~ and ~*** Kopf an Kopf (*a. fig.*); ***~ and crop*** mit Stumpf u. Stiel; ***~ or nothing*** a) (*adv.*) auf Biegen oder Brechen, b) (*attr.*) tollkühn, verzweifelt; ***it is ~ or nothing*** es geht um alles oder nichts; **3.** Hals-, Kammstück *n* (*Schlachtvieh*); **4.** Ausschnitt *m* (*Kleid*); **5.** *anat.* Hals *m e-s Organs*; **6.** △ Halsglied *n* (*Säule*); **7.** ⚙ a) Hals *m* (*Welle*), b) Schenkel *m* (*Achse*), c) (abgesetzter) Zapfen, d) Ansatz *m* (*Schraube*), e) Einfüllstutzen *m*; **8.** a) Landenge *f*, b) Engpaß *m*: ***~ of the woods*** ‚Ecke' *f e-s Landes*; **II** *v/t.* **9.** *e-m Huhn etc.* den Kopf abschlagen *od.* den Hals 'umdrehen; **10.** ⚙ *a.* ***~ out*** aushalsen; **11.** *sl.* ‚knutschen' *od.* ‚schmusen' mit; **III** *v/i.* **12.** *sl.* ‚knutschen'; **'~·cloth** *s.* Halstuch *n*.

neck·er·chief ['nekətʃɪf] *s.* Halstuch *n*.

neck·ing ['nekɪŋ] *s.* **1.** △ Säulenhals *m*; **2.** ⚙ a) Aushalsen *n e-s Hohlkörpers*, b) Querschnittverminderung *f*; **3.** *sl.* ‚Geknutsche' *n*.

neck·lace ['neklɪs], **'neck·let** [-lɪt] *s.* Halskette *f*.

neck| le·ver *s. Ringen*: Nackenhebel *m*; **'~·line** *s.* Ausschnitt *m* (*am Kleid*); **~ scis·sors** *s. pl. sg. konstr. Ringen*: Halsschere *f*; **'~·tie** *s.* Kra'watte *f*, Schlips *m*; **'~·wear** *s.* ✝ *coll.* Kra'watten *pl.*, Kragen *pl.*, Halstücher *pl.*

ne·crol·o·gy [ne'krɒlədʒɪ] *s.* **1.** Toten-, Sterbeliste *f*; **2.** Nachruf *m*; **nec·ro·man·cer** ['nekrəʊmænsə] *s.* **1.** Geister-, Totenbeschwörer *m*; **2.** *allg.* Schwarzkünstler *m*; **nec·ro·man·cy** ['nekrəʊmænsɪ] *s.* **1.** Geisterbeschwörung *f*, Nekroman'tie *f*; **2.** *allg.* Schwarze Kunst; **ne·croph·i·lism** [ne'krɒfɪlɪzəm] *s. psych.* Nekrophi'lie *f*; **ne·cro·sis** [ne'krəʊsɪs] *s.* ⚕ Ne'krose *f*, Brand *m* (*a.* ⚘): ***~ of the bone*** Knochenfraß *m*; **ne·crot·ic** [ne'krɒtɪk] *adj.* ⚘, ⚕ brandig.

nec·tar ['nektə] *s. myth.* Nektar *m* (*a.* ⚘ *u. fig.*), Göttertrank *m*; **'nec·ta·ry** [-ərɪ] *s.* ⚘, *zo.* Nek'tarium *n*, Honigdrüse *f*.

née, *bsd. Am.* **nee** [neɪ] *adj.* geborene (*vor dem Mädchennamen e-r Frau*).

need [ni:d] **I** *s.* **1.** (***of, for***) (dringendes) Bedürfnis (nach), Bedarf *m* (an *dat.*): ***one's own ~s*** Eigenbedarf; ***be*** (*od.* ***stand***) ***in ~ of s.th.*** et. dringend brauchen, et. sehr nötig haben; ***fill a ~*** e-m Bedürfnis entgegenkommen, e-m Mangel abhelfen; ***in ~ of repair*** reparaturbedürftig; ***have no ~ to do*** kein Bedürfnis *od.* keinen Grund haben zu tun; **2.** Mangel *m* (***of, for*** an *dat.*): ***feel the ~ of*** (*od.* ***for***) ***s.th.*** et. vermissen, Mangel an et. verspüren; **3.** dringende Notwendigkeit: ***there is no ~ for you to come*** du brauchst nicht zu kommen; **4.** Not(lage) *f*: ***in case of ~, if ~ be, if ~ arise*** nötigenfalls, im Notfall; **5.** Armut *f*, Not *f*; **6.** *pl.* Erfordernisse *pl.*, Bedürfnisse *pl.*; **II** *v/t.* **7.** benötigen, nötig haben, brauchen; **8.** erfordern: ***it ~s all your strength***; ***it ~ed doing*** es mußte (einmal) getan werden; **III** *v/aux.* **9.** müssen, brauchen: ***it ~s to be done*** es muß getan werden; ***it ~s but to become known*** es braucht nur bekannt zu werden; **10.** (*vor e-r Verneinung u. in Fragen, ohne* **to**; *3. sg. pres.* ***need***) brauchen, müssen: ***she ~ not do it***; ***you ~ not have come*** du hättest nicht zu kommen brauchen; **'need·ful** [-fʊl] **I** *adj.* □ nötig; **II** *s. das* Nötige: ***the ~*** F das nötige Kleingeld; **'need·i·ness** [-dɪnɪs] *s.* Bedürftigkeit *f*, Armut *f*.

nee·dle ['ni:dl] **I** *s.* **1.** (*Näh-, a. Grammophon-, Magnet- etc.*)Nadel *f* (*a.* ⚕, ⚘): ***knitting-~*** Stricknadel; ***as sharp as a ~*** *fig.* äußerst intelligent, ‚auf Draht'; ***~'s eye*** Nadelöhr *n*; ***get*** (*od.* ***take***) ***the ~*** F ‚hochgehen', e-e Wut kriegen; ***give s.o. the ~*** → 7; **2.** ⚙ a) Ven'tilnadel *f*, b) *mot.* Schwimmernadel *f* (*Vergaser*), c) Zeiger *m*, d) Zunge *f* (*Waage*), e) Radiernadel *f*; **3.** Nadel *f* (*Berg-, Felsspitze*); **4.** Obe'lisk *m*; **5.** *min.* Kri'stallnadel *f*; **II** *v/t.* **6.** (*mit e-r Nadel*) nähen, durch'stechen; ⚕ punktieren: ***~ one's way through*** *fig.* sich hindurchschlängeln; **7.** F *durch Sticheleien* aufbringen, reizen; **8.** anstacheln; **9.** F *Getränk durch Alkoholzusatz* schärfen; **~ bath** *s.* Strahldusche *f*; **'~·book** *s.* Nadelbuch *n*; **'~-gun** *s.* ⚔ Zündnadelgewehr *n*; **'~·like** *adj.* nadelartig; **~ point** *s.* **1.** Petit'point-Sticke̩rei *f*; **2.** → **'~-point lace** *s.* Nadelspitze *f* (*Ggs. Klöppelspitze*).

need·less ['ni:dlɪs] *adj.* unnötig, 'überflüssig: ***~ to say*** selbstredend, selbstverständlich; ***~ly*** *adv.* unnötig(erweise); **'need·less·ness** [-nɪs] *s.* Unnötigkeit *f*, 'Überflüssigkeit *f*.

nee·dle| valve *s.* ⚙ 'Nadelvenˌtil *n*; **'~ˌwom·an** *s.* [*irr.*] Näherin *f*; **'~·work I** *s.* Handarbeit *f*, Nähe'rei *f*; **II** *adj.* Handarbeits...: ***~ shop***.

needs [ni:dz] *adv.* unbedingt, notwendigerweise: ***if you must ~ do it*** wenn du es durchaus tun willst.

need·y ['ni:dɪ] *adj.* □ arm, bedürftig, notleidend.

ne'er [neə] *poet. für* ***never***; **'~-do-well I** *s.* Taugenichts *m*, Tunichtgut *m*; **II** *adj.* nichtsnutzig.

ne·far·i·ous [nɪ'feərɪəs] *adj.* □ ruchlos, schändlich; **ne'far·i·ous·ness** [-nɪs] *s.* Ruchlosigkeit *f*, Bosheit *f*.

ne·gate [nɪ'geɪt] *v/t.* **1.** verneinen, negieren, leugnen; **2.** annullieren, unwirksam machen, aufheben, verwerfen; **ne'ga·tion** [-eɪʃn] *s.* **1.** Verneinung *f*, Verneinen *n*, Negieren *n*; **2.** Verwerfung *f*, Annullierung *f*, Aufhebung *f*; **3.** *phls.* a) (*Logik*) Negati'on *f*, b) Nichts *n*.

neg·a·tive ['negətɪv] **I** *adj.* □ **1.** negativ, verneinend; **2.** abschlägig, ablehnend (*Antwort etc.*); **3.** erfolglos, ergebnislos; **4.** negativ (*ohne positive Werte*); **5.** ⚗, ⚡, ⚘, ⚕, *phot.*, *phys.* negativ: ***~ conductor*** ⚡ Minusleitung *f*; ***~ electrode*** Kathode *f*; ***~ lens*** *opt.* Zerstreuungslinse *f*; ***~ sign*** ⚘ Minuszeichen *n*, negatives Vorzeichen; ***~!*** Fehlanzeige!; **II** *s.* **6.** Verneinung *f*: ***answer in the ~*** verneinen; **7.** abschlägige Antwort; **8.** *ling.* Negati'on *f*; **9.** a) Einspruch *m*, Veto *n*, b) ablehnende Stimme; **10.** negative Eigenschaft, Negativum *n*; **11.** ⚡ negativer Pol; **12.** ⚘ a) Minuszeichen *n*, b) negative Zahl; **13.** *phot.* Negativ *n*; **III** *v/t.* **14.** negieren, verneinen; **15.** verwerfen, ablehnen; **16.** wider'legen; **17.** unwirksam machen, neutralisieren, aufheben; **'neg·a·tiv·ism** [-vɪzəm] *s.* Negati'vismus *m* (*a. phls., psych.*); **ne·ga·tor** [nɪ'geɪtə] *s.* Verneiner *m*; **'neg·a·to·ry** [-tərɪ] *adj.* verneinend, negativ.

neg·lect [nɪ'glekt] **I** *v/t.* **1.** vernachlässigen; **2.** miß'achten; **3.** versäumen, unter'lassen (***to do*** *od.* ***doing*** zu tun); **4.** über'sehen, -'gehen; außer acht lassen; **II** *s.* **5.** Vernachlässigung *f*, Hint'ansetzung *f*; **6.** 'Mißachtung *f*; **7.** Unter'lassung *f*, Versäumnis *n*, ⚖ *a.* Fahrlässigkeit *f*: ***~ of duty*** Pflichtversäumnis; **8.** Verwahrlosung *f*: ***in a state of ~*** verwahrlost; **9.** Über'gehen *n*, Auslassung *f*; **10.** Nachlässigkeit *f*; **neg'lect·ful** [-fʊl] *adj.* □ → ***negligent*** 1.

neg·li·gée ['negli:ʒeɪ] *s.* Negli'gé *n*: a) *ungezwungene Hauskleidung*, b) *dün-*

ner Morgenmantel.

neg·li·gence ['neglɪdʒəns] *s.* **1.** Nachlässigkeit *f*, Unachtsamkeit *f*; **2.** ⚖ Fahrlässigkeit *f*: ***contributory ~*** mitwirkendes Verschulden; '**neg·li·gent** [-nt] *adj.* ☐ **1.** nachlässig, gleichgültig, unachtsam (***of*** gegen): ***be ~ of s.th.*** et. vernachlässigen, et. außer acht lassen; **2.** ⚖ fahrlässig; **3.** lässig, sa'lopp.

neg·li·gi·ble ['neglɪdʒəbl] *adj.* ☐ **1.** nebensächlich, unwesentlich; **2.** geringfügig, unbedeutend; → ***quantity*** 2.

ne·go·ti·a·bil·i·ty [nɪˌgəʊʃjə'bɪlətɪ] *s.* † **1.** Verkäuflichkeit *f*; **2.** Begebbarkeit *f*; **3.** Bank-, Börsenfähigkeit *f*; **4.** Über'tragbarkeit *f*; **5.** Verwertbarkeit *f*; **ne·go·ti·a·ble** [nɪ'gəʊʃjəbl] *adj.* ☐ **1.** † a) verkäuflich, veräußerlich, b) verkehrsfähig, c) bank-, börsenfähig, d) (durch Indossa'ment) über'tragbar, begebbar, e) verwertbar: ***~ instrument*** begebbares (Wert)Papier; ***not ~*** nur zur Verrechnung; **2.** über'windbar (*Hindernis*); befahrbar (*Straße*); **3.** auf dem Verhandlungsweg erreichbar: ***salary ~*** Gehalt nach Vereinbarung.

ne·go·ti·ate [nɪ'gəʊʃɪeɪt] **I** *v/i.* **1.** ver-, unter'handeln, in Unter'handlung stehen (***with*** mit, ***for***, ***about*** um, wegen): ***negotiating table*** Verhandlungstisch *m*; **II** *v/t.* **2.** *Vertrag etc.* zu'stande bringen, (ab)schließen; **3.** verhandeln über (*acc.*); **4.** † *Wechsel* begeben: ***~ back*** zurückbegeben; **5.** *Hindernis etc.* über'winden, *a. Kurve* nehmen; **ne·go·ti·a·tion** [nɪˌgəʊʃɪ'eɪʃn] *s.* **1.** Ver-, Unter'handlung *f*: ***enter into ~s*** in Verhandlungen eintreten: ***by way of ~*** auf dem Verhandlungswege; **2.** Aushandeln *n* (*Vertrag*); **3.** † Begebung *f*, Über'tragung *f* (*Wechsel etc.*): ***further ~*** Weiterbegebung; **4.** Über'windung *f*, Nehmen *n von Hindernissen*; **ne'go·ti·a·tor** [-tə] *s.* **1.** 'Unterhändler *m*; **2.** Vermittler *m*.

ne·gress ['ni:grɪs] *s. obs.* Negerin *f*.

ne·gro ['ni:grəʊ] **I** *pl.* **-groes** *s.* Neger (-in); **II** *adj.* Neger...: ***~ question*** Negerfrage *f*, -problem *n*; ***~ spiritual*** → ***spiritual*** 8; '**ne·groid** [-rɔɪd] *adj.* negro'id, negerartig.

Ne·gus¹ ['ni:gəs] *s. hist.* Negus *m* (*äthiopischer Königstitel*).

ne·gus² ['ni:gəs] *s.* Glühwein *m*.

neigh [neɪ] **I** *v/t. u. v/i.* wiehern; **II** *s.* Gewieher *n*, Wiehern *n*.

neigh·bo(u)r ['neɪbə] **I** *s.* **1.** Nachbar (-in); **2.** Nächste(r) *m*, Mitmensch *m*; **II** *adj.* **3.** → ***neighbo(u)ring***; **III** *v/t.* **4.** (an)grenzen an (*acc.*); **IV** *v/i.* **5.** benachbart sein, in der Nachbarschaft wohnen; **6.** grenzen (***upon*** an *acc.*); '**neigh·bo(u)r·hood** [-hʊd] *s.* **1.** Nachbarschaft *f* (*a. fig.*), Um'gebung *f*, Nähe *f*: ***in the ~ of*** a) in der Umgebung von, b) *fig.* F ungefähr, etwa, um ... herum; **2.** *coll.* Nachbarn *pl.*, Nachbarschaft *f*; **3.** (Wohn)Gegend *f*: ***a fashionable ~***; '**neigh·bo(u)r·ing** [-bərɪŋ] *adj.* benachbart, angrenzend, Nachbar...: ***~ state*** *a.* Anliegerstaat *m*; '**neigh·bo(u)r·li·ness** [-lɪnɪs] *s.* (gut)'nachbarliches Verhalten; Freundlichkeit *f*; '**neigh·bo(u)r·ly** [-lɪ] *adj. u. adv.* **1.** (gut)'nachbarlich; **2.** freundlich, gesellig.

nei·ther ['naɪðə] **I** *adj. u. pron.* **1.** kein (von beiden): ***~ of you*** keiner von euch (beiden); **II** *cj.* **2.** weder: ***~ you nor he knows*** weder du weißt es noch er; **3.** noch (auch), auch nicht, ebensowenig: ***he does not know, ~ do I*** er weiß es nicht, noch *od.* ebensowenig weiß ich es.

nem·a·tode ['nemətəʊd] *zo. s.* Nema'tode *f*, Fadenwurm *m*.

nem con [ˌnem'kɒn] *adv.* einstimmig.

nem·e·sis, *a.* ♀ ['nemɪsɪs] *s. myth. u. fig.* Nemesis *f*, (die Göttin der) Vergeltung *f*.

ne·mo ['ni:məʊ] *s. Radio, TV*: 'Außenreporˌtage *f*.

neo- [ni:əʊ] *in Zssgn* neu, jung, neo..., Neo...

ne·o·lith ['ni:əʊlɪθ] *s.* jungsteinzeitliches Gerät; **ne·o·lith·ic** [ˌni:əʊ'lɪθɪk] *adj.* jungsteinzeitlich, neo'lithisch: ***♀ period*** Jungsteinzeit *f*.

ne·ol·o·gism [ni:'ɒlədʒɪzəm] *s.* **1.** *ling.* Neolo'gismus *m*, Wortneubildung *f*; **2.** *eccl.* neue Dok'trin; **ne'ol·o·gy** [-dʒɪ] *s.* **1.** → ***neologism*** 1 *u.* 2; **2.** *ling.* Neolo'gie *f*, Bildung *f* neuer Wörter.

ne·on ['ni:ən] *s.* ⚗ Neon *n*: ***~ lamp*** Neonlampe *f*, Leucht(stoff)röhre *f*; ***~ signs*** Leuchtreklame *f*.

ne·o·phyte ['ni:əʊfaɪt] *s.* **1.** *eccl.* Neubekehrte(r *m*) *f*, Konver'tit(in); **2.** *R.C.* a) No'vize *m*, *f*, b) Jungpriester *m*; **3.** *fig.* Neuling *m*, Anfänger(in).

ne·o·plasm ['ni:əʊplæzəm] *s.* ⚕ Neo'plasma *n*, Gewächs *n*.

ne·o·ter·ic [ˌni:əʊ'terɪk] *adj.* (☐ ***~ally***) neuzeitlich, mo'dern.

Ne·o·zo·ic [ˌni:əʊ'zəʊɪk] *geol.* **I** *s.* Neo'zoikum *n*, Neuzeit *f*; **II** *adj.* neo'zoisch.

Nep·a·lese [ˌnepɔ:'li:z] **I** *s.* Nepa'lese *m*, Nepalesin *f*, Bewohner(in) von Ne'pal; Nepa'lesen *pl.*; **II** *adj.* nepa'lesisch.

neph·ew ['nevju:] *s.* Neffe *m*.

ne·phol·o·gy [nɪ'fɒlədʒɪ] *s.* Wolkenkunde *f*.

ne·phrit·ic [ne'frɪtɪk] *adj.* ⚕ Nieren...; **ne·phri·tis** [ne'fraɪtɪs] *s.* ⚕ Ne'phritis *f*, Nierenentzündung *f*; **neph·ro·lith** ['nefrəʊlɪθ] *s.* ⚕ Nierenstein *m*; **ne·phrol·o·gist** [ne'frɒlədʒɪst] *s.* ⚕ Nierenfacharzt *m*, Uro'loge *m*.

nep·o·tism ['nepətɪzəm] *s.* Nepo'tismus *m*, Vetternwirtschaft *f*.

Nep·tune ['neptju:n] *s. myth. u. ast.* Neptun *m*.

Ne·re·id ['nɪərɪɪd] *s. myth.* Nere'ide *f*, Wassernymphe *f*.

ner·va·tion [nɜ:'veɪʃn], **nerv·a·ture** ['nɜ:vəˌtʃʊə] *s.* **1.** Anordnung *f* der Nerven; **2.** ♀ Aderung *f*.

nerve [nɜ:v] **I** *s.* **1.** Nerv(enfaser *f*) *m*: ***get on s.o.'s ~s*** j-m auf die Nerven gehen; ***be all ~s***, ***be a bag of ~s*** F ein Nervenbündel sein; ***a fit of ~s*** e-e Nervenkrise; ***strain every ~*** s-e ganze Kraft aufbieten; **2.** *fig.* a) Lebensnerv *m*, b) Stärke *f*, Ener'gie *f*, c) (innere) Ruhe, d) Mut *m*, e) *sl.* Frechheit *f*: ***lose one's ~*** die Nerven verlieren; ***have the ~ to do s.th.*** es wagen, et. zu tun; ***he has got a ~!*** *sl.* der hat vielleicht Nerven!; **3.** ♀ Nerv *m*, Ader *f* (*Blatt*); **4.** △ (Gewölbe)Rippe *f*; **II** *v/t.* **5.** *fig.* (*körperlich od. seelisch*) stärken, ermutigen: ***~ o.s.*** sich aufraffen; ***~ center*** *Am.*, ***~ cen·tre*** *Brit. s.* Nervenzentrum *n* (*a. fig.*); ***~ cord*** *s.* Nervenstrang *m*.

nerved [nɜ:vd] *adj.* **1.** nervig (*mst in Zssgn*): ***strong-~*** nervenstark; **2.** ♀, *zo.* geädert, gerippt.

nerve·less ['nɜ:vlɪs] *adj.* ☐ **1.** *fig.* kraft-, ener'gielos; **2.** ohne Nerven; **3.** ♀ ohne Adern, nervenlos.

nerve| poi·son *s.* Nervengift *n*; '**~-ˌrack·ing** *adj.* nervenaufreibend.

nerv·ine ['nɜ:vi:n] *adj. u. s.* ⚕ nervenstärkend(es Mittel).

nerv·ous ['nɜ:vəs] *adj.* **1.** Nerven...(*-system, -zusammenbruch etc.*): ***~ excitement*** nervöse Erregtheit; **2.** nervenreich; **3.** ner'vös: a) nervenschwach, erregbar, b) ängstlich, scheu, c) aufgeregt; **4.** aufregend; **5.** *obs.* kräftig, nervig; '**ner·vous·ness** [-nɪs] *s.* Nervosi'tät *f*.

nerv·y ['nɜ:vɪ] *adj.* F **1.** frech; **2.** ner'vös; **3.** nervenaufreibend.

nes·ci·ence ['nesɪəns] *s.* (vollständige) Unwissenheit; '**nes·ci·ent** [-nt] *adj.* unwissend (***of*** in *dat.*).

ness [nes] *s.* Vorgebirge *n*.

nest [nest] **I** *s.* **1.** *orn.*, *zo.*, *a. geol.* Nest *n*; **2.** *fig.* Nest *n*, Zufluchtsort *m*, behagliches Heim; **3.** *fig.* Schlupfwinkel *m*, Brutstätte *f*: ***~ of vice*** Lasterhöhle *f*; **4.** Brut *f* (*junger Tiere*): ***take a ~*** ein Nest ausnehmen; **5.** ⚔ (Widerstands-, M'G-)Nest *n*; **6.** Serie *f*, Satz *m* (*ineinanderpassender Dinge*, *z.B. Schüsseln*); **7.** ⚙ Satz *m*, Gruppe *f*: ***~ of boiler tubes*** Heizrohrbündel *n*; **II** *v/i.* **8.** a) ein Nest bauen, b) nisten; **9.** sich einnisten, sich 'niederlassen; **10.** Vogelnester ausnehmen; **III** *v/t.* **11.** *Töpfe etc.* inein'anderstellen, -setzen; ***~ egg*** *s.* **1.** Nestei *n*; **2.** *fig.* Spar-, Notgroschen *m*.

nes·tle ['nesl] **I** *v/i.* **1.** *a.* ***~ down*** sich behaglich 'niederlassen; **2.** sich anschmiegen *od.* kuscheln (***to***, ***against*** an *acc.*); **3.** sich einnisten; **II** *v/t.* **4.** schmiegen, kuscheln (***on***, ***to***, ***against*** an *acc.*); **nest·ling** ['nestlɪŋ] *s.* **1.** *orn.* Nestling *m*; **2.** *fig.* Nesthäkchen *n*.

net¹ [net] **I** *s.* **1.** (*a. weitS. Straßen- etc.*, Ā Koordi'naten)Netz *n*; → *a.* ***network*** 4; **2.** *fig.* Falle *f*, Netz *n*, Garn *n*; **3.** netzartiges Gewebe, Netz *n*; † Tüll *m*, Musse'lin *m*: ***~ curtain*** Store *m*; **4.** *Tennis*: Netzball *m*; **II** *v/t.* **5.** mit e-m Netz fangen; **6.** *fig.* (ein)fangen; **7.** mit e-m Netz um'geben *od.* bedecken; **8.** *Gewässer* mit Netzen abfischen; **9.** in Fi'let arbeiten, knüpfen; **10.** *Tennis*: Ball ins Netz schlagen; **III** *v/i.* **11.** Netz- *od.* Fi'letarbeit machen.

net² [net] **I** *adj.* † **1.** netto, Netto..., Rein..., Roh...: ***~ income*** Nettoeinkommen *n*; **II** *v/t.* **2.** netto einbringen, e-n Reingewinn von ... abwerfen; **3.** netto verdienen, e-n Reingewinn haben von; ***~ a·mount*** *s.* Nettobetrag *m*, Reinertrag *m*; ***~ cash*** *s.* † netto Kasse: ***~ in advance*** Nettokasse im voraus; ***~ ef·fi·cien·cy*** *s.* ⚙ Nutzleistung *f*.

neth·er ['neðə] *adj.* **1.** unter, Unter...: ***~ regions***, ***~ world*** Unterwelt *f*; **2.** nieder, Nieder...

Neth·er·land·er ['neðələndə] *s.* Niederländer(in); '**Neth·er·land·ish** [-dɪʃ] *adj.* niederländisch.

'**neth·er·most** *adj.* unterst, tiefst.

net| load *s.* †, ⚙ Nutzlast *f*; ***~ price*** *s.* † Nettopreis *m*; ***~ pro·ceeds*** *s. pl.* † Nettoeinnahme(n *pl.*) *f*, Reinerlös *m*; ***~***

prof·it *s.* † Reingewinn *m.*

net·ted ['netɪd] *adj.* **1.** netzförmig, maschig; **2.** von Netzen um'geben *od.* bedeckt; '**net·ting** [-tɪŋ] *s.* **1.** Netzstricken *n*, Fi'letarbeit *f*; **2.** Netz(werk) *n*, Geflecht *n* (*a. Draht*); ⚔ Tarnnetze *pl.*

net·tle ['netl] **I** *s.* **1.** ♀ Nessel *f*: ***grasp the ~*** *fig.* den Stier bei den Hörnern packen; **II** *v/t.* **2.** mit *od.* an Nesseln brennen; **3.** *fig.* ärgern, reizen: ***be ~d at*** aufgebracht sein über (*acc.*); **~ cloth** *s.* Nesseltuch *n*; **~ rash** *s.* ⚕ Nesselausschlag *m.*

net| weight *s.* † Netto-, Rein-, Eigen-, Trockengewicht *n*; '**~·work** *s.* **1.** Netz-, Maschenwerk *n*, Geflecht *n*, Netz *n*; **2.** Netz-, Fi'letarbeit *f*; **3.** *fig.* Netz *n*: ***~ of roads*** Straßennetz; ***~ of intrigues*** Netz von Intrigen; **4.** ϟ a) Leitungs-, Verteilungsnetz *n*, b) *Rundfunk*: Sendernetz *n*, -gruppe *f*; **~ yield** *s.* † effek'tive Ren'dite *od.* Verzinsung, Nettoertrag *m.*

neu·ral ['njʊərəl] *adj. physiol.* Nerven...: ***~ axis*** Nervenachse *f.*

neu·ral·gia [ˌnjʊə'rældʒə] *s.* ⚕ Neural'gie *f*, Nervenschmerz *m*; ˌ**neu'ral·gic** [-dʒɪk] *adj.* (□ **~ally**) neur'algisch.

neu·ras·the·ni·a [ˌnjʊərəs'θiːnɪə] *s.* ⚕ Neurasthe'nie *f*, Nervenschwäche *f*; ˌ**neu·ras'then·ic** [-'θenɪk] ⚕ **I** *adj.* (□ **~ally**) neura'sthenisch; **II** *s.* Neura'stheniker(in).

neu·ri·tis [ˌnjʊə'raɪtɪs] *s.* Nervenentzündung *f.*

neu·rol·o·gist [ˌnjʊə'rɒlədʒɪst] *s.* Neuro'loge *m*, Nervenarzt *m*; ˌ**neu'rol·o·gy** [-dʒɪ] *s.* Neurolo'gie *f.*

neu·ro·path ['njʊərəʊpæθ] *s.* ⚕ Nervenleidende(r *m*) *f*; **neu·ro·path·ic** [ˌnjʊərəʊ'pæθɪk] *adj.* (□ **~ally**) neuro'pathisch: a) ner'vös (*Leiden etc.*), b) nervenkrank; **neu·rop·a·thist** [ˌnjʊə'rɒpəθɪst] → ***neurologist***; **neu'rop·a·thy** [ˌnjʊə'rɒpəθɪ] *s.* Nervenleiden *n.*

neu·rop·ter·an [ˌnjʊə'rɒptərən] *zo.* **I** *adj.* Netzflügler...; **II** *s.* Netzflügler *m.*

neu·ro·sis [ˌnjʊə'rəʊsɪs] *pl.* **-ses** [-siːz] *s.* ⚕ Neu'rose *f*; ˌ**neu'rot·ic** [-'rɒtɪk] **I** *adj.* (□ **~ally**) **1.** neu'rotisch; **2.** Nerven...(*-mittel, -leiden etc.*); **II** *s.* **3.** Neu'rotiker(in); **4.** Nervenmittel *n*; ˌ**neu'rot·o·my** [-'rɒtəmɪ] *s.* **1.** 'Nervenanatoˌmie *f*; **2.** Nervenschnitt *m.*

neu·ter ['njuːtə] **I** *adj.* **1.** *ling.* a) sächlich, b) intransitiv (*Verb*); **2.** *biol.* geschlechtslos; **II** *s.* **3.** *ling.* a) Neutrum *n*, sächliches Hauptwort, b) intransitives Verb; **4.** ♀ Blüte *f* ohne Staubgefäße u. Stempel; **5.** *zo.* geschlechtsloses *od.* kastriertes Tier; **III** *v/t.* **6.** kastrieren.

neu·tral ['njuːtrəl] **I** *adj.* □ **1.** neu'tral (*a. pol.*), par'teilos, 'unparˌteiisch, unbeteiligt; **2.** neutral, unbestimmt, farblos; **3.** neutral (*a.* ⚗, ϟ), gleichgültig, 'indiffeˌrent; **4.** ♀, *zo.* geschlechtslos; **5.** ⚙, *mot.* a) Ruhe..., Null... (*Lage*), b) Leerlauf... (*Gang*); **II** *s.* **6.** a) Neu'trale(r *m*) *f*, Par'teilose(r *m*) *f*, b) neutraler Staat, c) Angehörige(r *m*) *f* e-s neutralen Staates; **7.** *mot.*, ⚙ Ruhelage *f*, Leerlaufstellung *f*: ***put the car in ~*** den Gang herausnehmen; **~ ax·is** *s.* ⩘, *phys.*, ⚙ neutrale Achse, Nullinie *f*; **~ con·duc·tor** *s.* ϟ Nulleiter *m*; **~ gear** *s.* ⚙ Leerlauf(gang) *m.*

neu·tral·ism ['njuːtrəlɪzəm] *s.* Neutra'lismus *m*; '**neu·tral·ist** [-ɪst] **I** *s.* Neutra'list *m*; **II** *adj.* neutra'listisch.

neu·tral·i·ty [njuː'trælətɪ] *s.* Neutrali'tät *f* (*a.* ⚗, *pol.*).

neu·tral·i·za·tion [ˌnjuːtrəlaɪ'zeɪʃn] *s.* **1.** Neutralisierung *f*, Ausgleichung *f*, (gegenseitige) Aufhebung; **2.** ⚗ Neutralisati'on *f*; **3.** *pol.* Neutrali'tätserklärung *f* e-s *Staates etc.*; **4.** ϟ Entkopplung *f*; **5.** ⚔ Niederhaltung *f*, Lahmlegung *f*, *a. sport*: Ausschaltung *f*; **neu·tral·ize** ['njuːtrəlaɪz] *v/t.* **1.** neutralisieren (*a.* ⚗), ausgleichen, aufheben: ***to ~ each other*** sich gegenseitig aufheben; **2.** *pol.* für neu'tral erklären; **3.** ϟ neutralisieren, entkoppeln; **4.** ⚔ niederhalten, -kämpfen, *a. sport*: *Gegner* ausschalten; *Kampfstoff* entgiften.

neu·tral| line *s.* **1.** ⩘, *phys.* Neu'trale *f*, neu'trale Linie; **2.** *phys.* Nullinie *f*; **3.** → ***neutral axis***; **~ po·si·tion** *s.* **1.** ⚙ Nullstellung *f*, -lage *f*; Ruhestellung *f*; **2.** ϟ neutrale Stellung (*Anker etc.*).

neu·tro·dyne ['njuːtrədaɪn] *s.* ϟ Neutro'dyn *n.*

neu·tron ['njuːtrɒn] *phys.* **I** *s.* Neu'tron *n*; **II** *adj.* Neutronen...(*-bombe, -zahl etc.*).

né·vé ['neveɪ] (*Fr.*) *s.* Firn(feld *n*) *m.*

nev·er ['nevə] *adv.* **1.** nie, niemals, nimmer(mehr); **2.** durch'aus nicht, nicht im geringsten; **3.** (doch) wohl nicht;

Besondere Redewendungen:

~ fear nur keine Bange!; ***~ mind*** das macht nichts!; ***well I ~!*** F nein, so was!, das ist ja unerhört!; ***~ so*** auch noch so; ***he ~ so much as answered*** er hat noch nicht einmal geantwortet; ***~ say die!*** nur nicht verzweifeln!

'**nev·er|-do-ˌwell** *s.* Taugenichts *m*, Tunichtgut *m*; ˌ**~-'end·ing** [-ər'e-] *adj.* endlos, nicht enden wollend; ˌ**~-'fail·ing** *adj.* **1.** unfehlbar, untrüglich; **2.** nie versiegend; ˌ**~'more** *adv.* nimmermehr, nie wieder; ˌ**~-'nev·er** *s.* F **1.** ***buy on the ~*** ‚abstottern', auf Pump kaufen; **2.** *a.* ***~ land*** a) ‚Arsch *m* der Welt', b) *fig.* Wolken'kuckucksheim *n.*

ˌ**nev·er·the'less** *adv.* nichtsdesto'weniger, dennoch, trotzdem.

ne·vus ['niːvəs] *s.* ⚕ Muttermal *n*, Leberfleck *m*: ***vascular ~*** Feuermal.

new [njuː] **I** *adj.* □ → ***newly***; **1.** *allg.* neu: ***nothing ~*** nichts Neues; → ***broom***[2]; **2.** *a. ling.* neu, mo'dern; *bsd. contp.* neumodisch; **3.** neu (*Obst etc.*), frisch (*Brot, Milch etc.*); **4.** neu (*Ggs. alt*), gut erhalten: ***as good as ~*** so gut wie neu; **5.** neu(entdeckt *od.* -erschienen *od.* -erstanden *od.* -geschaffen): ***~ facts***; ***~ star***; ***~ moon*** Neumond *m*; ***~ publications*** Neuerscheinungen *pl.*; ***the ~ woman*** die Frau von heute; ***the ≈ World*** die Neue Welt (*Amerika*); ***that is not ~ to me*** das ist mir nichts Neues; **6.** unerforscht: ***~ ground*** Neuland *n* (*a. fig.*); **7.** neu(gewählt, -ernannt): ***the ~ president***; **8.** (***to***) a) *j-m* unbekannt, b) nicht vertraut (mit *e-r Sache*), unerfahren (in *dat.*), c) *j-m* ungewohnt; **9.** neu, ander, besser: ***feel a ~ man*** sich wie neugeboren fühlen; **10.** erneut: ***a ~ start***; **11.** (*bsd. bei Ortsnamen*) Neu...; **II** *adv.* **12.** neu(erlich), so'eben, frisch (*bsd. in Zssgn*): ***~-built*** neuerbaut.

'**new|·born** *adj.* neugeboren (*a. fig.*); **~ build·ing** *s.* Neubau *m*; '**~-come** *adj.* neuangekommen; '**~ˌcom·er** *s.* **1.** Neuankömmling *m*, Fremde(r *m*) *f*; **2.** Neuling *m* (***to*** in *e-m Fach*); **≈ Deal** *s. hist.* New Deal *m* (*Wirtschafts- u. Sozialpolitik des Präsidenten F. D. Roosevelt*).

new·el ['njuːəl] *s.* ⚙ **1.** Spindel *f* (*Wendeltreppe, Gußform etc.*); **2.** Endpfosten *m* (*Geländer*).

'**new|ˌfan·gled** [-ˌfæŋgld] *adj. contp.* neu(modisch); '**~-fledged** *adj.* **1.** flügge geworden; **2.** *fig.* neugebacken; ˌ**~-'found** *adj.* **1.** neugefunden; neuerfunden; **2.** neuentdeckt.

New·found·land (dog) [njuː'faʊndlənd], **New'found·land·er** [-də] *s.* Neu'fundländer *m* (*Hund*).

new·ish ['njuːɪʃ] *adj.* ziemlich neu;

new·ly ['njuːlɪ] *adv.* **1.** neulich, kürzlich, jüngst: ***~ married*** neu-, jungvermählt; **2.** von neuem; **new·ness** ['njuːnɪs] *s.* Neuheit *f*, *das* Neue; *fig.* Unerfahrenheit *f.*

ˌ**new-'rich I** *adj.* neureich; **II** *s.* Neureiche(r *m*) *f*, Parve'nü *m.*

news [njuːz] *s. pl. sg. konstr.* **1.** *das* Neue, Neuigkeit(en *pl.*) *f*, Neues *n*, Nachricht(en *pl.*) *f*: ***a piece of ~*** e-e Nachricht *od.* Neuigkeit; ***at this ~*** bei dieser Nachricht; ***commercial ~*** † Handelsteil *m* (*Zeitung*); ***break the (bad) ~ to s.o.*** j-m die (schlechte) Nachricht (schonend) beibringen; ***have ~ from s.o.*** von j-m Nachricht haben; ***it is ~ to me*** das ist mir (ganz) neu; ***what('s the) ~?*** was gibt es Neues?; ***~ certainly travels fast!*** es spricht sich alles herum!; ***he is bad ~s Am. sl.*** mit ihm werden wir Ärger kriegen; **2.** neueste (Zeitungs-, Radio)Nachrichten *pl.*: ***be in the ~*** (in der Öffentlichkeit) von sich reden machen; **~ a·gen·cy** *s.* 'Nachrichtenagenˌtur *f*, -büˌro *n*; **~ a·gent** *s.* Zeitungshändler(in); **~ black·out** *s.* Nachrichtensperre *f*; '**~·boy** *s.* Zeitungsjunge *m*; **~ butch·er** *s.* 🚃 *Am.* Verkäufer *m* von Zeitungen, Süßigkeiten *etc.*; '**~·cast** *s. Radio, TV*: Nachrichtensendung *f*; '**~ˌcast·er** *s.* Nachrichtensprecher(in); **~ cin·e·ma** *s.* Aktuali'tätenkino *n*; **~ con·fer·ence** *s.* 'Pressekonfeˌrenz *f*; **~ deal·er** *Am.* → ***news agent***; **~ flash** *s.* (eingeblendete) Kurzmeldung; '**~·hawk** *s.*, '**~·hound** *s. Am.* F 'Zeitungsreˌporter (-in); **~ i·tem** *s.* 'Pressenoˌtiz *f*; '**~-ˌlet·ter** *s.* (Nachrichten)Rundschreiben *n*, Zirku'lar *n*; **~ mag·a·zine** *s.* 'Nachrichtenmagaˌzin *n*; '**~·man** [-mæn] *s.* [*irr.*] **1.** Zeitungshändler *m*, -austräger *m*; **2.** Journa'list *m*; '**~ˌmon·ger** *s.* Neuigkeitskrämer(in).

'**newsˌpa·per** *s.* Zeitung *f*; **~ ad·ver·tise·ment** *s.* 'Zeitungsanˌnonce *f*, -anzeige *f*; **~ clip·ping** *Am.*, **~ cut·ting** *s.* Zeitungsausschnitt *m*; '**~·man** [-mæn] *s.* [*irr.*] **1.** Zeitungsverkäufer *m*; **2.** Journa'list *m*; **3.** Zeitungsverleger *m.*

'**news|·print** *s.* 'Zeitungspaˌpier *n*; '**~ˌread·er** *s. Brit.* für ***newscaster***; '**~·reel** *s.* Wochenschau *f*; '**~·room** [-rʊm] *s.* **1.** 'Nachrichtenraum *m*, -zenˌtrale *f*; **2.** *Brit.* Zeitschriftenlesesaal *m*; **3.** *Am.* 'Zeitungsladen *m*, -kiˌosk *m*; **~ serv·ice** *s.* Nachrichtendienst *m*; '**~·sheet** *s.* Informati'onsblatt *n*; '**~-**

stall *s. Brit.*, **'~·stand** *s.* 'Zeitungski,osk *m*, -stand *m*.
New Style *s.* neue Zeitrechnung (*nach dem Gregorianischen Kalender*), neuer Stil.
news| ven·dor *s.* Zeitungsverkäufer(in); **'~,wor·thy** *adj.* von Inter'esse (für den Zeitungsleser), aktu'ell.
news·y ['nju:zɪ] *adj.* F voller Neuigkeiten.
newt [nju:t] *s. zo.* Wassermolch *m*.
new·ton ['nju:tn] *s. phys.* Newton *n* (*Maßeinheit*).
New·to·ni·an [nju:'təʊnjən] *adj.* Newton(i)sch: **~ *force*** Newtonsche Kraft.
new| year *s.* Neujahr *n*, *das* neue Jahr; **ℒ Year** *s.* Neujahrstag *m*; **ℒ Year's Day** *s.* Neujahrstag *m*; **ℒ Year's Eve** *s.* Sil'vesterabend *m*.
next [nekst] **I** *adj.* **1.** nächst, nächstfolgend, -stehend: ***the ~ house*** (***train***) das nächste Haus (der nächste Zug); (***the***) **~ *day*** am nächsten *od.* folgenden Tag; **~ *door*** (im Haus) nebenan; **~ *door to*** *fig.* beinahe, fast *unmöglich etc.*, so gut wie; **~ *to*** a) (gleich) neben, b) (gleich) nach (*Rang, Reihenfolge*), c) fast *unmöglich etc.*; **~ *to nothing*** fast gar nichts; **~ *to last*** zweitletzt; ***the ~ but one*** der (die, das) übernächste; **~ *in size*** a) nächstgrößer, b) nächstkleiner; **~ *friend*** ⚖ Prozeßpfleger *m*; ***the ~ of kin*** der (*pl.* die) nächste(n) Angehörige(n) *od.* Verwandte(n); ***be ~ best*** a) der (die, das) Zweitbeste sein, b) (***to***) *fig.* gleich kommen (nach), fast so gut sein (wie); ***week after ~*** übernächste Woche; ***what ~?*** was (denn) noch?; **II** *adv.* **2.** (*Ort, Zeit etc.*) zu'nächst, gleich dar'auf, als nächste(r) *od.* nächstes: ***come ~*** (als nächstes) folgen; **3.** nächstens, demnächst, das nächste Mal; **4.** (*bei Aufzählung*) dann, dar'auf; **III** *prp.* **5.** (gleich) neben (*dat.*) *od.* bei (*dat.*) *od.* an (*dat.*); **6.** zu'nächst nach, (*an Rang*) gleich nach; **IV** *s.* **7.** *der* (*die, das*) Nächste; **'next-door** *adj.* neben'an, im Nachbar- *od.* Nebenhaus, benachbart.
nex·us ['neksəs] *s.* Verknüpfung *f*, Zs.-hang *m*.
nib [nɪb] *s.* **1.** Schnabel *m* (*Vogel*); **2.** (Gold-, Stahl)Spitze *f* (*Schreibfeder*); **3.** *pl.* Kaffee- *od.* Ka'kaobohnenstückchen *pl.*
nib·ble ['nɪbl] **I** *v/t.* **1.** nagen, knabbern an (*dat.*): **~ *off*** abbeißen, -fressen; **2.** vorsichtig anbeißen (*Fische am Köder*); **II** *v/i.* **3.** nagen, knabbern (***at*** an *dat.*): **~ *at one's food*** im Essen herumstochern; **4.** *Kekse etc.* ‚knabbern', naschen; **5.** (fast) anbeißen (*Fisch*) (*a. fig. Käufer*); **6.** *fig.* kritteln, tadeln; **III** *s.* **7.** Nagen *n*, Knabbern *n*; **8.** (kleiner) Bissen, Happen *m*.
nib·lick ['nɪblɪk] *s. Golf: obs.* Niblick *m* (*Schläger*).
nibs [nɪbz] *s. pl. sg. konstr.* F ‚großes Tier': ***his ~*** ‚seine Hoheit'.
nice [naɪs] *adj.* ☐ **1.** fein (*Beobachtung, Sinn, Urteil, Unterschied etc.*); **2.** lekker, fein (*Speise etc.*); **3.** nett, freundlich (***to*** zu *j-m*); **4.** nett, hübsch, schön (*alle a. iro.*): **~ *girl***; **~ *weather***; ***a ~ mess*** *iro.* e-e schöne Bescherung; **~ *and fat*** schön fett; **~ *and warm*** hübsch warm; **5.** niedlich, nett; **6.** heikel, wählerisch (***about*** in *dat.*); **7.** (peinlich) genau, gewissenhaft; **8.** (*mst mit* ***not***) anständig; **9.** *fig.* heikel, schwierig; **'nice·ly** [-lɪ] *adv.* **1.** nett, fein: ***I was done ~*** *sl. iro.* ich wurde schön übers Ohr gehauen; **2.** gut, fein, befriedigend: ***that will do ~*** das paßt ausgezeichnet; ***she is doing ~*** F es geht ihr gut (*od.* besser), sie macht gute Fortschritte; **3.** sorgfältig, genau; **'nice·ness** [-nɪs] *s.* **1.** Feinheit *f*; **2.** Nettheit *f*; Niedlichkeit *f*; **3.** F Nettigkeit *f*; **4.** Schärfe *f des Urteils*; **5.** Genauigkeit *f*, Pünktlichkeit *f*; **'ni·ce·ty** [-sətɪ] **1.** Feinheit *f*, Schärfe *f des Urteils etc.*; **2.** peinliche Genauigkeit, Pünktlichkeit *f*: ***to a ~*** aufs genaueste, bis aufs Haar; **3.** Spitzfindigkeit *f*; **4.** *pl.* kleine 'Unterschiede *pl.*, Feinheiten *pl.*: ***not to stand upon niceties*** es nicht so genau nehmen; **5.** wählerisches Wesen; **6. *the niceties of life*** die Annehmlichkeiten des Lebens.
niche [nɪtʃ] **I** *s.* **1.** △, *a.* ⚕ Nische *f*; **2.** *fig.* Platz *m*, wo man hingehört: ***he finally found his ~ in life*** er hat endlich s-n Platz im Leben gefunden; **3.** *fig.* (ruhiges) Plätzchen; **II** *v/t.* **4.** mit e-r Nische versehen; **5.** in e-e Nische stellen.
ni·chrome ['naɪkrəʊm] *s.* ⚙ Nickelchrom *n*.
Nick¹ [nɪk] *npr.* **1.** Niki *m* (*Koseform zu* ***Nicholas***); **2. *Old ~*** *sl.* der Teufel.
nick² [nɪk] **I** *s.* **1.** Kerbe *f*, Einkerbung *f*, Einschnitt *m*; **2.** Kerbholz *n*; **3.** *typ.* Signa'tur(rinne) *f*; **4. *in the*** (***very***) **~** (***of time***) a) im richtigen Augenblick, wie gerufen, b) im letzten Moment; ***in good ~*** ‚gut in Schuß'; **5.** *Würfelspiel etc.*: (hoher) Wurf, Treffer *m*; **II** *v/t.* **6.** (ein)kerben, einschneiden: **~ *out*** auszacken, -furchen; **~ *o.s.*** sich *beim Rasieren* schneiden; **7.** *et.* glücklich treffen: **~ *the time*** gerade den richtigen Zeitpunkt treffen; **8.** erraten; **9.** *Zug etc.* erwischen, (noch) kriegen; **10.** *Brit. sl.* a) betrügen, reinlegen, b) ‚klauen', c) *j-n* ‚schnappen' *od.* ‚einlochen'.
nick·el ['nɪkl] **I** *s.* **1.** ⚗, *min.* Nickel *n*; **2.** *Am.* F Nickel *m*, Fünf'centstück *n*; **II** *adj.* **3.** Nickel…; **III** *v/t.* **4.** vernickeln; **~ *bloom*** *s. min.* Nickelblüte *f*; **'~-clad sheet** *s.* ⚙ nickelplattiertes Blech.
nick·el·o·de·on [,nɪkə'ləʊdɪən] *s. Am.* **1.** *hist.* billiges ('Film-, Varie'té)The,ater; **2.** Mu'sikauto,mat *m*.
'nick·el|-plate *v/t.* ⚙ vernickeln; **'~-,plat·ing** *s.* Vernickelung *f*; **~ sil·ver** *s.* Neusilber *n*; **~ steel** *s.* Nickelstahl *m*.
nick·nack ['nɪknæk] → ***knickknack***.
nick·name ['nɪkneɪm] **I** *s.* Spitzname *m*; ⚔ Deckname *m*; **II** *v/t.* mit e-m Spitznamen bezeichnen, *j-m* e-n *od.* den Spitznamen geben.
nic·o·tine ['nɪkəti:n] *s.* ⚗ Niko'tin *n*; **'nic·o·tin·ism** [-nɪzəm] *s.* Niko'tinvergiftung *f*.
nide [naɪd] *s.* (Fa'sanen)Nest *n*.
nid·i·fy ['nɪdɪfaɪ] *v/i.* nisten.
nid-nod ['nɪdnɒd] *v/i.* (mehrmals *od.* ständig) nicken.
ni·dus ['naɪdəs] *pl.* ***a.* -di** [-daɪ] *s.* **1.** *zo.* Nest *n*, Brutstätte *f*; **2.** *fig.* Lagerstätte *f*, Sitz *m*; **3.** ⚕ Herd *m e-r Krankheit*.
niece [ni:s] *s.* Nichte *f*.
nif·ty ['nɪftɪ] *adj. sl.* **1.** ‚sauber': a) hübsch, fesch, b) prima, c) raffiniert; **2.** *Brit.* stinkend.
nig·gard ['nɪgəd] **I** *s.* Knicker(in), Geizhals *m*, Filz *m*; **II** *adj.* ☐ geizig, knikk(er)ig, kärglich; **'nig·gard·li·ness** [-lɪnɪs] *s.* Knause'rei *f*, Geiz *m*; **'nig·gard·ly** [-lɪ] **I** *adv.* → ***niggard*** II; **II** *adj.* schäbig, kümmerlich: ***a ~ gift***.
nig·ger ['nɪgə] *s.* F *contp.* Nigger *m*, Neger(in), Schwarze(r *m*) *f*: ***work like a ~*** wie ein Pferd arbeiten, schuften; **~ *in the woodpile*** *sl. der* Haken an der Sache.
nig·gle ['nɪgl] *v/i.* **1.** pe'dantisch sein *od.* her'umtüfteln; **2.** trödeln; **3.** nörgeln, ‚meckern'.
nigh [naɪ] *obs. od. poet.* **I** *adv.* **1.** nahe (***to*** an *dat.*): **~ (*un*)*to death*** dem Tode nahe; **~ *but*** beinahe; ***draw ~ to*** sich nähern (*dat.*); **2.** *mst* ***well ~*** beinahe, nahezu; **II** *prp.* **3.** nahe bei, neben.
night [naɪt] *s.* **1.** Nacht *f*: ***at ~, by ~, in the ~***, F ***o'nights*** bei Nacht, nachts, des Nachts; ***~'s lodging*** Nachtquartier *n*; ***all ~*** (***long***) die ganze Nacht (hindurch); ***over ~*** über Nacht; ***bid*** (*od.* ***wish***) ***s.o. good ~*** *j-m* gute Nacht wünschen; ***make a ~ of it*** die ganze Nacht durchmachen, -feiern, sich die Nacht um die Ohren schlagen; ***stay the ~ at*** übernachten in *e-m Ort od.* bei *j-m*; **2.** Abend *m*: ***last ~*** gestern abend; ***the ~ before last*** vorgestern abend; ***first ~*** *thea.* Erstaufführung *f*, Premiere *f*; ***a ~ of Wagner*** Wagnerabend; ***on the ~ of May 4th*** am Abend des 4. Mai; **~ *out*** freier Abend; ***have a ~ out*** e-n Abend ausspannen, ausgehen; **3.** *fig.* Nacht *f*, Dunkelheit *f*; **~ at·tack** *s.* ⚔ Nachtangriff *m*; **~ bird** *s.* **1.** Nachtvogel *m*; **2.** *fig.* Nachtschwärmer *m*; **'~-blind** *adj.* ⚕ nachtblind; **'~·cap** *s.* **1.** Nachtmütze *f*, -haube *f*; **2.** *fig.* Schlummertrunk *m*; **~ club** *s.* Nachtklub *m*, 'Nachtlo,kal *n*; **'~·dress** *s.* Nachthemd *n* (*für Frauen u. Kinder*); **~ ex·po·sure** *s. phot.* Nachtaufnahme *f*; **'~·fall** *s.* Einbruch *m* der Nacht; **~ fight·er** *s.* ✈, ⚔ Nachtjäger *m*; **~ glass** *s.* Nachtfernrohr *n*, -glas *n*; **'~·gown** → ***nightdress***.
night·in·gale ['naɪtɪŋgeɪl] *s. orn.* Nachtigall *f*.
'night|·jar *s. orn.* Ziegenmelker *m*; **~ leave** *s.* ⚔ Urlaub *m* bis zum Wecken; **~ let·ter(-gram)** *s. Am.* (verbilligtes) 'Nachttele,gramm; **'~·life** *s.* Nachtleben *n*; **'~-long I** *adj.* e-e *od.* die ganze Nacht dauernd; **II** *adv.* die ganze Nacht (hin'durch).
night·ly ['naɪtlɪ] **I** *adj.* **1.** nächtlich, Nacht…; **2.** jede Nacht *od.* jeden Abend stattfindend; **II** *adv.* **3.** a) (all-) nächtlich, jede Nacht, b) jeden Abend, (all)abendlich.
night·mare ['naɪtmeə] *s.* **1.** Nachtmahr *m* (*böser Geist*); **2.** ⚕ Alp(drücken *n*) *m*, böser Traum; **3.** *fig.* Schreckgespenst *n*, Alptraum *m*, Spuk *m*; **'night·mar·ish** [-eərɪʃ] *adj.* beklemmend, schauerlich.
night| nurse *s.* Nachtschwester *f*; **~ owl** *s.* **1.** *orn.* Nachteule *f* (*a.* F *fig. Nachtmensch*); **2.** F Nachtschwärmer *m*; **~ por·ter** *s.* 'Nachtporti,er *m*.
nights [naɪts] *adv.* F bei Nacht, nachts.
night| school *s.* Abend-, Fortbildungsschule *f*; **'~·shade** *s.* ⚘ Nachtschatten *m*: ***deadly ~*** Tollkirsche *f*; **~ shift** *s.*

Nachtschicht *f*: ***be on ~*** Nachtschicht haben; **'~·shirt** *s.* Nachthemd *n* (*für Männer u. Knaben*); **'~·spot** *s.* F *für **nightclub***; **'~·stand** *s. Am.* Nachttisch *m*; **~ stick** *s. Am.* Schlagstock *m der Polizei*; **'~·stool** *s.* Nachtstuhl *m*; **'~·time** *s.* Nachtzeit *f*; **~ vi·sion** *s.* **1.** nächtliche Erscheinung; **2.** Nachtsehvermögen *n*; **~ watch** *s.* Nachtwache *f*; **ˌ~'watch·man** [-mən] *s.* [*irr.*] Nachtwächter *m*; **'~·wear** *s.* Nachtzeug *n*.

night·y ['naɪtɪ] *s.* F (Damen-, Kinder-) Nachthemd *n*.

ni·hil·ism ['naɪɪlɪzəm] *s. phls., pol.* Nihi'lismus *m*; **'ni·hil·ist** [-ɪst] **I** *s.* Nihi'list (-in); **II** *adj.* → **ni·hil·is·tic** [ˌnaɪɪ'lɪstɪk] *adj.* nihi'listisch.

nil [nɪl] *s.* Nichts *n*, Null *f* (*bsd. in Spielresultaten*): ***two goals to ~*** zwei zu null (2:0); ***~ report*** Fehlanzeige *f*; ***his influence is ~*** *fig.* sein Einfluß ist gleich null.

nim·ble ['nɪmbl] *adj.* □ flink, hurtig, gewandt, be'hend: ***~ mind*** *fig.* beweglicher Geist, rasche Auffassungsgabe; **ˌ~-'fin·gered** *adj.* **1.** geschickt; **2.** langfingerig, diebisch; **ˌ~-'foot·ed** *adj.* leicht-, schnellfüßig.

nim·ble·ness ['nɪmblnɪs] *s.* Flinkheit *f*, Gewandtheit *f*, *fig. a.* geistige Beweglichkeit.

nim·bus ['nɪmbəs] *pl.* **-bi** [-baɪ] *od.* **-bus·es** *s.* **1.** *a.* ***~ cloud*** graue Regenwolke; **2.** Nimbus *m*: a) Heiligenschein *m*, b) *fig.* Ruhm *m*.

nim·i·ny-pim·i·ny [ˌnɪmɪnɪ'pɪmɪnɪ] *adj.* affek'tiert, ‚etepe'tete'.

Nim·rod ['nɪmrɒd] *npr. Bibl. u. fig.* Nimrod *m* (*großer Jäger*).

nin·com·poop ['nɪnkəmpu:p] *s.* Einfaltspinsel *m*, Trottel *m*.

nine [naɪn] **I** *adj.* **1.** neun: ***~ days' wonder*** Tagesgespräch *n*, sensationelles Ereignis; ***~ times out of ten*** in neun von zehn Fällen; **II** *s.* **2.** Neun *f*, Neuner *m* (*Spielkarte etc.*): ***the ~ of hearts*** Herzneun; ***to the ~s*** in höchstem Maße; ***dressed up to the ~s*** piekfein gekleidet, aufgedonnert; **3.** ***the*** ℒ die neun Musen; **4.** *sport* Baseballmannschaft *f*; **'nine·fold I** *adj. u. adv.* neunfach; **II** *s. das* Neunfache; **'nine·pins** *s. pl.* **1.** Kegel *pl.*: ***~ alley*** Kegelbahn *f*; **2.** *a. sg. konstr.* Kegelspiel *n*: ***play ~*** Kegel spielen, kegeln.

nine·teen [ˌnaɪn'ti:n] **I** *adj.* neunzehn; → ***dozen*** 2; **II** *s.* Neunzehn *f*; **ˌnine'teenth** [-θ] **I** *adj.* neunzehnt; **II** *s.* Neunzehntel *n*; **nine·ti·eth** ['naɪntɪɪθ] **I** *adj.* neunzigst; **II** *s.* Neunzigstel *n*; **nine·ty** ['naɪntɪ] **I** *s.* Neunzig *f*: ***he is in his nineties*** er ist in den Neunzigern; ***in the nineties*** in den neunziger Jahren (*e-s Jahrhunderts*); **II** *adj.* neunzig.

nin·ny ['nɪnɪ] F *s.* Trottel *m*.

ninth [naɪnθ] **I** *adj.* **1.** neunt: ***in the ~ place*** neuntens, an neunter Stelle; **II** *s.* **2.** *der* (*die, das*) Neunte; **3.** *a.* ***~ part*** Neuntel *n*; **4.** ♪ None *f*; **'ninth·ly** [-lɪ] *adv.* neuntens.

nip[1] [nɪp] **I** *v/t.* **1.** kneifen, zwicken, klemmen: ***~ off*** abzwicken, -kneifen, -beißen; **2.** (*durch Frost etc.*) beschädigen, vernichten, ka'puttmachen: ***~ in the bud*** *fig.* im Keim ersticken; **3.** *sl.* → ***nick***[2] 10 b *u.* c; **II** *v/i.* **4.** schneiden (*Kälte, Wind*); ⚙ klemmen (*Maschine*); **5.** F ‚flitzen': ***~ in*** hineinschlüpfen; ***~ on ahead*** nach vorne flitzen; **III** *s.* **6.** Kneifen *n*, Kniff *m*, Biß *m*; **7.** Schneiden *n* (*Kälte etc.*); scharfer Frost; **8.** ⚘ Frostbrand *m*; **9.** Knick *m* (*Draht etc.*); **10.** ***~ and tuck***, *attr.* ***~-and-tuck*** *Am.* auf Biegen oder Brechen, scharf (*Kampf*), hart (*Rennen*).

nip[2] [nɪp] **I** *v/i. u. v/t.* nippen (an *dat.*); **II** *s.* Schlückchen *n*.

Nip [nɪp] *s. sl.* ‚Japs' *m*.

nip·per ['nɪpə] *s.* **1.** *zo.* a) Vorder-, Schneidezahn *m* (*bsd. des Pferdes*), b) Schere *f* (*Krebs etc.*); **2.** *mst pl.* ⚙ a) *a.* ***a pair of ~s*** (Kneif)Zange *f*, b) Pin'zette *f*; **3.** *pl.* Kneifer *m*; **4.** *Brit.* F Bengel *m*, ‚Stift' *m*; **5.** *pl.* F Handschellen *pl.*

nip·ping ['nɪpɪŋ] *adj.* □ **1.** kneifend; **2.** beißend, schneidend (*Kälte, Wind*); **3.** *fig.* bissig, scharf (*Worte*).

nip·ple ['nɪpl] *s.* **1.** *anat.* Brustwarze *f*; **2.** (Saug)Hütchen *n*, Sauger *m* (*e-r Saugflasche*); **3.** ⚙ (Speichen-, Schmier)Nippel *m*; (Rohr)Stutzen *m*.

nip·py ['nɪpɪ] **I** *adj.* **1.** → ***nipping*** 2, 3; **2.** F schnell, ‚fix'; spritzig (*Auto*); **II** *s.* **3.** *Brit.* F Kellnerin *f*.

ni·sei ['ni:ˌseɪ] *pl.* **-sei**, **-seis** *s.* Ja'paner (-in) geboren in den USA.

ni·si ['naɪsaɪ] (*Lat.*) *cj.* ⚖ wenn nicht: ***decree ~*** vorläufiges Scheidungsurteil.

Nis·sen hut ['nɪsn] *s.* ⚔ Nissenhütte *f*, 'Wellblechbaˌracke *f*.

nit [nɪt] *s. zo.* Nisse *f*, Niß *f*.

ni·ter *Am.* → ***nitre***.

'nitˌpick·ing I *adj.* F kleinlich, ‚pingelig'; **II** *s.* ‚Pingeligkeit' *f*.

ni·trate ['naɪtreɪt] **I** *s.* ⚗ Ni'trat *n*, sal'petersaures Salz: ***~ of silver*** salpetersaures Silber, Höllenstein *m*; ***~ of soda*** (*od.* ***sodium***) salpetersaures Natrium; **II** *v/t.* nitrieren; **III** *v/i.* sich in Sal'peter verwandeln.

ni·tre ['naɪtə] *s.* ⚗ Sal'peter *m*: ***~ cake*** Natriumkuchen *m*.

ni·tric ['naɪtrɪk] *adj.* ⚗ sal'petersauer, Salpeter..., Stickstoff...; ***~ ac·id*** *s.* Sal'petersäure *f*; ***~ ox·ide*** *s.* 'Stickstoffoˌxyd *n*.

ni·tride ['naɪtraɪd] **I** *s.* Ni'trid *n*; **II** *v/t.* nitrieren; **ni·trif·er·ous** [naɪ'trɪfərəs] *adj.* **1.** stickstoffhaltig; **2.** sal'peterhaltig; **'ni·tri·fy** [-trɪfaɪ] **I** *v/t.* nitrieren; **II** *v/i.* sich in Sal'peter verwandeln; **'ni·trite** [-aɪt] *s.* Ni'trit *n*, sal'pet(e)rigsaures Salz.

ni·tro·ben·zene [ˌnaɪtrəʊ'benzi:n], **ni·tro·ben·zol(e)** [ˌnaɪtrəʊ'benzɒl] *s.* ⚗ Nitroben'zol *n*.

ni·tro·cel·lu·lose [ˌnaɪtrəʊ'seljʊləʊs] *s.* ⚗ Nitrozellu'lose *f*: ***~ lacquer*** Nitro(zellulose)lack *m*.

ni·tro·gen ['naɪtrədʒən] *s.* ⚗ Stickstoff *m*: ***~ carbide*** Stickkohlenstoff *m*; ***~ chloride*** Chlorstickstoff; **ni·tro·gen·ize** [naɪ'trɒdʒɪnaɪz] *v/t.* mit Stickstoff verbinden *od.* anreichern *od.* sättigen: ***~d foods*** stickstoffhaltige Nahrungsmittel; **ni·trog·e·nous** [naɪ'trɒdʒɪnəs] *adj.* stickstoffhaltig.

ni·tro·glyc·er·in(e) [ˌnaɪtrəʊ'glɪsəri:n] *s.* ⚗ Nitroglyze'rin *n*.

ni·tro·hy·dro·chlo·ric ['naɪtrəʊˌhaɪdrəʊ'klɒrɪk] *adj.* Salpetersalz...

ni·trous ['naɪtrəs] *adj.* ⚗ Salpeter..., sal'peterhaltig, sal'petrig; ***~ ac·id*** *s.* sal'petrige Säure; ***~ ox·ide*** *s.* 'Stickstoffoxyˌdul *n*, Lachgas *n*.

nit·ty-grit·ty [ˌnɪtɪ'grɪtɪ] *s.*: ***get down to the ~*** F zur Sache kommen.

nit·wit ['nɪtwɪt] *s.* Schwachkopf *m*.

nix[1] [nɪks] *Am. sl. pron. adv.* ‚nix', nichts, *int. a.* nein.

nix[2] [nɪks] *pl.* **-es** *s.* Nix *m*, Wassergeist *m*; **'nix·ie** [-ksɪ] *s.* (Wasser)Nixe *f*.

no [nəʊ] **I** *adv.* **1.** nein: ***answer ~*** nein sagen; **2.** (*nach **or** am Ende e-s Satzes*) nicht (*jetzt mst **not***): ***whether ... or ~*** ob ... oder nicht; **3.** (*beim comp.*) um nichts, nicht: ***~ better a writer*** kein besserer Schriftsteller; ***~ longer*** (***ago***) ***than yesterday*** erst gestern; ***~!*** nicht möglich!, nein!; → ***more*** 2, 4; ***soon*** 1; **II** *adj.* **4.** kein(e): ***~ hope*** keine Hoffnung; ***~ one*** keiner; ***~ man*** niemand; ***~ parking*** Parkverbot; ***~ thoroughfare*** Durchfahrt gesperrt; ***in ~ time*** im Nu; ***~-claims bonus*** Vergütung *f* für Schadenfreiheit; **5.** kein, alles andere als ein(e): ***he is ~ artist***; ***~ such thing*** nichts dergleichen; **6.** (*vor ger.*): ***there is ~ denying*** es läßt sich *od.* man kann nicht leugnen; **III** *pl.* **noes** *s.* **7.** Nein *n*, verneinende Antwort, Absage *f*, Weigerung *f*; **8.** *parl.* Gegenstimme *f*: ***the ayes and ~es*** die Stimmen für u. wider; ***the ~es have it*** die Mehrheit ist dagegen, der Antrag ist abgelehnt.

'no-acˌcount *adj. Am. dial.* unbedeutend (*mst Person*).

nob[1] [nɒb] *s. sl.* ‚Birne' *f* (*Kopf*).

nob[2] [nɒb] *s. sl.* ‚feiner Pinkel' (*vornehmer Mann*), ‚großes Tier'.

nob·ble ['nɒbl] *v/t. sl.* **1.** betrügen, ‚reinlegen'; **2.** *j-n* auf s-e Seite ziehen, ‚her'umkriegen'; **3.** bestechen; **4.** ‚klauen'.

nob·by ['nɒbɪ] *adj. sl.* schick.

No·bel Prize [nəʊ'bel] *s.* No'belpreis *m*: ***~ winner*** Nobelpreisträger(in); ***Nobel Peace Prize*** Friedensnobelpreis.

no·bil·i·ar·y [nəʊ'bɪlɪərɪ] *adj.* adlig, Adels...

no·bil·i·ty [nəʊ'bɪlətɪ] *s.* **1.** *fig.* Adel *m*, Würde *f*, Vornehmheit *f*: ***~ of mind*** vornehme Denkungsart; ***~ of soul*** Seelenadel; **2.** Adel(sstand) *m*, *die* Adligen *pl.*; (*bsd. in England*) *der* hohe Adel: ***the ~ and gentry*** der hohe u. niedere Adel.

no·ble ['nəʊbl] **I** *adj.* □ **1.** adlig, von Adel; edel, erlaucht; **2.** *fig.* edel, nobel, erhaben, groß(mütig), vor'trefflich: ***the ~ art*** (***of self-defence***, *Am.* ***self-defense***) die edle Kunst der Selbstverteidigung (*Boxen*); **3.** prächtig, stattlich: ***a ~ edifice***; **4.** prächtig geschmückt (***with*** mit); **5.** *phys.* Edel...(*-gas, -metall*); **II** *s.* **6.** Edelmann *m*, (hoher) Adliger; **7.** *hist.* Nobel *m* (*Goldmünze*); **'~·man** [-mən] *s.* [*irr.*] **1.** Edelmann *m*, (hoher) Adliger; **2.** *pl. Schach*: Offi'ziere *pl.*; **ˌ~-'mind·ed** *adj.* edeldenkend; **ˌ~-'mind·ed·ness** *s.* vornehme Denkungsart, Edelmut *m*.

no·ble·ness ['nəʊblnɪs] *s.* **1.** Adel *m*, hohe Abstammung; **2.** *fig.* a) Adel *m*, Würde *f*, b) Edelsinn *m*, -mut *m*.

'no·bleˌwom·an *s.* [*irr.*] Adlige *f*.

no·bod·y ['nəʊbədɪ] **I** *adj. pron.* niemand, keiner: ***~ else*** sonst niemand, niemand anders; **II** *s. fig.* unbedeutende Per'son, ‚Niemand' *m*, ‚Null' *f*: ***be*** (***a***) ***~ a.*** nichts sein, nichts zu sagen haben.

nock [nɒk] **I** *s. Bogenschießen*: Kerbe *f*; **II** *v/t.* a) *Pfeil* auf die Kerbe legen, b) *Bogen* einkerben.

noc·tam·bu·la·tion [nɒkˌtæmbjʊˈleɪʃn], *a.* **noc·tam·bu·lism** [nɒkˈtæmbjʊlɪzəm] *s.* ⚕ Somnambuˈlismus *m*, Nachtwandeln *n*; **noc·tam·bu·list** [nɒkˈtæmbjʊlɪst] *s.* Schlafwandler(in), Somnamˈbule(r *m*) *f*.

noc·turn [ˈnɒktɜːn] *s. R.C.* Nachtmette *f*; **noc·tur·nal** [nɒkˈtɜːnl] *adj.* □ nächtlich, Nacht…; **noc·turne** [ˈnɒktɜːn] *s.* **1.** *paint.* Nachtstück *n*; **2.** ♪ Notˈturno *n*.

noc·u·ous [ˈnɒkjʊəs] *adj.* □ **1.** schädlich; **2.** giftig (*Schlangen*).

nod [nɒd] **I** *v/i.* **1.** nicken: **~ *to s.o.*** j-m zunicken, j-n grüßen; ***~ding acquaintance*** oberflächliche(r) Bekannte(r), Grußbekanntschaft *f*; ***we are on ~ding terms*** wir grüßen uns; **2.** sich neigen (*Blumen etc.*) (*a. fig.* ***to*** vor *dat.*); wippen (*Hutfeder*); **3.** nicken, (*sitzend*) schlafen: **~ *off*** einnicken; **4.** *fig.* unaufmerksam sein, ‚schlafen‘: ***Homer sometimes ~s*** auch dem Aufmerksamsten entgeht manchmal etwas; **II** *v/t.* **5. ~ *one's head*** (mit dem Kopf) nicken; **6.** (*durch Nicken*) andeuten: **~ *one's assent*** beifällig (zu)nicken; **~ *s.o. out*** j-n hinauswinken; **III** *s.* **7.** (Kopf)Nicken *n*, Wink *m*: ***give s.o. a ~*** j-m zunicken; ***go to the land of ~*** einschlafen; ***on the ~*** *Am. sl.* auf Pump.

nod·al [ˈnəʊdl] *adj.* Knoten…: **~ *point*** a) ♪, *phys.* Schwingungsknoten *m*, b) Ⓐ, *phys.* Knotenpunkt *m*.

nod·dle [ˈnɒdl] *s. sl.* Schädel *m*, ‚Birne‘ *f*, *fig.* ‚Grips‘ *m*.

node [nəʊd] *s.* **1.** *allg.* Knoten *m* (*a. ast.*, ⚘, Ⓐ; *a. fig. im Drama etc.*): **~ *of a curve*** Ⓐ Knotenpunkt *m* e-r Kurve; **2.** ⚕ Knoten *m*, Knötchen *n*: ***gouty ~*** Gichtknoten; **3.** *phys.* Schwingungsknoten *m*.

no·dose [ˈnəʊdəʊs] *adj.* knotig (*a.* ⚕), voller Knoten; **no·dos·i·ty** [nəʊˈdɒsətɪ] *s.* **1.** knotige Beschaffenheit; **2.** → ***node*** 2.

nod·u·lar [ˈnɒdjʊlə] *adj.* knoten-, knötchenförmig: ***~-ulcerous*** ⚕ tubero-ulzerös.

nod·ule [ˈnɒdjuːl] *s.* **1.** ⚘, ⚕ Knötchen *n*: ***lymphatic ~*** Lymphknötchen *n*; **2.** *geol.*, *min.* Nest *n*, Niere *f*.

no·dus [ˈnəʊdəs] *pl.* **-di** [-daɪ] *s.* Knoten *m*, Schwierigkeit *f*.

nog [nɒg] *s.* **1.** Holznagel *m*, -klotz *m*; **2.** △ a) Holm *m* (*querliegender Balken*), b) *Maurerei*: Riegel *m*.

nog·gin [ˈnɒgɪn] *s.* **1.** kleiner (Holz-)Krug; **2.** F ‚Birne‘ *f* (*Kopf*).

nog·ging [ˈnɒgɪŋ] *s.* △ Riegelmauer *f*, (ausgemauertes) Fachwerk.

ˈno-good *Am.* F **I** *s.* Lump *m*, Nichtsnutz *m*; **II** *adj.* nichtsnutzig, elend, miseˈrabel.

ˈno·how *adv.* F **1.** auf keinen Fall, durchˈaus nicht; **2.** nichtssagend, ungut: ***feel ~*** nicht auf der Höhe sein; ***look ~*** nach nichts aussehen.

noil [nɔɪl] *s. sg. u. pl.* ⚚, ⚙ Kämmling *m*, Kurzwolle *f*.

ˌno-ˈi·ron *adj.* bügelfrei (*Hemd etc.*).

noise [nɔɪz] **I** *s.* **1.** Geräusch *n*; Lärm *m*, Getöse *n*, Geschrei *n*: **~ *of battle*** Gefechtslärm; **~ *abatement***, **~ *control*** Lärmbekämpfung *f*; **~ *nuisance*** Lärmbelästigung *f*; ***hold your ~!*** F halt den Mund!; **2.** Rauschen *n* (*a.* ⚡ *Störung*), Summen *n*: **~ *factor*** ⚡ Rauschfaktor *m*; **3.** *fig.* Streit *m*, Krach *m*: ***make a ~*** Krach machen (***about*** wegen); → 4; **4.** *fig.* Aufsehen *n*, Geschrei *n*: ***make a great ~ in the world*** großes Aufsehen erregen; ***make a ~*** viel Tamtam machen (***about*** um); **5. *a big ~*** *sl.* ein hohes (*od.* großes) Tier (*wichtige Persönlichkeit*); **II** *v/i.* **6. ~ *it*** lärmen; **III** *v/t.* **7. ~ *abroad*** verbreiten, aussprengen.

noise·less [ˈnɔɪzlɪs] *adj.* □ laut-, geräuschlos (*a.* ⚙), still; **ˈnoise·less·ness** [-nɪs] *s.* Geräuschlosigkeit *f*.

noise| lev·el *s.* Lärm-, ⚡ Störpegel *m*; **~ sup·pres·sion** *s.* ⚡ **1.** Störschutz *m*; **2.** Entstörung *f*; **~ volt·age** *s.* ⚡ **1.** Geräuschspannung *f*; **2.** Störspannung *f*.

nois·i·ness [ˈnɔɪzɪnɪs] *s.* Lärm *m*, Getöse *n*; lärmendes Wesen.

noi·some [ˈnɔɪsəm] *adj.* □ **1.** schädlich, ungesund; **2.** widerlich.

nois·y [ˈnɔɪzɪ] *adj.* □ **1.** geräuschvoll, laut; lärmend: **~ *running*** ⚙ geräuschvoller Gang; **~ *fellow*** Krakeeler *m*, Schreier *m*; **2.** *fig.* grell, schreiend (*Farbe etc.*); laut, aufdringlich (*Stil*).

nol·le [ˈnɒlɪ], **nol·le·pros** [ˌnɒlɪˈprɒs] (*Lat.*) ⚖ *Am.* **I** *v/i.* a) die Zuˈrücknahme e-r Klage einleiten, b) *im Strafprozeß*: das Verfahren einstellen; **II** *s.* → ***nolle prosequi***.

nol·le pros·e·qui [ˌnɒlɪˈprɒsɪkwaɪ] (*Lat.*) *s.* ⚖ a) Zuˈrücknahme *f* der (*Zivil*)Klage, b) Einstellung *f* des (*Straf-*)Verfahrens.

ˌno-ˈload *s.* ⚡ Leerlauf *m*: **~ *speed*** Leerlaufdrehzahl *f*.

nol-pros [nɒlˈprɒs] → ***nolle*** I.

no·mad [ˈnɒməd] **I** *adj.* noˈmadisch, Nomaden…; **II** *s.* Noˈmade *m*, Noˈmadin *f*; **no·mad·ic** [nəʊˈmædɪk] *adj.* (□ ***~ally***) **1.** → ***nomad*** I; **2.** *fig.* unstet; **ˈno·mad·ism** [-dɪzəm] *s.* Noˈmadentum *n*, Wanderleben *n*.

ˈno-man's land *s.* ⚔ Niemandsland *n* (*a. fig.*).

nom·bril [ˈnɒmbrɪl] *s.* Nabel *m* (*des Wappenschilds*).

nom de plume [ˌnɔ̃mdəˈpluːm] (*Fr.*) *s.* Pseudoˈnym *n*, Schriftstellername *m*.

no·men·cla·ture [nəʊˈmenklətʃə] *s.* **1.** Nomenklaˈtur *f*: a) (*wissenschaftliche*) Namengebung, b) Namensverzeichnis *n*; **2.** (*fachliche*) Terminoloˈgie; **3.** *coll. die* Namen *pl.*, Bezeichnungen *pl.* (*a.* Ⓐ).

nom·i·nal [ˈnɒmɪnl] *adj.* □ **1.** Namen…; **2.** nomiˈnell, Nominal…: **~ *consideration*** ⚖ formale Gegenleistung; **~ *fine*** nominelle (*sehr geringe*) Geldstrafe; **~ *rank*** Titularrang *m*; **3.** *ling.* nomiˈnal; **4.** ⚙, ⚡ Nominal…, Nenn…, Soll…; **~ ac·count** *s.* ⚚ Sachkonto *n*; **~ a·mount** *s.* ⚚ Nennbetrag *m*; **~ bal·ance** *s.* ⚚ Sollbestand *m*; **~ ca·pac·i·ty** *s.* ⚡, ⚙ Nennleistung *f*; **~ cap·i·tal** *s.* ⚚ ˈGrund-, ˈStammkapiˌtal *n*; **~ fre·quen·cy** *s.* ⚡ ˈSollfreˌquenz *f*; **~ in·ter·est** *s.* ⚚ Nomiˈnalzinsfuß *m*.

nom·i·nal·ism [ˈnɒmɪnəlɪzəm] *s. phls.* Nominaˈlismus *m*.

nom·i·nal| out·put *s.* ⚙ Nennleistung *f*; **~ par** *s.* ⚚ Nenn-, Nomiˈnalwert *m*; **~ par·i·ty** *s.* ⚚ ˈNennwertpariˌtät *f*; **~ speed** *s.* ⚡ Nenndrehzahl *f*; **~ stock** *s.* ⚚ ˈGründungs-, ˈStammkapiˌtal *n*; **~ val·ue** *s.* ⚚, ⚙ Nennwert *m*.

nom·i·nate *v/t.* [ˈnɒmɪneɪt] **1.** (***to***) berufen, ernennen (zu *e-r Stelle*), einsetzen (in *ein Amt*); **2.** nominieren, als (ˈWahl)Kandiˌdaten aufstellen; **nom·i·na·tion** [ˌnɒmɪˈneɪʃn] *s.* **1.** (***to***) Berufung *f*, Ernennung *f* (zu), Einsetzung *f* (in): ***in ~*** vorgeschlagen (***for*** für); **2.** Vorschlagsrecht *n*; **3.** Nominierung *f*, Vorwahl *f* (*e-s Kandidaten*): **~ *day*** Wahlvorschlagstermin *m*; **nom·i·na·tive** [ˈnɒmɪnətɪv] **I** *adj. ling.* nominativ (-isch): **~ *case*** → ***II***; **II** *s. ling.* Nominativ *m*, erster Fall; **ˈnom·i·na·tor** [-tə] *s.* Ernenn(end)er *m*; **nom·i·nee** [ˌnɒmɪˈniː] *s.* **1.** Vorgeschlagene(r *m*) *f*, Kandiˈdat(in); **2.** ⚚ Begünstigte(r *m*) *f*, Empfänger(in) *e-r Rente etc.*

non- [nɒn] *in Zssgn*: nicht…, Nicht…, un…, miß…

ˌnon(-)acˈcept·ance *s.* Annahmeverweigerung *f*, Nichtannahme *f e-s Wechsels etc.*

ˌnon(-)aˈchiev·er *s.* Versager *m*.

non·age [ˈnəʊnɪdʒ] *s.* Unmündigkeit *f*, Minderjährigkeit *f*.

non·a·ge·nar·i·an [ˌnəʊnədʒɪˈneərɪən] **I** *adj.* neunzigjährig; **II** *s.* Neunzigjährige(r *m*) *f*.

ˌnon-agˈgres·sion *s.* Nichtangriff *m*: **~ *treaty*** *pol.* Nichtangriffspakt *m*.

non·a·gon [ˈnɒnəgən] *s.* Ⓐ Nonaˈgon *n*, Neuneck *n*.

ˌnon(-)al·coˈhol·ic *adj.* alkoholfrei.

ˌnon-aˈligned *adj. pol.* bündnis-, blockfrei.

ˌnon(-)apˈpear·ance *s.* Nichterscheinen *n vor Gericht etc.*

ˌnon(-)asˈsess·a·ble *adj.* nicht steuerpflichtig, steuerfrei.

ˌnon(-)atˈtend·ance *s.* Nichterscheinen *n*.

ˌnon(-)belˈlig·er·ent **I** *adj.* nicht kriegführend; **II** *s.* nicht am Krieg teilnehmende Perˈson *od.* Natiˈon.

nonce [nɒns] *s.* (*nur in*): ***for the ~*** a) für das ˈeine Mal, nur für diesen Fall, b) einstweilen; **~ word** *s. ling.* Ad-ˈhoc-Bildung *f*.

non·cha·lance [ˈnɒnʃələns] (*Fr.*) *s.* Nonchaˈlance *f*: a) (Nach)Lässigkeit *f*, Gleichgültigkeit *f*, b) Unbekümmertheit *f*; **ˈnon·cha·lant** [-nt] *adj.* □ lässig: a) gleichgültig, b) unbekümmert.

ˌnon(-)colˈle·gi·ate *adj.* **1.** *Brit. univ.* keinem College angehörend; **2.** nicht akaˈdemisch; **3.** nicht aus Colleges bestehend (*Universität*).

non·com [ˌnɒnˈkɒm] F *für* ***non-commissioned*** (***officer***).

ˌnon(-)ˈcom·bat·ant ⚔ **I** *s.* ˈNichtkämpfer *m*, -kombatˌtant *m*; **II** *adj.* am Kampf nicht beteiligt.

ˌnon(-)comˈmis·sioned *adj.* **1.** unbestallt, nicht beˈvollmächtigt; **2.** ˈUnteroffiˌziersˌrang besitzend; **~ of·fi·cer** *s.* ⚔ ˈUnteroffiˌzier *m*.

ˌnon-comˈmit·tal **I** *adj.* **1.** unverbindlich, nichtssagend, neuˈtral; **2.** zuˈrückhaltend, sich nicht festlegen wollend (*Person*); **II** *s.* Unverbindlichkeit *f*.

ˌnon(-)comˈmit·ted → ***non-aligned***.

ˌnon(-)comˈpli·ance *s.* **1.** Zuˈwiderhandeln *n* (***with*** gegen), Weigerung *f*; **2.**

Nichterfüllung *f*, Nichteinhaltung *f* (***with*** von *od. gen.*).

non com·pos (men·tis) [ˌnɒnˈkɒmpəs(ˈmentɪs)] (*Lat.*) *adj.* ⚖ unzurechnungsfähig.

ˌnon-conˈduc·tor *s.* ⚡ Nichtleiter *m.*

ˌnon·conˈform·ist I *s.* Nonkonforˈmist (-in): a) (soziˈaler *od.* poˈlitischer) Einzelgänger, b) *Brit. eccl.* Dissiˈdent(in), Freikirchler(in); **II** *adj.* ˈnonkonforˌmistisch; **ˌnon·conˈform·i·ty** *s.* **1.** mangelnde Überˈeinstimmung (***with*** mit) *od.* Anpassung (***to*** an *acc.*); **2.** Nonkonforˈmismus *m*; **3.** *eccl.* Dissiˈdententum *n.*

ˌnon-conˈtent *s. Brit. parl.* Neinstimme *f* (*im Oberhaus*).

ˌnon(-)conˈten·tious *adj.* □ nicht strittig: **~ *litigation*** ⚖ freiwillige Gerichtsbarkeit.

ˌnon-conˈtrib·u·to·ry *adj.* beitragsfrei (*Organisation*).

ˈnon(-)co(-)ˌop·erˈa·tion *s.* Verweigerung *f* der Mit- *od.* Zuˈsammenarbeit; *pol.* passiver ˈWiderstand.

ˌnon(-)corˈrod·ing *adj.* ⚙ **1.** korrosiˈonsfrei; **2.** rostbeständig (*Eisen*).

ˌnon(-)ˈcreas·ing *adj.* ✝ knitterfrei.

ˌnon(-)ˈcut·ting *adj.* ⚙ spanlos: **~ *shaping*** spanlose Formung.

ˌnon(-)ˈdaz·zling *adj.* ⚙ blendfrei.

ˌnon(-)deˈliv·er·y *s.* **1.** ✝, ⚖ Nichtauslieferung *f*, Nichterfüllung *f*; **2.** ✉ Nichtbestellung *f.*

ˈnon(-)deˌnom·iˈna·tion·al *adj.* nicht konfesˈsionsgebunden: **~ *school*** Simultan-, Gemeinschaftsschule *f.*

non·de·script [ˈnɒndɪskrɪpt] **I** *adj.* schwer zu beschreiben(d), unbestimmbar, nicht klassifizierbar (*mst contp.*); **II** *s.* Perˈson *od.* Sache, die schwer zu klassifizieren ist *od.* über die nichts Näheres bekannt ist, *etwas* ˈUndefiˌnierbares.

ˌnon-diˈrec·tion·al *adj. Funk, Radio*: ungerichtet: **~ *aerial*** (*bsd. Am.* ***antenna***) Rundstrahlantenne *f.*

none [nʌn] **I** *pron. u. s. mst pl. konstr.* kein, niemand: **~ *of them is here*** keiner von ihnen ist hier; ***I have ~*** ich habe keine(n); **~ *but fools*** nur Narren; ***it's ~ of your business*** das geht dich nichts an; **~ *of that*** nichts dergleichen; **~ *of your tricks!*** laß deine Späße!; ***he will have ~ of me*** er will von mir nichts wissen; → ***other*** 8; **II** *adv.* in keiner Weise, nicht im geringsten, keineswegs: **~ *too high*** keineswegs zu hoch; **~ *the less*** nichtsdestoweniger; **~ *too soon*** kein bißchen zu früh, im letzten Augenblick; → ***wise*** 3.

ˌnon-efˈfec·tive ⚔ **I** *adj.* dienstuntauglich; **II** *s.* Dienstuntaugliche(r) *m.*

ˌnon(-)ˈe·go *s. phls.* Nicht-Ich *n.*

non·en·ti·ty [nɒˈnentətɪ] *s.* **1.** Nicht(da)sein *n*; **2.** Unding *n*, Nichts *n*; *fig. contp.* Null *f* (*Person*).

nones [nəʊnz] *s. pl.* **1.** *antiq.* Nonen *pl.*; **2.** *R.C.* ˈMittagsofˌfizium *n.*

ˌnon(-)esˈsen·tial *Brit.* **I** *adj.* unwesentlich; **II** *s.* unwesentliche Sache, Nebensächlichkeit *f*: **~*s*** *a.* nicht lebenswichtige Dinge.

ˈnone·such I *adj.* **1.** unvergleichlich; **II** *s.* **2.** Perˈson *od.* Sache, die nicht ihresgleichen hat, Muster *n*; **3.** ⚘ a) Brennende Liebe, b) Nonpaˈreilleapfel *m.*

ˌnon·theˈless *adv.* nichtsdestoweniger, dennoch.

ˌnon(-)eˈvent *s.* F ‚Reinfall' *m.*

ˌnon(-)exˈist·ence *s.* Nicht(da)sein *n*; *weitS.* Fehlen *n*; **ˌnon(-)exˈist·ent** *adj.* nicht existierend.

ˌnon(-)ˈfad·ing *adj.* ⚙, ✝ lichtecht.

non(-)fea·sance [ˌnɒnˈfiːzəns] *s.* ⚖ pflichtwidrige Unterˈlassung.

ˌnon(-)ˈfer·rous *adj.* **1.** nicht eisenhaltig; **2.** Nichteisen…: **~ *metal.***

ˌnon(-)ˈfic·tion *s.* Sachbücher *pl.*

ˌnon(-)ˈfreez·ing *adj.* ⚙ kältebeständig: **~ *mixture*** Frostschutzmittel *n.*

ˌnon(-)ful·fil(l)·ment *s.* Nichterfüllung *f.*

ˌnon(-)ˈhu·man *adj.* nicht zur menschlichen Rasse gehörig.

ˌnon(-)inˈduc·tive *adj.* ⚡ induktiˈonsfrei.

ˌnon(-)inˈflam·ma·ble *adj.* nicht feuergefährlich.

ˌnon-ˈin·ter·est-ˌbear·ing *adj.* ✝ zinslos.

ˈnon(-)ˌin·terˈven·tion *s. pol.* Nichteinmischung *f.*

ˌnon-ˈi·ron *adj.* bügelfrei.

ˌnon(-)ˈju·ry *adj.*: **~ *trial*** ⚖ summarisches Verfahren.

ˌnon-ˈlad·der·ing *adj.* maschenfest.

ˌnon(-)ˈlead·ed [-ˈledɪd] *adj.* ⚗ bleifrei (*Benzin*).

ˌnon(-)ˈmet·al *s.* ⚗ ˈNichtmeˌtall *n*; **ˌnon(-)meˈtal·lic** *adj.* ˈnichtmeˌtallisch: **~ *element*** Metalloid *n.*

ˌnon(-)neˈgo·ti·a·ble *adj.* ✝ ˈunüberˌtragbar, nicht begebbar: **~ *bill*** (***cheque***, *Am.* ***check***) Rektawechsel *m* (-scheck *m*).

no-ˈnon·sense *adj.* sachlich, kühl.

ˌnon(-)ˈnu·cle·ar *adj.* **1.** a) *pol.* ohne Aˈtomwaffen, b) ⚔ konventioˈnell; **2.** ⚙ ohne Aˈtomkraft.

ˌnon(-)obˈjec·tion·a·ble *adj.* einwandfrei.

ˌnon(-)obˈserv·ance *s.* Nichtbe(ob)achtung *f*; Nichterfüllung *f.*

non·pa·reil [ˈnɒnpərəl] (*Fr.*) **I** *adj.* **1.** unvergleichlich; **II** *s.* **2.** *der* (*die, das*) Unvergleichliche; **3.** *typ.* Nonpaˈreille (-schrift) *f*; **4.** Liebesperlen(plätzchen *n*) *pl.*

ˌnon(-)ˈpar·ti·san *adj.* **1.** (parˈtei)unabhängig; ˈüberparˌteilich; **2.** objekˈtiv, ˈunparˌteiisch.

ˌnon(-)ˈpar·ty → ***non(-)partisan.***

ˌnon(-)ˈpay·ment *s.* Nicht(be)zahlung *f*, Nichterfüllung *f.*

ˌnon(-)perˈform·ance *s.* ⚖ Nichterfüllung *f.*

ˌnon(-)ˈper·ish·a·ble *adj.* haltbar: **~ *foods.***

ˌnon(-)ˈper·son *s.* ‚ˈUnperson' *f.*

ˌnonˈplus I *v/t.* verblüffen, verwirren: **be ~(*s*)*ed*** *a.* verdutzt sein; **II** *s.* Verlegenheit *f*, Klemme *f*: ***at a ~*** ratlos, verdutzt.

ˌnon(-)polˈlut·ing *adj.* ˈumweltfreundlich, ungiftig.

ˌnon(-)proˈduc·tive *adj.* ✝ ˈunproduk̦tiv (*a. Person*); unergiebig.

ˌnon(-)ˈprof·it (mak·ing) *adj.* gemeinnützig: ***a ~ institution.***

ˈnonˌpro·lif·erˈa·tion *s. pol.* Nichtweitergabe *f* von Aˈtomwaffen: **~ *treaty*** Atomsperrvertrag *m.*

non-pros [ˌnɒnˈprɒs] *v/t.* ⚖ *e-n Kläger* (*wegen Nichterscheinens*) abweisen;

non pro·se·qui·tur [ˌnɒnprəʊˈsekwɪtə] (*Lat.*) *s.* Abweisung *f* e-s Klägers *wegen Nichterscheinens.*

ˌnon(-)ˈquo·ta *adj.* ✝ nicht kontingenˈtiert: **~ *imports.***

ˌnon-reˈcur·ring *adj.* einmalig (*Zahlung etc.*).

ˈnon(-)ˌrep·re·senˈta·tion·al *adj. Kunst*: gegenstandslos, abˈstrakt.

ˌnon(-)ˈres·i·dent I *adj.* **1.** außerhalb des Amtsbezirks wohnend; abwesend (*Amtsperson*); **2.** nicht ansässig: **~ *traffic*** Durchgangsverkehr *m*; **3.** auswärtig (*Klubmitglied*); **II** *s.* **4.** Abwesende(r *m*) *f*; **5.** Nichtansässige(r *m*) *f*; nicht im Hause Wohnende(r *m*) *f*; **6.** ✝ Deˈvisenausländer *m.*

ˌnon(-)reˈturn·a·ble *adj.* ✝ Einweg…: **~ *bottle.***

ˌnon(-)ˈrig·id *adj. Brit.* ✈ unstarr (*Luftschiff*; *a. phys. Molekül*).

ˌnon(-)ˈsched·uled *adj.* **1.** außerplanmäßig; **2.** ✈ Charter…

non·sense [ˈnɒnsəns] **I** *s.* Unsinn *m*, dummes Zeug: ***talk ~***; ***stand no ~*** sich nichts gefallen lassen; ***make ~ of*** a) ad absurdum führen, b) illusorisch machen; ***there's no ~ about him*** er ist ein ganz kühler Bursche; **II** *int.* Unsinn!, Blödsinn!; **III** *adj.* a) Nonsens…: **~ *verses***, **~ *word***, b) → **non·sen·si·cal** [nɒnˈsensɪkl] *adj.* □ unsinnig, sinnlos, abˈsurd.

non se·qui·tur [ˌnɒnˈsekwɪtə] (*Lat.*) *s.* Trugschluß *m*, irrige Folgerung.

ˌnon(-)ˈskid *adj. mot.* rutschsicher, Gleitschutz…

ˌnon(-)ˈsmok·er *s.* **1.** Nichtraucher(in); **2.** Nichtraucher(abteil *n*) *m.*

ˌnon-ˈstart·er *s. fig.* F **1.** ‚Blindgänger' *m* (*Person*); **2.** ‚Pleite' *f*, ‚Reinfall' *m* (*Plan etc.*).

ˌnon(-)ˈstop *adj.* ohne Halt, pausenlos, Nonstop…, ˈdurchgehend (*Zug*), ohne Zwischenlandung (*Flug*), *adv. a.* nonˈstop: **~ *flight*** Nonstopflug *m*; **~ *operation*** ⚙ 24-Stunden-Betrieb *m*; **~ *run*** *mot.* Ohnehaltfahrt *f.*

ˈnon·such → ***nonesuch.***

ˌnon(-)ˈsuit ⚖ **I** *s.* **1.** (*gezwungene*) Zuˈrücknahme e-r Klage; **2.** Abweisung *f* e-r Klage; **II** *v/t.* **3.** *den Kläger* mit der Klage abweisen.

ˌnon(-)supˈport *s.* ⚖ Nichterfüllung *f* einer ˈUnterhaltsverpflichtung.

ˌnon-ˈsyn·chro·nous *adj.* ⚙ *Brit.* asynˈchron.

ˌnon-ˈU *adj. Brit.* F unfein.

ˌnon(-)ˈu·ni·form *adj.* ungleichmäßig (*a. phys.*, ⚗), uneinheitlich.

ˌnon(-)ˈun·ion *Brit. adj.* ✝ keiner Gewerkschaft angehörig, nicht organisiert: **~ *shop*** *Am.* gewerkschaftsfreier Betrieb; **ˌnon(-)ˈun·ion·ist** *s.* **1.** nicht organisierter Arbeiter; **2.** Gewerkschaftsgegner *m.*

ˌnon(-)ˈus·er *s.* ⚖ Nichtausübung *f* e-s Rechts.

ˌnon(-)ˈval·ue bill *s.* ✝ Gefälligkeitswechsel *m.*

ˌnon(-)ˈva·lent *adj.* ⚗, *phys.* nullwertig.

ˌnon(-)ˈvi·o·lent *adj.* gewaltlos.

ˌnon(-)ˈwar·ran·ty *s.* ⚖ Haftungsausschluß *m.*

noo·dle¹ [ˈnuːdl] *s.* **1.** F Trottel *m*; **2.** *sl.* ‚Birne' *f*, Schädel *m.*

noo·dle² [ˈnuːdl] *s.* Nudel *f*: **~ *soup*** Nudelsuppe *f*.
nook [nʊk] *s.* (Schlupf)Winkel *m*, Ecke *f*, (stilles) Plätzchen.
noon [nuːn] **I** *s. a.* **ˈ~·day**, **ˈ~·tide**, **ˈ~·time** Mittag(szeit *f*) *m*: ***at* ~** zu Mittag; ***at high* ~** am hellen Mittag; **II** *adj.* mittägig, Mittags…
noose [nuːs] **I** *s.* Schlinge *f* (*a. fig.*): ***running* ~** Lauf-, Gleitschlinge; ***slip one's head out of the hangman's* ~** *fig.* mit knapper Not dem Galgen entgehen; ***put one's head into the* ~** *fig.* den Kopf in die Schlinge stecken; **II** *v/t.* a) *et.* schlingen (***over*** über *acc.*, ***round*** um), b) (mit e-r Schlinge) fangen.
ˌno-ˈpar *adj.* † nennwertlos (*Aktie*).
nope [nəʊp] *adv.* F ‚ne(e)', nein.
nor [nɔː] *cj.* **1.** (*mst nach neg.*) noch: ***neither … ~*** weder … noch; **2.** (*nach e-m verneinten Satzglied od. zu Beginn e-s angehängten verneinten Satzes*) und nicht, auch nicht(s): **~ *do*** (*od.* ***am***) ***I*** ich auch nicht.
Nor·dic [ˈnɔːdɪk] **I** *adj.* nordisch: **~ *combined*** *Skisport*: Nordische Kombination; **II** *s.* nordischer Mensch.
norm [nɔːm] *s.* **1.** Norm *f* (*a.* Ꭿ, †); **2.** *biol.* Typus *m*; **3.** *bsd. ped.* ˈDurchschnittsleistung *f*; **ˈnor·mal** [-ml] **I** *adj.* □ → ***normally***; **1.** norˈmal, Normal…; gewöhnlich, üblich: **~ *school*** Pädagogische Hochschule; **~ *speed*** ⚙ Betriebsdrehzahl *f*; **2.** Ꭿ normal: a) richtig, b) lot-, senkrecht: **~ *line*** → 5; **II** *s.* **3.** → ***normalcy***; **4.** Norˈmaltyp *m*; **5.** Ꭿ Norˈmale *f*, Senkrechte *f*, (Einfalls)Lot *n*; **ˈnor·mal·cy** [-mlsɪ] *s.* Normaliˈtät *f*, Norˈmalzustand *m*, *das* Norˈmale: ***return to* ~** sich normalisieren; **nor·mal·i·ty** [nɔːˈmælətɪ] *s.* Normaliˈtät *f* (*a.* Ꭿ).
nor·mal·i·za·tion [ˌnɔːməlaɪˈzeɪʃn] *s.* **1.** Normalisierung *f*; **2.** Normung *f*, Vereinheitlichung *f*; **nor·mal·ize** [ˈnɔːməlaɪz] *v/t.* **1.** normalisieren; **2.** normen, vereinheitlichen; **3.** *metall.* norˈmalglühen; **nor·mal·ly** [ˈnɔːməlɪ] *adv.* norˈmalerweise, (für) gewöhnlich.
Nor·man [ˈnɔːmən] **I** *s.* **1.** *hist.* Norˈmanne *m*, Norˈmannin *f*; **2.** Bewohner(in) der Normanˈdie; **3.** *ling.* Norˈmannisch *n*; **II** *adj.* **4.** norˈmannisch.
nor·ma·tive [ˈnɔːmətɪv] *adj.* normaˈtiv.
Norse [nɔːs] **I** *adj.* **1.** skandiˈnavisch; **2.** altnordisch; **3.** (*bsd.* alt)norwegisch; **II** *s.* **4.** *ling.* a) Altnordisch *n*, b) (*bsd.* Alt)Norwegisch *n*; **5.** *coll.* a) *die* Skandinavier *pl.*, b) *die* Norweger *pl.*; **ˈ~·man** [-mən] *s.* [*irr.*] *hist.* Nordländer *m*, Norweger *m*.
north [nɔːθ] **I** *s.* **1.** *mst* ***the*** ℒ Nord(en *m*) (*Himmelsrichtung*, *Gegend etc.*): ***to the* ~ *of*** nördlich von; **~ *by east*** ⚓ Nord zu Ost; **2.** ***the*** ℒ a) *Brit.* Nordengland *n*, b) *Am.* die Nordstaaten *pl.*, c) die Arktis; **II** *adj.* **3.** nördlich, Nord…; **III** *adv.* **4.** nördlich, nach *od.* im Norden (***of*** von); ℒ **At·lan·tic Trea·ty** *s.* ˈNordatˌlantikˌpakt *m*; ℒ **Brit·ain** *s.* Schottland *n*; ℒ **Coun·try** *s.* Nord-England *n*; **~-east** [ˌnɔːθˈiːst; ⚓ nɔːrˈiːst] **I** *s.* Nordˈost(en *m*): **~ *by east*** ⚓ Nordost zu Ost; **II** *adj.* nordˈöstlich, Nordost…; **III** *adv.* nordöstlich, nach Nordosten; **~-east·er** [ˌnɔːθˈiːstə; ⚓ nɔːrˈiːstə] *s.* Nordˈostwind *m*; **~-east·er·ly** [ˌnɔːθˈiːstəlɪ; ⚓ nɔːrˈiːstəlɪ] *adj. u. adv.* nordöstlich, Nordost…; **ˌ~-ˈeast·ern** *adj.* nordöstlich; **ˌ~-ˈeast·ward I** *adj. u. adv.* nordöstlich; **II** *s.* nordöstliche Richtung.
north·er·ly [ˈnɔːðəlɪ] *adj. u. adv.* nördlich; **ˈnorth·ern** [-ðn] *adj.* **1.** nördlich, Nord…: **~ *Europe*** Nordeuropa *n*; **~ *lights*** Nordlicht *n*; **2.** nordisch; **ˈnorth·ern·er** [-ðənə] *s.* Bewohner(in) des nördlichen Landesteils, *bsd.* der amer. Nordstaaten; **ˈnorth·ern·most** *adj.* nördlichst; **north·ing** [ˈnɔːθɪŋ] *s.* **1.** *ast.* nördliche Deklinatiˈon (*Planet*); **2.** Weg *m od.* Diˈstanz *f* nach Norden, nördliche Richtung.
ˈNorth|·man [-mən] *s.* [*irr.*] Nordländer *m*; ℒ **point** *s. phys.* Nordpunkt *m*; **~ Pole** *s.* Nordpol *m*; **~ Sea** *s.* Nordsee *f*; **~ Star** *s. ast.* Poˈlarstern *m*.
north·ward [ˈnɔːθwəd] *adj. u. adv.* nördlich (***of***, ***from*** von), nordwärts, nach Norden; **ˈnorth·wards** [-dz] *adv.* → ***northward***.
north-west [ˌnɔːθˈwest; ⚓ nɔːˈwest] **I** *s.* Nordˈwest(en *m*); **II** *adj.* nordˈwestlich, Nordwest…: ℒ ***Passage*** *geogr.* Nordwestpassage *f*; **III** *adv.* nordwestlich, nach *od.* von Nordwesten; **north-west·er** [ˌnɔːθˈwestə; ⚓ nɔːˈwestə] *s.* **1.** Nordˈwestwind *m*; **2.** *Am.* Ölzeug *n*; **north-west·er·ly** [ˌnɔːθˈwestəlɪ; ⚓ nɔːˈwestəlɪ] *adj. u. adv.* nordwestlich; **ˌnorth-ˈwest·ern** *adj.* nordwestlich.
Nor·we·gian [nɔːˈwiːdʒən] **I** *adj.* **1.** norwegisch; **II** *s.* **2.** Norweger(in); **3.** *ling.* Norwegisch *n*.
nose [nəʊz] **I** *s.* **1.** *anat.* Nase *f* (*a. fig.* ***for*** für); **2.** *Brit.* Aˈroma *n*, starker Geruch (*Tee*, *Heu etc.*); **3.** ⚙ *etc.* a) Nase *f*, Vorsprung *m*, (⚔ Geschoß)Spitze *f*, Schnabel *m*, b) Schneidkopf *m* (*Drehstahl etc.*), Mündung *f*; **4.** a) ✈ (Rumpf)Nase *f*, (*a.* ⚓ Schiffs)Bug *m*, b) *mot.* ‚Schnauze' *f* (*Vorderteil*);
Besondere Redewendungen:
bite (*od.* ***snap***) ***s.o.'s* ~ *off*** j-n scharf anfahren; ***cut off one's* ~ *to spite one's face*** sich ins eigene Fleisch schneiden; ***follow one's* ~** a) immer der Nase nach gehen, b) s-m Instinkt folgen; ***have a good* ~ *for s.th.*** F e-e gute Nase *od.* e-n ‚Riecher' für et. haben; ***hold one's* ~** sich die Nase zuhalten; ***lead s.o. by the* ~** j-n völlig beherrschen; ***keep one's* ~ *clean*** F sich nichts zuschulden kommen lassen; ***look down one's* ~** ein verdrießliches Gesicht machen; ***look down one's* ~ *at*** *j-n od. et.* verachten; ***pay through the* ~** ‚bluten' *od.* übermäßig bezahlen müssen; ***poke*** (*od.* ***put***, ***thrust***) ***one's* ~ *into*** s-e Nase in *et.* stecken; ***put s.o.'s* ~ *out of joint*** a) j-n ausstechen, j-m die Freundin *etc.* ausspannen, b) j-m das Nachsehen geben; ***not to see beyond one's* ~** a) die Hand nicht vor den Augen sehen können, b) *fig.* e-n engen (*geistigen*) Horizont haben; ***turn up one's* ~** (***at***) die Nase rümpfen (über *acc.*); ***as plain as the* ~ *in your face*** sonnenklar; ***under s.o.'s*** (***very***) **~** direkt vor j-s Nase; **II** *v/t.* **5.** riechen, spüren, wittern; **6.** beschnüffeln; mit der Nase berühren *od.* stoßen; **7.** *fig.* a) sich *im Verkehr etc.* vorsichtig vortasten, b) *Auto etc.* vorsichtig (*aus der Garage etc.*) fahren; **8.** näseln(d aussprechen); **III** *v/i.* **9.** *a.* **~ *around*** (herˈum)schnüffeln (***after***, ***for*** nach) (*a. fig.*);
Zssgn mit adv.:
nose| down ✈ **I** *v/t. Flugzeug* (an-)drücken; **II** *v/i.* im Steilflug niedergehen; **~ out** *v/t.* **1.** ausschnüffeln, -spionieren, herˈausbekommen; **2.** um e-e Handbreit schlagen; **~ o·ver** *v/i.* ✈ (sich) überˈschlagen, e-n ‚Kopfstand' machen; **~ up** ✈ **I** *v/t. Flugzeug* hochziehen; **II** *v/i.* steil hochgehen.
nose| ape *s. zo.* Nasenaffe *m*; **ˈ~·bag** *s.* Futterbeutel *m*; **ˈ~·bleed** *s.* ⚕ Nasenbluten *n*; **ˈ~-cone** *s.* Raˈketenspitze *f*.
nosed [nəʊzd] *adj. mst in Zssgn* mit e-r *dicken etc.* Nase, …nasig.
ˈnose|·dive I *s.* **1.** ✈ Sturzflug *m*; **2.** † F (Kurs-, Preis)Sturz *m*; **II** *v/i.* **3.** e-n Sturzflug machen; **4.** † ‚purzeln' (*Kurs*, *Preis*); **ˈ~·gay** *s.* Sträußchen *n*; **ˈ~-ˌheav·y** *adj.* ✈ vorderlastig; **ˈ~-ˌo·ver** *s.* ✈ ‚Kopfstand' *m beim Landen*; **ˈ~·piece** *s.* ⚙ a) Mundstück *n* (*Blasebalg*, *Schlauch etc.*), b) Reˈvolver *m* (*Objektivende e-s Mikroskops*), c) Steg *m* (*e-r Brille*); Nasensteg *m* (*Schutzbrille*); **ˈ~·rag** *s. sl.* ‚Rotzfahne' *f* (*Taschentuch*); **~ tur·ret** *s.* ✈ vordere Kanzel; **ˈ~ˌwarm·er** *s. sl.* ‚Nasenwärmer' *m*, kurze Pfeife; **~ wheel** *s.* ✈ Bugrad *n*.
nos·ey → ***nosy***.
ˌno-ˈshow *s.* ✈ *Am. sl.* **1.** *zur Abflugszeit nicht erschienener Flugpassagier*; **2.** ‚Phantom' *n* (*fiktiver Arbeitnehmer etc.*).
nos·o·log·i·cal [ˌnɒsəʊˈlɒdʒɪkl] *adj.* □ ⚕ noso-, pathoˈlogisch; **no·sol·o·gist** [nəʊˈsɒlədʒɪst] *s.* Pathoˈloge *m*.
nos·tal·gi·a [nɒˈstældʒɪə] *s.* ⚕ Nostalˈgie *f* (*a.* ⚕): a) Heimweh *n*, b) Sehnsucht *f nach etwas Vergangenem*; **nos·tal·gic** [nɒˈstældʒɪk] *adj.* (□ **~*ally***) **1.** Heimweh…; **2.** noˈstalgisch, wehmütig.
nos·tril [ˈnɒstrɪl] *s.* Nasenloch *n*, *bsd. zo.* Nüster *f*: ***it stinks in one's* ~*s*** es ekelt einen an.
nos·trum [ˈnɒstrəm] *s.* **1.** ⚕ Geheimmittel *n*, ˈQuacksalbermediˌzin *f*; **2.** *fig.* (*soziales*, *politisches*) Heilmittel *n*, Paˈtentreˌzept *n*.
nos·y [ˈnəʊzɪ] *adj.* **1.** F neugierig: **~ *parker*** *Brit.* neugierige Person; **2.** *Brit.* a) aroˈmatisch, duftend (*bsd. Tee*), b) muffig.
not [nɒt] *adv.* **1.** nicht; **~ *that*** nicht, daß, nicht als ob; ***is it* ~?**, F ***isn't it?*** nicht wahr?; → ***at*** 7; **2. ~ *a*** kein(e): **~ *a few*** nicht wenige.
no·ta·bil·i·ty [ˌnəʊtəˈbɪlətɪ] *s.* **1.** wichtige Perˈsönlichkeit, ˈStandesperˌson *f*; **2.** herˈvorragende Eigenschaft, Bedeutung *f*; **no·ta·ble** [ˈnəʊtəbl] **I** *adj.* □ **1.** beachtens-, bemerkenswert, denkwürdig, wichtig; **2.** beträchtlich: ***a* ~ *difference***; **3.** angesehen, herˈvorragend; **4.** ⚗ merklich; **II** *s.* **5.** → ***notability*** 1.
no·tar·i·al [nəʊˈteərɪəl] *adj.* □ ⚖ **1.** Notariats…, notariˈell; **2.** notariell beglaubigt; **no·ta·rize** [ˈnəʊtəraɪz] *v/t.* notariell beˈurkunden *od.* beglaubigen; **no·ta·ry** [ˈnəʊtərɪ] *s. mst* **~ *public*** (öffentlicher) Notar.
no·ta·tion [nəʊˈteɪʃn] *s.* **1.** Aufzeichnung *f*, Notierung *f*; **2.** *bsd.* ⚗, Ꭿ Schreibweise *f*, Bezeichnung *f*: ***chemical* ~** chemisches Formelzeichen; **3.** ♪

(Aufzeichnen *n* in) Notenschrift *f*.

notch [nɒtʃ] **I** *s*. **1.** *a*. ⚙ Kerbe *f*, Einschnitt *m*, Aussparung *f*, Falz *m*, Nute *f*, Raste *f*: ***be a ~ above*** F e-e Klasse besser sein als; **2.** (Vi'sier)Kimme *f* (*Schußwaffe*): ***~ and bead sights*** Kimme und Korn; **3.** *Am*. Engpaß *m*; **II** *v/t*. **4.** *bsd*. ⚙ (ein)kerben, (ein)schneiden, einfeilen; **5.** ⚙ a) ausklinken, b) nuten, falzen; **notched** [-tʃt] *adj*. **1.** ⚙ (ein-)gekerbt, mit Nuten versehen; **2.** ⚘ grob gezähnt (*Blatt*).

note [nəʊt] **I** *s*. **1.** (Kenn)Zeichen *n*, Merkmal *n*; *fig*. Ansehen *n*, Ruf *m*, Bedeutung *f*: ***man of ~*** bedeutender Mann; ***nothing of ~*** nichts von Bedeutung; **2.** *mst pl*. No'tiz *f*, Aufzeichnung *f*: ***compare ~s*** Meinungen *od*. Erfahrungen austauschen, sich beraten; ***make a ~ of s.th.*** sich et. vormerken *od*. notieren; ***make a mental ~ of s.th.*** sich et. merken; ***take ~s of s.th.*** sich über et. Notizen machen; ***take ~ of s.th.*** *fig*. et. zur Kenntnis nehmen, et. berücksichtigen; **3.** *pol*. (diplo'matische) Note: ***exchange of ~s*** Notenwechsel *m*; **4.** Briefchen *n*, Zettelchen *n*; **5.** *typ*. a) Anmerkung *f*, b) (Satz-)Zeichen *n*; **6.** ✝ a) Nota *f*, Rechnung *f*: ***as per ~*** laut Nota, b) (Schuld)Schein *m*: ***~ of hand*** → ***promissory***; ***bought and sold ~*** Schlußschein; ***~s payable*** (***receivable***) *Am*. Wechselverbindlichkeiten (-forderungen), c) Banknote *f*, d) Vermerk *m*, Notiz *f*: ***urgent ~*** Dringlichkeitsvermerk *m*, e) Mitteilung *f*: ***advice ~*** Versandanzeige *f*; ***~ of exchange*** Kursblatt *n*; **7.** ♪ a) Note *f*, b) Ton *m*, c) Taste *f*; **8.** *weitS*. a) Klang *m*, Melo'die *f*; Gesang *m* (*Vogel*), b) *fig*. Ton(art *f*) *m*: ***change one's ~*** e-n anderen Ton anschlagen; ***strike the right ~*** den richtigen Ton treffen; ***strike a false ~*** a) sich im Ton vergreifen, b) sich danebenbenehmen; ***on this*** (***encouraging** etc.*) ***~*** mit diesen (ermutigenden *etc*.) Worten; **9.** *fig*. Brandmal *n*, Schandfleck *m*; **II** *v/t*. **10.** Kenntnis nehmen von, bemerken, be(ob)achten; **11.** besonders erwähnen; **12.** *a*. ***~ down*** niederschreiben, notieren, vermerken; **13.** ✝ *Wechsel* protestieren; *Preise* angeben.

note| bank *s*. ✝ Notenbank *f*; '**~·book** *s*. No'tizbuch *n*; ✝, ⚖ Kladde *f*; **~ broker** *s*. ✝ *Am*. Wechselhändler *m*, Dis'kontmakler *m*.

not·ed ['nəʊtɪd] *adj*. ☐ **1.** bekannt, berühmt (***for*** wegen); **2.** ✝ notiert: ***~ before official hours*** vorbörslich (*Kurs*); '**not·ed·ly** [-lɪ] *adv*. ausgesprochen, deutlich, besonders.

note| pa·per *s*. 'Briefpa,pier *n*; **~ press** *s*. ✝ 'Banknotenpresse *f*, -drucke,rei *f*; '**~,wor·thy** *adj*. bemerkens-, beachtenswert.

noth·ing ['nʌθɪŋ] **I** *pron*. **1.** nichts (***of*** von): ***~ much*** nichts Bedeutendes; **II** *s*. **2.** Nichts *n*: ***to ~*** zu *od*. in nichts; ***for ~*** vergebens, umsonst; **3.** *fig*. Nichts *n*, Unwichtigkeit *f*, Kleinigkeit *f*; *pl*. Nichtigkeiten *pl*.; Null *f* (*a. Person*): ***whisper sweet ~s*** Süßholz raspeln; **III** *adv*. **4.** durch'aus nicht, keineswegs: ***~ like complete*** alles andere als vollständig; **IV** *int*. **5.** F keine Spur!, Unsinn!; *Besondere Redewendungen*: ***good for ~*** zu nichts zu gebrauchen; ***~ doing*** F a) (das) kommt gar nicht in Frage, b) nichts zu machen; ***~ but*** nichts als, nur; ***~ else*** nichts anderes, sonst nichts; ***~ if not courageous*** überaus mutig; ***not for ~*** nicht umsonst, nicht ohne Grund; ***that is ~ to what we have seen*** das ist nichts gegen das, was wir gesehen haben; ***that's ~ to me*** das bedeutet mir nichts; ***that is ~ to you*** das geht dich nichts an; ***there is ~ like*** es geht nichts über; ***there is ~ to it*** a) da ist nichts dabei, b) an der Sache ist nichts dran; ***come to ~*** *fig*. zunichte werden, sich zerschlagen; ***feel like ~ on earth*** sich hundeelend fühlen; ***make ~ of s.th.*** nicht viel Wesens von et. machen, sich nichts aus et. machen; ***I can make ~ of it*** ich kann daraus nicht klug werden; → ***say*** 2, ***think*** 3 e.

noth·ing·ness ['nʌθɪŋnɪs] *s*. **1.** Nichts *n*; **2.** Nichtigkeit *f*; **3.** Leere *f*.

no·tice ['nəʊtɪs] **I** *s*. **1.** Wahrnehmung *f*: ***to avoid ~*** (*Redew*.) um Aufsehen zu vermeiden; ***come under s.o.'s ~*** j-m bekanntwerden; ***escape ~*** unbemerkt bleiben; ***take ~ of*** Notiz nehmen von *et. od. j-m*, beachten; ***~!*** zur Beachtung!; **2.** No'tiz *f*, (*a. Presse*)Nachricht *f*, Anzeige *f* (*a*. ✝), (An)Meldung *f*, Ankündigung *f*, Mitteilung *f*; ⚖ Vorladung *f*; (Buch)Besprechung *f*; Kenntnis *f*: ***~ of acceptance*** ✝ Annahmeerklärung *f*; ***~ of arrival*** ✝ Eingangsbestätigung *f*; ***~ of assessment*** Steuerbescheid *m*; ***~ of departure*** (polizeiliche) Abmeldung *f*; ***previous ~*** Voranzeige *f*; ***bring s.th. to s.o.'s ~*** j-m et. zur Kenntnis bringen; ***give ~ that*** bekanntgeben, daß; ***give s.o. ~ of s.th.*** j-n von et. benachrichtigen; ***give ~ of appeal*** ⚖ Berufung einlegen; ***give ~ of motion*** *parl*. e-n Initiativantrag stellen; ***give ~ of a patent*** ein Patent anmelden; ***have ~ of*** Kenntnis haben von; **3.** Warnung *f*; Kündigung(sfrist) *f*: ***give s.o. ~*** (***for Easter***) j-m (zu Ostern) kündigen; ***I am under ~ to leave*** mir ist gekündigt worden; ***at a day's ~*** binnen eines Tages; ***at a moment's ~*** sogleich, jederzeit; ***at short ~*** kurzfristig, auf (kurzen) Abruf, sofort; ***subject to a month's ~*** mit monatlicher Kündigung; ***without ~*** fristlos; ***until further ~*** bis auf weiteres; → ***quit*** 9; **II** *v/t*. **4.** bemerken, beobachten, wahrnehmen; **5.** beachten, achten auf (*acc*.); **6.** No'tiz nehmen von; **7.** *Buch* besprechen; **8.** anzeigen, melden, bekanntmachen, ⚖ benachrichtigen; **no·tice·a·ble** ['nəʊtɪsəbl] *adj*. ☐ **1.** wahrnehmbar, merklich, spürbar; **2.** bemerkenswert, beachtlich; **3.** auffällig, ins Auge fallend.

no·tice| board *s*. **1.** Anschlagtafel *f*, Schwarzes Brett; **2.** Warnschild *n*; **~ pe·ri·od** *s*. Kündigungsfrist *f*.

no·ti·fi·a·ble ['nəʊtɪfaɪəbl] *adj*. meldepflichtig; **no·ti·fi·ca·tion** [,nəʊtɪfɪ'keɪʃn] *s*. Anzeige *f*, Meldung *f*, Mitteilung *f*, Bekanntmachung *f*, Benachrichtigung *f*; **no·ti·fy** ['nəʊtɪfaɪ] *v/t*. **1.** bekanntgeben, anzeigen, avisieren, melden, (amtlich) mitteilen (***s.th. to s.o.*** j-m et.); **2.** *j-n* benachrichtigen, in Kenntnis setzen (***of*** von, ***that*** daß).

no·tion ['nəʊʃn] *s*. **1.** Begriff *m* (*a. phls.*, ℞), Gedanke *m*, I'dee *f*, Vorstellung *f* (***of*** von): ***not to have the vaguest ~ of s.th.*** nicht die leiseste Ahnung von et. haben; ***I have a ~ that*** ich denke mir, daß; **2.** Meinung *f*, Ansicht *f*: ***fall into the ~ that*** auf den Gedanken kommen, daß; **3.** Neigung *f*, Lust *f*, Absicht *f* (***of doing*** zu tun); **4.** *pl*. *Am*. a) Kurzwaren *pl*., b) Kinkerlitzchen *pl*.; '**no·tion·al** [-ʃənl] *adj*. ☐ **1.** begrifflich, Begriffs…; **2.** *phls*. rein gedanklich, spekula'tiv; **3.** theo'retisch; **4.** fik'tiv, angenommen, imagi'när.

no·to·ri·e·ty [,nəʊtə'raɪətɪ] *s*. **1.** *bsd. contp*. allgemeine Bekanntheit, (traurige) Berühmtheit, schlechter Ruf; **2.** Berüchtigtsein *n*, *das* No'torische; **3.** allbekannte Per'sönlichkeit *od*. Sache; **no·to·ri·ous** [nəʊ'tɔːrɪəs] *adj*. ☐ no'torisch: a) offenkundig, b) all-, stadt-, weltbekannt, c) berüchtigt (***for*** wegen).

not·with·stand·ing [,nɒtwɪθ'stændɪŋ] **I** *prp*. ungeachtet, trotz (*gen*.): ***~ the objections*** ungeachtet der Einwände; ***his great reputation ~*** trotz s-s hohen Ansehens; **II** *a*. ***~ that*** *cj*. ob'gleich; **III** *adv*. nichtsdesto'weniger, dennoch.

nou·gat ['nuːgɑː] *s*. *Art* türkischer Honig.

nought [nɔːt] *s. u. pron*. **1.** nichts: ***bring to ~*** ruinieren, zunichte machen; ***come to ~*** zunichte werden, mißlingen, fehlschlagen; **2.** Null *f* (*a. fig*.): ***set at ~*** *et*. in den Wind schlagen, verlachen, ignorieren.

noun [naʊn] *ling*. **I** *s*. Hauptwort *n*, Substantiv *n*: ***proper ~*** Eigenname *m*; **II** *adj*. substantivisch.

nour·ish ['nʌrɪʃ] *v/t*. **1.** (er)nähren, erhalten (***on*** von); **2.** *fig*. *Gefühl* nähren, hegen; '**nour·ish·ing** [-ʃɪŋ] *adj*. nahrhaft, Nähr…; '**nour·ish·ment** [-mənt] *s*. **1.** Ernährung *f*; **2.** Nahrung *f* (*a. fig*.), Nahrungsmittel *n*: ***take ~*** Nahrung zu sich nehmen.

nous [naʊs] *s*. **1.** *phls*. Vernunft *f*, Verstand *m*; **2.** F Mutterwitz *m*, ‚Grütze' *f*, ‚Grips' *m*.

no·va ['nəʊvə] *pl*. **-vae** [-viː], *a*. **-vas** *s*. *ast*. Nova *f*, neuer Stern.

no·va·tion [nəʊ'veɪʃn] *s*. ⚖ Nova'tion *f* (*Forderungsablösung od. -übertragung*).

nov·el ['nɒvl] **I** *adj*. neu(artig); ungewöhnlich, über'raschend; **II** *s*. Ro'man *m*: ***short ~*** Kurzroman; ***~-writer*** → ***novelist***; **no·vel·la** [nəʊ'velə] *s*. No'velle *f*; **nov·el·ette** [,nɒvə'let] *s*. **1.** kurzer Roman; **2.** *contp*. seichter Unter'haltungsro,man; **nov·el·ist** ['nɒvəlɪst] *s*. Ro'manschriftsteller(in); **nov·el·is·tic** [,nɒvə'lɪstɪk] *adj*. ro'manhaft, Roman…; '**nov·el·ty** [-tɪ] *s*. **1.** Neuheit *f*: a) *das* Neue, b) *et*. Neues: ***the ~ had soon worn off*** der Reiz des Neuen war bald verflogen; **2.** Ungewöhnlichkeit *f*, *et*. Ungewöhnliches; **3.** *pl*. ✝ (billige) Neuheiten *pl*.: ***~ item*** Neuheit *f*, Schlager *m*, (billiger) Modeartikel; **4.** Neuerung *f*.

No·vem·ber [nəʊ'vembə] *s*. No'vember *m*: ***in ~*** im November.

nov·ice ['nɒvɪs] *s*. **1.** Anfänger(in), Neuling *m* (***at*** auf *e-m Gebiet*); **2.** *R.C.* No'vize *m*, *f*, No'vizin *f*; **3.** *bibl*. Neubekehrte(r *m*) *f*.

now [naʊ] **I** *adv*. **1.** nun, gegenwärtig, jetzt: ***from ~*** von jetzt an; ***up to ~*** bis jetzt; **2.** so'fort, bald; **3.** eben, so'eben: ***just ~*** gerade eben, vor ein paar Minuten; **4.** nun, dann, dar'auf, damals; **5.** (*nicht zeitlich*) nun (aber); **II** *cj.* **6.** *a.* ***~ that*** nun aber, nun da, da nun, jetzt wo; **III** *s.* **7.** *poet.* Gegenwart *f*, Jetzt *n*; *Besondere Redewendungen*: ***before ~*** schon einmal, schon früher; ***by ~*** mittlerweile, jetzt; ***~ if*** wenn nun aber; ***how ~?*** nun?, was gibt's?, was soll das heißen?; ***what is it ~?*** was ist jetzt schon wieder los?; ***now ... now ...*** bald ... bald ...; ***~ and again***, (***every***) ***~ and then*** von Zeit zu Zeit, hie(r) und da, dann und wann, gelegentlich; ***~ then*** (nun) also; ***come ~!*** nur ruhig!, sachte, sachte!; ***what ~?*** was nun?; ***~ or never*** jetzt oder nie.

now·a·days ['naʊədeɪz] **I** *adv.* heutzutage, jetzt; **II** *s.* *das* Heute *od.* Jetzt.

'no·way(s) [-weɪ(z)] F → ***nowise***.

'no·where I *adv.* **1.** nirgends, nirgendwo: ***be ~*** a) *Sport*: unter ‚ferner liefen' enden, b) nichts erreicht haben; ***get ~*** nicht weiterkommen, nichts erreichen; ***~ near*** auch nicht annähernd; **2.** nirgendwohin; **II** *s.* **3.** Nirgendwo *n*: ***from ~*** aus dem Nichts; ***in the middle of ~*** 🚂 auf freier Strecke *halten*.

'no·wise *adv.* in keiner Weise.

nox·ious ['nɒkʃəs] *adj.* □ schädlich (***to*** für): ***~ substance*** Schadstoff *m*.

noz·zle ['nɒzl] *s.* **1.** Schnauze *f*, Rüssel *m*; **2.** *sl.* ‚Rüssel' *m* (*Nase*); **3.** ⚙ a) Schnauze *f*, Tülle *f*, Schnabel *m*, Mundstück *n*, Ausguß *m*, Röhre *f*, (*an Gefäßen etc.*), b) Stutzen *m*, Mündung *f* (*an Röhren etc.*), c) (*Kraftstoff- etc.*)Düse *f*, d) 'Zapfpis,tole *f*.

nth [enθ] *adj.* Ꭿ n-te(r), n-tes: ***to the ~ degree*** a) Ꭿ bis zum n-ten Grade, b) *fig.* im höchsten Maße; ***for the ~ time*** zum hundertsten Mal.

nu [nju:] *s.* Ny *n* (*griech. Buchstabe*).

nu·ance [nju:'ɑ̃:ns] (*Fr.*) *s.* Nu'ance *f*: a) Schattierung *f*, b) Feinheit *f*, feiner 'Unterschied.

nub [nʌb] *s.* **1.** Knopf *m*, Auswuchs *m*, Knötchen *n*; **2.** (kleiner) Klumpen, Nuß *f* (*Kohle etc.*); **3.** ***the ~*** F der springende Punkt (***of*** bei); **'nub·bly** [-blɪ] *adj.* knotig.

nu·bile ['nju:baɪl] *adj.* **1.** heiratsfähig, ehemündig (*Frau*); **2.** attrak'tiv; **nu·bil·i·ty** [nju:'bɪlətɪ] *s.* Heiratsfähigkeit *f etc.*

nu·cle·ar ['nju:klɪə] **I** *adj.* **1.** kernförmig; *a. biol. etc.* Kern...; **2.** *phys.* nukle'ar, Nuklear..., (Atom)Kern..., ato'mar, Atom...: ***~ test***; ***~ weapon*** Kernwaffe *f*; **3.** *a.* ***~-powered*** mit A'tomantrieb, Atom...: ***~ submarine***; **II** *s.* **4.** Kernwaffe *f*, A'tomra,kete *f*; **5.** *pol.* A'tommacht *f*; ***~ bomb*** *s.* A'tombombe *f*; ***~ charge*** *s. phys.* Kernladung *f*; ***~ chem·is·try*** *s.* 'Kernche,mie *f*; ***~ dis·in·te·gra·tion*** *s. phys.* Kernzerfall *m*; ***~ en·er·gy*** *s. phys.* **1.** 'Kernener,gie *f*; **2.** *allg.* A'tomener,gie *f*; ***~ fam·i·ly*** *s.* 'Kernfa,milie *f*; ***~ fis·sion*** *s. phys.* Kernspaltung *f*; ***~ fuel*** *s.* Kernbrennstoff *m*: ***~ rod*** Brennstab *m*; ***~ fu·sion*** *s. phys.* 'Kernfus,ion *f*; ***~ par·ti·cle*** *s. phys.* Kernteilchen *n*; ***~ phys·ics*** *s. pl. sg. konstr.* 'Kernphy,sik *f*; ***~ pow·er*** *s.* **1.** *phys.* A'tomkraft *f*; **2.** *pol.* A'tommacht *f*; ***~ re·ac·tor*** *s. phys.* 'Kernre,aktor *m*; ***~ re·search*** *s.* (A'tom)Kernforschung *f*; ***~ ship*** *s.* Re'aktorschiff *n*; ***~ the·o·ry*** *s. phys.* 'Kerntheo,rie *f*; ***~ war(·fare)*** *s.* A'tomkrieg(führung *f*) *m*; ***~ war·head*** *s.* ⚔ A'tomsprengkopf *m*; ***~ waste*** *s.* A'tommüll *m*.

nu·cle·i ['nju:klɪaɪ] *pl. von* ***nucleus***.

nu·cle·o·lus [nju:'kli:ələs] *pl.* **-li** [-laɪ] *s.* ⚘, *biol.* Kernkörperchen *n*.

nu·cle·on ['nju:klɪɒn] *s. phys.* Nukleon *n*, (A'tom)Kernbaustein *m*.

nu·cle·us ['nju:klɪəs] *pl.* **-e·i** [-ɪaɪ] *s.* **1.** *allg.* (*a.* A'tom-, Ko'meten-, Zell)Kern *m* (*a.* Ꭿ); **2.** *fig.* Kern *m*: a) Mittelpunkt *m*, b) Grundstock *m*; **3.** *opt.* Kernschatten *m*.

nude [nju:d] **I** *adj.* **1.** nackt (*a. fig. Tatsache etc.*), bloß; **2.** nackt, kahl: ***~ hill***; **3.** ⚖ unverbindlich, nichtig: ***~ contract***; **II** *s.* **4.** *paint. etc.* Akt *m*: ***study from the ~*** Aktstudie *f*; **5.** Nacktheit *f*: ***in the ~*** nackt.

nudge [nʌdʒ] **I** *v/t. j-n* anstoßen, ‚(an-)stupsen'; **II** *s.* Stups *m*.

nu·die ['nju:dɪ] *s. sl.* Nacktfilm *m*.

nud·ism ['nju:dɪzəm] *s.* 'Nackt-, 'Freikörperkul,tur *f*, Nu'dismus *m*; **'nud·ist** [-ɪst] *s.* Nu'dist(in), FK'K-Anhänger (-in): ***~ beach*** Nacktbadestrand *m*; ***~ camp***, ***~ colony*** FKK-Platz *m*; **'nu·di·ty** [-ətɪ] *s.* **1.** Nacktheit *f*, Blöße *f*; **2.** *fig.* Armut *f*; **3.** Kahlheit *f*; **4.** *paint. etc.* 'Akt(fi,gur *f*) *m*.

nu·ga·to·ry ['nju:gətərɪ] *adj.* **1.** wertlos, albern; **2.** unwirksam (*a.* ⚖), eitel, leer.

nug·get ['nʌgɪt] *s.* **1.** Nugget *n* (*Goldklumpen*); **2.** *fig.* Brocken *m*.

nui·sance ['nju:sns] *s.* **1.** Ärgernis *n*, Plage *f*, *et.* Lästiges *od.* Unangenehmes; Unfug *m*, 'Mißstand *m*: ***dust ~*** Staubplage; ***what a ~!*** wie ärgerlich!; **2.** ⚖ Poli'zeiwidrigkeit *f*: ***public ~*** Störung *f od.* Gefährdung *f* der öffentlichen Sicherheit u. Ordnung, *a. fig. iro.* öffentliches Ärgernis; ***private ~*** Besitzstörung *f*; ***commit no ~!*** das Verunreinigen (dieses Ortes) ist verboten!; **3.** (*von Personen*) ‚Landplage' *f*, Quälgeist *m*, Nervensäge *f*: ***be a ~ to s.o.*** j-m lästig fallen; ***make a ~ of o.s.*** anderen auf die Nerven gehen; ***~ raid*** *s.* ⚔, ✈ Störangriff *m*; ***~ tax*** *s. sl. ärgerliche kleine* (*Verbraucher*)*Steuer*: ***~ val·ue*** *s.* Wert *m od.* Wirkung *f* als störender Faktor.

nuke [nu:k] *Am. sl.* **I** *s.* **1.** Kernwaffe *f*; **2.** 'Kernre,aktor *m*; **II** *v/t.* **3.** mit Kernwaffen angreifen.

null [nʌl] **I** *adj.* **1.** ⚖ *u. fig.* nichtig, ungültig: ***declare ~ and void*** für null u. nichtig erklären; **2.** wertlos, leer, nichtssagend, unbedeutend; **II** *s.* **3.** Ꭿ, ϟ Null *f*: ***~ set*** Nullmenge *f*.

nul·li·fi·ca·tion [,nʌlɪfɪ'keɪʃn] *s.* **1.** Aufhebung *f*, Nichtigerklärung *f*; **2.** Zu'nichtemachen *n*; **nul·li·fy** ['nʌlɪfaɪ] *v/t.* **1.** ungültig machen, für null u. nichtig erklären, aufheben; **2.** zu'nichte machen; **nul·li·ty** ['nʌlətɪ] *s.* **1.** Unwirksamkeit *f*; ⚖ Ungültigkeit *f*, Nichtigkeit *f*: ***decree of ~*** Nichtigkeitsurteil *n od.* Annullierung *f e-r Ehe*; ***~ suit*** Nichtigkeitsklage *f*; ***be a ~*** (null u.) nichtig sein; **2.** Nichts *n*; *fig.* Null *f* (*Person*).

numb [nʌm] **I** *adj.* □ starr, erstarrt (***with*** vor *Kälte etc.*); taub (*empfindungslos*); *fig.* a) (wie) betäubt, starr (***with fear*** vor Angst), b) abgestumpft; **II** *v/t.* starr *od.* taub machen, erstarren lassen; *fig.* a) betäuben, b) abstumpfen.

num·ber ['nʌmbə] **I** *s.* **1.** Zahl(enwert *m*) *f*, Ziffer *f*; **2.** (Haus-, Tele'fon- *etc.*) Nummer *f*: ***by ~s*** nummernweise; ***~ engaged*** *teleph.* besetzt; ***have s.o.'s ~*** F j-n durchschaut haben; ***his ~ is up*** F s-e Stunde hat geschlagen, jetzt ist er dran; → ***number one***; **3.** (An)Zahl *f*: ***a ~ of*** e-e Anzahl von (*od. gen.*), mehrere; ***a great ~ of*** sehr viele *Leute etc.*; ***five in ~*** fünf an (der) Zahl; ***in large ~s*** in großen Mengen; ***in round ~*** rund; ***one of their ~*** einer aus ihrer Mitte; ***~s of times*** zu wiederholten Malen; ***times without ~*** unzählige Male; ***five times the ~ of people*** fünfmal so viele Leute; **4.** ⚕ a) (An)Zahl *f*, Nummer *f*, b) Ar'tikel *m*, Ware *f*; **5.** Heft *n*, Nummer *f*, Ausgabe *f* (*Zeitschrift etc.*), Lieferung *f e-s Werkes*: ***appear in ~s*** in Lieferungen erscheinen; **6.** *thea. etc.* (Pro'gramm)Nummer *f*; **7.** ♪ a) Nummer *f* (*Satz*), b) *sl.* Tanznummer *f*, Schlager *m*; **8.** *poet. pl.* Verse *pl.*; **9.** *ling.* Numerus *m*: ***plural*** (***singular***) ***~*** Mehrzahl (Einzahl) *f*; **10.** ⚙ Feinheitsnummer *f* (*Garn*); **11.** *sl.* ‚Type' *f*, ‚Nummer' *f* (*Person*); **12.** **2s** *bibl.* Numeri *pl.*, Viertes Buch Mose; **II** *v/t.* **13.** zs.-zählen, aufrechnen: ***~ off*** abzählen; ***his days are ~ed*** s-e Tage sind gezählt; **14.** zählen, rechnen (*a. fig.* ***among***, ***in***, ***with*** zu *od.* unter *acc.*); **15.** numerieren: ***~ consecutively*** durchnumerieren; **16.** zählen, sich belaufen auf (*acc.*); **17.** *Jahre* zählen, alt sein; **III** *v/i.* **18.** (auf)zählen; **19.** zählen (***among*** zu *j-s Freunden etc.*); **'num·ber·ing** [-bərɪŋ] *s.* Numerierung *f*; **'num·ber·less** [-lɪs] *adj.* unzählig, zahllos.

num·ber| one I *adj.* **1.** a) erstklassig, b) (aller)höchst: ***~ priority***; **II** *s.* **2.** Nummer *f* Eins; der (die, das) Erste; erste Klasse; **3.** F das liebe Ich: ***look after ~*** auf seinen Vorteil bedacht sein, nur an sich selbst denken; **4.** ***do ~*** F sein ‚kleines Geschäft' machen; **'~·plate** *s. mot.* Nummernschild *n*; ***~ pol·y·gon*** *s.* Ꭿ 'Zahlenvieleck *n*, -poly,gon *n*; ***~ two*** *s.*: ***do ~*** F sein ‚großes Geschäft' machen.

numb·ness ['nʌmnɪs] *s.* Erstarrung *f*, Starr-, Taubheit *f*; *fig.* Betäubung *f*.

nu·mer·a·ble ['nju:mərəbl] *adj.* zählbar; **'nu·mer·al** [-rəl] **I** *adj.* **1.** Zahl..., Zahlen..., nu'merisch: ***~ language*** Ziffernsprache *f*; **II** *s.* **2.** Ziffer *f*, Zahlzeichen *n*; **3.** *ling.* Zahlwort *n*; **'nu·mer·ar·y** [-ərɪ] *adj.* Zahl(en)...; **nu·mer·a·tion** [,nju:mə'reɪʃn] *s.* **1.** Zählen *n*; Rechenkunst *f*; **2.** Numerierung *f*; **3.** (Auf-) Zählung *f*; **'nu·mer·a·tive** [-ətɪv] *adj.* zählend, Zahl(en)...: ***~ system*** Zahlensystem *n*; **'nu·mer·a·tor** [-məreɪtə] *s.* Ꭿ Zähler *m e-s Bruchs*; **nu·mer·i·cal** [nju:'merɪkl] *adj.* □ nu'merisch: a) Ꭿ Zahl(en)...: ***~ value***; ***~ equation*** Zahlengleichung *f*, b) zahlenmäßig: ***~ superiority***.

nu·mer·ous ['nju:mərəs] *adj.* □ zahlreich: ***a ~ assembly***; **'nu·mer·ous·ness** [-nɪs] *s.* große Zahl, Menge *f*, Stärke *f*.

nu·mis·mat·ic [,nju:mɪz'mætɪk] *adj.* (□ ***~ally***) numis'matisch, Münz(en)...; **,nu·mis'mat·ics** [-ks] *s. pl. sg. konstr.*

Numis'matik *f*, Münzkunde *f*; **nu·mis·ma·tist** [nju:'mɪzmətɪst] *s*. Numis'matiker(in): a) Münzkenner(in), b) Münzsammler(in).
num·skull ['nʌmskʌl] *s*. Dummkopf *m*, Trottel *m*.
nun [nʌn] *s*. *eccl*. Nonne *f*.
nun·ci·a·ture ['nʌnʃɪətʃə] *s*. *eccl*. Nuntia'tur *f*; **nun·ci·o** ['nʌnʃɪəʊ] *pl*. **-os** *s*. Nuntius *m*.
nun·cu·pa·tive ['nʌnkjʊpeɪtɪv] *adj*. ⚖ mündlich: **~ *will*** mündliches Testament, *bsd*. ⚔ Not-, ⚓ Seetestament.
nun·ner·y ['nʌnərɪ] *s*. Nonnenkloster *n*.
nup·tial ['nʌptʃəl] **I** *adj*. hochzeitlich, Hochzeit(s)..., Ehe..., Braut...: **~ *bed*** Brautbett *n*; **~ *flight*** Hochzeitsflug *m der Bienen*; **II** *s*. *mst pl*. Hochzeit *f*.
nurse [nɜ:s] **I** *s*. **1.** *mst* ***wet ~*** (Säug-)Amme *f*; **2.** *a*. ***dry ~*** Kinderfrau *f*, -mädchen *n*; **3.** Krankenschwester *f*, *a*. ***~-attendant*** (Kranken)Pfleger(in): ***head ~*** Oberschwester; → ***male*** 1; **4.** a) Stillen *n*, Stillzeit *f*, b) Pflege *f*: ***at ~*** in Pflege; ***put out to ~*** *Kinder* in Pflege geben; **5.** *zo*. a) Amme *f*, b) Arbeiterin *f* (*Biene*); **6.** *fig*. Nährmutter *f*; **II** *v/t*. **7.** *Kind* säugen, nähren, stillen, *dem Kind* die Brust geben; **8.** *Kind* auf-, großziehen; **9.** a) *Kranke* pflegen, b) *Krankheit* auskurieren, c) *Glied*, *Stimme* schonen, d) *Knie etc*. (schützend) um'fassen: ***~ one's leg*** ein Bein über das andere schlagen, e) sparsam *od*. schonend 'umgehen mit: ***~ a glass of wine*** bedächtig ein Glas Wein trinken; **10.** *fig*. a) nähren, fördern, b) *Gefühl etc*. nähren, hegen; **11.** streicheln, hätscheln; *weitS*. *a*. *pol*. sich eifrig kümmern um, sich ‚warm halten': ***~ one's constituency***; **III** *v/i*. **12.** a) säugen, stillen, b) die Brust nehmen (*Säugling*); **13.** als (Kranken)Pfleger(in) arbeiten.
nurse·ling → ***nursling***.
'**nurse·maid** *s*. Kindermädchen *n*.
nurs·er·y ['nɜ:srɪ] *s*. **1.** Kinderzimmer *n*: ***day ~*** Spielzimmer *n*; ***night ~*** Kinderschlafzimmer; **2.** Kindertagesstätte *f*; **3.** Pflanz-, Baumschule *f*; Schonung *f*; *fig*. Pflanzstätte *f*, Schule *f*; **4.** Fischpflege *f*, Streckteich *m*; **5.** *a*. ***~ stakes*** (Pferde-)Rennen *n* für Zweijährige; **~ gov·er·ness** *s*. Kinderfräulein *n*; '**~·man** [-mən] *s*. [*irr*.] Pflanzenzüchter *m*; **~ rhyme** *s*. Kinderlied *n*, -reim *m*; **~ school** *s*. Kindergarten *m*; **~ slope** *s*. *Skisport*: ‚Idi'otenhügel' *m*, Anfängerhügel *m*; **~ tale** *s*. Ammenmärchen *n*.
nurs·ing ['nɜ:sɪŋ] **I** *s*. **1.** Säugen *n*, Stillen *n*; **2.** *a*. ***sick~***, ***~ care*** (Kranken-)Pflege *f*; **II** *adj*. **3.** Nähr..., Pflege..., Kranken...; **~ ben·e·fit** *s*. Stillgeld *n*; **~ bot·tle** *s*. Säuglingsflasche *f*; **~ home** *s*. **1.** *bsd*. *Brit*. a) Pri'vatklinik *f*, b) pri'vate Entbindungsklinik; **2.** Pflegeheim *n*; **~ moth·er** *s*. stillende Mutter; **~ staff** *s*. 'Pflegeperso͵nal *n*.
nurs·ling ['nɜ:slɪŋ] *s*. **1.** Säugling *m*; **2.** Pflegling *m*; **3.** *fig*. a) Liebling *m*, Hätschelkind *n*, b) Schützling *m*.
nur·ture ['nɜ:tʃə] **I** *v/t*. **1.** (er)nähren; **2.** auf-, erziehen; **3.** *fig*. *Gefühle etc*. hegen; **II** *s*. **4.** Nahrung *f*; *fig*. Pflege *f*, Erziehung *f*.
nut [nʌt] **I** *s*. **1.** ⚘ Nuß *f*; **2.** ⚙ a) Nuß *f*, b) (Schrauben)Mutter *f*: ***~s and bolts*** *fig*. praktische Grundlagen, wesentliche Details; **3.** ♪ a) Frosch *m* (*am Bogen*), b) Saitensattel *m*; **4.** *pl*. ✝ Nußkohle *f*; **5.** *fig*. schwierige Sache: ***a hard ~ to crack*** e-e harte Nuß; **6.** *sl*. a) ‚Birne' *f* (*Kopf*): ***be*** (***go***) ***off one's ~*** verrückt sein (werden), b) *contp*. ‚Knülch' *m*, Kerl *m*, c) komischer Kauz, ‚Spinner' *m*, d) Idi'ot *m*, e) Geck *m*; **7.** *sl*. ***be ~s*** verrückt sein (***on*** nach); ***he is ~s about her*** er ist in sie total verschossen; ***drive s.o. ~s*** j-n verrückt machen; ***go ~s*** überschnappen; ***that's ~s to him*** das ist genau sein Fall; ***~s!*** a) du spinnst wohl!, b) *a*. ***~ to you!*** ‚du kannst mich mal!'; **8.** *pl*. V ‚Eier' *pl*. (*Hoden*); **9.** ***not for ~s*** *sl*. überhaupt nicht; ***he can't play for ~s*** *sl*. er spielt miserabel; **II** *v/i*. **10.** Nüsse pflücken.
nut| **bolt** ⚙ **1.** Mutterbolzen *m*; **2.** Bolzen *m od*. Schraube *f* mit Mutter; '**~-**͵**but·ter** *s*. Nußbutter *f*; '**~·case** *s*. *sl*. ‚Spinner' *m*; '**~**͵**crack·er** *s*. **1.** *a*. *pl*. Nußknacker *m*; **2.** *orn*. Tannenhäher *m*; '**~·gall** *s*. Gallapfel *m*: ***~ ink*** Gallustinte *f*; '**~·hatch** *s*. *orn*. Kleiber *m*, Spechtmeise *f*; '**~·house** *s*. *sl*. ‚Klapsmühle' *f*.
nut·meg ['nʌtmeg] *s*. Mus'kat(nuß *f*) *m*: ***~ butter*** Muskatbutter *f*.
nu·tri·a ['nju:trɪə] *s*. **1.** *zo*. Biberratte *f*, Nutria *f*; **2.** ✝ Nutriafell *n*.
nu·tri·ent ['nju:trɪənt] **I** *adj*. **1.** nährend, nahrhaft; **2.** Ernährungs...: ***~ medium*** *biol*. Nährsubstanz *f*; ***~ solution*** Nährlösung *f*; **II** *s*. **3.** Nährstoff *m*; **4.** *biol*. Baustoff *m*; '**nu·tri·ment** [-ɪmənt] *s*. Nahrung *f*, Nährstoff *m* (*a*. *fig*.); *biol*. Baustoff *m*.
nu·tri·tion [nju:'trɪʃn] *s*. **1.** Ernährung *f*; **2.** Nahrung *f*: ***~ cycle*** Nahrungskreislauf *m*; **nu'tri·tion·al** [-ʃənl] Ernährungs...; **nu'tri·tion·ist** [-ʃnɪst] *s*. Ernährungswissenschaftler(in), Diä'tetiker(in); **nu'tri·tious** [-ʃəs] *adj*. □ nährend, nahrhaft; **nu'tri·tious·ness** [-ʃəsnɪs] *s*. Nahrhaftigkeit *f*.
nu·tri·tive ['nju:trətɪv] *adj*. □ **1.** nährend, nahrhaft: ***~ value*** Nährwert *m*; **2.** Ernährungs...: ***~ tract*** Ernährungsbahn *f*.
nuts [nʌts] → ***nut*** 7.
nut| **screw** *s*. ⚙ **1.** Schraube *f* mit Mutter; **2.** Innengewinde *n*; '**~·shell** *s*. ⚘ Nußschale *f*: (***to put it***) ***in a ~*** (*Redewendung*) mit 'einem Wort, kurz gesagt; '**~·tree** *s*. ⚘ **1.** Haselnußstrauch *m*; **2.** Nußbaum *m*.
nut·ty ['nʌtɪ] *adj*. **1.** voller Nüsse; **2.** nußartig, Nuß...; **3.** pi'kant; **4.** *sl*. verrückt (***on*** nach).
nuz·zle ['nʌzl] **I** *v/t*. **1.** mit der Schnauze aufwühlen; **2.** mit der Schnauze *od*. Nase reiben an (*dat*.); *fig*. *Kind* liebkosen, hätscheln; **3.** *e-m Schwein etc*. e-n Ring durch die Nase ziehen; **II** *v/i*. **4.** (mit der Schnauze) wühlen, schnüffeln (***in*** in *dat*., ***for*** nach); **5.** sich (an)schmiegen (***to*** an *acc*.).
ny·lon ['naɪlɒn] *s*. Nylon *n*: ***~s*** F Nylonstrümpfe, Nylons.
nymph [nɪmf] *s*. **1.** *myth*. Nymphe *f* (*a*. *poet*. *u*. *iro*. *Mädchen*); **2.** *zo*. a) Puppe *f*, b) Nymphe *f*; '**nymph·et** [nɪm'fet] *s*. ‚Nymphchen' *n*; **nym·pho** ['nɪmfəʊ] *pl*. **-phos** *s*. F *für* ***nymphomaniac*** II.
nym·pho·ma·ni·a [͵nɪmfəʊ'meɪnjə] *s*. ⚕ Nymphoma'nie *f*, Mannstollheit *f*; ͵**nym·pho'ma·ni·ac** [-nɪæk] **I** *adj*. nympho'man, mannstoll; **II** *s*. Nympho'manin *f*.

O

O, o¹ [əʊ] *s.* **1.** O *n*, o *n* (*Buchstabe*); **2.** *bsd. teleph.* Null *f*.

O, o² [əʊ] *int.* o(h)!, ah!, ach!

oaf [əʊf] *s.* **1.** Dummkopf *m*, ‚Esel' *m*; **2.** Lümmel *m*, Flegel *m*; **oaf·ish** ['əʊfɪʃ] *adj.* **1.** dumm, ‚blöd'; **2.** lümmel-, flegelhaft.

oak [əʊk] **I** *s.* **1.** ⚘ *a.* **~-tree** Eiche *f*, Eichbaum *m*; **2.** *poet.* Eichenlaub *n*; **3.** Eichenholz *n*; **4.** *Brit. univ. sl.* Eichentür *f*: **sport one's ~** die Tür verschlossen halten, nicht zu sprechen sein; **5. the** *𝔒***s** *sport Stutenrennen in Epsom*; **II** *adj.* **6.** eichen, Eichen…; **~ ap·ple** *s.* ⚘ Gallapfel *m*.

oak·en ['əʊkən] *adj.* **1.** *bsd. poet.* Eichen…; **2.** eichen, von Eichenholz; **oak·let** ['əʊklɪt], **oak·ling** ['əʊklɪŋ] *s.* ⚘ junge *od.* kleine Eiche.

oa·kum ['əʊkəm] *s.* Werg *n*: **pick ~** a) Werg zupfen, b) F ‚Tüten kleben', ‚Knast schieben'.

'oak·wood *s.* **1.** Eichenholz *n*; **2.** Eichenwald(ung *f*) *m*.

oar [ɔː] **I** *s.* **1.** Ruder *n* (*a. zo.*), *bsd. sport* Riemen *m*: **four-~** Vierer *m* (*Boot*); **pull a good ~** gut rudern; **put** (*od.* **shove**) **one's ~ in** F sich einmischen, *im Gespräch* ‚s-n Senf dazugeben'; **rest on one's ~s** *fig.* sich auf s-n Lorbeeren ausruhen; → **ship** 8; **2.** *sport* Ruderer *m*, Ruderin *f*: **a good ~**; **3.** *fig.* Flügel *m*, Arm *m*; **4.** *Brauerei*: Krücke *f*; **II** *v/t. u. v/i.* **5.** rudern; **oared** [ɔːd] *adj.* **1.** mit Rudern (versehen), Ruder…; **2.** *in Zssgn* …rud(e)rig; **oar·lock** ['ɔːlɒk] *s. Am.* Riemendolle *f*; **oars·man** ['ɔːzmən] *s.* [*irr.*] Ruderer *m*; **oars·wom·an** ['ɔːzˌwʊmən] *s.* [*irr.*] Ruderin *f*.

o·a·sis [əʊ'eɪsɪs] *pl.* **-ses** [-siːz] *s.* O'ase *f* (*a. fig.*).

oast [əʊst] *s. Brauerei*: Darre *f*.

oat [əʊt] *s. mst pl.* Hafer *m*: **be off one's ~s** F keinen Appetit haben; **he feels his ~s** F a) ihn sticht der Hafer, b) er ist ‚groß in Form'; **sow one's wild ~s** sich austoben, sich die Hörner abstoßen; **oat·en** ['əʊtn] *adj.* **1.** Hafer…; **2.** Hafermehl…

oath [əʊθ; *pl.* əʊðz] *s.* **1.** Eid *m*, Schwur *m*: **~ of allegiance** Fahnen-, Treueid; **~ of disclosure** ⚖ Offenbarungseid; **~ of office** Amts-, Diensteid; **false ~** Falsch-, Meineid *m*; **bind by ~** eidlich verpflichten; (**up**)**on ~** unter Eid, eidlich; **upon my ~!** das kann ich beschwören!; **administer** (*od.* **tender**) **an ~ to s.o., put s.o. to** (*od.* **on**) **his ~** j-m e-n Eid abnehmen, j-n schwören lassen; **swear** (*od.* **take**) **an ~** e-n Eid leisten, schwören (**on, to** auf *acc.*); **in lieu of an ~** an Eides Statt; **under ~** unter Eid, eidlich verpflichtet; **be on one's ~** unter Eid stehen; **2.** Fluch *m*, Verwünschung *f*.

'oat·meal *s.* **1.** Hafermehl *n*, -grütze *f*; **2.** Haferschleim *m*.

ob·bli·ga·to [ˌɒblɪ'gɑːtəʊ] ♪ **I** *adj.* obli'gat, hauptstimmig; **II** *pl.* **-tos** *s.* selbständige Begleitstimme.

ob·du·ra·cy ['ɒbdjʊrəsɪ] *s. fig.* Verstocktheit *f*, Halsstarrigkeit *f*; **'ob·du·rate** [-rət] *adj.* ☐ **1.** verstockt, halsstarrig; **2.** hartherzig.

o·be·di·ence [ə'biːdjəns] *s.* **1.** Gehorsam *m* (**to** gegen); **2.** *fig.* Abhängigkeit *f* (**to** von): **in ~ to** gemäß (*dat.*), im Verfolg (*gen.*); **in ~ to s.o.** auf j-s Verlangen; **o'be·di·ent** [-nt] *adj.* ☐ **1.** gehorsam (**to** *dat.*); **2.** ergeben, unter'würfig (**to** *dat.*): **Your ~ servant** Hochachtungsvoll (*Amtsstil*); **3.** *fig.* abhängig (**to** von).

o·bei·sance [əʊ'beɪsəns] *s.* **1.** Verbeugung *f*; **2.** Ehrerbietung *f*, Huldigung *f*: **do** (*od.* **make** *od.* **pay**) **~ to s.o.** j-m huldigen; **o'bei·sant** [-nt] *adj.* huldigend, unter'würfig.

ob·e·lisk ['ɒbəlɪsk] *s.* **1.** Obe'lisk *m*; **2.** *typ.* a) → **obelus**, b) Kreuz(zeichen) *n* (*für Randbemerkungen*).

ob·e·lus ['ɒbɪləs] *pl.* **-li** [-laɪ] *s. typ.* **1.** Obe'lisk *m* (*Zeichen für fragwürdige Stellen*); **2.** Verweisungszeichen *n auf Randbemerkungen*.

o·bese [əʊ'biːs] *adj.* fettleibig, korpu'lent, *a. fig.* fett, dick; **o'bese·ness** [-nɪs], **o'bes·i·ty** [-sətɪ] *s.* Fettleibigkeit *f*, Korpu'lenz *f*.

o·bey [ə'beɪ] **I** *v/t.* **1.** *j-m* gehorchen, folgen (*a. fig.*); **2.** *e-m Befehl etc.* Folge leisten, befolgen (*acc.*); **II** *v/i.* **3.** gehorchen, folgen (**to** *dat.*).

ob·fus·cate ['ɒbfʌskeɪt] *v/t.* **1.** verfinstern, trüben (*a. fig.*); **2.** *fig. Urteil etc.* trüben, verwirren; *die Sinne* benebeln; **ob·fus·ca·tion** [ˌɒbfʌs'keɪʃn] Verfinsterung *f etc.*

o·bit·u·ar·y [ə'bɪtjʊərɪ] **I** *s.* **1.** Todesanzeige *f*; **2.** Nachruf *m*; **3.** *eccl.* Totenliste *f*; **II** *adj.* **4.** Toten…, Todes…: **~ notice** Todesanzeige *f*.

ob·ject¹ [əb'dʒekt] **I** *v/t.* **1.** *fig.* einwenden, vorbringen (**to** gegen); **2.** vorhalten, vorwerfen (**to, against** *dat.*); **II** *v/i.* **3.** Einwendungen machen, Einsprüche erheben, protestieren, reklamieren (**to, against** gegen); **4.** et. einwenden, et. dagegen haben: **~ to s.th.** et. beanstanden; **do you ~ to my smoking?** haben Sie et. dagegen, wenn ich rauche?; **if you don't ~** wenn Sie nichts dagegen haben.

ob·ject² ['ɒbdʒɪkt] *s.* **1.** Ob'jekt *n* (*a. Kunst*), Gegenstand *m* (*a. fig. des Mitleids etc.*): **~ of invention** ⚖ Erfindungsgegenstand; **money is no ~** Geld spielt keine Rolle; **salary no ~** Gehalt Nebensache; **2.** Absicht *f*, Ziel *n*, Zweck *m*: **make it one's ~ to do s.th.** es sich zum Ziel setzen, et. zu tun; **3.** F komische *od.* scheußliche Per'son *od.* Sache: **what an ~ you are!** wie sehen Sie denn aus!; **4.** *ling.* a) Ob'jekt *n*: **direct ~** Akkusativobjekt; **~ clause** Objektsatz *m*, b) von e-r Präpositi'on abhängiges Wort; **~ draw·ing** *s.* Zeichnen *n* nach Vorlagen *od.* Mo'dellen; **'~-ˌfind·er** *s. phot.* (Objek'tiv)Sucher *m*; **'~-glass** *s. opt.* Objek'tiv(linse *f*) *n*.

ob·jec·ti·fy [ɒb'dʒektɪfaɪ] *v/t.* objektivieren.

ob·jec·tion [əb'dʒekʃn] *s.* **1.** a) Einwendung *f* (*a.* ⚖), Einspruch *m*, -wand *m*, -wurf *m*, Bedenken *n* (**to** gegen), b) *weitS.* Abneigung *f*, 'Widerwille *m* (**against** gegen): **I have no ~ to him** ich habe nichts gegen ihn *od.* an ihm nichts auszusetzen; **make** (*od.* **raise**) **an ~ to s.th.** gegen et. e-n Einwand erheben; **take ~ to s.th.** gegen et. protestieren; **2.** Beanstandung *f*, Reklamati'on *f*; **ob'jec·tion·a·ble** [-ʃnəbl] *adj.* ☐ **1.** nicht einwandfrei, zu beanstanden(d), unerwünscht, anrüchig; **2.** unangenehm (**to** *dat. od.* für); **3.** anstößig.

ob·jec·tive [əb'dʒektɪv] **I** *adj.* ☐ **1.** objek'tiv (*a. phls.*), sachlich, vorurteilslos; **2.** *ling.* Objekts…: **~ case** → 5; **~ genitive** objektiver Genitiv; **3.** Ziel…: **~ point** → 6; **II** *s.* **4.** *opt.* Objek'tiv(linse *f*) *n*; **5.** *ling.* Ob'jektsfall *m*; **6.** (*bsd.* ⚔ Kampf-, Angriffs)Ziel *n*; **ob'jec·tive·ness** [-nɪs], **ob·jec·tiv·i·ty** [ˌɒbdʒek'tɪvətɪ] *s.* Objektivi'tät *f*.

ob·ject lens *s. opt.* Objek'tiv(linse *f*) *n*.

ob·ject·less ['ɒbdʒɪktlɪs] *adj.* gegenstands-, zweck-, ziellos.

ob·ject les·son *s.* **1.** *ped. u. fig.* 'Anschauungsˌunterricht *m*; **2.** *fig.* Schulbeispiel *n*; **3.** *fig.* Denkzettel *m*.

ob·jec·tor [əb'dʒektə] *s.* Gegner(in) (**to** *gen*); → **conscientious**.

ob·ject| plate, ~ slide *s.* Ob'jektträger *m* (*Mikroskop etc.*); **~ teach·ing** *s.* 'Anschauungsˌunterricht *m*.

ob·jet d'art [ˌɒbʒeɪ'dɑː] (*Fr.*) *s.* (*bsd.* kleiner) Kunstgegenstand.

ob·jur·gate ['ɒbdʒɜːgeɪt] *v/t.* tadeln, schelten.

ob·late¹ ['ɒbleɪt] *adj.* ⩘, *phys.* (an den Polen) abgeplattet.

ob·late² ['ɒbleɪt] *R.C.* Ob'lat(in) (*Laienbruder od. -schwester*).

ob·la·tion [əʊ'bleɪʃn] *s. bsd. eccl.* Opfer (-gabe *f*) *n*.

ob·li·gate *v/t.* ['ɒblɪgeɪt] *a.* ⚖ verpflichten; **ob·li·ga·tion** [ˌɒblɪ'geɪʃn] *s.* **1.** Verpflichten *n*; **2.** Verpflichtung *f*, Verbindlichkeit *f*: ***of ~*** obligatorisch; ***be under an ~ to s.o.*** j-m (zu Dank) verpflichtet sein; **3.** † a) Schuldverschreibung *f*, Obligati'on *f*, b) (Schuld-)Verpflichtung *f*, Verbindlichkeit *f*: ***financial ~*** Zahlungsverpflichtung; ***~ to buy*** Kaufzwang *m*; ***no ~, without ~*** unverbindlich, freibleibend; **ob·li·ga·to·ry** [ə'blɪgətərɪ] *adj.* □ verpflichtend, bindend, (rechts)verbindlich, obliga'torisch (***on, upon*** für), Zwangs…

o·blige [ə'blaɪdʒ] **I** *v/t.* **1.** nötigen, zwingen: ***I was ~d to go*** ich mußte gehen; **2.** *fig.* *j-n* (zu Dank) verpflichten: ***much ~d!*** sehr verbunden!, danke bestens!; ***I am ~d to you for it*** ich habe es Ihnen zu verdanken; ***will you ~ me by*** (*ger.*)? wären Sie so freundlich, zu (*inf.*)?, *iro.* würden Sie gefälligst *et. tun*?; **3.** *j-m* gefällig sein, e-n Gefallen tun, dienen: ***to ~ you*** Ihnen zu Gefallen; ***~ the company with*** die Gesellschaft mit *e-m Lied etc.* erfreuen; **4.** ⚖ *j-n* (*durch Eid etc.*) binden (***to*** an *acc.*): ***~ o.s.*** sich verpflichten (***to do*** *et.* zu tun); **II** *v/i.* **5.** ***~ with*** F *Lied etc.* vortragen, zum besten geben; **6.** erwünscht sein: ***an early reply will ~*** um baldige Antwort wird gebeten; **ob·li·gee** [ˌɒblɪ'dʒiː] *s.* ⚖ Obligati'onsgläubiger (-in), Forderungsberechtigte(r *m*) *f*; **o'blig·ing** [-dʒɪŋ] *adj.* □ verbindlich, gefällig, zu'vor-, entgegenkommend; **o'blig·ing·ness** [-dʒɪŋnɪs] *s.* Gefälligkeit *f*, Zu'vorkommenheit *f*; **ob·li·gor** [ˌɒblɪ'gɔː] *s.* ⚖ (Obligati'ons)Schuldner(in).

ob·lique [ə'bliːk] *adj.* □ **1.** *bsd.* ⩓ schief, schräg: ***~(-angled)*** schiefwink(e)lig; ***at an ~ angle with*** im spitzen Winkel zu; **2.** 'indiˌrekt, versteckt, verblümt: ***~ accusation***; ***~ glance*** Seitenblick *m*; **3.** unaufrichtig, unredlich; **4.** *ling.* abhängig, 'indiˌrekt: ***~ case*** Beugefall *m*; ***~ speech*** indirekte Rede; **ob'lique·ness** [-nɪs], **ob·liq·ui·ty** [ə'blɪkwətɪ] *s.* **1.** Schiefe *f* (*a. ast.*), schiefe Lage *od.* Richtung, Schrägheit *f*; **2.** *fig.* Schiefheit *f*: ***moral ~*** Unredlichkeit *f*; ***~ of judg(e)ment*** Schiefe *f* des Urteils.

ob·lit·er·ate [ə'blɪtəreɪt] *v/t.* **1.** auslöschen, tilgen (*beide a. fig.*), *Schrift a.* ausstreichen, wegradieren; *Briefmarken* entwerten; **2.** ⚕ veröden; **ob·lit·er·a·tion** [əˌblɪtə'reɪʃn] *s.* **1.** Verwischung *f*, Auslöschung *f*; **2.** *fig.* Vernichtung *f*, Vertilgung *f*.

ob·liv·i·on [ə'blɪvɪən] *s.* **1.** Vergessenheit *f*: ***fall*** (*od.* ***sink***) ***into ~*** in Vergessenheit geraten; **2.** Vergessen *n*, Vergeßlichkeit *f*; **3.** ⚖, *pol.* Straferlaß *m*: (***Act of***) ☊ Amne'stie *f*; **ob'liv·i·ous** [-ɪəs] *adj.* □ vergeßlich: ***be ~ of s.th.*** *et.* vergessen (haben); ***be ~ to s.th.*** F *fig.* blind sein gegen et., et. nicht beachten.

ob·long ['ɒblɒŋ] **I** *adj.* **1.** länglich: ***~ hole*** ⚙ Langloch *n*; **2.** ⩓ rechteckig; **II** *s.* **3.** ⩓ Rechteck *n*.

ob·lo·quy ['ɒbləkwɪ] *s.* **1.** Verleumdung *f*, Schmähung *f*: ***fall into ~*** in Verruf kommen; **2.** Schmach *f*.

ob·nox·ious [əb'nɒkʃəs] *adj.* □ **1.** anstößig, anrüchig, verhaßt, ab'scheulich; **2.** (***to***) unbeliebt (bei), unangenehm (*dat.*); **ob'nox·ious·ness** [-nɪs] *s.* **1.** Anstößigkeit *f*, Anrüchigkeit *f*; **2.** Verhaßtheit *f*.

o·boe ['əʊbəʊ] *s.* ♪ O'boe *f*; **'o·bo·ist** [-əʊɪst] *s.* Obo'ist(in).

ob·scene [əb'siːn] *adj.* □ **1.** unzüchtig (*a.* ⚖), unanständig, zotig, ob'szön: ***~ libel*** ⚖ Veröffentlichung *f* unzüchtiger Schriften; ***~ talker*** Zotenreißer *m*; **2.** 'widerlich; **ob·scen·i·ty** [əb'senətɪ] *s.* **1.** Unanständigkeit *f*, Schmutz *m*, Zote *f*, *pl. a.* Obszöni'täten *pl.*; **2.** 'Widerlichkeit *f*.

ob·scur·ant ['ɒbskjʊərənt] *s.* Obsku'rant *m*, Dunkelmann, Bildungsfeind *m*; **ob·scur·ant·ism** [ˌɒbskjʊə'ræntɪzəm] *s.* Obskuran'tismus *m*, Bildungshaß *m*; **ob·scur·ant·ist** [ˌɒbskjʊə'ræntɪst] **I** *s.* → ***obscurant***; **II** *adj.* obskuran'tistisch.

ob·scu·ra·tion [ˌɒbskjʊ'reɪʃn] *s.* Verdunkelung *f* (*a. fig.*).

ob·scure [əb'skjʊə] **I** *adj.* □ **1.** dunkel, düster; **2.** *fig.* dunkel, unklar; **3.** *fig.* ob'skur, unbekannt, unbedeutend; **4.** *fig.* verborgen: ***live an ~ life***; **II** *v/t.* **5.** verdunkeln, verfinstern (*a. fig.*); **6.** *fig.* verkleinern, in den Schatten stellen; **7.** *fig.* unverständlich *od.* undeutlich machen; **8.** verbergen; **ob'scu·ri·ty** [-ərətɪ] *s.* **1.** Dunkelheit *f* (*a. fig.*); **2.** *fig.* Unklarheit *f*, Undeutlichkeit *f*, Unverständlichkeit *f*; **3.** *fig.* Unbekanntheit *f*, Verborgenheit *f*, Niedrigkeit *f der Herkunft*: ***be lost in ~*** vergessen sein.

ob·se·quies ['ɒbsɪkwɪz] *s. pl.* Trauerfeierlichkeit(en *pl.*) *f*.

ob·se·qui·ous [əb'siːkwɪəs] *adj.* □ unter'würfig (***to*** gegen), ser'vil, kriecherisch; **ob'se·qui·ous·ness** [-nɪs] *s.* Unter'würfigkeit *f*.

ob·serv·a·ble [əb'zɜːvəbl] *adj.* □ **1.** wahrnehmbar; **2.** bemerkenswert; **3.** zu be(ob)achten(d); **ob'serv·ance** [-vns] *s.* **1.** Befolgung *f*, Be(ob)achtung *f*, Ein-, Innehaltung *f von Gesetzen etc.*; **2.** *eccl.* Heilighaltung *f*, Feiern *n*; **3.** Brauch *m*, Sitte *f*; **4.** Regel *f*, Vorschrift *f*; **5.** *R.C.* Ordensregel *f*, Obser'vanz *f*; **ob'serv·ant** [-vnt] *adj.* □ **1.** beobachtend, befolgend (***of*** *acc.*): ***be very ~ of forms*** sehr auf Formen halten; **2.** aufmerksam, acht-, wachsam (***of*** auf *acc.*).

ob·ser·va·tion [ˌɒbzə'veɪʃn] **I** *s.* **1.** Beobachtung *f* (*a.* ⚕, ⚓ *etc.*), Über'wachung *f*, Wahrnehmung *f*: ***keep s.o. under ~*** j-n beobachten (lassen); **2.** ⚔ (Nah)Aufklärung *f*; **3.** Beobachtungsvermögen *n*; **4.** Bemerkung *f*; **5.** Befolgung *f*; **II** *adj.* **6.** Beobachtungs…, Aussichts…; ***~ bal·loon*** *s.* 'Fesselbalˌlon *m*; ***~ car*** *s.* 🚂 Aussichtswagen *m*; ***~ coach*** *s.* Omnibus *m* mit Aussichtsplattform; ***~ post*** *s.* ⚔ Beobachtungsstand *m*, -posten *m*; ***~ tow·er*** *s.* Beobachtungswarte *f*; Aussichtsturm *m*; ***~ ward*** *s.* ⚕ Be'obachtungsstatiˌon *f*; ***~ win·dow*** *s.* ⚙ *etc.* Beobachtungsfenster *n*.

ob·serv·a·to·ry [əb'zɜːvətrɪ] *s.* Observa'torium *n*: a) Wetterwarte *f*, b) Sternwarte *f*.

ob·serve [əb'zɜːv] **I** *v/t.* **1.** beobachten: a) über'wachen, b) (be)merken, wahrnehmen, c) *Gesetz etc.* befolgen, (ein-)halten, beachten, *Fest etc.* feiern, begehen: ***~ silence*** Stillschweigen bewahren; **2.** bemerken, äußern, sagen; **II** *v/i.* **3.** Beobachtungen machen; **4.** Bemerkungen machen, sich äußern (***on, upon*** über *acc.*); **ob'serv·er** [-və] *s.* **1.** Beobachter(in) (*a. pol.*), Zuschauer(in); **2.** Befolger(in); **3.** ⚔, ✈ a) Beobachter *m*, b) (*Flugmeldedienst*: Luftspäher *m*; **ob'serv·ing** [-vɪŋ] *adj.* □ aufmerksam, achtsam.

ob·sess [əb'ses] *v/t.* quälen, heimsuchen, verfolgen (*von Ideen etc.*): ***~ed by*** (*od.* ***with***) besessen von; **ob·ses·sion** [əb'seʃn] *s.* Besessenheit *f*, fixe I'dee; *psych.* Zwangsvorstellung *f*; **ob'ses·sive** [-sɪv] *adj. psych.* zwanghaft, Zwangs…: ***~ neurosis***.

ob·so·les·cence [ˌɒbsəʊ'lesns] *s.* Veralten *n*: ***planned ~*** †, ⚙ künstliche Veralterung; **ob·so'les·cent** [-nt] *adj.* veraltend.

ob·so·lete ['ɒbsəliːt] *adj.* □ **1.** veraltet, über'holt, altmodisch; **2.** abgenutzt, verbraucht; **3.** *biol.* zu'rückgeblieben, rudimen'tär.

ob·sta·cle ['ɒbstəkl] *s.* Hindernis *n* (***to*** für) (*a. fig.*): ***put ~s in s.o.'s way*** *fig.* j-m Hindernisse in den Weg legen; ***~ race*** *sport* Hindernisrennen *n*.

ob·stet·ric, ob·stet·ri·cal [ɒb'stetrɪk(l)] *adj.* Geburts(hilfe)…, Entbindungs…; **ob·ste·tri·cian** [ˌɒbste'trɪʃn] *s.* ⚕ Geburtshelfer(in); **ob'stet·rics** [-ks] *s. pl. mst sg. konstr.* Geburtshilfe *f*.

ob·sti·na·cy ['ɒbstɪnəsɪ] *s.* Hartnäckigkeit *f* (*a. fig.*, ⚕ *etc.*), Eigensinn *m*; **'ob·sti·nate** [-tənət] *adj.* □ hartnäckig (*a. fig.*), halsstarrig, eigensinnig.

ob·strep·er·ous [əb'strepərəs] *adj.* □ **1.** ungebärdig, tobend, 'widerspenstig; **2.** lärmend.

ob·struct [əb'strʌkt] **I** *v/t.* **1.** versperren, -stopfen, blockieren: ***~ s.o.'s view*** j-m die Sicht nehmen; **2.** *a. fig.* behindern, hemmen, lahmlegen; **3.** *fig.*, *a. pol.* blockieren, vereiteln; **4.** *sport*: sperren, (*a. Amtsperson*) behindern (***in*** bei); **II** *v/i.* **5.** *pol.* Obstrukti'on treiben; **ob'struc·tion** [-kʃn] *s.* **1.** Versperrung *f*, Verstopfung *f*; **2.** Behinderung *f*, Hemmung *f*; **3.** Hindernis *n* (***to*** für); **4.** *pol.* Obstrukti'on *f*; **ob'struc·tion·ism** [-kʃənɪzəm] *s. bsd. pol.* Obstrukti'onspoliˌtik *f*; **ob'struc·tion·ist** [-kʃənɪst] **I** *s.* Obstrukti'onspoˌlitiker(in); **II** *adj.* Obstruktions…; **ob'struc·tive** [-tɪv] **I** *adj.* □ **1.** versperrend (*etc.* → ***obstruct*** I); **2.** (***of, to***) hinderlich, hemmend (für): ***be ~ to s.th.*** et. behindern; **3.** Obstruktions…; **II** *s.* **4.** Hindernis *n*.

ob·tain [əb'teɪn] **I** *v/t.* **1.** erlangen, erhalten, bekommen, erwerben, sich verschaffen, *Sieg* erringen: ***~ by flattery*** sich erschmeicheln; ***~ legal force*** Rechtskraft erlangen; ***details can be ~ed from*** Näheres ist zu erfahren bei; **2.** *Willen, Wünsche etc.* 'durchsetzen; **3.** erreichen; **4.** † *Preis* erzielen; **II** *v/i.* **5.** (vor)herrschen, bestehen; Geltung haben, sich behaupten; **ob'tain·a·ble** [-nəbl] *adj.* erreichbar, erlangbar; erhältlich, zu erhalten(d) (***at*** bei); **ob'tain·ment** [-mənt] *s.* Erlangung *f*.

ob·trude [əb'truːd] **I** *v/t.* aufdrängen, -nötigen, -zwingen (***upon, on*** *dat.*): ***~***

o.s. upon → **II** *v/i.* sich aufdrängen (***upon***, ***on*** *dat.*); **ob'tru·sion** [-u:ʒn] *s.* **1.** Aufdrängen *n*, Aufnötigung *f*; **2.** Aufdringlichkeit *f*; **ob'tru·sive** [-u:sɪv] *adj.* □ aufdringlich (*a. Sache*).

ob·tu·rate ['ɒbtjʊəreɪt] *v/t.* **1.** *a.* ⚕ verstopfen, verschließen; **2.** ⚙ (ab)dichten, lidern; **ob·tu·ra·tion** [ˌɒbtjʊə'reɪʃn] *s.* **1.** Verstopfung *f*, Verschließung *f*; **2.** ⚙ (Ab)Dichtung *f*.

ob·tuse [əb'tju:s] *adj.* □ **1.** stumpf (*a.* ⩓): **~(-*angled*)** stumpfwink(e)lig; **2.** *fig.* begriffsstutzig, beschränkt; dumpf (*Ton, Schmerz etc.*); **ob'tuse·ness** [-nɪs] *s.* **1.** Stumpfheit *f* (*a. fig.*); **2.** Begriffsstutzigkeit *f*.

ob·verse ['ɒbvɜ:s] **I** *s.* **1.** Vorderseite *f*; Bildseite *f e-r Münze*; **2.** Gegenstück *n*, *die* andere Seite, Kehrseite *f*; **II** *adj.* □ **3.** Vorder…, dem Beobachter zugekehrt; **4.** entsprechend, 'umgekehrt; **ob·verse·ly** [ɒb'vɜ:slɪ] *adv.* 'umgekehrt.

ob·vi·ate ['ɒbvɪeɪt] *v/t.* **1.** *e-r Sache* begegnen, zu'vorkommen, vorbeugen, *et.* verhindern, verhüten; **2.** aus dem Weg räumen, beseitigen; **3.** erübrigen; **ob·vi·a·tion** [ˌɒbvɪ'eɪʃn] *s.* **1.** Vorbeugen *n*, Verhütung *f*; **2.** Beseitigung *f*.

ob·vi·ous ['ɒbvɪəs] *adj.* □ offensichtlich, augenfällig, klar, deutlich; naheliegend, einleuchtend: ***it is ~ that*** es liegt auf der Hand, daß; ***it was the ~ thing to do*** es war das Nächstliegende; ***he was the ~ choice*** kein anderer kam dafür in Frage; **'ob·vi·ous·ness** [-nɪs] *s.* Offensichtlichkeit *f*.

oc·ca·sion [ə'keɪʒn] **I** *s.* **1.** (günstige) Gelegenheit; **2.** (***of***) Gelegenheit *f* (zu), Möglichkeit *f* (*gen.*); **3.** (besondere) Gelegenheit, Anlaß *m*; (𝔉 festliches) Ereignis: ***on this ~*** bei dieser Gelegenheit; ***on the ~ of*** anläßlich (*gen.*); ***on ~*** a) bei Gelegenheit, b) gelegentlich, c) wenn nötig; ***for the ~*** für diese besondere Gelegenheit, eigens zu diesem Zweck; ***a great ~*** ein großes Ereignis; ***improve the ~*** die Gelegenheit (*bsd.* zu e-r Moralpredigt) benützen; ***rise to the ~*** sich der Lage gewachsen zeigen; **4.** Anlaß *m*, Anstoß *m*: ***give ~ to*** → 6; **5.** (***for***) Grund *m* (zu), Ursache *f* (*gen.*), Veranlassung *f* (zu); **II** *v/t.* **6.** verursachen (***s.o. s.th.***, ***s.th. to s.o.*** j-m et.), hervorrufen, bewirken, zeitigen; **7.** *j-n* veranlassen (***to do*** zu tun); **oc'ca·sion·al** [-ʒənl] *adj.* □ **1.** gelegentlich, Gelegenheits…(*-arbeit, -dichter, -gedicht etc.*); vereinzelt; **2.** zufällig; **oc'ca·sion·al·ly** [-ʒnəlɪ] *adv.* gelegentlich, hin u. wieder.

Oc·ci·dent ['ɒksɪdənt] *s.* **1.** 'Okzident *m*, Westen *m*, Abendland *n*; **2.** ⚘ Westen *m*; **Oc·ci·den·tal** [ˌɒksɪ'dentl] **I** *adj.* □ **1.** abendländisch, westlich; **2.** ⚘ westlich; **II** *s.* **3.** Abendländer(in).

oc·cip·i·tal [ɒk'sɪpɪtl] *anat.* **I** *adj.* Hinterhaupt(s)…; **II** *s.* 'Hinterhauptsbein *n*; **oc·ci·put** ['ɒksɪpʌt] *pl.* **oc·cip·i·ta** [ɒk'sɪpɪtə] *s. anat.* 'Hinterkopf *m*.

oc·clude [ɒ'klu:d] *v/t.* **1.** *a.* ⚕ verstopfen, verschließen; **2.** a) einschließen, b) ausschließen, c) abschließen (***from*** von); **3.** ⚗ okkludieren, adsorbieren; **oc'clu·sion** [-u:ʒn] *s.* **1.** *a.* ⚕ a) Verstopfung *f*, Verschließung *f*, b) Verschluß *m*; **2.** Okklusi'on *f*: a) ⚗ Adsorpti'on *f*, b) ⚕ Biß(stellung *f*) *m*; ***abnormal ~*** Bißanomalie *f*.

oc·cult [ɒ'kʌlt] **I** *adj.* □ ok'kult: a) geheimnisvoll, verborgen (*a.* ⚕), b) magisch, 'übersinnlich, c) geheim, Geheim…: ***~ sciences*** Geheimwissenschaften; **II** *v/t.* verdecken; *ast.* verfinstern; **III** *s.* ***the ~*** das Ok'kulte; **oc·cult·ism** ['ɒkəltɪzəm] *s.* Okkul'tismus *m*; **oc·cult·ist** ['ɒkəltɪst] **I** *s.* Okkul'tist (-in); **II** *adj.* okkul'tistisch.

oc·cu·pan·cy ['ɒkjʊpənsɪ] *s.* **1.** Besitzergreifung *f* (*a.* ⚖); Einzug *m* (***of*** in *e-e Wohnung*); **2.** Innehaben *n*, Besitz *m*: ***during his ~ of the post*** solange er die Stelle innehatte; **3.** In'anspruchnahme *f* (*von Raum etc.*); **'oc·cu·pant** [-nt] *s.* **1.** *bsd.* ⚖ Besitzergreifer(in); **2.** Besitzer (-in), Inhaber(in); **3.** Bewohner(in), Insasse *m*, Insassin *f* (*Haus etc.*); **oc·cu·pa·tion** [ˌɒkjʊ'peɪʃn] *s.* **1.** Besitz *m*, Innehaben *n*; **2.** Besitznahme *f*, -ergreifung *f*; **3.** ⚔, *pol.* Besetzung *f*, Besatzung *f*, Okkupati'on *f*: ***~ troops*** Besatzungstruppen; → ***zone*** 1; **4.** Beschäftigung *f*: ***without ~*** beschäftigungslos; **5.** Beruf *m*, Gewerbe *n*: ***by ~*** von Beruf; ***employed in an ~*** berufstätig; ***in*** (*od.* ***as a***) ***regular ~*** hauptberuflich; **oc·cu·pa·tion·al** [ˌɒkju:'peɪʃənl] *adj.* **1.** beruflich, Berufs…(*-gruppe, -krankheit etc.*), Arbeits…(*-psychologie, -unfall etc.*): ***~ hazard*** Berufsrisiko *n*; **2.** Beschäftigungs…: ***~ therapy***.

oc·cu·pi·er ['ɒkjʊpaɪə] → ***occupant***.

oc·cu·py ['ɒkjʊpaɪ] *v/t.* **1.** in Besitz nehmen, Besitz ergreifen von; *Wohnung* beziehen; ⚔ besetzen; **2.** besitzen, innehaben; *fig. Amt etc.* bekleiden, innehaben: ***~ the chair*** den Vorsitz führen; **3.** bewohnen; **4.** *Raum* einnehmen, (*a. Zeit*) in Anspruch nehmen; **5.** *j-n, j-s Geist* beschäftigen: ***~ o.s.*** sich beschäftigen *od.* befassen (***with*** mit); ***be occupied with*** (*od.* ***in***) ***doing*** damit beschäftigt sein, *et.* zu tun.

oc·cur [ə'kɜ:] *v/i.* **1.** sich ereignen, vorfallen, -kommen, passieren, eintreten; **2.** vorkommen (***in Poe*** bei Poe); **3.** zustoßen, vorkommen, begegnen (***to s.o.*** j-m); **4.** einfallen (***to*** *dat.*): ***it ~red to me that*** es fiel mir ein *od.* es kam mir der Gedanke, daß; **oc·cur·rence** [ə'kʌrəns] *s.* **1.** Vorkommen *n*, Auftreten *n*; **2.** Ereignis *n*, Vorfall *m*, Vorkommnis *n*.

o·cean ['əʊʃn] *s.* **1.** Ozean *m*, Meer *n*: ***~ lane*** Schiffahrtsroute *f*; ***~ liner*** Ozeandampfer *m*; **2.** *fig.* Meer *n*: ***~s of*** 𝔉 e-e Unmenge von; ***~ bill of lad·ing*** *s.* ⚓ Konnosse'ment *n*, Seefrachtbrief *m*; **'~-ˌgo·ing** *adj.* ⚓ Hochsee…, hochseetüchtig.

o·ce·an·ic [ˌəʊʃɪ'ænɪk] *adj.* oze'anisch, Ozean…, Meer(es)…

o·ce·a·no·graph·ic, **o·ce·a·no·graph·i·cal** [ˌəʊʃɪənəʊ'græfɪk(l)] *adj.* ozeano'graphisch; **o·ce·a·nog·ra·phy** [ˌəʊʃjə'nɒgrəfɪ] *s.* Meereskunde *f*; **o·ce·a·nol·o·gy** [ˌəʊʃjə'nɒlədʒɪ] *s.* Ozeanolo'gie *f*, Meereskunde *f*.

oc·el·lat·ed ['ɒsəleɪtɪd] *adj. zo.* **1.** augenfleckig; **2.** augenähnlich; **o·cel·lus** [əʊ'seləs] *pl.* **-li** [-laɪ] *s. zo.* **1.** Punktauge *n*; **2.** Augenfleck *m*.

o·cher *Am.* → ***ochre***.

och·loc·ra·cy [ɒk'lɒkrəsɪ] *s.* Ochlokra'tie *f*, Pöbelherrschaft *f*.

o·chre ['əʊkə] **I** *s.* **1.** *min.* Ocker *m*: ***blue*** (*od.* ***iron***) ***~*** Eisenocker *m*; ***brown*** (*od.* ***spruce***) ***~*** brauner Eisenocker; **2.** Okkerfarbe *f*, -gelb *n*; **II** *adj.* **3.** ockergelb; **o·chre·ous** ['əʊkrɪəs] *adj.* **1.** Ocker…; **2.** ockerhaltig *od.* -artig *od.* -farbig.

o'clock [ə'klɒk] Uhr (*bei Zeitangaben*): ***four ~*** vier Uhr.

oc·ta·gon ['ɒktəgən] *s.* ⩓ Achteck *n*; **oc·tag·o·nal** [ɒk'tægənl] *adj.* □ **1.** achteckig, -seitig; **2.** Achtkant…

oc·ta·he·dral [ˌɒktə'hedrəl] *adj.* ⩓, *min.* okta'edrisch, achtflächig; **ˌoc·ta'he·dron** [-drən] *pl.* **-drons** *od.* **-dra** [-drə] *s.* Okta'eder *n*.

oc·tal ['ɒktl] *adj.* ⚡ Oktal…

oc·tane ['ɒkteɪn] *s.* ⚗ Ok'tan *n*: ***~ number***, ***~ rating*** Oktanzahl *f*.

oc·tant ['ɒktənt] *s.* ⩓, ⚓ Ok'tant *m*.

oc·tave ['ɒktɪv; *eccl.* 'ɒkteɪv] *s.* ♪, *eccl.*, *phys.* Ok'tave *f*.

oc·ta·vo [ɒk'teɪvəʊ] *pl.* **-vos** *s.* **1.** Ok'tav(forˌmat) *n*; **2.** Ok'tavband *m*.

oc·til·lion [ɒk'tɪljən] *s.* ⩓ *Brit.* Oktilli'on *f*, *Am.* Quadrilli'arde *f*.

Oc·to·ber [ɒk'təʊbə] *s.* Ok'tober *m*: ***in ~*** im Oktober.

oc·to·dec·i·mo [ˌɒktəʊ'desɪməʊ] *pl.* **-mos** *s.* **1.** Okto'dezforˌmat *n*; **2.** Okto'dezband *m*.

oc·to·ge·nar·i·an [ˌɒktəʊdʒɪ'neərɪən] **I** *adj.* achtzigjährig; **II** *s.* Achtzigjährige(r *m*) *f*, Achtziger(in).

oc·to·pod ['ɒktəpɒd] *s. zo.* Okto'pode *m*, Krake *m*.

oc·to·pus ['ɒktəpəs] *pl.* **-pus·es** *od.* **'oc·to·pi** [-paɪ] *s.* **1.** *zo.* Krake *m*: a) 'Seepoˌlyp *m*, b) Okto'pode *m*; **2.** *fig.* Po'lyp *m*.

oc·to·syl·lab·ic [ˌɒktəʊsɪ'læbɪk] **I** *adj.* achtsilbig; **II** *s.* Achtsilb(l)er *m* (*Vers*); **oc·to·syl·la·ble** ['ɒktəʊˌsɪləbl] *s.* **1.** achtsilbiges Wort; **2.** → ***octosyllabic*** II.

oc·u·lar ['ɒkjʊlə] **I** *adj.* □ **1.** Augen…(*-bewegung, -zeuge etc.*); **2.** sichtbar (*Beweis*), augenfällig; **II** *s.* **3.** *opt.* Oku'lar *n*; **'oc·u·lar·ly** [-lɪ] *adv.* **1.** augenscheinlich; **2.** durch Augenschein, mit eigenen Augen; **'oc·u·list** [-lɪst] *s.* Augenarzt *m*.

odd [ɒd] **I** *adj.* □ → ***oddly***; **1.** sonderbar, seltsam, merkwürdig, kuri'os: ***an ~ fellow*** (*od.* 𝔉 ***fish***) ein sonderbarer Kauz; **2.** (*nach Zahlen etc.*) und etliche, und einige *od.* etwas dar'über: ***50 ~*** über 50, einige 50; ***fifty ~ thousand*** zwischen 50000 u. 60000; ***it cost five pounds ~*** es kostete etwas über 5 Pfund; **3.** (*noch*) übrig, 'überzählig, restlich; **4.** ungerade: ***~ and even*** gerade u. ungerade; ***an ~ number*** eine ungerade Zahl; ***~ man out*** Überzählige(r) *m*; ***the ~ man*** der Mann mit der entscheidenden Stimme (*bei Stimmengleichheit*) (→ 6); **5.** a) einzeln (*Schuh etc.*): ***~ pair*** Einzelpaar *n*, b) vereinzelt: ***some ~ volumes*** einige Einzelbände, c) ausgefallen, wenig gefragt (*Kleidergröße*); **6.** gelegentlich, Gelegenheits…: ***~ jobs*** Gelegenheitsarbeiten; ***at ~ moments***, ***at ~ times*** dann und wann, zwischendurch; ***~ man*** Gelegenheitsarbeiter *m*; **II** *s.* **7.** → ***odds***; **'odd·ball** *s. Am.* 𝔉 → ***oddity*** 2.

odd·i·ty ['ɒdɪtɪ] *s.* **1.** Seltsamkeit *f*, Wunderlichkeit *f*, Eigenartigkeit *f*; **2.** komischer Kauz, Unikum *n*; **3.** seltsame *od.* kuri'ose Sache; **odd·ly** ['ɒdlɪ] *adv.* **1.** → ***odd*** 1; **2.** *a.* ~ ***enough*** seltsamerweise; **odd·ments** ['ɒdmənts] *s. pl.* Reste *pl.*, 'Überbleibsel *pl.*; Krimskrams *m*; ✝ Einzelstücke *pl.*; **odd·ness** ['ɒdnɪs] *s.* Seltsamkeit *f*, Sonderbarkeit *f*.

'odd,num·bered *adj.* ungeradzahlig.

odds [ɒdz] *s. pl. oft sg. konstr.* **1.** Verschiedenheit *f*, 'Unterschied *m*: ***what's the ~?*** F was macht es (schon) aus?; ***it makes no ~*** es macht nichts (aus); **2.** Vorgabe *f* (*im Spiel*): ***give s.o. ~*** j-m et. vorgeben; ***take ~*** sich vorgeben lassen; ***take the ~*** e-e ungleiche Wette eingehen; **3.** (Gewinn)Chancen *pl.*: ***the ~ are 10 to 1*** die Chancen stehen 10 zu 1; ***the ~ are in our favo(u)r*** (*od.* ***on us***) *a. fig.* wir haben die besseren Chancen; ***the ~ are against us*** unsere Chancen stehen schlecht, wir sind im Nachteil; ***against long ~*** mit wenig Aussicht auf Erfolg; ***by long ~*** bei weitem; ***the ~ are that he will come*** es ist sehr wahrscheinlich, daß er kommt; **4.** Uneinigkeit *f*: ***at ~ with*** im Streit mit, uneins mit; ***set at ~*** uneinig machen, gegeneinander aufhetzen; **5.** ***~ and ends*** a) allerlei Kleinigkeiten, Krimskrams *m*, dies u. das, b) Reste, Abfälle; **,~-'on I** *adj.* aussichtsreich (*z. B. Rennpferd*): ***~ certainty*** sichere Sache; ***it's ~ that*** es ist so gut wie sicher, daß; **II** *s.* gute Chance.

ode [əʊd] *s.* Ode *f*.

o·di·ous ['əʊdjəs] *adj.* □ **1.** verhaßt, hassenswert, ab'scheulich; **2.** widerlich, ekelhaft; **'o·di·ous·ness** [-nɪs] *s.* **1.** Verhaßtheit *f*, Ab'scheulichkeit *f*; **2.** Widerlichkeit *f*; **'o·di·um** [-jəm] *s.* **1.** Verhaßtheit *f*; **2.** Odium *n*, Vorwurf *m*, Makel *m*; **3.** Haß *m*, Gehässigkeit *f*.

o·dom·e·ter [əʊ'dɒmɪtə] *s.* **1.** Weg(strecken)messer *m*; **2.** Kilo'meterzähler *m*.

o·don·tic [ɒ'dɒntɪk] *adj.* Zahn...: ***~ nerve***; **o·don·tol·o·gy** [,ɒdɒn'tɒlədʒɪ] *s.* Zahn(heil)kunde *f*, Odontolo'gie *f*.

o·dor(·less) *Am.* → ***odour(less)***.

o·dor·ant ['əʊdərənt] *adj.*, **o·dor·if·er·ous** [,əʊdə'rɪfərəs] *adj.* □ **1.** wohlriechend, duftend; **2.** *allg.* riechend.

o·dour ['əʊdə] *s.* **1.** Geruch *m*; **2.** Duft *m*, Wohlgeruch *m*; **3.** *fig.* Geruch *m*, Ruf *m*: ***the ~ of sanctity*** der Geruch der Heiligkeit; ***to be in bad ~ with s.o.*** bei j-m in schlechtem Rufe stehen; **'o·dour·less** [-lɪs] *adj.* geruchlos.

Od·ys·sey ['ɒdɪsɪ] *s. lit.* (*fig. oft* ♀) Odys'see *f*.

oe·col·o·gy [iː'kɒlədʒɪ] → ***ecology***.

oec·u·men·i·cal [,iːkjʊ'menɪkəl] *etc.* → ***ecumenical*** *etc.*

oe·de·ma [iː'diːmə] *pl.* **-ma·ta** [-mətə] *s.* ⚕ Ö'dem *n*.

oe·di·pal ['iːdɪpl] *adj. psych.* ödi'pal, Ödipus...

Oed·i·pus com·plex ['iːdɪpəs] *s. psych.* 'Ödipuskom,plex *m*.

oen·o·lo·gy [iː'nɒlədʒɪ] Wein(bau)kunde *f*, Önolo'gie *f*.

o'er ['əʊə] *poet. od. dial. für* ***over***.

oe·so·phag·e·al [iː,sɒfə'dʒiːəl] *adj. anat.* Speiseröhren..., Schlund...: ***~ orifice*** Magenmund *m*; **oe·soph·a·gus** [iː'sɒfəgəs] *pl.* **-gi** [-gaɪ] *od.* **-gus·es** *s. anat.* Speiseröhre *f*.

of [ɒv, əv] *prp.* **1.** *allg.* von; **2.** *zur Bezeichnung des Genitivs*: ***the tail ~ the dog*** der Schwanz des Hundes; ***the tail ~ a dog*** der Hundeschwanz; **3.** *Ort*: bei: ***the battle ~ Hastings***; **4.** *Entfernung, Trennung, Befreiung*: a) von: ***south ~*** (***within ten miles ~***) ***London***; ***cure*** (***rid***) ***~ s.th.***; ***free ~***, b) *gen.*: ***robbed ~ his purse*** s-r Börse beraubt, c) um: ***cheat s.o. ~ s.th.***; **5.** *Herkunft*: von, aus: ***~ good family***; ***Mr. X ~ London***; **6.** *Teil*: von *od. gen.*: ***the best ~ my friends***; ***a friend ~ mine*** ein Freund von mir, e-r m-r Freunde; ***that red nose ~ his*** diese rote Nase, die er hat; **7.** *Eigenschaft*: von, mit: ***a man ~ courage***; ***a man ~ no importance*** ein unbedeutender Mensch; **8.** *Stoff*: aus, von: ***a dress ~ silk*** ein Kleid aus *od.* von Seide, ein Seidenkleid; (***made***) ***~ steel*** aus Stahl (hergestellt), stählern, Stahl...; **9.** *Urheberschaft, Art u. Weise*: von: ***the works ~ Byron***; ***it was clever ~ him***; ***~ o.s.*** von selbst, von sich aus; **10.** *Ursache, Grund*: a) von, an (*dat.*): ***die ~ cancer*** an Krebs sterben, b) aus: ***~ charity***, c) vor (*dat.*): ***afraid ~***, d) auf (*acc.*): ***proud ~***, e) über (*acc.*): ***ashamed ~***, f) nach: ***smell ~***; **11.** *Beziehung*: hinsichtlich (*gen.*): ***quick ~ eye*** flinkäugig; ***nimble ~ foot*** leichtfüßig; **12.** *Thema*: a) von, über (*acc.*): ***speak ~ s.th.***, b) an (*acc.*): ***think ~ s.th.***; **13.** *Apposition, im Deutschen nicht ausgedrückt*: a) ***the city ~ London***; ***the University ~ Oxford***; ***the month ~ April***; ***the name ~ Smith***, b) *Maß*: ***two feet ~ snow***; ***a glass ~ wine***; ***a piece ~ meat***; **14.** *Genitivus objectivus*: a) zu: ***the love ~ God***, b) vor (*dat.*): ***the fear ~ God*** die Furcht vor Gott, die Gottesfurcht, c) bei: ***an audience ~ the king;*** **15.** *Zeit*: a) an (*dat.*), in (*dat.*), *mst gen.*: ***~ an evening*** e-s Abends; ***~ late years*** in den letzten Jahren, b) von: ***your letter ~ March 3rd*** Ihr Schreiben vom 3. März, c) *Am.* F vor (*bei Zeitangaben*): ***ten minutes ~ three***.

off [ɒf] **I** *adv.* **1.** *mst in Zssgn mit vb.* fort, weg, da'von: ***be ~*** a) weg *od.* fort sein, b) (weg)gehen, sich davonmachen, (ab)fahren, c) weg müssen; ***be ~!***, ***~ you go!***, ***~ with you!*** fort mit dir!, pack dich!, weg!; ***where are you ~ to?*** wo gehst du hin?; **2.** ab(*-brechen, -kühlen, -rutschen, -schneiden etc.*), her'unter(...), los(...): ***the apple is ~*** der Apfel ist ab; ***dash ~*** losrennen; ***have one's shoes*** *etc.* ***~*** s-e *od.* die Schuhe *etc.* ausgezogen haben; ***~ with your hat!*** herunter mit dem Hut!; **3.** entfernt, weg: ***3 miles ~***; **4.** *Zeitpunkt*: von jetzt an, hin: ***Christmas is a week ~*** bis Weihnachten ist es eine Woche; ***~ and on*** a) ab u. zu, hin u. wieder, b) ab u. an, mit (kurzen) Unterbrechungen; **5.** abgezogen, ab(züglich); **6.** a) aus(geschaltet), abgeschaltet, -gestellt (*Maschine, Radio etc.*), (ab)gesperrt (*Gas etc.*), zu (*Hahn etc.*), b) *fig.* aus, vor'bei, abgebrochen; gelöst (*Verlobung*): ***the bet is ~*** die Wette gilt nicht mehr; ***the whole thing is ~*** die ganze Sache ist abgeblasen *od.* ins Wasser gefallen; **7.** aus(gegangen), verkauft, nicht mehr vorrätig; **8.** frei (*von Arbeit*): ***take a day ~*** sich e-n Tag freinehmen; **9.** ganz, zu Ende: ***drink ~*** (ganz) austrinken; ***kill ~*** ausrotten; ***sell ~*** ausverkaufen; **10.** ✝ flau: ***the market is ~***; **11.** nicht frisch, (leicht) verdorben (*Nahrungsmittel*); **12.** *sport* außer Form; **13.** ⚓ vom Land *etc.* ab; **14.** ***well*** (***badly***) ***~*** gut (schlecht) d(a)ran *od.* gestellt *od.* situiert; ***how are you ~ for ...?*** wie bist du dran mit ...?; **II** *prp.* **15.** von ... (weg, ab, her'unter): ***climb ~ the horse*** vom Pferd (herunter)steigen; ***eat ~ a plate*** von e-m Teller essen; ***take 3 percent ~ the price*** 3 Prozent vom Preis abziehen; ***be ~ a drug*** *sl.* von e-r Droge ‚heruntersein'; **16.** abseits von *od. gen.*, von ... ab: ***~ the street***; ***a street ~ Piccadilly*** e-e Seitenstraße von Piccadilly; ***~ one's balance*** aus dem Gleichgewicht; ***~ form*** außer Form; **17.** frei von: ***~ duty*** dienstfrei; **18.** ⚓ auf der Höhe von *Trafalgar etc.*, vor *der Küste*; **III** *adj.* **19.** (weiter) entfernt; **20.** Seiten..., Neben...: ***~ street***; **21.** recht (*von Tieren, Fuhrwerken etc.*): ***the ~ horse*** das rechte Pferd, das Handpferd; **22.** *Kricket*: abseitig (*rechts vom Schlagmann*); **23.** ab(-), los(gegangen); **24.** (arbeits-, dienst)frei: ***an ~ day***; → **25.** (*verhältnismäßig*) schlecht: ***an ~ day*** ein schlechter Tag (*an dem alles mißlingt etc.*); ***an ~ year for fruit*** ein schlechtes Obstjahr; **26.** ✝ a) flau, still, tot (*Saison*), b) von schlechter Quali'tät: ***~ shade*** Fehlfarbe *f*; **27.** ‚ab', unwohl, nicht auf dem Damm: ***I am feeling rather ~ today***; **28.** ***on the ~ chance*** auf gut Glück: ***I went there on the ~ chance of seeing him*** ich ging in der vagen Hoffnung hin, ihn zu sehen; **IV** *int.* **29.** weg!, fort!, raus!: ***hands ~!*** Hände weg!; **30.** her'unter!, ab!

of·fal ['ɒfl] *s.* **1.** Abfall *m*; **2.** *sg. od. pl. konstr.* Fleischabfall *m*, Inne'reien *pl.*; **3.** billige *od.* minderwertige Fische *pl.*; **4.** *fig.* Schund *m*, Ausschuß *m*.

,off|'beat *adj.* F ausgefallen, extrava'gant (*Geschmack, Kleidung etc.*); **'~·cast I** *adj.* verworfen, abgetan; **II** *s.* abgetane Per'son *od.* Sache; **,~-'cen·ter** *Am.*, **,~-'cen·tre** *Brit. adj.* verrutscht; ⚙ außermittig, ex'zentrisch (*a. fig.*); **,~-'col·o(u)r** *adj.* **1.** a) farblich abweichend, b) nicht lupenrein: ***~ jewel***; **2.** *fig.* nicht (ganz) in Ordnung; unpäßlich; **3.** zweideutig, schlüpfrig: ***~ jokes***; **,~-'du·ty** *adj.* dienstfrei.

of·fence [ə'fens] *s.* **1.** *allg.* Vergehen *n*, Verstoß *m* (***against*** gegen); **2.** ⚖ a) *a.* ***criminal ~*** Straftat *f*, strafbare Handlung, De'likt *n*, b) *a.* ***lesser*** *od.* ***minor ~*** Über'tretung *f*; **3.** Anstoß *m*, Ärgernis *n*, Beleidigung *f*, Kränkung *f*: ***give ~*** Anstoß *od.* Ärgernis erregen (***to*** bei); ***take ~*** (***at***) Anstoß nehmen (an *dat.*), beleidigt *od.* gekränkt sein (durch, über *acc.*), (*et.*) übelnehmen; ***no ~*** (***meant***)***!*** nichts für ungut!; **4.** Angriff *m*: ***arms of ~*** Angriffswaffen *pl.*; **of'fence·less** [-lɪs] *adj.* harmlos.

of·fend [ə'fend] **I** *v/t.* **1.** *j-n, j-s Gefühle etc.* verletzen, beleidigen, kränken: ***it ~s the eye*** es beleidigt das Auge; ***be ~ed at*** (*od.* ***by***) ***s.th.*** sich durch et. beleidigt fühlen; ***be ~ed with*** (*od.* ***by***) ***s.o.*** sich durch j-n beleidigt fühlen; **II** *v/i.* **2.** Anstoß erregen; **3.** (***against***) verstoßen (gegen), sündigen, sich vergehen (an *dat.*); **of'fend·ed·ly** [-dɪdlɪ] *adv.* beleidigt; **of'fend·er** [-də] *s.* Übel-, Missetäter(in); ⚖ Straffällige(r *m*) *f*: ***first ~*** ⚖ nicht Vorbestrafte(r *m*) *f*, Ersttäter(in); ***second ~*** Rückfällige(r *m*) *f*; **of'fend·ing** [-dɪŋ] *adj.* **1.** verletzend, beleidigend; **2.** anstößig.

of·fense(·less) *Am.* → ***offence(less)***.

of·fen·sive [ə'fensɪv] **I** *adj.* ☐ **1.** beleidigend, anstößig, anstoß- *od.* ärgerniserregend; **2.** 'widerwärtig, ekelhaft, übel: ***~ smell***; **3.** angreifend, offen'siv: ***~ war*** Angriffs-, Offensivkrieg *m*; ***~ weapon*** Angriffswaffe *f*; **II** *s.* **4.** Offen'sive *f*, Angriff *m*: ***take the ~*** die Offensive ergreifen, zum Angriff übergehen; **of'fen·sive·ness** [-nɪs] *s.* **1.** *das* Beleidigende, Anstößigkeit *f*; **2.** 'Widerlichkeit *f*.

of·fer ['ɒfə] **I** *v/t.* **1.** *Geschenk*, *Ware etc.*, *a. Schlacht* anbieten; ✝ *a.* offerieren; *Preis*, *Summe* bieten: ***~ s.o. a cigarette***; ***~ one's hand*** (***to***) *j-m* die Hand bieten *od.* reichen; ***~ for sale*** zum Verkauf anbieten; **2.** *Ansicht*, *Entschuldigung etc.* vorbringen, äußern; **3.** *Anblick*, *Schwierigkeit etc.* bieten: ***no opportunity ~ed itself*** es bot sich keine Gelegenheit; **4.** sich bereit erklären zu, sich (an)erbieten zu; **5.** Anstalten machen zu, sich anschicken zu; **6.** *fig. Beleidigung* zufügen; *Widerstand* leisten; *Gewalt* antun (***to*** *dat.*); **7.** *a.* ***~ up*** opfern, *Opfer*, *Gebet*, *Geschenk* darbringen (***to*** *dat.*); **II** *v/i.* **8.** sich bieten, auftauchen: ***no opportunity ~ed*** es bot sich keine Gelegenheit; **III** *s.* **9.** *allg.* Angebot *n*, Anerbieten *n*; **10.** ✝ (An-)Gebot *n*, Of'ferte *f*, Antrag *m*: ***on ~*** zu verkaufen, verkäuflich; **11.** Vorbringen *n* (*e-s Vorschlags*, *e-r Meinung etc.*); **of·fer·ing** ['ɒfərɪŋ] *s.* **1.** *eccl.* Opfer *n*; **2.** *eccl.* Spende *f*; **3.** Angebot *n* (*Am. a.* ✝ *Börse*).

of·fer·to·ry ['ɒfətərɪ] *s.* *eccl.* **1.** *mst* ♀ Offer'torium *n*; **2.** Kol'lekte *f*, Geldsammlung *f*; **3.** Opfer(geld) *n*.

ˌoff|-'face *adj.* stirnfrei (*Damenhut*); **'~-fla·vo(u)r** *s.* (unerwünschter) Beigeschmack; **ˌ~'grade** *adj.* ✝ von geringerer Quali'tät: ***~ iron*** Ausfalleisen *n*.

off|·hand [ˌɒf'hænd] **I** *adv.* **1.** aus dem Stegreif *od.* Kopf, (so) ohne weiteres *sagen können etc.*; **II** *adj.* **2.** unvorbereitet, improvisiert, Stegreif…: ***an ~ speech***; **3.** lässig (*Art etc.*), 'hingeworfen (*Bemerkung*); **4.** kurz (angebunden); **ˌ~'hand·ed** [-dɪd] → ***offhand*** II; **ˌ~'hand·ed·ness** [-dɪdnɪs] *s.* Lässigkeit *f*.

of·fice ['ɒfɪs] *s.* **1.** Bü'ro *n*, Kanz'lei *f*, Kon'tor *n*; Geschäftsstelle *f* (*a.* ⚖ *des Gerichts*), Amt *n*; Geschäfts-, Amtszimmer *n od.* -gebäude *n*; **2.** Behörde *f*, Amt *n*, (Dienst)Stelle *f*; *mst* ♀ *bsd. Brit.* Mini'sterium *n*, (Ministeri'al)Amt *n*: ***Foreign ♀***; **3.** Zweigstelle *f*, Fili'ale *f*; **4.** (*bsd.* öffentliches, staatliches) Amt, Posten *m*, Stellung *f*: ***take ~***, ***enter upon an ~*** ein Amt antreten; ***be in ~*** im Amt *od.* an der Macht sein; ***hold an ~*** ein Amt bekleiden *od.* innehaben; ***resign one's ~*** zurücktreten, sein Amt niederlegen; **5.** Funkti'on *f*, Aufgabe *f*, Pflicht *f*: ***it is my ~ to advise him***; **6.** Dienst(leistung *f*) *m*, Gefälligkeit *f*: ***good ~s*** *pol.* gute Dienste; ***do s.o. a good ~*** j-m e-n guten Dienst erweisen; ***through the good ~s of*** durch die freundliche Vermittlung von; **7.** *eccl.* Gottesdienst *m*: ***♀ for the Dead*** Totenamt *n*; ***perform the last ~s to*** *e-n Toten* aussegnen; ***divine ~*** das Brevier; **8.** *pl. bsd. Brit.* Wirtschaftsteil *m*, -raum *m od.* -räume *pl. od.* -gebäude *n od. pl.*; **9.** *sl.* Wink *m*, Tip *m*.

of·fice| ac·tion *s.* (Prüfungs)Bescheid *m des Patentamts*; **'~-ˌbear·er** *s.* Amtsinhaber(in); **~ block** *s.* Bü'rogebäude *n*; **~ boy** *s.* Laufbursche *m*, Bü'rogehilfe *m*; **~ clerk** *s.* Konto'rist(in), Bü'roangestellte(r *m*) *f*; **~ girl** *s.* Bü'rogehilfin *f*; **'~ˌhold·er** *s.* Amtsinhaber(in), (Staats)Beamte(r) *m*, (Staats)Beamtin *f*; **~ hours** *s. pl.* Dienststunden *pl.*, Geschäftszeit *f*; **'~-ˌhunt·er** *s.* Postenjäger(in).

of·fi·cer ['ɒfɪsə] **I** *s.* **1.** ⚔, ⚓ Offi'zier *m*: ***~ of the day*** Offizier vom Tagesdienst; ***commanding ~*** Kommandeur *m*, Einheitsführer *m*; ***~ cadet*** Fähnrich *m*; ***~ candidate*** Offiziersanwärter *m*; ***♀s' Training Corps*** *Brit.* Offiziersausbildungskorps *n*; **2.** a) Poli'zist *m*, Poli'zeibeamte(r) *m*, b) Herr Wachtmeister (*Anrede*); **3.** Beamte(r) *m* (*a.* ✝ *etc.*), Beamtin *f*, Amtsträger(in): ***medical ~*** Amtsarzt *m*; ***public ~*** Beamte(r) im öffentlichen Dienst; **4.** Vorstandsmitglied *n*; **II** *v/t.* **5.** ⚔ a) mit Offizieren versehen, b) *e-e Einheit* als Offizier befehligen (*mst pass.*): ***be ~ed by*** befehligt werden von; **6.** *fig.* leiten, führen.

of·fice| seek·er *s. bsd. Am.* **1.** Stellungssuchende(r *m*) *f*; **2.** *b.s.* Postenjäger(in); **~ staff** *s.* Bü'roperso ˌnal *n*; **~ sup·plies** *s. pl.* Bü'romateriˌal *n*, -bedarf *m*.

of·fi·cial [ə'fɪʃl] **I** *adj.* ☐ **1.** offizi'ell, amtlich, dienstlich, behördlich: ***~ act*** Amtshandlung *f*; ***~ business*** ✉ Dienstsache *f*; ***~ call*** *teleph.* Dienstgespräch *n*; ***~ duties*** Amtspflichten; ***~ language*** Amtssprache *f*; ***~ oath*** Amtseid *m*; ***~ residence*** Amtssitz *m*; ***~ secret*** Amts-, Dienstgeheimnis *n*; ***through ~ channels*** auf dem Dienst- *od.* Instanzenweg; ***~ trip*** Dienstreise *f*; **2.** offiziell, amtlich (bestätigt *od.* autorisiert): ***an ~ report***; **3.** offizi'ell, for'mell: ***an ~ dinner***; **4.** ⚕ offizi'nell; **II** *s.* **5.** Beamte(r) *m*, Beamtin *f*; Funktio'när(in); **of'fi·cial·dom** [-dəm] *s.* → ***officialism*** 2 *u.* 3; **of·fi·cial·ese** [əˌfɪʃə'li:z] *s.* Behördensprache *f*, Amtsstil *m*; **of'fi·cial·ism** [-ʃəlɪzəm] *s.* **1.** Amtsme'thoden *pl.*; **2.** Bürokra'tie *f*, Amtsschimmel *m*; **3.** *coll. das* Beamtentum, *die* Beamten *pl.*

of·fi·ci·ate [ə'fɪʃɪeɪt] *v/i.* **1.** amtieren, fungieren (***as*** als); **2.** den Gottesdienst leiten: ***~ at the wedding*** die Trauung vornehmen.

of·fic·i·nal [ˌɒfɪ'saɪnl] **I** *adj.* ⚕ a) offizi'nell, als Arz'nei anerkannt, b) Arznei…: ***~ plants*** Heilkräuter *pl.*; **II** *s.* offizinelle Arznei.

of·fi·cious [ə'fɪʃəs] *adj.* ☐ **1.** aufdringlich, über'trieben diensteifrig, 'übereifrig; **2.** offizi'ös, halbamtlich; **of'fi·cious·ness** [-nɪs] *s.* Zudringlichkeit *f*, (aufdringlicher) Diensteifer.

of·fing ['ɒfɪŋ] *s.* ⚓ offene See, Seeraum *m*: ***in the ~*** a) auf offener See, b) *fig.* in (Aus)Sicht: ***be in the ~*** *a.* sich abzeichnen.

off·ish ['ɒfɪʃ] *adj.* F reserviert, unnahbar, kühl, steif.

'off|-key *adj. u. adv.* ♪ falsch; **'~-ˌli·cence** *s. Brit.* 'Schankkonzessiˌon *f* über die Straße; **ˌ~'load** *v/t. fig.* abladen (***on s.o.*** auf j-n); **ˌ~-'peak I** *adj.* abfallend, unter der Spitze liegend: ***~ charges*** *pl.* verbilligter Tarif; ***~ hours*** verkehrsschwache Stunden; ***~ tariff*** Nacht(strom)tarif *m*; **II** *s.* ⚡ Belastungstal *n*; ***~ po·si·tion*** *s.* ⚙ Ausschalt-, Nullstellung *f*; **'~·print I** *s.* Sonder(ab)druck *m* (***from*** aus); **II** *v/t.* als Sonder(ab)druck herstellen; **'~-ˌput·ting** *adj.* F störend, unangenehm; **'~ˌscour·ings** *s. pl.* **1.** Kehricht *m*, Schmutz *m*; **2.** Abschaum *m* (*bsd. fig.*): ***the ~s of humanity***; **'~·scum** *s. fig.* Abschaum *m*, Auswurf *m*; ***~ sea·son*** *s.* 'Nebensaiˌson *f*, stille Sai'son.

off·set ['ɒfset] **I** *s.* **1.** Ausgleich *m*, Kompensati'on *f*; ✝ Verrechnung *f*: ***~ account*** Verrechnungskonto *n*; **2.** ⚘ a) Ableger *m*, b) kurzer Ausläufer; **3.** Neben-, Seitenlinie *f* (*e-s Stammbaums etc.*); **4.** Abzweigung *f*; Ausläufer *m* (*bsd. e-s Gebirges*); **5.** *typ.* a) Offsetdruck *m*, b) Abziehen *n*, Abliegen *n* (*bsd. noch feuchten Druckes*), c) Abzug *m*, Pa'trize *f* (*Lithographie*); **6.** ⚙ a) Kröpfung *f*; Biegung *f e-s Rohrs*, b) ⚒ kurze Sohle, c) ⚡ (Ab)Zweigleitung *f*; **7.** *surv.* Ordi'nate *f*; **8.** △ Absatz *m e-r Mauer etc.*; **II** *v/t.* [*irr.* → ***set***] **9.** ausgleichen, aufwiegen, wettmachen: ***the gains ~ the losses***; **10.** ✝ *Am.* aufrechnen, ausgleichen; **11.** ⚙ kröpfen; **12.** △ *Mauer etc.* absetzen; **13.** *typ.* im Offsetverfahren drucken; ***~ bulb*** *s.* ⚘ Brutzwiebel *f*; ***~ sheet*** *s. typ.* 'Durchschußbogen *m*.

'off|·shoot *s.* **1.** ⚘ Sprößling *m*, Ausläufer *m*, Ableger *m*; **2.** Abzweigung *f*; **3.** *fig.* Seitenlinie *f* (*e-s Stammbaums etc.*); **'~·shore I** *adv.* **1.** von der Küste ab *od.* her; **2.** in einiger Entfernung von der Küste; **II** *adj.* **3.** küstennah: ***~ drilling*** Off-shore-Bohrung *f*; **4.** ablandig (*Wind*, *Strömung*); **5.** Auslands…: ***~ order*** *Am.* Off-shore-Auftrag *m*; **ˌ~'side** *adj. u. adv. sport* abseits; **'~·side I** *s.* **1.** *sport* Abseits(stellung *f*) *n*; **2.** *mot.* Fahrerseite *f*; **II** *adj. u. adv.* abseits: ***be ~*** im Abseits stehen; ***~ trap*** Abseitsfalle *f*; **'~·size** *s.* ⚙ Maßabweichung *f*; **'~·spring** *s.* **1.** Nachkommen(schaft *f*) *pl.*; **2.** (*pl.* ***offspring***) Nachkomme *m*, Abkömmling *m*; **3.** *fig.* Frucht *f*, Ergebnis *n*; **ˌ~'stage** *adj.* hinter der Bühne, hinter den Ku'lissen (*a. fig.*); **'~·take** *s.* **1.** ✝ Abzug *m*; Einkauf *m*; **2.** ⚙ Abzug(srohr *n*) *m*; **ˌ~-the-'cuff** *adj. fig.* aus dem Handgelenk *od.* Stegreif; **ˌ~-the-'peg** *adj.* von der Stange, Konfektions…; **ˌ~-the-'rec·ord** *adj.* nicht für die Öffentlichkeit bestimmt, 'inoffiziˌell; **ˌ~-the-'shelf** *adj.* ✝, ⚙ Standard…: ***~ accessories***; **ˌ~-'white** *adj.* gebrochen weiß.

oft [ɒft] *adv. obs.*, *poet. u. in Zssgn* oft: ***~-told*** oft erzählt.

of·ten ['ɒfn] *adv.* oft(mals), häufig: ***as ~ as not***, ***ever so ~*** sehr oft; ***more ~ than not*** meistens.

o·gee ['əʊdʒiː] *s.* **1.** S-Kurve *f*, S-förmige Linie; **2.** ⚠ a) Kar'nies *n*, Rinnleiste *f*, b) *a.* **~ arch** Eselsrücken *m* (*Bogenform*).

o·give ['əʊdʒaɪv] *s.* **1.** ⚠ a) Gratrippe *f e-s Gewölbes*, b) Spitzbogen *m*; **2.** ⚔ Geschoßspitze *f*; **3.** *Statistik*: Häufigkeitsverteilungskurve *f*.

o·gle ['əʊgl] **I** *v/t.* liebäugeln mit; **II** *v/i.* (**with**) liebäugeln (mit, *a. fig.*), ‚Augen machen' (*dat.*); **III** *s.* verliebter *od.* liebäugelnder Blick; **'o·gler** [-lə] *s.* Liebäugelnde(r *m*) *f*.

o·gre ['əʊgə] *s.* **1.** (menschenfressendes) Ungeheuer, *bsd.* Riese *m* (*im Märchen*); **2.** *fig.* Scheusal *n*, Ungeheuer *n* (*Mensch*); **o·gress** ['əʊgrɪs] *s.* Menschenfresserin *f*, Riesin *f* (*im Märchen*).

oh [əʊ] *int.* oh!; ach!

ohm [əʊm], **ohm·ad** ['əʊmæd] *s.* ⚡ Ohm *n*: **2's Law** Ohmsches Gesetz; **ohm·age** ['əʊmɪdʒ] *s.* Ohmzahl *f*; **ohm·ic** ['əʊmɪk] *adj.* Ohmsch: **~ resistance**; **ohm·me·ter** ['əʊmˌmiːtə] *s.* ⚡ Ohmmeter *n*.

oil [ɔɪl] **I** *s.* **1.** Öl *n*: **pour ~ on the flames** *fig.* Öl ins Feuer gießen; **pour ~ on troubled waters** *fig.* die Gemüter beruhigen; **smell of ~** *fig.* mehr Fleiß als Geist *od.* Talent verraten; **2.** (Erd-)Öl *n*, Pe'troleum *n*: **to strike ~** a) Erdöl finden, auf Öl stoßen, fündig werden (*a. fig.*), b) *fig.* Glück *od.* Erfolg haben; **3.** *mst pl.* Ölfarbe *f*: **paint in ~s** in Öl malen; **4.** *mst pl.* F Ölgemälde *n*; **5.** *pl.* Ölzeug *n*, -haut *f*; **II** *v/t.* **6.** ⚙ (ein-)ölen, einfetten, schmieren; → **palm**[1] 1; **'~ˌbear·ing** *adj.* *geol.* ölhaltig, -führend; **'~·berg** [-bɜːg] *s.* ⚓ Riesentanker *m*; **~ box** *s.* ⚙ Schmierbüchse *f*; **'~-brake** *s. mot.* Öldruckbremse *f*; **~ burn·er** *s.* ⚙ Ölbrenner *m*; **'~·cake** *s.* Ölkuchen *m*; **'~·can** *s.* 'Ölkaˌnister *m*, -kännchen *n*; **~ change** *s. mot.* Ölwechsel *m*; **'~·cloth** *s.* **1.** Wachstuch *n*; **2.** → **oilskin**; **~ col·o(u)r** *s. mst pl.* Ölfarbe *f*; **~ cri·sis** *s.* [*irr.*] ⚚ Ölkrise *f*; **'~·cup** *s.* ⚙ Öler *m*, Schmierbüchse *f*.

oiled [ɔɪld] *adj.* **1.** (ein)geölt; **2.** *bsd.* **well ~** *sl.* ‚blau', besoffen.

oil·er ['ɔɪlə] *s.* **1.** ⚓, ⚙ Öler *m*, Schmierer *m* (*Person u. Gerät*); **2.** ⚙ Öl-, Schmierkanne *f*; **3.** *Am.* F → **oilskin** 2; **4.** *Am.* Ölquelle *f*; **5.** ⚓ Öltanker *m*.

'oil|·field *s.* Ölfeld *n*; **'~ˌfired** *adj.* mit Ölfeuerung, ölbeheizt: **~ central heating** Ölzentralheizung *f*; **~ fu·el** *s.* **1.** Heizöl *n*; **2.** Öltreibstoff *m*; **~ gas** *s.* Ölgas *n*; **'~-ga(u)ge** *s.* ⚙ Ölstandsanzeiger *m*; **~ glut** *s.* Ölschwemme *f*.

oil·i·ness ['ɔɪlɪnɪs] *s.* **1.** ölige Beschaffenheit, Fettigkeit *f*, Schmierfähigkeit *f*; **2.** *fig.* Glattheit *f*, aalglattes Wesen; **3.** *fig.* Öligkeit *f*, salbungsvolles Wesen.

oil| lev·el *s. mot.* Ölstand *m*; **~ paint** *s.* Ölfarbe *f*; **~ paint·ing** *s.* **1.** 'Ölmaleˌrei *f*; **2.** Ölgemälde *n*; **3.** ⚙ Ölanstrich *m*; **~ pan** *s. mot.* Ölwanne *f*; **'~-proˌduc·ing coun·try** *s.* Ölförderland *n*; **~ rig** *s.* Bohrinsel *f*; **~ seal** *s.* ⚙ **1.** Öldichtung *f*; **2.** *a.* **~ ring** Simmerring *m*; **'~·skin** *s.* **1.** Ölleinwand *f*; **2.** *pl.* Ölzeug *n*, -kleidung *f*; **~ slick** *s.* **1.** ⚙ Ölschlick *m*; **2.** Ölteppich *m* (*auf dem Meer etc.*); **~ stove** *s.* Ölofen *m*; **~ sump** *s.* ⚙ Ölwanne *f*; **~ switch** *s.* ⚙ Ölschalter *m*; **~ var·nish** *s.* Öllack *m*; **~ well** *s.* Ölquelle *f*.

oil·y ['ɔɪlɪ] *adj.* ☐ **1.** ölig, ölhaltig, Öl...; **2.** fettig, schmierig; **3.** *fig.* glatt(züngig), aalglatt, schmeichlerisch; **4.** *fig.* ölig, salbungsvoll.

oint·ment ['ɔɪntmənt] *s.* ⚕ Salbe *f*; → **fly**[2] 1.

O.K., **OK**, **o·kay** [ˌəʊ'keɪ] F **I** *adj. u. int.* richtig, gut, in Ordnung, genehmigt; **II** *v/t.* genehmigen, gutheißen, *e-r Sache* zustimmen; **III** *s.* Zustimmung *f*, Genehmigung *f*.

old [əʊld] **I** *adj.* **1.** alt, betagt: **grow ~** alt werden, altern; **2.** *zehn Jahre etc.* alt: **ten years ~**; **3.** alt('hergebracht): **~ tradition**; **as ~ as the hills** uralt; **4.** alt, vergangen, früher: **the ~ masters** *paint. etc.* die alten Meister; → **old boy**; **5.** alt(bekannt, -bewährt): **an ~ friend**; **6.** alt, abgenutzt; (ab)getragen (*Kleider*): **that is ~ hat** das ist ein alter Hut; **7.** alt(modisch), verkalkt; **8.** alt, erfahren, gewitz(ig)t: **~ offender** alter Sünder; → **hand** 6; **9.** F (*guter*) alter, lieber: **~ chap** *od.* **man** ‚altes Haus'; **nice ~ boy** netter alter ‚Knabe'; **the ~ man** der ‚Alte' (*Chef*); **my ~ man** mein ‚Alter' (*Vater*); **my ~ woman** meine ‚Alte' (*Ehefrau*); **10.** *sl.* toll: **have a fine ~ time** sich toll amüsieren; **any ~ thing** irgend (et)was, egal was; **any ~ time** egal wann; **II** *s.* **11. the ~** die Alten *pl*; **12. of ~**, **in times of ~** ehedem, vor alters; **from of ~** seit alters; **times of ~** alte Zeiten; **a friend of ~** ein alter Freund.

old| age *s.* (hohes) Alter, Greisenalter *n*: **~ annuity**, **~ pension** (Alters)Rente *f*, Ruhegeld *n*; **~ insurance** Altersversicherung *f*; **~ pensioner** (Alters)Rentner(in), Ruhegeldempfänger(in); **~ boy** *s. Brit.* ehemaliger Schüler, Ehemalige(r) *m*; **~·clothes·man** [ˌəʊld'kləʊðzmæn] *s.* [*irr.*] Trödler *m*.

old·en ['əʊldən] *adj. Brit. obs. od. poet.* alt: **in ~ times**.

Old| Eng·lish *s. ling.* Altenglisch *n*; **ˌ2-es'tab·lished** *adj.* alteingesessen (*Firma etc.*), alt (*Brauch etc.*); **ˌ2-'fash·ioned** *adj.* **1.** altmodisch: **an ~ butler** ein Butler der alten Schule; **2.** altklug (*Kind*); **ˌ2-'fo·g(e)y·ish** *adj.* altmodisch, verknöchert, verkalkt; **2 girl** *s.* **1.** *Brit.* ehemalige Schülerin; **2.** F ‚altes Mädchen'; **~ Glo·ry** *s.* Sternenbanner *n* (*Flagge der USA*); **~ Guard** *s. pol.* ‚alte Garde': a) *Am. der ultrakonservative Flügel der Republikaner*, b) *allg. jede streng konservative Gruppe*.

old·ie ['əʊldɪ] *s.* F **1.** Oldie *m* (*alter Schlager*); **2.** alter Witz.

old·ish ['əʊldɪʃ] *adj.* ältlich.

ˌold|-'line *adj.* **1.** konserva'tiv; **2.** traditio'nell; **3.** e-r alten Linie entstammend; **ˌ~-'maid·ish** *adj.* alt'jüngferlich.

old·ster ['əʊldstə] *s.* F ‚alter Knabe'.

old| style *s.* **1.** alte Zeitrechnung (*nach dem Julianischen Kalender*); **2.** *typ.* Mediä'val(schrift) *f*; **'~-time** *adj.* aus alter Zeit, alt; **ˌ~-'tim·er** *s.* F **1.** Oldtimer *m*: a) altmodische Sache, *z.B.* altes Auto, b) ‚alter Hase', ‚Vete'ran' *m*; **2.** → **oldster**; **~ wives' tale** *s.* Ammenmärchen *n*; **ˌ~-'wom·an·ish** *adj.* alt'weiberhaft; **ˌ~-'world** *adj.* **1.** altertümlich, anheimelnd; **2.** alt, an'tik: **~ furniture**; **3.** altmodisch.

o·le·ag·i·nous [ˌəʊlɪ'ædʒɪnəs] *adj.* ölig (*a. fig.*), ölhaltig, Öl...

o·le·ate ['əʊlɪeɪt] *s.* ⚗ ölsaures Salz: **~ of potash** ölsaures Kali.

o·le·fi·ant ['əʊlɪfaɪənt] *adj.* ⚗ ölbildend: **~ gas**.

o·le·if·er·ous [ˌəʊlɪ'ɪfərəs] *adj.* ⚘ ölhaltig.

o·le·in ['əʊlɪɪn] *s.* ⚗ **1.** Ole'in *n*; **2.** (handelsübliche) Ölsäure.

o·le·o·graph ['əʊlɪəʊgrɑːf] *s.* Öldruck *m* (*Bild*); **o·le·og·ra·phy** [ˌəʊlɪ'ɒgrəfɪ] *s.* Öldruck(verfahren *n*) *m*.

o·le·o·mar·ga·rine ['əʊlɪəʊˌmɑːdʒə'riːn] *s.* Marga'rine *f*.

O lev·el *s. Brit. ped.* (*etwa*) mittlere Reife.

ol·fac·tion [ɒl'fækʃn] *s.* Geruchssinn *m*; **ol·fac·to·ry** [ɒl'fæktərɪ] *adj.* Geruchs...: **~ nerves**.

ol·i·garch ['ɒlɪgɑːk] *s.* Olig'arch *m*; **'ol·i·garch·y** [-kɪ] *s.* Oligar'chie *f*.

o·li·o ['əʊlɪəʊ] *pl.* **-os** *s.* **1.** Ra'gout *n* (*a. fig.*); **2.** ♪ Potpourri *n*.

ol·ive ['ɒlɪv] **I** *s.* **1.** *a.* **~-tree** O'live *f*, Ölbaum *m*: **Mount of 2s** *bibl.* Ölberg; **2.** O'live *f* (*Frucht*); **3.** Ölzweig *m*; **4.** *a.* **~-green** O'livgrün *n*; **II** *adj.* **5.** o'livenartig, Oliven...; **6.** o'livgrau, -grün; **'~-branch** *s.* Ölzweig *m* (*a. fig.*): **hold out the ~** s-n Friedenswillen zeigen; **~ drab** *s.* **1.** O'livgrün *n*; **2.** *Am.* o'livgrünes Uni'formtuch; **ˌ~-'drab** *adj.* o'livgrün; **~ oil** *s.* O'livenöl *n*.

ol·la po·dri·da [ˌɒləpɒ'driːdə] → **olio** 1.

ol·o·gy ['ɒlədʒɪ] *s. humor.* Wissenschaft(szweig *m*) *f*.

O·lym·pi·ad [əʊ'lɪmpɪæd] *s. allg.* Olympi'ade *f*; **O'lym·pi·an** [-ɪən] *adj.* o'lympisch; **O'lym·pic** [-ɪk] **I** *adj.* o'lympisch: **~ games** → **II** *s. pl.* O'lympische Spiele *pl*.

om·buds·man ['ɒmbʊdzmən] *s.* [*irr.*] **1.** *pol.* Ombudsmann *m* (*Beauftragter für Beschwerden von Staatsbürgern*); **2.** Beschwerdestelle *f*, Schiedsrichter *m*.

om·e·let(te) ['ɒmlɪt] *s.* Ome'lett *n*: **you cannot make an ~ without breaking eggs** *fig.* wo gehobelt wird, (da) fallen Späne.

o·men ['əʊmen] **I** *s.* Omen *n*, (*bsd.* schlechtes) Vorzeichen (**for** für): **a good** (**bad**, **ill**) **~**; **II** *v/i. u. v/t.* deuten (auf *acc.*), ahnen (lassen), prophe'zeien, (ver)künden.

o·men·tum [əʊ'mentəm] *pl.* **-ta** [-tə] *s. anat.* (Darm)Netz *n*.

om·i·nous ['ɒmɪnəs] *adj.* ☐ unheil-, verhängnisvoll, omi'nös, drohend.

o·mis·si·ble [əʊ'mɪsɪbl] *adj.* auslaßbar; **o·mis·sion** [ə'mɪʃn] *s.* **1.** Aus-, Weglassung *f* (**from** aus); **2.** Unter'lassung *f*, Versäumnis *n*, Über'gehung *f*: **sin of ~** Unterlassungssünde *f*; **o·mit** [ə'mɪt] *v/t.* **1.** aus-, weglassen (**from** aus *od.* von); über'gehen; **2.** unter'lassen, (es) versäumen (**doing**, **to do** *et.* zu tun).

om·ni·bus ['ɒmnɪbəs] **I** *s.* **1.** Omnibus *m*, (Auto)Bus *m*; **2.** Sammelband *m*, Antholo'gie *f*; **II** *adj.* **3.** Sammel... (*-konto*, *-klausel etc.*); **~ bar** *s.* ⚡ Sammelschiene *f*; **~ bill** *s. parl.* (Vorlage *f* zu e-m) Mantelgesetz *n*.

om·ni·di·rec·tion·al [ˌɒmnɪdɪ'rekʃənl] *s.* ⚡ Rundstrahl...(*-antenne*), Allrichtungs...(*-mikrofon*).

om·ni·far·i·ous [ˌɒmnɪ'feərɪəs] *adj.* von

aller(lei) Art, vielseitig.

om·nip·o·tence [ˌɒmˈnɪpətəns] *s.* Allmacht *f*; **omˈnip·o·tent** [-nt] *adj.* □ allˈmächtig.

om·ni·pres·ence [ˌɒmnɪˈprezns] *s.* Allˈgegenwart *f*; **ˌom·niˈpres·ent** [-nt] *adj.* allˈgegenwärtig, überˈall.

om·nis·cience [ɒmˈnɪsɪəns] *s.* Allˈwissenheit *f*; **omˈnis·cient** [-nt] *adj.* □ allˈwissend.

om·ni·um [ˈɒmnɪəm] *s.* ♱ *Brit.* Omnium *n*, Gesamtwert *m e-r fundierten öffentlichen Anleihe*; **ˌ~-ˈgath·er·um** [-ˈgæðərəm] *s.* **1.** Sammelˈsurium *n*; **2.** bunte Gesellschaft.

om·niv·o·rous [ɒmˈnɪvərəs] *adj.* alles fressend.

o·mo·plate [ˈəʊməʊpleɪt] *s. anat.* Schulterblatt *n*.

om·phal·ic [ɒmˈfælɪk] *adj. anat.* Nabel…; **om·pha·lo·cele** [ˈɒmfələʊsiːl] *s.* ⚕ Nabelbruch *m*.

om·pha·los [ˈɒmfəlɒs] *pl.* **-li** [-laɪ] *s.* **1.** *anat.* Nabel *m* (*a. fig. Mittelpunkt*); **2.** *antiq.* Schildbuckel *m*.

on [ɒn; ən] **I** *prp.* **1.** *mst* auf (*dat. od. acc.*): *siehe die mit* **on** *verbundenen Wörter*; **2.** *Lage*: a) (*getragen von*): auf (*dat.*), an (*dat.*), in (*dat.*): ***~ board*** an Bord; ***~ earth*** auf Erden; ***the scar ~ the face*** die Narbe im Gesicht; ***~ foot*** zu Fuß; ***~ all fours*** auf allen vieren; ***~ the radio*** im Radio; ***have you a match ~ you?*** haben Sie ein Streichholz bei sich?, b) (*festgemacht od. unmittelbar*) an (*dat.*): ***~ the chain***; ***~ the Thames***; ***~ the wall***; **3.** *Richtung*, *Ziel*: auf (*acc.*) … (hin) (*od.* los), nach … (hin), an (*acc.*), zu: ***a blow ~ the chin*** ein Schlag ans Kinn; ***throw s.o. od. s.th. ~ the floor*** j-n *od.* et. zu Boden werfen; **4.** *fig.* a) *Grund*: auf … (hin): ***~ his authority***; ***~ suspicion***; ***levy a duty ~ silk*** einen Zoll auf Seide erheben; ***~ his own theory*** nach s-r eigenen Theorie; ***~ these conditions*** unter diesen Bedingungen, b) *Aufeinanderfolge*: auf (*acc.*), über (*acc.*), nach: ***loss ~ loss*** Verlust auf *od.* über Verlust, ein Verlust nach dem andern, c) *gehörig* zu, *beschäftigt* bei, an (*dat.*): ***~ a committee*** zu e-m Ausschuß gehörend; ***be ~ the Stock Exchange*** an der Börse (beschäftigt) sein, d) *Zustand*: in, auf (*dat.*), zu: ***~ duty*** im Dienst; ***~ fire*** in Brand; ***~ leave*** auf Urlaub; ***~ sale*** verkäuflich, e) *gerichtet* auf (*acc.*): ***an attack ~***; ***~ business*** geschäftlich; ***a joke ~ me*** ein Spaß auf m-e Kosten; ***shut*** (***open***) ***the door ~ s.o.*** j-m die Tür verschließen (öffnen); ***have s.th. ~ s.o.*** *sl.* et. Belastendes über j-n wissen; ***have nothing ~ s.o.*** *sl.* j-m nichts anhaben können, *a.* j-m nichts voraus haben; ***this is ~ me*** F das geht auf m-e Rechnung; ***be ~ a pill*** e-e Pille (ständig) nehmen, f) *Thema*: über (*acc.*): ***agreement*** (***lecture***, ***opinion***) ***~***; ***talk ~ a subject***; **5.** *Zeitpunkt*: an (*dat.*): ***~ Sunday***; ***~ the 1st of April***; ***~ or before April 1st*** bis zum 1. April; ***~ his arrival*** bei *od.* (gleich) nach seiner Ankunft; ***~ being asked*** als ich *etc.* (danach) gefragt wurde; ***~ entering*** beim Eintritt; **II** *adv.* **6.** (*a. Zssgn mit vb.*) (dar)ˈauf(*-legen*, *-schrauben etc.*); **7.** *bsd. Kleidung*: a) an(*-haben*, *-ziehen*): ***have*** (***put***) ***a coat ~***, b) auf: ***keep one's hat ~***; **8.** (*a. in Zssgn mit vb.*) weiter(*-gehen*, *-sprechen etc.*): ***and so ~*** und so weiter; ***~ and ~*** immer weiter; ***~ and off*** a) ab u. zu, b) ab u. an, mit Unterbrechungen; ***from that day ~*** von dem Tage an; ***~ with the show!*** weiter im Programm!; ***~ to …*** auf (*acc.*) … (hinauf *od.* hinaus); **III** *adj. pred.* **9.** ***be ~*** a) im Gange sein (*Spiel etc.*), vor sich gehen: ***what's ~?*** was ist los?; ***have you anything ~ tomorrow?*** haben Sie morgen et. vor?; ***that's not ~!*** das ist nicht ‚drin'!, b) an sein (*Licht*, *Radio*, *Wasser etc.*), an-, eingeschaltet sein, laufen; auf sein (*Hahn*): ***~-off*** ⚙ An-Aus, c) *thea.* gegeben werden, laufen (*Film*), *Radio*, *TV*: gesendet werden, d) d(a)ran (*an der Reihe*) sein, e) (mit) dabeisein, mitmachen; **10.** ***be ~ to*** *sl. et.* ‚spitzgekriegt' haben, über *j-n od. et.* im Bilde sein; ***he is always ~ at me*** er ‚bearbeitet' mich ständig (***about*** wegen); **11.** *sl.* beschwipst: ***be a bit ~*** e-n Schwips haben.

o·nan·ism [ˈəʊnənɪzəm] *s.* ⚕ **1.** Coitus *m* interˈruptus; **2.** Onaˈnie *f*.

ˈon·board *adj.* ✈ bordeigen, Bord…: ***~ computer***.

once [wʌns] **I** *adv.* **1.** einmal: ***~ again*** (*od.* ***more***) noch einmal; ***~ and again*** (*od.* ***~ or twice***) einige Male, ab u. zu; ***~ in a while*** (*od.* ***way***) zuweilen, hin u. wieder; ***~*** (***and***) ***for all*** ein für allemal; ***if ~ he should suspect*** wenn er erst einmal mißtrauisch würde; ***not ~*** kein einziges Mal; **2.** einmal, einst: ***~*** (***upon a time***) ***there was*** es war einmal (*Märchenanfang*); **II** *s.* **3.** ***every ~ in a while*** von Zeit zu Zeit; ***for ~***, ***this ~*** dieses ˈeine Mal, (für) diesmal (*ausnahmsweise*); **4.** ***at ~*** a) auf einmal, zugleich, gleichzeitig: ***don't all speak at ~***; ***at ~ a soldier and a poet*** Soldat u. Dichter zugleich, b) sogleich, sofort: ***all at ~*** plötzlich, mit ˈeinem Male; **III** *cj.* **5.** *a.* ***~ that*** soˈbald *od.* wenn … (einmal), wenn erst; **ˈ-ˌo·ver** *s.* F ***give s.o. od. s.th. the ~*** a) *j-n* kurz mustern *od.* abschätzen, (sich) *j-n od. et.* (rasch) mal ansehen, b) *j-n* ‚in die Mache' nehmen.

ˈonˌcom·ing *adj.* **1.** (herˈan)nahend, entgegenkommend: ***~ traffic*** Gegenverkehr *m*; **2.** *fig.* kommend: ***the ~ generation***.

one [wʌn] **I** *adj.* **1.** ein (eine, ein): ***~ hundred*** (ein)hundert; ***~ man in ten*** jeder zehnte; ***~ or two*** ein paar, einige; **2.** (*betont*) ein (eine, ein), ein einziger (eine einzige, ein einziges): ***all were of ~ mind*** sie waren alle ˈeines Sinnes; ***for ~ thing*** (zunächst) einmal; ***his ~ thought*** sein einziger Gedanke; ***the ~ way to do it*** die einzige Möglichkeit (es zu tun); **3.** ein gewisser (e-e gewisse, ein gewisses), ein (eine, ein): ***~ day*** e-s Tages (*in Zukunft od. Vergangenheit*); ***~ of these days*** irgendwann (ein)mal; ***~ John Smith*** ein gewisser J. S.; **II** *s.* **4.** Eins *f*, eins: ***Roman ~*** römische Eins; ***~ and a half*** ein(und)einhalb, anderthalb; ***at ~ o'clock*** um ein Uhr; **5.** *der* (*die*) einzelne, *das* einzelne (Stück): ***~ by ~***, ***~ after another*** e-r nach dem andern, einzeln; ***I for ~*** ich zum Beispiel; **6.** Einheit *f*: ***be at ~ with s.o.*** mit j-m ˈeiner Meinung *od.* einig sein; ***~ and all*** alle miteinander; ***all in ~*** alles in ˈeinem; ***it is all ~*** (***to me***) es ist (mir) ganz einerlei; ***be made ~*** ein (*Ehe*)Paar werden; ***make ~*** mit von der Partie sein; **7.** *bsd.* Einˈdollar- *od.* Einˈpfundnote *f*; **III** *pron.* **8.** ein, einer, jemand: ***like ~ dead*** wie ein Toter; ***~ of the poets*** einer der Dichter; ***~ another*** einander; ***~ who*** einer, der; ***the ~ who*** der(jenige), der; ***~ of these days*** dieser Tage; ***~ in the eye*** F *fig.* ein Denkzettel; **9.** (*Stützwort*, *mst unübersetzt*): ***a sly ~*** ein (ganz) Schlauer; ***the little ~s*** die Kleinen; ***a red pencil and a blue ~*** ein roter Bleistift u. ein blauer; ***that ~*** der (die, das) da *od.* dort; ***the ~s you mention*** die (von Ihnen) erwähnten; → ***each*** *etc.*; **10.** man: ***~ knows***; **11.** ***~'s*** sein: ***break ~'s leg*** sich das Bein brechen; ***take ~'s walk*** s-n Spaziergang machen; **ˌ~-ˈact play** *s. thea.* Einakter *m*; **ˌ~-ˈarmed** *adj.* einarmig: ***~ bandit*** F Spielautomat *m*; **ˌ~-ˈcrop sys·tem** *s.* ⚘ ˈMonokulˌtur *f*; **ˌ~-ˈdig·it** *adj.* ⚙ einstellig (*Zahl*); **ˌ~-ˈeyed** *adj.* einäugig; **ˌ~-ˈhand·ed** *adj.* **1.** einhändig; **2.** mit nur ˈeiner Hand zu bedienen(d); **ˌ~-ˈhorse** *adj.* **1.** einspännig; **2.** ***~ town*** F (elendes) ‚Kaff' *n od.* ‚Nest' *n*; **ˌ~-ˈlegged** [-ˈlegd] *adj.* **1.** einbeinig; **2.** *fig.* einseitig; **ˌ~-ˈline busi·ness** *s.* ♱ Fachgeschäft *n*; **ˌ~-ˈman** *adj.* Einmann…: ***~ business*** ♱ Einzelunternehmen *n*; ***~ bus*** Einmannbus *m*; ***~ show*** a) One-man-Show *f* (*a. fig.*), b) Ausstellung *f* der Werke ˈeines Künstlers.

one·ness [ˈwʌnnɪs] *s.* **1.** Einheit *f*; **2.** Gleichheit *f*, Identiˈtät *f*; **3.** Einigkeit *f*, (völliger) Einklang.

ˌone|-ˈnight stand *s. thea.* einmaliges Gastspiel (*a. fig.* F *sexuelles Abenteuer*); **ˌ~-ˈpiece** *adj.* **1.** einteilig: ***~ bathing-suit***; **2.** ⚙ aus ˈeinem Stück, Voll…; **ˌ~-ˈprice shop** *s.* Einheitspreisladen *m*.

on·er [ˈwʌnə] *s.* **1.** *sl.* ‚Kaˈnone' *f* (*Könner*) (***at*** in *dat.*); **2.** *sl.* ‚Mordsding' *n* (*bsd. wuchtiger Schlag*).

on·er·ous [ˈɒnərəs] *adj.* □ lästig, drückend, beschwerlich (***to*** für); **ˈon·er·ous·ness** [-nɪs] *s.* Beschwerlichkeit *f*, Last *f*.

oneˈself *pron.* **1.** *refl.* sich (selber): ***by ~*** aus eigener Kraft, von selbst; **2.** selbst, selber; **3.** *mst* ***one's self*** man (selbst *od.* selber).

ˌone|-ˈsid·ed [-ˈsaɪdɪd] *adj.* □ einseitig (*a. fig.*); **ˈ~-time I** *adj.* einst-, ehemalig; **II** *adv.* einst-, ehemals; **ˈ~-track** *adj.* **1.** 🚂 eingleisig; **2.** *fig.* einseitig: ***you have a ~ mind*** du hast immer nur dasselbe im Kopf; **~-up·man·ship** [wʌnˈʌpmənʃɪp] *s.* die Kunst, dem andern immer (um eine Nasenlänge) vorˈaus zu sein; **ˌ~-ˈway** *adj.* **1.** Einweg…(*-flasche etc.*), Einbahn…(*-straße*, *-verkehr*): ***~ ticket*** *Am.* einfache Fahrkarte; **2.** *fig.* einseitig.

on·ion [ˈʌnjən] *s.* **1.** ⚘ Zwiebel *f*; **2.** *sl.* ‚Rübe' *f* (*Kopf*): ***off one's ~*** *sl.* (total) verrückt; **3.** ***know one's ~s*** F sein Geschäft verstehen; **ˈ~·skin** *s.* **1.** Zwiebelschale *f*; **2.** ˈDurchschlag- *od.* ˈLuftpostpaˌpier *n*.

ˈonˌlook·er *s.* Zuschauer(in) (***at*** bei); **ˈonˌlook·ing** *adj.* zuschauend.

on·ly [ˈəʊnlɪ] **I** *adj.* **1.** einzig, alˈleinig: ***the ~ son*** der einzige Sohn; ***my one and ~ hope*** meine einzige Hoffnung; ***the ~ begotten Son of God*** Gottes eingeborener Sohn; **2.** einzigartig: ***the ~ and only Mr. X*** *a. iro.* der unvergleichliche, einzigartige Mr. X; **II** *adv.* **3.** nur, bloß: ***not ~ ..., but (also)*** nicht nur ..., sondern auch; ***if ~*** wenn nur; **4.** erst: ***~ yesterday*** erst gestern, gestern noch; ***~ just*** eben erst, gerade, kaum; **III** *cj.* **5.** jeˈdoch, nur (daß), aber; **6.** ***~ that*** nur, daß; außer, wenn.

ˌ**on-ˈoff switch** *s.* ϟ Ein-Aus-Schalter *m.*

on·o·mat·o·poe·ia [ˌɒnəʊmætəʊˈpiːə] *s.* Lautmaleˈrei *f*; ˌ**on·o·mat·oˈpoe·ic** [-ˈpiːɪk], **on·o·mat·o·po·et·ic** [ˌɒnəʊmætəʊpəʊˈetɪk] *adj.* (☐ ***~ally***) lautnachahmend, onomatopoˈetisch.

ˈ**on|-poˌsi·tion** *s.* ⚙ Einschaltstellung *f*, -zustand *m*; ˈ**~·rush** *s.* Ansturm *m* (*a. fig.*); ˈ**~·set** *s.* **1.** Angriff *m*, Atˈtacke *f*; **2.** Anfang *m*, Beginn *m*, Einsetzen *n*: ***at the first ~*** gleich beim ersten Anlauf; **3.** ⚕ Ausbruch *m* (*e-r Krankheit*), Anfall *m*; **~ˈshore** *adj. u. adv.* **1.** landwärts; **2.** a) in Küstennähe, b) an Land; **3.** ✝ Inlands...: ***~ purchases***; **~·slaught** [ˈɒnslɔːt] *s.* (heftiger) Angriff *od.* Ansturm (*a. fig.*); ˌ**~-the-ˈjob** *adj.* praktisch: ***~ training***.

on·to [ˈɒntʊ; -tə] *prp.* **1.** auf (*acc.*); **2.** ***be ~ s.th.*** *sl.* hinter et. gekommen sein; ***he's ~ you*** *sl.* er hat dich durchschaut.

on·to·gen·e·sis [ˌɒntəʊˈdʒenɪsɪs] *s. biol.* Ontogeˈnese *f.*

on·tol·o·gy [ɒnˈtɒlədʒɪ] *s. phls.* Ontoloˈgie *f.*

o·nus [ˈəʊnəs] (*Lat.*) *s. nur sg.* **1.** *fig.* Last *f*, Verpflichtung *f*, Onus *n*; **2.** *a.* ***~ of proof***, ***~ probandi*** ⚖ Beweislast *f*: ***the ~ rests with him*** die Beweislast trifft ihn.

on·ward [ˈɒnwəd] **I** *adv.* vorwärts, weiter: ***from the tenth century ~*** vom 10. Jahrhundert an; **II** *adj.* vorwärts-, fortschreitend; ˈ**on·wards** [-dz] → ***onward*** I.

on·yx [ˈɒnɪks] *s.* **1.** *min.* Onyx *m*; **2.** ⚕ Nagelgeschwür *n* der Hornhaut, Onyx *m.*

o·o·blast [ˈəʊəblɑːst] *s. biol.* Eikeim *m*; **o·o·cyst** [ˈəʊəsɪst] *s.* Ooˈzyste *f.*

oo·dles [ˈuːdlz] *s. pl.* F Unmengen *pl.*, ‚Haufen' *m*: ***he has ~ of money*** er hat Geld wie Heu.

oof [uːf] *s. Brit. sl.* ‚Kies' *m* (*Geld*).

oomph [ʊmf] *s. sl.* ˈSex-Apˈpeal *m.*

o·o·sperm [ˈəʊəspɜːm] *s. biol.* befruchtetes Ei *od.* befruchtete Eizelle, Zyˈgote *f.*

ooze [uːz] **I** *v/i.* **1.** (ˈdurch-, aus-, ein)sikkern (***through, out of, into***); ein-, hinˈdurchdringen (*a. Licht etc.*): ***~ away*** a) versickern, b) *fig.* (dahin)schwinden; ***~ out*** a) entweichen (*Luft, Gas*), b) *fig.* durchsickern (*Geheimnis*); ***~ with sweat*** von Schweiß triefen; **II** *v/t.* **2.** ausströmen, -schwitzen; **3.** *fig.* ausstrahlen, *iro.* triefen von; **III** *s.* **4.** ⚙ Lohbrühe *f*: ***~ leather*** lohgares Leder; **5.** Schlick *m*, Schlamm(grund) *m*; **oo·zy** [ˈuːzɪ] *adj.* **1.** schlammig, schlikk(er)ig; **2.** schleimig; **3.** feucht.

o·pac·i·ty [əʊˈpæsətɪ] *s.* **1.** ˈUndurchˌsichtigkeit *f* (*a. fig.*); **2.** Dunkelheit *f* (*a. fig.*); **3.** *fig.* Borniertheit *f*; **4.** *phys.* (ˈLicht)ˌUndurchˌlässigkeit *f*; **5.** Deckfähigkeit *f* (*Farbe*).

o·pal [ˈəʊpl] *s. min.* Oˈpal *m*: ***~ blue*** Opalblau *n*; ***~ glass*** Opal-, Milchglas *n*; ***~ lamp*** Opallampe *f*; **o·pal·esce** [ˌəʊpəˈles] *v/i.* opalisieren, bunt schillern; **o·pal·es·cence** [ˌəʊpəˈlesns] *s.* Opalisieren *n*, Schillern *n*; **o·pal·es·cent** [ˌəʊpəˈlesnt] *adj.* opalisierend, schillernd.

o·paque [əʊˈpeɪk] *adj.* ☐ **1.** ˈundurchˌsichtig, oˈpak: ***~ colo(u)r*** Deckfarbe *f*; **2.** ˈundurchˌlässig (***to*** für *Strahlen*): ***~ meal*** ⚕ Kontrastmahlzeit *f*; **3.** glanzlos, trüb; **4.** *fig.* a) unklar, dunkel, b) borniert, dumm; **oˈpaque·ness** [-nɪs] *s.* (ˈLicht)ˌUndurchˌlässigkeit *f*; Deckkraft *f* (*Farben*).

op art [ɒp] *s. Kunst*: Op-art *f.*

o·pen [ˈəʊpən] **I** *adj.* ☐ **1.** *allg.* offen (*z. B. Buch, Flasche, ⚘ Kette, ϟ Stromkreis, ⚔ Stadt, Tür, ⚕ Wunde*); offenstehend, auf: ***~ prison*** offenes Gefängnis; ***~ warfare*** ⚔ Bewegungskrieg *m*; ***keep one's eyes ~*** *fig.* die Augen offenhalten; → ***arm***[1] 1, ***bowels*** 1, ***order*** 5; **2.** zugänglich, frei, offen (*Gelände, Straße, Meer etc.*): ***~ field*** freies Feld; ***~ spaces*** öffentliche Plätze (*Parkanlagen etc.*); **3.** frei, bloß, offen (*Wagen etc.*; *ϟ Motor*); → ***lay open***; **4.** offen, eisfrei (*Wetter, ⚓ Hafen, Gewässer*); ⚓ klar (*Sicht*): ***~ winter*** frostfreier Winter; **5.** ge-, eröffnet (*Laden, Theater etc.*), offen (*a. fig.* ***to*** *dat.*), öffentlich (*Sitzung, Versteigerung etc.*); (jedem) zugänglich: ***a career ~ to talent***; ***~ competition*** freier Wettbewerb; ***~ market*** ✝ offener *od.* freier Markt; ***~ position*** freie *od.* offene (*Arbeits*)Stelle; ***~ policy*** a) ✝ Offenmarktpolitik *f*, b) *Versicherung*: Pauschalpolice *f*; ***~ scholarship*** *Brit.* offenes Stipendium; ***~ for subscription*** ✝ zur Zeichnung aufgelegt; ***in ~ court*** in öffentlicher Verhandlung, vor Gericht; **6.** (***to***) *fig. der Kritik, dem Zweifel etc.* ausgesetzt, unterˈworfen: ***~ to question*** anfechtbar; ***~ to temptation*** anfällig gegen die Versuchung; ***leave o.s. wide ~*** (***to s.o.***) sich (j-m gegenüber) e-e (große) Blöße geben; **7.** zugänglich, aufgeschlossen (***to*** für *od. dat.*): ***an ~ mind***; ***be ~ to conviction*** (***an offer***) mit sich reden (handeln) lassen; ***that is ~ to argument*** darüber läßt sich streiten; **8.** offen(kundig), unverhüllt: ***~ contempt***; ***an ~ secret*** ein offenes Geheimnis; **9.** offen, freimütig: ***an ~ character***; ***~ letter*** offener Brief; ***I will be ~ with you*** ich will ganz offen mit dir reden; **10.** freigebig: ***with an ~ hand***; ***keep an ~ house*** ein offenes Haus führen, gastfrei sein; **11.** *fig.* unentschieden, offen (*Frage, Forderung, Kampf, Urteil etc.*); **12.** *fig.* frei (*ohne Verbote*): ***~ pattern*** ⚖ ungeschütztes Muster; ***~ season*** Jagd-, Fischzeit *f*; **13.** ✝ laufend (*Konto, Kredit, Rechnung*): ***~ cheque*** Barscheck *m*; **14.** ⚙ durchˈbrochen (*Gewebe, Handarbeit*); **15.** *ling.* offen (*Silbe, Vokal*): ***~ consonant*** Reibelaut *m*; **16.** ♪ a) weit (*Lage, Satz*), b) leer (*Saite etc.*): ***~ note*** Grundton *m*; **17.** *typ.* licht (*Satz*): ***~ type*** Konturschrift *f*; **II** *s.* **18.** ***the ~*** a) offenes Land, b) offene See: ***in the ~*** im Freien, unter freiem Himmel; ⚒ über Tag; ***bring into the ~*** *fig.* an die Öffentlichkeit bringen; ***come into the ~*** *fig.* sich erklären, offen reden, Farbe bekennen, (***with s.th.*** mit et.) an die Öffentlichkeit treten; **19.** ***the*** ♀ *bsd. Golf*: offenes Turnier *für Amateure u. Berufsspieler*; **III** *v/t.* **20.** *allg.* öffnen, aufmachen; *Buch a.* aufschlagen; ϟ *Stromkreis* ausschalten, unterˈbrechen: ***~ the bowels*** ⚕ den Leib öffnen; ***~ s.o.'s eyes*** *fig.* j-m die Augen öffnen; → ***throttle*** 2; **21.** *Aussicht*, ✝ *Akkreditiv, Debatte*, ⚔ *das Feuer*, ✝ *Konto, Geschäft*, ⚖ *die Verhandlung etc.* eröffnen; *Verhandlungen* anknüpfen, in *Verhandlungen* eintreten; ✝ *neue Märkte* erschließen: ***~ s.th. to traffic*** *e-e Straße etc.* dem Verkehr übergeben; **22.** *fig. Gefühle, Gedanken* enthüllen, *s-e Absichten* entdecken: ***~ o.s. to s.o.*** sich j-m mitteilen; → ***heart*** *Redew.*; **IV** *v/i.* **23.** sich öffnen *od.* auftun, aufgehen; *fig.* sich *dem Auge, Geist etc.* erschließen, zeigen, auftun; **24.** führen, gehen (*Tür, Fenster*) (***on to*** auf *acc.*, ***into*** nach *dat.*); **25.** *fig.* a) anfangen, beginnen (*Schule, Börse etc.*), öffnen, aufmachen (*Laden etc.*), b) (e-n Brief, s-e Rede) beginnen (***with*** mit *e-m Kompliment etc.*); **26.** *allg.* öffnen; (ein Buch) aufschlagen; ***~ out*** **I** *v/t.* **1.** *et.* ausbreiten; **II** *v/i.* **2.** sich ausbreiten, -dehnen, sich erweitern; **3.** *mot.* Vollgas geben; ***~ up*** **I** *v/t.* **1.** *Land*, ✝ *Markt etc.* erschließen; **II** *v/i.* **2.** ⚔ Das Feuer eröffnen; **3.** *fig.* a) ‚loslegen' (*mit Worten, Schlägen etc.*), b) ‚auftauen', mitteilsam werden; **4.** sich auftun *od.* zeigen.

ˌ**o·pen|-ˈac·cess li·brar·y** *s.* ˈFreihandbiblioˌthek *f*; ˌ**~-ˈair** *adj.* Freilicht..., Freiluft..., unter freiem Himmel: ***~ swimming pool*** Freibad *n*; ˌ**~-and-ˈshut** *adj.* ganz einfach, sonnenklar; ˌ**~-ˈarmed** *adj.* warm, herzlich (*Empfang*); ˌ**~-ˈdoor** *adj.* frei zugänglich: ***~ policy*** (Handels)Politik *f* der offenen Tür; ˌ**~-ˈend·ed** *adj.* **1.** zeitlich unbegrenzt: ***~ discussion*** Open-end-Diskussion *f*; **2.** ausbaufähig: ***~ program(me)***.

o·pen·er [ˈəʊpnə] *s.* **1.** (*fig.* Er)Öffner (-in); **2.** (*Büchsen- etc.*)Öffner *m*; *sport etc.* Eröffnung(sspiel *n*, *thea.* -nummer *f*) *f.*

ˌ**o·pen|-ˈeyed** *adj.* **1.** mit großen Augen, staunend; **2.** wachsam; ˌ**~-ˈhand·ed** *adj.* ☐ freigebig; ˌ**~-ˈheart** *adj.*: ***~ surgery*** ⚕ Offenherzchirurgie *f*; ˌ**~-ˈheart·ed** *adj.* ☐ offen(herzig), aufrichtig; ˌ**~-ˈhearth** *adj.* ⚙ Siemens-Martin(*-ofen, -stahl*).

o·pen·ing [ˈəʊpnɪŋ] **I** *s.* **1.** *das* Öffnen; Eröffnung *f* (*a. fig. Akkreditiv, Konto, Testament, Unternehmen*); *fig.* Inbetriebnahme *f* (*e-r Anlage etc.*); *fig.* Erschließung *f* (*Land*, ✝ *Markt*); **2.** Öffnung *f*, Loch *n*, Lücke *f*, Bresche *f*, Spalt *m*, ˈDurchlaß *m*; **3.** *Am.* (Wald-)Lichtung *f*; **4.** ⚙ (Spann)Weite *f*; **5.** *fig.* Eröffnung *f* (*a. Schach, Kampf etc.*), Beginn *m*, einleitender Teil (*a.* ⚖); **6.** Gelegenheit *f*, (✝ Absatz)Möglichkeit *f*; **7.** ✝ offene *od.* freie Stelle; **II** *adj.* **8.** Öffnungs...; **9.** Eröffnungs...: ***~ speech***; ***~ price*** ✝ Eröffnungskurs *m*;

~ ***night*** *thea.* Eröffnungsvorstellung *f.*
ˌo·pen|-ˈmar·ket *adj.* Freimarkt...: ~ ***paper*** marktgängiges Wertpapier; ~ ***policy*** Offenmarktpolitik *f*; **ˌ~-ˈmind·ed** *adj.* ☐ aufgeschlossen, vorurteilslos; **ˌ~-ˈmouthed** *adj.* mit offenem Mund, *fig. a.* gaffend; **ˌ~-ˈplan of·fice** *s.* ˈGroßraumbüˌro *n*; ~ **ses·a·me** *s.* Sesam öffne dich *n*; ~ **shop** *s. Am.* Betrieb *m*, der auch Nichtgewerkschaftsmitglieder beschäftigt; ♀ **U·ni·ver·si·ty** *s.* ˈFernsehuniversiˌtät *f*, ˈTelekolˌleg *n*; ˈ**~·work** *s.* ˈDurchbrucharbeit *f* (*Handarbeit*); ~ **work·ing** *s.* ⚒ Tagebau *m.*
op·er·a¹ [ˈɒpərə] *s.* Oper *f* (*a. Gebäude*): ***comic*** ~ komische Oper; ***grand*** ~ große Oper.
op·er·a² [ˈɒpərə] *pl. von* ***opus.***
op·er·a·ble [ˈɒpərəbl] *adj.* **1.** ˈdurchführbar; **2.** ⚙ betriebsfähig; **3.** ⚕ opeˈrabel.
op·er·a| cloak *s.* Abendmantel *m*; ~ **glass(·es** *pl.*) *s.* Opern-, Theˈaterglas *n*; ~ **hat** *s.* ˈKlappzyˌlinder *m*, Chapeauˈclaque *m*; ~ **house** *s.* Opernhaus *n*, Oper *f*; ~ **pump** *s. Am.* glatter Pumps.
op·er·ate [ˈɒpəreɪt] **I** *v/i.* **1.** arbeiten, in Betrieb sein, funktionieren, laufen (*Maschine etc.*): ***be operating*** in Betrieb sein; ~ ***on batteries*** von Batterien betrieben werden; ~ ***at a deficit*** † mit Verlust arbeiten; **2.** wirksam werden *od.* sein, (ein)wirken (***on, upon*** auf *acc.*, ***as*** als), hinwirken (***for*** auf *acc.*); **3.** ⚕ (***on, upon***) *j-n* operieren: ***be ~d on*** operiert werden; **4.** † F spekulieren, operieren: ~ ***for a fall*** auf e-e Baisse spekulieren; **5.** ⚔ operieren; **II** *v/t.* **6.** bewirken, verursachen, (mit sich) bringen; **7.** ⚙ *Maschine* laufen lassen, bedienen, *Gerät* handhaben, *Schalter, Bremse etc.* betätigen, *Auto* fahren: ***safe to*** ~ betriebssicher; **8.** *Unternehmen, Geschäft* betreiben, führen, *Vorhaben* ausführen.
op·er·at·ic [ˌɒpəˈrætɪk] *adj.* (☐ ***~ally***) opernhaft (*a. fig. contp.*), Opern...: ~ ***performance*** Opernaufführung *f*; ~ ***singer*** Opernsänger(in).
op·er·at·ing [ˈɒpəreɪtɪŋ] *adj.* **1.** *bsd.* ⚙ in Betrieb befindlich, Betriebs..., Arbeits...: ~ ***conditions*** Betriebsbedingungen; ~ ***instructions*** Bedienungsvorschrift *f*, Betriebsanweisung *f*; ~ ***lever*** Betätigungshebel *m*; ~ ***system*** *Computer*: Betriebssystem *n*; **2.** † Betriebs..., betrieblich: ~ ***assets*** Vermögenswerte; ~ ***costs*** (*od.* ***expenses***) Betriebs-, Geschäfts(un)kosten; ~ ***profit*** Betriebsgewinn *m*; ~ ***statement*** Betriebsbilanz *f*; **3.** ⚕ operierend, Operations...: ~ ***room*** *od.* ~ ***theatre*** (*Am.* ***theater***) Operationssaal *m*; ~ ***surgeon*** → ***operator*** 4; ~ ***table*** Operationstisch *m.*
op·er·a·tion [ˌɒpəˈreɪʃn] *s.* **1.** Wirken *n*, Wirkung *f* (***on*** auf *acc.*); **2.** *bsd.* ⚖ Wirksamkeit *f*, Geltung *f*: ***by*** ~ ***of law*** kraft Gesetzes; ***come into*** ~ in Kraft treten; **3.** ⚙ Betrieb *m*, Tätigkeit *f*, Lauf *m* (*Maschine etc.*): ***in*** ~ in Betrieb; ***put*** (*od.* ***set***) ***in*** (***out of***) ~ in (außer) Betrieb setzen; **4.** *bsd.* ⚙ Wirkungs-, Arbeitsweise *f*; Arbeits(vor)gang *m*, (*Arbeits-, Denk- etc. a. chemischer*) Proˈzeß *m*; **5.** ⚙ Inbetriebsetzung *f*, Bedienung *f* (*Maschine, Gerät*), Betätigung *f* (*Bremse, Schalter*); **6.** Arbeit *f*: ***building ~s*** Bauarbeiten; **7.** † a) Betrieb *m*: ***continuous*** ~ durchgehender Betrieb; ***in*** ~ in Betrieb, b) Unterˈnehmen *n*, -ˈnehmung *f*, c) Geschäft *n*: ***trading*** ~ Tauschgeschäft; **8.** *Börse*: Transaktiˈon *f*; **9.** ⚕ Operatiˈon *f*, (chirˈurgischer) Eingriff: ~ ***for appendicitis*** Blinddarmoperation; ~ ***to*** (*od.* ***on***) ***the neck*** Halsoperation; ***major*** ~ a) größere Operation, b) *fig.* F große Sache, ‚schwere Geburt'; **10.** ⚔ Operatiˈon *f*, Einsatz *m*, Unterˈnehmung *f*; **ˌop·erˈa·tion·al** [-ʃənl] *adj.* **1.** ⚙ a) Betriebs..., Arbeits..., b) betriebsbereit, -fähig; **2.** † betrieblich, Betriebs...; **3.** ⚔ Einsatz..., Operations..., einsatzfähig: ~ ***objective*** Operationsziel *n*; **4.** ⚓ klar, fahrbereit; **op·er·a·tive** [ˈɒpərətɪv] **I** *adj.* ☐ **1.** wirkend, treibend: ***an ~ motive***; **2.** wirksam: ***an ~ dose***; ***become*** ~ ⚖ (rechts)wirksam werden, in Kraft treten; ***the ~ word*** das Wort, auf das es ankommt, ⚖ *a.* das rechtsbegründende Wort; **3.** praktisch; **4.** †, ⚙ Arbeits..., Betriebs..., betriebsfähig; **5.** ⚕ operaˈtiv, chirˈurgisch: ~ ***dentistry*** Zahn- u. Kieferchirurgie *f*; **6.** arbeitend, tätig, beschäftigt; **II** *s.* **7.** (Fach)Arbeiter *m*, Meˈchaniker *m*; → ***operator*** 2; **8.** *Am.* Priˈvatdetekˌtiv(in); **op·er·a·tor** [ˈɒpəreɪtə] *s.* **1.** *der* (*die, das*) Wirkende; **2.** a) ⚙ Bedienungsperson *f*, Arbeiter(in), (*Kran- etc.*)Führer *m*: ***engine*** ~ Maschinist *m*; ***~'s license*** *Am.* Führerschein *m*, b) Telegraˈfist(in), c) Telefoˈnist(in), d) (Film)Vorführer *m*, *a.* Kameramann *m*; **3.** † a) Unterˈnehmer *m*, b) *Börse*: (berufsmäßiger) Spekuˈlant, *b.s.* Schieber *m*; **4.** ⚕ operierender Arzt, Operaˈteur *m*; **5.** *Computer*: Opeˈrator *m.*
o·per·cu·lum [əʊˈpɜːkjʊləm] *pl.* **-la** [-lə] *s.* **1.** ⚘ Deckel *m*; **2.** *zo.* a) Deckel *m* (*Schnecken*), b) Kiemendeckel *m* (*Fische*).
op·er·et·ta [ˌɒpəˈretə] *s.* Opeˈrette *f.*
oph·thal·mi·a [ɒfˈθælmɪə] *s.* ⚕ Bindehautentzündung *f*; **ophˈthal·mic** [-ɪk] *adj.* Augen...; augenkrank: ~ ***hospital*** Augenklinik *f*; **oph·thal·mol·o·gist** [ˌɒfθælˈmɒlədʒɪst] *s.* Augenarzt *m*, Augenärztin *f*; **oph·thal·mol·o·gy** [ˌɒfθælˈmɒlədʒɪ] *s.* Augenheilkunde *f*, Ophthalmoloˈgie *f*; **oph·thal·mo·scope** [ɒfˈθælməskəʊp] *s.* ⚕ Augenspiegel *m*, Ophthalmoˈskop *n.*
o·pi·ate [ˈəʊpɪət] **I** *s.* **1.** ⚕ Opiˈat *n*, ˈOpiumpräpaˌrat *n*; **2.** Schlaf- *od.* Beruhigungs- *od.* Betäubungsmittel *n* (*a. fig.*): ~ ***for the people*** Opium *n* fürs Volk; **II** *adj.* **3.** einschläfernd; betäubend (*a. fig.*).
o·pine [əʊˈpaɪn] **I** *v/i.* daˈfürhalten; **II** *v/t. et.* meinen.
o·pin·ion [əˈpɪnjən] *s.* **1.** Meinung *f*, Ansicht *f*, Stellungnahme *f*: ***in my*** ~ m-s Erachtens, nach m-r Meinung *od.* Ansicht; ***be of*** (***the***) ~ ***that*** der Meinung sein, daß; ***that is a matter of*** ~ das ist Ansichtssache *f*; ***public*** ~ die öffentliche Meinung; **2.** Achtung *f*, (gute) Meinung: ***have a high*** (***low*** *od.* ***poor***) ~ ***of*** e-e (keine) hohe Meinung haben von, (nicht) viel halten von; ***she has no*** ~ ***of Frenchmen*** sie hält nicht viel von (den) Franzosen; **3.** (schriftliches) Gutachten (***on*** über *acc.*): ***counsel's*** ~ Rechtsgutachten; **4.** *mst pl.* Überˈzeugung *f*: ***have the courage of one's ~s*** zu s-r Überzeugung stehen; **5.** ⚖ (Urteils)Begründung *f*; **oˈpin·ion·at·ed** [-neɪtɪd] *adj.* **1.** starr-, eigensinnig; dogˈmatisch; **2.** schulmeisterlich, überˈheblich.
oˈpin·ion|-ˌform·ing *adj.* meinungsbildend; ~ **form·er**, ~ **lead·er**, **~-ˌmak·er** *s.* Meinungsbildner *m*; ~ **poll** *s.* ˈMeinungsˌumfrage *f*; ~ **re·search** *s.* Meinungsforschung *f.*
o·pi·um [ˈəʊpjəm] *s.* Opium *n*: ***~-eater*** Opiumesser *m*; ~ ***poppy*** ⚘ Schlafmohn *m*; **ˈo·pi·um·ism** [-mɪzəm] *s.* ⚕ **1.** Opiumsucht *f*; **2.** Opiumvergiftung *f.*
o·pos·sum [əˈpɒsəm] *s. zo.* Oˈpossum *n*, Beutelratte *f.*
op·po·nent [əˈpəʊnənt] **I** *adj.* entgegenstehend, -gesetzt, gegnerisch (***to*** *dat.*); **II** *s.* Gegner(in) (*a.* ⚖, *sport*), Gegenspieler(in), ˈWidersacher(in), Oppoˈnent(in).
op·por·tune [ˈɒpətjuːn] *adj.* ☐ **1.** günstig, passend, gut angebracht, opporˈtun; **2.** rechtzeitig; **ˈop·por·tune·ness** [-nɪs] *s.* Opportuniˈtät *f*, Rechtzeitigkeit *f*; günstiger Zeitpunkt.
op·por·tun·ism [ˈɒpətjuːnɪzm] *s.* Opportuˈnismus *m*; **ˈop·por·tun·ist** [-ɪst] *s.* Opportuˈnist(in).
op·por·tu·ni·ty [ˌɒpəˈtjuːnətɪ] *s.* (*günstige*) Gelegenheit, Möglichkeit *f* (***of doing, to do*** zu tun; ***for s.th.*** zu et.): ***miss the*** ~ die Gelegenheit verpassen; ***seize*** (*od.* ***take***) ***an*** ~ e-e Gelegenheit ergreifen; ***at the first*** ~ bei der ersten Gelegenheit; ~ ***for advancement*** Aufstiegsmöglichkeit; ~ ***makes the thief*** Gelegenheit macht Diebe.
op·pose [əˈpəʊz] *v/t.* **1.** (*vergleichend*) gegenˈüberstellen; **2.** entgegensetzen, -stellen (***to*** *dat.*); **3.** entgegentreten (*dat.*), sich widerˈsetzen (*dat.*); angehen gegen, bekämpfen; **4.** ⚖ *Am.* gegen *e-e Patentanmeldung* Einspruch erheben; **opˈposed** [-zd] *adj.* **1.** gegensätzlich, entgegengesetzt (*a.* A); **2.** (***to***) abgeneigt (*dat.*), feind (*dat.*), feindlich (gegen): ***be ~ to*** *j-m od. e-r Sache* feindlich *od.* ablehnend gegenüberstehen, gegen *j-n od. et.* sein; **3.** ⚙ Gegen...: ~ ***piston engine*** Gegenkolben-, Boxermotor *m*; **opˈpos·ing** [-zɪŋ] *adj.* **1.** gegenˈüberliegend; **2.** opponierend, gegnerisch; **3.** *fig.* entgegengesetzt, unvereinbar.
op·po·site [ˈɒpəzɪt] **I** *adj.* ☐ **1.** gegenˈüberliegend, -stehend (***to*** *dat.*): ~ ***angle*** A Gegen-, Scheitelwinkel *m*; **2.** entgegengesetzt (gerichtet), ˈumgekehrt: ~ ***directions***; ~ ***signs*** A entgegengesetzte Vorzeichen; ***of ~ sign*** A ungleichnamig; ~ ***pistons*** ⚙ gegenläufige Kolben; **3.** gegensätzlich, entgegengesetzt, gegenteilig, (grund)verschieden, ander: ***words of ~ meaning***; **4.** gegnerisch, Gegen...: ~ ***side*** *sport* Gegenpartei *f*, gegnerische Mannschaft; ~ ***number*** *sport, pol. etc.* Gegenspieler(in), ‚Gegenüber' *n*, *weitS.* ‚Kollege' *m*, ‚Kollegin' *f* (von der anderen Seite); **5.** ⚘ gegenständig (*Blätter*); **II** *s.* **6.** Gegenteil *n* (*a.* A), -satz *m*: ***just the*** ~ das genaue Gegenteil; **III** *adv.* **7.** gegenˈüber; **IV** *prp.* **8.** gegenüber (*dat.*): ***the ~ house***; ***play ~ X.*** *sport,*

Film etc. (der, die) Gegenspieler(in) von X sein.

op·po·si·tion [ˌɒpəˈzɪʃn] *s.* **1.** Gegenˈüberstellung *f*; *das* Gegenˈüberstehen *od.* -liegen; ⚙ Gegenläufigkeit *f*; **2.** ˈWiderstand *m* (*to* gegen): ***offer ~*** (*to*) Widerstand leisten (gegen); ***meet with*** (*od.* ***face***) ***stiff ~*** auf heftigen Widerstand stoßen; **3.** Gegensatz *m*, ˈWiderspruch *m*: ***act in ~ to*** zuwiderhandeln (*dat.*); **4.** *pol.* (*a. ast. u. fig.*) Oppositiˈon *f*; **5.** ✝ Konkurˈrenz *f*; **6.** ⚖ a) ˈWiderspruch *m*, b) *Am.* Einspruch *m* (*to* gegen *e-e Patentanmeldung*); **7.** *Logik*: Gegensatz *m*; ˌ**op·poˈsi·tion·al** [-ʃənl] *adj.* **1.** *pol.* oppositioˈnell, Oppositions…, regierungsfeindlich; **2.** gegensätzlich, Widerstands…

op·press [əˈpres] *v/t.* **1.** *seelisch* bedrükken; **2.** unterˈdrücken, tyrannisieren, schikanieren; **opˈpres·sion** [-eʃn] *s.* **1.** Unterˈdrückung *f*, Tyrannisierung *f*; ⚖ a) Schiˈkane(n *pl.*) *f*, b) ˈMißbrauch *m* der Amtsgewalt; **2.** Druck *m*, Bedrängnis *f*, Not *f*; **3.** Bedrücktheit *f*; **4.** ⚕ Beklemmung *f*; **opˈpres·sive** [-sɪv] *adj.* □ **1.** *seelisch* (be)drückend; **2.** tyˈrannisch, grausam, hart; ⚖ schikaˈnös; **3.** drückend (schwül); **opˈpres·sive·ness** [-sɪvnɪs] *s.* **1.** Druck *m*; **2.** Schwere *f*, Schwüle *f*; **opˈpres·sor** [-sə] *s.* Unterˈdrücker *m*, Tyˈrann *m*.

op·pro·bri·ous [əˈprəʊbrɪəs] *adj.* □ **1.** schmähend, Schmäh…; **2.** schändlich, inˈfam; **opˈpro·bri·um** [-ɪəm] *s.* Schmach *f*, Schande *f*.

op·pugn [ɒˈpjuːn] *v/t.* anfechten.

opt [ɒpt] *v/i.* wählen (***between*** zwischen *dat.*), sich entscheiden (***for*** für, ***against*** gegen), *bsd. pol.* optieren (***for*** für); ***~ out*** a) sich dagegen entscheiden, b) ‚aussteigen' (***of***, ***on*** aus *der Gesellschaft*, *e-r Unternehmung etc.*); **op·ta·tive** [ˈɒptətɪv] **I** *adj.* Wunsch…, *ling.* optativ(isch): ***~ mood*** → **II** *s. ling.* Optativ *m*, Wunschform *f*.

op·tic [ˈɒptɪk] **I** *adj.* **1.** Augen…, Seh…, Gesichts…: ***~ angle*** Seh-, Gesichtswinkel *m*; ***~ axis*** a) optische Achse, b) Sehachse *f*; ***~ nerve*** Sehnerv *m*; **2.** → ***optical***; **II** *s.* **3.** *mst pl. humor.* Auge *n*; **4.** *pl. sg. konstr. phys.* Optik *f*, Lichtlehre *f*; ˈ**op·ti·cal** [-kl] *adj.* □ optisch: ***~ illusion*** optische Täuschung; ***~ microscope*** Lichtmikroskop *n*; ***~ viewfinder*** *TV* optischer Sucher; **op·ti·cian** [ɒpˈtɪʃn] *s.* Optiker(in).

op·ti·mal [ˈɒptɪml] → ***optimum*** II.

op·ti·mism [ˈɒptɪmɪzəm] *s.* Optiˈmismus *m*; ˈ**op·ti·mist** [-ɪst] *s.* Optiˈmist(in); **op·ti·mis·tic** [ˌɒptɪˈmɪstɪk] *adj.* (□ ***~ally***) optiˈmistisch.

op·ti·mize [ˈɒptɪmaɪz] *v/t.* ✝, ⚙ optimieren.

op·ti·mum [ˈɒptɪməm] **I** *pl.* **-ma** [-mə] *s.* **1.** Optimum *n*, günstigster Fall, Bestfall *m*; **2.** ✝, ⚙Bestwert *m*; **II** *adj.* **3.** optiˈmal, günstigst, best.

op·tion [ˈɒpʃn] *s.* **1.** Wahlfreiheit *f*, freie Wahl *od.* Entscheidung: ***~ of a fine*** Recht *n*, e-e Geldstrafe (*an Stelle der Haft*) zu wählen; **2.** Wahl *f*: ***at one's ~*** nach Wahl; ***make one's ~*** s-e Wahl treffen; **3.** Alternaˈtive *f*: ***I had no ~ but to*** ich hatte keine andere Wahl als; **4.** ✝ Optiˈon *f* (*a. Versicherung*), Vorkaufsrecht *n*: ***buyer's ~*** Kaufoption, Vorprämie *f*; ***~ for the call*** (***the put***) Vor- (Rück)prämiengeschäft *n*; ***~ rate*** Prämiensatz *m*; ***~ of repurchase*** Rückkaufsrecht *n*; **op·tion·al** [ˈɒpʃənl] *adj.* □ **1.** freigestellt, wahlfrei, freiwillig, fakultaˈtiv: ***~ bonds*** *Am.* kündbare Obligationen; ***~ subject*** *ped.* Wahlfach *n*; **2.** ✝ Options…: ***~ bargain*** Prämiengeschäft *n*.

op·u·lence [ˈɒpjʊləns] *s.* Reichtum *m*, (ˈÜber)Fülle *f*, ˈÜberfluß *m*: ***live in ~*** im Überfluß leben; ˈ**op·u·lent** [-nt] *adj.* □ **1.** (sehr) reich (*a. fig.*); **2.** üppig, opuˈlent: ***~ meal***.

o·pus [ˈəʊpəs] *pl.* **op·er·a** [ˈɒpərə] (*Lat.*) *s.* (*einzelnes*) Werk, Opus *n*; → ***magnum opus***; **o·pus·cule** [ɒˈpʌskjuːl] *s.* ♪, *lit.* kleines Werk.

or[1] [ɔː] *cj.* **1.** oder: ***~ else*** sonst, andernfalls; ***one ~ two*** ein bis zwei, einige; **2.** (*nach neg.*) noch, und kein, und auch nicht.

or[2] [ɔː] *s. her.* Gold *n*, Gelb *n*.

or·a·cle [ˈɒrəkl] **I** *s.* **1.** Oˈrakel(spruch *m*) *n*; *fig. a.* Weissagung *f*: ***work the ~*** F e-e Sache ‚drehen'; **2.** *fig.* oˈrakelhafter Ausspruch; **3.** *fig.* Proˈphet(in), unfehlbare Autoriˈtät; **II** *v/t. u. v/i.* **4.** oˈrakeln; **o·rac·u·lar** [ɒˈrækjʊlə] *adj.* □ **1.** oˈrakelhaft (*a. fig.*), Orakel…; **2.** *fig.* weise.

o·ral [ˈɔːrəl] **I** *adj.* □ **1.** mündlich: ***~ contract***; ***~ examination***; **2.** ⚕ oˈral (*a. ling.*), Mund…: ***for ~ use*** zum innerlichen Gebrauch; ***~ intercourse*** Oralverkehr *m*; ***~ stage*** *psych.* orale Phase; **II** *s.* **3.** F mündliche Prüfung.

or·ange [ˈɒrɪndʒ] **I** *s.* ⚘ Oˈrange *f*, Apfelˈsine *f*: ***bitter ~*** Pomeranze *f*; ***squeeze the ~ dry*** F j-n ausquetschen wie e-e Zitrone; **II** *adj.* Orangen…; oˈrange (-farben); ***~ lead*** [led] *s.* ⚙ Oˈrangemennige *f*, Bleisafran *m*; ***~ peel*** *s.* **1.** Oˈrangenschale *f*; **2.** *a.* ***~ effect*** ⚙ Oˈrangenschalenstrukˌtur *f* (*Lackierung*).

or·ange·ry [ˈɒrɪndʒərɪ] *s.* Orangeˈrie *f*.

o·rang-ou·tang [ɔːˌræŋuːˈtæŋ], **oˌrang-uˈtan** [-uːˈtæn] *s. zo.* ˈOrang-ˈUtan *m*.

o·rate [ɔːˈreɪt] *v/i.* **1.** e-e Rede halten; **2.** *humor. u. contp.* (lange) Reden halten *od.* ‚schwingen', reden; **oˈra·tion** [-eɪʃn] *s.* **1.** *förmliche od. feierliche* Rede; **2.** *ling.* (*direkte etc.*) Rede *f*; **or·a·tor** [ˈɒrətə] *s.* **1.** Redner(in); **2.** ⚖ *Am.* Kläger(in) (*in* ***equity****-Prozessen*); **or·a·tor·i·cal** [ˌɒrəˈtɒrɪkl] *adj.* □ rednerisch, Redner…, oraˈtorisch, rheˈtorisch, Rede…; **or·a·to·ri·o** [ˌɒrəˈtɔːrɪəʊ] *pl.* **-ri·os** *s.* ♪ Oraˈtorium *n*; **or·a·tor·ize** [ˈɒrətəraɪz] → ***orate*** 2; **or·a·to·ry** [ˈɒrətərɪ] *s.* **1.** Redekunst *f*, Beredsamkeit *f*, Rheˈtorik *f*; **2.** *eccl.* Kaˈpelle *f*, Andachtsraum *m*.

orb [ɔːb] **I** *s.* **1.** Kugel *f*, Ball *m*; **2.** *poet.* Gestirn *n*, Himmelskörper *m*; **3.** *poet.* a) Augapfel *m*, b) Auge *n*; **4.** *hist.* Reichsapfel *m*; **or·bic·u·lar** [ɔːˈbɪkjʊlə] *adj.* □ **1.** kugelförmig; **2.** rund, kreisförmig; **3.** ringförmig; **or·bit** [ˈɔːbɪt] **I** *s.* **1.** (*ast. etc.* Kreis-, *phys.* Elekˈtronen-) Bahn *f*: ***get into ~*** in e-e Umlaufbahn gelangen (*Erdsatellit*); ***put into ~*** → 5; **2.** *fig.* Bereich *m*, Wirkungskreis *m*; *pol.* Einflußsphäre *f*; **3.** *anat.* a) Augenhöhle *f*, b) Auge *n*; **II** *v/t.* **4.** *die Erde etc.* umˈkreisen; **5.** in e-e ˈUmlaufbahn bringen; **III** *v/i.* **6.** die Erde *etc.* umˈkreisen; **7.** ✈ (über dem Flugplatz) kreisen; ˈ**or·bit·al** [-bɪtl] **I** *adj.* **1.** *anat.* Augenhöhlen…: ***~ cavity*** Augenhöhle *f*; **2.** *ast.*, *phys.* Bahn…: ***~ electron***; **II** *s.* **3.** *Brit.* Ringstraße *f*.

or·chard [ˈɔːtʃəd] *s.* Obstgarten *m*; ˈObstplanˌtage *f*: ***in ~*** mit Obstbäumen bepflanzt; ˈ**or·chard·ing** [-dɪŋ] *s.* **1.** Obstbau *m*; **2.** *coll. Am.* ˈObstkulˌturen *pl.*

or·ches·tic [ɔːˈkestɪk] **I** *adj.* Tanz…; **II** *s. pl.* Orˈchestik *f*.

or·ches·tra [ˈɔːkɪstrə] *s.* **1.** ♪ Orˈchester *n*; **2.** *thea.* a) Orˈchester(raum *m*, -graben *m*) *n*, b) Parˈterre *n*, c) *a.* ***~ stalls*** Parˈkett *n*; **or·ches·tral** [ɔːˈkestrəl] *adj.* ♪ **1.** Orchester…; **2.** orcheˈstral; ˈ**or·ches·trate** [-reɪt] *v/t.* **1.** *a. v/i.* ♪ orchestrieren, instrumentieren; **2.** *fig. Am.* ordnen, aufbauen; **or·ches·tra·tion** [ˌɔːkeˈstreɪʃn] *s.* Instrumentatiˈon *f*.

or·chid [ˈɔːkɪd] *s.* ⚘ Orchiˈdee *f*.

or·chis [ˈɔːkɪs] *pl.* ˈ**or·chis·es** *s.* ⚘ **1.** Orchiˈdee *f*; **2.** Knabenkraut *n*.

or·dain [ɔːˈdeɪn] *v/t.* **1.** *eccl.* ordinieren, (*zum Priester*) weihen; **2.** bestimmen, fügen (*Gott*, *Schicksal*); **3.** anordnen, verfügen.

or·deal [ɔːˈdiːl] *s.* **1.** *hist.* Gottesurteil *n*: ***~ by fire*** Feuerprobe *f*; **2.** *fig.* Zerreiß-, Feuerprobe *f*, schwere Prüfung; **3.** *fig.* Qual *f*, Nervenprobe *f*, Torˈtur *f*, Marˈtyrium *n*.

or·der [ˈɔːdə] **I** *s.* **1.** Ordnung *f*, geordneter Zustand: ***love of ~*** Ordnungsliebe *f*; ***in ~*** in Ordnung (*a. fig.*); ***out of ~*** in Unordnung; → 8; **2.** (öffentliche) Ordnung: ***law and ~*** Ruhe *f* u. Ordnung; **3.** Ordnung *f* (*a.* ⚘ *Kategorie*), Syˈstem *n*: ***social ~*** soziale Ordnung; **4.** (An)Ordnung *f*, Reihenfolge *f*; *ling.* (Satz)Stellung *f*, Wortfolge *f*: ***in alphabetical ~*** in alphabetischer Ordnung; ***~ of priority*** Dringlichkeitsfolge *f*; ***~ of merit*** (*od.* ***precedence***) Rangordnung; **5.** Ordnung *f*, Aufstellung *f*; △ Stil *m*: ***in close*** (***open***) ***~*** ⚔ in geschlossener (geöffneter) Ordnung; ***~ of battle*** a) ⚔ Schlachtordnung, Gefechtsaufstellung, b) ⚓ Gefechtsformation *f*; ***Doric ~*** △ dorische Säulenordnung; **6.** ⚔ vorschriftsmäßige Uniˈform u. Ausrüstung; → ***marching***; **7.** (Geschäfts-) Ordnung *f*: ***standing ~s*** *parl.* feststehende Geschäftsordnung; ***a call to ~*** ein Ordnungsruf *m*; ***call to ~*** zur Ordnung rufen; ***rise to*** (***a point of***) ***~*** zur Geschäftsordnung sprechen; ***℞!, ℞!*** zur Ordnung!; ***in*** (***out of***) ***~*** (un)zulässig; ***~ of the day*** Tagesordnung; → 9; ***be the ~ of the day*** *fig.* an der Tagesordnung sein; ***pass to the ~ of the day*** zur Tagesordnung übergehen; → ***rule*** 15; **8.** Zustand *m*: ***in bad ~*** nicht in Ordnung, in schlechtem Zustand; ***out of ~*** nicht in Ordnung, defekt; ***in running ~*** betriebsfähig; **9.** Befehl *m*, Instruktiˈon *f*, Anordnung *f*: ***℞ in Council*** *pol.* Kabinettsbefehl; ***~ of the day*** ⚔ Tagesbefehl; ***~ for remittance*** Überweisungsauftrag *m*; ***doctor's ~s*** ärztliche Anordnung; ***by ~*** a) befehls-, auftragsgemäß, b) im Auftrag (*vor der Unterschrift*); ***by*** (*od.* ***on the***) ***~ of*** auf Befehl von, im Auftrag von; ***be under ~s to do s.th.*** Befehl haben, et. zu tun; ***till***

further ~s bis auf weiteres; ***in short ~*** *Am.* F sofort; **10.** ⚖ (Gerichts)Beschluß *m*, Befehl *m*, Verfügung *f*; **11.** ⚚ Bestellung *f* (*a. Ware*), Auftrag *m* (***for*** für): ***a large*** (*od.* ***tall***) **~** F e-e (arge) Zumutung, (zu)viel verlangt; ***~s on hand*** Auftragsbestand *m*; ***give*** (*od.* ***place***) ***an ~*** e-n Auftrag erteilen, e-e Bestellung aufgeben; ***make to ~*** a) auf Bestellung anfertigen, b) nach Maß anfertigen; ***shoes made to ~*** Maßschuhe; ***last ~s, please*** Polizeistunde!; **12.** ⚚ Order *f* (*Zahlungsauftrag*): ***pay to s.o.'s ~*** an j-s Order zahlen; ***pay to the ~ of*** für mich an … (*Wechselindossament*); ***payable to ~*** zahlbar an Order; ***own ~*** eigene Order; **13.** → ***post-office order***, ***postal*** I; **14.** A Ordnung *f*, Grad *m*: ***equation of the first ~*** Gleichung *f* ersten Grades; **15.** Größenordnung *f*: ***of*** (*od.* ***in***) ***the ~ of*** in der Größenordnung von; **16.** Art *f*, Rang *m*: ***of a high ~*** von hohem Rang; ***of quite another ~*** von ganz anderer Art; ***on the ~ of*** nach Art von; **17.** (Gesellschafts)Schicht *f*, Klasse *f*, Stand *m*: ***the higher ~s*** die höheren Klassen; ***the military ~*** der Soldatenstand; **18.** Orden *m* (*Gemeinschaft*): ***the Franciscan ~*** *eccl.* der Franziskanerorden; ***the Teutonic ~*** *hist.* der Deutsche (*Ritter-*) Orden; **19.** Orden(szeichen *n*) *m*; → ***Garter*** 2; **20.** *pl. mst* ***holy ~s*** *eccl.* (heilige) Weihen, Priesterweihe *f*: ***take*** (***holy***) ***~s*** die (heiligen) Weihen empfangen; ***major ~s*** höhere Weihen; **21.** Einlaßschein *m*, *thea.* Freikarte *f*; **22.** ***in ~ to*** *inf.* um zu *inf.*; ***in ~ that*** damit; **II** *v/t.* **23.** *j-m od. e-e Sache* befehlen, *et.* anordnen: ***he ~ed him to come*** er befahl ihm zu kommen; **24.** *j-n* schikken, beordern (***to*** nach); **25.** ⚕ *j-m et.* verordnen; **26.** bestellen (*a.* ⚚; *a. im Restaurant*); **27.** regeln, leiten, führen; **28.** ***~ arms!*** ⚔ Gewehr ab!; **29.** ordnen, einrichten: ***~ one's affairs*** s-e Angelegenheiten in Ordnung bringen; **~ a·bout** *v/t.* her'umkommandieren; **~ a·way** *v/t.* **1.** weg-, fortschicken; **2.** abführen lassen; **~ back** *v/t.* zu'rückbeordern; **~ in** *v/t.* her'einkommen lassen; **~ off** *v/t.* *sport* vom Platz stellen; **~ out** *v/t.* **1.** hin'ausbeordern; **2.** hin'ausweisen.

or·der| bill *s.* ⚚ 'Orderpa,pier *n*; **~ bill of lad·ing** *s.* ⚚, ⚓ 'Orderkonnosse,ment *n*; **~ book** *s.* **1.** ⚚ Auftragsbuch *n*; **2.** *Brit. parl.* Liste *f* der angemeldeten Anträge; **~ check** *Am.*, **~ cheque** *Brit. s.* ⚚ Orderscheck *m*; **~ form** *s.* ⚚ Bestellschein *m*; **~ in·stru·ment** *s.* ⚚ 'Orderpa,pier *n*.

or·der·less ['ɔːdəlıs] *adj.* unordentlich, regellos; **'or·der·li·ness** [-lınıs] *s.* **1.** Ordnung *f*, Regelmäßigkeit *f*; **2.** Ordentlichkeit *f*.

or·der·ly ['ɔːdəlı] **I** *adj.* **1.** ordentlich, (wohl)geordnet; **2.** plan-, regelmäßig, me'thodisch; **3.** *fig.* ruhig, friedlich: ***an ~ citizen***; **4.** ⚔ a) im *od.* vom Dienst, diensttuend, b) Ordonnanz…: ***on ~ duty*** auf Ordonnanz; **II** *adv.* **5.** ordnungsgemäß, planmäßig; **III** *s.* **6.** ⚔ a) Ordon'nanz *f*, b) Sani'täter *m*, Krankenträger *m*, c) (Offi'ziers)Bursche *m*; **7.** *allg.* (Kranken)Pfleger *m*; **~ of·fi·cer** *s.* ⚔ **1.** Ordon'nanzoffi,zier *m*; **2.** Offi'zier *m* vom Dienst; **~ room** *s.* ⚔ Schreibstube *f*.

or·der| num·ber *s.* ⚚ Bestellnummer *f*; **~ pad** *s.* ⚚ Bestell(schein)block *m*; **~ pa·per** *s.* **1.** 'Sitzungspro,gramm *n*, (*schriftliche*) Tagesordnung; **2.** ⚚ *Am.* 'Orderpa,pier *n*; **~ slip** *s.* ⚚ Bestellzettel *m*.

or·di·nal ['ɔːdınl] **I** *adj.* **1.** A Ordnungs…, Ordinal…: ***~ number***; **2.** ⚘, *zo.* Ordnungs…; **II** *s.* **3.** A Ordnungszahl *f*; **4.** *eccl.* a) Ordi'nale *n* (*Regelbuch für die Ordinierung anglikanischer Geistlicher*), b) *oft* ≈ Ordi'narium *n* (*Ritualbuch od. Gottesdienstordnung*).

or·di·nance ['ɔːdınəns] *s.* **1.** *amtliche* Verordnung; **2.** *eccl.* (*festgesetzter*) Brauch, Ritus *m*.

or·di·nand [,ɔːdı'nænd] *s. eccl.* Ordi'nandus *m*.

or·di·nar·i·ly ['ɔːdnrılı] *adv.* **1.** nor'malerweise, gewöhnlich; **2.** wie gewöhnlich *od.* üblich.

or·di·nar·y ['ɔːdnrı] **I** *adj.* □ → ***ordinarily***; **1.** gewöhnlich, nor'mal, üblich; **2.** gewöhnlich, mittelmäßig, Durchschnitts…: ***~ face*** Alltagsgesicht *n*; **3.** ständig; ordentlich (*Gericht*, *Mitglied*); **II** *s.* **4.** *das* Übliche, *das* Nor'male: ***nothing out of the ~*** nichts Ungewöhnliches; ***above the ~*** außergewöhnlich; **5.** ***in ~*** ordentlich, von Amts wegen; ***judge in ~*** ordentlicher Richter; ***physician in ~*** (***to a king***) Leibarzt *m* (e-s Königs); **6.** *eccl.* Ordi'narium *n*, Gottesdienst-, Meßordnung *f*; **7.** *a.* ≈ *eccl.* Ordi'narius *m* (*Bischof*); **8.** ⚖ a) ordentlicher Richter, b) *Am.* Nachlaßrichter *m*; **9.** *Brit. obs.* a) Hausmannskost *f*, b) Tagesgericht *n*; **10.** *Brit. obs.* Gaststätte *f*; **~ life in·sur·ance** *s.* Lebensversicherung *f* auf den Todesfall; **~ sea·man** *s.* 'Leichtma,trose *m*; **~ share** *s.* ⚚ Stammaktie *f*.

or·di·nate ['ɔːdnət] *s.* A Ordi'nate *f*.

or·di·na·tion [,ɔːdı'neıʃn] *s.* **1.** *eccl.* Priesterweihe *f*, Ordinati'on *f*; **2.** Ratschluß *m* (*Gottes etc.*).

ord·nance ['ɔːdnəns] *s.* ⚔ **1.** Artille'rie *f*, Geschütze *pl.*: ***a piece of ~*** ein (schweres) Geschütz; ***~ technician*** Feuerwerker *m*; **2.** 'Feldzeugmateri,al *n*; **3.** Feldzeugwesen *n*: ***Royal Army ≈ Corps*** Feldzeugkorps *n* des brit. Heeres; **≈ De·part·ment** *s.* ⚔ Zeug-, Waffenamt *n*; **~ de·pot** *s.* ⚔ 'Feldzeug-, *bsd.* Artille'riede,pot *n*; **~ map** *s.* ⚔ **1.** *Am.* Gene'ralstabskarte *f*; **2.** *Brit.* Meßtischblatt *n*; **~ of·fi·cer** *s.* **1.** ⚓ *Am.* Artille'rieoffi,zier *m*; **2.** Offi'zier *m* der Feldzeugtruppe; **3.** 'Waffenoffi,zier *m*; **~ park** *s.* ⚔ a) Geschützpark *m*, b) Feldzeugpark *m*; **~ ser·geant** *s.* ⚔ 'Waffen-, Ge'räte,unteroffi,zier *m*; **≈ Sur·vey** *s.* amtliche Landesvermessung: ***≈ map*** *Brit.* a) Meßtischblatt *n*, b) (*1:100000*) Generalstabskarte *f*.

or·dure ['ɔː,djʊə] *s.* Kot *m*, Schmutz *m*, Unflat *m* (*a. fig.*).

ore [ɔː] *s.* **1.** Erz *n*; **2.** *poet.* (kostbares) Me'tall; **'~-,bear·ing** *adj. geol.* erzführend, -haltig; **~ bed** *s.* Erzlager *n*.

or·gan ['ɔːgən] *s.* **1.** Or'gan *n*: a) *anat.* Körperwerkzeug *n*: ***~ of sight*** Sehorgan, b) *fig.* Werkzeug *n*, Hilfsmittel *n*, c) Sprachrohr *n* (*Zeitschrift*): ***party ~*** Parteiorgan, d) *laute etc.* Stimme; **2.** ♪ a) Orgel *f*: ***~ stop*** Orgelregister *n*, b) Kla'vier *n* (*e-r Orgel*), c) *a.* ***American ~ Art*** Har'monium *n*, d) → ***barrel-organ***: ***~-grinder*** Leier(kasten)mann *m*.

or·gan·die, **or·gan·dy** ['ɔːgəndı] *s.* Or'gandy *m* (*Baumwollgewebe*).

or·gan·ic [ɔː'gænık] *adj.* (□ ***~ally***) *allg.* **1.** or'ganisch; **2.** bio'logisch-or'ganisch: ***~ vegetables***; **~ chem·is·try** *s.* or'ganische Che'mie; **~ dis·ease** *s.* ⚕ or'ganische Krankheit; **~ e·lec·tric·i·ty** *s.* *zo.* tierische Elektrizi'tät; **~ law** *s. pol.* Grundgesetz *n*.

or·gan·ism ['ɔːgənızəm] *s. biol. u. fig.* Orga'nismus *m*.

or·gan·ist ['ɔːgənıst] *s.* ♪ Orga'nist(in).

or·gan·i·za·tion [,ɔːgənaı'zeıʃn] *s.* **1.** Organisati'on *f*: a) Organisierung *f*, Bildung *f*, Gründung *f*, b) (syste'matischer) Aufbau, Gliederung *f*, (Aus)Gestaltung *f*, c) Zs.-schluß *m*, Verband *m*, Gesellschaft *f*: ***administrative ~*** Verwaltungsapparat *m*; **2.** Orga'nismus *m*, Sy'stem *n*; **,or·gan·i'za·tion·al** [-ʃənl] *adj.* organisa'torisch; **or·gan·ize** ['ɔːgənaız] **I** *v/t.* **1.** organisieren: a) aufbauen, einrichten, b) gründen, ins Leben rufen, c) veranstalten, *sport a.* ausrichten: ***~d tour*** Gesellschaftsreise *f*, d) gestalten; **2.** in ein Sy'stem bringen; **3.** (gewerkschaftlich) organisieren: ***~d labo(u)r***; **II** *v/i.* **4.** sich organisieren; **or·gan·iz·er** ['ɔːgənaızə] *s.* Organi'sator *m*; Veranstalter *m*, *sport a.* Ausrichter *m*; ⚖ Gründer *m*.

or·gan loft *s.* △ Orgelchor *m*.

or·gan·zine ['ɔːgənziːn] *s.* Organ'sin (-seide *f*) *m*, *n*.

or·gasm ['ɔːgæzəm] *s. physiol.* **1.** Or'gasmus *m*, (sexu'eller) Höhepunkt; **2.** heftige Erregung; **or·gi·as·tic** [,ɔːdʒı'æstık] *adj.* orgi'astisch; **or·gy** ['ɔːdʒı] *s.* Orgie *f*.

o·ri·el ['ɔːrıəl] *s.* △ Erker *m*.

o·ri·ent ['ɔːrıənt] **I** *s.* **1.** Osten *m*; **2.** ***the ≈*** der (Ferne) Osten, der Orient; **II** *adj.* **3.** aufgehend (*Sonne*); **4.** östlich; **5.** glänzend; **III** *v/t.* [-ıent] **6.** orientieren, die Lage *od.* die Richtung bestimmen von, orten; *Landkarte* einnorden; *Instrument* einstellen; *Kirche* osten; **7.** *fig.* *geistig* (aus)richten, orientieren (***by*** an *dat.*): ***profit-~ed*** gewinnorientiert; **8.** ***~ o.s.*** sich orientieren (***by*** an *dat.*), sich zu'rechtfinden, sich informieren; **o·ri·en·tal** [,ɔːrı'entl] **I** *adj.* **1.** östlich; **2.** *mst* ≈ orien'talisch, *bsd. Am. a.* ostasiatisch, östlich; **II** *s.* **3.** Orien'tale *m*, Orien'talin *f*, *bsd. Am. a.* Ostasiat(in); **o·ri·en·tal·ist** [,ɔːrı'entəlıst] *s.* Orienta'list(in); **o·ri·en·tate** ['ɔːrıenteıt] → ***orient*** 6, 7, 8; **o·ri·en·ta·tion** [,ɔːrıen'teıʃn] *s.* **1.** △ Ostung *f* (*Kirche*); **2.** Anlage *f*, Richtung *f*; **3.** Orientierung *f* (*a.* ✈ *u. fig.*), Ortung *f*; Ausrichtung *f* (*a. fig.*); **4.** *a. fig.* Orientierung *f*, (Sich-) Zu'rechtfinden *n*: ***~ course*** Einführungskurs *m*; **5.** Orientierungssinn *m*; **or·i·en·teer·ing** [,ɔːrıen'tıːrıŋ] *s.* Orientierungslauf *m*.

or·i·fice ['ɒrıfıs] *s.* Öffnung *f* (*a. anat.*, ⚙), Mündung *f*.

or·i·flamme ['ɒrıflæm] *s.* Banner *n*, Fahne *f*; *fig.* Fa'nal *n*.

or·i·gin ['ɒrıdʒın] *s.* **1.** Ursprung *f*: a) Quelle *f*, b) *fig.* Herkunft *f*, Abstammung *f*: ***certificate of ~*** ⚚ Ursprungszeugnis *n*; ***country of ~*** ✝ Ursprungsland *n*, c) Anfang *m*, Entstehung *f*: ***the ~ of species*** der Ursprung der Arten; **2.** ⩓ Koordi'natenursprung *m*, -nullpunkt *m*.

o·rig·i·nal [ə'rɪdʒənl] **I** *adj.* □ → ***originally***; **1.** origi'nal, Original…, Ur…, ursprünglich, echt: ***the ~ text*** der Urod. Originaltext; **2.** erst, ursprünglich, Ur…: ***~ bill*** ✝ *Am.* Primawechsel *m*; ***~ capital*** ✝ Gründungskapital *n*; ***~ copy*** Erstausfertigung *f*; ***~ cost*** ✝ Selbstkosten *pl.*; ***~ inhabitants*** Ureinwohner; ***~ jurisdiction*** ⚖ erstinstanzliche Zuständigkeit; ***~ share*** ✝ Stammaktie *f*; → ***sin*** 1; **3.** origi'nell, neu(artig); ***an ~ idea***; **4.** schöpferisch, ursprünglich: ***~ genius*** Originalgenie *n*, Schöpfergeist *m*; ***~ thinker*** selbständiger Geist; **5.** urwüchsig, Ur…: ***~ nature*** Urnatur *f*; **II** *s.* **6.** Origi'nal *n*: a) Urbild *n*, -stück *n*, b) Urfassung *f*, -text *m*: ***in the ~*** im Original, im Urtext, ⚖ urschriftlich; **7.** Original *n* (*Mensch*); **8.** ⚘, *zo.* Stammform *f*; **o·rig·i·nal·i·ty** [ə'rɪdʒə'nælətɪ] *s.* **1.** Originali'tät *f*: a) Ursprünglichkeit *f*, Echtheit *f*, b) Eigenart *f*, origi'neller Cha'rakter, c) Neuheit *f*; **2.** *das* Schöpferische; **o'rig·i·nal·ly** [-dʒənəlɪ] *adv.* **1.** ursprünglich, zu'erst; **2.** hauptsächlich, eigentlich; **3.** von Anfang an, schon immer; **4.** origi'nell.

o·rig·i·nate [ə'rɪdʒəneɪt] **I** *v/i.* **1.** (***from***) entstehen (aus), s-n Ursprung haben (in *dat.*), herrühren (von *od.* aus); **2.** (***with***, ***from***) ausgehen (von *j-m*); **II** *v/t.* **3.** her'vorbringen, verursachen, erzeugen, schaffen; **4.** den Anfang machen mit, den Grund legen zu; **o·rig·i·na·tion** [əˌrɪdʒə'neɪʃn] *s.* **1.** Her'vorbringung *f*, Schaffung *f*, Veranlassung *f*; **2.** → ***origin*** 1 b *u.* c; **o'rig·i·na·tive** [-tɪv] *adj.* schöpferisch; **o'rig·i·na·tor** [-tə] *s.* Urheber(in), Begründer(in), Schöpfer(in).

o·ri·ole ['ɔːrɪəʊl] *s. orn.* Pi'rol *m*.

or·mo·lu ['ɔːməʊluː] *s.* a) Malergold *n*, b) Goldbronze *f*.

or·na·ment **I** *s.* ['ɔːnəmənt] Orna'ment *n*, Verzierung *f* (*a.* ♪), Schmuck *m*; *fig.* Zier(de) *f* (***to*** für *od. gen.*): ***rich in ~*** reich verziert; **II** *v/t.* [-ment] verzieren, schmücken; **or·na·men·tal** [ˌɔːnə'mentl] *adj.* □ ornamen'tal, schmükkend, dekora'tiv, Zier…: ***~ castings*** ⚙ Kunstguß *m*; ***~ plants*** Zierpflanzen; ***~ type*** Zierschrift *f*; **or·na·men·ta·tion** [ˌɔːnəmen'teɪʃn] *s.* Ornamentierung *f*, Verzierung *f*.

or·nate [ɔː'neɪt] *adj.* □ **1.** reich verziert; **2.** über'laden (*Stil etc.*); blumig (*Sprache*).

or·ni·tho·log·i·cal [ˌɔːnɪθə'lɒdʒɪkl] *adj.* □ ornitho'logisch; **or·ni·thol·o·gist** [ˌɔːnɪ'θɒlədʒɪst] *s.* Ornitho'loge *m*; **or·ni·thol·o·gy** [ˌɔːnɪ'θɒlədʒɪ] *s.* Ornitholo'gie *f*, Vogelkunde *f*; **or·ni·thop·ter** [ˌɔːnɪ'θɒptə] *s.* ✈ Schwingenflügler *m*; **ˌor·ni·tho'rhyn·chus** [-ə'rɪŋkəs] *s. zo.* Schnabeltier *n*.

o·rol·o·gy [ɒ'rɒlədʒɪ] *s.* Gebirgskunde *f*.

o·ro·pha·ryn·ge·al ['ɔːrəʊˌfærɪn'dʒiːəl] *adj.* ⚕ Mundrachen…

o·ro·tund ['ɔːrəʊtʌnd] *adj.* **1.** volltönend; **2.** bom'bastisch (*Stil*).

or·phan ['ɔːfn] **I** *s.* **1.** (Voll)Waise *f*, Waisenkind *n*: ***~s' home*** → ***orphanage*** 1; **II** *adj.* **2.** Waisen…: ***an ~ child***; **III** *v/t.* **3.** zur Waise machen: ***be ~ed*** (zur) Waise werden, verwaisen; **or·phan·age** ['ɔːfənɪdʒ] *s.* **1.** Waisenheim *n*, -haus *n*; **2.** Verwaistheit *f*; **or·phan·ize** ['ɔːfnaɪz] *v/t.* → ***orphan*** 3.

or·rer·y ['ɒrərɪ] *s.* Plane'tarium *n*.

or·tho·chro·mat·ic [ˌɔːθəʊkrəʊ'mætɪk] *adj. phot.* orthochro'matisch, farb(wert)richtig.

or·tho·don·ti·a [ˌɔːθəʊ'dɒnʃɪə] *s.* ⚕ 'Kieferorthopäˌdie *f*.

or·tho·dox ['ɔːθədɒks] *adj.* □ **1.** *eccl.* ortho'dox: a) streng-, recht-, altgläubig, b) ℒ 'griechisch-ortho'dox: ℒ ***Church***; **2.** *fig.* ortho'dox: a) streng: ***an ~ opinion***, b) anerkannt, üblich, konventio'nell; **'or·tho·dox·y** [-ksɪ] *s. eccl.* Ortho'do'xie *f* (*a. fig. orthodoxes Denken*).

or·thog·o·nal [ɔː'θɒgənl] *adj.* ⩓ ortho'go'nal, rechtwink(e)lig.

or·tho·graph·ic, **or·tho·graph·i·cal** [ˌɔːθəʊ'græfɪk(l)] *adj.* □ **1.** ortho'graphisch; **2.** ⩓ senkrecht, rechtwink(e)lig; **or·thog·ra·phy** [ɔː'θɒgrəfɪ] *s.* Orthogra'phie *f*, Rechtschreibung *f*.

or·tho·p(a)e·dic [ˌɔːθəʊ'piːdɪk] *adj.* ⚕ ortho'pädisch; **ˌor·tho'p(a)e·dics** [-ks] *s. pl. oft sg. konstr.* Orthopä'die *f*; **ˌor·tho'p(a)e·dist** [-ɪst] *s.* Ortho'päde *m*; **or·tho·p(a)e·dy** ['ɔːθəʊpiːdɪ] → ***orthop(a)edics***.

or·thop·ter [ɔː'θɒptə] *s.* **1.** ✈ → ***ornithopter***; **2.** → **or'thop·ter·on** [-ərɒn] *s. zo.* Geradflügler *m*.

or·tho·scope ['ɔːθəʊskəʊp] *s.* ⚕ Ortho'skop *n*.

Os·car ['ɒskə] *s.* Oskar *m* (*Filmpreis*).

os·cil·late ['ɒsɪleɪt] **I** *v/i.* **1.** oszillieren, schwingen, pendeln, vibrieren: ***oscillating axle*** *mot.* Schwingachse *f*; ***oscillating circuit*** ⚡ Schwingkreis *m*; **2.** *fig.* (hin- u. her) schwanken; **II** *v/t.* **3.** in Schwingungen versetzen; **os·cil·la·tion** [ˌɒsɪ'leɪʃn] *s.* **1.** Oszillati'on *f*, Schwingung *f*, Pendelbewegung *f*, Schwankung *f*; **2.** *fig.* Schwanken *n*; **3.** ⚡ a) Ladungswechsel *m*, b) Stoßspannung *f*, c) Peri'ode *f*; **'os·cil·la·tor** [-tə] *s.* ⚡ Oszil'lator *m*; **'os·cil·la·to·ry** [-lətərɪ] *adj.* oszilla'torisch, schwingend, schwingungsfähig: ***~ circuit*** ⚡ Schwingkreis *m*; **os·cil·lo·graph** [ə'sɪləʊgrɑːf] *s.* Oszillo'graph *m*; **os·cil·lo·scope** [ə'sɪləʊskəʊp] *s. phys.*, ⚡ Oszillo'skop *n*.

os·cu·late ['ɒskjʊleɪt] *v/t. u. v/i.* **1.** *humor.* (sich) küssen; **2.** ⩓ oskulieren.

o·sier ['əʊʒə] *s.* ⚘ Korbweide *f*: ***~ basket*** Weidenkorb *m*; ***~ furniture*** Korbmöbel *pl*.

os·mic ['ɒzmɪk] *adj.* ⚗ Osmium…

os·mo·sis [ɒz'məʊsɪs] *s. phys.* Os'mose *f*; **os·mot·ic** [ɒz'mɒtɪk] *adj.* (□ ***~ally***) os'motisch.

os·prey ['ɒsprɪ] *s.* **1.** *orn.* Fischadler *m*; **2.** ✝ Reiherfederbusch *m*.

os·se·in ['ɒsɪɪn] *s. biol.*, ⚗ Knochenleim *m*.

os·se·ous ['ɒsɪəs] *adj.* knöchern, Knochen…; **os·si·cle** ['ɒsɪkl] *s. anat.* Knöchelchen *n*; **os·si·fi·ca·tion** [ˌɒsɪfɪ'keɪʃn] Verknöcherung *f*; **os·si·fied** ['ɒsɪfaɪd] *adj.* verknöchert (*a. fig.*); **os·si·fy** ['ɒsɪfaɪ] **I** *v/t.* **1.** verknöchern (lassen); **2.** *fig.* verknöchern; (*in Konventionen*) erstarren lassen; **II** *v/i.* **3.** verknöchern; **4.** *fig.* verknöchern, (in Konventi'onen) erstarren; **os·su·ar·y** ['ɒsjʊərɪ] *s.* Beinhaus *n*.

os·te·i·tis [ˌɒstɪ'aɪtɪs] *s.* ⚕ Knochenentzündung *f*.

os·ten·si·ble [ɒ'stensəbl] *adj.* □ **1.** scheinbar; **2.** an-, vorgeblich: ***~ partner*** ✝ Strohmann *m*.

os·ten·ta·tion [ˌɒsten'teɪʃn] *s.* **1.** (protzige) Schaustellung; **2.** Protze'rei *f*, Prahle'rei *f*; **3.** Gepränge *n*; **ˌos·ten'ta·tious** [-ʃəs] *adj.* □ **1.** großtuerisch, prahlerisch, prunkend; **2.** (*absichtlich*) auffällig, ostenta'tiv, betont; **ˌos·ten'ta·tious·ness** [-ʃəsnɪs] → ***ostentation***.

os·te·o·blast ['ɒstɪəʊblɑːst] *s. biol.* Knochenbildner *m*; **os·te·oc·la·sis** [ˌɒstɪ'ɒkləsɪs] *s.* ⚕ (opera'tive) 'Knochenfrakˌtur; **os·te·ol·o·gy** [ˌɒstɪ'ɒlədʒɪ] *s.* Knochenlehre *f*; **os·te·o·ma** [ˌɒstɪ'əʊmə] *s.* ⚕ Oste'om *n*, gutartige Knochengeschwulst; **os·te·o·ma·la·ci·a** [ˌɒstɪəʊmə'leɪʃɪə] *s.* ⚕ Knochenerweichung *f*; **'os·te·o·path** [-ɪəʊpæθ] *s.* ⚕ Osteo'path *m*.

ost·ler ['ɒslə] *s.* Stallknecht *m*.

os·tra·cism ['ɒstrəsɪzəm] *s.* **1.** *antiq.* Scherbengericht *n*; **2.** *fig.* a) Verbannung *f*, b) Ächtung *f*; **'os·tra·cize** [-saɪz] *v/t.* **1.** verbannen (*a. fig.*); **2.** *fig.* ächten, (aus der Gesellschaft) ausstoßen, verfemen.

os·trich ['ɒstrɪtʃ] *s. orn.* Strauß *m*; **~ pol·i·cy** *s.* Vogel-'Strauß-Poliˌtik *f*.

oth·er ['ʌðə] **I** *adj.* **1.** ander; **2.** (*vor s. im pl.*) andere, übrige: ***the ~ guests***; **3.** ander, weiter, sonstig: ***one ~ person*** e-e weitere Person, (noch) j-d anders; **4.** anders (***than*** als): ***no person ~ than yourself*** niemand außer dir; **5.** (***from***, ***than***) anders (als), verschieden (von); **6.** zweit (*nur in*): ***every ~*** jeder (jede, jedes) zweite; ***every ~ day*** jeden zweiten Tag; **7.** (*nur in*): ***the ~ day*** neulich, kürzlich; ***the ~ night*** neulich abends; **II** *pron.* **8.** ander: ***the ~*** der (die, das) andere; ***each ~*** einander; ***the two ~s*** die beiden anderen; ***of all ~s*** vor allen anderen; ***no*** (*od.* ***none***) ***~ than*** kein anderer als; ***some day*** (*od.* ***time***) ***or ~*** eines Tages, irgendeinmal; ***some way or ~*** irgendwie, auf irgendeine Weise; → ***someone*** I; **III** *adv.* **9.** anders (***than*** als); **'~·wise** [-waɪz] *adv.* **1.** (*a. cj.*) sonst, andernfalls; **2.** sonst, im übrigen: ***stupid but ~ harmless***; **3.** anderweitig: ***~ occupied***; ***unless you are ~ engaged*** wenn du nichts anderes vorhast; **4.** anders (***than*** als): ***we think ~*** wir denken anders; ***berries edible and ~*** eßbare u. nicht eßbare Beeren; **ˌ~'world** *adj.* jenseitig; **ˌ~'world·ly** *adj.* **1.** jenseitig, Jenseits…; **2.** auf das Jenseits gerichtet; **3.** weltfremd.

o·ti·ose ['əʊʃɪəʊs] *adj.* □ müßig: a) untätig, b) zwecklos.

o·to·lar·yn·gol·o·gist ['əʊtəʊˌlærɪŋ'gɒlədʒɪst] *s.* ⚕ Hals-Nasen-Ohren-Arzt *m*; **o·tol·o·gy** [əʊ'tɒlədʒɪ] *s.* Ohrenheilkunde *f*; **o·to·rhi·no·lar·yn·gol·o·gist** ['əʊtəʊˌraɪnəʊˌlærɪŋ'gɒlədʒɪst] → ***otolaryngologist***; **o·to·scope** ['əʊtəskəʊp] *s.* ⚕ Ohr(en)spiegel *m*.

ot·ter ['ɒtə] *s.* **1.** *zo.* Otter *m*; **2.** Otterfell *n*, -pelz *m*; **'~·hound** *s. hunt.* Otterhund *m*.

Ot·to·man ['ɒtəʊmən] **I** *adj.* **1.** os'manisch, türkisch; **II** *s. pl.* **-mans 2.** Os'mane *m*, Türke *m*; **3.** ~ Otto'mane *f* (*Sofa*).

ouch [aʊtʃ] *int.* autsch!, au!

ought¹ [ɔːt] **I** *v/aux. ich, er, sie, es* sollte, *du* solltest, *ihr* solltet, *wir, sie, Sie* sollten: ***he ~ to do it*** er sollte es (eigentlich) tun; ***he ~ (not) to have seen it*** er hätte es (nicht) sehen sollen; ***you ~ to have known better*** du hättest es besser wissen sollen *od.* müssen; **II** *s.* (mo'ralische) Pflicht.

ought² [ɔːt] *s.* Null *f*.

ought³ [ɔːt] → ***aught***.

ounce¹ [aʊns] *s.* **1.** Unze *f* (*28,35 g*): ***by the ~*** nach (dem) Gewicht; **2.** *fig. ein* bißchen, Körnchen *n* (*Wahrheit etc.*): ***an ~ of practice is worth a pound of theory*** Probieren geht über Studieren.

ounce² [aʊns] *s.* **1.** *zo.* Irbis *m* (*Schneeleopard*); **2.** *poet.* Luchs *m*.

our ['aʊə] *poss. adj.* unser: ***~ Father*** *das* Vaterunser; **ours** ['aʊəz] *poss. pron.* **1.** *der* (*die, das*) uns(e)re: ***I like ~ better*** mir gefällt das unsere besser; ***a friend of ~*** ein Freund von uns; ***this world of ~*** diese unsere Welt; ***~ is a small group*** unsere Gruppe ist klein; **2.** unser, *der* (*die, das*) uns(e)re: ***it is ~*** es gehört uns, es ist unser; **ˌour'self** *pron.*: ***We ~*** Wir höchstselbst; **ˌour'selves** *pron.* **1.** *refl.* uns (selbst): ***we blame ~*** wir geben uns (selbst) die Schuld; **2.** (wir) selbst: ***let us do it ~***; **3.** uns (selbst): ***good for the others, not for ~*** gut für die andern, nicht für uns (selbst).

oust [aʊst] *v/t.* **1.** vertreiben, entfernen, verdrängen, hin'auswerfen (***from*** aus): ***~ s.o. from office***; ***~ from the market*** ♰ vom Markt verdrängen; **2.** ⚖ enteignen, um den Besitz bringen; **3.** berauben (***of*** *gen.*); **'oust·er** [-tə] *s.* ⚖ a) Enteignung *f*, b) Besitzvorenthaltung *f*.

out [aʊt] **I** *adv.* **1.** (*a. in Zssgn mit vb.*) hin'aus (*-gehen, -werfen etc.*), her'aus (*-kommen, -schauen etc.*), aus (*-brechen, -pumpen, -sterben etc.*): ***voyage ~*** Ausreise *f*; ***way ~*** Ausgang *m*; ***on the way ~*** beim Hinausgehen; ***~ with him!*** hinaus mit ihm!; ***~ with it!*** hinaus *od.* heraus damit!; ***have a tooth ~*** sich e-n Zahn ziehen lassen; ***insure ~ and home*** ♰ hin u. zurück versichern; ***have it ~ with s.o.*** *fig.* die Sache mit j-m ausfechten; ***that's ~!*** das kommt nicht in Frage!; **2.** außen, draußen, fort: ***some way ~*** ein Stück draußen; ***he is ~*** er ist draußen; **3.** nicht zu Hause, ausgegangen: ***be ~ on business*** geschäftlich verreist sein; ***a day ~*** ein freier Tag; ***an evening ~*** ein Ausgeh-Abend *m*; ***be ~ on account of illness*** wegen Krankheit der Arbeit fernbleiben; **4.** ausständig (*Arbeiter*): ***be ~*** streiken; **5.** a) ins Freie, b) draußen, im Freien, c) ⚓ draußen, auf See, d) ⚔ im Felde; **6.** a) ausgeliehen (*Buch*), b) verliehen (*Geld*), c) verpachtet, vermietet, d) (*aus dem Gefängnis etc.*) entlassen; **7.** her'aus *sein*: a) (***just***) ***~*** (soeben) erschienen (*Buch*), b) in Blüte (*Blumen*), entfaltet (*Blüte*), c) ausgeschlüpft (*Küken*), d) verrenkt (*Glied*), e) *fig.* enthüllt (*Geheimnis*): ***the girl is not yet ~*** das Mädchen ist noch nicht in die Gesellschaft eingeführt (worden); → ***blood*** 3, ***murder*** 1; **8.** *sport* aus, draußen: a) nicht (mehr) im Spiel, b) im Aus; **9.** *Boxen*: ausgezählt, kampfunfähig; **10.** *pol.* draußen, raus, nicht (mehr) im Amt, nicht (mehr) am Ruder; **11.** aus der Mode; **12.** aus, vor'bei (*zu Ende*): ***before the week is ~*** vor Ende der Woche; **13.** aus, erloschen (*Feuer, Licht*); **14.** aus(gegangen), verbraucht: ***the potatoes are ~***; **15.** aus der Übung: ***my hand is ~***; **16.** zu Ende, bis zum Ende, ganz: ***hear s.o. ~*** j-n bis zum Ende *od.* ganz anhören; **17.** ausgetreten, über die Ufer getreten (*Fluß*); **18.** löch(e)rig, 'durchgescheuert; → ***elbow*** 1; **19.** ärmer um *1 Dollar etc.*; **20.** unrichtig, im Irrtum (befangen): ***his calculations are ~*** s-e Berechnungen stimmen nicht; ***be (far) ~*** sich (gewaltig) irren, (ganz) auf dem Holzweg sein; **21.** entzweit, verkracht: ***be ~ with s.o.***; **22.** laut *lachen etc.*; **23.** ***~ for*** auf *e-e Sache* aus, auf der Jagd *od.* Suche nach: ***~ for prey*** auf Raub aus; **24.** ***~ to do s.th.*** darauf aus, et. zu tun; **25.** (*bsd. nach sup.*) *das Beste etc.* weit u. breit; **26.** ***~ and about*** (wieder) auf den Beinen; ***~ and away*** bei weitem; ***~ and ~*** durch u. durch; ***~ of*** → 31; **II** *adj.* **27.** Außen...: ***~ edge***; ***~ party*** Oppositionspartei *f*; **28.** *sport* auswärtig, Auswärts... (*-spiel*); **29.** *Kricket*: nicht schlagend: ***~ side*** → 34; **30.** 'übernorˌmal, Über...; → ***outsize***; **III** *prp.* **31.** ***~ of*** a) aus (... her'aus), zu ... hin'aus, b) *fig.* aus *Furcht, Mitleid etc.*, c) aus, von: ***two ~ of three*** zwei von drei *Personen etc.*, d) außerhalb, außer *Reichweite, Sicht etc.*, e) außer *Atem, Übung etc.*, ohne: ***be ~ of s.th.*** et. nicht (mehr) haben, ohne et. sein; → ***money*** 1, ***work*** 1, f) aus *der Mode, Richtung etc.*, nicht gemäß: ***~ of drawing*** verzeichnet; → ***focus*** 1, ***hand*** *Redew.*, ***question*** 4, g) außerhalb (*gen. od.* von): ***6 miles ~ of Oxford***; ***~ of doors*** im Freien, ins Freie; ***be ~ of it*** nicht dabeisein (dürfen); ***feel ~ of it*** sich ausgeschlossen *od.* nicht zugehörig fühlen, h) um *et. betrügen*: ***cheat s.o. ~ of s.th.***, i) aus, von: ***get s.th. ~ of s.o.*** et. von j-m bekommen; ***he got more (pleasure) ~ of it*** er hatte mehr davon, j) *hergestellt* aus: ***made ~ of paper***; **IV** *s.* **32.** *typ.* Auslassung *f*, ‚Leiche' *f*; **33.** *Tennis etc.*: Ausball *m*; **34.** ***the ~s*** *Kricket etc.*: die 'Feldparˌtei; **35.** ***the ~s*** *parl.* die Oppositi'on; **36.** *Am.* F Ausweg *m*, Schlupfloch *n*; **37.** → ***outage*** 2; **V** *v/t.* **38.** F rausschmeißen; **39.** *sport*: a) *den Gegner* ausschalten, b) *Boxen*: k.'o. schlagen, c) *Tennis*: *Ball* ins Aus schlagen; **VI** *int.* **40.** hin'aus!, raus!

ˌout'act *v/t. thea. etc. j-n* ‚an die Wand spielen'.

out·age ['aʊtɪdʒ] *s.* **1.** fehlende Menge; **2.** ⚙ (Strom- *etc.*)Ausfall *m*.

ˌout|-and-'out *adj.* abso'lut, völlig: ***an ~ villain*** ein Erzschurke; **ˌ~-and-'out·er** *s. sl.* **1.** 'Hundertproˌzentige(r *m*) *f*, ‚Waschechte(r' *m*) *f*; **2.** *et.* 'Hundertproˌzentiges *od.* ganz Typisches *s-r Art*; **'~·back** *s.* (*bsd. der* australische) Busch, *das* Hinterland; **ˌ~'bal·ance** *v/t.* über'wiegen; **ˌ~'bid** *v/t.* [*irr.* → ***bid***] über'bieten (*a. fig.*); **'~·board** ⚓ **I** *adj.* Außenbord...: ***~ motor***; **II** *adv.* außenbords; **'~·bound** *adj.* **1.** ⚓ nach auswärts bestimmt *od.* fahrend, auslaufend, ausgehend; **2.** ✈ im Abflug; **3.** ♰ nach dem Ausland bestimmt; **ˌ~'box** *v/t. j-n* ausboxen, *im Boxen* schlagen; **ˌ~'brave** *v/t.* **1.** trotzen (*dat.*); **2.** an Kühnheit *od.* Glanz über'treffen; **'~·break** *s. allg.* Ausbruch *m*; **'~ˌbuild·ing** *s.* Außen-, Nebengebäude *n*; **'~·burst** *s.* Ausbruch *m* (*a. fig.*); **'~·cast I** *adj.* **1.** ausgestoßen, verstoßen; **II** *s.* **2.** Ausgestoßene(r *m*) *f*; **3.** Abfall *m*, Ausschuß *m*; **ˌ~'class** *v/t. j-m* weit über'legen sein, *j-n* weit über'treffen, *sport a. j-n* deklassieren; **'~ˌclear·ing** *s.* ♰ Gesamtbetrag *m* der Wechsel- u. Scheckforderungen e-r Bank an das ***Clearing-House***; **'~·come** *s.* Ergebnis *n*, Resul'tat *n*, Folge *f*; **'~·crop I** *s.* **1.** *geol.* a) Zu'tageliegen *n*, Anstehen *n*, b) Anstehendes *n*, Ausbiß *m*; **2.** *fig.* Zu'tagetreten *n*; **II** *v/i.* **ˌout'crop 3.** *geol.* zu'tage liegen *od.* treten (*a. fig.*); **'~·cry** *s.* Aufschrei *m*, Schrei *m* der Entrüstung; **ˌ~'dat·ed** *adj.* über'holt, veraltet; **ˌ~'dis·tance** *v/t.* (weit) über'holen *od.* hinter sich lassen (*a. fig.*); **ˌ~'do** *v/t.* [*irr.* → ***do¹***] über'treffen (***o.s.*** sich selbst); **'~·door** *adj.* Außen..., draußen, außerhalb des Hauses, im Freien: ***~ aerial*** Außen-, Hochantenne *f*; ***~ dress*** Ausgehanzug *m*; ***~ exercise*** Bewegung *f* im Freien; ***~ performance*** *thea.* Freilichtaufführung *f*; ***~ season*** *bsd. sport* Freiluftsaison *f*; ***~ shot*** *phot.* Außen-, Freilichtaufnahme *f*; **ˌ~'doors I** *adv.* **1.** draußen, im Freien; **2.** hin'aus, ins Freie; **II** *adj.* **3.** → ***outdoor***; **III** *s.* **4.** das Freie; die freie Na'tur.

out·er ['aʊtə] *adj.* Außen...: ***~ garments***, ***~ wear*** Oberbekleidung *f*; ***~ cover*** ✈ Außenhaut *f*; ***~ diameter*** äußerer Durchmesser; ***~ harbo(u)r*** ⚓ Außenhafen *m*; ***the ~ man*** der äußere Mensch; ***~ skin*** Oberhaut *f*, Epidermis *f*; ***~ space*** Weltraum *m*; ***~ surface*** Außenfläche *f*, -seite *f*; ***~ world*** Außenwelt *f*; **'~·most** *adj.* äußerst.

ˌout|'face *v/t.* **1.** Trotz bieten (*dat.*), mutig *od.* gefaßt begegnen (*dat.*): ***~ a situation*** e-r Lage Herr werden; **2.** *j-n* mit Blicken aus der Fassung bringen; **'~·fall** *s.* Mündung *f*; **'~·field** *s.* **1.** *Baseball u. Kricket*: a) Außenfeld *n*, b) Außenfeldspieler *pl.*; **2.** *fig.* fernes Gebiet; **3.** weitabliegende Felder *pl.* (*e-r Farm*); **'~ˌfield·er** *s.* Außenfeldspieler(in); **ˌ~'fight** *v/t.* niederkämpfen, schlagen; **'~ˌfight·er** *s.* Di'stanzboxer *m*; **'~·fit I** *s.* **1.** Ausrüstung *f*, -stattung *f*: ***travel(l)ing ~***; ***~ of tools*** Werkzeug *n*; ***cooking ~*** Kochutensilien *pl.*; ***puncture ~*** Reifenflickzeug *n*; ***the whole ~*** F der ganze Kram; **2.** F a) ⚔ Einheit *f*, ‚Haufen' *m*, b) Gruppe *f*, c) F ‚Verein' *m*, ‚Laden' *m*, Gesellschaft *f*; **II** *v/t.* **3.** ausrüsten, -statten; **'~ˌfit·ter** *s.* ♰ **1.** 'Ausrüstungsliefer ˌant *m*; **2.** Herrenausstatter *m*; **3.** (Fach)Händler *m*: ***electrical ~*** Elektrohändler; **ˌ~'flank** *v/t.* **1.** ⚔ die Flanke um'fassen von: ***~ing attack*** Umfassungsangriff *m*; **2.** *fig.* über'listen; **'~·flow** *s.* Ausfluß *m* (*a.* ⚕): ***~ of gold*** ♰ Goldabfluß *m*; **ˌ~'gen·er·al** → ***outmanoeuvre***; **ˌ~'go I** *v/t.* [*irr.* → ***go***] *fig.* über'treffen; über'listen; **II** *s.* **'outgo** *pl.* **'~·goes** ♰ Ausgaben *pl.*; **ˌ~'go-**

ing I *adj.* weggehend; 🚂, ⚓, *teleph. etc.* abgehend (*a. Verkehr*, ⚡, *Strom*); ausziehend (*Mieter*); zu'rückgehend (*Flut*); abtretend (*Regierung*): **~ *mail*** Postausgang *m*; **II** *s.* Ausgehen *n*; *pl.* † Ausgaben *pl.*; **'~·group** *s.* Fremdgruppe *f*; **ˌ~'grow** *v/t.* [*irr.* → ***grow***] **1.** schneller wachsen als, hin'auswachsen über (*acc.*); **2.** *j-m* über den Kopf wachsen; **3.** her'auswachsen aus *Kleidern*; **4.** *fig. Gewohnheit etc.* (mit der Zeit) ablegen, her'auswachsen aus; **'~·growth** *s.* **1.** na'türliche Folge, Ergebnis *n*; **2.** Nebenerscheinung *f*; **3.** ⚕ Auswuchs *m*; **'~·guard** *s.* ⚔ Vorposten *m*, Feldwache *f*; **ˌ~-'Her·od** [-'herəd] *v/t.*: **~ *Herod*** der schlimmste Tyrann sein; **'~·house** *s.* **1.** Nebengebäude *n*, Schuppen *m*; **2.** *Am.* Außenabort *m*.

out·ing ['aʊtɪŋ] *s.* Ausflug *m*: ***go for an ~*** e-n Ausflug machen; ***works ~, company ~*** Betriebsausflug.

ˌout|'jump *v/t.* höher *od.* weiter springen als; **~'land·ish** [-'lændɪʃ] *adj.* **1.** fremdartig, seltsam, e'xotisch; **2.** a) unkultiviert, b) rückständig; **3.** abgelegen; **4.** ausländisch; **ˌ~'last** *v/t.* über'dauern, -'leben.

out·law ['aʊtlɔː] **I** *s.* **1.** *hist.* Geächtete(r *m*) *f*, Vogelfreie(r *m*) *f*; **2.** Ban'dit *m*, Verbrecher *m*; **3.** *Am.* bösartiges Pferd; **II** *v/t.* **4.** *hist.* ächten, für vogelfrei erklären; **5.** ⚖ *Am.* für verjährt erklären: ***~ed claim*** verjährter Anspruch; **6.** für ungesetzlich erklären, verbieten; *Krieg etc.* ächten; **'out·law·ry** [-rɪ] *s.* **1.** *hist.* a) Acht *f* (u. Bann *m*), b) Ächtung *f*; **2.** Verfemung *f*, Verbot *n*, Ächtung *f*; **3.** Ge'setzesmißˌachtung *f*; **4.** Verbrechertum *n*.

'out|·lay *s.* (Geld)Auslage(n *pl.*) *f*: ***initial ~*** Anschaffungskosten *pl.*; **'~·let** *s.* **1.** Auslaß *m*, Abzug *m*, Abzugsöffnung *f*, 'Durchlaß *m*; *mot.* Abluftstutzen *m*; **2.** ⚡ Steckdose *f*; *weitS.* (***electric ~***) Stromverbraucher *m*; **3.** *fig.* Ven'til *n*, Betätigungsfeld *n*: ***find an ~ for one's emotions*** s-n Gefühlen Luft machen können; **4.** † a) Absatzmarkt *m*, -möglichkeit *f*, b) Großabnehmer *m*, c) Verkaufsstelle *f*; **'~·line I** *s.* **1.** a) 'Umriß(linie *f*) *m*, b) *mst pl.* 'Umrisse *pl.*, Kon'turen *pl.*, Silhou'ette *f*; **2.** *Zeichnen*: a) Kon'turzeichnung *f*, b) 'Umriß-, Kon'turlinie *f*; **3.** Entwurf *m*, Skizze *f*; **4.** (***of***) *fig.* 'Umriß *m* (von), 'Überblick *m* (über *acc.*); **5.** Abriß *m*, Auszug *m*: ***an ~ of history***; **II** *v/t.* **6.** entwerfen, skizzieren; *fig. a.* um'reißen, e-n 'Überblick geben über (*acc.*), in groben Zügen darstellen; **7.** die 'Umrisse zeigen von: ***~d against*** scharf abgehoben von; **ˌ~'live** *v/t. j-n od. et.* über'leben; *et.* über'dauern; **'~·look** *s.* **1.** Aussicht *f*, (Aus-) Blick *m*; *fig.* Aussichten *pl.*; **2.** *fig.* Auffassung *f*, Einstellung *f*; Ansichten *pl.*, (Welt)Anschauung *f*; *pol.* Zielsetzung *f*; **3.** Ausguck *m*, Warte *f*; **4.** Wacht *f*, Wache *f*; **'~ˌly·ing** *adj.* **1.** außerhalb *od.* abseits gelegen, entlegen, Außen...: ***~ district*** Außenbezirk *m*; **2.** *fig.* am Rande liegend, nebensächlich; **ˌ~·ma'neu·ver** *Am.*, **ˌ~·ma'noeu·vre** *Brit.* *v/t.* ausmanövrieren (*a. fig. überlisten*); **ˌ~'match** *v/t.* über'treffen, (aus dem Felde) schlagen; **ˌ~'mod·ed** *adj.* 'unmoˌdern, veraltet, über'holt; **'~·most** [-məʊst] *adj.* äußerst (*a. fig.*); **ˌ~'num·ber** *v/t.* an Zahl über'treffen, zahlenmäßig über'legen sein (*dat.*): ***be ~ed*** in der Minderheit sein.

ˌout-of|-'bal·ance [ˌaʊtəv-] *adj.* ⚙ unausgeglichen: ***~ force*** Unwuchtkraft *f*; **ˌ~-'date** *adj.* veraltet, 'unmoˌdern; **ˌ~-'door(s)** → ***outdoor(s)***; **ˌ~-'pock·et ex·pens·es** *s. pl.* Barauslagen *pl.*; **ˌ~-the-'way** [ˌaʊtəvðə-] *adj.* **1.** abgelegen, versteckt; **2.** ausgefallen, ungewöhnlich; **3.** ungehörig; **ˌ~-'town** *adj.* auswärtig: ***~ bank*** † auswärtige Bank; ***~ bill*** Distanzwechsel *m*; **ˌ~-'turn** *adj.* unangebracht, taktlos, vorlaut; **ˌ~-'work pay** *s.* Er'werbslosenunterˌstützung *f*.

ˌout|'pace *v/t.* *j-n* hinter sich lassen; **'~ˌpa·tient** *s.* ⚕ ambu'lanter Pati'ent: ***~ treatment*** ambulante Behandlung; **ˌ~'play** *v/t.* besser spielen als, schlagen; **ˌ~'point** *v/t.* *sport* nach Punkten schlagen; **'~·port** *s.* ⚓ **1.** Vorhafen *m*; **2.** abgelegener Hafen; **'~·pour**, **'~ˌpour·ing** *s.* Erguß *m* (*a. fig.*); **'~·put** *s.* Output *m*: a) †, ⚙ (Arbeits)Leistung *f*, b) † Ausstoß *m*, Produkti'on *f*, Ertrag *m*, c) ⚒ Förderung *f*, Fördermenge *f*, d) ⚡ Ausgang(sleistung *f*) *m*, e) *Computer*: (Daten)Ausgabe *f*: ***~ capacity*** ⚙ Leistungsfähigkeit *f*, *e-r Maschine*: *a.* Stückleistung *f*; ***~ voltage*** ⚡ Ausgangsspannung *f*.

out·rage ['aʊtreɪdʒ] **I** *s.* **1.** Frevel(tat *f*) *m*, Greuel(tat *f*) *m*, Ausschreitung *f*, Verbrechen *n*, *a. fig.* Ungeheuerlichkeit *f*; **2.** (***on, upon***) Frevel(tat *f*) *m* (an *dat.*), Atten'tat *n* (auf *acc.*) (*bsd. fig.*): ***an ~ upon decency*** e-e grobe Verletzung des Anstandes; ***an ~ upon justice*** e-e Vergewaltigung der Gerechtigkeit; **3.** Schande *f*, Schmach *f*; **II** *v/t.* **4.** sich vergehen an (*dat.*), *j-m* Gewalt antun (*a. fig.*); **5.** *Gefühle etc.* mit Füßen treten, gröblich beleidigen *od.* verletzen; **6.** *j-n* em'pören, schockieren; **out·ra·geous** [aʊt'reɪdʒəs] *adj.* ☐ **1.** frevelhaft, abscheulich, verbrecherisch; **2.** schändlich, em'pörend, ungeheuerlich: ***~ behavio(u)r***; **3.** heftig, unerhört: ***~ heat***.

ˌout|'range *v/t.* **1.** ⚔ e-e größere Reichweite haben als; **2.** hin'ausreichen über (*acc.*); **3.** *fig.* über'treffen; **ˌ~'rank** *v/t.* **1.** im Rang höherstehen als; **2.** *fig.* wichtiger sein als; **ˌ~'reach** → ***outrange*** 2, 3; **ˌ~'ride** *v/t.* [*irr.* → ***ride***] **1.** besser *od.* schneller reiten *od.* fahren als; **2.** ⚓ *e-n Sturm* ausreiten; **'~ˌrid·er** *s.* Vorreiter *m*; **'~ˌrig·ger** *s.* **1.** ⚓, ⚙ *u. Rudern*: Ausleger *m*; **2.** Auslegerboot *n*; **'~·right I** *adj.* **1.** völlig, gänzlich, to'tal: ***an ~ loss***; ***an ~ lie*** e-e glatte Lüge; **2.** vorbehaltlos, offen: ***an ~ refusal*** e-e glatte Weigerung; **3.** gerade (her)'aus, di'rekt; **II** *adv.* ***out'right*** **4.** → 1; **5.** ohne Vorbehalt, ganz: ***refuse ~*** rundweg ablehnen; ***sell ~*** fest verkaufen; **6.** auf der Stelle, so'fort: ***kill ~***; ***buy ~ Am.*** gegen sofortige Lieferung kaufen; ***laugh ~*** laut lachen; **ˌ~'ri·val** *v/t.* über'treffen, über'bieten (***in*** an *od.* in *dat.*), ausstechen; **ˌ~'run I** *v/t.* [*irr.* → ***run***] **1.** schneller laufen als, (im Laufen) besiegen; **2.** *fig.* über'schreiten; **II** *s.* **'outrun** **3.** *Skisport*: Auslauf *m*; **'~ˌrun·ner** *s.* **1.** (Vor)Läufer *m* (*Bedienter*); **2.** Leithund *m*; **ˌ~'sell** *v/t.* [*irr.* → ***sell***] **1.** mehr verkaufen als; **2.** sich besser verkaufen als; mehr einbringen als; **'~·set** *s.* **1.** Anfang *m*, Beginn *m*: ***at the ~*** am Anfang; ***from the ~*** gleich von Anfang an; **2.** Aufbruch *m zu e-r Reise*; **ˌ~'shine** [*irr.* → ***shine***] *v/t.* über'strahlen, *fig. a.* in den Schatten stellen.

ˌout'side I *s.* **1.** *das* Äußere (*a. fig.*), Außenseite *f*: ***on the ~ of*** außerhalb, jenseits (*gen.*); **2.** *fig. das* Äußerste: ***at the ~*** äußerstenfalls, höchstens; **3.** *sport* Außenstürmer *m*: ***~ right*** Rechtsaußen *m*; **II** *adj.* **4.** äußer, Außen... (*-antenne, -durchmesser etc.*), von außen: ***~ broker*** † freier Makler; ***~ capital*** Fremdkapital *n*; ***an ~ opinion*** die Meinung e-s Außenstehenden; **5.** außerhalb, (dr)außen; **6.** *fig.* äußerst (*Schätzung, Preis*); **7.** ***~ chance*** winzige Chance, *sport* Außenseiterchance *f*; **III** *adv.* **8.** draußen, außerhalb: ***~ of*** a) außerhalb, b) *Am.* F außer, ausgenommen; **9.** her'aus, hin'aus; **10.** außen, an der Außenseite; **IV** *prp.* **11.** außerhalb, jenseits (*gen.*) (*a. fig.*); **ˌout'sid·er** *s.* **1.** *allg.* Außenseiter(in); **2.** † freier Makler.

ˌout|'sit *v/t.* [*irr.* → ***sit***] länger sitzen (bleiben) als; **'~·size I** *s.* 'Übergröße *f* (*a. Kleidungsstück*); **II** *adj. a.* **'~·sized** 'übergroß, -dimensioˌnal; **'~·skirts** *s. pl.* nahe Um'gebung, Stadtrand *m*, *a. fig.* Rand(gebiet *n*) *m*, Periphe'rie *f*; **ˌ~'smart** → ***outwit***; **ˌ~'speed** *v/t.* [*irr.* → ***speed***] schneller sein als.

ˌout|'spo·ken *adj.* ☐ offen, freimütig; unverblümt: ***she was very ~ about it*** sie äußerte sich sehr offen darüber; **ˌ~'spo·ken·ness** [-'spəʊkənnɪs] *s.* Offenheit *f*, Freimütigkeit *f*; Unverblümtheit *f*.

ˌout'stand·ing *adj.* **1.** her'vorragend (*bsd. fig. Leistung, Spieler etc.*); *fig.* her'vorstechend (*Eigenschaft etc.*), promi'nent (*Persönlichkeit*); **2.** *bsd.* † unerledigt, aus-, offenstehend (*Forderung etc.*), unbezahlt (*Zinsen*): ***~ capital stock*** ausgegebenes Aktienkapital; ***~ debts*** → **'outˌstand·ings** *s. pl.* † Außenstände *pl.*, Forderungen *pl.*

ˌout|'stare *v/t.* mit e-m Blick aus der Fassung bringen; **'~ˌsta·tion** *s.* **1.** 'Außenstatiˌon *f*; **2.** *Funk*: 'Gegenstatiˌon *f*; **ˌ~'stay** *v/t.* länger bleiben als; → ***welcome*** 1; **ˌ~'stretch** *v/t.* ausstrecken; **ˌ~'strip** *v/t.* über'holen, hinter sich lassen, *fig. a.* über'flügeln, (aus dem Feld) schlagen; **ˌ~'swim** *v/t.* [*irr.* → ***swim***] schneller schwimmen als, schlagen; **ˌ~'talk** *v/t.* in Grund u. Boden reden; ‚über'fahren'; **'~·turn** *s.* **1.** Ertrag *m*; **2.** † Ausfall *m*: ***~ sample*** Ausfallmuster *n*; **ˌ~'vote** *v/t.* über'stimmen.

out·ward ['aʊtwəd] **I** *adj.* ☐ → ***outwardly***; **1.** äußer, sichtbar; Außen...; **2.** äußerlich (*a.* ⚕ *u. fig. contp.*); **3.** nach (dr)außen gerichtet *od.* führend, Aus(wärts)..., Hin...: ***~ cargo, ~ freight*** ⚓ ausgehende Ladung, Hinfracht *f*; ***~ journey*** Aus-, Hinreise *f*; ***~ trade*** Ausfuhrhandel *m*; **II** *adv.* **4.** (nach) auswärts, nach außen: ***clear ~*** *Schiff* ausklarieren; → ***bound***[2]; **'out·ward·ly** [-lɪ] *adv.* äußerlich; außen, nach außen (hin); **'out·ward·ness** [-nɪs] *s.* Äußerlichkeit *f*; äußere Form; **'out·wards** [-dz] → ***outward*** II.

ˌoutˈ|ˈwear *v/t.* [*irr.* → ***wear***] **1.** abnutzen; **2.** *fig.* erschöpfen; **3.** *fig.* überˈdauern, haltbarer sein als; **ˌ~ˈweigh** *v/t.* **1.** mehr wiegen als; **2.** *fig.* überˈwiegen, gewichtiger sein als, *e-e Sache* aufwiegen; **ˌ~ˈwit** *v/t.* überˈlisten, ‚austricksen'; **ˈ~·work** *s.* **1.** ⚔ Außenwerk *n*; *fig.* Bollwerk *n*; **2.** ✝ Heimarbeit *f*; **ˈ~ˌwork·er** *s.* **1.** Außenarbeiter(in); **2.** Heimarbeiter(in); **ˈ~·worn** *adj.*, *pred.* ***ˌoutˈworn*** **1.** abgetragen, abgenutzt; **2.** veraltet, überˈholt; **3.** erschöpft.

ou·zel [ˈuːzl] *s. orn.* Amsel *f*.

o·va [ˈəʊvə] *pl. von* ***ovum***.

o·val [ˈəʊvl] **I** *adj.* oˈval; **II** *s.* Oˈval *n*.

o·var·i·an [ˌəʊˈveərɪən] *adj.* **1.** *anat.* Eierstock(s)...; **2.** ⚘ Fruchtknoten...; **o·va·ri·tis** [ˌəʊvəˈraɪtɪs] *s.* Eierstockentzündung *f*; **o·va·ry** [ˈəʊvərɪ] *s.* **1.** *anat.* Eierstock *m*; **2.** ⚘ Fruchtknoten *m*.

o·va·tion [əʊˈveɪʃn] *s.* Ovatiˈon *f*, begeisterte Huldigung.

ov·en [ˈʌvn] *s.* **1.** Backofen *m*, -rohr *n*; **2.** ⚙ Ofen *m*; **ˈ~·dry** *adj.* ofentrocken; **ˈ~ˌread·y** *adj.* bratfertig; **ˈ~·ware** *s.* feuerfestes Geschirr.

o·ver [ˈəʊvə] **I** *prp.* **1.** *Lage*: über (*dat.*): ***the lamp ~ his head***; ***be ~ the signature of Mr. N.*** von Herrn N. unterzeichnet sein; **2.** *Richtung, Bewegung*: über (*acc.*), über (*acc.*) ... hin *od.* (hin-) ˈweg: ***jump ~ the fence***; ***the bridge ~ the Danube*** die Brücke über die Donau; ***~ the radio*** im Radio; ***all ~ the town*** durch die ganze *od.* in der ganzen Stadt; ***from all ~ Germany*** aus ganz Deutschland; ***be all ~ s.o.*** *sl.* ganz hingerissen sein von j-m; **3.** über (*dat.*), auf der anderen Seite von (*od. gen.*): ***~ the sea*** in Übersee, jenseits des Meeres; ***~ the street*** über die Straße, auf der anderen Seite; ***~ the way*** gegenüber; **4.** a) über *der Arbeit einschlafen etc.*, bei *e-m Glase Wein etc.*, b) über (*acc.*), wegen: ***laugh ~*** über *et.* lachen; **5.** *Herrschaft, Rang*: über (*dat. od. acc.*): ***be ~ s.o.*** über j-m stehen; **6.** über (*acc.*), mehr als: ***~ a mile***: ***~ and above*** zusätzlich zu, außer; → 21; **7.** über (*acc.*), während (*gen.*): ***~ the weekend***; ***~ night*** die Nacht über; **8.** durch: ***he went ~ his notes*** er ging seine Notizen durch; **II** *adv.* **9.** hinˈüber, darˈüber: ***he jumped ~***; **10.** hinˈüber (***to*** zu), auf die andere Seite; **11.** herˈüber: ***come ~*** herüberkommen (*a. weitS. zu Besuch*); **12.** drüben: ***~ there*** da drüben; ***~ against*** gegenüber (*dat.*; *a. fig. im Gegensatz zu*); **13.** (*genau*) darˈüber: ***the bird is directly ~***; **14.** über (*acc.*) ...; darˈüber...(*-decken, -legen etc.*); überˈ...: ***to paint ~*** *et.* übermalen; **15.** (*mst in Verbindung mit vb.*) a) überˈ... (*-geben etc.*): ***hand s.th. ~***, b) ˈüber... (*-kochen etc.*): ***boil ~***; **16.** (*oft in Verbindung mit vb.*) a) ˈum... (*-fallen, -werfen etc.*), b) (her)ˈum... (*-drehen etc.*): ***see ~!*** siehe umstehend; **17.** ˈdurch(weg), vom Anfang bis zum Ende: ***the world ~*** a) in der ganzen Welt, b) durch die ganze Welt; ***read s.th. ~*** *et.* (ganz) durchlesen; **18.** (gründlich) überˈ... (*-denken, -legen*): ***think s.th. ~***; ***talk s.th. ~*** et. durchsprechen; **19.** nochmals, wieder: ***do s.th. ~***; (***all***) ***~ again*** nochmals, (ganz) von vorn; ***~ and ~*** (***again***) immer wieder; ***ten times ~*** zehnmal hintereinander; **20.** ˈübermäßig, allzu *sparsam etc.*, ˈüber...(*-vorsichtig etc.*); **21.** darˈüber, mehr: ***10 years and ~*** 10 Jahre und darüber; ***~ and above*** außerdem, überdies; → 6; **22.** übrig, über: ***left ~*** übrig (-gelassen *od.* -geblieben); ***have s.th. ~*** et. übrig haben; **23.** zu Ende, vorˈüber, vorˈbei: ***the lesson is ~***; ***~ with*** F erledigt, vorüber; ***it's all ~*** es ist aus und vorbei; ***get s.th. ~*** (***and done***) ***with*** F et. hinter sich bringen; *Funk*: ***~!*** over!, Ende!; ***~ and out!*** over and out!, Ende (*der Gesamtdurchsage*)!

ˌo·ver|-aˈbun·dant [-vərə-] *adj.* □ ˈüberreich(lich), ˈübermäßig; **ˌ~ˈact** [-vərˈæ-] **I** *v/t.* *e-e Rolle* überˈtreiben, überˈspielen; **II** *v/i.* (s-e Rolle) überˈtreiben; **ˈ~·all** [-ərɔːl] **I** *adj.* **1.** gesamt, Gesamt...: ***~ length***; ***~ efficiency*** ⚙ Totalnutzeffekt *m*; **II** *s.* **2.** *a. pl.* Arbeits-, Monˈteur-, Kombinatiˈonsanzug *m*; (*Arzt- etc.*)Kittel *m*; **3.** *Brit.* Kittelschürze *f*; **4.** *pl. obs.* ˈÜberzieh-, Arbeitshose *f*; **ˌ~-amˈbi·tious** [-əræ-] *adj.* □ allzu ehrgeizig; **ˌ~ˈanx·ious** [-ərˈæ-] *adj.* □ **1.** ˈüberängstlich; **2.** allzu begierig; **ˈ~·arm stroke** [-ərɑːm] *s. Schwimmen*: Hand-über-ˈHand-Stoß *m*; **ˌ~ˈawe** [-ərˈɔː] *v/t.* **1.** einschüchtern; **2.** tief beeindrucken; **ˌ~ˈbal·ance I** *v/t.* **1.** überˈwiegen (*a. fig.*); **2.** ˈumstoßen, -kippen; **II** *v/i.* **3.** ˈumkippen, das ˈÜbergewicht bekommen; **III** *s.* ***ˈoverbalance*** **4.** ˈÜbergewicht *n*; **5.** ✝ ˈÜberschuß *m*: ***~ of exports***; **ˌ~ˈbear** *v/t.* [*irr.* → ***bear***[1]] **1.** niederdrücken; **2.** überˈwinden; **3.** tyrannisieren; **4.** *fig.* schwerer wiegen als; **ˌ~ˈbear·ance** *s.* Anmaßung *f*, Arroˈganz *f*; **ˌ~ˈbear·ing** *adj.* □ **1.** anmaßend, arroˈgant, hochfahrend; **2.** von überˈragender Bedeutung; **ˌ~ˈbid** *v/t.* [*irr.* → ***bid***] **1.** ✝ überˈbieten; **2.** *Bridge*: überˈreizen; **ˈ~·blouse** *s.* Kasackbluse *f*; **ˌ~ˈblown** *adj.* **1.** am Verblühen (*a. fig.*); **2.** ♪ überˈblasen (*Ton*); **3.** *metall.* ˈübergar (*Stahl*); **4.** *fig.* schwülstig; **ˈ~·board** *adv.* ⚓ über Bord: ***throw ~*** über Bord werfen (*a. fig.*); ***go ~*** (***about*** *od.* ***for***) F hingerissen sein (von); **ˌ~ˈbrim** *v/i. u. v/t.* ˈüberfließen (lassen); **ˌ~ˈbuild** *v/t.* [*irr.* → ***build***] **1.** überˈbauen; **2.** zu dicht bebauen; **3.** ***~ o.s.*** sich ‚verbauen'; **ˌ~ˈbur·den** *v/t.* überˈbürden, -ˈladen, -ˈlasten; **ˌ~ˈbus·y** *adj.* **1.** zu sehr beschäftigt; **2.** ˈübergeschäftig; **ˌ~ˈbuy** [*irr.* → ***buy***] ✝ **I** *v/t.* zu viel kaufen von; **II** *v/i.* zu teuer *od.* über Bedarf (ein)kaufen; **ˌ~-ˈcap·i·tal·ize** *v/t.* ✝ **1.** e-n zu hohen Nennwert für das ˈStammkapiˌtal *e-s Unternehmens* angeben: ***~ a firm***; **2.** ˈüberkapitalisieren; **ˌ~ˈcast I** *v/t.* [*irr.* → ***cast***] **1.** *mit Wolken* überˈziehen, bedecken, verdunkeln, trüben (*a. fig.*); **2.** *Naht* umˈstechen; **II** *v/i.* [*irr.* → ***cast***] **3.** sich bewölken, sich beziehen (*Himmel*); **III** *adj.* ***ˈovercast*** **4.** bewölkt, bedeckt (*Himmel*); **5.** trüb(e), düster (*a. fig.*); **6.** überˈwendlich (genäht); **ˌ~ˈcharge I** *v/t.* **1.** a) *j-m* zuˈviel berechnen, b) *e-n Betrag* zuˈviel verlangen, c) zuˈviel anrechnen *od.* verlangen für *et.*; **2.** ⚙, ⚡ überˈladen (*a. fig.*); **II** *s.* **3.** ✝ a) Mehrbetrag *m*, Aufschlag *m*: ***~ for arrears*** Säumniszuschlag *m*, b) Überˈforderung *f*, Überˈteuerung *f*; **4.** Überˈladung *f*, ˈÜberbelastung *f*; **ˌ~ˈcloud** → ***overcast*** 1, 3; **ˈ~·coat** *s.* Mantel *m*; **ˌ~ˈcome** [*irr.* → ***come***] **I** *v/t.* überˈwinden, -ˈwältigen, -ˈmannen, bezwingen; *e-r Sache* Herr werden: ***he was ~ with*** (*od.* ***by***) ***emotion*** er wurde von s-n Gefühlen übermannt; **II** *v/i.* siegen, triumphieren: ***we shall ~!***; **ˌ~ˈcom·pen·sate** *v/t. psych.* ˈüberkompensieren; **ˌ~-ˈcon·fi·dence** *s.* **1.** übersteigertes Selbstvertrauen *od.* -bewußtsein; **2.** zu großes Vertrauen; **3.** zu großer Optiˈmismus; **ˌ~-ˈcon·fi·dent** *adj.* □ **1.** allzuˈsehr vertrauend (***of*** auf *acc.*); **2.** überˈtrieben selbstbewußt; **3.** (all)zu optiˈmistisch; **ˌ~ˈcrop** *v/t.* ⚒ Raubbau treiben mit; **ˌ~ˈcrowd** *v/t.* überˈfüllen: ***~ed profession*** überlaufener Beruf; **ˌ~-deˈvel·op** *v/t. bsd. phot.* ˈüberentwickeln; **ˌ~ˈdo** *v/t.* [*irr.* → ***do***[1]] **1.** überˈtreiben, zu weit treiben; **2.** *fig.* zu weit gehen mit *od.* in (*dat.*), *et.* zu arg treiben: ***~ it*** (*od.* ***things***) a) zu weit gehen, b) des Guten zuviel tun; **3.** ˈüberbeanspruchen; **4.** zu stark *od.* zu lange kochen *od.* braten; **ˌ~ˈdone** *adj.* ˈübergar; **ˈ~·dose I** *s.* ˈÜberdosis *f*; **II** *v/t.* ***ˌoverˈdose*** a) *j-m* e-e zu starke Dosis geben, b) *et.* ˈüberdosieren; **ˈ~·draft** *s.* ✝ a) (ˈKonto)ÜberˌZiehung *f*, b) Überˈziehung *f*, überˈzogener Betrag; **ˌ~ˈdraw** *v/t.* [*irr.* → ***draw***] **1.** *Konto* überˈziehen; **2.** *Bogen* überˈspannen; **3.** *fig.* überˈtreiben; **ˌ~ˈdress** *v/t. u. v/i.* (sich) überˈtrieben anziehen; **ˌ~ˈdrive I** *v/t.* [*irr.* → ***drive***] **1.** abschinden, -hetzen; **2.** *et.* zu weit treiben; **II** *s.* ***ˈoverdrive*** **3.** *mot.* Overdrive *m*, Schnell-, Schongang *m*; **ˌ~ˈdue** *adj.* ˈüberfällig (*a.* 🚂, ✝): ***the train is ~*** der Zug hat Verspätung; ***she is ~*** sie müßte längst hier sein; **ˌ~ˈeat** [-ərˈiːt] *v/i.* [*irr.* → ***eat***] (*a.* ***~ o.s.***) sich überˈessen; **ˌ~ˈem·pha·size** [-ərˈe-] *v/t.* ˈüberbetonen; **ˌ~-ˈes·ti·mate** [-ərˈestɪmeɪt] **I** *v/t.* überˈschätzen, ˈüberbewerten; **II** *s.* [-mət] Überˈschätzung *f*; **ˌ~-exˈcite** [-vərɪ-] *v/t.* **1.** überˈreizen; **2.** ⚡ ˈübererregen; **ˌ~-exˈert** [-vərɪ-] *v/t.* überˈanstrengen; **ˌ~-exˈpose** [-vərɪ-] *v/t. phot.* ˈüberbelichten; **ˌ~-exˈpo·sure** [-vərɪ-] *s. phot.* ˈÜberbelichtung *f*; **ˌ~-faˈtigue I** *v/t.* überˈmüden, überˈanstrengen; **II** *s.* Überˈmüdung *f*; **ˌ~ˈfeed** *v/t.* [*irr.* → ***feed***] überˈfüttern, ˈüberernähren; **ˌ~ˈflow I** *v/i.* **1.** ˈüberlaufen, ˈüberfließen, ˈüberströmen, sich ergießen (***into*** in *acc.*); **2.** *fig.* ˈüberquellen (***with*** von); **II** *v/t.* **3.** überˈfluten, überˈschwemmen; **4.** nicht mehr Platz finden in (*e-m Saal etc.*); **III** *s.* ***ˈoverflow*** **5.** Überˈschwemmung *f*, ˈÜberfließen *n*; **6.** ⚙ a) *a.* ⚡ ˈÜberlauf *m*, b) *a.* ***~ pipe*** Überlaufrohr *n*, c) *a.* ***~ basin*** ˈÜberlaufbasˌsin *n*: ***~ valve*** Überströmventil *n*; **7.** ˈÜberschuß *m*: ***~ meeting*** Parallelversammlung *f*; **ˌ~ˈflow·ing I** *adj.* **1.** ˈüberfließend, -quellend, -strömend (*a. fig. Güte, Herz etc.*); **2.** ˈüberreich (*Ernte etc.*); **II** *s.* **3.** ˈÜberfließen *n*: ***full to ~*** voll (bis) zum Überlaufen, *weitS.* zum Platzen voll; **ˌ~ˈfly** *v/t.* [*irr.* → ***fly***[1]] überˈfliegen; **ˌ~ˈfond** *adj.*: ***be ~ of doing s.th.*** et. leidenschaftlich gern tun; **ˈ~·freight** *s.* ✝ ˈÜberfracht *f*; **ˈ~·ground** *adj.* über der Erde (befindlich); **ˌ~ˈgrow** *v/t.* [*irr.* → ***grow***] **1.** überˈwachsen, -ˈwuchern; **2.** hinˈauswachsen über (*acc.*), zu groß werden für; ˌ~'**grown** *adj.* **1.** über'wachsen; **2.** 'übermäßig gewachsen, 'übergroß; '~·**growth** *s.* **1.** Über'wucherung *f*; **2.** 'übermäßiges Wachstum; '~·**hand** *adj. u. adv.* **1.** *Schlag etc.* von oben; **2.** *sport* 'überhand: ~ ***stroke*** a) *Tennis*: Überhandschlag *m*, b) *Schwimmen*: Hand-über-Hand-Stoß *m*; ~ ***service*** Hochaufschlag *m*; **3.** *Näherei*: über'wendlich; ˌ~'**hang I** *v/t.* [*irr.* → ***hang***] **1.** her'vorstehen *od.* -ragen *od.* 'überhängen über (*acc.*); **2.** *fig.* (drohend) schweben über (*dat.*), drohen (*dat.*); **II** *v/i.* [*irr.* → ***hang***] **3.** 'überhängen, -kragen (*a.* △), her'vorstehen, -ragen; **III** *s.* ***'overhang*** **4.** 'Überhang *m* (*a.* △, ⚓, ✈); ⚙ Ausladung *f*; ˌ~-'**hap·py** *adj.* 'überglücklich; ˌ~-'**hast·y** *adj.* über'eilt; ˌ~'**haul I** *v/t.* **1.** ⚙ *Maschine etc.* (gene'ral)überˌholen, (*a. fig.*) gründlich über'prüfen (*a. fig.*) u. in'stand setzen; **2.** ⚓ *Tau, Taljen etc.* 'überholen; **3.** a) einholen, b) über'holen; **II** *s.* ***'overhaul*** **4.** ⚙ Über'holung *f*, gründliche Über'prüfung (*a. fig.*); '~·**head I** *adj.* **1.** oberirdisch, Frei..., Hoch...(*-antenne, -behälter etc.*): ~ ***line*** Frei-, Oberleitung *f*; ~ ***railway*** Hochbahn *f*; **2.** *mot.* a) obengesteuert (*Motor, Ventil*), b) obenliegend (*Nockenwelle*); **3.** allgemein, Gesamt...: ~ ***costs***, ~ ***expenses*** → 5; **4.** *sport*: a) ~ ***stroke*** → 6, b) ~ ***kick*** (Fall-) Rückzieher *m*; **II** *s.* **5.** *a. pl.* allgemeine Unkosten *pl.*, Gemeinkosten *pl.*, laufende Geschäftskosten *pl.*; **6.** *Tennis*: Über'kopfball *m*; **III** *adv.* ***ˌover'head*** **7.** (dr)oben: ***works*** ~! Vorsicht, Dacharbeiten!; ˌ~'**hear** *v/t.* [*irr.* → ***hear***] belauschen, (zufällig) (mit'an)hören; ˌ~'**heat I** *v/t. Motor etc.*, *a. fig.* über'hitzen, *Raum* über'heizen: ~ ***itself*** → II; **II** *v/i.* ⚙ heißlaufen; '~·**house** *adj.* Dach...(*-antenne etc.*); ˌ~'**hung** *adj.* ⚙ fliegend (angeordnet), freitragend; 'überhängend; ˌ~·**in'dulge** [-vərɪ-] **I** *v/t.* **1.** zu nachsichtig behandeln; **2.** *e-r Leidenschaft etc.* 'übermäßig frönen; **II** *v/i.* **3.** ~ ***in*** sich allzu'sehr ergehen in (*dat.*); ˌ~·**in'dul·gence** [-vərɪ-] *s.* **1.** zu große Nachsicht; **2.** 'übermäßiger Genuß; ˌ~-**in'dul·gent** [-vərɪ-] *adj.* allzu nachsichtig; ˌ~·**in'sure** [-vərɪ-] *v/t. u. v/i.* (sich) 'überversichern; ˌ~-'**is·sue** [-ər'ɪ-] **I** *s.* 'Überemissiˌon *f*; **II** *v/t.* zu'viel *Banknoten etc.* ausgeben; ˌ~'**joyed** [-'dʒɔɪd] *adj.* außer sich vor Freude, 'überglücklich; '~·**kill** *s.* **1.** ⚔ Overkill *m*; **2.** *fig.* 'Übermaß *n*, Zu'viel *n* (***of*** an *dat.*); ˌ~'**lad·en** *adj.* über'laden (*a. fig.*); ˌ~'**land I** *adv.* über Land, auf dem Landweg; **II** *adj.* ***'overland*** Überland...: ~ ***route*** Landweg *m*; ~ ***transport*** Überland-, Fernverkehr *m*; ˌ~'**lap I** *v/t.* **1.** 'übergreifen auf (*acc.*) *od.* in (*acc.*), sich über'schneiden mit, teilweise zs.-fallen mit; ⚙ über'lappen; **2.** hin'ausgehen über (*acc.*); **II** *v/i.* **3.** sich *od.* ein'ander über'schneiden, sich teilweise decken, auf- *od.* inein'ander 'übergreifen; ⚙ über'lappen, 'übergreifen; **III** *s.* ***'overlap*** **4.** 'Übergreifen *n*, Über'schneiden *n*; ⚙ Über'lappung *f*; ˌ~'**lay I** *v/t.* [*irr.* → ***lay***[1]] **1.** belegen; ⚙ über'lagern; **2.** über'ziehen (***with*** mit *Gold etc.*); **3.** *typ.* zurichten; **II** *s.* ***'overlay*** **4.** Bedekkung *f*: ~ ***mattress*** Auflegematratze *f*; **5.** Auflage *f*, 'Überzug *m*; **6.** *typ.* Zurichtung *f*; **7.** Planpause *f*; ˌ~'**leaf** *adv.* 'umstehend, 'umseitig; ˌ~'**lie** *v/t.* [*irr.* → ***lie***[2]] **1.** liegen auf *od.* über (*dat.*); **2.** *geol.* über'lagern; ˌ~'**load I** *v/t.* über'laden, 'überbelasten, *a.* ↯ über'lasten; **II** *s.* ***'overload*** 'Überbelastung *f*, -beanspruchung *f*, *a.* ↯ Über'lastung *f*; ˌ~'**long** *adj. u. adv.* 'überlang, (all)zu lang; ˌ~'**look** *v/t.* **1.** *Fehler etc.* (geflissentlich) über'sehen, nicht beachten, *fig. a.* ignorieren, (nachsichtig) hin'wegsehen über (*acc.*); **2.** über'blicken; *weitS. a.* Aussicht gewähren auf (*acc.*); **3.** über'wachen; (prüfend) 'durchsehen; '~·**lord** *s.* Oberherr *m*; '~·**lord·ship** *s.* Oberherrschaft *f*.

o·ver·ly ['əʊvəlɪ] *adv.* allzu('sehr).

ˌo·ver|'ly·ing *adj.* da'rüberliegend; '~·**man** [-mæn] *s.* [*irr.*] Aufseher *m*, Vorarbeiter *m*; ⚒ Steiger *m*; ˌ~-'**manned** *adj.* 'überbelegt, zu stark bemannt; ˌ~'**much I** *adj.* allzu'viel; **II** *adv.* allzu('sehr, -'viel), 'übermäßig; ˌ~-'**nice** *adj.* 'überfein; ˌ~'**night I** *adv.* über Nacht; **II** *adj.* Nacht...; Übernachtungs...: ~ ***lodgings***; ~ ***bag*** Reisetasche *f*; ~ ***case*** Handkoffer *m*; ~ ***guests*** Übernachtungsgäste; ~ ***stay*** Übernachtung *f*; ~ ***stop*** Aufenthalt *m* für e-e Nacht; '~·**pass** *s.* ('Straßen-, 'Eisenbahn)ÜberˌführungF *f*; ˌ~'**pay** *v/t.* [*irr.* → ***pay***] **1.** zu teuer bezahlen; **2.** 'überreichlich belohnen; **3.** 'überbezahlen; ˌ~'**peo·pled** *adj.* über'völkert; ˌ~·**per'suade** *v/t.* *j-n* (gegen s-n Willen) über'reden; ˌ~'**play** *v/t.* **1.** über'treiben; **2.** ~ ***one's hand*** *fig.* sich über'nehmen, es über'treiben; '~·**plus** *s.* 'Überschuß *m*; '~ˌ**pop·u'la·tion** *s.* 'Über(be)völkerung *f*; ˌ~'**pow·er** *v/t.* über'wältigen (*a. fig.*); ˌ~'**print I** *v/t.* **1.** *typ.* a) über'drucken, b) e-e zu große Auflage drucken von; **2.** *phot.* 'überkopieren; **II** *s.* ***'overprint*** **3.** *typ.* 'Überdruck *m*; **4.** a) Aufdruck *m* (*auf Briefmarken*), b) Briefmarke *f* mit Aufdruck; ˌ~·**pro'duce** *v/t.* ⚚ 'überproduzieren; ˌ~·**pro'duc·tion** *s.* 'ÜberproduktiˌonF *f*; ˌ~'**proof** *adj.* 'überproˌzentig (*alkoholisches Getränk*); ˌ~'**rate** *v/t.* **1.** über'schätzen, 'überbewerten (*a. sport*); **2.** ⚚ zu hoch veranschlagen; ˌ~'**reach** *v/t.* **1.** zu weit gehen für: ~ ***one's purpose*** *fig.* über sein Ziel hinausschießen; ~ ***o.s.*** es zu weit treiben, sich übernehmen; **2.** *j-n* über'vorteilen, -'listen; ˌ~·**re'act** *v/i.* 'überreagieren; ˌ~'**ride** *v/t.* [*irr.* → ***ride***] **1.** über'reiten; **2.** *fig.* sich (rücksichtslos) hin'wegsetzen über (*acc.*); **3.** *fig.* 'umstoßen, aufheben, nichtig machen; **4.** den Vorrang haben vor (*dat.*); ˌ~'**rid·ing** *adj.* über'wiegend, hauptsächlich; vorrangig; ˌ~'**ripe** *adj.* 'überreif; ˌ~'**rule** *v/t.* **1.** *Vorschlag etc.* verwerfen, zu'rückweisen; ⚖ *Urteil* 'umstoßen; **2.** *fig.* die Oberhand gewinnen über (*acc.*); ˌ~'**rul·ing** *adj.* beherrschend, 'übermächtig; ˌ~'**run** *v/t.* [*irr.* → ***run***] **1.** *fig. Land etc.* über'fluten, -'schwemmen (*a. fig.*), einfallen in (*acc.*), über'rollen (*a. fig.*): ***be*** ~ ***with*** wimmeln von, überlaufen sein von; **2.** *fig.* rasch um sich greifen in (*dat.*); **3.** *typ.* um'brechen; ˌ~'**run·ning** *adj.* ⚙ Freilauf..., Überlauf...: ~ ***clutch***; ˌ~'**sea I** *adv. a.* ˌ~'**seas** nach *od.* in 'Übersee; **II** *adj.* 'überseeisch, Übersee...; ˌ~'**see** *v/t.* [*irr.* → ***see***[1]] beaufsichtigen, über'wachen; '~ˌ**se·er** [-ˌsɪə] *s.* **1.** Aufseher(in), In'spektor *m*, Inspek'torin *f*; **2.** Vorarbeiter(in); ⚒ Steiger *m*; ˌ~-'**sen·si·tive** *adj.* □ 'überempfindlich; ˌ~'**set** *v/t.* [*irr.* → ***set***] → ***upset***[1] I; ˌ~'**sew** *v/t.* [*irr.* → ***sew***] über'wendlich nähen; ˌ~'**sexed** *adj.* sexbesessen; ˌ~'**shad·ow** *v/t.* **1.** *fig.* in den Schatten stellen; **2.** *bsd. fig.* über'schatten, e-n Schatten werfen auf (*acc.*), verdüstern; '~·**shoe** *s.* 'Überschuh *m*; ˌ~'**shoot** *v/t.* [*irr.* → ***shoot***] **1.** über *ein Ziel* hin'ausschießen (*a. fig.*): ~ ***o.s.*** (*od.* ***the mark***) zu weit gehen, übers Ziel hinausschießen; '~·**shot** *adj.* oberschlächtig (*Wasserrad, Mühle*); '~·**sight** *s.* **1.** Versehen *n*: ***by an*** ~ aus Versehen; **2.** Aufsicht *f*; ˌ~'**sim·pli·fy** *v/t.* (zu) grob vereinfachen; '~·**size** *s.* 'Übergröße *f*; '~·**size(d)** *adj.* 'übergroß; ~·**slaugh** ['əʊvəslɔː] *v/t.* **1.** ⚔ abkommandieren; **2.** *Am. bei der Beförderung* über'gehen; ˌ~'**sleep I** *v/t.* [*irr.* → ***sleep***] *e-n Zeitpunkt* verschlafen: ~ ***o.s.*** → II; **II** *v/i.* [*irr.* → ***sleep***] (sich) verschlafen; '~·**sleeve** *s.* Ärmelschoner *m*; ˌ~'**speed** *v/t.* [*irr.* → ***speed***] *den Motor* über'drehen; ˌ~'**spend** [*irr.* → ***spend***] **I** *v/i.* **1.** zuviel ausgeben; **II** *v/t.* **2.** *Ausgabensumme* über'schreiten; **3.** ~ ***o.s.*** über s-e Verhältnisse leben; '~·**spill** *s.* (*bsd.* Be'völkerungs)ˌÜberschuß *m*; ˌ~'**spread** *v/t.* [*irr.* → ***spread***] **1.** über'ziehen, sich ausbreiten über (*acc.*); **2.** (***with***) über'ziehen *od.* bedekken (mit); ˌ~'**staffed** *adj.* (perso'nell) 'überbesetzt; ˌ~'**state** *v/t.* über'treiben: ~ ***one's case*** in s-n Behauptungen zu weit gehen; ˌ~'**state·ment** *s.* Über'treibung *f*; ˌ~'**stay** *v/t.* *e-e Zeit* über'schreiten: ~ ***one's time*** über s-e Zeit hinaus bleiben; → ***welcome*** 1; ˌ~'**steer** *v/i.* *mot.* über'steuern; ˌ~'**step** *v/t.* über'schreiten (*a. fig.*); ˌ~'**stock I** *v/t.* **1.** 'überreichlich eindecken, ⚚ *a.* 'überbeliefern, *den Markt* über'schwemmen: ~ ***o.s.*** → 3; **2.** ⚚ in zu großen Mengen auf Lager halten; **II** *v/i.* **3.** sich zu hoch eindecken; ˌ~'**strain I** *v/t.* über'anstrengen, 'überstrapazieren (*a. fig.*): ~ ***one's conscience*** übertriebene Skrupel haben; **II** *s.* ***'overstrain*** Über'anstrengung *f*; ˌ~'**strung** *adj.* **1.** über'reizt (*Nerven od. Person*); **2.** ***'overstrung*** ♪ kreuzsaitig (*Klavier*); ˌ~·**sub'scribe** *v/t.* ⚚ *Anleihe* über'zeichnen; ˌ~·**sub'scrip·tion** *s.* ⚚ Über'zeichnung *f*; ˌ~-**sup'ply** *s.* (***of*** an *dat.*) **1.** 'Überangebot *n*; **2.** zu großer Vorrat.

o·vert ['əʊvɜːt] *adj.* □ offen(kundig): ~ ***act*** ⚖ Ausführungshandlung *f*; ~ ***hostility*** offene Feindschaft; ~ ***market*** ⚚ offener Markt.

ˌo·ver|'take *v/t.* [*irr.* → ***take***] **1.** einholen (*a. fig.*); **2.** über'holen (*a. v/i.*); **3.** *fig.* über'raschen, -'fallen; **4.** *Versäumtes* nachholen; ˌ~'**task** *v/t.* **1.** über'bürden; **2.** über *j-s* Kräfte gehen; ˌ~'**tax** *v/t.* **1.** 'überbesteuern; **2.** zu hoch einschätzen; **3.** 'überbeanspruchen, zu hohe Anforderungen stellen an (*acc.*); *Geduld* strapazieren: ~ ***one's strength*** sich (kräftemäßig) übernehmen; ˌ~-**the-'count·er** *adj.* **1.** ⚚ freihändig (*Effektenverkauf*): ~ ***market*** Freiverkehrsmarkt *m*; **2.** *pharm.* re'zeptfrei; ˌ~'**throw I** *v/t.* [*irr.* → ***throw***] **1.** ('um-)

stürzen (*a. fig. Regierung etc.*); **2.** niederwerfen, besiegen; **3.** niederreißen, vernichten; **II** *s.* **'*overthrow* 4.** Sturz *m*, Niederlage *f* (*e-r Regierung etc.*); **5.** Vernichtung *f*, 'Untergang *m*; **'~·time I** *s.* ✝ a) 'Überstunden *pl.*, b) *a.* ***~ pay*** Mehrarbeitszuschlag *m*, 'Überstundenlohn *m*; **II** *adv.*: ***work ~*** Überstunden machen; **,~'tire** *v/t.* über'müden; **'~·tone** *s.* **1.** ♪ Oberton *m*; **2.** *fig.* a) 'Unterton *m*, b) *pl.* Neben-, Zwischentöne *pl.*: ***it had ~s of*** es schwang darin et. mit von; **,~'top**, **,~'tow·er** *v/t.* über'ragen (*a. fig.*); **,~'train** *v/t. u. v/i.* 'übertrainieren; **'~·trump** *v/t. u. v/i.* über'trumpfen.

o·ver·ture ['əʊvə,tjʊə] *s.* **1.** ♪ Ouver'türe *f*; **2.** *fig.* Einleitung *f*, Vorspiel *n*; **3.** (for'meller Heirats-, Friedens)Antrag *m*, Angebot *n*; **4.** *pl.* Annäherungsversuche *pl.*

,o·ver|'turn I *v/t.* ('um)stürzen (*a. fig.*); 'umstoßen, -kippen; **II** *v/i.* 'umkippen, -schlagen, -stürzen, kentern; **III** *s.* ***'overturn*** ('Um)Sturz *m*; **,~'val·ue** *v/t.* zu hoch einschätzen, 'überbewerten; **'~·view** *s. fig.* 'Überblick *m*; **,~'ween·ing** *adj.* **1.** anmaßend, über'heblich; **2.** über'trieben; **'~·weight I** *s.* 'Übergewicht *n* (*a. fig.*); **II** *adj.* ***,over'weight*** 'übergewichtig, mit 'Übergewicht.

o·ver·whelm [,əʊvə'welm] *v/t.* **1.** über'wältigen, -'mannen (*bsd. fig.*); **2.** *fig. mit Fragen, Geschenken etc.* über'schütten, -'häufen: ***~ed with work*** überlastet; **3.** erdrücken; **o·ver'whelm·ing** [-mɪŋ] *adj.* über'wältigend.

o·ver|·wind [,əʊvə'waɪnd] *v/t.* [*irr.* → ***wind²***] *Uhr etc.* über'drehen; **,~'work I** *v/t.* **1.** über'anstrengen, mit Arbeit über'lasten, 'überstrapazieren (*a. fig.*): ***~ o.s.*** → 2; **II** *v/i.* **2.** sich über'arbeiten; **III** *s.* **3.** 'Arbeitsüber,lastung *f*; **4.** Über'arbeitung *f*; **,~'wrought** *adj.* **1.** über'arbeitet, erschöpft; **2.** über'reizt; **,~'zeal·ous** *adj.* 'übereifrig.

o·vi·duct ['əʊvɪdʌkt] *s. anat.* Eileiter *m*; **'o·vi·form** [-ɪfɔːm] *adj.* eiförmig, o'val; **o·vip·a·rous** [əʊ'vɪpərəs] *adj.* ovi'par, eierlegend.

o·vo·gen·e·sis [,əʊvəʊ'dʒenɪsɪs] *s. biol.* Eibildung *f*; **o·void** ['əʊvɔɪd] *adj. u. s.* eiförmig(er Körper).

o·vu·lar ['ɒvjʊlə] *adj. biol.* Ei..., Ovular...; **o·vu·la·tion** [,ɒvjʊ'leɪʃn] *s.* Ovulati'on *f*, Eisprung *m*; **o·vule** ['əʊvjuːl] *s.* **1.** *biol.* Ovulum *n*, kleines Ei; **2.** ⚘ Samenanlage *f*; **o·vum** ['əʊvəm] *pl.* **o·va** ['əʊvə] *s. biol.* Ovum *n*, Ei(zelle *f*) *n*.

owe [əʊ] **I** *v/t.* **1.** *Geld, Achtung, e-e Erklärung etc.* schulden, schuldig sein: ***~ s.o. a grudge*** gegen j-n e-n Groll hegen; ***you ~ that to yourself*** das bist du dir schuldig; **2.** bei *j-m* Schulden haben (***for*** für); **3.** *et.* verdanken, zu verdanken haben, Dank schulden für: ***I ~ him much*** ich habe ihm viel zu verdanken; **II** *v/i.* **4.** Schulden haben; **5.** die Bezahlung schuldig sein (***for*** für); **ow·ing** ['əʊɪŋ] *adj.* **1.** geschuldet: ***be ~*** zu zahlen sein, noch offenstehen; ***have ~*** ausstehen haben; **2.** ***~ to*** infolge (*gen.*), wegen (*gen.*), dank (*dat.*): ***be ~ to*** zurückzuführen sein auf (*acc.*), zuzuschreiben sein (*dat.*).

owl [aʊl] *s.* **1.** *orn.* Eule *f*; **2.** *fig.* ‚alte Eule' (*Person*): ***wise old ~*** ‚kluges Kind'; **owl·ish** ['aʊlɪʃ] *adj.* □ eulenhaft.

own [əʊn] **I** *v/t.* **1.** besitzen; **2.** *Erben, Kind, Schuld etc.* anerkennen; **3.** zugeben, (ein)gestehen, einräumen: ***~ o.s. defeated*** sich geschlagen geben; **II** *v/i.* **4.** sich bekennen (***to*** zu): ***~ to*** → 3; **5.** ***~ up*** es zugeben *od.* gestehen; **III** *adj.* **6.** eigen: ***my ~ self*** ich selbst; ***~ brother to s.o.*** j-s leiblicher Bruder; **7.** eigen(-artig), besonder: ***it has a value all its ~*** es hat e-n ganz besonderen *od.* eigenen Wert; **8.** selbst: ***I cook my ~ breakfast*** ich mache mir das Frühstück selbst; **9.** (innig) geliebt, einzig: ***my ~ child!***; **IV** *s.* **10.** ***my ~*** a) mein Eigentum *n*, b) meine Angehörigen *pl.*: ***may I have it for my ~?*** darf ich es haben?; ***come into one's ~*** a) s-n rechtmäßigen Besitz erlangen, b) zur Geltung kommen; ***she has a car of her ~*** sie hat ein eigenes Auto; ***he has a way of his ~*** er hat e-e eigene Art; ***on one's ~*** F a) selbständig, unabhängig, ohne fremde Hilfe, b) von sich aus, aus eigenem Antrieb, c) auf eigene Verantwortung; ***be left on one's ~*** F sich selbst überlassen sein; ***get one's ~ back*** F sich revanchieren, sich rächen (***on*** an *dat.*); → ***hold*** 20.

-owned [əʊnd] *adj. in Zssgn* gehörig, gehörend (*dat.*), in *j-s* Besitz: ***state-~*** staatseigen, Staats...

own·er ['əʊnə] *s.* Eigentümer(in), Inhaber(in); ***at ~'s risk*** ✝ auf eigene Gefahr; ***~-driver*** j-d, der sein eigenes Auto fährt; ***~-occupation*** Eigennutzung *f* (*e-s Hauses etc.*); **'own·er·less** [-lɪs] *adj.* herrenlos; **'own·er·ship** [-ʃɪp] *s.* **1.** Eigentum(srecht) *n*, Besitzerschaft *f*; **2.** Besitz *m*.

ox [ɒks] *pl.* **ox·en** ['ɒksn] *s.* **1.** Ochse *m*; **2.** (Haus)Rind *n*.

ox·a·late ['ɒksəleɪt] *s.* ⚗ Oxa'lat *n*; **ox·al·ic** [ɒks'ælɪk] *adj.* ⚗ o'xalsauer: ***~ acid*** Oxalsäure *f*.

Ox·bridge ['ɒksbrɪdʒ] *s. Brit.* F (die Universi'täten) Oxford *u.* Cambridge *pl.*

Ox·ford| man *s.* [*irr.*] → ***Oxonian*** II; **~ move·ment** *s. eccl.* Oxfordbewegung *f*.

ox·i·dant ['ɒksɪdənt] *s.* ⚗ Oxydati'onsmittel *n*; **'ox·i·date** [-deɪt] → ***oxidize***; **ox·i·da·tion** [,ɒksɪ'deɪʃn] *s.* ⚗ Oxydati'on *f*, Oxydierung *f*; **ox·ide** ['ɒksaɪd] *s.* ⚗ O'xyd *n*; **'ox·i·dize** [-daɪz] *v/t. u. v/i.* ⚗ oxydieren; **'ox·i·diz·er** [-daɪzə] *s.* ⚗ Oxydati'onsmittel *n*.

'ox·lip *s.* ⚘ Hohe Schlüsselblume.

Ox·o·ni·an [ɒk'səʊnjən] **I** *adj.* Oxforder, Oxford...; **II** *s.* Mitglied *n od.* Graduierte(r *m*) *f* der Universi'tät Oxford; *weitS.* Oxforder(in).

'ox·tail *s.* Ochsenschwanz *m*: ***~ soup***.

ox·y·a·cet·y·lene [,ɒksɪə'setɪliːn] *adj.* ⚗, ⚙ Sauerstoff-Azetylen...: ***~ torch*** *od.* ***burner*** Schweißbrenner *m*; ***~ welding*** Autogenschweißen *n*.

ox·y·gen ['ɒksɪdʒən] *s.* ⚗ Sauerstoff *m*: ***~ apparatus*** Atemgerät *n*; ***~ tent*** ⚕ Sauerstoffzelt *n*; **ox·yg·e·nant** [ɒk'sɪdʒənənt] *s.* Oxydati'onsmittel *n*; **ox·y·gen·ate** [ɒk'sɪdʒəneɪt], **ox·y·gen·ize** [ɒk'sɪdʒənaɪz] *v/t.* **1.** oxydieren, mit Sauerstoff verbinden *od.* behandeln; **2.** mit Sauerstoff anreichern.

ox·y·hy·dro·gen [,ɒksɪ'haɪdrədʒən] ⚗, ⚙ **I** *adj.* Hydrooxygen..., Knallgas...; **II** *s.* Knallgas *n*.

o·yer ['ɔɪə] *s.* ⚖ **1.** *hist.* gerichtliche Unter'suchung; **2.** → **~ and ter·mi·ner** ['tɜːmɪnə] *s.* ⚖ **1.** *hist.* gerichtliche Unter'suchung *u.* Entscheidung; **2.** *mst* ***commission*** (*od.* ***writ***) ***of ~*** *Brit. königliche Ermächtigung an die Richter der Assisengerichte, Gericht zu halten.*

o·yez [əʊ'jes] *int.* hört (zu)!

oys·ter ['ɔɪstə] *s.* **1.** *zo.* Auster *f*: ***~s on the shell*** frische Austern; ***he thinks the world is his ~*** *fig.* er meint, er kann alles haben; **2.** F ‚zugeknöpfter Mensch'; **~ bank**, **~ bed** *s.* Austernbank *f*; **~ catch·er** *s. orn.* Austernfischer *m*; **~ farm** *s.* Austernpark *m*.

o·zone ['əʊzəʊn] *s.* **1.** ⚗ O'zon *m*, *n*: ***~ layer*** O'zonschicht *f*; **2.** F O'zon *m*, *n*, reine frische Luft; **o·zon·ic** [əʊ'zɒnɪk] *adj.* **1.** o'zonisch, Ozon...; **2.** o'zonhaltig; **o·zo·nif·er·ous** [,əʊzəʊ'nɪfərəs] *adj.* **1.** o'zonhaltig; **2.** o'zonerzeugend; **o·zo·nize** ['əʊzəʊnaɪz] **I** *v/t.* ozonisieren; **II** *v/i.* sich in O'zon verwandeln; **o·zo·niz·er** ['əʊzəʊnaɪzə] *s.* Ozoni'sator *m*.

P

P, p [piː] *s.* P *n*, p *n* (*Buchstabe*): ***mind one's P's and Q's*** sich sehr in acht nehmen.

pa [pɑː] *s.* F Pa'pa *m*, ‚Paps' *m*.

pab·u·lum ['pæbjʊləm] *s.* Nahrung *f* (*a. fig.*).

pace¹ [peɪs] **I** *s.* **1.** Schritt *m* (*a. als Maß*); **2.** Gang(art *f*) *m*: ***put a horse through its ~s*** ein Pferd alle Gangarten machen lassen; ***put s.o. through his ~s*** *fig.* j-n auf Herz u. Nieren prüfen; **3.** Paßgang *m* (*Pferd*); **4.** a) ⚔ Marschschritt *m*, b) (Marsch)Geschwindigkeit *f*, Tempo *n* (*a. sport*; *a. fig. e-r Handlung etc.*), Fahrt *f*, Schwung *m*: ***go the ~*** a) ein scharfes Tempo anschlagen, b) *fig.* flott leben; ***keep ~ with*** Schritt halten mit (*a. fig.*); ***set the ~*** *sport* das Tempo angeben (*a. fig.*) *od.* machen; ***at a great ~*** in schnellem Tempo; **II** *v/t.* **5.** *a.* ***~ out*** (*od.* ***off***) abschreiten; **6.** *Zimmer etc.* durch'schreiten, -'messen; **7.** *fig.* das Tempo (*gen.*) bestimmen; **8.** *sport* Schrittmacher sein für; **9.** *Pferd* im Paßgang gehen lassen; **III** *v/i.* **10.** (*auf u. ab etc.*) schreiten; **11.** im Paßgang gehen (*Pferd*).

pa·ce² ['peɪsɪ] (*Lat.*) *prp.* ohne (*dat.*) nahetreten zu wollen.

'pace|ˌmak·er *s. sport* (*a.* ⚕ Herz-) Schrittmacher *m*: ***~ race*** *Radsport*: Steherrennen *n*; **'~ˌmak·ing** *s. sport* Schrittmacherdienste *pl.*

pac·er ['peɪsə] *s.* **1.** → ***pacemaker***; **2.** Paßgänger *m* (*Pferd*).

pach·y·derm ['pækɪdɜːm] *s. zo.* Dickhäuter *m* (*a. humor. fig.*); **pach·y·der·ma·tous** [ˌpækɪ'dɜːmətəs] *adj.* **1.** *zo.* dickhäutig; *fig. a.* dickfellig; **2.** ⚘ dickwandig.

pa·cif·ic [pə'sɪfɪk] *adj.* (□ ***~ally***) **1.** friedfertig, versöhnlich, Friedens…: ***~ policy***; **2.** ruhig, friedlich; **3.** ℒ *geogr.* pa'zifisch, Pa'zifisch: ***the ℒ (Ocean)*** der Pazifische *od.* Stille Ozean, der Pa'zifik; **pac·i·fi·ca·tion** [ˌpæsɪfɪ'keɪʃn] *s.* **1.** Befriedung *f*; **2.** Beschwichtigung *f*.

pac·i·fi·er ['pæsɪfaɪə] *s.* **1.** Friedensstifter(in); **2.** *Am.* a) Schnuller *m*, b) Beißring *m für Kleinkinder*; **'pac·i·fism** [-fɪzəm] *s.* Pazi'fismus *m*; **'pac·i·fist** [-fɪst] **I** *s.* Pazi'fist *m*; **II** *adj.* pazi'fistisch; **'pac·i·fy** [-faɪ] *v/t.* **1.** *Land* befrieden; **2.** besänftigen, beschwichtigen.

pack [pæk] **I** *s.* **1.** Pack(en) *m*, Ballen *m*, Bündel *n*; **2.** *bsd. Am.* Packung *f*, Schachtel *f Zigaretten etc.*, Päckchen *n*: ***a ~ of films*** ein Filmpack *m*; **3.** ⚕, *Kosmetik*: Packung *f*: ***face ~***; **4.** (Karten)Spiel *n*; **5.** ⚔ a) Tor'nister *m*, b) Rückentrage *f* (*Kabelrolle etc.*); **6.** Verpackungsweise *f*; **7.** (Schub *m*) Kon'serven *pl.*; **8.** Menge *f*: ***a ~ of lies*** ein Haufen Lügen; ***a ~ of nonsense*** lauter Unsinn; **9.** Packeis *n*; **10.** Pack *n*, Bande *f* (*Diebe etc.*); **11.** Meute *f*, Koppel *f* (*Hunde*); Rudel *n* (*Wölfe*, ⚔ *U-Boote*); **12.** *Rugby*: Sturm(reihe *f*) *m*; **II** *v/t.* **13.** *oft* ***~ up*** einpacken (*a.* ⚕), zs.-, verpacken: ***~ it in!*** F *fig.* hör doch auf (damit)!; **14.** zs.-pressen, -pferchen; → ***sardine***; **15.** vollstopfen: ***a ~ed house*** *thea. etc.* ein zum Bersten volles Haus; **16.** eindosen, konservieren; **17.** ⚙ (ab)dichten; **18.** bepacken, -laden; **19.** *Geschworenenbank etc.* mit s-n Leuten besetzen; **20.** *Am.* F (bei sich) tragen: ***~ a hard punch*** *Boxen*: e-n harten Schlag haben; **21.** *a.* ***~ off*** (fort)schicken, (-)jagen; **III** *v/i.* **22.** packen (*oft* ***~ up***): ***~ up*** *fig.* ‚einpacken' (*es aufgeben*); **23.** sich *gut etc.* (ver)packen lassen; **24.** fest werden, sich fest zs.-ballen; **25.** *mst* ***~ off*** *fig.* sich packen *od.* da'vonmachen: ***send s.o. ~ing*** j-n fortjagen; **26.** ***~ up*** *sl.* ‚absterben', ‚verrecken' (*Motor*) (***on s.o.*** j-m).

pack·age ['pækɪdʒ] **I** *s.* **1.** Pack *m*, Ballen *m*; Frachtstück *n*; *bsd. Am.* Pa'ket *n*; **2.** Packung *f* (*Spaghetti etc.*); **3.** Verpackung *f*; **4.** ⚙ betriebsfertige Maschine *od.* Baueinheit; **5.** ☿, *pol.*, *fig.* Pa'ket *n* (*a. Computer*), *pol. a.* Junktim *n*: ***~ deal*** a) Kopplungsgeschäft *n*, b) Pau'schalarrangeˌment *n*, -angebot *n*: ***~ tour*** Pauschalreise *f*, c) *pol.* Junktim *n*, d) (als Ganzes *od.* en bloc verkauftes) ('Fernseh- *etc.*)Proˌgramm *n*; **II** *v/t.* **6.** verpacken; **7.** *Lebensmittel etc.* abpacken; **8.** ☿ en bloc anbieten *od.* verkaufen; **'pack·ag·ing** [-dʒɪŋ] **I** *s.* (Einzel-)Verpackung *f*; **II** *adj.* Verpackungs…: ***~ machine***.

'pack|-ˌan·i·mal *s.* Pack-, Lasttier *n*; **'~-cloth** *s.* Packleinwand *f*; **'~-drill** *s.* ⚔ Strafexerzieren *n* in voller Marschausrüstung.

pack·er ['pækə] *s.* **1.** (Ver)Packer(in); **2.** ☿ Verpacker *m*, Großhändler *m*; *Am.* Kon'servenˌhersteller *m*; **3.** Ver'packungsmaˌschine *f*.

pack·et ['pækɪt] **I** *s.* **1.** kleines Pa'ket, Päckchen *n*, Schachtel *f* (*Zigaretten etc.*); ***sell s.o. a ~*** F j-n ‚anschmieren'; **2.** ⚓ *a.* ***~ boat*** Postschiff *n*, Pa'ketboot *n*; **3.** *sl.* Haufen *m* Geld, *e-e* ‚(hübsche) Stange Geld'; **4.** *sl.* ‚Ding' *n* (*Schlag, Ärger etc.*); **II** *v/t.* **5.** verpacken, paketieren.

'pack|·horse *s.* **1.** Packpferd *n*; **2.** *fig.* Lastesel *m*; ***~ ice*** *s.* Packeis *n*.

pack·ing ['pækɪŋ] *s.* **1.** (Ver)Packen *n*: ***do one's ~*** packen; **2.** Konservierung *f*; **3.** Verpackung *f* (*a.* ☿); **4.** ⚙ a) (Ab-) Dichtung *f*, b) Dichtung *f*, c) 'Dichtungsmateriˌal *n*, d) Füllung *f*, e) *Computer*: Verdichtung *f*; **5.** Zs.-ballen *n*; ***~ box*** *s.* **1.** Packkiste *f*; **2.** ⚙ Stopfbüchse *f*; ***~ case*** *s.* Packkiste *f*; ***~ de·part·ment*** *s.* ☿ Packe'rei *f*; ***~ house*** *s.* **1.** *Am.* Abpackbetrieb *m*; **2.** Warenlager *n*; ***~ pa·per*** *s.* 'Packpaˌpier *n*; ***~ ring*** *s.* ⚙ Dichtring *m*, Man'schette *f*; ***~ sleeve*** *s.* ⚙ Dichtungsmuffe *f*.

pack| rat *s. zo.* Packratte *f*; **'~·sack** *s. Am.* Rucksack *m*, Tor'nister *m*; **'~ˌsad·dle** *s.* Pack-, Saumsattel *m*; **'~·thread** *s.* Packzwirn *m*, Bindfaden *m*; ***~ train*** *s.* 'Tragtierkoˌlonne *f*.

pact [pækt] s. Pakt *m*, Vertrag *m*.

pad¹ [pæd] **I** *s.* **1.** Polster *n*, (Stoß)Kissen *n*, Wulst *m*, Bausch *m*: ***oil ~*** ⚙ Schmierkissen *n*; **2.** *sport* Knie- *od.* Beinschützer *m*; **3.** 'Unterlage *f*; ⚙ Kon'sole *f für Hilfsgeräte*; **4.** ('Löschpaˌpier-, Brief-, Schreib)Block *m*; **5.** Stempelkissen *n*; **6.** *zo.* (Fuß)Ballen *m*; **7.** *hunt.* Pfote *f*; **8.** *sl.* ‚Bude' *f* (*Zimmer od. Wohnung*); **9.** ✈ a) Startrampe *f*, b) (Ra'keten)Abschußrampe *f*; **10.** *Am. sl.* a) Schutzgelder *pl.*, b) Schmiergelder *pl.*; **II** *v/t.* **11.** (aus)polstern, wattieren: ***~ded cell*** Gummizelle *f* (*für Irre*): **12.** *fig. Rede, Schrift* ‚garnieren', ‚aufblähen'.

pad² [pæd] *v/t. u. v/i. a.* ***~ along*** *sl.* (da'hin)trotten, (-)latschen.

pad·ding ['pædɪŋ] *s.* **1.** (Aus)Polstern *n*; **2.** Polsterung *f*, Wattierung *f*, Einlage *f*; **3.** (Polster)Füllung *f*; **4.** *fig.* leeres Füllwerk, (Zeilen)Füllsel *n*; **5.** *a.* ***~ capacitor*** ⚡ 'Paddingkondenˌsator *m*.

pad·dle ['pædl] **I** *s.* **1.** Paddel *n*: **2.** ⚓ a) Schaufel(rad *n*) *f*, b) Raddampfer *m*; **3.** *obs.* Waschbleuel *m*; **4.** ⚙ Kratze *f*, Rührstange *f*; **5.** ⚙ a) Schaufel *f* (*Wasserrad*), b) Schütz *n*, Falltor *n* (*Schleuse*); **II** *v/i.* **6.** rudern, *bsd.* paddeln; → ***canoe*** I; **7.** *im Wasser* planschen; **8.** watscheln; **III** *v/t.* **9.** paddeln; **10.** *Am.* F verhauen; ***~ steam·er*** *s.* ⚓ Raddampfer *m*; ***~ wheel*** *s.* Schaufelrad *n*.

pad·dling pool ['pædlɪŋ] *s.* Planschbecken *n*.

pad·dock¹ ['pædək] *s.* **1.** (Pferde)Koppel *f*; **2.** *sport* a) Sattelplatz *m*, b) *mot.* Fahrerlager *n*.

pad·dock² ['pædək] *s. zo.* **1.** *obs. od. dial.* Frosch *m*; **2.** *obs.* Kröte *f*.

Pad·dy¹ ['pædɪ] *s.* F ‚'Paddy' *m* (*Ire*).

pad·dy² ['pædɪ] *s.* ☿ roher Reis.

pad·dy³ ['pædɪ] *s.* F Wutanfall *m*; ***~ wag·on*** *s. Am.* F ‚grüne Minna' (*Polizeigefangenenwagen*).

pad·lock ['pædlɒk] **I** *s.* Vorhänge-, Vorlegeschloß *n*; **II** *v/t.* mit e-m Vorhängeschloß verschließen.

pa·dre ['pɑ:drɪ] *s.* Pater *m* (*Priester*); ⚔ Ka'plan *m*.

pae·an ['pi:ən] *s.* **1.** *antiq.* Pä'an *m*; **2.** *allg.* Freuden-, Lobgesang *m*.

paed·er·ast *etc.* → ***pederast*** *etc.*

pae·di·at·ric *etc.* → ***pediatric*** *etc.*

pa·gan ['peɪgən] **I** *s.* Heide *m*, Heidin *f*; **II** *adj.* heidnisch; '**pa·gan·ism** [-nɪzəm] *s.* Heidentum *n*.

page[1] [peɪdʒ] **I** *s.* **1.** Seite *f* (*Buch etc.*); *typ.* Schriftseite *f*, Ko'lumne *f*: **~ *printer*** *tel.* Blattdrucker *m*; **2.** *fig.* Chronik *f*, Buch *n*; **3.** *fig.* Blatt *n aus der Geschichte etc.*; **II** *v/t.* **4.** paginieren.

page[2] [peɪdʒ] **I** *s.* **1.** *hist.* Page *m*; Edelknabe *m*; **2.** *a.* **~ *boy*** (Ho'tel)Page *m*; **II** *v/t.* **3.** *j-n* (durch e-n Pagen *od.* per Lautsprecher) ausrufen lassen; **4.** mit *j-m* über Funkrufempfänger Kon'takt aufnehmen, *j-n* ,anpiepsen'.

pag·eant ['pædʒənt] *s.* **1.** a) (*bsd.* hi'storischer) Fest- *od.* Umzug, b) (historisches) Festspiel; **2.** (Schau)Gepränge *n*, Pomp *m*; **3.** *fig.* leerer Prunk; '**pag·eant·ry** [-rɪ] *s.* → ***pageant*** 2, 3.

pag·er ['peɪdʒə(r)] Funkrufempfänger *m*, ,Piepser' *m*.

pag·i·nal ['pædʒɪnl] *adj.* Seiten...; '**pag·i·nate** [-neɪt] *v/t.* paginieren; **pag·i·na·tion** [ˌpædʒɪ'neɪʃn], *a.* **pag·ing** ['peɪdʒɪŋ] *s.* Paginierung *f*, 'Seitennumeˌrierung *f*.

pa·go·da [pə'gəʊdə] *s.* Pa'gode *f*; **~ *tree*** *s.* ♀ So'phora *f*: ***shake the* ~** *obs. fig.* in Indien schnell ein Vermögen machen.

pah [pɑ:] *int. contp.* a) pfui!, b) pah!

paid [peɪd] **I** *pret. u. p.p. von* ***pay***; **II** *adj.* bezahlt: **~ *in*** → ***paid-in***; **~ *up*** → ***paid-up***; ***put* ~ *to s.th.*** e-r Sache ein Ende setzen; **ˌ~-'in** *adj.* **1.** ✝ (voll) eingezahlt: **~ *capital*** Einlagekapital *n*; **2.** → ***paid-up*** 2; **ˌ~-'up** *adj.* **1.** → ***paid-in*** 1; **2. *fully* ~ *member*** Mitglied *n* ohne Beitragsrückstände, vollwertiges Mitglied.

pail [peɪl] *s.* Eimer *m*, Kübel *m*; '**pail·ful** [-fʊl] *s. ein* Eimer(voll) *m*: ***by* ~*s*** eimerweise.

pail·lasse ['pælɪæs] *s.* Strohsack *m* (*Matratze*).

pain [peɪn] **I** *s.* **1.** Schmerz(en *pl.*) *m*, Pein *f*; *pl.* ⚕ (Geburts)Wehen *pl.*: ***be in* ~** Schmerzen haben, leiden; ***you are a* ~ *in the neck*** F du gehst mir auf die Nerven; **2.** Schmerz(en *pl.*) *m*, Leid *n*, Kummer *m*: ***give*** (*od.* ***cause***) ***s.o.* ~** j-m Kummer machen; **3.** *pl.* Mühe *f*, Bemühungen *pl.*: ***be at* ~*s*, *take* ~*s*** sich Mühe geben, sich anstrengen; ***spare no* ~*s*** keine Mühe scheuen; ***all he got for his* ~*s*** der (ganze) Dank (für s-e Mühe); **4.** Strafe *f*: (***up***)***on*** (*od.* ***under***) **~ *of*** bei Strafe von; ***on*** (*od.* ***under***) **~ *of death*** bei Todesstrafe; **II** *v/t.* **5.** *j-m* weh tun, *j-n* schmerzen; *fig. a. j-n* schmerzlich berühren, peinigen; **pained** [-nd] *adj.* gequält, schmerzlich; '**pain·ful** [-fʊl] *adj.* □ **1.** schmerzhaft; **2.** a) schmerzlich, quälend, b) peinlich: ***produce a* ~ *impression*** peinlich wirken; **3.** mühsam; '**pain·ful·ness** [-fʊlnɪs] *s.* Schmerzhaftigkeit *f etc.*; '**painˌkill·er** *s.* F schmerzstillendes Mittel; '**pain·less** [-lɪs] *adj.* □ schmerzlos (*a. fig.*).

pains·tak·ing ['peɪnzˌteɪkɪŋ] **I** *adj.* □ sorgfältig, gewissenhaft; eifrig; **II** *s.* Sorgfalt *f*, Mühe *f*.

paint [peɪnt] **I** *v/t.* **1.** *Bild* malen; *fig.* ausmalen, schildern: **~ *s.o.'s portrait*** j-n malen; **2.** an-, bemalen, (an)streichen; *Auto* lackieren: **~ *out*** übermalen; **~ *the town red*** *sl.* ,auf die Pauke hauen', ,(schwer) einen draufmachen'; → ***lily***; **3.** *Mittel* auftragen, *Hals*, *Wunde* (aus)pinseln; **4.** schminken: **~ *one's face*** sich schminken, sich ,anmalen'; **II** *v/i.* **5.** malen; **6.** streichen; **7.** sich schminken; **III** *s.* **8.** (Anstrich-, Öl)Farbe *f*; (Auto)Lack *m*; Tünche *f*; **9.** *a.* ***coat of* ~** Anstrich *m*: ***as fresh as* ~** F frisch u. munter; **10.** Schminke *f*; **11.** ⚕ Tink'tur *f*; '**~·box** *s.* **1.** Tusch-, Malkasten *m*; **2.** Schminkdose *f*; '**~·brush** *s.* Pinsel *m*.

paint·ed ['peɪntɪd] *p.p. u. adj.* **1.** ge-, bemalt, gestrichen; lackiert; **2.** *bsd.* ♀, *zo.* bunt, scheckig; **3.** *fig.* gefärbt; ≈ **La·dy** *s.* **1.** *zo.* Distelfalter *m*; **2.** ♀ Rote Wucherblume; **~ *wom·an*** *s.* Hure *f*, ,Flittchen' *n*.

paint·er[1] ['peɪntə] *s.* ⚓ Fangleine *f*: ***cut the* ~** *fig.* alle Brücken hinter sich abbrechen.

paint·er[2] ['peɪntə] *s.* **1.** (Kunst)Maler (-in); **2.** Maler *m*, Anstreicher *m*: **~*'s colic*** ⚕ Bleikolik *f*; **~*'s shop*** a) Malerwerkstatt *f*, b) (Auto)Lackiererei *f*; '**paint·ing** [-tɪŋ] *s.* **1.** Malen *n*, Male'rei *f*: **~ *in oil*** Ölmalerei *f*; **2.** Gemälde *n*, Bild *n*; **3.** ⚙ a) Farbanstrich *m*, b) Spritzlackieren *n*.

paint| re·fresh·er *s.* 'Neuglanzpoliˌtur *f*; **~ *re·mov·er*** *s.* (Farben)Abbeizmittel *n*.

paint·ress ['peɪntrɪs] *s.* Malerin *f*.

'**paint|-ˌspray·ing pis·tol** *s.* ⚙ ('Anstreich)ˌSpritzpiˌstole *f*; '**~·work** *s. mot.* Lackierung *f*, Lack *m*.

pair [peə] **I** *s.* **1.** Paar *n*: ***a* ~ *of boots*, *legs etc.***; **2.** (*Zweiteiliges*, *mst unübersetzt*): ***a* ~ *of scales*** (***scissors***, ***spectacles***) eine Waage (Schere, Brille); ***a* ~ *of trousers*** ein Paar Hosen, eine Hose; **3.** Paar *n*, Pärchen *n* (*Mann u. Frau; zo. Männchen u. Weibchen*): **~ *skating*** *sport* Paarlauf(en *n*) *m*; ***in* ~*s*** paarweise; **4.** Partner *m*; Gegenstück *n* (*von e-m Paar*); *der* (*die*, *das*) andere *od.* zweite: ***where is the* ~ *to this shoe?***; **5.** *pol.* a) *zwei Mitglieder verschiedener Parteien*, *die sich abgesprochen haben*, *sich der Stimme zu enthalten etc.*, b) *dieses Abkommen*, c) *e-r dieser Partner*; **6.** (Zweier)Gespann *n*: ***carriage and* ~** Zweispänner *m*; **7.** *sport* Zweier *m* (*Ruderboot*): **~ *with cox*** Zweier mit Steuermann; **8.** *a.* ***kinematic* ~** ⚙ Ele'mentenpaar *n*; **9.** *Brit.* **~ *of stairs*** (*od.* ***steps***) Treppe *f*: ***two* ~ *front*** (***back***) (Raum *m od.* Mieter *m*) im zweiten Stock nach vorn (hinten); **II** *v/t.* **10.** *a.* **~ *off*** a) paarweise anordnen, b) F *fig.* verheiraten; **11.** *Tiere* paaren (***with*** mit); **III** *v/i.* **12.** sich paaren (*Tiere*) (*a. fig.*); **13.** zs.-passen; **14.** **~ *off*** a) paarweise weggehen, b) F *fig.* sich verheiraten (***with*** mit), c) *pol.* (***with*** mit *e-m Mitglied e-r anderen Partei*) ein Abkommen treffen (→ 5a); **pair·ing** ['peərɪŋ] *s. biol.* Paarung *f* (*a. sport*): **~ *season*, ~ *time*** Paarungszeit *f*.

pair-oar ['peərɔ:] **I** *s.* Zweier *m* (*Boot*); **II** *adj.* zweiruderig.

pa·ja·mas [pə'dʒɑ:məs] *bsd. Am.* → ***pyjamas***.

Pak·i ['pækɪ] *s. Brit. sl.* Paki'stani *m*.

Pak·i·stan·i [ˌpɑ:kɪ'stɑ:nɪ] **I** *adj.* paki'stanisch; **II** *s.* Paki'staner(in), Paki'stani *m*.

pal [pæl] **I** *s.* F ,Kumpel' *m*, ,Spezi' *m*, Freund *m*; **II** *v/i. mst* **~ *up*** F sich anfreunden (***with s.o.*** mit j-m).

pal·ace ['pælɪs] *s.* Schloß *n*, Pa'last *m*, Pa'lais *n*: **~ *of justice*** Justizpalast; **~ *car*** *s.* 🚃 Sa'lonwagen *m*; **~ *guard*** *s.* **1.** Pa'lastwache *f*; **2.** *fig. contp.* Clique *f um e-n Regierungschef*, Kama'rilla *f*; **~ *rev·o·lu·tion*** *s. pol. fig.* Pa'lastrevoluˌtiˌon *f*.

pal·a·din ['pælədɪn] *s. hist.* Pala'din *m* (*a. fig.*).

pa·lae·og·ra·pher *etc.* → ***paleographer*** *etc.*

pal·at·a·ble ['pælətəbl] *adj.* □ wohlschmeckend, schmackhaft (*a. fig.*); '**pal·a·tal** [-tl] **I** *adj.* **1.** Gaumen...; **II** *s.* **2.** Gaumenknochen *m*; **3.** *ling.* Pala'tal (-laut) *m*; '**pal·a·tal·ize** [-təlaɪz] *v/t. ling. Laut* palatalisieren; **pal·ate** ['pælət] *s.* **1.** *anat.* Gaumen *m*: ***bony*** (*od.* ***hard***) **~** harter Gaumen, Vordergaumen; ***cleft* ~** Wolfsrachen *m*; ***soft* ~** weicher Gaumen, Gaumensegel *n*; **2.** *fig.* (***for***) Gaumen *m*, Sinn *m* (für), Geschmack *m* (an *dat.*).

pa·la·tial [pə'leɪʃl] *adj.* pa'lastartig, Palast..., Schloß..., Luxus...

pa·lat·i·nate [pə'lætɪnət] **I** *s.* **1.** *hist.* Pfalzgrafschaft *f*; **2.** ***the*** ≈ die (Rhein-) Pfalz; **II** *adj.* **3.** ≈ Pfälzer, pfälzisch.

pal·a·tine[1] ['pælətaɪn] **I** *adj.* **1.** *hist.* Pfalz..., pfalzgräflich: ***Count*** ≈ Pfalzgraf; ***County*** ≈ Pfalzgrafschaft *f*; **2.** ≈ pfälzisch, Pfälzer(...); **II** *s.* **3.** Pfalzgraf *m*; **4.** ≈ (Rhein)Pfälzer(in).

pal·a·tine[2] ['pælətaɪn] *anat.* **I** *adj.* Gaumen...: **~ *tonsil*** Gaumen-, Halsmandel *f*; **II** *s.* Gaumenbein *n*.

pa·lav·er [pə'lɑ:və] **I** *s.* **1.** Unter'handlung *f*, -'redung *f*, Konfe'renz *f*; **2.** F ,Pa'laver' *n*, Geschwätz *n*; **3.** F ,Wirbel' *m*; **II** *v/i.* **4.** unter'handeln; **5.** pa'lavern, ,quasseln'; **III** *v/t.* **6.** F *j-n* beschwatzen; *j-m* schmeicheln.

pale[1] [peɪl] **I** *s.* **1.** Pfahl *m* (*a. her.*); **2.** *bsd. fig.* um'grenzter Raum, Bereich *m*, (enge) Grenzen *pl.*: ***beyond the* ~** *fig.* jenseits der Grenzen des Erlaubten; ***within the* ~ *of the Church*** im Schoße der Kirche; **II** *v/t.* **3.** *a.* **~ *in*** einpfählen, -zäunen; *fig.* um'schließen; **4.** *hist.* pfählen.

pale[2] [peɪl] **I** *adj.* □ **1.** blaß, bleich, fahl: ***turn* ~** → 3; **~ *with fright*** schreckensbleich; ***as* ~ *as ashes*** (***clay***, ***death***) aschfahl (kreidebleich, totenblaß); **2.** hell, blaß, matt (*Farben*): **~ *ale*** helles Bier; **~ *green*** Blaß-, Zartgrün; **~ *pink*** (Blaß)Rosa; **II** *v/i.* **3.** blaß werden, erbleichen, erblassen; **4.** *fig.* verblassen (***before*** *od.* ***beside*** vor *dat.*); **III** *v/t.* **5.** bleich machen, erbleichen lassen.

'**pale·face** *s.* Bleichgesicht *n* (*Ggs. Indianer*).

pale·ness ['peɪlnɪs] *s.* Blässe *f*, Farblosigkeit *f* (*a. fig.*).

pa·le·og·ra·pher [ˌpælɪ'ɒgrəfə] *s.* Paläo'graph *m*; ˌ**pa·le'og·ra·phy** [-fɪ] *s.* **1.**

alte Schriftarten *pl.*, alte Schriftdenkmäler *pl.*; **2.** Paläogra'phie *f*, Handschriftenkunde *f*.
pa·le·o·lith·ic [ˌpælɪəʊ'lɪθɪk] **I** *adj.* paläo'lithisch, altsteinzeitlich; **II** *s.* Altsteinzeit *f*.
pa·le·on·tol·o·gist [ˌpælɪɒn'tɒlədʒɪst] *s.* Paläonto'loge *m*; ˌ**pa·le·on'tol·o·gy** [-dʒɪ] *s.* Paläontolo'gie *f*.
pa·le·o·zo·ic [ˌpælɪəʊ'zəʊɪk] *geol.* **I** *adj.* paläo'zoisch: **~ era** → II; **II** *s.* Paläo'zoikum *n*.
Pal·es·tin·i·an [ˌpæle'stɪnɪən] **I** *adj.* palästi'nensisch; **II** *s.* Palästi'nenser(in).
pal·e·tot ['pæltəʊ] *s.* **1.** 'Paletot *m*, 'Überzieher *m* (*für Herren*); **2.** loser (Damen)Mantel.
pal·ette ['pælət] *s. paint.* Pa'lette *f*, *fig. a.* Farbenskala *f*; **~ knife** *s.* Streichmesser *n*, Spachtel *m*, *f*.
pal·frey ['pɔːlfrɪ] *s.* Zelter *m*.
pal·ing ['peɪlɪŋ] *s.* Um'pfählung *f*, Pfahl-, Lattenzaun *m*, Sta'ket *n*.
pal·in·gen·e·sis [ˌpælɪn'dʒenɪsɪs] *s. bsd. eccl.* 'Wiedergeburt *f*, *a. biol.* Palinge'nese *f*.
pal·i·sade [ˌpælɪ'seɪd] **I** *s.* **1.** Pali'sade *f*; Pfahlzaun *m*, Sta'ket *n*; **2.** Schanzpfahl *m*; **II** *v/t.* **3.** mit Pfählen *od.* mit e-r Palisade um'geben.
pall[1] [pɔːl] *s.* **1.** Bahr-, Leichentuch *n*; **2.** *fig.* Mantel *m*, Hülle *f*, Decke *f*; **3.** a) (Rauch)Wolke *f*, b) Dunstglocke *f*; **4.** *eccl.* → ***pallium*** 2; **5.** *her.* Gabel(kreuz *n*) *f*.
pall[2] [pɔːl] **I** *v/i.* **1.** (***on***, ***upon***) jeden Reiz verlieren (für), *j-n* kalt lassen *od.* langweilen; **2.** schal *od.* fade werden, s-n Reiz verlieren; **II** *v/t.* **3.** *a. fig.* über'sättigen.
pal·la·di·um [pə'leɪdjəm] [-djə] *s.* Pal'ladium *n*: a) *pl.* **-di·a** *fig.* Hort *m*, Schutz *m*, b) ⚗ *ein Element.*
'**pallˌbear·er** *s.* Sargträger *m*.
pal·let[1] ['pælɪt] *s.* (Stroh)Lager *n*, Strohsack *m*, Pritsche *f*.
pal·let[2] ['pælɪt] *s.* **1.** ⚙ Dreh-, Töpferscheibe *f*; **2.** *paint.* Pa'lette *f*; **3.** Trokkenbrett *n* (*für Keramik*, *Ziegel etc.*); **4.** ⚙ Pa'lette: **~ truck** Gabelstapler *m*; '**pal·let·ize** [-lətaɪz] *v/t.* ⚙ palettieren.
pal·liasse ['pælɪæs] → ***paillasse***.
pal·li·ate ['pælɪeɪt] *v/t.* **1.** ⚕ lindern; **2.** *fig.* bemänteln, beschönigen; **pal·li·a·tion** [ˌpælɪ'eɪʃn] *s.* **1.** Linderung *f*; **2.** Bemäntelung *f*, Beschönigung *f*; '**pal·li·a·tive** [-ɪətɪv] **I** *adj.* **1.** ⚕ lindernd, pallia'tiv; **2.** *fig.* bemäntelnd, beschönigend; **II** *s.* **3.** ⚕ Linderungsmittel *n*; **4.** *fig.* Bemäntelung *f*.
pal·lid ['pælɪd] *adj.* □ *a. fig.* blaß, farblos; '**pal·lid·ness** [-nɪs] *s.* Blässe *f*.
pal·li·um ['pælɪəm] *pl.* **-li·a** [-lɪə], **-li·ums** *s.* **1.** *antiq.* 'Pallium *n*, Philo'sophenmantel *m*; **2.** *eccl.* a) Pallium *n* (*Schulterband des Erzbischofs*), b) Al'tartuch *n*; **3.** *anat.* (Ge)Hirnmantel *m*; **4.** *zo.* Mantel *m*.
pal·lor ['pælə] *s.* Blässe *f*.
pal·ly ['pælɪ] *adj.* F **1.** (eng) befreundet; **2.** kumpelhaft.
palm[1] [pɑːm] **I** *s.* **1.** Handfläche *f*, -teller *m*, hohle Hand: ***grease*** (*od.* ***oil***) ***s.o.'s ~*** j-n ‚schmieren', bestechen; **2.** Hand(-breite) *f* (*als Maß*); **3.** Schaufel *f* (*Anker*, *Hirschgeweih*); **II** *v/t.* **4.** betasten, streicheln; **5.** a) palmieren (*wegzaubern*), b) *Am. sl.* ‚klauen', stehlen; **6. ~ *s.th. off on s.o.*, ~ *s.o. off with s.th.*** j-m et. ‚aufhängen' *od.* ‚andrehen'; **~ *o.s. off*** (***as***) sich ausgeben (als).
palm[2] [pɑːm] *s.* **1.** ♆ Palme *f*; **2.** *fig.* Siegespalme *f*, Krone *f*, Sieg *m*: ***bear*** (*od.* ***win***) ***the ~*** den Sieg davontragen; → ***yield*** 4.
pal·mate ['pælmɪt] *adj.* **1.** ♆ handförmig (gefingert *od.* geteilt); **2.** *zo.* schwimmfüßig.
palm grease *s.* F Schmiergeld *n*.
pal·mi·ped ['pælmɪped], '**pal·mi·pede** [-ɪpiːd] *zo.* **I** *adj.* schwimmfüßig; **II** *s.* Schwimmfüßer *m*.
palm·ist ['pɑːmɪst] *s.* Handleser(in); '**palm·is·try** [-trɪ] *s.* Handlesekunst *f*, Chiroman'tie *f*.
palm| oil *s.* **1.** Palmöl *n*; **2.** → ***palm grease***; **♀ Sun·day** *s.* Palm'sonntag *m*; **~ tree** *s.* Palme *f*.
palm·y ['pɑːmɪ] *adj.* **1.** palmenreich; **2.** *fig.* glorreich, Glanz..., Blüte...
pa·loo·ka [pə'luːkə] *s. Am. sl.* **1.** *bsd. sport* ‚Niete' *f*, ‚Flasche' *f*; **2.** ‚Ochse' *m*; **3.** Lümmel *m*.
palp [pælp] *s. zo.* Taster *m*, Fühler *m*; **pal·pa·bil·i·ty** [ˌpælpə'bɪlətɪ] *s.* **1.** Fühl-, Greif-, Tastbarkeit *f*; **2.** *fig.* Handgreiflichkeit *f*, Augenfälligkeit *f*; '**pal·pa·ble** [-pəbl] *adj.* □ **1.** fühl-, greif-, tastbar; **2.** *fig.* handgreiflich, augenfällig; '**pal·pa·ble·ness** [-pəblnɪs] → ***palpability***; '**pal·pate** [-peɪt] *v/t.* befühlen, abtasten (*a.* ⚕); **pal·pa·tion** [pæl'peɪʃn] *s.* Abtasten *n* (*a.* ⚕).
pal·pe·bra ['pælpɪbrə] *s. anat.* Augenlid *n*: ***lower ~*** Unterlid *n*.
pal·pi·tant ['pælpɪtənt] *adj.* klopfend, pochend; **pal·pi·tate** ['pælpɪteɪt] *v/i.* **1.** klopfen, pochen (*Herz*); **2.** (er)zittern; **pal·pi·ta·tion** [ˌpælpɪ'teɪʃn] *s.* Klopfen *n*, (heftiges) Schlagen: **~ (*of the heart*)** ⚕ Herzklopfen *n*.
pal·sied ['pɔːlzɪd] *adj.* **1.** gelähmt; **2.** zittrig, wacklig; **pal·sy** ['pɔːlzɪ] **I** *s.* **1.** ⚕ Lähmung *f*: ***shaking ~*** Schüttellähmung; ***wasting ~*** progressive Muskelatrophie; → ***writer*** 1; **2.** *fig.* Ohnmacht *f*, Lähmung *f*; **II** *v/t.* **3.** lähmen.
pal·ter ['pɔːltə] *v/i.* **1.** (***with***) gemein handeln (an *dat.*), sein Spiel treiben (mit); **2.** feilschen.
pal·tri·ness ['pɔːltrɪnɪs] *s.* Armseligkeit *f*, Schäbigkeit *f*; **pal·try** ['pɔːltrɪ] *adj.* □ **1.** armselig, karg: ***a ~ sum***; **2.** dürftig, fadenscheinig: ***a ~ excuse***; **3.** schäbig, schofel, gemein: ***a ~ fellow***; ***a ~ lie***; ***a ~ ten dollars*** lumpige zehn Dollar.
pam·pas ['pæmpəs] *s. pl.* Pampas *pl.* (*südamer. Grasebene*[*n*]).
pam·per ['pæmpə] *v/t.* verwöhnen, -hätscheln; *fig. Stolz etc.* nähren, ‚hätscheln'; *e-m Gelüst* frönen.
pam·phlet ['pæmflɪt] *s.* **1.** Bro'schüre *f*, Druckschrift *f*, Heft *n*; **2.** Flugblatt *n*, -schrift *f*; **pam·phlet·eer** [ˌpæmflə'tɪə] *s.* Verfasser(in) von Flugschriften.
pan[1] [pæn] **I** *s.* **1.** Pfanne *f*: ***frying ~*** Bratpfanne; **2.** ⚙ Pfanne *f*, Tiegel *m*, Becken *n*, Mulde *f*, Trog *m*; **3.** Schale *f* (*e-r Waage*); **4.** ⚔ *hist.* (Zünd)Pfanne *f*; → ***flash*** 2; **5.** *sl.* Vi'sage *f*, Gesicht *n*; **6.** F ‚Verriß' *m*, vernichtende Kri'tik; **II** *v/t.* **7.** *oft* **~ *out***, **~ *off*** *Gold*(*sand*) auswaschen; **8.** F ‚verreißen', scharf kritisieren; **III** *v/i.* **9. ~ *out*** *Am. sl.* sich bezahlt machen, ‚klappen': **~ *out well*** a) *an Gold* ergiebig sein, b) *fig.* ‚hinhauen', ‚einschlagen'.
pan[2] [pæn] **I** *v/t. Filmkamera* schwenken, fahren; **II** *v/i.* a) panoramieren, die 'Filmˌkamera fahren *od.* schwenken, b) (her'um)schwenken (*Kamera*); **III** *s. Film*: Schwenk *m*.
pan- [pæn] *in Zssgn* all..., gesamt...; All..., Gesamt..., Pan...
pan·a·ce·a [ˌpænə'sɪə] *s.* All'heil-, Wundermittel *n*; *fig. a.* Pa'tentreˌzept *n*.
pa·nache [pə'næʃ] *s.* **1.** Helm-, Federbusch *m*; **2.** *fig.* Großtue'rei *f*.
Pan-A·mer·i·can [ˌpænə'merɪkən] *adj.* panameri'kanisch.
'**pan·cake I** *s.* **1.** Pfann-, Eierkuchen *m*; **2.** Leder *n* geringerer Qualität (*aus Resten hergestellt*); **3.** *a.* **~ *landing*** ✈ Bumslandung *f*; **II** *v/i.* **4.** ✈ *bei Landung* 'durchsacken; **III** *v/t.* **5.** ✈ *Maschine* 'durchsacken lassen; **IV** *adj.* **6.** Pfannkuchen...: **~ *Day*** F Fastnachtsdienstag *m*; **7.** flach: **~ *coil*** ⚡ Flachspule.
pan·chro·mat·ic [ˌpænkrəʊ'mætɪk] *adj.* ♪, *phot.* panchro'matisch.
pan·cre·as ['pæŋkrɪəs] *s. anat.* Bauchspeicheldrüse *f*, Pankreas *n*; **pan·cre·at·ic** [ˌpæŋkrɪ'ætɪk] *adj.* Bauchspeicheldrüsen...: **~ *juice*** Bauchspeichel *m*.
pan·da ['pændə] *s. zo.* Panda *m*, Katzenbär *m*; **~ car** *s. Brit.* (Funk-, Poli'zei)Streifenwagen *m*; **~ cros·sing** *s. Brit.* 'Fußgängerˌüberweg *m* mit Druckampel.
pan·dem·ic [pæn'demɪk] *adj.* ⚕ pan'demisch, ganz allgemein verbreitet.
pan·de·mo·ni·um [ˌpændɪ'məʊnjəm] *s. fig.* **1.** In'ferno *n*, Hölle *f*; **2.** Höllenlärm *m*.
pan·der ['pændə] **I** *s.* **1.** a) Kuppler(in), b) Zuhälter *m*; **2.** *fig.* j-d, der aus den Schwächen u. Lastern anderer Kapi'tal schlägt; j-d, der e-m Laster Vorschub leistet; **II** *v/t.* **3.** verkuppeln; **III** *v/i.* **4.** kuppeln; **5.** (***to***) *e-m Laster etc.* Vorschub leisten: **~ *to s.o.'s ambition*** j-s Ehrgeiz anstacheln.
Pan·do·ra's box [pæn'dɔːrəz] *s. myth. u. fig.* die Büchse der Pan'dora.
pane [peɪn] *s.* **1.** (Fenster)Scheibe *f*; **2.** ⚙ Feld *n*, Fach *n*, Platte *f*, Tafel *f*, Füllung *f* (*Tür*), ⚠ Kas'sette *f* (*Decke*): **~ *of glass*** *e-e* Tafel Glas; **3.** ebene Seitenfläche; Finne *f* (*Hammer*); Fa'cette *f* (*Edelstein*).
pan·e·gyr·ic [ˌpænɪ'dʒɪrɪk] **I** *s.* Lobrede *f*, -preisung *f*, -schrift *f*, Lobeshymne *f* (***on*** über *acc.*); **II** *adj.* → **pan·e'gyr·i·cal** [-kl] *adj.* □ lobpreisend, Lob(es)...; ˌ**pan·e'gyr·ist** [-ɪst] *s.* Lobredner *m*; **pan·e·gy·rize** ['pænɪdʒɪraɪz] **I** *v/t.* (lob)preisen, ‚in den Himmel heben'; **II** *v/i.* sich in Lobeshymnen ergehen.
pan·el ['pænl] **I** *s.* **1.** ⚠ (vertieftes) Feld, Fach *n*, Füllung *f* (*Tür*), Täfelung *f* (*Wand*); **2.** Tafel *f* (*Holz*), Platte *f* (*Blech etc.*); **3.** *paint.* Holztafel *f*, Gemälde *n* auf Holz; **4.** *phot.* (Bild *n* im) 'Hochforˌmat *n*; **5.** Einsatz(streifen) *m am Kleid*; **6.** ✈ a) ⚔ 'Flieger-, Si'gnaltuch *n*, b) Stoffbahn *f* (*Fallschirm*), c) Streifen *m* der Bespannung (*am Flugzeugflügel*), Verkleidung(sblech *n*) *f* (*Flügelbauteil*); **7.** ⚡, ⚙ a) → ***instru-***

ment 6, b) Schalttafel(feld *n*) *f*, c) *Radio etc.*: Feld *n*, Einschub *m*, d) → ***panel board*** 2; **8.** (Bau)Abteilung *f*, Abschnitt *m*; **9.** ⚒ (Abbau)Feld *n*; **10.** ⚖ a) Liste *f* der Geschworenen, b) Geschworene *pl.*; **11.** (ˈUnter)Ausschuß *m*, Kommissiˈon *f*, Gremium *n*, Kammer *f*; **12.** a) → ***panel discussion***, b) Diskussiˈonsteilnehmer *pl.*; **13.** *Meinungsforschung*: Befragtengruppe *f*; **II** *v/t.* **14.** täfeln, paneelieren, in Felder einteilen; **15.** *Kleid* mit Einsatzstreifen verzieren.

pan·el| board *s.* **1.** ⚙ Füllbrett *n*, (Wand-, Parˈkett)Tafel *f*; **2.** ⚡ Schaltbrett *n*, -tafel *f*; ~ **dis·cus·sion** *s.* Podiumsgespräch *n*, öffentliche Diskussiˈon; ~ **game** *s.* *TV etc.*: Ratespiel *n*, ˈQuiz(proˌgramm) *n*; ~ **heat·ing** *s.* Flächenheizung *f*.

pan·el·ist [ˈpænlɪst] *s.* **1.** Diskussiˈonsteilnehmer(in); **2.** *TV etc.* Teilnehmer (-in) an e-m ˈQuizproˌgramm.

pan·el·(l)ing [ˈpænlɪŋ] *s.* Täfelung *f*, Verkleidung *f*.

pan·el| sys·tem *s.* ˈListensyˌstem *n* (*für die Auswahl von Abgeordneten etc.*); ~ **saw** *s.* Laubsäge *f*; ~ **truck** *s.* *Am.* (kleiner) Lieferwagen; ˈ~**·work** *s.* Tafel-, Fachwerk *n*.

pang [pæŋ] *s.* **1.** plötzlicher Schmerz, Stechen *n*, Stich *m*: ***death ~s*** Todesqualen; ***~s of hunger*** nagender Hunger; ***~s of love*** Liebesschmerz *m*; **2.** *fig.* aufschießende Angst, plötzlicher Schmerz, Qual *f*, Weh *n*, Pein *f*: ***~s of remorse*** heftige Gewissensbisse.

ˌPan-ˈGer·man I *adj.* ˈpangerˌmanisch, all-, großdeutsch; **II** *s.* ˈPangermaˌnist *m*, Alldeutsche(r) *m*.

pan·han·dle [ˈpænˌhændl] **I** *s.* **1.** Pfannenstiel *m*; **2.** *Am.* schmaler Fortsatz (*bes. e-s Staatsgebiets*); **II** *v/t. u. v/i.* **3.** *Am. sl. j-n* (an)betteln, *et.* ‚schnorren', erbetteln (*a. fig.*); ˈ**panˌhan·dler** [-lə] *s. Am. sl.* Bettler *m*, ‚Schnorrer' *m*.

pan·ic[1] [ˈpænɪk] *s.* ⚘ (Kolben)Hirse *f*.

pan·ic[2] [ˈpænɪk] **I** *adj.* **1.** panisch: ~ ***fear***; ~ ***haste*** blinde Hast; ~ ***braking*** *mot.* scharfes Bremsen; ~ ***buying*** Angstkäufe; ***push the ~ button*** *fig.* F panisch reagieren; ***be at ~ stations*** F fast ‚ˈdurchdrehen'; **II** *s.* **2.** Panik *f*, panischer Schrecken; **3.** ✝ Börsenpanik *f*, Kurssturz *m*: ***~-proof*** krisenfest; **4.** *Am. sl.* etwas zum Totlachen; **III** *v/t. pret. u. p.p.* ˈ**pan·icked** [-kt] **5.** in Panik versetzen; **6.** in Panik geraten, *Am. sl. Publikum* hinreißen; **IV** *v/i.* **7.** von panischem Schrecken erfaßt werden: ***don't ~!*** nur die Ruhe!; **8.** sich zu e-r Kurzschlußhandlung hinreißen lassen, ‚ˈdurchdrehen'; ˈ**pan·ick·y** [-kɪ] *adj.* F **1.** ˈüberängstlich, -nerˌvös; **2.** in Panik.

pan·i·cle [ˈpænɪkl] *s.* ⚘ Rispe *f*.

ˈ**pan·ic|ˌmon·ger** *s.* Bange-, Panikmacher(in); ~ **re·ac·tion** *s.* Kurzschlußhandlung *f*; ˈ~**-ˌstrick·en**, ˈ~**-struck** *adj.* von panischem Schrecken gepackt.

pan·jan·drum [pənˈdʒændrəm] *s. humor.* Wichtigtuer *m*.

pan·nier [ˈpænɪə] *s.* **1.** (Trag)Korb *m*: ***a pair of ~s*** e-e Doppelpacktasche (*Fahr-, Motorrad*); **2.** a) Reifrock *m*, b) Reifrockgestell *n*.

pan·ni·kin [ˈpænɪkɪn] *s.* **1.** Pfännchen *n*; **2.** kleines Trinkgefäß.

pan·ning [ˈpænɪŋ] *s.* *Film*: Panoramierung *f*, (Kamera)Schwenkung *f*: ~ ***shot*** Schwenk *m*.

pan·o·plied [ˈpænəplɪd] *adj.* **1.** vollständig gerüstet (*a. fig.*); **2.** prächtig geschmückt; **pan·o·ply** [ˈpænəplɪ] *s.* **1.** vollständige Rüstung; **2.** *fig.* prächtige Umˈrahmung *od.* Aufmachung, Schmuck *m*.

pan·o·ra·ma [ˌpænəˈrɑːmə] *s.* **1.** Panoˈrama *n* (*a. paint.*), Rundblick *m*; **2.** a) *Film*: Schwenk *m*, b) *phot.* Rundbildaufnahme *f*: ~ ***lens*** Weitwinkelobjektiv *n*; **3.** *fig.* vollständiger ˈÜberblick (***of*** über *acc.*); ˌ**pan·oˈram·ic** [-ˈræmɪk] *adj.* (□ ***~ally***) panoˈramisch, Rundblick...: ~ ***camera*** Panoramenkamera; ~ ***sketch*** Ansichtsskizze; ~ ***windshield*** *mot. Am.* Rundsichtverglasung.

pan shot *s.* (Kamera)Schwenk *m*.

pan·sy [ˈpænzɪ] *s.* **1.** ⚘ Stiefmütterchen *n*; **2.** *a.* ~ ***boy*** F a) ‚Bubi' *m*, b) ‚Homo' *m*, ‚Schwule(r)' *m*.

pant [pænt] **I** *v/i.* **1.** keuchen, japsen, schnaufen: ~ ***for breath*** nach Luft schnappen; **2.** *fig.* lechzen, dürsten, gieren (***for*** *od.* ***after*** nach); **II** *v/t.* **3.** ~ ***out*** *Worte* (herˈvor)keuchen.

pan·ta·loon [ˌpæntəˈluːn] *s.* **1.** *thea.* Hansˈwurst *m*; **2.** *pl. hist.* Pantaˈlons *pl.* (*Herrenhose*).

pan·tech·ni·con [pænˈteknɪkən] *s. Brit.* **1.** Möbellager *n*; **2.** *a.* ~ ***van*** Möbelwagen *m*.

pan·the·ism [ˈpænθiːɪzəm] *s. phls.* Pantheˈismus *m*; ˈ**pan·the·ist** [-ɪst] *s.* Pantheˈist(in); **pan·the·is·tic** [ˌpænθiːˈɪstɪk] *adj.* pantheˈistisch.

pan·the·on [ˈpænθɪən] *s.* Pantheon *n*, Ehrentempel *m*, Ruhmeshalle *f*.

pan·ther [ˈpænθə] *s. zo.* Panther *m*.

pan·ties [ˈpæntɪz] *s. pl.* F **1.** Kinderhöschen *n od. pl.*; **2.** (Damen)Slip *m*.

pan·ti·hose [ˈpæntɪhəʊz] *s.* Strumpfhose *f*.

pan·tile [ˈpæntaɪl] *s.* Dachziegel *m*, -pfanne *f*, Hohlziegel *m*.

pan·to·graph [ˈpæntəʊgrɑːf] *s.* **1.** ⚡ Scherenstromabnehmer *m*; **2.** ⚙ Storchschnabel *m*.

pan·to·mime [ˈpæntəmaɪm] **I** *s.* **1.** *thea.* Pantoˈmime *f*; **2.** *Brit.* (Laien)Spiel *n*, englisches Weihnachtsspiel; **3.** Mienen-, Gebärdenspiel *n*; **II** *v/t.* **4.** pantoˈmimisch darstellen, mimen; **pan·to·mim·ic** [ˌpæntəˈmɪmɪk] *adj.* (□ ***~ally***) pantoˈmimisch.

pan·try [ˈpæntrɪ] *s.* Vorratskammer *f*, Speiseschrank *m*: ***butlers ~*** Anrichteraum *m*.

pants [pænts] *s. pl.* **1.** lange (Herren-) Hose; → ***wear***[1] 1; **2.** *Brit.* Herrenunterhose *f*.

ˈ**pant| skirt** [pænt] *s.* Hosenrock *m*; **pant(s) suit** *s. Am.* Hosenanzug *m*.

pant·y [ˈpæntɪ] → ***panties***; ~ **gir·dle** *s.* Miederhös-chen *n*; ~ **hose** *s.* Strumpfhose *f*; ˈ~**·waist** *Am. s.* **1.** Hemdhöschen *n*; **2.** *sl.* Schwächling *m*.

pap [pæp] *s.* **1.** (Kinder)Brei *m*, Papp *m*; **2.** *fig. Am.* F Protektiˈon *f*.

pa·pa [pəˈpɑː] *s.* Paˈpa *m*.

pa·pa·cy [ˈpeɪpəsɪ] *s.* **1.** päpstliches Amt; **2.** ☧ Papsttum *n*; **3.** Pontifiˈkat *n*; ˈ**pa·pal** [-pl] *adj.* □ **1.** päpstlich; **2.** ˈrömisch-kaˈtholisch; ˈ**pa·pal·ism** [-əlɪzəm] *s.* Papsttum *n*; ˈ**pa·pal·ist** [-əlɪst] *s.* Paˈpist(in).

pa·per [ˈpeɪpə] **I** *s.* **1.** ⚙ a) Paˈpier *n*, b) Pappe *f*, c) Taˈpete *f*; **2.** Blatt *n* Papier; **3.** Papier *n als Schreibmaterial*: ~ ***does not blush*** Papier ist geduldig; ***on ~*** *fig.* auf dem Papier, theoretisch; → ***commit*** 1; **4.** Dokuˈment *n*, Schriftstück *n*; **5.** ✝ a) (ˈWert)Paˌpier *n*, b) Wechsel *m*, c) Paˈpiergeld *n*: ***best ~*** erstklassiger Wechsel; ***convertible ~*** (*in Gold*) einlösbares Papiergeld; ~ ***currency*** Papierwährung *f*; **6.** *pl.* a) ˈAusweis- *od.* Beˈglaubigungspaˌpiere *pl.*, Dokuˈmente *pl.*: ***send in one's ~s*** den Abschied nehmen, b) Akten *pl.*, Schriftstücke *pl.*: ***~s on appeal*** ⚖ Berufungsakten; ***move for ~s*** *bsd. parl.* die Vorlage der Unterlagen *e-s Falles* beantragen; **7.** Prüfungsarbeit *f*; **8.** Aufsatz *m*, Abhandlung *f*, Vortrag *m*, -lesung *f*, Refeˈrat *n*: ***read a ~*** e-n Vortrag halten, referieren (***on*** über *acc.*); **9.** Zeitung *f*, Blatt *n*; **10.** Brief *m*, Heft *n mit Nadeln etc.*; **11.** *thea. sl.* a) Freikarte *f*, b) Besucher *m* mit Freikarte; **II** *adj.* **12.** paˈpieren, Papier..., Papp...; **13.** *fig.* (hauch)dünn, schwach; **14.** nur auf dem Paˈpier vorhanden: ~ ***team***; **III** *v/t.* **15.** in Papier einwickeln; mit Papier ausschlagen: ~ ***over*** überkleben, *fig.* (notdürftig) übertünchen; **16.** tapezieren; **17.** mit ˈSandpaˌpier polieren; **18.** *thea. sl. Haus* mit Freikarten füllen; ˈ~**·back** *s.* Paperback *n*, Taschenbuch *n*; ~ **bag** *s.* Tüte *f*; ˈ~**·board** *s.* Pappdeckel *m*, Pappe...; ~ **chase** *s.* Schnitzeljagd *f*; ~ **clip** *s.* Büˈro-, Heftklammer *f*; ~ **cup** *s.* Pappbecher *m*; ~ **cut·ter** *s.* **1.** Paˈpierˌschneidemaˌschine *f*; **2.** → ***paper knife***; ~ **ex·er·cise** *s.* ⚔ Planspiel *n*; ~ **fas·ten·er** *s.* Heftklammer *f*; ˈ~**ˌhang·er** *s.* Tapezierer *m*; ~ **knife** *s.* Paˈpiermesser *n*, Brieföffner *m*; ~ **mill** *s.* Paˈpierfaˌbrik *f*, -mühle *f*; ~ **mon·ey** *s.* Paˈpiergeld *n*; ~ **plate** *s.* Pappteller *m*; ~ **prof·it** *s.* ✝ rechnerischer Gewinn; ~ **stain·er** *s.* Taˈpetenmaler *m*, -macher *m*; ~ **tape** *s. Computer*: Lochstreifen *m*; ˈ~**·thin** *adj.* hauchdünn (*a. fig.*); ~ **ti·ger** *s. fig.* Paˈpiertiger *m*; ~ **war(·fare)** *s.* **1.** Pressekrieg *m*, -fehde *f*, Federkrieg *m*; **2.** Paˈpierkrieg *m*; ˈ~**-weight** *s.* **1.** Briefbeschwerer *m*; **2.** *sport* Paˈpiergewicht(ler *m*) *n*; ˈ~**-work** *s.* Schreib-, Büˈroarbeit *f*.

pa·per·y [ˈpeɪpərɪ] *adj.* paˈpierähnlich; (paˈpier)dünn.

pa·pier-mâ·ché [ˌpæpjeɪˈmæʃeɪ] *s.* Paˈpiermaˌché, ˈPappmaˌché *n*.

pa·pil·i·o·na·ceous [pəˌpɪlɪəʊˈneɪʃəs] *adj.* ⚘ schmetterlingsblütig.

pa·pil·la [pəˈpɪlə] *pl.* **-pil·lae** [-liː] *s. anat.* Paˈpille *f* (*a.* ⚘), Warze *f*; **papˈil·lar·y** [-ərɪ] *adj.* **1.** warzenartig, papilˈlär; **2.** mit Paˈpillen versehen.

pa·pist [ˈpeɪpɪst] *s. contp.* Paˈpist *m*; **pa·pis·tic** *adj.*; **pa·pis·ti·cal** [pəˈpɪstɪk(l)] *adj.* □ **1.** päpstlich; **2.** *contp.* paˈpistisch; ˈ**pa·pist·ry** [-rɪ] *s.* Paˈpismus *m*, Papisteˈrei *f*.

pa·poose [pəˈpuːs] *s.* **1.** Indiˈanerbaby *n*; **2.** *Am. humor.* ‚Balg' *m*.

pap·pus [ˈpæpəs] *pl.* **-pi** [-aɪ] *s.* **1.** ⚘ a) Haarkrone *f*, b) Federkelch *m*; **2.** Flaum *m*.

pap·py [ˈpæpɪ] *adj.* breiig, pappig.

Pap| test, ~ **smear** [pæp] *s.* ⚕ Abstrich

m.

pa·py·rus [pəˈpaɪərəs] *pl.* **-ri** [-raɪ] *s.* **1.** ⚘ Paˈpyrus(staude *f*) *m*; **2.** *antiq.* Paˈpyrus(rolle *f*, -text) *m.*

par [pɑː] **I** *s.* **1.** ✝ Nennwert *m*, Pari *n*: ***issue*** ~ Emissionskurs *m*; ***nominal*** (*od.* ***face***) ~ Nennbetrag *m* (*Aktie*), Nominalwert *m*; ~ ***of exchange*** Wechselpari(tät *f*) *n*, Parikurs *m*; ***at*** ~ zum Nennwert, al pari; ***above*** (***below***) ~ über (unter) Pari; **2.** *fig.* ***above*** ~ in bester Form; ***up to*** (***below***) ~ F (nicht) auf der Höhe; ***be on a*** ~ (***with***) ebenbürtig *od.* gewachsen sein (*dat.*), entsprechen (*dat.*); ***put on a*** ~ ***with*** gleichstellen (*dat.*); ***on a*** ~ *Brit.* im Durchschnitt; **3.** *Golf*: Par *n*, festgesetzte Schlagzahl; **II** *adj.* **4.** ✝ pari: ~ ***clearance*** *Am.* Clearing *n* zum Pariwert; ~ ***value*** Pari-, Nennwert *m.*

para- [pærə] *in Zssgn* **1.** neben, über … hinˈaus; **2.** ähnlich; **3.** falsch; **4.** ⚗ neben, ähnlich; Verwandtschaft bezeichnend; **5.** ⚕ a) fehlerhaft, abˈnorm, b) ergänzend, c) umˈgebend; **6.** Schutz…; **7.** Fallschirm…

pa·ra [ˈpærə] *s.* F **1.** ⚔ Fallschirmjäger *m*; **2.** *typ.* Absatz *m.*

par·a·ble [ˈpærəbl] *s.* Paˈrabel *f*, Gleichnis *n* (*a. bibl.*).

pa·rab·o·la [pəˈræbələ] *s.* Ⱥ Paˈrabel *f*: ~ ***compasses*** Parabelzirkel *m.*

par·a·bol·ic [ˌpærəˈbɒlɪk] *adj.* **1.** → ***parabolical***; **2.** Ⱥ paraˈbolisch, Parabel…: ~ ***mirror*** Parabolspiegel *m*; ˌ**par·aˈbol·i·cal** [-kl] *adj.* □ paraˈbolisch, gleichnishaft; **pa·rab·o·loid** [pəˈræbəlɔɪd] *s.* Ⱥ Paraboloˈid *n.*

ˈ**par·a·brake** *v/t.* ✈ durch Bremsfallschirm abbremsen.

par·a·chute [ˈpærəʃuːt] **I** *s.* **1.** ✈ Fallschirm *m*: ~ ***jumper*** Fallschirmspringer *m*; **2.** ⚘ Schirmflieger *m*; **3.** ⚙ Sicherheits-, Fangvorrichtung *f*; **II** *v/t.* **4.** (mit dem Fallschirm) absetzen, -werfen; **III** *v/i.* **5.** mit dem Fallschirm abspringen; **6.** (wie) mit e-m Fallschirm schweben; ~ ***flare*** *s.* ⚔ Leuchtfallschirm *m*; ~ ***troops*** *s. pl.* ⚔ Fallschirmtruppen *pl.*

par·a·chut·ist [ˈpærəʃuːtɪst] *s.* ✈ **1.** Fallschirmspringer(in); **2.** ⚔ Fallschirmjäger *m.*

pa·rade [pəˈreɪd] **I** *s.* **1.** Paˈrade *f*, Vorführung *f*, Zurˈschaustellen *n*; ***make a*** ~ ***of*** → 7; **2.** ⚔ a) Paˈrade *f* (*Truppenschau u. Vorbeimarsch*): ***be on*** ~ e-e Parade abhalten, b) Apˈpell *m*: ~ ***rest!*** Rührt Euch!, c) *a.* ~ ***ground*** Paˈrade-, Exerzierplatz *m*; **3.** (ˈUm)Zug *m*, (Auf-, Vorˈbei)Marsch *m*; **4.** *bsd. Brit.* Promeˈnade *f*; **5.** *fenc.* Paˈrade *f*; **II** *v/t.* **6.** zur Schau stellen, vorführen; **7.** zur Schau tragen, protzen mit; **8.** ⚔ auf-, vorˈbeimarschieren lassen; **9.** *Straße* entlangstolzieren; **III** *v/i.* **10.** ⚔ paradieren, (vorˈbei)marschieren; **11.** e-n Umzug veranstalten, durch die Straßen ziehen; **12.** sich zur Schau stellen, stolzieren.

par·a·digm [ˈpærədaɪm] *s. ling.* Paraˈdigma *n*, (Muster)Beispiel *n*; **par·a·dig·mat·ic** [ˌpærədɪgˈmætɪk] *adj.* (□ ~***ally***) paradigˈmatisch.

par·a·dise [ˈpærədaɪs] *s.* (*bibl.* ♀) Paraˈdies *n* (*a. fig.*): ***bird of*** ~ Paradiesvogel *m*; → ***fool's paradise***; **par·a·dis·i·ac** [ˌpærəˈdɪsɪæk], **par·a·di·si·a·cal** [ˌpærədɪˈsaɪəkl] *adj.* paraˈdiesisch.

par·a·dox [ˈpærədɒks] *s.* Paˈradoxon *n*, Paraˈdox *n*; **par·a·dox·i·cal** [ˌpærəˈdɒksɪkl] *adj.* □ paraˈdox.

ˈ**par·a·drop** *v/t.* ✈ mit dem Fallschirm abwerfen *od.* absetzen.

par·af·fin [ˈpærəfɪn], **par·af·fine** [ˈpærəfiːn] **I** *s.* Parafˈfin *n*: ***liquid*** ~, *Brit.* ~ (***oil***) Paraffinöl *n*; ***solid*** ~ Erdwachs *n*; ~ ***wax*** Paraffin (*für Kerzen*); **II** *v/t.* ⚙ paraffinieren.

par·a·glid·er [ˈpærəˌglaɪdə] *s. sport* Gleitschirm *m.*

par·a·gon [ˈpærəgən] *s.* **1.** Muster *n*, Vorbild *n*: ~ ***of virtue*** Muster *od. iro.* Ausbund *m* an Tugend; **2.** *typ.* Text *f* (*Schriftgrad*).

par·a·graph [ˈpærəgrɑːf] *s.* **1.** *typ.* a) Absatz *m*, Abschnitt *m*, Paraˈgraph *m*, b) Paraˈgraphzeichen *n*; **2.** kurzer (ˈZeitungs)Arˌtikel; ˈ**par·a·graph·er** [-fə] *s.* **1.** Verfasser *m* kleiner Zeitungsartikel; **2.** ˈLeitarˌtikler *m* (*e-r Zeitung*).

Par·a·guay·an [ˌpærəˈgwaɪən] **I** *adj.* paraˈguayisch; **II** *s.* Paraˈguayer(in).

par·a·keet [ˈpærəkiːt] *s. orn.* Sittich *m*: ***Australian grass*** ~ Wellensittich.

par·al·de·hyde [pəˈrældɪhaɪd] *s.* ⚗ Paraldeˈhyd *n.*

par·al·lac·tic [ˌpærəˈlæktɪk] *adj. ast.*, *phys.* paralˈlaktisch: ~ ***motion*** parallaktische Verschiebung; **par·al·lax** [ˈpærəlæks] *s.* Paralˈlaxe *f.*

par·al·lel [ˈpærəlel] **I** *adj.* **1.** (***with***, ***to***) paralˈlel (zu, mit), gleichlaufend (mit): ~ ***bars*** *Turnen*: Barren *m*; ~ ***connection*** ϟ Parallelschaltung *f*; ***run*** ~ ***to*** parallel verlaufen zu; **2.** *fig.* paralˈlel, gleich(gerichtet, -laufend), entsprechend: ~ ***case*** Parallelfall *m*; ~ ***passage*** Parallele *f in e-m Text*; **II** *s.* **3.** Ⱥ *u. fig.* Paralˈlele *f* (***to*** zu): ***in*** ~ ***with*** parallel zu; ***draw a*** ~ ***between*** *fig.* e-e Parallele ziehen zwischen (*dat.*), (miteinander) vergleichen; **4.** Ⱥ Paralleliˈtät *f* (*a. fig. Gleichheit*); **5.** *geogr.* Breitenkreis *m*; **6.** ϟ Paralˈlelschaltung *f*: ***connect*** (*od.* ***join***) ***in*** ~ parallelschalten; **7.** Gegenstück *n*, Entsprechung *f*: ***have no*** ~ nicht seinesgleichen haben; ***without*** ~ ohnegleichen; **III** *v/t.* **8.** (***with***, ***to***) anpassen, -gleichen (*dat.*); **9.** gleichkommen (*dat.*); **10.** et. Gleiches *od.* Entsprechendes finden zu; **11.** *bsd. Am.* F parallel laufen zu; ˈ**par·al·lel·ism** [-lɪzəm] *s.* Ⱥ Paralleˈlismus *m* (*a. ling.*, *phls.*, *fig.*), Paralleliˈtät *f*; **par·al·lel·o·gram** [ˌpærəˈleləʊgræm] *s.* Ⱥ Paralleloˈgramm *n*: ~ ***of forces*** *phys.* Kräfteparallelogramm *n.*

pa·ral·o·gism [pəˈrælədʒɪzəm] *s. phls.* Paraloˈgismus *m*, Trugschluß *m.*

par·a·ly·sa·tion [ˌpærəlaɪˈzeɪʃn] *s.* **1.** ⚕ Lähmung *f* (*a. fig.*); **2.** *fig.* Lahmlegung *f*; **par·a·lyse** [ˈpærəlaɪz] *v/t.* **1.** ⚕ paralysieren, lähmen (*a. fig.*); **2.** *fig.* lahmlegen, lähmen, zum Erliegen bringen; **pa·ral·y·sis** [pəˈrælɪsɪs] *pl.* **-ses** [-siːz] *s.* **1.** ⚕ Paraˈlyse *f*, Lähmung *f*; **2.** *fig.* a) Lähmung *f*, Lahmlegung *f*, b) Daˈniederliegen *n*, c) Ohnmacht *f*; **par·a·lyt·ic** [ˌpærəˈlɪtɪk] **I** *adj.* (□ ~***ally***) ⚕ paraˈlytisch: a) Lähmungs…, b) gelähmt (*a. fig.*); **II** *s.* ⚕ Paraˈlytiker(in).

par·a·lyze *bsd. Am.* → ***paralyse.***

par·a·med·ic [ˌpærəˈmedɪk] *s. Am.* **1.** ärztlicher Assiˈstent, *a.* Saniˈtäter *m*; **2.** Arzt, der sich in abgelegenen Gegenden mit dem Fallschirm absetzen läßt.

pa·ram·e·ter [pəˈræmɪtə] *s.* Ⱥ **1.** Paˈrmameter *m*; **2.** Nebenveränderliche *f.*

ˌ**par·aˈmil·i·tar·y** *adj.* ˈparamiliˌtärisch.

par·a·mount [ˈpærəmaʊnt] **I** *adj.* □ **1.** höher stehend (***to*** als), oberst, höchst; **2.** *fig.* an der Spitze stehend, größt, überˈragend, ausschlaggebend: ***of*** ~ ***importance*** von (aller)größter Bedeutung.

par·a·mour [ˈpærəˌmʊə] *s.* Geliebte(r *m*) *f*, Buhle *m*, *f.*

par·a·noi·a [ˌpærəˈnɔɪə] *s.* ⚕ Paraˈnoia *f*; ˌ**par·aˈnoi·ac** [-ɪæk] **I** *adj.* paraˈnoisch; **II** *s.* Paraˈnoiker(in); **par·a·noid** [ˈpærənɔɪd] *adj.* paranoˈid.

par·a·pet [ˈpærəpɪt] *s.* **1.** ⚔ Wall *m*, Brustwehr *f*; **2.** ▲ (Brücken)Geländer *n*, (Balˈkon-, Fenster)Brüstung *f.*

par·aph [ˈpærəf] *s.* Paˈraphe *f*, (ˈUnterschrifts)Schnörkel *m.*

par·a·pher·na·li·a [ˌpærəfəˈneɪljə] *s. pl.* **1.** Zubehör *n*, *m*, Utenˈsilien *pl.*, ‚Drum u. ˈDran' *n*; **2.** ⚖ Parapherˈnalgut *n der Ehefrau.*

par·a·phrase [ˈpærəfreɪz] **I** *s.* Paraˈphrase *f* (*a.* ♪), Umˈschreibung *f*; freie ˈWiedergabe, Interpretatiˈon *f*; **II** *v/t. u. v/i.* paraphrasieren (*a.* ♪), interpretieren, *e-n Text* frei ˈwiedergeben; umˈschreiben.

par·a·ple·gi·a [ˌpærəˈpliːdʒə] *s.* Parapleˈgie *f*, doppelseitige Lähmung; ˌ**paraˈpleg·ic** [-dʒɪk] *adj.* paraˈplegisch.

ˌ**par·a·psyˈchol·o·gy** [ˌpærəsaɪˈkɒlədʒɪ] *s.* ˈParapsycholoˌgie *f.*

par·a·scend·ing [ˌpærəˈsendɪŋ] *s.* Fallschirmsport *m*, -springen *n.*

par·a·sit·al [ˌpærəˈsaɪtl] *adj.* paraˈsitisch (*a. fig.*); **par·a·site** [ˈpærəsaɪt] **I** *s.* **1.** *biol. u. fig.* Schmaˈrotzer *m*, Paraˈsit *m*; **2.** *ling.* paraˈsitischer Laut; **II** *adj.* **3.** → ***parasitic*** 4; ˌ**par·aˈsit·ic**, ˌ**par·aˈsit·ic·al** [-ˈsɪtɪk(l)] *adj.* □ **1.** *biol.* paraˈsitisch (*a. ling.*), schmaˈrotzend; **2.** ⚕ paraˈsitisch, parasiˈtär; **3.** *fig.* schmaˈrotzerhaft, paraˈsitisch; **4.** ⚙, ϟ (*nur* ***parasitic***) störend, parasiˈtär: ~ ***current*** Fremdstrom *m*; **par·a·sit·ism** [ˈpærəsaɪtɪzəm] *s.* Parasiˈtismus *m* (*a.* ⚕), Schmaˈrotzertum *n.*

par·a·sol [ˈpærəsɒl] *s.* (Damen)Sonnenschirm *m*, *obs.* Paraˈsol *m*, *n.*

par·a·suit [ˈpærəsuːt] *s.* ✈ ˈFallschirmkombinatiˌon *f.*

par·a·thy·roid (**gland**) [ˌpærəˈθaɪrɔɪd] *s. anat.* Nebenschilddrüse *f.*

ˈ**par·aˌtroop·er** *s.* ⚔ Fallschirmjäger *m*; ˈ**par·a·troops** *s. pl.* ⚔ Fallschirmtruppen *pl.*

par·a·ty·phoid (**fe·ver**) [ˌpærəˈtaɪfɔɪd] *s.* ⚕ Paratyphus *m.*

par·a·vane [ˈpærəveɪn] *s.* ⚓ Minenabweiser *m*, Ottergerät *n.*

par·boil [ˈpɑːbɔɪl] *v/t.* **1.** halbgar kochen, ankochen; **2.** *fig.* überˈhitzen.

par·cel [ˈpɑːsl] **I** *s.* **1.** Paˈket *n*, Päckchen *n*; Bündel *n*; *pl.* Stückgüter *pl.*: ~ ***of shares*** Aktienpaket; ***do up in*** ~***s*** einpacken; **2.** ✝ Posten *m*, Parˈtie *f*, Los *n* (*Ware*): ***in*** ~***s*** in kleinen Posten, stück-, packweise; **3.** *contp.* Haufe(n) *m*; **4.** *a.* ~ ***of land*** Parˈzelle *f*; **II** *v/t.* **5.** *mst* ~ ***out*** auf-, aus-, abteilen, *Land* parzellieren; **6.** *a.* ~ ***up*** einpacken, (ver)packen; ~ ***of·fice*** *s.* Gepäckabfertigung(sstelle) *f*;

~ **post** *s.* Pa'ketpost *f.*
par·ce·nar·y ['pɑːsmərɪ] *s.* ⚖ Mitbesitz *m* (*durch Erbschaft*); '**par·ce·ner** [-nə] *s.* Miterbe *m.*
parch [pɑːtʃ] **I** *v/t.* **1.** rösten, dörren; **2.** ausdörren, -trocknen, (ver)sengen: ***be ~ed*** (***with thirst***), ‚am Verdursten' sein; **II** *v/i.* **3.** ausdörren, -trocknen, rösten, schmoren; '**parch·ing** [-tʃɪŋ] *adj.* **1.** brennend (*Durst*); **2.** sengend (*Hitze*); '**parch·ment** [-mənt] *s.* **1.** Perga'ment *n*; **2.** *a.* ***vegetable ~*** Perga'mentpaˌpier *n*; **3.** Per'gament(urkunde *f*) *n*, Urkunde *f.*
pard [pɑːd], '**pard·ner** [-dnə] *s. bsd. Am.* F Partner *m*, ‚Kumpel' *m.*
par·don ['pɑːdn] **I** *v/t.* **1.** *j-m od. e-e Sache* verzeihen, *j-n od. et.* entschuldigen: ***~ me!*** Verzeihung!, entschuldigen Sie!, verzeihen Sie!; ***~ me for interrupting you!*** entschuldigen Sie, wenn ich Sie unterbreche!; **2.** *Schuld* vergeben; **3.** *j-m* das Leben schenken, *j-m* die Strafe erlassen, *j-n* begnadigen; **II** *s.* **4.** Verzeihung *f*: ***a thousand ~s*** ich bitte Sie tausendmal um Entschuldigung; ***beg*** (*od.* ***ask***) ***s.o.'s ~*** j-n um Verzeihung bitten; (***I***) ***beg your ~*** a) entschuldigen Sie bitte!, Verzeihung!, b) F *a.* ***~?*** wie sagten Sie (doch eben)?, wie bitte?, c) *empört*: erlauben Sie mal!; **5.** Vergebung *f*; *R.C.* Ablaß *m*; ⚖ Begnadigung *f*, Straferlaß *m*: ***general ~*** (allgemeine) Amnestie; **6.** Par'don *m*, Gnade *f*; '**par·don·a·ble** [-nəbl] *adj.* □ verzeihlich (*Fehler*), läßlich (*Sünde*); '**par·don·er** [-nə] *s. eccl. hist.* Ablaßkrämer *m.*
pare [peə] *v/t. Äpfel etc.* schälen; *Fingernägel etc.* (be)schneiden: ***~ down*** *fig.* beschneiden, einschränken; ***~ off*** (ab-) schälen (*a.* ⚙); → ***claw*** 1 b.
par·e·gor·ic [ˌpærə'gɒrɪk] *adj. u. s.* ⚕ schmerzstillend(es Mittel).
par·en·ceph·a·lon [ˌpæren'sefəlɒn] *s. anat.* Kleinhirn *n.*
pa·ren·chy·ma [pə'reŋkɪmə] *s.* **1.** Paren'chym *n* (*biol.*, ⚘ *Grund-*, *anat. Organgewebe*); **2.** ⚕ Tumorgewebe *n.*
par·ent ['peərənt] **I** *s.* **1.** *pl.* Eltern *pl.*: ***~-teacher association*** *ped.* (*amer.*, *a. brit.*) Eltern-Lehrer-Ausschuß *m*; ***~-teacher meeting*** Elternabend *m*; **2.** *a.* ⚖ Elternteil *m*; **3.** Vorfahr *m*; **4.** *biol.* Elter *m*; **5.** *fig.* Ursache *f*: ***the ~ of vice*** aller Laster Anfang; **6.** ✝ F ‚Mutter' *f* (*Muttergesellschaft*); **II** *adj.* **7.** *biol.* Stamm…, Mutter…: ***~ cell*** Mutterzelle *f*; **8.** ursprünglich, Ur…: ***~ form*** Urform *f*; **9.** *fig.* Mutter…, Stamm…: ***~ company*** ✝ Stammhaus *n*, Muttergesellschaft *f*; ***~ material*** Urstoff *m*, *geol.* Ausgangsgestein *n*; ***~ organization*** Dachorganisation *f*; ***~ patent*** ✝ Stammpatent *n*; ***~ rock*** *geol.* Urgestein *n*; ***~ ship*** ⚓ Mutterschiff *n*; ***~ unit*** ⚔ Stammtruppenteil *m*; '**par·ent·age** [-tɪdʒ] *s.* **1.** Abkunft *f*, Abstammung *f*, Fa'milie *f*; **2.** Elternschaft *f*; **3.** *fig.* Urheberschaft *f*; **pa·ren·tal** [pə'rentl] *adj.* □ elterlich, Eltern…: ***~ authority*** ⚖ elterliche Gewalt.
pa·ren·the·sis [pə'renθɪsɪs] *pl.* **-the·ses** [-siːz] *s.* **1.** *ling.* Paren'these *f*, Einschaltung *f*: ***by way of ~*** *fig.* beiläufig; **2.** *mst pl. typ.* (runde) Klammer(n *pl.*): ***put in parentheses*** einklammern; **pa'ren·the·size** [-saɪz] *v/t.* **1.** einschalten, einflechten; **2.** *typ.* einklammern; **par·en·thet·ic**, **par·en·thet·i·cal** [ˌpærən'θetɪk(l)] *adj.* □ **1.** paren'thetisch, eingeschaltet; *fig.* beiläufig; **2.** eingeklammert.
par·ent·less ['peərəntlɪs] *adj.* elternlos.
pa·re·sis ['pærɪsɪs] *s.* ⚕ **1.** Pa'rese *f*, unvollständige Lähmung; **2.** *a.* ***general ~*** progres'sive Para'lyse.
par·get ['pɑːdʒɪt] **I** *s.* **1.** Gips(stein) *m*; **2.** Verputz *m*; **3.** Stuck *m*; **II** *v/t.* **4.** verputzen; **5.** mit Stuck verzieren.
par·he·li·on [pɑː'hiːljən] *pl.* **-li·a** [-ljə] *s.* Nebensonne *f*, Par'helion *n.*
pa·ri·ah ['pærɪə] *s.* Paria *m* (*a. fig.*).
pa·ri·e·tal [pə'raɪıtl] **I** *adj.* **1.** *anat.* parie'tal: a) (*a.* ⚘, *biol.*) wandständig, Wand…, b) seitlich, c) Scheitel(bein)…; **2.** *ped. Am.* in'tern, Haus…; **II** *s.* **3.** *a.* ***~ bone*** Scheitelbein *n.*
par·ing ['peərɪŋ] *s.* **1.** Schälen *n*; (Be-) Schneiden *n*, Stutzen *n* (*a. fig.*); **2.** *pl.* Schalen *pl.*: ***potato ~s***; **3.** *pl.* ⚙ Späne *pl.*, Schabsel *pl.*, Schnitzel *pl.*; ***~ knife*** *s.* **1.** Schälmesser *n* (*für Obst etc.*); **2.** Beschneidmesser.
pa·ri pas·su [ˌpɑːrɪ'pæsuː] (*Lat.*) *adv.* gleichrangig, -berechtigt.
Par·is ['pærɪs] *adj.* Pa'riser; ***~ blue*** *s.* Ber'liner Blau *n*; ***~ green*** *s.* Pa'riser *od.* Schweinfurter Grün *n.*
par·ish ['pærɪʃ] **I** *s.* **1.** *eccl.* a) Kirchspiel *n*, Pfarrbezirk *m*, b) Gemeinde *f* (*a. coll.*); **2.** *a.* ***civil*** (*od.* ***poor-law***) ***~*** *pol. Brit.* (po'litische) Gemeinde: ***go*** (*od.* ***be***) ***on the ~*** der Gemeinde zur Last fallen; **II** *adj.* **3.** Kirchen…, Pfarr…: ***~ church*** Pfarrkirche *f*; ***~ clerk*** Küster *m*; ***~ register*** Kirchenbuch *n*; **4.** *pol.* Gemeinde…: ***~ council*** Gemeinderat *m*; ***~-pump politics*** Kirchturmpolitik *f*; **pa·rish·ion·er** [pə'rɪʃənə] *s.* Gemeindeglied *n.*
Pa·ri·sian [pə'rɪzjən] **I** *s.* Pa'riser(in); **II** *adj.* Pa'riser.
par·i·syl·lab·ic [ˌpærɪsɪ'læbɪk] *ling.* **I** *adj.* parisyl'labisch, gleichsilbig; **II** *s.* Pari'syllabum *n.*
par·i·ty ['pærətɪ] *s.* **1.** Gleichheit *f*, *a.* gleichberechtigte Stellung; **2.** ✝ a) Pari'tät *f*, b) 'Umrechnungskurs *m*: ***at the ~ of*** zum Umrechnungskurs von; ***~ clause*** Paritätsklausel *f*; ***~ price*** Parikurs *m.*
park [pɑːk] **I** *s.* **1.** Park *m*, (Park)Anlagen *pl.*; **2.** Na'turschutzgebiet *n*, Park *m*: ***national ~***; **3.** *bsd.* ⚔ (Geschütz-, Fahrzeug- *etc.*)Park *m*; **4.** *Am.* Parkplatz *m*; **5.** a) *Am.* (Sport)Platz *m*, b) ***the ~*** *Brit.* F der Fußballplatz; **II** *v/t.* **6.** *mot. etc.* parken, ab-, aufstellen; F *et.* abstellen, *wo* lassen: ***~ o.s.*** sich ‚hinhocken'; **III** *v/i.* **7.** parken.
par·ka ['pɑːkə] *s.* Parka *m*, *f.*
ˌ**park-and-'ride sys·tem** *s.* 'Park-and-'ride-Syˌstem *n.*
park·ing ['pɑːkɪŋ] *s. mot.* **1.** Parken *n*: ***No ~!*** Parken verboten!; **2.** Parkplatz *m*, -plätze *pl.*, -fläche *f*; ***~ brake*** *s.* Feststellbremse *f*; ***~ disc*** *s.* Parkscheibe *f*; ***~ fee*** *s.* Parkgebühr *f*; ***~ ga·rage*** *s.* Parkhaus *n*; ***~ light*** *s.* Park-, Standlicht *n*; ***~ lot*** *s. Am.* Parkplatz *m*, -fläche *f*; ***~ me·ter*** *s.* Park(zeit)uhr *f*; ***~ place*** *s.* Parkplatz *m*, -fläche *f*; ***~ space*** *s.* **1.** → ***parking place***; **2.** Abstellfläche *f*; -lücke *f*; ***~ tick·et*** *s.* Strafzettel *m* (für unerlaubtes Parken).
par·lance ['pɑːləns] *s.* Ausdrucksweise *f*, Sprache *f*: ***in common ~*** auf gut deutsch; ***in legal ~*** in der Rechtssprache; ***in modern ~*** im modernen Sprachgebrauch.
par·lay ['pɑːlɪ] *Am.* **I** *v/t.* **1.** *Wett-*, *Spielgewinn* wieder einsetzen; **2.** *fig.* aus *j-m od. et.* Kapi'tal schlagen; **3.** erweitern, ausbauen (***into*** zu); **II** *v/i.* **4.** e-n Spielgewinn wieder einsetzen; **III** *s.* **5.** erneuter Einsatz e-s Gewinns; **6.** Auswertung *f*; **7.** Ausweitung *f*, Ausbau *m.*
par·ley ['pɑːlɪ] **I** *s.* **1.** Unter'redung *f*, Verhandlung *f*; **2.** ⚔ (Waffenstillstands)Verhandlung(en *pl.*) *f*, Unter'handlung(en *pl.*) *f*; **II** *v/i.* **3.** sich besprechen (***with*** mit); **4.** ⚔ unter'handeln; **III** *v/t.* **5.** *humor.* parlieren: ***~ French.***
par·lia·ment ['pɑːləmənt] *s.* Parla'ment *n*: ***enter*** (*od.* ***get into*** *od.* ***go into***) ♀ ins Parlament gewählt werden; ***Member of*** ♀ *Brit.* Mitglied des Unterhauses, Abgeordnete(r *m*) *f*; **par·lia·men·tar·i·an** [ˌpɑːləmen'teərɪən] *pol.* **I** *s.* (erfahrener) Parlamen'tarier; **II** *adj.* → ***parliamentary***; **par·lia·men·ta·rism** [ˌpɑːlə'mentərɪzəm] *s.* parlamen'tarisches Sy'stem, Parlamenta'rismus *m*; **par·lia·men·ta·ry** [ˌpɑːlə'mentərɪ] *adj.* **1.** parlamen'tarisch, Parlaments…: ♀ ***Commissioner*** *Brit.* → ***ombudsman*** 1; ***~ group*** (*od.* ***party***) Fraktion *f*; ***~ party leader*** *Brit.* Fraktionsvorsitzende(r) *m*; **2.** *fig.* höflich (*Sprache*).
par·lo(u)r ['pɑːlə] **I** *s.* **1.** Wohnzimmer *n*; **2.** *obs.* Besuchszimmer *n*, Sa'lon *m*; **3.** Empfangs-, Sprechzimmer *n*; **4.** Klub-, Gesellschaftszimmer *n* (*Hotel*); **5.** *bsd. Am.* Geschäftsraum *m*, Sa'lon *m*; → ***beauty parlo(u)r***; **II** *adj.* **6.** Wohnzimmer…: ***~ furniture***; **7.** *fig.* Salon…: ***~ radical***, *Am.* ***~ red*** *pol.* Salonbolschewist(in); ***~ car*** *s.* 🚃 *Am.* Sa'lonwagen *m*; ***~ game*** *s.* Gesellschaftsspiel *n*; '***~maid*** *s.* Stubenmädchen *n.*
par·lous ['pɑːləs] *obs.* **I** *adj.* **1.** pre'kär; **2.** schlau; **II** *adv.* **3.** ‚furchtbar'.
pa·ro·chi·al [pə'rəʊkjəl] *adj.* □ **1.** parochi'al, Pfarr…, Gemeinde…: ***~ church council*** Kirchenvorstand *m*; ***~ school*** *Am.* Konfessionsschule *f*; **2.** *fig.* beschränkt, eng(stirnig): ***~ politics*** Kirchturmpolitik *f*; **pa'ro·chi·al·ism** [-lɪzəm] *s.* **1.** Parochi'alsyˌstem *n*; **2.** *fig.* Beschränktheit *f*, Spießigkeit *f.*
par·o·dist ['pærədɪst] *s.* Paro'dist(in); **par·o·dy** ['pærədɪ] **I** *s. a. fig.* Paro'die *f* (***of*** auf *acc.*); **II** *v/t.* parodieren.
pa·rol [pə'rəʊl] *adj.* ⚖ a) (bloß) mündlich, b) unbeglaubigt, ungesiegelt: ***~ contract*** formloser (*mündlicher od. schriftlicher*) Vertrag; ***~ evidence*** Zeugenbeweis *m.*
pa·role [pə'rəʊl] **I** *s.* **1.** ⚖ a) bedingte Haftentlassung *od.* Strafaussetzung, b) Hafturlaub *m*: ***put s.o. on ~*** → 4; ***~ officer*** *Am.* Bewährungshelfer *m*; **2.** *a.* ***~ of hono(u)r*** *bsd.* ⚔ Ehrenwort *n*: ***on ~*** auf Ehrenwort; **3.** ⚔ Pa'role *f*, Kennwort *n*; **II** *v/t.* **4.** ⚖ a) *j-n* bedingt (aus der Haft) entlassen, j-s Strafe bedingt aussetzen, b) *j-m* Hafturlaub gewähren; **pa·rol·ee** [pərəʊ'liː] *s.* ⚖ bedingt Haftentlassene(r *m*) *f.*

par·o·nym ['pærənɪm] *s. ling.* **1.** Paro'nym *n*, Wortableitung *f*; **2.** 'Lehnüber,setzung *f*; **pa·ron·y·mous** [pə'rɒnɪməs] *adj.* □ a) (stamm)verwandt, b) 'lehnüber,setzt (*Wort*).
par·o·quet ['pærəket] → ***parakeet***.
pa·rot·id [pə'rɒtɪd] *s. a.* ~ ***gland*** *anat.* Ohrspeicheldrüse *f*; **par·o·ti·tis** [,pærəʊ'taɪtɪs] *s.* Mumps *m*.
par·ox·ysm ['pærəksɪzəm] *s.* ⚕ Paro'xysmus *m*, Krampf *m*, Anfall *m* (*a. fig.*): ~***s of laughter*** Lachkrampf *m*; ~***s of rage*** Wutanfall *m*; **par·ox·ys·mal** [,pærek'sɪzməl] *adj.* krampfartig.
par·quet ['pɑːkeɪ] **I** *s.* **1.** Par'kett(fußboden *m*) *n*; **2.** *thea. bsd. Am.* Par'kett *n*; **II** *v/t.* **3.** parkettieren; '**par·quet·ry** [-kɪtrɪ] *s.* Par'kett(arbeit *f*) *n*.
par·ri·cid·al [,pærɪ'saɪdl] *adj.* vater-, muttermörderisch; **par·ri·cide** ['pærɪsaɪd] *s.* **1.** Vater-, Muttermörder(in); **2.** Vater-, Mutter-, Verwandtenmord *m*.
par·rot ['pærət] **I** *s. orn.* Papa'gei *m*, *fig. a.* Nachschwätzer(in); **II** *v/t.* nachplappern; ~ **dis·ease**, ~ **fe·ver** *s.* ⚕ Papa'geienkrankheit *f*.
par·ry ['pærɪ] **I** *v/t. Stöße, Schläge, Fragen etc.* parieren, abwehren (*beide a. v/i.*); **II** *s. fenc. etc.* Pa'rade *f*, Abwehr *f*.
parse [pɑːz] *v/t. ling. Satz* gram'matisch zergliedern, *Satzteil* bestimmen, *Wort* grammatisch definieren.
par·sec ['pɑːsek] *s. ast.* Parsek *n*, Sternweite *f* (*3,26 Lichtjahre*).
par·si·mo·ni·ous [,pɑːsɪ'məʊnjəs] *adj.* □ **1.** sparsam, geizig, knauserig (***of*** mit); **2.** armselig, kärglich; ,**par·si'mo·ni·ous·ness** [-nɪs], **par·si·mo·ny** ['pɑːsɪmənɪ] *s.* Sparsamkeit *f*, Geiz *m*, Knauserigkeit *f*.
pars·ley ['pɑːslɪ] *s.* ♀ Peter'silie *f*.
pars·nip ['pɑːsnɪp] *s.* ♀ Pastinak *m*.
par·son ['pɑːsn] *s.* Pastor *m*, Pfarrer *m*; F *contp.* Pfaffe *m*: ~***'s nose*** Bürzel *m* (*e-r Gans etc.*); '**par·son·age** [-nɪdʒ] *s.* Pfar'rei *f*, Pfarrhaus *n*.
part [pɑːt] **I** *s.* **1.** Teil *m*, *n*, Stück *n*: ~ ***by volume*** (***weight***) *phys.* Raum(Gewichts)teil; ~ ***of speech*** *ling.* Redeteil, Wortklasse *f*; ***in*** ~ teilweise; ***payment in*** ~ Abschlagszahlung *f*; ***be*** ~ ***and parcel of*** e-n wesentlichen Bestandteil bilden von (*od. gen.*); ***for the best*** ~ ***of the year*** fast das ganze Jahr (über); **2.** ♗ Bruchteil *m*: ***three*** ~***s*** drei Viertel; **3.** ⚙ (Bau-, Einzel)Teil *n*: ~***s list*** Ersatzteil-, Stückliste *f*; **4.** ✝ Lieferung *f e-s Buches*; **5.** (Körper)Teil *m*, Glied *n*: ***soft*** ~ Weichteil *n*; ***the*** (***privy***) ~***s*** die Geschlechtsteile; **6.** Anteil *m* (***of***, ***in*** an *dat.*): ***have a*** ~ ***in*** teilhaben an (*dat.*); ***have neither*** ~ ***nor lot in*** nicht das geringste mit *et.* zu tun haben; ***take*** ~ (***in***) teilnehmen (an *dat.*), mitmachen (bei); ***he wanted no*** ~ ***of it*** er wollte davon nichts wissen *od.* damit zu tun haben; **7.** *fig.* Teil *m*, Seite *f*: ***the most*** ~ die Mehrheit, das Meiste *von et.*; ***for my*** ~ ich für mein(en) Teil; ***for the most*** ~ meistens, größtenteils; ***on the*** ~ ***of*** von seiten, seitens (*gen.*); ***take in good*** (***bad***) ~ *et.* gut (übel) aufnehmen; **8.** Seite *f*, Par'tei *f*: ***he took my*** ~ er ergriff m-e Partei; **9.** Pflicht *f*: ***do one's*** ~ das Seinige *od.* s-e Schuldigkeit tun; **10.** *thea.* Rolle *f* (*a. fig.*): ***act*** (*od. a. fig.* ***play***) ***a*** ~ e-e Rolle spielen; **11.** ♪ Sing- *od.* Instrumen'talstimme *f*, Par'tie *f*: ***for*** (*od.* ***in*** *od.* ***of***) ***several*** ~***s*** mehrstimmig; **12.** *pl.* (geistige) Fähigkeiten *pl.*, Ta'lent *n*: ***a man of*** ~***s*** ein fähiger Kopf; **13.** *oft pl.* Gegend *f*, Teil *m e-s Landes, der Erde*: ***in these*** ~***s*** hierzulande; ***in foreign*** ~***s*** im Ausland; **14.** *Am.* (Haar)Scheitel *m*; **II** *v/t.* **15.** teilen, ab-, ein-, zerteilen; trennen (***from*** von); **16.** *Streitende* trennen, *Metalle* scheiden, *Haar* scheiteln; **III** *v/i.* **17.** ausein'andergehen, sich lösen, zerreißen, brechen (*a.* ⚓), aufgehen (*Vorhang*); **18.** ausein'andergehen, sich trennen (*Menschen, Wege etc.*): ~ ***friends*** als Freunde auseinandergehen; ~ ***with*** sich von *j-m od. et.* trennen; ~ ***with one's money*** mit dem Geld herausrücken; **IV.** *adj.* **19.** Teil…: ~ ***damage*** Teilschaden *m*; ~ ***delivery*** Teillieferung *f*; **V** *adv.* **20.** teilweise, zum Teil: ***made*** ~ ***of iron***, ~ ***of wood*** teils aus Eisen, teils aus Holz.
part- [pɑːt] *in Zssgn* teilweise, zum Teil: ~***-done*** zum Teil erledigt; ***accept s.th. in*** ~***-exchange*** et. in Zahlung nehmen; ~***-finished*** halbfertig; ~***-opened*** ein Stück geöffnet.
par·take [pɑː'teɪk] **I** *v/i.* [*irr.* → ***take***] **1.** teilnehmen, -haben (***in***, ***of*** an *dat.*); **2.** (***of***) *et.* an sich haben (von), *et.* teilen (mit): ***his manner*** ~***s of insolence*** es ist et. Unverschämtes in s-m Benehmen; **3.** (***of***) mitessen, genießen, *j-s Mahlzeit* teilen; *Mahlzeit* einnehmen; **II** *v/t.* [*irr.* → ***take***] **4.** *obs.* teilen, teilhaben (an *dat.*).
par·terre [pɑː'teə] *s.* **1.** französischer Garten; **2.** *thea. bsd. Am.* Par'terre *n*.
par·the·no·gen·e·sis [,pɑːθɪnəʊ'dʒenɪsɪs] *s.* Parthenoge'nese *f*: a) ♀ Jungfernfrüchtigkeit *f*, b) *zo.* Jungfernzeugung *f*, c) *eccl.* Jungfrauengeburt *f*.
Par·thi·an ['pɑːθjən] *adj.* parthisch: ~ ***shot*** → ***parting shot***.
par·tial ['pɑːʃl] *adj.* □ → ***partially***; **1.** teilweise, parti'ell, Teil…: ~ ***eclipse*** *ast.* partielle Finsternis; ~ ***payment*** Teilzahlung *f*; ~ ***view*** Teilansicht *f*; **2.** par'teiisch, eingenommen (***to*** für), einseitig: ***be*** ~ ***to s.th.*** e-e besondere Vorliebe haben für et.; **par·ti·al·i·ty** [,pɑːʃɪ'ælətɪ] *s.* **1.** Par'teilichkeit *f*, Voreingenommenheit *f*; **2.** Vorliebe *f* (***to***, ***for*** für); '**par·tial·ly** [-ʃəlɪ] *adv.* teilweise, zum Teil.
par·tic·i·pant [pɑː'tɪsɪpənt] **I** *s.* Teilnehmer(in) (***in*** an *dat.*); **II** *adj.* teilnehmend, Teilnehmer…, (mit)beteiligt; **par·tic·i·pate** [pɑː'tɪsɪpeɪt] *v/i.* **1.** teilhaben, -nehmen, sich beteiligen (***in*** an *dat.*), mitmachen (bei); beteiligt sein (an *dat.*); ✝ am Gewinn beteiligt sein; **2.** ~ ***of*** *et.* an sich haben von; **par'tic·i·pat·ing** [-peɪtɪŋ] *adj.* **1.** ✝ gewinnberechtigt, mit Gewinnbeteiligung (*Versicherungspolice etc.*): ~ ***share*** dividendenberechtigte Aktie; ~ ***rights*** Gewinnbeteiligungsrechte; **2.** → ***participant*** II; **par·tic·i·pa·tion** [pɑː,tɪsɪ'peɪʃn] *s.* **1.** Teilnahme *f*, Beteiligung *f*, Mitwirkung *f*; **2.** ✝ Teilhaberschaft *f*, (Gewinn)Beteiligung *f*; **par'tic·i·pa·tor** [-peɪtə] *s.* Teilnehmer(in) (***in*** an *dat.*).
par·ti·cip·i·al [,pɑːtɪ'sɪpɪəl] *adj.* □ *ling.* partizipi'al; **par·ti·ci·ple** ['pɑːtɪsɪpl] *s. ling.* Parti'zip *n*, Mittelwort *n*.
par·ti·cle ['pɑːtɪkl] *s.* **1.** Teilchen *n*, Stückchen *n*; **2.** *phys.* Par'tikel *n* (*a. f*), (Stoff-, Masse-, Elemen'tar)Teilchen *n*; **3.** *fig.* Fünkchen *n*, Spur *f*: ***not a*** ~ ***of truth in it*** nicht ein wahres Wort daran; **4.** *ling.* Par'tikel *f*.
par·ti-col·o(u)red ['pɑːtɪ,kʌləd] *adj.* bunt, vielfarbig.
par·tic·u·lar [pə'tɪkjʊlə] **I** *adj.* □ → ***particularly***; **1.** besonder, einzeln, spezi'ell, Sonder…: ~ ***average*** ✝ kleine (besondere) Havarie; ***for no*** ~ ***reason*** aus keinem besonderen Grund; ***this*** ~ ***case*** dieser spezielle Fall; **2.** individu'ell, ausgeprägt; **3.** ausführlich; 'umständlich; **4.** peinlich genau, eigen: ***be*** ~ ***about*** es genau nehmen mit, Wert legen auf (*acc.*); **5.** wählerisch (***in***, ***about***, ***as to*** in *dat.*): ***none too*** ~ ***about*** *iro.* nicht gerade wählerisch (*in s-n Methoden etc.*); **6.** eigentümlich, sonderbar; **II** *s.* **7.** Einzelheit *f*, besonderer 'Umstand; *pl.* nähere Umstände *od.* Angaben *pl.*, *das* Nähere: ***in*** ~ insbesondere; ***enter into*** ~***s*** sich auf Einzelheiten einlassen; ***further*** ~***s from*** Näheres (erfährt man) bei; **8.** Perso'nalien *pl.*, Angaben *pl. zur Person*; **9.** F Speziali'tät *f*, *et.* Typisches; **par'tic·u·lar·ism** [-ərɪzəm] *s. pol.* Partikula'rismus *m*: a) Sonderbestrebungen *pl.*, b) ,Kleinstaate'rei *f*; **par·tic·u·lar·i·ty** [pə,tɪkjʊ'lærətɪ] *s.* **1.** Besonderheit *f*, Eigentümlichkeit *f*; **2.** besonderer 'Umstand, Einzelheit *f*; **3.** Ausführlichkeit *f*; **4.** (peinliche) Genauigkeit; **5.** Eigenheit *f*; **par·tic·u·lar·i·za·tion** [pə,tɪkjʊləraɪ'zeɪʃn] *s.* Detaillierung *f*, Spezifizierung *f*; **par'tic·u·lar·ize** [-əraɪz] **I** *v/t.* spezifizieren, einzeln (*a.* 'umständlich) anführen, ausführlich angeben; **II** *v/i.* ins einzelne gehen; **par'tic·u·lar·ly** [-lɪ] *adv.* **1.** besonders, im besonderen, insbesondere: ***not*** ~ nicht sonderlich; (***more***) ~ ***as*** um so mehr als, zumal; **2.** ungewöhnlich; **3.** ausdrücklich.
part·ing ['pɑːtɪŋ] **I** *adj.* **1.** Scheide…, Abschieds…: ~ ***kiss***; ~ ***breath*** letzter Atemzug; **2.** trennend, abteilend: ~ ***wall*** Trennwand *f*; **II** *s.* **3.** Abschied *m*, Scheiden *n*, Trennung *f* (***with*** von); *fig.* Tod *m*; **4.** Trennlinie *f*, (Haar)Scheitel *m*: ~ ***of the ways*** Weggabelung, *fig.* Scheideweg; **5.** ⚗, *phys.* Scheidung *f*: ~ ***silver*** Scheidesilber; **6.** ⚙ *Gießerei*: a) *a.* ~ ***sand*** Streusand *m*, trockener Formsand, b) *a.* ~ ***line*** Teilfuge *f* (*Gußform*); **7.** ⚓ Bruch *m*, Reißen *n*; ~ ***shot*** *s. fig.* letzte boshafte Bemerkung (*beim Abschied*).
par·ti·san[1] ['pɑːtɪzn] *s.* ⚔ *hist.* Parti'sane *f* (*Stoßwaffe*).
par·ti·san[2] [,pɑːtɪ'zæn] **I** *s.* **1.** Par'teigänger(in), -genosse *m*, -genossin *f*; **2.** ⚔ Parti'san *m*, Freischärler *m*; **II** *adj.* **3.** Partei…; **4.** par'teiisch: ~ ***spirit*** leidenschaftliche Parteilichkeit; **5.** ⚔ Partisanen…, ,**par·ti'san·ship** [-ʃɪp] *s.* **1.** *pl.* Par'teigängertum *n*; **2.** *fig.* Par'tei-, Vetternwirtschaft *f*.
par·tite ['pɑːtaɪt] *adj.* **1.** geteilt (*a.* ♀); **2.** *in Zssgn* …teilig.
par·ti·tion [pɑː'tɪʃn] **I** *s.* **1.** (Auf-, Ver-)Teilung *f*; **2.** ⚖ ('Erb)Ausein,andersetzung *f*; **3.** Trennung *f*, Absonderung *f*; **4.** Scheide-, Querwand *f*, Fach *n*

(*Schrank etc.*); (Bretter)Verschlag *m*: **~ wall** Zwischenwand *f*; **II** *v/t.* **5.** (auf-, ver)teilen; **6.** *Erbschaft* ausein'andersetzen; **7.** *mst* **~ off** abteilen, -fachen;
par·ti·tive ['pɑːtɪtɪv] **I** *adj.* teilend, Teil...; *ling.* parti'tiv: **~ genitive**; **II** *s. ling.* Parti'tivum *n.*
part·ly ['pɑːtlɪ] *adv.* zum Teil, teilweise, teils: **~ ..., ~ ...** teils ..., teils ...
part·ner ['pɑːtnə] **I** *s.* **1.** *allg.* (*a. sport, a.* Tanz)Partner(in); **2.** ✝ Gesellschafter *m*, (Geschäfts)Teilhaber(in), Kompagnon *m*: **general ~** (unbeschränkt) haftender Gesellschafter, Komplementär *m*; **special ~** *Am.* Kommanditist (-in); → **dormant** 3; **limited** I; **silent** 2; **sleeping partner**; **3.** 'Lebenskameˌrad (-in), Gatte *m*, Gattin *f*; **II** *v/t.* **4.** zs.-bringen, -tun; **5.** sich zs.-tun, sich assoziieren (**with** mit *j-m*): **be ~ed with** *j-n* zum Partner haben; **'part·ner·ship** [-ʃɪp] *s.* **1.** Teilhaberschaft *f*, Partnerschaft *f*, Mitbeteiligung *f* (**in** an *dat.*); **2.** ✝ a) Handelsgesellschaft *f*, b) Perso'nalgesellschaft *f*: **general** *od.* **ordinary ~** Offene Handelsgesellschaft; → **limited** I; **special ~** *Am.* Kommanditgesellschaft *f*; **deed of ~** Gesellschaftsvertrag *m*; **enter into a ~ with** → **partner** 5.
part| own·er *s.* **1.** Miteigentümer(in); **2.** ⚓ Mitreeder *m*; **~ pay·ment** *s.* Teil-, Abschlagszahlung *f*.
par·tridge ['pɑːtrɪdʒ] *pl.* **par·tridge** *u.* **par·tridg·es** *s. orn.* Rebhuhn *n*.
part| sing·ing *s.* ♪ mehrstimmiger Gesang; **'~-time I** *adj.* Teilzeit..., Halbtags...: **~ job**; **II** *adv.* halbtags; **'~-ˌtim·er** *s.* Teilzeitbeschäftigte(r *m*) *f*, Halbtagskraft *f*.
par·tu·ri·ent [pɑː'tjʊərɪənt] *adj.* **1.** gebärend, kreißend; **2.** *fig.* (*mit e-r Idee*) schwanger; **par·tu·ri·tion** [ˌpɑːtjʊə'rɪʃn] *s.* Gebären *n*.
par·ty ['pɑːtɪ] *s.* **1.** *pol.* Par'tei *f*: **~ boss** Parteibonze *m*; **~ spirit** Parteigeist *m*; → **whip** 4a; **2.** Par'tie *f*, Gesellschaft *f*: **hunting ~**; **make one of the ~** sich anschließen, mitmachen; **3.** Trupp *m*: a) ⚔ Kom'mando *n*, b) (Arbeits)Gruppe *f*, c) (Rettungs- *etc.*)Mannschaft *f*; **4.** Einladung *f*, Party *f*, Gesellschaft *f*: **give a ~**; **5.** ⚖ (Pro'zeß- *etc.*)Parˌtei *f*: **contracting ~**, **~ to a contract** Vertragspartei, Kontrahent *m*; **a third ~** ein Dritter; **6.** Teilhaber(in), -nehmer (-in), Beteiligte(r *m*) *f*: **be a ~ to** beteiligt sein an, *et.* mitmachen; **the parties concerned** die Beteiligten; **7.** F ,Typ' *m*, Per'son *f*; **~ card** *s.* Par'teibuch *n*; **~ line** *s.* **1.** *teleph.* Gemeinschaftsanschluß *m*; **2.** *pol.* Par'teilinie *f*, -direkˌtive *f*: **follow the ~** *parl.* linientreu sein; **voting was on ~s** bei der Abstimmung herrschte Fraktionszwang; **~ lin·er** *s. Am.* Linientreue(r *m*) *f*; **~ tick·et** *s.* **1.** Gruppenfahrkarte *f*; **2.** *pol. Am.* (Kandi'daten)liste *f e-r Partei*.
par·ve·nu ['pɑːvənjuː] (*Fr.*) *s.* Em'porkömmling *m*, Parve'nü *m*.
Pas·cal ['pæskl] Pas'cal *n*: a) *phys. Einheit des Drucks*, b) *e-e Computersprache*.
pa·sha ['pɑːʃə] *s.* Pascha *m*.
pasque·flow·er ['pæskˌflaʊə] *s.* ⚘ Küchenschelle *f*.
pass¹ [pɑːs] *s.* **1.** (Eng)Paß *m*, Zugang *m*, 'Durchgang *m*, -fahrt *f*, Weg *m*: **hold the ~** die Stellung halten (*a. fig.*); **sell the ~** *fig.* alles verraten; **2.** Joch *n*, Sattel *m* (*Berg*); **3.** schiffbarer Ka'nal; **4.** Fischgang *m* (*Schleuse etc.*).
pass² [pɑːs] **I** *s.* **1.** (Reise)Paß *m*; (Perso'nal)Ausweis *m*; Passierschein *m*; 🚆, *thea. a.* **free ~** Frei-, Dauerkarte *f*; **2.** ⚔ a) Urlaubsschein *m*, b) Kurzurlaub *m*: **be on ~** auf (Kurz)Urlaub sein; **3.** a) Bestehen *n*, 'Durchkommen *n im Examen etc.*, b) bestandenes Examen, c) Note *f*, Zeugnis *n*, d) *univ. Brit.* einfacher Grad; **4.** ✝, ⚙ Abnahme *f*, Genehmigung *f*; **5.** Bestreichung *f*, Strich *m beim Hypnotisieren etc.*; **6.** *Maltechnik*: Strich *m*; **7.** (Hand)Bewegung *f*, (Zauber)Trick *m*; **8.** *Fußball etc.*: Paß *m*, (Ball)Abgabe *f*, Vorlage *f*: **~ back** Rückgabe *f*; **low ~** Flachpaß; **9.** *fenc.* Ausfall *m*, Stoß *m*; **10.** *sl.* Annäherungsversuch *m*, *oft* **hard ~** Zudringlichkeit *f*: **make a ~ at** *e-r Frau gegenüber* zudringlich werden; **11.** *fig.* a) Zustand *m*, b) kritische Lage: **a pretty ~** F e-e ,schöne Geschichte'; **be at a desperate ~** hoffnungslos sein; **things have come to such a ~** die Dinge haben sich derart zugespitzt; **12.** ⚙ Arbeitsgang *m* (*Werkzeugmaschine*); **13.** ⚙ (Schweiß)Lage *f*; **14.** *Walzwesen*: a) Gang *m*, b) Zug *m*; **15.** ⚡ Paß *m* (*frequenzabhängiger Vierpol*); **II** *v/t.* **16.** *et.* passieren, vor'bei-, vor'übergehen, -fahren, -fließen, -kommen, -reiten, -ziehen an (*dat.*); **17.** über'holen (*a. mot.*), vor'beilaufen, -fahren an (*dat.*); **18.** durch-, über'schreiten, passieren, durch'gehen, -'reisen *etc.*: **~ s.o.'s lips** über j-s Lippen kommen; **19.** über'steigen, -'treffen, hin'ausgehen über (*acc.*) (*a. fig.*): **it ~es my comprehension** es geht über m-n Verstand; **20.** *fig.* über'gehen, -'springen, keine No'tiz nehmen von; ✝ *e-e Dividende* ausfallen lassen; **21.** *durch et.* hin'durchleiten, -führen (*a.* ⚙), gleiten lassen: **~ (through a sieve)** durch ein Sieb passieren, durchseihen; ; **~ one's hand over** mit der Hand über *et.* fahren; **22.** *Gegenstand* reichen, (*a.* ⚖ *Falschgeld*) weitergeben; *Geld* in 'Umlauf setzen; (über-) 'senden, (*a. Funkspruch*) befördern; *sport Ball* abspielen, abgeben (**to** an *acc.* passen), (zu): **~ the chair** (**to**) den Vorsitz abgeben (an *j-n*); **~ the hat** (**round** *Brit.*) e-e Sammlung veranstalten (**for** für *j-n*); **~ the time of day** guten Tag *etc.* sagen, grüßen; **~ to s.o.'s account** j-m *e-n Betrag* in Rechnung stellen; **~ to s.o.'s credit** j-m gutschreiben; → **word** 5; **23.** *Türschloß* öffnen; **24.** vor'bei-, 'durchlassen, passieren lassen; **25.** *fig.* anerkennen, gelten lassen, genehmigen; **26.** ⚕ a) *Eiter, Nierenstein etc.* ausscheiden, b) *Eingeweide* entleeren, *Wasser* lassen; **27.** *Zeit* verbringen, -leben, -treiben; **28.** *parl. etc.* a) *Vorschlag* 'durchbringen, -setzen, b) *Gesetz* verabschieden, ergehen lassen, c) *Resolution* annehmen; **29.** rechtskräftig machen; **30.** ⚖ *Eigentum, Rechtstitel* über'tragen, *letztwillig* zukommen lassen; **31.** a) *Examen* bestehen, b) *Prüfling* bestehen lassen, 'durchkommen lassen; **32.** *Urteil* äußern, *s-e Meinung* aussprechen (**upon** über *acc.*), *Bemerkung* fallenlassen, *Kompliment* machen: **~ criticism on** Kritik üben an (*dat.*); → **sentence** 2 a; **III** *v/i.* **33.** sich fortbewegen, von e-m Ort zum andern gehen *od.* fahren *od.* ziehen *etc.*; **34.** vor'bei-, vor'übergehen *etc.* (**by** an *dat.*); **35.** 'durchgehen, passieren (*a. Linie*): **it just ~ed through my mind** *fig.* es ging mir eben durch den Kopf; **36.** ⚕ abgehen, abgeführt werden; **37.** 'durchkommen: a) ein Hindernis *etc.* bewältigen, b) (e-e Prüfung) bestehen; **38.** her'umgereicht werden, von Hand zu Hand gehen, her'umgehen; im 'Umlauf sein: **harsh words ~ed between them** es fielen harte Worte bei ihrer Auseinandersetzung; **39.** a) *sport* passen, (den Ball) zuspielen *od.* abgeben, b) (*Kartenspiel u. fig.*) passen: **I ~ on that!** da muß ich passen!; **40.** *fenc.* ausfallen; **41.** 'übergehen (**from ...** [**in**]**to** von ... zu), werden (**into** zu); **42.** *in andere Hände* 'übergehen, über'tragen werden (*Eigentum*); fallen (**to** an *Erben etc.*); *unter j-s Aufsicht* kommen, geraten; **43.** an-, hin-, 'durchgehen, leidlich sein, unbeanstandet bleiben, geduldet werden: **let that ~** reden wir nicht mehr davon; **44.** *parl. etc.* 'durchgehen, bewilligt *od.* zum Gesetz erhoben werden, Rechtskraft erlangen; **45.** gangbar sein, Geltung finden (*Ideen, Grundsätze*); **46.** angesehen werden, gelten (**for** als); **47.** urteilen, entscheiden (**upon** über *acc.*); ⚖ *a.* gefällt werden (*Urteil*); **48.** vergehen (*a. Schmerz etc.*), verstreichen (*Zeit*); endigen; sterben: **fashions ~** Moden kommen u. gehen; **49.** sich zutragen *od.* abspielen, passieren: **what ~ed between you and him?**; **bring to ~** bewirken; **it came to ~ that** *bibl.* es begab sich, daß;
Zssgn mit prp.:
pass| be·yond *v/i.* hin'ausgehen über (*acc.*) (*a. fig.*); **~ by** *v/i.* **1.** vor'bei-, vor'übergehen an (*dat.*); **2.** *et. od. j-n* über'gehen (**in silence** stillschweigend); **3.** unter *dem Namen* ... bekannt sein; **~ for** → **pass** 46; **~ in·to I** *v/t.* **1.** *et.* einführen in (*acc.*); **II** *v/i.* **2.** (hin'ein)gehen *etc.* in (*acc.*); **3.** führen *od.* leiten in (*acc.*); **4.** 'übergehen in (*acc.*): **~ law** (zum) Gesetz werden; **~ through I** *v/t.* **1.** durch ... führen *od.* leiten *od.* stecken; 'durchschleusen; **II** *v/i.* **2.** durch'fahren, -'queren, -'schreiten *etc.*; durch ... gehen *etc.*; durch'fließen; **3.** durch ... führen (*Draht, Tunnel etc.*); **4.** durch'bohren; **5.** 'durchmachen, erleben;
Zssgn mit adv.:
pass| a·way I *v/t.* **1.** *Zeit* ver-, zubringen (**doing s.th.** mit et.); **II** *v/i.* **2.** vergehen (*Zeit etc.*); **3.** verscheiden, sterben; **~ by** *v/i.* **1.** vor'bei-, vor'übergehen (*a. Zeit*); **2.** → **pass over** 4; **~ down** *v/t. Bräuche etc.* über'liefern, weitergeben (**to** an *dat.*); **~ in** *v/t.* **1.** einlassen; **2.** einreichen, -händigen: **~ one's check** *Am. sl.* ,den Löffel abgeben' (*sterben*); **~ off I** *v/t.* **1.** *j-n od. et.* ausgeben (**for, as** für, als); **II** *v/i.* **2.** vergehen (*Schmerz etc.*); **3.** *gut etc.* vor'übergehen, von'statten gehen; **4.** 'durchgehen (**as** als); **~ on I** *v/t.* **1.** weitergeben, -reichen (**to** *dat. od.* an *acc.*); befördern; **2.** ✝ abwälzen (**to** auf *acc.*);

II *v/i.* **3.** weitergehen; **4.** 'übergehen (***to*** zu); **5.** → ***pass away*** 3; **~ out I** *v/i.* **1.** hin'ausgehen, -fließen, -strömen; **2.** *sl.* ‚umkippen', ohnmächtig werden; **II** *v/t.* **3.** ver-, austeilen; **~ o·ver I** *v/i.* **1.** hin'übergehen; **2.** 'überleiten, -führen; **II** *v/t.* **3.** über'reichen, -'tragen; **4.** über'gehen (***in silence*** stillschweigend), ignorieren; **5.** → ***pass up*** 1; **~ through** *v/i.* **1.** hin'durchführen; **2.** hin'durchgehen, -reisen *etc.*: ***be passing through*** auf der Durchreise sein; **~ up** *v/t. sl.* **1.** a) sich *e-e Chance* entgehen lassen, b) *et.* ‚sausen' lassen; verzichten auf (*acc.*); **2.** *j-n* über'gehen.

pass·a·ble ['pɑːsəbl] *adj.* □ **1.** passierbar; gang-, befahrbar; **2.** ✝ gangbar, gültig (*Geld etc.*); **3.** *fig.* leidlich, pas'sabel.

pas·sage ['pæsɪdʒ] *s.* **1.** Her'ein-, Her'aus-, Vor'über-, 'Durchgehen *n*, 'Durchgang *m*, -reise *f*, -fahrt *f*, 'Durchfließen *n*: ***no ~!*** kein Durchgang!, keine Durchfahrt!; → ***bird*** 1; **2.** ✝ ('Waren-)Tran,sit *m*, 'Durchgang *m*; **3.** Pas'sage *f*, ('Durch-, Verbindungs)Gang *m*; *bsd. Brit.* Korridor *m*; **4.** Ka'nal *m*, Furt *f*; **5.** ⚙ 'Durchlaß *m*, -tritt *m*; **6.** (See-, Flug)Reise *f*, ('Über)Fahrt *f*: ***book one's ~*** s-e Schiffskarte lösen (***to*** nach); ***work one's ~*** s-e Überfahrt durch Arbeit abverdienen; **7.** Vergehen *n*, Ablauf *m*: ***the ~ of time***; **8.** *parl.* 'Durchkommen *n*, Annahme *f*, In'krafttreten *n e-s Gesetzes*; **9.** Wortwechsel *m*; **10.** *pl.* Beziehungen *pl.*, *geistiger* Austausch; **11.** (Text)Stelle *f*, Passus *m*; **12.** ♪ Pas'sage *f* (*a. Reiten*); **13.** *fig.* 'Übergang *m*, -tritt *m* (***from ... to, into*** von ... in *acc.*, zu); **14.** a) (Darm)Entleerung *f*, Stuhlgang *m*, b) *anat.* (*Gehör- etc.*)Gang *m*, (*Harn- etc.*) Weg(e *pl.*) *m*: ***auditory*** (***urinary***) **~**; **~ at arms** *s.* **1.** Waffengang; **2.** Wortgefecht *n*, ‚Schlagabtausch' *m*; **~ boat** *s.* Fährboot *n*; '**~·way** *s.* 'Durchgang *m*, Korridor *m*, Pas'sage *f*.

'**pass|·book** *s.* **1.** *bsd. Brit.* a) Bank-, Kontobuch *n*, b) Sparbuch *n*; **2.** Buch *n* über kreditierte Waren; **~ check** *s. Am.* Pas'sierschein *m*; **~ de·gree** → ***pass²*** 3c.

pas·sé, pas·sée ['pɑːseɪ] (*Fr.*) *adj.* pas'sé: a) vergangen, b) veraltet, c) verblüht: ***a passée belle*** e-e verblühte Schönheit.

passe·men·terie ['pɑːsməntrɪ] (*Fr.*) *s.* Posamentierwaren *pl.*

pas·sen·ger ['pæsɪndʒə] *s.* **1.** Passa'gier *m*, Fahr-, Fluggast *m*, Reisende(r *m*) *f*, Insasse *m*: **~ *cabin*** ✈ Fluggastraum *m*; **2.** F a) Schma'rotzer *m*, b) Drückeberger *m*; **~ car** *s.* **1.** Per'sonen(kraft)wagen *m*, *abbr.* Pkw; **2.** 🚂 *Am.* Per'sonenwagen *m*, **~ lift** *s. Brit.* Per'sonenaufzug *m*; **~ pi·geon** *s. orn.* Wandertaube *f*; **~ plane** *s.* ✈ Passa'gierflugzeug *n*; **~ serv·ice** *s.* Per'sonenbeförderung *f*; **~ traf·fic** *s.* Per'sonenverkehr *m*; **~ train** *s.* 🚂 Per'sonenzug *m*.

passe-par·tout ['pæspɑːtuː] (*Fr.*) *s.* **1.** Hauptschlüssel *m*; **2.** Passepar'tout *n* (*Bildumrahmung*).

,**pass·er-'by** *pl.* ,**pass·ers-'by** *s.* Pas'sant(in).

pass ex·am·i·na·tion *s. univ. Brit.* unterstes 'Abschluße,xamen.

pas·sim ['pæsɪm] (*Lat.*) *adv.* passim, hier u. da, an verschiedenen Orten.

pass·ing ['pɑːsɪŋ] **I** *adj.* **1.** vor'über-, 'durchgehend: **~ *axle*** ⚙ durchgehende Achse; **2.** vergehend, vor'übergehend, flüchtig; **3.** beiläufig; **II** *s.* **4.** Vor'bei-, 'Durch-, Hin'übergehen *n*: ***in ~*** im Vorbeigehen, *fig.* beiläufig, nebenbei; ***no ~!*** *mot.* Überholverbot!; **5.** 'Übergang *m*: **~ *of title*** Eigentumsübertragung *f*; **6.** Da'hinschwinden *n*; **7.** Hinscheiden *n*, Ableben *n*; **8.** *pol.* 'Durchgehen *n e-s Gesetzes*; **~ beam** *s. mot.* Abblendlicht *n*; **~ lane** *s. mot.* Über'holspur *f*; **~ note** *s.* ♪ 'Durchgangston *m*; **~ shot** *s. Tennis*: Pas'sierschlag *m*; **~ zone** *s. Staffellauf*: Wechselzone *f*.

pas·sion ['pæʃn] *s.* **1.** Leidenschaft *f*, heftige Gemütserregung, (Gefühls-)Ausbruch *m*; **2.** Zorn *m*: ***fly into a ~*** e-n Wutanfall bekommen; → ***heat*** 6; **3.** Leidenschaft *f*: a) heiße Liebe, heftige Neigung, b) heißer Wunsch, c) Passi'on *f*, Vorliebe *f* (***for*** für), d) Liebhabe'rei *f*; Passi'on *f*: ***it has become a ~ with him*** es ist bei ihm zur Leidenschaft geworden, er tut es leidenschaftlich gern(e); **4.** ♀ *eccl.* Leiden *n* (Christi), Passion *f* (*a.* ♪, *paint. u. fig.*); **pas·sion·ate** ['pæʃənət] *adj.* □ **1.** leidenschaftlich (*a. fig.*); **2.** hitzig, jähzornig; **pas·sion·less** ['pæʃnlɪs] *adj.* □ leidenschaftslos.

pas·sion| play *s. eccl.* Passi'onsspiel *n*; ♀ **Sun·day** *s. eccl.* Passi'onssonntag *m*; **~ week** *s.* **1.** Karwoche *f*; **2.** Woche zwischen Passi'onssonntag u. Palm'sonntag.

pas·si·vate ['pæsɪveɪt] *v/t.* ⚙, ⚗ passivieren.

pas·sive ['pæsɪv] **I** *adj.* □ **1.** passiv (*a. ling.*, ⚡, ⚔, *sport*), leidend, teilnahmslos, 'widerstandslos: **~ *air defence*** Luftschutz; **~ *verb ling.*** passivisch konstruiertes Verb; **~ *voice*** → 3; **~ *vocabulary*** passiver Wortschatz; **2.** ✝ untätig, nicht zinstragend, passiv: **~ *debt*** unverzinsliche Schuld; **~ *trade*** Passivhandel *m*; **II** *s.* **3.** *ling.* Passiv *n*, Leideform *f*; '**pas·sive·ness** [-nɪs], **pas·siv·i·ty** [pæ'sɪvətɪ] *s.* Passivi'tät *f*, Teilnahmslosigkeit *f*.

'**pass·key** *s.* **1.** Hauptschlüssel *m*; **2.** Drücker *m*; **3.** Nachschlüssel *m*.

pas·som·e·ter [pæ'sɒmɪtə] *s.* ⚙ Schrittmesser *m*.

Pass·o·ver ['pɑːs,əʊvə] *s. eccl.* **1.** Passah(fest) *n*; **2.** ♀ Osterlamm *n*.

pass·port ['pɑːspɔːt] *s.* **1.** (Reise)Paß *m*: **~ *inspection*** Paßkontrolle *f*; **2.** ✝ Passierschein *m*; **3.** *fig.* Zugang *m*, Weg *m*, Schlüssel *m* (***to*** zu).

'**pass·word** *s.* Pa'role *f*, Losung *f*, Kennwort *n*.

past [pɑːst] **I** *adj.* **1.** vergangen, verflossen: ***for some time ~*** seit einiger Zeit; **2.** *ling.* Vergangenheits...: **~ *participle*** Mittelwort *n* der Vergangenheit, Partizip *n* Perfekt; **~ *tense*** Vergangenheit *f*, Präteritum *n*; **3.** vorig, früher, ehemalig, letzt: **~ *president***; **~ *master fig.*** Altmeister *m*, großer Könner; **II** *s.* **4.** Vergangenheit *f* (*a. ling.*), *weitS. a.* Vorleben *n*: ***a woman with a ~*** eine Frau mit Vergangenheit; **III** *adv.* **5.** vor'bei, vor'über: ***to run ~***; **IV** *prp.* **6.** (*Zeit*) nach, über (*acc.*): ***half ~ seven*** halb acht; ***she is ~ forty*** sie ist über vierzig; **7.** an ... vorbei: ***he ran ~ the house***; **8.** über ... hin'aus: **~ *comprehension*** unfaßbar, unfaßlich; **~ *cure*** unheilbar; **~ *hope*** hoffnungslos; ***he is ~ it*** F er ist ‚darüber hinaus'; ***she is ~ caring*** das kümmert sie alles nicht mehr; ***I would not put it ~ him sl.*** ich traue es ihm glatt zu.

pas·ta ['pæstə] *s.* Teigwaren *pl.*

past-'due *ad.* ✝ 'überfällig (*Wechsel etc.*); Verzugs...(*-zinsen*).

paste [peɪst] **I** *s.* **1.** Teig *m*, (*Fisch-, Zahn- etc.*)Paste *f*, Brei *m*; ⚙ Tonmasse *f*; Glasmasse *f*; **2.** Kleister *m*, Klebstoff *m*, Papp *m*; **3.** a) Paste *f* (*Diamantenherstellung*), b) künstlicher Edelstein, Simili *n*, *m*; **II** *v/t.* **4.** kleben, kleistern, pappen, bekleben (***with*** mit); **5.** **~ up** a) auf-, ankleben (***on, in*** auf, in *acc.*), b) verkleistern (*Loch*); **6.** *sl.* ('durch)hauen: **~ *s.o. one*** j-m ‚eine kleben'; '**~·board I** *s.* **1.** Pappe *f*, Pappendeckel *m*, Kar'ton *m*; **2.** *sl.* (Eintritts-, Spiel-, Vi'siten)Karte *f*; **II** *adj.* **3.** aus Pappe, Papp...: **~ *box*** Karton; **4.** *fig.* unecht, wertlos, kitschig, nachgemacht.

pas·tel I *s.* [pæ'stel] **1.** ⚘ Färberwaid *m*; **2.** ⚙ Waidblau *n*; **3.** Pa'stellstift *m*, -farbe *f*; **4.** Pa'stellzeichnung *f*, -bild *n*; **II** *adj.* ['pæstl] **5.** zart, duftig, Pastell... (*Farbe*); **pas·tel·ist** ['pæstəlɪst], **pas·tel·list** [pæ'stelɪst] *s.* Pa'stellmaler(in).

pas·tern ['pæstɜːn] *s. zo.* Fessel *f* (*vom Pferd*).

'**paste-up** *s. typ.* 'Klebe,umbruch *m*.

pas·teur·i·za·tion [,pæstəraɪ'zeɪʃn] *s.* Pasteurisierung *f*; **pas·teur·ize** ['pæstəraɪz] *v/t.* pasteurisieren.

pas·tille ['pæstəl] *s.* **1.** Räucherkerzchen *n*; **2.** *pharm* Pa'stille *f*.

pas·time ['pɑːstaɪm] *s.* (***as a ~*** zum) Zeitvertreib *m*.

past·i·ness ['peɪstɪnɪs] *s.* **1.** breiiger Zustand; breiiges Aussehen; **2.** *fig.* käsiges Aussehen.

past·ing ['peɪstɪŋ] *s.* **1.** Kleistern *n*, Kleben *n*; **2.** ⚙ Klebstoff *m*; **3.** *sl.* ‚Dresche' *f*, (Tracht *f*) Prügel *pl.*

pas·tor ['pɑːstə] *s.* Pfarrer *m*, Pastor *m*, Seelsorger *m*; '**pas·to·ral** [-tərəl] **I** *adj.* □ **1.** Schäfer..., Hirten..., i'dyllisch, ländlich; **2.** *eccl.* pasto'ral, seelsorgerlich: **~ *staff*** Krummstab; **II** *s.* **3.** Hirtengedicht *n*, I'dylle *f*; **4.** *paint.* ländliche Szene; **5.** ♪ a) Schäferspiel *n*, b) Pasto'rale *n*; **6.** *eccl.* a) Hirtenbrief *m*, b) *pl. a.* ♀ ***Epistles*** Pasto'ralbriefe *pl.* (*von Paulus*); '**pas·tor·ate** [-ərət] *s.* **1.** Pasto'rat *n*, Pfarramt *n*; **2.** *coll. die* Geistlichen *pl.*; **3.** *Am.* Pfarrhaus *n*.

past per·fect *ling. s.* Vorvergangenheit *f*, 'Plusquamper,fekt(um) *n*.

pas·try ['peɪstrɪ] *s.* **1.** a) *coll.* Kon'ditorwaren *pl.*, Feingebäck *n*, b) Kuchen *m*, Torte *f*; **2.** (Kuchen-, Torten)Teig *m*; **~ cook** *s.* Kon'ditor *m*.

pas·tur·age ['pɑːstjʊrɪdʒ] *s.* **1.** Weiden *n* (*Vieh*); **2.** Weidegras *n*; **3.** Weide(land *n*) *f*; **4.** Bienenzucht *f* u. -fütterung *f*.

pas·ture ['pɑːstʃə] **I** *s.* **1.** Weidegras *n*, Viehfutter *n*; **2.** Weide(land *n*) *f*: ***seek greener ~s fig.*** sich nach besseren Möglichkeiten umsehen; ***retire to ~*** (in den Ruhestand) abtreten; **II** *v/i.* **3.** grasen, weiden; **III** *v/t.* **4.** *Vieh* auf die Weide treiben, weiden; **5.** *Wiese* abweiden.

past·y¹ [ˈpeɪstɪ] *adj.* **1.** teigig, kleisterig; **2.** *fig.* ‚käsig', blaß.

past·y² [ˈpæstɪ] *s.* (ˈFleisch)Paˌstete *f.*

pat [pæt] **I** *s.* **1.** *Brit.* (*leichter*) Schlag, Klaps *m*: **~ on the back** *fig.* Schulterklopfen *n*, Lob *n*, Glückwunsch *m*; **2.** (Butter)Klümpchen *n*; **3.** Klopfen *n*, Getrappel *n*, Tapsen *n*; **II** *adj.* **4.** a) paˈrat, bereit, b) passend, treffend: **~ answer** schlagfertige Antwort; **~ solution** Patentlösung; **a ~ style** ein gekonnter Stil; **know s.th. off** (*od.* **have it down**) **~** F et. (wie) am Schnürchen können; **5.** fest: **stand ~** festbleiben, sich nicht beirren lassen; **6.** (*a. adv.*) im rechten Augenblick, rechtzeitig, wie gerufen; **III** *v/t.* **7.** *Brit.* klopfen, tätscheln: **~ s.o. on the back** j-m (anerkennend) auf die Schulter klopfen, *fig. a.* j-n beglückwünschen.

pat² [pæt] *s.* Ire *m* (*Spitzname*).

ˈpat-a-cake backe, backe Kuchen (*Kinderspiel*).

patch [pætʃ] **I** *s.* **1.** Fleck *m*, Flicken *m*, Lappen *m*; ⚔ *etc.* Tuchabzeichen *n*: **not a ~ on** F gar nicht zu vergleichen mit; **2.** a) ⚕ Pflaster *n*, b) Augenbinde *f*; **3.** Schönheitspflästerchen *n*; **4.** Stück *n* Land, Fleck *m*; Stück *n* Rasen; Stelle *f* (*a. im Buch*): **in ~es** stellenweise; **strike a bad ~** e-e Pechsträhne *od.* e-n schwarzen Tag haben; **5.** (Farb)Fleck *m* (*bei Tieren etc.*); **6.** *pl.* Bruchstücke *pl.*, *et.* Zs.-gestoppeltes; **II** *v/t.* **7.** flikken, ausbessern; mit Flicken versehen; **8. ~ up** *bsd. fig.* a) zs.-stoppeln: **~ up a textbook**, b) ‚zs.-flicken', c) *Ehe etc.* ‚kitten', d) *Streit* beilegen, e) überˈtünchen, beschönigen; **ˈ~·board** *s. Computer*: Schaltbrett; **~ kit** *s.* Flickzeug *n.*

patch·ou·li [ˈpætʃʊlɪ] *s.* ˈPatschuli *n* (*Pflanze u. Parfüm*).

patch| pock·et *s.* aufgesetzte Tasche; **~ test** *s.* ⚕ Tuberkuˈlinprobe *f*; **ˈ~·word** *s. ling.* Flickwort *n*; **ˈ~·work** *s. a. fig.* Flickwerk *n.*

patch·y [ˈpætʃɪ] *adj.* □ **1.** voller Flicken; **2.** *fig.* zs.-gestoppelt; **3.** fleckig; **4.** *fig.* ungleichmäßig.

pate [peɪt] *s.* F Schädel *m*, ‚Birne' *f.*

pâté [ˈpæteɪ] (*Fr.*) *s.* Paˈstete *f.*

pat·en [ˈpætən] *s. eccl.* Paˈtene *f*, Hostienteller *m.*

pa·ten·cy [ˈpeɪtənsɪ] *s.* **1.** Offenkundigkeit *f*; **2.** ⚕ ˈDurchgängigkeit *f* (*e-s Kanals etc.*).

pat·ent [ˈpeɪtənt; *bsd.* ⚖ *u. Am.* ˈpæ-] **I** *adj.* □ **1.** offen(kundig): **to be ~** auf der Hand liegen; **2. letters ~** → 6 *u.* 7; **3.** patentiert, gesetzlich geschützt: **~ article** Markenartikel *m*; **~ fuel** Preßkohlen *pl.*; **~ leather** Lack-, Glanzleder *n*; **~-leather shoe** Lackschuh *m*; **~ medicine** Marken-, Patentmedizin *f*; **4.** ⚖ Patent…: **~ agent** (*Am.* **attorney**) Patentanwalt *m*; **~ law** *objektives* Patentrecht; **℘ Office** Patentamt *n*; **~ right** *subjektives* Patentrecht; **~ roll** *Brit.* Patentregister *n*; **~ specification** Patentschrift *f*, -beschreibung *f*; **5.** *Brit.* F ‚paˈtent': **~ methods**; **II** *s.* **6.** Paˈtent *n*, Priviˈleg(ium) *n*, Freibrief *m*, Bestallung *f*; **7.** ⚖ Paˈtent(urkunde *f*) *n*: **~ of addition** Zusatzpatent; **~ applied for**, **~ pending** Patent angemeldet; **take out a ~ for** → 10; **8.** *Brit.* F ‚Reˈzept' *n*; **III** *v/t.* **9.** patentieren, gesetzlich schützen; **10.** patentieren lassen; **ˈpat·ent·a·ble** [-təbl] *adj.* paˈtentfähig; **pat·ent·ee** [ˌpeɪtənˈtiː] *s.* Paˈtentinhaber(in).

pa·ter [ˈpeɪtə] *s. ped. sl.* ‚alter Herr' (*Vater*).

pa·ter·nal [pəˈtɜːnl] *adj.* □ väterlich, Vater…: **~ grandfather** Großvater väterlicherseits; **paˈter·ni·ty** [-nətɪ] *s.* Vaterschaft *f* (*a. fig.*): **~ suit** ⚖ Vaterschaftsklage *f*; **declare ~** die Vaterschaft feststellen.

pa·ter·nos·ter [ˌpætəˈnɒstə] **I** *s.* **1.** *R.C.* a) Vaterˈunser *n*, b) Rosenkranz *m*; **2.** ⚙ Paterˈnoster *m* (*Aufzug*); **II** *adj.* **3.** ⚙ Paternoster…

path [pɑːθ] **~s** [pɑːðz] *s.* **1.** Pfad *m*, Weg *m* (*a. fig.*): **cross s.o.'s ~** j-m über den Weg laufen; **2.** ⚙, *phys.*, *sport* Bahn *f*: **~ of electrons** Elektronenbahn.

pa·thet·ic [pəˈθetɪk] *adj.* (□ **~ally**) **1.** *obs.* paˈthetisch, allzu gefühlvoll: **~ fallacy** Vermenschlichung *f* der Natur (*in der Literatur*); **2.** mitleiderregend; **3.** *Brit.* F kläglich, jämmerlich, ‚zum Weinen'.

ˈpathˌfind·er *s.* **1.** ✈, ⚔ Pfadfinder *m*; **2.** Forschungsreisende(r) *m*; **3.** *fig.* Bahnbrecher *m.*

path·less [ˈpɑːθlɪs] *adj.* weglos.

path·o·gen·ic [ˌpæθəˈdʒenɪk] *adj.* ⚕ pathoˈgen, krankheitserregend.

path·o·log·i·cal [ˌpæθəˈlɒdʒɪkl] *adj.* □ ⚕ pathoˈlogisch: a) krankhaft, b) *die Krankheitslehre betreffend*; **pa·thol·o·gist** [pəˈθɒlədʒɪst] *s.* ⚕ Pathoˈloge *m*; **pa·thol·o·gy** [pəˈθɒlədʒɪ] *s.* ⚕ **1.** Patholoˈgie *f*, Krankheitslehre *f*; **2.** pathologischer Befund.

pa·thos [ˈpeɪθɒs] *s.* **1.** *obs.* Pathos *n*; **2.** a) Mitleid *n*, b) *das* Mitleiderregende.

ˈpath·way *s.* Pfad *m*, Weg *m*, Bahn *f.*

pa·tience [ˈpeɪʃns] *s.* **1.** Geduld *f*; Ausdauer *f*: **lose one's ~** die Geduld verlieren; **be out of ~ with s.o.** aufgebracht sein gegen j-n; **have no ~ with s.o.** j-n nicht leiden können, nichts übrig haben für j-n; **try s.o.'s ~** j-s Geduld auf die Probe stellen; → **Job²**; **possess** 2 b; **2.** *bsd. Brit.* Patiˈence *f* (*Kartenspiel*); **ˈpa·tient** [-nt] **I** *adj.* □ **1.** geduldig; nachsichtig; beharrlich: **be ~ of** ertragen; **~ of two interpretations** *fig.* zwei Deutungen zulassend; **II** *s.* **2.** Patiˈent(in), Kranke(r *m*) *f*; **3.** ⚖ *Brit.* Geistesgestörte(r *m*) *f* (*in e-r Heil- und Pflegeanstalt*).

pat·i·o [ˈpætɪəʊ] *s.* **1.** Innenhof *m*, Patio *m*; **2.** Terˈrasse *f*, Veˈranda *f.*

pa·tri·arch [ˈpeɪtrɪɑːk] *s.* Patriˈarch *m*; **pa·tri·ar·chal** [ˌpeɪtrɪˈɑːkl] *adj.* patriarˈchalisch (*a. fig. ehrwürdig*); **ˈpa·tri·arch·ate** [-kɪt] *s.* Patriarˈchat *n.*

pa·tri·cian [pəˈtrɪʃn] **I** *adj.* paˈtrizisch; *fig.* aristoˈkratisch; **II** *s.* Paˈtrizier(in).

pat·ri·cide [ˈpætrɪsaɪd] → **parricide**.

pat·ri·mo·ni·al [ˌpætrɪˈməʊnjəl] *adj.* ererbt, Erb…; **pat·ri·mo·ny** [ˈpætrɪmənɪ] *s.* **1.** väterliches Erbteil (*a. fig.*); **2.** Vermögen *n*; **3.** Kirchengut *n.*

pa·tri·ot [ˈpætrɪət] *s.* Patriˈot(in); **pa·tri·ot·eer** [ˌpætrɪəˈtɪə] *s.* Hurˈrapatriˌot *m*; **pa·tri·ot·ic** [ˌpætrɪˈɒtɪk] *adj.* (□ **~ally**) patriˈotisch; **ˈpa·tri·ot·ism** [-tɪzəm] *s.* Patrioˈtismus *m*, Vaterlandsliebe *f.*

pa·trol [pəˈtrəʊl] **I** *v/i.* **1.** ⚔ patroullieren, ✈ Paˈtrouille fliegen; auf Streife sein (*Polizisten*), s-e Runde machen (*Wachmann*); **II** *v/t.* **2.** ⚔ abpatrouillieren, ✈ *Strecke* abfliegen; auf Streife sein in (*dat.*); **III** *s.* **3.** (**on ~** auf) Paˈtrouille *f*; Streife *f*; Runde *f*; **4.** ⚔ Paˈtrouille *f*, Späh-, Stoßtrupp *m*; (Poliˈzei)Streife *f*: **~ activity** ⚔ Spähtrupptätigkeit *f*; **~ car** a) ⚔ (Panzer-)Spähwagen *m*, b) (Funk-, Poliˈzei-)Streifenwagen *m*; **~ wagon** *Am.* Polizeigefangenenwagen *m*; **~·man** [-mæn] *s.* [*irr.*] Streifenbeamte(r) *m.*

pa·tron [ˈpeɪtrən] *s.* **1.** Paˈtron *m*, Schutz-, Schirmherr *m*; **2.** Gönner *m*, Förderer *m*; **3.** *R.C.* a) ˈKirchenpaˌtron *m*, b) → **patron saint**; **4.** a) ✝ (Stamm-)Kunde *m*, b) Stammgast *m*, *a. thea. etc.* regelmäßiger Besucher; **5.** *Brit. mot.* Pannenhelfer *m*; **pa·tron·age** [ˈpætrənɪdʒ] *s.* **1.** Schirmherrschaft *f*; **2.** Gönnerschaft *f*, Förderung *f*; **3.** ⚖ Patroˈnatsrecht *n*; **4.** Kundschaft *f*; **5.** gönnerhaftes Benehmen; **6.** *Am.* Recht *n* der Ämterbesetzung; **pa·tron·ess** [ˈpeɪtrənɪs] *s.* Paˈtronin *f etc.* (→ **patron**).

pa·tron·ize [ˈpætrənaɪz] *v/t.* **1.** beschirmen, beschützen; **2.** fördern, unterˈstützen; **3.** (Stamm)Kunde *od.* Stammgast sein bei, *Theater etc.* regelmäßig besuchen; **4.** gönnerhaft behandeln; **ˈpa·tron·iz·er** [-zə] *s.* → **patron** 2, 4; **ˈpa·tron·iz·ing** [-zɪŋ] *adj.* □ gönnerhaft, herˈablassend: **~ air** Gönnermiene *f.*

pa·tron saint *s. R.C.* Schutzheilige(r) *m.*

pat·sy [ˈpætsɪ] *s. sl.* **1.** Sündenbock *m*; **2.** Gimpel *m*; **3.** ˈWitzfiˌgur *f.*

pat·ten [ˈpætn] *s.* **1.** Holzschuh *m*; **2.** Stelzschuh *m*; **3.** ⚠ Säulenfuß *m.*

pat·ter¹ [ˈpætə] **I** *v/i. u. v/t.* **1.** schwatzen, (daˈher)plappern; ‚heˈrunterleiern'; **II** *s.* **2.** Geplapper *n*; **3.** (ˈFach-)Jargon *m*; **4.** Gaunersprache *f.*

pat·ter² [ˈpætə] **I** *v/i.* **1.** prasseln (*Regen etc.*); **2.** trappeln (*Füße*); **II** *s.* **3.** Prasseln *n* (*Regen*); **4.** (Fuß)Getrappel *n*; **5.** Klappern *n.*

pat·tern [ˈpætən] **I** *s.* **1.** (*a.* Schnitt-, Stick)Muster *n*, Vorlage *f*, Moˈdell *n*: **on the ~ of** nach dem Muster von *od. gen.*; **2.** ✝ Muster *n*: a) (Waren)Probe *f*, b) Desˈsin *n*, Moˈtiv *n* (*Stoff*): **by ~ post** als Muster ohne Wert; **3.** *fig.* Muster *n*, Vorbild *n*; **4.** *fig.* Plan *m*, Anlage *f*: **~ of one's life**; **5.** ⚙ a) Schaˈblone *f*, b) ˈGußmoˌdell *n*, c) Lehre *f*; **6.** *Weberei*: Paˈtrone *f*; **7.** (**behavio[u]r**) **~** *psych.* (Verhaltens)Muster *n*; **II** *adj.* **8.** musterhaft, Muster…: **a ~ wife**; **III** *v/t.* **9.** (nach)bilden, gestalten (**after**, **on** nach): **~ one's conduct on s.o.** sich (in s-m Benehmen) ein Beispiel an j-m nehmen; **10.** mit Muster(n) verzieren, mustern; **~ bomb·ing** *s.* ⚔ Flächenwurf *m*; **~ book** *s.* ✝ Musterbuch *n*; **~ mak·er** *s.* ⚙ Moˈdellmacher *m*; **~ paint·ing** *s.* ⚔ Tarnanstrich *m.*

pat·ty [ˈpætɪ] *s.* Paˈstetchen *n.*

pau·ci·ty [ˈpɔːsətɪ] *s.* geringe Zahl *od.* Menge, Knappheit.

Paul·ine [ˈpɔːlaɪn] *adj. eccl.* pauˈlinisch.

paunch [pɔːntʃ] *s.* **1.** (Dick)Bauch *m*,

Wanst *m*; **2.** *zo.* Pansen *m*; **'paunch·y** [-tʃɪ] *adj.* dickbäuchig.

pau·per ['pɔːpə] **I** *s.* **1.** Arme(r *m*) *f*; **2.** *Am.* a) Unter'stützungsempfänger(in), b) ⚖ unter Armenrecht Klagende(r *m*) *f*; **II** *adj.* **3.** Armen...; **'pau·per·ism** [-ərɪzəm] *s.* Verarmung *f*, Massenarmut *f*; **pau·per·i·za·tion** [ˌpɔːpəraɪ'zeɪʃn] *s.* Verarmung *f*, Verelendung *f*; **'pau·per·ize** [-əraɪz] *v/t.* bettelarm machen.

pause [pɔːz] **I** *s.* **1.** Pause *f*, Unter'brechung *f*: ***make a ~*** innehalten, pausieren; ***it gives one ~ to think*** es gibt e-m zu denken; **2.** *typ.* Gedankenstrich *m*; **3.** ♪ Fer'mate *f*; **II** *v/i.* **4.** pausieren, innehalten; stehenbleiben; zögern; **5.** verweilen (***on, upon*** bei): ***to ~ upon a note*** (*od.* ***tone***) ♪ e-n Ton aushalten.

pave [peɪv] *v/t. Straße* pflastern, *Fußboden* legen: ***~ the way for*** *fig.* den Weg ebnen für; → ***paving***; **'pave·ment** [-mənt] *s.* **1.** (Straßen)Pflaster *n*; **2.** *Brit.* Bürgersteig *m*, Trot'toir *n*: ***~ artist*** Pflastermaler *m*; ***~ café*** Straßencafé *n*; **3.** *Am.* Fahrbahn *f*; **4.** Fußboden(belag) *m*; **'pav·er** [-və] *s.* **1.** Pflasterer *m*; **2.** Fliesen-, Plattenleger *m*; **3.** Pflasterstein *m*, Fußbodenplatte *f*; **4.** *Am.* 'Straßenbeˌtonmischer *m*.

pa·vil·ion [pə'vɪljən] *s.* **1.** (großes) Zelt; **2.** Pavillon *m*, Gartenhäuschen *n*; **3.** ☤ (Messe)Pavillon *m*.

pav·ing ['peɪvɪŋ] *s.* Pflastern *n*; (Be)Pflasterung *f*, Straßendecke *f*; Fußbodenbelag *m*; ***~ stone*** *s.* Pflasterstein *m*; ***~ tile*** *s.* Fliese *f*.

pav·io(u)r ['peɪvjə] *s.* Pflasterer *m*.

paw [pɔː] **I** *s.* **1.** Pfote *f*, Tatze *f*; **2.** F ‚Pfote' *f* (*Hand*); **3.** F *humor.* ‚Klaue' *f* (*Handschrift*); **II** *v/t.* **4.** *mit dem Vorderfuß od. der Pfote* scharren; **5.** F ‚betatschen': a) derb *od.* ungeschickt anfassen, b) *j-n* ‚begrabschen': ***~ the air*** (in der Luft) herumfuchteln; **III** *v/i.* **6.** stampfen, scharren; **7.** ‚(he'rum)fummeln'.

pawl [pɔːl] *s.* **1.** ⚙ Sperrhaken *m*, -klinke *f*, Klaue *f*; **2.** ⚓ Pall *n*.

pawn¹ [pɔːn] *s.* **1.** *Schach:* Bauer *m*; **2.** *fig.* 'Schachfiˌgur *f*.

pawn² [pɔːn] **I** *s.* **1.** Pfand(sache *f*) *n*; ⚖ *u. fig. a.* Faustpfand *n*: ***in*** (*od.* ***at***) ***~*** verpfändet, versetzt; **II** *v/t.* **2.** verpfänden (*a. fig.*), versetzen; **3.** ☤ lombardieren; **'~ˌbro·ker** *s.* Pfandleiher *m*.

pawn·ee [ˌpɔː'niː] *s.* ⚖ Pfandinhaber *m*, -nehmer *m*; **pawn·er**, **pawn·or** ['pɔːnə] *s.* Pfandschuldner *m*.

'pawn|·shop *s.* Pfandhaus *n*, Pfandleihe *f*; ***~ tick·et*** *s.* Pfandschein *m*.

pay [peɪ] **I** *s.* **1.** Bezahlung *f*; (Arbeits-)Lohn *m*, Löhnung *f*; Gehalt *n*; Sold *m* (*a. fig.*); ⚔ (Wehr)Sold *m*: ***in the ~ of s.o.*** bei j-m beschäftigt, in j-s Sold; **2.** *fig.* Belohnung *f*, Lohn *m*; **II** *v/t.* [*irr.*] **3.** zahlen, entrichten; *Rechnung* bezahlen *od.* begleichen, *Wechsel* einlösen, *Hypothek* ablösen; *j-n* bezahlen, *Gläubiger* befriedigen: ***~ into*** einzahlen auf *ein Konto*; ***~ one's way*** ohne Verlust arbeiten, s-n Verbindlichkeiten nachkommen, auskommen mit dem, was man hat; **4.** *fig.* (be)lohnen, vergelten (***for*** *et.*): ***~ home*** heimzahlen; **5.** *fig. Achtung* zollen; *Aufmerksamkeit* schenken; *Besuch* abstatten; *Ehre* erweisen; *Kompliment* machen; → ***court*** 10; ***homage*** 2; **6.** *fig.* sich lohnen für *j-n*; **III** *v/i.* [*irr.*] **7.** zahlen, Zahlung leisten: ***~ for*** (für) *et.* bezahlen (*a. fig. et. büßen*), die Kosten tragen für; ***he had to ~ dearly for it*** *fig.* er mußte es bitter büßen, es kam ihn teuer zu stehen; **8.** *fig.* sich lohnen, sich rentieren, sich bezahlt machen;

Zssgn mit adv.:

pay| back *v/t.* **1.** zu'rückzahlen, -erstatten; **2.** *fig.* a) *Besuch etc.* erwidern, b) *j-m* heimzahlen (***for s.th.*** et.); → ***coin*** 1; ***~ down*** *v/t.* **1.** bar bezahlen; **2.** e-e Anzahlung machen von; ***~ in*** *v/t. u. v/i.* (*auf ein Konto*) einzahlen; → ***paid-in***; ***~ off*** **I** *v/t.* **1.** *j-n* auszahlen, entlohnen; ⚓ abmustern; **2.** *et.* abbezahlen, tilgen; **3.** *Am. für* ***pay back*** 2b; **II** *v/i.* **4.** F → ***pay*** 8; ***~ out*** *v/t.* **1.** auszahlen; **2.** F *fig.* → ***pay back*** 2b; **3.** (*pret. u. p.p.* **payed**) *Kabel, Kette etc.* ausstekken, -legen, abrollen; ***~ up*** *v/t. j-n od. et.* voll *od.* so'fort bezahlen; *Schuld* tilgen; ☤ *Anteile, Versicherung etc.* voll einzahlen; → ***paid-up***.

pay·a·ble ['peɪəbl] *adj.* **1.** zahlbar, fällig: ***~ to bearer*** auf den Überbringer lautend; ***make a cheque*** (*Am.* ***check***) ***~ to s.o.*** e-n Scheck auf j-n ausstellen; **2.** ☤ ren'tabel.

ˌpay|-as-you-'earn *s. Brit.* Lohnsteuerabzug *m*; **ˌ~-as-you-'see tel·e·vi·sion** *s.* Münzfernsehen *n*; ***~ bed*** *s.* ⚕ Pri'vatbett *n*; ***~ check*** *s. Am.* Lohn-, Gehaltsscheck *m*; ***~ claim*** *s.* Lohn-, Gehaltsforderung *f*; ***~ clerk*** *s.* **1.** ☤ Lohnauszahler *m*; **2.** ⚔ Rechnungsführer *m*; **'~·day** *s.* Zahl-, Löhnungstag *m*; ***~ desk*** *s.* ☤ Kasse *f* (*im Kaufhaus*); ***~ dirt*** *s.* **1.** *geol.* goldführendes Erdreich; **2.** *fig. Am.* Geld *n*, Gewinn *m*: ***strike ~*** Erfolg haben.

pay·ee [peɪ'iː] *s.* **1.** Zahlungsempfänger (-in); **2.** Wechselnehmer(in).

pay en·ve·lope *s.* Lohntüte *f*.

pay·er ['peɪə] *s.* **1.** (Be)Zahler *m*; **2.** (*Wechsel*)Bezogene(r) *m*, Tras'sat *m*.

pay freeze *s.* Lohnstopp *m*.

pay·ing ['peɪɪŋ] *adj.* **1.** lohnend, einträglich, ren'tabel: ***not ~*** unrentabel; ***~ concern*** lohnendes Geschäft; **2.** Kassen..., Zahl(ungs)...: ***~ guest*** zahlender Gast; **ˌ~-'in slip** *s.* Einzahlungsschein *m*.

pay| load *s.* **1.** ⚙, ⚓, ✈ Nutzlast *f*: ***~ capacity*** Ladefähigkeit *f*; **2.** ⚔ Sprengladung *f*; **3.** ☤ *Am.* Lohnanteil *m*; **'~ˌmas·ter** *s.* ⚔ Zahlmeister *m*.

pay·ment ['peɪmənt] *s.* **1.** (Ein-, Aus-, Be)Zahlung *f*, Entrichtung *f*, Abtragung *f von Schulden*, Einlösung *f e-s Wechsels*: ***~ in kind*** Sachleistung *f*; ***in ~ of*** zum Ausgleich (*gen.*); ***on ~ (of)*** nach Eingang (*gen.*), gegen Zahlung (von *od. gen.*); ***accept in ~*** in Zahlung nehmen; **2.** gezahlte Summe, Bezahlung *f*; **3.** Lohn *m*, Löhnung *f*, Besoldung *f*; **4.** *fig.* Lohn *m* (*a. Strafe*).

'pay|-off *s. sl.* **1.** Aus- *od.* Abzahlung *f*; **2.** *fig.* Abrechnung *f* (*Rache*); **3.** Resul'tat *n*; Entscheidung *f*; **4.** *Am.* Clou *m* (*Höhepunkt*); ***~ of·fice*** *s.* **1.** 'Lohnbüˌro *n*; **2.** Zahlstelle *f*.

pay·o·la [peɪ'əʊlə] *s. Am. sl.* Bestechungs-, Schmiergeld(er *pl.*) *n*.

pay| pack·et *s.* Lohntüte *f*; ***~ pause*** *s.* Lohnpause *f*; **'~·roll** *s.* Lohnliste *f*: ***have*** (*od.* ***keep***) ***s.o. on one's ~*** j-n (bei sich) beschäftigen; ***he is no longer on our ~*** er arbeitet nicht mehr für *od.* bei uns; ***~ slip*** *s.* Lohn-, Gehaltsstreifen *m*; ***~ tel·e·phone*** *s.* Münzfernsprecher *m*; ***~ tel·e·vi·sion*** *s.* Münzfernsehen *n*.

pea [piː] **I** *s.* ⚘ Erbse *f*: ***as like as two ~s*** sich gleichend wie ein Ei dem andern; → ***sweet pea***; **II** *adj.* erbsengroß, -förmig.

peace [piːs] **I** *s.* **1.** Friede(n) *m*: ***at ~*** a) in Frieden, im Friedenszustand, b) in Frieden ruhend (*tot*); **2.** *a.* ***the King's*** (*od.* ***Queen's***) ***~***, ***public ~*** Landfrieden *m*, öffentliche Ruhe und Ordnung, öffentliche Sicherheit: ***breach of the ~*** ⚖ (öffentliche) Ruhestörung; ***disturb the ~*** die öffentliche Ruhe stören; ***keep the ~*** die öffentliche Sicherheit wahren; **3.** *fig.* Ruhe *f*, Friede(n) *m*: ***~ of mind*** Seelenruhe; ***hold one's ~*** sich ruhig verhalten; ***leave in ~*** in Ruhe *od.* Frieden lassen; **4.** Versöhnung *f*, Eintracht *f*: ***make one's ~ with s.o.*** sich mit j-m versöhnen; **II** *int.* **5.** sst!, still!, ruhig!; **III** *adj.* **6.** Friedens...: ***~ conference***; ***~ feelers***; ***~ movement***; ***~ offensive***; ***~ corps*** Friedenstruppe *f*; **'peace·a·ble** [-səbl] *adj.* □ friedlich: a) friedfertig, -liebend, b) ruhig, ungestört; **'peace·ful** [-fʊl] *adj.* □ friedlich; **'~ˌkeep·ing** *adj.*: ***~ force*** *pol.* ⚔ Friedenstruppe *f*; **'peace·less** [-lɪs] *adj.* friedlos.

peace·nik ['piːsnɪk] *s. Am. sl.* Kriegsgegner(in).

peace| of·fer·ing *s.* **1.** *eccl.* Sühneopfer *n*; **2.** Versöhnungsgeschenk *n*, versöhnliche Geste, Friedenszeichen *n*; ***~ of·fi·cer*** *s.* Sicherheitsbeamte(r) *m*, Schutzmann *m*; ***~ re·search*** *s.* Friedensforschung *f*; ***~ set·tle·ment*** *s.* Friedensregelung *f*; **'~·time I** *s.* Friedenszeit *f*; **II** *adj.* in Friedenszeiten, Friedens...; ***~ trea·ty*** *s. pol.* Friedensvertrag *m*.

peach¹ [piːtʃ] *s.* **1.** ⚘ Pfirsich(baum) *m*; **2.** *sl.* ‚klasse' Per'son *od.* Sache: ***a ~ of a car*** ein ‚todschicker' Wagen; ***a ~ of a girl*** ein bildhübsches Mädchen.

peach² [piːtʃ] *v/i.*: ***~ against*** (*od.* ***on***) *Komplicen* ‚verpfeifen', *Schulkameraden* verpetzen.

peach·y ['piːtʃɪ] *adj.* **1.** pfirsichartig; **2.** *sl.* ‚prima', ‚schick', ‚klasse'.

pea·cock ['piːkɒk] *s.* **1.** *orn.* Pfau(hahn) *m*; **2.** *fig.* (eitler) Fatzke *m*; ***~ blue*** *s.* Pfauenblau *n* (*Farbe*).

'pea|·fowl *s. orn.* Pfau *m*; **'~·hen** *s. orn.* Pfauhenne *f*; ***~ jack·et*** *s.* ⚓ Ko'lani *m* (*Uniformjacke*).

peak¹ [piːk] **I** *s.* **1.** Spitze *f*; **2.** Bergspitze *f*; Horn *n*, spitzer Berg; **3.** (Mützen-)Schirm *m*; **4.** ⚓ Piek *f*; **5.** ⚗, *phys.* Höchst-, Scheitelwert *m*; **6.** *fig.* (Leistungs- *etc.*)Spitze *f*, Höchststand *m*; Gipfel *m des Glücks etc.*: ***~ of traffic*** Verkehrsspitze; ***reach the ~*** den Höchststand erreichen; **II** *adj.* **7.** Spitzen..., Höchst..., Haupt...: ***~ factor*** *phys.*, ⚡ Scheitelfaktor *m*; ***~ load*** Spitzenbelastung *f* (*a.* ⚡); ***~ season*** Hochsaison *f*, -konjunktur; ***~ time*** a) Hochkonjunktur *f*, b) Stoßzeit *f*, c) = ***~ (traffic) hours*** Hauptverkehrszeit *f*.

peak² [piːk] *v/i.* **1.** kränkeln, abmagern; **2.** spitz aussehen.

peaked [piːkt] *adj.* **1.** spitz(ig): ***~ cap***

Schirmmütze; **2.** F ‚spitz', kränklich.

peak·y ['pi:kɪ] *adj.* **1.** gipfelig; **2.** spitz (-ig); **3.** → ***peaked*** 2.

peal [pi:l] **I** *s.* **1.** (Glocken)Läuten *n*; **2.** Glockenspiel *n*; **3.** (*Donner*)Schlag *m*, Dröhnen *n*: **~ *of laughter*** schallendes Gelächter; **II** *v/i.* **4.** läuten; erschallen, dröhnen, schmettern; **III** *v/t.* **5.** erschallen lassen.

'pea·nut I *s.* **1.** ⚘ Erdnuß *f*; **2.** *Am. sl.* a) *pl.* ‚kleine Fische' *pl.* (*geringer Betrag*), b) ‚kleines Würstchen' (*Person*); **II** *adj.* **3.** *Am. sl.* klein, unbedeutend, lächerlich: ***a ~ politician***; **~ but·ter** *s.* Erdnußbutter *f*.

pear [peə] *s.* ⚘ **1.** Birne *f* (*a. weitS. Objekt*); **2.** *a.* **~ *tree*** Birnbaum *m*.

pearl [pɜ:l] **I** *s.* **1.** Perle *f* (*a. fig. u. pharm.*): ***cast ~s before swine*** Perlen vor die Säue werfen; **2.** Perl'mutt *n*; **3.** *typ.* Perl(schrift) *f*; **II** *adj.* **4.** Perlen...; Perlmutt(er)...; **III** *v/i.* **5.** Perlen bilden, perlen, tropfen; **~ bar·ley** *s.* Perlgraupen *pl.*; **~ div·er** *s.* Perlentaucher *m*; **'~-ˌoys·ter** *s. zo.* Perlmuschel *f*.

pearl·y ['pɜ:lɪ] *adj.* **1.** Perlen..., perlenartig, perlmutterartig; **2.** perlenreich.

'pear|-quince *s.* ⚘ Echte Quitte, Birnenquitte *f*; **'~-shaped** *adj.* birnenförmig.

peas·ant ['peznt] **I** *s.* **1.** (Klein)Bauer *m*; **2.** *fig.* F ‚Bauer' *m*; **II** *adj.* **3.** (klein-)bäuerlich, Bauern...: **~ *woman*** Bäuerin *f*; **'peas·ant·ry** [-rɪ] *s. die* (Klein-)Bauern *pl.*, Landvolk *n*.

pease [pi:z] *s. pl. Br. dial.* Erbsen *pl.*: **~ *pudding*** Erbs(en)brei *m*.

'pea|-ˌshoot·er *s.* **1.** Blas-, Pusterohr *n*; **2.** *Am.* Kata'pult *m, n*; **3.** *Am. sl.* ‚Ka'none' *f* (*Pistole*); **~ soup** *s.* **1.** Erbsensuppe *f*; **2.** *a.* **ˌ~-'soup·er** [-'su:pə] *s.* **1.** F ‚Waschküche' *f* (*dichter Nebel*); **2.** 'Frankokaˌnadier *m*; **ˌ~'soup·y** [-'su:pɪ] *adj.* F dicht u. gelb (*Nebel*).

peat [pi:t] *s.* **1.** Torf *m*: ***cut*** (*od.* ***dig***) **~** Torf stechen: **~ *bath*** ⚕ Moorbad *n*; **~ *coal*** Torfkohle *f*: **~ *moss*** Torfmoos *n*; **2.** Torfstück *n*, -sode *f*.

peb·ble ['pebl] **I** *s.* **1.** Kiesel(stein) *m*: ***you are not the only ~ on the beach*** F man (*od.* ich) kann auch ohne dich auskommen; **2.** A'chat *m*; **3.** 'Bergkriˌstall *m*; **4.** *opt.* Linse *f* aus 'Bergkriˌstall; **II** *v/t.* **5.** *Weg* mit Kies bestreuen; **6.** ⚙ *Leder* krispeln; **'peb·bly** [-lɪ] *adj.* kieselig.

pec·ca·dil·lo [ˌpekə'dɪləʊ] *pl.* **-loes** *s.* ‚kleine Sünde', Kava'liersdeˌlikt *n*.

peck¹ [pek] *s.* **1.** Viertelscheffel *m* (*Brit. 9,1, Am. 8,8 Liter*); **2.** *fig.* Menge *f*, Haufen *m*: ***a ~ of trouble***.

peck² [pek] **I** *v/t.* **1.** *mit dem Schnabel etc.* (auf)picken, (-)hacken; **2.** *j-m* ein Küßchen geben; **II** *v/i.* **3.** (***at***) picken, hacken (nach), einhacken (auf *acc.*): ***~ing order*** *zo.* u. *fig.* Hackordnung *f*; **~ *at s.o.*** *fig.* auf j-m ‚herumhacken'; **~ *at one's food*** *lustlos* im Essen herumstochern; **III** *s.* **4.** Schlag *m*, (Schnabel-)Hieb *m*; **5.** Loch *n*; **6.** leichter *od.* flüchtiger Kuß; **7.** *Brit. sl.* ‚Futter' *n* (*Essen*); **'peck·er** [-kə] *s.* **1.** Picke *f*, Haue *f*; **2.** ⚙ Abfühlnadel *f*; **3.** *sl.* ‚Zinken' *m* (*Nase*): ***keep your ~ up!*** halt die Ohren steif!; **4.** *Am. sl.* ‚Schwanz' *m* (*Penis*); **peck·ish** ['pekɪʃ] *adj.* F **1.** hungrig; **2.** *Am.* reizbar.

pec·to·ral ['pektərəl] **I** *adj.* **1.** *anat.*, ⚕ Brust...; **II** *s.* **2.** *hist.* Brustplatte *f*; **3.** *anat.* Brustmuskel *m*; **4.** *pharm.* Brustmittel *n*; **5.** *zo. a.* **~ *fin*** Brustflosse *f*; **6.** *R.C.* Brustkreuz *n*.

pec·u·late ['pekjʊleɪt] *v/t.* (*v/i.* öffentliche Gelder) unter'schlagen, veruntreuen; **pec·u·la·tion** [ˌpekjʊ'leɪʃn] *s.* Unter'schlagung *f*, Veruntreuung *f*, 'Unterschleif *m*; **'pec·u·la·tor** [-tə] *s.* Veruntreuer *m*.

pe·cul·iar [pɪ'kju:ljə] **I** *adj.* □ **1.** eigen (-tümlich) (***to*** *dat.*); **2.** eigen, seltsam, absonderlich; **3.** besonder; **II** *s.* **4.** ausschließliches Eigentum; **pe·cu·li·ar·i·ty** [pɪˌkju:lɪ'ærətɪ] *s.* **1.** Eigenheit *f*, Eigentümlichkeit *f*, Besonderheit *f*; **2.** Eigenartigkeit *f*, Seltsamkeit *f*.

pe·cu·ni·ar·y [pɪ'kju:njərɪ] *adj.* □ Geld..., pekuni'är, finanzi'ell: **~ *advantage*** Vermögensvorteil.

ped·a·gog·ic, ped·a·gog·i·cal [ˌpedə'gɒdʒɪk(l)] *adj.* □ päda'gogisch, erzieherisch, Erziehungs...; **ˌped·a'gog·ics** [-ks] *s. pl. sg. konstr.* Päda'gogik *f*; **ped·a·gogue** ['pedəgɒg] *s.* **1.** Päda'goge *m*, Erzieher *m*; **2.** *contp. fig.* Pe'dant *m*, Schulmeister *m*; **ped·a·go·gy** ['pedəgɒdʒɪ] *s.* Päda'gogik *f*.

ped·al ['pedl] **I** *s.* **1.** Pe'dal *n* (*a.* ♪), Fußhebel *m*, Tretkurbel *f*; → ***soft pedal***; **2.** *a.* **~ *note*** ♪ Pe'dal- *od.* Orgelton *m*; **II** *v/i.* **3.** ⚙, ♪ Pe'dal treten; **4.** radfahren, ‚strampeln'; **III** *v/t.* **5.** treten, fahren; **IV.** *adj.* **6.** Pedal..., Fuß...: **~ *bin*** Treteimer *m*; **~ *car*** Tretauto *n*; **~ *brake*** *mot.* Fußbremse *f*; **~ *control*** ✈ Pedalsteuerung *f*; **~ *switch*** ⚙ Fußschalter *m*.

ped·a·lo ['pedələʊ] *s.* Tretboot *n*.

ped·ant ['pedənt] *s.* Pe'dant(in), Kleinigkeitskrämer(in); **pe·dan·tic** [pɪ'dæntɪk] *adj.* (□ ***~ally***) pe'dantisch, kleinlich; **'ped·ant·ry** [-trɪ] *s.* Pedante'rie *f*.

ped·dle ['pedl] **I** *v/i.* **1.** hausieren gehen; **2.** sich mit Kleinigkeiten abgeben, tändeln; **II** *v/t.* **3.** hausieren gehen mit (*a. fig.*), handeln mit: **~ *drugs***; **~ *new ideas***; **'ped·dler** [-lə] *Am.* → ***pedlar***; **'ped·dling** [-lɪŋ] *adj. fig.* kleinlich; geringfügig, unbedeutend, wertlos.

ped·er·ast ['pedəræst] *s.* Päde'rast *m*; **'ped·er·as·ty** [-tɪ] *s.* Pädera'stie *f*, Knabenliebe *f*.

ped·es·tal ['pedɪstl] *s.* **1.** △ Sockel *m*, Posta'ment *n*, Säulenfuß *m*: ***set s.o. on a ~*** *fig.* j-n aufs Podest erheben; **2.** *fig.* Basis *f*, Grundlage *f*; **3.** ⚙ 'Untergestell *n*, Sockel *m*, (Lager)Bock *m*.

pe·des·tri·an [pɪ'destrɪən] **I** *adj.* **1.** zu Fuß, Fuß...; Spazier...; Fußgänger...: **~ *precinct*** (*od.* ***area***) Fußgängerzone *f*; **2.** *fig.* pro'saisch, nüchtern; langweilig; **II** *s.* **3.** Fußgänger(in); **pe'des·tri·an·ize** [-naɪz] *v/t.* in e-e Fußgängerzone verwandeln.

pe·di·at·ric [ˌpi:dɪ'ætrɪk] *adj.* ⚕ pädi'atrisch, Kinder(heilkunde)...; **pe·di·a·tri·cian** [ˌpi:dɪə'trɪʃn] *s.* Kinderarzt *m*, -ärztin *f*; **ˌpe·di'at·rics** [-ks] *s. pl. sg. konstr.* Kinderheilkunde *f*, Pädia'trie *f*; **ˌpe·di'at·rist** [-ɪst] → ***pediatrician***; **ped·i·at·ry** ['pi:dɪætrɪ] → ***pediatrics***.

ped·i·cel ['pedɪsəl] *s.* **1.** ⚘ Blütenstengel *m*; **2.** *anat.*, *zo.* Stiel(chen *n*) *m*; **'ped·i·cle** [-kl] *s.* **1.** ⚘ Blütenstengel *m*; **2.** ⚕ Stiel *m* (*Tumor*).

ped·i·cure ['pedɪkjʊə] **I** *s.* Pedi'küre *f*: a) Fußpflege *f*, b) Fußpfleger(in); **II** *v/t.* *j-s* Füße behandeln *od.* pflegen; **'ped·i·cur·ist** [-ərɪst] → ***pedicure*** I b.

ped·i·gree ['pedɪgri:] **I** *s.* **1.** Stammbaum *m* (*a. zo. u. fig.*), Ahnentafel *f*; **2.** Entwicklungstafel *f*; **3.** Ab-, Herkunft *f*; **4.** lange Ahnenreihe; **II** *adj. a.* **'ped·i·greed** [-i:d] **5.** mit Stammbaum, reinrassig, Zucht...

ped·i·ment ['pedɪmənt] *s.* △ **1.** Giebel (-feld *n*) *m*; **2.** Ziergiebel *m*.

ped·lar ['pedlə] *s.* Hausierer *m*.

pe·dom·e·ter [pɪ'dɒmɪtə] *s. phys.* Schrittmesser *m*, -zähler *m*.

pe·dun·cle [pɪ'dʌŋkl] *s.* **1.** ⚘ Blütenstandstiel *m*, Blütenzweig *m*; **2.** *zo.* Stiel *m*, Schaft *m*; **3.** *anat.* Zirbel-, Hirnstiel *m*.

pee [pi:] *v/i.* F ‚Pi'pi machen', ‚pinkeln'.

peek¹ [pi:k] **I** *v/i.* **1.** gucken, spähen (***into*** in *acc.*); **2.** **~ *out*** her'ausgucken (*a. fig.*); **II** *s.* **3.** flüchtiger *od.* heimlicher Blick.

peek² [pi:k] *s.* Piepsen *n* (*Vogel*).

peek·a·boo [ˌpi:kə'bu:] *s.* ‚Guck-Guck-Spiel' *n* (*kleiner Kinder*).

peel¹ [pi:l] **I** *v/t.* **1.** *Frucht, Kartoffeln, Bäume* schälen: **~ *off*** abschälen, -lösen; ***~ed barley*** Graupen *pl.*; ***keep your eyes ~ed*** *sl.* halt die Augen offen; **2.** *sl. Kleider* abstreifen; **II** *v/i.* **3.** *a.* **~ *off*** sich abschälen, sich abblättern, abbröckeln, abschilfern; **4.** *sl.* ‚sich entblättern', ‚strippen'; **5.** **~ *off*** ✈ *aus e-m Verband* ausscheren; **III** *s.* **6.** (*Zitronen- etc.*)Schale *f*; Rinde *f*; Haut *f*.

peel² [pi:l] *s.* **1.** Backschaufel *f*, Brotschieber *m*; **2.** *typ.* Aufhängekreuz *n*.

peel·er¹ ['pi:lə] *s.* **1.** (*Kartoffel- etc.*) Schäler *m*; **2.** *sl.* Stripperin *f*.

peel·er² ['pi:lə] *s. sl. obs.* ‚Bulle' *m* (*Polizist*).

peel·ing ['pi:lɪŋ] *s.* (*lose*) Schale, Rinde *f*, Haut *f*.

peen [pi:n] *s.* ⚙ Finne *f*, Hammerbahn *f*.

peep¹ [pi:p] **I** *v/i.* **1.** piep(s)en (*Vogel etc.*): ***he never dared ~ again*** er hat es nicht mehr gewagt, den Mund aufzumachen; **II** *s.* **2.** Piep(s)en *n*; **3.** *sl.* ‚Pieps' *m* (*Wort*).

peep² [pi:p] **I** *v/i.* **1.** gucken, neugierig *od.* verstohlen blicken (***into*** in *acc.*): **~ *at*** e-n Blick werfen auf (*acc.*); **2.** *oft* **~ *out*** her'vorgucken, -schauen, -lugen (*a. fig. sich zeigen, zum Vorschein kommen*); **II** *s.* **3.** neugieriger *od.* verstohlener Blick: ***have*** (*od.* ***take***) ***a ~*** → 1; **4.** Blick *m* (***of*** in *acc.*), ('Durch)Sicht *f*; **5.** ***at ~ of day*** bei Tagesanbruch; **'peep·er** [-pə] *s.* **1.** Spitzel *m*; **2.** *sl.* ‚Gucker' *m* (*Auge*); **3.** *sl.* Spiegel *m*; Fenster *n*; Brille *f*.

'peep-hole *s.* Guckloch *n*.

Peep·ing Tom ['pi:pɪŋ] *s.* ‚Spanner' *m* (*Voyeur*).

'peep|·scope *s.* ‚Spion' *m* (*an der Tür*); **~ show** *s.* **1.** Guckkasten *m*; **2.** Peep-Show *f*.

peer¹ [pɪə] *v/i.* **1.** spähen, gucken (***into*** in *acc.*): **~ *at*** sich *et.* genau an- *od.* begucken; **2.** *poet.* sich zeigen; **3.** → ***peep²*** 2.

peer² [pɪə] *s.* **1.** Gleiche(r *m*) *f*, Ebenbürtige(r *m*) *f*: ***without a ~*** ohnegleichen, unvergleichlich; ***he associates with his ~s*** er gesellt sich zu seinesgleichen; ***~ group*** *sociol.* Peer-group *f*; **2.** Angehörige(r) *m* des (brit.) Hochadels: ***~ of the realm*** *Brit.* Peer *m* (*Mitglied des Oberhauses*); **peer·age** ['pɪərɪdʒ] *s.* **1.** Peerage *f*: a) Peerswürde *f*, b) Hochadel *m*, (*die*) Peers *pl.*; **2.** 'Adelskaˌlender *m*; **peer·ess** ['pɪərɪs] *s.* **1.** Gemahlin *f* e-s Peers; **2.** hohe Adlige: ***~ in her own right*** Peereß *f* im eigenen Recht; **peer·less** ['pɪəlɪs] *adj.* □ unvergleichlich, einzig(artig).

peeve [pi:v] F *v/t.* (ver)ärgern; **peeved** [-vd] *adj.* F ‚eingeschnappt', verärgert; **'pee·vish** [-vɪʃ] *adj.* □ grämlich, übellaunig, verdrießlich.

peg [peg] **I** *s.* **1.** (Holz-, *surv.* Absteck-) Pflock *m*; (Holz)Nagel *m*; (Schuh)Stift *m*; ⚙ Dübel *m*; Sprosse *f* (*a. fig.*): ***take s.o. down a ~*** (***or two***) j-m ‚einen Dämpfer aufsetzen'; ***come down a ~*** gelindere Saiten aufziehen, ‚zurückstecken'; ***a round ~ in a square hole, a square ~ in a round hole*** ein Mensch am falschen Platze; **2.** (Kleider)Haken *m*: ***off the ~*** von der Stange (*Anzug*); **3.** (Wäsche)Klammer *f*; **4.** (Zelt)Hering *m*; **5.** ♪ Wirbel *m* (*Saiteninstrument*); **6.** *fig.* ‚Aufhänger' *m*: ***a good ~ on which to hang a story***; **7.** *Brit.* ‚Gläs-chen' *n*, *bsd.* Whisky *m* mit Soda; **II** *v/t.* **8.** anpflöcken, -nageln; **9.** ⚙ (ver)dübeln; **10.** *a.* ***~ out*** *surv. Grenze, Land* abstecken: ***~ out one's claim*** *fig.* s-e Ansprüche geltend machen; **11.** † *Löhne, Preise* stützen, halten: ***~ged price*** Stützkurs; **12.** F schmeißen (***at*** nach); **III** *v/i.* **13.** ***~ away*** (*od.* ***along***) F drauf'los arbeiten; **14.** ***~ out*** F a) ‚zs.-klappen', b) ‚abkratzen' (*sterben*); **'~·top** *s.* Kreisel *m*.

peign·oir ['peɪnwɑ:] (*Fr.*) *s.* Morgenrock *m*.

pe·jo·ra·tive ['pi:dʒərətɪv] **I** *adj.* □ abschätzig, her'absetzend, pejora'tiv; **II** *s. ling.* abschätziges Wort, Pejora'tivum *n*.

peke [pi:k] F *für* ***Pekingese*** 2.

Pe·king·ese [ˌpi:kɪŋ'i:z] *s. sg. u. pl.* **1.** Bewohner(in) von Peking; **2.** ♀ Peki'nese *m* (*Hund*).

pel·age ['pelɪdʒ] *s. zo.* Körperbedekkung *f* wilder Tiere (*Fell etc.*).

pel·ar·gon·ic [ˌpelɑ:'gɒnɪk] *adj.* ⚗ Pelargon…: ***~ acid***; **ˌpel·ar'go·ni·um** [-'gəʊnjəm] *s.* ⚘ Pelar'gonie *f*.

pelf [pelf] *s. contp.* Mammon *m*.

pel·i·can ['pelɪkən] *s. orn.* Pelikan *m*; **~ cross·ing** *s. mit Ampeln gesicherter* Fußgängerüberweg *m*.

pe·lisse [pe'li:s] *s.* (*langer*) Damen- *od.* Kindermantel.

pel·let ['pelɪt] *s.* **1.** Kügelchen *n*, Pille *f*; **2.** Schrotkorn *n* (*Munition*).

pel·li·cle ['pelɪkl] *s.* Häutchen *n*; Mem'bran *f*; **pel·lic·u·lar** [pe'lɪkjʊlə] *adj.* häutchenförmig, Häutchen…

pell-mell [ˌpel'mel] **I** *adv.* **1.** durchein'ander, ‚wie Kraut u. Rüben'; **2.** 'unterschiedslos; **3.** Hals über Kopf; **II** *adj.* **4.** verworren, kunterbunt; **5.** hastig, über'eilt; **III** *s.* **6.** Durchein'ander *n*.

pel·lu·cid [pe'lju:sɪd] *adj.* □ 'durchsichtig, klar (*a. fig.*).

pelt¹ [pelt] *s.* Fell *n*, (Tier)Pelz *m*; † *rohe* Haut.

pelt² [pelt] **I** *v/t.* **1.** *j-n mit Steinen etc.* bewerfen, (*fig. mit Fragen*) bombardieren; **2.** verhauen, prügeln; **II** *v/i.* **3.** *mit Steinen etc.* werfen (***at*** nach); **4.** niederprasseln: ***~ing rain*** Platzregen *m*; **III** *s.* **5.** Schlag *m*, Wurf *m*; **6.** Prasseln *n* (*Regen*); **7.** Eile *f*: (***at***) ***full ~*** in voller Geschwindigkeit.

pelt·ry ['peltrɪ] *s.* **1.** Rauch-, Pelzwaren *pl.*; **2.** Fell *n*, Haut *f*.

pel·vic ['pelvɪk] *adj. anat.* Becken…: ***~ cavity*** Beckenhöhle; **pel·vis** ['pelvɪs] *pl.* **-ves** [-vi:z] *s. anat.* Becken *n*.

pem·(m)i·can ['pemɪkən] *s.* Pemmikan *n* (*Dörrfleisch*).

pen¹ [pen] **I** *s.* **1.** Pferch *m*, Hürde *f* (*Schafe*), Verschlag *m* (*Geflügel*), Hühnerstall *m*; **2.** kleiner Behälter *od.* Raum; **3.** ⚓ (U-Boot)Bunker *m*; **4.** *Am. sl.* ‚Kittchen' *n*, ‚Knast' *m*; **II** *v/t.* **5.** *a.* ***~ in, ~ up*** einpferchen, -schließen, -sperren.

pen² [pen] **I** *s.* **1.** (Schreib)Feder *f*, *a.* Federhalter *m*; Füller *m*; Kugelschreiber *m*: ***set ~ to paper*** die Feder ansetzen; ***~ and ink*** Schreibzeug *n*; ***~ friend*** Brieffreund(in); **2.** *fig.* Feder *f*, Stil *m*: ***he has a sharp ~*** er führt e-e spitze Feder; **II** *v/t.* **3.** (nieder)schreiben; ab-, verfassen.

pe·nal ['pi:nl] *adj.* □ **1.** strafrechtlich, Straf…: ***~ code*** Strafgesetzbuch *n*; ***~ colony*** Sträflingskolonie *f*; ***~ duty*** Strafzoll *m*; ***~ institution*** Strafanstalt *f*; ***~ law*** Strafrecht *n*; ***~ reform*** Strafrechtsreform *f*; ***~ sum*** Vertrags-, Konventionalstrafe *f*; → ***servitude*** 2; **2.** sträflich, strafbar: ***~ act***; **'pe·nal·ize** [-nəlaɪz] *v/t.* **1.** mit e-r Strafe belegen, bestrafen; **2.** benachteiligen, ‚bestrafen'; **pen·al·ty** ['penltɪ] *s.* **1.** gesetzliche Strafe: ***on*** (*od.* ***under***) ***~ of*** bei Strafe von; → ***extreme*** 2; ***pay*** (*od.* ***bear***) ***the ~ of*** *et.* büßen; **2.** (Geld)Buße *f*, Vertragsstrafe *f*; **3.** *fig.* Nachteil *m*, Fluch *m des Ruhms etc.*; **4.** *sport* a) Strafe *f*, Strafpunkt *m*, b) *Fußball*: Elf'meter *m*, c) *Hockey*: Sieben'meter *m*, *Eishockey*: Penalty *m*: ***~ area*** *Fußball*: Strafraum *m*; ***~ box*** a) *Eishockey*: Strafbank, b) *Fußball*: Strafraum *m*; ***~ kick*** *Fußball*: Strafstoß *m*; ***~ shot*** *Eishockey*: Penalty *m*; ***~ spot*** a) *Fußball*: Elfmeterpunkt *m*, b) *Hockey*: Siebenmeterpunkt *m*.

pen·ance ['penəns] *s.* Buße *f*: ***do ~*** Buße tun.

ˌpen-and-'ink *adj.* Feder…, Schreiber…: ***~*** (***drawing***) Federzeichnung *f*.

pence [pens] *pl. von* ***penny***.

pen·chant ['pɑ̃:ŋʃɑ̃:ŋ] (*Fr.*) *s.* (***for***) Neigung *f*, Hang *m* (für, zu), Vorliebe *f* (für).

pen·cil ['pensl] **I** *s.* **1.** Blei-, Zeichen-, Farbstift *m*: ***red ~*** Rotstift; ***in ~*** mit Bleistift; **2.** *paint. obs.* Pinsel *m*; *fig.* Stil *m e-s Malers*; **3.** *rhet.* Griffel *m*, Stift *m*; **4.** ⚙, ⚕, *Kosmetik*: Stift *m*; **5.** ⚡, *phys.* (Strahlen)Büschel *m*, *n*: ***~ of light*** *phot.* Lichtbündel *n*; **II 6.** *v/t.* zeichnen; **7.** mit e-m Bleistift aufschreiben, anzeichnen *od.* anstreichen; **8.** mit e-m Stift behandeln, *z.B. die Augenbrauen* nachziehen; **'pen·cil(l)ed** [-ld] *adj.* **1.** fein gezeichnet *od.* gestrichelt; **2.** mit e-m Bleistift gezeichnet *od.* angestrichen; **3.** ⚡, *phys.* gebündelt (*Strahlen etc.*).

pen·cil push·er *s. humor.* ‚Bürohengst' *m*; **~ sharp·en·er** *s.* Bleistiftspitzer *m*.

'pen·craft *s.* **1.** → ***penmanship***; **2.** Schriftstelle'rei *f*.

pend·ant ['pendənt] **I** *s.* **1.** Anhänger *m*, (*Schmuckstück*), Ohrgehänge *n*; **2.** a) Behang *m*, b) Hängeleuchter *m*; **3.** Bügel *m* (*Uhr*); **4.** ⚠ Hängezierat *m*; **5.** *fig.* Anhang *m*, Anhängsel *n*; **6.** *fig.* Pen'dant *n*, Seiten-, Gegenstück *n* (***to*** zu); **7.** ⚓ → ***pennant*** 1; **II** *adj.* → ***pendent*** I; **'pend·en·cy** [-dənsɪ] *s. fig. bsd.* ⚖ Schweben *n*, Anhängigkeit *f* (*e-s Prozesses*); **'pen·dent** [-nt] **I** *adj.* **1.** (her'ab)hängend; 'überhängend; Hänge…; **2.** *fig.* → ***pending*** 3; **3.** *ling.* unvollständig; **II** *s.* **4.** → ***pendant*** I; **'pend·ing** [-dɪŋ] **I** *adj.* **1.** hängend; **2.** bevorstehend; **3.** *bsd.* ⚖ schwebend, (noch) unentschieden; anhängig (*Klage*); → ***patent*** 7; **II** *prp.* **4.** a) während, b) bis zu.

pen·du·late ['pendjʊleɪt] *v/i.* **1.** pendeln; **2.** *fig.* fluktuieren, schwanken; **'pen·du·lous** [-ləs] *adj.* hängend, pendelnd; Hänge…(*bauch etc.*), Pendel…(*-bewegung etc.*); **'pen·du·lum** [-ləm] **I** *s.* **1.** *phys.* Pendel *n*; **2.** ⚙ a) Pendel *n*, Perpen'dikel *m*, *n* (*Uhr*), b) Schwunggewicht *n*; **3.** *fig.* Pendelbewegung *f*, wechselnde Stimmung *od.* Haltung; → ***swing*** 20; **II** *adj.* **4.** Pendel… (*-säge, -uhr, -waage etc.*): ***~ wheel*** Unruh *f der Uhr*.

pen·e·tra·bil·i·ty [ˌpenɪtrə'bɪlətɪ] *s.* Durch'dringbarkeit *f*, Durch'dringlichkeit *f*; **pen·e·tra·ble** ['penɪtrəbl] *adj.* □ durch'dringlich, erfaßbar, erreichbar; **pen·e·tra·li·a** [ˌpenɪ'treɪljə] (*Lat.*) *s. pl.* **1.** *das* Innerste, *das* Aller'heiligste; **2.** *fig.* Geheimnisse *pl.*; in'time Dinge *pl.*

pen·e·trate ['penɪtreɪt] **I** *v/t.* **1.** durch'dringen, eindringen in (*acc.*), durch'bohren, *a.* ⚔ durch'stoßen; **2.** *fig. seelisch* durch'dringen, erfüllen; **3.** *fig. geistig* eindringen in (*acc.*), ergründen, durch'schauen; **II** *v/i.* **4.** eindringen, 'durchdringen (***into, to*** in *acc.*, zu); ✈, ⚔ einfliegen; **5.** 'durch-, vordringen (***to*** zu); **6.** *fig.* ergründen: ***~ into a secret***; **'pen·e·trat·ing** [-tɪŋ] *adj.* □ **1.** 'durchdringend, durch'bohrend (*a. Blick*): ***~ power*** ⚔ Durchschlagskraft *f*; **2.** *fig.* durch'dringend, scharf(sinnig); **pen·e·tra·tion** [ˌpenɪ'treɪʃn] *s.* **1.** Ein-, 'Durchdringen, Durch'bohren *n*; **2.** Eindringungsvermögen *n*, 'Durchschlagskraft *f* (*e-s Geschosses*); Tiefenwirkung *f*; **3.** ⚔ 'Durch-, Einbruch *m*; ✈ Einflug *m*; **4.** *phys.* Schärfe *f*, Auflösungsvermögen *n* (*Auge, Objektiv etc.*); **5.** *fig.* Ergründung *f*; **6.** *fig.* Einflußnahme *f*, Durchdringung *f*: ***peaceful ~*** friedliche Durchdringung *e-s Landes*; **7.** *fig.* Scharfsinn *m*, durch'dringender Verstand; **'pen·e·tra·tive** [-trətɪv] *adj.* □ → ***penetrating***.

pen friend *s.* Brieffreund(in).

pen·guin ['peŋgwɪn] *s.* **1.** Pinguin *m*; **2.** ✈ Übungsflugzeug *n*; **~ suit** *s.* Raumanzug *m*.

'penˌhold·er *s.* Federhalter *m*.

pen·i·cil·lin [ˌpenɪ'sɪlɪn] *s.* ⚕ Penicil'lin *n*.

pen·in·su·la [pɪ'nɪnsjʊlə] *s.* Halbinsel *f*; **pen'in·su·lar** [-lə] *adj.* **1.** Halbinsel…;

2. halbinselförmig.
pe·nis ['pi:nɪs] *s. anat.* Penis *m.*
pen·i·tence ['penɪtəns] *s.* Bußfertigkeit *f*, Buße *f*, Reue *f*; '**pen·i·tent** [-nt] **I** *adj.* ☐ **1.** bußfertig, reuig, zerknirscht; **II** *s.* **2.** Bußfertige(r *m*) *f*, Büßer(in); **3.** Beichtkind *n*; **pen·i·ten·tial** [ˌpenɪ'tenʃl] *eccl.* **I** *adj.* ☐ bußfertig, Buß...; **II** *s. a.* ~ ***book*** *R.C.* Buß-, Pöni'tenzbuch *n*; **pen·i·ten·tia·ry** [ˌpenɪ'tenʃərɪ] **I** *s.* **1.** *eccl.* Bußpriester *m*; **2.** *Am.* 'Straf(voll'zugs)anstalt *f*; **3.** *hist.* Besserungsanstalt *f*; **II** *adj.* **4.** *eccl.* Buß...
'**pen**|·**knife** *s.* [*irr.*] Feder-, Taschenmesser *n*; '~·**man** [-mən] *s.* [*irr.*] **1.** Kalli'graph *m*; **2.** Schriftsteller *m*; '~·**man·ship** [-mənʃɪp] *s.* **1.** Schreibkunst *f*; **2.** Stil *m*; schriftstellerisches Können; ~ **name** *s.* Schriftstellername *m*, Pseudo'nym *n.*
pen·nant ['penənt] *s.* **1.** ⚓, ⚔ Wimpel *m*, Stander *m*, kleine Flagge; **2.** (Lanzen)Fähnchen *n*; **3.** *sport Am.* Siegeswimpel *m*; *fig.* Meisterschaft *f*; **4.** ♪ *Am.* Fähnchen *n.*
pen·ni·less ['penɪlɪs] *adj.* ☐ ohne (e-n Pfennig) Geld, mittellos.
pen·non ['penən] *s.* **1.** *bsd.* ⚔ Fähnlein *n*, Wimpel *m*, Lanzenfähnchen *n*; **2.** Fittich *m*, Schwinge *f.*
Penn·syl·va·nia Dutch [ˌpensɪl'veɪnjə] *s.* **1.** *coll.* in Pennsyl'vania lebende 'Deutsch-Ameriˌkaner *pl.*; **2.** *ling.* Pennsyl'vanisch-Deutsch *n.*
pen·ny ['penɪ] *pl.* **-nies** *od. coll.* **pence** [pens] *s.* **1.** a) *Brit.* Penny *m* (= £ 0.01 = 1 p), b) *Am.* Centstück *n*: ***in for a ~, in for a pound*** wer A sagt, muß auch B sagen; ***the ~ dropped!*** *humor.* ‚der Groschen ist gefallen‘!; ***spend a ~*** F ‚mal verschwinden‘ (*auf die Toilette*); **2.** *fig.* Pfennig *m*, Heller *m*, Kleinigkeit *f*: ***not worth a ~*** keinen Heller wert; ***he hasn't a ~ to bless himself with*** er hat keinen roten Heller; ***a ~ for your thoughts!*** (an) was denkst du denn (eben)?; **3.** *fig.* Geld *n*: ***turn an honest ~*** sich et. (durch ehrliche Arbeit) (da'zu)verdienen; ***a pretty ~*** ein hübsches Sümmchen.
ˌ**pen·ny**|**-a-'lin·er** *s. bsd. Brit.* Schreiberling *m*, Zeilenschinder *m*; ~ **arcade** *s.* 'Spielsaˌlon *m*; ~ **dread·ful** *s.* 'Groschen-, 'Schauerroˌman *m*; Groschenblatt *n*; ˌ~**-in-the-'slot ma·chine** *s.* (Verkaufs)Automat *m*; '~-ˌ**pinch·er** *s.* F Pfennigfuchser *m*; '~·**weight** *s. Brit.* Pennygewicht *n* (*1½ Gramm*); ˌ~-'**wise** *adj.* am falschen Ende sparsam: ~ ***and pound-foolish*** im Kleinen sparsam, im Großen verschwenderisch; '~·**worth** ['penəθ] *s.* **1.** was man für e-n Penny kaufen kann: ***a ~ of tobacco*** für e-n Penny Tabak; **2.** (*bsd.* guter) Kauf: ***a good ~.***
pe·no·log·ic, **pe·no·log·i·cal** [ˌpi:nə'lɒdʒɪkl] *adj.* ☐ ⚖ krimi'nalkundlich, Strafvollzugs...; **pe·nol·o·gy** [pi:'nɒlədʒɪ] *s.* Krimi'nalstrafkunde *f*, *bsd.* Strafvollzugslehre *f.*
pen pal *Am. für* **pen friend.**
pen·sion[1] ['pɑ̃:ŋsɪɔ̃:ŋ] (*Fr.*) *s.* Pensi'on *f*: a) Fremdenheim *n*, b) 'Unterkunft u. Verpflegung *f*: ***full ~.***
pen·sion[2] ['penʃn] **I** *s.* Pensi'on *f*, Ruhegeld *n*, Rente *f*: ~ ***fund*** Pensionskasse *f*; ~ ***plan***, ~ ***scheme*** (Alters)Versorgungsplan *m*; ***entitled to a ~*** pensionsberechtigt; ***be on a ~*** in Rente *od.* Pension sein; **II** *v/t. oft* ~ ***off*** *j-n* pensionieren; '**pen·sion·a·ble** [-ʃnəbl] *adj.* pensi'onsberechtigt, -fähig: ***of ~ age*** im Renten- *od.* Pensionsalter; '**pen·sion·er** [-ʃənə] *s.* **1.** Pensio'när *m*, Ruhegeldempfänger(in), Rentner(in); **2.** *Brit.* Stu'dent *m* (*in Cambridge*), der für Kost u. Wohnung im College zahlt.
pen·sive ['pensɪv] *adj.* ☐ **1.** nachdenklich, sinnend, gedankenvoll; **2.** ernst, tiefsinnig; '**pen·sive·ness** [-nɪs] *s.* Nachdenklichkeit *f*; Tiefsinn *m*, Ernst *m.*
'**pen·stock** *s.* **1.** Wehr *n*, Stauanlage *f*; **2.** *Am.* Druckrohr *n.*
pen·ta·cle ['pentəkl] → ***pentagram.***
pen·ta·gon ['pentəgən] *s.* ⩓ Fünfeck *n*: ***the*** ♎ *Am.* das Pentagon (*das amer. Verteidigungsministerium*); **pen·tag·o·nal** [pen'tægənl] *adj.* fünfeckig; '**pen·ta·gram** [-græm] *s.* Penta'gramm *n*, Drudenfuß *m*; **pen·ta·he·dral** [ˌpentə'hi:drəl] *adj.* ⩓ fünfflächig; **pen·ta·he·dron** [ˌpentə'hi:drɒn] *pl.* **-drons** *od.* **-dra** [-drə] *s.* ⩓ ˌPenta'eder *n*; **pen·tam·e·ter** [pen'tæmɪtə] *s.* Pen'tameter *m.*
Pen·ta·teuch ['pentətju:k] *s. bibl.* Penta'teuch *m*, die Fünf Bücher Mose.
pen·tath·lete [pen'tæθli:t] *s. sport* Fünfkämpfer(in); **pen'tath·lon** [-lɒn] *s. sport* Fünfkampf *m.*
pen·ta·va·lent [ˌpentə'veɪlənt] *adj.* ⚗ fünfwertig.
Pen·te·cost ['pentɪkɒst] *s.* Pfingsten *n od. pl.*, Pfingstfest *n*; **Pen·te·cos·tal** [ˌpentɪ'kɒstl] *adj.* pfingstlich; Pfingst...
pent·house ['penthaʊs] *s.* ⚠ **1.** Wetter-, Vor-, Schirmdach *n*; **2.** Anbau *m*, Nebengebäude *n*, angebauter Schuppen; **3.** Penthouse *n*, 'Dachterˌrassenwohnung *f.*
pen·tode ['pentəʊd] *s.* ⚡ Pen'tode *f*, Fünfpolröhre *f.*
ˌ**pent-'up** *adj.* **1.** eingepfercht; **2.** *fig.* angestaut (*Gefühle*): ~ ***demand*** ✝ *Am.* Nachholbedarf *m.*
pe·nult [pe'nʌlt] *s. ling.* vorletzte Silbe; **pe'nul·ti·mate** [-tɪmət] **I** *adj.* vorletzt; **II** *s.* → ***penult.***
pe·num·bra [pɪ'nʌmbrə] *pl.* **-bras** *s.* Halbschatten *m.*
pe·nu·ri·ous [pɪ'njʊərɪəs] *adj.* ☐ **1.** geizig, knauserig; **2.** karg; **pen·u·ry** ['penjʊrɪ] *s.* Knappheit *f*, Armut *f*, Not *f*, Mangel *m.*
pe·on ['pi:ən] *s.* **1.** Sol'dat *m*, Poli'zist *m*, Bote *m* (*in Indien u. Ceylon*); **2.** Tagelöhner *m* (*in Südamerika*); **3.** (*durch Geldschulden*) zu Dienst verpflichteter Arbeiter (*Mexiko*); **4.** *Am.* zu Arbeit her'angezogener Sträfling; '**pe·on·age** [-nɪdʒ] '**pe·on·ism** [-nɪzəm] *s.* Dienstbarkeit *f*, Leibeigenschaft *f.*
pe·o·ny ['pi:ənɪ] *s.* ⚘ Pfingstrose *f.*
peo·ple ['pi:pl] **I** *s.* **1.** *pl. konstr.* die Leute *pl.*, die Menschen *pl.*: ***English ~*** (die) Engländer; ***London ~*** die Londoner (Bevölkerung); ***country ~*** Landleute, -bevölkerung; ***literary ~*** (die) Literaten; ***a great many ~*** sehr viele Leute; ***some ~*** manche; ***he of all ~*** ausgerechnet er; **2.** ***the ~*** a) *a. sg. konstr.* das *gemeine* Volk, b) die Bürger *pl.*, die Wähler *pl.*; **3.** *pl.* **~s** Volk *n*, Nati'on *f*: ***the ~s of Europe***; ***the chosen ~*** das auserwählte Volk; **4.** *pl. konstr.* F *j-s* Angehörige *pl.*, Fa'milie *f*: ***my ~*** m-e Leute; **5.** F man: ***~ say*** man sagt; **II** *v/t.* **6.** bevölkern (***with*** mit).
peo·ple's re·pub·lic *s. pol.* 'Volksrepuˌblik *f*: ***the*** ♎ ***of Poland.***
pep [pep] *sl.* **I** *s.* E'lan *m*, Schwung *m*, ‚Schmiß‘ *m*: ~ ***pill*** Aufputschtablette *f*; ~ ***talk*** Anfeuerung *f*, ermunternde Worte; **II** *v/t.* ~ ***up*** a) *j-n* ‚aufmöbeln‘, in Schwung bringen, b) *j-n* anfeuern, c) *Geschichte* ‚pfeffern‘, d) *et.* in Schwung bringen.
pep·per ['pepə] **I** *s.* **1.** Pfeffer *m* (*a. fig. et. Scharfes*); **2.** ⚘ Pfefferstrauch *m*, *bsd.* a) Spanischer Pfeffer, b) Roter Pfeffer, c) Paprika *m*; **3.** pfefferähnliches Gewürz: ~ ***cake*** Ingwerkuchen *m*; **II** *v/t.* **4.** pfeffern; **5.** *fig. Stil etc.* würzen; **6.** *fig.* sprenkeln, bestreuen; **7.** *fig.* ‚bepfeffern‘, bombardieren (*a. mit Fragen etc.*); **8.** *fig.* 'durchprügeln; ˌ~**-and-'salt** **I** *adj.* pfeffer-und-salz-farbig (*Stoff*); **II** *s.* a) Pfeffer u. Salz *n* (*Stoff*), b) Anzug *m* in Pfeffer u. Salz; '~·**box** *s. bsd. Brit.*, '~-ˌ**cast·or** *s.* Pfefferbüchse *f*, -streuer *m*; '~·**corn** *s.* Pfefferkorn *n*; '~·**mint** *s.* **1.** ⚘ Pfefferminze *f*; **2.** Pfefferminzöl *n*; **3.** *a.* ~ ***drop***, ~ ***lozenge*** Pfefferminzplätzchen *n.*
pep·per·y ['pepərɪ] *adj.* **1.** pfefferig, scharf; **2.** *fig.* hitzig, jähzornig; **3.** gepfeffert, scharf (*Stil*).
pep·py ['pepɪ] *adj. sl.* schwungvoll, ‚schmissig‘, forsch.
pep·sin ['pepsɪn] *s.* ⚗ Pep'sin *n*; **pep·tic** ['peptɪk] *anat. adj.* **1.** Verdauungs...: ~ ***gland*** Magendrüse *f*; ~ ***ulcer*** Magengeschwür *n*; **2.** verdauungsfördernd, peptisch; **pep·tone** ['peptəʊn] *s. physiol.* Pep'ton *n.*
per [pɜ:; pə] *prp.* **1.** per, durch: ~ ***bearer*** durch Überbringer; ~ ***post*** durch die Post; ~ ***rail*** per Bahn; **2.** pro, je, für: ~ ***annum*** [pər'ænəm] pro Jahr, jährlich; ~ ***capita*** ['kæpɪtə] pro Kopf, pro Person; ~ ***capita income*** Pro-Kopf-Einkommen *n*; ~ ***capita quota*** Kopfbetrag *m*; ~ ***cent*** pro *od.* vom Hundert; ~ ***second*** in der *od.* pro Sekunde; **3.** laut, gemäß (✝ *a.* ***as ~***).
per·ad·ven·ture [pərəd'ventʃə] *adv. obs.* viel'leicht, ungefähr.
per·am·bu·late [pə'ræmbjʊleɪt] **I** *v/t.* **1.** durch'wandern, -'reisen, -'ziehen; **2.** bereisen, besichtigen; **3.** die Grenzen *e-s Gebiets* abschreiten; **II** *v/i.* **4.** um'herwandern; **per·am·bu·la·tion** [pəˌræmbjʊ'leɪʃn] *s.* **1.** Durch'wanderung *f*; **2.** Bereisen *n*, Besichtigung(sreise) *f*; **3.** Grenzbegehung *f*; **per·am·bu·la·tor** [pə'ræmbjʊleɪtə] *s. bsd. Brit.* Kinderwagen *m.*
per·ceiv·a·ble [pə'si:vəbl] *adj.* ☐ **1.** wahrnehmbar, spürbar, merklich; **2.** verständlich; **per·ceive** [pə'si:v] *v/t. u. v/i.* **1.** wahrnehmen, empfinden, (be-)merken, spüren; **2.** verstehen, erkennen, begreifen.
per·cent, *Brit.* **per cent** [pə'sent] **I** *adj.* **1.** ...prozentig; **II** *s.* **2.** Pro'zent *n* (%); **3.** *pl.* 'Wertpaˌpiere *pl.* mit feststehendem Zinssatz: ***three per cents*** dreiprozentige Wertpapiere; **per'cent·age** [-tɪdʒ] *s.* **1.** Pro'zent-, Hundertsatz *m*; Prozentgehalt *m*: ~ ***by weight*** Ge-

wichtsprozent *n*; **2.** ⚚ Pro'zente *pl.*; **3.** *weitS.* Teil *m*, Anteil *m* (***of*** an *dat.*); **4.** ⚚ Gewinnanteil *m*, Provisi'on *f*, Tan'tieme *f*; **per'cen·tal** [-tl], **per'cen·tile** [-taɪl] *adj.* prozentu'al, Prozent…

per·cep·ti·bil·i·ty [pəˌseptə'bɪlətɪ] *s.* Wahrnehmbarkeit *f*; **per·cep·ti·ble** [pə'septəbl] *adj.* □ wahrnehmbar, merklich; **per·cep·tion** [pə'sepʃn] *s.* **1.** (sinnliche *od.* geistige) Wahrnehmung, Empfindung *f*; **2.** Wahrnehmungsvermögen *n*; **3.** Auffassung(skraft) *f*; **4.** Begriff *m*, Vorstellung *f*; **5.** Erkenntnis *f*; **per·cep·tion·al** [pə'sepʃənl] *adj.* Wahrnehmungs…, Empfindungs…; **per·cep·tive** [pə'septɪv] *adj.* □ **1.** wahrnehmend, Wahrnehmungs…; **2.** auffassungsfähig, scharfsichtig; **per·cep·tiv·i·ty** [ˌpɜːsep'tɪvətɪ] *s.* → ***perception*** 2.

perch¹ [pɜːtʃ] *pl.* **'perch·es** [-ɪz] *od.* **perch** *s. ichth.* Flußbarsch *m*.

perch² [pɜːtʃ] **I** *s.* **1.** (Auf)Sitzstange *f für Vögel*, Hühnerstange *f*; **2.** F *fig.* hoher (sicherer) Sitz, ‚Thron' *m*: ***knock s.o. off his ~*** *fig.* j-n von s-m Sockel herunterstoßen; ***come off your ~!*** F tu nicht so überlegen!; **3.** *surv.* Meßstange *f*; **4.** Rute *f* (*Längenmaß = 5,029 m*); **5.** ⚓ Pricke *f*; **6.** Lang-, Lenkbaum *m e-s Wagens*; **II** *v/i.* **7.** sich setzen *od.* niederlassen (***on*** auf *acc.*), sitzen (*Vögel*); *fig.* hoch sitzen *od.* ‚thronen'; **III** *v/t.* **8.** (*auf et. Hohes*) setzen: ***~ o.s.*** sich setzen; ***be ~ed*** sitzen, ‚thronen'.

per·chance [pə'tʃɑːns] *adv. poet.* viel'leicht, zufällig.

perch·er ['pɜːtʃə] *s. orn.* Sitzvogel *m*.

per·chlo·rate [pə'klɔːreɪt] *s.* ⚗ Perchlo'rat *n*; **per'chlo·ric** [-ɪk] *adj.* 'überchlorig: ***~ acid*** Über- *od.* Perchlorsäure *f*; **per'chlo·ride** [-raɪd] *s.* Perchlo'rid *n*.

per·cip·i·ence [pə'sɪpɪəns] *s.* **1.** Wahrnehmen *n*; **2.** Wahrnehmung(svermögen *n*) *f*; **per'cip·i·ent** [-nt] → ***perceptive*** 1.

per·co·late ['pɜːkəleɪt] **I** *v/t.* **1.** *Kaffee etc.* filtern, 'durchseihen, 'durchsickern lassen; **II** *v/i.* **2.** 'durchsickern (*a. fig.*): ***percolating tank*** Sickertank *m*; **3.** gefiltert werden; **per·co·la·tion** [ˌpɜːkə'leɪʃn] *s.* 'Durchseihung *f*, Filtrati'on *f*; **'per·co·la·tor** [-tə] *s.* Fil'triertrichter *m*, Perko'lator *m*, 'Kaffeemaˌschine *f*.

per·cuss [pə'kʌs] *v/t. u. v/i.* ⚕ perkutieren, abklopfen; **per'cus·sion** [-ʌʃən] **I** *s.* **1.** Schlag *m*, Stoß *m*, Erschütterung *f*, Aufschlag *m*; **2.** ⚕ a) Perkussi'on *f*, Abklopfen *n*, b) 'Klopfmasˌsage *f*; **3.** ♪ *coll.* 'Schlaginstruˌmente *pl.*, -zeug *n*; **II** *adj.* **4.** Schlag…, Stoß…, Zünd…: ***~ cap*** Zündhütchen *n*; ***~ drill*** ⚙ Schlagbohrer *m*; ***~ fuse*** ⚔ Aufschlagzünder *m*; ***~ instrument*** ♪ Schlaginstrument *n*; ***~ welding*** ⚙ Schlag-, Stoßschweißen *n*; **III** *v/t.* **5.** ⚕ a) perkutieren, abklopfen, b) durch Beklopfen massieren; **per'cus·sion·ist** [-ʌʃnɪst] *s.* ♪ Schlagzeuger *m*; **per'cus·sive** [-sɪv] → ***percussion*** 4.

per·cu·ta·ne·ous [ˌpɜːkjuː'teɪnjəs] *adj.* □ ⚕ perku'tan, durch die Haut.

per di·em [ˌpɜː'daɪem] **I** *adj. u. adv.* täglich, pro Tag: ***~ rate*** Tagessatz *m*; **II** *s.* Tagegeld *n*.

per·di·tion [pə'dɪʃn] *s.* **1.** Verderben *n*; **2.** a) ewige Verdammnis, b) Hölle *f*.

per·e·gri·nate ['perɪgrɪneɪt] **I** *v/i.* wandern, um'herreisen; **II** *v/t.* durch'wandern, bereisen; **per·e·gri·na·tion** [ˌperɪgrɪ'neɪʃn] *s.* **1.** Wanderschaft *f*; **2.** Wanderung *f*; **3.** *fig.* Weitschweifigkeit *f*.

per·emp·to·ri·ness [pə'rempt*ə*rɪnɪs] *s.* **1.** Entschiedenheit *f*, Bestimmtheit *f*; herrisches Wesen; **2.** Endgültigkeit *f*; **per·emp·to·ry** [pə'rempt*ə*rɪ] *adj.* □ **1.** entschieden, bestimmt; gebieterisch, herrisch; **2.** entscheidend, endgültig; zwingend, defini'tiv: ***a ~ command.***

per·en·ni·al [pə'renjəl] **I** *adj.* □ **1.** das ganze Jahr *od.* Jahre hin'durch dauernd, beständig; **2.** immerwährend, anhaltend; **3.** ⚘ perennierend, winterhart; **II** *s.* **4.** ⚘ perennierende Pflanze.

per·fect ['pɜːfɪkt] **I** *adj.* □ → ***perfectly***; **1.** per'fekt, voll'endet: a) fehler-, makellos, ide'al, b) fertig, abgeschlossen: ***make ~*** vervollkommnen; ***~ pitch*** ♪ absolutes Gehör; ***~ participle*** *ling.* Mittelwort *n* der Vergangenheit, Partizip *n* Perfekt; ***~ tense*** Perfekt *n*; **2.** gründlich (ausgebildet), per'fekt (***in*** in *dat.*); **3.** gänzlich, 'vollständig: ***a ~ circle***; ***~ strangers*** wildfremde Leute; **4.** F rein, ‚kom'plett': ***~ nonsense***; ***a ~ fool*** ein ausgemachter Narr; **II** *s.* **5.** *ling.* Perfekt *n*: ***past ~*** Plusquamperfekt; **III** *v/t.* [pə'fekt] **6.** voll'enden; ver'vollkommnen (***o.s.*** sich); **per·fect·i·ble** [pə'fektəbl] *adj.* ver'vollkommnungsfähig; **per·fec·tion** [pə'fekʃn] *s.* **1.** Ver'vollkommnung *f*; **2.** *fig.* Voll'kommenheit *f*, Voll'endung *f*, Perfekti'on *f*: ***bring to ~*** vervollkommnen; ***to ~*** vollkommen, meisterlich; **3.** Vor'trefflichkeit *f*; **4.** Fehler-, Makellosigkeit *f*; **5.** *fig.* Gipfel *m*; **6.** *pl.* Fertigkeiten *pl.*; **per·fec·tion·ist** [pə'fekʃnɪst] **I** *s.* Perfektio'nist *m*; **II** *adj.* perfektio'nistisch; **'per·fect·ly** [-ktlɪ] *adv.* **1.** vollkommen, fehlerlos; gänzlich, völlig; **2.** F ganz, abso'lut, einfach *wunderbar etc.*

per·fid·i·ous [pə'fɪdɪəs] *adj.* □ verräterisch, falsch, heimtückisch, per'fid; **per'fid·i·ous·ness** [-nɪs], **per·fi·dy** ['pɜːfɪdɪ] *s.* Falschheit *f*, Perfi'die *f*, Tücke *f*, Verrat *m*.

per·fo·rate **I** *v/t.* ['pɜːfəreɪt] durch'bohren, -'löchern, lochen, perforieren: ***~d disk*** ⚙ (Kreis)Lochscheibe *f*; ***~d tape*** Lochstreifen *m*; **II** *adj.* [-rɪt] durch'löchert, gelocht; **per·fo·ra·tion** [ˌpɜːfə'reɪʃn] *s.* **1.** Durch'bohrung *f*, -'lochung *f*, -'löcherung *f*, Perforati'on *f*: ***~ of the stomach*** ⚕ Magendurchbruch *m*; **2.** Lochung *f*, gelochte Linie; **3.** Loch *n*, Öffnung *f*; **'per·fo·ra·tor** [-tə] *s.* Locher *m*.

per·force [pə'fɔːs] *adv.* notgedrungen, gezwungenermaßen.

per·form [pə'fɔːm] **I** *v/t.* **1.** *Arbeit, Dienst etc.* verrichten, leisten, machen, tun, ausführen; ⚕ *e-e Operation* 'durchführen (***on*** bei); **2.** voll'bringen, -'ziehen, 'durchführen; *e-r Verpflichtung* nachkommen, *e-e Pflicht, a. e-n Vertrag* erfüllen; **3.** *Theaterstück, Konzert etc.* aufführen, geben, spielen; *e-e Rolle* spielen, darstellen; **II** *v/i.* **4.** et. ausführen *od.* leisten; ⚙ funktionieren, arbeiten: ***~ well*** e-e gute Leistung bringen; **5.** *thea. etc.* e-e Vorstellung geben, auftreten, spielen: ***~ on the piano*** Klavier spielen, auf dem Klavier et. vortragen; **per'form·ance** [-məns] *s.* **1.** Aus-, 'Durchführung *f*: ***in the ~ of his duty*** in Ausübung s-r Pflicht; **2.** Leistung *f* (*a.* ⚖, ⚙), Erfüllung *f* (*Pflicht, Versprechen, Vertrag*), Voll'ziehung *f*: ***~ in kind*** Sachleistung; ***~ data*** ⚙ Leistungswerte *pl.*; ***~ principle*** *sociol.* Leistungsprinzip *n*; ***~ test*** *ped.* Leistungsprüfung *f*; ***~ of a machine*** (Arbeits)Leistung *od.* Arbeitsweise *f* e-r Maschine; **3.** ♪, *thea.* Aufführung *f*, Vorstellung *f*, Vortrag *m*; **4.** *thea.* Darstellung(skunst) *f*, Spiel *n*; **5.** *ling.* Perfor'manz *f*; **per'form·er** [-mə] *s.* **1.** Ausführende(r *m*) *f*; **2.** Leistungsträger(in): ***top ~***; **3.** Schauspieler(in); Darsteller(in); Musiker(in); Künstler(in); **per'form·ing** [-mɪŋ] *adj.* **1.** *thea.* Aufführungs…: ***~ rights***; **2.** darstellend: ***~ arts***; **3.** dressiert (*Tier*).

per·fume **I** *v/t.* [pə'fjuːm] **1.** mit Duft erfüllen, parfümieren (*a. fig.*); **II** *s.* ['pɜːfjuːm] **2.** Duft *m*, Wohlgeruch *m*; **3.** Par'füm *n*, Duftstoff *m*; **per'fum·er** [-mə] *s.* Parfüme'riehändler *m*, Parfü'meur *m*; **per'fum·er·y** [-mərɪ] *s.* Parfüme'rien *pl.*; Parfüme'rie(geschäft *n*) *f*.

per·func·to·ry [pə'fʌŋkt*ə*rɪ] *adj.* □ **1.** oberflächlich, obenhin, flüchtig; **2.** me'chanisch, inter'esselos.

per·go·la ['pɜːgələ] *s.* Laube *f*, offener Laubengang, Pergola *f*.

per·haps [pə'hæps; præps] *adv.* viel'leicht.

per·i·car·di·tis [ˌperɪkɑː'daɪtɪs] *s.* ⚕ Herzbeutelentzündung *f*, Perikar'ditis *f*; **per·i·car·di·um** [ˌperɪ'kɑːdjəm] *pl.* **-di·a** [-djə] *s. anat.* **1.** Herzbeutel *m*; **2.** Herzfell *n*.

per·i·carp ['perɪkɑːp] *s.* ⚘ Fruchthülle *f*, Peri'karp *n*.

per·i·gee ['perɪdʒiː] *s. ast.* Erdnähe *f*.

per·i·he·li·on [ˌperɪ'hiːljən] *s. ast.* Sonnennähe *f e-s Planeten*.

per·il ['perəl] **I** *s.* Gefahr *f*, Risiko *n* (*a.* ⚚): ***in ~ of one's life*** in Lebensgefahr; ***at*** (***one's***) ***~*** auf eigene Gefahr; ***at the ~ of*** auf die Gefahr hin, daß; **II** *v/t.* gefährden; **'per·il·ous** [-rələs] *adj.* □ gefährlich.

per·im·e·ter [pə'rɪmɪtə] *s.* **1.** Periphe'rie *f*: a) △ 'Umkreis *m*, b) *allg.* Rand *m*: ***~ position*** ⚔ Randstellung *f*; **2.** ⚕, *opt.* Peri'meter *n* (*Instrument*).

per·i·ne·um [ˌperɪ'niːəm] *pl.* **-ne·a** [-ə] *s. anat.* Damm *m*, Peri'neum *n*.

pe·ri·od ['pɪərɪəd] **I** *s.* **1.** Peri'ode *f* (*a.* △, ϟ, ♪), Zeit(dauer *f*, -raum *m*, -spanne *f*) *f*, Frist *f*: ***~ of appeal*** ⚖ Berufungsfrist; ***~ of exposure*** *phot.* Belichtungszeit; ***~ of office*** Amtsdauer *f*; ***for a ~*** für einige Zeit; ***for a ~ of*** auf die Dauer von; **2.** *ast.* 'Umlaufszeit *f*; **3.** (vergangenes *od.* gegenwärtiges) Zeitalter: ***glacial ~*** Eiszeit *f*; ***dresses of the ~*** zeitgenössische Kleider; ***a girl of the ~*** ein modernes Mädchen; **4.** *ped.* ('Unterrichts)Stunde *f*; **5.** *Sport*: Spielabschnitt *m*, *z.B. Eishockey*: Drittel *n*; **6.** *a.* ***monthly ~*** (*od.* ***~s*** *pl.*) ⚕ Periode *f der Frau*; **7.** (Sprech)Pause *f*, Absatz *m*; **8.** *ling.* a) Punkt *m*: ***put a ~ to*** *fig. e-r Sache* ein Ende setzen, b) Satzgefüge *n*, c) *allg.* wohlgefügter Satz; **II** *adj.* **9.** a) zeitgeschichtlich, Zeit…: ***~ play*** Zeitstück *n*; b) Stil…: ***~ furniture***; ***~***

house Haus *n* im Zeitstil; **~ *dress*** historisches Kostüm.

pe·ri·od·ic¹ [ˌpɪərɪ'ɒdɪk] *adj.* (□ **~ *ally***) **1.** peri'odisch, Kreis…, regelmäßig 'wiederkehrend; **2.** *ling.* rhe'torisch, wohlgefügt (*Satz*).

per·i·od·ic² [ˌpɜːraɪ'ɒdɪk] *adj.* ⚗ per-, überjodsauer: **~ *acid*** Überjodsäure *f.*

pe·ri·od·i·cal [ˌpɪərɪ'ɒdɪkl] **I** *adj.* □ **1.** → ***periodic***¹; **2.** regelmäßig erscheinend; **3.** Zeitschriften…; **II** *s.* **4.** Zeitschrift *f*; **pe·ri·o·dic·i·ty** [ˌpɪərɪə'dɪsətɪ] *s.* **1.** Periodizi'tät *f* (*a.* ⚕); **2.** ⚗ Stellung *f* e-s Ele'ments in der A'tomgewichtstafel; **3.** ϟ Fre'quenz *f.*

per·i·os·te·um [ˌperɪ'ɒstɪəm] *pl.* **-te·a** [-ə] *s. anat.* Knochenhaut *f*; **per·i·os·ti·tis** [ˌperɪə'staɪtɪs] *s.* ⚕ Knochenhautentzündung *f.*

per·i·pa·tet·ic [ˌperɪpə'tetɪk] *adj.* (□ **~*ally***) **1.** um'herwandelnd; **2.** ♀ *phls.* peripa'tetisch; **3.** *fig.* weitschweifig.

pe·riph·er·al [pə'rɪfərəl] *adj.* □ **1.** peri'pherisch, Rand…; **2.** *anat.* peri'pher; **pe·riph·er·y** [pə'rɪfərɪ] *s.* Periphe'rie *f*; *fig. a.* Rand *m*, Grenze *f.*

pe·riph·ra·sis [pə'rɪfrəsɪs] *pl.* **-ses** [-siːz] *s.* Um'schreibung *f*, Peri'phrase *f*; **per·i·phras·tic** [ˌperɪ'fræstɪk] *adj.* (□ **~*ally***) um'schreibend, peri'phrastisch.

per·i·scope ['perɪskəʊp] *s.* ⚔ **1.** Sehrohr *n* (*U-Boot, Panzer*); **2.** Beobachtungsspiegel *m.*

per·ish ['perɪʃ] **I** *v/i.* **1.** 'umkommen, 'untergehen, zu'grunde gehen, sterben, (tödlich) verunglücken (***by, of, with*** durch, von, an *dat.*): ***to ~ by drowning*** ertrinken; **~ *the thought!*** Gott behüte!; **2.** hinschwinden, absterben, eingehen; **II** *v/t.* **3.** vernichten (*mst pass.*): ***be ~ed with*** F (fast) umkommen vor *Kälte etc.*; '**per·ish·a·ble** [-ʃəbl] **I** *adj.* □ vergänglich; leichtverderblich (*Lebensmittel etc.*); **II** *s. pl.* leichtverderbliche Waren *pl.*; '**per·ish·er** [-ʃə] *s. Brit.* ***little ~*** kleiner Räuber (*Kind*); '**per·ish·ing** [-ʃɪŋ] **I** *adj.* □ vernichtend, tödlich (*a. fig.*); **II** *adv.* F scheußlich, verflixt: **~ *cold.***

per·i·style ['perɪstaɪl] *s.* ⚠ Säulengang *m*, Peri'styl *n.*

per·i·to·n(a)e·um [ˌperɪtəʊ'niːəm] *pl.* **-ne·a** [-ə] *s. anat.* Bauchfell *n*; ˌ**per·i·to'ni·tis** [-tə'naɪtɪs] *s.* ⚕ Bauchfellentzündung *f.*

per·i·wig ['perɪwɪg] *s.* Pe'rücke *f.*

per·i·win·kle ['perɪˌwɪŋkl] *s.* **1.** ⚘ Immergrün *n.*; **2.** *zo.* (*eßbare*) Uferschnecke.

per·jure ['pɜːdʒə] *v/t.*: **~ *o.s.*** e-n Meineid leisten, meineidig werden; **~*d*** meineidig; '**per·jur·er** [-dʒərə] *s.* Meineidige(r *m*) *f*; '**per·ju·ry** [-dʒərɪ] *s.* Meineid *m.*

perk¹ [pɜːk] *s. mst pl. bsd. Brit* F *für* ***perquisite*** 1.

perk² [pɜːk] **I** *v/i. mst* **~ *up*** **1.** (lebhaft) den Kopf recken, munter werden; **2.** *fig.* die Nase hoch tragen, selbstbewußt *od.* forsch auftreten; **3.** *fig.* sich erholen, munter werden; **II** *v/t. mst* **~ *up*** **4.** *den Kopf* recken; *die Ohren* spitzen; **5.** **~ *up*** *j-n* ‚aufmöbeln'; **6.** **~ *o.s.*** (***up***) sich schön machen; '**perk·i·ness** [-kɪnɪs] *s.* Keckheit *f*, Selbstbewußtsein *n*; '**perk·y** [-kɪ] *adj.* □ **1.** flott, forsch; **2.** keck, dreist, frech.

perm [pɜːm] *s.* F Dauerwelle *f.*

per·ma·frost ['pɜːməfrɒst] *s.* Dauerfrostboden *m.*

per·ma·nence ['pɜːmənəns] *s.* **1.** Perma'nenz *f* (*a. phys.*), Ständigkeit *f*, (Fort)Dauer *f*; **2.** Beständigkeit *f*, Dauerhaftigkeit *f*; '**per·ma·nen·cy** [-sɪ] **1.** → ***permanence***; **2.** *et.* Dauerhaftes *od.* Bleibendes; feste Anstellung, Dauerstellung *f*; '**per·ma·nent** [-nt] *adj.* □ (fort)dauernd, bleibend, perma'nent; ständig (*Ausschuß, Bauten, Personal, Wohnsitz etc.*); dauerhaft, Dauer… (*-magnet, -stellung, -ton, -wirkung etc.*), mas'siv (*Bau*): **~ *assets*** ✝ Anlagevermögen *n*; **~ *call*** *teleph.* Dauerbelegung *f*; ♀ ***Secretary*** *Brit.* ständiger (*fachlicher*) Staatssekretär; **~ *situation*** ✝ Dauer-, Lebensstellung *f*; **~ *wave*** Dauerwelle *f*; **~ *way*** 🚂 Bahnkörper *m*; Oberbau *m.*

per·man·ga·nate [pɜː'mæŋgəneɪt] *s.* ⚗ Permanga'nat *n*: **~ *of potash*** Kaliumpermanganat; **per·man·gan·ic** [ˌpɜːmæŋ'gænɪk] *adj.* Übermangan…: **~ *acid.***

per·me·a·bil·i·ty [ˌpɜːmjə'bɪlətɪ] *s.* Durch'dringbarkeit *f*, *bsd. phys.* Permeabili'tät *f*: **~ *to gas(es)*** *phys.* Gasdurchlässigkeit *f.*

per·me·a·ble ['pɜːmjəbl] *adj.* □ 'durchlässig (***to*** für); **per·me·ance** ['pɜːmɪəns] *s.* **1.** Durch'dringung *f*; **2.** *phys.* ma'gnetischer Leitwert; **per·me·ate** ['pɜːmɪeɪt] **I** *v/t.* durch'dringen; **II** *v/i.* dringen (***into*** in *acc.*), sich verbreiten (***among*** unter *dat.*), 'durchsickern; **per·me·a·tion** [ˌpɜːmɪ'eɪʃn] *s.* Eindringen *n*, Durch'dringung *f.*

per·mis·si·ble [pə'mɪsəbl] *adj.* □ zulässig; **per'mis·sion** [-'mɪʃn] *s.* Erlaubnis *f*, Genehmigung *f*, Zulassung *f*: ***by special ~*** mit besonderer Erlaubnis; ***ask s.o. for ~, ask s.o.'s ~*** j-n um Erlaubnis bitten; **per'mis·sive** [-sɪv] *adj.* □ **1.** gestattend, zulassend; ⚖ fakulta'tiv; **2.** tole'rant, libe'ral; (sexu'ell) freizügig: **~ *society*** tabufreie Gesellschaft; **per'mis·sive·ness** [-sɪvnɪs] *s.* **1.** Zulässigkeit *f*; **2.** Tole'ranz *f*; **3.** (sexu'elle) Freizügigkeit *f.*

per·mit [pə'mɪt] **I** *v/t.* **1.** *et.* erlauben, gestatten, zulassen, dulden: ***am I ~ted to*** darf ich?; **~ *o.s. s.th.*** sich et. erlauben; **II** *v/i.* **2.** erlauben: ***weather*** (***time***) **~*ting*** wenn es das Wetter (die Zeit) erlaubt; **3.** **~ *of*** *fig.* zulassen: ***the rule ~s of no exception***; **III** *s.* ['pɜːmɪt] **4.** Genehmigung(sschein *m*) *f*, Li'zenz *f*, Zulassung *f* (***to*** für); ✝ Aus-, Einfuhrerlaubnis *f*; **5.** Aus-, Einreiseerlaubnis *f*; **6.** Passierschein *m*; **per·mit·tiv·i·ty** [ˌpɜːmɪ'tɪvətɪ] *s.* ϟ Dielektrizi'tätskonˌstante *f.*

per·mu·ta·tion [ˌpɜːmjuː'teɪʃn] *s.* **1.** Vertauschung *f*, Versetzung *f*: **~ *lock*** Vexierschloß; **2.** & Permutati'on *f.*

per·ni·cious [pə'nɪʃəs] *adj.* □ **1.** verderblich, schädlich; **2.** ⚕ bösartig, perni'ziös; **per'ni·cious·ness** [-nɪs] *s.* Schädlichkeit *f*; Bösartigkeit *f.*

per·nick·et·y [pə'nɪkətɪ] *adj.* **1.** F ‚pingelig', kleinlich, wählerisch, pe'dantisch (***about*** mit); **2.** heikel (*a. Sache*).

per·o·rate ['perəreɪt] *v/i.* **1.** große Reden schwingen; **2.** e-e Rede abschließen; **per·o·ra·tion** [ˌperə'reɪʃn] *s.* (zs.-fassender) Redeschluß.

per·ox·ide [pə'rɒksaɪd] ⚗ 'Superoˌxyd *n*; *engS.* 'Wasserstoffˌsuperoˌxyd *n*: **~ *blonde*** F ‚Wasserstoffblondine' *f*; **per'ox·i·dize** [-sɪdaɪz] *v/t. u. v/i.* peroxydieren.

per·pen·dic·u·lar [ˌpɜːpən'dɪkjʊlə] **I** *adj.* □ **1.** senk-, lotrecht (***to*** zu): **~ *style*** ⚠ englische Spätgotik; **2.** rechtwinklig (***to*** auf *dat.*); **3.** ⚒ seiger; **4.** steil; **5.** aufrecht (*a. fig.*); **II** *s.* **6.** (Einfalls)Lot *n*, Senkrechte *f*; Perpen'dikel *n*, *m*: ***out of (the) ~*** schief, nicht senkrecht; ***raise (let fall) a ~*** ein Lot errichten (fällen); **7.** ⚙ (Senk)Lot *n*, Senkwaage *f.*

per·pe·trate ['pɜːpɪtreɪt] *v/t. Verbrechen etc.* begehen, verüben; F *fig. Buch etc.* ‚verbrechen'; **per·pe·tra·tion** [ˌpɜːpɪ'treɪʃn] *s.* Begehung *f*, Verübung *f*; '**per·pe·tra·tor** [-tə] *s.* Täter *m.*

per·pet·u·al [pə'petʃʊəl] *adj.* □ **1.** fort-, immerwährend, unaufhörlich, beständig, ewig, andauernd: **~ *check*** Dauerschach *n*; **~ *motion machine*** Perpetuum mobile *n*; **~ *snow*** ewiger Schnee, Firn *m*; **2.** lebenslänglich, unabsetzbar: **~ *officer***; **3.** ✝ unablösbar, unkündbar: **~ *lease***; **~ *bonds*** Rentenanleihen; **4.** ⚘ perennierend; **per'pet·u·ate** *v/t.* [-tʃʊeɪt] verewigen, fortbestehen lassen, (immerwährend) fortsetzen; **per·pet·u·a·tion** [pəˌpetʃʊ'eɪʃn] *s.* Fortdauer *f*, endlose Fortsetzung, Verewigung *f*, Fortbestehenlassen *n*; **per·pe·tu·i·ty** [ˌpɜːpɪ'tjuːətɪ] *s.* **1.** Fortdauer *f*, unaufhörliches Bestehen, Unaufhörlichkeit *f*, Ewigkeit *f*: ***in*** (*od.* ***to*** *od.* ***for***) **~** auf ewig; **2.** ⚖ Unveräußerlichkeit(sverfügung) *f*; **3.** lebenslängliche (Jahres-) Rente.

per·plex [pə'pleks] *v/t.* verwirren, verblüffen, bestürzt machen; **per'plexed** [-kst] *adj.* □ **1.** verwirrt, verblüfft, verdutzt, bestürzt (*Person*); **2.** verworren, verwickelt (*Sache*); **per'plex·i·ty** [-ksətɪ] *s.* **1.** Verwirrung *f*, Bestürzung *f*, Verlegenheit *f*; **2.** Verworrenheit *f.*

per·qui·site ['pɜːkwɪzɪt] *s.* **1.** *mst pl. bsd. Brit.* a) Nebeneinkünfte *pl.*, -verdienst *m*, b) Vergünstigung *f*; **2.** Vergütung *f*, Gehalt *n*; **3.** per'sönliches Vorrecht.

per·se·cute ['pɜːsɪkjuːt] *v/t.* **1.** *bsd. pol., eccl.* verfolgen; **2.** a) plagen, belästigen, b) drangsalieren, schikanieren; **per·se·cu·tion** [ˌpɜːsɪ'kjuːʃn] *s.* **1.** Verfolgung *f*: **~ *mania***, **~ *complex*** Verfolgungswahn *m*; **2.** Drangsalierung *f*, Schi'kane(n *pl.*) *f*; '**per·se·cu·tor** [-tə] *s.* **1.** Verfolger *m*; **2.** Peiniger(in).

per·se·ver·ance [ˌpɜːsɪ'vɪərəns] *s.* Beharrlichkeit *f*, Ausdauer *f*; **per·sev·er·ate** [pə'sevəreɪt] *v/i. psych.* ständig *od.* immer 'wiederkehren (*Melodie, Motiv, Gedanken etc.*); **per·se·vere** [ˌpɜːsɪ'vɪə] *v/i.* (***in***) beharren, ausdauern, aushalten (bei), fortfahren (mit), festhalten (an *dat.*); ˌ**per·se'ver·ing** [-'vɪərɪŋ] *adj.* □ beharrlich, standhaft.

Per·sian ['pɜːʃn] **I** *adj.* **1.** persisch; **II** *s.* **2.** Perser(in); **3.** *ling.* Persisch *n*; **~ *blinds*** *s. pl.* Jalou'sien *pl.*; **~ *carpet*** *s.* Perserteppich *m*; **~ *cat*** *s.* An'gorakatze *f.*

per·si·flage [ˌpɜːsɪ'flɑːʒ] *s.* Persi'flage *f*, (*feine*) Verspottung *f.*

per·sim·mon [pɜː'sɪmən] *s.* ⚘ Persi'mone *f*, Kaki-, Dattelpflaume *f*.
per·sist [pə'sɪst] *v/i.* **1.** (**in**) aus-, verharren (bei), hartnäckig bestehen (auf *dat.*), beharren (auf *dat.*, bei), unbeirrt fortfahren (mit); **2.** weiterarbeiten (**with** an *dat.*); **3.** fortdauern, anhalten; fort-, weiterbestehen; **per'sist·ence** [-təns], **per'sist·en·cy** [-tənsɪ] *s.* **1.** Beharren *n* (**in** bei); Beharrlichkeit *f*; Fortdauer *f*; **2.** beharrliches *od.* hartnäckiges Fortfahren (**in** in *dat.*); **3.** Hartnäckigkeit *f*, Ausdauer *f*; **4.** *phys.* Beharrung(szustand *m*) *f*, Nachwirkung *f*; Wirkungsdauer *f*; *TV etc.* Nachleuchten *n*; *opt.* (Augen)Trägheit *f*; **per'sist·ent** [-tənt] *adj.* □ **1.** beharrlich, ausdauernd, hartnäckig; **2.** ständig, nachhaltig; anhaltend (*a.* ✝ *Nachfrage*; *a. Regen*); ⚔ seßhaft (*Kampfstoff*), schwerflüchtig (*Gas*).
per·son ['pɜːsn] *s.* **1.** Per'son *f* (*a. contp.*), (Einzel)Wesen *n*, Indi'viduum *n*; *weitS.* Per'sönlichkeit *f*: **any ~** irgend jemand: **in ~** in eigener Person, persönlich; **no ~** niemand; **natural ~** ⚖ natürliche Person; **~-to-~ call** *teleph.* Voranmeldung(sgespräch *n*) *f*; **2.** *das* Äußere, Körper *m*: **carry s.th. on one's ~** et. bei sich tragen; **3.** *thea.* Rolle *f*.
per·so·na [pɜː'səʊnə] *pl.* **-nae** [-niː] *s.* (*Lat.*) **1.** a) *thea.* Cha'rakter *m*, Rolle *f*, b) Gestalt *f* (*in der Literatur*); **2. ~ (non) grata** Persona (non) grata *f*, (nicht) genehme Person.
per·son·a·ble ['pɜːsnəbl] *adj.* **1.** von angenehmem Äußeren; **2.** sym'pathisch; **'per·son·age** [-nɪdʒ] *s.* **1.** (hohe) Per'sönlichkeit; **2.** → **persona** 1; **'per·son·al** [-nl] **I** *adj.* □ **1.** per'sönlich (*a. ling.*); Personal...(*-konto, -kredit, -steuer etc.*); Privat...(*-einkommen, -leben etc.*); eigen (*a. Meinung*): **~ call** *teleph.* Voranmeldung(sgespräch *n*) *f*; **~ column** → 5; **~ damage** Personenschaden *m*; **~ data** Personalien *pl.*; **~ file** Personalakte *f*; **~ injury** Körperverletzung *f*; **~ property** (*od.* **estate**) → **personalty**; **~ union** *pol.* Personalunion *f*; **2.** persönlich, pri'vat, vertraulich (*Brief etc.*); mündlich (*Auskunft etc.*): **~ matter** Privatsache *f*; **3.** äußer, körperlich: **~ charms**; **~ hygiene** Körperpflege *f*; **4.** persönlich, anzüglich (*Bemerkung etc.*): **become ~** anzüglich werden; **II** *s.* **5.** Per'sönliches *n* (*Zeitung*); **per·son·al·i·ty** [ˌpɜːsə'nælətɪ] *s.* **1.** Per'sönlichkeit *f* (*a. jur.*), Per'son *f*: **~ clash** *psych.* Persönlichkeitskonflikt *m*; **~ cult** *pol.* Personenkult *m*; **~ test** *psych.* Persönlichkeitstest *m*; **2.** Individuali'tät *f*; **3.** *pl.* Anzüglichkeiten *pl.*, anzügliche Bemerkungen *pl.*; **per·son·al·ize** ['pɜːsnəlaɪz] → **personify**; **'per·son·al·ty** [-nltɪ] ⚖ bewegliches Vermögen; **'per·son·ate** [-səneɪt] *v/t.* **1.** → **personify**; **2.** vor-, darstellen; **3.** nachahmen; **4.** sich (fälschlich) ausgeben als; **per·son·a·tion** [ˌpɜːsə'neɪʃn] *s.* **1.** Vor-, Darstellung *f*; **2.** Personifikati'on *f*, Verkörperung *f*; **3.** Nachahmung *f*; **4.** ⚖ fälschliches Sich'ausgeben.
per·son·i·fi·ca·tion [pɜːˌsɒnɪfɪ'keɪʃn] *s.* Verkörperung *f*; **per·son·i·fy** [pɜː'sɒnɪfaɪ] *v/t.* personifizieren, verkörpern, versinnbildlichen.
per·son·nel [ˌpɜːsə'nel] *s.* Perso'nal *n*, Belegschaft *f*; ⚔, ⚓ Mannschaft(en *pl.*) *f*, Besatzung *f*: **~ manager** ✝ Personalchef *m*.
per·spec·tiv·al [ˌpɜːspekt'taɪvl] *adj.* perspek'tivisch; **per·spec·tive** [pə'spektɪv] **I** *s.* **1.** ⩘, *paint. etc.* Perspek'tive *f*: **in (true) ~** in richtiger Perspektive; **2.** *a.* **~ drawing** perspektivische Zeichnung; **3.** Perspek'tive *f*: a) Aussicht *f*, -blick *m* (*beide a. fig.*), b) *fig.* klarer Blick: **he has no ~** er sieht die Dinge nicht im richtigen Verhältnis (zueinander); **II** *adj.* □ → **perspectival**.
per·spex ['pɜːspeks] (*TM*) *s. Brit.* Sicherheits-, Plexiglas *n*.
per·spi·ca·cious [ˌpɜːspɪ'keɪʃəs] *adj.* □ scharfsinnig, 'durchdringend; **ˌper·spi'cac·i·ty** [-'kæsətɪ] *s.* Scharfblick *m*, -sinn *m*; **ˌper·spi'cu·i·ty** [-'kjuːətɪ] *s.* Klarheit *f*, Verständlichkeit *f*; **per·spic·u·ous** [pə'spɪkjʊəs] *adj.* □ deutlich, klar, (leicht)verständlich.
per·spi·ra·tion [ˌpɜːspə'reɪʃn] *s.* **1.** Ausdünsten *n*, Schwitzen *n*; **2.** Schweiß *m*; **per·spir·a·to·ry** [pə'spaɪərətərɪ] *adj.* Schweiß...: **~ gland** Schweißdrüse *f*; **per·spire** [pə'spaɪə] **I** *v/i.* schwitzen, transpirieren; **II** *v/t.* ausschwitzen, -dünsten.
per·suade [pə'sweɪd] *v/t.* **1.** über'reden, bereden (**to** *inf.*, **into** *ger.* zu *inf.*); **2.** über'zeugen (**of** von, **that** daß): **~ o.s.** a) sich überzeugen, b) sich einbilden *od.* einreden; **be ~d that** überzeugt sein, daß; **per'suad·er** [-də] *s.* **1.** Überredungskünstler(in), ‚Verführer' *m*; **2.** *sl.* Über'redungsmittel *n* (*a. Pistole etc.*).
per·sua·sion [pə'sweɪʒn] *s.* **1.** Über'redung *f*; **2.** *a.* **powers of ~** Über'redungsgabe *f*, -künste *pl.*; **3.** Über'zeugung *f*, fester Glaube; **4.** *eccl.* Glaube(nsrichtung *f*) *m*; **5.** F *humor.* a) Art *f*, Sorte *f*, b) Geschlecht *n*: **female ~**; **per'sua·sive** [-eɪsɪv] *adj.* □ **1.** über'redend; **2.** über'zeugend; **per'sua·sive·ness** [-eɪsɪvnɪs] *s.* **1. persuasion** 2; **2.** über'zeugende Art.
pert [pɜːt] *adj.* □ keck (*a. fig. Hut etc.*), schnippisch, vorlaut.
per·tain [pɜː'teɪn] *v/i.* (**to**) a) gehören (*dat. od.* zu), b) betreffen (*acc.*), sich beziehen (auf *acc.*): **~ing to** betreffend.
per·ti·na·cious [ˌpɜːtɪ'neɪʃəs] *adj.* □ **1.** hartnäckig, zäh; **2.** beharrlich, standhaft; **ˌper·ti'nac·i·ty** [-'næsətɪ] *s.* Hartnäckigkeit *f*; Zähigkeit *f*, Beharrlichkeit *f*.
per·ti·nence ['pɜːtɪnəns], **'per·ti·nen·cy** [-sɪ] *s.* **1.** Angemessenheit *f*, Gemäßheit *f*; **2.** Sachdienlichkeit *f*, Rele'vanz *f*; **'per·ti·nent** [-nt] *adj.* □ **1.** angemessen, passend, gemäß; **2.** zur Sache gehörig, einschlägig, sachdienlich, gehörig (**to** zu): **be ~ to** Bezug haben auf (*acc.*).
pert·ness ['pɜːtnɪs] *s.* Keckheit *f*, schnippisches Wesen, vorlaute Art.
per·turb [pə'tɜːb] *v/t.* beunruhigen, stören, verwirren, ängstigen; **per·tur·ba·tion** [ˌpɜːtə'beɪʃn] *s.* **1.** Unruhe *f*, Bestürzung *f*; **2.** Beunruhigung *f*, Störung *f*; **3.** *ast.* Perturbati'on *f*.
pe·ruke [pə'ruːk] *s. hist.* Pe'rücke *f*.
pe·rus·al [pə'ruːzl] *s.* sorgfältiges 'Durchlesen, 'Durchsicht *f*, Prüfung *f*: **for ~** zur Einsicht; **pe·ruse** [pə'ruːz] *v/t.* ('durch)lesen; *weitS.* 'durchgehen, prüfen.
Pe·ru·vi·an [pə'ruːvjən] **I** *adj.* peru'anisch: **~ bark** ⚘ Chinarinde *f*; **II** *s.* Peru'aner(in).
per·vade [pə'veɪd] *v/t.* durch'dringen, -'ziehen, erfüllen (*a. fig.*); **per'va·sion** [-eɪʒn] *s.* Durch'dringung *f* (*a. fig.*); **per'va·sive** [-eɪsɪv] *adj.* □ 'durchdringend; *fig.* 'überall vor'handen, beherrschend.
per·verse [pə'vɜːs] *adj.* □ **1.** verkehrt, Fehl...; **2.** verderbt, böse; **3.** verdreht, wunderlich; **4.** verstockt; **5.** launisch; **6.** *psych.* per'vers (*a. fig.*), 'widernatürlich; **per'ver·sion** [-ɜːʒn] *s.* **1.** Verdrehung *f*, 'Umkehrung *f*; Entstellung *f*: **~ of justice** Rechtsbeugung *f*; **~ of history** Geschichtsklitterung *f*; **2.** *bsd. eccl.* Verirrung *f*, Abkehr *f vom Guten etc.*; **3.** *psych.* Perversi'on *f*; **4.** ⩘ 'Umkehrung *f* (*e-r Figur*); **per'ver·si·ty** [-sətɪ] *s.* **1.** Verdrehtheit *f*; **2.** Halsstarrigkeit *f*; **3.** Verderbtheit *f*; **4.** 'Widernaˌtürlichkeit *f*, Perversi'tät *f* (*a. fig.*); **per'ver·sive** [-sɪv] *adj.* verderblich (**of** für).
per·vert **I** *v/t.* [pə'vɜːt] **1.** verdrehen, verkehren, entstellen, fälschen, pervertieren (*a. psych.*); miß'brauchen; **2.** *j-n* verderben, verführen; **II** *s.* ['pɜːvɜːt] **3.** Abtrünnige(r *m*) *f*; **4.** *a.* **sexual ~** *psych.* per'verser Mensch; **per'vert·er** [-tə] *s.* Verdreher(in); Verführer(in).
per·vi·ous ['pɜːvjəs] *adj.* □ **1.** 'durchlässig (*a. phys.*), durch'dringbar, gangbar (**to** für); **2.** *fig.* zugänglich (**to** für), offen (**to** *dat.*); **3.** ⚙ undicht.
pes·ky ['peskɪ] *adj.* u. *adv. Am.* F ‚verflixt'.
pes·sa·ry ['pesərɪ] *s.* ⚕ Pes'sar *n*.
pes·si·mism ['pesɪmɪzəm] *s.* Pessi'mismus *m*, Schwarzsehe'rei *f*; **'pes·si·mist** [-ɪst] **I** *s.* Pessi'mist(in), Schwarzseher (-in); **II** *adj. a.* **pes·si·mis·tic** [ˌpesɪ'mɪstɪk] *adj.* (□ **~ally**) pessi'mistisch.
pest [pest] *s.* **1.** Pest *f*, Plage *f* (*a. fig.*); **2.** *fig.* Pestbeule *f*; **3.** *fig.* a) ‚Ekel' *n*, ‚Nervensäge' *f*, b) Plage *f*, lästige Sache; **4.** *bsd.* **insect ~** *biol.* Schädling *m*: **~ control** Schädlingsbekämpfung *f*.
pes·ter ['pestə] *v/t.* plagen, quälen, belästigen, *j-m* auf die Nerven gehen.
pes·ti·cide ['pestɪsaɪd] *s.* Schädlingsbekämpfungsmittel *n*.
pes·ti·lence ['pestɪləns] *s.* Seuche *f*, Pest *f*, Pesti'lenz *f* (*a. fig.*); **'pes·ti·lent** [-nt] *adj.* → **pes·ti·len·tial** [ˌpestɪ'lenʃl] *adj.* □ **1.** verpestend, ansteckend; **2.** *fig.* verderblich, schädlich; **3.** *oft humor.* ekelhaft.
pes·tle ['pesl] **I** *s.* **1.** Mörserkeule *f*, Stößel *m*; **2.** ⚗ Pi'still *n*; **II** *v/t.* **3.** zerstoßen.
pet¹ [pet] **I** *s.* **1.** (zahmes) Haustier; Stubentier *n*; **2.** gehätscheltes Tier *od.* Kind, Liebling *m*, ‚Schatz' *m*, ‚Schätzchen' *n*; **II** *adj.* **3.** Lieblings...: **~ dog** Schoßhund *m*; **~ mistake** Lieblingsfehler *m*; **~ name** Kosename *m*; **~ shop** Tierhandlung *f*; → **aversion** 3; **III** *v/t.* **4.** (ver)hätscheln, liebkosen; **5.** F ‚abfummeln', Petting machen mit; **IV** *v/i.* **6.** F ‚fummeln', knutschen, Petting machen.
pet² [pet] *s.* schlechte Laune: **in a ~** verärgert, schlecht gelaunt.

pet·al ['petl] *s.* ⚘ Blumenblatt *n.*

pe·tard [pe'tɑ:d] *s.* **1.** ⚔ *hist.* Pe'tarde *f*, Sprengbüchse *f*; → ***hoist¹***; **2.** Schwärmer *m* (*Feuerwerk*).

pe·ter¹ ['pi:tə] *v/i.*: **~ *out*** a) (allmählich) zu Ende gehen, b) sich verlieren, c) sich totlaufen, versanden.

Pe·ter² ['pi:tə] *npr. u. s. bibl.* 'Petrus *m*: (***the Epistles of***) **~** die Petrusbriefe.

pe·ter³ ['pi:tə] *s. sl.* ,Zipfel' *m* (*Penis*).

pe·ter⁴ ['pi:tə] *s. sl.* **1.** Geldschrank *m*; **2.** (Laden)Kasse *f*.

pet·it ['petɪ] → ***petty***.

pe·ti·tion [pɪ'tɪʃn] **I** *s.* Bitte *f*, *bsd.* Bittschrift *f*, Gesuch *n*; Eingabe *f* (*a. Patentrecht*); ⚖ (schriftlicher) Antrag: **~ *for divorce*** Scheidungsklage *f*; **~ *in bankruptcy*** Konkursantrag *m*; ***file one's ~ in bankruptcy*** Konkurs anmelden; **~ *for clemency*** Gnadengesuch *n*; **II** *v/i.* (*u. v/t. j-n*) bitten, an-, ersuchen (***for*** um), schriftlich einkommen (***s.o.*** bei j-m), e-e Bittschrift einreichen (***s.o.*** an j-n): **~ *for divorce*** die Scheidungsklage einreichen; **pe'ti·tion·er** [-ʃnə] *s.* Antragsteller(in): a) Bitt-, Gesuchsteller(in), Pe'tent *m*, b) ⚖ (Scheidungs)Kläger(in).

pet·rel ['petrəl] *s.* **1.** *orn.* Sturmvogel *m*; → ***stormy petrel***; **2.** Unruhestifter *m*.

pet·ri·fac·tion [ˌpetrɪ'fækʃn] *s.* Versteinerung *f* (*Vorgang u. Ergebnis*; *a. fig.*); **pet·ri·fy** ['petrɪfaɪ] **I** *v/t.* **1.** versteinern (*a. fig.*); **2.** *fig. durch Schrecken etc.* versteinern, erstarren lassen: ***petrified with horror*** starr vor Schrecken; **II** *v/i.* **3.** sich versteinern (*a. fig.*).

pe·tro·chem·is·try [ˌpetrəʊ'kemɪstrɪ] *s.* Petroche'mie *f*; **pe·trog·ra·phy** [pɪ'trɒgrəfɪ] *s.* Gesteinsbeschreibung *f*, -kunde *f*.

pet·rol ['petrəl] *s. mot. Brit.* Ben'zin *n*, Kraftstoff *m*: **~ *bomb*** Molotowcocktail *m*; **~ *coupon*** Benzingutschein *m*; **~ *engine*** Benzin-, Vergasermotor *m*; **~ *ga(u)ge*** Kraftstoffanzeige *f*; **~ *station*** Tankstelle *f*; **pet·ro·la·tum** [ˌpetrə'leɪtəm] *s.* **1.** ⚗ Petro'latum *n*, Vase'lin *n*; **2.** ⚕ Paraf'finöl *n*; **pe·tro·le·um** [pɪ'trəʊljəm] *s.* Pe'troleum *n*, Erd-, Mine'ralöl *n*: **~ *jelly*** → ***petrolatum***; **pe·trol·o·gy** [pɪ'trɒlədʒɪ] *s.* Gesteinskunde *f*.

pet·ti·coat ['petɪkəʊt] **I** *s.* **1.** 'Unterrock *m*; Petticoat *m*; **2.** *fig.* Frauenzimmer *n*, Weibsbild *n*, ,Unterrock' *m*; **3.** Kinderröckchen *n*; **4.** ⚙ Glocke *f*; **5.** ⚡ a) *a.* **~ *insulator*** 'Glockenisoˌlator *m*, b) Isolierglocke *f*; **6.** *mot.* (Ven'til)Schutzhaube *f*; **II** *adj.* **7.** Weiber…: **~ *government*** Weiberregiment *n*.

pet·ti·fog·ger ['petɪfɒgə] *s.* 'Winkeladvoˌkat *m*; Haarspalter *m*, Rabu'list *m*; **'pet·ti·fog·ging** [-gɪŋ] **I** *adj.* **1.** rechtsverdrehend; **2.** schika'nös, rabu'listisch; **3.** gemein, lumpig; **II** *s.* **4.** Rabu'listik *f*, Haarspalte'rei *f*, Rechtskniffe *pl.*

pet·ti·ness ['petɪnɪs] *s.* **1.** Geringfügigkeit *f*; **2.** Kleinlichkeit *f*.

pet·ting ['petɪŋ] *s.* F ,Fumme'lei' *f*, Petting *n*.

pet·tish ['petɪʃ] *adj.* □ reizbar, mürrisch; **'pet·tish·ness** [-nɪs] *s.* Gereiztheit *f*.

pet·ti·toes ['petɪtəʊz] *s. pl. Küche*: Schweinsfüße *pl.*

pet·ty ['petɪ] *adj.* □ **1.** unbedeutend, geringfügig, klein, Klein…: **~ *cash*** ✝ a) geringfügige Beträge, b) kleine Kasse, Portokasse; **~ *offence*** ⚖ Bagatelldelikt *n*; **~ *wares*** Kurzwaren; **2.** kleinlich; **~ bour·gois** ['bʊəʒwɑ:] **I** *s.* (*Fr.*) Kleinbürger(in); **II** *adj.* kleinbürgerlich; **~ bour·geoi·sie** [ˌbʊəʒwɑ:'zi:] *s.* (*Fr.*) Kleinbürgertum *n*; **~ ju·ry** *s.* ⚖ kleine Jury; **~ lar·ce·ny** *s.* ⚖ leichter Diebstahl; **~ of·fi·cer** *s.* ⚔, ⚓ Maat *m* (*Unteroffizier*); **~ ses·sions** *s. pl.* → ***magistrate***.

pet·u·lance ['petjʊləns] *s.* Gereiztheit *f*; **'pet·u·lant** [-nt] *adj.* □ gereizt.

pe·tu·ni·a [pɪ'tju:njə] *s.* ⚘ Pe'tunie *f*.

pew [pju:] *s.* **1.** Kirchenstuhl *m*, -sitz *m*, Bank(reihe) *f*; **2.** *Brit.* F Platz *m*: ***take a ~*** sich ,platzen'.

pe·wit ['pi:wɪt] *s. orn.* **1.** Kiebitz *m*; **2.** *a.* **~ *gull*** Lachmöwe *f*.

pew·ter ['pju:tə] **I** *s.* **1.** brit. Schüsselzinn *n*, Hartzinn *n*; **2.** *coll.* Zinngerät *n*; **3.** Zinnkrug *m*, -gefäß *n*; **4.** *Brit. sl. bsd. Sport*: Po'kal *m*; **II** *adj.* **5.** (Hart-) Zinn…, zinnern; **'pew·ter·er** [-ərə] *s.* Zinngießer *m*.

pha·e·ton ['feɪtn] *s.* Phaeton *m* (*Kutsche*; *mot. obs. Tourenwagen*).

phag·o·cyte ['fægəʊsaɪt] *s. biol.* Phago'cyte *f*, Freßzelle *f*.

phal·ange ['fælændʒ] *s.* **1.** *anat.* Finger-, Zehenknochen *m*; **2.** ⚘ Staubfädenbündel *n*; **3.** *zo.* Tarsenglied *n*.

pha·lanx ['fælæŋks] *pl.* **-lanx·es** *od.* **-lan·ges** [fæ'lændʒi:z] *s.* **1.** ⚔ *hist.* Phalanx *f*, *fig. a.* geschlossene Front; **2.** → ***phalange*** 1 *u.* 2.

phal·lic ['fælɪk] *adj.* phallisch, Phallus…: **~ *symbol***; **phal·lus** ['fæləs] *pl.* **-li** [-laɪ] *s.* Phallus *m*.

phan·tasm ['fæntæzəm] → ***phantom*** 1 a *u.* b; **phan·tas·ma·go·ri·a** [ˌfæntæzmə'gɒrɪə] *s.* Phantasmago'rie *f*, Gaukelbild *n*, Blendwerk *n*; **phan·tas·ma·gor·ic** [ˌfæntæzmə'gɒrɪk] *adj.* (□ **~*ally***) phantasma'gorisch, gespensterhaft, trügerisch; **phan·tas·mal** [fæn'tæzml] *adj.* □ **1.** halluzina'torisch, eingebildet; **2.** geisterhaft; **3.** illu'sorisch, unwirklich, trügerisch.

phan·tom ['fæntəm] **I** *s.* **1.** Phan'tom *n*: a) Erscheinung *f*, Gespenst *n*, *a. fig.* Geist *m*, b) Wahngebilde *n*, Hirngespinst *n*; Trugbild *n*, c) *fig.* Alptraum *m*, Schreckgespenst *n*; **2.** *fig.* Schatten *m*, Schein *m*; **3.** ⚕ Phantom *n* (*Körpermodell*); **II** *adj.* **4.** Phantom…, Gespenster…, Geister…; **5.** scheinbar, Schein…; **~ cir·cuit** *s.* ⚡ Phan'tomkreis *m*, Duplexleitung *f*; **~ (limb) pain** *s.* ⚕ Phan'tomschmerz *m*; **~ ship** *s.* Geisterschiff *n*; **~ view** *s.* ⚙ (Konstrukti'ons-) Durchsicht *f*.

phar·i·sa·ic, phar·i·sa·i·cal [ˌfærɪ'seɪɪk(l)] *adj.* □ phari'säisch, selbstgerecht, scheinheilig; **phar·i·sa·ism** ['færɪseɪɪzəm] *s.* Phari'säertum *n*, Scheinheiligkeit *f*; **Phar·i·see** ['færɪsi:] *s.* **1.** *eccl.* Phari'säer *m*; **2.** ♀ *fig.* Phari'säer(in), Selbstgerechte(r *m*) *f*, Heuchler(in).

phar·ma·ceu·ti·cal [ˌfɑ:mə'sju:tɪkl] *adj.* □ pharma'zeutisch; Apotheker…; **ˌphar·ma'ceu·tics** [-ks] *s. pl. sg. konstr.* Pharma'zeutik *f*, Arz'neimittelkunde *f*; **phar·ma·cist** ['fɑ:məsɪst] *s.* **1.** Pharma'zeut *m*, Apo'theker *m*; **2.** pharma'zeutischer Chemiker; **phar·ma·col·o·gy** *s.* [ˌfɑ:mə'kɒlədʒɪ] ˌPharmakolo'gie *f*, Arz'neimittellehre *f*; **phar·ma·co·poe·ia** [ˌfɑ:məkə'pi:ə] *s.* **1.** ˌPharmako'pöe *f*, amtliches Arz'neibuch; **2.** Arz'neimittelvorrat *m*; **phar·ma·cy** ['fɑ:məsɪ] *s.* **1.** → ***pharmaceutics***; **2.** Apo'theke *f*.

pha·ryn·gal [fə'rɪŋgl]; **pha·ryn·ge·al** [ˌfærɪn'dʒi:əl] **I** *adj. anat.* Rachen… (*-mandeln etc.*; *a. ling. -laut*); **II** *s. anat.* Schlundknochen *m*; **phar·yn·gi·tis** [ˌfærɪn'dʒaɪtɪs] *s.* 'Rachenkaˌtarrh *m*; **phaˌryn·go'na·sal** [-gəʊ'neɪzl] *adj.* Rachen u. Nase betreffend; **phar·ynx** ['færɪŋks] *s.* Schlund *m*, Rachen(höhle *f*) *m*.

phase [feɪz] **I** *s.* **1.** ⚗, ⚡, ✈, *ast., biol., phys.* Phase *f*: ***the ~s of the moon*** *ast.* Mondphasen; **~ *advancer*** (*od.* ***converter***) ⚡ Phasenverschieber *m*; ***in ~*** (***out of ~***) ⚡ phasengleich (phasenverschoben); **2.** (Entwicklungs)Stufe *f*, Stadium *n*, Phase *f* (*a. psych.*); **3.** ⚔ (Front)Abschnitt *m*; **II** *v/t.* **4.** ⚡ in Phase bringen; **5.** aufeinander abstimmen, ⚙ synchronisieren; **6.** stufenweise durchführen, staffeln: **~ *down*** einstellen; **~ *in*** stufenweise einführen; **~ *out*** *et.* stufenweise einstellen *od.* abwickeln *od.* auflösen, *Produkt etc.* auslaufen lassen; **III** *v/i.* **7.** **~ *out*** sich stufenweise zurückziehen (***of*** aus).

pheas·ant ['feznt] *s. orn.* Fa'san *m*; **'pheas·ant·ry** [-rɪ] *s.* Fasane'rie *f*.

phe·nic ['fi:nɪk] *adj.* ⚗ kar'bolsauer, Karbol…: **~ *acid*** → **phe·nol** ['fi:nɒl] *s.* ⚗ Phe'nol *n*, Kar'bolsäure *f*; **phe·nol·ic** [fɪ'nɒlɪk] **I** *adj.* Phenol…: **~ *resin*** → **II** *s.* Phe'nolharz *n*.

phe·nom·e·nal [fɪ'nɒmɪnl] *adj.* □ phänome'nal: a) *phls.* Erscheinungs… (*-welt etc.*), b) unglaublich, ,toll'; **phe'nom·e·nal·ism** [-nəlɪzəm] *s. phls.* Phänomena'lismus *m*; **phe·nom·e·non** [fɪ'nɒmɪnən] *pl.* **-na** [-nə] *s.* **1.** Phäno'men *n*, Erscheinung *f* (*a. phys. u. phls.*); **2.** *pl.* **-nons** *fig.* wahres Wunder; *a.* ***infant ~*** Wunderkind *n*.

phe·no·type ['fi:nəʊtaɪp] *s. biol.* 'Phänoˌtypus *m*, Erscheinungsbild *n*.

phen·yl ['fi:nɪl] *s.* Phe'nyl *n*; **phe·nyl·ic** [fɪ'nɪlɪk] *adj.* Phenyl…, phe'nolisch: **~ *acid*** → ***phenol***.

phew [fju:] *int.* puh!

phi·al ['faɪəl] *s.* Phi'ole *f* (*bsd.* Arz'nei-) Fläschchen *n*, Am'pulle *f*.

Phi Be·ta Kap·pa [ˌfaɪˌbi:tə'kæpə] *s. Am.* a) *studentische Vereinigung hervorragender Akademiker*, b) *ein Mitglied dieser Vereinigung*.

phi·lan·der [fɪ'lændə] *v/i.* ,poussieren', schäkern; **phi'lan·der·er** [-ərə] *s.* Schäker *m*, Schürzenjäger *m*.

phil·an·throp·ic, phil·an·throp·i·cal [ˌfɪlən'θrɒpɪk(l)] *adj.* □ philan'thropisch, menschenfreundlich; **phi·lan·thro·pist** [fɪ'lænθrəpɪst] **I** *s.* Philan'throp *m*, Menschenfreund *m*; **II** *adj.* → ***philanthropic***; **phi·lan·thro·py** [fɪ'lænθrəpɪ] *s.* Philanthro'pie *f*, Menschenliebe *f*.

phil·a·tel·ic [ˌfɪlə'telɪk] *adj.* philate'listisch; **phi·lat·e·list** [fɪ'lætəlɪst] **I** *s.* Philate'list *m*; **II** *adj.* philate'listisch; **phi·lat·e·ly** [fɪ'lætəlɪ] *s.* Philate'lie *f*.

phil·har·mon·ic [ˌfɪlɑ:'mɒnɪk] *adj.* philhar'monisch (*Konzert, Orchester*): **~**

society Philharmonie *f.*
Phi·lip·pi·ans [fɪˈlɪpɪənz] *s. pl. sg. konstr. bibl.* (Brief *m* des Paulus an die) Phiˈlipper *pl.*
phi·lip·pic [fɪˈlɪpɪk] *s.* Phiˈlippika *f*, Strafpredigt *f.*
Phil·ip·pine [ˈfɪlɪpi:n] *adj.* **1.** philipˈpinisch, Philippinen…; **2.** Filipino…
Phi·lis·tine [ˈfɪlɪstaɪn] **I** *s. fig.* Phiˈlister *m*, Spießbürger *m*, Spießer *m*; **II** *adj.* phiˈlisterhaft, spießbürgerlich; **ˈphi·lis·tin·ism** [-tɪnɪzəm] *s.* Phiˈlistertum *n*, Philisteˈrei *f*, Spießbürgertum *n*, Baˈnausentum *n.*
phil·o·log·i·cal [ˌfɪləˈlɒdʒɪkl] *adj.* □ philoˈlogisch, sprachwissenschaftlich; **phi·lol·o·gist** [fɪˈlɒlədʒɪst] *s.* Philoˈloge *m*, Philoˈlogin *f*, Sprachwissenschaftler (-in); **phi·lol·o·gy** [fɪˈlɒlədʒɪ] *s.* Philoloˈgie *f*, (Literaˈtur- u.) Sprachwissenschaft *f.*
phi·los·o·pher [fɪˈlɒsəfə] *s.* Philoˈsoph *m* (*a. fig. Lebenskünstler*): ***natural*** ~ Naturforscher *m*; ***~s' stone*** Stein *m* der Weisen; **phil·o·soph·ic**, **phil·o·soph·i·cal** [ˌfɪləˈsɒfɪk(l)] *adj.* □ philoˈsophisch (*a. fig. weise, gleichmütig*); **phiˈlos·o·phize** [-faɪz] *v/i.* philosophieren; **phiˈlos·o·phy** [-fɪ] *s.* **1.** Philosoˈphie *f*: ***natural*** ~ Naturwissenschaft *f*; ~ ***of history*** Geschichtsphilosophie; **2.** a) *a.* ~ ***of life*** (ˈLebens)Philosoˌphie *f*, Weltanschauung *f*, b) *fig.* (philoˈsophische) Gelassenheit, c) ‚Philosoˈphie' *f*, Denkbild *n*, -modell *n.*
phil·ter *Am.*, **phil·tre** *Brit.* [ˈfɪltə] *s.* **1.** Liebestrank *m*; **2.** Zaubertrank *m.*
phiz [fɪz] *s. sl.* Viˈsage *f*, Gesicht *n.*
phle·bi·tis [flɪˈbaɪtɪs] *s.* ⚕ Venenentzündung *f*, Phleˈbitis *f.*
phlegm [flem] *s.* **1.** *physiol.* Phlegma *n*, Schleim *m*; **2.** *fig.* Phlegma *n*: a) stumpfer Gleichmut, b) (geistige) Trägheit; **phleg·mat·ic** [flegˈmætɪk] **I** *adj.* (□ ***~ally***) *physiol. u. fig.* phlegˈmatisch; **II** *s.* Phlegˈmatiker(in).
pho·bi·a [ˈfəʊbɪə] *s. psych.* (***about***) Phoˈbie *f*, krankhafte Furcht (vor *dat.*) *od.* Abneigung (gegen).
Phoe·ni·cian [fɪˈnɪʃɪən] **I** *s.* **1.** Phöˈnizier (-in); **2.** *ling.* Phöˈnikisch *n*; **II** *adj.* **3.** phöˈnizisch.
phoe·nix [ˈfi:nɪks] *s. myth.* Phönix *m* (*legendärer Vogel*), *fig. a.* Wunder *n.*
phon [fɒn] *s. phys.* Phon *n.*
phone[1] [fəʊn] *s. ling.* (Einzel)Laut *m.*
phone[2] [fəʊn] *s.*, *v/t. u. v/i.* F → ***telephone***; ***~-in*** *Radio, TV* Sendung *f* mit telefonischer Publikumsbeteiligung.
pho·neme [ˈfəʊni:m] *s. ling.* **1.** Phoˈnem *n*; **2.** → ***phone***[1].
pho·net·ic [fəʊˈnetɪk] *adj.* (□ ***~ally***) phoˈnetisch, lautlich: ~ ***spelling***, ~ ***transcription*** Lautschrift *f*; **pho·ne·ti·cian** [ˌfəʊnɪˈtɪʃn] *s.* Phoˈnetiker *m*; **phoˈnet·ics** [-ks] *s. pl. mst sg. konstr.* Phoˈnetik *f*, Laut(bildungs)lehre *f.*
pho·ney [ˈfəʊnɪ] → ***phony.***
phon·ic [ˈfəʊnɪk] *adj.* **1.** lautlich, aˈkustisch; **2.** phoˈnetisch; **3.** ⚙ phonisch.
pho·no·gram [ˈfəʊnəgræm] *s.* Lautzeichen *n*; **ˈpho·no·graph** [-grɑ:f] *s.* ⚙ **1.** Phonoˈgraph *m*, ˈSprechmaˌschine *f*; **2.** *Am.* Plattenspieler *m*, Grammoˈphon *n*; **pho·no·graph·ic** [ˌfəʊnəˈgræfɪk] *adj.* (□ ***~ally***) phonoˈgraphisch.
pho·nol·o·gy [fəʊˈnɒlədʒɪ] *s. ling.* Phonoloˈgie *f*, Lautlehre *f.*
pho·nom·e·ter [fəʊˈnɒmɪtə] *s. phys.* Phonoˈmeter *n*, Schall(stärke)messer *m.*
pho·ny [ˈfəʊnɪ] F **I** *adj.* **1.** falsch, gefälscht, unecht; Falsch…, Schwindel…, Schein…: ~ ***war*** *hist.* ‚Sitzkrieg' *m*; **II** *s.* **2.** Schwindler(in), ‚Schauspieler(in)', Scharlatan *m*: ***he is*** ~ *a.* der ist nicht ‚echt'; **3.** Fälschung *f*, Schwindel *m.*
phos·gene [ˈfɒzdʒi:n] *s.* ⚗ Phosˈgen *n*, Chlorˈkohlenoˌxyd *n*; **phos·phate** [ˈfɒsfeɪt] *s.* ⚗ **1.** Phosˈphat *n*: ~ ***of lime*** phosphorsaurer Kalk; **2.** ✓ Phosˈphat (-düngemittel) *n*; **phos·phat·ic** [fɒsˈfætɪk] *adj.* ⚗ phosˈphathaltig; **phos·phide** [ˈfɒsfaɪd] *s.* ⚗ Phosˈphid *n*; **phos·phite** [ˈfɒsfaɪt] *s.* **1.** ⚗ Phosˈphit *n*; **2.** *min.* ˈPhosphormeˌtall *n*; **phos·phor** [ˈfɒsfə] **I** *s.* **1.** *poet.* Phosphor *m*; **2.** ⚙ Leuchtmasse *f*; **II** *adj.* **3.** Phosphor…; **phos·pho·rate** [ˈfɒsfəreɪt] *v/t.* ⚗ **1.** phosphorisieren; **2.** phosphoreszierend machen; **phos·pho·resce** [ˌfɒsfəˈres] *v/i.* phosphoreszieren, (nach)leuchten; **phos·pho·res·cence** [ˌfɒsfəˈresns] *s.* **1.** ⚗, *phys.* Chemolumiˈneszenz *f*; **2.** *phys.* Phosphoresˈzenz *f*, Nachleuchten *n*; **phos·pho·res·cent** [ˌfɒsfəˈresnt] *adj.* phosphoreszierend; **phos·phor·ic** [fɒsˈfɒrɪk] *adj.* phosphorsauer, -haltig, Phosphor…; **phos·pho·rous** [ˈfɒsfərəs] *adj.* ⚗ phosˈphorig(sauer); **phos·pho·rus** [ˈfɒsfərəs] *pl.* **-ri** [-raɪ] *s.* **1.** ⚗ Phosphor *m*; **2.** *phys.* ˈLeuchtphosˌphore *f*, -masse *f.*
phot [fɒt] *s. phys.* Phot *n.*
pho·to [ˈfəʊtəʊ] F → ***photograph.***
photo- [fəʊtəʊ] *in Zssgn* Photo…, Foto…: a) Licht…, b) photoˈgraphisch; **ˈ~·cell** *s.* ⚡ Photozelle *f*; **ˌ~ˈchem·i·cal** *adj.* □ photoˈchemisch; **ˌ~·comˈpose** *v/t.* im Photosatz herstellen; **ˈ~ˌcop·i·er** *s.* Fotokoˈpiergerät *n*; **ˈ~ˌcop·y** → ***photostat*** 1 *u.* 3; **ˌ~·eˈlec·tric** [-təʊ-] *adj.*; **ˌ~·eˈlec·tri·cal** [-təʊ-] *adj.* □ *phys.* photoeˈlektrisch: ~ ***barrier*** Lichtschranke *f*; ~ ***cell*** Photozelle *f*; **ˌ~-enˈgrav·ing** [-təʊ-] *s.* Lichtdruck(verfahren *n*) *m*; **~ fin·ish** *s. sport* a) Fotofinish *n*, b) äußerst knappe Entscheidung; **ˈ~·fit** *s. Polizei:* Phanˈtombild *n*; **ˈ~-flash (lamp)** *s.* Blitzlicht(birne *f*) *n.*
pho·to·gen·ic [ˌfəʊtəʊˈdʒenɪk] *adj.* **1.** photoˈgen, bildwirksam; **2.** *biol.* lichterzeugend, Leucht…; **~·gram·me·try** [ˌfəʊtəˈgræmɪtrɪ] *s.* Photogrammeˈtrie *f*, Meßbildverfahren *n.*
pho·to·graph [ˈfəʊtəgrɑ:f] **I** *s.* Fotograˈfie *f*, (Licht)Bild *n*, Aufnahme *f*: ***take a*** ~ e-e Aufnahme machen (***of*** von); **II** *v/t.* fotografieren, aufnehmen, ‚knipsen'; **III** *v/i.* fotografieren; fotografiert werden: ***he does not*** ~ ***well*** er wird nicht gut auf den Bildern, er läßt sich schlecht fotografieren; **pho·tog·ra·pher** [fəˈtɒgrəfə] *s.* Fotoˈgraf(in); **pho·to·graph·ic** [ˌfəʊtəˈgræfɪk] *adj.* (□ ***~ally***) **1.** fotoˈgrafisch; **2.** *fig.* fotografisch genau; **pho·tog·ra·phy** [fəˈtɒgrəfɪ] *s.* Fotograˈfie *f*, Lichtbildkunst *f.*
pho·to·gra·vure [ˌfəʊtəgrəˈvjʊə] *s.* ˈPhotograˌvüre *f*, Kupferlichtdruck *m*; **ˌpho·toˈjour·nal·ism** *s.* ˈBildjournaˌlismus *m*; **ˌpho·toˈlith·o·graph** *typ.* **I** *s.* ˌPhotolithograˈphie *f* (*Erzeugnis*); **II** *v/t.* photolithographieren; **ˌpho·to·liˈthog·ra·phy** *s.* ˌPhotolithograˈphie *f* (*Verfahren*).
pho·tom·e·ter [fəʊˈtɒmɪtə] *s. phys.* Photoˈmeter *n*, Lichtstärkemesser *m*; **phoˈtom·e·try** [-trɪ] *s.* Lichtstärkemessung *f.*
ˌpho·toˈmi·cro·graph *s. phot.* ˈMikrofotograˌfie *f* (*Bild*).
ˌpho·to|·monˈtage *s.* ˈFotomonˌtage *f*; **ˌ~ˈmu·ral** *s.* Riesenvergrößerung *f* (*Wandschmuck*), *a.* ˈFototaˌpete *f*; **ˌ~ˈoff·set** *s. typ.* fotoˈgrafischer Offsetdruck *m.*
pho·ton [ˈfəʊtɒn] *s.* **1.** *phys.* Photon *n*, Lichtquant *n*; **2.** *opt.* Troland *n.*
ˈpho·to-play *s.* Filmdrama *n.*
pho·to·stat [ˈfəʊtəʊstæt] *phot.* **I** *s.* **1.** Fotokoˈpie *f*, Ablichtung *f*; **2.** ℛ Fotokoˈpiergerät *n* (*Handelsname*); **II** *v/t.* **3.** fotokopieren, ablichten; **pho·to·stat·ic** [ˌfəʊtəʊˈstætɪk] *adj.* Kopier…, Ablichtungs…: ~ ***copy*** → ***photostat*** 1.
ˌpho·to·teˈleg·ra·phy *s.* ˈBildtelegraˌphie *f*; **ˈpho·to·type** *s. typ.* **I** *s.* Lichtdruck(bild *n*, -platte *f*) *m*; **II** *v/t.* im Lichtdruckverfahren vervielfältigen; **ˌpho·toˈtype·set** → ***photocompose.***
phrase [freɪz] **I** *s.* **1.** (Rede)Wendung *f*, Redensart *f*, Ausdruck *m*: ~ ***of civility*** Höflichkeitsfloskel *f*; ~ ***book*** a) Sammlung *f* von Redewendungen, b) Sprachführer *m*; **2.** Phrase *f*, Schlagwort *n*: ~ ***monger*** Phrasendrescher *m*; ***as the*** ~ ***goes*** wie man so schön sagt; **3.** *ling.* a) Wortverbindung *f*, b) kurzer Satz, c) Sprechtakt *m*; **4.** ♪ Satz *m*; Phrase *f*; **II** *v/t.* **5.** ausdrücken, formulieren; **6.** ♪ phrasieren; **phra·se·ol·o·gy** [ˌfreɪzɪˈɒlədʒɪ] *s.* Phraseoloˈgie *f* (*a. Buch*), Ausdrucksweise *f.*
phren·ic [ˈfrenɪk] *anat.* **I** *adj.* Zwerchfell…; **II** *s.* Zwerchfell *n.*
phre·nol·o·gist [frɪˈnɒlədʒɪst] *s.* Phrenoˈloge *m*; **phreˈnol·o·gy** [-dʒɪ] *s.* Phrenoloˈgie *f*, Schädellehre *f.*
phthi·sis [ˈθaɪsɪs] *s.* Tuberkuˈlose *f*, Schwindsucht *f.*
phut [fʌt] **I** *int.* fft!; **II** *adj. sl.*: ***go*** ~ a) futschgehen, b) ‚platzen'.
phy·col·o·gy [faɪˈkɒlədʒɪ] *f* Algenkunde *f.*
phyl·lox·e·ra [ˌfɪlɒkˈsɪərə] *pl.* **-rae** [-ri:] *s. zo.* Reblaus *f.*
phy·lum [ˈfaɪləm] *pl.* **-la** [-lə] *s.* **1.** *bot. zo.* ˈUnterabteilung *f*, Ordnung; **2.** *biol.* Stamm *m*; **3.** *ling.* Sprachstamm *m.*
phys·ic [ˈfɪzɪk] **I** *s.* **1.** Arzˈnei(mittel *n*) *f*, *bsd.* Abführmittel *n*; **2.** *obs.* Heilkunde *f*; **3.** *pl. sg. konstr.* (die) Phyˈsik; **II** *v/t. pret. u. p.p.* **ˈphys·icked** [-kt] **4.** *obs.* j-n (ärztlich) behandeln; **ˈphys·i·cal** [-kl] **I** *adj.* □ **1.** physisch, körperlich (*a. Liebe etc.*): ~ ***condition*** Gesundheitszustand *m*; ~ ***culture*** Körperkultur *f*; ~ ***education***, ~ ***training*** *ped.* Leibeserziehung *f*; ~ ***examination*** → 3; ~ ***force*** physische Gewalt; ~ ***impossibility*** absolute Unmöglichkeit; ~ ***inventory*** ✝ Bestandsaufnahme *f*; ~ ***stock*** ✝ Lagerbestand *m*; **2.** physiˈkalisch; naˈturwissenschaftlich: ~ ***geography*** physikalische Geographie; ~ ***science*** a) Physik *f*, b) Naturwissenschaft(en *pl.*) *f*; **II** *s.* **3.** ärztliche Unterˈsuchung, ⚔ Musterung *f*; **phy·si·cian** [fɪˈzɪʃn] *s.* Arzt *m*;

'phys·i·cist [-ɪsɪst] *s.* Physiker *m.*
ˌphys·i·co-'chem·i·cal [ˌfɪzɪkəʊ-] *adj.* □ physiko'chemisch.
phys·i·og·no·my [ˌfɪzɪ'ɒnəmɪ] *s.* **1.** Physiogno'mie *f* (*a. fig.*), Gesichtsausdruck *m*, -züge *pl.*; **2.** Phyio'gnomik *f*; **ˌphys·i'og·ra·phy** [-'ɒgrəfɪ] *s.* **1.** ˌPhysio(geo)gra'phie *f*; **2.** Na'turbeschreibung *f*; **phys·i·o·log·i·cal** [ˌfɪzɪə'lɒdʒɪkl] *adj.* □ physio'logisch; **ˌphys·i'ol·o·gist** [-'ɒlədʒɪst] *s.* Physio'loge *m*; **ˌphys·i-'ol·o·gy** [-'ɒlədʒɪ] *s.* Physiolo'gie *f*; **phys·i·o·ther·a·pist** [ˌfɪzɪəʊ'θerəpɪst] *s.* ⚕ Physiothera'peut(in), *weitS.* Heilgymnastiker(in); **phys·i·o·ther·a·py** [ˌfɪzɪəʊ'θerəpɪ] *s.* ˌPhysiothera'pie *f*, 'Heilgymˌnastik *f.*
phy·sique [fɪ'ziːk] *s.* Körperbau *m*, -beschaffenheit *f*, Konstituti'on *f.*
phy·to·gen·e·sis [ˌfaɪtəʊ'dʒenɪsɪs] *s.* ⚘ Lehre *f* von der Entstehung der Pflanzen; **phy·tol·o·gy** [faɪ'tɒlədʒɪ] *s.* Pflanzenkunde *f*; **phy·to·to·my** [faɪ'tɒtəmɪ] *s.* ⚘ 'Pflanzenanatoˌmie *f.*
pi·an·ist ['pɪənɪst] *s.* ♪ Pia'nist(in), Kla'vierspieler(in).
pi·an·o¹ [pɪ'ænəʊ] *pl.* **-os** *s.* ♪ Kla'vier *n*, Piˌano('forte) *n*: ***at*** (***on***) ***the ~*** am (auf dem) Klavier.
pi·a·no² ['pjɑːnəʊ] ♪ **I** *pl.* **-nos** *s.* Pi'ano *n* (*leises Spiel*): ***~ pedal*** Pianopedal *n*; **II** *adv.* pi'ano, leise.
pi·an·o·for·te [ˌpjænəʊ'fɔːtɪ] → ***piano¹***.
pi·an·o play·er 1. → ***pianist***; **2.** Pia'nola *n.*
pi·az·za [pɪ'ætsə] *pl.* **-zas** (*Ital.*) *s.* **1.** öffentlicher Platz; **2.** *Am.* (große) Ve'randa.
pi·broch ['piːbrɒk; -ɒx] *s.* 'Kriegsmuˌsik *f* der Bergschotten; 'Dudelsackvariatiˌonen *pl.*
pi·ca ['paɪkə] *s. typ.* Cicero *f*, Pica *f.*
pic·a·resque [ˌpɪkə'resk] *adj.* pika'resk: ***~ novel*** Schelmenroman *m.*
pic·a·roon [ˌpɪkə'ruːn] *s.* **1.** Gauner *m*, Abenteurer *m*; **2.** Pi'rat *m.*
pic·a·yune [ˌpɪkɪ'juːn] *Am.* **I** *s.* **1.** *mst fig.* Pfennig *m*, Groschen *m*; **2.** *fig.* Lap'palie *f*; Tinnef *m, n*; **3.** *fig.* ‚Null' *f* (*unbedeutender Mensch*); **II** *adj.*, *a.* **ˌpic·a'yun·ish** [-nɪʃ] **4.** unbedeutend, schäbig; klein(lich).
pic·ca·lil·li ['pɪkəlɪlɪ] *s. pl.* Picca'lilli *pl.* (*eingemachtes, scharf gewürztes Mischgemüse*).
pic·ca·nin·ny ['pɪkənɪnɪ] **I** *s. humor.* (*bsd.* Neger)Kind *n*, Gör *n*; **II** *adj.* kindlich; winzig.
pic·co·lo ['pɪkələʊ] *pl.* **-los** *s.* ♪ Pikkoloflöte *f*; ***~ pi·an·o*** *s.* ♪ Kleinklavier *n.*
pick [pɪk] **I** *s.* **1.** ⚙ a) Spitz-, Kreuzhacke *f*, Picke *f*, Pickel *m*, b) ⚒ (Keil)Haue *f*; **2.** Schlag *m*; **3.** Auswahl *f*, -lese *f*: ***the ~ of the bunch*** der (die, das) Beste von allen; ***take your ~!*** suchen Sie sich etwas aus!; Sie haben die Wahl!; **4.** *typ.* unreiner Buchstabe; **5.** ⚘ Ernte *f*; **II** *v/t.* **6.** aufhacken, -picken: → ***brain*** 2, ***hole*** 1; **7.** *Körner* aufpicken; auflesen; sammeln; *Blumen, Obst* pflücken; *Beeren* abzupfen; F lustlos essen, herumstochern in (*dat.*); **8.** *fig.* (sorgfältig) auswählen, -suchen: ***~ one's way*** (*od.* ***steps***) sich s-n Weg suchen *od.* bahnen, *fig.* sich durchlavieren; ***~ one's words*** s-e Worte (sorgfältig) wählen; ***~ a quarrel*** (***with s.o.***) (mit j-m) Streit suchen *od.* anbändeln; **9.** *Gemüse etc.* (ver)lesen, säubern; *Hühner* rupfen; *Metall* scheiden; *Wolle* zupfen; in *der Nase* bohren; in *den Zähnen* stochern; *e-n Knochen* (ab)nagen; → ***bone*** 1; **10.** *Schloß* mit e-m Dietrich öffnen, ‚knakken'; *j-m die Tasche* ausräumen (*Dieb*); **11.** ♪ *Am. Banjo etc.* spielen; **12.** ausfasern, zerpflücken: ***~ to pieces*** *fig. Theorie etc.* zerpflücken, herunterreißen; **III** *v/i.* **13.** hacken, picke(l)n; **14.** (lustlos) im Essen her'umstochern; **15.** sorgfältig wählen: ***~ and choose*** *a.* wählerisch sein; **16.** ‚sti'bitzen', stehlen;
Zssgn mit prp. u. adv.:
pick| at *v/i.* **1.** *im Essen* her'umstochern; **2.** F her'ummäkeln *od.* -nörgeln an (*dat.*); auf *j-m* her'umhacken; ***~ off*** *v/t.* **1.** (ab)pflücken, -rupfen; **2.** wegnehmen; **3.** (einzeln) abschießen, ‚wegputzen'; ***~ on*** *v/i.* **1.** aussuchen, sich entscheiden für; **2.** → ***pick at*** 2; ***~ out*** *v/t.* **1.** (sich) *et. od. j-n* auswählen; **2.** ausmachen, erkennen; *fig.* her'ausfinden, -bekommen; **3.** ♪ sich *e-e Melodie auf dem Klavier etc.* zs.-suchen; **4.** *mit e-r anderen Farbe* absetzen; ***~ o·ver*** *v/t.* **1.** (gründlich) 'durchsehen, -gehen; **2.** (das Beste) auslesen; ***~ up* I** *v/t.* **1.** *Boden* aufhacken; **2.** aufheben, -nehmen, -lesen; in die Hand nehmen: ***pick o.s. up*** sich ‚hochrappeln' (*a. fig.*); → ***gauntlet¹*** 2; **3.** *j-n im Fahrzeug* mitnehmen, abholen; **4.** F a) *j-n* ‚auflesen, -gabeln, -reißen', b) ‚hochnehmen' (*verhaften*), c) ‚klauen' (*stehlen*); **5.** *Strickmaschen* aufnehmen; **6.** a) *Rundfunksender* ‚(rein)kriegen', b) *Sendung* empfangen, aufnehmen, abhören, c) *Funkspruch etc.* auffangen; **7.** in Sicht bekommen; **8.** *fig. et.* ‚mitkriegen', *Wort, Sprache etc.* ‚aufschnappen'; **9.** erstehen, gewinnen: ***~ a livelihood*** sich mit Gelegenheitsarbeiten *etc.* durchschlagen; ***~ courage*** Mut fassen; ***~ speed*** auf Touren (*od.* in Fahrt) kommen; **II** *v/i.* **10.** sich (wieder) erholen (*a.* ✝); **11.** sich anfreunden (***with*** mit); **12.** auf Touren kommen, Geschwindigkeit aufnehmen; *fig.* stärker werden.
pick-a-back ['pɪkəbæk] *adj. u. adv.* huckepack *tragen etc.*: ***~ plane*** ✈ Hukkepackflugzeug *n.*
pick·a·nin·ny → ***piccaninny***.
'pick·ax(e) *s.* (Spitz)Hacke *f*, (Beil)Pike *f*, Pickel *m.*
picked [pɪkt] *adj. fig.* ausgewählt, -gesucht, (aus)erlesen: ***~ troops*** ⚔ Kerntruppen *pl.*
pick·er·el ['pɪkərəl] *s. ichth.* (*Brit.* junger) Hecht.
pick·et ['pɪkɪt] **I** *s.* **1.** (Holz-, Absteck-) Pfahl *m*; Pflock *m*; **2.** ⚔ Vorposten *m*; **3.** Streikposten *m*; **II** *v/t.* **4.** einpfählen; **5.** an e-n Pfahl binden, anpflocken; **6.** Streikposten aufstellen vor (*dat.*), mit Streikposten besetzen; (als Streikposten) anhalten *od.* belästigen; **7.** ⚔ als Vorposten ausstellen; **III** *v/i.* **8.** Streikposten stehen.
pick·ings ['pɪkɪŋz] *s. pl.* **1.** Nachlese *f*, 'Überbleibsel *pl.*, Reste *pl.*; **2.** *a.* ***~ and stealings*** a) unehrliche Nebeneinkünfte *pl.*, b) Diebesbeute *f*, Fang *m*; **3.** Pro'fit *m.*
pick·le ['pɪkl] **I** *s.* **1.** Pökel *m*, Salzlake *f*, Essigsoße *f* (*zum Einlegen*); **2.** Essig-, Gewürzgurke *f*; **3.** *pl.* Eingepökelte(s) *n*, Pickles *pl.*; → ***mixed pickles***; **4.** ⚙ Beize *f*; **5.** F *a.* ***nice*** (*od.* ***sad*** *od.* ***sorry***) ***~*** mißliche Lage, ‚böse Sache': ***be in a ~*** (schön) in der Patsche sitzen; **6.** F Balg *m, n*, Gör *n*; **II** *v/t.* **7.** einpökeln, -salzen, -legen; **8.** ⚙ *Metall* (ab)beizen; *Bleche* dekapieren: ***pickling agent*** Abbeizmittel *n*; **9.** ⚘ *Saatgut* beizen; **'pick·led** [-ld] *adj.* **1.** gepökelt, eingesalzen; Essig..., Salz...: ***~ herring*** Salzhering *m*; **2.** *sl.* ‚blau' (*betrunken*).
'pick|·lock *s.* **1.** Einbrecher *m*; **2.** Dietrich *m*; **'~-me-up** *s.* F Schnäps-chen *n*, *a. fig.* Stärkung *f*; **'~-off** *adj.* ⚙ *Am.* 'abmonˌtierbar, Wechsel...; **'~ˌpock·et** *s.* Taschendieb *m*; **'~·up** *s.* **1.** Ansteigen *n*; ✝ Erholung *f*: ***~*** (***in prices***) Anziehen *n* der Preise, Hausse *f*; **2.** *mot.* Start-, Beschleunigungsvermögen *n*; **3.** *a.* ***~ truck*** Kleinlastwagen; **4.** *Am.* → ***pick-me-up***; **5.** ⚙ Tonabnehmer *m*, Pick-up *m* (*am Plattenspieler*); Empfänger *m* (*Mikrophon*); Geber *m* (*Meßgerät*); **6.** *TV*: a) Abtasten *n*, b) Abtastgerät *n*, c) *a. Radio*: 'Aufnahme- und Über'tragungsapparaˌtur *f*; **7.** ϟ a) Schalldose *f*, b) Ansprechen *n* (*Relais*); **8.** F a) Zufallsbekanntschaft *f*, b) ‚Flittchen' *n*, c) ‚Anhalter' *m*; **9.** *mst* ***~ dinner*** *sl.* improvisierte Mahlzeit, Essen *n* aus (Fleisch)Resten; **10.** *sl.* a) Verhaftung *f*, b) Verhaftete(r *m*) *f*; **11.** *sl.* Fund *m.*
pick·y ['pɪkɪ] *adj.* F wählerisch.
pic·nic ['pɪknɪk] **I** *s.* **1.** a) Picknick *n*, b) Ausflug *m*; **2.** F a) (reines) Vergnügen, b) Kinderspiel *n*: ***no ~*** keine leichte Sache, kein Honiglecken; **II** *v/i.* **3.** ein Picknick *etc.* machen; picknicken.
pic·to·gram ['pɪktəʊgræm] Pikto'gramm *n.*
pic·to·ri·al [pɪk'tɔːrɪəl] **I** *adj.* □ **1.** malerisch, Maler...: ***~ art*** Malerei; **2.** Bild(er)..., illustriert: ***~ advertising*** Bildwerbung; **3.** *fig.* bildmäßig (*a. phot.*), -haft; **II** *s.* **4.** Illustrierte *f* (*Zeitung*).
pic·ture ['pɪktʃə] **I** *s.* **1.** *allg., a. TV* Bild *n*: (***clinical***) ***~*** ⚕ Krankheitsbild, Befund *m*; **2.** Abbildung *f*, Illustrati'on *f*, Bild *n*; **3.** Gemälde *n*, Bild *n*: ***sit for one's ~*** sich malen lassen; **4.** (geistiges) Bild, Vorstellung *f*: ***form a ~ of s.th.*** sich von et. ein Bild machen; **5.** *fig.* F Bild *n*, Verkörperung *f*: ***he looks the very ~ of health*** er sieht aus wie das blühende Leben; ***be the ~ of misery*** ein Bild des Jammers sein; **6.** Ebenbild *n*: ***the child is the ~ of his father***; **7.** *fig.* anschauliche Darstellung *od.* Schilderung (*in Worten*), Bild *n*; **8.** F bildschöne Sache *od.* Per'son: ***she is a perfect ~*** sie ist bildschön; ***the hat is a ~*** der Hut ist ein Gedicht; **9.** *fig.* F Blickfeld *n*: ***be in the ~*** a) sichtbar sein, e-e Rolle spielen, b) im Bilde (*informiert*) sein; ***come into the ~*** in Erscheinung treten; ***put s.o. in the ~*** j-n ins Bild setzen; ***quite out of the ~*** gar nicht von Interesse, ohne Belang; **10.** *phot.* Aufnahme *f*, Bild *n*; **11.** a) Film *m*, Streifen *m*, b) *pl.* F Kino *n*, Film *m* (*Filmvorführung od. Filmwelt*): ***go to the ~s*** *Brit.* ins Kino gehen; **II** *v/t.* **12.** abbilden, darstellen, malen; **13.** *fig.* anschaulich schildern, beschreiben, ausmalen; **14.**

a. ~ ***to o.s.*** *fig.* sich ein Bild machen von, sich *et.* ausmalen *od.* vorstellen; **15.** *s-e Empfindung etc.* spiegeln, zeigen; **III** *adj.* **16.** Bild..., Bilder...; **17.** Film...: ~ ***play*** Filmdrama *n*; ~ **book** *s.* Bilderbuch *n*; ~ **card** *s. Kartenspiel*: Fi'gurenkarte *f*, Bild *n*; ~ **ed·i·tor** *s.* 'Bildredakˌteur *m*; '~ˌ**go·er** *s. Brit.* Kinobesucher(in); ~ **post·card** *s.* Ansichtskarte *f*; ~ **puz·zle** *s.* **1.** Vexierbild *n*; **2.** Bilderrätsel *n*.

pic·tur·esque [ˌpɪktʃə'resk] *adj.* □ malerisch (*a. fig.*).

pic·ture| te·leg·ra·phy *s.* 'Bildtelegraˌphie *f*; ~ **the·a·ter** *Am.*, ~ **the·a·tre** *Brit. s.* 'Filmtheˌater *n*, Lichtspielhaus *n*, Kino *n*; ~ **trans·mis·sion** *s.* 'Bildüberˌtragung *f*, Bildfunk *m*; ~ **tube** *s. TV* Bildröhre *f*; ~ **writ·ing** *s.* Bilderschrift *f*.

pic·tur·ize ['pɪktʃəraɪz] *v/t.* **1.** *Am.* verfilmen; **2.** bebildern.

pid·dle ['pɪdl] *v/i.* **1.** (*v/t.* ver)trödeln; **2.** F ‚Pi'pi machen', ‚pinkeln'; '**pid·dling** [-lɪŋ] *adj.* ‚lumpig'.

pidg·in ['pɪdʒɪn] *s.* **1.** *sl.* Angelegenheit *f*: ***that is your*** ~ das ist deine Sache; **2.** ~ ***English*** Pidgin-Englisch *n* (*Verkehrssprache zwischen Europäern u. Ostasiaten*); *weitS.* Kauderwelsch *n*.

pie¹ [paɪ] *s.* **1.** *orn.* Elster *f*; **2.** *zo.* Scheck(e) *m* (*Pferd*).

pie² [paɪ] *s.* **1.** ('Fleisch-, 'Obst- *etc.*)Paˌstete *f*, Pie *f*: ~ ***in the sky*** F a) ein ‚schöner Traum', b) leere Versprechung(en); ***a share in the*** ~ ✝ F ein ‚Stück vom Kuchen'; ~***-flinging*** ‚Tortenschlacht' *f*; ***it's*** (***as easy as***) ~ *sl.* es ist kinderleicht; → ***finger*** 1; ***humble*** I; **2.** (Obst)Torte *f*; **3.** *pol. Am. sl.* Protekti'on *f*, Bestechung *f*: ~ ***counter*** ‚Futterkrippe' *f*; **4.** F *e-e* feine Sache, *ein* ‚gefundenes Fressen'.

pie³ [paɪ] **I** *s.* **1.** *typ.* Zwiebelfisch(e *pl.*) *m*; **2.** *fig.* Durchein'ander *n*; **II** *v/t.* **3.** *typ. Satz* zs.-werfen; **4.** *fig.* durchein'anderbringen.

pie·bald ['paɪbɔːld] **I** *adj.* scheckig, bunt; **II** *s.* scheckiges Tier; Schecke *m, f* (*Pferd*).

piece [piːs] **I** *s.* **1.** Stück *n*: ***a*** ~ ***of land*** ein Stück Land; ***a*** ~ ***of furniture*** ein Möbel(stück) *n*; ***a*** ~ ***of wallpaper*** e-e Rolle Tapete; ***a*** ~ je, das Stück (*im Preis*); ***by the*** ~ a) stückweise *verkaufen*, b) im Akkord *od.* Stücklohn *arbeiten od. bezahlen*; ***in*** ~***s*** entzwei, ‚kaputt'; ***of a*** ~ gleichmäßig; ***all of a*** ~ aus 'einem Guß; ***be all of a*** ~ ***with*** ganz passen zu; ***break*** (*od.* ***fall***) ***to*** ~***s*** entzweigehen, zerbrechen; ***go to*** ~***s*** a) in Stücke gehen (*a. fig.*), b) *fig.* zs.-brechen (*Person*); ***take to*** ~***s*** auseinandernehmen, zerlegen; → ***pick*** 12, ***pull*** 16; **2.** *fig.* Beispiel *n*, Fall *m*, *mst* ein(e): ***a*** ~ ***of advice*** ein Rat(schlag) *m*; ***a*** ~ ***of folly*** e-e Dummheit; ***a*** ~ ***of news*** e-e Neuigkeit; → ***mind*** 4; **3.** Teil *m* (*e-s Service etc.*): ***two-***~ ***set*** zweiteiliger Satz; **4.** (Geld)Stück *n*, Münze *f*; **5.** ⚔ Geschütz *n*; Gewehr *n*; **6.** a) *a.* ~ ***of work*** Arbeit *f*, Stück *n*: ***a nasty*** ~ ***of work*** *fig.* F ein ‚fieser' Kerl, b) *paint.* Stück *n*, Gemälde *n*, c) *thea.* (Bühnen-)Stück *n*, d) ♪ (Mu'sik)Stück *n*, e) (kleines) *literarisches* Werk; **7.** ('Spiel)Fiˌgur *f*, Stein *m*; *Schach*: Offi'zier *m*, Figur *f*: ***minor*** ~***s*** leichtere Figuren (*Läufer u. Springer*); **8.** F a) Stück *n* Wegs, kurze Entfernung, b) Weilchen *n*; **9.** V *a.* ~ ***of ass*** a) ‚heiße Biene', b) ‚Nummer' *f* (*Koitus*); **II** *v/t.* **10.** *a.* ~ ***up*** flicken, ausbessern, zs.-stücken; **11.** verlängern, anstücken, -setzen (***on to*** an *acc.*); **12.** *oft* ~ ***together*** zs.-setzen, -stücke(l)n (*a. fig.*); **13.** ver'vollständigen, ergänzen; ~ **goods** *pl.* ✝ Meter-, Schnittware *f*; '~**·meal** *adv. u. adj.* stückchenweise, all'mählich; ~ **rate** *s.* Ak'kordsatz *m*; ~ **wag·es** *s. pl.* Ak'kord-, Stücklohn *m*; '~**·work** *s.* Ak'kordarbeit *f*; '~ˌ**work·er** *s.* Ak'kordarbeiter(in).

pièce de ré·sis·tance [pjˌesdərezɪ'stɑ̃ːŋs] (*Fr.*) *s.* **1.** Hauptgericht *n*; **2.** *fig.* Glanzstück *n*, Krönung *f*.

pie| chart *s. Statistik*: 'Kreisdiaˌgramm *n*; '~**·crust** *s.* Pa'stetenkruste *f*, ungefüllte Pa'stete.

pied¹ [paɪd] *adj.* gescheckt, buntscheckig: ♀ ***Piper*** (***of Hamelin***) *der* Rattenfänger von Hameln.

pied² [paɪd] *pret. u. p.p. von* ***pie³*** II.

'**pie|-eyed** *adj. Am. sl.* ‚blau', ‚besoffen'; '~**·plant** *s. Am.* Rha'barber *m*.

pier [pɪə] *s.* **1.** Pier *m, f* (*feste Landungsbrücke*); **2.** Kai *m*; **3.** Mole *f*, Hafendamm *m*; (Brücken- *od.* Tor- *od.* Stütz-)Pfeiler *m*; **pier·age** ['pɪərɪdʒ] *s.* Kaigeld *n*.

pierce [pɪəs] **I** *v/t.* **1.** durch'bohren, -'dringen, -'stechen, -'stoßen; ⚙ lochen; ⚔ durch'brechen, -'stoßen, eindringen in (*acc.*); **2.** *fig.* durch'dringen (*Kälte, Schrei, Schmerz etc.*): ***to*** ~ ***s.o.'s heart*** j-m ins Herz schneiden; **3.** *fig.* durch'schauen, ergründen, eindringen in *Geheimnisse etc.*; **II** *v/i.* **4.** (ein)dringen (***into*** in *acc.*) (*a. fig.*); dringen (***through*** durch); '**pierc·ing** [-sɪŋ] *adj.* □ 'durchdringend, scharf, schneidend, stechend (*a. Kälte, Blick, Schmerz*); gellend (*Schrei*).

pier| glass *s.* Pfeilerspiegel *m*; '~**·head** *s.* Molenkopf *m*.

pi·er·rot ['pɪərəʊ] *s.* Pier'rot *m*, Hans'wurst *m*.

pi·e·tism ['paɪətɪzəm] *s.* **1.** Pie'tismus *m*; **2.** → ***piety*** 1; **3.** *contp.* Frömme'lei *f*; '**pi·e·tist** [-ɪst] *s.* **1.** Pie'tist(in); **2.** *contp.* Frömmler(in).

pi·e·ty ['paɪətɪ] *s.* **1.** Frömmigkeit *f*; **2.** Pie'tät *f*, Ehrfurcht *f* (***to*** vor *dat.*).

pi·e·zo·e·lec·tric [paɪˌiːzəʊɪ'lektrɪk] *adj. phys.* pi'ezoeˌlektrisch.

pif·fle ['pɪfl] F **I** *v/i.* Quatsch reden *od.* machen; **II** *s.* Quatsch *m*.

pig [pɪg] **I** *pl.* **pigs** *od. coll.* **pig** *s.* **1.** Ferkel *n*: ***sow in*** ~ trächtiges Mutterschwein; ***sucking*** ~ Spanferkel; ***buy a*** ~ ***in a poke*** *fig.* die Katze im Sack kaufen; ~***s might fly*** *iron.* ‚man hat schon Pferde kotzen sehen'; ***in a*** (*od.* ***the***) ~***'s eye!*** *Am. sl.* Quatsch!, ‚von wegen'!; **2.** *fig. contp.* a) ‚Freßsack' *m*, b) ‚Ekel' *n*, c) sturer Kerl, d) gieriger Kerl; **3.** *sl.* ‚Bulle' *m* (*Polizist*); **4.** ⚙ a) Massel *f*, (Roheisen)Barren *m*, b) Roheisen *n*, c) Block *m*, Mulde *f* (*bsd. Blei*); **II** *v/i.* **5.** ferkeln, frischen; **6.** *mst* ~ ***it*** F ‚aufein'anderhocken', eng zs.-hausen.

pi·geon ['pɪdʒɪn] *s.* **1.** *pl.* **-geons** *od. coll.* **-geon** Taube *f*: ***that's not my*** ~ F a) das ist nicht mein Fall, b) das ist nicht mein ‚Bier'; **2.** *sl.* ‚Gimpel' *m*; **3.** → ***clay pigeon***; ~ **breast** *s.* ⚕ Hühnerbrust *f*; '~**·hole I** *s.* **1.** (Ablege-, Schub-)Fach *n*; **2.** Taubenloch *n*; **II** *v/t.* **3.** in ein Schubfach legen, einordnen, *Akten* ablegen; **4.** *fig.* zu'rückstellen, zu den Akten legen, auf die lange Bank schieben, die Erledigung *e-r Sache* verschleppen; **5.** *fig. Tatsachen, Wissen* (ein)ordnen, klassifizieren; **6.** mit Fächern versehen; ~ **house**, ~ **loft** *s.* Taubenschlag *m*; '~**-ˌliv·ered** *adj.* feige.

pi·geon·ry ['pɪdʒɪnrɪ] *s.* Taubenschlag *m*.

pig·ger·y ['pɪgərɪ] *s.* **1.** Schweinezucht *f*; **2.** Schweinestall *m*; **3.** *fig. contp.* Saustall *m*; **pig·gish** ['pɪgɪʃ] *adj.* **1.** schweinisch, unflätig; **2.** gierig; **3.** dickköpfig; **pig·gy** ['pɪgɪ] **I** *s.* F **1.** Schweinchen *n*: ~ ***bank*** Sparschwein(chen); **2.** *Am.* Zehe *f*; **II** *adj.* **3.** → ***piggish***; '**pig·gy·back** → ***pick-a-back***.

ˌ**pig|'head·ed** *adj.* □ dickköpfig, stur; ~ **i·ron** *s.* Massel-, Roheisen *n*; ~ **Lat·in** *s. e-e Kindergeheimsprache*.

pig·let ['pɪglɪt] *s.* Ferkel *n*.

pig·ment ['pɪgmənt] **I** *s.* **1.** *a. biol.* Pig'ment *n*; **2.** Farbe *f*, Farbstoff *m*, -körper *m*; **II** *v/t. u. v/i.* **3.** (sich) pigmentieren, (sich) färben; '**pig·men·tar·y** [-tərɪ], *a.* **pig·men·tal** [pɪg'mentl] *adj.* Pigment...; **pig·men·ta·tion** [ˌpɪgmən'teɪʃn] *s.* **1.** *biol.* Pigmentati'on *f*, Färbung *f*; **2.** ⚕ Pigmentierung *f*.

pig·my ['pɪgmɪ] → ***pygmy***.

'**pig|·nut** *s.* ⚘ 'Erdkaˌstanie *f*, -nuß *f*; '~**·skin** *s.* **1.** Schweinehaut *f*; **2.** Schweinsleder *n*; '~ˌ**stick·ing** *s.* **1.** Wildschweinjagd *f*, Sauhatz *f*; **2.** Schweineschlachten *n*; '~**·sty** [-staɪ] *s.* Schweinestall *m* (*a. fig.*); '~**·tail** *s.* **1.** Zopf *m*; **2.** Rolle *f* ('Kau)ˌTabak.

pi-jaw ['paɪdʒɔː] *s. Brit. sl.* Mo'ralpredigt *f*, Standpauke *f*.

pike¹ [paɪk] *pl.* **pikes** *od. bsd. coll.* **pike** *s.* **1.** *ichth.* Hecht *m*; **2.** *Sport*: Hechtsprung *m*.

pike² [paɪk] *s.* **1.** ⚔ *hist.* Pike *f*, (Lang-)Spieß *m*; **2.** (Speer- *etc.*)Spitze *f*, Stachel *m*; **3.** a) Schlagbaum *m* (*Mautstraße*), b) Maut *f*, Straßenbenutzungsgebühr *f*, c) Mautstraße *f*, gebührenpflichtige Straße; **4.** *Brit. dial.* Bergspitze *f*.

'**pike·man** [-mən] *s.* [*irr.*] **1.** ⚒ Hauer *m*; **2.** Mauteinnehmer *m*; **3.** ⚔ *hist.* Pike'nier *m*.

pik·er ['paɪkə] *s. Am. sl.* **1.** Geizhals *m*; **2.** vorsichtiger Spieler.

'**pike·staff** *s.*: ***as plain as a*** ~ sonnenklar.

pi·las·ter [pɪ'læstə] *s.* ⚠ Pi'laster *m*, (*viereckiger*) Stützpfeiler.

pil·chard ['pɪltʃəd] *s.* Sar'dine *f*.

pile¹ [paɪl] **I** *s.* **1.** Haufen *m*, Stoß *m*, Stapel *m* (*Akten, Holz etc.*): ***a*** ~ ***of arms*** e-e Gewehrpyramide; **2.** Scheiterhaufen *m*; **3.** großes Gebäude, Ge'bäudekomˌplex *m*; **4.** F ‚Haufen' *m*, ‚Masse' *f* (*bsd. Geld*): ***make a*** (*od.* ***one's***) ~ e-e Menge Geld machen, ein Vermögen verdienen; ***make a*** ~ ***of money*** e-e Stange Geld verdienen; **5.** ⚡ a) (gal'vanische *etc.*) Säule: ***thermoelectrical*** ~ Thermosäule, b) Batte'rie *f*; **6.** *a.* ***atomic*** ~ (A'tom)Meiler *m*,

Re'aktor *m*; **7.** *metall.* 'Schweiß(eisen)pa'ket *n*; **8.** *Am. sl.* ‚Schlitten' *m* (*Auto*); **9.** → ***piles***; **II** *v/t.* **10.** *a.* ~ ***up*** (*od.* ***on***) (an-, auf)häufen, (auf)stapeln, aufschichten: ~ ***arms*** ⚔ Gewehre zs.-setzen; **11.** aufspeichern (*a. fig.*); **12.** über'häufen, -'laden (*a. fig.*): ~ ***a table with food***; ~ ***up*** (*od.* ***on***) ***the agony*** F Schrecken auf Schrecken häufen; ~ ***it on*** F dick auftragen; **13.** ~ ***up*** F a) ⚓ *Schiff* auflaufen lassen, b) ✈ mit *dem Flugzeug* ‚Bruch machen', c) *mot. sein Auto* ka'puttfahren; **III** *v/i.* **14.** *mst* ~ ***up*** sich (auf- *od.* an)häufen, sich ansammeln *od.* stapeln (*a. fig.*); **15.** F sich (scharenweise) drängen (***into*** in *acc.*); **16.** ~ ***up*** a) ⚓ auffahren, b) ✈ ‚Bruch machen', c) *mot.* aufein'anderprallen.

pile² [paɪl] **I** *s.* **1.** ⚙ (Stütz)Pfahl *m*, Pfeiler *m*; Bock *m*, Joch *n e-r Brücke*; **2.** *her.* Spitzpfahl *m*; **II** *v/t.* **3.** auspfählen, unter'pfählen, durch Pfähle verstärken; **4.** (hin'ein)treiben *od.* (ein)rammen in (*acc.*).

pile³ [paɪl] **I** *s.* **1.** Flaum *m*; **2.** (Woll-)Haar *n*, Pelz *m* (*des Fells*); **3.** *Weberei*: a) Samt *m*, Ve'lours *n*, b) Flor *m*, Pol *m* (*e-s Gewebes*); **II** *adj.* **4.** …fach gewebt (*Teppich etc.*): ***a three-~ carpet***.

pile| bridge (Pfahl)Jochbrücke *f*; ~ **driv·er** *s.* ⚙ **1.** (Pfahl)Ramme *f*; **2.** Rammklotz *m*; ~ **dwell·ing** *s.* Pfahlbau *m*; ~ **fab·ric** *s.* Samtstoff *m*; *pl.* Polgewebe *pl.*

piles [paɪlz] *s. pl.* ⚕ Hämorrho'iden *pl.*

'pile·up *s. mot.* 'Massenkarambo,lage *f.*

pil·fer ['pɪlfə] *v/t. u. v/i.* stehlen, sti'bitzen; **'pil·fer·age** [-ərɪdʒ] *s.* Diebe'rei *f*; **'pil·fer·er** [-ərə] *s.* Dieb(in).

pil·grim ['pɪlgrɪm] *s.* **1.** Pilger(in), Wallfahrer(in); **2.** *fig.* Pilger *m*, Wanderer *m*; **3.** 2 (*pl. a.* ***2 Fathers***) *hist.* Pilgervater *m*; **'pil·grim·age** [-mɪdʒ] **I** *s.* **1.** Pilger-, Wallfahrt *f* (*a. fig.*); **2.** *fig.* lange Reise; **II** *v/i.* **3.** pilgern, wallfahren.

pill [pɪl] **I** *s.* **1.** Pille *f* (*a. fig.*), Ta'blette *f*: ***swallow the ~*** die bittere Pille schlukken, in den sauren Apfel beißen; → ***gild²*** 2; **2.** *sl.* ‚Brechmittel' *n*, ‚Ekel' *n* (*Person*); **3.** *sport sl.* Ball *m*; *Brit. a.* Billard *n*; **4.** ⚔ *sl. od. humor.* ‚blaue Bohne' (*Gewehrkugel*), ‚Ei' *n*, ‚Koffer' *m* (*Granate, Bombe*); **5.** *sl.* ‚Stäbchen' *n* (*Zigarette*); **6.** ***the ~*** die (Anti'baby-)Pille: ***be on the ~*** die Pille nehmen; **II** *v/t.* **7.** *sl. bei e-r Wahl* durchfallen lassen.

pil·lage ['pɪlɪdʒ] **I** *v/t.* **1.** (aus)plündern; **2.** rauben, erbeuten; **II** *v/i.* **3.** plündern; **III** *s.* **4.** Plünderung *f*, Plündern *n*; **5.** Beute *f.*

pil·lar ['pɪlə] **I** *s.* **1.** Pfeiler *m*, Ständer *m* (*a. Reitsport*): ***a ~ of coal*** ⚒ Kohlenpfeiler; ***run from ~ to post*** *fig.* von Pontius zu Pilatus laufen; **2.** △ (*a. weitS.* Luft-, Rauch- *etc.*)Säule *f*; **3.** *fig.* Säule *f*, (Haupt)Stütze *f*: ***the ~s of society*** (***wisdom***) die Säulen der Gesellschaft (der Weisheit); ***he was a ~ of strength*** er stand da wie ein Fels in der Brandung; **4.** ⚙ Stütze *f*, Sup'port *m*, Sockel *m*; **II** *v/t.* **5.** mit Pfeilern *od.* Säulen stützen *od.* schmücken; **'~·box** *s. Brit.* Briefkasten *m* (in Säulenform).

pil·lared ['pɪləd] *adj.* **1.** mit Säulen *od.* Pfeilern (versehen); **2.** säulenförmig.

'pill·box *s.* **1.** Pillenschachtel *f*; **2.** ⚔ *sl.* Bunker *m*, 'Unterstand *m.*

pil·lion ['pɪljən] *s.* **1.** leichter (Damen-)Sattel; **2.** Sattelkissen *n*; **3.** *a.* ~ ***seat*** *mot.* Soziussitz *m*: ***ride ~*** auf dem Soziussitz (mit)fahren; ~ **rid·er** *s.* Soziusfahrer(in).

pil·lo·ry ['pɪlərɪ] **I** *s.* (***in the ~*** am) Pranger *m* (*a. fig.*); **II** *v/t.* an den Pranger stellen; *fig.* anprangern.

pil·low ['pɪləʊ] **I** *s.* **1.** (Kopf)Kissen *n*, Polster *n*: ***take counsel of one's ~*** *fig. die* Sache beschlafen; **2.** ⚙ (Zapfen)Lager *n*, Pfanne *f*; **II** *v/t.* **3.** (auf ein Kissen) betten, stützen (***on*** auf *acc.*): ~ ***up*** hoch betten; **'~·case** *s.* (Kopf)Kissenbezug *m*; ~ **fight** *s.* Kissenschlacht *f*; **'~·lace** *s.* Klöppel-, Kissenspitzen *pl.*; ~ **slip** → ***pillowcase***.

pi·lose ['paɪləʊs] *adj.* 🌿, *zo.* behaart.

pi·lot ['paɪlət] **I** *s.* **1.** ⚓ Lotse *m*: ***drop the ~*** *fig.* den Lotsen von Bord schikken; **2.** ✈ Flugzeug-, Bal'lonführer *m*, Pi'lot *m*: ***~'s licence*** Flug-, Pilotenschein *m*; ***second ~*** Kopilot *m*; **3.** *fig.* a) Führer *m*, Wegweiser *m*, b) Berater *m*; **4.** ⚙ a) Be'tätigungsele,ment *n*, b) Führungszapfen *m*; **5.** → a) ***pilot program***(***me***), b) ***pilot film***; **II** *v/t.* **6.** ⚓ lotsen (*a. mot. u. fig.*), steuern: ~ ***through*** durchlotsen (*a. fig.*); **7.** ✈ steuern, fliegen; **8.** *bsd. fig.* führen, lenken, leiten; **III** *adj.* **9.** Versuchs…, Pilot…; **10.** Hilfs-…: ~ ***parachute***; **11.** Steuer…, Kontroll…, Leit…: ~ ***relay*** Steuer-, Kontrollrelais *n*; **'pi·lot·age** [-tɪdʒ] *s.* **1.** ⚓ Lotsen(kunst *f*) *n*: ***certificate of ~*** Lotsenpatent *n*; **2.** Lotsengeld *n*; **3.** ✈ a) Flugkunst *f*, b) 'Bodennavigati,on *f*; **4.** *fig.* Leitung *f*, Führung *f.*

pi·lot| bal·loon *s.* ✈ Pi'lotbal,lon *m*; ~ **boat** *s.* Lotsenboot *n*; ~ **burn·er** *s.* ⚙ Sparbrenner *m*; ~ **cloth** *s.* dunkelblauer Fries; ~ **en·gine** *s.* 🚂 'Leerfahrtlokomo,tive *f*; ~ **film** *s.* Pi'lotfilm *m*; ~ **in·jec·tion** *s. mot.* Voreinspritzung *f*; ~ **in·struc·tor** *s.* ✈ Fluglehrer(in); ~ **jet** *s.* ⚙ Leerlaufdüse *f*; ~ **lamp** *s.* ⚙ Kon'trollampe *f.*

pi·lot·less ['paɪlətlɪs] *adj.* führerlos, unbemannt: ~ ***airplane***.

pi·lot| light *s.* **1.** → ***pilot burner***; **2.** → ***pilot lamp***; ~ **of·fi·cer** *s.* ⚔ Fliegerleutnant *m*; ~ **plant** *s.* **1.** Versuchsanlage *f*; **2.** Musterbetrieb *m*; ~ **pro·gram**(**me** *Brit.*) *s. Radio, TV*: Pi'lotsendung *f*; ~ **pro·ject** *s.*, ~ **scheme** *s.* Pi'lot-, Ver'suchspro,jekt *n*; ~ **stu·dy** *s.* Pi'lotstudie *f*; ~ **train·ee** *s.* Flugschüler (-in); ~ **valve** *s.* ⚙ 'Steuerven,til *n.*

pi·lous ['paɪləs] → ***pilose***.

pil·ule ['pɪlju:l] *s.* kleine Pille.

pi·men·to [pɪ'mentəʊ] *pl.* **-tos** *s.* 🌿 *bsd. Brit.* **1.** Pi'ment *m*, *n*, Nelkenpfeffer *m*; **2.** Pi'mentbaum *m.*

pimp [pɪmp] **I** *s.* a) Kuppler *m*, b) Zuhälter *m*; **II** *v/i.* Kuppler *od.* Zuhälter sein.

pim·per·nel ['pɪmpənel] *s.* 🌿 Pimper'nell *m.*

pim·ple ['pɪmpl] **I** *s.* Pustel *f*, (Haut)Pikkel *m*; **II** *v/i.* pickelig werden; **'pim·pled** [-ld], **'pim·ply** [-lɪ] *adj.* pickelig.

pin [pɪn] **I** *s.* **1.** (Steck)Nadel *f*: ***~s and needles*** ‚Kribbeln' (*in eingeschlafenen Gliedern*); ***sit on ~s and needles*** *fig.* wie auf Kohlen sitzen; ***I don't care a ~*** das ist mir völlig schnuppe; **2.** (Schmuck-, Haar-, Hut)Nadel *f*: ***scarf-~*** Krawattennadel; **3.** (Ansteck)Nadel *f*, Abzeichen *n*; **4.** ⚙ Pflock *m*, Dübel *m*, Bolzen *m*, Zapfen *m*, Stift *m*: ***split ~*** Splint *m*; ~ ***with thread*** Gewindezapfen *m*; ~ ***bearing*** Nadel-, Stiftlager *n*; **5.** ⚙ Dorn *m*; **6.** *a.* ***drawing ~*** *Brit.* Reißnagel *m*, -zwecke *f*; **7.** *a.* ***clothes-~*** Wäscheklammer *f*; **8.** *a.* ***rolling ~*** Nudel-, Wellholz *n*; **9.** F ‚Stelzen' *pl.* (*Beine*): ***that knocked him off his ~s*** das hat ihn ‚umgehauen'; **10.** ♪ Wirbel *m* (*Streichinstrument*); **11.** a) *Kegelsport*: Kegel *m*, b) *Bowling*: Pin *m*; **II** *v/t.* **12.** (an)heften, -stecken, befestigen (***to***, ***on*** an *acc.*): ~ ***up*** auf-, hochstecken; ~ ***one's faith on*** sein Vertrauen auf j-n setzen; ~ ***one's hopes on*** s-e (ganze) Hoffnung setzen auf (*acc.*); ~ ***a murder on s.o.*** F j-m e-n Mord ‚anhängen'; **13.** pressen, drücken, heften (***against***, ***to*** gegen, an *acc.*), festhalten; **14.** *a.* ~ ***down*** a) zu Boden pressen, b) *fig. j-n* festnageln (***to*** auf *ein Versprechen, e-e Aussage etc.*), c) ⚔ *Feindkräfte* fesseln (*a. Schach*), d) *et.* genau bestimmen *od.* definieren; **15.** ⚙ verbolzen, -dübeln, -stiften.

pin·a·fore ['pɪnəfɔ:] *s.* (Kinder)Lätzchen *n*, (-)Schürze *f.*

'pin|·ball ma·chine *s.* Flipper *m* (*Spielautomat*); ~ **bit** *s.* ⚙ Bohrspitze *f*; ~ **bolt** *s.* Federbolzen *m.*

pince-nez ['pæ:nsneɪ] (*Fr.*) *s.* Kneifer *m*, Klemmer *m.*

pin·cer ['pɪnsə] *adj.* Zangen…: ~ ***movement*** ⚔ Zangenbewegung *f*; **'pin·cers** [-əz] *s. pl.* **1.** (Kneif-, Beiß)Zange *f*: ***a pair of ~*** eine Kneifzange; **2.** ⚕, *typ.* Pin'zette *f*; **3.** *zo.* Krebsschere *f.*

pinch [pɪntʃ] **I** *v/t.* **1.** zwicken, kneifen, (ein)klemmen, quetschen: ~ ***off*** abkneifen; **2.** beengen, einengen, -zwängen; *fig.* (be)drücken, beengen, beschränken: ***be ~ed for time*** wenig Zeit haben; ***be ~ed*** in Bedrängnis sein, Not leiden, knapp sein (***for***, ***in***, ***of*** an *dat.*); ***be ~ed for money*** knapp bei Kasse sein; ***~ed circumstances*** beschränkte Verhältnisse; **3.** *fig.* quälen: ***be ~ed with hunger*** ausgehungert sein; ***a ~ed face*** ein spitzes *od.* abgehärmtes Gesicht; **4.** *sl. et.* ‚klauen' (*stehlen*); **5.** *sl. j-n* ‚schnappen' (*verhaften*); **II** *v/i.* **6.** drücken, kneifen, zwicken: ***~ing want*** drückende Not; → ***shoe*** 1; **7.** *fig. a.* ~ ***and scrape*** knausern, darben, sich nichts gönnen; **III** *s.* **8.** Kneifen *n*, Zwicken *n*; **9.** *fig.* Druck *m*, Qual *f*, Not(lage) *f*: ***at a ~*** im Notfall; ***if it comes to a ~*** wenn es zum Äußersten kommt; **10.** Prise *f* (*Tabak etc.*); **11.** Quentchen *n*, (kleines) bißchen: ***a ~ of butter***; ***with a ~ of salt*** *fig.* mit Vorbehalt; **12.** *sl.* Festnahme *f*, Verhaftung *f.*

pinch·beck ['pɪntʃbek] **I** *s.* **1.** Tombak *m*, Talmi *n* (*a. fig.*); **II** *adj.* **2.** Talmi… (*a. fig.*); **3.** unecht.

'pinch|·hit *v/i.* [*irr.* → ***hit***] *Am. Baseball u. fig.* einspringen (***for*** für); **'~·hit·ter** *s. Am.* Ersatz(mann) *m.*

'pinch,pen·ny I *adj.* knick(e)rig; **II** *s.* Knicker *m.*

'pin,cush·ion *s.* Nadelkissen *n.*

pine¹ [paɪn] *s.* **1.** 🌿 Kiefer *f*, Föhre *f*, Pinie *f*; **2.** Kiefernholz *n*; **3.** F Ananas *f.*

pine² [paɪn] *v/i.* **1.** sich sehnen,

schmachten (***after, for*** nach); **2.** *mst* ~ ***away*** verschmachten, vor Gram vergehen; **3.** sich grämen *od.* abhärmen (***at*** über *acc.*).
pin·e·al gland [ˈpɪnɪəl] *s. anat.* Zirbeldrüse *f.*
ˈpine|ˌap·ple *s.* **1.** ⚘ Ananas *f*; **2.** ⚔ *sl.* a) ˈHandgraˌnate *f*, b) (kleine) Bombe; ~ **cone** *s.* ⚘ Kiefernzapfen *m*; ~ **marten** *s. zo.* Baummarder *m*; ~ **nee·dle** *s.* ⚘ Fichtennadel *f*; ~ **oil** *s.* Kiefernöl *n.*
pine| tar *s.* Kienteer *m*; ~ **tree** → ***pine***[1] 1.
ping [pɪŋ] **I** *v/i.* **1.** pfeifen (*Kugel*), schwirren (*Mücke etc.*); *mot.* klingeln; **II** *s.* **2.** Peng *n*; **3.** Pfeifen *n*, Schwirren *n*; *mot.* Klingeln *n*; ˈ**~-pong** [-pɒŋ] *s.* Tischtennis *n.*
ˈpin|·head *s.* **1.** (Steck)Nadelkopf *m*; **2.** *fig.* Kleinigkeit *f*; **3.** F Dummkopf *m*; ˈ**~·hole** *s.* **1.** Nadelloch *n*; **2.** kleines Loch (*a. opt.*): ~ ***camera*** Lochkamera *f.*
pin·ion[1] [ˈpɪnjən] *s.* ⚙ **1.** Ritzel *n*, Antriebs(kegel)rad *n*: ***gear*** ~ Getriebezahnrad *n*; ~ ***drive*** Ritzelantrieb *m*; **2.** Kammwalze *f.*
pin·ion[2] [ˈpɪnjən] **I** *s.* **1.** *orn.* Flügelspitze *f*; **2.** *orn.* (Schwung)Feder *f*; **3.** *poet.* Schwinge *f*, Fittich *m*; **II** *v/t.* **4.** die Flügel stutzen (*dat.*) (*a. fig.*); **5.** fesseln (***to*** an *acc.*).
pink[1] [pɪŋk] **I** *s.* **1.** ⚘ Nelke *f*: ***plumed*** (*od.* ***feathered***) ~ Federnelke; **2.** Blaßrot *n*, Rosa *n*; **3.** *bsd. Brit.* (scharlach-) roter Jagdrock; **4.** *pol. Am. sl.* ‚rot Angehauchte(r)' *m*, Saˈlonbolscheˌwist *m*; **5.** *fig.* Gipfel *m*, Krone *f*, höchster Grad: ***in the*** ~ ***of health*** bei bester Gesundheit; ***the*** ~ ***of perfection*** die höchste Vollendung; ***be in the*** ~ (***of condition***) in ‚Hochform' sein; **II** *adj.* **6.** rosa(farben), blaßrot: ~ ***slip*** ‚blauer Brief', Kündigungsschreiben *n*; **7.** *pol. sl.* ‚rötlich', kommuˈnistisch angehaucht.
pink[2] [pɪŋk] *v/t.* **1.** *a.* ~ ***out*** auszacken: ~***ing shears*** *pl.* Zickzackschere *f*; **2.** durchˈbohren, -ˈstechen.
pink[3] [pɪŋk] *s.* ⚓ Pinke *f* (*Boot*).
pink[4] [pɪŋk] *v/i.* klopfen (*Motor*).
pink·ish [ˈpɪŋkɪʃ] *adj.* rötlich (*a. pol. sl.*), blaßrosa.
ˈpin-ˌmon·ey *s.* (*a.* selbstverdientes) Taschengeld (*der Frau*).
pin·na [ˈpɪnə] *pl.* **-nae** [-niː] *s.* **1.** *anat.* Ohrmuschel *f*; **2.** *zo.* a) Feder *f*, Flügel *m*, b) Flosse *f*; **3.** ⚘ Fieder(blatt *n*) *f.*
pin·nace [ˈpɪnɪs] *s.* ⚓ Piˈnasse *f.*
pin·na·cle [ˈpɪnəkl] *s.* **1.** ⩓ a) Spitzturm *m*, b) Zinne *f*; **2.** (Fels-, Berg)Spitze *f*, Gipfel *m*; **3.** *fig.* Gipfel *m*, Spitze *f*, Höhepunkt *m.*
pin·nate [ˈpɪnɪt] *adj.* gefiedert.
pin·ni·grade [ˈpɪnɪgreɪd], ˈ**pin·ni·ped** [-ped] *zo.* **I** *adj.* flossen-, schwimmfüßig; **II** *s.* Flossen-, Schwimmfüßer *m.*
pin·nule [ˈpɪnjuːl] *s.* **1.** Federchen *n*; **2.** *zo.* Flössel *n*; **3.** ⚘ Fiederblättchen *n.*
pin·ny [ˈpɪnɪ] F → ***pinafore.***
pi·noch·le, pi·noc·le [ˈpiːnʌkl] *s. Am.* Biˈnokel *n* (*Kartenspiel*).
ˈpin|·point **I** *v/t. Ziel* genau festlegen *od.* lokalisieren *od.* bombardieren; *fig. et.* genau bestimmen; **II** *adj.* genau, Punkt…: ~ ***bombing*** Bombenpunktwurf *m*; ~ ***strike*** ✝ Schwerpunktstreik *m*; ~ ***target*** Punktziel *n*; ˈ**~·prick** *s.* **1.** Nadelstich *m* (*a. fig.*): ***policy of*** **~*s*** Politik *f* der Nadelstiche; **2.** *fig.* Sticheˈlei *f*, spitze Bemerkung; ˈ**~-striped** *adj.* mit Nadelstreifen (*Anzug*).
pint [paɪnt] *s.* **1.** Pinte *f* (*Brit. 0,57*, *Am. 0,47 Liter*); **2.** F Halbe *f* (Bier); ˈ**pint-size(d)** *adj.* F winzig.
pin·tle [ˈpɪntl] *s.* **1.** ⚙ (Dreh)Bolzen *m*; **2.** *mot.* Düsennadel *f*, -zapfen *m*; **3.** ⚓ Fingerling *m*, Ruderhaken *m.*
pin·to [ˈpɪntəʊ] *Am. pl.* **-tos** *s.* Scheck(e) *m*, Schecke *f* (*Pferd*).
ˈpin-up (girl) *s.* Pin-ˈup-Girl *n.*
pi·o·neer [ˌpaɪəˈnɪə] **I** *s.* **1.** ⚔ Pioˈnier *m*; **2.** *fig.* Pioˈnier *m*, Bahnbrecher *m*, Vorkämpfer *m*, Wegbereiter *m*; **II** *v/i.* **3.** *fig.* den Weg bahnen, bahnbrechende Arbeit leisten; **III** *v/t.* **4.** den Weg bahnen für (*a. fig.*); **IV.** *adj.* **5.** Pionier…: ~ ***work***; **6.** *fig.* bahnbrechend, wegbereitend, Versuchs…, erst.
pi·ous [ˈpaɪəs] *adj.* □ **1.** fromm (*a. iro.*), gottesfürchtig: ~ ***fraud*** (***wish***) *fig.* frommer Betrug (Wunsch); ~ ***effort*** F gutgemeinter Versuch; **2.** lieb (*Kind*).
pip[1] [pɪp] *s.* **1.** *vet.* Pips *m* (*Geflügelkrankheit*); **2.** *Brit.* F miese Laune: ***he gives me the*** ~ er geht mir auf den ‚Wecker'.
pip[2] [pɪp] *s.* **1.** Auge *n* (*auf Spielkarten*), Punkt *m* (*auf Würfeln etc.*); **2.** (Obst-) Kern *m*; **3.** ⚔ *bsd. Brit. sl.* Stern *m* (*Rangabzeichen*); **4.** *Radar*: Blip *m* (*Bildspur*); **5.** *Brit. Radio*: Ton *m* (*Zeitzeichen*).
pip[3] [pɪp] *Brit.* F **I** *v/t.* **1.** ˈdurchfallen lassen (*bei e-r Wahl etc.*); **2.** *fig.* knapp besiegen, im Ziel abfangen; **3.** ‚abknallen' (*erschießen*); **II** *v/i.* **4.** *a.* ~ ***out*** ‚abkratzen' (*sterben*).
pipe [paɪp] **I** *s.* **1.** ⚙ a) Rohr *n*, Röhre *f*, b) (Rohr)Leitung *f*; **2.** (Tabaks)Pfeife *f*: ***put that in your*** ~ ***and smoke it*** F laß dir das gesagt sein; **3.** ♪ Pfeife *f* (*Flöte*); Orgelpfeife *f*; (ˈHolz)Blasinstruˌment *n*; *mst pl.* Dudelsack *m*; **4.** a) Pfeifen *n* (*e-s Vogels*), Piep(s)en *n*, b) Pfeifenton *m*, c) Stimme *f*; **5.** F Luftröhre *f*: ***clear one's*** ~ sich räuspern; **6.** *metall.* Lunker *m*; **7.** ⚒ (Wetter)Lutte *f*; **8.** ✝ Pipe *f* (*Weinfaß = Brit. 477,3, Am. 397,4 Liter*); **II** *v/t.* **9.** (durch Röhren, *weitS.* durch Kabel) leiten, *weitS. a.* schleusen, *a. e-e Radiosendung* überˈtragen: **~*d music*** Musik *f* aus dem Lautsprecher, Musikberieselung *f*; **10.** Röhren *od.* e-e Rohrleitung legen in (*acc.*); **11.** pfeifen, flöten; *Lied* anstimmen, singen; **12.** quieken, piepsen; **13.** ⚓ *Mannschaft* zs.-pfeifen; **14.** *Schneiderei*: paspelieren, mit Biesen besetzen; **15.** *Torte etc.* mit feinem Guß verzieren, spritzen; **16.** ~ ***one's eye*** F ‚flennen', weinen; **III** *v/i.* **17.** pfeifen (*a. Wind etc.*), flöten; piep(s)en: ~ ***down*** *sl.* ‚die Luft anhalten', ‚die Klappe halten'; ~ ***up*** loslegen, anfangen; ~ **bowl** *s.* Pfeifenkopf *m*; ~ **burst** *s.* Rohrbruch *m*; ~ **clamp** *s.* ⚙ Rohrschelle *f*; ˈ**~·clay** **I** *s.* **1.** *min.* Pfeifenton *m*; **2.** ⚔ *fig.* ‚Komˈmiß' *m*; **II** *v/t.* **3.** mit Pfeifenton weißen; ~ **clip** *s.* ⚙ Rohrschelle *f*; ~ **dream** *s.* F Luftschloß *n*, Hirngespinst *n*; ~ **fit·ter** *s.* ⚙ Rohrleger *m*; ˈ**~·line** *s.* **1.** Rohrleitung *f*; *für Erdöl, Erdgas*: Pipeline *f*: ***in the*** ~ *fig.* in Vorbereitung (*Pläne etc.*), im Kommen (*Entwicklung etc.*); **2.** *fig.* ‚Draht' *m*, (geheime) Verbindung *od.* (Informatiˈons)Quelle; **3.** (*bsd.* Verˈsorgungs)Syˌstem *n.*
pip·er [ˈpaɪpə] *s.* Pfeifer *m*: ***pay the*** ~ *fig.* die Zeche bezahlen, *weitS.* der Dumme sein.
pipe| rack *s.* Pfeifenständer *m*; ~ **tongs** *s. pl.* ⚙ Rohrzange *f.*
pi·pette [pɪˈpet] *s.* ⚗ Piˈpette *f.*
pipe wrench *s.* ⚙ Rohrzange *f.*
pip·ing [ˈpaɪpɪŋ] **I** *s.* **1.** ⚙ a) Rohrleitung *f*, -netz *n*, Röhrenwerk *n*, b) Rohrverlegung *f*; **2.** *metall.* a) Lunker *m*, b) Lunkerbildung *f*; **3.** Pfeifen *n*, Piep(s)en *n*; Pfiff *m*; **4.** *Schneiderei*: Paspel *f*, (*an Uniformen*) Biese *f*; **5.** (feiner) Zuckerguß, Verzierung *f* (*Kuchen*); **II** *adj.* **6.** pfeifend, schrill; **7.** friedlich, iˈdyllisch (*Zeit*); **III** *adv.* **8.** ~ ***hot*** siedend heiß, *fig.* ‚brühwarm'.
pip·pin [ˈpɪpɪn] *s.* **1.** Pippinapfel *m*; **2.** *sl.* a) ‚tolle Sache', b) ‚toller Kerl'.
ˈpip·squeak *s.* F ‚Grashüpfer' *m*, ‚Würstchen' *n* (*Person*).
pi·quan·cy [ˈpiːkənsɪ] *s.* Piˈkantheit *f*, *das* Piˈkante; ˈ**pi·quant** [-nt] *adj.* □ piˈkant (*a. fig.*).
pique [piːk] **I** *v/t.* **1.** (auf)reizen, sticheln, ärgern, *j-s Stolz etc.* verletzen: ***be*** **~*d at*** über *et.* pikiert *od.* verärgert sein; **2.** *Neugier etc.* reizen, wecken; **3.** ~ ***o.s.*** (***on***) sich et. einbilden (auf *acc.*), sich brüsten (mit); **II** *s.* **4.** Groll *m*; Gereiztheit *f*, Gekränktsein *n*, Ärger *m.*
pi·qué [ˈpiːkeɪ] *s.* Piˈkee *m* (*Gewebe*).
pi·quet [pɪˈket] *s.* Piˈkett *n* (*Kartenspiel*).
pi·ra·cy [ˈpaɪərəsɪ] *s.* **1.** Pirateˈrie *f*, Seeräubeˈrei *f*; **2.** Plagiˈat *n*, *bsd.* a) Raubdruck *m*, b) Raubpressung *f* (*e-r Schallplatte f*); **3.** Paˈtentverletzung *f*; **pi·rate** [ˈpaɪərət] **I** *s.* **1.** a) Piˈrat *m*, Seeräuber *m*, b) Seeräuberschiff *n*; **2.** Plagiˈator *m*, *bsd.* a) Raubdrucker *m*, b) Raubpresser *m* (*von Schallplatten*); **II** *adj.* **3.** Piraten…: ~ ***ship***; **4.** ⚖ Raub…: ~ ***record***; ~ ***edition*** Raubdruck *m*; **5.** Schwarz…: ~ ***listener***; ~ (***radio***) ***station*** Piˈraten-, Schwarzsender *m*; **III** *v/t.* **6.** kapern, (aus)plündern (*a. weitS.*); **7.** plagiieren, *bsd.* unerlaubt nachdrukken; **pi·rat·i·cal** [paɪˈrætɪkl] *adj.* □ **1.** (see)räuberisch, Piraten…; **2.** ~ ***edition*** Raubdruck *m.*
pir·ou·ette [ˌpɪrʊˈet] **I** *s. Tanz etc.*: Pirouˈette *f*; **II** *v/i.* pirouettieren.
Pis·ces [ˈpɪsiːz] *s. pl. ast.* **1.** Fische *pl.*; **2.** *Person*: *ein* Fisch *m.*
pis·ci·cul·ture [ˈpɪsɪkʌltʃə] *s.* Fischzucht *f*; **pis·ci·cul·tur·ist** [ˌpɪsɪˈkʌltʃərɪst] *s.* Fischzüchter *m.*
pish [pɪʃ] *int.* **1.** pfui!; **2.** pah!
pi·si·form [ˈpaɪsɪfɔːm] *adj.* erbsenförmig, Erbsen…
piss [pɪs] *sl.* **I** *v/i.* ‚pissen', ‚pinkeln': ~ ***on s.th.*** *fig.* ‚auf et. scheißen'; ~ ***off!*** hau ab!; **II** *v/t.* ‚be-, anpissen': ~ ***the bed*** ins Bett pinkeln; **III** *s.* ‚Pisse' *f*; **pissed** [-st] *adj. sl.* **1.** ‚blau', besoffen; **2.** ~ ***off*** ‚(stock)sauer'.
pis·tach·i·o [pɪˈstɑːʃɪəʊ] *pl.* **-i·os** *s.* ⚘ Piˈstazie *f.*
pis·til [ˈpɪstɪl] *s.* ⚘ Piˈstill *n*, Stempel *m*, Griffel *m*; ˈ**pis·til·late** [-lət] *adj.* mit Stempel(n), weiblich (*Blüte*).
pis·tol [ˈpɪstl] *s.* Piˈstole *f* (*a. phys.*):

hold a ~ to s.o.'s head *fig.* j-m die Pistole auf die Brust setzen; **~ point** *s.*: ***at ~*** mit vorgehaltener Pistole; **~ shot** *s.* **1.** Piˈstolenschuß *m*; **2.** *Am.* Piˈstolenschütze *m*.

pis·ton [ˈpɪstən] *s.* **1.** ⚙ Kolben *m*: **~ *engine*** Kolbenmotor *m*; **2.** ⚙ (Druck-)Stempel *m*; **~ dis·place·ment** *s.* Kolbenverdrängung *f*, Hubraum *m*; **~ rod** *s.* Kolben-, Pleuelstange *f*; **~ stroke** *s.* Kolbenhub *m*.

pit¹ [pɪt] **I** *s.* **1.** Grube *f* (*a. anat.*): ***refuse ~*** Müllgrube; ***~ of the stomach*** Magengrube; **2.** Abgrund *m* (*a. fig.*): (***bottomless***) **~**, **~** (***of hell***) (Abgrund der) Hölle *f*, Höllenschlund *m*; **3.** ⚒ a) (*bsd.* Kohlen)Grube *f*, Zeche *f*, b) (*bsd.* Kohlen)Schacht *m*; **4.** 🌾 (Rüben- *etc.*)Miete *f*; **5.** ⚙ a) *Gießerei*: Dammgrube *f*, b) Abstichherd *m*, Schlackengrube *f*; **6.** *thea.* a) *bsd. Brit.* Parˈkett *n*, b) Orˈchestergraben *m*; **7.** *mot. Sport*: Box *f*: **~ *stop*** Boxenstopp *m*; **8.** † *Am.* Börse *f*, Maklerstand *m*: ***grain ~*** Getreidebörse; **9.** ⚕ (Blattern-, Pokken)Narbe *f*; **10.** ⚙ Rostgrübchen *n*; **II** *v/t.* **11.** Löcher *od.* Vertiefungen bilden in (*dat.*) *od.* graben in (*acc.*); ⚙ an-, zerfressen (*Korrosion*); ⚕ mit Narben bedecken: ***~ted with smallpox*** pokkennarbig; **12.** 🌾 *Rüben etc.* einmieten; **13.** (***against***) a) *feindlich* gegenˈüberstellen (*dat.*), b) *j-n* ausspielen (gegen), c) *s-e Kraft etc.* messen (mit), *Argument* ins Feld führen (gegen); **III** *v/i.* **14.** Löcher *od.* Vertiefungen bilden; ⚕ narbig werden; ⚙ sich festfressen (*Kolben*).

pit² [pɪt] *Am.* **I** *s.* (Obst)Stein *m*; **II** *v/t.* entsteinen.

pit-a-pat [ˌpɪtəˈpæt] **I** *adv.* ticktack (*Herz*); klippklapp (*Schritte*); **II** *s.* Getrappel *n*, Getrippel *n*.

pitch¹ [pɪtʃ] **I** *s.* Pech *n*; **II** *v/t.* (ver)pichen, teeren (*a.* ⚓).

pitch² [pɪtʃ] **I** *s.* **1.** Wurf *m* (*a. sport*): ***queer s.o.'s ~*** F j-m ‚die Tour vermasseln', j-m e-n Strich durch die Rechnung machen; ***what's the ~?*** *Am. sl.* was ist los?; **2.** † (Waren)Angebot *n*; **3.** ⚓ Stampfen *n*; **4.** Neigung *f*, Gefälle *n* (*Dach etc.*); **5.** ⚙ a) Teilung *f* (*Gewinde, Zahnrad*), b) Schränkung *f* (*Säge*), c) Steigung *f* (*Luftschraube* ✈); **6.** ♪ a) Tonhöhe *f*, b) (*absolute*) Stimmung *e-s Instruments*, c) Norˈmalstimmung *f*, Kammerton *m*: ***above ~*** zu hoch; ***have absolute ~*** das absolute Gehör haben; ***sing true to ~*** tonrein singen; **7.** Grad *m*, Stufe *f*, Höhe *f* (*a. fig.*); *fig.* höchster Grad, Gipfel *m*: ***to the highest ~*** aufs äußerste; **8.** † a) Stand *m e-s Händlers*, b) *sl.* Anpreisung *f*, Verkaufsgespräch *n*, c) *sl.* ‚Platte' *f*, ‚Masche' *f*; **9.** *sport Brit.* Spielfeld *n*; *Kricket*: (Mittel)Feld *n*; **II** *v/t.* **10.** (*gezielt*) werfen (*a. sport*), schleudern; *Golf*: *den Ball* heben (*hoch schlagen*); **11.** *Heu etc.* aufladen, -gabeln; **12.** *Pfosten etc.* einrammen, befestigen; *Zelt, Verkaufsstand etc.* aufschlagen; *Leiter, Stadt etc.* anlegen; **13.** ♪ a) *Instrument* stimmen, b) *Grundton* angeben, c) *Lied etc. in e-r Tonart* anstimmen *od.* singen *od.* spielen: ***high-~ed voice*** hohe Stimme; ***~ one's hopes too high*** *fig.* s-e Hoffnungen zu hoch stecken; ***~ a yarn*** *fig.* ein Garn spinnen; **14.** *fig. Rede etc.* abstimmen (***on*** auf *acc.*), *et.* ausdrücken; **15.** *Straße* beschottern, *Böschung* verpacken; **16.** *Brit. Ware* ausstellen, feilhalten; **17.** ⚔ ***~ed battle*** regelrechte *od.* offene (Feld)Schlacht; **III** *v/i.* **18.** (kopfˈüber) hinstürzen, -schlagen; **19.** ⚔ (sich) lagern; **20.** † e-n (Verkaufs-)Stand aufschlagen; **21.** ⚓ stampfen (*Schiff*); *fig.* taumeln; **22.** sich neigen (*Dach etc.*); **23.** ***~ in*** F a) sich (tüchtig) ins Zeug legen, loslegen, b) tüchtig ‚zulangen' (*essen*); **24.** ***~ into*** F a) herfallen über *j-n* (*a. fig.*), b) herfallen über *das Essen*, c) sich (mit Schwung) an *die Arbeit* machen; **25.** ***~ on***, ***~ upon*** sich entscheiden für, verfallen auf (*acc.*); **ˌ~-and-ˈtoss** *s.* ‚Kopf oder Schrift' (*Spiel*); **~ an·gle** *s.* ⚙ Steigungswinkel *m*; **ˌ~-ˈblack** *adj.* pechschwarz; **ˈ~-blende** [-blend] *s. min.* (Uˈran)Pechblende *f*; **~ cir·cle** *s.* ⚙ Teilkreis *m* (*Zahnrad*); **ˌ~-ˈdark** *adj.* pechschwarz, stockdunkel (*Nacht*).

pitch·er¹ [ˈpɪtʃə] *s. sport* Werfer *m*.

pitch·er² [ˈpɪtʃə] *s.* (irdener) Krug (*mit Henkel*).

ˈpitch|·fork I *s.* **1.** 🌾 Heu-, Mistgabel *f*; **2.** ♪ Stimmgabel *f*; **II** *v/t.* **3.** mit der Heugabel werfen; **4.** *fig.* rücksichtslos werfen: ***~ troops into a battle***; **5.** ‚schubsen' (***into*** in *ein Amt etc.*); **~ pine** *s.* ⚘ Pechkiefer *f*; **~ pipe** *s.* ♪ Stimmpfeife *f*.

pitch·y [ˈpɪtʃɪ] *adj.* **1.** pechartig; **2.** voll Pech; **3.** pechschwarz (*a. fig.*).

pit coal *s.* Schwarz-, Steinkohle *f*.

pit·e·ous [ˈpɪtɪəs] → ***pitiable*** 1.

ˈpit·fall *s.* Fallgrube *f*, Falle *f*, *fig. a.* Fallstrick *m*.

pith [pɪθ] *s.* **1.** ⚘, *anat.* Mark *n*; **2.** *a.* ***~ and marrow*** *fig.* Mark *n*, Kern *m*, ˈQuintesˌsenz *f*; **3.** *fig.* Kraft *f*, Präˈgnanz *f* (*e-r Rede etc.*); **4.** *fig.* Gewicht *n*, Bedeutung *f*.

ˈpit·head *s.* ⚒ **1.** Füllort *m*, Schachtöffnung *f*; **2.** Fördergerüst *n*.

pith·e·can·thro·pus [ˌpɪθɪkænˈθrəʊpəs] *s.* Javamensch *m*.

pith| hat, **~ hel·met** *s.* Tropenhelm *m*.

pith·i·ness [ˈpɪθɪnɪs] *s.* **1.** *das* Markige, Markigkeit *f*; **2.** *fig.* Kernigkeit *f*, Präˈgnanz *f*, Kraft *f*; **pith·less** [ˈpɪθlɪs] *adj.* marklos; *fig.* kraftlos, schwach; **pith·y** [ˈpɪθɪ] *adj.* □ **1.** mark(art)ig; **2.** *fig.* markig, kernig, präˈgnant.

pit·i·a·ble [ˈpɪtɪəbl] *adj.* □ **1.** mitleiderregend, bedauernswert; *a. contp.* erbärmlich, jämmerlich, elend, kläglich; **2.** *contp.* armselig, dürftig; **ˈpit·i·ful** [-fʊl] *adj.* □ **1.** mitleidig, mitleidsvoll; **2.** → ***pitiable***; **ˈpit·i·less** [-lɪs] *adj.* □ **1.** unbarmherzig; **2.** erbarmungslos, mitleidlos.

ˈpit|·man [-mən] *s.* [*irr.*] Bergmann *m*, Knappe *m*, Grubenarbeiter *m*; **~ prop** *s.* ⚒ (Gruben)Stempel *m*; *pl.* Grubenholz *n*; **~ saw** *s.* ⚙ Schrot-, Längensäge *f*.

pit·tance [ˈpɪtəns] *s.* **1.** Hungerlohn *m*, ‚paar Pfennige' *pl.*; **2.** (kleines) bißchen: ***the small ~ of learning*** das kümmerliche Wissen.

pit·ting [ˈpɪtɪŋ] *s. metall.* Körnung *f*, Lochfraß *m*, ˈGrübchenkorrosiˌon *f*.

pi·tu·i·tar·y [pɪˈtjʊɪtərɪ] *physiol.* **I** *adj.* pituiˈtär, schleimabsondernd, Schleim…; **II** *s. a.* ***~ gland*** Hirnanhang(drüse *f*) *m*, Hypoˈphyse *f*.

pit·y [ˈpɪtɪ] **I** *s.* **1.** Mitleid *n*, Erbarmen *n*: ***feel ~ for***, ***have*** (*od.* ***take***) ***~ on*** Mitleid haben mit; ***for ~'s sake!*** um Himmels willen!; **2.** Jammer *m*: ***it is a*** (***great***) ***~*** es ist (sehr) schade; ***what a ~!*** wie schade!; ***it is a thousand pities*** es ist jammerschade; ***the ~ of it is that*** es ist ein Jammer, daß; **II** *v/t.* **3.** bemitleiden, bedauern, Mitleid haben mit: ***I ~ him*** er tut mir leid; **pit·y·ing** [ˈpɪtɪɪŋ] *adj.* □ mitleidig.

piv·ot [ˈpɪvət] **I** *s.* **1.** a) (Dreh)Punkt *m*, b) (Dreh)Zapfen *m*: **~ *bearing*** Zapfenlager, c) Stift *m*, d) Spindel *f*; **2.** (Tür-)Angel *f*; **3.** ⚔ stehender Flügel(mann), Schwenkungspunkt *m*; **4.** *fig.* a) Dreh-, Angelpunkt *m*, b) → ***pivot man***, c) *Fußball*: ˈSchaltstatiˌon *f* (*Spieler*); **II** *v/t.* **5.** ⚙ a) mit Zapfen *etc.* versehen, b) drehbar lagern, c) (ein)schwenken; **III** *v/i.* **6.** sich drehen (***upon***, ***on*** um) (*a. fig.*); ⚔ schwenken; **ˈpiv·ot·al** [-tl] *adj.* **1.** Zapfen…, Angel…: **~ *point*** Angelpunkt *m*; **2.** *fig.* zenˈtral, Kardinal…: ***a ~ question***.

piv·ot| bolt *s.* Drehbolzen *m*; **~ bridge** *s.* Drehbrücke *f*; **~ man** [-mən] *s.* [*irr.*] *fig.* ˈSchlüsselfiˌgur *f*; **ˈ~-ˌmount·ed** *adj.* schwenkbar; **~ tooth** *s.* ⚕ Stiftzahn *m*.

pix·el [ˈpɪksəl] *s. TV*, *Computer*: Bild(schirm)punkt *m*.

pix·ie → ***pixy***.

pix·i·lat·ed [ˈpɪksɪleɪtɪd] *adj. Am.* F **1.** ‚verdreht', leicht verrückt; **2.** ‚blau' (*betrunken*).

pix·y [ˈpɪksɪ] *s.* Fee *f*, Elf *m*, Kobold *m*.

piz·zle [ˈpɪzl] *s.* **1.** *zo.* Fiesel *m*; **2.** Ochsenziemer *m*.

pla·ca·ble [ˈplækəbl] *adj.* □ versöhnlich, nachgiebig.

plac·ard [ˈplækɑːd] **I** *s.* **1.** a) Plaˈkat *n*, b) Transpaˈrent *n*; **II** *v/t.* **2.** mit Plaˈkaten bekleben; **3.** durch Plaˈkate bekanntgeben, anschlagen.

pla·cate [pləˈkeɪt] *v/t.* beschwichtigen, besänftigen, versöhnlich stimmen.

place [pleɪs] **I** *s.* **1.** Ort *m*, Stelle *f*, Platz *m*: ***from ~ to ~*** von Ort zu Ort; ***in ~*** am Platze (*a. fig. angebracht*); ***in ~s*** stellenweise; ***in ~ of*** an Stelle (*gen.*), anstatt (*gen.*); ***out of ~*** *fig.* fehl am Platz, unangebracht; ***take ~*** stattfinden; ***take s.o.'s ~*** j-s Stelle einnehmen; ***take the ~ of*** ersetzen, an die Stelle treten von; ***if I were in your ~*** an Ihrer Stelle (*würde ich …*); ***put yourself in my ~*** versetzen Sie sich in meine Lage; **2.** Ort *m*, Stätte *f*: ***~ of amusement*** Vergnügungsstätte; ***~ of birth*** Geburtsort; ***~ of business*** † Geschäftssitz *m*; ***~ of delivery*** † Erfüllungsort; ***~ of worship*** Gotteshaus *n*, Kultstätte *f*; ***from this ~*** † ab hier; ***in*** (*od.* ***of***) ***your ~*** † dort; ***go ~s*** *Am.* a) ‚groß ausgehen', b) die Sehenswürdigkeiten *e-s Ortes* ansehen, c) *fig.* es weit bringen (*im Leben*); **3.** Wohnsitz *m*; F Wohnung *f*, Haus *n*: ***at his ~*** bei ihm (zu Hause); **4.** Wohnort *m*; Ort(schaft *f*) *m*, Stadt *f*, Dorf *n*: ***in this ~*** hier; **5.** ⚓ Platz *m*, Hafen *m*: ***~ for tran(s)shipment*** Umschlagplatz; **6.** ⚔ Festung *f*; **7.** F Gaststätte *f*, Loˈkal *n*; **8.** (Sitz)Platz *m*; **9.** *fig.* Platz *m* (*in e-r Reihenfolge*; *a. sport*), Stelle *f* (*a.*

in e-m Buch): ***in the first ~*** a) an erster Stelle, erstens, b) zuerst, von vornherein, c) in erster Linie, d) überhaupt (erst); ***in third ~*** *sport* auf dem dritten Platz; **10.** ⩚ (Dezi'mal)Stelle *f*; **11.** Raum *m* (*a. fig., a. für Zweifel etc.*); **12.** *thea.* Ort *m* (der Handlung); **13.** (An)Stellung *f*, (Arbeits)Stelle *f*: ***out of ~*** stellenlos; **14.** Dienst *m*, Amt *n*: ***it is not my ~*** *fig.* es ist nicht meines Amtes; **15.** (sozi'ale) Stellung, Rang *m*, Stand *m*: ***keep s.o. in his ~*** j-n in s-n Schranken *od.* Grenzen halten; ***know one's ~*** wissen, wohin man gehört; ***put s.o. in his ~*** j-n in s-e Schranken weisen; **16.** *univ.* (Studien)Platz *m*; **II** *v/t.* **17.** stellen, setzen, legen (*a. fig.*); *teleph. Gespräch* anmelden; → ***disposal*** 3; **18.** ⚔ *Posten* aufstellen, (***o.s.*** sich) postieren; **19.** *j-n* an-, einstellen; ernennen, in ein Amt einsetzen; **20.** *j-n* 'unterbringen (*a. Kind*), *j-m* Arbeit *od.* e-e Anstellung verschaffen; **21.** ✝ *Anleihe, Kapital* 'unterbringen; *Auftrag* erteilen *od.* vergeben; *Bestellung* aufgeben; *Vertrag* abschließen; → ***account*** 5, ***credit*** 1; **22.** ✝ *Ware* absetzen; **23.** (der Lage nach) näher bestimmen; *fig. j-n* ,'unterbringen' (*identifizieren*): ***I can't ~ him*** ich weiß nicht, wo ich ihn ,unterbringen' *od.* ,hintun' soll; **24.** *sport* plazieren: ***be ~d*** unter den ersten drei sein, sich plazieren; **~ bet** *s. Rennsport*: Platzwette *f*.

pla·ce·bo [plə'si:bəʊ] *pl.* **-bos** *s.* **1.** ⚕ Pla'cebo *n*, 'Blindpräpa,rat *n*; **2.** *fig.* Beruhigungspille *f*.

place| card *s.* Platz-, Tischkarte *f*; **~ hunt·er** *s.* Pöstchenjäger *m*; **~ hunt·ing** *s.* Pöstchenjäge'rei *f*; **~ kick** *s. sport* a) *Fußball*: Stoß *m* auf den ruhenden Ball (*Freistoß etc.*), b) *Rugby*: Platztritt *m*; **'~·man** [-mən] *s.* [*irr.*] *pol. contp.* ,Pöstcheninhaber' *m*, ,'Futterkrippenpo,litiker' *m*; **~ mat** *s.* Set *n*, Platzdeckchen *n*.

place·ment ['pleɪsmənt] *s.* **1.** (Hin-, Auf)Stellen *n*, Plazieren *n*; **2.** a) Einstellung *f e-s Arbeitnehmers*, b) Vermittlung *f e-s Arbeitsplatzes*, c) 'Unterbringung *f von Arbeitskräften, Waisen*; **3.** Stellung *f*, Lage *f*; Anordnung *f*; **4.** ✝ a) Anlage *f*, Unterbringung *f von Kapital*, b) Vergabe *f von Aufträgen*; **5.** *ped. Am.* Einstufung *f*.

place name *s.* Ortsname *m*.

pla·cen·ta [plə'sentə] *pl.* **-tae** [-ti:] *s.* **1.** *anat.* Pla'zenta *f*, Mutterkuchen *m*; **2.** ⚘ Samenleiste *f*.

plac·er ['plæsə] *s. min.* **1.** *bsd. Am.* (*Gold- etc.*)Seife *f*; **2.** seifengold- *od.* erzseifenhaltige Stelle; **'~-gold** *s.* Seifen-, Waschgold *n*; **'~-,min·ing** *s.* Goldwaschen *n*.

pla·cet ['pleɪset] (*Lat.*) *s.* Plazet *n*, Zustimmung *f*, Ja *n*.

plac·id ['plæsɪd] *adj.* □ **1.** (seelen)ruhig, ,gemütlich'; **2.** mild, sanft; **3.** selbstgefällig; **pla·cid·i·ty** [plæ'sɪdətɪ] *s.* Milde *f*, Gelassenheit *f*, (Seelen)Ruhe *f*.

plack·et ['plækɪt] *s. Mode*: a) Schlitz *m an Frauenkleid*, b) Tasche *f*.

pla·gi·a·rism ['pleɪdʒjərɪzəm] *s.* Plagi'at *n*; **'pla·gi·a·rist** [-ɪst] *s.* Plagi'ator *m*; **'pla·gi·a·rize** [-raɪz] **I** *v/t.* plagiieren, abschreiben; **II** *v/i.* ein Plagi'at begehen.

plague [pleɪg] **I** *s.* **1.** ⚕ Seuche *f*, Pest *f*: ***avoid like the ~*** *fig.* wie die Pest meiden; **2.** *bsd. fig.* Plage *f*, Heimsuchung *f*, Geißel *f*: ***the ten ~s*** *bibl.* die Zehn Plagen; ***a ~ on it!*** zum Henker damit!; **3.** *fig.* F a) Plage *f*, b) Quälgeist *m* (*Mensch*); **II** *v/t.* **4.** plagen, quälen; **5.** F belästigen, peinigen; **6.** *fig.* heimsuchen; **~ spot** *s. mst fig.* Pestbeule *f*.

plaice [pleɪs] *pl. coll.* **plaice** *s. ichth.* Scholle *f*.

plaid [plæd] **I** *s.* schottisches Plaid(tuch); **II** *adj.* 'buntka,riert.

plain [pleɪn] **I** *adj.* □ **1.** einfach, schlicht: ***~ clothes*** Zivil(kleidung *f*) *n*; ***~-clothes man*** Kriminalbeamte(r) *m od.* Polizist in Zivil; ***~ cooking*** bürgerliche Küche; ***~ fare*** Hausmannskost *f*; ***~ paper*** unliniertes Papier; ***~ postcard*** gewöhnliche Postkarte; **2.** schlicht, schmucklos, kahl (*Zimmer etc.*); ungemustert, einfarbig (*Stoff*): ***~ knitting*** Rechts-, Glattstrickerei *f*; ***~ sewing*** Weißnäherei *f*; **3.** unscheinbar, reizlos, hausbacken (*Gesicht, Mädchen etc.*); **4.** klar, leicht verständlich: ***in ~ language*** *tel.* im Klartext (*a. fig.*), offen; **5.** klar, offenbar, -kundig (*Irrtum etc.*); **6.** klar (und deutlich), 'unmißverständlich, 'unum,wunden: ***~ talk***; ***the ~ truth*** die nackte Wahrheit; **7.** offen, ehrlich: ***~ dealing*** ehrliche Handlungsweise; **8.** pur, unverdünnt (*Getränk*); *fig.* bar, rein (*Unsinn etc.*): ***~ folly*** heller Wahnsinn; **9.** *bsd. Am.* flach; ⚙ glatt: ***~ country*** *Am.* Flachland *n*; ***~ roll*** ⚙ Glattwalze *f*; ***~ bearing*** Gleitlager *n*; ***~ fit*** ⚙ Schlichtsitz *m*; *fig.* → ***sailing*** 1; **10.** ohne Filter (*Zigarette*); **II** *adv.* **11.** klar, deutlich; **III** *s.* **12.** Ebene *f*, Fläche *f*; Flachland *n*; *pl. bsd. Am.* Prä'rie *f*; **'plain·ness** [-nɪs] *s.* **1.** Einfachheit *f*, Schlichtheit *f*; **2.** Deutlichkeit *f*, Klarheit *f*; **3.** Offenheit *f*, Ehrlichkeit *f*; **4.** Reizlosigkeit *f* (*e-r Frau etc.*); **,plain-'spo·ken** *adj.* offen, freimütig: ***he is a ~ man*** er nimmt (sich) kein Blatt vor den Mund.

plaint [pleɪnt] *s.* **1.** Beschwerde *f*, Klage *f*; **2.** ⚖ (An)Klage(schrift) *f*; **'plain·tiff** [-tɪf] *s.* ⚖ (Zi'vil)Kläger(in): ***party ~*** klagende Partei; **'plain·tive** [-tɪv] *adj.* □ traurig, kläglich; wehleidig (*Stimme*); Klage...: ***~ song.***

plait [plæt] **I** *s.* **1.** Zopf *m*, Flechte *f*; (Haar-, Stroh)Geflecht *n*; **2.** Falte *f*; **II** *v/t.* **3.** *Haar, Matte etc.* flechten; **4.** verflechten.

plan [plæn] **I** *s.* **1.** (Spiel-, Wirtschafts-, Arbeits)Plan *m*, Entwurf *m*, Pro'jekt *n*, Vorhaben *n*: ***~ of action*** Schlachtplan (*a. fig.*); ***according to ~*** planmäßig; ***make ~s (for the future)*** (Zukunfts-) Pläne schmieden; **2.** (Lage-, Stadt-) Plan *m*: ***general ~*** Übersichtsplan; **3.** ⚙ (Grund)Riß *m*: ***~ view*** Draufsicht; **II** *v/t.* **4.** planen, entwerfen, e-n Plan entwerfen für *od.* zu: ***~ ahead*** (*a. v/i.*) vorausplanen; ***~ning board*** Planungsamt *n*; **5.** *fig.* planen, beabsichtigen.

plane¹ [pleɪn] *s.* ⚘ Pla'tane *f*.

plane² [pleɪn] **I** *adj.* **1.** flach, eben; ⚙ plan; **2.** ⩚ eben: ***~ figure***; ***~ curve*** einfach gekrümmte Kurve; **II** *s.* **3.** Ebene *f*, (ebene) Fläche: ***~ of refraction*** *phys.* Brechungsebene; ***on the upward ~*** *fig.* im Anstieg; **4.** *fig.* Ebene *f*, Stufe *f*, Ni'veau *n*, Bereich *m*: ***on the same ~ as*** auf dem gleichen Niveau wie; **5.** ⚙ Hobel *m*; **6.** ⚒ Förderstrecke *f*; **7.** ✈ a) Tragfläche *f*: ***elevating (depressing) ~s*** Höhen-(Flächen)steuer *n*, b) Flugzeug *n*; **III** *v/t.* **8.** (ein)ebnen, planieren, ⚙ *a.* schlichten, *Bleche* abrichten; **9.** (ab)hobeln; **10.** *typ.* bestoßen; **IV.** *v/i.* **11.** ✈ gleiten; fliegen; **'plan·er** [-nə] *s.* **1.** ⚙ 'Hobel(ma,schine *f*) *m*; **2.** *typ.* Klopfholz *n*.

plane sail·ing *s.* ⚓ Plansegeln *n*.

plan·et ['plænɪt] *s. ast.* Pla'net *m*.

'plane-,ta·ble *s. surv.* Meßtisch *m*: ***~ map*** Meßtischblatt *n*.

plan·e·tar·i·um [,plænɪ'teərɪəm] *s.* Plane'tarium *n*; **plan·e·tar·y** ['plænɪtərɪ] *adj.* **1.** *ast.* plane'tarisch, Planeten...; **2.** *fig.* um'herirrend; **3.** ⚙ Planeten...: ***~ gear*** Planetengetriebe *n*; ***~ wheel*** Umlaufrad *n*; **plan·et·oid** ['plænɪtɔɪd] *s. ast.* Planeto'id *m*.

'plane-tree → ***plane¹***.

pla·nim·e·ter [plæ'nɪmɪtə] *s.* ⚙ Plani'meter *n*, Flächenmesser *m*; **pla'nim·e·try** [-trɪ] *s.* Planime'trie *f*.

plan·ish ['plænɪʃ] ⚙ *v/t.* **1.** glätten, (ab-) schlichten, planieren; **2.** *Holz* glatthobeln; **3.** *Metall* glatthämmern; polieren.

plank [plæŋk] **I** *s.* **1.** (*a.* Schiffs)Planke *f*, Bohle *f*, (Fußboden)Diele *f*, Brett *n*: ***~ flooring*** Bohlenbelag *m*; ***walk the ~*** a) ⚓ *hist.* ertränkt werden, b) *fig. pol. etc.* ,abgeschossen' werden; **2.** *pol. bsd. Am.* (Pro'gramm)Punkt *m e-r Partei*; **3.** ⚒ Schwarte *f*; **II** *v/t.* **4.** mit Planken *etc.* belegen, beplanken, dielen; **5.** verschalen, ⚒ verzimmern; **6.** *Speise* auf e-m Brett servieren; **7.** ***~ down*** (*od.* ***out***) F *Geld* auf den Tisch legen, hinlegen, ,blechen'; **~ bed** *s.* (Holz)Pritsche *f* (*im Gefängnis etc.*).

plank·ing ['plæŋkɪŋ] *s.* Beplankung *f*, (Holz)Verschalung *f*, Bohlenbelag *m*; *coll.* Planken *pl.*

plank·ton ['plæŋktən] *s. zo.* Plankton *n*.

plan·less ['plænlɪs] *adj.* planlos; **'plan·ning** [-nɪŋ] *s.* **1.** Planen *n*, Planung *f*; **2.** ✝ Bewirtschaftung *f*, Planwirtschaft *f*.

pla·no-con·cave [,pleɪnəʊ'kɒnkeɪv] *adj. phys.* 'plan-kon,kav (*Linse*).

plant [plɑ:nt] **I** *s.* **1.** a) Pflanze *f*, Gewächs *n*, b) Setz-, Steckling *m*: ***in ~*** im Wachstum befindlich; **2.** ⚙ (Betriebs-, Fa'brik)Anlage *f*, Werk *n*, Fa'brik *f*, (Fabrikati'ons)Betrieb *m*: ***~ engineer*** Betriebsingenieur *m*; **3.** ⚙ (Ma'schinen)Anlage *f*, Aggre'gat *n*; Appara'tur *f*; **4.** (Be'triebs)Materi,al *n*, Betriebseinrichtung *f*, Inven'tar *n*: ***~ equipment*** Werksausrüstung *f*; **5.** *sl.* a) *et.* Eingeschmuggeltes, Schwindel *m*, (*a.* Poli'zei)Falle *f*, b) (Poli'zei)Spitzel *m*; **II** *v/t.* **6.** (ein-, an)pflanzen: ***~ out*** aus-, um-, verpflanzen; **7.** *Land* a) bepflanzen, b) besiedeln, kolonisieren; **8.** *Kolonisten* ansiedeln; **9.** *Garten etc.* anlegen; *et.* errichten; *Kolonie etc.* gründen; **10.** *fig.* (***o.s.*** sich) *wo* aufpflanzen, (auf-) stellen, postieren; **11.** *Faust, Fuß wohin* setzen, ,pflanzen'; **12.** *fig. Ideen etc.* (ein)pflanzen, einimpfen; **13.** *sl. Schlag* ,landen', ,verpassen'; *Schuß* setzen, knallen; **14.** *Spitzel* einschleusen; **15.** *sl. Belastendes etc.* (ein)schmuggeln, ,deponieren': ***~ s.th. on*** *j-m et.*

'unterschieben'; **16.** *j-n* im Stich lassen.

plan·tain¹ ['plæntɪn] *s.* ♀ Wegerich *m.*

plan·tain² ['plæntɪn] *s.* ♀ **1.** Pi'sang *m*; **2.** Ba'nane *f* (*Frucht*).

plan·ta·tion [plæn'teɪʃn] *s.* **1.** Pflanzung *f* (*a. fig.*), Plan'tage *f*; **2.** (Wald)Schonung *f*; **3.** *hist.* Ansiedlung *f*, Kolo'nie *f.*

plant·er ['plɑːntə] *s.* **1.** Pflanzer *m*, Plan'tagenbesitzer *m*; **2.** *hist.* Siedler *m*; **3.** 'Pflanzmaˌschine *f.*

plan·ti·grade ['plæntɪɡreɪd] *zo.* **I** *adj.* auf den Fußsohlen gehend; **II** *s.* Sohlengänger *m* (*Bär etc.*).

plant louse *s.* [*irr.*] *zo.* Blattlaus *f.*

plaque [plɑːk] *s.* **1.** (Schmuck)Platte *f*; **2.** A'graffe *f*, (Ordens)Schnalle *f*, Spange *f*; **3.** Gedenktafel *f*; **4.** (Namens-) Schild *n*; **5.** ⚕ Fleck *m*: ***dental ~*** Zahnbelag *m.*

plash¹ [plæʃ] *v/t. u. v/i.* (Zweige) zu e-r Hecke verflechten.

plash² [plæʃ] **I** *v/i.* **1.** platschen, plätschern (*Wasser*); *im Wasser* planschen; **II** *v/t.* **2.** platschen *od.* klatschen auf (*acc.*): ***~!*** platsch!; **III** *s.* **3.** Platschen *n*, Plätschern *n*, Spritzen *n*; **4.** Pfütze *f*, Lache *f*; **'plash·y** [-ʃɪ] *adj.* **1.** plätschernd, klatschend, spritzend; **2.** voller Pfützen, matschig, feucht.

plasm ['plæzəm], **'plas·ma** [-zmə] *s.* **1.** *biol.* ('Milch-, 'Blut-, 'Muskel)ˌPlasma *n*; **2.** *biol.* Proto'plasma *n*; **3.** *min.*, *phys.* 'Plasma *n*; **plas·mat·ic** [plæz'mætɪk], **'plas·mic** [-zmɪk] *adj. biol.* plas'matisch, Plasma…

plas·ter ['plɑːstə] **I** *s.* **1.** *pharm.* (Heft-, Senf)Pflaster *n*; **2.** a) Gips *m* (*a.* ⚕), b) ⚙ Mörtel *m*, Verputz *m*, Bewurf *m*, Tünche *f*: ***~ cast*** a) Gipsabdruck *m*, b) ⚕ Gipsverband *m*; **3.** *mst* ***~ of Paris*** a) (gebrannter) Gips (*a.* ⚕), b) Stuck *m*, Gips(mörtel) *m*; **II** *v/t.* **4.** ⚙ (ver)gipsen, (über)'tünchen, verputzen; **5.** bepflastern (*a. fig. mit Plakaten, Steinwürfen etc.*); **6.** *fig.* über'schütten (***with*** mit *Lob etc.*); **7.** ***be ~ed*** *sl.* 'besoffen' sein; **'plas·ter·er** [-ərə] *s.* Stukka'teur *m*; **'plas·ter·ing** [-ərɪŋ] *s.* **1.** Verputz *m*, Bewurf *m*; **2.** Stuck *m*; **3.** Gipsen *n*; **4.** Stukka'tur *f.*

plas·tic ['plæstɪk] **I** *adj.* (□ ***~ally***) **1.** plastisch: ***~ art*** bildende Kunst, Plastik *f*; **2.** formgebend, gestaltend; **3.** ⚙ (ver)formbar, knetbar, plastisch: ***~ clay*** bildfähiger Ton; **4.** Kunststoff…: ***~ bag*** Plastikbeutel *m*, -tüte *f*; (***synthetic***) ***~ material*** → 9; **5.** ⚕ plastisch: ***~ surgery***; ***~ surgeon*** Facharzt *m* für plastische Chirurgie; **6.** *fig.* plastisch, anschaulich; **7.** *fig.* formbar (*Geist*); **8.** ***~ bomb*** Plastikbombe *f*; **II** *s.* **9.** ⚙ (Kunstharz)Preßstoff *m*, Plastik-, Kunststoff *m*; **'plas·ti·cine** [-ɪsiːn] *s.* Plasti'lin *n*, Knetmasse *f*; **plas·tic·i·ty** [plæ'stɪsətɪ] *s.* Plastizi'tät *f* (*a. fig. Bildhaftigkeit*), (Ver)Formbarkeit *f*; **'plas·ti·ciz·er** [-ɪsaɪzə] *s.* ⚙ Weichmacher *m.*

plat [plæt] → ***plait***, ***plot*** 1.

plate [pleɪt] **I** *s.* **1.** *allg.* Platte *f* (*a. phot.*); (Me'tall)Schild *n*, Tafel *f*; (Namen-, Firmen-, Tür)Schild *n*; **2.** *paint.* (Kupfer- *etc.*)Stich *m*; *weitS.* Holzschnitt *m*: ***etched ~*** Radierung *f*; **3.** (Bild)Tafel *f* (*Buch*); **4.** (Eß-, *eccl.* Kol'lekten)Teller *m*; Platte *f* (*a. Gang e-r Mahlzeit*); *coll.* (Gold-, Silber-, Tafel-) Geschirr *n od.* (-)Besteck *n*: ***German ~*** Neusilber *n*; ***have a lot on one's ~*** F viel am Hals haben; ***hand s.o. s.th. on a ~*** j-m et. 'auf dem Tablett servieren'; **5.** ⚙ (Glas-, Me'tall)Platte *f*; Scheibe *f*, La'melle *f* (*Kupplung etc.*); Deckel *m*; **6.** ⚙ Grobblech *n*; Blechtafel *f*; **7.** ⚡ *Radio*: A'node *f e-r Röhre*; Platte *f*, Elek'trode *f e-s Kondensators*; **8.** *typ.* (Druck-, Stereo'typ)Platte *f*; **9.** Po'kal *m*, Preis *m beim Rennen*; **10.** *Am. Baseball*: (Schlag)Mal *n*; **11.** *a.* ***dental ~*** a) (Gaumen)Platte *f*, b) *weitS.* (künstliches) Gebiß; **12.** *Am. sl.* a) ('hyper)eleˌgante Per'son, b) 'tolle Frau'; **13.** *pl. sl.* 'Plattfüße' *pl.* (*Füße*); **II** *v/t.* **14.** mit Platten belegen; ⚔, ⚓ panzern, blenden; **15.** plattieren, (mit Me'tall) über'ziehen; **16.** *typ.* a) stereotypieren, b) *Typendruck*: in Platten formen; ***~ ar·mo(u)r*** *s.* ⚓, ⚙ Plattenpanzer(ung *f*) *m.*

pla·teau ['plætəʊ] *pl.* **-teaux**, **teaus** [-z] (*Fr.*) *s.* Pla'teau *n* (*a. fig. psych. etc.*), Hochebene *f.*

plate cir·cuit *s.* ⚡ An'odenkreis *m.*

plat·ed ['pleɪtɪd] *adj.* ⚙ plattiert, me'tallüberˌzogen, versilbert, -goldet, dubliert; **'plate·ful** [-fʊl] *pl.* **-fuls** *s. ein* Teller(voll) *m.*

plate| glass *s.* Scheiben-, Spiegelglas *n*; **'~ˌhold·er** *s. phot.* ('Platten)Kasˌsette *f*; **'~ˌlay·er** *s.* 🚂 Streckenarbeiter *m*; **'~mark** → ***hallmark***.

plat·en ['plætən] *s.* **1.** *typ.* Drucktiegel *m*, Platte *f*: ***~ press*** Tiegeldruckpresse *f*; **2.** ('Schreibmaˌschinen)Walze *f*; **3.** 'Druckzyˌlinder *m* (*Rotationsmaschine*).

plat·er ['pleɪtə] *s.* **1.** ⚙ Plattierer *m*; **2.** (minderwertiges) Rennpferd.

plate| shears *s. pl.* Blechschere *f*; **~ spring** *s.* ⚙ Blattfeder *f.*

plat·form ['plætfɔːm] *s.* **1.** Plattform *f*, ('Redner)Triˌbüne *f*, Podium *n*; **2.** ⚙ Rampe *f*; (Lauf-, Steuer)Bühne *f*: ***lifting ~*** Hebebühne *f*; **3.** Treppenabsatz *m*; **4.** *geogr.* a) Hochebene *f*, b) Ter'rasse *f* (*a. engS.*); **5.** 🚂 a) Bahnsteig *m*, b) Plattform *f am Wagenende*); **6.** ⚔ Bettung *f e-s Geschützes*; **7.** a) *a.* ***~ sole*** Pla'teausohle *f*, b) *pl*, *a.* ***~ shoes*** Schuhe *pl.* mit Plateausohle; **8.** *fig.* öffentliches Forum, Podiumsgespräch *n*; **9.** *pol.* Par'teiproˌgramm *n*, Plattform *f*; *bsd. Am.* program'matische Wahlerklärung; ***~ car*** *bsd. Am.* → ***flatcar***; ***~ scale*** *s.* ⚙ Brückenwaage *f*; ***~ tick·et*** *s.* Bahnsteigkarte *f.*

plat·ing ['pleɪtɪŋ] *s.* **1.** Panzerung *f*; **2.** ⚙ Beplattung *f*, Me'tallˌauflage *f*, Verkleidung *f* (*mit Metallplatten*); **3.** Plattieren *n*, Versilberung *f.*

pla·tin·ic [plə'tɪnɪk] *adj.* Platin…: ***~ acid*** ⚗ Platinchlorid *n*; **plat·i·nize** ['plætɪnaɪz] *v/t.* **1.** ⚙ platinieren, mit Platin über'ziehen; **2.** ⚗ mit Platin verbinden; **plat·i·num** ['plætɪnəm] *s.* Platin *n*: ***~ blonde*** F Platinblondine *f.*

plat·i·tude ['plætɪtjuːd] *s. fig.* Plattheit *f*, Gemeinplatz *m*, Plati'tüde *f*; **plat·i·tu·di·nar·i·an** ['plætɪˌtjuːdɪ'neərɪən] *s.* Phrasendrescher *m*, Schwätzer *m*; **plat·i·tu·di·nize** [ˌplætɪ'tjuːdɪnaɪz] *v/i.* sich in Gemeinplätzen ergehen, quatschen; **plat·i·tu·di·nous** [ˌplætɪ'tjuːdɪnəs] *adj.* □ platt, seicht, phrasenhaft.

Pla·ton·ic [plə'tɒnɪk] *adj.* (□ ***~ally***) pla'tonisch.

pla·toon [plə'tuːn] *s.* **1.** ⚔ Zug *m* (*Kompanieabteilung*): ***in*** (*od.* ***by***) ***~s*** zugweise; **2.** Poli'zeiaufgebot *n.*

plat·ter ['plætə] *s.* **1.** (Servier)Platte *f*: ***hand s.o. s.th. on a ~*** *fig.* F j-m et. 'auf e-m Tablett servieren'; **2.** *Am. sl.* Schallplatte *f.*

plat·y·pus ['plætɪpəs] *pl.* **-pus·es** *s. zo.* Schnabeltier *n.*

plat·y(r)·rhine ['plætɪraɪn] *zo.* **I** *adj.* breitnasig; **II** *s.* Breitnase *f* (*Affe*).

plau·dit ['plɔːdɪt] *s. mst pl.* lauter Beifall, Ap'plaus *m.*

plau·si·bil·i·ty [ˌplɔːzə'bɪlətɪ] *s.* **1.** Glaubwürdigkeit *f*, Wahr'scheinlichkeit *f*; **2.** gefälliges Äußeres, einnehmendes Wesen; **plau·si·ble** ['plɔːzəbl] *adj.* □ **1.** glaubhaft, einleuchtend, annehmbar, plau'sibel; **2.** einnehmend, gewinnend (*Äußeres*); **3.** glaubwürdig.

play [pleɪ] **I** *s.* **1.** (Glücks-, Wett-, Unter'haltungs)Spiel *n* (*a. sport*): ***be at ~*** a) spielen, b) *Kartenspiel*: am Ausspielen sein, c) *Schach*: am Zuge sein; ***it is your ~*** Sie sind am Spiel; ***in*** (***out of***) ***~*** *sport*: (noch) im Spiel (im Aus) (*Ball*); ***lose money at ~*** Geld verwetten; **2.** Spiel(weise *f*) *n*: ***that was pretty ~*** das war gut (gespielt); → ***fair¹*** 9, ***foul play***; **3.** Spiele'rei *f*, Kurzweil *f*, *a.* Liebesspiel(e *pl.*) *n*: ***a ~ of words*** ein Spiel mit Worten; ***a ~*** (***up***)***on words*** ein Wortspiel; ***in ~*** im Scherz; **4.** *thea.* (Schau)Spiel *n*, (The'ater)Stück *n*: ***at the ~*** im Theater; ***go to the ~*** ins Theater gehen; ***as good as a ~*** äußerst amüsant *od.* interessant; **5.** Spiel *n*, Vortrag *m*; **6.** *fig.* Spiel *n des Lichtes auf Wasser etc.*, spielerische Bewegung, (*Muskel- etc.*)Spiel *n*: ***~ of colo(u)rs*** Farbenspiel; **7.** Bewegung *f*, Gang *m*: ***bring into ~*** a) in Gang bringen, b) ins Spiel *od.* zur Anwendung bringen; ***come into ~*** ins Spiel kommen; ***make ~*** a) Wirkung haben, b) s-n Zweck erfüllen; ***make ~ with*** zur Geltung bringen, sich brüsten mit; ***make a ~ for*** *Am. sl. e-m Mädchen* den Kopf verdrehen wollen; **8.** Spielraum *m* (*a. fig.*); ⚙ *mst* Spiel *n*: ***allow*** (*od.* ***give***) ***full*** (*od.* ***free***) ***~ to*** *e-r Sache*, *s-r Phantasie etc.* freien Lauf lassen; **II** *v/i.* **9.** a) spielen (*a. sport*, *thea. u. fig.*) (***for*** um *Geld etc.*), b) mitspielen (*a. fig. mitmachen*): ***~ at*** a) *Ball*, *Karten etc.* spielen, b) *fig.* sich nur so nebenbei mit *et.* beschäftigen; ***~ at business*** ein bißchen in Geschäften machen; ***~ for time*** a) Zeit zu gewinnen suchen, b) *sport*: auf Zeit spielen; ***~ into s.o.'s hands*** j-m in die Hände spielen; ***~*** (***up***)***on*** a) ♪ auf *einem Instrument* spielen, b) mit *Worten* spielen, c) *fig. j-s Schwächen* ausnutzen; ***~ with*** spielen mit (*a. fig. e-m Gedanken*; *a. leichtfertig umgehen mit*; *a. engS. herumfingern an*); ***~ safe*** 'auf Nummer Sicher' gehen; ***~!*** *Tennis etc.*: bitte! (= *fertig*); → ***fair¹*** 15, ***false*** II, ***fast²*** 3, ***gallery*** 2; **10.** a) *Kartenspiel*: ausspielen, b) *Schach*: am Zug sein, ziehen; **11.** a) 'her'umspielen', sich amüsieren, b) Unsinn treiben, c) scherzen; **12.** a) sich tummeln, b) flattern, gaukeln, c) spielen (*Lächeln*, *Licht etc.*) (***on*** auf *dat.*), d) schillern (*Farbe*), e) in Tätigkeit sein (*Springbrunnen*); **13.** a) schießen, b) spritzen, c) strahlen, streichen: **~ on** gerichtet sein auf (*acc.*), bestreichen, bespritzen (*Schlauch, Wasserstrahl*), anstrahlen, absuchen (*Scheinwerfer*); **14.** ⚙ a) Spiel(raum) haben, b) sich bewegen (*Kolben etc.*); **15.** sich *gut etc.* zum Spielen eignen (*Boden etc.*); **III** *v/t.* **16.** *Karten, Tennis etc., a.* ♪, *a. thea. Rolle od. Stück, a. fig.* spielen: **~ (s.th. on) the piano** (et. auf dem) Klavier spielen; **~ both ends against the middle** *fig.* vorsichtig lavieren; **~ it safe** a) kein Risiko eingehen, b) (*Wendung*) um (ganz) sicher zu gehen; **~ it low down** *sl.* ein gemeines Spiel treiben (**on** mit *j-m*); **~ the races** bei (Pferde)Rennen wetten; → **deuce** 3, **fool**[1] 2, **game**[1] 4, **havoc**, **hooky**[2], **trick** 2, **truant** 1; **17.** a) *Karte* ausspielen (*a. fig.*): **~ one's cards well** s-e Chancen gut (aus)nutzen, b) *Schachfigur* ziehen; **18.** spielen, Vorstellungen geben in (*dat.*): **~ the larger cities**; **19.** *Geschütz, Scheinwerfer, Licht-, Wasserstrahl etc.* richten (**on** auf *acc.*): **~ a hose on** *et.* bespritzen; **~ colo(u)red lights on** *et.* bunt anstrahlen; **20.** *Fisch* auszappeln lassen;

Zssgn mit prp.:

play| at → **play** 9; **~ (up·)on** → **play** 9, 12, 13, 19; **~ up to** → **play** 9; **~ with** → **play** 9;

Zssgn mit adv.:

play| a·round *v/i.* → **play** 11a; **~ a·way I** *v/t. Geld* verspielen; **II** *v/i.* drauf'losspielen; **~ back** *v/t. Platte, Band* abspielen; **~ down** *v/t. fig.* ‚her'unterspielen'; **~ off** *v/t.* **1.** *sport Spiel* a) beenden, b) *durch Stichkampf* entscheiden; **2.** *fig. j-n* ausspielen (**against** gegen *e-n andern*); **3.** *Musik* her'unterspielen; **~ out** *v/t.* erschöpfen: **played out** erschöpft, ‚fertig'; **~ up I** *v/i.* **1.** ♪ lauter spielen; **2.** *sport* F ‚aufdrehen'; **3.** *Brit.* F ‚verrückt spielen' (*Auto etc.*); **4. ~ to** a) *j-m* schöntun, b) *j-n* unter'stützen; **II** *v/t.* **5.** *e-e Sache* ‚hochspielen'; **6.** F *j-n* ‚auf die Palme bringen' (*reizen*).

play·a·ble ['pleɪəbl] *adj.* **1.** spielbar; **2.** *thea.* bühnenreif, -gerecht.

'play|·act *v/i. contp.* ‚schauspielern'; **~ ac·tor** *s. mst contp.* Schauspieler *m* (*a. fig.*); **'~·back** *s.* ⚡ **1.** Playback *n*, Abspielen *n*: **~ head** Tonabnehmerkopf *m*; **2.** Wiedergabegerät *n*; **'~·bill** *s.* The'aterplaˌkat *n*; **'~·book** *s. thea.* Textbuch *n*; **'~·boy** *s.* Playboy *m*; **'~·day** *s.* (schul)freier Tag.

play·er ['pleɪə] *s.* **1.** *sport, a.* ♪ Spieler (-in); **2.** *Brit. sport* Berufsspieler *m*; **3.** (Glücks)Spieler *m*; **4.** Schauspieler(in); **~ pi·an·o** *s.* me'chanisches Kla'vier.

'playˌfel·low → **playmate**.

play·ful ['pleɪfʊl] *adj.* ☐ **1.** spielerisch; **2.** verspielt; **3.** ausgelassen, neckisch; **'play·ful·ness** [-nɪs] *s.* **1.** Munterkeit *f*; Ausgelassenheit *f*; **2.** Verspieltheit *f*.

'play|·girl *s.* Playgirl *n*; **'~ˌgo·er** *s.* The'aterbesucher(in); **'~·ground** *s.* **1.** Spiel-, Tummelplatz *m* (*a. fig.*); **2.** Schulhof *m*; **'~·house** *s.* **1.** *thea.* Schauspielhaus *n*; **2.** Spielhaus *n*, -hütte *f*.

play·ing| card ['pleɪɪŋ] *s.* Spielkarte *f*; **~ field** *s. Brit.* Sport-, Spielplatz *m*.

play·let ['pleɪlɪt] *s.* kurzes Schauspiel.

'play|·mate *s.* 'Spielkameˌrad(in), Gespiele *m*, Gespielin *f*; **'~-off** *s. sport* Entscheidungsspiel *n*; **'~·pen** Laufgitter *n*; **'~·suit** *s.* Spielhös-chen *n*; **'~·thing** *s.* Spielzeug *n* (*fig. a. Person*); **'~·time** *s.* **1.** Freizeit *f*; **2.** *ped.* große Pause; **'~·wright** *s.* Bühnenschriftsteller *m*, Dra'matiker *m*.

plea [pliː] *s.* **1.** Vorwand *m*, Ausrede *f*: **on the ~ of** (*od.* **that**) unter dem Vorwand (*gen.*) *od.* daß; **2.** ⚖ a) Verteidigung *f*, b) Antwort *f* des Angeklagten: **~ of guilty** Schuldgeständnis *n*; **3.** ⚖ Einrede *f*: **make a ~** Einspruch erheben; **~ of the crown** *Brit.* Strafklage *f*; **4.** *fig.* (dringende) Bitte (**for** um), Gesuch *n*; **5.** *fig.* Befürwortung *f*.

plead [pliːd] **I** *v/i.* **1.** ⚖ *u. fig.* plädieren (**for** für); **2.** ⚖ (*vor Gericht*) e-n Fall erörtern, Beweisgründe vorbringen; **3.** ⚖ sich zu s-r Verteidigung äußern: **~ guilty** sich schuldig bekennen (**to** *gen.*); **4.** dringend bitten (**for** um, **with s.o.** j-n); **5.** sich einsetzen *od.* verwenden (**for** für, **with s.o.** bei j-m); **6.** einwenden *od.* geltend machen (**that** daß); **II** *v/t.* **7.** ⚖ *u. fig.* als Verteidigung *od.* Entschuldigung anführen, *et.* vorschützen: **~ ignorance**; **8.** ⚖ erörtern; **9.** ⚖ a) *Sache* vertreten, verteidigen: **~ s.o.'s cause**, b) (als Beweisgrund) vorbringen, anführen; **'plead·er** [-də] *s.* ⚖ *u. fig.* Anwalt *m*, Sachwalter *m*; **'plead·ing** [-dɪŋ] **I** *s.* **1.** ⚖ a) Plädo'yer *n*, b) Plädieren *n*, Führen *n* e-r Rechtssache, c) Parteivorbringen *n*, d) *pl.*, gerichtliche Verhandlungen *pl.*, e) *bsd. Brit.* vorbereitete Schriftsätze *pl.*, Vorverhandlung *f*; **2.** Fürsprache *f*; **3.** Bitten *n* (**for** um); **II** *adj.* ☐ **4.** flehend, bittend, inständig.

pleas·ant ['pleznt] *adj.* ☐ **1.** angenehm (*a. Geruch, Traum etc.*), wohltuend, erfreulich (*Nachrichten etc.*), vergnüglich; **2.** freundlich (*a. Wetter, Zimmer*): **please look ~!** bitte recht freundlich!; **'pleas·ant·ness** [-nɪs] *s.* **1.** *das* Angenehme; angenehmes Wesen; **2.** Freundlichkeit *f*; **3.** Heiterkeit *f* (*a. fig.*); **'pleas·ant·ry** [-trɪ] *s.* **1.** Heiter-, Lustigkeit *f*; **2.** Scherz *m*: a) Witz *m*, b) Hänse'lei *f*.

please [pliːz] **I** *v/i.* **1.** gefallen, angenehm sein, befriedigen, Anklang finden: **~!** bitte (sehr)!; **as you ~** wie Sie wünschen; **if you ~** a) wenn ich bitten darf, wenn es Ihnen recht ist, b) *iro.* gefälligst, c) man stelle sich vor, denken Sie nur; **~ come in!** bitte, treten Sie ein!; **2.** befriedigen, zufriedenstellen: **anxious to ~** dienstbeflissen, sehr eifrig; **II** *v/t.* **3.** *j-m* gefallen *od.* angenehm sein *od.* zusagen, *j-n* erfreuen: **be ~d to do** sich freuen *et.* zu tun; **I am only too ~d to do it** ich tue es mit dem größten Vergnügen; **be ~d with** a) befriedigt sein von, b) Vergnügen haben an (*dat.*), c) Gefallen finden an (*dat.*): **I am ~d with it** es gefällt mir; **4.** befriedigen, zufriedenstellen: **~ o.s.** tun, was man will; **~ yourself** a) wie Sie wünschen, b) bitte, bedienen Sie sich; **only to ~ you** nur Ihnen zuliebe; → **hard** 3; **5.** (*a. iro.*) geruhen, belieben (**to do** *et.* zu tun): **~ God** so Gott will; **'pleased** [-zd] *adj.* zufrieden (**with** mit), erfreut (**at** über *acc.*); → **Punch**[4]; **'pleas·ing** [-zɪŋ] *adj.* ☐ angenehm, wohltuend, gefällig.

pleas·ur·a·ble ['pleʒərəbl] *adj.* ☐ angenehm, vergnüglich, ergötzlich.

pleas·ure ['pleʒə] **I** *s.* **1.** Vergnügen *n*, Freude *f*, (*a. sexueller*) Genuß, Lust *f*: **with ~!** mit Vergnügen!; **give s.o. ~** j-m Vergnügen (*od.* Freude) machen; **have the ~ of doing** das Vergnügen haben, *et.* zu tun; **take ~ in** (*od.* **at**) Vergnügen *od.* Freude finden an (*dat.*): **he takes (a) ~ in contradicting** es macht ihm Spaß zu widersprechen; **take one's ~** sich vergnügen; **a man of ~** ein Genußmensch; **2.** Gefallen *m*, Gefälligkeit *f*: **do s.o. a ~** j-m e-n Gefallen tun; **3.** Belieben *n*, Gutdünken *n*: **at ~** nach Belieben; **at the Court's ~** nach dem Ermessen des Gerichts; ⚖ **during Her Majesty's ~** *Brit.* auf unbestimmte Zeit (*Freiheitsstrafe*); **II** *v/i.* **4.** sich erfreuen *od.* vergnügen; **~ boat** *s.* Vergnügungsdampfer *m*; **~ ground** *s.* Vergnügungs-, Rasenplatz *m*; **~ prin·ci·ple** *s. psych.* 'Lustprinˌzip *n*; **'~-ˌseek·ing** *adj.* vergnügungssüchtig; **~ tour** *s.*, **~ trip** *s.* Vergnügungsreise *f*.

pleat [pliːt] **I** *s.* (Rock- *etc.*)Falte *f*; **II** *v/t.* falten, fälteln, plissieren.

ple·be·ian [plɪ'biːən] **I** *adj.* ple'bejisch; **II** *s.* Ple'bejer(in); **ple'be·ian·ism** [-nɪzəm] *s.* Ple'bejertum *n*.

pleb·i·scite ['plebɪsɪt] *s.* Plebis'zit *n*, Volksabstimmung *f*, -entscheid *m*.

plec·trum ['plektrəm] *pl.* **-tra** [-ə] *s.* ♪ Plektron *n*.

pledge [pledʒ] **I** *s.* **1.** (Faust-, 'Unter-) Pfand *n*, Pfandgegenstand *m*; Verpfändung *f*; Bürgschaft *f*, Sicherheit *f*; *hist.* Bürge *m*, Geisel *f*: **in ~ of** a) als Pfand für, b) *fig.* als Beweis für, zum Zeichen, daß; **hold in ~** als Pfand halten; **put in ~** verpfänden; **take out of ~** *Pfand* auslösen; **2.** Versprechen *n*, feste Zusage, Gelübde *n*, Gelöbnis *n*: **take the ~** dem Alkohol abschwören; **3.** *fig.* 'Unterpfand *n*, Beweis *m* (*der Freundschaft etc.*): **under the ~ of secrecy** unter dem Siegel der Verschwiegenheit; **4.** *a.* **~ of love** *fig.* Pfand *n* der Liebe (*Kind*); **5.** Zutrinken *n*, Toast *m*; **6.** *bsd. univ. Am.* a) Versprechen *n*, e-r Verbindung *od.* e-m (Geheim)Bund beizutreten, b) Anwärter(in) auf solche Mitgliedschaft; **II** *v/t.* **7.** verpfänden (**s.th. to s.o.** j-m et.); Pfand bestellen für, e-e Sicherheit leisten für; als Sicherheit *od.* zum Pfand geben: **~ one's word** *fig.* sein Wort verpfänden; **~d article** Pfandobjekt; **~d merchandise** ☤ sicherungsübereignete Ware(n); **~d securities** ☤ lombardierte Effekten; **8.** *j-n* verpflichten (**to** zu, auf *acc.*): **~ o.s.** geloben, sich verpflichten; **9.** *j-m* zutrinken, auf das Wohl (*gen.*) trinken; **'pledge·a·ble** [-dʒəbl] *adj.* verpfändbar; **pledg·ee** [ple'dʒiː] *s.* Pfandnehmer(in), -inhaber (-in), -gläubiger(in); **pledge·or** [ple'dʒɔː], **'pledg·er** [-dʒə], **pledg·or** [ple'dʒɔː] *s.* ⚖ Pfandgeber(in), -schuldner(in).

Ple·iad ['plaɪəd] *pl.* **'Ple·ia·des** [-diːz] *s. ast., fig.* Siebengestirn *n*.

Pleis·to·cene ['plaɪstəʊsiːn] *s. geol.* Pleisto'zän *n*, Di'luvium *n*.

ple·na·ry ['pliːnərɪ] *adj.* **1.** ☐ voll(ständig), Voll..., Plenar...: **~ session** Plenarsitzung *f*; **2.** voll('kommen), uneingeschränkt: ~ ***indulgence*** *R.C.* vollkommener Ablaß; ~ ***power*** Generalvollmacht *f*.

plen·i·po·ten·ti·ar·y [ˌplenɪpəʊˈtenʃərɪ] **I** *s*. **1.** (Geneˈral)BeˌvollmächtigteR(r *m*) *f*, bevollmächtigter Gesandter *od*. Miˈnister; **II** *adj*. **2.** bevollmächtigt; **3.** absoˈlut, unbeschränkt.

plen·i·tude [ˈplenɪtjuːd] *s*. **1.** → ***plenty*** 1; **2.** Vollkommenheit *f*.

plen·te·ous [ˈplentjəs] *adj*. □ *poet*. reich(lich); ˈ**plen·te·ous·ness** [-nɪs] *s*. *poet*. Fülle *f*.

plen·ti·ful [ˈplentɪfʊl] *adj*. □ reich(lich), im ˈÜberfluß (vorˈhanden); ˈ**plen·ti·ful·ness** [-nɪs] → ***plenty*** 1.

plen·ty [ˈplentɪ] **I** *s*. Fülle *f*, ˈÜberfluß *m*, Reichtum *m* (***of*** an *dat*.): ***have*** ~ ***of s.th.*** mit et. reichlich versehen sein, et. in Hülle u. Fülle haben; ***in*** ~ im Überfluß; ~ ***of money*** (***time***) jede Menge *od*. viel Geld (Zeit); ~ ***of times*** sehr oft; → ***horn*** 4; **II** *adj*. *bsd*. *Am*. reichlich, jede Menge; **III** *adv*. F a) bei weitem, ‚lange‘, b) *Am*. ‚mächtig‘.

ple·num [ˈpliːnəm] *s*. **1.** Plenum *n*, Vollversammlung *f*; **2.** *phys*. (vollkommen) ausgefüllter Raum.

ple·o·nasm [ˈplɪəʊnæzəm] *s*. Pleoˈnasmus *m*; **ple·o·nas·tic** [ˌplɪəʊˈnæstɪk] *adj*. (□ ~***ally***) pleoˈnastisch.

pleth·o·ra [ˈpleθərə] *s*. **1.** ⚕ Blutandrang *m*; **2.** *fig*. ˈÜberfülle *f*, Zuˈviel *n* (***of*** an *dat*.); **ple·thor·ic** [pleˈθɒrɪk] *adj*. (□ ~***ally***) **1.** ⚕ pleˈthorisch; **2.** *fig*. ˈübervoll, überˈladen.

pleu·ra [ˈplʊərə] *pl*. **-rae** [-riː] *s*. *anat*. Brust-, Rippenfell *n*; ˈ**pleu·ral** [-rəl] *adj*. Brust-, Rippenfell…; ˈ**pleu·ri·sy** [-rəsɪ] *s*. ⚕ Pleuˈritis *f*, Brustfell-, Rippenfellentzündung *f*.

pleu·ro·car·pous [ˌplʊərəʊˈkɑːpəs] *adj*. ⚘ seitenfrüchtig; ˌ**pleu·ro·pneuˈmo·ni·a** [-njʊˈməʊnjə] *s*. **1.** ⚕ Lungen- u. Rippenfellentzündung *f*; **2.** *vet*. Lungen- u. Brustseuche *f*.

plex·or [ˈpleksə] *s*. ⚕ Perkussiˈonshammer *m*.

plex·us [ˈpleksəs] *pl*. **-es** [-ɪz] *s*. **1.** *anat*. Plexus *m*, (Nerven)Geflecht *n*; **2.** *fig*. Flechtwerk *n*, Netz(werk) *n*, Komˈplex *m*.

pli·a·bil·i·ty [ˌplaɪəˈbɪlətɪ] *s*. Biegsamkeit *f*, Geschmeidigkeit *f* (*a*. *fig*.); **pli·a·ble** [ˈplaɪəbl] *adj*. □ **1.** biegsam, geschmeidig (*a*. *fig*.); **2.** *fig*. nachgiebig, fügsam, leicht zu beeinflussen(d).

pli·an·cy [ˈplaɪənsɪ] *s*. Biegsamkeit *f*, Geschmeidigkeit *f* (*a*. *fig*.); ˈ**pli·ant** [-nt] *adj*. □ → ***pliable***.

pli·ers [ˈplaɪəz] *s*. *pl*. (*a*. *als sg*. *konstr*.) ⚙ (***a pair of*** ~ e-e) (Draht-, Kneif)Zange: ***round***(***-nosed***) ~ Rundzange *f*.

plight[1] [plaɪt] *s*. (mißliche) Lage, Not-, Zwangslage *f*.

plight[2] [plaɪt] *bsd*. *poet*. **I** *v/t*. **1.** *Wort*, *Ehre* verpfänden, *Treue* geloben: ~***ed troth*** gelobte Treue; **2.** verloben (***to*** *dat*.); **II** *s*. **3.** *obs*. Gelöbnis *n*, feierliches Versprechen; **4.** *a*. ~ ***of faith*** Verlobung *f*.

plim·soll [ˈplɪmsəl] *s*. Turnschuh *m*.

plinth [plɪnθ] *s*. ⚠ **1.** Plinthe *f*, Säulenplatte *f*; **2.** Fußleiste *f*.

Pli·o·cene [ˈplaɪəʊsiːn] *s*. *geol*. Plioˈzän *n*.

plod [plɒd] **I** *v/i*. **1.** *a*. ~ ***along***, ~ ***on*** mühsam *od*. schwerfällig gehen, sich daˈhinschleppen, trotten, (einˈher)stapfen; **2.** ~ ***away*** *fig*. sich abmühen *od*. -plagen (***at*** mit), ‚schuften‘; **II** *v/t*. **3.** ~ ***one's way*** → 1; ˈ**plod·der** [-də] *s*. *fig*. Arbeitstier *n*; ˈ**plod·ding** [-dɪŋ] **I** *adj*. □ **1.** stapfend; **2.** arbeitsam, angestrengt *od*. unverdrossen (*arbeitend*); **II** *s*. **3.** Plackeˈrei *f*, Schufteˈrei *f*.

plonk[1] [plɒŋk] *s*. F billiger u. schlechter Wein.

plonk[2] [plɒŋk] F **I** *v/t*. **1.** *a*. ~ ***down*** *et*. ‚hinschmeißen‘; **2.** ♪ zupfen auf (*acc*.); **3.** ~ ***down*** *Am*. *sl*. ‚blechen‘, bezahlen; **II** *v/i*. **4.** ‚knallen‘; **III** *adv*. **5.** knallend; **6.** ‚zack‘, genau: ~ ***in the eye***; ~***!*** wamm!

plop [plɒp] **I** *v/i*. plumpsen; **II** *v/t*. plumpsen lassen; **III** *s*. Plumps *m*, Plumpsen *n*; **IV** *adv*. mit e-m Plumps; **V** *int*. plumps!

plo·sion [ˈpləʊʒn] *s*. *ling*. Verschluß (-sprengung *f*) *m*; **plo·sive** [ˈpləʊsɪv] **I** *adj*. Verschluß…; **II** *s*. Verschlußlaut *m*.

plot [plɒt] **I** *s*. **1.** Stück(chen) *n* Land, Parˈzelle *f*, Grundstück *n*: ***a garden-***~ ein Stück Garten; **2.** *bsd*. *Am*. (Lage-, Bau)Plan *m*, (Grund)Riß *m*, Diaˈgramm *n*, graphische Darstellung; **3.** ⚔ a) *Artillerie*: Zielort *m*, b) *Radar*: Standort *m*; **4.** (geheimer) Plan, Komˈplott *n*, Anschlag *m*, Verschwörung *f*, Inˈtrige *f*: ***lay a*** ~ ein Komplott schmieden; **5.** Handlung *f*, Fabel *f* (*Roman*, *Drama etc*.), *a*. Inˈtrige *f* (*Komödie*); **II** *v/t*. **6.** e-n Plan von *et*. anfertigen, *et*. planen, entwerfen; aufzeichnen (*a*. ~ ***down***) (***on*** in *dat*.); ⚓, ✈ *Kurs* abstecken, -setzen, ermitteln; ⩘ *Kurve* (graphisch) darstellen *od*. auswerten; *Luftbilder* auswerten: ~***ted fire*** ⚔ Planfeuer *n*; **7.** *a*. ~ ***out*** *Land* parzellieren; **8.** *Verschwörung* planen, aushecken, *Meuterei etc*. anzetteln; **9.** *Romanhandlung etc*. entwickeln, ersinnen; **III** *v/i*. **10.** (***against***) Ränke *od*. ein Komplott schmieden, intrigieren, sich verschwören (gegen), e-n Anschlag verüben (auf *acc*.); ˈ**plot·ter** [-tə] *s*. **1.** Planzeichner (-in); **2.** Anstifter(in); **3.** Ränkeschmied *m*, Intriˈgant(in), Verschwörer(in).

plough [plaʊ] **I** *s*. **1.** Pflug *m*: ***put one's hand to the*** ~ s-e Hand an den Pflug legen; **2.** ***the*** ♌ *ast*. der Große Bär *od*. Wagen; **3.** *Tischlerei*: Falzhobel *m*; **4.** *Buchbinderei*: Beschneidhobel *m*; **5.** *univ*. *Brit*. *sl*. ‚(ˈDurch)Rasseln‘ *n*, ‚ˈDurchfall‘ *m*; **II** *v/t*. **6.** *Boden* (ˈum-) pflügen: ~ ***back*** unterpflügen, *fig*. *Gewinn* wieder in das Geschäft stecken; → ***sand*** 2; **7.** *fig*. a) *Wasser*, *Gesicht* (durch)ˈfurchen, *Wellen* pflügen, b) sich (*e-n Weg*) bahnen: ~ ***one's way***; **8.** *univ*. *Brit*. *sl*. ˈdurchfallen lassen: ***be*** *od*. ***get*** ~***ed*** durchrasseln; **III** *v/i*. **9.** *fig*. sich e-n Weg bahnen: ~ ***through a book*** F ein Buch durchackern; ˈ~**-land** *s*. Ackerland *n*; ˈ~**·man** [-mən] *s*. [*irr*.] Pflüger *m*: ~***'s lunch*** Imbiß *m* aus Brot, Käse *etc*.; ~ **plane** *s*. ⚙ Nuthobel *m*; ˈ~**·share** *s*. ⚒ Pflugschar *f*.

plov·er [ˈplʌvə] *s*. *orn*. **1.** Regenpfeifer *m*; **2.** Gelbschenkelwasserläufer *m*; **3.** Kiebitz *m*.

plow [plaʊ] *etc*. *Am*. → ***plough*** *etc*.

ploy [plɔɪ] *s*. F Trick *m*, ‚Masche‘ *f*.

pluck [plʌk] **I** *s*. **1.** Rupfen *n*, Zupfen *n*, Zerren *n*; **2.** Ruck *m*, Zug *m*; **3.** Geschlinge *n von Schlachttieren*; **4.** *fig*. Schneid *m*, Mut *m*; **5.** → ***plough*** 5; **II** *v/t*. **6.** *Obst*, *Blumen etc*. pflücken, abreißen; **7.** *Federn*, *Haar*, *Unkraut etc*. ausreißen, -zupfen, *Geflügel* rupfen; ⚙ *Wolle* plüsen; → ***crow***[1] 1; **8.** zupfen, ziehen, zerren, reißen: ~ ***s.o. by the sleeve*** j-n am Ärmel zupfen; ~ ***up courage*** *fig*. Mut fassen; **9.** *sl*. *j-n* ‚rupfen‘, ausplündern; **10.** → ***plough*** 8; **III** *v/i*. **11.** (***at***) zupfen, ziehen, zerren (an *dat*.), schnappen, greifen (nach); ˈ**pluck·i·ness** [-kɪnɪs] *s*. Schneid *m*, Mut *m*; ˈ**pluck·y** [-kɪ] *adj*. □ F mutig, schneidig.

plug [plʌg] **I** *s*. **1.** Pflock *m*, Stöpsel *m*, Dübel *m*, Zapfen *m*, (Faß)Spund *m*; Pfropf(en) *m* (*a*. ⚕); Verschlußschraube *f*, (Hahn-, Venˈtil)Küken *n*: ***drain*** ~ Ablaßschraube; **2.** ⚡ Stecker *m*, Stöpsel *m*: ~***-ended cord*** Stöpselschnur *f*; ~ ***socket*** Steckdose *f*; **3.** *mot*. Zündkerze *f*; **4.** (ˈFeuer)Hyˌdrant *m*; **5.** (Kloˈsett-) Spülvorrichtung *f*; **6.** (Zahn)Plombe *f*; **7.** Priem *m* (*Kautabak*); **8.** → ***plug hat***; **9.** ✝ *sl*. Ladenhüter *m*; **10.** *sl*. alter Gaul; **11.** *sl*. a) (Faust)Schlag *m*, b) Schuß *m*, c) Kugel *f*: ***take a*** ~ ***at*** → 18; **12.** *Am*. *Radio*: Reˈklame(hinweis *m*) *f*; **13.** F falsches Geldstück; **II** *v/t*. **14.** *a*. ~ ***up*** zu-, verstopfen, zustöpseln; **15.** *Zahn* plombieren; **16.** ~ ***in*** ⚡ *Gerät* einstecken, -stöpseln, *durch Steckkontakt* anschließen; **17.** F *im Radio etc*. (ständig) Reklame machen für; *Lied etc*. ständig spielen (lassen); **18.** *sl*. *j-m* ‚eine (*e-n Schlag*, *e-e Kugel*) verpassen‘; **III** *v/i*. **19.** F *a*. ~ ***away*** ‚schuften‘ (***at*** an *dat*.); ~ **box** *s*. ˈSteckdose *f*, -konˌtakt *m*; ~ **fuse** *s*. Stöpselsicherung *f*; ~ **hat** *s*. *Am*. *sl*. ‚Angströhre‘ *f* (*Zylinder*); ˈ~**-in** *adj*. ⚙ Steck…, Einschub…; ˈ~**ˌug·ly I** *s*. *Am*. *sl*. Schläger *m*, Raˈbauke *m*; **II** *adj*. F abgrundhäßlich; ~ **wrench** *s*. *mot*. Zündkerzenschlüssel *m*.

plum [plʌm] *s*. **1.** Pflaume *f*, Zwetsch(g)e *f*; **2.** Roˈsine (*im Pudding etc*.): ~ ***cake*** Rosinenkuchen *m*; **3.** *fig*. a) ‚Roˈsine‘ *f* (*das Beste*), b) *a*. ~ ***job*** ‚Bombenjob‘ *m*, c) *Am*. *sl*. Belohnung *f für Unterstützung bei der Wahl* (*Posten*, *Titel etc*.); **4.** *Am*. *sl*. unverhoffter Gewinn, ✝ ˈSonderdiviˌdende *f*.

plum·age [ˈpluːmɪdʒ] *s*. Gefieder *n*.

plumb [plʌm] **I** *s*. **1.** (Blei)Lot *n*, Senkblei *n*: ***out of*** ~ aus dem Lot, nicht (mehr) senkrecht; **2.** ⚓ (Echo)Lot *n*; **II** *adj*. **3.** lot-, senkrecht; **4.** F völlig, rein (*Unsinn etc*.); **III** *adv*. **5.** *fig*. genau, ‚peng‘, platsch (*ins Wasser etc*.); **6.** *Am*. F ‚toˈtal‘ (*verrückt etc*.); **IV** *v/t*. **7.** lotrecht machen; **8.** ⚓ *Meerestiefe* (ab-, aus)loten, sondieren; **9.** *fig*. sondieren, ergründen; **10.** ⚙ (mit Blei) verlöten, verbleien; **11.** F Wasser- *od*. Gasleitungen legen in (*e-m Haus*); **V** *v/i*. **12.** klempnern; **plum·ba·go** [plʌmˈbeɪgəʊ] *s*. **1.** *min*. a) Graˈphit *m*, b) Bleiglanz *m*; **2.** ⚘ Bleiwurz *f*.

ˈ**plumb-bob** → ***plumb*** 1.

plum·be·ous [ˈplʌmbɪəs] *adj*. **1.** bleiartig; **2.** bleifarben; **3.** *Keramik*: mit Blei glasiert; **plumb·er** [ˈplʌmə(r)] *s*. **1.**

Klempner *m*, Installa'teur *m*; **2.** Bleiarbeiter *m*; '**plum·bic** [-bɪk] *adj.* Blei…: **~ *chloride*** ⚗ Bleitetrachlorid *n*; **plum·bif·erous** [plʌm'bɪfərəs] *adj.* bleihaltig; '**plumb·ing** [-mɪŋ] *s.* **1.** Klempner-, Installa'teurarbeit *f*; **2.** Rohr-, Wasser-, Gasleitung *f*; sani'täre Einrichtung; **3.** Blei(gießer)arbeit *f*; **4.** △, ⚓ Ausloten *n*; '**plum·bism** [-bɪzəm] *s.* ⚕ Bleivergiftung *f*.

'**plumb-line I** *s.* **1.** Senkschnur *f*, -blei *n*; **II** *v/t.* **2.** △, ⚓ ausloten; **3.** *fig.* sondieren, prüfen.

plumbo- [plʌmbəʊ] ⚗ *in Zssgn* Blei…, *z.B.* ***plumbosolvent*** bleizersetzend.

plumb rule *s.* ⚙ Lot-, Senkwaage *f*.

plume [pluːm] **I** *s.* **1.** *orn.* (*Straußen- etc.*) Feder *f*: ***adorn o.s. with borrowed ~s*** *fig.* sich mit fremden Federn schmükken; **2.** (Hut-, Schmuck)Feder *f*; **3.** Feder-, Helmbusch *m*; **4.** *fig.* **~ (*of cloud*)** Wolkenstreifen *m*; **~ (*of smoke*)** Rauchfahne *f*; **II** *v/t.* **5.** mit Federn schmücken: **~ *o.s.* (*up*)*on*** *fig.* sich brüsten mit; **~*d*** a) gefiedert, b) mit Federn geschmückt; **6.** *Gefieder* putzen; '**plume·less** [-lɪs] *adj.* ungefiedert.

plum·met ['plʌmɪt] **I** *s.* **1.** (Blei)Lot *n*, Senkblei *n*; **2.** ⚙ Senkwaage *f*; **3.** *Fischen*: (Blei)Senker *m*; **4.** *fig.* Bleigewicht *n*; **II** *v/i.* **5.** absinken, (ab)stürzen (*a. fig.*).

plum·my ['plʌmɪ] *adj.* **1.** pflaumenartig, Pflaumen…; **2.** reich an Pflaumen *od.* Ro'sinen; **3.** F ‚prima', ‚schick'; **4.** so'nor: **~ *voice***.

plu·mose ['pluːməʊs] *adj.* **1.** *orn.* gefiedert; **2.** ♀, *zo.* federartig.

plump¹ [plʌmp] **I** *adj.* drall, mollig, ‚pummelig': **~ *cheeks*** Pausbacken; **II** *v/t. u. v/i. oft* **~ *out*** prall *od.* fett machen (werden).

plump² [plʌmp] **I** *v/i.* **1.** (hin)plumpsen, schwer fallen, sich (*in e-n Sessel etc.*) fallen lassen; **2.** *pol.* kumulieren: **~ *for*** a) *e-m Wahlkandidaten* s-e Stimme ungeteilt geben, b) *j-n* rückhaltlos unterstützen, c) sich sofort für *et.* entscheiden; **II** *v/t.* **3.** plumpsen lassen; **4.** mit *s-r Meinung etc.* her'ausplatzen, unverblümt her'aussagen; **III** *s.* **5.** F Plumps *m*; **IV** *adv.* **6.** plumpsend, mit e-m Plumps; **7.** F unverblümt, gerade her'aus; **V** *adj.* □ **8.** F plump (*Lüge etc.*), deutlich, glatt (*Ablehnung etc.*); '**plump·er** [-pə] *s.* **1.** Plumps *m*; **2.** Bausch *m*; **3.** *pol.* ungeteilte Wahlstimme; **4.** *sl.* plumpe Lüge.

plum pud·ding *s.* Plumpudding *m*.

plum·y ['pluːmɪ] *adj.* **1.** gefiedert; **2.** federartig.

plun·der ['plʌndə] **I** *v/t.* **1.** *Land, Stadt etc.* plündern; **2.** rauben, stehlen; **3.** *j-n* ausplündern; **II** *v/i.* **4.** plündern, räubern; **III** *s.* **5.** Plünderung *f*; **6.** Beute *f*, Raub *m*; **7.** *Am.* F Plunder *m*; '**plun·der·er** [-ərə] *s.* Plünderer *m*, Räuber *m*.

plunge [plʌndʒ] **I** *v/t.* **1.** (ein-, 'unter-)tauchen, stürzen (***in, into*** in *acc.*); *fig. j-n in Schulden etc.* stürzen; *e-e Nation in e-n Krieg* stürzen *od.* treiben; *Zimmer in Dunkel* tauchen *od.* hüllen; **2.** *Waffe* stoßen; **II** *v/i.* **3.** (ein-, 'unter-)tauchen (***into*** in *acc.*); **4.** (ab)stürzen (*a. fig. Klippe etc.*, † *Preise*); **5.** *ins Zimmer etc.* stürzen, stürmen; *fig.* sich *in e-e Tätigkeit, in Schulden etc.* stürzen; **6.** ⚓ stampfen (*Schiff*); **7.** sich nach vorne werfen, ausschlagen (*Pferd*); **8.** *sl.* et. riskieren, alles auf 'eine Karte setzen; **III** *s.* **9.** (Ein-, 'Unter)Tauchen *n*; *sport* (Kopf)Sprung *m*: ***take the ~*** *fig.* den entscheidenden Schritt *od.* den Sprung wagen; **10.** Sturz *m*, Stürzen *n*; **11.** Ausschlagen *n e-s Pferdes*; **12.** Sprung-, Schwimmbekken *n*; **13.** Schwimmen *n*, Bad *n*; '**plung·er** [-dʒə] *s.* **1.** Taucher *m*; **2.** ⚙ Tauchkolben *m*; **3.** ϟ a) Tauchkern *m*, b) Tauchspule *f*; **4.** *mot.* Ven'tilkolben *m*; **5.** ⚔ Schlagbolzen *m*; **6.** *sl.* a) Hasar'deur *m*, Spieler *m*, b) wilder Speku'lant.

plunk [plʌŋk] → ***plonk²***.

plu·per·fect [ˌpluː'pɜːfɪkt] *s. a.* **~ *tense*** *ling.* Plusquamperfekt *n*, Vorvergangenheit *f*.

plu·ral ['plʊərəl] **I** *adj.* □ **1.** mehrfach: **~ *marriage*** Mehrehe *f*; **~ *society*** pluralistische Gesellschaft; **~ *vote*** Mehrstimmenwahlrecht *n*; **2.** *ling.* Plural…, im Plural, plu'ralisch: **~ *number*** → 3; **II** *s.* **3.** *ling.* Plural *m*, Mehrzahl *f*; '**plu·ral·ism** [-rəlɪzəm] *s.* **1.** Vielheit *f*; **2.** *eccl.* Besitz *m* mehrerer Pfründen *od.* Ämter; **3.** *phls.*, *pol.* Plura'lismus *m*; '**plu·ral·ist** [-rəlɪst] *adj. phls.*, *pol.* plura'listisch; **plu·ral·i·ty** [ˌplʊə'rælətɪ] *s.* **1.** Mehrheit *f*, 'Über-, Mehrzahl *f*; **2.** Vielheit *f*, -zahl *f*; **3.** *pol.* (*Am. bsd.* rela'tive) Stimmenmehrheit; **4.** → ***pluralism*** 2; '**plu·ral·ize** [-rəlaɪz] *v/t. ling.* **1.** in den Plural setzen; **2.** als *od.* im Plural gebrauchen.

plus [plʌs] **I** *prp.* **1.** plus, und; **2.** *bsd.* † zuzüglich (*gen.*); **II** *adj.* **3.** Plus…, *a.* extra, Extra…; **4.** ⚡, ϟ positiv, Plus…: **~ *quantity*** positive Größe; **5.** F plus, mit; **III** *s.* **6.** Plus(zeichen) *n*; **7.** Plus *n*, Mehr *n*, 'Überschuß *m*; **8.** *fig.* Plus (-punkt *m*) *n*; ˌ**~-'fours** *s. pl.* weite Knickerbocker- *od.* Golfhose.

plush [plʌʃ] **I** *s.* **1.** Plüsch *m*; **II** *adj.* **2.** Plüsch…; **3.** *sl.* (stink)vornehm, ‚feu'dal'; '**plush·y** [-ʃɪ] *adj.* **1.** plüschartig; **2.** → ***plush*** 3.

plus·(s)age ['plʌsɪdʒ] *s. Am.* 'Überschuß *m*.

Plu·to ['pluːtəʊ] *s. myth. u. ast.* Pluto *m* (*Gott u. Planet*).

plu·toc·ra·cy [pluː'tɒkrəsɪ] *s.* **1.** Plutokra'tie *f*, Geldherrschaft *f*; **2.** 'Geldaristokraˌtie *f*, *coll.* Pluto'kraten *pl.*; **plu·to·crat** ['pluːtəʊkræt] *s.* Pluto'krat *m*, Kapita'list *m*; **plu·to·crat·ic** [ˌpluːtəʊ'krætɪk] *adj.* pluto'kratisch.

plu·ton·ic [pluː'tɒnɪk] *adj. geol.* plu'tonisch; **plu'to·ni·um** [-'təʊnjəm] *s.* ⚗ Plu'tonium *n*.

plu·vi·al ['pluːvjəl] *adj.* regnerisch; Regen…; '**plu·vi·o·graph** [-əʊgrɑːf] *s. phys.* Regenschreiber *m*; **plu·vi·om·e·ter** [ˌpluːvɪ'ɒmɪtə] *s. phys.* Pluvio'meter *n*, Regenmesser *m*; '**plu·vi·ous** [-jəs] → ***pluvial***.

ply¹ [plaɪ] **I** *v/t.* **1.** *Arbeitsgerät* handhaben, hantieren mit; **2.** *Gewerbe* betreiben, ausüben; **3.** (***with***) bearbeiten (mit) (*a. fig.*); *fig. j-m* (mit *Fragen etc.*) zusetzen, *j-n* (mit *et.*) über'häufen: **~ *s.o. with drink*** j-n zum Trinken nötigen; **4.** *Strecke* (regelmäßig) befahren; **II** *v/i.* **5.** verkehren, fahren, pendeln (***between*** zwischen); **6.** ⚓ aufkreuzen.

ply² [plaɪ] **I** *s.* **1.** Falte *f*; (Garn)Strähne *f*; (Stoff-, Sperrholz- *etc.*)Lage *f*, Schicht *f*: ***three-~*** dreifach (*z.B. Garn, Teppich*); **2.** *fig.* Hang *m*, Neigung *f*; **II** *v/t.* **3.** falten; *Garn* fachen; '**ply·wood** *s.* Sperrholz *n*.

pneu·mat·ic [njuː'mætɪk] **I** *adj.* (□ **~*ally***) **1.** ⚙, *phys.* pneu'matisch, Luft…; ⚙ Druck-, Preßluft…: **~ *brake*** Druckluftbremse *f*; **~ *tool*** Preßluftwerkzeug *n*; **2.** *zo.* lufthaltig; **II** *s.* **3.** Luftreifen *m*; **4.** Fahrzeug *n* mit Luftbereifung; **~ dis·patch** *s.* Rohrpost *f*; **~ drill** *s.* Preßluftbohrer *m*; **~ float** *s.* Floßsack *m*; **~ ham·mer** *s.* Preßlufthammer *m*.

pneu·mat·ics [njuː'mætɪks] *s. pl. sg. konstr. phys.* Pneu'matik *f*.

pneu·mat·ic| tire (*od.* **tyre**) *s.* Luftreifen *m*; *pl. a.* Luftbereifung *f*; **~ tube** *s.* pneu'matische Röhre; *weitS.*, *a. pl.* Rohrpost *f*.

pneu·mo·ni·a [njuː'məʊnjə] *s.* ⚕ Lungenentzündung *f*, Pneumo'nie *f*; **pneu'mon·ic** [-'mɒnɪk] *adj.* pneu'monisch, die Lunge *od.* Lungenentzündung betreffend.

poach¹ [pəʊtʃ] **I** *v/t.* **1.** *a.* **~ *up*** *Erde* aufwühlen, *Rasen* zertrampeln; **2.** (zu e-m Brei) anrühren; **3.** wildern, unerlaubt jagen *od.* fangen; **4.** räubern (*a. fig.*); **5.** *sl.* wegschnappen; **6.** ⚙ *Papier* bleichen; **II** *v/i.* **7.** weich *od.* matschig werden (*Boden*); **8.** unbefugt eindringen (***on*** in *acc.*); → ***preserve*** 8b; **9.** *hunt.* wildern.

poach² [pəʊtʃ] *v/t. Eier* pochieren: **~*ed egg*** pochiertes *od.* verlorenes Ei.

poach·er¹ ['pəʊtʃə] *s.* Wilderer *m*, Wilddieb *m*.

poach·er² ['pəʊtʃə] *s.* Po'chierpfanne *f*.

poach·ing ['pəʊtʃɪŋ] *s.* Wildern *n*, Wilde'rei *f*.

PO Box [ˌpiː əʊ 'bɒks] *s.* Postfach *n*.

po·chette [pɒ'ʃet] (*Fr.*) *s.* Handtäschchen *n*.

pock [pɒk] *s.* ⚕ **1.** Pocke *f*, Blatter *f*; **2.** → ***pockmark***.

pock·et ['pɒkɪt] **I** *s.* **1.** (*Hosen- etc.*, *a. zo. Backen- etc.*)Tasche *f*: ***have s.o. in one's ~*** *fig.* j-n in der Tasche *od.* Gewalt haben; ***put s.o. in one's ~*** *fig.* j-n in die Tasche stecken; ***put one's pride in one's ~*** s-n Stolz überwinden, klein beigeben; **2.** *fig.* Geldbeutel *m*, Fi'nanzen *pl.*: ***be in ~*** gut bei Kasse sein; ***be 3 dollars in*** (***out of***) **~** drei Dollar profitiert (verloren) haben; ***put one's hand in one's ~*** (tief) in die Tasche greifen; → ***line²*** 2; **3.** *Brit.* Sack *m Hopfen, Wolle* (= *76 kg*); **4.** *geol.* Einschluß *m*; **5.** *min.* (*Erz-, Gold*)Nest *n*; **6.** *Billard*: Tasche *f*, Loch *n*; **7.** ✈ (Luft)Loch *n*, Fallbö *f*; **8.** ⚔ Kessel *m*: **~ *of resistance*** Widerstandsnest *n*; **II** *adj.* **9.** Taschen…, im (*fig.* Westen)Taschenformat; **III** *v/t.* **10.** in die Tasche stecken, einstecken (*a. fig. einheimsen*); **11.** a) *fig. Kränkung* einstecken, hinnehmen, b) *Gefühle* unter'drücken, *s-n Stolz* über'winden; **12.** *Billardkugel* einlochen; **13.** *pol. Am. Gesetzesvorlage* nicht unter'schreiben, sein Veto einlegen gegen (*Präsident etc.*); **14.** ⚔ *Feind* einkesseln; **~ bat·tle·ship** *s.* ⚓ Westentaschenkreuzer *m*; **~ bil·liards** *s. pl. sing. konstr.* Poolbillard *n*; **~**

book *s.* **1.** Taschen-, No'tizbuch *n*; **2.** a) Brieftasche *f*, b) Geldbeutel *m* (*beide a. fig.*); **3.** *Am.* Handtasche *f*; **4.** Taschenbuch *n*; **~ cal·cu·la·tor** *s.* Taschenrechner *m*; **~ e·di·tion** *s.* Taschenausgabe *f*.

pock·et·ful ['pɒkɪtfʊl] *pl.* **-fuls** *s. e-e* Tasche(voll): ***a ~ of money***.

'**pock·et|·knife** *s.* [*irr.*] Taschenmesser *n*; **~ lamp** *s.* Taschenlampe *f*; **~ light·er** *s.* Taschenfeuerzeug *n*; **~ mon·ey** *s.* Taschengeld *n*; '**~-size(d)** *adj.* im (*fig.* Westen)Taschenformat; **~ ve·to** *s. pol. Am.* Zu'rückhalten *n od.* Verzögerung *f* e-s Gesetzentwurfs (*bsd. durch den Präsidenten etc.*).

'**pock|·mark** *s.* Pockennarbe *f*; '**~-marked** *adj.* pockennarbig.

pod¹ [pɒd] *s. zo.* **1.** Herde *f* (*Wale, Robben*); **2.** Schwarm *m* (*Vögel*).

pod² [pɒd] **I** *s.* **1.** ⚘ Hülse *f*, Schale *f*, Schote *f*: ***~ pepper*** Paprika *f*; **2.** *zo.* (Schutz)Hülle *f*, *a.* Ko'kon *m* (*der Seidenraupe*), Beutel *m* (*des Moschustiers*); **3.** *sl.* ‚Wampe' *f*, Bauch *m*: ***in ~*** ‚dick' (*schwanger*); **II** *v/i.* **4.** Hülsen ansetzen; **5.** *Erbsen etc.* aushülsen, -schoten.

po·dag·ra [pəʊ'dægrə] *s.* ⚕ Podagra *n*, (Fuß)Gicht *f*.

podg·y ['pɒdʒɪ] *adj.* F unter'setzt, dicklich.

po·di·a·trist [pəʊ'daɪətrɪst] *s. Am.* Fußpfleger(in); **po'di·a·try** [-trɪ] *s.* Fußpflege *f*, Pedi'küre *f*.

Po·dunk ['pəʊdʌŋk] *s. Am. contp.* ‚Krähwinkel' *n*.

po·em ['pəʊɪm] *s.* Gedicht *n* (*a. fig.*), Dichtung *f*; **po·et** ['pəʊɪt] *s.* Dichter *m*, Po'et *m*: ***~ laureate*** a) Dichterfürst *m*, b) *Brit.* Hofdichter *m*; **po·et·as·ter** [pəʊɪ'tæstə] *s.* Dichterling *m*; **po·et·ess** ['pəʊɪtɪs] *s.* Dichterin *f*.

po·et·ic, po·et·i·cal [pəʊ'etɪk(l)] *adj.* □ **1.** po'etisch, dichterisch: ***~ justice*** *fig.* ausgleichende Gerechtigkeit; → ***licence*** 4; **2.** *fig.* po'etisch, ro'mantisch, stimmungsvoll; **po'et·ics** [-ks] *s. pl. sg. konstr.* Po'etik *f*; **po·et·ize** ['pəʊɪtaɪz] **I** *v/i.* **1.** dichten; **II** *v/t.* **2.** in Verse bringen; **3.** (im Gedicht) besingen; **po·et·ry** ['pəʊɪtrɪ] *s.* **1.** Poe'sie *f* (*a. Ggs. Prosa*) (*a. fig.*), Dichtkunst *f*; **2.** Dichtung *f*, *coll.* Dichtungen *pl.*, Gedichte *pl.*: ***dramatic ~*** dramatische Dichtung.

po-faced [ˌpəʊ'feɪst] *Brit.* F grimmig (dreinschauend).

po·grom ['pɒgrəm] *s.* Po'grom *m*, *n*, (*bsd.* Juden)Verfolgung *f*.

poign·an·cy ['pɔɪnənsɪ] *s.* **1.** Schärfe *f von Gerüchen etc.*; **2.** *fig.* Bitterkeit *f*, Heftigkeit *f*, Schärfe *f*; **3.** Schmerzlichkeit *f*; '**poign·ant** [-nt] *adj.* □ **1.** scharf, beißend (*Geruch, Geschmack*); **2.** pi'kant (*a. fig.*); **3.** *fig.* a) bitter, quälend (*Reue, Hunger etc.*), b) ergreifend: ***a ~ scene***, c) beißend, scharf: ***~ wit***, d) treffend, präg'nant: ***~ remark***; **4.** 'durchdringend: ***a ~ look***.

point [pɔɪnt] **I** *s.* **1.** (Nadel-, Messer-, Bleistift- *etc.*)Spitze *f*: (***not***) ***to put too fine a ~ upon s.th.*** *fig.* et. (nicht gerade) gewählt ausdrücken; ***at the ~ of the pistol*** → ***pistol point***; ***at the ~ of the sword*** *fig.* unter Zwang, mit Gewalt; **2.** ⚙ a) Stecheisen *n*, b) Grabstichel *m*, Griffel *m*, c) Radiernadel *f*, d) Ahle *f*; **3.** *geogr.* a) Landspitze *f*, b) Himmelsrichtung *f*: → ***cardinal*** 1; **4.** *hunt.* a) (Geweih)Ende *n*, b) Stehen *n des Jagdhundes*; **5.** *ling.* a) *a.* ***full ~*** Punkt *m am Satzende*, b) ***~ of exclamation*** Ausrufezeichen *n*; → ***interrogation*** 1; **6.** *typ.* a) Punk'tur *f*, b) typo'graphischer Punkt (= *0,376 mm im Didot-System*); **7.** ℞ a) Punkt *m*: ***~ of intersection*** Schnittpunkt, b) (Dezi'mal)Punkt *m*, Komma *n*; **8.** (Kompaß)Strich *m*; **9.** Auge *n*, Punkt *m auf Karten, Würfeln*; **10.** → ***point lace***; **11.** *phys.* Grad *m e-r Skala* (*a. ast.*), Stufe *f* (*a.* ⚙ *e-s Schalters*), Punkt *m*: ***~ of action*** Angriffspunkt (der Kraft); ***~ of contact*** Berührungspunkt; ***~ of culmination*** Kulminations-, Gipfelpunkt; ***boiling-~*** Siedepunkt; ***freezing-~*** Gefrierpunkt; ***3 ~s below zero*** 3 Grad unter Null; ***to bursting ~*** zum Bersten (*voll*); ***frankness to the ~ of insult*** *fig.* an Beleidigung grenzende Offenheit; ***up to a ~*** bis zu e-m gewissen Grad; ***when it came to the ~*** *fig.* als es so weit war, als es darauf ankam; → ***stretch*** 10; **12.** Punkt *m*, Stelle *f*, Ort *m*: ***~ of departure*** Ausgangsort; ***~ of destination*** Bestimmungsort; ***~ of entry*** ⚓ Eingangshafen *m*; ***~ of lubrication*** ⚙ Schmierstelle; ***~ of view*** *fig.* Gesichts-, Standpunkt; **13.** ⚡ a) Kon'takt(punkt) *m*, b) *Brit.* 'Steckkonˌtakt *m*; **14.** *Brit.* (Kon'troll)Posten *m e-s Verkehrspolizisten*; **15.** *pl.* 🚂 *Brit.* Weichen *pl.*; **16.** Punkt *m e-s Bewertungs- od. Bewirtschaftungssystems* (*a. Börse u. sport*): ***bad ~*** *sport* Strafpunkt; ***beat*** (***win***) ***on ~s*** nach Punkten schlagen (gewinnen); ***winner on ~s*** Punktsieger *m*; ***level on ~s*** punktgleich; ***give ~s to s.o.*** a) *sport* j-m vorgeben, b) *fig.* j-m überlegen sein; **17.** *Boxen*: ‚Punkt' *m* (*Kinnspitze*); **18.** *a.* ***~ of time*** Zeitpunkt *m*, Augenblick *m*: ***at the ~ of death***; ***at this ~*** a) in diesem Augenblick, b) an dieser Stelle, hier (*a. in e-r Rede etc.*); ***be on the ~ of doing s.th.*** im Begriff sein, et. zu tun; **19.** Punkt *m e-r Tagesordnung etc.*, (Einzel-, Teil)Frage *f*: ***a case in ~*** ein einschlägiger Fall, ein Beispiel; ***the case in ~*** der vorliegende Fall; ***at all ~s*** in allen Punkten, in jeder Hinsicht; ***~ of interest*** interessante Einzelheit; ***~ of law*** Rechtsfrage; ***~ of order*** a) (Punkt der) Tagesordnung *f*, b) Verfahrensfrage *f*; ***differ on many ~s*** in vielen Punkten nicht übereinstimmen; **20.** Kernpunkt *m*, -frage *f*, springender Punkt, Sache *f*: ***beside*** (*od.* ***off***) ***the ~*** nicht zur Sache gehörig, abwegig, unerheblich; ***come to the ~*** zur Sache kommen; ***the ~*** zur Sache gehörig, (zu)treffend, exakt; ***keep*** (*od.* ***stick***) ***to the ~*** bei der Sache bleiben; ***make*** (*od.* ***score***) ***a ~*** ein Argument anbringen, s-e Ansicht durchsetzen; ***make a ~ of s.th.*** Wert *od.* Gewicht auf et. legen, auf et. bestehen; ***make the ~ that*** die Feststellung machen, daß; ***that's the ~ I wanted to make*** darauf wollte ich hinaus; ***in ~ of*** hinsichtlich (*gen.*); ***in ~ of fact*** tatsächlich; ***that is the ~!*** das ist die Frage!; ***the ~ is that*** die Sache ist die, daß; ***it's a ~ of hono(u)r to him*** das ist Ehrensache für ihn; ***you have a ~ there!*** da haben Sie nicht unrecht!; ***I take your ~!*** ich verstehe, was Sie meinen!; → ***miss²*** 1, ***press*** 8; **21.** Pointe *f e-s Witzes etc.*; **22.** Zweck *m*, Ziel *n*, Absicht *f*: ***what's your ~ in coming?***; ***carry*** (*od.* ***gain*** *od.* ***make***) ***one's ~*** sich (*od.* s-e Ansicht) durchsetzen, sein Ziel erreichen; ***there is no ~ in doing*** es hat keinen Zweck *od.* es ist sinnlos, zu tun; **23.** Nachdruck *m*: ***give ~ to one's words*** s-n Worten Nachdruck *od.* Gewicht verleihen; **24.** (her'vorstechende) Eigenschaft, (Vor)Zug *m*: ***a noble ~ in her*** ein edler Zug an ihr; ***it has its ~s*** es hat so s-e Vorzüge; ***strong ~*** starke Seite, Stärke; ***weak ~*** schwache Seite, wunder Punkt; **II** *v/t.* **25.** (an-, zu)spitzen; **26.** *fig.* pointieren; **27.** *Waffe etc.* richten (***at*** auf *acc.*): ***~ one's finger at*** (mit dem Finger) auf *j-n* deuten *od.* zeigen; ***~*** (***up***)***on*** *Augen, Gedanken etc.* richten auf (*acc.*); ***~ to*** *Kurs, Aufmerksamkeit* lenken auf (*acc.*), *j-n* bringen auf (*acc.*); **28.** ***~ out*** a) zeigen, b) *fig.* hinweisen *od.* aufmerksam machen auf (*acc.*), betonen, c) *fig.* aufzeigen (*a. Fehler*), klarmachen, d) ausführen, darlegen; **29.** ***~ off places*** ℞ (Dezimal-) Stellen abstreichen; **30.** ***~ up*** a) △ verfugen, b) ⚙ *Fugen* glattstreichen, c) *Am. fig.* unter'streichen; **III** *v/i.* **31.** (mit dem Finger) zeigen, deuten, weisen (***at*** auf *acc.*); **32.** ***~ to*** nach *e-r Richtung* weisen *od.* liegen (*Haus etc.*); *fig.* a) hinweisen, -deuten auf (*acc.*), b) ab-, hinzielen auf (*acc.*); **33.** *hunt.* (vor)stehen (*Jagdhund*); **34.** ⚕ reifen (*Abszeß etc.*); ˌ**~-'blank I** *adj.* **1.** schnurgerade; **2.** ⚔ Kernschuß… (*weite etc.*): ***at ~ range*** aus kürzester Entfernung; ***~ shot*** Fleckschuß *m*; **3.** unverblümt, offen; glatt (*Ablehnung*); **II** *adv.* **4.** geradewegs; **5.** *fig.* 'rundher'aus, klipp u. klar; '**~-ˌdu·ty** *s. Brit.* (Verkehrs)Postendienst *m* (*Polizei*).

point·ed ['pɔɪntɪd] *adj.* □ **1.** spitz, zugespitzt, Spitz…(*-bogen, -geschoß etc.*); **2.** scharf, pointiert (*Stil, Bemerkung*), anzüglich; **3.** treffend; '**point·ed·ness** [-nɪs] *s.* **1.** Spitzigkeit *f*; **2.** *fig.* Schärfe *f*, Deutlichkeit *f*; **3.** Anzüglichkeit *f*, Spitze *f*; '**point·er** [-tə] *s.* **1.** ⚔ 'Richtschütze *m*, -kanoˌnier *m*; **2.** Zeiger *m*, Weiser *m* (*Uhr, Meßgerät*); **3.** Zeigestock *m*; **4.** Radiernadel *f*; **5.** *hunt.* Vorsteh-, Hühnerhund *m*; **6.** F Fingerzeig *m*, Tip *m*.

point lace *s.* genähte Spitze(n *pl.*).

point·less ['pɔɪntlɪs] *adj.* □ **1.** ohne Spitze, stumpf; **2.** *sport etc.* punktlos; **3.** *fig.* witzlos, ohne Pointe; **4.** *fig.* sinn-, zwecklos.

'**point-poˌlice·man** [-mən] *s.* [*irr.*] → ***pointsman*** 2; **points·man** ['pɔɪntsmən] *s.* [*irr.*] *Brit.* **1.** 🚂 Weichensteller *m*; **2.** Ver'kehrspoliˌzist *m*; **point sys·tem** *s.* **1.** *sport, ped. etc.* 'Punktsysˌtem *n* (*a. typ.*); **2.** Punktschrift *f für Blinde*; ˌ**point-to-'point** (**race**) *s.* Geländejagdrennen *n*.

poise [pɔɪz] **I** *s.* **1.** Gleichgewicht *n*; **2.** Schwebe *f* (*a. fig. Unentschiedenheit*); **3.** (*Körper-, Kopf*)Haltung *f*; **4.** *fig.* sicheres Auftreten; Gelassenheit *f*; Haltung *f*; **II** *v/t.* **5.** im Gleichgewicht halten; *et.* balancieren: ***be ~d*** a) im Gleichgewicht sein, b) gelassen *od.* ausgeglichen sein, c) *fig.* schweben: ***~d for***

bereit zu; **6.** *Kopf, Waffe etc.* halten; **III** *v/i.* **7.** schweben.

poi·son [ˈpɔɪzn] **I** *s.* **1.** Gift *n* (*a. fig.*): ***what is your ~?*** F was wollen Sie trinken?; **II** *v/t.* **2.** (***o.s.*** sich) vergiften (*a. fig.*); **3.** ⚕ infizieren; ˈ**poi·son·er** [-nə] *s.* **1.** Giftmörder(in), Giftmischer(in); **2.** *fig.* Vergifter(in), ‚Giftspritze' *f.*

ˈ**poi·son|-fang** *s. zo.* Giftzahn *m*; **~ gas** *s.* ⚔ Kampfstoff *m*, *bsd.* Giftgas *n.*

poi·son·ing [ˈpɔɪznɪŋ] *s.* **1.** Vergiftung *f*; **2.** Giftmord *m*; ˈ**poi·son·ous** [-nəs] *adj.* □ **1.** giftig (*a. fig.*) Gift...; **2.** F ekelhaft.

ˌ**poi·son-ˈpen let·ter** *s.* verleumderischer *od.* obˈszöner (*anonymer*) Brief.

poke¹ [pəʊk] **I** *v/t.* **1.** *j-n* stoßen, puffen, knuffen: **~ *s.o. in the ribs*** j-m e-n Rippenstoß geben; **2.** *Loch* stoßen (***in*** in *acc.*); **3.** *a.* **~ *up*** *Feuer* schüren; **4.** *Kopf* vorstrecken, *Nase etc. wohin* stecken: ***she ~s her nose into everything*** sie steckt überall ihre Nase hinein; **5. ~ *fun at s.o.*** sich über j-n lustig machen; **II** *v/i.* **6.** stoßen (***at*** nach); stöbern (***into*** in *dat.*): **~ *about*** (herum)tasten, -tappen (***for*** nach); **7.** *fig.* a) *a.* **~ *and pry*** (herˈum)schnüffeln, b) sich einmischen (***into*** in *acc.*); **8.** *a.* **~ *about*** F (herˈum)trödeln, bummeln; **III** *s.* **9.** (Rippen)Stoß *m*, Puff *m*, Knuff *m*; **10.** *Am.* → ***slowpoke.***

poke² [pəʊk] *s. obs.* Spitztüte *f*; → ***pig*** 1.

ˈ**poke-bon·net** *s.* Kiepe(nhut *m*) *f.*

pok·er¹ [ˈpəʊkə] *s.* Schürhaken *m*: ***be as stiff as a ~*** steif wie ein Stock sein.

po·ker² [ˈpəʊkə] *s.* Poker(spiel) *n.*

pok·er| face *s.* Pokergesicht *n* (*unbewegtes, undurchdringliches Gesicht, a. Person*); **~ work** *s.* Brandmaleˈrei *f.*

pok·y [ˈpəʊkɪ] *adj.* **1.** eng, winzig; **2.** ˈunelegant: **~ *dress***; **3.** langweilig, ‚lahm' (*a. Mensch*).

po·lar [ˈpəʊlə] **I** *adj.* □ **1.** poˈlar (*a. phys.*, ⚗), Polar...: **~ *air*** Polarluft *f*, polare Kaltluft; **~ *fox*** Polarfuchs *m*; **~ *lights*** Polarlicht *n*; ♀ ***Sea*** Polar-, Eismeer *n*; **2.** *fig.* poˈlar, genau entgegengesetzt (wirkend); **II** *s.* **3.** ⚗ Poˈlare *f*; **~ ax·is** *s.* ⚗, *ast.* Poˈlarachse *f*; **~ bear** *s. zo.* Eisbär *m*; **~ cir·cle** *s. geogr.* Poˈlarkreis *m.*

po·lar·i·ty [pəʊˈlærətɪ] *s. phys.* Polariˈtät *f* (*a. fig.*): **~ *indicator*** ⚡ Polsucher *m*; **po·lar·i·za·tion** [ˌpəʊləraɪˈzeɪʃn] *s.* ⚡, *phys.* Polarisatiˈon *f*; *fig.* Polarisierung *f*; **po·lar·ize** [ˈpəʊləraɪz] *v/t.* ⚡, *phys.* polarisieren (*a. fig.*); **po·lar·iz·er** [ˈpəʊləraɪzə] *s. phys.* Polariˈsator *m.*

pole¹ [pəʊl] **I** *s.* **1.** Pfosten *m*, Pfahl *m*; **2.** (*Bohnen-, Telegraphen-, Zelt- etc.*) Stange *f*; (*sport* Sprung)Stab *m*; (Wagen)Deichsel *f*; ⚡ (Leitungs)Mast *m*; (Schi)Stock *m*: **~ *jumper*** *sport* Stabhochspringer; ***be up the ~*** *sl.* a) in der Tinte sitzen, b) verrückt sein; **3.** ⚓ a) Flaggenmast *m*, b) Schifferstange *f*: ***under bare ~s*** ⚓ vor Topp und Takel; **4.** (Meß)Rute *f* (*5,029 Meter*); **II** *v/t.* **5.** *Boot* staken; **6.** *Bohnen etc.* stängen.

pole² [pəʊl] *s.* **1.** *ast., biol., geogr., phys.* Pol *m*: ***celestial ~*** Himmelspol; ***negative ~*** *phys.* negativer Pol, ⚡ *a.* Kathode *f*; → ***positive*** 8; **2.** *fig.* Gegenpol *m*, entgegengesetztes Exˈtrem: ***they are ~s apart*** Welten trennen sie.

Pole³ [pəʊl] *s.* Pole *m*, Polin *f.*

pole| aer·i·al *s.* ˈStabanˌtenne *f*; ˈ**~·ax(e)** *s.* **1.** Streitaxt *f*; **2.** ⚓ a) *hist.* Enterbeil *n*, b) Kappbeil *n*; **3.** Schlächterbeil *n*; ˈ**~·cat** *s. zo.* **1.** Iltis *m*; **2.** *Am.* Skunk *m*; **~ chang·er** *s.* ⚡ Polwechsler *m*; **~ charge** *s.* ⚔ gestreckte Ladung; **~ jump** *etc.* → ***polevault*** *etc.*

po·lem·ic [pɒˈlemɪk] **I** *adj.* (□ **~*ally***) **1.** poˈlemisch, Streit...; **II** *s.* **2.** Poˈlemiker (-in); **3.** Poˈlemik *f*; **poˈlem·i·cist** [-ɪsɪst] *s.* Poˈlemiker(in); **poˈlem·ics** [-ks] *s. pl. sg. konstr.* Poˈlemik *f.*

pole| star *s. ast.* Poˈlarstern *m*; *fig.* Leitstern *m*; **~ vault** *s. sport* Stabhochsprung *m*; ˈ**~-vault** *sport v/i.* stabhochspringen; **~ vault·er** *s. sport* Stabhochspringer *m.*

po·lice [pəˈliːs] **I** *s.* **1.** Poliˈzei(behörde, -truppe) *f*; **2.** *coll. pl. konstr.* Poliˈzei *f*, *einzelne* Poliˈzisten *pl.*: ***five ~***; **3.** ⚔ *Am.* Ordnungsdienst *m*: ***kitchen ~*** Küchendienst; **II** *v/t.* **4.** (poliˈzeilich) überˈwachen; **5.** *fig.* kontrollieren, überˈwachen; **6.** ⚔ *Am. Kaserne etc.* säubern, in Ordnung halten; **III** *adj.* **7.** poliˈzeilich, Polizei...(*-gericht, -gewalt, -staat etc.*): **~ blot·ter** *s. Am.* Dienstbuch *n*; **~ con·sta·ble** → ***policeman*** 1; **~ dog** *s.* **1.** Poliˈzeihund *m*; **2.** (deutscher) Schäferhund; **~ force** *s.* Poliˈzei(truppe) *f*; **~·man** [-mən] *s.* [*irr.*] **1.** Poliˈzist *m*, Schutzmann *m*; **2.** *zo.* Solˈdat *m* (*Ameise*); **~ of·fi·cer** *s.* Poliˈzeibeamte(r) *m*, Poliˈzist *m*; **~ rec·ord** *s.* ˈVorstrafenreˌgister *n*; **~ sta·tion** *s.* Poliˈzeiwache *f*, -reˌvier *n*; **~ trap** *s.* Autofalle *f*; **~ˌwo·man** *s.* Poliˈzistin *f.*

pol·i·clin·ic [ˌpɒlɪˈklɪnɪk] *s.* ⚕ Poliklinik *f*, Ambuˈlanz *f.*

pol·i·cy¹ [ˈpɒlɪsɪ] *s.* **1.** Verfahren(sweise *f*) *n*, Taktik *f*, Poliˈtik *f*: ***marketing ~*** ♆ Absatzpolitik *e-r Firma*; ***honesty is the best ~*** ehrlich währt am längsten; ***the best ~ would be to*** (*inf.*) das Beste *od.* Klügste wäre, zu (*inf.*); **2.** Poliˈtik *f* (*Wege u. Ziele der Staatsführung*), poˈlitische Linie: ***foreign ~*** Außenpolitik; **~ *adviser*** (politischer) Berater; **3. *public ~*** ⚖ Rechtsordnung *f*: ***against public ~*** sittenwidrig; **4.** Klugheit *f*: a) Zweckmäßigkeit *f*, b) Schlauheit *f.*

pol·i·cy² [ˈpɒlɪsɪ] *s.* **1.** (Verˈsicherungs-) Poˌlice *f*, Versicherungsschein *m*; **2.** *a.* **~ *racket*** *Am.* Zahlenlotto *n*; ˈ**~ˌhold·er** *s.* Versicherungsnehmer(in), Poˈliceninhaber(in); ˈ**~-ˌmak·ing** *adj.* die Richtlinien der Poliˈtik bestimmend.

pol·i·o [ˈpəʊlɪəʊ] *s.* ⚕ F **1.** Polio *f*; **2.** Polio-Fall *m.*

pol·i·o·my·e·li·tis [ˌpəʊlɪəʊmaɪəˈlaɪtɪs] *s.* ⚕ spiˈnale Kinderlähmung, Poliomyeˈlitis *f.*

Pol·ish¹ [ˈpəʊlɪʃ] **I** *adj.* polnisch; **II** *s. ling.* Polnisch *n.*

pol·ish² [ˈpɒlɪʃ] **I** *v/t.* **1.** polieren, glätten; *Schuhe etc.* wichsen; ⚙ abschleifen, -schmirgeln, glanzschleifen; **2.** *fig.* abschleifen, verfeinern: **~ *off*** F a) *Gegner* ‚erledigen', b) *Arbeit* ‚hinhauen' (*schnell erledigen*), c) *Essen* ‚wegputzen', ‚verdrücken' (*verschlingen*); **~ *up*** aufpolieren (*a. fig. Wissen auffrischen*); **II** *v/i.* **3.** glänzend werden; sich polieren lassen; **III** *s.* **4.** Poliˈtur *f*, (Hoch)Glanz *m*, Glätte *f*: ***give s.th. a ~*** et. polieren; **5.** Poliermittel *n*, Poliˈtur *f*; Schuhcreme *f*; Bohnerwachs *n*; **6.** *fig.* Schliff *m* (*feine Sitten*); **7.** *fig.* Glanz *m*; ˈ**pol·ished** [-ʃt] *adj.* **1.** poliert, glatt, glänzend; **2.** *fig.* geschliffen: a) höflich, b) gebildet, fein, c) brilˈlant; ˈ**pol·ish·er** [-ʃə] *s.* **1.** Polierer *m*, Schleifer *m*; **2.** ⚙ a) Polierfeile *f*, -stahl *m*, -scheibe *f*, -bürste *f*, b) Poˈliermaˌschine *f*; **3.** Poliermittel *n*, Poliˈtur *f*; ˈ**pol·ish·ing** [-ʃɪŋ] **I** *s.* Polieren *n*, Glätten *n*, Schleifen *n*; **II** *adj.* Polier..., Putz...: **~ *file*** Polierfeile *f*; **~ *powder*** Polier-, Schleifpulver *n*; **~ *wax*** Bohnerwachs *n.*

po·lite [pəˈlaɪt] *adj.* □ **1.** höflich, artig (***to*** gegen); **2.** verfeinert, fein: **~ *arts*** schöne Künste; **~ *letters*** schöne Literatur, Belletristik; **poˈlite·ness** [-nɪs] *s.* Höflichkeit *f.*

pol·i·tic [ˈpɒlɪtɪk] *adj.* □ **1.** diploˈmatisch; **2.** *fig.* diploˈmatisch, (welt)klug, berechnend, poˈlitisch; **3.** poˈlitisch: ***body ~*** Staatskörper *m*; **po·lit·i·cal** [pəˈlɪtɪkl] *adj.* □ **1.** poˈlitisch: **~ *economy*** Volkswirtschaft *f*; **~ *science*** Politologie *f*; **~ *scientist*** Politologe *m*, Politikwissenschaftler *m*; ***a ~ issue*** ein Politikum; **2.** staatlich, Staats...: **~ *system*** Regierungssystem *n*; **pol·i·ti·cian** [ˌpɒlɪˈtɪʃn] *s.* **1.** Poˈlitiker *m*; **2.** a) (Parˈtei)Poˌlitiker *m* (*a. contp.*), b) *Am.* poˈlitischer Opportuˈnist; **po·lit·i·cize** [pəˈlɪtɪsaɪz] *v/i. u. v/t. allg.* politisieren; **po·lit·i·co** [pəˈlɪtɪkəʊ] *Am.* F *für* ***politician*** 2.

politico- [pəlɪtɪkəʊ] *in Zssgn* politisch-...: ***~-economical*** wirtschaftspolitisch.

pol·i·tics [ˈpɒlɪtɪks] *s. pl. oft sg. konstr.* **1.** Poliˈtik *f*, Staatskunst *f*; **2.** (Parˈtei-, ˈStaats)Poliˌtik: ***enter ~*** ins politische Leben (ein)treten; **3.** poˈlitische Überˈzeugung *od.* Richtung: ***what are his ~?*** wie ist er politisch eingestellt?; **4.** *fig.* (Interˈessen)Poliˌtik *f*; **5.** *Am.* (politische) Machenschaften *pl.*: ***play ~*** Winkelzüge machen, manipulieren; ˈ**pol·i·ty** [-ɪtɪ] *s.* **1.** Regierungsform *f*, Verfassung *f*, politische Ordnung; **2.** Staats-, Gemeinwesen *n*, Staat *m.*

pol·ka [ˈpɒlkə] **I** *s.* ♪ Polka *f*; **II** *v/i.* Polka tanzen; **~ dot** *s.* Punktmuster *n* (*auf Textilien*).

poll¹ [pəʊl] **I** *s.* **1.** *bsd. dial. od. humor.* (Hinter)Kopf *m*; **2.** (ˈEinzel)Perˌson *f*; **3.** Abstimmung *f*, Stimmabgabe *f*, Wahl *f*: ***poor ~*** geringe Wahlbeteiligung; **4.** Wählerliste *f*; **5.** a) Stimmenzählung *f*, b) Stimmenzahl *f*; **6.** *mst pl.* ˈWahlloˌkal *n*: ***go to the ~s*** zur Wahl (-urne) gehen; **7.** (Ergebnis *n* e-r) (ˈMeinungs)ˌUmfrage *f*; **II** *v/t.* **8.** *Haar etc.* stutzen, (*a. Tier*) scheren; *Baum* kappen; *Pflanze* köpfen; *e-m Rind* die Hörner stutzen; **9.** in die Wahlliste eintragen; **10.** *Wahlstimmen* erhalten, auf sich vereinigen; **11.** *Bevölkerung* befragen; **III** *v/i.* **12.** s-e Stimme abgeben, wählen: **~ *for*** stimmen für.

poll² [pɒl] *s. univ. Brit. sl.* **1.** *coll.* ***the*** ♀ *Studenten, die sich nur auf den* ***poll degree*** (→ 2) *vorbereiten*; **2.** *a.* **~ *examination*** (leichteres) Bakkalaureˈatsexˌamen: **~ *degree*** *nach Bestehen dieses Examens erlangter Grad.*

poll³ [pəʊl] **I** *adj.* hornlos: **~ *cattle***; **II** *s.* hornloses Rind.

pol·lack [ˈpɒlək] *pl.* **-lacks**, *bsd. coll.*

-lack *s.* Pollack *m* (*Schellfisch*).
pol·lard [ˈpɒləd] **I** *s.* **1.** gekappter Baum; **2.** *zo.* a) hornloses Tier, b) Hirsch, der sein Geweih abgeworfen hat; **3.** (Weizen)Kleie *f*; **II** *v/t.* **4.** *Baum etc.* kappen, stutzen.
ˈ**poll·book** *s.* Wählerliste *f.*
pol·len [ˈpɒlən] *s.* ⚘ Pollen *m*, Blütenstaub *m*: ~ ***catarrh*** Heuschnupfen *m*; ~ ***sac*** Pollensack *m*; ~ ***tube*** Pollenschlauch *m*; ˈ**pol·li·nate** [-neɪt] *v/t. bot.* bestäuben, befruchten.
poll·ing [ˈpəʊlɪŋ] **I** *s.* **1.** Wählen *n*, Wahl *f*; **2.** Wahlbeteiligung *f*: ***heavy*** (***poor***) ~ starke (geringe) Wahlbeteiligung; **II** *adj.* **3.** Wahl…: ~ ***booth*** Wahlzelle *f*; ~ ***district*** Wahlkreis *m*; ~ ***place*** *Am.*, ~ ***station*** *bsd. Brit.* Wahllokal *n.*
pol·lock [ˈpɒlək] → ***pollack***.
poll·ster [ˈpəʊlstə] *s. Am.* Meinungsforscher *m*, Interˈviewer *m.*
ˈ**poll-tax** *s.* Kopfsteuer *f*, -geld *n.*
pol·lu·tant [pəˈluːtənt] *s.* Schadstoff *m*; **pol·lute** [pəˈluːt] *v/t.* **1.** beflecken (*a. fig. Ehre etc.*), beschmutzen; **2.** *Wasser etc.* verunreinigen, *Umwelt etc.* verschmutzen; **3.** *fig.* besudeln; *eccl.* entweihen; *moralisch* verderben; **polˈlu·ter** [-tə] *s.* ˈUmweltverschmutzer *m*, -sünder *m*; **polˈlu·tion** [-uːʃn] *s.* **1.** Befleckung *f*, Verunreinigung *f* (*a. fig.*); **2.** *fig.* Entweihung *f*, Schändung *f*; **3.** *physiol.* Pollutiˈon *f*; **4.** (ˈUmwelt-, Luft-, Wasser)Verschmutzung *f*: ~ ***control*** Umweltschutz *m*; **polˈlu·tive** [-tɪv] *adj.* ˈumweltverschmutzend, -feindlich.
po·lo [ˈpəʊləʊ] *s. sport* Polo *n*: ~ (***neck***) Rollkragen(pullover) *m*; ~ ***shirt*** Polohemd *n.*
po·lo·ny [pəˈləʊnɪ] *s.* grobe Zerveˈlatwurst.
pol·troon [pɒlˈtruːn] *s.* Feigling *m.*
poly- [pɒlɪ] *in Zssgn* Viel…, Mehr…, Poly…; **pol·y·an·drous** [ˌpɒlɪˈændrəs] *adj.* ⚘, *zo.*, *sociol.* polyˈandrisch; ˌ**pol·y·aˈtom·ic** *adj.* ⚗ ˈviel-, ˈmehraˌtomig; ˌ**pol·yˈbas·ic** *adj.* ⚗ mehrbasig; ˌ**pol·y·chroˈmat·ic** *adj.* (☐ ~***ally***) viel-, mehrfarbig; ˈ**pol·y·chrome I** *adj.* **1.** viel-, mehrfarbig, bunt: ~ ***printing*** Bunt-, Mehrfarbendruck; **II** *s.* **2.** Vielfarbigkeit *f*; **3.** buntbemalte Plastik; ˌ**pol·yˈclin·ic** *s.* Klinik *f* (für alle Krankheiten).
po·lyg·a·mist [pəˈlɪgəmɪst] *s.* Polygaˈmist(in); **poˈlyg·a·mous** [-məs] *adj.* polyˈgam(isch ⚘, *zo.*); **poˈlyg·a·my** [-mɪ] *s.* Polygaˈmie *f* (*a. zo.*), Mehrehe *f*, Vielweibeˈrei *f.*
pol·y·glot [ˈpɒlɪglɒt] **I** *adj.* **1.** vielsprachig; **II** *s.* **2.** Polyˈglotte *f* (*Buch in mehreren Sprachen*); **3.** Polyˈglotte(r *m*) *f* (*Person*).
pol·y·gon [ˈpɒlɪgən] *s.* ⩓ a) Polyˈgon *n*, Vieleck *n*, b) Polygoˈnalzahl *f*: ~ ***of forces*** *phys.* Kräftepolygon; **po·lyg·o·nal** [pɒˈlɪgənl] *adj.* polygoˈnal, vieleckig.
po·lyg·y·ny [pəˈlɪdʒɪnɪ] *s. allg.* Polygyˈnie *f.*
pol·y·he·dral [ˌpɒlɪˈhedrl] *adj.* ⩓ polyˈedrisch, vielflächig, Polyeder…; ˌ**pol·yˈhe·dron** [-rən] *s.* ⩓ Polyˈeder *n.*
pol·y·mer·ic [ˌpɒlɪˈmerɪk] *adj.* ⚗ ˌpolyˈmer; **po·lym·er·ism** [pəˈlɪmərɪzəm] *s.* Polymeˈrie *f*; **pol·y·mer·ize** [pəˈlɪməraɪz] ⚗ **I** *v/t.* polymerisieren; **II** *v/i.* polyˈmere Körper bilden.
pol·y·mor·phic [ˌpɒlɪˈmɔːfɪk] *adj.* polyˈmorph, vielgestaltig.
Pol·y·ne·sian [ˌpɒlɪˈniːzjən] **I** *adj.* **1.** polyˈnesisch; **II** *s.* **2.** Polyˈnesier(in); **3.** *ling.* Polyˈnesisch *n.*
pol·y·no·mi·al [ˌpɒlɪˈnəʊmjəl] **I** *adj.* ⩓ polyˈnomisch, vielglied(e)rig; **II** *s.* ⩓ Polyˈnom *n.*
pol·yp(**e**) [ˈpɒlɪp] *s.* ⚕, *zo.* Poˈlyp *m.*
ˈ**pol·y·phase** *adj.* ⚡ mehrphasig: ~ ***current*** Mehrphasen-, Drehstrom *m*; ˌ**pol·yˈphon·ic** [-ˈfɒnɪk] *adj.* **1.** vielstimmig, mehrtönig; **2.** ♪ polyˈphon, kontraˈpunktisch; **3.** *ling.* phoˈnetisch mehrdeutig; ˈ**pol·y·pod** [-pɒd] *s. zo.* Vielfüßer *m.*
pol·y·pus [ˈpɒlɪpəs] *pl.* **-pi** [-paɪ] *s.* **1.** *zo.* Poˈlyp *m*, Tintenfisch *m*; **2.** ⚕ Poˈlyp *m.*
pol·y·sty·rene [ˌpɒlɪˈstaɪriːn] *s.* ⚗ Styroˈpor *n.*
ˌ**pol·y·sylˈlab·ic** *adj.* mehr-, vielsilbig; ˈ**pol·yˌsyl·la·ble** *s.* vielsilbiges Wort; ˌ**pol·yˈtech·nic I** *adj.* polyˈtechnisch; **II** *s.* polyˈtechnische Schule, Polyˈtechnikum *n*; ˈ**pol·y·the·ism** *s.* Polytheˈismus *m*, Vielgötteˈrei *f*; **pol·y·thene** [ˈpɒlɪθiːn] *s.* ⚗ Polyäthyˈlen *n*: ~ ***bag*** Plastiktüte *f*; ˌ**pol·yˈtrop·ic** *adj.* ⩓, *biol.* polyˈtrop(isch); ˌ**pol·yˈva·lent** *adj.* ⚗ polyvaˈlent, mehrwertig.
pol·y·zo·on [ˌpɒlɪˈzəʊɒn] *pl.* **-ˈzo·a** [-ə] *s.* Moostierchen *n.*
pom [pɒm] → ***pommy***.
po·made [pəˈmɑːd] **I** *s.* Poˈmade *f*; **II** *v/t.* pomadisieren, mit Poˈmade einreiben.
po·man·der [pəʊˈmændə] *s.* Duftkugel *f.*
po·ma·tum [pəʊˈmeɪtəm] → ***pomade***.
pome [pəʊm] *s.* **1.** ⚘ Apfel-, Kernfrucht *f*; **2.** *hist.* Reichsapfel *m.*
pome·gran·ate [ˈpɒmɪˌgrænɪt] *s.* **1.** *a.* ~ ***tree*** Graˈnatapfelbaum *m*; **2.** *a.* ~ ***apple*** Graˈnatapfel *m.*
Pom·er·a·nian [ˌpɒməˈreɪnjən] **I** *adj.* **1.** pommer(i)sch; **II** *s.* **2.** Pommer(in); **3.** *a.* ~ ***dog*** Spitz *m.*
po·mi·cul·ture [ˈpəʊmɪˌkʌltʃə] *s.* Obstbaumzucht *f.*
pom·mel [ˈpʌml] **I** *s.* (Degen-, Sattel-, Turm)Knopf *m*, Knauf *m*; **II** *v/t.* mit den Fäusten bearbeiten, schlagen.
pom·my [ˈpɒmɪ] *s. sl. brit.* Einwanderer *m* (in Ausˈtralien *od.* Neuˈseeland).
pomp [pɒmp] *s.* Pomp *m*, Prunk *m.*
pom·pon [ˈpɔ̃ːmpɔ̃ːŋ] (*Fr.*) *s.* Troddel *f*, Quaste *f.*
pom·pos·i·ty [pɒmˈpɒsətɪ] *s.* **1.** Prunk *m*; Pomphaftigkeit *f*, Prahleˈrei *f*; wichtigtuerisches Wesen; **2.** Bomˈbast *m*, Schwülstigkeit *f* (*im Ausdruck*); **pomp·ous** [ˈpɒmpəs] *adj.* ☐ **1.** pomˈpös, prunkvoll; **2.** wichtigtuerisch, aufgeblasen; **3.** bomˈbastisch, schwülstig (*Sprache*).
ponce [pɒns] *Brit. sl.* **I** *s.* **1.** Zuhälter *m*; **2.** ‚Homo' *m*; **II** *v/i.* **3.** Zuhälter sein; ˈ**ponc·ing** [-sɪŋ] *s. Brit. sl.* Zuhälteˈrei *f.*
pon·cho [ˈpɒntʃəʊ] *pl.* **-chos** [-z] *s.* Poncho *m*, ˈUmhang *m.*
pond [pɒnd] *s.* Teich *m*, Weiher *m*: ***horse*** ~ Pferdeschwemme *f*; ***big*** ~ ‚Großer Teich' (*Atlantik*).
pon·der [ˈpɒndə] **I** *v/i.* nachdenken, -sinnen, (nach)grübeln (***on***, ***upon***, ***over*** über *acc.*): ~ ***over s.th.*** et. überlegen; **II** *v/t.* überˈlegen, nachdenken über (*acc.*): ~ ***one's words*** s-e Worte abwägen; ~***ing silence*** nachdenkliches Schweigen; **pon·der·a·bil·i·ty** [ˌpɒndərəˈbɪlətɪ] *s. phys.* Wägbarkeit *f*; ˈ**pon·der·a·ble** [-dərəbl] *adj.* wägbar (*a. fig.*); **pon·der·os·i·ty** [ˌpɒndəˈrɒsətɪ] *s.* **1.** Gewicht *n*, Schwere *f*, Gewichtigkeit *f*; **2.** *fig.* Schwerfälligkeit *f*; ˈ**pon·der·ous** [-dərəs] *adj.* ☐ **1.** schwer, massig, gewichtig; **2.** *fig.* schwerfällig (*Stil*); ˈ**pon·der·ous·ness** [-dərəsnɪs] → ***ponderosity***.
pone[1] [pəʊn] *s. Am.* Maisbrot *n.*
po·ne[2] [ˈpəʊnɪ] *s. Kartenspiel*: **1.** Vorhand *f*; **2.** Spieler, der abhebt.
pong [pɒŋ] **I** *s.* **1.** dumpfes Dröhnen; **2.** *Br. sl.* Gestank *m*, ‚Mief' *m*; **II** *v/i.* **3.** dröhnen; **4.** *Br. sl.* stinken; **5.** *sl. thea.* improvisieren.
pon·tiff [ˈpɒntɪf] *s.* **1.** Hoheˈpriester *m*; **2.** Papst *m*; **pon·tif·i·cal** [pɒnˈtɪfɪkl] *adj.* ☐ **1.** *antiq.* (ober)priesterlich; **2.** *R.C.* pontifiˈkal: a) bischöflich, b) *bsd.* päpstlich: ℒ ***Mass*** Pontifikalamt *n*; **3.** *fig.* a) feierlich, würdig, b) päpstlich, überˈheblich; **pon·tif·i·cate I** *s.* [pɒnˈtɪfɪkət] Pontifiˈkat *n*; **II** *v/i.* [-keɪt] a) sich päpstlich gebärden, b) ~ (***on***) sich dogmatisch auslassen (über); ˈ**pon·ti·fy** [-ɪfaɪ] → ***pontificate*** II.
pon·toon[1] [pɒnˈtuːn] *s.* **1.** Ponˈton *m*, Brückenkahn *m*: ~ ***bridge*** Ponton-, Schiffsbrücke *f*; ~ ***train*** ⚔ Brückenkolonne *f*; **2.** ⚓ Kielleichter *m*, Prahm *m*; **3.** ✈ Schwimmer *m.*
pon·toon[2] [pɒnˈtuːn] *s. Brit.* ˈSiebzehnundˈvier *n* (*Kartenspiel*).
po·ny [ˈpəʊnɪ] **I** *s.* **1.** *zo.* Pony *n*: a) kleines Pferd, b) *Am. a.* Mustang *m*, c) *pl. sl.* Rennpferde *pl.*; **2.** *Brit. sl.* £ 25; **3.** *Am.* F ‚Klatsche' *f*, Eselsbrücke *f* (*Übersetzungshilfe*); **4.** *Am.* F a) kleines (Schnaps- *etc.*)Glas, b) Gläs-chen *n* Schnaps *etc.*; **5.** *Am.* et. ‚im Westentaschenformat', Miniatur… (*z.B. Auto, Zeitschrift*); **II** *v/t.* **6.** ~ ***up*** *Am. sl.* berappen, bezahlen; ~ ***en·gine*** *s.* 🚂 Ranˈgierlokomoˌtive *f*; ~ ***tail*** *s.* Pferdeschwanz *m* (*Frisur*).
pooch [puːtʃ] *s. Am. sl.* Köter *m.*
poo·dle [ˈpuːdl] *s. zo.* Pudel *m.*
poof [puːf] *Brit. sl.* ‚Schwule(r)' *m*, ‚Homo' *m.*
pooh [puː] *int. contp.* pah!; ˌ~-ˈ**pooh** *v/t.* geringschätzig behandeln, *et.* als unwichtig abtun, die Nase rümpfen über (*acc.*), *et.* verlachen.
pool[1] [puːl] *s.* **1.** Teich *m*, Tümpel *m*; **2.** Pfütze *f*, Lache *f*: ~ ***of blood*** Blutlache; **3.** (Schwimm)Becken *n*; **4.** *geol.* peˈtroleumhaltige Geˈsteinsparˌtie; **5.** ⚙ Schmelzbad *n.*
pool[2] [puːl] **I** *s.* **1.** *Kartenspiel*: a) (Gesamt)Einsatz *m*, b) (Spiel)Kasse *f*; **2.** *mst pl.* (Fußball- *etc.*)Toto *m*, *n*; **3.** *Billard*: a) *Brit.* Poulespiel *n* (*mit Einsatz*), b) *Am.* Poolbillard *n*; **4.** *fenc.* Ausscheidungsrunde *f*; **5.** ✝ a) Pool *m*, Karˈtell *n*, Ring *m*, Interˈessengemeinschaft *f*, b) *a.* ***working*** ~ Arbeitsgemeinschaft *f*, c) (Preis- *etc.*)Abkommen *n*; **6.** ✝ gemeinsamer Fonds; **7.** ~ (***of players***) *sport* a) Kader *m*, b) Aufgebot *n*, Auswahl *f*; **II** *v/t.* **8.** ✝ *Geld*, *Kapital* zs.-legen: ~ ***funds*** zs.-schießen;

Gewinn unterein'ander (ver)teilen; *Geschäftsrisiko* verteilen; **9.** ✝ zu e-m Ring vereinigen; **10.** *fig. Kräfte, Wissen etc.* vereinigen, zs.-tun; **III** *v/i.* **11.** ein Kar'tell bilden; '**~room** *s. Am.* **1.** Billardzimmer *n*; **2.** 'Spielsaˌlon *m*; **3.** Wettannahmestelle *f*.

poop¹ [pu:p] ⚓ **I** *s.* **1.** Heck *n*; **2.** *a.* **~ deck** Achterdeck *n*; **3.** *obs.* Achterhütte *f*; **II** *v/t.* **4.** *Schiff* von hinten treffen (*Sturzwelle*): **be ~ed** e-e Sturzsee von hinten bekommen.

poop² [pu:p] **I** *v/i.* **1.** tuten; **2.** ‚pupen', furzen; **II** *v/t.* **3.** *sl. j-n* ‚auspumpen': **~ed (out)** ‚fix u. fertig'.

poor [pʊə] **I** *adj.* □ → **poorly** II; **1.** arm, mittellos, (unter'stützungs)bedürftig: **~ person** ⚖ Arme(r *m*) *f*; **2.** *fig.* arm(selig), ärmlich, dürftig (*Kleidung, Mahlzeit etc.*); **3.** dürr, mager (*Boden, Erz, Vieh etc.*), schlecht, unergiebig (*Ernte etc.*): **~ coal** Magerkohle *f*; **4.** *fig.* arm (**in** an *dat.*); schlecht, mangelhaft, schwach (*Gesundheit, Leistung, Spieler, Sicht, Verständigung etc.*): **~ consolation** schwacher Trost; **a ~ lookout** schlechte Aussichten; **a ~ night** e-e schlechte Nacht; **5.** *fig. contp.* jämmerlich, traurig: **in my ~ opinion** *iro.* m-r unmaßgeblichen Meinung nach; **6.** F arm, bedauernswert: **~ me!** *humor.* ich Ärmste(r)!; **II** *s.* **7. the ~** die Armen *pl.*; '**~-house** *s. hist.* Armenhaus *n*; **~ law** *s. hist.* **1.** ⚖ Armenrecht *n*; **2.** *pl.* öffentliches Fürsorgerecht.

poor·ly ['pʊəlɪ] **I** *adj.* **1.** unpäßlich, kränklich: **he looks ~** er sieht schlecht aus; **II** *adv.* **2.** armselig, dürftig: **he is ~ off** es geht ihm schlecht; **3.** *fig.* schlecht, dürftig, schwach: **~ gifted** schwachbegabt; **think ~ of** nicht viel halten von; '**poor·ness** [-nɪs] *s.* **1.** Armut *f*, Mangel *m*; *fig.* Armseligkeit *f*, Ärmlichkeit *f*, Dürftigkeit *f*; **2.** ✓ Magerkeit *f*, Unfruchtbarkeit *f* (*des Bodens*); *min.* Unergiebigkeit *f*.

poove [pu:v] *s.* → **poof**; '**poov·y** *adj.* ‚schwul'.

pop¹ [pɒp] **I** *v/i.* **1.** knallen, puffen, losgehen (*Flaschenkork, Feuerwerk etc.*); **2.** aufplatzen (*Kastanien, Mais*); **3.** F knallen, ‚ballern' (**at** auf *acc.*); **4.** *mit adv.* flitzen, huschen: **~ in** hereinplatzen, auf e-n Sprung vorbeikommen (*Besuch*); **~ off** F a) ‚abhauen', sich aus dem Staub machen, plötzlich verschwinden, b) einnicken, c) ‚abkratzen' (*sterben*), d) *Am. sl.* ‚das Maul aufreißen'; **~ up** (plötzlich) auftauchen; **5.** *a.* **~ out** aus den Höhlen treten (*Augen*); **II** *v/t.* **6.** knallen *od.* platzen lassen; *Am. Mais* rösten; **7.** F *Gewehr etc.* abfeuern; **8.** abknallen, -schießen; **9.** schnell *wohin* tun *od.* stecken: **~ one's head in the door**; **~ on** *Hut* aufstülpen; **10.** her'ausplatzen mit (*e-r Frage etc.*): **~ the question** F (**to** *e-r Dame*) e-n Heiratsantrag machen; **11.** *Brit. sl.* versetzen, verpfänden; **III** *s.* **12.** Knall *m*, Puff *m*, Paff *m*; **13.** F Schuß *m*: **take a ~ at** schießen nach; **14.** *Am. sl.* Pi'stole *f*; **15.** F ‚Limo' *f* (*Limonade*); **16. in ~** *Brit. sl.* versetzt, verpfändet; **IV** *int.* **17.** puff!, paff!, husch!, zack!; **V** *adv.* **18.** a) mit e-m Knall, b) plötzlich: **go ~** knallen, platzen.

pop² [pɒp] *s. Am.* F **1.** Pa'pa *m*, Papi *m*; **2.** ‚Opa' *m*, Alter *m*.

pop³ [pɒp] F **I** *s.* **1.** *a.* **~ music** 'Schlager-, 'Popmuˌsik *f*; **2.** *a.* **~ song** Schlager *m*; **II** *adj.* **3.** Schlager...: **~ group** Popgruppe *f*; **~ singer** Schlager-, Popsänger(in).

pop⁴ [pɒp] → **popsicle**.

pop art *s. Kunst*: Pop-art *f*.

'**pop·corn** *s.* Puffmais *m*, Popcorn *n*.

pope [pəʊp] *s. R.C.* Papst *m* (*a. fig.*); '**pope·dom** [-dəm] *s.* Papsttum *n*; '**pop·er·y** [-pərɪ] *s. contp.* Papiste'rei *f*, Pfaffentum *n*.

'**pop|-eyed** *adj.* F glotzäugig: **be ~** Stielaugen machen (**with** vor *dat.*); '**~-gun** *s.* Kindergewehr *n*; ‚Knallbüchse' *f* (*a. fig. schlechtes Gewehr*).

pop·in·jay ['pɒpɪndʒeɪ] *s. obs.* Geck *m*, Laffe *m*, Fatzke *m*.

pop·ish ['pəʊpɪʃ] *adj.* □ *contp.* pa'pistisch.

pop·lar ['pɒplə] *s.* ⚘ Pappel *f*.

pop·lin ['pɒplɪn] *s.* Pope'lin *m*, Pope'line *f* (*Stoff*).

pop·per ['pɒpə] *s.* F Druckknopf *m*.

pop·pet ['pɒpɪt] *s.* **1.** *obs. od. dial.* Püppchen *n* (*a. Kosewort*); **2.** ⚙ a) *a.* **~ head** Docke *f e-r Drehbank*, b) *a.* **~ valve** 'Schnüffelvenˌtil *n*.

pop·py ['pɒpɪ] *s.* **1.** ⚘ Mohn(blume *f*) *m*; **2.** a) Mohnsaft *m*, b) Mohnrot *n*; '**~cock** *s. Am.* F Quatsch *m*; ♀ **Day** *s. Brit.* F Volkstrauertag *m* (*Sonntag vor od. nach dem 11. November*); '**~-seed** *s.* Mohn(samen) *m*.

pops [pɒps] → **pop²** 2.

pop·si·cle ['pɒpsɪkl] *s. Am.* Eis *n* am Stiel.

pop·sy ['pɒpsɪ], *a.* ˌ**~-'wop·sy** [-'wɒpsɪ] *s.* ‚süße Puppe', ‚Mädchen' *n*, ‚Schatz' *m*.

pop·u·lace ['pɒpjʊləs] *s.* **1.** Pöbel *m*; **2.** (gemeines) Volk, *der* große Haufen.

pop·u·lar ['pɒpjʊlə] *adj.* □ → **popularly**; **1.** Volks...: **~ election** allgemeine Wahl; **~ front** *pol.* Volksfront *f*; **~ government** Volksherrschaft *f*; **2.** allgemein, weitverbreitet (*Irrtum, Unzufriedenheit etc.*); **3.** popu'lär, (allgemein) beliebt (**with** bei): **the ~ hero** der Held des Tages; **make o.s. ~ with** sich bei *j-m* beliebt machen; **4.** a) popu'lär, volkstümlich, b) gemeinverständlich, Popular...: **~ magazine** populäre Zeitschrift; **~ music** volkstümliche Musik; **~ science** Popularwissenschaft *f*; **~ song** Schlager *m*; **~ writer** Volksschriftsteller(in); **5.** (für jeden) erschwinglich, Volks...: **~ edition** Volksausgabe *f*; **~ prices** volkstümliche Preise; **pop·u·lar·i·ty** [ˌpɒpjʊ'lærətɪ] *s.* Populari'tät *f*, Volkstümlichkeit *f*, Beliebtheit *f* (**with** bei, **among** unter *dat.*); '**pop·u·lar·ize** [-əraɪz] *v/t.* **1.** popu'lär machen, (*beim Volk*) einführen; **2.** popularisieren, volkstümlich *od.* gemeinverständlich darstellen; '**pop·u·lar·ly** [-lɪ] *adv.* **1.** allgemein; im Volksmund; **2.** populär, volkstümlich, gemeinverständlich.

pop·u·late ['pɒpjʊleɪt] *v/t.* bevölkern, besiedeln; **pop·u·la·tion** [ˌpɒpjʊ'leɪʃn] *s.* **1.** Bevölkerung *f*, Einwohnerschaft *f*: **~ density** Bevölkerungsdichte *f*; **~ explosion** Bevölkerungsexplosion *f*; **2.** Bevölkerungszahl *f*; **3.** Gesamtzahl *f*, Bestand *m*: **swine ~** Schweinebestand (*e-s Landes*); '**pop·u·lous** [-ləs] *adj.* □ dichtbesiedelt, volkreich; '**pop·u·lous·ness** [-ləsnɪs] *s.* dichte Besied(e)lung, Bevölkerungsdichte *f*.

por·ce·lain ['pɔ:səlɪn] **I** *s.* Porzel'lan *n*; **II** *adj.* Porzellan...: **~ clay** *min.* Porzellanerde *f*, Kaolin *n*.

porch [pɔ:tʃ] *s.* **1.** (über'dachte) Vorhalle, Por'tal *n*; **2.** *Am.* Ve'randa *f*: **~ climber** *sl.* ‚Klettermaxe' *m*, Einsteigdieb *m*.

por·cine ['pɔ:saɪn] *adj.* **1.** *zo.* zur Fa'milie der Schweine gehörig; **2.** schweineartig; **3.** *fig.* schweinisch.

por·cu·pine ['pɔ:kjʊpaɪn] *s. zo.* Stachelschwein *n*.

pore¹ [pɔ:] *v/i.* **1.** (**over**) brüten (über *dat.*): **~ over one's books** über s-n Büchern hocken; **2.** (nach)grübeln (**on, upon** über *acc*).

pore² [pɔ:] *s. biol. etc.* Pore *f*.

pork [pɔ:k] *s.* **1.** Schweinefleisch *n*; **2.** *Am.* F *von der Regierung aus politischen Gründen gewährte (finanzielle) Begünstigung od. Stellung*; **~ bar·rel** *s. Am.* F *politisch berechnete* Geldzuwendung *der Regierung*; **~ butch·er** *s.* Schweineschlächter *m*; **~ chop** *s.* 'Schweinekoteˌlett *n*.

pork·er ['pɔ:kə] *s.* Mastschwein *n*; '**pork·ling** [-klɪŋ] *s.* Ferkel *n*.

pork pie *s.* 'Schweinefleischpaˌstete *f*.

'**pork-pie hat** *s.* runder Filzhut.

pork·y¹ ['pɔ:kɪ] *adj.* fett(ig), dick.

por·ky² ['pɔ:kɪ] *s. Am.* F Stachelschwein *n*.

porn [pɔ:n], **por·no** ['pɔ:nəʊ] *sl.* **I** *s.* **1.** Porno(gra'phie *f*) *m*; **2.** Porno(film) *m*; **II** *adj.* **3.** → **pornographic**.

por·no·graph·ic [ˌpɔ:nəʊ'græfɪk] *adj.* porno'graphisch, Porno...: **~ film** Porno(film) *m*; **por·nog·ra·phy** [pɔ:'nɒgrəfɪ] *s.* Pornogra'phie *f*.

por·ny ['pɔ:nɪ] *adj. sl.* → **pornographic**.

po·ros·i·ty [pɔ:'rɒsətɪ] *s.* **1.** Porosi'tät *f*, ('Luft-, 'Wasser)ˌDurchlässigkeit *f*; **2.** Pore *f*, po'röse Stelle; **po·rous** ['pɔ:rəs] *adj.* po'rös: a) löch(e)rig, porig, b) ('luft-, 'wasser)ˌdurchlässig.

por·poise ['pɔ:pəs] *pl.* **-pois·es**, *coll.* **-poise** *s. zo.* **1.** Tümmler *m*; **2.** Del'phin *m*.

por·ridge ['pɒrɪdʒ] *s.* Porridge *n, m*, Hafer(flocken)brei *m*, -grütze *f*: **pease-~** Erbsenbrei.

por·ri·go [pə'raɪgəʊ] *s.* ⚕ Grind *m*.

port¹ [pɔ:t] *s.* **1.** ⚓, ✈ (See-, Flug)Hafen *m*: **free ~** Freihafen; **inner ~** Binnenhafen; **~ of call** a) ⚓ Anlaufhafen, b) ✈ Anflughafen; **~ of delivery** (*od.* **discharge**) Löschhafen, -platz *m*; **~ of departure** a) ⚓ Abgangshafen, b) ✈ Abflughafen; **~ of destination** a) ⚓ Bestimmungshafen, b) ✈ Zielflughafen; **~ of entry** Einlaufhafen; **~ of registry** Heimathafen; **~ of tran(s)shipment** Umschlaghafen; **any ~ in a storm** *fig.* in der Not frißt der Teufel Fliegen; **2.** Hafenplatz *m*, -stadt *f*; **3.** *fig.* (sicherer) Hafen, Ziel *n*: **come safe to ~**.

port² [pɔ:t] ⚓ **I** *s.* Backbord(seite *f*) *n*: **on the ~ beam** an Backbord dwars; **on the ~ bow** an Backbord voraus; **on the ~ quarter** Backbord achtern; **cast to ~** nach Backbord abfallen; **II** *v/t. Ruder* nach der Backbordseite 'umlegen; **III**

v/i. nach Backbord drehen (*Schiff*); **IV** *adj.* a) ⚓ Backbord…, b) ✈ link.

port³ [pɔːt] *s.* **1.** Tor *n*, Pforte *f*; ***city ~*** Stadttor; **2.** ⚓ a) (Pfort-, Lade)Luke *f*, b) (Schieß)Scharte *f* (*a.* ⚔ *Panzer*); **3.** ⚙ (Auslaß-, Einlaß)Öffnung *f*, Abzug *m*.

port⁴ [pɔːt] *s.* Portwein *m*.

port⁵ [pɔːt] *v/t.* **1.** *obs.* tragen; **2.** ⚔ *Am.* ***~ arms!*** Gewehr in Schräghalte nach links!

port·a·ble [ˈpɔːtəbl] **I** *adj.* **1.** tragbar: ***~ radio*** (***set***) a) → 3a, b) ⚔ Tornisterfunkgerät; ***~ typewriter*** → 4; **2.** transporˈtabel, beweglich: ***~ derrick*** fahrbarer Kran; ***~ firearm*** Handfeuerwaffe *f*; ***~ railway*** Feldbahn *f*; ***~ search-light*** Handscheinwerfer *m*; **II** *s.* **3.** a) Kofferradio *n*, b) Portable *m*, *n*, tragbares Fernsehgerät, c) Phonokoffer *m*, d) Koffertonbandgerät *n*; **4.** ˈReiseschreibmaˌschine *f*.

por·tage [ˈpɔːtɪdʒ] *s.* **1.** (*bsd.* ˈTrage-)Transˌport *m*; **2.** ☤ Fracht *f*, Rollgeld *n*; **3.** ⚓ a) Porˈtage *f*, Trageplatz *m*, b) Tragen *n* (*von Kähnen etc.*) über e-e Portage.

por·tal¹ [ˈpɔːtl] *s.* **1.** ⚠ Porˈtal *n*, (Haupt)Eingang *m*, Tor *n*: ***~ crane*** ⚙ Portalkran *m*; **2.** *poet.* Pforte *f*, Tor *n*: ***~ of heaven***.

por·tal² [ˈpɔːtl] *anat.* **I** *adj.* Pfort(ader)…; **II** *s.* Pfortader *f*.

ˌpor·tal-to-ˈpor·tal pay *s.* ☤ *Arbeitslohn, berechnet für die Zeit vom Betreten der Fabrik etc. bis zum Verlassen.*

port·cul·lis [ˌpɔːtˈkʌlɪs] *s.* ⚔ *hist.* Fallgatter *n*.

por·tend [pɔːˈtend] *v/t.* vorbedeuten, anzeigen, deuten auf (*acc.*); **por·tent** [ˈpɔːtent] *s.* **1.** Vorbedeutung *f*; **2.** (*bsd.* schlimmes) (Vor-, An)Zeichen, Omen *n*; **3.** Wunder *n* (*Sache od. Person*); **porˈten·tous** [-ntəs] *adj.* □ **1.** omiˈnös, unheil-, verhängnisvoll; **2.** ungeheuer, wunderbar, *a. humor.* unheimlich.

por·ter¹ [ˈpɔːtə] *s.* a) Pförtner *m*, b) Porˈtier *m*.

por·ter² [ˈpɔːtə] *s.* **1.** 🚂 (Gepäck)Träger *m*, Dienstmann *m*; **2.** 🚂 *Am.* (Schlafwagen)Schaffner *m*.

por·ter³ [ˈpɔːtə] *s.* Porter(bier *n*) *m*.

ˈpor·ter-house *s.* **1.** *obs.* Bier-, Speisehaus *n*; **2.** *a.* ***~ steak*** Porterhousesteak *n*.

ˈport|ˌfire *s.* ⚔ Zeitzündschnur *f*, Lunte *f*; **ˌ~ˈfo·li·o** *s.* **1.** a) Aktentasche *f*, (*a.* Künstler- *etc.*)Mappe *f*, b) Porteˈfeuille *n* (*für Staatsdokumente*); **2.** *fig.* (Miˈnister)PorteˌfeuiIle *n*: ***without ~*** ohne Geschäftsbereich; **3.** ☤ (ˈWechsel-)Porteˌfeuille *n*; **ˈ~·hole** *s.* **1.** ⚓ a) (Pfort)Luke *f*, b) Bullauge *n*; **2.** ⚙ → ***port³*** 3.

por·ti·co [ˈpɔːtɪkəʊ] *pl.* **-cos** *s.* ⚠ Säulengang *m*.

por·tion [ˈpɔːʃn] **I** *s.* **1.** (An)Teil *m* (***of*** an *dat.*); **2.** Portiˈon *f* (*Essen*); **3.** Teil *m*, Stück *n* (*Buch, Gebiet, Strecke etc.*); **4.** Menge *f*, Quantum *n*; **5.** ⚖ a) Mitgift *f*, Aussteuer *f*, b) Erbteil *n*: ***legal ~*** Pflichtteil *n*; **6.** *fig.* Los *n*, Schicksal *n*; **II** *v/t.* **7.** aufteilen: ***~ out*** aus-, verteilen; **8.** zuteilen; **9.** *Tochter* aussteuern.

port·li·ness [ˈpɔːtlɪnɪs] *s.* **1.** Stattlichkeit *f*; **2.** Wohlbeleibtheit *f*; **port·ly** [ˈpɔːtlɪ] *adj.* **1.** stattlich, würdevoll; **2.** wohlbeleibt.

port·man·teau [ˌpɔːtˈmæntəʊ] *pl.* **-s** *u.* **-x** [-z] *s.* **1.** Handkoffer *m*; **2.** *obs.* Mantelsack *m*; **3.** *mst* ***~ word*** *ling.* Schachtelwort *n*.

por·trait [ˈpɔːtrɪt] *s.* **1.** a) Porˈträt *n*, Bild(nis) *n*, b) *phot.* Porˈträt(aufnahme *f*) *n*; ***take s.o.'s ~*** j-n porträtieren *od.* malen; → ***sit for*** 3; **2.** *fig.* Bild *n*, (lebenswahre) Schilderung *f*; **ˈpor·trait·ist** [-tɪst] *s.* Porˈträtmaler(in); **ˈpor·trai·ture** [-tʃə] *s.* **1.** → ***portrait***; **2.** a) Porˈträtmaleˌrei *f*, b) *phot.* Porˈträtphotograˌphie *f*; **por·tray** [pɔːˈtreɪ] *v/t.* **1.** porträˈtieren, (ab)malen; **2.** *fig.* schildern, darstellen; **por·tray·al** [pɔːˈtreɪəl] *s.* **1.** Porträtieren *n*; **2.** Porˈträt *n*; **3.** *fig.* Schilderung *f*.

Por·tu·guese [ˌpɔːtjʊˈgiːz] **I** *pl.* **-guese** *s.* **1.** Portuˈgiese *m*, Portuˈgiesin *f*; **2.** *ling.* Portuˈgiesisch *n*; **II** *adj.* **3.** portuˈgiesisch.

pose¹ [pəʊz] **I** *s.* **1.** Pose *f* (*a. fig.*), Posiˈtur *f*, Haltung *f*; **II** *v/t.* **2.** aufstellen, in Posiˈtur setzen; **3.** *Frage* stellen, aufwerfen; **4.** *Behauptung* aufstellen, *Anspruch* erheben; **5.** (***as***) hinstellen (als), ausgeben (für); **III** *v/i.* **6.** sich in Posiˈtur setzen; **7.** a) *paint etc.* Moˈdell stehen *od.* sitzen, b) sich photographieren lassen; **8.** posieren, sich in Pose werfen; **9.** auftreten *od.* sich ausgeben (***as*** als).

pose² [pəʊz] *v/t.* durch Fragen verwirren, verblüffen.

pos·er [ˈpəʊzə] *s.* **1.** → ***poseur***; **2.** ‚harte Nuß‘, knifflige Frage.

po·seur [pəʊˈzɜː] (*Fr.*) *s.* Poˈseur *m*, ‚Schauspieler‘ *m*.

posh [pɒʃ] *adj.* F ‚pikfein‘, ‚todschick‘, ‚feuˈdal‘.

pos·it [ˈpɒzɪt] *phls.* **I** *v/t.* postulieren; **II** *n* Postuˈlat *n*.

po·si·tion [pəˈzɪʃn] **I** *s.* **1.** Positiˈon *f*, Lage *f*, Standort *m*; ⚙ (Schalt- *etc.*) Stellung *f*: ***~ of the sun*** *ast.* Sonnenstand *m*; ***in*** (***out of***) ***~*** (nicht) in der richtigen Lage; **2.** *körperliche* Lage, Stellung *f*: ***horizontal ~***; **3.** ⚓, ✈ Positiˈon *f* (*a. sport*), ⚓ *a.* Besteck *n*: ***~ lights*** a) ⚓, ✈ Positionslichter, b) *mot.* Begrenzungslichter; **4.** ⚔ Stellung *f*: ***~ warfare*** Stellungskrieg *m*; **5.** (Arbeits-)Platz *m*, Stellung *f*, Posten *m*, Amt *n*: ***hold a responsible ~*** e-e verantwortliche Stellung innehaben; **6.** *fig.* (soziˈale) Stellung, (gesellschaftlicher) Rang: ***people of ~*** Leute von Rang; **7.** *fig.* Lage *f*, Situatiˈon *f*: ***an awkward ~***; ***be in a ~ to do s.th.*** in der Lage sein, et. zu tun; **8.** *fig.* (Sach)Lage *f*, Stand *m* *der Dinge*: ***financial ~*** Finanzlage, Vermögensverhältnisse *pl.*; ***legal ~*** Rechtslage; **9.** Standpunkt *m*, Haltung *f*: ***take up a ~ on a question*** zu e-r Frage Stellung nehmen; **10.** ⛪, *phls.* (Grund-, Lehr)Satz *m*; **II** *v/t.* **11.** *bsd.* ⚙ in die richtige Lage bringen, (ein-)stellen; anbringen; **12.** lokalisieren; **13.** *Polizisten etc.* postieren; **poˈsi·tion·al** [-ʃənl] *adj.* Stellungs…, Lage…: ***~ play*** *sport* Stellungsspiel *n*; **po·si·tion find·er** *s.* Ortungsgerät *n*; **po·si·tion pa·per** *s. pol.* ˈGrundsatzpaˌpier *n*.

pos·i·tive [ˈpɒzətɪv] **I** *adj.* □ **1.** bestimmt, definiˈtiv, ausdrücklich (*Befehl etc.*), fest (*Versprechen etc.*), unbedingt: ***~ law*** ⚖ positives Recht; **2.** sicher, ˈunumˌstößlich, eindeutig (*Beweis, Tatsache*); **3.** positiv, tatsächlich; **4.** positiv, zustimmend: ***~ reaction***; **5.** überˈzeugt, (absoˈlut) sicher: ***be ~ about s.th.*** e-r Sache ganz sicher sein; **6.** rechthaberisch; **7.** F ausgesprochen, absoˈlut: ***a ~ fool*** ein ausgemachter Narr; **8.** ⚡, ⛪, ⚗, *biol., phys., phot., phls.* positiv: ***~ electrode*** ⚡ Anode *f*; ***~ pole*** ⚡ Pluspol *m*; **9.** ⚙ zwangsläufig, Zwangs… (*Getriebe, Steuerung etc.*); **10.** *ling.* im Positiv stehend: ***~ degree*** Positiv *m*; **II** *s.* **11.** *et.* Positives, Positivum *n*; **12.** *phot.* Positiv *n*; **13.** *ling.* Positiv *m*; **ˈpos·i·tive·ness** [-nɪs] *s.* **1.** Bestimmtheit *f*, Wirklichkeit *f*; **2.** *fig.* Hartnäckigkeit *f*; **ˈpos·i·tiv·ism** [-vɪzəm] *s. phls.* Positiˈvismus *m*.

pos·se [ˈpɒsɪ] *s.* (Poliˈzei- *etc.*)Aufgebot *n*; *allg.* Haufen *m*, Schar *f*.

pos·sess [pəˈzes] *v/t.* **1.** *allg.* (*a. Eigenschaften, Kenntnisse etc.*) besitzen, haben; im Besitz haben, (inne)haben: ***~ed of*** im Besitz *e-r Sache*; ***~ o.s. of*** *et.* in Besitz nehmen, sich *e-r Sache* bemächtigen; ***~ed noun*** *ling.* Besitzsubjekt *n*; **2.** a) (*a. fig. e-e Sprache etc.*) beherrschen, Gewalt haben über (*acc.*), b) erfüllen (***with*** mit *e-r Idee*, mit *Unwillen etc.*): ***like a man ~ed*** wie ein Besessener, wie toll; ***~ one's soul in patience*** sich in Geduld fassen; **posˈses·sion** [-eʃn] *s.* **1.** *abstrakt*: Besitz *m* (*a.* ⚖): ***actual ~*** tatsächlicher *od.* unmittelbarer Besitz; ***adverse ~*** Ersitzung(sbesitz *m*) *f*; ***in the ~ of*** in *j-s* Besitz; ***in ~ of s.th.*** im Besitz e-r Sache; ***have ~ of*** im Besitze von *et.* sein; ***take ~ of*** Besitz ergreifen von, in Besitz nehmen; **2.** Besitz(tum *n*) *m*, Habe *f*; **3.** *pl.* Besitzungen *pl.*, Liegenschaften *pl.*: ***foreign ~s*** auswärtige Besitzungen; **4.** *fig.* Besessenheit *f*; **5.** *fig.* Beherrscht-, Erfülltsein *n* (***by*** von *e-r Idee etc.*); **6.** *mst* ***self-~*** *fig.* Fassung *f*, Beherrschung *f*; **posˈses·sive** [-sɪv] **I** *adj.* □ **1.** Besitz…; **2.** besitzgierig, -betonend: ***~ instinct*** Sinn *m* für Besitz; **3.** *fig.* besitzergreifend (*Mutter etc.*); **4.** *ling.* possesˈsiv, besitzanzeigend: ***~ case*** → 5 b; **II** *s.* **5.** *ling.* a) Possesˈsiv(um) *n*, besitzanzeigendes Fürwort, b) Genitiv *m*, zweiter Fall; **posˈses·sor** [-sə] *s.* Besitzer (-in), Inhaber(in); **posˈses·so·ry** [-sərɪ] *adj.* Besitz…: ***~ action*** ⚖ Besitzstörungsklage *f*; ***~ right*** Besitzrecht *n*.

pos·si·bil·i·ty [ˌpɒsəˈbɪlətɪ] *s.* **1.** Möglichkeit *f* (***of*** zu, für, ***of doing*** *et.* zu tun): ***there is no ~ of his coming*** es besteht keine Möglichkeit, daß er kommt; **2.** *pl.* (Entwicklungs)Möglichkeiten *pl.*, (-)Fähigkeiten *pl.*; **pos·si·ble** [ˈpɒsəbl] **I** *adj.* □ **1.** möglich (***with*** bei, ***to*** *dat.*, ***for*** für): ***this is ~ with him*** das ist bei ihm möglich; ***highest ~*** größtmöglich; **2.** eventuˈell, etwaig, denkbar; **3.** F annehmbar, pasˈsabel, leidlich; **II** *s.* **4.** ***the ~*** das (Menschen-)Mögliche, das Beste; *sport* die höchste Punktzahl; **5.** in Frage kommende Perˈson (*bei Wettbewerb etc.*); **pos·si·bly** [ˈpɒsəblɪ] *adv.* **1.** möglicherweise, vielˈleicht; **2.** (irgend) möglich: ***when I ~ can*** wenn ich irgend kann; ***I cannot ~ do this*** ich kann das unmöglich tun; ***how can I ~ do it?*** wie kann ich es nur *od.* bloß machen?

pos·sum ['pɒsəm] *s.* F *abbr. für* ***opossum***: ***to play ~*** sich nicht rühren, sich tot *od.* krank *od.* dumm stellen.

post¹ [pəʊst] **I** *s.* **1.** Pfahl *m*, Pfosten *m*, Ständer *m*, Stange *f*, Stab *m*: ***as deaf as a ~*** *fig.* stocktaub; **2.** Anschlagsäule *f*; **3.** *sport* (Start- *od.* Ziel)Pfosten *m*, Start- (*od.* Ziel)linie *f*: ***be beaten at the ~*** kurz vor dem Ziel geschlagen werden; **II** *v/t.* **4.** *mst* ***~ up*** *Plakate etc.* anschlagen, -kleben; **5.** *mst* ***~ over*** *Mauer mit Zetteln* bekleben; **6.** a) *et.* (durch Aushang *etc.*) bekanntgeben: ***~ as missing*** ⚓, ✈ als vermißt melden, b) *fig.* (öffentlich) anprangern.

post² [pəʊst] **I** *s.* **1.** ⚔ Posten *m* (*Stelle od. Soldat*): ***advanced ~*** vorgeschobener Posten; ***last ~*** *Brit.* Zapfenstreich *m*; ***at one's ~*** auf (s-m) Posten; **2.** ⚔ Standort *m*, Garni'son *f*: ***≈ Exchange*** (*abbr.* ***PX***) *Am.* Einkaufsstelle *f*; ***~ headquarters*** Standortkommandantur *f*; **3.** Posten *m*, Platz *m*, Stand *m*; ☨ Börsenstand *m*; **4.** Handelsniederlassung *f*, -platz *m*; **5.** ☨ (Rechnungs)Posten *m*; **6.** Posten *m*, (An)Stellung *f*, Stelle *f*, Amt *n*: ***~ of a secretary*** Sekretärsposten; **II** *v/t.* **7.** *Soldaten etc.* aufstellen, postieren; **8.** ⚔ a) ernennen, b) versetzen, (ab)kommandieren; **9.** ☨ eintragen, verbuchen; *Konto* (ins Hauptbuch) über'tragen: ***~ up*** *Bücher* nachtragen, in Ordnung bringen.

post³ [pəʊst] **I** *s.* **1.** ✉ *bsd. Brit.* Post *f*: a) *als Einrichtung*, b) *Brit.* Postamt *n*, c) *Brit.* Post-, Briefkasten *m*, d) Postzustellung *f*, e) Postsendung(en *pl.*) *f*, -sachen *pl.*, *f*) Nachricht *f*: ***by ~*** per (*od.* mit der) Post; **2.** *hist.* a) Post(kutsche) *f*, b) Ku'rier *m*; **3.** *bsd. Brit.* 'Brief,papier *n* (*Format*); **II** *v/t.* **4.** *Brit.* zur Post geben, mit der Post (zu)senden, aufgeben, in den Briefkasten werfen; **5.** F *mst* ***~ up*** *j-n* informieren: ***keep s.o. ~ed*** j-n auf dem laufenden halten; ***well ~ed*** gut unterrichtet.

post- [pəʊst] *in Zssgn* nach, später, hinter, post…

post·age ['pəʊstɪdʒ] *s.* Porto *n*, Postgebühr *f*, -spesen *pl.*: ***additional*** (*od.* ***extra***) ***~*** Nachporto, Portozuschlag *m*; ***~ free, ~ paid*** portofrei, franko; '**~-due** *s.* Nach-, Strafporto *n*; **~ stamp** *s.* Briefmarke *f*, Postwertzeichen *n*.

post·al ['pəʊstəl] **I** *adj.* po'stalisch, Post…: ***~ card*** → II; ***~ cash order*** Postnachnahme *f*; ***~ code*** → ***postcode***; ***~ district*** Postzustellbezirk *m*; ***~ order*** *Brit.* Postanweisung *f*; ***~ parcel*** Postpaket *n*; ***~ tuition*** Fernunterricht *m*; ***~ vote*** *Brit.* Briefwahl *f*; ***~ voter*** Briefwähler(in); ***≈ Union*** Weltpostverein *m*; **II** *s. Am.* Postkarte *f* (*mit aufgedruckter Marke*).

'**post|·card** [-stk] *s.* Postkarte *f*; '**~·code** *s. Brit.* Postleitzahl *f*.

ˌ**post|-'date** *v/t.* **1.** *Brief etc.* vo'rausdaˌtieren; **2.** nachträglich *od.* später datieren; 'ˌ**~ˌen·try** *s.* **1.** ☨ nachträgliche (Ver)Buchung; **2.** ☨ Nachverzollung *f*; **3.** *sport* Nachnennung *f*.

post·er ['pəʊstə] *s.* **1.** Pla'katankleber *m*; **2.** Pla'kat *n*: ***~ paint*** Plakatfarbe *f*; **3.** Poster *m*, *n*.

poste res·tante [ˌpəʊst'restɑ̃:nt] (*Fr.*) **I** *adj.* postlagernd; **II** *s. bsd. Brit.* Aufbewahrungsstelle *f* für postlagernde Sendungen.

pos·te·ri·or [pɒ'stɪrɪə] **I** *adj.* ☐ a) später (***to*** als), b) hinter, Hinter…: ***be ~ to*** *zeitlich od. örtlich* kommen nach, folgen auf (*acc.*); **II** *s.* Hinterteil *n*, Hintern *m*; **pos·ter·i·ty** [pɒ'sterətɪ] *s.* **1.** Nachkommen(schaft *f*) *pl.*; **2.** Nachwelt *f*.

pos·tern ['pəʊstɜ:n] *s. a.* ***~ door, ~ gate*** Hinter-, Neben-, Seitentür *f*.

ˌ**post-'free** *adj.* portofrei.

ˌ**post'grad·u·ate** [-st'g-] **I** *adj.* nach dem ersten aka'demischen Grad: ***~ studies***; **II** *s.* j-d, der nach dem ersten aka'demischen Grad weiterstudiert.

ˌ**post'haste** *adv.* eiligst.

post·hu·mous ['pɒstjʊməs] *adj.* ☐ po'stum, post'hum: a) *nach des Vaters Tod geboren*, b) nachgelassen, hinter'lassen (*Schriftwerk*), c) nachträglich (*Ordensverleihung etc.*): ***~ fame*** Nachruhm *m*.

pos·til·(l)ion [pə'stɪljən] *s. hist.* Postillion *m*.

post·ing ['pəʊstɪŋ] *s.* Versetzung *f*, ⚔ 'Abkommanˌdierung *f*.

post|·man ['pəʊstmən] *s.* [*irr.*] Briefträger *m*, Postbote *m*; '**~·mark** [-stm-] **I** *s.* Poststempel *m*; **II** *v/t.* (ab)stempeln; 'ˌ**~ˌmas·ter** [-stˌm-] *s.* Postamtsvorsteher *m*, Postmeister *m*: ***≈ General*** Postminister *m*.

post·me·rid·i·an [ˌpəʊstmə'rɪdɪən] *adj.* Nachmittags…, nachmittägig; **post me·rid·i·em** [-mə'rɪdɪəm] (*Lat.*) *adv.* (*abbr.* ***p.m.***) nachmittags.

'**postˌmis·tress** [-stˌm-] *s.* Postmeisterin *f*.

post|-mor·tem [ˌpəʊst'mɔ:təm] ⚖, ⚕ **I** *adj.* Leichen…, nach dem Tode (stattfindend); **II** *s.* (*abbr. für* ***~ examination***) Leichenöffnung *f*, Auto'psie *f*; *fig.* Ma'növerkriˌtik *f*, nachträgliche Ana'lyse; ˌ**~'na·tal** *adj.* nach der Geburt (stattfindend); ˌ**~'nup·tial** *adj.* nach der Hochzeit (stattfindend).

post of·fice *s.* **1.** Post(amt *n*) *f*: ***General ≈*** Hauptpost(amt); ***≈ Department*** *Am.* Postministerium *n*; **2.** *Am. ein Gesellschaftsspiel*; **~ box** *s.* Post(schließ)fach *n*; **~ or·der** *s.* Postanweisung *f*; **~ savings bank** *s.* Postsparkasse *f*.

ˌ**post'op·er·a·tive** *adj.* ⚕ postopera'tiv, nachträglich.

ˌ**post-'paid** *adj. u. adv.* freigemacht, frankiert.

post·pone [ˌpəʊst'pəʊn] *v/t.* **1.** verschieben, auf-, hin'ausschieben; **2.** 'unterordnen (***to*** *dat.*), hint'ansetzen; ˌ**post'pone·ment** [-mənt] *s.* **1.** Verschiebung *f*, Aufschub *m*; **2.** ⚙, *a. ling.* Nachstellung *f*.

ˌ**post·po'si·tion** *s.* **1.** Nachstellung *f* (*a. ling.*); **2.** *ling.* nachgestelltes (Verhältnis)Wort; ˌ**post'pos·i·tive** *ling.* **I** *adj.* nachgestellt; **II** *s.* → ***postposition*** 2.

ˌ**post'pran·di·al** *adj.* nach dem Essen, nach Tisch (*Rede, Schläfchen etc.*).

post·script ['pəʊsskrɪpt] *s.* **1.** Post'skriptum *n* (*zu e-m Brief*), Nachschrift *f*; **2.** Nachtrag *m* (*zu e-m Buch*); **3.** Nachbemerkung *f*.

pos·tu·lant ['pɒstjʊlənt] *s.* **1.** Antragsteller(in); **2.** *R.C.* Postu'lant(in); **pos·tu·late I** *v/t.* ['pɒstjʊleɪt] **1.** fordern, verlangen, begehren; **2.** postulieren, (als gegeben) vor'aussetzen; **II** *s.* [-lət] **3.** Postu'lat *n*, ('Grund)Vorˌaussetzung *f*.

pos·ture ['pɒstʃə] **I** *s.* **1.** (Körper)Haltung *f*, Stellung *f*; (*a. thea., paint.*) Posi'tur *f*, Pose *f*; **2.** Lage *f* (*a. fig. Situation*), Anordnung *f*; **3.** *fig. geistige* Haltung; **II** *v/t.* **4.** zu'rechtstellen, arrangieren; **III** *v/i.* **5.** sich in Posi'tur stellen *od.* in Pose werfen; posieren (*a. fig.* ***as*** als); '**pos·tur·er** [-ərə] *s.* **1.** Schlangenmensch *m* (*Artist*); **2.** → ***poseur***.

ˌ**post'war** *adj.* Nachkriegs…

po·sy ['pəʊzɪ] *s.* **1.** Sträußchen *n*; **2.** *obs.* Motto *n*, Denkspruch *m*.

pot [pɒt] **I** *s.* **1.** (*Blumen-, Koch-, Nacht- etc.*)Topf *m*: ***go to ~*** *sl.* a) kaputtgehen, b) ‚vor die Hunde gehen' (*Person*); ***keep the ~ boiling*** a) die Sache in Gang halten, b) sich über Wasser halten; ***the ~ calls the kettle black*** ein Esel schilt den andern Langohr; ***big ~*** *sl.* ‚großes Tier'; ***a ~ of money*** F ‚ein Heidengeld'; ***he has ~s of money*** F er hat Geld wie Heu; **2.** Kanne *f*; **3.** ⚙ Tiegel *m*, Gefäß *n*: ***~ annealing*** Kastenglühen *n*; ***~ galvanization*** Feuerverzinken *n*; **4.** *sport sl.* Po'kal *m*; **5.** (Spiel)Einsatz *m*; **6.** → ***pot shot***; **7.** *sl.* Pot *n*, Marihu'ana *n*; **II** *v/t.* **8.** in e-n Topf tun; *Pflanze* eintopfen; **9.** *Fleisch* einlegen, einmachen: ***~ted meat*** Fleischkonserven *pl.*; **10.** *Billardball* einlochen; **11.** *hunt.* (ab)schießen; **12.** F einheimsen, erbeuten; **13.** *Baby* aufs Töpfchen setzen; **14.** *fig.* F a) *Musik* ‚konservieren', b) *Stoff* mundgerecht machen; **III** *v/i.* **15.** (los)ballern, schießen (***at*** auf *acc.*).

po·ta·ble ['pəʊtəbl] **I** *adj.* trinkbar; **II** *s.* Getränk *n*.

po·tage [pɒ'tɑ:ʒ] (*Fr.*) *s.* (dicke) Suppe.

pot·ash ['pɒtæʃ] *s.* ⚗ **1.** Pottasche *f*, 'Kaliumkarboˌnat *n*: ***bicarbonate of ~*** doppeltkohlensaures Kali; ***~ fertilizer*** Kalidünger *m*; ***~ mine*** Kalibergwerk *n*; **2.** → ***caustic*** 1.

po·tas·si·um [pə'tæsjəm] *s.* ⚗ Kalium *n*; **~ bro·mide** *s.* 'Kaliumbroˌmid *n*; **~ car·bon·ate** *s.* 'Kaliumkarboˌnat *n*, Pottasche *f*; **~ cy·a·nide** *s.* 'Kaliumcyaˌnid *n*, Zyan'kali *n*; **~ hy·drox·ide** *s.* 'Kaliumhydroˌxyd *n*, Ätzkali *n*; **~ ni·trate** *s.* 'Kaliumniˌtrat *n*.

po·ta·tion [pəʊ'teɪʃn] *s.* **1.** Trinken *n*; Zeche'rei *f*; **2.** Getränk *n*.

po·ta·to [pə'teɪtəʊ] *pl.* **-toes** *s.* **1.** Kar'toffel *f*: ***fried ~es*** Bratkartoffeln; ***small ~es*** *Am.* F ‚kleine Fische'; ***hot ~*** F ‚heißes Eisen'; ***drop s.th. like a hot ~*** et. wie eine heiße Kartoffel fallen lassen; ***think o.s. no small ~es*** *sl.* sehr von sich eingenommen sein; **2.** *Am. sl.* a) ‚Rübe' *f* (*Kopf*), b) Dollar *m*; **~ bee·tle** *s. zo.* Kar'toffelkäfer *m*; **~ blight** → ***potato disease***; **~ bug** → ***potato beetle***; **~ chips** *s. pl.* a) *Brit.* Pommes frites *pl.*, b) *Am.* → **~ crisps** *s. pl.* Kar'toffelchips *pl.*; **~ dis·ease** *s.* Kar'toffelkrankheit *f*; **~ trap** *s. sl.* ‚Klappe' *f*, ‚Maul' *n*.

pot| bar·ley *s.* Graupen *pl.*; '**~-ˌbel·lied** *adj.* dickbäuchig; '**~-ˌbel·ly** *s.* Schmerbauch *m*; 'ˌ**~ˌboil·er** *s.* F *Kunst etc.*: reine Brotarbeit; '**~·boy** *s. Brit.* Schankkellner *m*.

po·teen [pɒ'ti:n] *s.* heimlich gebrannter Whisky (*in Irland*).

po·ten·cy ['pəʊtənsɪ] *s.* **1.** Stärke *f*, Macht *f*; *fig. a.* Einfluß *m*; **2.** Wirksamkeit *f*, Kraft *f*; **3.** *physiol.* Po'tenz *f*; '**po·tent** [-nt] *adj.* □ **1.** mächtig, stark; **2.** einflußreich; **3.** po'tent, fi'nanzstark: ***a ~ bidder***; **4.** zwingend, über'zeugend (*Argumente etc.*); **5.** stark (*Drogen*, *Getränk*); **6.** *physiol.* po'tent; '**po·ten·tate** [-teɪt] *s.* Poten'tat *m*, Machthaber *m*, Herrscher *m*; **po·ten·tial** [pəʊ'tenʃl] **I** *adj.* □ **1.** potenti'ell: a) möglich, eventu'ell, b) in der Anlage vorhanden, la'tent: ***~ market*** (***murderer***) potentieller Markt (Mörder); **2.** *ling.* Möglichkeits…: ***~ mood*** → 4; **3.** *phys.* potenti'ell, gebunden: ***~ energy*** potentielle Energie, Energie der Lage; **II** *s.* **4.** *ling.* Potenti'alis *m*, Möglichkeitsform *f*; **5.** *phys.* Potenti'al *n* (*a.* ⚡), ⚡ Spannung *f*: ***~ equation*** ⚘ Potentialgleichung *f*; **6.** (*Kriegs-*, *Menschen- etc.*)Potenti'al *n*, Re'serven *pl.*; **7.** Leistungsfähigkeit *f*, Kraftvorrat *m*; **po·ten·ti·al·i·ty** [pəʊtenʃɪ'ælətɪ] *s.* **1.** Potentiali'tät *f*, (Entwicklungs)Möglichkeit *f*; **2.** Wirkungsvermögen *n*, innere Kraft; **po·ten·ti·om·e·ter** [pəʊˌtenʃɪ'ɒmɪtə] *s.* ⚡ Potentio'meter *n* (*veränderbarer Widerstand*).

'**pot·head** *s. sl.* ‚Hascher' *m*.

po·theen [pɒ'θiːn] → ***poteen***.

poth·er ['pɒðə] **I** *s.* **1.** Aufruhr *m*, Lärm *m*, Aufregung *f*, ‚The'ater' *n*: ***be in a ~ about s.th.*** e-n großen Wirbel wegen et. machen; **2.** Rauch-, Staubwolke *f*, Dunst *m*; **II** *v/t.* **3.** verwirren, aufregen; **III** *v/i.* **4.** sich aufregen.

'**pot|·herb** *s.* Küchenkraut *n*; '**~·hole** *s.* **1.** *mot.* Schlagloch *n*; **2.** *geol.* Gletschertopf *m*, Strudelkessel *m*; '**~ˌhol·er** *s.* Höhlenforscher *m*; '**~·hook** *s.* **1.** Kesselhaken *m*; **2.** Schnörkel *m* (*Kinderschrift*); *pl.* Gekritzel *n*; '**~·house** *s.* Wirtschaft *f*, Kneipe *f*; '**~ˌhunt·er** *s. sl.* **1.** Aasjäger *m*; **2.** *sport* F Preisjäger *m*.

po·tion ['pəʊʃn] *s.* (Arz'nei-, Gift-, Zauber)Trank *m*.

pot luck *s.*: ***take ~*** a) (***with s.o.***) (bei j-m) mit dem vorliebnehmen, was es gerade (zu essen) gibt, b) es aufs Geratewohl probieren.

pot·pour·ri [ˌpəʊ'pʊrɪ] *s.* Potpourri *n*: a) Dufttopf *m*, b) musi'kalisches Aller'lei, c) *fig.* Kunterbunt *n*, Aller'lei *n*.

pot| roast *s.* Schmorfleisch *n*; '**~·sherd** [-ʃɜːd] *s.* (Topf)Scherbe *f*; **~ shot** *s.* **1.** unweidmännischer Schuß; **2.** Nahschuß *m*, 'hinterhältiger Schuß; **3.** (wahllos abgegebener) Schuß; **4.** *fig.* Seitenhieb *m*.

pot·tage ['pɒtɪdʒ] *s.* dicke Gemüsesuppe (mit Fleisch).

pot·ter[1] ['pɒtə] **I** *v/i.* **1.** *oft* ***~ about*** her'umwerkeln, -hantieren; **2.** (her'um-)trödeln: ***~ at*** herumspielen, -pfuschen an *od.* in (*dat.*); **II** *v/t.* **3.** ***~ away*** *Zeit* vertrödeln.

pot·ter[2] ['pɒtə] *s.* Töpfer(in): ***~'s clay*** Töpferton *m*; ***~'s lathe*** Töpferscheibentisch *m*; ***~'s wheel*** Töpferscheibe *f*; '**pot·ter·y** [-ərɪ] *s.* **1.** Töpfer-, Tonware(n *pl.*) *f*, Steingut *n*, Ke'ramik *f*; **2.** Töpfe'rei(werkstatt) *f*; **3.** Töpfe'rei *f* (*Kunst*), Ke'ramik *f*.

pot·ty ['pɒtɪ] *adj.* F **1.** verrückt; **2.** klein, unbedeutend.

'**pot-ˌval·o(u)r** *s.* angetrunkener Mut.

pouch [paʊtʃ] **I** *s.* **1.** Beutel (*a. zo.*, ♀), (Leder-, Trage-, *a.* Post)Tasche *f*, (kleiner) Sack; **2.** Tabaksbeutel *m*; **3.** Geldbeutel *m*; **4.** ⚔ Pa'tronentasche *f*; **5.** *anat.* (Tränen)Sack *m*; **II** *v/t.* **6.** in e-n Beutel tun; **7.** *fig.* einstecken; **8.** (*v/i.* sich) beuteln *od.* bauschen; **pouched** [-tʃt] *adj. zo.* Beutel…

pouf(fe) [puːf] *s.* **1.** a) Haarknoten *m*, -rolle *f*, b) Einlage *f*; **2.** Puff *m* (*Sitzpolster*); **3.** Tur'nüre *f*; **4.** → ***poof***.

poul·ter·er ['pəʊltərə] *s.* Geflügelhändler *m*.

poul·tice ['pəʊltɪs] ⚕ **I** *s.* 'Breiˌumschlag *m*, Packung *f*; **II** *v/t.* e-n 'Breiˌumschlag auflegen auf (*acc.*), e-e Packung machen um.

poul·try ['pəʊltrɪ] *s.* (Haus)Geflügel *n*, Federvieh *n*: ***~ farm*** Geflügelfarm *f*; '**~·man** [-mən] *s. irr.* Geflügelzüchter *m od.* -händler *m*.

pounce[1] [paʊns] **I** *s.* **1.** a) Her'abstoßen *n e-s Raubvogels*, b) Sprung *m*, Satz *m*: ***on the ~*** sprungbereit; **II** *v/i.* **2.** (her'ab)stoßen, sich stürzen (***on***, ***upon*** auf *acc.*) (*Raubvogel*); **3.** *fig.* a) (***on***, ***upon***) sich stürzen (auf *j-n*, *e-n Fehler*, *e-e Gelegenheit etc.*), losgehen (auf *j-n*), b) ‚zuschlagen'; **4.** (plötzlich) stürzen: ***~ into the room***.

pounce[2] [paʊns] **I** *s.* **1.** Glättpulver *n*, *bsd.* Bimssteinpulver *n*; **2.** Pauspulver *n*; **3.** 'durchgepaustes (*bsd.* Stick)Muster; **II** *v/t.* **4.** glatt abreiben, bimsen; **5.** 'durchpausen.

pound[1] [paʊnd] *s.* **1.** Pfund *n* (*abbr.* ***lb.*** *= 453,59 g*): ***~ cake*** *Am.* (reichhaltiger) Früchtekuchen *m*; **2.** *a.* ***~ sterling*** Pfund *n* (Sterling) (*abbr.* £): ***pay twenty shillings in the ~*** *fig. obs.* voll bezahlen.

pound[2] [paʊnd] **I** *s.* **1.** schwerer Stoß *od.* Schlag, Stampfen *n*; **II** *v/t.* **2.** (zer-)stoßen, (zer)stampfen; **3.** feststampfen, rammen; **4.** hämmern (auf), trommeln auf, schlagen: ***~ sense into s.o.*** *fig.* j-m Vernunft einhämmern; ***~ out*** a) glatthämmern, b) *Melodie* herunterhämmern (*auf dem Klavier*); **5.** ⚔ beschießen; **III** *v/i.* **6.** hämmern (*a. Herz*), pochen, schlagen; **7.** *mst* ***~ along*** (ein'her)stampfen, wuchtig gehen; **8.** stampfen (*Maschine etc.*); **9.** ***~*** (***away***) ***at*** ⚔ unter schweren Beschuß nehmen.

pound[3] [paʊnd] **I** *s.* **1.** 'Tieraˌsyl *n*; **2.** Hürde *f*, Pferch *m*; **3.** Abstellplatz *m* für abgeschleppte Autos; **II** *v/t.* **4.** *oft* ***~ up*** einpferchen.

pound·age ['paʊndɪdʒ] *s.* **1.** Anteil *m od.* Gebühr *f* pro Pfund (*Sterling*); **2.** Bezahlung *f* pro Pfund (*Gewicht*); **3.** Gewicht *n* in Pfund.

pound·er ['paʊndə] *s.* *in Zssgn* …pfünder.

ˌ**pound-'fool·ish** *adj.* unfähig, mit großen Summen *od.* Pro'blemen 'umzugehen; → ***penny-wise***.

pour [pɔː] **I** *s.* **1.** Strömen *n*; **2.** (Regen-)Guß *m*; **3.** *metall.* Einguß *m*: ***~ test*** Stockpunktbestimmung; **II** *v/t.* **4.** gießen, schütten (***from***, ***out of*** aus, ***into***, ***in*** in *acc.*, ***on***, ***upon*** auf *acc.*): ***~ forth*** (*od.* ***out***) a) ausgießen, (aus)strömen lassen, b) *fig. Herz* ausschütten, *Kummer* ausbreiten, c) *Flüche etc.* ausstoßen; ***~ out drinks*** Getränke eingießen, -schenken; ***~ off*** abgießen; ***~ it on*** *Am. sl.* a) ‚rangehen', b) *a.* ***~ on the speed*** ‚volle Pulle' fahren; **5.** ***~ itself*** sich ergießen (*Fluß*); **III** *v/i.* **6.** strömen, gießen: ***~ down*** niederströmen; ***~ forth*** (*od.* ***out***) (*a. fig.*) sich ergießen, strömen (***from*** aus); ***it ~s with rain*** es gießt in Strömen; ***it never rains but it ~s*** *fig.* ein Unglück kommt selten allein; **7.** *fig.* strömen (*Menschenmenge etc.*): ***~ in*** hereinströmen (*a. Aufträge*, *Briefe etc.*); **8.** *metall. in die Form* gießen; **pour·a·ble** ['pɔːrəbl] *adj.* ⚙ vergießbar: ***~ compound*** Gußmasse *f*; **pour·ing** ['pɔːrɪŋ] **I** *adj.* **1.** strömend (*a. Regen*); **2.** ⚙ Gieß…, Guß…: ***~ gate*** Gießtrichter *m*; **II** *s.* **3.** ⚙ (Ver)Gießen *n*, Guß *m*.

pout[1] [paʊt] **I** *v/i.* **1.** die Lippen spitzen *od.* aufwerfen; **2.** a) e-e Schnute *od.* e-n Flunsch ziehen, b) *fig.* schmollen; **3.** vorstehen (*Lippen*); **II** *v/t.* **4.** *Lippen*, *Mund* (schmollend) aufwerfen, (*a. zum Kuß*) spitzen; **5.** schmollen(d sagen); **III** *s.* **6.** Flunsch *m*, Schnute *f*, Schmollmund *m*; **7.** Schmollen *n*: ***have the ~s*** schmollen, im Schmollwinkel sitzen.

pout[2] [paʊt] *s. ein* Schellfisch *m*.

pout·er ['paʊtə] *s.* **1.** *a.* ***~ pigeon*** *orn.* Kropftaube *f*; **2.** → ***pout***[2].

pov·er·ty ['pɒvətɪ] *s.* **1.** (***of*** an *dat.*) Armut *f*, Mangel *m* (*beide a. fig.*): ***~ of ideas*** Ideenarmut; **2.** *fig.* Armseligkeit *f*, Dürftigkeit *f*; **3.** Armut *f*, geringe Ergiebigkeit (*des Bodens etc.*); '**~-ˌstrick·en** *adj.* **1.** in Armut lebend, verarmt; **2.** *fig.* armselig.

pow·der ['paʊdə] **I** *s.* **1.** (*Back-*, *Schieß- etc.*)Pulver *n*: ***not worth ~ and shot*** keinen Schuß Pulver wert; ***keep your ~ dry!*** sei auf der Hut!; ***take a ~*** *Am. sl.* ‚türmen'; **2.** Puder *m*: ***face ~***; **II** *v/t.* **3.** pulvern, pulverisieren: ***~ed milk*** Trockenmilch *f*; ***~ed sugar*** Staubzucker *m*; **4.** (be)pudern: ***~ one's nose*** a) sich die Nase pudern, b) F ‚mal kurz verschwinden'; **5.** bestäuben, bestreuen (***with*** mit); **III** *v/i.* **6.** zu Pulver werden; ***~ box*** *s.* Puderdose *f*; ***~ keg*** *s. fig.* Pulverfaß *n*; '**~-ˌmet·al·lur·gy** *s.* 'Sintermetallurˌgie *f*, Me'tallkeˌramik *f*; ***~ mill*** *s.* 'Pulvermühle *f*, -faˌbrik *f*; ***~ puff*** *s.* Puderquaste *f*; ***~ room*** *s.* 'Damentoiˌlette *f*.

pow·der·y ['paʊdərɪ] *adj.* **1.** pulverig, Pulver…: ***~ snow*** Pulverschnee *m*; **2.** bestäubt.

pow·er ['paʊə] **I** *s.* **1.** Kraft *f*, Stärke *f*, Macht *f*, Vermögen *n*: ***do all in one's ~*** alles tun, was in s-r Macht steht; ***it was out of*** (*od.* ***not in***) ***his ~*** es stand nicht in s-r Macht (***to do*** zu tun); ***more ~ to you***(***r elbow***)***!*** nur zu!, viel Erfolg!; **2.** Kraft *f*, Ener'gie *f*; *weitS.* Wucht *f*, Gewalt *f*; **3.** *mst pl. hypnotische etc.* Kräfte *pl.*, (geistige) Fähigkeiten *pl.*, Ta'lent *n*: ***reasoning ~*** Denkvermögen *n*; **4.** Macht *f*, Gewalt *f*, Herrschaft *f*, Einfluß *m* (***over*** über *acc.*): ***be in ~*** *pol.* an der Macht *od.* am Ruder sein; ***be in s.o.'s ~*** in j-s Gewalt sein; ***come into ~*** *pol.* an die Macht kommen; ***~ politics*** Machtpolitik *f*; **5.** *pol.* Gewalt *f als Staatsfunktion*: ***legislative ~***; ***separation of ~s*** Gewaltenteilung *f*; **6.** *pol.* (Macht)Befugnis *f*, (Amts)Gewalt *f*; **7.** ⚖ (Handlungs-, Vertretungs)Vollmacht *f*, Befugnis *f*, Recht *n*: ***~ of testation*** Testierfähigkeit *f*; → ***attorney***;

8. *pol.* Macht *f*, Staat *m*; **9.** Macht(faktor *m*) *f*, einflußreiche Stelle *od.* Per'son: ***the ~s that be*** die maßgeblichen (Regierungs)Stellen; ***~ behind the throne*** graue Eminenz; **10.** *mst pl.* höhere Macht: ***heavenly ~s***; **11.** F Masse *f*: ***a ~ of people***; **12.** ⩚ Po'tenz *f*: ***raise to the third ~*** in die dritte Potenz erheben; **13.** ϟ, *phys.* Kraft *f*, Ener'gie *f*, Leistung *f*; *a.* ***~ current*** ϟ (Stark)Strom *m*; *Funk*, *Radio*, *TV*: Sendestärke *f*; *opt.* Stärke *f e-r Linse*: ***~ cable*** Starkstromkabel *n*; ***~ economy*** Energiewirtschaft *f*; **14.** ⚙ me'chanische Kraft, Antriebskraft *f*: ***~-propelled*** kraftbetrieben, Kraft…; ***~ on*** (mit) Vollgas; ***~ off*** a) mit abgestelltem Motor, b) im Leerlauf; **II** *v/t.* **15.** mit (*elektrischer etc.*) Kraft versehen *od.* betreiben, antreiben: ***rocket-~ed*** raketengetrieben; **~ am·pli·fi·er** *s. Radio*: Kraft-, Endverstärker *m*; **'~-as,sis·ted** *adj. mot.* Servo… (*-lenkung etc.*); **~ brake** *s. mot.* 'Servobremse *f*; **~ con·sump·tion** *s.* ϟ Strom-, Ener'gieverbrauch *m*; **~ cut** *s.* ϟ **1.** Stromsperre *f*; **2.** → ***power failure***; **'~-drive** *s.* ⚙ Kraftantrieb *m*; **'~-,driv·en** *adj.* ⚙ kraftbetrieben, Kraft…; **~ en·gi·neer·ing** *s.* ϟ 'Starkstrom,technik *f*; **~ fac·tor** *s.* ϟ, *phys.* 'Leistungs,faktor *m*; **~ fail·ure** *s.* ϟ Strom-, Netzausfall *m*.

pow·er·ful ['paʊəfʊl] *adj.* □ **1.** mächtig (*a. Körper*, *Schlag*, *Mensch*), stark (*a. opt. u. Motor*), gewaltig, kräftig; **2.** *fig.* kräftig, wirksam (*a. Argument*); wuchtig (*Stil*); packend (*Roman etc.*); **3.** F ‚massig', gewaltig.

pow·er| glid·er *s.* ✈ Motorsegler *m*; **'~·house** *s.* **1.** → ***power station***; **2.** ⚙ Ma'schinenhaus *n*; **3.** *Am. sl.* a) *sport* ‚Bombenmannschaft' *f*, b) *sport* ‚Ka'none' *f* (*Spitzenspieler*), c) Riesenkerl *m*, d) ‚Wucht' *f*, ‚tolle' Person *od.* Sache; **~ lathe** *s.* ⚙ Hochleistungsdrehbank *f*.

pow·er·less ['paʊəlɪs] *adj.* □ kraft-, machtlos, ohnmächtig.

pow·er| line *s.* ϟ **1.** Starkstromleitung *f*; **2.** 'Überlandleitung *f*; **,~-'op·er·at·ed** *adj.* ⚙ kraftbetätigt, -betrieben; **~ out·put** *s.* ϟ, ⚙ Ausgangs-, Nennleistung *f*; **~ pack** *s.* ϟ Netzteil *n* (*Radio etc.*); **'~-plant** *s.* **1.** → ***power station***; **2.** Ma'schinensatz *m*, Aggre'gat *n*, Triebwerk(anlage *f*) *n*; **~ play** *s. sport* Powerplay *n*; **~ point** *s.* ϟ Steckdose *f*; **~ pol·i·tics** *s. pl. sg. konstr.* 'Machtpoli,tik *f*; **~ saw** *s.* ⚙ Motorsäge *f*; **~ shar·ing** *s.* Teilhabe *f* an der Macht; **'~-,shov·el** *s.* ⚙ Löffelbagger *m*; **~ sta·tion** *s.* ϟ Elektrizi'täts-, Kraftwerk *n*: ***long-distance ~*** Überlandzentrale *f*; **~ steer·ing** *s. mot.* Servolenkung *f*; **~ stroke** *s.* ⚙, ϟ, *mot.* Arbeitshub *m*, -takt *m*; **~ strug·gle** *s.* Machtkampf *m*; **~ sup·ply** *s.* ϟ **1.** Ener'gieversorgung *f*, Netz(anschluß *m*) *n*; **2.** → ***power pack***; **~ trans·mis·sion** *s.* ⚙ 'Leistungs-, Ener'gieüber,tragung *f*; **~ un·it** *s.* **1.** → ***power station***; **2.** → ***power plant*** 2.

pow·wow ['paʊwaʊ] **I** *s.* **1.** a) indi'anisches Fest, b) Ratsversammlung *f*, c) indi'anischer Medi'zinmann; **2.** *Am.* F a) (lärmende, *a.* po'litische) Versammlung, b) Konfe'renz *f*, Besprechung *f*; **II** *v/i.* **3.** *bsd. Am.* F e-e Versammlung *etc.* abhalten; debattieren.

pox [pɒks] *s.* ⚕ **1.** Pocken *pl.*, Blattern *pl.*; Pusteln *pl.*; **2.** V Syphilis *f*.

prac·ti·ca·bil·i·ty [,præktɪkə'bɪlətɪ] *s.* 'Durchführbarkeit *f etc.*; **prac·ti·ca·ble** ['præktɪkəbl] *adj.* □ **1.** 'durch-, ausführbar, möglich; **2.** anwendbar, brauchbar; **3.** gang-, (be)fahrbar (*Straße*, *Furt etc.*).

prac·ti·cal ['præktɪkl] *adj.* □ → ***practically***; **1.** (*Ggs. theoretisch*) praktisch (*Kenntnisse*, *Landwirtschaft etc.*); angewandt: ***~ chemistry***; ***~ fact*** Erfahrungstatsache *f*; **2.** praktisch (*Anwendung*, *Versuch etc.*); **3.** praktisch, geschickt (*Person*); **4.** praktisch, in der Praxis tätig, ausübend: ***~ politician***; ***~ man*** Mann der Praxis, Praktiker; **5.** praktisch (*Denken*); **6.** praktisch, faktisch, tatsächlich; **7.** sachlich; **8.** praktisch anwendbar, 'durchführbar; **9.** handgreiflich, grob: ***~ joke***; **prac·ti·cal·i·ty** [,præktɪ'kælətɪ] *s. das* Praktische, praktisches Wesen, Sachlichkeit *f*; praktische Anwendbarkeit; **'prac·ti·cal·ly** *adv.* **1.** [-kəlɪ] → ***practical***; **2.** [-klɪ] praktisch, so gut wie *nichts etc.*

prac·tice ['præktɪs] **I** *s.* **1.** Praxis *f* (*Ggs. Theorie*): ***in ~*** in der Praxis; ***put into ~*** in die Praxis umsetzen, ausführen, verwirklichen; **2.** Übung *f* (*a.* ♪, ⚔), *mot. sport* Training *n*: ***in*** (***out of***) ***~*** in (aus) der Übung; ***~ makes perfect*** Übung macht den Meister; **3.** Praxis *f* (*Arzt*, *Anwalt*): ***be in ~*** praktizieren, s-e Praxis ausüben (*Arzt*); **4.** Brauch *m*, Gewohnheit *f*, übliches Verfahren, Usus *m*; **5.** Handlungsweise *f*, Praktik *f*; *oft pl. contp.* (unsaubere) Praktiken *pl.*, Machenschaften *pl.*, Schliche *pl.*; **6.** Verfahren *n*; ⚙ *a.* Technik *f*: ***welding ~*** Schweißtechnik; **7.** ⚖ Verfahren(sregeln *pl.*) *n*, for'melles Recht; **8.** Übungs…, Probe…: ***~ alarm***, ***~ alert*** Probealarm *m*; ***~ ammunition*** ⚔ Übungsmunition *f*; ***~ cartridge*** ⚔ Exerzierpatrone *f*; ***~ flight*** ✈ Übungsflug *m*; ***~ run*** *mot.* Trainingsfahrt *f*; **II** *v/t. u. v/i.* **9.** *Am.* → ***practise***.

prac·tise ['præktɪs] **I** *v/t.* **1.** *Beruf* ausüben; *Geschäft etc.* betreiben; tätig sein als *od.* in (*dat.*), *als Arzt*, *Anwalt* praktizieren: ***~ medicine*** (***law***); **2.** ♪ *etc.* (ein)üben, sich üben in (*dat.*); *et. auf e-m Instrument* üben; *j-n* schulen: ***~ Bach*** Bach üben; **3.** *fig. Höflichkeit etc.* üben: ***~ politeness***; **4.** verüben: ***~ a fraud on*** *j-n* arglistig täuschen; **II** *v/i.* **5.** praktizieren (*als Arzt*, *Jurist*, *a. Katholik*); **6.** (sich) üben (***on the piano*** auf dem Klavier, ***at shooting*** im Schießen); **7.** ***~ on*** (*od.* ***upon***) a) *j-n* ‚bearbeiten', b) *j-s Schwäche etc.* ausnutzen, miß'brauchen; **'prac·tised** [-st] *adj.* geübt (*Person*, *a. Auge*, *Hand*).

prac·ti·tion·er [præk'tɪʃnə] *s.* **1.** Praktiker *m*; **2.** ***general*** (*od.* ***medical***) ***~*** praktischer Arzt; **3.** ***legal*** (*od.* ***general***) ***~*** (Rechts)Anwalt *m*.

prag·mat·ic [præg'mætɪk] *adj.* (□ ***~ally***) **1.** *phls.* prag'matisch; **2.** → **prag'mat·i·cal** [-kl] *adj.* □ **1.** *phls.* prag'matisch, *fig. a.* praktisch (denkend), sachlich; **2.** belehrend; **3.** geschäftig; **4.** 'übereifrig, aufdringlich; **5.** rechthaberisch; **prag·ma·tism** ['prægmətɪzəm] *s.* **1.** *phls.* Pragma'tismus *m*, *fig. a.* Sachlichkeit *f*, praktisches Denken; **2.** 'Übereifer *m*; **3.** rechthaberisches Wesen; **prag·ma·tize** ['prægmətaɪz] *v/t.* **1.** als re'al darstellen; **2.** vernunftmäßig erklären, rationalisieren.

prai·rie ['preərɪ] *s.* **1.** Grasebene *f*, Steppe *f*; **2.** Prä'rie *f* (*in Nordamerika*); **3.** *Am.* (grasbewachsene) Lichtung; **~ dog** *s. zo.* Prä'riehund *m*; **~ schoon·er** *s. Am.* Planwagen *m der frühen Siedler*.

praise [preɪz] **I** *v/t.* **1.** loben, rühmen, preisen; → ***sky*** 2; **2.** (*bsd. Gott*) (lob-) preisen, loben; **II** *s.* **3.** Lob *n*: ***sing s.o.'s ~*** j-s Lob singen; ***in ~ of s.o.***, ***in s.o.'s ~*** zu j-s Lob; **'~,wor·thi·ness** *s.* Löblichkeit *f*, lobenswerte Eigenschaft; **'~,wor·thy** *adj.* □ lobenswert, löblich.

pram¹ [præm] *s.* ⚓ Prahm *m*.

pram² [præm] *s.* F → ***perambulator***.

prance [prɑːns] *v/i.* **1.** a) sich bäumen, b) tänzeln (*Pferd*); **2.** (ein'her)stolzieren, paradieren; sich brüsten; **3.** F her'umtollen.

pran·di·al ['prændɪəl] *adj.* Essens…, Tisch…

prang [præŋ] *Brit.* F **I** *s.* **1.** ✈ Bruchlandung *f*; **2.** *mot.* schwerer Unfall; **3.** Luftangriff *m*; **4.** *fig.* ‚tolles Ding'; **II** *v/i.* **5.** ‚knallen', ‚krachen'.

prank¹ [præŋk] *s.* **1.** Streich *m*, Ulk *m*, Jux *m*; **2.** *weitS.* Kapri'ole *f*, Faxe *f e-r Maschine etc.*

prank² [præŋk] **I** *v/t. mst* ***~ out*** (*od.* ***up***) (her'aus)putzen, schmücken; **II** *v/i.* prunken, prangen.

prate [preɪt] **I** *v/i.* schwatzen, schwafeln (***of*** von); **II** *v/t.* (da'her)schwafeln; **III** *s.* Geschwätz *n*, Geschwafel *n*; **'prat·er** [-tə] *s.* Schwätzer(in); **'prat·ing** [-tɪŋ] *adj.* □ schwatzhaft, geschwätzig; **prat·tle** ['prætl] → ***prate***.

prawn [prɔːn] *s. zo.* Gar'nele *f*.

pray [preɪ] **I** *v/i.* **1.** beten (***to*** zu, ***for*** um, für); **2.** bitten, ersuchen (***for*** um); ⚖ beantragen (***that*** daß); **II** *v/t.* **3.** *j-n* inständig bitten, ersuchen, anflehen (***for*** um): ***~, consider!*** bitte, bedenken Sie doch!; **4.** *et.* erbitten, erflehen.

prayer [preə] *s.* **1.** Ge'bet *n*: ***put up a ~*** ein Gebet emporsenden; ***say one's ~s*** beten, s-e Gebete verrichten; ***he hasn't got a ~*** *Am. sl.* er hat nicht die geringste Chance; **2.** *oft pl.* Andacht *f*: ***evening ~*** Abendandacht; **3.** inständige Bitte, Flehen *n*; **4.** Gesuch *n*; ⚖ *a.* Antrag *m*, Klagebegehren *n*; **5.** ['preɪə] Beter(in); **~ book** *s.* Ge'betbuch *n*; **~ meet·ing** *s.* Ge'betsversammlung *f*; **~ wheel** *s.* Ge'betsmühle *f*.

pre- [priː; prɪ] *in Zssgn* a) (*zeitlich*) vor (-her); vor…; früher als, b) (*räumlich*) vor, da'vor.

preach [priːtʃ] **I** *v/i.* **1.** (***to***) predigen (zu *od.* vor *dat.*), e-e Predigt halten (*dat. od.* vor *dat.*); **2.** *fig.* ‚predigen': ***~ at s.o.*** j-m e-e (Moral)Predigt halten; **II** *v/t.* **3.** *et.* predigen: ***~ the gospel*** das Evangelium verkünden; ***~ a sermon*** e-e Predigt halten; **4.** ermahnen zu: ***~ charity*** Nächstenliebe predigen; **'preach·er** [-tʃə] *s.* Prediger(in); **'preach·i·fy** [-tʃɪfaɪ] *v/i.* sal'badern, Mo'ral predigen; **'preach·ing** [-tʃɪŋ] *s.* **1.** Predigen *n*; **2.** *bibl.* Lehre *f*; **'preach·y** [-tʃɪ] *adj.* □ F sal'badernd, moralisierend.

pre·am·ble [pri:ˈæmbl] *s.* **1.** Präˈambel *f* (*a.* ⚖), Einleitung *f*; Oberbegriff *m e-r Patentschrift*; Kopf *m e-s Funkspruchs etc.*; **2.** *fig.* Vorspiel *n*, Auftakt *m*.
pre·ar·range [ˌpri:əˈreɪndʒ] *v/t.* **1.** vorher abmachen *od.* anordnen *od.* bestimmen; **2.** vorbereiten.
preb·end [ˈprebənd] *s. eccl.* Präˈbende *f*, Pfründe *f*; **ˈpreb·en·dar·y** [-bəndərɪ] *s.* Pfründner *m*.
pre·cal·cu·late [ˌpri:ˈkælkjʊleɪt] *v/t.* vorˈausberechnen.
pre·car·i·ous [prɪˈkeərɪəs] *adj.* ☐ **1.** preˈkär, unsicher (*a. Lebensunterhalt*), bedenklich (*a. Gesundheitszustand*); **2.** gefährlich; **3.** anfechtbar; **4.** ⚖ ˈwiderruflich; **preˈcar·i·ous·ness** [-nɪs] *s.* **1.** Unsicherheit *f*; **2.** Gefährlichkeit *f*; **3.** Zweifelhaftigkeit *f*.
pre·cau·tion [prɪˈkɔ:ʃn] *s.* **1.** Vorkehrung *f*, Vorsichtsmaßregel *f*: ***take ~s*** Vorsichtsmaßregeln *od.* Vorsorge treffen; ***as a ~*** vorsichtshalber, vorsorglich; **2.** Vorsicht *f*; **preˈcau·tion·ar·y** [-ʃnərɪ] *adj.* **1.** vorbeugend, Vorsichts...: ***~ measures*** Vorkehrungen; **2.** Warn...: ***~ signal*** Warnsignal *n*.
pre·cede [ˌpri:ˈsi:d] **I** *v/t.* **1.** vorˈaus-, vorˈangehen (*dat.*) (*a. fig. Buchkapitel, Zeitraum etc.*); **2.** den Vorrang *od.* Vortritt *od.* Vorzug haben vor (*dat.*), vorgehen (*dat.*); **3.** *fig.* (***by***, ***with s.th.***) (durch et.) einleiten, (*e-r Sache* et.) vorˈausschicken; **II** *v/i.* **4.** vorˈan-, vorˈausgehen; **5.** den Vorrang *od.* Vortritt haben; **ˌpreˈced·ence** [-dəns] *s.* **1.** Vorˈhergehen *n*, Prioriˈtät *f*: ***have the ~ of*** *e-r Sache zeitlich* vorangehen; **2.** Vorrang *m*, Vorzug *m*, Vortritt *m*, Vorrecht *n*: ***take ~ of*** (*od.* ***over***) → ***precede*** 2; (***order of***) ***~*** Rangordnung *f*;
prec·e·dent [ˈpresɪdənt] **I** *s.* ⚖ Präzeˈdenzfall *m*, Präjuˈdiz *n*: ***without ~*** ohne Beispiel, noch nie dagewesen; ***set a ~*** e-n Präzedenzfall schaffen; **II** [prɪˈsi:dənt] *adj.* ☐ vorˈhergehend; **preˈced·ing** [-dɪŋ] **I** *adj.* vorˈhergehend: ***~ indorser*** † Vor(der)mann *m* (*Wechsel*); **II** *prp.* vor (*dat.*).
pre·cen·sor [ˌpri:ˈsensə] *v/t.* e-r ˈVorzenˌsur unterˈwerfen.
pre·cen·tor [ˌpri:ˈsentə] *s.* ♪, *eccl.* Kantor *m*, Vorsänger *m*.
pre·cept [ˈpri:sept] *s.* **1.** (*a.* göttliches) Gebot; **2.** Regel *f*, Richtschnur *f*; **3.** Lehre *f*, Unterˈweisung *f*; **4.** ⚖ Gerichtsbefehl *m*; **pre·cep·tor** [prɪˈseptə] *s.* Lehrer *m*.
pre·cinct [ˈpri:sɪŋkt] *s.* **1.** Bezirk *m*: ***cathedral ~s*** Domfreiheit *f*; **2.** *bsd. Am.* Poliˈzei-, Wahlbezirk *m*; **3.** *pl.* Bereich *m*, *pl. fig. a.* Grenzen *pl.*
pre·ci·os·i·ty [ˌpreʃɪˈɒsətɪ] *s.* Geziertheit *f*, Affektiertheit *f*.
pre·cious [ˈpreʃəs] **I** *adj.* ☐ **1.** kostbar, wertvoll (*a. fig.*): ***~ memories***; **2.** edel (*Steine etc.*): ***~ metals*** Edelmetalle; **3.** F ‚schön': a) *iro.* ‚nett': ***a ~ mess***, b) beträchtlich: ***a ~ lot better than*** bei weitem besser als; **4.** *fig.* preziˈös, affektiert, geziert: ***~ style***; **II** *adv.* **5.** F reichlich, äußerst: ***~ little***; **III** *s.* **6.** Schatz *m*, Liebling *m*: ***my ~!***; **ˈprecious·ness** [-nɪs] *s.* **1.** Köstlichkeit *f*, Kostbarkeit *f*; **2.** → ***preciosity***.
prec·i·pice [ˈpresɪpɪs] *s.* Abgrund *m*, *fig. a.* Klippe *f*.
pre·cip·i·ta·ble [prɪˈsɪpɪtəbl] *adj.* ⚗ abscheidbar, fällbar, niederschlagbar; **preˈcip·i·tance** [-təns], **pre·cip·i·tan·cy** [-tənsɪ] *s.* **1.** Eile *f*; **2.** Hast *f*, Überˈstürzung *f*; **preˈcip·i·tant** [-tənt] **I** *adj.* ☐ **1.** (steil) abstürzend, jäh; **2.** *fig.* hastig, eilig; **3.** *fig.* überˈeilt; **II** *s.* **4.** ⚗ Fällungsmittel *n*; **preˈcip·i·tate** [-teɪt] **I** *v/t.* **1.** hinˈabstürzen (*a. fig.*); **2.** *fig. Ereignisse* herˈaufbeschwören, (plötzlich) herˈbeiführen, beschleunigen; **3.** *j-n* (hinˈein)stürzen (***into*** in *acc.*): ***~ a country into war***; **4.** ⚗ (aus)fällen; **5.** *meteor.* niederschlagen, verflüssigen; **II** *v/i.* **6.** ⚗ *u. meteor.* sich niederschlagen; **III** *adj.* [-tət] **7.** jäh(lings) hinˈabstürzend, steil abfallend; **8.** *fig.* überˈstürzt, -ˈeilt, ˈvoreilig; eilig, hastig; **9.** plötzlich; **IV** *s.* [-teɪt] **10.** ⚗ Niederschlag *m*, ˈFällproˌdukt *n*; **preˈcip·i·tate·ness** [-tətnɪs] *s.* Überˈeilung *f*, ˈVoreiligkeit *f*; **pre·cip·i·ta·tion** [prɪˌsɪpɪˈteɪʃn] *s.* **1.** jäher Sturz, (Herˈab)Stürzen *n*; **2.** *fig.* Überˈstürzung *f*; Hast *f*; **3.** ⚗ Fällung *f*; **4.** *meteor.* Niederschlag *m*; **5.** *Spiritismus*: Materialisatiˈon *f*; **preˈcip·i·tous** [-təs] *adj.* ☐ **1.** jäh, steil (abfallend), abschüssig; **2.** *fig.* überˈstürzt.
pré·cis [ˈpreɪsi:] (*Fr.*) **I** *pl.* **-cis** [-si:z] *s.* (kurze) ˈÜbersicht, Zs.-fassung *f*; **II** *v/t.* kurz zs.-fassen.
pre·cise [prɪˈsaɪs] *adj.* ☐ **1.** präˈzis(e), klar, genau; **2.** exˈakt, (peinlich) genau, korˈrekt; *contp.* peˈdantisch; **3.** genau, richtig (*Betrag*, *Moment etc.*); **preˈcise·ly** [-lɪ] *adv.* **1.** → ***precise***; **2.** gerade, genau, ausgerechnet; **3.** ***~!*** genau!; **preˈcise·ness** [-nɪs] *s.* **1.** (überˈtriebene) Genauigkeit; **2.** (ängstliche) Gewissenhaftigkeit, Pedanteˈrie *f*; **pre·ci·sion** [prɪˈsɪʒn] **I** *s.* Genauigkeit *f*, Exˈaktheit *f*; *a.* ⚙, ⚔ Präzisiˈon *f*; **II** *adj.* ⚙, ⚔ Präzisions..., Fein...: ***~ adjustment*** a) ⚙ Feineinstellung, b) ⚔ genaues Einschießen; ***~ bombing*** gezielter Bombenwurf; ***~ instrument*** Präzisionsinstrument *n*; ***~ mechanics*** Feinmechanik *f*; ***~-made*** Präzisions...
pre·clude [prɪˈklu:d] *v/t.* **1.** ausschließen (***from*** von); **2.** *e-r Sache* vorbeugen *od.* zuˈvorkommen; *Einwände* vorˈwegnehmen; **3.** *j-n* hindern (***from*** an *dat.*, ***from doing*** zu tun); **preˈclu·sion** [-u:ʒn] *s.* **1.** Ausschließung *f*, Ausschluß *m* (***from*** von); **2.** Verhinderung *f*; **preˈclu·sive** [-u:sɪv] *adj.* ☐ **1.** ausschließend (***of*** von); **2.** (ver)hindernd.
pre·co·cious [prɪˈkəʊʃəs] *adj.* ☐ **1.** frühreif, frühzeitig (entwickelt); **2.** *fig.* frühreif, altklug; **preˈco·cious·ness** [-nɪs], **preˈcoc·i·ty** [-ˈkɒsətɪ] *s.* **1.** Frühreife *f*, -zeitigkeit *f*; **2.** *fig.* Frühreife *f*, Altklugheit *f*.
pre·cog·ni·tion [ˌpri:kɒgˈnɪʃn] *s.* Präkogniˈtiˈon *f*, Vorauswissen *n*.
pre·con·ceive [ˌpri:kənˈsi:v] *v/t.* (sich) vorher ausdenken, sich vorher vorstellen: ***~d opinion*** → **pre·con·cep·tion** [ˌpri:kənˈsepʃn] *s.* vorgefaßte Meinung, *a.* Vorurteil *n*.
pre·con·cert [ˌpri:kənˈsɜ:t] *v/t.* vorher vereinbaren: ***~ed*** verabredet, *b.s.* abgekartet.
pre·con·di·tion [ˌpri:kənˈdɪʃn] **I** *s.* **1.** Vorbedingung *f*, Vorˈaussetzung *f*; **II** *v/t.* **2.** ⚙ vorbehandeln; **3.** *fig.* j-n einstimmen.
pre·co·nize [ˈpri:kənaɪz] *v/t.* **1.** öffentlich verkündigen; **2.** *R. C. Bischof* präkonisieren.
pre·cook [ˌpri:ˈkʊk] *v/t.* vorkochen.
pre·cool [ˌpri:ˈku:l] *v/t.* vorkühlen.
pre·cur·sor [ˌpri:ˈkɜ:sə] *s.* **1.** Vorläufer (-in), Vorbote *m*, -botin *f*; **2.** (Amts-) Vorgänger(in); **ˌpreˈcur·so·ry** [-ərɪ] *adj.* **1.** vorˈausgehend; **2.** einleitend, vorbereitend.
pre·da·ceous *Am.*, **pre·da·cious** *Brit.* [prɪˈdeɪʃəs] *adj.* räuberisch: ***~ animal*** Raubtier *n*; ***~ instinct*** Raub(tier)instinkt *m*.
pre·date [ˌpri:ˈdeɪt] *v/t.* **1.** zuˈrück-, vordatieren; **2.** *zeitlich* vorˈangehen.
pred·a·to·ry [ˈpredətərɪ] *adj.* ☐ räuberisch, Raub...(*-krieg*, *-vogel etc.*).
pre·de·cease [ˌpri:dɪˈsi:s] *v/t.* früher sterben als *j-d*, vor *j-m* sterben: ***~d parent*** ⚖ vorverstorbener Elternteil.
pred·e·ces·sor [ˈpri:dɪsesə] *s.* **1.** Vorgänger(in) (*a. fig. Buch etc.*): ***~ in interest*** ⚖ Rechtsvorgänger; ***~ in office*** Amtsvorgänger; **2.** Vorfahr *m*.
pre·des·ti·nate [ˌpri:ˈdestɪneɪt] **I** *v/t. eccl. u. weitS.* prädestinieren, aus(er)wählen, (vorˈher)bestimmen, ausersehen (***to*** für, zu); **II** *adj.* [-neɪt] prädestiniert, auserwählt; **pre·des·ti·na·tion** [pri:ˌdestɪˈneɪʃn] *s.* **1.** Vorˈherbestimmung *f*; **2.** *eccl.* Prädestinatiˈon *f*, Gnadenwahl *f*; **ˌpreˈdes·tine** [-tɪn] → ***predestinate*** I.
pre·de·ter·mi·na·tion [ˈpri:dɪˌtɜ:mɪˈneɪʃn] *s.* Vorˈherbestimmung *f*; **pre·de·ter·mine** [ˌpri:dɪˈtɜ:mɪn] *v/t.* **1.** *eccl.*, *a.* ⚙ vorˈherbestimmen; **2.** *Kosten etc.* vorher festsetzen *od.* bestimmen: ***~ s.o. to s.th.*** j-n für et. vorbestimmen.
pred·i·ca·ble [ˈpredɪkəbl] **I** *adj.* aussagbar, *j-m* zuzuschreiben(d); **II** *s. pl. phls.* Prädikaˈbilien *pl.*, Allgemeinbegriffe *pl.*; **pre·dic·a·ment** [prɪˈdɪkəmənt] *s.* **1.** *phls.* Kategoˈrie *f*; **2.** (mißliche) Lage; **pred·i·cate** [ˈpredɪkeɪt] **I** *v/t.* **1.** behaupten, aussagen; **2.** *phls.* prädizieren, aussagen; **3.** gründen, basieren (***on*** auf *dat.*): ***be ~d on*** basieren auf (*dat.*); **II** *s.* [-kət] **4.** *phls.* Aussage *f*; **5.** *ling.* Prädiˈkat *n*, Satzaussage *f*: ***~ adjective*** prädikatives Adjektiv; ***~ noun*** Prädikatsnomen *n*; **pred·i·ca·tion** [ˌpredɪˈkeɪʃn] *s.* Aussage *f* (*a. ling. im Prädikat*), Behauptung *f*; **pred·i·ca·tive** [prɪˈdɪkətɪv] *adj.* ☐ **1.** aussagend, Aussage...; **2.** *ling.* prädikaˈtiv; **pred·i·ca·to·ry** [prɪˈdɪkətərɪ] *adj.* **1.** predigend, Prediger...; **2.** gepredigt.
pre·dict [prɪˈdɪkt] *v/t.* vorˈher-, vorˈaussagen, propheˈzeien; **preˈdict·a·ble** [-təbl] *adj.* vorˈaussagbar, berechenbar (*a. Person*, *Politik etc.*): ***he's so ~*** bei ihm weiß man immer genau, was er tun wird; **preˈdict·a·bly** [-təblɪ] *adv.* a) wie vorherzusehen war, b) man kann jetzt schon sagen, daß; **preˈdic·tion** [-kʃn] *s.* Vorˈher-, Vorˈaussage *f*, Weissagung *f*, Propheˈzeiung *f*; **preˈdic·tor** [-tə] *s.* **1.** Proˈphet(in); **2.** ✈ Komˈmandogerät *n*.
pre·di·lec·tion [ˌpri:dɪˈlekʃn] *s.* Vorliebe *f*, Voreingenommenheit *f*.
pre·dis·pose [ˌpri:dɪˈspəʊz] *v/t.* **1.** (***for***) *j-n* (im vorˈaus) geneigt *od.* empfäng-

lich machen *od.* einnehmen (für); **2.** (***to***) *bsd.* ⚕ prädisponieren, empfänglich *od.* anfällig machen (für); **pre·dis·po·si·tion** [ˈpriːˌdɪspəˈzɪʃn] *s.* (***to***) Neigung *f* (zu); Empfänglichkeit *f* (für); Anfälligkeit *f* (für) (*alle a.* ⚕).

pre·dom·i·nance [prɪˈdɒmɪnəns] *s.* **1.** Vorherrschaft *f*; Vormacht(stellung) *f*; **2.** *fig.* Vorherrschen *n*, Überˈwiegen *n*, ˈÜbergewicht *n* (***in*** in *dat.*, ***over*** über *acc.*); **3.** Überˈlegenheit *f*; **preˈdom·i·nant** [-nt] *adj.* □ **1.** vorherrschend, überˈwiegend, ˈvorwiegend; **2.** überˈlegen; **preˈdom·i·nate** [-neɪt] *v/i.* **1.** vorherrschen, überˈwiegen, vorwiegen; **2.** *zahlenmäßig, geistig, körperlich etc.* überˈlegen sein; **3.** die Oberhand *od.* das ˈÜbergewicht haben (***over*** über *acc.*); **4.** herrschen, die Herrschaft haben (***over*** über *acc.*).

pre-em·i·nence [ˌpriːˈemɪnəns] *s.* **1.** Herˈvorragen *n*, Überˈlegenheit *f* (***above, over*** über *acc.*); **2.** Vorrang *m*, -zug *m* (***over*** vor *dat.*); **3.** herˈvorragende Stellung; **ˌpre-ˈem·i·nent** [-nt] *adj.* □ herˈvorragend, überˈragend: ***be ~*** hervorstechen, sich hervortun.

pre·empt [ˌpriːˈempt] *v/t.* **1.** (*v/i.* Land) durch Vorkaufsrecht erwerben; **2.** (im voraus) mit Beschlag belegen; **ˌpreˈemp·tion** [-pʃn] *s.* Vorkauf(srecht *n*) *m*: ***~ price*** Vorkaufspreis *m*; **ˌpreˈemp·tive** [-tɪv] *adj.* **1.** Vorkaufs…: ***~ right***; **2.** ⚔ Präventiv…: ***~ strike*** Präventivschlag *m*; **ˌpreˈemp·tor** [-tə] *s.* Vorkaufsberechtigte(r *m*) *f*.

preen [priːn] *v/t.* *Gefieder etc.* putzen; *sein Haar* (her)richten: ***~ o.s.*** sich putzen (*a. Person*); ***~ o.s. on*** sich et. einbilden auf (*acc.*).

pre-en·gage [ˌpriːɪnˈgeɪdʒ] *v/t.* **1.** im vorˈaus *vertraglich* verpflichten; **2.** im vorˈaus in Anspruch nehmen; **3.** ✝ vorbestellen; **ˌpre-enˈgage·ment** [-mənt] *s.* vorher eingegangene Verpflichtung, frühere Verbindlichkeit.

pre-ex·am·i·na·tion [ˈpriːɪgˌzæmɪˈneɪʃn] *s.* vorˈherige Vernehmung, ˈVorunterˌsuchung *f*, -prüfung *f*.

pre-ex·ist [ˌpriːɪgˈzɪst] *v/i.* vorher vorˈhanden sein *od.* existieren; **ˌpre-exˈist·ence** [-təns] *s. bsd. eccl.* früheres Dasein, Präexiˈstenz *f*.

pre·fab [ˈpriːfæb] **I** *adj.* → ***prefabricated***; **II** *s.* Fertighaus *n*.

pre·fab·ri·cate [ˌpriːˈfæbrɪkeɪt] *v/t.* vorfabrizieren, *genormte* Fertigteile für *Häuser etc.* herstellen; **ˌpreˈfab·ri·cat·ed** [-tɪd] *adj.* vorgefertigt, zs.-setzbar, Fertig…: ***~ house*** Fertighaus *n*; ***~ piece*** Bauteil *n*.

pref·ace [ˈprefɪs] **I** *s.* Vorwort *n*, -rede *f*; Einleitung *f* (*a. fig.*); **II** *v/t. Rede etc.* einleiten (*a. fig.*), ein Vorwort schreiben zu *e-m Buch*.

pref·a·to·ry [ˈprefətərɪ] *adj.* □ einleitend, Einleitungs…

pre·fect [ˈpriːfekt] *s.* **1.** *pol.* Präˈfekt *m*; **2.** *Brit.* Vertrauensschüler *m*.

pre·fer [prɪˈfɜː] *v/t.* **1.** (es) vorziehen (***to*** *dat.*, ***rather than*** statt); bevorzugen: ***I ~ to go today*** ich gehe lieber heute; ***~red*** ✝ bevorzugt, Vorzugs…(*-aktie etc.*); **2.** befördern (***to*** [***the rank of***] zum); **3.** ⚖ *Gläubiger etc.* begünstigen, bevorzugt befriedigen; **4.** ⚖ *Gesuch, Klage* einreichen (***to*** bei, ***against*** gegen); *Ansprüche* erheben; **pref·er·a·ble** [ˈprefərəbl] *adj.* □ (***to***) vorzuziehen(d) (*dat.*); vorzüglicher (als); **pref·er·a·bly** [ˈprefərəblɪ] *adv.* vorzugsweise, lieber, am besten; **pref·er·ence** [ˈprefərəns] *s.* **1.** Bevorzugung *f*, Vorzug *m* (***above, before, over, to*** vor *dat.*); **2.** Vorliebe *f* (***for*** für): ***by ~*** mit (besonderer) Vorliebe; **3.** ✝, ⚖ a) Vor(zugs)recht *n*, Prioriˈtät *f*: ***~ bond*** Prioritätsobligation *f*; ***~ dividend*** *Brit.* Vorzugsdividende *f*; ***~ share*** (*od.* ***stock***) → e), b) Vorzug *m*, Bevorrechtigung *f*: ***~ as to dividends*** Dividendenbevorrechtigung *f*, c) bevorzugte Befriedigung (*a. Konkurs*): ***fraudulent ~*** Gläubigerbegünstigung *f*, d) *Zoll*: ˈMeistbegünstigung(staˌrif *m*) *f*, e) *Brit.* ˈVorzugsˌaktie *f*; **pref·er·en·tial** [ˌprefəˈrenʃl] *adj.* □ bevorzugt; *a.* ✝, ⚖ bevorrechtigt (*Forderung, Gläubiger etc.*), Vorzugs…(*-aktie, -dividende, -recht, -zoll*): ***~ treatment*** Vorzugsbehandlung *f*; **pref·er·en·tial·ly** [ˌprefəˈrenʃəlɪ] *adv.* vorzugsweise; **preˈfer·ment** [-mənt] *s.* **1.** Beförderung *f* (***to*** zu); **2.** höheres Amt, Ehrenamt *n* (*bsd. eccl.*); **3.** ⚖ Einreichung *f* (*Klage*).

pre·fig·u·ra·tion [ˈpriːˌfɪgjʊˈreɪʃn] *s.* **1.** vorbildhafte Darstellung, Vor-, Urbild *n*; **2.** vorˈherige Darstellung.

pre·fix **I** *v/t.* [ˌpriːˈfɪks] (*a. ling. Wort, Silbe*) vorsetzen, vorˈausgehen lassen (***to*** *dat.*); **II** *s.* [ˈpriːfɪks] *ling.* Präˈfix *n*, Vorsilbe *f*.

preg·gers [ˈpregəz] *adj.* F schwanger.

preg·nan·cy [ˈpregnənsɪ] *s.* **1.** Schwangerschaft *f*; *zo.* Trächtigkeit *f*; **2.** *fig.* Fruchtbarkeit *f*, Schöpferkraft *f*, Gedankenfülle *f*; **3.** *fig.* Präˈgnanz *f*, Bedeutungsgehalt *m*, -schwere *f*; **ˈpreg·nant** [-nt] *adj.* □ **1.** a) schwanger (*Frau*), b) trächtig (*Tier*); **2.** *fig.* fruchtbar, reich (***in*** an *dat.*); **3.** einfalls-, geistreich; **4.** *fig.* bedeutungsvoll, gewichtig; voll (***with*** von).

pre·heat [ˌpriːˈhiːt] *v/t.* vorwärmen (*a.* ⚙).

pre·hen·sile [prɪˈhensaɪl] *adj. zo.* Greif…: ***~ organ***.

pre·his·tor·ic, **pre·his·tor·i·cal** [ˌpriːhɪˈstɒrɪk(l)] *adj.* □ prähiˈstorisch, vorgeschichtlich; **pre·his·to·ry** [ˌpriːˈhɪstərɪ] *s.* Vor-, Urgeschichte *f*.

pre-ig·ni·tion [ˌpriːɪgˈnɪʃn] *s. mot.* Frühzündung *f*.

pre·judge [ˌpriːˈdʒʌdʒ] *v/t.* im vorˈaus *od.* vorschnell be- *od.* verurteilen.

prej·u·dice [ˈpredʒʊdɪs] **I** *s.* **1.** Vorurteil *n*, Voreingenommenheit *f*, *a.* ⚖ Befangenheit *f*; **2.** (*a.* ⚖) Nachteil *m*, Schaden *m*: ***to the ~ of*** zum Nachteil (*gen.*); ***without ~*** ohne Verbindlichkeit; ***without ~ to*** ohne Schaden für, unbeschadet (*gen.*); **II** *v/t.* **3.** mit e-m Vorurteil erfüllen, einnehmen (***in favo[u]r of*** für, ***against*** gegen): ***~d*** a) (vor)eingenommen, b) ⚖ befangen, c) vorgefaßt (*Meinung*); **4.** *a.* ⚖ beeinträchtigen, benachteiligen, schaden (*dat.*), *e-r Sache* abträglich sein; **prej·u·di·cial** [ˌpredʒʊˈdɪʃl] *adj.* □ nachteilig, schädlich (***to*** für): ***be ~ to*** → ***prejudice*** 4.

prel·a·cy [ˈpreləsɪ] *s. eccl.* **1.** Präläˈtur *f* (*Würde od. Amtsbereich*); **2.** *coll.* Präˈlaten(stand *m*, -tum *n*) *pl.*; **prel·ate** [ˈprelɪt] *s.* Präˈlat *m*.

pre·lect [prɪˈlekt] *v/i.* lesen, e-e Vorlesung *od.* Vorlesungen halten (***on, upon*** über *acc.*, ***to*** vor *dat.*); **preˈlec·tion** [-kʃn] *s.* Vorlesung *f*, Vortrag *m*; **preˈlec·tor** [-tə] *s.* Vorleser *m*, (Universiˈtäts)Lektor *m*.

pre·lim [ˈpriːlɪm] **1.** F → ***preliminary examination***; **2.** *pl. typ.* Titeˈlei *f*.

pre·lim·i·nar·y [prɪˈlɪmɪnərɪ] **I** *adj.* □ **1.** einleitend, vorbereitend, Vor…: ***~ discussion*** Vorbesprechung *f*; ***~ inquiry*** ⚖ Voruntersuchung *f*; ***~ measures*** vorbereitende Maßnahmen; ***~ round*** *sport* Vorrunde *f*; ***~ work*** Vorarbeit *f*; **2.** vorläufig: ***~ dressing*** ⚕ Notverband *m*; **II** *s.* **3.** *mst pl.* Einleitung *f*, Vorbereitung(en *pl.*) *f*, vorbereitende Maßnahmen *pl.*; *pl.* Prälimiˈnarien *pl.* (*a.* ⚖ *e-s Vertrags*); **4.** ⚖ Vorverhandlungen *pl.*; **5.** → ***~ ex·am·i·na·tion*** *s. univ.* **1.** Aufnahmeprüfung *f*; **2.** a) Vorprüfung *f*, b) ⚕ Physikum *n*.

prel·ude [ˈpreljuːd] **I** *s.* **1.** ♪ Vorspiel *n*, Einleitung *f* (*beide a. fig.*), Präˈludium *n*; *fig.* Auftakt *m*; **II** *v/t.* **2.** ♪ a) einleiten, b) als Präˈludium spielen; **3.** *bsd. fig.* einleiten, das Vorspiel *od.* der Auftakt sein zu; **III** *v/i.* **4.** ♪ a) ein Präˈludium spielen, b) als Vorspiel dienen (***to*** für, zu); **5.** *fig.* das Vorspiel *od.* die Einleitung bilden (***to*** zu).

pre·mar·i·tal [ˌpriːˈmærɪtl] *adj.* vorehelich.

pre·ma·ture [ˌpreməˈtjʊə] *adj.* □ **1.** früh-, vorzeitig, verfrüht: ***~ birth*** Frühgeburt *f*; ***~ ignition*** *mot.* Frühzündung *f*; **2.** *fig.* voreilig, -schnell, überˈeilt; **3.** frühreif; **ˌpre·maˈture·ness** [-nɪs], **ˌpre·maˈtu·ri·ty** [-ərətɪ] *s.* **1.** Frühreife *f*; **2.** Früh-, Vorzeitigkeit *f*; **3.** Überˈeiltheit *f*.

pre·med·i·cal [ˌpriːˈmedɪkl] *adj. univ. Am.* ˈvormediˌzinisch, in die Mediˈzin einführend: ***~ course*** Einführungskurs *m* in die Medizin; ***~ student*** Medizinstudent(in), der (die) e-n Einführungskurs besucht.

pre·me·di·e·val [ˈpriːˌmedɪˈiːvl] *adj.* frühmittelalterlich.

pre·med·i·tate [ˌpriːˈmedɪteɪt] *v/t. u. v/i.* vorher überˈlegen: ***~d murder*** vorsätzlicher Mord; **ˌpreˈmed·i·tat·ed·ly** [-tɪdlɪ] *adv.* mit Vorbedacht, vorsätzlich; **pre·med·i·ta·tion** [priːˌmedɪˈteɪʃn] *s.* Vorbedacht *m*; Vorsatz *m*.

pre·mi·er [ˈpremjə] **I** *adj.* erst; oberst, Haupt…; **II** *s.* Premiˈer(miˌnister) *m*, Miˈnisterpräsiˌdent(in).

pre·mière [prəˈmjeə] (*Fr.*) *thea.* **I** *s.* **1.** Premiˈere *f*, Ur-, Erstaufführung *f*; **2.** a) Darstellerin *f*, b) Primaballeˈrina *f*; **II** *v/t.* **3.** ur-, erstaufführen.

pre·mi·er·ship [ˈpremjəʃɪp] *s.* Amt *n* *od.* Würde *f* des Premiˈermiˌnisters.

prem·ise¹ [ˈpremɪs] *s.* **1.** *phls.* Präˈmisse *f*, Vorˈaussetzung *f*, Vordersatz *m e-s Schlusses*; **2.** ⚖ a) *pl. das* Obenerwähnte: ***in the ~s*** im Vorstehenden; ***in these ~s*** in Hinsicht auf das eben Erwähnte, b) obenerwähntes Grundstück; **3.** *pl.* a) Grundstück *n*, b) Haus *n* nebst Zubehör (*Nebengebäude, Grund u. Boden*), c) Loˈkal *n*, Räumlichkeiten *pl.*: ***business ~s*** Geschäftsräume *pl.*, Werksgelände *n*; ***licensed ~*** Schanklokal *n*; ***on the ~s*** an Ort u. Stelle, auf dem Grundstück, im Hause *od.* Lokal.

pre·mise² [prɪˈmaɪz] *v/t.* **1.** vorˈausschik-

ken; **2.** *phls.* postulieren.
pre·mi·um [ˈpriːmjəm] *s.* **1.** (Leistungs- *etc.*)Prämie *f*, Bonus *m*; Belohnung *f*, Preis *m*; Zugabe *f*: **~ offers** ✝ Verkauf *m* mit Zugaben; **~ system** Prämienlohnsystem *n*; **2.** (Versicherungs)Prämie *f*: **free of ~** prämienfrei; **3.** ✝ Aufgeld *n*, Agio *n*: **at a ~** a) ✝ über Pari, b) *fig.* hoch im Kurs (stehend), sehr gesucht; **sell at a ~** a) (*v/i.*) über Pari stehen, b) (*v/t.*) mit Gewinn verkaufen; **4.** Lehrgeld *n e-s Lehrlings*, ˈAusbildungshonoˌrar *n*.
pre·mo·ni·tion [ˌpriːməˈnɪʃn] *s.* **1.** Warnung *f*; **2.** (Vor)Ahnung *f*, (Vor)Gefühl *n*; **pre·mon·i·to·ry** [prɪˈmɒnɪtərɪ] *adj.* warnend: **~ symptom** ⚕ Frühsymptom *n*.
pre·na·tal [ˌpriːˈneɪtl] *adj.* ⚕ vor der Geburt, vorgeburtlich, pränaˈtal: **~ care** Schwangerenvorsorge *f*.
pre·oc·cu·pan·cy [ˌpriːˈɒkjʊpənsɪ] *s.* **1.** (Recht *n* der) frühere(n) Besitznahme; **2.** (**in**) Beschäftigtsein *n* (mit), Vertieftsein *n* (in *acc.*); **pre·oc·cu·pa·tion** [priːˌɒkjʊˈpeɪʃn] *s.* **1.** vorˈherige Besitznahme; **2.** (**with**) Beschäftigtsein *n* (mit), Vertieftsein *n* (in *acc.*), Inˈanspruchnahme *f* (durch); **3.** Hauptbeschäftigung *f*; **4.** Vorurteil *n*, Voreingenommenheit *f*; **ˌpreˈoc·cu·pied** [-paɪd] *adj.* vertieft (**with** in *acc.*), gedankenverloren; **pre·oc·cu·py** [ˌpriːˈɒkjʊpaɪ] *v/t.* **1.** vorher *od.* vor anderen in Besitz nehmen; **2.** *j-n* (völlig) in Anspruch nehmen, *j-s Gedanken* ausschließlich beschäftigen, erfüllen.
pre·or·dain [ˌpriːɔːˈdeɪn] *v/t.* vorher anordnen, vorˈherbestimmen.
prep [prep] *s.* F **1.** a) *a.* **~ school** → **preparatory school**, b) *Am.* Schüler (-in) e-r **preparatory school**; **2.** *Brit.* → **preparation** 5.
pre·pack [ˌpriːˈpæk], **pre·pack·age** [ˌpriːˈpækɪdʒ] *v/t.* ✝ abpacken.
pre·paid [ˌpriːˈpeɪd] *adj.* vorˈausbezahlt; ✉ frankiert, (porto)frei.
prep·a·ra·tion [ˌprepəˈreɪʃn] *s.* **1.** Vorbereitung *f*: **in ~ for** als Vorbereitung auf (*acc.*); **make ~s** Vorbereitungen *od.* Anstalten treffen (**for** für); **2.** (Zu-)Bereitung *f* (*von Tee, Speisen etc.*), Herstellung *f*; ⚒, ⚙ Aufbereitung *f* (*von Erz, Kraftstoff etc.*); Vorbehandlung *f*, Imprägnieren *n* (*von Holz etc.*); **3.** ⚗, ⚕ Präpaˈrat *n*, *pharm. a.* Arzˈnei (-mittel *n*) *f*; **4.** Abfassung *f e-r Urkunde etc.*; Ausfüllen *n e-s Formulars*; **5.** *ped. Brit.* (Anfertigung *f* der) Hausaufgaben *pl.*, Vorbereitung(sstunde) *f*; **6.** ♪ a) (Dissoˈnanz)Vorbereitung *f*, b) Einleitung *f*; **pre·par·a·tive** [prɪˈpærətɪv] **I** *adj.* □ → **preparatory** I; **II** *s.* Vorbereitung *f*, vorbereitende Maßnahme (**for** auf *acc.*, **to** zu).
pre·par·a·to·ry [prɪˈpærətərɪ] **I** *adj.* □ **1.** vorbereitend, als Vorbereitung dienend (**to** für); **2.** Vor(bereitungs)...; **3. ~ to** *adv.* im Hinblick auf (*acc.*), vor (*dat.*): **~ to doing s.th.** bevor *od.* ehe man etwas tut; **II** *s.* **4.** *Brit.* → **~ school** *s.* (*Am.* priˈvate) Vor(bereitungs)schule.
pre·pare [prɪˈpeə] **I** *v/t.* **1.** (*a. Rede, Schularbeiten, Schüler etc.*) vorbereiten; zuˈrecht-, fertigmachen, (her)richten; *Speise etc.* (zu)bereiten; **2.** (aus)rüsten, bereitstellen; **3.** *j-n seelisch* vorbereiten (**to do** zu tun, **for** auf *acc.*): a) geneigt *od.* bereit machen, b) gefaßt machen: **~ o.s. to do s.th.** sich anschikken, et. zu tun; **4.** anfertigen, ausarbeiten, *Plan* entwerfen, *Schriftstück* abfassen; **5.** ⚗, ⚙ a) herstellen, anfertigen, b) präparieren, zurichten; **6.** *Kohle* aufbereiten; **II** *v/i.* **7.** (**for**) sich (*a. seelisch*) vorbereiten (auf *acc.*), sich anschicken *od.* rüsten, Vorbereitungen *od.* Anstalten treffen (für): **~ for war** (sich) zum Krieg rüsten; **~ to ...!** ⚔ Fertig zum ...!; **preˈpared** [-eəd] *adj.* **1.** vor-, zubereitet, bereit; **2.** *fig.* bereit, gewillt; **3.** gefaßt (**for** auf *acc.*); **preˈpar·ed·ness** [-eədnɪs] *s.* **1.** Bereitschaft *f*, -sein *n*; **2.** Gefaßtsein *n* (**for** auf *acc.*).
pre·pay [ˌpriːˈpeɪ] *v/t.* [*irr.* → **pay**] vorˈausbezahlen, *Brief etc.* frankieren; **ˌpreˈpay·ment** [-mənt] *s.* Vorˈaus(be)zahlung *f*; ✉ Frankierung *f*.
pre·pense [prɪˈpens] *adj.* □ ⚖ vorsätzlich, vorbedacht: **with** (*od.* **of**) **malice ~** in böswilliger Absicht.
pre·pon·der·ance [prɪˈpɒndərəns] *s.* **1.** ˈÜbergewicht *n* (*a. fig.* **over** über *acc.*); **2.** *fig.* Überˈwiegen *n* (*an Zahl etc.*), überˈwiegende Zahl (**over** über *acc.*); **preˈpon·der·ant** [-nt] *adj.* □ überˈwiegend, entscheidend; **pre·pon·der·ate** [prɪˈpɒndəreɪt] *v/i. fig.* überˈwiegen, vorherrschen: **~ over** (an Zahl) übersteigen, überlegen sein (*dat.*).
prep·o·si·tion [ˌprepəˈzɪʃn] *s. ling.* Präpositiˈon *f*, Verhältniswort *n*; **ˌprep·o·ˈsi·tion·al** [-ʃənl] *adj.* □ präpositioˈnal.
pre·pos·sess [ˌpriːpəˈzes] *v/t.* **1.** *mst pass. j-n, j-s Geist* einnehmen (**in favo[u]r of** für): **~ed** voreingenommen; **~ing** einnehmend, anziehend; **2.** erfüllen (**with** mit *Ideen etc.*); **ˌpre·posˈses·sion** [-eʃn] *s.* Voreingenommenheit *f* (**in favo[u]r of** für), Vorurteil *n* (**against** gegen); vorgefaßte (günstige) Meinung (**for** von).
pre·pos·ter·ous [prɪˈpɒstərəs] *adj.* □ **1.** abˈsurd, un-, ˈwidersinnig; **2.** lächerlich, groˈtesk.
pre·po·tence [prɪˈpəʊtəns], **preˈpo·ten·cy** [-sɪ] *s.* **1.** Vorherrschaft *f*, Überˈlegenheit *f*; **2.** *biol.* stärkere Vererbungskraft; **preˈpo·tent** [-nt] *adj.* **1.** vorherrschend, (an Kraft) überˈlegen; **2.** *biol.* sich stärker fortpflanzend *od.* vererbend.
pre·print I *s.* [ˈpriːprɪnt] **1.** Vorabdruck *m* (*e-s Buches etc.*); **2.** Teilausgabe *f*; **II** *v/t.* [ˌpriːˈprɪnt] **3.** vorabdrucken.
pre·puce [ˈpriːpjuːs] *s. anat.* Vorhaut *f*.
Pre-Raph·a·el·ite [ˌpriːˈræfəlaɪt] *paint.* **I** *adj.* präraffaeˈlitisch; **II** *s.* Präraffaeˈlit(in).
pre·re·cord·ed [ˌpriːrɪˈkɔːdɪd] *adj.* bespielt (*Musikkassette etc.*).
pre·req·ui·site [ˌpriːˈrekwɪzɪt] **I** *adj.* vorˈauszusetzen(d), erforderlich (**for**, **to** für); **II** *s.* Vorbedingung *f*, (ˈGrund-)Vorˌaussetzung (**for**, **to** für).
pre·rog·a·tive [prɪˈrɒgətɪv] **I** *s.* Priviˈleg(ium) *n*, Vorrecht *n*: **royal ~** Hoheitsrecht *n*; **II** *adj.* bevorrechtigt: **~ right** Vorrecht.
pre·sage [ˈpresɪdʒ] **I** *v/t.* **1.** *mst Böses* ahnen; **2.** (vorher) anzeigen *od.* ankündigen; **3.** weissagen, propheˈzeien; **II** *s.* **4.** Omen *n*, Warnungs-, Anzeichen *n*; **5.** (Vor)Ahnung *f*, Vorgefühl *n*; **6.** Vorbedeutung *f*: **of evil ~**.
pres·by·op·ic [ˌprezbɪˈɒpɪk] *adj.* alters-(weit)sichtig.
pres·by·ter [ˈprezbɪtə] *s. eccl.* **1.** (Kirchen)Älteste(r) *m*; **2.** (Hilfs)Geistliche(r) *m* (*in Episkopalkirchen*); **Pres·by·te·ri·an** [ˌprezbɪˈtɪərɪən] **I** *adj.* presbyteriˈanisch; **II** *s.* Presbyteriˈaner(in); **ˈpres·by·ter·y** [-tərɪ] *s.* **1.** Presbyˈterium *n* (*a.* ⚠ *Chor*); **2.** Pfarrhaus *n*.
pre·school *ped.* **I** *adj.* [ˌpriːˈskuːl] vorschulisch, Vorschul...: **~ child** noch nicht schulpflichtiges Kind; **II** *s.* [ˈpriːskuːl] Vorschule *f*.
pre·sci·ence [ˈpresɪəns] *s.* Vorˈherwissen *n*, Vorˈaussicht *f*; **ˈpre·sci·ent** [-nt] *adj.* □ vorˈherwissend, -sehend (**of** *acc.*).
pre·scribe [prɪˈskraɪb] **I** *v/t.* **1.** vorschreiben (**to s.o.** j-m), *et.* anordnen: (**as**) **~d** (wie) vorgeschrieben, vorschriftsmäßig; **2.** ⚕ verordnen, -schreiben (**for** *od.* **to s.o.** j-m, **for s.th.** gegen et.); **II** *v/i.* **3.** ⚕ et. verschreiben, ein Reˈzept ausstellen (**for s.o.** j-m); **4.** ⚖ a) verjähren, b) Verjährung *od.* Ersitzung geltend machen (**for**, **to** für, auf *acc.*).
pre·scrip·tion [prɪˈskrɪpʃn] **I** *s.* **1.** Vorschrift *f*, Verordnung *f*; **2.** ⚕ a) Reˈzept *n*, b) verordnete Mediˈzin; **3.** ⚖ a) (**positive**) **~** Ersitzung *f*, b) (**negative**) **~** Verjährung *f*; **II** *adj.* **4.** ärztlich verordnet: **~ glasses**; **~ pad** Rezeptblock *m*; **preˈscrip·tive** [-ptɪv] *adj.* □ **1.** verordnend, vorschreibend; **2.** ⚖ a) ersessen: **~ right**, b) Verjährungs...: **~ period**; **~ debt** verjährte Schuld.
pre·se·lec·tion [ˌpriːsɪˈlekʃn] *s.* **1.** ⚙ Vorwahl *f*; **2.** *Radio*: ˈVorselektiˌon *f*; **ˌpre·seˈlec·tive** [-ktɪv] *adj.* ⚙, *mot.* Vorwähler...: **~ gears**; **ˌpre·seˈlec·tor** [-ktə] *s.* ⚙ Vorwähler *m*.
pres·ence [ˈprezns] *s.* **1.** Gegenwart *f*, Anwesenheit *f*, ⚔ *pol.* Präˈsenz *f*: **in the ~ of** in Gegenwart *od.* in Anwesenheit von *od. gen.*, *vor Zeugen*; **saving your ~** so sehr ich es bedaure, dies in Ihrer Gegenwart sagen zu müssen; → **mind** 2; **2.** (unmittelbare) Nähe, Vorˈhandensein *n*: **be admitted into the ~** (zur Audienz) vorgelassen werden; **in the ~ of danger** angesichts der Gefahr; **3.** hohe Perˈsönlichkeit(en *pl.*); **4.** Äußere(s) *n*, Aussehen *n*, (stattliche Erscheinung; *weitS.* Auftreten *n*, Haltung *f*; **5.** Anwesenheit *f* e-s unsichtbaren Geistes; **~ cham·ber** *s.* Audiˈenzsaal *m*.
pres·ent[1] [ˈpreznt] **I** *adj.* □ → **presently**; **1.** (*räumlich*) gegenwärtig, anwesend; vorˈhanden (*a.* ⚗ *etc.*): **~ company**, **those ~** die Anwesenden; **be ~ at** teilnehmen an (*dat.*), beiwohnen (*dat.*), zugegen sein bei; **~!** (*bei Namensaufruf*) hier!; **it is ~ to my mind** *fig.* es ist mir gegenwärtig; **2.** (*zeitlich*) gegenwärtig, jetzig, augenblicklich, momenˈtan: **the ~ day** (*od.* **time**) die Gegenwart; **~ value** Gegenwartswert *m*; **3.** heutig (*bsd. Tag*), laufend (*bsd. Jahr, Monat*); **4.** vorliegend (*Fall, Urkunde etc.*): **the ~ writer** der Schreiber *od.* Verfasser (dieser Zeilen); **5.** *ling.* **~ participle** Mittelwort *n* der Gegenwart, Partizip *n* Präsens; **~ perfect** Perfekt *n*, zweite Vergangenheit; **~ tense** → 7; **II** *s.* **6.** Gegenwart *f*: **at ~** gegenwärtig, im

Augenblick, jetzt, momentan; ***for the ~*** für den Augenblick, vorläufig, einstweilen; ***up to the ~*** bislang, bis dato; **7.** *ling.* Präsens *n*, Gegenwart *f*; **8.** *pl.* ⚖ (vorliegendes) Schriftstück *od.* Doku'ment: ***by these ~s*** hiermit, hierdurch; ***know all men by these ~s*** hiermit jedermann kund und zu wissen (*daß*).

pre·sent² [prɪ'zent] **I** *v/t.* **1.** (dar)bieten, (über)'reichen; *Nachricht etc.* über'bringen: ***~ one's compliments to*** sich *j-m* empfehlen; ***~ s.o. with*** j-n mit *et.* beschenken; ***~ s.th. to*** *j-m* et. schenken; **2.** *Gesuch etc.* einreichen, vorlegen, unter'breiten; ✝ *Scheck*, *Wechsel* (zur Zahlung) vorlegen, präsentieren; ⚖ *Klage* erheben: ***~ a case*** e-n Fall vor Gericht vertreten; **3.** *j-n für ein Amt* vorschlagen; **4.** *Bitte*, *Klage* vorbringen; *Gedanken*, *Wunsch etc.* äußern, unterbreiten; **5.** *j-n* vorstellen (***to*** *dat.*), einführen (***at*** bei *Hofe*): ***~ o.s.*** a) sich vorstellen, b) sich einfinden, erscheinen, sich melden (***for*** zu), c) *fig.* sich bieten (*Möglichkeit etc.*); **6.** *Schwierigkeiten* bieten, *Problem* darstellen; **7.** *thea. etc.* darbieten, *Film* vorführen, zeigen, *Sendung* bringen *od.* moderieren, *Rolle* spielen *od.* verkörpern; *fig.* vergegenwärtigen, darstellen, schildern; **8.** ⚔ a) *Gewehr* präsentieren, b) *Waffe* anlegen, richten (***at*** auf *acc.*).

pres·ent³ ['preznt] *s.* Geschenk *n*: ***make s.o. a ~ of s.th.*** j-m et. zum Geschenk machen.

pre·sent·a·ble [prɪ'zentəbl] *adj.* □ **1.** darstellbar; **2.** präsen'tabel (*Geschenk*); **3.** präsen'tabel (*Erscheinung*), anständig angezogen.

pres·en·ta·tion [ˌprezən'teɪʃn] *s.* **1.** Schenkung *f*, (feierliche) Über'reichung *od.* 'Übergabe: ***~ copy*** Widmungsexemplar *n*; **2.** Gabe *f*, Geschenk *n*; **3.** Vorstellung *f*, Einführung *f e-r Person*; **4.** Vorstellung *f*, Erscheinen *n*; **5.** *fig.* Darstellung *f*, Schilderung *f*, Behandlung *f e-s Falles*, *Problems etc.*; **6.** *thea.*, *Film*: Darbietung *f*, Vorführung *f*; *Radio*, *TV*: Moderati'on *f*; ⚕ Demonstrati'on *f* (*im Kolleg*); **7.** Einreichung *f e-s Gesuchs etc.*; ✝ Vorlage *f e-s Wechsels*: (***up***)***on ~*** gegen Vorlage; ***payable on ~*** zahlbar bei Sicht; **8.** Vorschlag(srecht *n*) *m*; Ernennung *f* (*Brit. a. eccl.*); **9.** ⚕ (Kinds)Lage *f im Uterus*; **10.** *psych.* a) Wahrnehmung *f*, b) Vorstellung *f*.

ˌ**pres·ent-'day** [ˌpreznt-] *adj.* heutig, gegenwärtig, mo'dern.

pre·sent·er [prɪ'zentə] *s. Brit.* ('Fernseh)Modeˌrator *m*.

pre·sen·tient [prɪ'senʃɪənt] *adj.* im vor'aus fühlend, ahnend (***of*** *acc.*); **pre·sen·ti·ment** [prɪ'zentɪmənt] *s.* (Vor-)Gefühl *n*, (*mst* böse Vor)Ahnung.

pres·ent·ly ['prezntlɪ] *adv.* **1.** (so-)'gleich, bald (dar'auf), als'bald; **2.** jetzt, gegenwärtig; **3.** so'fort.

pre·sent·ment [prɪ'zentmənt] *s.* **1.** Darstellung *f*, 'Wiedergabe *f*, Bild *n*; **2.** *thea. etc.* Darbietung *f*, Aufführung *f*; **3.** ✝ (*Wechsel- etc.*)Vorlage *f*; **4.** ⚖ Anklage(schrift) *f*; Unter'suchung *f* von Amts wegen.

pre·serv·a·ble [prɪ'zɜːvəbl] *adj.* erhaltbar, zu erhalten(d), konservierbar; **pres·er·va·tion** [ˌprezə'veɪʃn] *s.* **1.** Bewahrung *f*, (Er)Rettung *f*, Schutz *m* (***from*** vor *dat.*): ***~ of natural beauty*** Naturschutz; **2.** Erhaltung *f*, Konservierung *f*: ***in good ~*** gut erhalten: ***~ of evidence*** ⚖ Beweissicherung *f*; **3.** Einmachen *n*, -kochen *n*, Konservierung *f* (*von Früchten etc.*); **pre'serv·a·tive** [-vətɪv] **I** *adj.* **1.** bewahrend, Schutz...: ***~ coat*** ⚙ Schutzanstrich *m*; **2.** erhaltend, konservierend; **II** *s.* **3.** Konservierungsmittel *n* (*a.* ⚙); **pre·serve** [prɪ'zɜːv] **I** *v/t.* **1.** bewahren, behüten, (er)retten, (be)schützen (***from*** vor *dat.*); **2.** erhalten, vor dem Verderb schützen: ***well-~d*** gut erhalten; **3.** aufbewahren, -heben; ⚖ *Beweise* sichern; **4.** konservieren (*a.* ⚙), *Obst etc.* einkochen, -machen, -legen: ***~d meat*** Büchsenfleisch *n*, *coll.* Fleischkonserven *pl.*; **5.** *hunt. bsd. Brit. Wild*, *Fische* hegen; **6.** *fig. Haltung*, *Ruhe*, *Andenken etc.* (be)wahren: ***~ silence***; **II** *s.* **7.** *mst pl.* Eingemachte(s) *n*, Kon'serve(n *pl.*) *f*; **8.** *oft pl.* a) *hunt. bsd. Brit.* ('Wild)Reserˌvat *n*, (Jagd-, Fisch)Gehege *n*, b) *fig.* Gehege *n*: ***poach on s.o.'s ~s*** j-m ins Gehege kommen (*a. fig.*); **pre'serv·er** [-və] *s.* **1.** Bewahrer(in), Erhalter(in), (Er)Retter(in); **2.** Konservierungsmittel *n*; **3.** 'Einkochappaˌrat *m*; **4.** *hunt. Brit.* Heger *m*, Wildhüter *m*.

pre·set [ˌpriː'set] *v/t.* [*irr.* → ***set***] ⚙ voreinstellen.

pre·shrink [ˌpriː'ʃrɪŋk] *v/t.* [*irr.* → ***shrink***] ⚙ *Stoffe* krumpfen; vorwaschen.

pre·side [prɪ'zaɪd] *v/i.* **1.** den Vorsitz haben *od.* führen (***at*** bei, ***over*** über *acc.*), präsidieren: ***~ over*** (*od.* ***at***) ***a meeting*** e-e Versammlung leiten; ***presiding judge*** ⚖ Vorsitzende(r *m*) *f*; **2.** ♪ *u. fig.* führen.

pres·i·den·cy ['prezɪdənsɪ] *s.* **1.** Prä'sidium *n*, Vorsitz *m*, (Ober)Aufsicht *f*; **2.** *pol.* a) Präsi'dentschaft *f*, b) Amtszeit *f e-s Präsidenten*; **3.** *eccl.* (***First*** ♀ oberste) Mor'monenbehörde *f*; '**pres·i·dent** [-nt] *s.* **1.** Präsi'dent *m* (*a. pol. u.* ⚖), Vorsitzende(r *m*) *f*, Vorstand *m e-r* Körperschaft; *Am.* ✝ (Gene'ral)Diˌrektor *m*: ***♀ of the Board of Trade*** *Brit.* Handelsminister *m*; **2.** *univ. bsd. Am.* Rektor *m*; **pres·i·dent e·lect** *s. der* gewählte Präsi'dent (*vor Amtsantritt*); **pres·i·den·tial** [ˌprezɪ'denʃl] *adj.* □ Präsidenten..., Präsidentschafts...: ***~ message*** *Am.* Botschaft *f* des Präsidenten an den Kongreß; ***~ primary*** *Am.* Vorwahl *f* zur Nominierung des Präsidentschaftskandidaten *e-r Partei*; ***~ system*** Präsidialsystem *n*; ***~ term*** Amtsperiode *f* des Präsidenten; ***~ year*** *Am.* F Jahr *n* der Präsidentenwahl.

press [pres] **I** *v/t.* **1.** *allg.*, *a. j-m die Hand* drücken, pressen (*a.* ⚙); **2.** drükken auf (*acc.*): ***~ the button*** auf den Knopf drücken (*a. fig.*); **3.** *Saft*, *Frucht etc.* (aus)pressen, keltern; **4.** (*vorwärts-*, *weiter- etc.*)drängen, (-)treiben: ***~ on***; **5.** *j-n* (be)drängen: a) in die Enge treiben, zwingen (***to do*** zu tun), b) *j-m* zusetzen, *j-n* bestürmen: ***~ s.o. for*** j-n dringend um *et.* bitten, von j-m *Geld* erpressen; ***be ~ed for money*** (***time***) in Geldverlegenheit sein (unter Zeitdruck stehen, es eilig haben); ***hard ~ed*** in Bedrängnis; **6.** ([***up***]***on*** *j-m*) *et.* aufdrängen, -nötigen; **7.** *Kleidungsstück* plätten; **8.** Nachdruck legen auf (*acc.*): ***~ a charge*** Anklage erheben; ***~ one's point*** auf s-r Forderung *od.* Meinung nachdrücklich bestehen; ***~ the point that*** nachdrücklich betonen, daß; ***~ home*** a) *Forderung etc.* 'durchsetzen, b) *Angriff* energisch 'durchführen, c) *Vorteil* ausnutzen (wollen); **9.** ⚔, ⚓ *in den Dienst* pressen; **II** *v/i.* **10.** drücken, (e-n) Druck ausüben (*a. fig.*); **11.** drängen, pressieren: ***time ~es*** die Zeit drängt; **12.** ***~ for*** dringen *od.* drängen auf (*acc.*), fordern; **13.** (sich) *wohin* drängen: ***~ forward*** (sich) vor(wärts)drängen; ***~ on*** vorwärtsdrängen, weitereilen; ***~ in upon s.o.*** auf j-n eindringen (*a. fig.*); **III** *s.* **14.** (*Frucht-*, *Wein- etc.*)Presse *f*; **15.** *typ.* a) (Drucker-)Presse *f*, b) Drucke'rei(anstalt *f*, -raum *m*, -wesen *n*) *f*, c) Druck(en *n*) *m*: ***correct the ~*** Korrektur lesen; ***go to*** (***the***) ***~*** in Druck gehen; ***send to*** (***the***) ***~*** in Druck geben; ***in the ~*** im Druck; ***ready for the ~*** druckfertig; **16.** ***the ~*** die Presse (*Zeitungswesen*, *a. coll. die Zeitungen od. die Presseleute*): ***~ campaign*** Pressefeldzug *m*; ***~ conference*** Pressekonferenz *f*; ***~ photographer*** Pressephotograph *m*; ***have a good*** (***bad***) ***~*** e-e gute (schlechte) Presse haben; **17.** Spanner *m für Skier od. Tennisschläger*; **18.** (*Bücher- etc.*, *bsd. Wäsche*)Schrank *m*; **19.** *fig.* a) Druck *m*, Hast *f*, b) Dringlichkeit *f*, Drang *m der Geschäfte*: ***the ~ of business***; **20.** ⚔, ⚓ *hist.* Zwangsaushebung *f*; ***~ a·gen·cy*** *s.* 'Presseagenˌtur *f*; ***~ a·gent*** *s. thea. etc.* 'Presseaˌgent *m*; ***~ bar·on*** *s.* Pressezar *m*; '***~-box*** *s.* 'Pressetriˌbüne *f*; ***~ but·ton*** *s.* ϟ (Druck)Knopf *m*; ***~ clip·ping*** *Am.* → ***press cutting***; ***~ cop·y*** *s.* **1.** 'Durchschlag *m*; **2.** Rezensi'onsexemˌplar *n*; ***~ cor·rec·tor*** *s. typ.* Kor'rektor *m*; ***♀ Coun·cil*** *s. Brit.* Presserat *m*; ***~ cut·ting*** *s. Brit.* Zeitungsausschnitt *m*.

pressed [prest] *adj.* gepreßt, Preß... (*-glas*, *-käse*, *-öl*, *-ziegel etc.*); '**press·er** [-sə] *s.* **1.** ⚙ Presser(in); **2.** *typ.* Drukker *m*; **3.** Bügler(in); **4.** ⚙ Preßvorrichtung *f*; **5.** *typ. etc.* Druckwalze *f*.

press| gal·ler·y *s. parl. bsd. Brit.* 'Pressetriˌbüne *f*; '**~-gang I** *s.* ⚓ *hist.* 'Preßpaˌtrouille *f*; **II** *v/t.*: ***~ s.o. into doing s.th.*** F j-n zu et. zwingen.

press·ing ['presɪŋ] **I** *adj.* □ **1.** pressend, drückend; **2.** *fig.* a) (be)drückend, b) dringend, dringlich; **II** *s.* **3.** (Aus)Pressen *n*; **4.** ⚙ a) Stanzen *n*, b) *Papierfabrikation*: Satinieren *n*; **5.** ⚙ Preßling *m*; **6.** *Schallplattenfabrikation*: a) Preßplatte *f*, b) Pressung *f*, c) Auflage *f*.

press| law *s. mst pl.* Pressegesetz(e *pl.*) *n*; **~ lord** *s.* Pressezar *m*; '**~·man** [-mən] *s.* [*irr.*] **1.** (Buch)Drucker *m*; **2.** Zeitungsmann *m*, Pressevertreter *m*; '**~·mark** *s.* Signa'tur *f*, Biblio'theksnummer *f e-s Buches*; **~ proof** *s. typ.* letzte Korrek'tur, Ma'schinenrevisiˌon *f*; **~ re·lease** *s.* Presseverlautbarung *f*; **~ room** *s.* Drucke'rei(raum *m*) *f*, Ma'schinensaal *m*; '**~·stud** *s.* Druckknopf *m*; ˌ**~-to-'talk but·ton** *s.* Sprechtaste *f*; '**~-up** *s. sport* Liegestütz *m*.

pres·sure ['preʃə] **I** *s.* **1.** Druck *m* (*a.*

⚙, *phys.*): ~ ***hose*** (***pump***, ***valve***) ⚙ Druckschlauch *m*, (-pumpe *f*, -ventil *n*); ***work at high*** ~ mit Hochdruck arbeiten (*a. fig.*); **2.** *meteor.* (Luft)Druck *m*: ***high*** (***low***) ~ Hoch-(Tief)druck; **3.** *fig.* Druck *m* (*Last od. Zwang*): ***act under*** ~ unter Druck handeln; ***bring*** ~ ***to bear upon*** auf *j-n* Druck ausüben; ***the*** ~ ***of business*** der Drang *od.* Druck der Geschäfte; ~ ***of taxation*** Steuerdruck *m*, -last *f*; **4.** *fig.* Drangsal *f*, Not *f*: ***monetary*** ~ Geldknappheit *f*; ~ ***of conscience*** Gewissensnot *f*; **II** *v/t.* **5.** → ***pressurize*** 1; **6.** *fig. j-n* (dazu) treiben *od.* zwingen (***into doing*** et. zu tun); ~ **cab·in** *s.* ✈ 'Druckausgleichska,bine *f*; ~ **cook·er** *s.* Schnellkochtopf *m*; ~ **drop** *s.* **1.** ⚙ Druckgefälle *n*; **2.** ⚡ Spannungsabfall *m*; ~ **e·qual·i·za·tion** *s.* Druckausgleich *m*; ~ **ga(u)ge** *s.* ⚙ Druckmesser *m*, Mano'meter *n*; ~ **group** *s. pol.* Inter'essengruppe *f*; ~ **lu·bri·ca·tion** *s.* ⚙ 'Druck(,umlauf)-,schmierung *f*; '~-,**sen·si·tive** *adj.* ⚕ druckempfindlich; ~ **suit** *s.* ✈ ('Über-)Druckanzug *m*; ~ **tank** *s.* ⚙ Druckbehälter *m*.

pres·sur·ize ['preʃəraɪz] *v/t.* **1.** ⚗, ⚙ unter Druck setzen (*a. fig.*), unter 'Überdruck halten, *bsd.* ✈ druckfest machen: ~***d cabin*** → ***pressure cabin***; **2.** ⚗ belüften.

'**press·work** *s. typ.* Druckarbeit *f*.

pres·ti·dig·i·ta·tion ['prestɪ,dɪdʒɪ'teɪʃn] *s.* **1.** Fingerfertigkeit *f*; **2.** Taschenspielerkunst *f*; **pres·ti·dig·i·ta·tor** [,prestɪ'dɪdʒɪteɪtə] *s.* Taschenspieler *m* (*a. fig.*).

pres·tige [pre'stiːʒ] (*Fr.*) *s.* Pre'stige *n*, Geltung *f*, Ansehen *n*.

pres·tig·ious [pre'stɪdʒəs] *adj.* berühmt, renom'miert.

pres·to ['prestəʊ] (*Ital.*) **I** *adv.* ♪ presto, (sehr) schnell (*a. fig.*): ***hey*** ~, ***pass!*** Hokuspokus (Fidibus)! (*Zauberformel*); **II** *adj.* blitzschnell.

pre·stressed [,priː'strest] *adj.* ⚙ vorgespannt: ~ ***concrete*** Spannbeton *m*.

pre·sum·a·ble [prɪ'zjuːməbl] *adj.* □ vermutlich, mutmaßlich, wahr'scheinlich; **pre·sume** [prɪ'zjuːm] **I** *v/t.* **1.** *als wahr* annehmen, vermuten; vor'aussetzen; schließen (***from*** aus): ~***d dead*** verschollen; **2.** sich *et.* erlauben; **II** *v/i.* **3.** vermuten, mutmaßen: ***I*** ~ (wie) ich vermute, vermutlich; **4.** sich her'ausnehmen, sich erdreisten, (es) wagen (***to*** *inf.* zu *inf.*); anmaßend sein; **5.** ~ (***up***)***on*** ausnutzen *od.* miß'brauchen (*acc.*); **pre'sum·ed·ly** [-mɪdlɪ] *adv.* vermutlich; **pre'sum·ing** [-mɪŋ] *adj.* □ → ***presumptuous*** 1.

pre·sump·tion [prɪ'zʌmpʃn] *s.* **1.** Vermutung *f*, Annahme *f*, Mutmaßung *f*; **2.** ⚖ Vermutung *f*, Präsumti'on *f*: ~ ***of death*** Todesvermutung, Verschollenheit *f*; ~ ***of law*** Rechtsvermutung *f* (*der Wahrheit bis zum Beweis des Gegenteils*); **3.** Wahrscheinlichkeit *f*: ***there is a strong*** ~ ***of his death*** es ist (mit Sicherheit) anzunehmen, daß er tot ist; **4.** Vermessenheit *f*, Anmaßung *f*, Dünkel *m*; **pre'sump·tive** [-ptɪv] *adj.* □ vermutlich, mutmaßlich, präsum'tiv: ~ ***evidence*** ⚖ Indizienbeweis *m*; ~ ***title*** ⚖ präsumtives Eigentum; **pre'sump·tu·ous** [-ptjʊəs] *adj.* □ **1.** anmaßend, vermessen, dreist; **2.** über'heblich, dünkelhaft.

pre·sup·pose [,priːsə'pəʊz] *v/t.* vor'aussetzen: a) im vor'aus annehmen, b) zur Vor'aussetzung haben; **pre·sup·po·si·tion** [,priːsʌpə'zɪʃn] *s.* Vor'aussetzung *f*.

pre-tax [,priː'tæks] *adj.* ⚚ vor Abzug der Steuern, *a.* Brutto…

pre-teen [,priː'tiːn] *adj. u. s.* (Kind *n*) im Alter zwischen 10 u. 12.

pre·tence [prɪ'tens] *s.* **1.** Anspruch *m*: ***make no*** ~ ***to*** keinen Anspruch erheben auf (*acc.*); **2.** Vorwand *m*, Scheingrund *m*, Vortäuschung *f*: ***false*** ~***s*** ⚖ Arglist *f*; ***under false*** ~***s*** arglistig, unter Vorspiegelung falscher Tatsachen; **3.** *fig.* Schein *m*, Verstellung *f*: ***make*** ~ ***of doing s.th.*** sich den Anschein geben, als tue man etwas.

pre·tend [prɪ'tend] **I** *v/t.* **1.** vorgeben, -täuschen, -schützen, -heucheln; so tun als ob: ~ ***to be sick*** sich krank stellen, krank spielen; **2.** → ***presume*** 2–4; **II** *v/i.* **3.** sich verstellen, heucheln: ***he is only*** ~***ing*** er tut nur so; **4.** Anspruch erheben (***to*** auf *den Thron etc.*); **pre'tend·ed** [-dɪd] *adj.* □ vorgetäuscht, an-, vorgeblich; **pre'tend·er** [-də] *s.* **1.** Beanspruchende(r *m*) *f*; **2.** ('Thron-)Präten,dent *m*, Thronbewerber *m*.

pre·tense *Am.* → ***pretence***.

pre·ten·sion [prɪ'tenʃn] *s.* **1.** Anspruch *m* (***to*** auf *acc.*): ***of great*** ~***s*** anspruchsvoll; **2.** Anmaßung *f*, Dünkel *m*; **pre'ten·tious** [-ʃəs] *adj.* □ **1.** anmaßend; **2.** prätenti'ös, anspruchsvoll; **3.** protzig; **pre'ten·tious·ness** [-ʃəsnɪs] *s.* Anmaßung *f*.

preter- [priːtə] *in Zssgn* (hin'ausgehend) über (*acc.*), mehr als.

pret·er·it(e) ['pretərɪt] *ling.* **I** *adj.* Vergangenheits…; **II** *s.* Prä'teritum *n*, (erste) Vergangenheit; ,~-'**pres·ent** [-'preznt] *s.* Prä'terito,präsens *n*.

pre·ter·nat·u·ral [,priːtə'nætʃrəl] *adj.* □ **1.** ab'norm, außergewöhnlich; **2.** 'überna,türlich.

pre·text ['priːtekst] *s.* Vorwand *m*, Ausrede *f*: ***under*** (*od.* ***on***) ***the*** ~ ***of*** unter dem Vorwand (*gen.*).

pre·tri·al [,priː'traɪəl] ⚖ **I** *s.* Vorverhandlung *f*; **II** *adj.* vor der (Haupt)Verhandlung, Untersuchungs…

pret·ti·fy ['prɪtɪfaɪ] *v/t.* F verschönern, hübsch machen; '**pret·ti·ly** [-ɪlɪ] *adv.* → ***pretty*** 1; '**pret·ti·ness** [-ɪnɪs] *s.* **1.** Hübschheit *f*, Niedlichkeit *f*; Anmut *f*; **2.** Geziertheit *f*; **pret·ty** ['prɪtɪ] **I** *adj.* □ **1.** hübsch, nett, niedlich; **2.** (*a. iro.*) schön, fein, tüchtig: ***a*** ~ ***mess!*** e-e schöne Geschichte!; **3.** F ‚(ganz) schön', ‚hübsch', beträchtlich: ***it costs a*** ~ ***penny*** es kostet e-e schöne Stange Geld; **II** *adv.* **4.** a) ziemlich, ganz, b) einigermaßen, leidlich: ~ ***cold*** ganz schön kalt; ~ ***good*** recht gut, nicht schlecht; ~ ***much the same thing*** so ziemlich dasselbe; ~ ***near*** nahe daran, ziemlich nahe; **5.** ***sitting*** ~ *sl.* wie der Hase im Kohl, ‚warm' (sitzend); **II** *v/t.* **6.** ~ ***up*** *et.* hübsch machen, ‚aufpolieren'.

pret·zel ['pretsəl] *s.* (Salz)Brezel *f*.

pre·vail [prɪ'veɪl] *v/i.* **1.** (***over***, ***against***) die Oberhand *od.* das 'Übergewicht gewinnen *od.* haben (über *acc.*), (*a.* ⚖ ob)siegen; *fig. a.* sich 'durchsetzen *od.* behaupten (gegen); **2.** *fig.* ausschlag-, maßgebend sein; **3.** *fig.* (vor)herrschen; (weit) verbreitet sein; **4.** ~ (***up***)***on s.o. to do*** j-n dazu bewegen *od.* bringen, *et.* zu tun; **pre'vail·ing** [-lɪŋ] *adj.* □ **1.** über'legen: ~ ***party*** ⚖ obsiegende Partei; **2.** (vor)herrschend, maßgebend: ***the*** ~ ***opinion*** die herrschende Meinung; ***under the*** ~ ***circumstances*** unter den obwaltenden Umständen; ~ ***tone*** ⚚ Grundstimmung *f*; **prev·a·lence** ['prevələns] *s.* **1.** (Vor)Herrschen *n*; Über'handnehmen *n*; **2.** (allgemeine) Gültigkeit; **prev·a·lent** ['prevələnt] *adj.* □ (vor)herrschend, über'wiegend; häufig, weit verbreitet.

pre·var·i·cate [prɪ'værɪkeɪt] *v/i.* Ausflüchte machen; die Wahrheit verdrehen; **pre·var·i·ca·tion** [prɪ,værɪ'keɪʃn] *s.* **1.** Ausflucht *f*, Tatsachenverdrehung *f*, Winkelzug *m*; **2.** ⚖ Anwaltstreubruch *m*; **pre'var·i·ca·tor** [-tə] *s.* Ausflüchtemacher(in), Wortverdreher(in).

pre·vent [prɪ'vent] *v/t.* **1.** verhindern, -hüten; *e-r Sache* vorbeugen *od.* zu'vorkommen; **2.** (***from***) *j-n* hindern (an *dat.*), abhalten (von): ~ ***s.o. from coming*** j-n am Kommen hindern, j-n vom Kommen abhalten; **pre'vent·a·ble** [-təbl] *adj.* verhütbar, abwendbar; **pre'ven·tion** [-nʃn] *s.* **1.** Verhinderung *f*, Verhütung *f*: ~ ***of accidents*** Unfallverhütung; **2.** *bsd.* ⚕ Vorbeugung *f*; **pre'ven·tive** [-tɪv] **I** *adj.* □ **1.** *a.* ⚕ vorbeugend, prophy'laktisch, Vorbeugungs…: ~ ***medicine*** Vorbeugungsmedizin *f*; **2.** *bsd.* ⚖ präven'tiv: ~ ***arrest*** Schutzhaft *f*; ~ ***detention*** a) Sicherungsverwahrung, b) *Am.* Vorbeugehaft *f*; ~ ***war*** *pol.* Präventivkrieg *m*; **II** *s.* **3.** *a.* ⚕ Vorbeugungs-, Schutzmittel *n*; **4.** Schutz-, Vorsichtsmaßnahme *f*.

pre·view ['priːvjuː] *s.* **1.** Vorbesichtigung *f*; *Film*: a) Probeaufführung *f*, b) (Pro'gramm)Vorschau *f*; *Radio*, *TV*: Probe *f*; **2.** Vorbesprechung *f e-s Buches*; **3.** (Vor)'Ausblick *m*.

pre·vi·ous ['priːvjəs] **I** *adj.* □ → ***previously***; **1.** vor'her-, vor'ausgehend, früher, vor'herig, Vor…: ~ ***conviction*** ⚖ Vorstrafe *f*; ~ ***holder*** ⚚ Vor(der)mann *m*; ~ ***question*** *parl.* Vorfrage, ob ohne weitere Debatte abgestimmt werden soll; ***move the*** ~ ***question*** Übergang zur Tagesordnung beantragen; ***without*** ~ ***notice*** ohne vorherige Ankündigung; **2.** *mst* ***too*** ~ F verfrüht, voreilig; **II** *adv.* **3.** ~ ***to*** bevor, vor (*dat.*); ~ ***to that*** zuvor; '**pre·vi·ous·ly** [-lɪ] *adv.* vorher, früher.

pre·vo·ca·tion·al [,priːvəʊ'keɪʃənl] *adj.* vorberuflich.

pre·vue ['priːvjuː] *s. Am.* (Film)Vorschau *f*.

pre·war [,priː'wɔː] *adj.* Vorkriegs…

prey [preɪ] **I** *s.* **1.** *zo. u. fig.* Raub *m*, Beute *f*, Opfer *n*: → ***beast*** 1, ***bird*** 1; ***become*** (*od.* ***fall***) ***a*** ~ ***to*** *j-m od. e-r Sache* zum Opfer fallen; **II** *v/i.* **2.** auf Raub *od.* Beute ausgehen; **3.** ~ (***up***)***on*** a) *zo.* Jagd machen auf (*acc.*), erbeuten, fressen, b) *fig.* berauben, aussaugen, c) *fig.* nagen *od.* zehren an (*dat.*): ***it*** ~***ed upon his mind*** es ließ ihm keine Ruhe, der Gedanke quälte ihn.

price [praɪs] **I** *s.* **1.** ⚚ a) (Kauf)Preis *m*, Kosten *pl.*, b) *Börse*: Kurs(wert) *m*: ~

of issue Emissionspreis; ***bid ~*** gebotener Preis, *Börse*: Geldkurs; ***share*** (*od.* ***stock***) ~ Aktienkurs; ***secure a good ~*** e-n guten Preis erzielen; ***every man has his ~*** *fig.* keiner ist unbestechlich; (***not***) ***at any ~*** um jeden (keinen) Preis; **2.** (Kopf)Preis *m*: ***set a ~ on s.o.'s head*** e-n Preis auf j-s Kopf aussetzen; **3.** *fig.* Lohn *m*, Preis *m*; **4.** (Wett-)Chance(n *pl.*) *f*: ***what ~ ...?*** *sl.* wie steht es mit ...?, welche Chancen hat ...?; **II** *v/t.* **5.** † a) den Preis festsetzen für, b) *Waren* auszeichnen: ***~d*** mit Preisangaben (*Katalog*); ***high-~d*** hoch im Preis, teuer; **6.** bewerten: ***~ s.th. high*** (***low***) e-r Sache großen (geringen) Wert beimessen; **7.** F nach dem Preis *e-r Ware* fragen; **'~-ˌcon·scious** *adj.* preisbewußt; **~ con·trol** *s.* 'Preiskonˌtrolle *f*, -überˌwachung *f*; **~ cut** *s.* Preissenkung *f*; **~ cut·ting** *s.* Preisdrücke'rei *f*, -senkung *f*, 'Preisunterˌbietung *f*; **~ freeze** *s.* Preisstopp *m*.

price·less ['praɪslɪs] *adj.* unschätzbar, unbezahlbar (*a.* F *köstlich*).

price| lev·el *s.* 'Preisniˌveau *n*; **~ lim·it** *s.* (Preis)Limit *n*, Preisgrenze *f*; **~ list** *s.* **1.** Preisliste *f*; **2.** *Börse*: Kurszettel *m*; **'~-mainˌtained** *adj.* † preisgebunden (*Ware*); **~ main·te·nance** *s.* † Preisbindung *f*; **~ range** *s.* Preisklasse *f*; **~ tag**, **~ tick·et** *s.* Preisschild *n*, -zettel *m*.

pric·ey ['praɪsɪ] *adj.* F (ganz schön) teuer.

prick [prɪk] **I** *s.* **1.** (*Insekten-, Nadel- etc.*)Stich *m*; **2.** stechender Schmerz, Stich *m*: ***~s of conscience*** *fig.* Gewissensbisse; **3.** spitzer Gegenstand; Stachel *m* (*a. fig.*): ***kick against the ~s*** wider den Stachel löcken; **4.** V a) ‚Schwanz' *m*, b) ‚blöder Hund'; **II** *v/t.* **5.** (ein-, 'durch)stechen, ‚piken': ***~ one's finger*** sich in den Finger stechen; ***his conscience ~ed him*** *fig.* er bekam Gewissensbisse; **6.** *a.* ***~ out*** (aus)stechen, lochen; *Muster etc.* punktieren; **7.** ⸙ pikieren: ***~ in*** (***out***) ein-(aus)pflanzen; **8.** prickeln auf *od.* in (*dat.*); **9.** ***~ up one's ears*** die Ohren spitzen (*a. fig.*); **III** *v/i.* **10.** stechen (*a. Schmerzen*); **11.** prickeln; **12.** ***~ up*** sich aufrichten (*Ohren etc.*); **'prick·er** [-kə] *s.* **1.** ⚙ Pfriem *m*, Ahle *f*; **2.** *metall.* Schießnadel *f*; **'prick·et** [-kɪt] *s.* *zo.* Spießbock *m*.

prick·le ['prɪkl] **I** *s.* **1.** Stachel *m*, Dorn *m*; **2.** Prickeln *n*, Kribbeln *n* (*der Haut*); **II** *v/i.* **3.** stechen; **4.** prickeln, kribbeln; **'prick·ly** [-lɪ] *adj.* **1.** stachelig, dornig; **2.** stechend, pickelnd: ***~ heat*** ⚕ Frieselausschlag *m*, Hitzebläschen *pl.*; **3.** *fig.* reizbar.

pric·y ['praɪsɪ] → ***pricey***.

pride [praɪd] **I** *s.* **1.** Stolz *m* (*a. Gegenstand des Stolzes*): ***civic ~*** Bürgerstolz *m*; ***~ of place*** Ehrenplatz *m*, *fig.* Vorrang *m*, *b.s.* Standesdünkel *m*; ***take ~ of place*** die erste Stelle einnehmen; ***take*** (***a***) ***~ in*** stolz sein auf (*acc.*); ***he is the ~ of his family*** er ist der Stolz s-r Familie; **2.** *b.s.* Stolz *m*, Hochmut *m*: ***~ goes before a fall*** Hochmut kommt vor dem Fall; **3.** *rhet.* Pracht *f*; **4.** Höhe *f*, Blüte *f*: ***~ of the season*** beste Jahreszeit; ***in the ~ of his years*** in s-n besten Jahren; **5.** *zo.* (Löwen)Rudel *n*; **6.** ***in his ~*** *her.* radschlagend (*Pfau*); **II** *v/t.* **7.** ***~ o.s.*** (***on, upon***) stolz sein (auf *acc.*), sich et. einbilden (auf *acc.*), sich brüsten (mit).

priest [pri:st] *s.* Priester *m*, Geistliche(r) *m*; **'priest·craft** *s.* *contp.* Pfaffenlist *f*; **'priest·ess** [-tɪs] *s.* Priesterin *f*; **'priest·hood** [-hʊd] *s.* **1.** Priesteramt *n*, -würde *f*; **2.** Priesterschaft *f*, Priester *pl.*; **'priest·ly** [-lɪ] *adj.* priesterlich, Priester...

prig [prɪg] *s.* (selbstgefälliger) Pe'dant; eingebildeter Mensch; Tugendbold *m*; **'prig·gish** [-gɪʃ] *adj.* □ **1.** selbstgefällig, eingebildet; **2.** pe'dantisch; **3.** tugendhaft.

prim [prɪm] **I** *adj.* □ **1.** steif, for'mell, *a.* affektiert, gekünstelt; **2.** spröde, ‚etepe'tete'; **3.** → ***priggish***; **II** *v/t.* **4.** *Mund, Gesicht* affektiert verziehen.

pri·ma·cy ['praɪməsɪ] *s.* **1.** Pri'mat *m, n*, Vorrang *m*, Vortritt *m*; **2.** *eccl.* Pri'mat *m, n* (*Würde, Sprengel e-s Primas*); **3.** *R.C.* Pri'mat *m, n* (*Gerichtsbarkeit des Papstes*).

pri·ma don·na [ˌpri:mə'dɒnə] *s.* ♪ Prima'donna *f* (*a. fig.*).

pri·ma fa·ci·e [ˌpraɪmə'feɪʃi:] (*Lat.*) *adj. u. adv.* dem (ersten) Anschein nach: ***~ case*** ⚖ Fall, bei dem der Tatbestand einfach liegt; ***~ evidence*** ⚖ a) glaubhafter Beweis, b) Beweis des ersten Anscheins.

pri·mal ['praɪml] *adj.* □ **1.** erst, frühest, ursprünglich; **2.** wichtigst, Haupt...; **'pri·ma·ri·ly** [-mərəlɪ] *adv.* in erster Linie; **pri·ma·ry** ['praɪmərɪ] **I** *adj.* □ **1.** erst, ursprünglich, Anfangs..., Ur...: ***~ instinct*** Urinstinkt *m*; ***~ matter*** Urstoff *m*; ***~ rocks*** Urgestein *n*, -gebirge *n*; ***~ scream*** *psych.* Urschrei *m*; **2.** pri'mär, hauptsächlich, wichtigst, Haupt...: ***~ accent*** *ling.* Hauptakzent *m*; ***~ concern*** Hauptsorge *f*; ***~ industry*** Grundstoffindustrie *f*; ***~ liability*** ⚖ unmittelbare Haftung; ***~ road*** Straße *f* erster Ordnung; ***~ share*** † Stammaktie *f*; ***of ~ importance*** von höchster Wichtigkeit; **3.** grundlegend, elemen'tar, Grund...: ***~ education*** Volksschul-, *Am.* Grundschul(aus)bildung *f*; ***~ school*** Volks-, *Am.* Grundschule *f*; **4.** ϟ Primär...(*-batterie, -spule, -strom etc.*); **5.** ⚕ Primär...: ***~ tumo(u)r*** Primärtumor *m*; **II** *s.* **6.** *a.* ***~ colo(u)r*** Pri'mär-, Grundfarbe *f*; **7.** *a.* ***~ feather*** *orn.* Haupt-, Schwungfeder *f*; **8.** *pol. Am.* a) *a.* ***~ election*** Vorwahl *f* (*zur Aufstellung von Wahlkandidaten*), b) *a.* ***~ meeting*** (*innerparteiliche*) Versammlung zur Nominierung der 'Wahlkandiˌdaten; **9.** *a.* ***~ planet*** *ast.* 'Hauptplaˌnet *m*.

pri·mate ['praɪmət] *s.* *eccl. Brit.* Primas *m*: ***ℒ of England*** (*Titel des Erzbischofs von York*); ***ℒ of All England*** (*Titel des Erzbischofs von Canterbury*); **pri·ma·tes** [praɪ'meɪti:z] *s. pl. zo.* Pri'maten *pl.*

prime [praɪm] **I** *adj.* □ **1.** erst, wichtigst, wesentlichst, Haupt...(*-grund etc.*): ***of ~ importance*** von größter Wichtigkeit; **2.** erstklassig (*Kapitalanlage, Qualität etc.*), prima: ***~ bill*** † vorzüglicher Wechsel; ***~ rate*** Vorzugszins *m* für erste Adressen; ***~ time*** *TV* Haupteinschaltzeit *f*; **3.** pri'mär, grundlegend; **4.** erst, Erst..., Ur...; **5.** 𝔄 a) unteilbar, b) teilerfremd (***to*** zu): ***~ factor*** (***number***) Primfaktor *m* (Primzahl *f*); **II** *s.* **6.** Anfang *m*: ***~ of the day*** (***year***) Tagesanbruch *m* (Frühling *m*); **7.** *fig.* Blüte(zeit) *f*: ***in his ~*** in der Blüte s-r Jahre, im besten (Mannes)Alter; **8.** *das* Beste, höchste Voll'kommenheit; † Primasorte *f*, auserlesene Quali'tät; **9.** *eccl.* Prim *f*, erste Gebetsstunde; Frühgottesdienst *m*; **10.** 𝔄 a) Primzahl *f*, b) Strich *m* (*erste Ableitung e-r Funktion*): ***x ~*** (***x'***) x Strich (x'); **11.** Strichindex *m*; **12.** ♪ *u. fenc.* Prim *f*; **III** *v/t.* **13.** ⚔ *Bomben, Munition* scharfmachen: ***~d*** zündfertig; **14.** a) ⚙ *Pumpe* anlassen, b) *sl.* ‚vollaufen lassen': ***~d*** ‚besoffen'; **15.** *mot.* a) *Kraftstoff* vorpumpen, b) Anlaßkraftstoff einspritzen in (*acc.*); **16.** ⚙, *paint.* grundieren; **17.** mit Strichindex versehen; **18.** *fig.* instruieren, vorbereiten; **~ cost** *s.* † **1.** Selbstkosten(preis *m*) *pl.*, Gestehungskosten *pl.*; **2.** Einkaufspreis *m*, Anschaffungskosten *pl.*; **~ min·is·ter** *s.* Premi'ermiˌnister *m*, Mi'nisterpräsiˌdent *m*; **~ mov·er** *s.* **1.** *phys.* Antriebskraft *f*; *fig.* Triebfeder *f*, treibende Kraft; **2.** ⚙ 'Antriebsmaˌschine *f*; 'Zugmaˌschine *f* (*Sattelschlepper*); ⚔ *Am.* Geschützschlepper *m*; Triebwagen *m* (*Straßenbahn*).

prim·er¹ ['praɪmə] *s.* **1.** ⚔ Zündvorrichtung *f*, -hütchen *n*, -pille *f*; Sprengkapsel *f*; **2.** ⚔ Zündbolzen *m* (*am Gewehr*); **3.** ⚒ Zünddraht *m*; **4.** ⚙ Einspritzvorrichtung *f* (*bsd. mot.*): ***~ pump*** Anlaßeinspritzpumpe *f*; ***~ valve*** Anlaßventil *n*; **5.** ⚙ Grundier-, Spachtelmasse *f*: ***~ coat*** Voranstrich *m*; **6.** Grundierer *m*.

prim·er² ['praɪmə] *s.* **1.** a) Fibel *f*, b) Elemen'tarbuch *n*, c) *fig.* Leitfaden *m*; **2.** ['prɪmə] *typ.* a) ***great ~*** Tertia (-schrift) *f*, b) ***long ~*** Korpus(schrift) *f*, (-), Garmond(schrift) *f*.

pri·me·val [praɪ'mi:vl] *adj.* □ urzeitlich, Ur...(*-wald etc.*).

prim·ing ['praɪmɪŋ] *s.* **1.** ⚔ Zündmasse *f*, Zündung *f*: ***~ charge*** Zünd-, Initialladung *f*; **2.** ⚙ Grundierung *f*: ***~ colo(u)r*** Grundierfarbe *f*; **3.** *a.* ***~ material*** Spachtelmasse *f*; **4.** *mot.* Einspritzen *n* von Anlaßkraftstoff: ***~ fuel injector*** Anlaßeinspritzanlage *f*; **5.** ⚙ Angießen *n e-r Pumpe*; **6.** *a.* ***~ of the tide*** verfrühtes Eintreten der Flut; **7.** *fig.* Instrukti'on *f*, Vorbereitung *f*.

prim·i·tive ['prɪmɪtɪv] **I** *adj.* □ **1.** erst, ursprünglich, urzeitlich, Ur...: ***ℒ Church*** Urkirche; ***~ races*** Ur-, Naturvölker; ***~ rocks*** *geol.* Urgestein *n*; **2.** *allg.* (*a. contp.*) primi'tiv (*Kultur, Mensch, a. fig. Denkweise, Konstruktion etc.*); **3.** *ling.* Stamm...: ***~ verb***; **4.** ***~ colo(u)r*** Grundfarbe *f*; **II** *s.* **5.** *der* (*die, das*) Primi'tive: ***the ~s*** die Primitiven (*Naturvölker*); **6.** *Kunst*: a) primi'tiver Künstler, b) Frühmeister *m*, c) Früher Meister (*der Frührenaissance, a. Bild*); **7.** *ling.* Stammwort *n*; **'prim·i·tive·ness** [-nɪs] *s.* **1.** Ursprünglichkeit *f*; **2.** Primitivi'tät *f*; **'prim·i·tiv·ism** [-vɪzəm] *s.* **1.** Primitivi'tät *f*; **2.** *Kunst*: Primiti'vismus *m*.

prim·ness ['prɪmnɪs] *s.* **1.** Steifheit *f*, Förmlichkeit *f*; **2.** Sprödigkeit *f*, Zimperlichkeit *f*.

pri·mo·gen·i·tor [ˌpraɪməʊ'dʒenɪtə] *s.*

(Ur)Ahn *m*, Stammvater *m*; **ˌpri·mo·ˈgen·i·ture** [-ɪtʃə] *s.* Erstgeburt(srecht *n* ⚖) *f*.

pri·mor·di·al [praɪˈmɔːdjəl] □ primorˈdiˈal (*a. biol.*), Ur…

prim·rose [ˈprɪmrəʊz] *s.* **1.** ⚘ Primel *f*, gelbe Schlüsselblume: ***~ path*** *fig.* Rosenpfad *m*; **2.** ***evening ~*** ⚘ Nachtkerze *f*; **3.** *a.* ***~ yellow*** Blaßgelb *n*.

prim·u·la [ˈprɪmjʊlə] *s.* ⚘ Primel *f*.

prince [prɪns] *s.* **1.** Fürst *m* (*Landesherr u. Adelstitel*): ***ꝏ of the Church*** Kirchenfürst; ***ꝏ of Darkness*** Fürst der Finsternis (*Satan*); ***ꝏ of Peace*** Friedensfürst (*Christus*); ***~ of poets*** Dichterfürst; ***merchant ~*** Kaufherr *m*; ***~ consort*** Prinzgemahl *m*; **2.** Prinz *m*: ***~ of the blood*** Prinz von (königlichem) Geblüt; ***ꝏ Albert*** *Am.* Gehrock *m*; **prince·dom** [ˈprɪnsdəm] *s.* **1.** Fürstenwürde *f*; **2.** Fürstentum *n*; **ˈprince·ling** [-lɪŋ] *s.* **1.** Prinzchen *n*; **2.** kleiner Herrscher, Duoˈdezfürst *m*; **ˈprince·ly** [-lɪ] *adj.* fürstlich (*a. fig.*); prinzlich, königlich; **prin·cess** [prɪnˈses] **I** *s.* **1.** Prinˈzessin *f*: ***~ royal*** *älteste Tochter e-s Herrschers*; **2.** Fürstin *f*; **II** *adj.* **3.** *Damenmode*: Prinzeß…(*-kleid etc.*).

prin·ci·pal [ˈprɪnsəpl] **I** *adj.* □ → ***principally***; **1.** erst, hauptsächlich, Haupt…: ***~ actor*** Haupt(rollen)darsteller *m*; ***~ office***, ***~ place of business*** Hauptgeschäftsstelle *f*, -niederlassung *f*; **2.** ♪, *ling.* Haupt…, Stamm…: ***~ chord*** Stammakkord; ***~ clause*** Hauptsatz; ***~ parts*** Stammformen *des Verbs*; **3.** ☤ Kapital…: ***~ amount*** Kapitalbetrag *m*; **II** *s.* **4.** ˈHaupt(perˌson *f*) *n*; Vorsteher (-in), *bsd. Am.* (ˈSchul)Diˌrektor *m*, Rektor *m*; **5.** ☤ Chef(in), Prinziˈpal (-in); **6.** ☤, ⚖ Auftrag-, Vollmachtgeber (-in), Geschäftsherr *m*; **7.** ⚖ *a.* ***~ in the first degree*** Haupttäter(in), -schuldige(r *m*) *f*: ***~ in the second degree*** Mittäter(in); **8.** *a.* ***~ debtor*** Hauptschuldner(in); **9.** Duelˈlant *m* (*Ggs. Sekundant*); **10.** ☤ (ˈGrund)Kapiˌtal *n*, Hauptsumme *f*; (*Nachlaß- etc.*)Masse *f*: ***~ and interest*** Kapital u. Zins(en); **11.** *a.* ***~ beam*** △ Hauptbalken *m*; **prin·ci·pal·i·ty** [ˌprɪnsɪˈpæləti] *s.* Fürstentum *n*; **ˈprin·ci·pal·ly** [-plɪ] *adv.* hauptsächlich, in der Hauptsache.

prin·ci·ple [ˈprɪnsəpl] *s.* **1.** Prinˈzip *n*, Grundsatz *m*, -regel *f*: ***a man of ~s*** ein Mann mit Grundsätzen; ***~ of law*** Rechtsgrundsatz *m*; ***in ~*** im Prinzip, an sich; ***on ~*** aus Prinzip, grundsätzlich; ***on the ~ that*** nach dem Grundsatz, daß; **2.** *phys. etc.* Prinzip *n*, (Naˈtur-) Gesetz *n*, Satz *m*: ***~ of causality*** Kausalitätsprinzip; ***~ of averages*** Mittelwertsatz: ***~ of relativity*** Relativitätstheorie *f*; **3.** Grund(lage *f*) *m*; **4.** ⚗ Grundbestandteil *m*; **ˈprin·ci·pled** [-ld] *adj.* mit *hohen etc.* Grundsätzen.

prink [prɪŋk] **I** *v/i. a.* ***~ up*** sich (auf)putzen, sich schniegeln; **II** *v/t.* (auf)putzen: ***~ o.s. (up)***.

print [prɪnt] **I** *v/t.* **1.** *typ.* drucken (lassen), in Druck geben: ***~ in italics*** kursiv drucken; **2.** (ab)drucken: ***~ed form*** Vordruck *m*; ***~ed matter*** 📯 Drucksache(n *pl.*) *f*: ***~ed circuit*** ϟ gedruckte Schaltung; **3.** bedrucken: ***~ed goods*** bedruckte Stoffe; **4.** in Druckschrift schreiben: ***~ed characters*** Druckbuchstaben; **5.** *Stempel etc.* (auf)drükken (***on*** *dat.*), *Eindruck*, *Spur* hinterˈlassen (***on*** auf *acc.*), *Muster etc.* ab-, aufdrucken, drücken (***in*** in *acc.*); **6.** *fig.* einprägen (***on s.o.'s mind*** j-m); **7.** ***~ out*** a) *Computer*: ausdrucken, b) *a.* ***~ off*** *phot.* abziehen, kopieren; **II** *v/i.* **8.** *typ.* drucken; **9.** gedruckt werden, sich im Druck befinden: ***the book is ~ing***; **10.** sich drucken (*phot.* abziehen) lassen; **III** *s.* **11.** (*Finger- etc.*)Abdruck *m*, Eindruck *m*, Spur *f*, Mal *n*; **12.** *typ.* Druck *m*: ***colo(u)red ~*** Farbdruck; ***in ~*** a) im Druck (erschienen), b) vorrätig; ***out of ~*** vergriffen; ***in cold ~*** *fig.* schwarz auf weiß; **13.** Druckschrift *f*, *bsd. Am.* Zeitung *f*, Blatt *n*: ***rush into ~*** sich in die Öffentlichkeit flüchten; ***appear in ~*** im Druck erscheinen; **14.** Druckschrift *f*, -buchstaben *pl.*; **15.** ˈZeitungspaˌpier *n*; **16.** (*Stahl- etc.*) Stich *m*; Holzschnitt *m*; Lithograˈphie *f*; **17.** bedruckter Katˈtun, Druckstoff *m*: ***~ dress*** Kattunkleid *n*; **18.** *phot.* Abzug *m*, Koˈpie *f*; **19.** ⚙ Stempel *m*, Form *f*: ***~ cutter*** Formenschneider *m*; **20.** *metall.* Gesenk *n*; *Eisengießerei*: Kernauge *n*; **21.** *fig.* Stempel *m*; **ˈprint·a·ble** [-təbl] *adj.* **1.** druckfähig; **2.** druckfertig, -reif (*Manuskript*); **ˈprint·er** [-tə] *s.* **1.** (Buch- *etc.*)Drucker *m*: ***~'s devil*** Setzerjunge *m*; ***~'s error*** Druckfehler *m*; ***~'s flower*** Vignette *f*; ***~'s ink*** Druckerschwärze *f*; **2.** Druckeˈreibesitzer *m*; **3.** ⚙ ˈDruck-, Koˈpierappaˌrat *m*; **4.** → ***printing telegraph***; **ˈprint·er·y** [-tərɪ] *s. bsd. Am.* Druckeˈrei *f*.

print·ing [ˈprɪntɪŋ] *s.* **1.** Drucken *n*; (Buch)Druck *m*, Buchdruckerkunst *f*; **2.** Tuchdruck *m*; **3.** *phot.* Abziehen *n*, Kopieren *n*; ***~ block*** *s.* Kliˈschee *n*; ***~ frame*** *s. phot.* Koˈpierrahmen *m*; ***~ ink*** *s.* Druckerschwärze *f*, -farbe *f*; ***~ machine*** *s. typ.* Schnellpresse *f*, (ˈBuch-) ˌDruckmaˌschine *f*; ***~ of·fice*** *s.* (Buch-) Druckeˈrei *f*: ***lithographic ~*** lithographische Anstalt; **ˈ~-out** *adj. phot.* Kopier…; ***~ pa·per*** *s.* **1.** ˈDruckpaˌpier *n*; **2.** ˈLichtpauspaˌpier *n*; **3.** Koˈpierpaˌpier *n*; ***~ press*** *s.* Druckerpresse *f*: ***~ type*** Letter *f*, Type *f*; ***~ tel·e·graph*** *s.* ˈDrucktelegraph *m*; ***~ types*** *s. pl.* Lettern *pl.*; ***~ works*** *s. pl. oft sg. konstr.* Druckeˈrei *f*.

ˈprint|ˌmak·er *s.* Graphiker(in); **ˈ~·out** *s. Computer*: Ausdruck *m*, Printout *m*.

pri·or [ˈpraɪə] **I** *adj.* **1.** (***to***) früher, älter (als): ***~ art*** *Patentrecht*: Stand *m* der Technik, Vorwegnahme *f*; ***~ patent*** älteres Patent; ***~ use*** Vorbenutzung *f*; ***subject to ~ sale*** ☤ Zwischenverkauf vorbehalten; **2.** vordringlich, Vorzugs…: ***~ right*** (*od.* ***claim***) Vorzugsrecht *n*; ***~ condition*** erste Voraussetzung; **II** *adv.* **3.** ***~ to*** vor (*dat.*) (*zeitlich*); **III** *s. eccl.* **4.** Prior *m*; **ˈpri·or·ess** [-ərɪs] *s.* Priˈorin *f*; **pri·or·i·ty** [praɪˈɒrətɪ] *s.* **1.** Prioriˈtät *f* (*a.* ⚖), Vorrang *m* (*a. e-s Anspruchs etc.*), Vorzug *m* (***over, to*** vor *dat.*): ***take ~ of*** den Vorrang haben *od.* genießen vor (*dat.*); ***set priorities*** Prioritäten setzen, Schwerpunkte bilden; ***~ share*** ☤ Vorzugsaktie *f*; **2.** Dringlichkeit(sstufe) *f*: ***~ call*** *teleph.* Vorrangsgespräch *n*; ***~ list*** Dringlichkeitsliste *f*; ***of first*** (*od.* ***top***) ***~*** von größter Dringlichkeit; ***give ~ to*** *et.* vordringlich behandeln; **3.** Vorfahrt(srecht *n*) *f*; **ˈpri·o·ry** [-ərɪ] *s. eccl.* Prioˈrei *f*.

prism [ˈprɪzəm] *s.* Prisma *n* (*a. fig.*): ***~ binoculars*** Prismen(fern)glas *n*; **pris·mat·ic** [prɪzˈmætɪk] *adj.* (□ ***~ally***) prisˈmatisch, Prismen…: ***~ colo(u)rs*** Regenbogenfarben.

pris·on [ˈprɪzn] *s.* Gefängnis *n* (*a. fig.*), Strafanstalt *f*; **ˈ~-ˌbreak·ing** *s.* Ausbruch *m* aus dem Gefängnis; ***~ camp*** *s.* **1.** (Kriegs)Gefangenenlager *n*; **2.** ‚offenes' Gefängnis; ***~ ed·i·tor*** *s.* (*presserechtlich verantwortlicher*) ‚ˈSitzredakˌteur' *m*.

pris·on·er [ˈprɪznə] *s.* Gefangene(r *m*) *f* (*a. fig.*), Häftling *m*: ***~ (at the bar)*** Angeklagte(r *m*) *f*; ***~ (on remand)*** Untersuchungsgefangene(r); ***~ of state*** Staatsgefangene(r), politischer Häftling; ***~ (of war)*** Kriegsgefangene(r); ***hold (take) s.o. ~*** j-n gefangenhalten (-nehmen); ***he is a ~ to*** *fig.* er ist gefesselt an (*acc.*); ***~'s bar(s)***, ***~'s base*** *s.* Barlauf(spiel *n*) *m*.

pris·on| of·fi·cer *s.* Strafvollzugsbeamte(r) *m*; ***~ psy·cho·sis*** *s.* [*irr.*] ˈHaftpsyˌchose *f*.

pris·sy [ˈprɪsɪ] *adj. Am.* F zimperlich, etepeˈtete.

pris·tine [ˈprɪstaɪn] *adj.* **1.** ursprünglich, -tümlich, unverdorben; **2.** vormalig, alt.

pri·va·cy [ˈprɪvəsɪ] *s.* **1.** Zuˈrückgezogenheit *f*; Alleinsein *n*; Ruhe *f*: ***disturb s.o.'s ~*** j-n stören; **2.** Priˈvatleben *n*, *a.* ⚖ Priˈvat-, Inˈtimsphäre *f*: ***right of ~*** Persönlichkeitsrecht *n*; **3.** Heimlichkeit *f*, Geheimhaltung *f*: ***~ of letters*** ⚖ Briefgeheimnis *n*; ***talk to s.o. in ~*** mit j-m unter vier Augen sprechen; ***in strict ~*** streng vertraulich.

pri·vate [ˈpraɪvɪt] **I** *adj.* □ **1.** priˈvat, Privat…(*-konto*, *-leben*, *-person*, *-recht etc.*), perˈsönlich: ***~ affair*** Privatangelegenheit *f*; ***~ member's bill*** *parl.* Antrag *m* e-s Abgeordneten; ***~ eye*** *Am. sl.* Privatdetektiv *m*; ***~ firm*** ☤ Einzelfirma *f*; ***~ gentleman*** Privatier *m*; ***~ means*** Privatvermögen *n*; → ***nuisance*** 2; ***~ property*** Privateigentum *n*; -besitz *m*; **2.** priˈvat, Privat…(*-pension*, *-schule etc.*), nicht öffentlich: ***~ (limited) company*** ☤ *Brit.* Gesellschaft *f* mit beschränkter Haftung; ***~ corporation*** a) ⚖ privatrechtliche Körperschaft, b) ☤ *Am.* Gesellschaft *f* mit beschränkter Haftung; ***sell by ~ contract*** unter der Hand verkaufen; ***~ hotel*** Fremdenheim *n*; ***~ industry*** Privatwirtschaft *f*; ***~ road*** Privatweg *m*; ***~ theatre*** Liebhabertheater *n*; ***~ view*** Besichtigung *f* durch geladene Gäste; **3.** alˈlein, zuˈrückgezogen, einsam; **4.** geheim (*Gedanken*, *Verhandlungen etc.*), heimlich; vertraulich (*Mitteilung etc.*): ***~ parts*** → 10; ***~ prayer*** stilles Gebet; ***~ reasons*** Hintergründe; ***keep s.th. ~*** et. geheimhalten *od.* vertraulich behandeln; ***this is for your ~ ear*** dies sage ich Ihnen ganz im Vertrauen; **5.** außeramtlich (*Angelegenheit*); **6.** nicht beamtet; **7.** ⚖ außergerichtlich: ***~ arrangement*** gütlicher Vergleich; **8.** ***~ soldier*** → 9; **II** *s.* **9.** ⚔ (gewöhnlicher) Solˈdat; *pl.* Mannschaften *pl.*: ***~ 1st Class*** *Am.* Obergefreite(r) *m*; **10.** *pl.* Geschlechtsteile *pl.*;

11. ***in ~*** a) pri'vat(im), b) insge'heim, unter vier Augen.

pri·va·teer [ˌpraɪvə'tɪə] **I** *s.* **1.** ⚓ Freibeuter *m*, Kaperschiff *n*; **2.** Kapi'tän *m* e-s Kaperschiffes, Kaperer *m*; **3.** *pl.* Mannschaft *f* e-s Kaperschiffes; **II** *v/i.* **4.** Kape'rei treiben.

pri·va·tion [praɪ'veɪʃn] *s.* **1.** *a. fig.* Wegnahme *f*, Entziehung *f*, Entzug *m*; **2.** Not *f*, Entbehrung *f*.

priv·a·tive ['prɪvətɪv] **I** *adj.* □ **1.** entziehend, beraubend; **2.** *a. ling. od. phls.* verneinend, negativ; **II** *s.* **3.** *ling.* a) Ver'neinungsparˌtikel *f*, b) priva'tiver Ausdruck.

priv·et ['prɪvɪt] *s.* ⚘ Li'guster *m*.

priv·i·lege ['prɪvɪlɪdʒ] **I** *s.* **1.** Privi'leg *n*, Sonder-, Vorrecht *n*, Vergünstigung *f*, *Am. pol.* Grundrecht *n*; ***breach of a ~*** a) Übertretung *f* der Machtbefugnis, b) *parl.* Vergehen *n* gegen die Vorrechte des Parlaments; ***Committee of ~s*** Ausschuß *m* zur Untersuchung von Rechtsübergriffen; ***~ of Parliament*** *pol.* Immunität *f* e-s Abgeordneten; ***~ of self-defence*** (Recht *n* der) Notwehr *f*; ***with kitchen ~s*** mit Küchenbenutzung; **2.** *fig.* (besonderer) Vorzug: ***have the ~ of being admitted*** den Vorzug haben, zugelassen zu sein; ***it is a ~ to do*** es ist e-e besondere Ehre, *et.* zu tun; **3.** *pl.* ✝ Prämien- *od.* Stellgeschäft *n*; **II** *v/t.* **4.** privilegieren, bevorrecht(ig)en: ***the ~d classes*** die privilegierten Stände; ***~d debt*** bevorrechtigte Forderung; ***~d communication*** ⚖ a) vertrauliche Mitteilung (*für die Schweigepflicht besteht*), b) Berufsgeheimnis *n*.

priv·i·ty ['prɪvətɪ] *s.* **1.** ⚖ (Inter'essen-) Gemeinschaft *f*; **2.** ⚖ Rechtsbeziehung *f*; **3.** ⚖ Rechtsnachfolge *f*; **4.** Mitwisserschaft *f*.

priv·y ['prɪvɪ] **I** *adj.* □ **1.** eingeweiht (***to*** in *acc.*); **2.** ⚖ (mit)beteiligt (***to*** an *dat.*); **3.** *mst. poet.* heimlich, geheim: ***~ parts*** Scham-, Geschlechtsteile; ***~ stairs*** Hintertreppe *f*; **II** *s.* **4.** 'Mitinteresˌsent(in) (***to*** an *dat.*); **5.** A'bort *m*, Abtritt *m*; **2 Coun·cil** *s. Brit.* (Geheimer) Staats- *od.* Kronrat: ***Judicial Committee of the ~*** ⚖ Justizausschuß *m* des Staatsrats (*höchste Berufungsinstanz für die Dominions*); **2 Coun·cil·lor** *s. Brit.* Geheimer (Staats)Rat (*Person*); **2 Purse** *s. königliche* Pri'vatschaˌtulle; **2 Seal** *s. Brit.* Geheimsiegel *n*: ***Lord ~*** königlicher Geheimsiegelbewahrer.

prize¹ [praɪz] **I** *s.* **1.** (Sieger)Preis *m* (*a. fig.*), Prämie *f*: ***the ~s of a profession*** die höchsten Stellungen in e-m Beruf; **2.** (*a.* Lotte'rie)Gewinn *m*: ***the first ~*** das Große Los; **3.** Lohn *m*, Belohnung *f*; **II** *adj.* **4.** preisgekrönt, prämiiert; **5.** Preis…: ***~ medal***; **6.** a) erstklassig (*a. iro.*), b) F *contp.* Riesen…: ***~ idiot***; **III** *v/t.* **7.** (hoch)schätzen, würdigen.

prize² [praɪz] **I** *s.* ⚓ Prise *f*, Beute *f* (*a. fig.*): ***make ~ of*** → **II** *v/t.* (als Prise) aufbringen, kapern.

prize³ [praɪz] *bsd. Brit.* **I** *v/t.* **1.** (auf-) stemmen: ***~ open*** (mit e-m Hebel) aufbrechen; ***~ up*** hochwuchten *od.* -stemmen; **II** *s.* **2.** Hebelwirkung *f*, -kraft *f*; **3.** Hebel *m*.

prize| com·pe·ti·tion *s.* Preisausschreiben *n*; **~ court** *s.* ⚓ Prisengericht *n*; **~ fight** *s.* Preisboxkampf *m*; **~ fight·er** *s.* Preis-, Berufsboxer *m*; **~ list** *s.* Gewinnliste *f*; **'~·man** [-mən] *s.* [*irr.*] Preisträger *m*; **~ mon·ey** *s.* **1.** ⚓ Prisengeld(er *pl.*) *n*; **2.** Geldpreis *m*; **~ ques·tion** *s.* Preisfrage *f*; **~ ring** *s.* (Box)Ring *m*, *das* Berufsboxen; **~ win·ner** *s.* Preisträger(in); **'~-ˌwin·ning** *adj.* preisgekrönt, präm(i)iert.

pro¹ [prəʊ] *pl.* **pros I** *s.* Ja-Stimme *f*, Stimme *f* da'für: ***the ~s and cons*** das Für und Wider; **II** *adv.* (da)'für.

pro² [prəʊ] (*Lat.*) *prp.* für; pro, per; → ***pro forma***, ***pro rata***.

pro³ [prəʊ] *s.* F **1.** *sport* Profi *m* (*a. fig.*); **2.** ‚Nutte' *f*.

pro- [prəʊ] *in Zssgn*: **1.** pro…, …freundlich, *z.B.* ***~-German***; **2.** stellvertretend, Vize…, Pro…; **3.** vor (*räumlich u. zeitlich*).

prob·a·bil·i·ty [ˌprɒbə'bɪlətɪ] *s.* Wahrscheinlichkeit *f* (*a.* A̸): ***in all ~*** aller Wahrscheinlichkeit nach, höchstwahrscheinlich; ***theory of ~***, ***~ calculus*** A̸ Wahrscheinlichkeitsrechnung *f*; ***the ~ is that*** es besteht die Wahrscheinlichkeit, daß; **prob·a·ble** ['prɒbəbl] *adj.* □ **1.** wahrscheinlich, vermutlich, mutmaßlich: ***~ cause*** ⚖ hinreichender Verdacht; **2.** wahrscheinlich, glaubhaft, einleuchtend.

pro·bate ['prəʊbeɪt] ⚖ **I** *s.* **1.** gerichtliche (*bsd.* Testa'ments)Bestätigung; **2.** Testa'mentserˌöffnung *f*; **3.** Abschrift *f* e-s gerichtlich bestätigten Testaments; **II** *v/t.* **4.** *bsd. Am. Testament* a) bestätigen, b) eröffnen u. als rechtswirksam bestätigen lassen; **~ court** *s.* Nachlaßgericht *n*, (*in U.S.A. a. zuständig in Sachen der freiwilligen Gerichtsbarkeit, bsd. als*) Vormundschaftsgericht *n*; **~ du·ty** *s.* ⚖ Erbschaftssteuer *f*.

pro·ba·tion [prə'beɪʃn] *s.* **1.** (Eignungs-) Prüfung *f*, Probe(zeit) *f*: ***on ~*** auf Probe(zeit); **2.** ⚖ a) Bewährungsfrist *f*, b) bedingte Freilassung *f*: ***place s.o. on ~*** j-m Bewährungsfrist zubilligen, j-n unter Zubilligung von Bewährungsfrist freilassen: ***~ officer*** Bewährungshelfer (-in); **3.** *eccl.* Novizi'at *n*; **pro'ba·tion·ar·y** [-ʃnərɪ], **pro'ba·tion·al** [-ʃənl] *adj.* Probe…: ***~ period*** ⚖ Bewährungsfrist *f*; **pro'ba·tion·er** [-ʃnə] *s.* **1.** 'Probekandiˌdat(in), Angestellte(r *m*) *f* auf Probe, *z.B.* Lernschwester *f*; **2.** *fig.* Neuling *m*; **3.** *eccl.* No'vize *m*, *f*; **4.** ⚖ a) j-d, dessen Strafe zur Bewährung ausgesetzt ist, b) auf Bewährung bedingt Strafentlassene(r).

pro·ba·tive ['prəʊbətɪv] als Beweis dienend (***of*** für): ***~ facts*** ⚖ beweiserhebliche Tatsachen; ***~ force*** Beweiskraft *f*.

probe [prəʊb] **I** *v/t.* **1.** ⚕ sondieren (*a. fig.*); **2.** *fig.* eindringen in (*acc.*), erforschen, (gründlich) unter'suchen; **II** *v/i.* **3.** *fig.* (forschend) eindringen (***into*** in *acc.*); **III** *s.* **4.** ⚕, *a. Raumforschung etc.*: Sonde *f*; **5.** *fig.* Sondierung *f*; *bsd. Am.* Unter'suchung *f*.

prob·i·ty ['prəʊbətɪ] *s.* Rechtschaffenheit *f*, Redlichkeit *f*.

prob·lem ['prɒbləm] **I** *s.* **1.** Pro'blem *n* (*a. phls.*, *Schach etc.*), proble'matische Sache, Schwierigkeit *f*: ***set a ~*** ein Problem stellen; **2.** A̸ Aufgabe *f*, Problem *n*; **3.** *fig.* Rätsel *n* (***to*** für *j-n*); **II** *adj.* **4.** proble'matisch: ***~ play*** Problemstück *n*; ***~ child*** schwererziehbares Kind, Sorgenkind; ***~ drinker*** Alkoholiker(in); **prob·lem·at·ic**, **prob·lem·at·i·cal** [ˌprɒblə'mætɪk(l)] *adj.* □ proble'matisch, zweifelhaft.

pro·bos·cis [prəʊ'bɒsɪs] *pl.* **-cis·es** [-sɪsiːz] *s. zo.* Rüssel *m* (*a. humor.*).

pro·ce·dur·al [prə'siːdʒərəl] *adj.* ⚖ verfahrensrechtlich; Verfahrens…: ***~ law***; **pro·ce·dure** [prə'siːdʒə] *s.* **1.** *allg.* Verfahren *n* (*a.* ⚙), Vorgehen *n*; **2.** ⚖ (*bsd. prozeßrechtliches*) Verfahren: ***rules of ~*** Prozeßvorschriften, Verfahrensbestimmungen; **3.** Handlungsweise *f*, Verhalten *n*.

pro·ceed [prə'siːd] *v/i.* **1.** weitergehen, -fahren *etc.*; sich begeben (***to*** nach); **2.** *fig.* weitergehen (*Handlung etc.*), fortschreiten; **3.** vor sich gehen, von'statten gehen; **4.** *fig.* fortfahren (***with***, ***in*** mit, in *s-r Rede etc.*), s-e Arbeit *etc.* fortsetzen: ***~ on one's journey*** s-e Reise fortsetzen, weiterreisen; **5.** *fig.* vorgehen, verfahren: ***~ with*** *et.* durchführen *od.* in Angriff nehmen; ***~ on the assumption that*** davon ausgehen, daß; **6.** schreiten *od.* 'übergehen (***to*** zu), sich anschicken (***to do*** zu tun): ***~ to business*** an die Arbeit gehen, anfangen; **7.** (***from***) ausgehen *od.* herrühren *od.* kommen (von) (*Geräusch*, *Hoffnung*, *Krankheit etc.*), (*e-r Hoffnung etc.*) entspringen; **8.** ⚖ (gerichtlich) vorgehen, e-n Pro'zeß anstrengen (***against*** gegen); **9.** *univ. Brit.* promovieren (***to*** [***the degree of***] zum); **pro'ceed·ing** [-dɪŋ] *s.* **1.** Vorgehen *n*, Verfahren *n*; **2.** *pl.* ⚖ Verfahren *n*, (Gerichts)Verhandlung(en *pl.*) *f*: ***take*** (*od.* ***institute***) ***~s against*** ein Verfahren einleiten *od.* gerichtlich vorgehen gegen; **3.** *pl.* (Sitzungs-, Tätigkeits)Bericht(e *pl.*) *m*, (⚖ Pro'zeß)Akten *pl.*; **pro·ceeds** ['prəʊsiːdz] *s. pl.* **1.** Erlös *m* (***from a sale*** aus e-m Verkauf), Ertrag *m*, Gewinn *m*; **2.** Einnahmen *pl.*

pro·cess ['prəʊses] **I** *s.* **1.** Verfahren *n*, Pro'zeß *m* (*a.* ⚙, ⚗): ***~ engineering*** Verfahrenstechnik *f*; ***~ chart*** Arbeitsablaufdiagramm *n*; ***~ control*** *Computer*: Prozeßsteuerung *f*; ***~ of manufacture*** Herstellungsvorgang *m*, Werdegang *m*; ***in ~ of construction*** im Bau (befindlich); **2.** Vorgang *m*, Verlauf *m*, Pro'zeß *m* (*a. phys.*): ***~ of combustion*** Verbrennungsvorgang; ***mental ~*** Denkprozeß *m*; **3.** Arbeitsgang *m*; **4.** Fortgang *m*, -schreiten *n*, (Ver)Lauf *m*: ***in ~ of time*** im Laufe der Zeit; ***be in ~*** im Gange sein; **5.** *typ.* 'photomeˌchanisches Reprodukti'onsverfahren: ***~ printing*** Mehrfarbendruck *m*; **6.** *anat.* Fortsatz *m*; **7.** ⚘ Auswuchs *m*; **8.** ⚖ a) Zustellung(en *pl.*) *f*, *bsd.* Vorladung *f*, b) (ordentliches) Verfahren: ***due ~ of law*** rechtliches Gehör; **II** *v/t.* **9.** ⚙ *etc.* bearbeiten, (chemisch *etc.*) behandeln, e-m Verfahren unter'werfen; *Material*, *a. Daten* verarbeiten; *Lebensmittel* haltbar machen, *Milch etc.* sterilisieren: ***~ into*** verarbeiten zu; **10.** ⚖ *j-n* gerichtlich belangen; **11.** *Am. fig. j-n* 'durchschleusen, abfertigen, *j-s Fall etc.* bearbeiten; **III** *v/i.* [prəʊ'ses] **12.** F in e-r Prozessi'on (mit)gehen; **'proc·ess·ing** [-sɪŋ] *s.* **1.** ⚙ Vered(e)lung *f*: ***~ indus-***

try weiterverarbeitende Industrie, Veredelungsindustrie *f*; **2.** ⚙, *a. Computer*: Verarbeitung *f*; **3.** *bsd. Am. fig.* Bearbeitung *f*.

pro·ces·sion [prə'seʃn] *s.* **1.** Prozessi'on *f*, (feierlicher) (Auf-, 'Um)Zug: ***go in ~*** e-e Prozession abhalten *od.* machen; **2.** Reihe(nfolge) *f*; **3.** *a.* ***~ of the Holy Spirit*** *eccl.* Ausströmen *n* des Heiligen Geistes; **pro'ces·sion·al** [-ʃənl] **I** *adj.* Prozessions…; **II** *s. eccl.* a) Prozessi'onsbuch *n*, b) Prozessi'onshymne *f*.

pro·ces·sor ['prəʊsesə] *s.* **1.** ⚙ Verarbeiter *m*; Hersteller(in); **2.** *Am.* (Sach-) Bearbeiter(in); **3.** *Computer*: Pro'zessor *m*.

pro·claim [prə'kleɪm] *v/t.* **1.** proklamieren, (öffentlich) verkünd(ig)en, kundgeben: ***~ war*** den Krieg erklären; ***~ s.o. a traitor*** j-n zum Verräter erklären; ***~ s.o. king*** j-n zum König ausrufen; **2.** den Ausnahmezustand verhängen über *ein Gebiet etc.*; **3.** in die Acht erklären; **4.** *Versammlung etc.* verbieten.

proc·la·ma·tion [ˌprɒklə'meɪʃn] *s.* **1.** Proklamati'on *f* (***to*** an *acc.*), (öffentliche *od.* feierliche) Verkündigung *od.* Bekanntmachung, Aufruf *m*: ***~ of martial law*** Verhängung *f* des Standrechts; **2.** Erklärung *f*, Ausrufung *f zum König etc.*; **3.** Verhängung *f* des Ausnahmezustandes.

pro·cliv·i·ty [prə'klɪvətɪ] *s.* Neigung *f*, Hang *m* (***to, toward*** zu).

pro·cras·ti·nate [prəʊ'kræstɪneɪt] **I** *v/i.* zaudern, zögern; **II** *v/t.* hi'nausziehen, verschleppen.

pro·cre·ant ['prəʊkrɪənt] *adj.* (er)zeugend; **pro·cre·ate** ['prəʊkrɪeɪt] *v/t.* (er-) zeugen, her'vorbringen (*a. fig.*); **pro·cre·a·tion** [ˌprəʊkrɪ'eɪʃn] *s.* (Er)Zeugung *f*, Her'vorbringen *n*; **'pro·cre·a·tive** [-ɪeɪtɪv] *adj.* **1.** zeugungsfähig, Zeugungs…: ***~ capacity*** Zeugungsfähigkeit; **2.** fruchtbar; **'pro·cre·a·tor** [-ɪeɪtə] *s.* Erzeuger *m*.

Pro·crus·te·an [prəʊ'krʌstɪən] *adj.* Prokrustes… (*a. fig.*): ***~ bed.***

proc·tor ['prɒktə] **I** *s.* **1.** *univ. Brit.* a) Diszipli'narbeˌamte(r) *m*, b) Aufsichtsführende(r) *m*, (*bsd. bei Prüfungen*): ***~'s man, ~'s (bull)dog*** *sl.* Pedell; **2.** ⚖ a) Anwalt *m* (*an Spezialgerichten*), b) *a.* ***King's*** (*od.* ***Queen's***) ~ Proku'rator *m* der Krone; **II** *v/t.* **3.** beaufsichtigen.

pro·cur·a·ble [prə'kjʊərəbl] *adj.* zu beschaffen(d), erhältlich; **proc·u·ra·tion** [ˌprɒkjʊə'reɪʃn] *s.* **1.** → ***procurement*** 1 *u.* 3; **2.** (Stell)Vertretung *f*; **3.** ✝ Pro'kura *f*, Vollmacht *f*: ***by ~*** per Prokura; ***joint ~*** Gesamthandlungsvollmacht; ***single*** (*od.* ***sole***) ~ Einzelprokura; **4.** → ***procuring*** 2; **proc·u·ra·tor** ['prɒkjʊəreɪtə] *s.* **1.** ⚖ Anwalt *m*: ♀ ***General*** *Brit.* Königlicher Anwalt des Schatzamtes; **2.** ⚖ Bevollmächtigte(r) *m*, Sachwalter *m*; **3.** ***~ fiscal*** ⚖ *Scot.* Staatsanwalt *m*.

pro·cure [prə'kjʊə] **I** *v/t.* **1.** (sich) be-, verschaffen, besorgen (***s.th. for s.o., s.o. s.th.*** j-m et.); *a. Beweise etc.* liefern, beibringen; **2.** erwerben, erlangen; **3.** verkuppeln; **4.** *fig.* bewirken, her'beiführen; **5.** veranlassen: ***~ s.o. to commit a crime*** j-n zu e-m Verbrechen anstiften; **II** *v/i.* **6.** kuppeln; Zuhälte'rei treiben; **pro'cure·ment** [-mənt] *s.* **1.** Besorgung *f*, Beschaffung *f*; **2.** Erwerbung *f*; **3.** Vermittlung *f*; **4.** Veranlassung *f*; **pro'cur·er** [-ərə] *s.* **1.** Beschaffer(in), Vermittler(in); **2.** a) Kuppler *m*, b) Zuhälter *m*; **pro'cur·ess** [-ərɪs] *s.* Kupplerin *f*; **pro'cur·ing** [-ərɪŋ] *s.* **1.** Beschaffen *n etc.*; **2.** a) Kuppe'lei *f*, b) Zuhälte'rei *f*.

prod [prɒd] **I** *v/t.* **1.** stechen, stoßen; **2.** *fig.* anstacheln, -spornen (***into*** zu *et.*); **II** *s.* **3.** Stich *m*, Stechen *n*, Stoß *m* (*a. fig.*); **4.** *fig.* Ansporn *m*; **5.** Stachelstock *m*; **6.** Ahle *f*.

prod·i·gal ['prɒdɪgl] **I** *adj.* □ **1.** verschwenderisch (***of*** mit): ***be ~ of*** → ***prodigalize***; ***the ~ son*** *bibl.* der verlorene Sohn; **II** *s.* **2.** Verschwender(in); **3.** reuiger Sünder; **prod·i·gal·i·ty** [ˌprɒdɪ'gælətɪ] *s.* **1.** Verschwendung *f*; **2.** Üppigkeit *f*, Fülle *f* (***of*** an *dat.*); **'prod·i·gal·ize** [-gəlaɪz] *v/t.* verschwenden, verschwenderisch 'umgehen mit.

pro·di·gious [prə'dɪdʒəs] *adj.* □ **1.** erstaunlich, wunderbar, großartig; **2.** gewaltig, ungeheuer; **prod·i·gy** ['prɒdɪdʒɪ] *s.* **1.** Wunder *n* (***of*** *gen. od.* an *dat.*): ***a ~ of learning*** ein Wunder der *od.* an Gelehrsamkeit; **2.** *mst* ***infant ~*** Wunderkind *n*.

pro·duce[1] [prə'dju:s] *v/t.* **1.** *allg.* erzeugen, machen, schaffen; ✝ *Waren etc.* produzieren, herstellen, erzeugen; *Kohle etc.* gewinnen, fördern; *Buch* a) verfassen, b) her'ausbringen; *thea. Stück* a) inszenieren, b) aufführen; *Film* produzieren; *Brit. thea., Radio*: Re'gie führen bei: ***~ o.s.*** *fig.* sich produzieren; **2.** ♀ *Früchte etc.* her'vorbringen; **3.** ✝ *Gewinn, Zinsen* (ein)bringen, abwerfen; **4.** *fig.* erzeugen, bewirken, her'vorrufen, zeitigen; *Wirkung* erzielen; **5.** her'vorziehen, -holen (***from*** aus *der Tasche etc.*); *Ausweis etc.* (vor)zeigen, vorlegen; *Beweise, Zeugen etc.* beibringen; *Gründe* anführen; **6.** Å *Linie* verlängern.

prod·uce[2] ['prɒdju:s] *s.* (*nur sg.*) **1.** (*bsd.* 'Boden)Proˌdukt(e *pl.*) *n*, (Na'tur)Erzeugnis(se *pl.*) *n*: ***~ market*** Produkten-, Warenmarkt *m*; **2.** Ertrag *m*, Gewinn *m*.

pro·duc·er [prə'dju:sə] *s.* **1.** *a.* ✝ Erzeuger(in), 'Hersteller(in): ***~ country*** ✝ Erzeugerland *n*; **2.** ✝ Produ'zent *m*, Fabri'kant *m*: ***~ goods*** Produktionsgüter; **3.** *a)* *Film*: Produ'zent *m*, Produkti'onsleiter *m*, b) *Brit. thea., Radio*: Regis'seur *m*, Spielleiter *m*; **4.** ⚙ Gene'rator *m*: ***~ gas*** Generatorgas *n*; **pro'duc·i·ble** [-səbl] *adj.* **1.** erzeug-, herstellbar, produzierbar; **2.** vorzuzeigen(d), beizubringen(d); **pro'duc·ing** [-sɪŋ] *adj.* Produktions…, Herstellungs…

prod·uct ['prɒdəkt] *s.* **1.** *a.* ✝, ⚙ Pro'dukt *n* (*a.* Å, ⚗), Erzeugnis *n*: ***intermediate ~*** Zwischenprodukt *n*; ***~ line*** Erzeugnis(gruppe *f*) *n*; ***~ patent*** Stoffpatent *n*; **2.** *fig.* (*a.* 'Geistes)Proˌdukt *n*, Ergebnis *n*, Werk *n*; **3.** *fig.* Pro'dukt *n* (*Person*).

pro·duc·tion [prə'dʌkʃn] *s.* **1.** (*z.B. Kälte-, Strom*)Erzeugung *f*, (*z.B. Rauch*)Bildung *f*; **2.** ✝ Produkti'on *f*, Herstellung *f*, Erzeugung *f*, Fertigung *f*; ⚗, ⚒, *min.* Gewinnung *f*; ⚒ Förderleistung *f*: ***~ of gold*** Goldgewinnung; ***be in ~*** serienmäßig hergestellt werden; ***be in good ~*** genügend hergestellt werden; ***go into ~*** a) in Produktion gehen, b) die Produktion aufnehmen (*Fabrik*); **3.** (*Arbeits*)Erzeugnis *n*, (*a.* Na'tur)Proˌdukt *n*, Fabri'kat *n*; **4.** *fig.* (*mst* lite'rarisches) Pro'dukt, Ergebnis *n*, Werk *n*, Schöpfung *f*, Frucht *f*; **5.** Her'vorbringen *n*, Entstehung *f*; **6.** Vorlegung *f*, -zeigung *f e-s Dokuments etc.*, Beibringung *f e-s Zeugen*, Erbringen *n e-s Beweises*; Vorführen *n*, Aufweisen *n*; **7.** Her'vorholen *n*, -ziehen *n*; **8.** *thea.* Vor-, Aufführung *f*, Inszenierung *f*; **9.** a) *Brit. thea., Radio, TV*: Re'gie *f*, Spielleitung *f*, b) *Film*: Produkti'on *f*; **pro'duc·tion·al** [-ʃənl] *adj.* Produktions…

pro·duc·tion| ca·pac·i·ty *s.* Produkti'onskapaziˌtät *f*, Leistungsfähigkeit *f*; ***~ car*** *s. mot.* Serienwagen *m*; ***~ costs*** *s. pl.* Gestehungskosten *pl.*; ***~ di·rec·tor*** *s. Radio*: Sendeleiter *m*; ***~ en·gi·neer*** *s.* Be'triebsingeniˌeur *m*; ***~ goods*** *s. pl.* Produkti'onsgüter *pl.*; ***~ line*** *s.* ⚙ Fließband *n*, Fertigungsstraße *f*; ***~ man·ag·er*** *s.* ✝ 'Herstellungsleiter *m*.

pro·duc·tive [prə'dʌktɪv] *adj.* □ **1.** (***of*** *acc.*) her'vorbringend, erzeugend, schaffend: ***be ~ of*** führen zu, erzeugen; **2.** produk'tiv, ergiebig, ertragreich, fruchtbar, ren'tabel; **3.** produzierend, leistungsfähig; ⚒ abbauwürdig; **4.** *fig.* produk'tiv, fruchtbar, schöpferisch; **pro'duc·tive·ness** [-nɪs], **pro·duc·tiv·i·ty** [ˌprɒdʌk'tɪvətɪ] *s.* Produktivi'tät *f*: a) ✝ Rentabili'tät *f*, Ergiebigkeit *f*, b) ✝ Leistungs-, Ertragsfähigkeit *f*, c) *fig.* Fruchtbarkeit *f*.

pro·em ['prəʊem] *s.* Einleitung *f* (*a. fig.*), Vorrede *f*.

prof [prɒf] *s.* F Prof *m* (*Professor*).

prof·a·na·tion [ˌprɒfə'neɪʃn] *s.* Entweihung *f*, Profanierung *f*; **pro·fane** [prə'feɪn] **I** *adj.* □ **1.** weltlich, pro'fan, ungeweiht, Profan…(*-bau, -geschichte*); **2.** lästerlich, gottlos: ***~ language***; **3.** uneingeweiht (***to*** in *acc.*); **II** *v/t.* **4.** entweihen, profanieren; **pro·fan·i·ty** [prə'fænətɪ] *s.* **1.** Gott-, Ruchlosigkeit *f*; **2.** Weltlichkeit *f*; **3.** Fluchen *n*; *pl.* Flüche *pl.*

pro·fess [prə'fes] *v/t.* **1.** (*a.* öffentlich) erklären, *Reue etc.* bekunden, sich bezeichnen (***to be*** als), sich bekennen zu (*e-m Glauben etc.*) *od.* als (*Christ etc.*): ***~ o.s. a communist***; ***~ Christianity***; **2.** beteuern, versichern, *b.s.* heucheln, zur Schau tragen; **3.** eintreten für, *Grundsätze etc.* vertreten; **4.** (*als Beruf*) ausüben, betreiben; **5.** *Brit.* Pro'fessor sein in (*dat.*), lehren; **pro'fessed** [-st] *adj.* □ **1.** erklärt (*Feind etc.*), ausgesprochen; **2.** an-, vorgeblich; **3.** Berufs…, berufsmäßig; **4.** (in einen Orden) aufgenommen: ***~ monk*** Profeß *m*; **pro'fess·ed·ly** [-sɪdlɪ] *adv.* **1.** angeblich; **2.** erklärtermaßen; **3.** offenkundig; **pro'fes·sion** [-eʃn] *s.* **1.** (*bsd.* aka'demischer *od.* freier) Beruf, Stand *m*: ***learned ~*** gelehrter Beruf; ***the ~s*** die akademischen Berufe; ***the military ~*** der Soldatenberuf; ***by ~*** von Beruf; **2.** ***the ~*** *coll.* der Beruf *od.* Stand: ***the medical ~*** die Ärzteschaft; **3.** (*bsd.* Glaubens)Bekenntnis *n*; **4.** Bekundung *f*, (*a.* falsche) Versicherung *od.* Behauptung, Beteuerung *f*: ***~ of***

friendship Freundschaftsbeteuerung *f*; **5.** *eccl.* Pro'feß *f*, Gelübde(ablegung *f*) *n*; **pro'fes·sion·al** [-eʃənl] **I** *adj.* □ **1.** Berufs..., beruflich, Amts..., Standes...: **~ discretion** Schweigepflicht *f des Arztes etc.*; **~ ethics** Berufsethos *n*; **2.** Fach..., Berufs..., fachlich: **~ association** Berufsgenossenschaft *f*; **~ school** Fach-, Berufsschule *f*; **~ studies** Fachstudium *n*; **~ terminology** Fachsprache *f*; **~ man** Mann vom Fach (→ 4); **3.** professio'nell, Berufs... (*a. sport*): **~ player**; **4.** freiberuflich, aka'demisch; **~ man** Akademiker, Geistesarbeiter; **the ~ classes** die höheren Berufsstände; **5.** gelernt, fachlich ausgebildet: **~ gardener**; **6.** *fig. iro.* unentwegt, ‚Berufs...': **~ patriot**; **II** *s.* **7.** *sport* Berufssportler(in) *od.* -spieler (-in); **8.** Berufskünstler *m etc.*, Künstler *m* vom Fach; **9.** Fachmann *m*; **10.** Geistesarbeiter *m*; **pro'fes·sion·al·ism** [-eʃnəlɪzəm] *s.* Berufssportlertum *n*, -spielertum *n*, Profitum *n*.

pro·fes·sor [prə'fesə] *s.* **1.** Pro'fessor *m*, Profes'sorin *f*; → **associate** 8; **2.** *Am.* Hochschullehrer *m*; **3.** *a. humor.* Lehrmeister *m*; **4.** *bsd. Am. od. Scot.* (*a.* Glaubens)Bekenner *m*; **pro·fes·so·ri·al** [ˌprɒfɪ'sɔːrɪəl] *adj.* □ professo'ral; Professoren...: **~ chair** Lehrstuhl *m*, Professur *f*; **pro·fes·so·ri·ate** [ˌprɒfɪ'sɔːrɪət] *s.* **1.** Profes'soren(schaft *f*) *pl.*; **2.** → **pro'fes·sor·ship** [-ʃɪp] *s.* Profes'sur *f*, Lehrstuhl *m*.

prof·fer ['prɒfə] **I** *s.* Angebot *n*; **II** *v/t.* (an)bieten.

pro·fi·cien·cy [prə'fɪʃnsɪ] *s.* Können *n*, Tüchtigkeit *f*, (gute) Leistungen *pl.*; Fertigkeit *f*; **pro'fi·cient** [-nt] **I** *adj.* □ tüchtig, geübt, bewandert, erfahren (**in**, **at** in *dat.*); **II** *s.* Fachmann *m*, Meister *m*.

pro·file ['prəʊfaɪl] **I** *s.* **1.** Pro'fil *n*: a) Seitenansicht *f*, b) Kon'tur *f*: **keep a low ~** *fig.* sich ‚bedeckt' *od.* im Hintergrund halten; **2.** (*a.* △, ⚙) Pro'fil *n*, Längsschnitt *m*; **3.** Querschnitt *m* (*a. fig.*); **4.** 'Kurzbiograˌphie *f*; **II** *v/t.* **5.** im Profil darstellen, profilieren; ⚙ im Quer- *od.* Längsschnitt zeichnen; **6.** ⚙ profilieren, fassonieren; kopierfräsen: **~ cutter** Fassonfräser *m*.

prof·it ['prɒfɪt] **I** *s.* **1.** (✝ *oft pl.*) Gewinn *m*, Pro'fit *m*: **~ and loss account** Gewinn- u. Verlustkonto *n*, Erfolgsrechnung *f*; **~ margin** Gewinnspanne *f*; **~-sharing** Gewinnbeteiligung *f*; **~-taking** *Börse*: Gewinnmitnahme *f*; **sell at a ~** mit Gewinn verkaufen; **leave a ~** e-n Gewinn abwerfen; **2.** *oft pl.* a) Ertrag *m*, Erlös *m*, b) Reinertrag *m*; **3.** ⚖ Nutzung *f*, Früchte *pl.* (*aus Land*); **4.** Nutzen *m*, Vorteil *m*: **turn s.th. to ~** aus et. Nutzen ziehen; **to his ~** zu s-m Vorteil; **II** *v/i.* **5.** (**by**, **from**) (e-n) Nutzen *od.* Gewinn ziehen (aus), profitieren (von): **~ by** *a.* sich *et.* zunutze machen, *e-e Gelegenheit* ausnützen; **III** *v/t.* **6.** nützen, nutzen (*dat.*), von Nutzen sein für; **'prof·it·a·ble** [-təbl] *adj.* □ **1.** gewinnbringend, einträglich, lohnend, ren'tabel: **be ~** *a.* sich rentieren; **2.** vorteilhaft, nützlich (**to** für); **'prof·it·a·ble·ness** [-təblnɪs] *s.* **1.** Einträglichkeit *f*, Rentabili'tät *f*; **2.** Nützlichkeit *f*; **prof·it·eer** [ˌprɒfɪ'tɪə] **I** *s.* Pro'fitmacher *m*, (Kriegs- *etc.*)Gewinnler *m*, ‚Schieber' *m*, Wucherer *m*; **II** *v/i.* Schieber- *od.* Wuchergeschäfte machen, ‚schieben'; **prof·it·eer·ing** [ˌprɒfɪ'tɪərɪŋ] *s.* Schieber-, Wuchergeschäfte *pl.*, Preistreibe'rei *f*; **'prof·it·less** [-lɪs] *adj.* □ **1.** 'unrenˌtabel, ohne Gewinn; **2.** nutzlos.

prof·li·ga·cy ['prɒflɪgəsɪ] *s.* **1.** Lasterhaftigkeit *f*, Verworfenheit *f*; **2.** Verschwendung(ssucht) *f*; **'prof·li·gate** [-gət] **I** *adj.* □ **1.** verworfen, liederlich; **2.** verschwenderisch; **II** *s.* **3.** lasterhafter Mensch, Liederjan *m*; **4.** Verschwender(in).

pro for·ma [ˌprəʊ'fɔːmə] (*Lat.*) *adv. u. adj.* **1.** pro forma, zum Schein; **2.** ✝ Proforma...(*-rechnung*), Schein...(*-geschäft*): **~ bill** Proforma-, Gefälligkeitswechsel *m*.

pro·found [prə'faʊnd] *adj.* □ **1.** tief (*mst fig. Friede*, *Seufzer*, *Schlaf etc.*); **2.** tiefschürfend, inhaltsschwer, gründlich, pro'fund; **3.** *fig.* unergründlich, dunkel; **4.** *fig.* tief, groß (*Hochachtung etc.*), stark (*Interesse etc.*), vollkommen (*Gleichgültigkeit*); **pro'found·ness** [-nɪs], **pro'fun·di·ty** [-'fʌndətɪ] *s.* **1.** Tiefe *f*, Abgrund *m* (*a. fig.*); **2.** Tiefgründigkeit *f*, -sinnigkeit *f*; **3.** Gründlichkeit *f*; **4.** *pl.* tiefgründige Pro'bleme *od.* Theo'rien; **5.** *oft pl.* Weisheit *f*, pro'funder Ausspruch; **6.** Stärke *f*, hoher Grad (*der Erregung etc.*).

pro·fuse [prə'fjuːs] *adj.* □ **1.** (*a.* 'über-)reich (**of**, **in** an *dat.*), 'überfließend, üppig; **2.** (*oft* allzu) freigebig, verschwenderisch (**of**, **in** mit): **be ~ in one's thanks** überschwenglich danken; **~ly illustrated** reich(haltig) illustriert; **pro'fuse·ness** [-nɪs], **pro'fu·sion** [-uːʒn] *s.* **1.** ('Über)Fülle *f*, 'Überfluß *m* (**of** an *dat.*): **in ~** in Hülle u. Fülle; **2.** Verschwendung *f*, Luxus *m*, allzu große Freigebigkeit.

pro·gen·i·tive [prəʊ'dʒenɪtɪv] *adj.* **1.** Zeugungs...: **~ act**; **2.** zeugungsfähig; **pro'gen·i·tor** [-tə] *s.* **1.** Vorfahr *m*, Ahn *m*; **2.** *fig.* Vorläufer *m*; **pro'gen·i·tress** [-trɪs] *s.* Ahne *f*; **pro'gen·i·ture** [-tʃə] *s.* **1.** Zeugung *f*; **2.** Nachkommenschaft *f*; **prog·e·ny** ['prɒdʒənɪ] *s.* **1.** Nachkommen(schaft *f a.* ⚘) *pl.*; *zo. die Jungen pl.*, Brut *f*; **2.** *fig.* Frucht *f*, Pro'dukt *n*.

pro·gna·thy ['prɒgnəθɪ] *s.* ⚕ **1.** Progna'thie *f*; **2.** Proge'nie *f*.

prog·no·sis [prɒg'nəʊsɪs] *pl.* **-ses** [-siːz] *s.* ⚕ *etc.* Pro'gnose *f*, Vor'hersage *f*; **prog'nos·tic** [-'nɒstɪk] **I** *adj.* **1.** pro'gnostisch (*bsd.* ⚕), vor'aussagend (**of** *acc.*); **2.** warnend, vorbedeutend; **II** *s.* **3.** Vor'hersage *f*; **4.** (An-, Vor)Zeichen *n*; **prog·nos·ti·cate** [prɒg'nɒstɪkeɪt] *v/t.* **1.** (*a. v/i.*) vor'her-, vor'aussagen, prognostizieren; **2.** anzeigen; **prog·nos·ti·ca·tion** [prəgˌnɒstɪ'keɪʃn] *s.* **1.** Vor'her-, Vor'aussage *f*, Pro'gnose *f* (*a.* ⚕); **2.** Prophe'zeiung *f*; **3.** Vorzeichen *n*.

pro·gram(me) ['prəʊgræm] **I** *s.* **1.** ('Studien-, Par'tei- *etc.*)Proˌgramm *n*, Plan *m* (*a. fig.* F): **manufacturing ~** Herstellungsprogramm *n*; **2.** Pro'gramm *n*: a) *thea.* Spielplan *m*, b) Pro'grammheft *n*, c) Darbietung *f*, d) *Radio*, *TV*: Sendefolge *f*, Sendung *f*: **~ director** Programmdirektor *m*; **~ music** Programmmusik *f*; **~ picture** Beifilm *m*; **3.** *Computer*: Programm *n*: **~-controlled** programmgesteuert; **~ step** Programmschritt *m*; **II** *v/t.* **4.** ein Pro'gramm aufstellen für; **5.** auf das Pro'gramm setzen, planen, ansetzen; **6.** *Computer* programmieren; **'pro·grammed** [-md] *adj.* programmiert: **~ instruction**; **~ learning**; **'pro·gram·mer** [-mə] *s.* *Computer*: Program'mierer(in); **'pro·gram·ming** [-mɪŋ] *s.* **1.** *Rundfunk*, *TV*: Pro'grammgestaltung *f*; **2.** *Computer*: Programmierung *f*: **~ language** Programmiersprache *f*.

pro·gress I ['prəʊgres] *s.* (*nur sg. außer* 6) **1.** *fig.* Fortschritt(e *pl.*) *m*: **make ~** Fortschritte machen; **~ engineer** Entwicklungsingenieur *m*; **~ report** Zwischenbericht; **2.** (Weiter)Entwicklung *f*: **in ~** im Werden (begriffen); **3.** Fortschreiten *n*, Vorrücken *n*; ⚔ Vordringen *n*; **4.** Fortgang *m*, (Ver)Lauf *m*: **be in ~** im Gange sein; **5.** Über'handnehmen *n*, 'Umsichgreifen *n*: **the disease made rapid ~** die Krankheit griff schnell um sich; **6.** *obs.* Reise *f*, Fahrt *f*; *Brit. mst hist.* Rundreise *f e-s Herrschers etc.*; **II** [prəʊ'gres] *v/i.* **7.** fortschreiten, weitergehen, s-n Fortgang nehmen; **8.** sich (fort-, weiter)entwikkeln: **~ towards completion** s-r Vollendung entgegengehen; **9.** *fig.* Fortschritte machen, vo'ran-, vorwärtskommen.

pro·gres·sion [prəʊ'greʃn] *s.* **1.** Vorwärts-, Fortbewegung *f*; **2.** Weiterentwicklung *f*, Verlauf *m*; **3.** (Aufein'ander)Folge *f*; **4.** Progressi'on *f*: a) ⚹ Reihe *f*, b) Staffelung *f e-r Steuer etc.*; **5.** ♪ a) Se'quenz *f*, b) Fortschreitung *f* (*Stimmbewegung*); **pro'gres·sion·ist** [-ʃnɪst], **pro'gress·ist** [-esɪst] *s. pol.* Fortschrittler *m*; **pro'gres·sive** [-esɪv] **I** *adj.* □ **1.** fortschrittlich (*Person u. Sache*): **~ party** *pol.* Fortschrittspartei *f*; **2.** fortschreitend, -laufend, progres'siv: **a ~ step** *fig.* ein Schritt nach vorn; **~ assembly** ⚙ Fließbandmontage *f*; **3.** gestaffelt, progres'siv (*Besteuerung etc.*); **4.** (fort)laufend: **~ numbers**; **5.** *a.* ⚕ zunehmend, progres'siv: **~ paralysis**; **6.** *ling.* progres'siv: **~ form** Verlaufsform *f*; **II** *s.* **7.** *pol.* Progres'sive(r *m*) *f*, Fortschrittler *m*; **pro'gres·sive·ly** [-esɪvlɪ] *adv.* schritt-, stufenweise, nach u. nach, all'mählich.

pro·hib·it [prə'hɪbɪt] *v/t.* **1.** verbieten, unter'sagen (**s.th.** et., **s.o. from doing** j-m *et.* zu tun); **2.** verhindern (**s.th. being done** daß et. geschieht); **3.** hindern (**s.o. from doing** j-n daran, *et.* zu tun); **pro·hi·bi·tion** [ˌprəʊɪ'bɪʃn] *s.* **1.** Verbot *n*; **2.** (*hist. Am. mst* 2) Prohibiti'on(szeit) *f*, Alkoholverbot *n*; **pro·hi·bi·tion·ist** [ˌprəʊɪ'bɪʃnɪst] *s. hist. Am.* Prohibitio'nist *m*, Verfechter *m* des Alkoholverbots; **pro'hib·i·tive** [-tɪv] *adj.* □ **1.** verbietend, unter'sagend; **2.** ✝ Prohibitiv..., Schutz..., Sperr...: **~ duty** Prohibitivzoll *m*; **~ tax** Prohibitivsteuer *f*; **3.** unerschwinglich (*Preis*), untragbar (*Kosten*); **pro'hib·i·to·ry** [-tərɪ] → **prohibitive**.

pro·ject I *v/t.* [prə'dʒekt] **1.** planen, entwerfen, projektieren; **2.** werfen, schleudern; **3.** *Bild*, *Licht*, *Schatten etc.* werfen, projizieren; **4.** *fig.* projizieren (*a.* ♁): **~ o.s.** (*od.* **one's thoughts**) **into** sich versetzen in (*acc.*); **~ one's feelings into** s-e Gefühle übertragen auf (*acc.*); **II** *v/i.* **5.** vorspringen, -stehen, -ragen (**over** über *acc.*); **III** *s.* [ˈprɒdʒekt] **6.** Proˈjekt *n* (*a. Am. ped.*), Plan *m*, (*a.* Bau)Vorhaben *n*, Entwurf *m*: **~ engineer** Projektingenieur *m*.

pro·jec·tile [prəʊˈdʒektaɪl] **I** *s.* **1.** ⚔ Geschoß *n*, Projekˈtil *n*; **2.** (Wurf)Geschoß *n*; **II** *adj.* **3.** (an)treibend, Stoß..., Trieb...: **~ force**; **4.** Wurf...

pro·jec·tion [prəˈdʒekʃn] *s.* **1.** Vorsprung *m*, vorspringender Teil *od.* Gegenstand *etc.*; △ Auskragung *f*, -ladung *f*, ˈÜberhang *m*; **2.** Fortsatz *m*; **3.** Werfen *n*, Schleudern *n*, (Vorwärts)Treiben *n*; **4.** Wurf *m*, Stoß *m*; **5.** ♁, *ast.* Projektiˈon *f*: **upright ~** Aufriß *m*; **6.** *phot.* Projektiˈon *f*: a) Projizieren *n* (*Lichtbilder*), b) Lichtbild *n*; **7.** Vorführen *n* (*Film*): **~ booth** Vorführkabine *f*; **~ screen** Projektions-, Leinwand *f*, Bildschirm *m*; **8.** *psych.* Projektiˈon *f*; **9.** *fig.* ˈWiderspiegelung *f*; **10.** a) Planen *n*, Entwerfen *n*, b) Plan *m*, Entwurf *m*; **11.** *Statistik etc.*: Hochrechnung *f*; **proˈjec·tion·ist** [-kʃnɪst] *s.* Filmvorführer *m*; **proˈjec·tor** [-ktə] *s.* **1.** Projektiˈonsappaˌrat *m*, Vorführgerät *n*, Bildwerfer *m*, Proˈjektor *m*; **2.** ⚙ Scheinwerfer *m*; **3.** ⚔ (Raˈketen-, Flammen- *etc.*)Werfer *m*; **4.** a) Planer *m*, b) *contp.* Pläneschmied *m*, Proˈjektemacher *m*.

pro·lapse [ˈprəʊlæps] ⚕ **I** *s.* Vorfall *m*, Proˈlaps(us) *m*; **II** *v/i.* [prəˈlæps] prolabieren, vorfallen; **pro·lap·sus** [prəʊˈlæpsəs] → **prolapse** I.

prole [prəʊl] *s.* F Proˈlet(in).

pro·le·tar·i·an [ˌprəʊlɪˈteərɪən] **I** *adj.* proleˈtarisch, Proletarier...; **II** *s.* Proleˈtarier(in); **ˌpro·leˈtar·i·at(e)** [-ɪət] *s.* Proletariˈat *n*.

pro·li·cide [ˈprəʊlɪsaɪd] *s.* ⚖ Tötung *f* der Leibesfrucht, Abtreibung *f*.

pro·lif·er·ate [prəʊˈlɪfəreɪt] *v/i. biol.* **1.** wuchern; **2.** sich fortpflanzen (*durch Zellteilung etc.*); **3.** sich stark vermehren; **pro·lif·eˈra·tion** [prəʊˌlɪfəˈreɪʃn] *s.* **1.** Wuchern *n*; **2.** Fortpflanzung *f*; **3.** starke Vermehrung *od.* Ausbreitung; **proˈlif·ic** [-fɪk] *adj.* (□ **~ally**) **1.** *bsd. biol.* (*oft* ˈüberaus) fruchtbar; **2.** *fig.* reich (**of, in** an *dat.*); **3.** *fig.* fruchtbar, produkˈtiv (*Schriftsteller etc.*).

pro·lix [ˈprəʊlɪks] *adj.* □ weitschweifig; **pro·lix·i·ty** [ˌprəʊˈlɪksətɪ] *s.* Weitschweifigkeit *f*.

pro·log *Am.* → **prologue**.

pro·logue [ˈprəʊlɒg] *s.* **1.** *bsd. thea.* Proˈlog *m*, Einleitung *f* (**to** zu); **2.** *fig.* Vorspiel *n*, Auftakt *m*; **ˈpro·logu·ize** [-gaɪz] *v/i.* e-n Proˈlog verfassen *od.* sprechen.

pro·long [prəˈlɒŋ] *v/t.* **1.** verlängern, (aus)dehnen; **2.** ✝ *Wechsel* prolongieren; **proˈlonged** [-ŋd] *adj.* anhaltend (*Beifall, Regen etc.*): **for a ~ period** längere Zeit; **pro·lon·ga·tion** [ˌprəʊlɒŋˈgeɪʃn] *s.* **1.** Verlängerung *f*; **2.** Prolongierung *f e-s Wechsels etc.*, Fristverlängerung *f*, Aufschub *m*: **~ business** ✝ Prolongationsgeschäft *n*.

prom [prɒm] *s.* **1.** *Am.* F High-School-, College-Ball *m*; **2.** *bsd. Brit.* F a) ˈStrandpromeˌnade *f*, b) → **promenade concert**.

prom·e·nade [ˌprɒməˈnɑːd] **I** *s.* **1.** Proˈmeˈnade *f*: a) Spaziergang *m*, -fahrt *f*, -ritt *m*, b) Spazierweg *m*, Wandelhalle *f*; **2.** [*a.* -ˈneɪd] feierlicher Einzug der (Ball)Gäste, Poloˈnaise *f*; **3.** → **prom** 1; **4.** → **promenade concert**; **II** *v/i.* **5.** promenieren, spazieren(gehen *etc.*); **III** *v/t.* **6.** promenieren *od.* (herˈum)spazieren in (*dat.*) *od.* auf (*dat.*); **7.** spazierenführen, (umˈher)führen; **~ concert** *s. Konzert in ungezwungener Atmosphäre*; **~ deck** *s.* ⚓ Promeˈnadendeck *n*.

prom·i·nence [ˈprɒmɪnəns] *s.* **1.** (Her-)ˈVorragen *n*, -springen *n*; **2.** Vorsprung *m*, vorstehender Teil; *ast.* Protubeˈranz *f*; **3.** *fig.* a) Berühmtheit *f*, b) Bedeutung *f*: **bring into ~** a) berühmt machen, b) klar herausstellen, hervorheben; **come into ~** in den Vordergrund rücken, hervortreten; → **blaze** 7; **ˈprom·i·nent** [-nt] *adj.* □ **1.** vorstehend, -springend (*a. Nase etc.*); **2.** marˈkant, auffallend, herˈvorstechend (*Eigenschaft*); **3.** promiˈnent: a) führend (*Persönlichkeit*), herˈvorragend, b) berühmt.

prom·is·cu·i·ty [ˌprɒmɪˈskjuːətɪ] *s.* **1.** Vermischt-, Verworrenheit *f*, Durcheinˈander *n*; **2.** Wahllosigkeit *f*; **3.** Promiskuiˈtät *f*, wahllose *od.* ungebundene Geschlechtsbeziehungen *pl.*; **pro·mis·cu·ous** [prəˈmɪskjʊəs] *adj.* □ **1.** (kunter)bunt, verworren; **2.** wahl-, ˈunterschiedslos; **3.** gemeinsam (*beider Geschlechter*): **~ bathing**.

prom·ise [ˈprɒmɪs] **I** *s.* **1.** Versprechen *n*, -heißung *f*, Zusage *f* (**to** *j-m* gegenˈüber): **~ to pay** ✝ Zahlungsversprechen; **break** (**keep**) **one's ~** sein Versprechen brechen (halten); **make a ~** ein Versprechen geben; **breach of ~** Bruch *m* des Eheversprechens; **Land of ~** → **Promised Land**; **2.** *fig.* Hoffnung *f od.* Aussicht *f* (**of** auf *acc.*, zu *inf.*): **of great ~** vielversprechend (*Aussicht, junger Mann etc.*); **show some ~** gewisse Ansätze zeigen; **II** *v/t.* **3.** versprechen, zusagen, in Aussicht stellen (**s.o. s.th.**, **s.th. to s.o.** j-m et.): **I ~ you** a) das kann ich Ihnen versichern, b) ich warne Sie!; **4.** *fig.* versprechen, erwarten *od.* hoffen lassen, ankündigen; **5.** **be ~d** (in die Ehe) versprochen sein; **6.** **~ o.s. s.th.** sich et. versprechen *od.* erhoffen; **III** *v/i.* **7.** versprechen, zusagen; **8.** *fig.* Hoffnungen erwecken: **he ~s well** er läßt sich gut an; **the weather ~s fine** das Wetter verspricht gut zu werden; **Prom·ised Land** [ˈprɒmɪst] *s. bibl. u. fig. das* Gelobte Land, Land *n* der Verheißung; **prom·is·ee** [ˌprɒmɪˈsiː] *s.* ⚖ Versprechensempfänger(in), Berechtigte(r *m*) *f*; **ˈprom·is·ing** [-sɪŋ] *adj.* □ *fig.* vielversprechend, hoffnungs-, verheißungsvoll, aussichtsreich; **ˈprom·i·sor** [-sɔː] *s.* ⚖ Versprechensgeber(in); **ˈprom·is·so·ry** [-sərɪ] *adj.* versprechend: **~ note** ✝ Schuldschein *m*, Eigen-, Solawechsel *m*.

pro·mo [ˈprəʊməʊ] F **I** *adj.* Reklame...; **II** *s. Radio, TV*: (Werbe)Spot *m*; *Zeitung*: Anzeige *f*.

prom·on·to·ry [ˈprɒməntrɪ] *s.* Vorgebirge *n*.

pro·mote [prəˈməʊt] *v/t.* **1.** fördern, unterˈstützen; *b.s.* Vorschub leisten (*dat.*); **2.** *j-n* befördern: **be ~d** a) befördert werden, b) *sport* aufsteigen; **3.** *parl. Antrag* a) unterˈstützen, b) einbringen; **4.** ✝ *Gesellschaft* gründen; **5.** ✝ a) *Verkauf* (*durch Werbung*) steigern, b) werben für; **6.** *Boxkampf etc.* veranstalten; **7.** *ped. Am. Schüler* versetzen; **8.** *Schach*: *Bauern* verwandeln; **9.** *Am. sl.* ‚organisieren'; **proˈmot·er** [-tə] *s.* **1.** Förderer *m*; Befürworter *m*; *b.s.* Anstifter *m*; **2.** ✝ Gründer *m*: **~'s shares** Gründeraktien; **3.** *sport* Veranstalter *m*; **proˈmo·tion** [-əʊʃn] *s.* **1.** Beförderung *f* (*a.* ⚔): **~ list** Beförderungsliste *f*; **get one's ~** befördert werden; **~ prospects** *pl.* Aufstiegschancen *pl.*; **2.** Förderung *f*, Befürwortung *f*: **export ~** ✝ Exportförderung; **3.** ✝ Gründung *f*; **4.** ✝ Verkaufsförderung *f*, Werbung *f*; **5.** *ped. Am.* Versetzung *f*; **6.** *sport* Aufstieg *m*: **gain ~** aufsteigen; **7.** *Schach*: Umwandlung *f*; **proˈmo·tion·al** [-əʊʃənl] *adj.* **1.** Beförderungs...; **2.** fördernd; **3.** ✝ Reklame..., Werbe...; **proˈmo·tive** [-tɪv] *adj.* fördernd, begünstigend (**of** *acc.*).

prompt [prɒmpt] **I** *adj.* □ **1.** unverzüglich, prompt, soˈfortig, ˈumgehend: **a ~ reply** e-e prompte *od.* schlagfertige Antwort; **2.** schnell, rasch; **3.** bereit (-willig); **4.** ✝ a) pünktlich, b) bar, c) sofort liefer- u. zahlbar: **for ~ cash** gegen sofortige Kasse; **II** *adv.* **5.** pünktlich; **III** *v/t.* **6.** *j-n* antreiben, bewegen, (*a. et.*) veranlassen (**to** zu); **7.** *Gedanken, Gefühl etc.* eingeben, wecken; **8.** *j-m* das Stichwort geben, ein-, vorsagen; *thea. j-m* soufflieren: **~-book** Soufflierbuch *n*; **~ box** Souffleurkasten; **IV** *s.* **9.** ✝ Ziel *n*, Zahlungsfrist *f*; **ˈprompt·er** [-tə] *s.* **1.** *thea.* Soufˈfleur *m*, Soufˈfleuse *f*; **2.** Vorsager(in); **3.** Anreger(in), Urheber(in); *b.s.* Anstifter(in); **ˈprompt·ing** [-tɪŋ] *s.* (*oft pl.*) *fig.* Eingebung *f*, Stimme *f des Herzens*; **ˈpromp·ti·tude** [-tɪtjuːd], **ˈprompt·ness** [-nɪs] *s.* **1.** Schnelligkeit *f*; **2.** Bereitwilligkeit *f*; **3.** *bsd.* ✝ Promptheit *f*, Pünktlichkeit *f*.

ˈprompt-note *s.* ✝ Verkaufsnota *f* mit Angabe der Zahlungsfrist.

pro·mul·gate [ˈprɒmlgeɪt] *v/t.* **1.** *Gesetz etc.* (öffentlich) bekanntmachen *od.* verkündigen; **2.** *Lehre etc.* verbreiten; **pro·mul·ga·tion** [ˌprɒmlˈgeɪʃn] *s.* **1.** (öffentliche) Bekanntmachung, Verkündung *f*, -öffentlichung *f*; **2.** Verbreitung *f*.

prone [prəʊn] *adj.* □ **1.** auf dem Bauch *od.* mit dem Gesicht nach unten liegend, hingestreckt: **~ position** a) Bauchlage, b) ⚔ *etc.* Anschlag liegend; **2.** (vornˈüber)gebeugt; **3.** abschüssig; **4.** *fig.* (**to**) neigend (zu), veranlagt (zu), anfällig (für); **ˈprone·ness** [-nɪs] *s.* (**to**) Neigung *f*, Hang *m* (zu), Anfälligkeit *f* (für).

prong [prɒŋ] **I** *s.* **1.** Zinke *f e-r* (*Heu- etc.*)*Gabel*; Zacke *f*, Spitze *f*, Dorn *m*; **2.** (Geweih)Sprosse *f*, -ende *n*; **3.** Horn *n*; **4.** (Heu-, Mist- *etc.*)Gabel *f*; **II** *v/t.* **5.** mit e-r Gabel stechen *od.* heben; **6.** aufspießen; **pronged** [-ŋd] *adj.* gezinkt, zackig: **two-~** zweizinkig.

pro·nom·i·nal [prəˈnɒmɪnl] *adj.* □ *ling.* pronomiˈnal.

pro·noun ['prəʊnaʊn] *s. ling.* Pro'nomen *n*, Fürwort *n*.
pro·nounce [prə'naʊns] **I** *v/t.* **1.** aussprechen (*a. ling.*); **2.** erklären für, bezeichnen als; **3.** *Urteil* aussprechen *od.* verkünden, *Segen* erteilen: ~ ***sentence of death*** das Todesurteil fällen, auf Todesstrafe erkennen; **4.** behaupten (***that*** daß); **II** *v/i.* **5.** Stellung nehmen, s-e Meinung äußern (***on*** zu): ~ ***in favo(u)r of*** (***against***) ***s.th.*** sich für (gegen) et. aussprechen; **pro'nounced** [-st] *adj.* □ **1.** ausgesprochen, ausgeprägt, deutlich (*Tendenz etc.*), sichtlich (*Besserung etc.*); **2.** bestimmt, entschieden (*Ansicht etc.*); **pro'nounc·ed·ly** [-sɪdlɪ] *adv.* ausgesprochen *gut, schlecht etc.*; **pro'nounce·ment** [-mənt] *s.* **1.** Äußerung *f*; **2.** Erklärung *f*, (⚖ *Urteils*)Verkünd(ig)ung *f*; **3.** Entscheidung *f*.
pron·to ['prɒntəʊ] *adv. Am.* F fix, schnell, ‚aber dalli'.
pro·nun·ci·a·tion [prəˌnʌnsɪ'eɪʃn] *s.* Aussprache *f*.
proof [pru:f] **I** *adj.* **1.** fest (***against***, ***to*** gegen), 'undurchˌlässig, (*wasser- etc.*) dicht, (*hitze*)beständig, (*kugel*)sicher; **2.** gefeit (***against*** gegen) (*a. fig.*); *fig. a.* unzugänglich: ~ ***against bribes*** unbestechlich; **3.** ⚗ *obs.* probehaltig, nor'malstark (*alkoholische Flüssigkeit*); **II** *s.* **4.** Beweis *m*, Nachweis *m*: ***in*** ~ ***of*** zum *od.* als Beweis (*gen.*); ***give*** ~ ***of*** *et.* beweisen; **5.** (*a.* ⚖) Beweis(mittel *n*, -stück *n*) *m*; Beleg(e *pl.*) *m*; **6.** Probe *f* (*a.* ✗), (*a.* Materi'al)Prüfung *f*: ***put to*** (***the***) ~ auf die Probe stellen; ***the*** ~ ***of the pudding is in the eating*** Probieren geht über Studieren; **7.** *typ.* a) Korrek'turfahne *f*, -bogen *m*, b) Probeabzug *m* (*a. phot.*): ***clean*** ~ Revisionsbogen *m*; **8.** Nor'malstärke *f alkoholischer Getränke*; **III** *v/t.* **9.** ⚙ (*wasser- etc.*)dicht *od.* (*hitze- etc.*)beständig *od.* (*kugel- etc.*)fest machen, imprägnieren; '~-ˌ**read·er** *s. typ.* Kor'rektor *m*; '~ˌ**read·ing** *s. typ.* Korrek'turlesen *n*; ~ **sheet** → ***proof*** 7 a; ~ **spir·it** *s.* Nor'malweingeist *m*.
prop[1] [prɒp] **I** *s.* **1.** Stütze *f* (*a.* ⚓), (Stütz)Pfahl *m*; **2.** *fig.* Stütze *f*, Halt *m*; **3.** ⚠, ⚙ Stempel *m*, Stützbalken *m*, Strebe *f*; **4.** ⚙ Drehpunkt *m e-s Hebels*; **5.** *pl. sl.* ‚Stelzen' *pl.* (*Beine*); **II** *v/t.* **6.** stützen (*a. fig.*); **7.** *a.* ~ ***up*** a) (ab)stützen, ⚙ *a.* absteifen, verstreben, *mot.* aufbocken, b) *sich*, *et.* lehnen (***against*** gegen).
prop[2] [prɒp] *s. thea.* Requi'sit *n* (*a. fig.*).
prop[3] [prɒp] *s.* ✈ Pro'peller *m*.
prop·a·gan·da [ˌprɒpə'gændə] *s.* Propa'ganda *f*; ✝ Werbung *f*, Re'klame *f*: ***make*** ~ ***for***; ~ ***week*** Werbewoche *f*; ˌ**prop·a'gan·dist** [-dɪst] **I** *s.* Propagan'dist(in); **II** *adj.* propagan'distisch; **prop·a·gan·dis·tic** [ˌprɒpəgæn'dɪstɪk] *adj.* propagan'distisch; ˌ**prop·a'gan·dize** [-daɪz] **I** *v/t.* **1.** Propa'ganda machen für, propagieren; **2.** *j-n* durch Propa'ganda beeinflussen; **II** *v/i.* **3.** Propa'ganda machen.
prop·a·gate ['prɒpəgeɪt] **I** *v/t.* **1.** *biol.*, *a. phys. Ton, Bewegung, Licht* fortpflanzen; **2.** *Nachricht etc.* aus-, verbreiten, propagieren; **II** *v/i.* **3.** sich fortpflanzen; **prop·a·ga·tion** [ˌprɒpə'geɪʃn] *s.* **1.** Fortpflanzung *f* (*a. phys.*), Vermehrung *f*; **2.** Aus-, Verbreitung *f*; **prop·a·ga·tor** ['prɒpəgeɪtə] *s.* **1.** Fortpflanzer *m*; **2.** Verbreiter *m*, Propagan'dist *m*.
pro·pane ['prəʊpeɪn] *s.* ⚗ Pro'pan *n*.
pro·pel [prə'pel] *v/t.* (an-, vorwärts)treiben (*a. fig. od.* ⚙); **pro'pel·lant** [-lənt] *s.* ⚙ Treibstoff *m*, -mittel *n*: ~ (***charge***) Treibladung *f e-r Rakete etc.*; **pro'pel·lent** [-lənt] **I** *adj.* **1.** (an-, vorwärts-) treibend: ~ ***gas*** Treibgas; ~ ***power*** Antriebs-, Triebkraft *f*; **II** *s.* **2.** *fig.* treibende Kraft; **3.** → ***propellant***; **pro'pel·ler** [-lə] *s.* Pro'peller *m*: a) ✈ Luftschraube *f*, b) ⚓ Schiffsschraube *f*: ~ ***blade*** ✈ Luftschraubenblatt *n*; **pro'pel·ling** [-lɪŋ] *adj.* Antriebs..., Trieb..., Treib...: ~ ***charge*** Treibladung *f*, -satz *m e-r Rakete etc.*; ~ ***nozzle*** ✈ Schubdüse *f*; ~ ***pencil*** Drehbleistift *m*.
pro·pen·si·ty [prə'pensətɪ] *s. fig.* Hang *m*, Neigung *f* (***to***, ***for*** zu).
prop·er ['prɒpə] *adj.* □ **1.** richtig, passend, geeignet, angemessen, ordnungsgemäß, zweckmäßig: ***in*** ~ ***form*** in gebührender *od.* angemessener Form; ***in the*** ~ ***place*** am rechten Platz; ***do as you think*** (***it***) ~ tun Sie, was Sie für richtig halten; ~ ***fraction*** ✗ echter Bruch; **2.** anständig, schicklich, kor'rekt, einwandfrei (*Benehmen etc.*): ***it is*** ~ es (ge)ziemt *od.* schickt sich; **3.** zulässig; **4.** eigen(tümlich) (***to*** *dat.*), besonder; **5.** genau: ***in the*** ~ ***meaning of the word*** strenggenommen; **6.** (*mst nachgestellt*) eigentlich: ***philosophy*** ~ die eigentliche Philosophie; ***in the Middle East*** ~ im Mittleren Osten selbst; **7.** maßgebend, zuständig (*Dienststelle etc.*); **8.** F ‚richtig', ‚ordentlich', ‚anständig': ***a*** ~ ***licking*** e-e gehörige Tracht Prügel; **9.** *ling.* Eigen...: ~ ***name*** (*od.* ***noun***) Eigenname *m*; '**prop·er·ly** [-lɪ] *adv.* **1.** richtig (*etc.* → ***proper*** 1, 2), passend, wie es sich gehört: ***behave*** ~ sich (anständig) benehmen; **2.** genau: ~ ***speaking*** eigentlich, streng genommen; **3.** F gründlich, ‚anständig', ‚tüchtig'.
prop·er·tied ['prɒpətɪd] *adj.* besitzend, begütert: ***the*** ~ ***classes***.
prop·er·ty ['prɒpətɪ] *s.* **1.** Eigentum *n*, Besitz(tum *n*) *m*, Gut *n*, Vermögen *n*: ***common*** ~ Gemeingut; ***damage to*** ~ Sachschaden *m*; ***law of*** ~ ⚖ Sachenrecht *n*; ***left*** ~ Hinterlassenschaft *f*; ***lost*** ~ Fundsache *f*; ***man of*** ~ begüterter Mann; ***personal*** ~ → ***personalty***; **2.** *a.* ***landed*** ~ (Grund-, Land)Besitz *m*, Grundstück *n*, Liegenschaft *f*, Ländereien *pl.*; **3.** ⚖ Eigentum(srecht) *n*: ***industrial*** ~ gewerbliches Schutzrecht; ***intellectual*** ~ geistiges Eigentum; ***literary*** ~ literarisches Eigentum, Urheberrecht; **4.** *mst pl. thea.* Requi'sit(en *pl.*) *n*; **5.** Eigenart *f*, -heit *f*; Merkmal *n*; **6.** *phys. etc.* Eigenschaft *f*, ⚙ *a.* Fähigkeit *f*: ~ ***of material*** Werkstoffeigenschaft; ***insulating*** ~ Isolationsvermögen *n*; ~ **as·sets** *s. pl.* ✝ Vermögenswerte *pl.*; ~ **in·sur·ance** *s.* Sachversicherung *f*; ~ **man** [mæn] *s.* [*irr.*] *thea.* Requisi'teur *m*; ~ **mar·ket** *s.* Immo'bilienmarkt *m*; ~ **tax** *s.* **1.** Vermögenssteuer *f*; **2.** Grundsteuer *f*.
proph·e·cy ['prɒfɪsɪ] *s.* Prophe'zeiung *f*, Weissagung *f*; '**proph·e·sy** [-saɪ] *v/t.* prophe'zeien, weis-, vor'aussagen (***s.th. for s.o.*** j-m et.).
proph·et ['prɒfɪt] *s.* Pro'phet *m* (*a. fig.*): ***the Major*** (***Minor***) ***2s*** *bibl.* die großen (kleinen) Propheten; '**proph·et·ess** [-tɪs] *s.* Pro'phetin *f*; **pro·phet·ic**, **pro·phet·i·cal** [prə'fetɪk(l)] *adj.* □ pro'phetisch.
pro·phy·lac·tic [ˌprɒfɪ'læktɪk] **I** *adj. bsd.* ⚕ prophy'laktisch, vorbeugend, Vorbeugungs..., Schutz...; **II** *s.* ⚕ Prophy'laktikum *n*, vorbeugendes Mittel; *fig.* vorbeugende Maßnahme; ˌ**pro·phy'lax·is** [-ksɪs] *s.* ⚕ Prophy'laxe *f*, Präven'tivbeˌhandlung *f*, Vorbeugung *f*.
pro·pin·qui·ty [prə'pɪŋkwətɪ] *s.* **1.** Nähe *f*; **2.** nahe Verwandtschaft.
pro·pi·ti·ate [prə'pɪʃɪeɪt] *v/t.* versöhnen, besänftigen, günstig stimmen; **pro·pi·ti·a·tion** [prəˌpɪʃɪ'eɪʃn] *s.* **1.** Versöhnung *f*; Besänftigung *f*; **2.** *obs.* (Sühn-) Opfer *n*, Sühne *f*; **pro'pi·ti·a·to·ry** [-ɪətərɪ] *adj.* □ versöhnend, sühnend, Sühn...
pro·pi·tious [prə'pɪʃəs] *adj.* □ **1.** günstig, vorteilhaft (***to*** für); **2.** gnädig, geneigt.
'**prop·jet** *s.* ✈ **1.** *a.* ~ ***engine*** Pro'pellerturˌbine(n-Triebwerk *n*) *f*; **2.** *a.* ~ ***plane*** Flugzeug *n* mit Pro'pellerturˌbine(n).
pro·po·nent [prə'pəʊnənt] *s.* **1.** Vorschlagende(r *m*) *f*; *fig.* Befürworter(in); **2.** ⚖ präsum'tiver Testa'mentserbe.
pro·por·tion [prə'pɔ:ʃn] **I** *s.* **1.** (richtiges) Verhältnis; Gleich-, Ebenmaß *n*; *pl.* (Aus)Maße *pl.*, Größenverhältnisse *pl.*, Dimensi'onen *pl.*, Proporti'onen *pl.*: ***in*** ~ ***as*** in dem Maße wie, je nachdem wie; ***in*** ~ ***to*** im Verhältnis zu; ***be out of*** (***all***) ~ ***to*** in keinem Verhältnis stehen zu; ***sense of*** ~ *fig.* Augenmaß *n*; **2.** *fig.* a) Ausmaß *n*, Größe *f*, Umfang *m*, b) Symmet'rie *f*, Harmo'nie *f*; **3.** ✗, ⚗ Proporti'on *f*; **4.** ✗ a) Dreisatz(rechnung *f*) *m*, *obs.* Regelde'tri *f*, b) *a.* ***geometric*** ~ Verhältnisgleichheit *f*; **5.** Anteil *m*, Teil *m*: ***in*** ~ anteilig; **II** *v/t.* **6.** (***to***) in das richtige Verhältnis bringen (mit, zu), anpassen (*dat.*); **7.** verhältnismäßig verteilen; **8.** proportionieren, bemessen; **9.** sym'metrisch gestalten: ***well-~d*** ebenmäßig, wohlgestaltet; **pro'por·tion·al** [-ʃənl] **I** *adj.* □ **1.** proportio'nal, verhältnismäßig; anteilmäßig: ~ ***numbers*** ✗ Proportionalzahlen *pl.*; ~ ***representation*** *pol.* Verhältniswahl(system *n*) *f*; **2.** → ***proportionate***; **II** *s.* **3.** ✗ Proportio'nale *f*; **pro'por·tion·ate** [-ʃnət] *adj.* □ (***to***) im richtigen Verhältnis (stehend) (zu), angemessen (*dat.*), entsprechend (*dat.*): ~ ***share*** ✝ Verhältnisanteil *m*, anteilmäßige Befriedigung.
pro·pos·al [prə'pəʊzl] *s.* **1.** Vorschlag *m*, (*a.* ✝, *a. Friedens*)Angebot *n*, (*a.* Heirats)Antrag *m*; **2.** Plan *m*; **pro·pose** [prə'pəʊz] **I** *v/t.* **1.** vorschlagen (***s.th. to s.o.*** j-m et., ***s.o. for*** j-n zu *od.* als); **2.** *Antrag* stellen; *Resolution* einbringen; *Mißtrauensvotum* stellen *od.* beantragen; **3.** *Rätsel* aufgeben; *Frage* stellen; **4.** beabsichtigen, sich vornehmen; **5.** e-n Toast ausbringen auf (*acc.*), auf *et.* trinken; **II** *v/i.* **6.** beabsichtigen, vorhaben; planen: ***man*** ~***s*** (***but***) ***God disposes*** der Mensch denkt, Gott lenkt; **7.** e-n Heiratsantrag machen (***to*** *dat.*),

anhalten (***for*** um *j-n, j-s Hand*); **pro'pos·er** [-zə] *s. pol.* Antragsteller *m*; **prop·o·si·tion** [ˌprɒpə'zɪʃn] **I** *s.* **1.** Vorschlag *m*, Antrag *m*; **2.** (vorgeschlagener) Plan, Pro'jekt *n*; **3.** † Angebot *n*; **4.** Behauptung *f*; **5.** F a) Sache *f*, b) Geschäft *n*: ***an easy ~*** ‚kleine Fische', Kleinigkeit *f*; **6.** *phls.* Satz *m*; **7.** Å (Lehr)Satz *m*; **II** *v/t.* **8.** *j-m* e-n Vorschlag machen; **9.** *e-m Mädchen* e-n unsittlichen Antrag machen.

pro·pound [prə'paʊnd] *v/t.* **1.** *Frage etc.* vorlegen, -tragen (***to*** *dat.*); **2.** vorschlagen; **3.** ***~ a will*** ⚖ auf Anerkennung e-s Testaments klagen.

pro·pri·e·tar·y [prə'praɪətərɪ] **I** *adj.* **1.** Eigentums…(-*recht etc.*), Vermögens…; **2.** Eigentümer…, Besitzer…: ***~ company*** † a) *Am.* Holding-, Dachgesellschaft *f*, b) *Brit.* Familiengesellschaft *f*; ***the ~ classes*** die besitzenden Schichten; **3.** gesetzlich geschützt (*Arznei, Ware*): ***~ article*** Markenartikel *m*; ***~ name*** Markenbezeichnung *f*; **II** *s.* **4.** Eigentümer *m od. pl.*; **5.** ⚕ a) medi'zinischer 'Markenarˌtikel, b) nicht re'zeptpflichtiges Medika'ment; **pro·pri·e·tor** [prə'praɪətə] *s.* Eigentümer *m*, Besitzer *m*, (Geschäfts)Inhaber *m*, Anteilseigner *m*, Gesellschafter *m*: ***~s' capital*** Eigenkapital *n e-r Gesellschaft*; ***sole ~*** a) Alleininhaber(in), b) † *Am.* Einzelkaufmann *m*; **pro'pri·e·tor·ship** [-təʃɪp] *s.* **1.** Eigentum(srecht) *n* (***in*** an *dat.*); **2.** Verlagsrecht *n*; **3.** *Bilanz*: 'Eigenkapiˌtal *n*; **4.** ***sole ~*** a) al'leiniges Eigentumsrecht, b) † *Am.* 'Einzelunterˌnehmen *n*; **pro'pri·e·tress** [-trɪs] *s.* Eigentümerin *f etc.*; **pro'pri·e·ty** [-tɪ] *s.* **1.** Schicklichkeit *f*, Anstand *m*; **2.** *pl.* Anstandsformen *pl.*; **3.** Angemessenheit *f*, Richtigkeit *f*.

props [prɒps] *s. pl. thea. sl.* **1.** Requi'siten *pl.*; **2.** *sg. konstr.* Requisi'teur *m*.

pro·pul·sion [prə'pʌlʃn] *s.* **1.** ⚙ Antrieb *m* (*a. fig.*), Antriebskraft *f*: ***~ nozzle*** Rückstoßdüse *f*; **2.** Fortbewegung *f*; **pro'pul·sive** [-lsɪv] *adj.* (an-, vorwärts-) treibend (*a. fig.*): ***~ force*** Triebkraft *f*; ***~ jet*** Treibstrahl *m*.

pro ra·ta [ˌprəʊ'rɑːtə] (*Lat.*) *adj. u. adv.* verhältnis-, anteilmäßig, pro 'rata; **pro-rate** ['prəʊreɪt] *Am v/t.* anteilmäßig ver-, aufteilen.

pro·ro·ga·tion [ˌprəʊrə'geɪʃn] *s. pol.* Vertagung *f*; **pro·rogue** [prə'rəʊg] *v/t. u. v/i.* (sich) vertagen.

pro·sa·ic [prəʊ'zeɪk] *adj.* (□ ***~ally***) *fig.* pro'saisch: a) all'täglich, b) nüchtern, trocken, c) langweilig.

pro·sce·ni·um [prəʊ'siːnjəm] *pl.* **-ni·a** [-njə] *s. thea.* Pro'szenium *n*.

pro·scribe [prəʊ'skraɪb] *v/t.* **1.** ächten, für vogelfrei erklären; **2.** *mst fig.* verbannen; **3.** *fig.* a) verurteilen, b) verbieten; **pro'scrip·tion** [-'skrɪpʃn] *s.* **1.** Ächtung *f*, Acht *f*, Proskripti'on *f* (*mst hist.*); **2.** Verbannung *f*; **3.** *fig.* Verurteilung *f*, Verbot *n*; **pro'scrip·tive** [-'skrɪptɪv] *adj.* □ **1.** Ächtungs…, ächtend; **2.** verbietend, Verbots…

prose [prəʊz] **I** *s.* **1.** Prosa *f*; **2.** *fig.* Prosa *f*, Nüchternheit *f*, All'täglichkeit *f*; **3.** *ped.* Über'setzung *f in die Fremdsprache*; **II** *adj.* **4.** Prosa…: ***~ writer*** Prosaschriftsteller(in); **5.** *fig.* pro'saisch; **III** *v/t. u. v/i.* **6.** in Prosa schreiben; **7.** langweilig erzählen.

pros·e·cute ['prɒsɪkjuːt] **I** *v/t.* **1.** *Plan etc.* verfolgen, weiterführen: ***~ an action*** ⚖ e-n Prozeß führen; **2.** *Gewerbe, Studien etc.* betreiben; **3.** *Untersuchung* 'durchführen; **4.** ⚖ a) strafrechtlich verfolgen, b) gerichtlich verfolgen, belangen, anklagen (***for*** wegen), c) *Forderung* einklagen; **II** *v/i.* **5.** gerichtlich vorgehen; **6.** ⚖ als Kläger auftreten, die Anklage vertreten: ***prosecuting counsel*** (*Am.* ***attorney***) → ***prosecutor***; **pros·e·cu·tion** [ˌprɒsɪ'kjuːʃn] *s.* **1.** Verfolgung *f*, Fortsetzung *f*, 'Durchführung *f e-s Plans etc.*; **2.** Betreiben *n e-s Gewerbes etc.*; **3.** ⚖ a) strafrechtliche Verfolgung, Strafverfolgung *f*, b) Einklagen *n e-r Forderung etc.*: ***liable to ~*** strafbar; ***Director of Public ~s*** Leiter *m* der Anklagebehörde; **4.** ***the ~*** ⚖ die Staatsanwaltschaft, die Anklage(behörde); → ***witness*** 1; **'pros·e·cu·tor** [-tə] *s.* ⚖ (An)Kläger *m*, Anklagevertreter *m*: ***public ~*** Staatsanwalt *m*.

pros·e·lyte ['prɒsɪlaɪt] *s. eccl.* Prose'lyt (-in), Konver'tit(in), *a. fig.* Neubekehrte(r *m*) *f*; **'pros·e·lyt·ism** [-lɪtɪzəm] *s.* Prosely'tismus *m*: a) Bekehrungseifer *m*, b) Prose'lytentum *n*; **'pros·e·lyt·ize** [-lɪtaɪz] **I** *v/t.* (***to***) bekehren (zu), *fig. a.* gewinnen (für); **II** *v/i.* Anhänger gewinnen.

pros·i·ness ['prəʊzɪnɪs] *s.* **1.** Eintönigkeit *f*, Langweiligkeit *f*; **2.** Weitschweifigkeit *f*.

pros·o·dy ['prɒsədɪ] *s.* Proso'die *f* (*Silbenmessungslehre*).

pros·pect I *s.* ['prɒspekt] **1.** (Aus)Sicht *f*, (-)Blick *m* (***of*** auf *acc.*); **2.** *fig.* Aussicht *f*: ***hold out a ~ of*** *et.* in Aussicht stellen; ***have s.th. in ~*** auf et. Aussicht haben, et. in Aussicht haben; **3.** *fig.* Vor('aus)schau *f* (***of*** auf *acc.*); **4.** † *etc.* Interes'sent *m*, Reflek'tant *m*; † möglicher Kunde; **5.** ⚒ a) (*Erz- etc.*) Anzeichen *n*, b) Schürfprobe *f*, c) Schürfstelle *f*; **II** *v/t.* [prə'spekt] **6.** *Gebiet* durch'forschen, unter'suchen (***for*** nach *Gold etc.*); **III** *v/i.* [prə'spekt] **7.** (***for***) ⚒ suchen (nach, *a. fig.*), schürfen (nach); (nach *Öl*) bohren; **pro·spec·tive** [prə'spektɪv] *adj.* □ **1.** (zu)künftig, vor'aussichtlich, in Aussicht stehend, potenti'ell: ***~ buyer*** Kaufinteressent *m*, potentieller Käufer; **2.** *fig.* vor'ausschauend; **pros·pec·tor** [prə'spektə] *s.* Pro'spektor *m*, Schürfer *m*, Goldsucher *m*; **pro·spec·tus** [prə'spektəs] *s.* Pro'spekt *m*: a) Werbeschrift *f*, b) † Subskripti'onsanzeige *f*, c) *Brit.* 'Schulproˌspekt *m*.

pros·per ['prɒspə] **I** *v/i.* Erfolg haben (***in*** bei); gedeihen, florieren, blühen (*Unternehmen etc.*); **II** *v/t.* begünstigen, *j-m* hold *od.* gewogen sein; segnen, *j-m* gnädig sein (*Gott*); **pros·per·i·ty** [prɒ'sperətɪ] *s.* **1.** Wohlstand *m* (*a.* †), Gedeihen *n*, Glück *n*; **2.** † Prosperi'tät *f*, Blüte(zeit) *f*, (*a.* ***peak ~*** 'Hoch)Konjunkˌtur *f*; **'pros·per·ous** [-pərəs] *adj.* □ **1.** gedeihend, blühend, erfolgreich, glücklich; **2.** wohlhabend, Wohlstands…; **3.** günstig (*Wind etc.*).

pros·tate (gland) ['prɒsteɪt] *s. anat.* Prostata *f*, Vorsteherdrüse *f*.

pros·the·sis ['prɒsθɪsɪs] *pl.* **-ses** [-siːz] *s.* **1.** ⚕ Pro'these *f*, künstliches Glied; **2.** ⚕ Anfertigung *f* e-r Pro'these; **3.** *ling.* Pros'these *f* (*Vorsetzen e-s Buchstabens od. e-r Silbe vor ein Wort*).

pros·ti·tute ['prɒstɪtjuːt] **I** *s.* **1.** a) Prostituierte *f*, b) *a.* ***male ~*** Strichjunge *m*; **II** *v/t.* **2.** prostituieren: ***to ~ o.s.*** sich prostituieren *od.* verkaufen (*a. fig.*); **3.** *fig.* (für ehrlose Zwecke) her-, preisgeben, entwürdigen, *Talente etc.* wegwerfen; **pros·ti·tu·tion** [prɒstɪ'tjuːʃn] *s.* **1.** Prostituti'on *f*; **2.** *fig.* Her'ab-, Entwürdigung *f*.

pros·trate I *v/t.* [prɒ'streɪt] **1.** zu Boden werfen *od.* strecken, niederwerfen; **2.** ***~ o.s.*** *fig.* sich in den Staub werfen, sich demütigen (***before*** vor); **3.** entkräften, erschöpfen; *fig.* niederschmettern; **II** *adj.* ['prɒstreɪt] **4.** hingestreckt; **5.** *fig.* erschöpft (***with*** vor *dat.*), da'niederliegend, kraftlos; *weitS.* gebrochen (***with grief*** vom Gram); **6.** *fig.* a) demütig, b) fußfällig, im Staube liegend; **pros'tra·tion** [-eɪʃn] *s.* **1.** Fußfall *m* (*a. fig.*); **2.** *fig.* Niederwerfung *f*; Demütigung *f*; **3.** Erschöpfung, Entkräftung *f*; **4.** *fig.* Niedergeschlagenheit *f*.

pros·y ['prəʊzɪ] *adj.* □ **1.** langweilig, weitschweifig; **2.** nüchtern, pro'saisch.

pro·tag·o·nist [prəʊ'tægənɪst] *s.* **1.** *thea.* 'Hauptfiˌgur *f*, Held(in), Träger(in) der Handlung; **2.** *fig.* Vorkämpfer(in).

pro·te·an [prəʊ'tiːən] *adj.* **1.** *fig.* pro'teisch, vielgestaltig; **2.** *zo.* a'möbenartig: ***~ animalcule*** Amöbe *f*.

pro·tect [prə'tekt] *v/t.* **1.** (be)schützen (***from*** vor *dat.*, ***against*** gegen): ***~ interests*** Interessen wahren; **2.** † (durch Zölle) schützen; **3.** † a) *Sichtwechsel* honorieren, einlösen, b) *Wechsel mit Laufzeit* schützen; **4.** ⚙ (ab)sichern, abschirmen; *weitS.* schonen: ***~ed against corrosion*** korrosionsgeschützt; ***~ed motor*** ⚡ geschützter Motor; **5.** ⚔ (taktisch) sichern, abschirmen; **6.** *Schach*: *Figur* decken; **pro'tec·tion** [-kʃn] *s.* **1.** Schutz *m*, Beschützung *f* (***from*** vor *dat.*); Sicherheit *f*: ***~ of interests*** Interessenwahrung *f*; (***legal***) ***~ of registered designs*** ⚖ Gebrauchsmusterschutz *m*; ***~ of industrial property*** gewerblicher Rechtsschutz; **2.** † Wirtschaftsschutz *m*, 'Schutzzoll (-poliˌtik *f*, -syˌstem *n*) *m*; **3.** † Honorierung *f e-s Wechsels*: ***find due ~*** honoriert werden; **4.** Protekti'on *f*, Gönnerschaft *f*, Förderung *f*: ***~ (money)*** *Am.* ‚Schutzgebühr' *f*; **5.** ⚙ Schutz *m*, Abschirmung *f*; **pro'tec·tion·ism** [-kʃənɪzəm] *s.* † 'Schutzzollpoliˌtik *f*; **pro'tec·tion·ist** [-kʃənɪst] **I** *s.* **1.** Protektio'nist *m*, Verfechter *m* der Schutzzollpolitik; **2.** Na'turschützer *m*; **II** *adj.* **3.** protektio'nistisch, Schutzzoll…; **pro'tec·tive** [-tɪv] *adj.* □ **1.** (be)schützend, schutzgewährend, Schutz…: ***~ conveyance*** ⚖ Sicherungsübereignung *f*; ***~ custody*** ⚖ Schutzhaft *f*; ***~ duty*** † Schutzzoll *m*; ***~ goggles*** Schutzbrille *f*; **2.** † Schutzzoll…; **3.** beschützerisch; **pro'tec·tor** [-tə] *s.* **1.** Beschützer *m*, Schutz-, Schirmherr *m*, Gönner *m*; **2.** ⚙ *etc.* Schutz(vorrichtung *f*, -mittel *n*) *m*, Schützer *m*, Schoner *m*; **3.** *hist.* Pro'tektor *m*, Reichsverweser *m*; **pro'tec·tor·ate** [-tərət] *s.* Protekto'rat *n*: a) Schutzherrschaft *f*, b) Schutzgebiet *n*; **pro'tec·tress** [-trɪs] *s.* Beschützerin *f*,

Schutz-, Schirmherrin *f.*

pro·té·gé ['prəʊteʒeɪ] (*Fr.*) *s.* Schützling *m*, Prote'gé *m.*

pro·te·in ['prəʊtiːn] *s. biol.* Prote'in *n*, Eiweiß(körper *m od. pl.*) *n.*

pro·test I *s.* ['prəʊtest] **1.** Pro'test *m*, Ein-, 'Widerspruch *m*: ***in ~, as a ~*** aus (*od.* als) Protest; ***enter*** (*od.* ***lodge***) ***a ~*** Protest erheben *od.* Verwahrung einlegen (***with*** bei); ***accept under ~*** unter Vorbehalt *od.* Protest annehmen; **2.** ✝, ⚖ ('Wechsel)Pro,test *m*; **3.** ⚓, ⚖ 'See-pro,test *m*, Verklarung *f*; **II** *v/i.* [prə'test] **4.** protestieren, Verwahrung einlegen, sich verwahren (***against*** gegen); **III** *v/t.* [prə'test] **5.** protestieren gegen, reklamieren; **6.** beteuern (***s.th.*** et., ***that*** daß): ***~ one's loyalty***; **7.** ✝ *Wechsel* protestieren: ***have a bill ~ed*** e-n Wechsel zu Protest gehen lassen.

Prot·es·tant ['prɒtɪstənt] **I** *s.* Prote'stant (-in); **II** *adj.* prote'stantisch; '**Prot·es·tant·ism** [-tɪzəm] *s.* Protestan'tismus *m.*

prot·es·ta·tion [,prəʊte'steɪʃn] *s.* **1.** Beteuerung *f*; **2.** Pro'test *m.*

pro·to·col ['prəʊtəkɒl] **I** *s.* **1.** (Ver'handlungs)Proto,koll *n*; **2.** *pol.* Proto'koll *n*: a) *diplomatische Etikette*, b) *kleineres Vertragswerk*; **3.** *pol.* Einleitungs- u. Schlußformeln *pl. e-r Urkunde etc.*; **II** *v/t. u. v/i.* **4.** protokollieren.

pro·ton ['prəʊtɒn] *s. phys.* Proton *n.*

pro·to·plasm ['prəʊtəʊplæzəm] *s. biol.* **1.** Proto'plasma *n* (*Zellsubstanz*); **2.** Urschleim *m*; '**pro·to·plast** [-plæst] *s. biol.* Proto'plast *m.*

pro·to·type ['prəʊtəʊtaɪp] *s.* Proto'typ *m* (*a. biol.*): a) Urbild *n*, -typ *m*, -form *f*, b) (Ur)Muster *n*; ⚙ ('Richt)Mo,dell *n*, Ausgangsbautyp *m.*

pro·to·zo·on [,prəʊtəʊ'zəʊən] *pl.* **-'zo·a** [-'zəʊə] *s. zo.* Proto'zoon *n*, Urtierchen *n*, Einzeller *m.*

pro·tract [prə'trækt] *v/t.* **1.** in die Länge (*od.* hinaus)ziehen, verschleppen: ***~ed illness*** langwierige Krankheit; ***~ed defence*** ⚔ hinhaltende Verteidigung; **2.** A mit e-m Winkelmesser *od.* maßstabsgetreu zeichnen *od.* auftragen; **pro'trac·tion** [-kʃn] *s.* **1.** Hin'ausschieben *n*, -ziehen *n*, Verschleppen *n* (*a.* ⚕); **2.** A maßstabsgetreue Zeichnung; **pro'trac·tor** [-tə] *s.* **1.** A Transpor'teur *m*, Gradbogen *m*, Winkelmesser *m*; **2.** *anat.* Streckmuskel *m.*

pro·trude [prə'truːd] **I** *v/i.* her'aus-, (her)'vorstehen, -ragen, -treten; **II** *v/t.* her'ausstrecken, (her)'vortreten lassen; **pro'tru·sion** [-uːʒn] *s.* **1.** Her'vorstehen *n*, -treten *n*, Vorspringen *n*; **2.** Vorwölbung *f*, (her)'vorstehender Teil; **pro'tru·sive** [-uːsɪv] *adj.* □ vorstehend, her'vortretend.

pro·tu·ber·ance [prə'tjuːbərəns] *s.* **1.** Auswuchs *m*, Beule *f*, Höcker *m*; **2.** *ast.* Protube'ranz *f*; **3.** (Her)'Vortreten *n*, -stehen *n*; **pro'tu·ber·ant** [-nt] *adj.* □ (her)'vorstehend, -tretend, -quellend (*a. Augen*).

proud [praʊd] **I** *adj.* □ **1.** stolz (***of*** auf *acc.*, ***to*** *inf.* zu *inf.*): ***a ~ day*** *fig.* ein stolzer Tag *für uns etc.*; **2.** hochmütig, eingebildet; **3.** *fig.* stolz, prächtig; **4.** ***~ flesh*** ⚕ wildes Fleisch; **II** *adv.* **5.** F stolz: ***do s.o. ~*** a) j-m große Ehre erweisen, b) j-n königlich bewirten; ***do o.s. ~*** a) stolz auf sich sein können, b) es sich gutgehen lassen.

prov·a·ble ['pruːvəbl] *adj.* □ be-, nachweisbar, erweislich; **prove** [pruːv] **I** *v/t.* **1.** er-, nach-, beweisen, **2.** ⚖ *Testament* bestätigen (lassen); **3.** bekunden, unter Beweis stellen, zeigen; **4.** (*a.* ⚙) prüfen, erproben: ***a ~d remedy*** ein erprobtes *od.* bewährtes Mittel; ***~ o.s.*** a) sich bewähren, b) sich erweisen als; → ***proving*** 1; **5.** A die Probe machen auf (*acc.*); **II** *v/i.* **6.** sich her'ausstellen *od.* erweisen (als): ***he will ~*** (***to be***) ***the heir*** es wird sich herausstellen, daß er der Erbe ist; ***~ true*** (***false***) a) sich als richtig (falsch) herausstellen, b) sich (nicht) bestätigen (*Voraussage etc.*); **7.** ausfallen, sich ergeben; '**prov·en** [-vən] *adj.* be-, erwiesen, nachgewiesen; *fig.* bewährt.

prov·e·nance ['prɒvənəns] *s.* Herkunft *f*, Ursprung *m*, Proveni'enz *f.*

prov·en·der ['prɒvɪndə] *s.* **1.** ⚘ (Trokken)Futter *n*; **2.** F *humor.* ‚Futter' *n* (*Lebensmittel*).

prov·erb ['prɒvɜːb] **1.** *s.* Sprichwort *n*: ***he is a ~ for shrewdness*** s-e Schläue ist sprichwörtlich (*b.s.* berüchtigt); **2.** (***The Book of***) ***℞s*** *pl. bibl.* die Sprüche *pl.* (Salo'monis); **pro·ver·bi·al** [prə'vɜːbjəl] *adj.* □ sprichwörtlich (*a. fig.*).

pro·vide [prə'vaɪd] **I** *v/t.* **1.** versehen, -sorgen, ausstatten, beliefern (***with*** mit); **2.** ver-, beschaffen, besorgen, liefern; zur Verfügung (*od.* bereit)stellen; *Gelegenheit* schaffen; **3.** ⚖ vorsehen, -schreiben, bestimmen (*a. Gesetze, Vertrag etc.*); **II** *v/i.* **4.** Vorsorge *od.* Vorkehrungen treffen, vorsorgen, sich sichern (***against*** vor *dat.*, gegen): ***~ against*** a) sich schützen vor (*dat.*), b) *et.* unmöglich machen, verhindern; ***~ for*** a) sorgen für (*j-s Lebensunterhalt*), b) *Maßnahmen* vorsehen, *e-r Sache* Rechnung tragen, *Bedürfnisse* befriedigen, *Gelder etc.* bereitstellen; **5.** ⚖ den Vorbehalt machen (***that*** daß): ***unless otherwise ~d*** sofern nichts Gegenteiliges bestimmt ist; ***providing*** (***that***) → **pro'vid·ed** [-dɪd] *cj. a.* ***~ that* 1.** vor'ausgesetzt (daß), unter der Bedingung, daß; **2.** wenn, so'fern.

prov·i·dence ['prɒvɪdəns] *s.* **1.** (göttliche) Vorsehung; **2.** ***the ℞*** die Vorsehung, Gott *m*; **3.** Vorsorge *f*, (weise) Vor'aussicht; '**prov·i·dent** [-nt] *adj.* □ **1.** vor'ausblickend, vor-, fürsorglich: ***~ bank*** Sparkasse *f*; ***~ fund*** Unterstützungskasse *f*; ***~ society*** Versicherungsverein *m* auf Gegenseitigkeit; **2.** haushälterisch, sparsam; **prov·i·den·tial** [,prɒvɪ'denʃl] *adj.* □ **1.** schicksalhaft; **2.** glücklich, gnädig (*Geschick etc.*).

pro·vid·er [prə'vaɪdə] *s.* **1.** Versorger (-in), Ernährer *m*: ***good ~*** F treusorgende(r) Mutter (Vater); **2.** Liefe'rant *m.*

prov·ince ['prɒvɪns] *s.* **1.** Pro'vinz *f* (*a. Ggs. Stadt*), Bezirk *m*; **2.** *fig.* a) (Wissens)Gebiet *n*, Fach *n*, b) (Aufgaben-) Bereich *m*, Amt *n*: ***it is not within my ~*** a) es schlägt nicht in mein Fach, b) es ist nicht m-s Amtes (***to*** *inf.* zu *inf.*).

pro·vin·cial [prə'vɪnʃl] **I** *adj.* □ **1.** Provinz…, provinzi'ell (*a. fig. engstirnig, spießbürgerlich*): ***~ town***; **2.** provinzi'ell, ländlich, kleinstädtisch; **3.** *fig. contp.* pro'vinzlerisch (*ungebildet, plump*); **II** *s.* **4.** Pro'vinzbewohner(in); *contp.* Pro'vinzler(in); **pro'vin·cial·ism** [-ʃəlɪzəm] *s.* Provinzia'lismus *m* (*a. mundartlicher Ausdruck, a. contp. Kleingeisterei, Lokalpatriotismus, Plumpheit*); *contp.* Pro'vinzlertum *n.*

prov·ing ['pruːvɪŋ] *s.* **1.** Prüfen *n*, Erprobung *f*: ***~ flight*** Probe-, Erprobungsflug *m*; ***~ ground*** Versuchsgelände *n*; **2.** ***~ of a will*** ⚖ Eröffnung *f* u. Bestätigung *f* e-s Testaments.

pro·vi·sion [prə'vɪʒn] **I** *s.* **1.** a) Vorkehrung *f*, -sorge *f*, Maßnahme *f*, b) Vor-, Einrichtung *f*: ***make ~*** sorgen *od.* Vorkehrungen treffen (***for*** für), sich schützen (***against*** vor *dat. od.* gegen); **2.** ⚖ Bestimmung *f*, Vorschrift *f*: ***come within the ~s of the law*** unter die gesetzlichen Bestimmungen fallen; **3.** ⚖ Bedingung *f*, Vorbehalt *m*; **4.** Beschaffung *f*, Besorgung *f*, Bereitstellung *f*; **5.** *pl.* (Lebensmittel)Vorräte *pl.*, Vorrat *m* (***of*** an *dat.*), Nahrungsmittel *pl.*, Provi'ant *m*: ***~s dealer*** (*od.* ***merchant***) Lebensmittel-, Feinkosthändler *m*; ***~s industry*** Nahrungsmittelindustrie *f*; **6.** *oft pl.* Rückstellungen *pl.*, -lagen *pl.*, Re'serven *pl.*: ***~ for taxes*** Steuerrückstellungen *pl.*; **II** *v/t.* **7.** mit Lebensmitteln versehen, verproviantieren; **pro'vi·sion·al** [-ʒənl] *adj.* □ provi'sorisch, einstweilig, behelfsmäßig: ***~ agreement*** Vorvertrag *m*; ***~ arrangement*** Provisorium *n*; ***~ receipt*** Interimsquittung *f*; ***~ regulations*** Übergangsbestimmungen; ***~ result*** *sport* vorläufiges *od.* inoffizielles Endergebnis.

pro·vi·so [prə'vaɪzəʊ] *s.* ⚖ Vorbehalt *m*, (Bedingungs)Klausel *f*, Bedingung *f*: ***~ clause*** Vorbehaltsklausel *f*; **pro'vi·so·ry** [-zərɪ] *adj.* □ **1.** bedingend, bedingt, vorbehaltlich; **2.** provi'sorisch, vorläufig.

pro·vo ['prəʊvəʊ] *s. Mitglied der provisorischen irisch-republikanischen Armee.*

prov·o·ca·tion [,prɒvə'keɪʃn] *s.* **1.** Her'ausforderung *f*, Provokati'on *f* (*a.* ⚖); **2.** Aufreizung *f*, Erregung *f*; **3.** Verärgerung *f*, Ärger *m*: ***at the slightest ~*** beim geringsten Anlaß; **pro·voc·a·tive** [prə'vɒkətɪv] **I** *adj.* (*a.* zum 'Widerspruch) her'ausfordernd, aufreizend (***of*** zu), provozierend; **II** *s.* Reiz(mittel *n*) *m*, Antrieb *m* (***of*** zu).

pro·voke [prə'vəʊk] *v/t.* provozieren: a) erzürnen, aufbringen, b) *et.* her'vorrufen, *Gefühl a.* erregen, c) *j-n* (auf)reizen, her'ausfordern: ***~ s.o. to do s.th.*** j-n dazu bewegen, et. zu tun; **pro'vok·ing** [-kɪŋ] *adj.* □ **1.** → ***provocative*** I; **2.** unerträglich, unausstehlich.

prov·ost ['prɒvəst] *s.* **1.** Vorsteher *m* (*a. univ. Brit. e-s College*); **2.** *Scot.* Bürgermeister *m*; **3.** *eccl.* Propst *m*; **4.** [prə'vəʊ] ⚔ Pro'fos *m*, Offi'zier *m* der Mili'tärpoli,zei; ***~ mar·shal*** [prə'vəʊ] *s.* ⚔ Komman'deur *m* der Mili'tärpoli,zei.

prow [praʊ] *s.* ⚓, ✈ Bug *m.*

prow·ess ['praʊɪs] *s.* **1.** Tapferkeit *f*, Kühnheit *f*; **2.** über'ragendes Können, Tüchtigkeit *f.*

prowl [praʊl] **I** *v/i.* um'herschleichen, -streichen; **II** *v/t.* durch'streifen; **III** *s.* Um'herstreifen *n*, Streife *f*: ***be on the ~***

→ I; ~ ***car*** *Am.* (Polizei)Streifenwagen *m*; **ˈprowl·er** [-lə] *s.* Herˈumtreiber *m*.

prox·i·mal [ˈprɒksɪml] *adj.* ☐ *anat.* proxiˈmal, körpernah; **ˈprox·i·mate** [-mət] *adj.* ☐ **1.** nächst, folgend, (sich) unmittelbar (anschließend): ~ ***cause*** unmittelbare Ursache; **2.** naheliegend; **3.** annähernd; **prox·im·i·ty** [prɒkˈsɪmətɪ] *s.* Nähe *f*: ~ ***fuse*** ⚔ Annäherungszünder *m*; **ˈprox·i·mo** [-məʊ] *adv.* (des) nächsten Monats.

prox·y [ˈprɒksɪ] *s.* **1.** (Stell)Vertretung *f*, (Handlungs)Vollmacht *f*: ***by*** ~ in Vertretung (→ 2); ***marriage by*** ~ Ferntrauung *f*; **2.** (Stell)Vertreter(in), Bevollmächtigte(r *m*) *f*: ***by*** ~ durch e-n Bevollmächtigten; ***stand*** ~ ***for s.o.*** als Stellvertreter fungieren für j-n; **3.** Vollmacht(surkunde) *f*.

prude [pru:d] *s.* prüder Mensch: ***be a*** ~ prüde sein.

pru·dence [ˈpru:dəns] *s.* **1.** Klugheit *f*, Vernunft *f*; **2.** ˈUm-, Vorsicht *f*, Überˈlegtheit *f*: ***ordinary*** ~ ⚖ die im Verkehr erforderliche Sorgfalt; **ˈpru·dent** [-nt] *adj.* ☐ **1.** klug, vernünftig; **2.** ˈum-, vorsichtig, besonnen; **pru·den·tial** [prʊˈdenʃl] *adj.* ☐ a) → ***prudent***, b) sachverständig: ***for*** ~ ***reasons*** aus Gründen praktischer Überlegung.

prud·er·y [ˈpru:dərɪ] *s.* Prüdeˈrie *f*; **ˈprud·ish** [-dɪʃ] *adj.* ☐ prüde.

prune¹ [pru:n] *s.* **1.** (*a.* Back)Pflaume *f*; **2.** *sl.* ‚Blödmann' *m*.

prune² [pru:n] *v/t.* **1.** *Bäume etc.* (aus-)putzen, beschneiden; **2.** *a.* ~ ***off***, ~ ***away*** wegschneiden; **3.** *fig.* zu(ˈrecht-)stutzen, befreien (***of*** von), säubern, *Text etc.* zs.-streichen, straffen, kürzen, *Überflüssiges* entfernen.

pru·nel·la¹ [prʊˈnelə] *s.* ✝ Pruˈnell *m*, Lasting *m* (*Gewebe*).

pru·nel·la² [prʊˈnelə] *s.* ⚕ *obs.* Halsbräune *f*.

pru·nelle [prʊˈnel] *s.* Prüˈnelle *f* (*getrocknete entkernte Pflaume*).

pru·nel·lo [prʊˈneləʊ] → ***prunelle***.

prun·ing| knife [ˈpru:nɪŋ] *s.* [*irr.*] Gartenmesser *n*; ~ **shears** *s. pl.* Baumschere *f*.

pru·ri·ence [ˈprʊərɪəns], **ˈpru·ri·en·cy** [-sɪ] *s.* **1.** Geilheit *f*, Lüsternheit *f*; (Sinnen)Kitzel *m*; **2.** Gier *f* (***for*** nach); **ˈpru·ri·ent** [-nt] *adj.* ☐ geil, lüstern, lasˈziv.

Prus·sian [ˈprʌʃn] **I** *adj.* preußisch; **II** *s.* Preuße *m*, Preußin *f*; ~ **blue** *s.* Preußischblau *n*.

prus·si·ate [ˈprʌʃɪət] *s.* ⚗ Prussiˈat *n*; ~ **of pot·ash** *s.* ⚗ ˈKaliumferrocyaˌnid *n*.

prus·sic ac·id [ˈprʌsɪk] *s.* ⚗ Blausäure *f*, Zyˈanwasserstoff(säure *f*) *m*.

pry¹ [praɪ] *v/i.* neugierig gucken *od.* sein, (***about*** herˈum)spähen, (-)schnüffeln: ~ ***into*** a) *et.* zu erforschen suchen, b) *contp.* s-e Nase stecken in (*acc.*).

pry² [praɪ] **I** *v/t.* **1.** *a.* ~ ***open*** *mit e-m Hebel etc.* aufbrechen, -stemmen: ~ ***up*** hochstemmen, -heben; **2.** *fig.* herˈausholen; **II** *s.* **3.** Hebel *m*; Brecheisen *n*; **4.** Hebelwirkung *f*.

pry·ing [ˈpraɪɪŋ] *adj.* ☐ neugierig, naseweis.

psalm [sɑ:m] *s.* Psalm *m*: ***the*** (***Book of***) **℘s** *bibl.* die Psalmen; **ˈpsalm·ist** [-mɪst] *s.* Psalˈmist *m*; **psal·mo·dy** [ˈsælmədɪ] *s.* **1.** Psalmoˈdie *f*, Psalmengesang *m*; **2.** Psalmen *pl.*

Psal·ter [ˈsɔ:ltə] *s.* Psalter *m*, (Buch *n* der) Psalmen *pl.*; **psal·te·ri·um** [sɔ:lˈtɪərɪəm] *pl.* **-ri·a** [-rɪə] *s. zo.* Blättermagen *m*.

pse·phol·o·gy [*p*seˈfɒlədʒɪ] *s.* (wissenschaftliche) Anaˈlyse von Wahlergebnissen u. -trends.

pseudo- [ˈ*p*sju:dəʊ] *in Zssgn* Pseudo…, pseudo…, falsch, unecht; **ˌpseu·do-ˈcarp** [-ˈkɑ:p] *s.* ⚘ Scheinfrucht *f*; **ˈpseu·do·nym** [-dənɪm] *s.* Pseudoˈnym *n*, Deckname *m*; **ˌpseu·doˈnym·i·ty** [-dəˈnɪmətɪ] *s.* **1.** Pseudonymiˈtät *f*; **2.** Führen *n* e-s Pseudoˈnyms; **pseuˈdon·y·mous** [-ˈdɒnɪməs] *adj.* ☐ pseudoˈnym.

pshaw [pʃɔ:] *int.* pah!

psit·ta·co·sis [psɪtəˈkəʊsɪs] *s.* ⚕ Papaˈgeienkrankheit *f*.

pso·ri·a·sis [*p*sɒˈraɪəsɪs] *s.* ⚕ Schuppenflechte *f*, Psoˈriasis *f*.

Psy·che [ˈsaɪkɪ] *s.* **1.** *myth.* Psyche *f*; **2.** ℘ Psyche *f*, Seele *f*, Geist *m*.

psy·che·del·ic [ˌsaɪkɪˈdelɪk] *adj.* psycheˈdelisch, bewußtseinserweiternd.

psy·chi·at·ric, psy·chi·at·ri·cal [ˌsaɪkɪˈætrɪk(l)] *adj.* psychiˈatrisch; **psy·chi·a·trist** [saɪˈkaɪətrɪst] *s.* ⚕ Psychiˈater *m*; **psyˈchi·a·try** [saɪˈkaɪətrɪ] *s.* ⚕ Psychiaˈtrie *f*.

psy·chic [ˈsaɪkɪk] **I** *adj.* (☐ ~***ally***) **1.** psychisch, seelisch(-geistig), Seelen…; **2.** ˈübersinnlich: ~ ***forces***; **3.** mediˈal (veranlagt), F ‚hellseherisch'; **4.** parapsychoˈlogisch: ~ ***research*** Para-Forschung *f*; **II** *s.* **5.** mediˈal veranlagte Perˈson, Medium *n*; **6.** *das* Psychische; **7.** *pl. sg. konstr.* a) Seelenkunde *f*, -forschung *f*, b) Parapsycholoˈgie *f*; **ˈpsy·chi·cal** [-kl] *adj.* ☐ → ***psychic*** I.

psy·cho·a·nal·y·sis [ˌsaɪkəʊəˈnæləsɪs] *s.* ˌPsychoanaˈlyse *f*; **psy·cho·an·a·lyst** [ˌsaɪkəʊˈænəlɪst] *s.* ˌPsychoanaˈlytiker (-in).

psy·cho·graph [ˈsaɪkəʊgrɑ:f] *s.* Psychoˈgramm *n*.

psy·cho·log·ic [ˌsaɪkəˈlɒdʒɪk] → ***psychological***; **ˌpsy·choˈlog·i·cal** [-kl] *adj.* ☐ psychoˈlogisch: ~ ***moment*** richtiger Augenblick; ~ ***warfare*** a) psychologische Kriegführung, b) *fig.* Nervenkrieg *m*; **psy·chol·o·gist** [saɪˈkɒlədʒɪst] *s.* Psychoˈloge *m*, Psychoˈlogin *f*; **psy·chol·o·gy** [saɪˈkɒlədʒɪ] *s.* Psycholoˈgie *f* (*Wissenschaft od. Seelenleben*): ***good*** ~ *fig.* das psychologisch Richtige.

psy·cho·path [ˈsaɪkəʊpæθ] *s.* Psychoˈpath(in); **psy·cho·path·ic** [ˌsaɪkəʊˈpæθɪk] **I** *adj.* psychoˈpathisch; **II** *s.* Psychoˈpath(in); **psy·chop·a·thy** [saɪˈkɒpəθɪ] *s.* Psychopaˈthie *f*, Gemütskrankheit *f*.

psy·cho·sis [saɪˈkəʊsɪs] *pl.* **-ses** [-si:z] *s.* Psyˈchose *f* (*a. fig.*).

psy·cho·ther·a·py [ˌsaɪkəʊˈθerəpɪ] *s.* ⚕ ˌPsychotheraˈpie *f*.

psy·chot·ic [saɪˈkɒtɪk] **I** *adj.* ☐ psyˈchotisch; **II** *s.* Psyˈchotiker(in).

ptar·mi·gan [ˈtɑ:mɪgən] *s. zo.* Schneehuhn *n*.

pto·maine [ˈtəʊmeɪn] *s.* ⚗ Ptomaˈin *n*, Leichengift *n*.

pub [pʌb] *s. bsd. Brit.* F Pub *n od. m*, Kneipe *f*; **ˈ~-crawl** *s. bsd. Brit.* F Kneipenbummel *m*.

pu·ber·ty [ˈpju:bətɪ] *s.* **1.** Puberˈtät *f*, Geschlechtsreife *f*; **2.** *a.* ***age of*** ~ Puberˈtät(salter *n*) *f*: ~ ***vocal change*** Stimmbruch *m*.

pu·bes¹ [ˈpju:bi:z] *s. anat.* a) Schamgegend *f*, b) Schamhaare *pl.*

pu·bes² [ˈpju:bi:z] *pl. von* ***pubis***.

pu·bes·cence [pju:ˈbesns] *s.* **1.** Geschlechtsreife *f*; **2.** ⚘, *zo.* Flaumhaar *n*; **puˈbes·cent** [-nt] *adj.* **1.** geschlechtsreif (werdend); **2.** Pubertäts…; **3.** ⚘, *zo.* fein behaart.

pu·bic [ˈpju:bɪk] *adj. anat.* Scham…

pu·bis [ˈpju:bɪs] *pl.* **-bes** [-bi:z] *s. anat.* Schambein *n*.

pub·lic [ˈpʌblɪk] **I** *adj.* ☐ **1.** öffentlich *stattfindend* (*z.B. Verhandlung*, *Versammlung*, *Versteigerung*): ~ ***notice*** öffentliche Bekanntmachung, Aufgebot *n*; ***in the*** ~ ***eye*** im Lichte der Öffentlichkeit; **2.** öffentlich, allgemein bekannt: ~ ***figure*** Persönlichkeit *f* des öffentlichen Lebens, prominente Gestalt; ***go*** ~ a) sich an die Öffentlichkeit wenden, b) ✝ sich in e-e AG umwandeln; ***make*** ~ (allgemein) bekanntmachen; **3.** a) öffentlich (*z.B. Anstalt*, *Bad*, *Dienst*, *Feiertag*, *Kredit*, *Sicherheit*, *Straße*, *Verkehrsmittel*), b) Staats…, staatlich (*z.B. Anleihe*, *Behörde*, *Papiere*, *Schuld*, *Stellung*), c) Volks… (*-bücherei*, *-gesundheit etc.*), d) Gemeinde…, Stadt…: ~ ***accountant*** *Am.* Wirtschaftsprüfer *m*; ~***-address system*** öffentliche Lautsprecheranlage; ℘ ***Assistance*** *Am.* Sozialhilfe *f*; ~ ***charge*** Sozialhilfeempfänger(in); ~ (***limited***) ***company*** ✝ *Brit.* Aktiengesellschaft; ~ ***convenience*** öffentliche Bedürfnisanstalt; ~ ***corporation*** ⚖ öffentlich-rechtliche Körperschaft; ~ ***economy*** Volkswirtschaft(slehre) *f*; ~ ***enemy*** Staatsfeind *m*; ~ ***house*** *bsd. Brit.* → ***pub***; ~ ***information*** Unterrichtung der Öffentlichkeit; ~ ***law*** öffentliches Recht; ~ ***opinion*** öffentliche Meinung; ~ ***opinion poll*** öffentliche Umfrage, Meinungsbefragung *f*; ~ ***relations*** a) Public Relations *pl.*, Öffentlichkeitsarbeit *f*, b) *attr.* Presse…, Werbe…, Public-Relations-…; ~ ***revenue*** Staatseinkünfte *pl.*; ~ ***school*** a) *Brit.* Public School *f*, höhere Privatschule mit Internat, b) *Am.* staatliche Schule; ~ ***service*** a) Staatsdienst *m*, b) öffentliche Versorgung (*Gas*, *Wasser*, *Elektrizität etc.*); ~ ***servant*** a) (Staats)Beamte(r) *m*, b) Angestellte(r) *m* im öffentlichen Dienst: ~ ***works*** öffentliche (Bau-)Arbeiten; → ***nuisance*** 2, ***policy***¹ 3, ***prosecutor***, ***utility*** 3; **4.** natioˈnal: ~ ***disaster***; **II** *s.* **5.** Öffentlichkeit *f*: ***in*** ~ in der Öffentlichkeit, öffentlich; **6.** *sg. u. pl. konstr.* Öffentlichkeit *f*, *die* Leute *pl.*; *das* Publikum; Kreise *pl.*, Welt *f*: ***appear before the*** ~ an die Öffentlichkeit treten; ***exclude the*** ~ ⚖ die Öffentlichkeit ausschließen; **7.** *Brit.* F → ***pub***; **ˈpub·li·can** [-kən] *s.* **1.** *Brit.* (Gast)Wirt *m*; **2.** *hist.*, *bibl.* Zöllner *m*; **pub·li·ca·tion** [ˌpʌblɪˈkeɪʃn] *s.* **1.** Bekanntmachung *f*, -gabe *f*; **2.** Herˈausgabe *f*, Veröffentlichung *f* (*von Druckwerken*); **3.** Publikatiˈon *f*, Veröffentlichung *f*, Verlagswerk *n*; (Druck)Schrift *f*: ***monthly*** ~ Monatsschrift; ***new*** ~ Neuerscheinung *f*; **ˈpub·li·cist** [-ɪsɪst] *s.* **1.** Publiˈzist *m*, Tagesschriftsteller *m*; **2.** Völkerrechtler *m*; **pub·lic·i·ty** [pʌbˈlɪsətı] *s.* **1.** Publizi'tät *f*, Öffentlichkeit *f* (*a.* ⚖ *des Verfahrens*): *give s.th.* ~ et. allgemein bekanntmachen; ***seek*** ~ bekannt werden wollen; **2.** Re'klame *f*, Werbung *f*, Pu'blicity *f*: ~ ***agent***, ~ ***man*** Werbefachmann *m*; ~ ***campaign*** Werbefeldzug *m*; ~ ***manager*** Werbeleiter *m*; '**pub·li·cize** [-ısaız] *v/t.* **1.** publizieren, (öffentlich) bekanntmachen; **2.** Re'klame machen für, propagieren.

ˌ**pub·lic**|-'**pri·vate** *adj.* ✝ gemischt-wirtschaftlich; ˌ~-'**spir·it·ed** *adj.* gemeinsinnig, sozi'al gesinnt.

pub·lish ['pʌblıʃ] *v/t.* **1.** (offizi'ell) bekanntmachen, -geben; *Aufgebot etc.* verkünd(ig)en; **2.** publizieren, veröffentlichen; **3.** *Buch etc.* verlegen, her'ausbringen: ***just*** ~***ed*** (so)eben erschienen; ~***ed by Methuen*** im Verlag Methuen erschienen; ~***ed by the author*** im Selbstverlag; **4.** ⚖ *Beleidigendes* äußern, verbreiten; '**pub·lish·er** [-ʃə] *s.* **1.** Verleger *m*, Her'ausgeber *m*; *bsd. Am.* Zeitungsverleger *m*; **2.** *pl.* Verlag *m*, Verlagsanstalt *f*; '**pub·lish·ing** [-ʃıŋ] **I** *s.* Her'ausgabe *f*, Verlag *m*; **II** *adj.* Verlags...: ~ ***business*** Verlagsgeschäft *n*, -buchhandel *m*; ~ ***house*** → ***publisher*** 2.

puce [pju:s] *adj.* braunrot.

puck [pʌk] *s.* **1.** Kobold *m*; **2.** *Eishokkey*: Puck *m*, Scheibe *f*.

puck·a ['pʌkə] *adj. Brit.* F **1.** echt, wirklich; **2.** erstklassig, tadellos.

puck·er ['pʌkə] **I** *v/t. oft* ~ ***up*** **1.** runzeln, fälteln, Runzeln *od.* Falten bilden in (*dat.*); **2.** *Mund, Lippen etc.* zs.-ziehen, spitzen; *a. Stirn, Stoff* kräuseln; **II** *v/i.* **3.** sich kräuseln, sich zs.-ziehen, sich falten, Runzeln bilden; **III** *s.* **4.** Runzel *f*, Falte *f*; **5.** Bausch *m*; **6.** F Aufregung *f* (***about*** über *acc.*, wegen).

pud·ding ['pʊdıŋ] *s.* **1.** a) Pudding *m*, b) Nach-, Süßspeise *f*; → ***proof*** 6; **2.** *Art* 'Fleischpaˌstete *f*; **3.** *e-e Wurstsorte*: ***black*** ~ Blutwurst *f*; ***white*** ~ Preßsack *m*; '~-***faced*** *adj.* mit e-m Vollmondgesicht.

pud·dle ['pʌdl] **I** *s.* **1.** Pfütze *f*, Lache *f*; **2.** ⚙ Lehmschlag *m*; **II** *v/t.* **3.** mit Pfützen bedecken; in Matsch verwandeln; **4.** *Wasser* trüben (*a. fig.*); **5.** *Lehm* zu Lehmschlag verarbeiten; **6.** mit Lehmschlag abdichten *od.* auskleiden; **7.** *metall.* puddeln: ~***(d) steel*** Puddelstahl *m*; **III** *v/i.* **8.** her'umplanschen *od.* -waten; **9.** *fig.* her'umpfuschen; '**pud·dler** [-lə] *s.* ⚙ Puddler *m* (*Arbeiter od. Gerät*).

pu·den·cy ['pju:dənsı] *s.* Verschämtheit *f*.

pu·den·dum [pju:'dendəm] *mst im pl.* **-da** [-də] *s.* (weibliche) Scham, Vulva *f*.

pu·dent ['pju:dənt] *adj.* verschämt.

pudg·y ['pʌdʒı] *adj.* dicklich.

pu·er·ile ['pjʊəraıl] *adj.* □ pue'ril, knabenhaft, kindlich, *contp.* kindisch; **pu·er·il·i·ty** [pjʊə'rılətı] *s.* **1.** Puerili'tät *f*, kindliches *od.* kindisches Wesen; **2.** Kinde'rei *f*.

pu·er·per·al [pju:'ɜ:pərəl] *adj.* Kindbett...: ~ ***fever***.

puff [pʌf] **I** *s.* **1.** Hauch *m*; (leichter) Windstoß; **2.** Zug *m beim Rauchen*; Paffen *n der Pfeife etc.*; **3.** (Rauch-, Dampf)Wölkchen *n*; **4.** leichter Knall; **5.** *Bäckerei*: Windbeutel *m*; **6.** Puderquaste *f*; **7.** Puffe *f*, Bausch *m an Kleidern*; **8.** a) marktschreierische Anpreisung, aufdringliche Re'klame, b) lobhudelnde Kri'tik: ~ ***is part of the trade*** Klappern gehört zum Handwerk; **II** *v/t.* **9.** blasen, pusten (***away*** weg, ***out*** aus); **10.** auspuffen, -paffen, -stoßen; **11.** *Zigarre etc.* paffen; **12.** *oft* ~ ***out***, ~ ***up*** aufblasen, (-)blähen; *fig.* aufgeblasen machen: ~***ed up with pride*** stolzgeschwellt; ~***ed eyes*** geschwollene Augen; ~***ed sleeve*** Puffärmel *m*; **13.** außer Atem bringen: ~***ed*** außer Atem; **14.** marktschreierisch anpreisen: ~ ***up*** *Preise* hochtreiben; **III** *v/i.* **15.** paffen (***at*** an *e-r Zigarre etc.*); Rauch- od. Dampfwölkchen ausstoßen; **16.** pusten, schnaufen, keuchen; **17.** *Lokomotive etc.* (da'hin)dampfen, keuchen; **18.** ~ ***out*** (*od.* ***up***) sich (auf)blähen; ~ **ad·der** *s. zo.* Puffotter *f*; '~·**ball** *s.* ♀ Bofist *m*.

puff·er ['pʌfə] *s.* **1.** Paffer *m*; **2.** Marktschreier *m*; **3.** Preistreiber *m*, Scheinbieter *m bei Auktionen*; '**puff·er·y** [-ərı] *s.* Marktschreie'rei *f*; **puff·i·ness** ['pʌfınıs] *s.* **1.** Aufgeblähtheit *f*, Aufgeblasenheit *f* (*a. fig.*); **2.** (Auf)Gedunsenheit *f*; **3.** Schwulst *m*; **puff·ing** ['pʌfıŋ] *s.* **1.** Aufbauschung *f*, Aufblähung *f*; **2.** → ***puff*** 8 a; **3.** Scheinbieten *n bei Auktionen*, Preistreibe'rei *f*; **puff paste** *s.* Blätterteig *m*; **puff·y** ['pʌfı] *adj.* □ **1.** böig (*Wind*); **2.** kurzatmig, keuchend; **3.** aufgebläht, (an)geschwollen; **4.** bauschig (*Ärmel*); **5.** aufgedunsen, dick; **6.** *fig.* schwülstig.

pug[1] [pʌg] *s. a.* ~-***dog*** Mops *m*.

pug[2] [pʌg] *v/t.* **1.** *Lehm etc.* mischen u. kneten; schlagen; **2.** mit Lehmschlag *etc.* ausfüllen *od.* abdichten.

pug[3] [pʌg] *s. sl.* Boxer *m*.

pu·gil·ism ['pju:dʒılızəm] *s.* (Berufs-) Boxen *n*; '**pu·gil·ist** [-ıst] *s.* (Berufs-) Boxer *m*.

pug·na·cious [pʌg'neıʃəs] *adj.* □ **1.** kampflustig, kämpferisch; **2.** streitsüchtig; **pug'nac·i·ty** [-'næsətı] *s.* **1.** Kampflust *f*; **2.** Streitsucht *f*.

'**pug**|-**nose** *s.* Stupsnase *f*; '~-**nosed** *adj.* stupsnasig.

puis·ne ['pju:nı] **I** *adj.* ⚖ rangjünger, 'untergeordnet: ~ ***judge*** → II; **II** *s.* 'Unterrichter *m*, Beisitzer *m*.

puke [pju:k] **I** *v/t. u. v/i.* (sich) erbrechen, ,kotzen'; **II** *s.* ,Kotze' *f*.

puk·ka ['pʌkə] → ***pucka***.

pul·chri·tude ['pʌlkrıtju:d] *s. bsd. Am.* (weibliche) Schönheit; **pul·chri·tu·di·nous** [ˌpʌlkrı'tju:dınəs] *adj. Am.* schön.

pule [pju:l] *v/i.* **1.** wimmern, winseln; **2.** piepsen.

pull [pʊl] **I** *s.* **1.** Ziehen *n*, Zerren *n*; **2.** Zug *m*, Ruck *m*: ***give a strong*** ~ (***at***) kräftig ziehen (an *dat.*); **3.** *mot. etc.* Zug(kraft *f*) *m*, Ziehkraft *f*; **4.** Anziehungskraft *f* (*a. fig.*); **5.** *fig.* Zug-, Werbekraft *f*; **6.** Zug *m*, Schluck *m* (***at*** aus); **7.** Zug(griff) *m*, -leine *f*: ***bell*** ~ Glokkenzug; **8.** a) Bootfahrt *f*, Ruderpar'tie *f*, b) Ruderschlag *m*; **9.** (***long*** ~ große) Anstrengung, ,Schlauch' *m*, *fig.* Durststrecke *f*; **10.** ermüdende Steigung; **11.** Vorteil *m* (***over***, ***of*** vor *dat.*, gegen'über); **12.** *sl.* (***with***) (heimlicher) Einfluß (auf *acc.*), Beziehungen *pl.* (zu); **13.** *typ.* Fahne *f*, (erster) Abzug; **II** *v/t.* **14.** ziehen, schleppen; **15.** zerren (an *dat.*), zupfen (an *dat.*): ~ ***about*** umherzerren; ~ ***a muscle*** sich e-e Muskelzerrung zuziehen; → ***face*** 2, ***leg*** *Redew.*, ***string*** 3, ***trigger*** 2; **16.** reißen: ~ ***apart*** auseinanderreißen; ~ ***to pieces*** a) zerreißen, in Stücke reißen, b) *fig.* (in e-r Kritik *etc.*) ,verreißen'; ~ ***o.s. together*** *fig.* sich zs.-reißen; **17.** *Pflanze* ausreißen; *Korken*, *Zahn* ziehen; *Blumen*, *Obst* pflücken; *Flachs* raufen; *Gans etc.* rupfen; *Leder* enthaaren; **18.** ~ ***one's punches*** *Boxen*: verhalten schlagen, *fig.* sich zurückhalten; ***not to*** ~ ***one's punches*** *fig.* vom Leder ziehen, kein Blatt vor den Mund nehmen; **19.** *Pferd* zügeln; *Rennpferd* pullen; **20.** *Boot* rudern: ~ ***a good oar*** gut rudern; → ***weight*** 1; **21.** *Am. Messer etc.* ziehen: ~ ***a pistol on*** *j-n* mit der Pistole bedrohen; **22.** *typ. Fahne* abziehen; **23.** *sl. et.* ,drehen', ,schaukeln' (*ausführen*): ~ ***the job*** das Ding drehen; ~ ***a fast one on s.o.*** j-n ,reinlegen'; **24.** *sl.* ,schnappen' (*verhaften*); **25.** *sl.* e-e Razzia machen auf (*acc.*), *Spielhölle etc.* ausheben; **III** *v/i.* **26.** ziehen (***at*** an *dat.*); **27.** zerren, reißen (***at*** an *dat.*); **28.** *a.* ~ ***against the bit*** am Zügel reißen (*Pferd*); **29.** a) e-n Zug machen, trinken (***at*** aus *e-r Flasche*), b) ziehen (***at*** an *e-r Pfeife etc.*); **30.** *gut etc.* ziehen (*Pfeife etc.*); **31.** sich vorwärtsarbeiten, -bewegen, -schieben: ~ ***into the station*** 🚂 (in den Bahnhof) einfahren; **32.** rudern, pullen: ~ ***together*** *fig.* zs.-arbeiten; **33.** (her'an)fahren (***to the kerb*** an den Bordstein); **34.** *sl.* ,ziehen', Zugkraft haben (*Reklame*);

Zssgn mit adv.:

pull| **away I** *v/t.* **1.** wegziehen, -reißen; **II** *v/i.* **2.** anfahren (*Bus etc.*); **3.** sich losreißen; **4.** *a. sport* sich absetzen (von ***from***); ~ **down** *v/t.* **1.** her'unterziehen, -reißen; *Gebäude* abreißen; **2.** *fig.* her'unterreißen, her'absetzen; **3.** *j-n* schwächen; *j-n* entmutigen; ~ **in I** *v/t.* **1.** (her)'einziehen; **2.** *Pferd* zügeln, parieren; **II** *v/i.* **3.** anhalten, stehenbleiben; **4.** hin'einrudern; 🚂 einfahren; ~ **off I** *v/t.* **1.** wegziehen, -reißen; **2.** *Schuhe etc.* ausziehen; *Hut* abnehmen (***to*** vor *dat.*); **3.** *Preis, Sieg* da'vontragen, erringen; **4.** F *et.* ,schaukeln', ,schaffen'; **II** *v/i.* **5.** sich in Bewegung setzen, abfahren; abstoßen (*Boot*); ~ **on** *v/t. Kleid etc.* anziehen; ~ **out I** *v/t.* **1.** her'ausziehen; ⚔ *Truppen* abziehen; **2.** ✈ *Flugzeug* hochziehen, *aus dem Sturzflug* abfangen; **3.** *fig.* in die Länge ziehen; **II** *v/i.* **4.** hin'ausrudern; abfahren (*Zug etc.*); ausscheren (*Fahrzeug*); ⚔ abziehen; *fig.* ,aussteigen' (***of*** aus); ~ **round I** *v/t. Kranken* wieder ,hinkriegen', 'durchbringen; **II** *v/i.* wieder auf die Beine kommen, 'durchkommen, sich erholen; ~ **through I** *v/t.* **1.** (hin-) 'durchziehen; **2.** *fig.* a) *j-m* 'durchhelfen, b) → ***pull round*** I; **3.** *et.* erfolgreich 'durchführen; **II** *v/i.* **4.** → ***pull round*** II; sich 'durchschlagen; ~ **up I** *v/t.* **1.** hochziehen (*a.* ✈); ⚓ *Flagge* hissen; **2.** *Pferd, Wagen* anhalten; **3.** *j-n* zu'rückhalten, *j-m* Einhalt gebieten; *j-n* zur Rede stellen; **II** *v/i.* **4.** (an)halten, vorfahren; **5.** *fig.* bremsen; **6.** *sport* sich nach vorn schieben: ~ ***to*** (*od.* ***with***) *j-n* einholen.

'pull|·back *s.* **1.** Hemmnis *n*; **2.** ⚔ Rückzug *m*; **~ date** *s.* ☤ Haltbarkeitsdatum *n*.

pul·let ['pʊlɪt] *s.* Hühnchen *n*.

pul·ley ['pʊlɪ] ⚙ *s.* **1.** a) Rolle *f* (*bsd. Flaschenzug*): ***rope ~*** Seilrolle *f*; ***block and ~, set of ~s*** Flaschenzug *m*, b) Flasche *f* (*Verbindung mehrerer Rollen*), c) Flaschenzug *m*; **2.** ⚓ Talje *f*; **3.** *a.* ***belt ~*** Riemenscheibe *f*; **~ block** *s.* ⚙ (Roll)Kloben *m*; **~ chain** *s.* Flaschenzugkette *f*; **~ drive** *s.* Riemenscheibenantrieb *m*.

Pull·man (car) ['pʊlmən] *pl.* **-mans** *s.* 🚃 Pullmanwagen *m*.

'pull|-off I *s.* **1.** ✈ Lösen *n* des Fallschirms (*beim Absprung*); **2.** *leichter etc.* Abzug (*Schußwaffe*); **II** *adj.* **3.** ⚙ Abzieh…(*-feder*); **'~-out I** *s.* **1.** Faltblatt *n*; **2.** (Zeitschriften)Beilage *f*; **3.** ⚔ (Truppen)Abzug *m*; **II** *adj.* **4.** ausziehbar: ***~ map*** Faltkarte *f*; ***~ seat*** Schiebesitz *m*; **'~ˌo·ver** *s.* Pull'over *m*; **~ switch** *s.* ⚡ Zugschalter *m*.

pul·lu·late ['pʌljʊleɪt] *v/i.* **1.** (her'vor-)sprossen, knospen; **2.** Knospen treiben; **3.** keimen (*Samen*); **4.** *biol.* sich (*durch Knospung*) vermehren; **5.** *fig.* wuchern, grassieren; **6.** *fig.* wimmeln.

'pull-up *s.* **1.** *Brit. mot.* Raststätte *f*; **2.** Klimmzug *m*.

pul·mo·nar·y ['pʌlmənərɪ] *adj. anat.* Lungen…; **'pul·mo·nate** [-neɪt] *zo. adj.* Lungen…, mit Lungen (ausgestattet): **~ (*mollusc*)** Lungenschnecke *f*; **pul·mon·ic** [pʌl'mɒnɪk] **I** *adj.* Lungen…; **II** *s.* Lungenheilmittel *n*.

pulp [pʌlp] **I** *s.* **1.** Fruchtfleisch *n*, -mark *n*; **2.** ⚘ Stengelmark *n*; **3.** *anat.* (Zahn-)Pulpa *f*; **4.** Brei *m*, breiige Masse: ***beat to a ~*** *fig. j-n* zu Brei schlagen; **5.** ⚙ a) Pa'pierbrei *m*, Pulpe *f*, *bsd.* Ganzzeug *n*, b) Zellstoff *m*: ***~board*** Zellstoffpappe *f*; ***~ engine*** → ***pulper*** 1; ***~ factory*** Holzschleiferei *f*; **6.** Maische *f*, Schnitzel *pl.* (*Zucker*); **7.** *Am.* a) Schund *m*, b) *a.* ***~ magazine*** *Am.* Schundblatt *n*; **II** *v/t.* **8.** in Brei verwandeln; **9.** *Papier* einstampfen; **10.** *Früchte* entfleischen; **III** *v/i.* **11.** breiig werden *od.* sein; **'pulp·er** [-pə] *s.* **1.** ⚙ (Ganzzeug)Holländer *m* (*Papier*); **2.** ⚒ (Rüben)Breimühle *f*; **'pulp·i·fy** [-pɪfaɪ] *v/t.* in Brei verwandeln; **'pulp·i·ness** [-pɪnɪs] *s.* **1.** Weichheit *f*; **2.** Fleischigkeit *f*; **3.** Matschigkeit *f*.

pul·pit ['pʊlpɪt] *s.* **1.** Kanzel *f*: ***in the ~*** auf der Kanzel; ***~ orator*** Kanzelredner *m*; **2.** ***the ~*** *coll.* die Geistlichkeit; **3.** *fig.* Kanzel *f*; **4.** ⚙ Bedienungsstand *m*.

pulp·y ['pʌlpɪ] *adj.* □ **1.** weich u. saftig; **2.** fleischig; **3.** schwammig; **4.** breiig, matschig.

pul·sate [pʌl'seɪt] *v/i.* **1.** pulsieren (*a.* ⚡), (rhythmisch) pochen *od.* schlagen; **2.** vibrieren; **3.** *fig.* pulsieren (***with*** von *Leben, Erregung*); **pul·sa·tile** ['pʌlsətaɪl] *adj.* ♪ Schlag…: ***~ instrument***; **pul'sat·ing** [-tɪŋ] *adj.* **1.** ⚡ pulsierend (*a. fig.*), stoßweise; **2.** *fig.* beschwingt (*Rhythmus, Weise*); **pul'sa·tion** [-eɪʃn] *s.* **1.** Pulsieren *n* (*a. fig.*), Pochen *n*, Schlagen *n*; **2.** Pulsschlag *m* (*a. fig.*); **3.** Vibrieren *n*.

pulse¹ [pʌls] **I** *s.* **1.** Puls(schlag) *m* (*a. fig.*): ***quick ~*** schneller Puls; ***~-rate*** ⚕ Pulszahl *f*; ***feel s.o.'s ~*** a) j-m den Puls fühlen, b) *fig.* j-m auf den Zahn fühlen, bei j-m vorfühlen; **2.** ⚡, *phys.* Im'puls *m*, (Strom)Stoß *m*; **II** *v/i.* **3.** → ***pulsate***.

pulse² [pʌls] *s.* Hülsenfrüchte *pl.*

pul·ver·i·za·tion [ˌpʌlvəraɪ'zeɪʃn] *s.* **1.** Pulverisierung *f*, (Feinst)Mahlung *f*; **2.** Zerstäubung *f von Flüssigkeiten*; **3.** *fig.* Zermalmung *f*; **pul·ver·ize** ['pʌlvəraɪz] **I** *v/t.* **1.** pulverisieren, *zu Staub* zermahlen, -stoßen, -reiben: ***~d coal*** feingemahlene Kohlen *pl.*, Kohlenstaub *m*; **2.** *Flüssigkeit* zerstäuben; **3.** *fig.* zermalmen; **II** *v/i.* **4.** (in Staub) zerfallen; **pul·ver·iz·er** ['pʌlvəraɪzə] *s.* **1.** ⚙ Zerkleinerer *m*, Pulverisiermühle *f*, Mahlanlage *f*; **2.** Zerstäuber *m*; **pul·ver·u·lent** [pʌl'verjələnt] *adj.* **1.** (fein)pulverig; **2.** (leicht) zerbröckelnd; **3.** staubig.

pu·ma ['pjuːmə] *s. zo.* Puma *m*.

pum·ice ['pʌmɪs] **I** *s. a.* ***~-stone*** Bimsstein *m*; **II** *v/t.* mit Bimsstein abreiben, (ab)bimsen.

pum·mel ['pʌml] → ***pommel*** II.

pump¹ [pʌmp] **I** *s.* **1.** Pumpe *f*: (***dispensing***) ***~*** *mot.* Zapfsäule *f*; ***~ priming*** a) Anlassen *n* der Pumpe, b) ☤ Ankurbelung *f* der Wirtschaft; **2.** Pumpen(stoß *m*) *n*; **II** *v/t.* **3.** pumpen: ***~ dry*** aus-, leerpumpen; ***~ out*** auspumpen (*a. fig. erschöpfen*); ***~ up*** a) hochpumpen, b) *Reifen* aufpumpen (*a. fig.*); ***~ bullets into*** *fig. j-m* Kugeln in den Leib jagen; ***~ money into*** ☤ Geld in *et.* hineinpumpen; **4.** *fig. j-n* ausholen, -fragen, -horchen; **III** *v/i.* **5.** pumpen (*a. fig. Herz etc.*).

pump² [pʌmp] *s.* **1.** Pumps *m* (*Halbschuh*); **2.** *Brit.* Turnschuh *m*.

'pump-ˌhan·dle I *s.* Pumpenschwengel *m*; **II** *v/t.* F *j-s Hand* 'überschwenglich schütteln.

pump·kin ['pʌmpkɪn] *s.* ⚘ (*bsd.* Garten-)Kürbis *m*.

'pump-room *s.* Trinkhalle *f in Kurbädern*.

pun [pʌn] **I** *s.* Wortspiel *n* (***on*** über *acc.*, mit); **II** *v/i.* Wortspiele *od.* ein Wortspiel machen, witzeln.

punch¹ [pʌntʃ] **I** *s.* **1.** (Faust)Schlag *m*: ***beat s.o. to the ~*** *Am. fig.* j-m zuvorkommen; → ***pull*** 18; **2.** Schlagkraft *f* (*a. fig.*); → ***pack*** 20; **3.** F Wucht *f*, Schmiß *m*, Schwung *m*; **II** *v/t.* **4.** (*mit der Faust*) schlagen, boxen, knuffen; **5.** (ein)hämmern auf (*acc.*): ***~ the typewriter***.

punch² [pʌntʃ] ⚙ **I** *s.* **1.** Stanzwerkzeug *n*, Lochstanze *f*, -eisen *n*, Stempel *m*, 'Durchschlag *m*, Dorn *m*; **2.** Pa'trize *f*; **3.** Prägestempel *m*; **4.** Lochzange *f* (*a.* 🚃 *etc.*); **5.** (Pa'pier)Locher *m*; **II** *v/t.* **6.** (aus-, loch)stanzen, durch'schlagen, lochen; **7.** *Zahlen etc.* punzen, stempeln; **8.** *Fahrkarten etc.* lochen, knipsen: ***~ed card*** Lochkarte *f*; ***~ed tape*** Lochstreifen *m*.

punch³ [pʌntʃ] *s.* Punsch *m*.

Punch⁴ [pʌntʃ] *s.* Kasperle *n*, Hans'wurst *m*: ***~ and Judy show*** Kasperletheater *n*; ***he was as pleased as ~*** er hat sich königlich gefreut.

punch⁵ [pʌntʃ] *s. Brit.* **1.** kurzbeiniges schweres Zugpferd; **2.** F ‚Stöpsel' *m* (*kleine dicke Person*).

'punch|·ball *s. Boxen*: Punchingball *m*, (Mais)Birne *f*; **~ card** *s.* Lochkarte *f*; **ˌ~-'drunk** *adj.* **1.** (von vielen Boxhieben) blöde (geworden); **2.** groggy.

pun·cheon¹ ['pʌntʃən] *s.* **1.** (Holz-, Stütz)Pfosten *m*; **2.** ⚙ → ***punch²*** 1.

pun·cheon² ['pʌntʃən] *s. hist.* Puncheon *n* (*Faß von 315–540 l*).

punch·er ['pʌntʃə] *s.* **1.** ⚙ Locheisen *n*, Locher *m*; **2.** F Schläger *m* (*a. Boxer*); **3.** *Am.* F Cowboy *m*.

punch·ing| bag ['pʌntʃɪŋ] *s. Boxen*: Sandsack *m*; **'~-ball** *s. Boxen*: Punchingball *m*; **~ die** *s.* ⚙ 'Stanzmaˌtrize *f*.

punch| line *s. Am.* Po'inte *f*, 'Knalleffekt *m*; **~ press** *s.* ⚙ Lochpresse *f*; **'~-up** *s.* F Schläge'rei *f*.

punc·til·i·o [pʌŋk'tɪlɪəʊ] *pl.* **-i·os** *s.* **1.** Punkt *m* der Eti'kette; Feinheit *f des Benehmens etc.*; **2.** heikler *od.* kitzliger Punkt: ***~ of hono(u)r*** Ehrenpunkt *m*; **3.** → ***punctiliousness***; **punc'til·i·ous** [-ɪəs] *adj.* □ **1.** peinlich (genau), pe'dantisch, spitzfindig; **2.** (über'trieben) förmlich; **punc'til·i·ous·ness** [-ɪəsnɪs] *s.* pe'dantische Genauigkeit, Förmlichkeit *f*.

punc·tu·al ['pʌŋktjʊəl] *adj.* □ pünktlich; **punc·tu·al·i·ty** [ˌpʌŋktjʊ'ælətɪ] *s.* Pünktlichkeit *f*.

punc·tu·ate ['pʌŋktjʊeɪt] *v/t.* **1.** interpunktieren, Satzzeichen setzen in (*acc.*); **2.** *fig.* a) unter'brechen (***with*** durch, mit), b) unter'streichen; **punc·tu·a·tion** [ˌpʌŋktjʊ'eɪʃn] *s.* **1.** Interpunkti'on *f*, Zeichensetzung *f*: ***close*** (***open***) ***~*** (weniger) strikte Zeichensetzung; ***~ mark*** Satzzeichen *n*; **2.** *fig.* a) Unter'brechung *f*, b) Unter'streichung *f*.

punc·ture ['pʌŋktʃə] **I** *v/t.* **1.** durch'stechen, -'bohren; **2.** ⚕ punktieren; **II** *v/i.* **3.** ein Loch bekommen, platzen (*Reifen*); **4.** ⚡ 'durchschlagen; **III** *s.* **5.** (Ein-)Stich *m*, Loch *n*; **6.** Reifenpanne *f*: ***~ outfit*** Flickzeug *n*; **7.** ⚕ Punk'tur *f*; **8.** ⚡ 'Durchschlag *m*; **'~-proof** *adj. mot.* pannen-, ⚡ 'durchschlagsicher.

pun·dit ['pʌndɪt] *s.* **1.** Pandit *m* (*brahmanischer Gelehrter*); **2.** *humor.* a) ‚gelehrtes Haus', b) ‚Weise(r)' *m* (*Experte*).

pun·gen·cy ['pʌndʒənsɪ] *s.* Schärfe *f* (*a. fig.*); **'pun·gent** [-nt] *adj.* □ **1.** scharf (*im Geschmack*); **2.** stechend (*Geruch etc.*), *a. fig.* beißend, scharf; **3.** *fig.* prickelnd, pi'kant.

pu·ni·ness ['pjuːnɪnɪs] *s.* **1.** Schwächlichkeit *f*; **2.** Kleinheit *f*.

pun·ish ['pʌnɪʃ] *v/t.* **1.** *j-n* (be)strafen (***for*** für, wegen); **2.** *Vergehen* bestrafen, ahnden; **3.** F *fig. Boxer etc.* übel zurichten, arg mitnehmen (*a. weitS. strapazieren*): ***~ing*** ‚mörderisch', zermürbend; **4.** F ‚reinhauen' (*ins Essen*); **'pun·ish·a·ble** [-ʃəbl] *adj.* □ strafbar; **'pun·ish·ment** [-mənt] *s.* **1.** Bestrafung *f* (***by*** durch); **2.** Strafe *f* (*a.* ⚖): ***for*** (*od.* ***as***) ***a ~*** als *od.* zur Strafe; **3.** F a) grobe Behandlung, b) *Boxen*: ‚Prügel' *pl.*: ***take ~*** ‚schwer einstecken' müssen; c) Stra'paze *f*, ‚Schlauch' *m*, d) ⚙, ☤ harte Beanspruchung.

pu·ni·tive ['pjuːnətɪv] *adj.* Straf…

punk [pʌŋk] **I** *s.* **1.** Zunder(holz *n*) *m*; **2.** *sl. contp.* a) ‚Flasche' *f*, b) ‚Blödmann' *m*, c) ‚Mist' *m*; **3.** ‚Punk' *m* (*Bewegung u. Anhänger*), Punker(in); **II** *adj. sl.* **4.** mise'rabel; **5.** Punk… (*a.* ♪).

pun·ster [ˈpʌnstə] *s.* Wortspielmacher (-in), Witzbold *m.*

punt¹ [pʌnt] **I** *s.* Punt *n*, Stakkahn *m*; **II** *v/t. Boot* staken; **III** *v/i.* punten, im Punt fahren.

punt² [pʌnt] **I** *s. Rugby etc.*: Falltritt *m*; **II** *v/t. u. v/i.* (den Ball) aus der Hand (ab)schlagen.

punt³ [pʌnt] *v/i.* **1.** *Glücksspiel*: gegen die Bank setzen; **2.** (*auf ein Pferd*) setzen, *allg.* wetten.

pu·ny [ˈpjuːnɪ] *adj.* ☐ schwächlich; winzig, *a. fig.* kümmerlich.

pup [pʌp] **I** *s.* junger Hund: ***in ~*** trächtig (*Hündin*); ***conceited ~*** → ***puppy*** 2; ***sell s.o. a ~*** F j-m et. andrehen, j-n ‚reinlegen'; **II** *v/t. u. v/i.* (Junge) werfen.

pu·pa [ˈpjuːpə] *pl.* **-pae** [-piː] *s. zo.* Puppe *f*; ˈ**pu·pate** [-peɪt] *v/i. zo.* sich verpuppen; **pu·pa·tion** [pjuːˈpeɪʃən] *s. zo.* Verpuppung *f.*

pu·pil¹ [ˈpjuːpl] *s.* **1.** Schüler(in): ***~ teacher*** Junglehrer(in); **2.** ☤ Praktiˈkant(in); **3.** ⚖ Mündel *m, n.*

pu·pil² [ˈpjuːpl] *s. anat.* Puˈpille *f.*

pu·pil·(l)age [ˈpjuːpɪlɪdʒ] *s.* **1.** Schüler-, Lehrjahre *pl.*; **2.** Minderjährigkeit *f*, Unmündigkeit *f*; ˈ**pu·pil·(l)ar** [-lə] → ˈ**pu·pil·(l)ar·y** [-lərɪ] *adj.* **1.** ⚖ Mündel…; **2.** *anat.* Pupillen…

pup·pet [ˈpʌpɪt] *s. a. fig.* Marioˈnette *f*, Puppe *f*: ***~ government*** Marionettenregierung *f*; ***~ show*** (*od.* ***play***) Puppenspiel *n*, Marioˈnettentheˌater *n.*

pup·py [ˈpʌpɪ] *s.* **1.** *zo.* junger Hund, Welpe *m*, *a. weitS.* Junge(s) *n*: ***~ love*** → ***calf love***; **2.** *fig.* (junger) Schnösel, Fatzke *m*; ˈ**pup·py·hood** [-hʊd] *s.* Jugend-, Flegeljahre *pl.*

pup tent *s.* kleines Schutzzelt.

pur [pɜː] → ***purr.***

pur·blind [ˈpɜːblaɪnd] *adj.* **1.** *fig.* kurzsichtig, dumm; **2.** a) halb blind, b) *obs.* (ganz) blind.

pur·chas·a·ble [ˈpɜːtʃəsəbl] *adj.* käuflich (*a. fig.*); **pur·chase** [ˈpɜːtʃəs] **I** *v/t.* **1.** kaufen, erstehen, (käuflich) erwerben; **2.** *fig.* erkaufen, erringen (***with*** mit, durch); **3.** *fig.* kaufen (*bestechen*); **4.** ⚙, ⚓ a) hochwinden; b) (mit Hebelkraft) heben *od.* bewegen; **II** *s.* **5.** (An-, Ein)Kauf *m*: ***by ~*** durch Kauf, käuflich; ***make ~s*** Einkäufe machen; **6.** ˈKauf (-obˌjekt *n*) *m*, Anschaffung *f*: ***~s*** *Bilanz*: Wareneingänge; **7.** ⚖ Erwerbung *f*; **8.** (Jahres)Ertrag *m*: ***at ten years' ~*** zum Zehnfachen des Jahresertrages; ***his life is not worth a day's ~*** er lebt keinen Tag mehr, er macht es nicht mehr lange; **9.** ⚙ Hebevorrichtung *f*, *bsd.* a) Flaschenzug *m*, b) ⚓ Talje *f*; **10.** Hebelkraft *f*, -wirkung *f*; **11.** (guter) Angriffs- *od.* Ansatzpunkt; **12.** *fig.* a) Machtstellung *f*, Einfluß *m*, b) Machtmittel *n*, Handhabe *f.*

pur·chase| ac·count *s.* ☤ Wareneingangskonto *n*; **~ dis·count** *s.* ˈEinkaufsraˌbatt *m*; **~ mon·ey** *s.* Kaufsumme *f*; **~ pat·tern** *s.* Käuferverhalten *n*; **~ price** *s.* Kaufpreis *m.*

pur·chas·er [ˈpɜːtʃəsə] *s.* **1.** Käufer(in); Abnehmer(in); **2.** ⚖ Erwerber *m*: ***first ~*** Ersterwerber.

pur·chase tax *s. Brit.* Kaufsteuer *f.*

pur·chas·ing| a·gent [ˈpɜːtʃəsɪŋ] *s.* ☤ Einkäufer *m*; **~ as·so·ci·a·tion** *s.* Einkaufsgenossenschaft *f*; **~ de·part·ment** *s.* Einkauf(sabteilung *f*) *m*; **~ man·ag·er** *s.* Einkaufsleiter *m*; **~ pow·er** *s.* Kaufkraft *f.*

pure [pjʊə] *adj.* ☐ **1.** rein: a) sauber, makellos (*a. fig. Freundschaft, Sprache, Ton etc.*), b) unschuldig, unberührt: ***a ~ girl***, c) unvermischt: ***~ gold*** pures *od.* reines Gold, d) theoˈretisch: ***~ mathematics*** reine Mathematik, e) völlig, bloß, pur: ***~ nonsense***; ***~ly*** *adv. fig.* rein, bloß, ausschließlich; **2.** *biol.* reinrassig; ˈ**~·bred I** *adj.* reinrassig, rasserein; **II** *s.* reinrassiges Tier.

pu·rée [ˈpjʊəreɪ] (*Fr.*) *s.* **1.** Püˈree *n*; **2.** (Püˈree)Suppe *f.*

pur·ga·tion [pɜːˈgeɪʃn] *s.* **1.** *mst eccl. u. fig.* Reinigung *f*; **2.** ⚕ Darmentleerung *f*; **pur·ga·tive** [ˈpɜːgətɪv] **I** *adj.* ☐ **1.** reinigend; **2.** ⚕ abführend, Abführ…; **II** *s.* **3.** ⚕ Abführmittel *n*; **pur·ga·to·ry** [ˈpɜːgətərɪ] *s. R.C.* Fegefeuer *n* (*a. fig.*).

purge [pɜːdʒ] **I** *v/t.* **1.** *mst fig j-n* reinigen (***of, from*** von) *Schuld, Verdacht*); **2.** *Flüssigkeit* klären, läutern; **3.** ⚕ a) *Darm* abführen, entschlacken, b) *j-m* Abführmittel geben; **4.** *Verbrechen* sühnen; **5.** *pol.* a) *Partei etc.* säubern, b) (aus der Parˈtei) ausschließen, c) liquidieren (*töten*); **II** *v/i.* **6.** sich läutern; **7.** ⚕ a) abführen (*Medikament*), b) Stuhlgang haben; **III** *s.* **8.** Reinigung *f*; **9.** ⚕ a) Entleerung *f*, -schlackung *f*, b) Abführmittel *n*; **10.** *pol.* ˈSäuberung(s-aktiˌon) *f.*

pu·ri·fi·ca·tion [ˌpjʊərɪfɪˈkeɪʃn] *s.* **1.** Reinigung *f* (*a. eccl.*); **2.** ⚙ Reinigung *f* (*a. metall.*), Klärung *f*, Abläuterung *f*; Regenerierung *f von Altöl*; **pu·ri·fi·er** [ˈpjʊərɪfaɪə] *s.* ⚙ Reiniger *m*, ˈReinigungsappaˌrat *m*; **pu·ri·fy** [ˈpjʊərɪfaɪ] **I** *v/t.* **1.** reinigen (***of, from*** von) (*a. fig. läutern*); **2.** ⚙ reinigen, läutern, klären; aufbereiten, *Öl* regenerieren; **II** *v/i.* **3.** sich läutern.

pur·ism [ˈpjʊərɪzəm] *s. a. ling. u. Kunst*: Puˈrismus *m*; ˈ**pur·ist** [-ɪst] *s.* Puˈrist *m*, *bsd.* Sprachreiniger *m.*

Pu·ri·tan [ˈpjʊərɪtən] **I** *s.* **1.** *hist.* (*fig. mst* 2) Puriˈtaner(in); **II** *adj.* **2.** puriˈtanisch; **3.** *fig.* (*mst* 2) → ***puritanical***; **pu·ri·tan·i·cal** [ˌpjʊərɪˈtænɪkəl] *adj.* ☐ puritanisch, überˈtrieben sittenstreng; ˈ**Pu·ri·tan·ism** [-tənɪzəm] *s.* Puritaˈnismus *m.*

pu·ri·ty [ˈpjʊərətɪ] *s.* Reinheit *f*: ***2 Campaign*** *fig.* Sauberkeitskampagne *f.*

purl¹ [pɜːl] **I** *v/i.* murmeln, rieseln (*Bach*); **II** *s.* Murmeln *n.*

purl² [pɜːl] **I** *v/t.* **1.** (um)ˈsäumen, einfassen; **2.** (*a. v/i.*) linksstricken; **II** *s.* **3.** Gold-, Silberdrahtlitze *f*; **4.** Zäckchen (-borte *f*) *n*; **5.** Häkelkante *f*; **6.** Linksstricken *n.*

purl·er [ˈpɜːlə] *s.* F **1.** schwerer Sturz: ***come*** (*od.* ***take***) ***a ~*** schwer stürzen; **2.** schwerer Schlag.

pur·lieus [ˈpɜːljuːz] *s. pl.* Umˈgebung *f*, Randbezirk(e *pl.*) *m.*

pur·loin [pɜːˈlɔɪn] *v/t.* entwenden, stehlen (*a. fig.*); **purˈloin·er** [-nə] *s.* Dieb *m*; *fig.* Plagiˈator *m.*

pur·ple [ˈpɜːpl] **I** *adj.* **1.** purpurn, purpurrot: ***2 Heart*** a) ⚔ *Am.* Verwundetenabzeichen *n*, b) *Brit.* F Amphetamintablette *f*; **2.** *fig.* brilˈlant (*Stil*): ***~ passage*** Glanzsstelle *f*; **3.** *Am.* lästerlich; **II** *s.* **4.** Purpur *m* (*a. fig. Herrscher-, Kardinalswürde*): ***raise to the ~*** zum Kardinal ernennen; **III** *v/i.* **5.** sich purpurn färben.

pur·port [ˈpɜːpət] **I** *v/t.* **1.** behaupten, vorgeben: ***~ to be*** (***do***) angeblich sein (tun), sein (tun) wollen; **2.** besagen, beinhalten, zum Inhalt haben, ausdrükken (wollen); **II** *s.* **3.** Tenor *m*, Inhalt *m*, Sinn *m.*

pur·pose [ˈpɜːpəs] **I** *s.* **1.** Zweck *m*, Ziel *n*; Absicht *f*, Vorsatz *m*: ***for what ~?*** zu welchem Zweck?, wozu?; ***for all practical ~s*** praktisch; ***for the ~ of*** a) um zu, zwecks, b) im Sinne *e-s Gesetzes*; ***of set ~*** ⚖ vorsätzlich; ***on ~*** absichtlich; ***to the ~*** a) zur Sache (gehörig), b) zweckdienlich; ***to no ~*** vergeblich, umsonst; ***answer*** (*od.* ***serve***) ***the ~*** dem Zweck entsprechen; ***be to little ~*** wenig Zweck haben; ***turn to good ~*** gut anwenden *od.* nützen; ***novel with a ~***, ***~-novel*** Tendenzroman *m*; **2.** *a. **strength of ~*** Entschlußkraft *f*; **3.** Zielbewußtheit *f*; **4.** Wirkung *f*; **II** *v/t.* **5.** vorhaben, beabsichtigen, bezwecken; ˈ**~-built** *adj.* speziˈalgefertigt, Spezial…, Zweck…

pur·pose·ful [ˈpɜːpəsfʊl] *adj.* ☐ **1.** zielbewußt, entschlossen; **2.** zweckmäßig, -voll; **3.** absichtlich; ˈ**pur·pose·less** [-lɪs] *adj.* ☐ **1.** zwecklos; **2.** ziel-, planlos; ˈ**pur·pose·ly** [-lɪ] *adv.* absichtlich, vorsätzlich; ˈ**pur·pos·ive** [-sɪv] *adj.* **1.** zweckmäßig, -voll, -dienlich; **2.** absichtlich, bewußt, *a.* gezielt; **3.** zielstrebig.

ˈ**pur·pose-trained** *adj.* mit Speziˈalausbildung.

purr [pɜː] **I** *v/i.* **1.** schnurren (*Katze etc.*); **2.** *fig.* surren, summen (*Motor etc.*); **3.** *fig.* vor Behagen schnurren; **II** *v/t.* **4.** *et.* summen, säuseln (*sagen*); **III** *s.* **5.** Schnurren *n*; Surren *n.*

purse [pɜːs] **I** *s.* **1.** a) Geldbeutel *m*, Börse *f*, b) (Damen)Handtasche *f*: ***a light*** (***long***) ***~*** *fig.* ein magerer (voller) Geldbeutel; ***public ~*** Staatssäckel *m*; **2.** Fonds *m*: ***common ~*** gemeinsame Kasse; **3.** Geldsammlung *f*, -geschenk *n*: ***make up a ~ for*** Geld sammeln für; **4.** *sport*: a) Siegprämie *f*, b) *Boxen*: Börse *f*; **II** *v/t.* **5.** *oft **~ up*** in Falten legen; *Stirn* runzeln; *Lippen* schürzen, *Mund* spitzen; ˈ**~-proud** *adj.* geldstolz, protzig.

purs·er [ˈpɜːsə] *s.* **1.** ⚓ Zahl-, Proviˈantmeister *m*; **2.** ✈ Purser(in).

ˈ**purse-strings** *s. pl.*: ***hold the ~*** den Geldbeutel verwalten; ***tighten the ~*** den Daumen auf dem Beutel halten.

purs·lane [ˈpɜːslɪn] *s.* ⚘ Portulak(gewächs *n*) *m.*

pur·su·ance [pəˈsjʊəns] *s.* Verfolgung *f*, Ausführung *f*: ***in ~ of*** a) im Verfolg (*gen.*), b) → ***pursuant***; **purˈsu·ant** [-nt] *adj.* ☐: ***~ to*** gemäß *od.* laut *e-r Vorschrift etc.*

pur·sue [pəˈsjuː] **I** *v/t.* **1.** (*a.* ⚔) verfolgen, *j-m* nachsetzen, *j-n* jagen; **2.** *fig. Zweck, Ziel, Plan* verfolgen; **3.** nach *Glück etc.* streben; *dem Vergnügen* nachgehen; **4.** *Kurs, Weg* einschlagen, folgen (*dat.*); **5.** *Beruf, Studien etc.* betreiben, nachgehen (*dat.*); **6.** *et.* weiterführen, fortsetzen, fortfahren in; **7.**

Thema etc. weiterführen, (weiter) diskutieren; **II** *v/i.* **8.** *~* ***after*** → 1; **9.** *im Sprechen etc.* fortfahren; **pur'su·er** [-ju:ə] *s.* **1.** Verfolger(in); **2.** ⚖ *Scot.* (An)Kläger(in).

pur·suit [pə'sju:t] *s.* **1.** Verfolgung *f*, Jagd *f* (***of*** auf *acc.*): *~* ***action*** ⚔ Verfolgungskampf *m*; ***in hot*** *~* in wilder Verfolgung *od.* Jagd; **2.** *fig.* Streben *n*, Trachten *n*, Jagd *f* (***of*** nach); **3.** Verfolgung *f*, Verfolg *m e-s Plans etc.*: ***in*** *~* ***of*** im Verfolg *e-r Sache*; **4.** Beschäftigung *f*, Betätigung *f*; Ausübung *f e-s Gewerbes*, Betreiben *n von Studien etc.*; **5.** *pl.* Arbeiten *pl.*, Geschäfte *pl.*; Studien *pl.*; *~* **in·ter·cep·tor** *s.* ✈ Zerstörer *m*; *~* **plane** *s.* ✈ Jagdflugzeug *n*.

pur·sy¹ ['pɜ:sɪ] *adj.* **1.** kurzatmig; **2.** korpu'lent; **3.** protzig.

pur·sy² ['pɜ:sɪ] *adj.* zs.-gekniffen.

pu·ru·lence ['pjʊərʊləns] *s.* ⚕ **1.** Eitrigkeit *f*; **2.** Eiter *m*; **'pu·ru·lent** [-nt] *adj.* □ ⚕ eiternd, eit(e)rig; Eiter...: *~* ***matter*** Eiter *m*.

pur·vey [pə'veɪ] **I** *v/t.* (***to***) *mst Lebensmittel* liefern (an *acc.*), (*j-n*) versorgen mit; **II** *v/i.* (***for***) liefern (an *acc.*), sorgen (für): *~* ***for*** *j-n* beliefern; **pur'vey·ance** [-eɪəns] *s.* **1.** Lieferung *f*, Beschaffung *f*; **2.** (Mund)Vorrat *m*, Lebensmittel *pl.*; **pur'vey·or** [-eɪə] *s.* **1.** Liefe'rant *m*: ♀ ***to Her Majesty*** Hoflieferant; **2.** Lebensmittelhändler *m*.

pur·view ['pɜ:vju:] *s.* **1.** ⚖ verfügender Teil (*e-s Gesetzes*); **2.** *bsd.* ⚖ (Anwendungs)Bereich *m e-s Gesetzes*, b) Zuständigkeit(sbereich *m*) *f*; **3.** Wirkungskreis *m*, Sphäre *f*, Gebiet *n*; **4.** Gesichtskreis *m*, Blickfeld *n* (*a. fig.*).

pus [pʌs] *s.* ⚕ Eiter *m*.

push [pʊʃ] **I** *s.* **1.** Stoß *m*, Schub *m*: ***give s.o. a*** *~* a) j-m e-n Stoß versetzen, b) *mot.* j-n anschieben; ***give s.o. the*** *~ sl.* j-n ‚rausschmeißen' (*entlassen*); ***get the*** *~ sl.* ‚rausfliegen' (*entlassen werden*); **2.** ⚠, ⚙, *geol.* (horizon'taler) Druck, Schub *m*; **3.** Anstoß *m*, -trieb *m*; **4.** Anstrengung *f*, Bemühung *f*; **5.** *bsd.* ⚔ Vorstoß *m* (***for*** auf *acc.*); Offen'sive *f*; **6.** *fig.* Druck *m*, Drang *m der Verhältnisse*; **7.** kritischer Augenblick: ***at a*** *~* im Notfall; ***bring to the last*** *~* aufs Äußerste treiben; ***when it came to the*** *~* als es darauf ankam; **8.** F Schwung *m*, Ener'gie *f*, Tatkraft *f*, Draufgängertum *n*; **9.** Protekti'on *f*: ***get a job by*** *~*; **10.** F Menge *f*, Haufen *m Menschen*; **11.** *sl.* a) (exklu'sive) Clique, b) ‚Verein' *m*, ‚Bande' *f*; **II** *v/t.* **12.** stoßen, *Karren etc.* schieben: *~* ***open*** aufstoßen; **13.** stecken, schieben (***into*** in *acc.*); **14.** drängen: *~* ***one's way ahead*** (***through***) sich vor- (durch)drängen; **15.** *fig.* (an)treiben, drängen (***to*** zu, ***to do*** zu tun): *~* ***s.o. for*** j-n bedrängen *od.* j-m zusetzen wegen; *~* ***s.o. for payment*** bei j-m auf Zahlung drängen; *~* ***s.th. on s.o.*** j-m et. aufdrängen; ***be*** *~****ed for time*** in Zeitnot *od.* im Gedränge sein; ***be*** *~****ed for money*** in Geldverlegenheit sein; **16.** *a.* *~* ***ahead*** (*od.* ***forward*** *od.* ***on***) *Angelegenheit* (e'nergisch) betreiben *od.* verfolgen, vor'antreiben; **17.** *a.* *~* ***through*** 'durchführen, -setzen; *Anspruch* 'durchdrücken; *Vorteil* ausnutzen: *~* ***s.th. too far*** et. zu weit treiben; **18.** Re'klame machen für, die Trommel rühren für; **19.** F verkaufen, mit *Rauschgift etc.* handeln; **20.** F sich *e-m Alter* nähern: ***be*** *~****ing 70***; **III** *v/i.* **21.** stoßen, schieben; **22.** (sich) drängen; **23.** sich vorwärtsdrängen, sich vor'ankämpfen; **24.** sich tüchtig ins Zeug legen; **25.** *Billard*: schieben; *~* **a·round** *v/t.* her'umschubsen (*a. fig.*); *~* **off I** *v/t.* **1.** *Boot* abstoßen; **2.** ⚘ *Waren* abstoßen, losschlagen; **II** *v/i.* **3.** ⚓ abstoßen (***from*** von); **4.** F ‚abhauen'; **5.** *~!* F ‚schieß los'!; *~* **up** *v/t.* hoch-, hin'aufschieben, -stoßen; ⚘ *Preise* hochtreiben; *~* **un·der** *v/t.* F *j-n* ‚'unterbuttern'.

'push|·ball *s.* Pushball(spiel *n*) *m*; **'~-bike** *s. Brit.* F Fahrrad *n*; **'~-ˌbut·ton I** *s.* ⚙ Druckknopf *m*, -taste *f*; **II** *adj.* druckknopfgesteuert, Druckknopf...: *~* ***switch***; *~* ***telephone*** Tastentelefon *n*; *~* ***warfare*** automatische Kriegführung; **'~·cart** *s.* **1.** (Hand)Karren *m*; **2.** *Am.* Einkaufswagen *m*; **'~·chair** *s.* (Kinder-)Sportwagen *m*.

push·er ['pʊʃə] *s.* **1.** ⚙ Schieber *m* (*a. Kinderlöffel*); **2.** 🚂 'Hilfslokomoˌtive *f*; **3.** *a.* *~* ***airplane*** Flugzeug *n* mit Druckschraube; **4.** F Streber *m*; Draufgänger *m*; **5.** *sl.* ‚Pusher' *m*, ‚Dealer' *m* (*Rauschgifthändler*).

push·ful ['pʊʃfʊl] *adj.* □ e'nergisch, unter'nehmend, draufgängerisch.

push·ing ['pʊʃɪŋ] *adj.* □ **1.** → ***pushful***; **2.** streberisch; **3.** zudringlich.

'push|-off *s.* F Anfang *m*, Start *m*; **'~ˌo·ver** *s.* F **1.** leicht zu besiegender Gegner; **2.** Gimpel *m*: ***he is a*** *~* ***for that*** darauf fällt er prompt herein; **3.** leichte Sache, Kinderspiel *n*; **ˌ~-'pull** *adj.* ⚡ Gegentakt...; *~* **start** *s. mot.* Anschieben *n*; **ˌ~-to-'talk but·ton** *s.* ⚡ Sprechtaste *f*; **'~-up** *s.* Liegestütz *m*.

push·y ['pʊʃɪ] *adj.* F aufdringlich, pene'trant; aggres'siv.

pu·sil·la·nim·i·ty [ˌpju:sɪlə'nɪmətɪ] *s.* Kleinmütigkeit *f*, Verzagtheit *f*; **pu·sil·lan·i·mous** [ˌpju:sɪ'lænɪməs] *adj.* □ kleinmütig, verzagt.

puss¹ [pʊs] *s.* **1.** Mieze *f*, Kätzchen *n* (*a.* F *fig. Mädchen*): ♀ ***in Boots*** *der* Gestiefelte Kater; *~* ***in the corner*** Kämmerchen vermieten (*Kinderspiel*); **2.** *hunt.* Hase *m*.

puss² [pʊs] *s. sl.* ‚Fresse' *f*, Vi'sage *f*.

puss·l(e)y ['pʊslɪ] *s.* ⚘ *Am.* Kohlportulak *m*.

puss·y ['pʊsɪ] *s.* **1.** Mieze(kätzchen *n*) *f*, Kätzchen *n*; **2.** → ***tipcat***; **3.** *et.* Weiches u. Wolliges, *bsd.* ⚘ (Weiden)Kätzchen *n*; **4.** *vulg.* ‚Muschi' *f* (*Vulva*): ***have some*** *~* ‚bumsen'; **'~·cat 1.** → ***pussy*** 1; **2.** → ***pussy willow***; **'~·foot I** *v/i.* **1.** (wie e-e Katze) schleichen; **2.** *fig.* F a) leisetreten, b) sich nicht festlegen (***on*** auf *acc.*), her'umreden (um); **II** *pl.* **-foots** [-fʊts] *s.* **3.** Schleicher *m*; **4.** *fig.* F Leisetreter *m*; *~* **wil·low** *s.* ⚘ Verschiedenfarbige Weide.

pus·tule ['pʌstju:l] *s.* **1.** ⚕ Pustel *f*, Eiterbläschen *n*; **2.** ⚘, *zo.* Warze *f*.

put [pʊt] **I** *s.* **1.** *bsd. sport* Stoß *m*, Wurf *m*; **2.** ⚘, *Börse*: Rückprämie *f*: *~* ***and call*** Stellagegeschäft *n*; *~* ***of more*** Nochgeschäft *n* ‚auf Geben'; **II** *adj.* **3.** F an Ort u. Stelle, unbeweglich: ***stay*** *~* a) sich nicht (vom Fleck) rühren, b) festbleiben (*a. fig.*); **III** *v/t.* [*irr.*] **4.** legen, stellen, setzen, *wohin* tun; befestigen (***to*** an *dat.*): ***I shall*** *~* ***the matter before him*** ich werde ihm die Sache vorlegen; ***I*** *~* ***him above his brother*** ich stelle ihn über seinen Bruder; *~* ***s.th. in hand*** *fig.* et. in die Hand nehmen, anfangen; **5.** stecken (***in one's pocket*** in die Tasche, ***in prison*** ins Gefängnis); **6.** *j-n in e-e unangenehme Lage*, ⚘ *et. auf den Markt, in Ordnung, thea. ein Stück auf die Bühne etc.* bringen: *~* ***s.o. across a river*** j-n über e-n Fluß übersetzen; *~* ***it across s.o.*** F j-n ‚reinlegen'; *~* ***one's brain to it*** sich darauf konzentrieren, die Sache in Angriff nehmen; *~* ***s.o. in mind of*** j-n erinnern an (*acc.*); *~* ***s.th. on paper*** et. zu Papier bringen; *~* ***s.o. right*** j-n berichtigen; **7.** *ein Ende, in Kraft, in Umlauf, j-n auf Diät, in Besitz, in ein gutes od. schlechtes Licht, ins Unrecht, über ein Land, sich et. in den Kopf, j-n an e-e Arbeit* setzen: *~* ***one's signature to*** s-e Unterschrift darauf *od.* darunter setzen; *~* ***yourself in my place*** versetze dich in m-e Lage; **8.** *~* ***o.s.*** sich in *j-s Hände etc.* begeben: *~* ***o.s. under s.o.'s care*** sich in j-s Obhut begeben; *~* ***yourself in***(***to***) ***my hands*** vertraue dich mir ganz an; **9.** *~* ***out of*** aus … hin'ausstellen *etc.*; werfen *od.* verdrängen aus; außer *Betrieb od. Gefecht etc.* setzen; → ***action*** 2, 9, ***running*** 1; **10.** unter'werfen, -'ziehen (***to*** *e-r Probe etc.*; ***through*** *e-m Verhör etc.*): *~* ***s.o. through it*** j-n auf Herz u. Nieren prüfen; → ***confusion*** 3, ***death*** 1, ***expense*** 2, ***shame*** 2, ***sword***, ***test*** 1; **11.** *Land* bepflanzen (***into***, ***under*** mit): ***land was*** *~* ***under potatoes***; **12.** (***to***) setzen (an *acc.*), (an)treiben *od.* zwingen (zu): *~* ***s.o. to work*** j-n an die Arbeit setzen, j-n arbeiten lassen; *~* ***to school*** zur Schule schicken, einschulen; *~* ***to trade*** *j-n* ein Handwerk lernen lassen; *~* ***s.o. to a joiner*** j-n bei e-m Schreiner in die Lehre geben; *~* ***s.o. to it*** j-m zusetzen, j-n bedrängen; ***be hard*** *~* ***to it*** arg bedrängt werden; → ***flight¹***, ***pace¹*** 2; **13.** veranlassen, verlocken (***on***, ***to*** zu); **14.** *in Furcht, Wut etc.* versetzen; → ***countenance*** 2, ***ease*** 2, ***guard*** 11, ***mettle*** 2, ***temper*** 4; **15.** über'setzen (***into French*** *etc.* ins Französische *etc.*); **16.** (*un*)*klar etc.* ausdrükken, sagen *klug etc.* formulieren, *in Worte* fassen: ***the case was cleverly*** *~*; ***to*** *~* ***it mildly*** gelinde gesagt; ***how shall I*** *~* ***it?*** wie soll ich mich (*od.* es) ausdrücken; **17.** schätzen (***at*** auf *acc.*); **18.** (***to***) verwenden (für), anwenden (zu): *~* ***s.th. to a good use*** et. gut verwenden; **19.** *Frage, Antrag etc.* vorlegen, stellen; *den Fall* setzen: ***I*** *~* ***it to you*** a) ich appelliere an Sie, b) ich stelle es Ihnen anheim; ***I*** *~* ***it to you that*** geben Sie zu, daß; **20.** *Geld* setzen, wetten (***on*** auf *acc.*); **21.** (***into***) *Geld* stecken (in *acc.*), anlegen (in *dat.*), investieren (in *dat.*); **22.** *Schuld* zuschieben, geben (***on*** *dat.*): ***they*** *~* ***the blame on him***; **23.** *Uhr* stellen; **24.** *bsd. sport* werfen, schleudern; *Kugel, Stein* stoßen; **25.** *Waffe* stoßen, *Kugel* schießen (***in***[***to***] in *acc.*); **IV.** *v/i.* [*irr.*] **26.** sich begeben (***to land*** an Land), fahren: *~* ***to sea*** in See stechen; **27.** *Am.* münden, sich ergießen (*Fluß*) (***into*** in *e-n*

See etc.); **28.** **~ upon** *mst pass.* a) *j-m* zusetzen, b) *j-n* ausnutzen, c) *j-n* ‚reinlegen‘;
Zssgn mit prp.:
→ *Beispiele unter* **put** 4 → 28;
Zssgn mit adv.:
put| a·bout I *v/t.* **1.** ⚓ wenden; **2.** *Gerücht* verbreiten; **3.** a) beunruhigen, b) quälen, c) ärgern; **II** *v/i.* **4.** ⚓ wenden; **~ a·cross** *v/t.* **1.** ⚓ 'übersetzen; **2.** *sl. et.* ‚schaukeln‘, erfolgreich 'durchführen, *Idee etc.* ‚verkaufen‘: **put it across** ‚es schaffen‘, Erfolg haben; **~ a·side** *v/t.* **1.** → **put away** 1 *u.* 3; **2.** *fig.* bei'seite schieben; **~ a·way I** *v/t.* **1.** weglegen, -stecken, -tun, beiseite legen; **2.** auf-, wegräumen; **3.** *Geld* zu'rücklegen, ‚auf die hohe Kante legen‘; **4.** *Laster etc.* ablegen; **5.** F *Speisen* ‚verdrücken‘, *Getränke* ‚runterstellen‘; **6.** F *j-n* ‚einsperren‘; **7.** F *j-n* ‚beseitigen‘ (*umbringen*); **8.** *sl. et.* versetzen; **II** *v/i.* **9.** ⚓ auslaufen (**for** nach); **~ back I** *v/t.* **1.** zu'rückschieben, -stellen, -tun; **2.** *Uhr* zu'rückstellen, *Zeiger* zu'rückdrehen; **3.** *fig.* aufhalten, hemmen; → **clock**[1] 1; **4.** *Schüler* zu'rückversetzen; **II** *v/i.* **5.** ⚓ 'umkehren; **~ by** *v/t.* **1.** → **put away** 1 *u.* 3; **2.** *e-r Frage etc.* ausweichen; **3.** *fig.* bei'seite schieben, *j-n* über'gehen; **~ down** *v/t.* **1.** hin-, niederlegen, -stellen, -setzen; → **foot** 1; **2.** *j-n auf der Fahrt* absetzen, aussteigen lassen; **3.** *Weinkeller* anlegen; **4.** *Aufstand* niederwerfen, *a. Mißstand* unter'drücken; **5.** *j-n* demütigen, ducken; kurz abweisen; her'untersetzen; **6.** zum Schweigen bringen; **7.** a) *Preise* heruntersetzen, b) *Ausgaben* einschränken; **8.** (auf-, nieder)schreiben; **9.** (**to**) ⚚ a) *j-m* anschreiben, b) auf *j-s Rechnung* setzen: **put s.th. down to s.o.'s account**; **10.** *j-n* eintragen *od.* vormerken (**for** für *e-e Spende etc.*): **put o.s. down** sich eintragen; **11.** zuschreiben (**to** *dat.*); **12.** schätzen (**at**, **for** auf *acc.*); **13.** ansehen (**as**, **for** als); **~ forth** *v/t.* **1.** her'vor-, hin'auslegen, -stellen, -schieben; **2.** *Hand etc.* ausstrecken; **3.** *Kraft etc.* aufbieten; **4.** ⚘ *Knospen etc.* treiben; **5.** veröffentlichen, *bsd. Buch* her'ausbringen; **6.** behaupten; **~ for·ward** *v/t.* **1.** vorschieben; *Uhr* vorstellen, *Zeiger* vorrücken; **2.** in den Vordergrund schieben: **put o.s. forward** a) sich hervortun, b) sich vordrängen; **3.** *fig.* vor'anbringen, weiterhelfen (*dat.*); **4.** *Meinung etc.* vorbringen, *et.* vorlegen, unter'breiten; *Theorie* aufstellen; **~ in I** *v/t.* **1.** her'ein-, hin'einlegen *etc.*; **2.** einschieben, -schalten: **~ a word** a) e-e Bemerkung einwerfen *od.* anbringen, b) ein Wort mitsprechen, c) ein Wort einlegen (**for** für); **~ an extra hour's work** e-e Stunde mehr arbeiten; **3.** *Schlag etc.* anbringen; **4.** *Gesuch etc.* einreichen, *Dokument* vorlegen; *Anspruch* stellen *od.* erheben (**to**, **for** auf *acc.*); **5.** *j-n* anstellen, *in ein Amt* einsetzen; **6.** *Annonce* einrücken; **7.** F *Zeit* verbringen; **II** *v/i.* **8.** ⚓ einlaufen; **9.** einkehren (**at** in *e-m Gasthaus etc.*); **10.** sich bewerben (**for** um): **~ for s.th.** et. fordern *od.* verlangen; **~ in·side** *v/t.* F *j-n* ‚einlochen‘; **~ off I** *v/t.* **1.** weg-, bei'seite legen, -stellen; **2.** *Kleider*, *bsd. fig. Zweifel etc.* ablegen; **3.** auf-, verschieben; **4.** *j-n* vertrösten, abspeisen (**with** mit *Worten etc.*); **5.** *j-m* absagen; **6.** sich drücken vor (*dat.*); **7.** *j-n* abbringen, *j-m* abraten (**from** von); **8.** hindern (**from** an *dat.*); **9.** **put s.th. off** (**up**)**on s.o.** j-m et. ‚andrehen‘; **10.** F a) *j-n* aus der Fassung *od.* aus dem Kon'zept bringen, b) j-m die Lust nehmen, *j-n* abstoßen; **II** *v/i.* **11.** ⚓ auslaufen; **~ on** *v/t.* **1.** *Kleider* anziehen; *Hut*, *Brille* aufsetzen; *Rouge* auflegen; **2.** *Fett* ansetzen; → **weight** 1; **3.** *Charakter*, *Gestalt* annehmen; **4.** vortäuschen, -spiegeln, (er)heucheln: → **air**[1] 7, **dog** *Redew.*; **put it on** F a) angeben, b) übertreiben, c) ‚schwer draufschlagen‘ (*auf den Preis*), d) heucheln; **put it on thick** F dick auftragen; **his modesty is all ~** s-e Bescheidenheit ist nur Mache; **5.** *Summe* aufschlagen (**on** auf *den Preis*); **6.** *Uhr* vorstellen, *Zeiger* vorrücken; **7.** an-, einschalten, *Gas etc.* aufdrehen, *Dampf* anlassen, *Tempo* beschleunigen; **8.** *Kraft*, *a. Arbeitskräfte*, *Sonderzug etc.* einsetzen; **9.** *Schraube*, *Bremse* anziehen; **10.** *thea. etc. Stück*, *Sendung* bringen; **11.** **put s.o. on to** j-m e-n Tip geben für, j-n auf *e-e Idee* bringen; **12.** *sport Tor etc.* erzielen; **~ out I** *v/t.* **1.** hin'auslegen, -stellen *etc.*; **2.** *Hand*, *Fühler* ausstrecken; *Zunge* her'ausstrecken; *Ankündigung etc.* aushängen; **3.** *sport* zum Ausscheiden zwingen, ‚aus dem Rennen werfen‘; **4.** *Glied* aus-, verrenken; **5.** *Feuer*, *Licht* (aus-)löschen; **6.** a) verwirren, außer Fassung bringen, b) verstimmen, ärgern: **be ~ about s.th.**, c) *j-m* Ungelegenheiten bereiten, *j-n* stören; **7.** *Kraft etc.* aufbieten; **8.** *Geld* ausleihen (**at interest** auf Zinsen), investieren; **9.** *Boot* aussetzen; **10.** *Augen* ausstechen; **11.** *Arbeit*, *a. Kind*, *Tier* außer Haus geben; ⚚ in Auftrag geben; → **grass** 3, **nurse** 4; **12.** *Knospen etc.* treiben; **II** *v/i.* **13.** ⚓ auslaufen: **~** (**to sea**) in See stechen; **~ o·ver I** *v/t.* **1.** *sl.* → **put across** 2; **2.** *e-m Film etc.* Erfolg sichern, popu'lär machen (*acc.*): **put o.s. over** sich durchsetzen, ‚ankommen‘; **3.** **put it over on** *j-n* ‚reinlegen‘; **II** *v/i.* **4.** ⚓ hin'überfahren; **~ through** *v/t.* **1.** 'durch-, ausführen; **2.** *teleph. j-n* verbinden (**to** mit); **~ to** *v/t. Pferd* anspannen, *Lokomotive* vorspannen; **~ to·geth·er** *v/t.* **1.** zs.-setzen (*a. Schriftwerk*) zs.-stellen; **2.** zs.-zählen: → **two** 2; **3.** zs.-stecken; → **head** *Redew.*; **~ up I** *v/t.* **1.** hin'auflegen, -stellen; **2.** hochschieben, -ziehen; → **back**[1] 7, **shutter** 1; **3.** *Hände* a) heben, b) *zum Kampf* hochnehmen; **4.** *Bild etc.* aufhängen; *Plakat* anschlagen; **5.** *Haar* aufstecken; **6.** *Schirm* aufspannen; **7.** *Zelt etc.* aufstellen, *Gebäude* errichten; **8.** F *et.* aushecken; *et.* ‚drehen‘, fingieren; **9.** *Gebet* em'porsenden; **10.** *Gast* (bei sich) aufnehmen, 'unterbringen; **11.** weglegen; **12.** aufbewahren; **13.** ein-, ver-, wegpacken; zs.-legen; **14.** *Schwert* einstecken; **15.** konservieren, einkochen, -machen; **16.** *Spiel etc.* zeigen; *e-n Kampf* liefern; *Widerstand* leisten; **17.** (als Kandi'daten) aufstellen; **18.** *Auktion*: an-, ausbieten: **~ for sale** meistbietend verkaufen; **19.** *Preis etc.* hin'aufsetzen, erhöhen; **20.** *Wild* aufjagen; **21.** *Eheaufgebot* verkünden; **22.** bezahlen; **23.** (ein)setzen (*Wette etc.*), *Geld* bereitstellen, *od.* hinter'legen; **24.** **~ to** a) *j-n* anstiften zu, b) *j-n* informieren über (*acc.*), *a. j-m* e-n Tip geben für; **II** *v/i.* **25.** absteigen, einkehren (**at** in); **26.** (**for**) sich aufstellen lassen, kandidieren (für), sich bewerben (um); **27.** **~ with** sich abfinden mit, sich gefallen lassen, hinnehmen.

pu·ta·tive ['pju:tətɪv] *adj.* □ **1.** vermeintlich; **2.** mutmaßlich; **3.** ⚖ puta'tiv.

'put|·down *s.*: **that was a ~** damit wollte er *etc.* mich *etc.* fertigmachen; **'~·off** *s.* **1.** Ausflucht *f*; **2.** Verschiebung *f*; **'~-on I** *adj.* **1.** vorgetäuscht; **II** *s. Am. sl.* **2.** Bluff *m*; **3.** Getue *n*, ‚Mache‘ *f*, ‚Schau‘ *f*.

put-put ['pʌtpʌt] *s.* Tuckern *n* (*e-s Motors etc.*).

pu·tre·fa·cient [ˌpju:trɪ'feɪʃənt] → **putrefactive**; ˌ**pu·tre'fac·tion** [-'fækʃn] *s.* **1.** Fäulnis *f*, Verwesung *f*; **2.** Faulen *n*; ˌ**pu·tre'fac·tive** [-'fæktɪv] **I** *adj.* **1.** faulig, Fäulnis…; **2.** fäulniserregend; **II** *s.* **3.** Fäulniserreger *m*; **pu·tre·fy** ['pju:trɪfaɪ] **I** *v/i.* (ver)faulen, verwesen; **II** *v/t.* verfaulen lassen.

pu·tres·cence [pju:'tresns] *s.* (Ver-)Faulen *n*, Fäulnis *f*; **pu'tres·cent** [-nt] *adj.* **1.** (ver)faulend, verwesend; **2.** faulig, Fäulnis…

pu·trid ['pju:trɪd] *adj.* □ **1.** verfault, verwest; faulig (*Geruch*), stinkend; **2.** *fig.* verderbt, kor'rupt; **3.** *fig.* verderblich; **4.** *fig.* ekelhaft; **5.** *sl.* mise'rabel.

putsch [pʊtʃ] (*Ger.*) *s. pol.* Putsch *m*, Staatsstreich *m*.

putt [pʌt] *Golf*: **I** *v/t. u. v/i.* putten; **II** *s.* Putt *m*.

put·tee ['pʌtɪ] *s.* 'Wickelgaˌmasche *f*.

putt·er ['pʌtə] *s. Golf*: Putter *m* (*Schläger od. Spieler*).

'putt·ing-green ['pʌtɪŋ] *s. Golf*: Putting green *n* (*Platzteil*).

put·ty ['pʌtɪ] **I** *s.* **1.** ⚙ Kitt *m*, Spachtel *m*: (**glaziers'**) **~** Glaserkitt; (**plasterers'**) **~** Kalkkitt; (**jewellers'**) **~** Zinnasche *f*; **2.** *fig.* Wachs *n*: **he is ~ in her hand**; **II** *v/t.* **3.** *a.* **~ up** (ver)kitten; **~ knife** *s.* [*irr.*] Spachtelmesser *n*.

'put-up *adj.* F abgekartet: **a ~ job** e-e ‚Schiebung‘.

puz·zle ['pʌzl] **I** *s.* **1.** Rätsel *n*; **2.** Puzzle-, Geduldspiel *n*; **3.** schwierige Sache, Prob'lem *n*; **4.** Verwirrung *f*, Verlegenheit *f*; **II** *v/t.* **5.** verwirren, vor ein Rätsel stellen, verdutzen; **6.** *et.* komplizieren, durchein'anderbringen; **7.** *j-m* Kopfzerbrechen machen, zu schaffen machen: **~ one's brains** (*od.* **head**) sich den Kopf zerbrechen (**over** über *acc.*); **8.** **~ out** austüfteln, -knobeln, her'ausbekommen; **III** *v/i.* **9.** verwirrt sein (**over**, **about** über *acc.*); **10.** sich den Kopf zerbrechen (**over** über *acc.*); **'~-ˌhead·ed** *adj.* wirrköpfig, kon'fus; **~ lock** *s.* Vexier-, Buchstabenschloß *n*.

puz·zle·ment ['pʌzlmənt] *s.* Verwirrung *f*; **'puz·zler** [-lə] → **puzzle** 3; **'puz·zling** [-lɪŋ] *adj.* □ **1.** rätselhaft; **2.** verwirrend.

py·e·li·tis [paɪə'laɪtɪs] *s.* ⚕ Nierenbeckenentzündung *f*.

pyg·m(a)e·an [pɪg'mi:ən] → **pygmy** II.

pyg·my ['pɪgmɪ] **I** *s.* **1.** ♀ Pyg'mäe *m*,

Pyg'mäin *f* (*Zwergmensch*); **2.** *fig.* Zwerg *m*; **II** *adj.* **3.** Pygmäen…; **4.** winzig, Zwerg…; **5.** unbedeutend.

py·ja·mas [pə'dʒɑːməz] *s. pl.* Schlafanzug *m*, Py'jama *m*.

py·lon ['paɪlən] *s.* **1.** ϟ (freitragender) Mast (*für Hochspannungsleitungen etc.*); **2.** ✈ Orientierungsturm *m*, *bsd.* Wendeturm *m*.

py·lo·rus [paɪ'lɔːrəs] *pl.* **-ri** [-raɪ] *s. anat.* Py'lorus *m*, Pförtner *m*.

pyr·a·mid ['pɪrəmɪd] *s.* Pyra'mide *f* (*a.* ⩓ *u. fig.*); **py·ram·i·dal** [pɪ'ræmɪdl] *adj.* □ **1.** Pyramiden…; **2.** pyrami'dal (*a. fig. gewaltig*), pyra'midenartig, -förmig.

pyre ['paɪə] *s.* Scheiterhaufen *m*.

py·ret·ic [paɪ'retɪk] *adj.* ⚕ fieberhaft, Fieber…; **py'rex·i·a** [-eksɪə] *s.* ⚕ Fieberzustand *m*.

py·rite ['paɪraɪt] *s. min.* Py'rit *m*, Schwefel-, Eisenkies *m*; **py·ri·tes** [paɪ'raɪtiːz] *s. min.* Py'rit *m*: ***copper*** **~** Kupferkies; ***iron*** **~** → ***pyrite***.

pyro- [paɪərəʊ] *in Zssgn* Feuer…, Brand…, Wärme…, Glut…; **'py·ro·gen** [-rədʒən] *s.* ⚕ fiebererregender Stoff; **py·rog·e·nous** [paɪ'rɒdʒɪnəs] *adj.* **1.** a) wärmeerzeugend, b) durch Wärme erzeugt; **2.** ⚕ a) fiebererregend, b) durch Fieber verursacht; **3.** *geol.* pyro'gen; **py·rog·ra·phy** [paɪ'rɒgrəfɪ] *s.* Brandmale'rei *f*; **py·ro·ma·ni·a** [ˌpaɪrəʊ'meɪnɪə] *s.* Pyroma'nie *f*, Brandstiftungstrieb *m*; **py·ro·ma·ni·ac** [ˌpaɪrəʊ'meɪnɪæk] *s.* Pyro'mane *m*, Pyro'manin *f*.

py·ro·tech·nic, **py·ro·tech·ni·cal** [ˌpaɪrəʊ'teknɪk(l)] *adj.* □ **1.** pyro'technisch; **2.** Feuerwerks…, feuerwerkartig; **3.** *fig.* bril'lant; **ˌpy·ro'tech·nics** [-ks] *s. pl.* **1.** Pyro'technik *f*, Feuerwerke'rei *f*; **2.** *fig.* Feuerwerk *n von Witz etc.*; **ˌpy·ro'tech·nist** [-ɪst] *s.* Pyro'techniker *m*.

Pyr·rhic vic·to·ry ['pɪrɪk] *s.* Pyrrhussieg *m*.

Py·thag·o·re·an [paɪˌθægə'rɪən] **I** *adj.* pythago'reisch; **II** *s. phls.* Pythago'reer *m*.

py·thon ['paɪθn] *s. zo.* **1.** Python(schlange *f*) *m*; **2.** *allg.* Riesenschlange *f*.

pyx [pɪks] **I** *s.* **1.** *R.C.* Pyxis *f*, Mon'stranz *f*; **2.** *Brit.* Büchse *f* mit Probemünzen; **II** *v/t.* **3.** *Münze* a) in der ***Pyx*** hinter'legen, b) auf Gewicht u. Feinheit prüfen.

Q

Q, q [kju:] *s.* Q *n*, q *n* (*Buchstabe*).

ˈ**Q-boat** *s.* ⚓ U-Boot-Falle *f*.

quack¹ [kwæk] **I** *v/i.* **1.** quaken; **2.** *fig.* schnattern, schwatzen; **II** *s.* **3.** Quaken *n*; *fig.* Geplapper *n*.

quack² [kwæk] **I** *s.* **1.** *a.* ~ ***doctor*** Quacksalber *m*, Kurpfuscher *m*; **2.** Scharlatan *m*; Marktschreier *m*; **II** *adj.* **3.** quacksalberisch, Quacksalber…; **4.** marktschreierisch; **5.** Schwindel…; **III** *v/i. u. v/t.* **6.** quacksalbern, herˈumpfuschen (an *dat.*); **7.** marktschreierisch auftreten (*v/t.* anpreisen); ˈ**quack·er·y** [-kərɪ] *s.* **1.** Quacksalbeˈrei *f*, Kurpfuscheˈrei *f*; **2.** Scharlataneˈrie *f*; **3.** marktschreierisches Auftreten.

quad¹ [kwɒd] F → ***quadrangle***, ***quadrat***, ***quadruped***, ***quadruplet***.

quad² [kwɒd] **I** *s.* ⚡ Viererkabel *n*; **II** *v/t.* zum Vierer verseilen.

quad·ra·ble [ˈkwɒdrəbl] *adj.* Ⱥ quadrierbar.

quad·ra·ge·nar·i·an [kwɒdrədʒɪˈneərɪən] **I** *adj.* a) vierzigjährig, b) in den Vierzigern; **II** *s.* Vierziger(in), Vierzigjährige(r *m*) *f*.

quad·ran·gle [ˈkwɒdræŋgl] *s.* **1.** Ⱥ *u. weitS.* Viereck *n*; **2.** a) (*bsd.* Schul)Hof *m*, b) viereckiger Geˈbäudekomˌplex; **quad·ran·gu·lar** [kwɒˈdræŋgjʊlə] *adj.* □ Ⱥ viereckig.

quad·rant [ˈkwɒdrənt] *s.* **1.** Ⱥ Quaˈdrant *m*, Viertelkreis *m*, (ˈKreis)Segˌment *n*; **2.** ⚓, *ast.* Quaˈdrant *m*.

quad·ra·phon·ic [ˌkwɒdrəˈfɒnɪk] *adj.* ♪, *phys.* quadroˈphonisch; ˌ**quad·raˈphon·ics** [-ks] *s. pl. sg. konstr.* Quadrophoˈnie *f*.

quad·rat [ˈkwɒdrət] *s. typ.* Quaˈdrat *n*, (großer) Ausschluß: ***em*** ~ Geviert *n*; ***en*** ~ Halbgeviert *n*.

quad·rate [ˈkwɒdrət] **I** *adj.* (annähernd) quaˈdratisch, *bsd. anat.* Quadrat…; **II** *v/t.* [kwɒˈdreɪt] in Überˈeinstimmung bringen (***with***, ***to*** mit); **III** *v/i.* [kwɒˈdreɪt] überˈeinstimmen; **quad·rat·ic** [kwɒˈdrætɪk] **I** *adj.* quaˈdratisch (*Form*, Ⱥ *Gleichung*): ~ ***curve*** Kurve *f* zweiter Ordnung; **II** *s.* Ⱥ quaˈdratische Gleichung; **quad·ra·ture** [ˈkwɒdrətʃə] *s.* **1.** Ⱥ, *ast.* Quadraˈtur *f* (***of the circle*** des Kreises); **2.** ⚡ (Phasen)Verschiebung *f* um 90 Grad.

quad·ren·ni·al [kwɒˈdrenɪəl] **I** *adj.* □ **1.** vierjährig, vier Jahre dauernd; **2.** vierjährlich, alle vier Jahre stattfindend; **II** *s.* **3.** Zeitraum *m* von vier Jahren; **4.** vierter Jahrestag.

quad·ri·lat·er·al [ˌkwɒdrɪˈlætərəl] **I** *adj.* vierseitig; **II** *s.* Vierseit *n*, -eck *n*.

qua·drille [kwəˈdrɪl] *s.* Quaˈdrille *f* (*Tanz*).

quad·ril·lion [kwɒˈdrɪljən] *s.* Ⱥ **1.** *Brit.* Quadrilliˈon *f*; **2.** *Am.* Billiˈarde *f*.

quad·ri·par·tite [ˌkwɒdrɪˈpɑ:taɪt] *adj.* **1.** vierteilig (*a.* ⚘); **2.** Vierer…, zwischen vier Partnern abgeschlossen *etc.*: ~ ***pact*** Viererpakt *m*.

quad·ro [ˈkwɒdrəʊ] *adj. u. adv.* ♪, *Radio*: quadro.

quadro- [kwɒdrəʊ] *in Zssgn* quadro…

ˌ**quad·roˈphon·ic** [-ˈfɒnɪk] *etc.* → ***quadraphonic*** *etc.*

quad·ru·ped [ˈkwɒdrʊped] **I** *s.* Vierfüßer *m*; **II** *adj. a.* **quad·ru·pe·dal** [ˌkwɒdrəˈpi:dl] vierfüßig; ˈ**quad·ru·ple** [-pl] **I** *adj.* **1.** *a.* ~ ***to*** (*od.* ***of***) vierfach, -fältig; viermal so groß wie; **2.** Vierer…: ~ ***machinegun*** ⚔ Vierlings-MG *n*; ~ ***measure*** ♪ Viervierteltakt *m*; ~ ***thread*** ⚙ viergängiges Gewinde; **II** *adv.* **3.** vierfach; **III** *s.* **4.** *das* Vierfache; **IV** *v/t.* **5.** vervierfachen; **6.** viermal so groß *od.* so viel sein wie; **V** *v/i.* **7.** sich vervierfachen; ˈ**quad·ru·plet** [-plɪt] *s.* **1.** Vierling *m* (*Kind*); **2.** Vierergruppe *f*; ˈ**quad·ru·plex** [-pleks] **I** *adj.* **1.** vierfach; **2.** ⚡ Quadruplex…, Vierfach…: ~ ***system*** Vierfachbetrieb *m*, Doppelgegensprechen *n*; **II** *s.* **3.** ˈQuadruplextеleˌgraph *m*; **quad·ru·pli·cate** **I** *v/t.* [kwɒˈdru:plɪkeɪt] **1.** vervierfachen; **2.** *Dokument* vierfach ausfertigen; **II** *adj.* [kwɒˈdru:plɪkət] **3.** vierfach; **III** *s.* [-kət] **4.** vierfache Ausfertigung.

quaff [kwɑ:f] **I** *v/i.* zechen; **II** *v/t.* schlürfen, in langen Zügen (aus)trinken: ~ ***off*** *Getränk* hinunterstürzen.

quag [kwæg] → ***quagmire***; ˈ**quag·gy** [-gɪ] *adj.* **1.** sumpfig; **2.** schwammig; ˈ**quag·mire** [-maɪə] *s.* Moˈrast *m*, Moor(boden *m*) *n*, Sumpf(land *n*) *m*: ***be caught in a*** ~ *fig.* in der Patsche sitzen.

quail¹ [kweɪl] *pl.* **quails**, *coll.* **quail** *s. orn.* Wachtel *f*.

quail² [kweɪl] *v/i.* **1.** verzagen; **2.** (vor Angst) zittern (***before*** vor *dat.*; ***at*** bei).

quaint [kweɪnt] *adj.* □ **1.** wunderlich, drollig, kuriˈos; **2.** malerisch, anheimelnd (*altmodisch*); **3.** seltsam, merkwürdig; ˈ**quaint·ness** [-nɪs] *s.* **1.** Wunderlichkeit *f*; Seltsamkeit *f*; **2.** anheimelndes (*bsd.* altmodisches) Aussehen.

quake [kweɪk] **I** *v/i.* zittern, beben (***with***, ***for*** vor *dat.*); **II** *s.* Zittern *n*, (*a.* Erd)Beben *n*, Erschütterung *f*.

Quak·er [ˈkweɪkə] *s.* **1.** *eccl.* Quäker *m*: ~***(sʼ) meeting*** *fig.* schweigsame Versammlung; **2.** *a.* ~ ***gun*** ⚔ *Am.* Geˈschützatˌtrappe *f*; **3.** *2*, *a.* ***2-bird*** *orn.* schwarzer Albatros; ˈ**Quak·er·ess** [-ərɪs] *s.* Quäkerin *f*; ˈ**Quak·er·ism** [-ərɪzəm] *s.* Quäkertum *n*.

ˈ**quak·ing-grass** [ˈkweɪkɪŋ-] *s.* ⚘ Zittergras *n*.

qual·i·fi·ca·tion [ˌkwɒlɪfɪˈkeɪʃn] *s.* **1.** Qualifikatiˈon *f*, Befähigung *f*, Eignung *f* (***for*** für, zu): ~ ***test*** Eignungsprüfung *f*; ***have the necessary*** ~***s*** den Anforderungen entsprechen; **2.** Vorbedingung *f*, (notwendige) Vorˈaussetzung (***of***, ***for*** für); **3.** Eignungszeugnis *n*; **4.** Einschränkung *f*, Modifikatiˈon *f*: ***without any*** ~ ohne jede Einschränkung; **5.** *ling.* nähere Bestimmung; **6.** ☤ ˈMindestˌaktienkapiˌtal *n* (*e-s Aufsichtsratsmitglieds*); **qual·i·fied** [ˈkwɒlɪfaɪd] *adj.* **1.** qualifiziert, geeignet, befähigt (***for*** für); **2.** berechtigt: ~ ***for a post*** anstellungsberechtigt; ~ ***voter*** Wahlberechtigte(r *m*) *f*; **3.** eingeschränkt, bedingt, modifiziert: ~ ***acceptance*** ☤ bedingte Annahme (*e-s Wechsels*); ~ ***sale*** ☤ Konditionskauf *m*; ***in a*** ~ ***sense*** mit Einschränkungen; **qual·i·fy** [ˈkwɒlɪfaɪ] **I** *v/t.* **1.** qualifizieren, befähigen, geeignet machen (***for*** für; ***for being***, ***to be*** zu sein); **2.** berechtigen (***for*** zu); **3.** bezeichnen, charakterisieren (***as*** als); **4.** einschränken, modifizieren; **5.** abschwächen, mildern; **6.** *Getränke* verdünnen; **7.** *ling.* modifizieren, näher bestimmen; **II** *v/i.* **8.** sich qualifizieren *od.* eignen, die Eignung besitzen *od.* nachweisen, in Frage kommen (***for*** für; ***as*** als): ~***ing examination*** Eignungsprüfung *f*; ~***ing period*** Anwartschafts-, Probezeit *f*; **9.** *sport* sich qualifizieren (***for*** für): ~***ing round*** Ausscheidungsrunde *f*; **10.** die nötigen Fähigkeiten erwerben; **11.** die (juˈristischen) Vorbedingungen erfüllen, *bsd. Am.* den Eid ablegen; **qual·i·ta·tive** [ˈkwɒlɪtətɪv] *adj.* □ qualitaˈtiv (*a.* ⚗ *Analyse*, *a.* Ⱥ *Verteilung*); **qual·i·ty** [ˈkwɒlətɪ] *s.* **1.** Eigenschaft *f* (*Person u. Sache*): (***good***) ~ gute Eigenschaft; ***in the*** ~ ***of*** (in der Eigenschaft) als; **2.** Art *f*, Naˈtur *f*, Beschaffenheit *f*; **3.** Fähigkeit *f*, Taˈlent *n*; **4.** *bsd.* ☤, ⚙ Qualiˈtät *f*: ***in*** ~ qualitativ; **5.** ☤ (Güte)Sorte *f*, Klasse *f*; **6.** gute Qualiˈtät, Güte *f*: ~ ***goods*** Qualitätswaren; ~ ***of life*** Lebensqualität; **7.** a) ♪ ˈTonqualiˌtät *f*, -farbe *f*, b) *ling.* Klangfarbe *f*; **8.** *phls.* Qualiˈtät *f*; **9.** vornehmer Stand: ***person of*** ~ Standesperson *f*; ***the people of*** ~ die vornehme Welt.

qualm [kwɑ:m] *s.* **1.** Übelkeitsgefühl *n*, Schwäche(anfall *m*) *f*; **2.** Bedenken *pl.*, Zweifel *pl.*; Skrupel *m*; ˈ**qualm·ish** [-mɪʃ] *adj.* □ **1.** (sich) übel (fühlend), unwohl; **2.** Übelkeits…: ~ ***feelings***.

quan·da·ry [ˈkwɒndərɪ] *s.* Verlegenheit *f*, verzwickte Lage: ***be in a*** ~ sich in e-m

Dilemma befinden; nicht wissen, was man tun soll.

quan·ta ['kwɒntə] *pl. von* ***quantum***.

quan·ti·ta·tive ['kwɒntɪtətɪv] *adj.* □ quantita'tiv (*a. ling.*), Mengen...: ***~ analysis*** ⚗ quantitative Analyse; ***~ ratio*** Mengenverhältnis *n*; **quan·ti·ty** ['kwɒntətɪ] *s.* **1.** Quanti'tät *f*, (bestimmte *od.* große) Menge, Quantum *n*: ***~ of heat*** *phys.* Wärmemenge; ***a ~ of cigars*** e-e Anzahl Zigarren; ***in*** (***large***) ***quantities*** in großen Mengen; ***~ discount*** † Mengenrabatt *m*; ***~ production*** Massenerzeugung *f*, Serienfertigung *f*; ***~ purchase*** Großeinkauf *m*; ***~ surveyor*** *Brit.* Bausachverständige(r) *m*; **2.** 𝔄 Größe *f*: ***negligible ~*** a) unwesentliche Größe, b) *fig.* völlig unbedeutende Person *etc.*; ***numerical ~*** Zahlengröße; (***un***)***known ~*** (un)bekannte Größe (*a. fig.*); **3.** *ling.* Quanti'tät *f*, Lautdauer *f*; (Silben)Zeitmaß *n*.

quan·ti·za·tion [ˌkwɒntɪ'zeɪʃn] *s. phys.* Quantelung *f*; **quan·tize** ['kwɒntaɪz] *v/t.* **1.** *phys.* quanteln; **2.** *Computer*: quantisieren.

quan·tum ['kwɒntəm] *pl.* **-ta** [-tə] *s.* **1.** Quantum *n*, Menge *f*; **2.** (An)Teil *m*; **3.** *phys.* Quant *n*: ***~ of radiation*** Lichtquant; **~ me·chan·ics** *s. pl.* 'Quantenmeˌchanik *f*; **~ or·bit**, **~ path** *s.* Quantenbahn *f*.

quar·an·tine ['kwɒrəntiːn] **I** *s.* ⚕ **1.** Quaran'täne *f*: ***absolute ~*** Isolierung *f*; ***~ flag*** ⚓ Quarantäneflagge *f*; ***put in ~*** → 2; **II** *v/t.* **2.** unter Quaran'täne stellen; **3.** *fig. pol.*, † *Land* völlig isolieren.

quar·rel ['kwɒrəl] **I** *s.* **1.** Streit *m*, Zank *m*, Hader *m* (***with*** mit; ***between*** zwischen): ***have no ~ with*** (*od.* ***against***) keinen Grund zum Streit haben mit, nichts auszusetzen haben an (*dat.*); → ***pick*** 8; **II** *v/i.* **2.** (sich) streiten, (sich) zanken (***with*** mit; ***for*** wegen; ***about*** über *acc.*); **3.** sich entzweien; **4.** hadern (***with one's lot*** mit s-m Schicksal); **5.** et. auszusetzen haben (***with*** an *dat.*); → ***bread*** 2; **'quar·rel·(l)er** [-rələ] *s.* Zänker(in), ‚Streithammel' *m*; **'quar·rel·some** [-səm] *adj.* □ streitsüchtig; **'quar·rel·some·ness** [-səmnɪs] *s.* Streitsucht *f*.

quar·ri·er ['kwɒrɪə] *s.* Steinbrecher *m*.

quar·ry¹ ['kwɒrɪ] *s.* **1.** *hunt.* (verfolgtes) Wild, Jagdbeute *f*; **2.** *fig.* Wild *n*, Opfer *n*, Beute *f*.

quar·ry² ['kwɒrɪ] **I** *s.* **1.** Steinbruch *m*; **2.** Quaderstein *m*; **3.** 'unglasierte Kachel; **4.** *fig.* Fundgrube *f*, Quelle *f*; **II** *v/t.* **5.** *Steine* brechen, abbauen; **6.** *fig.* zs.-tragen, (mühsam) erarbeiten, ausgraben; stöbern (***for*** nach); **'~·man** [-mən] *s.* [*irr.*] → ***quarrier***; **'~·stone** *s.* Bruchstein *m*.

quart¹ [kwɔːt] *s.* **1.** Quart *n* (*Maß* = *Brit. 1,14 l*, *Am. 0,95 l*); **2.** *a.* ***~-pot*** Quartkrug *m*.

quart² [kɑːt] *s.* **1.** *fenc.* Quart *f*; **2.** *Kartenspiel*: Quart *f* (*Sequenz von 4 Karten gleicher Farbe*); **3.** ♪ Quart(e) *f*.

quar·tan ['kwɔːtn] ⚕ **I** *adj.* viertägig: ***~ fever*** → **II** *s.* Quar'tan-, Vier'tagefieber *n*.

quar·ter ['kwɔːtə] **I** *s.* **1.** Viertel *n*, vierter Teil: ***~ of a century*** Vierteljahrhundert *n*; ***for a ~ the price*** zum viertel Preis; ***not a ~ as good*** nicht annähernd so gut; **2.** *a.* ***~ of an hour*** Viertel(stunde *f*) *n*: ***a ~ to six*** (ein) Viertel vor sechs, drei Viertel sechs; **3.** *a.* ***~ of a year*** Vierteljahr *n*, Quar'tal *n*; **4.** Viertel(pfund *n*, -zentner *m*) *n*; **5.** *bsd.* Hinter)Viertel *n e-s Schlachttieres*; Kruppe *f e-s Pferdes*; **6.** *sport* a) (Spiel)Viertel *n*, b) Viertelmeile(nlauf *m*, *a.* ***~-mile race***) *f*, c) → ***quarterback*** I; **7.** *Am.* Vierteldollar *m*, 25 Cent; **8.** Quarter *n*: a) *Handelsgewicht* (*Brit. 12,7 kg*, *Am. 11,34 kg*), b) *Hohlmaß* (*2,908 hl*); **9.** Himmelsrichtung *f*; **10.** Gegend *f*, Teil *m e-s Landes etc.*: ***at close ~s*** nahe aufeinander; ***come to close ~s*** handgemein werden; ***from all ~s*** von überall(her); ***in this ~*** hierzulande, in dieser Gegend; **11.** (Stadt)Viertel *n*: ***poor ~*** Armenviertel; ***residential ~*** Wohnbezirk *m*; **12.** *mst pl.* Quar'tier *n*, 'Unterkunft *f*, Wohnung *f*: ***have free ~s*** freie Wohnung haben; **13.** *mst pl.* ⚔ Quar'tier *n*, ('Truppen)ˌUnterkunft *f*: ***be confined to ~s*** Stubenarrest haben; **14.** Stelle *f*, Seite *f*, Quelle *f*: ***higher ~s*** höhere Stellen; ***in the proper ~*** bei der zuständigen Stelle; ***from official ~s*** von amtlicher Seite; ***from a good ~*** aus guter Quelle; → ***informed*** 1; **15.** *bsd.* ⚔ Par'don *m*, Schonung *f*: ***find no ~*** keine Schonung finden; ***give no ~*** keinen Pardon geben; ***give fair ~*** *fig.* Nachsicht üben; **16.** ⚓ Achterschiff *n*; **17.** ⚓ Posten *m*; **18.** *her.* Quar'tier *n*, (Wappen)Feld *n*; **19.** ⚙, △ Stollenholz *n*; **II** *v/t.* **20.** *et.* vierteln; *weitS.* aufteilen, zerstückeln; **21.** *j-n* vierteilen; **22.** *Wappenschild* vieren; **23.** *j-n* beherbergen; ⚔ einquartieren, *Truppen* 'unterbringen ([***up***]***on*** bei): ***~ed in barracks*** kaserniert; ***be ~ed at*** (*od.* ***in***) in Garnison liegen in (*dat.*); ***be ~ed*** (***up***)***on*** bei *j-m* in Quartier liegen; ***~ o.s. upon s.o.*** *fig.* sich bei j-m einquartieren; **24.** *Gegend* durch'stöbern (*Jagdhunde*).

'quar·ter|·back I *s. American Football*: ‚'Angriffsdiriˌgent' *m*; **II** *v/t. den Angriff* dirigieren (*a. fig.*); **~ bind·ing** *s. Buchbinderei*: Halbfranz(band *m*) *n*; **~ cir·cle** *s.* **1.** 𝔄 Viertelkreis *m*; **2.** ⚙ Abrundung *f*; **~ day** *s.* Quar'talstag *m für fällige Zahlungen* (*in England*: *25. 3.*, *24. 6.*, *29. 9.*, *25. 12.*; *in USA*: *1. 1.*, *1. 4.*, *1. 7.*, *1. 10.*); **'~·deck** *s.* ⚓ **1.** Achterdeck *n*; **2.** *coll.* Offi'ziere *pl.*; **ˌ~'fi·nal** *s. sport* **1.** *mst pl.* 'Viertelfiˌnale *n*; **2.** 'Viertelfiˌnalspiel *n*; **ˌ~'fi·nal·ist** *s. sport* Teilnehmer(in) am Viertelfinale.

quar·ter·ly ['kwɔːtəlɪ] **I** *adj.* **1.** Viertel...; **2.** vierteljährlich, Quartals...; **II** *adv.* **3.** in *od.* nach Vierteln; **4.** vierteljährlich, quar'talsweise; **III** *s.* **5.** Viertel'jahresschrift *f*.

'quar·terˌmas·ter *s.* **1.** ⚔ Quar'tiermeister *m*; **2.** ⚓ a) Steuerer *m* (*Handelsmarine*), b) Steuermannsmaat *m* (*Kriegsmarine*); **'~-'Gen·er·al** *s.* ⚔ Gene'ralquarˌtiermeister *m*.

quar·tern ['kwɔːtən] *s. bsd. Brit.* **1.** Viertel *n* (*bsd. e-s Maßes od. Gewichtes*): a) Viertelpinte *f*, b) Viertel *n* e-s engl. Pfunds; **2.** *a.* ***~ loaf*** Vier'pfundbrot *n*.

quar·ter| ses·sions *s. pl.* ⚖ **1.** *Brit. obs.* Krimi'nalgericht *n* (*mit vierteljährlichen Sitzungen*, *a. Berufungsinstanz für Zivilsachen*; *bis 1971*); **2.** *Am.* (*in einigen Staaten*) *ein ähnliches* Gericht für Strafsachen; **'~-tone** *s.* ♪ **1.** 'Vierteltoninterˌvall *n*; **2.** Viertelton *m*.

quar·tet(te) [kwɔː'tet] *s.* **1.** ♪ Quar'tett *n* (*a. humor. 4 Personen*); **2.** Vierergruppe *f*.

quar·tile ['kwɔːtaɪl] *s.* **1.** *ast.* Quadra'tur *f*, Geviertschein *m*; **2.** *Statistik*: Quar'til *n*, Viertelswert *m*.

quar·to ['kwɔːtəʊ] *pl.* **-tos** *typ.* **I** *s.* 'Quartforˌmat *n*; **II** *adj.* im 'Quartforˌmat.

quartz [kwɔːts] *s. min.* Quarz *m*: ***crystallized ~*** Bergkristall *m*; ***~ clock*** Quarzuhr *f*; ***~ lamp*** a) ⚙ Quarz(glas)lampe *f*, b) ⚕ Quarzlampe *f* (*Höhensonne*).

qua·sar ['kweɪzɑː] *s. ast.* Qua'sar *m*.

quash¹ [kwɒʃ] *v/t.* ⚖ **1.** *Verfügung etc.* aufheben, annullieren, verwerfen; **2.** *Klage* abweisen; **3.** *Verfahren* niederschlagen.

quash² [kwɒʃ] *v/t.* **1.** zermalmen, -stören; **2.** *fig.* unter'drücken.

qua·si ['kweɪzaɪ] *adv.* gleichsam, gewissermaßen, sozu'sagen; (*mst mit Bindestrich*) Quasi..., Schein..., ...ähnlich: ***~ contract*** vertragsähnliches Verhältnis; ***~-judicial*** quasigerichtlich; ***~-official*** halbamtlich.

qua·ter·na·ry [kwə'tɜːnərɪ] **I** *adj.* **1.** aus vier bestehend; **2.** ~ *geol.* Quartär...; **3.** ⚗ vierbindig, quater'När; **II** *s.* **4.** Gruppe *f* von 4 Dingen; **5.** Vier *f* (*Zahl*); **6.** *geol.* Quar'tär(periˌode *f*) *n*.

quat·rain ['kwɒtreɪn] *s.* Vierzeiler *m*.

quat·re·foil ['kætrəfɔɪl] *s.* **1.** △ Vierpaß *m*; **2.** ⚘ vierblättriges (Klee)Blatt.

qua·ver ['kweɪvə] **I** *v/i.* **1.** zittern; **2.** ♪ tremolieren (*weitS. a. beim Sprechen*); **II** *v/t. mst* ***~ out*** **3.** mit über'triebenem Vi'brato singen; **4.** mit zitternder Stimme sagen, stammeln; **III** *s.* **5.** ♪ Trillern *n*, Tremolo *n*; **6.** ♪ *Brit.* Achtelnote *f*; **'qua·ver·y** [-vərɪ] *adj.* zitternd.

quay [kiː] *s.* ⚓ (***on the ~*** am) Kai *m*; **quay·age** ['kiːɪdʒ] *s.* **1.** Kaigeld *n*, -gebühr *f*; **2.** Kaianlagen *pl*.

quea·si·ness ['kwiːzɪnɪs] *s.* **1.** Übelkeit *f*; **2.** ('Über)Empfindlichkeit *f*; **quea·sy** ['kwiːzɪ] *adj.* □ **1.** ('über)empfindlich (*Magen etc.*); **2.** heikel, mäkelig (*beim Essen etc.*); **3.** ekelerregend; **4.** unwohl: ***I feel ~*** mir ist übel; **5.** bedenklich.

queen [kwiːn] **I** *s.* **1.** Königin *f* (*a. fig.*): ***~ of*** (***the***) ***May*** Maikönigin; ***the ~ of the watering-places*** *fig.* die Königin *od.* Perle der Badeorte; ***~'s metal*** Weißmetall *n*; ***~'s ware*** gelbes Steingut; ***~ Anne is dead!*** *humor.* so'n Bart!; **2.** *zo.* Königin *f*: a) *a.* ***~ bee*** Bienenkönigin, b) *a.* ***~ ant*** Ameisenkönigin; **3.** *Kartenspiel*, *Schach*: Dame *f*: ***~'s pawn*** Damenbauer *m*; **4.** *sl.* a) ‚Schwule(r)' *m*, ‚Tunte' *f*, b) *Am.* ‚Prachtweib' *n*; **II** *v/i.* **5.** *mst* ***~ it*** die große Dame spielen: ***~ it over*** *j-n* von oben herab behandeln; **6.** *Schach*: in e-e Dame verwandelt werden (*Bauer*); **III** *v/t.* **7.** zur Königin machen; **8.** *Bienenstock* beweiseln; **9.** *Schach*: *Bauern* (in e-e Dame) verwandeln; **~ dow·a·ger** *s.* Königinwitwe *f*; **'~·like** → ***queenly***.

queen·ly ['kwi:nlɪ] *adj. u. adv.* wie e-e Königin, maje'stätisch.
queen moth·er *s.* Königinmutter *f.*
Queen's| Bench → ***King's Bench***; **~ Coun·sel** → ***King's Counsel***; **~ Eng·lish** → ***English*** 3; **~ Speech** → ***King's Speech***.
queer [kwɪə] **I** *adj.* ☐ **1.** seltsam, sonderbar, wunderlich, kuri'os, ‚komisch': **~ (*in the head*)** F leicht verrückt; **~ *fellow*** komischer Kauz; **2.** F fragwürdig, ‚faul' (*Sache*): ***be in* ♀ *Street*** a) ‚auf dem trockenen sitzen', b) ‚in der Tinte sitzen'; **3.** unwohl, schwummerig: ***feel* ~** sich ‚komisch' fühlen; **4.** *sl.* gefälscht; **5.** *sl.* ‚schwul' (*homosexuell*); **II** *v/t.* **6.** *sl.* verpfuschen, verderben; → ***pitch***² 1; **7.** *sl. j-n* in ein falsches Licht setzen (***with*** bei); **III** *s.* **8.** *sl.* ‚Blüte' *f* (*Falschgeld*); **9.** *sl.* ‚Schwule(r)' *m*, ‚Homo' *m*.
quell [kwel] *v/t. rhet.* **1.** bezwingen; **2.** *Aufstand etc., a. Gefühle* unter'drükken, ersticken.
quench [kwentʃ] *v/t.* **1.** *rhet. Flammen, Durst etc.* löschen; **2.** *fig.* a) → ***quell*** 2, b) *Hoffnung* zu'nichte machen, c) *Verlangen* stillen; **3.** ⚙ *Asche, Koks etc.* (ab)löschen; **4.** *metall.* abschrecken, härten: **~*ing and tempering*** (Stahl-) Vergütung *f*; **5.** ⚡ *Funken* löschen: **~*ed spark gap*** Löschfunkenstrecke *f*; **6.** *fig. j-m* den Mund stopfen; '**quench·er** [-tʃə] *s.* F Schluck *m*; '**quench·less** [-lɪs] *adj.* ☐ un(aus)löschbar.
que·nelle [kə'nel] *s.* Fleisch- *od.* Fischknödel *m*.
que·rist ['kwɪərɪst] *s.* Fragesteller(in).
quer·u·lous ['kwerʊləs] *adj.* ☐ quengelig, nörgelnd, verdrossen.
que·ry ['kwɪərɪ] **I** *s.* **1.** (*bsd.* zweifelnde *od.* unangenehme) Frage; † Rückfrage *f*: **~ (*abbr.* *qu.*), *was the money ever paid?*** Frage, wurde das Geld je bezahlt?; **2.** *typ.* (anzweifelndes) Fragezeichen; **3.** *fig.* Zweifel *m*; **II** *v/t.* **4.** fragen; **5.** *j-n* (aus-, be)fragen; **6.** *et.* in Zweifel ziehen, in Frage stellen, beanstanden; **7.** *typ.* mit e-m Fragezeichen versehen.
quest [kwest] **I** *s.* **1.** Suche *f*, Streben *n*, Trachten *n* (***for, of*** nach): ***knightly* ~** Ritterzug *m*; ***the* ~ *for the (Holy) Grail*** die Suche nach dem (Heiligen) Gral; ***in* ~ *of*** auf der Suche nach; **2.** Nachforschung(en *pl.*) *f*; **II** *v/i.* **3.** suchen (***for, after*** nach); **4.** Wild suchen (*Jagdhund*); **III** *v/t.* **5.** suchen *od.* trachten nach.
ques·tion ['kwestʃən] **I** *s.* **1.** Frage *f* (*a. ling.*): ***beg the* ~** die Antwort auf eine Frage schuldig bleiben; ***put a* ~ *to s.o.*** j-m e-e Frage stellen; ***the* ~ *does not arise*** die Frage ist belanglos; → ***pop***¹ 10; **2.** Frage *f*, Pro'blem *n*, Thema *n*, (Streit)Punkt *m*: ***the social* ~** die soziale Frage; **~*s of the day*** Tagesfragen; **~ *of fact*** ⚖ Tatfrage; **~ *of law*** ⚖ Rechtsfrage; ***the point in* ~** die fragliche *od.* vorliegende *od.* zur Debatte stehende Sache; ***come into* ~** in Frage kommen, wichtig werden; ***there is no* ~ *of*** *s.th. od. ger.* es ist nicht die Rede von *et. od.* davon, daß; **~!** *parl.* zur Sache!; **3.** Frage *f*, Sache *f*, Angelegenheit *f*: ***only a* ~ *of time*** nur e-e Frage der Zeit; **4.** Frage *f*, Zweifel *m*: ***beyond (all)* ~** ohne Frage, fraglos; ***call in* ~** → 8; ***there is no* ~ *but*** (*od.* ***that***) es steht außer Frage, daß; ***out of* ~** außer Frage; ***that is out of the* ~** das kommt nicht in Frage; **5.** *pol.* Anfrage *f*: ***put to the* ~** zur Abstimmung über *e-e Sache* schreiten; **6.** ⚖ Vernehmung *f*; Unter'suchung *f*: ***put to the* ~** *hist. j-n* foltern; **II** *v/t.* **7.** *j-n* (aus-, be)fragen; ⚖ vernehmen, -hören; **8.** *et.* an-, bezweifeln, in Zweifel ziehen; '**ques·tion·a·ble** [-tʃənəbl] *adj.* ☐ **1.** fraglich, zweifelhaft, ungewiß; **2.** bedenklich, fragwürdig; '**ques·tion·ar·y** [-tʃənərɪ] → ***questionnaire***; '**ques·tion·er** [-tʃənə] *s.* Fragesteller(in), Frager(in); '**ques·tion·ing** [-tʃənɪŋ] **I** *adj.* ☐ fragend (*a. Blick, Stimme*); **II** *s.* Befragung *f*; ⚖ Vernehmung *f*.
ques·tion| mark *s.* Fragezeichen *n*; **~ mas·ter** *s.* Mode'rator *m* e-r Quizsendung.
ques·tion·naire [ˌkwestɪə'neə] (*Fr.*) *s.* Fragebogen *m*.
ques·tion time *s. parl.* Fragestunde *f*.
queue [kju:] **I** *s.* **1.** (Haar)Zopf *m*; **2.** *bsd. Brit.* Schlange *f*, Reihe *f vor Geschäften etc.*: ***stand (od. wait) in a* ~** Schlange stehen; → ***jump*** 25; **II** *v/i.* **3.** *mst* **~ *up*** *Brit.* Schlange stehen, sich anstellen; '**~-ˌjump·er** *s.* F j-d., der sich vordrängelt, *mot.* Ko'lonnenspringer *m*.
quib·ble ['kwɪbl] **I** *s.* **1.** Spitzfindigkeit *f*, Wortklaube'rei *f*, Ausflucht *f*; **2.** *obs.* Wortspiel *n*; **II** *v/i.* **3.** her'umreden, Ausflüchte machen; **4.** spitzfindig sein, Haarspalte'rei betreiben; **5.** witzeln; '**quib·bler** [-lə] *s.* **1.** Wortklauber(in), -verdreher(in); **2.** Krittler(in); '**quib·bling** [-lɪŋ] *adj.* ☐ spitzfindig, haarspalterisch, wortklauberisch.
quick [kwɪk] **I** *adj.* ☐ **1.** schnell, so'fortig: **~ *answer (service)*** prompte Antwort (Bedienung); **~ *returns*** † schneller Umsatz; **2.** schnell, hurtig, geschwind, rasch: ***be* ~!** mach schnell!, beeile dich!; ***be* ~ *about s.th.*** sich mit et. beeilen; **3.** (geistig) gewandt, flink, aufgeweckt, schlagfertig, ‚fix'; beweglich, flink (*Geist*): **~ *wit*** Schlagfertigkeit *f*; **4.** scharf (*Auge, Ohr, Verstand*): ***a* ~ *ear*** ein feines Gehör; **5.** scharf (*Geruch, Geschmack, Schmerz*); **6.** voreilig, hitzig: ***a* ~ *temper***; **7.** *obs.* lebend (*a.* ⚘ *Hecke*), lebendig: **~ *with child*** (hoch)schwanger; **8.** *fig.* lebhaft (*a. Gefühle; a. Handel etc.*); **9.** lose, treibend (*Sand etc.*); **10.** *min.* erzhaltig, ergiebig; **11.** † flüssig (*Anlagen, Aktiva*); **II** *s.* **12.** ***the* ~** die Lebenden *pl.*; **13.** (lebendes) Fleisch; *fig.* Mark *n*: ***to the* ~** a) (bis) ins Fleisch, b) *fig.* bis ins Mark *od.* Herz, c) durch u. durch; ***cut s.o. to the* ~** j-n tief verletzen; ***touched to the* ~** bis ins Mark getroffen; ***a Socialist to the* ~** ein Sozialist bis auf die Knochen; ***paint s.o. to the* ~** j-n malen wie er leibt u. lebt; **14.** *Am.* → ***quicksilver***; **III** *adv.* **15.** schnell, geschwind; ˌ**~-'ac·tion** *adj.* ⚙ Schnell...; '**~-break switch** *s.* ⚡ Mo'mentschalter *m*; '**~-change** *adj.* **1.** **~ *artist*** *thea.* Verwandlungskünstler(in); **2.** ⚙ Schnellwechsel...(*-futter, -getriebe etc.*); '**~-ˌdry·ing** *adj.* schnelltrocknend (*Lack*); ä'therisch (*Öl*); '**~-eared** *adj.* mit e-m feinen Gehör.
quick·en ['kwɪkən] **I** *v/t.* **1.** beschleunigen; **2.** (wieder) lebendig machen; beseelen; **3.** *Interesse etc.* an-, erregen; **4.** beleben, *j-m* neuen Auftrieb geben; **II** *v/i.* **5.** sich beschleunigen (*Puls, Schritte etc.*); **6.** (wieder) lebendig werden; **7.** gekräftigt werden; **8.** hoch'schwanger werden; **9.** sich bewegen (*Fötus*).
'**quick|-eyed** *adj.* scharfsichtig (*a. fig.*); '**~-ˌfire**, '**~-ˌfir·ing** *adj.* ⚔ Schnellfeuer...; '**~-freeze** *v/t.* einfrieren, tiefkühlen; '**~-ˌfreez·ing** *s.* Tiefkühl-, Gefrierverfahren *n*; '**~-ˌfro·zen** *adj.* tiefgekühlt.
quick·ie ['kwɪkɪ] *s.* F **1.** *et.*, 'Hingehauenes', ‚auf die Schnelle' gemachte Sache, *z. B.* billiger, improvisierter Film; **2.** ‚kurze Sache', *z. B.* kurzer Werbefilm; **3.** ***have a* ~** F rasch einen ‚kippen'.
'**quick|·lime** *s.* ⚗ gebrannter, ungelöschter Kalk, Ätzkalk *m*; **~ march** *s.* ⚔ Eilmarsch *m*; '**~-match** *s.* ⚔, ⚒ Zündschnur *f*; **~ mo·tion** *s.* ⚙ Schnellgang *m*; ˌ**~-'mo·tion cam·er·a** *s. phot.* Zeitraffer(kamera *f*) *m*.
quick·ness ['kwɪknɪs] *s.* **1.** Schnelligkeit *f*; **2.** (geistige) Beweglichkeit *od.* Flinkheit; **3.** Hitzigkeit *f*: **~ *of temper***; **4.** **~ *of sight*** gutes Sehvermögen; **5.** Lebendigkeit *f*, Kraft *f*.
'**quick|·sand** *s. geol.* Treibsand *m*; '**~·set** *s.* **1.** heckenbildende Pflanze, *bsd.* Weißdorn *m*; **2.** Setzling *m*; **3.** *a.* **~ *hedge*** lebende Hecke; ˌ**~-'set·ting** *adj.* ⚙ schnell abbindend (*Zement etc.*); ˌ**~-'sight·ed** *adj.* scharfsichtig; '**~ˌsil·ver** *s.* Quecksilber *n* (*a. fig.*); '**~·step** *s.* **1.** ⚔ Schnellschritt *m*; **2.** ♪ Quickstep *m* (*schneller Foxtrott*); ˌ**~-'tem·pered** *adj.* hitzig, jäh; **~ time** *s.* ⚔ **1.** schnelles Marschtempo; **2.** exerziermäßiges Marschtempo: **~ *march!*** Im Gleichschritt, marsch!; ˌ**~-'wit·ted** *adj.* schlagfertig, aufgeweckt, ‚fix'.
quid¹ [kwɪd] *s.* **1.** Priem *m* (*Kautabak*); **2.** wiedergekäutes Futter.
quid² [kwɪd] *pl. mst* **quid** *s. Brit. sl.* Pfund *n* (Sterling).
quid·di·ty ['kwɪdətɪ] *s.* **1.** *phls.* Es'senz *f*, Wesen *n*; **2.** Feinheit *f*; **3.** Spitzfindigkeit *f*.
quid·nunc ['kwɪdnʌŋk] *s.* Neuigkeitskrämer *m*, Klatschtante *f*.
quid pro quo [ˌkwɪdprəʊ'kwəʊ] *pl.* **quid pro quos** (*Lat.*) *s.* Gegenleistung *f*, Vergütung *f*.
qui·es·cence [kwaɪ'esns] *s.* Ruhe *f*, Stille *f*; **qui'es·cent** [-nt] *adj.* ☐ **1.** ruhig, bewegungslos; *fig.* ruhig, still: **~ *state*** Ruhezustand *m*; **2.** *ling.* stumm (*Buchstabe*).
qui·et ['kwaɪət] **I** *adj.* ☐ **1.** ruhig, still (*a. fig. Person, See, Straße etc.*); **2.** ruhig, leise, geräuschlos (*a.* ⚙): **~ *running*** *mot.* ruhiger Gang; ***be* ~!** sei still!; **~, *please!*** ich bitte um Ruhe!; ***keep* ~** a) sich ruhig verhalten, b) den Mund halten; **3.** bewegungslos, still; **4.** ruhig, friedlich (*a. Leben, Zeiten*); behaglich, beschaulich: **~ *conscience*** ruhiges Gewissen; **~ *enjoyment*** ⚖ ruhiger Besitz, ungestörter Genuß; **5.** ruhig, unauffällig (*Farbe etc.*); **6.** versteckt, geheim, leise: ***keep s.th.* ~** et. geheimhalten, et. für sich behalten; **7.** † ruhig, still, ‚flau' (*Geschäft etc.*); **II** *s.* **8.** Ruhe *f*, Stille *f*;

Frieden *m*: ***on the ~*** (*od.* ***on the q.t.***) F ‚klammheimlich', stillschweigend; **III** *v/t.* **9.** beruhigen, zur Ruhe bringen; **10.** besänftigen; **11.** zum Schweigen bringen; **IV** *v/i.* **12.** *mst* ***~ down*** ruhig *od.* still werden, sich beruhigen; **'qui·et·en** [-tn] → ***quiet*** III *u.* IV.

qui·et·ism ['kwaııtızəm] *s. eccl.* Quie'tismus *m.*

qui·et·ness ['kwaıətnıs] *s.* **1.** → ***quietude***; **2.** Geräuschlosigkeit *f*; **qui·e·tude** ['kwaııtju:d] *s.* **1.** Stille *f*, Ruhe *f*; **2.** *fig.* Friede(n) *m*; **3.** (Gemüts)Ruhe *f.*

qui·e·tus [kwaı'i:təs] *s.* **1.** Ende *n*, Tod *m*; **2.** Todesstoß *m*: ***give s.o. his ~*** j-m den Garaus machen; **3.** (restlose) Tilgung *e-r Schuld*; **4.** ⚖ a) *Brit.* Endquittung *f*, b) *Am.* Entlastung *f des Nachlaßverwalters.*

quill [kwıl] **I** *s.* **1.** *a.* ***~-feather*** *orn.* (Schwung-, Schwanz)Feder *f*; **2.** *a.* ***~ pen*** Federkiel *m*; *fig.* Feder *f*; **3.** *zo.* Stachel *m* (*Igel etc.*); **4.** ♪ a) *hist.* Panflöte *f*, b) Plektrum *n*; **5.** Zahnstocher *m*; **6.** Zimtstange *f*; **7.** ⚙ Weberspule *f*; **8.** ⚙ Hohlwelle *f*; **II** *v/t.* **9.** rund fälteln, kräuseln; **10.** *Faden* aufspulen; **'~-ˌdriv·er** *s. contp.* Federfuchser *m.*

quilt [kwılt] **I** *s.* **1.** Steppdecke *f*; **2.** gesteppte (Bett)Decke; **II** *v/t.* **3.** steppen, 'durchnähen; **4.** wattieren, (aus)polstern; **'quilt·ing** [-tıŋ] *s.* **1.** 'Durchnähen *n*, Steppen *n*: ***~ seam*** Steppnaht *f*; **2.** gesteppte Arbeit; **3.** Füllung *f*, Wattierung *f*; **4.** Pi'kee *m* (*Gewebe*).

quim [kwım] *s.* V ‚Möse' *f.*

quince [kwıns] *s.* ⚘ Quitte *f.*

qui·nine [*Brit.* kwı'ni:n; *Am.* 'kwaınaın] *s.* ⚗, *pharm.* Chi'nin *n.*

quin·qua·ge·nar·i·an [ˌkwıŋkwədʒı'neərıən] **I** *adj.* fünfzigjährig, in den Fünfzigern; **II** *s.* Fünfzigjährige(r *m*) *f*, Fünfziger(in); **quin·quen·ni·al** [kwıŋ'kwenıəl] *adj.* □ fünfjährig; fünfjährlich (*wiederkehrend*).

quins [kwınz] *s. pl.* F Fünflinge *pl.*

quin·sy ['kwınzı] *s.* ⚕ (Hals)Bräune *f*, Mandelentzündung *f.*

quint *s.* **1.** [kınt] *Pikett*: Quinte *f*; **2.** [kwınt] ♪ Quint(e) *f.*

quin·tal ['kwıntl] *s.* Doppelzentner *m.*

quinte [kɛ̃t; kænt] (*Fr.*) *s. fenc.* Quinte *f.*

quint·es·sence [kwın'tesns] *s.* **1.** ⚗ 'Quintessenz *f* (*a. phls. u. fig.*); **2.** *fig.* Kern *m*, Inbegriff *m*; **3.** a) Urtyp *m*, b) klassisches Beispiel, c) (höchste) Voll'kommenheit *f.*

quin·tet(te) [kwın'tet] *s.* **1.** ♪ Quin'tett *n* (*a. humor. 5 Personen*); **2.** Fünfergruppe *f.*

quin·tu·ple ['kwıntjʊpl] **I** *adj.* fünffach; **II** *s. das* Fünffache; **III** *v/t. u. v/i.* (sich) verfünffachen; **'quin·tu·plets** [-plıts] *s. pl.* Fünflinge *pl.*

quip [kwıp] **I** *s.* **1.** witziger Einfall, geistreiche Bemerkung, Bon'mot *n*; **2.** (Seiten)Hieb *m*, Stich(e'lei *f*) *m*; **II** *v/i.* **3.** witzeln, spötteln.

quire ['kwaıə] *s.* **1.** *typ.* Buch *n* (*24 Bogen*); **2.** *Buchbinderei*: Lage *f.*

quirk [kwɜ:k] *s.* **1.** → ***quip*** 1, 2; **2.** Kniff *m*, Trick *m*; **3.** Zucken *n des Mundes etc.*; **4.** Eigenart *f*, seltsame Angewohnheit: ***by a ~ of fate*** durch e-n verrückten Zufall, wie das Schicksal so spielt; **5.** Schnörkel *m*; **6.** ⚠ Hohlkehle *f*; **'quirk·y** [-kı] *adj.* F **1.** ‚gerissen' (*Anwalt etc.*); **2.** eigenartig, schrullig, ‚komisch'.

quis·ling ['kwızlıŋ] *s. pol.* F Quisling *m*, Kollabora'teur *m.*

quit [kwıt] **I** *v/t.* **1.** verzichten auf (*acc.*); **2.** *a. Stellung* aufgeben; *Dienst* quittieren; sich vom *Geschäft* zu'rückziehen; **3.** F aufhören (***s.th.*** mit et.; ***doing*** zu tun); **4.** verlassen; **5.** *Schuld* bezahlen, tilgen; **6.** ***~ o.s.*** sich befreien (***of*** von); **7.** *poet.* vergelten (***love with hate*** Liebe mit Haß); **II** *v/i.* **8.** aufhören; **9.** weggehen; **10.** ausziehen (*Mieter*): ***notice to ~*** Kündigung *f*; ***give notice to ~*** (*j-m* die Wohnung) kündigen; **III** *adj. pred.* **11.** quitt, frei: ***go ~*** frei ausgehen; ***be ~ for*** davonkommen mit; **12.** frei, los (***of*** von): ***~ of charges*** ✝ nach Abzug der Kosten, spesenfrei; **'~·claim** *s.* ⚖ **1.** Verzicht(leistung *f*) *m auf Rechte*; **2.** ***~ deed*** a) Grundstückskaufvertrag *m*, b) *Am.* Zessi'onsurkunde *f* (*beide: ohne Haftung für Rechts- od. Sachmängel*).

quite [kwaıt] *adv.* **1.** ganz, völlig: ***~ another*** ein ganz anderer; ***~ wrong*** völlig falsch; **2.** wirklich, tatsächlich, ziemlich: ***~ a disappointment*** e-e ziemliche Enttäuschung; ***~ good*** recht gut; ***~ a few*** ziemlich viele; ***~ a gentleman*** wirklich ein feiner Herr; **3.** F ganz, durch'aus: ***~ nice*** ganz *od.* sehr nett; ***~ the thing*** genau das Richtige; ***~ (so)!*** ganz recht!

quit rent *s.* ⚖ Miet-, Pachtzins *m.*

quits [kwıts] *adj.* quitt (*mit j-m*): ***call it ~*** quitt sein; ***get ~ with s.o.*** mit j-m quitt werden; → ***double*** 10.

quit·tance ['kwıtəns] *s.* **1.** Vergeltung *f*, Entgelt *n*; **2.** Erledigung *f e-r Schuld etc.*; **3.** ✝ Quittung *f.*

quit·ter ['kwıtə] *s. Am. u.* F **1.** Drückeberger *m*; **2.** Feigling *m.*

quiv·er¹ ['kwıvə] **I** *v/i.* beben, zittern (***with*** vor *dat.*); **II** *s.* Beben *n*, Zittern *n*: ***in a ~ of excitement*** *fig.* zitternd vor Aufregung.

quiv·er² ['kwıvə] *s.* Köcher *m*: ***have an arrow left in one's ~*** *fig.* noch ein Eisen im Feuer haben; ***a ~ full of children*** *fig.* e-e ganze Schar Kinder.

qui vive [ˌki:'vi:v] (*Fr.*) *s.*: ***be on the ~*** auf dem Quivive *od.* auf der Hut sein.

quix·ot·ic [kwık'sɒtık] *adj.* (□ ***~ally***) donqui'chotisch (*weltfremd, überspannt*); **quix·ot·ism** ['kwıksətızəm], **quix·ot·ry** ['kwıksətrı] *s.* Donquichotte'rie *f*, Narre'tei *f.*

quiz [kwız] **I** *v/t.* **1.** *Am. j-n* prüfen, abfragen; **2.** (aus)fragen; **3.** *bsd. Brit.* aufziehen, hänseln; **4.** (spöttisch) anstarren, fixieren; **II** *pl.* **'quiz·zes** [-zız] *s.* **5.** *ped. Am.* Prüfung *f*, Klassenarbeit *f*; **6.** Ausfragen *n*; **7.** *Radio, TV*: Quiz *n*: ***~ game*** Ratespiel *n*, Quiz; ***~master*** Quizmaster *m*; ***~ program(me)***, ***~ show*** Quizsendung *f*; **8.** Denksportaufgabe *f*; **9.** *obs.* Foppe'rei *f*, Ulk *m.*

quiz·zi·cal ['kwızıkl] *adj.* □ **1.** seltsam, komisch; **2.** spöttisch.

quod [kwɒd] *s. sl.* ‚Kittchen' *n*: ***be in ~*** *a.* ‚sitzen'.

quoin [kɔın] **I** *s.* **1.** ⚠ a) (vorspringende) Ecke, b) Eckstein *m*; **2.** *typ.* Schließkeil *m*; **II** *v/t.* **3.** *typ. Druckform* schließen; **4.** ⚙ verkeilen; **5.** ⚠ *Ecke* mit Keilsteinen versehen.

quoit [kɔıt] *s.* **1.** Wurfring *m*; **2.** *pl. sg. konstr.* Wurfringspiel *n.*

quon·dam ['kwɒndæm] *adj.* ehemalig, früher.

Quon·set hut ['kwɒnsıt] *s. Am.* (*Warenzeichen*) *e-e* Nissenhütte.

quo·rum ['kwɔ:rəm] *s.* **1.** beschlußfähige Anzahl *od.* Mitgliederzahl: ***be*** (*od.* ***constitute***) ***a ~*** beschlußfähig sein; **2.** ⚖ handlungsfähige Besetzung *e-s Gerichts.*

quo·ta ['kwəʊtə] *s.* **1.** *bsd.* ✝ Quote *f*, Anteil *m*; **2.** ✝ (*Einfuhr- etc.*)Kontin'gent *n*: ***~ goods*** kontingentierte Waren; ***~ system*** Zuteilungssystem *n*; **3.** ⚖ Kon'kursdividende(nquote) *f*; **4.** *Am.* Einwanderungsquote *f.*

quot·a·ble ['kwəʊtəbl] *adj.* zi'tierbar.

quo·ta·tion [kwəʊ'teıʃn] *s.* **1.** Zi'tat *n*; Anführung *f*, Her'anziehung *f* (*a.* ⚖): ***familiar ~s*** geflügelte Worte; **2.** Beleg (-stelle *f*) *m*; **3.** ✝ a) Preisangabe *f*, -ansatz *m*, b) (Börsen-, Kurs)Notierung *f*, Kurs *m*: ***final ~*** Schlußnotierung; **4.** *typ.* Steg *m*; ***~ marks*** *s. pl.* Anführungszeichen *pl.*, ‚Gänsefüßchen' *pl.*

quote [kwəʊt] **I** *v/t.* **1.** zitieren (***from*** aus), (*a. als Beweis*) anführen, *weitS. a.* Bezug nehmen auf (*acc.*), sich auf *ein Dokument etc.* berufen, *e-e Quelle, e-n Fall* her'anziehen; **2.** ✝ *Preis* aufgeben, ansetzen, berechnen; **3.** *Börse*: notieren: ***be ~d at*** (*od.* ***with***) notieren *od.* im Kurs stehen mit; **4.** *Am.* in Anführungszeichen setzen; **II** *v/i.* **5.** zitieren (***from*** aus): ***~: ...*** ich zitiere ..., Zitat...; **III** *s.* F **6.** Zi'tat *n*; **7.** *pl.* → ***quotation marks.***

quoth [kwəʊθ] *obs. ich, er, sie, es* sprach, sagte.

quo·tid·i·an [kwɒ'tıdıən] **I** *adj.* **1.** täglich: ***~ fever*** → 3; **2.** all'täglich, gewöhnlich; **II** *s.* **3.** ⚕ Quotidi'anfieber *n.*

quo·tient ['kwəʊʃnt] *s.* ⅍ Quoti'ent *m.*

R

R, r [ɑː] *s.* R *n*, r *n* (*Buchstabe*): ***the three Rs*** (*reading*, [*w*]*riting*, [*a*]*rithmetic*) (das) Lesen, Schreiben, Rechnen.
rab·bet [ˈræbɪt] ⚙ **I** *s.* **1.** a) Fuge *f*, Falz *m*, Nut *f*, b) Falzverbindung *f*; **2.** Stoßstahl *m*; **II** *v/t.* **3.** einfügen, (zs.-)fugen, falzen; **~ joint** *s.* Fuge *f*, Falzverbindung *f*; **~ plane** *s.* Falzhobel *m*.
rab·bi [ˈræbaɪ] *s.* **1.** Rabˈbiner *m*; **2.** Rabbi *m* (*Schriftgelehrter*); **rab·bin·ate** [ˈræbɪnət] *s.* **1.** Rabbiˈnat *n*; **2.** *coll.* Rabˈbiner *pl.*; **rab·bin·i·cal** [ræˈbɪnɪkl] *adj.* □ rabˈbinisch.
rab·bit [ˈræbɪt] *s.* **1.** *zo.* Kaˈninchen *n*; **2.** *zo. Am. allg.* Hase *m*; **3.** → ***Welsh rabbit***; **4.** *sport* F a) Anfänger(in), b) ‚Flasche' *f*, c) *Laufsport*: Tempomacher *m*; **~ fe·ver** *s.* Hasenpest *f*; **~ hutch** *s.* Kaˈninchenstall *m*; **~ punch** *s. Boxen*: Genickschlag *m*.
rab·ble¹ [ˈræbl] *s.* **1.** Mob *m*, Pöbelhaufen *m*; **2. *the ~*** der Pöbel: ***~-rousing*** aufwieglerisch, demagogisch.
rab·ble² [ˈræbl] ⚙ **I** *s.* Rührstange *f*, Kratze *f*; **II** *v/t.* ˈumrühren.
Rab·e·lai·si·an [ˌræbəˈleɪzɪən] *adj.* **1.** des Rabeˈlais; **2.** im Stil von Rabeˈlais (*grob-satirisch*, *geistvoll-frech*).
rab·id [ˈræbɪd] *adj.* □ **1.** wütend (*a. Haß etc.*), rasend (*a. fig. Hunger etc.*); **2.** rabiˈat, faˈnatisch: ***a ~ anti-Semite***; **3.** toll(wütig): ***a ~ dog***; **ˈrab·id·ness** [-nɪs] *s.* **1.** Rasen *n*, Wut *f*; **2.** (wilder) Fanaˈtismus.
ra·bies [ˈreɪbiːz] *s. vet.* Tollwut *f*.
rac·coon [rəˈkuːn] *s.* Waschbär *m*.
race¹ [reɪs] *s.* **1.** Rasse *f*: ***the white ~***; **2.** Rasse *f*: a) Rassenzugehörigkeit *f*, b) rassische Eigenart: ***differences of ~*** Rassenunterschiede; **3.** a) Geschlecht *n*, Faˈmilie *f*, b) Volk *n*; **4.** *biol.* Rasse *f*, Gattung *f*, ˈUnterart *f*; **5.** (*Menschen- etc.*)Geschlecht *n*: ***the human ~***; **6.** *fig.* Kaste *f*, Schlag *m*: ***the ~ of politicians***; **7.** Rasse *f des Weins etc.*
race² [reɪs] **I** *s.* **1.** *sport* (Wett)Rennen *n*, (Wett)Lauf *m*: ***motor ~*** Autorennen; **2.** *pl. sport* Pferderennen *n*; → ***play*** 16; **3.** *fig.* (***for***) Wettlauf *m*, Kampf *m* (um), Jagd *f* (nach): ***~ against time*** Wettlauf mit der Zeit; **4.** *ast.* Lauf *m* (*a. fig. des Lebens etc.*): ***his ~ is run*** er hat die längste Zeit gelebt; **5.** a) starke Strömung, b) Stromschnelle *f*, c) Flußbett *n*, d) Kaˈnal *m*, Gerinne *n*, e) Kaˈnalgewässer *n*; **6.** ⚙ a) Laufring *m* (*Kugellager*), (Gleit)Bahn *f*, b) *Weberei*: Schützenbahn *f*; **7.** → ***slipstream***; **II** *v/i.* **8.** an e-m Rennen teilnehmen, *bsd.* um die Wette laufen *od.* fahren (***with*** mit); laufen *etc.* (***for*** um); **9.** (daˈhin)rasen, (-)schießen, rennen; **10.** ⚙ ˈdurchdrehen (*Rad*); **III** *v/t.* **11.** um die Wette laufen *od.* fahren *etc.* mit; **12.** *Pferde* rennen *od.* laufen lassen; **13.** *Fahrzeug* rasen lassen, rasen mit; **14.** *fig.* (ˈdurch)hetzen, (-)jagen; *Gesetz* ˈdurchpeitschen; **15.** ⚙ a) *Motor* ˈdurchdrehen lassen, b) *Motor* hochjagen: ***~ up*** *Flugzeugmotor* abbremsen; **~ boat** *s.* Rennboot *n*; **ˈ~·course** *s.* (Pferde)Rennbahn *f*; **~ di·rec·tor** *s. mot.* Rennleiter *m*; **ˈ~ˌgo·er** *s.* Rennplatzbesucher(in); **ˈ~·horse** *s.* Rennpferd *n*.
ra·ceme [rəˈsiːm] *s.* ⚘ Traube *f* (*Blütenstand*).
race meet·ing *s.* (Pferde)Rennen *n*.
rac·er [ˈreɪsə] *s.* **1.** a) (Renn)Läufer(in), b) Rennfahrer(in); **2.** Rennpferd *n*; **3.** Rennrad *n*, -boot *n*, -wagen *m*.
Race Re·la·tions Board *s. Brit.* Ausschuß *m* zur Verhinderung von Rassendiskriminierung.
race| ri·ot *s.* ˈRassenkraˌwall *m*; **ˈ~·track** *s.* **1.** *mot.* Rennstrecke *f*; **2.** → ***racecourse***; **ˈ~·way** *s.* **1.** (Mühl)Gerinne *n*; **2.** ⚙ Laufring *m*.
ra·chis [ˈreɪkɪs] *pl.* **rach·i·des** [ˈreɪkɪdiːs] *s.* **1.** ⚘, *zo.* Rhachis *f*, Spindel *f*; **2.** *anat.*, *zo.* Rückgrat *n*; **ra·chi·tis** [ræˈkaɪtɪs] *s.* ⚕ Raˈchitis *f*.
ra·cial [ˈreɪʃl] *adj.* □ rassisch, Rassen…: ***~ equality*** Rassengleichheit *f*; ***~ discrimination*** Rassendiskriminierung *f*; ***~ segregation*** Rassentrennung *f*; **ˈra·cial·ism** [-ʃəlɪzəm] *s.* **1.** Rasˈsismus *m*; **2.** Rassenkult *m*; **3.** ˈRassenpoliˌtik *f*; **ˈra·cial·ist** [-ʃəlɪst] **I** *s.* Rasˈsist(in); **II** *adj.* rasˈsistisch.
rac·i·ness [ˈreɪsɪnɪs] *s.* **1.** Rassigkeit *f*, Rasse *f*; **2.** Urwüchsigkeit *f*; **3.** *das* Piˈkante, Würze *f*; **4.** Schwung *m*, ‚Schmiß' *m*.
rac·ing [ˈreɪsɪŋ] **I** *s.* **1.** Rennen *n*; **2.** (Pferde)Rennsport *m*; **II** *adj.* **3.** Renn…(*-boot*, *-wagen etc.*): ***~ circuit*** *mot.* Rennstrecke *f*; ***~ cyclist*** Radrennfahrer *m*; ***~ driver*** Rennfahrer(in); ***~ man*** Pferdesport-Liebhaber *m*; ***~ world*** *die* Rennwelt.
rac·ism [ˈreɪsɪzəm] → ***racialism***; **ˈrac·ist** → ***racialist***.
rack¹ [ræk] **I** *s.* **1.** Gestell *n*, Gerüst *n*; (*Gewehr-*, *Kleider- etc.*)Ständer *m*; (Streck-, Stütz)Rahmen *m*; ✓ Raufe *f*, Futtergestell *n*; 🚂 Gepäcknetz *n*; (Handtuch)Halter *m*; **2.** ˈFächerreˌgal *n*; **3.** *typ.* ˈSetzreˌgal *n*; **4.** ⚙ Zahnstange *f*: ***~(-and-pinion) gear*** Zahnstangengetriebe *n*; **5.** *hist.* Folterbank *f*, (Streck)Folter *f*; *fig.* (Folter)Qualen *pl.*: ***put on the ~*** *bsd. fig. j-n* auf die Folter spannen; **II** *v/t.* **6.** (aus)recken, strecken; **7.** auf *od.* in ein Gestell *od.* Reˈgal legen; **8.** *bsd. fig.* foltern, martern: ***~ one's brains*** sich den Kopf zermartern; ***~ed with pain*** schmerzgequält; ***~ing pains*** rasende Schmerzen; **9.** a) *Miete* (wucherisch) hochschrauben, b) → ***rack-rent*** 3; **10. ~ *up*** ✓ mit Futter versehen.
rack² [ræk] *s.*: ***go to ~ and ruin*** *a. fig.* kaˈputtgehen.
rack³ [ræk] *s.* Paßgang *m* (*Pferd*).
rack⁴ [ræk] **I** *s.* fliegendes Gewölk; **II** *v/i.* (daˈhin)ziehen (*Wolken*).
rack⁵ [ræk] *v/t. oft* **~ *off*** *Wein etc.* abziehen, -füllen.
rack·et¹ [ˈrækɪt] *s.* **1.** *sport* Raˈkett *n*, (*Tennis- etc.*)Schläger *m*: ***~ press*** Spanner *m*; **2.** *pl. oft sg. konstr.* Raˈkettspiel *n*, Wandballspiel *n*; **3.** Schneeteller *m*.
rack·et² [ˈrækɪt] **I** *s.* **1.** Krach *m*, Lärm *m*, Raˈdau *m*, Spekˈtakel *m*; **2.** ‚Wirbel' *m*, Aufregung *f*; **3.** a) ausgelassene Gesellschaft, rauschendes Fest, b) Vergnügungstaumel *m*, c) Trubel *m des Gesellschaftslebens*: ***go on the ~*** ‚auf die Pauke hauen'; **4.** harte (Nerven-) Probe, ‚Schlauch' *m*: ***stand the ~*** F a) die Sache durchstehen, b) die Folgen zu tragen haben, c) (alles) berappen; **5.** *sl.* a) Schwindel *m*, ‚Schiebung' *f*, b) Erpresserbande *f*, Racket *n*, c) organisierte Erpressung, d) ‚Masche' *f*, (einträgliches) Geschäft, e) *Am.* Beruf *m*, Branche *f*; **II** *v/i.* **6.** Krach machen, lärmen; **7.** *mst* **~ *about*** ‚(herum)sumpfen'; **rack·et·eer** [ˌrækəˈtɪə] **I** *s.* **1.** Gangster *m*, Erpresser *m*; **2.** Schieber *m*, Geschäftemacher *m*; **II** *v/i.* **3.** dunkle Geschäfte machen; **4.** organisierte Erpressung betreiben; **rack·et·eer·ing** [ˌrækəˈtɪərɪŋ] *s.* **1.** Gangstertum *n*, organisierte Erpressung; **2.** Geschäftemacheˈrei *f*; **ˈrack·et·y** [-tɪ] *adj.* **1.** lärmend; **2.** turbuˈlent; **3.** ausgelassen, ausschweifend.
rack| rail·way *s.* Zahnradbahn *f*; **ˈ~-rent** **I** *s.* **1.** Wuchermiete *f*; **2.** *Brit.* höchstmögliche Jahresmiete; **II** *v/t.* **3.** e-e Wuchermiete für *et. od.* von *j-m* verlangen; **~ wheel** *s.* Zahnrad *n*.
ra·coon → ***raccoon***.
rac·y [ˈreɪsɪ] *adj.* **1.** rassig (*a. fig. Auto*, *Stil etc.*), feurig (*Pferd*, *a. Musik etc.*); **2.** urtümlich, kernig: ***~ of the soil*** urwüchsig, bodenständig; **3.** *fig.* a) leˈbendig, geistreich, ‚spritzig', b) schwungvoll, schmissig: ***~ melody***; **4.** piˈkant, würzig (*Geruch etc.*) (*a. fig.*); **5.** F *u. Am.* schlüpfrig, gewagt.
rad [ræd] *s. pol.* Radiˈkale(r *m*) *f*.
ra·dar [ˈreɪdɑː] **I** *s.* **1.** Raˈdar *m*, *n*, Funkmeßtechnik *f*, -ortung *f*; **2.** *a.* **~**

set Radargerät *n*; **II** *adj.* **3.** Radar…: ~ ***display*** Radarschirmbild *n*; ~ ***scanner*** Radarsuchgerät *n*; ~ ***screen*** Radarschirm *m*; ~ ***scope*** Radarsichtgerät *n*; ~ ***trap*** Radarfalle *f* (*der Polizei*).

rad·dle ['rædl] **I** *s.* **1.** *min.* Rötel *m*; **II** *v/t.* **2.** mit Rötel bemalen; **3.** rot anmalen.

ra·di·al ['reɪdjəl] **I** *adj.* ☐ **1.** radi'al, Radial…, Strahl(en)…; sternförmig; **2.** *anat.* Speichen…; **3.** ⚘, *zo.* radi'alsym,metrisch; **II** *s.* **4.** *anat.* → a) ***radial artery***, b) ***radial nerve***; ~ **ar·ter·y** *s.* Speichenschlagader *f*; ~ **drill** *s.* ⚙ Radi'albohrma,schine *f*; ~ **en·gine** *s.* Sternmotor *m*; '~**-flow tur·bine** *s.* Radi'altur,bine *f*; ~ **nerve** *s.* Speichennerv *m*; '~**(-ply) tire** (*Brit.* **tyre**) *s.* ⚙ Gürtelreifen *m*; ~ **route** *s.* Ausfallstraße *f*.

ra·di·ance ['reɪdjəns], '**ra·di·an·cy** [-sɪ] *s.* **1.** *a. fig.* Strahlen *n*, strahlender Glanz; **2.** → ***radiation***; '**ra·di·ant** [-nt] **I** *adj.* ☐ **1.** strahlend (*a. fig.* ***with*** vor *dat.*, von): ~ ***beauty***; ~ ***with joy*** freudestrahlend; ***be*** ~ ***with health*** vor Gesundheit strotzen; **2.** *phys.* Strahlungs…(*-energie etc.*): ~ ***heating*** ⚙ Flächenheizung *f*; **3.** strahlenförmig (angeordnet); **II** *s.* **4.** Strahl(ungs)punkt *m*; '**ra·di·ate** [-dɪeɪt] **I** *v/i.* **1.** ausstrahlen (***from*** von) (*a. fig.*); **2.** *a. fig.* strahlen, leuchten; **II** *v/t.* **3.** *Licht, Wärme etc.* ausstrahlen; **4.** *fig. Liebe etc.* ausstrahlen, -strömen: ~ ***health*** vor Gesundheit strotzen; **5.** *Radio, TV*: ausstrahlen, senden; **III** *adj.* [-dɪət] **6.** radi'al, strahlig, Strahl(en)…; **ra·di·a·tion** [,reɪdɪ'eɪʃn] *s.* **1.** *phys.* (Aus)Strahlung *f* (*a. fig.*): ~ ***detection team*** ⚔ Strahlenspürtrupp *m*; **2.** *a.* ~ ***therapy*** ⚕ Strahlenbehandlung *f*, Bestrahlung *f*; '**ra·di·a·tor** [-dɪeɪtə] *s.* **1.** ⚙ Heizkörper *m*; Strahlkörper *m*, -ofen *m*; **2.** ⚡ 'Raumstrahlan,tenne *f*; **3.** *mot.* Kühler *m*: ~ ***core*** Kühlerblock *m*; ~ ***grid***, ~ ***grill*** Kühlergrill *m*; ~ ***mascot*** Kühlerfigur *f*.

rad·i·cal ['rædɪkl] **I** *adj.* ☐ → ***radically***; **1.** radi'kal (*pol. oft* ♀); *weitS. a.* drastisch, gründlich: ~ ***cure*** Radikal-, Roßkur *f*; ***undergo a*** ~ ***change*** sich von Grund auf ändern; **2.** ursprünglich, eingewurzelt; fundamen'tal (*Fehler etc.*); grundlegend, Grund…: ~ ***difference***; ~ ***idea***; **3.** *bsd.* ⚘, ⅍ Wurzel…: ~ ***sign*** → 8b; ~ ***plane*** ⅍ Potenzebene *f*; **4.** *ling.* Wurzel…, Stamm…: ~ ***word*** Stamm(wort *n*) *m*; **5.** ♪ Grund(ton)…; **6.** *a.* ⚗ Radikal…; **II** *s.* **7.** *pol.* (*a.* ♀) Radi'kale(r *m*) *f*; **8.** ⅍ a) Wurzel *f*, b) Wurzelzeichen *n*; **9.** *ling.* Wurzel(buchstabe *m*) *f*; **10.** ♪ Grundton *m* (*Akkord*); **11.** ⚗ Radi'kal *n*; '**rad·i·cal·ism** [-kəlɪzəm] *s.* Radika'lismus *m*; '**rad·i·cal·ize** [-kəlaɪz] *v/t.* (*v/i.* sich) radikalisieren; '**rad·i·cal·ly** [-kəlɪ] *adv.* **1.** radi'kal, von Grund auf; **2.** ursprünglich.

rad·i·ces ['reɪdɪsiːz] *pl. von* ***radix***.

rad·i·cle ['rædɪkl] *s.* **1.** ⚘ a) Keimwurzel *f*, b) Würzelchen *n*; **2.** *anat.* (Gefäß-, Nerven)Wurzel *f*.

ra·di·i ['reɪdɪaɪ] *pl. von* ***radius***.

ra·di·o ['reɪdɪəʊ] **I** *pl.* **-di·os** *s.* **1.** Funk(-betrieb) *m*; **2.** Radio *n*, Rundfunk *m*: ***on the*** ~ im Rundfunk; **3.** a) Radio(gerät) *n*, Rundfunkempfänger *m*, b) Funkgerät *n*; **4.** (Radio)Sender *m*; **5.** Rundfunkgesellschaft *f*; **6.** F Funkspruch *m*; **II** *v/t.* **7.** senden, funken, *e-e Funkmeldung* 'durchgeben; **8.** ⚕ a) e-e Röntgenaufnahme machen von, b) durch'leuchten; **9.** ⚕ mit Radium bestrahlen.

,**ra·di·o**|'**ac·tive** *adj.* radioak'tiv: ~ ***waste*** radioaktiver Müll, Atom-Müll *m*; ,~**ac'tiv·i·ty** *s.* Radioaktivi'tät *f*; ~ **am·a·teur** *s.* 'Funkama,teur *m*; ~ **bea·con** *s.* Funkbake *f*; ~ **beam** *s.* Funk-, Richtstrahl *m*; ~ **bear·ing** *s.* **1.** Funkpeilung *f*; **2.** Peilwinkel *m*; ~ **car** *s.* Funk(streifen)wagen *m*; ,~'**car·bon dat·ing** *s.* Radiokar'bonme,thode, C-'14-Me,thode *f*; ,~'**chem·is·try** *s.* 'Radio-, 'Strahlenche,mie *f*; ,~**-con'trol** **I** *s.* Funksteuerung *f*; **II** *v/t.* fernsteuern; ,~'**el·e·ment** *s.* radioak'tives Ele'ment; ~ **en·gi·neer·ing** *s.* Funktechnik *f*; ~ **fre·quen·cy** *s.* ⚡ 'Hochfre,quenz *f*.

ra·di·o·gram ['reɪdɪəʊgræm] *s.* **1.** 'Funkmeldung *f*, -tele,gramm *n*; **2.** *Brit.* a) → ***radiograph*** I, b) Mu'siktruhe *f*.

ra·di·o·graph ['reɪdɪəʊgrɑːf] ⚕ **I** *s.* Radio'gramm *n*, *bsd.* Röntgenaufnahme *f*; **II** *v/t.* ein Radio'gramm *etc.* machen von; **ra·di·o·gra·phy** [,reɪdɪ'ɒgrəfɪ] *s.* Röntgenogra'phie *f*.

ra·di·o·log·i·cal [,reɪdɪəʊ'lɒdʒɪkl] *adj.* ⚕ radio'logisch, Röntgen…; **ra·di·ol·o·gist** [,reɪdɪ'ɒlədʒɪst] *s.* Röntgeno'loge *m*; **ra·di·ol·o·gy** [,reɪdɪ'ɒlədʒɪ] *s.* Strahlen-, 'Röntgenkunde *f*.

ra·di·o| **mark·er** *s.* ✈ (Anflug)Funkbake *f*; ~ **mes·sage** *s.* Funkmeldung *f*; ~ **op·er·a·tor** *s.* (✈ Bord)Funker *m*.

ra·di·o·phone ['reɪdɪəʊfəʊn] *s.* **1.** *phys.* Radio'phon *n*; **2.** → ***radiotelephone***.

,**ra·di·o**|'**pho·no·graph** *s. Am.* Mu'siktruhe *f*; ,~'**pho·to·graph** *s.* Funkbild *n*; ,~**pho'tog·ra·phy** *s.* Bildfunk *m*.

ra·di·os·co·py [,reɪdɪ'ɒskəpɪ] *s.* ⚕ Röntgenosko'pie *f*, 'Röntgenunter,suchung *f*.

ra·di·o| **set** *s.* → ***radio*** 3; ~ **sonde** [sɒnd] *s. meteor.* Radiosonde *f*; ,~'**tel·e·gram** *s.* 'Funktele,gramm *n*; ,~**te'leg·ra·phy** *s.* drahtlose Telegra'fie; ,~'**tel·e·phone** *s.* Funksprechgerät *n*; ,~**te'leph·o·ny** *s.* drahtlose Telefo'nie; ,~'**ther·a·py** *s.* 'Strahlen-, 'Röntgenthera,pie *f*.

rad·ish ['rædɪʃ] *s.* **1.** *a.* ***large*** ~ Rettich *m*; **2.** *a.* ***red*** ~ Ra'dieschen *n*.

ra·di·um ['reɪdjəm] *s.* ⚗ Radium *n*.

ra·di·us ['reɪdjəs] *pl.* **-di·i** [-dɪaɪ] *od.* **-di·us·es** *s.* **1.** ⅍ Radius *m*, Halbmesser *m*: ~ ***of turn*** *mot.* Wendehalbmesser; **2.** ⚙, *anat.* Speiche *f*; **3.** ⚘ Strahl (-blüte *f*) *m*; **4.** 'Umkreis *m*: ***within a*** ~ ***of***; **5.** *fig.* (Wirkungs-, Einfluß)Bereich *m*: ~ (***of action***) Aktionsradius *m*, *mot.* Fahrbereich *m*.

ra·dix ['reɪdɪks] *pl.* **rad·i·ces** ['reɪdɪsiːz] *s.* **1.** ⅍ Basis *f*, Grundzahl *f*; **2.** ⚘, *a. ling.* Wurzel *f*.

raf·fi·a ['ræfɪə] *s.* Raffiabast *m*.

raff·ish ['ræfɪʃ] *adj.* ☐ **1.** liederlich; **2.** pöbelhaft, ordi'när.

raf·fle ['ræfl] **I** *s.* Tombola *f*, Verlosung *f*; **II** *v/t. oft* ~ ***off*** *et.* (in e-r Tombola) verlosen; **III** *v/i.* losen (***for*** um).

raft [rɑːft] **I** *s.* **1.** Floß *n*; **2.** zs.-gebundenes Holz; **3.** *Am.* Treibholz(ansammlung *f*) *n*; **4.** F Unmenge *f*, ‚Haufen' *m*, ‚Latte' *f*; **II** *v/t.* **5.** flößen, als *od.* mit dem Floß befördern; **6.** zu e-m Floß zs.-binden; **7.** mit e-m Floß befahren; '**raft·er** [-tə] *s.* **1.** Flößer *m*; **2.** ⚙ (Dach-)Sparren *m*; **rafts·man** ['rɑːftsmən] *s.* [*irr.*] Flößer *m*.

rag[1] [ræg] *s.* **1.** Fetzen *m*, Lumpen *m*, Lappen *m*: ***in*** ~***s*** a) in Fetzen (*Stoff etc.*), b) zerlumpt (*Person*); ***not a*** ~ ***of evidence*** nicht den geringsten Beweis; ***chew the*** ~ a) ‚quatschen', plaudern, b) ‚meckern'; ***cook to*** ~***s*** zerkochen; ***it's a red*** ~ ***to him*** *fig.* es ist für ihn ein rotes Tuch; → ***ragtag***; **2.** *pl. Papierherstellung*: Hadern *pl.*, Lumpen *pl.*; **3.** *humor.* ‚Fetzen' *m* (*Kleid*, *Anzug*): ***not a*** ~ ***to put on*** keinen Fetzen zum Anziehen *haben*; → ***glad*** 2; **4.** *humor.* ‚Lappen' *m* (*Geldschein*, *Taschentuch etc.*); **5.** (*contp.* Käse-, Wurst)Blatt *n* (*Zeitung*); **6.** ♪ F → ***ragtime***.

rag[2] [ræg] *sl.* **I** *v/t.* **1.** *j-n* ‚anschnauzen'; **2.** *j-n* ‚aufziehen'; **3.** *j-m* e-n Streich spielen; **4.** *j-n* ‚piesacken', übel mitspielen (*dat.*); **II** *v/i.* **5.** Ra'dau machen; **III** *s.* **6.** Ra'dau *m*; **7.** Ulk *m*, Jux *m*.

rag·a·muf·fin ['rægə,mʌfɪn] *s.* **1.** zerlumpter Kerl; **2.** Gassenkind *n*.

,**rag**|**-and-'bone man** [-gən'b-] *s.* Lumpensammler *m*; ~ **bag** *s.* Lumpensack *m*; *fig.* Sammel'surium *n*: ***out of the*** ~ aus der ‚Klamottenkiste'; ~ **doll** *s.* Stoffpuppe *f*.

rage [reɪdʒ] **I** *s.* **1.** Wut(anfall *m*) *f*, Zorn *m*, Rage *f*: ***be in a*** ~ vor Wut schäumen, toben; ***fly into a*** ~ in Wut geraten; **2.** Wüten *n*, Toben *n*, Rasen *n* (*der Elemente*, *der Leidenschaft etc.*); **3.** Sucht *f*, Ma'nie *f*, Gier *f* (***for*** nach): ~ ***for collecting things*** Sammelwut *f*; **4.** Begeisterung *f*, Taumel *m*, Rausch *m*, Ek'stase *f*: ***it is all the*** ~ es ist jetzt die große Mode, alles ist wild darauf; **II** *v/i.* **5.** (*a. fig.*) toben, rasen, wüten (***at***, ***against*** gegen).

rag fair *s.* Trödelmarkt *m*.

rag·ged ['rægɪd] *adj.* ☐ **1.** zerlumpt, abgerissen (*Person*, *Kleidung*); **2.** zottig, struppig; **3.** zerfetzt, ausgefranst (*Wunde*); **4.** zackig, gezackt (*Glas*, *Stein*); **5.** holp(e)rig: ~ ***rhymes***; **6.** verwildert: ***a*** ~ ***garden***; **7.** roh, unfertig, fehler-, mangelhaft; zs.-hanglos; **8.** rauh (*Stimme*, *Ton*).

'**rag·man** [-mən] *s.* [*irr.*] Lumpensammler *m*.

ra·gout ['ræguː] *s.* Ra'gout *n*.

rag| **pa·per** *s.* ⚙ 'Hadernpa,pier *n*; '~**pick·er** *s.* Lumpensammler(in); '~**tag** *s.* Pöbel *m*, Gesindel *n*: ~ ***and bobtail*** Krethi u. Plethi *pl.*; '~**time** *s.* ♪ Ragtime *m* (*Jazzstil*).

raid [reɪd] **I** *s.* **1.** Ein-, 'Überfall *m*; Raub-, Streifzug *m*; ⚔ 'Stoßtruppunter,nehmen *n*; ⚓ Kaperfahrt *f*; ✈ (Luft-)Angriff *m*; **2.** (Poli'zei),Razzia *f*; **3.** *fig.* a) (An)Sturm *m* (***on***, ***upon*** auf *acc.*), b) *sport* Vorstoß *m*; **II** *v/t.* **4.** e-n 'Überfall machen auf (*acc.*), über'fallen, angreifen (*a.* ✈): ~***ing party*** ⚔ Stoßtrupp *m*; **5.** stürmen, plündern; **6.** e-e Razzia machen in (*dat.*); **7.** ~ ***the market*** ✝ den Markt drücken.

rail[1] [reɪl] **I** *s.* **1.** ⚙ Schiene *f*, Riegel *m*, Querstange *f*; **2.** Geländer *n*; (***main***) ~ ⚓ Reling *f*; **3.** 🚂 a) Schiene *f*, b) *pl.* Gleis *n*: ***by*** ~ mit der Bahn; ***run off the*** ~***s*** entgleisen; ***off the*** ~***s*** *fig.* aus dem Geleise, durcheinander; **4.** *pl.* ✝ 'Eisenbahn,aktien *pl.*; **II** *v/t.* **5.** *a.* ~ **in** mit e-m Geländer um'geben: ~ **off** durch ein Geländer (ab)trennen.

rail² [reɪl] *s. orn.* Ralle *f.*

rail³ [reɪl] *v/i.* schimpfen, lästern, fluchen (**at, against** über *acc.*): ~ **at** (*od.* **against**) über *et.* herziehen, gegen *et.* wettern.

rail| bus *s.* Schienenbus *m*; **'~·car** *s.* Triebwagen *m*; **'~·head** *s.* **1.** Kopfbahnhof *m*, ⚔ Ausladebahnhof *m*; **2.** 🚂 a) Schienenkopf *m*, b) im Bau befindliches Ende (*e-r neuen Strecke*).

rail·ing ['reɪlɪŋ] *s.* **1.** *a. pl.* Geländer *n*, Gitter *n*; **2.** ⚓ Reling *f.*

rail·ler·y ['reɪlərɪ] *s.* Necke'rei *f*, Stiche'lei *f*, (gutmütiger) Spott.

rail·road ['reɪlrəʊd] *bsd. Am.* **I** *s.* **1.** *allg.* Eisenbahn *f*; **2.** *pl.* ✝ 'Eisenbahn,aktien *pl.*; **II** *adj.* **3.** Eisenbahn…: ~ **accident**; **II** *v/t.* **4.** mit der Eisenbahn befördern; **5.** F *Gesetzesvorlage etc.* 'durchpeitschen; **6.** F a) *j-n* ‚über'fahren', zwingen (**into doing** et. zu tun), b) *j-n* ‚abservieren'; **'rail·road·er** [-də] *s. Am.* Eisenbahner *m.*

rail·way ['reɪlweɪ] **I** *s.* **1.** *bsd. Brit. allg.* Eisenbahn *f*; **2.** Lo'kalbahn *f*; **II** *adj.* **3.** Eisenbahn…: ~ **accident**; ~ **car·riage** *s.* Per'sonenwagen *m*; ~ **guard** *s.* Zugbegleiter *m*; ~ **guide** *s.* Kursbuch *n*; **'~·man** [-weɪmən] *s.* [*irr.*] Eisenbahner *m.*

rai·ment ['reɪmənt] *s. poet.* Kleidung *f*, Gewand *n.*

rain [reɪn] **I** *s.* **1.** Regen *m*; *pl.* Regenfälle *pl.*, -güsse *pl.*: **the ~s** die Regenzeit (*in den Tropen*); ~ **or shine** bei jedem Wetter; **as right as** ~ F ganz richtig, in Ordnung; **II** *v/i.* **2.** *impers.* regnen; → **pour** 6; **3.** *fig.* regnen; niederprasseln (*Schläge*); strömen (*Tränen*); **III** *v/t.* **4.** *Tropfen etc.* (her)'niedersenden, regnen: **it's ~ing cats and dogs** es gießt in Strömen; **5.** *fig.* (nieder)regnen *od.* (-)hageln lassen; **'~·bow** [-bəʊ] *s.* Regenbogen *m*; ~ **check** *s. Am.* Einlaßkarte *f* für die Neuansetzung e-r wegen Regens abgebrochenen (Sport)Veranstaltung: **may I take a ~ on it?** *fig.* darf ich darauf (*auf Ihr Angebot etc.*) später einmal zurückkommen?; **'~·coat** *s.* Regenmantel *m*; **'~·drop** *s.* Regentropfen *m*; **'~·fall** *s.* **1.** Regen(schauer) *m*; **2.** *meteor.* Niederschlagsmenge *f*; ~ **for·est** *s.* Regenwald *m.*

rain·i·ness ['reɪnɪnɪs] *s.* **1.** Regenneigung *f*; **2.** Regenwetter *n.*

'rain|·proof I *adj.* wasserdicht; **II** *s.* Regenmantel *m*; **'~·storm** *s.* heftiger Regenguß.

rain·y ['reɪnɪ] *adj.* □ regnerisch, verregnet; Regen…(*-wetter, -wind etc.*): **save up for a ~ day** *fig.* e-n Notgroschen zurücklegen.

raise [reɪz] **I** *v/t.* **1.** *oft* ~ **up** (in die Höhe) heben, auf-, em'por-, hochheben, erheben, erhöhen; *mit Kran etc.* hochwinden, -ziehen; *Augen* erheben, aufschlagen; ⚕ *Blasen* ziehen; *Kohle* fördern; *Staub* aufwirbeln; *Vorhang* hochziehen; *Teig, Brot* treiben: ~ **one's glass to** auf *j-n* das Glas erheben, *j-m* zutrinken; ~ **one's hat** (**to s.o.**) den Hut ziehen (vor j-m, *a. fig.*); → **power** 12; **2.** aufrichten, -stellen, aufrecht stellen; **3.** errichten, erstellen, (er)bauen; **4.** *Familie* gründen; *Kinder* auf-, großziehen; **5.** a) *Pflanzen* ziehen, b) *Tiere* züchten; **6.** aufwecken: ~ **from the dead** von den Toten erwecken; **7.** *Geister* zitieren, beschwören; **8.** *Gelächter, Sturm etc.* her'vorrufen, verursachen; *Erwartungen, Verdacht, Zorn* erwekken, erregen; *Gerücht* aufkommen lassen; *Schwierigkeiten* machen; **9.** *Geist, Mut* beleben, anfeuern; **10.** aufwiegeln (**against** gegen); *Aufruhr* anstiften, -zetteln; **11.** *Geld etc.* beschaffen; *Anleihe, Hypothek, Kredit* aufnehmen; *Steuern* erheben; *Heer* aufstellen; **12.** *Stimme, Geschrei* erheben; **13.** *Anspruch* erheben, *Einwand a.* vorbringen, geltend machen, *Forderung a.* stellen; *Frage* aufwerfen; *Sache* zur Sprache bringen; **14.** (ver)stärken, vergrößern, vermehren; **15.** *Lohn, Preis, Wert etc.* erhöhen, hin'aufsetzen; *Temperatur, Wette etc.* steigern; **16.** (im Rang) erhöhen: ~ **to the throne** auf den Thron erheben; **17.** *Belagerung, Blockade etc., a. Verbot* aufheben; **18.** ⚓ sichten; **II** *s.* **19.** Erhöhung *f*; *Am.* Steigung *f* (*Straße*); **20.** *bsd. Am.* (Gehalts-, Lohn)Erhöhung *f*, Aufbesserung *f*; **raised** [-zd] *adj.* **1.** erhöht; **2.** gesteigert; **3.** ⚙ erhaben; **4.** Hefe…: ~ **cake.**

rai·sin ['reɪzn] *s.* Ro'sine *f.*

rai·son| d'é·tat [,reɪzɔ̃:n'deɪ'tɑ:] (*Fr.*) *s.* 'Staatsrä,son *f*; ~ **d'ê·tre** [-'deɪtrə] (*Fr.*) *s.* Daseinsberechtigung *f*, -zweck *m.*

raj [rɑ:dʒ] *s. Brit. Ind.* Herrschaft *f.*

ra·ja(h) ['rɑ:dʒə] *s.* Radscha *m* (*indischer Fürst*).

rake¹ [reɪk] **I** *s.* **1.** Rechen *m* (*a. des Croupiers etc.*), Harke *f*; **2.** ⚙ a) Rührstange *f*, b) Kratze *f*, c) Schürhaken *m*; **II** *v/t.* **3.** (glatt-, zs.-)rechen, (-)harken; **4.** *mst* ~ **together** zs.-scharren (*a. fig. zs.-raffen*); **5.** durch'stöbern (*a.* ~ **up**, ~ **over**): ~ **up** *fig. alte Geschichten* aufrühren; **6.** ⚔ (mit Feuer) bestreichen, ‚beharken'; **7.** über'blicken, absuchen; **III** *v/i.* **8.** rechen, harken; **9.** *fig.* her'umstöbern, -suchen (**for** nach).

rake² [reɪk] *s.* Lebemann *m.*

rake³ [reɪk] **I** *v/i.* **1.** Neigung haben; **2.** ⚓ a) 'überhängen (*Steven*), b) Fall haben (*Mast, Schornstein*); **II** *v/t.* **3.** (nach rückwärts) neigen; **III** *s.* **4.** Neigung(swinkel *m*) *f.*

'rake-off *s.* F (Gewinn)Anteil *m.*

rak·ish¹ ['reɪkɪʃ] *adj.* □ ausschweifend, liederlich, wüst.

rak·ish² ['reɪkɪʃ] *adj.* **1.** ⚓, *mot.* schnittig (gebaut); **2.** *fig.* flott, verwegen, keck.

ral·ly¹ ['rælɪ] **I** *v/t.* **1.** *Truppen etc.* (wieder) sammeln *od.* ordnen; **2.** vereinigen, scharen (**round, to** um *acc.*), zs.-trommeln; **3.** aufrütteln, -muntern, in Schwung bringen; **4.** *Kräfte etc.* sammeln, zs.-raffen; **II** *v/i.* **5.** sich (wieder) sammeln; **6.** *a. fig.* sich scharen (**round, to** um *acc.*); sich zs.-tun; sich anschließen (**to** *dat. od.* an *acc.*); **7.** *a.* ~ **round** sich erholen (*a. fig. u.* ✝), neue Kräfte sammeln; *sport etc.* sich (wieder) ‚fangen'; **8.** *Tennis etc.*: a) e-n Ballwechsel ausführen, b) sich einschlagen; **III** *s.* **9.** ⚔ Sammeln *n*; **10.** Zs.-kunft *f*, Treffen *n*, Tagung *f*, Kundgebung *f*, (Massen)Versammlung *f*; **11.** Erholung *f* (*a.* ✝ *der Preise, des Marktes*); **12.** *Tennis*: Ballwechsel *m*; **13.** *mot.* Rallye *f*, Sternfahrt *f.*

ral·ly² ['rælɪ] *v/t.* hänseln.

ral·ly·ing ['rælɪɪŋ] *adj.* Sammel…: ~ **cry** Parole *f*, Schlagwort *n*; ~ **point** Sammelpunkt *m*, -platz *m.*

ram [ræm] **I** *s.* **1.** *zo.* (*ast.* ♈) Widder *m*; **2.** ⚔ *hist.* Sturmbock *m*; **3.** ⚙ a) Ramme *f*, b) Rammbock *m*, -bär *m*, c) Preßkolben *m*; **4.** ⚓ Rammsporn *m*; **II** *v/t.* **5.** (fest-, ein)rammen (*a.* ~ **down** *od.* **in**); *weitS.* (gewaltsam) stoßen, drükken; **6.** (hin'ein)stopfen: ~ **up** a) vollstopfen, b) verrammeln, verstopfen; **7.** *fig.* eintrichtern, -pauken: ~ **s.th. into s.o.** j-m et. einbleuen; → **throat** 1; **8.** ⚓, ✈ *etc.* rammen; *weitS.* stoßen, schmettern, ‚knallen'.

ram·ble ['ræmbl] **I** *v/i.* **1.** um'herwandern, -streifen, bummeln; **2.** sich winden (*Fluß etc.*); **3.** ⚘ wuchern, (üppig) ranken; **4.** *fig.* (vom Thema) abschweifen; drauf'losreden; **II** *s.* **5.** (Fuß)Wanderung *f*, Streifzug *m*; Bummel *m*; **'ram·bler** [-lə] *s.* **1.** Wand(e)rer *m*, Wand(r)erin *f*; **2.** *a.* **crimson** ~ ⚘ Kletterrose *f*; **'ram·bling** [-lɪŋ] **I** *adj.* □ **1.** um'herwandernd, -streifend: ~ **club** Wanderverein *m*; **2.** ⚘ (üppig) rankend, wuchernd; **3.** weitläufig, verschachtelt (*Gebäude*); **4.** *fig.* abschweifend, weitschweifig, planlos; **II** *s.* **5.** Wandern *n*, Um'herstreifen *n.*

ram·bunc·tious [ræm'bʌŋkʃəs] *adj.* laut, lärmend, wild.

ram·ie ['ræmi:] *s.* Ra'mie(faser) *f.*

ram·i·fi·ca·tion [,ræmɪfɪ'keɪʃn] *s.* Verzweigung *f*, -ästelung *f* (*a. fig.*); **ram·i·fy** ['ræmɪfaɪ] *v/t. u. v/i.* (sich) verzweigen (*a. fig.*).

ram·jet (en·gine) ['ræmdʒet] *s.* ⚙ Staustrahltriebwerk *n.*

ramp¹ [ræmp] **I** *s.* **1.** Rampe *f* (*a.* △ *Abdachung*); **2.** (schräge) Auffahrt, (Lade)Rampe *f*; **3.** Krümmling *m* (*am Treppengeländer*); **4.** ✈ (fahrbare) Treppe; **II** *v/i.* **5.** sich (drohend) aufrichten, zum Sprung ansetzen (*Tier*); **6.** toben, wüten; **7.** ⚘ wuchern; **III** *v/t.* **8.** mit e-r Rampe versehen.

ramp² [ræmp] *s. Brit. sl.* Betrug *m.*

ram·page [ræm'peɪdʒ] **I** *v/i.* toben, wüten; **II** *s.*: **be on the** ~ a) (sich aus)toben, b) *fig.* grassieren, um sich greifen, wüten; **ram'pa·geous** [-dʒəs] *adj.* □ wild, wütend.

ramp·an·cy ['ræmpənsɪ] *s.* **1.** Über'handnehmen *n*, 'Umsichgreifen *n*, Grassieren *n*; **2.** *fig.* wilde Ausgelassenheit, Wildheit *f*; **'ramp·ant** [-nt] *adj.* □ **1.** wild, zügellos, ausgelassen; **2.** über'handnehmend: **be** ~ → **rampage** II b; **3.** üppig, wuchernd (*Pflanzen*); **4.** (drohend) aufgerichtet, sprungbereit (*Tier*); **5.** *her.* steigend.

ram·part ['ræmpɑ:t] *s.* ⚔ a) Brustwehr *f*, b) (Schutz)Wall *m* (*a. fig.*).

ram·rod ['ræmrɒd] *s.* ⚔ *hist.* Ladestock *m*: **as stiff as a** ~ als hätte *er etc.* e-n Ladestock verschluckt.

ram·shack·le ['ræm,ʃækl] *adj.* baufällig, wack(e)lig; klapp(e)rig.

ran¹ [ræn] *pret. von* **run.**

ran² [ræn] *s.* **1.** Docke *f* Bindfaden; **2.** ⚓ aufgehaspeltes Kabelgarn.

ranch [rɑ:ntʃ; *bsd. Am.* ræntʃ] **I** *s.*

Ranch *f*, (*bsd.* Vieh)Farm *f*; **II** *v/i.* Viehzucht treiben; **ˈranch·er** [-tʃə] *s. Am.* **1.** Rancher *m*, Viehzüchter *m*; **2.** Farmer *m*; **3.** Rancharbeiter *m*.

ran·cid [ˈrænsɪd] *adj.* **1.** ranzig (*Butter etc.*); **2.** *fig.* widerlich; **ran·cid·i·ty** [rænˈsɪdətɪ], **ˈran·cid·ness** [-nɪs] *s.* Ranzigkeit *f*.

ran·cor *Am.* → ***rancour***.

ran·cor·ous [ˈræŋkərəs] *adj.* □ erbittert, voller Groll, giftig; **ran·cour** [ˈræŋkə] *s.* Groll *m*, Haß *m*.

ran·dom [ˈrændəm] **I** *adj.* □ ziel-, wahllos, zufällig, aufs Carateˈwohl, Zufalls…: **~ *mating*** *biol.* Zufallspaarung *f*; **~ *sample*** (*od.* ***test***) Stichprobe *f*; **~ *shot*** Schuß *m* ins Blaue; **~ *access*** *Computer*: wahlfreier *od.* direkter Zugriff; **II** *s.*: ***at* ~** aufs Geratewohl, auf gut Glück, blindlings, zufällig: ***talk at* ~** (wild) drauflosreden.

rand·y [ˈrændɪ] *adj.* F geil.

ra·nee [ˌrɑːˈniː] *s.* Rani *f* (*indische Fürstin*).

rang [ræŋ] *pret. von* ***ring***[2].

range [reɪndʒ] **I** *s.* **1.** Reihe *f*; (*a.* Berg-)Kette *f*; **2.** (Koch-, Küchen)Herd *m*; **3.** Schießstand *m*, -platz *m*; **4.** Entfernung *f zum Ziel*, Abstand *m*: ***at a* ~ *of*** aus (*od.* in) e-r Entfernung von; ***at close* ~** aus der Nähe; ***find the* ~** ⚔ sich einschießen; ***take the* ~** die Entfernung schätzen; **5.** *bsd.* ⚔ Reich-, Trag-, Schußweite *f*; ⚓ Laufstrecke *f* (*Torpedo*); ✈ Flugbereich *m*: ***at close* ~** aus nächster Nähe; ***out of* ~** außer Schußweite; ***within* ~ *of vision*** in Sichtweite; → ***long-range***; **6.** Ausdehnung *f*, (ausgedehnte) Fläche; **7.** *fig.* Bereich *m*, Spielraum *m*, Grenzen *pl.*; (⚘, *zo.* Verbreitungs)Gebiet *n*: **~ (*of action*)** Aktionsbereich; **~ (*of activities*)** (Betätigungs)Feld *n*; **~ *of application*** Anwendungsbereich; **~ *of prices*** ☤ Preislage *f*, -klasse *f*; **~ *of reception*** *Funk*: Empfangsbereich; ***boiling* ~** *phys.* Siedebereich; **8.** ☤ Kollektiˈon *f*, Sortiˈment *n*: ***a wide* ~ (*of goods*)** e-e große Auswahl, ein großes Angebot; **9.** Bereich *m*, Gebiet *n*, Raum *m*: **~ *of knowledge*** Wissensbereich; **~ *of thought*** Ideenkreis *m*; **10.** ♪ a) ˈTon-, ˈStimmˌumfang *m*, b) Ton-, Stimmlage *f*; **II** *v/t.* **11.** (in Reihen) aufstellen *od.* anordnen; **12.** einreihen, -ordnen: **~ *o.s. with*** (*od.* ***on the side of***) zu *j-m* halten; **13.** *Gebiet etc.* durchˈstreifen, -ˈwandern; **14.** längs *der Küste* fahren, entlangfahren; **15.** *Teleskop etc.* einstellen; **16.** ⚔ a) *Geschütz* richten (***on*** auf *acc.*), b) e-e Reichweite haben von, tragen; **III** *v/i.* **17.** (***with***) e-e Reihe *od.* Linie bilden (mit), in e-r Reihe *od.* Linie stehen (mit); **18.** sich erstrecken, verlaufen, reichen; **19.** *fig.* rangieren (***among*** unter), im gleichen Rang stehen (***with*** mit); zählen, gehören (***with*** zu); **20.** (umˈher)streifen, (-)schweifen, wandern (*a. Auge, Blick*); **21.** ⚘, *zo.* vorkommen, verbreitet *od.* zu finden sein; **22.** schwanken, sich bewegen (***from … to …*** *od.* ***between … and …*** zwischen … und …) (*Zahlenwert, Preis etc.*); **23.** ⚔ sich einschießen (*Geschütz*).

ˈrange-ˌfind·er *s.* ⚔, *phot.* Entfernungsmesser *m* (⚔ *a. Mann*).

rang·er [ˈreɪndʒə] *s.* **1.** *Am.* Ranger *m*: a) *Wächter e-s Nationalparks*, b) *mst* ♀ *Angehöriger e-r Schutztruppe e-s Bundesstaates*, c) ⚔ *Angehöriger e-r Kommandotruppe*; **2.** *Brit.* Aufseher *m* e-s königlichen Forsts *od.* Parks (*Titel*); **3.** *a.* **~ *guide*** *Brit.* Ranger *f* (*Pfadfinderin über 16 Jahre*).

rank[1] [ræŋk] **I** *s.* **1.** Reihe *f*, Linie *f*; **2.** ⚔ a) Glied *n*, b) Rang *m*, Dienstgrad *m*: ***the* ~*s*** (Unteroffiziere und) Mannschaften; **~ *and file*** ⚔ *der* Mannschaftsstand, *pol.* die Basis (*e-r Partei*); ***in* ~ *and file*** in Reih und Glied; ***close the* ~*s*** die Reihen schließen; ***join the* ~*s*** ins Heer eintreten; ***rise from the* ~*s*** von der Pike auf dienen (*a. fig.*); **3.** (soziˈale) Klasse, Stand *m*, Schicht *f*, Rang *m*: ***man of* ~** Mann von Stand; **~ *and fashion*** die vornehme Welt; ***of second* ~** zweitrangig; ***take* ~ *of*** den Vorrang haben vor (*dat.*); ***take* ~ *with*** mit *j-m* gleichrangig sein; **II** *v/t.* **4.** (ein-)reihen, (-)ordnen, klassifizieren; **5.** *Truppe etc.* aufstellen, formieren; **6.** *fig.* rechnen, zählen (***with***, ***among*** zu): ***I* ~ *him above Shaw*** ich stelle ihn über Shaw; **III** *v/i.* **7.** sich reihen *od.* ordnen; ⚔ (in geschlossener Formatiˈon) marschieren; **8.** e-n Rang *od.* e-e Stelle einnehmen, rangieren (***above*** über *dat.*, ***below*** unter *dat.*, ***next to*** hinter *dat.*): **~ *as*** gelten als; **~ *first*** an erster Stelle stehen; **~ *high*** e-n hohen Rang einnehmen, *a.* e-n hohen Stellenwert haben; **~*ing officer*** *Am.* rangältester Offizier; **9.** **~ *among*, ~ *with*** gehören *od.* zählen zu.

rank[2] [ræŋk] *adj.* □ **1.** a) üppig, geil wachsend (*Pflanzen*), b) verwildert (*Garten*); **2.** fruchtbar, fett (*Boden*); **3.** stinkend, ranzig; **4.** widerlich, scharf (*Geruch od. Geschmack*); **5.** kraß: **~ *outsider*; ~ *beginner*** blutiger Anfänger; **~ *nonsense*** blühender Unsinn; **6.** ekelhaft, unanständig.

rank·er [ˈræŋkə] *s.* ⚔ a) einfacher Solˈdat, b) aus dem Mannschaftsstand herˈvorgegangener Offiˈzier.

ran·kle [ˈræŋkl] *v/i.* **1.** eitern, schwären (*Wunde*); **2.** *fig.* nagen, fressen, weh tun: **~ *with*** *j-n* wurmen, *j-m* weh tun.

ran·sack [ˈrænsæk] *v/t.* **1.** durchˈwühlen; **2.** plündern, ausrauben.

ran·som [ˈrænsəm] **I** *s.* **1.** Loskauf *m*, Auslösung *f*; **2.** Lösegeld *n*: ***a king's* ~** e-e Riesensumme; ***hold to* ~** a) *j-n* gegen Lösegeld gefangenhalten, b) *fig. j-n* erpressen; **3.** *eccl.* Erlösung *f*; **II** *v/t.* **4.** los-, freikaufen; **5.** *eccl.* erlösen.

rant [rænt] **I** *v/i.* **1.** toben, lärmen; **2.** schwadronieren, Phrasen dreschen; **3.** *obs.* geifern (***at***, ***against*** über *acc.*); **II** *v/t.* **4.** paˈthetisch vortragen; **III** *s.* **5.** Wortschwall *m*; Schwulst *m*, leeres Gerede, ˌPhrasendrescheˈrei *f*; **ˈrant·er** [-tə] *s.* **1.** paˈthetischer Redner, Kanzelpauker *m*; **2.** Schwadroˈneur *m*, Großsprecher *m*.

ra·nun·cu·lus [rəˈnʌŋkjʊləs] *pl.* **-lus·es, -li** [-laɪ] *s.* ⚘ Raˈnunkel *f*.

rap[1] [ræp] **I** *v/t.* **1.** klopfen *od.* pochen an *od.* auf (*acc.*): **~ *s.o.'s fingers*, ~ *s.o. over the knuckles*** *bsd. fig.* j-m auf die Finger klopfen; **2.** *Am. sl.* a) *j-m* e-e ‚Ziˈgarre' verpassen, b) *j-n*, *et.* scharf kritisieren, c) *j-n* ‚verdonnern', d) *j-n* ‚schnappen'; **3.** **~ *out*** a) durch Klopfen mitteilen (*Geist*), b) *Worte* herˈauspoltern, ‚bellen'; **II** *v/i.* **4.** klopfen, pochen, schlagen (***at*** an *acc.*); **III** *s.* **5.** Klopfen *n*; **6.** Schlag *m*; **7.** *Am.* F a) scharfe Kriˈtik, b) ‚Ziˈgarre' *f*, Rüge *f*; **8.** *Am. sl.* a) Anklage *f*, b) Strafe *f*, c) Schuld *f*: **~ *sheet*** Strafregister *n*; ***beat the* ~** sich rauswinden; ***take the* ~** (zu e-r Strafe) ‚verdonnert' werden; **9.** *Am.* F ‚Plausch' *m*: **~ *session*** (Gruppen-)Diskussion *f*.

rap[2] [ræp] *s. fig.* Heller *m*, Deut *m*: ***I don't care*** (*od.* ***give***) ***a* ~** (***for it***) das ist mir ganz egal; ***it is not worth a* ~** es ist keinen Pfifferling wert.

ra·pa·cious [rəˈpeɪʃəs] *adj.* □ raubgierig, Raub…(*-tier*, *-vogel*); *fig.* (hab)gierig; **raˈpa·cious·ness** [-nɪs], **raˈpac·i·ty** [-ˈpæsətɪ] *s.* **1.** Raubgier *f*; **2.** *fig.* Habgier *f*.

rape[1] [reɪp] **I** *s.* **1.** Vergewaltigung *f* (*a. fig.*), ⚖ Notzucht *f*: **~ *and murder*** Lustmord *m*; ***statutory* ~** *Am.* ⚖ Unzucht mit Minderjährigen; **2.** Entführung *f*, Raub *m*; **II** *v/t.* **3.** vergewaltigen; **4.** *obs.* rauben.

rape[2] [reɪp] *s.* ⚘ Raps *m*.

rape[3] [reɪp] *s.* Trester *pl.*

rape|·oil *s.* Rüb-, Rapsöl *n*; **ˈ~·seed** *s.* Rübsamen *m*.

rap·id [ˈræpɪd] **I** *adj.* □ **1.** schnell, rasch, raˈpid(e); reißend (*Fluß*; ☤ *Absatz*); Schnell…: **~ *fire*** ⚔ Schnellfeuer *n*; **~ *transit*** *Am.* Nahschnellverkehr *m*; **2.** jäh, steil (*Hang*); **3.** *phot.* a) lichtstark (*Objektiv*), b) hochempfindlich (*Film*); **II** *s.* **4.** *pl.* Stromschnelle(n *pl.*) *f*; **ra·pid·i·ty** [rəˈpɪdətɪ] *s.* Schnelligkeit *f*, (rasende) Geschwindigkeit.

ra·pi·er [ˈreɪpjə] *s. fenc.* Raˈpier *n*: **~ *thrust*** *fig.* sarˈkastische Bemerkung.

rap·ist [ˈreɪpɪst] *s.* Vergewaltiger *m*: **~-*killer*** Lustmörder *m*.

rap·port [ræˈpɔː] *s.* (enge, perˈsönliche) Beziehung: ***be in*** (*od.* ***en***) **~ *with*** mit *j-m* in Verbindung stehen, *fig.* gut harmonieren mit.

rap·proche·ment [ræˈprɒʃmɑ̃ːŋ] (*Fr.*) *s. bsd. pol.* (Wieder)ˈAnnäherung *f*.

rapt [ræpt] *adj.* **1.** versunken, verloren (***in*** in *acc.*): **~ *in thought***; **2.** hingerissen, entzückt (***with***, ***by*** von); **3.** verzückt (*Lächeln etc.*); gespannt (***upon*** auf *acc.*) (*a. Aufmerksamkeit*).

rap·to·ri·al [ræpˈtɔːrɪəl] *orn.* **I** *adj.* Raub…; **II** *s.* Raubvogel *m*.

rap·ture [ˈræptʃə] *s.* **1.** Entzücken *n*, Verzückung *f*, Begeisterung *f*, Taumel *m*: ***in* ~*s*** hingerissen (***at*** von); ***go into* ~*s*** in Verzückung geraten (***over*** über *acc.*); **~ *of the deep*** ⚓ Tiefenrausch *m*; **2.** *pl.* Ausbruch *m* des Entzückens, Begeisterungstaumel *m*; **ˈrap·tur·ous** [-tʃərəs] *adj.* □ **1.** entzückt, hingerissen; **2.** stürmisch, begeistert (*Beifall etc.*); **3.** verzückt (*Gesicht*).

rare[1] [reə] *adj.* □ **1.** selten, rar (*a. fig. ungewöhnlich, hervorragend, köstlich*): **~ *earth*** ⚗ seltene Erde; **~ *fun*** F Mordsspaß *m*; **~ *gas*** Edelgas *n*; **2.** *phys.* dünn (*Luft*).

rare[2] [reə] *adj.* halbgar, nicht ˈdurchgebraten (*Fleisch*); englisch (*Steak*).

rare·bit [ˈreəbɪt] *s.*: ***Welsh* ~** überbackene Käseschnitte.

rar·ee show [ˈreəriː] *s.* **1.** Guckkasten *m*; **2.** Straßenzirkus *m*; **3.** *fig.* Schauspiel *n.*

rar·e·fac·tion [ˌreərɪˈfækʃn] *s. phys.* Verdünnung *f*; **rar·e·fy** [ˈreərɪfaɪ] **I** *v/t.* **1.** verdünnen; **2.** *fig.* verfeinern; **II** *v/i.* **3.** sich verdünnen.

rare·ness [ˈreənɪs] → ***rarity.***

rar·ing [ˈreərɪŋ] *adj.*: ***~ to do s.th.*** F ganz wild darauf, et. zu tun.

rar·i·ty [ˈreərətɪ] *s.* **1.** Seltenheit *f*: a) *seltenes Vorkommen*, b) Rariˈtät *f*, Kostbarkeit *f*; **2.** Vorˈtrefflichkeit *f*; **3.** *phys.* Verdünnung *f.*

ras·cal [ˈrɑːskəl] *s.* **1.** Schuft *m*, Schurke *m*, Haˈlunke *m*; **2.** *humor.* a) Gauner *m*, b) Frechdachs *m* (*Kind*); **ras·cal·i·ty** [rɑːˈskælətɪ] *s.* Schurkeˈrei *f*; **ˈras·cal·ly** [-kəlɪ] *adj u. adv.* niederträchtig, gemein.

rash¹ [ræʃ] *adj.* ☐ **1.** hastig, überˈeilt, -ˈstürzt, vorschnell: ***a ~ decision***; **2.** unbesonnen.

rash² [ræʃ] *s.* ⚕ (Haut)Ausschlag *m.*

rash·er [ˈræʃə] *s.* (dünne) Scheibe Frühstücksspeck *od.* Schinken.

rash·ness [ˈræʃnɪs] *s.* **1.** Hast *f*, Überˈeiltheit *f*, -ˈstürztheit *f*; **2.** Unbesonnenheit *f.*

rasp [rɑːsp] **I** *v/t.* **1.** raspeln, feilen, schaben; **2.** *fig. Gefühle etc.* verletzen; *Ohren* beleidigen; *Nerven* reizen; **3.** krächzen(d äußern); **II** *s.* **4.** Raspel *f*, Grobfeile *f*; Reibeisen *n.*

rasp·ber·ry [ˈrɑːzbərɪ] *s.* **1.** ♀ Himbeere *f*; **2.** *a.* ***~ cane*** ♀ Himbeerstrauch *m*; **3.** ***give*** (*od.* ***blow***) ***a ~*** *fig. sl.* verächtlich schnauben.

rasp·ing [ˈrɑːspɪŋ] **I** *adj.* ☐ **1.** kratzend, krächzend (*Stimme etc.*); **II** *s.* **2.** Raspeln *n*; **3.** *pl.* Raspelspäne *pl.*

ras·ter [ˈræstə] *s. opt., TV* Raster *m.*

rat [ræt] **I** *s.* **1.** *zo.* Ratte *f*: ***smell a ~*** *fig.* Lunte *od.* den Braten riechen, Unrat wittern; ***like a drowned ~*** pudelnaß; ***~s!*** ‚Quatschʻ!; **2.** *pol.* F ˈÜberläufer *m*, Abtrünnige(r *m*) *f*; **3.** F a) *allg.* Verräter *m*, b) ‚Schweinʻ *n*, c) Spitzel *m*, d) Streikbrecher *m*; **II** *v/i.* **4.** *pol.* F ˈüberlaufen, *allg.* Verrat begehen: ***~ on*** a) *j-n* verraten *od.* im Stich lassen, b) *Kumpane* ‚verpfeifenʻ, c) *et.* widerrufen, d) aus *et.* ‚aussteigenʻ; **5.** Ratten fangen.

rat·a·bil·i·ty [ˌreɪtəˈbɪlətɪ] *s.* **1.** (Ab-)Schätzbarkeit *f*; **2.** Verhältnismäßigkeit *f*; **3.** *bsd. Brit.* Steuerbarkeit *f*, ˈUmlagepflicht *f*; **rat·a·ble** [ˈreɪtəbl] *adj.* ☐ **1.** (ab)schätzbar, abzuschätzen(d), bewertbar; **2.** anteilmäßig, proportioˈnal; **3.** *bsd. Brit.* (kommuˈnal)steuerpflichtig; zollpflichtig: ***~ value*** Einheitswert *m.*

ratch [rætʃ] *s.* ⚙ **1.** (gezahnte) Sperrstange; **2.** Auslösung *f* (*Uhr*).

ratch·et [ˈrætʃɪt] *s.* ⚙ Sperrklinke *f*; ***~ wheel*** *s.* ⚙ Sperrad *n.*

rate¹ [reɪt] **I** *s.* **1.** (Verhältnis)Ziffer *f*, Quote *f*, Maß(stab *m*) *n*, (*Wachstums-, Inflations- etc.*)Rate *f*: ***birth ~*** Geburtenziffer; ***death ~*** Sterblichkeitsziffer; ***at the ~ of*** im Verhältnis von (→ 2 *u.* 6); ***at a fearful ~*** in erschreckendem Ausmaß; **2.** (*Diskont-, Lohn-, Steuer- etc.*)Satz *m*, Kurs *m*, Taˈrif *m*: ***~ of exchange*** (Umrechnungs-, Wechsel-)Kurs; ***~ of the day*** Tageskurs; ***at the ~ of*** zum Satze von; **3.** (festgesetzter) Preis, Betrag *m*, Taxe *f*: ***at any ~*** *fig.* a) auf jeden Fall, b) wenigstens; ***at that ~*** unter diesen Umständen; **4.** (Post- *etc.*) Gebühr *f*, Porto *n*; (Gas-, Strom-) Preis *m*: ***inland ~*** Inlandporto; **5.** *Brit.* (Kommuˈnal)Steuer *f*, (Gemeinde)Abgabe *f*; **6.** (relaˈtive) Geschwindigkeit: ***~ of climb*** ✈ Steiggeschwindigkeit; ***~ of energy*** *phys.* Energiemenge *f* pro Zeiteinheit; ***~ of an engine*** Motorleistung *f*; ***~ plate*** ⚙ Leistungsschild *n*; ***at the ~ of*** mit e-r Geschwindigkeit von; **7.** Grad *m*, Rang *m*, Klasse *f*; **8.** ⚓ a) Klasse *f* (*Schiff*), b) Dienstgrad *m* (*Matrose*); **II** *v/t.* **9.** *et.* abschätzen, taxieren (***at*** auf *acc.*); **10.** *j-n* einschätzen, beurteilen; ⚓ *Seemann* einstufen; **11.** *Preis etc.* bemessen, ansetzen; *Kosten* veranschlagen: ***~ up*** höher versichern; **12.** *j-n* betrachten als, halten für; **13.** rechnen, zählen (***among*** zu); **14.** *Brit.* a) (zur Steuer) veranlagen, b) besteuern; **15.** *Am. sl. et.* wert sein, Anspruch haben auf (*acc.*); **III** *v/i.* **16.** angesehen werden, gelten (***as*** als): ***~ high*** (***low***) hoch (niedrig) ‚im Kurs stehenʻ, e-n hohen Stellenwert haben; ***~ above*** (***below***) rangieren, stehen über (unter) *j-m od. e-r Sache*; ***~ with s.o.*** bei j-m e-n Stein im Brett haben; ***she*** (***it***) ***~d high with him*** sie (es) galt viel bei ihm; **17.** ***~ among*** zählen zu.

rate² [reɪt] **I** *v/t.* ausschelten (***for, about*** wegen); **II** *v/i.* schimpfen (***at*** auf *acc.*).

rate·a·bil·i·ty *etc.* → ***ratability*** *etc.*

rat·ed [ˈreɪtɪd] *adj.* **1.** (gemeinde)steuerpflichtig; **2.** ⚙ Nenn…: ***~ power*** Nennleistung *f.*

ˈrate|pay·er *s. Brit.* (Gemeinde)Steuerzahler(in).

rath·er [ˈrɑːðə] *adv.* **1.** ziemlich, fast, etwas: ***~ cold*** ziemlich kalt; ***I would ~ think*** ich möchte fast glauben; ***I ~ expected it*** ich habe es fast erwartet; **2.** lieber, eher (***than*** als): ***I would*** (*od.* ***had***) ***much ~ go*** ich möchte viel lieber gehen; **3.** (***or*** oder) vielmehr, eigentlich, besser gesagt; **4.** *bsd. Brit.* F (ja) freilich!, allerˈdings!

rat·i·fi·ca·tion [ˌrætɪfɪˈkeɪʃn] *s.* **1.** Bestätigung *f*, Genehmigung *f*; **2.** *pol.* Ratifizierung *f*; **rat·i·fy** [ˈrætɪfaɪ] *v/t.* **1.** bestätigen, genehmigen, gutheißen; **2.** *pol.* ratifizieren.

rat·ing¹ [ˈreɪtɪŋ] *s.* **1.** (Ab)Schätzung *f*, Bewertung *f*, (*a.* Leistungs)Beurteilung *f*; *ped. Am.* (Zeugnis)Note *f*; *Radio, TV*: Einschaltquote *f*; **2.** (Leistungs-)Stand *m*, Niˈveau *n*; **3.** *fig.* Stellenwert *m*; **4.** ⚓ a) Dienstgrad *m*, b) *Brit.* Maˈtrose *m*, c) *pl. Brit.* Leute *pl.* e-s bestimmten Dienstgrades; **5.** ⚓ (Segel-)Klasse *f*; **6.** ☤ Kreˈditwürdigkeit *f*; **7.** Taˈrif *m*; **8.** *Brit.* a) (Gemeindesteuer-)Veranlagung *f*, b) Steuersatz *m*; **9.** ⚙ (Nenn)Leistung *f*, Betriebsdaten *pl.*

rat·ing² [ˈreɪtɪŋ] *s.* heftige Schelte.

ra·tio [ˈreɪʃɪəʊ] *s.* **1.** A *etc.* Verhältnis *n*: ***~ of distribution*** Verteilungsschlüssel *m*; ***be in the inverse ~*** a) im umgekehrten Verhältnis stehen, b) A umgekehrt proportional sein (***to*** zu); **2.** A Quotiˈent *m*; **3.** ☤ Wertverhältnis *n* zwischen Gold u. Silber; **4.** ⚙ Überˈsetzungsverhältnis *n* (*e-s Getriebes*).

ra·ti·oc·i·na·tion [ˌrætɪɒsɪˈneɪʃn] *s.* **1.** logisches Denken; **2.** logischer Gedankengang *od.* Schluß.

ra·tion [ˈræʃn] **I** *s.* **1.** Ratiˈon *f*, Zuteilung *f*: ***~ card*** Lebensmittelkarte *f*; ***off the ~*** markenfrei; **2.** ✕ (Tages)Verpflegungssatz *m*; **3.** *pl.* Lebensmittel *pl.*, Verpflegung *f*; **II** *v/t.* **4.** rationieren, (zwangs)bewirtschaften; **5.** *a.* ***~ out*** (in Rationen) zuteilen; **6.** ✕ verpflegen.

ra·tion·al [ˈræʃənl] *adj.* ☐ **1.** vernünftig: a) vernunftmäßig, ratioˈnal, b) vernunftbegabt, c) verständig; **2.** zweckmäßig, ratioˈnal (*a.* A); **ra·tion·ale** [ˌræʃəˈnɑːl] *s.* **1.** ˈGrundprinˌzip *n*; **2.** vernunftmäßige Erklärung.

ra·tion·al·ism [ˈræʃnəlɪzəm] *s.* Rationaˈlismus *m*; **ˈra·tion·al·ist** [-ɪst] **I** *s.* Rationaˈlist *m*; **II** *adj.* → **ra·tion·al·is·tic** [ˌræʃnəˈlɪstɪk] *adj.* (☐ ***~ally***) rationaˈlistisch; **ra·tion·al·i·ty** [ˌræʃəˈnælətɪ] *s.* **1.** Vernünftigkeit *f*; **2.** Vernunft *f*, Denkvermögen *n*; **ra·tion·al·i·za·tion** [ˌræʃnəlaɪˈzeɪʃn] *s.* **1.** Rationalisieren *n*; **2.** ☤ Rationalisierung *f*; **ˈra·tion·al·ize** [-laɪz] **I** *v/t.* **1.** ratioˈnal erklären, vernunftgemäß deuten; **2.** ☤ rationalisieren; **II** *v/i.* **3.** ratioˈnell verfahren; **4.** rationaˈlistisch denken.

ra·tion·ing [ˈræʃnɪŋ] *s.* Rationierung *f.*

rat race *s.* **1.** ‚Hetzjagdʻ *f* (*des Lebens*); **2.** harter (Konkurˈrenz)Kampf; **3.** Teufelskreis *m.*

rats·bane [ˈrætsbeɪn] *s.* Rattengift *n.*

rat-tat [ˌrætˈtæt], *a.* **rat-tat-tat** [ˌrætəˈtæt] **I** *s.* Rattern *n*, Geknatter *n*; **II** *v/i.* knattern.

rat·ten [ˈrætn] *v/i. bsd. Brit.* (die Arbeit) sabotieren, Saboˈtage treiben.

rat·ter [ˈrætə] *s.* Rattenfänger *m* (*Hund od. Katze*).

rat·tle [ˈrætl] **I** *v/i.* **1.** rattern, klappern, rasseln, klirren: ***~ at the door*** an der Tür rütteln; ***~ off*** losrattern, davonjagen; **2.** röcheln; rasseln (*Atem*); **3.** *a.* ***~ away*** *od.* ***on*** plappern; **II** *v/t.* **4.** rasseln mit *od.* an (*dat.*); an *der Tür etc.* rütteln; mit *Geschirr etc.* klappern; → ***sabre*** 1; **5.** *a.* ***~ off*** *Rede etc.* ‚herˈunterrasselnʻ; **6.** F *j-n* aus der Fassung bringen, verunsichern; **III** *s.* **7.** Rattern *n*, Gerassel *n*, Klappern *n*; **8.** Rassel *f*, (Kinder)Klapper *f*; **9.** Röcheln *n*; **10.** Lärm *m*, Trubel *m*; **11.** ♀ a) ***red ~*** Sumpfläusekraut *n*, b) ***yellow ~*** Klappertopf *m*; **ˈ~·brain** *s.* Hohl-, Wirrkopf *m*; **ˈ~·brained** [-breɪnd] **ˈ~ˌpat·ed** [-ˌpeɪtɪd] *adj.* hohl-, wirrköpfig; **ˈ~·snake** *s.* Klapperschlange *f*; **ˈ~·trap** F **I** *s.* **1.** Klapperkasten *m* (*Fahrzeug etc.*); **2.** *mst pl.* (Trödel)Kram *m*; **II** *adj.* **3.** klapperig.

rat·tling [ˈrætlɪŋ] **I** *adj.* **1.** ratternd, klappernd; **2.** lebhaft; **3.** F schnell: ***at a ~ pace*** in rasendem Tempo; **4.** F ‚tollʻ; **II** *adv.* **5.** äußerst.

rat·ty [ˈrætɪ] *adj.* **1.** rattenverseucht; **2.** Ratten…; **3.** *sl.* gereizt, bissig.

rau·cous [ˈrɔːkəs] *adj.* ☐ rauh, heiser.

rav·age [ˈrævɪdʒ] **I** *s.* **1.** Verwüstung *f*, Verheerung *f*; **2.** *pl.* verheerende (Aus-)Wirkungen *pl.*: ***the ~s of time*** der Zahn der Zeit; **II** *v/t.* **3.** verwüsten, verheeren; plündern: ***a face ~d by grief*** *fig.* ein gramzerfurchtes Gesicht; **III** *v/i.* **4.** Verheerungen anrichten.

rave [reɪv] **I** *v/i.* **1.** a) phantasieren, irrereden, b) toben, wüten (*a. fig. Sturm etc.*), c) *fig.* wettern; **2.** schwärmen (***about, of*** von); **II** *s.* **3.** Pracht *f*; **4.** F

Schwärme'rei *f*: **~ *review*** ‚Bombenkritik' *f*; **5.** *Brit. sl.* a) Mode *f*, b) → ***rave-up***.

rav·el ['rævl] **I** *v/t.* **1.** *a.* **~ *out*** ausfasern, auftrennen; entwirren (*a. fig.*); **2.** verwirren, -wickeln (*a. fig.*); **II** *v/i.* **3.** *a.* **~ *out*** sich auftrennen, sich ausfasern; sich entwirren (*a. fig.*); **III** *s.* **4.** Verwirrung *f*, -wicklung *f*; **5.** loser Faden.

ra·ven¹ ['reɪvn] **I** *s. orn.* Rabe *m*; **II** *adj.* (kohl)rabenschwarz.

rav·en² ['rævn] **I** *v/i.* **1.** rauben, plündern; **2.** gierig (fr)essen; **3.** Heißhunger haben; **4.** lechzen (***for*** nach); **II** *v/t.* **5.** (gierig) verschlingen.

rav·en·ous ['rævənəs] *adj.* □ **1.** ausgehungert, heißhungrig (*beide a. fig.*); **2.** gierig (***for*** auf *acc.*): **~ *hunger*** Bärenhunger *m*; **3.** gefräßig; **4.** raubgierig (*Tier*).

'rave-up *s. Brit. sl.* ‚tolle Party'.

ra·vine [rə'vi:n] *s.* (Berg)Schlucht *f*, Klamm *f*; Hohlweg *m*.

rav·ing ['reɪvɪŋ] **I** *adj.* □ **1.** tobend, rasend; **2.** phantasierend, delirierend; **3.** F ‚toll', phan'tastisch: ***a ~ beauty***; **II** *s.* **4.** *mst pl.* a) Rase'rei *f*, b) De'lirien *pl.*, Fieberwahn *m*.

rav·ish ['rævɪʃ] *v/t.* **1.** entzücken, hinreißen; **2.** *obs. Frau* a) vergewaltigen, schänden, b) entführen; **3.** *rhet.* rauben, entreißen; **'rav·ish·er** [-ʃə] *s. obs.* **1.** Schänder *m*; **2.** Entführer *m*; **'rav·ish·ing** [-ʃɪŋ] *adj.* □ hinreißend, entzückend.

raw [rɔ:] **I** *adj.* □ **1.** roh (*a. fig. grob*); **2.** roh, ungekocht; **3.** ⚙, ✝ roh, Roh…, unbearbeitet, *a.* ungegerbt (*Leder*), ungewalkt (*Tuch*), ungesponnen (*Wolle etc.*), unvermischt, unverdünnt (*Spirituosen*): **~ *material*** Rohmaterial *n*, -stoff *m* (*a. fig.*); **~ *silk*** Rohseide *f*; **4.** *phot.* unbelichtet; **5.** roh, noch nicht ausgewertet: **~ *data***; **6.** *Am.* nagelneu; **7.** wund(gerieben); offen (*Wunde*); **8.** unwirtlich, rauh, naßkalt (*Wetter*, *Klima etc.*); **9.** unerfahren, ‚grün'; **10.** *sl.* gemein: ***a ~ deal*** e-e Gemeinheit; **II** *s.* **11.** wund(gerieben)e Stelle; **12.** *fig.* wunder Punkt: ***touch s.o. on the ~*** j-n an s-r empfindlichen Stelle treffen; **13.** ✝ Rohstoff *m*; **14.** ***in the ~*** a) im Naturzustand, b) nackt: ***life in the ~*** *fig.* die grausame Härte des Lebens; **'~-boned** *adj.* hager, (grob)knochig; **'~-hide** *s.* **1.** Rohhaut *f*, -leder *n*; **2.** Peitsche *f*.

raw·ness ['rɔ:nɪs] *s.* **1.** Rohzustand *m*; **2.** Unerfahrenheit *f*; **3.** Wundsein *n*; **4.** Rauheit *f des Wetters*.

ray¹ [reɪ] **I** *s.* **1.** (Licht)Strahl *m*; **2.** *fig.* (*Hoffnungs- etc.*)Strahl *m*, Schimmer *m*; **3.** *phys.*, ⚡, ⚕ Strahl *m*: **~ *treatment*** ⚕ Strahlenbehandlung *f*, Bestrahlung *f*; **II** *v/i.* **4.** Strahlen aussenden; **5.** sich strahlenförmig ausbreiten; **III** *v/t.* **6.** *a.* **~ *out*** ausstrahlen; **7.** bestrahlen (*a. phys.*, ⚕), ⚕ F röntgen.

ray² [reɪ] *s. ichth.* Rochen *m*.

ray·on ['reɪɒn] *s.* ✝ 'Kunstseide(npro,dukt *n*) *f*: **~ *staple*** Zellwolle *f*.

raze [reɪz] *v/t.* **1.** *Gebäude* niederreißen; *Festung* schleifen: **~ *s.th. to the ground*** et. dem Erdboden gleichmachen; **2.** *fig.* ausmerzen; **3.** ritzen, kratzen, streifen.

ra·zor ['reɪzə] *s.* Rasiermesser *n*: (***safety***) **~** Rasierapparat *m*; **~ *blade*** Rasierklinge *f*; ***as sharp as a ~*** messerscharf; ***be on the ~'s edge*** auf des Messers Schneide stehen; **~ *cut*** *s.* Messerschnitt *m* (*a. Frisur*); **~ *strop*** *s.* Streichriemen *m*.

razz [ræz] *v/t. Am. sl.* hänseln, ‚aufziehen'.

raz·zi·a ['ræzɪə] *s. hist.* Raubzug *m*.

raz·zle-daz·zle ['ræzl,dæzl] *s. sl.* **1.** Saufe'rei *f*: ***go on the ~*** ‚auf die Pauke hauen'; **2.** ‚Rummel' *m*; **3.** *Am. sl.* a) ‚Kuddelmuddel' *m*, *n*, b) ‚Wirbel' *m*, Tam'tam *n*.

re [ri:] (*Lat.*) *prp.* **1.** ⚖ in Sachen; **2.** *bsd.* ✝ betrifft, betreffs, bezüglich.

re- *in Zssgn* **1.** [ri:] wieder, noch einmal, neu: ***reprint***, ***rebirth***; **2.** [rɪ] zu'rück, wider: ***revert***, ***retract***.

're [ə] F *für* ***are***.

re·ab·sorb [,ri:əb'sɔ:b] *v/t.* resorbieren.

reach [ri:tʃ] **I** *v/t.* **1.** (hin-, her)reichen, über'reichen, geben (***s.o. s.th.*** j-m et.); *j-m e-n Schlag* versetzen; **2.** (her)langen, nehmen: **~ *s.th. down*** et. herunterlangen; **3.** *oft* **~ *out*** (*od.* ***forth***) *Hand etc.* reichen, 'ausstrecken; **4.** reichen *od.* sich erstrecken bis an (*acc.*) *od.* zu: ***the water ~ed his knees*** das Wasser ging ihm bis an die Knie; **5.** *Zahl*, *Alter* erreichen; sich belaufen auf (*acc.*); *Auflagenzahl* erleben; **6.** erreichen, erzielen, gelangen zu: **~ *an understanding***; **~ *no conclusion*** zu keinem Schluß gelangen; **7.** *Ziel* erreichen, treffen; **8.** *Ort* erreichen, eintreffen in *od.* an (*dat.*): **~ *home*** nach Hause gelangen; **~ *s.o.'s ear*** j-m zu Ohren kommen; **9.** *j-n* erreichen (*Brief etc.*); **10.** *fig.* (ein)wirken auf (*acc.*), *durch Werbung etc.* ansprechen *od.* gewinnen *od.* erreichen, bei j-m (*geistig*) 'durchdringen; **II** *v/i.* **11.** (mit der Hand) reichen *od.* greifen *od.* langen; **12.** *a.* **~ *out*** langen, greifen (***after***, ***for***, ***at*** nach); **13.** reichen, sich erstrecken *od.* ausdehnen (***to*** bis [zu]): ***as far as the eye can ~*** soweit das Auge reicht; **14.** sich belaufen (***to*** auf *acc.*); **III** *s.* **15.** Griff *m*: ***make a ~ for s.th.*** nach et. greifen *od.* langen; **16.** Reich-, Tragweite *f* (*Geschoß*, *Waffe*, *Stimme etc.*) (*a. fig.*): ***within ~*** erreichbar; ***within s.o.'s ~*** in j-s Reichweite, für j-n erreichbar *od.* erschwinglich, j-m zugänglich; ***above*** (*od.* ***beyond*** *od.* ***out of***) **~** unerreichbar *od.* unerschwinglich (***of*** für); ***within easy ~ of the station*** vom Bahnhof aus leicht zu erreichen; **17.** Bereich *m*, 'Umfang *m*, Ausdehnung *f*; **18.** (geistige) Fassungskraft, Hori'zont *m*; **19.** a) Ka'nalabschnitt *m* (*zwischen zwei Schleusen*), b) Flußstrecke *f*; **'reach·a·ble** [-tʃəbl] *adj.* erreichbar.

'reach-me-,down F **I** *adj.* **1.** Konfektions…, von der Stange; **2.** abgelegt (*Kleider*); **II** *s.* **3.** *mst pl.* Konfekti'onsanzug *m*, Kleid *n* von der Stange, *pl.* Konfekti'onskleidung *f*; **4.** abgelegtes Kleidungsstück *n* (*das von jüngeren Geschwistern etc. weiter getragen wird*).

re·act [rɪ'ækt] **I** *v/i.* **1.** ⚗, ⚕ reagieren (***to*** auf *acc.*): ***slow to ~*** reaktionsträge; **2.** *fig.* (***to***) reagieren, antworten, eingehen (auf *acc.*), aufnehmen (et.); sich verhalten (auf *acc.*, bei): **~ *against*** *e-r Sache* entgegenwirken *od.* widerstreben; **3.** ein-, zu'rückwirken, Rückwirkungen haben (([***up***]***on*** auf *acc.*): **~ *on each other*** sich gegenseitig beeinflussen; **4.** ⚔ e-n Gegenschlag führen; **II** *v/t.* **5.** ⚗ zur Reakti'on bringen.

re-act [,ri:'ækt] *v/t. thea. etc.* wieder'aufführen.

re·act·ance [rɪ'æktəns] *s.* ⚡ Reak'tanz *f*, 'Blind,widerstand *m*.

re·ac·tion [rɪ'ækʃn] *s.* **1.** ⚗, ⚕, *phys.* Reakti'on *f*; **2.** Rückwirkung *f*, -schlag *m*, Gegen-, Einwirkung *f* (***from***, ***against*** gegen, [***up***]***on*** auf *acc.*); **3.** *fig.* (***to***) Reakti'on *f* (auf *acc.*), Verhalten *n* (bei), Stellungnahme *f* (zu); **4.** *pol.* Reakti'on *f* (*a. Bewegung*), Rückschritt (-lertum *n*) *m*; **5.** ✝ rückläufige Bewegung, (*Kurs-*, *Preis- etc.*)Rückgang *m*; **6.** ⚔ Gegenstoß *m*, -schlag *m*; **7.** ⚙ Gegendruck *m*; **8.** ⚡ Rückkopplung *f*, -wirkung *f*; **re'ac·tion·ar·y** [-ʃnərɪ] **I** *adj. bsd. pol.* reaktio'när; **II** *s. pol.* Reaktio'när(in).

re·ac·tion| drive *s.* ⚙ Rückstoßantrieb *m*; **~ *time*** *s. psych.* Reakti'onszeit *f*.

re'ac·ti·vate [rɪ'æktɪveɪt] *v/t.* reaktivieren; **re·ac·tive** [rɪ'æktɪv] *adj.* □ **1.** reak'tiv, rück-, gegenwirkend; **2.** empfänglich (***to*** für), Reaktions…; **3.** ⚡ Blind… (*-strom*, *-leistung etc.*); **re·ac·tor** [rɪ'æktə] *s.* **1.** *phys.* ('Kern)Re,aktor *m*; **2.** ⚡ Drossel(spule) *f*.

read¹ [ri:d] **I** *v/t.* [*irr.*] **1.** lesen (*a. fig.*): **~ *s.th. into*** et. in *e-n Text* hineinlesen; **~ *off*** *et.* ablesen; **~ *out*** a) *et.* (laut) vorlesen, b) *Buch etc.* auslesen; **~ *over*** a) durchlesen, b) *formell* vor-, verlesen (*Notar etc.*); **~ *up*** a) sich in *et.* einlesen, b) *et.* nachlesen; **~ *s.o.'s face*** in j-s Gesicht lesen; **2.** vor-, verlesen; *Rede etc.* ablesen; **3.** *parl. Vorlage* lesen: ***was read for the third time*** *die Vorlage* wurde in dritter Lesung behandelt; **4.** *Kurzschrift etc.* lesen können; *die Uhr* kennen: **~ *music*** a) Noten lesen, b) nach Noten spielen *etc.*; **5.** *Traum etc.* deuten; → ***fortune*** 3; **6.** *et.* auslegen, auffassen, verstehen: ***do you ~ me?*** a) *Funk*: können Sie mich verstehen?, b) *fig.* haben Sie mich verstanden?; ***we can take it as ~ that*** wir können (also) davon ausgehen, daß; **7.** *Charakter etc.* durch'schauen: ***I ~ you like a book*** ich lese in dir wie in e-m Buch; **8.** ⚙ a) anzeigen (*Meßgerät*), b) *Barometerstand etc.* ablesen; **9.** *Rätsel* lösen; **II** *v/i.* [*irr.*] **10.** lesen: **~ *to s.o.*** j-m vorlesen; **11.** e-e Vorlesung *od.* e-n Vortrag halten; **12.** *bsd. Brit.* (***for***) sich vorbereiten (auf *e-e Prüfung etc.*), *et.* studieren: **~ *for the bar*** sich auf den Anwaltsberuf vorbereiten; **~ *up on*** sich in *et.* einlesen *od.* einarbeiten; **13.** sich *gut etc.* lesen lassen; **14.** *so u. so.* lauten, heißen: ***the passage ~s as follows***.

read² [red] **I** *pret. u. p.p. von* ***read¹***; **II** *adj.* **1.** gelesen: ***the most-~ book*** das meistgelesene Buch; **2.** belesen (***in*** in *dat.*); → ***well-read***.

read·a·ble ['ri:dəbl] *adj.* □ lesbar: a) lesenswert, b) leserlich.

re·ad·dress [,ri:ə'dres] *v/t.* **1.** *Brief* neu adressieren; **2.** **~ *o.s.*** sich nochmals wenden (***to*** an *j-n*).

read·er ['ri:də] *s.* **1.** Leser(in); **2.** Vorleser(in); **3.** (Verlags)Lektor *m*, (Ver-

ˈlags)Lekˌtorin *f*; **4.** *typ.* Korˈrektor *m*; **5.** *univ. Brit.* außerordentlicher Proˈfessor, Doˈzent(in); **6.** a) *ped.* Lesebuch *n*, b) Antholoˈgie *f*; **7.** *Computer*: Lesegerät *n*; ˈ**read·er·ship** [-ʃɪp] *s.* **1.** Vorleseramt *n*; **2.** *univ. Brit.* Doˈzentenstelle *f*.

read·i·ly [ˈredɪlɪ] *adv.* **1.** soˈgleich, prompt; **2.** bereitwillig, gern; **3.** leicht, ohne weiteres; ˈ**read·i·ness** [-ɪnɪs] *s.* **1.** Bereitschaft *f*: **~ *for war*** Kriegsbereitschaft; ***in ~*** bereit, in Bereitschaft; ***place in ~*** bereitstellen; **2.** Schnelligkeit *f*, Raschheit *f*, Promptheit *f*: **~ *of mind*** *od.* ***wit*** Geistesgegenwart *f*; **3.** Gewandtheit *f*; **4.** Bereitwilligkeit *f*: **~ *to help others*** Hilfsbereitschaft *f*.

read·ing [ˈriːdɪŋ] **I** *s.* **1.** Lesen *n*; *weitS.* Bücherstudium *n*; **2.** (Vor)Lesung *f*, Vortrag *m*; **3.** *parl.* Lesung *f*; **4.** Belesenheit *f*: ***a man of vast ~*** ein sehr belesener Mann; **5.** Lekˈtüre *f*, Lesestoff *m*: ***this book makes good ~*** dieses Buch liest sich gut; **6.** Lesart *f*, Versiˈon *f*; **7.** Deutung *f*, Auslegung *f*, Auffassung *f*; **8.** ⚙ Anzeige *f*, Ablesung *f* (*Meßgerät*), (*Barometer- etc.*)Stand *m*; **II** *adj.* **9.** Lese…: **~ *lamp***; **~ desk** *s.* Lesepult *n*; **~ glass** *s.* Vergrößerungsglas *n*, Lupe *f*; **~ glas·ses** *s. pl.* Lesebrille *f*; **~ head** *s. Computer*: Lesekopf *m*; **~ mat·ter** *s.* **1.** Lesestoff *m*; **2.** redaktioˈneller Teil (*e-r Zeitung*); **~ pub·lic** *s.* Leserschaft *f*, ˈLeserˌpublikum *n*; **~ room** *s.* Lesezimmer *n*, -saal *m*.

re·ad·just [ˌriːəˈdʒʌst] *v/t.* **1.** wiederˈanpassen; ⚙ nachstellen, -richten; **2.** wieder in Ordnung bringen; ☤ sanieren; *pol. etc.* neu orientieren; ˌ**re·adˈjust·ment** [-stmənt] *s.* **1.** Wiederˈanpassung *f*; **2.** Neuordnung *f*; ☤ wirtschaftliche Sanierung; **3.** ⚙ Korrekˈtur *f*.

re·ad·mis·sion [ˌriːədˈmɪʃn] *s.* Wiederˈzulassung *f* (***to*** zu); ˌ**re·adˈmit** [-ˈmɪt] *v/t.* wieder zulassen.

ˈ**read|·out** *s. Computer*: Ausgabe *f* (*von lesbaren Worten*): **~ *pulse*** Leseimpuls *m*; ˈ**~-through** *s. thea.* Leseprobe *f*.

read·y [ˈredɪ] **I** *adj.* ☐ → ***readily***; **1.** bereit, fertig (***for*** zu *et.*): **~ *for action*** ⚔ einsatzbereit; **~ *for sea*** ⚓ seeklar; **~ *for service*** ⚙ betriebsfertig; **~ *for take-off*** ✈ startbereit; **~ *to operate*** ⚙ betriebsbereit; ***be ~ with s.th.*** et. bereithaben *od.* -halten; ***get*** *od.* ***make ~*** (sich) bereit- *od.* fertigmachen; ***are you ~? go!*** *sport* Achtung-fertig-los!; **2.** bereit(willig), willens, geneigt (***to*** zu); **3.** schnell, rasch, prompt: ***find a ~ market*** (*od.* ***sale***) ☤ raschen Absatz finden, gut gehen; **4.** schlagfertig, prompt (*Antwort*), geschickt (*Arbeiter etc.*), gewandt: ***a ~ pen*** e-e gewandte Feder; **~ *wit*** Schlagfertigkeit *f*; **5.** im Begriff, nahe darˈan (***to do*** zu tun); **6.** ☤ verfügbar, greifbar (*Vermögenswerte*), bar (*Geld*): **~ *cash*** *od.* ***money*** Bargeld *n*, -zahlung *f*; **~ *money business*** Bar-, Kassageschäft *n*; **7.** bequem, leicht: **~ *at*** (*od.* ***to***) ***hand*** gleich zur Hand; **II** *v/t.* **8.** bereit-, fertigmachen; **III** *s.* **9.** *mst* ***the ~*** *sl.* Bargeld *n*; **10.** ⚔ ***at the ~*** schußbereit (*a. Kamera*); **IV** *adv.* **11.** fertig: **~*-built house*** Fertighaus *n*; **12.** ***readier*** schneller; ***readiest*** am schnellsten; ˌ**~-ˈmade** *adj.* **1.** Konfektions…, von der Stange: **~ *clothes*** Konfektion(sbekleidung *f*) *f*; **~ *shop*** Konfektionsgeschäft *n*; **2.** gebrauchsfertig, Fertig…; **3.** *fig.* schablonisiert, ‚fertig', ‚vorgekaut'; **4.** *fig.* Patent…: **~ *solution***; **~ reck·on·er** *s.* ˈRechentaˌbelle *f*; ˌ**~-to-ˈserve** *adj.* tischfertig (*Speise*); ˌ**~-to-ˈwear** → ***ready-made*** 1; ˌ**~ˈwit·ted** *adj.* schlagfertig.

re·af·firm [ˌriːəˈfɜːm] *v/t.* nochmals versichern *od.* beteuern.

re·af·for·est [ˌriːæˈfɒrɪst] *v/t.* wieder aufforsten.

re·a·gent [riːˈeɪdʒənt] *s.* **1.** ⚗ Reˈagens *n*; **2.** *fig.* Gegenkraft *f*, -wirkung *f*; **3.** *psych.* ˈTestperson *f*.

re·al [rɪəl] **I** *adj.* ☐ → ***really***; **1.** reˈal (*a. phls.*), tatsächlich, wirklich, wahr, eigentlich: **~ *life*** das wirkliche Leben; ***the ~ thing*** *sl.* das einzig Wahre; **2.** echt (*Seide etc., a. fig. Gefühle, Mann etc.*); **3.** ⚖ a) dinglich, b) unbeweglich: **~ *account*** ☤ Sach(wert)konto *n*; **~ *action*** dingliche Klage; **~ *assets*** unbewegliches Vermögen; **~ *estate*** *od.* ***property*** Grundeigentum *n*, Liegenschaften *pl.*, Immobilien *pl.*; **~ *stock*** ☤ Ist-Bestand *m*; **~ *time*** *Computer*: Echtzeit *f*; **~ *wage*** Reallohn *m*; **4.** *phys.*, A reˈell (*Bild, Zahl etc.*); **5.** ↯ ohmsch, Wirk…: **~ *power*** Wirkleistung *f*; **II** *adv.* **6.** *bsd. Am.* F sehr, äußerst, ‚richtig': ***for ~*** echt, im Ernst; **III** *s.* **7.** ***the ~*** *phls.* das Reˈale, die Wirklichkeit; ˈ**re·al·ism** [-lɪzəm] *s.* Reaˈlismus *m* (*a. phls., lit., paint.*); ˈ**re·al·ist** [-lɪst] **I** *s.* Reaˈlist(in); **II** *adj.* → **re·al·is·tic** [ˌrɪəˈlɪstɪk] *adj.* (☐ **~*ally***) reaˈlistisch (*a. phls., lit., paint.*), wirklichkeitsnah, -getreu, sachlich; **re·al·i·ty** [rɪˈælətɪ] *s.* **1.** Realiˈtät *f*, Wirklichkeit *f*: ***in ~*** in Wirklichkeit, tatsächlich; **2.** Wirklichkeits-, Naˈturtreue *f*; **3.** Tatsache *f*, Faktum *n*, Gegebenheit *f*; **re·al·iz·a·ble** [ˈrɪəlaɪzəbl] *adj.* ☐ **1.** realisierbar, aus-, ˈdurchführbar; **2.** ☤ realisierbar, verwertbar, kapitalisierbar, verkäuflich; **re·al·i·za·tion** [ˌrɪəlaɪˈzeɪʃn] *s.* **1.** Realisierung *f*, Verwirklichung *f*, Aus-, ˈDurchführung *f*; **2.** Vergegenˈwärtigung *f*, Erkenntnis *f*; **3.** ☤ a) Realisierung *f*, Verwertung *f*, b) Liquidatiˈon *f*, Glattstellung *f*, c) Erzielung *f* *e-s Gewinns*: **~ *account*** Liquidationskonto *n*; **re·al·ize** [ˈrɪəlaɪz] *v/t.* **1.** (klar) erkennen, sich klarmachen, begreifen, erfassen: ***he ~d that*** er sah ein, daß; ihm wurde klar *od.* es kam ihm zum Bewußtsein, daß; **2.** verwirklichen, realisieren, aus-, ˈdurchführen; **3.** sich vergegenˈwärtigen, sich (lebhaft) vorstellen; **4.** ☤ a) realisieren, verwerten, zu Geld *od.* flüssig machen, b) *Gewinn, Preis* erzielen; **re·al·ly** [ˈrɪəlɪ] *adv.* **1.** wirklich, tatsächlich, eigentlich: ***not ~*** eigentlich nicht; ***not ~!*** nicht möglich!; **2.** (*rügend*) **~*!*** ich muß schon sagen!; **3.** unbedingt: ***you ~ must come!***

realm [relm] *s.* **1.** Königreich *n*: ***Peer of the* ♀** Mitglied *n* des Oberhauses; **2.** *fig.* Reich *n*, Sphäre *f*; **3.** Bereich *m*, (Fach-) Gebiet *n*.

re·al·tor [ˈrɪəltə] *s. Am.* Immoˈbilienmakler *m*; ˈ**re·al·ty** [-tɪ] *s.* Grundeigentum *n*, -besitz *m*, Liegenschaften *pl.*

ream¹ [riːm] *s.* Ries *n* (*480 Bogen Papier*): ***printer's ~***, ***long ~*** 516 Bogen Druckpapier; **~*s and ~s of*** *fig.* zahllose, große Mengen von.

ream² [riːm] *v/t.* ⚙ **1.** *Bohrloch etc.* erweitern; **2.** *oft* **~ *out*** a) *Bohrung* (auf-, aus)räumen, b) *Kaliber* ausbohren, c) nachbohren; ˈ**ream·er** [-mə] *s.* **1.** ⚙ Reib-, Räumahle *f*; **2.** *Am.* Fruchtpresse *f*.

re·an·i·mate [ˌriːˈænɪmeɪt] *v/t.* **1.** ˈwiederbeleben; **2.** *fig.* neu beleben.

reap [riːp] **I** *v/t.* **1.** *Getreide etc.* schneiden, ernten; **2.** *Feld* mähen, abernten; **3.** *fig.* ernten; **II** *v/i.* **4.** mähen, ernten: ***he ~s where he has not sown*** *fig.* er erntet, wo er nicht gesät hat; ˈ**reap·er** [-pə] *s.* **1.** Schnitter(in), Mäher(in): ***the Grim* ♀** *fig.* der Sensenmann; **2.** ˈMähmaˌschine *f*: **~*-binder*** Mähbinder *m*.

re·ap·pear [ˌriːəˈpɪə] *v/i.* wieder erscheinen; ˌ**re·apˈpear·ance** [-ərəns] *s.* ˈWiedererscheinen *n*.

re·ap·pli·ca·tion [ˈriːˌæplɪˈkeɪʃn] *s.* **1.** wiederˈholte Anwendung; **2.** erneutes Gesuch; **re·ap·ply** [ˌriːəˈplaɪ] **I** *v/t.* wieder *od.* wiederˈholt anwenden; **II** *v/i.* (***for***) (*et.*) wiederholt beantragen, erneut e-n Antrag stellen (auf *acc.*); sich erneut bewerben (um).

re·ap·point [ˌriːəˈpɔɪnt] *v/t.* wieder ernennen *od.* einsetzen *od.* anstellen.

re·ap·prais·al [ˌriːəˈpreɪzl] *s.* Neubewertung *f*, -beurteilung *f*.

rear¹ [rɪə] **I** *v/t.* **1.** *Kind* auf-, großziehen, erziehen; *Tiere* züchten; *Pflanzen* ziehen; **2.** *Leiter etc.* aufrichten, -stellen; **3.** *rhet. Gebäude* errichten; **4.** *Haupt, Stimme etc.* (er)heben; **II** *v/i.* **5.** *a.* **~ *up*** sich (auf)bäumen (*Pferd etc.*); **6.** *oft* **~ *up*** (auf-, hoch)ragen.

rear² [rɪə] **I** *s.* **1.** ˈHinter-, Rückseite *f*; *mot.*, ⚓ Heck *n*: ***at*** (*Am.* in) ***the ~ of*** hinter (*dat.*); **2.** ˈHintergrund *m*: ***in the ~ of*** im Hintergrund (*gen.*); **3.** ⚔ Nachhut *f*: ***bring up the ~*** *allg.* die Nachhut bilden, den Zug beschließen; ***take in the ~*** *den Feind* im Rücken fassen; **4.** F a) ‚Hintern' *m*, b) *Brit.* ‚Lokus' *m* (*Abort*); **II** *adj.* **5.** hinter, Hinter…, Rück…: **~ *axle***: *mot.* Hinterachse *f*; **~ *echelon*** ⚔ rückwärtiger Stab; **~ *engine*** *mot.* Heckmotor *m*; **~ ad·mi·ral** *s.* ⚓ ˈKonteradmiˌral *m*; **~ drive** *s. mot.* Heckantrieb *m*; **~ end** *s.* **1.** hinter(st)er Teil, Ende *n*; **2.** F ‚Hinternˈ *m*; ˈ**~-guard** *s.* ⚔ Nachhut *f*: **~ *action*** Rückzugsgefecht *n* (*a. fig.*); **~ gun·ner** *s.* ✈ Heckschütze *m*; **~ lamp**, **~ light** *s. mot.* Schlußlicht *n*.

re·arm [ˌriːˈɑːm] **I** *v/t.* ˈwiederbewaffnen; **II** *v/i.* wiederˈaufrüsten; ˌ**reˈar·ma·ment** [-məmənt] *s.* Wiederˈaufrüstung *f*, ˈWiederbewaffnung *f*.

re·ar·range [ˌriːəˈreɪndʒ] *v/t.* neu-, ˈumordnen, ändern; ˌ**re·arˈrange·ment** [-mənt] *s.* **1.** ˈUm-, Neuordnung *f*, Neugestaltung *f*; Änderung *f*; **2.** ⚗ ˈUmlagerung *f*; **3.** A ˈUmschreibung *f*.

rear| sight *s.* ⚔ Kimme *f*; ˈ**~-view mir·ror**, ˈ**~-ˌvi·sion mir·ror** *s. mot.* Rückspiegel *m*.

rear·ward [ˈrɪəwəd] **I** *adj.* **1.** hinter, rückwärtig; **2.** Rückwärts…; **II** *adv. a.* ˈ**rear·wards** [-dz] nach hinten, rückwärts, zuˈrück.

rea·son [ˈriːzn] **I** *s.* **1.** *ohne art.* Vernunft *f* (*a. phls.*), Verstand *m*, Einsicht *f*: ***Age of* ♀** *hist. die* Aufklärung; ***bring s.o. to ~*** j-n zur Vernunft bringen; ***listen to ~***

Vernunft annehmen; ***lose one's ~*** den Verstand verlieren; ***it stands to ~*** es ist klar, es leuchtet ein (***that*** daß); ***there is ~ in what you say*** was du sagst, hat Hand u. Fuß; ***in (all) ~*** a) in Grenzen, mit Maß u. Ziel, b) mit Recht; ***do everything in ~*** sein möglichstes tun (in gewissen Grenzen); **2.** Grund *m* (***of***, ***for*** *gen. od.* für), Ursache *f* (***for*** *gen.*), Anlaß *m*: ***the ~ why*** (der Grund) weshalb; ***by ~ of*** wegen (*gen.*), infolge (*gen.*); ***for this ~*** aus diesem Grund, deshalb; ***with ~*** aus gutem Grund, mit Recht; ***have ~ to do*** Grund *od.* Anlaß haben, zu tun; ***there is no ~ to suppose*** es besteht kein Grund zu der Annahme; ***there is every ~ to believe*** alles spricht dafür (***that*** daß); ***for ~s best known to oneself*** *iro.* aus unerfindlichen Gründen; **3.** Begründung *f*, Rechtfertigung *f*: ***~ of state*** Staatsräson *f*; **II** *v/i.* **4.** logisch denken; vernünftig urteilen; **5.** schließen, folgern (***from*** aus); **6.** (***with***) vernünftig reden (mit *j-m*), (*j-m*) gut zureden, (*j-n*) zu über'zeugen suchen: ***he is not to be ~ed with*** er läßt nicht mit sich reden; **III** *v/t.* **7.** *a.* ***~ out*** durch'denken: ***~ed*** wohldurchdacht; **8.** ergründen (***why*** warum, ***what*** was); **9.** erörtern: ***~ away*** *et.* wegdisputieren; ***~ s.o. into (out of) s.th.*** j-m et. ein- (aus)reden; **10.** schließen, geltend machen (***that*** daß); **'rea·son·a·ble** [-nəbl] *adj.* □ → ***reasonably***; vernünftig: a) vernunftgemäß, b) verständig, einsichtig (*Person*), c) angemessen, annehmbar, tragbar, billig (*Forderung*), zumutbar (*Bedingung*, *Frist*, *Preis etc.*): ***~ doubt*** berechtigter Zweifel; ***~ care and diligence*** ⚖ die im Verkehr erforderliche Sorgfalt; **'rea·son·a·ble·ness** [-nəblnɪs] *s.* **1.** Vernünftigkeit *f*, Verständigkeit *f*; **2.** Annehmbarkeit *f*, Zumutbarkeit *f*, Billigkeit *f*; **'rea·son·a·bly** [-nəblɪ] *adv.* **1.** vernünftig; **2.** vernünftiger-, billigerweise; **3.** ziemlich, leidlich: ***~ good***; **'rea·son·er** [-nə] *s.* logischer Geist (*Person*); **'rea·son·ing** [-nɪŋ] **I** *s.* **1.** Denken *n*, Folgern *n*, Urteilen *n*; **2.** *a.* ***line of ~*** Gedankengang *m*; **3.** Argumentati'on *f*, Beweisführung *f*; **4.** Schluß(folgerung *f*) *m*, Schlüsse *pl.*; **5.** Argu'ment *n*, Beweis *m*; **II** *adj.* **6.** Denk…, Urteils…

re·as·sem·ble [ˌriːə'sembl] *v/t.* **1.** (*v/i.* sich) wieder versammeln; **2.** ⚙ wieder zs.-bauen.

re·as·sert [ˌriːə'sɜːt] *v/t.* **1.** erneut feststellen; **2.** wieder behaupten; **3.** wieder geltend machen.

re·as·sess·ment [ˌriːə'sesmənt] *s.* **1.** neuerliche (Ab)Schätzung; **2.** ⚚ Neuveranlagung *f*; **3.** *fig.* Neubeurteilung *f*.

re·as·sur·ance [ˌriːə'ʃʊərəns] *s.* **1.** Beruhigung *f*; **2.** nochmalige Versicherung, Bestätigung *f*; **3.** ⚚ Rückversicherung *f*; **re·as·sure** [ˌriːə'ʃʊə] *v/t.* **1.** *j-n* beruhigen; **2.** *et.* nochmals versichern *od.* beteuern; **3.** ⚚ wieder versichern; **ˌre·as'sur·ing** [-ərɪŋ] *adj.* □ beruhigend.

re·bap·tism [ˌriː'bæptɪzəm] *s.* 'Wiedertaufe *f*; **re·bap·tize** [ˌriːbæp'taɪz] *v/t.* **1.** 'wiedertaufen; **2.** 'umtaufen.

re·bate¹ ['riːbeɪt] *s.* **1.** Ra'batt *m*, (Preis-)Nachlaß *m*, Abzug *m*; **2.** Zu'rückzahlung *f*, (Rück)Vergütung *f*.

re·bate² ['ræbɪt] → ***rabbet***.

reb·el ['rebl] **I** *s.* Re'bell(in), Empörer (-in) (*beide a. fig.*), Aufrührer(in); **II** *adj.* re'bellisch, aufrührerisch; Rebellen…; **III** *v/i.* [rɪ'bel] rebellieren, sich empören *od.* auflehnen (***against*** gegen); **re·bel·lion** [rɪ'beljən] *s.* **1.** Rebelli'on *f*, Aufruhr *m*, Aufstand *m*, Empörung *f* (***against***, ***to*** gegen); **2.** Auflehnung *f*, offener 'Widerstand; **re'bel·lious** [rɪ'beljəs] *adj.* □ **1.** re'bellisch: a) aufrührerisch, -ständisch, b) *fig.* aufsässig, 'widerspenstig (*a. Sache*); **2.** ⚕ hartnäckig (*Krankheit*).

re·birth [ˌriː'bɜːθ] *s.* 'Wiedergeburt *f* (*a. fig.*).

re·bore [ˌriː'bɔː] *v/t.* ⚙ **1.** *Loch* nachbohren; **2.** *Motorzylinder* ausschleifen.

re·born [ˌriː'bɔːn] *adj.* 'wiedergeboren, neugeboren (*a. fig.*).

re·bound¹ **I** *v/i.* [rɪ'baʊnd] **1.** zu'rückprallen, -schnellen; **2.** *fig.* zu'rückfallen (***upon*** auf *acc.*); **II** *s.* ['riːbaʊnd] **3.** Zu'rückprallen *n*; **4.** Rückprall *m*; **5.** 'Widerhall *m*; **6.** *fig.* Reakti'on *f* (***from*** auf *e-n Rückschlag etc.*): ***on the ~*** a) als Reaktion darauf, b) in e-r Krise (befindlich); ***take s.o. on*** (*od.* ***at***) ***the ~*** j-s Enttäuschung ausnutzen; **7.** *sport* Abpraller *m*.

re·bound² [ˌriː'baʊnd] *adj.* neugebunden (*Buch*).

re·broad·cast [ˌriː'brɔːdkɑːst] **I** *v/t.* [*irr.* → ***cast***] **1.** *Radio*, *TV*: *e-e Sendung* wieder'holen; **2.** durch Re'lais(statiˌonen) über'tragen; **II** *v/i.* [*irr.* → ***cast***] **3.** über Re'lais(statiˌonen) senden: ***~ing station*** Ballsender *m*; **III** *s.* **4.** Wieder'holungssendung *f*; **5.** Re'laisüberˌtragung *f*, Ballsendung *f*.

re·buff [rɪ'bʌf] **I** *s.* **1.** (schroffe) Abweisung, Abfuhr *f*: ***meet with a ~*** abblitzen; **II** *v/t.* **2.** zu'rück-, abweisen, abblitzen lassen; **3.** *Angriff* abweisen, zu'rückschlagen.

re·build [ˌriː'bɪld] *v/t.* [*irr.* → ***build***] **1.** wieder'aufbauen (*a. fig.*); **2.** 'umbauen; **3.** *fig.* wieder'herstellen.

re·buke [rɪ'bjuːk] **I** *v/t.* **1.** *j-n* rügen, rüffeln, zu'rechtweisen, *j-m* e-n scharfen Verweis erteilen; **2.** *et.* scharf tadeln, rügen; **II** *s.* **3.** Rüge *f*, (scharfer) Tadel, Rüffel *m*.

re·bus ['riːbəs] *pl.* **-bus·es** [-sɪz] *s.* Rebus *m*, *n*, Bilderrätsel *n*.

re·but [rɪ'bʌt] *bsd.* ⚖ **I** *v/t.* wider'legen, entkräften; **II** *v/i.* den Gegenbeweis antreten; **re'but·tal** [-tl] *s. bsd.* ⚖ Wider'legung *f*, Entkräftung *f*; **re'but·ter** [-tə] *s. bsd.* ⚖ Gegenbeweis *m*.

re·cal·ci·trance [rɪ'kælsɪtrəns] *s.* 'Widerspenstigkeit *f*; **re'cal·ci·trant** [-nt] *adj.* 'widerspenstig.

re·call [rɪ'kɔːl] **I** *v/t.* **1.** zu'rückrufen, *Gesandten etc.* abberufen; ⚚ *defekte Autos etc.* (in die Werkstatt) zu'rückrufen; **2.** sich erinnern an (*acc.*), sich ins Gedächtnis zurückrufen; **3.** *j-n* erinnern (***to*** an *acc.*): ***~ s.th. to s.o.*** (*od.* ***to s.o.'s mind***) j-m et. ins Gedächtnis zurückrufen; **4.** *poet. Gefühl* wieder wachrufen; **5.** *Versprechen etc.* zu'rücknehmen, wider'rufen: ***until ~ed*** bis auf Widerruf; **6.** ⚚ *Kapital*, *Kredit etc.* (auf)kündigen; **II** *s.* **7.** Zu'rückrufung *f*; Abberufung *f e-s Gesandten etc.*; ⚙, ⚚ Rückruf *m* (*in die Werkstatt*); **8.** 'Widerruf *m*, Zu'rücknahme *f*: ***beyond*** (*od.* ***past***) ***~*** unwiderruflich, unabänderlich; **9.** ⚚ (Auf)Kündigung *f*, Aufruf *m*; **10.** ⚔ Si'gnal *n* zum Sammeln; **11.** (***total*** abso'lutes) Gedächtnis; ***~ test*** *s. ped.* Nacherzählung *f*.

re·cant [rɪ'kænt] **I** *v/t.* *Behauptung* (for'mell) zu'rücknehmen, wider'rufen; **II** *v/i.* (öffentlich) wider'rufen, Abbitte tun; **re·can·ta·tion** [ˌriːkæn'teɪʃn] *s.* Wider'rufung *f*.

re·cap¹ [ˌriː'kæp] *v/t.* ⚙ *Am. Autoreifen* runderneuern.

re·cap² ['riːkæp] *F für* ***recapitulate***, ***recapitulation***.

re·cap·i·tal·i·za·tion [ˈriːˌkæpɪtəlaɪ'zeɪʃn] *s.* ⚚ Neukapitalisierung *f*.

re·ca·pit·u·late [ˌriːkə'pɪtjʊleɪt] *v/t. u. v/i.* rekapitulieren (*a. biol.*), (kurz) zs.-fassen *od.* wieder'holen; **re·ca·pit·u·la·tion** ['riːkəˌpɪtjʊ'leɪʃn] *s.* ˌRekapitulati'on *f* (*a. biol.*), kurze Wieder'holung *od.* Zs.-fassung.

re·cap·ture [ˌriː'kæptʃə] **I** *v/t.* **1.** *et.* wieder (in Besitz) nehmen, 'wiedererlangen; *j-n* wieder ergreifen; **2.** ⚔ zu'rückerobern; **II** *s.* **3.** 'Wiedererlangung *f*, -ergreifung *f*; ⚔ Zu'rückeroberung *f*.

re·cast [ˌriː'kɑːst] **I** *v/t.* [*irr.* → ***cast***] **1.** ⚙ 'umgießen; **2.** 'umformen, neu-, 'umgestalten; **3.** *thea. Stück*, *Rolle* 'umbesetzen; *Rollen* neu verteilen; **4.** 'durchrechnen; **II** *s.* **5.** ⚙ 'Umguß *m*; **6.** 'Umarbeitung *f*, 'Umgestaltung *f*; **7.** *thea.* Neu-, 'Umbesetzung *f*.

re·cede [rɪ'siːd] *v/i.* **1.** zu'rücktreten, -weichen: ***receding*** fliehend (*Kinn*, *Stirn*); **2.** ent-, verschwinden; *fig. in den Hintergrund* treten; **3.** *fig.* (***from***) zurücktreten (von *e-m Amt*, *Vertrag*), (von *e-r Sache*) Abstand nehmen, (*e-e Ansicht*) aufgeben; *bsd.* ⚚ zu'rückgehen, im Wert fallen.

re·ceipt [rɪ'siːt] **I** *s.* **1.** Empfang *m e-s Briefes etc.*, Erhalt *m*; Annahme *f e-r Sendung*; Eingang *m von Waren*: ***on ~ of*** bei *od.* nach Empfang (*gen.*); ***be in ~ of*** im Besitz *e-r Sendung etc.* sein; **2.** Empfangsbestätigung *f*, Quittung *f*, Beleg *m*: ***~ stamp*** Quittungsstempel *m*; **3.** *pl.* ⚚ Einnahmen *pl.*, Eingänge *pl.*, eingehende Gelder *pl. od.* Waren *pl.*; **4.** *obs.* ('Koch)Reˌzept *n*; **II** *v/t. u. v/i.* **5.** quittieren.

re·ceiv·a·ble [rɪ'siːvəbl] *adj.* **1.** annehmbar, zulässig (*Beweis etc.*): ***to be ~*** als gesetzliches Zahlungsmittel gelten; **2.** ⚚ ausstehend (*Forderung*, *Gelder*, *Guthaben*), debi'torisch (*Posten*): ***accounts ~, ~s*** *s. pl.* Außenstände, Forderungen; ***bills ~*** Rimessen; **re·ceive** [rɪ'siːv] **I** *v/t.* **1.** *Brief etc.*, *a weitS. Befehl*, *Eindruck*, *Radiosendung*, *Sakramente*, *Wunde* empfangen, *a. Namen*, *Schock*, *Treffer* erhalten, bekommen; *Aufmerksamkeit* finden, auf sich ziehen; *Neuigkeit* erfahren; **2.** in Empfang nehmen, annehmen, *a. Beichte*, *Eid* entgegennehmen; *Geld etc.* einnehmen: ***~ stolen goods*** ⚖ Hehlerei treiben; **3.** *j-n* bei sich aufnehmen, beherbergen; **4.** *Besucher*, *a. weitS. Schauspieler etc.* empfangen (***with applause*** mit Beifall); **5.** *j-n* aufnehmen (***into*** in *e-e Gemeinschaft*); *j-n* zulassen; **6.** *Nachricht etc.* aufnehmen, reagieren auf (*acc.*): ***how did he ~ this offer?***; **7.** *et.* erleben, erleiden, erfahren; *Beleidigung* einstecken; *Armbruch etc.* da'vontragen; **8.** ⚙ *Flüssigkeit, Schraube etc.* aufnehmen; **9.** *et.* (als gültig) anerkennen; **II** *v/i.* **10.** (Besuch) empfangen; **11.** *eccl.* das Abendmahl empfangen, *R.C.* kommunizieren; **re'ceived** [-vd] *adj.* **1.** erhalten: ***~ with thanks*** dankend erhalten; **2.** allgemein anerkannt: ***~ text*** echter *od.* authentischer Text; **3.** gültig, kor'rekt, vorschriftsmäßig; **re'ceiv·er** [-və] *s.* **1.** Empfänger(in); **2.** (Steuer-, Zoll)Einnehmer *m*; **3.** *a.* ***official ~*** ⚖ a) (gerichtlich bestellter) Zwangs- *od.* Kon'kurs- *od.* Masseverwalter, b) Liqui'dator *m*, c) Treuhänder *m*; **4.** *a.* ***~ of stolen goods*** ⚖ Hehler (-in); **5.** (Radio-, Funk)Empfänger *m*, Empfangsgerät *n*; **6.** *teleph.* Hörer *m*; **7.** ⚙ (Sammel)Becken *n*, (-)Behälter *m*; **8.** ⚗, *phys.* Rezipi'ent *m*; **re'ceiv·er·ship** [-vəʃɪp] *s.* ⚖ Zwangs-, Kon'kursverwaltung *f*, Geschäftsaufsicht *f*; **re'ceiv·ing** [-vɪŋ] *s.* **1.** Annahme *f*: ***~ hopper*** ⚙ Schüttrumpf *m*; ***~ office*** Annahmestelle *f*; ***~ order*** ⚖ Konkurseröffnungsbeschluß *m*; **2.** *Funk*: Empfang *m*: ***~ set*** → ***receiver*** 5; ***~ station*** Empfangsstation *f*; **3.** ⚖ Hehle'rei *f*.

re·cen·cy ['riːsnsɪ] *s.* Neuheit *f*.

re·cen·sion [rɪ'senʃn] *s.* **1.** Prüfung *f*, Revisi'on *f*, 'Durchsicht *f e-s Textes etc.*; **2.** revidierter Text.

re·cent ['riːsnt] *adj.* ☐ **1.** vor kurzem *od.* unlängst (geschehen *od.* entstanden *etc.*): ***the ~ events*** die jüngsten Ereignisse; **2.** neu, jung, frisch: ***of ~ date*** neueren *od.* jüngeren Datums; **3.** neu, mo'dern; **'re·cent·ly** [-lɪ] *adv.* kürzlich, vor kurzem, unlängst, neulich.

re·cep·ta·cle [rɪ'septəkl] *s.* **1.** Behälter *m*, Gefäß *n*; **2.** *a.* ***floral ~*** ✿ Fruchtboden *m*; **3.** ⚡ a) Steckdose *f*, b) Gerätbuchse *f*.

re·cep·tion [rɪ'sepʃn] *s.* **1.** Empfang *m* (*a. Funk, TV*), Annahme *f*; **2.** Zulassung *f*; **3.** Aufnahme *f* (*a. fig.*): ***meet with a favo(u)rable ~*** e-e günstige Aufnahme finden (*Buch etc.*); **4.** (offizi'eller) Empfang, *a.* Empfangsabend *m*: ***a warm (cool) ~*** ein herzlicher (kühler) Empfang; ***~ room*** Empfangszimmer *n*; **re'cep·tion·ist** [-ʃənɪst] *s.* **1.** Empfangsdame *f*; **2.** ⚕ Sprechstundenhilfe *f*.

re·cep·tive [rɪ'septɪv] *adj.* ☐ aufnahmefähig, empfänglich (***of*** für); **re·cep·tiv·i·ty** [ˌresep'tɪvətɪ] *s.* Aufnahmefähigkeit *f*, Empfänglichkeit *f*.

re·cess [rɪ'ses] **I** *s.* **1.** (zeitweilige) Unter'brechung (*a.* ⚖ *der Verhandlung*), (*Am. a.* Schul)Pause *f*, *bsd. parl.* Ferien *pl.*; **2.** Schlupfwinkel *m*, stiller Winkel; **3.** △ (Wand)Aussparung *f*, Nische *f*, Al'koven *m*; **4.** ⚙ Aussparung *f*, Vertiefung *f*, Einschnitt *m*; **5.** *pl. fig. das* Innere, Tiefe(n *pl.*) *f*, geheime Winkel *pl. des Herzens etc.*; **II** *v/t.* **6.** in e-e Nische stellen, zu'rücksetzen; **7.** aussparen; ausbuchten, einsenken, vertiefen; **III** *v/i.* **8.** *Am.* e-e Pause *od.* Ferien machen, unter'brechen, sich vertagen.

re·ces·sion [rɪ'seʃn] *s.* **1.** Zu'rücktreten *n*; **2.** *eccl.* Auszug *m*; **3.** △ *etc.* Vertiefung *f*; **4.** ✝ Rezessi'on *f*, (leichter) Konjunk'turrückgang: ***period of ~*** Rezessionsphase *f*; **re'ces·sion·al** [-ʃənl] **I** *adj.* **1.** *eccl.* Schluß…; **2.** *parl.* Ferien…; **3.** ✝ Rezessions…; **II** *s.* **4.** *a.* ***~ hymn*** 'Schlußchoˌral *m*.

re·charge [ˌriː'tʃɑːdʒ] *v/t.* **1.** wieder (be-)laden; **2.** ⚔ a) von neuem angreifen, b) nachladen; **3.** ⚡ *Batterie* wieder aufladen.

re·cher·ché [rə'ʃeəʃeɪ] (*Fr.*) *adj. fig.* **1.** ausgesucht, exqui'sit; **2.** *iro.* gesucht, prezi'ös.

re·chris·ten [ˌriː'krɪsn] → ***rebaptize***.

re·cid·i·vism [rɪ'sɪdɪvɪzəm] *s.* ⚖ Rückfall *m*, -fälligkeit *f*; **re'cid·i·vist** [-ɪst] *s.* Rückfällige(r *m*) *f*; **re'cid·i·vous** [-vəs] *adj.* rückfällig.

rec·i·pe ['resɪpɪ] *s.* ('Koch)ReˌZept *n*.

re·cip·i·ent [rɪ'sɪpɪənt] **I** *s.* **1.** Empfänger (-in); **II** *adj.* **2.** aufnehmend; **3.** empfänglich (***of, to*** für).

re·cip·ro·cal [rɪ'sɪprəkl] **I** *adj.* ☐ **1.** wechsel-, gegenseitig, *Vertrag, Versicherung* auf Gegenseitigkeit: ***~ service*** Gegendienst *m*; ***~ relationship*** Wechselbeziehung *f*; **2.** 'umgekehrt; **3.** 𝒜, *ling., phls.* rezi'prok; **II** *s.* **4.** Gegenstück *n*; **5.** *a.* ***~ value*** 𝒜 reziproker Wert, Kehrwert *m*; **re'cip·ro·cate** [-keɪt] **I** *v/t.* **1.** *Gefühle etc.* erwidern, vergelten; *Glückwünsche etc.* austauschen; **II** *v/i.* **2.** sich erkenntlich zeigen, sich revanchieren (***for*** für, ***with*** mit): ***glad to ~*** zu Gegendiensten gern bereit; **3.** in Wechselbeziehung stehen; **4.** ⚙ sich hin- u. herbewegen: ***reciprocating engine*** Kolbenmaschine *f*, -motor *m*; **re·cip·ro·ca·tion** [rɪˌsɪprə'keɪʃn] *s.* **1.** Erwiderung *f*; **2.** Erkenntlichkeit *f*; **3.** Austausch *m*; **4.** Wechselwirkung *f*; **5.** ⚙ ˌHinund'herbewegung *f*; **rec·i·proc·i·ty** [ˌresɪ'prɒsətɪ] *s.* Reziprozi'tät *f*; Gegenseitigkeit *f* (*a.* ✝ *in Verträgen etc.*): ***~ clause*** Gegenseitigkeitsklausel *f*.

re·cit·al [rɪ'saɪtl] *s.* **1.** Vortrag *m*, -lesung *f*; **2.** ♪ (Solo)Vortrag *m*, (*Orgel- etc.*) Kon'zert *n*: ***lieder ~*** Liederabend *m*; **3.** Bericht *m*, Schilderung *f*; **4.** Aufzählung *f*; **5.** ⚖ a) *a.* ***~ of fact*** Darstellung *f* des Sachverhalts, b) Prä'ambel *f e-s Vertrags etc.*; **rec·i·ta·tion** [ˌresɪ'teɪʃn] *s.* **1.** Auf-, Hersagen *n*, Rezitieren *n*; **2.** Vortrag *m*, Rezitati'on *f*; **3.** *ped. Am.* Abfrage-, Übungsstunde *f*; **4.** Vortragsstück *n*, rezitierter Text; **rec·i·ta·tive** [ˌresɪtə'tiːv] ♪ **I** *adj.* rezita'tivartig; **II** *s.* Rezita'tiv *n*, Sprechgesang *m*; **re·cite** [rɪ'saɪt] *v/t.* **1.** (auswendig) her- *od.* aufsagen; **2.** rezitieren, vortragen, deklamieren; **3.** ⚖ a) *Sachverhalt* darstellen, b) anführen, zitieren; **re'cit·er** [-tə] *s.* **1.** Rezi'tator *m*, Rezita'torin *f*, Vortragskünstler(in); **2.** Vortragsbuch *n*.

reck·less ['reklɪs] *adj.* ☐ **1.** unbesorgt, unbekümmert (***of*** um); ***be ~ of*** sich nicht kümmern um; **2.** sorglos; leichtsinnig; verwegen; **3.** rücksichtslos; ⚖ (bewußt *od.* grob) fahrlässig; **'reck·less·ness** [-nɪs] *s.* **1.** Unbesorgtheit *f*, Unbekümmertheit *f* (***of*** um); **2.** Sorglosigkeit *f*, Leichtsinn *m*, Verwegenheit *f*; **3.** Rücksichtslosigkeit *f*.

reck·on ['rekən] **I** *v/t.* **1.** (be-, er)rechnen: ***~ in*** einrechnen; ***~ over*** nachrechnen; ***~ up*** a) auf-, zs.-zählen, b) *j-n* einschätzen; **2.** halten für: ***~ as*** *od.* ***for*** betrachten als; ***~ among*** *od.* ***with*** rechnen *od.* zählen zu (*od.* unter *acc.*); **3.** der Meinung sein (***that*** daß); **II** *v/i.* **4.** zählen, rechnen: ***~ with*** a) rechnen mit (*a. fig.*), b) abrechnen mit (*a. fig.*); ***he is to be ~ed with*** mit ihm muß man rechnen; ***~ without*** nicht rechnen mit; ***~ (up)on*** *fig.* rechnen *od.* zählen auf *j-n, j-s Hilfe etc.*; ***I ~*** schätze ich, glaube ich; → ***host²*** 2; **reck·on·er** ['reknə] *s.* **1.** Rechner(in); **2.** → ***ready reckoner***; **reck·on·ing** ['reknɪŋ] *s.* **1.** Rechnen *n*; **2.** Berechnung *f*, Kalkulati'on *f*; ⚓ Gissung *f*: ***dead ~*** gegißtes Besteck; ***be out of*** (*od.* ***out in***) ***one's ~*** sich verrechnet haben (*a. fig.*); **3.** Abrechnung *f*: ***day of ~*** a) *bsd. fig.* Tag *m* der Abrechnung, b) *eccl. der* Jüngste Tag; **4.** *obs.* Rechnung *f*, Zeche *f*.

re·claim [rɪ'kleɪm] *v/t.* **1.** *Eigentum, Rechte etc.* zu'rückfordern, her'ausverlangen, reklamieren; **2.** *Land* urbar machen, kultivieren, trockenlegen; **3.** *Tiere* zähmen; **4.** *Volk* zivilisieren; **5.** ⚙ *aus Altmaterial* gewinnen, *Altöl, Gummi etc.* regenerieren; **6.** *fig.* a) *j-n* bekehren, bessern, b) *j-n* zu'rückbringen, -führen (***from*** von, ***to*** zu); **re'claim·a·ble** [-məbl] *adj.* ☐ **1.** (ver)besserungsfähig; **2.** kul'turfähig (*Land*); **3.** ⚙ regenerierfähig.

rec·la·ma·tion [ˌreklə'meɪʃn] *s.* **1.** Reklamati'on *f*: a) Rückforderung *f*, b) Beschwerde *f*; **2.** *fig.* Bekehrung *f*, Besserung *f*, Heilung *f* (***from*** von); **3.** Urbarmachung *f*, Neugewinnung *f* (*von Land*); **4.** ⚙ Rückgewinnung *f*.

re·cline [rɪ'klaɪn] **I** *v/i.* **1.** sich (an-, zu'rück)lehnen: ***reclining chair*** (verstellbarer) Lehnstuhl; **2.** ruhen, liegen (***on, upon*** an, auf *dat.*); **3.** *fig.* ***~ upon*** sich stützen auf (*acc.*); **II** *v/t.* **4.** (an-, zu'rück)lehnen, legen (***on, upon*** auf *acc.*).

re·cluse [rɪ'kluːs] **I** *s.* **1.** Einsiedler(in); **II** *adj.* **2.** einsam, abgeschieden (***from*** von); **3.** einsiedlerisch.

rec·og·ni·tion [ˌrekəg'nɪʃn] *s.* **1.** ('Wieder)Erkennen *n*: ***~ vocabulary*** *ling.* passiver Wortschatz; ***beyond ~, out of ~, past (all) ~*** (bis) zur Unkenntlichkeit *verändert, verstümmelt etc.*; ***the capital has changed beyond (all) ~*** die Hauptstadt ist (überhaupt) nicht wiederzuerkennen; **2.** Erkenntnis *f*; **3.** Anerkennung *f* (*a. pol.*): ***in ~ of*** als Anerkennung für; ***win ~*** sich durchsetzen, Anerkennung finden; **rec·og·niz·a·ble** ['rekəgnaɪzəbl] *adj.* ☐ ('wieder-)erkennbar, kenntlich; **re·cog·ni·zance** [rɪ'kɒgnɪzəns] *s.* **1.** ⚖ schriftliche Verpflichtung; (Schuld)Anerkenntnis *n*, *f*: ***enter into ~s*** sich gerichtlich binden; **2.** ⚖ Sicherheitsleistung *f*, Kauti'on *f*; **re·cog·ni·zant** [rɪ'kɒgnɪzənt] *adj.*: ***be ~ of*** anerkennen; **rec·og·nize** ['rekəgnaɪz] *v/t.* **1.** ('wieder)erkennen; **2.** *j-n, e-e Regierung, Schuld etc., a. lobend* anerkennen: ***~ that*** zugeben, daß; **3.** No'tiz nehmen von; **4.** *auf der Straße* grüßen; **5.** *j-m* das Wort erteilen.

re·coil **I** *v/i.* [rɪ'kɔɪl] **1.** zu'rückprallen; zu'rückstoßen (*Gewehr etc.*); **2.** *fig.* zu'rückprallen, -schrecken, -schaudern (***at, from*** vor *dat.*); **3.** ***~ on*** *fig.* zu'rückfallen auf (*acc.*); **II** *s.* ['riːkɔɪl] **4.** Rückprall *m*; **5.** ⚔ a) Rückstoß *m* (*Gewehr*),

b) (Rohr)Rücklauf *m* (*Geschütz*); **re'coil·less** [-lɪs] *adj.* ⚔ rückstoßfrei.

rec·ol·lect [ˌrekəˈlekt] *v/t.* sich erinnern (*gen.*) *od.* an (*acc.*), sich ins Gedächtnis zu'rückrufen.

re-col·lect [ˌriːkəˈlekt] *v/t.* wieder sammeln (*a. fig.*): **~ o.s.** sich fassen.

rec·ol·lec·tion [ˌrekəˈlekʃn] *s.* Erinnerung *f* (*Vermögen u. Vorgang*), Gedächtnis *n*: **it is within my ~** es ist mir erinnerlich; **to the best of my ~** soweit ich mich (daran) erinnern kann.

re·com·mence [ˌriːkəˈmens] *v/t. u. v/i.* wieder beginnen.

rec·om·mend [ˌrekəˈmend] *v/t.* **1.** empfehlen (**s.th. to s.o.** j-m et.): **~ s.o. for a post** j-n für e-n Posten empfehlen; **~ caution** Vorsicht empfehlen, zu Vorsicht raten; **2.** empfehlen, anziehend machen: **his manners ~ him**; **3.** (an-) empfehlen, anvertrauen: **~ o.s. to s.o.**; **ˌrec·omˈmend·a·ble** [-dəbl] *adj.* ☐ empfehlenswert; **rec·om·men·da·tion** [ˌrekəmenˈdeɪʃn] *s.* **1.** Empfehlung *f* (*a. fig. Eigenschaft*), Befürwortung *f*, Vorschlag *m*: **on the ~ of** auf Empfehlung von; **2.** *a.* **letter of ~** Empfehlungsschreiben *n*; **ˌrec·omˈmend·a·to·ry** [-dətərɪ] *adj.* empfehlend, Empfehlungs…

re·com·mis·sion [ˌriːkəˈmɪʃn] *v/t.* **1.** wieder anstellen *od.* beauftragen; ⚔ *Offizier* reaktivieren; **2.** ⚓ *Schiff* wieder in Dienst stellen.

re·com·mit [ˌriːkəˈmɪt] *v/t.* **1.** *parl.* (an e-n Ausschuß) zu'rückverweisen; **2.** ⚖ a) *j-n* wieder *dem Gericht* über'antworten, b) *j-n* wieder in *e-e* (*Straf- od. Heil-*) *Anstalt* einweisen.

re·com·pense [ˈrekəmpens] **I** *v/t.* **1.** *j-n* belohnen, entschädigen (**for** für); **2.** *et.* vergelten, belohnen (**to s.o.** j-m); **3.** *et.* erstatten, ersetzen, wieder'gutmachen; **II** *s.* **4.** Belohnung *f*; *a. b.s.* Vergeltung *f*; **5.** Entschädigung *f*, Ersatz *m*.

re·com·pose [ˌriːkəmˈpəʊz] *v/t.* **1.** wieder zs.-setzen; **2.** neu (an)ordnen, 'umgestalten, -gruppieren; **3.** *fig.* wieder beruhigen; **4.** *typ.* neu setzen.

rec·on·cil·a·ble [ˈrekənsaɪləbl] *adj.* **1.** versöhnbar; **2.** vereinbar (**with** mit); **rec·on·cile** [ˈrekənsaɪl] *v/t.* **1.** *j-n* ver-, aussöhnen (**to**, **with** mit): **~ o.s. to**, **become ~d to** *fig.* sich versöhnen *od.* abfinden *od.* befreunden mit *et.*, sich fügen *od.* finden in (*acc.*); **2.** *fig.* in Einklang bringen, abstimmen (**with**, **to** mit); **3.** *Streit* beilegen, schlichten; **rec·on·cil·i·a·tion** [ˌrekənsɪlɪˈeɪʃn] *s.* **1.** Ver-, Aussöhnung *f* (**to**, **with** mit); **2.** Beilegung *f*, Schlichtung *f*; **3.** Ausgleich(ung *f*) *m*, Einklang *m* (**between** zwischen *dat.*, unter *dat.*).

rec·on·dite [rɪˈkɒndaɪt] *adj.* ☐ *fig.* tief (-gründig), ab'strus, dunkel.

re·con·di·tion [ˌriːkənˈdɪʃn] *v/t. bsd.* ⚙ wieder in'standsetzen, über'holen, erneuern.

re·con·nais·sance [rɪˈkɒnɪsəns] *s.* ⚔ a) Erkundung *f*, Aufklärung *f*, b) *a.* **~ party** *od.* **patrol** Spähtrupp *m*: **~ car** Spähwagen *m*; **~ plane** Aufklärungsflugzeug *n*, Aufklärer *m*.

rec·on·noi·ter *Am.*, **rec·on·noi·tre** *Brit.* [ˌrekəˈnɔɪtə] *v/t.* ⚔ erkunden, aufklären, auskundschaften (*a. fig.*), rekognoszieren (*a. geol.*).

re·con·quer [ˌriːˈkɒŋkə] *v/t.* 'wieder-, zu'rückerobern; **ˌreˈcon·quest** [-kwest] *s.* 'Wiedereroberung *f*.

re·con·sid·er [ˌriːkənˈsɪdə] *v/t.* **1.** von neuem erwägen, nochmals über'legen, nachprüfen; **2.** *pol.*, ⚖ *Antrag*, *Sache* nochmals behandeln; **re·con·sid·er·a·tion** [ˈriːkənˌsɪdəˈreɪʃn] *s.* nochmalige Über'legung *od.* Erwägung *od.* Prüfung.

re·con·stit·u·ent [ˌriːkənˈstɪtjʊənt] **I** *s.* ⚕ 'Roborans *n*; **II** *adj. bsd.* ⚕ wieder'aufbauend.

re·con·sti·tute [ˌriːˈkɒnstɪtjuːt] *v/t.* **1.** wieder einsetzen; **2.** wieder'herstellen; neu bilden; ⚔ neu aufstellen; **3.** im Wasser auflösen.

re·con·struct [ˌriːkənˈstrʌkt] *v/t.* **1.** wieder aufbauen (*a. fig.*), wieder herstellen; **2.** 'umbauen (*a.* ⚙ *neu konstruieren*), 'umformen, -bilden; **3.** ✝ wieder'aufbauen, sanieren; **ˌre·conˈstruc·tion** [ˌriːkənˈstrʌkʃn] *s.* **1.** Wieder'aufbau *m*, -'herstellung *f*; **2.** 'Umbau *m* (*a.* ⚙ *Neukonstruktion*), 'Umformung *f*; **3.** Rekonstrukti'on *f* (*a. e-s Verbrechens etc.*); **4.** ✝ Sanierung *f*, Wieder'aufbau *m*.

re·con·ver·sion [ˌriːkənˈvɜːʃn] *s.* (ˈRück)ˌUmwandlung *f*, 'Umstellung *f* (*bsd.* ✝ *e-s Betriebs*, *auf Friedensproduktion etc.*); **ˌre·conˈvert** [-ˈvɜːt] *v/t.* (wieder) 'umstellen.

rec·ord[1] [ˈrekɔːd] *s.* **1.** Aufzeichnung *f*, Niederschrift *f*: **on ~** a) (geschichtlich *etc.*) verzeichnet, schriftlich belegt, b) → 4 b, c) *fig. das beste etc.* aller Zeiten, bisher; **off the ~** inoffiziell, nicht für die Öffentlichkeit bestimmt; **on the ~** offiziell; **matter of ~** verbürgte Tatsache; **2.** (schriftlicher) Bericht; **3.** *a.* ⚖ Urkunde *f*, Doku'ment *n*, 'Unterlage *f*; **4.** ⚖ a) Proto'koll *n*, Niederschrift *f*, b) (Gerichts)Akte *f*, Aktenstück *n*: **on ~** aktenkundig; **on the ~ of the case** nach Aktenlage; **go on ~** *fig.* a) sich erklären *od.* festlegen, b) sich erweisen (**as** als); **place on ~** aktenkundig machen; **court of ~** ordentliches Gericht; **~ office** Archiv *n*; (**just**) **to put the ~ straight!** (nur) um das mal klarzustellen!; **just for the ~!** (nur) um das mal festzuhalten!; **5.** Re'gister *n*, Liste *f*, Verzeichnis *n*: **criminal ~** a) Strafregister, b) *weitS.* Vorstrafen *pl.*; **have a** (**criminal**) **~** vorbestraft sein; **6.** *a.* ⚙ Registrierung *f*; **7.** a) Ruf *m*, Leumund *m*, Vergangenheit *f*: **a bad ~**, b) *gute etc.* Leistung(en *pl.*) *in der Vergangenheit*; **8.** *fig.* Urkunde *f*, Zeugnis *n*: **be a ~ of** *et.* bezeugen; **9.** (Schall)Platte *f*: **~ changer** Plattenwechsler *m*; **~ library** a) Plattensammlung *f*, -archiv *n*, b) Plattenverleih *m*; **~ machine** *Am.* Musikautomat *m*; **~ player** Plattenspieler *m*; **10.** *sport*, *a. weitS.* Re'kord *m*, Best-, Höchstleistung *f*: **~ high** (**low**) ✝ Rekordhoch (-tief) *n*; **~ performance** *allg.* Spitzenleistung *f*; **~ prices** ✝ Rekordpreise; **in ~ time** in Rekordzeit.

re·cord[2] [rɪˈkɔːd] *v/t.* **1.** schriftlich niederlegen; (*a.* ⚙) aufzeichnen, -schreiben; ⚖ beurkunden, protokollieren; zu den Akten nehmen; ✝ *etc.* eintragen, registrieren, erfassen: **by ~ed delivery** ✉ per Einschreiben; **2.** ⚙ *Meßwerte* registrieren, verzeichnen; **3.** (*auf Tonband etc.*) aufnehmen, -zeichnen, *Sendung* mitschneiden, *a. fotografisch* festhalten; **4.** *fig.* aufzeichnen, festhalten, der Nachwelt über'liefern; **5.** *Stimme* abgeben; **re·cord·er** [rɪˈkɔːdə] *s.* **1.** Regi'strator *m*; *weitS.* Chro'nist *m*; **2.** Schrift-, Proto'kollführer(in); **3.** ⚖ *Brit. obs.* Einzelrichter *m* der **Quarter Sessions**; **4.** ⚙ Aufnahmegerät *n*: a) Regi'strierappaˌrat *m*, (Bild-, Selbst-) Schreiber *m*, b) 'Wiedergabegerät *n*; → **tape recorder** *etc.*; **5.** ♪ Blockflöte *f*; **re·cord·ing** [rɪˈkɔːdɪŋ] **I** *s.* **1.** *a.* ⚙ Aufzeichnung *f*, Registrierung *f*; **2.** Beurkundung *f*; Protokollierung *f*; **3.** *Radio etc.*: Aufnahme *f*, Aufzeichnung *f*, Mitschnitt *m*; **II** *adj.* **4.** Protokoll…; **5.** registrierend: **~ chart** Registrierpapier *n*; **~ head** a) ϟ Tonkopf *m* (*Tonbandgerät*), b) Schreibkopf *m* (*Computer*).

re·count[1] [rɪˈkaʊnt] *v/t.* **1.** (im einzelnen) erzählen; **2.** aufzählen.

re-count[2] [ˌriːˈkaʊnt] *v/t.* nachzählen.

re·coup [rɪˈkuːp] *v/t.* **1.** 'wiedergewinnen, *Verlust etc.* wieder'einbringen; **2.** *j-n* entschädigen (**for** für); **3.** ✝, ⚖ einbehalten.

re·course [rɪˈkɔːs] *s.* **1.** Zuflucht *f* (**to** zu): **have ~ to s.th.** s-e Zuflucht zu et. nehmen; **have ~ to foul means** zu unredlichen Mitteln greifen; **2.** ✝, ⚖ Re'greß *m*, Re'kurs *m*: **with** (**without**) **~** mit (ohne) Rückgriff; **liable to ~** regreßpflichtig.

re·cov·er [rɪˈkʌvə] **I** *v/t.* **1.** (*a. fig. Appetit*, *Bewußtsein*, *Fassung etc.*) 'wiedererlangen, -finden; zu'rückerlangen, -gewinnen; ⚔ 'wieder-, zu'rückerobern; *Fahrzeug*, *Schiff* bergen: **~ one's breath** wieder zu Atem kommen; **~ one's legs** wieder auf die Beine kommen; **~ land from the sea** dem Meer Land abringen; **2.** *Verluste etc.* wieder'gutmachen, wieder'einbringen, ersetzen; *Zeit* wieder'aufholen; **3.** ⚖ a) *Schuld etc.* einziehen, beitreiben, b) *Urteil* erwirken (**against** gegen): **~ damages for** Schadensersatz erhalten für; **4.** ⚙ *aus Altmaterial* regenerieren, 'wiedergewinnen; **5. ~ o.s.** → 8 *u.* 9.: **be ~ed from** wiederhergestellt sein von; **6.** (er)retten, befreien (**from** aus *dat.*); **7.** *fenc. etc.* in die Ausgangsstellung bringen; **II** *v/i.* **8.** genesen, wieder gesund werden; **9.** sich erholen (**from**, **of** von *e-m Schock etc.*) (*a.* ✝); **10.** wieder zu sich kommen, das Bewußtsein 'wiedererlangen; **11.** ⚖ a) Recht bekommen, b) entschädigt werden, sich schadlos halten: **~ in one's** (**law-**) **suit** s-n Prozeß gewinnen, obsiegen.

re·cov·er·a·ble [rɪˈkʌvərəbl] *adj.* **1.** 'wiedererlangbar; **2.** wieder'gutzumachen(d); **3.** ⚖ ein-, beitreibbar (*Schuld*); **4.** wieder'herstellbar; **5.** ⚙ regenerierbar; **re·cov·er·y** [rɪˈkʌvərɪ] *s.* **1.** (Zu)'Rück-, 'Wiedererlangung *f*, -gewinnung *f*; **2.** ⚖ a) Ein-, Beitreibung *f*, b) *mst* **~ of damages** (Erlangung *f* von) Schadenersatz *m*; **3.** ⚙ Rückgewinnung *f aus Abfallstoffen etc.*; **4.** ⚓ *etc.* Bergung *f*, Rettung *f*: **~ vehicle** *mot.* Bergungsfahrzeug *n*; Abschleppwagen *m*; **5.** *fig.* Rettung *f*, Bekehrung *f*; **6.** Genesung *f*, Gesundung *f*, Erholung *f* (*a.* ✝), (*gesundheitliche*) Wieder'herstellung: **economic ~** Konjunkturaufschwung *m*, -belebung *f*; **be past** (*od.* **beyond**) ~ unheilbar krank sein, *fig.* hoffnungslos darniederliegen; **7.** *sport* a) *fenc. etc.* Zu'rückgehen *n* in die Ausgangsstellung, b) *Golf*: Bunkerschlag *m*.

rec·re·an·cy ['rekrɪənsɪ] *s.* **1.** Feigheit *f*; **2.** Abtrünnigkeit *f*; **'rec·re·ant** [-nt] **I** *adj.* □ **1.** feig(e); **2.** abtrünnig, treulos; **II** *s.* **3.** Feigling *m*; **4.** Abtrünnige(r *m*) *f*.

rec·re·ate ['rekrɪeɪt] **I** *v/t.* **1.** erfrischen, *j-m* Erholung *od.* Entspannung gewähren; **2.** erheitern, unter'halten; **3.** ~ ***o.s.*** a) ausspannen, sich erholen, b) sich ergötzen *od.* unterhalten; **II** *v/i.* **4.** → 3.

re-cre·ate [ˌriːkrɪ'eɪt] *v/t.* neu *od.* wieder (er)schaffen.

rec·re·a·tion [ˌrekrɪ'eɪʃn] *s.* Erholung *f*, Entspannung *f*, Erfrischung *f*; Belustigung *f*, Unter'haltung *f*: ~ ***area*** Erholungsgebiet *n*; ~ ***centre***, *Am.* ~ ***center*** Freizeitzentrum *n*; ~ ***ground*** Spiel-, Sportplatz *m*; ˌ**rec·re'a·tion·al** [-ʃənl] *adj.* Erholungs…, Entspannungs…, *Ort etc.* der Erholung; Freizeit…: ~ ***value*** Freizeitwert *m*; **rec·re·a·tive** ['rekrɪeɪtɪv] *adj.* **1.** erholsam, entspannend, erfrischend; **2.** unter'haltend.

re·crim·i·nate [rɪ'krɪmɪneɪt] *v/i. u. v/t.* Gegenbeschuldigungen vorbringen (gegen); **re·crim·i·na·tion** [rɪˌkrɪmɪ'neɪʃn] *s.* Gegenbeschuldigung *f*.

re·cru·desce [ˌriːkruː'des] *v/i.* **1.** wieder aufbrechen (*Wunde*); **2.** sich wieder verschlimmern (*Zustand*); **3.** *fig.* wieder'ausbrechen, -'aufflackern (*Übel*); ˌ**re·cru'des·cence** [-sns] *s.* **1.** Wieder'aufbrechen *n* (*e-r Wunde etc.*); **2.** *fig.* a) Wieder'ausbrechen *n*, b) Wieder'aufleben *n*.

re·cruit [rɪ'kruːt] **I** *s.* **1.** ⚔ a) Re'krut *m*, b) *Am.* (einfacher) Sol'dat; **2.** Neuling *m* (*a. contp.*); **II** *v/t.* **3.** ⚔ rekrutieren: a) *Rekruten* ausheben, einziehen, b) anwerben, c) *Einheit* ergänzen, erneuern, d) *weitS. Leute* her'anziehen: **be ~ed from** sich rekrutieren aus, *fig. a.* sich zs.-setzen *od.* ergänzen aus; **4.** *j-n, j-s Gesundheit* wieder'herstellen; **5.** *fig.* stärken, erfrischen; **III** *v/i.* **6.** Rekruten ausheben *od.* anwerben; **7.** sich erholen; **re'cruit·al** [-tl] *s.* Erholung *f*, Wieder'herstellung *f*; **re'cruit·ing** [-tɪŋ] ⚔ **I** *s.* Rekrutierung *f*, (An)Werben *n*; **II** *adj.* Werbe…(*-büro, -offizier etc.*); Rekrutierungs…(*-stelle*); **re'cruit·ment** [-mənt] *s.* **1.** Verstärkung *f*, Auffrischung *f*; **2.** *bsd.* ⚔ Rekrutierung *f*; **3.** Erholung *f*.

rec·tal ['rektəl] *adj.* □ *anat.* rek'tal: ~ ***syringe*** Klistierspritze *f*.

rec·tan·gle ['rekˌtæŋgl] *s.* A Rechteck *n*; **rec·tan·gu·lar** [rek'tæŋgjʊlə] *adj.* □ A **1.** rechteckig; **2.** rechtwink(e)lig.

rec·ti·fi·a·ble ['rektɪfaɪəbl] *adj.* **1.** zu berichtigen(d), korrigierbar; **2.** A, ⚙, ⚗ rektifizierbar; **rec·ti·fi·ca·tion** [ˌrektɪfɪ'keɪʃn] *s.* **1.** Berichtigung *f*, Verbesserung *f*, Richtigstellung *f*; **2.** A, ⚗ Rektifikati'on *f*; **3.** ⚡ Gleichrichtung *f*; **4.** *phot.* Entzerrung *f*; **'rec·ti·fi·er** [-aɪə] *s.* **1.** Berichtiger *m*; **2.** ⚗ *etc.* Rektifizierer *m*; **3.** ⚡ Gleichrichter *m*; **4.** *phot.* Entzerrungsgerät *n*; **rec·ti·fy** ['rektɪfaɪ] *v/t.* berichtigen, korrigieren, richtigstellen; *Mißstand etc.* beseitigen; A, ⚗, ⚙ rektifizieren; ⚡ gleichrichten.

rec·ti·lin·e·al [ˌrektɪ'lɪnɪəl] *adj.*, ˌ**rec·ti'lin·e·ar** [-ɪə] *adj.* □ geradlinig; **rec·ti·tude** ['rektɪtjuːd] *s.* Geradheit *f*, Rechtschaffenheit *f*.

rec·tor ['rektə] *s.* **1.** *eccl.* Pfarrer *m*; **2.** *univ.* Rektor *m*; **3.** *Scot.* ('Schul)Diˌrektor *m*; **'rec·tor·ate** [-ərət], **'rec·tor·ship** [-ʃɪp] *s.* **1.** *ped.* Rekto'rat *n*; **2.** *eccl.* a) Pfarrstelle *f*, b) Amt *n od.* Amtszeit *f* e-s Pfarrers; **'rec·to·ry** [-tərɪ] *s.* Pfar'rei *f*, Pfarre *f*: a) Pfarrhaus *n*, b) *Brit.* Pfarrstelle *f*, c) Kirchspiel *n*.

rec·tum ['rektəm] *pl.* **-ta** [-tə] *s. anat.* Mastdarm *m*, Rektum *n*.

re·cum·ben·cy [rɪ'kʌmbənsɪ] *s.* **1.** liegende Stellung, Liegen *n*; **2.** *fig.* Ruhe *f*; **re'cum·bent** [-nt] *adj.* □ (sich zu'rück)lehnend, liegend, *a. fig.* ruhend.

re·cu·per·ate [rɪ'kjuːpəreɪt] **I** *v/i.* **1.** sich erholen (*a.* ☤); **II** *v/t.* **2.** 'wiedererlangen; **3.** *Verluste etc.* wettmachen; **re·cu·per·a·tion** [rɪˌkjuːpə'reɪʃn] *s.* Erholung *f* (*a. fig.*); **re'cu·per·a·tive** [-rətɪv] *adj.* **1.** stärkend, kräftigend; **2.** Erholungs…

re·cur [rɪ'kɜː] *v/i.* **1.** 'wiederkehren, wieder'auftreten (*Ereignis*, *Erscheinung etc.*); **2.** *fig. in Gedanken*, *im Gespräch* zu'rückkommen (**to** auf *acc.*); **3.** *fig.* 'wiederkehren (*Gedanken*); **4.** zu'rückgreifen (**to** auf *acc.*); **5.** A (peri'odisch) wiederkehren (*Kurve etc.*): **~ring decimal** periodische Dezimalzahl; **re·currence** [rɪ'kʌrəns] *s.* **1.** 'Wiederkehr *f*, Wieder'auftreten *n*; **2.** Zu'rückgreifen *n* (**to** auf *acc.*); **3.** *fig.* Zu'rückkommen *n* (*im Gespräch etc.*) (**to** auf *acc.*); **re·cur·rent** [rɪ'kʌrənt] *adj.* □ **1.** 'wiederkehrend (*a. Zahlungen*, *Träume*), sich wieder'holend; **2.** peri'odisch auftretend: ~ ***fever*** ⚕ Rückfallfieber *n*; **3.** ♀, *anat.* rückläufig (*Nerv*, *Arterie etc.*).

re·cy·cle [ˌriː'saɪkl] *v/t.* **1.** ⚙ *Abfälle* 'wiederverwerten; **2.** ☤ *Kapital* zu'rückschleusen; **re'cy·cling** [-lɪŋ] *s.* ⚙, ☤ Re'cycling *n*: a) ⚙ 'Wiederverwertung *f*: ~ ***of waste material***, b) ☤ Rückschleusung *f*: ~ ***of funds***.

red [red] **I** *adj.* **1.** rot: ~ ***ant*** rote Waldameise; ≈ ***Book*** a) Adelskalender *m*, b) *pol.* Rotbuch *n*; ~ ***cabbage*** Rotkohl *m*; ≈ ***Cross*** Rotes Kreuz; ~ ***currant*** Johannisbeere *f*; ~ ***deer*** Edel-, Rothirsch *m*; ≈ ***Ensign*** brit. Handelsflagge *f*; ~ ***hat*** Kardinalshut *m*; ~ ***heat*** Rotglut *f*; ~ ***herring*** a) Bückling *m*, b) *fig.* Ablenkungsmanöver *n*, falsche Spur; ***draw a ~ herring across the path*** a) ein Ablenkungsmanöver durchführen, b) e-e falsche Spur zurücklassen; ~ ***lead*** *min.* Mennige *f*; ~ ***lead ore*** Rotbleierz *n*; ~ ***light*** Warn-, Stopplicht *n*; ***see the ~ light*** *fig.* die Gefahr erkennen; ***the lights are at ~*** *mot.* die Ampel steht auf Rot; ~ ***tape*** Amtsschimmel *m*, Bürokratismus *m*, Papierkrieg *m*; ***see ~*** ,rotsehen', wild werden; → ***paint*** 2; ***rag***[1] 1; **2.** rot(glühend); **3.** rot(haarig); **4.** rot(häutig); **5.** *oft* ≈ *pol.* rot: a) kommu'nistisch, sozia'listisch, b) sow'jetisch: ***the ≈ Army*** die Rote Armee; **II** *s.* **6.** Rot *n*; **7.** *a.* **~*skin*** Rothaut *f* (*Indianer*); **8.** *oft* ≈ *pol.* Rote(r *m*) *f*; **9.** *bsd.* ☤ ***be in the ~*** in den roten Zahlen sein; ***get out of the ~*** aus den roten Zahlen herauskommen.

re·dact [rɪ'dækt] *v/t.* **1.** redigieren, her'ausgeben; **2.** *Erklärung etc.* abfassen; **re'dac·tion** [-kʃn] *s.* **1.** Redakti'on *f* (*Tätigkeit*), Her'ausgabe *f*; **2.** (Ab)Fassung *f*; **3.** Neubearbeitung *f*.

ˌ**red|-'blood·ed** *adj. fig.* lebensprühend, vi'tal, feurig; **'~·breast** *s. orn.* Rotkehlchen *n*; **'~·cap** *s.* ,Rotkäppchen' *n*: a) *Brit. sl.* Mili'tärpoliˌzist *m*, b) *Am.* (Bahnhofs)Gepäckträger *m*; ~ **car·pet** *s.* roter Teppich: ~ ***treatment*** ,großer Bahnhof'.

red·den ['redn] **I** *v/t.* röten, rot färben; **II** *v/i.* rot werden: a) sich röten, b) erröten (***at*** über *acc.*, ***with*** vor *dat.*).

red·dish ['redɪʃ] *adj.* rötlich.

red·dle ['redl] *s.* Rötel *m*.

re·dec·o·rate [ˌriː'dekəreɪt] *v/t. Zimmer etc.* renovieren, neu streichen *od.* tapezieren.

re·deem [rɪ'diːm] *v/t.* **1.** *Verpflichtung* abzahlen, -lösen, tilgen, amortisieren; **2.** zu'rückkaufen; **3.** ☤ *Staatspapier* auslosen; **4.** *Pfand* einlösen; **5.** *Gefangene etc.* los-, freikaufen; **6.** *Versprechen* erfüllen, einlösen; **7.** *Fehler etc.* wieder'gutmachen, *Sünde* abbüßen; **8.** *schlechte Eigenschaft* aufwiegen, wettmachen, versöhnen mit: **~*ing feature*** a) versöhnender Zug, b) ausgleichendes Moment; **9.** *Ehre*, *Rechte* 'wiedererlangen, wieder'herstellen; **10.** (***from***) bewahren (vor *dat.*); (er)retten (von); befreien (von); **11.** *eccl.* erlösen (***from*** von); **12.** *Zeitverlust* wettmachen; **re'deem·a·ble** [-məbl] *adj.* □ **1.** abzahlbar, -lösbar, tilgbar; kündbar (*Anleihe*); rückzahlbar (*Wertpapier*): ~ ***loan*** Tilgungsdarlehen *n*; **2.** zu'rückkaufbar; **3.** ☤ auslosbar (*Staatspapier*); **4.** einlösbar (*Pfand*, *Versprechen etc.*); **5.** wieder'gutzumachen(d) (*Fehler*), abzubüßen(d) (*Sünde*); **6.** 'wiedererlangbar; **7.** *eccl.* erlösbar; **re'deem·er** [-mə] *s.* **1.** Einlöser(in) *etc.*; **2.** ≈ *eccl.* Erlöser *m*, Heiland *m*.

re·de·liv·er [ˌriːdɪ'lɪvə] *v/t.* **1.** *j-n* wieder befreien; **2.** *et.* zu'rückgeben; rückliefern.

re·demp·tion [rɪ'dempʃn] *s.* **1.** Abzahlung *f*, Ablösung *f*, Tilgung *f*, Amortisati'on *f e-r Schuld etc.*: ~ ***fund*** *Am.* ☤ Tilgungsfonds *m*; ~ ***loan*** ☤ Ablösungsanleihe *f*; **2.** Rückkauf *m*; **3.** Auslosung *f von Staatspapieren*; **4.** Einlösung *f e-s Pfandes* (*fig. e-s Versprechens*); **5.** Los-, Freikauf *m e-r Geisel etc.*; **6.** Wieder'gutmachung *f e-s Fehlers*; Abbüßung *f e-r Sünde*; **7.** Ausgleich *m* (***of*** für), Wettmachen *n e-s Nachteils*; **8.** 'Wiedererlangung *f*, Wieder'herstellung *f e-s Rechts etc.*; **9.** *bsd. eccl.* Erlösung *f* (***from*** von): ***past*** *od.* ***beyond ~*** hoffnungs- *od.* rettungslos (verloren); **re'demp·tive** [-ptɪv] *adj. eccl.* erlösend, Erlösungs…

re·de·ploy [ˌriːdɪ'plɔɪ] *v/t.* **1.** *bsd.* ⚔ 'umgrupˌpieren; **2.** ⚔, *a.* ☤ verlegen; ˌ**re·de'ploy·ment** [-mənt] *s.* **1.** 'Umgrupˌpierung *f*; (Truppen)Verschiebung *f*; **2.** Verlegung *f*.

re·de·vel·op [ˌriːdɪ'veləp] *v/t.* **1.** neu entwickeln; **2.** *phot.* nachentwickeln; **3.** *Stadtteil etc.* sanieren; ˌ**re·de'vel·op·ment** [-mənt] *s.* **1.** Neuentwicklung *f etc.*; **2.** (Stadt- *etc.*)Sanierung *f*: ~ ***area*** Sanierungsgebiet *n*.

ˌ**red-ˈhand·ed** *adj.*: ***catch s.o.*** **~** j-n auf frischer Tat ertappen.

red·hi·bi·tion [ˌredhɪˈbɪʃn] *s.* ⚖ Wandlung *f beim Kauf*; **red·hib·i·to·ry** [redˈhɪbɪtərɪ] *adj.* Wandlungs…(*-klage etc.*): ***~ defect*** Fehler *m* der Sache beim Kauf.

ˌ**red-ˈhot** *adj.* **1.** rotglühend; **2.** glühend heiß; **3.** *fig.* wild, toll; **4.** hitzig, jähzornig; **5.** allerneuest, ˈbrandaktuˌell: ***~ news.***

red·in·te·grate [reˈdɪntɪgreɪt] *v/t.* **1.** wiederˈherstellen; **2.** erneuern.

re·di·rect [ˌriːdɪˈrekt] *v/t.* **1.** *Brief etc.* ˈumadresˌsieren; **2.** *Verkehr* ˈumleiten; **3.** *fig.* e-e neue Richtung geben (*dat.*), ändern.

re·dis·count [ˌriːˈdɪskaʊnt] ✝ **I** *v/t.* **1.** rediskontieren; **II** *s.* **2.** Rediskonˈtierung *f*; **3.** Redisˈkont *m*: ***~ rate*** *Am.* Rediskontsatz *m*; **4.** rediskonˈtierter Wechsel.

re·dis·cov·er [ˌriːdɪˈskʌvə] *v/t.* ˈwiederentdecken.

re·dis·trib·ute [ˌriːdɪˈstrɪbjuːt] *v/t.* **1.** neu verteilen; **2.** wieder verteilen.

ˌ**red**|**-ˈlet·ter day** *s. fig.* Freuden-, Glückstag *m*; ˌ**~-ˈlight dis·trict** *s.* Borˈdellviertel *n*.

red·ness [ˈrednɪs] *s.* Röte *f*.

re·do [ˌriːˈduː] *v/t.* [*irr.* → ***do***] **1.** nochmals tun *od.* machen; **2.** *Haar etc.* nochmals richten *etc.*

red·o·lence [ˈredəʊləns] *s.* Duft *m*, Wohlgeruch *m*; ˈ**red·o·lent** [-nt] *adj.* duftend (***of, with*** nach): ***be ~ of*** *fig. et.* atmen, stark gemahnen an (*acc.*), umˈwittert sein von.

re·dou·ble [ˌriːˈdʌbl] **I** *v/t.* **1.** verdoppeln; **2.** *Bridge*: *j-m* Reˈkontra geben; **II** *v/i.* **3.** sich verdoppeln; **4.** *Bridge*: Reˈkontra geben.

re·doubt [rɪˈdaʊt] *s.* ⚔ **1.** Reˈdoute *f*; **2.** Schanze *f*; **reˈdoubt·a·ble** [-təbl] *adj. rhet. od. iro.* **1.** furchtbar, schrecklich; **2.** gewaltig.

re·dound [rɪˈdaʊnd] *v/i.* **1.** ausschlagen *od.* gereichen (***to*** zu *j-s Ehre, Vorteil etc.*); **2.** zuˈteil werden, erwachsen (***to*** *dat.*, ***from*** aus); **3.** zuˈrückfallen, -wirken (***upon*** auf *acc.*).

re·draft [ˌriːˈdrɑːft] **I** *s.* **1.** neuer Entwurf; **2.** ✝ Rück-, Riˈkambiowechsel *m*; **II** *v/t.* **3.** → ***redraw*** I.

re·draw [ˌriːˈdrɔː] [*irr.* → ***draw***] **I** *v/t.* neu entwerfen; **II** *v/i.* ✝ zuˈrücktrasˌsieren (***on*** auf *acc.*).

re·dress [rɪˈdres] **I** *s.* **1.** Abhilfe *f* (*a.* ⚖): ***legal ~*** Rechtshilfe *f*: ***obtain ~ from s.o.*** gegen j-n Regreß nehmen; **2.** Behebung *f*, Beseitigung *f e-s Übelstandes*; **3.** Wiederˈgutmachung *f e-s Unrechts, Fehlers etc.*; **4.** Entschädigung *f* (***for*** für); **II** *v/t.* **5.** *Mißstand* beheben, beseitigen, (*dat.*) abhelfen; *Unrecht* wiederˈgutmachen; *Gleichgewicht etc.* wiederˈherstellen; **6.** ✈ *Flugzeug* in die norˈmale Fluglage zuˈrückbringen.

ˌ**red**|**-ˈshort** *adj. metall.* rotbrüchig; ˈ**~-start** *s. orn.* Rotschwänzchen *n*; ˌ**~-ˈtape** *adj.* büroˈkratisch; ˌ**~-ˈtap·ism** [-ˈteɪpɪzəm] *s.* Bürokraˈtismus *m*; ˌ**~-ˈtap·ist** [-ˈteɪpɪst] *s.* Büroˈkrat(in), Aktenmensch *m*.

re·duce [rɪˈdjuːs] **I** *v/t.* **1.** herˈabsetzen, vermindern, -ringern, -kleinern, reduzieren, *fig. a.* abbauen: ***~d scale*** verjüngter Maßstab; ***on a ~d scale*** in verkleinertem Maßstab; **2.** *Preise* herˈabsetzen, ermäßigen: ***at ~d prices*** zu herabgesetzten Preisen; ***at a ~d fare*** zu ermäßigtem Fahrpreis; **3.** *im Rang, Wert etc.* herˈabsetzen, -mindern, -drücken, erniedrigen; *a.* ***~ to the ranks*** ⚔ degradieren; **4.** schwächen, erschöpfen; (*finanziell*) erschüttern: ***in ~d circumstances*** in beschränkten Verhältnissen, verarmt; **5.** (***to***) verwandeln (in *acc.*, zu), machen (zu): ***~ to pulp*** zu Brei machen; ***~d to a skeleton*** zum Skelett abgemagert; **6.** bringen (***to*** zu): ***~ to a system*** in ein System bringen; ***~ to rules*** in Regeln fassen; ***~ to writing*** schriftlich niederlegen, aufzeichnen; ***~ theories into practice*** Theorien in die Praxis umsetzen; **7.** zuˈrückführen, reduzieren (***to*** auf *acc.*): ***~ to absurdity*** ad absurdum führen; **8.** zerlegen (***to*** in *acc.*); **9.** einteilen (***to*** in *acc.*); **10.** anpassen (***to*** *dat. od.* an *acc.*); **11.** ⚗, ⚗, *biol.* reduzieren; *Gleichung* auflösen; ***~ to a common denominator*** auf e-n gemeinsamen Nenner bringen; **12.** *metall.* (aus)schmelzen (***from*** aus); **13.** zwingen, *zur Verzweiflung etc.* bringen: ***~ to obedience*** zum Gehorsam zwingen; ***he was ~d to sell (-ing) his house*** er war gezwungen, sein Haus zu verkaufen; ***~d to tears*** zu Tränen gerührt; **14.** unterˈwerfen, erobern; *Festung* zur ˈÜbergabe zwingen; **15.** beschränken (***to*** auf *acc.*); **16.** *Farben etc.* verdünnen; **17.** *phot.* abschwächen; **18.** ⚕ einrenken, (wieder) einrichten; **II** *v/i.* **19.** (an Gewicht) abnehmen; e-e Abmagerungskur machen; **reˈduc·er** [-sə] *s.* **1.** ⚗ Reduktiˈonsmittel *n*; **2.** *phot.* a) Abschwächer *m*, b) Entwickler *m*; **3.** ⚙ a) Reduˈzierstück *n od.* -maˌschine *f*, b) → ***reducing gear***; **reˈduc·i·ble** [-səbl] *adj.* **1.** reduzierbar (*a.* ⚕), zuˈrückführbar (***to*** auf *acc.*): ***be ~ to*** sich reduzieren *od.* zurückführen lassen auf (*acc.*); **2.** verwandelbar (***to, into*** in *acc.*); **3.** herˈabsetzbar.

re·duc·ing| **a·gent** [rɪˈdjuːsɪŋ] *s.* ⚗ Reduktiˈonsmittel *n*; **~ di·et** *s.* Abmagerungskur *f*; **~ gear** *s.* ⚙ Unterˈsetzungsgetriebe *n*.

re·duc·tion [rɪˈdʌkʃn] *s.* **1.** Herˈabsetzung *f*, Verminderung *f*, -ringerung *f*, -kleinerung *f*, Reduzierung *f*, *fig. a.* Abbau *m*: ***~ in (od. of) prices*** Preisherabsetzung, -ermäßigung *f*; ***~ in (od. of) wages*** Lohnkürzung *f*; ***~ of interest*** Zinsherabsetzung; ***~ of staff*** Personalabbau *m*; **2.** (Preis)Nachlaß *m*, Abzug *m*, Raˈbatt *m*; **3.** Verminderung *f*, Rückgang *m*: ***import ~*** ✝ Einfuhrrückgang; **4.** Verwandlung *f* (***into, to*** in *acc.*): ***~ into gas*** Vergasung *f*; **5.** Zuˈrückführung *f*, Reduzierung *f* (***to*** auf *acc.*); **6.** Zerlegung *f* (***to*** in *acc.*); **7.** ⚗ Reduktiˈon *f*; **8.** ⚗ Reduktiˈon *f*, Kürzung *f*, Vereinfachung *f*; Auflösung *f von Gleichungen*; **9.** *metall.* (Aus-)Schmelzung *f*; **10.** Unterˈwerfung *f* (***to*** unter *acc.*); Bezwingung *f*, ⚔ Niederkämpfung *f*; **11.** *phot.* Abschwächung *f*; **12.** *biol.* Reduktiˈon *f*; **13.** ⚕ Einrenkung *f*; **14.** Verkleinerung *f* (*e-s Bildes etc.*); **~ com·pass·es** *s. pl.* Reduktiˈonszirkel *m*; **~ di·vi·sion** *s. biol.* Reduktiˈonsteilung *f*; **~ gear** *s.* ⚙ Reduktiˈons-, Unterˈsetzungsgetriebe *n*; **~ ra·tio** *s.* ⚙ Unterˈsetzungsverhältnis *n*.

re·dun·dance [rɪˈdʌndəns], **reˈdun·dan·cy** [-sɪ] *s.* **1.** ˈÜberfluß *m*, -fülle *f*; **2.** ˈÜberflüssigkeit *f*, ✝ *a.* Arbeitslosigkeit *f*: ***~ letter*** *od.* ***notice*** Entlassungsschreiben *n*; **3.** Wortfülle *f*; **4.** *ling., Informatik*: Redunˈdanz *f*; **reˈdun·dant** [-nt] *adj.* □ **1.** ˈüberreichlich, -mäßig; **2.** ˈüberschüssig, -zählig: ***~ workers*** freigesetzte (*entlassene*) Arbeitskräfte; ***make s.o. ~*** j-n freisetzen, -stellen; **3.** ˈüberflüssig; **4.** üppig; **5.** ˈüberfließend (***of, with*** von); **6.** überˈladen (*Stil etc.*), *bsd.* weitschweifig; **7.** *ling., Informatik*: redunˈdant.

re·du·pli·cate [rɪˈdjuːplɪkeɪt] *v/t.* **1.** verdoppeln; **2.** wiederˈholen; **3.** *ling.* reduplizieren.

re·dye [ˌriːˈdaɪ] *v/t.* **1.** nachfärben; **2.** ˈumfärben.

re·ech·o [riːˈekəʊ] **I** *v/i.* ˈwiderhallen (***with*** von); **II** *v/t.* widerhallen lassen.

reed [riːd] *s.* **1.** ⚘ Schilf *n*; (Schilf)Rohr *n*; Ried(gras) *n*: ***broken ~*** *fig.* schwankes Rohr; **2.** *pl. Brit.* (Dachdecker-)Stroh *n*; **3.** Pfeil *m*; **4.** Rohrflöte *f*; **5.** ♪ a) (Rohr)Blatt *n*: ***~ instruments, the ~s*** Rohrblattinstrumente, b) *a.* ***~-stop*** Zungenstimme *f* (*Orgel*); **6.** ⚙ Weberkamm *m*, Blatt *n*.

re-ed·it [ˌriːˈedɪt] *v/t.* neu herˈausgeben; **re-e·di·tion** [ˌriːɪˈdɪʃn] *s.* Neuausgabe *f*.

re-ed·u·cate [ˌriːˈedjʊkeɪt] *v/t.* ˈumschulen; **re-ed·u·ca·tion** [ˈriːˌedjʊˈkeɪʃn] *s.* ˈUmschulung *f*.

reed·y [ˈriːdɪ] *adj.* **1.** schilfig, schilfreich; **2.** lang u. schlank; **3.** dünn, quäkend (*Stimme*).

reef[1] [riːf] *s.* **1.** (Felsen)Riff *n*; **2.** *min.* Ader *f*, (Quarz)Gang *m*.

reef[2] [riːf] ⚓ **I** *s.* Reff *n*; **II** *v/t.* *Segel* reffen.

reef·er [ˈriːfə] *s.* **1.** ⚓ a) Reffer *m*, b) *sl.* ˈSeekaˌdett *m*, c) Bord-, Maˈtrosenjakke *f*, d) *Am. sl.* Kühlschiff *n*; **2.** *Am. sl.* a) 🚃, *mot.* Kühlwagen *m*, b) Kühlschrank *m*; **3.** *sl.* Marihuˈana-Zigaˌrette *f*.

reek [riːk] **I** *s.* **1.** Gestank *m*, (üble) Ausdünstung, Geruch *m*; **2.** Dampf *m*, Dunst *m*, Qualm *m*; **II** *v/i.* **3.** stinken, riechen (***of, with*** nach), üble Dünste ausströmen; **4.** dampfen, rauchen (***with*** von); **5.** *fig.* (***of, with***) stark riechen (nach), voll sein (von); ˈ**reek·y** [-kɪ] *adj.* **1.** dampfend, dunstend; **2.** rauchig.

reel[1] [riːl] **I** *s.* **1.** Haspel *f*, (*Garn- etc.*) Winde *f*; **2.** (*Garn-, Schlauch- etc.*) Rolle *f*, (*Bandmaß-, Farbband-, Film- etc.*)Spule *f*; ⚡ Kabeltrommel *f*; **3.** a) Film(streifen) *m*, b) (Film)Akt *m*; **II** *v/t.* **4.** *a.* ***~ up*** aufspulen, -wickeln, -rollen: ***~ off*** abhaspeln, -spulen, *fig.* ‚herunterrasseln‘: ***~ off a poem.***

reel[2] [riːl] *v/i.* **1.** sich (schnell) drehen, wirbeln: ***my head ~s*** mir schwindelt; **2.** wanken, taumeln: ***~ back*** zurücktaumeln.

reel[3] [riːl] *s.* Reel *m* (*schottischer Volkstanz*).

re-e·lect [ˌriːɪˈlekt] *v/t.* ˈwiederwählen; ˌ**re-eˈlec·tion** [-kʃn] *s.* ˈWiederwahl *f*; **re-el·i·gi·ble** [ˌriːˈelɪdʒəbl] *adj.* ˈwiederwählbar.

re·em·bark [ˌriːɪmˈbɑːk] *v/t.* (*v/i.* sich) wieder einschiffen.
re·e·merge [ˌriːɪˈmɜːdʒ] *v/i.* wiederˈauftauchen, -ˈauftreten.
re·en·act [ˌriːɪˈnækt] *v/t.* **1.** wieder in Kraft setzen; **2.** *thea.* neu inszenieren; **3.** *fig.* wiederˈholen; ˌ**re·enˈact·ment** [-mənt] *s.* **1.** ˌWiederinˈkraftsetzung *f*; **2.** *thea.* Neuinszenierung *f*.
re·en·gage [ˌriːɪnˈgeɪdʒ] *v/t. j-n* wieder an- *od.* einstellen.
re·en·list [ˌriːɪnˈlɪst] ⚔ *v/t. u. v/i.* (sich) weiter-, ˈwiederverpflichten; (*nur v/i.*) kapitulieren: **~ed man** Kapitulant *m*; ˌ**re·enˈlist·ment** [-mənt] *s.* Wiederˈanwerbung *f*.
re·en·ter [ˌriːˈentə] *v/t.* **1.** wieder betreten, wieder eintreten in (*acc.*); **2.** wieder eintragen (*in e-e Liste etc.*); **3.** ⚙ *Farben* auftragen; **re·en·trant** [riːˈentrənt] **I** *adj.* ⩓ einspringend (*Winkel*); **II** *s.* einspringender Winkel; **re·en·try** [riːˈentrɪ] *s.* Wiederˈeintritt *m* (*a. Raumfahrt: in die Erdatmosphäre*; *a.* ⚖ *in den Besitz*).
re·es·tab·lish [ˌriːɪˈstæblɪʃ] *v/t.* **1.** wiederˈherstellen; **2.** wiederˈeinführen, neu gründen.
reeve¹ [riːv] *s. Brit.* a) *hist.* Vogt *m*, b) Gemeindevorsteher *m*.
reeve² [riːv] *v/t.* ⚓ *Tauende* einscheren; *das Tau* ziehen (**around** um).
re·ex·am·i·na·tion [ˈriːɪgˌzæmɪˈneɪʃn] *s.* **1.** Nachprüfung *f*, Wiederˈholungsprüfung *f*; **2.** ⚖ a) nochmaliges (Zeugen-) Verhör, b) nochmalige Unterˈsuchung.
re·ex·change [ˌriːɪksˈtʃeɪndʒ] *s.* **1.** Rücktausch *m*; **2.** † Rück-, Gegenwechsel *m*; **3.** † Rückwechselkosten *pl.*
re·ex·port † **I** *v/t.* [ˌriːekˈspɔːt] **1.** wiederˈausführen; **II** *s.* [ˌriːˈekspɔːt] **2.** Wiederˈausfuhr *f*; **3.** wiederˈausgeführte Ware.
re·fash·ion [ˌriːˈfæʃn] *v/t.* ˈumgestalten, -modeln.
re·fec·tion [rɪˈfekʃn] *s.* **1.** Erfrischung *f*; **2.** Imbiß *m*; **reˈfec·to·ry** [-ktərɪ] *s.* **1.** *R.C.* Refekˈtorium *n* (*Speiseraum*); **2.** *univ.* Mensa *f*.
re·fer [rɪˈfɜː] **I** *v/t.* **1.** verweisen, hinweisen (**to** auf *acc.*); **2.** *j-n um Auskunft, Referenzen etc.* verweisen (**to** an *j-n*); **3.** (zur Entscheidung *etc.*) überˈgeben, -ˈweisen (**to** an *acc.*): **~ back to** ⚖ *Rechtssache* zurückverweisen an *die Unterinstanz*; **~ to drawer** † an Aussteller zurück; **4.** (**to**) zuschreiben (*dat.*), zuˈrückführen (auf *acc.*); **5.** zuordnen, -weisen (**to** *e-r Klasse etc.*); **II** *v/i.* **6.** (**to**) verweisen, hinweisen, sich beziehen, Bezug haben (auf *acc.*), betreffen (*acc.*): **~ to s.th. briefly** et. kurz berühren; **~ring to my letter** Bezug nehmend auf mein Schreiben; **the point ~red to** der erwähnte *od.* betreffende Punkt; **7.** sich beziehen *od.* berufen, Bezug nehmen (**to** auf *j-n*); **8.** (**to**) sich wenden (an *acc.*), (*a. Uhr, Wörterbuch etc.*) befragen; (in *e-m Buch*) nachschlagen, -sehen; **ref·er·a·ble** [rɪˈfɜːrəbl] *adj.* **1.** (**to**) zuzuschreiben(d) (*dat.*), zuˈrückführen(d) (auf *acc.*); **2.** (**to**) zu beziehen(d) (auf *acc.*), bezüglich (*gen.*); **ref·er·ee** [ˌrefəˈriː] **I** *s.* **1.** ⚖, *sport* Schiedsrichter *m*, ⚖ *a.* beauftragter Richter; *Boxen*: Ringrichter *m*; **2.** *parl. etc.* Refeˈrent *m*, Berichterstatter *m*; **3.** ⚖ *etc.* Sachbearbeiter(in), -verständige(r *m*) *f*; **II** *v/i. u. v/t.* **4.** als Schiedsrichter *etc.* fungieren (bei); **ref·er·ence** [ˈrefrəns] **I** *s.* **1.** Verweis(ung *f*) *m*, Hinweis *m* (**to** auf *acc.*): **cross-~** Querverweis: (**list of**) **~s** Quellenangabe *f*, Literaturverzeichnis *n*; **mark of ~** → 2 a *u.* 4; **2.** a) Verweiszeichen *n*, b) Verweisstelle *f*, c) Beleg *m*, ˈUnterlage *f*; **3.** Bezugnahme *f* (**to** auf *acc.*); *Patentrecht*: Entgegenhaltung *f*: **in** (*od.* **with**) **~ to** bezüglich (*gen.*); **for future ~** zu späterer Verwendung; **terms of ~** Richtlinien; **have ~ to** sich beziehen auf (*acc.*); **4.** *a.* **~ number** Akten-, Geschäftszeichen *n*; **5.** (**to**) Anspielung *f* (auf *acc.*), Erwähnung *f* (*gen.*): **make ~ to** auf *et.* anspielen, *et.* erwähnen; **6.** (**to**) Zs.-hang *m* (mit), Beziehung *f* (zu): **have no ~ to** nichts zu tun haben mit; **with ~ to him** was ihn betrifft; **7.** Rücksicht *f* (**to** auf *acc.*): **without ~ to** ohne Berücksichtigung (*gen.*); **8.** (**to**) Nachschlagen *n*, -sehen *n* (in *dat.*), Befragen *n* (*gen.*): **book** (*od.* **work**) **of ~** Nachschlagewerk *n*; **~ library** Handbibliothek *f*; **9.** (**to**) Befragung *f* (*gen.*), Rückfrage *f* (bei); **10.** ⚖ Überˈweisung *f e-r Sache* (**to** an *ein Schiedsgericht etc.*); **11.** a) Refeˈrenz *f*, Empfehlung *f*, *allg.* Zeugnis *n*, b) Refeˈrenz *f* (*Auskunftgeber*); **II** *adj.* **12.** ⚙, ⩓ Bezugs…: **~ frequency**; **~ value**; **III** *v/t.* **13.** Verweise anbringen in *e-m Buch*; **ref·er·en·dum** [ˌrefəˈrendəm] *pl.* **-dums** *s. pol.* Volksentscheid *m*, -befragung *f*, Refeˈrendum *n*.
re·fill [ˌriːˈfɪl] **I** *v/t.* wieder füllen, nach-, auffüllen; **II** *v/i.* sich wieder füllen; **III** *s.* [ˈriːfɪl] Nach-, Ersatzfüllung *f*; ⚡ Erˈsatzbatteˌrie *f*; Ersatzmine *f* (*Bleistift etc.*); Einlage *f* (*Ringbuch*).
re·fine [rɪˈfaɪn] **I** *v/t.* **1.** ⚙ veredeln, raffinieren, *bsd.* a) *Eisen* frischen, b) *Metall* feinen, c) *Stahl* gar machen, d) *Glas* läutern, e) *Petroleum, Zucker* raffinieren; **2.** *fig.* bilden, verfeinern, kultivieren; **3.** *fig.* läutern, vergeistigen; **II** *v/i.* **4.** sich läutern; **5.** sich verfeinern *od.* kultivieren; **6.** (herˈum)tüfteln ([**up**]**on** an *dat.*); **7.** **~** (**up**)**on** verbessern, weiterentwickeln; **reˈfined** [-nd] *adj.* ☐ **1.** geläutert, raffiniert: **~ sugar** Feinzucker *m*, Raffinade *f*; **~ steel** Raffinierstahl *m*; **2.** *fig.* fein, gebildet, kultiviert; **3.** *fig.* raffiniert, subˈtil; **4.** (ˈüber)fein, (-)genau; **reˈfine·ment** [-mənt] *s.* **1.** ⚙ Veredelung *f*, Vergütungs-, Raffinaˈtionsbehandlung *f*; **2.** Verfeinerung *f*; **3.** Feinheit *f der Sprache, e-r Konstruktion etc.*, Raffiˈnesse *f* (*des Luxus etc.*); **4.** Vornehm-, Feinheit *f*, Kultiviertheit *f*, gebildetes Wesen; **5.** Klügeˈlei *f*, Spitzfindigkeit *f*; **reˈfin·er** [-nə] *s.* **1.** ⚙ a) (Eisen)Frischer *m*, b) Raffiˈneur *m*, (Zucker)Sieder *m*, c) *metall.* Vorfrischofen *m*; **2.** Verfeinerer *m*; **3.** Klügler (-in), Haarspalter(in); **reˈfin·er·y** [-nərɪ] *s.* ⚙ **1.** (*Öl-, Zucker- etc.*)Raffineˈrie *f*; **2.** *metall.* (Eisen-, Frisch)Hütte *f*; **reˈfin·ing fur·nace** [-nɪŋ] *s. metall.* Frisch-, Feinofen *m*.
re·fit [ˌriːˈfɪt] **I** *v/t.* **1.** wieder inˈstand setzen, ausbessern; **2.** neu ausrüsten; **II** *v/i.* **3.** ausgebessert *od.* überˈholt werden; **III** *s.* **4.** *a.* **re·fit·ment** [rɪˈfɪtmənt] Wiederinˈstandsetzung *f*, Ausbesserung *f*.
re·fla·tion [riːˈfleɪʃn] *s.* † Reflatiˈon *f*.
re·flect [rɪˈflekt] **I** *v/t.* **1.** *Strahlen etc.* reflektieren, zuˈrückwerfen, -strahlen: **~ing power** Reflexionsvermögen *n*; **2.** *Bild etc.* (ˈwider)spiegeln: **~ing telescope** Spiegelteleskop *n*; **3.** *fig.* (ˈwider)spiegeln, zeigen: **be ~ed in** sich (wider)spiegeln in (*dat.*); **~ credit on s.o.** j-m Ehre machen; **our prices ~ your commission** † unsere Preise enthalten Ihre Provision; **4.** überˈlegen (**that** daß, **how** wie); **II** *v/i.* **5.** ([**up**]**on**) nachdenken, -sinnen (über *acc.*), (*et.*) überˈlegen; **6.** **~** (**up**)**on** a) sich abfällig äußern über (*acc.*), *et.* herˈabsetzen, b) ein schlechtes Licht werfen auf (*acc.*), *j-m* nicht gerade zur Ehre gereichen, c) *et.* ungünstig beeinflussen; **reˈflec·tion** [-kʃn] *s.* **1.** *phys.* Reflexiˈon *f*, Zuˈrückstrahlung *f*; **2.** (ˈWider)Spiegelung *f* (*a. fig.*); Reˈflex *m*, ˈWiderschein *m*: **a faint ~ of** *fig.* ein schwacher Abglanz (*gen.*); **3.** Spiegelbild *n*; **4.** *fig.* Nachwirkung *f*, Einfluß *m*; **5.** a) Überˈlegung *f*, Erwägung *f*, b) Betrachtung *f*, Gedanke *m* (**on** über *acc.*): **on ~** nach einigem Nachdenken; **6.** abfällige Bemerkung (**on** über *acc.*), Anwurf *m*: **cast ~s upon** herabsetzen, in ein schlechtes Licht setzen; **7.** *anat.* a) Zuˈrückbiegung *f*, b) zuˈrückgebogener Teil; **8.** *physiol.* Reˈflex *m*; **reˈflec·tive** [-tɪv] *adj.* ☐ **1.** reflektierend, zuˈrückstrahlend; **2.** nachdenklich; **reˈflec·tor** [-tə] *s.* **1.** Reˈflektor *m*; **2.** Spiegel *m*; **3.** *mot. etc.* Rückstrahler *m*; Katzenauge *n* (*Fahrrad etc.*); **4.** Scheinwerfer *m*; **re·flex** [ˈriːfleks] **I** *s.* **1.** *physiol.* Reˈflex *m*: **~ action** (*od.* **movement**) Reflexbewegung *f*; **2.** (ˈLicht)Reˌflex *m*, ˈWiderschein *m*; *fig.* Abglanz *m*: **~ camera** (Spiegel)Reflexkamera *f*; **3.** Spiegelbild *n* (*a. fig.*); **II** *adj.* **4.** zuˈrückgebogen; **5.** Reflex…, Rück…; **re·flex·i·ble** [rɪˈfleksəbl] *adj.* reflektierbar; **re·flex·ion** [rɪˈflekʃn] *s.* → **reflection**; **re·flex·ive** [rɪˈfleksɪv] **I** *adj.* ☐ **1.** zuˈrückwirkend; **2.** *ling.* refleˈxiv, rückbezüglich, Reflexiv…; **II** *s.* **3.** *ling.* a) rückbezügliches Fürwort *od.* Zeitwort, b) reflexive Form.
re·float [ˌriːˈfləʊt] ⚓ **I** *v/t.* wieder flottmachen; **II** *v/i.* wieder flott werden.
re·flux [ˈriːflʌks] *s.* Zuˈrückfließen *n*, Rückfluß *m* (*a.* † *von Kapital*).
re·for·est [ˌriːˈfɒrɪst] *v/t. Land* aufforsten.
re·form¹ [rɪˈfɔːm] **I** *s.* **1.** *pol. etc.* Reˈform *f*, Verbesserung *f*; **2.** Besserung *f*: **~ school** Besserungsanstalt *f*; **II** *v/t.* **3.** reformieren, verbessern; **4.** *j-n* bessern; **5.** *Mißstand etc.* beseitigen; **6.** ⚖ *Am. Urkunde* berichtigen; **III** *v/i.* **7.** sich bessern.
re·form², re-form [ˌriːˈfɔːm] **I** *v/t.* ˈumformen, -gestalten, -bilden, neu gestalten; **II** *v/i.* sich ˈumformen, sich neu gestalten.
ref·or·ma·tion¹ [ˌrefəˈmeɪʃn] *s.* **1.** Reformierung *f*, Verbesserung *f*; **2.** Besserung *f des Lebenswandels etc.*; **3.** ♀ *eccl.* Reformatiˈon *f*; **4.** ⚖ *Am.* Berichtigung *f e-r Urkunde*.
re·for·ma·tion², re-for·ma·tion [ˌriːfɔːˈmeɪʃn] *s.* ˈUmbildung *f*, ˈUm-, Neuge-

staltung *f*.

re·form·a·to·ry [rɪˈfɔːmətərɪ] **I** *adj.* **1.** Besserungs...: **~ *measures*** Besserungsmaßnahmen; **2.** Reform...; **II** *s.* **3.** Besserungsanstalt *f*; **reˈformed** [-md] *adj.* **1.** verbessert, neu u. besser gestaltet; **2.** gebessert: **~ *drunkard*** geheilter Trinker; **3.** ♀ *eccl.* reformiert; **reˈform·er** [-mə] *s.* **1.** *bsd. eccl.* Reforˈmator *m*; **2.** *pol.* Reˈformer(in); **reˈform·ist** [-mɪst] *s.* **1.** *eccl.* Reformierte(r *m*) *f*; **2.** → ***reformer***.

re·fract [rɪˈfrækt] *v/t. phys. Strahlen* brechen; **reˈfract·ing** [-tɪŋ] *adj. phys.* lichtbrechend, Brechungs..., Refraktions...: **~ *angle*** Brechungswinkel *m*; **~ *telescope*** Refraktor *m*; **reˈfrac·tion** [-kʃn] *s. phys.* **1.** (*Licht-*, *Strahlen*)Brechung *f*, Refraktiˈon *f*; **2.** *opt.* Brechungskraft *f*; **reˈfrac·tive** [-tɪv] *adj. phys.* Brechungs..., Refraktions...; **reˈfrac·tor** [-tə] *s. phys.* **1.** Lichtbrechungskörper *m*; **2.** Reˈfraktor *m*; **reˈfrac·to·ri·ness** [-tərɪnɪs] *s.* **1.** ˈWiderspenstigkeit *f*; **2.** ˈWiderstandskraft *f*, *bsd.* a) ⚗ Strengflüssigkeit *f*, b) ⚙ Feuerfestigkeit *f*; **3.** ⚕ a) ˈWiderstandsfähigkeit *f gegen Krankheiten*, b) Hartnäckigkeit *f e-r Krankheit*; **reˈfrac·to·ry** [-tərɪ] **I** *adj.* **1.** ˈwiderspenstig, aufsässig; **2.** ⚗ strengflüssig; **3.** ⚙ feuerfest: **~ *clay*** Schamotte(ton *m*) *f*; **4.** ⚕ a) ˈwiderstandsfähig (*Person*), b) hartnäckig (*Krankheit*); **II** *s.* **5.** ⚙ feuerfester Baustoff.

re·frain¹ [rɪˈfreɪn] *v/i.* (***from***) Abstand nehmen *od.* absehen (von), sich (*gen.*) enthalten: **~ *from doing s.th.*** et. unterlassen, es unterlassen, et. zu tun.

re·frain² [rɪˈfreɪn] *s.* Reˈfrain *m*.

re·fran·gi·ble [rɪˈfrændʒɪbl] *adj. phys.* brechbar.

re·fresh [rɪˈfreʃ] **I** *v/t.* **1.** erfrischen, erquicken (*a. fig.*); **2.** *fig. sein Gedächtnis* auffrischen; *Vorrat etc.* erneuern; **II** *v/i.* **3.** sich erfrischen; **4.** frische Vorräte fassen (*Schiff etc.*); **reˈfresh·er** [-ʃə] *s.* **1.** Erfrischung *f*; ‚Gläs-chen' *n* (*Trunk*); **2.** *fig.* Auffrischung *f*: **~ *course*** Auffrischungs-, Wiederholungskurs *m*; ***paint* ~** Neuglanzpolitur *f*; **3.** ⚖ ˈNachschuß (-honoˌrar *n*) *m e-s Anwalts*; **reˈfresh·ing** [-ʃɪŋ] *adj.* □ erfrischend (*a. fig. wohltuend*); **reˈfresh·ment** [-mənt] *s.* Erfrischung *f* (*a. Getränk etc.*): **~ *room*** (Bahnhofs)Büfett *n*.

re·frig·er·ant [rɪˈfrɪdʒərənt] **I** *adj.* **1.** kühlend, Kühl...; **II** *s.* **2.** ⚕ kühlendes Mittel, Kühltrank *m*; **3.** ⚙ Kühlmittel *n*; **re·frig·er·ate** [rɪˈfrɪdʒəreɪt] *v/t.* ⚙ kühlen; **reˈfrig·er·at·ing** [-reɪtɪŋ] *adj.* ⚙ Kühl...(*-raum etc.*), Kälte...(*-maschine etc.*); **re·frig·er·a·tion** [rɪˌfrɪdʒəˈreɪʃn] *s.* Kühlung *f*; Kälteerzeugung *f*, -technik *f*; **reˈfrig·er·a·tor** [-reɪtə] *s.* ⚙ Kühlschrank *m*, -raum *m*, -anlage *f*; ˈKältemaˌschine *f*: **~ *van Brit.***, **~ *car Am.*** 🚃 Kühlwagen *m*; **~ *van od. lorry Brit.***, **~ *truck Am. mot.*** Kühlwagen *m*; **~ *vessel*** ⚓ Kühlschiff *n*.

re·fu·el [ˌriːˈfjʊəl] *v/t. u. v/i. mot.*, ✈ (auf)tanken.

ref·uge [ˈrefjuːdʒ] **I** *s.* **1.** Zuflucht *f* (*a. fig. Ausweg*, *a. Person*, *Gott*), Schutz *m* (***from*** vor): ***seek*** (*od.* ***take***) **~ *in fig.*** s-e Zuflucht suchen in *od.* nehmen zu; ***house of* ~** Obdachlosenasyl *n*; **2.** Zuflucht *f*, Zufluchtsort *m*; **3.** *a.* **~ *hut mount.*** Schutzhütte *f*; **4.** Verkehrsinsel *f*; **II** *v/i.* **5.** Schutz suchen; **ref·u·gee** [ˌrefjʊˈdʒiː] *s.* Flüchtling *m*: **~ *camp*** Flüchtlingslager *n*.

re·ful·gent [rɪˈfʌldʒənt] *adj.* □ glänzend, strahlend.

re·fund¹ **I** *v/t.* [riːˈfʌnd] **1.** *Geld* zuˈrückzahlen, -erstatten, *Verlust*, *Auslagen* ersetzen, rückvergüten; **2.** *j-m* Rückzahlung leisten, *j-m* seine Auslagen ersetzen; **II** *s.* [ˈriːfʌnd] **3.** Rückvergütung *f*.

re·fund² [ˌriːˈfʌnd] *v/t.* ✝ *Anleihe etc.* neu fundieren.

re·fund·ment [rɪˈfʌndmənt] *s.* Rückvergütung *f*.

re·fur·bish [ˌriːˈfɜːbɪʃ] *v/t.* ˈaufpoˌlieren (*a. fig.*).

re·fur·nish [ˌriːˈfɜːnɪʃ] *v/t.* wieder *od.* neu möblieren *od.* ausstatten.

re·fu·sal [rɪˈfjuːzl] *s.* **1.** Ablehnung *f*, Zuˈrückweisung *f e-s Angebots etc.*; **2.** Verweigerung *f e-r Bitte*, *des Gehorsams etc.*, *a. Reitsport*; **3.** abschlägige Antwort: ***he will take no* ~** er läßt sich nicht abweisen; **4.** Weigerung *f* (***to do s.th.*** et. zu tun); **5.** ✝ Vorkaufsrecht *n*, Vorhand *f*: ***first* ~ *of*** erstes Anrecht auf (*acc.*); ***give s.o. the* ~ *of s.th.*** j-m das Vorkaufsrecht auf e-e Sache einräumen.

re·fuse¹ [rɪˈfjuːz] **I** *v/t.* **1.** *Amt*, *Antrag*, *Kandidaten etc.* ablehnen; *Angebot* ausschlagen; *et. od. j-n* zuˈrückweisen; *j-n* abweisen; *j-m e-e Bitte* abschlagen; **2.** *Befehl*, *Forderung*, *Gehorsam* verweigern; *Bitte* abschlagen; **3.** *Kartenspiel*: *Farbe* verweigern; **4.** *Hindernis* verweigern, scheuen vor (*dat.*) (*Pferd*); **II** *v/i.* **5.** sich weigern, es ablehnen (***to do*** zu tun): ***he* ~*d to believe it*** er wollte es einfach nicht glauben; ***he* ~*d to be bullied*** er ließ sich nicht tyrannisieren; ***it* ~*d to work*** es wollte nicht funktionieren, es ‚streikte'; **6.** absagen (*Gast*); **7.** scheuen (*Pferd*).

ref·use² [ˈrefjuːs] **I** *s.* **1.** ⚙ Abfall *m*, Ausschuß *m*; **2.** (Küchen)Abfall *m*, Müll *m*; **II** *adj.* **3.** wertlos; **4.** Abfall..., Müll...

ref·u·ta·ble [ˈrefjʊtəbl] *adj.* □ widerˈlegbar; **ref·u·ta·tion** [ˌrefjuːˈteɪʃn] *s.* Widerˈlegung *f*; **re·fute** [rɪˈfjuːt] *v/t.* widerˈlegen.

re·gain [rɪˈgeɪn] *v/t.* ˈwiedergewinnen; *a. Bewußtsein etc.* ˈwiedererlangen: **~ *one's feet*** wieder auf die Beine kommen; **~ *the shore*** den Strand wiedergewinnen (*erreichen*).

re·gal [ˈriːgl] *adj.* □ königlich (*a. fig. prächtig*); Königs...

re·gale [rɪˈgeɪl] **I** *v/t.* **1.** erfreuen, ergötzen; **2.** festlich bewirten: **~ *o.s. on*** sich laben an (*dat.*); **II** *v/i.* **3.** (***on***) schwelgen (in *dat.*), sich gütlich tun (an *dat.*).

re·ga·li·a [rɪˈgeɪljə] *s. pl.* (ˈKrönungs-, ˈAmts)Inˌsignien *pl.*

re·gard [rɪˈgɑːd] **I** *v/t.* **1.** ansehen; betrachten (*a. fig.* ***with*** mit *Abneigung etc.*); **2.** *fig.* **~ *as*** betrachten als, halten für: ***be* ~*ed as*** gelten als *od.* für; **3.** *fig.* beachten, berücksichtigen; **4.** respektieren; **5.** achten, (hoch)schätzen; **6.** betreffen, angehen: ***as* ~*s*** was ... betrifft; **II** *s.* **7.** (*fester od. bedeutsamer*) Blick; **8.** Hinblick *m*, -sicht *f* (***to*** auf *acc.*): ***in this* ~** in dieser Hinsicht; ***in* ~ *to*** (*od.* ***of***), ***with* ~ *to*** hinsichtlich, bezüglich, was ... betrifft; ***have* ~ *to*** a) sich beziehen auf (*acc.*), b) in Betracht ziehen; **9.** (***to***, ***for***) Rücksicht(nahme) *f* (auf *acc.*), Beachtung *f* (*gen.*): ***pay no* ~ *to s.th.*** sich um et. nicht kümmern; ***without* ~ *to*** (*od.* ***for***) ohne Rücksicht auf (*acc.*); ***have no* ~ *for s.o.'s feelings*** auf j-s Gefühle keine Rücksicht nehmen; **10.** (Hoch)Achtung *f* (***for*** vor *dat.*); **11.** *pl.* Grüße *pl.*, Empfehlungen *pl.*: ***with kind* ~*s to*** mit herzlichen Grüßen an (*acc.*); ***give him my*** (***best***) **~*s*** grüße ihn (herzlich) von mir; **reˈgard·ful** [-fʊl] *adj.* □ **1.** achtsam, aufmerksam (***of*** auf *acc.*); **2.** rücksichtsvoll (***of*** gegen); **reˈgard·ing** [-dɪŋ] *prp.* bezüglich, betreffs, hinsichtlich (*gen.*); **reˈgard·less** [-lɪs] **I** *adj.* □ **1.** **~ *of*** ungeachtet (*gen.*), ohne Rücksicht auf (*acc.*); **2.** rücksichts-, achtlos; **II** *adv.* **3.** F trotzdem, dennoch; ganz gleich, was passiert *od.* passieren würde; ohne Rücksicht auf Kosten *etc.*

re·gat·ta [rɪˈgætə] *s.* Reˈgatta *f*.

re·gen·cy [ˈriːdʒənsɪ] *s.* **1.** Reˈgentschaft *f* (*Amt*, *Gebiet*, *Periode*); **2.** ♀ *hist.* Regentschaft(szeit) *f*, *bsd.* a) Réˈgence *f* (*in Frankreich*, *des Herzogs Philipp von Orléans* [*1715–23*]), b) *in England* (*1811–30*), *von Georg*, *Prinz von Wales* (*später Georg IV.*).

re·gen·er·ate [rɪˈdʒenəreɪt] **I** *v/t. u. v/i.* **1.** (sich) regenerieren (*a. biol.*, *phys.*, ⚙) (sich) erneuern, (sich) neu *od.* wieder bilden; (sich) wieder erzeugen: ***to be* ~*d eccl.*** wiedergeboren werden; **2.** *fig.* (sich) bessern *od.* reformieren; **3.** *fig.* (sich) neu beleben; **4.** ⚡ rückkoppeln; **II** *adj.* [-rət] **5.** ge- *od.* verbessert, reformiert; ˈwiedergeboren; **re·gen·er·a·tion** [rɪˌdʒenəˈreɪʃn] *s.* **1.** Regeneratiˈon *f* (*a. biol.*), Erneuerung *f*; **2.** *eccl.* ˈWiedergeburt *f*; **3.** Besserung *f*; **4.** ⚡ Rückkopplung *f*; **5.** ⚙ Regenerierung *f*, ˈWiedergewinnung *f*; **reˈgen·er·a·tive** [-nərətɪv] *adj.* □ **1.** (ver)bessernd; **2.** neuschaffend; **3.** Erneuerungs..., Verjüngungs...; **4.** ⚡ Rückkopplungs...

re·gent [ˈriːdʒənt] *s.* **1.** Reˈgent(in): ***Queen* ♀** Regentin *f*; ***Prince* ♀** Prinzregent *m*; **2.** *univ. Am.* Mitglied *n* des ˈAufsichtskomiˌtees; **ˈre·gent·ship** [-ʃɪp] *s.* Reˈgentschaft *f*.

reg·i·cide [ˈredʒɪsaɪd] *s.* **1.** Königsmörder *m*; **2.** Königsmord *m*.

re·gime, *a.* **ré·gime** [reɪˈʒiːm] *s.* **1.** *pol.* Reˈgime *n*, Regierungsform *f*; **2.** (vor-)herrschendes Syˈstem: ***matrimonial* ~** ⚖ eheliches Güterrecht; **3.** → ***regimen*** 1.

reg·i·men [ˈredʒɪmən] *s.* **1.** ⚕ gesunde Lebensweise, *bsd.* Diˈät *f*; **2.** Regierung *f*, Herrschaft *f*; **3.** *ling.* Rektiˈon *f*.

reg·i·ment **I** *s.* [ˈredʒɪmənt] **1.** ⚔ Regiˈment *n*; **2.** *fig.* (große) Schar; **II** *v/t.* [ˈredʒɪment] **3.** *fig.* reglementieren, bevormunden; **4.** organisieren, systeˈmatisch einteilen.

reg·i·men·tal [ˌredʒɪˈmentl] *adj.* □ Regiments...: **~ *officer Brit.*** Truppenoffizier *m*; **reg·i·men·tals** [ˌredʒɪˈmentlz] *s. pl.* ⚔ (Regiˈments)Uniˌform *f*; **reg·i·men·ta·tion** [ˌredʒɪmenˈteɪʃn] *s.* **1.** Organisierung *f*, Einteilung *f*; **2.** Reglementierung *f*, Diriˈgismus *m*, Bevormundung *f.*

Re·gi·na [rɪˈdʒaɪnə] (*Lat.*) *s. Brit.* ⚖ *die* Königin; *weitS. die* Krone, *der* Staat: ~ *versus John Doe*.

re·gion [ˈriːdʒən] *s.* **1.** Gebiet *n* (*a. meteor.*), (*a.* ✱ *Körper*)Gegend *f*, (*a. Höhen-, Tiefen*)Regiˈon *f*, Landstrich *m*; (Verwaltungs)Bezirk *m*; **2.** *fig.* Gebiet *n*, Bereich *m*, Sphäre *f*; (*a. himmlische etc.*) Regiˈon: *in the ~ of* von ungefähr …; ˈ**re·gion·al** [-dʒənl] *adj.* □ regioˈnal; örtlich, loˈkal (*beide a.* ✱); Orts…; Bezirks…: ~ (***station***) *Radio*: Regioˈnalsender *m*; ˈ**re·gion·al·ism** [-dʒənəlɪzəm] *s.* **1.** Regionaˈlismus *m*, Loˈkalpatriotismus *m*; **2.** Heimatkunst *f*; **3.** *ling.* nur regioˈnal gebrauchter Ausdruck.

reg·is·ter [ˈredʒɪstə] **I** *s.* **1.** Reˈgister *n* (*a. Computer*), (Eintragungs)Buch *n*, (*a.* Inhalts)Verzeichnis *n*; (*Wähler- etc.*)Liste *f*: ~ ***of births, marriages, and deaths*** Personenstandsregister; ~ ***of companies*** Handelsregister; (***ship's***) ~ Schiffsregister; ~ ***ton*** ⚓ Registertonne *f*; **2.** ⚙ a) Registriervorrichtung *f*, Zählwerk *n*: ***cash*** ~ Registrier-, Kontrollkasse *f*, b) Schieber *m*, Klappe *f*, Venˈtil *n*; **3.** ♪ a) (ˈOrgel)Reˌgister *n*, b) Stimm-, Tonlage *f*, c) ˈStimmˌumfang *m*; **4.** *typ.* Reˈgister *n*; **5.** *phot.* genaue Einstellung; **6.** → ***registrar***; **II** *v/t.* **7.** registrieren, (in ein Register *etc.*) eintragen *od.* -schreiben (lassen), anmelden (***for school*** zur Schule); *weitS.* amtlich erfassen; (*a. fig. Erfolg etc.*) verzeichnen, -buchen: ~ ***a company*** e-e Firma handelsgerichtlich eintragen; **8.** ✝ *Warenzeichen* anmelden; *Artikel* gesetzlich schützen; **9.** *Postsachen* einschreiben (lassen); *Gepäck* aufgeben; **10.** ⚙ *Meßwerte* registrieren, anzeigen; **11.** *fig. Empfindung* zeigen, ausdrükken, registrieren; **12.** *typ.* in das Reˈgister bringen; **13.** ⚔ *Geschütz* einschießen; **III** *v/i.* **14.** sich (in das Hoˈtelreˌgister, in die Wählerliste *etc.*) eintragen (lassen); *univ. etc.* sich einschreiben (***for*** für); **15.** sich (an)melden (***at, with*** bei *der Polizei etc.*); **16.** *typ.* Reˈgister halten; **17.** ⚙ a) sich decken, genau passen, b) einrasten; **18.** ♪ registrieren; **19.** ⚔ sich einschießen; ˈ**reg·is·tered** [-əd] *adj.* **1.** eingetragen (✝ *Geschäftssitz, Gesellschaft, Warenzeichen*); **2.** ✝ gesetzlich geschützt: ~ ***design*** (*od.* ***pattern***) Gebrauchsmuster *n*; **3.** ✝ registriert, Namens…: ~ ***bonds*** Namensschuldverschreibungen; ~ ***capital*** autorisiertes (Aktien)Kapital; ~ ***share*** (*Am.* ***stock***) Namensaktie *f*; **4.** ✉ eingeschrieben, Einschreibe…(*-brief etc.*): ~***!*** Einschreiben!; **reg·is·trar** [ˌredʒɪˈstrɑː] *s.* Regiˈstrator *m*, Archiˈvar(in), Urkundsbeamte(r) *m*; *Brit.* Standesbeamte(r) *m*; ✱ *Brit.* Krankenhausarzt *m*, -ärztin *f*: ~***'s office*** a) Standesamt *n*, b) Registratur *f*; ***2-General*** *Brit.* oberster Standesbeamter; ~ ***in bankruptcy*** ⚖ *Brit.* Konkursrichter *m*; **reg·is·tra·tion** [ˌredʒɪˈstreɪʃn] *s.* **1.** (*bsd.* amtliche) Registrierung, Erfassung *f*; Eintragung *f* (*a.* ✝ *e-r Gesellschaft, e-s Warenzeichens*); *mot.* Zulassung *f e-s Fahrzeugs*; **2.** (*polizeiliche, a. Hotel-, Schul- etc.*) Anmeldung, Einschreibung *f*: ***compulsory*** ~ (An)Meldepflicht *f*; ~ ***fee*** Anmelde-, Einschreibgebühr *f*; ✝ Umschreibungsgebühr *f* (*Aktien*); ~ ***form*** (An)Meldeformular *n*; ~ ***office*** Meldestelle *f*, Einwohnermeldeamt *n*; **3.** Zahl *f* der Erfaßten, registrierte Zahl; **4.** ✉ Einschreibung *f*; **5.** *a.* ~ ***of luggage*** *bsd. Brit.* Gepäckaufgabe *f*: ~ ***window*** Gepäckschalter *m*; ˈ**reg·is·try** [-trɪ] *s.* **1.** Registrierung *f* (*a. e-s Schiffs*): ~ ***fee*** *Am.* Anmelde-, Einschreibegebühr *f*; ***port of*** ~ ⚓ Registerhafen *m*; **2.** Reˈgister *n*; **3.** *a.* ~ ***office*** a) Registraˈtur *f*, b) Standesamt *n*, c) ˈStellenverˌmittlungsbüˌro *n*.

reg·let [ˈreglɪt] *s.* **1.** ⌂ Leistchen *n*; **2.** *typ.* a) Reˈglette *f*, b) (ˈZeilen)ˌDurchschuß *m*.

reg·nant [ˈregnənt] *adj.* regierend; *fig.* (vor)herrschend.

re·gress I *v/i.* [rɪˈgres] **1.** sich rückwärts bewegen; **2.** *fig.* a) sich rückläufig entwickeln, b) *biol., psych.* sich zuˈrückbilden *od.* -entwickeln; **II** *s.* [ˈriːgres] **3.** Rückwärtsbewegung *f*; **4.** rückläufige Entwicklung; **reˈgres·sion** [-eʃn] *s.* **1.** → ***regress*** II; **2.** Regressiˈon *f*: a) *biol. psych.* Rückentwicklung *f*, b) ⚗ Beziehung *f*; **reˈgres·sive** [-sɪv] *adj.* □ **1.** rückläufig; **2.** rückwirkend (*Steuer etc., a. ling. Akzent*); **3.** *biol.* regresˈsiv.

re·gret [rɪˈgret] **I** *s.* **1.** Bedauern *n* (***at*** über *acc.*): ***to my*** ~ zu m-m Bedauern, leider; **2.** Reue *f*; **3.** Schmerz *m*, Trauer *f* (***for*** um); **II** *v/t.* **4.** bedauern, bereuen: ***it is to be ~ted*** es ist bedauerlich; ***I ~ to say*** ich muß leider sagen; **5.** *Vergangenes etc., a. Tote* beklagen, trauern um, *j-m od. e-r Sache* nachtrauern; **reˈgret·ful** [-fʊl] *adj.* □ bedauernd, reue-, kummervoll; **reˈgret·ta·ble** [-təbl] *adj.* □ **1.** bedauerlich; **2.** bedauernswert, zu bedauern(d); **reˈgret·ta·bly** [-təblɪ] *adv.* bedauerlicherweise.

re·grind [ˌriːˈgraɪnd] *v/t.* [*irr.* → ***grind***] ⚙ nachschleifen.

re·group [ˌriːˈgruːp] *v/t.* ˈum-, neugruppieren, (*a.* ✝ *Kapital*) ˈumschichten; **reˈgroup·ment** [-mənt] *s.* ˈUmgrupˌpierung *f*.

reg·u·lar [ˈregjʊlə] **I** *adj.* □ **1.** *zeitlich* regelmäßig; 🚂 *etc.* fahrplanmäßig: ~ ***air service*** regelmäßige Flugverbindung; ~ ***business*** ✝ laufende Geschäfte; ~ ***customer*** → 14; ***at ~ intervals*** in regelmäßigen Abständen; **2.** regelmäßig (*in Form od. Anordnung*), ebenmäßig; symˈmetrisch; **3.** regelmäßig, geregelt, geordnet (*Lebensweise etc.*); **4.** pünktlich, genau; **5.** reguˈlär, norˈmal, gewohnt; **6.** richtig, geprüft, gelernt: ***a ~ cook***; ~ ***doctor*** approbierter Arzt; **7.** richtig, vorschriftsmäßig, formgerecht; **8.** F ‚richtig(gehend)': ~ ***rascal***; ***a ~ guy*** *Am.* ein Pfundskerl; **9.** ⚔ a) reguˈlär (*Kampftruppe*), b) Berufs…, akˈtiv (*Heer, Soldat*); **10.** *sport*: Stamm…: ~ ***player***; ***make the ~ team*** sich e-n Stammplatz (*in der Mannschaft*) erobern; *eccl.* Ordens…; **II** *s.* **11.** Ordensgeistliche(r) *m*; **12.** ⚔ akˈtiver Solˈdat, Beˈrufssolˌdat *m*; *pl.* reguˈläre Truppen *pl.*; **13.** *pol. Am.* treuer Parˈteianhänger; **14.** F Stammkunde *m*, -kundin *f*, -gast *m*; **reg·u·lar·i·ty** [ˌregjʊˈlærətɪ] *s.* **1.** Regelmäßigkeit *f*: a) Gleichmäßigkeit *f*, Stetigkeit *f*, b) regelmäßige Form; **2.** Ordnung *f*, Richtigkeit *f*; ˈ**reg·u·lar·ize** [-əraɪz] *v/t.* regeln, festlegen.

reg·u·late [ˈregjʊleɪt] *v/t.* **1.** *Geschäft, Verdauung, Verkehr etc.* regeln; ordnen; (*a.* ✝ *Wirtschaft*) lenken; **2.** ⚖ (gesetzlich) regeln; **3.** ⚙ a) *Geschwindigkeit etc.* regulieren, regeln, b) *Gerät, Uhr* (ein)stellen; **4.** anpassen (***according to*** an *acc.*); ˈ**reg·u·lat·ing** [-tɪŋ] *adj.* ⚙ Regulier…, (Ein)Stell…: ~ ***screw*** Stellschraube *f*; ~ ***switch*** Regelschalter *m*; **reg·u·la·tion** [ˌregjʊˈleɪʃn] **I** *s.* **1.** Regelung *f*, Regulierung *f* (*a.* ⚙); ⚙ Einstellung *f*; **2.** Verfügung *f*, (Ausführungs)Verordnung *f*; *pl.* a) ˈDurchführungsbestimmungen *pl.*, b) Satzung(en *pl.*) *f*, Staˈtuten *pl.*, c) (Dienst-, Betriebs)Vorschrift *f*: ~***s of the works*** Betriebsordnung *f*; ***traffic ~s*** Verkehrsvorschriften; ***according to ~s*** nach Vorschrift, vorschriftsmäßig; ***contrary to ~s*** vorschriftswidrig; **II** *adj.* **3.** vorschriftsmäßig; ⚔ *a.* Dienst…(*-mütze etc.*); ˈ**reg·u·la·tive** [-lətɪv] *adj.* regelnd, regulierend, *a. phls.* regulaˈtiv; ˈ**reg·u·la·tor** [-tə] *s.* **1.** ⚡ Regler *m*; **2.** *Uhrmacherei*: Reguˈlator *m* (*a. Uhr*); **3.** ⚙ Regulier-, Stellvorrichtung *f*: ~ ***valve*** Reglerventil *n*; **4.** ⚘ Reguˈlator *m*; ˈ**reg·u·la·to·ry** [-leɪtərɪ] *adj.* Durch-, Ausführungs…

re·gur·gi·tate [rɪˈgɜːdʒɪteɪt] **I** *v/i.* zuˈrückfließen; **II** *v/t.* wieder ausströmen, -speien; *Essen* erbrechen.

re·ha·bil·i·tate [ˌriːəˈbɪlɪteɪt] *v/t.* **1.** rehabilitieren: a) wiederˈeinsetzen (***in*** in *acc.*), b) *j-s* Ruf wiederˈherstellen, c) *e-n Versehrten* wieder ins Berufsleben eingliedern; **2.** *et. od. j-n* wiederˈherstellen; **3.** ⚖ *Strafentlassenen* resozialisieren; **4.** *Altbauten*, ✝ *e-n Betrieb etc.* sanieren; **re·ha·bil·i·ta·tion** [ˈriːəˌbɪlɪˈteɪʃn] *s.* **1.** Rehabilitierung *f*: a) Wiederˈeinsetzung *f* (*in frühere Rechte*), b) Ehrenrettung *f*, c) *a.* ***vocational*** ~ Wiederˈeingliederung *f* ins Berufsleben: ~ ***centre*** (*Am.* ***center***) Rehabilitationszentrum *n*; **2.** Wiederˈherstellung *f*; ✝ Sanierung *f*: ***industrial*** ~ wirtschaftlicher Wiederaufbau; **3.** *a.* ***social*** ~ ⚖ Resozialisierung *f*.

re·hash [ˈriːhæʃ] **I** *s.* **1.** *fig. et.* Aufgewärmtes, Wiederˈholung *f*, ‚Aufguß' *m*; **2.** Wiederˈaufwärmen *n*; **II** *v/t.* [ˌriːˈhæʃ] **3.** *fig.* wiederˈaufwärmen, ˈwiederkäuen.

re·hear·ing [ˌriːˈhɪərɪŋ] *s.* ⚖ erneute Verhandlung.

re·hears·al [rɪˈhɜːsl] *s.* **1.** *thea.*, ♪ *u. fig.* Probe *f*: ***be in*** ~ einstudiert werden; ***final*** ~ Generalprobe; **2.** Einstudierung *f*; **3.** Wiederˈholung *f*; **4.** Aufsagen *n*, Vortrag *m*; **5.** *fig.* Litaˈnei *f*; **re·hearse** [rɪˈhɜːs] *v/t.* **1.** *thea.*, ♪ *et.* proben (*a. v/i. u. fig.*), *Rolle etc.* einstudieren; **2.** wiederˈholen; **3.** aufzählen; **4.** aufsagen, rezitieren; **5.** *fig. Möglichkeiten etc.* ˈdurchspielen.

reign [reɪn] **I** *s.* **1.** Regierung *f*, Regierungszeit *f*: ***in*** (*od.* ***under***) ***the ~ of*** unter der Regierung (*gen.*); **2.** Herrschaft *f* (*a. fig. der Mode etc.*): ~ ***of law*** Rechtsstaatlichkeit *f*; ***2 of terror*** Schreckensherrschaft; **II** *v/i.* **3.** regieren, herrschen (***over*** über *acc.*); **4.** *fig.* (vor)herrschen: ***silence ~ed*** es herrschte Stille.

re·im·burs·a·ble [ˌriːɪmˈbɜːsəbl] *adj.* rückzahlbar; **re·im·burse** [ˌriːɪmˈbɜːs] *v/t.* **1.** *j-n* entschädigen (**for** für): **~ o.s.** sich entschädigen *od.* schadlos halten; **2.** *et.* zuˈrückzahlen, vergüten, *Auslagen* erstatten, *Kosten* decken; **ˌre·imˈburse·ment** [-mənt] *s.* **1.** Entschädigung *f*; **2.** (ˈWieder)Erstattung *f*, (Rück)Vergütung *f*, (Kosten)Deckung *f*: **~ credit** † Rembourskredit *m*.

re·im·port † **I** *v/t.* [ˌriːɪmˈpɔːt] **1.** wiederˈeinführen; **II** *s.* [ˌriːˈɪmpɔːt] **2.** ˈWiedereinfuhr *f*; **3.** *pl.* wiederˈeingeführte Waren *pl.*

rein [reɪn] **I** *s.* **1.** *oft pl.* Zügel *m mst pl.* (*a. fig.*): **draw ~** (an)halten, zügeln (*a. fig.*); **give a horse the ~(s)** die Zügel locker lassen; **give free ~(s) to** *s-r Phantasie* freien Lauf lassen *od.* die Zügel schießen lassen; **keep a tight ~ on** *j-n* fest an der Kandare haben; **take** (*od.* **assume**) **the ~s of government** die Zügel (der Regierung) in die Hand nehmen; **II** *v/t.* **2.** *Pferd* aufzäumen; **3.** lenken: **to ~ back** (*od.* **in**, **up**) (*a. v/i.*) a) anhalten, b) verhalten; **4.** *a.* **~ in** *fig.* zügeln, im Zaum halten.

re·in·car·na·tion [ˌriːɪnkɑːˈneɪʃn] *s.* Reinkarnatiˈon *f*: a) (Glaube *m* an die) Seelenwanderung *f*, b) ˈWiederverkörperung *f*, -geburt *f*.

rein·deer [ˈreɪnˌdɪə] *pl.* **-deer** *od.* **-deers** *s. zo.* Ren(ntier) *n*.

re·in·force [ˌriːɪnˈfɔːs] **I** *v/t.* **1.** verstärken (*a.* ⚙, *Gewebe etc.*, *a.* ⚔ *u. fig.* ⚙ *Beton* armieren: **~d concrete** Eisen-, Stahlbeton *m*; **2.** *fig. Gesundheit* kräftigen, *Worte* bekräftigen, *Beweis* unterˈmauern; **II** *s.* **3.** ⚙ Verstärkung *f*; **ˌre·inˈforce·ment** [-mənt] *s.* **1.** Verstärkung *f*; Armierung *f* (*Beton*); *pl.* ⚔ Verstärkungstruppen *pl.*; **2.** *fig.* Unterˈmauerung *f*, Bekräftigung *f*.

re·in·stall [ˌriːɪnˈstɔːl] *v/t.* wiederˈeinsetzen; **ˌre·inˈstal(l)·ment** [-mənt] *s.* Wiederˈeinsetzung *f*.

re·in·state [ˌriːɪnˈsteɪt] *v/t.* **1.** *j-n* wiederˈeinsetzen (**in** in *acc.*); **2.** *et.* (wieder) inˈstand setzen; **3.** *j-n od. et.* wiederˈherstellen; *Versicherung etc.* wiederˈaufleben lassen; **ˌre·inˈstate·ment** [-mənt] *s.* **1.** Wiederˈeinsetzung *f*; **2.** Wiederˈherstellung *f*.

re·in·sur·ance [ˌriːɪnˈʃʊərəns] *s.* † Rückversicherung *f*; **re·in·sure** [ˌriːɪnˈʃʊə] *v/t.* **1.** rückversichern; **2.** nachversichern.

re·in·vest·ment [ˌriːɪnˈvestmənt] *s.* † Neu-, ˈWiederanlage *f*.

re·is·sue [ˌriːˈɪʃuː] **I** *v/t.* **1.** *Banknoten etc.* wieder ausgeben; **2.** *Buch* neu herˈausgeben; **II** *s.* **3.** ˈWieder-, Neuausgabe *f*: **~ patent** Abänderungspatent *n*.

re·it·er·ate [riːˈɪtəreɪt] *v/t.* (ständig) wiederˈholen; **re·it·er·a·tion** [riːˌɪtəˈreɪʃn] *s.* Wiederˈholung *f*.

re·ject I *v/t.* [rɪˈdʒekt] **1.** *Antrag, Kandidaten, Lieferung, Verantwortung etc.* ablehnen; *Ersuchen, Freier etc.* ab-, zuˈrückweisen; *Bitte* abschlagen; *et.* verwerfen; *Nahrung* verweigern: **be ~ed** *pol. u. thea.* durchfallen; **2.** (als wertlos) ausscheiden; **3.** *Essen* wieder von sich geben (*Magen*); **4.** ⚕ *körperfremdes Gewebe etc.* abstoßen; **II** *s.* [ˈriːdʒekt] **5.** ⚔ Ausgemusterte(r) *m*, Untaugliche(r) *m*; **6.** † ˈAusschußarˌtikel *m*; **re·jec·ta·men·ta** [rɪˌdʒektəˈmentə] *s. pl.* **1.** Abfälle *pl.*; **2.** Strandgut *n*; **3.** *physiol.* Exkreˈmente *pl.*; **reˈjec·tion** [-kʃn] *s.* **1.** Ablehnung *f*, Zuˈrückweisung *f*, Verwerfung *f*; †, ⚙ Abnahmeverweigerung *f*; **2.** Ausscheidung *f*; **3.** *pl.* Ausschußartikel *pl.*; **4.** ⚕ Abstoßung *f*; **5.** *pl. physiol.* Exkreˈmente *pl.*; **reˈjec·tor** [-tə] *s. a.* **~ circuit** ⚡ Sperrkreis *m*.

re·joice [rɪˈdʒɔɪs] **I** *v/i.* **1.** sich freuen, frohˈlocken (**in**, **at** über *acc.*); **2.** **~ in** sich *e-r Sache* erfreuen; **II** *v/t.* **3.** erfreuen: **~d at** (*od.* **by**) erfreut über (*acc.*); **reˈjoic·ing** [-sɪŋ] **I** *s.* **1.** Freude *f*, Frohˈlocken *n*; **2.** *oft pl.* (Freuden)Fest *n*, Lustbarkeit(en *pl.*) *f*; **II** *adj.* □ **3.** erfreut, froh (**in**, **at** über *acc.*).

re·join [ˌriːˈdʒɔɪn] *v/t. u. v/i.* (sich) ˈwiedervereinigen (**to**, **with** mit), (sich) wieder zs.-fügen.

re·join¹ [ˌriːˈdʒɔɪn] *v/t.* sich wieder anschließen (*dat.*) *od.* an (*acc.*), wieder eintreten in *e-e Partei etc.*; wieder zuˈrückkehren zu, *j-n* wieder treffen.

re·join² [rɪˈdʒɔɪn] *v/t.* **1.** erwidern; **2.** ⚖ e-e Gegenerklärung auf e-e Reˈplik abgeben; **reˈjoin·der** [-ndə] *s.* Erwiderung *f*; ⚖ Gegenerklärung *f* (*des Beklagten auf e-e Replik*).

re·ju·ve·nate [rɪˈdʒuːvɪneɪt] *v/t.* (*v/i.* sich) verjüngen; **re·ju·ve·na·tion** [rɪˌdʒuːvɪˈneɪʃn] *s.* Verjüngung *f*.

re·ju·ve·nesce [ˌriːdʒuːvɪˈnes] *v/t. u. v/i.* (sich) verjüngen (*a. biol.*); **ˌre·ju·veˈnes·cence** [-sns] *s.* (*biol.* Zell)Verjüngung *f*.

re·kindle [ˌriːˈkɪndl] **I** *v/t.* **1.** wieder anzünden; **2.** *fig.* wieder entfachen, neu beleben; **II** *v/i.* **3.** sich wieder entzünden; **4.** *fig.* wieder entbrennen, wiederˈaufleben.

re·lapse [rɪˈlæps] **I** *v/i.* **1.** zuˈrückfallen, wieder (ver)fallen (**into** in *acc.*); **2.** rückfällig werden; ⚕ e-n Rückfall bekommen; **II** *s.* **3.** ⚕ Rückfall *m*.

re·late [rɪˈleɪt] **I** *v/t.* **1.** berichten, erzählen (**to s.o.** j-m); **2.** in Beziehung *od.* Zs.-hang bringen, verbinden (**to**, **with** mit); **II** *v/i.* **3.** sich beziehen, Bezug haben (**to** auf *acc.*): **relating to** in bezug auf (*acc.*), bezüglich (*gen.*); **4.** **~ to s.o.** a) sich j-m gegenüber verhalten, b) zu j-m e-e (*gute, innere etc.*) Beziehung haben; **reˈlat·ed** [-tɪd] *adj.* verwandt (**to**, **with** mit) (*a. fig.*): **~ by marriage** verschwägert.

re·la·tion [rɪˈleɪʃn] *s.* **1.** Bericht *m*, Erzählung *f*; **2.** Beziehung *f* (*a. pol.*, †, A), (*a. Vertrags-, Vertrauens- etc.*)Verhältnis *n*; (*kausaler etc.*) Zs.-hang; Bezug *m*: **business ~s** Geschäftsbeziehungen; **human ~s** a) zwischenmenschliche Beziehungen, b) (innerbetriebliche) Kontaktpflege; **in ~ to** in bezug auf (*acc.*); **be out of all ~ to** in keinem Verhältnis stehen zu; **bear no ~ to** nichts zu tun haben mit; → **public** 3; **3.** a) Verwandte(r *m*) *f*, b) Verwandtschaft *f* (*a. fig.*): **what ~ is he to you?** wie ist er mit dir verwandt?; **reˈla·tion·ship** [-ʃɪp] *s.* **1.** Beziehung *f*, (*a. Rechts*)Verhältnis *n* (**to** zu); **2.** Verwandtschaft *f* (**to** mit) (*a. coll. u. fig.*).

rel·a·tive [ˈrelətɪv] **I** *adj.* □ **1.** bezüglich, sich beziehend (**to** auf *acc.*): **~ value** A Bezugswert *m*; **~ to** bezüglich, hinsichtlich (*gen.*); **2.** relaˈtiv, verhältnismäßig, Verhältnis…; **3.** (**to**) abhängig (von), bedingt (durch); **4.** gegenseitig, entsprechend, jeweilig; **5.** *ling.* bezüglich, Relativ…; **6.** ♪ paralˈlel (*Tonart*); **II** *s.* **7.** Verwandte(r *m*) *f*; **8.** *ling.* a) Relaˈtivproˌnomen *n*, b) Relaˈtivsatz *m*; **ˈrel·a·tive·ness** [-nɪs] *s.* Relativiˈtät *f*; **ˈrel·a·tiv·ism** [-vɪzəm] *s. phls.* Relatiˈvismus *m*; **rel·a·tiv·i·ty** [ˌreləˈtɪvətɪ] *s.* **1.** Relativiˈtät *f*: **theory of ~** *phys.* Relativitätstheorie *f*; **2.** Abhängigkeit *f* (**to** von).

re·lax [rɪˈlæks] **I** *v/t.* **1.** *Muskeln etc.*, ⚙ *Feder* entspannen; (*a. fig. Disziplin, Vorschrift etc.*) lockern: **~ing climate** Schonklima *n*; **2.** in *s-n Anstrengungen etc.* nachlassen; **3.** ⚕ abführend wirken; **II** *v/i.* **4.** sich entspannen (*Muskeln etc.*, *a. Geist, Person*); ausspannen, sich erholen (*Person*); es sich bequem machen: **~ing** entspannend, erholsam, Erholungs…; **5.** sich lockern (*Griff, Seil etc.*) (*a. fig.*); **6.** nachlassen (**in** in *e-r Bemühung etc.*) (*a. Sturm etc.*); **7.** milder *od.* freundlicher werden; **re·lax·a·tion** [ˌriːlækˈseɪʃn] *s.* **1.** Entspannung *f* (*a. fig. Erholung*); Lockerung *f* (*a. fig.*); Erschlaffung *f*; **2.** Nachlassen *n*; **3.** Milderung *f e-r Strafe etc.*

re·lay [ˈriːleɪ] **I** *s.* **1.** a) frisches Gespann, b) Pferdewechsel *m*, c) *fig.* †, ⚔ Ablösung(smannschaft) *f*: **~ attack** ⚔ rollender Angriff; **in ~s** ⚔ in rollendem Einsatz; **2.** *sport a.* **~ race** Staffel(lauf *m*, -wettbewerb *m*) *f*: **~ team** Staffel *f*; **3.** a) [ˌriːˈleɪ] ⚡ Reˈlais *n*: **~ station** Relais-, Zwischensender *m*, **~ switch** Schaltschütz *n*, b) *Radio*: Überˈtragung *f*; **II** *v/t.* **4.** *allg.* weitergeben; **5.** [ˌriːˈleɪ] ⚡ mit Reˈlais steuern; *Radio*: (mit Reˈlais) überˈtragen.

re·lease [rɪˈliːs] **I** *s.* **1.** (Haft)Entlassung *f*, Freilassung *f* (**from** aus); **2.** *fig.* Befreiung *f*, Erlösung *f* (**from** von); **3.** Entlastung *f* (*a. e-s Treuhänders etc.*), Entbindung *f* (**from** von *e-r Pflicht*); **4.** Freigabe *f* (*Buch, Film, Vermögen etc.*): **first ~** *Film*: Uraufführung *f*; (**press**) **~** (Presse)Verlautbarung *f*; **~ of energy** Freiwerden *n* von Energie; **5.** ⚖ a) Verzicht(leistung *f*, -urkunde *f*) *m*, b) (ˈRechts)ÜberˌtragungRef *f*, c) Quittung *f*; **6.** ⚙, *phot.* a) Auslöser *m*, b) Auslösung *f*: **~ of bombs** ⚔ Bombenabwurf *m*; **II** *v/t.* **7.** *Häftling* ent-, freilassen; **8.** *fig.* (**from**) a) befreien, erlösen (von), b) entbinden, -lasten (von *e-r Pflicht, Schuld etc.*); **9.** *Buch, Film, Guthaben* freigeben; **10.** ⚖ verzichten auf (*acc.*), *Recht* aufgeben *od.* überˈtragen; *Hypothek* löschen; **11.** ⚗, *phys.* freisetzen; **12.** ⚙ a) auslösen (*a. phot.*); *Bomben* abwerfen; *Gas* abblasen, b) ausschalten: **~ the clutch** auskuppeln.

rel·e·gate [ˈrelɪgeɪt] *v/t.* **1.** relegieren, verbannen (**out of** aus): **be ~d** *sport* absteigen; **2.** verweisen (**to** an *acc.*); **3.** (**to**) verweisen (in *acc.*), zuschreiben (*dat.*): **~ to the sphere of legend** in das Reich der Fabel verweisen; **he was ~d to fourth place** *sport* er wurde auf den vierten Platz verwiesen; **re·le·ga·tion** [ˌrelɪˈgeɪʃn] *s.* **1.** Verbannung *f* (**out of** aus); **2.** Verweisung *f* (**to** an *acc.*); **3.** *sport* Abstieg *m*: **in danger of ~** in Abstiegsgefahr.

re·lent [rɪˈlent] *v/i.* weicher *od.* mitleidig werden, sich erweichen lassen; **reˈlent·less** [-lɪs] *adj.* □ unbarmherzig, schonungslos, hart.

rel·e·vance [ˈreləvəns], **ˈrel·e·van·cy** [-sɪ] *s.* Releˈvanz *f*, (*a.* Beweis)Erheblichkeit *f*; Bedeutung *f* (**to** für); **ˈrel·e·vant** [-nt] *adj.* □ **1.** einschlägig, sachdienlich; anwendbar (**to** auf *acc.*); **2.** (beweis-, rechts- *etc.*)erheblich, belangvoll, von Bedeutung (**to** für).

re·li·a·bil·i·ty [rɪˌlaɪəˈbɪlətɪ] *s.* Zuverlässigkeit *f*, ⚙ *a.* Betriebssicherheit *f*: ~ **test** Zuverlässigkeitsprüfung *f*; **re·li·a·ble** [rɪˈlaɪəbl] *adj.* □ **1.** zuverlässig (*a.* ⚙ *betriebssicher*), verläßlich; **2.** glaubwürdig; **3.** vertrauenswürdig, reˈell (*Firma etc.*); **re·li·ance** [rɪˈlaɪəns] *s.* Vertrauen *n*: **in** ~ (**up**)**on** unter Verlaß auf (*acc.*), bauend auf; **place** ~ **on** (*od.* **in**) Vertrauen in *j-n* setzen; **re·li·ant** [rɪˈlaɪənt] *adj.* **1.** vertrauensvoll; **2.** zuversichtlich.

rel·ic [ˈrelɪk] *s.* **1.** (ˈÜber)Rest *m*, ˈÜberbleibsel *n*, Reˈlikt *n*: **~s of the past** *fig.* Zeugen der Vergangenheit; **2.** *R.C.* Reˈliquie *f*.

re·lief[1] [rɪˈliːf] *s.* **1.** Erleichterung *f* (*a.* ⚕); → **sigh** 5; **2.** (angenehme) Unterˈbrechung, Abwechslung *f*, Wohltat *f* (**to** für *das Auge etc.*); **3.** Trost *m*; **4.** Entlastung *f*; (*Steuer- etc.*)Erleichterung *f*; **5.** a) Unterˈstützung *f*, Hilfe *f*, b) *Am.* Soziˈalhilfe *f*; ~ **fund** Unterstützungsfonds *m*, -kasse *f*; **be on** ~ Sozialhilfe beziehen; **6.** ⚖ a) Rechtshilfe *f*: **the** ~ **sought** das Klagebegehren, b) Rechtsbehelf *m*, -mittel *n*; **7.** ⚔ a) *a. allg.* Ablösung *f*, b) Entsatz *m*, Entlastung *f*, c) *in Zssgn* Entlastungs…: ~ **attack** (**road**, **train**); ~ **driver** *mot.* Beifahrer *m*.

re·lief[2] [rɪˈliːf] *s.* ⚠ *etc.* Reliˈef *n*; erhabene Arbeit: ~ **map** Relief-, Höhenkarte *f*; **be in** ~ **against** sich (scharf) abheben gegen; **set into vivid** ~ *fig. et.* plastisch schildern; **stand out in** (**bold**) ~ deutlich hervortreten (*a. fig.*); **throw into** ~ hervortreten lassen (*a. fig.*).

re·lieve [rɪˈliːv] *v/t.* **1.** *Schmerzen etc.*, *a. Gewissen* erleichtern: ~ **one's feelings** s-n Gefühlen Luft machen; ~ **s.o.'s mind** j-n beruhigen; → **nature** 7; **2.** *j-n* entlasten: ~ **s.o. from** (*od.* **of**) j-m *et.* abnehmen, j-n von *e-r Pflicht etc.* entbinden, j-n *e-r Verantwortung etc.* entheben, j-n von *et.* befreien; ~ **s.o. of** *humor.* j-n um *et.* ‚erleichtern', j-m *et.* stehlen; **3.** *j-n* erleichtern, beruhigen, trösten: **I am ~d to hear** es beruhigt mich, zu hören; **4.** ⚔ a) *Platz* entsetzen, b) *Kampftruppe* entlasten, c) *Posten*, *Einheit* ablösen; **5.** *Bedürftige* unterˈstützen, *Armen* helfen; **6.** *Eintöniges* beleben, Abwechslung bringen in (*acc.*); **7.** herˈvor-, abheben; **8.** *j-m* Recht verschaffen; *e-r Sache* abhelfen; **9.** ⚙ a) entlasten (*a.* ⚠), *Feder* entspannen, b) ˈhinterdrehen.

re·lie·vo [rɪˈliːvəʊ] *pl.* **-vos** *s.* Reliˈefarbeit *f*.

re·li·gion [rɪˈlɪdʒən] *s.* **1.** Religiˈon *f* (*a. iro.*): **get** ~ F fromm werden; **2.** Frömmigkeit *f*; **3.** Ehrensache *f*, Herzenspflicht *f*; **4.** moˈnastisches Leben: **enter** ~ in e-n Orden eintreten; **reˈli·gion·ist** [-dʒənɪst] *s.* religiˈöser Schwärmer *od.* Eiferer; **re·lig·i·os·i·ty** [rɪˌlɪdʒɪˈɒsətɪ] *s.* **1.** Religiosiˈtät *f*; **2.** Frömmeˈlei *f*.

re·li·gious [rɪˈlɪdʒəs] *adj.* □ **1.** Religions…, religiˈös (*Buch*, *Pflicht etc.*); **2.** religiˈös, fromm; **3.** Ordens…: ~ **order** geistlicher Orden; **4.** *fig.* gewissenhaft, peinlich genau; **5.** *fig.* andächtig: ~ **silence**.

re·lin·quish [rɪˈlɪŋkwɪʃ] *v/t.* **1.** *Hoffnung*, *Idee*, *Plan etc.* aufgeben; **2.** (**to**) *Besitz*, *Recht* abtreten (*dat. od.* an *acc.*), preisgeben (*dat.*), überˈlassen (*dat.*); **3.** *et.* loslassen, fahrenlassen; **4.** verzichten auf (*acc.*); **reˈlin·quish·ment** [-mənt] *s.* **1.** Aufgabe *f*; **2.** Überˈlassung *f*; **3.** Verzicht *m* (**of** auf *acc.*).

rel·i·quar·y [ˈrelɪkwərɪ] *s.* *R.C.* Reˈliquienschrein *m*.

rel·ish [ˈrelɪʃ] **I** *v/t.* **1.** gern essen, sich schmecken lassen; *a. fig.* (mit Behagen) genießen, Geschmack finden an (*dat.*): **I do not much ~ the idea** ich bin nicht gerade begeistert davon (**of doing** zu tun); **2.** *fig.* schmackhaft machen; **II** *v/i.* **3.** schmecken *od.* (*fig.*) riechen (**of** nach); **III** *s.* **4.** (Wohl)Geschmack *m*; **5.** *fig.* a) Kostprobe *f*, b) Beigeschmack *m* (**of** von); **6.** a) Gewürz *n*, Würze *f* (*a. fig.*), b) Horsd'œuvre *n*, Appeˈtithappen *m*; **7.** *fig.* (**for**) Geschmack *m* (an *dat.*), Sinn *m* (für): **have no ~ for** sich nichts machen aus; **with** (**great**) ~ mit (großem) Behagen, mit Wonne (*a. iro.*).

re·live [ˌriːˈlɪv] *v/t. et.* noch einmal durchˈleben *od.* erleben.

re·lo·cate [ˌriːləʊˈkeɪt] **I** *v/t.* **1.** ˈumsiedeln, *Betrieb*, *Werk*: *a.* verlegen; **2.** *Computer*: verschieben; **II** *v/i.* **3.** ˈumziehen (**to** nach).

re·luc·tance [rɪˈlʌktəns] *s.* **1.** Widerˈstreben *n*, Abneigung *f* (**to** gegen, **to do s.th.** et. zu tun): **with** ~ widerstrebend, ungern, zögernd; **2.** *phys.* maˈgnetischer ˈWiderstand; **reˈluc·tant** [-nt] *adj.* □ ˈwiderwillig, widerˈstrebend, zögernd, ungern: **be** ~ **to do s.th.** sich sträuben, et. zu tun; et. nur ungern tun.

re·ly [rɪˈlaɪ] *v/i.* **1.** ~ (**up**)**on** sich verlassen, vertrauen *od.* bauen *od.* zählen auf (*acc.*): ~ **on s.th.** (**for**) auf et. angewiesen sein (hinsichtlich *gen.*), et. (ausschließlich) beziehen (von); **2.** ~ (**up**)**on** sich auf *e-e Quelle etc.* stützen *od.* berufen.

re·main [rɪˈmeɪn] **I** *v/i.* **1.** *allg.* bleiben; **2.** (übrig)bleiben (*a. fig.* **to s.o.** j-m); zuˈrück-, verbleiben, noch übrig sein: **it now ~s for me to explain** es bleibt mir nur noch übrig, zu erklären; **nothing ~s** (**to us**) **but to** (*inf.*) es bleibt (uns) nichts anderes übrig, als zu (*inf.*); **that ~s to be seen** das bleibt abzuwarten; **3.** (bestehen) bleiben: ~ **in force** in Kraft bleiben; **4.** *im Briefschluß*: verbleiben; **II** *s. pl.* **5.** *a. fig.* Reste *pl.*, ˈÜberreste *pl.*, -bleibsel *pl.*; **6.** *die* sterblichen Überreste *pl.*; **7.** *a.* **literary ~s** hinterˈlassene Werke *pl.*, liteˈrarischer Nachlaß; **reˈmain·der** [-də] **I** *s.* **1.** Rest *m* (*a.* Ꝑ), *das* übrige; **2.** ✝ Restbestand *m*, -betrag *m*: ~ **of a debt** Restschuld *f*; **3.** ⚙ Rückstand *m*; **4.** *Buchhandel*: Restauflage *f*, Remitˈtenden *pl.*; **5.** ⚖ a) Anwartschaft *f* (auf Grundeigentum), b) Nacherbenrecht *n*; **II** *v/t.* **6.** *Bücher* billig abgeben; **reˈmain·der·man** [-dəmæn] *s.* [*irr.*] ⚖ a) Anwärter *m*, b) Nacherbe *m*; **reˈmain·ing** [-nɪŋ] *adj.* übrig(geblieben), Rest…, verbleibend, restlich.

re·make [ˌriːˈmeɪk] **I** *v/t.* [*irr.* → **make**] wieder *od.* neu machen, *Film*: *a.* neu drehen; **II** *s.* [ˈriːmeɪk] ˈNeuverfilmung *f*, Reˈmake *n*.

re·mand [rɪˈmɑːnd] **I** *v/t.* ⚖ a) (in Unterˈsuchungshaft) zuˈrückschicken, b) *Rechtssache* (an die untere Inˈstanz) zuˈrückverweisen; **II** *s.* (Zuˈrücksendung *f* in die) Unterˈsuchungshaft *f*: ~ **prison** Untersuchungsgefängnis *n*; **prisoner on** ~ Untersuchungsgefangene(r *m*) *f*; **be brought up on** ~ aus der Untersuchungshaft vorgeführt werden; ~ **centre** (*od.* **home**) Unterˈsuchungshaftanstalt *f* für Jugendliche.

re·mark [rɪˈmɑːk] **I** *v/t.* **1.** (be)merken, beobachten; **2.** bemerken, äußern (**that** daß); **II** *v/i.* **3.** e-e Bemerkung *od.* Bemerkungen machen, sich äußern ([**up**]**on** über *acc.*, zu); **III** *s.* **4.** Bemerkung *f*, Äußerung *f*: **without** ~ ohne Kommentar; **worthy of** ~ → **reˈmark·a·ble** [-kəbl] *adj.* □ bemerkenswert: a) beachtlich, b) ungewöhnlich; **reˈmark·a·ble·ness** [-kəblnɪs] *s.* **1.** Ungewöhnlichkeit *f*, Merkwürdigkeit *f*; **2.** Bedeutsamkeit *f*.

re·mar·riage [ˌriːˈmærɪdʒ] *s.* ˈWiederverˌheiratung *f*; **ˌreˈmar·ry** [-rɪ] *v/i.* wieder heiraten.

re·me·di·a·ble [rɪˈmiːdjəbl] *adj.* □ heil-, abstellbar: **this is** ~ dem ist abzuhelfen; **reˈme·di·al** [-jəl] *adj.* □ **1.** heilend, Heil…: ~ **gymnastics** Heilgymnastik *f*; ~ **teaching** Förderunterricht *m* (für *Lernschwache*); **2.** abhelfend: ~ **measure** Abhilfsmaßnahme *f*.

rem·e·dy [ˈremɪdɪ] **I** *s.* **1.** ⚕ (Heil-)Mittel *n*, Arzˈnei *f* (**for**, **against** für, gegen); **2.** *fig.* (Gegen)Mittel *n* (**for**, **against** gegen); Abhilfe *f*; ⚖ Rechtsmittel *n*, -behelf *m*; **3.** *Münzwesen*: Reˈmedium *n*, Toleˈranz *f*; **II** *v/t.* **4.** *Mangel*, *Schaden* beheben; **5.** *Mißstand* abstellen, abhelfen (*dat.*), in Ordnung bringen.

re·mem·ber [rɪˈmembə] **I** *v/t.* **1.** sich entsinnen (*gen.*) *od.* an (*acc.*), sich besinnen auf (*acc.*), sich erinnern an (*acc.*): **I ~ that** es fällt mir (gerade) ein, daß; **2.** sich merken, nicht vergessen; **3.** eingedenk sein (*gen.*), denken an (*acc.*), beherzigen, sich *et.* vor Augen halten; **4.** *j-n mit e-m Geschenk*, *in s-m Testament* bedenken; **5.** empfehlen, grüßen: ~ **me to him** grüßen Sie ihn von mir; **II** *v/i.* **6.** sich erinnern *od.* entsinnen: **not that I** ~ nicht, daß ich wüßte; **reˈmem·brance** [-brəns] *s.* **1.** Erinnerung *f*, Gedächtnis *n* (**of** an *acc.*); **2.** Gedächtnis *n*, An-, Gedenken *n*: **in ~ of** im Gedenken *od.* zur Erinnerung an (*acc.*); **℞ Day** Volkstrauertag *m* (*11. November*); **3.** Andenken *n* (*Sache*); **4.** *pl.* Grüße *pl.*, Empfehlungen *pl.*

re·mi·gra·tion [ˌriːmaɪˈgreɪʃn] *s.* Rückwanderung *f*.

re·mil·i·ta·ri·za·tion [ˈriːˌmɪlɪtəraɪˈzeɪʃn] *s.* Remilitarisierung *f*.

re·mind [rɪˈmaɪnd] *v/t. j-n* erinnern (**of** an *acc.*, **that** daß): **that ~s me** da(bei) fällt mir (et.) ein; ***this ~s me of home*** das erinnert mich an zu Hause; **re'mind·er** [-də] *s.* **1.** Mahnung *f*: ***a gentle ~*** ein (zarter) Wink; **2.** Erinnerung *f* (*of* an *acc.*); **3.** Gedächtnishilfe *f*.

rem·i·nisce [ˌremɪ'nɪs] *v/i.* in Erinnerungen schwelgen; **ˌrem·i'nis·cence** [-sns] *s.* **1.** Erinnerung *f*; **2.** *pl.* (Lebens)Erinnerungen *pl.*, Reminis'zenzen *pl.*; **3.** *fig.* Anklang *m*; **ˌrem·i'nis·cent** [-snt] *adj.* □ **1.** sich erinnernd (*of* an *acc.*), Erinnerungs...; **2.** Erinnerungen wachrufend (*of* an *acc.*), erinnerungsträchtig; **3.** sich (gern) erinnernd, in Erinnerungen schwelgend.

re·mise¹ [rɪ'maɪz] *s.* ⚖ Aufgabe *f e-s Anspruchs*, Rechtsverzicht *m*.

re·mise² [rə'miːz] *s.* **1.** *obs.* a) Re'mise *f*, Wagenschuppen *m*, b) Mietkutsche *f*; **2.** *fenc.* Ri'messe *f*.

re·miss [rɪ'mɪs] *adj.* □ (nach)lässig, säumig; lax, träge: ***be ~ in one's duties*** s-e Pflichten vernachlässigen; **re'mis·si·ble** [-səbl] *adj.* **1.** erläßlich; **2.** verzeihlich; *R.C.* läßlich (*Sünde*); **re'mis·sion** [-ɪʃn] *s.* **1.** Vergebung *f* (der Sünden); **2.** a) (teilweiser) Erlaß *e-r Strafe, Schuld, Gebühr etc.*, b) Nachlaß *m*, Ermäßigung *f*; **3.** Nachlassen *n der Intensität etc.*; ⚕ Remissi'on *f*; **re'miss·ness** [-nɪs] *s.* (Nach)Lässigkeit *f*.

re·mit [rɪ'mɪt] **I** *v/t.* **1.** *Sünden* vergeben; **2.** *Schulden, Strafe* (ganz *od.* teilweise) erlassen; **3.** hin'aus-, verschieben (***till, to*** bis, ***to*** auf *acc.*); **4.** a) nachlassen in *s-n Anstrengungen etc.*, b) *Zorn etc.* mäßigen, c) aufhören mit, einstellen; **5.** ✝ *Geld etc.* über'weisen, -'senden; **6.** *bsd.* ⚖ a) (*Fall etc. zur Entscheidung*) über'tragen, b) → ***remand*** I b; **II** *v/i.* **7.** ✝ Zahlung leisten, remittieren; **re'mit·tal** [-tl] → ***remission***; **re'mit·tance** [-təns] *s.* **1.** (*bsd.* Geld)Sendung *f*, Über'weisung *f*; **2.** ✝ (Geld-, Wechsel-) Sendung *f*, Überweisung *f*, Ri'messe *f*: ***~ account*** Überweisungskonto *n*; ***make ~*** remittieren, Deckung anschaffen; **re·mit·tee** [ˌremɪ'tiː] *s.* ✝ (Zahlungs-, Über'weisungs)Empfänger *m*; **re'mit·tent** [-tənt] *bsd.* ⚕ **I** *adj.* (vor'übergehend) nachlassend; remittierend (*Fieber*); **II** *s.* remittierendes Fieber; **re'mit·ter** [-tə] *s.* **1.** ✝ Geldsender *m*, Über'sender *m*; Remit'tend *m*; **2.** ⚖ a) Wieder'einsetzung *f* (***to*** in *frühere Rechte etc.*), b) Über'weisung *f e-s Falles*.

rem·nant ['remnənt] *s.* **1.** ('Über)Rest *m*, 'Überbleibsel *n*; kläglicher Rest; *fig.* (letzter) Rest, Spur *f*; **2.** ✝ (Stoff)Rest *m*; *pl.* Reste(r) *pl.*: ***~ sale*** Resteverkauf *m*.

re·mod·el [ˌriː'mɒdl] *v/t.* 'umbilden, -bauen, -formen, -gestalten.

re·mon·e·ti·za·tion [riːˌmʌnɪtaɪ'zeɪʃn] *s.* ✝ Wiederin'kurssetzung *f*.

re·mon·strance [rɪ'mɒnstrəns] *s.* (Gegen)Vorstellung *f*, Vorhaltung *f*, Einspruch *m*, Pro'test *m*; **re'mon·strant** [-nt] **I** *adj.* □ protestierend; **II** *s.* Einsprucherheber *m*; **re·mon·strate** ['remənstreɪt] **I** *v/i.* **1.** protestieren (***against*** gegen); **2.** Vorhaltungen *od.* Vorwürfe machen (***on*** über *acc.*, ***with s.o.*** j-m); **II** *v/t.* **3.** einwenden (***that*** daß).

re·morse [rɪ'mɔːs] *s.* Gewissensbisse *pl.*, Reue *f* (***at*** über *acc.*, ***for*** wegen): ***without ~*** unbarmherzig, kalt; **re'morse·ful** [-fʊl] *adj.* □ reumütig, reuevoll; **re'morse·less** [-lɪs] *adj.* □ unbarmherzig, hart(herzig).

re·mote [rɪ'məʊt] **I** *adj.* □ **1.** *räumlich u. zeitlich, a. fig.* fern, (weit) entfernt (***from*** von); *fig.* schwach, vage: ***~ antiquity*** graue Vorzeit; ***a ~ chance*** e-e winzige Chance; ***~ control*** ⚙ a) Fernsteuerung *f*, b) Fernbedienung *f*; ***~-control(led)*** ferngesteuert, -gelenkt, mit Fernbedienung; ***~ future*** ferne Zukunft; ***not the ~st idea*** keine blasse Ahnung; ***~ possibility*** vage Möglichkeit; ***~ relation*** entfernte(r) *od.* weitläufige(r) Verwandte(r); ***~ resemblance*** entfernte *od.* schwache Ähnlichkeit; **2.** abgelegen, entlegen; **3.** mittelbar, 'indiˌrekt: ***~ damages*** ⚖ Folgeschäden; **4.** distan'ziert, unnahbar; **II** *s.* **5.** *Am. TV*: Außenübertragung *f*; **re'mote·ness** [-nɪs] *s.* Ferne *f*, Entlegenheit *f*.

re·mount [ˌriː'maʊnt] **I** *v/t.* **1.** *Berg, Pferd etc.* wieder besteigen; **2.** ⚔ neue Pferde beschaffen für; **3.** ⚙ *Maschine* wieder aufstellen; **II** *v/i.* **4.** wieder aufsteigen; wieder aufsitzen (*Reiter*); **5.** *fig.* zu'rückgehen (***to*** auf *acc.*); **III** *s.* ['riːmaʊnt] **6.** frisches Reitpferd; ⚔ Re'monte *f*.

re·mov·a·ble [rɪ'muːvəbl] *adj.* □ **1.** absetzbar; **2.** ⚙ abnehmbar, auswechselbar; **3.** behebbar (*Übel*); **re'mov·al** [-vl] *s.* **1.** Fort-, Wegschaffen *n*, -räumen *n*; Entfernen *n*; Abfuhr *f*, 'Abtransˌport *m*; Beseitigung *f* (*a. fig. Behebung von Fehlern, Mißständen, e-s Gegners*); **2.** 'Umzug *m* (***to*** in *acc.*, nach): ***~ of business*** Geschäftsverlegung *f*; ***~ man*** a) Spediteur *m*, b) Möbelpacker *m*; ***~ van*** Möbelwagen *m*; **3.** a) Absetzung *f*, Enthebung *f* (***from office*** aus dem Amt), b) (Straf)Versetzung *f*; **4.** ⚖ Verweisung *f* (***to*** an *acc.*); **re·move** [rɪ'muːv] **I** *v/t.* **1.** *allg.* (weg-) nehmen, entfernen (***from*** aus); ⚙ abnehmen, abmontieren, ausbauen; *Kleidungsstück* ablegen; *Hut* abnehmen; *Hand* zu'rückziehen; *fig. Furcht, Zweifel etc.* nehmen: ***~ from the agenda*** *et.* von der Tagesordnung absetzen; ***~ o.s.*** sich entfernen (***from*** von); **2.** wegräumen, -rücken, -bringen, fortschaffen, abtransportieren; (*a. fig. j-n*) aus dem Wege räumen: ***~ furniture*** (Wohnungs)Umzüge besorgen; ***~ a prisoner*** e-n Gefangenen abführen (lassen); ***~ mountains*** *fig.* Berge versetzen; ***~ by suction*** ⚙ absaugen; ***a first cousin once ~d*** Kind e-s Vetters *od.* e-r Kusine; **3.** *Fehler, Gegner, Hindernis, Spuren etc.* beseitigen; *Flecken* entfernen; *fig. Schwierigkeiten* beheben; **4.** *wohin* bringen, schaffen, verlegen; **5.** *Beamten* absetzen, entlassen, *s-s Amtes* entheben; **II** *v/i.* **6.** (aus-, 'um-, ver)ziehen (***to*** nach); **III** *s.* **7.** Entfernung *f*, Abstand *m*: ***at a ~*** *fig.* mit einigem Abstand; **8.** Schritt *m*, Stufe *f*, Grad *m*; **9.** *Brit.* nächster Gang (*beim Essen*); **re'mov·er** [-və] *s.* **1.** Abbeizmittel *n*; **2.** ('Möbel)Spediˌteur *m*.

re·mu·ner·ate [rɪ'mjuːnəreɪt] *v/t.* **1.** *j-n* entschädigen, belohnen (***for*** für); **2.** *et.* vergüten, Entschädigung zahlen für, ersetzen; **re·mu·ner·a·tion** [rɪˌmjuːnə'reɪʃn] *s.* **1.** Entschädigung *f*, Vergütung *f*; **2.** Belohnung *f*; **3.** Hono'rar *n*, Lohn *m*, Entgelt *n*; **re'mu·ner·a·tive** [-nərətɪv] *adj.* □ einträglich, lohnend, lukra'tiv, vorteilhaft.

Ren·ais·sance [rə'neɪsəns] (*Fr.*) *s.* **1.** Renais'sance *f*; **2.** ♀ 'Wiedergeburt *f*, -erwachen *n*.

re·nal ['riːnl] *adj. anat.* Nieren...

re·name [ˌriː'neɪm] *v/t.* **1.** 'umbenennen; **2.** neu benennen.

re·nas·cence [rɪ'næsns] *s.* **1.** 'Wiedergeburt *f*, Erneuerung *f*; **2.** ♀ Renais'sance *f*; **re'nas·cent** [-nt] *adj.* sich erneuernd, wieder auflebend, 'wiedererwachend.

rend [rend] [*irr.*] **I** *v/t.* **1.** (zer)reißen: ***~ from*** *j-m* entreißen; ***~ the air*** die Luft zerreißen (*Schrei etc.*); **2.** spalten (*a. fig.*); **II** *v/i.* **3.** (zer)reißen.

ren·der ['rendə] *v/t.* **1.** *a.* ***~ back*** zu'rückgeben, -erstatten: ***~ up*** herausgeben, *fig.* vergelten (***good for evil*** Böses mit Gutem); **2.** (*a.* ⚔ *Festung*) über'geben; ✝ *Rechnung* (vor)legen: ***per account ~ed*** ✝ laut (erteilter) Rechnung; ***~ a profit*** Gewinn abwerfen; → *a.* ***account*** 6 *u.* 7; **3.** (***to s.o.*** j-m) *e-n Dienst, Hilfe etc.* leisten; *Aufmerksamkeit, Ehre, Gehorsam* erweisen; *Dank* abstatten: ***for services ~ed*** für geleistete Dienste; **4.** *Grund* angeben; **5.** ⚖ *Urteil* fällen; **6.** *berühmt, schwierig, sichtbar etc.* machen: ***~ audible*** hörbar machen; ***~ possible*** möglich machen, ermöglichen; **7.** *künstlerisch* 'wiedergeben, interpretieren; **8.** *sprachlich, sinngemäß* 'wiedergeben, über'setzen; **9.** ⚙ *Fett* auslassen; **10.** ⚠ roh bewerfen; **'ren·der·ing** [-dərɪŋ] *s.* **1.** 'Übergabe *f*: ***~ of account*** ✝ Rechnungslegung *f*; **2.** *künstlerische* 'Wiedergabe, ˌInterpretati'on *f*, Gestaltung *f*, Vortrag *m*; **3.** Über'setzung *f*, 'Wiedergabe *f*; **4.** ⚠ Rohbewurf *m*.

ren·dez·vous ['rɒndɪvuː] *pl.* **-vous** [-vuːz] (*Fr.*) *s.* **1.** a) Rendez'vous *n*, Verabredung *f*, Stelldichein *n*, b) Zs.-kunft *f*; **2.** Treffpunkt *m* (*a.* ⚔).

ren·di·tion [ren'dɪʃn] *s.* **1.** → ***rendering*** 2 *u.* 3; **2.** *Am.* (Urteils)Fällung *f*, (-)Verkündung *f*.

ren·e·gade ['renɪgeɪd] *s.* Rene'gat(in), Abtrünnige(r *m*) *f*, 'Überläufer(in).

re·nege [rɪ'niːg] **I** *v/i.* **1.** sein Wort brechen: ***~ on*** *et.* nicht (ein)halten, *e-r Sache* untreu werden; **2.** *Kartenspiel*: nicht bedienen; **II** *v/t.* **3.** ab-, verleugnen.

re·new [rɪ'njuː] *v/t.* **1.** *allg.* erneuern (*z.B. Bekanntschaft, Angriff, Autoreifen, Gelöbnis*): ***~ed*** erneut; **2.** *Briefwechsel etc.* wieder'aufnehmen: ***~ one's efforts*** sich erneut bemühen; **3.** *Jugend, Kraft* 'wiedererlangen; *biol.* regenerieren; **4.** ✝ *Vertrag etc.* erneuern, verlängern; *Wechsel* prolongieren; **5.** ergänzen, -setzen; **6.** wieder'holen; **re'new·a·ble** [-juːəbl] *adj.* **1.** erneuerbar, zu erneuern(d); **2.** ✝ erneuerungs-, verlängerungsfähig; prolongierbar (*Wechsel*); **re'new·al** [-juːəl] *s.* **1.** Erneuerung *f*; **2.** ✝ a) Erneuerung *f*, Verlängerung *f*, b) Prolongati'on *f*.

ren·i·form ['riːnɪfɔːm] *adj.* nierenförmig.

ren·net¹ [ˈrenɪt] *s.* ⚗, *zo.* Lab *n.*

ren·net² [ˈrenɪt] *s.* ⚘ *Brit.* Reˈnette *f.*

re·nounce [rɪˈnaʊns] **I** *v/t.* **1.** verzichten auf (*acc.*), *et.* aufgeben; entsagen (*dat.*); **2.** verleugnen; *dem Glauben etc.* abschwören; *Freundschaft* aufsagen; ⚚ *Vertrag* kündigen; *et.* von sich weisen, ablehnen; sich von *j-m* lossagen; *j-n* verstoßen; **3.** *Kartenspiel*: *Farbe* nicht bedienen (können); **II** *v/i.* **4.** Verzicht leisten; **5.** *Kartenspiel*: nicht bedienen (können), passen.

ren·o·vate [ˈrenəʊveɪt] *v/t.* **1.** erneuern; wiederˈherstellen; **2.** renovieren; **ren·o·va·tion** [ˌrenəʊˈveɪʃn] *s.* Renovierung *f*, Erneuerung *f*; ˈ**ren·o·va·tor** [-tə] *s.* Erneuerer *m.*

re·nown [rɪˈnaʊn] *s. rhet.* Ruhm *m*, Ruf *m*, Berühmtheit *f*; **reˈnowned** [-nd] *adj.* berühmt, namhaft.

rent¹ [rent] **I** *s.* **1.** (Wohnungs)Miete *f*, Mietzins *m*: ***for ~*** *bsd. Am.* a) zu vermieten, b) zu verleihen; ***~-control(l)ed*** miet(preis)gebunden; ***~ tribunal*** Mieterschiedsgericht *n*; **2.** Pacht(geld *n*, -zins *m*) *f*; **II** *v/t.* **3.** vermieten; **4.** verpachten; **5.** mieten; **6.** (ab)pachten; **7.** *Am.* a) *et.* ausleihen, b) sich *et.* leihen; **III** *v/i.* **8.** vermietet *od.* verpachtet werden (***at*** *od.* ***for*** zu).

rent² [rent] **I** *s.* Riß *m*; Spalt(e *f*) *m*; **II** *pret. u. p.p. von* ***rend***.

rent·a·ble [ˈrentəbl] *adj.* (ver)mietbar.

ˌrent-a-ˈcar (serv·ice) *s. mot.* Autoverleih *m.*

ren·tal [ˈrentl] *s.* **1.** Miet-, Pachtbetrag *m*, -satz *m*: ***~ car*** Mietwagen *m*; ***~ library*** *Am.* Leihbücherei *f*: ***~ value*** Miet-, Pachtwert *m*; **2.** (Brutto)Mietertrag *m*; **3.** Zinsbuch *n.*

rent charge *pl.* **rents charge** *s.* Grundrente *f.*

rent·er [ˈrentə] *s. bsd. Am.* **1.** Pächter (-in), Mieter(in); **2.** Verpächter(in), -mieter(in), -leiher(in); **ˌrent-ˈfree** *adj.* miet-, pachtfrei.

re·nun·ci·a·tion [rɪˌnʌnsɪˈeɪʃn] *s.* **1.** (***of***) Verzicht *m* (auf *acc.*), Aufgabe *f* (*gen.*); **2.** Entsagung *f*; **3.** Ablehnung *f.*

re·o·pen [ˌriːˈəʊpən] **I** *v/t.* **1.** ˈwiedereröffnen; **2.** wieder beginnen, wiederˈaufnehmen; **II** *v/i.* **3.** sich wieder öffnen; **4.** ˈwiedereröffnen (*Geschäft etc.*); **5.** wieder beginnen.

re·or·gan·i·za·tion [ˈriːˌɔːgənaɪˈzeɪʃn] *s.* **1.** ˈUmbildung *f*, Neuordnung *f*, -gestaltung *f*; **2.** ⚚ Sanierung *f*; **re·or·gan·ize** [ˌriːˈɔːgənaɪz] *v/t.* **1.** reorganisieren, neu gestalten, ˈumgestalten, ˈumgliedern; **2.** ⚚ sanieren.

rep¹ [rep] *s.* Rips *m* (*Stoff*).

rep² [rep] *s. sl.* **1.** Wüstling *m*; **2.** *Am.* Ruf *m.*

re·pack [ˌriːˈpæk] *v/t.* ˈumpacken.

re·paint [ˌriːˈpeɪnt] *v/t.* neu (an)streichen, überˈmalen.

re·pair¹ [rɪˈpeə] **I** *v/t.* **1.** reparieren, (wieder) inˈstand setzen; ausbessern, flicken; **2.** wiederˈherstellen; **3.** wiederˈgutmachen; *Verlust* ersetzen; **II** *s.* **4.** Reparaˈtur *f*, Inˈstandsetzung *f*, Ausbesserung *f*; *pl.* Inˈstandsetzungsarbeit(en *pl.*) *f*: ***state of ~*** (baulicher *etc.*) Zustand; ***in good ~*** in gutem Zustand; ***in need of ~*** reparaturbedürftig; ***out of ~*** a) betriebsunfähig, b) baufällig; ***under ~*** in Reparatur; ***~ kit***, ***~ outfit*** Reparaturwerkzeug *n*, Flickzeug *n.*

re·pair² [rɪˈpeə] **I** *v/i.* sich begeben (***to*** nach, zu); **II** *s.* Zufluchtsort *m*, (beliebter) Aufenthaltsort.

re·pair·a·ble [rɪˈpeərəbl] *adj.* **1.** reparaˈturbedürftig; **2.** zu reparieren(d), reparierbar; **3.** → ***reparable***.

reˈpair|·man [-mæn] *s.* [*irr.*] *bsd. Am.* Meˈchaniker *m*, Autoschlosser *m*, (*Fernseh- etc.*)Techniker *m*; ***~-shop*** *s.* Reparaˈturwerkstatt *f.*

rep·a·ra·ble [ˈrepərəbl] *adj.* ☐ wiederˈgutzumachen(d); ersetzbar (*Verlust*);

rep·a·ra·tion [ˌrepəˈreɪʃn] *s.* **1.** Wiederˈgutmachung *f*: ***make ~*** Genugtuung leisten; **2.** Entschädigung *f*, Ersatz *m*; **3.** *pol.* Wiederˈgutmachungsleistung *f*; *pl.* Reparatiˈonen *pl.*

rep·ar·tee [ˌrepɑːˈtiː] *s.* schlagfertige Antwort, Schlagfertigkeit *f*: ***quick at ~*** schlagfertig.

re·par·ti·tion [ˌriːpɑːˈtɪʃn] **I** *s.* Aufteilung *f*, (Neu)Verteilung *f*; **II** *v/t.* (neu) auf-, verteilen.

re·pass [ˌriːˈpɑːs] *v/i.* (*u. v/t.*) wieder vorˈbeikommen (***an*** *dat.*).

re·past [rɪˈpɑːst] *s.* Mahl(zeit *f*) *n.*

re·pa·tri·ate [riːˈpætrɪeɪt] **I** *v/t.* repatriieren, (in die Heimat) zuˈrückführen; **II** *s.* Repatriierte(r *m*) *f*, Heimkehrer (-in); **re·pa·tri·a·tion** [ˌriːpætrɪˈeɪʃn] *s.* Rückführung *f.*

re·pay [*irr.* → ***pay***] **I** *v/t.* [riːˈpeɪ] **1.** *Geld etc.* zuˈrückzahlen, (zuˈrück)erstatten; **2.** *fig. Besuch*, *Gruß*, *Schlag etc.* erwidern; *Böses* heimzahlen, vergelten (***to s.o.*** j-m); **3.** *j-n* belohnen, (*a.* ⚚) entschädigen (***for*** für); **4.** *et.* lohnen, vergelten (***with*** mit); **II** *v/i.* [ˌriːˈpeɪ] **5.** nochmals (be)zahlen; **reˈpay·a·ble** [-ˈpeɪəbl] *adj.* rückzahlbar; **reˈpay·ment** [-mənt] *s.* **1.** Rückzahlung *f*; **2.** Erwiderung *f*; **3.** Vergeltung *f.*

re·peal [rɪˈpiːl] **I** *v/t.* **1.** *Gesetz etc.* aufheben, außer Kraft setzen; **2.** widerˈrufen; **II** *s.* **3.** Aufhebung *f von Gesetzen*; **reˈpeal·a·ble** [-ləbl] *adj.* ˈwiderruflich, aufhebbar.

re·peat [rɪˈpiːt] **I** *v/t.* **1.** wiederˈholen: ***~ an experience*** et. nochmals durchmachen *od.* erleben; ***~ an order*** (***for s.th.*** et.) nachbestellen; **2.** nachsprechen, wiederˈholen; weitererzählen; **3.** *ped. Gedicht* aufsagen; **II** *v/i.* **4.** sich wiederˈholen (*Vorgang*); **5.** repetieren (*Uhr*, *Gewehr*); **6.** aufstoßen (*Speisen*); **III** *s.* **7.** Wiederˈholung *f* (*a. TV etc.*); **8.** *et.* sich Wiederˈholendes (*z.B. Muster*), *bsd. Stoff*, *Tapete*: Rapˈport *m*; **9.** ♪ a) Wiederˈholung *f*, b) Wiederˈholungszeichen *n*: **10.** ⚚ *oft* ***~ order*** Nachbestellung *f*; **reˈpeat·ed** [-tɪd] *adj.* ☐ wiederˈholt, mehrmalig; neuerlich; **reˈpeat·er** [-tə] *s.* **1.** Wiederˈholende(r *m*) *f*; **2.** Repetieruhr *f*; **3.** Repetier-, Mehrladegewehr *n*; **4.** *Am. Wähler, der widerrechtlich mehrere Stimmen abgibt*; **5.** Ⱥ periˈodische Deziˈmalzahl *f*; **6.** ⚖ Rückfällige(r *m*) *f*; **7.** ⚓ Tochterkompaß *m*; **8.** ⚡ a) (Leitungs)Verstärker *m*, b) Überˈtrager *m*; **reˈpeat·ing** [-tɪŋ] *adj.* wiederˈholend: ***~ decimal*** → ***repeater*** 5; ***~ rifle*** → ***repeater*** 3; ***~ watch*** → ***repeater*** 2.

re·pel [rɪˈpel] *v/t.* **1.** *Angreifer* zuˈrückschlagen, -treiben; **2.** *Angriff* abschlagen, abweisen, *a. Schlag* abwehren; **3.** *fig.* ab-, zuˈrückweisen; **4.** *phys.* abstoßen; **5.** *fig. j-n* abstoßen, anwidern; **reˈpel·lent** [-lənt] *adj.* ☐ **1.** ab-, zuˈrückstoßend; **2.** *fig.* abstoßend.

re·pent [rɪˈpent] *v/t.* (*a. v/i.* ***of***) *et.* bereuen; **reˈpent·ance** [-təns] *s.* Reue *f*; **reˈpent·ant** [-tənt] *adj.* ☐ reuig (***of*** über *acc.*), bußfertig.

re·per·cus·sion [ˌriːpəˈkʌʃn] *s.* **1.** Rückprall *m*, -stoß *m*; **2.** ˈWiderhall *m*; **3.** *mst pl. fig.* Rück-, Auswirkungen *pl.* (***on*** auf *acc.*).

rep·er·toire [ˈrepətwɑː] → ***repertory*** 1.

rep·er·to·ry [ˈrepətərɪ] *s.* **1.** *thea.* Reperˈtoire *n*, Spielplan *m*: ***~ theatre*** (*Am.* ***theater***) Repertoirebühne *f*, -theater *n*; **2.** → ***repository*** 3.

rep·e·ti·tion [ˌrepɪˈtɪʃn] *s.* **1.** Wiederˈholung *f*: ***~ order*** ⚚ Nachbestellung *f*; ***~ work*** ⚙ Reihenfertigung *f*; **2.** *ped.* (Stück *n* zum) Aufsagen *n*; **3.** Koˈpie *f*, Nachbildung *f*; **rep·e·ti·tious** [ˌrepɪˈtɪʃəs] *adj.* ☐ sich ständig wiederˈholend; ewig gleichbleibend; **re·pet·i·tive** [rɪˈpetətɪv] *adj.* ☐ **1.** sich wiederˈholend, wiederˈholt; **2.** → ***repetitious***.

re·pine [rɪˈpaɪn] *v/i.* murren, ˈmißvergnügt *od.* unzufrieden sein (***at*** über *acc.*); **reˈpin·ing** [-nɪŋ] *adj.* ☐ unzufrieden, murrend, mürrisch.

re·place [rɪˈpleɪs] *v/t.* **1.** wieder hinstellen, -legen; *teleph. Hörer* auflegen; **2.** *et. Verlorenes*, *Veraltetes* ersetzen, an die Stelle treten von; ⚙ austauschen, ersetzen, *a.* wieder einsetzen; **3.** *j-n* ersetzen *od.* ablösen *od.* vertreten, *j-s* Stelle einnehmen; **4.** *Geld* zuˈrückerstatten, ersetzen; **5.** Ⱥ vertauschen; **reˈplace·a·ble** [-səbl] *adj.* ersetzbar; ⚙ auswechselbar; **reˈplace·ment** [-mənt] *s.* **1.** a) Ersetzung *f*, b) Ersatz *m*: ***~ engine*** ⚙ Austauschmotor *m*; ***~ part*** Ersatzteil *n*; **2.** ⚔ a) Ersatzmann *m*, b) Ersatz *m*, Auffüllung *f*: ***~ unit*** Ersatztruppenteil *m*; **3.** *med.* Proˈthese *f*: ***~ surgery*** Ersatzteilchirurgie *f.*

re·plant [ˌriːˈplɑːnt] *v/t.* **1.** ˈumpflanzen; **2.** neu pflanzen.

re·play [ˈriːpleɪ] *s. sport* **1.** Wiederˈholungsspiel *n*; **2.** *TV*: Wiederˈholung *f e-r Spielszene*.

re·plen·ish [rɪˈplenɪʃ] *v/t.* (wieder) auffüllen, ergänzen; **reˈplen·ish·ment** [-mənt] *s.* **1.** Auffüllung *f*, Ersatz *m*; **2.** Ergänzung *f.*

re·plete [rɪˈpliːt] *adj.* **1.** (***with***) (zum Platzen) voll (von), angefüllt (von); **2.** reichlich versehen (***with*** mit); **reˈpletion** [-iːʃn] *s.* (ˈÜber)Fülle *f*: ***full to ~*** bis zum Rande voll.

re·plev·in [rɪˈplevɪn] *s.* ⚖ **1.** (Klage *f* auf) Herˈausgabe *f* gegen Sicherheitsleistung; **2.** einstweilige Verfügung (auf Herausgabe).

rep·li·ca [ˈreplɪkə] *s.* **1.** *paint.* Reˈplik *f*, Origiˈnalkoˌpie *f*; **2.** Koˈpie *f*; **3.** *fig.* Ebenbild *n.*

rep·li·ca·tion [ˌreplɪˈkeɪʃn] *s.* **1.** Erwiderung *f*; **2.** Echo *n*; **3.** ⚖ Reˈplik *f*; **4.** Reproduktiˈon *f*, Koˈpie *f.*

re·ply [rɪˈplaɪ] **I** *v/i.* **1.** antworten, erwidern (***to s.th.*** auf et., ***to s.o.*** j-m) (*a. fig.*); **2.** ⚖ replizieren; **II** *s.* **3.** Antwort *f*, Erwiderung *f*: ***in ~ to*** (als Antwort) auf; ***in ~ to your letter*** in Beantwortung Ihres Schreibens; ***~-paid telegram*** Telegramm *n* mit bezahlter

Rückantwort; ~ (***postal***) ***card*** Postkarte *f* mit Rückantwort; ~ ***postage*** Rückporto *n*; (***there is***) ***no*** ~ *teleph.* der Teilnehmer meldet sich nicht; **4.** *Funk*: Rückmeldung *f*; **5.** ⚖ Re'plik *f*.

re·port [rɪ'pɔːt] **I** *s.* **1.** *allg.* Bericht *m* (***on*** über *acc.*); ☤ (Geschäfts-, Sitzungs-, Verhandlungs)Bericht *m*: ***month under*** ~ Berichtsmonat *m*; ~ ***stage*** *parl.* Erörterungsstadium *n e-r Vorlage*; **2.** Gutachten *n*, Refe'rat *n*; **3.** ⚔ Meldung *f*; **4.** ⚖ Anzeige *f*; **5.** Nachricht *f*, (Presse)Bericht *m*, (-)Meldung *f*; **6.** (Schul)Zeugnis *n*; **7.** Gerücht *n*; **8.** Ruf *m*, Leumund *m*; **9.** Knall *m*; **II** *v/t.* **10.** berichten (***to s.o.*** j-m); Bericht erstatten, berichten über (*acc.*); erzählen: ***it is ~ed that*** es heißt, daß; ***he is ~ed as saying*** er soll gesagt haben; ***~ed speech*** *ling.* indirekte Rede; **11.** *Vorkommnis*, *Schaden etc.* melden; **12.** *j-n* (***o.s.*** sich) melden; anzeigen (***to*** bei, ***for*** wegen); **13.** *parl.* *Gesetzesvorlage* (wieder) vorlegen (*Ausschuß*); **III** *v/i.* **14.** (e-n) Bericht geben *od.* erstatten, berichten (***on***, ***of*** über *acc.*); **15.** als Berichterstatter(in) arbeiten (***for*** für *e-e Zeitung*); **16.** (***to***) sich melden (bei); sich stellen (*dat.*): ~ ***for duty*** sich zum Dienst melden; **17.** ~ ***to*** *Am.* *j-m* unter'stellt sein; **re'port·a·ble** [-təbl] *adj.* **1.** ⚕ meldepflichtig (*Krankheit*); **2.** steuerpflichtig (*Einkommen*); **re'port·ed·ly** [-tɪdlɪ] *adv.* wie verlautet; **re'port·er** [-tə] *s.* **1.** Re'porter(in), (Presse)Berichterstatter(in); **2.** Berichterstatter (-in), Refe'rent(in); **3.** Proto'kollführer(in).

re·pose [rɪ'pəʊz] **I** *s.* **1.** Ruhe *f* (*a. fig.*); Erholung *f* (***from*** von): ***in*** ~ in Ruhe, untätig (*a. Vulkan*); **2.** *fig.* Gelassenheit *f*, (Gemüts)Ruhe *f*; **II** *v/i.* **3.** ruhen (*a. Toter*); (sich) ausruhen, schlafen; **4.** ~ ***on*** a) liegen *od.* ruhen auf (*dat.*), b) *fig.* beruhen auf (*dat.*), c) verweilen bei (*Gedanken*); **5.** ~ ***in*** *fig.* vertrauen auf (*acc.*); **III** *v/t.* **6.** *j-m* Ruhe gewähren, *j-n* (sich aus)ruhen lassen: ~ ***o.s.*** sich zur Ruhe legen; **7.** ~ ***on*** legen *od.* betten auf (*acc.*); **8.** ~ ***in*** *fig.* *Vertrauen*, *Hoffnung* setzen auf (*acc.*); **re·pos·i·to·ry** [rɪ'pɒzɪtərɪ] *s.* **1.** Behältnis *n*, Gefäß *n* (*a. fig.*); **2.** Verwahrungsort *m*; ☤ (Waren)Lager *n*, Niederlage *f*; **3.** *fig.* Fundgrube *f*, Quelle *f*; **4.** Vertraute(r *m*) *f*.

re·pos·sess [ˌriːpə'zes] *v/t.* **1.** wieder in Besitz nehmen; **2.** ~ ***of*** *j-n* wieder in den Besitz *e-r Sache* setzen.

rep·re·hend [ˌreprɪ'hend] *v/t.* tadeln, rügen; **ˌrep·re'hen·si·ble** [-nsəbl] *adj.* □ tadelnswert, sträflich; **ˌrep·re'hen·sion** [-nʃn] *s.* Tadel *m*, Rüge *f*, Verweis *m*.

rep·re·sent [ˌreprɪ'zent] *v/t.* **1.** *j-n od. j-s Sache* vertreten: ***be ~ed at*** bei *e-r Sache* vertreten sein; **2.** (bildlich, graphisch) dar-, vorstellen, abbilden; **3.** *thea.* a) *Rolle* darstellen, verkörpern, b) *Stück* aufführen; **4.** *fig.* (*symbolisch*) darstellen, verkörpern, bedeuten, repräsentieren; *e-r Sache* entsprechen; **5.** darlegen, -stellen, schildern, vor Augen führen (***to*** *dat.*): ~ ***to o.s.*** sich *et.* vorstellen; **6.** hin-, darstellen (***as*** *od.* ***to be*** als); behaupten, vorbringen: ~ ***that*** behaupten, daß; es so hinstellen, als ob; ~ ***to s.o. that*** j-m vorhalten, daß; **rep·re·sen·ta·tion** [ˌreprɪzen'teɪʃn] *s.* **1.** ⚖, ☤, *pol.* Vertretung *f*; → ***proportional*** 1; **2.** (*bildliche*, *graphische*) Darstellung, Bild *n*; **3.** *thea.* a) Darstellung *f e-r Rolle*, b) Aufführung *f e-s Stückes*; **4.** Schilderung *f*, Darstellung *f des Sachverhalts*: ***false ~s*** ⚖ falsche Angaben; **5.** Vorhaltung *f*: ***make ~s to*** bei *j-m* vorstellig werden, Vorstellungen erheben bei; **6.** ⚖ a) Anzeige *f* von Ge'fahrˌumständen (*Versicherung*), b) Rechtsnachfolge *f* (*bsd. Erbrecht*); **7.** *phls.* Vorstellung *f*, Begriff *m*; **ˌrep·re'sent·a·tive** [-tətɪv] **I** *s.* **1.** Vertreter (-in); Stellvertreter(in), Beauftragte(r *m*) *f*, Repräsen'tant(in): ***authorized*** ~ Bevollmächtigte(r *m*) *f*; (***commercial***) ~ Handelsvertreter(in); **2.** *parl.* (Volks-) Vertreter(in), Abgeordnete(r *m*) *f*: ***House of 2s*** *Am.* Repräsentantenhaus *n*; **3.** *fig.* typischer Vertreter, Musterbeispiel *n* (***of*** *gen.*); **II** *adj.* □ **4.** (***of***) vertretend (*acc.*), stellvertretend (für): ***in a*** ~ ***capacity*** als Vertreter(in); **5.** *pol.* repräsenta'tiv: ~ ***government*** parlamentarische Regierung; **6.** darstellend (***of*** *acc.*): ~ ***arts***; **7.** (***of***) *fig.* verkörpernd (*acc.*), sym'bolisch (für); **8.** typisch, kennzeichnend (***of*** für); *Statistik etc.*: repräsenta'tiv (*Auswahl*, *Querschnitt*): ~ ***sample*** ☤ Durchschnittsmuster *n*; **9.** ✿, *zo.* entsprechend (***of*** *dat.*).

re·press [rɪ'pres] *v/t.* **1.** *Gefühle*, *Tränen etc.* unter'drücken; **2.** *psych.* verdrängen; **re'pres·sion** [-eʃn] *s.* **1.** Unter'drückung *f*; **2.** *psych.* Verdrängung *f*; **re'pres·sive** [-sɪv] *adj.* □ **1.** repres'siv, unter'drückend; **2.** hemmend, Hemmungs...

re·prieve [rɪ'priːv] **I** *s.* **1.** ⚖ a) Begnadigung *f*, b) (Straf-, Voll'streckungs)Aufschub *m*; **2.** *fig.* (Gnaden)Frist *f*, Atempause *f*; **II** *v/t.* **3.** ⚖ *j-s* 'Urteilsvollˌstreckung aussetzen, (*a. fig.*) *j-m* e-e Gnadenfrist gewähren; **4.** *j-n* begnadigen; **5.** *fig.* *j-m* e-e Atempause gönnen.

rep·ri·mand ['reprɪmɑːnd] **I** *s.* Verweis *m*, Rüge *f*, Maßregelung *f*; **II** *v/t.* *j-m* e-n Verweis erteilen, *j-n* rügen *od.* maßregeln.

re·print [ˌriː'prɪnt] **I** *v/t.* neu drucken, nachdrucken, neu auflegen; **II** *s.* ['riːprɪnt] Nach-, Neudruck *m*, Re'print *m*, Neuauflage *f*.

re·pris·al [rɪ'praɪzl] *s.* Repres'salie *f*, Vergeltungsmaßnahme *f*: ***make ~s*** (***up***)***on*** Repressalien ergreifen gegen.

re·pro ['reprəʊ] *s.* F **1.** *typ.* ‚Repro' *f*, Reprodukti'on(svorlage) *f*; **2.** → ***reproduction*** 8.

re·proach [rɪ'prəʊtʃ] **I** *s.* **1.** Vorwurf *m*, Tadel *m*: ***without fear or*** ~ ohne Furcht u. Tadel; ***heap ~es on*** *j-n* mit Vorwürfen überschütten; **2.** *fig.* Schande *f* (***to*** für): ***bring*** ~ (***up***)***on*** *j-m* Schande machen; **II** *v/t.* **3.** vorwerfen, -halten, zum Vorwurf machen (***s.o. with s.th.*** j-m et.); **4.** *j-m* Vorwürfe machen, *j-n* tadeln (***for*** wegen); **5.** *et.* tadeln; **6.** *fig.* ein Vorwurf sein für, *et.* mit Schande bedecken; **re'proach·ful** [-fʊl] *adj.* □ vorwurfsvoll, tadelnd.

rep·ro·bate ['reprəʊbeɪt] **I** *adj.* **1.** ruchlos, lasterhaft; **2.** *eccl.* verdammt; **II** *s.* **3.** a) verkommenes Sub'jekt, b) Schurke *m*, c) Taugenichts *m*; **4.** (*von Gott*) Verworfene(r *m*) *f*; Verdammte(r *m*) *f*; **III** *v/t.* **5.** miß'billigen, verurteilen, verwerfen; verdammen (*Gott*); **rep·ro·ba·tion** [ˌreprəʊ'beɪʃn] *s.* 'Mißbilligung *f*, Verurteilung *f*.

re·pro·cess [ˌriː'prəʊses] *v/t.* ⚙ wieder'aufbereiten: ***~ing plant*** Wiederaufbereitungsanlage *f* (*für Kernbrennstoffe*).

re·pro·duce [ˌriːprə'djuːs] **I** *v/t.* **1.** *biol.* *u. fig.* ('wieder)erzeugen, (wieder) her'vorbringen; (***o.s.*** sich) fortpflanzen; **2.** *biol.* *Glied* regenerieren, neu bilden; **3.** *Bild etc.* reproduzieren; (*a.* ⚙) nachbilden, kopieren; *typ.* ab-, nachdrucken, vervielfältigen; **4.** *Stimme etc.* reproduzieren, 'wiedergeben; **5.** *Buch*, *Schauspiel* neu her'ausbringen; **6.** *et.* wieder'holen; **II** *v/i.* **7.** sich fortpflanzen *od.* vermehren; **ˌre·pro'duc·er** [-sə] *s.* **1.** ϟ a) 'Tonˌwiedergabegerät *n*, b) Tonabnehmer *m*; **2.** *Computer*: (Loch)Kartendoppler *m*; **ˌre·pro'duc·i·ble** [-səbl] *adj.* reproduzierbar; **ˌre·pro'duc·tion** [-'dʌkʃn] *s.* **1.** *allg.* 'Wiedererzeugung *f*; **2.** *biol.* Fortpflanzung *f*; **3.** *typ.*, *phot.* Reprodukti'on *f* (*a. psych. früherer Erlebnisse*); **4.** *typ.* Nachdruck *m*, Vervielfältigung *f*; **5.** ⚙ Nachbildung *f*; **6.** ♪, ϟ *etc.* 'Wiedergabe *f*; **7.** *ped.* Nacherzählung *f*; **8.** Reproduktion *f*: a) Nachbildung *f*, b) *paint.* Ko'pie *f*; **ˌre·pro'duc·tive** [-'dʌktɪv] *adj.* □ **1.** sich vermehrend, fruchtbar; **2.** *biol.* Fortpflanzungs...: ~ ***organs***; **3.** *psych.* reproduk'tiv, nachschöpferisch.

re·proof [rɪ'pruːf] *s.* Tadel *m*, Rüge *f*, Verweis *m*.

re·prov·al [rɪ'pruːvl] → ***reproof***; **re·prove** [rɪ'pruːv] *v/t.* *j-n* tadeln, rügen; *et.* miß'billigen; **re'prov·ing·ly** [-vɪŋlɪ] *adv.* tadelnd *etc.*

reps [reps] → ***rep***[1].

rep·tant ['reptənt] *adj.* ✿, *zo.* kriechend; **'rep·tile** [-taɪl] **I** *s.* **1.** *zo.* Rep'til *n*, Kriechtier *n*; **2.** *fig.* a) Kriecher(in), b) ‚falsche Schlange'; **II** *adj.* **3.** kriechend, Kriech...; **4.** *fig.* a) kriecherisch, b) gemein, niederträchtig, **rep·til·i·an** [rep'tɪlɪən] **I** *adj.* **1.** *zo.* Reptilien..., Kriechtier..., rep'tilisch; **2.** → ***reptile*** 4 b; **II** *s.* **3.** → ***reptile*** 1 *u.* 2.

re·pub·lic [rɪ'pʌblɪk] *s.* *pol.* Repu'blik *f*: ***the*** ~ ***of letters*** *fig.* die Gelehrtenwelt, die literarische Welt; **re'pub·li·can** [-kən] (*USA pol.* 2) **I** *adj.* republi'kanisch; **II** *s.* Republi'kaner(in); **re'pub·li·can·ism** [-kənɪzəm] *s.* **1.** republi'kanische Staatsform; **2.** republi'kanische Gesinnung.

re·pub·li·ca·tion ['riːˌpʌblɪ'keɪʃn] *s.* **1.** 'Wiederveröffentlichung *f*; **2.** Neuauflage *f* (*a. Erzeugnis*); **re·pub·lish** [ˌriː'pʌblɪʃ] *v/t.* neu veröffentlichen.

re·pu·di·ate [rɪ'pjuːdɪeɪt] **I** *v/t.* **1.** *Autorität*, *Schuld etc.* nicht anerkennen; *Vertrag* für unverbindlich erklären; **2.** *als unberechtigt* zu'rückweisen, verwerfen; **3.** *et.* ablehnen, nicht glauben; **4.** *Sohn etc.* verstoßen; **II** *v/i.* **5.** Staatsschulden nicht anerkennen; **re·pu·di·a·tion** [rɪˌpjuːdɪ'eɪʃn] *s.* **1.** Nichtanerkennung *f* (*bsd. e-r Staatsschuld*); **2.** Ablehnung *f*, Zu'rückweisung *f*, Verwerfung *f*; **3.** Verstoßung *f*.

re·pug·nance [rɪ'pʌgnəns] *s.* **1.** 'Widerwille *m*, Abneigung *f* (***to***, ***against*** gegen); **2.** Unvereinbarkeit *f*, (innerer)

ˈWiderspruch (***of*** *gen. od.* von, ***to, with*** mit); **reˈpug·nant** [-nt] *adj.* **1.** widerlich, zuˈwider(laufend), ˈwiderwärtig (***to*** *dat.*); **2.** unvereinbar (***to, with*** mit); **3.** widerˈstrebend.

re·pulse [rɪˈpʌls] **I** *v/t.* **1.** *Feind* zuˈrückschlagen, -werfen; *Angriff* abschlagen, -weisen; **2.** *fig. j-n* abweisen; *Bitte* abschlagen; **II** *s.* **3.** Zurückschlagen *n*, Abwehr *f*; **4.** *fig.* Zuˈrückweisung *f*, Absage *f*: ***meet with a ~*** abgewiesen werden (*a. fig.*); **5.** *phys.* Rückstoß *m*; **reˈpul·sion** [-lʃn] *s.* **1.** *phys.* Abstoßung *f*, Repulsiˈon *f*: ***~ motor*** ⚡ Repulsionsmotor *m*; **2.** *fig.* Abscheu *m, f*; **reˈpul·sive** [-sɪv] *adj.* □ *fig.* abstoßend (*a. phys.*), ˈwiderwärtig; **reˈpul·sive·ness** [-sɪvnɪs] *s.* ˈWiderwärtigkeit *f*.

re·pur·chase [ˌriːˈpɜːtʃəs] **I** *v/t.* ˈwieder-, zuˈrückkaufen; **II** *s.* ✝ Rückkauf *m*.

rep·u·ta·ble [ˈrepjʊtəbl] *adj.* □ **1.** achtbar, geachtet, angesehen, ehrbar; **2.** anständig; **rep·u·ta·tion** [ˌrepjʊˈteɪʃn] *s.* **1.** (guter) Ruf, Name *m*: ***a man of ~*** ein Mann von Ruf *od.* Namen; **2.** Ruf *m*: ***good*** (***bad***) ***~***; ***have the ~ of being*** im Ruf stehen, *et.* zu sein; ***have a ~ for*** bekannt sein für *od.* wegen.

re·pute [rɪˈpjuːt] **I** *s.* **1.** Ruf *m*, Leumund *m*: ***by ~*** dem Rufe nach, wie es heißt; ***of ill ~*** von schlechtem Ruf, übelbeleumdet; ***house of ill ~*** Bordell *n*; **2.** → ***reputation*** 1: ***be held in high ~*** hohes Ansehen genießen; **II** *v/t.* **3.** halten für: ***be ~d*** (***to be***) gelten als; ***be well*** (***ill***) ***~d*** in gutem (üblem) Rufe stehen; **reˈput·ed** [-tɪd] *adj.* □ **1.** angeblich; **2.** ungeeicht, landesüblich (*Maß*); **3.** bekannt, berühmt; **reˈput·ed·ly** [-tɪdlɪ] *adv.* angeblich, dem Vernehmen nach.

re·quest [rɪˈkwest] **I** *s.* **1.** Bitte *f*, Wunsch *m*; (*a. formelles*) Ersuchen, Gesuch *n*, Antrag *m*; (*Zahlungs- etc.*) Aufforderung *f*: ***at*** (*od.* ***by***) (***s.o.'s***) ***~*** auf (j-s) Ansuchen *od.* Bitte hin, auf (j-s) Veranlassung; ***by ~*** auf Wunsch; ***no flowers by ~*** Blumenspenden dankend verbeten; ***~ denied!*** *a. iro.* (Antrag) abgelehnt!; (***musical***) ***~ program***(***me***) Wunschkonzert *n*; ***~ stop*** 🚌 *etc.* Bedarfshaltestelle *f*; **2.** Nachfrage *f* (*a.* ✝): ***to be in*** (***great***) ***~*** (sehr) gefragt *od.* begehrt sein; **II** *v/t.* **3.** bitten *od.* ersuchen um: ***~ s.th. from s.o.*** j-n um et. ersuchen; ***it is ~ed*** es wird gebeten; **4.** *j-n* (höflich) bitten, *j-n* (*a. amtlich*) ersuchen (***to do*** zu tun).

re·qui·em [ˈrekwɪem] *s.* Requiem *n* (*a.* ♪), Seelen-, Totenmesse *f*.

re·quire [rɪˈkwaɪə] **I** *v/t.* **1.** erfordern (*Sache*): ***be ~d*** erforderlich sein; ***if ~d*** erforderlichenfalls, wenn nötig; **2.** brauchen, nötig haben, *e-r Sache* bedürfen: ***a task which ~s to be done*** e-e Aufgabe, die noch erledigt werden muß; **3.** verlangen, fordern (***of s.o.*** von j-m): ***~*** (***of***) ***s.o. to do s.th.*** j-n auffordern, et. zu tun; von j-m verlangen, daß er et. tue; ***~d subject*** *ped. Am.* Pflichtfach *n*; **4.** *Brit.* wünschen; **II** *v/i.* **5.** (es) verlangen; **reˈquire·ment** [-mənt] *s.* **1.** (*fig.* An)Forderung *f*; *fig.* Bedingung *f*, Vorˈaussetzung *f*: ***meet the ~s*** den Anforderungen entsprechen; **2.** Erfordernis *n*, Bedürfnis *n*; *mst pl.* Bedarf *m*: ***~s of raw materials*** Rohstoffbedarf *m*.

req·ui·site [ˈrekwɪzɪt] **I** *adj.* **1.** erforderlich, notwendig (***for, to*** für); **II** *s.* **2.** Erfordernis *n*, Vorˈaussetzung *f* (***for*** für); **3.** (Beˈdarfs-, Geˈbrauchs)Arˌtikel *m*: ***office ~s*** Büroartikel; **req·ui·si·tion** [ˌrekwɪˈzɪʃn] **I** *s.* **1.** Anforderung *f* (***for*** an *dat.*): ***~ number*** Bestellnummer *f*; **2.** (amtliche) Aufforderung; *Völkerrecht*: Ersuchen *n*; **3.** ⚔ Requisitiˈon *f*, Beschlagnahme *f*; Inˈanspruchnahme *f*; **4.** Einsatz *m*, Beanspruchung *f*; **5.** Erfordernis *n*; **II** *v/t.* **6.** verlangen; **7.** in Anspruch nehmen; ⚔ requirieren.

re·quit·al [rɪˈkwaɪtl] *s.* **1.** Belohnung *f* (***for*** für); **2.** Vergeltung *f* (***of*** für); **3.** Vergütung *f* (***for*** für); **re·quite** [rɪˈkwaɪt] *v/t.* **1.** belohnen: ***~ s.o.*** (***for s.th.***); **2.** vergelten.

re·read [ˌriːˈriːd] *v/t.* [*irr.* → ***read***] nochmals (ˈdurch)lesen.

re·route [ˌriːˈruːt] *v/t.* ˈumleiten.

re·run [ˌriːˈrʌn] **I** *v/t.* [*irr.*] *thea. Film*: wieder aufführen; *Radio, TV, a. Computer*: *Programm* wiederˈholen; **II** *s.* [ˈriːrʌn] ˈWiederaufführung *f*; Wiederˈholung *f*.

res [riːz] *pl.* **res** (*Lat.*) *s.* ⚖ Sache *f*: ***~ judicata*** rechtskräftig entschiedene Sache, *weitS.* (materielle) Rechtskraft; ***~ gestae*** (beweiserhebliche) Tatsachen, Tatbestand *m*.

re·sale [ˈriːseɪl] *s.* ˈWieder-, Weiterverkauf *m*: ***~ price maintenance*** Preisbindung *f* der zweiten Hand.

re·scind [rɪˈsɪnd] *v/t. Gesetz, Urteil etc.* aufheben, für nichtig erklären; *Kauf etc.* rückgängig machen; von *e-m Vertrag* zuˈrücktreten; **reˈscis·sion** [-ɪʒn] *s.* **1.** Aufhebung *f e-s Urteils etc.*; **2.** Rücktritt *m vom Vertrag*.

res·cue [ˈreskjuː] **I** *v/t.* **1.** (***from***) retten (aus), (*bsd.* ⚖ gewaltsam) befreien (von); (*bsd. et.*) bergen: ***~ from oblivion*** der Vergessenheit entreißen; **2.** (gewaltsam) zuˈrückholen; **II** *s.* **3.** Rettung *f* (*a. fig.*); Bergung *f*: ***come to s.o.'s ~*** j-m zu Hilfe kommen; **4.** (gewaltsame) Befreiung; **III** *adj.* **5.** Rettungs…: ***~ operation*** *a. fig.* Rettungsaktion *f*; ***~ party*** Rettungs-, Bergungsmannschaft *f*; ***~ vessel*** ⚓ Bergungsfahrzeug *f*; **ˈres·cu·er** [-jʊə] *s.* Befreier(in), Retter(in).

re·search [rɪˈsɜːtʃ] **I** *s.* **1.** Forschung(sarbeit) *f*, (wissenschaftliche) Unterˈsuchung (***on*** über *acc.*, auf dem Gebiet *gen.*); **2.** (genaue) Unterˈsuchung, (Nach)Forschung *f* (***after, for*** nach); **II** *v/i.* **3.** forschen, Forschungen anstellen, wissenschaftlich arbeiten (***on*** über *acc.*): ***~ into*** → 4; **III** *v/t.* **4.** erforschen, unterˈsuchen; **IV** *adj.* **5.** Forschungs…: **reˈsearch·er** [-tʃə] *s.* Forscher(in).

re·seat [ˌriːˈsiːt] *v/t.* **1.** *Saal etc.* neu bestuhlen; **2.** *j-n* ˈumsetzen; **3.** ***~ o.s.*** sich wieder setzen; **4.** ⚙ *Ventile* nachschleifen.

re·sect [riːˈsekt] *v/t.* ✂ herˈausschneiden; **reˈsec·tion** [-kʃn] *s.* ✂ Resektiˈon *f*.

re·se·da [ˈresɪdə] *s.* **1.** ♀ Reˈseda *f*; **2.** Reˈsedagrün *n*.

re·sell [ˌriːˈsel] *v/t.* [*irr.* → ***sell***] wieder verkaufen, weiterverkaufen; **ˌreˈsell·er** [-lə] *s.* ˈWiederverkäufer *m*.

re·sem·blance [rɪˈzembləns] *s.* Ähnlichkeit *f* (***to*** mit, ***between*** zwischen): ***bear*** (*od.* ***have***) ***~ to*** → **re·sem·ble** [rɪˈzembl] *v/t.* (*dat.*) ähnlich sein *od.* sehen, gleichen, ähneln.

re·sent [rɪˈzent] *v/t.* übelnehmen, verübeln, sich ärgern über (*acc.*); **reˈsent·ful** [-fʊl] *adj.* □ **1.** (***against, of***) aufgebracht (gegen), ärgerlich *od.* voller Groll (auf *acc.*); **2.** übelnehmerisch, reizbar; **reˈsent·ment** [-mənt] *s.* **1.** Ressentiˈment *n*, Groll *m* (***against, at*** gegen); **2.** Verstimmung *f*, Unmut *m*, Unwille *m*.

res·er·va·tion [ˌrezəˈveɪʃn] *s.* **1.** Vorbehalt *m*; ⚖ *a.* Vorbehaltsrecht *n od.* -klausel *f*: ***without ~*** ohne Vorbehalt; → ***mental*** 1; **2.** *oft pl. Am.* Vorbestellung *f*, Reservierung *f von Zimmern etc.*; **3.** *Am.* Reserˈvat *n*: a) Naˈturschutzgebiet *n*, b) Indiˈanerreservatiˌon *f*.

re·serve [rɪˈzɜːv] **I** *s.* **1.** *allg.* Reˈserve *f* (*a. fig.*), Vorrat *m*: ***in ~*** in Reserve, vorrätig; ***~ seat*** Notsitz *m*; **2.** ✝ Reserve *f*, Rücklage *f*, -stellung *f*: ***~ account*** Rückstellungskonto *n*: ***~ currency*** Leitwährung *f*; **3.** ⚔ a) Reˈserve *f*: ***~ officer*** Reserveoffizier *m*; b) *pl. taktische* Reˈserven *pl.*; **4.** *sport* Ersatz (-mann) *m*, Reˈservespieler *m*; **5.** Reserˈvat *n*, Schutzgebiet *n*: ***~ game*** geschützter Wildbestand; **6.** Vorbehalt *m* (*a.* ⚖): ***without ~*** vorbehalt-, rückhaltlos; ***with certain ~s*** mit gewissen Einschränkungen; ***~ price*** ✝ Mindestgebot *n* (*bei Versteigerungen*); **7.** *fig.* Zuˈrückhaltung *f*, Reˈserve *f*, zuˈrückhaltendes Wesen: ***receive s.th. with ~*** *e-e Nachricht etc.* mit Zurückhaltung aufnehmen; **II** *v/t.* **8.** (sich) aufsparen *od.* -bewahren, (zuˈrück)behalten, in Reˈserve halten; ⚔ *j-n* zuˈrückstellen; **9.** (sich) zuˈrückhalten mit, warten mit, *et.* verschieben: ***~ judg***(***e***)***ment*** ⚖ die Urteilsverkündung aussetzen; **10.** reservieren (lassen), vorbestellen, vormerken (***to, for*** für); **11.** *bsd.* ⚖ a) vorbehalten (***to s.o.*** j-m), b) sich vorbehalten: ***~ the right to do*** (*od.* ***of doing***) ***s.th.*** sich das Recht vorbehalten, et. zu tun; ***all rights ~d*** alle Rechte vorbehalten; **reˈserved** [-vd] *adj.* □ *fig.* zuˈrückhaltend, reserviert; **reˈserv·ist** [-vɪst] *s.* ⚔ Reserˈvist *m*.

res·er·voir [ˈrezəvwɑː] *s.* **1.** Behälter *m* für Wasser *etc.*; Speicher *m*; **2.** (ˈWasser)Reserˌvoir *n*: a) Wasserturm *m*, b) Sammel-, Staubecken *n*, Basˈsin *n*; **3.** *fig.* Reserˈvoir *n* (***of*** an *dat.*).

re·set [ˌriːˈset] *v/t.* [*irr.* → ***set***] **1.** *Edelstein* neu fassen; **2.** *Messer* neu abziehen; **3.** *typ.* neu setzen; **4.** ⚙ nachrichten, -stellen; *Computer*: rücksetzen, nullstellen.

re·set·tle [ˌriːˈsetl] **I** *v/t.* **1.** *Land* wieder besiedeln; **2.** *j-n* wieder ansiedeln, ˈumsiedeln; **3.** wieder in Ordnung bringen; **II** *v/i.* **4.** sich wieder ansiedeln; **5.** *fig.* sich wieder setzen *od.* legen *od.* beruhigen; **ˌreˈset·tle·ment** [-mənt] *s.* **1.** ˈWiederansiedlung *f*, ˈUmsiedlung *f*; **2.** Neuordnung *f*.

re·shape [ˌriːˈʃeɪp] *v/t.* neu formen, ˈumgestalten.

re·ship [ˌriːˈʃɪp] *v/t.* **1.** *Güter* wieder verschiffen; **2.** ˈumladen; **ˌreˈship·ment** [-mənt] *s.* **1.** ˈWiederverladung *f*; **2.**

Rückladung *f*, -fracht *f*.

re·shuf·fle [ˌriːˈʃʌfl] **I** *v/t.* **1.** *Spielkarten* neu mischen; **2.** *bsd. pol.* ˈumgruppieren, -bilden; **II** *s.* **3.** *pol.* ˈUmbildung *f*, ˈUmgruppierung *f*.

re·side [rɪˈzaɪd] *v/i.* **1.** wohnen, ansässig sein, s-n (ständigen) Wohnsitz haben (*in*, *at* in *dat.*); **2.** *fig.* (*in*) a) wohnen (in *dat.*), b) innewohnen (*dat.*), c) zustehen (*dat.*), liegen, ruhen (bei *j-m*).

res·i·dence [ˈrezɪdəns] *s.* **1.** Wohnsitz *m*, -ort *m*; Sitz *m e-r Behörde etc.*: ***take up one's ~*** s-n Wohnsitz nehmen *od.* aufschlagen, sich niederlassen; **2.** Aufenthalt *m*: ***~ permit*** Aufenthaltsgenehmigung *f*; ***place of ~*** Wohn-, Aufenthaltsort *m*; **3.** (herrschaftliches) Wohnhaus; **4.** Wohnung *f*: ***official ~*** Dienstwohnung *f*; **5.** Wohnen *n*; **6.** Ortsansässigkeit *f*: ***~ is required*** es besteht Residenzpflicht; ***be in ~*** am Amtsort ansässig sein; **ˈres·i·dent** [-nt] **I** *adj.* **1.** (orts-)ansässig, (ständig) wohnhaft; **2.** im (*Schul- od. Kranken- etc.*)Haus wohnend: ***~ physician***; **3.** *fig.* innewohnend (*in dat.*); **4.** *zo.* seßhaft: ***~ birds*** Standvögel; **II** *s.* **5.** Ortsansässige(r *m*) *f*, Einwohner(in); *mot.* Anlieger *m*; **6.** ⚕ *Am.* Assisˈtenzarzt *m*, -ärztin *f*; *pol. a.* ***minister-~*** Miˈnisterresiˌdent *m* (*Gesandter*); **res·i·den·tial** [ˌrezɪˈdenʃl] *adj.* **1.** a) Wohn…: ***~ allowance*** Ortszulage *f*; ***~ area*** (*a.* vornehme) Wohngegend; ***~ university*** Internatsuniversität *f*, b) herrschaftlich; **2.** Wohnsitz…

re·sid·u·al [rɪˈzɪdjʊəl] **I** *adj.* **1.** Ѧ zuˈrückbleibend, übrig; **2.** übrig(geblieben), Rest… (*a. phys. etc.*): ***~ product*** ⚗, ⚙ Nebenprodukt *n*; ***~ soil*** *geol.* Eluvialboden *m*; **3.** *phys.* remaˈnent: ***~ magnetism***; **II** *s.* **4.** Rückstand *m*, Rest *m*; **5.** Ѧ Rest(wert) *m*, Diffeˈrenz *f*; **reˈsid·u·ar·y** [-ərɪ] *adj.* restlich, übrig(geblieben): ***~ estate*** ⚖ Reinnachlaß *m*; ***~ legatee*** Nachvermächtnisnehmer(in); **res·i·due** [ˈrezɪdjuː] *s.* **1.** Rest *m* (*a.* Ѧ, ✝); **2.** ⚗ Rückstand *m*; **3.** ⚖ reiner (Erb)Nachlaß; **reˈsid·u·um** [-jʊəm] *pl.* **-u·a** [-jʊə] (*Lat.*) *s.* **1.** *bsd.* ⚗ Rückstand *m*, (*a.* Ѧ) Reˈsiduum *n*; **2.** *fig.* Bodensatz *m*, Hefe *f e-s Volkes etc.*

re·sign [rɪˈzaɪn] **I** *v/t.* **1.** *Besitz*, *Hoffnung etc.* aufgeben; verzichten auf (*acc.*); *Amt* niederlegen; **2.** überˈlassen (*to dat.*); **3.** ***~ o.s.*** sich anvertrauen *od.* überlassen (*to dat.*); **4.** ***~ o.s.*** (*to*) sich ergeben (in *acc.*), sich abfinden *od.* versöhnen (mit *s-m Schicksal etc.*); **II** *v/i.* **5.** (*to* in *acc.*) sich ergeben, sich fügen; **6.** (*from*) a) zuˈrücktreten (von *e-m Amt*), abdanken; b) austreten (aus); **res·ig·na·tion** [ˌrezɪgˈneɪʃn] *s.* **1.** Aufgabe *f*, Verzicht *m*; **2.** Rücktritt(sgesuch *n*) *m*, Amtsniederlegung *f*, Abdankung *f*: ***send in*** (*od.* ***tender***) ***one's ~*** s-n Rücktritt einreichen; **3.** Ergebung *f* (*to* in *acc.*); **reˈsigned** [-nd] *adj.* ☐ ergeben: ***he is ~ to his fate*** er hat sich mit s-m Schicksal abgefunden.

re·sil·i·ence [rɪˈzɪlɪəns] *s.* Elastiziˈtät *f*: a) *phys.* Prallkraft *f*, b) *fig.* Spannkraft *f*; **reˈsil·i·ent** [-nt] *adj.* eˈlastisch: a) federnd, b) *fig.* spannkräftig, unverwüstlich.

res·in [ˈrezɪn] **I** *s.* **1.** Harz *n*; **2.** → ***rosin*** I; **II** *v/t.* **3.** harzen, mit Harz behandeln; **ˈres·in·ous** [-nəs] *adj.* harzig, Harz…

re·sist [rɪˈzɪst] **I** *v/t.* **1.** widerˈstehen (*dat.*): ***I cannot ~ doing it*** ich muß es einfach tun; **2.** ˈWiderstand leisten (*dat. od.* gegen), sich widerˈsetzen (*dat.*), sich sträuben gegen: ***~ing a public officer in the excecution of his duty*** ⚖ Widerstand *m* gegen die Staatsgewalt; **II** *v/i.* **3.** ˈWiderstand leisten, sich widerˈsetzen; **III** *s.* **4.** ⚙ Deckmittel *n*, Schutzlack *m*; **reˈsist·ance** [-təns] *s.* **1.** Widerstand *m* (*to* gegen): ***air ~*** *phys.* Luftwiderstand; ***~ movement*** *pol.* Widerstandsbewegung *f*; ***offer ~*** Widerstand leisten (*to dat.*); ***take the line of least ~*** den Weg des geringsten Widerstandes einschlagen; **2.** ˈWiderstandskraft *f* (*a.* ⚕); ⚙ (*Hitze-*, *Kälte- etc.*)Beständigkeit *f*, (*Biegungs-*, *Säure-*, *Stoß- etc.*)Festigkeit *f*: ***~ to wear*** Verschleißfestigkeit *f*; **3.** ⚡ Widerstand *m*; **reˈsist·ant** [-tənt] *adj.* **1.** widerˈstehend, -ˈstrebend; **2.** ⚙ ˈwiderstandsfähig (*to* gegen), beständig; **re·sis·tiv·i·ty** [rɪzɪˈstɪvətɪ] *s.* ⚡ speˈzifischer Widerstand; **reˈsis·tor** [-tə] *s.* ⚡ Widerstand *m* (*Bauteil*).

re·sit I *s.* [ˈriːsɪt] *ped.* Wiederˈholungsprüfung *f*; **II** *v/t.* [ˌriːˈsɪt] [*irr.* → ***sit***] *Prüfung* wiederˈholen; **III** *v/i.* [ˌriːˈsɪt] [*irr.* → ***sit***] die Prüfung wiederˈholen.

re·sole [ˌriːˈsəʊl] *v/t.* neu besohlen.

res·o·lu·ble [rɪˈzɒljʊbl] *adj.* **1.** ⚗ auflösbar; **2.** *fig.* lösbar.

res·o·lute [ˈrezəluːt] *adj.* ☐ entschieden, entschlossen, resoˈlut; **ˈres·o·lute·ness** [-nɪs] *s.* Entschlossenheit *f*; resoˈlute Art.

res·o·lu·tion [ˌrezəˈluːʃn] *s.* **1.** Entschlossenheit *f*, Entschiedenheit *f*; **2.** Entschluß *m*: ***good ~s*** gute Vorsätze; **3.** ✝, *parl.* Beschluß(fassung *f*) *m*, Entschließung *f*, Resolutiˈon *f*; **4.** ⚗, Ѧ, ♪, *phys.*, *opt.* (*a. Metrik*) Auflösung *f* (*into* in *acc.*); **5.** ⚙ Rasterung *f* (*Bild*); **6.** ⚕ a) Lösung *f e-r Entzündung etc.*, b) Zerteilung *f e-s Tumors*; **7.** *fig.* Lösung *f e-r Frage*; Behebung *f von Zweifeln*.

re·solv·a·ble [rɪˈzɒlvəbl] *adj.* (auf)lösbar (*into* in *acc.*); **reˈsolve** [rɪˈzɒlv] **I** *v/t.* **1.** *a. opt.*, ⚗, ♪, Ѧ auflösen (*into* in *acc.*): ***be ~d into*** sich auflösen in (*acc.*); ***~d into dust*** in Staub verwandelt; ***resolving power*** *opt.*, *phot.* Auflösungsvermögen *n*; → ***committee***; **2.** analysieren; **3.** *fig.* zuˈrückführen (*into*, *to* auf *acc.*); **4.** *fig. Frage etc.* lösen; **5.** *fig. Bedenken*, *Zweifel* zerstreuen; **6.** a) beschließen, sich entschließen (*to do et.* zu tun), b) entscheiden; **II** *v/i.* **7.** sich auflösen (*into* in *acc.*, *to* zu); **8.** (*on*, *upon s.th.*) (et.) beschließen, sich entschließen (zu et.); **III** *s.* **9.** Entschluß *m*, Vorsatz *m*; **10.** *Am.* → ***resolution*** 3; **11.** *rhet.* Entschlossenheit *f*; **reˈsolved** [-vd] *p.p. u. adj.* ☐ (fest) entschlossen.

res·o·nance [ˈrezənəns] *s.* Resoˈnanz *f* (*a.* ♪, ⚕, *phys.*), Nach-, ˈWiderhall *m*, Mitschwingen *n*: ***~ box*** Resonanzkasten *m*; **ˈres·o·nant** [-nt] *adj.* ☐ **1.** ˈwider-, nachhallend (*with* von); **2.** volltönend (*Stimme*); **3.** *phys.* mitschwingend, Resonanz…; **ˈres·o·na·tor** [-neɪtə] *s.* **1.** *phys.* Resoˈnator *m*; **2.** ⚡ Resoˈnanzkreis *m*.

re·sorb [rɪˈsɔːb] *v/t.* (wieder) aufsaugen, resorbieren; **reˈsorb·ence** [-bəns], **reˈsorp·tion** [-ɔːpʃn] *s.* Resorptiˈon *f*.

re·sort [rɪˈzɔːt] **I** *s.* **1.** Zuflucht *f* (*to* zu); Mittel *n*: ***in the*** (*od.* ***as a***) ***last ~*** als letzter Ausweg, ‚wenn alle Stricke reißen'; ***have ~ to*** → 5; ***without ~ to force*** ohne Gewaltanwendung; **2.** Besuch *m*, Zustrom *m*: ***place of ~*** (beliebter) Treffpunkt; **3.** (Aufenthalts-, Erholungs)Ort *m*: ***health ~*** Kurort; ***summer ~*** Sommerurlaubsort; **II** *v/i.* **4.** ***~ to*** a) sich begeben zu *od.* nach, b) *Ort* oft besuchen; **5.** ***~ to*** s-e Zuflucht nehmen zu, zuˈrückgreifen auf (*acc.*), greifen zu, Gebrauch machen von.

re·sound [rɪˈzaʊnd] **I** *v/i.* **1.** ˈwiderhallen (*with*, *to* von): ***~ing*** schallend; **2.** erschallen, ertönen (*Klang*); **II** *v/t.* **3.** ˈwiderhallen lassen.

re·source [rɪˈsɔːs] *s.* **1.** (Hilfs)Quelle *f*, (-)Mittel *n*; **2.** *pl.* a) Mittel *pl.*, Reichtümer *pl. e-s Landes*: ***natural ~s*** Bodenschätze, b) Geldmittel *pl.*, c) ✝ *Am.* Akˈtiva *pl.*; **3.** → ***resort*** 1; **4.** Findig-, Wendigkeit *f*; Taˈlent *n*: ***he is full of ~*** er weiß sich immer zu helfen; **5.** Entspannung *f*, Unterˈhaltung *f*; **reˈsource·ful** [-fʊl] *adj.* ☐ **1.** reich an Hilfsquellen; **2.** findig, wendig, einfallsreich.

re·spect [rɪˈspekt] **I** *s.* **1.** Rücksicht *f* (*to*, *of* auf *acc.*): ***without ~ to persons*** ohne Ansehen der Person; **2.** Hinsicht *f*, Beziehung *f*: ***in every*** (***some***) ***~*** in jeder (gewisser) Hinsicht; ***in ~ of*** (*od.* ***to***), ***with ~ to*** (*od.* ***of***) hinsichtlich (*gen.*), bezüglich (*gen.*), in Anbetracht (*gen.*); ***have ~ to*** sich beziehen auf (*acc.*); **3.** (Hoch)Achtung *f*, Ehrerbietung *f*, Reˈspekt *m* (*for* vor *dat.*); **4.** ***one's ~s*** *pl.* s-e Empfehlungen *pl. od.* Grüße *pl.* (*to* an *acc.*): ***give him my ~s*** grüßen Sie ihn von mir; ***pay one's ~s to*** a) *j-n* bestens grüßen, b) *j-m* s-e Aufwartung machen; **II** *v/t.* **5.** sich beziehen auf (*acc.*), betreffen; **6.** (hoch)achten, ehren; **7.** *Gefühle*, *Gesetze etc.* respektieren, (be)achten; ***~ o.s.*** etwas auf sich halten; **re·spect·a·bil·i·ty** [rɪˌspektəˈbɪlətɪ] *s.* **1.** Ehrbarkeit *f*, Achtbarkeit *f*; **2.** Ansehen *n*; ✝ Solidiˈtät *f*; **3.** a) *pl.* Reˈspektsperˌsonen *pl.*, Honoratiˈoren *pl.*, b) Reˈspektsperˌson *f*; **4.** *pl.* Anstandsregeln *pl.*; **reˈspect·a·ble** [-təbl] *adj.* ☐ **1.** ansehnlich, (recht) beachtlich; **2.** acht-, ehrbar; anständig, soˈlide; **3.** angesehen, geachtet; **4.** korˈrekt, konventioˈnell; **reˈspect·er** [-tə] *s.*: ***be no ~ of persons*** ohne Ansehen der Person handeln; **reˈspect·ful** [-fʊl] *adj.* ☐ reˈspektvoll (*a. iro. Entfernung*), ehrerbietig, höflich: ***Yours ~ly*** mit vorzüglicher Hochachtung (*Briefschluß*); **reˈspect·ing** [-tɪŋ] *prp.* bezüglich (*gen.*), hinsichtlich (*gen.*), über (*acc.*); **reˈspec·tive** [-tɪv] *adj.* ☐ jeweilig (*jedem einzeln zukommend*), verschieden: ***to our ~ places*** *wir gingen* jeder an s-n Platz; **reˈspec·tive·ly** [-tɪvlɪ] *adv.* a) beziehungsweise, b) in dieser Reihenfolge.

res·pi·ra·tion [ˌrespəˈreɪʃn] *s.* Atmung *f*, Atmen *n*, Atemholen *n*: ***artificial ~*** künstliche Beatmung; **res·pi·ra·tor** [ˈrespəreɪtə] *s.* **1.** *Brit.* Gasmaske *f*; **2.** Atemfilter *m*; **3.** ⚕ Atemgerät *n*, ˈSauerstoffappaˌrat *m*; **re·spir·a·to·ry**

[rɪ'spaɪərətərɪ] *adj. anat.* Atmungs...
re·spire [rɪ'spaɪə] **I** *v/i.* **1.** atmen; **2.** *fig.* aufatmen; **II** *v/t.* **3.** (ein)atmen; *poet.* atmen.
res·pite ['respaɪt] **I** *s.* **1.** Frist *f*, (Zahlungs)Aufschub *m*, Stundung *f*; **2.** ⚖ a) Aussetzung *f* des Voll'zugs (*der Todesstrafe*), b) Strafaufschub *m*; **3.** *fig.* (Atem-, Ruhe)Pause *f*; **II** *v/t.* **4.** auf-, verschieben; **5.** *j-m* Aufschub gewähren, e-e Frist einräumen; **6.** ⚖ die Voll'streckung des Urteils an *j-m* aufschieben; **7.** Erleichterung von *Schmerz etc.* verschaffen.
re·splend·ence [rɪ'splendəns], **re'splend·en·cy** [-sɪ] *s.* Glanz *m* (*a. fig. Pracht*); **re'splend·ent** [-nt] *adj.* □ glänzend, strahlend, prangend.
re·spond [rɪ'spɒnd] *v/i.* **1.** (*to*) antworten (auf *acc.*) (*a. eccl.*), *Brief etc.* beantworten; **2.** *fig.* antworten, er'widern (*with* mit); **3.** *fig.* (*to*) reagieren *od.* ansprechen (auf *acc.*), empfänglich sein (für), eingehen auf (*acc.*): **~ to a call** e-m Rufe folgen; **4.** ⚙ ansprechen (*Motor*), gehorchen; **re'spond·ent** [-dənt] **I** *adj.* **1. ~ to** reagierend auf (*acc.*), empfänglich für; **2.** ⚖ beklagt; **II** *s.* **3.** ⚖ a) (Scheidungs)Beklagte(r *m*) *f*, b) Berufungsbeklagte(r *m*) *f*.
re·sponse [rɪ'spɒns] *s.* **1.** Antwort *f*, Erwiderung *f*: **in ~ to** als Antwort auf (*acc.*), in Erwiderung (*gen.*); **2.** *fig.* a) Reakti'on *f* (*a. biol.*, *psych.*), Antwort *f*, b) 'Widerhall *m* (*alle*: **to** auf *acc.*): **meet with a good ~** Widerhall *od.* e-e gute Aufnahme finden; **3.** *eccl.* Antwort(strophe) *f*; **4.** ⚙ Ansprechen *n* (*des Motors etc.*).
re·spon·si·bil·i·ty [rɪˌspɒnsə'bɪlətɪ] *s.* **1.** Verantwortlichkeit *f*; **2.** Verantwortung *f* (*for, of* für): **on one's own ~** auf eigene Verantwortung; **3.** ⚖ a) Zurechnungsfähigkeit *f*, b) Haftbarkeit *f*; **4.** Vertrauenswürdigkeit *f*; ✝ Zahlungsfähigkeit *f*; **5.** *oft pl.* Verbindlichkeit *f*, Verpflichtung *f*; **re·spon·si·ble** [rɪ'spɒnsəbl] *adj.* □ **1.** verantwortlich (**to** *dat.*, **for** für): **~ partner** ✝ persönlich haftender Gesellschafter; **2.** ⚖ a) zurechnungsfähig, b) geschäftsfähig, c) haftbar; **3.** verantwortungsbewußt, zuverlässig; ✝ so'lide, zahlungsfähig; **4.** verantwortungsvoll, verantwortlich (*Stellung*): **used to ~ work** an selbständiges Arbeiten gewöhnt; **5.** (*for*) a) schuld (an *dat.*), verantwortlich (für), b) die Ursache (*gen. od.* von); **re·spon·sive** [rɪ'spɒnsɪv] *adj.* □ **1.** Antwort..., antwortend (**to** auf *acc.*); **2.** (**to**) (leicht) reagierend (auf *acc.*), ansprechbar; *weitS.* empfänglich *od.* zugänglich *od.* aufgeschlossen (für): **be ~ to** a) ansprechen *od.* reagieren auf (*acc.*), b) eingehen auf (*j-n*), (*e-m Bedürfnis etc.*) entgegenkommen; **3.** ⚙ e'lastisch (*Motor*).
rest¹ [rest] **I** *s.* **1.** (*a.* Nacht)Ruhe *f*, Rast *f*; *fig.* a) Ruhe *f* (*Frieden*, *Untätigkeit*), b) Ruhepause *f*, Erholung *f*, c) ewige *od.* letzte Ruhe (*Tod*); *phys.* Ruhe(lage *f*): **at ~** in Ruhe, ruhig; **be at ~** a) ruhen (*Toter*), b) beruhigt sein, c) ⚙ sich in Ruhelage befinden; **give a ~ to** a) *Maschine etc.* ruhen lassen, b) F *et.* auf sich beruhen lassen; **have a good night's ~** gut schlafen; **lay to ~** zur letzten Ruhe betten; **set s.o.'s mind at ~** j-n beruhigen; **set a matter at ~** e-e Sache (endgültig) entscheiden *od.* erledigen; **take a ~** sich ausruhen; **2.** Ruheplatz *m* (*a. Grab*), Raststätte *f*; Aufenthalt *m*; Herberge *f*, Heim *n*; **3.** ⚙ a) Auflage *f*, Stütze *f*, (Arm)Lehne *f*, (Fuß)Raste *f*, *teleph.* Gabel *f*, b) Sup'port *m e-r Drehbank*, c) ⚔ (Gewehr)Auflage *f*; **4.** ♪ Pause *f*; **5.** *Metrik*: Zä'sur *f*; **II** *v/i.* **6.** ruhen, schlafen (*a. Toter*); **7.** (sich aus-) ruhen, rasten, e-e (Ruhe)Pause einlegen: **let a matter ~** *fig.* e-e Sache auf sich beruhen lassen; **the matter cannot ~ there** damit kann es nicht sein Bewenden haben; **8.** sich stützen: **~ against** sich stützen *od.* lehnen gegen, ⚙ anliegen an (*acc.*); **~ (up)on** a) ruhen auf (*dat.*) (*a. Last*, *Blick*, *Schatten etc.*), b) *fig.* beruhen auf (*dat.*), sich stützen auf (*acc.*), c) *fig.* sich verlassen auf (*acc.*); **9. ~ with** bei *j-m* liegen (*Entscheidung*, *Schuld*), in *j-s* Händen liegen, von *j-m* abhängen, *j-m* über'lassen bleiben; **10.** ⚖ *Am.* → 16; **III** *v/t.* **11.** (aus)ruhen lassen, *j-m* Ruhe gönnen: **~ o.s.** sich ausruhen; **God ~ his soul** Gott hab' ihn selig; **12.** *Augen*, *Stimme* schonen; **13.** legen, lagern (**on** auf *acc.*); **14.** *Am.* F *Hut etc.* ablegen; **15. ~ one's case** ⚖ *Am.* den Beweisvortrag abschließen.
rest² [rest] **I** *s.* **1.** Rest *m*; (*das*) übrige, (*die*) übrigen: **and all the ~ of it** und alles übrige; **the ~ of us** wir übrigen; **for the ~** im übrigen; **2.** ✝ *Brit.* Re'serveˌfonds *m*; **3.** ✝ *Brit.* a) Bilanzierung *f*, b) Restsaldo *m*; **II** *v/i.* **4.** *in e-m Zustand* bleiben, weiterhin sein: **~ assured that** seien Sie versichert *od.* verlassen Sie sich darauf, daß; **5. ~ with** → **rest¹** 9.
re·state [ˌriː'steɪt] *v/t.* neu (u. besser) formulieren; ˌ**re'state·ment** [-mənt] *s.* neue Darstellung *od.* Formulierung.
res·tau·rant ['restərɔ̃ːŋ] (*Fr.*) *s.* Restau'rant *n*, Gaststätte *f*: **~ car** Speisewagen *m*.
rest| cure ⚕ Liegekur *f*; **~ home** *s.* Alten- *od.* Pflegeheim *n*.
rest·ed ['restɪd] *p.p. u. adj.* ausgeruht, erholt; **rest·ful** ['restfʊl] *adj.* □ **1.** ruhig, friedlich; **2.** erholsam, gemütlich; **3.** bequem, angenehm.
rest house *s.* Rasthaus *n*.
rest·ing place ['restɪŋ] *s.* **1.** Ruheplatz *m*; **2.** (letzte) Ruhestätte, Grab *n*.
res·ti·tu·tion [ˌrestɪ'tjuːʃn] *s.* **1.** Restitu'tion *f*: a) (Zu)'Rückerstattung *f*, b) Entschädigung *f*, c) Wieder'gutmachung *f*, d) Wieder'herstellung *f von Rechten etc.*: **make ~** Ersatz leisten (**of** für); **2.** *phys.* (e'lastische) Rückstellung; **3.** *phot.* Entzerrung *f*.
res·tive ['restɪv] *adj.* □ **1.** unruhig, ner'vös; **2.** störrisch, 'widerspenstig, bokkig (*a. Pferd*); **'res·tive·ness** [-nɪs] *s.* **1.** Unruhe *f*, Ungeduld *f*; **2.** 'Widerspenstigkeit *f*.
rest·less ['restlɪs] *adj.* □ **1.** ruhe-, rastlos; **2.** unruhig; **3.** schlaflos (*Nacht*); **'rest·less·ness** [-nɪs] *s.* **1.** Ruhe-, Rastlosigkeit *f*; **2.** (ner'vöse) Unruhe, Unrast *f*.
re·stock [ˌriː'stɒk] **I** *v/t.* **1.** ✝ a) *Lager* wieder auffüllen, b) *Ware* wieder auf Lager nehmen; **2.** *Gewässer* wieder mit Fischen besetzen; **II** *v/i.* **3.** neuen Vorrat einlagern.
res·to·ra·tion [ˌrestə'reɪʃn] *s.* **1.** Wieder'herstellung *f* (*e-s Zustandes*, *der Gesundheit etc.*); **2.** Restaurierung *f e-s Kunstwerks etc.*; **3.** Rückerstattung *f*, -gabe *f*; **4.** Wieder'einsetzung *f* (**to** in *ein Amt*); **5. the ~** *hist.* die Restaura'ti'on; **re·stor·a·tive** [rɪ'stɒrətɪv] ⚕ **I** *adj.* □ **1.** stärkend; **II** *s.* **2.** Stärkungsmittel *n*; **3.** 'Wiederbelebungsmittel *n*.
re·store [rɪ'stɔː] *v/t.* **1.** *Einrichtung*, *Gesundheit*, *Ordnung etc.* wieder'herstellen; **2.** a) *Kunstwerk etc.* restaurieren, b) ⚙ in'stand setzen; **3.** *j-n* wieder'einsetzen (**to** in *acc.*); **4.** zu'rückerstatten, -bringen, -geben: **~ s.th. to its place** et. an s-n Platz zurückstellen; **~ the receiver** *teleph.* den Hörer auflegen *od.* einhängen; **~ s.o. (to health)** j-n gesund machen *od.* wiederherstellen; **~ s.o. to liberty** j-m die Freiheit wiedergeben; **~ s.o. to life** j-n ins Leben zurückrufen; **~ a king (to the throne)** e-n König wieder auf den Thron setzen; **re'stor·er** [-ɔːrə] *s.* **1.** Wieder'hersteller (-in); **2.** Restau'rator *m*, Restaura'torin *f*; **3.** Haarwuchsmittel *n*.
re·strain [rɪ'streɪn] *v/t.* **1.** zu'rückhalten: **~ s.o. from doing s.th.** j-n davon abhalten, et. zu tun; **~ing order** ⚖ Unterlassungsurteil *n*; **2.** a) in Schranken halten, Einhalt gebieten (*dat.*), b) *Pferd* im Zaum halten, zügeln (*a. fig.*); **3.** *Gefühl* unter'drücken, bezähmen; **4.** a) einsperren, -schließen, b) *Geisteskranken* in e-r Anstalt 'unterbringen; **5.** *Macht etc.* be-, einschränken; **6.** ✝ *Produktion etc.* drosseln; **re'strained** [-nd] *adj.* □ **1.** zu'rückhaltend, beherrscht, maßvoll; **2.** verhalten, gedämpft; **re'straint** [-nt] *s.* **1.** Einschränkung *f*, Beschränkung(en *pl.*) *f*; Hemmnis *n*, Zwang *m*: **~ of** (*od.* **upon**) **liberty** Beschränkung der Freiheit; **~ of trade** a) Beschränkung des Handels, b) Einschränkung des freien Wettbewerbs, Konkurrenzverbot *n*; **~ clause** Konkurrenzklausel *f*; **call for ~** Maßhalteappell *m*; **without ~** frei, ungehemmt, offen; **2.** ⚖ Freiheitsbeschränkung *f*, Haft *f*: **place s.o. under ~** j-n in Gewahrsam nehmen; **3.** a) Zu'rückhaltung *f*, Beherrschtheit *f*, b) (künstlerische) Zucht.
re·strict [rɪ'strɪkt] *v/t.* a) einschränken, b) beschränken (**to** auf *acc.*): **be ~ed to doing** sich darauf beschränken müssen, *et.* zu tun; **re'strict·ed** [-tɪd] *adj.* □ eingeschränkt, beschränkt, begrenzt: **~!** nur für den Dienstgebrauch!; **~ area** Sperrgebiet *n*; **~ district** Gebiet *n* mit bestimmten Baubeschränkungen; **re'stric·tion** [-kʃn] *s.* **1.** Ein-, Beschränkung *f* (**of, on** *gen.*): **~s on imports** Einfuhrbeschränkungen; **~s of space** räumliche Beschränktheit; **without ~s** uneingeschränkt; **2.** Vorbehalt *m*; **re'stric·tive** [-tɪv] **I** *adj.* □ be-, einschränkend (**of** *acc.*): **~ clause** a) *ling.* einschränkender Relativsatz, b) ✝ einschränkende Bestimmung; **II** *s. ling.* Einschränkung *f*.
rest room *s. Am.* Toi'lette *f* (*Hotel etc.*).
re·struc·ture [ˌriː'strʌktʃə] *v/t.* 'umstrukturieren.
re·sult [rɪ'zʌlt] **I** *s.* **1.** *a.* 𝔄 Ergebnis *n*,

Resul'tat *n*; (*a.* guter) Erfolg: ***without ~*** ergebnislos; **2.** Folge *f*, Aus-, Nachwirkung *f*: ***as a ~*** a) die Folge war, daß, b) folglich; ***get ~s*** Erfolge erzielen, et. erreichen; **II** *v/i.* **3.** sich ergeben, resultieren (***from*** aus): ***~ in*** hinauslaufen auf (*acc.*), zur Folge haben (*acc.*), enden mit (*dat.*); **re'sult·ant** [-tənt] **I** *adj.* **1.** sich ergebend, (dabei *od.* daraus) entstehend, resultierend (***from*** aus); **II** *s.* **2.** *phys.*, Å Resul'tante *f*; **3.** (End)Ergebnis *n*.

re·sume [rɪ'zjuːm] **I** *v/t.* **1.** *Tätigkeit etc.* wieder'aufnehmen, wieder anfangen; fortsetzen: ***he ~d painting*** er begann wieder zu malen, er malte wieder; **2.** 'wiedererlangen; *Platz* wieder einnehmen; *Amt*, *Kommando* wieder über'nehmen; *Namen* wieder annehmen; **3.** resümieren, zs.-fassen; **II** *v/i.* **4.** s-e Tätigkeit wieder'aufnehmen; **5.** *in s-r Rede* fortfahren; **6.** wieder beginnen.

ré·su·mé ['rezjuːmeɪ] (*Fr.*) *s.* **1.** Resü'mee *n*, Zs.-fassung *f*; **2.** *bsd. Am.* Lebenslauf *m*.

re·sump·tion [rɪ'zʌmpʃn] *s.* **1.** a) Zu'rücknahme *f*, b) ⚚ Li'zenzentzug *m*; **2.** Wieder'aufnahme *f e-r Tätigkeit*, *von Zahlungen etc.*

re·sur·gence [rɪ'sɜːdʒəns] *s.* Wiederem'porkommen *n*, Wieder'aufleben *n*, -'aufstieg *m*, 'Wiedererweckung *f*; **re'sur·gent** [-nt] *adj.* wieder'auflebend, 'wiedererwachend.

res·ur·rect [ˌrezə'rekt] *v/t.* **1.** F wieder zum Leben erwecken; **2.** *fig. Sitte* wieder'aufleben lassen; **3.** *Leiche* ausgraben; ˌ**res·ur'rec·tion** [-kʃn] *s.* **1.** (*eccl.* ⚲) Auferstehung *f*; **2.** *fig.* Wieder'aufleben *n*, 'Wiedererwachen *n*; **3.** Leichenraub *m*.

re·sus·ci·tate [rɪ'sʌsɪteɪt] **I** *v/t.* **1.** 'wiederbeleben; **2.** *fig.* 'wiedererwecken, wieder'aufleben lassen; **II** *v/i.* **3.** das Bewußtsein 'wiedererlangen; **4.** wieder'aufleben; **re·sus·ci·ta·tion** [rɪˌsʌsɪ'teɪʃn] *s.* **1.** 'Wiederbelebung *f* (*a. fig. Erneuerung*); **2.** Auferstehung *f*.

ret [ret] **I** *v/t. Flachs etc.* rösten, rötten; **II** *v/i.* verfaulen (*Heu*).

re·tail ['riːteɪl] **I** *s.* Einzel-, Kleinhandel *m*, Kleinverkauf *m*, De'tailgeschäft *n*: ***by*** (*Am.* ***at***) ***~*** → III; **II** *adj.* Einzel-, Kleinhandels...: ***~ bookseller*** Sortimentsbuchhändler *m*; ***~ dealer*** Einzelhändler *m*; ***~ price*** Einzelhandels-, Ladenpreis *m*; ***~ trade*** → I; **III** *adv.* im Einzelhandel, einzeln, en de'tail: ***sell ~***; **IV** *v/t.* [riː'teɪl] a) *Waren* im kleinen *od.* en de'tail verkaufen, b) *Klatsch* weitergeben, (haarklein) weitererzählen; **V** *v/i.* [riː'teɪl] im Einzelhandel verkauft werden (***at*** zu *6 Dollar etc.*); **re·tail·er** [riː'teɪlə] *s.* **1.** ⚚ Einzel-, Kleinhändler (-in); **2.** Erzähler(in), Verbreiter(in) *von Klatsch etc.*

re·tain [rɪ'teɪn] *v/t.* **1.** zu'rück(be)halten, einbehalten; **2.** *Eigenschaft*, *Posten etc.*, *a. im Gedächtnis* behalten; *a. Geduld etc.* bewahren; **3.** *Brauch* beibehalten; **4.** *j-n* in s-n Diensten halten: ***~ a lawyer*** e-n Anwalt nehmen; ***~ing fee*** → ***retainer*** 2 a; **5.** ⚙ halten, sichern, stützen; *Wasser* stauen: ***~ing nut*** Befestigungsmutter *f*; ***~ing ring*** Sprengring *m*; ***~ing wall*** Stütz-, Staumauer *f*; **re'tain·er** [-nə] *s.* **1.** *hist.* Gefolgsmann *m*: ***old ~*** F altes Faktotum; **2.** ⚖ a) Verpflichtung *f* e-s Anwalts, b) Hono'rarvorschuß *m*: ***general ~*** Pauschalhonorar *n*, c) Pro'zeßvollmacht *f*; **3.** ⚙ a) Befestigungsteil *n*, b) Käfig *m e-s Kugellagers*.

re·take [ˌriː'teɪk] **I** *v/t.* [*irr.* → ***take***] **1.** wieder (an-, ein-, zu'rück)nehmen; **2.** ⚔ wieder'einnehmen; **3.** *Film*: *Szene etc.* wieder'holen, nochmals (ab)drehen; **II** *s.* ['riːteɪk] **4.** *Film*: Re'take *n*, Wieder'holung *f*.

re·tal·i·ate [rɪ'tælɪeɪt] **I** *v/i.* Vergeltung üben, sich rächen (***upon s.o.*** an j-m); **II** *v/t.* vergelten, sich rächen für, heimzahlen; **re·tal·i·a·tion** [rɪˌtælɪ'eɪʃn] *s.* Vergeltung *f*: ***in ~*** als Vergeltung(smaßnahme); **re'tal·i·a·to·ry** [-ɪətərɪ] *adj.* Vergeltungs...: ***~ duty*** ⚚ Kampfzoll *m*.

re·tard [rɪ'tɑːd] *v/t.* **1.** verzögern, -langsamen, aufhalten; **2.** *phys.* retardieren, verzögern; *Elektronen* bremsen: ***be ~ed*** nacheilen; **3.** *biol.* retardieren; **4.** *psych. j-s.* Entwicklung hemmen: ***~ed child*** zurückgebliebenes Kind; ***mentally ~ed*** geistig zurückgeblieben; **5.** *mot. Zündung* nachstellen: ***~ed ignition*** a) Spätzündung *f*, b) verzögerte Zündung; **re·tar·da·tion** [ˌriːtɑː'deɪʃn] *s.* **1.** Verzögerung *f* (*a. phys.*), -langsamung *f*, -spätung *f*; Aufschub *m*; **2.** Å, *phys.*, *biol.* Retardati'on *f*; *phys.* (*Elektronen-*) Bremsung *f*; **3.** *psych.* a) Entwicklungshemmung *f*, b) 'Unterentwickeltheit *f*; **4.** ♪ a) Verlangsamung *f*, b) aufwärtsgehender Vorhalt.

retch [retʃ] *v/i.* würgen (*beim Erbrechen*).

re·tell [ˌriː'tel] *v/t.* [*irr.* → ***tell***] **1.** nochmals erzählen *od.* sagen, wieder'holen; **2.** *ped.* nacherzählen.

re·ten·tion [rɪ'tenʃn] *s.* **1.** Zu'rückhalten *n*; **2.** Einbehaltung *f*; **3.** Beibehaltung *f* (*a. von Bräuchen etc.*), Bewahrung *f*; **4.** ⚕ Verhalten *n*; **5.** Festhalten *n*, Halt *m*: ***~ pin*** ⚙ Arretierstift *m*; **6.** Merken *n*, Merkfähigkeit *f*; **re'ten·tive** [-ntɪv] *adj.* □ **1.** (zu'rück)haltend (***of*** *acc.*); **2.** erhaltend, bewahrend; gut (*Gedächtnis*); **3.** Wasser speichernd.

re·think [ˌriː'θɪŋk] *v/t.* [*irr.* → ***think***] *et.* nochmals über'denken; ˌ**re'think·ing** [-kɪŋ] *s.* 'Umdenken *n*.

ret·i·cence ['retɪsəns] *s.* **1.** Verschwiegenheit *f*, Schweigsamkeit *f*; **2.** Zu'rückhaltung *f*; '**ret·i·cent** [-nt] *adj.* □ verschwiegen (***about***, ***on*** über *acc.*), schweigsam; zu'rückhaltend.

ret·i·cle ['retɪkl] *s. opt.* Fadenkreuz *n*.

re·tic·u·lar [rɪ'tɪkjʊlə] *adj.* □ netzartig, -förmig, Netz...; **re'tic·u·late I** *adj.* □ [-lət] netzartig, -förmig; **II** *v/t.* [-leɪt] netzförmig mustern *od.* bedecken; **III** *v/i.* [-leɪt] sich verästeln; **re'tic·u·lat·ed** [-leɪtɪd] *adj.* netzförmig, maschig, Netz...: ***~ glass*** Filigranglas *n*; **re·tic·u·la·tion** [rɪˌtɪkjʊ'leɪʃn] *s.* Netzwerk *n*; **ret·i·cule** ['retɪkjuːl] *s.* **1.** → ***reticle***; **2.** Damentasche *f*; Arbeitsbeutel *m*; **re·ti·form** ['riːtɪfɔːm] *adj.* netz-, gitterförmig.

ret·i·na ['retɪnə] *s. anat.* Retina *f*, Netzhaut *f*.

ret·i·nue ['retɪnjuː] *s.* Gefolge *n*.

re·tire [rɪ'taɪə] **I** *v/i.* **1.** *allg.* sich zu'rückziehen (*a.* ⚔): ***~*** (***from business***) *a.* sich zur Ruhe setzen; ***~ into o.s.*** sich verschließen; ***~*** (***to rest***) sich zur Ruhe begeben, schlafen gehen; **2.** ab-, zu'rücktreten; in den Ruhestand treten, in Pensi'on *od.* Rente gehen, s-n Abschied nehmen (*Beamter*); **3.** *fig.* zu'rücktreten (*Hintergrund*, *Ufer etc.*); **II** *v/t.* **4.** zu'rückziehen (*a.* ⚔); **5.** ⚚ *Noten* aus dem Verkehr ziehen; *Wechsel* einlösen; **6.** *bsd.* ⚔ verabschieden, pensionieren; → ***retired*** 1; **re'tired** [-əd] *p.p. u. adj.* □ **1.** pensioniert, im Ruhestand (lebend): ***~ general*** General a.D. *od.* außer Dienst; ***~ pay*** Ruhegeld *n*, Pension *f*; ***be placed on the ~ list*** ⚔ den Abschied erhalten; **2.** im Ruhestand (lebend); **3.** zu'rückgezogen (*Leben*); **4.** abgelegen, einsam (*Ort*): **re'tire·ment** [-mənt] *s.* **1.** (Sich)Zu'rückziehen *n*; **2.** Aus-, Rücktritt *m*, Ausscheiden *n*; **3.** Ruhestand *m*: ***early ~*** vorzeitiger Ruhestand; ***~ pension*** (Alters)Rente *f*, Ruhegeld *n*; ***~ pensioner*** (Alters)Rentner(in), Ruhegeldempfänger(in); ***go into ~*** sich ins Privatleben zurückziehen; **4.** *j-s* Zu'rückgezogenheit *f*; **5.** a) Abgeschiedenheit *f*, b) abgelegener Ort, Zuflucht *f*; **6.** ⚔ (planmäßige) Absetzbewegung, Rückzug *m*; **7.** ⚚ Einziehung *f*; **re'tir·ing** [-ərɪŋ] *adj.* □ **1.** Ruhestands...: ***~ age*** Renten-, Pensionsalter *n*; ***~ pension*** Ruhegeld *n*; **2.** *fig.* zu'rückhaltend, bescheiden; **3.** unauffällig, de'zent (*Farbe etc.*); **4.** ***~ room*** a) Privatzimmer *n*, b) Toilette *f*.

re·tool [ˌriː'tuːl] *v/t. Fabrik* mit neuen Ma'schinen ausrüsten.

re·tort[1] [rɪ'tɔːt] **I** *s.* **1.** (scharfe *od.* treffende) Entgegnung, (schlagfertige) Antwort; Erwiderung *f*; **II** *v/t.* **2.** (darauf) erwidern; **3.** *Beleidigung etc.* zu'rückgeben (***on s.o.*** j-m); **III** *v/i.* **4.** (scharf *od.* treffend) erwidern, entgegnen.

re·tort[2] [rɪ'tɔːt] *s.* ⚗, ⚙ Re'torte *f*.

re·tor·tion [rɪ'tɔːʃn] *s.* **1.** (Sich)'Umwenden *n*, Zu'rückströmen *n*, -biegen *n*, -beugen *n*; **2.** *Völkerrecht*: Retorsi'on *f* (*Vergeltungsmaßnahme*).

re·touch [ˌriː'tʌtʃ] **I** *v/t. et.* über'arbeiten; *phot.* retuschieren; **II** *s.* Re'tusche *f*.

re·trace [rɪ'treɪs] **I** *v/t.* (*a. fig. Stammbaum etc.*) zu'rückverfolgen; *fig.* zu'rückführen (***to*** auf *acc.*): ***~ one's steps*** a) (denselben Weg) zurückgehen, b) *fig.* die Sache ungeschehen machen; **II** *s.* ϟ Rücklauf *m*.

re·tract [rɪ'trækt] **I** *v/t.* **1.** *Behauptung* zu'rücknehmen, (*a.* ⚖ *Aussage*) wider'rufen; **2.** *Haut*, *Zunge etc.*, *a.* ⚖ *Anklage* zu'rückziehen; **3.** *zo. Klauen etc.*, *a.* ✈ *Fahrgestell* einziehen; **II** *v/i.* **4.** sich zurückziehen; **5.** widerrufen, es zurücknehmen; **6.** zu'rücktreten (***from*** von *e-m Entschluß*, *e-m Vertrag etc.*); **re'tract·a·ble** [-təbl] *adj.* **1.** einziehbar: ***~ landing gear*** ✈ einziehbares Fahrgestell; **2.** zu'rückziehbar; **3.** zu'rücknehmbar, zu wider'rufen(d); **re·trac·ta·tion** [ˌriːtræk'teɪʃn] → ***retraction*** 1; **re'trac·tile** [-taɪl] *adj.* **1.** einziehbar; **2.** *a. anat.* zu'rückziehbar; **re'trac·tion** [-kʃn] *s.* **1.** Zu'rücknahme *f*, 'Widerruf *m*; **2.** Zu'rück-, Einziehen *n*; **3.** ⚕, *zo.* Retrakti'on *f*; **re'trac·tor** [-tə] *s.* **1.** *anat.* Retrakti'onsmuskel *m*;

2. ⚕ Re'traktor *m*, Wundhaken *m*.

re·train [ˌriː'treɪn] *v/t. j-n* 'umschulen; ˌ**re'train·ing** [-nɪŋ] *s. a.* ***occupational*** ~ 'Umschulung *f*.

re·trans·late [ˌriːtræns'leɪt] *v/t.* (zu-) 'rücküberˌsetzen; ˌ**re·trans'la·tion** [-eɪʃn] *s.* 'Rücküberˌsetzung *f*.

re·tread [ˌriː'tred] **I** *v/t.* ⚙ *Reifen* runderneuern; **II** ['riːtred] *s.* runderneuerter Reifen.

re·treat [rɪ'triːt] **I** *s.* **1.** *bsd.* ⚔ Rückzug *m*: ***beat a*** ~ *fig.* das Feld räumen, klein beigeben; ***sound the*** (*od.* ***a***) ~ zum Rückzug blasen; ***there was no*** ~ es gab kein Zurück; **2.** Zufluchtsort *m*, Schlupfwinkel *m*; **3.** Anstalt *f für Geisteskranke etc.*; **4.** Zu'rückgezogenheit *f*, Abgeschiedenheit *f*; **5.** ⚔ Zapfenstreich *m*; **II** *v/i.* **6.** *a.* ⚔ sich zu'rückziehen; **7.** zu'rücktreten, -weichen (*z.B. Meer*): ~***ing chin*** fliehendes Kinn; **III** *v/t.* **8.** *bsd. Schachfigur* zu'rückziehen.

re-treat [ˌriː'triːt] *v/t. allg.* erneut behandeln.

re·trench [rɪ'trentʃ] **I** *v/t.* **1.** *Ausgaben etc.* einschränken, *a. Personal* abbauen; **2.** beschneiden, kürzen; **3.** a) *Textstelle* streichen, b) *Buch* zs.-streichen; **4.** *Festungswerk* mit inneren Verschanzungen versehen; **II** *v/i.* **5.** sich einschränken, Sparmaßnahmen 'durchführen, sparen; **re'trench·ment** [-mənt] *s.* **1.** Einschränkung *f*, (*Kosten-*, *Personal-*) Abbau *m*; Sparmaßnahme *f*; (Gehalts-) Kürzung *f*; **2.** Streichung *f*, Kürzung *f*; **3.** ⚔ Verschanzung *f*, innere Verteidigungsstellung.

re·tri·al [ˌriː'traɪəl] *s.* **1.** nochmalige Prüfung; **2.** ⚖ Wieder'aufnahmeverfahren *n*.

ret·ri·bu·tion [ˌretrɪ'bjuːʃn] *s.* Vergeltung *f*, Strafe *f*; **re·trib·u·tive** [rɪ'trɪbjʊtɪv] *adj.* □ vergeltend, Vergeltungs…

re·triev·a·ble [rɪ'triːvəbl] *adj.* □ **1.** 'wiederzugewinnen(d); **2.** wieder'gutzumachen(d), wettzumachen(d); **re'trieve** [rɪ'triːv] **I** *v/t.* **1.** *hunt.* apportieren; **2.** 'wiederfinden, -bekommen; **3.** (sich *et.*) zu'rückholen; **4.** *et.* her'ausholen, -fischen (***from*** aus); **5.** *fig.* 'wiedergewinnen, -erlangen; *Fehler* wieder'gutmachen; *Verlust* wettmachen; **6.** *j-n* retten (***from*** aus); **7.** *et.* der Vergessenheit entreißen; **II** *s.* **8.** ***beyond*** (*od.* ***past***) ~ unwiederbringlich dahin; **re'triev·er** [-və] *s. hunt.* Re'triever *m*, *allg.* Apportierhund *m*.

retro- [retrəʊ] *in Zssgn* zurück…, rück (-wärts)…, Rück…; entgegengesetzt; hinter…; ˌ**ret·ro'ac·tive** *adj.* □ **1.** ⚖ rückwirkend; **2.** zu'rückwirkend; ˌ**ret·ro'ces·sion** *s.* **1.** a) *a.* ⚕ Zu'rückgehen *n*, b) ⚕ Nach'innenschlagen *n*; **2.** ⚖ 'Wieder-, Rückabtretung *f*; ˌ**ret·ro·gra'da·tion** *s.* **1.** → ***retrogression*** 1; **2.** Zu'rückgehen *n*; **3.** *fig.* Rück-, Niedergang *m*; **ret·ro·grade** ['retrəʊgreɪd] **I** *adj.* **1.** ⚕, ♪, *ast.*, *zo.* rückläufig; **2.** *fig.* rückgängig, -läufig, Rückwärts…, rückschrittlich; **II** *v/i.* **3.** a) rückläufig sein, b) zu'rückgehen; **4.** rückwärts gehen; **5.** *bsd. biol.* entarten.

ret·ro·gres·sion [ˌretrəʊ'greʃn] *s.* **1.** *ast.* rückläufige Bewegung; **2.** *bsd. biol.* Rückentwicklung *f*; **3.** *fig.* Rückgang *m*, -schritt *m*; ˌ**ret·ro'gres·sive** [-esɪv] *adj.* □ **1.** *bsd. biol.* rückschreitend: ~ ***metamorphosis*** *biol.* Rückbildung *f*; **2.** *fig.* rückschrittlich; **3.** *fig.* nieder-, zu'rückgehend; **ret·ro·rock·et** ['retrəʊˌrɒkɪt] *s.* 'Bremsraˌkete *f*; **ret·ro·spect** ['retrəʊspekt] *s.* Rückblick *m*, -schau *f* (***of***, ***on*** auf *acc.*): ***in*** (***the***) ~ rückschauend, im Rückblick; **ret·ro·spec·tion** [ˌretrəʊ'spekʃn] *s.* Erinnerung *f*; Zu'rückblicken *n*; **ret·ro·spec·tive** [ˌretrəʊ'spektɪv] *adj.* □ **1.** zu'rückblickend; **2.** nach rückwärts *od.* hinten (gerichtet); **3.** ⚖ rückwirkend.

ret·rous·sé [rə'truːseɪ] (*Fr.*) *adj.* nach oben gebogen: ~ ***nose*** Stupsnase *f*.

re·try [ˌriː'traɪ] *v/t.* ⚖ a) *Prozeß* wieder'aufnehmen, b) neu verhandeln gegen *j-n*.

re·turn [rɪ'tɜːn] **I** *v/i.* **1.** zu'rückkehren, -kommen (***to*** zu); 'wiederkehren (*a. fig.*); *fig.* wieder auftreten (*Krankheit etc.*): ~ ***to*** *fig.* a) auf *ein Thema* zurückkommen, b) zu *e-m Vorhaben* zurückkommen, c) in *e-e Gewohnheit etc.* zurückfallen, d) in *e-n Zustand* zurückkehren; ~ ***to dust*** zu Staub werden; ~ ***to health*** wieder gesund werden; **2.** zu'rückfallen (*Besitz*) (***to*** an *acc.*); **3.** erwidern, antworten; **II** *v/t.* **4.** *Gruß etc.*, *a. Besuch*, ⚔ *Feuer*, *Liebe*, *Schlag etc.* erwidern: ~ ***thanks*** danken; **5.** zu'rückgeben, *Geld a.* zu'rückzahlen, -erstatten; **6.** zu'rückschicken, -senden: ~***ed empties*** ☤ zurückgesandtes Leergut; ~***ed letter*** unzustellbarer Brief; **7.** (an s-n Platz) zu'rückstellen, -tun; **8.** (ein-) bringen, *Gewinn* abwerfen, *Zinsen* tragen; **9.** *Bericht* erstatten; ⚖ a) Voll'zugsbericht erstatten über (*acc.*), b) *Gerichtsbefehl* mit Vollzugsbericht rückvorlegen; **10.** ⚖ Schuldspruch fällen *od.* aussprechen: ***be*** ~***ed guilty*** schuldig gesprochen werden; **11.** *Votum* abgeben; **12.** amtlich erklären für *od.* als, *j-n arbeitsunfähig etc.* schreiben; **13.** *Einkommen* zur Steuerveranlagung erklären, angeben (***at*** mit); **14.** *amtliche Liste etc.* vorlegen *od.* veröffentlichen; **15.** *parl. Brit. Wahlergebnis* melden; **16.** *parl. Brit.* als Abgeordneten wählen (***to Parliament*** ins Parlament); **17.** *sport Ball* zu'rückschlagen; **18.** *Echo*, *Strahlen* zu'rückwerfen; **19.** ⚙ zu'rückführen, -leiten; **III** *s.* **20.** Rückkehr *f*, -kunft *f*; 'Wiederkehr *f* (*a. fig.*): ~ ***of health*** Genesung *f*; ***by*** ~ ***of post*** *Brit.*, ***by*** ~ ***mail*** *Am.* postwendend, umgehend; ***many happy*** ~***s of the day!*** herzlichen Glückwunsch zum Geburtstag!; ***on my*** ~ bei m-r Rückkehr; **21.** Wieder'auftreten *n* (*Krankheit etc.*): ~ ***of influenza*** Gripperückfall *m*; ~ ***of cold weather*** Kälterückfall *m*; **22.** 🚂 Rückfahrkarte *f*; **23.** Rück-, Her'ausgabe *f*: ***on sale or*** ~ ☤ in Kommission; **24.** *oft pl.* ☤ Rücksendung *f* (*a. Ware*): ~***s*** a) Rückgut, b) *Buchhandel*: *a.* ~ ***copies*** Remittenden; **25.** ☤ Rückzahlung *f*, (-)Erstattung *f*; *Versicherung*: ~ (***of premium***) Ri'storno *n*; **26.** Entgelt *n*, Gegenleistung *f*, Entschädigung *f*: ***in*** ~ dafür, dagegen; ***in*** ~ ***for*** (als Gegenleistung) für; ***without*** ~ unentgeltlich; **27.** *oft pl.* ☤ a) (*Kapital-etc.*)'Umsatz *m*: ***quick*** ~***s*** schneller Umsatz, b) Ertrag *m*, Einnahme *f*, Verzinsung *f*, Gewinn *m*: ***yield*** (*od.* ***bring***) ***a*** ~ Nutzen abwerfen, sich rentieren; **28.** Erwiderung *f* (*a. fig. e-s Grußes etc.*): ~ ***of affection*** Gegenliebe *f*; **29.** (amtlicher) Bericht, (sta'tistischer) Ausweis, Aufstellung *f*; *pol. Brit.* Wahlbericht *m*, -ergebnis *n*: ***annual*** ~ Jahresbericht *m*, -ausweis *m*; ***bank*** ~ Bankausweis *m*; ***official*** ~***s*** amtliche Ziffern; **30.** Steuererklärung *f*; **31.** ⚖ a) Rückvorlage *f* (*e-s Vollstreckungsbefehls etc.*) (mit Voll'zugsbericht), b) Voll'zugsbericht *m* (*des Gerichtsvollziehers etc.*); **32.** *a.* ~ ***day*** ⚖ Ver'handlungsterˌmin *m*; **33.** ⚙ a) Rückführung *f*, -leitung *f*, b) Rücklauf *m*, c) ϟ Rückleitung *f*; **34.** Biegung *f*, Krümmung *f*; **35.** △ a) 'Wiederkehr *f*, b) vorspringender *od.* zu'rückgesetzter Teil, c) (Seiten)Flügel *m*; **36.** *Tennis*: Re'turn *m*, Rückschlag *m* (*a. Ball*); **37.** *sport a.* ~ ***match*** Rückspiel *n*; **38.** (leichter) Feinschnitt (*Tabak*); **IV** *adj.* **39.** Rück…(*-porto*, *-reise*, *-spiel etc.*): ~ ***cable*** ϟ Rückleitung *f*; ~ ***cargo*** Rückfracht *f*, -ladung *f*; ~ ***current*** ϟ Rück-, Erdstrom *m*; ~ ***ticket*** a) Rückfahrkarte *f*, b) ✈ Rückflugkarte *f*; ~ ***valve*** ⚙ Rückschlagventil *n*; ~ ***visit*** Gegenbesuch *m*; ~ ***wire*** ϟ Nulleiter *m*; **re'turn·a·ble** [-nəbl] *adj.* **1.** zu'rückzugeben(d); einzusenden(d); **2.** ☤ rückzahlbar.

re·turn·ing of·fi·cer [rɪ'tɜːnɪŋ] *s. pol. Brit.* 'Wahlkommisˌsar *m*.

re·u·ni·fi·ca·tion [ˌriːjuːnɪfɪ'keɪʃn] *s. pol.* 'Wiedervereinigung *f*.

re·un·ion [ˌriː'juːnjən] *s.* **1.** 'Wiedervereinigung *f*; *fig.* Versöhnung *f*; **2.** (*Familien-*, *Klassen- etc.*)Treffen *n*, Zs.-kunft *f*.

re·u·nite [ˌriːjuː'naɪt] **I** *v/t.* 'wiedervereinigen; **II** *v/i.* sich wieder vereinigen.

rev [rev] *mot.* F **I** *s.* Umdrehung *f*: ~***s per minute*** Dreh-, Tourenzahl *f*; **II** *v/t. mst* ~ ***up*** auf Touren bringen; **III** *v/i.* laufen, auf Touren sein (*Motor*): ~ ***up*** a) auf Touren kommen, b) den Motor ‚hochjagen' *od.* auf Touren bringen.

re·vac·ci·nate [ˌriː'væksɪneɪt] *v/t.* ⚕ 'wieder-, nachimpfen.

re·val·or·i·za·tion ['riːˌvælərаɪ'zeɪʃn] *s.* ☤ Aufwertung *f*; **re·val·or·ize** [ˌriː'væləraɪz] *v/t.* aufwerten.

re·val·u·ate [ˌriː'væljʊeɪt] *v/t.* ☤ **1.** neu bewerten; **2.** aufwerten; **re·val·u·a·tion** ['riːˌvæljʊ'eɪʃn] *s.* **1.** Neubewertung *f*; **2.** Aufwertung *f*.

re·val·ue [ˌriː'væljuː] → ***revaluate***.

re·vamp [ˌriː'væmp] *v/t.* F ‚aufpolieren'.

re·vanch·ist [rɪ'væntʃɪst] **I** *adj.* revan'chistisch; **II** *s.* Revan'chist *m*.

re·veal [rɪ'viːl] **I** *v/t.* (***to***) **1.** *eccl.*, *a. fig.* offenbaren (*dat.*); **2.** enthüllen, zeigen (*dat.*) (*a. fig. erkennen lassen*), sehen lassen; **3.** *fig. Geheimnis etc.* enthüllen, verraten, aufdecken (*dat.*); **II** *s.* **4.** ⚙ a) innere Laibung (*Tür etc.*), b) Fensterrahmen *m* (*Auto*); **re'veal·ing** [-lɪŋ] *adj.* **1.** enthüllend, aufschlußreich; **2.** ‚offenherzig' (*Kleid*).

rev·eil·le [rɪ'vælɪ] *s.* ⚔ (Si'gnal *n* zum) Wecken *n*.

rev·el ['revl] **I** *v/i.* **1.** (lärmend) feiern, ausgelassen sein; **2.** (***in***) *fig.* a) schwelgen (in *dat.*), *et.* in vollen Zügen genießen, b) sich weiden *od.* ergötzen (***in*** an *dat.*); **II** *s.* **3.** *oft pl.* → ***revelry***.

rev·e·la·tion [ˌrevəˈleɪʃn] *s.* **1.** Enthüllung *f*, Offenˈbarung *f*: ***it was a ~ to me*** es fiel mir wie Schuppen von den Augen; ***what a ~!*** welch überraschende Entdeckung!, ach so ist das!; **2.** (göttliche) Offenbarung: ***the 2 (of St. John)*** *bibl.* die (Geheime) Offenbarung (des Johannes); **3.** F ‚Offenbarung' *f* (*et. Ausgezeichnetes*).

rev·el·(l)er [ˈrevlə] *s.* **1.** Feiernde(r *m*) *f*; **2.** Zecher *m*; **3.** Nachtschwärmer *m*; **ˈrev·el·ry** [-lrɪ] *s.* lärmende Festlichkeit, Rummel *m*, Trubel *m*.

re·venge [rɪˈvendʒ] **I** *v/t.* **1.** *et.*, *a. j-n* rächen ([***up***]***on*** an *dat.*): ***~ o.s. for s.th.*** sich für et. rächen; ***be ~d*** a) gerächt sein *od.* werden, b) sich rächen; **2.** sich rächen für, vergelten (***upon***, ***on*** an *dat.*); **II** *s.* **3.** Rache *f*: ***take one's ~*** Rache nehmen, sich rächen; ***in ~ for it*** dafür; **4.** Reˈvanche *f* (*beim Spiel*): ***have one's ~*** sich revanchieren; **5.** Rachsucht *f*, -gier *f*; **reˈvenge·ful** [-fʊl] *adj.* □ rachsüchtig; **reˈvenge·ful·ness** [-fʊlnɪs] → ***revenge*** 5.

rev·e·nue [ˈrevənjuː] *s.* **1.** *a.* ***public ~*** öffentliche Einnahmen *pl.*, Staatseinkünfte *pl.*; **2.** a) Fiˈnanzverwaltung *f*, b) Fiskus *m*: ***defraud the ~*** Steuern hinterziehen; ***~ board*** → ***revenue office***; **3.** *pl.* Einnahmen *pl.*, Einkünfte *pl.*; **4.** Ertrag *m*, Nutzung *f*; **5.** Einkommensquelle *f*; **~ cut·ter** *s.* ⚓ Zollkutter *m*; **~ of·fice** *s.* Fiˈnanzamt *n*; **~ of·fi·cer** *s.* Zollbeamte(r) *m*; Fiˈnanzbeamte(r) *m*; **~ stamp** *s.* ✝ Bandeˈrole *f*, Steuermarke *f*.

re·ver·ber·ate [rɪˈvɜːbəreɪt] *phys.* **I** *v/i.* **1.** zuˈrückstrahlen; **2.** (nach-, ˈwider-) hallen; **II** *v/t.* **3.** *Strahlen*, *Hitze*, *Klang* zuˈrückwerfen; von *e-m Klange* widerhallen; **re·ver·ber·a·tion** [rɪˌvɜːbəˈreɪʃn] *s.* **1.** Zuˈrückwerfen *n*, -strahlen *n*; **2.** ˈWiderhall(en *n*) *m*; Nachhall *m*; **reˈver·ber·a·tor** [-tə] *s.* ⚙ **1.** Reˈflektor *m*; **2.** Scheinwerfer *m*.

re·vere [rɪˈvɪə] *v/t.* (ver)ehren.

rev·er·ence [ˈrevərəns] **I** *s.* **1.** Verehrung *f* (***for*** für *od. gen.*); **2.** Ehrfurcht *f* (***for*** vor *dat.*); **3.** Ehrerbietung *f*; **4.** Reveˈrenz *f* (*Verbeugung od. Knicks*); **5.** *dial. od. humor.* ***Your*** (***His***) ***~*** Euer (Seine) Ehrwürden; **II** *v/t.* **6.** (ver)ehren; **ˈrev·er·end** [-nd] **I** *adj.* **1.** ehrwürdig; **2.** 2 *eccl.* hochwürdig (*Geistlicher*): ***Very 2*** (*im Titel e-s Dekans*); ***Right 2*** (*Bischof*); ***Most 2*** (*Erzbischof*): ***2 Mother*** Mutter Oberin *f*; **II** *s.* **3.** Geistliche(r) *m*; **ˈrev·er·ent** [-nt] *adj.* □, **rev·er·en·tial** [ˌrevəˈrenʃl] *adj.* □ ehrerbietig, ehrfurchtsvoll.

rev·er·ie [ˈrevərɪ] *s.* Träumeˈrei *f* (*a.* ♪): ***be lost in*** (***a***) ***~*** in Träumen versunken sein.

re·ver·sal [rɪˈvɜːsl] *s.* **1.** ˈUmkehr(ung) *f*; ˈUmschwung *m*, -schlagen *n*: ***~ of opinion*** Meinungsumschwung; ***~ process*** *phot.* Umkehrentwicklung *f*; **2.** ⚖ (Urteils)Aufhebung *f*, ˈUmstoßung *f*; **3.** ⚙ ˈUmsteuerung *f*; **4.** ⚡ (ˈStrom)ˌUmkehr *f*; **5.** ✝ Stornierung *f*; **reˈverse** [rɪˈvɜːs] **I** *s.* **1.** Gegenteil *n*, *das* ˈUmgekehrte; **2.** Rückschlag *m*: ***~ of fortune*** Schicksalsschlag *m*; **3.** ⚔ Niederlage *f*, Schlappe *f*; **4.** Rückseite *f*, *bsd. fig.* Kehrseite *f*: ***~ of a coin*** Rückseite *od.* Revers *m* e-r Münze; ***~ of the medal*** *fig.* Kehrseite der Medaille; ***on the ~*** umstehend; ***take in ~*** ⚔ im Rücken packen; **5.** *mot.* Rückwärtsgang *m*; **6.** ⚙ ˈUmsteuerung *f*; **II** *adj.* □ **7.** ˈumgekehrt, verkehrt, entgegengesetzt (***to*** *dat.*): ***~-charge call*** *teleph.* R-Gespräch *n*; ***~ current*** ⚡ Gegenstrom *m*; ***~ flying*** ✈ Rückenflug *m*; ***~ order*** umgekehrte Reihenfolge; ***~ side*** a) Rückseite *f*, b) linke (*Stoff*)Seite; **8.** rückläufig, rückwärts…: ***~ gear*** → 5; **III** *v/t.* **9.** ˈumkehren (*a.* A, ⚡), ˈumdrehen; *fig. Politik* (ganz) ˈumstellen; *Meinung* völlig ändern: ***~ the charge(s)*** *teleph.* ein R-Gespräch führen; ***~ the order of things*** die Weltordnung auf den Kopf stellen; **10.** ⚖ *Urteil* aufheben, ˈumstoßen; **11.** ✝ stornieren; **12.** ⚙ im Rückwärtsgang *od.* rückwärts fahren *od.* laufen (lassen); **13.** ⚡ a) ˈumpolen, b) ˈumsteuern; **IV** *v/i.* **14.** rückwärts fahren; **15.** *beim Walzer* ˈlinksherˌum tanzen; **reˈvers·i·ble** [-səbl] *adj.* **1.** *a.* A, ⚗, *phys.* ˈumkehrbar; **2.** doppelseitig, wendbar (*Stoff*, *Mantel*); **3.** ⚙ ˈumsteuerbar; **4.** ⚖ ˈumstoßbar; **reˈvers·ing** [-sɪŋ] *adj.* ⚙, *phys.* Umkehr…, Umsteuerungs…: ***~ gear*** a) Umsteuerung *f*, b) Wendegetriebe *n*, c) Rückwärtsgang *m*; ***~ pole*** ⚡ Wendepol *m*; ***~ switch*** ⚡ Wendeschalter *m*; **reˈver·sion** [-ɜːʃn] *s.* **1.** *a.* A ˈUmkehrung *f*; **2.** ⚖ a) Heim-, Rückfall *m*, b) *a.* ***right of ~*** Heimfallsrecht *n*; **3.** ⚖ a) Anwartschaft *f* (***of*** auf *acc.*), b) Anwartschaftsrente *f*; **4.** *biol.* a) Rückartung *f*, b) Ataˈvismus *m*; **5.** ⚡ ˈUmpolung *f*; **reˈver·sion·ar·y** [-ɜːʃnərɪ] *adj.* **1.** ⚖ anwartschaftlich, Anwartschafts…: ***~ annuity*** Rente *f* auf den Überlebensfall; ***~ heir*** Nacherbe *m*; **2.** *biol.* ataˈvistisch; **reˈver·sion·er** [-ɜːʃnə] *s.* ⚖ **1.** Anwartschaftsberechtigte(r *m*) *f*, Anwärter(in); **2.** Nacherbe *m*, -erbin *f*; **re·vert** [rɪˈvɜːt] **I** *v/i.* **1.** zuˈrückkehren (***to*** zu *s-m Glauben etc.*); **2.** zuˈrückkommen (***to*** auf *e-n Brief*, *ein Thema etc.*); **3.** wieder zuˈrückfallen (***to*** in *acc.*): ***~ to barbarism***; **4.** ⚖ zuˈrück-, heimfallen (***to s.o.*** an j-n); **5.** *biol.* zuˈrückschlagen (***to*** zu); **II** *v/t.* **6.** *Blick* (zuˈrück)wenden; **reˈvert·i·ble** [-ɜːtəbl] *adj.* ⚖ heimfällig (*Besitz*).

re·vet·ment [rɪˈvetmənt] *s.* **1.** ⚙ Verkleidung *f*, Futtermauer *f* (*Ufer etc.*); **2.** ⚔ Splitterschutzwand *f*.

re·view [rɪˈvjuː] **I** *s.* **1.** ˈNachprüfung *f*, (Über)ˈPrüfung *f*, Revisiˈon *f*: ***court of ~*** ⚖ Rechtsmittelgericht *n*; ***be under ~*** überprüft werden; **2.** (Buch)Besprechung *f*, Rezensiˈon *f*, Kriˈtik *f*: ***~ copy*** Rezensionsexemplar *n*; **3.** Rundschau *f*, kritische Zeitschrift; **4.** ⚔ Paˈrade *f*, Truppenschau *f*: ***naval ~*** Flottenparade; ***pass in ~*** a) mustern, b) (vorbei-) defilieren (lassen), c) → **5.** Rückblick *m*, -schau *f* (***of*** auf *acc.*): ***pass in ~*** a) Rückschau halten über (*acc.*), b) *im Geiste* Revue passieren lassen; **6.** Bericht *m*, ˈÜbersicht *f*, -blick *m* (***of*** über *acc.*): ***market ~*** ✝ Markt-, Börsenbericht; ***month under ~*** Berichtsmonat *m*; **7.** ˈDurchsicht *f*; **8.** → ***revue***; **II** *v/t.* **9.** nachprüfen, (über)ˈprüfen, e-r Revisiˈon unterˈziehen; **10.** ⚔ besichtigen, inspizieren; **11.** *fig.* zuˈrückblicken auf (*acc.*); **12.** überˈblicken, -ˈschauen: ***~ the situation***; **13.** e-n ˈÜberblick geben über (*acc.*); **14.** *Buch* besprechen, rezensieren; **III** *v/i.* **15.** (Buch)Besprechungen schreiben; **reˈview·er** [-juːə] *s.* Kritiker(in), Rezenˈsent(in): ***~'s copy*** Rezensionsexemplar *n*.

re·vile [rɪˈvaɪl] *v/t. u. v/i.*: ***~*** (***at*** *od.* ***against***) ***s.th.*** et. schmähen *od.* verunglimpfen; **reˈvile·ment** [-mənt] *s.* Schmähung *f*, Verunglimpfung *f*.

re·vis·al [rɪˈvaɪzl] *s.* **1.** (Nach)Prüfung *f*; **2.** (nochmalige) ˈDurchsicht; **3.** *typ.* zweite Korrekˈtur; **re·vise** [rɪˈvaɪz] **I** *v/t.* **1.** revidieren: a) *typ.* in zweiter Korrektur lesen, b) *Buch* überˈarbeiten: ***~ed edition*** verbesserte Auflage, c) *fig. Ansicht* ändern; **2.** überˈprüfen, (wieder)ˈdurchsehen; **II** *s.* **3.** *a.* ***~ proof*** *typ.* Revisiˈonsbogen *m*, Korrekˈturabzug *m*; **4.** → ***revision***; **reˈvis·er** [-zə] *s.* **1.** *typ.* Korˈrektor *m*; **2.** Bearbeiter *m*; **re·vi·sion** [rɪˈvɪʒn] *s.* **1.** Revisiˈon *f*: a) ˈDurchsicht *f*, b) Überˈarbeitung *f*, c) Korrekˈtur *f*; **2.** verbesserte Ausgabe *od.* Auflage.

re·vis·it [ˌriːˈvɪzɪt] *v/t.* nochmals *od.* wieder besuchen: ***London ~ed*** Wiedersehen *n* mit London.

re·vi·tal·ize [ˌriːˈvaɪtəlaɪz] *v/t.* neu beleben, ˈwiederbeleben.

re·viv·al [rɪˈvaɪvl] *s.* **1.** ˈWiederbelebung *f* (*a.* ✝; *a.* ⚖ *von Rechten*): ***~ of architecture*** Neugotik *f*; ***2 of Learning*** *hist.* Renaissance *f*; **2.** Wiederˈaufleben *n*, -ˈaufblühen *n*, Erneuerung *f*; **3.** *eccl.* a) Erweckung *f*, b) *a.* ***~ meeting*** Erwekkungsversammlung *f*; **4.** Wiederˈaufgreifen *n e-s veralteten Worts etc.*; *thea.* Wiederˈaufnahme *f e-s vergessenen Stücks*; **reˈviv·al·ism** [-vəlɪzəm] *s. bsd. U.S.A.* a) (religiˈöse) Erweckungsbewegung, ˌEvangelisatiˈon *f*, b) Erwekkungseifer *m*; **re·vive** [rɪˈvaɪv] **I** *v/t.* **1.** ˈwiederbeleben (*a. fig.*); **2.** *Anspruch*, *Gefühl*, *Hoffnung*, *Streit etc.* wiederˈaufleben lassen; *Gefühle* ˈwiedererwecken; *Brauch*, *Gesetz* wiederˈeinführen; *Vertrag* erneuern; *Gerechtigkeit*, *Ruf* wiederˈherstellen; *Thema* wiederˈaufgreifen; **3.** *thea. Stück* wieder auf die Bühne bringen; **4.** ⚙ *Metall* frischen; **II** *v/i.* **5.** wieder (zum Leben) erwachen; **6.** das Bewußtsein ˈwiedererlangen; **7.** *fig.* wiederˈaufleben (*a. Rechte*); ˈwiedererwachen (*Haß etc.*); wiederˈaufblühen; ✝ sich erholen; **8.** wiederˈauftreten; wiederˈaufkommen (*Brauch etc.*); **reˈviv·er** [-və] *s.* **1.** ⚙ Auffrischungs-, Regenerierungsmittel *n*; **2.** *sl.* (*alkoholische*) Stärkung; **re·viv·i·fy** [riːˈvɪvɪfaɪ] *v/t.* **1.** ˈwiederbeleben; **2.** *fig.* wiederˈaufleben lassen, neu beleben.

rev·o·ca·ble [ˈrevəkəbl] *adj.* □ ˈwiderruflich; **rev·o·ca·tion** [ˌrevəˈkeɪʃn] *s.* ⚖ ˈWiderruf *m*, Aufhebung *f*; (*Lizenz- etc.*)Entzug *m*.

re·voke [rɪˈvəʊk] **I** *v/t.* widerˈrufen, aufheben, rückgängig machen; **II** *v/i.* *Kartenspiel*: nicht Farbe bekennen, nicht bedienen.

re·volt [rɪˈvəʊlt] **I** *s.* **1.** Reˈvolte *f*, Aufruhr *m*, Aufstand *m*; **II** *v/i.* **2.** a) (*a. fig.*) revoltieren, sich emˈpören, sich auflehnen (***against*** gegen), b) abfallen (***from*** von); **3.** *fig.* ˈWiderwillen emp-

finden (***at*** über *acc.*), sich sträuben *od.* empören (***against***, ***at***, ***from*** gegen); **III** *v/t.* **4.** *fig.* empören, mit Abscheu erfüllen, abstoßen; **re'volt·ing** [-tɪŋ] *adj.* □ em'pörend, abstoßend, widerlich.
rev·o·lu·tion [ˌrevə'lu:ʃn] *s.* **1.** 'Umwälzung *f*, Um'drehung *f*, Rotati'on *f*: **~s per minute** ⚙ Umdrehungen pro Minute, Dreh-, Tourenzahl *f*; **~ counter** Drehzahlmesser *m*, Tourenzähler *m*; **2.** *ast.* a) Kreislauf *m* (*a. fig.*), b) Um'drehung *f*, c) 'Umlauf(zeit *f*) *m*; **3.** *fig.* Revoluti'on *f*: a) 'Umwälzung *f*, 'Umschwung *m*, b) *pol.* 'Umsturz *m*; ˌ**rev·o-'lu·tion·ar·y** [-ʃnərɪ] **I** *adj.* revolutio'när: a) *pol.* Revolutions..., Umsturz..., b) *fig.* 'umwälzend, e'pochemachend; **II** *s. a.* ˌ**rev·o'lu·tion·ist** [-ʃnɪst] Revolutio'när(in) (*a. fig.*); ˌ**rev·o'lu·tion·ize** [-ʃnaɪz] *v/t.* **1.** aufwiegeln, in Aufruhr bringen; **2.** *Staat* revolutionieren (*a. fig. von Grund auf umgestalten*).
re·volve [rɪ'vɒlv] **I** *v/i.* **1.** *bsd.* A, ⚙, *phys.* sich drehen, kreisen, rotieren (***on***, ***about*** um *e-e Achse*, ***round*** um *e-n Mittelpunkt*); **2.** e-n Kreislauf bilden, da'hinrollen (*Jahre etc.*); **II** *v/t.* **3.** drehen, rotieren lassen; **4.** *fig.* (hin u. her) über'legen, *Gedanken*, *Problem* wälzen; **re'volv·er** [-və] *s.* Re'volver *m*; **re'volv·ing** [-vɪŋ] *adj.* a) sich drehend, kreisend, drehbar (***about***, ***round*** um), b) Dreh...(*-bleistift*, *-brücke*, *-bühne*, *-tür etc.*): **~ credit** ✝ Revolving-Kredit *m*; **~ shutter** Rolladen *m*.
re·vue [rɪ'vju:] *s. thea.* **1.** Re'vue *f*; **2.** (zeitkritisches) Kaba'rett, sa'tirische Kaba'rettvorführung.
re·vul·sion [rɪ'vʌlʃn] *s.* **1.** ⚕ Ableitung *f*; **2.** *fig.* 'Umschwung *m*; **3.** *fig.* Abscheu *m* (***against*** vor *dat.*); **re'vul·sive** [-lsɪv] *adj. u. s.* ableitend(es Mittel).
re·ward [rɪ'wɔ:d] **I** *s.* **1.** Entgelt *n*; Belohnung *f*, *a.* Finderlohn *m*; **2.** Vergeltung *f*, (gerechter) Lohn; **II** *v/t.* **3.** *j-n od. et.* belohnen (*a. fig.*); *fig. j-m* vergelten (***for s.th.*** et.); *j-n od. et.* bestrafen; **re'ward·ing** [-dɪŋ] *adj.* □ lohnend (*a. fig.*); *fig. a.* dankbar (*Aufgabe*).
re·wind [ˌri:'waɪnd] **I** *v/t. Film*, *Tonband etc.* (zu')rückspulen, 'umspulen; *Garn etc.* wieder'aufspulen; *Uhr* wieder aufziehen; **II** *s.* Rückspulung *f etc.*; Rücklauf *m* (*am Tonbandgerät etc.*): **~ button** Rücklauftaste *f*.
re·word [ˌri:'wɜ:d] *v/t.* neu *od.* anders formulieren.
re·write [ˌri:'raɪt] **I** *v/t. u. v/i.* [*irr.* → ***write***] **1.** nochmals *od.* neu schreiben; **2.** 'umschreiben; *Am. Pressebericht* redigieren, über'arbeiten; **II** *s.* **3.** *Am.* redigierter Bericht: **~ man** Überarbeiter *m*.
Rex [reks] (*Lat.*) *s.* ⚖ *Brit. der* König.
rhap·sod·ic, **rhap·sod·i·cal** [ræp'sɒdɪk(l)] *adj.* □ **1.** rhap'sodisch; **2.** *fig.* begeistert, 'überschwenglich, ek'statisch; **rhap·so·dist** ['ræpsədɪst] *s.* **1.** Rhap'sode *m*; **2.** *fig.* begeisterter Schwärmer; **rhap·so·dize** ['ræpsədaɪz] *v/i. fig.* schwärmen (***about***, ***on*** von); **rhap·so·dy** ['ræpsədɪ] *s.* **1.** Rhapso'die *f* (*a.* ♪); **2.** *fig.* (Wort)Schwall *m*, Schwärme'rei *f*: ***go into rhapsodies over*** in Ekstase geraten über (*acc.*).
rhe·o·stat ['rɪəʊstæt] *s.* ⚡ Rheo'stat *m*, 'Regelˌwiderstand *m*.
rhet·o·ric ['retərɪk] *s.* **1.** Rhe'torik *f*, Redekunst *f*; **2.** *fig. contp.* schöne Reden *pl.*, (leere) Phrasen *pl.*, Schwulst *m*; **rhe·tor·i·cal** [rɪ'tɒrɪkl] *adj.* □ **1.** rhe'torisch, Redner...: **~ question** rhetorische Frage; **2.** *contp.* schönrednerisch, phrasenhaft, schwülstig; **rhet·o·ri·cian** [ˌretə'rɪʃn] *s.* **1.** guter Redner, Redekünstler *m*; **2.** *contp.* Schönredner *m*, Phrasendrescher *m*.
rheu·mat·ic [ru:'mætɪk] ⚕ **I** *adj.* (□ **~ally**) **1.** rheu'matisch: **~ fever** Gelenkrheumatismus *m*; **II** *s.* **2.** Rheu'matiker(in); **3.** *pl.* F Rheuma *n*; **rheu·ma·tism** ['ru:mətɪzəm] *s.* Rheuma'tismus *m*, Rheuma *n*: ***articular ~*** Gelenkrheumatismus.
Rhine·land·er ['raɪnlændə] *s.* Rheinländer(in).
rhine·stone ['raɪnstəʊn] *s. min.* Rheinkiesel *m* (*Bergkristall*).
rhi·no[1] ['raɪnəʊ] *s. sl.* ‚Kies' *m* (*Geld*).
rhi·no[2] ['raɪnəʊ] *pl.* **-nos** *s.* F, **rhi·noc·er·os** [raɪ'nɒsərəs] *pl.* **-os·es**, *coll.* **-os** *s. zo.* Rhi'nozeros *n*, Nashorn *n*.
rhi·zoph·a·gous [raɪ'zɒfəgəs] *adj. zo.* wurzelfressend.
Rho·de·si·an [rəʊ'di:zjən] **I** *adj.* rho'desisch; **II** *s.* Rho'desier(in).
rho·do·cyte ['rəʊdəsaɪt] *s. physiol.* rotes Blutkörperchen.
rho·do·den·dron [ˌrəʊdə'dendrən] *s.* ⚘ Rhodo'dendron *n*, *m*.
rhomb [rɒm] → ***rhombus***; **rhom·bic** ['rɒmbɪk] *adj.* rhombisch, rautenförmig; **rhom·bo·he·dron** [ˌrɒmbə'hedrən] *pl.* **-he·dra** [-drə], **-he·drons** *s.* A Rhombo'eder *n*; **rhom·boid** ['rɒmbɔɪd] **I** *s.* **1.** A Rhombo'id *n*, Parallelo'gramm *n*; **II** *adj.* **2.** rautenförmig; **3.** → ***rhomboidal***; **rhom·boi·dal** [rɒm'bɔɪdl] *adj.* A rhombo'idförmig, rhombo'idisch; **rhom·bus** ['rɒmbəs] *pl.* **-bus·es**, **-bi** [-baɪ] *s.* A Rhombus *m*, Raute *f*.
rhu·barb ['ru:bɑ:b] *s.* **1.** ⚘ Rha'barber *m*; **2.** *Am. sl.* ‚Krach' *m*.
rhumb [rʌm] *s.* **1.** Kompaßstrich *m*; **2.** *a.* **~-line** a) A loxo'dromische Linie, b) ⚓ Dwarslinie *f*.
rhyme [raɪm] **I** *s.* **1.** Reim *m* (***to*** auf *acc.*): ***without ~ or reason*** ohne Sinn und Zweck; **2.** *sg. od. pl.* a) Vers *m*, b) Reim *m*, Gedicht *n*, Lied *n*; **II** *v/i.* **3.** reimen, Verse machen; **4.** sich reimen (***with*** mit, ***to*** auf *acc.*); **III** *v/t.* **5.** reimen, in Reime bringen; **6.** *Wort* reimen lassen (***with*** auf *acc.*); '**rhyme·less** [-lɪs] *adj.* reimlos; '**rhym·er** [-mə], '**rhyme·ster** [-stə] *s.* Verseschmied *m*; **rhym·ing dic·tion·ar·y** ['raɪmɪŋ] *s.* Reimwörterbuch *n*.
rhythm ['rɪðəm] *s.* **1.** ♪ Rhythmus *m* (*a. Metrik u. fig.*); Takt *m*: ***three-four ~***; ***dance ~s*** Tanzrhythmen, beschwingte Weisen; **~ method** Knaus-Ogino-Methode *f* (*Empfängnisverhütung*); **2.** Versmaß *n*; **3.** ⚕ Pulsschlag *m*; **rhythmic**, **rhyth·mi·cal** ['rɪðmɪk(l)] *adj.* □ rhythmisch: a) taktmäßig, b) *fig.* regelmäßig ('wiederkehrend); **rhyth·mics** ['rɪðmɪks] *s. pl. sg. konstr.* ♪ Rhythmik *f* (*a. Metrik*).
ri·al·to [rɪ'æltəʊ] *s.* **1.** *Am.* The'aterviertel *n*; **2.** Börse *f*, Markt *m*.
rib [rɪb] **I** *s.* **1.** *anat.* Rippe *f*: **~ cage** Brustkorb *m*; **2.** *Küche*: a) *a.* **~ roast** Rippenstück *n*, b) Rippe(n)speer *m*; **3.** *humor.* ‚Ehehälfte' *f*; **4.** ⚘ (Blatt)Rippe *f*, (-)Ader *f*; **5.** ⚙ Stab *m*, Stange *f*, (*a. Heiz-*, *Kühl- etc.*)Rippe *f*; **6.** ▲ (*Gewölbe- etc.*)Rippe *f*, Strebe *f*; **7.** ⚓ a) (Schiffs)Rippe *f*, Spant *n*, b) Spiere *f*; **8.** ♪ Zarge *f*; **9.** (*Stoff*)Rippe *f*: **~ stitch** *Stricken*: linke Masche; **II** *v/t.* **10.** mit Rippen versehen; **11.** *Stoff etc.* rippen; **12.** *sl.* ‚aufziehen', hänseln.
rib·ald ['rɪbəld] **I** *adj.* **1.** lästerlich, frech; **2.** zotig, ‚saftig', ob'szön; **II** *s.* **3.** Spötter(in), Lästermaul *n*; **4.** Zotenreißer *m*; '**rib·ald·ry** [-drɪ] *s.* Zoten(reiße'rei *f*) *pl.*, ‚saftige' Späße *pl.*
rib·and ['rɪbənd] *s.* (Zier)Band *n*.
ribbed [rɪbd] *adj.* gerippt, geriffelt, Rippen...: **~ cooler** ⚙ Rippenkühler *m*; **~ glass** Riffelglas *n*.
rib·bon ['rɪbən] *s.* **1.** Band *n*, Borte *f*; **2.** Ordensband *n*; **3.** (schmaler) Streifen; **4.** Fetzen *m*: ***tear to ~s*** in Fetzen reißen; **5.** Farbband *n* (*Schreibmaschine*); **6.** ⚙ a) (Me'tall)Band *n*, (-)Streifen *m*, b) (Holz)Leiste *f*: **~ microphone** Bändchenmikrophon *n*; **~ saw** Bandsäge *f*; **7.** *pl.* Zügel *pl.*; **~ build·ing**, **~ de·vel·op·ment** *s. Brit.* Stadtrandsiedlung *f* entlang e-r Ausfallstraße.
rib·bon·ed ['rɪbənd] *adj.* **1.** bebändert; **2.** gestreift.
ri·bo·fla·vin [raɪbəʊ'fleɪvɪn] *s.* ⚕ Ribofla'vin *n* (*Vitamin B_2*).
rice [raɪs] *s.* ⚘ Reis *m*; **~ flour** *s.* Reismehl *n*; **~ pad·dy** *s.* Reisfeld *n*; **~ pa·per** *s.* 'Reispaˌpier *n*; **~ pud·ding** *s.* Milchreis *m*.
ric·er ['raɪsə] *s. Am.* Kar'toffelpresse *f*.
rich [rɪtʃ] **I** *adj* (□ → ***richly***) **1.** reich (***in*** an *dat.*) (*a. fig.*), wohlhabend: **~ *in cattle*** viehreich; **~ *in hydrogen*** wasserstoffreich; **~ *in ideas*** ideenreich; **2.** schwer (*Stoff*), prächtig, kostbar (*Seide*, *Schmuck etc.*); **3.** reich(lich), reichhaltig, ergiebig (*Ernte etc.*); **4.** fruchtbar, fett (*Boden*); **5.** a) *geol.* (erz)reich, fündig (*Lagerstätte*), b) *min.* reich, fett (*Erz*): ***strike it ~*** *min.* a) auf Öl *etc.* stoßen, b) *fig.* arrivieren, zu Geld kommen, c) *fig.* das große Los ziehen, e-n Volltreffer landen; **6.** ⛏ schwer; *mot.* fett, gasreich (*Luftgemisch*); **7.** schwer, fett (*Speise*); **8.** schwer, kräftig (*Wein*, *Duft etc.*); **9.** satt, voll (*Farbton*); **10.** voll, satt (*Ton*); voll(tönend), klangvoll (*Stimme*); **11.** inhalt(s)reich; **12.** F ‚köstlich', ‚großartig'; **II** *s.* **13.** *coll.* ***the ~*** die Reichen *pl.*; **rich·es** ['rɪtʃɪz] *s. pl.* Reichtum *m*, -tümer *pl.*; '**rich·ly** [-lɪ] *adv.* reichlich, in reichem Maße; '**rich·ness** [-nɪs] *s.* **1.** Reichtum *m*, Reichhaltigkeit *f*, Fülle *f*; **2.** Pracht *f*; **3.** Ergiebigkeit *f*; **4.** Nahrhaftigkeit *f*; **5.** (Voll)Gehalt *m*, Schwere *f* (*Wein etc.*); **6.** Sattheit *f* (*Farbton*); **7.** Klangfülle *f*.
rick[1] [rɪk] ↗ *bsd. Brit.* **I** *s.* (Getreide-, Heu)Schober *m*; **II** *v/t.* schobern.
rick[2] [rɪk] *v/t. bsd. Brit.* verrenken.
rick·ets ['rɪkɪts] *s. sg. od. pl. konstr.* ⚕ Ra'chitis *f*; '**rick·et·y** [-tɪ] *adj.* **1.** ⚕ ra'chitisch; **2.** gebrechlich (*Person*), wack(e)lig (*a. Möbel u. fig.*), klapp(e)rig (*Auto etc.*).
ric·o·chet ['rɪkəʃeɪ] **I** *s.* **1.** Abprallen *n*; **2.** ⚔ a) Rikoschettieren *n*, b) *a.* **~ shot** Abpraller *m*, Querschläger *m*; **II** *v/i.* **3.**

abprallen.

rid [rɪd] *v/t.* [*irr.*] befreien, frei machen (***of*** von): ***get ~ of*** *j-n od. et.* loswerden; ***be ~ of*** *j-n od. et.* los sein; **rid·dance** [ˈrɪdəns] *s.* Befreiung *f*, Erlösung *f*: (***he is a***) ***good ~!*** man ist froh, daß man ihn (wieder) los ist!, den wären wir los!

rid·den [ˈrɪdn] **I** *p.p. von* **ride**; **II** *adj. in Zssgn.* bedrückt, geplagt, gepeinigt von: ***fever-~***; ***pest-~*** von der Pest heimgesucht.

rid·dle¹ [ˈrɪdl] **I** *s.* **1.** Rätsel *n* (*a. fig.*): ***speak in ~s*** → 4; **II** *v/t.* **2.** enträtseln: ***~ me*** rate mal; **3.** *fig. j-n* vor ein Rätsel stellen; **III** *v/i.* **4.** *fig.* in Rätseln sprechen.

rid·dle² [ˈrɪdl] **I** *s.* **1.** Schüttelsieb *n*; **II** *v/t.* **2.** (ˈdurch-, aus)sieben; **3.** *fig.* durchˈsieben, durchˈlöchern: ***~ s.o. with bullets***; **4.** *fig. Argument etc.* zerpflücken; **5.** *fig.* mit Fragen bestürmen.

ride [raɪd] **I** *s.* **1.** a) Ritt *m*, b) Fahrt *f* (*bsd. auf e-m* [*Motor*]*Rad od. in e-m öffentlichen Verkehrsmittel*): ***go for a ~, take a ~*** a) ausreiten, b) ausfahren; ***give s.o. a. ~*** j-n reiten *od.* fahren lassen, j-n *im Auto etc.* mitnehmen; ***take s.o. for a ~*** F a) j-n (im Auto entführen und) umbringen, b) j-n ‚reinlegen' (*betrügen*), c) j-n ‚auf den Arm nehmen' (*hänseln*); **2.** Reitweg *m*, Schneise *f*; **II** *v/i.* [*irr.*] **3.** reiten (*a. fig. rittlings sitzen*): ***~ out*** F ausreiten; ***~ for*** zustreben (*dat.*), entgegeneilen (*dat.*); ***~ for a fall*** halsbrecherisch reiten, *fig.* in sein Verderben rennen; ***~ up*** hochrutschen (*Kragen etc.*); ***let it ~!*** F laß die Karre laufen!; ***he let the remark ~*** er ließ die Bemerkung hingehen; ***Nixon ~s again!*** *iro.* N. ist wieder da!; **4.** fahren: ***~ on a bicycle*** radfahren; ***~ in a train*** mit e-m Zug fahren; **5.** sich (fort)bewegen, daˈhinziehen (*a. Mond, Wolken etc.*); **6.** (auf dem Wasser) treiben, schwimmen; *fig.* schweben: ***~ at anchor*** ⚓ vor Anker liegen; ***~ on the waves of popularity*** *fig.* von der Woge der Volksgunst getragen werden; ***~ on the wind*** sich vom Wind tragen lassen (*Vogel*); ***be riding on air*** *fig.* selig sein (*vor Glück*); **7.** *fig.* ruhen, liegen, sich drehen (***on*** auf *dat.*); **8.** sich überˈlagern (*z.B.* ⚕ *Knochenfragmente*); ⚓ unklar laufen (*Tau*); **9.** ⚙ fahren, laufen, gleiten; **10.** zum Reiten *gut etc.* geeignet sein (*Boden*); **11.** im Reitdreß wiegen; **III** *v/t.* [*irr.*] **12.** reiten: ***~ at*** *sein Pferd* lenken nach *od.* auf (*acc.*); ***~ to death*** zu Tode reiten (*a. fig. Theorie, Witz etc.*); ***~ a race*** an e-m Rennen teilnehmen; **13.** reiten *od.* rittlings sitzen (lassen) auf (*dat.*); *j-n auf den Schultern* tragen; **14.** *Motorrad etc.* fahren, lenken: ***~ over*** a) *j-n* überfahren, b) → 17; c) über *e-e Sache* rücksichtslos hinweggehen; **15.** *fig.* reiten *od.* schwimmen *od.* schweben auf (*dat.*): ***~ the waves*** auf den Wellen reiten; **16.** aufliegen *od.* ruhen auf (*dat.*); **17.** tyrannisieren, beherrschen; *weitS.* heimsuchen, plagen, quälen; *j-m* bös zusetzen (*a. mit Kritik*); *Am.* F *j-n* reizen, hänseln: ***the devil ~s him*** ihn reitet der Teufel; → **ridden** II; **18.** *Land* durchˈreiten; **~ down** *v/t.* **1.** überˈholen; **2.** a) niederreiten, b) überˈfahren; **~ out** *v/t. Sturm etc.* (gut) überˈstehen (*a. fig.*).

rid·er [ˈraɪdə] *s.* **1.** Reiter(in); **2.** (Mit-)Fahrer(in); **3.** ⚙ a) Oberteil *n*, b) Laufgewicht *n* (*Waage*); **4.** △ Strebe *f*; **5.** ⚓ Binnenspant *n*; **6.** ⚖ a) Zusatz (-klausel *f*) *m*, b) Beiblatt *n*, c) (ˈWechsel)Alˌlonge *f*, d) zusätzliche Empfehlung; **7.** ∡ Zusatzaufgabe *f*; **8.** ⚒ Salband *n*.

ridge [rɪdʒ] **I** *s.* **1.** a) (Gebirgs)Kamm *m*, Grat *m*, Kammlinie *f*, b) Berg-, Hügelkette *f*, c) Wasserscheide *f*; **2.** Kamm *m e-r Welle*; **3.** Rücken *m der Nase, e-s Tiers*; **4.** △ (Dach)First *m*; **5.** ⚘ a) (Furchen)Rain *m*, b) erhöhtes Mistbeet; **6.** ⚙ Wulst *m*; **7.** *meteor.* Hochdruckgürtel *m*; **II** *v/t. u. v/i.* **8.** (sich) furchen; **~ pole** *s.* **1.** △ Firstbalken *m*; **2.** Firststange *f* (*Zelt*); **~ tent** *s.* Hauszelt *n*; **~ tile** *s.* △ Firstziegel *m*; ˈ**~·way** *s.* Kammlinien-, Gratweg *m*.

rid·i·cule [ˈrɪdɪkjuːl] **I** *s.* Spott *m*: ***hold up to ~*** → II; ***turn*** (***in***)***to ~*** *et.* ins Lächerliche ziehen; **II** *v/t.* lächerlich machen, verspotten; **ri·dic·u·lous** [rɪˈdɪkjʊləs] *adj.* □ lächerlich; **ri·dic·u·lous·ness** [rɪˈdɪkjʊləsnɪs] *s.* Lächerlichkeit *f*.

rid·ing [ˈraɪdɪŋ] **I** *s.* **1.** Reiten *n*; Reitsport *m*; **2.** Fahren *n*; **3.** Reitweg *m*; **4.** *Brit.* Verwaltungsbezirk *m*; **II** *adj.* **5.** Reit…: ***~ horse*** (***school, whip*** *etc.*); ***~ breeches*** *pl.* Reithose *f*; ***~ habit*** Reitkleid *n*.

rife [raɪf] *adj. pred.* **1.** weit verbreitet, häufig: ***be ~*** (vor)herrschen, grassieren; ***grow*** (*od.* ***wax***) ***~*** überhandnehmen; **2.** (***with***) voll (von), angefüllt (mit).

rif·fle [ˈrɪfl] **I** *s.* **1.** ⚙ Rille *f*, Riefelung *f*; **2.** *Am.* a) seichter Abschnitt (*Fluß*), b) Stromschnelle *f*; **3.** Stechen *n* (*Mischen von Spielkarten*); **II** *v/t.* **4.** ⚙ riffeln; **5.** *Spielkarten* stechen (*mischen*); **6.** ˈdurchblättern; *Zettel etc.* durcheinˈanderbringen.

riff-raff [ˈrɪfræf] *s.* Pöbel *m*, Gesindel *n*, Pack *n*.

ri·fle¹ [ˈraɪfl] **I** *s.* **1.** Gewehr *n* (*mit gezogenem Lauf*), Büchse *f*; **2.** *pl.* ⚔ Schützen *pl.*; **II** *v/t.* **3.** *Gewehrlauf* ziehen.

ri·fle² [ˈraɪfl] *v/t.* (aus)plündern, *Haus a.* durchˈwühlen.

ri·fle| corps *s.* Schützenkorps *n*; **~ grenade** *s.* Geˈwehrgranate *f*; ˈ**~·man** [-mən] *s.* [*irr.*] ⚔ Schütze *m*, Jäger *m*; **~ pit** *s.* ⚔ Schützenloch *n*; **~ prac·tice** *s.* ⚔ Schießübung *f*; **~ range** *s.* **1.** Schießstand *m*; **2.** Schußweite *f*; **~ shot** *s.* **1.** Gewehrschuß *m*; **2.** Schußweite *f*.

ri·fling [ˈraɪflɪŋ] *s.* **1.** Ziehen *n e-s Gewehrlaufs etc.*; **2.** Züge *pl.*

rift [rɪft] **I** *s.* **1.** Spalte *f*, Spalt *m*, Ritze *f*; **2.** Sprung *m*, Riß *m*: ***a little ~ within the lute*** *fig.* der Anfang vom Ende; **II** *v/t.* **3.** (zer)spalten; **~ saw** *s.* ⚙ Gattersäge *f*; **~ val·ley** *s. geol.* Senkungsgraben *m*.

rig¹ [rɪg] **I** *s.* **1.** ⚓ Takelung *f*, Takeˈlage *f*; ✈ (Auf)Rüstung *f*; **2.** Ausrüstung *f*; Vorrichtung *f*; **3.** F *fig.* Aufmachung *f* (*Kleidung*): ***in full ~*** in voller Montur; **4.** *Am.* a) Fuhrwerk *n*, b) Sattelschlepper *m*; **5.** Bohranlage *f*; **II** *v/t.* **6.** ⚓ a) *Schiff* auftakeln, b) *Segel* anschlagen; **7.** ✈ (auf)rüsten, montieren; **8.** ***~ out, ~ up*** a) ⚓ *etc.* ausrüsten, -statten, b) F *fig. j-n* ‚auftakeln', ausstaffieren; **9.** *oft* ***~ up*** (behelfsmäßig) zs.-bauen, zs.-basteln.

rig² [rɪg] **I** *v/t.* ⚚ *Markt etc., pol. Wahl* manipulieren; **II** *s.* (ˈSchwindel)Maˌnöver *n*, Schiebung *f*.

rig·ger [ˈrɪgə] *s.* **1.** ⚓ Takler *m*; **2.** ✈ Monˈteur *m*, (ˈRüst)Meˌchaniker *m*; **3.** ⚡ Kabelleger *m*; **4.** △ Schutzgerüst *n*; **5.** ⚙ Schnur-, Riemenscheibe *f*; **6.** ⚚ Kurstreiber *m*.

rig·ging [ˈrɪgɪŋ] *s.* **1.** ⚓ Takeˈlage *f*, Takelwerk *n*: ***running*** (***standing***) ***~*** laufendes (stehendes) Gut; **2.** ✈ Verspannung *f*; **3.** → **rig²** II; **~ loft** *s. thea.* Schnürboden *m*.

right [raɪt] **I** *adj.* □ → ***rightly***; **1.** richtig, recht, angemessen: ***it is only ~*** es ist nicht mehr als recht und billig; ***he is ~ to do so*** er tut recht daran (, so zu handeln); ***the ~ thing*** das Richtige; ***say the ~ thing*** das rechte Wort finden; **2.** richtig: a) korˈrekt, b) wahr(heitsgemäß): ***the solution is ~*** die Lösung stimmt *od.* ist richtig; ***is your watch ~?*** geht Ihre Uhr richtig?; ***be ~*** recht haben; ***get s.th. ~*** et. klarlegen, et. in Ordnung bringen; ***~?*** F klar?; ***all ~!*** a) alles in Ordnung, b) ganz recht!, c) abgemacht!, in Ordnung!, gut!, (na) schön! (→ *a.* 4); ***~ you are!*** F richtig!, jawohl!; ***that's ~!*** ganz recht!, stimmt!; **3.** richtig, geeignet: ***he is the ~ man*** er ist der Richtige; ***he is all ~*** F er ist in Ordnung (→ *a.* 4); ***the ~ man in the ~ place*** der rechte Mann am rechten Platz; **4.** gesund, wohl: ***he is all ~*** a) es geht ihm gut, er fühlt sich wohl, b) ihm ist nichts passiert; ***out of one's ~ mind, not ~ in one's*** (*od.* ***the***) ***head*** F nicht ganz bei Trost; ***in one's ~ mind*** bei klarem Verstand; **5.** richtig, in Ordnung: ***come ~*** in Ordnung kommen; ***put*** (*od.* ***set***) ***~*** a) in Ordnung bringen, b) *j-n* (über e-n Irrtum) aufklären, c) *Irrtum* richtigstellen, d) *j-n* gesund machen; ***put o.s. ~ with s.o.*** a) sich vor j-m rechtfertigen, b) sich mit j-m gut stellen; **6.** recht, Rechts… (*a. pol.*): ***~ arm*** (*od.* ***hand***) *fig.* rechte Hand; ***~ side*** rechte Seite, Oberseite *f* (*a. Münze, Stoff etc.*); ***on*** (*od.* ***to***) ***the ~ side*** rechts, rechter Hand; ***on the ~ side of 40*** noch nicht 40 (Jahre alt); ***~ turn*** Rechtswendung *f* (um 90 Grad); ***~ wing*** a) *sport u. pol.* rechter Flügel, b) *sport* Rechtsaußen *m* (*Spieler*); **7.** ∡ a) recht(*er Winkel*), b) rechtwink(e)lig (*Dreieck*), c) gerade (*Linie*), d) senkrecht (*Figur*): ***at ~ angles*** rechtwink(e)lig; **8.** *obs.* rechtmäßig (*Erbe*); echt (*Kognak etc.*); **II** *adv.* **9.** richtig, recht: ***act*** (*od.* ***do***) ***~***; ***guess ~*** richtig (er)raten; **10.** recht, richtig, gut: ***nothing goes ~ with me*** (bei) mir geht alles schief; ***turn out ~*** gut ausgehen; → 5; **11.** rechts (***from*** von); nach rechts; auf der rechten Seite: ***~ and left*** a) rechts und links, b) *fig. a.* ***~, left and centre*** (*Am.* ***center***) überall, von *od.* auf *od.* nach allen Seiten; ***~ about face!*** ⚔ (ganze Abteilung,) kehrt!; **12.** gerade (-wegs), (schnur)stracks, soˈfort: ***~ ahead, ~ on*** geradeaus; ***~ away*** (*od.* ***off***) *bsd. Am.* sofort, gleich; ***~ now*** *Am.* jetzt (gleich); **13.** völlig, ganz (und gar), diˈrekt: ***rotten ~ through*** durch und durch faul; **14.** genau, gerade: ~ ***in the middle***; **15.** F ‚richtig', ‚ordentlich': ***I was ~ glad***; ***he's a big shot all ~*** (***but***) er ist schon ein ‚großes Tier' (, aber); **16.** *obs.* recht, sehr: ***know ~ well*** sehr wohl wissen; **17.** ♀ *in Titeln*: hoch, sehr: ~ ***Hono***(***u***)***rable*** Sehr Ehrenwert; → ***reverend*** 2; **III** *s.* **18.** Recht *n*: ***of*** (*od.* ***by***) ~***s*** von Rechts wegen, rechtmäßig, eigentlich; ***in the ~*** im Recht; ~ ***and wrong*** Recht und Unrecht; ***do s.o. ~*** j-m Gerechtigkeit widerfahren lassen; ***give s.o. his ~s*** j-m sein Recht geben *od.* lassen; **19.** ⚖ (subjek'tives) Recht, Anrecht *n*, (Rechts)Anspruch *m* (***to*** auf *acc.*); Berechtigung *f*: ~***s and duties*** Rechte und Pflichten; ~ ***of inheritance*** Erbschaftsanspruch; ~ ***of possession*** Eigentumsrecht; ~ ***of sale*** Verkaufsrecht; ~ ***of way*** → ***right-of-way***; ***industrial ~s*** gewerbliche Schutzrechte; ***by ~ of*** kraft (*gen.*), auf Grund (*gen.*); ***in ~ of his wife*** a) im Namen s-r Frau, b) von seiten s-r Frau; ***in one's own ~*** aus eigenem Recht; ***be within one's ~s*** das Recht auf s-r Seite haben; **20.** *das* Rechte *od.* Richtige: ***do the ~***; **21.** *pl.* (richtige) Ordnung: ***bring*** (*od.* ***put*** *od.* ***set***) ***s.th. to ~s*** et. (wieder) in Ordnung bringen; **22.** wahrer Sachverhalt: ***know the ~s of a case***; **23.** *die* Rechte, rechte Seite (*a. Stoff*): ***on*** (*od.* ***to***) ***the ~*** rechts, zur Rechten; ***on the ~ of*** rechts von; ***keep to the ~*** sich rechts halten, *mot.* rechts fahren; ***turn to the ~*** (sich) nach rechts wenden; **24.** rechte Hand, Rechte *f*; **25.** *Boxen*: Rechte *f* (*Faust od. Schlag*); **26.** ♀ *pol.* a) rechter Flügel, b) 'Rechtspar,tei *f*; **IV** *v/t.* **27.** (⚓ auf)richten, ins Gleichgewicht bringen; ✈ *Maschine* abfangen; **28.** *Fehler*, *Irrtum* berichtigen: ~ ***itself*** a) sich wieder ausgleichen, b) (wieder) in Ordnung kommen; **29.** *Unrecht etc.* wieder'gutmachen, in Ordnung bringen; **30.** *Zimmer etc.* in Ordnung bringen; **31.** *j-m* zu s-m Recht verhelfen: ~ ***o.s.*** sich rehabilitieren; **V** *v/i.* **32.** sich wieder aufrichten.

'right|·a·bout *s. a.* ~ ***face*** (*od.* ***turn***) Kehrtwendung *f* (*a. fig.*): ***send s.o. to the ~*** j-m ‚heimleuchten'; **'~-,an·gled** → ***right*** 7 b; **'~·down** *adj. u. adv.* ‚regelrecht', ausgesprochen.

right·eous ['raɪtʃəs] **I** *adj.* □ gerecht (*a. Sache*, *Zorn*), rechtschaffen; **II** *s. coll.* ***the ~*** die Gerechten *pl.*; **'right·eous·ness** [-nɪs] *s.* Rechtschaffenheit *f*.

'right|·ful [-fʊl] *adj.* □ rechtmäßig; **'~-hand** *adj.* **1.** recht: ~ ***bend*** Rechtskurve *f*; ~ ***man*** a) ⚔ rechter Nebenmann, b) *fig.* rechte Hand; **2.** rechtshändig: ~ ***blow*** *Boxen*: Rechte *f*; **3.** ⚙ Rechts…; rechtsgängig (*Schraube*); rechtsläufig (*Motor*): ~ ***drive*** Rechtssteuerung *f*; ~ ***thread*** Rechtsgewinde *n*; **,~-'hand·ed** *adj.* **1.** rechtshändig: ~ ***person*** Rechtshänder(in); **2.** → ***right-hand*** 3; **,~-'hand·er** [-'hændə] *s.* F **1.** Rechtshänder(in); **2.** *Boxen*: Rechte *f* (*Schlag*).

right·ist ['raɪtɪst] **I** *adj. pol.* 'rechtsgerichtet, -stehend; **II** *s.* 'Rechtspar,teiler *m*, Rechte(r *m*) *f*.

right·ly ['raɪtlɪ] *adv.* **1.** richtig; **2.** mit Recht; **3.** F (*nicht*) genau.

,right-'mind·ed *adj.* rechtschaffen.

right·ness ['raɪtnɪs] *s.* **1.** Richtigkeit *f*; **2.** Rechtmäßigkeit *f*; **3.** Geradheit *f* (*Linie*).

right·o [,raɪt'əʊ] *int. Brit.* F gut!, schön!, in Ordnung!

,right|-of-'way *pl.* **,rights-of-'way** *s.* **1.** *Verkehr*: a) Vorfahrt(srecht *n*) *f*, b) Vorrang *m* (*e-r Straße*, *a. fig.*): ***yield the ~*** (die) Vorfahrt gewähren (***to*** *dat.*); **2.** Wegerecht *n*; **3.** öffentlicher Weg; **4.** *Am.* zu öffentlichen Zwecken beanspruchtes (*z.B.* Bahn)Gelände; **,~-'wing** *adj. pol.* Rechts…, dem rechten Flügel angehörend, rechtsstehend; **,~'wing·er** *s.* **1.** → ***rightist*** II; **2.** *sport* Rechtsaußen *m*.

right·oh → ***righto***.

rig·id ['rɪdʒɪd] *adj.* □ **1.** starr, steif; **2.** ⚙ a) starr, unbeweglich, b) (stand-, form-) fest, sta'bil: ~ ***airship*** Starrluftschiff *n*; **3.** *fig.* a) streng (*Disziplin*, *Glaube*, *Sparsamkeit etc.*), b) starr (*Politik*, ✝ *Preise etc.*), c) streng, hart, unbeugsam (*Person*); **ri·gid·i·ty** [rɪ'dʒɪdətɪ] *s.* **1.** Starr-, Steifheit *f* (*a. fig.*), Starre *f*; **2.** ⚙ a) Starrheit *f*, Unbeweglichkeit *f*, b) (Stand-, Form)Festigkeit *f*, Stabili'tät *f*; **3.** *fig.* Strenge *f*, Härte *f*, Unnachgiebigkeit *f*.

rig·ma·role ['rɪgmərəʊl] *s.* **1.** Geschwätz *n*: ***tell a long ~*** lang u. breit erzählen; **2.** *iro.* Brim'borium *n*.

rig·or[1] ['rɪgə] *Am.* → ***rigour***.

rig·or[2] ['rɪgə] *s.* ⚕ **1.** Schüttel-, Fieberfrost *m*; **2.** Starre *f*; → **ri·gor mor·tis** ['raɪgɔː 'mɔːtɪs] *s.* ⚕ Leichenstarre *f*.

rig·or·ous ['rɪgərəs] *adj.* □ **1.** streng, hart, rigo'ros: ~ ***measures***; **2.** streng (*Winter*); rauh (*Klima etc.*); **3.** (peinlich) genau, strikt, ex'akt.

rig·our ['rɪgə] *s.* **1.** Strenge *f*, Härte *f* (*a. des Winters*); Rauheit *f* (*Klima*): ~***s of the weather*** Unbilden der Witterung; **2.** Ex'aktheit *f*, Schärfe *f*.

rile [raɪl] *v/t.* F ärgern: ***be ~d at*** aufgebracht sein über (*acc.*).

rill [rɪl] *s.* Bächlein *n*, Rinnsal *n*.

rim [rɪm] **I** *s.* **1.** *allg.* Rand *m*; **2.** ⚙ a) Felge *f*, b) (Rad)Kranz *m*: ~ ***brake*** Felgenbremse *f*; **3.** (Brillen)Rand *m*, Fassung *f*; **II** *v/t.* **4.** mit e-m Rand versehen; einfassen; **5.** ⚙ *Rad* befelgen.

rime [raɪm] *s. poet.* (Rauh)Reif *m*.

rim·less ['rɪmlɪs] *adj.* randlos.

rim·y ['raɪmɪ] *adj.* bereift, voll Reif.

rind [raɪnd] *s.* **1.** ⚘ (Baum)Rinde *f*, Borke *f*; **2.** (Brot-, Käse)Rinde *f*, Kruste *f*; **3.** (Speck)Schwarte *f*; **4.** (Obst-, Gemüse)Schale *f*; **5.** *fig.* Schale *f*, *das* Äußere.

ring[1] [rɪŋ] **I** *s.* **1.** *allg.* Ring *m* (*a.* ⚘, ⚗): ***form a ~*** *fig.* e-n Kreis bilden (*Personen*); **2.** ⚙ Öse *f*; **3.** *ast.* Hof *m*; **4.** (Zirkus)Ring *m*, Ma'nege *f*; **5.** (Box-) Ring *m*, *weitS.* (*das*) (Berufs)Boxen: ***be in the ~ for*** *fig.* kämpfen um; **6.** *Rennsport*: a) Buchmacherstand *m*, b) *coll. die* Buchmacher *pl.*; **7.** ✝ Ring *m*, Kar'tell *n*; **8.** (*Verbrecher-*, *Spionage- etc.*)Ring *m*, Organisati'on *f*; *weitS.* Clique *f*; **II** *v/t.* **9.** beringen; *e-m Tier* e-n Ring durch die Nase ziehen; **10.** ⚒ *Baum* ringeln; **11.** in Ringe schneiden: ~ ***onions***; **12.** *mst* ~ ***in*** (*od.* ***round*** *od.* ***about***) um'ringen, -'kreisen, einschließen; *Vieh* um'reiten, zs.-treiben.

ring[2] [rɪŋ] **I** *s.* **1.** a) Glockenklang *m*, -läuten *n*, b) Glockenspiel *n*, Läutwerk *n* (*Kirche*); **2.** Läut-, Rufzeichen *n*, Klingeln *n*; **3.** *teleph.* Anruf *m*: ***give me a ~*** rufe mich an; **4.** Klang *m*, Schall *m*: ***the ~ of truth*** der Klang der Wahrheit, der echte Klang; **II** *v/i.* [*irr.*] **5.** läuten (*Glocke*), klingeln (*Glöckchen*): ~ ***at the door*** klingeln; ~ ***for*** nach *j-m* klingeln; ~ ***off*** *teleph.* (den Hörer) auflegen; **6.** klingen (*Münze*, *Stimme*, *Ohr etc.*): ~ ***true*** wahr klingen; **7.** *oft* ~ ***out*** erklingen, -schallen (***with*** von), ertönen (*a. Schuß*): ~ ***again*** widerhallen; **III** *v/t.* [*irr.*] **8.** *Glocke* läuten: ~ ***the bell*** a) klingeln, läuten, b) *fig.* → ***bell***[1] 1; ~ ***down*** (***up***) ***the curtain*** *thea.* den Vorhang nieder- (hoch)gehen lassen; ~ ***in the new year*** das neue Jahr einläuten; ~ ***s.o. up*** *teleph. bsd. Brit.* j-n *od.* bei j-m anrufen; **9.** erklingen lassen; *fig. j-s Lob* erschallen lassen.

'ring|-a,round-a-'ros·y *s.* ‚Ringelreihen' *n* (*Kinderspiel*); ~ **bind·er** *s.* Ringbuch *n*; ~ **com·pound** *s.* ⚗ Ringverbindung *f*; **'~·dove** *s. orn.* **1.** Ringeltaube *f*; **2.** Lachtaube *f*.

ringed [rɪŋd] *adj.* **1.** beringt (*Hand etc.*); *fig.* verheiratet; **2.** *zo.* Ringel…

ring·er ['rɪŋə] *s.* **1.** Glöckner *m*; **2.** *Am. sl.* a) *Pferderennen*: ‚Ringer' *m vertauschtes Pferd*, b) *fig. a.* ***dead ~*** Doppelgänger(in), (genaues) Ebenbild, ‚Zwilling' *m* (***for*** von).

ring·ing ['rɪŋɪŋ] **I** *s.* **1.** (Glocken)Läuten *n*; **2.** Klinge(l)n *n*: ***he has a ~ in his ears*** ihm klingen die Ohren; **II** *adj.* □ **3.** klinge(l)nd, schallend: ~ ***cheers*** brausende Hochrufe; ~ ***laugh*** schallendes Gelächter.

'ring,lead·er *s.* Rädelsführer *m*.

ring·let ['rɪŋlɪt] *s.* **1.** Ringlein *n*; **2.** (Ringel)Löckchen *n*.

'ring|,mas·ter *s.* 'Zirkusdi,rektor *m*; **'~-road** *s. mot. bsd. Brit.* Ring-, Um'gehungsstraße *f*; **'~·side** *s.*: ***at the ~*** *Boxen*: am Ring; ~ ***seat*** Ringplatz *m*, *weitS.* guter Platz; ***have a ~ seat*** *fig.* die Sache aus nächster Nähe verfolgen (können); ~ **snake** *s. zo.* Ringelnatter *f*.

ring·ster ['rɪŋstə] *s. Am.* F *bsd. pol.* Mitglied *n* e-s Ringes *od.* e-r Clique.

'ring|-wall *s.* Ringmauer *f*; **'~-worm** *s.* ⚕ Ringelflechte *f*.

rink [rɪŋk] *s.* **1.** a) (*bsd.* Kunst)Eisbahn *f*, b) Rollschuhbahn *f*; **2.** a) *Bowls*: Spielfeld *n*, b) *Curling*: Rink *m*, Bahn *f*.

rinse [rɪns] **I** *v/t.* **1.** *oft* ~ ***out*** (ab-, aus-, nach)spülen; **2.** *Haare* tönen; **II** *s.* **3.** Spülung *f*: ***give s.th. a good ~*** et. gut (ab- *od.* aus)spülen; **4.** Spülmittel *n*; **5.** Tönung *f* (*Haar*); **'rins·ing** [-sɪŋ] *s.* **1.** (Aus)Spülen *n*, Spülung *f*; **2.** *mst pl.* Spülwasser *n*.

ri·ot ['raɪət] **I** *s.* **1.** *bsd.* ⚖ Aufruhr *m*, Zs.-rottung *f*: ♀ ***Act*** *hist. Brit.* Aufruhrakte *f*; ***read the*** ♀ ***Act to*** *fig. humor. j-n* (ernstlich) warnen, *j-m* die Leviten lesen; ~ ***call*** *Am.* Hilfeersuchen *n* (der Polizei bei Aufruhr *etc.*); ~ ***gun*** Straßenkampfwaffe *f*; ~ ***squad***, ~ ***police*** Überfallkommando *n*; ~ ***stick*** Schlagstock *m*; **2.** Tu'mult *m*, Aufruhr *m*, (*a. fig. der Gefühle*), Kra'wall *m* (*a.* = Lärm *m*); **3.** *fig.* Ausschweifung *f*, 'Orgie *f* (*a. weitS. in Farben etc.*): ***run ~*** a) (sich aus)toben, b) durchgehen (*Phantasie etc.*), c) *hunt.* e-e falsche Fährte verfolgen (*Hund*), d) ♀ wuchern; ***he (it) is a ~*** F er (es) ist einfach ‚toll' *od.* ‚zum Schreien' (komisch); **II** *v/i.* **4.** a) an e-m Aufruhr teilnehmen, b) e-n Aufruhr anzetteln; **5.** randalieren, toben; **6.** *a. fig.* schwelgen (***in*** in *dat.*); **'ri·ot·er** [-tə] *s.* Aufrührer *m*; Randalierer *m*, Kra'wallmacher *m*; **'ri·ot·ous** [-təs] *adj.* ☐ **1.** aufrührerisch: ***~ assembly*** ⚖ Zs.-rottung *f*; **2.** tumultu'arisch, tobend; **3.** ausgelassen, wild (*a. Farbe etc.*); **4.** zügellos, toll.

rip [rɪp] **I** *v/t.* **1.** (zer)reißen, (-)schlitzen; *Naht etc.* (auf-, zer)trennen: ***~ off*** los-, wegreißen, *fig. sl.* ***sich*** *et.* ‚unter den Nagel reißen'; *Bank etc.* ausrauben; *j-n* ‚ausnehmen', neppen; ***~ up*** (*od.* ***open***) aufreißen, -schlitzen, -trennen; **II** *v/i.* **2.** reißen, (auf)platzen; **3.** F sausen: ***let her ~!*** gib Gas!; ***~ into*** *fig.* auf *j-n* losgehen; **4.** ***~ out with*** *Fluch etc.* ausstoßen; **III** *s.* **5.** Schlitz *m*, Riß *m*.

ri·par·i·an [raɪ'peərɪən] **I** *adj.* **1.** Ufer...: ***~ owner*** → 3; **II** *s.* **2.** Uferbewohner (-in); **3.** ⚖ Uferanlieger *m*.

'rip·cord *s.* ✈ Reißleine *f*.

ripe [raɪp] *adj.* ☐ **1.** reif (*Obst, Ernte etc.*); ausgereift (*Käse, Wein*); schlachtreif (*Tier*); *hunt.* abschußreif; ⚕ operati'onsreif (*Abszeß etc.*): ***~ beauty*** *fig.* reife Schönheit; **2.** *körperlich, geistig* reif, voll entwickelt; **3.** *fig.* reif, gereift, (*Alter, Urteil etc.*); voll'endet (*Künstler etc.*); ausgereift (*Plan etc.*); **4.** (*zeitlich*) reif (***for*** für); **5.** reif, bereit, fertig (***for*** für); **6.** F deftig (*Witz etc.*); **'rip·en** [-pən] **I** *v/i.* **1.** *a. fig.* reifen, reif werden; **2.** sich (voll) entwickeln, her'anreifen (***into*** zu); **II** *v/t.* **3.** reifen lassen; **'ripe·ness** [-nɪs] *s.* Reife *f* (*a. fig.*).

'rip-off *s. sl.* **1.** a) Diebstahl *m*, b) Raub *m*; **2.** ‚Nepp' *m*, *allg.* ‚Beschiß' *m*.

ri·poste [rɪ'pɒst] **I** *s.* **1.** *fenc.* Ri'poste *f*, Nachstoß *m*; **2.** *fig.* a) schlagfertige Erwiderung, b) scharfe Antwort; **II** *v/i.* **3.** *fenc.* ripostieren; Gegenstoß machen (*a. fig.*); **4.** *fig.* (schlagfertig *od.* hart) kontern.

rip·per ['rɪpə] *s.* **1.** ⚙ a) Trennmesser *n*, b) 'Trennma,schine *f*, c) → ***rip saw***; **2.** *sl.* a) 'Prachtexem,plar *n*, b) Prachtkerl *m*; **3.** *blutrünstiger Mörder*; **rip·ping** ['rɪpɪŋ] *obs. Brit. sl. adj.* ☐ prächtig, ‚prima', ‚toll'.

rip·ple[1] ['rɪpl] **I** *s.* **1.** kleine Welle(n *pl.*), Kräuselung *f* (*Wasser, Sand etc.*): ***~ of laughter*** *fig.* leises Lachen; ***cause a ~*** *fig.* ein kleines Aufsehen erregen; **2.** Rieseln *n*, (Da'hin)Plätschern *n* (*a. fig. Gespräch*); **3.** *fig.* Spiel(en) *n* (*der Muskeln etc.*); **II** *v/i.* **4.** kleine Wellen schlagen, sich kräuseln; **5.** rieseln, (da'hin-) plätschern (*a. fig. Gespräch*); **6.** *fig.* spielen (*Muskeln etc.*); **III** *v/t.* **7.** *Wasser etc.* leicht bewegen, kräuseln.

rip·ple[2] ['rɪpl] ⚙ **I** *s.* Riffelkamm *m*; **II** *v/t. Flachs* riffeln.

'rip·ple| cloth *s.* Zibe'line *f* (*Wollstoff*); ***~ cur·rent*** *s.* ⚡ Brummstrom *m*; ***~ fin·ish*** *s.* ⚙ Kräusellack *m*.

,rip|-'roar·ing *adj.* F ‚toll'; ***~ saw*** *s.* ⚙ Spaltsäge *f*; **'~,snort·er** [-,snɔːtə] *s. sl.* a) ‚tolle Sache', b) ‚toller Kerl'; **'~-'snort·ing** [-'snɔːtɪŋ] *adj. sl.* ‚toll'.

rise [raɪz] **I** *v/i.* [*irr.*] **1.** sich erheben, *vom Bett, Tisch etc.* aufstehen: ***~ (from the dead)*** *eccl.* (von den Toten) auferstehen; **2.** a) aufbrechen, b) die Sitzung schließen, sich vertagen; **3.** auf-, em'por-, hochsteigen (*Vogel, Rauch etc.*; *a. Geruch*; *a. fig. Gedanke, Zorn etc.*): ***the curtain ~s*** *thea.* der Vorhang geht auf; ***my hair ~s*** die Haare stehen mir zu Berge; ***her colo(u)r rose*** die Röte stieg ihr ins Gesicht; ***land ~s to view*** Land kommt in Sicht; ***spirits rose*** die Stimmung hob sich; ***the word rose to her lips*** das Wort kam ihr auf die Lippen; **4.** steigen, sich bäumen (*Pferd*): ***~ to a fence*** zum Sprung über ein Hindernis ansetzen; **5.** sich erheben, em'porragen (*Berg etc.*); **6.** aufgehen (*Sonne etc.*; *a. Saat, Teig*); **7.** (an)steigen (*Gelände etc.*; *a. Wasser*; *a. Temperatur etc.*); **8.** (an)steigen, anziehen (*Preise etc.*); **9.** ⚕ sich bilden (*Blasen*); **10.** sich erheben, aufkommen (*Sturm*); **11.** sich erheben *od.* em'pören, revoltieren: ***~ in arms*** zu den Waffen greifen; ***my stomach ~s against*** (*od.* ***at***) ***it*** mein Magen sträubt sich dagegen, (*a. fig.*) es ekelt mich an; **12.** *beruflich od. gesellschaftlich* aufsteigen: ***~ in the world*** vorwärtskommen, es zu et. bringen; **13.** *fig.* sich erheben: a) erhaben sein (***above*** über *acc.*), b) sich em'porschwingen (*Geist*); → ***occasion*** 3; **14.** ♪ (an)steigen, anschwellen; **II** *v/t.* [*irr.*] **15.** aufsteigen lassen; *Fisch* an die Oberfläche locken; **16.** *Schiff* sichten; **III** *s.* **17.** (Auf)Steigen *n*, Aufstieg *m*; **18.** *ast.* Aufgang *m*; **19.** Auferstehung *f von den Toten*; **20.** Steigen *n* (*Fisch*), Schnappen *n* nach dem Köder: ***get*** (*od.* ***take***) ***a ~ out of s.o.*** *sl.* j-n ‚auf die Palme bringen'; **21.** *fig.* Aufstieg *m* (*Person, Nation etc.*): ***a young man on the ~*** ein aufstrebender junger Mann; **22.** (An)Steigen *n*, Erhöhung *f* (*Flut, Temperatur etc.*; † *Preise etc.*); *Börse*: Aufschwung *m*, Hausse *f*; *bsd. Brit.* Aufbesserung *f*, Lohn-, Gehaltserhöhung *f*: ***buy for a ~*** auf Hausse spekulieren; ***on the ~*** im Steigen (begriffen) (*Preise*); **23.** Zuwachs *m*, -nahme *f*: ***~ in population*** Bevölkerungszuwachs; **24.** Ursprung *m* (*a. fig. Entstehung*): ***take*** (*od.* ***have***) ***its ~*** entspringen, entstehen; **25.** Anlaß *m*: ***give ~ to*** verursachen, hervorrufen, erregen; **26.** a) Steigung *f* (*Gelände*), b) Anhöhe *f*, Erhebung *f*; **27.** Höhe *f*; △ Pfeilhöhe *f* (*Bogen*); **ris·en** ['rɪzn] *p.p. von* ***rise***; **'ris·er** [-zə] *s.* **1.** ***early ~*** Frühaufsteher (-in); ***late ~*** Langschläfer(in); **2.** Steigung *f e-r Treppenstufe*; **3.** a) ⚙ Steigrohr *n*, b) ⚡ Steigleitung *f*, c) *Gießerei*: Steiger *m*.

ris·i·bil·i·ty [,rɪzɪ'bɪlətɪ] *s.* **1.** *a. pl.* Lachlust *f*; **2.** Gelächter *n*; **ris·i·ble** ['rɪzɪbl] *adj.* **1.** lachlustig; **2.** Lach...: ***~ muscles***; **3.** lachhaft.

ris·ing ['raɪzɪŋ] **I** *adj.* **1.** (an)steigend (*a. fig.*): ***~ ground*** (Boden)Erhebung *f*, Anhöhe *f*; ***~ gust*** Steigbö *f*; ***~ main*** a) ⚙ Steigrohr *n*, b) ⚡ Steigleitung *f*; ***~ rhythm*** *Metrik*: steigender Rhythmus; **2.** her'anwachsend, kommend (*Generation*); **3.** aufstrebend: ***a ~ lawyer***; **II** *prp.* **4.** *Am.* F ***~ of*** a) (etwas) mehr als, b) genau; **III** *s.* **5.** Aufstehen *n*; **6.** (An-) Steigen *n* (*a. fig. Preise, Temperatur etc.*); **7.** Steigung *f*, Anhöhe *f*; **8.** *ast.* Aufgehen *n*; **9.** Aufstand *m*, Erhebung *f*; **10.** Steigerung *f*, Zunahme *f*; **11.** Aufbruch *m e-r Versammlung*; **12.** ⚕ a) Geschwulst *f*, b) Pustel *f*.

risk [rɪsk] **I** *s.* **1.** Wagnis *n*, Gefahr *f*, Risiko *n*: ***at one's own ~*** auf eigene Gefahr; ***at the ~ of one's life*** unter Lebensgefahr; ***at the ~ of*** (*ger.*) auf die Gefahr hin, zu (*inf.*); ***be at ~*** gefährdet sein, auf dem Spiel stehen; ***put at ~*** gefährden; ***run the ~ of doing s.th.*** Gefahr laufen, et. zu tun; ***run*** (*od.* ***take***) ***a ~*** ein Risiko eingehen; **2.** † a) Risiko *n*, Gefahr *f*, b) versichertes Wagnis (*Ware od. Person*): ***security ~*** *pol.* Sicherheitsrisiko; **II** *v/t.* **3.** riskieren, wagen, aufs Spiel setzen: ***~ one's life***; **4.** *Verlust, Verletzung etc.* riskieren; **'risk·y** [-kɪ] *adj.* ☐ **1.** ris'kant, gewagt, gefährlich; **2.** → ***risqué***.

ris·qué ['riːskeɪ] *adj.* gewagt, schlüpfrig: ***a ~ story***.

ris·sole ['rɪsəʊl] (*Fr.*) *s. Küche*: Briso'lett *n*.

rite [raɪt] *s.* **1.** *bsd. eccl.*: Ritus *m*, Zere'mo'nie *f*, feierliche Handlung: ***funeral ~s*** Totenfeier *f*, Leichenbegängnis *n*; ***last ~s*** Sterbesakramente; **2.** *oft* ♀ *eccl.* Ritus *m*: a) Religi'onsform *f*, b) Litur'gie *f*; **3.** Gepflogenheit *f*, Brauch *m*.

rit·u·al ['rɪtʃʊəl] **I** *s.* **1.** *eccl. etc., a. fig.* Ritu'al *n*; **2.** *eccl.* Ritu'albuch *n*; **II** *adj.* ☐ **3.** ritu'al, Ritual...: ***~ murder*** Ritualmord *m*; **4.** ritu'ell, feierlich: ***~ dance***.

ritz·y ['rɪtsɪ] *adj. sl.* **1.** ‚stinkvornehm', ‚feu'dal'; **2.** angeberisch.

ri·val ['raɪvl] **I** *s.* **1.** Ri'vale *m*, Ri'valin *f*, Nebenbuhler(in), Konkur'rent(in): ***without a ~*** *fig.* ohnegleichen, unerreicht; **II** *adj.* **2.** rivalisierend, wetteifernd: ***~ firm*** † Konkurrenzfirma *f*; **III** *v/t.* **3.** rivalisieren *od.* wetteifern *od.* konkurrieren mit, *j-m* den Rang streitig machen; **4.** *fig.* es aufnehmen mit; gleichkommen (*dat.*); **'ri·val·ry** [-rɪ] *s.* **1.** Rivali'tät *f*, Nebenbuhlerschaft *f*; **2.** Wettstreit *m*, -eifer *m*, Konkur'renz *f*: ***enter into ~ with s.o.*** j-m Konkurrenz machen.

rive [raɪv] **I** *v/t.* [*irr.*] **1.** (zer)spalten; **2.** *poet.* zerreißen; **II** *v/i.* [*irr.*] **3.** sich spalten; *fig.* brechen (*Herz*); **riv·en** ['rɪvən] *p.p. von* ***rive***.

riv·er ['rɪvə] *s.* **1.** Fluß *m*, Strom *m*: ***~ police*** Wasserschutzpolizei *f*; ***the ~ Thames*** die Themse; ***Hudson*** ♀ der Hudson; ***down the ~*** stromab(wärts); ***sell s.o. down the ~*** F j-n ‚verkaufen'; ***up the ~*** a) stromauf(wärts), b) *Am.* F in den *od.* im ‚Knast'; **2.** *fig.* Strom *m*, Flut *f*.

riv·er·ain ['rɪvəreɪn] **I** *adj.* Ufer..., Fluß...; **II** *s.* Ufer- *od.* Flußbewohner(in).

riv·er| ba·sin *s. geol.* Einzugsgebiet *n*; **'~-bed** *s.* Flußbett *n*; ***~ dam*** *s.* Staudamm *m*, Talsperre *f*; **'~-front** *s.* (Fluß-) Hafenviertel *n*; **'~-head** *s.* (Fluß)Quelle *f*, Quellfluß *m*; ***~ horse*** *s. zo.* Flußpferd *n*.

riv·er·ine ['rɪvəraɪn] *adj.* am Fluß (gelegen *od.* wohnend); Fluß...

riv·er| po·lice *s.* 'Wasserschutzpoli,zei *f*; **'~-side I** *s.* Flußufer *n*; **II** *adj.* am Ufer (gelegen), Ufer...

riv·et ['rɪvɪt] **I** *s.* ⚙ **1.** Niete *f*, Niet *m*: ***~ joint*** Nietverbindung *f*; **II** *v/t.* **2.** ⚙

(ver)nieten; **3.** befestigen (***to*** an *acc.*); **4.** *fig.* a) *Blick, Aufmerksamkeit* heften, richten (***on*** auf *acc.*), b) *Aufmerksamkeit, a. j-n* fesseln: ***stand ~ed to the spot*** wie angewurzelt stehenbleiben; **'riv·et·ing** [-tɪŋ] *s.* ⚙ **1.** Nietnaht *f*; **2.** (Ver)Nieten *n*: ***~ hammer*** Niethammer *m*.

riv·u·let ['rɪvjʊlɪt] *s.* Flüßchen *n*.

roach¹ [rəʊtʃ] *s. ichth.* Plötze *f*, Rotauge *n*: ***sound as a ~*** kerngesund.

roach² [rəʊtʃ] *s.* ⚓ Gilling *f*.

roach³ [rəʊtʃ] → ***cockroach***.

road [rəʊd] **I** *s.* **1.** a) (Land)Straße *f*, b) Weg *m* (*a. fig.*), c) Strecke *f*, d) Fahrbahn *f*: ***by ~*** a) auf dem Straßenweg, b) per Achse, mit dem Fahrzeug; ***on the ~*** a) auf der Straße, b) auf Reisen, unterwegs, c) *thea.* auf Tournee; ***hold the ~ well*** *mot.* e-e gute Straßenlage haben; ***take*** (*sl.* ***hit***) ***the ~*** aufbrechen; ***rule of the ~*** Straßenverkehrsordnung *f*; ***the ~ to success*** *fig.* der Weg zum Erfolg; ***be in s.o.'s ~*** *fig.* j-m im Wege stehen; ***~ up!*** Straßenarbeiten!; **2.** *mst pl.* ⚓ Reede *f*; **3.** 🚂 *Am.* Bahn(strecke) *f*; **4.** ⚒ Förderstrecke *f*; **II** *adj.* **5.** Straßen…, Weg…: ***~ conditions*** Straßenzustand *m*; ***~ haulage*** Güterkraftverkehr *m*; ***~ junction*** Straßenknotenpunkt *m*, -einmündung *f*; ***~ sign*** Straßenschild *n*, Wegweiser *m*.

road·a·bil·i·ty [ˌrəʊdə'bɪlətɪ] *s. mot.* Fahreigenschaften *pl.*; *engS.* Straßenlage *f*.

road| ac·ci·dent *s.* Verkehrsunfall *m*; **'~·bed** *s.* a) 🚂 Bahnkörper *m*, b) Straßenbettung *f*; **'~·block** *s.* **1.** Straßensperre *f*; **2.** Verkehrshindernis *n*; **3.** *fig.* Hindernis *n*; **'~·book** *s.* Reisehandbuch *n*; **~ hog** *s.* Verkehrsrowdy *m* (*rücksichtsloser Fahrer*); **'~ˌhold·ing** *s. mot.* Straßenlage *f*; **~ hole** *s.* Schlagloch *n*; **~ house** *s.* Rasthaus *n*; **'~·man** [-mən] *s.* [*irr.*] **1.** Straßenarbeiter *m*; **2.** Straßenhändler *m*; **~ man·a·ger** *s.* Roadmanager *m* (*e-r Rockgruppe*); **~ map** *s.* Straßen-, Autokarte *f*; **~ met·al** *s.* Straßenbeschotterung *f*, -schotter *m*; **~ roll·er** *s.* ⚙ Straßenwalze *f*; **~ sense** *s. mot.* Fahrverstand *m*; **'~·side I** *s.* (***by the ~*** am) Straßenrand *m*; **II** *adj.* an der Landstraße (gelegen): ***~ inn***; **'~·stead** *s.* ⚓ Reede *f*.

road·ster ['rəʊdstə] *s.* **1.** *Am.* Roadster *m*, (offener) Sportzweisitzer; **2.** *sport* (starkes) Tourenrad.

road| tank·er *s. mot.* Tankwagen *m*; **'~-test** *mot.* **I** *s.* Probefahrt *f*; **II** *v/t.* *ein Auto* probefahren; **~ us·er** *s.* Verkehrsteilnehmer(in); **'~·way** *s.* Fahrdamm *m*, -bahn *f*; **'~·work** *s. sport* Lauftraining *n*; **~ works** *s. pl.* Straßenarbeiten *pl.*, Baustelle *f auf e-r Straße*; **'~ˌwor·thi·ness** *s. mot.* Verkehrssicherheit *f* (*Auto*); **'~ˌwor·thy** *adj. mot.* verkehrssicher (*Auto*).

roam [rəʊm] **I** *v/i. a.* ***~ about*** (um'her)streifen, (-)wandern; **II** *v/t.* durch'streifen (*a. fig. Blick etc.*); **III** *s.* Wandern *n*, Um'herstreifen *n*.

roan [rəʊn] **I** *adj.* **1.** rötlichgrau; **2.** gefleckt; **II** *s.* **3.** Rotgrau *n*; **4.** *zo.* a) Rotschimmel *m*, b) rotgraue Kuh; **5.** Schafleder *n*.

roar [rɔː] **I** *v/i.* **1.** brüllen: ***~ at*** a) *j-n* anbrüllen, b) über *et.* schallend lachen; ***~ with*** vor *Schmerz, Lachen etc.* brüllen; **2.** *fig.* tosen, toben, brausen (*Wind, Meer*); krachen, (g)rollen (*Donner*); (er)dröhnen, donnern (*Geschütz, Motor etc.*); brausen, donnern (*Fahrzeug*); **3.** *vet.* keuchen (*Pferd*); **II** *v/t.* **4.** *et.* brüllen: ***~ out*** *Freude, Schmerz etc.* hinausbrüllen; ***~ s.o. down*** j-n niederschreien; **III** *s.* **5.** Brüllen *n*, Gebrüll *n* (*a. fig.*): ***set the table in a ~*** (***of laughter***) bei der Gesellschaft schallendes Gelächter hervorrufen; **6.** *fig.* Tosen *n*, Toben *n*, Brausen *n* (*Wind, Meer*); Krachen *n*, Rollen *n* (*Donner*); Donner *m* (*Geschütze*); Dröhnen *n*, Lärm *m* (*Motor, Maschinen etc.*); Getöse *n*; **'roar·ing** [-rɪŋ] **I** *adj.* □ **1.** brüllend (*a. fig.* ***with*** vor *dat.*); **2.** lärmend, laut; **3.** tosend (*etc.* → ***roar*** 2); **4.** brausend, stürmisch (*Nacht, Fest*); **5.** a) großartig, ‚phan'tastisch': ***a ~ business*** (*od.* ***trade***) ein schwunghafter Handel, ein ‚Bombengeschäft'; ***in ~ health*** vor Gesundheit strotzend, b) ‚wild', ‚fa'natisch': ***a ~ Christian***; **II** *s.* **6.** → ***roar*** 5 *u.* 6; **7.** *vet.* Keuchen *n* (*Pferd*).

roast [rəʊst] **I** *v/t.* **1.** *Fleisch etc.* braten, rösten; schmoren: ***be ~ed alive*** a) bei lebendigem Leibe verbrannt werden *od.* verbrennen, b) *fig.* vor Hitze fast umkommen; **2.** *Kaffee etc.* rösten; **3.** *metall.* rösten, abschwelen; **4.** F a) ‚durch den Kakao ziehen', b) ‚verreißen' (*kritisieren*); **II** *v/i.* **5.** rösten, braten; schmoren (*a. fig. in der Sonne etc.*): ***I am simply ~ing*** *fig.* mir ist wahnsinnig heiß; **III** *s.* **6.** Braten *m*; → ***rule*** 13; **IV** *adj.* **7.** geröstet, gebraten, Röst…: ***~ beef*** Rinderbraten *m*; ***~ meat*** Braten *m*; ***~ pork*** Schweinebraten *m*; **'roast·er** [-tə] *s.* **1.** Röster *m*, 'Röstappaˌrat *m*; **2.** *metall.* Röstofen *m*; **3.** Spanferkel *n*, Brathähnchen *n etc.*; **'roast·ing** [-tɪŋ] *s.*: ***give s.o. a. ~*** F → ***roast*** 4.

rob [rɒb] *v/t.* **1.** a) *et.* rauben, stehlen, b) *Haus etc.* ausrauben, (-)plündern, c) *fig.* berauben (***of*** *gen.*); **2.** *j-n* berauben: ***~ s.o. of*** a) j-n *e-r Sache* berauben (*a. fig.*), b) *fig.* j-n um *et.* bringen, j-m *et.* nehmen; **rob·ber** ['rɒbə] *s.* Räuber *m*; **rob·ber·y** ['rɒbərɪ] *s.* **1.** *a.* ⚖ Raub *m* (***from*** an *dat.*); 'Raubˌüberfall *m*; **2.** *fig.* ‚Diebstahl' *m*, ‚Beschiß' *m*.

robe [rəʊb] **I** *s.* **1.** (Amts)Robe *f*, Ta'lar *m* (*Geistlicher, Richter etc.*): ***~s*** Amtstracht *f*; ***state ~*** Staatskleid *n*; (***the gentlemen of***) ***the*** (***long***) ***~*** *fig.* die Juristen; **2.** Robe *f*: a) wallendes Gewand, b) Festkleid *n*, c) Abendkleid *n*, d) ✝ *einteiliges Damenkleid*, e) Bademantel *m*; **3.** *bsd.* Taufkleid *n* (*Säugling*); **II** *v/t.* **4.** *j-n* (feierlich an)kleiden, *j-m* die Robe anlegen; **5.** *fig.* (ein)hüllen; **III** *v/i.* **6.** die Robe anlegen.

rob·in ['rɒbɪn] *s.* **1.** *a.* ***~ red-breast*** *orn.* a) Rotkehlchen *n*, b) amer. Wanderdrossel *f*; **2.** → ***round robin***.

rob·o·rant ['rɒbərənt] ⚕ **I** *adj.* stärkend; **II** *s.* Stärkungsmittel *n*, Roborans *n*.

ro·bot ['rəʊbɒt] **I** *s.* **1.** Roboter *m* (*a. fig.*), ⚙ *a.* Auto'mat *m*; **2.** *a.* ***~ bomb*** ⚔ V-Geschoß *n*; **II** *adj.* **3.** auto'matisch: ***~ pilot*** ✈ Selbststeuergerät *n*.

ro·bust [rəʊ'bʌst] *adj.* □ **1.** ro'bust: a) kräftig, stark (*Gesundheit, Körper, Person etc.*), b) kernig, gerade (*Geist*), c) derb (*Humor*); **2.** ⚙ sta'bil, 'widerstandsfähig; **3.** hart, schwer (*Arbeit etc.*); **ro'bust·ness** [-nɪs] *s.* Ro'bustheit *f*.

roc [rɒk] *s. myth.* (Vogel *m*) Rock *m*.

rock¹ [rɒk] *s.* **1.** Fels *m* (*a. fig.*), Felsen *m*; *coll.* Felsen *pl.*, (Fels)Gestein *n*: ***the ~*** *geogr.* Gibraltar; ***volcanic ~*** *geol.* vulkanisches Gestein; (***as***) ***firm as a ~*** *fig.* wie ein Fels, zuverlässig; **2.** Klippe *f* (*a. fig.*): ***on the ~s*** a) F ‚pleite', in Geldnot, b) F ‚kaputt', in die Brüche gegangen (*Ehe etc.*), c) on the rocks, mit Eiswürfeln (*Getränk*); ***see ~s ahead*** mit Schwierigkeiten rechnen; **3.** *Am.* Stein *m*: ***throw ~s at s.o.***; **4.** Pfefferminzstange *f*; **5.** *sl.* Stein, *bsd.* Diamant *m*, *pl.* ‚Klunkern' *pl.*; **6.** *Am. sl.* a) Geldstück *n*, *bsd.* Dollar *m*, b) *pl.* ‚Kies' *m* (*Geld*); **7.** *pl.* V ‚Eier' *pl.* (*Hoden*).

rock² [rɒk] **I** *v/t.* **1.** wiegen, schaukeln; *Kind* (in den Schlaf) wiegen: ***~ in security*** *fig. j-n* in Sicherheit wiegen; **2.** ins Wanken bringen, erschüttern: ***~ the boat*** *fig.* die Sache gefährden; **3.** *Sieb, Sand etc.* rütteln; **II** *v/i.* **4.** (sich) schaukeln, sich wiegen; **5.** (sch)wanken, wackeln, taumeln (*a. fig.*); **6.** ♪ a) Rock 'n' Roll tanzen, b) ‚rocken' (*spielen*); **III** *s.* **7.** → ***rock 'n' roll***.

rock| and roll [ˌrɒkən'rəʊl] → ***rock 'n' roll***; **~ bed** Felsengrund *m*; **~ bot·tom** *s. fig.* Tief-, Nullpunkt *m*: ***get down to ~*** der Sache auf den Grund gehen; ***his supplies touched ~*** s-e Vorräte waren erschöpft; **ˌ~-'bot·tom** *adj.* F allerniedrigst, äußerst (*Preis etc.*); **'~-bound** *adj.* von Felsen um'schlossen; **~ cake** *s.* hartgebackenes Plätzchen; **~ can·dy** → ***rock¹*** 4; **~ climb·ing** *s.* Felsenklettern *n*; **~ cork** *s. min.* 'Bergasˌbest *m*, -kork *m*; **~ crys·tal** *s. min.* 'Bergkriˌstall *m*; **~ de·bris** *geol.* Felsgeröll *n*; **~ draw·ings** *s. pl.* Felszeichnungen *pl.*; **~ drill** *s.* ⚙ Steinbohrer *m*.

rock·er ['rɒkə] *s.* **1.** Kufe *f* (*Wiege etc.*): ***off one's ~*** *sl.* ‚übergeschnappt', verrückt; **2.** a) Schaukelpferd *n*, b) *Am.* Schaukelstuhl *m*; **3.** ⚙ a) Wippe *f*, b) Wiegemesser *n*, c) Schwing-, Kipphebel *m*; **4.** Schwingtrog *m* (*zur Goldwäsche*); **5.** *Eislauf*: a) Holländer(schlittschuh) *m*, b) Kehre *f*; **6.** *pl. Brit.* Rokker *pl.*, ‚Lederjacken' *pl.* (*Jugendliche*); **~ arm** *s.* ⚙ Kipphebel *m*; **~ switch** *s.* ⚡ Wippschalter *m*.

rock·er·y ['rɒkərɪ] *s.* Steingarten *m*.

rock·et¹ ['rɒkɪt] **I** *s.* **1.** *allg.* Ra'kete *f*; **2.** *fig.* F ‚Zi'garre' *f*, Anpfiff *m*; **II** *adj.* **3.** Raketen…: ***~ bomb***; ***~ aircraft***, ***~-driven airplane*** Raketenflugzeug *n*; ***~-assisted take-off*** ✈ Raketenstart *m*; **III** *v/i.* **4.** (wie e-e Ra'kete) hochschießen; **5.** ✝ hochschnellen (*Preise*); **6.** *fig.* e-n ko'metenhaften Aufstieg nehmen; **IV** *v/t.* **7.** ⚔ mit Raketen beschießen; **8.** mit e-r Ra'kete *in den Weltraum etc.* befördern.

rock·et² ['rɒkɪt] *s.* ♀ **1.** 'Nachtviˌole *f*; **2.** Rauke *f*; **3.** → ***~ salad***; **4.** *a.* ***~ cress*** (echtes) Barbarakraut.

rock·et·eer [ˌrɒkɪ'tɪə] *s.* ⚔ **1.** Ra'ketenkanoˌnier *m od.* -piˌlot *m*; **2.** Ra'ketenforscher *m*, -fachmann *m*.

rock·et| jet *s.* Ra'ketentriebwerk *n*; **~**

launch·er *s.* ⚔ Ra'ketenwerfer *m*; '~-ˌ**launch·ing site** *s.* ⚔ Ra'ketenabschußbasis *f*; '~-ˌ**pow·ered** *adj.* mit Ra'ketenantrieb; ~ **pro·jec·tor** *s.* ⚔ (Ra'keten)Werfer *m*.

rock·et·ry ['rɒkɪtrɪ] *s.* **1.** Ra'ketentechnik *f od.* -forschung *f*; **2.** *coll.* Ra'keten *pl.*

rock·et sal·ad *s.* ⚘ Senfkohl *m*.

rock| flour *s. min.* Bergmehl *n*; ~ **garden** *s.* Steingarten *m*.

rock·i·ness ['rɒkɪnɪs] *s.* felsige *od.* steinige Beschaffenheit.

rock·ing| chair ['rɒkɪŋ] *s.* Schaukelstuhl *m*; ~ **horse** *s.* Schaukelpferd *n*; ~ **le·ver** *s.* Schwinghebel *m*.

rock| leath·er → ***rock cork***; ~ **'n' roll** [ˌrɒkən'rəʊl] *s.* Rock 'n' Roll *m* (*Musik u. Tanz*); ~ **oil** *s.* Stein-, Erdöl *n*, Pe'troleum *n*; ~ **plant** *s.* ⚘ Felsen-, Alpen-, Steingartenpflanze *f*; '~·**rose** *s.* ⚘ Cistrose *f*; ~ **salt** *s.* ⚒ Steinsalz *n*; '~·**slide** *s.* Steinschlag *m*, Felssturz *m*; '~·**wood** *s. min.* 'Holzasˌbest *m*; '~·**work** *s.* **1.** Gesteinsmasse *f*; **2.** a) Steingarten *m*, b) Grottenwerk *n*; **3.** ⚠ Quaderwerk *n*.

rock·y[1] ['rɒkɪ] *adj.* **1.** felsig; **2.** steinhart (*a. fig.*).

rock·y[2] ['rɒkɪ] *adj.* □ F wack(e)lig (*a. fig.*), wankend.

ro·co·co [rəʊ'kəʊkəʊ] **I** *s.* **1.** Rokoko *n*; **II** *adj.* **2.** Rokoko...; **3.** verschnörkelt, über'laden.

rod [rɒd] *s.* **1.** Rute *f*, Gerte *f*; *a. fig. bibl.* Reis *n*; **2.** (Zucht)Rute *f* (*a. fig.*): ***have a ~ in pickle for s.o.*** mit j-m noch ein Hühnchen zu rupfen haben; ***kiss the ~*** sich unter die Rute beugen; ***make a ~ for one's own back*** *fig.* sich die Rute selber flechten; ***spare the ~ and spoil the child*** wer die Rute spart, verzieht das Kind; **3.** a) Zepter *n*, b) Amtsstab *m*, c) *fig.* Amtsgewalt *f*, d) *fig.* Knute *f*, Tyran'nei *f*; → ***Black Rod***; **4.** (Holz)Stab *m*, Stock *m*; **5.** ⚙ (Rund-) Stab *m*, (Treib-, Verbindungs- *etc.*) Stange *f*: ~ ***aerial*** ϟ Stabantenne *f*; *Kernkraft*: Brennstab *m*; **6.** a) Angelrute *f*, b) Angler *m*; **7.** Meßlatte *f*, -stab *m*; **8.** a) Rute *f* (*Längenmaß*), b) Qua'dratrute *f* (*Flächenmaß*); **9.** *Am. sl.* ‚Ka'none' *f* (*Pistole*); **10.** *anat.* Stäbchen *n* (*Netzhaut*); **11.** *biol.* 'Stäbchenbakˌterie *f*; **12.** *Am. sl.* → ***hot rod***.

rode [rəʊd] *pret. von* ***ride***.

ro·dent ['rəʊdənt] **I** *adj.* **1.** *zo.* nagend; Nage...: ~ ***teeth***; **2.** ⚕ fressend (*Geschwür*); **II** *s.* **3.** Nagetier *n*.

ro·de·o [rəʊ'deɪəʊ] *pl.* **-s** *s. Am.* Ro'deo *m, n*: a) Zs.-treiben *n* von Vieh, b) *Sammelplatz für diesen Zweck*, c) 'Cowboy-Turˌnier *n*, Wildwest-Vorführung *f*, d) 'Motorrad-, 'Autoroˌdeo *m, n*.

roe[1] [rəʊ] *s. zo.* **1.** *a.* ***hard ~*** Rogen *m*, Fischlaich *m*: ~ ***corn*** Fischei *n*; **2.** *a.* ***soft ~*** Milch *f*; **3.** Eier *pl.* (*vom Hummer etc.*).

roe[2] [rəʊ] *pl.* **roes**, *coll.* **roe** *s. zo.* **1.** Reh *n*; **2.** a) Ricke *f* (*weibliches Reh*), b) Hirschkuh *f*; '~·**buck** *s.* Rehbock *m*; '~·**deer** *s.* Reh *n*.

roent·gen → ***röntgen***.

ro·ga·tion [rəʊ'geɪʃn] *s. eccl.* a) (Für-) Bitte *f*, ('Bitt)Litaˌnei *f*, b) *mst pl.* Bittgang *m*: ***℞ Sunday*** Sonntag *m* Rogate; ***℞ week*** Himmelfahrts-, Bittwoche *f*;

rog·a·to·ry ['rɒgətərɪ] *adj.* ⚖ Untersuchungs...: ~ ***commission***; ***letters ~*** Amtshilfeersuchen *n*.

rog·er ['rɒdʒə] **1.** *int. Funk*: Roger!, Verstanden!; **2.** F in Ordnung!

rogue [rəʊg] *s.* **1.** Schurke *m*, Gauner *m*: ***~s' gallery*** Verbrecheralbum *n*; **2.** *humor.* Schelm *m*, Schlingel *m*, Spitzbube *m*; **3.** ⚘ a) aus der Art schlagende Pflanze, b) 'Mißbildung *f*; **4.** *zo. a.* ~ ***elephant***, ~ ***buffalo*** *etc.* bösartiger Einzelgänger; **5.** *Pferderennen*: a) bockendes Pferd, b) Ausreißer *m* (*Pferd*); '**ro·guer·y** [-gərɪ] *s.* **1.** Schurke'rei *f*, Gaune'rei *f*; **2.** Spitzbübe'rei *f*; '**ro·guish** [-gɪʃ] *adj.* □ **1.** schurkisch; **2.** schelmisch, schalkhaft, spitzbübisch.

roist·er ['rɔɪstə] *v/i.* **1.** kra'keelen; **2.** aufschneiden, prahlen; '**roist·er·er** [-tərə] *s.* **1.** Kra'keeler *m*; **2.** Großmaul *n*.

role, **rôle** [rəʊl] (*Fr.*) *s. thea. u. fig.* Rolle *f*: ***play a ~*** e-e Rolle spielen.

roll [rəʊl] **I** *s.* **1.** (*Haar-*, *Kragen-*, *Papier- etc.*)Rolle *f*; **2.** a) *hist.* Schriftrolle *f*, Perga'ment *n*, b) Urkunde *f*, c) (*bsd.* Namens)Liste *f*, Verzeichnis *n*, d) ⚖ Anwaltsliste *f*: ~ ***of hono(u)r*** Ehrenliste, -tafel *f* (*bsd. der Gefallenen*); ***the ℞s*** Staatsarchiv *n* (*Gebäude in London*); ***call the ~*** die (Namens- *od.* Anwesenheits)Liste verlesen, Appell abhalten; ***strike s.o. off the ~*** j-n von der Anwaltsliste streichen; → ***master*** 13; **3.** ⚠ a) *a.* ***~-mo(u)lding*** Rundleiste *f*, Wulst *m*, b) *antiq.* Vo'lute *f*; **4.** ⚙ Rolle *f*, Walze *f*; **5.** Brötchen *n*, Semmel *f*; **6.** (*bsd.* 'Fleisch)Rouˌlade *f*; **7.** *sport* Rolle *f* (*a.* ✈ *Kunstflug*); **8.** ⚓ Rollen *n*, Schlingern *n* (*Schiff*); **9.** wiegender Gang, Seemannsgang *m*; **10.** Fließen *n*, Fluß *m* (*des Wassers*; *a. fig. der Rede*, *von Versen etc.*); **11.** (*Orgel- etc.*)Brausen *n*; (*Donner*)Rollen *n*; (*Trommel-*) Wirbel *m*; Dröhnen *n* (*Stimme etc.*); Rollen *n*, Trillern *n* (*Vogel*); **12.** *Am. sl.* a) Geldscheinbündel *n*, b) *fig.* (*e-e* Masse) Geld *n*; **II** *v/i.* **13.** rollen (*Ball etc.*): ***start ~ing*** ins Rollen kommen; **14.** rollen, fahren (*Fahrzeug*); **15.** *a.* ~ ***along*** sich (da'hin)wälzen, da'hinströmen (*Fluten*) (*a. fig.*); **16.** da'hinziehen (*Gestirn*, *Wolken*); **17.** sich wälzen: ***be ~ing in money*** F im Geld schwimmen; **18.** *sport*, *a.* ✈ e-e Rolle machen; **19.** ⚓ schlingern; **20.** wiegend gehen: ***~ing gait*** → 9; **21.** (g)rollen (*Donner*); brausen (*Orgel*); dröhnen (*Stimme*); wirbeln (*Trommel*); trillern (*Vogel*); **22.** a) ⚙ sich walzen lassen, b) *typ.* sich verteilen (*Druckfarbe*); **III** *v/t.* **23.** *Faß*, *Rad etc.*, *a. Augen* rollen; (her'um)wälzen, (-)drehen: ~ ***a problem round in one's mind*** *fig.* ein Problem wälzen; *Film*: ~ ***film!***, ~ ***it*** *Am.* Kamera an!; **24.** *Wagen etc.* rollen, fahren, schieben; **25.** *Wassermassen* wälzen (*Fluß*); **26.** (zs.-, auf-, ein)rollen, (-)wickeln; **27.** *Teig* (aus)rollen; *Zigarette* drehen; *Schneeball etc.* formen: ***~ed ham*** Rollschinken *m*; **28.** ⚙ *Metalle* walzen, strecken; *Rasen*, *Straße* walzen: ***~ed glass*** gezogenes Glas; ***~ed gold*** Walzgold *n*, Golddublee *n*; ***~ed iron*** (*od.* ***products***) Walzeisen *n*; ~ ***on*** *et.* aufwalzen; **29.** *typ.* a) *Papier* ka'landern, glätten, b) *Druckfarbe* auftragen; **30.** rollen(d sprechen): ~ ***one's r's***; ***~ed r*** Zungen-R *n*; **31.** *Trommel* wirbeln; **32.** ⚓ *Schiff* zum Rollen bringen; **33.** *Körper etc. beim Gehen* wiegen; **34.** *Am. sl. Betrunkenen etc.* ausplündern;

Zssgn mit adv.:

roll| back *v/t. fig.* her'unterschrauben, reduzieren; ~ **in** *v/i.* **1.** *fig.* her'einströmen, eintreffen (*Angebote*, *Geld etc.*); **2.** F schlafen gehen; ~ **out** *v/t.* **1.** *metall.* auswalzen, strecken; **2.** *Teig* ausrollen; **3.** a) *Lied etc.* (hin'aus)schmettern, b) *Verse* deklamieren; ~ **o·ver** *v/t.* (*v/i.* sich) he'rumwälzen, -drehen; ~ **up I** *v/i.* **1.** (her)'anrollen, (-)'anfahren; F vorfahren; **2.** F ‚aufkreuzen', auftauchen; **3.** sich zs.-rollen; **4.** *fig.* sich ansammeln *od.* (-)häufen; **II** *v/t.* **5.** her'anfahren; **6.** aufrollen, -wickeln; **7.** ⚔ *gegnerische Front* aufrollen; **8.** *sl.* ansammeln: ~ ***a fortune***.

'**roll|·back** *s. Am.* **1.** ⚔ Zu'rückwerfen *n* (*des Feinds*); **2.** ✝ Zu'rückschrauben *n* (*der Preise*); '~·**bar** *s. mot.* 'Überrollbügel *m*; ~ **call** *s.* **1.** Namensaufruf *m*: ~ (***vote***) *pol.* namentliche Abstimmung; **2.** ⚔ 'Anwesenheitsapˌpell *m*.

roll·er ['rəʊlə] *s.* **1.** ⚙ a) Walzwerkarbeiter *m*, b) Fördermann *m*; **2.** (Stoff-, Garn- *etc.*)Rolle *f*; **3.** ⚙ a) (Gleit-, Lauf-, Führungs)Rolle *f*, b) (Gleit)Rolle *f*, Rädchen *n* (*unter Möbeln*, *an Rollschuhen etc.*); **4.** a) Walze *f*, b) Zy'linder *m*, Trommel *f*; **5.** *typ.* Druckwalze *f*; **6.** Rollstab *m* (*Landkarte etc.*); **7.** ⚓ Roller *m*, Sturzwelle *f*; **8.** *orn.* a) Flug-, Tümmlertaube *f*, b) *e-e* Racke: ***common ~*** Blauracke, c) Harzer Roller *m*; ~ **band·age** *s.* ⚕ Rollbinde *f*; ~ **bearing** *s.* ⚙ Rollen-, Wälzlager *n*; ~ **clutch** *s.* ⚙ Rollen-, Freilaufkupplung *f*; ~ **coast·er** *s.* Achterbahn(wagen *m*) *f*; '~·**mill** *s.* ⚙ **1.** Mahl-, Quetschwerk *n*; **2.** → ***rolling mill***; '~·**skate I** *s.* Rollschuh *m*; **II** *v/i.* rollschuhlaufen; ~ **skating** *s.* Rollschuhlaufen *n*; ~ **tow·el** *s.* Rollhandtuch *n*.

roll| film *s. phot.* Rollfilm *m*; '~·**front cab·i·net** *s.* Rollschrank *m*.

rol·lick ['rɒlɪk] *v/i.* **1.** a) ausgelassen *od.* 'übermütig sein, b) her'umtollen; **2.** das Leben genießen; '**rol·lick·ing** [-kɪŋ] *adj.* ausgelassen, 'übermütig.

roll·ing ['rəʊlɪŋ] **I** *s.* **1.** Rollen *n*; **2.** Da'hinfließen *n* (*Wasser etc.*); **3.** Rollen *n* (*Donner*); Brausen *n* (*Wasser*); **4.** *metall.* Walzen *n*, Strecken *n*; **5.** ⚓ Schlingern *n*; **II** *adj.* **6.** rollend *etc.*; → ***roll*** II; ~ **bar·rage** *s.* ⚔ Feuerwalze *f*; ~ **cap·i·tal** *s.* ✝ Be'triebskapiˌtal *n*; ~ **chair** *s.* ⚕ Rollstuhl *m*; ~ **kitch·en** *s.* ⚔ Feldküche *f*; ~ **mill** *s.* ⚙ **1.** Walzwerk *n*, Hütte *f*; **2.** 'Walzmaˌschine *f*; **3.** Walz(en)straße *f*; ~ **pin** *s.* Nudel-, Wellholz *n*; ~ **press** *s.* ⚙ **1.** Walzen-, Rotati'onspresse *f*; **2.** *Papierfabrikation*: Sati'niermaˌschine *f*; ~ **stock** *s.* 🚂 rollendes Materi'al, Betriebsmittel *pl.*; ~ **stone** *s. fig.* Zugvogel *m*: ***a ~ gathers no moss*** wer rastet, der rostet; ~ **ti·tle** *s. Film*: Rolltitel *m*.

roll| lathe *s.* ⚙ Walzendrehbank *f*; '~·**mop** *s.* Rollmops *m*; '~·**neck** *s.* 'Rollkragen(pulˌlover) *m*; '~·**on** *s.* **1.** E'lastikschlüpfer *m*; **2.** Deorollstift *m*; '~·**top desk** *s.* Rollpult *n*; ~ **train** *s. metall.* Walzenstrecke *f*.

ro·ly-po·ly [ˌrəʊlɪˈpəʊlɪ] **I** *s.* **1.** *a.* **~ *pudding*** *Art* Pudding *m*; **2.** Pummelchen *n* (*Person*); **II** *adj.* **3.** mollig, pummelig.

Ro·ma·ic [rəʊˈmeɪɪk] **I** *adj.* roˈmaisch, neugriechisch; **II** *s. ling.* Neugriechisch *n*.

Ro·man [ˈrəʊmən] **I** *adj.* **1.** römisch: **~ *arch*** △ romanischer Bogen; **~ *candle*** Leuchtkugel *f* (*Feuerwerk*); **~ *holiday*** *fig.* a) blutrünstiges Vergnügen, b) Vergnügen *n* auf Kosten anderer, c) Riesenskandal *m*; **~ *law*** römisches Recht; **~ *nose*** Römer-, Adlernase *f*; **~ *numeral*** römische Ziffer; **2.** (römisch-)kaˈtholisch; **3.** *mst* ♀ *typ.* Antiqua...; **II** *s.* **4.** Römer(in); **5.** *mst* ♀ *typ.* Anˈtiqua *f*; **6.** *eccl.* Kathoˈlik(in); **7.** *pl. bibl.* (Brief *m* des Paulus an die) Römer *pl.*

ro·man à clef [rəʊˌmɑːnɑːˈkleɪ] (*Fr.*) *s.* ˈSchlüsselroˌman *m*.

Ro·man Cath·o·lic *eccl.* **I** *adj.* (römisch-)kaˈtholisch; **II** *s.* Kathoˈlik(in); **~ *Church*** *s.* Römische *od.* (Römisch-)Kaˈtholische Kirche.

ro·mance¹ [rəʊˈmæns] **I** *s.* **1.** *hist.* (ˈRitter-, ˈVers)Roˌman *m*; **2.** Roˈmanze *f*: a) (roˈmantischer) ˈLiebes-, ˈAbenteuerroˌman, b) *fig.* ˈLiebesafˌfäre *f*, c) ♪ *Lied od. lyrisches Instrumentalstück*; **3.** *fig.* Märchen *n*, Phantasteˈrei *f*; **4.** *fig.* Roˈmantik *f*: a) Zauber *m*, b) roˈmantische Iˈdeen *pl.*; **II** *v/i.* **5.** (Roˈmanzen) dichten; **6.** *fig.* a) fabulieren, ‚Roˈmane erzählen', b) ins Schwärmen geraten.

Ro·mance² [rəʊˈmæns] *bsd. ling.* **I** *adj.* roˈmanisch: **~ *peoples*** Romanen; **~ *philologist*** Romanist(in); **II** *s.* a) Roˈmanisch *n*, b) *a.* ***the ~ languages*** die romanischen Sprachen *pl.*

ro·manc·er [rəʊˈmænsə] *s.* **1.** Roˈmanzendichter(in); Verfasser(in) e-s (ˈVers-)Roˌmans; **2.** a) Phanˈtast(in), b) Aufschneider(in).

Rom·a·nes [ˈrɒmənes] *s.* Ziˈgeunersprache *f*.

Ro·man·esque [ˌrəʊməˈnesk] **I** *adj.* **1.** △, *ling.* roˈmanisch; **2.** *ling.* provenˈzalisch; **3.** ♀ *fig.* roˈmantisch; **II** *s.* **4.** *a.* **~ *style*** romanischer (Bau)Stil; *das* Roˈmanische; **5.** → ***Romance²*** II.

ro·man-fleuve [rəʊˌmɑ̃ːŋˈflɜːv] (*Fr.*) *s.* Faˈmilienroˌman *m*.

Ro·man·ic [rəʊˈmænɪk] *adj.* **1.** → ***Romance²*** I; **2.** römisch (*Kulturform*).

Ro·man·ism [ˈrəʊmənɪzəm] *s.* **1.** a) Romaˈnismus *m*, römisch-kaˈtholische Einstellung, b) Poliˈtik *f od.* Gebräuche *pl.* der römischen Kirche; **2.** *hist.* das Römertum; ˈ**Ro·man·ist** [-ɪst] *s.* **1.** *ling.*, ⚖ Romaˈnist(in); **2.** (ˈRömisch-)KaˌtholischeⁿRömisch-)Kaˌtholische(r *m*) *f*.

ro·man·tic [rəʊˈmæntɪk] **I** *adj.* (☐ **~*ally***) **1.** *allg.* roˈmantisch: a) Kunst *etc.*: *die Romantik betreffend*: ***the ~ movement*** die Romantik, b) roˈmanhaft, phanˈtastisch (*a. iro.*): ***a ~ tale***, c) roˈmantisch veranlagt: ***a ~ girl***, d) malerisch: ***a ~ town***, e) gefühlvoll: ***a ~ scene***; **II** *s.* **2.** Roˈmantiker(in) (*a. fig.*); **3.** *das* Roˈmantische; **4.** *pl.* romantische Iˈdeen *pl. od.* Gefühle *pl.*; **roˈman·ti·cism** [-ɪsɪzəm] *s.* **1.** *Kunst*: Roˈmantik *f*; **2.** (Sinn *m* für) Romantik *f*; **roˈman·ti·cist** [-ɪsɪst] *s. Kunst*: Roˈmantiker(in); **roˈman·ti·cize** [-ɪsaɪz] **I** *v/t.* **1.** romantisieren; **2.** in roˈmantischem Licht sehen; **II** *v/i.* **3.** *fig.* schwärmen.

Rom·a·ny [ˈrɒmənɪ] *s.* **1.** Ziˈgeuner(in); **2.** *coll. die* Zigeuner *pl.*; **3.** Romani *n*, Ziˈgeunersprache *f*.

Rome [rəʊm] *npr.* Rom *n* (*a. fig. hist. das Römerreich*; *eccl. die Katholische Kirche*): **~ *was not built in a day*** Rom ist nicht an einem Tag erbaut worden; ***do in ~ as the Romans do!*** man sollte sich immer s-r Umgebung anpassen!

romp [rɒmp] **I** *v/i.* **1.** umˈhertollen, sich balgen, toben: **~ *through*** *fig.* spielend durchkommen; **2.** ‚rasen', flitzen: **~ *away*** davonziehen (*Rennpferd etc.*); **II** *s.* **3.** *obs.* Wildfang *m*, Range *f*; **4.** Tollen *n*, Balgeˈrei *f*; **5.** F *sport* leichter Sieg; **6.** F ‚(wilde) Schmuseˈrei'; ˈ**romp·ers** [-pəz] *s. pl.* Spielanzug *m* (*für Kinder*); ˈ**romp·y** [-pɪ] *adj.* ausgelassen, wild.

ron·deau [ˈrɒndəʊ] *pl.* **-deaus** [-dəʊz] *s. Metrik*: Ronˈdeau *n*, Ringelgedicht *n*; **ron·del** [ˈrɒndl] *s.* vierzehnzeiliges Rondeau.

ron·do [ˈrɒndəʊ] *s.* ♪ Rondo *n*.

rönt·gen [ˈrɒntjən] **I** *s. phys.* Röntgen *n* (*Maßeinheit*); **II** *adj. mst* ♀ Röntgen...: **~ *rays***; **III** *v/t.* → ˈ**rönt·gen·ize** [-tgənaɪz] *v/t.* röntgen; **rönt·gen·o·gram** [rɒntˈgenəgræm] *s.* Röntgenaufnahme *f*; **rönt·gen·og·ra·phy** [ˌrɒntgəˈnɒgrəfɪ] *s.* ˈRöntgenphotograˌphie *f* (*Verfahren*); **rönt·gen·ol·o·gist** [ˌrɒntgəˈnɒlədʒɪst] *s.* Röntgenoˈloge *f*; **rönt·gen·os·co·py** [ˌrɒntgəˈnɒskəpɪ] *s.* ˈRöntgendurchˌleuchtung *f*, -unterˌsuchung *f*; **rönt·gen·o·ther·a·py** [ˌrɒntgənəˈθerəpɪ] *s.* ˈRöntgentheraˌpie *f*.

rood [ruːd] **I** *s.* **1.** *eccl.* Kruziˈfix *n*; **2.** Viertelacre *m* (*Flächenmaß*); **3.** Rute *f* (*Längenmaß*); **II** *adj.* **4.** △ Lettner...: **~ *altar***; **~ *loft*** Chorbühne *f*; **~ *screen*** Lettner *m*.

roof [ruːf] **I** *s.* **1.** △ (Haus)Dach *n*: ***under my ~*** *fig.* unter m-m Dach, in m-m Haus; ***raise the ~*** F Krach schlagen; **2.** *mot.* Verdeck *n*; **3.** *fig.* (*Blätter-, Zelt- etc.*)Dach *n*, (*Himmels*)Gewölbe *n*, (-)Zelt *n*: **~ *of the mouth*** *anat.* Gaumen(dach *n*) *m*; ***the ~ of the world*** das Dach der Welt; **4.** ⚒ Hangende(s) *n*; **II** *v/t.* **5.** bedachen: **~ *in*** *Haus* (ein)dekken; **~ *over*** überdachen: **~*ed-in*** überdacht, umbaut; ˈ**roof·age** [-fɪdʒ] → ***roofing*** 2; ˈ**roof·er** [-fə] *s.* Dachdecker *m*; **roof gar·den** *s.* **1.** Dachgarten *m*; **2.** *Am.* ˈDachrestauˌrant *n*; ˈ**roof·ing** [-fɪŋ] **I** *s.* **1.** Bedachen *n*, Dachdeckerarbeit *f*; **2.** a) ˈDeckmateriˌalien *pl.*, b) Dachwerk *n*; **II** *adj.* **3.** Dach...: **~ *felt*** Dachpappe *f*; ˈ**roof·less** [-lɪs] *adj.* **1.** ohne Dach, unbedeckt; **2.** *fig.* obdachlos; **roof rack** *s. mot.* Dachgepäckträger *m*; **roof tree** *s.* **1.** △ Firstbalken *m*; **2.** *fig.* Dach *n*.

rook¹ [rʊk] **I** *s.* **1.** *orn.* Saatkrähe *f*; **2.** *fig.* Gauner *m*, Bauernfänger *m*; **II** *v/t.* **3.** *j-n* betrügen.

rook² [rʊk] *s. Schachspiel*: Turm *m*.

rook·er·y [ˈrʊkərɪ] *s.* **1.** a) Krähenhorst *m*, b) ˈKrähenkoloˌnie *f*; **2.** *orn.*, *zo.* Brutplatz *m*; **3.** *fig.* a) ˈElendsquarˌtier *n*, -viertel *n*, b) ˈMietskaˌserne *f*.

rook·ie [ˈrʊkɪ] *s. sl.* **1.** ⚔ Reˈkrut *m*; **2.** Neuling *m*, Anfänger(in).

room [ruːm] **I** *s.* **1.** Raum *m*, Platz *m*: ***make ~ (for)*** *a. fig.* Platz machen (*dat.*); ***no ~ to swing a cat (in)*** sehr wenig Platz; ***in the ~ of*** an Stelle von (*od. gen.*); **2.** Raum *m*, Zimmer *n*, Stube *f*: ***next ~*** Nebenzimmer; **~ *heating*** Raumheizung *f*; **~ *temperature*** (*a. normale*) Raum-, Zimmertemperatur *f*; **3.** *pl. Brit.* Wohnung *f*; **4.** *fig.* (Spiel-)Raum *m*; Gelegenheit *f*, Anlaß *m*: **~ *for complaint*** Anlaß zur Klage; ***there is no ~ for hope*** es besteht keinerlei Hoffnung; ***there is ~ for improvement*** es ließe sich noch manches besser machen; **II** *v/i.* **5.** *bsd. Am.* wohnen, logieren (***at*** in *dat.*, ***with*** bei): **~ *together*** zs.-wohnen; **-roomed** [ruːmd] *adj. in Zssgn.* ...zimmerig; **room·er** [ˈruːmə] *s. bsd. Am.* ˈUntermieter(in); ˈ**room·ful** [-fʊl] *pl.* **-fuls** *s.*: ***a ~ of people*** ein Zimmer voll(er) Leute; **room·i·ness** [ˈruːmɪnɪs] *s.* Geräumigkeit *f*.

room·ing| house [ˈruːmɪŋ] *s. Am.* Fremdenheim *n*, Pensiˈon *f*; ˌ**~-ˈin** *n* ⚕ Rooming-ˈin *n* (*gemeinsame Unterbringung von Mutter und Kind*).

ˈ**room·mate** *s.* ˈStubenkameˌrad(in).

room·y [ˈruːmɪ] *adj.* ☐ geräumig.

roost [ruːst] **I** *s.* a) Schlafplatz *m*, -sitz *m* (*Vogel*), b) Hühnerstange *f od.* -stall *m*: ***at ~*** auf der Stange; ***come home to ~*** *fig.* auf den Urheber zurückfallen; → ***rule*** 13; **II** *v/i. orn.* a) auf der Stange sitzen, b) sich (zum Schlafen) niederhocken; ˈ**roost·er** [-tə] *s. bsd. Am.* (Haus)Hahn *m*.

root¹ [ruːt] **I** *s.* **1.** ⚘ Wurzel *f* (*a. weitS. Wurzelgemüse, Knolle, Zwiebel*): **~ *and branch*** *fig.* mit Stumpf u. Stiel; ***pull out by the ~*** mit der Wurzel herausreißen (*a. fig. ausrotten*); ***put down ~s*** *fig.* Wurzel schlagen, seßhaft werden; ***strike at the ~ of*** *fig. et.* an der Wurzel treffen; ***strike*** (*od.* ***take***) **~** Wurzel schlagen (*a. fig.*); **~*s of a mountain*** *der* Fuß e-s Berges; **2.** *anat.* (*Haar-, Nagel-, Zahn-, Zungen- etc.*) Wurzel *f*; **3.** ⩚ a) Wurzel *f*, b) eingesetzter *od.* gesuchter Wert (*Gleichung*): **~ *extraction*** Wurzelziehen *n*; **4.** *ling.* Wurzel(wort *n*) *f*, Stammwort *n*; **5.** ♪ Grundton *m*; **6.** *fig.* a) Quelle *f*, Ursache *f*, Wurzel *f*: **~ *of all evil*** Wurzel alles Bösen; ***get at the ~ of*** *e-r Sache* auf den Grund gehen; ***have its ~ in, take its ~ from*** → 8, b) *pl.* Wurzeln *pl.*, Ursprung *m*, c) Kern *m*, Wesen *n*, Gehalt *m*: **~ *of the matter*** Kern der Sache; **~ *idea*** Grundgedanke *m*; **II** *v/i.* **7.** Wurzel fassen *od.* schlagen, (ein)wurzeln (*a. fig.*): ***deeply ~ed*** *fig.* tief verwurzelt; ***stand ~ed to the ground*** wie angewurzelt dastehen; **8.** **~ *in*** beruhen auf (*dat.*), s-n Grund *od.* Ursprung haben in (*dat.*); **III** *v/t.* **9.** tief einpflanzen, einwurzeln lassen: ***fear ~ed him to the ground*** *fig.* er stand vor Furcht wie angewurzelt; **10.** **~ *up***, **~ *out***, **~ *away*** a) ausreißen, b) *fig.* ausrotten, vertilgen.

root² [ruːt] **I** *v/i.* **1.** wühlen (***for*** nach) (*Schwein*); **2.** **~ *about*** *fig.* herˈumwühlen; **II** *v/t.* **3.** *Boden* auf-, ˈumwühlen; **4.** **~ *out***, **~ *up*** *a. fig.* ausgraben, aufstöbern.

root³ [ruːt] *v/i.* **~ *for*** *Am. sl.* a) *sport j-n* anfeuern, b) *fig.* Stimmung machen für *j-n od. et.*

ˌ**root-and-ˈbranch** *adj.* radiˈkal, restlos.

root·ed [ˈruːtɪd] *adj.* ☐ (fest) eingewur-

zelt (*a. fig.*); **ˈroot·ed·ly** [-lɪ] *adv.* von Grund auf, zuˈtiefst; **ˈroot·ed·ness** [-nɪs] *s.* Verwurzelung *f*, Eingewurzeltsein *n*.
root·er [ˈruːtə] *s. sport Am.* F begeisterter Anhänger, ‚Faˈnatiker' *m*.
root·less [ˈruːtlɪs] *adj.* wurzellos (*a. fig.*); **root·let** [ˈruːtlɪt] *s.* ♀ Wurzelfaser *f*.
ˌ**root|-mean-ˈsquare** *s.* 𝔄 quaˈdratischer Mittelwert; ˈ**~-stock** *s.* **1.** ♀ Wurzelstock *m*; **2.** *fig.* Wurzel *f*; **~ treatment** *s.* ✱ (Zahn)Wurzelbehandlung *f*.
rope [rəʊp] **I** *s.* **1.** Seil *n*, Tau *n*; Strick *m*, Strang *m* (*beide a. zum Erhängen*); ⚓ (Tau)Ende *n*: ***the ~*** *fig.* der Strick (*Tod durch den Strang*); ***be at the end of one's ~*** mit s-m Latein am Ende sein; ***know the ~s*** sich auskennen, ‚den Bogen raushaben'; ***learn the ~s*** sich einarbeiten; ***show s.o. the ~s*** j-m die Kniffe beibringen; **2.** *mount.* (Kletter)Seil *n*: ***on the ~*** angeseilt; ***~ (team)*** Seilschaft *f*; **3.** (Arˈtisten)Seil *n*: ***on the high ~s*** *fig.* a) hochgestimmt, b) hochmütig; **4.** *Am.* Lasso *n, m*; **5.** *pl. Boxen*: (Ring)Seile *pl.*: ***be on the ~s*** a) (angeschlagen) in den Seilen hängen, b) *fig.* am Ende *od.* ‚fertig' sein; ***have s.o. on the ~s*** *sl.* j-n ‚zur Schnecke' gemacht haben; **6.** *fig.* Strang *m Tabak etc.*; Bund *n Zwiebeln etc.*; Schnur *f Perlen etc.*: ***~ of sand*** *fig.* Illusion *f*; **7.** Faden *m* (*Flüssigkeit*); **8.** *fig.* Spielraum *m*, Handlungsfreiheit *f*: ***give s.o. (plenty of) ~***; **II** *v/t.* **9.** (mit e-m Seil) zs.-binden; festbinden; **10.** *mst* ***~ in*** (*od.* ***off*** *od.* ***out***) *Platz* (durch ein Seil) absperren *od.* abgrenzen; **11.** *mount.* anseilen: ***~ down (up)*** *j-n* ab- (auf)seilen; **12.** *Am.* mit dem Lasso einfangen: ***~ in*** *sl. Wähler, Kunden etc.* fangen, *j-n* ‚an Land ziehen', sich *ein Mädchen etc.* ‚anlachen'; **III** *v/i.* **13.** Fäden ziehen (*Flüssigkeit*); **14.** *a.* ***~ up*** *mount.* sich anseilen: ***~ down*** sich abseilen; **~ danc·er** *s.* Seiltänzer(in); **~ lad·der** *s.* **1.** Strickleiter *f*; **2.** ⚓ Seefallreep *n*; **~ mo(u)ld·ing** *s.* △ Seilleiste *f*; **~ quoit** *s.* ⚓, *sport* Seilring *m*; **~ rail·way** → ***ropeway***.
rop·er·y [ˈrəʊpərɪ] *s.* Seileˈrei *f*.
ˈ**rope's-end** ⚓ **I** *s.* Tauende *n*; **II** *v/t.* mit dem Tauende prügeln.
rope| tow *s. Skisport*: Schlepplift *m*; ˈ**~·walk** *s.* Seiler-, Reeperbahn *f*; ˈ**~ˌwalk·er** *s.* Seiltänzer(in); ˈ**~·way** *s.* (Seil)Schwebebahn *f*; ˈ**~·yard** *s.* Seileˈrei *f*; **~ yarn** *s.* **1.** ⚙ Kabelgarn *n*; **2.** *fig.* Bagaˈtelle *f*.
rop·i·ness [ˈrəʊpɪnɪs] *s.* Dickflüssigkeit *f*, Klebrigkeit *f*; ˈ**rop·y** [-pɪ] *adj.* □ **1.** klebrig, zäh, fadenziehend: ***~ sirup***; **2.** kahmig: ***~ wine***; **3.** F ‚mies'.
ror·qual [ˈrɔːkwəl] *s. zo.* Finnwal *m*.
ro·sace [ˈrəʊzeɪs] (*Fr.*) *s.* △ **1.** Roˈsette *f*; **2.** → ***rose window***.
ro·sa·ceous [rəʊˈzeɪʃəs] *adj.* **1.** ♀ a) zu den Rosaˈzeen gehörig, b) rosenblütig; **2.** Rosen…
ro·sar·i·an [rəʊˈzeərɪən] *s.* **1.** Rosenzüchter *m*; **2.** *R.C.* Mitglied *n* einer Rosenkranzbruderschaft.
ro·sa·ry [ˈrəʊzərɪ] *s.* **1.** *R.C.* Rosenkranz *m*: ***say the 2*** den Rosenkranz beten; **2.** Rosengarten *m*, -beet *n*.
rose¹ [rəʊz] **I** *s.* **1.** ♀ Rose *f*: ***~ of Jericho*** Jerichorose; ***~ of May*** Weiße Narzisse; ***~ of Sharon*** a) *bibl.* Sharon-Tulpe *f*, b) Großblumiges Johanniskraut; ***the ~ of*** *fig.* die Rose (*das schönste Mädchen*) von; ***gather (life's) ~s*** sein Leben genießen; ***on a bed of ~s*** *fig.* auf Rosen gebettet; ***it is no bed of ~s*** es ist kein Honiglecken; ***it is not all ~s*** es ist nicht so rosig, wie es aussieht; ***under the ~*** im Vertrauen; **2.** → ***rose colo(u)r***; **3.** *her. hist.* Rose *f*: ***Red 2*** Rote Rose (*Haus Lancaster*); ***White 2*** Weiße Rose (*Haus York*); ***Wars of the 2s*** Rosenkriege; **4.** △ Roˈsette *f* (*a. Putz*; *a. Edelstein[schliff]*); **5.** Brause *f* (*Gießkanne etc.*); **6.** *phys.* ˈKreisˌskala *f*; **7.** ⚓ *etc.* Windrose *f*; **8.** ✱ Wundrose *f*; **II** *adj.* **9.** Rosen…; **10.** rosenfarbig.
rose² [rəʊz] *pret. von* ***rise***.
ro·se·ate [ˈrəʊzɪət] *adj.* □ → ***rosecolo(u)red***.
rose| bit *s.* ⚙ Senkfräser *m*; ˈ**~·bud** *s.* ♀ Rosenknospe *f* (*a. fig. Mädchen*); ˈ**~·bush** *s.* Rosenstrauch *m*; **~ col·o(u)r** *s.* Rosa-, Rosenrot *n*: ***life is not all ~*** *fig.* das Leben besteht nicht nur aus Annehmlichkeiten; ˈ**~-ˌcol·o(u)red** *adj.* **1.** rosa-, rosenfarbig, rosenrot; **2.** *fig.* rosig, optiˈmistisch: ***see things through ~ spectacles*** die Dinge durch e-e rosa (-rote) Brille sehen; ˈ**~·hip** *s.* ♀ Hagebutte *f*.
rose·mar·y [ˈrəʊzmərɪ] *s.* ♀ Rosmarin *m*.
ro·se·o·la [rəʊˈziːələ] *s.* ✱ **1.** Roseˈole *f* (*Ausschlag*); **2.** → ***German measles***.
ˌ**rose|-ˈpink I** *s.* ⚙ Rosenlack *m*, roter Farbstoff; **II** *adj.* rosa, rosenrot (*a. fig.*); **~ rash** → ***roseola*** 1; ˌ**~-ˈred** *adj.* rosenrot.
ro·ser·y → ***rosary*** 2.
rose tree *s.* Rosenstock *m*.
ro·sette [rəʊˈzet] *s.* Roˈsette *f* (*a.* △); **roˈset·ted** [-tɪd] *adj.* **1.** mit Rosetten geschmückt; **2.** roˈsettenförmig.
ˈ**rose|-ˌwa·ter I** *s.* **1.** Rosenwasser *n*; **2.** *fig.* a) Schmeicheˈleien *pl.*, b) Gefühlsduseˈlei *f*; **II** *adj.* **3.** *fig.* a) (ˈüber)fein, (-)zart, b) affekˈtiert, c) sentimenˈtal; **~ win·dow** *s.* △ (ˈFenster)RoˌSette *f*, (-)Rose *f*; ˈ**~·wood** *s.* Rosenholz *n*.
ros·in [ˈrɒzɪn] **I** *s.* ⚗ (Terpenˈtin)Harz *n*, *bsd.* Koloˈphonium *n*, Geigenharz *n*; **II** *v/t.* mit Koloˈphonium einreiben.
ros·i·ness [ˈrəʊzɪnɪs] *s.* Rosigkeit *f*, rosiges Aussehen.
ros·ter [ˈrəʊstə] *s.* ⚔ **1.** (Dienst-, Namens)Liste *f*; **2.** Dienstplan *m*.
ros·tral [ˈrɒstrəl] *adj.* (schiffs)schnabelförmig; ˈ**ros·trate(d)** [-reɪt(ɪd)] *adj.* **1.** ♀, *zo.* geschnäbelt; **2.** → ***rostral***.
ros·trum [ˈrɒstrəm] *pl.* **-tra** [-trə] *s.* **1.** a) Rednerbühne *f*, Podium *n*, b) Kanzel *f*, c) *fig.* Plattform *f*; **2.** ⚓ *hist.* Schiffsschnabel *m*; **3.** ♀, *zo.* Schnabel *m*; **4.** *zo.* a) Kopfspitze *f*, b) Rüssel *m* (*Insekt*).
ros·y [ˈrəʊzɪ] *adj.* □ **1.** rosenrot, -farbig; ***~ red*** Rosenrot *n*; **2.** rosig, blühend (*Wangen etc.*); **3.** *fig.* rosig.
rot [rɒt] **I** *v/i.* **1.** (ver)faulen, (-)modern (*a. fig. im Gefängnis*); verrotten, verwesen; *geol.* verwittern; **2.** *fig.* verkommen, verrotten; **3.** *Brit. sl.* ‚quatschen', Unsinn reden; **II** *v/t.* **4.** faulen lassen; **5.** *bsd. Flachs* rotten; **6.** *Brit. sl. Plan etc.* vermurksen; **7.** *Brit. sl.* j-n ‚anpflaumen' (*hänseln*); **III** *s.* **8.** a) Fäulnis *f*, Verwesung *f*, b) Fäule *f*, c) *et.* Verfaultes; → ***dry-rot***; **9.** ♀, *zo.* a) Fäule *f*, b) *vet.* Leberfäule *f* (*Schaf*); **10.** *Brit. sl.*, *a. int.* ‚Quatsch' *m*, Blödsinn *m*.
ro·ta [ˈrəʊtə] *s.* **1.** → ***roster***; **2.** *Brit.* a) ˈDienstˌturnus *m*, b) *a.* ***~ system*** Turnusplan *m*; **3.** *mst* 2 *R.C.* Rota *f* (*oberster Gerichtshof der römisch-katholischen Kirche*).
Ro·tar·i·an [rəʊˈteərɪən] **I** *s.* Roˈtarier *m*; **II** *adj.* Rotary…, Rotarier…
ro·ta·ry [ˈrəʊtərɪ] **I** *adj.* **1.** rotierend, kreisend, sich drehend, ˈumlaufend; Rotations…, Dreh…: ***~ crane*** Dreh-, Schwenkkran *m*; ***~ file*** Drehkartei *f*; ***~ pump*** Umlaufpumpe *f*; ***~ switch*** ϟ Drehschalter *m*; ***~ traffic*** Kreisverkehr *m*; **II** *s.* **2.** ⚙ *durch Rotation arbeitende Maschine, bsd.* a) → ***rotary engine***, b) → ***rotary machine***, c) → ***rotary press***; **3.** 2 → 2 **Club** *s.* Rotary-Club *m*; **~ cur·rent** *s.* ϟ Drehstrom *m*; **~ en·gine** *s.* Drehkolbenmotor *m*; **~ hoe** *s.* ✓ Hackfräse *f*; 2 **In·ter·na·tion·al** *s.* Weltvereinigung *f* der Rotary-Clubs; **~ ma·chine** *s. typ.* Rotatiˈonsmaˌschine *f*; **~ pis·ton en·gine** *s.* → ***rotary engine***; **~ press** *s. typ.* Rotatiˈons(druck)presse *f*.
ro·tate¹ [rəʊˈteɪt] **I** *v/i.* **1.** rotieren, kreisen, sich drehen; **2.** der Reihe nach *od.* turnusmäßig wechseln: ***~ in office***; **II** *v/t.* **3.** rotieren *od.* (um)ˈkreisen lassen; **4.** *Personal* turnusmäßig *etc.* auswechseln; **5.** ✓ *Frucht* wechseln: ***~ crops*** im Fruchtwechsel anbauen.
ro·tate² [ˈrəʊteɪt] *adj.* ♀, *zo.* radförmig.
ro·ta·tion [rəʊˈteɪʃn] *s.* **1.** ⚙, *phys.* Rotatiˈon *f*, (Achsen-, ˈUm)Drehung *f*, ˈUm-, Kreislauf *m*, Drehbewegung *f*: ***~ of the earth*** (tägliche) Erdumdrehung (*um die eigene Achse*); **2.** Wechsel *m*, Abwechslung *f*: ***in*** (*od.* ***by***) ***~*** der Reihe nach, abwechselnd, im Turnus; ***~ in office*** turnusmäßiger Wechsel im Amt; ***~ of crops*** ✓ Fruchtwechsel, -folge *f*; **ro·ta·tive** [ˈrəʊtətɪv] *adj.* **1.** → ***rotary*** 1; **2.** abwechselnd, regelmäßig ˈwiederkehrend; **ro·ta·to·ry** [ˈrəʊtətərɪ] *adj.* **1.** → ***rotary*** 1; **2.** *fig.* abwechselnd *od.* turnusmäßig (aufeinˈanderfolgend): ***~ assemblies***; **3.** ***~ muscle*** *anat.* Dreh-, Rollmuskel *m*.
rote [rəʊt] *s.*: ***by ~*** *fig.* a) (rein) mechanisch, b) auswendig.
ˈ**rot·gut** *s. sl.* Fusel *m*.
ro·ti·fer [ˈrəʊtɪfə] *s. zo.* Rädertier(chen) *n*; **Ro·tif·er·a** [rəʊˈtɪfərə] *s. pl. zo.* Rädertiere *pl.*
ro·to·gra·vure [ˌrəʊtəʊgrəˈvjʊə] *s. typ.* **1.** Kupfer(tief)druck *m*; **2.** → ***roto section***.
ro·tor [ˈrəʊtə] *s.* **1.** ✈ Rotor *m*, Drehflügel *m*; **2.** ϟ Rotor *m*, Anker *m*; **3.** ⚙ Rotor *m* (*Drehteil e-r Maschine*); **4.** ⚓ (Flettner)Rotor *m*.
ro·to sec·tion [ˈrəʊtəʊ] *s.* Kupfertiefdruckbeilage *f e-r Zeitung*.
rot·ten [ˈrɒtn] *adj.* □ **1.** faul, verfault: ***~ to the core*** a) kernfaul, b) *fig.* durch u. durch korrupt; **2.** morsch, mürbe; **3.** brandig, stockig (*Holz*); **4.** ✱ faul(ig) (*Zahn*); **5.** *fig.* a) verderbt, korˈrupt, b) niederträchtig, gemein; **6.** *sl.* (‚ˈhunds-)miseˌrabel': ***~ luck*** Saupech *n*; ***~ weather*** Sauwetter *n*; ˈ**rot·ten·ness**

[-nɪs] *s.* **1.** Fäule *f*, Fäulnis *f*; **2.** *fig.* Verderbtheit *f*, Kor'ruptheit *f*; **rot·ter** ['rɔtə] *s. Brit. sl.* Schweinehund *m*, ‚Scheißkerl' *m*.

ro·tund [rəʊ'tʌnd] *adj.* ☐ **1.** *obs.* rund, kreisförmig; **2.** rundlich (*Mensch*); **3.** *fig.* a) voll(tönend) (*Stimme*), b) hochtrabend, blumig, pom'pös (*Ausdruck*); **4.** *fig.* ausgewogen (*Stil*); **ro'tun·da** [-də] *s.* △ Rundbau *m*; **ro'tun·date** [-deɪt] *adj. bsd.* ⚘ abgerundet; **ro'tun·di·ty** [-dətɪ] *s.* **1.** Rundheit *f*; **2.** Rundlichkeit *f*; **3.** Rundung *f*; **4.** *fig.* Ausgewogenheit *f* (*des Stils etc.*).

rou·ble ['ru:bl] *s.* Rubel *m* (*russische Währung*).

rou·é ['ru:eɪ] (*Fr.*) *s. obs.* Rou'é *m*, Lebemann *m*.

rouge [ru:ʒ] **I** *s.* Rouge *n*, (rote) Schminke; ⚙ Polierrot *n*; **II** *adj. her.* rot; **III** *v/i.* Rouge auflegen, sich schminken; **IV** *v/t.* (rot) schminken.

rough [rʌf] **I** *adj.* ☐ → ***roughly***; **1.** rauh (*Oberfläche, a. Haut, Tuch etc.*; *a. Stimme*); **2.** rauh, struppig (*Fell, Haar*); **3.** holp(e)rig, uneben (*Gelände, Weg*); **4.** rauh, unwirtlich, zerklüftet (*Landschaft*); **5.** rauh (*Wind etc.*); stürmisch (*See, Überfahrt, Wetter*): ***~ sea*** ⚓ grobe See; **6.** grob, roh (*Mensch, Manieren etc.*); rauhbeinig, ungehobelt (*Person*); heftig (*Temperament etc.*): ***~ play*** rohes *od.* hartes Spiel; ***~ stuff*** F Gewalttätigkeit(en *pl.*) *f*; **7.** rauh, barsch, schroff (*Person od. Redeweise*): ***~ words***; ***have a ~ tongue*** e-e rauhe Sprache sprechen; **8.** F rauh (*Behandlung, Empfang etc.*), hart (*Leben, Tag etc.*), garstig, böse: ***it was ~*** es war e-e böse Sache; ***I had a ~ time*** es ist mir ziemlich ‚mies' ergangen; ***that's ~ luck for him*** da hat er aber Pech (gehabt); **9.** roh, grob: a) ohne Feinheit, b) unbearbeitet, im Rohzustand: ***~ cloth*** ungewalktes Tuch; ***~ food*** grobe Kost; ***~ rice*** unpolierter Reis; ***~ style*** grober *od.* ungeschliffener Stil; ***~ stone*** a) unbehauener Stein, b) ungeschliffener (Edel-)Stein; → ***diamond*** 1, ***rough-and-ready***; **10.** ⚙ Grob…: ***~ carpenter*** Grobtischler *m*; ***~ file*** Schruppfeile *f*; **11.** unfertig, Roh…: ***~ copy*** Konzept *n*; ***~ draft*** (*od.* ***sketch***) Faustskizze *f*, Rohentwurf *m*; ***in a ~ state*** im Rohzustand; **12.** *fig.* grob: a) annähernd (richtig), ungefähr, b) flüchtig, im 'Überschlag: ***~ analysis*** Rohanalyse *f*; ***~ calculation*** Überschlag *m*; ***~ size*** ⚙ Rohmaß *n*; **13.** *typ.* noch nicht beschnitten (*Buchrand*); **14.** herb, sauer (*bsd. Wein*); **15.** stark (wirkend) (*Arznei*); **16.** *Brit. sl.* schlecht, ungenießbar (*Fisch*); **II** *adv.* **17.** rauh, hart, roh: ***play ~***; ***cut up ~*** ‚massiv' werden; **18.** grob, flüchtig; **III** *s.* **19.** Rauheit *f*, *das* Rauhe: ***over ~ and smooth*** über Stock und Stein; ***take the ~ with the smooth*** *fig.* das Leben nehmen, wie es ist; → ***rough-and-tumble*** II; **20.** *bsd. Brit.* ‚Schläger' *m*, Rowdy *m*, Rohling *m*; **21.** Rohzustand *m*: ***from the ~*** aus dem Rohen *arbeiten*; ***in the ~*** im Groben, im Rohzustand; ***take s.o. in the ~*** j-n nehmen, wie er ist; **22.** a) holperiger Boden, b) *Golf*: Rough *n*; **23.** Stollen *m* (*am Pferdehufeisen*); **IV** *v/t.* **24.** an-, aufrauhen; **25.** *j-n* miß'handeln, übel zurichten; **26.** *mst ~* ***out*** *Material* roh *od.* grob bearbeiten, vorbearbeiten; *metall.* vorwalzen; *Linse, Edelstein* grob schleifen; **27.** *Pferd* zureiten; **28.** *Pferd(ehuf)* mit Stollen versehen; **29.** ***~ in***, ***~ out*** entwerfen, flüchtig skizzieren; **30.** ***~ up*** *Haare etc.* gegen den Strich streichen: ***~ the wrong way*** *fig. j-n* reizen *od.* verstimmen; **31.** *sport Gegner* hart ‚nehmen'; **V** *v/i.* **32.** rauh werden; **33.** *sport* (über'trieben) hart spielen; **34.** ***~ it*** F primi'tiv *od.* anspruchslos leben, ein spar'tanisches Leben führen.

rough·age ['rʌfɪdʒ] *s.* a) ⚒ Rauhfutter *n*, b) grobe Nahrung, c) *biol.* Ballaststoffe *pl.*

,rough|-and-'read·y *adj.* **1.** grob (gearbeitet), Not…, Behelfs…: ***~ rule*** Faustregel *f*; **2.** rauh *od.* grob, aber zuverlässig (*Person*); **3.** schludrig: ***a ~ worker***; **,~-and-'tum·ble I** *adj.* **1.** wild, heftig, verworren: ***a ~ fight***; **II** *s.* **2.** wildes Handgemenge, wüste Keile'rei; **3.** *fig.* Wirren *pl. des Krieges, des Lebens etc.*; **'~·cast I** *s.* **1.** *fig.* roher Entwurf; **2.** △ Rohputz *m*, Berapp *m*; **II** *adj.* **3.** im Entwurf, unfertig; **4.** roh verputzt, angeworfen; **III** *v/t.* [*irr.* → ***cast***] **5.** im Entwurf anfertigen, roh entwerfen; **6.** △ berappen, (*mit Rohputz*) anwerfen; **'~·dry** *v/t. Wäsche* (nur) trocknen (*ohne sie zu bügeln od. mangeln*).

rough·en ['rʌfən] **I** *v/i.* rauh(er) werden; **II** *v/t. a.* ***~ up*** an-, aufrauhen, rauh machen.

,rough|-'grind *v/t.* [*irr.* → ***grind***] **1.** ⚙ vorschleifen; **2.** *Korn* schroten; **~-'han·dle** *v/t.* grob *od.* bru'tal behandeln; **,~-'hew** *v/t.* [*irr.* → ***hew***] **1.** *Holz, Stein etc.* roh behauen, grob bearbeiten; **2.** *fig.* in groben Zügen entwerfen; **,~-'hewn** *adj.* **1.** ⚙ roh behauen; **2.** *fig.* in groben Zügen entworfen *od.* gestaltet; **3.** *fig.* grobschlächtig, ungehobelt; **'~·house** *sl.* **I** *s.* a) Ra'dau *m*, b) wüste Keile'rei; **II** *v/t.* → ***rough*** 25; **III** *v/i.* Ra'dau machen, toben.

rough·ly ['rʌflɪ] *adv.* **1.** rauh, roh, grob; **2.** a) grob, ungefähr, annähernd: ***~ speaking*** etwa, ungefähr, b) ganz allgemein (gesagt).

,rough|-ma'chine *v/t.* ⚙ grob bearbeiten; **'~·neck** *s. Am. sl.* **1.** Rauhbein *n*, Grobian *m*; **2.** Rowdy *m*.

rough·ness ['rʌfnɪs] *s.* **1.** Rauheit *f*, Unebenheit *f*; **2.** ⚙ rauhe Stelle; **3.** *fig.* Roheit *f*, Grobheit *f*, Ungeschliffenheit *f*; **4.** Wildheit *f*, Heftigkeit *f*; **5.** Herbheit *f* (*Wein*).

,rough|-'plane *v/t.* ⚙ vorhobeln; **'~·rid·er** *s.* **1.** Zureiter *m*; **2.** verwegener Reiter; **3.** *Am.* ⚔ *hist.* a) 'irregu,lärer Kavalle'rist, b) ♀ *Angehöriger e-s im spanisch-amer. Krieg aufgestellten Kavallerie-Freiwilligenregiments*; **'~·shod** *adj.* scharf beschlagen (*Pferd*): ***ride ~ over*** *fig.* a) *j-n* rücksichtslos behandeln, *j-n* schikanieren, b) rücksichtslos über *et.* hinweggehen.

rou·lade [ru:'lɑ:d] (*Fr.*) *s.* **1.** ♪ Rou'lade *f*, Pas'sage *f*; **2.** *Küche*: Rou'lade *f*.

rou·lette [ru:'let] *s.* **1.** Rou'lett *n* (*Glücksspiel*); **2.** ⚙ Rollrädchen *n*.

Rou·ma·ni·an → ***Rumanian***.

round [raʊnd] **I** *adj.* ☐ → ***roundly***; **1.** *allg.* rund: a) kugelrund, b) kreisrund, c) zy'lindrisch, d) abgerundet, e) bogenförmig, f) e-n Kreis beschreibend (*Bewegung, Linie etc.*), g) rundlich, dick (*Arme, Wangen etc.*): → ***round angle*** (***hand***, ***robin*** *etc.*); **2.** *ling.* gerundet (*Vokal*); **3.** weich, vollmundig (*Wein*); **4.** 𝔄 ganz (*ohne Bruch*): ***in ~ numbers*** a) in ganzen Zahlen, b) auf- *od.* abgerundet; **5.** *fig.* rund, voll: ***a ~ dozen***; **6.** rund, annähernd (richtig); **7.** rund, beträchtlich (*Summe*); **8.** (ab)gerundet, flüssig (*Stil*); **9.** voll(tönend) (*Stimme*); **10.** flott, scharf: ***at a ~ pace***; **11.** offen, unverblümt: ***a ~ answer***; ***~ lie*** freche Lüge; **12.** kräftig, derb, ‚saftig': ***in ~ terms*** in unmißverständlichen Ausdrücken; **II** *s.* **13.** Rund *n*, Kreis *m*, Ring *m*; **14.** Rund (-teil *n*, -bau *m*) *n*, *et.* Rundes; **15.** a) (runde) Stange, b) ⚙ Rundstab *m*, c) (Leiter)Sprosse *f*; **16.** Rundung *f*: ***out of ~*** ⚙ unrund; ***worked on the ~*** über e-n Leisten gearbeitet (*Schuh*); **17.** *Kunst*: Rundplastik *f*: ***in the ~*** a) plastisch, b) *fig.* vollkommen; **18.** *a.* ***~ of beef*** Rindskeule *f*; **19.** *Brit.* Scheibe *f*, Schnitte *f* (*Brot etc.*); **20.** Kreislauf *m*, Runde *f*: ***the ~ of the seasons***; ***the daily ~*** der tägliche Trott; **21.** a) (Dienst)Runde *f*, Rundgang *m* (*Briefträger, Polizist etc.*), b) ⚔ Streife *f*: ***make the ~ of*** e-n Rundgang machen um; **22.** a) (Inspekti'ons)Rundgang *m*, -fahrt *f*, b) Rundreise *f*, Tour *f*; **23.** *fig.* Reihe *f*, Folge *f von Besuchen, Pflichten etc.*: ***a ~ of pleasures***; **24.** a) *Boxen, Golf etc.*: Runde *f*, b) (Verhandlungs- *etc.*)Runde *f*: ***first ~ to him!*** die erste Runde geht an ihn!, *fig. humor. a.* eins zu null für ihn!; **25.** Runde *f*, Lage *f* (*Bier etc.*): ***stand a ~*** (***of drinks***) ‚e-n ausgeben' (*für alle*); **26.** Runde *f*, Kreis *m* (*Personen*): ***go*** (*od.* ***make***) ***the ~*** (***of***) die Runde machen, kursieren (bei, in *dat.*) (*Gerücht, Witz etc.*); **27.** a) ⚔ Salve *f*, b) Schuß *m*: ***20 ~s*** (***of cartridge***) 20 Schuß (Patronen); **28.** *fig.* Lach-, Beifallssalve *f*: ***~ after ~ of applause*** nicht enden wollender Beifall; **29.** ♪ a) Rundgesang *m*, Kanon *m*, b) Rundtanz *m*, Reigen *m*; **III** *adv.* **30.** *a.* ***~ about*** rund-, rings(her)'um; **31.** rund(her)'um, im ganzen 'Umkreis, auf *od.* von allen Seiten: ***all ~*** a) ringsum, überall, b) *fig.* durch die Bank, auf der ganzen Linie; ***for a mile ~*** im Umkreis von e-r Meile; **32.** rundherum, im Kreise: ***~ and ~*** immer rundherum; ***hand s.th. ~*** et. herumreichen; ***look ~*** um sich blicken; ***turn ~*** (sich) umdrehen; ***the wheels go ~*** die Räder drehen sich; **33.** außen her'um: ***a long way ~*** ein weiter Umweg; **34.** *zeitlich*: her'an: ***comes ~ again*** *der Sommer etc.* kehrt wieder; **35.** e-e Zeit lang: ***all the year ~*** das ganze Jahr lang *od.* hindurch; ***the clock ~*** volle 24 Stunden; **36.** a) hin'über, b) her'über: ***ask s.o. ~*** j-n zu sich bitten; ***order one's car ~*** (den Wagen) vorfahren lassen; **IV** *prp.* **37.** (rund) um: ***a tour ~ the world***; **38.** um (… her'um): ***sail ~ the Cape***; ***just ~ the corner*** gleich um die Ecke; **39.** in *od.* auf (*dat.*) … herum: ***~ all the shops*** in allen Läden herum; **40.** um (… herum), im 'Umkreis von (*od. gen.*); **41.** um (… herum): ***write a book ~ a story***; ***argue ~ and ~ a subject*** um ein

Thema herumreden; **42.** *zeitlich*: durch, während (*gen.*); **V** *v/t.* **43.** rund machen, (*a. fig.* ab)runden: **~ed edge** abgerundete Kante; **~ed number** auf- *od.* abgerundete Zahl; **~ed teaspoon** gehäufter Teelöffel; **~ed vowel** *ling.* gerundeter Vokal; **44.** um'kreisen; **45.** um'geben, -'schließen; **46.** *Ecke, Landspitze etc.* um'fahren, -'segeln, her'umfahren *od.* biegen um; **47.** *mot. Kurve* ausfahren; **VI** *v/i.* **48.** rund werden, sich runden; **49.** *fig.* sich abrunden, voll'kommen werden; **50.** ⚓ drehen, wenden; **51. ~ on** F a) *j-n* ‚anfahren', b) über *j-n* herfallen;

Zssgn mit adv.:

round| off *v/t.* **1.** abrunden (*a. fig.*); **2.** *Fest, Rede etc.* beschließen, krönen; **3.** *Zahlen* auf *od.* abrunden; **4.** *Schiff* wenden; **~ out I** *v/t.* **1.** (*v/i.* sich) runden *od.* ausfüllen; **2.** *fig.* abrunden; **II** *v/i.* **3.** rundlich werden (*Person*); **~ to** *v/i.* ⚓ beidrehen; **~ up** *v/t.* **1.** *Vieh* zs.-treiben; **2.** F a) *Verbrecherbande* ausheben, b) *Leute etc.* zs.-trommeln, *a. et.* auftreiben, c) zs.-klauben; **3.** *Zahl etc.* aufrunden.

'round·a·bout I *adj.* **1.** 'umständlich, weitschweifig (*Erklärung etc.*): **~ way** Umweg *m*; **2.** rundlich (*Person*); **II** *s.* **3.** 'Umweg *m*; **4.** *fig.* 'Umschweife *pl.*; **5.** *bsd. Brit.* Karus'sell *n*; → **swing** 24; **6.** *Brit.* Kreisverkehr *m.*

round| an·gle *s.* ⩓ Vollwinkel *m*; **~ arch** *s.* ⚠ (ro'manischer) Rundbogen; **~ dance** *s.* Rundtanz *m*; Dreher *m.*

roun·del ['raʊndl] *s.* **1.** kleine runde Scheibe; **2.** Medail'lon *n* (*a. her.*), runde Schmuckplatte; **3.** ⚠ a) rundes Feld *od.* Fenster, b) runde Nische; **4.** *Metrik*: → **rondel.**

roun·de·lay ['raʊndɪleɪ] *s.* **1.** ♪ Re'frainliedchen *n*, Rundgesang *m*; **2.** Rundtanz *m*; **3.** (Vogel)Lied *n.*

round·er ['raʊndə] *s.* **1.** *Brit. sport* a) *pl. sg. konstr.* Rounders *n*, Rundball *m* (*Art Baseball*), b) ganzer 'Umlauf; **2.** *Am. sl.* a) liederlicher Kerl, b) Säufer *m.*

'round|-eyed *adj.* mit großen Augen, staunend; **~ hand** *s.* Rundschrift *f*; **'~·head** *s.* **1.** ℒ *hist.* Rundkopf *m* (*Puritaner*); **2.** Rundkopf *m* (*Person*; *a.* ⚙): **~ screw** Rundkopfschraube *f*; **'~·house** *s.* **1.** 🚂 Lokomo'tivschuppen *m*; **2.** ⚓ *hist.* Achterhütte *f*; **3.** *hist.* Turm *m*, Gefängnis *n*; **4.** *Am. sl.* (wilder) Schwinger (*Schlag*).

round·ing ['raʊndɪŋ] *s.* Rundung *f* (*a. ling.*): **~-off** Abrundung *f*; **'round·ish** [-ɪʃ] *adj.* rundlich; **'round·ly** [-dlɪ] *adv.* **1.** rund, ungefähr; **2.** rundweg, rundher'aus; **3.** gründlich, gehörig; **'round·ness** [-dnɪs] *s.* **1.** Rundheit *f* (*a. fig.*); Rundung *f*; **2.** *fig.* Unverblümtheit *f*; **'round·nose(d)** *adj.* ⚙ Rund...: **~ pliers** Rundzange *f*; **round rob·in** *s.* **1.** Petiti'on *f*, Denkschrift *f* (*bsd. mit im Kreis herum geschriebenen Unterschriften*); **2.** *sport Am. Turnier, bei dem jeder gegen jeden antritt*; **round shot** *s.* ⚔ *hist.* Ka'nonenkugel *f.*

rounds·man ['raʊndzmən] *s.* [*irr.*] *Brit.* Austräger *m*, Laufbursche *m*: **milk ~** Milchmann *m.*

round| steak *s. aus der Keule geschnittenes Beefsteak*; **~ ta·ble** *s.* **1.** a) runder Tisch, b) Tafelrunde *f*: **the ℒ** die Tafelrunde (des König Artus); **2. round-table conference** Konfe'renz *f* am runden Tisch, 'Round-table-Konfe,renz *f*; **'~-the-clock** *adj.* 24stündig, rund um die Uhr; **'~·top** *s.* ⚓ Krähennest *n*; **~ tow·el** *s.* Rollhandtuch *n*; **~ trip** *s. Am.* 'Hin- u. 'Rückfahrt *f od.* -flug *m*; **,~-'trip** *adj.*: **~ ticket** *Am.* a) Rückfahrkarte *f*, b) ✈ Rückflugticket *n*; **~ turn** *s.* ⚓ Rundtörn *m* (*Knoten*): **bring up with a ~** *j-n* jäh unterbrechen; **'~·up** *s.* **1.** Zs.-treiben *n von Vieh*; **2.** *fig.* a) Zs.-treiben *n*, Sammeln *n*, b) Razzia *f*, Aushebung *f* von Verbrechern, c) Zs.-fassung *f*, 'Übersicht *f*: **football ~**; **~ of the news** Nachrichtenüberblick *m*; **'~·worm** *s. zo.*, ⚕ Spulwurm *m.*

roup [ru:p] *s. vet.* a) Darre *f der Hühner*, b) Pips *m.*

rouse [raʊz] **I** *v/t.* **1.** *oft* **~ up** wachrütteln, (auf)wecken (**from** aus); **2.** *Wild etc.* aufjagen; **3.** *fig. j-n* auf-, wachrütteln, ermuntern: **~ o.s.** sich aufraffen; **4.** *fig. j-n* in Wut bringen, aufbringen, reizen; **5.** *fig. Gefühle etc.* erwecken, wachrufen, *Haß* entflammen, *Zorn* erregen; **6.** ⚙ *Bier etc.* ('um)rühren; **II** *v/i.* **7.** *mst* **~ up** aufwachen (*a. fig.*); **8.** aufschrecken; **III** *s.* **9.** ⚔ *Brit.* Wecken *n*; **'rous·er** [-zə] *s.* F **1.** Sensati'on *f*; **2.** faustdicke Lüge, Schwindel *m*; **'rous·ing** [-zɪŋ] *adj.* ☐ **1.** *fig.* aufrüttelnd, zündend, mitreißend (*Ansprache, Lied etc.*); **2.** brausend, stürmisch (*Beifall etc.*); **3.** aufregend, spannend; **4.** F ‚toll'.

roust·a·bout ['raʊstəbaʊt] *s.* **1.** *Am.* a) Werft-, Hafenarbeiter *m*, b) *oft contp.* Gelegenheitsarbeiter *m*; **2.** Handlanger *m*, Hilfsarbeiter *m.*

rout¹ [raʊt] **I** *s.* **1.** Rotte *f*, wilder Haufen; **2.** ⚖ Zs.-rottung *f*, Auflauf *m*; **3.** *bsd.* ⚔ a) wilde Flucht, b) Schlappe *f*, Niederlage *f*: **put to ~** → 5; **4.** *obs.* (große) Abendgesellschaft; **II** *v/t.* **5.** ⚔ in die Flucht *od.* vernichtend schlagen.

rout² [raʊt] *v/t.* **1.** → **root²** II; **2. ~ out, ~ up** *j-n aus dem Bett od. e-m Versteck etc.* (her'aus)treiben, (-)jagen; **3.** vertreiben; **4.** ⚙ ausfräsen (*a. typ.*), ausschweifen.

route [ru:t; ⚔ *a.* raʊt] **I** *s.* **1.** (Reise-, Fahrt)Route *f*, (-)Weg *m*: **en ~** (*Fr.*) unterwegs; **2.** (Bahn-, Bus-, Flug-) Strecke *f*, Route *f*; (Verkehrs)Linie *f*; ⚓ Schiffahrtsweg *m*; (Fern)Straße *f*; **3.** ϟ Leit(ungs)weg *m*; **4.** ⚔ a) Marschroute *f*, b) *Brit.* Marschbefehl *m*: **~ march** *Brit.* Übungsmarsch *m*, *Am.* Marsch *m* mit Marscherleichterungen; **~ step, march!** ohne Tritt(, marsch)!; **5.** ✝ *Am.* Versand(art *f*) *m*; **II** *v/t.* **6.** *Truppen* in Marsch setzen; *Transportgüter etc.* befördern, *a. weitS.* leiten (**via** über *acc.*); **7.** die Route (*od.* ⚙ den Arbeitsgang) festlegen von (*od. gen.*); **8.** *Anträge etc.* (auf dem Dienstweg) weiterleiten; **9.** a) ϟ legen, führen: **~ lines**, b) *tel.* leiten.

rou·tine [ru:'ti:n] **I** *s.* **1.** a) (Ge'schäfts-, 'Amts- *etc.*)Rou,tine *f*, übliche *od.* gleichbleibende Proze'dur, gewohnter Gang, b) me'chanische Arbeit, (ewiges) Einerlei, c) Rou'tinesache *f*, d) *contp.* Scha'blone *f*, e) *contp.* (alter) Trott; **2.** *Am.* a) (Zirkus- *etc.*)Nummer *f*, b) *contp.* ‚Platte' *f*, Geschwätz *n*; **3.** *Computer etc.*: Rou'tine *f*, (Unter)Pro'gramm *n*; **II** *adj.* **4.** a) all'täglich, immer gleichbleibend, üblich, b) laufend, regel-, rou'tinemäßig: **~ check**; **5.** *contp.* me'chanisch, scha'blonenhaft; **rou'tine·ly** [-lɪ] *adv.* **1.** rou'tinemäßig; **2.** *contp.* mechanisch; **rou'tin·ist** [-nɪst] *s.* Gewohnheitsmensch *m*; **rou'tin·ize** [-naɪz] *v/t.* **1.** e-r Rou'tine *etc.* unter'werfen; **2.** *et.* zur Routine machen.

roux [ru:] *s. pl.* **roux** [ru:z] Mehlschwitze *f*, Einbrenne *f.*

rove¹ [rəʊv] **I** *v/i. a.* **~ about** um'herstreifen, -schweifen, -wandern (*a. fig. Augen etc.*); **II** *v/t.* durch'streifen; **III** *s.* (Um'her)Wandern *n*; Wanderschaft *f.*

rove² [rəʊv] **I** *v/t.* **1.** ⚙ vorspinnen; **2.** *Wolle etc.* ausfasern; *Gestricktes* auftrennen, aufräufeln; **II** *s.* **3.** Vorgespinst *n*; **4.** (*Woll- etc.*)Strähne *f.*

rov·er¹ ['rəʊvə] *s.* ⚙ 'Vorspinnma,schine *f.*

rov·er² ['rəʊvə] *s.* **1.** Wanderer *m*; **2.** Pi'rat(enschiff *n*) *m*; **3.** Wandertier *n*; **4.** *obs. Brit. Pfadfinder über 17.*

rov·ing ['rəʊvɪŋ] *adj.* **1.** um'herziehend, -streifend; **2.** *fig.* ausschweifend: **~ fancy**; **have a ~ eye** gern ein Auge riskieren; **3.** *fig.* ‚fliegend': **~ reporter**, **~ force** (Polizei)Einsatztruppe *f.*

row¹ [rəʊ] *s.* **1.** *allg.* (*a. Häuser-, Sitz-*) Reihe *f*: **in ~s** in Reihen, reihenweise; **a hard ~ to hoe** *fig.* e-e schwierige Sache; **2.** Straße *f*: **Rochester ℒ**; **3.** ⚠ Baufluchtlinie *f.*

row² [rəʊ] **I** *v/i.* **1.** rudern; **II** *v/t.* **2.** *Boot, a. Rennen, a. j-n* rudern: **~ down** *j-n* (*beim Rudern*) überholen; **3.** rudern gegen, mit *j-m* (wett)rudern; **III** *s.* **4.** Rudern *n*; 'Ruderpar,tie *f*: **go for a ~** rudern gehen.

row³ [raʊ] F **I** *s.* Krach *m*: a) Kra'wall *m*, Spek'takel *m*, b) Streit *m*, c) Schläge'rei *f*: **get into a ~** a) ‚eins aufs Dach bekommen', b) Krach bekommen (**with** mit); **have a ~ with** Krach haben mit; **kick up a ~** Krach schlagen; **what's the ~?** was ist denn los?; **II** *v/t. j-n* ‚zs.-stauchen'; **III** *v/i.* randalieren.

row·an ['raʊən] *s.* ⚘ Eberesche *f*; **'~,ber·ry** *s.* Vogelbeere *f.*

row·di·ness ['raʊdɪnɪs] *s.* Pöbelhaftigkeit *f*, rüpelhaftes Benehmen *od.* Wesen; **row·dy** ['raʊdɪ] **I** *s.* 'Rowdy *m*, Ra'bauke *m*, Schläger *m*; **II** *adj.* rüpel-, rowdyhaft, gewalttätig; **'row·dy·ism** [-ɪɪzəm] *s.* **1.** Rowdytum *n*, rüpelhaftes Benehmen; **2.** Gewalttätigkeit *f*, Rüpe'lei *f.*

row·el ['raʊəl] **I** *s.* Spornrädchen *n*; **II** *v/t.* e-m *Pferd* die Sporen geben.

row·en ['raʊən] *s.* ↗ Grummet *n.*

row·ing ['rəʊɪŋ] **I** *s.* Rudern *n*, Rudersport *m*; **II** *adj.* Ruder...: **~ boat**; **~ machine** Ruderapparat *m.*

row·lock ['rɒlək] *s.* ⚓ Dolle *f.*

roy·al ['rɔɪəl] **I** *adj.* ☐ **1.** königlich, Königs...: **His ℒ Highness** S-e Königliche Hoheit; **~ prince** Prinz *m* von königlichem Geblüt; → **princess** 1; **ℒ Academy** Königliche Akademie der Künste (*Großbritanniens*); **~ blue** Königsblau *n*; **ℒ Exchange** *die* Londoner Börse (*Gebäude*); **~ flush** *Poker*: Royal Flush *m*; **ℒ Navy** (Königlich-Brit.) Marine *f*;

~ paper → 6; *~ road fig.* leichter *od.* bequemer Weg (*to* zu); *~ speech* Thronrede *f*; **2.** fürstlich (*a. fig.*): *the ~ and ancient game* das Golfspiel; **3.** *fig.* (*a.* F) prächtig, großartig: *in ~ spirits* F in glänzender Stimmung; *~ stag hunt.* Kapitalhirsch *m*; *~ tiger zo.* Königstiger *m*; **4.** edel (*a. Gas*); **II** *s.* **5.** F Mitglied *n* des Königshauses; **6.** Roy'alpa,pier *n* (*Format*); **7.** *a. ~ sail* ⚓ Ober-(bram)segel *n*; **roy·al·ist** ['rɔɪəlɪst] **I** *s.* Roya'list(in), Königstreue(r *m*) *f*; **II** *adj.* königstreu; **'roy·al·ty** [-ltɪ] *s.* **1.** Königtum *n*: a) Königswürde *f*, b) Königreich *n*: *insignia of ~* Kroninsignien *pl.*; **2.** königliche Abkunft; **3.** a) fürstliche Per'sönlichkeit, b) *pl.* Fürstlichkeiten *pl.*, c) Königshaus *n*; **4.** Krongut *n*; **5.** Re'gal *n*, königliches Privi'leg; **6.** Abgabe *f* an die Krone, Pachtgeld *n*: *mining ~* Bergwerksabgabe *f*; **7.** mon'archische Regierung; **8.** ⚖ (Au'toren- *etc.*)Tanti,eme *f*, Gewinnanteil *m*; **9.** ⚖ a) Li'zenz *f*, b) Li'zenzgebühr *f*: *~ fees* Pa'tentgebühren; *subject to payment of royalties* lizenzpflichtig.

rub [rʌb] **I** *s.* **1.** (Ab)Reiben *n*, Polieren *n*: *give it a ~* reibe es (doch einmal); *have a ~ with a towel* sich (mit dem Handtuch) abreiben *od.* abtrocknen; **2.** *fig.* Schwierigkeit *f*, Haken *m*: *there's the ~!* F da liegt der Hase im Pfeffer!; *there's a ~ in it* F die Sache hat e-n Haken; **3.** Unannehmlichkeit *f*; **4.** *fig.* Stiche'lei *f*; **5.** rauhe *od.* aufgeriebene Stelle; **6.** Unebenheit *f*; **II** *v/t.* **7.** reiben: *~ one's hands* sich die Hände reiben (*mst fig.*); *~ shoulders with fig.* verkehren mit, (*dat.*) nahe stehen; *~ it in, ~ s.o.'s nose in it* es j-m ,unter die Nase reiben'; → *rub up*; **8.** reiben, (reibend) streichen; massieren; **9.** einreiben (*with* mit *e-r Salbe etc.*); **10.** streifen, reiben an (*dat.*); (wund) scheuern; **11.** a) scheuern, schaben, b) *Tafel etc.* abwischen, c) polieren, d) wichsen, bohnern, e) abreiben, frottieren; **12.** ⚙ (ab)schleifen, (ab)feilen: *~ with emery* (*pumice*) abschmirgeln (abbimsen); **13.** *typ.* abklatschen; **III** *v/i.* **14.** reiben, streifen (*against od.* [*up*]*on* an *dat.*, gegen); **15.** *fig.* sich schlagen (*through* durch);

Zssgn mit adv.:

rub| a·long *v/i.* **1.** sich (mühsam) 'durchschlagen; **2.** (gut) auskommen (*with* mit *j-m*); *~* **down** *v/t.* **1.** abreiben, frottieren; *Pferd* striegeln; **2.** her'unter-, wegreiben; *~* **in** *v/t.* **1.** *a. Zeichnung* einreiben; **2.** *sl.* ,her'umreiten' auf (*dat.*); → *rub* 7; *~* **off I** *v/t.* **1.** ab-, wegreiben; abschleifen; **II** *v/i.* **2.** abgehen (*Lack etc.*); **3.** *fig.* sich abnützen; **4.** *fig.* F abfärben (*onto* auf *acc.*); *~* **out I** *v/t.* **1.** ausradieren; **2.** wegwischen, -reiben; **3.** *Am. sl.* ,'umlegen' (*töten*); **II** *v/i.* **4.** weggehen (*Fleck etc.*); *~* **up** *v/t.* **1.** (auf)polieren; **2.** *fig.* a) *Kenntnisse etc.* auffrischen, b) *Gedächtnis etc.* stärken; **3.** *fig.* F *rub s.o. up the right way* j-n richtig behandeln; *rub s.o. up the wrong way* j-n ,verschnupfen' *od.* verstimmen; *it rubs me up the wrong way* es geht mir gegen den Strich; **4.** *Farben etc.* verreiben.

rub-a-dub ['rʌbədʌb] *s.* Ta'ramtamtam *n*, Trommelwirbel *m*.

rub·ber¹ ['rʌbə] **I** *s.* **1.** Gummi *n*, *m*, (Na'tur)Kautschuk *m*; **2.** (Radier-)Gummi *m*; **3.** *a. ~ band* Gummiring *m*, -band *n*; **4.** *~ tyre* (*od. bsd. Am. tire*) Gummireifen *m*; **5.** *pl.* a) *Am.* ('Gummi),Überschuhe *pl.*, b) *Brit.* Turnschuhe *pl.*; **6.** *sl.* ,Gummi' *m*, ,Pa'riser' *m* (*Kondom*); **7.** Reiber *m*, Polierer *m*; **8.** Mas'seur(in), Mas'seuse *f*; **9.** Reibzeug *n*; **10.** a) Frottier(hand)tuch *n*, -handschuh *m*, b) Wischtuch *n*, c) Polierkissen *n*, d) *Brit.* Geschirrtuch *n*; **11.** Reibfläche *f*; **12.** ⚙ a) Schleifstein *m*, b) Putzfeile *f*; **13.** *typ.* Farbläufer *m*; **14.** 'Schmirgelpa,pier *n*; 'Glaspa,pier *n*; **15.** (weicher) Formziegel; **16.** F *Eishockey*: Puck *m*, Scheibe *f*; **17.** *Baseball*: Platte *f*; **II** *v/t.* **18.** → *rubberize*; **III** *v/i.* **19.** → *rubberneck* 4, 5; **IV** *adj.* **20.** Gummi...: *~ solution* Gummilösung *f*.

rub·ber² ['rʌbə] *s.* *Kartenspiel*: Robber *m*.

rub·ber| boat *s.* Gummi-, Schlauchboot *n*; *~* **ce·ment** *s.* ⚙ Gummilösung *f*; *~* **check** *s. Am.*, *~* **cheque** *s. Brit.* F geplatzter Scheck; *~* **coat·ing** *s.* Gummierung *f*; *~* **din·ghi** *s.* Schlauchboot *n*.

rub·ber·ize ['rʌbəraɪz] *v/t.* ⚙ mit Gummi imprägnieren, gummieren.

'rub·ber|·neck *Am.* F **I** *s.* **1.** Gaffer(in), Neugierige(r *m*) *f*; **2.** Tou'rist(in); **II** *adj.* **3.** neugierig, schaulustig; **III** *v/i.* **4.** neugierig gaffen, ,sich den Hals verrenken'; **5.** die Sehenswürdigkeiten (*e-r Stadt etc.*) ansehen; **IV** *v/t.* **6.** neugierig betrachten; *~* **plant** *s.* ♀ Kautschukpflanze *f*, *bsd.* Gummibaum *m*; *~* **stamp** *s.* **1.** Gummistempel *m*; **2.** F a) sturer Beamter, b) bloßes Werkzeug, c) Nachbeter *m*; **3.** *bsd. Am.* F (abgedroschene) Phrase; **,~-'stamp** *v/t.* **1.** abstempeln; **2.** F (rou'tinemäßig) genehmigen; *~* **tree** *s.* ♀ a) Gummibaum *m*, b) Kautschukbaum *m*.

rub·bing ['rʌbɪŋ] *s.* **1.** a) *phys.* Reibung *f*, b) ⚙ Abrieb *m*; **2.** *typ.* Reiberdruck *m*; *~* **cloth** *s.* Frottier-, Wisch-, Scheuertuch *n*; *~* **con·tact** *s.* ⚡ 'Reibe-, 'Schleifkon,takt *m*; **'~·stone** *s.* Schleif-, Wetzstein *m*; *~* **var·nish** *s.* ⚙ Schleiflack *m*.

rub·bish ['rʌbɪʃ] **I** *s.* **1.** Abfall *m*, Kehricht *m*, Müll *m*: *~ bin* Abfalleimer *m*; *~ chute* Müllschlucker *m*; **2.** (Gesteins-)Schutt *m* (*a. geol.*); **3.** F Schund *m*, Plunder *m*; **4.** F *a. int.* Blödsinn *m*, Quatsch *m*; **5.** ⚒ a) *über Tage*: Abraum *m*, b) *unter Tage*: taubes Gestein; **'rub·bish·y** [-ʃɪ] *adj.* **1.** schuttbedeckt; **2.** F Schund..., wertlos.

rub·ble ['rʌbl] *s.* **1.** Bruchstein(e *pl.*) *m*, Schotter *m*; **2.** *geol.* (Stein)Schutt *m*, Geröll *n*, Geschiebe *n*; **3.** (rohes) Bruchsteinmauerwerk; **4.** loses Packeis; *~* **ma·son·ry** → *rubble* 3; **'~·stone** *s.* Bruchstein *m*; **'~·work** → *rubble* 3.

'rub·down *s.* Abreibung *f*: *have a ~* sich trockenreiben *od.* frottieren.

rube [ru:b] *s. Am. sl.* ,Lackel' *m*.

ru·be·fa·cient [,ru:bɪ'feɪʃjənt] ⚕ **I** *adj.* (*bsd.* haut)rötend; **II** *s.* (*bsd.* haut)rötendes Mittel; **,ru·be'fac·tion** [-'fækʃn] *s.* ⚕ Hautröte *f*, -rötung *f*.

ru·bi·cund ['ru:bɪkənd] *adj.* rötlich, rot, rosig (*Person*).

ru·bric ['ru:brɪk] **I** *s.* **1.** *typ.* Ru'brik *f* ([*roter*] *Titelkopf od. Buchstabe*; *Abschnitt*); **2.** *eccl.* Rubrik *f*, li'turgische Anweisung; **II** *adj.* **3.** rot (gedruckt *etc.*), rubriziert; **'ru·bri·cate** [-keɪt] *v/t.* **1.** rot bezeichnen; **2.** rubrizieren.

'rub·stone *s.* Schleifstein *m*.

ru·by ['ru:bɪ] **I** *s.* **1.** *a. true ~, Oriental ~ min.* Ru'bin *m*; **2.** (Ru'bin)Rot *n*; **3.** *fig.* Rotwein *m*; **4.** *fig.* roter (Haut)Pikkel; **5.** *Uhrmacherei*: Stein *m*; **6.** *typ.* Pa'riser Schrift *f*, Fünfein'halbpunktschrift *f*; **II** *adj.* **7.** (kar'min-, ru'bin)rot.

ruche [ru:ʃ] *s.* Rüsche *f*; **ruched** [-ʃt] *adj.* mit Rüschen besetzt; **'ruch·ing** [-ʃɪŋ] *s.* **1.** *coll.* Rüschen(besatz *m*) *pl.*; **2.** Rüschenstoff *m*.

ruck¹ [rʌk] *s.* **1.** *sport das* (Haupt)Feld; **2.** *the* (*common*) *~ fig.* die breite Masse: *rise out of the ~ fig.* sich über den Durchschnitt erheben.

ruck² [rʌk] **I** *s.* Falte *f*; **II** *v/t. oft ~ up* hochschieben, zerknüllen, -knittern; **III** *v/i. oft ~ up* Falten werfen, hochrutschen.

ruck·sack ['rʌksæk] (*Ger.*) *s.* Rucksack *m*.

ruck·us ['rʌkəs] → *ruction*.

ruc·tion ['rʌkʃn] *s. oft pl.* F a) Tohuwa'bohu *n*, b) Krach *m*, Kra'wall *m*, c) Schläge'rei *f*.

rud·der ['rʌdə] *s.* **1.** ⚓ (Steuer)Ruder *n*, Steuer *n*; **2.** ✈ Seitenruder *n*, -steuer *n*: *~ controls* Seitensteuerung *f*; **3.** *fig.* Richtschnur *f*; **4.** *Brauerei*: Rührkelle *f*; **'rud·der·less** [-lɪs] *adj.* **1.** ohne Ruder; **2.** *fig.* führer-, steuerlos.

rud·di·ness ['rʌdɪnɪs] *s.* Röte *f*; **rud·dy** ['rʌdɪ] *adj.* □ **1.** rot, rötlich, gerötet; gesund (*Gesichtsfarbe*); **2.** *Brit. sl.* verflixt.

rude [ru:d] *adj.* □ **1.** grob, unverschämt; rüde, ungehobelt; **2.** roh, unsanft (*a. fig. Erwachen*); **3.** wild, heftig (*Kampf*, *Leidenschaft*); rauh (*Klima etc.*); hart (*Los*, *Zeit etc.*); **4.** wild (*Landschaft*); holp(e)rig (*Weg*); **5.** wirr (*Masse etc.*): *~ chaos* chaotischer Urzustand; **6.** *allg.* primi'tiv: a) unzivilisiert, b) ungebildet, c) kunstlos, d) behelfsmäßig; **7.** ro'bust, unverwüstlich (*Gesundheit*): *be in ~ health* vor Gesundheit strotzen; **8.** roh, unverarbeitet (*Stoff*); **9.** plump, ungeschickt; **10.** a) ungefähr, b) flüchtig, grob: *~ sketch*; *a ~ observer* ein oberflächlicher Beobachter; **'rude·ness** [-nɪs] *s.* **1.** Grobheit *f*; **2.** Roheit *f*; **3.** Heftigkeit *f*; **4.** Wild-, Rauheit *f*; **5.** Primitivi'tät *f*; **6.** Unebenheit *f*.

ru·di·ment ['ru:dɪmənt] *s.* **1.** Rudi'ment *n* (*a. biol. rudimentäres Organ*), Ansatz *m*; **2.** *pl.* Anfangsgründe *pl.*, Grundlagen *pl.*, Rudi'mente *pl.*; **ru·di·men·tal** [,ru:dɪ'mentl], **ru·di·men·ta·ry** [,ru:dɪ'mentərɪ] *adj.* □ **1.** elemen'tar, Anfangs...; **2.** rudimen'tär (*a. biol.*).

rue¹ [ru:] *s.* ♀ Gartenraute *f*.

rue² [ru:] *v/t.* bereuen, bedauern; *Ereignis* verwünschen: *he will live to ~ it* er wird es noch bereuen; **'rue·ful** [-fʊl] *adj.* □ **1.** kläglich, jämmerlich: *the Knight of the ⁓ Countenance* der Ritter von der traurigen Gestalt (*Don Quichotte*); **2.** wehmütig; **3.** reumütig; **'rue·ful·ness** [-fʊlnɪs] *s.* **1.** Gram *m*, Traurigkeit *f*; **2.** Jammer *m*.

ruff¹ [rʌf] *s.* **1.** Halskrause *f* (*a. zo., orn.*); **2.** (Pa'pier)Krause *f* (*Topf etc.*); **3.** Rüsche *f*; **4.** *orn.* a) Kampfläufer *m*, b) Haustaube *f* mit Halskrause.

ruff² [rʌf] **I** *s. Kartenspiel*: Trumpfen *n*; **II** *v/t. u. v/i.* mit Trumpf stechen.

ruff(e)³ [rʌf] *s. ichth.* Kaulbarsch *m*.

ruf·fi·an ['rʌfjən] *s.* **1.** Rüpel *m*; **2.** Raufbold *m*; **'ruf·fi·an·ism** [-nɪzəm] *s.* Roheit *f*, Brutali'tät *f*; **'ruf·fi·an·ly** [-lɪ] *adj.* **1.** roh, bru'tal; **2.** wild.

ruf·fle ['rʌfl] **I** *v/t.* **1.** *Wasser etc., a. Tuch* kräuseln; *Stirn* kraus ziehen; **2.** *Federn, Haare* sträuben: **~ one's feathers** sich aufplustern (*a. fig.*); **3.** *Papier* zerknittern; **4.** durchein'anderbringen, -werfen; **5.** *fig. j-n* aus der Fassung bringen; *j-n* (ver)ärgern: **~ s.o.'s temper** j-n verstimmen; **II** *v/i.* **6.** sich kräuseln; **7.** zerknüllt *od.* zerzaust werden; **8.** *fig.* die Ruhe verlieren; **9.** *fig.* sich aufspielen, anmaßend auftreten; **III** *s.* **10.** Kräuseln *n*; **11.** Rüsche *f*, Krause *f*; **12.** *orn.* Halskrause *f*; **13.** *fig.* Aufregung *f*, Störung *f*: **without ~ or excitement** in aller Ruhe.

ru·fous ['ru:fəs] *adj.* rotbraun.

rug [rʌg] *s.* **1.** (kleiner) Teppich, (Bett-, Ka'min)Vorleger *m*, Brücke *f*: **pull the ~ from under s.o.** *fig.* j-m den Boden unter den Füßen wegziehen; **2.** *bsd. Brit.* dicke wollene (Reise- *etc.*)Decke.

rug·by (foot·ball) ['rʌgbɪ] *s. sport* Rugby *n*.

rug·ged ['rʌgɪd] *adj.* ☐ **1.** zerklüftet, wild (*Landschaft etc.*), zackig, schroff (*Fels etc.*), felsig; **2.** durch'furcht (*Gesicht etc.*), uneben (*Boden etc.*), holperig (*Weg etc.*), knorrig (*Gestalt*); **3.** rauh (*Rinde, Tuch, a. fig. Manieren, Sport etc.*): **life is ~** das Leben ist hart; **~ individualism** krasser Individualismus; **4.** ruppig, grob; **5.** *bsd. Am. a.* ⚙ ro'bust, stark, sta'bil; **'rug·ged·ness** [-nɪs] *s.* **1.** Rauheit *f*; **2.** Grobheit *f*; **3.** *Am.* Ro'bustheit *f*.

rug·ger ['rʌgə] *Brit.* F *für* **Rugby**.

ru·in ['rʊɪn] **I** *s.* **1.** Ru'ine *f* (*a. fig. Person etc.*); *pl.* Ruine(n *pl.*) *f*, Trümmer *pl.*: **lay in ~s** in Schutt u. Asche legen; **lie in ~s** in Trümmern liegen; **2.** Verfall *m*: **go to ~** verfallen; **3.** Ru'in *m*, 'Untergang *m*, Zs.-bruch *m*, Verderben *n*: **bring to ~** → 5; **the ~ of my hopes** (**plans**) das Ende m-r Hoffnungen (Pläne); **it will be the ~ of him** es wird sein Untergang sein; **II** *v/t.* **4.** vernichten, zerstören; **5.** *j-n, a. Sache, Gesundheit etc.* ruinieren, zu'grunde richten; *Hoffnungen, Pläne* zu'nichte machen; *Augen, Aussichten etc.* verderben; *Sprache* verhunzen; **6.** *Mädchen* verführen; **ru·in·a·tion** [rʊɪ'neɪʃn] *s.* **1.** Zerstörung *f*, Verwüstung *f*; **2.** F *j-s* Ru'in *m*, Verderben *n*, 'Untergang *m*; **'ru·in·ous** [-nəs] *adj.* ☐ **1.** verfallen(d), baufällig, ru'inenhaft; **2.** verderblich, mörderisch, ruinierend, rui'nös: **a ~ price** a) ruinöser *od.* enormer Preis, b) Schleuderpreis *m*; **'ru·in·ous·ness** [-nəsnɪs] *s.* **1.** Baufälligkeit *f*; **2.** Verderblichkeit *f*.

rule [ru:l] **I** *s.* **1.** Regel *f*, Nor'malfall *m*: **as a ~** in der Regel; **as is the ~** wie es allgemein üblich ist; **become the ~** zur Regel werden; **make it a ~ to** (*inf.*) es sich zur Regel machen, zu (*inf.*); **by all the ~s** eigentlich; → **exception** 1; **2.** Regel *f*, Richtschnur *f*, Grundsatz *m*; *sport etc.* Spielregel *f* (*a. fig.*): **against the ~s** regelwidrig; **~s of action** (*od.* **conduct**) Verhaltensmaßregeln, Richtlinien; **~ of thumb** Faustregel, praktische Erfahrung; **by ~ of thumb** über den Daumen gepeilt; **serve as a ~** als Richtschnur *od.* Maßstab dienen; **3.** ⚖ a) Vorschrift *f*, (gesetzliche) Bestimmung, Norm *f*, b) gerichtliche Entscheidung, c) Rechtsgrundsatz *m*: **~s of the air** Luftverkehrsregeln; **work to ~** Dienst nach Vorschrift tun (*als Streikmittel*); → **road** 1; **4.** *pl.* (Geschäfts-, Gerichts- *etc.*)Ordnung *f*: (**standing**) **~s of court** ⚖ Prozeßordnung; **~s of procedure** a) Verfahrensordnung, b) Geschäftsordnung; **5.** *a.* **standing ~** Satzung *f*: **against the ~s** satzungswidrig; **the ~s** (**and by-laws**) die Satzungen, die Statuten; **6.** *eccl.* Ordensregel *f*; **7.** † U'sance *f*, Handelsbrauch *m*; **8.** A Regel *f*, Rechnungsart *f*: **~ of proportion**, **~ of three** Regeldetri *f*, Dreisatz *m*; **9.** Herrschaft *f*, Regierung *f*: **during** (**under**) **the ~ of** während (unter) der Regierung (*gen.*); **~ of law** Rechtsstaatlichkeit *f*; **10.** a) Line'al *n*, b) *a.* **folding ~** Zollstock *m*; **11.** a) Richtmaß *n*, b) Winkel(eisen *n*, -maß *n*) *m*; **12.** *typ.* a) (Messing)Linie *f*: **~ case** Linienkasten *m*, b) Ko'lumnenmaß *n* (*Satzspiegel*), c) *Brit.* Strich *m*: **em ~** Gedankenstrich; **en ~** Halbgeviert *n*; **II** *v/t.* **13.** *a.* **~ over** *Land, Gefühl etc.* beherrschen, herrschen über (*acc.*), regieren: **~ the roast** (*od.* **roost**) *fig.* das Regiment führen, Herr im Haus sein; **14.** lenken, leiten: **be ~d by** sich leiten lassen von; **15.** *bsd.* ⚖ anordnen, verfügen, entscheiden: **~ out** a) *j-n od. et.* ausschließen (*a. sport*), b) *et.* ablehnen; **~ s.o. out of order** *parl.* j-m das Wort entziehen; **~ s.th. out of order** et. nicht zulassen; **16.** a) *Papier* linieren, b) *Linie* ziehen: **~ s.th. out** et. durchstreichen; **~d paper** liniertes Papier; **III** *v/i.* **17.** herrschen *od.* regieren (**over** über *acc.*); **18.** entscheiden (**that** daß); **19.** † *hoch etc.* stehen, liegen, notieren (*Preise*): **~ high** (**low**); weiterhin hoch notieren; **20.** vorherrschen; **21.** gelten, in Kraft sein (*Recht etc.*); **'rul·er** [-lə] *s.* **1.** Herrscher(in); **2.** Line'al *n*; ⚙ Richtscheit *n*; **3.** ⚙ Li'niermaˌschine *f*; **'rul·ing** [-lɪŋ] **I** *s.* **1.** ⚖ (gerichtliche) Entscheidung; Verfügung *f*; **2.** Linie(n *pl.*) *f*; **3.** Herrschaft *f*; **II** *adj.* **4.** herrschend; *fig.* (vor-)herrschend; **5.** maßgebend, grundlegend: **~ case**; **6.** † bestehend, laufend: **~ price** Tagespreis *m*.

rum¹ [rʌm] *s.* Rum *m*, *Am. a.* Alkohol *m*.

rum² [rʌm] *adj.* ☐ *bsd. Brit. sl.* **1.** ‚komisch' (*eigenartig*): **~ customer** komischer Kauz; **~ go** dumme Geschichte; **~ start** (tolle) Überraschung; **2.** ulkig, drollig.

Ru·ma·ni·an [ru:'meɪnjən] **I** *adj.* **1.** ru'mänisch; **II** *s.* **2.** Ru'mäne *m*, Ru'mänin *f*; **3.** *ling.* Ru'mänisch *n*.

rum·ba ['rʌmbə] *s.* Rumba *m*, *f*.

rum·ble¹ ['rʌmbl] **I** *v/i.* **1.** poltern (*a. Stimme*); rattern (*Gefährt, Zug etc.*), rumpeln, rollen (*Donner*), knurren (*Magen*); **II** *v/t.* **2.** *a.* **~ out** *Worte* her'auspoltern, *Lied* grölen; **III** *s.* **3.** Gepolter *n*, Rattern *n*, Rumpeln *n*, Rollen *n* (*Donner*); **4.** ⚙ Poliertrommel *f*; **5.** a) Bedientensitz *m*, b) Gepäckraum *m*, c) → **rumble seat**; **6.** *Am.* (Straßen-) Schlacht *f* (*zwischen jugendlichen Banden*).

rum·ble² ['rʌmbl] *v/t. sl.* **1.** *j-n* durch'schauen; **2.** *et.* ‚spitzkriegen'; **3.** *Am. j-n* argwöhnisch machen.

rum·ble seat *s. Am. mot.* Not-, Klappsitz *m*.

rum·bus·tious [rʌm'bʌstɪəs] *adj.* F **1.** laut, lärmend; **2.** wild, ausgelassen.

ru·men ['ru:men] *pl.* **-mi·na** [-mɪnə] *s. zo.* Pansen *m*; **'ru·mi·nant** [-mɪnənt] **I** *adj.* ☐ **1.** *zo.* 'wiederkäuend; **2.** *fig.* grübelnd; **II** *s.* **3.** *zo.* 'Wiederkäuer *m*; **'ru·mi·nate** [-mɪneɪt] **I** *v/i.* **1.** 'wiederkäuen; **2.** *fig.* grübeln (**about**, **over** über *acc.*); **II** *v/t.* **3.** *fig.* grübeln über (*acc., dat.*); **ru·mi·na·tion** [ˌru:mɪ'neɪʃn] *s.* **1.** 'Wiederkäuen *n*; **2.** *fig.* Grübeln *n*; **'ru·mi·na·tive** [-mɪnətɪv] *adj.* ☐ nachdenklich, grüblerisch.

rum·mage ['rʌmɪdʒ] **I** *v/t.* **1.** durch'stöbern, -'wühlen, wühlen in (*dat.*); **2.** *a.* **~ out**, **~ up** aus-, her'vorkramen; **II** *v/i.* **3.** *a.* **~ about** (her'um)stöbern *od.* (-)wühlen (**in** in *dat.*); **III** *s.* **4.** *mst* **~ goods** Ramsch *m*, Ausschuß *m*, Restwaren *pl.*; **~ sale** *s.* **1.** Ramschverkauf *m*; **2.** 'Wohltätigkeitsbaˌzar *m*.

rum·mer ['rʌmə] *s.* Römer *m*, ('Wein-) Poˌkal *m*.

rum·my¹ ['rʌmɪ] *s.* Rommé *n* (*Kartenspiel*).

rum·my² ['rʌmɪ] *adj.* ☐ → **rum²** 1 *u.* 2.

ru·mo(u)r ['ru:mə] **I** *s.* a) Gerücht *n*, b) Gerede *n*: **~ has it**, **the ~ runs** es geht das Gerücht; **II** *v/t.* (als Gerücht) verbreiten (*mst pass.*): **it is ~ed that** man sagt *od.* es geht das Gerücht, daß; **he is ~ed to be** man munkelt *od.* es heißt, er sei.

rump [rʌmp] *s.* **1.** *zo.* Steiß *m*, 'Hinterteil *n* (*a. des Menschen*); *orn.* Bürzel *m*; **~ steak** *Küche*: Rumpsteak *n*; **2.** *fig.* Rumpf *m*, kümmerlicher Rest: **the** 2 (**Parliament**) *hist.* das Rumpfparlament.

rum·pie ['rʌmpɪ] *s.* Aufsteiger *m*, der auf dem Lande wohnt (= **rural upwardly-mobile professional**).

rum·ple ['rʌmpl] *v/t.* **1.** zerknittern, -knüllen; **2.** *Haar etc.* zerwühlen.

rum·pus ['rʌmpəs] *s.* F **1.** Krach *m*, Kra'wall *m*; **2.** Trubel *m*; **3.** Streit *m*, ‚Krach' *m*; **~ room** *s. Am.* Hobby- *od.* Partyraum *m*.

'rum-ˌrun·ner *s. Am.* Alkoholschmuggler *m*.

run [rʌn] **I** *s.* **1.** Laufen *n*, Rennen *n*; **2.** Lauf *m* (*a. sport u. fig.*); Lauf-, ⚔ Sturmschritt *m*: **at the ~** im Lauf (-schritt), im Dauerlauf; **in the long ~** *fig.* auf die Dauer, am Ende, schließlich; **in the short ~** fürs nächste; **on the ~** a) auf der Flucht, b) (immer) auf den Beinen (*tätig*); **be in the ~** *bsd. Am. pol. bei e-r Wahl* in Frage kommen *od.* im Rennen liegen, kandidieren; **come down with a ~** schnell *od.* plötzlich fallen (*a. Barometer, Preis*); **go for** (*od.* **take**) **a ~** e-n Lauf machen; **have a ~ for one's money** sich abhetzen müssen; **have s.o. on the ~** j-n herumjagen, -hetzen; **3.** a) Anlauf *m*: ***take a ~*** (e-n) Anlauf nehmen, b) *Baseball, Kricket*: erfolgreicher Lauf; **4.** *Reiten*: schneller Ga'lopp; **5.** ⚓, *mot.* Fahrt *f*; **6.** *oft* ***short ~*** Spazierfahrt *f*; **7.** Abstecher *m*, kleine Reise (***to*** nach); **8.** ✈ (Bomben)Zielanflug *m*; **9.** ♪ Lauf *m*; **10.** Zulauf *m*, ✝ Ansturm *m*, Run *m* (***on*** auf *e-e Bank etc.*); ✝ stürmische Nachfrage (***on*** nach *e-r Ware*); **11.** *fig.* Lauf *m*, (Fort)Gang *m*: ***the ~ of events***; **12.** *fig.* Verlauf *m*: ***the ~ of the hills***; **13.** *fig.* a) Ten'denz *f*, b) Mode *f*; **14.** Folge *f*, (*sport* Erfolgs-, Treffer)Serie *f*: ***a ~ of bad*** (***good***) ***luck*** e-e Pechsträhne (e-e Glückssträhne); **15.** *Am.* kleiner Wasserlauf; **16.** *bsd. Am.* Laufmasche *f*; **17.** (Bob-, Rodel)Bahn *f*; **18.** ✈ Rollstrecke *f*; **19.** a) (Vieh-)Trift *f*, Weide *f*, b) (Hühner)Hof *m*, Auslauf *m*; **20.** ⚙ a) Bahn *f*, b) Laufschiene *f*, c) Rinne *f*; **21.** Mühl-, Mahlgang *m*; **22.** ⚙ a) Herstellungsgröße *f*, (Rohr- *etc.*)Länge *f*, b) (Betriebs)Leistung *f*, Ausstoß *m*, c) Gang *m*, 'Arbeitsperi‚ode *f*, d) 'Durchlauf *m* (*von Beschickungsgut*), e) Charge *f*, Menge *f*, f) Bedienung *f*; **23.** Auflage *f* (*Zeitung*); **24.** *Kartenspiel*: Se'quenz *f*; **25.** (Amts-, Gültigkeits-, Zeit)Dauer *f*: ***~ of office***; **26.** *thea.*, *Film*: Laufzeit *f*: ***have a ~ of 20 nights*** 20mal nacheinander gegeben werden; **27.** a) Art *f*, Schlag *m*; Sorte *f* (*a.* ✝), b) *mst* ***common*** (*od.* ***general*** *od.* ***ordinary***) ***~*** 'Durchschnitt *m*, *die* große Masse: ***~ of the mill*** Durchschnitt *m*; **28.** Herde *f*; **29.** Schwarm *m* (*Fische*); **30.** ⚓ (Achter)Piek *f*; **31.** (***of***) a) freie Benutzung (*gen.*), b) freier Zutritt (zu); **II** *v/i.* [*irr.*] **32.** laufen, rennen; eilen, stürzen; **33.** da'vonlaufen, Reiß'aus nehmen; **34.** *sport* a) (um die Wette) laufen, b) (an e-m Lauf *od.* Rennen) teilnehmen, laufen, c) als *Zweiter etc.* einlaufen: ***also ran*** ferner liefen; **35.** *fig.* laufen (*Blick, Feuer, Finger, Schauer etc.*): ***his eyes ran over ...*** sein Blick überflog ...; ***the tune keeps ~ning through my head*** die Melodie geht mir nicht aus dem Kopf; **36.** *pol.* kandidieren (***for*** für); **37.** ⚓ *etc.* fahren; (*in den Hafen*) einlaufen: ***~ before the wind*** vor dem Wind segeln; **38.** wandern (*Fische*); **39.** 🚂 *etc.* verkehren, *auf e-r Strecke* fahren, gehen; **40.** fließen, strömen (*beide a. fig. Blut in den Adern, Tränen, a. Verse*): ***it ~s in the blood*** (***family***) es liegt im Blut (in der Familie); **41.** lauten (*Schriftstück*); **42.** gehen (*Melodie*); **43.** verfließen, -streichen (*Zeit etc.*); **44.** dauern: ***three days ~ning*** drei Tage hintereinander; **45.** laufen, gegeben werden (*Theaterstück etc.*); **46.** verlaufen (*Straße etc.*, *a. Vorgang*), sich erstrecken; führen, gehen (*Weg etc.*): ***my taste*** (***talent***) ***does not ~ that way*** dafür habe ich keinen Sinn (keine Begabung); **47.** ⚙ laufen, gleiten (*Seil etc.*); **48.** ⚙ laufen: a) in Gang sein, arbeiten, b) gehen (*Uhr etc.*), funktionieren; **49.** in Betrieb sein (*Fabrik, Hotel etc.*); **50.** aus-, zerlaufen (*Farbe*); **51.** tropfen, strömen, triefen (***with*** vor *dat.*) (*Gesicht etc.*); laufen (*Nase, Augen*); 'übergehen (*Augen*): ***~ with tears*** in Tränen schwimmen; **52.** rinnen, laufen (*Gefäß*); **53.** schmelzen (*Metall*); tauen (*Eis*); **54.** ⚕ eitern, laufen; **55.** fluten, wogen: ***a heavy sea was ~ning*** es ging e-e schwere See; **56.** *Am.* a) laufen, fallen (*Masche*), b) Laufmaschen bekommen (*Strumpf*); **57.** ⚖ laufen, gelten, in Kraft sein *od.* bleiben: ***the period ~s*** die Frist läuft; **58.** ✝ sich stellen (*Preis, Ware*); **59.** *mit adj.*: werden, sein: ***~ dry*** a) versiegen, b) keine Milch mehr geben, c) erschöpft sein, d) sich ausgeschrieben haben (*Schriftsteller*); → 80; ***~ low*** (*od.* ***short***) zur Neige gehen, knapp werden; → ***high*** 22, ***riot*** 3, ***wild*** 2; **60.** *im Durchschnitt* sein, *klein etc.* ausfallen (*Früchte etc.*); **III** *v/t.* [*irr.*] **61.** *Weg etc.* laufen; *Strecke* durch'laufen, zu'rücklegen; *Weg* einschlagen; **62.** fahren (*a.* ⚓); *Strecke* be-, durch'fahren: ***~ a car against a tree*** mit e-m Wagen gegen e-n Baum fahren; **63.** *Rennen* austragen, laufen, *Wettlauf* machen; **64.** um die Wette laufen mit: ***~ s.o. close*** dicht an j-n herankommen (*a. fig.*); **65.** *Pferd* treiben; **66.** *hunt.* hetzen, *a. Spur* verfolgen (*a. fig.*); **67.** *Botschaften* über'bringen; *Botengänge od. Besorgungen* machen: ***~ errands***; **68.** *Blokkade* brechen; **69.** a) *Pferd etc.* laufen lassen, b) *pol. j-n* als Kandi'daten aufstellen (***for*** für); **70.** a) *Vieh* treiben, b) weiden lassen; **71.** 🚂, ⚓ *etc.* fahren *od.* verkehren lassen; **72.** *Am. Annonce* veröffentlichen; **73.** transportieren; **74.** *Schnaps etc.* schmuggeln; **75.** *Augen, Finger etc.* gleiten lassen: ***~ one's hand through one's hair*** (sich) mit den Fingern durchs Haar fahren; **76.** *Film* laufen lassen; **77.** ⚙ *Maschine etc.* laufen lassen, bedienen; **78.** *Betrieb etc.* führen, leiten, verwalten; *Geschäft etc.* betreiben; *Zeitung* her'ausgeben; **79.** hin'eingeraten (lassen) in (*acc.*): ***~ debts*** Schulden machen; ***~ a firm into debt*** e-e Firma in Schulden stürzen; ***~ the danger of*** (*ger.*) Gefahr laufen zu (*inf.*); → ***risk*** 1; **80.** ausströmen, fließen lassen; *Wasser etc.* führen (*Leitung*): ***~ dry*** leerlaufen lassen; → 59; **81.** *Gold etc.* (mit sich) führen (*Fluß*); **82.** *Metall* schmelzen; **83.** *Blei, Kugel* gießen; **84.** *Fieber, Temperatur* haben; **85.** stoßen, stechen, stecken; **86.** *Graben, Linie, Schnur etc.* ziehen; *Straße etc.* anlegen; *Brücke* schlagen; *Leitung* legen; **87.** leicht (ver)nähen, heften; **88.** *j-n* belangen (***for*** wegen);

Zssgn mit prp.:

run| a·cross *v/i. j-n* zufällig treffen, stoßen auf (*acc.*); ***~ aft·er*** *v/i.* hinter ... (*dat.*) herlaufen *od.* sein, nachlaufen (*dat.*) (*alle a. fig.*); ***~ a·gainst*** **I** *v/i.* **1.** zs.-stoßen mit, laufen *od.* rennen *od.* fahren gegen; **2.** *pol.* kandidieren gegen; **II** *v/t.* **3.** *et.* stoßen gegen: ***run one's head against*** mit dem Kopf gegen *die Wand etc.* stoßen; ***~ at*** *v/i.* losstürzen auf (*acc.*); ***~ for*** *v/i.* **1.** auf ... (*acc.*) zulaufen *od.* -rennen; laufen nach; **2.** ***~ it*** Reiß'aus nehmen; **3.** *fig.* sich bemühen *od.* bewerben um; *pol.* → ***run*** 36; ***~ in·to*** **I** *v/i.* **1.** (hin'ein)laufen *od.* (-)rennen in (*acc.*); **2.** ⚓ in *den Hafen* einlaufen; **3.** → ***run against*** 1; **4.** → ***run across***; **5.** geraten *od.* sich stürzen in (*acc.*): ***~ debt***; **6.** werden *od.* sich entwickeln zu; **7.** sich belaufen auf (*acc.*): ***~ four editions*** vier Auflagen erleben; ***~ money*** ins Geld laufen; **II** *v/t.* **8.** *Messer etc.* stoßen *od.* rennen in (*acc.*); ***~ off*** *v/i.* her'unterfahren *od.* -laufen von: ***~ the rails*** entgleisen; ***~ on*** *v/i.* **1.** sich drehen um, betreffen; **2.** sich beschäftigen mit; **3.** losfahren auf (*acc.*); **4.** → ***run across***; **5.** mit *e-m Treibstoff* fahren, (an)getrieben werden von; ***~ o·ver*** *v/i.* **1.** laufen *od.* gleiten über (*acc.*); **2.** über'fahren; **3.** 'durchgehen, -lesen, über'fliegen; ***~ through*** *v/i.* **1.** → ***run over*** 3; **2.** kurz erzählen, streifen; **3.** 'durchmachen, erleben; **4.** sich hin'durchziehen durch; **5.** *Vermögen* 'durchbringen; ***~ to*** *v/i.* **1.** sich belaufen auf (*acc.*); **2.** (aus)reichen für (*Geldmittel*); **3.** sich entwickeln zu, neigen zu; **4.** F sich *et.* leisten; **5.** allzusehr *Blätter etc.* treiben (*Pflanze*); → ***fat*** 5, ***seed*** 1; ***~ up·on*** → ***run on***; ***~ with*** *v/i.* über'einstimmen mit;

Zssgn mit adv.:

run| a·way *v/i.* **1.** da'vonlaufen (***from*** von *od. dat.*): ***~ from a subject*** von einem Thema abschweifen; **2.** 'durchgehen (*Pferd etc.*): ***~ with*** a) durchgehen mit *j-m* (*a. Phantasie, Temperament*); ***don't ~ with the idea that*** glauben Sie bloß nicht, daß, b) *et.* ‚mitgehen lassen', c) *viel Geld* kosten *od.* verschlingen, d) *sport Satz etc.* klar gewinnen; ***~ down*** **I** *v/i.* **1.** hin'unterlaufen (*a. Träne etc.*); **2.** ablaufen (*Uhr*); **3.** *fig.* her'unterkommen; **II** *v/t.* **4.** über'fahren; **5.** ⚓ in den Grund bohren; **6.** *j-n* einholen; **7.** *Wild, Verbrecher* zur Strecke bringen; **8.** aufstöbern, ausfindig machen; **9.** erschöpfen, *Batterie a.* zu stark entladen: ***be ~*** *fig.* erschöpft *od.* ab(gearbeitet, -gespannt) sein; **10.** *Betrieb etc.* her'unterwirtschaften; ***~ in*** **I** *v/i.* **1.** hin'ein, her'einlaufen; **2.** ***~ with*** *fig.* über'einstimmen mit; **II** *v/t.* **3.** hin'einlaufen lassen; **4.** einfügen (*a. typ.*); **5.** F *Verbrecher* ‚einlochen'; **6.** ⚙ *Maschine* (sich) einlaufen lassen, *Auto etc.* einfahren; ***~ off*** **I** *v/i.* **1.** → ***run away***; **2.** ablaufen, -fließen; **II** *v/t.* **3.** *et.* schnell erledigen; *Gedicht etc.* her'unterrasseln; **4.** *typ.* abdrucken, -ziehen; **5.** *Rennen etc.* a) austragen, b) zur Entscheidung bringen; ***~ on*** *v/i.* **1.** weiterlaufen; **2.** *fig.* fortlaufen, fortgesetzt werden (***to*** bis); **3.** a) (unaufhörlich) reden, fortplappern, b) *in der Rede* fortfahren; **4.** anwachsen (***into*** zu); **5.** *typ.* (ohne Absatz) fortlaufen; ***~ out*** **I** *v/i.* **1.** hin'aus-, her'auslaufen; **2.** her'ausfließen, -laufen; **3.** (aus)laufen (*Gefäß*); **4.** *fig.* ablaufen, zu Ende gehen; **5.** ausgehen, knapp werden (*Vorrat*): ***I have ~ of tobacco*** ich habe keinen Tabak mehr; **6.** her'ausragen; sich erstrecken; **II** *v/t.* **7.** hin'ausjagen, -treiben; **8.** erschöpfen: ***run o.s. out*** bis zur Erschöpfung laufen; ***be ~*** a) *vom Laufen* ausgepumpt sein, b) ausverkauft sein; ***~ o·ver*** **I** *v/i.* **1.** hin'überlaufen; **2.** 'überlaufen, -fließen; **II** *v/t.* **3.** über'fahren; ***~ through*** *v/t.* **1.** durch'bohren, -'stoßen; **2.** *Wort* 'durchstreichen; **3.** *Zug* 'durchfahren lassen; ***~ up*** **I** *v/i.* **1.** hin'auflaufen, -fahren; **2.** zulaufen (***to*** auf *acc.*); **3.** schnell anwachsen, hochschießen; **4.** einlaufen, -gehen (*Kleider*); **II** *v/t.* **5.** *Vermögen etc.* anwachsen lassen; **6.** *Rechnung* auflaufen lassen; **7.** *Angebot, Preis* in die Höhe treiben; **8.** *Flagge* hissen; **9.** schnell zs.-zählen; **10.** *Haus etc.* schnell hochziehen; **11.** *Kleid etc.* ‚zs.-hauen‘ (*schnell nähen*).

'run|·a·bout *s.* **1.** Her'umtreiber(in); **2.** *a.* ~ ***car*** *mot.* Kleinwagen *m*, Stadtauto *n*; **3.** leichtes Motorboot; **'~-a·round** *s. Am.* F: ***give s.o. the*** ~ a) j-n von Pontius zu Pilatus schicken, b) j-n hinhalten, c) *j-n* ‚an der Nase herumführen‘; **'~·a·way I** *s.* **1.** Ausreißer(in), 'Durchgänger *m* (*a. Pferd*); **2.** 'Durchgehen *n e-s Atomreaktors*; **II** *adj.* **3.** 'durchgebrannt, flüchtig (*Häftling etc.*): ~ ***car*** Wagen, der sich selbständig gemacht hat; ~ ***inflation*** ✝ galoppierende Inflation; ~ ***match*** Heirat *f* e-s durchgebrannten Liebespaares; ~ ***victory*** *sport* Kantersieg *m*; **'~-down I** *adj.* **1.** erschöpft (*a.* ⚡ *Batterie*), abgespannt, ‚erledigt‘; **2.** heruntergekommen, baufällig; **3.** abgelaufen (*Uhr*); **II** ['rʌndaʊn] *s.* **4.** F (ausführlicher) Bericht.

rune [ruːn] *s.* Rune *f.*

rung¹ [rʌŋ] *p.p. von* ***ring²***.

rung² [rʌŋ] *s.* **1.** (*bsd.* Leiter)Sprosse *f*; **2.** *fig.* Stufe *f*, Sprosse *f*; **3.** (Rad)Speiche *f*; **4.** Runge *f.*

ru·nic ['ruːnɪk] **I** *adj.* **1.** runisch; Runen…; **II** *s.* **2.** Runeninschrift *f*; **3.** *typ.* Runenschrift *f.*

'run-in *s.* **1.** *sport Brit.* Einlauf *m*; **2.** *typ.* Einschiebung *f*; **3.** ⚙ a) Einfahren *n* (*Auto etc.*), b) Einlaufen *n* (*Maschine*); **4.** *Am.* F ‚Krach‘ *m*, Zs.-stoß *m* (*Streit*); ~ **groove** *s.* Einlaufrille *f* (*Schallplatte*).

run·let ['rʌnlɪt] *s.* Bach *m.*

run·nel ['rʌnl] *s.* **1.** Rinnsal *n*; **2.** Rinne *f*, Rinnstein *m.*

run·ner ['rʌnə] *s.* **1.** (*a.* Wett)Läufer (-in); **2.** Rennpferd *n*; **3.** a) Bote *m*, b) Laufbursche *m*, c) ⚔ Melder *m*; **4.** ✝ *Am.* a) Unter'nehmer *m*, b) F Vertreter *m*, c) F ‚Renner‘ *m*, Verkaufsschlager *m*; **5.** *mst in Zssgn* Schmuggler *m*; **6.** Läufer *m* (*Teppich*); **7.** (*Schlitten- etc.*) Kufe *f*; **8.** ⚙ a) Laufschiene *f*, b) Seilring *m*, c) (*Turbinen- etc.*) Laufrad *n*, d) (Gleit-, Lauf)Rolle *f*, e) Rollwalze *f*; **9.** *typ.* Zeilenzähler *m*; **10.** ⛏ Drillschar *f*; **11.** ⚓ Drehreep *n*; **12.** ⚘ a) Ausläufer *m*, b) Kletterpflanze *f*, c) Stangenbohne *f*; **13.** *orn.* Ralle *f*; **14.** *ichth.* Goldstöcker *m*; **ˌ~-'up** *s.* (***to*** hinter *dat.*) Zweite(r *m*) *f*, *sport a.* Vizemeister(in).

run·ning ['rʌnɪŋ] **I** *s.* **1.** Laufen *n*, Lauf *m* (*a.* ⚙): ***be still in the*** ~ noch gut im Rennen liegen (*a. fig.* ***for*** um); ***be out of the*** ~ aus dem Rennen sein (*a. fig.* ***for*** um); ***make the*** ~ a) das Tempo machen, b) das Tempo angeben; ***put s.o. out of the*** ~ j-n aus dem Rennen werfen (*a. fig.*); ***take*** (***up***) ***the*** ~ sich an die Spitze setzen (*a. fig.*); **2.** Schmuggel *m*; **3.** Leitung *f*, Aufsicht *f*; Bedienung *f*, Über'wachung *f e-r Maschine*; **4.** Durch'brechen *n e-r Blockade*; **II** *adj.* **5.** laufend (*a.* ⚙): ~ ***fight*** ⚔ a) Rückzugsgefecht *n*, b) laufendes Gefecht (*a. fig.*); ~ ***gear*** ⚙ Laufwerk *n*; ~ ***glance*** *fig.* flüchtiger Blick; ~ ***jump*** Sprung *m* mit Anlauf; ~ ***knot*** laufender Knoten; ~ ***mate*** *pol. Am.* 'Vizepräsiˌdentschaftsbewerber(in); ~ ***shot*** *Film*: Fahraufnahme *f*; ~ ***speed*** Fahr- *od.* Umlaufgeschwindigkeit *f*; ~ ***start*** *sport* fliegender Start; ***in*** ~ ***order*** ⚙ betriebsfähig; **6.** *fig.* laufend (*ständig*), fortlaufend: ~ ***account*** ✝ a) laufende Rechnung, b) Kontokorrent *n*; ~ ***commentary*** a) laufender Kommentar, b) (Funk)Reportage *f*; ~ ***debts*** laufende Schulden; ~ ***hand*** Schreibschrift *f*; ~ ***head***(***line***), ~ ***title*** Kolumnentitel *m*; ~ ***pattern*** fortlaufendes Muster; ~ ***text*** fortlaufender Text; **7.** fließend (*Wasser*); **8.** ⚕ laufend, eiternd (*Wunde*); **9.** aufein'anderfolgend: ***five times*** (***for three days***) ~ fünfmal (drei Tage) hintereinander; ~ ***fire*** ⚔ Lauffeuer *n*; **10.** line'ar gemessen: ***per*** ~ ***metre*** pro laufenden Meter; **11.** ⚘ a) rankend, b) kriechend; **12.** ♪ laufend: ~ ***passages*** Läufe; ~ **board** *s. mot.*, 🚂 *etc.* Tritt-, Laufbrett *n*; **ˌ~-'in test** *s.* ⚙ Probelauf *m.*

'run|-off *s. sport* Entscheidungslauf *m*, -rennen *n*; **'~-off vote** *s. pol.* Stichwahl *f*; **ˌ~-of-the-'mill** *adj.* Durchschnitts…, mittelmäßig; **'~·proof** *adj.* maschenfest; **'~-on** *typ.* **I** *adj.* angehängt, fortlaufend gesetzt; **II** *s.* angehängtes Wort.

runs [rʌnz] *s. pl.* F *bsd. Brit.* Durchfall *m*, ‚Scheißerei‘ *f.*

runt [rʌnt] *s.* **1.** *zo.* Zwergrind *n*, -ochse *m*; **2.** *fig.* (*contp.* lächerlicher) Zwerg; **3.** *orn. große kräftige Haustaubenrasse.*

'run|·through *s.* **1.** a) Überfliegen *n* (*e-s Briefs etc.*), b) kurze Zs.-fassung; **2.** *thea.* schnelle Probe; **'~-up** *s.* **1.** *sport.* Anlauf *m*: ***in the*** ~ ***to*** *fig.* im Vorfeld *der Wahlen etc.*; **2.** ⚔ (Ziel)Anflug *m*; **3.** ✈ kurzer Probelauf *der Motoren*; **'~·way** *s.* **1.** ✈ Start-, Lande-, Rollbahn *f*; **2.** *sport* Anlaufbahn *f*; **3.** *hunt.* Wildpfad *m*, (-)Wechsel *m*: ~ ***watching*** Ansitzjagd *f*; **4.** *bsd. Am.* Laufsteg *m.*

ru·pee [ruː'piː] *s.* Rupie *f* (*Geld*).

rup·ture ['rʌptʃə] **I** *s.* **1.** Bruch *m* (*a.* ⚕ *u. fig.*), (*a.* ⚕ *Muskel- etc.*)Riß *m*: ***diplomatic*** ~ Abbruch *m* der diplomatischen Beziehungen; ~ ***support*** ⚕ Bruchband *n*; **2.** Brechen *n* (*a.* ⚙): ~ ***limit*** ⚙ Bruchgrenze *f*; **II** *v/t.* **3.** brechen (*a. fig.*), zersprengen, -reißen (*a.* ⚕): ~ ***o.s.*** → 6; **4.** *fig.* abbrechen, trennen; **III** *v/i.* **5.** zerspringen, (-)reißen; **6.** ⚕ sich e-n Bruch heben.

ru·ral ['rʊərəl] *adj.* ☐ **1.** ländlich, Land…; **2.** landwirtschaftlich; **'ru·ral·ize** [-rəlaɪz] **I** *v/t.* **1.** e-n ländlichen Cha'rakter geben; **2.** auf das Landleben 'umstellen; **II** *v/i.* **3.** auf dem Lande leben; **4.** sich auf das Landleben umstellen; **5.** ländlich werden, verbauern.

Ru·ri·ta·ni·an [ˌrʊərɪ'teɪnjən] *adj. fig.* abenteuerlich.

ruse [ruːz] *s.* List *f*, Trick *m.*

rush¹ [rʌʃ] *s.* ⚘ Binse *f*; *coll.* Binsen *pl.*: ***not worth a*** ~ *fig.* keinen Pfifferling wert.

rush² [rʌʃ] **I** *v/i.* **1.** rasen, stürzen, (da'hin)jagen, stürmen, (he'rum)hetzen: ~ ***at s.o.*** auf j-n losstürzen; ~ ***in*** hereinstürzen, -stürmen; ~ ***into extremes*** *fig.* ins Extrem verfallen: ~ ***through*** a) hasten durch, b) *et.* hastig erledigen *etc.*; ***an idea*** ~***ed into my mind*** ein Gedanke schoß mir durch den Kopf; ***blood*** ~***ed to her face*** das Blut schoß ihr ins Gesicht; **2.** (da'hin)brausen (*Wind*); **3.** *fig.* sich (*vorschnell*) stürzen (***into*** in *od.* auf *acc.*); → ***conclusion*** 3, ***print*** 13; **II** *v/t.* **4.** (an)treiben, drängen, hetzen, jagen: ***I refuse to be*** ~***ed*** ich lasse mich nicht drängen; ~ ***up prices*** *Am.* die Preise in die Höhe treiben; ***be*** ~***ed for time*** F unter Zeitdruck stehen; **5.** schnell *od.* auf dem schnellsten Wege *wohin* bringen *od.* schaffen: ~ ***s.o. to the hospital***; **6.** schnell erledigen, *Arbeit etc.* her'unterhasten, hinhauen: ~ ***a bill*** (***through***) e-e Gesetzesvorlage durchpeitschen; **7.** über'stürzen, -'eilen; **8.** losstürmen auf (*acc.*), angreifen; **9.** im Sturm nehmen (*a. fig.*), stürmen (*a. fig.*): ~ ***s.o. off his feet*** j-n in Trab halten; **10.** über *ein Hindernis* hin'wegsetzen; **11.** *Am. sl.* mit Aufmerksamkeiten über'häufen, um'werben; **12.** *Brit. sl.* ‚neppen‘, ‚bescheißen‘ (***£5*** um 5 Pfund); **III** *s.* **13.** Vorwärtsstürmen *n*, Da'hinschießen *n*; Brausen *n* (*Wind*): ***on the*** ~ F in aller Eile; ***with a*** ~ plötzlich; **14.** ⚔ a) Sturm *m*, b) Sprung *m*: ***by*** ~***es*** sprungweise; **15.** *American Football*: Vorstoß *m*, 'Durchbruch *m*; **16.** *fig.* a) (An)Sturm *m* (***for*** auf *acc.*), b) (Massen)Andrang *m*, c) *a.* ✝ stürmische Nachfrage (***on*** *od.* ***for*** nach): ***make a*** ~ ***for*** losstürzen auf (*acc.*); **17.** ⚕ a) (Blut)Andrang *m*, b) (Adrena'lin- *etc.*)Stoß *m*; **18.** *fig.* plötzlicher Ausbruch (*von Tränen etc.*); plötzliche Anwandlung, Anfall *m*: ~ ***of pity***; **19.** a) Drang *m der Geschäfte*, ‚Hetze‘ *f*, b) Hochbetrieb *m*, -druck *m*, c) Über'häufung *f* (***of*** mit *Arbeit*); ~ **hour** *s.* Hauptverkehrs-, Stoßzeit *f*; **'~-ˌhour** *adj.* Hauptverkehrs…, Stoß…: ~ ***traffic*** Stoßverkehr *m*; ~ **job** *s.* eilige Arbeit, dringende Sache; ~ **or·der** *s.* ✝ Eilauftrag *m.*

rusk [rʌsk] *s.* **1.** Zwieback *m*; **2.** Sandkuchengebäck *n.*

rus·set ['rʌsɪt] **I** *adj.* **1.** a) rostbraun, b) rotgelb, -grau; **2.** *obs.* grob; **II** *s.* **3.** a) Rostbraun *n*, b) Rotgelb *n*, -grau *n*; **4.** grobes handgewebtes Tuch; **5.** Boskop *m* (*rötlicher Winterapfel*).

Rus·sia leath·er ['rʌʃə] *s.* Juchten(leder) *n*; **'Rus·sian** [-ʃn] **I** *s.* **1.** Russe *m*, Russin *f*; **2.** *ling.* Russisch *n*; **II** *adj.* **3.** russisch; **'Rus·sian·ize** [-ʃənaɪz] *v/t.* russifizieren.

Russo- [rʌsəʊ] *in Zssgn* a) russisch, b) russisch-…

rust [rʌst] **I** *s.* **1.** Rost *m* (*a. fig.*): ***gather*** ~ Rost ansetzen; **2.** Rost- *od.* Moderfleck *m*; **3.** ⚘ a) Rost *m*, Brand *m*, b) *a.* ~***-fungus*** Rostpilz *m*; **II** *v/i.* **4.** (ver-) rosten, einrosten (*a. fig.*), rostig werden; **5.** moderfleckig werden; **III** *v/t.* **6.** rostig machen; **7.** *fig.* einrosten lassen.

rus·tic ['rʌstɪk] **I** *adj.* ☐ (~***ally***) **1.** ländlich, rusti'kal, Land…, Bauern…; **2.** simpel, schlicht, anspruchslos; **3.** grob, ungehobelt, bäurisch; **4.** rusti'kal, roh (gearbeitet): ~ ***furniture***; **5.** △ a) Rustika…, b) mit Bossenwerk verziert; **6.** *typ.* unregelmäßig geformt; **II** *s.* **7.** (einfacher) Bauer, Landmann *m*; **8.** *fig.* Bauer *m*; **'rus·ti·cate** [-keɪt] **I** *v/i.* **1.** auf dem Lande leben; **2.** a) ein ländliches Leben führen, b) verbauern; **II** *v/t.*

3. aufs Land senden; **4.** *Brit. univ.* relegieren, (zeitweilig) von der Universi'tät verweisen; **5.** ⚠ mit Bossenwerk verzieren; **rus·ti·ca·tion** [ˌrʌstɪ'keɪʃn] *s.* **1.** Landaufenthalt *m*; **2.** Verbauerung *f*; **3.** *Brit. univ.* (zeitweise) Relegati'on; **rus·tic·i·ty** [rʌ'stɪsətɪ] *s.* **1.** ländlicher Cha'rakter; **2.** grobe *od.* bäurische Art; **3.** (ländliche) Einfachheit.

rus·tic| ware *s.* hellbraune Terra'kotta; **~ work** *s.* **1.** ⚠ Bossenwerk *n*, Rustika *f*; **2.** *roh gezimmerte Möbel etc.*

rust·i·ness ['rʌstɪnɪs] *s.* **1.** Rostigkeit *f*; **2.** *fig.* Eingerostetsein *n*.

rus·tle ['rʌsl] **I** *v/i.* **1.** rascheln (*Blätter etc.*), rauschen, knistern (*Seide etc.*); **2.** *Am. sl.* ‚rangehen', (e'nergisch) zupakken; **II** *v/t.* **3.** rascheln mit (*od.* in *dat.*), rascheln machen; **4.** *Am. sl. Vieh* stehlen; **5. ~ up** F a) *et.* ‚organisieren', auftreiben, b) *Essen* ‚zaubern'; **III** *s.* **6.** Rauschen *n*, Rascheln *n*, Knistern *n*; **'rus·tler** [-lə] *s. Am. sl.* **1.** Viehdieb *m*; **2.** Mordsanstrengung *f*.

rust·less ['rʌstlɪs] *adj.* rostfrei, nicht rostend: **~ *steel*.**

rust·y ['rʌstɪ] *adj.* □ **1.** rostig, verrostet; **2.** *fig.* eingerostet (*Kenntnisse etc.*); **3.** rostfarben; **4.** ⚘ vom Rost(pilz) befallen; **5.** schäbig (*Kleidung*); **6.** rauh (*Stimme*).

rut¹ [rʌt] **I** *s.* **1.** (Wagen-, Rad)Spur *f*, Furche *f*; **2.** *fig.* altes Geleise, alter Trott: ***be in a ~*** sich in ausgefahrenem Gleis bewegen; ***get into a ~*** in e-n (immer gleichen) Trott verfallen; **II** *v/t.* **3.** furchen.

rut² [rʌt] *zo.* **I** *s.* **1.** a) Brunst *f*, b) Brunft *f* (*Hirsch*); **2.** Brunst-, Brunftzeit *f*; **II** *v/i.* **3.** brunften, brunsten.

ru·ta·ba·ga [ˌru:tə'beɪgə] *s.* ⚘ *Am.* Gelbe Kohlrübe.

Ruth¹ [ru:θ], *a.* **book of ~** *s. bibl.* (das Buch) Ruth *f*.

ruth² [ru:θ] *s. obs.* Mitleid *n*.

ruth·less ['ru:θlɪs] *adj.* □ **1.** unbarmherzig, mitleidlos; **2.** rücksichts-, skrupellos; **'ruth·less·ness** [-nɪs] *s.* **1.** Unbarmherzigkeit *f*; **2.** Rücksichts-, Skrupellosigkeit *f*.

rut·ting ['rʌtɪŋ] *zo.* **I** *s.* Brunst *f*; **II** *adj.* Brunst…, Brunft…: **~ *time***; **rut·tish** ['rʌtɪʃ] *adj. zo.* brunftig, brünstig.

rut·ty ['rʌtɪ] *adj.* durch'furcht, ausgefahren (*Weg*).

rye [raɪ] *s.* **1.** ⚘ Roggen *m*; **2.** *a.* **~-*whisky*** Roggenwhisky *m*.

S

S, s [es] *s.* S *n*, s *n* (*Buchstabe*).
's [z] **1.** F *für* ***is***: ***he's here***; **2.** F *für* ***has***: ***she's just come***; **3.** [s] F *für* ***us***: ***let's go***; **4.** [s] F *für* ***does***: ***what's he think about it?***
Sab·bath ['sæbəθ] *s.* Sabbat *m*; *weitS.* 2 Sonn-, Ruhetag *m*: ***break*** (***keep***) ***the*** ~ den Sabbat entheiligen (heiligen); ***witches'*** ~ Hexensabbat; **'~break·er** *s.* Sabbatschänder(in).
Sab·bat·ic [sə'bætɪk] *adj.* (□ ***~ally***) → ***sabbatical*** I; **sab'bat·i·cal** [-kl] **I** *adj.* □ 2 Sabbat…; **II** *s. a.* ~ ***year*** a) Sabbatjahr *n*, b) *univ.* Ferienjahr *n e-s Professors.*
sa·ber ['seɪbə] *Am.* → ***sabre.***
sa·ble ['seɪbl] **I** *s.* **1.** *zo.* a) Zobel *m*, b) (*bsd.* Fichten)Marder *m*; **2.** Zobelfell *n*, -pelz *m*; **3.** *her.* Schwarz *n*; **4.** *mst pl. poet.* Trauer(kleidung) *f*; **II** *adj.* **5.** Zobel…; **6.** *her.* schwarz; **7.** *poet.* schwarz, finster.
sa·bot ['sæbəʊ] *s.* **1.** Holzschuh *m*; **2.** ⚔ Geschoß-, Führungsring *m*.
sab·o·tage ['sæbətɑːʒ] **I** *s.* Sabo'tage *f*; **II** *v/t.* sabotieren; **III** *v/i.* Sabo'tage treiben; **sa·bo·teur** [ˌsæbə'tɜː] (*Fr.*) *s.* Sabo'teur *m*.
sa·bre ['seɪbə] **I** *s.* **1.** Säbel *m*: ***rattle the*** ~ *fig.* mit dem Säbel rasseln; **2.** ⚔ *hist.* Kavalle'rist *m*; **II** *v/t.* **3.** niedersäbeln; ~ **rat·tling** *s. fig.* Säbelrasseln *n*.
sab·u·lous ['sæbjʊləs] *adj.* sandig, Sand…: ~ ***urine*** ⚕ Harngrieß *m*.
sac [sæk] *s.* **1.** ♀, *anat.*, *zo.* Sack *m*, Beutel *m*; **2.** ⚙ (Tinten)Sack *m* (*Füllhalter*).
sac·cha·rate ['sækəreɪt] *s.* ⚗ Saccha'rat *n*; **sac·char·ic** [sə'kærɪk] *adj.* ⚗ Zukker…: ~ ***acid***; **sac·cha·rif·er·ous** [ˌsækə'rɪfərəs] *adj.* ⚗ zuckerhaltig *od.* -erzeugend; **sac·char·i·fy** [sə'kærɪfaɪ] *v/t.* **1.** verzuckern, saccharifizieren; **2.** süßen; **sac·cha·rim·e·ter** [ˌsækə'rɪmɪtə] *s.* Zuckermesser *m*, Sacchari'meter *n*.
sac·cha·rin(e) ['sækərɪn] *s.* ⚗ Saccha'rin *n*; **'sac·cha·rine** [-raɪn] *adj.* **1.** Zucker…, Süßstoff…: **2.** *fig.* süßlich: ***a*** ~ ***smile***; **'sac·cha·roid** [-rɔɪd] *adj.* ⚗, *min.* zuckerartig, körnig; **sac·cha·rom·e·ter** [ˌsækə'rɒmɪtə] → ***saccharimeter***; **'sac·cha·rose** [-rəʊs] *s.* ⚗ Rohrzucker *m*, Saccha'rose *f*.
sac·cule ['sækjuːl] *s. bsd. anat.* Säckchen *n*.
sac·er·do·tal [ˌsæsə'dəʊtl] *adj.* □ priesterlich, Priester…; **ˌsac·er'do·tal·ism** [-təlɪzəm] *s.* **1.** Priestertum *n*; **2.** *contp.* Pfaffentum *n*.
sa·chem ['seɪtʃəm] *s.* **1.** Indi'anerhäuptling *m*; **2.** *Am. humor.* ‚großes Tier', *bsd. pol.* ‚Par'teiboß' *m*.

sa·chet ['sæʃeɪ] *s.* **1.** Säckchen *n*, Tütchen *n*; **2.** Duftkissen *n*.
sack¹ [sæk] **I** *s.* **1.** Sack *m*; **2.** F ‚Laufpaß' *m*: ***get the*** ~ a) ‚fliegen', ‚an die Luft gesetzt (*entlassen*) werden', b) *von e-m Mädchen* den Laufpaß bekommen; ***give s.o. the*** ~ → 7; **3.** *Am.* a) (Verpackungs)Beutel *m*, Tüte *f*, b) Beutel (-inhalt) *m*; **4.** a) 'Umhang *m*, b) (kurzer) loser Mantel, c) → ***sack coat***, ***sack dress***; **5.** *sl.* ‚Falle' *f*, ‚Klappe' *f* (*Bett*): ***hit the*** ~ sich ‚hinhauen'; **II** *v/t.* **6.** einsacken, in Säcke *od.* Beutel abfüllen; **7.** F a) *j-n* ‚rausschmeißen' (*entlassen*), b) *e-m Liebhaber* den Laufpaß geben.
sack² [sæk] **I** *s.* Plünderung *f*: ***put to*** ~ → **II** *v/t. Stadt etc.* (aus)plündern.
sack³ [sæk] *s.* heller Südwein.
'sack|·but [-bʌt] *s.* ♪ **1.** *hist.* 'Zugpoˌsaune *f*; **2.** *bibl.* Harfe *f*; **'~·cloth** *s.* Sackleinen *n*: ***in*** ~ ***and ashes*** *fig.* in Sack u. Asche *Buße tun od. trauern*; ~ **coat** *s. Am.* Sakko *m*, *n*; ~ **dress** *s.* Sackkleid *n*; **'~·ful** [-fʊl] *pl.* **-fuls** *s.* Sack(voll) *m*; ~ **race** *s.* Sackhüpfen *n*.
sa·cral ['seɪkrəl] **I** *adj.* **1.** *eccl.* sa'kral, Sakral…; **2.** *anat.* Sakral…, Kreuz(bein)…; **II** *s.* **3.** Sa'kralwirbel *m*; **4.** Sa'kralnerv *m*.
sac·ra·ment ['sækrəmənt] *s.* **1.** *eccl.* Sakra'ment *n*: ***the*** (***Blessed*** *od.* ***Holy***) ~ a) das (heilige) Abendmahl, b) *R.C.* die heilige Kommunion; ***the last*** ~***s*** die Sterbesakramente; **2.** Sym'bol *n* (***of*** für); **3.** My'sterium *n*; **4.** feierlicher Eid; **sac·ra·men·tal** [ˌsækrə'mentl] **I** *adj.* □ sakramen'tal, Sakraments…; *fig.* heilig, weihevoll; **II** *s. R.C.* heiliger *od.* sakramen'taler Ritus *od.* Gegenstand; *pl.* Sakramen'talien *pl.*
sa·cred ['seɪkrɪd] *adj.* □ **1.** *eccl. u. fig.* heilig (*a. Andenken*, *Pflicht*, *Recht etc.*), geheiligt, geweiht (***to*** *dat.*): ~ ***cow*** *fig.* ‚heilige Kuh'; **2.** geistlich, kirchlich, Kirchen… (*Dichtung*, *Musik*); **'sa·cred·ness** [-nɪs] *s.* Heiligkeit *f*.
sac·ri·fice ['sækrɪfaɪs] **I** *s.* **1.** *eccl. u. fig.* a) Opfer *n* (*Handlung u. Sache*), b) *fig.* Aufopferung *f*, Verzicht *m* (***of*** auf *acc.*): ~ ***of the Mass*** Meßopfer *n*; ***the great*** (*od.* ***last***) ~ das höchste Opfer, *bsd.* der Heldentod; ***make a*** ~ ***of*** *et.* opfern; ***make*** ~***s*** → 6; ***at some*** ~ ***of accuracy*** unter einigem Verzicht auf Genauigkeit; **2.** ♆ Verlust *m*: ***sell at a*** ~ → 4; **II** *v/t.* **3.** *eccl. u. fig.*, *a. Schach*: opfern (***to*** *dat.*): ~ ***one's life***; **4.** ♆ mit Verlust verkaufen; **III** *v/i.* **5.** *eccl.* opfern; **6.** *fig.* Opfer bringen; **sac·ri·fi·cial** [ˌsækrɪ'fɪʃl] *adj.* □ **1.** *eccl.* Opfer…; **2.** aufopferungsvoll.

sac·ri·lege ['sækrɪlɪdʒ] *s.* Sakri'leg *n*: a) Kirchenschändung *f*, -raub *m*, b) Entweihung *f*, c) *allg.* Frevel *m*; **sac·ri·le·gious** [ˌsækrɪ'lɪdʒəs] *adj.* □ sakri'legisch, *allg.* frevlerisch.
sa·crist ['seɪkrɪst], **sac·ris·tan** ['sækrɪstən] *s. eccl.* Sakri'stan *m*, Mesner *m*, Küster *m*; **sac·ris·ty** ['sækrɪstɪ] *s. eccl.* Sakri'stei *f*.
sac·ro·sanct ['sækrəʊsæŋkt] *adj.* (*a. iro.*) sakro'sankt, hochheilig.
sa·crum ['seɪkrəm] *s. anat.* Kreuzbein *n*, Sakrum *n*.
sad [sæd] *adj.* □ → ***sadly***; **1.** (***at***) traurig (über *acc.*), bekümmert, niedergeschlagen (wegen); melan'cholisch: ***a*** ~***der and a wiser man*** j-d, der durch Schaden klug geworden ist; **2.** traurig (*Pflicht*), tragisch (*Unfall etc.*): ~ ***to say*** bedauerlicherweise; **3.** schlimm, arg (*Zustand*); **4.** *contp.* elend, mise'rabel, jämmerlich, F arg, ‚furchtbar': ***a*** ~ ***dog*** ein mieser Kerl; **5.** dunkel, matt (*Farbe*); **6.** teigig, klitschig: ~ ***bread***; **sadden** ['sædn] **I** *v/t.* traurig machen, betrüben; **II** *v/i.* traurig werden (***at*** über *acc.*).
sad·dle ['sædl] **I** *s.* **1.** (*Pferde-*, *Fahrrad- etc.*)Sattel *m*: ***in the*** ~ im Sattel, *fig.* fest im Sattel, im Amt, an der Macht; ***put the*** ~ ***on the wrong*** (***right***) ***horse*** *fig.* die Schuld dem Falschen (Richtigen) geben *od.* zuschreiben; **2.** a) (*Pferde*)Rücken *m*, b) Rücken(stück *n*) *m* (*Schlachtvieh etc.*): ~ ***of mutton*** Hammelrücken; **3.** (Berg)Sattel *m*; **4.** Buchrücken *m*; **5.** ⚙ a) Querholz *n*, b) Bettschlitten *m*, Sup'port *m* (*Werkzeugmaschine*), c) Lager *n*, d) Türschwelle *f*; **II** *v/t.* **6.** *Pferd* satteln; **7.** *bsd. fig.* a) belasten, b) *Aufgabe etc.* aufbürden, -halsen (***on***, ***upon*** *dat.*), c) *et.* zur Last legen (***on***, ***upon*** *dat.*); **'~·back** *s.* **1.** Bergsattel *m*; **2.** △ Satteldach *n*; **3.** *zo. Tier mit sattelförmiger Rückenzeichnung*, *bsd.* a) Nebelkrähe *f*, b) männliche Sattelrobbe; **4.** hohlrückiges Pferd; **'~·backed** *adj.* **1.** hohlrückig (*Pferd etc.*); **2.** sattelförmig; **'~·bag** *s.* Satteltasche *f*; ~ **blan·ket** *s.* Woilach *m*; ~ **horse** *s.* Reitpferd *n*; **'~·nose** *s.* Sattelnase *f*.
sad·dler·y ['sædlərɪ] *s.* **1.** Sattle'rei *f*; **2.** Sattelzeug *n*.
sad·ism ['seɪdɪzəm] *s. psych.* Sa'dismus *m*; **'sad·ist** [-ɪst] **I** *s.* Sa'dist(in); **II** *adj.* → **sa·dis·tic** [sə'dɪstɪk] *adj.* (□ ***~ally***) sa'distisch.
sad·ly ['sædlɪ] *adv.* **1.** traurig, betrübt; **2.** *a.* ~ ***enough*** unglücklicherweise, leider; **3.** erbärmlich, arg, schmählich *ver-*

nachlässigt etc.
sad·ness ['sædnɪs] *s.* Traurigkeit *f.*
sa·fa·ri [sə'fɑːrɪ] *s.* (**on ~** auf) Sa'fari *f.*
safe [seɪf] **I** *adj.* □ **1.** sicher (**from** vor *dat.*): **we are ~ now** jetzt sind wir in Sicherheit; **keep s.th. ~** et. sicher aufbewahren; **better to be ~ than sorry!** ‚Vorsicht ist die Mutter der Porzellankiste!'; **2.** sicher, unversehrt, heil; außer Gefahr (*a. Patient*): **~ and sound** heil u. gesund *ankommen etc.*; **3.** sicher, ungefährlich: **~ period** ⚕ unfruchtbare Tage *pl.* (*der Frau*); **~ (to operate)** ⚙ betriebssicher; **~ stress** ⚙ zulässige Beanspruchung; **the rope is ~** das Seil hält; **is it ~ to go there?** ist es ungefährlich, da hinzugehen?; **in ~ custody** → 7; **as ~ as houses** F absolut sicher; **it is ~ to say** man kann (ruhig) sagen; **to be on the ~ side** um ganz sicher zu gehen; → **play** 9; **4.** vorsichtig (*Fahrer, Schätzung etc.*); **5.** sicher, zuverlässig: **a ~ leader**; **a ~ method**; **6.** sicher, wahrscheinlich: **a ~ winner**; **he is ~ to be there** er wird sicher *od.* bestimmt da sein; **7.** in sicherem Gewahrsam (*a. Verbrecher*); **II** *s.* **8.** Safe *m*, Tre'sor *m*, Geldschrank *m*; **9.** → **meat-safe**; **'~blow·er**, **'~ˌcrack·er** *s.* F Geldschrankknacker *m*; **~ con·duct** *s.* **1.** Geleitbrief *m*; **2.** freies *od.* sicheres Geleit; **~ de·pos·it** *s.* Stahlkammer *f*, Tre'sor(raum) *m*; **'~-deˌpos·it box** *s.* Tre'sor(fach *n*) *m*, Safe *m*; **'~·guard I** *s.* Sicherung *f*: a) Schutz (**against** gegen, vor *dat.*), Vorsichtsmaßnahme *f* (gegen), b) Sicherheitsklausel *f*, c) ⚙ Schutzvorrichtung *f*; **II** *v/t.* sichern, schützen; *Interessen* wahrnehmen: **~ing duty** Schutzzoll *m*; **~ keep·ing** *s.* sichere Verwahrung, Gewahrsam *m.*
safe·ness ['seɪfnɪs] → **safety** 1–3.
safe·ty ['seɪftɪ] *s.* **1.** Sicherheit *f*: **be in ~**; **jump to ~** sich durch e-n Sprung retten; **2.** Sicherheit *f*, Gefahrlosigkeit *f*: **~ (of operation)** ⚙ Betriebssicherheit; **~ glass** Sicherheitsglas *n*; **~ measure** Sicherheitsmaßnahme *f*, -vorkehrung *f*; **~ in flight** ✈ Flugsicherheit; **~ on the road** Verkehrssicherheit; **there is ~ in numbers** zu mehreren ist man sicherer; **~ first!** Sicherheit über alles!; **~ first scheme** Unfallverhütungsprogramm *n*; **play for ~** sichergehen (wollen), Risiken vermeiden; **3.** Sicherheit *f*, Zuverlässigkeit *f*, Verläßlichkeit *f* (*Mechanismus, Verfahren etc.*); **4.** *a.* **~ device** ⚙ Sicherung *f*, Schutz-, Sicherheitsvorrichtung *f*; **5.** Sicherung(sflügel *m*) *f* (*Gewehr etc.*): **at ~** gesichert; **~ belt** *s.* **1.** Rettungsgürtel *m*; **2.** ✈, *mot.* Sicherheitsgurt *m*; **~ bolt** *s.* ⚙, ⚔ Sicherheitsbolzen *m*; **~ buoy** *s.* Rettungsboje *f*; **~ catch** *s.* **1.** ⚙ Sicherung *f* (*Lift etc.*); **2.** Sicherungsflügel *m* (*Gewehr etc.*): **release the ~** entsichern; **~ curtain** *s. thea.* eiserner Vorhang; **~ fuse** *s.* **1.** ⚙ Sicherheitszünder *m*, -zündschnur *f*; **2.** ⚡ a) (Schmelz)Sicherung *f*, b) Sicherheitsausschalter *m*; **~ is·land** *s.* Verkehrsinsel *f*; **~ lamp** *s.* ⚒ Grubenlampe *f*; **~ lock** *s.* **1.** Sicherheitsschloß *n*; **2.** Sicherung *f* (*Gewehr, Mine etc.*); **~ match** *s.* Sicherheitszündholz *n*; **~ net** *s. Zirkus etc.* (*a. fig. soziales*) Netz; **~ pin** *s.* Sicherheitsnadel *f*; **~ razor** *s.* Ra'sierappaˌrat *m*; **~ rules** *pl.* ⚙ Sicherheits-, Unfallverhütungsvorschriften *pl.*; **~ sheet** *s.* Sprungtuch *n* (*Feuerwehr*); **~ valve** *s.* **1.** ⚙ 'Überdruck-, 'Sicherheitsvenˌtil *n*; **2.** *fig.* Ven'til *n*: **sit on the ~** Unterdrückungspolitik treiben; **~ zone** *s.* Verkehrsinsel *f.*
saf·fi·an ['sæfjən] *s.* Saffian(leder *n*) *m.*
saf·flow·er ['sæflaʊə] *s.* **1.** ⚘ Sa'flor *m*, Färberdistel *f*; **2.** getrocknete Sa'florblüten *pl.*: **~ oil** Safloröl *n.*
saf·fron ['sæfrən] *s.* **1.** ⚘ echter Safran; **2.** *pharm., Küche*: Safran *m*; **3.** Safrangelb *n.*
sag [sæg] **I** *v/i.* **1.** sich senken, ab-, 'durchsacken; *bsd.* ⚙ 'durchhängen; **2.** (he'rab)hängen (*a. Unterkiefer etc.*): **~ging shoulders** hängende *od.* abfallende Schultern; **3.** schief hängen (*Rocksaum etc.*); **4.** *fig.* sinken, nachlassen, abfallen; † nachgeben (*Markt, Preise*): **~ging spirits** sinkender Mut; **5.** ⚓ (*mst* **~ to leeward** nach Lee) (ab-)treiben; **II** *s.* **6.** 'Durch-, Absacken *n*; **7.** Senkung *f*; ⚙ 'Durchhang *m*; **8.** † (Preis)Abschwächung *f.*
sa·ga ['sɑːgə] *s.* **1.** Saga *f* (*Heldenerzählung*); **2.** Sage *f*, Erzählung *f*; **3.** *a.* **~ novel** Fa'milienroˌman *m.*
sa·ga·cious [sə'geɪʃəs] *adj.* □ scharfsinnig, klug (*a. Tier*); **sa·gac·i·ty** [sə'gæsɪtɪ] *s.* Scharfsinn *m.*
sage[1] [seɪdʒ] **I** *s.* Weise(r) *m*; **II** *adj.* □ weise, klug, verständig.
sage[2] [seɪdʒ] *s.* ⚘ Salbei *m*, *f*: **~ tea.**
Sag·it·ta·ri·us [ˌsædʒɪ'teərɪəs] *s. ast.* Schütze *m.*
sa·go ['seɪgəʊ] *s.* Sago *m.*
said [sed; səd] **I** *pret. u. p.p. von* **say**: **he is ~ to have been ill** er soll krank gewesen sein; es heißt, er sei krank gewesen; **II** *adj. bsd.* ⚖ vorerwähnt, besagt.
sail [seɪl] **I** *s.* **1.** ⚓ a) Segel *n*, b) *coll.* Segel(werk *n*) *pl.*: **make ~** a) die Segel (bei)setzen, b) mehr Segel beisetzen, c) *a.* **set ~** unter Segel gehen, auslaufen (**for** nach); **take in ~** a) Segel einholen, b) *fig.* zurückstecken; **under ~** unter Segel, auf der Fahrt; **under full ~** mit vollen Segeln; → **trim** 9; **2.** ⚓ (Segel-)Schiff(e *pl.*) *n*: **a fleet of 20 ~**; **~ ho!** Schiff ho! (*in Sicht*); **3.** ⚓ Fahrt *f*: **have a ~** segeln gehen; **4.** ⚙ a) Segel *n e-s Windmühlenflügels*, b) Flügel *m e-r Windmühle*; **II** *v/i.* **5.** a) *allg.* mit e-m Schiff *od.* zu Schiff fahren *od.* reisen, b) fahren (*Schiff*), c) *bsd. sport* segeln; → **wind**[1] 1; **6.** ⚓ a) auslaufen (*Schiff*), b) abfahren, -segeln (**for** *od.* **to** nach): **ready to ~** seeklar; **7.** a) ✈ fliegen, b) *a.* **~ along** *fig.* da'hinschweben, (-)segeln (*Wolke, Vogel*); **8.** *fig.* (*bsd. stolz*) schweben, ‚rauschen', schreiten; **9. ~ in** F ‚sich ranmachen', zupacken; **10. ~ into** F a) *j-n od. et.* attackieren, 'herfallen über (*acc.*), b) ‚rangehen' an (*acc.*), *et.* tüchtig anpacken; **III** *v/t.* **11.** durch'segeln, befahren; **12.** *Segelboot* segeln, *allg. Schiff* steuern; **13.** *poet.* durch *die Luft* schweben; **'~·boat** → **sailing boat.**
sail·er ['seɪlə] *s.* ⚓ Segler *m* (*Schiff*).
sail·ing ['seɪlɪŋ] **I** *s.* **1.** ⚓ (Segel-)Schiffahrt *f*, Navigati'on *f*: **plain** (*od.* **smooth**) **~** *fig.* ‚klare Sache'; **from now on it is all plain ~** von jetzt an geht alles glatt (über die Bühne); **2.** Segelsport *m*, Segeln *n*; **3.** Abfahrt *f* (**for** nach); **II** *adj.* **4.** Segel…; **~ boat** *s.* Segelboot *n*; **~ mas·ter** *s.* Navi'gator *m e-r Jacht*; **~ or·ders** *s. pl.* ⚓ **1.** Fahrtauftrag *m*; **2.** Befehl *m* zum Auslaufen; **~ ship**, **~ ves·sel** *s.* ⚓ Segelschiff *n.*
sail loft *s.* ⚓ Segelmacherwerkstatt *f* (*an Bord*).
sail·or ['seɪlə] *s.* **1.** Ma'trose *m*, Seemann *m*: **~ hat** Matrosenhut *m*; **~s' home** Seemannsheim *n*; **~'s knot** Schifferknoten *m*; **2.** *von Seereisenden*: **be a good ~** seefest sein; **be a bad ~** leicht seekrank werden; **3.** Ma'trosenanzug *m od.* -hut *m für Kinder*; **'sail·or·ly** [-lɪ] *adj.* seemännisch.
'sail·plane I *s.* Segelflugzeug *n*; **II** *v/i.* segelfliegen.
saint [seɪnt] **I** *s.* (*vor Eigennamen* ♀, *abbr.* **St** *od.* **S** [snt]) *eccl.* (*a. fig., iro. a.* **~ on wheels**) Heilige(r *m*) *f*: **St Bernard (dog)** Bernhardiner *m* (*Hund*); **St Anthony's fire** ⚕ *die* Wundrose; **St Elmo's fire** *meteor. das* Elmsfeuer; **(the Court of) St James('s)** der brit. Hof; **St-John's-wort** ⚘ *das* Johanniskraut; **St Monday** *Brit.* F ‚blauer Montag'; **St Martin's summer** Altweibersommer *m*; **St Paul's** *die* Paulskathedrale (*in London*); **St Peter's** *die* Peterskirche (*in Rom*); **St Valentine's day** *der* Valentinstag; **St Vitus's dance** ⚕ *der* Veitstanz; **II** *v/t.* heiligsprechen; **III** *v/i. mst* **~ it** a) wie ein Heiliger leben, b) den Heiligen spielen; **'saint·ed** [-tɪd] *p.p. u. adj.* **1.** *eccl.* heilig(gesprochen); **2.** heilig, fromm; **3.** anbetungswürdig; **4.** geheiligt, geweiht (*Ort*); **5.** selig (*Verstorbener*); **'saint·hood** [-hʊd] *s.* (Stand *m* der) Heiligkeit *f.*
'saint·like → **saintly.**
saint·li·ness ['seɪntlɪnɪs] *s.* Heiligkeit *f* (*a. iro.*); **saint·ly** ['seɪntlɪ] *adj.* **1.** heilig; **2.** fromm; **3.** heiligmäßig (*Leben*).
saith [seθ] *obs. od. poet. 3. sg. pres. von* **say.**
sake [seɪk] *s.*: **for the ~ of** um … (*gen.*) willen, *j-m* zuliebe; wegen (*gen.*), halber (*gen.*): **for heaven's ~** um Himmels willen; **for his ~** ihm zuliebe, seinetwegen; **for my own ~ as well as yours** um meinetwillen ebenso wie um deinetwillen; **for peace(') ~** um des lieben Friedens willen; **for old times' ~**, **for old ~'s ~** eingedenk alter Zeiten.
sal [sæl] *s.* ⚗, *pharm.* Salz *n*: **~ ammoniac** Salmiak(salz) *n.*
sa·laam [sə'lɑːm] **I** *s.* Selam *m* (*orientalischer Gruß*); **II** *v/t. u. v/i.* mit e-m Selam *od.* e-r tiefen Verbeugung (be-)grüßen.
sal·a·bil·i·ty [ˌseɪlə'bɪlətɪ] *s.* † Verkäuflichkeit *f*, Marktfähigkeit *f*; **sal·a·ble** ['seɪləbl] *adj.* □ † **1.** verkäuflich; **2.** marktfähig, gangbar.
sa·la·cious [sə'leɪʃəs] *adj.* □ **1.** geil, lüstern; **2.** ob'szön, zotig; **sa'la·cious·ness** [-nɪs], **sa·lac·i·ty** [sə'læsətɪ] *s.* **1.** Geilheit *f*, Wollust *f*; **2.** Obszöni'tät *f.*
sal·ad ['sæləd] *s.* **1.** Sa'lat *m* (*a. fig. Durcheinander*); **2.** ⚘ Sa'lat(gewächs *n*, -pflanze *f*) *m*; **~ days** *s. pl.*: **in my ~** in m-n wilden Jugendtagen; **~ dress·ing** *s.* Sa'latsoße *f*; **~ oil** *s.* Sa'latöl *n.*
sal·a·man·der ['sæləˌmændə] *s.* **1.** *zo.* Sala'mander *m*; **2.** Sala'mander *m* (*Feu-*

ergeist); **3.** *j-d der große Hitze ertragen kann*; **4.** a) rotglühendes (Schür)Eisen (*zum Anzünden*), b) *glühende Eisenschaufel, die über Gebäck gehalten wird, um es zu bräunen*; **5.** *metall.* Ofensau *f*.

sa·la·mi [sə'lɑːmɪ] *s.* Sa'lami *f*; **~ tac·tics** *s. pl. pol.* Sa'lamitaktik *f*.

sa·lar·i·at [sə'leərɪæt] *s.* (Klasse *f* der) Gehaltsempfänger *pl*.

sal·a·ried ['sælərɪd] *adj.* **1.** (fest)bezahlt, festangestellt: **~ *employee*** Gehaltsempfänger(in), Angestellte(r *m*) *f*; **2.** bezahlt (*Stellung*); **sal·a·ry** ['sælərɪ] **I** *s.* Gehalt *n*, Besoldung *f*; **II** *v/t.* (mit e-m Gehalt) bezahlen, *j-m* ein Gehalt zahlen.

sale [seɪl] *s.* **1.** Verkauf *m*, -äußerung *f*: ***by private ~*** unter der Hand; ***for ~*** zu verkaufen; ***not for ~*** unverkäuflich; ***be on ~*** angeboten *od.* verkauft werden; ***forced ~*** Zwangsverkauf *m*; ***~ of work*** Basar *m*; **2.** ☤ Verkauf *m*, Vertrieb *m*; → ***return*** 23; **3.** ☤ Ab-, 'Umsatz *m*, Verkaufsziffer *f*: ***slow ~*** schleppender Absatz; ***meet with a ready ~*** schnellen Absatz finden, gut ‚gehen'; **4.** (öffentliche) Versteigerung, Aukti'on *f*: ***put up for ~*** versteigern, meistbietend verkaufen; **5.** ☤ *a. pl.* (Sai'son)Schlußverkauf *m*; **sale·a·bil·i·ty** *etc. bsd. Brit.* → ***salability*** *etc.*; **'sale·room** → ***salesroom***.

sales| ac·count [seɪlz] *s.* ☤ Verkaufskonto *n*; **~ a·gent** *s.* (Handels)Vertreter *m*; **~ ap·peal** *s.* Zugkraft *f e-r Ware*; **'~·clerk** *s.* ☤ *Am.* (Laden)Verkäufer (-in); **~ de·part·ment** *s.* ☤ Verkauf(s-abteilung *f*) *m*; **~ drive** *s.* ☤ Ver'kaufskam,pagne *f*; **~ en·gi·neer** *s.* ☤ Ver'kaufsingeni,eur *m*; **~ fi·nance com·pa·ny** *s. Am.* **1.** Absatzfinanzierungsgesellschaft *f*; **2.** 'Teilzahlungskre,ditinsti,tut *n*; **'~·girl** *s.* (Laden)Verkäuferin *f*; **'~,la·dy** *Am.* → ***saleswoman***; **'~·man** [-mən] *s.* [*irr.*] **1.** ☤ a) Verkäufer *m*, b) *Am.* (Handlungs)Reisende(r) *m*, (Handels)Vertreter *m*; **2.** *fig. Am.* Reisende(r) *m* (***of*** in *dat.*); **~ man·ag·er** *s.* ☤ Verkaufsleiter *m*.

sales·man·ship ['seɪlzmənʃɪp] *s.* **1.** a) Verkaufstechnik, b) ☤ Verkaufsgewandtheit *f*, Geschäftstüchtigkeit *f*; **2.** *fig.* Über'zeugungskunst *f*, wirkungsvolle Art, e-e Idee *etc.* zu ‚verkaufen' *od.* ‚an den Mann zu bringen'.

sales| pro·mo·tion *s.* ☤ Verkaufsförderung *f*; **~ re·sist·ance** *s.* ☤ Kaufabneigung *f*, 'Widerstand *m* (des potenti'ellen Kunden); **'~·room** [-rʊm] *s.* Ver'kaufs-, *bsd.* Aukti'onsraum *m*, -lo,kal *n*; **~ slip** *s. Am.* Kassenbeleg *m*; **~ talk** *s.* **1.** ☤ Verkaufsgespräch *n*; **2.** anpreisende Worte *pl.*; **~ tax** *s.* ☤ 'Umsatzsteuer *f*; **'~,wom·an** *s.* [*irr.*] ☤ **1.** Verkäuferin *f*; **2.** *Am.* (Handels)Vertreterin *f*.

Sal·ic[1] ['sælɪk] *adj. hist.* salisch: **~ *law*** Salisches Gesetz.

sal·ic[2] ['sælɪc] *adj. min.* salisch.

sal·i·cyl·ic [,sælɪ'sɪlɪk] *adj.* Salizyl...

sa·li·ence ['seɪljəns], **'sa·li·en·cy** [-sɪ] *s.* **1.** Her'vorspringen *n*, Her'ausragen *n*; **2.** vorspringende Stelle, Vorsprung *m*: ***give ~ to*** *fig.* e-e *Sache* herausstellen; **'sa·li·ent** [-nt] **I** *adj.* **1.** (her)'vorspringend, her'ausragend: **~ *angle*** ausspringender Winkel; **~ *point*** *fig.* springender Punkt; **2.** *fig.* her'vorstechend, ins Auge springend; **3.** *her. u. humor.* springend; **4.** *poet.* (her'vor)sprudelnd; **II** *s.* **5.** ⚔ Frontausbuchtung *f*.

sa·lif·er·ous [sə'lɪfərəs] *adj.* **1.** salzbildend; **2.** *bsd. geol.* salzhaltig.

sa·line I *adj.* ['seɪlaɪn] **1.** salzig, salzhaltig, Salz...; **2.** *pharm.* sa'linisch; **II** *s.* [sə'laɪn] **3.** Salzsee *m od.* -sumpf *m od.* -quelle *f*; **4.** Sa'line *f*, Salzwerk *n*; **5.** ⚗ a) *pl.* Salze *pl.*, b) Salzlösung *f*; **6.** *pharm.* sa'linisches Mittel; **sa·lin·i·ty** [sə'lɪnətɪ] *s.* **1.** Salzigkeit *f*; **2.** Salzhaltigkeit *f*, Salzgehalt *m*.

sa·li·va [sə'laɪvə] *s.* Speichel(flüssigkeit *f*) *m*; **sal·i·var·y** ['sælɪvərɪ] *adj.* Speichel...; **sal·i·vate** ['sælɪveɪt] **I** *v/t.* **1.** (vermehrten) Speichelfluß her'vorrufen bei *j-m*; **II** *v/i.* **2.** Speichelfluß haben; **3.** Speichel absondern; **sal·i·va·tion** [,sælɪ'veɪʃn] *s.* **1.** Speichelabsonderung *f*; **2.** (vermehrter) Speichelfluß.

sal·low[1] ['sæləʊ] *s.* ⚘ (*bsd.* Sal)Weide *f*.

sal·low[2] ['sæləʊ] *adj.* bläßlich, fahl.

sal·ly ['sælɪ] **I** *s.* **1.** ⚔ Ausfall *m*: **~ *port*** *hist.* Ausfallstor *n*; **2.** *fig.* geistreicher Ausspruch *od.* Einfall, Geistesblitz *m*, *a.* (Seiten)Hieb *m*; **3.** (Zornes)Ausbruch *m*; **II** *v/i.* **4.** *oft* **~ *out*** ⚔ e-n Ausfall machen, her'vorbrechen; **5.** *mst* **~ *forth*** (*od.* ***out***) sich aufmachen, aufbrechen.

Sal·ly Lunn [,sælɪ'lʌn] *s. leichter Teekuchen.*

sal·ma·gun·di [,sælmə'gʌndɪ] *s.* **1.** bunter Teller (*Salat, kalter Braten etc.*); **2.** *fig.* Mischmasch *m*.

salm·on ['sæmən] *pl.* **-mons**, *coll.* **-mon I** *s.* **1.** *ichth.* Lachs *m*, Salm *m*: **~ *ladder*** (*od.* ***leap***, ***pass***) Lachsleiter *f*; **~ *peal***, **~ *peel*** junger Lachs; **~ *trout*** Lachsforelle *f*; **2.** *a.* **~ *colo*(*u*)*r***, **~ *pink*** Lachs(farbe *f*) *n*; **II** *adj.* **3.** *a.* **~*-colo*(*u*)*red***, **~*-pink*** lachsfarben, -rot.

sal·mo·nel·la [,sælmə'nelə] *pl.* **-lae** [-liː] *s. biol.* Salmo'nelle *f*.

sa·lon ['sælɔ̃ːŋ] (*Fr.*) *s.* Sa'lon *m* (*a. Ausstellungsraum, vornehmes Geschäft*; *a. fig. schöngeistiger Treffpunkt*).

sa·loon [sə'luːn] *s.* **1.** Sa'lon *m* (*bsd. in Hotels etc.*), (Gesellschafts)Saal *m*: ***billiard ~*** *Brit.* Billiardzimmer *n*; ***shaving ~*** Rasiersalon; **2.** a) ✈ Sa'lon *m* (*Aufenthaltsraum*), b) ⚓ *a.* **~ *cabin*** Ka'bine *f* erster Klasse, c) → ***saloon car***, d) → ***saloon bar***: ***sleeping ~*** 🚂 (Luxus-)Schlafwagen *m*; **3.** *Am.* Kneipe *f*; **4.** *obs.* Sa'lon *m*, Empfangszimmer *n*; **~ bar** *s. Brit. vornehmerer Teil e-s Lokals*; **~ car** *s.* **1.** *mot. Brit.* a) Limou'sine *f*, b) *sport* Tourenwagen *m*; **2.** → **~ car·riage** *s.* 🚂 Sa'lonwagen *m*; **~ deck** *s.* ⚓ Sa'londeck *n*; **~ pis·tol** *s. Brit.* 'Übungspi,stole *f*.

salt [sɔːlt] **I** *s.* **1.** (Koch)Salz *n*: ***eat s.o.'s ~*** *fig.* a) j-s Gast sein, b) von j-m abhängen; ***with a grain of ~*** *fig.* mit Vorbehalt, cum grano salis; ***not to be worth one's ~*** keinen Schuß Pulver wert sein; ***the ~ of the earth*** *bibl. u. fig.* das Salz der Erde; **2.** Salz(fäßchen) *n*: ***above*** (***below***) ***the ~*** am oberen (unteren) Ende der Tafel; **3.** ⚗ Salz *n*; **4.** *oft pl. pharm.* a) (*bsd.* Abführ)Salz *n*, b) *mst* ***smelling ~s*** Riechsalz, c) F → ***Epsom salt***; **5.** *fig.* Würze *f*, Salz *n*; **6.** *fig.* Witz *m*, E'sprit *m*; **7.** *bsd.* ***old ~*** F alter Seebär; **II** *v/t.* **8.** salzen, würzen (*beide a. fig.*); **9.** (ein)salzen, *bsd.* pökeln: **~*ed meat*** Pökel-, Salzfleisch *n*; **10.** ☤ F a) *Bücher etc.* ‚frisieren', b) *Bohrloch etc.* (betrügerisch) ‚anreichern'; **11.** *fig.* durch'setzen mit; **12.** **~ *away*** (*od.* ***down***) a) einsalzen, -pökeln, b) F *Geld etc.* ‚auf die hohe Kante legen'; **III** *adj.* **13.** salzig, Salz...: **~ *spring*** Salzquelle *f*; **14.** ⚘ halo'phil, Salz...; **15.** → ***salted*** 1.

sal·tant ['sæltənt] *adj. her.* springend; **sal·ta·tion** [sæl'teɪʃn] *s.* **1.** Springen *n*; **2.** Sprung *m*; **3.** plötzlicher 'Umschwung; **4.** *biol.* Erbsprung *m*; **'sal·ta·to·ry** [-ətərɪ] *adj.* **1.** springend; **2.** Spring..., Sprung...; **3.** Tanz...; **4.** *fig.* sprunghaft.

'salt,cel·lar *s.* **1.** Salzfäßchen *n*; **2.** *Brit.* F ‚Salzfäßchen' *n* (*Vertiefung über dem Schlüsselbein*).

salt·ed ['sɔːltɪd] *adj.* **1.** gesalzen; **2.** (ein-)gesalzen, gepökelt: **~ *herring*** Salzhering *m*; **3.** *sl.* routi'niert, ausgekocht, erfahren; **'salt·ern** [-tən] *s.* ⚙ **1.** Sa'line *f*; **2.** Salzgarten *m* (*Bassins*).

'salt-free *adj.* salzlos.

salt·i·ness ['sɔːltɪnɪs] *s.* Salzigkeit *f*.

salt| lick *s.* Salzlecke *f* (*für Wild*); **~ marsh** *s.* **1.** Salzsumpf *m*; **2.** Butenmarsch *f*; **~ mine** *s.* Salzbergwerk *n*.

salt·ness ['sɔːltnɪs] *s.* Salzigkeit *f*.

'salt·pan *s.* **1.** ⚙ Salzsiedepfanne *f*; **2.** (*geol.* na'türliches) Ver'dunstungsbas,sin.

salt·pe·ter *Am.*, **salt·pe·tre** *Brit.* ['sɔːlt,piːtə] *s.* ⚗ Sal'peter *m*.

salt| pit *s.* Salzgrube *f*; **'~,wa·ter** *adj.* Salzwasser...; **'~·works** *s. pl. oft sg. konstr.* Sa'line *f*.

salt·y ['sɔːltɪ] *adj.* **1.** salzig; **2.** *fig.* gesalzen, gepfeffert: **~ *remarks***.

sa·lu·bri·ous [sə'luːbrɪəs] *adj.* □ heilsam, gesund, zuträglich, bekömmlich; **sa'lu·bri·ty** [-rətɪ] *s.* Heilsamkeit *f*, Zuträglichkeit *f*.

sal·u·tar·i·ness ['sæljʊtərɪnɪs] → ***salubrity***; **sal·u·tar·y** ['sæljʊtərɪ] *adj.* heilsam, gesund (*a. fig.*).

sal·u·ta·tion [,sælju:'teɪʃn] *s.* **1.** Begrüßung *f*, Gruß *m*: ***in ~*** zum Gruß; **2.** Anrede *f* (*im Brief*); **sa·lu·ta·to·ry** [sə'luːtətərɪ] *adj.* Begrüßungs...: **~ (*oration*)** *bsd. ped. Am.* Begrüßungsrede *f*; **sa·lute** [sə'luːt] **I** *v/t.* **1.** grüßen, begrüßen (*durch e-e Geste etc.*); *weitS.* empfangen, *j-m* begegnen; **~ *with a smile***; **2.** (*dem Auge, dem Ohr*) begegnen, *j-n* begrüßen (*Anblick, Geräusch etc.*); **3.** ⚔, ⚓ salutieren vor (*dat.*), grüßen; **4.** *fig.* grüßen, ehren, feiern; **II** *v/i.* **5.** grüßen (***to*** *acc.*); **6.** ⚔ (***to***) salutieren (vor *dat.*), grüßen (*acc.*); **7.** Sa'lut schießen; **III** *s.* **8.** Gruß *m* (*a. fenc.*), Begrüßung *f*; **9.** ⚔, ⚓ a) Gruß *m*, Ehrenbezeigung *f*, b) Sa'lut *m* (***of six guns*** von 6 Schuß): **~ *of colo*(*u*)*rs*** ⚓ Flaggensalut; ***stand at the ~*** salutieren; ***take the ~*** a) den Gruß erwidern, b) die Parade abnehmen, c) die Front (der Ehrenkompanie) abschreiten; **10.** *obs.* (Begrüßungs)Kuß *m*; **11.** *Am.* Frosch *m* (*Feuerwerk*).

sal·vage ['sælvɪdʒ] **I** *s.* **1.** a) Bergung *f*, Rettung *f* (*Schiff, Ladung etc.*), b) Bergungsgut *n*, c) *a.* **~ *money*** Bergegeld *n*: **~ *vessel*** Bergungs-, *a.* Hebeschiff *n*, d) *Versicherung*: Wert *m* der geretteten Güter; **2.** *a.* ~ ***work*** Aufräumungsarbeiten *pl.*; **3.** ⚙ a) verwertbares 'Altmateri,al, b) 'Wiederverwertung *f*: ~ ***value*** Schrottwert *m*; **4.** *fig.* (Er-)Rettung *f* (***from*** aus); **II** *v/t.* **5.** bergen, retten (*a.* ⚓ *u. fig.*); **6.** *Schrott etc.* verwerten.

sal·va·tion [sæl'veɪʃn] *s.* **1.** (Er)Rettung *f*; **2.** a) Heil *n*, Rettung *f*, b) Retter *m*; **3.** *eccl.* a) (Seelen)Heil *n*, b) Erlösung *f*: ***2 Army*** Heilsarmee *f*; **sal'va·tion·ist** [-nɪst] *s. eccl.* Mitglied *n* der 'Heilsar,mee.

salve¹ [sælv] **I** *s.* **1.** (Heil)Salbe *f*; **2.** *fig.* Balsam *m*, Pflaster *n*, Trost *m*; **3.** *fig.* Beruhigungsmittel *n fürs Gewissen etc.*; **II** *v/t.* **4.** (ein)salben; **5.** *fig. Gewissen etc.* beschwichtigen; **6.** *fig. Mangel* beschönigen; **7.** *Schaden*, *Zweifel etc.* beheben.

salve² [sælv] → ***salvage*** 5.

sal·ver ['sælvə] *s.* Ta'blett *n*.

sal·vo¹ ['sælvəʊ] *pl.* **-vos, -voes** *s.* **1.** ⚔ a) Salve *f*, Lage *f*, b) *a.* ~ ***bombing*** ✈ Schüttwurf *m*; ~ ***fire*** a) ⚔ Laufsalve, b) ⚓ Salvenfeuer; **2.** *fig.* (*Beifalls*)Salve *f*.

sal·vo² ['sælvəʊ] *pl.* **-vos** *s.* **1.** Ausrede *f*; **2.** *bsd.* ⚖ Vorbehalt(sklausel *f*) *m*.

sal·vor ['sælvə] *s.* ⚓ **1.** Berger *m*; **2.** Bergungsschiff *n*.

Sa·mar·i·tan [sə'mærɪtən] **I** *s.* Samari'taner(in), Sama'riter(in): ***good*** ~ *bibl. u. fig.* barmherziger Samariter; **II** *adj.* sama'ritisch; *fig.* barmherzig.

same [seɪm] **I** *adj.* **1.** selb, gleich, nämlich: ***at the*** ~ ***price as*** zu demselben Preis wie; ***it comes to the*** ~ ***thing*** es läuft auf dasselbe hinaus; ***the very*** (*od.* ***just the*** *od.* ***exactly the***) ~ ***thing*** genau dasselbe; ***one and the*** ~ ***thing*** ein u. dasselbe; ***he is no longer the*** ~ ***man*** er ist nicht mehr der gleiche *od.* der alte; → ***time*** 4; **2.** *ohne Artikel fig.* eintönig; **II** *pron.* **3.** der-, die-, dasselbe, der *od.* die *od.* das gleiche: ***it is much the*** ~ es ist (so) ziemlich das gleiche; ~ ***here*** F so geht es mir auch, ‚ganz meinerseits'; ***it is all the*** ~ ***to me*** es ist mir ganz gleich *od.* einerlei; **4.** ***the*** ~ a) *a.* ⚖ der- *od.* dieselbe, die besagte Person, b) ⚖ der- *od.* dieselbe, die erwähnte Person, *a. eccl.* er, sie, es, dieser, diese, dies(es); **5.** *ohne Artikel* ⚓ *od.* F der- *od.* die- *od.* dasselbe: ***£5 for alterations to*** ~; **III** *adv.* **6.** ***the*** ~ in derselben Weise, genau so, ebenso (***as*** wie): ***all the*** ~ gleichviel, trotzdem; ***just the*** ~ F a) genau so, b) trotzdem; (***the***) ~ ***to you!*** (*danke*,) gleichfalls!; **'same·ness** [-nɪs] *s.* **1.** Gleichheit *f*, Identi'tät *f*; **2.** Einförmigkeit *f*, -tönigkeit *f*.

sam·let ['sæmlɪt] *s.* junger Lachs.

sam·pan ['sæmpæn] *s.* Sampan *m* (*chinesisches* [*Haus*]*Boot*).

sam·ple ['sɑːmpl] **I** *s.* **1.** ⚓ a) (Waren-, Quali'täts)Probe *f*, (Stück-, Typen-) Muster *n*, b) Probepackung *f*, c) (Ausstellungs)Muster *n*, d) Stichprobe(nmuster *n*) *f*: ***by*** ~ ***post*** (als) Muster ohne Wert; ***up to*** ~ dem Muster entsprechend; ~***s only*** Muster ohne Wert; **2.** *Statistik*: Sample *n*, Stichprobe *f*; **3.** *fig.* Probe *f*: ***a*** ~ ***of his courage***; ***that's a*** ~ ***of her behavio(u)r*** das ist typisch für sie; **II** *v/t.* **4.** probieren, e-e Probe nehmen von, *bsd. Küche*: kosten; **5.** e-e Stichprobe machen bei; **6.** e-e Probe zeigen von; ⚓ *et.* bemustern; **7.** als Muster dienen für; **8.** *Computer*: a) abfragen, b) abtasten; **III** *v/i.* **9.** ~ ***out*** ausfallen; **IV** *adj.* **10.** Muster…(*-buch*, *-karte*, *-koffer etc.*), Probe…; **'sam·pler** [-lə] *s.* **1.** Probierer(in), Prüfer *m*; **2.** *Stickerei*: Sticktuch *n*; **3.** *TV* Farbschalter *m*; **4.** *Computer*: Abtaster *m*; **'sam·pling** [-lɪŋ] *s.* **1.** ⚓ a) 'Musterkollekti,on *f*, b) Bemusterung *f*; **2.** Stichprobenerhebung *f*.

Sam·son ['sæmsn] *s. fig.* Samson *m*, Herkules *m*.

Sam·u·el ['sæmjʊəl] *npr. u. s. bibl.* (das Buch) Samuel *m*.

san·a·tive ['sænətɪv] *adj.* heilend, heilsam, -kräftig; **san·a·to·ri·um** [,sænə'tɔːrɪəm] *pl.* **-ri·ums, -ri·a** [-rɪə] *s.* ⚕ **1.** Sana'torium *n*, *bsd.* a) Lungenheilstätte *f*, b) Erholungsheim *n*; **2.** (*bsd.* Höhen-) Luftkurort *m*; **3.** *Brit.* (Inter'nats-) Krankenzimmer *n*; **'san·a·to·ry** [-tərɪ] → ***sanative***.

sanc·ti·fi·ca·tion [,sæŋktɪfɪ'keɪʃn] *s. eccl.* **1.** Heilig(mach)ung *f*; **2.** Weihung *f*, Heiligung *f*; **sanc·ti·fied** ['sæŋktɪfaɪd] *adj.* **1.** geheiligt, geweiht; **2.** heilig u. unverletzlich; **3.** → ***sanctimonious***; **sanc·ti·fy** ['sæŋktɪfaɪ] *v/t.* heiligen: a) weihen, b) (von Sünden) reinigen, c) *fig.* rechtfertigen: ***the end sanctifies the means*** der Zweck heiligt die Mittel.

sanc·ti·mo·ni·ous [,sæŋktɪ'məʊnjəs] *adj.* □ frömmelnd, scheinheilig; **,sanc·ti'mo·ni·ous·ness** [-nɪs], **sanc·ti·mo·ny** ['sæŋktɪmənɪ] *s.* Scheinheiligkeit *f*, Frömme'lei *f*.

sanc·tion ['sæŋkʃn] **I** *s.* **1.** Sankti'on *f*, (nachträgliche) Billigung *od.* Zustimmung: ***give one's*** ~ ***to*** → 3 a; **2.** ⚖ a) Sanktionierung *f e-s Gesetzes etc.*, b) *pol.* Sankti'on *f*, Zwangsmittel *n*, c) *gesetzliche* Strafe, d) *hist.* De'kret *n*; **II** *v/t.* **3.** sanktionieren: a) billigen, gutheißen, b) dulden, c) *Eid etc.* bindend machen, d) Gesetzeskraft verleihen (*dat.*).

sanc·ti·ty ['sæŋktətɪ] *s.* **1.** Heiligkeit *f* (*a. fig. Unverletzlichkeit*); **2.** *pl.* heilige Ide'ale *pl. od.* Gefühle *pl.*

sanc·tu·ar·y ['sæŋktjʊərɪ] *s.* **1.** Heiligtum *n* (*a. fig.*); **2.** *eccl.* Heiligtum *n*, heilige Stätte; *bsd. bibl.* Aller'heiligste(s) *n*; **3.** Frei- (*fig. a.* Zufluchts)stätte *f*, A'syl *n*: (***rights of***) ~ Asylrecht *n*; ***break the*** ~ das Asylrecht verletzen; **4.** *hunt.* a) Schonzeit *f*, b) Schutzgebiet *n*.

sanc·tum ['sæŋktəm] *s.* Heiligtum *n*: a) heilige Stätte, b) *fig.* Pri'vat-, Studierzimmer *n*, c) innerste Sphäre; ~ **sanc·to·rum** [sæŋk'tɔːrəm] *s. eccl.*, *a. humor. das* Aller'heiligste.

sand [sænd] **I** *s.* **1.** Sand *m*: ***built on*** ~ *fig.* auf Sand gebaut; ***rope of*** ~ *fig.* trügerische Sicherheit; **2.** *oft pl.* a) Sandbank *f*, b) Sand(fläche *f*, -wüste *f*) *m*: ***plough the*** ~(***s***) *fig.* s-e Zeit verschwenden; **3.** *mst pl.* Sand(körner *pl.*) *m*: ***his*** ~***s are running out*** s-e Tage sind gezählt; **4.** *Am. sl.* ‚Mumm' *m*; **II** *v/t.* **5.** mit Sand bestreuen; **6.** (ab-) schmirgeln.

san·dal¹ ['sændl] *s.* San'dale *f*.

san·dal² ['sændl], **'~·wood** *s.* **1.** (rotes) Sandelholz; **2.** Sandelbaum *m*.

'sand|·bag [-ndb-] **I** *s.* **1.** Sandsack *m*; **II** *v/t.* **2.** *bsd.* ⚔ mit Sandsäcken befestigen; **3.** mit e-m Sandsack niederschlagen; **'~·bank** [-ndb-] *s.* Sandbank *f*; **'~·blast** [-ndb-] ⚙ **I** *s.* Sandstrahl(gebläse *n*) *m*; **II** *v/t.* sandstrahlen; **'~·box** [-ndb-] *s.* **1.** *hist.* Streusandbüchse *f*; **2.** *Gießerei*: Sandform *f*; **3.** Sandkasten *m*; **'~·boy** [-ndb-] *s.*: (***as***) ***happy as a*** ~ kreuzfidel; ~ **drift** *s. geol.* Flugsand *m*.

sand·er ['sændə] *s.* ⚙ **1.** Sandstrahlgebläse *n*; **2.** 'Sandpa,pier,schleifma,schine *f*.

'sand|·fly *s.* a) Sandfliege *f*, b) Gnitze *f*, c) Kriebelmücke *f*; **'~·glass** *s.* Sanduhr *f*, Stundenglas *n*; **'~·grouse** *s. orn.* Flughuhn *n*; **'~·lot** *s. Am.* Sandplatz *m* (*Behelfsspielplatz für Baseball etc.*); **'~·man** [-ndmæn] *s.* [*irr.*] Sandmann *m*, -männchen *n*; **'~-,mar·tin** [-nd,m-] *s. orn.* Uferschwalbe *f*; **'~,pa·per** [-nd,p-] **I** *s.* 'Sandpa,pier *n*; **II** *v/t.* (ab)schmirgeln; **'~,pip·er** [-nd,p-] *s. orn.* Flußuferläufer *m*; **'~·pit** [-ndp-] *s.* **1.** Sandgrube *f*; **2.** Sandkasten *m*; ~ **shoes** *s. pl.* Strandschuhe *pl.*; ~ **spout** *s.* Sandhose *f*; **'~·stone** [-nds-] *s. geol.* Sandstein *m*; **'~·storm** [-nds-] *s.* Sandsturm *m*; ~ **ta·ble** *s.* ⚔ Sandkasten *m*; ~ **trap** *s. Golf*: Sandhindernis *n*.

sand·wich ['sænwɪdʒ] **I** *s.* Sandwich *n* (*belegtes Doppelbrot*): ***open*** ~ belegtes Brot; ***sit*** ~ *fig.* eingezwängt sitzen; **II** *v/t. a.* ~ ***in*** *fig.* einlegen, schieben; einklemmen, -zwängen; *sport Gegner* ‚in die Zange nehmen'; ~ **cake** *s.* Schichttorte *f*; ~ **course** *s. ped. Kurs, bei dem sich theoretische u. praktische Ausbildung abwechseln*; ~ **man** [-mæn] *s.* [*irr.*] Sandwichman *m*, Pla'katträger *m*.

sand·y¹ ['sændɪ] *adj.* **1.** sandig, Sand…: ~ ***desert*** Sandwüste *f*; **2.** *fig.* sandfarben; rotblond (*Haare*); **3.** sandartig; **4.** *fig.* a) unsicher, b) *Am. sl.* frech.

Sand·y² ['sændɪ] *s.* **1.** *bsd. Scot. Kurzform für* ***Alexander***; **2.** (*Spitzname für*) Schotte *m*.

sand yacht *s.* Strandsegler *m*.

sane [seɪn] *adj.* □ **1.** geistig gesund *od.* nor'mal; **2.** vernünftig, gescheit.

San·for·ize ['sænfəraɪz] *v/t.* sanforisieren (*Gewebe schrumpffest machen*).

sang [sæŋ] *pret. u. p.p. von* ***sing***.

sang·froid [,sɑ̃ːŋ'frwɑː] (*Fr.*) *s.* Kaltblütigkeit *f*.

San·grail [sæŋ'greɪl], **San·gre·al** ['sæŋgrɪəl] *s.* der Heilige Gral.

san·gui·nar·y ['sæŋgwɪnərɪ] *adj.* □ **1.** blutig, mörderisch (*Kampf etc.*); **2.** blutdürstig, grausam: ***a*** ~ ***person***; ~ ***laws***; **3.** blutig, Blut…; **4.** *Brit.* unflätig; **san·guine** ['sæŋgwɪn] **I** *adj.* □ **1.** heiter, lebhaft, leichtblütig; **2.** 'voll-, heißblütig, hitzig; **3.** zuversichtlich (*a. Bericht*, *Hoffnung etc.*): ***be*** ~ ***of success*** zuversichtlich auf Erfolg rechnen; **4.** rot, blühend, von gesunder Gesichtsfarbe; **5.** ⚕ *hist.* sangu'inisch; **6.** (blut-) rot; **II** *s.* **7.** Rötelstift *m*; **8.** Rötelzeichnung *f*; **san·guin·e·ous** [sæŋ'gwɪnɪəs] *adj.* → ***sanguine*** I.

sa·ni·es ['seɪnɪiːz] *s.* ⚕ pu'trider Eiter, Jauche *f*.

san·i·tar·i·an [,sænɪ'teərɪən] **I** *adj.* **1.** → ***sanitary*** 1; **II** *s.* **2.** Hygi'eniker *m*; **3.** Ge'sundheitsa,postel *m*; **,san·i'tar·i·um** [-rɪəm] *pl.* **-i·ums, -i·a** [-rɪə] *s. bsd. Am. für* ***sanatorium***; **san·i·tar·y** ['sænɪtərɪ]

I *adj.* □ **1.** hygi'enisch, Gesundheits…, (*a.* ⚙) sani'tär: ~ ***towel*** (*Am.* ***napkin***) Damenbinde *f*; **2.** hygi'enisch (einwandfrei), gesund; **II** *s.* **3.** *Am.* öffentliche Bedürfnisanstalt; **ˌsan·i'ta·tion** [-'teɪʃn] *s.* **1.** sani'täre Einrichtungen *pl.* (*in Gebäuden*); **2.** Gesundheitspflege *f*, -wesen *n*, Hygi'ene *f*.

san·i·tize ['sænɪtaɪz] *v/t.* **1.** → ***sterilize*** a; **2.** *fig. Image etc.* ‚aufpolieren'.

san·i·ty ['sænətɪ] *s.* **1.** geistige Gesundheit; *bsd.* ⚖ Zurechnungsfähigkeit *f*; **2.** gesunder Verstand.

sank [sæŋk] *pret. von* ***sink***.

san·se·rif [ˌsæn'serɪf] *s. typ.* Gro'tesk *f*.

San·skrit ['sænskrɪt] *s.* Sanskrit *n*.

San·ta Claus [ˌsæntə'klɔːz] *npr.* der Nikolaus, der Weihnachtsmann.

sap¹ [sæp] **I** *s.* **1.** ♀ Saft *m*; **2.** *fig.* (Lebens)Saft *m*, (-)Kraft *f*, Mark *n*; **3.** *a.* ~-***wood*** Splint(holz *n*) *m*; **II** *v/t.* **4.** entsaften.

sap² [sæp] **I** *s.* **1.** ⚔ Sappe *f*, Grabenkopf *m*; **II** *v/t.* **2.** (*a. fig. Gesundheit etc.*) unter'graben, -mi'nieren; **3.** *Kräfte etc.* erschöpfen, schwächen.

sap³ [sæp] *s.* F Trottel *m*.

sap⁴ [sæp] *Am. sl.* **I** *s.* Totschläger *m* (*Waffe*); **II** *v/t.* *j-n* (mit e-m Totschläger) bewußtlos schlagen.

'sap·head *s.* **1.** ⚔ Sappenkopf *m*; **2.** F Trottel *m*.

sap·id ['sæpɪd] *adj.* **1.** e-n Geschmack habend; **2.** schmackhaft; **3.** *fig.* interes'sant; **sa·pid·i·ty** [sə'pɪdətɪ] *s.* Schmackhaftigkeit *f*.

sa·pi·ence ['seɪpjəns] *s. mst iro.* Weisheit *f*; **'sa·pi·ent** [-nt] *adj.* □ *mst iro.* weise.

sap·less ['sæplɪs] *adj.* saftlos (*a. fig. kraftlos*).

sap·ling ['sæplɪŋ] *s.* **1.** junger Baum, Schößling *m*; **2.** *fig.* Grünschnabel *m*, Jüngling *m*.

sap·o·na·ceous [ˌsæpəʊ'neɪʃəs] *adj.* **1.** seifenartig, seifig; **2.** *fig.* glatt.

sa·pon·i·fi·ca·tion [səˌpɒnɪfɪ'keɪʃn] *s.* ⚗ Verseifung *f*; **sa·pon·i·fy** [sə'pɒnɪfaɪ] *v/t. u. v/i.* verseifen.

sap·per ['sæpə] *s.* ⚔ Pio'nier *m*, Sap'peur *m*.

Sap·phic ['sæfɪk] **I** *adj.* **1.** sapphisch; **2.** ♀ lesbisch; **II** *s.* **3.** sapphischer Vers.

sap·phire ['sæfaɪə] **I** *s.* **1.** *min.* Saphir *m* (*a. am Plattenspieler*); **2.** *a.* ~ ***blue*** Saphirblau *n*; **3.** *orn.* Saphirkolibri *m*; **II** *adj.* **4.** saphirblau; **5.** Saphir…

sap·py ['sæpɪ] *adj.* **1.** saftig; **2.** *fig.* kraftvoll, markig; **3.** *sl.* blöd, doof.

Sar·a·cen ['særəsn] **I** *s.* Sara'zene *m*, Sara'zenin *f*; **II** *adj.* sara'zenisch.

sar·casm ['sɑːkæzəm] *s.* Sar'kasmus *m*: a) beißender Spott, b) sar'kastische Bemerkung; **sar·cas·tic** [sɑː'kæstɪk] *adj.* (□ ~***ally***) sarkastisch.

sar·co·ma [sɑː'kəʊmə] *pl.* **-ma·ta** [-mətə] *s.* ⚕ Sar'kom *n* (*Geschwulst*); **sar'coph·a·gous** [-'kɒfəgəs] *adj. zo.* fleischfressend; **sar'coph·a·gus** [-'kɒfəgəs] *pl.* **-gi** [-gaɪ] *s.* Sarko'phag *m* (*Steinsarg*).

sard [sɑːd] *s. min.* Sard(er) *m*.

sar·dine¹ [sɑː'diːn] *pl.* **sar·dines** *od. coll.* **sar·dine** *s. ichth.* Sar'dine *f*: ***packed like*** ~***s*** zs.-gepfercht wie die Heringe.

sar·dine² ['sɑːdaɪn] → ***sard***.

sar·don·ic [sɑː'dɒnɪk] *adj.* (□ ~***ally***) ⚕ *u. fig.* sar'donisch.

sa·ri ['sɑːrɪ] *s.* Sari *m*.

sark [sɑːk] *s. Scot. od. dial.* Hemd *n*.

sark·y ['sɑːkɪ] F *für* ***sarcastic***.

sa·rong [sə'rɒŋ] *s.* Sarong *m*.

sar·sen ['sɑːsn] *s. geol.* großer Sandsteinblock.

sar·to·ri·al [sɑː'tɔːrɪəl] *adj.* □ **1.** Schneider…; **2.** Kleidung(s)…: ~ ***elegance*** Eleganz der Kleidung; **sar'to·ri·us** [-rɪəs] *s. anat.* Schneidermuskel *m*.

sash¹ [sæʃ] *s.* Schärpe *f*.

sash² [sæʃ] *s.* **1.** (schiebbarer) Fensterrahmen; **2.** schiebbarer Teil *e-s Schiebefensters*; ~ **saw** *s.* ⚙ Schlitzsäge *f*; ~ **win·dow** *s.* Schiebe-, Fallfenster *n*.

Sas·se·nach ['sæsənæk] *Scot. u. Irish* **I** *s.* ‚Sachse' *m*, Engländer *m*; **II** *adj.* englisch.

sat [sæt] *pret. u. p.p. von* ***sit***.

Sa·tan ['seɪtən] *s.* Satan *m*, Teufel *m* (*fig.* ♀); **sa·tan·ic** [sə'tænɪk] *adj.* (□ ~***ally***) sa'tanisch, teuflisch.

satch·el ['sætʃəl] *s.* Schultasche *f*, -mappe *f*, *bsd.* Schulranzen *m*.

sate¹ [seɪt] *v/t.* über'sättigen: ***be*** ~***d with*** übersättigt sein von.

sate² [sæt; seɪt] *obs. für* ***sat***.

sa·teen [sæ'tiːn] *s.* ('Baum)Wollsaˌtin *m*.

sat·el·lite ['sætəlaɪt] *s.* **1.** *ast.* a) Satel'lit *m*, Tra'bant *m*, b) (*künstlicher*) ('Erd-)Satelˌlit *m*: ~ ***picture*** Satellitenbild *n*; ~ ***transmission*** *TV etc.* Satellitenübertragung *f*; **2.** Tra'bant *m*, Anhänger *m*; **3.** *fig.* a) *a.* ~ ***state*** *od.* ***nation*** *pol.* Satel'lit(enstaat) *m*, b) *a.* ~ ***town*** Tra'bantenstadt *f*, c) *a.* ~ ***airfield*** Ausweichflugplatz *m*, d) ✝ Zweigfirma *f*.

sa·ti·ate ['seɪʃɪeɪt] *v/t.* **1.** über'sättigen; **2.** vollauf sättigen *od.* befriedigen; **sa·ti·a·tion** [ˌseɪʃɪ'eɪʃn] *s.* (Über)'Sättigung *f*; **sa·ti·e·ty** [sə'taɪətɪ] *s.* **1.** (***of***) Übersättigung *f* (mit), 'Überdruß *m* (an *dat.*): ***to*** ~ bis zum Überdruß; **2.** Sattheit *f*.

sat·in ['sætɪn] **I** *s.* ⚙ **1.** Sa'tin *m*, Atlas *m* (*Stoff*); **2.** *a.* ***white*** ~ *sl.* Gin *m*; **II** *adj.* **3.** Satin…; **4.** a) seidenglatt, b) glänzend; **III** *v/t.* **5.** ⚙ satinieren, glätten; **sat·i·net(te)** [ˌsætɪ'net] *s.* Halbatlas *m*.

'sat·in|-ˌfin·ished *adj.* ⚙ mattiert; ~ **pap·er** *s.* satiniertes Pa'pier, 'Atlaspaˌpier *n*.

sat·in·y ['sætɪnɪ] *adj.* seidig.

sat·ire ['sætaɪə] *s.* **1.** Sa'tire *f*, *bsd.* a) Spottgedicht *n*, -schrift *f* ([***up***]***on*** auf *acc.*), b) sa'tirische Litera'tur, c) Spott *m*; **2.** *fig.* Hohn *m* ([***up***]***on*** auf *acc.*); **sa·tir·ic, sa·tir·i·cal** [sə'tɪrɪk(l)] *adj.* □ sa'tirisch; **sat·i·rist** ['sætərɪst] *s.* Sa'tiriker(in); **sat·i·rize** ['sætəraɪz] *v/t.* verspotten, e-e Sa'tire machen auf (*acc.*).

sat·is·fac·tion [ˌsætɪs'fækʃn] *s.* **1.** Befriedigung *f*, Zu'friedenstellung *f*: ***find*** ~ ***in*** Befriedigung finden in (*dat.*); ***give*** ~ befriedigen; **2.** (***at, with***) Zufriedenheit *f* (mit), Befriedigung *f*, Genugtuung *f* (über *acc.*): ***to the*** ~ ***of all*** zur Zufriedenheit aller; **3.** *eccl.* Sühne *f*; **4.** Satisfakti'on *f*, Genugtuung *f* (*Duell etc.*); **5.** ⚖, ✝ Befriedigung *f e-s Anspruchs*; Erfüllung *f e-r Verpflichtung*; (Be)Zahlung *f e-r Schuld*; **6.** Gewißheit *f*: ***show to the court's*** ~ ⚖ einwandfrei glaubhaft machen; **ˌsat·is'fac·to·ri·ness** [-ktərɪnɪs] *s. das* Befriedigende; **ˌsat·is'fac·to·ry** [-ktərɪ] *adj.* □ **1.** befriedigend, zu'friedenstellend; **2.** *eccl.* sühnend; **sat·is·fy** ['sætɪsfaɪ] **I** *v/t.* **1.** befriedigen, zu'friedenstellen, genügen (*dat.*): ***be satisfied with s.th.*** mit et. zufrieden sein; **2.** a) *j-n* sättigen, b) *Hunger etc.*, *a. Neugier* stillen, c) *fig. Wunsch* erfüllen, *Bedürfnis*, *a. Trieb* befriedigen; **3.** ✝ *Anspruch* befriedigen; *Schuld* begleichen, tilgen; *e-r Verpflichtung* nachkommen; *Bedingungen*, ⚖ *a. Urteil* erfüllen; **4.** a) *j-n* entschädigen, b) *Gläubiger* befriedigen; **5.** *den Anforderungen* entsprechen, genügen; **6.** 𝒜 *Bedingung*, *Gleichung* erfüllen; **7.** *j-n* über'zeugen (***of*** von): ~ ***o.s. that*** sich überzeugen *od.* vergewissern, daß; ***I am satisfied that*** ich bin davon (*od.* habe mich) überzeugt, daß; **II** *v/i.* **8.** befriedigen; **sat·is·fy·ing** ['sætɪsfaɪɪŋ] *adj.* □ **1.** befriedigend, zu'friedenstellend; **2.** sättigend.

sa·trap ['sætrəp] *s. hist.* Sa'trap *m* (*a. fig.*), Statthalter *m*.

sat·u·rant ['sætʃərənt] **I** *adj.* **1.** *bsd.* ⚗ sättigend; **II** *s.* **2.** neutralisierender Stoff; **3.** ⚕ Mittel *n* gegen Magensäure; **sat·u·rate** ['sætʃəreɪt] *v/t.* **1.** ⚗ *u. fig.* sättigen, saturieren (*a.* ✝ *Markt*); **2.** (durch)'tränken, durch'setzen: ***be*** ~***d with*** *fig.* erfüllt *od.* durchdrungen sein von; **3.** ⚔ mit Bombenteppichen belegen; **sat·u·rat·ed** ['sætʃəreɪtɪd] *adj.* **1.** durch'tränkt, -'setzt; **2.** tropfnaß; **3.** satt (*Farbe*); **4.** ⚗ a) *a. fig.* saturiert, gesättigt, b) reakti'onsträge.

sat·u·ra·tion [ˌsætʃə'reɪʃn] *s.* **1.** *bsd.* ⚗, *phys. u. fig.* Sättigung *f*, Saturierung *f*; **2.** (Durch)'Tränkung *f*, Durch'setzung *f*; **3.** Sattheit *f* (*Farbe*); ~ **bomb·ing** *s.* ⚔ Bombenteppich(e *pl.*) *m*; ~ **point** *s.* ⚗ Sättigungspunkt *m*.

Sat·ur·day ['sætədɪ] *s.* Sonnabend *m*, Samstag *m*: ***on*** ~ am Sonnabend *od.* Samstag; ***on*** ~***s*** sonnabends, samstags.

Sat·urn ['sætən] *s.* **1.** *antiq.* Sa'turn(us) *m* (*Gott*); **2.** *ast.* Sa'turn *m* (*Planet*); **3.** ⚗ *hist.* Blei *n*; **4.** *her.* Schwarz *n*; **Sat·ur·na·li·a** [ˌsætə'neɪljə] *s. pl. antiq.* Satur'nalien *pl.*; **Sat·ur·na·li·an** [ˌsætə'neɪljən] *adj.* **1.** *antiq.* satur'nalisch; **2.** ♀ *fig.* orgi'astisch; **Sa·tur·ni·an** [sæ'tɜːnjən] *adj.* **1.** *ast.* Saturn…; **2.** *myth*, *a. fig. poet.* sa'turnisch: ~ ***age*** *fig.* goldenes Zeitalter; **'sat·ur·nine** [-naɪn] *adj.* □ **1.** düster, finster (*Person*, *Gesicht etc.*); **2.** ♀ im Zeichen des Sa'turn geboren; **3.** *min.* Blei…

sat·yr ['sætə] *s.* **1.** *oft* ♀ *myth.* Satyr *m* (*Waldgott*); **2.** *fig.* Satyr *m* (*geiler Mensch*); **3.** ⚕ Satyro'mane *m*; **sat·y·ri·a·sis** [ˌsætə'raɪəsɪs] *s.* ⚕ Saty'riasis *f*; **sa·tyr·ic** [sə'tɪrɪk] *adj.* Satyr…, satyrhaft.

sauce [sɔːs] **I** *s.* **1.** Sauce *f*, Soße *f*, Tunke *f*: ***hunger is the best*** ~ Hunger ist der beste Koch; ***what is*** ~ ***for the goose is*** ~ ***for the gander*** was dem einen recht ist, ist dem andern billig; **2.** *fig.* Würze *f*; **3.** *Am.* Kom'pott *n*; **4.** F Frechheit *f*; **5.** ⚙ a) Beize *f*, b) (Tabak-)Brühe *f*; **II** *v/t.* **6.** mit Soße würzen; **7.** *fig.* würzen; **8.** F frech sein zu; **'~·boat** *s.* Saucière *f*, Soßenschüssel *f*; **'~·dish** *s. Am.* Kom'pottschüssel *f*, -schale *f*; **'~·pan** [-pən] *s.* Kochtopf *m*, Kasse'rolle *f.*

sau·cer ['sɔːsə] *s.* 'Untertasse *f*; → ***flying saucer***; ~ **eye** [-əraɪ] *s.* Glotz-, Kulleraugе *n*; '**~-eyed** [-əraɪd] *adj.* glotzäugig.

sau·ci·ness ['sɔːsɪnɪs] *s.* **1.** Frechheit *f*; **2.** Keßheit *f*; **sau·cy** ['sɔːsɪ] *adj.* ☐ **1.** frech, unverschämt; **2.** F keß, flott, fesch: ***a ~ hat***.

sau·na ['sɔːnə] *s.* Sauna *f.*

saun·ter ['sɔːntə] **I** *v/i.* schlendern: ***~ about*** um'herschlendern, (-)bummeln; **II** *s.* (Um'her)Schlendern *n*, Bummel *m.*

sau·ri·an ['sɔːrɪən] *zo.* **I** *s.* Saurier *m*; **II** *adj.* Saurier…, Echsen…

sau·sage ['sɒsɪdʒ] *s.* **1.** Wurst *f*; **2.** *a.* ***~ balloon*** ⚔ F 'Fesselbal,lon *m*; **3.** *sl.* Deutsche(r *m*) *f*; **~ dog** *s. Brit.* F Dakkel *m*; **~ meat** *s.* Wurstmasse *f*, Brät *n.*

sau·té ['səʊteɪ] *(Fr.)* **I** *adj. Küche:* sau'té, sautiert; **II** *s.* Sau'té *n.*

sav·age ['sævɪdʒ] **I** *adj.* ☐ **1.** *allg.* wild: a) primi'tiv (*Volk etc.*), b) ungezähmt (*Tier*), c) bru'tal, grausam, d) F wütend, e) wüst (*Landschaft*); **II** *s.* **2.** Wilde(r *m*) *f*; **3.** Rohling *m*; **4.** bösartiges Tier, *bsd.* bissiges Pferd; **III** *v/t.* **5.** *j-n* übel zurichten, *a. fig. j-m* übel mitspielen; **6.** *j-n* anfallen, beißen (*Pferd etc.*); '**sav·age·ness** [-nɪs] *s.* **1.** Wildheit *f*, Roheit *f*, Grausamkeit *f*; **2.** Wut *f*, Bissigkeit *f*; '**sav·age·ry** [-dʒərɪ] *s.* **1.** Unzivilisiertheit *f*, Wildheit *f*; **2.** Roheit *f*, Grausamkeit *f.*

sa·van·na(h) [sə'vænə] *s. geogr.* Sa'vanne *f.*

sa·vant ['sævənt] *s.* großer Gelehrter.

save¹ [seɪv] **I** *v/t.* **1.** (er)retten (***from*** von, vor *dat.*): ***~ s.o.'s life*** j-m das Leben retten; **2.** ⚓ bergen; **3.** bewahren, schützen (***from*** vor *dat.*): ***God ~ the Queen*** Gott erhalte die Königin; ***~ the situation*** die Situation retten; → ***appearance*** 3, ***face*** 4, ***harmless*** 2; **4.** *Geld etc.* sparen, einsparen: ***~ time*** Zeit gewinnen *od.* sparen; **5.** (auf)sparen, aufheben, -bewahren: ***~ it!*** *sl.* ‚geschenkt'!, halt's Maul!; → ***breath*** 1; **6.** *a. Augen* schonen; schonend *od.* sparsam 'umgehen mit; **7.** *j-m e-e Mühe etc.* ersparen: ***it ~d me the trouble of going there***; **8.** *eccl.* (***from***) retten (aus), erlösen (von); **9.** *Brit.* ausnehmen: ***~ the mark!*** verzeihen Sie die Bemerkung!; ***~ your presence*** (*od.* ***reverence***) mit Verlaub; **10.** *a.* ***~ up*** aufsparen; **11.** *sport:* a) *Schuß* halten, b) *Tor* verhindern; **II** *v/i.* **12.** sparen; **13.** *sport* ‚retten', halten; **III** *s.* **14.** *sport* Pa'rade *f* (*Tormann*).

save² [seɪv] *prp. u. cj.* außer (*dat.*), mit Ausnahme von (*od. gen.*), ausgenommen (*nom.*), abgesehen von: ***~ for*** bis auf (*acc.*); ***~ that*** abgesehen davon, daß; nur, daß.

sav·e·loy [,sævə'lɔɪ] *s.* Zerve'latwurst *f.*

sav·er ['seɪvə] *s.* **1.** Retter(in); **2.** Sparer (-in); **3.** sparsames Gerät *etc.*

sav·ing ['seɪvɪŋ] **I** *adj.* ☐ **1.** sparsam (***of*** mit); **2.** …sparend: ***time-~***; **3.** rettend: ***~ grace*** *eccl.* seligmachende Gnade; ***~ humo(u)r*** befreiender Humor; **4.** ⚖ Vorbehalts…: ***~ clause***; **II** *s.* **5.** (Er-) Rettung *f*; **6.** a) Sparen *n*, b) Ersparnis *f*, Einsparung *f*: ***~ of time*** Zeitersparnis; **7.** *pl.* Ersparnis(se *pl.*) *f*; Spargeld (-er *pl.*) *n*; **8.** ⚖ Vorbehalt *m*; **III** *prp. u. cj.* **9.** außer (*dat.*), ausgenommen: ***~ your presence*** (*od.* ***reverence***) mit Verlaub.

sav·ings| ac·count ['seɪvɪŋz] *s.* Sparkonto *n*; **~ bank** *s.* Sparkasse *f*: ***~ (deposit) book*** Spar(kassen)buch *n*; **~ de·pos·it** *s.* Spareinlage *f.*

sav·io(u)r ['seɪvjə] *s.* (Er)Retter *m*, Erlöser *m*: ***the*** ℒ *eccl.* der Heiland *od.* Erlöser.

sa·voir| faire [,sævwɑː'feə] *(Fr.) s.* Gewandtheit *f*, Takt(gefühl *n*) *m*, Savoir-'faire *n*; **~ vi·vre** [-'viːvr] *(Fr.) s.* feine Lebensart, Savoir-'vivre *n.*

sa·vor·y ['seɪvərɪ] *s.* ⚘ Bohnenkraut *n*, Kölle *f.*

sa·vo(u)r ['seɪvə] **I** *s.* **1.** (Wohl)Geschmack *m*; **2.** *bsd. fig.* Würze *f*, Reiz *m*; **3.** *fig.* Beigeschmack *m*, Anstrich *m*; **II** *v/t.* **4.** *bsd. fig.* genießen, auskosten; **5.** *bsd. fig.* würzen; **6.** *fig.* e-n Beigeschmack *od.* Anstrich haben von, riechen nach; **III** *v/i.* **7.** ***~ of*** a) *a. fig.* schmecken *od.* riechen nach, b) → 6; '**sa·vo(u)r·i·ness** [-vərɪnɪs] *s.* Wohlgeschmack *m*, -geruch *m*, Schmackhaftigkeit *f*; '**sa·vo(u)r·less** [-lɪs] *adj.* geschmack-, geruchlos, fade; '**sa·vo(u)r·y** [-vərɪ] **I** *adj.* ☐ **1.** wohlschmeckend, -riechend, schmackhaft; **2.** *a. fig.* appe'titlich, angenehm; **3.** würzig, pi'kant (*a. fig.*); **II** *s.* **4.** *Brit.* pi'kante Vor- *od.* Nachspeise.

sa·voy [sə'vɔɪ] *s.* Wirsing(kohl) *m.*

sav·vy ['sævɪ] *sl.* **I** *v/t.* ‚kapieren', verstehen; **II** *s.* ‚Köpfchen' *n*, ‚'Durchblick' *m*, Verstand *m.*

saw¹ [sɔː] *pret. von* ***see¹***.

saw² [sɔː] *s.* Sprichwort *n.*

saw³ [sɔː] **I** *s.* **1.** ⚙ Säge *f*: ***singing*** (*od.* ***musical***) ***~*** ♪ singende Säge; **II** *v/t.* **2.** [*irr.*] sägen: ***~ down*** *Baum* umsägen; ***~ off*** absägen; ***~ out*** *Bretter* zuschneiden; ***~ up*** zersägen; ***~ the air*** (***with one's hands***) (mit den Händen) herumfuchteln; **III** *v/i.* [*irr.*] **3.** sägen; **4.** (auf der Geige) ‚kratzen'.

'**saw|·bones** *s. pl. sg. konstr. sl.* a) ‚Bauchaufschneider' *m* (*Chirurg*), b) ‚Medi'zinmann' *m* (*Arzt*); '**~·buck** *s. Am.* **1.** Sägebock *m*; **2.** *sl.* 10-Dollar-Note *f*; '**~·dust** *s.* Sägemehl *n*: ***let the ~ out of*** *fig.* die Hohlheit zeigen von; '**~·fish** *s. ichth.* Sägefisch *m*; '**~·fly** *s. zo.* Blattwespe *f*; **~ frame**, **~ gate** *s.* ⚙ Sägegatter *n*; '**~·horse** *s.* Sägebock *m*; '**~·mill** *s.* Sägewerk *n*, -mühle *f.*

sawn [sɔːn] *p.p. von* ***saw³***.

Saw·ney ['sɔːnɪ] *s.* F **1.** (*Spitzname für*) Schotte *m*; **2.** ℒ Trottel *m.*

saw| set *s.* ⚙ Schränkeisen *n*; '**~·tooth I** *s.* **1.** Sägezahn *m*; **II** *adj.* **2.** Sägezahn…: ***~ roof*** Säge-, Scheddach *n*; **3.** ⚡ Sägezahn…, Kipp…(*-spannung etc.*); '**~·wort** *s.* ⚘ Färberdistel *f.*

saw·yer ['sɔːjə] *s.* Säger *m.*

Saxe [sæks] *s.* Sächsischblau *n.*

sax·horn ['sækshɔːn] *s.* ♪ Saxhorn *n.*

sax·i·frage ['sæksɪfrɪdʒ] *s.* ⚘ Steinbrech *m.*

Sax·on ['sæksn] **I** *s.* **1.** Sachse *m*, Sächsin *f*; **2.** *hist.* (Angel)Sachse *m*, (Angel-) Sächsin *f*; **3.** *ling.* Sächsisch *n*; **II** *adj.* **4.** sächsisch; **5.** (alt-, angel)sächsisch, *ling. oft* ger'manisch: ***~ genitive*** sächsischer Genitiv; **~ blue** → ***Saxe***; '**Sax·o·ny** [-nɪ] *s.* **1.** *geogr.* Sachsen *n*; **2.** ℒ feiner, glänzender Wollstoff.

sax·o·phone ['sæksəfəʊn] *s.* ♪ Saxo'phon *n*; **sax·o·phon·ist** [sæk'sɒfənɪst] *s.* Saxopho'nist(in).

say [seɪ] **I** *v/t.* [*irr.*] **1.** *et.* sagen, sprechen; **2.** sagen, äußern, berichten: ***he has nothing to ~ for himself*** a) er ist sehr zurückhaltend, b) *contp.* mit ihm ist nicht viel los; ***have you nothing to ~ for yourself?*** hast du nichts zu deiner Rechtfertigung zu sagen?; ***to ~ nothing of*** ganz zu schweigen von, geschweige; ***the Bible ~s*** die Bibel sagt, in der Bibel heißt es; ***people*** (*od.* ***they***) ***~ he is ill***, ***he is said to be ill*** man sagt *od.* es heißt, er sei krank, er soll krank sein; **3.** sagen, behaupten, versprechen: ***you said you would come***; → ***soon*** 2; **4.** a) *a.* ***~ over*** *Gedicht etc.* auf-, hersagen, b) *Gebet* sprechen, c) *R.C. Messe* lesen; **5.** (be)sagen, bedeuten: ***that is to ~*** das heißt; ***$500, ~, five hundred dollars*** $500, in Worten: fünfhundert Dollar; ***that is ~ing a great deal*** das will viel heißen; **6.** annehmen: (***let us***) ***~ it happens*** angenommen, es passiert; ***a sum of, ~, $20*** e-e Summe von, sagen wir (mal), *od.* von etwa $20; ***I should ~*** ich dächte, ich würde sagen; **II** *v/i.* [*irr.*] **7.** sagen, meinen: ***you may well ~ so!*** das kann man wohl sagen!; ***it is hard to ~*** es ist schwer zu sagen; ***what do you ~*** (*od.* ***what ~ you***) ***to …?*** was hältst du von …?, wie wäre es mit …?; ***you don't ~ (so)!*** was Sie nicht sagen!, nicht möglich!; ***it ~s*** es lautet (*Schreiben etc.*); ***it ~s here*** hier steht (*geschrieben*), hier heißt es; **8.** ***I ~!*** *int.* a) hör(en Sie) mal!, sag(en Sie) mal!, b) *erstaunt od. beifällig:* Donnerwetter!; **III** *s.* **9.** ***have one's ~*** (***to*** *od.* ***on***) s-e Meinung äußern (über *acc. od.* zu); **10.** Mitspracherecht *n*: ***have a*** (***no***) ***~ in*** et. (nichts) zu sagen haben bei; ***it is my ~ now!*** jetzt rede ich!; **11.** *a.* ***final ~*** endgültige Entscheidung: ***who has the ~ in this matter?*** wer hat in dieser Sache zu entscheiden *od.* das letzte Wort zu reden?

say·est ['seɪɪst] *obs. 2. sg. pres. von* ***say***: ***thou ~*** du sagst.

say·ing ['seɪɪŋ] *s.* **1.** Reden *n*: ***it goes without ~*** es ist selbstverständlich; ***there is no ~*** man kann nicht sagen *od.* wissen (*ob, wann etc.*); **2.** Ausspruch *m*; **3.** Sprichwort *n*, Redensart *f*: ***as the ~ goes*** (*od.* ***is***) wie es (im Sprichwort) heißt, wie man sagt.

says [sez; səz] *3. sg. pres. von* ***say***: ***he ~*** er sagt.

'**say-so** *s.* F **1.** (bloße) Behauptung; **2.** → ***say*** 11.

scab [skæb] **I** *s.* **1.** ⚕ a) Grind *m*, (Wund)Schorf *m*, b) Krätze *f*; **2.** *vet.* Räude *f*; **3.** ⚘ Schorf *m*; **4.** *sl.* Ha'lunke *m*; **5.** *sl.* a) Streikbrecher(in), b) Nichtgewerkschaftler *m*: ***~ work*** Schwarzarbeit *f*, *a.* Arbeit unter Tariflohn; **6.** ⚙ Gußfehler *m*; **II** *v/i.* **7.** verschorfen, sich verkrusten; **8.** *a.* ***~ it*** *sl.* als Streikbrecher *od.* unter Ta'riflohn arbeiten.

scab·bard ['skæbəd] *s.* (Schwert- *etc.*) Scheide *f.*

scabbed [skæbd] *adj.* **1.** → ***scabby***; **2.** ⚘ schorfig.

scab·by ['skæbɪ] *adj.* ☐ **1.** ⚕ schorfig, grindig; **2.** *vet.* räudig; **3.** F schäbig, schuftig.

sca·bi·es ['skeɪbiːz] → ***scab*** 1 b *u.* 2.

sca·bi·ous¹ ['skeɪbjəs] *adj.* **1.** ⚕ skabi'ös, krätzig; **2.** *vet.* räudig.

sca·bi·ous² ['skeɪbjəs] *s.* ⚘ Skabi'ose *f.*

sca·brous ['skeɪbrəs] *adj.* **1.** rauh, schuppig (*Pflanze etc.*); **2.** heikel, kniff(e)lig: ***a ~ question***; **3.** *fig.* schlüpfrig, anstößig.

scaf·fold ['skæfəld] **I** *s.* **1.** (Bau-, Arbeits)Gerüst *n*; **2.** Blutgerüst *n*, (*a.* Tod *m* auf dem) Scha'fott *n*; **3.** ('Redner-, 'Zuschauer)Tri,büne *f*; **4.** *anat.* a) Knochengerüst *n*, b) Stützgewebe *n*; **5.** ⚙ Ansatz *m* (*im Hochofen*); **II** *v/t.* **6.** ein Gerüst anbringen an (*dat.*); **7.** auf e-m Gestell aufbauen; **'scaf·fold·ing** [-dɪŋ] *s.* **1.** (Bau)Gerüst *n*; **2.** Ge'rüstmateri,al *n*; **3.** Errichtung *f* des Gerüsts.

scal·a·ble ['skeɪləbl] *adj.* ersteigbar.

scal·age ['skeɪlɪdʒ] *s.* **1.** ✝ *Am.* Schwundgeld *n*; **2.** Holzmaß *n.*

sca·lar ['skeɪlə] 𝔄 **I** *adj.* ska'lar, ungerichtet; **II** *s.* Ska'lar *m.*

scal·a·wag ['skæləwæg] *s.* **1.** Kümmerling *m* (*Tier*); **2.** F Lump *m.*

scald¹ [skɔːld] *s.* Skalde *m* (*nordischer Sänger*).

scald² [skɔːld] **I** *v/t.* **1.** verbrühen; **2.** *Milch etc.* abkochen: ***~ing hot*** a) kochendheiß, b) glühendheiß (*Tag etc.*); ***~ing tears*** *fig.* heiße Tränen; **3.** *Obst etc.* dünsten; **4.** *Geflügel*, *Schwein etc.* abbrühen; **5.** *a.* ***~ out*** *Gefäß*, *Instrumente* auskochen; **II** *s.* **6.** Verbrühung *f.*

scale¹ [skeɪl] **I** *s.* **1.** *zo.* Schuppe *f*; *coll.* Schuppen *pl.*; **2.** ⚕ Schuppe *f*: ***come off in ~s*** → 11; ***the ~s fell from my eyes*** es fiel mir wie Schuppen von den Augen; **3.** a) ⚘ Schuppenblatt *n*, b) (*Erbsen- etc.*)Hülse *f*, Schale *f*; **4.** (*Messer*)Schale *f*; **5.** Ablagerung *f*, *bsd.* a) Kesselstein *m*, b) ⚕ Zahnstein *m*; **6.** *a. pl. metall.* Zunder *m*: ***iron ~*** Hammerschlag *m*, Glühspan *m*; **II** *v/t.* **7.** *a.* ***~ off*** *Fisch* (ab)schuppen; *Schicht etc.* ablösen, -schälen, -häuten; **8.** a) abklopfen, den Kesselstein entfernen aus, b) *Zähne* vom Zahnstein befreien; **9.** e-e Kruste *od.* Kesselstein ansetzen in (*dat.*) *od.* an (*dat.*); **10.** *metall.* zunderfrei machen, ausglühen; **III** *v/i.* **11.** *a.* ***~ off*** sich abschuppen *od.* -lösen, abblättern; **12.** Kessel- *od.* Zahnstein ansetzen.

scale² [skeɪl] **I** *s.* **1.** Waagschale *f* (*a. fig.*): ***hold the ~s even*** *fig.* gerecht urteilen; ***throw into the ~*** *fig. Argument*, *Schwert etc.* in die Waagschale werfen; ***turn*** (*od.* ***tip***) ***the ~(s)*** *fig.* den Ausschlag geben; ***turn the ~ at 55 lbs*** 55 Pfund wiegen; → ***weight*** 4; **2.** *mst pl.* Waage *f*: ***a pair of ~s*** eine Waage; ***go to ~*** *sport* gewogen werden (*Jockey*, *Boxer*); ***go to ~ at 90 lbs*** 90 Pfund auf die Waage bringen; **3.** ⁀**s** *pl. ast.* Waage *f*; **II** *v/t.* **4.** wiegen; **5.** F (ab-, aus-)wiegen; **III** *v/i.* **6.** ***~ in*** (***out***) vor (nach) dem Rennen gewogen werden (*Jokkey*).

scale³ [skeɪl] **I** *s.* **1.** ⚙, *phys.* Skala *f*: ***~ division*** Gradeinteilung *f*; ***~ disk*** Skalenscheibe *f*; ***~ line*** Teilstrich *m*; **2.** a) Stufenleiter *f*, Staffelung *f*, b) Skala *f*, Ta'rif *m*: ***~ of fees*** Gebührenordnung *f*; ***~ of wages*** Lohnskala, -tabelle *f*; **3.** Stufe *f* (*auf e-r Skala*, *Tabelle etc.*; *a. fig.*): ***social ~*** Gesellschaftsstufe; **4.** 𝔄, ⚙ a) Maßstab(angabe *f*) *m*, b) loga'rithmischer Rechenstab: ***in*** (*od.* ***to***) ***~*** maßstab(s)gerecht: ***drawn to a ~ of 1:5*** im Maßstab 1:5 gezeichnet; ***~ model*** maßstab(s)getreues Modell; **5.** *fig.* Maßstab *m*, 'Umfang *m*: ***on a large ~*** in großem Umfang, im großen; **6.** 𝔄 (nu'merische) Zahlenreihe: ***decimal ~*** Dezimalreihe *f*; **7.** ♪ a) Tonleiter *f*, b) 'Ton,umfang *m* (*Instrument*): ***learn one's ~s*** Tonleitern üben; **8.** *Am. Börse*: ***on a ~*** zu verschiedenen Kurswerten (*Wertpapiere*); **9.** *fig.* Leiter *f*: ***a ~ to success***; **II** *v/t.* **10.** erklimmen, erklettern (*a. fig.*); **11.** maßstab(s)getreu zeichnen: ***~ down*** (***up***) maßstäblich verkleinern (vergrößern); **12.** einstufen: ***~ down*** *Löhne* herunterschrauben, drücken; ***~ up*** *Preise etc.* hochschrauben; **III** *v/i.* **13.** *auf e-r Skala od. fig.* klettern, steigen: ***~ down*** fallen.

scale| ar·mo(u)r *s.* Schuppenpanzer *m*; ***~ beam*** *s.* Waagebalken *m*; ***~ buy·ing*** *s.* ✝ (spekula'tiver) Aufkauf von 'Wertpa,pieren.

scaled [skeɪld] *adj.* **1.** *zo.* schuppig, Schuppen...; **2.** abgeschuppt: ***~ herring***; **3.** mit e-r Skala (versehen).

'scale-down *s.* maßstab(s)gerechte Verkleinerung.

scale·less ['skeɪllɪs] *adj.* schuppenlos.

sca·lene ['skeɪliːn] 𝔄 **I** *adj.* ungleichseitig (*Figur*), schief (*Körper*); **II** *s.* schiefwinkliges Dreieck.

scal·ing ['skeɪlɪŋ] *s.* **1.** (Ab)Schuppen *n*; **2.** Kesselstein- *od.* Zahnsteinentfernung *f*; **3.** Erklettern *n*, Aufstieg *m* (*a. fig.*); **4.** ✝ (spekula'tiver) Auf- u. Verkauf *m* von 'Wertpa,pieren.

scall [skɔːl] *s.* ⚕ (Kopf)Grind *m.*

scal·la·wag → ***scalawag.***

scal·lion ['skæljən] *s.* ⚘ Scha'lotte *f.*

scal·lop ['skɒləp] **I** *s.* **1.** *zo.* Kammuschel *f*; **2.** *a.* ***~ shell*** Muschelschale *f* (*a. aus Porzellan zum Servieren von Speisen*); **3.** *Näherei*: Lan'gette *f*; **II** *v/t.* **4.** ⚙ ausbogen, bogenförmig verzieren; **5.** *Näherei*: langettieren; **6.** *Speisen* in der (Muschel)Schale über'backen.

scalp [skælp] **I** *s.* **1.** *anat.* Kopfhaut *f*; **2.** Skalp *m* (*abgezogene Kopfhaut als Siegeszeichen*): ***be out for ~s*** sich auf dem Kriegspfad befinden, *fig.* kampf-, angriffslustig sein; **3.** *fig.* ('Sieges)Tro,phäe *f*; **II** *v/t.* **4.** skalpieren; **5.** ✝ *Am.* F *Wertpapiere* mit kleinem Pro'fit weiterverkaufen; **6.** *Am. sl. Eintrittskarten* auf dem schwarzen Markt verkaufen.

scal·pel ['skælpəl] *s.* ⚕ Skal'pell *n.*

scal·y ['skeɪlɪ] *adj.* **1.** schuppig, geschuppt; **2.** Schuppen...; **3.** schuppenförmig; **4.** sich abschuppend, schilferig.

scamp [skæmp] **I** *s.* Ha'lunke *m*; *humor. a.* Spitzbube *m*; **II** *v/t. Arbeit etc.* schlud(e)rig ausführen, hinschlampen.

scam·per ['skæmpə] **I** *v/i.* **1.** *a.* ***~ about*** (he'rum)tollen, her'umhüpfen; **2.** hasten: ***~ away*** (*od.* ***off***) sich davonmachen; **II** *s.* **3.** (He'rum)Tollen *n.*

scan [skæn] **I** *v/t.* **1.** genau *od.* kritisch prüfen, forschend *od.* scharf ansehen; **2.** *Horizont etc.* absuchen; **3.** über'fliegen: ***~ the headlines***; **4.** *Vers* skandieren; **5.** ϟ *Computer*, *Radar*, *TV*: abtasten; **II** *v/i.* **6.** *Metrik*: a) skan'dieren, b) sich *gut etc.* skandieren (lassen).

scan·dal ['skændl] *s.* **1.** Skan'dal *m*: a) skanda'löses Ereignis, b) (öffentliches) Ärgernis: ***cause ~*** Anstoß erregen, c) Schande *f*, Schmach *f* (***to*** für); **2.** Verleumdung *f*, (böswilliger) Klatsch: ***talk ~*** klatschen; ***~ sheet*** Skandal-, Revolverblatt *n*; **3.** ⚖ üble Nachrede (*im Prozeß*); **4.** ‚unmöglicher' Mensch.

scan·dal·ize¹ ['skændəlaɪz] *v/t.* Anstoß erregen bei (*dat.*), *j-n* schockieren: ***be ~d at*** Anstoß nehmen an (*dat.*), empört sein über (*acc.*).

scan·dal·ize² ['skændəlaɪz] *v/t.* ⚓ *Segel* verkleinern, ohne zu reffen.

'scan·dal,mon·ger *s.* Lästermaul *n*, Klatschbase *f.*

scan·dal·ous ['skændələs] *adj.* ☐ **1.** skanda'lös, anstößig, schockierend; **2.** schändlich, schimpflich; **3.** verleumderisch, Schmäh...: ***~ stories***; **4.** klatschsüchtig (*Person*).

Scan·di·na·vi·an [,skændɪ'neɪvjən] **I** *adj.* **1.** skandi'navisch; **II** *s.* **2.** Skandi'navier(in); **3.** *ling.* a) Skandi'navisch *n*, b) Altnordisch *n.*

scan·ner ['skænə] *s.* **1.** *Computer*, *Radar*: Abtaster *m*; **2.** → ***scanning disk.***

scan·ning ['skænɪŋ] *s. allg.* Abtastung *f*; ***~ disk*** *s. TV* Abtastscheibe *f*; ***~ lines*** *s. pl. TV* Rasterlinien *pl.*

scan·sion ['skænʃn] *s. Metrik*: Skandierung *f*, Skansi'on *f.*

Scan·so·res [skæn'sɔːriːz] *s. pl. orn.* Klettervögel *pl.*; **scan'so·ri·al** [-rɪəl] *adj. orn.* **1.** Kletter...; **2.** zu den Klettervögeln gehörig.

scant [skænt] *adj.* knapp (***of*** an *dat.*), spärlich, dürftig, gering: ***a ~ 2 hours*** knapp 2 Stunden; **'scan·ties** [-tɪz] *s. pl.* Damenslip *m*; **'scant·i·ness** [-tɪnɪs], **'scant·ness** [-nɪs] *s.* **1.** Knappheit *f*, Kargheit *f*; **2.** Unzulänglichkeit *f*; **'scant·y** [-tɪ] *adj.* ☐ **1.** → ***scant***; **2.** unzureichend; **3.** eng, beengt (*Raum etc.*).

scape [skeɪp] *s.* **1.** ⚘, *zo.* Schaft *m*; **2.** △ (Säulen)Schaft *m.*

'scape·goat *s. fig.* Sündenbock *m.*

'scape·grace *s.* Taugenichts *m.*

scaph·oid ['skæfɔɪd] *anat.* **I** *adj.* scapho'id, Kahn...; **II** *s. a.* ***~ bone*** Kahnbein *n.*

scap·u·la ['skæpjʊlə] *pl.* **-lae** [-liː] *s. anat.* Schulterblatt *n*; **'scap·u·lar** [-lə] **I** *adj.* **1.** *anat.* Schulter(blatt)...; **II** *s.* **2.** → ***scapulary***; **3.** ⚕ Schulterbinde *f*; **'scap·u·lar·y** [-lərɪ] *s. eccl.* Skapu'lier *n.*

scar¹ [skɑː] **I** *s.* **1.** Narbe *f* (*a.* ⚘; *a. fig. u. psych.*); **2.** Schramme *f*, Kratzer *m*; **3.** *fig.* (Schand)Fleck *m*, Makel *m*; **II** *v/t.* **4.** e-e Narbe *od.* Narben hinter'lassen auf (*dat.*); **5.** *fig.* bei *j-m* ein Trauma hinter'lassen; **6.** *fig.* entstellen, verunstalten; **III** *v/i.* **7.** *a.* ***~ over*** vernarben (*a. fig.*).

scar² [skɑː] *s. Brit.* Klippe *f*, steiler (Felsen)Abhang.

scar·ab ['skærəb] *s.* **1.** *zo.* Skara'bäus *m* (*a. Schmuck etc.*); **2.** *zo.* Mistkäfer *m.*

scarce [skeəs] **I** *adj.* ☐ **1.** knapp, spärlich: ***~ commodities*** ✝ Mangelwaren; **2.** selten, rar: ***make o.s. ~*** F a) sich rar machen, b) ‚sich dünnmachen'; **II** *adv.* **3.** *obs.* → **'scarce·ly** [-lɪ] *adv.* **1.** kaum, gerade erst: ***~ anything*** kaum etwas, fast nichts; ***~ ... when*** kaum ... als; **2.**

wohl nicht, kaum, schwerlich; **'scarce·ness** [-nɪs], **'scar·ci·ty** [-sətɪ] *s.* **1.** a) Knappheit *f*, Mangel *m* (***of*** an *dat.*), b) Verknappung *f*; **2.** (Hungers)Not *f*; **3.** Seltenheit *f*: ***~ value*** Seltenheitswert *m*.

scare [skeə] **I** *v/t.* **1.** erschrecken, *j-m* e-n Schrecken einjagen, ängstigen: ***be ~d of s.th.*** sich vor et. fürchten; **2.** *a.* ***~ away*** verscheuchen, -jagen; **3.** ***~ up*** a) *Wild etc.* aufscheuchen, b) F *Geld etc.* auftreiben, *et.* ‚organisieren'; **II** *v/i.* **4.** erschrecken: ***he does not ~ easily*** er läßt sich nicht leicht ins Bockshorn jagen; **III** *s.* **5.** Schreck(en) *m*, Panik *f*: ***~ buying*** Angstkäufe *pl.*; ***~ news*** Schreckensnachricht(en *pl.*) *f*; **6.** blinder A'larm; **'~·crow** *s.* **1.** Vogelscheuche *f* (*a. fig. Person*); **2.** *fig.* Schreckgespenst *n*; **'~-ˌhead(·ing)** *s.* (riesige) Sensati'onsschlagzeile; **'~ˌmon·ger** *s.* Panikmacher(in); **'~ˌmon·ger·ing** *s.* Panikmache *f*.

scarf¹ [skɑːf] *pl.* **scarfs, scarves** [-vz] *s.* **1.** Hals-, Kopf-, Schultertuch *n*, Schal *m*; **2.** (breite) Kra'watte (*für Herren*); **3.** ✕ Schärpe *f*; **4.** *eccl.* Seidenstola *f*; **5.** Tischläufer *m*.

scarf² [skɑːf] **I** *s.* **1.** ⚙ Laschung *f*, Blatt *n* (*Hölzer*); ⚓ Lasch *m*; **2.** ⚙ → ***scarf joint***; **II** *v/t.* **3.** ⚙ zs.-blatten; ⚓ (ver)laschen; **4.** *e-n Wal* aufschneiden.

scarf| joint *s.* ⚙ Blattfuge *f*, Verlaschung *f*; **'~·pin** *s.* Kra'wattennadel *f*; **'~·skin** *s. anat.* Oberhaut *f*.

scar·i·fi·ca·tion [ˌskeərɪfɪ'keɪʃn] *s.* ⚕ Hautritzung *f*; **scar·i·fi·ca·tor** ['skeərɪfɪkeɪtə], **scar·i·fi·er** ['skeərɪfaɪə] *s.* **1.** ⚕ Stichelmesser *n*; **2.** ⚒ Messeregge *f*; **3.** ⚙ Straßenaufreißer *m*; **scar·i·fy** ['skeərɪfaɪ] *v/t.* **1.** *Haut* ritzen, ⚕ skarifizieren; **2.** ⚒ a) *Boden* auflockern, b) *Samen* anritzen; **3.** *fig.* a) *Gefühle etc.* verletzen, b) scharf kritisieren.

scar·la·ti·na [ˌskɑːlə'tiːnə] *s.* ⚕ Scharlach(fieber *n*) *m*.

scar·let ['skɑːlət] **I** *s.* **1.** Scharlach(rot *n*) *m*; **2.** Scharlach(tuch *n*, -gewand *n*) *m*; **II** *adj.* **3.** scharlachrot: ***flush*** (*od.* ***turn***) **~** dunkelrot werden; **4.** *fig.* unzüchtig; **~ fe·ver** *s.* ⚕ Scharlach(fieber *n*) *m*; **~ hat** *s.* **1.** Kardi'nalshut *m*; **2.** *fig.* Kardi'nalswürde *f*; **~ run·ner** *s.* ♀ Scharlach-, Feuerbohne *f*; ♀ **Wom·an** *s.* **1.** *bibl. die* (scharlachrot gekleidete) Hure; **2.** *fig. contp.* (*das* heidnische *od.* päpstliche) Rom.

scarp [skɑːp] **I** *s.* **1.** steile Böschung; **2.** ✕ Es'karpe *f*; **II** *v/t.* **3.** abböschen, abdachen; **scarped** [-pt] *adj.* steil, abschüssig.

scarred [skɑːd] *adj.* narbig.

scarves [skɑːvz] *pl. von* ***scarf¹***.

scar·y ['skeərɪ] *adj.* F **1.** a) grus(e)lig, schaurig, b) unheimlich; **2.** schreckhaft, ängstlich.

scat¹ [skæt] F **I** *int.* **1.** ‚hau ab'!; **2.** Tempo!; **II** *v/i.* **3.** ‚verduften'; **4.** flitzen.

scat² [skæt] *s. Jazz:* Scat *m* (*Singen zs.-hangloser Silben*).

scathe [skeɪð] **I** *v/t.* **1.** *poet.* versengen; **2.** *obs. od. Scot.* verletzen; **3.** *fig.* vernichtend kritisieren; **II** *s.* **4.** Schaden *m*: ***without ~***; **5.** Beleidigung *f*; **'scathe·less** [-lɪs] *adj.* unversehrt; **'scath·ing** [-ðɪŋ] *adj.* □ *fig.* **1.** vernichtend, ätzend (*Kritik etc.*); **2.** verletzend.

sca·tol·o·gy [skə'tɒlədʒɪ] *s.* **1.** ⚕ Skatolo'gie *f*, Kotstudium *n*; **2.** *fig.* Beschäftigung *f* mit dem Ob'szönen (in der Litera'tur).

scat·ter ['skætə] **I** *v/t.* **1.** *a.* ***~ about*** (aus-, um'her-, ver)streuen; **2.** verbreiten, -teilen; **3.** bestreuen (***with*** mit); **4.** *Menge etc.* zerstreuen, *a. Vögel etc.* ausein'anderscheuchen: ***be ~ed to the four winds*** in alle Winde zerstreut werden *od.* sein; **5.** *Geld* verschleudern, verzetteln: ***~ one's strength*** *fig.* sich verzetteln; **6.** *phys. Licht etc.* zerstreuen; **II** *v/i.* **7.** sich zerstreuen (*Menge*), ausein'anderstieben (*a. Vögel etc.*), sich zerteilen (*Nebel*); **8.** a) sich verbreiten (***over*** über *acc.*), b) verstreut sein; **III** *s.* **9.** *allg.*, *a. phys. etc.* Streuung *f*; **'~-brain** *s.* Wirrkopf *m*; **'~·brained** *adj.* wirr, kon'fus.

scat·tered ['skætəd] *adj.* **1.** ver-, zerstreut (liegend *od.* vorkommend *etc.*); **2.** vereinzelt (auftretend): ***~ rain showers***; **3.** *fig.* wirr; **4.** *phys.* dif'fus, Streu…

'scat·ter|·gun *s. Am.* Schrotflinte *f*; **~ rug** *s. Am.* Brücke *f* (*Teppich*).

scaur [skɔː] *bsd. Scot. für* ***scar²***.

scav·enge ['skævɪndʒ] **I** *v/t.* **1.** *Straßen etc.* reinigen, säubern; **2.** *mot. Zylinder von Gasen* reinigen, spülen: ***~ stroke*** Spültakt *m*, Auspuffhub *m*; **3.** *Am.* a) *Abfälle etc.* auflesen, b) *et.* auftreiben, c) *et.* durch'stöbern (***for*** nach); **II** *v/i.* **4.** ***~ for*** (her'um)suchen nach; **'scav·en·ger** [-dʒə] *s.* **1.** Straßenkehrer *m*; **2.** Müllmann *m*; **3.** a) Trödler *m*, b) Lumpensammler *m*; **4.** ⚗ Reinigungsmittel *n*; **5.** *zo.* Aasfresser *m*: ***~ beetle*** aasfressender Käfer.

sce·nar·i·o [sɪ'nɑːrɪəʊ] *pl.* **-ri·os** *s.* **1.** a) *thea.* Sze'nar(io) *n*, b) *Film:* Drehbuch *n*; **2.** *fig.* Sze'nario *n*, Plan *m*; **sce·na·rist** ['siːnərɪst] *s.* Drehbuchautor *m*.

scene [siːn] *s.* **1.** *thea.*, *Film*, *TV:* a) Szene *f*, Auftritt *m*, b) Ort *m* der Handlung, Schauplatz *m* (*a. Roman etc.*); → ***lay*** 6, c) Ku'lisse *f*, d) → ***scenery*** b: ***behind the ~s*** hinter den Kulissen (*a. fig.*); ***change of ~*** Szenenwechsel *m*, *fig.* ‚Tapetenwechsel' *m*; **2.** Szene *f*, Epi'sode *f* (*Roman etc.*); **3.** 'Hintergrund *m e-r Erzählung etc.*; **4.** *fig.* Szene *f*, Schauplatz *m*: ***~ of accident*** (***crime***) Unfallort *m* (Tatort *m*); **5.** Szene *f*, Anblick *m*; *paint.* (Landschafts-) Bild *n*: ***~ of destruction*** *fig.* Bild der Zerstörung; **6.** Szene *f*: a) Vorgang *m*, b) (heftiger) Auftritt: ***make*** (***s.o.***) ***a. ~*** (j-m) e-e Szene machen; **7.** *fig.* (Welt-) Bühne *f*: ***quit the ~*** von der Bühne abtreten, sterben; **8.** *sl.* (Drogen-, Pop- *etc.*)Szene *f*: ***that's not my ~*** *fig.* das ist nicht mein Fall; **~ dock** *s. thea.* Requi'sitenraum *m*; **~ paint·er** *s.* Bühnenmaler(in).

scen·er·y ['siːnərɪ] *s.* Szene'rie *f*: a) Landschaft *f*, Gegend *f*, b) *thea.* Bühnenbild *n*, -ausstattung *f*.

'sceneˌshift·er *s. thea.* Bühnenarbeiter *m*, Ku'lissenschieber *m*.

sce·nic ['siːnɪk] **I** *adj.* (□ ***~ally***) **1.** landschaftlich, Landschafts…; **2.** (landschaftlich) schön, malerisch: ***~ railway*** (in e-r künstlichen Landschaft angelegte) Liliputbahn; ***~ road*** landschaftlich schöne Strecke (*Hinweis auf Autokarte*); **3.** *thea.* a) szenisch, Bühnen…: ***~ designer*** Bühnenbildner(in), b) dra'matisch (*a. Gemälde etc.*), c) Ausstattungs…; **II** *s.* **4.** Na'turfilm *m*.

sce·no·graph·ic, sce·no·graph·i·cal [ˌsiːnə'græfɪk(l)] *adj.* □ szeno'graphisch, perspek'tivisch.

scent [sent] **I** *s.* **1.** (*bsd.* Wohl)Geruch *m*, Duft *m*; **2.** Par'füm *n*; **3.** *hunt.* a) Witterung *f*, b) Spur *f*, Fährte *f* (*a. fig.*): ***blazing ~*** warme Fährte; ***on the*** (***wrong***) ***~*** auf der (falschen) Fährte; ***put on the ~*** auf die Fährte setzen; ***put*** (*od.* ***throw***) ***off the ~*** von der (richtigen) Spur ablenken; **4.** a) Geruchssinn *m*, b) *zo. u. fig.* Spürsinn *m*, *gute etc.* Nase: ***have a ~ for s.th.*** *fig.* e-e Nase für et. haben; **II** *v/t.* **5.** *et.* riechen; **6.** *a.* ***~ out*** *hunt. u. fig.* wittern, (auf)spüren; **7.** mit Wohlgeruch erfüllen; **8.** parfümieren; **scent bag** *s.* **1.** *zo.* Duftdrüse *f*; **2.** *Fuchsjagd:* künstliche Schleppe; **3.** Duftkissen *n*; **scent bot·tle** *s.* Par'fümfläschchen *n*; **'scent·ed** [-tɪd] *adj.* **1.** duftend; **2.** parfümiert; **scent gland** *s. zo.* Duft-, Moschusdrüse *f*; **'scent·less** [-lɪs] *adj.* **1.** geruchlos; **2.** *hunt.* ohne Witterung (*Boden*).

scep·sis ['skepsɪs] *s.* **1.** Skepsis *f*; **2.** *phls.* Skepti'zismus *m*.

scep·ter ['septə] *etc. Am.* → ***sceptre*** *etc.*

scep·tic ['skeptɪk] *s.* **1.** (*phls. mst* ♀) Skeptiker(in); **2.** *eccl.* Zweifler(in), *allg.* Ungläubige(r *m*) *f*, Athe'ist(in); **'scep·ti·cal** [-kl] *adj.* □ skeptisch (*a. phls.*), mißtrauisch, ungläubig: ***be ~ about*** (*od.* ***of***) ***s.th.*** e-r Sache skeptisch gegenüberstehen, et. bezweifeln, an et. zweifeln; **'scep·ti·cism** [-ɪzɪzəm] → ***scepsis***.

scep·tre ['septə] *s.* Zepter *n*: ***wield the ~*** das Zepter führen, herrschen; **'scep·tered** [-əd] *adj.* **1.** zeptertragend, herrschend (*a. fig.*); **2.** *fig.* königlich.

sched·ule [*Brit.* 'ʃedjuːl; *Am.* 'skedʒʊl] **I** *s.* **1.** Liste *f*, Ta'belle *f*, Aufstellung *f*, Verzeichnis *n*; **2.** *bsd.* ⚖ Anhang *m*; **3.** *bsd. Am.* a) (Arbeits-, Lehr-, Stunden-) Plan *m*, b) Fahrplan *m*: ***be behind ~*** Verspätung haben, *weitS.* im Verzug sein; ***on ~*** (fahr)planmäßig, pünktlich; **4.** Formblatt *n*, Vordruck *m*, Formu'lar *n*; **5.** Einkommensteuerklasse *f*; **II** *v/t.* **6.** *et.* in e-r Liste *etc. od.* tabel'larisch zs.-stellen; **7.** (in e-e Liste *etc.*) eintragen, -fügen: ***~d departure*** (fahr)planmäßige Abfahrt; ***~d flight*** ✈ Linienflug *m*; ***the train is ~d to leave at 6*** der Zug fährt fahrplanmäßig um 6; **8.** *bsd.* ⚖ (als Anhang) beifügen (***to*** *dat.*); **9.** a) festlegen, b) planen.

sche·mat·ic [skɪ'mætɪk] *adj.* (□ ***~ally***) sche'matisch; **sche·ma·tize** ['skiːmətaɪz] *v/t. u. v/i.* schematisieren.

scheme [skiːm] **I** *s.* **1.** Schema *n*, Sy'stem *n*, Anlage *f*: ***~ of colo(u)r*** Farbenzusammenstellung *f*, -skala *f*; ***~ of philosophy*** philosophisches System; **2.** a) Schema *n*, Aufstellung *f*, Ta'belle *f*, b) 'Übersicht *f*, c) sche'matische Darstellung; **3.** Plan *m*, Pro'jekt *n*, Pro'gramm *n*: ***irrigation ~***; **4.** (dunkler) Plan, In'trige *f*, Kom'plott *n*; **II** *v/t.* **5.** *a.* ***~ out*** planen, entwerfen; **6.** *Böses* planen, aushecken; **7.** in ein Schema *od.* Sy'stem bringen; **III** *v/i.* **8.** Pläne schmieden, *bsd. b.s.* Ränke schmieden, intrigieren; **'schem·er** [-mə] *s.* **1.** Plänemacher *m*; **2.** Ränkeschmied *m*, Intri'gant *m*; **'schem·ing** [-mɪŋ] *adj.* □ ränkevoll, intri'gant.

scher·zan·do [skeət'sændəʊ] (*Ital.*) *adv.* ♪ scher'zando, heiter; **scher·zo** ['skeətsəʊ] *s.* ♪ Scherzo *n*.

schism ['sɪzəm] *s.* **1.** *eccl.* a) Schisma *n*, Kirchenspaltung *f*, b) Lossagung *f*; **2.** *fig.* Spaltung *f*, Riß *m*; **schis·mat·ic** [sɪz'mætɪk] *bsd. eccl.* **I** *adj.* (□ **~ally**) schis'matisch, abtrünnig; **II** *s.* Schis'matiker *m*, Abtrünnige(r) *m*; **schis'mat·i·cal** [sɪz'mætɪkl] *adj.* □ → **schismatic** I.

schist [ʃɪst] *s. geol.* Schiefer *m*.

schiz·oid ['skɪtsɔɪd] *psych.* **I** *adj.* schizo'id; **II** *s.* Schizo'ide(r *m*) *f*.

schiz·o·my·cete [ˌskɪtsəʊmaɪ'si:t] *s.* ♀ Spaltpilz *m*, Schizomy'zet *m*.

schiz·o·phrene ['skɪtsəʊfri:n] *s. psych.* Schizo'phrene(r *m*) *f*; **schiz·o·phre·ni·a** [ˌskɪtsəʊ'fri:njə] *s. psych.* Schizophre'nie *f*; **schiz·o·phren·ic** [ˌskɪtsəʊ'frenɪk] *psych.* **I** *s.* Schizophrene(r *m*) *f*; **II** *adj.* schizo'phren.

schle·miel, schle·mihl [ʃle'mi:l] *s. Am. sl.* **1.** Pechvogel *m*; **2.** Tolpatsch *m*.

schlep(p) [ʃlep] *Am. sl.* **I** *v/t.* (*v/i.* sich) schleppen; **II** *s.* → **'schlep·per** [-pə] *s. Am. sl.* ‚Blödmann' *m*.

schmaltz [ʃmɔ:lts] (*Ger.*) *s. sl.* **1.** ‚Schmalz' *m* (*a. Musik*); **2.** Kitsch *m*; **'schmaltz·y** [-tsɪ] *adj.* ‚schmalzig', sentimen'tal.

schnap(p)s [ʃnæps] (*Ger.*) *s.* Schnaps *m*.

schnit·zel ['ʃnɪtsəl] (*Ger.*) *s. Küche*: Wiener Schnitzel *n*.

schnor·kel ['ʃnɔ:kəl] → **snorkel**.

schol·ar ['skɒlə] *s.* **1.** a) Gelehrte(r) *m*, *bsd.* Geisteswissenschaftler *m*, b) Gebildete(r) *m*; **2.** Studierende(r *m*) *f*: **he is an apt ~** er lernt gut; **he is a good French ~** er ist im Französischen gut beschlagen; **he is not much of a ~** F mit s-r Bildung ist es nicht weit her; **3.** *ped. univ.* Stipendi'at *m*; **4.** *obs. od. poet.* Schüler(in), Jünger(in); **'schol·ar·ly** [-lɪ] *adj. u. adv.* **1.** gelehrt; **2.** gelehrtenhaft; **'schol·ar·ship** [-ʃɪp] *s.* **1.** Gelehrsamkeit *f*: **classical ~** humanistische Bildung; **2.** *ped.* Sti'pendium *n*.

scho·las·tic [skə'læstɪk] **I** *adj.* (□ **~ally**) **1.** aka'demisch (*Bildung etc.*); **2.** schulisch, Schul..., Schüler...; **3.** erzieherisch: **~ profession** Lehr(er)beruf *m*; **4.** *phls.* scho'lastisch (*a. fig. contp. spitzfindig, pedantisch*); **II** *s.* **5.** *phls.* Scho'lastiker *m*; **6.** *fig.* Schulmeister *m*, Pe'dant *m*; **scho'las·ti·cism** [-ɪsɪzəm] *s.* **1.** *a.* ℒ Scho'lastik *f*; **2.** *fig.* Pedante'rie *f*.

school¹ [sku:l] **I** *s.* **1.** Schule *f* (*Anstalt*): **at ~** auf der Schule; → **high school** *etc.*; → 4; **2.** (Schul)Stufe *f*: **lower ~** Unterstufe; **senior** (*od.* **upper**) **~** Oberstufe; **3.** Lehrgang *m*, Kurs(us) *m*; **4.** *mst ohne art.* ('Schul)ˌUnterricht *m*, Schule *f*: **at** (*od.* **in**) **~** in der Schule, im Unterricht; **go to ~** zur Schule gehen; **put to ~** einschulen; → **tale** 5; **5.** Schule *f*, Schulhaus *n*, -gebäude *n*; **6.** *univ.* a) Fakul'tät *f*: **the law ~** die juristische Fakultät, b) Fachbereich *m*, (selbständige) Abteilung innerhalb e-r Fakul'tät; **7.** *Am.* Hochschule *f*; **8.** *pl.* 'Schlußexˌamen *n* (*für den Grad e-s* **Bachelor of Arts**; *Oxford*); **9.** *fig. harte etc.* Schule, Lehre *f*: **a severe ~**; **10.** *phls., paint. etc.* Schule *f* (*Richtung u. Anhängerschaft*): **~ of thought** (geistige) Richtung; **the Hegelian ~** *phls.* die hegelianische Schule *od.* Richtung, die Hegelianer *pl.*; **a gentleman of the old ~** ein Kavalier der alten Schule; **11.** ♪ Schule *f*: a) Lehrbuch *n*, b) Lehre *f*, Sy'stem *n*; **II** *v/t.* **12.** einschulen; **13.** schulen, unter'richten, ausbilden, trainieren; **14.** *Temperament, Zunge etc.* zügeln; **15. ~ o.s.** (**to**) sich erziehen (zu), sich üben (in *dat.*); **~ o.s. to do s.th.** lernen *od.* sich daran gewöhnen et. zu tun; **16.** *Pferd* dressieren; **17.** *obs.* tadeln.

school² [sku:l] *s. ichth.* Schwarm *m* (*a. fig.*), Schule *f*, Zug *m* (*Wale etc.*).

school| age *s.* schulpflichtiges Alter; **'~-age** *adj.* schulpflichtig; **'~·board** *s.* (lo'kale) Schulbehörde; **'~·boy** *s.* Schüler *m*, Schuljunge *m*; **'~·bus** *s.* Schulbus *m*; **~ days** *pl.* (alte) Schulzeit; **'~ˌfel·low** → **schoolmate**; **'~·girl** *s.* Schülerin *f*, Schulmädchen *n*; **'~ˌgirl·ish** *adj.* schulmädchenhaft; **'~·house 1.** (*bsd.* Dorf-) Schulhaus *n*; **2.** *Brit.* (Wohn)Haus *n* des Schulleiters.

school·ing ['sku:lɪŋ] *s.* **1.** ('Schul)ˌUnterricht *m*; **2.** Schulung *f*, Ausbildung *f*; **3.** Schulgeld *n*; **4.** *sport* Schulreiten *n*; **5.** *obs.* Verweis *m*.

school| leav·er ['li:və] *s.* Schulabgänger (-in); **~ leav·ing cer·tif·i·cate** *s.* Abgangszeugnis *n*; **'~·ma'am** [-mæm] *s. Am. für* **schoolmarm**; **'~·man** [-mən] *s.* [*irr.*] **1.** Päda'goge *m*; **2.** *hist.* Scho'lastiker *m*; **'~·marm** [-mɑ:m] F **1.** Lehrerin *f*; **2.** *fig. contp.* Schulmeisterin *f*; **'~ˌmas·ter** *s.* **1.** Schulleiter *m*; **2.** Lehrer *m*; **3.** *fig. contp.* Schulmeister *m*; **'~ˌmas·ter·ly** *adj.* schulmeisterlich; **'~·mate** *s.* 'Schulkameˌrad(in); **'~ˌmis·tress** *s.* **1.** Schulleiterin *f*; **2.** Lehrerin *f*; **~ re·port** *s.* Schulzeugnis *n*; **'~·room** [-rʊm] *s.* Klassenzimmer *n*; **~ ship** *s.* ⚓ Schulschiff *n*; **~ tie** *s.*: **old ~** *Brit.* a) Krawatte *f* mit den Farben e-r **Public School**, b) *Spitzname für e-n ehemaligen Schüler e-r* **Public School**, c) sentimentale Bindung an die alte Schule, d) *der* Einfluß der **Public Schools** auf das öffentliche Leben in England, e) *contp.* Cliquenwirtschaft *f* unter ehemaligen Schülern e-r **Public School**, f) *contp.* arrogantes Gehabe solcher Schüler; **~ u·ni·form** *s.* (einheitliche) Schulkleidung; **'~·work** *s.* (in der Schule zu erledigende) Aufgaben *pl.*; **'~·yard** *s. Am.* Schulhof *m*.

schoon·er ['sku:nə] *s.* **1.** ⚓ Schoner *m*; **2.** *bsd. Am.* → **prairie schooner**; **3.** großes Bierglas.

schorl [ʃɔ:l] *s. min.* Schörl *m*, (schwarzer) Turma'lin.

schot·tische [ʃɒ'ti:ʃ] *s.* ♪ Schottische(r) *m* (*a. Tanz*).

schuss [ʃʊs] (*Ger.*) *Skisport*: **I** *s.* Schuß (-fahrt *f*) *m*; **II** *v/i.* Schuß fahren.

schwa [ʃwɑ:] *s. ling.* Schwa *n*: a) *kurzer Vokal von unbestimmter Klangfarbe*, b) *das phonetische Symbol* ə.

sci·a·gram ['skaɪəgræm], **'sci·a·graph** [-grɑ:f] *s.* ⚕ Röntgenbild *n*; **sci·ag·ra·phy** [skaɪ'ægrəfɪ] *s.* **1.** ⚕ Herstellung *f* von Röntgenaufnahmen; **2.** Schattenmale'rei *f*, Schattenriß *m*.

sci·at·ic [saɪ'ætɪk] *adj.* ⚕ **1.** Ischias...; **2.** an Ischias leidend; **sci'at·i·ca** [-kə] *s.* ⚕ Ischias *f*.

sci·ence ['saɪəns] *s.* **1.** Wissenschaft *f*: **man of ~** Wissenschaftler *m*; **2.** *a.* **natural ~** *coll. die* Na'turwissenschaft(en *pl.*); **3.** *fig.* Lehre *f*, Kunde *f*: **~ of gardening** Gartenbaukunst *f*; **4.** *phls., eccl.* Erkenntnis *f* (**of** von); **5.** Kunst (-fertigkeit) *f*, (gute) Technik (*a. sport*); **6.** ℒ → **Christian Science**; **~ fic·tion** *s.* 'Science-'fiction *f*.

sci·en·ter [saɪ'entə] (*Lat.*) ⚖ *adv.* wissentlich.

sci·en·tif·ic [ˌsaɪən'tɪfɪk] *adj.* (□ **~ally**) **1.** (*engS.* na'tur)wissenschaftlich; **2.** wissenschaftlich, ex'akt, syste'matisch; **3.** *fig. sport etc.* kunstgerecht; **sci·en·tist** ['saɪəntɪst] *s.* (Na'tur)Wissenschaftler *m*.

sci-fi [ˌsaɪ'faɪ] F *für* **science fiction**.

scil·i·cet ['saɪlɪset] *adv.* (*abbr.* **scil.** *od.* **sc.**) nämlich, d.h. (das heißt).

scim·i·tar, scim·i·ter ['sɪmɪtə] *s.* (orien'talischer) Krummsäbel.

scin·til·la [sɪn'tɪlə] *s. bsd. fig.* Fünkchen *n*: **not a ~ of truth**; **scin·til·lant** ['sɪntɪlənt] *adj.* funkelnd, schillernd; **scin·til·late** ['sɪntɪleɪt] **I** *v/i.* **1.** Funken sprühen; **2.** funkeln (*a. fig. Augen*), sprühen (*a. fig. Geist, Witz*); **II** *v/t.* **3.** *Funken, fig. Geistesblitze* (ver)sprühen; **scin·til·la·tion** [ˌsɪntɪ'leɪʃn] *s.* **1.** Funkensprühen *n*, Funkeln *n*; **2.** Schillern *n*; **3.** *fig.* Geistesblitz *m*.

sci·o·lism ['saɪəʊlɪzəm] *s.* Halbwissen *n*; **'sci·o·list** [-lɪst] *s.* Halbgebildete(r) *m*, -wisser *m*.

sci·on ['saɪən] *s.* **1.** ♀ Ableger *m*, Steckling *m*, (Pfropf)Reis *n*; **2.** *fig.* Sproß *m*, Sprößling *m*.

scir·rhous ['sɪrəs] *adj.* ⚕ szir'rhös, hart geschwollen; **'scir·rhus** [-rəs] *pl.* **-rhus·es** *s.* ⚕ Szirrhus *m*, harte Krebsgeschwulst.

scis·sor ['sɪzə] *v/t.* **1.** (*mit der Schere*) (zer-, zu-, aus)schneiden; **2.** scherenartig bewegen *etc.*; **~ kick** *s. Fußball, Schwimmen*: Scherenschlag *m*.

scis·sors ['sɪzəz] *s. pl.* **1.** *a.* **pair of ~** Schere *f*; **2.** *sg. konstr. sport* (*Hochsprung*: *a.* **~ jump**, *Ringen*: *a.* **~ hold**) Schere *f*.

scis·sure ['sɪʒə] *s. bsd.* ⚕ Fis'sur *f*, Riß *m*.

scle·ra ['sklɪərə] *s. anat.* Sklera *f*, Lederhaut *f* des Auges.

scle·ro·ma [ˌsklɪə'rəʊmə] *pl.* **-ma·ta** [-mətə] *s.* ⚕ Skle'rom *n*, Verhärtung *f*; **ˌscle'ro·sis** [-'rəʊsɪs] *pl.* **-ro·ses** [-si:z] *s.* **1.** ⚕ Skle'rose *f*, Verhärtung *f* (*des Zellgewebes*); **2.** ♀ Verhärtung *f* (*der Zellwand*); **scle'rot·ic** [-'rɒtɪk] **I** *adj.* ⚕, *anat.* skle'rotisch; *fig.* verkalkt; **II** *s. anat.* → **sclera**; **scle·rous** ['sklɪərəs] *adj.* ⚕ skle'rös, verhärtet.

scoff [skɒf] **I** *s.* **1.** Spott *m*, Hohn *m*; **2.** Zielscheibe *f* des Spotts; **II** *v/i.* **3.** spotten (**at** über *acc.*); **'scoff·er** [-fə] *s.* Spötter(in).

scold [skəʊld] **I** *v/t.* *j-n* (aus)schelten, auszanken; **II** *s.* zänkisches Weib, (Haus)Drachen *m*; **'scold·ing** [-dɪŋ] *s.*

1. Schelten *n*; **2.** Schelte *f*: ***get a*** (***good***) **~** (tüchtig) ausgeschimpft werden.

scol·lop ['skɒləp] → ***scallop***.

sconce¹ [skɒns] *s*. **1.** (Wand-, Kla'vier-) Leuchter *m*; **2.** Kerzenhalter *m*.

sconce² [skɒns] *s*. ⚔ Schanze *f*.

sconce³ [skɒns] *univ*. **I** *v/t*. *zu e-r Strafe* verdonnern; **II** *s*. Strafe *f*.

sconce⁴ [skɒns] *s*. *sl*. ‚Birne' *f*, Schädel *m*.

scone [skɒn] *s*. weiches Teegebäck.

scoop [sku:p] **I** *s*. **1.** a) Schöpfkelle *f*, (*a*. Wasser)Schöpfer *m*, b) (*a*. *Zucker- etc.*) Schaufel *f*, Schippe *f*, c) ⚙ Baggereimer *m*, -löffel *m*; **2.** *Apfel-*, *Käse*-Stecher *m*; **3.** ⚕ Spatel *m*; **4.** (Aus)Schöpfen *n*; **5.** Schub *m*: ***in one* ~** mit 'einem Schub; **6.** *sport* Schlenzer *m*; **7.** *sl*. a) ‚Schnitt' *m*, (großer) Fang, b) *Zeitung*: sensatio'nelle Erstmeldung, Exklu'sivbericht *m*, ‚Knüller' *m*; **II** *v/t*. **8.** schöpfen, schaufeln: **~ *out water*** Wasser ausschöpfen; **~ *up*** (auf)schaufeln, *fig*. *Geld* scheffeln; **9.** *mst* **~ *out*** *Loch* (aus-) graben; **10.** *oft* **~ *in*** *sl*. *Gewinn* einstekken, *Geld* scheffeln; **11.** *sl*. *Konkurrenzzeitung* durch e-e Erstmeldung ausstechen, *j-m* zu'vorkommen (***on*** bei, mit).

scoot [sku:t] F *v/t*. **1.** rasen, flitzen; **2.** ‚abhauen'; '**scoot·er** [-tə] *s*. **1.** (Kinder-, *a*. Motor)Roller *m*; **2.** *sport Am*. Eisjacht *f*.

scope [skəʊp] *s*. **1.** Bereich *m*, Gebiet *n*; ⚖ Anwendungsbereich *m*; Reichweite *f*: ***within the* ~ *of*** im Rahmen (*gen*.); ***come within the* ~ *of*** unter *ein Gesetz etc*. fallen; ***an undertaking of wide* ~** ein großangelegtes Unternehmen; **2.** Ausmaß *n*, 'Umfang *m*: **~ *of authority*** ⚖ Vollmachtsumfang; **3.** (Spiel)Raum *m*, Bewegungsfreiheit *f*: ***give one's fancy full* ~** s-r Phantasie freien Lauf lassen; ***have free* ~** freie Hand haben (***for*** bei); **4.** (geistiger) Hori'zont, Gesichtskreis *m*.

scor·bu·tic [skɔ:'bju:tɪk] ⚕ **I** *adj*. (□ **~*ally***) **1.** skor'butisch, Skorbut…; **II** *s*. **2.** Skor'butkranke(r *m*) *f*.

scorch [skɔ:tʃ] **I** *v/t*. **1.** versengen, -brennen: **~*ed earth*** ⚔ verbrannte Erde; **2.** (aus)dörren; **3.** ϟ verschmoren; **4.** *fig*. (durch scharfe Kritik *od*. beißenden Spott) verletzen; **II** *v/i*. **5.** versengt werden; **6.** ausdörren; **7.** F *mot*. *etc*. rasen; '**scorch·er** [-tʃə] *s*. **1.** F et. sehr Heißes, *bsd*. glühendheißer Tag; **2.** *sl*. ‚Ding' *n*: a) beißende Bemerkung, b) scharfe Kritik, c) böser Brief, d) ‚tolle' Sache; **3.** F *mot*. ‚Raser' *m*; **4.** *sport sl*. a) ‚Bombenschuß' *m*, b) knallharter Schlag; '**scorch·ing** [-tʃɪŋ] *adj*. □ **1.** sengend, brennend (heiß); **2.** vernichtend (*Kritik etc*.).

score [skɔ:] **I** *s*. **1.** Kerbe *f*, Rille *f*; **2.** (Markierungs)Linie *f*; *sport* Start-, Ziellinie *f*: ***get off at full* ~** a) losrasen, b) *fig*. außer sich geraten; **3.** Zeche *f*, Rechnung *f*: ***run up a* ~** Schulden machen; ***settle old* ~*s*** *fig*. e-e alte Rechnung begleichen; ***on the* ~ *of*** *fig*. auf Grund von, wegen; ***on that* ~** in dieser Hinsicht; ***on what* ~?** aus welchem Grund?; **4.** *bsd*. *sport* a) (Spiel)Stand *m*, b) *erzielte* Punkt- *od*. Trefferzahl, (Spiel)Ergebnis *n*, (Be)Wertung *f*, c) Punktliste *f*: ***know the* ~** F Bescheid wissen; ***make a* ~ *off s.o.*** F *fig*. j-m ‚eins auswischen'; ***what is the* ~?** a) wie steht das Spiel?, b) *fig*. *Am*. wie ist die Lage?; **~ *one for me!*** *humor*. eins zu null für mich!; **5.** (Satz *m* von) 20, 20 Stück: ***four* ~ *and seven years*** 87 Jahre; **6.** *pl*. große (An)Zahl *f*, Menge *f*: **~*s of times*** *fig*. hundert-, x-mal; **7.** ♪ Parti'tur *f*; **II** *v/t*. **8.** einkerben; **9.** markieren: **~ *out*** aus-, durchstreichen; **10.** *oft* **~ *up*** *Schulden*, *Zechen* anschreiben, -rechnen: **~** (***up***) ***s.th. against*** (*od*. ***to***) ***s.o.*** *fig*. j-m et. ankreiden; **11.** *ped*. *psych*. *j-s Leistung etc*. bewerten; **12.** *sport* a) *Punkte*, *Treffer* erzielen, sammeln, *Tore* schießen, *fig*. *Erfolge*, *Sieg* verzeichnen, erringen, b) *Punkte*, *Spielstand etc*. aufschreiben: **~ *a hit*** a) e-n Treffer erzielen, b) *fig*. e-n Bombenerfolg haben; **~ *s.o. off*** F *fig*. j-m ‚eins auswischen'; **13.** *sport* zählen: ***a try* ~*s 6 points***; **14.** ♪ a) in Parti'tur setzen, b) instrumentieren; **15.** *Am*. *fig*. scharf kritisieren *od*. angreifen; **III** *v/i*. **16.** *sport* a) e-n Punkt *od*. Treffer erzielen, Punkte sammeln, b) die Punkte zählen *od*. aufschreiben; **17.** F Erfolg *od*. Glück haben, e-n Vorteil erzielen: **~ *over*** *j-n*, *et*. übertreffen; **18.** zählen, gezählt werden: ***that* ~*s for us***; '**~-board** *s*. Anzeigetafel *f im Stadion etc*.; '**~-card** *s*. *sport* **1.** Spielberichtsbogen *m*; **2.** *Boxen etc*.: Punktzettel *m*; *Golf*: Zählkarte *f*.

score·less ['skɔ:lɪs] *adj*. *sport* torlos.

scor·er ['skɔ:rə] *s*. *sport* a) Schreiber *m*, b) Torschütze *m*.

sco·ri·a ['skɔ:rɪə] *pl*. **-ri·ae** [-rɪi:] *s*. (⚙ Me'tall-, *geol*. Gesteins)Schlacke *f*; **sco·ri·a·ceous** [ˌskɔ:rɪ'eɪʃəs] *adj*. schlackig; '**sco·ri·fy** [-ɪfaɪ] *v/t*. verschlacken.

scorn [skɔ:n] **I** *s*. **1.** Verachtung *f*: ***think* ~ *of*** verachten; **2.** Spott *m*, Hohn *m*: ***laugh to* ~** verlachen; **3.** Zielscheibe *f* des Spottes, *das* Gespött (*der Leute etc*.); **II** *v/t*. **4.** verachten: a) geringschätzen, b) verschmähen; '**scorn·ful** [-fʊl] *adj*. □ **1.** verächtlich; **2.** spöttisch.

Scor·pi·o ['skɔ:pɪəʊ] *s*. *ast*. Skorpi'on *m*; '**scor·pi·on** [-pjən] *s*. *zo*. Skorpi'on *m*.

Scot¹ [skɒt] *s*. Schotte *m*, Schottin *f*.

scot² [skɒt] *s*. **1.** (Zahlungs)Beitrag *m*: ***pay*** (***for***) ***one's* ~*s*** s-n Beitrag leisten; **2.** *a*. **~ *and lot*** *hist*. Gemeindeabgabe *f*: ***pay* ~ *and lot*** *fig*. alles auf Heller u. Pfennig bezahlen.

Scotch¹ [skɒtʃ] **I** *adj*. **1.** schottisch (*bsd*. *Whisky etc*.): **~ *broth*** *dicke Rindfleischsuppe mit Gemüse u. Graupen*; **~ *mist*** dichter, nasser Nebel; **~ *tape*** durchsichtiger Klebestreifen; **~ *terrier*** Scotchterrier *m*; **~ *woodcock*** *heißer Toast mit Anchovispaste u. Rührei*; **II** *s*. **2.** Scotch *m*, schottischer Whisky; **3.** ***the* ~** *coll*. die Schotten *pl*.; **4.** *ling*. Schottisch *n*.

scotch² [skɒtʃ] **I** *v/t*. **1.** (leicht) verwunden, schrammen; **2.** *fig*. *et*. im Keim ersticken: **~ *s.o.'s plans*** j-m e-n Strich durch die Rechnung machen; **3.** *Rad etc*. *mit e-m Bremsklotz* blockieren; **II** *s*. **4.** (Ein)Schnitt *m*, Kerbe *f*; **5.** ⚙ Bremsklotz *m*, Hemmschuh *m* (*a*. *fig*.).

'**Scotch·man** [-mən] *s*. [*irr*.] → ***Scotsman***.

ˌ**scot-'free** [ˌskɒt-] *adj*.: ***go*** (*od*. ***get off***) **~** *fig*. ungeschoren davonkommen.

Scot·land Yard ['skɒtlənd] *s*. Scotland Yard *m* (*die Londoner Kriminalpolizei*).

Scots [skɒts] **I** *s*. *ling*. Schottisch *n*; **II** *adj*. schottisch: **~ *law***; '**~·man** [-mən] *s*. [*irr*.] *bsd*. *Scot*. Schotte *m*; '**~ˌwom·an** *s*. [*irr*.] *bsd*. *Scot*. Schottin *f*.

Scot·ti·cism ['skɒtɪsɪzəm] *s*. schottische (Sprach)Eigenheit.

Scot·tish ['skɒtɪʃ] *adj*. schottisch.

scoun·drel ['skaʊndrəl] *s*. Schurke *m*, Schuft *m*, Ha'lunke *m*; '**scoun·drel·ly** [-rəlɪ] *adj*. schurkisch, niederträchtig, gemein.

scour¹ ['skaʊə] *v/t*. **1.** scheuern, schrubben; *Messer etc*. polieren; **2.** *Kleider etc*. säubern, reinigen; **3.** *Kanal etc*. schlämmen, *Rohr etc*. (aus)spülen; **4.** *Pferd etc*. putzen, striegeln; **5.** ⚙ *Wolle* waschen: **~*ing mill*** Wollwäscherei *f*; **6.** *Darm* entschlacken; **7.** *a*. **~ *away***, **~ *off*** *Flecken etc*. entfernen, *Schmutz* abreiben.

scour² ['skaʊə] **I** *v/i*. **1.** *a*. **~ *about*** (um-'her)rennen, (-)jagen; **2.** (suchend) um-'herstreifen; **II** *v/t*. **3.** durch'suchen, -'stöbern, *Gegend a*. -'kämmen, *Stadt a*. ‚abklappern' (***for*** nach).

scourge [skɜ:dʒ] **I** *s*. **1.** Geißel *f*: a) Peitsche *f*, b) *fig*. Plage *f*; **II** *v/t*. **2.** geißeln, (aus)peitschen; **3.** *fig*. a) *durch Kritik etc*. geißeln, b) züchtigen, c) quälen, peinigen.

scouse¹ [skaʊs] *s*. Labskaus *n*.

scouse² [skaʊs] *s*. *Brit*. F *s*. **1.** Liverpooler(in); **2.** Liverpooler Jar'gon *m*.

scout [skaʊt] **I** *s*. **1.** Kundschafter *m*, Späher *m*; **2.** ⚔ a) Erkundungsfahrzeug *n*: **~ *car*** Spähwagen *m*, b) ⚓ *a*. **~ *vessel*** Aufklärungsfahrzeug *n*, c) ✈ *a*. **~** (***air***)***plane*** Aufklärer *m*; **3.** Kundschaften *n*; ⚔ Erkundung *f*: ***on the* ~** auf Erkundung; **4.** Pfadfinder *m*, *Am*. Pfadfinderin *f*; **5.** ***a good* ~** F ein feiner Kerl; **6.** *univ*. *Brit*. Hausdiener *m* e-s College (*Oxford*); **7.** *mot*. *Brit*. Straßenwachtfahrer *m* (*Automobilklub*); **8.** a) *sport* ‚Späher' *m*, Beobachter *m* (*gegnerischer Mannschaften*), b) *a*. ***talent* ~** Ta'lentsucher *m*; **II** *v/i*. **9.** auf Erkundung sein: **~ *about*** (*od*. ***around***) sich umsehen (***for*** nach); **~*ing party*** ⚔ Spähtrupp *m*; **III** *v/t*. **10.** auskundschaften, erkunden; '**~ˌmas·ter** *s*. Führer *m* (e-r Pfadfindergruppe).

scow [skaʊ] *s*. ⚓ (See)Leichter *m*.

scowl [skaʊl] **I** *v/i*. finster blicken: **~ *at*** finster anblicken; **II** *s*. finsterer Blick *od*. (Gesichts)Ausdruck; '**scowl·ing** [-lɪŋ] *adj*. □ finster.

scrab·ble ['skræbl] **I** *v/i*. **1.** kratzen, scharren: **~ *about*** *bsd*. *fig*. (herum)suchen (***for*** nach); **2.** *fig*. sich (ab)plagen (***for*** für, um); **3.** krabbeln; **4.** kritzeln; **II** *v/t*. **5.** scharren nach; **6.** bekritzeln.

scrag [skræg] **I** *s*. **1.** *fig*. ‚Gerippe' *n* (*dürrer Mensch etc*.); **2.** *mst* **~ *end*** (***of mutton***) (Hammel)Hals *m*; **3.** F ‚Kragen' *m*, Hals *m*; **II** *v/t*. **4.** *sl*. a) *j-n* ‚abmurksen', *j-m* den Hals 'umdrehen, b) *j-n* aufhängen; '**scrag·gi·ness** [-gɪnɪs] *s*. Magerkeit *f*; '**scrag·gy** [-gɪ] *adj*. □ **1.** dürr, hager, knorrig; **2.** zerklüftet, rauh.

scram [skræm] *v/i. sl.* ‚abhauen', verduften: ***~!*** hau ab!, raus!

scram·ble ['scræmbl] **I** *v/i.* **1.** krabbeln, klettern: ***~ to one's feet*** sich aufrappeln; **2.** *a. fig.* sich raufen *od.* balgen (***for*** um): ***~ for a living*** sich (um s-n Lebensunterhalt) ‚abstrampeln'; **II** *v/t.* **3.** *oft* ***~ up***, ***~ together*** zs.-scharren, -raffen; **4.** ϟ *Funkspruch etc.* zerhakken; **5.** *Eier* verrühren: ***~d eggs*** Rührei *n*; **6.** *Karten etc.* durchein'anderwerfen; *Flugplan etc.* durchein'anderbringen; **III** *s.* **7.** Krabbe'lei *f*, Klette'rei *f*; **8.** *a. fig.* (***for***) Balge'rei *f* (um), Jagd *f* (nach *Geld etc.*); **9.** *Brit.* Moto-'Cross-Rennen *n*; **10.** ✈ a) A'larmstart *m*, b) Luftkampf *m*; **'scram·bler** [-lə] *s. tel.* Zerhacker *m*.

scrap¹ [skræp] **I** *s.* **1.** Stück(chen) *n*, Brocken *m*, Fetzen *m*, Schnitzel *n*, *m*: ***a ~ of paper*** ein Fetzen Papier (*a. fig.*); ***not a ~*** kein bißchen; **2.** *pl.* Abfall *m*, (*bsd.* Speise)Reste *pl.*; **3.** (Zeitungs-) Ausschnitt *m*; ausgeschnittenes Bild *etc. zum Einkleben*; **4.** *mst pl. fig.* Bruchstück *n*, (Gesprächs- *etc.*)Fetzen *m*: ***~s of conversation***; **5.** *mst pl.* (Fett)Grieben *pl.*; **6.** ⚙ a) Schrott *m*, b) Ausschuß *m*, c) Abfall *m*: ***~ value*** Schrottwert *m*; **II** *v/t.* **7.** (als unbrauchbar) ausrangieren; **8.** *fig.* zum alten Eisen *od.* über Bord werfen: ***~ methods***; **9.** ⚙ verschrotten.

scrap² [skræp] *sl.* **I** *s.* **1.** Streit *m*, Ausein'andersetzung *f*; **2.** Keile'rei *f*, Prüge'lei *f*; **3.** (Box)Kampf *m*; **II** *v/i.* **4.** streiten; **5.** sich prügeln; kämpfen (***with*** mit).

'scrap·book *s.* Sammelalbum *n*, Einklebebuch *n*.

scrape [skreɪp] **I** *s.* **1.** Kratzen *n*, Scharren *n*; **2.** Kratzer *m*, Schramme *f*; **3.** *fig. obs.* Kratzfuß *m*; **4.** *fig.* ‚Klemme' *f*: ***be in a ~*** in der Klemme sein *od.* sitzen; **5.** ***bread and ~*** F dünngeschmiertes Butterbrot; **II** *v/t.* **6.** kratzen, schaben: ***~ off*** ab-, wegkratzen; ***~ together*** (*od.* ***up***) *a. fig. Geld etc.* zs.-kratzen; ***~ (an) acquaintance with*** a) oberflächlich bekannt werden mit, b) *contp.* sich bei *j-m* anbiedern; ***~ a living*** → 11; **7.** kratzen *od.* scharren mit *den Füßen etc.*; **III** *v/i.* **8.** kratzen, schaben, scharren; **9.** scheuern, sich reiben (***against*** an *dat.*); **10.** kratzen (***on*** auf *e-r Geige etc.*); **11.** *mst* ***~ along*** *fig.* sich (mühsam) 'durchschlagen: ***~ through (an examination)*** mit Ach u. Krach durchkommen (durch e-e Prüfung); **'scrap·er** [-pə] *s.* **1.** Fußabstreifer *m*; **2.** ⚙ a) Schaber *m*, Kratzer *m*, Streichmesser *n*, b) ⚠ *etc.* Schrapper *m*, c) Planierpflug *m*.

scrap heap *s.* Abfall-, Schrotthaufen *m*: ***fit only for the ~*** völlig wertlos; ***throw on the ~*** *fig. a. j-n* zum alten Eisen werfen.

scrap·ing ['skreɪpɪŋ] *s.* **1.** Kratzen *n etc.*; **2.** *pl.* (Ab)Schabsel *pl.*, Späne *pl.*; **3.** *pl. fig. contp.* Abschaum *m*.

scrap| i·ron *s.*, **~ met·al** *s.* ⚙ (Eisen-) Schrott *m*, Alteisen *n*.

scrap·per ['skræpə] *s. sl.* Raufbold *m*.

scrap·py¹ ['skræpɪ] *adj.* ☐ *sl.* rauflustig.

scrap·py² ['skræpɪ] *adj.* ☐ **1.** aus (Speise)Resten (hergestellt): ***~ dinner***; **2.** bruchstückhaft; **3.** zs.-gestoppelt.

'scrap·yard *s.* Schrottplatz *m*.

scratch [skrætʃ] **I** *s.* **1.** Kratzer *m*, Schramme *f* (*beide a. fig. leichte Verwundung*), Riß *m*; **2.** Kratzen *n* (*a. Geräusch*): ***by the ~ of a pen*** mit 'einem Federstrich; **3.** *sport* a) Startlinie *f*, b) nor'male Startbedingungen *pl.*: ***come up to (the) ~*** a) sich stellen, s-n Mann stehen, b) den Erwartungen entsprechen; ***keep s.o. up to (the) ~*** j-n bei der Stange halten; ***start from ~*** a) ohne Vorgabe starten, b) *fig.* ganz von vorne anfangen; ***up to ~*** auf der Höhe, in Form; **4.** *pl. mst sg. konstr. vet.* Mauke *f*; **II** *adj.* **5.** Konzept…, Schmier…: ***~ paper***; ***~ pad*** a) Notizblock *m*, b) *Computer*: Notizblockspeicher *m*; **6.** *sport* a) ohne Vorgabe: ***~ race***, b) zs.-gewürfelt: ***~ team***; **III** *v/t.* **7.** (zer)kratzen: ***~ the surface of*** *fig. et.* (nur) oberflächlich behandeln; **8.** kratzen; *Tier* kraulen: ***~ one's head*** sich (*aus Verlegenheit etc.*) den Kopf kratzen; ***~ together*** (*od.* ***up***) *bsd. fig.* zs.-kratzen, -scharren; **9.** kritzeln; **10.** *a.* ***~ out***, ***~ through*** aus-, 'durchstreichen; **11.** *sport Pferd etc.* vom Rennen, *a. Nennung* zu'rückziehen; **12.** *pol. Kandidaten* streichen; **IV** *v/i.* **13.** kratzen (*a. Schreibfeder etc.*); **14.** sich kratzen *od.* scheuern; **15.** scharren (***for*** nach); **16.** ***~ along***, ***~ through*** → ***scrape*** 11; **17.** *sport* s-e Meldung zu'rückziehen, ausscheiden; **'scratch·y** [-tʃɪ] *adj.* ☐ **1.** kratzend; **2.** zerkratzt; **3.** kritzelig; **4.** *sport* a) → ***scratch*** 6, b) unausgeglichen; **5.** *vet.* an Mauke erkrankt.

scrawl [skrɔːl] **I** *v/t.* kritzeln, hinschmieren; **II** *v/i.* kritzeln; **III** *s.* Gekritzel *n*; Geschreibsel *n*.

scray [skreɪ] *s. Brit.* Seeschwalbe *f*.

scream [skriːm] **I** *s.* **1.** (gellender) Schrei; **2.** Gekreisch(e) *n*: ***~s of laughter*** brüllendes Gelächter; ***he (it) was a (perfect) ~*** *sl.* er (es) war zum Schreien (komisch); **3.** Heulen *n* (*Sirene etc.*); **II** *v/i.* **4.** schreien (*a. fig. Farben etc.*), gellen; kreischen: ***~ out*** aufschreien; ***~ with laughter*** vor Lachen brüllen; **5.** heulen (*Wind etc.*), schrill pfeifen; **III** *v/t.* **6.** *oft* ***~ out*** (her'aus)schreien; **'scream·er** [-mə] *s.* **1.** Schreiende(r *m*) *f*; **2.** *sl.* a) ‚tolle Sache', b) *bsd. Am.* F Riesenschlagzeile *f*; **'scream·ing** [-mɪŋ] *adj.* ☐ **1.** schrill, gellend; **2.** *fig.* schreiend, grell: ***~ colo(u)rs***; **3.** F a) ‚toll', großartig, b) *a.* ***~ly funny*** zum Schreien (komisch).

scree [skriː] *s. geol. Brit.* **1.** Geröll *n*; **2.** Geröllhalde *f*.

screech [skriːtʃ] **I** *v/i.* (gellend) schreien; kreischen (*a. weitS. Bremsen etc.*); **II** *v/t. et.* kreischen; **III** *s.* ('durchdringender) Schrei; ***~ owl*** *s. orn.* schreiende Eule.

screed [skriːd] *s.* **1.** lange Liste; **2.** langatmige Rede *etc.*, Ti'rade *f*.

screen [skriːn] **I** *s.* **1.** (Schutz)Schirm *m*, (-)Wand *f*; **2.** ⚠ a) Zwischenwand *f*, b) *eccl.* Lettner *m*; **3.** a) (Film)Leinwand *f*, b) *coll.* ***the ~*** der Film, das Kino: ***~ star*** Filmstar *m*; ***on the ~*** im Film; **4.** a) *TV*, *Radar*, *Computer*: Bildschirm *m*, b) ⚕ Röntgenschirm *m*; **5.** Drahtgitter *n*, -netz *n*; **6.** Fliegenfenster *n*; **7.** ⚙ Gittersieb *n für Sand etc.*; **8.** ⚔ a) *taktische* Abschirmung, (⚓ Geleit-) Schutz *m*, b) (Rauch-, Schützen-) Schleier *m*, Nebelwand *f*, c) Tarnung *f*; **9.** *fig.* a) Schutz *m*, Schirm *m*, b) Tarnung *f*, Maske *f*; **10.** *phys.* a) *a.* ***optical ~*** Filter *m*, Blende *f*, b) *a.* ***electric ~*** Abschirmung *f*, c) *a.* ***ground ~*** Erdungsebene *f*; **11.** *phot.*, *typ.* Raster (-platte *f*) *m*; **12.** *mot.* Windschutzscheibe *f*; **II** *v/t.* **13.** *a.* ***~ off*** abschirmen, verdecken; *Licht* abblenden; **14.** (be-) schirmen (***from*** vor *dat.*); **15.** *fig. j-n* decken; **16.** ⚔ a) tarnen (*a. fig.*), b) einnebeln; **17.** ⚙ *Sand etc.* ('durch)sieben: ***~ed coal*** Würfelkohle *f*; **18.** *phot. Bild* projizieren; **19.** *Film*: a) verfilmen, b) für den Film bearbeiten; **20.** *fig. Personen* (aus)sieben, (über)'prüfen; **III** *v/i.* **21.** sich (ver)filmen lassen; sich für den Film eignen (*a. Person*); ***~ grid*** *s.* ϟ Schirmgitter *n*; **'~·land** [-lənd] *s. Am.* Filmwelt *f*; **'~·play** *s. Film*: Drehbuch *n*; **'~·print I** *s.* Siebdruck *m*; **II** *v/t.* im Siebdruckverfahren herstellen; **~ test** *s. Film*: Probeaufnahme *f*; **'~-test** *v/t. Film*: Probeaufnahmen machen von; **~ wash·er** *s. mot.* Scheibenwaschanlage *f*; **~ wire** *s.* ⚙ Maschendraht *m*.

screw [skruː] **I** *s.* **1.** ⚙ Schraube *f* (*ohne Mutter*): ***there is a ~ loose (somewhere)*** *fig.* da stimmt et. nicht; ***he has a ~ loose*** F bei ihm ist e-e Schraube locker; **2.** ⚙ Spindel *f* (*Presse*); **3.** (Flugzeug-, Schiffs)Schraube *f*; **4.** ⚓ Schraubendampfer *m*; **5.** F *fig.* Druck *m*: ***apply the ~ to***, ***put the ~(s) on*** *j-n* unter Druck setzen; ***give another turn to the ~*** *a. fig.* die Schraube anziehen; **6.** *Brit.* Tütchen *n Tabak etc.*; **7.** *bsd. sport* Ef'fet *m*; **8.** *Brit.* Geizhals *m*; **9.** *Brit.* alter Klepper (*Pferd*); **10.** *Brit. sl.* Lohn *m*, Gehalt *n*; **11.** Korkenzieher *m*; **12.** *sl.* Gefängniswärter *m*; **13.** V ‚Nummer' *f*: ***have a ~*** ‚bumsen'; ***be a good ~*** gut ‚bumsen'; **II** *v/t.* **14.** schrauben: ***~ down*** ein-, festschrauben; ***~ on*** an-, aufschrauben; ***~ up*** a) zuschrauben, b) *Papier* zerknüllen; ***his head is ~ed on the right way*** F er ist nicht auf den Kopf gefallen; **15.** *fig. Augen*, *Körper etc.* (ver)drehen; *Mund etc.* verziehen; **16.** ***~ down (up)*** ✝ *Preise* her'unter- (hoch)schrauben; ***~ s.th. out of*** et. aus *j-m* herauspressen; ***~ up one's courage*** Mut fassen; **17.** *sport dem Ball* Ef'fet geben; **18.** F *j-n* ‚reinlegen'; **19.** ***~ up*** F ‚vermasseln'; **20.** V ‚bumsen', ‚vögeln': ***~ you!***, ***get ~ed*** *bsd. Am.* geh zum Teufel!; **III** *v/i.* **21.** sich (ein)schrauben lassen; **22.** knausern; **23.** V ‚bumsen', ‚vögeln'; **24.** ***~ around*** *Am. sl.* sich he'rumtreiben.

'screw|·ball *Am.* **I** *s.* **1.** *Baseball*: Ef'fetball *m*; **2.** *sl.* ‚Spinner' *m*; **II** *adj.* **3.** *sl.* verrückt; **~ bolt** *s.* ⚙ Schraubenbolzen *m*; **~ cap** *s.* **1.** Schraubdeckel *m*, Verschlußkappe *f*; **2.** 'Überwurfmutter *f*; **~ con·vey·er** *s.* Förderschnecke *f*; **~ die** *s.* Gewindeschneideeisen *n*; **'~·driv·er** *s.* Schraubenzieher *m*.

screw·ed [skruːd] *adj.* **1.** verschraubt; **2.** mit Gewinde; **3.** verdreht, gewunden; **4.** F ‚besoffen'.

screw| gear(·ing) *s.* ⚙ **1.** Schneckenrad *n*; **2.** Schneckengetriebe *n*; **~ jack** *s.* **1.** Hebespindel *f*; **2.** Wagenheber *m*; **~ nut** *s.* Mutterschraube *f*; **~ press** *s.* Spindel- *od.* Schraubenpresse *f*; **~**

steam·er → *screw* 4; **~ tap** *s.* ⚙ Gewindebohrer *m*; **~ top** *s.* Schraubverschluß *m*; **~ wrench** *s.* ⚙ Schraubenschlüssel *m*.

screw·y ['skru:ɪ] *adj.* **1.** schraubenartig; **2.** F ‚beschwipst'; **3.** *Am. sl.* verrückt; **4.** knickerig.

scrib·ble ['skrɪbl] **I** *v/t.* **1.** *a.* **~ down** (hin)kritzeln, (-)schmieren: **~ over** bekritzeln; **2.** ⚙ *Wolle* krempeln; **II** *v/i.* **3.** kritzeln; **III** *s.* **4.** Gekritzel *n*, Geschreibsel *n*; **'scrib·bler** [-lə] *s.* **1.** Kritzler *m*, Schmierer *m*; **2.** Schreiberling *m*; **3.** ⚙ 'Krempelma,schine *f*.

scrib·bling| block, **~ pad** ['skrɪblɪŋ] *s. Brit.* Schmier-, No'tizblock *m*.

scribe [skraɪb] **I** *s.* **1.** Schreiber *m* (*a. hist.*), Ko'pist *m*; **2.** *bibl.* Schriftgelehrte(r) *m*; **3.** *humor.* a) Schriftsteller *m*, b) Journa'list *m*; **4.** ⚙ *a.* **~ awl** Reißnadel *f*; **II** *v/t.* **5.** ⚙ anreißen; **'scrib·er** [-bə] → *scribe* 4.

scrim [skrɪm] *s.* leichter Leinen- *od.* Baumwollstoff.

scrim·mage ['skrɪmɪdʒ] *s.* **1.** Handgemenge *n*, Getümmel *n*; **2.** a) *American Football*: Scrimmage *n* (*Rückpaß*), b) *Rugby*: Gedränge *n*.

scrimp [skrɪmp] **I** *v/t.* **1.** knausern mit, knapp bemessen; **2.** *j-n* knapp halten (*for* mit); **II** *v/i.* **3.** *a.* **~ and save** knausern (*on* mit); **III** *adj.* **4.** → **'scrimp·y** [-pɪ] knapp, eng.

'scrim·shank *v/i. bsd.* ⚔ *Brit. sl.* sich drücken.

scrip¹ [skrɪp] *s. hist.* (Pilger-, Schäfer-) Tasche *f*, Ränzel *n*.

scrip² [skrɪp] *s.* **1.** ⚚ a) Berechtigungsschein *m*, b) Scrip *m*, Interimsschein *m*, -aktie *f*, *coll. die* Scrips *pl. etc.*; **2.** *a.* **~ money** a) Er'satzpa,piergeldwährung *f*, b) ⚔ Besatzungsgeld *n*.

script [skrɪpt] *s.* **1.** Handschrift *f*; **2.** Schrift(art) *f*: **phonetic ~** Lautschrift; **3.** *typ.* (Schreib)Schrift *f*; **4.** a) Text *m*, b) *thea. etc.* Manu'skript *n*, c) *Film*: Drehbuch *n*; **5.** ⚖ Urschrift *f*; **6.** *ped. Brit.* (schriftliche) Prüfungsarbeit; **~ ed·i·tor** *s. Film, thea., TV*: Drama'turg *m*; **~ girl** *s. Film*: Scriptgirl *n* (*Ateliersekretärin*).

scrip·tur·al ['skrɪptʃərəl] *adj.* **1.** Schrift...; **2.** *a.* ♀ biblisch, der Heiligen Schrift; **scrip·ture** ['skrɪptʃə] *s.* **1.** ♀, *mst* **the ♀s** *die* Heilige Schrift, *die* Bibel; **2.** *obs.* ♀ Bibelstelle *f*; **3.** heilige (nichtchristliche) Schrift: **Buddhist ~**; **4.** *a.* **~ class** (*od.* **lesson**) *ped.* Religi'onsstunde *f*.

'script,writ·er *s.* **1.** *Film, TV*: Drehbuchautor(in); **2.** *Radio*: Hörspielautor(in).

scrive·ner ['skrɪvnə] *s. hist.* **1.** (öffentlicher) Schreiber; **2.** No'tar *m*.

scrof·u·la ['skrɒfjʊlə] *s.* ⚕ Skrofu'lose *f*; **'scrof·u·lous** [-ləs] *adj.* □ ⚕ skrofu'lös.

scroll [skrəʊl] *s.* **1.** Schriftrolle *f*; **2.** a) ⚠ Vo'lute *f*, b) ♪ Schnecke *f*, c) Schnörkel *m* (*Schrift*); **3.** Liste *f*, Verzeichnis *n*; **4.** ⚙ Triebkranz *m*; **~ chuck** *s.* ⚙ Univer'salspannfutter *n*; **~ gear** *s.* ⚙ Schneckenrad *n*; **~ saw** *s.* ⚙ Laubsäge *f*; **'~·work** *s.* **1.** Schneckenverzierung *f*; **2.** Laubsägearbeit *f*.

scro·tum ['skrəʊtəm] *pl.* **-ta** [-tə] *s. anat.* Hodensack *m*, Skrotum *n*.

scrounge [skraʊndʒ] F **I** *v/t.* **1.** ‚organisieren': a) ‚klauen', b) beschaffen; **2.** schnorren; **II** *v/i.* **3.** ‚klauen'; **4.** schnorren, nassauern; **'scroung·er** [-dʒə] *s.* F **1.** Dieb *m*; **2.** Schnorrer *m*, Nassauer *m*.

scrub¹ [skrʌb] **I** *v/t.* **1.** schrubben, scheuern; **2.** ⚙ *Gas* reinigen; **3.** F *fig.* streichen, ausfallen lassen; **II** *v/i.* **4.** schrubben, scheuern; **III** *s.* **5.** Schrubben *n*: **that wants a good ~** das muß tüchtig gescheuert werden; **6.** *sport* a) Re'servespieler *m*, b) *a.* **~ team** zweite Mannschaft *od.* ‚Garni'tur', c) *a.* **~ game** Spiel *n* der Re'servemannschaften.

scrub² [skrʌb] *s.* **1.** Gestrüpp *n*, Buschwerk *n*; **2.** Busch *m* (*Gebiet*); **3.** a) verkümmerter Baum, b) Tier *n* minderwertiger Abstammung, c) Knirps *m*, d) *fig. contp.* ‚Null' *f* (*Person*).

'scrub(·bing) brush ['skrʌbɪŋ] *s.* Scheuerbürste *f*.

scrub·by ['skrʌbɪ] *adj.* **1.** verkümmert, -krüppelt; **2.** gestrüppreich; **3.** armselig, schäbig; **4.** stopp(e)lig.

scruff [skrʌf], **~ of the neck** *s.* Genick *n*: **take s.o. by the ~ of the neck** j-n beim Kragen packen.

scruff·y ['skrʌfɪ] *adj.* F schmudd(e)lig, dreckig.

scrum·mage ['skrʌmɪdʒ] → **scrimmage**.

scrump·tious ['skrʌmpʃəs] *adj.* F ‚toll', ‚prima'.

scrunch [skrʌntʃ] **I** *v/t.* **1.** knirschend (zer)kauen; **2.** zermalmen; **II** *v/i.* **3.** knirschen; **4.** knirschend kauen; **III** *s.* **5.** Knirschen *n*.

scru·ple ['skru:pl] **I** *s.* **1.** Skrupel *m*, Zweifel *m*, Bedenken *n* (*alle mst pl.*): **have ~s about doing** Bedenken haben, *et.* zu tun; **without ~** skrupellos; **2.** *pharm.* Skrupel *n* (= *20 Gran od. 1,296 Gramm*); **II** *v/i.* **3.** Skrupel *od.* Bedenken haben; **'scru·pu·lous** [-pjʊləs] *adj.* □ **1.** voller Skrupel *od.* Bedenken, (allzu) bedenklich (**about** in *dat.*); **2.** ('über)gewissenhaft, peinlich (genau); **3.** ängstlich, vorsichtig.

scru·ti·neer [,skru:tɪ'nɪə] *s. pol.* Wahlprüfer *m*; **scru·ti·nize** ['skru:tɪnaɪz] *v/t.* **1.** (genau) prüfen, unter'suchen; **2.** genau ansehen, studieren; **scru·ti·ny** ['skru:tɪnɪ] *s.* **1.** (genaue) Unter'suchung, *pol.* Wahlprüfung *f*; **2.** prüfender *od.* forschender Blick.

scu·ba ['sku:bə] *s.* (Schwimm)Tauchgerät *n*: **~ diving** Sporttauchen *n*.

scud [skʌd] **I** *v/i.* **1.** eilen, jagen; **2.** ⚓ lenzen; **II** *s.* **3.** (Da'hin)Jagen *n*; **4.** (tieftreibende) Wolkenfetzen *pl.*; **5.** (Wind)Bö *f*.

scuff [skʌf] **I** *v/i.* **1.** schlurfen(d gehen); **2.** ab-, aufscharren; **II** *v/t.* **3.** *bsd. Am.* abstoßen, abnutzen; **4.** boxen.

scuf·fle ['skʌfl] **I** *v/i.* **1.** sich balgen, raufen; **2.** → *scuff* 1; **II** *s.* **3.** Balge'rei *f*, Raufe'rei *f*, Handgemenge *n*; **4.** Schlurfen *n*.

scull [skʌl] ⚓ **I** *s.* **1.** Heck-, Wriggriemen *m*; **2.** Skullboot *n*; **II** *v/i. u. v/t.* **3.** wriggen; **4.** skullen; **'scul·ler** [-lə] *s.* **1.** Skuller *m* (*Ruderer*); **2.** → *scull* 2.

scul·ler·y ['skʌlərɪ] *s. Brit.* Spülküche *f*: **~-maid** Spül-, Küchenmädchen *n*; **'scul·lion** [-ljən] *s. hist. Brit.* Küchenjunge *m*.

sculp(t) [skʌlp(t)] F *für* **sculpture** II *u.* III.

sculp·tor ['skʌlptə] *s.* Bildhauer *m*; **'sculp·tress** [-trɪs] *s.* Bildhauerin *f*; **'sculp·tur·al** [-tʃərəl] *adj.* □ bildhauerisch, Skulptur...; **'sculp·ture** [-tʃə] **I** *s.* Plastik *f*: a) Bildhauerkunst *f*, b) Skulp'tur *f*, Bildhauerwerk *n*; **II** *v/t.* formen, (her'aus)meißeln *od.* (-)schnitzen; **III** *v/i.* bildhauern.

scum [skʌm] **I** *s.* (⚙ *u. fig.* Ab)Schaum *m*: **the ~ of the earth** *fig.* der Abschaum der Menschheit; **II** *v/t. u. v/i.* abschäumen.

scum·ble ['skʌmbl] *paint.* **I** *v/t.* **1.** *Farben*, *Umrisse* vertreiben, dämpfen; **II** *s.* **2.** Gedämpftheit *f*; **3.** La'sur *f*.

scum·my ['skʌmɪ] *adj.* **1.** schaumig; **2.** *fig.* gemein, ‚fies'.

scup·per ['skʌpə] **I** *s.* **1.** ⚓ Speigatt *n*; **II** *v/t.* ⚔ *Brit. sl.* **2.** niedermetzeln; **3.** *Schiff* versenken; **4.** *fig.* ka'puttmachen.

scurf [skɜ:f] *s.* **1.** ⚕ a) Schorf *m*, Grind *m*, b) *bsd. Brit.* (Kopf)Schuppen *pl.*; **2.** abblätternde Kruste; **'scurf·y** [-fɪ] *adj.* schorfig, grindig; schuppig.

scur·ril·i·ty [skʌ'rɪlətɪ] *s.* **1.** zotige Scherzhaftigkeit; **2.** Zotigkeit *f*; **3.** Zote *f*; **scur·ril·ous** ['skʌrɪləs] *adj.* □ **1.** ordi'när-scherzhaft, ‚frech'; **2.** unflätig, zotig.

scur·ry ['skʌrɪ] **I** *v/i.* **1.** huschen, hasten; **II** *s.* **2.** Hasten *n*; Getrippel *n*; **3.** *sport* a) Sprint *m*, b) *Pferdesport*: Fliegerrennen *n*; **4.** Schneetreiben *n*.

scur·vy ['skɜ:vɪ] **I** *s.* ⚕ Skor'but *m*; **II** *adj.* (hunds)gemein, ‚fies'.

scut [skʌt] *s.* **1.** *hunt.* Blume *f*, kurzer Schwanz (*Hase*), Wedel *m* (*Rotwild*); **2.** Stutzschwanz *m*.

scu·tage ['skju:tɪdʒ] *s.* ⚔ *hist.* Schildpfennig *m*, Rittersteuer *f*.

scutch [skʌtʃ] ⚙ **I** *v/t.* **1.** *Flachs* schwingen; **2.** *Baumwolle od. Seidenfäden* (durch Schlagen) entwirren; **II** *s.* **3.** (Flachs)Schwingmesser *n*, ('Flachs-) ,Schwingma,schine *f*.

scutch·eon ['skʌtʃən] *s.* **1.** → **escutcheon**; **2.** → **scute**.

scute [skju:t] *s. zo.* Schuppe *f*.

scu·tel·late(d) ['skju:təleɪt(ɪd)] *adj. zo.* schuppig; **scu'tel·lum** [skju:'teləm] *pl.* **-la** [-lə] *s.* ♀, *zo.* Schildchen *n*.

scut·tle¹ ['skʌtl] *s.* **1.** Kohlenkasten *m*, -eimer *m*; **2.** (flacher) Korb.

scut·tle² ['skʌtl] **I** *v/i.* **1.** hasten, flitzen; **2.** **~ out of** ⚔ *u. fig.* sich hastig zu'rückziehen aus *od.* von; **II** *s.* **3.** hastiger Rückzug.

scut·tle³ ['skʌtl] **I** *s.* **1.** (Dach-, Boden-) Luke *f*; **2.** ⚓ (Spring)Luke *f*; **3.** *mot.* Stirnwand *f*, Spritzbrett *n*; **II** *v/t.* **4.** ⚓ a) *Schiff* anbohren *od.* die 'Bodenven,tile öffnen, b) (selbst) versenken; **'~·butt** *s.* **1.** ⚓ Trinkwassertonne *f od.* -anlage *f*; **2.** *Am.* F Gerücht *n*.

scythe [saɪð] **I** *s.* **1.** Sense *f*; **II** *v/t.* **2.** (ab)mähen; **3.** **~ down** *Fußball*: ‚umsäbeln'.

sea [si:] *s.* **1.** a) See *f*, Meer *n* (*a. fig.*), b) Ozean *m*, Weltmeer *n*: **at ~** auf *od.* zur See; *mst* **all at ~** *fig.* ratlos, im dunkeln tappend; **beyond the ~**, **over ~(s)** nach *od.* in Übersee; **by ~** auf dem Seeweg; **on the ~** a) auf *od.* zur See, b) an der See *od.* Küste (gelegen); **follow the**

~ zur See fahren; ***put** (**out**) **to** ~* in See stechen; ***the four ~s*** die vier (*Großbritannien umgebenden*) Meere; ***the high ~s*** die hohe See, die Hochsee; **2.** ⚓ See(gang *m*) *f*: ***heavy ~***; ***long** (**short**) ~* lange (kurze) See; **3.** ⚓ See *f*, hohe Welle; → ***ship*** 7; ~ **an·chor** *s.* **1.** ⚓ Treibanker *m*; **2.** ✈ Wasseranker *m*; ~ **bear** *s. zo.* **1.** Eisbär *m*; **2.** Seebär *m*; **'~·board I** *s.* (See)Küste *f*; **II** *adj.* Küsten...; **'~-born** *adj.* **1.** aus dem Meer stammend; **2.** *poet.* meergeboren; **'~·borne** *adj.* auf dem Seewege befördert, See...: ~ ***goods*** Seehandelsgüter; ~ ***invasion*** ⚔ Landungsunternehmen *n* von See aus; ~ ***trade*** Seehandel *m*; ~ **calf** → ***sea dog*** 1a; ~ **cap·tain** *s.* ('Schiffs)Kapiˌtän *m*; ~ **cock** *s.* ⚓ 'Bordvenˌtil *n*; ~ **cow** *s. zo.* **1.** Seekuh *f*, Si'rene *f*; **2.** Walroß *n*; ~ **dog** *s.* **1.** *zo.* a) Gemeiner Seehund, Meerkalb *n*, b) → ***dogfish***; **2.** *fig.* ⚓ (alter) Seebär; **'~·drome** [-drəʊm] *s.* ✈ Wasserflughafen *m*; ~ **el·e·phant** *s. zo.* 'See-Eleˌfant *m*; **'~ˌfar·er** [-ˌfeərə] *s.* Seefahrer *m*, -mann *m*; **'~ˌfar·ing** [-ˌfeərɪŋ] **I** *adj.* seefahrend: ~ ***man*** Seemann *m*; ~ ***nation*** Seefahrernation *f*; **II** *s.* Seefahrt *f*; ~ **farm·ing** *s.* 'Aquakulˌtur *f*; **'~·food** *s.* Meeresfrüchte *pl.*; **'~·fowl** *s.* Seevogel *m*; ~ **front** *s.* Seeseite *f* (*e-r Stadt etc.*); ~ **ga(u)ge** *s.* ⚓ **1.** Tiefgang *m*; **2.** Lotstock *m*; **'~·girt** *adj. poet.* 'meerumˌschlungen; ~ **god** *s.* Meeresgott *m*; **'~ˌgo·ing** *adj.* ⚓ seetüchtig, Hochsee...; ~ **green** *s.* Meergrün *n*; ~ **gull** *s. orn.* Seemöwe *f*; ~ **hog** *s. zo.* Schweinswal *m*, *bsd.* Meerschwein *n*; ~ **horse** *s.* **1.** *zo.* a) Seepferdchen *n*, b) Walroß *n*; **2.** *myth.* Seepferd *n*; **3.** große Welle.

seal¹ [siːl] **I** *s.* **1.** *pl.* **seals**, *bsd. coll.* **seal** *zo.* Robbe *f*, *engS.* Seehund *m*; **2.** → ***sealskin***; **II** *v/i.* **3.** auf Robbenjagd gehen.

seal² [siːl] **I** *s.* **1.** Siegel *n*: ***set one's ~ to*** sein Siegel auf *et.* drücken, *bsd. fig. et.* besiegeln (*bekräftigen*); ***under the ~ of secrecy*** *fig.* unter dem Siegel der Verschwiegenheit; **2.** Siegel(prägung *f*) *n*; **3.** Siegel(stempel *m*) *n*, Petschaft *n*; → ***Great Seal***; **4.** ⚖ *etc.* Siegel *n*, Verschluß *m*; *Zollverkehr etc.*: Plombe *f*: ***under ~*** unter Verschluß; **5.** ⚙ a) (wasser-, luftdichter) Verschluß, b) (Ab-)Dichtung *f*, c) Versiegelung *f* (*Kunststoff etc.*); **6.** *fig.* Siegel *n*, Besiegelung *f*, Bekräftigung *f*; **7.** Zeichen *n*, Garan'tie *f*; **8.** *fig.* Stempel *m*, Zeichen *n des Todes etc.*; **II** *v/t.* **9.** *Urkunde* siegeln; **10.** *Rechtsgeschäft etc.* besiegeln (*bekräftigen*); **11.** *fig.* besiegeln: ***his fate is ~ed***; **12.** *fig.* zeichnen, s-n Stempel aufdrücken (*dat.*); **13.** versiegeln: ***~ed offer*** ☤ versiegeltes Angebot; ***under ~ed orders*** ☤ mit versiegelter Order; **14.** *Verschluß etc.* plombieren; **15.** *oft* ~ ***up*** her'metisch (*od.* ⚙ wasser-, vakuumdicht) abschließen *od.* abdichten, *Holz, Kunststoff etc.* versiegeln, ⚙ *a.* einzementieren, zuschmelzen, *mit Klebestreifen etc.* verschließen: ***it is a ~ed book to me*** *fig.* es ist mir ein Buch mit sieben Siegeln; ~ ***a letter*** e-n Brief zukleben; **16.** ~ ***off*** *fig.* a) ⚔ *etc.* abriegeln, b) dichtmachen: ~ ***off the border***.

sea lane *s.* See-, Schiffahrtsweg *m*.

seal·ant ['siːlənt] *s.* ⚙ Dichtungsmittel *n*.

sea| law·yer *s.* ⚓ F Queru'lant *m*; **'~-legs** *s. pl.*: ***get** od. **find one's** ~* ⚓ seefest werden.

seal·er¹ ['siːlə] *s.* ⚓ Robbenfänger *m* (*Mann od. Schiff*).

seal·er² ['siːlə] *s.* ⚙ a) Versiegler *m*, b) Verschließvorrichtung *f*, c) Versiegelungsmasse *f*.

'seal·er·y [-ərɪ] *s.* **1.** Robbenfang *m*; **2.** Robbenfangplatz *m*.

sea lev·el *s.* Meeresspiegel *m*, -höhe *f*: ***corrected to ~*** auf Meereshöhe umgerechnet.

'seal-ˌfish·er·y → ***sealery*** 1.

seal·ing ['siːlɪŋ] *s.* **1.** (Be)Siegeln *n*; **2.** Versiegeln *n*, ⚙ *a.* (Ab)Dichtung *f*: ~ (***compound***) Dichtungsmasse *f*; ~ ***machine*** → ***sealer²*** b; ~ ***ring*** Dichtungsring *m*; ~ **wax** *s.* Siegellack *m*.

sea| li·on *s. zo.* Seelöwe *m*; **♀ Lord** *s.* ⚓ *Brit.* Seelord *m* (*Amtsleiter in der brit. Admiralität*).

'seal|-ˌrook·er·y *s. zo.* Brutplatz *m* von Robben; **'~·skin** *s.* **1.** Seal(skin) *m*, *n*, Seehundsfell *n*; **2.** Sealmantel *m*, -cape *n*.

seam [siːm] **I** *s.* **1.** Saum *m*, Naht *f* (*a.* ⚕): ***burst at the ~s*** aus den Nähten platzen (*a. fig.*); **2.** ⚙ a) (Guß-, Schweiß)Naht *f*: ~ ***welding*** Nahtschweißen *n*, b) *bsd.* ⚓ Fuge *f*, c) Sprung *m*, d) Falz *m*; **3.** Runzel *f*; **4.** Narbe *f*; **5.** *geol.* (Nutz)Schicht *f*, Flöz *n*; **II** *v/t.* **6.** *a.* ~ ***up***, ~ ***together*** zs.-nähen; **7.** säumen; **8.** *bsd. fig.* (durch-)'furchen; **9.** (zer)schrammen; **10.** ⚙ durch e-e (Guß- *od.* Schweiß)Naht verbinden.

sea·man ['siːmən] *s.* [*irr.*] ⚓ **1.** Seemann *m*, Ma'trose *m*; **2.** ⚔ *Am.* (Ma'rine)Obergefreite(r) *m*: ~ ***recruit*** Matrose; **'sea·man·like** *adj. u. adv.* seemännisch; **'sea·man·ship** [-ʃɪp] *s.* Seemannschaft *f*.

sea| mark *s.* Seezeichen *n*; ~ **mew** *s. orn.* Sturmmöwe *f*; ~ **mile** *s.* Seemeile *f*; ~ **mine** *s.* ⚔ Seemine *f*.

seam·less ['siːmlɪs] *adj.* □ **1.** naht-, saumlos: ***~-drawn tube*** ⚙ nahtlos gezogene Röhre; **2.** fugenlos.

sea mon·ster *s.* Meeresungeheuer *n*.

seam·stress ['semstrɪs] *s.* Näherin *f*.

sea mud *s.* Seeschlamm *m*, Schlick *m*.

seam·y ['siːmɪ] *adj.* gesäumt: ***the ~ side*** a) die linke Seite, b) *fig.* die Kehr- *od.* Schattenseite.

se·ance, sé·ance ['seɪɑ̃ːns] (*Fr.*) *s.* Sé'ance *f*, (spiri'tistische) Sitzung.

'sea|·piece *s. paint.* Seestück *n*; **'~-plane** *s.* See-, Wasserflugzeug *n*; **'~·port** *s.* Seehafen *m*, Hafenstadt *f*; ~ **pow·er** *s.* Seemacht *f*; **'~·quake** *s.* Seebeben *n*.

sear¹ [sɪə] **I** *v/t.* **1.** versengen; **2.** ⚕ (aus-)brennen; **3.** *Fleisch* anbraten; **4.** *bsd. fig.* brandmarken; **5.** *fig.* abstumpfen: ***a ~ed conscience***; **6.** verdorren lassen; **II** *v/i.* **7.** verdorren; **III** *adj.* **8.** *poet.* verdorrt, -welkt: ***the ~ and yellow leaf*** *fig.* der Herbst des Lebens.

sear² [sɪə] *s.* ⚔ Abzugsstollen *m* (*Gewehr*).

search [sɜːtʃ] **I** *v/t.* **1.** durch'suchen, -'stöbern (***for*** nach); **2.** ⚖ *Person, Haus etc.* durch'suchen, visitieren; **3.** unter'suchen; **4.** *fig. Gewissen etc.* erforschen, prüfen; **5.** *mst* ~ ***out*** auskundschaften, ausfindig machen; **6.** durch'dringen (*Wind, Geschosse etc.*); **7.** ⚔ mit Tiefenfeuer belegen *od.* bestreichen; **8.** *sl.* ~ ***me!*** keine Ahnung!; **II** *v/i.* **9.** (***for***) suchen, forschen (nach); ⚖ fahnden (nach): ~ ***into*** ergründen, untersuchen; **10.** ~ ***after*** streben nach; **III** *s.* **11.** Suchen *n*, Forschen *n* (***for, of*** nach): ***in ~ of*** auf der Suche nach; ***go in ~ of*** auf die Suche gehen nach; **12.** ⚖ a) Fahndung *f*, b) Haussuchung *f*, c) ('Leibes)Visitatiˌon *f*, d) Einsichtnahme *f in öffentliche Bücher*, e) Überprüfung *f*, *Patentwesen*: Re'cherche *f*: ***right of** (**visit and**) ~* ⚓ Recht *n* auf Durchsuchung neutraler Schiffe; **'search·er** [-tʃə] *s.* **1.** Sucher *m*, (Er)Forscher *m*; **2.** (*Zoll- etc.*)Prüfer *m*; **3.** ⚕ Sonde *f*; **'search·ing** [-tʃɪŋ] *adj.* □ **1.** gründlich, eingehend, tiefschürfend; **2.** forschend (*Blick*); durch'dringend (*Wind etc.*): ~ ***fire*** ⚔ Tiefen-, Streufeuer *n*.

'search|·light *s.* (Such)Scheinwerfer *m*; ~ **par·ty** *s.* Suchtrupp *m*; ~ **ra·dar** *s.* ⚔ Ra'dar-Suchgerät *n*; ~ **war·rant** *s.* ⚖ Haussuchungsbefehl *m*.

'sea|-ˌres·cue *adj.* Seenot...; ~ **risk** *s.* ⚖ Seegefahr *f*; ~ **room** *s.* ⚓ Seeräumte *f*; ~ **route** *s.* See-, Schiffahrtsweg *m*; **'~·scape** *s.* **1.** *paint.* Seestück *n*; **2.** (Aus)Blick *m* auf das Meer; ~ **ser·pent** *s. zo. u. myth.* Seeschlange *f*; **'~·shore** *s.* Seeküste *f*; **'~·sick** *adj.* seekrank; **'~·sick·ness** *s.* Seekrankheit *f*; **'~·side I** *s.* See-, Meeresküste *f*: ***go to the ~*** an die See fahren; **II** *adj.* an der See gelegen, See...: ~ ***place***, ~ ***resort*** Seebad *n*.

sea·son ['siːzn] **I** *s.* **1.** (Jahres)Zeit *f*; **2.** a) (Reife- *etc.*)Zeit *f*, rechte Zeit (*für et.*), b) *hunt.* (*Paarungs- etc.*)Zeit *f*: ***in ~*** a) (gerade) reif, (günstig auf dem Markt) zu haben (*Frucht*), b) zur rechten Zeit, c) *hunt.* jagdbar, d) brünstig (*Tier*); ***out of ~*** a) nicht (auf dem Markt) zu haben, b) *fig.* unpassend; ***in and out of ~*** jederzeit; ***cherries are now in ~*** jetzt ist Kirschenzeit; ***a word in ~*** ein Rat zur rechten Zeit; ***for a ~*** e-e Zeitlang; → ***close season***; **3.** ☤ Sai'son *f*, Haupt(betriebs-, -geschäfts-)zeit *f*: ***dull** (od. **slack**) ~* stille Saison, tote Jahreszeit; ***height of the ~*** Hochsaison; **4.** (*Veranstaltungs*)Sai'son *f*: ***theatrical ~*** Theatersaison, Spielzeit *f*; **5.** (*Bade-, Kur- etc.*)Sai'son *f*: ***holiday ~*** Ferienzeit *f*; **6.** Festzeit *f*; → ***compliment*** 3; **7.** F → ***season ticket***; **II** *v/t.* **8.** *Speisen* würzen (*a. fig.*): ***~ed with wit*** geistreich; **9.** *Tabak etc.* (aus)reifen lassen: ***~ed wine*** abgelagerter *od.* ausgereifter Wein; **10.** *Holz* ablagern; **11.** *Pfeife* einrauchen; **12.** gewöhnen (***to*** an *acc.*), abhärten: ***be ~ed to*** an *ein Klima etc.* gewöhnt sein; ***~ed soldiers*** fronterfahrene Soldaten; ***~ed by battle*** kampfgewohnt; **13.** *obs.* mildern; **III** *v/i.* **14.** reifen; **15.** ablagern (*Holz*); **'sea·son·a·ble** [-nəbl] *adj.* □ **1.** rechtzeitig; **2.** jahreszeitlich; **3.** zeitgemäß; **4.** passend, angebracht, oppor'tun, günstig; **'sea·son·al** [-zənl] *adj.* □ **1.** jahreszeitlich; **2.** sai'sonbedingt, -gemäß: ~ ***closing-out sale*** ☤ Saisonschlußverkauf *m*; ~ ***trade*** Saisongewerbe *n*; ~ ***work(er)*** Saisonarbeit(er *m*) *f*;

ˈsea·son·ing [-nɪŋ] *s.* **1.** Würze *f* (*a. fig.*), Gewürz *n*; **2.** Reifen *n etc.*; **sea·son tick·et** *s.* **1.** 🚂 *etc. Brit.* Dauer-, Zeitkarte *f*; **2.** *thea. etc.* Abonneˈment(skarte *f*) *n*.

seat [siːt] **I** *s.* **1.** Sitz(gelegenheit *f*, -platz *m*) *m*; Stuhl *m*, Sessel *m*, Bank *f*; **2.** (*Stuhl- etc.*)Sitz *m*; **3.** Platz *m bei Tisch etc.*: ***take a ~*** Platz nehmen; ***take one's ~*** s-n Platz einnehmen; ***take your ~s!*** 🚂 einsteigen!; **4.** *thea. etc.* Platz *m*, Sitz *m*: ***book a ~*** e-e (*Theater- etc.*)Karte kaufen; **5.** (Präsiˈdenten- *etc.*) Sitz *m* (*a. fig. Amt*); **6.** (Amts-, Regierungs-, ☤ Geschäfts)Sitz *m*; **7.** *parl. etc.* Sitz *m* (*a. Mitgliedschaft*), *parl. a.* Manˈdat *n*: ***a ~ in parliament***; ***have ~ and vote*** Sitz u. Stimme haben; **8.** Wohn-, Faˈmilien-, Landsitz *m*; **9.** *fig.* Sitz *m*: a) Stätte *f*, (Schau)Platz *m*: ***~ of war*** Kriegsschauplatz, b) ⚕ Herd *m e-r Krankheit* (*a. fig.*); **10.** Gesäß *n*, Sitzfläche *f*; Hosenboden *m*; **11.** *Reitsport etc.*: Sitz *m* (*Haltung*); **12.** ⚙ Auflager *n*, Fundaˈment *n*; **II** *v/t.* **13.** *j-n wohin* setzen, *j-m* e-n Sitz anweisen: ***~ o.s.*** sich setzen; ***be ~ed*** sitzen; **14.** Sitzplätze bieten für: ***the hall ~s 600 persons***; **15.** *Raum* bestuhlen, mit Sitzplätzen versehen; **16.** *Stuhl* mit e-m (neuen) Sitz versehen; **17.** ⚙ a) auflegen, lagern (***on*** auf *dat.*), b) einpassen, *Ventil* einschleifen; **18.** *pass.* sitzen, s-n Sitz haben, liegen (***in*** in *dat.*); **seat belt** *s.* ✈, *mot.* Sicherheitsgurt *m*; **ˈseat·ed** [-tɪd] *adj.* **1.** sitzend: ***be ~*** → ***seat*** 18; ***be ~!*** nehmen Sie Platz!; ***remain ~*** sitzen bleiben, Platz behalten; **2.** *in Zssgn* ...sitzig: ***two-~***; **ˈseat·er** [-tə] *s. in Zssgn* ...sitzer *m*: ***two-~***; **ˈseat·ing** [-tɪŋ] **I** *s.* **1.** a) Anweisen *n* von Sitzplätzen, b) Platznehmen *n*; **2.** Sitzgelegenheit(en *pl.*) *f*, Bestuhlung *f*; **II** *adj.* **3.** Sitz...: ***~ accommodation*** Sitzgelegenheiten; **seat mile** *s.* ⚓ Passaˈgiermeile *f*.

sea| trout *s.* ˈMeer-, ˈLachsfoˌrelle *f*; **~ ur·chin** *s. zo.* Seeigel *m*; **ˈ~·wall** *s.* Deich *m*; (Hafen)Damm *m*.

sea·ward [ˈsiːwəd] **I** *adj. u. adv.* seewärts; **II** *s.* Seeseite *f*; **ˈsea·wards** [-dz] *adv.* seewärts.

sea| wa·ter *s.* See-, Meerwasser *n*; **ˈ~·way** *s.* **1.** ⚓ Fahrt *f*; **2.** Seeweg *m*; **3.** Seegang *m*; **ˈ~·weed** *s.* **1.** (See)Tang *m*, Alge *f*; **2.** *allg.* Meerespflanze(n *pl.*) *f*; **ˈ~ˌwor·thy** *adj.* seetüchtig.

se·ba·ceous [sɪˈbeɪʃəs] *adj. physiol.* Talg...

sec [sek] (*Fr.*) *adj.* sec, trocken (*Wein*).

se·cant [ˈsiːkənt] **I** *s.* A a) Seˈkante *f*, b) Schnittlinie *f*; **II** *adj.* schneidend.

sec·a·teur [ˈsekətɜː] (*Fr.*) *s. mst* (***a pair of***) ***~s*** *pl.* (e-e) Baumschere.

se·cede [sɪˈsiːd] *v/i. bsd. eccl., pol.* sich trennen *od.* lossagen, abfallen (***from*** von); **seˈced·er** [-də] *s.* Abtrünnige(r *m*) *f*, Separaˈtist *m*.

se·ces·sion [sɪˈseʃn] *s.* **1.** Sezessiˈon *f* (*USA hist. oft* 2), (Ab-, *eccl.* Kirchen-) Spaltung *f*, Abfall *m*, Lossagung *f*; **2.** ˈÜbertritt *m* (***to*** zu); **seˈces·sion·al** [-ʃənl] *adj.* Sonderbunds..., Abfall..., Sezessions...; **seˈces·sion·ist** [-nɪst] *s.* Abtrünnige(r *m*) *f*, Sonderbündler *m*, Sezessioˈnist *m* (*Am. hist. oft* 2).

se·clude [sɪˈkluːd] *v/t.* (***o.s.*** sich) abschließen, absondern (***from*** von); **seˈclud·ed** [-dɪd] *adj.* □ einsam, abgeschieden: a) zuˈrückgezogen (*Lebensweise*), b) abgelegen (*Ort*); **seˈclu·sion** [-uːʒn] *s.* **1.** Abschließung *f*; **2.** Zuˈrückgezogenheit *f*, Abgeschiedenheit *f*: ***live in ~*** zurückgezogen leben.

sec·ond [ˈsekənd] **I** *adj.* □ → ***secondly***; **1.** zweit; nächst: ***~ Advent*** (*od.* ***Coming***) *eccl.* ˈWiederkunft *f* (Christi); ***~ ballot*** Stichwahl *f*; ***~ Chamber*** *parl.* Oberhaus *n*; ***~ floor*** a) *Brit.* zweiter Stock, b) *Am.* erster Stock (*über dem Erdgeschoß*); ***~ in height*** zweithöchst; ***at ~ hand*** aus zweiter Hand; ***in the ~ place*** zweitens; ***it has become ~ nature with him*** es ist ihm zur zweiten Natur geworden *od.* in Fleisch u. Blut übergegangen; → ***self*** 1, ***sight*** 1, ***thought*** 3, ***wind***[1] 6; **2.** (***to***) ˈuntergeordnet (*dat.*), geringer (als): ***~ cabin*** ⚓ Kabine *f* zweiter Klasse; ***~ cousin*** Vetter *m* zweiten Grades; ***~ lieutenant*** ⚔ Leutnant *m*; ***come ~*** *fig.* an zweiter Stelle kommen; ***~ to none*** unerreicht; ***he is ~ to none*** er ist unübertroffen; → ***fiddle*** 1; **II** *s.* **3.** *der* (*die, das*) Zweite: ***~ in command*** ⚔ a) stellvertretender Kommandeur, b) ⚓ erster Offizier; **4.** *sport* Zweite(r *m*) *f*, zweiter Sieger: ***run ~*** den zweiten Platz belegen; ***be a good ~*** nur knapp geschlagen werden; **5.** *univ.* → ***second class*** 2; **6.** F 🚂 *etc.* zweite Klasse; **7.** *Duell, Boxen*: Sekunˈdant *m*; *fig.* Beistand *m*; **8.** Seˈkunde *f*; *weitS. a.* Augenblick *m*, Moˈment *m*; **9.** ♪ a) Seˈkunde *f*, b) Begleitstimme *f*; **10.** *pl.* ☤ Ware(n *pl.*) *f* zweiter Qualiˈtät *od.* Wahl; **11.** ***~ of exchange*** ☤ Seˈkundawechsel *m*; **III** *v/t.* **12.** sekundieren (*dat.*) (*a. fig.*); **13.** *fig.* unterˈstützen (*a. parl.*), beistehen (*dat.*); **14.** [sɪˈkɒnd] ⚔ *Brit. Offizier* abstellen, abkommandieren.

sec·ond·ar·i·ness [ˈsekəndərɪnɪs] *s. das* Sekunˈdäre, Zweitrangigkeit *f*; **sec·ond·ar·y** [ˈsekəndərɪ] **I** *adj.* □ **1.** sekunˈdär, zweitrangig, ˈuntergeordnet, nebensächlich: ***of ~ importance***; **2.** ↯, ⚗, *biol., geol., phys.* sekunˈdär, Sekundär...: ***~ electron***; **3.** Neben...: ***~ colo(u)r***, ***~ effect***; **4.** Neben..., Hilfs...: ***~ line*** 🚂 Nebenbahn; **5.** *ling.* a) sekunˈdär, abgeleitet, b) Neben...: ***~ accent*** Nebenakzent *m*; ***~ derivative*** Sekundärableitung *f*; ***~ tense*** Nebentempus *n*; **6.** *ped.* Oberschul...: ***~ education*** höhere Schulbildung; ***~ school*** höhere Schule; **II** *s.* **7.** ˈUntergeordnete(r *m*) *f*, Stellvertreter(in); **8.** ↯ a) Sekunˈdär(strom)kreis *m*, b) Sekunˈdärwicklung *f*; **9.** *ast. a.* ***~ planet*** Satelˈlit *m*; **10.** *orn.* Nebenfeder *f*.

ˈsec·ond|-best *adj.* zweitbest: ***come off ~*** *fig.* den kürzeren ziehen; **~ class** *s.* **1.** 🚂 *etc.* zweite Klasse; **2.** *univ. Brit. akademischer Grad zweiter Klasse*; **ˌ~-ˈclass** [-ndˈk-] *adj.* **1.** zweitklassig, -rangig; **2.** 🚂 *etc. Wagen etc.* zweiter Klasse: ***~ mail*** a) *Am.* Zeitungspost *f*, b) *Brit.* gewöhnliche Inlandspost; **ˌ~-deˈgree** *adv.* **1.** zweiten Grades: ***~ burns***; **2.** ***~ murder*** ⚖ Totschlag *m*; **ˌ~ˈguess** *v/t. Am.* **1.** im nachhinein kritisieren; **2.** a) durchˈschauen, b) vorˈhersehen; **ˈ~·hand I** *adj.* **1.** überˈnommen, *a. Wissen etc.* aus zweiter Hand; **2.** ˈindiˌrekt; **3.** gebraucht, alt; antiˈquarisch (*Bücher*): ***~ bookshop*** Antiquariat *n*; ***~ car*** Gebrauchtwagen *m*; ***~ dealer*** Altwarenhändler *m*; **II** *adv.* **4.** gebraucht: ***buy s.th. ~***; ***~ hand*** *s.* Seˈkundenzeiger *m*.

sec·ond·ly [ˈsekəndlɪ] *adv.* zweitens.

se·cond·ment [sɪˈkɒndmənt] *s. Brit.* **1.** ⚔ Abkommandierung *f*; **2.** Versetzung *f*.

ˌsec·ond|-ˈrate *adj.* zweitrangig, -klassig, mittelmäßig; **ˌ~-ˈrat·er** *s.* mittelmäßige Perˈson *od.* Sache.

se·cre·cy [ˈsiːkrəsɪ] *s.* **1.** Verborgenheit *f*; **2.** Heimlichkeit *f*: ***in all ~***, ***with absolute ~*** ganz im geheimen, insgeheim; **3.** Verschwiegenheit *f*; Geheimhaltung(spflicht) *f*; (*Wahl- etc.*)Geheimnis *n*: ***official ~*** Amtsverschwiegenheit *f*; ***professional ~*** Berufsgeheimnis *n*, Schweigepflicht *f*; → ***swear*** 6; **se·cret** [ˈsiːkrɪt] **I** *adj.* □ **1.** geheim, heimlich, Geheim...(*-dienst, -diplomatie, -tür etc.*): ***~ ballot*** geheime Wahl; → ***keep*** 13; **2.** a) verschwiegen, b) verstohlen (*Person*); **3.** verschwiegen (*Ort*); **4.** unerforschlich, verborgen; **II** *s.* **5.** Geheimnis *n* (***from*** vor *dat.*): ***the ~ of success*** *fig.* das Geheimnis des Erfolgs, der Schlüssel zum Erfolg; ***in ~*** a) heimlich, im geheimen, b) im Vertrauen; ***be in the ~*** (in das Geheimnis) eingeweiht sein; ***let s.o. into the ~*** j-n (in das Geheimnis) einweihen; ***make no ~ of*** kein Geheimnis *od.* Hehl aus *et.* machen.

se·cre·taire [ˌsekrəˈteə] (*Fr.*) *s.* Sekreˈtär *m*, Schreibschrank *m*.

sec·re·tar·i·al [ˌsekrəˈteərɪəl] *adj.* **1.** Sekretärs...: ***~ help*** Schreibkraft *f*; **2.** Schreib..., Büro...; **ˌsec·reˈtar·i·at(e)** [-ɪət] *s.* Sekretariˈat *n*.

sec·re·tar·y [ˈsekrətrɪ] *s.* **1.** Sekreˈtär (-in): ***~ of embassy*** Botschaftsrat *m*; **2.** Schriftführer *m*; ☤ a) Geschäftsführer *m*, b) Syndikus *m*; **3.** *pol. Brit.* a) ***~*** (***of state***) Miˈnister *m*, b) ˈStaatssekreˌtär *m*: ***2 of State for Foreign Affairs***, ***Foreign 2*** Außenminister *m*; ***2 of State for Home Affairs***, ***Home 2*** Innenminister; **4.** *pol. Am.* Miˈnister *m*: ***2 of Defense*** Verteidigungsminister; ***2 of State*** a) Außenminister, b) Staatssekretär *m e-s Bundesstaats*; **5.** → ***secretaire***; **~ bird** *s. orn.* Sekreˈtär *m*; **ˌ~-ˈgen·er·al** *pl.* **ˌsec·re·tar·ies-ˈgen·er·al** *s.* Geneˈralsekreˌtär *m*.

sec·re·tar·y·ship [ˈsekrətrɪʃɪp] *s.* **1.** Posten *m od.* Amt *n* e-s Sekreˈtärs *etc.*; **2.** Miˈnisteramt *n*.

se·crete [sɪˈkriːt] *v/t.* **1.** *physiol.* absondern, abscheiden; **2.** verbergen (***from*** vor *dat.*); ⚖ *Vermögensstücke* beiˈseite schaffen; **seˈcre·tion** [-iːʃn] *s.* **1.** *physiol.* a) Sekretiˈon *f*, Absonderung *f*, b) Seˈkret *n*; **2.** Verheimlichung *f*; **seˈcre·tive** [-tɪv] *adj.* □ heimlich, verschlossen, geheimnistuerisch: ***be ~ about*** mit *et.* geheim tun; **seˈcre·tive·ness** [-tɪvnɪs] *s.* Heimlichtueˈrei *f*; Verschwiegenheit *f*.

ˈse·cretˌmon·ger *s.* Geheimniskrämer(in).

se·cre·to·ry [sɪˈkriːtərɪ] *physiol.* **I** *adj.* sekreˈtorisch, Sekretions...; **II** *s.* sekretorische Drüse.

sect [sekt] *s.* **1.** Sekte *f*; **2.** Religiˈonsge-

meinschaft *f*.
sec·tar·i·an [sekˈteərɪən] **I** *adj.* **1.** sekˈtiererisch; **2.** Konfessions…; **II** *s.* **3.** Anhänger(in) e-r Sekte; **4.** Sekˈtierer (-in); **secˈtar·i·an·ism** [-nɪzəm] *s.* Sekˈtierertum *n*.
sec·tion [ˈsekʃn] **I** *s.* **1.** a) Durchˈschneidung *f*, b) (*a. mikroskopischer*) Schnitt, c) ⚕ Sektiˈon *f*, Schnitt *m*; **2.** Ab-, Ausschnitt *m*, Teil *m* (*a. der Bevölkerung etc.*); **3.** Abschnitt *m*, Absatz *m* (*Buch etc.*); ⚖ (*Gesetzes- etc.*)Paraˈgraph *m*; **4.** *a.* ~ **mark** Paraˈgraph(enzeichen *n*) *m*; **5.** ⚙ Teil *m*, *n*; **6.** △, ⚙ Schnitt(bild *n*) *m*, Querschnitt *m*, Proˈfil *n*: ***horizontal*** ~ Horizontalschnitt *m*; **7.** 🚂 *Am.* a) Streckenabschnitt *m*, b) Abˈteil *n e-s Schlafwagens*; **8.** *Am.* Bezirk *m*; **9.** *Am.* ˈLandparˌzelle *f* von e-r Quaˈdratmeile; **10.** ⚘, *zo.* ˈUntergruppe *f*; **11.** Abˈteilung *f*, Refeˈrat *n* (*Verwaltung*); **12.** ⚔ a) *Brit.* Gruppe *f*, b) *Am.* Halbzug *m*, c) ✈ Halbstaffel *f*, d) Stabsabteilung *f*; **II** *v/t.* **13.** (ab-, ein-) teilen, unterˈteilen; **14.** e-n Schnitt machen von; ˈ**sec·tion·al** [-ʃənl] *adj.* □ **1.** Schnitt…(*-fläche*, *-zeichnung etc.*); **2.** Teil…(*-ansicht*, *-streik etc.*); **3.** zs.-setzbar, montierbar: ~ ***furniture*** Anbaumöbel *pl.*; **4.** ⚙ Profil…, Form… (*-draht*, *-stahl*); **5.** regioˈnal, *contp.* partikulaˈristisch: ~ ***pride*** Lokalpatriotismus *m*; ˈ**sec·tion·al·ism** [-nəlɪzəm] *s.* Partikulaˈrismus *m*.
sec·tor [ˈsektə] *s.* **1.** △ (Kreis- *od.* Kugel)Sektor *m*; **2.** △, *ast.* Sektor *m* (*a. fig. Bereich*); **3.** ⚔ Sektor *m*, Frontabschnitt *m*.
sec·u·lar [ˈsekjʊlə] **I** *adj.* □ **1.** weltlich: a) diesseitig, b) proˈfan: ~ ***music***, c) nicht kirchlich (*Erziehung etc.*): ~ ***arm*** weltliche Gerichtsbarkeit; **2.** ˈfreireliˌgiˌös, -denkerisch; **3.** *eccl.* weltgeistlich, Säkular…: ~ ***clergy*** Weltgeistlichkeit *f*; **4.** säkuˈlar: a) hundertjährlich, b) hundertjährig, c) säkuˈlar; **5.** jahrˈhundertelang; **6.** *ast.*, *phys.* säkuˈlar; **II** *s.* **7.** *R.C.* Weltgeistliche(r) *m*; ˈ**sec·u·lar·ism** [-ərɪzəm] *s.* **1.** Säkulaˈrismus *m* (*a. phls.*), Weltlichkeit *f*; **2.** Antiklerikaˈlismus *m*; **sec·u·lar·i·ty** [ˌsekjʊˈlærətɪ] *s.* **1.** Weltlichkeit *f*; **2.** *pl.* weltliche Dinge *pl.*; **sec·u·lar·i·za·tion** [ˌsekjʊləraɪˈzeɪʃn] *s.* **1.** *eccl.* Säkularisierung *f*; **2.** Verweltlichung *f*; ˈ**sec·u·lar·ize** [-əraɪz] *v/t.* **1.** kirchlichem Einfluß entziehen; **2.** *kirchlichen Besitz*, *a. Ordensgeistliche* säkularisieren; **3.** verweltlichen; *Sonntag etc.* entheiligen; **4.** mit freidenkerischen Iˈdeen durchˈdringen.
sec·un·dine [ˈsekəndɪn] *s.* **1.** *mst pl.* ⚕ Nachgeburt *f*; **2.** ⚘ inneres Integuˈment der Samenanlage.
se·cure [sɪˈkjʊə] **I** *adj.* □ **1.** sicher: a) geschützt (***from*** vor *dat.*), b) fest (*Grundlage etc.*), c) gesichert (*Existenz*), d) gewiß (*Hoffnung*, *Sieg etc.*); **2.** ruhig, sorglos: ***a*** ~ ***life***; **II** *v/t.* **3.** sichern, schützen (***from***, ***against*** vor *dat.*); **4.** sichern, garantieren (***s.th. to s.o.*** *od.* ***s.o. s.th.*** j-m et.); **5.** sich *et.* sichern *od.* beschaffen; erreichen, erlangen; *Patent*, *Urteil etc.* erwirken; **6.** ⚙ *etc.* sichern, befestigen; *Türe etc.* (fest) (ver)schließen: ~ ***by bolts*** festschrauben; **7.** *Wertsachen* sicherstellen; **8.** *Verbrecher* festnehmen; **9.** *bsd.* ✝ sicherstellen: a) *et.* sichern (***on***, ***by*** durch *Hypothek etc.*), b) *j-m* Sicherheit bieten: ~ ***a creditor***; **10.** ⚕ *Ader* abbinden.
se·cu·ri·ty [sɪˈkjʊərətɪ] *s.* **1.** Sicherheit *f* (*Zustand od. Schutz*) (***against***, ***from*** vor *dat.*, gegen): 2 Sicherheit(sabteilung) *f*; ✝ *a.* Werkspolizei *f*; 2 ***Council*** *pol.* Sicherheitsrat *m*; ~ ***check*** Sicherheitsüberprüfung *f*; ~ ***clearance*** Unbedenklichkeitsbescheinigung *f*; 2 ***Force*** Friedenstruppe *f*; → ***risk*** 2; **2.** (innere) Sicherheit, Sorglosigkeit *f*; **3.** Gewißheit *f*; **4.** ⚖, ✝ a) Bürge *m*, b) Sicherheit *f*, Bürgschaft *f*, Kautiˈon *f*: ~ ***bond*** Bürgschaftswechsel *m*; ***give*** (*od.* ***put up***, ***stand***) ~ Bürgschaft leisten, Kaution stellen; **5.** ✝ a) Schuldverschreibung *f*, b) Aktie *f*, c) *pl.* ˈWertpaˌpiere *pl.*: ~ ***market*** Effektenmarkt *m*; ***public securities*** Staatspapiere.
se·dan [sɪˈdæn] *s.* **1.** *mot.* Limouˈsine *f*; **2.** *a.* ~ ***chair*** Sänfte *f*.
se·date [sɪˈdeɪt] *adj.* □ **1.** ruhig, gelassen; **2.** gesetzt, ernst; **seˈdate·ness** [-nɪs] *s.* **1.** Gelassenheit *f*; **2.** Gesetztheit *f*; **seˈda·tion** [-eɪʃn] *s.*: ***be under*** ~ ⚕ unter dem Einfluß von Beruhigungsmitteln stehen.
sed·a·tive [ˈsedətɪv] *bsd.* ⚕ **I** *adj.* beruhigend; **II** *s.* Beruhigungsmittel *n*.
sed·en·tar·i·ness [ˈsedntərɪnɪs] *s.* **1.** sitzende Lebensweise; **2.** Seßhaftigkeit *f*; **sed·en·tar·y** [ˈsedntərɪ] *adj.* □ **1.** sitzend (*Beschäftigung*, *Statue etc.*): ~ ***life*** sitzende Lebensweise; **2.** seßhaft: ~ ***birds*** Standvögel.
sedge [sedʒ] *s.* ⚘ **1.** Segge *f*; **2.** *allg.* Riedgras *n*.
sed·i·ment [ˈsedɪmənt] *s.* Sediˈment *n*: a) (Boden)Satz *m*, Niederschlag *m*, b) *geol.* Schichtgestein *n*; **sed·i·men·ta·ry** [ˌsedɪˈmentərɪ] *adj.* sedimenˈtär, Sediment…; **sed·i·men·ta·tion** [ˌsedɪmenˈteɪʃn] *s.* **1.** Sedimentatiˈon *f*: a) Ablagerung *f*, b) *geol.* Schichtenbildung *f*; **2.** *a.* ***blood*** ~ ⚕ Blutsenkung *f*: ~ ***rate*** Senkungsgeschwindigkeit *f*.
se·di·tion [sɪˈdɪʃn] *s.* **1.** Aufwiegelung *f*, *a.* ⚖ Volksverhetzung *f*; **2.** Aufruhr *m*; **seˈdi·tious** [-ʃəs] *adj.* □ aufrührerisch, ˈumstürzlerisch, staatsgefährdend.
se·duce [sɪˈdjuːs] *v/t.* **1.** *Frau etc.* verführen (*a. fig. verleiten*; ***into***, ***to*** zu; ***into doing s.th.*** dazu, et. zu tun); **2.** ~ ***from*** *j-n* von *s-r Pflicht etc.* abbringen; **seˈduc·er** [-sə] *s.* Verführer *m*; **se·duc·tion** [sɪˈdʌkʃn] *s.* **1.** (*a. sexuelle*) Verführung; Verlockung *f*; **2.** *fig.* Versuchung *f*, verführerischer Zauber; **se·duc·tive** [sɪˈdʌktɪv] *adj.* □ verführerisch (*a. fig.*).
se·du·li·ty [sɪˈdjuːlətɪ] *s.* Emsigkeit *f*, (emsiger) Fleiß; **sed·u·lous** [ˈsedjʊləs] *adj.* □ emsig, fleißig.
see¹ [siː] **I** *v/t.* [*irr.*] **1.** sehen: ~ ***page 15*** siehe Seite 15; ***I*** ~ ***him come*** (*od.* ***coming***) ich sehe ihn kommen; ***I cannot*** ~ ***myself doing it*** *fig.* ich kann mir nicht vorstellen, daß ich es tue; ***I*** ~ ***things otherwise*** *fig.* ich sehe *od.* betrachte die Dinge anders; ~ ***o.s. obliged to*** *fig.* sich gezwungen sehen zu; **2.** (ab)sehen, erkennen: ~ ***danger ahead***; **3.** ersehen, entnehmen (***from*** aus *der Zeitung etc.*); **4.** (ein)sehen, verstehen: ***as I*** ~ ***it*** wie ich es sehe, in m-n Augen; ***I do not*** ~ ***the use of it*** ich weiß nicht, wozu es gut sein soll; → ***joke*** 2; **5.** (sich) ansehen, besuchen: ~ ***a play***; **6.** a) *j-n* besuchen: ***go*** (***come***) ***to*** ~ ***s.o.*** j-n besuchen (gehen *od.* kommen), b) *Anwalt etc.* aufsuchen, konsultieren (***about*** wegen), *j-n* sprechen (***on business*** geschäftlich); **7.** *j-n* empfangen: ***he refused to*** ~ ***me***; **8.** nachsehen, herˈausfinden; **9.** dafür sorgen (daß): ~ (***to it***) ***that it is done!*** sorge dafür *od.* sieh zu, daß es geschieht!; ~ ***justice done to s.o.*** dafür sorgen, daß j-m Gerechtigkeit widerfährt; **10.** sehen, erleben: ***live to*** ~ erleben; ~ ***action*** ⚔ im Einsatz sein, Kämpfe mitmachen; ***he has seen better days*** er hat (schon) bessere Tage gesehen; **11.** *j-n* begleiten, geleiten, bringen (***to the station*** zum Bahnhof); → ***see off***, ***see out***; **II** *v/i.* [*irr.*] **12.** sehen; → ***fit¹*** 3; **13.** verstehen, einsehen: ***I*** ~***!*** (ich) verstehe!, aha!, ach so!; (***you***) ~ wissen Sie, weißt du; (***you***) ~***?*** F verstehst du?; **14.** nachsehen; **15.** sehen, sich überˈlegen: ***let me*** ~***!*** warte mal!, laß mich überlegen!; ***we'll*** ~ wir werden sehen, mal abwarten.
Zssgn mit prp.:
see| a·bout *v/i.* **1.** sich kümmern um; **2.** F sich *et.* überlegen; ~ **aft·er** *v/i.* sehen nach, sich kümmern um; ~ **in·to** *v/i.* e-r Sache auf den Grund gehen; ~ **o·ver** *v/i.* sich ansehen; ~ **through I** *v/i. j-n od. et.* durchˈschauen; **II** *v/t. j-m* über *et.* hinˈweghelfen; ~ **to** *v/i.* sich kümmern um; → ***see¹*** 9.
Zssgn mit adv.:
see| off *v/t. j-n* fortbegleiten, verabschieden; ~ **out** *v/t.* **1.** *j-n* hinˈausbegleiten; **2.** F *et.* bis zum Ende ansehen *od.* mitmachen; ~ **through I** *v/t.* **1.** *j-m* ˈdurchhelfen (***with*** in *e-r Sache*); **2.** *et.* (bis zum Ende) ˈdurchhalten *od.* -fechten; **II** *v/i.* **3.** F durchhalten.
see² [siː] *s. eccl.* **1.** (Erz)Bischofssitz *m*; → ***Holy See***; **2.** (Erz)Bistum *n*.
seed [siːd] **I** *s.* **1.** ⚘ a) Same *m*, b) (Obst-) Kern *m*, c) *coll.* Samen *pl.*, d) ⚒ Saat (-gut *n*) *f*: ***go*** (*od.* ***run***) ***to*** ~ in Samen schießen, *fig.* herunterkommen; **2.** *zo.* a) Ei *n od.* Eier *pl.* (*des Hummers etc.*), b) Austernbrut *f*; **3.** *physiol.* Samen *m*; *fig.* Nachkommenschaft *f*: ***the*** ~ ***of Abraham*** *bibl.* der Same Abrahams; **4.** *pl. fig.* Saat *f*, Keim *m*: ***sow the*** ~***s of discord*** (die Saat der) Zwietracht säen; **II** *v/t.* **5.** entsamen; *Obst* entkernen; **6.** *Acker* besäen; **7.** *sport Spieler* setzen; **III** *v/i.* **8.** ⚘ a) Samen tragen, b) in Samen schießen, c) sich aussäen; ˈ~**·bed** *s.* Treibbeet *n*; *fig.* Pflanz-, *contp.* Brutstätte *f*; ˈ~**·cake** *s.* Kümmelkuchen *m*; ˈ~**·case** *s.* ⚘ Samenkapsel *f*; ~ **corn** *s.* **1.** Saatkorn *n*; **2.** *Am.* Saatmais *m*; ~ **drill** → ***seeder*** 1.
seed·er [ˈsiːdə] *s.* **1.** ⚒ ˈSämaˌschine *f*; **2.** (Frucht)Entkerner *m*.
seed·i·ness [ˈsiːdɪnɪs] *s.* F **1.** Schäbigkeit *f*, Abgerissenheit *f*; verwahrloster Zustand; **2.** ‚Flauheit' *f des Befindens*.
seed leaf *s.* [*irr.*] ⚘ Keimblatt *n*.
seed·less [ˈsiːdlɪs] *adj.* kernlos; ˈ**seed·ling** [-lɪŋ] *s.* ⚘ Sämling *m*.
seed| oys·ter *s. zo.* **1.** Saatauster *f*; **2.** *pl.* Austernlaich *m*; ~ **pearl** *s.* Staub-

perle *f*; **~ plot** *s.* → ***seedbed***; **~ po·ta·to** *s.* 'Saatkar,toffel *f.*

seed·y ['si:dɪ] *adj.* **1.** ⚘ samentragend, -reich; **2.** F schäbig: a) fadenscheinig, b) her'untergekommen (*Person*); **3.** F ‚flau', ‚mies' (*Befinden*): ***look ~*** elend aussehen.

see·ing ['si:ɪŋ] **I** *s.* Sehen *n*: ***worth ~*** sehenswert; **II** *cj. a.* ***~ that*** da doch; in Anbetracht dessen, daß; **III** *prp.* angesichts (*gen.*), in Anbetracht (*gen.*); **'~-eye dog** *s. Am.* Blindenhund *m.*

seek [si:k] **I** *v/t.* [*irr.*] **1.** suchen; **2.** *Bett, Schatten, j-n* aufsuchen; **3.** (***of***) *Rat, Hilfe etc.* suchen (bei), erbitten (von); **4.** begehren, erstreben, nach *Ruhm etc.* trachten; ⚖ *etc.* beantragen, begehren: ***~ divorce***; → ***life*** *Redew.*; **5.** (ver)suchen, trachten (*et. zu tun*); **6.** zu ergründen suchen; **7.** ***be to ~*** *obs.* (noch) fehlen, zu wünschen übrig lassen; **8.** *a.* ***~ out*** her'ausfinden, aufspüren, *fig.* aufs Korn nehmen; **II** *v/i.* [*irr.*] **9.** suchen, fragen, forschen (***for***, ***after*** nach): ***~ after*** *a.* begehren; **'seek·er** [-kə] *s.* **1.** Sucher(in): ***~ after truth*** Wahrheitssucher; **2.** ⚕ Sonde *f.*

seem [si:m] *v/i.* **1.** (zu sein) scheinen, anscheinend sein, erscheinen: ***it ~s impossible to me*** es (er)scheint mir unmöglich; **2.** *mit inf.* scheinen: ***you ~ to believe it*** du scheinst es zu glauben; ***apples ~ not to grow here*** Äpfel wachsen hier anscheinend nicht; ***I ~ to hear voices*** mir ist, als hörte ich Stimmen; **3.** *impers.* ***it ~s that*** es scheint, daß; anscheinend; ***it ~s as if*** (*od.* ***though***) es sieht so aus *od.* es scheint so als ob; ***it ~s to me that it will rain*** mir scheint, es wird regnen; ***it should*** (*od.* ***would***) ***~ that*** man sollte glauben, daß; ***I can't ~ to open this door*** ich bringe diese Tür einfach nicht auf; **'seem·ing** [-mɪŋ] *adj.* □ **1.** scheinbar: ***a ~ friend***; **2.** anscheinend; **'seem·li·ness** [-lɪnɪs] *s.* Anstand *m*, Schicklichkeit *f*; **'seem·ly** [-lɪ] *adj. u. adv.* geziemend, schicklich.

seen [si:n] *p.p. von* ***see***[1].

seep [si:p] *v/i.* ('durch)sickern (*a. fig.*), tropfen, lecken: ***~ away*** versickern; ***~ in*** *a. fig.* einsickern, -dringen; **'seep·age** [-pɪdʒ] *s.* **1.** ('Durch-, Ver)Sickern *n*; **2.** 'Durchgesickertes *n*; **3.** Leck *n.*

se·er ['si:ə] *s.* Seher(in).

seer·suck·er ['sɪə,sʌkə] *s.* leichtes, kreppartiges Leinen.

see·saw ['si:sɔ] **I** *s.* **1.** Wippen *n*, Schaukeln *n*; **2.** Wippe *f*, Wippschaukel *f*; **3.** *fig.* (ständiges) Auf u. Ab *od.* Hin u. Her; **II** *adj.* **4.** schaukelnd, (*a. fig.*) Schaukel...(*-bewegung, -politik*); **III** *v/i.* **5.** wippen, schaukeln; **6.** sich auf u. ab *od.* hin u. her bewegen; **7.** *fig.* (hin u. her) schwanken.

seethe [si:ð] *v/i.* **1.** kochen, sieden, wallen (*alle a. fig.* ***with*** vor *dat.*); **2.** *fig.* brodeln, gären (***with*** vor *dat.*): ***seething with rage*** vor Wut kochend; **3.** wimmeln (***with*** von).

'see-through *adj.* **1.** 'durchsichtig: ***~ blouse***; **2.** Klarsicht...: ***~ package***.

seg·ment ['segmənt] **I** *s.* **1.** Abschnitt *m*, Teil *m, n*; **2.** *bsd.* ⟂ (*Kreis- etc.*) Seg'ment *n*; **3.** *biol.* a) *allg.* Glied *n*, Seg'ment *n*, b) 'Körperseg,ment *n*, Ring *m* (*Wurm etc.*); **II** *v/t.* [seg'ment] **4.** (*v/i.* sich) in Segmente teilen; **seg·men·tal** [seg'mentl] *adj.* □, **'seg·men·tar·y** [-tərɪ] *adj.* segmen'tär; **seg·men·ta·tion** [,segmən'teɪʃn] *s.* **1.** Segmentati'on *f*; **2.** *biol.* Zellteilung *f*, (Ei)Furchung *f.*

seg·ment| gear *s.* Seg'ment(zahnrad)-getriebe *n*; **~ saw** *s.* **1.** Baumsäge *f*; **2.** Bogenschnittsäge *f.*

seg·re·gate ['segrɪgeɪt] **I** *v/t.* **1.** trennen (*a. nach Rassen etc.*), absondern; **2.** ⚙ ausseigern, -scheiden; **II** *v/i.* **3.** sich absondern *od.* abspalten (*a. fig.*); ⚗ sich abscheiden; **4.** *biol.* mendeln; **III** *adj.* [-gɪt] **5.** abgesondert, isoliert; **seg·re·ga·tion** [,segrɪ'geɪʃn] *s.* **1.** Absonderung *f*, -trennung *f*; **2.** Rassentrennung *f*; **3.** ⚗ Ausscheidung *f*; **4.** abgespaltener Teil; **seg·re·ga·tion·ist** [,segrɪ'geɪʃnɪst] **I** *s.* Verfechter(in) der Rassentrennung; **II** *adj.* die Rassentrennung befürwortend; **'seg·re·ga·tive** [-gətɪv] *adj.* sich absondernd, Trennungs...

sei·gneur [se'njɜ:], **sei·gnor** ['seɪnjə] *s.* **1.** *hist.* Lehns-, Feu'dalherr *m*; **2.** Herr *m*; **seign·ior·age** ['seɪnjərɪdʒ] *s.* **1.** Re'gal *n*, Vorrecht *n*; **2.** a) *königliche* Münzgebühr, b) Schlagschatz *m*; **sei'gno·ri·al** [-'njɔ:rɪəl] *adj.* feu'dalherrschaftlich; **seign·ior·y** ['seɪnjərɪ] *s.* **1.** Feu'dalrechte *pl.*; **2.** (feu'dal)herrschaftliche Do'mäne.

seine [seɪn] *s.* ⚓ Schlagnetz *n.*

seise [si:z] → ***seize*** 4; **'sei·sin** [-zɪn] → ***seizin***.

seis·mic ['saɪzmɪk] *adj.* seismisch.

seis·mo·graph ['saɪzməgrɑ:f] *s.* Seismo'graph *m*, Erdbebenmeßgerät *n*; **seis·mol·o·gist** [saɪz'mɒlədʒɪst] *s.* Seismo'loge *m*; **seis·mol·o·gy** [saɪz'mɒlədʒɪ] *s.* Erdbebenkunde *f*, Seismik *f*; **seis·mom·e·ter** [saɪz'mɒmɪtə] *s.* Seismo'meter *n*; **'seis·mo·scope** [-əskəʊp] *s.* Seismo'skop *n.*

seiz·a·ble ['si:zəbl] *adj.* **1.** (er)greifbar; **2.** ⚖ pfändbar; **seize** [si:z] **I** *v/t.* **1.** *et. od. j-n* (er)greifen, packen, fassen (*alle a. fig. Panik etc.*): ***~d with*** ⚕ von *e-r Krankheit* befallen; ***~d with apoplexy*** ⚕ vom Schlag getroffen; **2.** ⚔ (ein-)nehmen, erobern; **3.** sich *e-r Sache* bemächtigen, *Macht etc.* an sich reißen; **4.** ⚖ *j-n* in den Besitz setzen (***of*** von *od. gen.*): ***be ~d with***, ***stand ~d of*** im Besitz *e-r Sache* sein; **5.** *j-n* ergreifen, festnehmen; **6.** beschlagnahmen; **7.** *Gelegenheit* ergreifen, wahrnehmen; **8.** *geistig* erfassen, begreifen; **9.** ⚓ (bei)zeisen, zurren; **II** *v/i.* **10.** ***~*** (***up***)***on*** *Gelegenheit* ergreifen, *Idee* (begierig) aufgreifen, *a.* einhaken bei; **11.** *oft* ***~ up*** ⚙ sich festfressen; **'sei·zin** [-zɪn] *s.* ⚖ *Am.* (Grund)Besitz *m*, verbunden mit Eigentumsvermutung; **'seiz·ings** [-zɪŋz] *s. pl.* ⚓ Zurrtau *n*; **sei·zure** ['si:ʒə] *s.* **1.** Ergreifung *f*; **2.** Inbesitznahme *f*; **3.** ⚖ a) Beschlagnahme *f*, b) Festnahme *f*; **4.** ⚕ Anfall *m.*

sel·dom ['seldəm] *adv.* selten.

se·lect [sɪ'lekt] **I** *v/t.* **1.** auswählen, -lesen; **II** *adj.* **2.** ausgewählt: ***~ committee*** *parl. Brit.* Sonderausschuß *m*; **3.** erlesen (*Buch, Geist, Speise etc.*); exklu'siv (*Gesellschaft etc.*); **4.** wählerisch; **se·lect·ee** [sɪ,lek'ti:] *s.* ⚔ *Am.* Einberufene(r) *m*; **se'lec·tion** [-kʃn] *s.* **1.** Wahl *f*; **2.** Auswahl *f*, -lese *f*; **3.** *biol.* Zuchtwahl *f*: ***natural ~*** natürliche Auslese; **4.** Auswahl *f* (***of*** an *dat.*); **se'lec·tive** [-tɪv] *adj.* □ **1.** auswählend, Auswahl...: ***~ service*** ⚔ *Am.* a) Wehrpflicht *f*, -dienst *m*, b) Einberufung; **2.** ⚡ trennscharf, selek'tiv: ***~ circuit*** Trennkreis *m*; **se·lec·tiv·i·ty** [,sɪlek'tɪvətɪ] *s. Radio, TV*: Trennschärfe *f*; **se'lect·man** [-mən] *s.* [*irr.*] *Am.* Stadtrat *m*; **se'lec·tor** [-tə] *s.* **1.** Auswählende(r *m*) *f*; **2.** Sortierer(in); **3.** ⚙ a) *a.* ⚡ Wähler *m*, b) Schaltgriff *m*, c) *mot.* Gangwähler *m*, d) *Computer*: Se'lektor *m.*

se·le·nic [sɪ'lenɪk] *adj.* ⚗ se'lensauer, Selen...; **se·le·ni·um** [sɪ'li:njəm] *s.* ⚗ Se'len *n.*

sel·e·nog·ra·phy [,selɪ'nɒgrəfɪ] *s.* Mondbeschreibung *f*; **,sel·e'nol·o·gy** [-'nɒlədʒɪ] *s.* Selenolo'gie *f*, Mondkunde *f.*

self [self] **I** *pl.* **selves** [selvz] *s.* **1.** Selbst *n*, Ich *n*: ***my better*** (***second***) ***~*** mein besseres Selbst (mein zweites Ich); ***my humble*** (*od.* ***poor***) ***~*** meine Wenigkeit; ***the study of the ~*** *phls.* das Studium des Ich; → ***former***[2] 1; **2.** Selbstsucht *f*, das eigene *od.* liebe Ich; **3.** *biol.* a) Tier *n od.* Pflanze *f* von einheitlicher Färbung, b) auto'games Lebewesen; **II** *adj.* **4.** einheitlich, *bsd.* ⚘ einfarbig; **III** *pron.* **5.** ✝ *od.* F → ***myself*** *etc.*

,self|-a'ban·don·ment *s.* (Selbst)Aufopferung *f*, (bedingungslose) Hingabe; **,~-a'base·ment** *s.* Selbsterniedrigung *f*; **,~-ab'sorbed** *adj.* **1.** mit sich selbst beschäftigt; **2.** ego'zentrisch; **,~-a'buse** *s.* Selbstbefleckung *f*; **,~-'act·ing** *adj.* ⚙ selbsttätig; **,~-ad'he·sive** *adj.* selbstklebend; **,~-ad'just·ing** *adj.* ⚙ selbstregelnd, -einstellend; **,~-ap'point·ed** *adj.* selbsternannt; **,~-as'ser·tion** *s.* **1.** Geltendmachung *f* s-r Rechte, s-s Willens, s-r Meinung *etc.*; **2.** anmaßendes Auftreten; **,~-as'sert·ive** *adj.* **1.** anmaßend, über'heblich; **2.** ***~ person*** j-d, der sich 'durchzusetzen weiß; **,~-as'sur·ance** *s.* Selbstsicherheit *f*, -bewußtsein *n*; **,~-as'sured** *adj.* selbstbewußt; **,~-'ca·ter·ing** *adj.* für Selbstversorger, mit Selbstverpflegung; **,~-'cen·t(e)red** *adj.* ichbezogen, ego'zentrisch; **,~-'col·o(u)red** *adj.* **1.** einfarbig; **2.** na'turfarben; **,~-com'mand** *s.* Selbstbeherrschung *f*; **,~-com'pla·cent** *adj.* selbstgefällig, -zufrieden; **,~-con'ceit** *s.* Eigendünkel *m*; **,~-con'fessed** *adj.* selbsterklärt: ***a ~ racist*** j-d, der zugibt, Rassist zu sein; **,~-'con·fi·dence** *s.* Selbstvertrauen *n*, -bewußtsein *n*; **,~-'con·scious** *adj.* befangen, gehemmt; **,~-'con·scious·ness** *s.* Befangenheit *f*; **,~-con'tained** *adj.* **1.** *a.* ⚙ (in sich) geschlossen, unabhängig, selbständig: ***~ country*** Selbstversorgerland *n*; ***~ flat*** abgeschlossene Wohnung; ***~ house*** Einfamilienhaus *n*; **2.** reserviert, zu'rückhaltend (*Charakter, Person*); **3.** selbstbeherrscht; **'~-,con·tra'dic·tion** *s.* innerer 'Widerspruch; **'~-,con·tra'dic·to·ry** *adj.* 'widersprüchlich; **,~-con'trol** *s.* Selbstbeherrschung *f*; **,~-de'ceit**, **,~-de'cep·tion** *s.* Selbsttäuschung *f*, -betrug *m*; **,~-de'feat·ing** *adj.* genau das Gegenteil bewirkend, sinn- und zwecklos; **,~-de'fence** *Brit.*, **,~-de'fense** *Am. s.* **1.** Selbstverteidigung *f*; **2.** ⚖ Notwehr *f*; **,~-de'ni·al** *s.*

Selbstverleugnung *f*; **ˌ~-deˈny·ing** *adj.* selbstverleugnend; **ˌ~-deˈspair** *s.* Verzweiflung *f* an sich selbst; **ˌ~-deˈstruc·tion** *s.* **1.** Selbstzerstörung *f*; **2.** Selbstvernichtung *f*, -mord *m*; **ˈ~-deˌter·mi·ˈna·tion** *s.* **1.** *pol. etc.* Selbstbestimmung *f*; **2.** *phls.* freier Wille; **ˌ~-deˈvo·tion** → ***self-abandonment***; **ˌ~-disˈtrust** *s.* Mangel *m* an Selbstvertrauen; **ˌ~-ˈdoubt** *s.* Selbstzweifel *pl.*; **ˌ~-ˈed·u·cat·ed** → ***self-taught*** 1; **ˌ~-emˈployed** *adj.* ♱ selbständig (*Handwerker etc.*); **ˌ~-esˈteem** *s.* **1.** Selbstachtung *f*; **2.** Eigendünkel *m*; **ˌ~-ˈev·i·dent** *adj.* □ selbstverständlich; **ˌ~-exˈplan·a·to·ry** *adj.* ohne Erläuterung verständlich, für sich (selbst) sprechend; **ˌ~-exˈpres·sion** *s.* Ausdruck *m* der eigenen Perˈsönlichkeit; **ˌ~-ˈfeed·ing** *adj.* ⚙ autoˈmatisch (*Material od. Brennstoff*) zuführend; **ˌ~-forˈget·ful** *adj.* □ selbstvergessen, -los; **ˌ~-fulˈfil(l)·ment** *s.* Selbstverwirklichung *f*; **ˌ~-ˈgov·ern·ing** *adj. pol.* ˈselbstverwaltet, autoˈnom, unabhängig; **ˌ~-ˈgov·ern·ment** *s. pol.* Selbstverwaltung *f*, -regierung *f*, Autonoˈmie *f*; **ˌ~-ˈhelp** *s.* Selbsthilfe *f*: ***~ group***; **ˌ~-igˈni·tion** *s. mot.* Selbstzündung *f*; **ˌ~-ˈim·age** *s. psych.* Selbstverständnis *n*; **ˌ~-imˈpor·tance** *s.* ˈSelbstüberˌhebung *f*, Wichtigtueˈrei *f*; **ˌ~-imˈpor·tant** *adj.* überˈheblich, wichtigtuerisch; **ˌ~-inˈduced** *adj.* **1.** ⚡ selbstinduziert; **2.** selbstverursacht; **ˌ~-inˈdul·gence** *s.* **1.** Sichˈgehenlassen *n*; **2.** Zügellosigkeit *f*, Maßlosigkeit *f*; **ˌ~-inˈdul·gent** *adj.* **1.** schwach, nachgiebig gegen sich selbst; **2.** zügellos; **ˌ~-inˈflict·ed** *adj.* selbstzugefügt: ***~ wounds*** ⚔ Selbstverstümmelung *f*; **ˌ~-inˈstruc·tion** *s.* ˈSelbstˌunterricht *m*; **ˌ~-inˈstruc·tion·al** *adj.* Selbstlehr…, Selbstunterrichts…: ***~ manual***; **ˌ~-ˈin·ter·est** *s.* Eigennutz *m*, eigenes Interˈesse.

self·ish [ˈselfɪʃ] *adj.* □ selbstsüchtig, egoˈistisch, eigennützig; **ˈself·ish·ness** [-nɪs] *s.* Selbstsucht *f*, Egoˈismus *m*.

ˌself|-ˈknowl·edge *s.* Selbst(er)kenntnis *f*; **ˈ~-ˌlac·erˈa·tion** *s.* Selbstzerfleischung *f*.

self·less [ˈselflɪs] *adj.* selbstlos; **ˈself·less·ness** [-nɪs] *s.* Selbstlosigkeit *f*.

ˌself|-ˈload·ing *adj.* Selbstlade…; **ˌ~-ˈlove** *s.* Eigenliebe *f*; **ˌ~-ˈlu·bri·cat·ing** *adj.* ⚙ selbstschmierend; **ˌ~-ˈmade** *adj.* selbstgemacht: ***~ man*** j-d, der durch eigene Kraft hochgekommen ist, Selfmademan *m*; **ˌ~-negˈlect** *s.* **1.** Selbstlosigkeit *f*; **2.** Vernachlässigung *f* s-s Äußeren; **ˌ~-oˈpin·ion·at·ed** *adj.* **1.** eingebildet; **2.** rechthaberisch; **ˌ~-ˈpit·y** *s.* Selbstmitleid *n*; **ˌ~-ˈpor·trait** *s.* ˈSelbstporˌträt *n*, -bildnis *n*; **ˌ~-posˈses·sion** *s.* Selbstbeherrschung *f*; **ˌ~-ˈpraise** *s.* Eigenlob *n*; **ˈ~-ˌpres·erˈva·tion** *s.* Selbsterhaltung *f*: ***instinct of ~*** Selbsterhaltungstrieb *m*; **ˌ~-proˈpelled** *adj.* ⚙ Selbstfahr…, mit Eigenantrieb; **ˈ~-ˌre·al·iˈza·tion** *s.* Selbstverwirklichung *f*; **ˌ~-reˈcord·ing** *adj.* ⚙ selbstschreibend; **ˌ~-reˈgard** *s.* **1.** Eigennutz *m*; **2.** Selbstachtung *f*; **ˌ~-reˈli·ance** *s.* Selbstvertrauen *n*, -sicherheit *f*; **ˌ~-reˈli·ant** *adj.* selbstbewußt, -sicher; **ˌ~-reˈproach** *s.* Selbstvorwurf *m*; **ˌ~-reˈspect** *s.* Selbstachtung *f*; **ˌ~-reˈspect·ing** *adj.*: ***every ~ craftsman*** jeder Handwerker, der etwas auf sich hält; **ˌ~-reˈstraint** *s.* Selbstbeherrschung *f*; **ˌ~-ˈright·eous** *adj.* selbstgerecht; **ˌ~-ˈsac·ri·fice** *s.* Selbstaufopferung *f*; **ˌ~-ˈsac·ri·fic·ing** *adj.* aufopferungsvoll; **ˈ~-same** *adj.* ebenderselbe, -dieselbe, -dasselbe; **ˌ~-ˈsat·is·fied** *adj.* selbstzufrieden; **ˌ~-ˈseal·ing** *adj.* **1.** ⚙ selbstdichtend; **2.** selbstklebend (*bsd. Briefumschlag*); **3.** schußsicher; **ˌ~-ˈseek·er** *s.* Egoˈist(in); **ˌ~-ˈserv·ice I** *adj.* Selbstbedienungs…: ***~ shop***; **II** *s.* Selbstbedienung *f*; **ˌ~-ˈstart·er** *s. mot.* (Selbst-) Anlasser *m*; **ˌ~-ˈstyled** *adj. iron.* von eigenen Gnaden; **ˌ~-sufˈfi·cien·cy** *s.* **1.** Unabhängigkeit *f* (von fremder Hilfe); **2.** ♱ Autarˈkie *f*; **3.** Eigendünkel *m*; **ˌ~-sufˈfi·cient** *adj.* **1.** unabhängig, Selbstversorger…, ♱ *a.* auˈtark; **2.** dünkelhaft; **ˌ~-sugˈges·tion** *s. psych.* ˌAutosuggestiˈon *f*; **ˌ~-supˈpli·er** *s.* Selbstversorger *m*; **ˌ~-supˈport·ing** *adj.* **1.** → ***self-sufficient*** 1; **2.** ⚙ freitragend (*Brücke etc.*); **ˌ~-ˈtaught** *adj.* **1.** autodiˈdaktisch: ***~ person*** Autodidakt *m*; **2.** selbsterlernt; **ˌ~-ˈtim·er** *s. phot.* Selbstauslöser *m*; **ˌ~-ˈwill** *s.* Eigensinn *m*; **ˌ~-ˈwilled** *adj.* eigensinnig; **ˌ~-ˈwind·ing** *adj.* autoˈmatisch (*Uhr*).

sell [sel] **I** *s.* **1.** F a) Reinfall *m*, b) Schwindel *m*; **2.** ♱ F (***hard ~*** aggresˈsive) Verˈkaufsmeˌthode; → ***soft*** 1; **II** *v/t.* [*irr.*] **3.** verkaufen, -äußern (***to*** an *acc.*), ♱ *a. Ware* absetzen; → ***life*** *Redew.*; **4.** ♱ *Waren* führen, handeln mit, vertreiben; **5.** *fig.* verkaufen, e-n guten Absatz sichern (*dat.*): ***his name will ~ the book***; **6.** *fig.* ‚verkaufen', verraten; **7.** *sl.* ‚anschmieren'; **8.** F *j-m et.* ‚verkaufen', aufschwatzen, schmackhaft machen: ***~ s.o. on*** j-m *et.* andrehen, j-n zu *et.* überreden; ***be sold on*** *fig.* von *et.* überzeugt *od.* begeistert sein; **III** *v/i.* [*irr.*] **9.** verkaufen; **10.** verkauft werden (***at*** für); **11.** sich *gut etc.* verkaufen, *gut etc.* gehen, ‚ziehen'; ***~ off*** *v/t.* ausverkaufen, *Lager* räumen; ***~ out*** *v/t.* **1.** → ***sell off***: ***be sold out*** ausverkauft sein; **2.** *Wertpapiere* realisieren; **3.** *fig.* → ***sell*** 6; ***~ up*** *v/t.* **1.** (*v/i.* sein) *Geschäft etc.* verkaufen; **2.** ***~ s.o. up*** j-n auspfänden.

sell·er [ˈselə] *s.* **1.** Verkäufer(in); Händler(in): ***~s' market*** ♱ Verkäufermarkt *m*; ***~'s option*** Verkaufsoption *f*, *Börse*: Rückprämie(ngeschäft *n*) *f*; **2.** ***good ~*** ♱ gutgehende Ware, zugkräftiger Arˈtikel.

sell·ing [ˈselɪŋ] **I** *adj.* **1.** Verkaufs…, Absatz…, Vertriebs…: ***~ area*** *od.* ***space*** Verkaufsfläche *f*; **II** *s.* **2.** Verkauf *m*; **3.** → ***sell*** 2.

ˈsell·out *s.* **1.** Ausverkauf *m* (*a. fig. pol.*); **2.** ausverkaufte Veranstaltung, volles Haus; **3.** *fig.* Verrat *m*.

Selt·zer (wa·ter) [ˈseltsə] *s.* Selters (-wasser) *n*.

sel·vage [ˈselvɪdʒ] *s. Weberei*: Salband *n*.

selves [selvz] *pl. von* ***self***.

se·man·tic [sɪˈmæntɪk] *adj. ling.* seˈmantisch; **seˈman·tics** [-ks] *s. pl. mst sg. konstr.* Seˈmantik *f*, (Wort)Bedeutungslehre *f*.

sem·a·phore [ˈseməfɔː] **I** *s.* **1.** ⚙ Semaˈphor *m*: a) 🚂 (ˈFlügel)Siˌgnalmast *m*, b) optischer Teleˈgraph; **2.** ⚔, ⚓ (Flaggen)Winken *n*: ***~ message*** Winkspruch *m*; **II** *v/t. u. v/i.* **3.** signalisieren.

sem·blance [ˈsembləns] *s.* **1.** (äußere) Gestalt, Erscheinung *f*: ***in the ~ of*** in Gestalt (*gen.*); **2.** Ähnlichkeit *f* (***to*** mit); **3.** (An)Schein *m*: ***the ~ of honesty***; ***under the ~ of*** unter dem Deckmantel (*gen.*).

se·mei·ol·o·gy [ˌsemɪˈɒlədʒɪ] *s.*, **ˌse·meiˈot·ics** [-ˈɒtɪks] *s. pl. sg. konstr.* Semiˈotik *f*: a) *Lehre von den Zeichen*, b) ⚕ Symptomatoloˈgie *f*.

se·men [ˈsiːmen] *s. physiol.* Samen *m* (*a.* ⚘), Sperma *n*, Samenflüssigkeit *f*.

se·mes·ter [sɪˈmestə] *s. univ. bsd. Am.* Seˈmester *n*, Halbjahr *n*.

sem·i [ˈsemɪ] *s.* F *für* a) ***semidetached*** II, b) ***semifinal*** I, c) *Am.* ***semitrailer***.

semi- [semɪ] *in Zssgn* halb…, Halb…; **ˌ~-ˈan·nu·al** *adj.* □ halbjährlich; **ˈ~ˌau·toˈmat·ic** *adj.* (□ ***~ally***) ˈhalbautoˌmatisch; **ˌ~ˈbold** *adj. u. s. typ.* halbfett(e Schrift); **ˈ~·breve** *s.* ♪ ganze Note: ***~ rest*** ganze Pause; **ˈ~ˌcir·cle** *s.* **1.** Halbkreis *m*; **2.** ⟂ Winkelmesser *m*; **ˌ~ˈcir·cu·lar** *adj.* halbkreisförmig; **ˌ~ˈco·lon** *s.* Semiˈkolon *n*, Strichpunkt *m*; **ˌ~·conˈduc·tor** *s.* ⚡ Halbleiter *m*; **ˌ~ˈcon·scious** *adj.* nicht bei vollem Bewußtsein; **ˌ~·deˈtached I** *adj.*: ***~ house*** → **II** *s.* Doppelhaushälfte *f*; **ˌ~ˈfi·nal** *sport* **I** *s.* **1.** ˈSemi-, ˈHalbfiˌnale *n*, Vorschlußrunde *f*; **2.** ˈHalbfiˌnalspiel *n*; **II** *adj.* **3.** Halbfinal…; **ˌ~ˈfi·nal·ist** *s. sport* ˈHalbfinaˌlist(in); **ˌ~ˈfin·ished** *adj.* ⚙ halbfertig: ***~ product*** Halbfabrikat *n*; **ˌ~ˈflu·id**, **ˌ~ˈliq·uid** *adj.* halb-, zähflüssig; **ˈ~ˌman·uˈfac·tured** → ***semifinished***; **ˌ~ˈmonth·ly I** *adj. u. adv.* halbmonatlich; **II** *s.* Halbmonatsschrift *f*.

sem·i·nal [ˈsemɪnl] *adj.* □ **1.** ⚘, *physiol.* Samen…: ***~ duct*** Samengang *m*, -leiter *m*; ***~ fluid*** Samenflüssigkeit *f*, Sperma *n*; ***~ leaf*** ⚘ Keimblatt *n*; ***~ power*** Zeugungsfähigkeit *f*; **2.** *fig.* a) zukunftsträchtig, fruchtbar, b) folgenreich; **3.** noch unentwickelt: ***in the ~ state*** im Entwicklungsstadium.

sem·i·nar [ˈsemɪnɑː] *s. univ.* Semiˈnar *n*.

sem·i·nar·y [ˈsemɪnərɪ] *s.* **1.** (*eccl.* ˈPriester)Semiˌnar *n*, Bildungsanstalt *f*; **2.** *fig.* Schule *f*, Pflanzstätte *f*, *contp.* Brutstätte *f*.

sem·i·na·tion [ˌsemɪˈneɪʃn] *s.* (Aus)Säen *n*.

ˌsem·i·ofˈfi·cial *adj.* □ halbamtlich, offiziˈös.

se·mi·ol·o·gy [ˌsemɪˈɒlədʒɪ] *s.*, **ˌse·miˈot·ics** [-ˈɒtɪks] *s. pl. sg. konstr.* → ***semeiology***.

ˈsem·i|ˌpre·cious *adj.* halbedel: ***~ stone*** Halbedelstein *m*; **ˌ~·proˈfes·sion·al I** *adj.* ˈhalbprofessioˌnell; **II** *s. sport* ‚Halbprofi' *m*; **ˈ~ˌqua·ver** *s.* ♪ Sechzehntel(note *f*) *n*: ***~ rest*** Sechzehntelpause *f*; **ˌ~ˈrig·id** *adj.* halbstarr (*Luftschiff*); **ˌ~ˈskilled** *adj.* angelernt (*Arbeiter*).

Sem·ite [ˈsiːmaɪt] **I** *s.* Seˈmit(in); **II** *adj.* seˈmitisch; **Se·mit·ic** [sɪˈmɪtɪk] **I** *adj.* seˈmitisch; **II** *s. ling.* Seˈmitisch *n*.

ˈsem·i|·steel *s.* ⚙ Halb-, *Am.* Puddelstahl *m*; **ˈ~·tone** *s.* ♪ Halbton *m*; **ˈ~ˌtrail·er** *s. mot.* Sattelschlepper(anhänger) *m*; **ˈ~ˌvow·el** *s. ling.* ˈHalbvoˌkal *m*; **ˌ~ˈweek·ly I** *adj. u. adv.* halbwöchentlich; **II** *s.* halbwöchentlich erscheinende Veröffentlichung.

sem·o·li·na [ˌseməˈliːnə] *s.* Grieß(mehl *n*) *m*.

sem·pi·ter·nal [ˌsempɪˈtɜːnl] *adj. rhet.* immerwährend, ewig.

semp·stress [ˈsempstrɪs] → ***seamstress***.

sen·ate [ˈsenɪt] *s.* **1.** Seˈnat *m* (*a. univ.*); **2.** ♀ *parl. Am.* Seˈnat *m* (*Oberhaus*); **sen·a·tor** [ˈsenətə] *s.* Seˈnator *m*; **sen·a·to·ri·al** [ˌsenəˈtɔːrɪəl] *adj.* □ **1.** senaˈtorisch, Senats…; **2.** *Am.* zur Wahl von Senaˈtoren berechtigt.

send [send] [*irr.*] **I** *v/t.* **1.** *j-n, Brief, Hilfe etc.* senden, schicken (***to*** *dat.*): ~ ***s.o. to bed*** (***to a school, to prison***) j-n ins Bett (auf e-e Schule, ins Gefängnis) schicken; → ***word*** 6; **2.** *Ball, Kugel etc. wohin* senden, schießen, jagen; **3.** *mit adj. od. pres.p.* machen: ~ ***s.o. mad***; ~ ***s.o. flying*** a) j-n verjagen, b) j-n hinschleudern; ~ ***s.o. reeling*** j-n taumeln machen *od.* lassen; **4.** *sl. Zuhörer etc.* in Ekˈstase versetzen, ˈhinreißen; **II** *v/i.* **5.** ~ ***for*** a) nach *j-m* schicken, *j-n* kommen lassen, *j-n* holen *od.* rufen (lassen), b) (sich) *et.* kommen lassen, bestellen; **6.** ⚡, *Radio etc.*: senden; *Zssgn mit adv.*:

send| a·way I *v/t.* **1.** weg-, fortschicken; **2.** *Brief etc.* absenden; **II** *v/i.* **3.** ~ ***for*** (***to s.o.***) sich (von j-m) *et.* kommen lassen; ~ **down** *v/t.* **1.** *fig. Preise, Temperatur* (herˈab)drücken; **2.** *univ.* relegieren; **3.** F *j-n* einsperren; ~ **forth** *v/t.* **1.** *j-n, et., a. Licht* aussenden; *Wärme etc.* ausstrahlen; **2.** *Laut etc.* von sich geben; **3.** herˈvorbringen; **4.** *fig.* veröffentlichen, verbreiten; ~ **in** *v/t.* **1.** einsenden, -schicken, -reichen; → ***name*** *Redew.*; **2.** *sport Ersatzmann* aufs Feld schicken; ~ **off** *v/t.* **1.** → ***send away*** I; **2.** *j-n* (herzlich) verabschieden; **3.** *sport* vom Platz stellen; ~ **on** *v/t.* vorˈaus-, nachschicken; ~ **out** → ***send forth***; ~ **up** *v/t.* **1.** *j-n, a. Ball etc.* hinˈaufsenden; **2.** *Schrei* ausstoßen; **3.** *fig. Preise, Fieber* in die Höhe treiben; **4.** *Brit.* F ‚durch den Kaˈkao' ziehen, parodieren; **5.** F ‚einlochen'.

send·er [ˈsendə] *s.* **1.** Absender(in); **2.** (Über)ˈSender(in); **3.** *tel.* Geber *m* (*Sendegerät*).

ˈsend|-off *s.* F **1.** Abschied *m*, Abschiedsfeier *f*, Geleit(e) *n*; **2.** gute Wünsche *pl.* zum Anfang; **3.** *sport u. fig.* Start *m*; **ˈ~-up** *s. Brit.* F Verulkung *f*, Paroˈdie *f*.

se·nes·cence [sɪˈnesns] *s.* Altern *n*; **seˈnes·cent** [-nt] *adj.* **1.** alternd; **2.** Alters…

sen·es·chal [ˈsenɪʃl] *s. hist.* Seneschall *m*, Majorˈdomus *m*.

se·nile [ˈsiːnaɪl] *adj.* **1.** seˈnil: a) greisenhaft, b) ‚verkalkt', kindisch; **2.** Alters…: ~ ***decay*** Altersabbau *m*; ~ ***speckle*** ⚕ Altersfleck *m*; **se·nil·i·ty** [sɪˈnɪlətɪ] *s.* Seniliˈtät *f*.

sen·ior [ˈsiːnjə] **I** *adj.* **1.** (*nachgestellt, abbr. in England* ***sen.***, *in USA* ***Sr.***) senior: ***Mr. John Smith sen.*** (***Sr.***) Herr John Smith sen.; **2.** älter (***to*** als): ~ ***citizen*** älterer Mitbürger, Rentner(in); ~ ***citizens*** Senioren *pl.*; ~ ***partner*** ✝ Seniorchef *m*, Hauptteilhaber; **3.** rang-, dienstälter, ranghöher, Ober…: ***a*** ~ ***man*** *Brit.* ein höheres Semester (*Student*); ~ ***officer*** a) höherer Offizier, *mein etc.* Vorgesetzter, b) Rangälteste(r); ~ ***service*** *Brit. die* Kriegsmarine; **4.** *ped.* Ober…: ~ ***classes*** Oberklassen; **5.** *Am.* im letzten Schuljahr (stehend): ***the*** ~ ***class*** die oberste Klasse; ~ ***high*** (***school***) *Am. die obersten Klassen der High-School*; ~ ***college*** College, *an dem das 3. und 4. Jahr eines Studiums absolviert wird*; **II** *s.* **6.** Ältere(r *m*) *f*; Älteste(r *m*) *f*: ***he is my*** ~ ***by four years, he is four years my*** ~ er ist vier Jahre älter als ich; **7.** Rang-, Dienstälteste(r *m*) *f*; **8.** Vorgesetzte(r *m*) *f*; **9.** *Am.* Stuˈdent *m od.* Schüler *m* im letzten Studienjahr.

sen·ior·i·ty [ˌsiːnɪˈɒrətɪ] *s.* **1.** höheres Alter; **2.** höheres Dienstalter: ***by*** ~ *Beförderung* nach dem Dienstalter.

sen·na [ˈsenə] *s. pharm.* Sennesblätter *pl.*

sen·sate [ˈsenseɪt] *adj.* sinnlich (wahrgenommen).

sen·sa·tion [senˈseɪʃn] *s.* **1.** (Sinnes-) Wahrnehmung *f*, (-)Empfindung *f*; **2.** Gefühl *n*: ***pleasant*** ~; ~ ***of thirst*** Durstgefühl *n*; **3.** Empfindungsvermögen *n*; **4.** Sensatiˈon *f* (*a. Ereignis*), (großer) Eindruck, Aufsehen *n*: ***make*** (*od.* ***create***) ***a*** ~ großes Aufsehen erregen; **senˈsa·tion·al** [-ʃənl] *adj.* □ **1.** sensatioˈnell, Sensations…; **2.** sinnlich, Sinnes…; **3.** *phls.* sensuaˈlistisch; **senˈsa·tion·al·ism** [-ʃnəlɪzəm] *s.* **1.** Sensatiˈonsgier *f*, -lust *f*; **2.** ‚Sensatiˈonsmache' *f*; **3.** *phls.* Sensuaˈlismus *m*.

sense [sens] **I** *s.* **1.** Sinn *m*, ˈSinnesorˌgan n: ***the five*** ~***s*** die fünf Sinne; ~ ***of smell*** (***touch***) Geruchs- (Tast)sinn; ~ ***organ*** Sinnesorgan *n*; → ***sixth*** 1; **2.** *pl.* Sinne *pl.*, (klarer) Verstand: ***in*** (***out of***) ***one's*** ~***s*** bei (von) Sinnen; ***in one's right*** ~***s*** bei Verstand; ***lose one's*** ~***s*** den Verstand verlieren; ***bring s.o. to his*** ~***s*** j-n zur Besinnung bringen; **3.** *fig.* Vernunft *f*, Verstand *m*: ***a man of*** ~ ein vernünftiger *od.* kluger Mensch; ***common*** (*od.* ***good***) ~ gesunder Menschenverstand; ***have the*** ~ ***to do s.th.*** so klug sein, et. zu tun; ***knock some*** ~ ***into s.o.*** j-m den Kopf zurechtsetzen; **4.** Sinne *pl.*, Empfindungsvermögen *n*; **5.** Gefühl *n*, Empfindung *f* (***of*** für): ~ ***of pain*** Schmerzgefühl, -empfindung; ~ ***of security*** Gefühl der Sicherheit; **6.** Sinn *m*, Gefühl *n* (***of*** für): ~ ***of beauty*** Schönheitssinn; ~ ***of duty*** Pflichtgefühl; ~ ***of humo***(***u***)***r*** (Sinn für) Humor *m*; ~ ***of justice*** Gerechtigkeitssinn; ~ ***of locality*** Ortssinn; ~ ***of purpose*** Zielstrebigkeit *f*; **7.** Sinn *m*, Bedeutung *f* (*e-s Wortes etc.*): ***in a*** ~ gewissermaßen; **8.** Sinn *m* (*et. Vernünftiges*): ***what is the*** ~ ***of doing this?*** was hat es für e-n Sinn, das zu tun?; ***talk*** ~ vernünftig reden; ***it does not make*** ~ es hat keinen Sinn; **9.** (allgemeine) Ansicht, Meinung *f*: ***take the*** ~ ***of*** die Meinung (*gen.*) einholen; **10.** ⩘ Richtung *f*: ~ ***of rotation*** Drehsinn *m*; **II** *v/t.* **11.** fühlen, spüren, ahnen; **12.** *Am.* F ‚kapieren', begreifen; **13.** *Computer*: a) abtasten, ⚡ *a.* (ab)fühlen, b) abfragen; **ˈsense·less** [-lɪs] *adj.* □ **1.** a) besinnungslos, b) gefühllos; **2.** unvernünftig, dumm, verrückt (*Mensch*); **3.** sinnlos, unsinnig (*Sache*); **ˈsense·less·ness** [-lɪsnɪs] *s.* **1.** Unempfindlichkeit *f*; **2.** Bewußtlosigkeit *f*; **3.** Unvernunft *f*; **4.** Sinnlosigkeit *f*.

sen·si·bil·i·ty [ˌsensɪˈbɪlətɪ] *s.* **1.** Sensibiliˈtät *f*, Empfindungsvermögen *n*; **2.** *phys. etc.* Empfindlichkeit *f*: ~ ***to light*** Lichtempfindlichkeit; **3.** *fig.* Empfänglichkeit *f* (***to*** für); **4.** Sensibiliˈtät *f*, Empfindsamkeit *f*; **5.** *a. pl.* Fein-, Zartgefühl *n*; **sen·si·ble** [ˈsensəbl] *adj.* □ **1.** vernünftig (*Person, Sache*); **2.** fühl-, spürbar; **3.** merklich, wahrnehmbar; **4.** bei Bewußtsein; **5.** bewußt (***of*** *gen.*): ***be*** ~ ***of*** a) sich *e-r Sache* bewußt sein, b) *et.* empfinden; **sen·si·ble·ness** [ˈsensəblnɪs] *s.* Vernünftigkeit *f*, Klugheit *f*.

sens·ing| el·e·ment [ˈsensɪŋ] *s.* ⚙ (Meß)Fühler *m*; ~ **head** *s. Computer*: Abtastkopf *m*.

sen·si·tive [ˈsensɪtɪv] **I** *adj.* □ **1.** fühlend (*Kreatur etc.*); **2.** Empfindungs…: ~ ***nerves***; **3.** sensiˈtiv, (ˈüber)empfindlich (***to*** gegen): ***be*** ~ ***to*** empfindlich reagieren auf (*acc.*); **4.** senˈsibel, feinfühlig, empfindsam; **5.** *phys. etc.* (*phot.* licht-) empfindlich: ~ ***to heat*** wärmeempfindlich; ~ ***plant*** 🌿 Sinnpflanze *f*; ~ ***spot*** *fig.* empfindliche Stelle, neuralgischer Punkt; ~ ***subject*** *fig.* heikles Thema; **6.** schwankend (*a.* ✝ *Markt*); **7.** ⚔ gefährdet; **II** *s.* **8.** sensiˈtiver Mensch; **ˈsen·si·tive·ness** [-nɪs], **sen·si·tiv·i·ty** [ˌsensɪˈtɪvətɪ] *s.* **1.** → ***sensibility*** 1 *u.* 2: ~ ***group*** *psych.* Trainingsgruppe *f*; ~ ***training*** *psych.* Sensitivitätstraining *n*; **2.** Sensitiviˈtät *f*, Feingefühl *n*.

sen·si·tize [ˈsensɪtaɪz] *v/t.* sensibilisieren, (*phot.* licht)empfindlich machen.

sen·sor [ˈsensə] *s.* ⚡, ⚙ Sensor *m*.

sen·so·ri·al [senˈsɔːrɪəl] → ***sensory***; **senˈso·ri·um** [-əm] *pl.* **-ri·a** [-rɪə] *s. anat., psych.* **1.** Senˈsorium *n*, ˈSinnesappaˌrat *m*; **2.** Sitz *m* des Empfindungsvermögens, Bewußtsein *n*; **sen·so·ry** [ˈsensərɪ] *adj.* senˈsorisch, Sinnes…: ~ ***perception***.

sen·su·al [ˈsensjʊəl] *adj.* □ **1.** sinnlich: a) Sinnes…, b) wollüstig, *bsd. bibl.* fleischlich; **2.** *phls.* sensuaˈlistisch; **ˈsen·su·al·ism** [-lɪzəm] *s.* **1.** Sinnlichkeit *f*, Lüsternheit *f*; **2.** *phls.* Sensuaˈlismus *m*; **ˈsen·su·al·ist** [-lɪst] *s.* **1.** sinnlicher Mensch; **2.** *phls.* Sensuaˈlist *m*; **sen·su·al·i·ty** [ˌsensjʊˈælətɪ] *s.* Sinnlichkeit *f*; **ˈsen·su·al·ize** [-laɪz] *v/t.* **1.** sinnlich machen; **2.** versinnlichen.

sen·su·ous [ˈsensjʊəs] *adj.* □ sinnlich: a) Sinnes…, b) sinnenfroh; **ˈsen·su·ous·ness** [-nɪs] *s.* Sinnlichkeit *f*.

sent [sent] *pret. u. p.p. von* ***send***.

sen·tence [ˈsentəns] **I** *s.* **1.** *ling.* Satz (-verbindung *f*) *m*: ***complex*** ~ Satzgefüge *n*; ~ ***stress*** Satzbetonung *f*; **2.** ⚖ a) (*bsd.* Straf)Urteil *n*: ***pass*** ~ (***up***)***on*** das (*fig.* ein) Urteil fällen über (*acc.*), verurteilen (*a. fig.*), b) Strafe *f*: ***under*** ~ ***of death*** zum Tode verurteilt; ***serve a*** ~ ***of imprisonment*** e-e Freiheitsstrafe verbüßen; **3.** *obs.* Senˈtenz *f*, Sinnspruch *m*; **II** *v/t.* **4.** ⚖ *u. fig.* verurteilen (***to*** zu).

sen·ten·tious [senˈtenʃəs] *adj.* □ **1.** sententiˈös, präˈgnant, kernig; **2.** spruchreich, lehrhaft; *contp.* aufgeblasen, salbungsvoll; **senˈten·tious·ness** [-nɪs] *s.* **1.** Präˈgnanz *f*; **2.** Spruchreichtum *m*, Lehrhaftigkeit *f*; **3.** Großsprecheˈrei *f*.

sen·ti·ence ['senʃəns] *s.* **1.** Empfindungsvermögen *n*; **2.** Empfindung *f*; '**sen·tient** [-nt] *adj.* □ **1.** empfindungsfähig; **2.** fühlend.
sen·ti·ment ['sentɪmənt] *s.* **1.** Empfindung *f*, (Gefühls)Regung *f*, Gefühl *n* (***towards** j-m* gegenüber); **2.** *pl.* Gedanken *pl.*, Meinung *f*, (Geistes)Haltung *f*: ***noble ~s*** edle Gesinnung; ***them's my ~s*** *humor.* (so) denke ich; **3.** (Fein)Gefühl *n*, Innigkeit *f* (*a. Kunst*); **4.** *contp.* Sentimentali'tät *f*.
sen·ti·men·tal [ˌsentɪ'mentl] *adj.* □ **1.** sentimen'tal: a) gefühlvoll, empfindsam, b) *contp.* rührselig; **2.** gefühlsmäßig, Gefühls..., emotio'nal: ***~ value*** ✝ Liebhaberwert *m*; ˌ**sen·ti'men·tal·ism** [-təlɪzəm] **1.** Empfindsamkeit *f*; **2.** → ***sentimentality***; ˌ**sen·ti'men·tal·ist** [-təlɪst] *s.* Gefühlsmensch *m*; **sen·ti·men·tal·i·ty** [ˌsentɪmen'tælətɪ] *s. contp.* Sentimentali'tät *f*, Rührseligkeit *f*, Gefühlsduse'lei *f*; ˌ**sen·ti'men·tal·ize** [-təlaɪz] **I** *v/t.* sentimen'tal gestalten; **II** *v/i.* (***about**, **over***) in Gefühlen schwelgen (bei), sentimen'tal werden (bei, über *dat.*).
sen·ti·nel ['sentɪnl] *s.* **1.** Wächter *m*: ***stand ~ over*** bewachen; **2.** ⚔ → ***sentry*** 1; **3.** *Computer*: 'Trennsymˌbol *n*.
sen·try ['sentrɪ] ⚔ *s.* **1.** (Wach)Posten *m*, Wache *f*; **2.** Wache *f*, Wachdienst *m*; '**~-box** *s.* Wachhäus-chen *n*; '**~-go** *s.* Wachdienst *m*.
se·pal ['sepəl] *s.* ⚘ Kelchblatt *n*.
sep·a·ra·ble ['sepərəbl] *adj.* □ (ab-) trennbar; '**sep·a·rate** ['sepəreɪt] **I** *v/t.* **1.** trennen (***from*** von): a) *Freunde, a. Kämpfende etc.* ausein'anderbringen, ⚖ (ehelich) trennen, b) abtrennen, -schneiden, c) (ab)sondern, (aus)scheiden, d) ausein'anderhalten, unter'scheiden zwischen; **2.** (auf-, zer)teilen (***into*** in *acc.*); **3.** ⚗, ⚙ a) scheiden, (ab)spalten, b) sortieren, c) aufbereiten; **4.** *Milch* zentrifugieren; **5.** ⚔ *Am.* entlassen; **II** *v/i.* **6.** sich (⚖ ehelich) trennen (***from*** von), ausein'andergehen; **7.** ⚗, ⚙ sich absondern; **III** *adj.* ['seprət] □ **8.** getrennt, besonder, sepa'rat, Separat..., Sonder...: ***~ account*** ✝ Sonderkonto *n*; ***~ estate*** ⚖ eingebrachtes Sondergut (*der Ehefrau*); **9.** einzeln, gesondert, getrennt, Einzel...: ***~ questions*** gesondert zu behandelnde Fragen; **10.** einzeln, isoliert; **IV** *s.* ['seprət] **11.** *typ.* Sonder(ab)druck *m*; **sep·a·rate·ness** ['seprətnɪs] *s.* **1.** Getrenntheit *f*; **2.** Besonderheit *f*; **3.** Abgeschiedenheit *f*, Isoliertheit *f*; **sep·a·ra·tion** [ˌsepə'reɪʃn] *s.* **1.** (⚖ eheliche) Trennung, Absonderung *f*: ***judicial ~*** (gerichtliche) Aufhebung der ehelichen Gemeinschaft; ***~ of powers*** *pol.* Gewaltenteilung *f*; ***~ allowance*** Trennungszulage *f*; **2.** ⚙, ⚗ a) Abscheidung *f*, -spaltung *f*, b) Scheidung *f*, Klassierung *f von Erzen*; **3.** ⚔ *Am.* Entlassung *f*; '**sep·a·ra·tism** [-ətɪzəm] *s.* Separa'tismus *m*; '**sep·a·ra·tist** [-ətɪst] **I** *s.* **1.** Separa'tist(in); **2.** *eccl.* Sektierer (-in); **II** *adj.* **3.** separa'tistisch; '**sep·a·ra·tive** [-ətɪv] *adj.* trennend, Trennungs...; **sep·a·ra·tor** ['sepəreɪtə] *s.* **1.** ⚙ a) (Ab)Scheider *m*, b) (*bsd.* 'Milch-) Zentriˌfuge *f*; **2.** *a.* ***~ stage*** ⚡ Trennstufe *f*; **3.** *bsd.* ⚕ Spreizvorrichtung *f*.
Se·phar·dim [se'fɑːdɪm] (*Hebrew*) *s. pl.* Se'phardim *pl.*
se·pi·a ['siːpjə] *s.* **1.** *zo.* Sepia *f*, (Gemeiner) Tintenfisch *m*; **2.** Sepia *f* (*Sekret od. Farbstoff*); **3.** *paint.* a) Sepia *f* (*Farbe*), b) Sepiazeichnung *f*; **4.** *phot.* Sepiadruck *m*.
sep·sis ['sepsɪs] *s.* ⚕ Sepsis *f*.
sept- [sept] *in Zssgn* sieben...
sep·ta ['septə] *pl. von* ***septum***.
sep·tan·gle ['septæŋgl] *s.* ⩓ Siebeneck *n*.
Sep·tem·ber [sep'tembə] *s.* Sep'tember *m*: ***in ~*** im September.
sep·te·mi·a [sep'tiːmɪə] → ***septic(a)emia***.
sep·te·nar·y [sep'tiːnərɪ] **I** *adj.* **1.** aus sieben bestehend, Sieben...; **2.** → ***septennial***; **II** *s.* **3.** Satz *m* von sieben Dingen; **4.** Sieben *f*.
sep·ten·ni·al [sep'tenjəl] *adj.* □ **1.** siebenjährlich; **2.** siebenjährig.
sep·tet(te) [sep'tet] *s.* ♪ Sep'tett *n*.
sep·tic ['septɪc] **I** *adj.* (□ ***~ally***) ⚕ septisch: ***~ sore throat*** septische Angina; **II** *s.* Fäulniserreger *m*.
sep·ti·c(a)e·mi·a [ˌseptɪ'siːmɪə] *s.* ⚕ Blutvergiftung *f*, Sepsis *f*.
sep·tu·a·ge·nar·i·an [ˌseptjʊədʒɪ'neərɪən] **I** *s.* Siebzigjährige(r *m*) *f*, Siebziger(in); **II** *adj.* a) siebzigjährig, b) in den Siebzigern; **Sep·tu·a·ges·i·ma (Sun·day)** [ˌseptjʊə'dʒesɪmə] *s.* Septua'gesima *f* (*9. Sonntag vor Ostern*).
sep·tum ['septəm] *pl.* **-ta** [-tə] *s.* ⚘, *anat., zo.* (Scheide)Wand *f*, Septum *n*.
sep·tu·ple ['septjʊpl] **I** *adj.* siebenfach; **II** *s. das* Siebenfache; **III** *v/t.* (*v/i.* sich) versiebenfachen.
sep·tu·plet ['septjʊplɪt] *s.* **1.** Siebenergruppe *f*; **2.** *mst pl.* Siebenling *m* (*Kind*).
sep·ul·cher *Am.* → ***sepulchre***; **se·pul·chral** [sɪ'pʌlkrəl] *adj.* □ **1.** Grab..., Begräbnis...; **2.** *fig.* düster, Grabes... (*-stimme etc.*); **sep·ul·chre** ['sepəlkə] *s.* **1.** Grab(stätte *f*, -mal *n*) *n*; **2.** *a.* ***Easter ~*** *R.C.* Ostergrab *n* (*Schrein*).
sep·ul·ture ['sepəltʃə] *s.* (Toten)Bestattung *f*.
se·quel ['siːkwəl] *s.* **1.** (Aufein'ander-) Folge *f*: ***in the ~*** in der Folge; **2.** Folge (-erscheinung) *f*, (Aus)Wirkung *f*, Konse'quenz *f*, (*gerichtliches etc.*) Nachspiel; **3.** (Ro'man- *etc.*)Fortsetzung *f*, (*a.* Hörspiel- *etc.*)Folge *f*.
se·quence ['siːkwəns] *s.* **1.** (Aufein'ander)Folge *f*: ***~ of operations*** ⚙ Arbeitsablauf *m*; ***~ of tenses*** *ling.* Zeitenfolge; **2.** (Reihen)Folge *f*: ***in ~*** der Reihe nach; **3.** Folge *f*, Reihe *f*, Serie *f*; **4.** → ***sequel*** 2; **5.** ♪, *eccl., a. Kartenspiel*: Se'quenz *f*; **6.** *Film*: Szene *f*; **7.** Folgerichtigkeit *f*; **8.** *fig.* Vorgang *m*; '**se·quent** [-nt] **I** *adj.* **1.** (aufein'ander)folgend; **2.** (logisch) folgend; **II** *s.* **3.** (*zeitliche od. logische*) Folge; **se·quen·tial** [sɪ'kwenʃl] *adj.* □ **1.** (*regelmäßig*) (aufein'ander)folgend; **2.** folgend (***to*** auf *acc.*); **3.** folgerichtig, konse'quent.
se·ques·ter [sɪ'kwestə] *v/t.* **1.** (***o.s.*** sich) absondern (***from*** von); **2.** ⚖ → ***sequestrate***; **se'ques·tered** [-əd] *adj.* einsam, weltabgeschieden; zu'rückgezogen; **se'ques·trate** [-treɪt] *v/t.* ⚖ beschlagnahmen: a) unter Treuhänderschaft stellen, b) konfiszieren; **se·ques·tra·tion** [ˌsiːkwe'streɪʃn] *s.* **1.** Absonderung *f*; Ausschluß *m* (***from*** von, *eccl.* aus *der Kirche*); **2.** ⚖ Beschlagnahme *f*: a) Zwangsverwaltung *f*, b) Einziehung *f*; **3.** Zu'rückgezogenheit *f*.
se·quin ['siːkwɪn] *s.* **1.** *hist.* Ze'chine *f* (*Goldmünze*); **2.** Ziermünze *f*; **3.** Pail'lette *f*.
se·quoi·a [sɪ'kwɔɪə] *s.* ⚘ Mammutbaum *m*.
se·ra·glio [se'rɑːlɪəʊ] *s.* Se'rail *n*.
se·rai [se'raɪ] *s.* Karawanse'rei *f*.
ser·aph ['serəf] *pl.* '**ser·aphs**, '**ser·a·phim** [-fɪm] *s.* Seraph *m* (*Engel*); **se·raph·ic** [se'ræfɪk] *adj.* (□ ***~ally***) se'raphisch, engelhaft, verzückt.
Serb [sɜːb], '**Ser·bian** [-bjən] **I** *s.* **1.** Serbe *m*, Serbin *f*; **2.** *ling.* Serbisch *n*; **II** *adj.* **3.** serbisch.
sere [sɪə] → ***sear***[1] 7.
ser·e·nade [ˌserə'neɪd] ♪ **I** *s.* **1.** Sere'nade *f*, Ständchen *n*, 'Nachtmuˌsik *f*; **2.** Sere'nade *f* (*vokale od. instrumentale Abendmusik*); **II** *v/i. u. v/t.* **3.** (*j-m*) ein Ständchen bringen; ˌ**ser·e'nad·er** [-də] *s.* j-d, der ein Ständchen bringt.
se·rene [sɪ'riːn] *adj.* □ **1.** heiter, klar (*Himmel, Wetter etc.*), ruhig (*See*), friedlich (*Natur etc.*): ***all ~*** *sl.* ‚alles in Butter'; **2.** heiter, gelassen (*Person, Gemüt etc.*); **3.** ♀ durch'lauchtig: ***His ♀ Highness*** Seine Durchlaucht; **se·ren·i·ty** [sɪ'renətɪ] *s.* **1.** Heiterkeit *f*, Klarheit *f*; **2.** Gelassenheit *f*, heitere (Gemüts)Ruhe; **3.** (***Your***) ♀ (Eure) 'Durchlaucht *f* (*Titel*).
serf [sɜːf] *s.* **1.** *hist.* Leibeigene(r *m*) *f*; **2.** *obs. od. fig.* Sklave *m*; '**serf·age** [-fɪdʒ], '**serf·dom** [-dəm] *s.* **1.** Leibeigenschaft *f*; **2.** *obs. od. fig.* Sklave'rei *f*.
serge [sɜːdʒ] *s.* Serge *f* (*Stoff*).
ser·geant ['sɑːdʒənt] *s.* **1.** ⚔ Feldwebel *m*; *Artillerie, Kavallerie*: Wachtmeister *m*: ***~ first class*** *Am.* Oberfeldwebel; ***first ~*** Hauptfeldwebel; **2.** (Poli'zei-) Wachtmeister *m*; **3.** → ***serjeant***; ***~ major*** *s.* ⚔ Hauptfeldwebel *m*.
se·ri·al ['sɪərɪəl] **I** *s.* **1.** in Fortsetzungen *od.* in regelmäßiger Folge erscheinende Veröffentlichung, *bsd.* 'Fortsetzungsroˌman *m*; **2.** (Veröffentlichungs)Reihe *f*; Lieferungswerk *n*; peri'odische Zeitschrift; **3.** a) Sendereihe *f*, b) (Hörspiel-, Fernseh)Folge *f*, Serie *f*; **II** *adj.* □ **4.** Serien..., Fortsetzungs...: ***~ story***; ***~ rights*** Copyright *n* e-s Fortsetzungsromans; **5.** serienmäßig, Serien..., Reihen...: ***~ manufacture***; ***~ number*** a) laufende Nummer, b) Fabrikationsnummer *f*; ***~ photograph*** Reihenbild *n*; **6.** ♪ Zwölfton...; '**se·ri·al·ize** [-laɪz] *v/t.* **1.** peri'odisch *od.* in Fortsetzungen veröffentlichen; **2.** reihenweise anordnen; **se·ri·a·tim** [ˌsɪərɪ'eɪtɪm] (*Lat.*) *adv.* der Reihe nach.
se·ri·ceous [sɪ'rɪʃəs] *adj.* **1.** Seiden...; **2.** seidig; **3.** ⚘, *zo.* seidenhaarig; **ser·i·cul·ture** ['serɪˌkʌltʃə] *s.* Seidenraupenzucht *f*.
se·ries ['sɪəriːz] *pl.* **-ries** *s.* **1.** Serie *f*, Folge *f*, Kette *f*, Reihe *f*: ***in ~*** der Reihe nach (→ 3 *u.* 9); **2.** (Ar'tikel-, Buch- *etc.*)Serie *f*, Reihe *f*, Folge *f*; **3.** ⚙ Serie *f*, Baureihe *f*: ***~ production*** Reihen-, Serienbau *m*; ***in ~*** serienmäßig; **4.** (*Briefmarken- etc.*)Serie *f*; **5.** ⩓ Reihe

f; **6.** ⚗ homo'loge Reihe; **7.** *geol.* Schichtfolge *f*; **8.** *zo.* Ab'teilung *f*; **9.** *a.* **~ connection** ⚡ Serien-, Reihenschaltung *f*: **~ motor** Reihen(schluß)motor *m*; **connect in ~** hintereinanderschalten.

ser·if ['serɪf] *s. typ.* Se'rife *f.*

ser·in ['serɪn] *s. orn.* wilder Ka'narienvogel.

se·ri·o·com·ic [ˌsɪərɪəʊ'kɒmɪk] *adj.* (☐ **~ally**) ernst-komisch.

se·ri·ous ['sɪərɪəs] *adj.* ☐ **1.** ernst(haft): a) feierlich, b) von ernstem Cha'rakter, seri'ös, c) schwerwiegend, bedeutend: **~ dress** seriöse Kleidung; **~ music** ernste Musik; **~ problem** ernstes Problem; **~ artist** ernsthafter Künstler; **2.** ernstlich, bedenklich, gefährlich: **~ illness**; **~ rival** ernstzunehmender Rivale; **3.** ernst(haft, -lich), ernstgemeint (*Angebot etc.*): **are you ~?** meinst du das im Ernst?; **'se·ri·ous·ly** [-lɪ] *adv.* ernst (-lich); im Ernst: **~ ill** ernstlich krank; **~ wounded** schwerverwundet; **now, ~!** im Ernst!; **'se·ri·ous·ness** [-nɪs] *s.* **1.** Ernst *m*, Ernsthaftigkeit *f*; **2.** Wichtigkeit *f*, Bedeutung *f.*

ser·jeant ['sɑːdʒənt] *s.* ⚖ **1.** Gerichtsdiener *m*; **2. Common** ♀ Stadtsyndikus *m* (*London*); **3.** *a.* **~ at law** höherer Barrister (des Gemeinen Rechts); **~ at arms** *s. parl.* Ordnungsbeamte(r) *m.*

ser·mon ['sɜːmən] *s.* **1.** Predigt *f*: ♀ **on the Mount** *bibl.* Bergpredigt; **2.** *iro.* (Mo'ral-, Straf)Predigt *f*; **'ser·mon·ize** [-naɪz] **I** *v/i.* (*a. iro.*) predigen; **II** *v/t.* *j-m* e-e (Mo'ral)Predigt halten.

se·rol·o·gist [ˌsɪə'rɒlədʒɪst] *s.* ⚕ Sero'loge *m*; **se'rol·o·gy** [-dʒɪ] *s.* Serolo'gie *f*, Serumkunde *f*; **se'ros·i·ty** [-ɒsətɪ] *s.* ⚕ **1.** se'röser Zustand; **2.** se'röse Flüssigkeit; **se·rous** ['sɪərəs] *adj.* ⚕ se'rös.

ser·pent ['sɜːpənt] *s.* **1.** (*bsd. große*) Schlange; **2.** *fig.* (Gift)Schlange *f* (*Person*); **3.** ♀ *ast.* Schlange *f*; **'ser·pen·tine** [-taɪn] **I** *adj.* **1.** schlangenförmig, Schlangen...; **2.** sich schlängelnd *od.* windend, geschlängelt, Serpentinen...: **~ road**; **3.** *fig.* falsch, tückisch; **II** *s.* **4.** *geol.* Serpen'tin *m*; **5.** *Eislauf*: Schlangenbogen *m*; **6.** ♀ *Teich im Hyde Park.*

ser·pi·go [sɜː'paɪgəʊ] *s.* ⚕ fressende Flechte.

ser·rate ['serɪt], **ser·rat·ed** [se'reɪtɪd] *adj.* (sägeförmig) gezackt; ˌ**ser·rate-'den·tate** *adj.* ⚘ gesägt-gezähnt.

ser·ra·tion [se'reɪʃn] *s.* (sägeförmige) Auszackung.

ser·ried ['serɪd] *adj.* dichtgeschlossen (*Reihen*).

se·rum ['sɪərəm] *s.* **1.** *physiol.* (Blut-) Serum *n*; **2.** ⚕ (Heil-, Schutz)Serum *n.*

ser·val ['sɜːvəl] *s. zo.* Serval *m.*

serv·ant ['sɜːvənt] *s.* **1.** Diener *m* (*a. fig. Gottes, der Kunst etc.*); (**domestic**) **~** Dienstbote *m*, -mädchen *n*, Hausangestellte(r *m*) *f*; **~s' hall** Gesindestube *f*; **your obedient ~** hochachtungsvoll (*Amtsstil*); **2.** *bsd.* **public ~** Beamte(r) *m*, Angestellte(r) *m* (*im öffentlichen Dienst*); → **civil** 2; **3.** ⚖ (Handlungs-) Gehilfe *m*, Angestellte(r) *m* (*Ggs.* **master** 5 b); **~ girl**, **~ maid** *s.* Dienstmädchen *n.*

serve [sɜːv] **I** *v/t.* **1.** *j-m, a. Gott, s-m Land etc.* dienen; arbeiten für, im Dienst stehen bei; **2.** *j-m* dienlich sein, helfen (*a. Sache*); **3.** *Dienstzeit* (*a.* ⚔) ableisten; *Lehre* 'durchmachen; ⚖ *Strafe* absitzen, verbüßen; **4.** a) *Amt* ausüben, innehaben, b) Dienst tun in (*dat.*), *Gebiet, Personenkreis* betreuen, versorgen; **5.** *e-m Zweck* dienen *od.* entsprechen, *e-n Zweck* erfüllen, *e-r Sache* nützen: **it ~s no purpose** es hat keinen Zweck; **6.** genügen (*dat.*), ausreichen für: **enough to ~ us a month**; **7.** *j-m bei Tisch* aufwarten; *j-n*, ✝ *Kunden* bedienen; **8.** *a.* **~ up** *Essen etc.* servieren, auftragen, reichen: **dinner is ~d!** es ist serviert *od.* angerichtet!; **~ up** F *fig.* ‚auftischen'; **9.** ⚔ *Geschütz* bedienen; **10.** versorgen (**with** mit): **~ the town with gas**; **11.** *oft* **~ out** austeilen; **12.** *mst* F a) *j-n schändlich etc.* behandeln, b) *j-m et.* zufügen: **~ s.o. a trick** j-m e-n Streich spielen; **~ s.o. out** es j-m heimzahlen; (**it**) **~s him right** (das) geschieht ihm recht; **13.** *Verlangen* befriedigen, frönen (*dat.*); **14.** *Stute etc.* decken; **15.** ⚖ *Vorladung etc.* zustellen (*dat.*): **~ s.o. a writ**, **~ a writ on s.o.**; **16.** ⚙ um'wickeln; **17.** ⚓ *Tau* bekleiden; **II** *v/i.* **18.** dienen, Dienst tun (*beide a.* ⚔); in Dienst stehen, angestellt sein (**with** bei); **19.** servieren, bedienen: **~ at table**; **20.** fungieren, amtieren (**as** als): **~ on a committee** in e-m Ausschuß tätig sein; **21.** dienen, nützen: **it ~s to** *inf.* es dient dazu, zu *inf.*; **it ~s to show his cleverness** daran kann man s-e Klugheit erkennen; **22.** dienen (**as**, **for** als): **a blanket ~d as a curtain**; **23.** genügen, den Zweck erfüllen; **24.** günstig sein, passen: **as occasion ~s** bei passender Gelegenheit; **the tide ~s** ⚓ der Wasserstand ist (*zum Auslaufen etc.*) günstig; **25.** *sport* a) *Tennis etc.*: aufschlagen, b) *Volleyball*: aufgeben: **X to ~!** Aufschlag X; **26.** *R.C.* ministrieren; **III** *s.* **27.** → **service** 20; **'serv·er** [-və] *s.* **1.** *R.C.* Mini'strant *m*; **2.** a) *Tennis*: Aufschläger *m*, b) *Volleyball*: Aufgeber *m*; **3.** a) Tab'lett *n*, b) Warmhalteplatte *f*, c) Serviertischchen *n od.* -wagen *m*, d) Tortenheber *m.*

serv·ice[1] ['sɜːvɪs] *s.* ⚘ **1.** Spierbaum *m*; **2.** *a.* **wild ~**(**tree**) Elsbeerbaum *m.*

serv·ice[2] ['sɜːvɪs] **I** *s.* **1.** Dienst *m*, Stellung *f* (*bsd. v. Hausangestellten*): **be in ~** in Stellung sein; **take s.o. into ~** j-n einstellen; **2.** a) Dienstleistung *f* (*a.* ✝, ⚖), Dienst *m* (**to** an *dat.*), b) (guter) Dienst, Gefälligkeit *f*: **do** (*od.* **render**) **s.o. a ~** j-m e-n Dienst erweisen; **at your ~** zu Ihren Diensten; **be** (**place**) **at s.o.'s ~** j-m zur Verfügung stehen (stellen); **3.** ✝ Bedienung *f*: **prompt ~**; **4.** Nutzen *m*: **be of ~ to** *j-m* nützen; **5.** (*Nacht-, Nachrichten-, Presse-, Telefon- etc.*)Dienst *m*; **6.** a) Versorgungsdienst *m*, b) Versorgungsbetrieb *m*: **water ~** Wasserversorgung *f*; **7.** Funkti'on *f*, Amt *n* (*e-s Beamten*); **8.** (öffentlicher) Dienst, Staatsdienst *m*: **diplomatic ~**; **on Her Majesty's** ♀ *Brit.* ✉ Dienstsache *f*; **9.** 🚂 *etc.* Verkehr *m*, Betrieb *m*: **twenty-minute ~** Zwanzig-Minuten-Takt *m*; **10.** ⚙ Betrieb *m*: **in** (**out of**) **~** in (außer) Betrieb; **~ conditions** Betriebsbeanspruchung *f*; **~ life** Lebensdauer *f*; **11.** ⚙ Wartung *f*, Kundendienst *m*, Service *m*; **12.** ⚔ a) (Wehr-) Dienst *m*, b) Waffengattung *f*, c) *pl.* Streitkräfte *pl.*, d) *Brit.* Ma'rine *f*: **be on active ~** aktiv dienen; **~ pistol** Dienstpistole *f*; **13.** ⚔ *Am.* (technische) Versorgungstruppe; **14.** ⚔ Bedienung *f* (*Geschütz*); **15.** *mst pl.* Hilfsdienst *m*: **medical ~**(**s**); **16.** *eccl.* a) *a.* **divine ~** Gottesdienst *m*, b) Litur'gie *f*; **17.** Ser'vice *n*, Tafelgerät *n*; **18.** ⚖ Zustellung *f*; **19.** ⚓ Bekleidung *f* (*Tau*); **20.** *sport* a) *Tennis etc.*: Aufschlag, b) *Volleyball*: Aufgabe *f*; **II** *v/t.* **21.** ⚙ a) warten, pflegen, b) über'holen; **22.** ✝ *bsd. Am.* Kundendienst verrichten für *od.* bei; **23.** *zo. Stute* decken; **'serv·ice·a·ble** [-səbl] *adj.* ☐ **1.** brauch-, verwendbar, nützlich; betriebs-, leistungsfähig; **2.** zweckdienlich; **3.** haltbar, strapazierfähig.

serv·ice| a·re·a *s.* **1.** *Radio, TV*: Sendebereich *m*; **2.** *Brit.* (Autobahn)Raststätte *f* (mit Tankstelle); **~ book** *s. eccl.* Gebet-, Gesangbuch *n*; **~ box** *s.* ⚡ Anschlußkasten *m*; **~ brake** *s. mot.* Betriebsbremse *f*; **~ charge** *s.* **1.** *econ.* Bedienungszuschlag *m*; **2.** ✝ Bearbeitungsgebühr *f*; **~ court** *s. Tennis etc.*: Aufschlagfeld *n*; **~ dress** → **service uniform**; **~ flat** *s. Brit.* E'tagenwohnung *f* mit Bedienung; **~ hatch** *s. Brit.* 'Durchreiche *f* (*für Speisen*); **~ in·dus·try** *s.* **1.** *mst pl.* Dienstleistungsbetriebe *pl.*, -gewerbe *n*; **2.** 'Zulieferindusˌtrie *f*; **~ life** *s.* ⚙ Lebensdauer *f*; **~ line** *s. Tennis etc.*: Aufschlaglinie *f*; **'~·man** [-mən] *s.* [*irr.*] **1.** Sol'dat *m*, Mili'tärangehörige(r) *m*; **2.** ⚙ a) 'Kundendienst-meˌchaniker *m*, b) 'Wartungsmonˌteur *m*; **~ mod·ule** *s.* Versorgungsteil *m e-s Raumschiffs*; **~ so·ci·e·ty** *s.* Dienstleistungsgesellschaft *f*; **~ sta·tion** *s.* **1.** Kundendienst- *od.* Repara'turwerkstatt *f*; **2.** (Groß)Tankstelle *f*; **~ trade** *s.* Dienstleistungsgewerbe *n*; **~ u·ni·form** *s.* ⚔ Dienstanzug *m.*

ser·vi·ette [sɜːvɪ'et] *s.* Servi'ette *f.*

ser·vile ['sɜːvaɪl] *adj.* ☐ **1.** ser'vil, unter'würfig, kriecherisch; **2.** *fig.* sklavisch (*Gehorsam, Genauigkeit etc.*); **ser·vil·i·ty** [sɜː'vɪlətɪ] *s.* Unter'würfigkeit *f*; Krieche'rei *f.*

serv·ing ['sɜːvɪŋ] *s.* Porti'on *f.*

ser·vi·tor ['sɜːvɪtə] *s.* **1.** *obs.* Diener(in) (*a. fig.*); **2.** *obs. od. poet.* Gefolgsmann *m*; **3.** *univ. hist.* Stipendi'at *m.*

ser·vi·tude ['sɜːvɪtjuːd] *s.* **1.** Sklave'rei *f*, Knechtschaft *f* (*a. fig.*); **2.** ⚖ Zwangsarbeit *f*: **penal ~** Zuchthausstrafe *f*; **3.** ⚖ Servi'tut *n*, Nutzungsrecht *n.*

'ser·vo|-asˌsist·ed ['sɜːvəʊ-] *adj.* ⚙ Servo...; **~ brake** *s.* Servobremse *f*; **~ steer·ing** *s.* Servolenkung *f.*

ses·a·me ['sesəmɪ] *s.* **1.** ⚘ Indischer Sesam; **2.** → **open sesame.**

ses·a·moid ['sesəmɔɪd] *adj. anat.* Sesam...: **~ bones** Sesamknöchelchen.

sesqui- [seskwɪ] *in Zssgn* 'andert'halb; ˌ**~'al·ter** [-'æltə], ˌ**~'al·ter·al** [-'æltərəl] *adj.* im Verhältnis 3:2 *od.* 1:1½ stehend; ˌ**~·cen'ten·ni·al I** *adj.* 150jährig; **II** *s.* 150-Jahr-Feier *f*; ˌ**~·pe'da·li·an** [-pɪ'deɪljən] *adj.* **1.** 'andert'halb Fuß lang; **2.** *fig. humor.* sehr lang, mon'strös: **~ word**; **3.** *fig.* schwülstig; **'~·plane** [-pleɪn] *s.* ✈ Anderthalbdecker *m.*

ses·sile ['sesıl] *adj.* **1.** ⚘ stiellos; **2.** *zo.* ungestielt.

ses·sion ['seʃn] *s.* **1.** *parl.* ⚖ a) Sitzung *f*, b) 'Sitzungsperi,ode *f*: **be in ~** e-e Sitzung abhalten, tagen; **2.** (*einzelne*) Sitzung (*a.* ⚕ *psych.*), Konfe'renz *f*; **3.** *&s pl.* → **magistrates' court**, **Quarter Sessions**; **4.** a) **Court of &** *oberstes schottisches Zivilgericht*, b) **Court of &s** *Am.* (*einzelstaatliches*) *Gericht für Strafsachen*; **5.** *univ.* a) *Brit.* aka'demisches Jahr, b) *Am.* ('Studien)Se,mester *n*; **'ses·sion·al** [-ʃənl] *adj.* □ **1.** Sitzungs...; **2.** *univ. Brit.* Jahres...: **~ course**.

ses·tet [ses'tet] *s.* **1.** ♪ Sex'tett *n*; **2.** *Metrik*: sechszeilige Strophe.

set [set] **I** *s.* **1.** Satz *m Briefmarken*, *Dokumente*, *Werkzeuge etc.*; (*Möbel-*, *Toiletten- etc.*)Garni'tur *f*; (*Speise- etc.*) Ser'vice *n*, Besteck *n*; (*Farben- etc.*) Sorti'ment *n*; **2.** ✝ Kollekti'on *f*; **3.** Sammlung *f*: **a ~ of Shakespeare's works**; **4.** (Schriften)Reihe *f*, (Ar'tikel-) Serie *f*; **5.** ⚙ (Ma'schinen)Anlage *f*; **6.** (Häuser)Gruppe *f*; **7.** (Zimmer)Flucht *f*; **8.** ⚙ a) (Ma'schinen)Satz *m*, (-)Anlage *f*, Aggre'gat *n*, b) (*Radio- etc.*)Gerät *n*, Appa'rat *m*; **9.** a) *thea.* Bühnenausstattung *f*, b) *Film*: Szenenaufbau *m*; **10.** *Tennis etc.*: Satz *m*; **11.** 𝔄 a) Zahlenreihe *f*, b) Menge *f*; **12. ~ of teeth** Gebiß *n*; **13.** (Per'sonen)Kreis *m*: a) Gesellschaft(sschicht) *f*, *vornehme*, *literarische etc.* Welt, b) *contp.* Klüngel *m*, Clique *f*: **the chic ~** die ‚Schickeria'; **the fast ~** die Lebewelt; **14.** Sitz *m*, Schnitt *m von Kleidern*; **15.** Haltung *f*; **16.** Richtung *f*, (Ver)Lauf *m e-r Strömung etc.*; **17.** Neigung *f*, Ten'denz *f*; **18.** *poet.* 'Untergang *m der Sonne etc.*: **the ~ of the day** das Tagesende; **19.** ⚙ → **setting** 10; **20.** *hunt.* Vorstehen *n des Hundes*: **make a dead ~ at** *fig.* a) über *j-n* herfallen, b) es auf *e-n Mann* abgesehen haben (*Frau*); **21.** *hunt.* (*Dachs- etc.*)Bau *m*; **22.** ⚘ Setzling *m*, Ableger *m*; **II** *adj.* **23.** starr (*Gesicht*, *Lächeln*); **24.** fest (*Meinung*); **25.** festgesetzt: **at the ~ day**; **26.** vorgeschrieben, festgelegt: **~ rules**; **~ books** *od.* **reading** Pflichtlektüre *f*; **27.** for'mell, konventio'nell: **~ party**; **28.** 'wohlüber,legt, einstudiert: **~ speech**; **29.** a) bereit, b) fest entschlossen (**on doing** zu tun); **30.** zs.-gebissen (*Zähne*); **31.** eingefaßt (*Edelstein*); **32. ~ piece** *paint. etc.* Gruppenbild *n*; **33. ~ fair** beständig (*Barometer*); **34.** *in Zssgn* ...gebaut; **III** *v/t.* [*irr.*] **35.** setzen, stellen, legen: **~ the glass to one's lips** das Glas an die Lippen setzen; **~ a match to** ein Streichholz halten an (*acc.*), *et.* in Brand stecken; → **hand** 7, **sail** 1 *etc.*; **36.** (ein-, her)richten, (an)ordnen, zu'rechtmachen; *thea.* *Bühne* aufbauen; *Tisch* decken; ⚙ *etc.* (ein)stellen, (-) richten, regulieren; *Uhr*, *Wecker* stellen; ⚙ *Säge* schränken; *hunt.* *Falle* (auf-)stellen; ⚕ *Bruch*, *Knochen* (ein)richten; *Messer* abziehen; *Haar* legen; **37.** ♪ a) vertonen, b) arrangieren; **38.** *typ.* absetzen; **39.** ⚒ a) *a.* **~ out** *Setzlinge* (aus)pflanzen, b) *Boden* bepflanzen; **40.** a) *Bruthenne* setzen, b) *Eier* 'unterlegen; **41.** a) *Edelstein* fassen, b) *mit Edelsteinen etc.* besetzen; **42.** *Wache* (auf)stellen; **43.** *Aufgabe*, *Frage* stellen; **44.** *j-n* anweisen (**to do s.th.** et. zu tun), *j-n* an (*e-e Sache*) setzen: **~ o.s. to do s.th.** sich daran machen, et. zu tun; **45.** vorschreiben; **46.** *Zeitpunkt* festlegen; **47.** *Hund etc.* hetzen (**on** auf *j-n*): **~ spies on** *j-n* bespitzeln lassen; **48.** (veran)lassen (**doing** zu tun): **~ going** in Gang setzen; **~ s.o. laughing** j-n zum Lachen bringen; **~ s.o. thinking** j-m zu denken geben; **49.** *in e-n Zustand* versetzen; → **ease** 2; **50.** *Flüssiges* fest werden lassen; *Milch* gerinnen lassen; **51.** *Zähne* zs.-beißen; **52.** *Wert* bemessen, festsetzen; **53.** *Preis* aussetzen (**on** auf *acc.*); **54.** *Geld*, *Leben* riskieren; **55.** *Hoffnung*, *Vertrauen* setzen (**on** auf *acc.*; **in** in *acc.*); **56.** *Grenzen*, *Schranken etc.* setzen (**to** *dat.*); **IV** *v/i.* [*irr.*] **57.** 'untergehen (*Sonne etc.*); **58.** a) auswachsen (*Körper*), b) ausreifen (*Charakter*); **59.** fest werden (*Flüssiges*); abbinden (*Zement etc.*); erstarren (*a. Gesicht*, *Muskel*); gerinnen (*Milch*); ⚕ sich einrenken; **60.** sitzen (*Kleidung*); **61.** fließen, laufen (*Flut etc.*); wehen, kommen (**from** aus, von) (*Wind*) *fig.* sich neigen *od.* richten (**against** gegen); **62.** ⚘ Frucht ansetzen (*Blüte*, *Baum*); **63.** *hunt.* (vor)stehen (*Hund*);

Zssgn mit prp.:

set| a·bout *v/i.* **1.** sich an *et.* machen, *et.* in Angriff nehmen; **2.** F über *j-n* herfallen; **~ a·gainst** *v/t.* **1.** entgegen- *od.* gegen'überstellen (*dat.*): **set o.s.** (*od.* **one's face**) **against** sich *e-r Sache* widersetzen; **2.** *j-n* aufhetzen gegen; **~ (up·)on** *v/i.* herfallen über *j-n*.

Zssgn mit adv.:

set| a·part *v/t.* **1.** *Geld etc.* bei'seite legen; **2. set s.o. apart** (**from**) j-n unter'scheiden (von); **~ a·side** *v/t.* **1.** a) bei'seite legen, b) → **set apart** 1; **2.** *Plan etc.* fallenlassen; **3.** außer acht lassen, ausklammern; **4.** verwerfen, *bsd.* ⚖ aufheben; **~ back I** *v/t.* **1.** *Uhr* zu'rückstellen; **2.** *Haus etc.* zu'rücksetzen; **3.** *fig.* *j-n*, *et.* zu'rückwerfen; **4.** *j-n* ärmer machen (um); **II** *v/i.* **5.** zu'rückfließen (*Flut etc.*); **~ by** *v/t.* *Geld etc.* zu'rücklegen, sparen; **~ down** *v/t.* **1.** *Last*, *a. Fahrgast*, *a. das Flugzeug* absetzen; **2.** (schriftlich) niederlegen, aufzeichnen; **3.** *j-m* e-n ‚Dämpfer' aufsetzen; **4. ~ as** *j-n* abtun *od.* betrachten als; **5.** *et.* zuschreiben (**to** *dat.*); **6.** *et.* festlegen, -setzen; **~ forth I** *v/t.* **1.** bekanntmachen; **2.** → **set out** 1; **3.** zur Schau stellen; **II** *v/i.* **4.** aufbrechen: **~ on a journey** e-e Reise antreten; **5.** *fig.* ausgehen (**from** von); **~ for·ward I** *v/t.* **1.** *Uhr* vorstellen; **2.** a) *et.* vor'antreiben, b) *j-n od. et.* weiterbringen; **3.** vorbringen, darlegen; **II** *v/i.* **4.** sich auf den Weg machen; **~ in** *v/i.* einsetzen (*beginnen*); **~ off I** *v/t.* **1.** her'vortreten lassen, abheben (**from** von); **2.** her'vorheben; **3.** a) *Rakete* abschießen, b) *Sprengladung* zur Explosi'on bringen, c) *Feuerwerk* abbrennen; **4.** *Alarm etc.* auslösen (*a. Streik etc.*), führen zu; **5.** ✝ auf-, anrechnen (**against** gegen); **6.** ⚖ als Ausgleich nehmen (**against** für); **7.** *Verlust etc.* ausgleichen; **II** *v/i.* **8.** → **set forth** 4; **9.** *fig.* anfangen; **~ on** *v/t.* **1.** a) *j-n* drängen (**to do** zu tun), b) *j-n* aufhetzen (**to** zu); **2.** *Hund etc.* hetzen (**to** auf *acc.*); **~ out I** *v/t.* **1.** (ausführlich) darlegen, aufzeigen; **2.** anordnen, arrangieren; **II** *v/i.* **3.** aufbrechen, sich aufmachen, sich auf den Weg machen (**for** nach); **4.** sich vornehmen, da'rangehen (**to do** *et.* zu tun); **~ to** *v/i.* **1.** sich dar'anmachen, sich ‚da'hinterklemmen', ‚loslegen'; **2.** aufein'ander losgehen; **~ up I** *v/t.* **1.** errichten: **~ a monument**; **2.** ⚙ *Maschine etc.* aufstellen, montieren; **3.** *Geschäft etc.* gründen; *Regierung* bilden, einsetzen; **4.** *j-m* zu e-m (guten) Start verhelfen, *j-n* etablieren: **~ s.o. up in business**; **~ o.s. up** (**as**) → 15; **5.** *Behauptung etc.*, *a. Rekord* aufstellen; ⚖ *Anspruch* geltend machen, *a. Verteidigung* vorbringen; **6.** *Kandidaten* aufstellen; **7.** *j-n* erhöhen (**over** über *acc.*), *a. j-n* auf den Thron setzen; **8.** *Stimme*, *Geschrei* erheben; **9.** *a. Krankheit* verursachen; **10.** a) *j-n* kräftigen, b) *gesundheitlich* wieder'herstellen; **11.** *j-m* (finanzi'ell) ‚auf die Beine helfen'; **12.** *j-n* versehen, -sorgen (**with** mit); **13.** F a) *j-m* e-e Falle stellen, b) *j-m* et. ‚anhängen'; **14.** *typ.* (ab-) setzen: **~ in type**; **II** *v/i.* **15.** sich niederlassen *od.* etablieren (**as** als): **~ for o.s.** sich selbständig machen; **16. ~ for** sich ausgeben für *od.* als, sich aufspielen als.

se·ta·ceous [sı'teıʃəs] *adj.* borstig.

'set|·a,side *s. Am.* Rücklage *f*; **'~·back** *s.* **1.** *fig.* a) Rückschlag *m*, b) ‚Schlappe' *f*; **2.** △ a) Rücksprung *m e-r Wand*, b) zu'rückgesetzte Fas'sade; **'~·down** *s.* **1.** Dämpfer *m*; **2.** Rüffel *m*; **'~·off** *s.* **1.** Kon'trast *m*; **2.** ⚖ a) Gegenforderung *f*, b) Ausgleich *m* (*a. fig*; **against** für); **3.** ✝ Aufrechnung *f*; **'~·out** *s.* **1.** a) Aufbruch *m*, b) Anfang *m*; **2.** Aufmachung *f*; **3.** F a) Vorführung *f*, b) Party *f*; **~ piece** *s.* **1.** *Kunst*: formvollendetes Werk; **2.** ⚔ sorgfältig geplante Operati'on; **3.** → **set** 32; **~ point** *s.* **1.** *Tennis etc.*: Satzball *m*; **2.** ⚙ Sollwert *m*; **'~·screw** *s.* ⚙ Stellschraube *f*; **~ square** *s.* Winkel *m*, Zeichendreieck *n*.

sett [set] *s.* Pflasterstein *m*.

set·tee [se'ti:] *s.* **1.** Sitz-, Polsterbank *f*; **2.** kleineres Sofa: **~ bed** Bettcouch *f*.

set·ter ['setə] *s.* **1.** *allg.* Setzer(in), Einrichter(in); **2.** *typ.* (Schrift)Setzer *m*; **3.** Setter *m* (*Vorstehhund*); **4.** (Poli'zei-) Spitzel *m*; **,~-'on** [-ər'ɒn] *pl.* **,~s-'on** *s.* Aufhetzer(in).

set the·o·ry *s.* 𝔄 Mengenlehre *f*.

set·ting ['setıŋ] *s.* **1.** (*typ.* Schrift)Setzen *n*; Einrichten *n*; (Ein)Fassen *n* (*Edelstein*); **2.** Schärfen *n* (*Messer*); **3.** (*Gold- etc.*)Fassung *f*; **4.** Lage *f*, 'Hintergrund *m* (*a. fig. Rahmen*); **5.** Schauplatz *m*, 'Hintergrund *m e-s Romans etc.*; **6.** *thea.* szenischer 'Hintergrund, Bühnenbild *n*; *a. Film*: Ausstattung *f*; **7.** ♪ a) Vertonung *f*, b) Satz *m*; **8.** (*Sonnen- etc.*)'Untergang *m*; **9.** ⚙ Einstellung *f*; **10.** ⚙ Hartwerden *n*, Abbinden *n von Zement etc.*: **~ point** Stockpunkt *m*; **11.** ⚙ Schränkung *f* (*Säge*); **12.** Gedeck *n*; **~ lo·tion** *s.* (Haar)Festiger *m*; **'~-rule** *s. typ.* Setzlinie *f*; **'~-stick** *s. typ.* Winkelhaken *m*; **'~-up** *s.* **1.** *bsd.* ⚙ Einrichtung *f*, Aufstellung *f*; **2. ~ exercises** *Am.* Gymnastik *f*, Freiübungen *pl.*

set·tle ['setl] **I** *v/i.* **1.** sich niederlassen *od.* setzen (*a. Vogel etc.*); **2.** a) sich ansiedeln, b) **~ in** sich *in e-r Wohnung etc.* einrichten, c) **~ in** sich einleben *od.* eingewöhnen; **3.** a) *a.* **~ down** sich *in e-m Ort* niederlassen, b) sich (häuslich) niederlassen, c) *a.* ***marry and ~ down*** e-n Hausstand gründen, d) seßhaft werden, zur Ruhe kommen, sich einleben; **4. ~ *down to*** sich widmen (*dat.*), sich an *e-e Arbeit etc.* machen; **5.** sich legen *od.* beruhigen (*Wut etc.*); **6. ~ *on*** sich zuwenden (*dat.*), fallen auf (*acc.*) (*Zuneigung etc.*); **7.** ⚕ sich festsetzen (**on**, ***in*** in *dat.*), sich legen (**on** auf *acc.*) (*Krankheit*); **8.** beständig werden (*Wetter*): ***it ~d in for rain*** es regnete sich ein; ***it is settling for a frost*** es wird Frost geben; ***the wind has ~d in the west*** der Wind steht im Westen; **9.** sich senken (*Mauern etc.*); **10.** langsam absakken (*Schiff*); **11.** sich klären (*Flüssigkeit*); **12.** sich setzen (*Trübstoff*); **13.** sich legen (*Staub*); **14.** (**upon**) sich entscheiden (für), sich entschließen (zu); **15. ~ *for*** sich begnügen *od.* abfinden mit; **16.** e-e Vereinbarung treffen; **17.** a) **~ *up*** zahlen *od.* abrechnen (***with*** mit), b) **~ *with*** e-n Vergleich schließen mit, *Gläubiger* abfinden; **II** *v/t.* **18.** *Füße, Hut etc.* (fest) setzen (**on** auf *acc.*): **~ *o.s.*** sich niederlassen; **~ *o.s. to*** sich an *e-e Arbeit etc.* machen, sich anschikken zu; **19.** a) *Menschen* ansiedeln, b) *Land* besiedeln; **20.** *j-n beruflich, häuslich etc.* etablieren, 'unterbringen; *Kind etc.* versorgen, ausstatten, *a.* verheiraten; **21.** a) *Flüssigkeit* ablagern lassen, klären, b) *Trübstoff* sich setzen lassen; **22.** *Boden etc., a. fig. Glauben, Ordnung etc.* festigen; **23.** *Institutionen* gründen, aufbauen (**on** auf *dat.*); **24.** *Zimmer etc.* in Ordnung bringen; **25.** *Frage etc.* klären, regeln, erledigen: ***that ~s it*** a) damit ist der Fall erledigt, b) *iro.* jetzt ist es endgültig aus; **26.** *Streit* schlichten, beilegen; *strittigen Punkt* beseitigen; **27.** *Nachlaß* regeln, *s-e Angelegenheiten* in Ordnung bringen: **~ *one's affairs***; **28.** ([**up**]**on**) *Besitz* über'schreiben, -'tragen (auf *acc.*), *letztwillig* vermachen (*dat.*), *Legat, Rente* aussetzen (für); **29.** bestimmen, festlegen, -setzen; **30.** vereinbaren, sich einigen auf (*acc.*); **31.** *a.* **~ *up*** † erledigen, in Ordnung bringen: a) *Rechnung* begleichen, b) *Konto* ausgleichen, c) *Anspruch* befriedigen, d) *Geschäft* abwickeln; → ***account*** 5; **32.** ⚖ *Prozeß* durch Vergleich beilegen; **33.** *Magen, Nerven* beruhigen; **34.** *j-n* ‚fertigmachen', zum Schweigen bringen (F *a. töten*); **III** *s.* **35.** Sitzbank *f* (mit hoher Lehne); **'set·tled** [-ld] *adj.* **1.** fest, bestimmt; entschieden; feststehend (*Tatsache*); **2.** fest begründet (*Ordnung*); **3.** fest, ständig (*Wohnsitz, Gewohnheit*); **4.** beständig (*Wetter*); **5.** ruhig, gesetzt (*Person, Leben*).

set·tle·ment ['setlmənt] *s.* **1.** Ansied(e)lung *f*; **2.** Besied(e)lung *f e-s Landes*; **3.** Siedlung *f*, Niederlassung *f*; **4.** 'Unterbringung *f*, Versorgung *f* (*Person*); **5.** Regelung *f*, Klärung *f*, Erledigung *f e-r Frage etc.*; **6.** Schlichtung *f*, Beilegung *f e-s Streits*; **7.** Festsetzung *f*; **8.** (endgültige) Entscheidung; **9.** Über'einkommen *n*, Abmachung *f*; **10.** † a) Begleichung *f von Rechnungen*, b) Ausgleich(ung *f*) *m von Konten*, c) *Börse*: Abrechnung *f*, d) Abwicklung *f e-s Geschäfts*, e) Vergleich *m*, Abfindung *f*: **~ *day*** Abrechnungstag *m*; ***day of ~*** *fig.* Tag *m* der Abrechnung; ***in ~ of all claims*** zum Ausgleich aller Forderungen; **11.** ⚖ a) (*Eigentums*)Über'tragung *f*, b) Vermächtnis *n*, c) Aussetzung *f e-r Rente etc.*, d) Schenkung *f*, Stiftung *f*; **12.** ⚖ Ehevertrag *m*; **13.** a) ständiger Wohnsitz, b) Heimatberechtigung *f*; **14.** sozi'ales Hilfswerk.

set·tler ['setlə] *s.* **1.** (An)Siedler(in), Kolo'nist(in); **2.** F a) entscheidender Schlag, b) *fig.* vernichtendes Argu'ment, c) Abfuhr *f*; **'set·tling** [-lɪŋ] *s.* **1.** Festsetzen *n etc.*; → ***settle***; **2.** ⚙ Ablagerung *f*; **3.** *pl.* (Boden)Satz *m*; **4.** † Abrechnung *f*: **~ *day*** Abrechnungstag *m*; **'set·tlor** [-lə] *s.* ⚖ Verfügende(r *m*) *f*.

set-to [ˌset'tu:] *pl.* **-tos** *s.* F **1.** Schläge'rei *f*; **2.** (kurzer) heftiger Kampf; **3.** heftiger Wortwechsel.

set-up ['setʌp] *s.* **1.** Aufbau *m*; **2.** Anordnung *f* (*a.* ⚙); **3.** ⚙ Mon'tage *f*; **4.** *Film, TV*: a) (Kamera)Einstellung *f*, b) Bauten *pl.*; **5.** *Am.* Konstituti'on *f*; **6.** *Am.* F a) Situati'on *f*, b) Pro'jekt *n*; **7.** *Am.* F ‚Laden' *m* (*Firma etc.*), ‚Bude' *f* (*Wohnung etc.*); **8.** *Am.* F a) Schiebung *f*, b) Gimpel *m*, leichtes Opfer.

sev·en ['sevn] **I** *adj.* sieben: ***~-league boots*** Siebenmeilenstiefel; ***the ~ Years' War*** der Siebenjährige Krieg; **II** *s.* Sieben *f* (*Zahl, Spielkarte etc.*); **'~·fold** *adj. u. adv.* siebenfach.

sev·en·teen ['sevnti:n] **I** *adj.* siebzehn; **II** *s.* Siebzehn *f*: ***sweet ~*** ‚göttliche Siebzehn' (*Mädchenalter*); **ˌsev·en'teenth** [-nθ] **I** *adj.* **1.** siebzehnt; **II** *s.* **2.** *der* (*die, das*) Siebzehnte; **3.** Siebzehntel *n*.

sev·enth ['sevnθ] **I** *adj.* **1.** siebent; **II** *s.* **2.** *der* (*die, das*) Sieb(en)te: ***the ~ of May*** der 7. Mai; **3.** Sieb(en)tel *n*; **4.** ♪ Sep'time *f*; **'sev·enth·ly** [-lɪ] *adv.* sieb(en)tens.

sev·en·ti·eth ['sevntɪɪθ] **I** *adj.* **1.** siebzigst; **II** *s.* **2.** *der* (*die, das*) Siebzigste; **3.** Siebzigstel *n*; **sev·en·ty** ['sevntɪ] **I** *adj.* siebzig; **II** *s.* Siebzig *f*: ***the seventies*** a) die siebziger Jahre (*e-s Jahrhunderts*), b) die Siebziger(jahre) (*Alter*).

sev·er ['sevə] **I** *v/t.* **1.** (ab)trennen (***from*** von); **2.** ('durch)trennen; **3.** *fig. Freundschaft etc.* lösen, *Beziehungen* abbrechen; **4. ~ *o.s.*** (***from***) sich trennen *od.* lösen (von), (aus *der Kirche etc.*) austreten; **5.** (vonein'ander) trennen; **6.** ⚖ *Besitz etc.* teilen; **II** *v/i.* **7.** (zer)reißen; **8.** sich trennen (***from*** von); **9.** sich (vonein'ander) trennen; **sev·er·al** ['sevrəl] **I** *adj.* □ **1.** mehrere: **~ *people***; **2.** verschieden, getrennt: ***three ~ occasions***; **3.** einzeln, verschieden: ***the ~ reasons***; **4.** besonder, eigen: ***we went our ~ ways*** wir gingen jeder seinen (eigenen) Weg; → ***joint*** 6; **II** *s.* **5.** mehrere *pl.*: **~ *of you***; **sev·er·al·ly** ['sevrəlɪ] *adv.* **1.** einzeln, getrennt; **2.** beziehungsweise; **'sev·er·ance** [-ərəns] *s.* **1.** (Ab)Trennung *f*; **2.** Lösung *f e-r Freundschaft etc.*, Abbruch *m von Beziehungen*: **~ *pay*** † Entlassungsabfindung *f*.

se·vere [sɪ'vɪə] *adj.* □ **1.** streng: a) hart, scharf (*Kritik, Richter, Strafe etc.*), b) ernst(haft) (*Miene, Person*), c) rauh (*Wetter*), hart (*Winter*), d) herb (*Schönheit, Stil*), schmucklos, e) ex'akt, strikt; **2.** schwer, schlimm (*Krankheit, Verlust etc.*); **3.** heftig (*Schmerz, Sturm etc.*); **4.** scharf (*Bemerkung*); **se'vere·ly** [-lɪ] *adv.* **1.** streng, strikt; **2.** schwer, ernstlich: **~ *ill***; **se·ver·i·ty** [sɪ'verətɪ] *s.* **1.** *allg.* Strenge *f*: a) Schärfe *f*, Härte *f*, b) Rauheit *f* (*des Wetters etc.*), c) Ernst *m*, d) (herbe) Schlichtheit *f* (*Stil*), e) Ex'aktheit *f*; **2.** Heftigkeit *f*.

sew [səʊ] *v/t.* [*irr.*] **1.** nähen (*a. v/i.*): **~ *on*** annähen; **~ *up*** zu-, vernähen (→ 3); **2.** *Bücher* heften, broschieren; **3. ~ *up*** F a) *Brit. j-n* ‚restlos fertigmachen', b) *Am.* sich *et. od. j-n* sichern, c) *et.* ‚per'fekt machen': **~ *up a deal***.

sew·age ['sju:ɪdʒ] *s.* **1.** Abwasser *n*: **~ *farm*** Rieselfeld *n*; **~ *sludge*** Klärschlamm *m*; **~ *system*** Kanalisation *f*; **~ *works*** Kläranlage *f*; **2.** → ***sewerage***; **sew·er** ['sjʊə] **I** *s.* **1.** 'Abwasserkaˌnal *m*, Klo'ake *f*: **~ *gas*** Faulschlammgas *n*; **~ *pipe*** Abzugrohr *n*; **~ *rat*** *zo.* Wanderratte *f*; **2.** Gosse *f*; **II** *v/t.* **3.** kanalisieren; **sew·er·age** ['sjʊərɪdʒ] *s.* **1.** Kanalisati'on *f* (*System u. Vorgang*); **2.** → ***sewage*** 1.

sew·in ['sju:ɪn] *s.* 'Lachsfoˌrelle *f*.

sew·ing ['səʊɪŋ] *s.* Näharbeit *f*; **~ *machine*** *s.* 'Nähmaˌschine *f*.

sex [seks] **I** *s.* **1.** *biol.* Geschlecht *n*; **2.** (*männliches od. weibliches*) Geschlecht (*als Gruppe*): ***the ~*** *humor.* die Frauen; ***the gentle*** (*od.* ***weaker*** *od.* ***softer***) **~** das zarte *od.* schwache Geschlecht; ***of both ~es*** beiderlei Geschlechts; **3.** a) Geschlechtstrieb *m*, b) e'rotische Anziehungskraft, 'Sex(-Apˌpeal) *m*, c) Sexu'al-, Geschlechtsleben *n*, d) Sex(uali'tät *f*) *m*, e) Geschlechtsteil(e *pl.*) *n*, f) (Geschlechts)Verkehr *m*, ‚Sex' *m*: ***have ~ with*** mit *j-m* schlafen; **II** *v/t.* **4.** das Geschlecht bestimmen von; **5. ~ *up*** F a) *Film etc.* ‚sexy' gestalten, b) *j-n* ‚scharf machen'; **III** *adj.* **6.** a) Sexual...: **~ *crime*** (***education***, ***hygiene*** *etc.*); **~ *appeal*** → 3b; **~ *life*** → 3c; **~ *object*** Lustobjekt *n*, b) Geschlechts...: **~ *act*** (***hormone***, ***organ***, *etc.*), c) Sex...: **~ *film*** (***magazine***, *etc.*).

sex- [seks] *in Zssgn* sechs.

sex·a·ge·nar·i·an [ˌseksədʒɪ'neərɪən] **I** *adj.* a) sechzigjährig, b) in den Sechzigern; **II** *s.* Sechzigjährige(r *m*) *f*; Sechziger(in).

sex·ag·e·nar·y [sek'sædʒənərɪ] **I** *adj.* **1.** sechzigteilig; **2.** → ***sexagenarian*** I; **II** *s.* **3.** → ***sexagenarian*** II.

Sex·a·ges·i·ma (**Sun·day**) [ˌseksə'dʒesɪmə] *s.* Sonntag *m* Sexa'gesima (*8. Sonntag vor Ostern*); **ˌsex·a'ges·i·mal** [-məl] A **I** *adj.* Sexagesimal...; **II** *s.* Sexagesi'malbruch *m*.

sex·an·gu·lar [sek'sæŋgjʊlə] *adj.* □ sechseckig.

sex·cen·te·nar·y [ˌsekssen'ti:nərɪ] **I** *adj.* sechshundertjährig; **II** *s.* Sechshundert'jahrfeier *f*.

sex·en·ni·al [sek'senɪəl] *adj.* □ **1.** sechsjährig; **2.** sechsjährlich.

sex·i·ness ['seksɪnɪs] *s.* F *für* ***sex*** 3b.

sex·ism ['seksɪzəm] *s.* Se'xismus *m*; '**sex·ist** [-ɪst] **I** *adj.* se'xistisch; **II** *s.* Se'xist *m*.

sex·less ['sekslɪs] *adj. biol.* geschlechtslos (*a. fig.*), a'gamisch.

sex·ol·o·gy [sek'sɒlədʒɪ] *s. biol.* Sexu'alwissenschaft *f*.

sex·par·tite [seks'pɑːtaɪt] *adj.* sechsteilig.

'**sex·pot** *s. sl.* a) ‚Sexbombe' *f*, b) ‚Sexbolzen' *m*.

sex·tain ['sekstem] *s. Metrik*: sechszeilige Strophe.

sex·tant ['sekstənt] *s.* **1.** ⚓, *ast.* Sex'tant *m*; **2.** ♈ Kreissechstel *n*.

sex·tet(te) [seks'tet] *s.* ♪ Sex'tett *n*.

sex·to ['sekstəʊ] *pl.* **-tos** *s. typ.* 'Sexto (-forˌmat) *n*; **sex·to·dec·i·mo** [ˌsekstəʊ'desɪməʊ] *pl.* **-mos** *s.* **1.** Se'dez(forˌmat) *n*; **2.** Se'dezband *m*.

sex·ton ['sekstən] *s.* Küster *m* (u. Totengräber *m*); ~ **bee·tle** *s. zo.* Totengräber *m* (*Käfer*).

sex·tu·ple ['sekstjʊpl] **I** *adj.* sechsfach; **II** *s. das* Sechsfache; **III** *v/t. u. v/i.* (sich) versechsfachen.

sex·u·al ['seksjʊəl] *adj.* □ sexu'ell, geschlechtlich, Geschlechts…, Sexual…: ~ ***intercourse*** Geschlechtsverkehr *m*; **sex·u·al·i·ty** [ˌseksjʊ'ælətɪ] *s.* **1.** Sexuali'tät *f*; **2.** Sexu'al-, Geschlechtsleben *n*; '**sex·y** [-sɪ] *adj.* ‚sexy', ‚scharf'.

shab·bi·ness ['ʃæbɪnɪs] *s.* Schäbigkeit *f* (*a. fig.*).

shab·by ['ʃæbɪ] *adj.* □ *allg.* schäbig: a) fadenscheinig (*Kleider*), b) abgenutzt (*Sache*), c) ärmlich, her'untergekommen (*Person, Haus, Gegend etc.*), d) niederträchtig, e) geizig; ˌ~-**gen'teel** *adj.* vornehm, aber arm: ***the*** ~ die verarmten Vornehmen.

shab·rack ['ʃæbræk] *s.* ⚔ Scha'bracke *f*, Satteldecke *f*.

shack [ʃæk] **I** *s.* Hütte *f*, Ba'racke *f* (*a. contp.*); **II** *v/i.* ~ ***up*** *sl.* zs.-leben (***with*** mit).

shack·le ['ʃækl] **I** *s.* **1.** *pl.* Fesseln *pl.*, Ketten *pl.* (*a. fig.*); **2.** ⚙ Gelenkstück *n e-r Kette*; Bügel *m*, Lasche *f*; ⚓ (Anker-)Schäkel *m*; ⚡ Schäkel *m*; **II** *v/t.* **3.** fesseln (*a. fig. hemmen*); **4.** ⚓, ⚙ laschen.

'**shack·town** *s. Am.* → ***shantytown***.

shad [ʃæd] *pl.* **shads**, *coll.* **shad** *s. ichth.* Alse *f*.

shade [ʃeɪd] **I** *s.* **1.** Schatten *m* (*a. paint. u. fig.*): ***put*** (*od.* ***throw***) ***into the*** ~ *fig.* in den Schatten stellen; (***the***) ~***s of Goethe!*** *iro.* (das) erinnert doch sehr an Goethe!; **2.** schattiges Plätzchen; **3.** *myth.* a) Schatten *m* (*Seele*), b) *pl.* Schatten(reich *n*) *pl.*; **4.** a) Farbton *m*, Schattierung *f* (*a. fig.*), b) dunkle Tönung; **5.** *fig.* Spur *f*, ‚I'dee' *f*: ***a*** ~ ***better*** ein kleines bißchen besser; **6.** (*Schutz-, Lampen-, Sonnen- etc.*)Schirm *m*; **7.** *Am.* Rou'leau *n*; **8.** *pl.* F Sonnenbrille *f*; **II** *v/t.* **9.** beschatten, verdunkeln (*a. fig.*); **10.** *Augen etc.* abschirmen, schützen (***from*** gegen); **11.** *paint.* a) schattieren, b) schraffieren, c) dunkel tönen; **12.** *a.* ~ ***off*** a) *fig.* abstufen, b) ✝ *Preise* nach u. nach senken, c) *a.* ~ ***away*** all'mählich übergehen lassen (***into*** in *acc.*), d) *a.* ~ ***away*** all'mählich verschwinden lassen; **III** *v/i.* **13.** *a.* ~ ***off*** (*od.* ***away***) a) all'mählich 'übergehen (***into*** in *acc.*), b) nach u. nach verschwinden; '**shade·less** [-lɪs] *adj.* schattenlos; '**shad·i·ness** [-dɪnɪs] *s.* **1.** Schattigkeit *f*; **2.** *fig.* Anrüchigkeit *f*; '**shad·ing** [-dɪŋ] *s. paint. u. fig.* Schattierung *f*.

shad·ow ['ʃædəʊ] **I** *s.* **1.** Schatten *m* (*a. paint. u. fig.*); Schattenbild *n*: ***live in the*** ~ im Verborgenen leben; ***worn to a*** ~ zum Skelett abgemagert; ***he is but the*** ~ ***of his former self*** er ist nur noch ein Schatten s-r selbst; ***coming events cast their*** ~***s before*** kommende Ereignisse werfen ihre Schatten voraus; ***may your*** ~ ***never grow less*** *fig.* möge es dir immer gut gehen; **2.** Schemen *m*, Phan'tom *n*: ***catch*** (*od.* ***grasp***) ***at*** ~***s*** Phantomen nachjagen; **3.** *fig.* Spur *f*, Kleinigkeit *f*: ***without a*** ~ ***of doubt*** ohne den leisesten Zweifel; **4.** *fig.* Schatten *m*, Trübung *f* (*e-r Freundschaft etc.*); **5.** *fig.* Schatten *m* (*Begleiter od. Verfolger*); **II** *v/t.* **6.** e-n Schatten werfen auf (*acc.*), verdunkeln (*beide a. fig.*); **7.** *j-n* beschatten, verfolgen; **8.** *mst* ~ ***forth*** (*od.* ***out***) a) dunkel andeuten, b) versinnbildlichen; '~ˌ**box·ing** *s. sport* Schattenboxen *n*, *fig. a.* Spiegelfechte'rei *f*; ~ **cab·i·net** *s. pol.* 'Schattenkabiˌnett *n*; ~ **fac·to·ry** *s.* Schatten-, Ausweichbetrieb *m*.

shad·ow·less ['ʃædəʊlɪs] *adj.* schattenlos; '**shad·ow·y** [-əʊɪ] *adj.* **1.** schattig: a) dämmerig, düster, b) schattenspendend; **2.** *fig.* schattenhaft, vage; **3.** *fig.* unwirklich.

shad·y ['ʃeɪdɪ] *adj.* □ **1.** → ***shadowy*** 1 *u.* 2: ***on the*** ~ ***side of forty*** *fig.* über die Vierzig hinaus; **2.** F anrüchig, zwielichtig, fragwürdig.

shaft [ʃɑːft] *s.* **1.** (*Pfeil- etc.*)Schaft *m*; **2.** *poet.* Pfeil *m* (*a. fig. des Spottes*), Speer *m*; **3.** (Licht)Strahl *m*; **4.** ⚘ Stamm *m*; **5.** a) Stiel *m* (*Werkzeug etc.*), b) Deichsel(arm *m*) *f*, c) Welle *f*, Spindel *f*; **6.** (Fahnen)Stange *f*; **7.** Säulenschaft *m*, *a.* Säule *f*; **8.** (*Aufzugs-, Bergwerks- etc.*)Schacht *m*; → ***sink*** 17.

shag [ʃæg] **I** *s.* **1.** Zotte(l) *f*; zottiges Haar; **2.** a) (lange, grobe) Noppe, b) Plüsch(stoff) *m*; **3.** Shag(tabak) *m*; **4.** *orn.* Krähenscharbe *f*; **II** *v/t.* **5.** zottig machen, aufrauhen; **III** *v/i.* **6.** *sl.* ‚bumsen'; **shag·gy** ['ʃægɪ] *adj.* □ **1.** zottig, struppig; rauhhaarig: ~-***dog story*** a) surrealistischer Witz, b) kalauerhafte Geschichte; **2.** verwildert, verwahrlost; **3.** *fig.* verschroben.

sha·green [ʃæ'griːn] *s.* Cha'grin *n*, Körnerleder *n*.

shah [ʃɑː] *s.* Schah *m*.

shake [ʃeɪk] **I** *s.* **1.** Schütteln *n*, Rütteln *n*: ~ ***of the hand*** Händeschütteln; ~ ***of the head*** Kopfschütteln; ***give s.th. a good*** ~ et. tüchtig schütteln; ***give s.o. the*** ~ *Am. sl.* j-n ‚abwimmeln'; ***in two*** ~***s*** (***of a lamb's tail***) F im Nu; **2.** (*a.* seelische) Erschütterung; (*Wind- etc.*) Stoß *m*; *Am.* F Erdstoß *m*: ***he*** (***it***) ***is no great*** ~***s*** F mit ihm (damit) ist nicht viel los; **3.** Beben *n*: ***the*** ~***s*** ‚Tatterich' *m*; ***all of a*** ~ am ganzen Leibe zitternd; **4.** (*Milch- etc.*)Shake *m*; **5.** ♪ Triller *m*; **6.** Riß *m*, Spalt *m*; **II** *v/i.* [*irr.*] **7.** (sch)wanken; **8.** zittern, beben (*a. Stimme*) (***with*** vor *Furcht etc.*); **9.** ♪ trillern; **III** *v/t.* [*irr.*] **10.** schütteln: ~ ***one's head*** den Kopf schütteln; ~ ***one's finger at s.o.*** j-m mit dem Finger drohen; ***be shaken before taken!*** vor Gebrauch schütteln!; → ***hand*** *Redew.*, ***side*** 4; **11.** (*a. fig. Entschluß, Gegner, Glauben, Zeugenaussage*) erschüttern; **12.** a) *j-n* (seelisch) erschüttern, b) *j-n* aufrütteln; **13.** rütteln an (*dat.*) (*a. fig.*); **14.** ♪ *Ton* trillern;

Zssgn mit adv.:

shake| down I *v/t.* **1.** *Obst etc.* her'unterschütteln; **2.** *Stroh etc.* (zu e-m Nachtlager) ausbreiten; **3.** *Gefäßinhalt* zu'rechtschütteln; **4.** *Am. sl.* a) *j-n* ausplündern (*a. fig.*), b) erpressen, c) ‚filzen', durch'suchen; **5.** *bsd. Am.* F *Schiff, Flugzeug* testen; **II** *v/i.* **6.** sich setzen (*Masse*); **7.** a) sich ein (Nacht-)Lager zu'rechtmachen, b) ‚sich hinhauen'; **8.** *Am.* F a) sich vor'übergehend niederlassen (*an e-m Ort*), b) sich einleben, -gewöhnen, c) sich ‚einpendeln' (*Sache*), d) sich beschränken (***to*** auf *acc.*); ~ **off** *v/t.* **1.** *Staub etc., a. fig. Joch, a. Verfolger etc.* abschütteln; **2.** *fig. j-n od. et.* loswerden; ~ **out** *v/t.* **1.** ausschütteln; **2.** *Fahne etc.* ausbreiten; ~ **up** *v/t.* **1.** *Bett, Kissen* aufschütteln; **2.** *et.* zs.-, 'umschütteln, mischen; **3.** *fig.* a) *j-n* aufrütteln, b) *j-n* arg mitnehmen; **4.** *Betrieb etc.* 'umkrempeln.

'**shake|·down** *s.* **1.** (Not)Lager *n*; **2.** *Am. sl.* a) Ausplünderung *f*, b) Erpressung *f*, c) Durch'suchung *f*; **3.** *bsd. Am.* F Testfahrt *f*, -flug *m*; ˌ~-'**hands** *s.* Händedruck *m*.

shak·en ['ʃeɪkən] **I** *p.p. von* ***shake***; **II** *adj.* **1.** erschüttert, (sch)wankend (*a. fig.*): (***badly***) ~ arg mitgenommen; **2.** → ***shaky*** 5.

'**shake-out** *s.* ✝ *Am.* F Rezessi'on *f*.

shak·er ['ʃeɪkə] *s.* **1.** Mixbecher *m*, (*Cocktail- etc.*)Shaker *m*; **2.** ♀ *eccl.* Zitterer *m* (*Sektierer*).

Shake·spear·i·an [ʃeɪk'spɪərɪən] **I** *adj.* shakespearisch; **II** *s.* Shakespeareforscher(in).

'**shake-up** *s.* **1.** F Aufrütt(e)lung *f*; **2.** drastische (*bsd.* perso'nelle) Veränderungen *pl.*, 'Umkrempelung *f*, -gruppierung *f*.

shak·i·ness ['ʃeɪkɪnɪs] *s.* Wack(e)ligkeit *f* (*a. fig.*).

shak·ing ['ʃeɪkɪŋ] **I** *s.* **1.** Schütteln *n*; Erschütterung *f*; **II** *adj.* **2.** Schüttel…; → ***palsy*** 1; **3.** zitternd; **4.** wackelnd.

shak·y ['ʃeɪkɪ] *adj.* □ **1.** wack(e)lig (*a. fig. Person, Gesundheit, Kredit, Kenntnisse*): ***in rather*** ~ ***English*** in ziemlich holprigem Englisch; **2.** zitt(e)rig, bebend: ~ ***hands***; ~ ***voice***; **3.** *fig.* (sch)wankend; **4.** *fig.* unsicher, zweifelhaft; **5.** (kern)rissig (*Holz*).

shale [ʃeɪl] *s. geol.* Schiefer(ton) *m*: ~ ***oil*** Schieferöl *n*.

shall [ʃæl; ʃəl] *v/aux.* [*irr.*] **1.** *Futur*: *ich* werde, *wir* werden; **2.** *Befehl, Pflicht*: *ich, er, sie, es* soll, *du* sollst, *ihr* sollt, *wir, Sie, sie* sollen: ~ ***I come?***; **3.** ⚖ *Mußbestimmung* (*im Deutschen durch Indikativ wiederzugeben*): ***any person*** ~ ***be liable*** jede Person ist verpflichtet …; **4.** → ***should*** 1.

shal·lop ['ʃæləp] *s.* ⚓ Scha'luppe *f*.

shal·low ['ʃæləʊ] **I** *adj.* □ seicht, flach (*beide a. fig. oberflächlich*); **II** *s.* (*a. pl.*) seichte Stelle, Untiefe *f*; **III** *v/t. u. v/i.* (sich) verflachen; '**shal·low·ness** [-nɪs]

s. Seichtheit *f* (*a. fig.*).
shalt [ʃælt; ʃəlt] *obs. 2. sg. pres. von* ***shall***: ***thou ~*** du sollst.
sham [ʃæm] **I** *s.* **1.** (Vor)Täuschung *f*, (Be)Trug *m*, Heuche'lei *f*; **2.** Schwindler(in), Scharlatan *m*; **3.** Heuchler(in); **II** *adj.* **4.** vorgetäuscht, fingiert, Schein...: ***~ battle*** Scheingefecht *n*; **5.** unecht, falsch: ***~ diamond***; ***~ piety***; **III** *v/t.* **6.** vortäuschen, -spiegeln, fingieren, simulieren; **IV** *v/i.* **7.** sich (ver)stellen, heucheln: ***~ ill*** simulieren, krank spielen.
sha·man ['ʃæmən] *s.* Scha'mane *m*.
sham·a·teur ['ʃæmətə] *s.* F *sport* 'Scheinama,teur *m*.
sham·ble ['ʃæmbl] **I** *v/i.* watscheln; **II** *s.* watschelnder Gang.
sham·bles ['ʃæmblz] *s. pl. sg. konstr.* **1.** a) Schlachthaus *n*, b) Fleischbank *f*; **2.** *fig.* a) Schlachtfeld *n* (*a. iro. wüstes Durcheinander*), b) Trümmerfeld *n*, Bild *n* der Verwüstung, c) Scherbenhaufen *m*: ***his marriage was a ~.***
shame [ʃeɪm] **I** *s.* **1.** Scham(gefühl *n*) *f*: ***for ~!*** pfui, schäm dich!; ***feel ~ at*** sich über *et.* schämen; **2.** Schande *f*, Schmach *f*: ***be a ~ to*** → 5; ***~ on you!*** schäm dich!, pfui!; ***put s.o. to ~*** a) Schande über j-n bringen, b) j-n beschämen (*übertreffen*); ***to cry ~ upon s.o.*** pfui über j-n rufen; **3.** F Schande *f* (*Gemeinheit*): ***what a ~!*** a) es ist e-e Schande!, b) es ist ein Jammer!; **II** *v/t.* **4.** *j-n* beschämen, mit Scham erfüllen: ***~ s.o. into doing s.th.*** j-n so beschämen, daß er et. tut; **5.** *j-m* Schande machen; **6.** Schande bringen über (*acc.*); '**~-faced** [-feɪst] *adj.* ☐ **1.** verschämt, schamhaft; **2.** schüchtern; **3.** schamrot.
shame·ful ['ʃeɪmfʊl] *adj.* ☐ **1.** schmachvoll, schändlich; **2.** schimpflich; **3.** unanständig, anstößig; '**shame·ful·ness** [-nɪs] *s.* **1.** Schändlichkeit *f*; **2.** Anstößigkeit *f*; '**shame·less** [-lɪs] *adj.* ☐ schamlos (*a. fig. unverschämt*); '**shame·less·ness** [-lɪsnɪs] *s.* Schamlosigkeit *f* (*a. fig. Unverschämtheit*).
sham·mer ['ʃæmə] *s.* **1.** Schwindler(in); **2.** Heuchler(in); **3.** Simu'lant(in).
sham·my (**leath·er**) ['ʃæmɪ] *s.* Sämisch-, Wildleder *n*.
sham·poo [ʃæm'pu:] **I** *v/t.* **1.** *Kopf, Haare* schamponieren, waschen; **2.** *j-m* den Kopf *od.* das Haar waschen; **II** *s.* **3.** Haar-, Kopfwäsche *f*: ***~ and set*** Waschen u. Legen *n*; **4.** Sham'poo *n*, Schampon *n* (*Haarwaschmittel*).
sham·rock ['ʃæmrɒk] *s.* **1.** ⚘ Weißer Feldklee; **2.** Shamrock *m* (*Kleeblatt als Wahrzeichen Irlands*).
sham·us ['ʃeɪməs] *s. Am. sl.* **1.** ‚Schnüffler' *m* (*Detektiv*); **2.** ‚Bulle' *m* (*Polizist*).
shan·dy ['ʃændɪ] *s. Mischgetränk aus Bier u. Limonade.*
shang·hai [ʃæŋ'haɪ] *v/t.* F **1.** ⚓ schang'haien (*gewaltsam anheuern*); **2.** *fig. j-n* zwingen (***into doing*** *et.* zu tun).
shank [ʃæŋk] *s.* **1.** a) 'Unterschenkel *m*, Schienbein *n*, b) F Bein *n*, c) Hachse *f* (*vom Schlachttier*): ***go on* ℒ*'s pony*** (*od.* ***mare***) auf Schusters Rappen reiten; **2.** (Anker-, Bolzen-, Säulen- *etc.*) Schaft *m*; **3.** (Schuh)Gelenk *n*; **4.** *typ.* (Schrift)Kegel *m*; **5.** ⚘ Stiel *m*;
shanked [-kt] *adj.* **1.** ...schenk(e)lig; **2.** gestielt.
shan't [ʃɑ:nt] F *für* ***shall not.***
shan·ty[1] ['ʃæntɪ] *s.* Shanty *n*, Seemannslied *n*.
shan·ty[2] ['ʃæntɪ] *s.* Hütte *f*, Ba'racke *f*; '**~·town** *s.* Barackensiedlung *f*, -stadt *f*.
shape [ʃeɪp] **I** *s.* **1.** Gestalt *f*, Form *f* (*a. fig.*): ***in the ~ of*** in Form *e-s Briefes etc.*; ***in human ~*** in Menschengestalt; ***put*** *od.* ***get into ~*** formen, gestalten, *s-e Gedanken* ordnen; ***in no ~*** in keiner Weise; **2.** Fi'gur *f*, Gestalt *f*; **3.** feste Form, Gestalt *f*: ***take ~*** Gestalt annehmen (*a. fig.*); → ***lick*** 1; **4.** *körperliche od. geistige* Verfassung, Form *f*: ***be in*** (***good***) ***~*** in (guter) Form sein; **5.** ⚙ a) Form *f*, Fas'son *f*, Mo'dell *n*, b) Formteil *n*; **6.** *Küche*: a) (Pudding- *etc.*)Form *f*, b) Stürzpudding *m*; **II** *v/t.* **7.** gestalten, formen, bilden (*alle a. fig.*), *Charakter a.* prägen; **8.** anpassen (***to*** *dat.*); **9.** planen, entwerfen: ***~ the course for*** ⚓ *u. fig.* den Kurs setzen auf (*acc.*); **10.** ⚙ formen; **III** *v/i.* **11.** Gestalt *od.* Form annehmen, sich formen; **12.** sich entwickeln, sich gestalten: ***~*** (***up***) ***well*** sich ‚machen' *od.* gut anlassen, vielversprechend sein; ***~ up*** F e-e endgültige Form annehmen, sich (gut) entwickeln; **13.** ***~ up to*** a) Boxstellung einnehmen gegen, b) *fig. j-n* herausfordern; **shaped** [-pt] *adj.* geformt, ...gestaltet, ...förmig; '**shape·less** [-lɪs] *adj.* ☐ **1.** form-, gestaltlos; **2.** unförmig; '**shape·less·ness** [-lɪsnɪs] *s.* **1.** Fom-, Gestaltlosigkeit *f*; **2.** Unförmigkeit *f*; '**shape·li·ness** [-lɪnɪs] *s.* Wohlgestalt *f*, schöne Form; '**shape·ly** [-lɪ] *adj.* wohlgeformt, schön, hübsch; '**shap·er** [-pə] *s.* **1.** Former(in), Gestalter(in); **2.** ⚙ a) 'Waagrecht-'Stoßma,schine *f*, b) Schnellhobler *m*.
shard [ʃɑ:d] *s.* **1.** (Ton)Scherbe *f*; **2.** *zo.* (harte) Flügeldecke (*Insekt*).
share[1] [ʃeə] *s.* (Pflug)Schar *f*.
share[2] [ʃeə] **I** *s.* **1.** (An)Teil *m* (*a. fig.*): ***fall to s.o.'s ~*** j-m zufallen; ***go ~s with*** mit *j-m* teilen (***in s.th.*** et.); ***~ and ~ alike*** zu gleichen Teilen; **2.** (An)Teil *m*, Beitrag *m*; Kontin'gent *n*: ***do one's ~*** sein(en) Teil leisten; ***take a ~ in*** sich beteiligen an (*dat.*); ***have*** (*od.* ***take***) ***a large ~ in*** e-n großen Anteil haben an (*dat.*); **3.** ✝ Beteiligung *f*; Geschäftsanteil *m*; Kapi'taleinlage *f*: ***~ in a ship*** Schiffspart *m*; **4.** ✝ a) Gewinnanteil *m*, b) Aktie *f*, c) ⚒ Kux *m*: ***hold ~s in*** Aktionär in *e-r Gesellschaft* sein; **II** *v/t.* **5.** (*a. fig. sein Bett, e-e Ansicht, den Ruhm etc.*) teilen (***with*** mit); **6.** *mst* ***~ out*** aus-, verteilen; **7.** teilnehmen, -haben an (*dat.*); sich an *den Kosten etc.* beteiligen; **III** *v/i.* **8.** ***~ in*** → 7; **9.** sich teilen (***in*** in *acc.*); ***~ cer·tif·i·cate*** *s.* ✝ *Brit.* 'Aktienzertifi,kat *n*; '**~,crop·per** *s. Am. kleiner* Farmpächter (*der s-e Pacht mit e-m Teil der Ernte entrichtet*); '**~,hold·er** *s.* ✝ *Brit.* Aktio'när(in); ***~ list*** *s.* ✝ *Brit.* (Aktien)Kurszettel *m*; ***~ mark·et*** *s.* ✝ *Brit.* Aktienmarkt *m*; '**~·out** [-əraʊt] *s.* Aus-, Verteilung *f*.
shark [ʃɑ:k] *s.* **1.** *ichth.* Hai(fisch) *m*; **2.** *fig.* Gauner *m*, Betrüger *m*; **3.** *fig.* Schma'rotzer *m*; **4.** *Am. sl.* ‚Ka'none' *f* (*Könner*).
sharp [ʃɑ:p] **I** *adj.* ☐ **1.** scharf (*Messer etc., a. Gesichtszüge, Kurve etc.*); **2.** spitz (*Giebel etc.*); **3.** steil; **4.** *fig. allg.* scharf: a) deutlich (*Gegensatz, Umrisse etc.*), b) herb (*Geschmack*), c) schneidend (*Befehl, Stimme*), schrill (*Schrei, Ton*), d) heftig (*Schmerz etc.*), schneidend (*a. Frost, Wind*), e) hart (*Antwort, Kritik*), spitz (*Bemerkung, Zunge*), f) schnell (*Tempo, Spiel etc.*): ***~'s the word*** F mach fix!; **5.** scharf, wachsam (*Auge, Ohr*); angespannt (*Aufmerksamkeit*); **6.** scharfsinnig, gescheit, aufgeweckt, ‚auf Draht': ***~ at figures*** gut im Rechnen; **7.** gerissen, raffiniert: ***~ practice*** Gaunerei *f*; **8.** F ele'gant, schick; **9.** ♪ a) (zu) hoch, b) (*durch Kreuz* um e-n Halbton) erhöht, c) Kreuz...: ***C ~*** Cis *n*; **10.** *ling.* stimmlos (*Konsonant*); **II** *adv.* **11.** scharf; **12.** plötzlich; **13.** pünktlich, genau: ***at 3 o'clock ~*** Punkt 3 Uhr, genau um 3 Uhr; **14.** schnell: ***look ~*** mach schnell!; **15.** ♪ zu hoch; **III** *v/i. u. v/t.* **16.** ♪ zu hoch singen *od.* spielen; **17.** betrügen; **IV** *s.* **18.** *pl.* lange Nähnadeln *pl.*; **19.** *pl.* ✝ *Brit.* grobes Kleienmehl; **20.** ♪ a) Kreuz *n*, b) Erhöhung *f*, Halbton *m*, c) nächsthöhere Taste; **21.** F → ***sharper***; **,~-'cut** *adj.* **1.** scharf (geschnitten); **2.** festum'rissen, deutlich; **,~-'edged** *adj.* scharfkantig.
sharp·en ['ʃɑ:pən] **I** *v/t.* **1.** *Messer etc.* schärfen, schleifen, wetzen; *Bleistift etc.* (an)spitzen; **2.** *fig. j-n* ermuntern *od.* anspornen; *Sinn, Verstand* schärfen; *Appetit* anregen; **3.** *Rede etc.* verschärfen; *s-r Stimme etc.* e-n scharfen Klang geben; **II** *v/i.* **4.** scharf *od.* schärfer werden, sich verschärfen (*a. fig.*); '**sharp·en·er** [-pnə] *s.* (*Bleistift- etc.*) Spitzer *m*.
sharp·er ['ʃɑ:pə] *s.* **1.** Gauner *m*, Betrüger *m*; **2.** Falschspieler *m*.
,sharp-'eyed → ***sharp-sighted.***
sharp·ness ['ʃɑ:pnɪs] *s.* **1.** Schärfe *f*, Spitzigkeit *f*; **2.** *fig.* Schärfe *f* (*Herbheit, Strenge, Heftigkeit*); **3.** (Geistes)Schärfe *f*, Scharfsinn *m*; Gerissenheit *f*; **4.** (*phot.* Rand)Schärfe *f*, Deutlichkeit *f*.
,sharp|-'set *adj.* **1.** (heiß)hungrig; **2.** *fig.* scharf, erpicht (***on*** auf *acc.*); '**~-,shoot·er** *s.* Scharfschütze *m*; **,~-'sight·ed** *adj.* **1.** scharfsichtig; **2.** *fig.* scharfsinnig; **,~-'tongued** *adj. fig.* scharfzüngig (*Person*); **,~-'wit·ted** *adj.* scharfsinnig.
shat·ter ['ʃætə] **I** *v/t.* **1.** zerschmettern, -schlagen, -trümmern (*alle a. fig.*); *fig. Hoffnungen* zerstören; **2.** *Gesundheit, Nerven* zerrütten: ***I was*** (***absolutely***) ***~ed*** F ich war ‚am Boden zerstört'; **II** *v/i.* **3.** in Stücke brechen, zerspringen; '**shat·ter·ing** [-ərɪŋ] *adj.* ☐ **1.** vernichtend (*a. fig.*); **2.** *fig.* a) 'umwerfend, e'norm, b) entsetzlich, verheerend; '**shat·ter-proof** *adj.* ⚙ a) bruchsicher, b) splitterfrei, -sicher (*Glas*).
shave [ʃeɪv] **I** *v/t.* **1.** (***o.s.*** sich) rasieren: ***~*** (***off***) *Bart* abrasieren; ***get ~d*** rasiert werden; **2.** *Rasen etc.* (kurz) scheren; *Holz* (ab)schälen *od.* glatthobeln; *Häute* abschaben; **3.** streifen, *a.* knapp vor'beikommen an (*dat.*); **II** *v/i.* **4.** sich rasieren; **5.** ***~ through*** F (gerade noch) ‚'durchrutschen' (*in e-r Prüfung*); **III** *s.* **6.** Ra'sur *f*, Rasieren *n*: ***have*** (*od.* ***get***) ***a ~*** sich rasieren (lassen); ***have a close***

(*od.* ***narrow***) ~ F *fig.* mit knapper Not davonkommen; ***that was a close*** ~ F ‚das hätte ins Auge gehen können'; ***by a*** ~ F um ein Haar; **7.** (Ab)Schabsel *n*, Span *m*; **8.** ⚙ Schabeisen *n*; **9.** *obs.* F Schwindel *m*, Betrug *m*; **'shave·ling** [-lɪŋ] *s. obs. contp.* **1.** Pfaffe *m*; **2.** Mönch *m*; **'shav·en** [-vn] *adj.* **1.** (***clean-***~ glatt)rasiert; **2.** (kahl)geschoren (*Kopf*); **'shav·er** [-və] *s.* **1.** Bar'bier *m*; **2.** Ra'sierappa,rat *m*; **3.** *mst* ***young*** ~ F Grünschnabel *m*.

Sha·vi·an ['ʃeɪvjən] *adj.* Shawsch, für G. B. Shaw charakte'ristisch: ~ ***humo(u)r*** Shawscher Humor.

shav·ing ['ʃeɪvɪŋ] *s.* **1.** Rasieren *n*: ~ ***brush*** (***cream***, ***mirror***) Rasierpinsel *m* (-creme *f*, -spiegel *m*); ~ ***head*** Scherkopf *m*; ~ ***soap***, ~ ***stick*** Rasierseife *f*; **2.** *mst pl.* Schnitzel *m*, *n*, (Hobel)Span *m*.

shawl [ʃɔ:l] *s.* **1.** 'Umhängetuch *n*; **2.** Kopftuch *n*.

shawm [ʃɔ:m] *s.* ♪ Schal'mei *f*.

she [ʃi:; ʃɪ] **I** *pron.* **1.** a) sie (*3. sg. für alle weiblichen Lebewesen*), b) (*beim Mond*) er, (*bei Ländern*) es, (*bei Schiffen mit Namen*) sie, (*bei Schiffen ohne Namen*) es, (*bei Motoren u. Maschinen, wenn personifiziert*) er, es; **2.** sie, die (-jenige); **II** *s.* **3.** Sie *f*: a) Mädchen *n*, Frau *f*, b) Weibchen *n* (*Tier*); **III** *adj. in Zssgn* **4.** weiblich: ***~-bear*** Bärin *f*; ***~-dog*** Hündin *f*; **5.** *contp.* Weibs...: ***~-devil*** Weibsteufel *m*.

sheaf [ʃi:f] **I** *pl.* **-ves** [-vz] *s.* **1.** 🌾 Garbe *f*; **2.** (*Papier-*, *Pfeil-*, *phys. Strahlen-*) Bündel *n*: ~ ***of fire*** ⚔ Feuer-, Geschoßgarbe *f*; **II** *v/t.* **3.** → ***sheave***[1].

shear [ʃɪə] **I** *v/t.* [*irr.*] **1.** scheren: ~ ***sheep***; **2.** *a.* ~ ***off*** (ab)scheren, abschneiden; **3.** *fig.* berauben; → ***shorn***; **4.** *fig. j-n* ‚schröpfen'; **5.** *poet. mit dem Schwert* (ab)hauen; **II** *v/i.* [*irr.*] **6.** 🌾 sicheln, mähen; **III** *s.* **7.** *pl.* große Schere; ⚙ Me'tall-, Blechschere *f*; **8.** → ***shearing force***, ***shearing stress***; **'shear·er** [-ərə] *s.* **1.** (Schaf)Scherer *m*; **2.** Schnitter *m*.

shear·ing ['ʃɪərɪŋ] *s.* **1.** Schur *f* (*Schafescheren od. Schurertrag*); **2.** *phys.* (Ab-) Scherung *f*; **3.** *Scot. od. dial.* Mähen *n*, Mahd *f*; ~ **force** *s. phys.* Scher-, Schubkraft *f*; ~ **strength** *s. phys.* Scherfestigkeit *f*; ~ **stress** *s. phys.* Scherbeanspruchung *f*.

shear·ling ['ʃɪəlɪŋ] *s.* erst 'einmal geschorenes Schaf.

shear| pin *s.* ⚙ Scherbolzen *m*; ~ **stress** → ***shearing stress***; **'~,wa·ter** *s. orn.* Sturmtaucher *m*.

sheath [ʃi:θ] *s.* **1.** (*Schwert- etc.*)Scheide *f*; **2.** Futte'ral *n*, Hülle *f*; **3.** ⚘, *zo.* Scheide *f*; **4.** *zo.* Flügeldecke *f* (*Käfer*); **5.** Kon'dom *n*, *m*; **6.** Futte'ralkleid *n*; **sheathe** [ʃi:ð] *v/t.* **1.** *das Schwert* in die Scheide stecken; **2.** in e-e Hülle *od.* ein Futte'ral stecken; **3.** *bsd.* ⚙ um'hüllen, -'manteln, über'ziehen; *Kabel* armieren; **sheath·ing** ['ʃi:ðɪŋ] *s.* ⚙ Verschalung *f*, -kleidung *f*; Beschlag *m*; 'Überzug *m*, Mantel *m*; (Kabel)Bewehrung *f*.

sheave[1] [ʃi:v] *v/t.* 🌾 in Garben binden.

sheave[2] [ʃi:v] *s.* ⚙ Scheibe *f*, Rolle *f*.

sheaves [ʃi:vz] **1.** *pl. von* ***sheaf***; **2.** *pl. von* ***sheave***[2].

she·bang [ʃə'bæŋ] *s. Am. sl.* **1.** ‚Bude' *f*, ‚Laden' *m*; **2.** ***the whole*** ~ der ganze Plunder *od.* Kram.

shed[1] [ʃed] *s.* **1.** Schuppen *m*; **2.** Stall *m*; **3.** ✈ *kleine* Flugzeughalle; **4.** Hütte *f*.

shed[2] [ʃed] *v/t.* [*irr.*] F **1.** verschütten, *a. Blut*, *Tränen* vergießen; **2.** ausstrahlen, -strömen, *Duft*, *Licht*, *Frieden etc.* verbreiten; → ***light*** 1; **3.** *Wasser* abstoßen (*Stoff*); **4.** *biol. Laub*, *Federn etc.* abwerfen, *Hörner* abstoßen, *Zähne* verlieren: ~ ***one's skin*** sich häuten; **5.** *Winterkleider etc.*, *a. fig. Gewohnheit*, *a. iro. Freunde* ablegen.

she'd [ʃi:d] F *für* a) ***she would***, b) ***she had***.

sheen [ʃi:n] *s.* Glanz *m* (*bsd. von Stoffen*), Schimmer *m*.

sheen·y[1] ['ʃi:nɪ] *adj.* glänzend.

sheen·y[2] ['ʃi:nɪ] *s. sl.* ‚Itzig' *m* (*Jude*).

sheep [ʃi:p] *pl. coll.* **sheep** *s.* **1.** *zo.* Schaf *n*: ***cast ~'s eyes at s.o.*** j-m schmachtende Blicke zuwerfen; ***separate the ~ and the goats*** *bibl.* die Schafe von den Böcken trennen; ***you might as well be hanged for a ~ as (for) a lamb!*** wenn schon, denn schon!; → ***black sheep***; **2.** *fig. contp.* Schaf *n* (*Person*); **3.** *pl. fig.* Schäflein *pl.*, Herde *f* (*Gemeinde e-s Pfarrers etc.*); **4.** Schafleder *n*; **'~-dip** *s.* Desinfekti'onsbad *n* für Schafe; **'~·dog** *s.* Schäferhund *m*; **'~·farm** *s. Brit.* Schaf(zucht)farm *f*; **'~,farm·ing** *s. Brit.* Schafzucht *f*; **'~-fold** *s.* Schafhürde *f*.

sheep·ish ['ʃi:pɪʃ] *adj.* □ **1.** schüchtern; **2.** einfältig, blöd(e); **3.** verlegen, ‚belämmert'.

'sheep|·man [-mən] *s.* [*irr.*] *Am.* Schafzüchter *m*; **'~·pen** → ***sheepfold***; ~ **run** → ***sheepwalk***; **'~,shear·ing** *s.* Schafschur *f*; **'~·skin** *s.* **1.** Schaffell *n*; **2.** (*a.* Perga'ment *n* aus) Schafleder *n*; **3.** F a) Urkunde *f*, b) Di'plom *n*; **'~·walk** *s.* Schafweide *f*.

sheer[1] [ʃɪə] **I** *adj.* □ **1.** bloß, rein, pur, nichts als: ~ ***nonsense***; ***by*** ~ ***force*** mit bloßer *od.* nackter Gewalt; **2.** völlig, glatt: ~ ***impossibility***; **3.** rein, unvermischt, pur: ~ ***ale***; **4.** steil, jäh; **5.** hauchdünn (*Textilien*); **II** *adv.* **6.** völlig; **7.** senkrecht; **8.** di'rekt.

sheer[2] [ʃɪə] **I** *s.* **1.** ⚓ a) Ausscheren *n*, b) Sprung *m* (*Deckerhöhung*); **II** *v/i.* **2.** ⚓ abscheren, (ab)gieren (*Schiff*); **3.** *fig. a.* ~ ***away*** (***from***) a) abweichen (von), b) sich losmachen (von); ~ **off** *v/i.* **1.** → ***sheer***[2] 2; **2.** abhauen; **3.** ~ ***from*** aus dem Wege gehen (*dat.*).

sheet [ʃi:t] **I** *s.* **1.** Bettuch *n*, (Bett)Laken *n*; Leintuch *n*: ***stand in a white*** ~ reumütig s-e Sünden bekennen; (***as***) ***white as a*** ~ *fig.* kreidebleich; **2.** (*typ.* Druck)Bogen *m*, Blatt *n* (*Papier*): ***a blank*** ~ *fig.* ein unbeschriebenes Blatt; ***a clean*** ~ *fig.* e-e reine Weste; ***in*** (***the***) ***~s*** (noch) nicht gebunden, ungefalzt (*Buch*); **3.** Bogen *m* (*von Briefmarken*); **4.** a) Blatt *n*, Zeitung *f*, b) (Flug-) Schrift *f*; **5.** ⚙ (dünne) (*Blech-*, *Glas-etc.*)Platte *f*; **6.** *metall.* (Fein)Blech *n*; **7.** weite Fläche (*von Wasser etc.*); (wogende) Masse; (*Feuer-*, *Regen*)Wand *f*; *geol.* Schicht *f*: ***rain came down in ~s*** es regnete in Strömen; **8.** ⚓ Schot(e) *f*, Segelleine *f*: ***have three ~s in the wind*** *sl.* ‚sternhagelvoll' sein; **9.** ⚓ Vorder- (*u.* Achter)Teil *m*, *n* (*Boot*); **II** *v/t.* **10.** *Bett* beziehen; **11.** (in Laken) (ein)hüllen; **12.** ⚙ mit Blech verkleiden; **13.** *a.* ~ ***home*** *Segel* anholen; ~ **an·chor** *s.* ⚓ Notanker *m* (*a. fig.*); ~ **cop·per** *s.* Kupferblech *n*; ~ **glass** *s.* Tafelglas *n*.

sheet·ing ['ʃi:tɪŋ] *s.* **1.** Bettuchstoff *m*; **2.** Blechverkleidung *f*.

sheet| i·ron *s.* Eisenblech *n*; ~ **light·ning** *s.* **1.** Wetterleuchten *n*; **2.** Flächenblitz *m*; ~ **met·al** *s.* (Me'tall)Blech *n*; ~ **mu·sic** *s.* Noten(blätter) *pl.*; ~ **steel** *s.* Stahlblech *n*.

sheik(h) [ʃeɪk] *s.* **1.** Scheich *m*; **2.** *fig.* F a) ‚Scheich' *m* (*Freund*), b) *Am.* ‚Schwarm' *m* (*Person*); **'sheik(h)·dom** [-dəm] *s.* Scheichtum *n*.

shek·el ['ʃekl] *s.* **1.** a) S(ch)ekel *m* (*hebräische Gewichts- u. Münzeinheit*), b) Schekel *m* (*Münzeinheit in Israel*); **2.** *pl.* F ‚Zaster' *m* (*Geld*).

shel·drake ['ʃeldreɪk] *s. orn.* Brandente *f*.

shelf [ʃelf] *pl.* **shelves** [-vz] *s.* **1.** (Bücher-, Wand-, Schrank)Brett *n*; ('Bücher-, 'Waren- *etc.*)Re,gal *n*, Bord *n*, Fach *n*, Sims *m*: ***be put*** (*od.* ***laid***) ***on the*** ~ *fig.* a) ausrangiert werden (*a. Beamter etc.*), b) auf die lange Bank geschoben werden; ***get on the*** ~ ‚sitzenbleiben' (*Mädchen*); **2.** Riff *n*, Felsplatte *f*; **3.** ⚓ a) Schelf *m*, *n*, Küstensockel *m*, b) Sandbank *f*; **4.** *geol.* Festlandssockel *m*, Schelf *m*, *n*; ~ **life** *s.* † Lagerfähigkeit *f*; **'~,warm·er** *s.* ‚Ladenhüter' *m*.

shell [ʃel] **I** *s.* **1.** *allg.* Schale *f*; **2.** *zo.* a) Muschelschale *f*, b) Schneckenhaus *n*, c) Flügeldecke *f* (*Käfer*), d) Rückenschild *m* (*Schildkröte*): ***come out of one's*** ~ *fig.* aus sich herausgehen; ***retire into one's*** ~ *fig.* sich in sein Schneckenhaus zurückziehen; **3.** (Eier-) Schale *f*: ***in the*** ~ a) (noch) unausgebrütet, b) *fig.* noch in der Entwicklung; **4.** a) Muschel *f*, b) Perlmutt *n*, c) Schildpatt *n*; **5.** (Nuß- *etc.*)Schale *f*, Hülse *f*; **6.** ⚓, ✈ Schale *f*, Außenhaut *f*; (Schiffs)Rumpf *m*; **7.** Gerippe *n*, Gerüst *n* (*a. fig.*), △ *a.* Rohbau *m*; **8.** ⚙ Kapsel *f*, (*Scheinwerfer- etc.*)Gehäuse *n*; **9.** ⚔ a) Gra'nate *f*, b) Hülse *f*, c) *Am.* Pa'trone *f*; **10.** ('Feuerwerks)Ra,kete *f*; **11.** *Küche*: (Pa'steten)Hülle *f*; **12.** *phys.* (Elek'tronen)Schale *f*; **13.** *sport* (leichtes) Renn(ruder)boot; **14.** (*Degen- etc.*)Korb *m*; **15.** *fig. das* (bloße) Äußere; **16.** *ped. Brit.* Mittelstufe *f*; **II** *v/t.* **17.** schälen; *Erbsen etc.* enthülsen; *Nüsse* knacken; *Körner* von der Ähre *od.* vom Kolben entfernen; **18.** ⚔ (mit Gra'naten) beschießen; ~ **out** *v/t. u. v/i. sl.* ‚blechen' (*bezahlen*).

shel·lac [ʃə'læk] **I** *s.* **1.** ⚗ Schellack *m*; **II** *v/t. pret. u. p.p.* **shel'lacked** [-kt] **2.** mit Schellack behandeln; **3.** *fig. Am. sl. j-n* ‚vermöbeln'.

'shell,cra·ter *s.* ⚔ Gra'nattrichter *m*.

shelled [ʃeld] *adj.* ...schalig.

shell| egg *s.* Frischei *n*; **'~·fish** *s. zo.* Schalentier *n*; ~ **game** *s. Am.* Falschspielertrick *m* (*a. fig.*).

shell·ing ['ʃelɪŋ] *s.* ⚔ Beschuß *m*, (Artille'rie)Feuer *n*.

shell shock *s.* ⚔ 'Kriegsneu,rose *f*.

shel·ter ['ʃeltə] **I** *s.* **1.** Schutzhütte *f*, -dach *n*; Schuppen *m*; **2.** Obdach *n*,

Herberge *f*; **3.** Zuflucht *f*; **4.** Schutz *m*: ***take*** (*od.* ***seek***) ~ Schutz suchen (***with*** bei, ***from*** vor *dat.*); **5.** ⚔ a) Bunker *m*, 'Unterstand *m*, b) Deckung *f*; **II** *v/t.* **6.** (be)schützen, beschirmen (***from*** vor): ***a ~ed life*** ein behütetes Leben; **7.** schützen, bedecken, über'dachen; **8.** *j-m* Schutz *od.* Zuflucht gewähren: ***~ o.s.*** *fig.* sich verstecken (***behind*** hinter *j-m etc.*); ***~ed trade*** ⚚ *Brit.* (*durch Zölle*) geschützter Handelszweig; ***~ed workshop*** beschützende Werkstatt; **9.** *j-n* beherbergen; **III** *v/i.* **10.** Schutz suchen; sich 'unterstellen; ~ **half** *s.* ⚔ *Am.* Zeltbahn *f*.

shelve¹ [ʃelv] *v/t.* **1.** *Bücher* (in ein Re'gal) einstellen, auf ein (Bücher)Brett stellen; **2.** *fig.* a) *et.* zu den Akten legen, bei'seite legen, b) *j-n* ausrangieren; **3.** aufschieben; **4.** mit Fächern *od.* Re'galen versehen.

shelve² [ʃelv] *v/i.* (sanft) abfallen.

shelves [ʃelvz] *pl. von* ***shelf***.

shelv·ing¹ ['ʃelvɪŋ] *s.* (Bretter *pl.* für) Fächer *pl. od.* Re'gale *pl.*

shelv·ing² ['ʃelvɪŋ] *adj.* schräg, abfallend.

she·nan·i·gan [ʃɪ'nænɪgən] *s. mst pl.* F **1.** ‚Mumpitz' *m*, ‚fauler Zauber'; **2.** Trick *m*; **3.** ‚Blödsinn' *m*, Streich *m*.

shep·herd ['ʃepəd] **I** *s.* **1.** (Schaf)Hirt *m*, Schäfer *m*; **2.** *fig. eccl.* (Seelen)Hirt *m* (*Geistlicher*): ***the*** (***good***) ♀ *bibl.* der Gute Hirte (*Christus*); **II** *v/t.* **3.** *Schafe etc.* hüten; **4.** *fig. Menschenmenge etc.* treiben, führen, ‚bugsieren'; '**shep·herd·ess** [-dɪs] *s.* (Schaf)Hirtin *f*, Schäferin *f*.

shep·herd's| crook *s.* Hirtenstab *m*; ~ **dog** *s.* Schäferhund *m*; ~ **pie** *s.* Auflauf *m* aus Hackfleisch u. Kar'toffelbrei; ˌ~-'**purse** *s.* ⚘ Hirtentäschel *n*.

sher·bet ['ʃɜːbət] *s.* **1.** Sor'bett *n*, *m* (*Frucht-, Eisgetränk*); **2.** *bsd. Am.* Fruchteis *n*; **3.** *a.* ~ ***powder*** Brausepulver *n*.

sherd [ʃɜːd] → ***shard***.

sher·iff ['ʃerɪf] *s.* ⚖ Sheriff *m*: a) *in England, Wales u. Irland der höchste Verwaltungsbeamte e-r Grafschaft*, b) *in den USA der gewählte höchste Exekutivbeamte e-s Verwaltungsbezirkes*, c) *in Schottland e-e Art Amtsrichter.*

sher·ry ['ʃerɪ] *s.* Sherry *m*.

she's [ʃiːz; ʃɪz] F *für* a) ***she is***, b) ***she has***.

shew [ʃəʊ] *obs. für* ***show***.

shib·bo·leth ['ʃɪbəleθ] *s. fig.* **1.** Schib'boleth *n*, Erkennungszeichen *n*, -wort *n*; **2.** Kastenbrauch *m*; **3.** Plati'tüde *f*.

shield [ʃiːld] **I** *s.* **1.** Schild *m*; **2.** Schutzschild *m*, -schirm *m*; **3.** *fig.* a) Schutz *m*, Schirm *m*, b) (Be)Schützer(in); **4.** ⚡, ⚙ (Ab)Schirmung *f*; **5.** Arm-, Schweißblatt *n*; **6.** *zo.* (Rücken)Schild *m*, Panzer *m* (*Insekt etc.*); **7.** *her.* (Wappen-) Schild *m*; **II** *v/t.* **8.** (be)schützen, (be-) schirmen (***from*** vor *dat.*); **9.** *bsd. b.s. j-n* decken; **10.** ⚡, ⚙ (ab)schirmen; '~-ˌ**bear·er** *s.* Schildknappe *m*; ~ **fern** *s.* ⚘ Schildfarn *m*; ~ **forc·es** *s. pl.* ⚔ Schildstreitkräfte *pl.*

shiel·ing ['ʃiːlɪŋ] *s. Scot.* **1.** (Vieh)Weide *f*; **2.** Hütte *f*.

shift [ʃɪft] **I** *v/i.* **1.** den Platz *od.* die Lage wechseln, sich bewegen; **2.** sich verlagern (*a.* ⚖ *Beweislast*), sich verwandeln (*a. Szene*), sich verschieben (*a. ling.*), wechseln; **3.** ⚓ 'überschießen, sich verlagern (*Ballast, Ladung*); **4.** die Wohnung wechseln; **5.** 'umspringen (*Wind*); **6.** *mot.* schalten: ~ ***up*** (***down***) hinaufschalten (herunterschalten); **7.** *Kugelstoßen*: angleiten; **8.** ~ ***for o.s.*** a) auf sich selbst gestellt sein, b) sich selbst (weiter)helfen, sich durchschlagen; **9.** Ausflüchte machen; **10.** *mst* ~ ***away*** F sich da'vonmachen; **II** *v/t.* **11.** (aus-, 'um)wechseln, (aus)tauschen; → ***ground*** 2; **12.** (*a. fig.*) verschieben, -lagern, (*a. Schauplatz*, ⚔ *das Feuer*) verlegen; *Betrieb* 'umstellen (***to*** auf *acc.*); *thea. Kulissen* schieben; **13.** ⚙ schalten, ausrücken, verstellen, *Hebel* 'umlegen: ~ ***gears*** *mot.* schalten; **14.** ⚓ a) *Schiff* verholen, b) *Ladung* 'umstauen; **15.** *Kleidung* wechseln; **16.** *Schuld, Verantwortung* (ab)schieben, abwälzen ([***up***]***on*** auf *acc.*); **17.** *j-n* loswerden; **18.** *Am.* F a) *Essen etc.* ‚wegputzen', b) *Schnaps etc.* ‚kippen'; **III** *s.* **19.** Verschiebung *f*, -änderung *f*, -lagerung *f*, Wechsel *m*; **20.** ⚚ (Arbeits)Schicht *f* (*Arbeiter od. Arbeitszeit*); **21.** Ausweg *m*, Hilfsmittel *n*, Notbehelf *m*: ***make*** (***a***) ~ a) sich durchschlagen, b) es fertigbringen, es möglich machen (***to do*** zu tun), c) sich behelfen (***with*** mit, ***without*** ohne); **22.** Kniff *m*, List *f*, Ausflucht *f*; **23.** ~ ***of crop*** ⚒ *Brit.* Fruchtwechsel *m*; **24.** *geol.* Verwerfung *f*; **25.** ♪ a) Lagenwechsel *m* (*Streichinstrumente*), b) Zugwechsel *m* (*Posaune*), c) Verschiebung *f* (*Klavierpedal etc.*); **26.** *ling.* Lautverschiebung *f*; **27.** *Kugelstoßen*: Angleiten *n*; **28.** *obs.* ('Unter-) Hemd *n der Frau*; '**shift·er** [-tə] *s.* **1.** *thea.* Ku'lissenschieber *m*; **2.** *fig.* schlauer Fuchs; **3.** ⚙ a) Schalter *m*, b) Ausrückvorrichtung *f*; '**shift·i·ness** [-tɪnɪs] *s.* **1.** Gewandtheit *f*; **2.** Verschlagenheit *f*; **3.** Unzuverlässigkeit *f*; '**shift·ing** [-tɪŋ] *adj.* sich verschiebend, veränderlich: ~ ***sand*** Treib-, Flugsand *m*.

shift key *s.* 'Umschalter *m* (*Schreibmaschine*).

shift·less ['ʃɪftlɪs] *adj.* □ **1.** hilflos (*a. fig. unfähig*); **2.** unbeholfen, einfallslos; **3.** träge, faul.

shift| work *s.* **1.** Schichtarbeit *f*; **2.** *ped.* 'Schichtˌunterricht *m*; ~ **work·er** *s.* Schichtarbeiter(in).

shift·y ['ʃɪftɪ] *adj.* □ **1.** a) wendig, b) schlau, gerissen, c) verschlagen, falsch; **2.** *fig.* unstet.

shil·ling ['ʃɪlɪŋ] *s. Brit. obs.* Schilling *m*: ***a ~ in the pound*** 5 Prozent; ***pay twenty ~s in the pound*** s-e Schulden *etc.* auf Heller u. Pfennig bezahlen; ***cut s.o. off with a ~*** j-n enterben; ~ **shock·er** *s.* 'Schundroˌman *m*.

shil·ly-shal·ly ['ʃɪlɪˌʃælɪ] **I** *v/i.* zögern, schwanken; **II** *s.* Schwanken *n*, Zögern *n*; **III** *adj. u. adv.* zögernd, schwankend.

shim [ʃɪm] ⚙ *s.* Keil *m*, Klemmstück *n*, Ausgleichsscheibe *f*.

shim·mer ['ʃɪmə] **I** *v/i.* schimmern; **II** *s.* Schimmer *m*; '**shim·mer·y** [-ərɪ] *adj.* schimmernd.

shim·my ['ʃɪmɪ] **I** *s.* **1.** Shimmy *m* (*Tanz*); **2.** ⚙ Flattern *n* (*der Vorderräder*); **3.** F (Damen)Hemd *n*; **II** *v/i.* **4.** Shimmy tanzen; **5.** ⚙ flattern (*Vorderräder*).

shin [ʃɪn] **I** *s.* **1.** Schienbein *n*; **2.** ~ ***of beef*** Rinderhachse *f*; **II** *v/i.* **3.** ~ ***up*** *e-n Baum etc.* hin'aufklettern; **4.** *Am.* rennen; **III** *v/t.* **5.** *j-n* ans Schienbein treten; **6.** ~ ***o.s.*** sich das Schienbein verletzen; '~·**bone** *s.* Schienbein(knochen *m*) *n*.

shin·dig ['ʃɪndɪg] *s.* **1.** *sl.* ‚Schwof' *m*, Tanz(veranstaltung *f*) *m*; *weitS.* (‚wilde') Party; **2.** → ***shindy***.

shin·dy ['ʃɪndɪ] *s.* F Krach *m*, Ra'dau *m*.

shine [ʃaɪn] **I** *v/i.* [*irr.*] **1.** scheinen; leuchten, strahlen (*a. Augen etc.*; ***with joy*** vor Freude): ~ ***out*** hervorleuchten, *fig.* herausragen; ~ (***up***)***on*** *et.* beleuchten; ~ ***up to*** *Am. sl.* sich bei *j-m* anbiedern; **2.** glänzen (*a. fig. sich hervortun* ***as*** als, ***at*** in *dat.*); **II** *v/t.* **3.** F *Schuhe etc.* polieren; **III** *s.* **4.** (*Sonnen- etc.*) Schein *m*; → ***rain*** 1; **5.** Glanz *m*: ***take the ~ out of*** a) *e-r Sache* den Glanz nehmen, b) *et. od. j-n* in den Schatten stellen; **6.** Glanz *m* (*bsd. auf Schuhen*): ***have a ~?*** Schuhputzen gefällig?; **7.** ***kick up a ~*** F Radau machen; **8.** ***take a ~ to s.o.*** F j-n ins Herz schließen; '**shin·er** [-nə] *s.* **1.** glänzender Gegenstand; **2.** *sl.* a) Goldmünze *f* (*bsd. Sovereign*), b) Dia'mant *m*, c) *pl.* ‚Kies' *m* (*Geld*); **3.** *sl.* ‚Veilchen' *n*, blau(geschlagen)es Auge.

shin·gle¹ ['ʃɪŋgl] **I** *s.* **1.** (Dach)Schindel *f*; **2.** Herrenschnitt *m* (*Damenfrisur*); **3.** *Am.* F (Firmen)Schild *n*: ***hang out one's ~*** sich (als Arzt *etc.*) etablieren, ‚s-n eigenen Laden aufmachen'; **II** *v/t.* **4.** mit Schindeln decken; **5.** *Haar* (sehr) kurz schneiden: ***~d hair*** → 2.

shin·gle² ['ʃɪŋgl] *s. Brit.* **1.** grober Strandkies(el) *m*; **2.** Kiesstrand *m*.

shin·gle³ ['ʃɪŋgl] *v/t. metall.* zängen.

shin·gles ['ʃɪŋglz] *s. pl. sg. konstr.* ⚕ Gürtelrose *f*.

shin·gly ['ʃɪŋglɪ] *adj.* kies(el)ig.

shin·ing ['ʃaɪnɪŋ] *adj.* □ leuchtend (*a. fig. Beispiel*), strahlend; glänzend (*a. fig.*): ***a ~ light*** e-e Leuchte (*Person*).

shin·ny ['ʃɪnɪ] *v/i. Am.* F klettern.

shin·y ['ʃaɪnɪ] *adj. allg.* glänzend: a) leuchtend (*a. fig.*), funkelnd (*a. Auto etc.*), b) strahlend (*Tag etc.*), c) blank (-geputzt), d) abgetragen: ***a ~ jacket***.

ship [ʃɪp] **I** *s.* **1.** ⚓ *allg.* Schiff *n*: ***~'s articles*** → ***shipping articles***; ***~'s company*** Besatzung *f*; ***~'s husband*** Mitreeder *m*; ***~'s papers*** Schiffspapiere; ***~ of the desert*** *fig.* Wüstenschiff (*Kamel*); ***take ~*** sich einschiffen (***for*** nach); ***about ~!*** klar zum Wenden!; ***when my ~ comes home*** *fig.* wenn ich mein Glück mache; **2.** ⚓ Vollschiff *n* (*Segelschiff*); **3.** Boot *n*; **4.** *Am.* a) Luftschiff *n*, b) Flugzeug *n*, c) Raumschiff *n*; **II** *v/t.* **5.** an Bord bringen *od.* (*a. Passagiere*) nehmen, verladen; **6.** ⚓ verschiffen, transportieren; **7.** ⚚ a) verladen, b) versenden, -frachten, (aus-) liefern (*a. zu Lande*), c) *Ware zur Verladung* abladen, d) ⚓ *Ladung* über'nehmen: ~ ***a sea*** e-e See (*Sturzwelle*) übernehmen; **8.** ⚓ *Ruder* einlegen, *Mast* einsetzen: ~ ***the oars*** die Riemen einlegen; **9.** ⚓ *Matrosen* (an)heuern; **10.** F *a.* ~ ***off*** fortschicken; **III** *v/i.* **11.** sich einschiffen; **12.** sich anheuern lassen; ~ **bis·cuit** *s.* Schiffszwieback *m*; **'~·board** *s.*: ***on*** ~ an Bord; **'~·borne air·craft** *s.* ✈ Bordflugzeug *n*; **'~ˌbuild·er** *s.* ⚓ 'Schiffsarchiˌtekt *m*, -bauer *m*; **'~ˌbuild·ing** *s.* ⚓ Schiff(s)bau *m*; ~ **ca·nal** *s.* ⚓ 'Seekaˌnal *m*; ~ **chan·dler** *s.* Schiffsausrüster *m*; **'~·load** *s.* (volle) Schiffsladung (*als Maß*); **'~ˌmas·ter** *s.* ⚓ ('Handels)Kapiˌtän *m*.

ship·ment ['ʃɪpmənt] *s.* **1.** ⚓ a) Verladung *f*, b) Verschiffung *f*, 'Seetransˌport *m*, c) (Schiffs)Ladung *f*; **2.** ✝ (*a. zu Lande*) a) Versand *m*, b) (Waren)Sendung *f*, Lieferung *f*.

'shipˌown·er *s.* Reeder *m*.

ship·per ['ʃɪpə] *s.* ✝ **1.** Verschiffer *m*, Ablader *m*; **2.** Spedi'teur *m*.

ship·ping ['ʃɪpɪŋ] *s.* **1.** Verschiffung *f*; **2.** ✝ a) Abladung *f* (*Anbordnahme*), b) Verfrachtung *f*, Versand *m* (*a. zu Lande etc.*); **3.** ⚓ *coll.* Schiffsbestand *m* (*e-s Landes etc.*); ~ **a·gent** *s.* **1.** 'Schiffsaˌgent *m*; **2.** Schiffsmakler *m*; ~ **ar·ti·cles** *s. pl.* ⚓ 'Schiffsarˌtikel *pl.*, Heuervertrag *m*; ~ **bill** *s. Brit.* Mani'fest *n*; ~ **clerk** *s.* ✝ Leiter *m* der Versandabteilung; ~ **com·pa·ny** *s.* ⚓ Reede'rei *f*; ~ **fore·cast** *s.* Seewetterbericht *m*.

'ship|·shape *pred. adj. u. adv.* in tadelloser Ordnung, blitzblank; **ˌ~-to-'ship** *adj.* Bord-Bord-…; **ˌ~-to-'shore** *adj.* Bord-Land-…; **'~·way** *s.* Stapel *m*, Helling *f*; **'~·wreck I** *s.* **1.** ⚓ Wrack *n*; **2.** Schiffbruch *m*, *fig. a.* Scheitern *n von Plänen etc.*: ***make*** ~ ***of*** → 4; **II** *v/t.* **3.** scheitern lassen: ***be*** ~***ed*** schiffbrüchig werden *od.* sein; **4.** *fig.* zum Scheitern bringen, vernichten; **III** *v/i.* **5.** Schiffbruch erleiden, scheitern (*beide a. fig.*); **'~·wright** *s.* **1.** → ***shipbuilder***; **2.** Schiffszimmermann *m*; **'~·yard** *s.* (Schiffs)Werft *f*.

shir [ʃɜː] → ***shirr***.

shire ['ʃaɪə] *s.* **1.** brit. Grafschaft *f*; **2.** au'stralischer Landkreis; **3.** *a.* ~ ***horse*** *ein schweres Zugpferd*.

shirk [ʃɜːk] **I** *v/t.* sich drücken vor (*dat.*); **II** *v/i.* sich drücken (***from*** vor *dat.*); **'shirk·er** [-kə] *s.* Drückeberger *m*.

shirr [ʃɜː] **I** *s.* e'lastisches Gewebe, eingewebte Gummischnur, Zugband *n*; **II** *v/t.* *Gewebe* kräuseln; **shirred** [ʃɜːd] *adj.* e'lastisch, gekräuselt.

shirt [ʃɜːt] *s.* **1.** (Herren-, Ober-, *a.* 'Unter-, Nacht)Hemd *n*: ***get s.o.'s*** ~ ***out*** j-n ‚auf die Palme bringen'; ***give away the*** ~ ***off one's back*** sein letztes Hemd *für j-n* hergeben; ***keep one's*** ~ ***on*** *sl.* sich nicht aufregen; ***lose one's*** ~ ‚sein letztes Hemd verlieren'; ***put one's*** ~ ***on*** *sl.* alles auf *ein Pferd etc.* setzen; **2.** *a.* ~ ***blouse*** Hemdbluse *f*; ~ **front** *s.* Hemdbrust *f*.

shirt·ing ['ʃɜːtɪŋ] *s.* Hemdenstoff *m*.

'shirt-sleeve I *s.* Hemdsärmel *m*: ***in one's*** ~***s*** in Hemdsärmeln; **II** *adj. fig.* ‚hemdsärmelig', ungezwungen, le'ger: ~ ***diplomacy*** offene Diplomatie.

shirt·y ['ʃɜːtɪ] *adj. sl.* unverschämt, ungehobelt.

shit [ʃɪt] V **I** *s.* **1.** Scheiße *f*: ***have a*** ~ scheißen; **2.** *fig.* ‚Scheiße' *f*, ‚Scheiß (-dreck)' *m*; **3.** *fig.* Arschloch *n*; **4.** *pl.* ‚Scheiße'rei' *f*; **5.** *sl.* ‚Shit' *n* (*Haschisch*); **II** *v/i.* [*irr.*] **6.** scheißen: ~ ***on*** a) auf *j-n od. et.* scheißen, b) *fig. j-n* ‚verpfeifen'; **III** *v/t.* **7.** vollscheißen, scheißen in (*acc.*); **shit·ty** ['ʃɪtɪ] *adj.* ‚beschissen'.

shiv·er¹ ['ʃɪvə] **I** *s.* **1.** Splitter *m*, (Bruch-) Stück *n*, Scherbe *f*; **2.** *min.* Dachschiefer *m*; **II** *v/t.* **3.** zersplittern, zerschmettern; **III** *v/i.* **4.** (zer)splittern.

shiv·er² ['ʃɪvə] **I** *v/i.* **1.** (***with*** vor *dat.*) zittern, (er)schauern, frösteln; **2.** flattern (*Segel*); **II** *s.* **3.** Schauer *m*, Zittern *n*, Frösteln *n*: ***the*** ~***s*** a) ⚕ der Schüttelfrost, b) F *fig.* das kalte Grausen; **'shiv·er·ing** [-vərɪŋ] *s.* Schauer(n *n*) *m*: ~ ***fit*** Schüttelfrost *m*; **'shiv·er·y** [-ərɪ] *adj.* **1.** fröstelnd; **2.** fiebrig.

shoal¹ [ʃəʊl] **I** *s.* Schwarm *m*, Zug *m von Fischen*; *fig.* Unmenge *f*, Masse *f*; **II** *v/i.* in Schwärmen auftreten.

shoal² [ʃəʊl] **I** *s.* **1.** Untiefe *f*, seichte Stelle; Sandbank *f*; **2.** *fig.* Klippe *f*; **II** *adj.* **3.** seicht; **III** *v/i.* **4.** seicht(er) werden; **'shoal·y** [-lɪ] *adj.* seicht.

shock¹ [ʃɒk] **I** *s.* **1.** Stoß *m*, Erschütterung *f* (*a. fig. des Vertrauens etc.*); **2.** Zs.-stoß *m*, Zs.-prall *m*, Anprall *m*; **3.** ⚕ (Nerven)Schock *m*, Schreck *m*, (plötzlicher) Schlag (***to*** für), *seelische* Erschütterung (***to*** *gen.*): ***be in*** (***a state of***) ~ e-n Schock haben; ***get the*** ~ ***of one's life*** a) zu Tode erschrecken, b) sein blaues Wunder erleben; ***with a*** ~ mit Schrecken; **4.** Schock *m*, Ärgernis *n* (***to*** für); **5.** ⚡ Schlag *m*, (*a.* ⚕ E'lektro-) Schock *m*; **II** *v/t.* **6.** erschüttern, erbeben lassen; **7.** *fig.* schockieren, em'pören: ~***ed*** empört *od.* entrüstet (***at*** über *acc.*, ***by*** durch); **8.** *fig. j-m* e-n Schock versetzen, *j-n* erschüttern: ***I was*** ~***ed to hear*** zu m-m Entsetzen hörte ich; **9.** *j-m* e-n e'lektrischen Schlag versetzen; ⚕ *j-n* schocken.

shock² [ʃɒk] ⚘ **I** *s.* Mandel *f*, Hocke *f*; **II** *v/t.* in Mandeln aufstellen.

shock³ [ʃɒk] **I** *s.* (~ ***of hair*** Haar)Schopf *m*; **II** *adj.* zottig: ~ ***head*** Strubbelkopf *m*.

shock| ab·sorb·er *s.* ⚙ **1.** Stoßdämpfer *m*; **2.** 'Schwingmeˌtall *n*; ~ **ab·sorp·tion** *s.* ⚙ Stoßdämpfung *f*.

shock·er ['ʃɒkə] *s.* **1.** *allg.* ‚Schocker' *m*; **2.** Elektri'sierappaˌrat *m*.

'shock-ˌhead·ed *adj.* strubb(e)lig: ~ ***Peter*** (der) Struwwelpeter.

shock·ing ['ʃɒkɪŋ] **I** *adj.* □ **1.** schockierend, em'pörend, unerhört, anstößig; **2.** entsetzlich, haarsträubend; **3.** F scheußlich, schrecklich, mise'rabel; **II** *adv.* F **4.** schrecklich, unheimlich (*groß etc.*).

'shock|·proof *adj.* ⚙ stoß-, erschütterungsfest; ~ **tac·tics** *s. pl. sg. konstr.* ⚔ 'Durchbruchs-, Stoßtaktik *f*; ~ **ther·a·py**, ~ **treat·ment** *s.* ⚕ 'Schocktheraˌpie *f*, -behandlung *f*; ~ **troops** *s. pl.* ⚔ Stoßtruppen *pl.*; ~ **wave** *s.* Druckwelle *f*; *fig.* Erschütterung *f*, Schock *m*; ~ **work·er** *s. DDR etc.*: Stoßarbeiter *m*.

shod [ʃɒd] **I** *pret. u. p.p. von* ***shoe***; **II** *adj.* **1.** beschuht; **2.** beschlagen (*Pferd, Stock etc.*); **3.** bereift.

shod·dy ['ʃɒdɪ] **I** *s.* **1.** Shoddy *n*, (langfaserige) Reißwolle; **2.** Shoddytuch *n*; **3.** *fig.* Schund *m*, Kitsch *m*; **4.** *fig.* Protzentum *n*; **II** *adj.* **5.** Shoddy…; **6.** *fig.* a) unecht, falsch: ~ ***aristocracy*** Talmiaristokratie *f*, b) kitschig, Schund…: ~ ***literature***, c) protzig.

shoe [ʃuː] **I** *s.* **1.** (*bsd. Brit.* Halb)Schuh *m*: ***dead men's*** ~***s*** *fig.* ungeduldig erwartetes Erbe; ***be in s.o.'s*** ~***s*** *fig.* in j-s Haut stecken; ***know where the*** ~ ***pinches*** *fig.* wissen, wo der Schuh drückt; ***shake in one's*** ~***s*** *fig.* vor Angst schlottern; ***step into s.o.'s*** ~***s*** j-s Stelle einnehmen; ***that is another pair of*** ~***s*** *fig.* das sind zwei Paar Stiefel; ***now the*** ~ ***is on the other foot*** F jetzt will er *etc.* (plötzlich) nichts mehr davon wissen; **2.** Hufeisen *n*; **3.** ⚙ Schuh *m*, (Schutz)Beschlag *m*; **4.** ⚙ a) Bremsschuh *m*, -klotz *m*, b) Bremsbacke *f*; **5.** ⚙ (Reifen)Decke *f*; **6.** ⚡ Gleitschuh *m*; **II** *v/t.* [*irr.*] **7.** a) beschuhen, b) *Pferd, a. Stock* beschlagen; **'~·black** *s.* Schuhputzer *m*; **'~·horn** *s.* Schuhlöffel *m*; **'~·lace** *s.* Schnürsenkel *m*; **'~ˌmak·er** *s.* Schuhmacher *m*: ~***'s thread*** Pechdraht *m*; **'~·shine** *s. Am.* Schuhputzen *n*: ~ ***boy*** Schuhputzer *m*; **'~·string I** *s.* → ***shoelace***: ***on a*** ~ F mit ein paar Groschen, praktisch mit nichts *anfangen etc.*; **II** *adj.* F a) fi'nanzschwach, b) ‚klein', c) armselig.

shone [ʃɒn] *pret. u. p.p. von* ***shine***.

shoo [ʃuː] **I** *int.* **1.** husch!, sch!, fort!; **II** *v/t.* **2.** *a.* ~ ***away*** *Vögel etc.* verscheuchen; **3.** *Am.* F *j-n* ‚scheuchen'; **III** *v/i.* **4.** husch! *od.* sch! rufen.

shook¹ [ʃʊk] *bsd. Am. s.* **1.** Bündel *n* Faßdauben; **2.** Pack *m* Kistenbretter; **3.** → ***shock²*** I.

shook² [ʃʊk] *pret. von* ***shake***.

shoot [ʃuːt] **I** *s.* **1.** a) (*a.* Wett)Schießen *n*, b) Schuß *m*; **2.** *hunt.* a) Jagd *f*, b) 'Jagd(reˌvier *n*) *f*, c) Jagdgesellschaft *f*, d) *Am.* Strecke *f*; **3.** *Am.* Ra'ketenabschuß *m*; **4.** *phot.* (Film)Aufnahme *f*; **5.** (Holz- *etc.*)Rutsche *f*, Rutschbahn *f*; **6.** Stromschnelle *f*; **7.** ⚘ Schößling *m*, Trieb *m*; **II** *v/t.* [*irr.*] **8.** *Pfeil, Kugel etc.* (ab)schießen, (-)feuern: ~ ***questions at s.o.*** j-n mit Fragen bombardieren; → ***shoot off*** I; **9.** a) *Wild* schießen, erlegen, b) *a. j-n* anschießen, c) *a.* ~ ***dead*** *j-n* erschießen (***for*** wegen); **10.** *hunt.* in *e-m Revier* jagen; **11.** *sport Ball, Tor* schießen; **12.** ⚓ *Sonne etc.* schießen (*Höhe messen*); → ***moon*** 1; **13.** *fig. Strahl etc.* schießen, senden: ~ ***a glance at*** e-n schnellen Blick werfen auf (*acc.*); **14.** a) *Film, Szene* drehen, b) ‚schießen', aufnehmen, fotografieren; **15.** *fig.* stoßen, schleudern, werfen; **16.** *fig.* unter *e-r Brücke etc.* hin'durchschießen, über *e-e Stromschnelle etc.* hin'wegschießen; **17.** *Riegel* vorschieben; **18.** *mit Fäden* durch'schießen, -'wirken; **19.** *a.* ~ ***forth*** ⚘ *Knospen etc.* treiben; **20.** *Müll, Karren etc.* abladen, auskippen; **21.** *Faß* schroten; **22.** ⚕ (ein)spritzen; → ***shoot up*** 2; **III** *v/i.* [*irr.*] **23.** *a. sport* schießen, feuern (***at*** nach, auf *acc.*): ~! *Am. sl.* schieß los! (*sprich!*); **24.** *hunt.* jagen, schießen: ***go*** ~***ing*** auf die Jagd gehen; **25.** *fig.* (da'hin-, vor'bei- *etc.*)schießen, (-)jagen, (-)rasen: ~ ***ahead*** nach vorn schießen, voranstürmen; ~ ***ahead of*** vorbeischießen an (*dat.*), überholen; **26.** stechen (*Schmerz, Glied*); **27.** *a.* ~ ***forth*** ⚘ sprossen, keimen; **28.** a) filmen, b) fotografieren; **29.** ⚓ 'überschießen (*Ballast*);

Zssgn mit adv.:

shoot| down *v/t.* **1.** *j-n* niederschießen; **2.** *Flugzeug etc.* abschießen; **3.** F ‚abschmettern'; **~ off I** *v/t. Waffe* abschießen: **~ one's mouth** a) ‚blöd daherreden', b) ‚quatschen', ‚(weiter-)tratschen'; **II** *v/i.* stechen (*bei gleicher Trefferzahl*); **~ out I** *v/t.* **1.** *Auge etc.* ausschießen; **2. shoot it out** die Sache mit ‚blauen Bohnen' entscheiden; **3.** her'ausschleudern, hin'auswerfen; **4.** *Faust, Fuß* vorschnellen (lassen); *Zunge* her'ausstrecken; **5.** her'ausragen lassen; **II** *v/i.* **6.** ⚘ her'vorsprießen; **7.** vor-, her'ausschnellen; **~ up I** *v/t.* **1.** *sl.* zs.-schießen; **2.** *sl. Heroin etc.* ‚drücken'; **II** *v/i.* **3.** in die Höhe schießen, rasch wachsen (*Pflanze, Kind*); **4.** em'porschnellen (*a.* † *Preise*); **5.** (jäh) aufragen (*Klippe etc.*).

shoot·er ['ʃu:tə] *s.* **1.** Schütze *m*, Schützin *f*; **2.** F ‚Schießeisen' *n*.

shoot·ing ['ʃu:tɪŋ] **I** *s.* **1.** a) Schießen *n*, b) Schieße'rei *f*; **2.** Erschießen *n*; **3.** *fig.* Stechen *n* (*Schmerz*); **4.** *hunt.* a) Jagd *f*, b) Jagdrecht *n*, c) 'Jagdreˌvier *n*; **5.** Aufnahme(n *pl.*) *f zu e-m Film*, Dreharbeiten *pl.*; **II** *adj.* **6.** schießend, Schieß…; **7.** *fig.* stechend (*Schmerz*); **8.** Jagd…; **~ box** *s.* Jagdhütte *f*; **~ gal·ler·y** *s.* **1.** ⚔, *sport* Schießstand *m*; **2.** Schießbude *f*; **~ i·ron** *s. sl.* ‚Schießeisen' *n*; **~ li·cense** *s.* Jagdschein *m*; **~ match** *s.* Preis-, Wettschießen *n*: **the whole ~** F der ganze ‚Kram'; **~ range** *s.* Schießstand *m*; **~ star** *s. ast.* Sternschnuppe *f*; **~ war** *s.* heißer Krieg, Schießkrieg *m*.

shop [ʃɒp] **I** *s.* **1.** (Kauf)Laden *m*, Geschäft *n*: **set up ~** ein Geschäft eröffnen; **shut up ~** das Geschäft schließen, den Laden dichtmachen (*a. für immer*); **come to the wrong ~** F an die falsche Adresse geraten; **all over the ~** *sl.* a) überall verstreut, b) in alle Himmelsrichtungen; **2.** ⚙ Werkstatt *f*; **3.** a) Betrieb *m*, Fa'brik *f*, b) Ab'teilung *f in e-r Fabrik*: **talk ~** fachsimpeln; **sink the ~** F a) nicht vom Geschäft reden, b) s-n Beruf verheimlichen; → **closed shop**, **open shop**; **4.** *bsd. Brit. sl.* a) ‚Laden' *m* (*Institut etc.*), ‚Penne' *f* (*Schule*), ‚Uni' *f* (*Universität*), b) ‚Kittchen' *n* (*Gefängnis*); **II** *v/i.* **5.** einkaufen, Einkäufe machen: **go ~ping**; **~ around** F a) *vor dem Einkauf* die Preise vergleichen, b) *fig.* sich umsehen (**for** nach); **III** *v/t.* **6.** *bsd. Brit. sl.* a) *j-n* ‚verpfeifen', b) *j-n* ‚ins Kittchen bringen'; **~ as·sist·ant** *s. Brit.* Verkäufer(in); **~ com·mit·tee** *s.* † *Am.* Betriebsrat *m*; **'~ˌfit·ter** *s.* Ladeneinrichter *m*, -ausstatter *m*; **~ floor** *s.* **1.** Produkti'onsstätte *f*; **2.** Arbeiter *pl.*, Belegschaft *f*; **'~·girl** *s.* Ladenmädchen *n*; **'~ˌkeep·er** *s.* Ladenbesitzer(in): **nation of ~s** *fig. contp.* Krämervolk *n*; **'~ˌkeep·ing** *s.* **1.** Kleinhandel *m*; **2.** Betrieb *m e-s* (Laden)Geschäfts; **'~ˌlift·er** *s.* Ladendieb(in); **'~ˌlift·ing** *s.* Ladendiebstahl *m*.

shop·per ['ʃɒpə] *s.* (Ein)Käufer(in); **shop·ping** ['ʃɒpɪŋ] *s.* **1.** Einkauf *m*, Einkaufen *n* (*in Läden*): **~ centre** *Brit.*, **~ center** *Am.* Einkaufszentrum *n*; **~ list** Einkaufsliste *f*; **do one's ~** (seine) Einkäufe machen; **2.** Einkäufe *pl.* (*Ware*).

ˌ**shop|-'soiled** *adj.* **1.** † angestaubt, beschädigt; **2.** *fig.* abgenutzt; **~ stew·ard** *s.* † (gewerkschaftlicher) Vertrauensmann; **'~·talk** *s.* Fachsimpe'lei *f*; **'~ˌwalk·er** *s. Brit.* (aufsichtführender) Ab'teilungsleiter (*im Kaufhaus*); ˌ**~'win·dow** *s.* Schaufenster *n*, Auslage *f*: **put all one's goods in the ~** *fig.* ‚ganz auf Wirkung machen'; **'~·worn** → **shop-soiled**.

shore¹ [ʃɔ:] **I** *s.* **1.** Stütz-, Strebebalken *m*, Strebe *f*; **2.** ⚓ Schore *f* (*Spreizholz*); **II** *v/t.* **3.** *mst* **~ up** a) abstützen, b) *fig.* (unter)'stützen.

shore² [ʃɔ:] **I** *s.* **1.** Küste *f*, Strand *m*, Ufer *n*, Gestade *n*: **my native ~** *fig.* mein Heimatland; **2.** ⚓ Land *n*: **on ~** an(s) Land; **in ~** in Küstennähe; **II** *adj.* **3.** Küsten…, Strand…, Land…: **~ battery** ⚔ Küstenbatterie *f*; **~ leave** ⚓ Landurlaub *m*; **'shore·less** [-lɪs] *adj.* ohne Ufer, uferlos (*a. poet. fig.*); **'shore·ward** [-wəd] **I** *adj.* küstenwärts gelegen *od.* gerichtet *etc.*; **II** *adv. a.* **~s** küstenwärts, (nach) der Küste zu.

shorn [ʃɔ:n] *p.p. von* **shear**: **~ of** *fig. e-r Sache* beraubt.

short [ʃɔ:t] **I** *adj.* □ → **shortly**; **1.** *räumlich u. zeitlich* kurz: **a ~ life**; **a ~ memory**; **a ~ street**; **a ~ time ago** vor kurzer Zeit, vor kurzem; **~ sight** Kurzsichtigkeit *f* (*a. fig.*); **get the ~ end of the stick** *Am.* F schlecht wegkommen (*bei e-r Sache*); **have by the ~ hairs** *Am.* F *j-n od. et.* ‚in der Tasche' haben; **2.** kurz, gedrungen, klein; **3.** zu kurz (**for** für): **fall** (*od.* **come**) **~ of** *fig. et.* nicht erreichen, *den Erwartungen etc.* nicht entsprechen, hinter (*dat.*) zurückbleiben; **4.** *fig.* kurz, knapp: **a ~ speech**; **be ~ for** die Kurzform sein von; **5.** kurz angebunden, barsch (**with** gegen); **6.** knapp, unzureichend: **~ rations**; **~ weight** Fehlgewicht *n*; **run ~** knapp werden; **7.** knapp (**of** an *dat.*): **~ of breath** kurzatmig; **~ of cash** knapp bei Kasse; **they ran ~ of bread** das Brot ging ihnen aus; **8.** knapp, nicht ganz: **a ~ hour** (**mile**); **9.** geringer, weniger (**of** als): **nothing ~ of** nichts weniger als, geradezu (→ *a.* 17); **10.** mürbe (*Gebäck etc.*): **~ pastry** Mürbeteig *m*; **11.** *metall.* brüchig; **12.** *bsd.* † kurzfristig, *Wechsel etc.* auf kurze Sicht: **at ~ date** kurzfristig; **at ~ notice** a) kurzfristig (kündbar), b) schnell, prompt; **13.** † *Börse*: a) Baisse…, b) ungedeckt, dekkungslos: **sell ~**; **14.** a) klein, in e-m Gläs-chen serviert, b) stark (*Getränk*); **II** *adv.* **15.** kurz(erhand), plötzlich, ab'rupt: **cut s.o. ~**, **take s.o. up ~** j-n (jäh) unterbrechen; **be taken ~** F ‚dringend (austreten) müssen'; **stop ~** plötzlich innehalten (→ *a.* 17); **16.** zu kurz; **17. ~ of** a) knapp *od.* kurz vor (*dat.*), b) *fig.* abgesehen von, außer (*dat.*): **anything ~ of murder**; **~ of lying** ehe ich lüge; **stop ~ of** zurückschrecken vor (*dat.*); **III** *s.* **18.** *et.* Kurzes, *z. B.* Kurzfilm *m*; **19. in ~** kurzum; **called Bill for ~** kurz *od.* der Kürze halber Bill genannt; **20.** ⚡ F ‚Kurze(r)' *m* (*Kurzschluß*); **21.** † a) 'Baissespekuˌlant *m*, b) *pl.* ohne Deckung verkaufte 'Wertpaˌpiere *pl. od.* Waren *pl.*; **22.** *ling.* a) kurzer Vo'kal, b) kurze Silbe; **23.** *pl.* a) Shorts *pl.*, kurze Hose, b) *Am.* kurze 'Unterhose; **IV** *v/t.* **24.** F → **short-circuit** 1, 2; **'short·age** [-tɪdʒ] *s.* **1.** Knappheit *f*, Mangel *m* (**of** an *dat.*); **2.** Fehlbetrag *m*, Defizit *n*.

'short|·bread, **'~·cake** *s.* Mürbe-, Teekuchen *m*; ˌ**~'change** *v/t.* F *j-m* zu'wenig (Wechselgeld) her'ausgeben; *fig. j-n* ‚übers Ohr hauen'; **~ cir·cuit** *s.* ⚡ Kurzschluß *m*; ˌ**~-'cir·cuit** *v/t.* **1.** ⚡ e-n Kurzschluß verursachen in (*dat.*); **2.** ⚡ kurzschließen; **3.** *fig.* F a) *et.* ‚torpedieren', b) *et.* um'gehen; ˌ**~'com·ing** *s.* **1.** Unzulänglichkeit *f*; **2.** Fehler *m*, Mangel *m*; **3.** Pflichtversäumnis *n*; **4.** Fehlbetrag *m*; **~ cut** *s.* Abkürzung *f* (*Weg*); *fig.* abgekürztes Verfahren: **take a ~** (den Weg) abkürzen; ˌ**~'dat·ed** *adj.* † kurzfristig: **~ bond**; ˌ**~'dis·tance** *adj.* Nah…

short·en ['ʃɔ:tn] **I** *v/t.* **1.** (ab-, ver)kürzen, kürzer machen; *Bäume etc.* stutzen; *fig.* vermindern; **2.** ⚓ *Segel* reffen; **3.** *Teig* mürbe machen; **II** *v/i.* **4.** kürzer werden; **5.** fallen (*Preise*); **'short·en·ing** [-nɪŋ] *s.* **1.** (Ab-, Ver)Kürzung *f*; **2.** (Ver)Minderung *f*; **3.** Backfett *n*.

'short|·fall *s.* Fehlbetrag *m*; **'~·hand I** *s.* **1.** Kurzschrift *f*; **II** *adj.* **2.** in Kurzschrift (geschrieben), stenographiert; **3.** Kurzschrift…: **~ typist** Stenotypistin *f*; **~ writer** Stenograph(in); ˌ**~-'hand·ed** *adj.* knapp an Arbeitskräften; **~ haul** *s.* Nahverkehr *m*; **'~·horn** *s. zo.* Shorthorn *n*, Kurzhornrind *n*.

short·ie ['ʃɔ:tɪ] → **shorty**.

short·ish ['ʃɔ:tɪʃ] *adj.* etwas *od.* ziemlich kurz (geraten).

short| list *s.*: **be on the ~** in der engeren Wahl sein; **'~-list** *v/t. j-n* in die engere Wahl ziehen; ˌ**~'lived** [-'lɪvd] *adj.* kurzlebig, *fig. a.* von kurzer Dauer.

short·ly ['ʃɔ:tlɪ] *adv.* **1.** in Kürze, bald: **~ after** kurz (da)nach; **2.** in kurzen Worten; **3.** kurz (angebunden), schroff; **short·ness** ['ʃɔ:tnɪs] *s.* **1.** Kürze *f*; **2.** Schroffheit *f*; **3.** Knappheit *f*, Mangel *m* (**of** an *dat.*): **~ of breath** Kurzatmigkeit *f*; **4.** Mürbe *f* (*Gebäck etc.*).

'short|-range *adj.* **1.** Kurzstrecken…, Nah…, ⚔ *a.* Nahkampf…; **2.** *fig.* kurzfristig; **~ rib** *s. anat.* falsche Rippe; **~ sale** *s.* † Leerverkauf *m*; ˌ**~-'sight·ed** [-'saɪtɪd] *adj.* □ kurzsichtig (*a. fig.*); ˌ**~-'sight·ed·ness** [-'saɪtɪdnɪs] *s.* Kurzsichtigkeit *f* (*a. fig.*); ˌ**~-'spo·ken** *adj.* kurz angebunden, schroff; **~ sto·ry** *s.* Kurzgeschichte *f*; **~ tem·per** *s.* Reizbarkeit *f*, Heftigkeit *f*; ˌ**~-'tem·pered** *adj.* reizbar, aufbrausend; **'~-term** *adj. bsd.* † kurzfristig: **~ credit**; **~ time** *s.* † Kurzarbeit *f*: **work** (*od.* **be on**) **~** kurzarbeiten; **~ ton** *s. bsd. Am.* Tonne *f* (*2000 lbs.*); **~ wave** *s.* ⚡ Kurzwelle *f*; ˌ**~-'wave** *adj.* ⚡ **1.** kurzwellig; **2.** Kurzwellen…; **~ wind** *s.* Kurzatmigkeit *f* (*a. fig.*); ˌ**~-'wind·ed** *adj.* kurzatmig (*a. fig.*).

short·y ['ʃɔ:tɪ] *s.* F **1.** ‚Knirps' *m*; **2.** a) kleines Ding, b) kurze Sache.

shot¹ [ʃɒt] **I** *pret. u. p.p. von* **shoot**; **II** *adj.* **1.** *a.* **~ through** durch'schossen, gesprenkelt (*Seide etc.*); **2.** changierend, schillernd (*Stoff, Farbe*); **3.** *sl.* ‚ka'putt', erschöpft.

shot² [ʃɒt] *s.* **1.** Schuß *m* (*a. Knall*): **a long ~** *fig.* ein kühner Versuch; **by a long ~** *sl.* weitaus; **not by a long ~** längst nicht, kein bißchen; **call the ~s**

fig. ,am Drücker sein', das Sagen haben; ***like a ~*** F wie der Blitz, sofort; ***take a ~ at*** schießen auf (*acc.*); **2.** Schußweite *f*: ***out of ~*** außer Schußweite; **3.** *a.* ***small ~*** a) Schrotkugel *f*, -korn *n*, b) *coll.* Schrot(kugeln *pl.*) *m*; **4.** (Ka'nonen)Kugel *f*, Geschoß *n*: ***a ~ in the locker*** F Geld in der Tasche; **5.** *guter etc.* Schütze: ***big ~*** F ,großes *od.* hohes Tier'; **6.** *sport* Schuß *m*, Wurf *m*, Stoß *m*, Schlag *m*; **7.** *sport* Kugel *f*: → ***shot put***; **8.** a) (Film)Aufnahme *f*, (-)Szene *f*, b) *phot.* F Aufnahme *f*, Schnappschuß *m*; **9.** *fig.* Versuch *m*: ***at the third ~*** beim dritten Versuch; ***have a ~ at*** es (einmal) mit *et.* versuchen; **10.** *fig.* (Seiten)Hieb *m*; **11.** ⚕ Spritze *f* (*Injektion*): ***~ in the arm*** F *fig.* ,Spritze' *f* (*bsd.* † *finanzielle Hilfe*); **12.** F Schuß *m Rum etc.*; ,Gläs-chen' *n Schnaps*: ***stand ~*** die Zeche (für alle) bezahlen; **13.** ⚙ a) Sprengladung *f*, b) Sprengung *f*; **14.** *Am. sl.* Chance *f*; **'~·gun** *s.* Schrotflinte *f*: ***~ wedding*** F ,Mußheirat' *f*; **~ put** *s. sport* a) Kugelstoßen *n*, b) Stoß *m*; **'~-ˌput·ter** *s. sport* Kugelstoßer(in).

shot·ten ['ʃɒtn] *adj. ichth.* gelaicht habend: ***~ herring*** Laichhering *m*.

shot weld·ing *s.* ⚙ Schußschweißen *n*.

should [ʃʊd; ʃəd] **1.** *pret. von* **shall**, *a. konditional futurisch*: *ich*, *er*, *sie*, *es* sollte, *du* solltest, *wir*, *Ihr*, *Sie*, *sie* sollten: ***I ~ have gone*** ich hätte gehen sollen; ***if he ~ come*** falls er kommen sollte; ***~ it prove false*** sollte es sich als falsch erweisen; **2.** *konditional*: *ich* würde, *wir* würden: ***I ~ go if ...***; ***I ~ not have come if*** ich wäre nicht gekommen, wenn; ***I ~ like to*** ich würde *od.* möchte gern; **3.** *nach Ausdrücken des Erstaunens*: ***it is incredible that he ~ have failed*** es ist unglaublich, daß er versagt hat.

shoul·der ['ʃəʊldə] **I** *s.* **1.** Schulter *f*, Achsel *f*: ***~ to ~*** *bsd. fig.* Schulter an Schulter; ***put one's ~ to the wheel*** *fig.* sich tüchtig ins Zeug legen; (***straight***) ***from the ~*** *fig.* unverblümt, geradeheraus; ***give s.o. the cold ~*** *fig.* j-m die kalte Schulter zeigen; → ***rub*** 7; ***he has broad ~s*** *fig.* er hat e-n breiten Rükken; **2.** Bug *m*, Schulterstück *n* (*von Tieren*): ***~ of mutton*** Hammelkeule *f*; **3.** *fig.* Schulter *f*, Vorsprung *m*; **4.** *a.* ***hard ~*** a) Ban'kett *n*, Seitenstreifen *m*, b) *mot.* Standspur *f*; **5.** ✈ 'Übergangsstreifen *m* (*Flugplatz*); **II** *v/t.* **6.** (mit der Schulter) stoßen *od.* drängen: ***~ one's way through the crowd*** sich e-n Weg durch die Menge bahnen; **7.** *et.* schultern, auf die Schulter nehmen; ⚔ *Gewehr* 'übernehmen; *Aufgabe*, *Verantwortung etc.* auf sich nehmen; **~ bag** *s.* 'Umhängetasche *f*; **~ belt** *s.* **1.** ⚔ Schulterriemen *m*; **2.** *mot.* Schultergurt *m*; **~ blade** *s. anat.* Schulterblatt *n*; **~ strap** *s.* **1.** Träger *m* (*bsd. an Damenunterwäsche*); **2.** ⚔ Schulterstück *n*.

should·n't ['ʃʊdnt] F *für* ***should not***.

shout [ʃaʊt] **I** *v/i.* **1.** (laut) rufen, schreien (***for*** nach): ***~ to s.o.*** j-m zurufen; **2.** schreien, brüllen (***with*** vor *Schmerz*, *Lachen*): ***~ at s.o.*** j-n anschreien; **3.** jauchzen (***for***, ***with*** vor *dat.*); **II** *v/t.* **4.** (laut) rufen, schreien: ***~ disapproval*** laut sein Mißfallen äußern; ***~ s.o. down*** j-n niederbrüllen; ***~ out*** a) herausschreien, b) *Namen etc.* ausrufen; **III** *s.* **5.** Schrei *m*, Ruf *m*; **6.** Geschrei *n*, Gebrüll *n*: ***a ~ of laughter*** brüllendes Lachen; **7.** ***my ~!*** F jetzt bin ich dran! (*zum Stiften von Getränken*); **'shout·ing** [-tɪŋ] *s.* Schreien *n*, Geschrei *n*: ***all is over but*** *od.* ***bar the ~*** es ist so gut wie gelaufen.

shove [ʃʌv] **I** *v/t.* **1.** *beiseite etc.* schieben, stoßen: ***~ s.o. around*** *bsd. fig.* F j-n ,herumschubsen'; **2.** (achtlos *od.* rasch) *wohin* schieben, stecken; **II** *v/i.* **3.** schieben, stoßen; **4.** (sich) dränge(l)n; **5.** ***~ off*** a) vom Ufer abstoßen, b) *sl.* ,abschieben', sich da'vonmachen; **III** *s.* **6.** Stoß *m*, Schubs *m*.

shov·el ['ʃʌvl] **I** *s.* **1.** Schaufel *f*; **2.** ⚙ a) Löffel *m* (*e-s Löffelbaggers*), b) Löffelbagger *m*; **II** *v/t.* **3.** schaufeln: ***~ up*** (*od.* ***in***) ***money*** Geld scheffeln; **'shov·el·ful** [-fʊl] *pl.* **-fuls** *s. e-e* Schaufel(voll).

show [ʃəʊ] **I** *s.* **1.** (Her)Zeigen *n*: ***vote by ~ of hands*** durch Handzeichen wählen; **2.** Schau *f*, Zur'schaustellung *f*: ***a ~ of force*** *fig.* e-e Demonstration der Macht; **3.** *künstlerische etc.* Darbietung, Vorführung *f*, -stellung *f*, Show *f*: ***put on a ~*** F *fig.* ,e-e Schau abziehen'; ***steal s.o. the ~*** F *fig.* j-m ,die Schau stehlen'; **4.** F (The'ater-, Film)Vorstellung *f*; **5.** Schau *f*, Ausstellung *f*: ***flower ~***; ***on ~*** ausgestellt, zu besichtigen(d); **6.** *prunkvoller* 'Umzug; **7.** Schaubude *f auf Jahrmärkten*; **8.** Anblick *m*: ***make a sorry ~*** e-n traurigen Eindruck hinterlassen; ***make a good ~*** (e-e) ,gute Figur' machen; **9.** F *gute etc.* Leistung: ***good ~!*** gut gemacht!, bravo!; **10.** Protze'rei *f*, Angebe'rei *f*: ***for ~*** um Eindruck zu machen, (nur) fürs Auge; ***be fond of ~*** gern großtun; ***make a ~ of*** mit *et.* protzen (→ *a.* 11); **11.** (leerer) Schein: ***in outward ~*** nach außen hin; ***make a ~ of rage*** sich wütend stellen; **12.** Spur *f*: ***no ~ of*** keine Spur von; **13.** F Chance *f*: ***give s.o. a ~***; **14.** F ,Laden' *m*, ,Kiste' *f*, ,Kram' *m*: ***run the ~*** *sl.* ,den Laden schmeißen'; ***give the*** (***whole***) ***~ away*** F den ganzen Schwindel verraten; ***a dull*** (***poor***) ***~*** e-e langweilige (armselige) Sache; **II** *v/t.* [*irr.*] **15.** zeigen (***s.o. s.th.***, ***s.th. to s.o.*** j-m et.), sehen lassen, *Fahrkarten etc. a.* vorzeigen, -weisen: ***~ o.s.*** *od.* ***one's face*** sich zeigen *od.* blicken lassen, *fig.* sich *grausam etc.* zeigen, sich erweisen als; ***~ s.o. the door*** j-m die Tür weisen; ***we had nothing to ~ for it*** wir hatten nichts vorzuweisen; **16.** ausstellen, (auf e-r Ausstellung) zeigen; **17.** *thea. etc.* zeigen, vorführen; **18.** *j-n ins Zimmer etc.* geleiten, führen: ***~ s.o. over the house*** j-n durch das Haus führen; **19.** *Absicht etc.* (auf)zeigen, kundtun, darlegen; **20.** zeigen, beweisen, nachweisen; ⚖ *a.* glaubhaft machen: ***~ proof*** den Beweis erbringen; ***that goes to ~ that*** das zeigt *od.* beweist, daß; **21.** zeigen, erkennen lassen, verraten: ***~ bad taste***; **22.** *Gunst etc.* erweisen; **23.** *j-m* zeigen *od.* erklären (*wie et. gemacht wird*): ***~ s.o. how to write*** j-m das Schreiben beibringen; **III** *v/i.* [*irr.*] **24.** sich zeigen, sichtbar werden *od.* sein: ***it ~s*** man sieht es; **25.** F sich *in Gesellschaft* zeigen, erscheinen;

Zssgn mit adv.:

show| forth *v/t.* darlegen, kundtun; **~ in** *v/t. j-n* her'einführen; **~ off I** *v/t.* **1.** protzen mit; **2.** *a.* ***~ to advantage*** vorteilhaft zur Geltung bringen; **II** *v/i.* **3.** angeben; **~ out** *v/t.* hin'ausgeleiten, -bringen; **~ up I** *v/t.* **1.** her'auf-, hin'aufführen; **2.** F a) *j-n* bloßstellen, entlarven, b) *et.* aufdecken; **II** *v/i.* **3.** F ,aufkreuzen', -tauchen, erscheinen; **4.** sich abheben (***against*** gegen).

show| biz F → ***show business***; **'~·boat** *s.* The'aterschiff *n*; **~ busi·ness** *s.* Showbusineß *n*, Show-, Schaugeschäft *n*; **~ card** *s.* † **1.** Musterkarte *f*; **2.** 'Werbeplaˌkat *n* (*im Schaufenster*); **'~·case** *s.* Schaukasten *m*; **'~·down** *s.* **1.** Aufdecken *n* der Karten (*a. fig.*); **2.** entscheidende Kraftprobe, endgültige Ausein'andersetzung, ,Showdown' *m*.

show·er ['ʃaʊə] **I** *s.* **1.** (*Regen-*, *Hagel- etc.*)Schauer *m*; **2.** Guß *m*; **3.** *fig.* a) (*Funken-*, *Kugel- etc.*)Regen *m*, (*Geschoß-*, *Stein*)Hagel *m*, b) Schwall *m*, Unmenge *f*; **4.** *Am.* a) Brautgeschenke *pl.*, b) *a.* ***~ party*** Party *f* zur Über'reichung der Brautgeschenke; **5.** → ***shower bath***; **II** *v/t.* **6.** über'schütten, begießen: ***~ gifts*** *etc.* ***upon s.o.*** j-n mit Geschenken *etc.* überhäufen; **7.** *j-n* duschen; **8.** niederprasseln lassen; **III** *v/i.* **9.** (***~ down*** nieder)prasseln; **10.** (sich) duschen; **show·er bath** *s.* **1.** Dusche *f*: a) Brausebad *n*, b) Brause *f* (*Vorrichtung*); **2.** Duschraum *m*; **show·er·y** ['ʃaʊərɪ] *adj.* **1.** mit einzelnen (Regen-)Schauern; **2.** schauerartig.

show| girl *s.* Re'vuegirl *n*; **~ glass** → ***showcase***.

show·i·ness ['ʃəʊɪnɪs] *s.* **1.** Prunkhaftigkeit *f*, Gepränge *n*; **2.** Protzigkeit *f*, Auffälligkeit *f*; **3.** pom'pöses Auftreten.

show·ing ['ʃəʊɪŋ] *s.* **1.** Zur'schaustellung *f*; **2.** Ausstellung *f*; **3.** Vorführung *f* (*e-s Films etc.*); **4.** Darlegung *f*, Erklärung *f*; Beweis(e *pl.*) *m*: ***on*** (*od.* ***by***) ***your own ~*** nach Ihrer eigenen Darstellung; ***upon proper ~*** ⚖ nach erfolgter Glaubhaftmachung; **5.** *gute etc.* Leistung; **6.** Stand *m* der Dinge: ***on present ~*** so wie es derzeit aussieht; **ˌ~-'off** *s.* Angebe'rei *f*.

show| jump·er *s. sport* **1.** Springreiter (-in); **2.** Springpferd *n*; **~ jump·ing** *s.* Springreiten *n*.

'show·man [-mən] *s.* [*irr.*] **1.** Schausteller *m*; **2.** ,Showman' *m*: a) *j-d der im Showgeschäft tätig ist*, b) *fig.* geschickter Propagan'dist, wirkungsvoller Redner *etc.*, j-d, der sich gut ,zu verkaufen' versteht, *contp.* ,Schauspieler' *m*; **'show·man·ship** [-ʃɪp] *s.* ,Showmanship' *f*: a) ef'fektvolle Darbietung, b) *die* Kunst, sich in Szene zu setzen, Publikumswirksamkeit *f*.

shown [ʃəʊn] *p.p. von* ***show***.

'show|-off *s.* F **1.** ,Angabe' *f*, Protze'rei *f*; **2.** ,Angeber(in)' *m*; **'~·piece** *s.* Schau-, Pa'radestück *n*; **'~·place** *s.* Ort *m* mit vielen Sehenswürdigkeiten; **'~·room** *s.* **1.** Ausstellungsraum *m*; **2.** Vorführungssaal *m*; **~ tri·al** *s.* ⚖ 'Schauproˌzeß *m*; **~ win·dow** *s.* Schaufenster *n*.

show·y ['ʃəʊɪ] *adj.* □ **1.** a) prächtig, b) protzig; **2.** auffällig, grell.

shrank [ʃræŋk] *pret. von* ***shrink***.
shrap·nel [ˈʃræpnl] *s.* ⚔ **1.** Schrapˈnell *n*; **2.** Schrapˈnelladung *f*.
shred [ʃred] **I** *s.* **1.** Fetzen *m* (*a. fig.*), Lappen *m*: ***in ~s*** in Fetzen; ***tear to ~s*** a) → 4, b) *fig. Argument etc.* zerpflükken, -reißen; **2.** Schnitzel *m, n*; **3.** *fig.* Spur *f*, Aˈtom *n*: ***not a ~ of doubt*** nicht der leiseste Zweifel; **II** *v/t.* [*irr.*] **4.** zerfetzen, in Fetzen reißen; **5.** in Streifen schneiden, *Küche*: *a.* schnetzeln; **III** *v/i.* [*irr.*] **6.** zerreißen, in Fetzen gehen; ˈ**shred·der** [-də] *s.* **1.** ⚙ Reißwolf *m*; **2.** *Küche*: a) ˈSchnitzelmaˌschine *f*, -einsatz *m*, b) Reibeisen *n*.
shrew¹ [ʃruː] *s.* Xanˈthippe *f*, zänkisches Weib.
shrew² [ʃruː] *s. zo.* Spitzmaus *f*.
shrewd [ʃruːd] *adj.* ☐ **1.** schlau, gerieben; **2.** scharfsinnig, klug, gescheit: ***this was a ~ guess*** das war gut geraten; **3.** *obs.* scharf; ˈ**shrewd·ness** [-nɪs] *s.* **1.** Schlauheit *f*; **2.** Scharfsinn *m*, Klugheit *f*.
shrew·ish [ˈʃruːɪʃ] *adj.* ☐ zänkisch.
shriek [ʃriːk] **I** *s.* **1.** schriller *od.* spitzer Schrei; **2.** Kreischen *n* (*a. von Bremsen etc.*): ***~s of laughter*** kreischendes Lachen; **II** *v/i.* **3.** schreien, schrille Schreie ausstoßen; **4.** (gellend) aufschreien (***with*** vor *Schmerz etc.*): ***~ with laughter*** kreischen vor Lachen; **5.** schrill klingen; kreischen (*Bremsen etc.*); **III** *v/t.* **6.** ***~ out*** *et.* kreischen *od.* gellend schreien.
shriev·al·ty [ˈʃriːvltɪ] *s.* Amt *n* des Sheriffs.
shrift [ʃrɪft] *s.* **1.** *obs. eccl.* Beichte *f* (u. Absolutiˈon *f*); **2.** ***give s.o. short ~*** *fig.* mit j-m kurzen Prozeß machen, j-n kurz abfertigen.
shrike [ʃraɪk] *s. orn.* Würger *m*.
shrill [ʃrɪl] **I** *adj.* ☐ **1.** schrill, gellend; **2.** *fig.* grell (*Farbe etc.*); **3.** *fig.* heftig; **II** *v/t.* **4.** *et.* kreischen *od.* gellend schreien; **III** *v/i.* **5.** schrillen; ˈ**shrill·ness** [-nɪs] *s.* schriller Klang.
shrimp [ʃrɪmp] **I** *s.* **1.** *pl. coll.* **shrimp** *zo.* Garˈnele *f*; **2.** *fig. contp.* Knirps *m*, ‚Gartenzwerg' *m*; **II** *v/i.* **3.** Garˈnelen fangen.
shrine [ʃraɪn] *s.* **1.** *eccl.* a) (Reˈliquien-) Schrein *m*, b) Heiligengrab *n*, c) Alˈtar *m*; **2.** *fig.* Heiligtum *n*.
shrink [ʃrɪŋk] **I** *v/i.* [*irr.*] **1.** sich zs.-ziehen, (zs.-, ein)schrumpfen; **2.** einlaufen, -gehen (*Stoff*); **3.** abnehmen, schwinden; **4.** *fig.* zuˈrückweichen (***from*** vor *dat.*): ***~ from doing s.th.*** et. höchst widerwillig tun; **5.** *a.* ***~ back*** zuˈrückschrecken, -schaudern, -beben (***from, at*** vor *dat.*); **6.** sich scheuen *od.* fürchten (***from*** vor *dat.*); **7.** ***~ away*** sich daˈvonschleichen; **II** *v/t.* [*irr.*] **8.** (ein-, zs.-)schrumpfen lassen; **9.** *Stoffe* einlaufen lassen, krump(f)en; **10.** *fig.* zum Schwinden bringen; **11.** ***~ on*** ⚙ aufschrumpfen: ***~ fit*** Schrumpfsitz *m*; **III** *s.* **12.** *sl.* Psychiˈater *m*; ˈ**shrink·age** [-kɪdʒ] *s.* **1.** (Zs.-, Ein)Schrumpfen *n*; **2.** Schrumpfung *f*; **3.** Verminderung *f*; Schwund *m* (*a.* ✝, ⚙); **4.** Einlaufen *n* (*Textilien*); ˈ**shrink·ing** [-kɪŋ] *adj.* ☐ **1.** schrumpfend; **2.** abnehmend; **3.** ˈwiderwillig; **4.** scheu; ˈ**shrink·proof** *adj.* nicht einlaufend (*Gewebe*); ˈ**shrink-wrap** *v/t. Bücher etc.* einschweißen.
shriv·el [ˈʃrɪvl] **I** *v/t.* **1.** *a.* ***~ up*** (ein-, zs.-) schrumpfen lassen; **2.** (ver)welken lassen, ausdörren; **3.** runzeln; **II** *v/i.* **4.** *oft* ***~ up*** (zs.-, ein)schrumpfen, schrumpeln; **5.** runz(e)lig werden; **6.** (ver)welken; **7.** *fig.* verkümmern.
shroud [ʃraʊd] **I** *s.* **1.** Leichentuch *n*, Totenhemd *n*; **2.** *fig.* Hülle *f*, Schleier *m*; **3.** *pl.* ⚓ Wanten *pl.*; **4.** *a.* ***~ line*** Fangleine *f* (*am Fallschirm*); **II** *v/t.* **5.** in ein Leichentuch (ein)hüllen; **6.** *fig. in Nebel, Geheimnis* hüllen; **7.** *fig. et.* verschleiern.
Shrove| Mon·day [ʃrəʊv] *s.* Rosenˈmontag *m*; ˈ**~·tide** *s.* Faschings-, Fastnachtszeit *f*; **~ Tues·day** *s.* Faschings-, Fastnachtsˈdienstag *m*.
shrub¹ [ʃrʌb] *s.* Strauch *m*, Busch *m*.
shrub² [ʃrʌb] *s. Art* Punsch *m*.
shrub·ber·y [ˈʃrʌbərɪ] *s.* ♀ Strauchwerk *n*, Sträucher *pl.*, Gebüsch *n*; ˈ**shrub·by** [-bɪ] *adj.* ♀ strauchig, buschig, Strauch..., Busch...
shrug [ʃrʌg] **I** *v/t.* **1.** *die Achseln* zucken: ***she ~ged her shoulders***; **2.** ***~ s.th. off*** *fig.* et. mit e-m Achselzucken abtun; **II** *v/i.* **3.** die Achseln zucken; **III** *s.* **4.** *a.* ***~ of the shoulders*** Achselzucken *n*.
shrunk [ʃrʌŋk] **I** *p.p. von* ***shrink***; **II** *adj.* **1.** (ein-, zs.-)geschrumpft; **2.** eingelaufen, dekatiert (*Stoff*); ˈ**shrunk·en** [-kən] **I** → ***shrunk*** 1; **II** *adj.* abgemagert, -gezehrt; eingefallen (*Wangen*).
shuck [ʃʌk] *bsd. Am.* **I** *s.* **1.** Hülse *f*, Schote *f* (*von Bohnen etc.*); **2.** grüne Schale (*von Nüssen etc.*), *a.* Austernschale *f*; **3.** ***I don't care ~s!*** F das ist mir völlig ‚schnurz'!; ***~s!*** F Quatsch!; **II** *v/t.* **4.** enthülsen, -schoten; schälen.
shud·der [ˈʃʌdə] **I** *v/i.* schaudern, (er-) zittern (***at*** bei, ***with*** vor *dat.*): ***I ~ at the thought, I ~ to think of it*** es schaudert mich bei dem Gedanken; **II** *s.* Schauder(n *n*) *m*.
shuf·fle [ˈʃʌfl] **I** *s.* **1.** Schlurfen *n*, schlurfender Gang; **2.** *Tanz*: a) Schleifschritt *m*, b) Schleifer *m* (*Tanz*); **3.** (Karten-) Mischen *n*; **4.** Ausflucht *f*; Trick *m*; **II** *v/i.* **5.** schlurfen; (mit den Füßen) scharren: ***~ through s.th.*** *fig.* et. flüchtig erledigen; **6.** *fig.* a) Ausflüchte machen, sich herˈauszureden suchen, b) sich herˈauswinden (***out of*** aus); **7.** (die Karten) mischen; **III** *v/t.* **8.** hin- u. herschieben, *fig. a.* ‚jonglieren' mit: ***~ one's feet*** → 5; **9.** schmuggeln: ***~ away*** wegpraktizieren; **10.** ***~ off*** a) *Kleider* abstreifen, b) *fig.* abschütteln, sich befreien von, sich *e-r Verpflichtung* entziehen, *Schuld etc.* abwälzen (***on***[***to***] auf *acc.*); **11.** ***~ on*** *Kleider* mühsam anziehen; **12.** *Karten* mischen: ***~ together*** *et.* zs.-werfen, -raffen; ˈ**shuf·fle·board** *s.* a) Beilkespiel *n*, b) ⚓ *ein ähnliches Bordspiel*; ˈ**shuf·fler** [-lə] *s.* **1.** Schlurfende(r *m*) *f*; **2.** Ausflüchtemacher *m*; Schwindler(in); ˈ**shuf·fling** [-lɪŋ] *adj.* ☐ **1.** schlurfend, schleppend; **2.** unaufrichtig, unredlich; **3.** ausweichend: ***a ~ answer***.
shun [ʃʌn] *v/t.* (ver)meiden, ausweichen (*dat.*), sich fernhalten von.
shunt [ʃʌnt] **I** *v/t.* **1.** beiˈseite schieben; **2.** 🚂 *Zug etc.* rangieren, auf ein anderes Gleis fahren; **3.** ⚡ nebenschließen, shunten; **4.** *fig. et.* aufschieben; **5.** *fig.* *j-n* beiseite schieben, *j-n* kaltstellen; **6.** abzweigen; **II** *v/i.* **7.** 🚂 rangieren; **8.** *fig. von e-m Thema, Vorhaben etc.* abkommen, -springen; **III** *s.* **9.** 🚂 a) Rangieren *n*, b) Weiche *f*; **10.** ⚡ a) Nebenschluß *m*, b) ˈNebenˌwiderstand *m*; ˈ**shunt·er** [-tə] *s.* 🚂 a) Weichensteller *m*, b) Rangierer *m*; ˈ**shunt·ing** [-tɪŋ] 🚂 **I** *s.* Rangieren *n*; Weichenstellen *n*; **II** *adj.* Rangier..., Verschiebe...: ***~ engine***.
shush [ʃʌʃ] **I** *int.* sch!, pst!; **II** *v/i.* ‚sch' *od.* ‚pst' machen; **III** *v/t.* *j-n* zum Schweigen bringen.
shut [ʃʌt] **I** *v/t.* [*irr.*] **1.** (ver)schließen, zumachen: ***~ one's mind*** (*od.* ***heart***) ***to s.th.*** *fig.* sich gegen et. verschließen; → *Verbindungen mit anderen Substantiven*; **2.** einschließen, -sperren (***into, in*** in *dat., acc.*); **3.** ausschließen, -sperren (***out of*** aus); **4.** *Finger etc.* (ein)klemmen; **5.** *Taschenmesser, Buch etc.* schließen, zs.-, zuklappen; **II** *v/i.* [*irr.*] **6.** sich schließen, zugehen; **7.** schließen (*Fenster etc.*); **III** *p.p. u. adj.* **8.** ge-, verschlossen, zu: ***the shops are ~*** die Geschäfte sind geschlossen *od.* zu; *Zssgn mit adv.*:
shut| down I *v/t.* **1.** *Fenster etc.* schließen; **2.** *Fabrik etc.* schließen, stillegen; **II** *v/i.* **3.** die Arbeit *od.* den Betrieb einstellen, ‚zumachen'; **4.** ***~ (up)on*** F ein Ende machen mit; ***~ in*** *v/t.* **1.** einschließen (*a. fig.*); **2.** *Aussicht* versperren; ***~ off*** *v/t.* **1.** *Wasser, Motor etc.* abstellen; **2.** abschließen (***from*** von); ***~ out*** *v/t.* **1.** *j-n, a. Licht, Luft etc.* ausschließen, -sperren; **2.** *Landschaft* den Blicken entziehen; **3.** *sport Am. Gegner* (ohne Gegentor *etc.*) besiegen; ***~ to I*** *v/t.* → ***shut*** 1; **II** *v/i.* → ***shut*** 6; ***~ up I*** *v/t.* **1.** *Haus etc.* (fest) verschließen, -riegeln; → ***shop*** 1; **2.** *j-n* einsperren, -schließen; **3.** F *j-m* den Mund stopfen; **II** *v/i.* **4.** F die ‚Klappe' halten: ***~!*** halt's Maul!
ˈ**shut|·down** *s.* **1.** Arbeitsniederlegung *f*; **2.** Schließung *f*, (Betriebs)Stillegung *f*; **3.** *Radio, TV*: Sendeschluß *m*; ˈ**~·eye** *s.*: ***catch some ~*** *sl.* ein Schläfchen machen; ˈ**~·off** *s.* **1.** ⚙ Abstell-, Absperrvorrichtung *f*; **2.** *hunt.* Schonzeit *f*; ˈ**~·out** *s.* **1.** Ausschließung *f*; **2.** *sport* Zu-ˈNull-Niederlage *f od.* -Sieg *m*.
shut·ter [ˈʃʌtə] **I** *s.* **1.** Fensterladen *m*, Rolladen *m*: ***put up the ~s*** *fig.* das Geschäft (*am Abend od. für immer*) schließen; **2.** Klappe *f*; Verschluß *m* (*a. phot.*); **3.** ⚠ Schalung *f*; **4.** *Wasserbau*: Schütz(e *f*) *n*; **5.** ♪ Jalouˈsie *f* (*Orgel*); **II** *v/t.* **6.** mit Fensterläden versehen *od.* verschließen; ˈ**~·bug** *s.* F ‚Fotonarr' *m*; **~ speed** *s. phot.* Belichtung(szeit) *f*.
shut·tle [ˈʃʌtl] **I** *s.* **1.** ⚙ a) Weberschiff (-chen) *n*, (Web)Schütze(n) *m*, b) Schiffchen *n* (*Nähmaschine*); **2.** Schütz (-entor) *n* (*Schleuse*); **3.** Pendelroute *f*; → *a.* ***shuttle service, shuttle train***; **4.** (Raum)Fähre *f*; **II** *v/t.* **5.** (schnell) hin- u. herbewegen *od.* -befördern; **III** *v/i.* **6.** sich (schnell) hin- u. herbewegen; **7.** 🚂 *etc.* pendeln (***between*** zwischen); ˈ**~·cock I** *s. sport* Federball(spiel *n*) *m*; **II** *v/t. fig.* ˈhin- u. ˈherjagen; **~ di·plo·ma·cy** *s.* ˈReisediplomaˌtie *f*; **~ race** *s. sport* Pendelstaffel(lauf *m*) *f*; **~ ser·vice** *s.* Pendelverkehr *m*; **~ train** *s.* Pendel-, Vorortzug *m*.

shy¹ [ʃaɪ] **I** *adj.* □ **1.** scheu (*Tier*); **2.** scheu, schüchtern; **3.** zu'rückhaltend: ***be*** (*od.* ***fight***) ***~ of s.o.*** j-m aus dem Weg gehen; **4.** argwöhnisch; **5.** zaghaft: ***be ~ of doing s.th.*** Hemmungen haben, et. zu tun; **6.** *sl.* knapp (***of*** an *dat.*); **7.** ***I'm ~ of one dollar*** *sl.* mir fehlt (noch) ein Dollar; **II** *v/i.* **8.** scheuen (*Pferd etc.*); **9.** *fig.* zu'rückscheuen, -schrecken (***at*** vor *dat.*); **III** *s.* **10.** Scheuen *n* (*Pferd etc.*).

shy² [ʃaɪ] **I** *v/t. u. v/i.* **1.** werfen; **II** *s.* **2.** Wurf *m*; **3.** *fig.* Hieb *m*, Stiche'lei *f*; **4.** ***have a ~ at*** (***doing***) ***s.th.*** F es (mal) mit et. versuchen.

shy·ness ['ʃaɪnɪs] *s.* **1.** Scheu *f*; **2.** Schüchternheit *f*; **3.** Zu'rückhaltung *f*; **4.** 'Mißtrauen *n*.

shy·ster ['ʃaɪstə] *s. Am. sl.* **1.** 'Winkeladvo͵kat *m*; **2.** *fig.* Gauner *m*.

Si·a·mese [͵saɪə'mi:z] **I** *adj.* **1.** sia'mesisch; **II** *pl.* ͵**Si·a'mese** *s.* **2.** Sia'mese *m*, Sia'mesin *f*; **3.** *ling.* Sia'mesisch *n*; **~ cat** *s. zo.* Siamkatze *f*; **~ twins** *s. pl.* Sia'mesische Zwillinge *pl.* (*a. fig.*).

Si·be·ri·an [saɪ'bɪərɪən] **I** *adj.* si'birisch; **II** *s.* Si'birier(in).

sib·i·lance ['sɪbɪləns] *s.* **1.** Zischen *n*; **2.** *ling.* Zischlaut *m*; '**sib·i·lant** [-nt] **I** *adj.* **1.** zischend; **2.** *ling.* Zisch…: ***~ sound***; **II** *s.* **3.** *ling.* Zischlaut *m*; '**sib·i·late** [-leɪt] *v/t. u. v/i.* zischen; **sib·i·la·tion** [͵sɪbɪ'leɪʃn] *s.* **1.** Zischen *n*; **2.** *ling.* Zischlaut *m*.

sib·ling ['sɪblɪŋ] *s. biol.* Bruder *m*, Schwester *f*; *pl.* Geschwister *pl.*

sib·yl ['sɪbɪl] *s.* **1.** *myth.* Si'bylle *f*; **2.** *fig.* a) Seherin *f*, b) Hexe *f*; **sib·yl·line** [sɪ'bɪlaɪn] *adj.* **1.** sibyl'linisch; **2.** pro'phetisch; geheimnisvoll, dunkel.

sic·ca·tive ['sɪkətɪv] **I** *adj.* trocknend; **II** *s.* Trockenmittel *n*.

Si·cil·ian [sɪ'sɪljən] **I** *adj.* si'zilisch, sizili'anisch; **II** *s.* Si'zilier(in), Sizili'aner(in).

sick¹ [sɪk] **I** *adj.* **1.** (*Brit. nur attr.*) krank (***of*** an *dat.*): ***fall ~*** krank werden, erkranken; ***go ~*** *bsd.* ⚔ sich krank melden; **2.** Brechreiz verspürend: ***be ~*** sich erbrechen *od.* übergeben; ***I feel ~*** mir ist schlecht *od.* übel; ***she turned ~*** ihr wurde übel, sie mußte (sich er)brechen; ***it makes me ~*** mir wird übel davon, *fig. a.* es widert *od.* ekelt mich an; **3.** *fig.* krank (***of*** vor *dat.*; ***for*** nach); **4.** *fig.* enttäuscht, ärgerlich (***with*** über *j-n*; ***at*** über *et.*): ***~ at heart*** a) todunglücklich, b) angsterfüllt; **5.** F *fig.* (***of***) 'überdrüssig (*gen.*), angewidert (von): ***I am ~*** (***and tired***) ***of it*** ich habe es satt, es hängt mir zum Hals heraus; **6.** fahl (*Farbe, Licht*); **7.** F matt (*Lächeln*); **8.** schlecht (*Nahrungsmittel, Luft*); trüb (*Wein*); **9.** F grausig, ma'kaber: ***~ jokes***; ***~ humo(u)r*** ‚schwarzer' Humor; **II** *s.* **10.** ***the ~*** *pl.* die Kranken *pl.*

sick² [sɪk] *v/t. Hund, Polizei etc.* hetzen (***on*** auf *acc.*): ***~ him!*** faß!

sick| bay *s.* ⚓ ('Schiffs)Laza͵rett *n*; '**~·bed** *s.* Krankenbett *n*; **~ ben·e·fit** *s. Brit.* Krankengeld *n*; **~ call** *s.* ⚔ Re'vierstunde *f*: ***go on ~*** sich krank melden; **~ cer·tif·i·cate** *s.* 'Krankheitsat͵test *n*.

sick·en ['sɪkn] **I** *v/i.* **1.** erkranken, krank werden: ***be ~ing for*** *e-e Krankheit* ‚ausbrüten'; **2.** kränkeln; **3.** sich ekeln (***at*** vor *dat.*); **4.** 'überdrüssig *od.* müde sein *od.* werden (***of*** *gen.*): ***be ~ed with*** *e-r Sache* überdrüssig sein; **II** *v/t.* **5.** *j-m* Übelkeit verursachen, *j-n* zum Erbrechen reizen; **6.** anekeln, anwidern; '**sick·en·er** [-nə] *s. fig.* Brechmittel *n*; '**sick·en·ing** [-nɪŋ] *adj.* □ **1.** Übelkeit erregend: ***this is ~*** dabei kann einem (ja) übel werden; **2.** *fig.* ekelhaft, widerlich.

sick| head·ache *s.* **1.** Kopfschmerz(en *pl.*) *m* mit Übelkeit; **2.** Mi'gräne *f*; **~ in·sur·ance** *s.* Krankenversicherung *f*, -kasse *f*.

sick·ish ['sɪkɪʃ] *adj.* □ **1.** kränklich, unpäßlich, unwohl; **2.** → ***sickening***.

sick·le ['sɪkl] *s.* ⚘ *u. fig.* Sichel *f*.

sick leave *s.* Fehlen *n* wegen Krankheit: ***be on ~*** wegen Krankheit fehlen; ***request ~*** sich krank melden.

sick·li·ness ['sɪklɪnɪs] *s.* **1.** Kränklichkeit *f*; **2.** kränkliches Aussehen; **3.** Unzuträglichkeit *f*.

sick list *s.* ⚓, ⚔ Krankenliste *f*: ***be on the ~*** krank (gemeldet) sein.

sick·ly ['sɪklɪ] *adj. u. adv.* **1.** kränklich, schwächlich; **2.** kränklich, blaß (*Aussehen etc.*); matt (*Lächeln*); **3.** ungesund (*Gebiet, Klima*); **4.** 'widerwärtig (*Geruch etc.*); **5.** *fig.* wehleidig, süßlich: ***~ sentimentality***.

sick·ness ['sɪknɪs] *s.* **1.** Krankheit *f*: ***~ insurance*** → ***sick insurance***; **2.** Übelkeit *f*, Erbrechen *n*.

sick| nurse *s.* Krankenschwester *f*; **~ pay** *s.* Krankengeld *n*; **~ re·port** *s.* ⚔ **1.** Krankenbericht *m*, -liste *f*; **2.** Krankmeldung *f*; '**~·room** *s.* Krankenzimmer *n*, -stube *f*.

side [saɪd] **I** *s.* **1.** *allg.* Seite *f*: ***~ by ~*** Seite an Seite (***with*** mit); ***at*** (*od.* ***by***) ***the ~ of*** an der Seite von (*od. gen.*); ***by the ~ of*** *fig.* neben (*dat.*), verglichen mit; ***stand by s.o.'s ~*** *fig.* j-m zur Seite stehen; ***on all ~s*** überall; ***on the ~*** *sl.* nebenbei *verdienen etc.*; ***on the ~ of*** a) auf der Seite von, b) seitens (*gen.*); ***on this*** (***the other***) ***~ of*** diesseits (jenseits) (*gen.*); ***this ~ up!*** Vorsicht, nicht stürzen!; ***be on the small ~*** ziemlich klein sein; ***keep on the right ~ of*** sich mit *j-m* gut stellen; ***put on one ~*** *Frage etc.* zurückstellen, ausklammern; → ***dark*** 5, ***right*** 6, ***sunny***, ***wrong*** 2; **2.** & Seite *f* (*a. Gleichung*); Seitenlinie *f*, -fläche *f*; **3.** (Seiten)Rand *m*; **4.** (Körper)Seite *f*: ***shake*** (*od.* ***split***) ***one's ~s with laughter*** sich schütteln vor Lachen; **5.** (Speck-, Hammel- *etc.*)Seite *f*; **6.** Seite *f*: a) Hang *m*, Flanke *f*, *a.* Wand *f e-s Berges*, b) Ufer(seite *f*) *n*; **7.** Seite *f*, (Abstammungs)Linie *f*: ***on one's father's ~***, ***on the paternal ~*** väterlicherseits; **8.** *fig.* Seite *f*, (Cha'rakter)Zug *m*; **9.** Seite *f*: a) Par'tei *f* (*a.* ⚖ *u. sport*), b) *sport* Spielfeld(hälfte *f*) *n*: ***be on s.o.'s ~*** auf j-s Seite stehen; ***change ~s*** a) ins andere Lager überwechseln, b) *sport* die Seiten wechseln; ***take ~s*** → 16; ***win s.o. over to one's ~*** j-n auf s-e Seite ziehen; **10.** *sport Brit.* Mannschaft *f*; **11.** *ped. Brit.* Ab'teilung *f*: ***classical ~*** humanistische Abteilung; **12.** *Billiard*: Ef'fet *n*; **13.** ***put on ~*** *sl.* ‚angeben'; **II** *adj.* **14.** seitlich (liegend, stehend *etc.*), Seiten…; **15.** Seiten…, Neben…: ***~ door***; **III** *v/i.* **16.** (***with***) Par'tei ergreifen (*gen. od.* für), es halten (mit); **~ aisle** *s.* ⚠ Seitenschiff *n* (*Kirche*); **~ arms** *s. pl.* ⚔ Seitenwaffen *pl.*; **~ band** *s.* ⚡, *Radio*: 'Seiten(fre͵quenz)band *n*; '**~·board** *s.* **1.** Anrichtetisch *m*; **2.** Sideboard *n*: a) Bü'fett *n*, b) Anrichte *f*; **3.** *pl.* → '**~·burns** *s. pl.* Kote'letten *pl.* (*Backenbart*); '**~·car** *s.* **1.** Beiwagen *m*: ***~ motorcycle*** Seitenwagenmaschine *f*; **2.** → ***jaunting-car***; **3.** *ein Cocktail*.

sid·ed ['saɪdɪd] *adj. in Zssgn* …seitig: ***four-~***.

side| dish *s.* **1.** Zwischengang *m*; **2.** Beilage *f*; **~ ef·fect** *s.* Nebenwirkung *f*; **~ face** *s.* Pro'fil *n*; **~ glance** *s.* Seitenblick *m* (*a. fig.*); **~ is·sue** *s.* Nebenfrage *f*, -sache *f*, 'Randpro͵blem *n*; '**~·kick** *s. Am. sl.* Kum'pan *m*, Kumpel *m*, ‚Spezi' *m*; '**~·light** *s.* **1.** Seitenleuchte *f*; ⚓ Seitenlampe *f*; ✈ Positi'onslicht *n*; *mot.* Begrenzungslicht *n*; **2.** Seitenfenster *n*; **3.** *fig.* Streiflicht *n*: ***~s*** interessante Aufschlüsse (***on*** über *acc.*); '**~·line** *s.* **1.** Seitenlinie *f* (*a. sport*): ***on the ~s*** am Spielfeldrand; ***keep on the ~s*** *fig.* sich im Hintergrund halten; **2.** 🚂 Nebenstrecke *f*; **3.** Nebenbeschäftigung *f*, -verdienst *m*; **4.** ✝ a) Nebenzweig *m e-s Gewerbes*, b) 'Nebenar͵tikel *m*; '**~·long** *adj. u. adv.* seitlich, seitwärts, schräg: ***~ glance*** Seitenblick *m*.

si·de·re·al [saɪ'dɪərɪəl] *adj. ast.* si'derisch, Stern(en)…: ***~ day*** Sterntag *m*.

sid·er·ite ['saɪdəraɪt] *s.* ⚒, *min.* **1.** Side'rit *m*; **2.** Mete'orgestein *n*.

'**side|͵sad·dle** *s.* Damensattel *m*; '**~·show** *s.* **1.** a) Nebenvorstellung *f*, -ausstellung *f*, b) kleine Schaubude; **2.** *fig.* a) Nebensache *f*, b) Epi'sode *f* (am Rande); '**~·slip** *v/i.* **1.** seitwärts rutschen; **2.** ✈ seitlich abrutschen; **3.** *mot.* (seitlich) ausbrechen.

sides·man ['saɪdzmən] *s.* [*irr.*] Kirchenrat *m*.

'**side|͵split·ting** *adj.* zwerchfellerschütternd; '**~·step I** *s.* **1.** Seit(en)schritt *m*; **II** *v/t.* **2.** *Boxen*: *e-m Schlag* (durch Seitschritt) ausweichen; **3.** ausweichen (*dat.*) (*a. fig.*): ***~ a decision***; **III** *v/i.* **4.** e-n Seit(en)schritt machen; **5.** ausweichen (*a. fig.*); '**~·stroke** *s.* Seitenschwimmen *n*; '**~·swipe I** *v/t. Am.* F **1.** *j-m* e-n ‚Wischer' verpassen; **2.** *mot. Fahrzeug* streifen, *a.* seitlich abdrängen (*beim Überholen*); **II** *s.* **3.** ‚Wischer' *m* (*Streifschlag*); **4.** *fig.* Seitenhieb *m*; '**~·track I** *s.* **1.** → ***siding*** 1; **II** *v/t.* **2.** 🚂 *Waggon* auf ein Nebengleis schieben; **3.** *fig.* a) *et.* aufschieben, abbiegen, b) *j-n* ablenken (*a. v/i.*), c) *j-n* kaltstellen; **~ view** *s.* Seitenansicht *f*; '**~·walk** *s. bsd. Am.* Bürgersteig *m*: ***~ artist*** Pflastermaler *m*; ***~ superintendent*** *humor.* (besserwisserischer) Zuschauer *bei Bauarbeiten*.

side·ward ['saɪdwəd] **I** *adj.* seitlich; **II** *adv.* seitwärts; '**side·wards** [-dz] → ***sideward*** II; '**side·ways** → ***sideward***.

side| whis·kers *pl.* → ***sideburns***; '**~͵wind·er** [-͵waɪndə] *s. Am. sl.* **1.** (harter) Haken (*Schlag*); **2.** *Art* Klapperschlange *f*.

side·wise ['saɪdwaɪz] → ***sideward***.

sid·ing ['saɪdɪŋ] *s.* **1.** 🚂 Neben-, Anschluß-, Rangiergleis *n*; **2.** *fig.* Par'teinahme *f*.

si·dle ['saɪdl] *v/i.* sich schlängeln: ~ **away** sich davonschleichen; ~ **up to** sich an *j-n* heranmachen.

siege [siːdʒ] *s.* **1.** ⚔ Belagerung *f*: **state of** ~ Belagerungszustand *m*; **lay** ~ **to** a) *Stadt etc.* belagern, b) *fig. j-n* bestürmen; **2.** *fig.* a) heftiges Zusetzen, Bestürmen *n*, b) Zermürbung *f*; **3.** ⚙ a) Werktisch *m*, b) Glasschmelzofenbank *f*.

si·es·ta [sɪ'estə] *s.* Si'esta *f*, Mittagsruhe *f*, -schlaf *m*.

sieve [sɪv] **I** *s.* **1.** Sieb *n*: **have a memory like a** ~ ein Gedächtnis wie ein Sieb haben; **2.** *fig.* Klatschmaul *n*; **3.** Weidenkorb *m* (*a. Maß*); **II** *v/t. u. v/i.* **4.** ('durch-, aus)sieben.

sift [sɪft] **I** *v/t.* **1.** ('durch)sieben: ~ **out** a) aussieben, b) erforschen, ausfindig machen; **2.** *Zucker etc.* streuen; **3.** *fig.* sichten, sorgfältig (über)'prüfen; **II** *v/i.* **4.** 'durchrieseln, -dringen (*a. Licht etc.*); '**sift·er** [-tə] *s.* Sieb(vorrichtung *f*) *n*; '**sift·ing** [-tɪŋ] *s.* **1.** ('Durch)Sieben *n*; **2.** Sichten *n*, (sorgfältige) Unter'suchung; **3.** *pl.* a) *das* 'Durchgesiebte, b) Siebabfälle *pl*.

sigh [saɪ] **I** *v/i.* **1.** (auf)seufzen; tief (auf-)atmen; **2.** schmachten, seufzen (**for** nach): ~**ed-for** heißbegehrt; **3.** *fig.* seufzen, ächzen (*Wind*); **II** *v/t.* **4.** *oft* ~ **out** seufzen(d äußern); **III** *s.* **5.** Seufzer *m*: **a** ~ **of relief** ein Seufzer der Erleichterung, ein erleichtertes Aufatmen.

sight [saɪt] **I** *s.* **1.** Sehvermögen *n*, -kraft *f*, Auge(nlicht) *n*: **good** ~ gute Augen; **long** (**near**) ~ Weit- (Kurz)Sichtigkeit *f*; **second** ~ Zweites Gesicht; **lose one's** ~ das Augenlicht verlieren, erblinden; **2.** *fig.* Auge *n*: **in my** ~ in m-n Augen; **in the** ~ **of God** vor Gott; **find favo(u)r in s.o.'s** ~ Gnade vor j-s Augen finden; **3.** (An)Blick *m*, Sicht *f*: **at** (*od.* **on**) ~ beim ersten Anblick, auf Anhieb; sofort (*er*)*schießen etc.*; **at** ~ vom Blatt *singen*, *spielen*, *übersetzen*; **at first** ~ auf den ersten Blick; **by** ~ vom Sehen *kennen*; **catch** (*od.* **get**) ~ **of** zu Gesicht bekommen, erblicken; **lose** ~ **of** a) aus den Augen verlieren (*a. fig.*), b) *et.* übersehen; **4.** Sicht(weite) *f*: (**with**)**in** ~ a) in Sicht(weite), b) *fig.* in Sicht; **within** ~ **of** kurz vor *dem Sieg etc.*; **out of** ~ außer Sicht; **out of** ~, **out of mind** aus den Augen, aus dem Sinn; (**get**) **out of my** ~! geh mir aus den Augen!; **come in** ~ in Sicht kommen; **put out of** ~ wegtun; **5.** † Sicht *f*: **payable at** ~ bei Sicht fällig; **30 days** (**after**) ~ 30 Tage (nach) Sicht; ~ **unseen** unbesehen *kaufen*; ~ **bill** (*od.* **draft**) Sichtwechsel *m*, -tratte *f*; **6.** Anblick *m*: **a sorry** ~; **a** ~ **for sore eyes** ein erfreulicher Anblick, eine Augenweide; **be** (*od.* **look**) **a** ~ F gräßlich *od.* ‚verboten' aussehen; **I did look a** ~! F ich sah vielleicht aus!; **what a** ~ **you are!** F wie siehst denn du aus!; → **god** 1; **7.** Sehenswürdigkeit *f*: **the** ~**s of a town**; **8.** F Menge *f*, Masse *f Geld etc.*: **a long** ~ **better** zehnmal besser; **not by a long** ~ bei weitem nicht; **9.** ⚔ *etc.* Visier *n*; Zielvorrichtung *f*: **take** ~ (an-)visieren, zielen; **have in one's** ~**s** im Visier haben (*a. fig.*); **lower one's** ~**s** *fig.* zurückstecken; **raise one's** ~**s** höhere Ziele anstreben; **10.** *Am. sl.* Aussicht *f*, Chance *f*; **II** *v/t.* **11.** sichten, zu Gesicht bekommen; **12.** ⚔ a) anvisieren (*a.* ⚓, *ast.*), b) *Geschütz* richten; **13.** † *Wechsel* präsentieren; '**sight·ed** [-tɪd] *adj.* *in Zssgn* ...sichtig; '**sight·ing** [-tɪŋ] *adj.* ⚔ Ziel..., Visier...: ~ **mechanism** Zieleinrichtung *f*, -gerät *n*; ~ **shot** Anschuß *m* (*Probeschuß*); ~ **telescope** Zielfernrohr *n*; '**sight·less** [-lɪs] *adj.* □ blind; '**sight·li·ness** [-lɪnɪs] *s.* Ansehnlichkeit *f*, Stattlichkeit *f*; '**sight·ly** [-lɪ] *adj.* gutaussehend, stattlich.

'**sight**|**-read** *v/t. u. v/i.* [*irr.* → **read**] **1.** ♪ vom Blatt singen *od.* spielen; **2.** *ling.* vom Blatt über'setzen; '~ˌ**see·ing** **I** *s.* Besichtigung *f* von Sehenswürdigkeiten; **II** *adj.* Besichtigungs...: ~ **bus** Rundfahrtautobus *m*; ~ **tour** Stadtrundfahrt *f*, Besichtigungstour *f*; '~ˌ**se·er** [-ˌsiːə] *s.* Tou'rist(in).

sign [saɪn] **I** *s.* **1.** (*a.* Schrift)Zeichen *n*, Sym'bol *n* (*a. fig.*): ~ (**of the cross**) *eccl.* Kreuzzeichen; **in** ~ **of** *fig.* zum Zeichen (*gen.*); **2.** A, ♪ (Vor)Zeichen *n*; **3.** Zeichen *n*, Wink *m*: **give s.o. a** ~, **make a** ~ **to s.o.** j-m ein Zeichen geben; **4.** (An)Zeichen *n*, Sym'ptom *n* (*a.* ⚕): **no** ~ **of life** kein Lebenszeichen; **the** ~**s of the times** die Zeichen der Zeit; **make no** ~ sich nicht rühren; **5.** Kennzeichen *n*; **6.** *ast.* (Tierkreis)Zeichen *n*; **7.** (Aushänge-, Wirtshaus-)Schild *n*: **at the** ~ **of** im Wirtshaus zum *Hirsch etc.*; **8.** (Wunder)Zeichen *n*: ~**s and wonders** Zeichen u. Wunder; **9.** *hunt. etc.* Spur *f*; **II** *v/t.* **10.** unter'zeichnen, -'schreiben, (*a. typ. u. paint.*) signieren; **11.** mit *s-m Namen* unter'zeichnen: ~ **one's name** unterschreiben; **12.** ~ **away** *Vermögen etc.* über'tragen, -'schreiben; **13.** ~ **on** (*od.* **up**) (vertraglich) verpflichten, anstellen, -mustern, ⚓ anheuern; **14.** *eccl.* das Kreuzzeichen machen über (*acc. od. dat.*); *Täufling* segnen; **15.** *j-m* bedeuten (**to do** zu tun), *j-m et.* (durch Gebärden) zu verstehen geben: ~ **one's assent**; **III** *v/i.* **16.** unter'zeichnen, -'schreiben: ~ **in** a) sich eintragen, b) *bei Arbeitsbeginn* einstempeln; ~ **out** a) sich austragen, b) ausstempeln; **17.** ~ **on** (**off**) *Radio*, *TV*: sein Pro'gramm beginnen (beenden); ~ **off** *fig.* F *a.* Schluß machen; ~ **on** (*od.* **up**) a) sich (vertraglich) verpflichten (**for** zu), e-e Arbeit annehmen, b) ⚓ anheuern, ⚔ sich verpflichten (**for** auf *3 Jahre etc.*).

sig·nal ['sɪgnl] **I** *s.* **1.** *a.* ⚔ *etc.* Si'gnal *n*, (*a.* verabredetes) Zeichen: ~ **of distress** Notzeichen *n*; **2.** (Funk)Spruch *m*: **the** ≈**s** *Brit.* Fernmeldetruppe *f*; **3.** *fig.* Si'gnal *n*, (*auslösendes*) Zeichen (**for** für, zu); **4.** *Kartenspiel*: Si'gnal *n*; **II** *adj.* □ **5.** Signal...: ~ **beacon**; ≈ **Corps** *Am.* Fernmeldetruppe *f*; ~ **communications** ⚔ Fernmeldewesen *n*; **6.** *fig.* beachtlich, außerordentlich; **III** *v/t.* **7.** *j-m* Zeichen geben, winken; **8.** *Nachricht* signalisieren (*a. fig.*); *et.* melden; **IV** *v/i.* **9.** signalisieren; ~ **book** *s.* ⚓ Si'gnalbuch *n*; ~ **box** *s.* 🚂 Stellwerk *n*; ~ **check** *s.* Sprechprobe *f* (*Mikrophon*); ~ **code** *s.* Zeichenschlüssel *m*.

sig·nal·er *Am.* → **signaller**.

sig·nal·ize ['sɪgnəlaɪz] *v/t.* **1.** aus-, kennzeichnen: ~ **o.s. by** sich hervortun durch; **2.** her'vorheben; **3.** *a. fig.* ankündigen, signalisieren.

sig·nal·ler ['sɪgnələ] *s.* Si'gnalgeber *m*, *bsd.* a) ⚔ Blinker *m*, Melder *m*, b) ⚓ Si'gnalgast *m*.

'**sig·nal**|**·man** [-mən] *s.* [*irr.*] **1.** 🚂 Stellwärter *m*; **2.** ⚓ Si'gnalgast *m*; ~ **of·fi·cer** *s.* ⚔ *Am.* **1.** 'Fernmeldeoffiˌzier *m*; **2.** Leiter *m* des Fernmeldedienstes; ~ **rock·et** *s.* ⚔ Leuchtkugel *f*; ~ **tow·er** *s.* **1.** ⚙ Si'gnalturm *m*; **2.** 🚂 *Am.* Stellwerk *n*.

sig·na·ry ['sɪgnərɪ] *s.* ('Schrift)Zeichensyˌstem *n*.

sig·na·to·ry ['sɪgnətərɪ] **I** *adj.* **1.** unter'zeichnend, vertragschließend, Signatar...: ~ **powers** → 3c; **2.** † Zeichnungs...: ~ **power** Unterschriftsvollmacht *f*; **II** *s.* **3.** a) ('Mit)Unterˌzeichner (-in), b) *pol.* Signa'tar *m* (*Unterzeichnerstaat*), c) *pl. pol.* Signa'tarmächte *pl.* (**to a treaty** e-s Vertrags).

sig·na·ture ['sɪgnɪtʃə] *s.* **1.** 'Unterschrift(sleistung) *f*, Namenszug *m*; **2.** Signa'tur *f* (*e-s Buchs etc., a. pharm. Aufschrift*); **3.** ♪ Signa'tur *f*, Vorzeichnung *f*; **4.** *a.* ~ **tune** *Radio*: 'Kennmeloˌdie *f*; **5.** *typ.* a) *a.* ~ **mark** Signa'tur *f*, Bogenzeichen *n*, b) signierter Druckbogen.

'**sign·board** *s.* (*bsd.* Firmen-, Aushänge)Schild *n*.

sign·er ['saɪnə] *s.* Unter'zeichner(in).

sig·net ['sɪgnɪt] *s.* Siegel *n*, Petschaft *n*: **privy** ~ Privatsiegel des Königs; ~ **ring** *s.* Siegelring *m*.

sig·nif·i·cance [sɪg'nɪfɪkəns], *a.* **sig'nif·i·can·cy** [-sɪ] *s.* **1.** Bedeutung *f*, (tieferer) Sinn; **2.** Bedeutung *f*, Wichtigkeit *f*: **of no** ~ nicht von Belang; **sig'nif·i·cant** [-nt] *adj.* □ **1.** bedeutsam, wichtig, von Bedeutung; **2.** merklich; **3.** bezeichnend (**of** für); **4.** *fig.* vielsagend: **a** ~ **gesture**; **5.** A geltend; **sig·ni·fi·ca·tion** [ˌsɪgnɪfɪ'keɪʃn] *s.* **1.** (*bestimmte*) Bedeutung, Sinn *m*; **2.** Bezeichnung *f*, Bekundung *f*; **sig'nif·i·ca·tive** [-ətɪv] *adj.* □ **1.** Bedeutungs..., bedeutsam; **2.** bezeichnend, kennzeichnend (**of** für).

sig·ni·fy ['sɪgnɪfaɪ] **I** *v/t.* **1.** an-, bedeuten, kundtun, zu verstehen geben; **2.** bedeuten, ankündigen; **3.** bedeuten; **II** *v/i.* **4.** F wichtig sein: **it does not** ~ es hat nichts auf sich.

sign| **lan·guage** *s.* Zeichen-, *bsd.* Fingersprache *f*; ~ **man·u·al** *s.* **1.** (eigenhändige) 'Unterschrift; **2.** Handzeichen *n*; ~ **paint·er** *s.* Schilder-, Pla'katmaler *m*; '~**·post** **I** *s.* **1.** Wegweiser *m*; **2.** (Straßen)Schild *n*, (Verkehrs)Zeichen *n*; **II** *v/t.* **3.** *Straße etc.* aus-, beschildern.

si·lage ['saɪlɪdʒ] 🌾 **I** *s.* Silofutter *n*; **II** *v/t.* *Gärfutter* silieren.

si·lence ['saɪləns] **I** *s.* **1.** (Still)Schweigen *n* (*a. fig.*), Ruhe *f*, Stille *f*: **keep** ~ a) schweigen, still sein, b) Stillschweigen wahren (**on** über *acc.*); **in** ~ (still-)schweigend; ~ **gives consent** wer schweigt, scheint zuzustimmen; ~ **is golden** Schweigen ist Gold; ~! Ruhe!; → **pass over** 4; **2.** Schweigsamkeit *f*; **3.** Verschwiegenheit *f*; **4.** Vergessenheit *f*; **5.** *a.* ⚙ Geräuschlosigkeit *f*; **II** *v/t.* **6.** zum Schweigen bringen (*a.* ⚔ *u. fig.*); '**si·lenc·er** [-sə] *s.* **1.** ⚔, ⚙ Schalldämpfer *m*; **2.** *mot.* Auspufftopf *m*; '**si-**

lent [-nt] *adj.* □ **1.** still, ruhig, schweigsam: ***be ~*** (sich aus)schweigen (***on*** über *acc.*) (*a. fig.*); **2.** still (*Gebet etc.*), stumm (*Schmerz etc.*; *a. ling. Buchstabe*): ***~ film*** Stummfilm *m*; ***~ partner*** ☤ stiller Teilhaber (mit unbeschränkter Haftung); **3.** *fig.* stillschweigend: ***~ consent***; ***~ majority*** *die* schweigende Mehrheit; **4.** *a.* ⚙ geräuschlos, leise.

Si·le·sian [saɪˈliːzjən] **I** *adj.* schlesisch; **II** *s.* Schlesier(in).

sil·hou·ette [ˌsɪluːˈet] **I** *s.* **1.** Silhouˈette *f*: a) Schattenbild *n*, -riß *m*, b) ˈUmriß *m* (*a. fig.*): ***~ (target)*** ⚔ Kopfscheibe *f*; ***stand out in ~ against*** → 4; **2.** Scherenschnitt *m*; **II** *v/t.* **3.** silhouettieren; **4.** ***be ~d*** sich abheben (***against*** gegen).

sil·i·ca [ˈsɪlɪkə] *s.* ⚗ **1.** Kieselerde *f*; **2.** Quarz(glas *n*) *m*; **ˈsil·i·cate** [-kɪt] *s.* ⚗ Siliˈkat *n*; **ˈsil·i·cat·ed** [-keɪtɪd] *adj.* siliziert; **si·li·ceous** [sɪˈlɪʃəs] *adj.* kiesel(erde-, -säure)haltig, -artig, Kiesel...; **siˈlic·ic** [sɪˈlɪsɪk] *adj.* Kiesel(erde)...; **si·lic·i·fy** [sɪˈlɪsɪfaɪ] *v/t. u. v/i.* verkieseln; **si·li·cious** → ***siliceous***; **ˈsil·i·con** [-kən] *s.* ⚗ Siˈlizium *n*; **sil·i·co·sis** [ˌsɪlɪˈkəʊsɪs] *s.* ⚕ Siliˈkose *f*, Staublunge *f*.

silk [sɪlk] **I** *s.* **1.** Seide *f*: a) Seidenfaser *f*, b) Seidenfaden *m*, c) Seidenstoff *m*, -gewebe *n*; **2.** Seide(nkleid *n*) *f*: ***in ~s and satins*** in Samt u. Seide; **3.** ⚖ *Brit.* a) → ***silk gown***, b) F Kronanwalt *m*: ***take ~*** Kronanwalt werden; **4.** *fig.* Seide *f*, *zo. bsd.* Spinnfäden *pl.*; **5.** Seidenglanz *m* (*von Edelsteinen*); **II** *adj.* **6.** seiden, Seiden...: ***make a ~ purse out of a sow's ear*** *fig.* aus e-m Kieselstein e-n Diamanten schleifen; ***~ culture*** Seidenraupenzucht *f*; **ˈsilk·en** [-kən] *adj.* **1.** *poet.* seiden, Seiden...; **2.** → ***silky*** 1 *u.* 2.

silk| gown *s. Brit.* ˈSeidentaˌlar *m* (*e-s* ***King's*** *od.* ***Queen's Counsel***); ***~ hat*** *s.* Zyˈlinder(hut) *m*.

silk·i·ness [ˈsɪlkɪnɪs] *s.* **1.** *das* Seidige, seidenartige Weichheit; **2.** *fig.* Sanftheit *f*.

silk| moth *s. zo.* Seidenspinner *m*; **ˈ~-screen print·ing** *s. typ.* Seidensiebdruck *m*; **~ stock·ing** *s.* **1.** Seidenstrumpf *m*; **2.** *fig. Am.* eleˈgante *od.* vornehme Perˈson; **ˈ~·worm** *s. zo.* Seidenraupe *f*.

silk·y [ˈsɪlkɪ] *adj.* □ **1.** seidig (glänzend), seidenweich: ***~ hair***; **2.** *fig.* sanft, einschmeichelnd, zärtlich (*Person*, *Stimme etc.*), *contp.* ölig, (aal)glatt; **3.** lieblich (*Wein*).

sill [sɪl] *s.* **1.** (Tür)Schwelle *f*; **2.** Fensterbrett *n*; **3.** ⚙ Schwellbalken *m*; **4.** *geol.* Lagergang *m*.

sil·la·bub [ˈsɪləbʌb] *s. Getränk aus Wein, Sahne u. Gewürzen.*

sil·li·ness [ˈsɪlɪnɪs] *s.* **1.** Dummheit *f*, Albernheit *f*; **2.** Verrücktheit *f*.

sil·ly [ˈsɪlɪ] **I** *adj.* □ **1.** dumm, albern, blöd(e), verrückt (*Person u. Sache*); **2.** dumm, unklug (*Handlungsweise*); **3.** benommen, betäubt; **II** *s.* **4.** Dummkopf *m*, Dummerchen *n*; ***~ sea·son*** *s.* ‚Saureˈgurkenzeit' *f*.

si·lo [ˈsaɪləʊ] **I** *pl.* **-los** *s.* **1.** ⚒, ⚙ Silo *m*; **2.** ⚔ ˈunterirdische Raˈketenabschußrampe; **II** *v/t.* **3.** ⚒ *Futter* a) in e-m Silo aufbewahren, b) einmieten.

silt [sɪlt] **I** *s.* Treibsand *m*, Schlamm *m*, Schlick *m*; **II** *v/i. u. v/t. mst* ***~ up*** verschlammen.

sil·van [ˈsɪlvən] → ***sylvan***.

sil·ver [ˈsɪlvə] **I** *s.* **1.** ⚗, *min.* Silber *n*; **2.** a) Silber(geld) *n*, b) *allg.* Geld *n*; **3.** Silber(geschirr *n*, -zeug *n*) *n*; **4.** Silber (-farbe *f*, -glanz *m*) *n*; **5.** *phot.* ˈSilbersalz *n*, -niˌtrat *n*; **II** *adj.* **6.** silbern, Silber...: ***~ paper*** *phot.* Silberpapier *n*; **7.** silb(e)rig, silberglänzend; **8.** *fig.* silberhell (*Stimme etc.*); **III** *v/t.* **9.** versilbern; *Spiegel* belegen; **10.** silbern färben; **IV** *v/i.* **11.** silberweiß werden (*Haar etc.*); ***~ fir*** *s.* ⚘ Edel-, Weißtanne *f*; ***~ foil*** *s.* **1.** Silberfolie *f*; **2.** ˈSilberpaˌpier *n*; ***~ fox*** *s. zo.* Silberfuchs *m*; ***~ gilt*** *s.* vergoldetes Silber; ***~ glance*** *s.* Schwefelsilber *n*; **ˌ~-ˈgray** *bsd. Am.*, **ˌ~-ˈgrey** *adj.* silbergrau; ***~ leaf*** *s.* ⚙ Blattsilber *n*; ***~ lin·ing*** *s. fig.* Silberstreifen *m* am Horiˈzont, Lichtblick *m*: ***every cloud has its ~*** jedes Unglück hat auch sein Gutes; ***~ med·al*** *s.* ˈSilbermeˌdaille *f*; ***~ med·al·(l)ist*** *s.* ˈSilbermeˌdaillengewinner(in); ***~ ni·trate*** *s.* ⚗, *phot.* ˈSilberniˌtrat *n*; *bsd.* ⚕ Höllenstein *m*; ***~ plate*** *s.* **1.** Silberauflage *f*; **2.** Silber(geschirr *n*, -zeug *n*) *n*, Tafelsilber *n*; **ˈ~-plate** *v/t.* versilbern; ***~ point*** *s. paint.* Silberstiftzeichnung *f*; ***~ screen*** *s.* **1.** (Film)Leinwand *f*; **2.** *coll. der* Film; **ˈ~·side** *s.* bester Teil der Rindskeule; **ˈ~·smith** *s.* Silberschmied *m*; ***~ spoon*** *s.* Silberlöffel *m*: ***be born with a ~ in one's mouth*** *fig.* ein Glückskind *od.* das Kind reicher Eltern sein; **ˌ~-ˈtongued** *adj.* redegewandt; **ˈ~·ware** → ***silver plate*** 2; ***~ wed·ding*** *s.* silberne Hochzeit.

sil·ver·y [ˈsɪlvərɪ] → ***silver*** 7 *u.* 8.

sil·vi·cul·ture [ˈsɪlvɪkʌltʃə] *s.* Waldbau *m*, ˈForstkulˌtur *f*.

sim·i·an [ˈsɪmɪən] **I** *adj. zo.* affenartig, Affen...; **II** *s.* (*bsd.* Menschen)Affe *m*.

sim·i·lar [ˈsɪmɪlə] **I** *adj.* □ → ***similarly***; **1.** ähnlich (*a.* Ꭿ), (annähernd) gleich (***to*** *dat.*); **2.** gleichartig, entsprechend; **3.** *phys.*, ϟ gleichnamig; **II** *s.* **4.** *das* Ähnliche *od.* Gleichartige; **5.** *pl.* ähnliche *od.* gleichartige Dinge *pl.*; **sim·i·lar·i·ty** [ˌsɪmɪˈlærətɪ] *s.* **1.** Ähnlichkeit *f* (***to*** mit), Gleichartigkeit *f*; **2.** *pl.* Ähnlichkeiten *pl.*; **ˈsim·i·lar·ly** [-lɪ] *adv.* ähnlich, entsprechend.

sim·i·le [ˈsɪmɪlɪ] *s.* Gleichnis *n*, Vergleich *m*; **si·mil·i·tude** [sɪˈmɪlɪtjuːd] *s.* **1.** Ähnlichkeit *f* (*a.* Ꭿ); **2.** Gleichnis *n*; **3.** (Eben)Bild *n*.

sim·mer [ˈsɪmə] **I** *v/i.* **1.** sieden, wallen, brodeln; **2.** *fig.* kochen (***with*** vor *dat.*), gären (*Gefühl*, *Aufstand*): ***~ down*** sich ‚abregen' *od.* beruhigen; **II** *v/t.* **3.** zum Brodeln *od.* Wallen bringen; **III** *s.* **4.** ***keep at a*** (*od.* ***on the***) ***~*** sieden lassen.

Si·mon [ˈsaɪmən] *npr.* Simon *m*: ***Simple ~*** *fig.* F Einfaltspinsel *m*.

si·mo·ny [ˈsaɪmənɪ] *s.* Simoˈnie *f*, Ämterkauf *m*.

simp [sɪmp] *s. Am. sl.* Simpel *m*.

sim·per [ˈsɪmpə] **I** *v/i.* albern *od.* geziert lächeln; **II** *s.* einfältiges *od.* geziertes Lächeln.

sim·ple [ˈsɪmpl] **I** *adj.* □ → ***simply***; **1.** *allg.* einfach: a) simpel, leicht: ***a ~ explanation***; ***a ~ task***, b) schlicht (*Person*, *Lebensweise*, *Stil etc.*): ***~ beauty***, c) unkompliziert: ***a ~ design***; ***~ fracture*** ⚕ einfacher (Knochen)Bruch, d) nicht zs.-gesetzt, unzerlegbar: ***~ equation*** Ꭿ einfache Gleichung; ***~ fraction*** Ꭿ einfacher *od.* gemeiner Bruch; ***~ fruit*** ⚘ einfache Frucht; ***~ interest*** ☤ Kapitalzinsen *pl.*; ***~ larceny*** einfacher Diebstahl; ***~ sentence*** *ling.* einfacher Satz, e) niedrig: ***of ~ birth***; **2.** ♪ einfach; **3.** a) einfältig, simpel, b) naˈiv, leichtgläubig; **4.** gering(fügig): ***~ efforts***; **5.** rein, glatt: ***~ madness***; **II** *s.* **6.** *pharm.* Heilkraut *n*, -pflanze *f*; **ˌ~-ˈheart·ed**, **ˌ~-ˈmind·ed** *adj.* **1.** schlicht, einfach; **2.** → ***simple*** 3; **ˌ~-ˈmind·ed·ness** *s.* **1.** Schlichtheit *f*; **2.** Einfalt *f*; **3.** Arglosigkeit *f*.

sim·ple·ton [ˈsɪmpltən] *s.* Einfaltspinsel *m*.

sim·plex [ˈsɪmpleks] **I** *adj.* **1.** ⚙, ϟ Simplex...; **II** *s.* **2.** *ling.* Simplex *n*; **3.** ϟ, *teleph. etc.* Simplex-, Einfachbetrieb *m*.

sim·plic·i·ty [sɪmˈplɪsətɪ] *s.* **1.** Einfachheit *f*; **2.** Einfalt *f*.

sim·pli·fi·ca·tion [ˌsɪmplɪfɪˈkeɪʃn] *s.* Vereinfachung *f*; **sim·pli·fi·ca·tive** [ˈsɪmplɪfɪkətɪv] *adj.* vereinfachend; **sim·pli·fy** [ˈsɪmplɪfaɪ] *v/t.* **1.** vereinfachen (*a. erleichtern*, *a. als einfach hinstellen*); **2.** ⚙, ☤ *Am.* normieren.

sim·plis·tic [sɪmˈplɪstɪk] *adj.* (zu) stark vereinfachend.

sim·ply [ˈsɪmplɪ] *adv.* **1.** einfach (*etc.* → ***simple***); **2.** bloß, nur; **3.** F einfach (*großartig etc.*).

sim·u·la·crum [ˌsɪmjʊˈleɪkrəm] *pl.* **-cra** [-krə] *s.* **1.** (Ab)Bild *n*; **2.** Scheinbild *n*, Abklatsch *m*; **3.** leerer Schein.

sim·u·lant [ˈsɪmjʊlənt] *adj. bsd. biol.* ähnlich (***of*** *dat.*); **sim·u·late** [ˈsɪmjʊleɪt] *v/t.* **1.** vortäuschen, (-)heucheln, *bsd. Krankheit* simulieren: ***~d account*** ☤ fingierte Rechnung; **2.** *j-n od. et.* nachahmen; **3.** sich tarnen als; **4.** ähneln (*dat.*); **5.** *ling.* sich angleichen an (*acc.*); **6.** ⚙ simulieren; **sim·u·la·tion** [ˌsɪmjʊˈleɪʃn] *s.* **1.** Vorspiegelung *f*, -täuschung *f*; **2.** Heucheˈlei *f*, Verstellung *f*; **3.** Nachahmung *f*; **4.** Simulieren *n*, Krankspielen *n*; **5.** ⚙ Simulierung *f*; **sim·u·la·tor** [ˈsɪmjʊleɪtə] *s.* **1.** Heuchler(in); **2.** Simuˈlant(in); **3.** ⚙ *allg.* Simuˈlator *m*.

si·mul·ta·ne·i·ty [ˌsɪməltəˈnɪətɪ] *s.* Gleichzeitigkeit *f*; **si·mul·ta·ne·ous** [ˌsɪməlˈteɪnjəs] *adj.* □ gleichzeitig, simulˈtan (***with*** mit): ***~ translation*** Simultandolmetschen *n*.

sin [sɪn] **I** *s.* **1.** *eccl.* Sünde *f*: ***cardinal ~*** Hauptsünde; ***deadly*** (*od.* ***mortal***) ***~*** Todsünde; ***original ~*** Erbsünde; ***like ~*** F wie der Teufel; ***live in ~*** *obs. od. humor.* in Sünde leben; **2.** *fig.* (***against***) Sünde *f* (*Verstoß*) (gegen), Versündigung *f* (an *dat.*); **II** *v/i.* **3.** sündigen; **4.** *fig.* (***against***) sündigen, verstoßen (gegen *et.*), sich versündigen (an *j-m*).

sin·a·pism [ˈsɪnəpɪzəm] *s.* ⚕ Senfpflaster *n*.

since [sɪns] **I** *adv.* **1.** seitˈdem, -ˈher: ***ever ~*** seit der Zeit, seitdem: ***long ~*** seit langem, schon lange; ***how long ~?*** seit wie langer Zeit?; ***a short time ~*** vor kurzem; **2.** inˈzwischen, mittlerˈweile; **II** *prp.* **3.** seit: ***~ 1945***; ***~ Friday***; ***~ seeing you*** seitdem ich dich sah; **III** *cj.* **4.** seit(dem): ***how long is it ~ it hap-***

pened? wie lange ist es her, daß das geschah?; **5.** da (ja), weil.

sin·cere [sɪnˈsɪə] *adj.* □ **1.** aufrichtig, ehrlich, offen: ***a ~ friend*** ein wahrer Freund; **2.** aufrichtig, echt (*Gefühl etc.*); **3.** rein, lauter; **sinˈcere·ly** [-lɪ] *adv.* aufrichtig: ***Yours ~*** Mit freundlichen Grüßen (*Briefschluß*); **sinˈcere·ness** [-nɪs], **sin·cer·i·ty** [sɪnˈserətɪ] *s.* **1.** Aufrichtigkeit *f*; **2.** Lauterkeit *f*, Echtheit *f*.

sin·ci·put [ˈsɪnsɪpʌt] *s. anat.* Schädeldach *n*, *bsd.* Vorderhaupt *n*.

sine[1] [saɪn] *s.* ⩓ Sinus *m*: ***~ of angle*** Winkelsinus; ***~ curve*** Sinuskurve *f*; ***~ wave*** *phys.* Sinuswelle *f*.

si·ne[2] [ˈsaɪnɪ] (*Lat.*) *prp.* ohne.

si·ne·cure [ˈsaɪnɪkjʊə] *s.* Sineˈkure *f*: a) *eccl. hist.* Pfründe *f* ohne Seelsorge, b) einträglicher Ruheposten.

si·ne di·e [ˌsaɪnɪˈdaɪiː] (*Lat.*) *adv.* ⚖ auf unbestimmte Zeit; **si·ne qua non** [ˌsaɪnɪkweɪˈnɒn] (*Lat.*) *s.* unerläßliche Bedingung, Conˈditio *f* sine qua non.

sin·ew [ˈsɪnjuː] *s.* **1.** *anat.* Sehne *f*, Flechse *f*; **2.** *pl.* Muskeln *pl.*, (Muskel-)Kraft *f*: ***the ~s of war*** *fig.* das Geld *od.* die Mittel (zur Kriegführung *etc.*); **ˈsin·ewed** [-juːd] → ***sinewy***; **ˈsin·ew·less** [-lɪs] *adj. fig.* kraftlos, schwach; **ˈsin·ew·y** [-juːɪ] *adj.* **1.** sehnig; **2.** zäh (*Fleisch*); **3.** *fig.* a) stark, zäh, b) kräftig, kraftvoll (*a. Stil*).

sin·ful [ˈsɪnfʊl] *adj.* □ sündig, sündhaft.

sing [sɪŋ] **I** *v/i.* [*irr.*] **1.** singen (*a. fig. dichten*): ***~ of*** → 9; ***~ to s.o.*** j-m vorsingen; ***~ small*** *fig.* F kleinlaut werden, klein beigeben; **2.** summen (*Biene, Wasserkessel etc.*); **3.** krähen (*Hahn*); **4.** *fig.* pfeifen, sausen (*Geschoß*); heulen (*Wind*); **5.** ***~ out*** F (laut) rufen, schreien; **6.** *a.* ***~ out*** *sl.* gestehen, alle(s) verraten, ‚singen' (*Verbrecher*); **7.** sich *gut etc.* singen lassen; **II** *v/t.* [*irr.*] **8.** *Lied* singen: ***~ a child to sleep*** ein Kind in den Schlaf singen; ***~ out*** ausrufen, schreien; **9.** *poet.* (be)singen; **III** *s.* **10.** *Am.* F (Gemeinschafts)Singen *n*.

singe [sɪndʒ] **I** *v/t.* **1.** ver-, ansengen; → ***wing*** 1; **2.** *Geflügel, Schwein* sengen; **3.** *a.* ***~ off*** *Borsten etc.* absengen; **4.** *Haar* sengen (*Friseur*); **II** *v/i.* **5.** versengen; **III** *s.* **6.** Versengung *f*; **7.** versengte Stelle.

sing·er [ˈsɪŋə] *s.* **1.** Sänger(in); **2.** *poet.* Sänger *m* (*Dichter*).

sing·ing [ˈsɪŋɪŋ] **I** *adj.* **1.** singend *etc.*; **2.** Sing…, Gesangs…: ***~ lesson***; **II** *s.* **3.** Singen *n*, Gesang *m*; **4.** *fig.* Klingen *n*, Summen *n*, Pfeifen *n*, Sausen *n*: ***a ~ in the ears*** (ein) Ohrensausen; ***~ bird*** *s.* Singvogel *m*; ***~ voice*** *s.* Singstimme *f*.

sin·gle [ˈsɪŋgl] **I** *adj.* □ → ***singly***; **1.** einzig: ***not a ~ one*** kein *od.* nicht ein einziger; **2.** einzeln, einfach, Einzel…, Ein(fach)…: ***~-decker*** ✈ Eindecker *m* (*a. Bus*); ***~-stage*** einstufig; (***bookkeeping by***) ***~ entry*** ☤ einfache Buchführung; ***~(-trip) ticket*** → 10; **3.** einzeln, alˈlein, Einzel…: ***~ bed*** Einzelbett *n*; ***~ bill*** ☤ Solawechsel *m*; ***~ combat*** ⚔ Einzel-, Zweikampf *m*; ***~ game*** *sport* Einzel(spiel) *n*; ***~ house*** Einfamilienhaus *n*; **4.** a) allein, einsam, für sich (lebend), b) alˈleinstehend, ledig, unverheiratet; → *a.* 14; **5.** einmalig: ***~ payment***; **6.** ⚘ einfach; **7.** *fig.* ungeteilt, einzig: ***~ purpose***; ***have a ~ eye for*** nur Sinn haben für, nur denken an (*acc.*); ***with a ~ voice*** wie aus ˈeinem Munde; **8.** *fig.* aufrichtig: ***~ mind***; **II** *s.* **9.** *der* (*die, das*) Einzelne *od.* Einzige; Einzelstück *n*; **10.** *Brit.* a) 🚂 einfache Fahrkarte, b) ✈ einfaches (Flug)Ticket *n*; **11.** *pl. sg. konstr. sport* Einzel *n*: ***play a ~s***; ***men's ~s*** Herreneinzel; **12.** Single *f* (*Schallplatte*); **13.** Einbettzimmer *n*; **14.** Single *m*, alˈleinstehende Perˈson; **III** *v/t.* **15.** ***~ out*** a) auslesen, -suchen, -wählen (***from*** aus), b) bestimmen (***for*** für *e-n Zweck*), c) herˈausheben; **ˌ~-ˈact·ing** *adj.* ⚙ einfach wirkend; **ˌ~-ˈbreast·ed** *adj.*: ***~ suit*** Einreiher *m*; **ˌ~-ˈen·gined** *adj.* ˈeinmoˌtorig (*Flugzeug*); **ˌ~-ˈeyed** → ***single-minded***; **ˌ~-ˈhand·ed** *adj. u. adv.* **1.** einhändig; mit ˈeiner Hand; **2.** *fig.* eigenhändig, alˈlein, ohne (fremde) Hilfe; auf eigene Faust; **ˌ~-ˈheart·ed** *adj.* □ → ***single-minded***; **ˌ~-ˈline** *adj.* 🚂 eingleisig; **ˌ~-ˈmind·ed** *adj.* **1.** aufrichtig, redlich; **2.** zielbewußt, -strebig.

sin·gle·ness [ˈsɪŋglnɪs] *s.* **1.** Einmaligkeit *f*; **2.** Ehelosigkeit *f*; **3.** *a.* ***~ of purpose*** Zielstrebigkeit *f*; **4.** *fig.* Aufrichtigkeit *f*.

ˌsin·gle-ˈphase *adj.* ⚡ einphasig, Einphasen…; **ˌ~-ˈseat·er** *bsd.* ✈ **I** *s.* Einsitzer *m*; **II** *adj.* Einsitzer…, einsitzig; **ˈ~·stick** *s. sport* ˈStockraˌpier(fechten) *n*.

sin·glet [ˈsɪŋglɪt] *s.* ärmelloses ˈUnter- *od.* Triˈkothemd *n*.

sin·gle·ton [ˈsɪŋgltən] *s.* **1.** *Kartenspiel*: Singleton *m* (*einzige Karte e-r Farbe*); **2.** einziges Kind; **3.** Indiˈviduum *n*; **4.** Einzelgegenstand *m*.

ˌsin·gle-ˈtrack *adj.* **1.** einspurig (*Straße*); **2.** 🚂 eingleisig (*a. fig.* F *einseitig*).

sin·gly [ˈsɪŋglɪ] *adv.* **1.** einzeln, alˈlein; **2.** → ***single-handed*** 2.

ˈsing·song I *s.* **1.** Singsang *m*; **2.** *Brit.* Gemeinschaftssingen *n*; **II** *adj.* **3.** eintönig; **III** *v/t. u. v/i.* **4.** eintönig sprechen *od.* singen.

sin·gu·lar [ˈsɪŋgjʊlə] **I** *adj.* □ **1.** *ling.* singuˈlarisch: ***~ number*** → 6; **2.** ⩓, *phls.* singuˈlär; **3.** *bsd.* ⚖ einzeln: ***all and ~*** jeder (jede, jedes) einzelne; **4.** *fig.* einzigartig, außer-, ungewöhnlich, einmalig; **5.** *fig.* eigentümlich, seltsam; **II** *s.* **6.** *ling.* Singular *m*, Einzahl *f*; **sin·gu·lar·i·ty** [ˌsɪŋgjʊˈlærətɪ] *s.* **1.** Eigentümlichkeit *f*, Seltsamkeit *f*; **2.** Einzigartigkeit *f*; **ˈsin·gu·lar·ize** [-əraɪz] *v/t.* **1.** herˈausstellen; **2.** *ling.* in die Einzahl setzen.

sin·is·ter [ˈsɪnɪstə] *adj.* □ **1.** böse, drohend, unheilvoll, schlimm; **2.** finster, unheimlich; **3.** *her.* link.

sink [sɪŋk] **I** *v/i.* [*irr.*] **1.** sinken, ˈuntergehen (*Schiff, Gestirn etc.*); **2.** (herˈab-, nieder)sinken (*Arm, Kopf, Person etc.*): ***~ into a chair***, ***~ into the grave*** ins Grab sinken; **3.** *im Wasser, Schnee etc.* versinken, ein-, ˈuntersinken: ***~ or swim*** *fig.* egal, was passiert; **4.** sich senken: a) herˈabsinken (*Dunkelheit, Wolken etc.*), b) abfallen (*Gelände*), c) einsinken (*Haus, Grund*), d) sinken (*Preise, Wasserspiegel, Zahl etc.*); **5.** ˈumsinken; **6.** ***~ under*** erliegen (*dat.*); **7.** (***into***) a) (ein)dringen, (ein)sickern (in *acc.*), b) *fig.* (in *j-s Geist*) eindringen, sich einprägen (*dat.*): ***he allowed his words to ~ in*** er ließ s-e Worte wirken; **8.** ***~ into*** in *Ohnmacht* fallen *od.* sinken, in *Schlaf, Schweigen etc.* versinken; **9.** nachlassen, schwächer werden; **10.** sich dem Ende nähern (*Kranker*): ***he is ~ing fast*** er verfällt zusehends; **11.** *im Wert, in j-s Achtung etc.* sinken; **12.** *b.s.* (ver)sinken (***into*** in *acc.*), *in Armut, Vergessenheit* geraten, *dem Laster etc.* verfallen; **13.** sich senken (*Blick, Stimme*); **14.** sinken (*Mut*): ***his heart sank*** ihn verließ der Mut; **II** *v/t.* [*irr.*] **15.** *Schiff etc.* versenken; **16.** *bsd. in den Boden* ver-, einsenken; **17.** *Grube etc.* ausheben; *Brunnen, Loch* bohren: ***~ a shaft*** ⚒ e-n Schacht abteufen; **18.** ⚙ a) einlassen, -betten, b) eingravieren, c) *Stempel* schneiden; **19.** *Wasserspiegel etc., a. Preis, Wert* senken; **20.** *Blick, Kopf, Stimme* senken; **21.** *fig. Niveau, Stand* herˈabdrücken; **22.** zuˈgrunde richten: ***we are sunk*** *sl.* wir sind ‚erledigt'; **23.** *Tatsache* unterˈdrücken, vertuschen; **24.** *et.* ignorieren; *Streit* beilegen; *Ansprüche, Namen etc.* aufgeben; **25.** a) ☤ *Kapital* fest (*bsd.* ungünstig) anlegen, ‚stecken' (***into*** in *acc.*), b) (*bsd.* durch ˈFehlinvestiˌtiˌon) verlieren; **26.** ☤ *Schuld* tilgen; **III** *s.* **27.** Ausguß(becken *n*, -loch *n*) *m*, Spülstein *m* (*Küche*); **28.** a) Abfluß *m* (*Rohr*), b) Senkgrube *f*, c) *fig.* Pfuhl *m*: ***~ of iniquity*** *fig.* Sündenpfuhl, Lasterhöhle *f*; **29.** *thea.* Versenkung *f*; **ˈsink·a·ble** [-kəbl] *adj.* zu versenken(d), versenkbar (*bsd. Schiff*); **ˈsink·er** [-kə] *s.* **1.** ⚒ Abteufer *m*; **2.** ⚙ Stempelschneider *m*; **3.** *Weberei*: Plaˈtine *f*; **4.** ⚓ a) Senkblei *n* (*Lot*), b) Senkgewicht *n* (*Angelleine, Fischnetz*); **5.** *Am. sl.* Krapfen *m*; **ˈsink·ing** [-kɪŋ] **I** *s.* **1.** (Ver)Sinken *n*; **2.** Versenken *n*; **3.** ⚕ a) Schwächegefühl *n*, b) Senkung *f e-s Organs*; **4.** ☤ Tilgung *f*; **II** *adj.* **5.** sinkend (*a. Mut etc.*): ***a ~ feeling*** Beklommenheit *f*, flaues Gefühl (im Magen); **6.** ☤ Tilgungs…: ***~ fund*** Amortisationsfonds *m*.

sin·less [ˈsɪnlɪs] *adj.* □ sünd(en)los, unschuldig, schuldlos.

sin·ner [ˈsɪnə] *s. eccl.* Sünder(in) (*a. fig. Übeltäter*; *a. humor. Halunke*).

Sinn Fein [ˌʃɪnˈfeɪn] *s. pol.* Sinn Fein *m* (*nationalistische Bewegung u. Partei in Irland*).

Sino- [sɪnəʊ] *in Zssgn* chiˈnesisch, Chinesen…, China…; **si·nol·o·gy** [sɪˈnɒlədʒɪ] *s.* Sinoloˈgie *f* (*Erforschung der chinesischen Sprache, Kultur etc.*).

sin·ter [ˈsɪntə] **I** *s. geol. u. metall.* Sinter *m*; **II** *v/t. Erz* sintern.

sin·u·ate [ˈsɪnjʊət] *adj.* □ ⚘ gebuchtet (*Blatt*); **sin·u·os·i·ty** [ˌsɪnjʊˈɒsətɪ] *s.* **1.** Biegung *f*, Krümmung *f*; **2.** Gewundenheit *f* (*a. fig.*); **ˈsin·u·ous** [-jʊəs] *adj.* □ **1.** gewunden, sich schlängelnd: ***~ line*** Wellen-, Schlangenlinie *f*; **2.** ⩓ sinusförmig gekrümmt; **3.** *fig.* a) verwickelt, b) winkelzügig; **4.** geschmeidig.

si·nus [ˈsaɪnəs] *s.* **1.** Krümmung *f*, Kurve *f*; **2.** Ausbuchtung *f* (*a.* ⚘, ⚕); **3.** *anat.* Sinus *m*, (Knochen-, Neben)Höhle *f*; **4.** ⚕ Fistelgang *m*; **si·nus·i·tis** [ˌsaɪnəˈsaɪtɪs] *s.* ⚕ Sinuˈsitis *f*, Nebenhöhlenentzündung *f*: ***frontal ~*** Stirnhöhlenkatarrh *m*; **si·nus·oi·dal** [ˌsaɪnəˈsɔɪdl] *adj.*

⚕, ⚡, *phys.* sinusförmig: **~ *wave*** Sinuswelle *f.*

Sioux [suː] *pl.* **Sioux** [suː; suːz] *s.* **1.** 'Sioux(indi,aner[in]) *m, f;* **2.** *pl. die* 'Sioux(indi,aner) *pl.*

sip [sɪp] **I** *v/t.* **1.** nippen an (*acc.*) *od.* von, schlürfen (*a. fig.*); **II** *v/i.* **2.** (*of*) nippen (an *dat. od.* von), schlückchenweise trinken (von); **III** *s.* **3.** Nippen *n;* **4.** Schlückchen *n.*

si·phon ['saɪfn] **I** *s.* **1.** (Saug)Heber *m;* Siphon *m;* **2.** *a.* **~ *bottle*** Siphonflasche *f;* **3.** *zo.* Sipho *m;* **II** *v/t.* **4. ~ *out*** (*a.* ⚕ *Magen*) aushebe(r)n; **5. ~ *off*** a) absaugen, b) *fig.* abziehen, *Gewinne etc.* abschöpfen; **6.** *fig.* (weiter)leiten; **III** *v/i.* **7.** ablaufen.

sip·pet ['sɪpɪt] *s.* **1.** (Brot-, Toast)Brokken *m* (*zum Eintunken*); **2.** geröstete Brotschnitte.

sir [sɜː] *s.* **1.** (mein) Herr! (*respektvolle Anrede*): ***yes, ~!*** ja(wohl)!; **2(*s*)** *Anrede in* (*Leser*)*Briefen* (*unübersetzt*); ***Dear 2s*** Sehr geehrte Herren! (*Anrede in Briefen*); ***my dear ~!*** *iro.* mein Verehrtester!; **2.** **2** *Brit.* Sir *m* (*Titel e-s* ***baronet*** *od.* ***knight***); **3.** *Brit. Anrede für den* ***Speaker*** *im Unterhaus.*

sire ['saɪə] **I** *s.* **1.** *poet.* a) Vater *m,* Erzeuger *m,* b) Vorfahr *m;* **2.** *zo.* Vater (-tier *n*) *m, bsd.* Zuchthengst *m;* **3.** ***2!*** Sire!, Eure Maje'stät!; **II** *v/t.* **4.** zeugen: ***be ~d by*** abstammen von (*bsd. Zuchtpferd*).

si·ren ['saɪərən] *s.* **1.** *myth.* Si'rene *f* (*a. fig. verführerische Frau, bezaubernde Sängerin*); **2.** ⚙ Si'rene *f;* **3.** *zo.* a) Armmolch *m,* b) → **si·re·ni·an** [saɪ'rɪnjən] *s. zo.* Seekuh *f,* Si'rene *f.*

sir·loin ['sɜːlɔɪn] *s.* Lendenstück *n.*

si·roc·co [sɪ'rɒkəʊ] *pl.* **-cos** *s.* Schi'rokko *m* (*Wind*).

sir·up ['sɪrəp] → ***syrup.***

sis [sɪs] *s.* F Schwester *f.*

si·sal (hemp) ['saɪsl] *s.* ♀ Sisal(hanf) *m.*

sis·sy ['sɪsɪ] *s.* F **1.** Weichling *m,* ‚Heulsuse' *f;* **2.** ‚Waschlappen' *m,* Feigling *m.*

sis·ter ['sɪstə] **I** *s.* **1.** Schwester *f* (*a. fig. Genossin*): ***the three 2s*** *myth.* die drei Schicksalsschwestern; ***Hey, ~!*** *Am. sl.* He, Kleine!; **2.** *fig.* Schwester *f* (*Gleichartiges*); **3.** *eccl.* (Ordens)Schwester *f:* ***2s of Mercy*** Barmherzige Schwestern; **4.** ⚕ *bsd. Brit.* a) Oberschwester *f,* b) (Kranken)Schwester *f;* **5.** *a.* **~ *company*** ✝ Schwester(gesellschaft) *f;* **II** *adj.* **6.** Schwester... (*a. fig.*); **'sis·ter·hood** [-hʊd] *s.* **1.** schwesterliches Verhältnis; **2.** *eccl.* Schwesternschaft *f;* **'sis·ter-in-law** [-ərɪn-] *pl.* **'sis·ters-in-law** *s.* Schwägerin *f;* **'sis·ter·ly** [-lɪ] *adj.* schwesterlich.

Sis·tine ['sɪstaɪn] *adj.* six'tinisch: **~ *Chapel*; ~ *Madonna*.**

Sis·y·phe·an [,sɪsɪ'fiːən] *adj.*: **~ *task*** (*od.* ***labo[u]r***) Sisyphusarbeit *f.*

sit [sɪt] [*irr.*] **I** *v/i.* **1.** sitzen; **2.** sich setzen; **3.** (*to j-m*) (Por'trät *od.* Mo'dell) sitzen; **4.** sitzen, brüten (*Henne*); **5.** sitzen (*Sache, a. Wind*); **6.** Sitzung (ab-) halten, tagen; **7.** (*on*) beraten (über *acc.*), (*e-n Fall etc.*) unter'suchen; **8.** sitzen, e-n Sitz (inne)haben (***in Parliament*** im Parlament): **~ *on a committee*** e-m Ausschuß angehören; **~ *on the bench*** Richter sein; **~ *on a jury*** Geschworener sein; **9.** (*on*) sitzen, passen (*dat.*) (*Kleidung*); *fig.* (*j-m*) *gut etc.* zu Gesicht stehen; **II** *v/t.* **10. ~ *o.s.*** sich setzen; **11.** sitzen auf (*dat.*): **~ *a horse well*** gut zu Pferde sitzen;

Zssgn mit adv.:

sit| back *v/i.* **1.** sich zu'rücklehnen; **2.** *fig.* die Hände in den Schoß legen; **~ by** *v/i.* untätig zusehen; **~ down I** *v/i.* **1.** sich (hin)setzen, sich niederlassen, Platz nehmen: **~ *to work*** sich an die Arbeit machen; **2. ~ *under*** *e-e Beleidigung etc.* hinnehmen; **3.** ✈ aufsetzen; **II** *v/t.* **4.** *j-n* (hin)setzen; **~ in** *v/i.* F **1.** babysitten; **2.** F mitmachen (***at, on*** bei); **3. ~ *for*** für *j-n* einspringen; **4.** a) ein Sit-'in veranstalten, b) an e-m Sit-'in teilnehmen; **~ out I** *v/t.* **1.** *e-r Vorstellung etc.* bis zu Ende beiwohnen; **2.** länger bleiben *od.* aushalten als; **3.** *Spiel, Tanz* auslassen; **II** *v/i.* **4.** aussetzen, nicht mitmachen (*bei e-m Spiel etc.*); **5.** im Freien sitzen; **~ up I** *v/i.* **1.** aufrecht sitzen; **2.** sich aufsetzen: **~ (*and beg*)** ‚schönmachen' (*Hund*); ***make s.o. ~*** a) j-n aufrütteln, b) j-n aufhorchen lassen; **~ (*and take notice*)** F aufhorchen; **3.** sich *im Bett etc.* aufrichten; **4.** aufsitzen, -bleiben; wachen (***with*** bei *e-m Kranken*);

Zssgn mit prp.:

sit| for *v/i.* **1.** *e-e Prüfung* machen; **2.** *parl. e-n Wahlkreis* vertreten; **3. ~ *one's portrait*** sich porträtieren lassen; **~ on** → ***sit*** 7, 8, 9, ***sit upon***; **~ through** → ***sit out*** 1 (*Zssgn mit adv.*); **~ un·der** *v/i.* **1.** *eccl.* zu *j-s* Gemeinde gehören; **2.** *j-s* Schüler sein; **~ up·on** *v/i.* **1.** lasten auf *j-m*; im *Magen* liegen; **2.** *sl. j-m* ‚aufs Dach steigen'; **3.** F *Nachricht etc.* zu'rückhalten; auf *e-m Antrag* ‚sitzen'.

sit|·com ['sɪtkɒm] *s. thea.* F Situati'onsko,mödie *f;* **'~-down** *s.* **1.** Verschnaufpause *f;* **2.** a) *a.* **~ *strike*** ✝ Sitzstreik *m,* b) 'Sitzdemonstrati,on *f.*

site [saɪt] **I** *s.* **1.** Lage *f* (*e-s Gebäudes, e-r Stadt etc.*): **~ *plan*** Lageplan *m;* **2.** Stelle *f* (*a.* ⚕), Örtlichkeit *f;* **3.** Bauplatz *m,* Grundstück *n;* **4.** ✝ a) (Ausstellungs)Gelände *n,* b) Sitz *m* (*e-r Industrie*); **5.** Stätte *f,* Schauplatz *m;* **II** *v/t.* **6.** plazieren, legen, 'unterbringen: ***well-~d*** gutgelegen, in guter Lage (*Haus*).

'sit-in *s.* Sit-'in *n.*

sit·ter ['sɪtə] *s.* **1.** Sitzende(r *m*) *f;* **2.** a) Glucke *f:* ***a good ~*** e-e gute Brüterin, b) brütender Vogel; **3.** *paint.* Mo'dell *n;* **4.** *a.* **~*-in*** Babysitter *m;* **5.** *sl.* a) *hunt.* leichter Schuß, b) *fig.* leichte Beute, c) ‚todsichere Sache'.

sit·ting ['sɪtɪŋ] **I** *s.* **1.** Sitzen *n;* **2.** *bsd.* ⚖, *parl.* Sitzung *f,* Tagung *f;* **3.** *paint., phot. etc.* Sitzung *f:* ***at a ~*** *fig.* in 'einem Zug; **4.** a) Brutzeit *f,* b) Gelege *n;* **5.** *eccl., thea.* Sitz(platz) *m;* **II** *adj.* **6.** sitzend, Sitz...: **~ *duck*** *fig.* leichtes Opfer; **7.** brütend; **~ room** *s.* **1.** Platz *m* zum Sitzen; **2.** Wohnzimmer *n.*

sit·u·ate ['sɪtjʊeɪt] **I** *v/t.* **1.** aufstellen, *e-r Sache* e-n Platz geben, den Platz festlegen (*gen.*); **2.** in e-e Lage bringen; **II** *adj.* **3.** ⚖ *od. obs.* → ***situated*** 1; **'sit·u·at·ed** [-tɪd] *adj.* **1.** gelegen: ***be ~*** liegen *od.* sein (*Haus etc.*); **2.** in e-r *schwierigen etc.* Lage: ***thus ~*** in dieser Lage; ***well ~*** gutsituiert, wohlhabend.

sit·u·a·tion [,sɪtjʊ'eɪʃn] *s.* **1.** Lage *f e-s Hauses etc.*; **2.** Situati'on *f:* a) Lage *f,* Zustand *m,* b) Sachlage *f,* 'Umstände *pl.*: ***difficult ~***; **3.** *thea.* dra'matische Situati'on, Höhepunkt *m:* **~ *comedy*** Situationskomödie *f;* **4.** Stellung *f,* Stelle *f,* Posten *m:* ***~s offered*** Stellenangebote; ***~s wanted*** Stellengesuche.

si·tus ['saɪtəs] (*Lat.*) *s.* **1.** ⚕ Situs *m,* Lage *f* (*e-s Organs*); **2.** Sitz *m,* Lage *f:* ***in situ*** an Ort u. Stelle.

six [sɪks] **I** *adj.* **1.** sechs: ***it is ~ of one and half a dozen of the other*** *fig.* das ist gehupft wie gesprungen; **2.** *in Zssgn* sechs...: **~*-cylinder(ed)*** sechszylindrig, Sechszylinder... (*Motor*); **II** *s.* **3.** Sechs *f* (*Zahl, Spielkarte etc.*): ***at ~es and sevens*** a) ganz durcheinander, b) uneins; **4.** *Kricket: a.* **six·er** ['sɪksə] *s.* F Sechserschlag *m;* **'six·fold** [-fəʊld] *adj. u. adv.* sechsfach.

,six|-'foot·er *s.* F sechs Fuß langer *od.* ‚baumlanger' Mensch; **'~·pence** *s. Brit. obs.* Sixpencestück *n,* ½ Schilling *m:* ***it does not matter (a) ~*** das ist ganz egal; **,~-'shoot·er** *s.* F sechsschüssiger Re'volver.

six·teen [,sɪks'tiːn] **I** *s.* Sechzehn *f;* **II** *adj.* sechzehn; **,six'teenth** [-nθ] **I** *adj.* **1.** sechzehnt; **2.** sechzehntel; **II** *s.* **3.** *der* (*die, das*) Sechzehnte; **4.** Sechzehntel *n;* **5.** *a.* **~ *note*** ♪ Sechzehntel(note *f*) *n.*

sixth [sɪksθ] **I** *adj.* **1.** sechst: **~ *sense*** *fig.* sechster Sinn; **II** *s.* **2.** *der* (*die, das*) Sechste; **3.** Sechstel *n;* **4.** ♪ Sext *f;* **5.** *a.* **~ *form*** *ped. Brit.* Abschlußklasse *f;* **'sixth·ly** [-lɪ] *adv.* sechstens.

six·ti·eth ['sɪkstɪɪθ] **I** *adj.* **1.** sechzigst; **2.** sechzigstel; **II** *s.* **3.** *der* (*die, das*) Sechzigste; **4.** Sechzigstel *n.*

Six·tine ['sɪkstaɪn] → ***Sistine.***

six·ty ['sɪkstɪ] **I** *adj.* **1.** sechzig; **II** *s.* **2.** Sechzig *f;* **3.** *pl.* a) *die* sechziger Jahre *pl.* (*e-s Jahrhunderts*), b) *die* Sechziger (-jahre) *pl.* (*Alter*).

'six-,wheel·er *s. mot.* Dreiachser *m.*

siz·a·ble ['saɪzəbl] *adj.* (ziemlich) groß, ansehnlich, beträchtlich.

siz·ar ['saɪzə] *s. univ.* Stipendi'at *m* (*in Cambridge od. Dublin*).

size[1] [saɪz] **I** *s.* **1.** Größe *f,* Maß *n,* For'mat *n,* 'Umfang *m:* ***all of a ~*** (alle) gleich groß; ***of all ~s*** in allen Größen; ***the ~ of*** so groß wie; ***that's about the ~ of it*** F (genau) so ist es; ***cut s.o. down to ~*** *fig.* j-n in die Schranken verweisen; **2.** (Schuh-, Kleider- *etc.*) Größe *f,* Nummer *f:* ***two ~s too big*** zwei Nummern zu groß; ***what ~ do you take?*** welche Größe haben Sie?; **3.** *fig.* a) Größe *f,* Ausmaß *n,* b) *geistiges etc.* For'mat *e-r Person;* **II** *v/t.* **4.** nach Größen ordnen; **5. ~ *up*** F ab-, einschätzen, taxieren (*alle a. fig.*); **III** *v/i.* **6. ~ *up*** F gleichkommen (***to, with*** *dat.*).

size[2] [saɪz] **I** *s.* **1.** (*paint.* Grundier)Leim *m,* Kleister *m;* **2.** a) *Weberei:* Appre'tur *f,* b) *Hutmacherei:* Steife *f;* **II** *v/t.* **3.** leimen; **4.** *paint.* grundieren; **5.** *Stoff* appretieren; **6.** *Hutfilz* steifen.

-size [saɪz] → ***-sized.***

size·a·ble ['saɪzəbl] → ***sizable.***

-sized [saɪzd] *adj. in Zssgn* ...groß, von *od.* in ... Größe.

siz·er[1] ['saɪzə] *s.* **1.** Sortierer(in); **2.** ⚙

a) (ˈGrößen)Sorˌtiermaˌschine *f*, b) (ˈHolz)ˌZuschneidemaˌschine *f*.
siz·er² [ˈsaɪzə] *s.* ⚙ **1.** Leimer *m*; **2.** *Textilindustrie*: Schlichter *m*.
siz·zle [ˈsɪzl] **I** *v/i.* zischen; *Radio etc.*: knistern; **II** *s.* Zischen *n*; ˈ**siz·zling** [-lɪŋ] *adj.* **1.** zischend, brutzelnd; **2.** glühend heiß.
skald [skɔ:ld] → ***scald¹***.
skat [skæt] *s.* Skat(spiel *n*) *m*.
skate¹ [skeɪt] *pl.* **skates**, *bsd. coll.* **skate** *s. ichth.* (Glatt)Rochen *m*.
skate² [skeɪt] **I** *s.* **1.** a) Schlittschuh *m*, b) Kufe *f*; **2.** Rollschuh *m*; **II** *v/i.* **3.** Schlittschuh *od.* Rollschuh laufen: ***~ over*** *fig. Schwierigkeiten etc.* überspielen; → ***ice*** 1; ˈ**skate·board** *s.* Skateboard *n*; ˈ**skat·er** [-tə] *s.* **1.** Schlittschuh-, Eisläufer(in); **2.** Rollschuhläufer(in); **skate sail·ing** *s.* Eissegeln *n*.
skat·ing [ˈskeɪtɪŋ] *s.* **1.** Schlittschuhlauf(en *n*) *m*, Eislauf(en *n*) *m*; **2.** Rollschuhlauf((en *n*) *m*; **~ rink** *s.* **1.** Eisbahn *f*; **2.** Rollschuhbahn *f*.
ske·dad·dle [skɪˈdædl] F **I** *v/i.* ‚türmen', ‚abhauen'; **II** *s.* ‚Türmen' *n*.
skeet (shoot·ing) [ski:t] *s. sport* Skeetschießen *n*.
skein [skeɪn] *s.* **1.** Strang *m*, Docke *f* (*Wolle etc.*); **2.** Skein *n*, Warp *n* (*Baumwollmaß*); **3.** Kette *f*, Schwarm *m* (*Wildenten etc.*); **4.** *fig.* Gewirr *n*.
skel·e·tal [ˈskelɪtl] *adj.* **1.** ⚕ Skelett...; **2.** skeˈlettartig; **skel·e·tol·o·gy** [ˌskelɪˈtɒlədʒɪ] *s.* Knochenlehre *f*.
skel·e·ton [ˈskelɪtn] **I** *s.* **1.** Skeˈlett *n*, Knochengerüst *n*, Gerippe *n* (*alle a. fig.*): ***~ in the cupboard*** (*Am.* ***closet***), ***family ~*** *fig.* dunkler Punkt, (düsteres) Familiengeheimnis; ***~ at the feast*** Gespenst *n* der Vergangenheit; **2.** ⚘ Rippenwerk *n* (*Blatt*); **3.** Δ, ⚙ (*Stahl- etc.*)Skeˈlett *n*, (*a. Schiffs-, Flugzeug-*) Gerippe *n*; (*a. Schirm*)Gestell *n*; **4.** *fig.* a) Entwurf *m*, Rohbau *m*, b) Rahmen *m*; **5.** a) ˈStamm(persoˌnal *n*) *m*, b) ⚔ Kader *m*, Stammtruppe *f*; **6.** *sport* Skeleton *m* (*Schlitten*); **II** *adj.* **7.** Skelett...: ***~ construction*** Δ Skelettbauweise *f*; ***~-face type*** *typ.* Skelettschrift *f*; **8.** ⚚, ⚖ Rahmen...: ***~ agreement***; ***~ law***; ***~ bill*** Wechselblankett *n*; ***~ wage agreement*** Manteltarif(vertrag) *m*; **9.** ⚔ Stamm...: ***~ crew*** Stamm-, Restmannschaft *f*, *weitS.* Notbelegschaft *f*; ˈ**skel·e·ton·ize** [-tənaɪz] *v/t.* **1.** skelettieren; **2.** *fig.* skizzieren, in großen ˈUmrissen darstellen; **3.** *fig.* zahlenmäßig reduzieren.
skel·e·ton| key *s.* Dietrich *m*, Nachschlüssel *m*; **~ ser·vice** *s.* Bereitschaftsdienst *m*.
skep [skep] *s.* **1.** (Weiden)Korb *m*; **2.** Bienenkorb *m*.
skep·tic [ˈskeptɪk] *etc. Am.* → ***sceptic*** *etc.*
sker·ry [ˈskerɪ] *s. bsd. Scot.* kleine Felseninsel.
sketch [sketʃ] **I** *s.* **1.** *paint. etc.* Skizze *f*, Studie *f*: ***~ block***; **2.** Grundriß *m*, Schema *n*, Entwurf *m*; **3.** *fig.* (*a. literarische*) Skizze; **4.** *thea.* Sketch *m*; **II** *v/t.* **5.** *oft* ***~ in*** (*od.* ***out***) skizzieren; **6.** *fig.* skizzieren, in großen Zügen darstellen; **III** *v/i.* **7.** e-e Skizze *od.* Skizzen machen; ˈ**sketch·i·ness** [-tʃɪnɪs] *s.* Skizzenhaftigkeit *f*, *fig. a.* Oberflächlichkeit *f*; ˈ**sketch·y** [-tʃɪ] *adj.* □ **1.** skizzenhaft, flüchtig; **2.** *fig.* a) oberflächlich, b) unzureichend: ***a ~ meal***; **3.** *fig.* unklar, vage.
skew [skju:] **I** *adj.* **1.** schief, schräg: ***~ bridge***; **2.** abschüssig; **3.** 𝔄 ˈasymˌmetrisch; **II** *s.* **4.** Schiefe *f*; **5.** 𝔄 Asymmeˈtrie *f*; **6.** Δ a) schräger Kopf (*Strebepfeiler*), b) ˈUntersatzstein *m*; ˈ**~·back** *s.* Δ schräges ˈWiderlager; ˈ**~·bald I** *adj.* scheckig (*bsd. Pferd*); **II** *s.* Schecke *m*.
skewed [skju:d] *adj.* schief, abgeschrägt, verdreht; **skew·er** [ˈskju:ə] **I** *s.* **1.** Fleischspieß *m*; **2.** *humor.* Schwert *n*, Dolch *m*; **II** *v/t.* **3.** *Fleisch* spießen, *Wurst* speilen; **4.** *fig.* aufspießen.
ˈ**skew|-eyed** *adj. Brit.* schielend; **~gear·ing** *s.* ⚙ Stirnradgetriebe *n*.
ski [ski:] **I** *pl.* **ski**, **skis** *s.* **1.** *sport* Ski *m*; **2.** ✈ (Schnee)Kufe *f*; **II** *v/i. pret. u. p.p. Brit.* **ski'd**, *Am.* **skied 3.** *sport* Ski laufen *od.* fahren; ˈ**~·bob** *s.* Skibob *m*.
skid [skɪd] **I** *s.* **1.** Stützbalken *m*; **2.** Ladebalken *m*, (Lasten)Rolle *f*: ***put the ~s under*** *od.* ***on s.o.*** *fig.* F j-n ‚fertigmachen' *od.* ‚abschießen'; ***he is on the ~s*** *sl.* mit ihm geht's abwärts; **3.** Hemmschuh *m*, Bremsklotz *m*; **4.** ✈ (Gleit)Kufe *f*, Sporn(rad *n*) *m*; **5.** *a. mot.* Rutschen *n*, Schleudern *n*: ***go into a ~*** ins Schleudern geraten (*a. fig.* F); ***~ chain*** Schneekette *f*; ***~ mark*** Bremsspur *f*; **II** *v/t.* **6.** *Rad* bremsen, hemmen; **III** *v/i.* **7.** *a. mot. etc.* a) rutschen, b) schleudern; ˈ**~·lid** *s. sl.* Sturzhelm *m*; ˈ**~·proof** *adj.* rutschfest; **~ row** [rəʊ] *s. Am.* F a) billiges Vergnügungsviertel, b) ‚Pennergegend' *f*.
ski·er [ˈski:ə] *s. sport* Skiläufer(in), -fahrer(in).
skies [skaɪz] *pl. von* ***sky***.
skiff [skɪf] *s.* Skiff *n* (*Ruderboot*).
ski·ing [ˈski:ɪŋ] *s.* Skilaufen *n*, -fahren *n*, -sport *m*.
ski|-jor·ing [ˈski:ˌdʒɔ:rɪŋ] *s. sport* Ski-(k)jöring *n*; **~ jump** *s.* **1.** Skisprung *m*; **2.** Sprungschanze *f*; **~ jump·ing** *s.* Skispringen *n*, Sprunglauf *m*.
skil·ful [ˈskɪlfʊl] *adj.* □ geschickt: a) gewandt, b) kunstgerecht (*Arbeit, Operation etc.*), c) geübt, (sach)kundig (***at, in*** in *dat.*): ***be ~ at*** sich verstehen auf (*acc.*); ˈ**skil·ful·ness** [-nɪs] → ***skill***.
skill [skɪl] *s.* **1.** Geschick(lichkeit *f*) *n*: a) (Kunst)Fertigkeit *f*, Können *n*, b) Gewandtheit *f*; **2.** (Fach-, Sach)Kenntnis *f* (***at, in*** in *dat.*); **skilled** [-ld] *adj.* **1.** geschickt, gewandt, erfahren (***in*** in *dat.*); **2.** Fach...: ***~ labo(u)r*** Facharbeiter *pl.*; ***~ trades*** Fachberufe; ***~ workman*** gelernter Arbeiter, Facharbeiter *m*.
skil·let [ˈskɪlɪt] *s.* **1.** a) Tiegel *m*, b) Kasseˈrolle *f*; **2.** *Am.* Bratpfanne *f*.
skill·ful(·ness) *Am.* → ***skilful(ness)***.
skil·ly [ˈskɪlɪ] *s. Brit.* dünne Hafergrütze.
skim [skɪm] **I** *v/t.* **1.** (*a. fig.* ⚚ *Gewinne*) abschöpfen: ***~ the cream off*** den Rahm abschöpfen (*oft fig.*); **2.** abschäumen; **3.** *Milch* entrahmen: ***~med milk*** → ***skim milk***; **4.** *fig.* (hin)gleiten über (*acc.*); **5.** *fig. Buch etc.* überˈfliegen, flüchtig lesen; **II** *v/i.* **6.** gleiten, streichen (***over*** über *acc.*, ***along*** entlang); **7.** ***~ over*** → 5; ˈ**skim·mer** [-mə] *s.* **1.** Schaum-, Rahmkelle *f*; **2.** ⚙ Abstreicheisen *n*; **3.** ⚓ *Brit.* leichtes Rennboot; **skim milk** *s.* entrahmte Milch, Magermilch *f*; ˈ**skim·ming** [-mɪŋ] *s.* **1.** *mst pl. das* Abgeschöpfte; **2.** *pl.* Schaum *m* (*auf Kochgut etc.*); **3.** *pl.* ⚙ Schlacken *pl.*; **4.** Abschöpfen *n*, -schäumen *n*: ***~ of excess profit*** ⚚ Gewinnabschöpfung *f*.
skimp [skɪmp] *etc.* → ***scrimp*** *etc.*
skin [skɪn] **I** *s.* **1.** Haut *f* (*a. biol.*): ***dark*** (***fair***) ***~*** dunkle (helle) Haut(farbe); ***he is mere ~ and bone*** er ist nur noch Haut u. Knochen; ***be in s.o.'s ~*** *fig.* in j-s Haut stecken; ***get under s.o.'s ~*** F a) j-m ‚unter die Haut' gehen, b) j-n ärgern; ***have a thick*** (***thin***) ***~*** dickfellig (zartbesaitet) sein; ***save one's ~*** mit heiler Haut davonkommen; ***by the ~ of one's teeth*** mit knapper Not; ***that's no ~ off my nose*** F das ‚juckt' mich nicht; → ***jump*** 12; **2.** Fell *n*, Pelz *m*, Balg *m* (*von Tieren*); **3.** (*Obst- etc.*) Schale *f*, Haut *f*, Hülse *f*, Rinde *f*; **4.** ⚙ *etc.* dünne Schicht, Haut *f* (*auf der Milch etc.*); **5.** Oberfläche *f*, *bsd.* a) ⚓ Außenhaut *f*, b) ✈ Bespannung *f*, c) (*Ballon*)Hülle *f*; **6.** (*Wein- etc.*) Schlauch *m*; **7.** *sl.* Klepper *m* (*Pferd*); **II** *v/t.* **8.** enthäuten, (ab)häuten, schälen: ***keep one's eyes ~ned*** F die Augen offenhalten; **9.** *a.* ***~ out*** *Tier* abbalgen, -ziehen; **10.** *Knie etc.* aufschürfen; **11.** *sl. j-m* das Fell über die Ohren ziehen, *j-n* ‚rupfen' (*beim Spiel etc.*); **12.** F *Strumpf etc.* abstreifen; **III** *v/i.* **13.** ***~ over*** (zu)heilen (*Wunde*); **14.** ***~ out*** *Am. sl.* ‚abhauen'; ˌ**~-ˈdeep** *adj. u. adv.* (nur) oberflächlich; **~ dis·ease** *s.* Hautkrankheit *f*; **~ div·ing** *s.* Sporttauchen *n*; ˈ**~·flicks** *s.* F Sexfilm *m*; ˈ**~·flint** *s.* Knicker *m*, Geizhals *m*; **~ food** *s.* Nährcreme *f*; **~ fric·tion** *s. phys.* Oberflächenreibung *f*; **~ game** *s.* F Schwindel *m*, Bauernfängeˈrei *f*; **~ graft** *s.* ⚕ ˈHauttransplanˌtat *n*; ˈ**~-ˌgraft·ing** *s.* ⚕ ˈHauttransplantatiˌon *f*.
skinned [skɪnd] *adj.* **1.** häutig; **2.** ent-, gehäutet; **3.** *in Zssgn* ...häutig, ...fellig; ˈ**skin·ner** [-nə] *s.* **1.** Pelzhändler *m*, Kürschner *m*; **2.** Abdecker *m*; ˈ**skin·ny** [-nɪ] *adj.* **1.** häutig; **2.** mager, abgemagert, dünn; **3.** *fig.* knauserig.
ˌ**skin|ˈtight** *adj.* hauteng (*Kleidung*); **~ wool** *s.* Schlachtwolle *f*.
skip¹ [skɪp] **I** *v/i.* **1.** hüpfen, hopsen, springen; **2.** seilhüpfen; **3.** *fig.* Sprünge machen, *von e-m Thema zum andern* springen; *ped. Am.* e-e Klasse überˈspringen; Seiten überˈschlagen (*in e-m Buch*): ***~ off*** abschweifen; ***~ over*** *et.* übergehen; **4.** aussetzen, e-n Sprung tun (*Herz etc.*, *a.* ⚙); **5.** *oft* ***~ out*** F ‚abhauen'; ***~*** (***over***) ***to*** e-n Abstecher nach *e-m Ort* machen; **II** *v/t.* **6.** springen über (*acc.*): ***~*** (***a***) ***rope*** seilhüpfen; **7.** *fig.* (*ped. Am. a. e-e Klasse*) überˈspringen, auslassen, *Buchseite* überˈschlagen: ***~ it!*** ‚geschenkt'!; **8.** F a) verschwinden aus *e-r Stadt etc.*, b) sich vor *e-r Verabredung etc.* drücken, *Schule etc.* schwänzen; **9.** F ***~ it*** ‚abhauen'; **III** *s.* **10.** Hopser *m*; *Tanzen*: Hüpfschritt *m*.
skip² [skɪp] → ***skipper*** 2.
skip³ [skɪp] *s.* (Stuˈdenten)Diener *m*.
skip⁴ [skɪp] *s.* ⚙ Förderkorb *m*.
ˈ**skip·jack** *s.* **1.** *coll. pl. ichth.* a) *ein*

Thunfisch *m*, b) Blaufisch *m*; **2.** *zo.* Springkäfer *m*; **3.** Stehaufmännchen *n* (*Spielzeug*).

ski plane *s.* Flugzeug *n* mit Schneekufen.

skip·per ['skɪpə] *s.* **1.** ⚓, ✈ Kapi'tän *m*, ⚓ *a.* Schiffer *m*; **2.** *sport* a) 'Mannschaftskapi,tän *m*, b) *Am.* Manager *m od.* Trainer *m*.

skip·ping ['skɪpɪŋ] *s.* Hüpfen *n*, (*bsd.* Seil)Springen *n*; **~ rope** *s.* Springseil *n*.

skirl [skɜːl] *dial.* **I** *v/i.* **1.** pfeifen (*bsd. Dudelsack*); **2.** Dudelsack spielen; **II** *s.* **3.** Pfeifen *n* (*des Dudelsacks*).

skir·mish ['skɜːmɪʃ] **I** *s.* ⚔ *u. fig.* Geplänkel *n*: **~ line** Schützenlinie *f*; **II** *v/i.* plänkeln; **'skir·mish·er** [-ʃə] *s.* ⚔ Plänkler *m* (*a. fig.*).

skirt [skɜːt] **I** *s.* **1.** (Frauen)Rock *m*; **2.** *sl.* ‚Weibsbild' *n*, ‚Schürze' *f*; **3.** (Rock-, Hemd-, *etc.*)Schoß *m*; **4.** Saum *m*, Rand *m* (*fig. oft pl.*); **5.** *pl.* Außenbezirk *m*, Randgebiet *n*; **6.** Kutteln *pl.*: **~ of beef**; **II** *v/t.* **7.** a) (um)'säumen, b) sich entlangziehen an (*dat.*); **8.** entlang- *od.* her'umgehen *od.* -fahren um; **9.** *fig.* um'gehen; **III** *v/i.* **10.** **~ along** am Rande entlanggehen *od.* -fahren, sich entlangziehen; **'skirt·ed** [-tɪd] *adj.* **1.** e-n Rock tragend; **2.** *in Zssgn* a) mit e-m *langen etc.* Rock: **long-~**, b) *fig.* eingesäumt; **'skirt·ing** [-tɪŋ] *s.* **1.** Rand *m*, Saum *m*; **2.** Rockstoff *m*; **3.** *mst* **~ board** △ (*bsd.* Fuß-, Scheuer)Leiste *f*.

'ski-run *s.* Skipiste *f*.

skit [skɪt] *s.* **1.** Stiche'lei *f*, Seitenhieb *m*; **2.** Paro'die *f*, Sa'tire *f* (**on** über, auf *acc.*).

ski tow *s.* Schlepplift *m*.

skit·ter ['skɪtə] *v/i.* **1.** jagen, rennen; **2.** rutschen; **3.** hopsen; **4.** den Angelhaken an der Wasseroberfläche hinziehen.

skit·tish ['skɪtɪʃ] *adj.* □ **1.** ungebärdig, scheu (*Pferd*); **2.** ner'vös, ängstlich; **3.** *fig.* a) lebhaft, wild, b) (kindisch) ausgelassen (*bsd. Frau*), c) fri'vol, d) sprunghaft, kaprizi'ös.

skit·tle ['skɪtl] **I** *s.* **1.** *bsd. Brit.* Kegel *m*; **2.** *pl. sg. konstr.* Kegeln *n*, Kegelspiel *n*: **play (at) ~s** kegeln; **II** *int.* **3.** **~s!** F Quatsch!, Unsinn!; **III** *v/t.* **4.** **~ out** *Kricket: Schläger od. Mannschaft* (rasch) ‚erledigen'; **~ al·ley** *s.* Kegelbahn *f*.

skive¹ [skaɪv] **I** *v/t.* **1.** *Leder, Fell* spalten; **2.** *Edelstein* abschleifen; **II** *s.* **3.** Dia'mantenschleifscheibe *f*.

skive² [skaɪv] *Brit. sl.* **I** *v/t.* ‚sich drükken' vor (*dat.*); **II** *v/i. a.* **~ off** sich drücken.

skiv·vy ['skɪvɪ] *s. Brit. contp.* Dienstmagd *f*.

sku·a ['skjuːə] *s. orn.* (**great ~** Riesen-) Raubmöwe *f*.

skul·dug·ger·y [skʌl'dʌgərɪ] *s.* F Gaune'rei *f*, Schwindel *m*.

skulk [skʌlk] *v/i.* **1.** lauern; **2.** (um'her-) schleichen: **~ after s.o.** j-m nachschleichen; **3.** *fig.* sich drücken; **'skulk·er** [-kə] *s.* **1.** Schleicher(in); **2.** Drückeberger(in).

skull [skʌl] *s.* **1.** *anat.* Schädel *m*, Hirnschale *f*: **fractured ~** ⚕ Schädelbruch *m*; **2.** Totenschädel *m*: **~ and crossbones** a) Totenkopf *m* (*Giftzeichen etc.*), b) *hist.* Totenkopf-, Piratenflagge *f*; **3.** *fig.* Schädel *m* (*Verstand*): **have a thick ~** ein Brett vor dem Kopf haben; **'~·cap** *s.* **1.** *anat.* Schädeldach *n*; **2.** Käppchen *n*.

skunk [skʌŋk] **I** *s.* **1.** *zo.* Skunk *m*, Stinktier *n*; **2.** Skunk(s)pelz *m*; **3.** *fig. sl.* ‚Scheißkerl' *m*, ‚Schwein' *n*; **II** *v/t.* **4.** *Am.* F a) ‚vermöbeln' (*a. sport*), b) ‚bescheißen'.

sky [skaɪ] **I** *s.* **1.** *oft pl.* (*Wolken*)Himmel *m*: **in the ~** am Himmel; **out of a clear ~** *bsd. fig.* aus heiterem Himmel; **2.** *oft pl.* Himmel *m* (*a. fig.*), Himmelszelt *n*: **under the open ~** unter freiem Himmel; **praise to the skies** *fig.* in den Himmel heben; **the ~ is the limit** F nach oben sind keine Grenzen gesetzt; **3.** a) Klima *n*, b) Himmelsstrich *m*, Gegend *f*, c) ⚔, ✈ Luftraum *m*; **II** *v/t.* **4.** *Ball etc.* hoch in die Luft schlagen *od.* werfen; **5.** F *Bild* (zu) hoch aufhängen (*in e-r Ausstellung*); **~ ad·ver·tis·ing** *s.* † Luftwerbung *f*; **,~-'blue** *adj.* himmelblau; **'~·coach** *s.* ✈ *Am. Passagierflugzeug ohne Service*; **'~,div·er** *s. sport* Fallschirmspringer(in); **'~,div·ing** *s. sport* Fallschirmspringen *n*; **,~-'high** *adj. u. adv.* himmelhoch (*a. fig.*): **blow ~** a) sprengen, b) *fig. Theorie etc.* über den Haufen werfen; **'~·jack** **I** *v/t. Flugzeug* entführen; **II** *s.* Flugzeugentführung *f*; **'~,jack·er** *s.* Flugzeugentführer (-in); **'~,jack·ing** *s.* → **skyjack** II; **'~·lab** *s.* 'Raumla,bor *n*; **'~·lark** **I** *s.* **1.** *orn.* (Feld)Lerche *f*; **2.** Spaß *m*, Ulk *m*; **II** *v/i.* **3.** he'rumtollen, ‚Blödsinn' treiben; um'hertollen; **'~·light** *s.* Oberlicht *n*, Dachfenster *n*; **'~·line** *s.* Hori'zont (-linie *f*) *m*, (*Stadt- etc.*)Silhou'ette *f*; **'~-,lin·er** → **airliner**; **~ mar·shal** *s. Am. Bundespolizist, der zur Verhinderung von Flugzeugentführungen eingesetzt wird*; **~ pi·lot** *s. sl.* ‚Schwarzrock' *m* (*Geistlicher*); **'~,rock·et** **I** *s. Feuerwerk*: Ra'kete *f*; **II** *v/i.* in die Höhe schießen (*Preise etc.*), sprunghaft ansteigen; **III** *v/t.* sprunghaft ansteigen lassen; **'~·scape** [-skeɪp] *s. paint.* Wolkenlandschaft *f* (*Bild*); **'~,scrap·er** *s.* Wolkenkratzer *m*; **~ sign** *s.* † 'Leuchtre,klame *f* (*auf Häusern etc.*).

sky·ward ['skaɪwəd] **I** *adv.* himmel'an, -wärts; **II** *adj.* himmelwärts gerichtet; **'sky·wards** [-dz] → **skyward** I.

'sky|·way *s. bsd. Am.* **1.** ✈ Luftroute *f*; **2.** Hochstraße *f*; **'~,writ·er** *s.* Himmelsschreiber *m*; **'~,writ·ing** *s.* Himmelsschrift *f*.

slab [slæb] **I** *s.* **1.** (Me'tall-, Stein-, Holz- *etc.*)Platte *f*, Tafel *f*, Fliese *f*: **on the ~** F a) auf dem Operationstisch, b) im Leichenschauhaus; **2.** (dicke) Scheibe (*Brot, Fleisch etc.*); **3.** ⚙ Schwarten-, Schalbrett *n*; **4.** *metall.* Bramme *f* (*Roheisenblock*); **5.** *Am. sl. Baseball*: Schlagmal *n*; **6.** (*westliche USA*) Be'tonstraße *f*; **II** *v/t.* **7.** ⚙ a) *Stamm* abschwarten, b) in Platten *od.* Bretter zersägen.

slack¹ [slæk] **I** *adj.* □ **1.** schlaff, locker, lose (*alle a. fig.*): **keep a ~ rein** (*od.* **hand**) die Zügel locker lassen (*a. fig.*); **2.** a) langsam, träge (*Strömung etc.*), b) flau (*Brise*); **3.** † flau, lustlos; → **season** 3; **4.** (nach)lässig, lasch, schlaff: **be ~ in one's duties** s-e Pflichten vernachlässigen; **~ performance** schlappe Leistung; **5.** *ling.* locker: **~ vowel** offener Vokal; **II** *s.* **6.** ⚓ Lose *n* (*loses Tauende*); **7.** ⚙ Spiel *n*: **take up the ~** Druckpunkt nehmen (*beim Schießen*); **8.** ⚓ Stillwasser *n*; **9.** Flaute *f* (*a.* †); **10.** F (Ruhe)Pause *f*; **11.** *pl.* Freizeithose *f*; **III** *v/t.* **12.** *a.* **~ off** → **slacken** 1; **13.** *a.* **~ up** → **slacken** 2 u. 3; **14.** → **slake** 2; **IV** *v/i.* **15.** → **slacken** 5; **16.** *oft* **~ off** a) nachlassen, b) F trödeln; **17.** **~ up** langsamer werden *od.* fahren.

slack² [slæk] *s.* ⚒ Kohlengrus *m*.

slack·en ['slækən] **I** *v/t.* **1.** *Seil, Muskel etc.* lockern, locker machen, entspannen; **2.** lösen; ⚓ *Segel* lose machen; (*Tau*)*Ende* fieren; **3.** *Tempo* verlangsamen, her'absetzen; **4.** nachlassen *od.* nachlässig werden in (*dat.*); **II** *v/i.* **5.** sich lockern, schlaff werden; **6.** *fig.* erlahmen, nachlassen, nachlässig werden; **7.** langsamer werden; **8.** † stocken; **'slack·er** [-kə] *s.* Bumme'lant *m*, Faulpelz *m*; **'slack·ness** [-knɪs] *s.* **1.** Schlaffheit *f*, Lockerheit *f*; **2.** Flaute *f*, Stille *f* (*a. fig.*); **3.** † Flaute *f*, (Geschäfts)Stockung *f*; Unlust *f*; **4.** *fig.* Schlaffheit *f*, (Nach)Lässigkeit *f*, Trägheit *f*; **5.** ⚙ Spiel *n*, toter Gang.

slack| suit *s. Am.* Freizeitanzug *m*; **~ wa·ter** → **slack¹** 8.

slag [slæg] **I** *s.* **1.** ⚙ (*geol.* vul'kanische) Schlacke: **~ concrete** Schlackenbeton *m*; **2.** *Brit. sl.* Schlampe *f*; **II** *v/t. u. v/i.* **3.** verschlacken; **'slag·gy** [-gɪ] *adj.* schlackig.

slain [sleɪn] *p.p. von* **slay**.

slake [sleɪk] *v/t.* **1.** *Durst, a. fig. Begierde etc.* stillen; **2.** ⚙ *Kalk* löschen: **~d lime** ⚗ Löschkalk *m*.

sla·lom ['slɑːləm] *s. sport* Slalom *m*, Torlauf *m*.

slam¹ [slæm] **I** *v/t.* **1.** *a.* **~ to** *Tür, Deckel* zuschlagen, zuknallen; **2.** *et. auf den Tisch etc.* knallen: **~ down** *et.* hinknallen; **3.** *j-n* schlagen; **4.** *sl. sport* ‚über'fahren' (*besiegen*); **5.** F *j-n od. et.* ‚in die Pfanne hauen'; **II** *v/i.* **6.** *a.* **~ to** zuschlagen (*Tür*); **III** *s.* **7.** Knall *m*; **IV** *adv.* **8.** *a. int.* bums(!), peng(!).

slam² [slæm] *s. Kartenspiel*: Schlemm *m*: **grand ~** Groß-Schlemm.

slan·der ['slɑːndə] **I** *s.* **1.** ⚖ *mündliche* Verleumdung, üble Nachrede; **2.** *allg.* Verleumdung *f*, Klatsch *m*; **II** *v/t.* **3.** verleumden; **'slan·der·er** [-dərə] *s.* Verleumder(in); **'slan·der·ous** [-dərəs] *adj.* □ verleumderisch.

slang [slæŋ] **I** *s.* Slang *m*, Jar'gon *m*: a) Sonder-, Berufssprache *f*: **schoolboy ~** Schülersprache; **thieves' ~** Gaunersprache, *das* Rotwelsch, b) sa'loppe 'Umgangssprache; **II** *v/t. j-n* (wüst) beschimpfen: **~ing match** wüste gegenseitige Beschimpfungen *pl.*; **'slang·y** [-ɪ] *adj.* sa'lopp, Slang...

slant [slɑːnt] **I** *s.* **1.** Schräge *f*, schräge Fläche *od.* Richtung *od.* Linie: **on the** (*od.* **on a**) **~** schräg, schief; **2.** Abhang *m*; **3.** *fig.* a) Ten'denz *f*, ‚Färbung' *f*, b) Einstellung *f*, Gesichtspunkt *m*: **take a ~ at** *Am.* F e-n (Seiten)Blick werfen auf (*acc.*); **II** *adj.* □ **4.** schräg; **III** *v/i.* **5.** schräg liegen; sich neigen, kippen; **6.** *fig.* tendieren (**towards** zu *et.* hin); **IV** *v/t.* **7.** schräg legen, kippen, e-e schräge Richtung geben (*dat.*): **~ed** schräg; **8.** *fig.* e-e Ten'denz geben, ‚färben'; **'~-**

eye *s.* Schlitzauge *n* (*Asiate etc.*); ˈ**slant-eyed** *adj.* schlitzäugig; ˈ**slant·ing** [-tɪŋ] *adj.* □ schräg; ˈ**slant·wise** *adj. u. adv.* schräg, schief.

slap [slæp] **I** *s.* **1.** Schlag *m*, Klaps *m*: ***give s.o. a ~ on the back*** j-m anerkennend auf den Rücken klopfen; ***a ~ in the face*** e-e Ohrfeige, ein Schlag ins Gesicht (*a. fig.*); ***have a*** (***bit of***) ***~ and tickle*** F ‚knutschen'; **II** *v/t.* **2.** schlagen, e-n Klaps geben (*dat.*): ***~ s.o.'s face*** j-n ohrfeigen; **3.** → ***slam***¹ 2; **4.** scharf tadeln; **5.** ***~ on*** F a) *et.* draufklatschen, b) *Zuschlag etc.* ‚draufhauen'; **III** *v/i.* **6.** schlagen, klatschen (*a. Regen etc.*); **IV** *adv.* **7.** F genau, bums, ‚zack': ***I ran ~ into him***; ˌ**~-ˈbang** *adv.* **1.** → ***slap*** 7; **2.** Knall u. Fall; ˈ**~·dash I** *adv.* **1.** blindlings, Hals über Kopf; **2.** hoppla'hopp, ‚auf die Schnelle'; **3.** aufs Gerate'wohl; **II** *adj.* **4.** heftig, ungestüm; **5.** schlampig, schlud(e)rig: ***~ work***; ˈ**~ˌhap·py** *adj.* unbekümmert; ˈ**~·jack** *s. Am.* **1.** Pfannkuchen *m*; **2.** *ein Kinderkartenspiel*; ˈ**~·stick I** *s.* **1.** (Narren)Pritsche *f*; **2.** *thea.* a) Slapstick *m*, Kla'mauk *m*, b) 'Slapstickkoˌmödie *f*; **II** *adj.* **3.** Slapstick…, Klamauk…: ***~ comedy*** → 2 b; ˈ**~-up** *adj. sl.* ‚todschick', prima, ‚toll'.

slash [slæʃ] **I** *v/t.* **1.** (auf)schlitzen; zerfetzen; **2.** *Kleid etc.* schlitzen: ***~ed sleeve*** Schlitzärmel *m*; **3.** a) peitschen, b) *Peitsche* knallen lassen; **4.** *Ball etc.* ‚dreschen'; **5.** *fig.* geißeln, scharf kritisieren; **6.** *fig.* drastisch kürzen *od.* her'absetzen, zs.-streichen; **II** *v/i.* **7.** hauen (***at*** nach): ***~ out*** um sich hauen (*a. fig.*); **III** *s.* **8.** Hieb *m*, Streich *m*; **9.** Schnitt (-wunde *f*) *m*; **10.** Schlitz *m*; **11.** Holzschlag *m*; **12.** a) drastische Kürzung, b) drastischer Preisnachlaß; ˈ**slash·ing** [-ʃɪŋ] **I** *s.* **1.** ⚔ Verhau *m*; **II** *adj.* **2.** schneidend, schlitzend: ***~ weapon*** ⚔ Hiebwaffe *f*; **3.** *fig.* vernichtend, beißend (*Kritik etc.*); **4.** F ‚toll'.

slat [slæt] *s.* **1.** Leiste *f*, (*a.* Jalou'sie-) Stab *m*; **2.** *pl. sl.* a) Rippen *pl.*, b) ‚Arschbacken' *pl.*

slate¹ [sleɪt] **I** *s.* **1.** *geol.* Schiefer *m*; **2.** (Dach)Schiefer *m*, Schieferplatte *f*; **3.** Schiefertafel *f* (*zum Schreiben*): ***have a clean ~ fig.*** e-e reine Weste haben; ***clean the ~ fig.*** reinen Tisch machen; → ***wipe off*** 2; **4.** *Film*: Klappe *f*; **5.** *pol. etc. Am.* Kandi'datenliste *f*; **6.** Schiefergrau *n* (*Farbe*); **II** *v/t.* **7.** *Dach* mit Schiefer decken; **8.** *Am.* a) *Kandidaten* (vorläufig) aufstellen, vorschlagen: ***be ~d for*** für *e-n Posten* vorgesehen sein, b) *zeitlich* ansetzen; **III** *adj.* **9.** schieferartig, -farbig; Schiefer…

slate² [sleɪt] *v/t. sl.* **1.** ‚vermöbeln'; **2.** *fig.* a) *et.* ‚verreißen' (*kritisieren*), b) *j-n* abkanzeln.

ˌ**slate|-ˈblue** *adj.* schieferblau; ˈ**~-club** *s. Brit.* Sparverein *m*; ˌ**~-ˈgray**, ˌ**~-ˈgrey** *adj.* schiefergrau; **~ pen·cil** *s.* Griffel *m*.

slath·er [ˈslæðə] *Am.* F **I** *v/t.* **1.** dick schmieren *od.* auftragen; **2.** verschwenden; **II** *s.* **3.** *mst pl.* große Menge.

slat·ing [ˈsleɪtɪŋ] *s. sl.* **1.** ‚Verriß' *m*, beißende Kri'tik; **2.** Standpauke *f*.

slat·tern [ˈslætɜːn] *s.* **1.** Schlampe *f*; **2.** *Am.* ‚Nutte' *f*; ˈ**slat·tern·ly** [-lɪ] *adj. u. adv.* schlampig, schmudd(e)lig.

slat·y [ˈsleɪtɪ] *adj.* schief(e)rig.

slaugh·ter [ˈslɔːtə] **I** *s.* **1.** Schlachten *n*; **2.** *fig.* a) Abschlachten *n*, Niedermetzeln *n*, b) Gemetzel *n*, Blutbad *n*; → ***innocent*** 7; **II** *v/t.* **3.** *Vieh* schlachten; **4.** *fig.* a) (ab)schlachten, niedermetzeln, b) F *j-n* ‚auseinandernehmen' (*a. sport*); ˈ**slaugh·ter·er** [-ərə] *s.* Schlächter *m*; ˈ**slaugh·ter·house** *s.* **1.** Schlachthaus *n*; **2.** *fig.* Schlachtbank *f*.

Slav [slɑːv] **I** *s.* Slawe *m*, Slawin *f*; **II** *adj.* slawisch, Slawen…

slave [sleɪv] **I** *s.* **1.** Sklave *m*, Sklavin *f*; **2.** *fig.* Sklave *m*, Arbeitstier *n*, Kuli *m*: ***work like a ~*** → 4; **3.** *fig.* Sklave *m* (***to***, ***of*** *gen.*): ***a ~ to one's passions***; ***a ~ to drink*** alkoholsüchtig; **II** *v/i.* **4.** schuften, wie ein Kuli arbeiten; **~ driv·er** *s.* **1.** Sklavenaufseher *m*; **2.** *fig.* Leuteschinder *m*.

slav·er¹ [ˈsleɪvə] *s.* **1.** Sklavenschiff *n*; **2.** Sklavenhändler *m*.

slav·er² [ˈslævə] **I** *v/i.* **1.** geifern, sabbern (*a. fig.*): ***~ for*** *fig.* lechzen nach; **2.** *fig.* katzbuckeln; **II** *v/t.* **3.** *obs.* besabbern; **III** *s.* **4.** Geifer *m*.

slav·er·y [ˈsleɪvərɪ] *s.* **1.** Sklave'rei *f* (*a. fig.*): ***~ to*** *fig.* sklavische Abhängigkeit von; **2.** Sklavenarbeit *f*; *fig.* Placke'rei *f*, Schinde'rei *f*.

slave| ship *s.* Sklavenschiff *n*; **~ trade** *s.* Sklavenhandel *m*; **~ trad·er** *s.* Sklavenhändler *m*.

slav·ey [ˈsleɪvɪ] *s. Brit.* F ‚dienstbarer Geist'.

Slav·ic [ˈslɑːvɪk] **I** *adj.* slawisch; **II** *s. ling.* Slawisch *n*.

slav·ish [ˈsleɪvɪʃ] *adj.* **1.** □ sklavisch, Sklaven…; **2.** *fig.* knechtisch, kriecherisch, unter'würfig; **3.** *fig.* sklavisch: ***~ imitation***; ˈ**slav·ish·ness** [-nɪs] *s. das* Sklavische, sklavische Gesinnung.

slaw [slɔː] *s. Am.* 'Krautsaˌlat *m*.

slay [sleɪ] [*irr.*] **I** *v/t.* töten, erschlagen, ermorden; **II** *v/i.* morden; **slay·er** [ˈsleɪə] *s.* Mörder(in).

slea·zy [ˈsliːzɪ] *adj.* **1.** dünn (*a. fig.*), verschlissen (*Gewebe*); **2.** → ***shabby***.

sled [sled] → ***sledge***¹ 1; ˈ**sled·ding** [-dɪŋ] *s. bsd. Am.* 'Schlittenfahren *n*, -transˌport *m*: ***hard*** (***smooth***) ***~ fig.*** schweres (glattes) Vorankommen.

sledge¹ [sledʒ] **I** *s.* **1.** a) *a.* ⚙ Schlitten *m*, b) (Rodel)Schlitten *m*; **2.** *bsd. Brit.* (leichterer) Pferdeschlitten; **II** *v/t.* **3.** mit e-m Schlitten befördern *od.* fahren; **III** *v/i.* **4.** Schlitten fahren, rodeln.

sledge² [sledʒ] ⚙ *s.* **1.** Vorschlag-, Schmiedehammer *m*; **2.** schwerer Treibfäustel; **3.** ⚒ Schlägel *m*; ˈ**~ˌham·mer I** *s.* → ***sledge***² 1; **II** *adj. fig.* a) Holzhammer…(*-argumente etc.*), b) wuchtig, vernichtend (*Schlag*), c) ungeschlacht (*Stil*).

sleek [sliːk] **I** *adj.* □ **1.** glatt, glänzend (*Haar*); **2.** geschmeidig, glatt (*Körper*; *a. fig. Wesen*); **3.** *fig.* a) gepflegt, ele'gant, schick, b) schnittig (*Form*); **4.** *fig. b.s.* aalglatt, ölig; **II** *v/t.* **5.** *a.* ⚙ glätten; *Haar* glatt kämmen *od.* bürsten; ⚙ *Leder* schlichten; ˈ**sleek·ness** [-nɪs] *s.* Glätte *f*, Geschmeidigkeit *f* (*a. fig.*).

sleep [sliːp] **I** *v/i.* [*irr.*] **1.** schlafen, ruhen (*beide a. fig. Dorf*, *Streit*, *Toter etc.*): ***~ late*** lange schlafen; ***~ like a log*** (*od.* ***top*** *od.* ***dormouse***) schlafen wie ein Murmeltier; ***~*** [***up***]***on*** (*od.* ***over***) ***s.th.*** *fig.* et. überschlafen; **2.** schlafen, über'nachten: ***~ in*** (***out***) im (außer) Haus schlafen; **3.** stehen (*Kreisel*); **4.** ***~ with*** mit *j-m* schlafen; ***~ around*** mit vielen Männern ins Bett gehen; **II** *v/t.* [*irr.*] **5.** schlafen: ***~ the ~ of the just*** den Schlaf des Gerechten schlafen; **6.** ***~ away*** *Zeit* verschlafen; **7.** ***~ off*** *Kopfweh etc.* ausschlafen: ***~ it off*** s-n Rausch *etc.* ausschlafen; **8.** Schlafgelegenheit bieten für; *j-n* 'unterbringen; **III** *s.* **9.** Schlaf *m*, Ruhe *f* (*a. fig.*): ***in one's ~*** im Schlaf; ***the last ~*** *fig.* die letzte Ruhe, der Tod(esschlaf); ***get some ~*** ein wenig schlafen; ***go to ~*** a) schlafen gehen, b) einschlafen (*a. fig. sterben*); ***put to ~*** *allg.*, *a.* ⚕ einschläfern; **10.** *zo.* (Winter)Schlaf *m*; **11.** ⚘ Schlafbewegung *f*; ˈ**sleep·er** [-pə] *s.* **1.** Schläfer(in): ***be a light*** (***sound***) ***~*** e-n leichten (festen) Schlaf haben; **2.** 🚃 a) Schlafwagen *m*, b) *Brit.* Schwelle *f*; **3.** *Am.* Lastwagen *m* mit Schlafkoje; **4.** *Am.* a) ('Kinder-) Pyˌjama *m*, b) (Baby)Schlafsack *m*; **5.** *Am.* F über'raschender Erfolg; **6.** ✝ *Am.* Ladenhüter *m*; ˈ**sleep-in** *s.* Sleep-in *n*, 'Schlafdemonstratiˌon *f*; ˈ**sleep·i·ness** [-pɪnɪs] *s.* **1.** Schläfrigkeit *f*; **2.** *a. fig.* Verschlafenheit *f*.

sleep·ing [ˈsliːpɪŋ] *adj.* **1.** schlafend; **2.** Schlaf…: ***~ accommodation*** Schlafgelegenheit *f*; **~ bag** *s.* Schlafsack *m*; ♀ **Beau·ty** *s.* Dorn'rös-chen *n*; **~ car** *s.* 🚃 Schlafwagen *m*; **~ draught** *s.* Schlaftrunk *m*, -mittel *n*; **~ part·ner** *s.* ✝ *Brit.* stiller Teilhaber (mit unbeschränkter Haftung); **~ sick·ness** *s.* ⚕ Schlafkrankheit *f*; **~ suit** *s.* → ***sleeper*** 4 a; **~ tab·let** *s.* ⚕ 'Schlaftaˌblette *f*.

sleep·less [ˈsliːplɪs] *adj.* □ **1.** schlaflos; **2.** *fig.* a) rast-, ruhelos, b) wachsam; ˈ**sleep·less·ness** [-nɪs] *s.* **1.** Schlaflosigkeit *f*; **2.** *fig.* Rast-, Ruhelosigkeit *f*; **3.** Wachsamkeit *f*.

ˈ**sleep|ˌwalk·er** *s.* Nachtwandler(in); ˈ**~ˌwalk·ing I** *s.* Nacht-, Schlafwandeln *n*; **II** *adj.* schlafwandelnd; nachtwandlerisch.

sleep·y [ˈsliːpɪ] *adj.* □ **1.** schläfrig, müde; **2.** *fig.* schläfrig, schlafmützig, träge; **3.** *fig.* verschlafen, verträumt (*Dorf etc.*); **4.** teigig (*Obst*); ˈ**~·head** *s. fig.* Schlafmütze *f*.

sleet [sliːt] *meteor.* **I** *s.* **1.** Graupel(n *pl.*) *f*, Schloße(n *pl.*) *f*; **2.** a) *Brit.* Schneeregen *m*, b) *Am.* Graupelschauer *m*; **3.** F 'Eisˌüberzug *m auf Bäumen etc.*; **II** *v/i.* **4.** graupeln; ˈ**sleet·y** [-tɪ] *adj.* graupelig.

sleeve [sliːv] *s.* **1.** Ärmel *m*: ***have s.th. up*** (*od.* ***in***) ***one's ~*** a) et. auf Lager *od.* in petto haben, b) et. im Schild führen; ***laugh in one's ~*** sich ins Fäustchen lachen; ***roll up one's ~s*** die Ärmel hochkrempeln (*a. fig.*); **2.** ⚙ Muffe *f*, Buchse *f*, Man'schette *f*; **3.** (Schutz-) Hülle *f*; **sleeved** [-vd] *adj.* **1.** mit Ärmeln; **2.** *in Zssgn* …ärmelig; ˈ**sleeve·less** [-lɪs] *adj.* ärmellos.

sleeve| link *s.* Man'schettenknopf *m*; **~ tar·get** *s.* ⚔ Schleppsack *m*; **~ valve** *s.* ⚙ 'Muffenvenˌtil *n*.

sleigh [sleɪ] **I** *s.* (Pferde- *od.* Last)Schlitten *m*; **II** *v/i.* (im) Schlitten fahren; **~ bell** *s.* Schlittenschelle *f*.

sleight [slaɪt] *s.* **1.** Geschicklichkeit *f*; **2.** Trick *m*; ˌ**~-of-ˈhand** *s.* **1.** (Taschen-

spieler)Kunststück *n*, (-)Trick *m* (*a. fig.*); **2.** (Finger)Fertigkeit *f*.
slen·der ['slendə] *adj.* □ **1.** schlank; **2.** schmal, schmächtig; **3.** *fig.* a) schmal, dürftig: **~ *income***, b) gering, schwach: ***a ~ hope***; **4.** mager, karg (*Essen*); **'slen·der·ize** [-əraɪz] *v/t. u. v/i.* schlank (-er) machen *od.* werden; **'slen·der·ness** [-nɪs] *s.* **1.** Schlankheit *f*, Schmalheit *f*; **2.** *fig.* Dürftigkeit *f*; **3.** Kargheit *f* (*des Essens*).
slept [slept] *pret. u. p.p. von* ***sleep***.
sleuth [slu:θ] **I** *s. a.* ***~hound*** Spürhund *m* (*a. fig. Detektiv*); **II** *v/i.* ‚(he'rum-) schnüffeln'; **III** *v/t. j-s* Spur verfolgen.
slew¹ [slu:] *pret. von* ***slay***.
slew² [slu:] *s. Am. od. Canad.* Sumpf (-land *n*, -stelle *f*) *m*.
slew³ [slu:] **I** *v/t. a.* ***~ round*** her'umdrehen, (-)schwenken; **II** *v/i.* sich her'umdrehen.
slew⁴ [slu:] *s. Am.* F (große) Menge, Haufe(n) *m*: ***a ~ of people***.
slice [slaɪs] **I** *s.* **1.** Scheibe *f*, Schnitte *f*, Stück *n*: ***a ~ of bread***; **2.** *fig.* Stück *n Land etc.*; (An)Teil *m*: ***a ~ of the profits*** ein Anteil am Gewinn; ***a ~ of luck*** *fig.* e-e Portion Glück; **3.** (*bsd.* Fisch-) Kelle *f*; **4.** ⚙ Spa(ch)tel *m*; **5.** *Golf, Tennis*: Slice *m* (*Schlag u. Ball*); **II** *v/t.* **6.** in Scheiben schneiden, aufschneiden: ***~ off*** *Stück* abschneiden; **7.** *a. Luft, Wellen* durch'schneiden; **8.** *fig.* aufteilen; **9.** *Golf, Tennis*: *den Ball* slicen; **III** *v/i.* **10.** Scheiben schneiden; **11.** *Golf, Tennis*: slicen; **'slic·er** [-sə] *s.* (*Brot-, Gemüse- etc.*)'Schneidemaˌschine *f*; (*Gurken-, Kraut- etc.*)Hobel *m*.
slick [slɪk] F **I** *adj.* □ **1.** glatt, glitschig; **2.** *Am.* Hochglanz...; → *a.* 8; **3.** F a) geschickt, raffiniert, b) ‚schick', ‚flott'; **II** *adv.* **4.** geschickt; **5.** flugs; **6.** genau, ‚peng': ***~ in the eye***; **III** *v/t.* **7.** glätten; **8.** ‚auf Hochglanz bringen'; **IV** *s.* **9.** Ölfläche *f*; **10.** F *a.* ***~ paper*** *Am.* F ele'gante Zeitschrift; **'slick·er** [-kə] *s. Am.* **1.** Regenmantel *m*; **2.** F a) raffinierter Kerl, Schwindler *m*, b) ‚Großstadtpinkel' *m*.
slid [slɪd] *pret. u. p.p. von* ***slide***.
slide [slaɪd] **I** *v/i.* [*irr.*] **1.** gleiten (*a. Riegel etc.*): ***~ down*** hinunterrutschen, -gleiten; ***~ from*** entgleiten (*dat.*); ***let things ~*** *fig.* die Dinge laufen lassen; **2.** *auf Eis* schlittern; **3.** (aus)rutschen; **4.** ***~ over*** *fig.* leicht über *ein Thema* hin'weggehen; **5.** ***~ into*** *fig.* in *et.* hin'einschlittern; **II** *v/t.* [*irr.*] **6.** *Gegenstand, s-e Hände etc. wohin* gleiten lassen, schieben: ***~ in*** *fig. Wort* einfließen lassen; **III** *s.* **7.** Gleiten *n*; **8.** Schlittern *n auf Eis*; **9.** a) Schlitterbahn *f*, b) Rodelbahn *f*, c) (*a.* Wasser)Rutschbahn *f*; **10.** *geol.* Erd-, Fels-, Schneerutsch *m*; **11.** ⚙ a) Rutsche *f*, b) Schieber *m*, c) Schlitten *m* (*Drehbank etc.*), Führung *f*; **12.** ♪ Zug *m*; **13.** Spange *f*; **14.** *phot.* Dia(posi'tiv) *n*: ***~ lecture*** Lichtbildervortrag *m*; **15.** *Mikroskop*: Ob'jektträger *m*; **16.** (*Haar- etc.*)Spange *f*; ***~ cal·i·per*** *s.* ⚙ Schieb-, Schublehre *f*; ***~ rest*** *s.* ⚙ Sup'port *m*; ***~ rule*** *s.* ⚙ Rechenschieber *m*; ***~ valve*** *s.* ⚙ 'Schieber(venˌtil *n*) *m*.
slid·ing ['slaɪdɪŋ] *adj.* □ **1.** gleitend; **2.** Schiebe...: ***~ door***; ***~ fit*** *s.* ⚙ Gleitsitz *m*; ***~ roof*** *s. mot.* Schiebedach *n*; ***~ rule*** → ***slide rule***; ***~ scale*** *s.* ✝ **1.** gleitende (Lohn- *od.* Preis)Skala; **2.** 'Staffeltaˌrif *m*; ***~ seat*** *s. Rudern*: Gleit-, Rollsitz *m*; ***~ ta·ble*** *s.* Ausziehtisch *m*; ***~ time*** *s.* ✝ *Am.* Gleitzeit *f*.
slight [slaɪt] **I** *adj.* □ → ***slightly***; **1.** schmächtig, dünn; **2.** schwach (*Konstruktion*); **3.** leicht, schwach (*Geruch etc.*); **4.** leicht, gering(fügig), unbedeutend: ***a ~ increase***; ***not the ~est doubt*** nicht der geringste Zweifel; **5.** schwach, gering (*Intelligenz etc.*); **6.** flüchtig, oberflächlich (*Bekanntschaft etc.*); **II** *v/t.* **7.** *j-n* kränken; **8.** *et.* auf die leichte Schulter nehmen; **III** *s.* **9.** Kränkung *f*; **'slight·ing** [-tɪŋ] *adj.* □ abschätzig, kränkend; **'slight·ly** [-lɪ] *adv.* leicht, schwach, etwas, ein bißchen; **'slight·ness** [-nɪs] *s.* **1.** Geringfügigkeit *f*; **2.** Schmächtigkeit *f*; **3.** Schwäche *f*.
sli·ly ['slaɪlɪ] *adv. von* ***sly***.
slim [slɪm] **I** *adj.* □ **1.** schlank, dünn; **2.** *fig.* gering, dürftig, schwach: ***a ~ chance***; **3.** schlau, gerieben; **II** *v/t.* **4.** schlank(er) machen; **5.** ***~ down*** F *fig.* ‚abspecken', *a.* gesundschrumpfen; **III** *v/i.* **6.** schlank(er) werden; **7.** e-e Schlankheitskur machen; **'slim·down** *s. fig.* ‚Schlankheitskur' *f*, Gesundschrumpfung *f*.
slime [slaɪm] **I** *s.* **1.** *bsd.* ⚘, *zo.* Schleim *m*; **2.** Schlamm *m*; *fig.* Schmutz *m*; **II** *v/t.* **3.** mit Schlamm *od.* Schleim über'ziehen *od.* bedecken; **'slim·i·ness** [-mɪnɪs] *s.* **1.** Schleimigkeit *f*, *das* Schleimige; **2.** Schlammigkeit *f*.
'slim·line *v/t.* (*v/i.* sich) gesundschrumpfen.
slim·ming ['slɪmɪŋ] **I** *s.* Abnehmen *n*; Schlankheitskur *f*; **II** *adj.* Schlankheits...: ***~ cure***; ***~ diet***; **'slim·ness** [-mnɪs] *s.* **1.** Schlankheit *f*; **2.** *fig.* Dürftigkeit *f*.
slim·y ['slaɪmɪ] *adj.* □ **1.** schleimig, glitschig; **2.** schlammig; **3.** *fig.* a) ‚schleimig', kriecherisch, b) schmierig, schmutzig, c) widerlich, ‚fies'.
sling¹ [slɪŋ] **I** *s.* **1.** Schleuder *f*; **2.** (Schleuder)Wurf *m*; **II** *v/t.* [*irr.*] **3.** schleudern: ***~ ink*** F schriftstellern.
sling² [slɪŋ] **I** *s.* **1.** Schlinge *f zum Heben von Lasten*; **2.** ⚕ (Arm)Schlinge *f*, Binde *f*; **3.** Tragriemen *m*; **4.** *mst pl.* ⚓ Stropp *m*, Tauschlinge *f*; **II** *v/t.* [*irr.*] **5.** a) e-e Schlinge legen um *e-e Last*, b) *Last* hochziehen; **6.** aufhängen: ***be slung from*** hängen *od.* baumeln von; **7.** ⚔ *Gewehr* 'umhängen; **8.** ⚕ *Arm* in die Schlinge legen.
sling³ [slɪŋ] *s. Art* Punsch *m*.
'sling·shot *s.* **1.** (Stein)Schleuder *f*; **2.** *Am.* Kata'pult *n*, *m*.
slink [slɪŋk] **I** *v/i.* [*irr.*] **1.** schleichen, sich *wohin* stehlen: ***~ off*** wegschleichen, sich fortstehlen; **2.** *zo.* fehlgebären, *bsd.* verkalben (*Kuh*); **II** *v/t.* [*irr.*] **3.** *Junges* vor der Zeit werfen, zu früh zur Welt bringen; **'slink·y** [-kɪ] *adj.* **1.** aufreizend; **2.** geschmeidig; **3.** hauteng (*Kleid*).
slip [slɪp] **I** *s.* **1.** (Aus)Gleiten *n*, (-)Rutschen *n*; Fehltritt *m* (*a. fig.*); **2.** *fig.* (Flüchtigkeits)Fehler *m*, Schnitzer *m*, Lapsus *m*: ***~ of the pen*** Schreibfehler *m*; ***~ of the tongue*** ‚Versprecher' *m*; ***it was a ~ of the tongue*** ich habe mich (er hat sich *etc.*) versprochen; **3.** *fig.* ‚Panne' *f*: a) Mißgeschick *n*, b) Fehler *m*, Fehlleistung *f*; **4.** 'Unterkleid *n*, -rock *m*; **5.** (Kissen)Bezug *m*; **6.** (Hunde)Leine *f*, Koppel *f*: ***give s.o. the ~*** *fig.* j-m entwischen; **7.** ⚓ (Schlipp)Helling *f*; **8.** ⚙ Schlupf *m* (*Nachbleiben der Drehzahl*); **9.** *geol.* Erdrutsch *m*; **10.** ⚘ Pfropfreis *n*, Setzling *m*; **11.** *fig.* Sprößling *m*; **12.** Streifen *m*, Stück *n Holz od. Papier*, Zettel *m*: ***a ~ of a boy*** *fig.* ein schmächtiges Bürschchen; ***a ~ of a room*** ein winziges Zimmer; **13.** (Kon'troll- *etc.*)Abschnitt *m*; **14.** *typ.* Fahne *f*; **15.** *Kricket*: Eckmann *m*; **II** *v/i.* **16.** gleiten, rutschen: ***~ from*** *der Hand*, *a. dem Gedächtnis* entgleiten; **17.** sich (hoch- *etc.*)schieben, (ver)rutschen; **18.** sich lösen (*Knoten*); **19.** *wohin* schlüpfen: ***~ away*** a) *a.* ***~ off*** entschlüpfen, -wischen, sich davonstehlen, b) *a.* ***~ by*** verstreichen (*Tage, Zeit*); ***~ in*** sich einschleichen (*a. fig. Fehler etc.*), hineinschlüpfen; ***~ into*** in *ein Kleid, Zimmer etc.* schlüpfen *od.* gleiten; ***let an opportunity ~*** sich e-e Gelegenheit entgehen lassen; **20.** *a.* F ***~ up*** e-n Fehler machen, sich vertun: ***he is ~ping*** F er läßt nach; **III** *v/t.* **21.** *Gegenstand, s-e Hand etc. wohin* gleiten lassen, (*bsd.* heimlich) *wohin* stecken *od.* schieben: ***~ s.o. s.th.*** j-m et. zustecken; ***~ in*** a) *et.* hineingleiten lassen, b) *Bemerkung* einfließen lassen; **22.** *Ring, Kleid etc.* 'über- *od.* abstreifen: ***~ on*** (***off***); **23.** *j-m* entwischen; **24.** *j-s Aufmerksamkeit* entgehen: ***have ~ped s.o.'s memory*** (*od.* ***mind***) j-m entfallen sein; **25.** *et.* fahrenlassen; **26.** a) *Hundehalsband, a. Fessel etc.* abstreifen, b) *Hund etc.* loslassen; **27.** *Knoten* lösen; **28.** → ***slink*** 3; **'~·case** *s.* **1.** ('Bücher)Kasˌsette *f*; **2.** → **'~ˌcov·er** *s.* Schutzhülle *f* (*für Bücher*); Schonbezug *m* (*für Möbel*); **'~·knot** *s.* Laufknoten *m*; **'~-on I** *s.* Kleidungsstück *n* zum 'Überstreifen, *bsd.* a) Slipon *m* (*Mantel*), b) Pull'over *m*, c) Slipper *m*; **II** *adj.* a) Umhänge..., Überzieh..., b) ⚙ Aufsteck...
slip·per ['slɪpə] **I** *s.* **1.** a) Pan'toffel *m*, b) Slipper *m* (*leichter Haus- od. Straßenschuh*); **2.** ⚙ Hemmschuh *m*; **II** *v/t.* **3.** mit e-m Pantoffel schlagen.
slip·per·i·ness ['slɪpərɪnɪs] *s.* **1.** Schlüpfrigkeit *f*; **2.** *fig.* Gerissenheit *f*.
slip·per·y ['slɪpərɪ] *adj.* □ **1.** schlüpfrig, glatt, glitschig; **2.** *fig.* gerissen (*Person*); **3.** *fig.* zweifelhaft, unsicher; **4.** *fig.* heikel (*Thema*); **slip·py** ['slɪpɪ] *adj.* F **1.** → ***slippery*** 1; **2.** fix, flink: ***look ~!*** mach fix!
slip| ring *s.* ↯ Schleifring *m*; ***~ road*** *s. Brit.* (Autobahn)Zubringerstraße *f*; **'~·shod** *adj.* schlampig, schludrig; **'~·slop** *s.* F labberiges Zeug (*Getränk*; *a. fig. leeres Gewäsch*); ***~ sole*** *s.* Einlegesohle *f*; **'~·stick** *s. Am.* Rechenschieber *m*; **'~·stream** *s.* **1.** ✈ Luftschraubenstrahl *m*; **2.** *sport* Windschatten *m*; **'~-up** *s.* → ***slip*** 2, 3; **'~·way** *s.* ⚓ Helling *f*.
slit [slɪt] **I** *v/t.* [*irr.*] **1.** aufschlitzen, -schneiden; **2.** zerschlitzen; **3.** spalten; **4.** ritzen; **II** *v/i.* [*irr.*] **5.** reißen, schlitzen, e-n Riß bekommen; **III** *s.* **6.** Schlitz *m*; **'~-eyed** *adj.* schlitzäugig.
slith·er ['slɪðə] *v/i.* **1.** schlittern, rut-

schen, gleiten; **2.** (schlangenartig) gleiten; **'slith·er·y** [-ðərɪ] *adj.* schlüpfrig.
sliv·er ['slɪvə] **I** *s.* **1.** Splitter *m*, Span *m*; **2.** *Spinnerei*: a) Kammzug *m*, b) Florband *n*; **II** *v/t.* **3.** *Span etc.* abspalten; **4.** zersplittern; **III** *v/i.* **5.** zersplittern.
slob [slɒb] *s.* **1.** *bsd. Ir.* Schlamm *m*; **2.** *sl.* a) ‚fieser Typ', b) ordi'närer Kerl, c) ‚Blödmann' *m*.
slob·ber ['slɒbə] **I** *v/i.* **1.** geifern, sabbern; **2.** *~ over fig.* kindisch schwärmen von; **II** *v/t.* **3.** begeifern, -sabbern; **4.** *j-n* abküssen; **III** *s.* **5.** Geifer *m*; **6.** *fig.* sentimen'tales Gewäsch; **'slob·ber·y** [-ərɪ] *adj.* **1.** sabbernd; **2.** besabbert; **3.** *fig.* gefühlsduselig; **4.** schlampig.
sloe [sləʊ] *s.* ⚘ **1.** Schlehe *f*; **2.** *a. ~ bush, ~ tree* Schleh-, Schwarzdorn *m*; **'~·worm** → ***slowworm***.
slog [slɒg] F **I** *v/t.* **1.** hart schlagen; **2.** (ver)prügeln; **II** *v/i.* **3.** *~ on, ~ away* a) sich da'hinschleppen, b) sich ‚'durchbeißen'; **4.** *a. ~ away* sich plagen, schuften; **III** *s.* **5.** harter Schlag; **6.** *fig.* Schinde'rei *f*: ***a long ~*** e-e ‚Durststrecke'.
slo·gan ['sləʊgən] *s.* **1.** *Scot.* Schlachtruf *m*; **2.** Slogan *m*: a) Schlagwort *n*, b) ✝ Werbespruch *m*.
slog·ger ['slɒgə] *s.* **1.** *sport* harter Schläger; **2.** *fig.* ‚Arbeitstier' *n*.
sloop [slu:p] *s.* ⚓ Scha'luppe *f*.
slop¹ [slɒp] **I** *s.* **1.** Pfütze *f*; **2.** *pl.* a) Spülwasser *n*, b) Schmutzwasser *n*; **3.** Schweinetrank *m*; **4.** *pl.* a) Krankensüppchen *n*, b) ‚labberiges Zeug', ‚Spülwasser' *n*; **5.** F rührseliges Zeug; **II** *v/t.* **6.** (ver)schütten; **7.** *a. ~ up* geräuschvoll essen *od.* trinken; **III** *v/i.* **8.** *~ over* 'überschwappen; **9.** *~ over* F kindisch schwärmen; **10.** patschen, waten; **11.** *a. ~ around* ‚her'umhängen, -schlurfen'.
slop² [slɒp] *s.* **1.** Kittel *m*, lose Jacke; **2.** *pl.* (billige) Konfekti'onskleider *pl.*; **3.** ⚓ ‚Kla'motten' *pl.* (*Kleidung u. Bettzeug*).
slop ba·sin *s.* Schale *f* für Tee- *od.* Kaffeereste.
slope [sləʊp] **I** *s.* **1.** (Ab)Hang *m*; **2.** Böschung *f*; **3.** a) Neigung *f*, Gefälle *n*, b) Schräge *f*, geneigte Ebene: ***on the ~*** schräg, abfallend; **4.** *geol.* Senke *f*; **5.** ***at the ~*** ⚔ mit Gewehr über; **II** *v/i.* **6.** sich neigen; (schräg) abfallen; **III** *v/t.* **7.** neigen, senken; **8.** abschrägen (*a.* ⚙); **9.** schräg legen; **10.** (ab)böschen; **11.** ⚔ *Gewehr* 'übernehmen; **12.** F a) *a. ~ off* ‚abhauen', b) *~ around* her'umschlendern; **'slop·ing** [-pɪŋ] *adj.* ☐ schräg, abfallend; ansteigend.
'slop-pail *s.* Toi'letteneimer *m*.
slop·pi·ness ['slɒpɪnɪs] *s.* **1.** Matschigkeit *f*; **2.** Matsch *m*; **3.** Schlampigkeit *f*; **4.** F Rührseligkeit *f*; **slop·py** ['slɒpɪ] *adj.* ☐ **1.** matschig (*Boden etc.*); **2.** naß, bespritzt (*Tisch etc.*); **3.** *fig.* labberig (*Speisen*); **4.** schlampig, nachlässig (*Arbeit etc.*), sa'lopp (*Sprache*); **5.** rührselig.
'slop·shop *s. Laden mit billiger Konfektionsware.*
slosh [slɒʃ] **I** *s.* **1.** → ***slush*** 1 *u.* 2; **II** *v/i.* **2.** im (Schmutz)Wasser her'umpatschen; **3.** schwappen; **III** *v/t.* **4.** bespritzen: *~ on Farbe etc.* a) draufklatschen, b) klatschen auf (*acc.*); **5.** *Bier im Glas etc.* schwenken; **6.** *a. ~ down* F *Bier etc.* ‚hin'unterschütten'; **'sloshed** [-ʃt] *adj. sl.* ‚besoffen'.
slot¹ [slɒt] **I** *s.* **1.** Schlitz(einwurf) *m*; Spalte *f*; **2.** ⚙ Nut *f*: ***~ and key*** Nut u. Feder (*Metall*); **3.** F (freie) Stelle, Platz *m*: ***find a ~ for*** (***in***) → 5; **II** *v/t.* **4.** ⚙ nuten, schlitzen: ***~ting-machine*** Nutenstoßmaschine *f*; **5.** F *j-n od. et.* 'unterbringen (***into*** in *dat.*); **III** *v/i.* **6.** ***~ into*** F *a. fig.* (hin'ein)passen in (*acc.*).
slot² [slɒt] *s. hunt.* Spur *f*.
sloth [sləʊθ] *s.* **1.** Faulheit *f*; **2.** *zo.* Faultier *n*; **'sloth·ful** [-fʊl] *adj.* ☐ faul, träge.
slot ma·chine *s.* ('Waren-, 'Spiel)Auto₁mat *m*.
slouch [slaʊtʃ] **I** *s.* **1.** krumme, nachlässige Haltung; **2.** latschiger Gang; **3.** a) her'abhängende Hutkrempe, b) → ***slouch hat***; **4.** F ‚Flasche' *f*, ‚Niete' *f* (*Nichtskönner*): ***he is no ~*** ‚er ist auf Draht'; ***the show is no ~*** das Stück ist nicht ohne; **II** *v/i.* **5.** krumm dasitzen *od.* -stehen; **6.** *a. ~ along* latschen, latschig gehen; **7.** her'abhängen (*Krempe*); **III** *v/t.* **8.** *Schultern* hängen lassen; **9.** *Krempe* her'unterbiegen; **slouch hat** *s.* Schlapphut *m*; **'slouch·ing** [-tʃɪŋ] *adj.* ☐, **'slouch·y** [-tʃɪ] *adj.* **1.** krumm (*Haltung*); latschig (*Gang, Haltung, Person*); **2.** her'abhängend (*Krempe*); **3.** lax, faul.
slough¹ [slaʊ] *s.* **1.** Sumpf-, Schmutzloch *n*; **2.** Mo'rast *m* (*a. fig.*): ***2 of Despond*** Sumpf *m* der Verzweiflung.
slough² [slʌf] **I** *s.* **1.** abgestreifte Haut (*bsd. Schlange*); **2.** ⚕ Schorf *m*; **II** *v/i.* **3.** *oft ~ away* (*od.* ***off***) sich häuten; **4.** sich ablösen (*Schorf etc.*); **III** *v/t.* **5.** *a. ~ off Haut etc.* abstreifen, -werfen; *fig. Gewohnheit etc.* ablegen; **'slough·y** [-fɪ] *adj.* ⚕ schorfig.
slov·en ['slʌvn] *s.* a) Schlamper *m*, b) Schlampe *f*; **'slov·en·ly** [-lɪ] *adj. u. adv.* schlampig, schlud(e)rig.
slow [sləʊ] **I** *adj.* ☐ **1.** *allg.* langsam: ***~ and sure*** langsam, aber sicher; ***~ train*** 🚂 Personenzug *m*; ***be ~ in arriving*** lange ausbleiben, auf sich warten lassen; ***be ~ to write*** sich mit dem Schreiben Zeit lassen; ***be ~ to take offence*** nicht leicht et. übelnehmen; ***not to be ~ to do s.th.*** et. prompt tun, nicht lange mit et. fackeln; ***the clock is 20 minutes ~*** die Uhr geht 20 Minuten nach; **2.** all'mählich, langsam: ***~ growth***; **3.** säumig (*a. Zahler*); unpünktlich; **4.** schwach (*Feuer*); **5.** schleichend (*Fieber, Gift*); **6.** ✝ schleppend, schlecht (*Geschäft*); **7.** schwerfällig, schwer von Begriff, begriffsstutzig: ***be ~ in learning s.th.*** et. nur schwer lernen; ***be ~ of speech*** e-e schwere Zunge haben; **8.** langweilig, fad(e), ‚müde'; **9.** langsam (*Rennbahn*); schwer (*Boden*); **10.** *mot.* Leerlauf…; **II** *adv.* **11.** langsam: ***go ~*** *fig.* a) ‚langsam treten', b) ✝ e-n Bummelstreik machen; **III** *v/t.* **12.** *mst ~ down* (*od.* ***off, up***) a) *Geschwindigkeit* verlangsamen, verringern, b) *et.* verzögern; **IV** *v/i.* **13.** *~ down od. up* sich verlangsamen, langsamer werden, *fig.* ‚langsamer tun'; **'~-₁burn·ing stove** *s.* Dauerbrandofen *m*; **'~·coach** *s. contp.* ‚Schlafmütze' *f*; **'~·down** *s.* **1.** Verlangsamung *f*; **2.** *Am.* Bummelstreik *m*; **~ lane** *s. mot.* Kriechspur *f*; **~ march** *s.* ♪ Trauermarsch *m*; **~ match** *s.* ⚔ Zündschnur *f*, Lunte *f*; **~ mo·tion** *s.* Zeitlupentempo *n*; **₁~-'mo·tion** *adj.* Zeitlupen…: ***~ picture*** Zeitlupe(naufnahme) *f*.
slow·ness ['sləʊnɪs] *s.* **1.** Langsamkeit *f*; **2.** Schwerfälligkeit *f*, Begriffsstutzigkeit *f*; **3.** Langweiligkeit *f*, ‚Lahmheit' *f*.
'slow|·poke *Am.* F Langweiler *m*; **₁~-'speed** *adj.* ⚙ langsam(laufend); **~ train** *s.* Bummel-, Per'sonenzug *m*; **₁~-'wit·ted** → ***slow*** 7; **'~·worm** *s. zo.* Blindschleiche *f*.
sloyd [slɔɪd] *s. ped.* 'Werk₁unterricht *m* (*bsd. Schnitzen*).
sludge [slʌdʒ] *s.* **1.** Schlamm *m*, (*a.* Schnee)Matsch *m*; **2.** ⚙ Schlamm *m*, Bodensatz *m*; **3.** Klärschlamm *m*; **4.** Treibeis *n*; **'sludg·y** [-dʒɪ] *adj.* schlammig, matschig.
slue [slu:] → ***slew***[3] *u.* ***slew***[4].
slug¹ [slʌg] **I** *s. zo.* **1.** (Weg)Schnecke *f*; **2.** F Faulpelz *m*; **II** *v/i.* **3.** faulenzen.
slug² [slʌg] *s.* **1.** Stück *n* 'Rohme₁tall; **2.** a) *hist.* Mus'ketenkugel *f*, b) grobes Schrot, c) (Luftgewehr-, *Am.* Pi'stolen-) Kugel *f*; **3.** *Am.* a) falsche Münze, b) Gläs-chen *n Schnaps etc.*; **4.** *typ.* a) Re'glette *f*, b) 'Setzma₁schinenzeile *f*, c) Zeilenguß *m*; **5.** *phys.* Masseneinheit *f*.
slug³ [slʌg] **I** *bsd. Am.* harter Schlag; **II** *v/t. j-m* ‚ein Ding verpassen'.
slug·a·bed ['slʌgəbed] *s.* Langschläfer(in).
slug·gard ['slʌgəd] **I** *s.* Faulpelz *m*; **II** *adj.* ☐ faul.
slug·ger ['slʌgə] *s. Am.* F *Baseball, Boxen*: harter Schläger.
slug·gish ['slʌgɪʃ] *adj.* ☐ **1.** träge (*a.* ⚕ *Organ*), langsam, schwerfällig; **2.** ✝ *etc.* schleppend; **3.** träge fließend (*Fluß etc.*); **'slug·gish·ness** [-nɪs] *s.* Trägheit *f*, Langsamkeit *f*, Schwerfälligkeit *f*.
sluice [slu:s] **I** *s.* ⚙ **1.** Schleuse *f* (*a. fig.*); **2.** Stauwasser *n*; **3.** 'Schleusenka₁nal *m*; **4.** *min.* (Erz-, Gold)Waschrinne *f*; **II** *v/t.* **5.** *Wasser* ablassen; **6.** *min. Erz etc.* waschen; **7.** (aus)spülen; **III** *v/i.* **8.** (aus)strömen; **~ gate** *s.* Schleusentor *n*; **'~·way** → ***sluice*** 3.
slum [slʌm] **I** *s.* **1.** schmutzige Gasse; **2.** *mst pl.* Slums *pl.*, Elendsviertel *n*; **II** *v/i.* **3.** *mst go ~ming* die Slums aufsuchen (*bsd. aus Neugierde*); **4.** in primi'tiven Verhältnissen leben; **III** *v/t.* **5.** *~ it* → 4.
slum·ber ['slʌmbə] **I** *v/i.* **1.** *bsd. poet.* schlummern (*a. fig.*); **2.** da'hindösen; **II** *v/t.* **3.** *~ away Zeit* verschlafen; **III** *s. mst pl.* **4.** (*fig.* tiefer) Schlummer; **'slum·ber·ous** [-bərəs] *adj.* ☐ **1.** schläfrig; **2.** einschläfernd.
slump [slʌmp] **I** *v/i.* **1.** (hin'ein)plumpsen; **2.** *mst ~ down* (in sich) zs.-sacken (*Person*); **3.** ✝ stürzen (*Preise*); **4.** völlig versagen; **II** *s.* **5.** ✝ a) (Börsen-, Preis)Sturz *m*, Baisse *f*, b) starker Konjunk'turrückgang, Wirtschaftskrise *f*; **6.** *allg.* plötzlicher Rückgang.
slung [slʌŋ] *pret. u. p.p. von* ***sling***.
slung shot *s. Am.* Schleudergeschoß *n*.
slunk [slʌŋk] *pret. u. p.p. von* ***slink***.
slur¹ [slɜ:] **I** *v/t.* **1.** verunglimpfen, verleumden; **II** *s.* **2.** Makel *m* (Schand-) Fleck *m*: ***put*** *od.* ***cast a ~*** (***up***)***on*** a) → 1, b) *j-s Ruf etc.* schädigen; **3.** Verunglimpfung *f*.

slur² [slɜː] **I** *v/t.* **1.** a) undeutlich schreiben, b) *typ.* schmitzen, verwischen; **2.** undeutlich aussprechen; *Silbe etc.* verschleifen, -schlucken; **3.** ♪ a) *Töne* binden, b) *Noten* mit Bindebogen bezeichnen; **4.** *oft* ~ ***over*** (leicht) über *ein Thema* hin'weggehen; **II** *v/i.* **5.** undeutlich schreiben *od.* sprechen; **6.** ♪ le'gato singen *od.* spielen; **III** *s.* **7.** Undeutlichkeit *f*, ‚Genuschel' *n*; **8.** ♪ a) Bindung *f*, b) Bindebogen *m*; **9.** *typ.* Schmitz *m*.

slurp [slɜːp] *v/t. u. v/i.* schlürfen.

slush [slʌʃ] **I** *s.* **1.** Schneematsch *m*; **2.** Schlamm *m*, Matsch *m*; **3.** ⚙ Schmiere *f*, Rostschutzmittel *n*; **4.** ⚙ Pa'pierbrei *m*; **5.** *fig.* Gefühlsduse'lei *f*; **6.** *fig.* Kitsch *m*, Schund *m*; **II** *v/t.* **7.** bespritzen; **8.** ⚙ schmieren; **III** *v/i.* **9.** → ***slosh*** 2 *u.* 3; **slush fund** *s. pol. Am.* Schmiergelderfonds *m*; **'slush·y** [-ʃɪ] *adj.* **1.** matschig, schlammig; **2.** rührselig, kitschig.

slut [slʌt] *s.* **1.** Schlampe *f*; **2.** Hure *f*, ‚Nutte' *f*; **3.** *humor.* ‚kleines Luder' (*Mädchen*); **4.** *Am.* Hündin *f*; **'slut·tish** [-tɪʃ] *adj.* □ schlampig, liederlich.

sly [slaɪ] *adj.* □ **1.** schlau, verschlagen, listig; **2.** verstohlen, heimlich, 'hinterhältig: ***a*** ~ ***dog*** ein ganz Schlauer; ***on the*** ~ ‚klammheimlich'; **3.** durch'trieben, pfiffig; **'sly·boots** *s. humor.* Pfiffikus *m*, Schlauberger *m*; **'sly·ness** [-nɪs] *s.* Schlauheit *f etc.*

smack¹ [smæk] **I** *s.* **1.** (Bei)Geschmack *m* (***of*** von); **2.** Prise *f Salz etc.*; **3.** *fig.* Beigeschmack *m*, Anflug *m* (***of*** von); **II** *v/i.* **4.** schmecken (***of*** nach); **5.** *fig.* schmecken *od.* riechen (***of*** nach).

smack² [smæk] **I** *s.* **1.** Klatsch *m*, Klaps *m*: ***a*** ~ ***in the eye*** *fig.* a) ein Schlag ins Gesicht, b) ein Schlag ins Kontor; **2.** Schmatzen *n*; **3.** (*Peitschen- etc.*)Knall *m*; **4.** Schmatz *m* (*Kuß*); **II** *v/t.* **5.** *et.* schmatzend genießen; **6.** ~ ***one's lips*** a) (mit den Lippen) schmatzen, b) sich die Lippen lecken; **7.** *Hände etc.* zs.-schlagen; **8.** mit *der Peitsche* knallen; **9.** *j-m* e-n Klaps geben; **10.** *et.* hinklatschen; **III** *v/i.* **11.** schmatzen; **12.** knallen (*Peitsche etc.*); **13.** (hin)klatschen (***on*** auf *acc.*); **IV** *adv. u. int.* **14.** F a) klatsch(!), platsch(!), b) ‚zack', di'rekt: ***run*** ~ ***into s.th.***

smack³ [smæk] *s.* ⚓ Schmack(e) *f*.

smack·er ['smækə] *s.* **1.** F Schmatz *m* (*Kuß*); **2.** *sl.* a) *Brit.* Pfund *n*, b) *Am.* Dollar *m*; **'smack·ing** [-kɪŋ] *s.* Tracht *f* Prügel.

small [smɔːl] **I** *adj.* **1.** *allg.* klein; **2.** klein, schmächtig; **3.** klein, gering (*Anzahl, Ausdehnung, Grad etc.*): ***they came in*** ~ ***numbers*** es kamen nur wenige; **4.** klein, armselig, dürftig; **5.** wenig: ~ ***blame to him*** das macht ihm kaum Schande; ~ ***wonder*** kein Wunder; ***have*** ~ ***cause for*** kaum Anlaß zu *Dankbarkeit etc.* haben; **6.** klein, mit wenig Besitz: ~ ***farmer*** Kleinbauer *m*; **7.** klein, (sozi'al) niedrig: ~ ***people*** kleine Leute; **8.** klein, unbedeutend: ***a*** ~ ***man***; ***a*** ~ ***poet***; **9.** trivi'al, klein: ***the*** ~ ***worries*** die kleinen Sorgen: ***a*** ~ ***matter*** e-e Kleinigkeit; **10.** klein, bescheiden: ***a*** ~ ***beginning***; ***in a*** ~ ***way*** a) bescheiden *leben etc.*, b) im Kleinen handeln *etc.*; **11.** *contp.* kleinlich; **12.** *b.s.* niedrig (*Gesinnung etc.*): ***feel*** ~ sich schämen; ***make s.o. feel*** ~ j-n beschämen; **13.** dünn (*Bier*); **14.** schwach (*Stimme, Puls*); **II** *s.* **15.** schmal(st)er *od.* verjüngter Teil: ~ ***of the back*** *anat.* das Kreuz; **16.** *pl. Brit.* F 'Unterwäsche *f*, Taschentücher *pl. etc.*; ~ **arms** *s. pl.* ⚔ Hand(feuer)waffen *pl.*; ~ **beer** *s.* **1.** *obs.* Dünnbier *n*; **2.** *bsd. Brit.* F a) Lap'palie *f*, b) ‚Null' *f*, unbedeutende Per'son: ***think no*** ~ ***of o.s.*** F e-e hohe Meinung von sich haben; ~ **cap·i·tals** *s. pl. typ.* Kapi'tälchen *pl.*; ~ **change** *s.* **1.** Kleingeld *n*; **2.** → ***small beer*** 2; **'~·clothes** *s.* **1.** *pl. hist.* Kniehosen *pl.*; **2.** 'Unterwäsche *f*; **3.** Kinderkleidung *f*; ~ **coal** *s.* Feinkohle *f*, Grus *m*; ~ **fry** *s.* **1.** junge, kleine Fische *pl.*; **2.** ‚junges Gemüse', *die* Kleinen *pl.*; **3.** → ***small beer*** 2; **'~ˌhold·er** *s. Brit.* Kleinbauer *m*; **'~ˌhold·ing** *s. Brit.* Kleinlandbesitz *m*; ~ **hours** *s. pl. die* frühen Morgenstunden *pl.*

small·ish ['smɔːlɪʃ] *adj.* ziemlich klein.

small| let·ter *s.* Kleinbuchstabe *m*; **ˌ~-'mind·ed** *adj.* engstirnig, kleinlich, ‚kleinkariert'.

small·ness ['smɔːlnɪs] *s.* **1.** Kleinheit *f*; **2.** geringe Anzahl; **3.** Geringfügigkeit *f*; **4.** Kleinlichkeit *f*; **5.** niedrige Gesinnung.

small| pi·ca *s. typ.* kleine Cicero (-schrift); **'~·pox** [-pɒks] *s.* ⚕ Pocken *pl.*, Blattern *pl.*; ~ **print** *s. das* Kleingedruckte *e-s Vertrags*; ~ **shot** *s.* Schrot *m*, *n*; **'~·sword** *s. fenc.* Flo'rett *n*; ~ **talk** *s.* oberflächliche Konversati'on, Geplauder *n*: ***he has no*** ~ er kann nicht (unverbindlich) plaudern; **'~·time** *adj. Am. sl.* unbedeutend, klein, ‚Schmalspur...'; **'~·ware** *s.* Kurzwaren *pl.*

smalt [smɔːlt] *s.* **1.** ⚗ S(ch)malte *f*, Kobaltblau *n*; **2.** Kobaltglas *n*.

smar·agd ['smærægd] *s. min.* Sma'ragd *m*.

smarm·y ['smɑːmɪ] *adj.* □ *Brit.* F **1.** ölig; **2.** kriecherisch; **3.** kitschig.

smart [smɑːt] **I** *adj.* □ **1.** klug, gescheit, intelli'gent, pa'tent; **2.** geschickt, gewandt; **3.** geschäftstüchtig; **4.** *b.s.* gerissen, raffiniert; **5.** witzig, geistreich; **6.** *contp.* ‚superklug', ‚klugscheißerisch'; **7.** flink, fix; **8.** schmuck, gepflegt; **9.** a) ele'gant, fesch, schick, b) modisch (*Person, Kleidung, Wort etc.*): ***the*** ~ ***set*** die elegante Welt, die ‚Schickeria'; **10.** forsch, schneidig: ~ ***pace***; ***salute*** ~***ly*** zackig grüßen; **11.** hart, empfindlich (*Schlag, Strafe*); **12.** scharf (*Schmerz, Kritik etc.*); **13.** F beträchtlich; **II** *v/i.* **14.** schmerzen, brennen; **15.** leiden (***from, under*** unter *dat.*): ***he*** ~***ed under the insult*** die Kränkung nagte an s-m Herzen; **III** *s.* **16.** Schmerz *m*; **smart al·eck** ['ælɪk] *s.* F ‚Klugscheißer' *m*; **'smart-ˌal·eck·y** [-kɪ] → ***smart*** 6; **'smart·en** [-tn] **I** *v/t.* **1.** *a.* ~ ***up*** her'ausputzen; **2.** *fig. j-n* ‚auf Zack' bringen; **II** *v/i. mst* ~ ***up*** **3.** sich schönmachen, sich ‚in Schale werfen'; **4.** *fig.* aufwachen; **'smart-ˌmon·ey** *s.* Schmerzensgeld *n*; **'smart·ness** [-nɪs] *s.* **1.** Klugheit *f*, Gescheitheit *f*; **2.** Gewandtheit *f*; **3.** *b.s.* Gerissenheit *f*; **4.** flotte Ele'ganz, Schick *m*; **5.** Forschheit *f*; **6.** Schärfe *f*, Heftigkeit *f*; **'smart·y** [-tɪ] → ***smart aleck***.

smash [smæʃ] **I** *v/t.* **1.** *oft* ~ ***up*** zertrümmern, -schmettern, -schlagen: ~ ***in*** einschlagen; **2.** *j-n* (zs.-)schlagen; *Feind* vernichtend schlagen; *fig. Argument* restlos wider'legen, *Gegner* ‚fertigmachen'; **3.** *j-n* (finanzi'ell) ruinieren; **4.** *Faust, Stein etc. wohin* schmettern; **5.** *Tennis*: *Ball* schmettern; **II** *v/i.* **6.** zersplittern, in Stücke springen; **7.** krachen, knallen (***against*** gegen, ***through*** durch); **8.** zs.-stoßen, -krachen (*Autos etc.*); ✈ Bruch machen; **9.** a) *oft* ~ ***up*** ‚zs.-krachen', bank'rott gehen, b) zu'schanden werden, c) (gesundheitlich) ka'puttgehen; **III** *adv.* (*a. int.*) **10.** krachend, krach(!); **IV** *s.* **11.** Zerkrachen *n*; **12.** Krach *m*; **13.** (*a.* finanzi'eller) Zs.-bruch, Ru'in *m*: ***go*** ~ a) völlig zs.-brechen, ‚kaputtgehen', b) → 9; **14.** F voller Erfolg; **15.** *Tennis*: Schmetterball *m*; **16.** *kaltes Branntwein-Mischgetränk*; **ˌsmash-and-'grab raid** [-ʃn'g-] *s.* Schaufenstereinbruch *m*; **smashed** [-ʃt] *adj. sl.* **1.** ‚blau', besoffen; **2.** ‚high' (*unter Drogeneinfluß*); **'smash·er** [-ʃə] *s. sl.* **1.** schwerer Schlag (*a. fig.*); **2.** vernichtendes Argu'ment; **3.** ‚Wucht' *f*: a) ‚tolle Sache', b) ‚tolle Person': ***a*** ~ (***of a girl***) ein tolles Mädchen; **smash hit** *s.* F Schlager *m*, Bombenerfolg *m*; **'smash·ing** [-ʃɪŋ] *adj.* **1.** F ‚toll', sagenhaft; **2.** vernichtend (*Schlag, Niederlage*); **'smash-up** *s.* **1.** völliger Zs.-bruch; **2.** Bank'rott *m*; **3.** *mot. etc.* Zs.-stoß *m*; **4.** ✈ Bruch(landung *f*) *m*.

smat·ter·er ['smætərə] *s.* Stümper *m*, Halbwisser *m*; Dilet'tant *m*; **'smat·ter·ing** [-tərɪŋ] *s.* oberflächliche Kenntnis: ***he has a*** ~ ***of French*** er kann ein bißchen Französisch.

smear [smɪə] **I** *v/t.* **1.** *Fett etc.* schmieren (***on*** auf *acc.*); **2.** *et.* beschmieren, bestreichen (***with*** mit); **3.** (ein)schmieren; **4.** *Schrift* verschmieren; **5.** beschmieren, besudeln; **6.** *fig.* a) *j-s Ruf etc.* besudeln, b) *j-n* verleumden, ‚durch den Dreck ziehen'; **7.** *sport Am.* F ‚über'fahren'; **II** *v/i.* **8.** schmieren; **9.** sich verwischen; **III** *s.* **10.** Schmiere *f*; **11.** (Fett-, Schmutz)Fleck *m*; **12.** *fig.* Besudelung *f*; **13.** ⚕ Abstrich *m*; ~ **cam·paign** *s. pol.* Ver'leumdungskamˌpagne *f*; **'~·case** *s. Am.* Quark *m*; ~ **sheet** *s.* Skan'dalblatt *n*; ~ **test** *s.* ⚕ Abstrich *m*.

smear·y ['smɪərɪ] *adj.* □ **1.** schmierig; **2.** verschmiert.

smell [smel] **I** *v/t.* [*irr.*] **1.** *et.* riechen; **2.** *et.* beriechen, riechen an (*dat.*); **3.** *fig. Verrat etc.* wittern; → ***rat*** 1; **4.** *fig.* sich *et.* genauer besehen; **5.** ~ ***out*** *hunt.* aufspüren (*a. fig. entdecken, ausschnüffeln*); **II** *v/i.* [*irr.*] **6.** riechen (***at*** an *dat.*): ~ ***about*** (*od.* ***round***) *fig.* herumschnüffeln; **7.** *gut etc.* riechen: ***his breath*** ~***s*** er riecht aus dem Mund; **8.** ~ ***of*** riechen nach (*a. fig.*); **III** *s.* **9.** Geruch(ssinn) *m*; **10.** Geruch *m*: a) Duft *m*, b) Gestank *m*; **11.** *fig.* Anflug *m*, -strich *m* (***of*** von); **12.** ***take a*** ~ ***at s.th.*** *et.* beriechen (*a. fig.*); **'smell·er** [-lə] *s. sl.* **1.** ‚Riechkolben' *m* (*Nase*); **2.** Schlag *m* auf die Nase; Sturz *m*; **'smell·y** [-lɪ] *adj.* F übelriechend, muffig: ~ ***feet*** Schweißfüße.

smelt¹ [smelt] *pl.* **smelts** *coll. a.* **smelt** *s. ichth.* Stint *m*.

smelt² [smelt] *v/t.* **1.** *Erz* (ein)schmelzen, verhütten; **2.** *Kupfer etc.* ausschmelzen.
smelt³ [smelt] *pret. u. p.p. von* **smell**.
smelt·er [ˈsmeltə] *s.* Schmelzer *m*; **ˈsmelt·er·y** [-ərɪ] *s.* Schmelzhütte *f*; **ˈsmelt·ing** [-tɪŋ] *s.* ⚙ Verhüttung *f*: **~ furnace** Schmelzofen *m*.
smile [smaɪl] **I** *v/i.* **1.** lächeln (*a. fig. Sonne etc.*): **~ at** a) *j-m* zulächeln, b) *et.* belächeln, lächeln über (*acc.*); **come up smiling** *fig.* die Sache leicht überstehen; **2. ~ (up)on** *fig. j-m* lächeln, hold sein: **fortune ~d on him**; **II** *v/t.* **3. ~ away** *Tränen etc.* hinˈweglächeln; **4. ~ approval (consent)** beifällig (zustimmend) lächeln; **III** *s.* **5.** Lächeln *n*: **be all ~s** (über das ganze Gesicht) strahlen; **6.** *mst pl.* Gunst *f*; **ˈsmil·ing** [-lɪŋ] *adj.* ☐ **1.** lächelnd (*a. fig. heiter*); **2.** *fig.* huldvoll.
smirch [smɜːtʃ] **I** *v/t.* besudeln (*a. fig.*); **II** *s.* Schmutzfleck *m*; *fig.* Schandfleck *m*.
smirk [smɜːk] **I** *v/i.* affektiert *od.* blöd lächeln, grinsen; **II** *s.* einfältiges Lächeln, Grinsen *n*.
smite [smaɪt] [*irr.*] **I** *v/t.* **1.** *bibl., rhet., a. humor.* schlagen (*a. erschlagen, heimsuchen*): **smitten with the plague** von der Pest befallen; **2.** *j-n* quälen, peinigen (*Gewissen*); **3.** *fig.* packen: **smitten with** von *Begierde etc.* gepackt; **4.** *fig.* hinreißen: **he was smitten with** (*od.* **by**) **her charms** er war hingerissen von ihrem Charme; **be smitten by** (sinnlos) verliebt sein in (*acc.*); **II** *v/i.* **5. ~ upon** *bsd. fig.* an *das Ohr etc.* schlagen.
smith [smɪθ] *s.* Schmied *m*.
smith·er·eens [ˌsmɪðəˈriːnz] *s. pl.* F Fetzen *pl.*, Splitter *pl.*: **smash to ~** in (tausend) Stücke schlagen.
smith·er·y [ˈsmɪðərɪ] *s.* **1.** Schmiedearbeit *f*; **2.** Schmiedekunst *f*.
smith·y [ˈsmɪðɪ] *s.* Schmiede *f*.
smit·ten [ˈsmɪtn] **I** *p.p. von* **smite**; **II** *adj.* **1.** betroffen, befallen; **2.** (**by**) hingerissen (von), ‚verknallt', verliebt (in *acc.*); → **smite** 4.
smock [smɒk] **I** *s.* **1.** (Arbeits)Kittel *m*: **~ frock** *Art* Fuhrmannskittel *m*; **2.** Kinderkittel *m*; **II** *v/t.* **3.** *Bluse etc.* smoken, mit Smokarbeit verzieren; **ˈsmock·ing** [-kɪŋ] *s.* Smokarbeit *f* (*Vorgang u. Verzierung*).
smog [smɒg] *s.* (*aus* **smoke** *u.* **fog**) Smog *m*, Dunstglocke *f*; **ˈ~·bound** *adj.* von Smog eingehüllt.
smok·a·ble [ˈsməʊkəbl] *adj.* rauchbar; **smoke** [sməʊk] **I** *s.* **1.** Rauch *m* (*a.* ⚗, *phys.*): **like ~** *sl.* wie der Teufel; **no ~ without a fire** *fig.* irgend etwas ist immer dran (*an e-m Gerücht*); **2.** Qualm *m*, Dunst *m*: **end** (*od.* **go up**) **in ~** *fig.* in nichts zerrinnen, zu Wasser werden; **3.** ⚔ (Tarn)Nebel *m*; **4.** Rauchen *n e-r Zigarre etc.*: **have a ~** ‚eine' rauchen; **5.** F ‚Glimmstengel' *m*, Ziˈgarre *f*, Zigaˈrette *f*; **6.** *sl.* a) ‚Hasch' *n*, b) Marihuˈana *n*; **II** *v/i.* **7.** rauchen, qualmen (*Schornstein, Ofen etc.*); **8.** dampfen (*a. Pferd*); **9.** rauchen: **do you ~?**; **III** *v/t.* **10.** *Pfeife etc.* rauchen; **11. ~ out** a) ausräuchern (*a. fig.*), b) *fig.* ans Licht bringen; **12.** *Fisch etc.* räuchern; **13.** *Glas etc.* schwärzen; **~ ball**, **~ bomb** *s.* Nebel-, Rauchbombe *f*; **~ con·sum·er** *s.* Rauchverzehrer *m*; **ˈ~-dried** *adj.* geräuchert; **~ hel·met** *s.* Rauchmaske *f* (*Feuerwehr*).
smoke·less [ˈsməʊklɪs] *adj.* ☐ *a.* ⚔ rauchlos.
smok·er [ˈsməʊkə] *s.* **1.** Raucher(in): **~'s cough** Raucherhusten *m*; **~'s heart** ⚕ Nikotinherz *n*; **2.** 🚃 Raucher(abteil *n*) *m*.
smoke| room [rʊm] *s.* Herren-, Rauchzimmer *n*; **~ screen** *s.* ⚔ Rauch-, Nebelvorhang *m*; *fig.* Tarnung *f*, Nebel *m*; **ˈ~·stack** *s.* ⚓, 🚃, ⚙ Schornstein *m*.
smok·ing [ˈsməʊkɪŋ] **I** *s.* **1.** Rauchen *n*; **II** *adj.* **2.** Rauch…; **3.** Raucher…; **~ car**, **~ com·part·ment** *s.* 🚃 ˈRaucherabˌteil *n*.
smok·y [ˈsməʊkɪ] *adj.* ☐ **1.** qualmend; **2.** dunstig, verräuchert; **3.** rauchig (*a. Stimme*); rauchgrau.
smol·der [ˈsməʊldə] *Am.* → **smoulder**.
smooch [smuːtʃ] *v/i. sl.* **1.** schmusen, knutschen; **2.** *Brit.* engumˈschlungen tanzen.
smooth [smuːð] **I** *adj.* ☐ **1.** *allg.* glatt; **2.** glatt, ruhig (*See*): **I am in ~ water now** *fig.* jetzt habe ich es geschafft; **3.** ⚙ ruhig (*Gang*); *mot. a.* zügig (*Fahren, Schalten*); ✈ glatt (*Landung*); **4.** *fig.* glatt, reibungslos: **make things ~ for** *j-m* den Weg ebnen; **5.** fließend, geschliffen (*Rede etc.*); schwungvoll (*Melodie, Stil*); **6.** *fig.* sanft, weich (*Stimme, Ton*); **7.** glatt, gewandt (*Manieren, Person*); *b.s.* aalglatt: **a ~ tongue** e-e glatte Zunge; **8.** *Am. sl.* a) fesch, schick, b) ‚sauber', prima; **9.** geschmeidig, nicht klumpig (*Teig etc.*); **10.** lieblich (*Wein*); **II** *adv.* **11.** glatt, ruhig: **things have gone ~ with me** bei mir ging alles glatt; **III** *v/t.* **12.** glätten (*a. fig.*): **~ the way for** *fig. j-m od. e-r Sache* den Weg ebnen; **13.** besänftigen; **IV** *v/i.* **14.** → **smooth down** 1;
Zssgn mit adv.:
smooth| a·way *v/t. Schwierigkeiten etc.* wegräumen, ‚ausbügeln'; **~ down I** *v/i.* **1.** sich glätten *od.* beruhigen (*Meer etc.*) (*a. fig.*); **II** *v/t.* **2.** glattstreichen, glätten; **3.** *fig.* besänftigen; **4.** *Streit* schlichten; **~ out** *v/t.* **1.** *Falte* ausplätten (**from** aus); **2.** → **smooth away**; **~ o·ver** *v/t.* **1.** *Fehler etc.* bemänteln; **2.** *Streit* schlichten.
ˈsmooth|·bore *adj. u. s.* (Gewehr *n*) mit glattem Lauf; **ˈ~-faced** *adj.* **1.** a) bartlos, b) glattrasiert; **2.** *fig.* glatt, schmeichlerisch; **~ file** *s.* ⚙ Schlichtfeile *f*.
smooth·ie [ˈsmuːðɪ] *s.* F **1.** ‚dufter Typ'; **2.** aalglatter Bursche.
smooth·ing| i·ron [ˈsmuːðɪŋ] *s.* Plätt-, Bügeleisen *n*; **~ plane** *s.* ⚙ Schlichthobel *m*.
smooth·ness [ˈsmuːðnɪs] *s.* **1.** Glätte *f* (*a. fig.*); **2.** Reibungslosigkeit *f* (*a. fig.*); **3.** *fig.* glatter Fluß, Eleˈganz *f e-r Rede etc.*; **4.** Glätte *f*, Gewandtheit *f*; **5.** Sanftheit *f*.
ˈsmooth-tongued *adj.* glattzüngig, schmeichlerisch, aalglatt.
smote [sməʊt] *pret. von* **smite**.
smoth·er [ˈsmʌðə] **I** *v/t.* **1.** *j-n, a. Feuer, Rebellion, Ton* ersticken; **2.** *bsd. fig.* überˈhäufen (**with** mit *Arbeit etc.*): **~ s.o. with kisses** j-n abküssen; **3. ~ in** (*od.* **with**) völlig bedecken mit, einhüllen in (*dat.*), begraben unter (*Blumen, Decken etc.*); **4.** *oft* **~ up** *Gähnen, Wut etc., a. Geheimnis etc.* unterˈdrücken, *Skandal* vertuschen; **II** *v/i.* **5.** ersticken; **6.** *sport* F ‚überˈfahren'; **III** *s.* **7.** dicker Qualm; **8.** Dampf-, Dunst-, Staubwolke *f*; **9.** (erdrückende) Masse.
smoul·der [ˈsməʊldə] **I** *v/i.* **1.** glimmen, schwelen (*a. fig. Feindschaft, Rebellion etc.*); **2.** glühen (*a. fig. Augen*); **II** *s.* **3.** schwelendes Feuer.
smudge [smʌdʒ] **I** *s.* **1.** Schmutzfleck *m*, Klecks *m*; **2.** qualmendes Feuer (*gegen Mücken, Frost etc.*); **II** *v/t.* **3.** beschmutzen; **4.** be-, verschmieren, ˈvollklecksen; **5.** *fig. Ruf etc.* besudeln; **III** *v/i.* **6.** schmieren (*Tinte, Papier etc.*); **7.** schmutzig werden; **ˈsmudg·y** [-dʒɪ] *adj.* ☐ verschmiert, schmierig, schmutzig.
smug [smʌg] *adj.* ☐ **1.** *obs.* schmuck; **2.** geschniegelt u. gebügelt; **3.** selbstgefällig, blasiert.
smug·gle [ˈsmʌgl] **I** *v/t. Waren, a. weitS. Brief, j-n etc.* schmuggeln: **~ in** einschmuggeln; **II** *v/i.* schmuggeln; **ˈsmug·gler** [-lə] *s.* **1.** Schmuggler *m*; **2.** Schmuggelschiff *n*; **ˈsmug·gling** [-lɪŋ] *s.* Schmuggel *m*.
smut [smʌt] **I** *s.* **1.** Ruß-, Schmutzflocke *f od.* -fleck *m*; **2.** *fig.* Zote(n *pl.*) *f*, Schmutz *m*, Schweineˈrei(en *pl.*) *f*: **talk ~** Zoten reißen, ‚schweinigeln'; **3.** ⚘ (*bsd.* Getreide)Brand *m*; **II** *v/t.* **4.** beschmutzen; **5.** ⚘ brandig machen.
smutch [smʌtʃ] **I** *v/t.* beschmutzen; **II** *s.* schwarzer Fleck.
smut·ty [ˈsmʌtɪ] *adj.* ☐ **1.** schmutzig, rußig; **2.** *fig.* zotig, obˈszön: **~ joke** Zote *f*; **3.** ⚘ brandig.
snack [snæk] *s.* **1.** a) Imbiß *m*, b) Happen *m*, Bissen *m*; **2.** Anteil *m*: **go ~s** teilen; **~ bar** *s.* Imbißstube *f*.
snaf·fle [ˈsnæfl] **I** *s.* **1.** *a.* **~ bit** Trense(ngebiß *n*) *f*; **II** *v/t.* **2.** *e-m Pferd* die Trense anlegen; **3.** mit der Trense lenken; **4.** *Brit. sl.* ‚klauen'.
sna·fu [snæˈfuː] *Am. sl.* **I** *adj.* in heillosem Durcheinˈander, ‚beschissen'; **II** *s.* ‚beschissene Lage'; **III** *v/t.* ‚versauen'.
snag [snæg] **I** *s.* **1.** Aststumpf *m*; **2.** Baumstumpf *m* (*in Flüssen*); *fig.* ‚Haken' *m*: **strike a ~** auf Schwierigkeiten stoßen; **3.** a) Zahnstumpf *m*, b) *Am.* Raffzahn *m*; **II** *v/t.* **4.** *Boot* gegen e-n Stumpf fahren lassen; **5.** *Fluß* von Baumstümpfen befreien; **snagged** [-gd], **ˈsnag·gy** [-gɪ] *adj.* **1.** ästig, knorrig; **2.** voller Baumstümpfe (*Fluß*).
snail [sneɪl] *s.* **1.** *zo.* Schnecke *f* (*a. fig. lahmer Kerl*): **at a ~'s pace** im Schneckentempo; **2.** → **snail wheel**; **~ shell** *s.* Schneckenhaus *n*; **~ wheel** *s.* Schnecke(nrad *n*) *f* (*Uhr*).
snake [sneɪk] **I** *s.* **1.** Schlange *f* (*a. fig.*): **~ in the grass** a) verborgene Gefahr, b) (falsche) Schlange; **see ~s** F weiße Mäuse sehen; **2.** ⚚ Währungsschlange *f*; **II** *v/i.* **3.** sich schlängeln (*a. Weg*); **snake charm·er** *s.* Schlangenbeschwörer *m*; **snake pit** *s.* **1.** Schlangengrube *f*; **2.** Irrenanstalt *f*; **3.** *fig.* Hölle *f*; **ˈsnake·skin** *s.* **1.** Schlangenhaut *f*; **2.** Schlangenleder *n*; **snak·y** [ˈsneɪkɪ] *adj.* ☐ **1.** Schlangen…; **2.** schlangenartig, gewunden; **3.** *fig.* ˈhinterhältig.
snap [snæp] **I** *s.* **1.** Schnappen *n*, Biß *m*;

2. Knacken *n*, Knacks *m*, Klicken *n*; **3.** (*Peitschen- etc.*)Knall *m*; **4.** Reißen *n*; **5.** Schnappschloß *n*, Schnapper *m*; **6.** *phot.* Schnappschuß *m*; **7.** *etwa*: Schnipp-Schnapp *n* (*Kartenspiel*); **8.** *fig.* Schwung *m*, Schmiß *m*; **9.** kurze Zeit: ***in a ~*** im Nu; ***cold ~*** Kältewelle *f*; **10.** (knuspriges) Plätzchen; **11.** *Am.* F Kleinigkeit *f*, ‚Kinderspiel' *n*; **II** *adj.* **12.** Schnapp...; **13.** spontan, Schnell...: ***~ decision*** rasche Entscheidung; ***~ judgement*** (vor)schnelles Urteil; ***~ vote*** Blitzabstimmung *f*; **III** *adv. u. int.* **14.** knack(s)(!), krach(!), schnapp(!); **IV** *v/i.* **15.** schnappen (***at*** nach *a. fig. e-m Angebot etc.*), zuschnappen: ***~ at the chance*** zugreifen, die Gelegenheit beim Schopfe fassen; ***~ at s.o.*** j-n anschnauzen; **16.** *a.* ***~ to*** zuschnappen, zuknallen (*Schloß, Tür*); **17.** knacken, klicken; **18.** knallen (*Peitsche etc.*); **19.** (zer)springen, (-)reißen, entzweigehen: ***there something ~ped in me*** da ‚drehte ich durch'; **20.** schnellen: ***~ to attention*** ⚔ ‚Männchen bauen'; ***~ to it!*** F mach Tempo!; ***~ out of it!*** F komm, komm!, laß das (sein)!; **V** *v/t.* **21.** (er)schnappen; beißen: ***~ off*** abbeißen; ***~ s.o.'s head*** (*od.* ***nose***) ***off*** → ***snap up*** 4; **22.** (zu)schnappen lassen; **23.** *phot.* knipsen; **24.** zerknicken, -knacken, -brechen, -reißen: ***~ off*** abbrechen; **25.** mit *der Peitsche* knallen; mit *den Fingern* schnalzen: ***~ one's fingers at*** *fig.* auslachen, verhöhnen; **26.** *a.* ***~ out*** *Wort* her'vorstoßen, bellen; ***~ up*** *v/t.* **1.** auf-, wegschnappen; **2.** (gierig) an sich reißen, *Angebot* schnell annehmen: ***snap it up!*** F mach fix!; **3.** *Häuser etc.* aufkaufen; **4.** a) *j-n* anschnauzen, b) *j-m* das Wort abschneiden.

snap| catch *s.* ⚙ Schnapper *m*; **'~drag·on** *s.* **1.** ⚘ Löwenmaul *n*; **2.** Ro'sinenfischen *n aus brennendem Branntwein* (*Spiel*); **~ fas·ten·er** *s.* Druckknopf *m*; **~ hook** *s.* Kara'binerhaken *m*; **~ lock** *s.* Schnappschloß *n*.

snap·pish ['snæpɪʃ] *adj.* ☐ **1.** bissig (*Hund, a. Person*); **2.** schnippisch.

snap·py ['snæpɪ] *adj.* ☐ **1.** → ***snappish***; **2.** F a) schnell, fix, b) ‚zackig', forsch, c) schwungvoll, schmissig, d) schick: ***make it ~!, look ~!*** mach mal fix!

snap| shot *s.* ⚔ Schnellschuß *m*; **'~shot** *phot.* **I** *s.* Schnappschuß *m*; **II** *v/t.* e-n Schnappschuß machen von, *et.* knipsen.

snare [sneə] **I** *s.* **1.** Schlinge (*a.* ⚕), Fallstrick *m*, *fig. a.* Fußangel *f*: ***set a ~ for s.o.*** j-m e-e Falle stellen; **2.** ♪ Schnarrsaite *f*; **II** *v/t.* **3.** mit e-r Schlinge fangen; **4.** *fig.* um'stricken, fangen, *j-m* e-e Falle stellen; **5.** sich *et.* ‚angeln' *od.* unter den Nagel reißen; **~ drum** *s.* ♪ kleine Trommel, Schnarrtrommel *f*.

snarl¹ [snɑ:l] *bsd. Am.* **I** *s.* **1.** Knoten *m*, ‚Fitz' *m*; **2.** *fig.* wirres Durchein'ander, Gewirr *n*, *a.* Verwicklung *f*: (***traffic***) **~** Verkehrschaos *n*; **II** *v/t.* **3.** *a.* ***~ up*** verwirren, durchein'anderbringen; **III** *v/i.* **4.** *a.* ***~ up*** sich verwirren; (völlig) durchein'andergeraten.

snarl² [snɑ:l] **I** *v/i.* wütend knurren, die Zähne fletschen (*Hund, a. Person*): ***~ at j-n*** anfauchen; **II** *v/t. et.* knurren, wütend her'vorstoßen; **III** *s.* Knurren *n*, Zähnefletschen *n*.

'snarl-up *s.* F → ***snarl¹*** 2.

snatch [snætʃ] **I** *v/t.* **1.** *et.* schnappen, packen, (er)haschen, fangen: ***~ up*** aufraffen; **2.** *fig. Gelegenheit etc.* ergreifen; *et.*, *a. Schlaf* ergattern: ***~ a hurried meal*** rasch et. zu sich nehmen; **3.** *et.* an sich reißen; *a. Kuß* rauben; **4.** **~** (***away***) ***from*** *j-m et.*, *a. j-n dem Meer, dem Tod, durch den Tod* entreißen: ***he was ~ed away from us*** er wurde uns *durch e-n frühen Tod etc.* entrissen; **5.** ***~ off*** weg-, her'unterreißen; **6.** *Am. sl. Kind* rauben; **7.** *Gewichtheben*: reißen; **II** *v/i.* **8.** ***~ at*** schnappen *od.* greifen *od.* haschen nach: ***~ at the offer*** *fig.* mit beiden Händen zugreifen; **III** *s.* **9.** Schnappen *n*, schneller Griff: ***make a ~ at*** → 8; **10.** *fig.* (kurzer) Augenblick: ***~es of sleep***; **11.** *pl.* Bruchstücke *pl.*, ‚Brokken' *pl.*, Aufgeschnappte(s) *n*: ***~es of conversation*** Gesprächsfetzen *pl.*; ***by*** (*od.* ***in***) ***~es*** a) hastig, ruckweise, b) ab und zu; **12.** *Am.* V a) ‚Möse' *f*, b) ‚Nummer' *f* (*Koitus*); **'snatch·y** [-tʃɪ] *adj.* ☐ abgehackt, ruckweise, spo'radisch.

snaz·zy ['snæzɪ] *adj.* F ‚todschick'.

sneak [sni:k] **I** *v/i.* **1.** (sich *wohin*) schleichen: ***~ about*** herumschleichen, -schnüffeln; ***~ out of*** *fig.* sich von *et.* drücken, sich aus *e-r Sache* herauswinden; **2.** *ped. Brit. sl.* ‚petzen': ***~ on s.o.*** j-n verpetzen; **II** *v/t.* **3.** *et.* (heimlich) *wohin* schmuggeln; **4.** *sl.* ‚sti'bitzen'; **III** *s.* **5.** *contp.* ‚Leisetreter' *m*, Kriecher *m*; **6.** *Brit.* F ‚Petze' *f*; **~ at·tack** *s.* ⚔ Über'raschungsangriff *m*.

sneak·ers ['sni:kəz] *s. pl. bsd. Am.* leichte Turnschuhe *pl.*; **'sneak·ing** [-kɪŋ] *adj.* ☐ **1.** verstohlen; **2.** 'hinterlistig, gemein; **3.** *fig.* heimlich, leise (*Verdacht etc.*).

sneak| pre·view *s. Am.* F *inoffizielle erste Vorführung e-s neuen Films*; **~ thief** *s.* Einsteig- *od.* Gelegenheitsdieb *m*.

sneak·y ['sni:kɪ] → ***sneaking***.

sneer [snɪə] **I** *v/i.* **1.** höhnisch grinsen, ‚feixen' (***at*** über *acc.*); **2.** spötteln (***at*** über *acc.*); **II** *v/t.* **3.** *et.* höhnen(d äußern); **III** *s.* **4.** Hohnlächeln *n*; **5.** Hohn *m*, Spott *m*, höhnische Bemerkung; **'sneer·er** [-ərə] *s.* Spötter *m*, ‚Feixer' *m*; **'sneer·ing** [-ərɪŋ] *adj.* ☐ höhnisch, spöttisch, ‚feixend'.

sneeze [sni:z] **I** *v/i.* niesen: ***not to be ~d at*** F nicht zu verachten; **II** *s.* Niesen *n*; **'~wort** *s.* ⚘ Sumpfgarbe *f*.

snick [snɪk] **I** *v/t.* (ein)kerben; **II** *s.* Kerbe *f*.

snick·er ['snɪkə] **I** *v/i.* **1.** kichern; **2.** wiehern; **II** *v/t.* **3.** F *et.* kichern; **III** *s.* **4.** Kichern *n*; **,~'snee** [-'sni:] *s. humor.* ‚Dolch' *m* (*Messer*).

snide [snaɪd] *adj.* abfällig, höhnisch.

sniff [snɪf] **I** *v/i.* **1.** schniefen; **2.** schnüffeln (***at*** an *dat.*); **3.** *fig.* die Nase rümpfen (***at*** über *acc.*); **II** *v/t.* **4.** *a.* ***~ in*** (*od.* ***up***) durch die Nase einziehen; **5.** schnuppern an (*dat.*); **6.** riechen (*a. fig. wittern*); **III** *s.* **7.** Schnüffeln *n*; **8.** kurzer Atemzug; **9.** Naserümpfen *n*.

snif·fle ['snɪfl] *Am.* **I** *v/i.* **1.** schniefen; **2.** greinen, heulen; **II** *s.* **3.** Schnüffeln *n*; **4.** ***the ~s*** *pl.* F Schnupfen *m*.

sniff·y ['snɪfɪ] *adj.* ☐ F **1.** naserümpfend, hochnäsig, verächtlich; **2.** muffig.

snif·ter ['snɪftə] *s.* **1.** Schnäps-chen *n*, ‚Gläs-chen' *n*; **2.** *Am.* Kognakschwenker *m*.

snift·ing valve ['snɪftɪŋ] *s.* ⚙ 'Schnüffelven,til *n*.

snig·ger ['snɪgə] → ***snicker***.

snip [snɪp] **I** *v/t.* **1.** schnippeln, schnipseln, schneiden; **2.** *Fahrkarte* knipsen; **II** *s.* **3.** Schnitt *m*; **4.** Schnippel *m*, Schnipsel *m, n*; **5.** *sl.* a) todsichere Sache, b) günstige (Kauf)Gelegenheit: ***it's a ~!***; **6.** *Am.* F (frecher) Knirps.

snipe [snaɪp] **I** *s.* **1.** *orn.* (Sumpf-)Schnepfe *f*; **II** *v/i.* **2.** *hunt.* Schnepfen jagen *od.* schießen; **3.** ⚔ aus dem 'Hinterhalt schießen (***at*** auf *acc.*); **III** *v/t.* **4.** ⚔ abschießen, ‚wegputzen'; **'snip·er** [-pə] *s.* **1.** ⚔ Scharf-, Heckenschütze *m*: ***~scope*** ⚔ 'Infrarotvi,sier *n*; **2.** Todesschütze *m*, Killer *m*.

snip·pet ['snɪpɪt] *s.* **1.** (Pa'pier)Schnipsel *m, n*; **2.** *pl. fig.* Bruchstücke *pl.*, ‚Brokken' *pl.*

snitch [snɪtʃ] *sl.* **I** *v/t.* ‚klauen', sti'bitzen; **II** *v/i.* ***~ on*** *j-n* ‚verpfeifen'.

sniv·el ['snɪvl] **I** *v/i.* **1.** schniefen; **2.** greinen, plärren; **3.** wehleidig tun; **II** *v/t.* **4.** *et.* (her'aus)schluchzen; **III** *s.* **5.** Greinen *n*, Plärren *n*; **6.** wehleidiges Getue; **'sniv·el·(l)er** [-lə] *s.* ‚Heulsuse' *f*; **'sniv·el·(l)ing** [-lɪŋ] **I** *adj.* **1.** triefnasig; **2.** wehleidig; **II** *s.* **3.** → ***snivel*** 5 *u.* 6.

snob [snɒb] *s.* Snob *m*: ***~ appeal*** Snob-Appeal *m*; **'snob·ber·y** [-bərɪ] *s.* Sno'bismus *m*; **'snob·bish** [-bɪʃ] *adj.* ☐ sno'bistisch, versnobt.

snog [snɒg] *v/i.* F knutschen.

snook [snu:k] *s.*: ***cock a ~ at*** *j-m* e-e lange Nase machen, *fig. j-n* auslachen.

snook·er ['snu:kə] *s. a.* ***~ pool*** *Billard*: Snooker Pool *m*; **'snook·ered** [-əd] *adj.* F ‚to'tal erledigt'.

snoop [snu:p] *bsd. Am.* F **I** *v/i.* **1.** *a.* ***~ around*** her'umschnüffeln; **II** *s.* **2.** Schnüffe'lei *f*; **3.** → **'snoop·er** [-pə] ‚Schnüffler' *m*; **'snoop·y** [-pɪ] *adj.* F schnüffelnd, neugierig.

snoot [snu:t] *s. Am.* F **1.** ‚Schnauze' *f* (*Nase, Gesicht*); **2.** Gri'masse *f*, ‚Schnute' *f*; **'snoot·y** [-tɪ] *adj. Am.* F ‚großkotzig', hochnäsig, patzig.

snooze [snu:z] **I** *v/i.* **1.** ein Nickerchen machen; **2.** dösen; **II** *v/t.* **3.** ***~ away*** *Zeit* vertrödeln; **III** *s.* **4.** Nickerchen *n*: ***have a ~*** → 1.

snore [snɔ:] **I** *v/i.* schnarchen; **II** *s.* Schnarchen *n*; **snor·er** ['snɔ:rə] *s.* Schnarcher *m*.

snor·kel ['snɔ:kl] **I** *s.* ⚓, ⚔ *etc.* Schnorchel *m*; **II** *v/i.* schnorcheln.

snort [snɔ:t] **I** *v/i.* (*a.* wütend *od.* verächtlich) schnauben; prusten; **II** *v/t. a.* ***~ out*** *Worte* (wütend) schnauben; **III** *s.* Schnauben *n*; Prusten *n*; **'snort·er** [-tə] *s.* F **1.** heftiger Sturm; **2.** Mordsding *n*; **3.** Mordskerl *m*.

snot [snɒt] *s.* **1.** Rotz *m*; **2.** ‚Schwein' *n*; **'snot·ty** [-tɪ] *adj.* ☐ **1.** V rotzig, Rotz...; **2.** F ‚dreckig', gemein; **3.** *Am. sl.* patzig.

snout [snaʊt] *s.* **1.** *zo.* Schnauze *f* (*a.* F *fig. Nase, Gesicht*); **2.** ‚Schnauze' *f*, Vorderteil *n* (*Auto etc.*); **3.** ⚙ Schnabel *m*, Tülle *f*.

snow [snəʊ] **I** *s.* **1.** Schnee *m* (*a.* ☂ *u. Küche*; *a. TV*); **2.** Schneefall *m*; **3.** *pl.*

Schneemassen *pl.*; **4.** *sl.* ‚Snow' *m*, ‚Schnee' *m* (*Kokain, Heroin*); **II** *v/i.* **5.** schneien: **~ *in*** hereinschneien (*a. fig.*); ***~ed in*** (*od.* ***up***, ***under***) eingeschneit; ***be ~ed under*** *fig.* a) *mit Arbeit etc.* überhäuft sein, *von Sorgen etc.* erdrückt werden, b) *pol. Am. in e-r Wahl* vernichtend geschlagen werden; **6.** *fig.* regnen, hageln; **III** *v/t.* **7.** her'unterrieseln lassen; **'~·ball I** *s.* **1.** Schneeball *m* (*a.* ⚘): **~ *fight*** Schneeballschlacht *f*; **2.** *fig.* La'wine *f*: **~ *system*** Schneeballsystem *n*; **3.** *Getränk aus Eierlikör u. Zitronenlimonade*; **II** *v/t.* **4.** Schneebälle werfen auf; **III** *v/i.* **5.** sich mit Schneebällen bewerfen; **6.** *fig.* la'winenartig anwachsen; **'~·bank** *s.* Schneewehe *f*; **'~·bird** *s.* **1.** → ***snow bunting***; **2.** *sl.* ‚Kokser' *m*, Koka'inschnupfer *m*; **'~-blind** *adj.* schneeblind; **'~·bound** *adj.* eingeschneit, durch Schnee(massen) abgeschnitten; **~ bun·ny** *s.* F ‚Skihaserl' *n*; **~ bun·ting** *s. orn.* Schneeammer *f*; **'~·cap** *s. orn. ein* Kolibri *m*; **'~-capped** *adj.* schneebedeckt; **'~·drift** *s.* Schneewehe *f*; **'~·drop** *s.* ⚘ Schneeglöckchen *n*; **'~·fall** *s.* Schneefall *m*, -menge *f*; **'~·field** *s.* Schneefeld *n*; **'~·flake** *s.* Schneeflocke *f*; **~ gog·gles** *s. pl.* Schneebrille *f*; **~ line** *s.* Schneegrenze *f*; **'~·man** *s.* [*irr.*] Schneemann *m*: ***Abominable*** ♀ Schneemensch *m*, *der* Jeti; **'~·mo,bile** [-məʊ,bi:l] *s.* Motorschlitten *m*; **'~·plough**, *Am.* **'~·plow** *s.* Schneepflug *m* (*a. beim Skifahren*); **'~·shoe I** *s.* Schneeschuh *m*; **II** *v/i.* auf Schneeschuhen gehen; **'~·slide**, **'~·slip** *s.* Schneerutsch *m*; **'~·storm** *s.* Schneesturm *m*; **~ tire** (*Brit.* **tyre**) *s. mot.* Winterreifen *m*; **,~-'white** *adj.* schneeweiß; ♀ **White** *npr.* Schnee'wittchen *n*.

snow·y ['snəʊɪ] *adj.* ☐ **1.** schneeig, Schnee…: **~ *weather***; **2.** schneebedeckt, Schnee…; **3.** schneeweiß.

snub¹ [snʌb] **I** *v/t.* **1.** *j-n* brüskieren, vor den Kopf stoßen; **2.** *j-n* kurz abfertigen; **3.** *j-m* über den Mund fahren; **II** *s.* **4.** Brüskierung *f*.

snub² [snʌb] *adj.* stumpf: **~ *nose*** Stupsnase *f*; **'~-nosed** *adj.* stupsnasig.

snuff¹ [snʌf] **I** *v/t.* **1.** *a.* **~ *up*** durch die Nase einziehen; **2.** beschnüffeln; **II** *v/i.* **3.** schnüffeln (***at*** an *dat.*); **4.** (Schnupftabak) schnupfen; **III** *s.* **5.** Atemzug *m*, Einziehen *n*; **6.** Schnupftabak *m*, Prise *f*: ***take*** **~** schnupfen; ***be up to*** **~** F a) ‚schwer auf Draht sein', b) (toll) in Form sein; ***give s.o.*** **~** F j-m ‚Saures geben'.

snuff² [snʌf] **I** *s.* **1.** Schnuppe *f e-r Kerze*; **II** *v/t.* **2.** *Kerze* putzen; **3.** **~ *out*** auslöschen (*a. fig.*); *fig.* ersticken, vernichten; **4.** **~ *it*** *Brit.* F ‚abkratzen' (*sterben*).

'snuff|·box *s.* Schnupftabaksdose *f*; **'~-,col·o(u)red** *adj.* gelbbraun, tabakfarben.

snuf·fle ['snʌfl] **I** *v/i.* **1.** schnüffeln, schnuppern; **2.** schniefen; **3.** näseln; **II** *v/t.* **4.** *mst* **~ *out*** *et.* näseln; **III** *s.* **5.** Schnüffeln *n*; **6.** Näseln; **7.** ***the ~s*** *pl.* Schnupfen *m*.

'snuff|-,tak·er *s.* Schnupfer(in); **'~-,tak·ing** *s.* (Tabak)Schnupfen *n*.

snug [snʌg] **I** *adj.* ☐ **1.** gemütlich, behaglich, traulich; **2.** geborgen, gut versorgt: ***as ~ as a bug in a rug*** F wie die Made im Speck; **3.** angenehm; **4.** auskömmlich, ‚hübsch' (*Einkommen etc.*); **5.** kom'pakt; **6.** ordentlich; **7.** eng anliegend (*Kleid*): **~ *fit*** a) guter Sitz, b) ⚙ Paßsitz *m*; **8.** ⚓ schmuck, seetüchtig (*Schiff*); **9.** verborgen: ***keep s.th.*** **~** et. geheimhalten; ***lie*** **~** sich verborgen halten; **II** *v/i.* **10.** → ***snuggle*** I; **III** *v/t.* **11.** *oft* **~ *down*** gemütlich *od.* bequem machen; **12.** *mst* **~ *down*** ⚓ *Schiff* auf Sturm vorbereiten; **'snug·ger·y** [-gərɪ] *s.* **1.** behagliche Bude, warmes Nest (*Zimmer etc.*); **2.** kleines Nebenzimmer; **'snug·gle** [-gl] **I** *v/i.* sich schmiegen *od.* kuscheln ([***up***] ***in*** in *e-e Decke*, ***up to*** an *acc.*): **~ *down*** (***in bed***) sich ins Bett kuscheln; **II** *v/t.* an sich schmiegen, (lieb)'kosen.

so [səʊ] **I** *adv.* **1.** (*mst vor adj. u. adv.*) so, dermaßen: ***I was ~ surprised***; ***not ~ ... as*** nicht so … wie; **~ *great a man*** ein so großer Mann; → ***far*** 3, ***much*** *Redew.*; **2.** (*mst exklamatorisch*) (ja) so, 'überaus: ***I am ~ glad!***; **3.** so, in dieser Weise: ***and ~ on*** (*od.* ***forth***) und so weiter; ***is that ~?*** wirklich?; **~ *as to*** so daß, um zu; **~ *that*** so daß; ***or ~*** etwa, oder so; **~ *saying*** mit *od.* bei diesen Worten; → ***if*** 1; **4.** (*als Ersatz für ein Prädikativum od. e-n Satz*) a) es, das: ***I hope ~*** ich hoffe (es); ***I have never said ~*** das habe ich nie behauptet, b) auch: ***you are tired, ~ am I*** du bist müde, ich (bin es) auch, c) allerdings, ja: ***are you tired? ~ I am*** bist du müde? ja *od.* allerdings; ***I am stupid! ~ you are*** ich bin dumm! allerdings (das bist du); **~ *what?*** F na und?; **5.** so … daß: ***it was ~ hot I took my coat off***; **II** *cj.* **6.** daher, folglich, also, und so: ***it was necessary ~ we did it*** es war nötig, und so taten wir es (denn); **~ *you came after all!*** du bist also doch (noch) gekommen!

soak [səʊk] **I** *v/i.* **1.** sich vollsaugen, durch'tränkt werden: ***~ing wet*** tropfnaß; **2.** ('durch)sickern; **3.** *fig.* langsam *ins Bewußtsein* einsickern *od.* -dringen; **4.** *sl.* ‚saufen'; **II** *v/t.* **5.** *et.* einweichen; **6.** durch'tränken, -'nässen, -'feuchten; ⚙ *a.* imprägnieren (***in*** mit); **7.** **~ *o.s. in*** *fig.* sich ganz versenken in; **8.** **~ *in*** einsaugen: **~ *up*** a) aufsaugen, b) *fig. Wissen etc.* in sich aufnehmen; **9.** *sl. et.* ‚saufen'; **10.** *sl. j-n* ‚schröpfen'; **11.** *sl. j-n* verdreschen; **III** *s.* **12.** Einweichen *n*, Durch'tränken *n*; ⚙ Imprägnieren *n*; **13.** *sl.* a) Säufer *m*, b) Saufe'rei *f*; **14.** F Regenguß *m*, ‚Dusche' *f*; **'soak·age** [-kɪdʒ] *s.* **1.** 'Durchsickern *n*; **2.** 'durchgesickerte Flüssigkeit, Sickerwasser *n*; **'soak·er** [-kə] → ***soak*** 14.

'so-and-so ['səʊənsəʊ] *pl.* **-sos** *s.* **1.** (Herr *etc.*) Soundso: ***Mr. ~***; **2.** F ‚(blöder) Hund'.

soap [səʊp] **I** *s.* Seife *f* (*a.* ⚗): ***no ~!*** *Am.* F nichts zu machen!; **II** *v/t.* *a.* **~ *down*** a) (ein-, ab)seifen, b) → ***soft-soap***; **'~·box I** *s.* **1.** 'Seifenkiste *f*, -kar,ton *m*; **2.** ‚Seifenkiste' *f* (*improvisierte Rednerbühne od. Fahrzeug*); **II** *adj.* **3.** Seifenkisten…: **~ *derby*** Seifenkistenrennen *n*; **~ *orator*** Straßenredner *m*; **~ *bub·ble*** *s.* Seifenblase *f* (*a. fig.*); **~ *dish*** *s.* Seifenschale *f*; **~ *op·er·a*** *s. Radio, TV*: ‚Seifenoper' *f* (*rührselige Serie*); **'~·stone** *s. min.* Seifen-, Speckstein *m*; **'~·suds** *s. pl.* Seifenlauge *f*, -wasser *n*; **'~·works** *s. pl. oft sg. konstr.* Seifensiede'rei *f*.

soap·y ['səʊpɪ] *adj.* ☐ **1.** seifig, Seifen…; **2.** *fig.* ölig, schmeichlerisch.

soar [sɔ:] *v/i.* **1.** (hoch) aufsteigen, sich erheben (*Vogel, Berge etc.*); **2.** in großer Höhe schweben; **3.** ✈ segelfliegen, segeln; **4.** *fig.* sich em'porschwingen (*Geist*): ***~ing thoughts*** hochfliegende Gedanken; **5.** ✝ in die Höhe schnellen (*Preise*); **soar·ing** ['sɔ:rɪŋ] **I** *adj.* ☐ **1.** hochfliegend (*a. fig.*); **2.** *fig.* em'porstrebend; **II** *s.* **3.** ✈ Segeln *n*.

sob [sɒb] **I** *v/i.* schluchzen; **II** *v/t.* *a.* **~ *out*** *Worte* (her'aus)schluchzen; **III** *s.* Schluchzen *n*; schluchzender Laut: **~ *sister*** *sl.* a) Briefkastenonkel *m*, -tante *f* (*Frauenzeitschrift*), b) Verfasser(in) rührseliger Romane *etc.*; **~ *stuff*** *sl.* rührseliges Zeug, Schnulze(n *pl.*) *f*.

so·ber ['səʊbə] **I** *adj.* ☐ **1.** nüchtern: a) nicht betrunken, b) *fig.* sachlich: **~ *facts*** nüchterne Tatsachen; ***in ~ fact*** nüchtern betrachtet, c) unauffällig, gedeckt (*Farbe etc.*); **2.** mäßig; **II** *v/t.* **3.** *oft* **~ *up*** ernüchtern; **III** *v/i.* **4.** *oft* **~ *down*** *od.* ***up*** a) (wieder) nüchtern werden, b) *fig.* vernünftig werden; **,~-'mind·ed** *adj.* besonnen, nüchtern; **'~·sides** *s.* fader Kerl, ‚Trauerkloß' *m*, Spießer *m*.

so·bri·e·ty [səʊ'braɪətɪ] *s.* **1.** Nüchternheit *f* (*a. fig.*); **2.** Mäßigkeit *f*; **3.** Ernst (-haftigkeit *f*) *m*.

so·bri·quet ['səʊbrɪkeɪ] (*Fr.*) *s.* Spitzname *m*.

soc·age ['sɒkɪdʒ] *s.* ⚖ *hist.* **1.** Lehensleistung *f* (*ohne Ritter- u. Heeresdienst*); **2.** Frongut *n*.

,so-'called [,səʊ-] *adj.* sogenannt (*a. angeblich*).

socc·age ['sɒkɪdʒ] → ***socage***.

soc·cer ['sɒkə] **I** *s. sport* Fußball *m* (*Spiel*); **II** *adj.* Fußball…: **~ *team***; **~ *ball*** Fußball *m*.

so·cia·bil·i·ty [,səʊʃə'bɪlətɪ] *s.* Geselligkeit *f*, 'Umgänglichkeit *f*; **so·cia·ble** ['səʊʃəbl] **I** *adj.* ☐ **1.** gesellig (*a. zo. etc.*), 'umgänglich, freundlich; **2.** gesellig, gemütlich, ungezwungen: **~ *evening***; **II** *s.* **3.** Kremser *m* (*Kutschwagen*); **4.** Zweisitzer *m* (*Dreirad etc.*); **5.** Plaudersofa *n*; **6.** *bsd. Am.* → ***social*** 7.

so·cial ['səʊʃl] **I** *adj.* ☐ **1.** *zo. etc.* gesellig; **2.** gesellschaftlich, Gesellschafts…, sozi'al, Sozial…: **~ *action*** Bürgerinitiative *f*; **~ *climber*** *contp.* gesellschaftlicher ‚Aufsteiger'; **~ *contract*** *hist.* Gesellschaftsvertrag *m*; **~ *criticism*** Sozialkritik *f*; **~ *engineering*** angewandte Sozialwissenschaft; **~ *evil*** *die* Prostitution; **~ *order*** Gesellschaftsordnung *f*; **~ *rank*** gesellschaftlicher Rang, soziale Stellung; **~ *register*** Prominentenliste *f*; **~ *science*** Sozialwissenschaft *f*; **3.** sozi'al, Sozial…: **~ *insurance*** Sozialversicherung *f*; **~ *insurance contribution*** Sozialversicherungsbeitrag *m*; **~ *policy*** Sozialpolitik *f*; **~ *security*** a) soziale Sicherheit, b) Sozialversicherung *f*, c) Sozialhilfe *f*; ***be on ~ security*** Sozialhilfe beziehen; **~ *services*** a) Sozialeinrichtungen, b) staatliche Sozialleistungen; **~ *studies*** Gemeinschaftskunde *f*; **~ *work*** Sozialarbeit *f*; **~ *worker*** Sozialarbeiter(in); **4.** *pol.* Sozial...: ♀ ***Democrat*** Sozialdemokrat(in); **5.** gesellschaftlich, gesellig: **~ *activities*** gesellschaftliche Veranstaltungen; **6.** → ***sociable*** 1; **II** *s.* **7.** geselliges Bei'sammensein; **'so·cial·ism** [-ʃəlɪzəm] *s. pol.* Sozia'lismus *m*; **'so·cial·ist** [-ʃəlɪst] **I** *s.* Sozia'list(in); **II** *adj. a.* **so·cial·is·tic** [ˌsəʊʃə'lɪstɪk] *adj.* (□ **~*ally***) sozia'listisch; **'so·cial·ite** [-ʃəlaɪt] *s. Am.* F Angehörige(r *m*) *f* der oberen Zehn'tausend, Promi'nente(r *m*) *f*.

so·cial·i·za·tion [ˌsəʊʃəlaɪ'zeɪʃn] *s. pol.*, ✝ Sozialisierung *f*; **so·cial·ize** ['səʊʃəlaɪz] *v/t. pol.*, ✝ sozialisieren, verstaatlichen, vergesellschaften.

so·ci·e·ty [sə'saɪətɪ] *s. allg.* Gesellschaft *f*: a) Gemeinschaft *f*: ***human* ~**, b) Kul'turkreis *m*, c) (*die* große *od.* ele'gante) Welt: **~ *lady*** Dame *f* der großen Gesellschaft; ***not fit for good* ~** nicht salon-*od.* gesellschaftsfähig, d) (gesellschaftlicher) 'Umgang, e) Anwesenheit *f*, f) Verein(igung *f*) *m*: ♀ ***of Friends*** Gesellschaft der Freunde (*die Quäker*); ♀ ***of Jesus*** Gesellschaft Jesu.

socio- [səʊsjəʊ] *in Zssgn* a) Sozial..., b) sozio'logisch: **~*biology*** Soziobiologie *f*; **~*critical*** sozialkritisch; **~*political*** sozialpolitisch; **~*psychology*** Sozialpsychologie *f*.

so·ci·og·e·ny [ˌsəʊsɪ'ɒdʒənɪ] *s.* Wissenschaft *f* vom Ursprung der menschlichen Gesellschaft; **so·ci·o·gram** ['səʊsjəgræm] *s.* Sozio'gramm *n*; **so·ci·o·log·ic**, **so·ci·o·log·i·cal** [ˌsəʊsjə'lɒdʒɪk(l)] *adj.* □ sozio'logisch; **so·ci·ol·o·gist** [ˌsəʊsɪ'ɒlədʒɪst] *s.* Sozio'loge *m*; **so·ci·ol·o·gy** [ˌsəʊsɪ'ɒlədʒɪ] *s.* Soziolo'gie *f*.

sock¹ [sɒk] *s.* **1.** Socke *f*: ***pull up one's* ~*s*** *Brit.* F ,sich am Riemen reißen', sich anstrengen; ***put a* ~ *in it!*** *Brit. sl.* hör auf!, halt's Maul!; **2.** *Brit.* Einlegesohle *f*.

sock² [sɒk] *sl.* **I** *v/t. j-m* ,eine knallen *od.* reinhauen': **~ *it to s.o.*** j-m ,Bescheid stoßen', j-m ,Saures geben'; **II** *s.* (Faust)Schlag *m*; **III** *adj. Am.* ,toll'.

sock·et ['sɒkɪt] *s.* **1.** *anat.* a) (Augen-, Zahn)Höhle *f*, b) (Gelenk)Pfanne *f*; **2.** ⚙ Muffe *f*, Rohransatz *m*; **3.** ⚡ a) Steckdose *f*, b) Fassung *f*, c) Sockel *m* (*für Röhren etc.*), d) Anschluß *m*; **~ joint** *s.* ⚙, *anat.* Kugelgelenk *n*; **~ wrench** *s.* ⚙ Steckschlüssel *m*.

so·cle ['sɒkl] *s.* △ Sockel *m*.

sod¹ [sɒd] **I** *s.* **1.** Grasnarbe *f*: ***under the* ~** unterm Rasen (*tot*); **2.** Rasenstück *n*; **II** *v/t.* **3.** mit Rasen bedecken.

sod² [sɒd] *sl.* **I** *s.* **1.** ,Heini' *m*, Blödmann *m*; **2.** Kerl *m*: ***the poor* ~**; **II** *v/t.* **3.** **~ *it!*** ,Mist!'

so·da ['səʊdə] *s.* ⚗ **1.** Soda *f*, *n*, kohlensaures Natrium: (***bicarbonate of***) **~** → ***sodium bicarbonate***; **2.** → ***sodium hydroxide***; **3.** 'Natriumoˌxyd *n*; **4.** Soda(wasser *n*) *f*, *n*: ***whisky and* ~**; **5.** → ***soda water*** 2; **~ foun·tain** *s.* **1.** Siphon *m*; **2.** *Am.* Erfrischungshalle *f*, Eisbar *f*; **~ jerk(·er)** *s. Am.* F Verkäufer *m* in e-r Erfrischungshalle *od.* Eisbar; **~ lye** *s.* Natronlauge *f*; **~ pop** *s. Am.* ,Limo' *f*; **~ wa·ter** *s.* **1.** Sodawasser *n*; **2.** Selters (-wasser) *n*, Sprudel *m*.

sod·den ['sɒdn] *adj.* **1.** durch'weicht, -'näßt; **2.** teigig, klitschig (*Brot etc.*); **3.** *fig.* a) ,voll', ,besoffen', b) blöd(e) (*vom Trinken*); **4.** aufgedunsen; **5.** *sl.* a) ,blöd', ,doof', b) fad.

so·di·um ['səʊdjəm] *s.* ⚗ Natrium *n*; **~ bi·car·bon·ate** *s.* 'Natriumbikarboˌnat *n*, doppeltkohlensaures Natrium; **~ car·bon·ate** *s.* Soda *f*, *n*, 'Natriumkarboˌnat *n*; **~ chlor·ide** *s.* 'Natriumchloˌrid *n*, Kochsalz *n*; **~ hy·drox·ide** *s.* 'Natriumhydroˌxyd *n*, Ätznatron *n*; **~ ni·trate** *s.* 'Natriumniˌtrat *n*.

sod·o·my ['sɒdəmɪ] *s.* **1.** Sodo'mie *f*; **2.** *allg.* 'widernaˌtürliche Unzucht.

so·ev·er [səʊ'evə] *adv.* (*mst in Zssgn wer etc.*) auch immer.

so·fa ['səʊfə] *s.* Sofa *n*; **~ bed** *s.* Bettcouch *f*.

sof·fit ['sɒfɪt] *s.* △ Laibung *f*.

soft [sɒft] **I** *adj.* □ **1.** *allg.* weich (*a. fig. Person, Charakter etc.*): ***as* ~ *as silk*** seidenweich; **~ *currency*** ✝ weiche Währung; **~ *prices*** ✝ nachgiebige Preise; **~ *sell*** ✝ weiche Verkaufstaktik; **2.** ⚙ weich, *bsd.* a) ungehärtet (*Eisen*), b) schmiedbar (*Metall*), c) enthärtet (*Wasser*): **~ *coal*** ⚒ Weichkohle *f*; **~ *solder*** Weichlot *n*; **3.** *fig.* weich, sanft (*Augen, Worte etc.*); → ***spot*** 5; **4.** mild, sanft (*Klima, Regen, Schlaf, Wind, a. Strafe etc.*): ***be* ~ *with*** sanft umgehen mit *j-m*; **5.** leise, sacht (*Bewegung, Geräusch, Rede*); **6.** sanft, gedämpft (*Licht, Farbe, Musik*); **7.** schwach, verschwommen: **~ *outlines***; **~ *negative*** *phot.* weiches Negativ; **8.** mild, lieblich (*Wein*); **9.** *Brit.* schwül, feucht, regnerisch; **10.** höflich, ruhig, gewinnend; **11.** zart, zärtlich, verliebt: **~ *nothings*** zärtliche Worte; → ***sex*** 2; **12.** schlaff (*Muskeln*); **13.** *fig.* verweichlicht, schlapp; **14.** angenehm, leicht, ,gemütlich': **~ *job***; ***a* ~ *thing*** e-e ruhige Sache, e-e ,Masche' (*einträgliches Geschäft*); **15.** *a.* **~ *in the head*** F ,leicht bescheuert', ,doof'; **16.** a) alkoholfrei: **~ *drinks***, b) weich: **~ *drug*** Soft drug *f*, weiche Droge; **II** *adv.* **17.** sanft, leise; **III** *s.* **18.** F Trottel *m*; **'~·ball** *s. Am. sport Form des Baseball mit weicherem Ball u. kleinerem Feld*; **'~-boiled** *adj.* **1.** weich(gekocht) (*Ei*); **2.** F weichherzig; **'~-ˌcen·tred** *adj. Brit.* mit Cremefüllung.

sof·ten ['sɒfn] **I** *v/t.* **1.** weich machen; ⚙ *Wasser* enthärten; **2.** *Ton, Farbe* dämpfen; **3.** *a.* **~ *up*** ⚔ a) *Gegner* zermürben, b) *Festung etc.* sturmreif schießen; **4.** *fig.* mildern; *j-n* erweichen; *j-s Herz* rühren; *contp. j-n* ,kleinkriegen'; **5.** *fig.* verweichlichen; **II** *v/i.* **6.** weich(er) werden, sich erweichen; **'sof·ten·er** [-nə] *s.* ⚙ **1.** Enthärtungsmittel *n*; **2.** Weichmacher *m* (*bei Kunststoff, Öl etc.*); **'sof·ten·ing** [-nɪŋ] *s.* **1.** Erweichen *n*: **~ *of the brain*** ⚕ Gehirnerweichung *f*; **~ *point*** ⚙ Erweichungspunkt *m*; **2.** *fig.* Besänftigung *f*.

soft| goods *s. pl.* Tex'tilien *pl.*; **~ hail** *s.* Eisregen *m*; **'~·head** *s.* Schwachkopf *m*; **ˌ~'heart·ed** *adj.* weichherzig; **ˌ~-'land** *v/t. u. v/i.* weich landen.

soft·ness ['sɒftnɪs] *s.* **1.** Weichheit *f*; **2.** Sanftheit *f*; **3.** Milde *f*; **4.** Zartheit *f*; **5.** *contp.* Weichlichkeit *f*.

soft| ped·al *s.* ♪ (Pi'ano)Peˌdal *n*; **ˌ~-'ped·al** *v/t.* **1.** (*a. v/i.*) mit dem Pi'anopeˌdal spielen; **2.** F *et.* ,her'unterspielen'; **~ sci·ence** *s. Ggs. exakte Wissenschaft, z.B. Soziologie, Psychologie etc.*; **~ soap** *s.* **1.** Schmierseife *f*; **2.** *sl.* ,Schmus' *m*, Schmeiche'lei(en *pl.*) *f*; **ˌ~-'soap** *v/t. sl. j-m* ,um den Bart gehen', *j-m* Honig ums Maul schmieren; **ˌ~-'sol·der** *v/t.* ⚙ weichlöten; **'~-ˌspo·ken** *adj.* **1.** leise sprechend; **2.** *fig.* gewinnend, freundlich; **'~·ware** *s. Computer*: Software *f*; **'~·wood** *s.* **1.** Weichholz *n*; **2.** Nadelbaumholz *n*; **3.** Baum *m* mit weichem Holz.

soft·y ['sɒftɪ] *s.* F **1.** ,Softie' *m*; **2.** ,Schlappschwanz' *m*.

sog·gy ['sɒgɪ] *adj.* **1.** feucht, sumpfig (*Land*); **2.** durch'näßt, -'weicht; **3.** klitschig (*Brot etc.*); **4.** F ,doof'.

soi-di·sant [ˌswɑːdiː'zɑ̃ːŋ] (*Fr.*) *adj.* angeblich, sogenannt.

soil [sɔɪl] **I** *v/t.* **1.** a) schmutzig machen, verunreinigen, b) *bsd. fig.* besudeln, beflecken, beschmutzen; **II** *v/i.* **2.** schmutzig werden, *leicht etc.* schmutzen; **III** *s.* **3.** Verschmutzung *f*; **4.** Schmutzfleck *m*; **5.** Schmutz *m*; **6.** Dung *m*.

soil² [sɔɪl] *s.* **1.** (Erd)Boden *m*, Erde *f*, (Acker)Krume *f*, Grund *m*; **2.** *fig.* (Heimat)Erde *f*, Land *n*: ***on British* ~** auf britischem Boden; ***one's native* ~** die heimatliche Erde.

soil³ [sɔɪl] *v/t.* ✓ mit Grünfutter füttern; **'soil·age** [-lɪdʒ] *s.* ✓ Grünfutter *n*.

soil pipe *s.* ⚙ Abflußrohr *n*.

soi·rée ['swɑːreɪ] (*Fr.*) *s.* Soi'ree *f*, Abendgesellschaft *f*.

so·journ ['sɒdʒɜːn] **I** *v/i.* sich (vor'übergehend) aufhalten, (ver)weilen (***in*** in *od.* an *dat.*, ***with*** bei); **II** *s.* (vor'übergehender) Aufenthalt; **'so·journ·er** [-nə] *s.* Gast *m*, Besucher(in).

soke [səʊk] *s.* ⚖ *hist. Brit.* Gerichtsbarkeit(sbezirk *m*) *f*.

sol·ace ['sɒləs] **I** *s.* Trost *m*: ***she found* ~ *in religion***; **II** *v/t.* trösten.

so·la·num [səʊ'leɪnəm] *s.* ⚘ Nachtschatten *m*.

so·lar ['səʊlə] *adj.* **1.** *ast.* Sonnen...(*-system, -tag, -zeit etc.*), Solar...: **~ *eclipse*** Sonnenfinsternis *f*; **~ *plexus*** *anat.* Solarplexus *m*, F Magengrube *f*; **2.** ⚙ a) Sonnen...: **~ *cell*** (***energy*** *etc.*); **~ *collector*** *od.* ***panel*** Sonnenkollektor *m*, b) durch 'Sonnenenerˌgie angetrieben: **~ *power station*** Sonnen-, Solarkraftwerk *n*.

so·lar·i·um [səʊ'leərɪəm] *pl.* **-i·a** [-ɪə], **-i·ums** *s. allg.* So'larium *n*, ⚕ *a.* Sonnenliegehalle *f*.

so·lar·ize ['səʊləraɪz] *v/t.* **1.** ⚕ *j-n* mit Lichtbädern behandeln; **2.** ⚙ *Haus* auf 'Sonnenenerˌgie 'umstellen; **3.** *phot.* solarisieren (*a. v/i.*).

sold [səʊld] *pret. u. p.p. von* ***sell***.

sol·der ['sɒldə] **I** *s.* **1.** ⚙ Lot *n*, 'Lötmeˌtall *n*; **II** *v/t.* **2.** (ver)löten: **~*ed joint*** Lötstelle *f*; **~*ing iron*** Lötkolben *m*; **3.** *fig.* zs.-schweißen; **III** *v/i.* **4.** löten.

sol·dier ['səʊldʒə] **I** *s.* **1.** Sol'dat *m* (*a. engS. Feldherr*): **~ *of Christ*** Streiter *m* Christi; **~ *of fortune*** Glücksritter *m*; ***old* ~** a) F ,alter Hase', b) *sl.* leere Flasche; **2.** ⚔ (einfacher) Sol'dat, Schütze *m*, Mann *m*; **3.** *fig.* Kämpfer *m*; **4.** *zo.* Krieger *m*, Sol'dat *m* (*bei Ameisen etc.*); **II** *v/i.* **5.** (als Sol'dat) dienen: ***go* ~*ing*** Soldat werden; **6.** **~ *on*** *fig.* (unbeirrt) weitermachen; **'sol·dier·ly** [-lɪ] *adj.* **1.** sol'datisch; **2.** Soldaten...; **'sol·dier·y** [-ərɪ] *s.* **1.** Mili'tär *n*; **2.** Sol'daten *pl.*, *contp.* Solda'teska *f.*

sole¹ [səʊl] **I** *s.* **1.** (Fuß- *od.* Schuh)Sohle *f*: **~ leather** Sohlleder *n*; **2.** Bodenfläche *f*, Sohle *f*; **II** *v/t.* **3.** besohlen.

sole² [səʊl] *adj.* □ → **solely**; **1.** einzig, al'leinig, Allein...: **~ agency** Alleinvertretung *f*; **~ bill** ✝ Solawechsel *m*; **~ heir** Allein-, Universalerbe *m*; **2.** ⚖ unverheiratet.

sole³ [səʊl] *pl.* **soles**, *coll.* **sole** *s. ichth.* Seezunge *f.*

sol·e·cism ['sɒlɪsɪzəm] *s.* Schnitzer *m*, Verstoß *m*, ‚Sünde' *f*: a) *ling.* Sprachsünde, b) Faux'pas *m*; **sol·e·cis·tic** [ˌsɒlɪ'sɪstɪk] *adj.* **1.** *ling.* 'unkorˌrekt; **2.** ungehörig.

sole·ly ['səʊllɪ] *adv.* (einzig u.) al'lein, ausschließlich, nur.

sol·emn ['sɒləm] *adj.* □ **1.** *allg.* feierlich, ernst, so'lenn; **2.** feierlich (*Eid etc.*); ⚖ for'mell (*Vertrag*); **3.** gewichtig, ernst: **a ~ warning**; **4.** hehr, erhaben: **~ building**; **5.** düster; **so·lem·ni·ty** [sə'lemnətɪ] *s.* **1.** Feierlichkeit *f*, (feierlicher *od.* würdevoller) Ernst; **2.** *oft pl.* feierliches Zeremoni'ell; **3.** *bsd. eccl.* Festlich-, Feierlichkeit *f*; **'sol·em·nize** [-mnaɪz] *v/t.* **1.** feierlich begehen; **2.** *Trauung* (feierlich) voll'ziehen.

so·le·noid ['səʊlənɔɪd] *s.* ⚡, ⚙ Soleno'id *n*, Zy'linderspule *f*: **~ brake** Solenoidbremse *f.*

sol-fa [ˌsɒl'fɑː] ♪ **I** *s.* **1.** *a.* **~ syllables** Solmisati'onssilben *pl.*; **2.** Tonleiter *f*; **3.** Solmisati'on(sübung) *f*; **II** *v/t.* **4.** auf Solmisati'onssilben singen; **III** *v/i.* **5.** solmisieren.

so·lic·it [sə'lɪsɪt] **I** *v/t.* **1.** (dringend) bitten, angehen (**s.o.** j-n; **s.th.** um et.; **s.o. for s.th.** *od.* **s.th. of s.o.** j-n um et.); **2.** sich um *ein Amt etc.* bemühen; ✝ um *Aufträge*, *Kundschaft* werben; **3.** *j-n* ansprechen (*Prostituierte*); **4.** ⚖ anstiften; **II** *v/i.* **5.** dringend bitten (**for** um); **6.** ✝ Aufträge sammeln; **7.** sich anbieten (*Prostituierte*); **so·lic·i·ta·tion** [səˌlɪsɪ'teɪʃn] *s.* **1.** dringende Bitte; **2.** ✝ (Auftrags-, Kunden)Werbung *f*; **3.** Ansprechen *n* (*durch Prostituierte*); **4.** ⚖ Anstiftung *f* (**of** zu).

so·lic·i·tor [sə'lɪsɪtə] *s.* **1.** ⚖ *Brit.* So'licitor *m*, Anwalt *m* (*der nur vor niederen Gerichten plädieren darf*); **2.** *Am.* 'Rechtsrefeˌrent *m e-r Stadt etc.*; **3.** *Am.* ✝ A'gent *m*, Werber *m*; **~ gen·er·al** *pl.* **so·lic·i·tors gen·er·al** *s.* **1.** ⚖ zweiter Kronanwalt (*in England*); **2.** *USA* a) stellvertretender Ju'stizmiˌnister, b) oberster Ju'stizbeamter (*in einigen Staaten*).

so·lic·it·ous [sə'lɪsɪtəs] *adj.* □ **1.** besorgt (**about** um, **for** um, wegen); **2.** fürsorglich; **3.** (**of**) eifrig bedacht (auf *acc.*), begierig (nach); **4.** bestrebt *od.* eifrig bemüht (**to do** zu tun); **so'lic·i·tude** [-tjuːd] *s.* **1.** Besorgtheit *f*, Sorge *f*; **2.** (über'triebener) Eifer; **3.** *pl.* Sorgen *pl.*

sol·id ['sɒlɪd] **I** *adj.* □ **1.** *allg.* fest (*Eis*, *Kraftstoff*, *Speise*, *Wand etc.*): **~ body** Festkörper *m*; **~ lubricant** ⚙ Starrschmiere *f*; **~ state** *phys.* fester (Aggregat)Zustand; **~ waste** Festmüll *m*; **on ~ ground** auf festem Boden (*a. fig.*); **2.** kräftig, sta'bil, derb, fest: **~ build** kräftiger Körperbau; **~ leather** Kernleder *n*; **a ~ meal** ein kräftiges Essen; **a ~ blow** ein harter Schlag; **3.** mas'siv (*Ggs. hohl*), Voll...(*-gummi*, *-reifen*); **4.** mas'siv, gediegen: **~ gold**; **5.** *fig.* so'lid(e), gründlich: **~ learning**; **6.** *fig.* gewichtig, triftig (*Grund etc.*), stichhaltig, handfest (*Argument etc.*); **7.** so'lid(e), gediegen, zuverlässig (*Person*); **8.** ✝ so'lid(e), gutfundiert; **9.** a) soli'darisch, b) einmütig, geschlossen (**for** für *j-n od. et.*): **be ~ for s.o.**; **be ~ly behind s.o.** geschlossen hinter j-m stehen; **a ~ vote** e-e einstimmige Wahl; **10. be ~ (with s.o.)** *Am.* F (mit j-m) auf gutem Fuß stehen; **11.** *Am. sl.* ‚prima', erstklassig; **12.** ⩘ a) körperlich, räumlich, b) Kubik..., Raum...: **~ capacity**; **~ geometry** Stereometrie *f*; **~ measure** Raummaß *n*; **13.** geschlossen: **a ~ row of buildings**; **14.** F voll, ‚geschlagen': **a ~ hour**; **15.** F to'tal: **booked ~** total ausgebucht; **II** *s.* **16.** ⩘ Körper *m*; **17.** *phys.* Festkörper *m*; **18.** *pl.* feste Bestandteile *pl.*: **the ~s of milk**.

sol·i·dar·i·ty [ˌsɒlɪ'dærətɪ] *s.* Solidari'tät *f*, Zs.-halt *m*, Zs.-gehörigkeitsgefühl *n*; **sol·i·dar·y** ['sɒlɪdərɪ] *adj.* soli'darisch.

'sol·id|-drawn *adj.* ⚙ gezogen: **~ axle**; **~ tube** nahtlos gezogenes Rohr; **'~-hoofed** *adj. zo.* einhufig.

so·lid·i·fi·ca·tion [səˌlɪdɪfɪ'keɪʃn] *s. phys. etc.* Erstarrung *f*, Festwerden *n*; **so·lid·i·fy** [sə'lɪdɪfaɪ] **I** *v/t.* **1.** fest werden lassen; **2.** verdichten; **3.** *fig. Partei* festigen, konsolidieren; **II** *v/i.* **4.** fest werden, erstarren.

so·lid·i·ty [sə'lɪdətɪ] *s.* **1.** Festigkeit *f* (*a. fig.*); kom'pakte *od.* mas'sive Struk'tur; Dichtigkeit *f*; **2.** *fig.* Gediegenheit *f*, Zuverlässigkeit *f*, Solidi'tät *f*; ✝ Kre'ditfähigkeit *f.*

'sol·id-state chem·is·try *s.* 'Festkörperche,mie *f.*

sol·id·un·gu·late [ˌsɒlɪd'ʌŋgjʊleɪt] *adj. zo.* einhufig.

so·lil·o·quize [sə'lɪləkwaɪz] **I** *v/i.* Selbstgespräche führen, *bsd. thea.* monologisieren; **II** *v/t. et.* zu sich selbst sagen; **so'lil·o·quy** [-kwɪ] *s.* Selbstgespräch *n*, *bsd. thea.* Mono'log *m.*

sol·i·ped ['sɒlɪped] *zo.* **I** *s.* Einhufer *m*; **II** *adj.* einhufig.

sol·i·taire ['sɒlɪteə] *s.* **1.** Soli'tär(spiel) *n*; **2.** Pa'tience *f*; **3.** Soli'tär *m* (*einzeln gefaßter Edelstein*).

sol·i·tar·y ['sɒlɪtərɪ] *adj.* □ **1.** einsam (*Leben*, *Spaziergang etc.*); → **confinement** 2; **2.** einsam, abgelegen (*Ort*); **3.** einsam, einzeln (*Baum*, *Reiter etc.*); **4.** ⚘, *zo.* soli'tär; **5.** *fig.* einzig: **~ exception**; **'sol·i·tude** [-tjuːd] *s.* **1.** Einsamkeit *f*; **2.** (Ein)Öde *f.*

sol·mi·za·tion [ˌsɒlmɪ'zeɪʃn]*s.* ♪ a) Solmisati'on *f*, b) Solmisati'onsübung *f.*

so·lo ['səʊləʊ] *pl.* **-los I** *s.* **1.** *bsd.* ♪ Solo(gesang *m*, -spiel *n*, -tanz *m etc.*) *n*; **2.** *Kartenspiele*: Solo *n*; **3.** ✈ Al'leinflug *m*; **II** *adj.* **4.** *bsd.* ♪ Solo...; **5.** Allein...: **~ flight** → 3; **~ run** *sport* Alleingang *m*; **III** *adv.* **6.** al'lein, ‚solo': **fly ~** e-n Alleinflug machen; **'so·lo·ist** [-əʊɪst] *s.* So'list(in).

sol·stice ['sɒlstɪs] *s. ast.* Sonnenwende *f*: **summer ~**; **sol·sti·tial** [sɒl'stɪʃl] *adj.* Sonnenwende...: **~ point** Umkehrpunkt *m.*

sol·u·bil·i·ty [ˌsɒljʊ'bɪlətɪ] *s.* **1.** ⚗ Löslichkeit *f*; **2.** *fig.* Lösbarkeit *f*; **sol·u·ble** ['sɒljʊbl] *adj.* **1.** ⚗ löslich; **2.** *fig.* (auf-) lösbar.

so·lu·tion [sə'luːʃn] *s.* **1.** ⚗ a) Auflösung *f*, b) Lösung *f*: **aqueous ~** wässerige Lösung; (**rubber**) **~** Gummilösung *f*; **2.** ⩘ *etc.* (Auf)Lösung *f*; **3.** *fig.* Lösung *f* (*e-s Problems etc.*); (Er)Klärung *f.*

solv·a·ble ['sɒlvəbl] → **soluble**.

solve [sɒlv] *v/t.* **1.** *Aufgabe*, *Problem* lösen; **2.** lösen, (er)klären: **~ a mystery**; **~ a crime** ein Verbrechen aufklären; **'sol·ven·cy** [-vənsɪ] *s.* ✝ Zahlungsfähigkeit *f*; **'sol·vent** [-vənt] **I** *adj.* **1.** ⚗ (auf)lösend; **2.** *fig.* zersetzend; **3.** *fig.* erlösend: **the ~ power of laughter**; **4.** ✝ zahlungsfähig, sol'vent, li'quid; **II** *s.* **5.** ⚗ Lösungsmittel *n*; **6.** *fig.* zersetzendes Ele'ment.

so·mat·ic [səʊ'mætɪk] *adj. biol.*, ⚕ **1.** körperlich, physisch; **2.** so'matisch: **~ cell** Somazelle *f.*

so·ma·tol·o·gy [ˌsəʊmə'tɒlədʒɪ] *s.* ⚕ Somatolo'gie *f*, Körperlehre *f*; **so·ma·to·psy·chic** [ˌsəʊmətəʊ'saɪkɪk] *adj.* ⚕, *psych.* psychoso'matisch.

som·ber *Am.*, **som·bre** *Brit.* ['sɒmbə] *adj.* □ **1.** düster, trübe (*a. fig.*); **2.** dunkel(farbig); **3.** *fig.* melan'cholisch; **'som·ber·ness** *Am.*, **'som·bre·ness** *Brit.* [-nɪs] *s.* **1.** Düsterkeit *f*, Trübheit *f* (*a. fig.*); **2.** *fig.* Trübsinnigkeit *f.*

some [sʌm; səm] **I** *adj.* **1.** (*vor Substantiven*) (irgend)ein: **~ day** eines Tages; **~ day (or other)**, **~ time** irgendwann (einmal), mal; **2.** (*vor pl.*) einige, ein paar: **~ few** einige wenige; **3.** manche; **4.** ziemlich (viel), beträchtlich, e-e ganze Menge; **5.** gewiß: **to ~ extent** in gewissem Grade, einigermaßen; **6.** etwas, ein (klein) wenig: **~ bread** (etwas) Brot; **take ~ more!** nimm noch etwas!; **7.** ungefähr, gegen: **a village of ~ 60 houses** ein Dorf von etwa 60 Häusern; **8.** *sl.* beachtlich, ‚ganz hübsch': **~ race!** das war vielleicht ein Rennen!; **~ teacher!** *contp.* ein ‚schöner' Lehrer (ist das)!; **II** *adv.* **9.** *bsd. Am.* etwas, ziemlich; **10.** F ‚e'norm', ‚toll'; **III** *pron.* **11.** (irgend)ein: **~ of these days** dieser Tage, demnächst; **12.** etwas: **~ of it** etwas davon; **~ of these people** einige dieser Leute; **13.** welche: **will you have ~?**; **14.** *Am. sl.* dar'über hin'aus, noch mehr; **15. some ... some** die einen ... die anderen.

some|·bod·y ['sʌmbədɪ] **I** *pron.* jemand, (irgend)einer; **II** *s.* e-e bedeutende Per'sönlichkeit: **he thinks he is ~** er bildet sich ein, er sei jemand; **'~·how** *adv. oft* **~ or other 1.** irgend'wie, auf irgendeine Weise; **2.** aus irgendeinem Grund(e), ‚irgendwie': **~ (or other) I don't trust him**; **'~·one I** *pron.* jemand, (irgend)einer: **~ or other** irgendeiner; **II** *s.* → **somebody** II; **'~·place** *adv. Am.* irgendwo('hin).

som·er·sault ['sʌməsɔːlt] **I** *s.* a) Salto *m*, b) Purzelbaum *m* (*a. fig.*): **turn** *od.* **do a ~** → **II** *v/i.* e-n Salto machen *od.* e-n Purzelbaum schlagen.

Som·er·set House ['sʌməsɪt] *s. Verwaltungsgebäude in London mit Personenstandsregister, Notariats- u. Inlandssteuerbehörden etc.*

'some|·thing ['sʌm-] **I** *s.* **1.** (irgend) etwas, was: ***~ or other*** irgend etwas; ***a certain ~*** ein gewisses Etwas; **2.** ***~ of*** so etwas wie: ***he is ~ of a mechanic***; **3.** ***or ~*** oder so (etwas Ähnliches); **II** *adv.* **4.** ***~ like*** a) so etwas wie, so ungefähr, b) F wirklich, mal: ***that's ~ like a pudding!***; ***that's ~ like!*** das lasse ich mir gefallen!; **'~·time I** *adv.* **1.** irgend(-wann) einmal (*bsd. in der Zukunft*): ***write ~!*** schreib (ein)mal!; **2.** früher, ehemals; **II** *adj.* **3.** ehemalig, weiland (*Professor etc.*); **'~·times** *adv.* manchmal, hie und da, gelegentlich, zu'weilen; **'~·what** *adv. u. s.* etwas, ein wenig, ein bißchen: ***she was ~ puzzled***; ***~ of a shock*** ein ziemlicher Schock; **'~·where** *adv.* **1.** irgend'wo; **2.** irgendwo'hin: ***~ else*** sonstwohin, woandershin; **3.** ***~ about*** so etwa, um … her'um.

som·nam·bu·late [sɒm'næmbjʊleɪt] *v/i.* schlaf-, nachtwandeln; **som'nam·bu·lism** [-lɪzəm] *s.* Schlaf-, Nachtwandeln *n*; **som'nam·bu·list** [-lɪst] *s.* Schlaf-, Nachtwandler(in); **som·nam·bu·lis·tic** [sɒmˌnæmbjʊ'lɪstɪk] *adj.* schlaf-, nachtwandlerisch.

som·nif·er·ous [sɒm'nɪfərəs] *adj.* einschläfernd.

som·no·lence ['sɒmnələns] *s.* **1.** Schläfrigkeit *f*; **2.** ⚕ Schlafsucht *f*; **'som·no·lent** [-nt] *adj.* □ **1.** schläfrig; **2.** einschläfernd.

son [sʌn] *s.* **1.** Sohn *m*: ***~ and heir*** Stammhalter *m*; ***~ of God*** (*od.* ***man***), ***the* ℒ** *eccl.* Gottes-, Menschensohn (*Christus*); **2.** *fig.* Sohn *m*, Abkomme *m*: ***~ of a bitch*** *Am. sl.* a) ‚Scheißkerl' *m*, b) ‚Scheißding' *n*; ***~ of a gun*** *Am. sl.* a) ‚toller Hecht', b) ‚(alter) Gauner'; **3.** *fig. pl. coll.* Schüler *pl.*, Jünger *pl.*; Söhne *pl.* (*e-s Volks, e-r Gemeinschaft etc.*); **4.** → ***sonny***.

so·nance ['səʊnəns] *s.* **1.** Stimmhaftigkeit *f*; **2.** Laut *m*; **'so·nant** [-nt] *ling.* **I** *adj.* stimmhaft; **II** *s.* a) So'nant *m*, b) stimmhafter Laut.

so·nar ['səʊnɑ:] *s.* ⚓ Sonar *n*, S-Gerät *n* (*aus* ***sound navigation and ranging***).

so·na·ta [sə'nɑ:tə] *s.* ♪ So'nate *f*; **so·na·ti·na** [ˌsɒnə'ti:nə] *s.* ♪ Sona'tine *f*.

song [sɒŋ] *s.* **1.** ♪ Lied *n*, Gesang *m*: ***~ (and dance)*** F *fig.* Getue *n*, ‚The'ater' *n* (***about*** wegen); ***for a ~*** *fig.* für ein Butterbrot; **2.** Song *m*; **3.** *poet.* a) Lied *n*, Gedicht *n*, b) Dichtung *f*: ***ℒ of Solomon***, ***ℒ of Songs*** *bibl. das* Hohelied (Salomonis); ***ℒ of the Three Children*** *bibl. der* Gesang der drei Männer *od.* Jünglinge im Feuerofen; **4.** Singen *n*, Gesang *m*: ***break*** (*od.* ***burst***) ***into ~*** zu singen anfangen; **'~·bird** *s.* **1.** Singvogel *m*; **2.** ‚Nachtigall' *f* (*Sängerin*); **'~·book** *s.* Liederbuch *n*.

song·ster ['sɒŋstə] *s.* **1.** ♪ Sänger *m*; **2.** Singvogel *m*; **3.** *Am.* (*bsd.* volkstümliches) Liederbuch; **'song·stress** [-trɪs] *s.* Sängerin *f*.

'song-thrush *s. orn.* Singdrossel *f*.

son·ic ['sɒnɪk] *adj.* ⚙ Schall…; **~ bang** → ***sonic boom***; **~ bar·ri·er** → ***sound barrier***; **~ boom** *s.* ✈ Düsen-, 'Überschallknall *m*; **~ depth find·er** *s.* ⚓ Echolot *n*.

'son-in-law *pl.* **'sons-in-law** *s.* Schwiegersohn *m*.

son·net ['sɒnɪt] *s.* So'nett *n*.

son·ny ['sʌnɪ] *s.* Junge *m*, Kleiner *m* (*Anrede*).

son·o·buoy ['səʊnəbɔɪ] *s.* ⚓ Schallboje *f*.

so·nom·e·ter [səʊ'nɒmɪtə] *s.* Schallmesser *m*.

so·nor·i·ty [sə'nɒrətɪ] *s.* **1.** Klangfülle *f*, (Wohl)Klang *m*; **2.** *ling.* (Ton)Stärke *f* (*e-s Lauts*); **so·no·rous** [sə'nɔ:rəs] *adj.* □ **1.** tönend, reso'nant (*Holz etc.*); **2.** volltönend (*a. ling.*), klangvoll, so'nor (*Stimme, Sprache*); **3.** *phys.* Schall…, Klang…

son·sy ['sɒnsɪ] *adj. Scot.* **1.** drall (*Mädchen*); **2.** gutmütig.

soon [su:n] *adv.* **1.** bald, unverzüglich; **2.** (sehr) bald, (sehr) schnell: ***no ~er … than*** kaum … als; ***no ~er said than done*** gesagt, getan; **3.** bald, früh: ***as ~ as*** sobald als *od.* wie; ***~er or later*** früher oder später; ***the ~er the better*** je früher desto besser; **4.** gern: (***just***) ***as ~*** ebenso gern; ***I would ~er … than*** ich möchte lieber … als; **'soon·er** [-nə] *comp. adv.* **1.** früher, eher; **2.** schneller; **3.** lieber; → ***soon*** 2, 3, 4; **'soon·est** [-nɪst] *sup. adv.* frühestens.

soot [sʊt] **I** *s.* Ruß *m*; **II** *v/t.* mit Ruß bedecken, be-, verrußen.

sooth [su:θ] *s. Brit. obs.*: ***in ~***, ***~ to say*** fürwahr, wahrlich.

soothe [su:ð] *v/t.* **1.** besänftigen, beruhigen, beschwichtigen; **2.** *Schmerz etc.* mildern, lindern; **'sooth·ing** [-ðɪŋ] *adj.* □ **1.** besänftigend; **2.** lindernd; **3.** wohltuend, sanft: ***~ light***; ***~ music***.

sooth·say·er ['su:θˌseɪə] *s.* Wahrsager(in).

soot·y ['sʊtɪ] *adj.* □ **1.** rußig; **2.** geschwärzt; **3.** schwarz.

sop [sɒp] **I** *s.* **1.** eingetunkter Bissen (*Brot etc.*); **2.** *fig.* Beschwichtigungsmittel *n*, ‚Schmiergeld' *n*, ‚Brocken' *m*; → ***Cerberus***; **3.** *fig.* Weichling *m*; **II** *v/t.* **4.** *Brot etc.* eintunken; **5.** durch'nässen, -'weichen; **6.** ***~ up*** *Wasser* aufwischen.

soph [sɒf] F *für* ***sophomore***.

soph·ism ['sɒfɪzəm] *s.* **1.** So'phismus *m*, Spitzfindigkeit *f*, 'Scheinarguˌment *n*; **2.** Trugschluß *m*; **'Soph·ist** [-ɪst] *s. phls.* So'phist *m* (*a. fig. spitzfindiger Mensch*); **'soph·ist·er** [-ɪstə] *s. univ. hist. Student im 2. od. 3. Jahr* (*in Cambridge, Dublin*).

so·phis·tic, **so·phis·ti·cal** [sə'fɪstɪk(l)] *adj.* □ so'phistisch; **so'phis·ti·cate** [-keɪt] **I** *v/t.* **1.** verfälschen; **2.** *j-n* verbilden; **3.** *j-n* verfeinern; **II** *v/i.* **4.** So'phismen gebrauchen; **III** *s.* **5.** weltkluge (*etc.*) Per'son (→ ***sophisticated*** 1 *u.* 2); **so'phis·ti·cat·ed** [-keɪtɪd] *adj.* **1.** weltklug, intellektu'ell, (geistig) anspruchsvoll; **2.** *contp.* blasiert, ‚auf mo'dern *od.* intellektuell machend', ‚hochgestochen'; **3.** verfeinert, kultiviert, raffiniert (*Stil etc.*); hochentwickelt (*a.* ⚙ *Maschinen*); **4.** anspruchsvoll, exqui'sit (*Roman etc.*); **5.** unecht, verfälscht; **so·phis·ti·ca·tion** [səˌfɪstɪ'keɪʃn] *s.* **1.** Intellektua'lismus *m*, Kultiviertheit *f*; **2.** Blasiertheit *f*, hochgestochene Art; **3.** *das* (geistig) Anspruchsvolle; **4.** ⚙ Ausgereiftheit, (technisches) Raffine'ment; **5.** (Ver)Fälschung *f*; **6.** → ***sophistry***; **soph·ist·ry** ['sɒfɪstrɪ] *s.* **1.** Spitzfindigkeit *f*, Sophiste'rei *f*; **2.** So'phismus *m*, Trugschluß *m*.

soph·o·more ['sɒfəmɔ:] *s. ped. Am.* 'College-Stuˌdent(in) *od.* Schüler(in) e-r ***High School*** im 2. Jahr.

so·po·rif·ic [ˌsɒpə'rɪfɪk] **I** *adj.* einschläfernd, schlaffördernd; **II** *s. bsd. pharm.* Schlafmittel *n*.

sop·ping ['sɒpɪŋ] *adj. a.* ***~ wet*** patschnaß, triefend (naß); **'sop·py** [-pɪ] *adj.* □ **1.** durch'weicht (*Boden etc.*); **2.** regnerisch; **3.** F saftlos, fad(e); **4.** F rührselig, ‚schmalzig'; **5.** F ‚verknallt' (***on s.o.*** in j-n).

so·pran·o [sə'prɑ:nəʊ] *pl.* **-nos I** *s.* **1.** So'pran *m* (*Singstimme*); **2.** So'pranstimme *f*, -parˌtie *f* (*e-r Komposition*); **3.** Sopra'nist(in); **II** *adj.* **4.** Sopran…

sorb [sɔ:b] *s.* ⚘ **1.** Eberesche *f*; **2.** *a.* ***~ apple*** Elsbeere *f*.

sor·be·fa·cient [ˌsɔ:bɪ'feɪʃənt] **I** *adj.* absorbierend, absorpti'onsfördernd; **II** *s.* ⚕ Ab'sorbens *n*.

sor·bet ['sɔ:bɪt] *s.* Fruchteis *n*.

sor·cer·er ['sɔ:sərə] *s.* Zauberer *m*; **'sor·cer·ess** [-rɪs] *s.* Zauberin *f*, Hexe *f*; **'sor·cer·ous** [-rəs] *adj.* Zauber…, Hexen…; **'sor·cer·y** [-rɪ] *s.* Zaube'rei *f*, Hexe'rei *f*.

sor·did ['sɔ:dɪd] *adj.* □ *bsd. fig.* schmutzig, schäbig; **'sor·did·ness** [-nɪs] *s.* Schmutzigkeit *f* (*a. fig.*).

sor·dine ['sɔ:di:n], **sor·di·no** [sɔ:'di:nəʊ] *pl.* **-ni** [-ni:] ♪ Dämpfer *m*, Sor'dine *f*.

sore [sɔ:] **I** *adj.* □ → ***sorely***; **1.** weh(e), wund: ***~ feet***; ***~ heart*** *fig.* wundes Herz, Leid *n*; ***like a bear with a ~ head*** *fig.* brummig, bärbeißig; → ***spot*** 5; **2.** entzündet, schlimm, ‚böse': ***~ finger***; ***~ throat*** Halsentzündung *f*; → ***sight*** 6; **3.** *fig.* schlimm, arg: ***~ calamity***; **4.** F verärgert, beleidigt, böse (***about*** über *acc.*, wegen); **5.** heikel (*Thema*); **II** *s.* **6.** Wunde *f*, wunde Stelle, Entzündung *f*: ***an open ~*** a) e-e offene Wunde (*a. fig.*), b) *fig.* ein altes Übel, ein ständiges Ärgernis; **III** *adv.* **7.** → ***sorely*** 1; **'sore·head** *s. Am.* F mürrischer Mensch; **'sore·ly** [-lɪ] *adv.* **1.** arg, ‚bös': a) sehr, bitter, b) schlimm; **2.** dringend; **3.** bitterlich *weinen etc.*

so·ror·i·ty [sə'rɒrətɪ] *s.* **1.** *Am.* Verbindung *f* von Stu'dentinnen; **2.** *eccl.* Schwesternschaft *f*.

sorp·tion ['sɔ:pʃn] *s.* ⚗, *phys.* (Ab-)Sorpti'on *f*.

sor·rel[1] ['sɒrəl] **I** *s.* **1.** Rotbraun *n*; **2.** (Rot)Fuchs *m* (*Pferd*); **II** *adj.* **3.** rotbraun.

sor·rel[2] ['sɒrəl] *s.* ⚘ **1.** Sauerampfer *m*; **2.** Sauerklee *m*.

sor·row ['sɒrəʊ] **I** *s.* **1.** Kummer *m*, Leid *n*, Gram *m* (***at*** über *acc.*, ***for*** um): ***to my ~*** zu m-m Kummer *od.* Leidwesen; **2.** Leid *n*, Unglück *n*; *pl.* Leid(en *pl.*) *n*; **3.** Reue *f* (***for*** über *acc.*); **4.** *bsd. iro.* Bedauern *n*: ***without much ~***; **5.** Klage *f*, Jammer *m*; **II** *v/i.* **6.** sich grämen *od.* härmen (***at***, ***over***, ***for*** über *acc.*, wegen, um); **7.** klagen, trauern (***after***, ***for*** um, über *acc.*); **sor·row·ful** ['sɒrəʊfʊl] *adj.* □ **1.** sorgen-, kummervoll, bekümmert; **2.** klagend, traurig: ***a ~ song***; **3.** traurig, beklagenswert: ***a ~ accident***.

sor·ry ['sɒrɪ] *adj.* □ **1.** betrübt: ***I am*** (*od.* ***feel***) ***~ for him*** er tut mit leid; ***be ~ for o.s.*** sich selbst bedauern; (***I am***) (**so**) **~!** (es) tut mir (sehr) leid!, (ich) bedaure!, Verzeihung!; ***we are ~ to say*** wir müssen leider sagen; **2.** reuevoll: ***be ~ about*** *et.* bereuen *od.* bedauern; **3.** *contp.* traurig, erbärmlich (*Anblick, Zustand etc.*): ***a ~ excuse*** ,e-e faule Ausrede'.

sort [sɔːt] **I** *s.* **1.** Sorte *f*, Art *f*, Klasse *f*, Gattung *f*; ✝ *a.* Marke *f*, Quali'tät *f*: ***all ~s of people*** allerhand *od.* alle möglichen Leute; ***all ~s of things*** alles mögliche; **2.** Art *f*: ***after a ~*** gewissermaßen; ***nothing of the ~*** nichts dergleichen; ***something of the ~*** so etwas, et. Derartiges; ***he is not my ~*** er ist nicht mein Fall *od.* Typ; ***he is not the ~ of man who ...*** er ist nicht der Mann, der *so et. tut*; ***what ~ of a ...?*** was für ein ...?; ***he is a good ~*** er ist ein guter *od.* anständiger Kerl; (***a***) ***~ of a peace*** so etwas wie ein Frieden; ***I ~ of expected it*** F ich habe es irgendwie *od.* halb erwartet; ***he ~ of hinted*** F er machte so eine *od.* e-e vage Andeutung; **3.** ***of a ~, of ~s*** *contp.* so was wie: ***a politician of ~s***; **4.** ***out of ~s*** a) unwohl, nicht auf der Höhe, b) verstimmt; → 5; **5.** *typ.* 'Schriftgarniˌtur *f*: ***out of ~*** ausgegangen; **II** *v/t.* **6.** sortieren, (ein)ordnen, sichten; **7.** sondern, trennen (***from*** von); **8.** *oft* ***~ out*** auslesen, -suchen, -sortieren; **9.** ***~ s.th. out*** *fig.* a) et. ,auseinanderklauben', sich Klarheit verschaffen über et., b) e-e Lösung finden für et.; ***~ itself out*** sich von selbst erledigen; **10.** ***~ s.o. out*** F a) j-m den Kopf zurechtsetzen, b) j-n ,zur Schnecke machen'; ***~ o.s. out*** zur Ruhe kommen, mit sich ins reine kommen; **11.** *a.* ***~ together*** zs.-stellen, -tun (***with*** mit); **'sort·er** [-tə] *s.* Sortierer(in).

sor·tie ['sɔːtiː] **I** *s.* ✕ a) Ausfall *m*, b) ✈ (Einzel)Einsatz *m*, Feindflug *m*; **II** *v/i.* ✕ a) e-n Ausfall machen, b) ✈ e-n Einsatz fliegen, c) ⚓ auslaufen.

sor·ti·lege ['sɔːtɪlɪdʒ] *s.* Wahrsagen *n* (aus Losen).

so-so, so so ['səʊsəʊ] *adj. u. adv.* F so la'la (*leidlich, mäßig*).

sot [sɒt] **I** *s.* Säufer *m*; **II** *v/i.* (sich be-) saufen; **sot·tish** ['sɒtɪʃ] *adj.* □ **1.** ,versoffen'; **2.** ,besoffen'; **3.** ,blöd' (*albern*).

sot·to vo·ce [ˌsɒtəʊ'vəʊtʃɪ] (*Ital.*) *adv.* ♪ *u. fig.* leise, gedämpft.

sou·brette [suː'bret] (*Fr.*) *s. thea.* Sou'brette *f*.

sou·bri·quet ['suːbrɪkeɪ] → ***sobriquet***.

souf·fle ['suːfl] *s.* ⚕ Geräusch *n*.

souf·flé ['suːfleɪ] (*Fr.*) *s.* Auflauf *m*, Souf'flé *n*.

sough [saʊ] **I** *s.* Rauschen *n* (*des Windes*); **II** *v/i.* rauschen.

sought [sɔːt] *pret. u. p.p. von* ***seek***.

soul [səʊl] *s.* **1.** *eccl., phls.* Seele *f*: ***upon my ~!*** ganz bestimmt!; **2.** Seele *f*, Herz *n*, *das* Innere: ***he has a ~ above mere money-grubbing*** er hat auch noch Sinn für andere Dinge als Geldraffen; **3.** *fig.* Seele *f* (*Triebfeder*): ***he was the ~ of the enterprise***; **4.** *fig.* Geist *m* (*Person*): ***the greatest ~s of the past***; **5.** Seele *f*, Mensch *m*: ***the ship went down with 300 ~s***; ***a good ~*** e-e gute Seele, e-e Seele von e-m Menschen; ***poor ~*** armer Kerl; ***not a ~*** keine Menschenseele, niemand; **6.** Inbegriff *m*, *ein* Muster (***of*** *an dat.*): ***the ~ of generosity*** *er ist* die Großzügigkeit selbst; **7.** Inbrunst *f*, Kraft *f*, *künstlerischer* Ausdruck; **8.** *a.* ***~ music*** ♪ Soul *m*; **9.** ***~ brother, ~ sister*** *Am.* Schwarze(r *m*) *f*; **'soul-deˌstroy·ing** *adj.* geisttötend (*Arbeit etc.*); **'soul·ful** [-fʊl] *adj.* □ seelenvoll (*a. fig. u. iro.*); **'soul·less** [-lɪs] *adj.* □ seelenlos (*a. fig. gefühllos, egoistisch, ausdruckslos*); **'soul-ˌstir·ring** *adj.* ergreifend.

sound¹ [saʊnd] **I** *adj.* □ **1.** gesund: ***as ~ as a bell*** kerngesund; ***~ in mind and body*** körperlich u. geistig gesund; ***of ~ mind*** ⚖ voll zurechnungs- *od.* handlungsfähig; **2.** fehlerfrei (*Holz etc.*), tadellos, in'takt: ***~ fruit*** unverdorbenes Obst; **3.** gesund, fest (*Schlaf*); **4.** ✝ gesund, so'lide (*Firma, Währung*); sicher (*Kredit*); **5.** gesund, vernünftig (*Urteil etc.*); gut, brauchbar (*Rat, Vorschlag*); kor'rekt, folgerichtig (*Denken etc.*); ⚖ begründet, gültig; **6.** zuverlässig (*Freund etc.*); **7.** gut, tüchtig (*Denker, Schläfer, Stratege etc.*); **8.** tüchtig, kräftig, gehörig: ***a ~ slap*** e-e saftige Ohrfeige; **II** *adv.* **9.** fest, tief *schlafen*.

sound² [saʊnd] *s.* **1.** Sund *m*, Meerenge *f*; **2.** *ichth.* Fischblase *f*.

sound³ [saʊnd] **I** *v/t.* **1.** ⚓ (aus)loten, peilen; **2.** *Meeresboden etc.* erforschen (*a. fig.*); **3.** ⚕ a) sondieren, b) → ***sound⁴*** 14; **4.** *fig.* a) sondieren, erkunden, b) *j-n* ausholen, *j-m* auf den Zahn fühlen; **II** *v/i.* **5.** ⚓ loten; **6.** (weg)tauchen (*Wal*); **7.** *fig.* sondieren; **III** *s.* **8.** ⚕ Sonde *f*.

sound⁴ [saʊnd] **I** *s.* **1.** Schall *m*, Laut *m*, Ton *m*: ***~ amplifier*** Lautverstärker *m*; ***faster than ~*** mit Überschallgeschwindigkeit; ***~ and fury*** *fig.* a) Schall und Rauch, b) hohles Getöse; ♀ ***Peter Brown*** *Film, TV*: Ton: Peter Brown; ***within ~*** in Hörweite; **2.** Geräusch *n*, Laut *m*: ***without a ~*** geräusch-, lautlos; **3.** Ton *m*, Klang *m*, *a. fig.* Tenor *m* (*e-s Briefes, e-r Rede etc.*); **4.** ♪ Klang *m*, *Jazz etc.*: Sound *m*; **5.** *ling.* Laut *m*; **II** *v/i.* **6.** (er)schallen, (-)tönen, (-)klingen; **7.** (*a. fig. gut, unwahrscheinlich etc.*) klingen; **8.** ***~ off*** F ,tönen' (***about, on*** von): ***~ off against*** ,herziehen' über (*acc.*); **9.** ***~ in*** ⚖ auf *Schadenersatz etc.* gehen *od.* lauten (*Klage*); **III** *v/t.* **10.** *Trompete etc.* erschallen *od.* ertönen *od.* erklingen lassen: ***~ s.o.'s praises*** *fig.* j-s Lob singen; **11.** *durch ein Signal* verkünden; → ***alarm*** 1; ***retreat*** 1; **12.** äußern, von sich geben: ***~ a note of fear***; **13.** *ling.* aussprechen; **14.** ⚕ abhorchen, -klopfen; ***~ bar·rier*** *s.* ✈, *phys.* Schallgrenze *f*, -mauer *f*; ***~ board*** *s.* ♪ Reso'nanzboden *m*, Schallbrett *n*; ***~ box*** *s.* **1.** ♪ Reso'nanzkasten *m*; **2.** *Film etc.*: 'Tonkaˌbine *f*; ***~ broad·cast·ing*** *s.* Hörfunk *m*; ***~ ef·fects*** *s. pl. Film, TV*: 'Tonefˌfekte *pl.*, Geräusche *pl.*; ***~ en·gi·neer*** *s. Film*: Tonmeister *m*.

sound·er ['saʊndə] *s.* **1.** ⚓ a) Lot *n*, b) ✕ Lotgast *m*; **2.** *tel.* Klopfer *m*.

sound film *s.* Tonfilm *m*.

sound·ing¹ ['saʊndɪŋ] *adj.* □ **1.** tönend, schallend; **2.** wohlklingend; **3.** *contp.* lautstark, bom'bastisch.

sound·ing² ['saʊndɪŋ] *s.* **1.** Loten *n*; **2.** *pl.* (ausgelotete *od.* auslotbare) Wassertiefe: ***take a ~*** loten, *fig.* sondieren.

sound·ing| bal·loon *s.* Ver'suchsbalˌlon *m*, Bal'lonsonde *f*; ***~ board*** *s.* ♪ **1.** → ***sound board***; **2.** Schallmuschel *f* (*für Orchester etc. im Freien*); **3.** Schalldämpfungsbrett *n*; **4.** *fig.* Podium *n*.

sound·less ['saʊndlɪs] *adj.* □ laut-, geräuschlos.

sound mix·er *s. Film etc.*: Tonmeister *m*.

sound·ness ['saʊndnɪs] **1.** Gesundheit *f* (*a. fig.*); **2.** Vernünftigkeit *f*; **3.** Brauchbarkeit *f*; **4.** Folgerichtigkeit *f*; **5.** Zuverlässigkeit *f*; **6.** Tüchtigkeit *f*; **7.** ⚖ Rechtmäßigkeit *f*, Gültigkeit *f*.

'sound|-on-film *s.* Tonfilm *m*; **'~·proof** [-ndp-] **I** *adj.* schalldicht; **II** *v/t.* schalldicht machen, isolieren; **'~ˌproof·ing** [-ndp-] *s.* ⚙ Schalldämpfung *f*, Schallisolierung *f*; ***~ rang·ing*** **I** *s.* ✕ Schallmessen *n*; **II** *adj.* Schallmeß...; ***~ re·cord·er*** *s.* Tonaufnahmegerät *n*; ***~ shift*** *s. ling.* Lautverschiebung *f*; ***~ track*** *s. Film*: Tonstreifen *m*, -spur *f*; ***~ truck*** *s. Am.* Lautsprecherwagen *m*; ***~ wave*** *s. phys.* Schallwelle *f*.

soup [suːp] **I** *s.* **1.** Suppe *f*, Brühe *f*: ***be in the ~*** F ,in der Tinte sitzen'; ***from ~ to nuts*** F von A bis Z; **2.** *fig.* dicker Nebel, ,Waschküche' *f*; **3.** *phot.* F Entwickler *m*; **4.** *mot. sl.* P'S *f*; **II** *v/t.* **5.** *Am. sl.* ***~ up*** a) *Motor* ,frisieren', b) *fig. et.* ,aufmöbeln', c) *fig.* Dampf hinter *e-e Sache* machen.

soup·çon ['suːpsɔ̃ːŋ] *s.* Spur *f* (***of*** *Knoblauch, a. Ironie etc.*).

soup| kitch·en *s.* **1.** Armenküche *f*; **2.** ✕ Feldküche *f*; **'~·mix** *s.* 'Suppenpräpaˌrat *n*.

sour ['saʊə] **I** *adj.* □ **1.** sauer (*a. Geruch, Milch*); herb, bitter: ***~ grapes*** *fig.* saure Trauben; ***turn*** *od.* ***go ~*** → 8 *u.* 9; **2.** *fig.* sauer (*Gesicht etc.*); **3.** *fig.* sauertöpfisch, mürrisch, bitter; **4.** naßkalt (*Wetter*); **5.** ⚘ sauer (*kalkarm, naß*) (*Boden*); **II** *s.* **6.** Säure *f*; **7.** *fig.* Bitternis *f*: ***take the sweet with the ~*** das Leben nehmen, wie es (eben) ist; **III** *v/i.* **8.** sauer werden; **9.** *fig.* a) verbittert *od.* ,sauer' werden, b) die Lust verlieren (***on*** an *dat.*), c) ,mies' werden, d) ,ka'puttgehen'; **IV** *v/t.* **10.** sauer machen, säuern; **11.** *fig.* verbittern.

source [sɔːs] *s.* **1.** Quelle *f*, *poet.* Quell *m*; **2.** Quellfluß *m*; **3.** *poet.* Strom *m*; **4.** *fig.* (*Licht-, Strom- etc.*)Quelle *f*: ***~ impedance*** ⚡ Quellwiderstand *m*; ***~ material*** Ausgangsstoff *m* (→ *a.* 6); **5.** *fig.* Quelle *f*, Ursprung *m*: ***~ of information*** Nachrichtenquelle *f*; ***from a reliable ~*** aus zuverlässiger Quelle; ***have its ~ in*** s-n Ursprung haben in (*dat.*); ***take its ~ from*** entspringen (*dat.*); **6.** *fig. literarische* Quelle: ***~ material*** Quellenmaterial *n*; **7.** ✝ (*Einnahme-, Kapital- etc.*)Quelle *f*: ***~ of supply*** Bezugsquelle; ***levy a tax at the ~*** e-e Steuer an der Quelle erheben; ***~ lan·guage*** *s. ling.* Ausgangssprache *f* (*Übersetzung etc.*).

sour| cream *s. Brit.* Sauerrahm *m*; **'~·dough** *s. Am.* **1.** Sauerteig *m*; **2.** A'laska-Schürfer *m*.

sour·ing ['saʊərɪŋ] *s.* ⚗ Säuerung *f*; **'sour·ish** [-ərɪʃ] *adj.* säuerlich, angesäuert; **'sour·ness** [-ənɪs] *s.* **1.** Herbheit *f*; **2.** Säure *f* (*als Eigenschaft*); **3.** *fig.* Bitterkeit *f*.

'**sour·puss** *s.* F ‚Sauertopf' *m.*
souse [saʊs] **I** *s.* **1.** Pökelfleisch *n*; **2.** Pökelbrühe *f*, Lake *f*; **3.** Eintauchen *n*; **4.** Sturz *m* ins Wasser; **5.** ‚Dusche' *f*, (Regen)Guß *m*; **6.** *sl.* a) Saufe'rei *f*, b) *Am.* Säufer *m*, c) *Am.* ‚Suff' *m*; **II** *v/t.* **7.** eintauchen; **8.** durch'tränken, einweichen; **9.** *Wasser etc.* ausgießen (***over*** über *acc.*); **10.** (ein)pökeln; **11.** ***~d*** *sl.* ‚voll', besoffen.
sou·tane [suː'tɑːn] *s. R.C.* Sou'tane *f.*
sou·ten·eur [ˌsuːtə'nɜː] (*Fr.*) *s.* Zuhälter *m.*
south [saʊθ] **I** *s.* **1.** Süden *m*: ***in the ~ of*** im Süden von; ***to the ~ of*** → 6; **2.** *a.* 2 Süden *m* (*Landesteil*): ***from the*** 2 aus dem Süden (*Person, Wind*); ***the*** 2 der Süden, die Südstaaten (*der USA*); **3.** *poet.* Südwind *m*; **II** *adj.* **4.** südlich, Süd...: 2 ***Pole*** Südpol *m*; 2 ***Sea*** Südsee *f*; **III** *adv.* **5.** nach Süden, südwärts; **6.** ***~ of*** südlich von; **7.** aus dem Süden (*Wind*); 2 **Af·ri·can I** *adj.* 'südafri'kanisch; **II** *s.* 'Südafri'kaner(in): ***~ Dutch*** Afrikaander(in); **~ by east** *s.* Südsüd'ost *m*; **~·east** [ˌsaʊθ'iːst, ⚓ saʊ'iːst] **I** *s.* Süd'osten *m*; **II** *adj.* süd'östlich, Südost...; **III** *adv.* süd'östlich; nach Süd'osten.
south|·east·er [ˌsaʊθ'iːstə] *s.* Süd'ostwind *m*, -'oststurm *m*; **ˌ~-'east·er·ly** [-lɪ] **I** *adj.* → ***southeast*** II; **II** *adv.* von *od.* nach Süd'osten; **ˌ~-'east·ern** [-ən] → ***southeast*** II; **ˌ~-'east·ward** [-stwəd] **I** *adj. u. adv.* nach Süd'osten, süd'östlich; **II** *s.* süd'östliche Richtung; **ˌ~-'east·wards** [-stwədz] *adv.* nach Süd'osten.
south·er·ly ['sʌðəlɪ] **I** *adj.* südlich, Süd...; **II** *adv.* von *od.* nach Süden.
south·ern ['sʌðən] **I** *adj.* **1.** südlich, Süd...: 2 ***Cross*** *ast. das* Kreuz des Südens; ***~ lights*** *ast. das* Südlicht; **2.** 2 südstaatlich, ... der Südstaaten (*der USA*); **II** *s.* **3.** → ***southerner***; '**south·ern·er** [-nə] *s.* **1.** Bewohner(in) des Südens (*e-s Landes*); **2.** 2 Südstaatler(in) (*in den USA*); '**south·ern·ly** [-lɪ] → ***southerly***; '**south·ern·most** *adj.* südlichst.
south·ing ['saʊθɪŋ] *s.* **1.** ⚓ a) Südrichtung *f*, südliche Fahrt, b) 'Breitenˌunterschied *m* bei südlicher Fahrt; **2.** *ast.* a) Kulminati'on *f* (*des Mondes etc.*), b) südliche Deklinati'on (*e-s Gestirns*).
'**south|·most** *adj.* südlichst; '**~·paw** *sport* **I** *adj.* linkshändig; **II** *s.* Linkshänder *m*; *Boxen*: Rechtsausleger *m*; **ˌ~-south'east** [⚓ ˌsaʊsaʊ'iːst] **I** *adj.* südsüd'östlich, Südsüdost...; **II** *adv.* nach *od.* aus Südsüd'osten; **III** *s.* Südsüd'osten *m*; '**~·ward** [-wəd] *adj. u. adv.* nach Süden, südwärts.
south|-west [ˌsaʊθ'west; ⚓ saʊ'west] **I** *adj.* süd'westlich, Südwest...; **II** *adv.* nach *od.* aus Süd'westen; **III** *s.* Süd'westen *m*; **ˌ~'west·er** [-tə] *s.* **1.** Süd'westwind *m*; **2.** → ***sou'wester*** 1; **ˌ~'west·er·ly** [-təlɪ] *adj.* nach *od.* aus Süd'westen; **ˌ~'west·ern** [-tən] *adj.* süd'westlich, Südwest...; **ˌ~-'west·ward** [-wəd] *adj. u. adv.* nach Süd'westen.
sou·ve·nir [ˌsuːvə'nɪə] *s.* Andenken *n*, Souve'nir *n*: ***~ shop.***
sou'·west·er [saʊ'westə] *s.* **1.** Süd'wester *m* (*wasserdichter Hut*); **2.** → ***southwester*** 1.
sov·er·eign ['sɒvrɪn] **I** *s.* **1.** Souve'rän *m*, Mon'arch(in); **2.** *die* Macht im Staate (*Person od. Gruppe*); **3.** souve'räner Staat; **4.** † *Brit.* Sovereign *m* (*alte 20-Schilling-Münze aus Gold*); **II** *adj.* **5.** höchst, oberst; **6.** 'unumˌschränkt, souve'rän, königlich: ***~ power***; **7.** souve'rän (*Staat*); **8.** äußerst, größt: ***~ contempt*** tiefste Verachtung; **9.** 'unüberˌtrefflich; '**sov·er·eign·ty** [-rəntɪ] *s.* **1.** höchste (Staats)Gewalt; **2.** Landeshoheit *f*, Souveräni'tät *f*; **3.** Oberherrschaft *f.*
so·vi·et ['səʊvɪət] **I** *s. oft* 2 **1.** So'wjet *m*: ***Supreme*** 2 Oberster Sowjet; **2.** 2 So'wjetsyˌstem *n*; **3.** *pl. die* So'wjets; **II** *adj.* **4.** 2 so'wjetisch, Sowjet...; '**so·vi·et·ize** [-taɪz] *v/t.* sowjetisieren.
sow¹ [saʊ] *s.* **1.** Sau *f*, (Mutter)Schwein *n*: ***get the wrong ~ by the ear*** a) den Falschen erwischen, b) sich gewaltig irren; **2.** *metall.* a) (Ofen)Sau *f*, b) Massel *f* (*Barren*).
sow² [səʊ] [*irr.*] **I** *v/t.* **1.** säen; **2.** *Land* besäen; **3.** *fig.* säen, ausstreuen; → ***seed*** 4, ***wind¹*** 1; **4.** *et.* verstreuen; **II** *v/i.* **5.** säen.
sown [səʊn] *p.p. von* ***sow²***.
soy [sɔɪ] *s.* **1.** Sojabohnenöl *n*; **2.** → '**so·ya (bean)** ['sɔɪə], '**soy·bean** *s.* Sojabohne *f.*
soz·zled ['sɒzld] *adj. Brit. sl.* ‚blau'.
spa [spɑː] *s.* a) Mine'ralquelle *f*, b) Badekurort *m*, Bad *n.*
space [speɪs] **I** *s.* **1.** Raum *m* (*Ggs. Zeit*): ***disappear into ~*** ins Nichts verschwinden; ***look into ~*** ins Leere starren; **2.** Raum *m*, Platz *m*: ***require much ~***; ***for ~ reasons*** aus Platzgründen; **3.** (Welt)Raum *m*; **4.** (Zwischen-)Raum *m*, Stelle *f*, Lücke *f*; **5.** Zwischenraum *m*, Abstand *m*; **6.** Zeitraum *m*: ***a ~ of three hours***; ***after a ~*** nach e-r Weile; ***for a ~*** e-e Zeitlang; **7.** *typ.* Spatium *n*, Ausschlußstück *n*; **8.** *tel.* Abstand *m*, Pause *f*; **9.** *Am.* a) Raum *m* für Re'klame (*Zeitung*), b) *Radio, TV*: (Werbe)Zeit *f*; **II** *v/t.* **10.** räumlich *od.* zeitlich einteilen: ***~d out over 10 years*** auf 10 Jahre verteilt; **11.** in Zwischenräumen anordnen; **12.** *mst* ***~ out*** *typ.* a) ausschließen, b) gesperrt setzen, sperren: ***~d type*** Sperrdruck *m*; **13.** gesperrt schreiben (*auf der Schreibmaschine*); **~ age** *s.* Weltraumzeitalter *n*; **~ bar** *s.* Leertaste *f*; '**~·borne** *adj.* **1.** Weltraum...: ***~ satellite***; **2.** über Satel'lit, Satelliten...: ***~ television***; **~ capsule** *s.* Raumkapsel *f*; '**~·craft** *s.* Raumfahrzeug *n*, -schiff *n*; **~ flight** *s.* Raumflug *m*; **~ heat·er** *s.* Raumerhitzer *m*, -strahler *m*; '**~·lab** *s.* 'Raumlaˌbor *n*; '**~·man** *s.* [*irr.*] **1.** Raumfahrer *m*, Astro'naut *m*; **2.** Außerirdische(r) *m*; **~ med·i·cine** *s.* ⚕ 'Raumfahrtmediˌzin *f*; **~ probe** *s.* Raumsonde *f.*
spac·er ['speɪsə] *s.* ⚙ **1.** Di'stanzstück *n*; **2.** → ***space bar.***
space| race *s.* Wettlauf *m* um die Eroberung des Weltraums; **~ re·search** *s.* (Welt)Raumforschung *f*; '**~-ˌsav·ing** *adj.* raumsparend; '**~·ship** *s.* Raumschiff *n*; **~ shut·tle** *s.* Raumfähre *f*; **~ sta·tion** *s.* 'Raumstatiˌon *f*; '**~·suit** *s.* Raumanzug *m*; **ˌ~-'time I** *s.* ⚖, *phls.* Zeit-Raum *m*; **II** *adj.* Raum-Zeit-...; **~ trav·el** *s.* (Welt)Raumfahrt *f*; '**~·walk** *s.* Weltraumspaziergang *m*; '**~ˌwom·an** *s.* [*irr.*] **1.** Raumfahrerin *f*, Astro'nautin *f*; **2.** Außerirdische *f*; **~ writ·er** *s.* (Zeitungs- *etc.*)Schreiber, der nach dem 'Umfang s-s Beitrags bezahlt wird.
spa·cious ['speɪʃəs] *adj.* □ **1.** geräumig, weit, ausgedehnt; **2.** *fig.* weit, 'umfangreich, um'fassend; '**spa·cious·ness** [-nɪs] *s.* **1.** Geräumigkeit *f*; **2.** *fig.* Weite *f*, 'Umfang *m*, Ausmaß *n.*
spade¹ [speɪd] **I** *s.* **1.** Spaten *m*: ***call a ~ a ~*** *fig.* das Kind beim (rechten) Namen nennen; ***dig the first ~*** den ersten Spatenstich tun; **2.** ⚔ La'fettensporn *m*; **II** *v/t.* **3.** 'umgraben, mit e-m Spaten bearbeiten; **III** *v/i.* **4.** graben.
spade² [speɪd] *s.* **1.** Pik(karte *f*) *n*, Schippe *f* (*französisches Blatt*), Grün *n* (*deutsches Blatt*): ***seven of ~s*** Piksieben *f*; ***in ~s*** *Am.* F mit Zins u. Zinseszinsen; **2.** *mst pl.* Pik(farbe *f*) *n.*
spade·ful ['speɪdfʊl] *pl.* **-fuls** *s. ein* Spaten(voll) *m.*
'**spade·work** *s. fig.* (mühevolle) Vorarbeit, Kleinarbeit *f.*
spa·dix ['speɪdɪks] *pl.* **spa·di·ces** [speɪ'daɪsiːz] *s.* ♆ (Blüten)Kolben *m.*
spa·do ['speɪdəʊ] *pl.* **spa·do·nes** [spɑː'dəʊniːz] (*Lat.*) *s.* **1.** Ka'strat *m*; **2.** kastriertes Tier.
spa·ghet·ti [spə'getɪ] (*Ital.*) *s.* **1.** Spa'ghetti *pl.*; **2.** *sl.* 'Filmsaˌlat *m.*
spake [speɪk] *obs. pret. von* ***speak.***
spall [spɔːl] **I** *s.* (Stein-, Erz)Splitter *m*; **II** *v/t.* ⚙ *Erz* zerstückeln; **III** *v/i.* zerbröckeln, absplittern.
span [spæn] **I** *s.* **1.** Spanne *f*: a) *gespreizte Hand*, b) *engl. Maß = 9 inches*; **2.** △ a) Spannweite *f* (*Brückenbogen*), b) Stützweite *f* (*e-r Brücke*), c) (einzelner) Brückenbogen; **3.** ✈ Spannweite *f*; **4.** ⚓ Spann *n*, *m* (*Haltetau, -kette*); **5.** *fig.* Spanne *f*, 'Umfang *m*; **6.** *fig.* (kurze) Zeitspanne; **7.** Lebensspanne *f*, -zeit *f*; **8.** ⚕, *psych.* (*Gedächtnis-, Seh- etc.*) Spanne *f*; **9.** Gewächshaus *n*; **10.** *Am.* Gespann *n*; **II** *v/t.* **11.** abmessen; **12.** um'spannen (*a. fig.*); **13.** sich erstrecken über (*acc.*) (*a. fig.*), über'spannen; **14.** *Fluß* über'brücken; **15.** *fig.* überspannen, bedecken.
span·drel ['spændrəl] *s.* **1.** △ Span'drille *f*, (Gewölbe-, Bogen)Zwickel *m*; **2.** ⚙ Hohlkehle *f.*
span·gle ['spæŋgl] **I** *s.* **1.** Flitter(plättchen *n*) *m*, Pail'lette *f*; **2.** ♆ Gallapfel *m*; **II** *v/t.* **3.** mit Flitter besetzen; **4.** *fig.* schmücken, über'säen (***with*** mit): ***the ~d heavens*** der gestirnte Himmel.
Span·iard ['spænjəd] *s.* Spanier(in).
span·iel ['spænjəl] *s. zo.* Spaniel *m*, Wachtelhund *m*: ***a (tame) ~*** *fig.* ein Kriecher.
Span·ish ['spænɪʃ] **I** *adj.* **1.** spanisch; **II** *s.* **2.** *coll. die* Spanier; **3.** *ling.* Spanisch *n*; **~ A·mer·i·can I** *adj.* la'teinameriˌkanisch; **II** *s.* La'teinameriˌkaner(in); **~ chest·nut** *s.* ♆ 'Eßkaˌstanie *f*; **~ pa·pri·ka** *s.* ♆ Spanischer Pfeffer, Paprika *m.*
spank [spæŋk] F **I** *v/t.* **1.** verhauen, *j-m* ‚den Hintern versohlen'; **2.** *Pferde etc.* antreiben; **II** *v/i.* **3.** ***~ along*** da'hinflitzen; **III** *s.* **4.** Schlag *m*, Klaps *m*; '**spank·er** [-kə] *s.* **1.** F Renner *m* (*Pferd*); **2.** ⚓ Be'san *m*; **3.** *sl.* a) Prachtkerl *m*, b) 'Prachtexemˌplar *n*;

ˈ**spank·ing** [-kɪŋ] F **I** *adj.* □ **1.** schnell, tüchtig; **2.** scharf, stark: **~ *breeze*** steife Brise; **3.** prächtig, ‚toll'; **II** *adv.* **4.** prächtig; **III** *s.* **5.** ‚Haue' *f*, Schläge *pl.*

span·ner [ˈspænə] *s.* ⚙ Schraubenschlüssel *m*: ***throw a ~ in(to) the works*** F ‚querschießen'.

spar¹ [spɑː] *s. min.* Spat *m.*

spar² [spɑː] *s.* **1.** ⚓ Rundholz *n*, Spiere *f*; **2.** ✈ Holm *m.*

spar³ [spɑː] **I** *v/i.* **1.** *Boxen*: sparren: **~ *for time*** *fig.* Zeit schinden; **2.** (mit Sporen) kämpfen (*Hähne*); **3.** sich streiten (***with*** mit), sich in den Haaren liegen; **II** *s.* **4.** *Boxen*: Sparringskampf *m*; **5.** Hahnenkampf *m*; **6.** (Wort)Geplänkel *n.*

spare [speə] **I** *v/t.* **1.** *j-n od. et.* verschonen; *Gegner, j-s Gefühle, j-s Leben etc.* schonen: ***if we are ~d*** wenn wir verschont *od.* am Leben bleiben; **~ *his blushes!*** bring ihn doch nicht in Verlegenheit!; **2.** sparsam ˈumgehen mit, schonen; kargen mit: **~ *neither trouble nor expense*** weder Mühe noch Kosten scheuen; (***not to***) **~ *o.s.*** sich (nicht) schonen; **3.** *j-m et.* ersparen, *j-n* verschonen mit; **4.** entbehren: ***we cannot ~ him just now***; **5.** *et.* erübrigen, übrig haben: ***can you ~ me a cigarette*** (***a moment***)***?*** hast du e-e Zigarette (e-n Augenblick Zeit) für mich (übrig)?; ***no time to ~*** keine Zeit (zu verlieren); → ***enough*** II; **II** *v/i.* **6.** sparen; **7.** Gnade walten lassen; **III** *adj.* □ **8.** Ersatz…, Reserve…: **~ *part*** → 14; **~ *tyre*** (*od.* ***tire***) a) Ersatzreifen *m*, b) *humor.* ‚Rettungsring' *m* (*Fettwulst*); **9.** ˈüberflüssig, übrig: **~ *hours*** (*od.* ***time***) Freizeit *f*, Mußestunden *pl.*; **~ *moment*** freier Augenblick; **~ *room*** Gästezimmer *n*; **~ *money*** übriges Geld; **10.** sparsam, kärglich; **11.** → ***sparing*** 2; **12.** sparsam (*Person*); **13.** hager, dürr (*Person*); **IV** *s.* **14.** ⚙ Ersatzteil *n*; **15.** *Bowling*: Spare *m*; ˈ**spare·ness** [-nɪs] *s.* **1.** Magerkeit *f*; **2.** Kärglichkeit *f.*

ˈ**spare|-part sur·ger·y** *s.* ⚕ Erˈsatzteilchirurˌgie *f*; ˈ**~·rib** *s.* Rippe(n)speer *m.*

spar·ing [ˈspeərɪŋ] *adj.* □ **1.** sparsam (***in, of*** mit), karg; mäßig: ***be ~ of*** sparsam umgehen mit, mit *et., a. Lob* kargen; **2.** spärlich, dürftig, knapp, gering; ˈ**spar·ing·ness** [-nɪs] *s.* **1.** Sparsamkeit *f*; **2.** Spärlichkeit *f*, Dürftigkeit *f.*

spark¹ [spɑːk] **I** *s.* **1.** Funke(n) *m* (*a. fig.*): ***the vital ~*** der Lebensfunke; ***strike ~s out of s.o.*** j-n in Fahrt bringen; **2.** *fig.* Funke(n) *m*, Spur *f* (***of*** von *Intelligenz, Leben etc.*); **3.** ⚡ a) (eˈlektrischer) Funke, b) Entladung *f*, c) (Licht-)Bogen *m*; **4.** *mot.* (Zünd)Funke *m*: ***advance*** (***retard***) ***the ~*** die Zündung vor- (zurück)stellen; **5.** → ***sparks***; **II** *v/i.* **6.** Funken sprühen, funke(l)n; **7.** ⚙ zünden; **III** *v/t.* **8.** *fig. j-n* befeuern; **9.** *fig. et.* auslösen.

spark² [spɑːk] **I** *s.* **1.** flotter Kerl; **2.** ***bright ~*** *Brit. iro.* ‚Intelliˈgenzbolzen' *m*; **II** *v/t.* **3.** *j-m* den Hof machen.

spark| ad·vance *s. mot.* Vor-, Frühzündung *f*; **~ *ar·rest·er*** *s.* ⚡ Funkenlöscher *m*; **~ dis·charge** *s.* ⚡ Funkenentladung *f*; **~ gap** *s.* ⚡ (Meß)Funkenstrecke *f.*

spark·ing plug [ˈspɑːkɪŋ] *s. mot.* Zündkerze *f.*

spar·kle [ˈspɑːkl] **I** *v/i.* **1.** funkeln (*a. fig. Augen etc.*; ***with*** vor *Zorn etc.*); **2.** *fig.* a) funkeln, sprühen (*Geist, Witz*), b) brillieren, glänzen (*Person*): ***his conversation ~d with wit*** s-e Unterhaltung sprühte vor Witz; **3.** Funken sprühen; **4.** perlen (*Wein*); **II** *v/t.* **5.** *Licht* sprühen; **III** *s.* **6.** Funkeln *n*, Glanz *m*; **7.** Funke(n) *m*; **8.** *fig.* Brilˈlanz *f*; ˈ**spar·kler** [-lə] *s.* **1.** *sl.* Diaˈmant *m*; **2.** Wunderkerze *f* (*Feuerwerk*); ˈ**spark·let** [-lɪt] *s.* **1.** Fünkchen *n* (*a. fig.*); **2.** Kohlenˈdioxydkapsel *f* (*für Siphonflaschen*); ˈ**spar·kling** [-lɪŋ] *adj.* □ **1.** funkelnd, sprühend (*beide a. fig. Witz etc.*); **2.** *fig.* geistsprühend (*Person*); **3.** schäumend, moussierend: **~ *wine*** Schaumwein *m*, Sekt *m.*

ˈ**spark|ˌo·ver** *s.* ⚡ (ˈFunken)ˌÜberschlag *m*; **~ plug** *s.* **1.** *mot.* Zündkerze *f*; **2.** F ‚Motor' *m*, treibende Kraft.

sparks [spɑːks] *s.* F **1.** ⚓ Funker *m*; **2.** Eˈlektriker *m.*

spar·ring [ˈspɑːrɪŋ] *s.* **1.** *Boxen*: Sparring *n*: **~ *partner*** Sparringspartner *m*; **2.** *fig.* Wortgefecht *n.*

spar·row [ˈspærəʊ] *s. orn.* Spatz *m*, Sperling *m*; ˈ**~·grass** *s.* F Spargel *m*; **~ hawk** *s. orn.* Sperber *m.*

sparse [spɑːs] *adj.* □ spärlich, dünn(gesät); ˈ**sparse·ness** [-nɪs], ˈ**spar·si·ty** [-sətɪ] *s.* Spärlichkeit *f.*

Spar·tan [ˈspɑːtən] **I** *adj. antiq. u. fig.* sparˈtanisch; **II** *s.* Sparˈtaner(in).

spasm [ˈspæzəm] *s.* **1.** ⚕ Krampf *m*, Spasmus *m*, Zuckung *f*; **2.** *a. fig.* Anfall *m*; **spas·mod·ic** [spæzˈmɒdɪk] *adj.* (□ ***~ally***) **1.** ⚕ krampfhaft, -artig, spasˈmodisch; **2.** *fig.* sprunghaft, vereinzelt; **spas·tic** [ˈspæstɪk] ⚕ **I** *adj.* (□ ***~ally***) spastisch, Krampf…; **II** *s.* Spastiker(in).

spat¹ [spæt] *zo.* **I** *s.* **1.** Muschel-, Austernlaich *m*; **2.** a) *coll.* junge Schaltiere *pl.*, b) junge Auster; **II** *v/i.* **3.** laichen (*bsd. Muscheln*).

spat² [spæt] *s.* Gaˈmasche *f.*

spat³ [spæt] F **I** *s.* **1.** Klaps *m*; **2.** *Am.* Kabbeˈlei *f*; **II** *v/i.* **3.** *Am.* sich kabbeln.

spat⁴ [spæt] *pret. u. p.p. von* ***spit***.

spatch·cock [ˈspætʃkɒk] **I** *s.* sofort nach dem Schlachten gegrilltes Huhn *etc.*; **II** *v/t.* F *Worte etc.* einflicken.

spate [speɪt] *s.* **1.** Überˈschwemmung *f*, Hochwasser *n*; **2.** *fig.* Flut *f*, (Wort-)Schwall *m.*

spathe [speɪð] *s.* ⚘ Blütenscheide *f.*

spa·tial [ˈspeɪʃl] *adj.* □ räumlich, Raum…

spat·ter [ˈspætə] **I** *v/t.* **1.** bespritzen (***with*** mit); **2.** (ver)spritzen; **3.** *fig. j-s Namen* besudeln, *j-n* ‚mit Dreck bewerfen'; **II** *v/i.* **4.** spritzen; **5.** prasseln, klatschen; **III** *s.* **6.** Spritzen *n*; **7.** Klatschen *n*, Prasseln *n*; **8.** Spritzer *m*, Spritzfleck *m*; ˈ**~·dash** → ***spat²***.

spat·u·la [ˈspætjʊlə] *s.* ⚙, ⚕ Spatel *m*, Spachtel *m, f*; ˈ**spat·u·late** [-lɪt] *adj.* spatelförmig.

spav·in [ˈspævɪn] *s. vet.* Spat *m*; ˈ**spav·ined** [-nd] *adj.* spatig, lahm.

spawn [spɔːn] **I** *s.* **1.** *ichth.* Laich *m*; **2.** ⚘ Myˈzel(fäden *pl.*) *n*; **3.** *fig. contp.* Brut *f*; **II** *v/i.* **4.** *ichth.* laichen; **5.** *fig. contp.* a) sich wie Kaˈninchen vermehren, b) wie Pilze aus dem Boden schießen; **III** *v/t.* **6.** *ichth. Laich* ablegen; **7.** *fig. contp. Kinder* massenweise in die Welt setzen; **8.** *fig.* ausbrüten, herˈvorbringen; ˈ**spawn·er** [-nə] *s. ichth.* Rogener *m*, Fischweibchen *n* zur Laichzeit; ˈ**spawn·ing** [-nɪŋ] **I** *s.* **1.** Laichen *n*; **II** *adj.* **2.** Laich…; **3.** *fig.* sich stark vermehrend.

spay [speɪ] *v/t. vet.* die Eierstöcke (*gen.*) entfernen, kastrieren.

speak [spiːk] [*irr.*] **I** *v/i.* **1.** reden, sprechen (***to*** mit, zu, ***about***, ***of***, ***on*** über *acc.*): ***spoken*** *thea.* gesprochen (*Regieanweisung*); ***so to ~*** sozusagen; ***the portrait ~s*** *fig.* das Bild ist sprechend ähnlich; → ***speak of*** *u.* ***to***, ***speaking*** I; **2.** (öffentlich) sprechen *od.* reden; **3.** *fig.* ertönen (*Trompete etc.*); **4.** ⚓ signalisieren; **II** *v/t.* **5.** sprechen, sagen; **6.** *Gedanken, s-e Meinung etc.* aussprechen, äußern, *die Wahrheit etc.* sagen; **7.** verkünden (*Trompete etc.*); **8.** *Sprache* sprechen (können): ***he ~s French*** er spricht Französisch; **9.** *fig. Eigenschaft etc.* verraten; **10.** ⚓ *Schiff* ansprechen;

Zssgn mit prp.:

speak| for *v/i.* **1.** sprechen *od.* eintreten für: ***that speaks well for him*** das spricht für ihn; **~ *o.s.*** a) selbst sprechen, b) s-e eigene Meinung äußern; ***that speaks for itself*** das spricht für sich selbst; **2.** zeugen von; **~ of** *v/i.* **1.** sprechen von *od.* über (*acc.*): ***nothing to ~*** nicht der Rede wert; ***not to ~*** ganz zu schweigen von; **2.** *et.* verraten, zeugen von; **~ to** *v/i.* **1.** *j-n* ansprechen; mit *j-m* reden (*a. mahnend etc.*); **2.** *et.* bestätigen, bezeugen; **3.** zu sprechen kommen auf (*acc.*);

Zssgn mit adv.:

speak| out I *v/i.* → ***speak up*** 1 *u.* 2; **II** *v/t.* aussprechen; **~ up** *v/i.* **1.** laut u. deutlich sprechen: ***~!*** (sprich) lauter!; **2.** kein Blatt vor den Mund nehmen, frei herˈaussprechen: ***~!*** heraus mit der Sprache!; **3.** sich einsetzen (***for*** für).

ˈ**speakˌeas·y** *pl.* **-ˌeas·ies** *s. Am. sl.* Flüsterkneipe *f* (*ohne Konzession*).

speak·er [ˈspiːkə] *s.* **1.** Sprecher(in), Redner(in); **2.** ♀ *parl.* Sprecher *m*, Präsiˈdent *m*: ***the ♀ of the House of Commons***; ***Mr ♀!*** Herr Vorsitzender!; **3.** ⚡ Lautsprecher *m.*

speak·ing [ˈspiːkɪŋ] **I** *adj.* □ **1.** sprechend (*a. fig. Ähnlichkeit*): ***~!*** *teleph.* am Apparat!; ***Brown ~!*** *teleph.* (hier) Brown!; ***have a ~ knowledge of*** *e-e Sprache* (*nur*) sprechen können; **~ *acquaintance*** flüchtige(r) Bekannte(r); → ***term*** 9; **2.** Sprech…, Sprach…: ***a ~ voice*** e-e (gute) Sprechstimme; **II** *s.* **3.** Sprechen *n*, Reden *n*; **III** (*adverbial*) **4.** ***generally ~*** allgemein; ***legally ~*** vom rechtlichen Standpunkt aus (gesehen); ***strictly ~*** strenggenommen; **~ clock** *s. teleph.* Zeitansage *f*; **~ trum·pet** *s.* Sprachrohr *n*; **~ tube** *s.* **1.** Sprechverbindung *f* zwischen zwei Räumen *etc.*; **2.** Sprachrohr *n.*

spear [spɪə] **I** *s.* **1.** (Wurf)Speer *m*, Lanze *f*; Spieß *m*: **~ *side*** männliche Linie *e-r Familie*; **2.** *poet.* Speerträger *m*; **3.** ⚘ Halm *m*, Sproß *m*; **II** *v/t.* **4.** durchˈbohren, aufspießen; **III** *v/i.* **5.** ⚘ (auf-)sprießen; **~ gun** *s.* Harˈpunenbüchse *f*; ˈ**~·head I** *s.* **1.** Lanzenspitze *f*; **2.** ⚔ a) Angriffsspitze *f*, b) Stoßkeil *m*; **3.** *fig.*

a) Anführer *m*, Vorkämpfer *m*, b) Spitze *f*; **II** *v/t*. **4.** *fig*. an der Spitze (*gen.*) stehen, die Spitze (*gen.*) bilden; **'~·mint** *s*. ⚘ Grüne Minze.

spec [spek] *s*. F Spekulati'on *f*: ***on*** **~** auf ‚Verdacht', auf gut Glück.

spe·cial ['speʃl] **I** *adj*. □ → ***specially***; **1.** spezi'ell: a) (ganz) besonder: ***a*** **~** ***occasion***; ***his*** **~** ***charm***; ***my*** **~** ***friend***; ***on*** **~** ***days*** an bestimmten Tagen, b) spezialisiert, Spezial..., Fach...: **~** ***knowledge*** Fachkenntnis(se *pl.*) *f*; **2.** Sonder...(*-erlaubnis*, *-fall*, *-schule*, *-steuer*, *-zug etc.*), Extra..., Ausnahme...: **~** ***area*** *Brit*. Notstandsgebiet *n*; **2** ***Branch*** *Brit*. Staatssicherheitspolizei *f*; **~** ***constable*** → 3a; **~** ***correspondent*** → 3b; **~** ***delivery*** ✉ *Am*. Eilzustellung *f*, ‚durch Eilboten'; **~** ***edition*** → 3c; **~** ***offer*** † Sonderangebot *n*; **II** *s*. **3.** a) 'Hilfspoli,zist *m*, b) Sonderberichterstatter *m*, c) Sonderausgabe *f*, d) Sonderzug *m*, e) Sonderprüfung *f*, f) † *Am*. Sonderangebot *n*, g) *Radio*, *TV*: Sondersendung *f*, h) *Am*. Tagesgericht (*im Restaurant*); **'spe·cial·ist** [-ʃəlɪst] **I** *s*. **1.** Spezia'list *m*: a) Fachmann *m*, b) ⚕ Facharzt *m* (***in*** für); **2.** *Am*. *Börse*: Jobber *m* (*der sich auf e-e bestimmte Kategorie von Wertpapieren beschränkt*); **II** *adj*. **3.** → **spe·cial·ist·ic** [ˌspeʃə'lɪstɪk] *adj*. spezialisiert, Fach..., Spezial...; **spe·ci·al·i·ty** [ˌspeʃɪ'ælətɪ] *s*. *bsd. Brit*. **1.** Besonderheit *f*; **2.** besonderes Merkmal; **3.** Spezi'alfach *n*, -gebiet *n*; **4.** Speziali'tät *f* (*a*. †); **5.** † a) Spezi'alar,tikel *m*, b) Neuheit *f*; **spe·cial·i·za·tion** [ˌspeʃəlaɪ'zeɪʃn] *s*. Spezialisierung *f*; **'spe·cial·ize** [-ʃəlaɪz] **I** *v/i*. **1.** sich spezialisieren (***in*** auf *acc.*); **II** *v/t*. **2.** spezialisieren: **~*d*** spezialisiert, Spezial..., Fach...; **3.** näher bezeichnen; **4.** *biol*. *Organe* besonders entwikkeln; **'spe·cial·ly** [-ʃəlɪ] *adv*. **1.** besonders, im besonderen; **2.** eigens, extra, ausdrücklich; **'spe·cial·ty** [-tɪ] *s*. **1.** *bsd. Am*. → ***speciality***; **2.** ⚖ a) besiegelte Urkunde, b) formgebundener Vertrag.

spe·cie ['spi:ʃi] *s*. **1.** Hartgeld *n*, Münze *f*; **2.** Bargeld *n*: **~** ***payments*** Barzahlung *f*; ***in*** **~** a) in bar, b) in natura, c) *fig*. in gleicher Münze.

spe·cies ['spi:ʃi:z] *s. sg. u. pl.* **1.** *allg*. Art *f*, Sorte *f*; **2.** *biol*. Art *f*, Spezies *f*: ***our*** (*od*. ***the***) **~** die Menschheit; **3.** *Logik*: Art *f*, Klasse *f*; **4.** *eccl*. (sichtbare) Gestalt (von Brot u. Wein).

spe·cif·ic [spɪ'sɪfɪk] **I** *adj*. (□ **~*ally***) **1.** spe'zifisch, spezi'ell, bestimmt; **2.** eigen(tümlich); **3.** typisch, kennzeichnend, besonder; **4.** wesentlich; **5.** genau, defini'tiv, prä'zis(e), kon'kret: ***a*** **~** ***statement***; **6.** *biol*. Art...: **~** ***name***; **7.** ⚕ spe'zifisch (*Heilmittel*, *Krankheit*); **8.** *phys*. spe'zifisch: **~** ***gravity*** spezifisches Gewicht, *die* Wichte; **II** *s*. **9.** ⚕ Spe'zifikum *n*.

spec·i·fi·ca·tion [ˌspesɪfɪ'keɪʃn] *s*. **1.** Spezifizierung *f*; **2.** genaue Aufzählung, Einzelaufstellung *f*; **3.** *mst pl*. Einzelangaben *pl*., -vorschriften *pl*., *bsd*. a) ⚠ Baubeschrieb *m*, b) ⚙ (technische) Beschreibung; **4.** ⚖ Pa'tentbeschreibung *f*, -schrift *f*; **5.** ⚖ Spezifikati'on *f* (*Eigentumserwerb durch Verarbeitung*); **spec·i·fy** ['spesɪfaɪ] **I** *v/t*. **1.** (einzeln) angeben *od*. aufführen, (be)nennen, spezifizieren; **2.** bestimmen, (im einzelnen) festsetzen; **3.** in e-r Aufstellung besonders anführen; **II** *v/i*. **4.** genaue Angaben machen.

spec·i·men ['spesɪmɪn] *s*. **1.** Exem'plar *n*: ***a fine*** **~**; **2.** Muster *n* (*a*. *typ*.), Probe(stück *n*) *f*, ⚙ Prüfstück *n*: **~** ***of s.o.'s handwriting*** Handschriftenprobe; **3.** *fig*. Probe *f*, Beispiel *n* (***of*** *gen*.); **4.** *fig*. *contp*. a) ‚Exem'plar' *n*, ‚Muster' *n* (***of*** an), b) ‚Type' *f*, komischer Kauz; **~** **cop·y** *s*. 'Probeexem,plar *n*; **~** **sig·na·ture** *s*. 'Unterschriftsprobe *f*.

spe·cious ['spi:ʃəs] *adj*. □ *äußerlich* blendend, bestechend, trügerisch, Schein...(*Argument etc.*): **~** ***prosperity*** scheinbarer Wohlstand; **'spe·cious·ness** [-nɪs] *s*. **1.** *das* Bestechende; **2.** trügerischer Schein.

speck [spek] **I** *s*. **1.** Fleck(en) *m*, Fleckchen *n*; **2.** Stückchen *n*, *das* bißchen: ***a*** **~** ***of dust*** ein Stäubchen; **3.** faule Stelle (*im Obst*); **4.** *fig*. Pünktchen *n*; **II** *v/t*. **5.** sprenkeln; **'speck·le** [-kl] **I** *s*. Fleck (-en) *m*, Sprenkel *m*, Tupfen *m*, Punkt *m*; **II** *v/t*. → ***speck*** 5; **'speck·led** [-ld] *adj*. **1.** gefleckt, gesprenkelt, getüpfelt; **2.** (bunt)scheckig; **'speck·less** [-lɪs] *adj*. □ fleckenlos, sauber, rein (*a*. *fig*.).

specs [speks] *s*. *pl*. F Brille *f*.

spec·ta·cle ['spektəkl] *s*. **1.** Schauspiel *n* (*a*. *fig*.); **2.** Schaustück *n*: ***make a*** **~** ***of o.s.*** sich zur Schau stellen, (unangenehm) auffallen; **3.** *trauriger etc*. Anblick; **4.** *pl*. *a*. ***a pair of*** **~*s*** e-e Brille; **'spec·ta·cled** [-ld] *adj*. **1.** bebrillt; **2.** *zo*. Brillen...(*-bär etc*.): **~** ***cobra*** Brillenschlange *f*; **spec·tac·u·lar** [spek'tækjʊlə] **I** *adj*. □ **1.** Schau..., schauspielartig; **2.** spektaku'lär, aufsehenerregend, sensatio'nell; **II** *s*. **3.** *Am*. große (Fernseh)Schau, 'Galare,vue *f*; **spec·ta·tor** [spek'teɪtə] *s*. Zuschauer(in): **~** ***sport*** Zuschauersport *m*.

spec·ter ['spektə] *Am*. → ***spectre***.

spec·tra ['spektrə] *pl*. *von* ***spectrum***; **'spec·tral** [-trəl] *adj*. □ **1.** geisterhaft, gespenstisch; **2.** *phys*. Spektral...: **~** ***colo(u)r*** Spektral-, Regenbogenfarbe *f*; **'spec·tre** [-tə] *s*. **1.** Geist *m*, Gespenst *n*; **2.** *fig*. a) (Schreck)Gespenst *n*, b) *fig*. Hirngespinst *n*.

spec·tro·gram ['spektrəʊgræm] *s*. *phys*. Spektro'gramm *n*; **'spec·tro·graph** [-grɑ:f] *s*. *phys*. **1.** Spektro'graph *m*; **2.** Spektro'gramm *n*; **spec·tro·scope** ['spektrəskəʊp] *s*. *phys*. Spektro'skop *n*.

spec·trum ['spektrəm] *pl*. **-tra** [-trə] *s*. **1.** *phys*. Spektrum *n*: **~** ***analysis*** Spektralanalyse *f*; **2.** *a*. ***radio*** **~** ϟ (Fre'quenz)Spektrum *n*; **3.** *a*. ***ocular*** **~** *opt*. Nachbild *n*; **4.** *fig*. Spektrum *n*, Skala *f*: ***all across the*** **~** auf der ganzen Linie.

spec·u·la ['spekjʊlə] *pl*. *von* ***speculum***; **'spec·u·lar** [-lə] *adj*. **1.** spiegelnd, Spiegel...: **~** ***iron*** *min*. Eisenglanz *m*; **2.** ⚕ Spekulum...

spec·u·late ['spekjʊleɪt] *v/i*. **1.** nachsinnen, -denken, theoretisieren, Vermutungen anstellen, ‚spekulieren' (***on***, ***upon***, ***about*** über *acc*.); **2.** † spekulieren (***for***, ***on*** auf *Baisse etc*., ***in*** in *Kupfer etc*.); **spec·u·la·tion** [ˌspekjʊ'leɪʃn] *s*. **1.** Nachdenken *n*, Grübeln *n*; **2.** Betrachtung *f*, Theo'rie *f*, Spekulati'on *f* (*a*. *phls*.); **3.** Vermutung *f*, Mutmaßung *f*, Rätselraten *n*, Spekulati'on *f*: ***mere*** **~**; **4.** † Spekulati'on *f*; **'spec·u·la·tive** [-lətɪv] *adj*. □ **1.** *phls*. spekula'tiv; **2.** theo'retisch; **3.** nachdenkend, grüblerisch; **4.** forschend, abwägend (*Blick etc*.); **5.** † spekula'tiv, Spekulations...; **'spec·u·la·tor** [-leɪtə] *s*. † Speku'lant *m*.

spec·u·lum ['spekjʊləm] *pl*. **-la** [-lə] *s*. **1.** (Me'tall)Spiegel *m* (*bsd. für Teleskope*); **2.** ⚕ Spekulum *n*, Spiegel *m*.

sped [sped] *pret*. *u*. *p.p.* *von* ***speed***.

speech [spi:tʃ] **I** *s*. **1.** Sprache *f*, Sprechvermögen *n*: ***recover one's*** **~** die Sprache wiedergewinnen; **2.** Reden *n*, Sprechen *n*: ***freedom of*** **~** Redefreiheit *f*; **3.** Rede *f*, Äußerung *f*: ***direct one's*** **~** ***to*** das Wort an *j-n* richten; **4.** Gespräch *n*: ***have*** **~** ***with*** mit *j-m* reden; **5.** Rede *f*, Ansprache *f*, Vortrag *m*; ⚖ Plädoy'er *n*; **6.** a) (Landes)Sprache *f*, b) Dia'lekt *m*: ***in common*** **~** in der Umgangssprache, landläufig; **7.** Sprech-, Ausdrucksweise *f*, Sprache *f* (*e-r Person*); **8.** ♪ Klang *m e-r Orgel etc*.; **II** *adj*. **9.** Sprach..., Sprech...: **~** ***area*** *ling*. Sprachraum *m*; **~** ***centre*** (*Am*. ***center***) *anat*. Sprechzentrum *n*; **~** ***clinic*** ⚕ Sprachklinik *f*; **~** ***day*** *ped*. (Jahres-) Schlußfeier *f*; **~** ***defect*** Sprachfehler *m*; **~** ***island*** Sprachinsel *f*; **~** ***map*** Sprachenkarte *f*; **~** ***record*** Sprechplatte *f*; **~** ***therapist*** Logopäde *m*; **~** ***therapy*** Logopädie *f*.

speech·i·fi·ca·tion [ˌspi:tʃɪfɪ'keɪʃn] *s*. *contp*. Redenschwingen *n*; **speech·i·fi·er** ['spi:tʃɪfaɪə] *s*. Viel-, Volksredner *m*; **speech·i·fy** ['spi:tʃɪfaɪ] *v/i*. Reden schwingen.

speech·less ['spi:tʃlɪs] *adj*. □ **1.** *fig*. sprachlos (***with*** vor *Empörung etc*.): ***that left him*** **~** das verschlug ihm die Sprache; **2.** stumm, wortkarg; **3.** *fig*. unsäglich: **~** ***grief***; **'speech·less·ness** [-nɪs] *s*. Sprachlosigkeit *f*.

speed [spi:d] **I** *s*. **1.** Geschwindigkeit *f*, Schnelligkeit *f*, Eile *f*, Tempo *n*: ***at a*** **~** ***of*** mit e-r Geschwindigkeit von; ***at full*** **~** mit Höchstgeschwindigkeit; ***at the*** **~** ***of light*** mit Lichtgeschwindigkeit; ***full*** **~** ***ahead*** ⚓ volle Kraft voraus; ***that's not my*** **~*!*** *sl*. das ist nicht mein Fall!; **2.** ⚙ a) Drehzahl *f*, b) *mot*. *etc*. Gang *m*: ***three-~ bicycle*** Fahrrad mit Dreigangschaltung; **3.** *phot*. a) Lichtempfindlichkeit *f*, b) Verschlußgeschwindigkeit *f*; **4.** *obs*.: ***good*** **~*!*** viel Erfolg!, viel Glück!; **5.** *sl*. ‚Speed' *m* (*Aufputschmittel*); **II** *adj*. **6.** Schnell..., Geschwindigkeits...; **III** *v/t*. [*irr*.] **7.** *Gast* (rasch) verabschieden, *j-m* Lebe'wohl sagen; **8.** *j-m* beistehen: ***God*** **~** ***you!*** Gott sei mit dir!; **9.** rasch befördern; **10.** *Lauf etc*. beschleunigen; **11.** *mst* **~** ***up*** (*pret*. *u*. *p.p.* ***speeded***) *Maschine* beschleunigen, *fig*. *Sache* vo'rantreiben; *Produktion* erhöhen; **IV** *v/i*. [*irr*.] **12.** (da'hin-) eilen, rasen; **13.** *mot*. (zu) schnell fahren; → ***speeding***; **14.** **~** ***up*** (*pret*. *u*. *p.p.* ***speeded***) die Geschwindigkeit erhöhen; **15.** *obs*. gedeihen, Glück haben; **'~·boat** *s*. **1.** ⚓ Schnellboot *n*; **2.** *sport* Rennboot *n*; **~** **cop** *s*. F motorisierter Ver'kehrspoli,zist; **~** **count·er** *s*. ⚙ Drehzahlmesser *m*, Tourenzähler *m*.

speed·er ['spi:də] *s*. **1.** ⚙ Geschwindig-

keitsregler *m*; **2.** *mot.* ‚Raser' *m.*
speed in·di·ca·tor *s.* **1.** → ***speedometer***; **2.** → ***speed counter***.
speed·i·ness ['spi:dɪnɪs] *s.* Schnelligkeit *f*, Zügigkeit *f*.
speed·ing ['spi:dɪŋ] *s. mot.* zu schnelles Fahren, Ge'schwindigkeitsüber,tretung *f*: ***no ~!*** Schnellfahren verboten!
speed| lathe *s.* ⚙ Schnelldrehbank *f*; **~ lim·it** *s. mot.* Geschwindigkeitsbegrenzung *f*, Tempolimit *n*; **~ mer·chant** *s. mot. Brit. sl.* ‚Raser' *m.*
speed·o ['spi:dəʊ] *s. mot.* F ‚Tacho' *m.*
speed·om·e·ter [spɪ'dɒmɪtə] *s. mot.* Tacho'meter *m, n.*
'speed|-,read·ing *s.* 'Schnelleseme,thode *f*; **~ skat·er** *s. sport* Eisschnelläufer(in); **~ skat·ing** *s.* Eisschnellauf *m.*
speed·ster ['spi:dstə] *s.* **1.** → ***speeder*** 2; **2.** ‚Flitzer' *m* (*Sportwagen*).
speed| trap *s.* Ra'darfalle *f*; **'~-up** *s.* **1.** Beschleunigung *f*; **2.** Produkti'onserhöhung *f*; **'~·way** *s.* **1.** *sport* a) Speedwayrennen *pl.*, b) *a.* **~ *track*** Speedwaybahn *f*; **2.** *Am.* a) Schnellstraße *f*, b) Autorennstrecke *f*.
speed·well ['spi:dwel] *s.* ⚘ Ehrenpreis *n, m.*
speed·y ['spi:dɪ] *adj.* □ schnell, zügig, rasch, prompt: ***wish s.o. a ~ recovery*** j-m gute Besserung wünschen.
speiss [spaɪs] *s.* ⚒, *metall.* Speise *f*.
spe·le·ol·o·gist [,spelɪ'ɒlədʒɪst] *s.* Höhlenforscher *m*; **,spe·le'ol·o·gy** [-dʒɪ] *s.* Speläolo'gie *f*, Höhlenforschung *f*.
spell¹ [spel] **I** *v/t.* [*a. irr.*] **1.** buchstabieren: **~ *backward*** a) rückwärts buchstabieren, b) *fig.* völlig verdrehen; **2.** (ortho'graphisch richtig) schreiben; **3.** *Wort* bilden, ergeben: ***l-e-d ~s led***; **4.** *fig.* bedeuten: ***it ~s trouble***; **5. ~ *out*** (*od.* ***over***) (mühsam) entziffern; **6.** *oft* **~ *out*** *fig.* a) darlegen, b) (***for s.o.*** j-m) *et.* ‚ausein'anderklauben'; **II** *v/i.* [*a. irr.*] **7.** (richtig) schreiben; **8.** geschrieben werden, sich schreiben.
spell² [spel] **I** *s.* **1.** Arbeit(szeit) *f*: ***have a ~ at*** sich e-e Zeitlang mit *et.* beschäftigen; **2.** (Arbeits)Schicht *f*: ***give s.o. a ~*** → 7; **3.** *Am.* (*Husten- etc.*)Anfall *m*, (ner'vöser) Zustand; **4.** a) Zeit(abschnitt *m*) *f*, b) *ein* Weilchen *n*: ***for a ~***; **5.** *Am.* F Katzensprung *m* (*kurze Strekke*); **6.** *meteor.* Peri'ode *f*: ***a ~ of fine weather*** e-e Schönwetterperiode; ***hot ~*** Hitzewelle *f*; **II** *v/t.* **7.** *Am. j-n* (bei der Arbeit) ablösen.
spell³ [spel] **I** *s.* **1.** Zauber(wort *n*) *m*; **2.** *fig.* Zauber *m*, Bann *m*, Faszinati'on *f*: ***be under a ~*** a) verzaubert sein, b) *fig.* gebannt *od.* fasziniert sein; ***break the ~*** den Zauberbann (*fig.* das Eis) brechen; ***cast a ~ on*** → 3; **II** *v/t.* **3.** *j-n* a) verzaubern, b) *fig.* bezaubern, fesseln, faszinieren; **'~·bind** *v/t.* [*irr.* → ***bind***] → ***spell³*** 3; **'~,bind·er** *s.* faszinierender Redner, fesselnder Ro'man *etc.*; **'~·bound** *adj. u. adv.* (wie) gebannt, fasziniert.
spell·er ['spelə] *s.* **1.** ***he is a good ~*** er ist in der Orthographie gut beschlagen; **2.** Fibel *f*; **'spell·ing** [-lɪŋ] *s.* **1.** Buchstabieren *n*; **2.** Rechtschreibung *f*, Orthogra'phie *f*: **~ *bee*** Rechtschreibewettbewerb *m.*
spelt¹ [spelt] *s.* ⚘ Spelz *m*, Dinkel *m.*
spelt² [spelt] *pret. u. p.p. von **spell¹***.
spel·ter ['speltə] *s.* **1.** ⚒ (Handels-, Roh)Zink *n*; **2.** *a.* **~ *solder*** ⚙ Messingschlaglot *n.*
spe·lunk [spɪ'lʌŋk] *v/i. Am.* Höhlen erforschen (*als Hobby*).
spen·cer¹ ['spensə] *s. hist. u. Damenmode*: Spenzer *m* (*kurze Überjacke*).
spen·cer² ['spensə] *s.* ⚓ *hist.* Gaffelsegel *n.*
spend [spend] [*irr.*] **I** *v/t.* **1.** verbrauchen, aufwenden, ausgeben (***on*** für): **~ *money***; → ***penny*** 1; **2.** *Geld, Zeit etc.* verwenden, anlegen (***on*** für): **~ *time on s.th.*** Zeit für et. verwenden; **3.** verschwenden, -geuden, 'durchbringen; **4.** *Zeit* zu-, verbringen; **5.** (***o.s.*** sich) erschöpfen, verausgaben: ***the storm is spent*** der Sturm hat sich gelegt *od.* ausgetobt; **II** *v/i.* **6.** Geld ausgeben, Ausgaben machen; **7.** laichen (*Fische*).
spend·ing ['spendɪŋ] *s.* **1.** (*das*) Geldausgeben; **2.** Ausgabe(n *pl.*) *f*; **~ mon·ey** *s.* Taschengeld *n*; **~ pow·er** *s.* Kaufkraft *f*.
spend·thrift ['spendθrɪft] **I** *s.* Verschwender(in); **II** *adj.* verschwenderisch.
Spen·ser·i·an [spen'sɪərɪən] *adj.* (Edmund) Spenser betreffend: **~ *stanza*** Spenserstanze *f*.
spent [spent] **I** *pret. u. p.p. von **spend***; **II** *adj.* **1.** matt, verausgabt, erschöpft, entkräftet: **~ *bullet*** matte Kugel; **~ *liquor*** ⚙ Ablauge *f*; **2.** verbraucht; **3.** *zo.* (*von Eiern od. Samen*) entleert (*Insekten, Fische*): **~ *herring*** Hering *m* nach dem Laichen.
sperm¹ [spɜ:m] *s. physiol.* **1.** Sperma *n*, Samenflüssigkeit *f*; **2.** Samenzelle *f*.
sperm² [spɜ:m] *s.* **1.** Walrat *m, n*; **2.** → ***sperm whale***; **3.** → ***sperm oil***.
sper·ma·ce·ti [,spɜ:mə'setɪ] *s.* Walrat *m, n.*
sper·ma·ry ['spɜ:mərɪ] *s. physiol.* Keimdrüse *f*; **sper·mat·ic** [spɜ:'mætɪk] *adj. physiol.* sper'matisch, Samen...: **~ *cord*** Samenstrang *m*; **~ *filament*** Samenfaden *m*; **~ *fluid*** → ***sperm¹*** 1.
sper·ma·to·blast ['spɜ:mətəʊblæst] *s. biol.* Ursamenzelle *f*; **,sper·ma·to'gen·e·sis** [-əʊ'dʒenɪsɪs] *s. biol.* Samenbildung *f*; **,sper·ma·to'zo·on** [-əʊ'zəʊɒn] *pl.* **-'zo·a** [-'zəʊə] *s. biol.* Spermato'zoon *n*, Spermium *n.*
spermo- [spɜ:məʊ] *in Zssgn* Samen...
sperm oil *s.* Walratöl *n.*
sper·mo·log·i·cal [,spɜ:mə'lɒdʒɪkl] *adj.* **1.** ⚕ spermato'logisch; **2.** ⚘ samenkundlich.
sperm whale *s. zo.* Pottwal *m.*
spew [spju:] **I** *v/i.* sich erbrechen, ‚spukken', ‚speien'; **II** *v/t.* (er)brechen: **~ *forth*** (*od.* ***out***, ***up***) (aus)speien, (-)spucken, (-)werfen; **III** *s. das* Erbrochene.
sphac·e·la·tion [,sfæsɪ'leɪʃn] *s.* ⚕ Brandbildung *f*; **sphac·e·lous** ['sfæsɪləs] *adj.* ⚕ gangrä'nös, ne'krotisch.
sphaero- [sfɪərəʊ] *in Zssgn* Kugel..., Sphaero...
sphe·nog·ra·phy [sfɪ'nɒgrəfɪ] *s.* Keilschriftkunde *f*; **sphe·noid** ['sfi:nɔɪd] **I** *adj.* **1.** keilförmig; **2.** *anat.* Keilbein...; **II** *s.* **3.** *min.* Spheno'id *n* (*Kristallform*).
sphere [sfɪə] *s.* **1.** Kugel *f* (*a.* ⅍; *a. sport Ball*), kugelförmiger Körper; Erd-, Himmelskugel *f*; Himmelskörper *m*: ***doctrine of the ~*** ⅍ Sphärik *f*; **2.** *antiq. ast.* Sphäre *f*: ***music of the ~s*** Sphärenmusik *f*; **3.** *poet.* Himmel *m*, Sphäre *f*; **4.** *fig.* (*Einfluß-, Interessen- etc.*)Sphäre *f*, Gebiet *n*, Bereich *m*, Kreis *m*: **~ *of influence***; **~** (***of activity***) Wirkungskreis; **5.** Mili'eu *n*, (gesellschaftliche) Um'gebung; **spher·ic** ['sferɪk] **I** *adj.* **1.** *poet.* himmlisch; **2.** kugelförmig; **3.** sphärisch; **II** *s. pl.* **4.** → ***spherics¹***; **spher·i·cal** ['sferɪkl] *adj.* □ **1.** kugelförmig; **2.** ⅍ Kugel...(*-ausschnitt, -vieleck etc.*), sphärisch: **~ *astronomy***; **~ *trigonometry***; **sphe·ric·i·ty** [sfɪ'rɪsətɪ] *s.* Kugelgestalt *f*, sphärische Gestalt.
spher·ics¹ ['sferɪks] *s. pl. sg. konstr.* ⅍ Sphärik *f*, Kugellehre *f*.
spher·ics² ['sferɪks] *s. pl. sg. konstr.* Wetterbeobachtung *f* mit elek'tronischen Geräten.
sphero- → ***sphaero-***.
sphe·roid ['sfɪərɔɪd] **I** *s.* ⅍ Sphäro'id *n*; **II** *adj.* → **sphe·roi·dal** [,sfɪə'rɔɪdl] *adj.* □ sphäro'idisch, kugelig; **sphe·roi·dic**, **sphe·roi·di·cal** [,sfɪə'rɔɪdɪk(l)] *adj.* □ → ***spheroidal***.
spher·ule ['sferju:l] *s.* Kügelchen *n.*
sphinc·ter ['sfɪŋktə] *s. a.* **~ *muscle*** *anat.* Schließmuskel *m.*
sphinx [sfɪŋks] *pl.* **'sphinx·es** *s.* **1.** *mst* ♀ *myth. u.* ⚠ Sphinx *f* (*a. fig. rätselhafter Mensch*); **2.** a) *a.* **~ *moth*** Sphinx *f* (*Nachtfalter*), b) *a.* **~ *baboon*** Sphinxpavian *m*; **'~·like** *adj.* sphinxartig (*a. fig. rätselhaft*).
spi·ca ['spaɪkə] *pl.* **-cae** [-si:] *s.* **1.** ⚘ Ähre *f*; **2.** ⚕ Kornährenverband *m*; **'spi·cate** [-keɪt] *adj.* ⚘ a) ährentragend (*Pflanze*), b) ährenförmig (angeordnet) (*Blüte*).
spice [spaɪs] **I** *s.* **1.** a) Gewürz *n*, Würze *f*, b) *coll.* Gewürze *pl.*; **2.** *fig.* Würze *f*; **3.** *fig.* Beigeschmack *m*, Anflug *m*; **II** *v/t.* **4.** würzen (*a. fig.*); **spiced** [-st] → ***spicy*** 1 *u.* 2; **'spic·er·y** [-sərɪ] *s. coll.* Gewürze *pl.*; **'spic·i·ness** [-sɪnɪs] *s. fig. das* Würzige, *das* Pi'kante.
spick-and-span [,spɪkən'spæn] *adj.* **1.** funkelnagelneu; **2.** a) blitzsauber, b) ‚wie aus dem Ei gepellt' (*Person*).
spic·u·lar ['spaɪkjʊlə] *adj.* **1.** *zo.* nadelförmig; **2.** ⚘ ährchenförmig; **spic·ule** ['spaɪkju:l] *s.* **1.** (Eis- *etc.*)Nadel *f*; **2.** *zo.* nadelartiger Fortsatz, *bsd.* Ske'lettnadel *f* (*e-s Schwammes etc.*); **3.** ⚘ Ährchen *n.*
spic·y ['spaɪsɪ] *adj.* □ **1.** gewürzt; **2.** würzig, aro'matisch (*Duft etc.*); **3.** Gewürz...; **4.** *fig.* a) gewürzt, witzig, b) pi'kant, gepfeffert, schlüpfrig; **5.** *sl.* a) ‚gewieft', geschickt, b) schick.
spi·der ['spaɪdə] *s.* **1.** *zo.* Spinne *f*; **2.** ⚙ a) Armkreuz *n*, b) Drehkreuz *n*, c) Armstern *m* (*Rad*); **3.** ⚡ Ständerkörper *m*; **4.** *Am.* Dreifuß *m* (*Untersatz*); **~ catch·er** *s. orn.* **1.** Spinnenfresser *m*; **2.** Mauerspecht *m*; **~ line** *s. mst pl.* ⚙, *opt.* Faden(kreuz *n*) *m*, Ableselinie *f*; **~ web**, *a.* **~'s web** *s.* Spinn(en)gewebe *n* (*a. fig.*).
spi·der·y ['spaɪdərɪ] *adj.* **1.** spinnenartig; **2.** spinnwebartig; **3.** voll von Spinnen.
spiel [spi:l] *s. Am. sl.* **1.** Werbesprüche *pl.*; **2.** ‚Platte' *f*, Gequassel *n.*
spiff·ing ['spɪfɪŋ] *adj. sl.* ‚toll', ‚(tod-)schick'.
spif·(f)li·cate ['spɪflɪkeɪt] *v/t. sl.* ‚es *j-m*

besorgen‘.

spig·ot [ˈspɪgət] *s.* ⚙ **1.** (Faß)Zapfen *m*; **2.** Zapfen *m* (*e-s Hahns*); **3.** (Faß-, Leitungs)Hahn *m*; **4.** Muffenverbindung *f* (*bei Röhren*).

spike¹ [spaɪk] *s.* ⚘ **1.** (Gras-, Korn)Ähre *f*; **2.** (Blüten)Ähre *f*.

spike² [spaɪk] **I** *s.* **1.** Stift *m*, Spitze *f*, Dorn *m*, Stachel *m*; **2.** ⚙ (Haken-, Schienen)Nagel *m*, Bolzen *m*; **3.** (Zaun)Eisenspitze *f*; **4.** a) *mst pl.* Spike *m* (*am Rennschuh etc.*), b) *pl. mot.* Spikes *pl.* (*am Reifen*); **5.** *hunt.* Spieß *m* (*e-s Junghirsches*); **6.** *ichth.* junge Ma'krele; **II** *v/t.* **7.** festnageln; **8.** mit (Eisen)Spitzen versehen; **9.** aufspießen; **10.** *sport* mit den Spikes verletzen; **11.** ⚔ *Geschütz* vernageln: **~ *s.o.'s guns*** *fig.* j-m e-n Strich durch die Rechnung machen; **12.** a) e-n Schuß Alkohol geben in *ein Getränk*, b) *fig.* ‚pfeffern‘.

spiked¹ [spaɪkt] *adj.* ⚘ ährentragend.

spiked² [spaɪkt] *adj.* **1.** mit Nägeln *od.* (Eisen)Spitzen (versehen): **~ *shoes***; **~ *helmet*** Pickelhaube *f*; **2.** mit ‚Schuß‘ (*Getränk*).

spike·nard [ˈspaɪknɑːd] *s.* **1.** La'vendelöl *n*; **2.** ⚘ Indische Narde; **3.** ⚘ Traubige A'ralie.

spike oil → ***spikenard*** 1.

spik·y [ˈspaɪkɪ] *adj.* **1.** spitz, dornenartig, stachelig; **2.** *Brit.* F a) eigensinnig, b) empfindlich.

spile [spaɪl] **I** *s.* **1.** (Faß)Zapfen *m*, Spund *m*; **2.** Pflock *m*, Pfahl *m*; **II** *v/t.* **3.** verspunden; **4.** anzapfen; **ˈ~·hole** *s.* Spundloch *n*.

spill¹ [spɪl] *s.* **1.** (Holz)Splitter *m*; **2.** Fidibus *m*.

spill² [spɪl] **I** *v/t.* [*irr.*] **1.** aus-, verschütten, 'überlaufen lassen; **2.** *Blut* vergießen; **3.** um'her-, verstreuen; **4.** ⚓ *Segel* killen lassen; **5.** a) *Reiter* abwerfen, b) *j-n* schleudern; **6.** *sl.* ausplaudern, verraten; → ***bean*** 1; **II** *v/i.* [*irr.*] **7.** 'überlaufen, verschüttet werden; **8.** *a.* **~ *over*** sich ergießen (*a. fig.*); **9.** **~ *over with*** *fig.* wimmeln von; **10.** *sl.* ‚auspacken‘, ‚singen‘; **III** *s.* **11.** F Sturz *m* (*vom Pferd etc.*); **12.** ☤ Preissturz *m*.

spil·li·kin [ˈspɪlɪkɪn] *s.* **1.** (*bsd.* Mi'kado-)Stäbchen *n*; **2.** *pl. sg. konstr.* Mi'kado *n*.

ˈspill·way *s.* ⚙ 'Überlauf(rinne *f*) *m*, 'Abflußkaˌnal *m*.

spilt [spɪlt] *pret. u. p.p. von* ***spill²***; → ***milk*** 1.

spin [spɪn] **I** *v/t.* [*irr.*] **1.** *Wolle, Flachs etc.* (zu Fäden) spinnen; **2.** *Fäden, Garn* spinnen; **3.** schnell drehen, (her'um)wirbeln; *Kreisel* treiben; ✈ *Flugzeug* trudeln lassen; *Münze* hochwerfen; *Wäsche* schleudern; *Schallplatte* ‚laufen lassen‘; **4.** a) sich *et.* ausdenken, *Pläne* aushecken, b) erzählen; → ***yarn*** 3; **5.** **~ *out*** in die Länge ziehen, *Geschichte* ausspinnen, *a. Suppe etc.* ‚strecken‘; **6.** *sport Ball* mit Ef'fet schlagen; **7.** *sl. Kandidaten* ‚'durchrasseln‘ lassen; **II** *v/i.* [*irr.*] **8.** spinnen; **9.** *a.* **~ *round*** sich (im Kreis um die eigene Achse) drehen, her'umwirbeln: ***send s.o. ~ning*** j-n hinschleudern; ***my head ~s*** mir dreht sich alles; **10.** **~ *along*** da'hinsausen (*fahren*); **11.** ✈ trudeln; **12.** *mot.* 'durchdrehen (*Räder*); **13.** *sl.* ‚durchrasseln‘ (*Prüfungskandidat*); **III** *s.* **14.** *das* Her'umwirbeln; **15.** schnelle Drehung, Drall *m*; **16.** *phys.* Spin *m*, Drall *m* (*des Elektrons*); **17.** ***go for a ~*** F e-e Spritztour machen; **18.** ✈ a) (Ab)Trudeln *n*, b) 'Sturzspiˌrale *f*; **19.** *sport* Ef'fet *m*.

spin·ach [ˈspɪnɪdʒ] *s.* **1.** ⚘ Spi'nat *m*; **2.** *Am. sl.* ‚Mist‘ *m*.

spi·nal [ˈspaɪnl] *adj. anat.* spi'nal, Rückgrat…, Rückenmarks…; **~ *col·umn*** *s.* Wirbelsäule *f*, Rückgrat *n*; **~ *cord***, **~ *mar·row*** *s.* Rückenmark *n*; **~ *nerve*** *s.* Spi'nalnerv *m*.

spin·dle [ˈspɪndl] **I** *s.* **1.** ⚙ a) (Hand-, *a.* Drehbank)Spindel *f*, b) Welle *f*, Achszapfen *m*, c) Triebstock *m*, d) Hydro'meter *n*; **2.** *ein Garnmaß*; **3.** *biol.* Kernspindel *f*; **4.** ⚘ Spindel *f*; **II** *v/i.* **5.** (auf)schießen (*Pflanze*); **6.** in die Höhe schießen (*Person*); **ˈ~-legged** *adj.* storchbeinig; **ˈ~·legs**, **ˈ~·shanks** *s. pl.* **1.** ‚Storchbeine‘ *pl.*; **2.** *sg. konstr.* ‚Storchbein‘ *n* (*Person*).

spin·dling [ˈspɪndlɪŋ], **ˈspin·dly** [-lɪ] *adj.* lang u. dünn, spindeldürr.

ˌspin|-ˈdry *v/t. Wäsche* schleudern; **ˌ~-ˈdry·er**, *a.* **ˌ~-ˈdri·er** *s.* Wäscheschleuder *f*.

spine [spaɪn] *s.* **1.** ⚘, *zo.* Stachel *m*; **2.** *anat.* Rückgrat *n* (*a. fig. fester Charakter*), Wirbelsäule *f*; **3.** (Gebirgs)Grat *m*; **4.** Buchrücken *m*; **spined** [-nd] *adj.* **1.** *bot.*, *zo.* stachelig, Stachel…; **2.** Rückgrat…, Wirbel…; **ˈspine·less** [-lɪs] *adj.* **1.** stachellos; **2.** rückgratlos (*a. fig.*).

spin·et [spɪˈnet] *s.* ♪ Spi'nett *n*.

spin·na·ker [ˈspɪnəkə] *s.* ⚓ Spinnaker *m* (*großes Dreiecksegel*).

spin·ner [ˈspɪnə] *s.* **1.** *poet. od. dial.* Spinne *f*; **2.** Spinner(in); **3.** ⚙ 'Spinnmaˌschine *f*; **4.** Kreisel *m*; **5.** (Polier-)Scheibe *f*; **6.** → **ˈspin·ner·et** [-əret] *s. zo.* Spinndrüse *f*.

spin·ney [ˈspɪnɪ] *pl.* **-neys** *s. Brit.* Dikkicht *n*.

spin·ning| jen·ny [ˈspɪnɪŋ] *s.* 'Feinspinnmaˌschine *f*; **~ *mill*** *s.* Spinne'rei *f*; **~ *wheel*** *s.* Spinnrad *n*.

ˈspin-off *s.* ⚙ 'Nebenproˌdukt *n* (*a. fig.*).

spi·nose [ˈspaɪnəʊs], **ˈspi·nous** [-nəs] *adj.* stach(e)lig.

spin·ster [ˈspɪnstə] *s.* **1.** älteres Fräulein, alte Jungfer; **2.** *Brit.* ⚖ a) unverheiratete Frau, b) *nach dem Namen*: ledig: **~ *aunt*** unverheiratete Tante; **ˈspin·ster·hood** [-hʊd] *s.* **1.** Alt'jüngferlichkeit *f*; **2.** Alt'jungfernstand *m*; **3.** lediger Stand; **ˈspin·ster·ish** [-ərɪʃ], **ˈspin·ster·ly** [-lɪ] *adj.* alt'jüngferlich.

spin·y [ˈspaɪnɪ] *adj.* **1.** ⚘, *zo.* stach(e)lig; **2.** *fig.* heikel (*Thema etc.*).

spi·ra·cle [ˈspaɪərəkl] *s.* **1.** Atem-, Luftloch *n*, *bsd. zo.* Tra'chee *f*; **2.** *zo.* Spritzloch *n* (*bei Walen etc.*).

spi·ral [ˈspaɪərəl] **I** *adj.* ☐ **1.** gewunden, schrauben-, schneckenförmig, spi'ral, Spiral…: **~ *balance*** ⚙ (Spiral)Federwaage *f*; **~ *staircase*** Wendeltreppe *f*; **2.** ⊿ spi'ralig, Spiral…; **II** *s.* **3.** ⊿ *etc.* Spi'rale *f*; **4.** Windung *f e-r Spirale*; **5.** ⚙ a) *a.* **~ *conveyer*** Förderschnecke *f*, b) *a.* **~ *spring*** Spi'ralfeder *f*; **6.** ⚡ a) Spule *f*, b) Wendel *f* (*Glühlampe*); **7.** *a.* **~ *nebula*** *ast.* Spi'ralnebel *m*; **8.** ✈ Spi'ralflug *m*, Spi'rale *f*; **9.** ☤ (*Preis-, Lohn- etc.*)Spi'rale *f*: ***wage-price ~*** Lohn-Preis-Spirale; **III** *v/t.* **10.** spi'ralig machen; **11.** **~ *up*** (***down***) *Preise etc.* hin'auf- (her'unter)schrauben; **IV** *v/i.* **12.** sich spi'ralförmig nach oben *od.* unten bewegen, *a.* ✈, ☤ sich hoch- *od.* niederschrauben.

spi·rant [ˈspaɪərənt] *ling.* **I** *s.* Spirans *f*, Reibelaut *m*; **II** *adj.* spi'rantisch.

spire¹ [ˈspaɪə] *s.* **1.** → ***spiral*** 4; **2.** Spi'rale *f*; **3.** *zo.* Gewinde *n*.

spire² [ˈspaɪə] **I** *s.* **1.** (*Dach-, Turm-, a. Baum-, Berg- etc.*)Spitze *f*; **2.** Spitzturm *m*; **3.** Kirchturm(spitze *f*) *m*; **4.** spitz zulaufender Körper *od.* Teil, *z.B.* (Blüten)Ähre *f*, Grashalm *m*, (Geweih)Gabel *f*; **II** *v/i. u. v/t.* **5.** spitz zulaufen (lassen).

spired¹ [ˈspaɪəd] *adj.* spi'ralförmig.

spired² [ˈspaɪəd] *adj.* **1.** spitz (zulaufend); **2.** spitztürmig.

spir·it [ˈspɪrɪt] **I** *s.* **1.** *allg.* Geist *m*: a) Odem *m*, Lebenshauch *m*, b) innere Vorstellung: ***in*** (***the***) **~** im Geiste, c) Seele *f* (*a. e-s Toten*), d) Gespenst *n*, e) Gesinnung *f*, (*Gemein- etc.*)Sinn *m*, f) Cha'rakter *m*, g) Sinn *m*: ***the ~ of the law***; → ***enter into*** 4; **2.** Stimmung *f*, Gemütsverfassung *f*, *pl. a.* Lebensgeister *pl.*: ***in high*** (***low***) ***~s*** gehobener (in gedrückter) Stimmung; **3.** Feuer *n*, Schwung *m*, E'lan *m*; Ener'gie *f*, Mut *m*; **4.** (Mann *m* von) Geist *m*, Kopf *m*, Ge'nie *n*; **5.** Seele *f e-s Unternehmens*; **6.** (Zeit)Geist *m*: **~ *of the age***; **7.** ⚗ Destil'lat *n*, Geist *m*, Spiritus *m*: ***~(s) of hartshorn*** Hirschhornspiritus, -geist; ***~(s) of turpentine*** Terpentinöl *n*; ***~(s) of wine*** Weingeist; **8.** *pl.* alko'holische *od.* geistige Getränke *pl.*, Spiritu'osen *pl.*; **9.** *a. pl.* ⚗ *Am.* Alkohol *m*; **II** *v/t.* **10.** *a.* **~ *up*** aufmuntern, anstacheln; **11.** **~ *away***, **~ *off*** wegschaffen, -zaubern, verschwinden lassen; **ˈspir·it·ed** [-tɪd] *adj.* ☐ **1.** le'bendig, lebhaft, schwungvoll, tempera'mentvoll; **2.** e'nergisch, beherzt; **3.** feurig (*Pferd etc.*); **4.** (geist)sprühend, le'bendig (*Rede, Buch etc.*).

-spir·it·ed [spɪrɪtɪd] *adj. in Zssgn* **1.** …gesinnt: → ***public-~***; **2.** …gestimmt: → ***low-~***.

spir·it·ed·ness [ˈspɪrɪtɪdnɪs] *s.* **1.** Lebhaftigkeit *f*, Le'bendigkeit *f*; **2.** Ener'gie *f*, Beherztheit *f*; **3.** *in Zssgn*: ***low-~*** Niedergeschlagenheit *f*; ***public-~*** Gemeinsinn *m*.

spir·it·ism [ˈspɪrɪtɪzəm] *s.* Spiri'tismus *m*; **ˈspir·it·ist** [-ɪst] *s.* Spiri'tist(in); **spir·it·is·tic** [ˌspɪrɪˈtɪstɪk] *adj.* (☐ ***~al·ly***) spiri'tistisch.

spir·it·less [ˈspɪrɪtlɪs] *adj.* ☐ **1.** geistlos; **2.** leb-, lust-, schwunglos, schlapp; **3.** niedergeschlagen, mutlos; **ˈspir·it·less·ness** [-nɪs] *s.* **1.** Geistlosigkeit *f*; **2.** Lust-, Schwunglosigkeit *f*; **3.** Kleinmut *m*.

spir·it| lev·el *s.* ⚙ Nivellier-, Wasserwaage *f*; **~ *rap·ping*** *s.* Geisterklopfen *n*.

spir·it·u·al [ˈspɪrɪtjʊəl] **I** *adj.* ☐ **1.** geistig, unkörperlich; **2.** geistig, innerlich, seelisch: **~ *life*** Seelenleben *n*; **3.** vergeistigt (*Person, Gesicht etc.*); **4.** göttlich (inspiriert); **5.** a) religi'ös, b) kirchlich, c) geistlich (*Gericht, Lied etc.*); **6.** geistig, intellektu'ell; **7.** geistreich, -voll; **II** *s.* **8.** ♪ (Neger)Spiritual *n*; **ˈspir·it·u·al-**

ism [-lɪzəm] *s.* **1.** Geisterglaube *m*, Spiri'tismus *m*; **2.** *phls.* a) Spiritua'lismus *m*, b) meta'physischer Idea'lismus; **3.** *das* Geistige; **'spir·it·u·al·ist** [-lɪst] *s.* **1.** Spiritua'list *m*, Idea'list *m*; **2.** Spiri'tist *m*; **spir·it·u·al·i·ty** [ˌspɪrɪtjʊ'ælətɪ] *s.* **1.** *das* Geistige; **2.** *das* Geistliche; **3.** Unkörperlichkeit *f*, geistige Na'tur; **4.** *oft pl. hist.* geistliche Rechte *pl. od.* Einkünfte *pl.*; **'spir·it·u·al·ize** [-laɪz] *v/t.* **1.** vergeistigen; **2.** im über'tragenen Sinne deuten.

spir·it·u·ous ['spɪrɪtjʊəs] *adj.* **1.** alko'holisch: **~ *liquors*** Spirituosen; **2.** destilliert.

spir·y¹ ['spaɪərɪ] → ***spired¹***.

spir·y² ['spaɪərɪ] *adj.* **1.** spitz zulaufend; **2.** vieltürmig.

spit¹ [spɪt] **I** *v/i.* [*irr.*] **1.** spucken: **~ *on*** *fig.* auf *et.* spucken; **~ *on*** (*od.* ***at***) ***s.o.*** j-n anspucken; **~ *s.o. in the eye*** j-m ins Gesicht spucken (*a. fig.*); **2.** spritzen, klecksen (*Federhalter*); **3.** sprühen (*Regen*); **4.** fauchen, zischen (*Katze etc.*): **~ *at s.o.*** j-n anfauchen; **5.** (her'aus)sprudeln, (-)spritzen (*kochendes Wasser etc.*); **II** *v/t.* [*irr.*] **6.** *a.* **~ *out*** (aus)spukken; **7.** *Feuer etc.* speien; **8.** *a.* **~ *out*** *fig. Worte* (heftig) her'vorstoßen, zischen: **~ *it out!*** F nun sag's schon!; **III** *s.* **9.** Spucke *f*, Speichel *m*: **~ *and polish*** ⚓, ⚔ *sl.* a) Putz- u. Flickstunde *f*, b) peinliche Sauberkeit, c) Leuteschinderei *f*; **~-*and-polish*** F *attr.* ‚wie aus dem Ei gepellt'; **10.** Fauchen *n* (*e-r Katze*); **11.** Sprühregen *m*; **12.** F Eben-, Abbild *n*: ***she is the ~*** (***and image***) ***of her mother*** sie ist ihrer Mutter wie aus dem Gesicht geschnitten.

spit² [spɪt] **I** *s.* **1.** (Brat)Spieß *m*; **2.** *geogr.* Landzunge *f*; **3.** spitz zulaufende Sandbank; **II** *v/t.* **4.** an e-n Bratspieß stecken; **5.** aufspießen.

spit³ [spɪt] *s.* Spatenstich *m*.

spite [spaɪt] **I** *s.* **1.** Boshaftigkeit *f*, Gehässigkeit *f*: ***from pure*** (*od.* ***in*** *od.* ***out of***) **~** aus reiner Bosheit; **2.** Groll *m*: ***have a ~ against*** *j-m* grollen; **~ *vote*** *pol.* Protest-, Trotzwahl *f*; **3.** (***in***) **~ *of*** trotz, ungeachtet (*gen.*): ***in ~ of that*** dessenungeachtet; ***in ~ of o.s.*** unwillkürlich; **II** *v/t.* **4.** *j-m* ‚eins auswischen'; → ***nose*** *Redew.*; **'spite·ful** [-fʊl] *adj.* □ boshaft, gehässig; **'spite·ful·ness** [-fʊlnɪs] → ***spite*** 1.

'spitˌfire *s.* **1.** Feuer-, Hitzkopf *m*, *bsd.* ‚Drachen' *m* (*Frau*); **2.** feuerspeiender Vul'kan.

spit·tle ['spɪtl] *s.* Spucke *f*, Speichel *m*.

spit·toon [spɪ'tu:n] *s.* Spucknapf *m*.

spitz (**dog**) [spɪts] *s. zo.* Spitz *m* (*Hund*).

spiv [spɪv] *s. Brit. sl.* Schieber *m*, Schwarzhändler *m*.

splanch·nic ['splæŋknɪk] *adj. anat.* Eingeweide…

splash [splæʃ] **I** *v/t.* **1.** (mit Wasser *od.* Schmutz *etc.*) bespritzen; **2.** *Wasser etc.* spritzen, gießen, *Farbe etc.* klatschen (***on, over*** über *acc. od.* auf *acc.*); **3.** *s-n Weg* patschend bahnen; **4.** *Plakate* anbringen; **5.** F *in der Zeitung* in großer Aufmachung bringen; **II** *v/i.* **6.** spritzen; **7.** platschen: a) planschen, b) klatschen (*Regen etc.*), c) plumpsen: **~ *down*** wassern (*Raumkapsel*); **III** *adv. u. int.* **8.** p(l)atsch(!), klatsch(!); **IV** *s.* **9.** a) Spritzen *n*, b) Platschen *n*, Klatschen *n*, c) Schwapp *m*, Guß *m*; **10.** Spritzer *m*, (Spritz)Fleck *m*; **11.** (Farb-, Licht)Fleck *m*; **12.** F a) Aufsehen *n*, Sensati'on *f*, b) große Aufmachung, c) großer Aufwand: ***get a ~*** groß herausgestellt werden; ***make a ~*** Aufsehen erregen, Furore machen; **13.** *Brit.* F Schuß *m* (Soda)Wasser (*zum Whisky etc.*); **'~·board** *s.* ⚙ Schutzblech *n*; **'~·down** *s.* Wasserung *f*, Eintauchen *n* (*e-r Raumkapsel*).

splash·er ['splæʃə] *s.* **1.** Schutzblech *n*; **2.** Wandschoner *m*.

splash| guard *s.* ⚙ Spritzschutz *m*; **'~·proof** *adj.* ⚙ spritzwassergeschützt.

splash·y ['splæʃɪ] *adj.* **1.** spritzend; **2.** klatschend, platschend; **3.** bespritzt, beschmutzt; **4.** matschig; **5.** F sensatio'nell, ‚toll'.

splat·ter ['splætə] → ***splash*** 1, 2, 6, 7.

splay [spleɪ] **I** *v/t.* **1.** ausbreiten, -dehnen; **2.** △ ausschrägen; **3.** (ab)schrägen; **4.** *bsd. vet. Schulterknochen* ausrenken (*bei Pferden*); **II** *v/i.* **5.** ausgeschrägt sein; **III** *adj.* **6.** breit u. flach; **7.** gespreizt, auswärts gebogen (*Fuß*); **8.** schief, schräg; **9.** *fig.* linkisch; **IV** *s.* **10.** △ Ausschrägung *f*; **splayed** [-eɪd] → ***splay*** 7.

'splay|·foot I *s.* ⚕ Spreiz-, Plattfuß *m*; **II** *adj. a.* **ˌ~'foot·ed** spreiz- *od.* plattfüßig.

spleen [spli:n] *s.* **1.** *anat.* Milz *f*; **2.** *fig.* schlechte Laune; **3.** *obs.* Hypochon'drie *f*, Melancho'lie *f*; **4.** *obs.* Spleen *m*, ‚Tick' *m*; **'spleen·ful** [-fʊl], **'spleen·ish** [-nɪʃ] *adj.* □ **1.** mürrisch, übelgelaunt; **2.** hypo'chondrisch.

splen·dent ['splendənt] *adj. min. u. fig.* glänzend, leuchtend.

splen·did ['splendɪd] *adj.* □ **1.** *alle a.* F glänzend, großartig, herrlich, prächtig: **~ *isolation*** *pol. hist.* Splendid isolation *f*; **2.** glorreich; **3.** wunderbar, her'vorragend: **~ *talents***; **'splen·did·ness** [-nɪs] *s.* **1.** Glanz *m*, Pracht *f*; **2.** Großartigkeit *f*.

splen·dif·er·ous [splen'dɪfərəs] *adj.* F *od. humor.* herrlich, prächtig.

splen·do(u)r ['splendə] *s.* **1.** heller Glanz; **2.** Pracht *f*; **3.** Großartigkeit *f*, Bril'lanz *f*, Größe *f*.

sple·net·ic [splɪ'netɪk] **I** *adj.* (□ **~*ally***) **1.** ⚕ Milz…; **2.** milzkrank; **3.** → ***spleenish***; **II** *s.* **4.** ⚕ Milzkranke(r *m*) *f*; **5.** Hypo'chonder *m*.

splen·ic ['splenɪk] *adj.* ⚕ Milz…: **~ *fever*** Milzbrand *m*.

splice [splaɪs] **I** *v/t.* **1.** spleißen, zs.-splissen; **2.** (ein)falzen; **3.** verbinden, zs.-fügen, *bsd. Filmstreifen, Tonband* (zs.-)kleben; **4.** F verheiraten: ***get ~d*** getraut werden; **II** *s.* **5.** ⚓ Spleiß *m*, Splissung *f*; **6.** ⚙ (Ein)Falzung *f*; **7.** Klebestelle *f* (*an Filmen etc.*).

spline [splaɪn] *s.* **1.** längliches, dünnes Stück Holz *od.* Me'tall; **2.** *Art* 'Kurvenlineˌal *n*; **3.** ⚙ a) Keil *m*, Splint *m*, b) (Längs)Nut *f*.

splint [splɪnt] **I** *s.* **1.** ⚕ Schiene *f*: ***in ~s*** geschient; **2.** ⚙ Span *m*; **3.** → ***splint bone*** 1; **4.** *vet.* a) → ***splint bone*** 2, b) Knochenauswuchs *m*, Tumor *m* (*Pferdefuß*); **5.** *a.* **~ *coal*** Schieferkohle *f*; **II** *v/t.* **6.** ⚕ schienen; **~ *bone*** *s.* **1.** *anat.* Wadenbein *n*; **2.** *vet. Knochen des Pferdefußes hinter dem Schienbein.*

splin·ter ['splɪntə] **I** *s.* **1.** (*a. Bomben-, Knochen- etc.*)Splitter *m*, Span *m*: ***go*** (***in***)***to ~s*** → 4; **2.** *fig.* Splitter *m*, Bruchstück *n*; **II** *v/t.* **3.** zersplittern (*a. fig.*); **III** *v/i.* **4.** zersplittern (*a. fig.*): **~ *off*** (*fig.* sich) absplittern; **~ *group*** *s.* Splittergruppe *f*; **~ *par·ty*** *s. pol.* 'Splitterparˌtei *f*; **'~·proof** *adj.* splittersicher.

splin·ter·y ['splɪntərɪ] *adj.* **1.** *bsd. min.* splitterig, schieferig; **2.** leicht splitternd; **3.** Splitter…

split [splɪt] **I** *v/t.* [*irr.*] **1.** (zer)spalten, zerteilen, schlitzen; *Holz, fig. Haare* spalten; **2.** zerreißen; → ***side*** 4; **3.** *fig.* zerstören; **4.** *Gewinn, Flasche Wein etc.* (unterein'ander) teilen, sich in *et.* teilen; ✝ *Aktien* splitten: **~ *the difference*** a) ✝ sich in die Differenz teilen, b) sich auf halbem Wege entgegenkommen *od.* einigen; → ***ticket*** 7; **5.** trennen, entzweien, *Partei etc.* spalten; **6.** *sl. Plan etc.* verraten; **7.** *Am.* F *Whisky etc.* ‚spritzen' (*mit Wasser verdünnen*); **8.** ⚛, *phys. Atome etc.* (auf)spalten: **~ *off*** abspalten; **II** *v/i.* [*irr.*] **9.** sich aufspalten, reißen; platzen, bersten, zerspringen: ***my head is ~ing*** *fig.* ich habe rasende Kopfschmerzen; **10.** zerschellen (*Schiff*); **11.** sich spalten (***into*** in *acc.*): **~ *off*** sich abspalten; **12.** sich entzweien *od.* trennen (***over*** wegen *e-r Sache*); **13.** sich teilen (***on*** in *acc.*); **14.** **~ *on*** *j-n* ‚verpfeifen'; **15.** a) F sich schütteln vor Lachen, b) *sl.* ‚abhauen'; **16.** *pol. Am.* panaschieren; **III** *s.* **17.** Spalt *m*, Riß *m*, Sprung *m*; **18.** *fig.* Spaltung *f*, Zersplitterung *f* (*e-r Partei etc.*); **19.** *fig.* Entzweiung *f*, Bruch *m*; **20.** *pol.* Splittergruppe *f*; **21.** ⚙ Schicht *f von Spaltleder*; **22.** (*bsd.* Ba'nanen)Split *m*; **23.** F a) halbe Flasche (*Mineralwasser etc.*), b) halbgefülltes (Schnaps- *etc.*) Glas; **24.** *pl.* a) *Akrobatik*: Spa'gat *m*: ***do the ~s*** e-n Spagat machen, b) *sport* Grätsche *f*; **25.** *sl.* Spitzel *m*; **IV** *adj.* **26.** zer-, gespalten, Spalt…: **~ *infinitive*** *ling.* gespaltener Infinitiv; **~-*level house*** Halbgeschoßhaus *n*; **~ *peas*(*e*)** getrocknete halbe Erbsen (*für Püree etc.*); **~ *personality*** *psych.* gespaltene Persönlichkeit; **~ *second*** Bruchteil *m* e-r Sekunde; **~-*second watch*** *sport* Stoppuhr *f*; **~ *ticket*** *Am.* Wahlzettel *m* mit Stimmen für Kandidaten mehrerer Parteien; **'split·ting** [-tɪŋ] **I** *adj.* **1.** (*ohren- etc.*)zerreißend; **2.** rasend, heftig (*Kopfschmerzen*); **3.** blitzschnell; **4.** zwerchfellerschütternd: ***a ~ farce***; **II** *s.* **5.** Spaltung *f*; **6.** ✝ Splitting *n*: a) Aktienteilung *f*, b) *Besteuerung e-s Ehepartners zur Hälfte des gemeinsamen Einkommens*; **'split-up** *s.* **1.** → ***split*** 17–19; **2.** ✝ (Aktien)Split *m*.

splodge [splɒdʒ], **splotch** [splɒtʃ] **I** *s.* Fleck *m*, Klecks *m*; **II** *v/t.* beklecksen; **splotch·y** ['splɒtʃɪ] *adj.* fleckig, schmutzig.

splurge [splɜ:dʒ] F **I** *s.* **1.** ‚Angabe' *f*, protziges Getue; **2.** verschwenderischer Aufwand; **II** *v/i.* **3.** protzen, angeben; **4.** prassen.

splut·ter ['splʌtə] **I** *v/i.* **1.** stottern; **2.** ‚stottern', ‚kotzen' (*Motor*); **3.** zischen (*Braten etc.*); **4.** klecksen (*Schreibfeder*); **5.** spritzen, platschen (*Wasser etc.*); **II** *v/t.* **6.** *Worte* her'aussprudeln, -stottern; **7.** verspritzen; **8.** bespritzen;

9. *j-n* (*beim Sprechen*) bespucken; **III** *s.* **10.** Geplapper *m*; **11.** Spritzen *n*; Sprudeln *n*; Zischen *n*.

spoil [spɔɪl] **I** *v/t.* [*irr.*] **1.** *et., a. Appetit, Spaß* verderben, ruinieren, vernichten; *Plan* vereiteln; **2.** *Charakter etc.* verderben, *Kind* verziehen, -wöhnen: ***a ~ed brat*** ein verzogener Fratz; **3.** (*pret. u. p.p. nur **~ed***) berauben, entblößen (***of*** *gen.*); **4.** (*pret. u. p.p. nur **~ed***) *obs.* (aus)plündern; **II** *v/i.* [*irr.*] **5.** verderben, ‚ka'puttgehen', schlecht werden (*Obst etc.*); **6.** ***be ~ing for*** brennen auf (*acc.*); ***~ing for a fight*** streitlustig; **III** *s.* **7.** *mst pl.* (Sieges)Beute *f*, Raub *m*; **8.** Beute(stück *n*) *f*; **9.** *mst pl. bsd. Am.* a) Ausbeute *f*, b) *pol.* Gewinn *m*, Einkünfte *pl.* (*e-r Partei nach dem Wahlsieg*); **10.** Errungenschaft *f*, Gewinn *m*; **11.** *pl.* 'Überreste *pl.*, -bleibsel *pl.* (*von Mahlzeiten*); **'spoil·age** [-lɪdʒ] *s.* **1.** *typ.* Makula'tur *f*; **2.** ✝ Verderb *m von Waren*; **'spoil·er** [-lə] *s.* **1.** *mot.* Spoiler *m*; **2.** ✈ Störklappe *f*.

spoils·man ['spɔɪlzmən] *s.* [*irr.*] *pol. Am.* j-d, der nach der ‚Futterkrippe' strebt.

'spoil·sport *s.* Spielverderber(in).

spoils sys·tem *s. pol. Am.* 'Futterkrippensyˌstem *n*.

spoilt [spɔɪlt] *pret. u. p.p. von* ***spoil***.

spoke¹ [spəʊk] **I** *s.* **1.** (Rad)Speiche *f*; **2.** (Leiter)Sprosse *f*; **3.** ⚓ Spake *f* (*des Steuerrads*); **4.** Bremsvorrichtung *f*: ***put a ~ in s.o.'s wheel*** *fig.* j-m e-n Knüppel zwischen die Beine werfen; **II** *v/t.* **5.** *Rad* a) verspeichen, b) (ab)bremsen.

spoke² [spəʊk] *pret. u. obs. p.p. von* ***speak***.

spoke bone *s. anat.* Speiche *f*.

spo·ken ['spəʊkən] **I** *p.p. von* ***speak***; **II** *adj.* **1.** gesprochen, mündlich: ***~ English*** gesprochenes Englisch; **2.** *in Zssgn* ...sprechend.

spokes·man ['spəʊksmən] *s.* [*irr.*] Wortführer *m*, Sprecher *m*: ***government ~*** *pol.* Regierungssprecher.

spo·li·ate ['spəʊlɪeɪt] *v/t. u. v/i.* plündern; **spo·li·a·tion** [ˌspəʊlɪ'eɪʃn] *s.* **1.** Plünderung *f*, Beraubung *f*; **2.** ⚓, ⚔ *kriegsrechtliche Plünderung neutraler Schiffe*; **3.** ⚖ *unberechtigte Änderung e-s Dokuments*.

spon·da·ic [spɒn'deɪɪk] *adj. Metrik*: spon'deisch; **spon·dee** ['spɒndi:] *s.* Spon'deus *m*.

spon·dyl(e) ['spɒndɪl] *s. anat., zo.* Wirbelknochen *m*.

sponge [spʌndʒ] **I** *s.* **1.** *zo. u. weitS.* Schwamm *m*: ***pass the ~ over*** *fig.* aus dem Gedächtnis löschen, vergessen; ***throw up the ~*** *Boxen*: das Handtuch werfen (*a. fig. sich geschlagen geben*); **2.** ⚔ Wischer *m*; **3.** *fig.* Schma'rotzer *m*, ‚Nassauer' *m* (*Person*); **4.** *Küche*: a) aufgegangener Teig, b) *lockerer, gekochter Pudding*; **II** *v/t.* **5.** *a.* ***~ down*** (mit e-m Schwamm) reinigen, abwaschen: ***~ off***, ***~ away*** weg-, abwischen; ***~ out*** auslöschen (*a. fig.*); **6.** ***~ up*** *Wasser etc.* (mit e-m Schwamm) aufsaugen, -nehmen; **7.** (kostenlos) ergattern, ‚schnorren'; **III** *v/i.* **8.** Schwämme sammeln; **9.** F schma'rotzen, ‚nassauern': ***~ on s.o.*** auf j-s Kosten leben; ***~ bag*** *s.* Kul'turbeutel *m*; ***~ cake*** *s.* Bis'kuitkuchen *m*; ***~ cloth*** *s.* ✝ *Art* Frot'tee *n*; **'~-down** *s.* Abreibung *f* (mit e-m Schwamm).

spong·er ['spʌndʒə] *s.* **1.** ⚙ Dekatierer *m*; **2.** ⚙ Deka'tiermaˌschine *f*; **3.** Schwammtaucher *m*; **4.** → ***sponge*** 3.

sponge rub·ber *s.* Schaumgummi *m*.

spon·gi·ness ['spʌndʒɪnɪs] *s.* Schwammigkeit *f*; **spon·gy** ['spʌndʒɪ] *adj.* **1.** schwammig, po'rös, Schwamm...; **2.** *metall.* locker, porös; **3.** sumpfig, matschig.

spon·sal ['spɒnsəl] *adj.* Hochzeits...

spon·sion ['spɒnʃn] *s.* **1.** ('Übernahme *f* e-r) Bürgschaft *f*; **2.** ⚖, *pol.* (*von e-m nicht bsd. bevollmächtigten Vertreter*) *für e-n Staat übernommene Verpflichtung*.

spon·sor ['spɒnsə] **I** *s.* **1.** Bürge *m*, Bürgin *f*; **2.** (Tauf)Pate *m*, (-)Patin *f*: ***stand ~ to*** (*od.* ***for***) Pate stehen bei; **3.** Förderer *m*, Gönner(in); **4.** Schirmherr(in); **5.** Sponsor *m*, Geldgeber *m*; **II** *v/t.* **6.** bürgen für; **7.** fördern; **8.** die Schirmherrschaft (*gen.*) über'nehmen; **9.** *Radio, TV, sport etc.* sponsern, (als Sponsor) finanzieren; **spon·so·ri·al** [spɒn'sɔ:rɪəl] *adj.* Paten...; **'spon·sor·ship** [-ʃɪp] *s.* **1.** Bürgschaft *f*; **2.** Gönnerschaft *f*, Schirmherrschaft *f*; **3.** Patenschaft *f*.

spon·ta·ne·i·ty [ˌspɒntə'neɪətɪ] *s.* **1.** Spontanei'tät *f*, Freiwilligkeit *f*, eigener *od.* freier Antrieb; **2.** *das* Impul'sive, impul'sives *od.* spon'tanes Handeln; **3.** Ungezwungenheit *f*, Na'türlichkeit *f*;

spon·ta·ne·ous [spɒn'teɪnjəs] □ *adj.* **1.** spon'tan: a) plötzlich, impul'siv, b) freiwillig, von innen her'aus (erfolgend), c) ungekünstelt, ungezwungen (*Stil etc.*); **2.** auto'matisch, 'unwillˌkürlich; **3.** ⚘ wildwachsend; **4.** selbsttätig, von selbst (entstanden): ***~ combustion*** *phys.* Selbstverbrennung *f*; ***~ generation*** *biol.* Urzeugung *f*; ***~ ignition*** ⚙ Selbstentzündung *f*; **spon·ta·ne·ous·ness** [spɒn'teɪnjəsnɪs] → ***spontaneity***.

spoof [spu:f] F **I** *s.* **1.** Humbug *m*, Schwindel *m*; **2.** Ulk *m*; **II** *v/t.* **3.** beschwindeln; **4.** verulken.

spook [spu:k] **I** *s.* F **1.** Spuk *m*, Gespenst *n*; **2.** *Am. sl.* Ghostwriter *m*; **II** *v/i.* **3.** (her'um)geistern, spuken; **'spook·ish** [-kɪʃ], **'spook·y** [-kɪ] *adj.* **1.** gespenstisch, spukhaft, schaurig; **2.** *Am.* schreckhaft.

spool [spu:l] **I** *s.* Rolle *f*, Spule *f*, Haspel *f*; **II** *v/t.* (auf)spulen.

spoon [spu:n] **I** *s.* **1.** Löffel *m*; **2.** ⚓ Löffelruder(blatt) *n*; **3.** ⚓, ⚔ Führungsschaufel *f* (*Torpedorohr*); **4.** → ***spoon bait***; **5.** *sport* Spoon *m* (*Golfschläger*); **6.** F Einfaltspinsel *m*; **II** *v/t.* **7.** *mst* ***~ up***, ***~ out*** auslöffeln: ***~ out*** *a.* (löffelweise) austeilen; **8.** *sport Ball* schlenzen; **III** *v/i.* **9.** mit e-m Blinker angeln; **10.** *sl. obs.* ‚schmusen'; ***~ bait*** *s. Angeln*: Blinker *m*; **'~-bill** *s. orn.* **1.** Löffelreiher *m*; **2.** Löffelente *f*.

spoon·er·ism ['spu:nərɪzəm] *s.* (*un*)*beabsichtigtes Vertauschen von Buchstaben od. Silben* (*z.B.* ***queer old dean*** *statt* ***dear old queen***).

'spoon|·feed *v/t.* [*irr.* → ***feed***] **1.** mit dem Löffel füttern; **2.** *fig. j-n* auf-, hochpäppeln, *a.* verwöhnen; **3.** ***~ s.th. to s.o.*** *fig.* a) j-m et. ‚vorkauen', b) j-m et. eintrichtern; **4.** ***~ s.o.*** *fig.* j-n (geistig) bevormunden; **'~·ful** [-fʊl] *pl.* **-fuls** *s. ein* Löffel(voll) *m*; ***~ meat*** *s.* (Kinder-, Kranken)Brei *m*, ‚Papp' *m*.

spoor [spʊə] *hunt.* **I** *s.* Spur *f*, Fährte *f*; **II** *v/t.* aufspüren; **III** *v/i.* e-e Spur verfolgen.

spo·rad·ic [spə'rædɪk] *adj.* (□ ***~ally***) spo'radisch, vereinzelt (auftretend).

spore [spɔ:] *s.* **1.** *biol.* Spore *f*, Keimkorn *n*; **2.** *fig.* Keim(zelle *f*) *m*.

spo·rif·er·ous [spɔ:'rɪfərəs] *adj.* sporentragend, -bildend.

spo·ro·zo·a [ˌspɔ:rə'zəʊə] *s. pl. zo.* Sporentierchen *pl.*, Sporo'zoen *pl.*

spor·ran ['spɒrən] *s.* beschlagene Felltasche (*Schottentracht*).

sport [spɔ:t] **I** *s.* **1.** *oft pl.* Sport *m*: ***go in for ~s*** Sport treiben; **2.** 'Sport(art *f*, -disziˌplin *f*) *m*, *engS.* Jagd-, Angelsport *m*; **3.** Kurzweil *f*, Zeitvertreib *m*; **4.** Spaß *m*, Scherz *m*: ***in ~*** im Spaß, zum Scherz; ***make ~ of*** sich lustig machen über (*acc.*); **5.** Zielscheibe *f* des Spottes; **6.** *fig.* Spielball *m* (*des Schicksals, der Wellen etc.*); **7.** feiner *od.* anständiger Kerl: ***be a*** (***good***) ***~*** a) sei kein Spielverderber, b) sei ein guter Kerl, nimm es nicht übel; **8.** *Am.* F a) Sportbegeisterte(r *m*) *f*, *bsd.* Spieler *m*, b) Genießer *m*; **9.** *biol.* Spiel-, Abart *f*; **II** *adj.* **10.** sportlich, Sport...; **III** *v/i.* **11.** sich belustigen; **12.** sich tummeln, her'umtollen; **13.** sich lustig machen (***at***, ***over***, ***upon*** über *acc.*); **IV** *v/t.* **14.** stolz (zur Schau) tragen, protzen mit; **'sport·ing** [-tɪŋ] *adj.* □ **1.** a) Sport...: ***~ editor***, b) Jagd...: ***~ gun***; **2.** sportlich (*a. fig. fair, anständig*): ***a ~ chance*** e-e faire Chance; **3.** unter'nehmungslustig, mutig; **'spor·tive** [-tɪv] *adj.* □ **1.** a) mutwillig, b) verspielt; **2.** spaßhaft.

sports [spɔ:ts] *adj.* Sport...: ***~ car*** Sportwagen *m*; ***~ coat***, ***~ jacket*** Sportsakko *m, n*; **'~·cast** *s. Radio, TV*: *Am.* Sportsendung *f*; **'~ˌcast·er** *s. Am.* 'Sportreˌporter *m*; **'~·man** [-mən] *s.* [*irr.*] **1.** Sportsmann *m*, Sportler *m*; **2.** *fig.* fairer, anständiger Kerl; **'~·man·like** [-mənlaɪk] *adj.* sportlich, fair; **'~·man·ship** [-mənʃɪp] *s.* sportliches Benehmen, Fairneß *f*; **'~·wear** *s.* Sport- *od.* Freizeitkleidung *f*; **'~ˌwom·an** *s.* [*irr.*] Sportlerin *f*.

sport·y ['spɔ:tɪ] *adj.* F **1.** angeberisch, auffallend; **2.** sportlich: a) sporttreibend, b) fair, c) schick.

spor·ule ['spɒrju:l] *s. biol.* (kleine) Spore.

spot [spɒt] **I** *s.* **1.** (Schmutz-, Rost- *etc.*) Fleck(en) *m*; **2.** *fig.* Schandfleck *m*, Makel *m*; **3.** (Farb)Fleck *m*, Tupfen *m* (*a. zo.*); **4.** ⚕ a) Leberfleck *m*, Hautmal *n*, b) Pustel *f*, Pickel *m*; **5.** Stelle *f*, Ort *m*, Platz *m*: ***on the ~*** a) zur Stelle, da, b) an Ort u. Stelle, ‚vor Ort', c) auf der Stelle, sofort, d) ‚auf Draht', e) *sl.* in der ‚Tinte' *od.* Klemme; ***put on the ~*** F a) *j-n* in Verlegenheit bringen, b) *j-n* ‚umlegen' (*töten*); ***on the ~ of four*** Punkt 4 Uhr; ***in ~s*** stellenweise; ***soft ~*** *fig.* Schwäche (***for*** für); ***sore*** (*od.* ***tender***) ***~*** *fig.* wunder Punkt, empfindliche Stelle; **6.** Fleckchen *n*, Stückchen *n* (*Erde*); **7.** *bsd. Brit.* F a) Bissen *m*, Häppchen *n* (*Essen*), b) Tropfen *m*, Schluck *m* (*Whisky etc.*); **8.** *Billard*: Point *m*; **9.** *Am.* Auge *n* (*Würfel etc.*);

10. *pl.* † Lokowaren *pl.*; **11.** †, *Radio*, *TV*: (Werbe)Spot *m*; **12.** *Am.* F Nachtklub *m*; **13.** → ***spotlight*** I; **II** *adj.* **14.** † a) so'fort lieferbar, b) so'fort zahlbar (*bei Lieferung*), c) bar, Bar...: ~ ***business*** Lokogeschäft *n*; ~ ***goods*** → 10; → ***spot cash***; **III** *v/t.* **15.** beflekken (*a. fig.*); **16.** tüpfeln, sprenkeln; **17.** F entdecken, erspähen, her'ausfinden; **18.** placieren: ~ ***a billiard ball***; **19.** ⚔, ✈ (genau) ausmachen; **IV** *v/i.* **20.** e-n Fleck *od.* Flecke machen; **21.** flecken, fleckig werden.

spot| an·nounce·ment → ***spot*** 11; ~ **ball** *s. Billard*: auf dem Point stehender Ball; ~ **cash** *s.* † Barzahlung *f*, so'fortige Kasse; ~ **check** *s.* Stichprobe *f*; '~-**check** *v/t.* stichprobenweise über'prüfen.

spot·less ['spɒtlɪs] *adj.* □ fleckenlos (*a. fig.*); '**spot·less·ness** [-nɪs] *s.* Flekken-, Makellosigkeit *f* (*a. fig.*).

'**spot|·light I** *s.* **1.** *thea.* (Punkt)Scheinwerfer(licht *n*) *m*; **2.** *fig.* Rampenlicht *n* (der Öffentlichkeit): ***in the*** ~ im Brennpunkt des Interesses; **3.** *mot.* Suchscheinwerfer *m*; **II** *v/t.* **4.** anstrahlen; **5.** *fig.* die Aufmerksamkeit lenken auf (*acc.*); ~ **news** *s. pl.* Kurznachrichten *pl.*; ˌ~-'**on** *adj. Brit.* F haargenau; ~ **price** *s.* † Kassapreis *m*; ~ **re·mov·er** *s.* Fleckentferner *m*.

spot·ted ['spɒtɪd] *adj.* **1.** fleckig, gefleckt, getüpfelt, gesprenkelt; **2.** *fig.* besudelt, befleckt; **3.** ⚕ Fleck...: ~ ***fever*** a) Fleckfieber *n*, b) Genickstarre *f*; '**spot·ter** [-tə] *s.* **1.** *Am.* F Detek'tiv *m*; **2.** ⚔ a) (Luft)Aufklärer *m*, Artille'riebeobachter *m*, b) *Luftschutz*: Flugmelder *m*.

spot test → ***spot check***.

spot·ty ['spɒtɪ] *adj.* □ **1.** → ***spotted*** 1; **2.** uneinheitlich; **3.** pickelig.

'**spot-weld** *v/t.* ⚙ punktschweißen.

spous·al ['spaʊzl] **I** *adj.* **1.** a) Hochzeits..., b) ehelich; **II** *s.* **2.** *mst pl.* Hochzeit *f*; **3.** *obs.* Ehe(stand *m*) *f*; **spouse** [spaʊz] *s.* (*a.* ⚖ Ehe)Gatte *m*, Gattin *f*, Gemahl(in).

spout [spaʊt] **I** *v/t.* **1.** *Wasser etc.* (aus-)speien, (her'aus)spritzen; **2.** a) *Gedicht etc.* deklamieren, b) ‚her'unterrasseln', c) *Fragen etc.* her'aussprudeln; **3.** *sl.* versetzen, -pfänden; **II** *v/i.* **4.** Wasser speien, spritzen (*a. Wal*); **5.** her'vorsprudeln, her'ausschießen, -spritzen (*Blut*, *Wasser etc.*); **6.** a) deklamieren, b) *contp.* sal'badern; **III** *s.* **7.** Tülle *f*, Schnauze *f e-r Kanne*; **8.** Abfluß-, Speirohr *n*; **9.** (kräftiger) Wasserstrahl; **10.** *zo.* a) Fon'täne *f* (*e-s Wals*); b) → ***spout hole***; **11.** ***up the*** ~ *fig.* F a) versetzt, verpfändet, b) ‚im Eimer', futsch, c) ‚in Schwulitäten' (*Person*); ***she's up the*** ~ bei ihr ist was ‚unterwegs'; '**spout·er** [-tə] *s.* **1.** (spritzender) Wal; **2.** Ölquelle *f*; **3.** ‚Redenschwinger' *m*.

spout hole *s. zo.* Spritzloch *m* (*Wal*).

sprag¹ [spræg] *s.* **1.** Bremsklotz *m*; **2.** ⚙ Spreizholz *n*.

sprag² [spræg] *s. ichth.* Dorsch *m*.

sprain [spreɪn] **I** *v/t.* verstauchen; **II** *s.* ⚕ Verstauchung *f*.

sprang [spræŋ] *pret. von* ***spring***.

sprat [spræt] *s. ichth.* Sprotte *f*: ***throw a*** ~ ***to catch a whale*** (*od.* ***mackerel***) *fig.* mit der Wurst nach der Speckseite werfen.

sprawl [sprɔːl] **I** *v/i.* **1.** ausgestreckt daliegen: ***send s.o.*** ~***ing*** j-n zu Boden strecken; **2.** sich spreizen; **3.** sich (hin-)rekeln *od.* (-)lümmeln; **4.** sich ausbreiten: ~***ing town***; ~ ***ing hand*** ausladende Handschrift; **5.** ⚘ wuchern; **II** *v/t.* **6.** *mst* ~ ***out*** ausstrecken, -spreizen; **III** *s.* **7.** Rekeln *n*, Sich'breitmachen *n*; **8.** Ausbreitung *f des Stadtgebiets etc.*: ***urban*** ~.

spray¹ [spreɪ] *s.* **1.** Zweig(chen *n*) *m*, Reis *n*; **2.** *coll.* a) Gezweig *n*, b) Reisig *n*; **3.** Zweigverzierung *f*.

spray² [spreɪ] **I** *s.* **1.** Gischt *m*, *f*, Schaum *m*; Sprühnebel *m*, -regen *m*, -wasser *n*; **2.** ⚙, *pharm.* a) Spray *m*, *n*, b) Zerstäuber *m*, Sprüh-, Spraydose *f*; **II** *v/t.* **3.** zerstäuben, (ver)sprühen; *vom Flugzeug* abregnen; **4.** *a.* ~ ***on*** ⚙ aufsprühen, -spritzen; **5.** *et.* besprühen, -spritzen, *Haar* sprayen; *mot. etc.* spritzlackieren; '**spray·er** [-eɪə] → ***spray***² 2b.

spray| gun *s.* ⚙ 'Spritzpiˌstole *f*; ~ **noz·zle** *s.* **1.** (Gießkannen)Brause *f*; **2.** Brause *f*; **3.** *mot.* Spritzdüse *f*; '~-**paint** *v/t. Parolen etc.* sprühen (***on*** auf *acc.*).

spread [spred] **I** *v/t.* [*irr.*] **1.** *oft* ~ ***out*** *Hände*, *Flügel*, *Teppich etc.* ausbreiten, *Arme etc. a.* ausstrecken: ~ ***the table*** den Tisch decken; ***the peacock*** ~***s its tail*** der Pfau schlägt ein Rad; **2.** *oft* ~ ***out*** ausdehnen; *Beine etc.* spreizen (*a.* ⚙); **3.** bedecken, über'ziehen, -'säen (***with*** mit); **4.** *Heu etc.* ausbreiten; **5.** *Butter etc.* aufstreichen, *Farbe*, *Mörtel etc.* auftragen; **6.** *Brot* streichen, schmieren; **7.** breitschlagen; **8.** *Krankheit*, *Geruch etc.*, *a. Furcht* verbreiten; **9.** *a.* ~ ***abroad*** *Gerücht*, *Nachricht* verbreiten, aussprengen, -streuen; **10.** *zeitlich* verteilen; **11.** ~ ***o.s.*** *sl.* a) sich *als Gastgeber etc.* mächtig anstrengen, b) ‚angeben'; **II** *v/i.* [*irr.*] **12.** *a.* ~ ***out*** sich ausbreiten *od.* verteilen; **13.** sich ausbreiten (*Fahne etc.*; *a. Lächeln etc.*); sich spreizen (*Beine etc.*); **14.** sich *vor den Augen* ausbreiten *od.* -dehnen, sich erstrecken (*Landschaft*); **15.** ⚙ sich strecken *od.* dehnen (lassen) (*Werkstoff*); **16.** sich streichen *od.* auftragen lassen (*Butter*, *Farbe*); **17.** sich ver- *od.* ausbreiten (*Geruch*, *Pflanze*, *Krankheit*, *Gerücht etc.*), 'übergreifen (***to*** auf *acc.*) (*Feuer*, *Epidemie etc.*); **III** *s.* **18.** Ausbreitung *f*, -dehnung *f*; **19.** Aus-, Verbreitung *f* (*e-r Krankheit*, *von Wissen etc.*); **20.** Ausdehnung *f*, Weite *f*, 'Umfang *m*; **21.** (weite) Fläche; **22.** *orn.*, ✈ (Flügel)Spanne *f*; **23.** ⚛, *phys.*, *a. Ballistik*: Streuung *f*; **24.** (Zwischen)Raum *m*, Abstand *m*, Lücke *f* (*a. fig.*); (*a.* Zeit)Spanne *f*; **25.** Dehnweite *f*; **26.** Körperfülle *f*; **27.** (Bett- *etc.*)Decke *f*; **28.** Brotaufstrich *m*; **29.** F fürstliches Mahl; **30.** *typ.* Doppelseite *f*; **31.** † Stel'lagegeschäft *n*; **32.** † *Am.* Marge *f*, (Verdienst-)Spanne *f*, Differ'enz *f*; **IV** *adj.* **33.** verbreitet; ausgebreitet; **34.** gespreizt; **35.** Streich...: ~ ***cheese***.

spread| ea·gle *s.* **1.** *her.* Adler *m*; **2.** *Am.* F Chauvi'nismus *m*; **3.** *Eiskunstlauf*: Mond *m*; ˌ~-'**ea·gle I** *adj.* **1.** F angeberisch, bom'bastisch; **2.** F chauvi'nistisch; **II** *v/t.* **3.** ausbreiten, spreizen.

spread·er ['spredə] *s.* Streu- *od.* Spritzgerät *n*, *bsd.* a) ('Dünger)Streumaˌschine *f*, b) Abstandsstütze *f*, c) Zerstäuber *m*, d) Spritzdüse *f*, e) Buttermesser *n*.

spree [spriː] F *s.* (*Kauf- etc.*)Orgie *f*: ***go on a*** ~ a) ‚einen draufmachen', b) e-e ‚Sauftour' machen; ***go on a buying*** (*od.* ***shopping***, ***spending***) ~ wie verrückt einkaufen.

sprig [sprɪg] **I** *s.* **1.** Zweigchen *n*, Schößling *m*, Reis *n*; **2.** F Sprößling *m*, ‚Ableger' *m*; **3.** Bürschchen *n*; **4.** → ***spray***¹ 3; **5.** ⚙ Zwecke *f*, Stift *m*; **II** *v/t.* **6.** mit e-m Zweigmuster verzieren; **7.** anheften.

spright·li·ness ['spraɪtlɪnɪs] *s.* Lebhaftigkeit *f*, Munterkeit *f*; **spright·ly** ['spraɪtlɪ] *adj. u. adv.* lebhaft, munter, ‚spritzig'.

spring [sprɪŋ] **I** *v/i.* [*irr.*] **1.** springen: ~ ***at*** (*od.* [***up***]***on***) auf *j-n* losspringen, *j-n* anfallen; **2.** aufspringen; **3.** springen, schnellen, hüpfen: ~ ***open*** aufspringen (*Tür*); ***the trap sprang*** die Falle schnappte zu; **4.** *oft* ~ ***forth*** (*od.* ***out***) a) her'ausschießen, (-)sprudeln (*Wasser*, *Blut etc.*), b) (her'aus)sprühen, springen (*Funken etc.*); **5.** (***from***) entspringen (*dat.*): a) quellen (aus), b) *fig.* herkommen, abstammen (von): ***be sprung from*** entstanden sein aus; **6.** *mst* ~ ***up*** a) aufkommen (*Wind*), b) *fig.* plötzlich entstehen *od.* aufkommen (*Ideen*, *Industrie etc.*): ~ ***into existence***; ~ ***into fame*** plötzlich berühmt werden; **7.** aufschießen (*Pflanzen etc.*); **8.** (hoch) aufragen; **9.** auffliegen (*Rebhühner etc.*); **10.** ⚙ a) sich werfen, b) springen, platzen (*Holz*); **11.** ⚔ explodieren (*Mine*); **II** *v/t.* [*irr.*] **12.** *Falle* zuschnappen lassen, *et.* zu'rückschnellen lassen; **13.** *Riß etc.*, ⚓ *Leck* bekommen; **14.** explodieren lassen; → ***mine***² 8; **15.** mit *e-r Neuigkeit etc.* ‚her'ausplatzen': ~ ***s.th. on s.o.*** j-m et. plötzlich eröffnen; **16.** △ *Bogen* wölben; **17.** ⚙ (ab)federn; **18.** *Brit.* F *Geld etc.* springen lassen; **19.** *Brit.* F *j-n* erleichtern (***for*** um *Geld etc.*); **20.** *sl.* *j-n* ‚rausholen' (*befreien*); **III** *s.* **21.** Sprung *m*, Satz *m*; **22.** Frühling *m*, Lenz *m* (*beide a. fig.*); **23.** Elastizi'tät *f*, Sprung-, Schnellkraft *f*; **24.** *fig.* (geistige) Spannkraft; **25.** Sprung *m*, Riß *m im Holz etc.*; Krümmung *f e-s Bretts*; **26.** (*a. Mineral-*, *Öl*)Quelle *f*, Brunnen *m*: ***hot*** ~***s*** heiße Quellen; **27.** *fig.* Quelle *f*, Ursprung *m*; **28.** *fig.* Triebfeder *f*, Beweggrund *m*; **29.** △ a) (Bogen)Wölbung *f*, b) Gewölbeanfang *m*; **30.** ⚙ (*bsd.* Sprung)Feder *f*, Federung *f*; **IV** *adj.* **31.** Sprung..., Schwung...; **32.** Feder...; **33.** Frühlings...; ~ **bal·ance** *s.* ⚙ Federwaage *f*; ~ **bed** *s.* 'Sprungfedermaˌtratze *f*; '~**board** *s. sport* Sprungbrett *n* (*a. fig.*): ~ ***diving*** Kunstspringen *n*; '~**bok** [-bɒk] *pl.* **-boks**, *bsd. coll.* **-bok** *s. zo.* Springbock *m*; ~ **bows** [bəʊz] *s. pl.* ⚙ Federzirkel *m*; ~ **chick·en** *s.* Brathühnchen *n*: ***she is no*** ~ *fig.* F a) sie ist nicht mehr die jüngste, b) sie ist nicht von gestern; ˌ~-'**clean·ing** *s.* Frühjahrsputz *m*.

springe [sprɪndʒ] **I** *s.* **1.** *hunt.* Schlinge *f*; **2.** *fig.* Falle *f*; **II** *v/t.* **3.** *Tier* mit e-r Schlinge fangen.

spring·er ['sprɪŋə] *s.* **1.** *a.* ~ ***spaniel*** *hunt.* Springerspaniel *m*; **2.** △ (Bogen-)Kämpfer *m*.

spring| fe·ver *s.* **1.** Frühjahrsmüdigkeit *f*; **2.** (*rastlose*) Frühlingsgefühle *pl.*; ~ **gun** *s.* Selbstschuß *m*.

spring·i·ness ['sprɪŋɪnɪs] → ***spring*** 23.

spring·ing ['sprɪŋɪŋ] *s.* **1.** ⚙ Federung *f*; **2.** △ Kämpferlinie *f*.

spring| leaf *s.* ⚙ Federblatt *n*; ~ **lock** *s.* ⚙ Schnappschloß *n*; ~ **mat·tress** → ***spring bed***; ~ **sus·pen·sion** *s.* ⚙ federnde Aufhängung, Federung *f*; '~**·tide** → ***spring*** 22; ~ **tide** *s.* ⚓ Springflut *f*; *fig.* Flut *f*, Über'schwemmung *f*; '~**·time** → ***spring*** 22; ~ **wheat** *s.* ⚘ Sommerweizen *m*.

spring·y ['sprɪŋɪ] *adj.* □ **1.** federnd, e'lastisch; **2.** *fig.* schwungvoll.

sprin·kle ['sprɪŋkl] **I** *v/t.* **1.** *Wasser etc.* sprenkeln, (ver)sprengen (***on*** auf *acc.*); **2.** *Salz, Pulver etc.* sprenkeln, streuen; **3.** (ver-, zer)streuen, verteilen; **4.** *et.* besprenkeln, besprengen, bestreuen, (be)netzen (***with*** mit); **5.** *Stoff etc.* sprenkeln; **II** *v/i.* **6.** sprenkeln; **7.** (nieder)sprühen; **III** *s.* **8.** Sprühregen *m*; **9.** leichter Schneefall; **10.** Prise *f Salz etc.*; **11.** → ***sprinkling*** 2; '**sprin·kler** [-lə] *s.* **1.** a) 'Spreng-, Be'rieselungsappa,rat *m*: ~ ***system*** Sprinkler-, Beregnungsanlage *f*, b) Sprinkler *m*, Rasensprenger *m*, c) Brause *f*, Gießkannenkopf *m*, d) Sprinkler *m* (*e-r Feuerlöschanlage*), e) Sprengwagen *m*, f) Streuer *m*, Streudose *f*; **2.** *R.C.* Weihwasserwedel *m*; '**sprin·kling** [-lɪŋ] *s.* **1.** → ***sprinkle*** 8–10; **2.** *a.* ~ ***of*** *fig.* ein bißchen, etwas, e-e Spur, ein paar *Leute etc.*, ein wenig *Salz etc.*

sprint [sprɪnt] **I** *v/i.* **1.** rennen; **2.** *sport* sprinten (*Läufer*), *allg.* spurten; **II** *s.* **3.** *sport* a) Sprint *m*, Kurzstreckenlauf *m*, b) *allg.* Spurt *m* (*a. fig.*); c) *Pferde-, Radsport*: Fliegerrennen *n*; '**sprint·er** [-tə] *s.* *sport* **1.** Sprinter(in), *a. allg.* Spurter(in); **2.** *Radsport*: Flieger *m*.

sprit [sprɪt] *s.* ⚓ Spriet *n*.

sprite [spraɪt] *s.* **1.** Elfe *f*, Fee *f*; Kobold *m*; **2.** Geist *m*, Schemen *n*.

sprit·sail ['sprɪtsl] *s.* ⚓ Sprietsegel *n*.

sprock·et ['sprɒkɪt] *s.* ⚙ **1.** Zahn *m* e-s (Ketten)Rades; **2.** *a.* ~ ***wheel*** (Ketten-)Zahnrad *n*, Kettenrad *n*; **3.** 'Filmtrans,porttrommel *f*.

sprout [spraʊt] **I** *v/i.* **1.** *a.* ~ ***up*** sprießen, (auf)schießen, aufgehen; **2.** keimen; **3.** schnell wachsen, sich schnell entwikkeln; in die Höhe schießen (*Person*); wie Pilze aus dem Boden schießen (*Gebäude etc.*); **II** *v/t.* **4.** (her'vor)treiben, wachsen *od.* keimen lassen, entwikkeln; **III** *s.* **5.** Sproß *m*, Sprößling *m* (*a. fig.*), Schößling *m*; **6.** *pl.* → ***Brussels sprouts***.

spruce¹ [spru:s] *s.* ⚘ **1.** *a.* ~ ***fir*** Fichte *f*, Rottanne *f*; **2.** Fichte(nholz *n*) *f*.

spruce² [spru:s] **I** *adj.* □ **1.** schmuck, (blitz)sauber, a'drett; **2.** geschniegelt; **II** *v/t.* **3.** *oft* ~ ***up*** *j-n* feinmachen, (her'aus)putzen: ~ ***o.s. up*** → 4; **III** *v/i.* **4.** *oft* ~ ***up*** sich feinmachen, sich ‚in Schale werfen'; '**spruce·ness** [-nɪs] *s.* A'drettheit *f*; *contp.* Affigkeit *f*.

sprung [sprʌŋ] **I** *pret. u. p.p. von* ***spring***; **II** *adj.* **1.** ⚙ gefedert; **2.** rissig (*Holz*).

spry [spraɪ] *adj.* **1.** flink, hurtig; **2.** lebhaft, munter.

spud [spʌd] **I** *s.* **1.** ⚘ a) Jätmesser *n*, Reutspaten *m*, b) Stoßeisen *n*; **2.** Spachtel *m, f*; **3.** F Kar'toffel *f*; **II** *v/t.* **4.** *mst* ~ ***up***, ~ ***out*** ausgraben, -jäten; **5.** *Ölquelle* anbohren.

spue [spju:] → ***spew***.

spume [spju:m] *s.* Schaum *m*, Gischt *m, f*; '**spu·mous** [-məs], '**spu·my** [-mɪ] *adj.* schäumend.

spun [spʌn] **I** *pret. u. p.p. von* ***spin***; **II** *adj.* gesponnen: ~ ***glass*** Glasgespinst *n*; ~ ***gold*** Goldgespinst *n*; ~ ***silk*** Schappseide *f*.

spunk [spʌŋk] *s.* **1.** Zunderholz *n*; **2.** Zunder *m*, Lunte *f*; **3.** F a) Feuer *n*, Schwung *m*, b) ‚Mumm' *m*, Mut *m*; '**spunk·y** [-kɪ] *adj.* **1.** schwungvoll; **2.** mutig, draufgängerisch; **3.** *Am.* reizbar.

spur [spɜ:] **I** *s.* **1.** (Reit)Sporn *m*: ~***s to*** → 8; ***win one's*** ~***s*** *fig.* sich die Sporen verdienen; **2.** *fig.* Ansporn *m*, -reiz *m*: ***on the*** ~ ***of the moment*** der Eingebung des Augenblicks folgend, ohne Überlegung, spontan; **3.** ⚘ a) Dorn *m*, Stachel *m* (*kurzer Zweig etc.*), b) Sporn *m* (*Nektarbehälter*); **4.** *zo.* Sporn *m*, Stachel *m* (*des Hahns*); **5.** *geogr.* Ausläufer *m*, (Gebirgs)Vorsprung *m*; **6.** △ a) Strebe *f*, Stütze *f*, b) Strebebalken *m*, c) (Mauer)Vorsprung *m*; **7.** ⚔ *hist.* Außen-, Vorwerk *n*; **II** *v/t.* **8.** *Pferd* spornen, die Sporen geben (*dat.*); **9.** *oft* ~ ***on*** *fig. j-n* anspornen, -stacheln: ~ ***s.o. into action***; **10.** mit Sporen versehen, Sporen (an)schnallen an (*acc.*); **III** *v/i.* **11.** (das Pferd) spornen; **12.** a) sprengen, eilen, b) *fig.* (vorwärts)drängen.

spurge [spɜ:dʒ] *s.* ⚘ Wolfsmilch *f*.

spur| gear *s.* ⚙ **1.** Geradstirnrad *n*; **2.** → ~ **gear·ing** *s.* Geradstirnradgetriebe *n*.

spu·ri·ous ['spjʊərɪəs] *adj.* □ **1.** falsch, unecht, Pseudo..., *a.* ⚘, *zo.* Schein...: ~ ***fruit***; **2.** nachgemacht, gefälscht; **3.** unehelich; '**spu·ri·ous·ness** [-nɪs] *s.* Unechtheit *f*.

spurn [spɜ:n] *v/t.* **1.** *obs.* mit dem Fuß (weg)stoßen; **2.** verschmähen, verächtlich zu'rückweisen, *j-n a.* abweisen.

spurred [spɜ:d] *adj.* gespornt; *a.* ⚘, *zo.* sporentragend.

spurt¹ [spɜ:t] **I** *s.* **1.** *sport* (*a.* Zwischen-)Spurt *m*; **2.** plötzliche Aktivi'tät, ruckartige Anstrengung; **3.** † plötzliches Anziehen (*von Preisen etc.*); **II** *v/i.* **4.** *sport* spurten; **5.** plötzlich ak'tiv werden.

spurt² [spɜ:t] **I** *v/t. u. v/i.* (her'aus)spritzen; **II** *s.* (*Wasser- etc.*)Strahl *m*.

spur| track *s.* 🚂 Neben-, Seitengleis *n*; ~ **wheel** → ***spur gear*** 1.

sput·ter ['spʌtə] → ***splutter***.

spu·tum ['spju:təm] *pl.* **-ta** [-tə] *s.* ⚕ Sputum *n*, Auswurf *m*.

spy [spaɪ] **I** *v/t.* **1.** *a.* ~ ***out*** ausspionieren, -spähen, -kundschaften: ~ ***out*** *a.* herausfinden; ~ ***the land*** *fig.* ‚die Lage peilen'; **2.** erspähen, entdecken; **II** *v/i.* **3.** ⚔ *etc.* spionieren, Spio'nage treiben: ~ (***up***)***on*** *j-m* nachspionieren, *j-n* bespitzeln, *Gespräch etc.* abhören; **4.** her'umspionieren; **III** *s.* **5.** Späher(in), Kundschafter(in); **6.** ⚔, *pol.* Spi'on(in) (*a. fig. Spitzel*); '~**·glass** *s.* Fernglas *n*; '~**·hole** *s.* Guckloch *n*; ~ **ring** *s.* Spio'nagering *m*; ~ **sat·el·lite** *s.* ⚔ ,'Himmelsspi,on' *m*.

squab·ble ['skwɒbl] **I** *v/i.* sich zanken *od.* kabbeln; **II** *v/t. typ.* verquirlen; **III** *s.* Zank *m*, Kabbe'lei *f*; '**squab·bler** [-lə] *s.* ‚Streithammel' *m*.

squab·by ['skwɒbɪ] *adj.* unter'setzt, feist, plump.

squad [skwɒd] *s.* **1.** ⚔ Gruppe *f*, Korpo'ralschaft *f*: ***awkward*** ~ a) ‚patschnasse' Re'kruten, b) *fig.* ‚Flaschenverein' *m*; **2.** (Arbeits- *etc.*)Trupp *m*; **3.** *Polizei*: a) ('Überfall- *etc.*)Kom,mando *n*, b) ('Raub- *etc.*)Dezer,nat *n*; → ***murder squad*** *etc.*; ~ ***car*** *Am.* (Funk)Streifenwagen *m*; **4.** *sport* Riege *f*, Kader *m*.

squad·ron ['skwɒdrən] *s.* **1.** ⚔ a) ('Reiter)Schwa,dron *f*, b) ('Panzer)Batail,lon *n*; **2.** ⚓, ⚔ (Flotten)Geschwader *n*; **3.** ✈ Staffel *f*; **4.** *allg.* Gruppe *f*, Ab'teilung *f*, Mannschaft *f*; ~ **lead·er** *s.* ('Flieger)Ma,jor *m*.

squail [skweɪl] *s.* **1.** *pl. sg. konstr.* Flohhüpfen *n*; **2.** Spielplättchen *n*.

squal·id ['skwɒlɪd] *adj.* □ schmutzig, verkommen (*beide a. fig.*), verwahrlost; **squa·lid·i·ty** [skwɒ'lɪdətɪ], '**squal·id·ness** [-nɪs] *s.* Schmutz *m*, Verkommenheit *f* (*beide a. fig.*), Verwahrlosung *f*.

squall¹ [skwɔ:l] **I** *s.* **1.** *meteor.* Bö *f*, heftiger Windstoß: ***white*** ~ Sturmbö aus heiterem Himmel; **2.** F ‚Sturm' *m*, ‚Gewitter' *n*: ***look out for*** ~***s*** die Augen offen halten, auf der Hut sein; **II** *v/i.* **3.** stürmen.

squall² [skwɔ:l] **I** *v/i.* kreischen, schreien (*a. Kind*); **II** *v/t.* *oft* ~ ***out*** *et.* kreischen; **III** *s.* schriller Schrei: ~***s*** Geschrei *n*; '**squall·er** [-lə] *s.* Schreihals *m*.

squall·y ['skwɔ:lɪ] *adj.* böig, stürmisch (*a.* F *fig.*).

squal·or ['skwɒlə] → ***squalidity***.

squa·ma ['skweɪmə] *pl.* **-mae** [-mi:] *s.* ⚘, *anat., zo.* Schuppe *f*, schuppenartige Or'ganbildung; '**squa·mate** [-meɪt], '**squa·mous** [-məs] *adj.* schuppig.

squan·der ['skwɒndə] *v/t.* *oft* ~ ***away*** *Geld, Zeit etc.* verschwenden, -geuden: ~ ***o.s.*** *od.* ***one's energies*** sich verzetteln *od.* ‚verplempern'; '**squan·der·er** [-dərə] *s.* Verschwender(in); '**squan·der·ing** [-dərɪŋ] **I** *adj.* □ verschwenderisch; **II** *s.* Verschwendung *f*, -geudung *f*.

squan·der·ma·ni·a [,skwɒndə'meɪnjə] *s.* Verschwendungssucht *f*.

square [skweə] **I** *s.* **1.** & Qua'drat *n* (*Figur*); **2.** Qua'drat *n*, Viereck *n*, qua'dratisches Stück (*Glas, Stoff etc.*), Karo *n*; **3.** Feld *n* (*Schachbrett etc.*): ***be back to*** ~ ***one*** *fig.* wieder da sein, wo man angefangen hat; **4.** Häuserblock *m*; **5.** (öffentlicher) Platz; **6.** ⚙ a) Winkel(maß *n*) *m*, b) *bsd. Zimmerei*: Geviert *n*: ***on the*** ~ a) rechtwink(e)lig, b) F ehrlich, anständig, in Ordnung; ***out of*** ~ a) nicht rechtwink(e)lig, b) *fig.* nicht in Ordnung; **7.** & Qua'drat(zahl *f*) *n*: ***in the*** ~ im Quadrat; **8.** ⚔ *hist.* Kar'ree *n*; **9.** ('Wort-, 'Zahlen)Qua,drat *n*; **10.** △ Säulenplatte *f*; **11.** *sl.* Spießer *m*; **II** *v/t.* **12.** rechtwink(e)lig *od.* qua'dratisch machen; **13.** *a.* ~ ***off*** in Qua'drate einteilen, *Papier etc.* karieren:

~d paper Millimeterpapier *n*; **14.** auf s-e Abweichung vom rechten Winkel prüfen; **15.** A a) den Flächeninhalt berechnen von (*od. gen.*), b) *Zahl* quadrieren, ins Qua'drat erheben, c) *Figur* quadrieren; → ***circle*** 1; **16.** ⚙ vierkantig behauen; **17.** *Schultern* straffen; **18.** *fig.* in Einklang bringen (***with*** mit), anpassen (***to*** an *acc.*); **19.** (*a.* † *Konten*) ausgleichen; → ***account*** 5; **20.** *Schuld* begleichen; **21.** *Gläubiger* befriedigen; **22.** *sl. j-n* ‚schmieren', bestechen; **23.** *sport Kampf* unentschieden beenden; **III** *v/i.* **24.** ~ ***up*** (*Am. a.* ***off***) in Boxerstellung *od.* in Auslage gehen: ~ ***up to*** sich vor *j-m* aufpflanzen, *fig. Problem* anpacken; **25.** (***with***) über'einstimmen (mit), passen (zu); **26.** ~ ***up*** † *u. fig.* abrechnen (***with*** mit); **IV** *adj.* □ **27.** A qua'dratisch, Quadrat…(*-meile, -wurzel, -zahl etc.*); **28.** im Qua'drat: ***2 feet*** ~; **29.** rechtwink(e)lig, im rechten Winkel (stehend) (***to*** zu); **30.** (vier)eckig; **31.** ⚙ Vierkant…; **32.** gerade, gleichmäßig; **33.** breit(schulterig), stämmig, vierschrötig; **34.** *fig.* in Einklang (stehend) (***with*** mit), stimmend, in Ordnung: ***get things*** ~ die Sache in Ordnung bringen; **35.** † abgeglichen (*Konten*): ***get*** ~ ***with*** mit *j-m* quitt werden (*a. fig.*); **36.** F a) re'ell, anständig, b) offen, ehrlich: ~ ***deal*** a) reeller Handel, b) anständige Behandlung; **37.** klar, deutlich: ***a*** ~ ***refusal***; **38.** F ordentlich, reichlich: ***a*** ~ ***meal***; **39.** *sl.* ‚spießig'; **40.** zu viert: ~ ***game***; **V** *adv.* **41.** qua'dratisch, viereckig; rechtwink(e)lig; **42.** F anständig, ehrlich; **43.** *Am.* di'rekt, gerade; ˌ~-'**built** → ***square*** 33; ~ **dance** *s. Am.* Square dance *m*; '~**-head** *s. contp.* ‚Qua'dratschädel' *m* (*Skandinavier od. Deutscher in U.S.A. od. Kanada*); ~ **meas·ure** *s.* Flächenmaß *n.*

square·ness ['skweənɪs] *s.* **1.** *das* Qua'dratische *od.* Viereckige; **2.** Vierschrötigkeit *f*; **3.** F Ehrlichkeit *f*; **4.** *sl.* ‚Spießigkeit' *f.*

ˌ**square**|-'**rigged** *adj.* ⚓ mit Rahen getakelt; '~-ˌ**rig·ger** *s.* ⚓ Rahsegler *m*; ~ **root** *s.* A (Qua'drat)Wurzel *f*; ~ **sail** *s.* ⚓ Rahsegel *n*; ~ **shoot·er** *s. Am.* F ehrlicher *od.* anständiger Kerl; ˌ~-'**shoul·dered** *adj.* breitschultrig; ˌ~-'**toed** *adj. fig.* a) altmodisch, b) steif.

squash [skwɒʃ] **I** *v/t.* **1.** (zu Brei) zerquetschen, zs.-drücken; breitschlagen; **2.** *fig. Aufruhr etc.* niederschlagen, im Keim ersticken; **3.** F *j-n* ‚fertigmachen'; **II** *v/i.* **4.** zerquetscht werden; **5.** glucksen (*Schuhe im Morast etc.*); **III** *s.* **6.** Matsch *m*, Brei *m*; **7.** Gedränge *n*; **8.** ⚘ Kürbis *m*; **9.** (Zi'tronen- *etc.*)Saft *m*; **10.** Glucksen *n*, Platsch(en *n*) *m*; **11.** *sport* a) *a.* ~ ***tennis*** Squash *n*, b) *a.* ~ ***rackets*** *ein dem Squash ähnliches Spiel*; '**squash·y** [-ʃɪ] *adj.* □ **1.** weich, breiig; **2.** matschig (*Boden*).

squat [skwɒt] **I** *v/t.* **1.** hocken, kauern: ~ ***down*** sich hinhocken; **2.** sich ducken (*Tier*); **3.** F ‚hocken' (*sitzen*); **4.** sich ohne Rechtstitel ansiedeln; **II** *v/t.* **5.** *leerstehendes Haus* besetzen; **III** *adj.* **6.** unter'setzt, vierschrötig (*Person*); **7.** flach, platt; **IV** *s.* **8.** Hockstellung *f*, Hocke *f* (*a. sport*); **9.** Sitz *m*, Platz *m*; '**squat·ter** [-tə] *s.* **1.** Hockende(r *m*) *f*; **2.** Hausbesetzer *m*; **3.** Squatter *m*, Ansiedler *m* ohne Rechtstitel; **4.** Siedler *m* auf regierungseigenem Land; **5.** *Austral.* Schafzüchter *m.*

squaw [skwɔː] *s.* **1.** Squaw *f*, Indi'anerfrau *f*; **2.** *Am.* F (Ehe)Frau *f.*

squawk [skwɔːk] **I** *v/i.* **1.** *bsd. orn.* kreischen; **2.** *fig.* F zetern, aufbegehren; **II** *s.* **3.** *bsd. orn.* Kreischen *n*; **4.** F Gezeter *n.*

squeak [skwiːk] **I** *v/i.* **1.** quiek(s)en, piep(s)en; **2.** quietschen (*Bremsen, Türangel etc.*); **3.** *sl.* → ***squeal*** 5; **II** *v/t.* **4.** *et.* quiek(s)en; **III** *s.* **5.** Gequiek(s)e *n*, Piep(s)en *n*; **6.** Quietschen *n*; **7.** ***have a narrow*** (*od.* ***close***) ~ F mit knapper Not davonkommen; '**squeak·y** [-kɪ] *adj.* □ **1.** quiek(s)end; **2.** quietschend.

squeal [skwiːl] **I** *v/i.* **1.** kreischen, (auf-)schreien; **2.** quietschen (*Bremsen etc.*); **3.** quieken, piepsen; **4.** F zetern, schimpfen (***about, against*** gegen); **5.** *sl.* ‚pfeifen', ‚singen' (*verraten*): ~ ***on s.o.*** j-n verpetzen *od.* ‚verpfeifen' (***to*** bei); **II** *v/t.* **6.** *et.* schreien, kreischen; **III** *s.* **7.** schriller Schrei; **8.** Kreischen *n*, Quieken *n*; **9.** F *fig.* Aufschrei *m*; '**squeal·er** [-lə] *s.* **1.** Schreier *m*; **2.** Täubchen *n*, *allg.* junger Vogel; **3.** *sl.* Verräter *m.*

squeam·ish ['skwiːmɪʃ] *adj.* □ **1.** ('über)empfindlich, zimperlich; **2.** a) heikel (*im Essen*), b) (leicht) Ekel empfindend; **3.** 'übergewissenhaft, pe'nibel; '**squeam·ish·ness** [-nɪs] **1.** 'Überempfindlichkeit *f*, Zimperlichkeit *f*; **2.** 'Übergewissenhaftigkeit *f*; **3.** a) heikle Art, b) Ekel *m*, Übelkeit *f.*

squee·gee [ˌskwiː'dʒiː] *s.* **1.** Gummischrubber *m*; **2.** *phot. etc.* (Gummi-)Quetschwalze *f.*

squeez·a·ble ['skwiːzəbl] *adj.* **1.** zs.-drückbar; **2.** *fig.* gefügig; '**squeeze** [skwiːz] **I** *v/t.* **1.** (zs.-)drücken; **2.** a) *Frucht* auspressen, -quetschen, *Schwamm* ausdrücken, b) F *j-n* ‚ausnehmen', ‚schröpfen'; **3.** *oft* ~ ***out*** *Saft etc.* (her)'auspressen, -quetschen (***from*** aus): ~ ***a tear*** *fig.* e-e Träne zerdrükken, ein paar Krokodilstränen weinen; **4.** drücken, quetschen, zwängen (***into*** in *acc.*); eng (zs.-)packen: ~ ***o.s.*** (*od.* ***one's way***) ***into*** (***through***) sich hinein- (hindurch)zwängen; **5.** F fest *od.* innig an sich drücken; **6.** F a) unter Druck setzen, erpressen, b) *Geld etc.* her'auspressen, *Vorteil etc.* her'ausschinden (***out of*** aus); **7.** e-n Abdruck machen von (*e-r Münze etc.*); **II** *v/i.* **8.** quetschen, drücken, pressen; **9.** sich zwängen: ~ ***through*** (***in***) sich durch- (hinein)zwängen; **III** *s.* **10.** Druck *m*, Pressen *n*, Quetschen *n*; **11.** Händedruck *m*; **12.** (innige) Um'armung; **13.** Gedränge *n*; **14.** F a) Klemme *f*, *bsd.* Geldverlegenheit *f*, b) ‚Druck' *m*, Erpressung *f*: ***put the*** ~ ***on s.o.*** j-n unter Druck setzen; **15.** † wirtschaftlicher Engpaß, (*a.* Geld)Knappheit *f*; **16.** (*bsd.* Wachs)Abdruck *m*; **squeeze bot·tle** *s.* (Plastik)Spritzflasche *f*; **squeeze box** *s.* ♪ F ‚Quetschkomˌmode' *f*; '**squeez·er** [-zə] *s.* **1.** (Frucht-)Presse *f*; **2.** ⚙ a) ('Aus)Preßmaˌschine *f*, b) Quetschwerk *n*, c) 'Preßformmaˌschine *f.*

squelch [skweltʃ] **I** *v/t.* **1.** zermalmen; **2.** *fig.* F *j-n* ‚kurz fertigmachen', *j-m* den Mund stopfen, *Kritik etc.* abwürgen; **II** *v/i.* **3.** p(l)atschen; **4.** glucksen (*nasser Schuh etc.*); **III** *s.* **5.** Matsch *m*; **6.** P(l)atschen *n*, Glucksen *n*; **7.** → '**squelch·er** [-tʃə] *s.* F **1.** vernichtender Schlag; **2.** vernichtende Antwort.

squib [skwɪb] *s.* **1.** a) Frosch *m*, (Feuerwerks)Schwärmer *m*, b) *Brit. allg.* (Hand)Feuerwerkskörper *m*: ***damp*** ~ *fig.* ‚Flop' *m*, Schlag *m* ins Wasser; **2.** ⚒, *a.* ⚔ *hist.* Zündladung *f*; **3.** Spottgedicht *n*, Sa'tire *f.*

squid [skwɪd] *pl.* **squids**, *bsd. coll.* **squid** *s.* **1.** *zo. ein* zehnarmiger Tintenfisch; **2.** *künstlicher Köder in Tintenfischform.*

squif·fy ['skwɪfɪ] *adj. sl.* beschwipst.

squig·gle ['skwɪgl] **I** *s.* **1.** Schnörkel *m*; **II** *v/i.* **2.** kritzeln; **3.** sich winden.

squill [skwɪl] *s.* **1.** ⚘ a) Meerzwiebel *f*, b) Blaustern *m*; **2.** *zo.* Heuschreckenkrebs *m.*

squint [skwɪnt] **I** *v/i.* **1.** schielen (*a. weitS.*); **2.** ~ ***at*** a) schielen nach, b) e-n Blick werfen auf (*acc.*), c) scheel *od.* argwöhnisch blicken auf (*acc.*); **3.** blinzeln, zwinkern; **II** *v/t.* **4.** *Augen* a) verdrehen, b) zs.-kneifen; **III** *s.* **5.** Schielen *n* (*a. fig.*): ***have a*** ~ schielen; **6.** F (rascher *od.* verstohlener) Blick: ***have a*** ~ ***at*** → 2b; **IV** *adj.* **7.** schielend; **8.** schief, schräg; '~**-eyed** *adj.* **1.** schielend; **2.** *fig.* scheel, böse.

squir·arch·y ['skwaɪərɑːkɪ] *s.* → ***squirearchy.***

squire ['skwaɪə] **I** *s.* **1.** *englischer* Landjunker, *a.* Gutsherr *m*, Großgrundbesitzer *m*; **2.** *bsd.* F (*a. Am.*) a) (Friedens)Richter *m*, b) *andere Person mit lokaler Obrigkeitswürde*; **3.** *hist.* Edelknabe *m*, (Schild)Knappe *m*; **4.** Kava'lier *m*: a) Begleiter *m* (*e-r Dame*), b) Ga'lan *m*: ~ ***of dames*** Frauenheld *m*; **II** *v/t. u. v/i.* **5.** *obs.* a) (e-e Dame) begleiten, b) (e-r Dame) Ritterdienste leisten *od.* den Hof machen; '**squire·arch·y** [-ərɑːkɪ] *s.* Junkertum *n*: a) *coll. die* (Land)Junker *pl.*, b) (Land-)Junkerherrschaft *f*; '**squire·ling** [-əlɪŋ] *s. contp.* Krautjunker *m.*

squirm [skwɜːm] **I** *v/i.* **1.** sich krümmen, sich winden (*a. fig.* ***with*** vor *Scham etc.*): ~ ***out of*** a) sich (mühsam) aus *e-m Kleid* ‚herausschälen', b) *fig.* sich aus *e-r Notlage etc.* (heraus)winden; **II** *s.* **2.** Krümmen *n*, Sich'winden *n*; **3.** ⚓ Kink *m im Tau*; '**squirm·y** [-mɪ] *adj.* **1.** sich windend; **2.** *fig.* eklig.

squir·rel ['skwɪrəl] *s.* **1.** *zo.* Eichhörnchen *n*: ***flying*** ~ Flughörnchen *n*; **2.** Feh *n* (*Pelzwerk*); ~ **cage** *s.* **1.** a) Laufradkäfig *m*, b) *fig.* ‚Tretmühle' *f*; **2.** ⚡ Käfiganker *m*; '~**-cage** *adj.* ⚡ Käfig…, Kurzschluß…

squirt [skwɜːt] **I** *v/i.* **1.** spritzen; **2.** her'vorspritzen, -sprudeln; **II** *v/t.* **3.** *Flüssigkeit etc.* her'vor-, her'ausspritzen; **4.** bespritzen; **III** *s.* **5.** (Wasser- *etc.*)Strahl *m*; **6.** Spritze *f*: ~ ***can*** ⚙ Spritzkanne *f*; **7.** *a.* ~ ***gun*** 'Wasserpiˌstole *f*; **8.** F ‚kleiner Scheißer'.

squish [skwɪʃ] F **I** *v/t.* zermatschen; **II** *v/i.* → ***squelch*** 4.

stab [stæb] **I** *v/t.* **1.** *j-n* a) (nieder)stechen, b) erstechen, erdolchen; **2.** *Mes-*

ser etc. bohren, stoßen (***into*** in *acc.*); **3.** *fig.* verletzen: **~ *s.o. in the back*** j-m in den Rücken fallen; **~ *s.o.'s reputation*** an j-m Rufmord begehen; **4.** ⚙ *Mauer* rauh hauen; **II** *v/i.* **5.** stechen (***at*** nach); **6.** *mit den Fingern etc.* stoßen (***at*** nach, auf *acc.*); **7.** stechen (*Schmerz*); **III** *s.* **8.** (Dolch- *etc.*)Stoß *m*, Stich *m*: **~ *in the back*** *fig.* Dolchstoß; ***have*** (*od.* ***make***) ***a ~ at*** F *et.* probieren; **9.** Stich (-wunde *f*) *m*; **10.** *fig.* Stich *m* (*Schmerz, jähes Gefühl*); **~ cell** *s. biol.* Stabzelle *f.*

sta·bil·i·ty [stəˈbɪlətɪ] *s.* **1.** Stabiliˈtät *f*: a) Standfestigkeit *f*, b) (Wert)Beständigkeit *f*, Festigkeit *f*, Haltbarkeit *f*, c) Unveränderlichkeit *f* (*a.* ⚗), d) ⚗ Resiˈstenz *f*: ***monetary*** **~** ☤ Währungsstabilität; **2.** *fig.* Beständigkeit *f*, Standhaftigkeit *f*, (Chaˈrakter)Festigkeit *f*; **3.** a) ⚙ Kippsicherheit *f*, b) ✈ dyˈnamisches Gleichgewicht, c) **~ *on curves*** *mot.* Kurvenstabilität *f.*

sta·bi·li·za·tion [ˌsteɪbɪlaɪˈzeɪʃn] *s. allg., bsd.* ⚙, ☤ Stabilisierung *f*; **sta·bi·lize** [ˈsteɪbɪlaɪz] *v/t.* stabilisieren (*a.* ⚙, ⚓, ✈): a) festigen, stützen, b) konˈstant halten: **~*d warfare*** ⚔ Stellungskrieg *m*; **sta·bi·liz·er** [ˈsteɪbɪlaɪzə] *s.* ⚙, ✈, ⚓, ⚗ Stabiliˈsator *m.*

sta·ble¹ [ˈsteɪbl] *adj.* □ **1.** staˈbil (*a.* ☤): a) standfest, -sicher (*a.* ⚙), b) (wert-) beständig, fest, dauerhaft, haltbar, c) unveränderlich (*a.* ⚗), d) ⚗ resiˈstent; **2.** ☤, *pol.* staˈbil: **~ *currency***; **3.** *fig.* beständig, (*a.* chaˈrakterlich) gefestigt.

sta·ble² [ˈsteɪbl] **I** *s.* **1.** (Pferde-, Kuh-) Stall *m*; **2.** Stall(bestand) *m*; **3.** Rennstall *m* (*bsd. coll. Pferde, a. Rennfahrer*); **4.** *fig.* ‚Stall' *m* (*Mannschaft etc., a. Familie*); **5.** *pl.* ⚔ *Brit.* a) Stalldienst *m*, b) → ***stable call***; **II** *v/t.* **6.** *Pferd* einstallen; **III** *v/i.* **7.** im Stall stehen (*Pferd*); **8.** *fig.* hausen; **ˈ~·boy** *s.* Stalljunge *m*; **~ call** *s.* ⚔ Siˈgnal *n* zum Stalldienst; **~ com·pan·ion** → ***stablemate***; **ˈ~·man** [-mən] *s.* [*irr.*] Stallknecht *m*; **ˈ~·mate** *s.* Stallgefährte *m* (*a. fig. Radsport etc.*).

sta·ble·ness [ˈsteɪblnɪs] → ***stability***.

sta·bling [ˈsteɪblɪŋ] *s.* **1.** Einstallung *f*; **2.** Stallung(en *pl.*) *f*, Ställe *pl.*

stac·ca·to [stəˈkɑːtəʊ] (*Ital.*) *adv.* **1.** ♪ stakˈkato; **2.** *fig.* abgehackt.

stack [stæk] **I** *s.* **1.** Schober *m*, Feim *m*; **2.** Stoß *m*, Stapel *m* (*Holz, Bücher etc.*); **3.** *Brit. Maßeinheit für Holz u. Kohlen* (*3,05814 m³*); **4.** *Am.* (ˈBücher-) Reˌgal *n*; *pl.* ˈHauptmagaˌzin *n e-r Bibliothek*; **5.** ⚔ (Geˈwehr)Pyraˌmide *f*; **6.** a) *bsd.* 🚂, ⚓ Schornstein *m*, Kaˈmin *m*, b) (Schmiede)Esse *f*, c) *mot.* Auspuffrohr *n*, d) Aggreˈgat *n*, Satz *m*, e) (gestockte) Anˈtennenkombinatiˌon, f) *Computer*: Stapelspeicher *m*: ***blow one's ~*** F ‚in die Luft gehen'; **7.** Felssäule *f*; **II** *v/t.* **8.** *Heu etc.* aufschobern; **9.** aufschichten, -stapeln; **10.** *et.* ˈvollstapeln; **11.** ⚔ *Gewehre* zs.-setzen: **~ *arms***; **12.** **~ *the cards*** die Karten ‚packen' (*um zu betrügen*): ***the cards are ~ed against him*** *fig.* er hat kaum e-e Chance; **ˈstack·er** [-kə] *s.* Stapler *m* (*Person u. Gerät*).

sta·di·a¹ [ˈsteɪdjə] *pl. von* ***stadium***.

sta·di·a² [ˈsteɪdjə] *s. a.* **~ *rod*** *surv.* Meßlatte *f.*

sta·di·um [ˈsteɪdjəm] *pl.* **-di·a** [-djə] *s.* **1.** *antiq.* Stadion *n* (*Kampfbahn u. Längenmaß*); **2.** *pl. mst* **ˈsta·di·ums** *sport* Stadion *n*; **3.** *bsd.* ⚕, *biol.* Stadium *n.*

staff¹ [stɑːf] **I** *s.* **1.** Stock *m*, Stecken *m*; **2.** (*a.* Amts-, Bischofs-, Komˈmando-, Meß-, Wander)Stab *m*; **3.** (Fahnen-) Stange *f*, ⚓ Flaggenstock *m*; **4.** *fig.* a) Stütze *f des Alters etc.*, b) *das* Nötige *od.* Wichtigste: **~ *of life*** Brot *n*, Nahrung *f*; **5.** Unruhewelle *f* (*Uhr*); **6.** a) (Assiˈstenten-, Mitarbeiter)Stab *m*, b) Beamtenkörper *m*, -stab *m*, c) Lehrkörper *m*, ˈLehrerkolˌlegium *n*, d) Persoˈnal *n*, Belegschaft *f*: ***editorial*** **~** Redaktion(sstab *m*) *f*; ***nursing*** **~** ⚕ Pflegepersonal; ***the senior*** **~** ☤ die leitenden Angestellten; ***be on the*** **~** (***of***) zum Stab *od.* Lehrkörper *od.* Personal gehören (*gen.*), Mitarbeiter sein (bei), fest angestellt sein (bei); **7.** ⚔ Stab *m*: **~ *order*** Stabsbefehl *m*; **8.** *pl.* **staves** [steɪvz] ♪ ˈNoten(linien)syˌstem *n*; **II** *adj.* **9.** *bsd.* ⚔ Stabs…; **10.** Personal…; **III** *v/t.* **11.** (mit Persoˈnal) besetzen: ***well ~ed*** gut besetzt; **12.** mit e-m Stab *od.* Lehrkörper *etc.* versehen; **13.** den Lehrkörper *e-r Schule* bilden.

staff² [stɑːf] *s.* ⚙ *Baustoff aus Gips u.* (*Hanf*)*Fasern.*

staff| car *s.* ⚔ Befehlsfahrzeug *n*; **~ col·lege** *s.* ⚔ Geneˈralstabsakadeˌmie *f*; **~ man·a·ger** *s.* ☤ Persoˈnalchef *m*; **~ mem·ber** *s.* Mitarbeiter(in); **~ no·ta·tion** *s.* ♪ Liniennotenschrift *f*; **~ of·fi·cer** *s.* ⚔ ˈStabsoffiˌzier *m*; **~ re·duc·tions** *pl.* ☤ Persoˈnalabbau *m*; **~ room** *s. ped.* Lehrerzimmer *n*; **~ ser·geant** *s.* ⚔ (*Brit.* Ober)Feldwebel *m.*

stag [stæg] **I** *s.* **1.** *hunt., zo.* a) Rothirsch *m*, b) Hirsch *m*; **2.** *zo. bsd. dial.* Männchen *n*; **3.** *nach der Reife kastriertes männliches Tier*; **4.** F a) ‚Unbeweibte(r)' *m*, Herr *m* ohne Damenbegleitung, b) *bsd. Am.* → ***stag party***; **5.** ☤ *Brit.* Konˈzertzeichner *m*; **II** *adj.* **6.** F a) Herren…: **~ *dinner***, b) Sex…: **~ *film***; **III** *v/i.* **7.** ☤ *Brit. sl.* in neu ausgegebenen Aktien spekulieren; **8.** *a.* ***go*** **~** F ohne Damenbegleitung *od.* ‚solo' gehen; **~ bee·tle** *s. zo.* Hirschkäfer *m.*

stage [steɪdʒ] **I** *s.* **1.** Bühne *f*, Gerüst *n*; ⚓ Landungsbrücke *f*; **2.** *thea.* Bühne *f* (*a. fig. Theaterwelt, Bühnenlaufbahn*): ***the ~*** *fig.* die Bühne, das Theater; ***be on the ~*** Schauspieler(in) *od.* beim Theater sein; ***bring on the ~*** → 11a; ***go on the ~*** zur Bühne gehen; ***hold the ~*** sich auf der Bühne halten; ***set the ~ for*** *fig.* alles vorbereiten für; **3.** *hist.* a) (ˈPost)Statiˌon *f*, b) Postkutsche *f*; **4.** a) *Brit.* Teilstrecke *f*, Fahrzone *f* (*Bus etc.*), b) (Reise)Abschnitt *m*, Eˈtappe *f* (*a. fig. u. Radsport*): ***by*** (*od.* ***in***) (***easy***) **~*s*** etappenweise; **5.** ⚕, ☤, *biol. etc.* Stadium *n*, (Entwicklungs)Stufe *f*, Phase *f*: ***at this ~*** zum gegenwärtigen Zeitpunkt; ***critical*** (***experimental***, ***initial***) **~** kritisches (Versuchs-, Anfangs-) Stadium; **~*s of appeal*** ⚖ Instanzenweg *m*; **6.** ⚙ (Schalt- *etc.*, ⚡ Verstärker-, *a.* Raˈketen)Stufe *f*; **7.** *geol.* Stufe *f e-r Formation*; **8.** Obˈjektträger *m* (*am Mikroskop*); **9.** ⚙ Farbläufer *m*; **10.** *Am.* Höhe *f* des Spiegels (*e-s Flusses*); **II** *v/t.* **11.** *Theaterstück* a) auf die Bühne bringen, inszenieren, b) für die Bühne bearbeiten; **12.** *fig.* a) *allg.* veranstalten, b) inszenieren, aufziehen: **~ *a demonstration***; **13.** ⚙ berüsten; **14.** ⚔ *Am. Personen* ˈdurchschleusen; **~ box** *s. thea.* Proˈszeniumsloge *f*; **ˈ~·coach** *s. hist.* Postkutsche *f*; **ˈ~·craft** *s.* dramaˈturgisches *od.* schauspielerisches Können; **~ de·sign·er** *s.* Bühnenbildner(in); **~ di·rec·tion** *s.* Bühnen-, Reˈgieanweisung *f*; **~ di·rec·tor** *s.* Regisˈseur *m*; **~ door** *s.* Bühneneingang *m*; **~ ef·fect** *s.* **1.** ˈBühnenwirkung *f*, -efˌfekt *m*; **2.** *fig.* Theaˈtralik *f*; **~ fe·ver** *s.* Theˈaterbesessenheit *f*; **~ fright** *s.* Lampenfieber *n*; **ˈ~·hand** *s.* Bühnenarbeiter *m*; **ˌ~-ˈman·age** → ***stage*** 12; **~ man·ag·er** *s.* Inspiziˈent *m*; **~ name** *s.* Bühnen-, Künstlername *m*; **~ play** *s.* Bühnenstück *n.*

stag·er [ˈsteɪdʒə] *s. mst* ***old*** **~** ‚alter Hase'.

stage| race *s. Radsport*: Eˈtappenrennen *n*; **~ rights** *s. pl.* ⚖ Aufführungs-, Bühnenrechte *pl.*; **ˈ~-struck** *adj.* theˈaterbesessen; **~ ver·sion** *s. thea.* Bühnenfassung *f*; **~ whis·per** *s.* **1.** *thea.* nur für das Publikum bestimmtes Flüstern; **2.** *fig.* weithin hörbares Geflüster; **ˈ~ˌworth·y** *adj.* bühnenfähig, -gerecht (*Schauspiel*).

stage·y [ˈsteɪdʒɪ] *adj. Am. für* ***stagy***.

stag·fla·tion [stægˈfleɪʃn] *s.* ☤ Stagflaˈtiˈon *f.*

stag·ger [ˈstægə] **I** *v/i.* **1.** (sch)wanken, taumeln, torkeln; **2.** *fig.* wanken(d werden); **II** *v/t.* **3.** ins Wanken bringen, erschüttern (*a. fig.*); **4.** *fig.* verblüffen, *stärker*: ˈumwerfen, überˈwältigen; **5.** ⚙ gestaffelt *od.* versetzt anordnen; (*a. fig. Arbeitszeit*) staffeln; **III** *s.* **6.** Schwanken *n*, Taumeln *n*; **7.** *pl. sg. konstr.*: a) Schwindel *m*, b) *vet.* Schwindel *m* (*von Rindern*), Koller *m* (*von Pferden*), Drehkrankheit *f* (*von Schafen*); **8.** ⚙, ✈ *u. fig.* Staffelung *f*; **9.** *Leichtathletik*: Kurvenvorgabe *f*; **ˈstag·gered** [-əd] *adj.* **1.** ⚙ versetzt (angeordnet), gestaffelt; **2.** gestaffelt (*Arbeitszeit etc.*); **ˈstag·ger·ing** [-ərɪŋ] *adj.* □ **1.** (sch)wankend, taumelnd; **2.** wuchtig, heftig (*Schlag*); **3.** *fig.* a) ˈumwerfend, phanˈtastisch, b) schwindelerregend (*Preise etc.*).

stag·i·ness [ˈsteɪdʒɪnɪs] *s.* Theaˈtralik *f*, Effekthascheˈrei *f.*

stag·ing [ˈsteɪdʒɪŋ] *s.* **1.** *thea.* a) Inszenierung *f* (*a. fig.*), b) Bühnenbearbeitung *f*; **2.** (Bau)Gerüst *n*; **3.** ⚓ Hellinggerüst *n* (*e-r Werft*); **~ a·re·a** *s.* ⚔ **1.** Bereitstellungsraum *m*; **2.** Auffangraum *m.*

stag·nan·cy [ˈstægnənsɪ] *s.* Stagnatiˈon *f*: a) Stockung *f*, Stillstand *m*, b) *bsd.* ☤ Flauheit *f*, c) *fig.* Trägheit *f*; **ˈstag·nant** [-nt] *adj.* □ stagnierend: a) stockend (*a.* ☤), stillstehend, b) abgestanden (*Wasser*), c) *fig.* träge; **ˈstag·nate** [-neɪt] *v/i.* stagnieren, stocken; **stag·na·tion** [stægˈneɪʃn] → ***stagnancy***.

stag par·ty *s.* F (*bsd.* feuchtfröhlicher) Herrenabend *m.*

stag·y [ˈsteɪdʒɪ] *adj.* □ **1.** bühnenmäßig, Bühnen…; **2.** *fig.* theaˈtralisch.

staid [steɪd] *adj.* □ gesetzt, seriˈös; ruhig (*a. Farbe*), gelassen; **ˈstaid·ness** [-nɪs] *s.* Gesetztheit *f.*

stain [steɪn] **I** *s.* **1.** (Schmutz-, *a.* Farb-) Fleck *m*: **~*-resistant*** schmutzabweisend; **2.** *fig.* Schandfleck *m*, Makel *m*; **3.** Färbung *f*; **4.** ⚙ Farbe *f*, Färbemittel *n* (*a. beim Mikroskopieren*); **5.** (Holz-)Beize *f*; **II** *v/t.* **6.** beschmutzen, beflekken, besudeln (*alle a. fig.*); **7.** färben; *Holz* beizen; *Glas etc.* bemalen; *Stoff etc.* bedrucken: **~ed glass** buntes (Fenster)Glas; **III** *v/i.* **8.** Flecken verursachen; **9.** Flecken bekommen, schmutzen; **'stain·ing** [-nɪŋ] **I** *s.* **1.** (Ver)Färbung *f*; **2.** Verschmutzung *f*; **3.** ⚙ Färben *n*, Beizen *n*: **~ of glass** Glasmalerei *f*; **II** *adj.* **4.** Färbe…; **'stain·less** [-lɪs] *adj.* □ **1.** *bsd. fig.* fleckenlos, unbefleckt; **2.** rostfrei, nichtrostend (*Stahl*).

stair [steə] *s.* **1.** Treppe *f*, Stiege *f*; **2.** (Treppen)Stufe *f*; **3.** *pl.* Treppe(nhaus *n*) *f*: **below ~s** a) unten, b) *Br. obs.* beim Hauspersonal; **'~·case** → **stair** 3; **'~·head** *s.* oberster Treppenabsatz; **'~·way** → **stair** 3.

stake¹ [steɪk] **I** *s.* **1.** (*a.* Grenz)Pfahl *m*, Pfosten *m*: **pull up ~s** *Am.* F *fig.* s-e Zelte abbrechen; **2.** Marter-, Brandpfahl *m*: **the ~** *fig.* der (Tod auf dem) Scheiterhaufen; **3.** Pflock *m* (*zum Anbinden von Tieren*); **4.** (Wagen)Runge *f*; **5.** Absteckpfahl *m*, -pflock *m*; **6.** kleiner (Hand)Amboß; **II** *v/t.* **7.** *oft* **~ off, ~ out** abstecken (*a. fig.*): **~ out a claim** *fig.* s-e Ansprüche anmelden (**to** auf *acc.*); **~ in** (*od.* **out**) mit Pfählen einzäunen; **8.** *Pflanze* mit e-m Pfahl stützen; **9.** *Tier* anpflocken; **10.** a) mit e-m Pfahl durch'bohren, aufspießen, b) pfählen (*als Strafe*).

stake² [steɪk] **I** *s.* **1.** (Wett-, Spiel)Einsatz *m*: **place one's ~s on** setzen auf (*acc.*); **be at ~** *fig.* auf dem Spiel stehen; **play for high ~s** a) um hohe Einsätze spielen, b) *fig.* ein hohes Spiel spielen, allerhand riskieren; **sweep the ~s** den ganzen Gewinn kassieren; **2.** *fig.* Inter'esse *n*, Anteil *m* (*a.* †): **have a ~ in** interessiert *od.* beteiligt sein an (*dat.*); **3.** *pl. Pferderennen*: a) Dotierung *f*, b) Rennen *n*; **II** *v/t.* **4.** *Geld* setzen (**on** auf *acc.*); **5.** *fig.* (ein)setzen, aufs Spiel setzen, riskieren: **I'd ~ my life on that** darauf gehe ich jede Wette ein; **6.** *Am.* F Geld in *j-n od. et.* investieren.

'stake|,hold·er *s.* 'Unpar,teiische(r), der die Wetteinsätze verwahrt; **~ net** *s.* ⚓ Staknetz *n*; **'~·out** *s.* F (poli'zeiliche) Über'wachung (**on** *gen.*).

Sta·kha·no·vism [stæ'kænəvɪzəm] *s.* Sta'chanow-Sy,stem *n*.

sta·lac·tic, sta·lac·ti·cal [stə'læktɪk(l)] *adj.* → **stalactitic**; **sta·lac·tite** ['stæləktaɪt] *s.* Stalak'tit *m*, hängender Tropfstein; **stal·ac·tit·ic** [,stælək'tɪtɪk] *adj.* (□ **~ally**) stalak'titisch, Stalaktiten…

sta·lag·mite ['stæləgmaɪt] *s. min.* Stalag'mit *m*, stehender Tropfstein; **stal·ag·mit·ic** [,stæləg'mɪtɪk] *adj.* (□ **~ally**) stalag'mitisch.

stale¹ [steɪl] **I** *adj.* □ **1.** *allg.* alt (*Ggs. frisch*), *bsd.* a) schal, abgestanden (*Wasser, Wein*), b) alt(backen) (*Brot*), c) schlecht, verdorben (*Lebensmittel*); **2.** verbraucht (*Luft*); **3.** schal (*Geruch, Geschmack, fig. Vergnügen*); **4.** fad, abgedroschen, (ur)alt (*Witz*); **5.** a) verbraucht (*Person, Geist*), über'anstrengt, b) ‚eingerostet', aus der Übung (gekommen); **6.** ⚖ verjährt (*Scheck, Schuld etc.*), gegenstandslos (geworden); **II** *v/i.* **7.** schal *etc.* werden.

stale² [steɪl] **I** *v/i.* stallen, harnen (*Vieh*); **II** *s.* Harn *m*.

stale·mate ['steɪlmeɪt] **I** *s.* **1.** *Schach*: Patt *n*; **2.** *fig.* 'Patt(situati,on *f*) *n*, Sackgasse *f*; **II** *v/t.* **3.** patt setzen; **4.** *fig.* a) in e-e Sackgasse führen, b) matt setzen.

stale·ness ['steɪlnɪs] *s.* **1.** Schalheit *f* (*a. fig.*); **2.** a) Verbrauchtheit *f*, b) Abgedroschenheit *f*.

Sta·lin·ism ['stɑːlɪnɪzəm] *s. pol.* Stali'nismus *m*; **'Sta·lin·ist** [-nɪst] **I** *s.* Stali'nist(in); **II** *adj.* stali'nistisch.

stalk¹ [stɔːk] *s.* **1.** ⚘ Stengel *m*, Stiel *m*, Halm *m*; **2.** *biol., zo.* Stiel *m* (*Träger e-s Organs*); **3.** *zo.* Federkiel *m*; **4.** Stiel *m* (*e-s Weinglases etc.*); **5.** (Fa'brik-)Schlot *m*.

stalk² [stɔːk] **I** *v/i.* **1.** *hunt.* (sich an)pirschen; **2.** (ein'her)schreiten, (-)stolzieren; **3.** *fig.* 'umgehen (*Krankheit, Gespenst etc.*); **4.** staken, steifbeinig gehen; **II** *v/t.* **5.** *hunt. u. fig.* sich her'anpirschen an (*acc.*); **6.** *hunt.* durch'jagen; **7.** *j-n* verfolgen; **8.** 'umgehen in (*dat.*) (*Gespenst etc.*); **III** *s.* **9.** Pirsch (-jagd) *f*.

stalked [stɔːkt] *adj.* ⚘, *zo.* gestielt, …stielig.

stalk·er ['stɔːkə] *s.* Pirschjäger *m*.

'stalk·ing-horse ['stɔːkɪŋ] *s.* **1.** *hunt., hist.* Versteckpferd *n*; **2.** *fig.* Deckmantel *m*; **3.** *pol.* Strohmann *m*.

stalk·less ['stɔːklɪs] *adj.* **1.** ungestielt; **2.** ⚘ stengellos, sitzend.

stalk·y ['stɔːkɪ] *adj.* **1.** stengel-, stielartig; **2.** hochaufgeschossen.

stall¹ [stɔːl] **I** *s.* **1.** Box *f* (*im Stall*); **2.** (Verkaufs)Stand *m*, (Markt)Bude *f*: **~ money** Standgeld *n*; **3.** Chor-, Kirchenstuhl *m*; **4.** *pl. thea. Brit.* Sperrsitz *m*; **5.** Hülle *f*, Schutz *m*; **6.** ⚒ Arbeitsstand *m*; **7.** ✈ Sackflug *m*; **8.** (markierter) Parkplatz; **II** *v/t.* **9.** *Tiere* in Boxen 'unterbringen; **10.** im Stall füttern *od.* mästen; **11.** a) *Wagen* durch ‚Abwürgen' des Motors zum Stehen bringen, b) *Motor* abwürgen, c) ✈ über'ziehen: **~ing speed** kritische Geschwindigkeit; **III** *v/i.* **12.** steckenbleiben (*Wagen*); **13.** absterben (*Motor*); **14.** ✈ abrutschen.

stall² [stɔːl] **I** *s.* **1.** Ausflucht *f*, 'Hinhaltema,növer *n*; **2.** *Am.* Kom'plize *m*; **II** *v/i.* **3.** a) Ausflüchte machen, ausweichen, b) *a.* **~ for time** Zeit schinden; **4.** *sport* a) auf Zeit spielen, b) ‚kurztreten'; **III** *v/t.* **5.** *a.* **~ off** a) *j-n* hinhalten, b) *et.* hin'auszögern.

stall·age ['stɔːlɪdʒ] *s. Brit.* Standgeld *n*.

stal·lion ['stæljən] *s. zo.* (Zucht)Hengst *m*.

stal·wart ['stɔːlwət] **I** *adj.* □ **1.** ro'bust, stramm, (hand)fest; **2.** *bsd. pol.* unentwegt, treu; **II** *s.* **3.** strammer Kerl; **4.** *bsd. pol.* treuer Anhänger, Unentwegte(r *m*) *f*.

sta·men ['steɪmən] *s.* ⚘ Staubblatt *n*, -gefäß *n*, -faden *m*.

stam·i·na ['stæmɪnə] *s.* **1.** a) Lebenskraft *f* (*a. fig.*), b) Vitali'tät *f*; **2.** Zähigkeit *f*, Ausdauer *f*, 'Durchhalte-, Stehvermögen *n*; **3.** *a.* ⚔ 'Widerstandskraft *f*; **'stam·i·nal** [-nl] *adj.* **1.** Lebens…, vi'tal; **2.** Widerstands…, Konditions…; **3.** ⚘ Staubblatt…

stam·mer ['stæmə] **I** *v/i.* (*v/t. a.* **~ out**) stottern, stammeln; **II** *s.* Stottern *n* (*a.* ⚕), Gestammel *n*; **'stam·mer·er** [-ərə] *s.* Stotterer *m*, Stotterin *f*; **'stam·mer·ing** [-ərɪŋ] **I** *adj.* □ stotternd; **II** *s.* → **stammer** II.

stamp [stæmp] **I** *v/t.* **1.** stampfen (auf *acc.*): **~ one's foot** → 12; **~ down** a) feststampfen, b) niedertrampeln; **~ out** a) *Feuer* austreten, b) zertrampeln, c) ausmerzen, d) *Aufstand* niederschlagen; **2.** *Geld* prägen; **3.** aufprägen (**on** auf *acc.*); **4.** *Namen etc.* aufstempeln; **5.** *Urkunde etc.* stempeln; **6.** *Gewichte* eichen; **7.** *Brief etc.* frankieren, e-e Brief- *od.* Gebührenmarke (auf)kleben auf (*acc.*): **~ed envelope** Freiumschlag *m*; **8.** kennzeichnen; **9.** *fig.* stempeln, kennzeichnen, charakterisieren (**as** als); **10.** *fig.* (fest) einprägen: **~ed on s.o.'s memory** j-s Gedächtnis eingeprägt, unverrückbar in j-s Erinnerung; **11.** ⚙ a) *a.* **~ out** (aus)stanzen, b) pressen, c) *Erz* pochen, d) *Lumpen etc.* einstampfen; **II** *v/i.* **12.** (auf)stampfen; **13.** stampfen, trampeln (**upon** auf *acc.*); **III** *s.* **14.** Stempel *m*, (*Dienst-etc.*)Siegel *n*; **15.** *fig.* Stempel *m* (*der Wahrheit etc.*), Gepräge *n*: **bear the ~ of** den Stempel *des Genies etc.* tragen, das Gepräge *j-s od. e-r Sache* haben; **16.** (Brief)Marke *f*, (Post)Wertzeichen *n*; **17.** (Stempel-, Steuer-, Gebühren-)Marke *f*; **18.** † Ra'battmarke *f*; **19.** † (Firmen)Zeichen *n*, Eti'kett *n*; **20.** *fig.* Art *f*, Schlag *m*: **a man of his ~** ein Mann s-s Schlages; **of a different ~** aus e-m andern Holz geschnitzt; **21.** ⚙ a) Prägestempel *m*, b) Stanze *f*, c) Stampfe *f*, d) Presse *f*, e) Pochstempel *m*, f) Pa'trize *f*; **22.** Prägung *f*; **23.** Aufdruck *m*; **24.** Eindruck *m*, Spur *f*; **~ Act** *s. hist.* Stempelakte *f*; **~ col·lec·tor** *s.* Briefmarkensammler *m*; **~ du·ty** *s.* Stempelgebühr *f*.

stam·pede [stæm'piːd] **I** *s.* **1.** a) wilde, panische Flucht, Panik *f*, b) wilder Ansturm; **2.** (Massen)Ansturm *m* (*von Käufern etc.*); **3.** *Am. pol.* a) (krasser) 'Meinungs,umschwung, b) ‚Erdrutsch' *m*; **II** *v/i.* **4.** (in wilder Flucht) da'vonstürmen, 'durchgehen; **5.** (in Massen) losstürmen; **III** *v/t.* **6.** in wilde Flucht jagen; **7.** a) in Panik versetzen, b) *j-n* treiben (**into doing** dazu, *et.* zu tun), c) über'rumpeln, d) *Am. pol.* e-n Erdrutsch her'vorrufen bei.

stamp·ing ['stæmpɪŋ] *s.* ⚙ **1.** Ausstanzen *n etc.*; **2.** Stanzstück *n*; **3.** Preßstück *n*; **4.** Prägung *f*; **~ die** *s.* ⚙ 'Schlagma'trize *f*; **~ ground** *s. zo. u. fig.* Tummelplatz *m*, Re'vier *n*.

stamp(·ing) mill *s.* ⚙ a) Stampfwerk *n*, b) Pochwerk *n*.

stance [stæns] *s.* Stellung *f*, Haltung *f* (*a. sport*).

stanch¹ [stɑːntʃ] *v/t. Blutung* stillen.

stanch² [stɑːntʃ] → **staunch²**.

stan·chion ['stɑːnʃn] **I** *s.* Pfosten *m*, Stütze *f* (*a.* ⚓); **II** *v/t.* (ab)stützen, verstärken.

stand [stænd] **I** *s.* **1.** Stillstand *m*, Halt *m*; **2.** Standort *m*, Platz *m*, *fig.* Standpunkt *m*: **take one's ~** a) sich (auf)stellen (**at** bei, auf *dat.*), b) Stellung beziehen; **3.** *fig.* Eintreten *n*: ***make a ~ for*** sich einsetzen für; ***make a ~ against*** sich entgegenstellen *od.* -stemmen (*dat.*); **4.** (Verkaufs-, Messe)Stand *m*; **5.** Stand(platz) *m für Taxis*; **6.** ('Zuschauer)Tri,büne *f*; **7.** Podium *n*; **8.** *Am.* ⚖ Zeugenstand *m*: ***take the ~*** a) den Zeugenstand betreten, b) als Zeuge aussagen; **9.** (Kleider-, Noten- *etc.*) Ständer *m*; **10.** Gestell *n*; **11.** *phot.* Sta'tiv *n*; **12.** (Baum)Bestand *m*; **13.** ⸙ Stand *m des Getreides etc.*, (zu erwartende) Ernte: ***~ of wheat*** stehender Weizen; **14.** ***~ of arms*** ⚔ ('vollständige) Ausrüstung *e-s Soldaten*; **II** *v/i.* [*irr.*] **15.** *allg.* stehen: ***~ alone*** a) allein (da)stehen *mit e-r Ansicht etc.*, b) unerreicht dastehen *od.* sein; ***~ fast*** (*od.* ***firm***) hart bleiben (***on*** in *e-r Sache*); ***~ or fall*** siegen oder untergehen; ***~s at 78*** *das Thermometer* steht auf 78 Grad (Fahrenheit); ***the wind ~s in the west*** der Wind weht von Westen; ***~ well with s.o.*** mit j-m gut stehen; ***~ to lose*** (***win***) (mit Sicherheit) verlieren (gewinnen); ***as matters ~*** (so) wie die Dinge (jetzt) liegen, nach Lage der Dinge; ***I want to know where I ~*** ich will wissen, woran ich bin; **16.** aufstehen, sich erheben; **17.** sich *wohin* stellen, treten: ***~ back*** (*od.* ***clear***) zurücktreten; **18.** sich *wo* befinden, stehen, liegen (*Sache*); **19.** *a.* ***~ still*** stehenbleiben, stillstehen: ***~!*** halt!; ***~ fast!*** ⚔ *Brit.* stillgestanden!, *Am.* Abteilung halt!; **20.** *bestürzt etc.* sein: ***~ aghast***; ***~ convicted*** überführt sein; ***~ corrected*** s-n Irrtum *od.* sein Unrecht zugeben; ***~ in need of*** benötigen; **21.** groß sein, messen: ***he ~s six feet*** (***tall***); **22.** *neutral etc.* bleiben: ***~ unchallenged*** unbeanstandet bleiben; ***and so it ~s*** und dabei bleibt es; **23.** *a.* ***~ good*** gültig bleiben, (weiterhin) gelten: ***my offer ~s*** mein Angebot bleibt bestehen; **24.** bestehen, sich behaupten: ***~ through*** *et.* überstehen, -dauern; **25.** ⚓ *auf e-m Kurs* liegen, steuern; **26.** zu'statten kommen (***to*** *dat.*); **27.** *hunt.* vorstehen (***upon*** *dat.*) (*Hund*); **III** *v/t.* [*irr.*] **28.** *wohin* stellen; **29.** *e-m Angriff etc.* standhalten; **30.** *Beanspruchung, Kälte etc.* aushalten; *Klima, Person* (v)ertragen: ***I cannot ~ him*** ich kann ihn nicht ausstehen; **31.** sich *et.* gefallen lassen, dulden: ***I won't ~ it any longer***; **32.** sich *e-r Sache* unter'ziehen; *Pate* stehen; → ***trial*** 2; **33.** a) aufkommen für *et.*; *Bürgschaft* leisten, b) *j-m ein Essen etc.* spendieren: ***~ a drink*** ‚einen ausgeben'; → ***treat*** 11; **34.** *e-e Chance* haben;

Zssgn mit prp.:

stand| by *v/i.* **1.** *fig. j-m* zur Seite stehen, zu *j-m* halten *od.* stehen; **2.** *s-m Wort, s-n Prinzipien etc.* treu bleiben, stehen zu; **~ for** *v/i.* **1.** stehen für, bedeuten; **2.** eintreten für, vertreten; **3.** *bsd. Brit.* sich um *ein Amt* bewerben; **4.** *pol. Brit.* kandidieren für *e-n Sitz im Parlament*: ***~ election*** kandidieren, sich zur Wahl stellen; **5.** → ***stand*** 31; **~ on** *v/i.* **1.** bestehen *od.* halten auf (*acc.*); → ***ceremony*** 2; **2.** auf *sein Recht etc.* pochen; **3.** ⚓ *Kurs* beibehalten; **~ o·ver** *v/i. j-m* auf die Finger sehen; **~ to** *v/i.* **1.** → ***stand by*** 1; **2.** zu *s-m Versprechen etc.* stehen, bei *s-m Wort* bleiben: ***~ it that*** dabei bleiben *od.* darauf beharren, daß; ***~ one's duty*** (treu) s-e Pflicht tun; **~ up·on** → ***stand on***;

Zssgn mit adv.:

stand| a·loof, **~ a·part** *v/i.* **1.** a) abseits *od.* für sich stehen, b) sich ausschließen, nicht mitmachen; **2.** *fig.* sich distanzieren (***from*** von); **~ a·side** *v/i.* **1.** bei'seite treten; **2.** *fig. zu j-s Gunsten* verzichten, zu'rücktreten; **3.** tatenlos her'umstehen; **~ by** *v/i.* **1.** da'bei sein u. zusehen (müssen), (ruhig) zusehen; **2.** a) *bsd.* ⚔ bereitstehen, sich in Bereitschaft halten, b) ***~!*** Achtung!, ⚓ klar zum Manöver!; **3.** *Funk*: a) auf Empfang bleiben, b) sendebereit sein; **~ down** *v/i.* **1.** ⚖ den Zeugenstand verlassen; **2.** → ***stand aside*** 2; **~ in** *v/i.* **1.** einspringen (***for*** für *j-n*): ***~ for s.o.*** *Film*: j-n doubeln; **2.** ***~ with*** ‚unter e-r Decke stecken' mit *j-m*; **3.** ⚓ landwärts anliegen; **~ off I** *v/i.* **1.** sich entfernt halten (***from*** von); **2.** *fig.* Abstand halten (*im Umgang*); **3.** ⚓ seewärts anliegen; **II** *v/t.* **4.** † *j-n* (vor'übergehend) entlassen; **5.** sich *j-n* vom Leibe halten; **~ out** *v/i.* **1.** (*a. fig.* deutlich) her'vortreten: ***~ against*** sich gut abheben von; → 4; **2.** abstehen (*Ohren*); **3.** *fig.* her'ausragen, her'vorstechen; **4.** aus-, 'durchhalten: ***~ against*** sich hartnäckig wehren gegen; **5.** ***~ for*** bestehen auf (*dat.*); **6.** ***~ to sea*** ⚓ in See stechen; **~ o·ver I** *v/i.* **1.** (***to*** auf *acc.*) a) sich vertagen, b) verschoben werden; **2.** *für später* liegenbleiben, warten; **II** *v/t.* **3.** vertagen, verschieben (***to*** auf *acc.*); **~ to** ⚔ **I** *v/t.* in Bereitschaft versetzen; **II** *v/i.* in Bereitschaft stehen; **~ up I** *v/i.* **1.** aufstehen, sich erheben (*beide a. fig.*); **2.** sich aufrichten (*Stachel etc.*); **3.** eintreten *od.* sich einsetzen (***for*** für); **4.** ***~ to*** (mutig) gegen'übertreten (*dat.*); **5.** (***under***, ***to***) sich (gut) halten (unter, gegen), standhalten (*dat.*); **II** *v/t.* **6.** F *j-n* ‚versetzen'.

stand·ard¹ ['stændəd] **I** *s.* **1.** Standard *m*, Norm *f*; **2.** Muster *n*, Vorbild *n*; **3.** Maßstab *m*: ***apply another ~*** e-n anderen Maßstab anlegen; ***~ of value*** Wertmaßstab; ***by present-day ~s*** nach heutigen Begriffen; ***double ~*** doppelte Moral; **4.** Richt-, Eichmaß *n*; **5.** Richtlinie *f*; **6.** (Mindest)Anforderungen *pl.*: ***be up to*** (***below***) ***~*** den Anforderungen (nicht) genügen *od.* entsprechen; ***set a high ~*** hohe Anforderungen stellen, viel verlangen; ***~ of living*** Lebensstandard *m*; **7.** † 'Standard(quali,tät *f od.* -ausführung *f*) *m*; **8.** (*Gold- etc.*) Währung *f*, (-)Standard *m*; **9.** Standard *m*: a) (gesetzlich vorgeschriebener) Feingehalt (*der Edelmetalle*), b) Münzfuß *m*; **10.** Ni'veau *n*, Grad *m*: ***be of a high ~*** ein hohes Niveau haben; ***~ of knowledge*** Bildungsgrad, -stand *m*; ***~ of prices*** Preisniveau; **11.** *ped. bsd. Brit.* Stufe *f*, Klasse *f*; **II** *adj.* **12.** nor'mal, Normal...(*-film, -wert, -zeit etc.*); Standard..., Einheits...(*-modell etc.*); Durchschnitts...(*-wert etc.*): ***~ ga(u)ge*** 🚂 Normalspur *f*; ***~ set*** Seriengerät *n*; ***~ size*** gängige Größe (*Schuhe etc.*); **13.** gültig, maßgebend, Standard...(*-muster, -werk*), *ling.* hochsprachlich: ***~ German*** Hochdeutsch *n*; **14.** klassisch: ***~ novel***; ***~ author*** Klassiker *m*.

stand·ard² ['stændəd] **I** *s.* **1.** a) *pol. u.* ⚔ Stan'darte *f*, b) Fahne *f*, Flagge *f*, c) Wimpel *m*, d) *fig.* Banner *n*: ***~-bearer*** Fahnen-, *a. fig.* Bannerträger *m*; **2.** ⚙ a) Ständer *m*, b) Pfosten *m*, Pfeiler *m*, Stütze *f*; **3.** ⸙ Hochstämmchen *n*, Bäumchen *n*; **II** *adj.* **4.** Steh...: ***~ lamp***; **5.** ⸙ hochstämmig: ***~ rose***.

stand·ard·i·za·tion [,stændədaɪ'zeɪʃn] *s.* **1.** Normung *f*, Standardisierung *f*: ***~ committee*** Normenausschuß *m*; **2.** ⚗ Titrierung *f*; **3.** Eichung *f*; **stand·ard·ize** ['stændədaɪz] *v/t.* **1.** normen, normieren, standardisieren; **2.** ⚗ einstellen, titrieren; **3.** eichen.

'stand|-by [-ndb-] **I** *pl.* **-bys** *s.* **1.** Stütze *f*, Beistand *m*, Hilfe *f*: (***old***) ***~*** altbewährte Sache; (***on ~*** in) (A'larm- *etc.*) Bereitschaft *f*; **2.** ⚙ Hilfs-, Re'servegerät *n*; **II** *adj.* **3.** Hilfs..., Ersatz..., Reserve...: ***~ unit*** ⚡ Notaggregat *n*; ***~ credit*** † Beistandskredit *m*; **4.** *bsd.* ⚔ Bereitschafts...(*-dienst etc.*); **'~-down** *s.* Pause *f*.

stand·ee [stæn'di:] *s. Am.* F Stehplatzinhaber(in).

'stand-in *s.* **1.** *Film*: Double *n*; **2.** Vertreter(in), Ersatzmann *m*.

stand·ing ['stændɪŋ] **I** *s.* **1.** Stehen *n*: ***no ~*** keine Stehplätze; **2.** a) Stand *m*, Rang *m*, Stellung *f*, b) Ruf *m*, Ansehen *n*: ***of high ~*** hochangesehen, -stehend; **3.** Dauer *f*: ***of long ~*** alt (*Brauch, Freundschaft etc.*); **II** *adj.* **4.** stehend, Steh...: ***~ army*** stehendes Heer; ***~ corn*** Getreide *n* auf dem Halm; ***~ jump*** Sprung *m* aus dem Stand; ***~ ovation*** stürmischer Beifall; ***~ rule*** stehende Regel; ***~ start*** stehender Start; **5.** *fig.* ständig (*a. Ausschuß etc.*); **6.** † laufend (*Unkosten etc.*); **7.** üblich, gewohnt: ***a ~ dish***; **8.** bewährt, alt (*Witz etc.*); ***~ order*** *s.* **1.** † Dauerauftrag *m*; **2.** *pl. parl. etc.* Geschäftsordnung *f*; **3.** ⚔ Dauerbefehl *m*; ***~ room*** *s.* Platz *m* zum Stehen: ***~ only!*** nur Stehplätze!

'stand|·off *s.* **1.** *Am.* Distanzierung *f*; **2.** *fig.* Sackgasse *f*; **,~'off·ish** [-'ɒfɪʃ] *adj.* ☐ reserviert, (sehr) ablehnend, unnahbar; **,~'pat(·ter)** [-nd'pæt(ə)] *s. pol. Am.* F sturer Konserva'tiver; **'~·pipe** [-ndp-] *s.* ⚙ Standrohr *n*; **'~·point** [-ndp-] *s.* Standpunkt *m* (*a. fig.*); **'~·still** [-nds-] **I** *s.* Stillstand *m*: ***be at a ~*** stillstehen, stocken, ruhen; ***to a ~*** zum Stillstand *kommen, bringen*; **II** *adj.* stillstehend: ***~ agreement*** *pol.* Stillhalteabkommen *n*; **'~-up** *adj.* **1.** stehend: ***~ collar*** Stehkragen *m*; **2.** F im Stehen eingenommen: ***~ meal***; **3.** wild, wüst (*Schlägerei*).

stank [stæŋk] *pret. von* **stink**.

stan·na·ry ['stænərɪ] *Brit.* **I** *s.* **1.** Zinngrubengebiet *n*; **2.** Zinngrube *f*; **II** *adj.* **3.** Zinn(gruben)...; **'stan·nate** [-nət] *s.* ⚗ Stan'nat *n*; **'stannic** [-nɪk] *adj.* ⚗ Zinn...; **'stan·nite** [-naɪt] *s.* **1.** *min.* Zinnkies *m*, Stan'nin *n*; **2.** ⚗ Stan'nit *n*; **'stan·nous** [-nəs] *adj.* ⚗ Zinn...

stan·za ['stænzə] *pl.* **-zas** *s.* **1.** Strophe *f*; **2.** Stanze *f*.

sta·ple¹ ['steɪpl] **I** *s.* **1.** † Haupterzeugnis *n e- Landes etc.*; **2.** † Stapelware *f*: a) 'Hauptar,tikel *m*, b) Massenware *f*; **3.** † Rohstoff *m*; **4.** ⚙ Stapel *m*: a) *Fadenlänge od. -qualität*: ***of short ~***

kurzstapelig, b) *Büschel Schafwolle*; **5.** ⚙ a) Rohwolle *f*, b) Faser *f*: ~ ***fibre*** (*Am.* ***fiber***) Zellwolle *f*; **6.** *fig.* Hauptgegenstand *m*, -thema *n*; **7.** ☤ a) Stapelplatz *m*, b) Handelszentrum *n*, c) *hist.* Markt *m* (mit Stapelrecht); **II** *adj.* **8.** Stapel...: ~ ***goods***; **9.** Haupt...: ~ ***food***; ~ ***industry***; ~ ***topic*** Hauptthema *n*; **10.** ☤ a) Haupthandels..., b) gängig, c) Massen...; **III** *v/t.* **11.** *Wolle* (nach Stapel) sortieren.

sta·ple² [steɪpl] ⚙ **I** *s.* **1.** (Draht)Öse *f*; **2.** Krampe *f*; **3.** Heftdraht *m*, -klammer *f*; **II** *v/t.* **4.** (mit Draht) heften; klammern (***to*** an *acc.*): ***stapling machine*** → ***stapler***¹.

sta·pler¹ [ˈsteɪplə] *s.* ⚙ ˈHeftmaˌschine *f*.

sta·pler² [ˈsteɪplə] *s.* ☤ **1.** (Baumwoll-)Sortierer *m*; **2.** Stapelkaufmann *m*.

star [stɑː] **I** *s.* **1.** *ast.* a) Stern *m*, b) *mst* ***fixed*** ~ Fixstern *m*; **2.** Stern *m*: a) sternähnliche Figur, b) *fig.* Größe *f*, Berühmtheit *f* (*Person*), c) Orden *m*, d) *typ.* Sternchen *n*, e) *weißer Stirnfleck*, *bsd. e-s Pferdes*: ***ℒs and Stripes*** *das* Sternenbanner (*Nationalflagge der USA*); ***see*** ~***s*** F Sterne sehen (*nach e-m Schlag*); **3.** a) Stern *m* (*Schicksal*), b) *a.* ***lucky*** ~ Glücksstern *m*: ***unlucky*** ~ Unstern *m*; ***his*** ~ ***is in the ascendant*** (***is*** *od.* ***has set***) sein Stern ist im Aufgehen (ist untergegangen); ***my good*** ~ mein guter Stern; ***you may thank your*** ~***s*** Sie können von Glück sagen (, daß); **4.** *thea.* (Bühnen-, *bsd.* Film)Star *m*; **5.** *sport* Star *m*; **II** *adj.* **6.** Stern...; **7.** Haupt...: ~ ***prosecution witness*** ⚖ Hauptbelastungszeuge *m*; **8.** *thea.*, *sport* Star...: ~ ***performance*** Elitevorstellung *f*; ~ ***turn*** Hauptattraktion *f*; **9.** *Segeln*: Star *m* (*Boot*); **III** *v/t.* **10.** mit Sternen schmücken, besternen; **11.** *j-n* in der Hauptrolle zeigen: ~***ring X.*** mit X. in der Hauptrolle; **12.** *typ.* *Wort* mit Sternchen versehen; **IV** *v/i.* **13.** die *od.* e-e Hauptrolle spielen: ~ ***in a film.***

star·board [ˈstɑːbəd] ⚓ **I** *s.* Steuerbord *n*; **II** *adj.* Steuerbord...; **III** *adv.* a) nach Steuerbord, b) steuerbord(s).

starch [stɑːtʃ] **I** *s.* **1.** Stärke *f*: a) Stärkemehl *n*, b) Wäschestärke *f*, c) Stärkekleister *m*, d) ⚗ Aˈmylum *n*; **2.** *pl.* stärkereiche Nahrungsmittel *pl.*, ˈKohle(n)hyˌdrate *pl.*; **3.** *fig.* Steifheit *f*, Förmlichkeit *f*; **4.** *Am.* F ‚Mumm' *m*: ***take the*** ~ ***out of s.o.*** j-m ‚die Gräten ziehen'; **II** *v/t.* **5.** *Wäsche* stärken.

Star Cham·ber *s.* ⚖ *hist.* Sternkammer *f* (*nur dem König verantwortliches Willkürgericht bis 1641*).

starched [stɑːtʃt] *adj.* □ **1.** gestärkt, gesteift; **2.** → ***starchy*** 4; ˈ**starch·i·ness** [-tʃɪnɪs] *s. fig.* F Steifheit *f*, Förmlichkeit *f*; ˈ**starch·y** [-tʃɪ] *adj.* □ **1.** stärkehaltig: ~ ***food***; **2.** Stärke...; **3.** gestärkt; **4.** *fig.* F steif, förmlich.

ˈ**star-crossed** *adj. poet.* von e-m Unstern verfolgt, unglückselig.

star·dom [ˈstɑːdəm] *s.* **1.** Welt *f* der Stars; **2.** *coll.* Stars *pl.*; **3.** Berühmtheit *f*: ***rise to*** ~ ein Star werden.

star dust *s. ast.* **1.** Sternennebel *m*; **2.** kosmischer Staub.

stare [steə] **I** *v/i.* **1.** (~ ***at*** an)starren, (-)stieren; **2.** große Augen machen, erstaunt blicken: ~ ***at*** anstaunen, angaffen; ***make s.o.*** ~ j-n in Erstaunen versetzen; **II** *v/t.* **3.** ~ ***s.o. out*** (*od.* ***down***) j-n durch Anstarren aus der Fassung bringen; **4.** ~ ***s.o. in the face*** *fig.* a) j-m in die Augen springen, b) j-m deutlich *od.* drohend vor Augen stehen; **III** *s.* **5.** (starrer *od.* erstaunter) Blick, Starrblick *m*, Starren *n*.

ˈ**star|·finch** *s. orn.* Rotschwänzchen *n*; ˈ~ˌ**gaz·er** *s. humor.* **1.** Sterngucker *m*; **2.** Träumer(in); **3.** ‚Anbeter(in)' (*von Idolen*).

star·ing [ˈsteərɪŋ] **I** *adj.* □ **1.** stier, starrend: ~ ***eyes***; **2.** auffallend: ***a*** ~ ***tie***; **3.** grell (*Farbe*); **II** *adv.* **4.** toˈtal.

stark [stɑːk] **I** *adj.* □ **1.** steif, starr; **2.** rein, völlig: ~ ***folly***; ~ ***nonsense*** barer Unsinn; **3.** *fig.* rein sachlich (*Bericht*); **4.** kahl, öde (*Landschaft*); **II** *adv.* **5.** ganz, völlig: ~ (***staring***) ***mad*** ‚total' verrückt; ~ ***naked*** → **stark·ers** [ˈstɑːkəz] *adj.* F splitternackt.

star·less [ˈstɑːlɪs] *adj.* sternlos.

star·let [ˈstɑːlɪt] *s.* **1.** Sternchen *n*; **2.** *fig.* Starlet(t) *n*, Filmsternchen *n*.

ˈ**star·light I** *s.* Sternenlicht *n*; **II** *adj.* → ***starlit.***

star·ling¹ [ˈstɑːlɪŋ] *s. orn.* Star *m*.

star·ling² [ˈstɑːlɪŋ] *s.* ⚙ Pfeilerkopf *m* (*Eisbrecher e-r Brücke*).

ˈ**star·lit** *adj.* sternhell, -klar.

star map *s. ast.* Sternkarte *f*, -tafel *f*.

starred [stɑːd] *p.p. u. adj.* **1.** gestirnt (*Himmel*); **2.** sternengeschmückt; **3.** *typ. etc.* mit (e-m) Sternchen bezeichnet.

star·ry [ˈstɑːrɪ] *adj.* **1.** Sternen..., Stern...; **2.** → a) ***starlit***, b) ***starred*** 2; **3.** strahlend: ~ ***eyes***; **4.** sternförmig; ˌ~-ˈ**eyed** *adj.* **1.** mit strahlenden Augen; **2.** *fig.* a) ‚blauäugig', naˈiv, b) roˈmantisch.

star| shell *s.* ⚔ Leuchtgeschoß *n*; ˈ~-ˌ**span·gled** *adj.* sternenbesät: ***Star-Spangled Banner*** *Am. das* Sternenbanner (*Nationalflagge od. -hymne der USA*).

start [stɑːt] **I** *s.* **1.** *sport* Start *m* (*a. fig.*): ***good*** ~; ~***-and-finish line*** Start u. Ziel; ***give s.o. a*** ~ (***in life***) j-m zu e-m Start ins Leben verhelfen; **2.** Startzeichen *n* (*a. fig.*): ***give the*** ~; **3.** a) Aufbruch *m*, b) Abreise *f*, c) Abfahrt *f*, d) ✈ Abflug *m*, Start *m*, e) Abmarsch *m*; **4.** Beginn *m*, Anfang *m*: ***at the*** ~ am Anfang; ***from the*** ~ von Anfang an; ***from*** ~ ***to finish*** von Anfang bis Ende; ***make a fresh*** ~ e-n neuen Anfang machen, noch einmal von vorn anfangen; **5.** *sport* a) Vorgabe *f*, b) Vorsprung *m* (*a. fig.*): ***get*** (*od.* ***have***) ***the*** ~ ***of one's rivals*** s-n Rivalen zuvorkommen; **6.** Auf-, Zs.-fahren *n*, -schrecken *n*; Schreck *m*: ***give a*** ~ → 12; ***give s.o. a*** ~ j-n erschrecken; ***with a*** ~ jäh, erschrokken; **II** *v/i.* **7.** aufbrechen, sich aufmachen (***for*** nach): ~ ***on a journey*** e-e Reise antreten; **8.** a) abfahren, abgehen (*Zug etc.*), b) auslaufen (*Schiff*), ✈ abfliegen, starten (***for*** nach); **9.** anfangen, beginnen (***on*** mit *e-r Arbeit etc.*, ***doing*** zu tun): ~ ***in business*** ein Geschäft anfangen *od.* eröffnen; ***to*** ~ ***with*** (*Redew.*) a) erstens, als erstes, b) zunächst, c) um es gleich zu sagen, d) ... als Vorspeise; **10.** *fig.* ausgehen (***from*** von *e-m Gedanken*); **11.** entstehen, aufkommen; **12.** a) auffahren, -schrekken, b) zs.-fahren, -zucken (***at*** vor *dat.*, bei *e-m Laut etc.*); **13.** a) aufspringen, b) losstürzen; **14.** stutzen (***at*** bei); **15.** aus den Höhlen treten (*Augen*); **16.** sich lockern *od.* lösen; **17.** ⚙, *mot.* anspringen, anlaufen; **III** *v/t.* **18.** in Gang *od.* in Bewegung setzen; ⚙ *a.* anlassen; *Feuer* anzünden, in Gang bringen; **19.** *Brief*, *Streit etc.* anfangen; *Aktion* starten; *Geschäft*, *Zeitung* gründen, aufmachen; **20.** *Frage* aufwerfen, *Thema* anschneiden; **21.** *Gerücht* in ˈUmlauf setzen; **22.** *sport* starten (lassen); **23.** *Läufer*, *Pferd* aufstellen, an den Start bringen; **24.** 🚂 *Zug* abfahren lassen; **25.** *fig. j-m* zu e-m Start verhelfen: ~ ***s.o. in business***; **26.** *j-n* (veran)lassen (***doing*** zu tun); **27.** lockern, lösen; **28.** aufscheuchen; ~ **in** (*Am. a.* **out**) *v/i.* F anfangen (***to do*** zu tun); ~ **off** → ***start*** 9, 18; ~ **up** → ***start*** 12 a, 13 a, 17, 18.

start·er [ˈstɑːtə] *s.* **1.** *sport* a) Starter *m* (*Kampfrichter u. Wettkampfteilnehmer [-in]*); **2.** *mot.* Starter *m*, Anlasser *m*; **3.** *fig.* Initiˈator *m*; **4.** F *bsd. Brit.* Vorspeise *f*; **5.** ***for*** ~***s*** F a) als erstes, b) zunächst, c) um es gleich zu sagen.

start·ing [ˈstɑːtɪŋ] **I** *s.* **1.** Starten *n*, Ablauf *m*; **2.** ⚙ Anlassen *n*, Inˈgangsetzen *n*, Starten *n*: ***cold*** ~ *mot.* Kaltstart *m*; **II** *adj.* **3.** Start...(*-block*, *-geld*, *-linie*, *-schuß etc.*); *mot. etc.* Anlaß...(*-kurbel*, *-motor*, *-schalter*); ~ **gate** *s. Pferderennen*: ˈStartmaˌschine *f*; ~ **point** *s.* Ausgangspunkt *m* (*a. fig.*); ~ **price** *s.* **1.** *Pferderennen*: Eventuˈalquote *f*; **2.** *Auktion*: Mindestgebot *n*; ~ **sal·a·ry** *s.* Anfangsgehalt *n*.

star·tle [ˈstɑːtl] **I** *v/t.* **1.** erschrecken; **2.** aufschrecken; **3.** überˈraschen: a) bestürzen, b) verblüffen; **II** *v/i.* **4.** auf-, erschrecken: ~ ***easily*** sehr schreckhaft sein; ˈ**star·tling** [-lɪŋ] *adj.* □ **1.** erschreckend, bestürzend; **2.** verblüffend, aufsehenerregend.

star·va·tion [stɑːˈveɪʃn] *s.* **1.** Hungern *n*: ~ ***diet*** Hungerkur *f*; ~ ***wages*** Hungerlohn *m*, -löhne *pl.*; **2.** Hungertod *m*, Verhungern *n*.

starve [stɑːv] **I** *v/i.* **1.** *a.* ~ ***to death*** verhungern: ***I am simply starving*** F ich komme fast um vor Hunger; **2.** hungern (*a. fig.* ***for*** nach), Hunger (*fig.* Not) leiden; **3.** fasten; **4.** *fig.* verkümmern; **II** *v/t.* **5.** *a.* ~ ***to death*** verhungern lassen; **6.** aushungern; **7.** hungern lassen: ***be*** ~***d*** Hunger leiden, ausgehungert sein (*a. fig.* ***for*** nach); **8.** darben lassen (*a. fig.*): ***be*** ~***d of*** *od.* ***for*** knapp sein an (*dat.*); ˈ**starve·ling** [-lɪŋ] *obs.* **I** *s.* **1.** Hungerleider *m*; **2.** Kümmerling *m*; **II** *adj.* **3.** hungrig; **4.** abgemagert; **5.** kümmerlich.

star wheel *s.* ⚙ Sternrad *n*.

stash [stæʃ] *v/t. sl.* **1.** *mst* ~ ***away*** verstecken, beiˈseite tun; **2.** aufhören mit.

sta·sis [ˈsteɪsɪs] *pl.* **-ses** [-siːz] *s.* ⚕ Stase *f*, (*Blut- etc.*)Stauung *f*.

state [steɪt] **I** *s.* **1.** *mst* ℒ *pol.*, *a. zo.* Staat *m*: ***affairs of*** ~ Staatsgeschäfte; **2.** *pol. Am.* (Bundes-, Einzel)Staat *m*: ***the*** ℒ***s*** die (Vereinigten) Staaten; ~ ***law*** Rechtsordnung *f* des Einzelstaates; ℒ***'s attorney*** ⚖ Staatsanwalt *m*; ***turn*** ~***'s evidence*** ⚖ als Kronzeuge auftreten, gegen s-e Komplizen aussagen; **3.** (*Gesundheits-*, *Geistes- etc.*)Zustand *m*: ~

of health; ~ ***of aggregation*** *phys.* Aggregatzustand; ~ ***of war*** Kriegszustand; ***in a*** ~ F a) in e-m schrecklichen Zustand, b) ‚ganz aus dem Häuschen'; → ***emergency*** I; **4.** Stand *m*, Lage *f* (***of affairs*** der Dinge): ~ ***of the art*** neuester Stand der Technik; **5.** (Fa'milien-) Stand *m*: ***married*** ~ Ehestand; **6.** ⚕, *zo.* Stadium *n*; **7.** (gesellschaftliche) Stellung, Stand *m*: ***in a style befitting one's*** ~ standesgemäß; **8.** Pracht *f*, Staat *m*: ***in*** ~ feierlich, mit großem Zeremoniell *od.* Pomp; ***lie in*** ~ feierlich aufgebahrt liegen; ***live in*** ~ großen Aufwand treiben; **9.** *pl. pol. hist.* (Land- *etc.*)Stände *pl.*; **10.** *Kupferstecherei*: (Ab)Druck *m*; **II** *adj.* **11.** Staats..., staatlich, po'litisch: ~ ***capitalism*** Staatskapitalismus *m*; ~ ***funeral*** Staatsbegräbnis *n*; ~ ***mourning*** Staatstrauer *f*; ~ ***prison*** staatliche Strafanstalt (*in U.S.A. e-s Bundesstaates*); ~ ***prisoner*** politischer Häftling *od.* Gefangener; **12.** Staats..., Prunk..., Parade..., feierlich: ~ ***apartment*** → ***stateroom*** 1; ~ ***carriage*** Prunk-, Staatskarosse *f*; **III** *v/t.* **13.** festsetzen, -legen; *e-e Regel* aufstellen; → ***stated*** 1; **14.** erklären: a) darlegen, b) *a.* ⚖ (aus)sagen, *Gründe, Klage etc.* vorbringen, *Tatsachen etc.* anführen; → ***case***[1] 1, c) *Einzelheiten etc.* angeben; **15.** feststellen, konstatieren; **16.** behaupten; **17.** erwähnen, bemerken; **18.** *Problem etc.* stellen; **19.** ℞ (mathe'matisch) ausdrücken.

ˌstate|-con'trolled *adj.* staatlich gelenkt, unter staatlicher Aufsicht: ~ ***economy*** Zwangswirtschaft *f*; **'~-craft** *s. pol.* Staatskunst *f*.

stat·ed ['steɪtɪd] *p.p. u. adj.* **1.** festgesetzt: ***at the*** ~ ***time***; ***at*** ~ ***intervals*** in regelmäßigen Abständen; ~ ***meeting*** *bsd. Am.* ordentliche Versammlung; **2.** festgestellt; **3.** bezeichnet, (*a.* amtlich) anerkannt; **4.** angegeben: ***as*** ~ ***above***; ~ ***case*** ⚖ Sachdarstellung *f*.

State| De·part·ment *s. pol. Am.* 'Außenminiˌsterium *n*; **~·hood** ['steɪthʊd] *s. pol. bsd. Am.* Eigenstaatlichkeit *f*, Souveräni'tät *f*; **'~·house** *s. pol. Am.* Parla'mentsgebäude *n od.* Kapi'tol *n* (*e-s Bundesstaats*).

state·less ['steɪtlɪs] *adj. pol.* staatenlos: ~ ***person*** Staatenlose(r *m*) *f*.

state·li·ness ['steɪtlɪnɪs] *s.* **1.** Stattlichkeit *f*; Vornehmheit *f*; **2.** Würde *f*; **3.** Pracht *f*; **'state·ly** [-lɪ] *adj.* **1.** stattlich, impo'sant; prächtig; **2.** würdevoll; **3.** erhaben, vornehm.

state·ment ['steɪtmənt] *s.* **1.** (*a.* amtliche *etc.*) Erklärung: ***make a*** ~ e-e Erklärung abgeben; **2.** a) (Zeugen- *etc.*) Aussage *f*, b) Angabe(n *pl.*) *f*: ***false*** ~; ~ ***of facts*** Sachdarstellung *f*, Tatbestand *m*; ~ ***of contents*** Inhaltsangabe; **3.** Behauptung *f*; **4.** *bsd.* ⚖ (schriftliche) Darlegung, (Par'tei)Vorbringen *n*: ~ ***of claim*** Klageschrift *f*; ~ ***of defence*** (*Am.* ***defense***) a) Klagebeantwortung *f*, b) Verteidigungsschrift *f*; **5.** *bsd.* ✝ (*Geschäfts-, Monats-, Rechenschafts- etc.*)Bericht *m*, (*Bank-, Gewinn-, Jahres- etc.*)Ausweis *m*, (*statistische etc.*) Aufstellung: ~ ***of affairs*** Situationsbericht, Status *m e-r Firma*; ~ ***of account*** Kontoauszug *m*; ***financial*** ~ Gewinn- und Verlustrechnung *f*; **6.** *Am.* ✝ Bi'lanz *f*: ~ ***of assets and liabilities***; **7.** Darstellung *f*, Darlegung *f e-s Sachverhalts*; **8.** ✝ Lohn *m*, Ta'rif *m*; **9.** *fig.* Aussage *f*, Statement *n e-s Autors etc.*

'state·room *s.* **1.** Staats-, Prunkzimmer *n*; **2.** ⚓ ('Einzel)Kaˌbine *f*; **3.** 🚂 *Am.* Pri'vatabteil *n* (*mit Betten*).

'state·side *oft* ♀ *Am.* **I** *adj.* ameri'kanisch, Heimat...; ~ ***duty*** *bsd.* ⚔ Dienst *m* in der Heimat; **II** *adv.* in den *od.* in die Staaten (zurück).

states·man ['steɪtsmən] *s.* [*irr.*] **1.** *pol.* Staatsmann *m*; **2.** (bedeutender) Po'litiker; **'states·man·like** [-laɪk], **'states·man·ly** [-lɪ] *adj.* staatsmännisch; **'states·man·ship** [-ʃɪp] *s.* Staatskunst *f*.

States' rights *s. pl.* Staatsrechte *pl.* (*der Einzelstaaten der USA*).

stat·ic ['stætɪk] **I** *adj.* (□ ***~ally***) **1.** *phys. u. fig.* statisch: ~ ***sense*** ⚕ Gleichgewichtssinn *m*; **2.** ⚡ (elektro)'statisch; **3.** *Funk*: a) atmo'sphärisch (*Störung*), b) Störungs...; **II** *s.* **4.** ⚡ statische *od.* atmo'sphärische Elektrizi'tät; **5.** *pl. sg. konstr. phys.* Statik *f*; **6.** *pl. Funk*: atmo'sphärische Störung(en *pl.*).

sta·tion ['steɪʃn] **I** *s.* **1.** Platz *m*, Posten *m* (*a. sport*); **2.** (*Rettungs-, Unfall- etc.*) Stati'on *f*, (*Beratungs-, Dienst-, Tank- etc.*)Stelle *f*; (Tele'grafen)Amt *n*; (Tele'fon)Sprechstelle *f*; ('Wahl)Loˌkal *n*; (Handels)Niederlassung *f*; (Feuer)Wache *f*; **3.** (Poli'zei)Wache *f*; **4.** 🚂 a) Bahnhof *m*, b) ('Bahn)Statiˌon *f*; **5.** *Am.* (Bus- *etc.*)Haltestelle *f*; **6.** (Zweig-) Postamt *n*; **7.** ('Forschungs)Statiˌon *f*; (Erdbeben)Warte *f*; **8.** (Rundfunk-) Sender *m*, Stati'on *f*; **9.** Kraftwerk *n*; **10.** ⚔ a) Posten *m*, (⚓ Flotten)Stützpunkt *m*, b) Standort *m*, c) ✈ *Brit.* Fliegerhorst *m*; **11.** *biol.* Standort *m*; **12.** ⚓, ⚔ Positi'on *f*; **13.** Stati'on *f* (*Rastort*); **14.** *R.C.* a) *a.* ~ ***of the cross*** ('Kreuzweg)Statiˌon *f*, b) Stati'onskirche *f*; **15.** *eccl. a.* ~ ***day*** Wochen-Fasttag *m*; **16.** *surv.* a) Stati'on *f* (*Ausgangspunkt*), b) Basismeßstrecke *f*; **17.** *Austral.* (Rinder-, Schafs)Zuchtfarm *f*; **18.** *fig.* a) *gesellschaftliche etc.* Stellung: ~ ***in life***, b) Stand *m*, Rang *m*: ***below one's*** ~ nicht standesgemäß *heiraten etc.*; ***men of*** ~ Leute von Rang; **II** *v/t.* **19.** aufstellen, postieren; **20.** ⚔, ⚓ stationieren: ***be*** ***~ed*** stehen.

sta·tion·ar·y ['steɪʃnərɪ] *adj.* **1.** ⚙ *etc.* statio'när (*a. ast.*, ⚕), ortsfest, fest(stehend): ~ ***treatment*** ⚕ stationäre Behandlung; ~ ***warfare*** Stellungskrieg *m*; **2.** seßhaft; **3.** gleichbleibend, stationär, unveränderlich: ***remain*** ~ unverändert sein *od.* bleiben; **4.** (still)stehend: ***be*** ~ stehen; ~ **dis·ease** *s.* ⚕ lo'kal auftretende u. jahreszeitlich bedingte Krankheit.

sta·tion·er ['steɪʃnə] *s.* Pa'pier-, Schreibwarenhändler *m*; **'sta·tion·er·y** [-ərɪ] *s.* **1.** Schreib-, Pa'pierwaren *pl.*: ***office*** ~ Büromaterial *n*, -bedarf *m*; **2.** 'Brief-, 'Schreibpaˌpier *n*.

sta·tion| hos·pi·tal *s.* ⚔ 'Standortlazaˌrett *n*; **~ house** *s.* **1.** a) Poli'zeiwache *f*, b) Feuerwache *f*; **2.** 🚂 'Bahnstatiˌon *f*; **'~ˌmas·ter** *s.* 🚂 Stati'onsvorsteher *m*; **~ se·lec·tor** *s.* ⚡ Stati'onswähler *m*, Sendereinstellung *f*; **~ wag·on** *s. mot. Am.* Kombiwagen *m*.

stat·ism ['steɪtɪzəm] *s.* ✝, *pol.* Diri'gismus *m*, Planwirtschaft *f*; **'stat·ist** [-tɪst] **I** *s.* **1.** Sta'tistiker *m*; **2.** Anhänger(in) der Planwirtschaft; **II** *adj.* **3.** *pol.* diri'gistisch.

sta·tis·tic, **sta·tis·ti·cal** [stə'tɪstɪk(l)] *adj.* □ sta'tistisch; **stat·is·ti·ci·an** [ˌstætɪ'stɪʃn] *s.* Sta'tistiker *m*; **sta'tis·tics** [-ks] *s. pl.* **1.** *sg. konstr. allg.* Sta'tistik *f*; **2.** Sta'tistik(en *pl.*) *f*.

sta·tor ['steɪtə] *s.* ⚙, ⚡ Stator *m*.

stat·u·ar·y ['stætjʊərɪ] **I** *s.* **1.** Bildhauerkunst *f*; **2.** (Rund)Plastiken *pl.*, Statuen *pl.*, Skulp'turen *pl.*; **3.** Bildhauer *m*; **II** *adj.* **4.** Bildhauer...; **5.** (rund)plastisch; **6.** Statuen...: ~ ***marble***; **stat·ue** ['stætʃuː] Statue *f*, Standbild *n*, Plastik *f*; **stat·u·esque** [ˌstætjʊ'esk] *adj.* □ statuenhaft (*a. fig.*); **stat·u·ette** [ˌstætjʊ'et] *s.* Statu'ette *f*.

stat·ure ['stætʃə] *s.* **1.** Sta'tur *f*, Wuchs *m*, Gestalt *f*; **2.** Größe *f*; **3.** *fig.* (geistige *etc.*) Größe, For'mat *n*, Ka'liber *n*.

sta·tus ['steɪtəs] *pl.* **-es** [-ɪz] *s.* **1.** ⚖ a) Status *m*, Rechtsstellung *f*, b) *a.* ***legal*** ~ Rechtsfähigkeit *f*, c) Ak'tivlegitimatiˌon *f*: ~ ***of ownership*** Eigentumsverhältnisse *pl.*; ***equality of*** ~ (politische) Gleichberechtigung; ***national*** ~ Staatsangehörigkeit *f*; **2.** (Fa'milien-, Per'sonen)Stand *m*; **3.** *a.* ***military*** ~ (Wehr-) Dienstverhältnis *n*; **4.** (gesellschaftliche *etc.*) Stellung *f*, (Sozi'al)Preˌstige *n*, Status *m*: ~ ***symbol*** Statussymbol *n*; **5.** ✝ (geschäftliche) Lage: ***financial*** ~ Vermögenslage; **6.** *a.* ⚕ Zustand *m*, Status *m*; ~ **quo** [kwəʊ] (*Lat.*) *s. der* Status quo (*der jetzige Zustand*); ~ **quo an·te** [kwəʊ'æntɪ] (*Lat.*) *s. der* Status quo ante (*der vorherige Zustand*).

stat·ute ['stætjuːt] *s.* **1.** ⚖ a) Gesetz *n* (*vom Parlament erlassene Rechtsvorschrift*), b) Gesetzesvorschrift *f*, c) *parl.* Parla'mentsakte *f*: ~ ***of bankruptcy*** Konkursordnung *f*; **2.** ~ (***of limitations***) ⚖ (Gesetz *n* über) Verjährung *f*: ***not subject to the*** ~ unverjährbar; **3.** Sta'tut *n*, Satzung *f*; **'~-barred** *adj.* ⚖ verjährt; ~ **book** *s.* Gesetzessammlung *f*; ~ **law** *s.* Gesetzesrecht *n* (*Ggs.* ***common law***); ~ **mile** *s.* (gesetzliche) Meile (*1,60933 km*).

stat·u·to·ry ['stætjʊtərɪ] *adj.* □ **1.** ⚖ gesetzlich (*Erbe, Feiertag, Rücklage etc.*): ~ ***corporation*** Körperschaft *f* des öffentlichen Rechts; ~ ***declaration*** eidesstattliche Erklärung; **2.** Gesetzes...; **3.** ⚖ (dem Gesetz nach) strafbar; → ***rape***[1] 1; **4.** ⚖ Verjährungs...; **5.** satzungsgemäß.

staunch[1] [stɔːntʃ] → ***stanch***[1].

staunch[2] [stɔːntʃ] *adj.* □ **1.** (ge)treu, zuverlässig; **2.** standhaft, fest, eisern; **'staunch·ness** [-ʃnɪs] *s.* Festigkeit *f*, Zuverlässigkeit *f*.

stave [steɪv] **I** *s.* **1.** (Faß)Daube *f*; **2.** (Leiter)Sprosse *f*; **3.** Stock *m*; **4.** Strophe *f*, Vers *m*; **5.** ♪ 'Noten(linien)syˌstem *n*; **II** *v/t.* [*irr.*] **6.** *mst* ~ ***in*** a) einschlagen, b) *Loch* schlagen; **7.** ~ ***off*** a) *j-n* hinhalten *od.* abweisen, b) *Unheil etc.* abwenden, abwehren, c) *et.* aufschieben; **8.** mit Dauben *od.* Sprossen versehen; ~ **rhyme** *s.* Stabreim *m*.

staves [steɪvz] *pl. von* ***staff***[1] 8.

stay [steɪ] **I** *v/i.* **1.** bleiben (***with*** bei *j-m*): ~ ***away*** fernbleiben (***from*** *dat.*); ~

behind zurückbleiben; ~ ***clean*** rein bleiben; ***come to*** ~ (für immer) bleiben; ~ ***in*** zu Hause *od.* drinnen bleiben; ~ ***on*** (noch länger) bleiben; ~ ***for*** (*od.* ***to***) ***dinner*** zum Essen bleiben; **2.** sich (vor'übergehend) aufhalten, wohnen, weilen (***at***, ***in*** in *dat.*, ***with*** bei *j-m*); **3.** stehenbleiben; **4.** (sich) verweilen; **5.** warten (***for s.o.*** auf j-n); **6.** *bsd. sport* F a) 'durchhalten, b) ~ ***with*** *Am.* mithalten (können) mit; **II** *v/t.* **7.** a) aufhalten, hemmen, Halt gebieten (*dat.*), b) zu'rückhalten (***from*** von): ~ ***one's hand*** sich zurückhalten; **8.** ⚖ *Urteilsvollstreckung*, *Verfahren* aussetzen; *Verfahren*, *Zwangsvollstreckung* einstellen; **9.** *Hunger etc.* stillen; **10.** *a.* ~ ***up*** stützen (*a. fig.*); **11.** ⚙ a) absteifen, b) abverspannen, c) verankern; **III** *s.* **12.** (vor'übergehender) Aufenthalt; **13.** a) Halt *m*, Stockung *f*, b) Hemmnis *n* (***upon*** für): ***put a*** ~ ***on*** *s-e Gedanken etc.* zügeln; **14.** ⚖ Aussetzung *f*, Einstellung *f*, (Voll'streckungs)Aufschub *m*; **15.** F Ausdauer *f*; **16.** ⚙ a) Stütze *f*, b) Strebe *f*, c) Verspannung *f*, d) Anker *m*; **17.** ⚓ Stag *n*, Stütztau *n*; **18.** *pl.* Kor'sett *n*; **19.** *fig.* Stütze *f des Alters etc.*

stay|-at-home ['steɪəthəʊm] **I** *s.* Stubenhocker(in); **II** *adj.* stubenhockerisch; '**~-down (strike)** *s.* ⚒ *Brit.* Sitzstreik *m.*

stay·er ['steɪə] *s.* **1.** ausdauernder Mensch; **2.** *Pferdesport*: Steher *m.*

stay·ing pow·er ['steɪɪŋ] *s.* Stehvermögen *n*, Ausdauer *f.*

'**stay-in strike** *s.* Sitzstreik *m.*

stead [sted] *s.* **1.** Stelle *f*: ***in his*** ~ an s-r Statt, statt seiner; **2.** Nutzen *m*: ***stand s.o. in good*** ~ j-m (gut) zustatten kommen (*Kenntnisse etc.*).

stead·fast ['stedfəst] *adj.* ☐ fest: a) unverwandt (*Blick*), b) standhaft, unentwegt, treu (*Person*), c) unerschütterlich (*Person*, *a. Entschluß*, *Glaube etc.*); '**stead·fast·ness** [-nɪs] *s.* Standhaftigkeit *f*, Festigkeit *f.*

stead·i·ness ['stedɪnɪs] *s.* **1.** Festigkeit *f*; **2.** Beständigkeit *f*, Stetigkeit *f*; **3.** so'lide Art; **stead·y** ['stedɪ] **I** *adj.* ☐ **1.** (stand)fest, sta'bil: ***a*** ~ ***ladder***; ***not*** ~ ***on one's legs*** nicht fest auf den Beinen; **2.** gleichbleibend, -mäßig, unveränderlich; ausgeglichen (*Klima*); ✝ fest, sta'bil (*Preise*); **3.** stetig, ständig: ~ ***progress***; ~ ***work***; **4.** regelmäßig: ~ ***customer*** Stammkunde *m*; ***go*** ~ ***with*** F mit *e-m Mädchen* (fest) ‚gehen'; **5.** ruhig (*Augen*, *Nerven*), sicher (*Hand*); **6.** → ***steadfast***; **7.** so'lide, ordentlich, zuverlässig (*Person*, *Lebensweise*); **II** *int.* **8.** sachte!, ruhig Blut!; **9.** ~ ***on!*** halt!; **III** *v/t.* **10.** festigen, fest *od.* sicher *etc.* machen: ~ ***o.s.*** sich stützen; **11.** *Pferd* zügeln; **12.** *j-n* zur Vernunft bringen; **IV** *v/i.* **13.** fest *od.* ruhig *od.* sicher *etc.* werden; sich festigen (*a.* ✝ *Kurse*); **V** *s.* **14.** Stütze *f* (*für Hand od. Werkzeug*); **15.** F fester Freund *od.* feste Freundin; ~ ***state*** *s. phys.* Fließgleichgewicht *n.*

steak [steɪk] *s.* **1.** (*bsd.* Beef)Steak *n*; **2.** ('Fisch)Kote,lett *n*, (-)Fi,let *n*; ~ **hammer** *s.* Fleischklopfer *m.*

steal [stiːl] **I** *v/t.* [*irr.*] **1.** (***from s.o.*** j-m) stehlen (*a. fig. plagiieren*); **2.** *fig.* stehlen, erhaschen, ergattern: ~ ***a kiss*** e-n Kuß rauben; ~ ***a look*** e-n verstohlenen Blick werfen; → ***march***[1] 10, ***show*** 3, ***thunder*** 1; **3.** *fig. wohin* schmuggeln; **II** *v/i.* [*irr.*] **4.** stehlen; **5.** schleichen: ~ ***away*** sich davonstehlen; ~ ***into*** sich einschleichen *od.* sich stehlen in (*acc.*); **6.** ~ ***over*** *od.* (***up***)***on*** *fig. j-n* beschleichen, über'kommen (*Gefühl*); **III** *s.* **7.** F a) Diebstahl *m*, b) *Am.* Schiebung *f.*

stealth [stelθ] *s.* Heimlichkeit *f*: ***by*** ~ heimlich; '**stealth·i·ness** [-θɪnɪs] *s.* Heimlichkeit *f*; '**stealth·y** [-θɪ] *adj.* ☐ verstohlen, heimlich.

steam [stiːm] **I** *s.* **1.** (Wasser)Dampf *m*: ***at full*** ~ mit Volldampf (*a. fig.*); ***get up*** ~ Dampf aufmachen (*a. fig.*); ***let*** (*od.* ***blow***) ***off*** ~ Dampf ablassen, *fig. a.* sich *od.* s-m Zorn Luft machen; ***put on*** ~ a) Dampf anlassen, b) *fig.* Dampf dahinter machen; ***he ran out of*** ~ ihm ging die Puste aus; ***under one's own*** ~ mit eigener Kraft (*a. fig.*); **2.** Dunst *m*, Dampf *m*, Schwaden *pl.*; **3.** *fig.* Kraft *f*, Wucht *f*; **II** *v/i.* **4.** dampfen (*a. Pferd etc.*); **5.** verdampfen; **6.** ⚓, 🚂 dampfen (*fahren*): ~ ***ahead*** F *fig.* a) sich (mächtig) ins Zeug legen, b) gut vorankommen; **7.** ~ ***over*** *od.* ***up*** (sich) beschlagen (*Glas*); **8.** F vor Wut kochen (***about*** wegen); **III** *v/t.* **9.** a) *Speisen etc.* dämpfen, dünsten, b) *Holz etc.* mit Dampf behandeln, dämpfen, *Stoff* dekatieren; **10.** ~ ***up*** *Glas* beschlagen; **11.** ~ ***up*** F a) ankurbeln, b) *j-n* in Rage bringen: ***be*** **~*ed up*** → 8; ~ **bath** *s.* Dampfbad *n*; '**~·boat** *s.* Dampfboot *n*; ~ **boil·er** *s.* Dampfkessel *m*; ~ **en·gine** *s.* 'Dampfma,schine *f od.* -lokomo,tive *f.*

steam·er ['stiːmə] *s.* **1.** Dampfer *m*, Dampfschiff *n*; **2.** a) Dampfkochtopf *m*, b) 'Dämpfappa,rat *m.*

steam| fit·ter *s.* ('Heizungs)Installa,teur *m*; ~ **ga(u)ge** *s.* Mano'meter *n*; ~ **hammer** *s.* Dampfhammer *m*; ~ **heat** *s.* **1.** durch Dampf erzeugte Hitze; **2.** *phys.* spe'zifische Verdampfungswärme; ~ **nav·vy** *Brit.* → ***steam-shovel***; '~,**roll·er I** *s.* **1.** Dampfwalze *f* (*a. fig.*); **II** *v/t.* **2.** glattwalzen; **3.** *fig.* a) *Opposition etc.* niederwalzen, ‚über'fahren', b) *Antrag etc.* 'durchpeitschen; '**~·ship** → ***steamer*** 1; '~-,**shov·el** *s.* ⚙ (Dampf)Löffelbagger *m*; ~ **tug** *s.* Schleppdampfer *m.*

steam·y ['stiːmɪ] *adj.* ☐ dampfig, dunstig, dampfend, Dampf...

ste·a·rate ['stɪəreɪt] *s.* ⚗ Stea'rat *n.*

ste·ar·ic [stɪ'ærɪk] *adj.* ⚗ Stearin...;

ste·a·rin ['stɪərɪn] *s.* **1.** Stea'rin *n*; **2.** *der feste Bestandteil e-s Fettes.*

ste·a·tite ['stɪətaɪt] *s. min.* Stea'tit *m.*

steed [stiːd] *s. rhet.* (Streit)Roß *n.*

steel [stiːl] **I** *s.* **1.** Stahl *m*: **~*s*** ✝ Stahlaktien *pl.*; ***of*** ~ → 3; **2.** Stahl *m*: a) *oft* ***cold*** ~ kalter Stahl, Schwert *n*, Dolch *m*, b) Wetzstahl *m*, c) Feuerstahl *m*, d) Korsettstäbchen *n*; **II** *adj.* **3.** stählern (*a. fig.*), aus Stahl, Stahl...; **III** *v/t.* **4.** ⚙ (ver)stählen; **5.** *fig.* stählen, (ver)härten, wappnen: ~ ***o.s. for*** (***against***) ***s.th.*** sich für (gegen) et. wappnen; '**~-clad** *adj.* stahlgepanzert; ~ **en·grav·ing** *s.* Stahlstich *m*; ~ **mill** *s.* Stahl(walz)werk *n*; ~ **wool** *s.* Stahlspäne *pl.*, -wolle *f*; '**~·works** *s. pl. mst sg. konstr.* Stahlwerk(e *pl.*) *n.*

steel·y ['stiːlɪ] *adj.* → ***steel*** 3.

steel·yard ['stiːljɑːd] *s.* Laufgewichtswaage *f.*

steep[1] [stiːp] **I** *adj.* ☐ **1.** steil, jäh; **2.** F *fig.* a) ‚happig', ‚gepfeffert', unverschämt (*Preis etc.*), b) ‚toll', unglaublich; **II** *s.* **3.** steiler Abhang.

steep[2] [stiːp] **I** *v/t.* **1.** eintauchen, -weichen; **2.** (***in***, ***with***) (durch)'tränken (mit); imprägnieren (mit); **3.** (***in***) *fig.* durch'dringen (mit), versenken (in *acc.*), erfüllen (von): ~ ***o.s. in*** sich in *ein Thema etc.* versenken; **~*ed in*** versunken in (*dat.*), *b.s.* tief in *et.* verstrickt; **II** *s.* **4.** Einweichen *n*, -tauchen *n*; **5.** (Wasch)Lauge *f.*

steep·en ['stiːpən] *v/t. u. v/i.* steil(er) machen (werden); *fig.* (sich) erhöhen.

stee·ple ['stiːpl] *s.* **1.** Kirchturm(spitze *f*) *m*; **2.** Spitzturm *m*; '**~·chase** *sport s.* **1.** *Pferdesport*: Steeplechase *f*, Hindernis-, Jagdrennen *n*; **2.** Hindernislauf *m.*

stee·pled ['stiːpld] *adj.* **1.** betürmt (*Gebäude*); **2.** vieltürmig (*Stadt*).

'**stee·ple·jack** *s.* Schornstein- *od.* Turmarbeiter *m.*

steep·ness ['stiːpnɪs] *s.* **1.** Steilheit *f*, Steile *f*; **2.** steile Stelle.

steer[1] [stɪə] *s.* (*bsd.* junger) Ochse.

steer[2] [stɪə] **I** *v/t.* **1.** *Schiff*, *Fahrzeug*, *a. fig. Staat etc.* steuern, lenken; **2.** *Weg*, *Kurs* verfolgen, einhalten; **3.** *j-n wohin* lotsen, dirigieren; **II** *v/i.* **4.** steuern: ~ ***clear of*** *fig.* vermeiden, aus dem Wege gehen (*dat.*); ~ ***for*** lossteuern auf (*acc.*) (*a. fig.*); '**steer·a·ble** [-ərəbl] *adj.* lenkbar; '**steer·age** [-ərɪdʒ] *s. mst* ⚓ **1.** Steuerung *f*; **2.** Steuerwirkung *f*: **~*way*** ⚓ Steuerfahrt *f*; **3.** Zwischendeck *n.*

steer·ing ['stɪərɪŋ] **I** *s.* **1.** Steuern *n*; **2.** Steuerung *f*; **II** *adj.* **3.** Steuer...; ~ **column** *s. mot.* Lenksäule *f*: ~ ***lock*** Lenk(-rad)schloß *n*; ~ **com·mit·tee** *s.* Lenkungsausschuß *m*; (Kon'greß- *etc.*)Leitung *f*; ~ **gear** *s.* **1.** *mot.*, ✈ Steuerung *f*, Lenkung *f*; **2.** ⚓ Steuergerät *n*, Ruderanlage *f*; ~ **lock** *s. mot.* Lenkungseinschlag *m*; ~ **wheel** *s.* ⚓ Steuer-, *mot. a.* Lenkrad *n.*

steeve[1] [stiːv] ⚓ *v/t.* traven, *Ballenladung* zs.-pressen.

steeve[2] [stiːv] *s.* ⚓ Steigung *f* (*des Bugspriets*).

stein [staɪn] (*Ger.*) *s.* Bier-, Maßkrug *m.*

stel·lar ['stelə] *adj.* stel'lar, Stern(en)...

stel·late ['stelət] *adj.* sternförmig: ~ ***leaves*** ⚘ quirlständige Blätter.

stem[1] [stem] **I** *s.* **1.** (Baum)Stamm *m*; **2.** a) Stengel *m*, b) (Blüten-, Blatt-, Frucht)Stiel *m*, c) Halm *m*; **3.** Bündel *n* Bananen; **4.** (*Pfeifen-*, *Weinglas- etc.*) Stiel *m*; (Lampen)Fuß *m*; (Ven'til-) Schaft *m*; (Thermo'meter)Röhre *f*; **5.** (Aufzieh)Welle *f* (*Uhr*); **6.** Geschlecht *n*, Stamm *m*; **7.** *ling.* (Wort)Stamm *m*; **8.** ♪ (Noten)Hals *m*; **9.** *typ.* Grundstrich *m*; **10.** ⚓ (Vorder)Steven *m*: ***from*** ~ ***to stern*** von vorn bis achtern; **II** *v/t.* **11.** entstielen; **III** *v/i.* **12.** stammen (***from*** von).

stem[2] [stem] **I** *v/t.* **1.** *Fluß etc.* eindämmen (*a. fig.*); **2.** *Blutung* stillen; **3.** ⚓ ankämpfen gegen *die Strömung etc.*; **4.** *fig.* a) aufhalten, Einhalt gebieten (*dat.*), b) ankämpfen gegen, sich entgegenstemmen (*dat.*); **II** *v/i.* **5.** *Skisport*: stemmen.

stem·less ['stemlɪs] *adj.* stengellos, un-

gestielt.
stem| turn *s. Skisport*: Stemmbogen *m*; '**~ˌwind·er** *s.* Remon'toiruhr *f*.
stench [stentʃ] *s.* Gestank *m*.
sten·cil ['stensl] **I** *s.* **1.** *a.* **~ plate** ('Maler)Schaˌblone *f*, Pa'trone *f*; **2.** *typ.* ('Wachs)Maˌtrize *f*; **3.** Scha'blonenzeichnung *f*, -muster *n*; **4.** Ma'trizenabzug *m*; **II** *v/t.* **5.** *Oberfläche, Buchstaben* schablonieren; **6.** auf Matrize(n) schreiben.
Sten gun [sten] *s.* ⚔ leichtes Ma'schinengewehr, LMG *n*.
sten·o ['stenəʊ] F → a) **stenograph** 4, b) *Am.* **stenographer**.
sten·o·graph ['stenəgrɑːf] **I** *s.* **1.** Steno'gramm *n*; **2.** Kurzschriftzeichen *n*; **3.** Stenogra'phiermaˌschine *f*; **II** *v/t.* **4.** stenographieren; **ste·nog·ra·pher** [ste'nɒgrəfə] *s.* **1.** Steno'graph(in); **2.** *Am.* Stenoty'pistin *f*; **sten·o·graph·ic** [ˌstenə'græfɪk] *adj.* (□ **~ally**) steno'graphisch; **ste·nog·ra·phy** [ste'nɒgrəfɪ] *s.* Stenogra'phie *f*, Kurzschrift *f*.
sten·o·type ['stenəʊtaɪp] → **stenograph** 2 *u.* 3.
sten·to·ri·an [sten'tɔːrɪən] *adj.* 'überlaut: **~ voice** Stentorstimme *f*.
step [step] **I** *s.* **1.** Schritt *m* (*a. Geräusch, Maß*): **~ by ~** Schritt für Schritt (*a. fig.*); **take a ~** e-n Schritt machen; **2.** Fußstapfen *m*: **tread in s.o.'s ~s** *fig.* in j-s Fußstapfen treten; **3.** *eiliger etc.* Schritt, Gang *m*; **4.** (Tanz)Schritt *m*; **5.** (Gleich)Schritt *m*: **in ~** im Gleichschritt; **out of ~** außer Tritt; **out of ~ with** *fig.* nicht im Einklang mit; **fall in ~** Tritt fassen; **keep ~** (**with**) Schritt halten (mit); **6.** ein paar Schritte *pl.*, *ein* ‚Katzensprung' *m*: **it is only a ~ to the inn**; **7.** *fig.* Schritt *m*, Maßnahme *f*: **take ~s** Schritte unternehmen; **take legal ~s against** gegen *j-n* gerichtlich vorgehen; **a false ~** ein Fehler, e-e Dummheit; → **watch** 17; **8.** *fig.* Schritt *m*, Stufe *f*: **a great ~ forward** ein großer Schritt vorwärts; **9.** Stufe *f* (*e-r Treppe etc.*; *a.* ϟ *e-s Verstärkers etc.*); (Leiter)Sprosse *f*; ⚙, ϟ Schaltschritt *m*; **10.** (**pair of**) **~s** *pl.* Trittleiter *f*; **11.** Tritt(brett *n*) *m*; **12.** *geogr.* Stufe *f*, Ter'rasse *f*; Pla'teau *n*; **13.** ♪ a) (Ton-, Inter'vall)Schritt *m*, b) Inter'vall *n*, c) (Tonleiter)Stufe *f*; **14.** *fig.* a) (Rang-) Stufe *f*, Grad *m*, b) *bsd.* ⚔ Beförderung *f*; **II** *v/i.* **15.** schreiten, treten: **~ into a fortune** *fig.* unverhofft zu e-m Vermögen kommen; **16.** *wohin* gehen, treten: **~ in!** herein!; **17.** → **step out** 2; **18.** treten ([**up**]**on** auf *acc.*): **~ on the gas** (*od.* **~ on it**) (F *a. fig.*) Gas geben; **~ on it!** F Tempo!; **III** *v/t.* **19.** *Schritt* machen: **~ it** zu Fuß gehen; **20.** *Tanz* tanzen; **21.** *a.* **~ off** (*od.* **out**) *Entfernung etc.* a) abschreiten, b) abstecken; **22.** abstufen;
Zssgn mit adv.:
step| a·side *v/i.* **1.** zur Seite treten; **2.** → **step down** 2; **~ back I** *v/i. a. fig.* zu'rücktreten; **II** *v/t.* abstufen; **~ down I** *v/i.* **1.** her'unter-, hin'unterschreiten; **2.** *fig.* zu'rücktreten (**in favo[u]r of** zu'gunsten); **II** *v/t.* **3.** verringern, verzögern; **4.** ϟ her'untertransformieren; **~ in** *v/i.* **1.** eintreten, -steigen; **2.** *fig.* einschreiten, -greifen; **~ out I** *v/i.* **1.** her'austreten, aussteigen; **2.** (forsch) ausschreiten; **3.** F (viel) ausgehen; **II** *v/t.* **4.** → **step** 21a; **~ up I** *v/i.* **1.** hin'auf-, her'aufsteigen; **2.** zugehen (**to** auf *acc.*); **II** *v/t.* **3.** *Produktion etc.* steigern, ankurbeln; **4.** ϟ hochtransformieren.
step- [step] *in Zssgn* Stief...: **~child** Stiefkind *n*; **~father** Stiefvater *m*.
step| dance *s.* Step(tanz) *m*; '**~-down** *adj.* ϟ Umspann...: **~ transformer** Abwärtstransformator *m*; '**~-in I** *adj.* **1.** zum Hin'einschlüpfen, Schlupf...; **II** *s.* **2.** *mst pl.* Schlüpfer *m*; **3.** *pl. a.* **~ shoes** Slipper *pl.*; '**~ˌlad·der** *s.* Trittleiter *f*; '**~ˌmoth·er·ly** *adj. a. fig.* stiefmütterlich.
steppe [step] *s. geogr.* Steppe *f*.
step·ping stone ['stepɪŋ] *s.* **1.** (Tritt-) Stein *m im Wasserlauf etc.*; **2.** *fig.* Sprungbrett *n* (**to** zu).
'**step-up I** *adj.* stufenweise erhöhend: **~ transformer** ϟ Aufwärtstransformator *m*; **II** *s.* Steigerung *f*.
'**step·wise** *adv.* schritt-, stufenweise.
ster·e·o ['sterɪəʊ] F **I** *s.* **1.** a) → **stereotype** 1, b) → **stereoscope**; **2.** a) Stereogerät *n*, b) Stereo(schall)platte *f*; **II** *adj.* **3.** → **stereoscopic**; **4.** stereo, Stereo...: **~ record** → 2b.
stereo- [sterɪəʊ] *in Zssgn* a) starr, fest, b) 'dreidimensioˌnal, stereo..., Stereo..., Raum...; **ster·e·o·chem·is·try** [ˌsterɪəʊ'kemɪstrɪ] *s.* 'Stereo-, 'Raumcheˌmie *f*; **ster·e·og·ra·phy** [ˌsterɪ'ɒgrəfɪ] *s.* ⩚ Stereogra'phie *f*, Körperzeichnung *f*; **ster·e·om·e·try** [ˌsterɪ'ɒmɪtrɪ] *s.* **1.** *phys.* Stereome'trie *f*; **2.** ⩚ Geome'trie *f* des Raumes.
ster·e·o·phon·ic [ˌsterɪəʊ'fɒnɪk] *adj.* (□ **~ally**) stereo'phonisch, Stereoton...: **~ sound** Raumton *m*.
ster·e·o·plate ['sterɪəpleɪt] *s. typ.* Stereo'typplatte *f*, Stereo *n*.
ster·e·o·scope ['sterɪəskəʊp] *s.* Stereo'skop *n*; **ster·e·o·scop·ic** [ˌsterɪə'skɒpɪk] *adj.* (□ **~ally**) stereo'skopisch, Stereo...; **ster·e·os·co·py** [ˌsterɪ'ɒskəpɪ] *s.* Stereosko'pie *f*.
ster·e·o·type ['stɪərɪətaɪp] **I** *s.* **1.** *typ.* a) Steroty'pie *f*, Plattendruck *m*, b) Stereo'type *f*, Druckplatte *f*; **2.** *fig.* Kli'schee *n*, Scha'blone *f*; **II** *v/t.* **3.** *typ.* stereotypieren; **4.** *fig. Redensart etc.* stereo'typ wieder'holen; **5.** e-e feste Form geben (*dat.*); '**ster·e·o·typed** [-pt] *adj.* **1.** *typ.* stereotypiert; **2.** *fig.* stereo'typ, scha'blonenhaft; **ster·e·o·ty·pog·ra·phy** [ˌstɪərɪəʊtaɪ'pɒgrəfɪ] *s. typ.* Stereo'typdruck(verfahren *n*) *m*; '**ster·e·o·ˌtyp·y** [-pɪ] *s. typ.* Stereoty'pie *f*.
ster·ile ['steraɪl] *adj.* **1.** ste'ril: a) ⚕ keimfrei, b) ♀, *physiol.* unfruchtbar (*a. fig. Geist etc.*); **2.** *fig.* fruchtlos (*Arbeit, Diskussion etc.*); leer, gedankenarm (*Stil*); **ste·ril·i·ty** [ste'rɪlətɪ] *s.* Sterili'tät *f* (*a. fig.*).
ster·i·li·za·tion [ˌsterəlaɪ'zeɪʃn] *s.* **1.** Sterilisati'on *f*: a) Entkeimung *f*, b) Unfruchtbarmachung *f*; **2.** Sterili'tät *f*;
ster·i·lize ['sterəlaɪz] *v/t.* sterilisieren: a) keimfrei machen, b) unfruchtbar machen; '**ster·i·li·zer** ['sterəlaɪzə] *s.* Sterili'sator *m* (*Apparat*).
ster·ling ['stɜːlɪŋ] **I** *adj.* **1.** ⚜ Sterling(...): **ten pounds ~** 10 Pfund Sterling; **~ area** Sterlinggebiet *n*, -block *m*; **2.** von Standardwert (*Gold, Silber*); **3.** *fig.* echt, gediegen, bewährt; **II** *s.* **4.** ⚜ Sterling *m*.
stern[1] [stɜːn] *adj.* □ **1.** streng, hart: **~ discipline**; **~ penalty**; **2.** unnachgiebig; **3.** streng, finster: **a ~ face**.
stern[2] [stɜːn] **I** *s.* **1.** ⚓ Heck *n*, Achterschiff *n*: (**down**) **by the ~** hecklastig; **2.** *zo.* a) 'Hinterteil *n*, b) Schwanz *m*; **3.** *allg.* hinterer Teil; **II** *adj.* **4.** ⚓ Heck...
ster·nal ['stɜːnl] *adj. anat.* Brustbein...
'**stern|-ˌchas·er** *s.* ⚓ *hist.* Heckgeschütz *n*; '**~-fast** *s.* ⚓ Achtertau *n*.
stern·ness ['stɜːnnɪs] *s.* Strenge *f*, Härte *f*, Düsterkeit *f*.
'**stern·post** *s.* ⚓ Achtersteven *m*.
ster·num ['stɜːnəm] *pl.* **-na** [-nə] *s. anat.* Brustbein *n*.
ster·to·rous ['stɜːtərəs] *adj.* □ röchelnd.
stet [stet] (*Lat.*) *typ.* **I** *imp.* stehenlassen!, bleibt!; **II** *v/t.* mit ‚stet' markieren.
steth·o·scope ['steθəskəʊp] ⚕ **I** *s.* Stetho'skop *n*, Hörrohr *n*; **II** *v/t.* abhorchen; **steth·o·scop·ic** [ˌsteθə'skɒpɪk] *adj.* (□ **~ally**) stetho'skopisch.
ste·ve·dore ['stiːvədɔː] *s.* ⚓ **1.** Stauer *m*, Schauermann *m*; **2.** Stauer *m* (*Unternehmer*).
stew[1] [stjuː] **I** *v/t.* **1.** schmoren, dämpfen, langsam kochen; → **stewed** 1; **II** *v/i.* **2.** schmoren; → **juice** 1; **3.** *fig.* ‚schmoren', vor Hitze (fast) 'umkommen; **4.** F sich aufregen; **III** *s.* **5.** Schmor-, Eintopfgericht *n*; **6.** F Aufregung *f*.
stew[2] [stjuː] *s. Brit.* a) Fischteich *m*, b) Fischbehälter *m*.
stew·ard ['stjʊəd] *s.* **1.** Verwalter *m*; **2.** Haushalter *m*, Haushofmeister *m*; **3.** Tafelmeister *m*, Kämmerer *m* (*e-s College, Klubs etc.*); **4.** ⚓, ✈ Steward *m*; **5.** (Fest- *etc.*)Ordner *m*; *mot.* 'Rennkommisˌsar *m*; → **shop steward**; '**stew·ard·ess** [-dɪs] *s.* ⚓, ✈ Stewardeß *f*; '**stew·ard·ship** [-ʃɪp] *s.* Verwalteramt *n*.
stewed [stjuːd] *adj.* **1.** geschmort, gedämpft, gedünstet; **2.** *sl.* ‚besoffen'.
'**stew|·pan** *s.* Schmorpfanne *f*; '**~·pot** *s.* Schmortopf *m*.
stick[1] [stɪk] **I** *s.* **1.** Stecken *m*, Stock *m*, (trockener) Zweig; *pl.* Klein-, Brennholz *n*: **dry ~s** (dürres) Reisig; **2.** Scheit *n*, Stück *n* Holz; **3.** Gerte *f*, Rute *f*; **4.** Stengel *m*, Stiel *m* (*Rhabarber, Sellerie*); **5.** Stock *m* (*a. fig. Schläge*), Stab *m*: **get** (**give**) **the ~** e-e Tracht Prügel bekommen (verabreichen); **get hold of the wrong end of the ~** *fig.* die Sache falsch verstehen; **6.** (Besen- *etc.*)Stiel *m*; **7.** (Spazier)Stock *m*; **8.** (Zucker-, Siegellack)Stange *f*; **9.** a) (Stück *n*) Rasierseife *f*, b) (Lippen- *etc.*)Stift *m*; **10.** ♪ a) Taktstock *m*, b) (Trommel)Schlegel *m*, c) (Geigen)Bogen *m*; **11.** *sport* a) Schläger *m*, *Hockey etc.*: Stock *m*, b) *Pferdesport*: Hürde *f*; **12.** a) ✈ Steuerknüppel *m*, b) *mot.* Schalthebel *m*; **13.** ⚔ Bombenreihe *f*; **14.** *typ.* Winkelhaken *m*; **15.** F *a.* **dry** (*od.* **dull**) **~** Stockfisch *m*, *allg.* Kerl *m*; **16.** *pl. Am.* F finsterste Pro'vinz; **II** *v/t.* **17.** *Pflanze* mit e-m Stock stützen; **18.** *typ.* a) setzen, b) in e-m Winkelhaken anein'anderreihen.
stick[2] [stɪk] **I** *v/t.* [*irr.*] **1.** durch'stechen, -'bohren; *Schweine* (ab)stechen; **2.** ste-

chen mit *e-r Nadel etc.* (**in**, **into** in *acc.*); *et.* stecken, stoßen; **3.** *auf e-e Gabel etc.* stecken, aufspießen; **4.** *Kopf, Hand etc. wohin* stecken *od.* strecken; **5.** F legen, setzen, *in die Tasche etc.* stecken; **6.** (an)stecken, anheften; **7.** ˈvollstecken (**with** mit); **8.** *Briefmarke, Plakat etc.* ankleben, *Fotos etc.* (ein)kleben: **~ together** *et.* zs.-kleben; **9.** bekleben; **10.** zum Stecken bringen, festfahren: **be stuck** *im Schlamm etc.* stecken(bleiben *a. fig.*), festsitzen (*a. fig.*); **be stuck on** F vernarrt sein in (*acc.*); **be stuck with s.th.** et. ‚am Hals haben'; **be stuck for s.th.** um et. verlegen sein; **11.** *j-n* verwirren; **12.** F *j-n* ‚blechen' lassen (**for** für); **13.** *sl. j-n* ‚leimen' (*betrügen*); **14.** *sl. et. od. j-n* aushalten, -stehen, (v)ertragen: **I can't ~ him**; **15. ~ it** (**out**) F ˈdurchhalten, es aushalten; **16. ~ it on** F a) e-n unverschämten Preis verlangen, b) ‚dick auftragen', überˈtreiben; **II** *v/i.* [*irr.*] **17.** stecken; **18.** (fest)kleben, haften: **~ together** zs.-kleben; **19.** sich festklammern *od.* heften (**to** an *acc.*); **20.** haften, hängenbleiben (*a. fig. Spitzname etc.*): **some of it will ~** et. (*von e-r Verleumdung*) bleibt immer hängen; **~ in the mind** im Gedächtnis haftenbleiben; **make s.th. ~** *fig.* dafür sorgen, daß et. ‚sitzt'; **21. ~ to** bei *j-m od. e-r Sache* bleiben, *j-m* nicht von der Seite weichen: **~ to the point** *fig.* bei der Sache bleiben; **~ to it** dranbleiben; → **gun** 1; **22. ~ to** treu bleiben (*dat.*), zu *j-m, s-m Wort etc.* stehen, bei *s-r Ansicht etc.* bleiben, sich an *e-e Regel etc.* halten; **~ together** zs.-halten (*Freunde*); **23.** *im Hals, im Schmutz, a. fig. beim Lesen etc.* stekkenbleiben; → **mud** 2; **24. ~ at nothing** vor nichts zurückschrecken; **25.** herˈvorstehen (**from**, **out of** aus);

Zssgn mit adv.:

stick| a·round *v/i.* F in der Nähe bleiben; **~ out I** *v/i.* **1.** ab-, herˈvor-, herˈausstehen; **2.** *fig.* auffallen; **3.** bestehen (**for** auf *dat.*); **II** *v/t.* **4.** *Arm, Brust, a. Kopf, Zunge* herˈausstrecken; **5.** → **stick²** 15; **~ up I** *v/t.* **1.** *sl.* überˈfallen, ausrauben; **2. ~ 'em up!** *sl.* Hände hoch!; **II** *v/i.* **3.** in die Höhe stehen; **4. ~ for** sich für *j-n* einsetzen; **5. ~ to** mutig gegenˈübertreten (*dat.*), Paˈroli bieten (*dat.*).

stick·er [ˈstɪkə] *s.* **1.** a) (Schweine-) Schlächter *m*, b) Schlachtmesser *n*; **2.** Klebezettel *m*, Aufkleber *m*; **3.** *Am.* (*angeklebter*) Strafzettel; **4.** *fig.* zäher Kerl; **5.** F ‚Hocker' *m*, (zu) lange bleibender Gast; **6.** F ‚Ladenhüter' *m*; **7.** ‚harte Nuß'.

stick·i·ness [ˈstɪkɪnɪs] *s.* **1.** Klebrigkeit *f*; **2.** Schwüle *f*; **3.** F Schwierigkeit *f*.

stick·ing plas·ter [ˈstɪkɪŋ] *s.* Heftpflaster *n*.

stick-in-the-mud [ˈstɪkɪnðəmʌd] F **I** *adj.* rückständig, -schrittlich; **II** *s.* Rückschrittler *m*, *bsd. pol.* Reaktioˈnär *m*.

ˈ**stick·jaw** *s.* F ‚Plombenzieher' *m* (*zäher Bonbon etc.*).

stick·le [ˈstɪkl] *v/i.* **1.** harnäckig zanken *od.* streiten: **~ for s.th.** et. hartnäckig verfechten; **2.** Bedenken äußern, Skrupel haben.

stick·le·back [ˈstɪklbæk] *s. ichth.* Stichling *m*.

stick·ler [ˈstɪklə] *s.* **1.** Eiferer *m*; **2.** Verfechter *m* (**for** *gen.*); **3.** Kleinigkeitskrämer *m*, Peˈdant *m*, j-d, der es ganz genau nimmt (**for** mit).

stick-to-it·ive [ˌstɪkˈtuːətɪv] *adj. Am.* F hartnäckig, zäh.

ˈ**stick-up I** *adj.* **1. ~ collar** → 2; **II** *s.* **2.** F Stehkragen *m*; **3.** *sl.* (ˈRaub)ˌÜberfall *m*.

stick·y [ˈstɪkɪ] *adj.* □ **1.** klebrig, zäh: **~ charge** ⚔ Haftladung *f*; **~ label** *Brit.* Klebezettel *m*; **2.** schwül, stickig (*Wetter etc.*); **3.** F *fig.* a) klebrig, b) eklig, c) schwierig, heikel (*Sache*), d) kritisch, e) kitschig: **be ~ about doing s.th.** et. nur ungern tun.

stiff [stɪf] **I** *adj.* □ **1.** *allg.* steif, starr (*a. Gesicht, Person*): **~ collar** steifer Kragen; **~ neck** steifer Hals; → **lip** 1; **2.** zäh, dick, steif (*Teig etc.*); **3.** steif (*Brise*), stark (*Wind, Strömung*); **4.** stark (*Dosis, Getränk*), steif (*Grog*); **5.** *fig.* starrköpfig; **6.** *fig.* hart (*Gegner, Kampf etc.*), scharf (*Konkurrenz, Opposition*); **7.** schwierig (*Aufstieg, Prüfung etc.*); **8.** hart (*Strafe*); **9.** steif, forˈmell, gezwungen (*Benehmen, Person etc.*); **10.** steif, linkisch (*Stil*); **11.** F unglaublich: **a bit ~** ziemlich stark, allerhand; **12.** F ‚zu Tode' *gelangweilt, erschrocken*; **13.** † a) staˈbil, fest (*Preis, Markt*), b) hoch, unverschämt (*Forderung, Preis*); **II** *s. sl.* **14.** a) Leiche *f*, b) Besoffene(r) *m*; **15.** a) Langweiler *m*, b) Blödmann *m*; **16.** *Am.* a) ‚Lappen' *m* (*Banknote*), b) ‚Blüte' *f* (*Falschgeld*), c) ‚Kasˈsiber' *m* (*im Gefängnis*); ˈ**stiff·en** [-fn] **I** *v/t.* **1.** (ver)steifen, (ver)stärken; *Stoff etc.* stärken, steifen; **2.** steif *od.* starr machen (*Flüssigkeit, Glieder etc.*), verdicken (*Flüssiges*); **3.** *fig.* a) *et.* verschärfen, b) (be)stärken, *j-m* den Nacken steifen; **II** *v/i.* **4.** sich versteifen, -stärken; starr werden; **5.** *fig.* hart werden, sich versteifen; **6.** steif *od.* förmlich werden; **7.** † sich festigen (*Preise etc.*); ˈ**stiff·en·er** [-fnə] *s.* **1.** Versteifung *f*; **2.** F ‚Seelenwärmer' *m*, Stärkung *f* (*Getränk*); ˈ**stiff·en·ing** [-fnɪŋ] *s.* Versteifung *f*: a) Steifwerden *n*, b) ˈSteifmateriˌal *n*.

ˌ**stiff-ˈnecked** *adj. fig.* halsstarrig.

stiff·ness [ˈstɪfnɪs] *s.* **1.** Steifheit *f* (*a. fig. Förmlichkeit*), Steife *f*, Starrheit *f*; **2.** Zähigkeit *f*, Dickflüssigkeit *f*; **3.** *fig.* Härte *f*, Schärfe *f*.

sti·fle¹ [ˈstaɪfl] **I** *v/t.* **1.** *j-n* ersticken; **2.** *Fluch etc., a. Gefühl, a. Aufstand etc.* ersticken, unterˈdrücken, *Diskussion etc.* abwürgen; **II** *v/i.* **3.** (*weitS.* schier) ersticken.

sti·fle² [ˈstaɪfl] *s. zo.* **1.** *a.* **~ joint** Kniegelenk *n* (*Pferd, Hund*); **2.** *vet.* Kniegelenkgalle *f* (*Pferd*); **~ bone** *s.* Kniescheibe *f* (*Pferd*).

sti·fling [ˈstaɪflɪŋ] *adj.* □ erstickend (*a. fig.*), stickig.

stig·ma [ˈstɪgmə] *pl.* **-mas**, **-ma·ta** [-mətə] *s.* **1.** *fig.* Brand-, Schandmal *n*, Stigma *n*; **2.** ⚕ Symˈptom *n*; **3.** ⚕ (*pl.* **-mata**) Mal *n*, roter Hautfleck; **4. stigmata** *pl. eccl.* Wundmale *pl.*, Stigmata *pl.*; **5.** ⚘ Narbe *f* (*Blüte*); **6.** *zo.* Luftloch *n* (*Insekt*); **stig·mat·ic** [stɪgˈmætɪk] *adj.* (□ **~ally**) **1.** stigˈmatisch (*a. opt.*); **2.** ⚘ narbenartig; **3.** *opt.* (ana-) stigˈmatisch; ˈ**stig·ma·tize** [-ətaɪz] *v/t.* **1.** ⚕, *eccl.* stigmatisieren; **2.** *bsd. fig.* brandmarken.

stile¹ [staɪl] *s.* Zauntritt *m*.

stile² [staɪl] *s.* Seitenstück *n* (*e-r Täfelung*), Höhenfries *m* (*e-r Tür*).

sti·let·to [stɪˈletəʊ] *pl.* **-tos** [-z] *s.* Stiˈlett *n*: **~ (heel)** Pfennigabsatz *m*.

still¹ [stɪl] **I** *adj.* □ **1.** *allg.* still: a) reglos, unbeweglich, b) ruhig, lautlos, c) leise, gedämpft, d) friedlich, ruhig: **keep ~!** sei ruhig!; → **water** 11; **2.** nicht moussierend: **~ wine** Stillwein *m*; **3.** *phot.* Stand…, Steh…, Einzel(aufnahme)…; **II** *s.* **4.** *poet.* Stille *f*; **5.** *phot.* Standfoto *n*, Einzelaufnahme *f*; **III** *v/t.* **6.** *Geräusche etc.* zum Schweigen bringen; **7.** *j-n* beruhigen, *Verlangen etc.* stillen; **IV** *v/i.* **8.** still werden.

still² [stɪl] **I** *adv.* **1.** (immer) noch, noch immer, bis jetzt; **2.** (*beim comp.*) noch, immer: **~ higher**, **higher ~** noch höher; **~ more so because** um so mehr als; **3.** dennoch, doch; **II** *cj.* **4.** (und) dennoch, und doch, inˈdes(sen).

still³ [stɪl] *s.* a) Destillierkolben *m*, b) Destilˈlierappaˌrat *m*.

stil·lage [ˈstɪlɪdʒ] *s.* Gestell *n*.

ˈ**still|·birth** *s.* Totgeburt *f*; ˈ**~·born** *adj.* totgeboren (*a. fig.*); ˈ**~-fish** *v/i.* vom verankerten Boot aus angeln; **~ hunt** *s.* Pirsch(jagd) *f*; ˈ**~-hunt** *v/i.* (*v/t.* an)pirschen; **~ life** *s. paint.* Stilleben *n*.

still·ness [ˈstɪlnɪs] *s.* Stille *f*.

still room *s. bsd. Brit.* **1.** *hist.* Destillatiˈonsraum *m*; **2.** a) Vorratskammer *f*, b) Servierraum *m*.

stilt [stɪlt] *s.* **1.** Stelze *f*; **2.** △ Pfahl *m*, Pfeiler *m*; **3.** *a.* **~ bird** *orn.* Stelzenläufer *m*; ˈ**stilt·ed** [-tɪd] *adj.* □ **1.** gestelzt, gespreizt, geschraubt (*Rede, Stil etc.*); **2.** △ erhöht; ˈ**stilt·ed·ness** [-tɪdnɪs] *s.* Gespreiztheit *f*.

stim·u·lant [ˈstɪmjʊlənt] **I** *s.* **1.** ⚕ Stimulans *n*, Anregungs-, Weckmittel *n*; **2.** Genußmittel *n*, *bsd.* Alkohol *m*; **3.** Anreiz *m* (**of** für); **II** *adj.* **4.** → **stimulating** 1; **stim·u·late** [ˈstɪmjʊleɪt] *v/t.* **1.** ⚕ *etc., a. fig.* stimulieren, anregen (**s.o. into** j-n zu *et.*); *fig. a.* anspornen, anstacheln; beleben, ankurbeln; **2.** *Nerv* reizen; ˈ**stim·u·lat·ing** [-leɪtɪŋ] *adj.* **1.** *a. fig.* stimulierend, anregend, belebend; **2.** *fig.* anspornend; **stim·u·la·tion** [ˌstɪmjʊˈleɪʃn] *s.* **1.** Anreiz *m*, Antrieb *m*, Anregung *f*, Belebung *f*; **2.** ⚕ Reizung *f*, Reiz *m*; ˈ**stim·u·la·tive** [-lətɪv] → **stimulating**; ˈ**stim·u·lus** [-ləs] *pl.* **-li** [-laɪ] *s.* **1.** Stimulus *m*: a) (An)Reiz *m*, Antrieb *m*, Ansporn *m* (**to** zu), b) ⚕ Reiz *m*: **~ threshold** Reizschwelle *f*; **2.** → **stimulant** 1; **3.** ⚘ Nesselhaar *n*.

sti·my [ˈstaɪmɪ] → **stymie**.

sting [stɪŋ] **I** *v/t.* [*irr.*] **1.** stechen (*Insekt, Nessel etc.*); **2.** brennen, beißen in *od.* auf (*dat.*); **3.** schmerzen, weh tun (*Schlag etc.*): **stung by remorse** *fig.* von Reue geplagt; **4.** *fig. j-n* verletzen, kränken; **5.** anstacheln, reizen (**into** zu); **6.** *sl.* ‚neppen' (**for** um *Geld*); **II** *v/i.* [*irr.*] **7.** stechen; **8.** brennen, beißen (*Pfeffer etc.*); **9.** *a. fig.* schmerzen, weh tun; **III** *s.* **10.** Stachel *m* (*Insekt*; *a. fig. des Todes, der Eifersucht etc.*); **11.** ⚘ Brennborste *f*; **12.** Stich *m*, Biß *m*: **~ of conscience** *fig.* Gewissensbisse *pl.*; **13.** Schärfe *f*; **14.** Pointe *f*, Spitze *f* (*e-s*

Witzes); **15.** Schwung *m*, Wucht *f*; **ˈsting·er** [-ŋə] *s*. **1.** a) stechendes Inˈsekt, b) stechende Pflanze; **2.** F a) schmerzhafter Schlag, b) beißende Bemerkung.
sting·i·ness [ˈstɪndʒɪnɪs] *s*. Geiz *m*.
sting·ing [ˈstɪŋɪŋ] *adj*. □ **1.** ⚘, *zo*. stechend; **2.** *fig*. schmerzhaft (*Schlag etc.*); schneidend (*Kälte, Wind*); scharf, beißend, verletzend (*Worte, Tadel*); **~ net·tle** *s*. ⚘ Brennessel *f*.
stin·gy [ˈstɪndʒɪ] *adj*. □ **1.** geizig, knickerig: ***be ~ of s.th.*** mit et. knausern; **2.** dürftig, kärglich.
stink [stɪŋk] **I** *v/i*. [*irr*.] **1.** stinken, übel riechen (***of*** nach): ***~ of money*** *fig*. F vor Geld stinken; **2.** *fig*. verrufen sein, ‚stinken': ***~ to high heaven*** zum Himmel stinken; → ***nostril***; **3.** *fig*. F (ˈhunds)miseˌrabel sein; **II** *v/t*. [*irr*.] **4.** *a*. ***~ out, up*** verstänkern; **5.** ***~ out*** a) *Höhle, Tiere* ausräuchern, b) *j-n* durch Gestank vertreiben; **6.** *sl*. (den Gestank *gen*.) riechen: ***you can ~ it a mile off***; **III** *s*. **7.** Gestank *m*; **8.** Stunk *m*, Krach *m*: ***raise*** (*od*. ***kick up***) ***a ~*** Stunk machen (***about*** wegen); **9.** *pl*. *Brit*. *sl*. Cheˈmie *f*; **10.** *Am*. F (billiges) Parˈfüm; **ˈstink·ard** [-kəd] *s*. **1.** *zo*. Stinktier *n*; **2.** → ***stinker*** 1; **ˈstink·er** [-kə] *s*. **1.** a) ‚Stinker' *m*, b) *sl*. Dreckskerl *m*; **2.** a) ‚Stinkaˈdores' *m* (*Käse*), b) ‚Stinkaˈdores' *f* (*Zigarre*); **3.** *sl*. a) gemeiner Brief, b) böse Bemerkung *od*. Kriˈtik, c) ‚böse' (*schwierige etc*.) Sache, d) ‚Mist' *m*; **ˈstink·ing** [-kɪŋ] **I** *adj*. □ **1.** stinkend; **2.** *sl*. a) widerlich, b) miseˈrabel; **3.** → ***stinko***; **II** *adv*. **4.** ***~ rich*** *sl*. ‚stinkreich'.
stinko [ˈstɪŋkəʊ] *adj*. *Am*. *sl*. ‚(stink)besoffen', (toˈtal) ‚blau'.
ˈstink·pot *s*. **1.** ⚓ *hist*. Stinktopf *m*; **2.** F → ***stinker*** 1.
stint [stɪnt] **I** *v/t*. **1.** *j-n od*. *et*. einschränken, *j-n* kurz *od*. knapp halten (***in, of*** mit): ***~ o.s. of*** sich einschränken mit, sich *et*. versagen; **2.** knausern *od*. kargen mit (*Geld, Lob etc*.); **II** *s*. **3.** Be-, Einschränkung *f*: ***without ~*** ohne Einschränkung, rückhaltlos; **4.** a) (zugewiesene) Arbeit, Pensum *n*, b) (vorgeschriebenes) Maß; **5.** ⚒ Schicht *f*; **ˈstint·ed** [-tɪd] *adj*. □ knapp, karg.
stipe [staɪp] *s*. ⚘, *zo*. Stiel *m*.
sti·pend [ˈstaɪpend] *s*. Gehalt *n* (*bsd*. *e-s Geistlichen*); **sti·pen·di·ar·y** [staɪˈpendjərɪ] **I** *adj*. besoldet: ***~ magistrate*** → **II** *s*. *Brit*. Richter *m an e-m* ***magistrates' court***.
stip·ple [ˈstɪpl] **I** *v/t*. **1.** *paint*. tüpfeln, punktieren; **II** *s*. **2.** Punkˈtiermaˌnier *f*, Pointilˈlismus *m*; **3.** Punktierung *f*.
stip·u·late [ˈstɪpjʊleɪt] *bsd*. ⚖, ☤ **I** *v/i*. **1.** (***for***) a) e-e Vereinbarung treffen (über *acc*.), b) *et*. zur Bedingung machen; **II** *v/t*. **2.** festsetzen, vereinbaren, ausbedingen; **3.** ⚖ *Tatbestand* einverständlich feststellen, außer Streit stellen; **stip·u·la·tion** [ˌstɪpjʊˈleɪʃn] *s*. **1.** ☤, ⚖ (vertragliche) Abmachung, Überˈeinkunft *f*; **2.** Klausel *f*, Bedingung *f*; **3.** ⚖ Parˈteienüberˌeinkunft *f*.
stip·ule [ˈstɪpjuːl] *s*. ⚘ Nebenblatt *n*.
stir¹ [stɜː] **I** *v/t*. **1.** *Kaffee, Teig etc*. rühren: ***~ up*** a) (gut) umrühren, b) *Schlamm* aufwühlen; **2.** *Feuer* (an-)schüren; **3.** *Glied etc*. rühren, bewegen: ***not to ~ a finger*** keinen Finger krumm machen; **4.** *Blätter, See etc*. bewegen (*Wind*); **5.** ***~ up*** *a*. *fig*. *j-n* auf-, wachrütteln; **6.** ***~ up*** *fig*. a) *j-n* aufreizen, -hetzen, b) *Neugier etc*. erregen, c) *Streit etc*. entfachen; **7.** *fig*. aufwühlen, bewegen, erregen; *j-s Blut* in Wallung bringen; **II** *v/i*. **8.** sich rühren *od*. regen (*a*. *fig*. *geschäftig sein*): ***not to ~ from the spot*** sich nicht von der Stelle rühren; ***he never ~red abroad*** er ging nie aus; ***he is not ~ring yet*** er ist noch nicht auf(gestanden); **9.** a) im Gange *od*. ˈUmlauf sein, b) geschehen, sich ereignen; **III** *s*. **10.** Rühren *n*; **11.** Bewegung *f*; **12.** Aufregung *f*; **13.** Aufsehen *n*, Sensatiˈon *f*: ***create*** *od*. ***make a ~*** Aufsehen erregen.
stir² [stɜː] *s*. *sl*. ‚Kittchen' *n*, ‚Knast' *m* (*Gefängnis*): ***in ~*** im Knast.
stirps [stɜːps] *pl*. **stir·pes** [ˈstɜːpiːz] *s*. **1.** Faˈmilie(nzweig *m*) *f*; **2.** ⚖ a) Stammvater *m*, b) Stamm *m*: ***by stirpes*** *Erbfolge* nach Stämmen.
stir·rer [ˈstɜːrə] *s*. a) Rührlöffel *m*, b) Rührwerk *n*.
stir·ring [ˈstɜːrɪŋ] *adj*. □ **1.** bewegt; **2.** *fig*. rührig; **3.** erregend, aufwühlend; zündend (*Rede*); bewegt (*Zeiten*).
stir·rup [ˈstɪrəp] *s*. **1.** Steigbügel *m*; **2.** ⚙ Bügel *m*; **3.** ⚓ Springpferd *n* (*Haltetau*); **~ bone** *s*. *anat*. Steigbügel *m* (*im Ohr*); **~ i·ron** *s*. Steigbügel *m* (*ohne Steigriemen*); **~ leath·er** *s*. Steig(bügel)riemen *m*.
stitch [stɪtʃ] **I** *s*. **1.** *Nähen etc*.: Stich *m*: ***a ~ in time saves nine*** gleich getan ist viel gespart; ***put ~es in*** → 7; **2.** *Strikken, Häkeln etc*.: Masche *f*; → ***take up*** 14; **3.** Stich(art *f*) *m*, Strick-, Häkelart *f*; **4.** F Faden *m*: ***not to have a dry ~ on one*** keinen trockenen Faden am Leibe haben; ***without a ~ on*** splitternackt; **5.** a) Stich *m*, Stechen *n* (*Schmerz*), b) *a*. ***~es in the side*** Seitenstechen *n*: ***be in ~es*** F sich kaputtlachen; **II** *v/t*. **6.** nähen, steppen, (be)sticken; **7.** ***~ up*** vernähen (*a*. ⚕), (zs.-)flicken; **8.** *Buchbinderei*: (zs.-)heften, broschieren.
sto·a [ˈstəʊə] *pl*. **-ae** [-iː] *s*. *antiq*. Stoa *f*: a) ⌂ Säulenhalle *f*, b) ♀ stoische Philosoˈphie.
stoat [stəʊt] *s*. *zo*. **1.** Hermeˈlin *n*; **2.** Wiesel *n*.
stock [stɒk] **I** *s*. **1.** (*Baum-, Pflanzen-*) Strunk *m*; **2.** *fig*. ‚Klotz' *m* (*steifer Mensch*); **3.** ⚘ Levˈkoje *f*; **4.** ✓ (ˈPfropf)ˌUnterlage *f*; **5.** (*Peitschen-, Werkzeug*)Griff *m*; **6.** ⚔ a) (Gewehr-) Schaft *m*, b) Schulterstütze *f* (*MG*); **7.** ⚙ ˈUnterlage *f*, Block *m*; (Amboß-) Klotz *m*; **8.** ⚓ Stapel *m*: ***on the ~s*** im Bau, im Werden (*a*. *fig*.); **9.** *hist*. Stock *m* (*Strafmittel*); **10.** ⚙ (Grund-, Werk)Stoff *m*: ***paper ~*** Papierstoff; **11.** a) ⚙ (*Füll- etc*.)Gut *n*, Materiˈal *n*, b) (Fleisch-, Gemüse)Brühe *f* (*als Suppengrundlage*); **12.** steifer Kragen; *bsd*. ⚔ Halsbinde *f*; **13.** Stamm *m*, Rasse *f*, Her-, Abkunft *f*; **14.** *allg*. Vorrat *m*; ☤ (Waren)Lager *n*, Invenˈtar *n*: ***~*** (***on hand***) Warenbestand *m*; ***in*** (***out of***) ***~*** (nicht) vorrätig; ***take ~*** Inventur machen, *a*. *fig*. (e-e) Bestandsaufnahme machen; ***take ~ of*** *fig*. sich klarwerden über (*acc*.), *j-n od*. *et*. abschätzen; **15.** ☤ Ware(n *pl*.) *f*; **16.** *fig*. (*Wissens- etc*.) Schatz *m*: ***a ~ of information***; **17.** a) *a*. ***live ~*** lebendes Invenˈtar, Vieh(bestand *m*) *n*, b) *a*. ***dead ~*** totes Inventar, Materiˈal *n*: ***fat ~*** Schlachtvieh *n*; **18.** a) ☤ ˈAnleihekapiˌtal *n*, b) ˈGrundkapiˌtal *n*, c) ˈAktienkapiˌtal *n*, d) Geschäftsanteil *m*; **19.** ☤ a) *Am*. Aktie(n *pl*.) *f*: ***issue ~*** Aktien ausgeben, b) *pl*. Aktien *pl*., c) *pl*. Efˈfekten *pl*., ˈWertpaˌpiere *pl*.: ***his ~ has gone up*** s-e Aktien sind gestiegen (*a*. *fig*. F); **20.** ☤ a) Schuldverschreibung *f*, b) *pl*. *Brit*. ˈStaatspaˌpiere *pl*.; **21.** *thea*. Reperˈtoire(theˌater) *n*; **II** *adj*. **22.** (stets) vorrätig, Lager..., Serien...: ***~ size*** Standardgröße *f*; **23.** *fig*. stehend, stereoˈtyp: ***~ phrase***; **24.** ✓ Vieh..., Zucht...; **25.** ☤ *bsd*. *Am*. Aktien...; **26.** *thea*. Repertoire...; **III** *v/t*. **27.** versehen, -sorgen, ausstatten, füllen (***with*** mit); **28.** *a*. ***~ up*** auf Lager legen, (auf)speichern; **29.** ☤ *Ware* vorrätig haben, führen; **30.** ✓ anpflanzen; **31.** *Gewehr, Werkzeug* schäften; **IV** *v/i*. **32.** *a*. ***~ up*** sich eindecken; **~ account** *s*. ☤ *Brit*. Kapiˈtal-, Efˈfektenkonto *n*, -rechnung *f*.
stock·ade [stɒˈkeɪd] **I** *s*. **1.** Staˈket *n*, Einpfählung *f*; **2.** ⚔ a) Paliˈsade *f*, b) *Am*. Miliˈtärgefängnis *n*; **II** *v/t*. **3.** einpfählen, mit Staˈket umˈgeben.
stock| book *s*. ☤ **1.** Lagerbuch *n*; **2.** *Am*. Aktienbuch *n*; **ˈ~ˌbreed·er** *s*. Viehzüchter *m*; **ˈ~ˌbro·ker** *s*. Efˈfekten-, Börsenmakler *m*; **ˈ~car** *s*. 🚃 *Am*. Viehwagen *m*; **~ car** *s*. *mot*. Serienwagen *m*, *sport* Stock-Car *m*; **~ cer·tif·i·cate** *s*. ˈAktienzertifiˌkat *n*; **~ com·pa·ny** *s*. **1.** ☤ *Am*. Aktiengesellschaft *f*; **2.** *thea*. Reperˈtoiregruppe *f*, Enˈsemble *n*; **~ cor·po·ra·tion** *s*. ☤ *Am*. **1.** Kapiˈtalgesellschaft *f*; **2.** Aktiengesellschaft *f*; **~ div·i·dend** *s*. ☤ *Am*. Diviˈdende *f* in Form von Gratisaktien *pl*.; **~ exchange** *s*. ☤ (Efˈfekten-, Aktien-) Börse *f*; **~ farm·er** *s*. Viehzüchter *m*; **~ farm·ing** *s*. Viehzucht *f*; **ˈ~fish** *s*. Stockfisch *m*; **ˈ~ˌhold·er** *s*. ☤ *bsd*. *Am*. Aktioˈnär *m*; **ˈ~ˌhold·ing** *s*. ☤ *Am*. Aktienbesitz *m*.
stock·i·net [ˌstɒkɪˈnet] *s*. Stockiˈnett *n*, Triˈkot *m*, *n*.
stock·ing [ˈstɒkɪŋ] *s*. **1.** Strumpf *m*; **2.** *zo*. Färbung *f* am Fuß; **~ mask** *s*. Strumpfmaske *f*; **ˈ~ˌweav·er** *s*. Strumpfwirker *m*.
ˌstock|-in-ˈtrade *s*. **1.** ☤ a) Warenbestand *m*, b) Betriebsmittel *pl*., c) ˈArbeitsmateriˌal *n*; **2.** *fig*. a) Rüstzeug *n*, b) ‚Reperˈtoire' *n*; **ˈ~ˌjob·ber** → ***jobber*** 3, 4; **~ ledg·er** *s*. ☤ *Am*. Aktienbuch *n*; **ˈ~list** *s*. (Aktien- *od*. Börsen)Kurszettel *m*; **~ mar·ket** *s*. ☤ **1.** → ***stock exchange***; **2.** Börsenkurse *pl*.; **ˈ~pile I** *s*. Vorrat *m* (***of*** an *dat*.); **II** *v/t*. e-n Vorrat anlegen von, aufstapeln; **ˈ~pot** *s*. Suppentopf *m*; **~ room** *s*. Lager (-raum *m*) *n*; **~ shot** *s*. *phot*. Arˈchivaufnahme *f*; **ˌ~-ˈstill** *adj*. stockstill, -steif; **ˈ~ˌtak·ing** *s*. ☤ Bestandsaufnahme *f* (*a*. *fig*.), Invenˈtur *f*.
stock·y [ˈstɒkɪ] *adj*. □ stämmig, unterˈsetzt.
ˈstock·yard *s*. Viehhof *m*.
stodge [stɒdʒ] *sl*. **I** *v/i*. *u*. *v/t*. sich (*den Magen*) vollstopfen; **II** *s*. a) dicker Brei, b) schwerverdauliches Zeug (*a*. *fig*.); **ˈstodg·y** [-dʒɪ] *adj*. □ **1.** schwerverdau-

lich (*a. fig. Stil etc.*), *fig. a.* schwerfällig (*a. Person*); langweilig; **2.** *fig.* ‚spießig'.

sto·gie, sto·gy ['stəʊgɪ] *s. Am.* billige Zi'garre.

Sto·ic ['stəʊɪk] **I** *s. phls.* Stoiker *m* (*a. fig.* 𝔖); **II** *adj.*, *a.* **'Sto·i·cal** [-kl] ☐ *phls.* stoisch (*a. fig.* 𝔖 *unerschütterlich, gleichmütig*); **'Sto·i·cism** [-ɪsɪzəm] *s.* Stoi'zismus *m*: a) *phls.* Stoa *f*, b) 𝔖 *fig.* Gleichmut *m*.

stoke [stəʊk] **I** *v/t.* **1.** *Feuer etc.* schüren (*a. fig.*); **2.** *Ofen etc.* (an)heizen, beschicken; **3.** F a) 'vollstopfen, b) *Essen etc.* hin'einstopfen; **II** *v/i.* **4.** schüren, stochern; **5.** heizen, feuern; **'~·hold** *s.* ⚓ Heizraum *m*; **'~·hole 1.** → ***stokehold***; **2.** Schürloch *n*.

stok·er ['stəʊkə] *s.* **1.** Heizer *m*; **2.** (auto'matische) Brennstoffzuführung.

stole[1] [stəʊl] *s. eccl. u. Damenkleidung*: Stola *f*.

stole[2] [stəʊl] *pret.*, **'sto·len** [-lən] *p.p. von* ***steal***.

stol·id ['stɒlɪd] *adj.* ☐ **1.** stur, stumpf; **2.** gleichmütig, unerschütterlich; **sto·lid·i·ty** [stɒ'lɪdətɪ] *s.* **1.** Gleichmut *m*, Unerschütterlichkeit *f*; **2.** Stur-, Stumpfheit *f*.

sto·ma ['stəʊmə] *pl.* **-ma·ta** ['stɒmətə] *s.* **1.** ⚘ Stoma *n*, Spaltöffnung *f*; **2.** *zo.* Atmungsloch *n*.

stom·ach ['stʌmək] **I** *s.* **1.** Magen *m*: ***on an empty ~*** auf leeren Magen, nüchtern; **2.** Bauch *m*, Leib *m*; **3.** Appe'tit *m* (***for*** auf *acc.*); **4.** Lust *f* (***for*** zu); **II** *v/t.* **5.** verdauen (*a. fig.*); **6.** *fig.* a) (v)ertragen, b) ‚einstecken', hinnehmen; **'~·ache** *s.* Magenschmerz(en *pl.*) *m*.

stom·ach·er ['stʌməkə] *s. hist.* Mieder *n*, Brusttuch *n*.

sto·mach·ic [stəʊ'mækɪk] **I** *adj.* **1.** Magen...; **2.** magenstärkend; **II** *s.* **3.** ⚕ Magenmittel *n*.

sto·ma·ti·tis [ˌstəʊmə'taɪtɪs] *s.* ⚕ Mundschleimhautentzündung *f*, Stoma'titis *f*.

stomp [stɒmp] → ***stamp*** 1, 12, 13.

stone [stəʊn] **I** *s.* **1.** *allg.* (*a. Grab-, Schleif- etc.*)Stein *m*: ***a ~'s throw*** ein Steinwurf (weit), (nur) ein ‚Katzensprung'; ***leave no ~ unturned*** nichts unversucht lassen; ***throw ~s at*** *fig.* mit Steinen nach *j-m* werfen; → ***rolling stone***; **2.** *a.* ***precious ~*** (Edel)Stein *m*; **3.** (*Obst*)Kern *m*, Stein *m*; **4.** ⚕ a) (Gallen- *etc.*)Stein *m*, b) Steinleiden *n*; **5.** (Hagel)Korn *n*; **6.** *brit. Gewichtseinheit* (= *6,35 kg*); **II** *adj.* **7.** steinern, Stein...; **III** *v/t.* **8.** mit Steinen bewerfen; **9.** *a.* ***~ to death*** steinigen; **10.** *Obst* entkernen, -steinen; **11.** ⚙ schleifen, glätten; 𝔖 **Age** *s.* Steinzeit *f*; **'~-blind** *adj.* stockblind; **ˌ~-'broke** *adj.* ‚pleite', völlig ‚abgebrannt'; **~ coal** *s.* Steinkohle *f*, *bsd.* Anthra'zit *m*; **'~·crop** *s.* ⚘ Steinkraut *n*; **'~ˌcut·ter** *s.* **1.** Steinmetz *m*, -schleifer *m*; **2.** 'Steinschneidemaˌschine *f*.

stoned [stəʊnd] *adj.* **1.** entsteint, -kernt; **2.** *sl.* a) ‚(stink)besoffen', b) ‚high' (*im Drogenrausch*).

ˌstone|-'dead *adj.* mausetot; **ˌ~-'deaf** *adj.* stocktaub; **~ fruit** *s.* Steinfrucht *f*; *coll.* Steinobst *n*.

stone·less ['stəʊnlɪs] *adj.* steinlos (*Obst*).

stone| mar·ten *s. zo.* Steinmarder *m*; **'~ˌma·son** *s.* Steinmetz *m*; **~ pit** *s.* Steinbruch *m*; **ˌ~'wall I** *v/i.* **1.** *sport* mauern (*defensiv spielen*); **2.** *pol.* Obstrukti'on treiben (***on*** gegen); **II** *v/t.* **3.** *pol. Antrag* durch Obstrukti'on zu Fall bringen; **ˌ~'wall·ing** *s.* **1.** *sport* Mauern *n*; **2.** *pol.* Obstrukti'on *f*; **'~·ware** *s.* Steinzeug *n*.

ston·i·ness ['stəʊnɪnɪs] *s.* **1.** steinige Beschaffenheit; **2.** *fig.* Härte *f*; **ston·y** ['stəʊnɪ] *adj.* ☐ **1.** steinig; **2.** steinern (*a. fig. Herz*), Stein...; **3.** starr (*Blick*); **4.** *a.* ***~-broke*** → ***stone-broke***.

stood [stʊd] *pret. u. p.p. von* ***stand***.

stooge [stu:dʒ] *s.* **1.** *thea.* Stichwortgeber *m*; **2.** *sl.* Handlanger *m*, Krea'tur *f*; **3.** *Am. sl.* (Lock)Spitzel *m*; **4.** *Brit. sl.* ‚Heini' *m*.

stool [stu:l] *s.* **1.** Hocker *m*; (Bü'ro-, Kla'vier)Stuhl *m*: ***fall between two ~s*** sich zwischen zwei Stühle setzen; **2.** Schemel *m*; **3.** Nachtstuhl *m*; **4.** ⚕ Stuhl *m*: a) Kot *m*, b) Stuhlgang *m*: ***go to ~*** Stuhlgang haben; **5.** ⚘ a) Wurzelschößling *m*, b) Wurzelstock *m*, c) Baumstumpf *m*; **~ pi·geon** *s.* **1.** Lockvogel *m* (*a. fig.*); **2.** *bsd. Am. sl.* (Lock-)Spitzel *m*.

stoop[1] [stu:p] **I** *v/i.* **1.** sich bücken, sich (vorn'über)beugen; **2.** sich krumm halten, gebeugt gehen; **3.** *fig. contp.* a) sich her'ablassen, b) sich erniedrigen, die Hand reichen (***to*** zu *et.*, ***to do*** zu tun); **4.** her'abstoßen (*Vogel*); **II** *v/t.* **5.** neigen, beugen; *Schultern* hängen lassen; **III** *s.* **6.** (Sich)Beugen *n*; **7.** gebeugte *od.* krumme Haltung; krummer Rücken; **8.** Niederstoßen *n* (*Vogel*).

stoop[2] [stu:p] *s. Am.* kleine Ve'randa (*vor dem Haus*).

stop [stɒp] **I** *v/t.* **1.** aufhören (***doing*** zu tun): ***~ it!*** hör auf (damit)!; **2.** aufhören mit, *Besuche*, ⚚ *Lieferung*, *Zahlung*, *Tätigkeit*, ⚖ *Verfahren* einstellen; *Kampf*, *Verhandlungen etc.* abbrechen; **3.** ein Ende machen *od.* bereiten (*dat.*), Einhalt gebieten (*dat.*); **4.** *Angriff*, *Fortschritt*, *Gegner*, *Verkehr etc.* aufhalten, zum Stehen bringen, *Ball* stoppen; *Wagen*, *Zug*, *a. Uhr* anhalten, stoppen; *Maschine*, *a. Gas*, *Wasser* abstellen; *Fabrik* stillegen; *Lohn*, *Scheck etc.* sperren; *Redner etc.* unter'brechen; *Lärm etc.* unter'binden; **5.** verhindern; hindern (***from*** an *dat.*, ***from doing*** zu tun); **6.** *Boxen etc.*: a) *Schlag* parieren, b) *Gegner* besiegen, stoppen: ***~ a bullet*** e-e (Kugel) ‚verpaßt' kriegen; **7.** *a.* ***~ up*** *Ohren etc.* verstopfen: ***~ s.o.'s mouth*** *fig.* j-m den Mund stopfen; → ***gap*** 4; **8.** *Weg* versperren; **9.** *Blut*, *Wunde* stillen; **10.** *Zahn* plombieren, füllen; **11.** ♪ a) *Saite*, *Ton* greifen, b) *Griffloch* zuhalten, c) *Instrument*, *Ton* stopfen; **12.** *ling.* interpunktieren; **13.** ***~ down*** *phot. Objektiv* abblenden; **14.** ***~ out*** *Ätzkunst*: abdecken; **II** *v/i.* **15.** (an)halten, haltmachen, stehenbleiben, stoppen; **16.** aufhören, an-, innehalten, e-e Pause machen: ***~ dead*** (*od.* ***short***) jäh aufhören; ***~ at nothing*** *fig.* vor nichts zurückschrecken; **17.** aufhören (*Vorgang*, *Lärm etc.*); **18.** ***~ for*** warten auf (*acc.*); **19.** F *im Bett etc.* bleiben: ***~ away*** (***from***) fernbleiben (*dat.*); ***~ by*** *Am.* (rasch) bei *j-m* ‚reinschauen'; ***~ in*** zu Hause bleiben; ***~ off*** *od.* ***over*** Zwischenstation machen; ***~ out*** a) wegbleiben, nicht heimkommen, b) ⚚ weiterstreiken; **III** *s.* **20.** Halt *m*, Stillstand *m*: ***come to a ~*** anhalten; ***come to a full ~*** aufhören, zu e-m Ende kommen; ***put a ~ to*** → 3; **21.** Pause *f*; **22.** 🚂 *etc.* Aufenthalt *m*, Halt *m*; **23.** a) Stati'on *f* (*Zug*), b) Haltestelle *f* (*Autobus*), c) Anlegestelle *f* (*Schiff*); **24.** 'Absteigequarˌtier *n*; **25.** ⚙ Anschlag *m*, Sperre *f*, Hemmung *f*; **26.** ⚚ Sperrung *f*, Sperrauftrag *m* (*für Scheck etc.*); → *a.* ***stop order***; **27.** ♪ a) Griff *m*, Greifen *n* (*e-r Saite etc.*), b) Griffloch *n*, c) Klappe *f*, d) Ven'til *n*, e) Re'gister *n* (*Orgel etc.*), f) *a.* ***~ knob*** Re'gisterzug *m*: ***pull out all the ~s*** *fig.* alle Register ziehen; ***pull out the pathetic ~*** *fig.* pathetisch werden; **28.** *phot.* f-stop Blende *f* (*Einstellmarke*); **29.** *ling.* a) Knacklaut *m*, b) Verschlußlaut *m*; **30.** a) Satzzeichen *n*, b) Punkt *m*; **ˌ~-and-'go** *adj.* durch Verkehrsampeln geregelt: ***~ traffic*** Stop-and-go-Verkehr *m*; **'~·cock** *s.* ⚙ Absperrhahn *m*; **'~·gap I** *s.* Lückenbüßer *m*, Notbehelf *m*; ⚚ Über'brückung *f*; **II** *adj.* Not...; Behelfs...; ⚚ Überbrückungs...(*-hilfe*, *-kredit*); **'~·light** *s.* **1.** *mot.* Bremslicht *n*; **2.** rotes (Verkehrs)Licht; **'~-loss** *adj.* ⚚ zur Vermeidung weiterer Verluste: ***~ order*** → ***~ or·der*** *s.* ⚚ Stopp-loss-Auftrag *m*; **'~ˌo·ver** *s.* **1.** 'Reise-, 'Fahrtunterˌbrechung *f*, (kurzer) Aufenthalt; **2.** 'Zwischenstatiˌon *f*.

stop·page ['stɒpɪdʒ] *s.* **1.** a) (An)Halten *n*, b) Stillstand *m*, c) Aufenthalt *m*; **2.** (Verkehrs- *etc.*)Stockung *f*; **3.** ⚙ a) (Betriebs)Störung *f*, Hemmung *f*, b) *a.* ⚕ Verstopfung *f*; **4.** Sperrung *f*, (⚚ *Kredit- etc.*, ⚡ *Strom*)Sperre *f*; **5.** (Arbeits-, Betriebs-, Zahlungs)Einstellung *f*; **6.** (Gehalts)Abzug *m*.

stop pay·ment *s.* ⚚ Zahlungssperre *f* (*für Schecks etc.*).

stop·per ['stɒpə] **I** *s.* **1.** a) Stöpsel *m*, Pfropf(en) *m*, b) Stopfer *m*: ***put a ~ on*** *fig. e-r Sache* ein Ende setzen; **2.** ⚙ Absperrvorrichtung *f*; Hemmer *m*: ***~ circuit*** ⚡ Sperrkreis *m*; **3.** *Werbung*: F Blickfang *m*; **II** *v/t.* **4.** zustöpseln.

stop·ping ['stɒpɪŋ] *s.* ⚕ (Zahn)Füllung *f*, Plombe *f*; **~ dis·tance** *s. mot.* Anhalteweg *m*; **~ place** *s.* Haltestelle *f*; **~ train** *s.* 🚂 Bummelzug *m*.

stop·ple ['stɒpl] **I** *s.* Stöpsel *m*; **II** *v/t.* zustöpseln.

stop| press *s.* (Spalte *f* für) letzte (nach Redakti'onsschluß eingelaufene) Meldungen *pl.*; **~ screw** *s.* ⚙ Anschlagschraube *f*; **~ sign** *s. mot.* Stoppschild *n*; **~ valve** *s.* ⚙ 'Absperrvenˌtil *n*; **~ vol·ley** *s. Tennis*: Stoppflugball *m*; **'~·watch** *s.* Stoppuhr *f*.

stor·a·ble ['stɔ:rəbl] **I** *adj.* lagerfähig, Lager...; **II** *s.* lagerfähige Ware.

stor·age ['stɔ:rɪdʒ] *s.* **1.** (Ein)Lagerung *f*, Lagern *n*; *a.* ⚡ *u. Computer*: Speicherung *f*; → ***cold storage***; **2.** Lager(raum *m*) *n*, De'pot *n*; **3.** Lagergeld *n*; **~ bat·ter·y** *s.* ⚡ Akku(mu'lator) *m*; **~ cam·er·a** *s.* Speicherkamera *f*; **~ heat·er** *s.* Speicherofen *m*.

store [stɔ:] **I** *s.* **1.** (Vorrats)Lager *n*, Vorrat *m*: ***in ~*** vorrätig, auf Lager; ***be in ~ for s.o.*** *fig.* j-m bevorstehen, auf j-n warten; ***have*** (*od.* ***hold***) ***in ~ for*** *fig.*

Überraschung etc. bereithalten für *j-n*, *j-m e-e Enttäuschung etc.* bringen; **2.** *pl.* a) Vorräte *pl.*, Ausrüstung *f* (u. Verpflegung *f*), Provi'ant *m*, b) *a.* ***military ~s*** Mili'tärbedarf *m*, Versorgungsgüter *pl.*, c) *a.* ***naval*** (*od.* ***ship's***) ***~s*** Schiffsbedarf *m*; **3.** *a. pl. bsd. Brit.* Kauf-, Warenhaus *n*; **4.** *Am.* (Kauf)Laden *m*, Geschäft *n*; **5.** *bsd. Brit.* Lagerhaus *n*, Speicher *m* (*a. Computer*); **6.** *a. pl. fig.* (große) Menge, Fülle *f*, Reichtum *m* (***of*** an *dat.*): ***a great ~ of knowledge*** ein großer Wissensschatz; **7.** ***set great*** (***little***) ***~ by*** *fig.* a) hoch (gering) einschätzen, b) großen (wenig) Wert legen auf (*acc.*); **II** *v/t.* **8.** versorgen, -sehen, eindecken (***with*** mit); *Schiff* verproviantieren; *fig. s-n Kopf mit Wissen etc.* anfüllen; **9.** *a.* ***~ up*** einlagern, (auf-) speichern; *fig. im Gedächtnis* bewahren; **10.** *Möbel etc.* einstellen, -lagern; **11.** fassen, aufnehmen, 'unterbringen; **12.** ϟ, *phys.*, *a. Computer*: speichern; **~ cat·tle** *s.* Mastvieh *n*; **'~·house** *s.* **1.** Lagerhaus *n*; **2.** *fig.* Fundgrube *f*; **'~ˌkeep·er** *s.* **1.** Lagerverwalter *m*; ⚔ Kammer-, Geräteverwalter *m*; **2.** *Am.* Ladenbesitzer(in); **'~·room** *s.* **1.** Lagerraum *m*; **2.** Verkaufsraum *m*.

sto·rey ['stɔːrɪ] → ***story²***; **'sto·reyed** [-ɪd] → ***storied²***.

sto·ried¹ ['stɔːrɪd] *adj.* **1.** geschichtlich, berühmt; **2.** 'sagenumˌwoben; **3.** mit Bildern aus der Geschichte geschmückt: ***a ~ frieze***.

sto·ried² ['stɔːrɪd] *adj.* mit Stockwerken: ***two-~*** zweistöckig (*Haus*).

stork [stɔːk] *s. orn.* Storch *m*; **'~s·bill** *s.* ⚘ Storchschnabel *m*.

storm [stɔːm] **I** *s.* **1.** Sturm *m* (*a.* ⚔ *u. fig.*), Unwetter *n*: ***~ of applause*** Beifallssturm *m*; ***~ and stress*** *hist.* Sturm u. Drang; ***~ in a teacup*** *fig.* Sturm im Wasserglas; ***take by ~*** im Sturm erobern (*a. fig.*); **2.** (Hagel-, Schnee-) Sturm *m*, Gewitter *n*; **II** *v/i.* **3.** stürmen, wüten, toben (*Wind etc.*) (*a. fig.* ***at*** gegen, über *acc.*); **4.** ⚔ stürmen; **5.** *wohin* stürmen, stürzen; **III** *v/t.* **6.** ⚔ (er-) stürmen; **7.** *fig.* bestürmen; **8.** *et.* wütend ausstoßen; **~ an·chor** *s. bsd. fig.* Notanker *m*; **'~-ˌbeat·en** *adj.* sturmgepeitscht; **'~·bird** → ***stormy petrel*** 1; **'~·bound** *adj.* vom Sturm aufgehalten; **~ cen·ter** *Am.*, **~ cen·tre** *Brit. s.* **1.** *meteor.* Sturmzentrum *n*; **2.** *fig.* Unruheherd *m*; **~ cloud** *s.* Gewitterwolke *f* (*a. fig.*); **'~-tossed** *adj.* sturmgepeitscht; **'~-troops** *s. pl.* **1.** ⚔ Schock-, Sturmtruppe(n *pl.*) *f*; **2.** *hist.* (*Nazi-*)'Sturmabˌteilung *f*, S'A *f*.

storm·y ['stɔːmɪ] *adj.* □ stürmisch (*a. fig.*); **~ pet·rel** *s.* **1.** *orn.* Sturmschwalbe *f*; **2.** *fig.* a) Unruhestifter *m*, b) Unglücksbote *m*.

sto·ry¹ ['stɔːrɪ] *s.* **1.** (*a.* amü'sante) Geschichte, Erzählung *f*: ***the same old ~*** *fig.* das alte Lied; **2.** Fabel *f*, Handlung *f*, Story *f e-s Dramas etc.*; **3.** Bericht *m*, Geschichte *f*: ***the ~ goes*** man erzählt sich; ***to cut*** (*od.* ***make***) ***a long ~ short*** (*Redewendung*) um es kurz zu machen, kurz u. gut; ***tell the full ~*** *fig.* ‚auspakken'; ***that's quite another ~*** das ist et. ganz anderes; **4.** (Lebens)Geschichte *f*, Story *f*: ***the Glenn Miller ℒ***; **5.** *bsd. Am.* ('Zeitungs)Arˌtikel *m*; **6.** F (Lügen-, Ammen)Märchen *n*.

sto·ry² ['stɔːrɪ] *s.* Stock(werk *n*) *m*, Geschoß *n*, E'tage *f*; → ***upper*** I.

'sto·ry|·book I *s.* Geschichten-, Märchenbuch *n*; **II** *adj. fig.* ‚Bilderbuch...', märchenhaft; **'~ˌtell·er** *s.* **1.** (Märchen-, Geschichten)Erzähler(in); **2.** F Lügenbold *m*.

stoup [stuːp] *s.* **1.** *R.C.* Weihwasserbekken *n*; **2.** *Scot.* Eimer *m*; **3.** *dial.* a) Becher *m*, b) Krug *m*.

stout [staʊt] **I** *adj.* □ **1.** dick, beleibt; **2.** stämmig, kräftig; **3.** ausdauernd, zäh; **4.** mannhaft, beherzt, tapfer; **5.** heftig (*Angriff*, *Wind*); **6.** kräftig, ro'bust (*Material etc.*); **II** *s.* **7.** Stout *m* (*dunkles Bier*); **ˌstout'heart·ed** *adj.* □ → ***stout*** 4; **'stout·ness** [-nɪs] *s.* **1.** Stämmigkeit *f*; **2.** Beleibtheit *f*, Korpu'lenz *f*; **3.** Tapferkeit *f*, Mannhaftigkeit *f*; **4.** Ausdauer *f*.

stove¹ [stəʊv] **I** *s.* **1.** Ofen *m*; **2.** (Koch-) Herd *m*; **3.** ⚙ a) Brennofen *m*, b) Trokkenraum *m*; **4.** ✓ Treibhaus *n*; **II** *v/t.* **5.** trocknen, erhitzen; **6.** ⚘ im Treibhaus ziehen.

stove² [stəʊv] *pret. u. p.p. von* ***stave***.

stove| en·am·el *s.* ⚙ Einbrennlack *m*; **'~·pipe** *s.* **1.** Ofenrohr *n*; **2.** *a.* ***~ hat*** *bsd. Am.* F Zy'linder *m*, ‚Angströhre' *f*; **3.** *pl.* F Röhrenhose *f*.

stow [stəʊ] **I** *v/t.* **1.** ⚓ (ver)stauen; **2.** verstauen, packen: ***~ away*** a) wegräumen, -stecken, b) F *Essen* ‚verdrücken'; **3.** *sl.* aufhören mit: ***~ it!*** hör auf (damit)!, halt's Maul!; **II** *v/i.* **4.** *a.* ***~ away*** sich an Bord schmuggeln; **stow·age** ['stəʊɪdʒ] *s. bsd.* ⚓ **1.** Stauen *n*; **2.** Laderaum *m*; **3.** Ladung *f*; **4.** Staugeld *n*; **'stow·a·way** [-əʊə-] *s.* blinder Passa'gier.

stra·bis·mus [strə'bɪzməs] *s.* ⚕ Schielen *n*; **stra'bot·o·my** [-'bɒtəmɪ] *s.* ⚕ 'Schieloperatiˌon *f*.

strad·dle ['strædl] **I** *v/i.* **1.** a) die Beine spreizen, grätschen, b) breitbeinig *od.* mit gespreizten Beinen gehen *od.* stehen *od.* sitzen, c) rittlings sitzen; **2.** sich spreizen; **3.** sich (aus)strecken; **4.** *Am. fig.* schwanken, es mit beiden Par'teien halten; **II** *v/t.* **5.** rittlings sitzen auf (*dat.*); **6.** mit gespreizten Beinen stehen über (*dat.*); **7.** *die Beine* spreizen; **8.** *fig.* sich nicht festlegen wollen bei *e-r Streitfrage etc.*; **9.** ⚔ *Ziel* eingabeln; **10.** *Poker*: *den Einsatz* blind verdoppeln; **III** *s.* **11.** a) (Beine)Spreizen *n*, b) breitbeiniges *od.* ausgreifendes Gehen, c) breitbeiniges (Da)Stehen, d) Rittlingssitzen *n*; **12.** a) *Turnen*: Grätsche *f*, b) *Hochsprung*: Straddle *m*; **13.** † Stel'lage(geschäft *n*) *f*.

strafe [*Brit.* strɑːf; *Am.* streɪf] **I** *v/t.* **1.** ⚔, ✈ im Tiefflug mit Bordwaffen angreifen; **2.** *fig.* F *j-n* anschnauzen; **II** *s.* **3.** → **'straf·ing** [-fɪŋ] *s.* **1.** (Bordwaffen)Beschuß *m*; **2.** *fig.* ‚Anpfiff' *m*.

strag·gle ['strægl] *v/i.* **1.** um'herstreifen; **2.** (hinter'drein- *etc.*)bummeln, (-)zotteln; **3.** ⚘ wuchern; **4.** zerstreut liegen *od.* stehen (*Häuser etc.*); sich hinziehen (*Vorstadt etc.*); **5.** *fig.* abschweifen; **'strag·gler** [-lə] *s.* **1.** Bummler(in); **2.** Nachzügler *m* (*a.* ⚓); **3.** ⚔ Versprengte(r) *m*; **4.** ⚘ wilder Schößling; **'strag·gling** [-lɪŋ] *adj.* □, **'strag·gly** [-lɪ] *adj.* **1.** *beim Marsch etc.* zu'rückgeblieben; **2.** ausein'andergezogen (*Kolonne*); **3.** zerstreut (liegend); **4.** weitläufig; **5.** ⚘ wuchernd; **6.** lose, 'widerspenstig (*Haar etc.*).

straight [streɪt] **I** *adj.* □ **1.** gerade: ***~ angle*** ∢ gestreckter Winkel; ***~ hair*** glattes Haar; ***~ left*** *Boxen*: linke Gerade; ***~ line*** gerade Linie, ∢ Gerade *f*; ***keep a ~ face*** das Gesicht nicht verziehen; **2.** ordentlich: ***put ~*** in Ordnung bringen; ***put things ~*** Ordnung schaffen; ***set s.o. ~ on*** j-n berichtigen hinsichtlich (*gen.*); → ***record¹*** 4; **3.** gerade, di'rekt; **4.** *fig.* gerade, offen, ehrlich, re'ell: ***as ~ as a die*** a) grundehrlich, b) kerzengerade; **5.** anständig; **6.** F zuverlässig: ***a ~ tip***; **7.** pur: ***~ whisk(e)y***; **8.** *pol. Am.* 'hundertproˌzentig: ***a ~ Republican***; → ***ticket*** 7; **9.** † *Am. sl.* ohne ('Mengen)Raˌbatt; **10.** *thea.* a) konventio'nell (*Stück*), b) ef'fektlos (*Spiel*); **11.** nor'mal, konventio'nell (*Roman etc.*); **II** *adv.* **12.** gerade('aus); **13.** di'rekt, gerade(s)wegs: ***~ from London***; **14.** anständig, ordentlich: ***live ~***; **15.** richtig: ***get s.o. ~*** j-n richtig verstehen; ***I can't think ~*** ich kann nicht (richtig) denken; **16.** ***~ away***, ***~ off*** so'fort, auf der Stelle; **17.** ***~ out*** 'rundherˌaus; **III** *s.* **18.** Geradheit *f*: ***out of the ~*** krumm, schief; **19.** *sport* a) Gerade *f*: ***back ~*** Gegengerade; ***home ~*** Zielgerade, b) (Erfolgs-, Treffer- *etc.*) Serie *f*; **20.** *Poker*: Straight *m*; **21.** ***be on the ~ and narrow*** auf dem Pfad der Tugend wandeln; **22.** ***the ~ of it*** *Am.* F die (reine) Wahrheit; **23.** *sl.* ‚Spießer' *m*; **ˌ~·a'way I** *adv.* → ***straight*** 16; **II** *s. Am.* → ***straight*** 19a; **'~-edge** *s.* ⚙ Line'al *n*, Richtscheit *n*.

straight·en ['streɪtn] **I** *v/t.* **1.** gerade machen, -biegen, (gerade-, aus)richten; ⚔ *Front* begradigen: ***~ one's face*** e-e ernste Miene aufsetzen; ***~ o.s. up*** sich aufrichten; **2.** *oft* ***~ out*** in Ordnung bringen: ***~ one's affairs***; ***things will ~ themselves out*** das wird von allein (wieder) in Ordnung kommen; **3.** *oft* ***~ out*** entwirren, klarstellen; **4.** ***~ s.o. out*** j-m den Kopf zurechtsetzen; **II** *v/i.* **5.** geade werden; **6.** ***~ up*** *Am.* a) sich aufrichten, b) F ein anständiges Leben beginnen.

'straight|-faced *adj.* mit unbewegtem Gesicht; **~ flush** *s. Poker*: Straightflush *m*; **ˌ~'for·ward** [-'fɔːwəd] **I** *adj.* □ **1.** di'rekt, offen, freimütig; **2.** ehrlich, redlich, aufrichtig; **3.** einfach, ganz nor'mal, unkompliziert (*Aufgabe etc.*); **II** *adv.* **4.** → I; **ˌ~'for·ward·ness** [-'fɔːwədnɪs] *s.* Geradheit *f*, Offenheit *f*, Ehrlichkeit *f*, Aufrichtigkeit *f*; **ˌ~-from-the-'shoul·der** *adj.* unverblümt; **'~-line** *adj.* ∢, ⚙ geradlinig, line'ar (*a.* †).

straight·ness ['streɪtnɪs] *s.* Geradheit *f*: a) Geradlinigkeit *f*, b) *fig.* Offenheit *f*, Aufrichtigkeit *f*.

'straight-out *adj. Am.* F **1.** rückhaltlos; **2.** offen, aufrichtig.

strain¹ [streɪn] **I** *s.* **1.** Beanspruchung *f*, Spannung *f*, Zug *m*; **2.** ⚙ (verformende) Spannung, Verdehnung *f*; **3.** ⚕ a) Zerrung *f*, b) Über'anstrengung *f* (***on*** *gen.*); **4.** Anstrengung *f*, -spannung *f*, Kraftaufwand *m*; **5.** (***on***) Anstrengung *f*, Stra'paze *f* (für); starke In'anspruchnahme (*gen.*); *nervliche, finanzielle etc.* Belastung (für); Druck *m* (auf *acc.*); Last *f der Verantwortung etc.*: ***be a ~ on, put a (great) ~ on*** stark beanspruchen *od.* belasten, strapazieren; **6.** *mst pl.* ♪ Weise *f*, Melo'die *f*: ***to the ~s of*** unter den Klängen (*gen.*); **7.** *fig.* Ton *m*, Ma'nier *f*: ***a humorous ~***; **8.** Laune *f*; **II** *v/t.* **9.** (an)spannen; **10.** ⚙ verformen, -dehnen; **11.** ⚕ *Muskel etc.* zerren; *Handgelenk etc.* verstauchen; *s-e Augen, das Herz etc.* über'anstrengen; → ***nerve*** 1; **12.** *fig.* über'spannen, strapazieren, *j-s Geduld, Kräfte etc.* über'fordern; *Befugnisse* über'schreiten; *Recht, Sinn* vergewaltigen, strapazieren: ***~ a point*** zu weit gehen; **13.** ('durch)seihen, filtrieren: ***~ off*** (*od.* ***out***) abseihen; **14.** ***~ s.o. to one's breast*** j-n ans Herz drücken; **III** *v/i.* **15.** sich (an)spannen; **16.** ⚙ sich verdehnen, -formen; **17.** ***~ at*** zerren an (*dat.*); → ***gnat*** 1; **18.** sich anstrengen: ***~ after*** sich abmühen um, streben nach; → ***effect*** 3; **19.** drücken, pressen.

strain² [streɪn] *s.* **1.** Abstammung *f*; **2.** Linie *f*, Geschlecht *n*; **3.** *biol.* a) Rasse *f*, b) (Spiel)Art *f*; **4.** (Rassen)Merkmal *n*, Zug *m*, Schuß *m* (*indischen Bluts etc.*); **5.** (Erb)Anlage *f*, (Cha'rakter-)Zug *m*; **6.** Anflug *m* (***of*** von).

strained [streɪnd] *adj.* ☐ **1.** gezwungen: ***~ smile***; **2.** gespannt: ***~ relations***; **'strain·er** [-nə] *s.* Sieb *n*, Filter *m*, *n*.

strait [streɪt] **I** *s.* **1.** *oft pl.* Straße *f*, Meerenge *f*: ***the* 2*s of Dover*** die Straße von Dover; **2*s Settlements*** *ehemalige brit. Kronkolonie* (*Malakka, Penang, Singapur*); ***the* 2*s*** a) (*früher*) die Meerenge von Gibraltar, b) (*heute*) die Malakkastraße; **2.** *oft pl.* Not *f*, *bsd. finanzielle* Verlegenheit, Engpaß *m*: ***in dire ~s*** in e-r ernsten Notlage; **II** *adj.* ☐ **3.** *obs.* eng, schmal; **4.** streng, hart; **'strait·en** [-tn] *v/t.* beschränken, beengen: ***in ~ed circumstances*** in beschränkten Verhältnissen; ***~ed for*** verlegen um.

'strait|ˌjack·et **I** *s.* Zwangsjacke *f* (*a. fig.*); **II** *v/t.* in e-e Zwangsjacke stecken (*a. fig.*); **'~-laced** *adj.* sittenstreng, puri'tanisch, prüde.

strand¹ [strænd] **I** *s.* **1.** *poet.* Gestade *n*, Ufer *n*; **II** *v/t.* **2.** ⚓ auf den Strand setzen, auf Grund treiben; **3.** *fig.* stranden *od.* scheitern lassen: ***~ed*** a) gestrandet (*a. fig.*), b) *mot.* steckengeblieben, c) *fig.* arbeits-, mittellos; ***be (left) ~ed*** a) auf dem trockenen sitzen, b) ‚aufgeschmissen' sein; **III** *v/i.* **4.** stranden.

strand² [strænd] **I** *s.* **1.** Strang *m* (*e-s Taus od. Seils*); **2.** (*Draht-, Seil*)Litze *f*; **3.** *biol.* (Gewebe)Faser *f*; **4.** (Haar-)Strähne *f*; **5.** (Perlen)Schnur *f*; **6.** *fig.* Faden *m*, Zug *m* (*e-s Ganzen*); **II** *v/t.* **7.** ⚙ *Seil* drehen; *Kabel* verseilen: ***~ed wire*** Litzendraht *m*, Drahtseil *n*; **8.** *Tau etc.* brechen.

strange [streɪndʒ] *adj.* ☐ **1.** fremd, neu, unbekannt, ungewohnt (***to*** *j-m*); **2.** seltsam, sonderbar, merkwürdig: ***~ to say*** seltsamerweise; **3.** (***to***) nicht gewöhnt (an *acc.*), nicht vertraut (mit); **'strange·ness** [-nɪs] *s.* **1.** Fremdheit *f*; Fremdartigkeit *f*; **2.** Seltsamkeit *f*, *das* Merkwürdige; **'stran·ger** [-dʒə] *s.* **1.** Fremde(r *m*) *f*, Unbekannte(r *m*) *f*, Fremdling *m*: ***I am a ~ here*** ich bin hier fremd; ***you are quite a ~*** Sie sind ein seltener Gast; ***he is no ~ to me*** er ist mir kein Fremder; ***I spy*** (*od.* ***see***) ***~s*** *parl. Brit.* ich beantrage die Räumung der Zuschauertribüne; ***the little ~*** der kleine Neuankömmling (*Kind*); **2.** Neuling *m* (***to*** in *dat.*): ***be a ~ to*** nicht vertraut sein mit; ***he is no ~ to poverty*** die Armut ist ihm nicht unbekannt.

stran·gle ['stræŋgl] **I** *v/t.* **1.** erwürgen, erdrosseln; **2.** *j-n* würgen, *den Hals* einschnüren (*Kragen etc.*); **3.** *fig.* a) *Seufzer etc.* ersticken, b) *et.* abwürgen; **II** *v/i.* **4.** ersticken; **'~·hold** *s.* Würgegriff *m*, *fig. a.* to'tale Gewalt (***on*** über *acc.*).

stran·gu·late ['stræŋgjʊleɪt] *v/t.* **1.** ⚕ abschnüren, abbinden; **2.** → ***strangle*** 1; **stran·gu·la·tion** [ˌstræŋgjʊ'leɪʃn] *s.* **1.** Erdrosselung *f*, Strangulierung *f*; **2.** ⚕ Abschnürung *f*.

stran·gu·ry ['stræŋgjʊrɪ] *s.* ⚕ Harnzwang *m*.

strap [stræp] **I** *s.* **1.** (Leder-, *a.* Trag-, ⚙ Treib)Riemen *m*, Gurt *m*, Band *n*; **2.** a) Halteriemen *m im Bus etc.*, b) (Stiefel)Schlaufe *f*; **3.** a) Träger *m am Kleid*, b) Steg *m an der Hose*; **4.** Achselklappe *f*; **5.** Streichriemen *m*; **6.** ⚙ a) (Me'tall-)Band *n*, b) Bügel *m* (*a. am Kopfhörer*); **7.** ⚓ Stropp *m*; **8.** ✿ Blatthäutchen *n*; **II** *v/t.* **9.** festschnallen (***to*** an *dat.*): ***~ o.s. in*** sich anschnallen; **10.** *Messer* abziehen; **11.** mit e-m Riemen schlagen; **12.** ⚕ ein (Heft)Pflaster kleben auf *e-e Wunde*; **'~ˌhang·er** *s.* F Stehplatzinhaber(in) *im Omnibus etc.*; **~ i·ron** *s.* ⚙ *Am.* Bandeisen *n*.

strap·less ['stræplɪs] *adj.* trägerlos (*Kleid*); **'strap·per** [-pə] *s.* a) strammer Bursche, b) strammes *od.* dralles Mädchen; **'strap·ping** [-pɪŋ] **I** *adj.* **1.** stramm (*Bursche, Mädchen*), drall (*Mädchen*); **II** *s.* **2.** Riemen *pl.*; **3.** Tracht *f* Prügel; **4.** ⚕ Heftpflaster(verband *m*) *n*.

stra·ta ['strɑːtə] *pl. von* ***stratum***.

strat·a·gem ['strætɪdʒəm] *s.* **1.** Kriegslist *f*; **2.** List *f*, Kunstgriff *m*.

stra·te·gic [strə'tiːdʒɪk] *adj.* (☐ ***~ally***) *allg.* stra'tegisch, *a.* stra'tegisch wichtig, *a.* kriegswichtig, *a.* Kriegs…(*-lage, -plan*): ***~ arms*** strategische Waffen; **strat·e·gist** ['strætɪdʒɪst] *s.* Stra'tege *m*; **strat·e·gy** ['strætɪdʒɪ] *s.* Strate'gie *f*: a) Kriegskunst *f*, b) (Art *f* der) Kriegsführung *f*, c) *fig.* Taktik *f* (*a. sport*), d) *fig.* List *f*.

strat·i·fi·ca·tion [ˌstrætɪfɪ'keɪʃn] *s.* Schichtung *f* (*a. fig. Gliederung*); **strat·i·fied** ['strætɪfaɪd] *adj.* geschichtet, schichtenförmig: ***~ rock*** *geol.* Schichtgestein *n*; **strat·i·form** ['strætɪfɔːm] *adj.* schichtenförmig; **strat·i·fy** ['strætɪfaɪ] **I** *v/t.* schichten, *fig. a.* gliedern; **II** *v/i.* (*a. fig.* gesellschaftliche) Schichten bilden, *fig. a.* sich gliedern.

stra·tig·ra·phy [strə'tɪgrəfɪ] *s. geol.* Formati'onskunde *f*.

strat·o·cruis·er ['strætəʊˌkruːzə] *s.* ✈ Strato'sphärenflugzeug *n*.

strat·o·sphere ['strætəʊˌsfɪə] *s.* Strato'sphäre *f*; **strat·o·spher·ic** [ˌstrætəʊ'sferɪk] *adj.* **1.** strato'sphärisch; **2.** *Am.* F ‚astro'nomisch', e'norm.

stra·tum ['strɑːtəm] *pl.* **-ta** [-tə] *s.* **1.** *allg.* (*a.* Gewebe-, Luft)Schicht *f*, Lage *f*; **2.** *geol.* (Gesteins- *etc.*)Schicht *f*, Formati'on *f*; **3.** *fig.* (gesellschaftliche *etc.*) Schicht.

stra·tus ['streɪtəs] *pl.* **-ti** [-taɪ] *s.* Stratus *m*, Schichtwolke *f*.

straw [strɔː] **I** *s.* **1.** Strohhalm *m*: ***draw ~s*** Strohhalme ziehen (*als Lose*); ***catch*** (*od.* ***grasp***) ***at a ~*** sich an e-n Strohhalm klammern; ***the last ~ that breaks the camel's back*** der Tropfen, der das Faß zum Überlaufen bringt; ***that's the last ~!*** das hat gerade noch gefehlt!, jetzt reicht es mir aber!; ***he doesn't care a ~*** es ist ihm völlig ‚schnurz'; **2.** Stroh *n*; → ***man*** 3; **3.** Trinkhalm *m*; **4.** Strohhut *m*; **II** *adj.* **5.** Stroh…

straw·ber·ry ['strɔːbərɪ] *s.* **1.** ✿ Erdbeere *f*; **2.** F ‚Knutschfleck' *m*; **~ mark** *s.* ⚕ rotes Muttermal; **~ tongue** *s.* ⚕ Himbeerzunge *f* (*bei Scharlach*).

straw| bid *s.* ✝ *Am.* Scheingebot *n*; **'~-ˌcol·o(u)red** *adj.* strohfarbig, -farben; **~ hat** *s.* Strohhut *m*; **~ mat·tress** *s.* Strohsack *m*; **~ vote** *s. bsd. Am.* Probeabstimmung *f*.

straw·y ['strɔːɪ] *adj.* **1.** strohern; **2.** mit Stroh bestreut.

stray [streɪ] **I** *v/i.* **1.** (um'her)streunen (*a. Tier*): ***~ to*** *j-m* zulaufen; **2.** weglaufen (***from*** von); **3.** a) abirren (***from*** von), sich verlaufen, b) her'umirren, c) *fig.* in die Irre gehen, vom rechten Weg abkommen; **4.** *fig.* abirren, -schweifen (*Gedanken etc.*); **5.** ϟ streuen, vagabundieren; **II** *s.* **6.** verirrtes *od.* streunendes Tier; **7.** Her'umirrende(r *m*) *f*, Heimatlose(r *m*) *f*; **8.** *pl.* ϟ atmo'sphärische Störungen *pl.*; **III** *adj.* **9.** *a.* ***strayed*** verirrt (*a. Kugel*), verlaufen, streunend (*Hund, Kind*); **10.** vereinzelt: ***~ customers***; **11.** beiläufig: ***a ~ remark***; **12.** ϟ Streu…, vagabundierend (*Strom*).

streak [striːk] **I** *s.* **1.** Streif(en) *m*, Strich *m*; (Licht)Streifen *m*, (-)Strahl *m*: ***~ of lightning*** Blitzstrahl; ***like a ~*** (***of lightning***) F blitzschnell; **2.** Maser *f*, Ader *f* (*im Holz*); **3.** *fig.* Spur *f*, Anflug *m*; **4.** Anlage *f*, *humoristische etc.* Ader; **5.** ***~ of (bad) luck*** (Pech-)Glückssträhne *f*; **6.** ⚗ Schliere *f*; **7.** ⚕ Aufstreichimpfung *f*: ***~ culture*** Strichkultur *f*; **II** *v/t.* **8.** streifen; **9.** adern; **III** *v/i.* **10.** F flitzen; **streaked** [-kt] *adj.*, **'streak·y** [-kɪ] *adj.* ☐ **1.** gestreift; **2.** gemasert (*Holz*); **3.** durch'wachsen (*Speck*; *a. Am. fig.* F).

stream [striːm] **I** *s.* **1.** Wasserlauf *m*, Flüßchen *n*, Bach *m*; **2.** Strom *m*, Strömung *f*: ***against*** (***with***) ***the ~*** gegen den (mit dem) Strom *schwimmen* (*a. fig.*); **3.** (*a. Blut-, Gas-, Menschen- etc.*) Strom *m*, (*Licht-, Tränen- etc.*)Flut *f*: ***~ of words*** Wortschwall *m*; ***~ of consciousness*** *psych.* Bewußtseinsstrom; **4.** *ped.* Leistungsgruppe *f*; **5.** *fig.* a) Strömung *f*, Richtung *f*, b) Strom *m*, Lauf *m der Zeit etc.*; **II** *v/i.* **6.** strömen, fluten (*a. Licht, Menschen etc.*); **7.** strömen (*Tränen*), tränen (*Augen*): ***~ with*** triefen vor (*dat.*); **8.** *im Wind* flattern; **9.** fließen (*langes Haar*); **III** *v/t.* **10.** aus-, verströmen; **'stream·er** [-mə] *s.* **1.** Wimpel *m*; flatternde Fahne; **2.** (langes, flatterndes) Band; Pa'pierschlange *f*; **3.** Lichtstreifen *m* (*bsd. des Nordlichts*); **4.** *a.* **~ *headline*** *Zeitung*: breite Schlagzeile; **'stream·ing** [-mɪŋ] *s. ped.* Einteilung *f e-r Klasse* in Leistungsgruppen; **'stream·let** [-lɪt] *s.* Bächlein *n.*

'stream|·line I *s.* **1.** *phys.* Stromlinie *f*; **2.** *a.* **~ *shape*** Stromlinienform *f*, *weitS.* schnittige Form; **II** *adj.* **3.** → ***streamlined*** 1; **III** *v/t.* **4.** ⚙ stromlinienförmig konstruieren; windschnittig gestalten *od.* verkleiden; **5.** *fig.* a) modernisieren, b) rationalisieren, 'durchorganisieren, c) *pol.* ‚gleichschalten'; **'~·lined** *adj.* **1.** ⚙ stromlinienförmig, windschnittig, Stromlinien…; **2.** schnittig, formschön; **3.** *fig.* a) modernisiert, fortschrittlich, b) ratio'nell, c) *pol.* ‚gleichgeschaltet'; **'~ˌlin·er** *s. Am.* Stromlinienzug *m.*

street [striːt] *s.* **1.** Straße *f*: ***in the ~*** auf der Straße; ***~s ahead*** F haushoch überlegen (***of*** *dat.*); ***~s apart*** F völlig verschieden; ***not in the same ~ as*** F nicht zu vergleichen mit; ***walk the ~s*** ‚auf den Strich' gehen (*Prostituierte*); ***that's (right) up my ~*** das ist genau mein Fall; → ***man*** 3; **2. *the ~*** a) Hauptgeschäfts- *od.* Börsenviertel *n*, b) *Brit.* → ***Fleet Street***, c) *Am.* → ***Wall Street***, d) Finanzwelt *f*; **~ Ar·ab** *s.* Gassenjunge *m*; **'~·car** *s. Am.* Straßenbahn(wagen *m*) *f*; **'~ˌclean·er** → ***streetsweeper***; **~ map** *s.* Stadtplan *m*; **~ mar·ket** *s.* ☤ **1.** Freiverkehrsmarkt *m*; **2.** *Brit.* Nachbörse *f*; **'~ˌsweep·er** *s. bsd. Brit.* **1.** Straßenkehrer *m*; **2.** Kehrfahrzeug *n*; **~ the·a·ter** *Am.*, **~ the·a·tre** *Brit. s.* 'Straßentheˌater *n*; **'~ˌwalk·er** *s.* Straßen-, Strichmädchen *n*, Prostituierte *f.*

strength [streŋθ] *s.* **1.** Kraft *f*, Kräfte *pl.*, Stärke *f*: **~ *of body (mind, will)*** Körper- (Geistes-, Willens)kraft, -stärke: ***go from ~ to ~*** immer stärker werden; **2.** *fig.* Stärke *f*: ***his ~ is*** (*od.* ***lies***) ***in endurance*** s-e Stärke ist die Ausdauer; **3.** ⚔ (Truppen)Stärke *f*, Bestand *m*: ***actual ~*** Iststärke; ***in full ~*** in voller Stärke, vollzählig; ***in (great) ~*** in großer Zahl; **4.** ⚔ Stärke *f*, (Heeres- *etc.*)Macht *f*, Schlagkraft *f*; **5.** ⚙ (⚡ *Strom-, Feld- etc.*)Stärke *f*, (*Bruch-, Zerreiß- etc.*)Festigkeit *f*; ⚗, *phys.* Stärke *f* (*a. e-s Getränks*), Wirkungsgrad *m*; **6.** Stärke *f*, Intensi'tät *f* (*Farbe, Gefühl etc.*); **7.** (Beweis-, Über'zeugungs)Kraft *f*: ***on the ~ of*** auf Grund (*gen.*), kraft (*gen.*), auf (*acc.*) … hin; **'strength·en** [-θn] **I** *v/t.* **1.** stärken: **~ *s.o.'s hand*** *fig.* j-m Mut machen; **2.** *fig.* bestärken; **3.** (*zahlenmäßig, a.* ⚙, ⚡) verstärken; **II** *v/i.* **4.** stark *od.* stärker werden, sich verstärken; **'strength·en·er** [-θənə] *s.* **1.** ⚙ Verstärkung *f*; **2.** ⚕ Stärkungsmittel *n*; **3.** *fig.* Stärkung *f*; **'strength·en·ing** [-θənɪŋ] **I** *s.* **1.** Stärkung *f*; **2.** Verstärkung *f* (*a.* ⚙, ⚡); **II** *adj.* **3.** stärkend; **4.** verstärkend; **'strength·less** [-lɪs] *adj.* kraftlos.

stren·u·ous ['strenjʊəs] *adj.* □ **1.** emsig, rührig; **2.** eifrig, tatkräftig; **3.** e'nergisch: **~ *opposition***; **4.** anstrengend, mühsam; **'stren·u·ous·ness** [-nɪs] *s.* **1.** Emsigkeit *f*; **2.** Eifer *m*, Tatkraft *f*; **3.** Ener'gie *f*; **4.** *das* Anstrengende.

stress [stres] **I** *s.* **1.** ♪, *ling.* a) Ton *m*, ('Wort-, 'Satz)Akˌzent *m*, b) Betonung *f*: ***the ~ is on …*** der Ton liegt auf *der zweiten Silbe*; **2.** *fig.* Nachdruck *m*: ***lay ~ (up)on*** → 7; **3.** ⚙, *phys.* a) Beanspruchung *f*, Druck *m*, b) Spannung *f*, Dehnung *f*: **~ *analyst*** Statiker *m*; **4.** *seelische etc.* Belastung, Druck *m*, Streß *m*: **~ *disease*** ⚕ Streß-, Managerkrankheit *f*; **5.** Zwang *m*, Druck *m*: ***under (the) ~ of circumstances*** unter dem Druck der Umstände; **6.** Ungestüm *n*; Unbilden *pl. der Witterung*; **II** *v/t.* **7.** ♪, *ling.*, *a. fig.* betonen, den Ak'zent legen auf (*acc.*); *fig.* Nachdruck *od.* Gewicht legen auf (*acc.*), her'vorheben; **8.** ⚙, *phys. u. fig.* beanspruchen, belasten; **'stress·ful** [-fʊl] *adj.* anstrengend, ‚stressig', Streß…

stretch [stretʃ] **I** *v/t.* **1.** *oft* **~ *out*** (aus-) strecken, *bsd. Kopf, Hals* recken: **~ *o.s.* (*out*)** → 11; **~ *one's legs*** sich die Beine vertreten; **2. ~ *out*** *Hand etc.* aus-, hinstrecken; **3.** *j-n* niederstrecken; **4.** *Seil, Saite, Tuch etc.* spannen (***over*** über *dat. od. acc.*), straff ziehen; *Teppich etc.* ausbreiten; **5.** strecken; *Handschuhe etc.* ausweiten; *Hosen* spannen; **6.** ⚙ spannen, dehnen; **7.** *Nerven, Muskel* anspannen; **8.** *fig.* über'spannen, -'treiben: **~ *a principle***; **9.** 'überbeanspruchen, *Befugnisse, Kredit etc.* über'schreiten; **10.** *fig.* es mit *der Wahrheit, e-r Vorschrift etc.* nicht allzu genau nehmen: **~ *a point*** fünf gerade sein lassen, ein Auge zudrücken; **II** *v/i.* **11.** sich (aus)strecken; sich dehnen *od.* rekeln; **12.** langen (***for*** nach); **13.** sich erstrecken *od.* hinziehen (***to*** [bis] zu) (*Gebirge etc., a. Zeit*): **~ *down to*** zurückreichen *od.* -gehen (bis) zu *od.* in (*acc.*) (*Zeitalter, Erinnerung etc.*); **14.** sich *vor dem Blick* ausbreiten; **15.** sich dehnen (lassen); **16.** *mst* **~ *out*** a) *sport* im gestreckten Galopp reiten, b) F sich ins Zeug legen, c) reichen (*Vorrat*); **III** *s.* **17. *have a ~, give o.s. a ~*** sich strecken; **18.** Strecken *n*, (Aus-) Dehnen *n*; **19.** Spannen *n*; **20.** (An-) Spannung *f*, (Über)'Anstrengung *f*: ***by every ~ of the imagination*** unter Aufbietung aller Phantasie; ***on the ~*** (an-) gespannt (*Nerven etc.*); **21.** Über'treiben *n*; **22.** Über'schreiten *n von Befugnissen, Mitteln etc.*; **23.** (Weg)Strecke *f*; Fläche *f*, Ausdehnung *f*; **24.** *sport*: Gerade *f*; **25.** Zeit(spanne) *f*: ***a ~ of 10 years***; ***at a ~*** ununterbrochen, hintereinander, auf 'einen Sitz; **26. *do a ~*** *sl.* ‚Knast schieben', ‚sitzen'; **'stretch·er** [-tʃə] *s.* **1.** ⚕ (Kranken)Trage *f*: **~-*bearer*** Krankenträger *m*; **2.** (*Schuh- etc.*) Spanner *m*; **3.** ⚙ Streckvorrichtung *f*; **4.** *paint.* Keilrahmen *m*; **5.** Fußleiste *f im Boot*; **6.** △ Läufer(stein) *m*; **'stretch·y** [-tʃɪ] *adj.* dehnbar.

strew [struː] *v/t.* [*irr.*] **1.** (aus)streuen; **2.** bestreuen; **strewn** [struːn] *p.p. von* ***strew.***

stri·a ['straɪə] *pl.* **stri·ae** ['straɪiː] *s.* **1.** Streifen *m*, Furche *f*, Riefe *f*; **2.** *pl.* ⚕ Striemen *pl.*, Streifen *pl.*, Striae *pl.*; **3.** *zo.* Stria *f*; **4.** *pl. geol.* (Gletscher-) Schrammen *pl.*; **5.** △ Riffel *m* (*an Säulen*); **stri·ate I** *v/t.* [straɪ'eɪt] **1.** streifen, furchen, riefeln; **2.** *geol.* kritzen; **II** *adj.* ['straɪɪt] **3.** → **stri·at·ed** [straɪ'eɪtɪd] *adj.* **1.** gestreift, geriefelt; **2.** *geol.* gekritzt; **stri·a·tion** [straɪ'eɪʃn] *s.* **1.** Streifenbildung *f*, Riefung *f*; **2.** Streifen *m*, *pl.*, Riefe(n *pl.*) *f*; **3.** *geol.* Schramme(n *pl.*) *f.*

strick·en ['strɪkən] **I** *p.p. von* ***strike***; **II** *adj.* **1.** *obs.* verwundet; **2.** (***with***) heimgesucht, schwer betroffen (von *Unglück etc.*), befallen (von *Krankheit*), ergriffen (von *Schrecken, Schmerz etc.*); schwergeprüft (*Person*): **~ *in years*** hochbetagt, vom Alter gebeugt; **~ *area*** Katastrophengebiet *n*; **3.** *fig.* (nieder)geschlagen, (gram)gebeugt; verzweifelt (*Blick*); **4.** *allg.* angeschlagen: ***a ~ ship***; **5.** gestrichen (voll).

strick·le ['strɪkl] ⚙ **I** *s.* **1.** Abstreichlatte *f*; **2.** Streichmodel *m*; **II** *v/t.* **3.** ab-, glattstreichen.

strict [strɪkt] *adj.* □ → ***strictly***; **1.** strikt, streng (*Person*; *Befehl, Befolgung, Disziplin*; *Wahrheit etc.*); streng (*Gesetz, Moral, Untersuchung*): ***be ~ with*** mit *j-m* streng sein; ***in ~ confidence*** streng vertraulich; **2.** streng, genau: ***in the ~ sense*** im strengen Sinne; **'strict·ly** [-lɪ] *adv.* **1.** streng *etc.*; **2.** *a.* **~ *speaking*** genaugenommen; **3.** völlig, ausgesprochen; **4.** ausschließlich, rein; **'strict·ness** [-nɪs] *s.* Strenge *f*: a) Härte *f*, b) Genauigkeit *f.*

stric·ture ['strɪktʃə] *s.* **1.** *oft pl.* (***on, upon***) scharfe Kri'tik (an *dat.*), kritische Bemerkung (über *acc.*); **2.** ⚕ Strik'tur *f*, Verengung *f.*

strid·den ['strɪdn] *p.p. von* ***stride.***

stride [straɪd] **I** *v/i.* [*irr.*] **1.** schreiten; **2.** *a.* **~ *out*** ausschreiten; **II** *v/t.* [*irr.*] **3.** *et.* entlang-, abschreiten; **4.** über-, durch'schreiten; **5.** mit gespreizten Beinen stehen über (*dat.*) *od.* gehen über (*acc.*); **6.** rittlings sitzen auf (*dat.*); **III** *s.* **7.** (langer *od.* großer) Schritt: ***get into one's ~*** *fig.* (richtig) in Schwung kommen; ***take s.th. into*** (*od.* ***hit***) ***one's ~*** *fig.* et. spielend (leicht) schaffen; **8.** Schritt(weite *f*) *m*; **9.** *mst pl. fig.* Fortschritt(e *pl.*) *m*: ***with rapid ~s*** mit Riesenschritten.

stri·dent ['straɪdnt] *adj.* □ **1.** 'durchdringend, schneidend, grell (*Stimme, Laut*); **2.** knirschend; **3.** *fig.* scharf, heftig.

strife [straɪf] *s.* Streit *m*: a) Hader *m*, b) Kampf *m*: ***be at ~*** sich streiten, uneins sein.

stri·gose ['straɪgəʊs] *adj.* **1.** ⚘ Borsten…; **2.** *zo.* fein gestreift.

strike [straɪk] **I** *s.* **1.** (*a. Glocken*)Schlag *m*, Hieb *m*, Stoß *m*; **2.** a) *Bowling*: Strike *m* (*Abräumen beim 1. Wurf*), b) *Am. Baseball*: (Verlustpunkt *m* bei) Schlagfehler *m*; **3.** *fig.* ‚Treffer' *m*, Glücksfall *m*; **4.** ☤ Streik *m*, Ausstand *m*: ***be on ~*** streiken; ***go on ~*** in (den) Streik *od.* in den Ausstand treten; ***on ~*** streikend; **5.** ⚔ a) (*bsd.* Luft)Angriff *m*, b) A'tomschlag *m*; **II** *v/t.* [*irr.*] **6.** schlagen, Schläge *od.* e-n Schlag versetzen (*dat.*); *allg.* treffen: **~ *off*** abschlagen, -hauen; ***struck by a stone*** von e-m Stein getroffen; **7.** *Waffe* stoßen (***into*** in *acc.*); **8.** *Schlag* führen; → ***blow***[2] 1; **9.** ♪ *Ton, a. Glocke, Saite, Taste* anschlagen; → ***note*** 8; **10.** *Zündholz* anzünden, *Feuer* machen, *Funken* schlagen; **11.** *Kopf, Fuß etc.* (an)stoßen, schlagen (***against*** gegen); **12.** stoßen *od.* schlagen gegen *od.* auf (*acc.*);

zs.-stoßen mit; ⚓ auflaufen auf; einschlagen in (*acc.*) (*Geschoß*, *Blitz*); fallen auf (*acc.*) (*Strahl*); *Auge*, *Ohr* treffen (*Lichtstrahl*, *Laut*): **~ s.o.'s eye** j-m ins Auge fallen; **13.** *j-m* einfallen, in den Sinn kommen; **14.** *j-m* auffallen; **15.** *j-n* beeindrucken, Eindruck machen auf (*acc.*); **16.** *j-m wie* vorkommen: ***how does it ~ you?*** was hältst du davon?; ***it ~s me as ridiculous*** es kommt mir lächerlich vor; **17.** stoßen auf (*acc.*): a) (zufällig) treffen *od.* entdecken, b) *Gold etc.* finden; → ***oil*** 2, ***rich*** 5; **18.** *Wurzeln* schlagen; **19.** *Lager*, *Zelt* abbrechen; **20.** ⚓ *Flagge*, *Segel* streichen; **21.** *Angeln*: *Fisch* mit e-m Ruck auf den Haken spießen; **22.** *Giftzähne* schlagen in (*acc.*) (*Schlange*); **23.** ⚙ glattstreichen; **24.** a) 🟰 *Durchschnitt*, *Mittel* nehmen, b) ✝ *Bilanz*: *den Saldo* ziehen; → ***balance*** 6; **25.** (***off*** von *e-r Liste etc.*) streichen; **26.** *Münze* schlagen, prägen; **27.** *Stunde* schlagen (*Uhr*); **28.** *fig.* *j-n* schlagen, treffen (*Unglück etc.*), befallen (*Krankheit*); **29.** (***with*** mit *Schrecken*, *Schmerz etc.*) erfüllen; **30.** *blind etc.* machen; → ***blind*** 1, ***dumb*** 1; **31.** *Haltung*, *Pose* einnehmen; **32.** *Handel* abschließen; → ***bargain*** 2; **33.** ***~ work*** die Arbeit niederlegen: a) Feierabend machen, b) in Streik treten; **III** *v/i.* [*irr.*] **34.** (zu)schlagen, (-)stoßen; **35.** schlagen, treffen: ***~ at*** a) *j-n od.* nach *j-m* schlagen, b) *fig.* zielen auf (*acc.*); **36.** ([***up***]***on***) a) (an)schlagen, stoßen (an *acc.*, gegen), b) ⚓ auflaufen (auf *acc.*), auf Grund stoßen; **37.** fallen (*Licht*), auftreffen (*Lichtstrahl*, *Schall etc.*) ([***up***]***on*** auf *acc.*); **38.** *fig.* stoßen ([***up***]***on*** auf *acc.*); **39.** schlagen (*Uhrzeit*): ***the hour has struck*** die Stunde hat geschlagen (*a. fig.*); **40.** sich entzünden, angehen (*Streichholz*); **41.** einschlagen (*Geschoß*, *Blitz*); **42.** Wurzel schlagen; **43.** den Weg einschlagen, sich (plötzlich) *nach links etc.* wenden: ***~ for home*** F heimzu gehen; ***~ into*** a) einbiegen in (*acc.*), *Weg* einschlagen, b) *fig.* plötzlich verfallen in (*acc.*), *et.* beginnen, *a.* sich *e-m Thema* zuwenden; **44.** ✝ streiken (***for*** für); **45.** ⚓ die Flagge streichen (***to*** vor *dat.*) (*a. fig.*); **46.** (zu)beißen (*Schlange*); **47.** *fig.* zuschlagen (*Feind etc.*);
Zssgn mit adv.:

strike| back *v/i.* zu'rückschlagen (*a. fig.*); **~ down** *v/t.* niederschlagen, -strecken (*a. fig.*); **~ in** *v/i.* **1.** beginnen, einfallen (*a.* ♪); **2.** ⚕ (sich) nach innen schlagen; **3.** einfallen, unter'brechen (***with*** mit *e-r Frage etc.*); **4.** sich einmischen, -schalten, *a.* mitmachen: ***~ with*** a) sich richten nach, b) mitmachen bei; **~ in·wards** → ***strike in*** 2; **~ off** *v/t.* **1.** → ***strike*** 6; **2.** a) *Wort etc.* ausstreichen, *Eintragung* löschen, b) *j-n von e-r Liste etc.* streichen, *j-m die Berufserlaubnis etc.* entziehen; **3.** *typ.* abziehen; **~ out I** *v/t.* **1.** → ***strike off*** 2 a; **2.** *fig.* *et.* ersinnen; **3.** *mst fig.* *e-n Weg* einschlagen; **II** *v/i.* **4.** a) (los-, zu)schlagen, b) (zum Schlag) ausholen; **5.** (forsch) ausschreiten, *a.* (los)schwimmen (***for*** nach, auf *e-n Ort* zu); **6.** *fig.* loslegen; **7.** *mit den Armen beim Schwimmen* ausgreifen; **~ through** *v/t.* *Wort etc.* 'durchstreichen; **~ up I** *v/i.* **1.** ♪ einsetzen (*Spieler*, *Melodie*); **II** *v/t.* **2.** ♪ a) *Lied etc.* anstimmen, b) *Kapelle* einsetzen lassen; **3.** *Bekanntschaft*, *Freundschaft* schließen, *a.* *Gespräch* anknüpfen (***with*** mit).

strike| bal·lot *s.* Urabstimmung *f*; **'~-bound** *adj.* bestreikt (*Fabrik etc.*); **'~ˌbreak·er** *s.* Streikbrecher *m*; **~ call** *s.* Streikaufruf *m*; **~ pay** *s.* Streikgeld *n*; **'~-prone** *adj.* streikanfällig.

strik·er ['straɪkə] *s.* **1.** Schläger(in); **2.** Streikende(r *m*) *f*, Ausständige(r *m*) *f*; **3.** Hammer *m*, Klöppel *m* (*Uhr*); **4.** ⚔ Schlagbolzen *m*; **5.** ⚡ Zünder *m*; **6.** *bsd. Fußball*: Stürmer *m*, ‚Spitze' *f*: ***be ~*** Spitze spielen.

strike vote → ***strike ballot***.

strik·ing ['straɪkɪŋ] *adj.* □ **1.** schlagend, Schlag...; **2.** *fig.* a) bemerkenswert, auffallend, eindrucksvoll, b) über'raschend, verblüffend, c) treffend: ***~ example***; **3.** streikend.

string [strɪŋ] **I** *s.* **1.** Schnur *f*, Bindfaden *m*; **2.** (*Schürzen-*, *Schuh- etc.*)Band *n*, Kordel *f*: ***have s.o. on a ~*** j-n am Gängelband *od.* in s-r Gewalt haben; **3.** (Puppen)Draht *m*: ***pull ~s*** *fig.* s-e Beziehungen spielen lassen; ***pull the ~s*** *fig.* der Drahtzieher sein; **4.** (Bogen-)Sehne *f*: ***have two ~s to one's bow*** *fig.* zwei Eisen im Feuer haben; ***be a second ~*** das zweite Eisen im Feuer sein (→ 5); **5.** ♪ a) Saite *f*, b) *pl.* 'Streichinstruˌmente *pl.*, *die* Streicher *pl.*; ***first*** (***second*** *etc.*) ***~*** *sport etc.* erste (zweite *etc.*) ‚Garnitur'; ***be a second ~*** zur zweiten Garnitur gehören; ***harp on one ~*** *fig.* immer auf derselben Sache herumreiten; **6.** Schnur *f* (*Perlen etc.*); **7.** *fig.* Reihe *f*, Kette *f* (*von Fragen*, *Fahrzeugen etc.*); **8.** Koppel *f* (*Pferde etc.*); **9.** ⚘ a) Faser *f*, Fiber *f*, b) Faden *m von Bohnen*; **10.** *zo. obs.* Flechse *f*; **11.** ⚠ Fries *m*, Sims *m*; **12.** F Bedingung *f*, ‚Haken' *m*: ***no ~s attached*** ohne Bedingungen; **II** *v/t.* [*irr.*] **13.** *Schnur etc.* spannen; **14.** (zu-, ver-)schnüren, zubinden; **15.** *Perlen etc.* aufreihen; **16.** *fig.* anein'anderreihen: ***~ s.th. out*** et. ‚strecken', et. ‚ausspinnen'; **17.** *Bogen* spannen; **18.** ♪ a) besaiten, bespannen (*a. Tennisschläger*), b) *Instrument* stimmen; **19.** *mit Girlanden etc.* behängen; **20.** *Bohnen* abziehen; **21.** ***~ up*** *sl.* ‚aufknüpfen', -hängen; **22.** ***~ up*** *Nerven* anspannen: ***~ o.s. up to*** a) sich in *e-e Erregung etc.* hineinsteigern, b) sich aufraffen (***to do*** *et.* zu tun); → ***high-strung***; **23.** *Am. sl.* *j-n* ‚verkohlen', aufziehen; **24.** ***~ along*** F a) *j-n* hinhalten, b) *j-n* ‚einwickeln'; **III** *v/i.* [*irr.*] **25.** Fäden ziehen (*Flüssigkeit*); **26.** ***~ along*** mitmachen (***with*** mit, bei); **~ bag** *s.* Einkaufsnetz *n*; **~ band** *s.* ♪ 'Streichorˌchester *n*; **~ bean** *s.* ⚘ Gartenbohne *f*; **'~-course** → ***string*** 11.

stringed [strɪŋd] *adj.* **1.** ♪ Saiten..., Streich...: ***~ instruments***; ***~ music*** Streichmusik *f*; **2.** ♪ *in Zssgn* ...saitig; **3.** aufgereiht (*Perlen etc.*).

strin·gen·cy ['strɪndʒənsɪ] *s.* **1.** Strenge *f*, Schärfe *f*; **2.** Bündigkeit *f*, zwingende Kraft: ***the ~ of an argument***; **3.** ✝ (Geld-, Kre'dit)Verknappung *f*, Knappheit *f*; **'strin·gent** [-nt] *adj.* □ **1.** streng, scharf; **2.** zwingend: ***~ necessity***; **3.** zwingend, über'zeugend, bündig: ***~ arguments***; **4.** ✝ knapp (*Geld*), gedrückt (*Geldmarkt*).

string·er ['strɪŋə] *s.* **1.** ♪ Saitenaufzieher *m*; **2.** ⚙ Längs-, Streckbalken *m*; ⚠ (Treppen)Wange *f*; 🚂 Langschwelle *f*; ✈ Längsversteifung *f*; ⚓ Stringer *m*.

string·i·ness ['strɪŋɪnɪs] *s.* **1.** Faserigkeit *f*; **2.** Zähigkeit *f*.

string| or·ches·tra *s.* ♪ 'Streichorˌchester *n*; **~ quar·tet(te)** *s.* ♪ 'Streichquarˌtett *n*.

string·y ['strɪŋɪ] *adj.* **1.** faserig, zäh, sehnig; **2.** zäh(flüssig), klebrig, Fäden ziehend.

strip [strɪp] **I** *v/t.* **1.** *Haut etc.* abziehen, (-)schälen; *Baum* abrinden; **2.** *Bett* abziehen; **3.** *a.* ***~ off*** *Kleid etc.* ausziehen, abstreifen; **4.** *j-n* entkleiden, ausziehen (***to the skin*** bis auf die Haut): ***~ped*** a) nackt, entblößt, b) *mot.* ‚nackt' (*ohne Extras*); **5.** *fig.* entblößen, berauben (***of*** *gen.*), (aus)plündern: ***~ s.o. of his office*** j-n s-s Amtes entkleiden; **6.** *Haus etc.* ausräumen; *Fabrik* demontieren; **7.** ⚓ abtakeln; **8.** ⚙ zerlegen; **9.** ⚙ *Gewinde* über'drehen; **10.** *Kuh* ausmelken; **11.** *Kohlenlager etc.* freilegen; **II** *v/i.* **12.** a) sich ausziehen, b) ‚strippen': ***~ to the waist*** den Oberkörper frei machen; **III** *s.* **13.** a) (Sich)Ausziehen *n*, b) → ***striptease***; **14.** ✈ Start- u. Landestreifen *m*; **15.** *sport* F Dreß *m*; **16.** Streifen *m* (*Papier etc.*, *a. Land*); **17.** ⚙ a) Walzrohling *m*, b) Bandeisen *n*, -stahl *m*; **18.** → ***~ car·toon*** *s.* Comic strip *m*.

stripe [straɪp] **I** *s.* **1.** *mst andersfarbiger* Streifen (*a. zo.*), Strich *m*; **2.** ⚔ Tresse *f*, (Ärmel)Streifen *m*: ***get one's ~s*** (zum Unteroffizier) befördert werden; ***lose one's ~s*** degradiert werden; **3.** Striemen *m*; **4.** (Peitschen- *etc.*)Hieb *m*; **5.** *fig. Am.* Sorte *f*, Schlag *m*; **II** *v/t.* **6.** streifen: ***~d*** gestreift, streifig.

strip light·ing *s.* Sof'fittenbeleuchtung *f*.

strip·ling ['strɪplɪŋ] *s.* Bürschchen *n*.

strip| min·ing *s.* ⚒ Tagebau *m*; **'~·tease** *s.* Striptease *m*, *n*; **'~ˌteas·er** *s.* Stripteasetänzerin *f*, ‚Stripperin' *f*.

strive [straɪv] *v/i.* [*irr.*] **1.** sich (be)mühen, bestrebt sein (***to do*** zu tun); **2.** (***for***, ***after***) streben (nach), ringen, sich mühen (um); **3.** (erbittert) kämpfen (***against*** gegen, ***with*** mit), ringen (***with*** mit); **striv·en** ['strɪvn] *p.p. von* ***strive***.

strobe [strəʊb] *s.* **1.** *phot.* Röhrenblitz *m*; **2.** *Radar*: Schwelle *f*.

strode [strəʊd] *pret. von* ***stride***.

stroke [strəʊk] **I** *s.* **1.** (*a. Blitz-*, *Flügel-*, *Schicksals*)Schlag *m*; Hieb *m*, Streich *m*, Stoß *m*: ***at a*** (*od.* ***one***) ***~*** *a. fig.* mit 'einem Schlag, auf 'einen Streich; ***a good ~ of business*** ein gutes Geschäft; ***~ of luck*** Glückstreffer *m*, -fall *m*; ***not to do a ~ of work*** keinen Finger rühren; **2.** (Glocken-, Hammer-, Herz- *etc.*)Schlag *m*: ***on the ~*** pünktlich; ***on the ~ of nine*** Punkt neun; **3.** ⚕ Anfall *m*, *bsd.* Schlag(anfall) *m*; **4.** *mot.* a) (Kolben)Hub *m*, b) Hubhöhe *f*, c) Takt *m*; **5.** *sport* a) *Schwimmen*: Stoß *m*, (Bein)Schlag *m*, (Arm)Zug *m*, b) *Golf*, *Rudern*, *Tennis etc.*: Schlag *m*, c) *Ru-*

dern: Schlagzahl *f*; **6.** *Rudern*: Schlagmann *m*: ***row ~*** → 11; **7.** (Pinsel-, Feder)Strich *m* (*a. typ.*), (Feder)Zug *m*: ***with a ~ of the pen*** mit einem Federstrich (*a. fig.*); **8.** *fig.* (glänzender) Einfall, Leistung *f*: ***a clever ~*** ein geschickter Schachzug; ***a ~ of genius*** ein Geniestreich; **9.** ♪ a) Bogenstrich *m*, b) Anschlag *m*, c) (Noten)Balken *m*; **10.** Streicheln *n*; **II** *v/t.* **11.** ***~ a boat*** *Rudern*: am Schlag (e-s Bootes) sitzen; **12.** streichen über (*acc.*); glattstreichen; **13.** streicheln.

stroll [strəʊl] **I** *v/i.* **1.** schlendern, (um'her)bummeln, spazieren(gehen); **2.** um'herziehen: ***~ing actor*** (*od.* ***player***) → ***stroller*** 2; **II** *s.* **3.** Spaziergang *m*, Bummel *m*: ***go for a ~, take a ~*** e-n Bummel machen; **'stroll·er** [-lə] *s.* **1.** Bummler(in), Spaziergänger(in); **2.** Wanderschauspieler(in); **3.** (Kinder-)Sportwagen *m*.

stro·ma ['strəʊmə] *pl.* **-ma·ta** [-mətə] *s. biol.* Stroma *n* (*a.* ⚘).

strong [strɒŋ] **I** *adj.* □ → ***strongly***; **1.** *allg.* stark (*a. Gift, Kandidat, Licht, Nerven, Schlag, Verdacht, Gefühl etc.*); kräftig (*a. Farbe, Gesundheit, Stimme, Wort*): ***~ face*** energisches *od.* markantes Gesicht; ***~ man*** *pol.* starker Mann; ***have ~ feelings about*** sich erregen über (*acc.*); ***use ~ language*** Kraftausdrücke gebrauchen; → ***point*** 24; **2.** stark (an Zahl *od.* Einfluß), mächtig: ***a company 200 ~*** e-e 200 Mann starke Kompanie; **3.** *fig.* scharf (*Verstand*), klug (*Kopf*): ***~ in*** tüchtig in (*dat.*); **4.** fest (*Glaube, Überzeugung*); **5.** eifrig, über'zeugt: ***a ~ Tory***; **6.** gewichtig, zwingend: ***~ arguments***; **7.** stark, gewaltsam, e'nergisch (*Anstrengung, Maßnahmen*): ***with a ~ hand*** mit starker Hand; **8.** stark, schwer (*Getränk, Speise, Zigarre*); **9.** a) stark (*Geruch, Geschmack, Parfüm*), b) übelriechend *od.* -schmeckend, *a.* ranzig; **10.** *ling.* stark: ***~ declination***; ***~ verb***; **11.** ✝ a) anziehend (*Preis*), b) fest (*Markt*), c) lebhaft (*Nachfrage*); **II** *adv.* **12.** stark, e'nergisch, nachdrücklich; **13.** F tüchtig, mächtig: ***be going ~*** gut in Schuß *od.* Form sein; ***come*** (*od.* ***go***) ***it ~*** mächtig ‚rangehen', auftrumpfen; **'~·arm** F **I** *adj.* Gewalt…: ***~ methods***; ***~ man*** Schläger *m*; **II** *v/t.* a) *j-n* einschüchtern, b) über'fallen, c) zs.-schlagen; **'~·box** *s.* ('Geld-, 'Stahl)Kas‚sette *f*; Tre'sorfach *n*; **‚~'head·ed** *adj.* starrköpfig; **'~·hold** *s.* **1.** ⚔ Feste *f*; **2.** *fig.* Bollwerk *n*; **3.** *fig.* Hochburg *f*.

strong·ly ['strɒŋlɪ] *adv.* **1.** kräftig, stark; heftig: ***feel ~ about*** sich erregen über (*acc.*); **2.** nachdrücklich, sehr.

‚strong|-'mind·ed *adj.* willensstark, e'nergisch; **~ point** *s.* **1.** ⚔ Stützpunkt *m*; **2.** *fig.* → ***point*** 24; **~ room** *s.* Tre'sor(raum) *m*; **‚~-'willed** *adj.* **1.** willensstark; **2.** eigenwillig, -sinnig.

stron·ti·um ['strɒntɪəm] *s.* ⚗ Strontium *n*.

strop [strɒp] **I** *s.* **1.** Streichriemen *m* (*für Rasiermesser*); **2.** ⚓ Stropp *m*; **II** *v/t.* **3.** *Rasiermesser etc.* abziehen.

stro·phe ['strəʊfɪ] *s.* Strophe *f*; **stroph·ic** ['strɒfɪk] *adj.* strophisch.

strop·py ['strɒpɪ] *adj.* F 'widerspenstig, -borstig.

strove [strəʊv] *pret. von* ***strive***.

struck [strʌk] **I** *pret. u. p.p. von* ***strike***; **II** *adj.* ✝ *Am.* bestreikt.

struc·tur·al ['strʌktʃərəl] *adj.* □ **1.** struktu'rell (bedingt), Struktur… (*a. fig.*): ***~ unemployment*** strukturelle Arbeitslosigkeit; **2.** ⚙ baulich, Bau… (*-stahl, -teil, -technik etc.*), Konstruktions…; **3.** *biol.* a) morpho'logisch, Struktur…, b) or'ganisch (*Krankheit etc.*); **4.** *geol.* tek'tonisch; **5.** ⚗ Struktur…; **'struc·tur·al·ism** [-lɪzəm] *s. ling., phls.* Struktura'lismus *m*.

struc·ture ['strʌktʃə] **I** *s.* **1.** Struk'tur *f* (*a.* ⚗, *biol., phys., psych., sociol.*), Gefüge *n*, (Auf)Bau *m*, Gliederung *f* (*alle a. fig.*): ***~ of a sentence*** Satzbau *m*; ***price ~*** ✝ Preisstruktur, -gefüge; **2.** ⚙, ⚠ Bau(art *f*) *m*, Konstrukti'on *f*; **3.** Bau(werk *n*) *m*, Gebäude *n* (*a. fig.*); *pl.* Bauten *pl.*; **4.** *fig.* Gebilde *n*; **II** *v/t.* **5.** strukturieren; **'struc·ture·less** [-tʃəlɪs] *adj.* struk'turlos; **'struc·tur·ize** [-raɪz] *v/t.* strukturieren.

strug·gle ['strʌgl] **I** *v/i.* **1.** (***against, with***) kämpfen (gegen, mit), ringen (mit) (***for*** um *Atem, Macht etc.*); **2.** sich winden, zappeln, sich sträuben (***against*** gegen); **3.** sich (ab)mühen (***with*** mit, ***to do*** *et.* zu tun), sich anstrengen *od.* quälen: ***~ through*** sich durchkämpfen; ***~ to one's feet*** mühsam aufstehen, sich ‚hochrappeln'; **II** *s.* **4.** Kampf *m*, Ringen *n*, Streit *m* (***for*** um, ***with*** mit): ***~ for existence*** a) *biol.* Kampf ums Dasein, b) Existenzkampf; **5.** Anstrengung(en *pl.*) *f*, Streben *n*; **6.** Zappeln *n*, Sich'aufbäumen *n*; **'strug·gler** [-lə] *s.* Kämpfer *m*.

strum [strʌm] **I** *v/t.* **1.** klimpern auf (*dat.*): ***~ a piano***; **2.** *Melodie* (her'unter)klimpern *od.* (-)hämmern; **II** *v/i.* **3.** klimpern (***on*** auf *dat.*); **III** *s.* **4.** Geklimper *n*.

stru·ma ['struːmə] *pl.* **-mae** [-miː] *s.* ⚕ **1.** Struma *f*, Kropf *m*; **2.** Skrofu'lose *f*; **'stru·mose** [-məʊs], **'stru·mous** [-məs] *adj.* **1.** ⚕ stru'mös; **2.** ⚕ skrofu'lös; **3.** ⚘ kropfig.

strum·pet ['strʌmpɪt] *s. obs.* Metze *f*, Dirne *f*, Hure *f*.

strung [strʌŋ] *pret. u. p.p. von* ***string***.

strut¹ [strʌt] **I** *v/i.* **1.** (ein'her)stolzieren; **2.** *fig.* großspurig auftreten, sich spreizen; **II** *s.* **3.** Stolzieren *n*, stolzer Gang; **4.** *fig.* großspuriges Auftreten.

strut² [strʌt] ⚠, ⚙ **I** *s.* Strebe *f*, Stütze *f*, Spreize *f*; **II** *v/t.* verstreben, abspreizen, -stützen.

strut·ting¹ ['strʌtɪŋ] **I** *adj.* □ großspurig, -tuerisch; **II** *s.* → ***strut¹*** II.

strut·ting² ['strʌtɪŋ] *s.* ⚙, ⚠ Verstrebung *f*, Abstützung *f*.

strych·nic ['strɪknɪk] *adj.* ⚗ Strychnin…; **'strych·nin(e)** [-niːn] *s.* ⚗ Strych'nin *n*.

stub [stʌb] **I** *s.* **1.** (Baum)Stumpf *m*; **2.** (Kerzen-, Bleistift- *etc.*)Stummel *m*, Stumpf *m*; **3.** Ziga'retten-, Zi'garrenstummel *m*, ‚Kippe' *f*; **4.** kurzer stumpfer Gegenstand, *z.B.* Kuppnagel *m*; **5.** *Am.* Kon'trollabschnitt *m*; **II** *v/t.* **6.** *Land* roden; **7.** *mst* ***~ up*** *Bäume etc.* ausroden; **8.** mit *der Zehe etc.* (an)stoßen; **9.** *mst* ***~ out*** *Zigarette* ausdrücken.

stub·ble ['stʌbl] *s.* **1.** Stoppel *f*; **2.** *coll.* (Getreide-, Bart- *etc.*)Stoppeln *pl.*; **3.** *a.* ***~ field*** Stoppelfeld *n*; **'stub·bly** [-lɪ] *adj.* stopp(e)lig, Stoppel…

stub·born ['stʌbən] *adj.* □ **1.** eigensinnig, halsstarrig, störrisch, stur; 'widerspenstig (*a. Sache*); **2.** hartnäckig (*a. Widerstand etc.*); **3.** standhaft, unbeugsam; **4.** spröde, hart; *metall.* strengflüssig; **'stub·born·ness** [-nɪs] *s.* **1.** Eigen-, Starrsinn *m*, Halsstarrigkeit *f*; **2.** Hartnäckigkeit *f*; **3.** Standhaftigkeit *f*.

stub·by ['stʌbɪ] *adj.* **1.** stummelartig, kurz; **2.** unter'setzt, kurz und dick; **3.** stopp(e)lig.

stuc·co ['stʌkəʊ] ⚠ **I** *pl.* **-coes** *s.* **1.** Stuck *m* (*Gipsmörtel*); **2.** Stuck(arbeit *f*, -verzierung *f*) *m*, Stucka'tur *f*; **II** *v/t.* **3.** mit Stuck verzieren, stuckieren; **'~·work** → ***stucco*** 2.

stuck [stʌk] *pret. u. p.p. von* ***stick***.

‚stuck-'up *adj.* F hochnäsig.

stud¹ [stʌd] **I** *s.* **1.** Beschlagnagel *m*, Knopf *m*, Knauf *m*, Buckel *m*; **2.** ⚠ (Wand)Pfosten *m*, Ständer *m*; **3.** ⚙ a) Kettensteg *m*, b) Stift *m*, Zapfen *m*, c) Stiftschraube *f*, d) Stehbolzen *m*; **4.** ⚔ (Führungs)Warze *f* (*e-s Geschosses*); **5.** Kragen- *od.* Man'schettenknopf *m*; **6.** ⚡ a) Kon'taktbolzen *m*, b) Brücke *f*; **7.** Stollen *m* (*am Fußballschuh etc.*); **II** *v/t.* **8.** (mit Beschlagnägeln *etc.*) beschlagen *od.* verzieren; **9.** *a. fig.* besetzen, über'säen; **10.** verstreut sein über (*acc.*).

stud² [stʌd] **I** *s.* **1.** Gestüt *n*; **2.** *coll.* a) Zucht *f* (*Tiere*), b) Stall *m* (*Pferde*); **3.** a) (Zucht)Hengst *m*, b) *allg.* männliches Zuchttier, c) *sl.* ‚Zuchtbulle' *m*, ‚Aufreißer' *m*; **II** *adj.* **4.** Zucht…; **5.** Stall…; **'~·book** *s.* **1.** Gestütbuch *n für Pferde*; **2.** *allg.* Zuchtstammbuch *n*.

stu·dent ['stjuːdnt] *s.* **1.** a) *univ.* Stu'dent(in), b) *ped. bsd. Am. u. allg.* Schüler(in), c) Lehrgangs-, Kursteilnehmer(in): ***~ adviser*** Studienberater (-in); ***~ driver*** *Am.* Fahrschüler(in); ***~ hostel*** Studentenwohnheim *n*; ***~ teacher*** *ped.* Praktikant(in); **2.** Gelehrte(r *m*) *f*, Forscher(in); Büchermensch *m*; **3.** Beobachter(in), Erforscher(in) *des Lebens etc.*; **'stu·dent·ship** [-ʃɪp] *s.* **1.** Stu'dentenzeit *f*; **2.** *Brit.* Sti'pendium *n*.

stud| farm *s.* Gestüt *n*; **~ horse** *s.* Zuchthengst *m*.

stud·ied ['stʌdɪd] *adj.* □ **1.** gewollt, gesucht, gekünstelt; **2.** absichtlich, geflissentlich; **3.** wohlüberlegt.

stu·di·o ['stjuːdɪəʊ] *s.* **1.** *paint., phot. etc.* Ateli'er *n*, *a. thea. etc.* Studio *n*; **2.** ('Film)Ateli‚er *n*: ***~ shot*** Atelieraufnahme *f*; **3.** (Fernseh-, Rundfunk)Studio *n*, Aufnahme-, Senderaum *m*; ***~ couch*** *s.* Schlafcouch *f*.

stu·di·ous ['stjuːdɪəs] *adj.* □ **1.** gelehrtenhaft; **2.** fleißig, beflissen, lernbegierig; **3.** (eifrig) bedacht (***of*** auf *acc.*), bemüht (***to do*** zu tun); **4.** sorgfältig, peinlich (gewissenhaft); **5.** → ***studied***; **'stu·di·ous·ness** [-nɪs] *s.* **1.** Fleiß *m*, (Studier)Eifer *m*, Beflissenheit *f*; **2.** Sorgfalt *f*.

stud·y ['stʌdɪ] **I** *s.* **1.** Studieren *n*; **2.** Studium *n*: ***studies*** Studien *pl.*, Studium *n*; ***make a ~ of*** *et.* sorgfältig studieren; ***make a ~ of doing s.th.*** *fig.* bestrebt sein, et. zu tun; ***in a*** (***brown***) ***~*** *fig.* in Gedanken versunken, geistesabwesend; **3.** Studie *f*, Unter'suchung *f* (***of, in*** über *acc.*, zu); **4.** ˈStudienfach *n*, -zweig *m*, -obˌjekt *n*, Studium *n*: ***his face was a perfect ~*** *fig.* sein Gesicht war sehenswert; **5.** Studier-, Arbeitszimmer *n*; **6.** *Kunst, Literatur*: Studie *f*, Entwurf *m*; **7.** ♪ Eˈtüde *f*; **8.** ***be a good*** (***slow***) ***~*** *thea.* s-e Rolle leicht (schwer) lernen; **II** *v/t.* **9.** *allg.* studieren: a) *Fach etc.* erlernen, b) unterˈsuchen, erforschen, genau lesen: ***~ out*** *sl.* ausknobeln, c) mustern, prüfen(d ansehen), d) *sport etc. Gegner* abschätzen; **10.** *thea. Rolle* einstudieren; **11.** *Brit. j-m* gegenüber aufmerksam *od.* rücksichtsvoll sein; **12.** sich bemühen um *et.* (*od.* ***to do*** zu tun), bedacht sein auf (*acc.*): ***~ one's own interests***; **III** *v/i.* **13.** studieren; ***~ group*** *s.* Arbeitsgruppe *f*, -gemeinschaft *f*.

stuff [stʌf] **I** *s.* **1.** (*a.* Roh)Stoff *m*, Materiˈal *n*; **2.** a) (Woll)Stoff *m*, Zeug *n*, b) *Brit.* (*bsd.* Kamm)Wollstoff *m*; **3.** ⚙ Bauholz *n*; **4.** ⚙ Ganzzeug *n* (*Papier*); **5.** Lederschmiere *f*; **6.** *coll.* Zeug *n*, Sachen *pl.* (*Gepäck, Ware etc.*): ***green ~*** Grünzeug, Gemüse *n*; **7.** *contp.* (wertloses) Zeug, Kram *m* (*a. fig.*): ***~*** (***and nonsense***) dummes Zeug; **8.** *fig.* Zeug *n*, Stoff *m*: ***the ~ that heroes are made of*** das Zeug, aus dem Helden gemacht sind; ***he is made of sterner ~*** er ist aus härterem Holz geschnitzt; ***do your ~!*** F zeig mal, was du kannst!; ***he knows his ~*** F er kennt sich aus (*ist gut bewandert*); ***good ~!*** bravo!, prima!; ***that's the ~*** (***to give them***)! F so ist's richtig!; → ***rough*** 6; **9.** F a) ‚Zeug' *n*, ‚Stoff' *m* (*Schnaps etc.*), b) ‚Stoff' *m* (*Drogen*); **II** *v/t.* **10.** (*a. fig. sich den Kopf mit Tatsachen etc.*) vollstopfen; *e-e Pfeife* stopfen: ***~ o.s.*** (***on***) sich vollstopfen (mit *Essen*); ***~ s.o.*** (***with lies***) F j-m die Hucke voll lügen; ***~ed shirt*** *sl.* Fatzke *m*, Wichtigtuer *m*, ‚lackierter Affe'; **11.** *a.* ***~ up*** ver-, zustopfen; **12.** *Sofa etc.* polstern; **13.** *Geflügel* a) stopfen, nudeln, b) *Küche*: füllen; **14.** *Tiere* ausstopfen; **15.** *Am. Wahlurne* mit gefälschten Stimmzetteln füllen; **16.** *Leder* mit Fett imprägnieren; **17.** *et. wohin* stopfen; **18.** V *Frau* ‚bumsen': ***get ~ed!*** leck mich (am Arsch)!; **III** *v/i.* **19.** sich (den Magen) vollstopfen; ˈ**stuff·i·ness** [-fɪnɪs] *s.* **1.** Dumpfheit *f*, Schwüle *f*, Stickigkeit *f*; **2.** Langweiligkeit *f*; **3.** F a) Spießigkeit *f*, b) Steifheit *f*, c) Verstaubtheit *f*, d) ‚Muffigkeit' *f*.

stuff·ing [ˈstʌfɪŋ] *s.* **1.** Füllung *f*, ˈFüllmateriˌal *n*; Füllhaar *n*, ˈPolstermateriˌal *n*: ***knock the ~ out of*** *fig.* a) *j-n* ‚zur Schnecke machen', b) *j-n* fix u. fertig machen, c) *j-n gesundheitlich* kaputtmachen; **2.** *Küche*: Füllung *f*, Farce *f*; **3.** *fig.* Füllsel *n*; **4.** Lederschmiere *f*; ***~ box*** *s.* ⚙ Stopfbüchse *f*.

stuff·y [ˈstʌfɪ] *adj.* ☐ **1.** stickig, dumpf, schwül; **2.** *fig.* langweilig, fad; **3.** F a) beschränkt, spießig, b) peˈdantisch, c) verknöchert, d) F ‚muffig', e) prüde.

stul·ti·fi·ca·tion [ˌstʌltɪfɪˈkeɪʃn] *s.* Verdummung *f*; **stul·ti·fy** [ˈstʌltɪfaɪ] *v/t.* **1.** *a.* ***~ the mind*** verdummen; **2.** *j-n* veralbern; **3.** wirkungslos *od.* zuˈnichte machen.

stum·ble [ˈstʌmbl] **I** *v/i.* **1.** stolpern, straucheln (***at*** *od.* ***over*** über *acc.*) (*a. fig.*): ***~ in***(***to***) *fig.* in *e-e Sache* (hinein-)stolpern, (-)schlittern; ***~*** (***up***)***on*** (*od.* ***across***) *fig.* zufällig stoßen auf (*acc.*); **2.** stolpern, wanken; **3.** *fig.* e-n Fehltritt tun, straucheln; **4.** stottern, stokken: ***~ through*** *Rede etc.* herunterstottern; **II** *s.* **5.** Stolpern *n*, Straucheln *n*; *fig. a.* Fehltritt *m*; **6.** *fig.* ‚Schnitzer' *m*, Fehler *m*; **stum·bling block** [ˈstʌmblɪŋ] *s. fig.* **1.** Hindernis *n* (***to*** für); **2.** Stolperstein *m*.

stu·mer [ˈstjuːmə] *s. Brit. sl.* **1.** Fälschung *f*; **2.** gefälschter *od.* ungedeckter Scheck.

stump [stʌmp] **I** *s.* **1.** (*Baum-, Kerzen-, Zahn- etc.*)Stumpf *m*, Stummel *m*; (*Ast*)Strunk *m*: ***~ foot*** ⚕ Klumpfuß *m*; ***up a ~*** *Am. sl.* in der Klemme; **2.** ***go on*** (*od.* ***take***) ***the ~*** *bsd. Am. pol.* e-e Propagandareise machen, öffentliche Reden halten; **3.** *Kricket*: Torstab *m*: ***draw*** (***the***) ***~s*** das Spiel beenden; **4.** *sl.* ‚Stelzen' *pl.* (*Beine*): ***stir one's ~s*** ‚Tempo machen', sich beeilen; **5.** *Zeichnen*: Wischer *m*; **II** *v/t.* **6.** *a.* ***~ out*** *Kricket*: *den Schläger* ‚aus' machen; **7.** F *j-n durch e-e Frage etc.* verblüffen: ***he was ~ed*** er war verblüfft *od.* aufgeschmissen; ***~ed for*** verlegen um *e-e Antwort etc.*; **8.** *bsd. Am.* F *Gegend* als Wahlredner bereisen; ***~ it*** F → 2; **9.** F sta(m)pfen über (*acc.*); **10.** *Zeichnung* abtönen; **11.** *Am.* F *j-n* herˈausfordern (***to do*** zu tun); **12.** ***~ up*** *Brit.* F ‚berappen', ‚blechen'; **III** *v/i.* **13.** (daˈher-) sta(m)pfen; **14.** → 12; **15.** → 2; ˈ**stump·er** [-pə] *s.* **1.** *Kricket*: Torwächter *m*; **2.** F harte Nuß; **3.** *Am.* F a) Wahlredner *m*, b) Agiˈtator *m*; **stump speech** *s. Am.* Wahlrede *f*; ˈ**stump·y** [-pɪ] *adj.* ☐ **1.** stumpfartig; **2.** gedrungen, unterˈsetzt; **3.** plump.

stun [stʌn] *v/t.* **1.** *durch Schlag etc., a. durch Lärm etc.* betäuben; **2.** *fig.* betäuben: a) verblüffen, b) niederschmettern, c) überˈwältigen: ***~ned*** wie betäubt *od.* gelähmt.

stung [stʌŋ] *pret. u. p.p. von* ***sting***.

stunk [stʌŋk] *pret. u. p.p. von* ***stink***.

stun·ner [ˈstʌnə] *s.* F a) ‚toller Kerl', b) ‚tolle Frau', c) ‚tolle Sache'; ˈ**stun·ning** [-nɪŋ] *adj.* ☐ **1.** betäubend (*a. fig. niederschmetternd*); **2.** *sl.* ‚toll', phänomeˈnal.

stunt[1] [stʌnt] *v/t.* **1.** (im Wachstum, in der Entwicklung *etc.*) hemmen; **2.** verkümmern lassen, verkrüppeln: ***~ed*** verkümmert, verkrüppelt.

stunt[2] [stʌnt] **I** *s.* **1.** Kunst-, Glanzstück *n*; Kraftakt *m*; **2.** Sensatiˈon *f*: a) Schaunummer *f*, b) Braˈvourstück *n*, c) Schlager *m*; **3.** ✈ Flugkunststück *n*; *pl. a.* Kunstflug *m*; **4.** (Reˈklame- *etc.*)Trick *m*, ‚tolle Iˈdee', *weitS.* ‚tolles Ding'; **II** *v/i.* **5.** (Flug)Kunststücke machen, kunstfliegen; ˈ**stunt·er** [-tə] *s.* F **1.** Kunstflieger(in); **2.** Akroˈbat(in).

stunt| fly·ing *s.* ✈ Kunstflug *m*; ***~ man*** *s.* [*irr.*] *Film*: Stuntman *m*, Double *n* (*für gefährliche Szenen*).

stupe [stjuːp] ⚕ **I** *s.* heißer ˈUmschlag *od.* Wickel; **II** *v/t.* heiße ˈUmschläge legen auf (*acc.*), *j-m* heiße ˈUmschläge machen.

stu·pe·fa·cient [ˌstjuːpɪˈfeɪʃnt] **I** *adj.* betäubend, abstumpfend; **II** *s.* ⚕ Betäubungsmittel *n*; ˌ**stu·peˈfac·tion** [-ˈfækʃn] *s.* **1.** Betäubung *f*; **2.** Abstumpfung *f*; **3.** Abgestumpftheit *f*; **4.** Bestürzung *f*, Verblüffung *f*; **stu·pe·fy** [ˈstjuːpɪfaɪ] *v/t.* **1.** betäuben; **2.** verdummen; **3.** abstumpfen; **4.** verblüffen, bestürzen.

stu·pen·dous [stjuːˈpendəs] *adj.* ☐ erstaunlich; riesig, gewaltig, eˈnorm.

stu·pid [ˈstjuːpɪd] **I** *adj.* ☐ **1.** dumm; **2.** stumpfsinnig, blöd, fad; **3.** betäubt, benommen; **II** *s.* **4.** Dummkopf *m*; **stu·pid·i·ty** [stjuːˈpɪdətɪ] *s.* **1.** Dummheit *f* (*a. Handlung, Idee*); **2.** Stumpfsinn *m*; **stu·por** [ˈstjuːpə] *s.* **1.** Erstarrung *f*, Betäubung *f*; **2.** Stumpfheit *f*; **3.** ⚕, *psych.* Stupor *m*: a) Benommenheit *f*, b) Stumpfsinn *m*.

stur·di·ness [ˈstɜːdɪnɪs] *s.* **1.** Roˈbustheit *f*, Kräftigkeit *f*; **2.** Standhaftigkeit *f*; **stur·dy** [ˈstɜːdɪ] *adj.* ☐ **1.** roˈbust, kräftig, staˈbil (*a. Material etc.*); **2.** *fig.* standhaft, fest.

stur·geon [ˈstɜːdʒən] *pl.* ˈ**stur·geons**, *coll.* ˈ**stur·geon** *s. ichth.* Stör *m*.

stut·ter [ˈstʌtə] **I** *v/i.* **1.** stottern (*a. Motor*); **2.** keckern (*MG etc.*); **II** *v/t.* **3.** *a.* ***~ out*** (herˈvor)stottern; **III** *s.* **4.** Stottern *n*: ***have a ~*** stottern; ˈ**stut·ter·er** [-ərə] *s.* Stotterer *m*.

sty[1] [staɪ] *s.* Schweinestall *m* (*a. fig.*).

sty[2], **stye** [staɪ] *s.* ⚕ Gerstenkorn *n*.

Styg·i·an [ˈstɪdʒɪən] *adj.* **1.** stygisch; **2.** finster; **3.** höllisch.

style [staɪl] **I** *s.* **1.** *allg.* Stil *m*: a) Art *f*, Typ *m*, b) Manier *f*, Art *f* u. Weise *f*, *sport* Technik *f*: ***~ of singing*** Gesangsstil; ***in superior ~*** in überlegener Manier, souverän; ***it cramps my ~*** dabei kann ich mich nicht recht entfalten, c) guter Stil: ***in ~*** stilvoll (→ e, f), d) Lebensart *f*, -stil: ***in good*** (***bad***) ***~*** stil-, geschmackvoll (-los), e) vornehme Lebensart, Eleˈganz *f*: ***in ~*** vornehm; ***put on ~*** *Am.* F vornehm tun, f) Mode *f*: ***in ~*** modisch, g) *literarische etc.* Ausdrucksweise *od.* -kraft: ***commercial ~*** Geschäftsstil, h) Kunst-, Baustil: ***in proper ~*** stilecht; **2.** (Mach)Art *f*, Ausführung *f*, Fasˈson *f*; **3.** a) Titel *m*, Anrede *f*, b) ⚖ (Firmen)Bezeichnung *f*, Firma *f*: ***under the ~ of*** unter dem Namen …, ⚖ unter der Firma …; **4.** a) *antiq.* (Schreib)Griffel *m*, b) (Schreib-, Ritz)Stift *m*, c) Radiernadel *f*, d) Feder *f e-s Dichters*, e) Nadel *f* (*Plattenspieler*); **5.** ⚕ Sonde *f*; **6.** Zeiger *m* der Sonnenuhr; **7.** Zeitrechnung *f*, Stil *m*: ***Old*** (***New***) ♎; **8.** ⚘ Griffel *m*; **9.** *anat.* Griffelfortsatz *m*; **II** *v/t.* **10.** betiteln, benennen, bezeichnen, anreden (mit *od.* als); **11.** a) ⚙, ⚖ entwerfen, gestalten, b) modisch zuschneiden; ˈ**styl·er** [-lə] *s.* **1.** Modezeichner(in), -schöpfer (-in); **2.** ⚙ (Form)Gestalter *m*, Designer *m*.

sty·let [ˈstaɪlɪt] *s.* **1.** Stiˈlett *n* (*Dolch*); **2.** ⚕ Manˈdrin *m*, Sondenführer *m*.

styl·ing [ˈstaɪlɪŋ] *s.* **1.** Stilisierung *f*; **2.** ⚖, ⚙ Styling *n*, (Form)Gestaltung *f*.

styl·ish [ˈstaɪlɪʃ] *adj.* ☐ **1.** stilvoll; **2.** modisch, eleˈgant, flott; ˈ**styl·ish·ness** [-nɪs] *s.* Eleˈganz *f*.

styl·ist [ˈstaɪlɪst] *s.* **1.** Stiˈlist(in); **2.** → ***styler***; **sty·lis·tic** [staɪˈlɪstɪk] *adj.* (☐ ***~ally***) stiˈlistisch, Stil…

sty·lite [ˈstaɪlaɪt] *s. eccl.* Styˈlit *m*, Säulenheilige(r) *m*.

styl·ize [ˈstaɪlaɪz] *v/t.* **1.** *allg.* stilisieren;

2. der Konventi'on unter'werfen.

sty·lo ['staɪləʊ] *pl.* **-los** F, **'sty·lo·graph** [-ləgrɑːf], **sty·lo·graph·ic pen** [ˌstaɪləʊ'græfɪk] *s.* **1.** Tintenkuli *m*; **2.** Füll(feder)halter *m*.

sty·lus ['staɪləs] *s.* **1.** → ***style*** 4 a *u.* e, 6, 8, 9; **2.** Kopierstift *m*; **3.** Schreibstift *m e-s Registriergeräts.*

sty·mie, *a.* **sty·my** ['staɪmɪ] **I** *s. Golf:* **1.** a) *Situation, wenn der gegnerische Ball zwischen dem Ball des Spielers u. dem Loch liegt, auf das er spielt*, b) *Lage des gegnerischen Balles wie in 1a*; **2.** *den Gegner (durch die Ballage von 1)* hindern; **3.** *fig.* a) *Gegner* matt setzen, b) *Plan etc.* vereiteln: ***be stymied*** ‚aufgeschmissen' sein.

styp·tic ['stɪptɪk] *adj. u. s.* ⚕ blutstillend (-es Mittel).

Styr·i·an ['stɪrɪən] **I** *adj.* stei(e)risch, steiermärkisch; **II** *s.* Steiermärker(in).

Sua·bi·an ['sweɪbjən] → ***Swabian***.

su·a·ble ['sjuːəbl] *adj.* ⚖ **1.** (ein)klagbar (*Sache*); **2.** (passiv) pro'zeßfähig (*Person*).

sua·sion ['sweɪʒn] *s.* **1.** (***moral*** ~ gütliches) Zureden; **2.** Über'redung(sversuch *m*) *f*; **sua·sive** ['sweɪsɪv] *adj.* ☐ **1.** über'redend, zuredend; **2.** über'zeugend.

suave [swɑːv] *adj.* ☐ **1.** verbindlich, höflich, zu'vorkommend, sanft; *contp.* ölig; **2.** lieblich, mild (*Wein etc.*); **suav·i·ty** ['swɑːvətɪ] *s.* **1.** Höflichkeit *f*, Verbindlichkeit *f*; **2.** Lieblichkeit *f*, Milde *f*; **3.** *pl.* a) Artigkeiten *pl.*, b) Annehmlichkeiten *pl.*

sub[1] [sʌb] **I** *s.* F *abbr. für* ***submarine***, ***subordinate***, ***subway***, ***subaltern***, ***sublieutenant*** *etc.*; **II** *adj.* Aushilfs..., Not...; **III** *v/i.* F (***for***) einspringen (für), vertreten (*acc.*).

sub[2] [sʌb] (*Lat.*) *prp.* unter: ~ ***finem*** am Ende (*e-s zitierten Kapitels*); ~ ***judice*** (noch) anhängig, (noch) nicht entschieden (*Rechtsfall*); ~ ***rosa*** unter dem Siegel der Verschwiegenheit, vertraulich; ~ ***voce*** unter dem angegebenen Wort (*in e-m Wörterbuch etc.*).

sub- [sʌb; səb] *in Zssgn* a) Unter..., Grund..., Sub..., b) 'untergeordnet, Neben..., Unter..., c) annähernd, d) ⚗ basisch, e) 𝔄 'umgekehrt.

ˌsub'ac·e·tate [ˌsʌb-] *s.* ⚗ basisch essigsaures Salz.

ˌsub'ac·id [ˌsʌb-] *adj.* **1.** säuerlich; **2.** *fig.* bissig, säuerlich.

ˌsub'a·gent [ˌsʌb-] *s.* **1.** ✝ a) 'Untervertreter *m*, b) 'Zwischenspediˌteur *m*; **2.** ⚖ 'Unterbevollmächtigte(r *m*) *f*.

ˌsub'al·pine [ˌsʌb-] ♀, *zo.* **I** *adj.* subal'pin(isch); **II** *s.* a) subal'pines Tier, b) subal'pine Pflanze.

sub·al·tern ['sʌbltən] **I** *adj.* **1.** subal'tern, 'untergeordnet, Unter...; **II** *s.* **2.** Subal'terne(r *m*) *f*, Unter'gebene(r *m*) *f*; **3.** ⚔ *bsd. Brit.* Subal'ternoffiˌzier *m*.

sub·a·qua [səb'ækwə] *adj.* **1.** Unterwasser...; **2.** (Sport)Taucher...

ˌsub'arc·tic [ˌsʌb-] *adj. geogr.* sub'arktisch.

sub'au·di·ble [səb-] *adj.* **1.** *phys.* unter der Hörbarkeitsgrenze; **2.** kaum hörbar.

sub'cal·i·ber *Am.*, **sub'cal·i·bre** *Brit.* [səb-] *adj.* **1.** Kleinkaliber...; **2.** ⚔ *Artillerie*: Abkommkaliber...

'sub·comˌmit·tee ['sʌb-] *s.* 'Unterausschuß *m*.

ˌsub'com·pact (car) [ˌsʌb-] *s. mot.* Kleinwagen *m*.

ˌsub'con·scious [ˌsʌb-] ⚕, *psych.* **I** *adj.* ☐ 'unterbewußt; **II** *s.* 'Unterbewußtsein *n*, *das* 'Unterbewußte.

ˌsub'con·ti·nent [ˌsʌb-] *s. geogr.* 'Subkontiˌnent *m*.

sub'con·tract [səb-] *s.* Nebenvertrag *m*; **ˌsub·con'trac·tor** [ˌsʌb-] *s.* ✝ 'Subunterˌnehmer(in), *a.* Zulieferer *m*.

ˌsub'cul·ture [ˌsʌb-] *s. sociol.* 'Subkulˌtur *f*.

sub·cu·ta·ne·ous [ˌsʌbkjuː'teɪnjəs] *adj.* ☐ *anat.* subku'tan, unter der *od.* die Haut.

sub·deb [ˌsʌb'deb] *s. Am.* F **1.** → ***subdebutante***; **2.** Teenager *m*; **ˌsub'deb·u·tante** [ˌsʌb-] *s. Am.* noch nicht in die Gesellschaft eingeführtes junges Mädchen.

ˌsub·di'vide [ˌsʌb-] *v/t.* (*v/i.* sich) unter'teilen; **'sub·diˌvi·sion** *s.* **1.** Unter'teilung *f*; **2.** 'Unterabˌteilung *f*.

sub·due [səb'djuː] *v/t.* **1.** unter'werfen (***to*** *dat.*), unter'jochen; **2.** über'winden, -'wältigen, **3.** *fig.* besiegen, bändigen, zähmen: ~ ***one's passions***; **4.** *Farbe, Licht, Stimme, Wirkung etc., a. Begeisterung, Stimmung etc.* dämpfen; **5.** *fig. j-m* e-n Dämpfer aufsetzen; **sub'dued** [-juːd] *adj.* **1.** unter'worfen, -'jocht; **2.** gebändigt; **3.** gedämpft (*a. fig.*).

ˌsub'ed·it [ˌsʌb-] *v/t. Zeitung etc.* redigieren; **ˌsub'ed·i·tor** *s.* Redak'teur *m*.

'subˌhead(·ing) ['sʌb-] *s.* **1.** 'Unter-, Zwischentitel *m*; **2.** 'Unterabˌteilung *f e-s Buches etc.*

ˌsub'hu·man [ˌsʌb-] *adj.* **1.** halbtierisch; **2.** unmenschlich.

sub·ja·cent [sʌb'dʒeɪsənt] *adj.* **1.** dar'unter *od.* tiefer liegend; **2.** *fig.* zu'grunde liegend.

sub·ject ['sʌbʒɪkt] **I** *s.* **1.** (*Gesprächs-etc.*)Gegenstand *m*, Thema *n*, Stoff *m*: ~ ***of conversation***; ***on the ~ of*** über (*acc.*), bezüglich (*gen.*); **2.** *ped.* (Lehr-, Schul-, Studien)Fach *n*, Fachgebiet *n*: ***compulsory*** ~ Pflichtfach; **3.** Grund *m*, Anlaß *m* (***for complaint*** zur Beschwerde); **4.** Ob'jekt *n*, Gegenstand *m* (***of ridicule*** des Spotts); **5.** *paint. etc.* Thema *n* (*a.* ♪), Su'jet *n*, Vorwurf *m*; **6.** *ling.* Sub'jekt *n*, Satzgegenstand *m*; **7.** 'Untertan(in), *a.* Staatsbürger(in), -angehörige(r *m*) *f*: ***a British*** ~; **8.** *bsd.* ⚕ a) Ver'suchsperˌson *f*, -tier *n*, b) Leichnam *m für Sektionszwecke*, c) Pati'ent (-in), *hysterische etc.* Per'son; **9.** *ohne Artikel* die betreffende Person *etc.* (*in Informationen*); **10.** *phls.* a) Sub'jekt *n*, Ich *n*, b) Sub'stanz *f*; **II** *adj. pred.* **11.** 'untertan, unter'geben (***to*** *dat.*); **12.** abhängig (***to*** von); **13.** ausgesetzt (***to*** *dem Gespött etc.*); **14.** (***to***) unter'worfen, -'liegend (*dat.*), abhängig (von), vorbehaltlich (*gen.*): ~ ***to approval*** genehmigungspflichtig; ~ ***to your consent*** vorbehaltlich Ihrer Zustimmung; ~ ***to change without notice*** Änderungen vorbehalten; ~ ***to being unsold***, ~ ***to (prior) sale*** ✝ freibleibend, Zwischenverkauf vorbehalten; **15.** (***to***) neigend (zu), anfällig (für): ~ ***to headaches***; **III** *v/t.* [səb'dʒekt] **16.** (***to***) a) unter'werfen (*dat.*), abhängig machen (von), b) *e-r Behandlung, Prüfung etc.* unter'ziehen, c) *dem Gespött, der Hitze etc.* aussetzen; ~ **cat·a·logue** *s.* 'Schlagwortkataˌlog *m*; ~ **head·ing** *s.* Ru'brik *f* in e-m 'Sachreˌgister; ~ **in·dex** *s.* 'Sachreˌgister *n*.

sub·jec·tion [səb'dʒekʃn] *s.* **1.** Unter'werfung *f*; **2.** Unter'worfensein *n*; **3.** Abhängigkeit *f*: ***be in ~ to s.o.*** von j-m abhängig sein.

sub·jec·tive [səb'dʒektɪv] **I** *adj.* ☐ **1.** *allg., a.* ⚕, *phls.* subjek'tiv; **2.** *ling.* Subjekts...; **II** *s.* **3.** *a.* ~ ***case*** *ling.* Nominativ *m*; **sub'jec·tive·ness** [-nɪs] *s.* Subjektivi'tät *f*; **sub'jec·tiv·ism** [-vɪzəm] *s. bsd. phls.* Subjekti'vismus *m*.

sub·jec·tiv·i·ty [ˌsʌbdʒek'tɪvətɪ] *s.* Subjektivi'tät *f*.

sub·ject| mat·ter *s.* **1.** Gegenstand *m* (*e-r Abhandlung etc., a.* ⚖); **2.** Stoff *m*, Inhalt *m* (*Ggs. Form*); ~ **ref·er·ence** *s.* Sachverweis *m*.

ˌsub'join [ˌsʌb-] *v/t.* **1.** hin'zufügen, -setzen; **2.** beilegen, -fügen.

sub·ju·gate ['sʌbdʒʊgeɪt] *v/t.* **1.** unter'jochen, -'werfen (***to*** *dat.*); **2.** *bsd. fig.* bezwingen, bändigen; **sub·ju·ga·tion** [ˌsʌbdʒʊ'geɪʃn] *s.* Unter'werfung *f*, -'jochung *f*.

sub·junc·tive [səb'dʒʌŋktɪv] *ling.* **I** *adj.* ☐ **1.** konjunktiv(isch); **II** *s.* **2.** *a.* ~ ***mood*** Konjunktiv *m*; **3.** Konjunktivform *f*.

ˌsub'lease [ˌsʌb-] **I** *s.* 'Untermiete *f*, -pacht *f*, -vermietung *f*, -verpachtung *f*; **II** *v/t.* 'untervermieten, -verpachten; **ˌsub·les'see** *s.* 'Untermieter(in), -pächter(in); **ˌsub·les'sor** [-'sɔː] *s.* 'Untervermieter(in), -verpächter(in).

sub·let [ˌsʌb'let] *v/t.* [*irr.* → ***let***[1]] 'unter-, weitervermieten.

sub·lieu·ten·ant [ˌsʌblef'tenənt] *s.* ⚓ *Brit.* Oberleutnant *m* zur See.

sub·li·mate ['sʌblɪmeɪt] **I** *v/t.* **1.** ⚗ sublimieren; **2.** *fig.* sublimieren (*a. psych.*), veredeln, vergeistigen; **II** *s.* [-mɪt] **3.** ⚗ Subli'mat *n*; **sub·li·ma·tion** [ˌsʌblɪ'meɪʃn] *s.* **1.** ⚗ Sublimati'on *f*; **2.** *fig.* Sublimierung *f* (*a. psych.*).

sub·lime [sə'blaɪm] **I** *adj.* ☐ **1.** erhaben, hehr, su'blim; **2.** a) großartig (*a. iro.*): ~ ***ignorance***, b) *iro.* kom'plett: ***a ~ idiot***, c) kraß: ~ ***indifference***; **II** *s.* **3.** ***the ~*** das Erhabene; **III** *v/t.* **4.** → ***sublimate*** 1 *u.* 2; **IV** *v/i.* **5.** ⚗ sublimiert werden; **6.** *fig.* sich läutern.

sub·lim·i·nal [ˌsʌb'lɪmɪnl] *psych.* **I** *adj.* **1.** 'unterbewußt: ~ ***self*** → 3; **2.** 'unterschwellig (*Reiz etc.*, ✝ *Werbung*); **II** *s.* **3.** *das* 'Unterbewußte.

ˌsub·ma'chine-gun [ˌsʌb-] *s.* ⚔ Ma'schinenpiˌstole *f*.

sub·man ['sʌbmæn] *s.* [*irr.*] **1.** tierischer Kerl; **2.** Idi'ot *m*.

ˌsub·ma'rine [ˌsʌb-] **I** *s.* **1.** ⚓, ⚔ 'Unterseeboot *n*, U-Boot *n*; **II** *adj.* **2.** 'unterseeisch, Untersee..., subma'rin; **3.** ⚓, ⚔ Unterseeboot..., U-Boot-...: ~ ***warfare***; ~ ***chaser*** U-Boot-Jäger *m*; ~ ***pen*** U-Boot-Bunker *m*.

sub·merge [səb'mɜːdʒ] **I** *v/t.* **1.** ein-, 'untertauchen; **2.** über'schwemmen, unter Wasser setzen; **3.** *fig.* a) unter'drücken, b) über'tönen; **II** *v/i.* **4.** 'untertauchen, -sinken; **5.** ⚓ tauchen (*U-Boot*); **sub'merged** [-dʒd] *adj.* **1.** 'untergetaucht; ⚓, ⚔ *Angriff etc.* unter

Wasser; **2.** über'schwemmt; **3.** *fig.* verelendet, verarmt.

sub·mersed [səb'mɜ:st] *adj.* **1.** → **sub-merged** 1 *u.* 2; **2.** *bsd.* ⚘ Unterwasser...: **~ plants**; **sub'mers·i·ble** [-səbl] **I** *adj.* **1.** 'untertauch-, versenkbar; **2.** über'schwemmbar; **3.** ⚓ tauchfähig; **II** *s.* **4.** ⚓ 'Unterseeboot *n*; **sub'mer·sion** [-ɜ:ʃn] *s.* **1.** Ein-, 'Untertauchen *n*; **2.** Über'schwemmung *f.*

sub·mis·sion [səb'mɪʃn] *s.* **1.** (**to**) Unter'werfung *f* (unter *acc.*), Ergebenheit *f* (in *acc.*), Gehorsam *m* (gegen); **2.** Unter'würfigkeit *f*: **with all due ~** mit allem schuldigen Respekt; **3.** *bsd.* ⚖ Vorlage *f e-s Dokuments etc.*, Unter'breitung *f e-r Frage etc.*; **4.** ⚖ a) Sachvorlage *f*, Behauptung *f*, b) Kompro'miß *m, n*; **sub'mis·sive** [-ɪsɪv] *adj.* □ **1.** ergeben, gehorsam; **2.** unter'würfig; **sub'mis·sive·ness** [-ɪsɪvnɪs] *s.* **1.** Ergebenheit *f*; **2.** Unter'würfigkeit *f*; **sub'mit** [-'mɪt] **I** *v/t.* **1.** unter'werfen, -'ziehen, aussetzen (**to** *dat.*): **~ o.s.** (**to**) → 4; **2.** *bsd.* ⚖ unter'breiten, vortragen, -legen (**to** *dat.*); **3.** *bsd.* ⚖ beantragen, behaupten, zu bedenken geben, an'heimstellen (**to** *dat.*); *bsd. parl.* ergebenst bemerken; **II** *v/i.* **4.** (**to**) gehorchen (*dat.*), sich fügen (*dat. od.* in *acc.*); sich *j-m, e-m Urteil etc.* unter'werfen, sich *e-r Operation etc.* unter'ziehen; **sub'mit·tal** [-'mɪtl] *s.* Vorlage *f*, Unter'breitung *f.*

ˌsub'nor·mal [ˌsʌb-] *adj.* □ **1.** a) 'unterˌdurchschnittlich, b) minderbegabt, c) schwachsinnig; **2.** ⩚ 'subnorˌmal.

'subˌor·der ['sʌb-] *s. biol.* 'Unterordnung *f.*

sub·or·di·nate [sə'bɔ:dnɪt] **I** *adj.* □ **1.** 'untergeordnet: a) unter'stellt (**to** *dat.*): **~ position** untergeordnete Stellung, b) zweitrangig, nebensächlich: **~ clause** *ling.* Nebensatz *m*; **be ~ to** *e-r Sache* an Bedeutung nachstehen; **II** *s.* **2.** Unter'gebene(r *m*) *f*; **III** [-dɪneɪt] *v/t.* **3.** *a. ling.* 'unterordnen (**to** *dat.*); **4.** zu'rückstellen (**to** hinter *acc.*); **sub·or·di·na·tion** [səˌbɔ:dɪ'neɪʃn] *s.* 'Unterordnung *f* (**to** unter *acc.*); **sub'or·di·na·tive** [-dɪnətɪv] *adj. ling.* 'unterordnend: **~ conjunction**.

sub·orn [sʌ'bɔ:n] *v/t.* ⚖ (*bsd.* zum Meineid) anstiften; *Zeugen* bestechen; **sub·or·na·tion** [ˌsʌbɔ:'neɪʃn] *s.* ⚖ Anstiftung *f*, Verleitung *f* (**of** zum *Meineid*, zu *falscher Zeugenaussage*), (Zeugen)Bestechung *f.*

sub·pe·na *Am.* → **subpoena**.

'sub·plot ['sʌb-] *s.* Nebenhandlung *f.*

sub·poe·na [səb'pi:nə] ⚖ **I** *s.* (Vor)Ladung *f* (unter Strafandrohung); **II** *v/t.* vorladen.

sub·ro·gate ['sʌbrəʊgeɪt] *v/t.* ⚖ einsetzen (**for s.o.** an j-s Stelle; **to the rights of** in *j-s* Rechte); **sub·ro·ga·tion** [ˌsʌbrəʊ'geɪʃn] *s.* ⚖ 'Forderungsˌübergang *m* (kraft Gesetzes); Ersetzung *f e-s Gläubigers durch e-n anderen*: **~ of rights** Rechtseintritt *m.*

sub·scribe [səb'skraɪb] **I** *v/t.* **1.** *Vertrag etc.* unter'zeichnen, ('unterschriftlich) anerkennen; **2.** *et.* mit *s-m Namen etc.* (unter)'zeichnen; **3.** *Geldbetrag* zeichnen (**for** für *Aktien*, **to** für *e-n Fonds*); **II** *v/i.* **4.** e-n Geldbetrag zeichnen (**to** für *e-n Fonds*, **for** für *e-e Anleihe etc.*); **5. ~ for** *Buch* vorbestellen; **6. ~ to** *Zeitung etc.* abonnieren; **7.** unter'schreiben, -'zeichnen (**to** *acc.*); **8. ~ to** *fig. et.* unter'schreiben, gutheißen, billigen; **sub'scrib·er** [-bə] *s.* **1.** Unter'zeichner (-in), -'zeichnete(r *m*) *f* (**to** *gen.*); **2.** Befürworter(in) (**to** *gen.*); **3.** Subskri'bent(in), Abon'nent(in); *teleph.* Teilnehmer(in); **4.** Zeichner *m*, Spender *m* (**to** *e-s Geldbetrages*).

sub·scrip·tion [səb'skrɪpʃn] *s.* **1.** a) Unter'zeichnung *f*, b) 'Unterschrift *f*; **2.** (**to**) ('unterschriftliche) Einwilligung (in *acc.*), Zustimmung *f* (zu); **3.** (**to**) Beitrag *m* (zu, für), Spende *f* (für), (gezeichneter) Betrag; (*teleph.* Grund)Gebühr *f*; **4.** *Brit.* (Mitglieds)Beitrag *m*; **5.** Abonne'ment *n*, Bezugsrecht *n*, Subskripti'on *f* (**to** auf *acc.*): **by ~** im Abonnement; **take out a ~ to** *Zeitung etc.* abonnieren; **6.** ✝ Zeichnung *f* (**of** *e-r Summe, Anleihe etc.*): **~ for shares** Aktienzeichnung; **open for ~** zur Zeichnung aufgelegt; **invite ~s for a loan** e-e Anleihe (zur Zeichnung) auflegen; **~ list** *s.* **1.** ✝ Subskripti'onsliste *f*; **2.** *Zeitung*: Zeichnungsliste *f*; **~ price** *s.* Bezugspreis *m.*

'subˌsec·tion ['sʌb-] *s.* 'Unterabˌteilung *f*, -abschnitt *m.*

sub·se·quence ['sʌbsɪkwəns] *s.* **1.** späteres Eintreten; **2.** ⩚ Teilfolge *f*; **'sub·se·quent** [-nt] *adj.* □ (nach)folgend, später, nachträglich, Nach...: **~ to** a) später als, b) nach, im Anschluß an (*acc.*), folgend (*dat.*); **~ upon** a) infolge (*gen.*), b) *nachgestellt*: (daraus) entstehend, (daraufhin) erfolgend; **'sub·se·quent·ly** [-ntlɪ] *adv.* **1.** 'hinterher, nachher; **2.** anschließend; **3.** später.

sub·serve [səb'sɜ:v] *v/t.* dienlich *od.* förderlich sein (*dat.*); **sub'ser·vi·ence** [-vjəns] *s.* **1.** Dienlich-, Nützlichkeit *f* (**to** für); **2.** Abhängigkeit *f* (**to** von); **3.** Unter'würfigkeit *f*; **sub'ser·vi·ent** [-vjənt] *adj.* □ **1.** dienstbar, 'untergeordnet (**to** *dat.*); **2.** unter'würfig (**to** gegenüber); **3.** dienlich, förderlich (**to** *dat.*).

sub·side [səb'saɪd] *v/i.* **1.** sich senken: a) sinken (*Flut etc.*), b) (ein)sinken, absacken (*Boden etc.*), sich setzen (*Haus*); **2.** ⚗ sich niederschlagen; **3.** *fig.* abklingen, abflauen, sich legen: **~ into** verfallen in (*acc.*); **4.** *in e-n Stuhl etc.* sinken.

sub·sid·i·ar·y [səb'sɪdjərɪ] **I** *adj.* □ **1.** Hilfs..., Unterstützungs..., Subsidien...: **be ~ to** ergänzen, unterstützen; **2.** 'untergeordnet (**to** *dat.*), Neben...: **~ company** → 4; **~ stream** Nebenfluß *m*; **II** *s.* **3.** *oft pl.* Hilfe *f*, Stütze *f*; **4.** ✝ Tochtergesellschaft *f.*

sub·si·dize ['sʌbsɪdaɪz] *v/t.* subventionieren; **'sub·si·dy** [-dɪ] *s.* **1.** Beihilfe *f* (aus öffentlichen Mitteln), Subventi'on *f*; **2.** *oft pl. pol.* Sub'sidien *pl.*, Hilfsgelder *pl.*

sub·sist [səb'sɪst] **I** *v/i.* **1.** existieren, bestehen; **2.** weiterbestehen, fortdauern; **3.** sich ernähren *od.* erhalten, leben ([**up**]**on** von *e-r Nahrung*, **by** von *e-m Beruf*); **II** *v/t.* **4.** *j-n* er-, unter'halten; **sub'sist·ence** [-təns] *s.* **1.** Dasein *n*, Exi'stenz *f*; **2.** ('Lebens)ˌUnterhalt *m*, Auskommen *n*, Exi'stenz(möglichkeit) *f*: **~ level** Existenzminimum *n*; **3.** *bsd.* ⚔ Verpflegung *f*, -sorgung *f*; **4.** *a.* **~ money** a) (Lohn)Vorschuß *m*, b) 'Unterhaltsbeihilfe *f*, -zuschuß *m.*

'sub·soil ['sʌb-] *s.* 'Untergrund *m.*

ˌsub'son·ic [ˌsʌb-] **I** *adj.* Unterschall...; **II** *s.* 'Unterschallflug(zeug *n*) *m.*

'subˌspe·cies ['sʌb-] *s. biol.* 'Unterart *f*, Sub'spezies *f.*

sub·stance ['sʌbstəns] *s.* **1.** Sub'stanz *f*, Ma'terie *f*, Stoff *m*, Masse *f*; **2.** feste Konsi'stenz, Körper *m* (*Tuch etc.*); **3.** *fig.* Sub'stanz *f*: a) Wesen *n*, b) *das* Wesentliche, wesentlicher Inhalt *od.* Bestandteil, Kern *m*: **this essay lacks ~**; **in ~** im wesentlichen *übereinstimmen etc.*, c) Gehalt *m*: **arguments of little ~** wenig stichhaltige Argumente; **4.** *phls.* a) Sub'stanz *f*, b) Wesen *n*, Ding *n*; **5.** Vermögen *n*, Kapi'tal *n*: **a man of ~** ein vermögender Mann.

sub·stand·ard [səb-] *adj.* **1.** unter der Norm, klein..., Klein...; **2.** *ling.* 'umgangssprachlich.

sub·stan·tial [səb'stænʃl] *adj.* □ → **substantially**; **1.** materi'ell, stofflich, wirklich; **2.** fest, kräftig; **3.** nahrhaft, kräftig: **a ~ meal**; **4.** beträchtlich, wesentlich (*Fortschritt, Unterschied etc.*), namhaft (*Summe*); **5.** wesentlich: **in ~ agreement** im wesentlichen übereinstimmend; **6.** vermögend, kapi'talkräftig; **7.** *phls.* substanti'ell, wesentlich; **sub·stan·ti·al·i·ty** [səbˌstænʃɪ'ælətɪ] *s.* **1.** Wirklichkeit *f*, Stofflichkeit *f*; **2.** Festigkeit *f*; **3.** Nahrhaftigkeit *f*; **4.** Gediegenheit *f*; **5.** Stichhaltigkeit *f*; **6.** *phls.* Substantiali'tät *f*; **sub'stan·tial·ly** [-ʃəlɪ] *adv.* **1.** dem Wesen nach; **2.** im wesentlichen, wesentlich; **3.** beträchtlich, wesentlich, in hohem Maße; **4.** wirklich; **sub'stan·ti·ate** [-ʃɪeɪt] *v/t.* **1.** a) begründen, b) erhärten, beweisen, c) glaubhaft machen; **2.** Gestalt *od.* Wirklichkeit verleihen (*dat.*), konkretisieren; **3.** stärken, festigen; **sub·stan·ti·a·tion** [səbˌstænʃɪ'eɪʃn] *s.* **1.** a) Begründung *f*, b) Erhärtung *f*, Beweis *m*, c) Glaubhaftmachung *f*: **in ~ of** zur Erhärtung *od.* zum Beweis von (*od. gen.*); **2.** Verwirklichung *f.*

sub·stan·ti·val [ˌsʌbstən'taɪvl] *adj.* □ *ling.* substantivisch, Substantiv...; **sub·stan·tive** ['sʌbstəntɪv] **I** *s.* **1.** *ling.* a) Substantiv *n*, Hauptwort *n*, b) substantivisch gebrauchte Form; **II** *adj.* □ **2.** *ling.* substantivisch (gebraucht); **3.** selbständig; **4.** wesentlich; **5.** wirklich, re'al; **6.** fest; **7.** ⚖ materi'ell: **~ law**.

'subˌsta·tion ['sʌb-] *s.* **1.** Neben-, Außenstelle *f*: **post office ~** Zweigpostamt *n*; **2.** ⚡ 'Unterwerk *n*; **3.** *teleph.* (Teilnehmer)Sprechstelle *f.*

sub·sti·tute ['sʌbstɪtju:t] **I** *s.* **1.** Ersatz (-mann) *m*: a) (Stell)Vertreter(in), b) *sport* Auswechselspieler(in): **act as a ~ for** *j-n* vertreten; **2.** Ersatz(stoff) *m*, Surro'gat *n* (**for** für); **3.** *ling.* Ersatzwort *n*; **II** *adj.* **4.** Ersatz...: **~ driver**; **~ material** ⚙ Austausch(werk)stoff *m*; **~ power of attorney** ⚖ Untervollmacht *f*; **III** *v/t.* **5.** (**for**) einsetzen (für, an Stelle von), an die Stelle setzen (von *od. gen.*): **~ A for B** B durch A ersetzen, B gegen A austauschen *od.* auswechseln (*alle a. sport*); **6.** ersetzen, an *j-s* Stelle treten; **IV** *v/i.* **7.** (**for**) als Ersatz dienen, als Stellvertreter fungieren (für), vertreten (*acc.*), an die Stelle treten (von *od. gen.*); **sub·sti·tu·tion** [ˌsʌbstɪˈtjuːʃn] *s.* **1.** Einsetzung *f* (⚖ *e-s Ersatzerben, Unterbevollmächtigten*); *bsd. b.s.* (*Kindes- etc.*)ˈUnterschiebung *f*; **2.** Ersatz *m*, Ersetzung *f*; (ersatzweise) Verwendung; **3.** Stellvertretung *f*; **4.** &, ⚗, *ling.* Substitutiˈon *f*; **sub·sti·tu·tion·al** [ˌsʌbstɪˈtjuːʃənl] *adj.* □ **1.** stellvertretend, Stellvertretungs...; **2.** Ersatz...

ˌ**subˈstra·tum** [ˌsʌb-] *s.* [*irr.*] **1.** ˈUnter-, Grundlage *f* (*a. fig.*); **2.** *geol.* ˈUnterschicht *f*; **3.** *biol.* a) Subˈstrat *n*, Nähr-, Keimboden *m*, b) *a.* ⚗ Träger *m*, Medium *n*; **4.** *phot.* Grundschicht *f*; **5.** *ling.* Subˈstrat *n*; **6.** *phls.* Subˈstanz *f*.

ˈ**subˌstruc·ture** [ˈsʌb-] *s.* **1.** ⚠ Fundaˈment *n*, ˈUnterbau *m* (*a.* 🚂); **2.** *fig.* Grundlage *f*.

sub·sume [səbˈsjuːm] *v/t.* **1.** zs.-fassen, ˈunterordnen (***under*** unter *dat. od. acc.*); **2.** einordnen, -reihen, -schließen (***in*** in *acc.*); **3.** *phls. als Prämisse* vorˈausschicken; **subˈsump·tion** [-ˈsʌmpʃn] *s.* **1.** Zs.-fassung *f* (***under*** unter *dat. od. acc.*); **2.** Einordnung *f*.

ˌ**subˈten·ant** [ˌsʌb-] *s.* ˈUntermieter *m*, -pächter *m*.

sub·ter·fuge [ˈsʌbtəfjuːdʒ] *s.* **1.** Vorwand *m*, Ausflucht *f*; **2.** List *f*.

sub·ter·ra·ne·an [ˌsʌbtəˈreɪnjən] *adj.*, ˌ**sub·terˈra·ne·ous** [-njəs] *adj.* □ **1.** ˈunterirdisch (*a. fig.*); **2.** *fig.* verborgen, heimlich.

sub·tile [ˈsʌtl], **sub·til·i·ty** [sʌbˈtɪlətɪ] → ***subtle***, ***subtlety***; **sub·til·i·za·tion** [ˌsʌtɪlaɪˈzeɪʃn] *s.* **1.** Verfeinerung *f*; **2.** Spitzfindigkeit *f*; **3.** ⚗ Verflüchtigung *f*; **sub·til·ize** [ˈsʌtɪlaɪz] **I** *v/t.* **1.** verfeinern; **2.** spitzfindig diskutieren *od.* erklären; ausklügeln; **3.** ⚗ verflüchtigen, -dünnen; **II** *v/i.* **4.** spitzfindig argumentieren.

ˈ**subˌti·tle** [ˈsʌb-] **I** *s.* ˈUntertitel *m* (*Buch, Film*); **II** *v/t. Film* unterˈtiteln.

sub·tle [ˈsʌtl] *adj.* □ **1.** *allg.* fein: **~ *delight***; **~ *odo(u)r***; **~ *smile***; **2.** fein(sinnig), subˈtil: **~ *distinction***; **~ *irony***; **3.** scharf(sinnig), spitzfindig; **4.** heikel, schwierig: ***a* ~ *point***; **5.** raffiniert; **6.** schleichend (*Gift*); ˈ**sub·tle·ty** [-tɪ] *s.* **1.** Feinheit *f*; subˈtile Art; **2.** Spitzfindigkeit *f*; **3.** Scharfsinn(igkeit *f*) *m*; **4.** Gerissenheit *f*, Raffiˈnesse *f*; **5.** schlauer Einfall, Fiˈnesse *f*.

sub·to·pi·a [sʌbˈtəʊpɪə] *s. Brit.* zersiedelte Landschaft.

subˈto·tal [səb-] *s.* & Zwischen-, Teilsumme *f*.

sub·tract [səbˈtrækt] **I** *v/t.* & abziehen, subtrahieren; **II** *v/i. fig.* (***from***) Abstriche machen (von), schmälern (*acc.*); **subˈtrac·tion** [-kʃn] *s.* **1.** & Subtraktiˈon *f*, Abziehen *n*; **2.** *fig.* Abzug *m*.

sub·tra·hend [ˈsʌbtrəhənd] *s.* & Subtraˈhend *m*.

sub·trop·i·cal [ˌsʌbˈtrɒpɪkl] *adj. geogr.* subtropisch; ˌ**subˈtrop·ics** [-ks] *s. pl. geogr.* Subtropen *pl.*

sub·urb [ˈsʌbɜːb] *s.* Vorstadt *f*, -ort *m*; **sub·ur·ban** [səˈbɜːbən] **I** *adj.* **1.** vorstädtisch, Vorstadt..., Vororts...; **2.** *contp.* kleinstädtisch, spießig; **II** *s.* **3.** → ***suburbanite***; **sub·ur·ban·ite** [səˈbɜːbənaɪt] *s.* Vorstadtbewohner(in); **sub·ur·bi·a** [səˈbɜːbɪə] *s. oft contp.* **1.** Vorstadt *f*; **2.** *coll. die* Vorstädter *pl.*

ˈ**sub·vaˌri·e·ty** [ˈsʌb-] *s.* ⚘, *zo.* ˈuntergeordnete Abart.

sub·ven·tion [səbˈvenʃn] *s.* (staatliche) Subventiˈon, (geldliche) Beihilfe, Unterˈstützung *f*; **subˈven·tioned** [-nd] *adj.* subventioniert.

sub·ver·sion [səbˈvɜːʃn] *s.* **1.** *pol.* a) ˈUmsturz *m*, Sturz *m e-r Regierung*, b) Staatsgefährdung *f*, Verfassungsverrat *m*; **2.** Unterˈgrabung *f*, Zerrüttung *f*; **subˈver·sive** [-ɜːsɪv] *adj.* **1.** *pol.* ˈumstürzlerisch, staatsgefährdend, Wühl..., subverˈsiv; **2.** zerstörerisch; **3.** zerrüttend; **subˈvert** [-ɜːt] *v/t.* **1.** *Regierung* stürzen; *Gesetz* ˈumstoßen; *Verfassung* gewaltsam ändern; **2.** *Glauben, Moral, Ordnung etc.* unterˈgraben, zerrütten.

ˈ**sub·way** [ˈsʌb-] *s.* **1.** (ˈStraßen-, ˈFußgänger)Unterˌführung *f*; **2.** *Am.* U-Bahn *f*.

ˌ**subˈze·ro** [ˌsʌb-] *adj.* unter dem Gefrierpunkt.

suc·ceed [səkˈsiːd] **I** *v/i.* **1.** glücken, gelingen, erfolgreich sein *od.* verlaufen, Erfolg haben (*Sache*); **2.** Erfolg haben, erfolgreich sein, sein Ziel erreichen (*Person*) (***as*** als, ***in*** mit *et.*, ***with*** bei *j-m*): ***he* ~*ed in doing s.th.*** es gelang ihm, et. zu tun; **~ *in an action*** ⚖ obsiegen; **3.** (***to***) a) Nachfolger werden (in *e-m Amt etc.*), b) erben (*acc.*): **~ *to the throne*** auf den Thron folgen; **~ *to s.o.'s rights*** in j-s Rechte eintreten; **4.** (***to***) *unmittelbar* folgen (*dat. od.* auf *acc.*), nachfolgen (*dat.*); **II** *v/t.* **5.** nachfolgen (*dat.*), folgen (*dat. od.* auf *acc.*); *j-s* (Amts-, Rechts)Nachfolger werden, an *j-s* Stelle treten; *j-n* beerben: **~ *s.o. in office*** j-s Amt übernehmen.

suc·cès d'es·time [sʊkˌseɪdesˈtiːm] (*Fr.*) *s.* Achtungserfolg *m*.

suc·cess [səkˈses] *s.* **1.** (guter) Erfolg, Gelingen *n*: ***with* ~** erfolgreich; ***without* ~** erfolglos; ***be a (great)* ~** ein (großer) Erfolg sein (*Sache u. Person*), (gut) einschlagen; ***crowned with* ~** von Erfolg gekrönt (*Bemühung*); **~ *rate*** Erfolgsquote *f*; **2.** Erfolg *m*, Glanzleistung *f*; **3.** *beruflicher etc.* Erfolg; **sucˈcess·ful** [-fʊl] *adj.* □ **1.** erfolgreich: ***be* ~ *in doing s.th.*** et. mit Erfolg tun, Erfolg haben bei *od.* mit et.; **2.** erfolgreich, glücklich (*Sache*): ***be* ~** → ***succeed*** 1.

suc·ces·sion [səkˈseʃn] *s.* **1.** (Aufeinˈander-, Reihen)Folge *f*: ***in* ~** nach-, auf-, hintereinander; ***in rapid* ~** in rascher Folge; **2.** Reihe *f*, Kette *f*, (ˈununterˌbrochene) Folge (***of*** *gen. od.* von); **3.** Nach-, Erbfolge *f*, Sukzessiˈon *f*: **~ *to the throne*** Thronfolge; ***in* ~ *to*** als Nachfolger von; ***be next in* ~ *to s.o.*** als nächster auf j-n folgen; **~ *to an office*** Übernahme *f* e-s Amtes, Amtsnachfolge; ***Apostolic*** ♀ *eccl.* Apostolische Sukzession; ***the War of the Spanish*** ♀ *hist.* der Spanische Erbfolgekrieg; **4.** ⚖ a) Rechtsnachfolge *f*, b) Erbfolge *f*, c) *a.* ***order of* ~** Erbfolgeordnung *f*, d) *a.* ***law of* ~** *objektives* Erb(folge)recht, e) **~ *to*** ˈÜbernahme *f e-s Erbes*: **~ *duties*** Erbschaftssteuer *f* (*für unbewegliches Vermögen*); **~ *rights*** *subjektive* Erbrechte; **5.** *coll.* Nachkommenschaft *f*, Erben *pl.*; **sucˈces·sive** [-esɪv] *adj.* □ (aufeinˈander)folgend, sukzesˈsiv: ***3* ~ *days*** 3 Tage hintereinander; **sucˈces·sive·ly** [-esɪvlɪ] *adv.* nach-, hintereinˈander, der Reihe nach; **sucˈces·sor** [-esə] *s.* **1.** Nachfolger(in), (***to***, ***of*** *j-s*, für *j-n*): **~ *in office*** Amtsnachfolger; **~ *to the throne*** Thronfolger *m*; **2.** *a.* **~ *in interest*** (*od.* ***title***) ⚖ Rechtsnachfolger(in).

suc·cinct [səkˈsɪŋkt] *adj.* □ kurz (und bündig), knapp, laˈkonisch, präˈgnant; **sucˈcinct·ness** [-nɪs] *s.* Kürze *f*, Bündigkeit *f*, Präˈgnanz *f*.

suc·cor [ˈsʌkə] *Am.* → ***succour***.

suc·co·ry [ˈsʌkərɪ] *s.* ⚘ Ziˈchorie *f*.

suc·cour [ˈsʌkə] **I** *s.* Hilfe *f*, Beistand *m*; ⚔ Entsatz *m*; **II** *v/t.* beistehen (*dat.*), zu Hilfe kommen (*dat.*); ⚔ entsetzen.

suc·cu·lence [ˈsʌkjʊləns], ˈ**suc·cu·len·cy** [-sɪ] *s.* Saftigkeit *f*; ˈ**suc·cu·lent** [-nt] *adj.* □ **1.** saftig, fleischig, sukkuˈlent (*Frucht etc.*); **2.** *fig.* kraftvoll, saftig.

suc·cumb [səˈkʌm] *v/i.* **1.** zs.-brechen (***to*** unter *dat.*); **2.** (***to***) (*j-m*) unterˈliegen, (*e-r Krankheit, s-n Verletzungen etc., a. der Versuchung*) erliegen; **3.** (***to***, ***under***, ***before***) nachgeben (*dat.*).

such [sʌtʃ; sətʃ] **I** *adj.* **1.** solch, derartig: ***no* ~ *thing*** nichts dergleichen; ***there are* ~ *things*** so etwas gibt es *od.* kommt vor; **~ *people as you see here*** die(jenigen) *od.* alle Leute, die man hier sieht; ***a system* ~ *as this*** ein derartiges System; **~ *a one*** ein solcher, eine solche, ein solches; **~ *and* ~ *persons*** die u. die Personen; **2.** ähnlich, derartig: ***silk and* ~ *luxuries***; ***poets* ~ *as Spenser*** Dichter wie Spenser; **3.** *pred.* so (beschaffen), derart(ig) (***as to*** daß): **~ *is life*** so ist das Leben; **~ *as it is*** wie es nun einmal ist; **~ *being the case*** da es sich so verhält; **4.** solch, so (groß *od.* klein *etc.*), dermaßen: **~ *a fright that*** e-n derartigen Schrecken, daß...; **~ *was the force of the explosion*** so groß war die Gewalt der Explosion; **5.** F so (gewaltig), solch: ***we had* ~ *fun*** wir hatten e-n Riesenspaß; **II** *adv.* **6.** so, derart: **~ *a nice day*** so ein schöner Tag; **~ *a long time*** e-e so lange Zeit; **III** *pron.* **7.** solch, der, die das, die *pl.*: **~ *as*** a) diejenigen welche, alle die, b) wie (zum Beispiel); **~ *was not my intention*** das war nicht meine Absicht; ***man as* ~** der Mensch als solcher; ***and* ~ (*like*)** u. dergleichen; **8.** F *u.* ✝ der-, die-, dasˈselbe, dieˈselben *pl.*; ˈ**~·like** *adj. u. pron.* dergleichen.

suck [sʌk] **I** *v/t.* **1.** saugen (***from***, ***out of*** aus *dat.*); **2.** saugen an (*dat.*), aussaugen; **3.** *a.* **~ *in***, **~ *up*** ein-, aufsaugen, absorbieren (*a. fig.*); **4.** **~ *in*** einsaugen, verschlingen; **5.** lutschen (an *dat.*): **~ *one's thumb*** (am) Daumen lutschen; **6.** schlürfen: **~ *soup***; **7.** *fig.* holen, gewinnen, ziehen: **~ *advantage out of*** Vorteil ziehen aus; **8.** *fig.* aussaugen: **~ *s.o.'s brain*** j-n ausholen, j-m s-e Ideen stehlen; **II** *v/i.* **9.** saugen, lutschen (***at*** an *dat.*); **10.** Luft saugen *od.* ziehen (*Pumpe*); **11.** **~ *up to*** *sl. j-m* ‚in den Arsch kriechen'; **III** *s.* **12.** Saugen *n*, Lutschen *n*: ***give* ~ *to*** → ***suckle*** 1; **13.** Sog *m*, Saugkraft *f*; **14.** saugendes Geräusch; **15.** Strudel *m*; **16.** F kleiner Schluck; **17.** *sl.* ‚Arschkriecher' *m*; ˈ**suck·er** [-kə] *s.* **1.** *zo.* saugendes Jungtier, *bsd.* Spanferkel *n*; **2.** *zo.* a) Saugrüssel *m*, b) Saugnapf *m*; **3.** *ichth.* a) *ein* Karpfenfisch *m*, b) Neunauge *n*, c) Lumpenfisch *m*, d) Schildfisch *m*; **4.** ⚙ 'Saugven,til *n od.* -kolben *m od.* -rohr *n*; **5.** Lutscher *m* (*Bonbon*); **6.** ⚘ (*a. Wurzel*)Schößling *m*; **7.** *sl.* Dumme(r) *m*, Gimpel *m*: ***be a ~ for*** a) stets hereinfallen auf (*acc.*), b) scharf sein auf (*acc.*); ***play s.o. for a ~*** j-n ‚anschmieren'; ***there's a ~ born every minute*** die Dummen werden nicht alle.

suck·ing ['sʌkɪŋ] *adj.* **1.** saugend; Saug...; **2.** *fig.* angehend, ‚grün', Anfänger...; **~ coil** *s.* ⚙ Tauchkernspule *f*; **~ disk** *s. zo.* Saugnapf *m*; **~ pig** *s. zo.* (Span)Ferkel *n*.

suck·le ['sʌkl] *v/t.* **1.** *Kind, a. Jungtier* säugen, *Kind* stillen; **2.** *fig.* nähren, pflegen; **'suck·ling** [-lɪŋ] *s.* **1.** Säugling *m*; **2.** *zo.* (noch nicht entwöhntes) Jungtier.

su·crose ['sju:krəʊs] *s.* Rohr-, Rübenzucker *m*, Su'crose *f*.

suc·tion ['sʌkʃn] **I** *s.* **1.** (An)Saugen *n*; ⚙ *a.* Saugwirkung *f*; *phys.* Saugfähigkeit *f*; **2.** ⚙, *phys.* Sog *m*; **3.** *mot.* Hub (-höhe *f*, -kraft *f*) *m*; **II** *adj.* **4.** Saug... (*-leistung*, *-pumpe etc.*): ***~ cleaner*** (*od.* ***sweeper***) Staubsauger *m*; **~ cup** *s.* ⚙ Saugnapf *m*; **~ pipe** *s.* ⚙ Ansaugrohr *n*; **~ plate** *s.* ⚕ Saugplatte *f* (*für Zahnprothese*); **~ stroke** *s. mot.* (An)Saughub *m*.

Su·da·nese [ˌsu:də'ni:z] **I** *adj.* suda'nesisch; **II** *s.* Suda'nese *m*, Suda'nesin *f*; *pl.* Suda'nesen *pl.*

su·dar·i·um [sju:'deərɪəm] *s. eccl.* Schweißtuch *n* (der Heiligen Ve'ronika); **su·da·to·ri·um** [ˌsju:də'tɔ:rɪəm] *pl.* **ri·a** [-rɪə] → ***sudatory*** 3; **su·da·to·ry** ['sju:dətərɪ] **I** *adj.* **1.** Schwitz(bad)...; **2.** ⚕ schweißtreibend; **II** *s.* **3.** Schwitzbad *n*; **4.** ⚕ schweißtreibendes Mittel.

sud·den ['sʌdn] **I** *adj.* □ plötzlich, jäh, unvermutet, ab'rupt, über'stürzt; **II** *s.*: ***on a ~***, (***all***) ***of a ~*** (ganz) plötzlich; **'sud·den·ness** [-nɪs] *s.* Plötzlichkeit *f*.

su·dor·if·er·ous [ˌsju:də'rɪfərəs] *adj.* Schweiß absondernd: ***~ glands*** Schweißdrüsen; ˌ**su·dor'if·ic** [-fɪk] *adj. u. s.* schweißtreibend(es Mittel).

suds [sʌdz] *s. pl.* **1.** Seifenwasser *n*, -lauge *f*; **2.** *Am.* F Bier *n*; **'suds·y** [-zɪ] *adj. Am.* schaumig, seifig.

sue [sju:] **I** *v/t.* **1.** ⚖ *j-n* (gerichtlich) belangen, verklagen (***for*** auf *acc.*, wegen); **2.** ***~ out*** *Gerichtsbeschluß etc.* erwirken; **3.** *j-n* bitten (***for*** um); **4.** *obs.* werben *od.* anhalten um *j-n*; **II** *v/i.* **5.** (***for***) klagen (auf *acc.*), Klage einreichen (wegen); (*e-e Schuld*) einklagen: ***~ for a divorce*** auf Scheidung klagen; **6.** nachsuchen (***to s.o.*** bei j-m, ***for s.th.*** um et.).

suede, **suède** [sweɪd] *s.* Wildleder *n*, Ve'lours(leder) *n*.

su·et ['sjʊɪt] *s.* Nierenfett *n*, Talg *m*.

suf·fer ['sʌfə] **I** *v/i.* **1.** leiden (***from*** an *e-r Krankheit etc.*); **2.** leiden (***under*** [*od.* ***from***] unter *dat.*) (*Handel*, *Ruf*, *Maschine etc.*), Schaden leiden, zu Schaden kommen (*a. Person*); **3.** ⚔ Verluste erleiden; **4.** büßen, bezahlen müssen (***for*** für); **5.** hingerichtet werden; **II** *v/t.* **6.** *Strafe*, *Tod*, *Verlust etc.* erleiden, *Durst etc.* leiden, erdulden; **7.** *et. od. j-n* ertragen *od.* aushalten; **8.** a) dulden, (zu)lassen, b) erlauben, gestatten: ***he ~ed himself to be cheated*** er ließ sich betrügen; **'suf·fer·a·ble** [-fərəbl] *adj.* □ erträglich; **'suf·fer·ance** [-fərəns] *s.* **1.** Duldung *f*, Einwilligung *f*: ***on ~*** unter stillschweigender Duldung, nur geduldet(erweise); **2.** *obs.* a) Ergebung *f*, (Er)Dulden *n*, b) Leiden *n*, Not *f*: ***remain in ~*** ✝ weiter Not leiden (*Wechsel*); **'suf·fer·er** [-fərə] *s.* **1.** Leidende(r *m*) *f*, Dulder(in): ***be a ~ by*** (***from***) leiden durch (an *dat.*); **2.** Geschädigte(r *m*) *f*; **3.** Märtyrer(in); **'suf·fer·ing** [-fərɪŋ] **I** *s.* Leiden *n*, Dulden *n*; **II** *adj.* leidend.

suf·fice [sə'faɪs] **I** *v/i.* genügen, (aus)reichen: ***~ it to say*** es genüge zu sagen; **II** *v/t.* *j-m* genügen.

suf·fi·cien·cy [sə'fɪʃnsɪ] *s.* **1.** Hinlänglichkeit *f*, Angemessenheit *f*; **2.** hinreichende Menge *od.* Zahl: ***a ~ of money*** genug Geld; **3.** hinreichendes Auskommen, auskömmliches Vermögen; **suf'fi·cient** [-nt] **I** *adj.* □ **1.** genügend, genug, aus-, hin-, zureichend (***for*** für): ***be ~*** genügen, (aus)reichen; ***~ reason*** zureichender Grund; ***I am not ~ of a scientist*** ich bin in den Naturwissenschaften nicht bewandert genug; **2.** *obs.* tauglich, fähig; **II** *s.* **3.** F genügende Menge, genug; **suf'fi·cient·ly** [-ntlɪ] *adv.* genügend, genug, hinlänglich.

suf·fix ['sʌfɪks] **I** *s.* **1.** *ling.* Suf'fix *n*, Nachsilbe *f*; **II** *v/t.* **2.** *ling.* als Nachsilbe anfügen; **3.** anfügen, -hängen.

suf·fo·cate ['sʌfəkeɪt] **I** *v/t.* ersticken (*a. fig.*); **II** *v/i.* (***with***) ersticken (an *dat.*), (fast) 'umkommen (vor *dat.*); **'suf·fo·cat·ing** [-tɪŋ] *adj.* □ erstickend, stikkig; **suf·fo·ca·tion** [ˌsʌfə'keɪʃn] *s.* Ersticken *n*, Erstickung *f*.

suf·fra·gan ['sʌfrəgən] *eccl.* **I** *adj.* Hilfs..., Suffragan...; **II** *s. a.* ***~ bishop*** Weihbischof *m*.

suf·frage ['sʌfrɪdʒ] *s.* **1.** *pol.* Wahl-, Stimmrecht *n*: ***female ~*** Frauenstimmrecht; ***universal ~*** allgemeines Wahlrecht; **2.** (Wahl)Stimme *f*; **3.** Abstimmung *f*, Wahl *f*; **4.** Zustimmung *f*; **suf·fra·gette** [ˌsʌfrə'dʒet] *s.* Suffra'gette *f*, Stimmrechtlerin *f*.

suf·fuse [sə'fju:z] *v/t.* **1.** über'strömen, benetzen; über'gießen, -'ziehen, bedekken (***with*** mit *e-r Farbe*); durch'fluten (*Licht*): ***a face ~d with blushes*** ein von Schamröte übergossenes Gesicht; **2.** *fig.* (er)füllen; **suf'fu·sion** [-ju:ʒn] *s.* **1.** Über'gießen *n*, -'flutung *f*; **2.** 'Überzug *m*; **3.** ⚕ 'Blutunter,laufung *f*; **4.** *fig.* Schamröte *f*.

sug·ar ['ʃʊgə] **I** *s.* **1.** Zucker *m* (*a.* ⚗, *physiol.*); **2.** ⚗ 'Kohlehy,drat *n*; **3.** *fig.* honigsüße Worte *pl.*; **4.** *sl.* ‚Zaster' *m* (*Geld*); **5.** F ‚Schätzchen' *n*; **II** *v/t.* **6.** zuckern, süßen; (über)'zuckern; **7.** *a.* ***~ over*** *fig.* a) versüßen, b) über'tünchen; **~ ba·sin** *s. Brit.* Zuckerdose *f*; **~ beet** *s.* ⚘ Zuckerrübe *f*; **~ bowl** *s. Am.* Zukkerdose *f*; **~ can·dy** *s.* Kandis(zucker) *m*; **~ cane** *s.* ⚘ Zuckerrohr *n*; **'~-coat** *v/t.* mit Zuckerguß über'ziehen; verzukkern (*a. fig.*): ***~ed pill*** Dragée *n*, verzuckerte Pille (*a. fig.*); **'~-,coat·ing** *s.* **1.** Über'zuckerung *f*, Zuckerguß *m*; **2.** *fig.* Versüßen *n*; Beschönigung *f*; **~ dad·dy** *s.* alter ‚Knacker', der ein junges Mädchen aushält.

sug·ared ['ʃʊgəd] *adj.* **1.** gezuckert, gesüßt; **2.** mit Zuckerguß; **3.** *fig.* (honig)süß.

sug·ar| loaf *s.* Zuckerhut *m*; **~ ma·ple** *s.* ⚘ Zuckerahorn *m*; **'~·plum** *s.* **1.** Bon'bon *m, n*, Süßigkeit *f*; **2.** *fig.* Lockspeise *f*, Schmeiche'lei *f*; **~ re·fin·er·y** *s.* 'Zuckerraffine,rie *f*; **~ tongs** *s. pl.* Zukkerzange *f*.

sug·ar·y ['ʃʊgərɪ] *adj.* **1.** zuckerhaltig, zuck(e)rig, süß; **2.** süßlich (*a. fig.*); **3.** *fig.* zuckersüß.

sug·gest [sə'dʒest] *v/t.* **1.** *et. od. j-n* vorschlagen, empfehlen; *et.* anregen; *et.* nahelegen (***to*** *dat.*); **2.** *Idee etc.* eingeben, -flüstern, suggerieren: ***the idea ~s itself*** der Gedanke drängt sich auf (***to*** *dat.*); **3.** hindeuten, -weisen, schließen lassen auf (*acc.*); **4.** denken lassen *od.* erinnern *od.* gemahnen an (*acc.*); **5.** *et.* andeuten, anspielen auf (*acc.*); zu verstehen geben (***that*** daß); **6.** behaupten, meinen (***that*** daß); **sug'gest·i·ble** [-təbl] *adj.* **1.** beeinflußbar, sugge'stibel; **2.** suggerierbar; **sug'ges·tion** [-tʃn] *s.* **1.** Vorschlag *m*, Anregung *f*: ***at the ~ of*** auf Vorschlag von (*od. gen.*); **2.** Wink *m*, Hinweis *m*; **3.** Spur *f*, I'dee *f*: ***not even a ~ of fatigue*** nicht die leiseste Spur von Müdigkeit; **4.** Vermutung *f*: ***a mere ~***; **5.** Erinnerung *f* (***of*** an *acc.*); **6.** Andeutung *f*, Anspielung *f* (***of*** auf *acc.*); **7.** Suggesti'on *f*, Beeinflussung *f*; **8.** Eingebung *f*, -flüsterung *f*; **sug'ges·tive** [-tɪv] *adj.* □ **1.** anregend, gehaltvoll; **2.** (***of***) andeutend (*acc.*), erinnernd (an *acc.*): ***be ~ of*** → ***suggest*** 3, 4; **3.** vielsagend; *b.s.* zweideutig, schlüpfrig; **4.** *psych.* sugge'stiv; **sug'ges·tive·ness** [-tɪvnɪs] *s.* **1.** *das* Anregende *od.* Vielsagende, Gedanken-, Beziehungsreichtum *m*; **2.** Schlüpfrigkeit *f*, Zweideutigkeit *f*.

su·i·cid·al [sjʊɪ'saɪdl] *adj.* □ selbstmörderisch (*a. fig.*), Selbstmord...; **su·i·cide** ['sjʊɪsaɪd] **I** *s.* **1.** Selbstmord *m* (*a. fig.*), Freitod *m*: ***commit ~*** Selbstmord begehen; **2.** Selbstmörder(in); **II** *adj.* **3.** Selbstmord...

su·int [swɪnt] *s.* Wollfett *n*.

suit [su:t] **I** *s.* **1.** Satz *m*, Garni'tur *f*: ***~ of armo(u)r*** Rüstung *f*; **2.** a) *a.* ***~ of clothes*** (Herren)Anzug *m*, b) ('Damen)Ko,stüm *n*: ***cut one's ~ according to one's cloth*** *fig.* sich nach der Decke strecken; **3.** *Kartenspiel*: Farbe *f*: ***long ~*** lange Hand; ***follow ~*** a) Farbe bekennen, b) *fig.* ‚nachziehen', dasselbe tun, j-s Beispiel folgen; **4.** ⚖ Rechtsstreit *m*, Pro'zeß *m*, Klage(sache) *f*; **5.** Werbung *f*, (Heirats)Antrag *m*; **6.** Anliegen *n*, Bitte *f*; **II** *v/t.* **7.** (***to***) anpassen (*dat. od.* an *acc.*), einrichten (nach): ***~ the action to the word*** das Wort in die Tat umsetzen; ***~ one's style to*** sich im Stil nach *dem Publikum* richten; ***a task ~ed to his powers*** e-e s-n Kräften angemessene Aufgabe; **8.** entsprechen (*dat.*): ***~ s.o.'s purpose***; **9.** passen zu; *j-m* stehen, *j-n* kleiden; **10.** passen für, sich eignen zu *od.* für; → ***suited*** 1; **11.** sich schicken *od.* ziemen für *j-n*; **12.** *j-m* bekommen, zusagen (*Klima*, *Speise etc.*); **13.** *j-m* gefallen, *j-n* zufriedenstellen: ***try to ~ everybody*** es allen Leuten recht machen wollen; ~ ***o.s.*** nach Belieben handeln; ~ ***yourself*** mach, was du willst; ***are you ~ed?*** haben Sie et. Passendes gefunden?; **14.** *j-m* recht sein *od.* passen; **III** *v/i.* **15.** passen, (an)genehm sein; **16.** (***with***, ***to***) passen (zu), über'einstimmen (mit); **suit·a·bil·i·ty** [ˌsuːtəˈbɪlətɪ] *s.* **1.** Eignung *f*; **2.** Angemessenheit *f*; **3.** Schicklichkeit *f*; **'suit·a·ble** [-təbl] *adj.* ☐ passend, geeignet; angemessen (***to***, ***for*** für, zu): ***be ~*** a) passen, sich eignen, b) sich schicken; **'suit·a·ble·ness** [-təblnɪs] → ***suitability***.

'suit·case *s.* Handkoffer *m*.

suite [swiːt] *s.* **1.** Gefolge *n*; **2.** Folge *f*, Reihe *f*, Serie *f*; **3.** *a.* ~ ***of rooms*** a) Suite *f*, Zimmerflucht *f*, b) Apparte'ment *n*; **4.** ('Möbel)Garniˌtur *f*, (Zimmer)Einrichtung *f*; **5.** Fortsetzung *f* (*Roman etc.*); **6.** ♪ Suite *f*.

suit·ed ['suːtɪd] *adj.* **1.** passend, geeignet (***to***, ***for*** für): ***he is not ~ for*** (*od.* ***to be***) ***a teacher*** er eignet sich nicht zum Lehrer; **2.** *in Zssgn*: gekleidet; **'suit·ing** [-ɪŋ] *s.* Anzugstoff *m*.

suit·or ['suːtə] *s.* **1.** Freier *m*; **2.** ⚖ Kläger *m*, (Pro'zeß)Parˌtei *f*; **3.** Bittsteller *m*.

sulfa drugs, **sul·fate** *etc.* → ***sulpha drugs***, ***sulphate*** *etc.*

sulk [sʌlk] **I** *v/i.* schmollen (***with*** mit), trotzen, schlechter Laune *od.* ‚eingeschnappt' sein; **II** *s. mst pl.* Schmollen *n*, (Anfall *m* von) Trotz *m*, schlechte Laune: ***be in the ~s*** → I; **'sulk·i·ness** [-kɪnɪs] *s.* Schmollen *n*, Trotzen *n*, schlechte Laune, mürrisches Wesen; **'sulk·y** [-kɪ] **I** *adj.* ☐ **1.** mürrisch, launisch; **2.** schmollend, trotzend; **3.** *Am.* für 'eine Per'son (bestimmt): ***a ~ set of China***; **4.** 🌾, ⚙ *Am. Pflug* mit Fahrersitz; **II** *s.* **5.** a) zweirädriger, einsitziger Einspänner, b) *sport* Sulky *n*, Traberwagen *m*.

sul·len ['sʌlən] *adj.* ☐ **1.** mürrisch, grämlich, verdrossen; **2.** düster (*Miene, Landschaft etc.*); **3.** 'widerspenstig, störrisch (*bsd. Tiere u. Dinge*); **4.** langsam, träge (*Schritt etc.*); **'sul·len·ness** [-nɪs] *s.* **1.** mürrisches Wesen, Verdrossenheit *f*; **2.** Düsterkeit *f*; **3.** 'Widerspenstigkeit *f*; **4.** Trägheit *f*.

sul·ly ['sʌlɪ] *v/t. mst fig.* besudeln, beflecken.

sul·pha drugs ['sʌlfə] *s. pl. pharm.* Sulfona'mide *pl*.

sul·phate ['sʌlfeɪt] ⚗ **I** *s.* schwefelsaures Salz, Sul'fat *n*: ~ ***of copper*** Kupfervitriol *n*, -sulfat; **II** *v/t.* sulfatieren; **'sul·phide** [-faɪd] *s.* ⚗ Sul'fid *n*; **'sul·phite** [-faɪt] *s.* ⚗ schwefeligsaures Salz, Sul'fit *n*.

sul·phur ['sʌlfə] *s.* **1.** ⚗ Schwefel *m*; **2.** *a.* ~ ***yellow*** Schwefelgelb *n* (*Farbe*); **3.** *zo. ein* Weißling *m* (*Falter*); **'sul·phu·rate** [-fjʊreɪt] → ***sulphurize***; **sul·phu·re·ous** [sʌl'fjʊərɪəs] *adj.* **1.** schwef(e)lig, schwefelhaltig, Schwefel…; **2.** schwefelfarben; **'sul·phu·ret** [-fjʊret] ⚗ **I** *s.* Sul'fid *n*; **II** *v/t.* schwefeln: ~***ted*** geschwefelt; ~***ted hydrogen*** Schwefelwasserstoff *m*; **sul·phu·ric** [sʌl'fjʊərɪk] *adj.* ⚗ Schwefel…; **'sul·phu·rize** [-jʊəraɪz] ⚗, ⚙ *v/t.* **1.** schwefeln; **2.** vulkanisieren; **'sul·phu·rous** [-fərəs] *adj.* **1.** ⚗ → ***sulphureous***; **2.** *fig.* hitzig, heftig.

sul·tan ['sʌltən] *s.* Sultan *m*; **sul·tan·a** [sʌl'tɑːnə] *s.* **1.** Sultanin *f*; **2.** [səl'tɑːnə] *a.* ~ ***raisin*** ⚘ Sulta'nine *f*; **'sul·tan·ate** [-tənɪt] *s.* Sulta'nat *n*.

sul·tri·ness ['sʌltrɪnɪs] *s.* Schwüle *f*; **sul·try** ['sʌltrɪ] *adj.* ☐ **1.** schwül (*a. fig. erotisch*); **2.** *fig.* heftig, heiß, hitzig (*Temperament etc.*).

sum [sʌm] **I** *s.* **1.** *allg.* Summe *f*: a) *a.* ~ ***total*** (Gesamt-, End)Betrag *m*, b) (Geld)Betrag *m*, c) *fig.* Ergebnis *n*, d) *fig.* Gesamtheit *f*: ***in ~*** insgesamt, *fig.* mit 'einem Wort; **2.** F a) Rechenaufgabe *f*, b) *pl.* Rechnen *n*: ***do ~s*** rechnen; ***he is good at ~s*** er kann gut rechnen; **3.** *fig.* Inbegriff *m*, Kern *m*, Sub'stanz *f*; **4.** Zs.-fassung *f*; **II** *v/t.* **5.** *a.* ~ ***up*** summieren, zs.-zählen; **6.** ~ ***up*** *Ergebnis* ausmachen; **7.** ~ ***up*** *fig.* (kurz) zs.-fassen, rekapitulieren; **8.** ~ ***up*** (kurz) ein-, abschätzen, (mit Blicken) messen; **III** *v/i.* **9.** ~ ***up*** (das Gesagte) zs.-fassen, resümieren.

sum·ma·ri·ness ['sʌmərɪnɪs] *s. das* Sum'marische, Kürze *f*; **'sum·ma·rize** [-raɪz] *v/t. u. v/i.* (kurz) zs.-fassen; **'sum·ma·ry** [-rɪ] **I** *s.* Zs.-fassung *f*, (gedrängte) 'Übersicht, Abriß *m*, (kurze) Inhaltsangabe; **II** *adj.* sum'marisch: a) knapp, gedrängt, b) ⚖ abgekürzt, Schnell…: ~ ***procedure***; ~ ***offence*** Übertretung *f*; ~ ***dismissal*** fristlose Entlassung; **sum·ma·tion** [sʌ'meɪʃn] *s.* **1.** a) Zs.-zählen *n*, b) Summierung *f*, c) (Gesamt)Summe *f*; **2.** ⚖ Resü'mee *n*.

sum·mer[1] ['sʌmə] **I** *s.* **1.** Sommer *m*: ***in*** (***the***) ~ im Sommer; **2.** Lenz *m* (*Lebensjahr*): ***a lady of 20 ~s***; **II** *v/t.* **3.** *Vieh etc.* über'sommern lassen; **III** *v/i.* **4.** den Sommer verbringen; **IV** *adj.* **5.** Sommer…

sum·mer[2] ['sʌmə] *s.* ⚠ **1.** Oberschwelle *f*; **2.** Trägerbalken *m*; **3.** Tragstein *m auf Pfeilern*.

'sum·mer|·house *s.* **1.** Gartenhaus *n*, (-)Laube *f*; **2.** Landhaus *n*; ~ **light·ning** *s.* Wetterleuchten *n*.

'sum·mer·like [-laɪk], **sum·mer·ly** ['sʌməlɪ] *adj.* sommerlich.

sum·mer| re·sort *s.* Sommerfrische *f*, -kurort *m*; ~ **school** *s. bsd. univ.* Ferien-, Sommerkurs *m*; ~ **term** *s. univ.* 'Sommerseˌmester *n*; **'~·time** *s.* Sommer *m*, Sommerzeit *f*; ~ **time** *s.* Sommerzeit *f* (*Uhrzeit*).

sum·mer·y ['sʌmərɪ] *adj.* sommerlich.

ˌsum·ming-'up [ˌsʌmɪŋ-] (kurze) Zs.-fassung, Resü'mee *n* (*a.* ⚖).

sum·mit ['sʌmɪt] *s.* **1.** Gipfel *m* (*a. fig. pol.*), Kuppe *f e-s Berges*: ~ ***conference*** *pol.* Gipfelkonferenz *f*; **2.** Scheitel *m e-r Kurve etc.*; Kappe *f*, Krone *f e-s Dammes etc.*; **3.** *fig.* Gipfel *m*, Höhepunkt *m*: ***at the ~ of power*** auf dem Gipfel der Macht; **4.** höchstes Ziel; **'sum·mit·ry** [-trɪ] *s. pol.* 'Gipfelpoliˌtik *f*.

sum·mon ['sʌmən] *v/t.* **1.** auffordern, -rufen (***to do*** *et.* zu tun); **2.** rufen, kommen lassen, (her)zitieren; **3.** ⚖ vorladen; **4.** *Konferenz etc.* zs.-rufen, einberufen; **5.** *oft* ~ ***up*** *Kräfte*, *Mut etc.* zs.-nehmen, zs.-raffen, aufbieten; **'sum·mon·er** [-nə] *s.* (*hist.* Gerichts)Bote *m*; **'sum·mons** [-nz] *s.* **1.** Ruf *m*, Berufung *f*; **2.** Aufforderung *f*, Aufruf *m*; **3.** ⚖ (Vor)Ladung *f*: ***take out a ~ against s.o.*** j-n (vor)laden lassen; **4.** Einberufung *f*.

sump [sʌmp] *s.* **1.** Sammelbehälter *m*, Senkgrube *f*; **2.** ⚙, *mot.* Ölwanne *f*; **3.** ⚒ (Schacht)Sumpf *m*.

sump·ter ['sʌmptə] **I** *s.* Saumtier *n*; **II** *adj.* Pack…: ~ ***horse***; ~ ***saddle***.

sump·tion ['sʌmpʃn] *s. phls.* **1.** Prä'misse *f*; **2.** Obersatz *m*.

sump·tu·ar·y ['sʌmptjʊərɪ] *adj.* Aufwands…, Luxus…; **'sump·tu·ous** [-əs] *adj.* ☐ **1.** kostspielig; **2.** kostbar, prächtig, herrlich; **3.** üppig; **'sump·tu·ous·ness** [-əsnɪs] *s.* **1.** Kostspieligkeit *f*; **2.** Pracht *f*; Aufwand *m*, Luxus *m*.

sun [sʌn] **I** *s.* **1.** Sonne *f*: ***a place in the ~*** *fig.* ein Platz an der Sonne; ***under the ~*** *fig.* unter der Sonne, auf Erden; ***with the ~*** bei Tagesanbruch; ***his ~ is set*** *fig.* sein Stern ist erloschen; **2.** Sonne *f*, Sonnenwärme *f*, -licht *n*, -schein *m*: ***have the ~ in one's eyes*** die Sonne genau im Gesicht haben; **3.** *poet.* a) Jahr *n*, b) Tag *m*; **II** *v/t. u. v/i.* **4.** (sich) sonnen; **ˌ~-and-'plan·et** (**gear**) *s.* ⚙ Pla'netengetriebe *n*; **'~·baked** *adj.* von der Sonne ausgedörrt *od.* getrocknet; ~ **bath** *s.* Sonnenbad *n*; **'~·bathe** *v/i.* Sonnenbäder *od.* ein Sonnenbad nehmen; **'~·beam** *s.* Sonnenstrahl *m*; ~ **blind** *s. Brit.* Mar'kise *f*; **'~·burn** *s.* **1.** Sonnenbrand *m*; **2.** Sonnenbräune *f*; **'~·burned**, **'~·burnt** *adj.* **1.** sonn(en)verbrannt: ***be ~*** *a.* e-n Sonnenbrand haben; **2.** sonnengebräunt; **'~·burst** *s.* **1.** plötzlicher 'Durchbruch der Sonne; **2.** Sonnenbanner *n* (*Japans*).

sun·dae ['sʌndeɪ] *s.* Eisbecher *m*.

Sun·day ['sʌndɪ] **I** *s.* **1.** Sonntag *m*: ***on ~*** (am) Sonntag; ***on ~(s)*** sonntags; ~ ***evening***, ~ ***night*** Sonntagabend *m*; **II** *adj.* **2.** sonntäglich, Sonntags…: ~ ***best*** F Sonntagsstaat *m*, -kleider *pl.*; ~ ***school*** *eccl.* Sonntagsschule *f*; **3.** F Sonntags…: ~ ***driver***; ~ ***painter***.

sun·der ['sʌndə] *poet.* **I** *v/t.* **1.** trennen, sondern (***from*** von); **2.** *fig.* entzweien; **II** *v/i.* **3.** sich trennen; **III** *s.* **4.** ***in ~*** entzwei, auseinander.

'sun|·di·al *s.* Sonnenuhr *f*; **'~·down** → ***sunset***; **'~ˌdown·er** *s.* F **1.** *Austral.* Landstreicher *m*; **2.** Dämmerschoppen *m*.

sun·dries ['sʌndrɪz] *s. pl.* Di'verses *n*, Verschiedenes *n*, allerlei Dinge; di'verse Unkosten; **sun·dry** ['sʌndrɪ] *adj.* verschiedene, di'verse, allerlei, -hand: ***all and ~*** all u. jeder, alle miteinander.

'sun|·fast *adj. Am.* lichtecht; **'~ˌflow·er** *s.* Sonnenblume *f*.

sung [sʌŋ] *pret. u. p.p. von* ***sing***.

'sun|ˌglass·es *s. pl. a.* ***pair of ~*** Sonnenbrille *f*; **'~·glow** *s.* **1.** Morgen- *od.* Abendröte *f*; **2.** Sonnenhof *m*; ~ **god** *s.* Sonnengott *m*; ~ **hel·met** *s.* Tropenhelm *m*.

sunk [sʌŋk] **I** *pret. u. p.p. von* ***sink***; **II** *adj.* **1.** vertieft; **2.** *bsd.* ⚙ eingelassen, versenkt: ~ ***screw***; **'sunk·en** [-kn] **I** *obs. p.p. von* ***sink***; **II** *adj.* **1.** versunken; **2.** eingesunken: ~ ***rock*** blinde Klippe; **3.** tiefliegend, vertieft (angelegt); **4.** ⚙ → ***sunk*** 2; **5.** *fig.* hohl (*Augen, Wangen*), eingefallen (*Gesicht*).

sun| lamp *s.* **1.** ⚡ Ultravio'lettlampe *f*; **2.** *Film*: Jupiterlampe *f*; **'~·light** *s.* Sonnenschein *m*, -licht *n*; **'~·lit** *adj.* sonnenbeschienen.

sun·ni·ness ['sʌnɪnɪs] *fig. das* Sonnige; **sun·ny** ['sʌnɪ] *adj.* □ sonnig (*a. fig. Gemüt, Lächeln etc.*), Sonnen...: **~ side** Sonnenseite *f* (*a. fig. des Lebens*), *fig. a. die* heitere Seite; **be on the ~ side of forty** noch nicht 40 (Jahre alt) sein.

sun| par·lor, ~ porch *s. Am.* 'Glasveˌranda *f*; **~ pow·er** *s. phys.* 'Sonnenenerˌgie *f*; **'~·proof** *adj.* **1.** für Sonnenstrahlen 'unˌdurchlässig; **2.** lichtfest; **'~·rise** *s.* (**at ~** bei) Sonnenaufgang *m*; **'~·roof** *s.* **1.** 'Dachterˌrasse *f*; **2.** *mot.* Schiebedach *n*; **'~·set** *s.* (**at ~** bei) 'Sonnenˌuntergang *m*: **~ of life** *fig.* Lebensabend *m*; **'~·shade** *s.* **1.** Sonnenschirm *m*; **2.** Mar'kise *f*; **3.** *phot.* Gegenlichtblende *f*; **4.** *pl.* Sonnenbrille *f*; **'~·shine** *s.* Sonnenschein *m* (*a. fig.*); sonniges Wetter: **~ roof** *mot.* Schiebedach *n*; **~ show·er** *s.* F leichter Schauer bei Sonnenschein; **~ spot** *s.* **1.** *ast.* Sonnenfleck *m*; **2.** Sommersprosse *f*; **3.** *Brit.* F sonnige Gegend; **'~·stroke** *s.* ⚕ Sonnenstich *m*; **'~-struck** *adj.*: **be ~** e-n Sonnenstich haben; **'~·tan** *s.* (Sonnen-) Bräune *f*: **~ lotion** Sonnenöl *n*; **'~·trap** *s.* sonniges Plätzchen; **'~·up** *s. dial.* Sonnenaufgang *m*; **~ vi·sor** *s. mot.* Sonnenblende *f*; **~ wor·ship·(p)er** *s.* Sonnenanbeter *m*.

sup¹ [sʌp] *v/i. obs.* zu Abend essen (**off** *od.* **on s.th.** et).

sup² [sʌp] **I** *v/t. a.* **~ off, ~ out** löffeln, schlürfen: **~ sorrow** *fig.* leiden; **II** *v/i.* nippen, löffeln; **III** *s.* Mundvoll *m*, kleiner Schluck: **a bite and a ~** et. zu essen u. zu trinken; **neither bit** (*od.* **bite**) **nor ~** nichts zu nagen u. zu beißen.

super- [su:pə] *in Zssgn* a) 'übermäßig, Über..., über..., b) oberhalb (von *od. gen.*) *od.* über (*dat.*) befindlich, c) Super... (*bsd. in wissenschaftlichen Ausdrücken*), d) 'übergeordnet, Ober...

su·per ['su:pə] **I** *s.* **1.** F *für* a) **superintendent**, b) **supernumerary**, c) **superhet**(**erodyne**); **2.** ✝ F a) Spitzenklasse *f*, b) Quali'tätsware *f*; **II** *adj.* **3.** *a. iro.* Super...; **4.** F ‚super', ‚toll'; **III** *v/i. thea.* als Sta'tist(in) mitspielen.

su·per·a·ble ['su:pərəbl] *adj.* über'windbar, besiegbar.

ˌsu·per|·a'bound [-ərə-] *v/i.* **1.** im 'Überfluß vor'handen sein; **2.** Überfluß *od.* e-e 'Überfülle haben (**in, with** an *dat.*); **ˌ~·a'bun·dance** [-ərə-] *s.* 'Überfülle *f*, -fluß *m* (**of** an *dat.*); **ˌ~·a'bun·dant** [-ərə-] *adj.* □ **1.** 'überreichlich; **2.** 'überschwenglich; **ˌ~'add** [-ər'æd] *v/t.* noch hin'zufügen (**to** zu): **be ~ed** (**to**) noch dazukommen (zu *et.*).

su·per|·an·nu·ate [ˌsu:pə'rænjʊeɪt] *v/t.* **1.** pensionieren, in den Ruhestand versetzen; **2.** (als zu alt *od.* als veraltet) ausscheiden *od.* zurückweisen; **ˌ~'an·nu·at·ed** [-tɪd] *adj.* **1.** a) pensioniert, b) über'altert (*Person*); **2.** veraltet, über'holt; **3.** ausgedient (*Sache*); **~·an·nu·a·tion** ['su:pəˌrænjʊ'eɪʃn] *s.* **1.** Pensionierung *f*; **2.** Ruhestand *m*; **3.** (Alters)Rente *f*, Ruhegeld *n*, Pensi'on *f*: **~ fund** Pensionskasse *f*.

su·perb [sju:'pɜ:b] *adj.* □ **1.** herrlich, prächtig; **2.** vor'züglich.

ˌsu·per|'cal·en·der ⚙ **I** *s.* 'Hochkaˌlander *m*; **II** *v/t. Papier* hochsatinieren; **'~ˌcar·go** *s.* Frachtaufseher *m*, Super'kargo *m*; **'~·charge** *v/t.* **1.** über'laden; **2.** ⚙, *mot.* vor-, 'überverdichten: **~d engine** Lader-, Kompressormotor *m*; **'~ˌcharg·er** *s.* ⚙ Kom'pressor *m*, Gebläse *n*.

su·per·cil·i·ous [ˌsu:pə'sɪlɪəs] *adj.* □ hochmütig, her'ablassend; **ˌsu·per'cil·i·ous·ness** [-nɪs] *s.* Hochmut *m*, Hochnäsigkeit *f*.

ˌsu·per|·con'duc·tive *adj. phys.* supraleitend; **ˌ~·con'duc·tor** *s. phys.* Supraleiter *m*; **ˌ~-'du·ty** *adj.* ⚙ Höchstleistungs...; **ˌ~·el·e'va·tion** [-əre-] *s.* ⚙ Über'höhung *f*; **ˌ~'em·i·nence** [-ər'e-] *s.* **1.** Vorrang(stellung *f*) *m*; **2.** über'ragende Bedeutung *od.* Quali'tät, Vortrefflichkeit *f*.

su·per·er·o·ga·tion ['su:pərˌerə'geɪʃn] *s.* Mehrleistung *f*: **works of ~** *eccl.* überschüssige (gute) Werke; **work of ~** *fig.* Arbeit über die Pflicht hinaus; **su·per·e·rog·a·to·ry** [ˌsu:pəre'rɒgətərɪ] *adj.* **1.** über das Pflichtmaß hin'ausgehend, 'übergebührlich; **2.** 'überflüssig.

su·per·fi·ci·al [ˌsu:pə'fɪʃl] *adj.* □ **1.** oberflächlich, Oberflächen...; **2.** Flächen..., Quadrat...: **~ measurement** Flächenmaß *n*; **3.** äußerlich, äußer: **~ characteristics**; **4.** *fig.* oberflächlich: a) flüchtig, b) *contp.* seicht; **su·per·fi·ci·al·i·ty** ['su:pəˌfɪʃɪ'ælətɪ] *s.* **1.** Oberflächenlage *f*; **2.** *fig.* Oberflächlichkeit *f*; **su·per·fi·ci·es** [ˌsu:pə'fɪʃi:z] *s.* **1.** (Ober)Fläche *f*; **2.** *fig.* Oberfläche *f*, äußerer Anschein.

'su·per|-film *s.* Monumen'talfilm *m*; **ˌ~'fine** *adj.* **1.** *bsd.* ✝ extra-, hochfein; **2.** über'feinert.

su·per·flu·i·ty [ˌsu:pə'flʊətɪ] *s.* **1.** 'Überfluß *m*, Zu'viel *n* (**of** an *dat.*); **2.** *mst pl.* Entbehrlichkeit *f*, 'Überflüssigkeit *f*; **su·per·flu·ous** [su:'pɜ:flʊəs] *adj.* □ 'überflüssig.

ˌsu·per|'heat *v/t.* ⚙ über'hitzen; **'~ˌhe·ro** *s.* Superheld *m*; **'~·het** [-het], **ˌ~'het·er·o·dyne** [-'hetərədaɪn] **I** *adj.* Überlagerungs..., Superhet...; **II** *s.* Über'lagerungsempfänger *m*, Super(het) *m*; **'~·high fre·quen·cy** *s.* ⚡ 'Höchstfreˌquenz(bereich *m*) *f*; **ˌ~'high·way** *s. Am.* Autobahn *f*; **ˌ~'hu·man** *adj.* 'übermenschlich: **~ beings**; **~ efforts**; **ˌ~·im'pose** [-ərɪ-] *v/t.* **1.** dar'auf-, dar'übersetzen *od.* -legen; **2.** setzen, legen, lagern (**on** auf, über *acc.*): **one ~d on the other** übereinandergelagert; **3.** (**on**) hin'zufügen (zu), folgen lassen (*dat.*); **4.** ⚡, *phys.* über'lagern; **5.** *Film etc.*: 'durch-, einblenden, einkopieren.

su·per·in·tend [ˌsu:pərɪn'tend] *v/t.* die (Ober)Aufsicht haben über (*acc.*), beaufsichtigen, über'wachen, leiten; **ˌsu·per·in'tend·ence** [-dəns] *s.* (Ober-) Aufsicht *f* (**over** über *acc.*), Leitung *f* (**of** *gen.*); **ˌsu·per·in'ten·dent** [-dənt] **I** *s.* **1.** Leiter *m*, Vorsteher *m*, Di'rektor *m*: **~ of public works**; **2.** Oberaufseher *m*, Aufsichtsbeamte(r) *m*, In'spektor *m*: **~ of schools**; **3.** a) *Brit. etwa* 'Hauptkommisˌsar *m*, b) *Am.* Poli'zeichef *m*; **4.** *eccl.* Superinten'dent *m*; **5.** Hausverwalter *m*; **II** *adj.* **6.** aufsichtführend, leitend, Aufsichts...

su·pe·ri·or [su:'pɪərɪə] **I** *adj.* □ **1.** höherliegend, ober: **~ planets** *ast.* äußere Planeten; **~ wings** *zo.* Flügeldecken; **2.** höher(stehend), Ober..., vorgesetzt: **~ court** ⚖ höhere Instanz; **~ officer** vorgesetzter *od.* höherer Beamter *od.* Offizier, Vorgesetzte(r) *m*; **3.** über'legen, -'ragend: **~ man**; **~ skill**; → **style** 1b; **4.** besser (**to** als), her'vorragend, erlesen: **~ quality**; **5.** (**to**) größer, stärker (als), über'legen (*dat.*): **~ forces** ⚔ Übermacht *f*; **~ in number** zahlenmäßig überlegen, in der Überzahl; **6.** *fig.* erhaben (**to** über *acc.*): **~ to prejudice**; **rise ~ to** sich über *et.* erhaben zeigen; **7.** *fig.* über'legen, -'heblich: **~ smile**; **8.** *iro.* vornehm: **~ persons** bessere *od.* feine Leute; **9.** *typ.* hochgestellt; **II** *s.* **10. be s.o.'s ~** j-m überlegen sein (**in** im *Denken etc.*, an *Mut etc.*); **11.** Vorgesetzte(r *m*) *f*; **12.** *eccl.* a) Su'perior *m*, b) *mst* **lady ~** Oberin *f*; **su·pe·ri·or·i·ty** [su:ˌpɪərɪ'ɒrətɪ] *s.* **1.** Erhabenheit *f* (**to, over** über *acc.*); **2.** Über'legenheit *f*, 'Übermacht *f* (**to, over** über *acc.*, **in** in *od.* an *dat.*); **3.** Vorrecht *n*, -rang *m*, -zug *m*; **4.** Über'heblichkeit *f*: **~ complex** *psych.* Superioritätskomplex *m*.

su·per·la·tive [su:'pɜ:lətɪv] **I** *adj.* □ **1.** höchst; **2.** über'ragend, 'unüberˌtrefflich; **3.** *ling.* superlativisch, Superlativ...: **~ degree** → 5; **II** *s.* **4.** höchster Grad, Gipfel *m*; *contp.* Ausbund *m* (**of** von *od.* an *dat.*); **5.** *ling.* Superlativ *m*: **talk in ~s** *fig.* in Superlativen reden.

'su·per|·man [-mæn] *s.* [*irr.*] **1.** 'Übermensch *m*; **2.** a) ♀ *ein Comics-Held*, b) *iro.* Supermann *m*; **'~ˌmar·ket** *s.* Supermarkt *m*; **ˌ~'nat·u·ral** **I** *adj.* □ 'übernaˌtürlich; **II** *s. das* 'Übernaˌtürliche; **ˌ~'nor·mal** *adj.* □ **1.** 'überˌdurchschnittlich; **2.** außer-, ungewöhnlich; **ˌ~'nu·mer·ar·y** [-'nju:mərərɪ] **I** *adj.* **1.** 'überzählig, außerplanmäßig, extra; **2.** 'überflüssig; **II** *s.* **3.** 'überzählige Per'son *od.* Sache; **4.** außerplanmäßiger Beamter *od.* Offi'zier; **5.** Hilfskraft *f*, -arbeiter(in); **6.** *thea. etc.* Sta'tist(in); **ˌ~'ox·ide** [-ər'ɒ-] *s.* ⚗ 'Super-, 'Peroˌxyd *n*; **ˌ~'phos·phate** *s.* ⚗ 'Superphosˌphat *n*.

su·per·pose [ˌsu:pə'pəʊz] *v/t.* **1.** (auf)legen, lagern, schichten (**on** über, auf *acc.*); **2.** überein'anderlegen, -lagern (*a.* ⚡); **3.** ⚡ über'lagern; **ˌsu·per·po'si·tion** *s.* **1.** Aufschichtung *f*, -lagerung *f*; **2.** Überein'andersetzen *n*; **3.** *geol.* Schichtung *f*; **4.** ⚘, ⚡ Superpositi'on *f*; **5.** ⚡ Über'lagerung.

'su·per|ˌpow·er **I** *s. pol.* Supermacht *f*; **II** *adj.* ⚡ Groß...: **~ station** Großkraftwerk *n*; **'~·race** *s.* Herrenvolk *n*.

su·per·sede [ˌsu:pə'si:d] *v/t.* **1.** *j-n od. et.* ersetzen (**by** durch); **2.** *et.* abschaffen, beseitigen, *Gesetz etc.* aufheben; **3.** *j-n* absetzen, s-s Amtes entheben; **4.** *j-n in der Beförderung etc.* über'gehen; **5.** *et.* verdrängen, ersetzen, 'überflüssig machen; **6.** an die Stelle treten von (*od. gen.*), *j-n od. et.* ablösen: **be ~d by** abgelöst werden von; **ˌsu·per'se·de·as** [-dıæs] *s.* **1.** ⚖ Sistierungsbefehl *m*, 'Widerruf *m e-r Anordnung*; **2.** *fig.* aufschiebende Wirkung, Hemmnis *n*; **ˌsu·per'sed·ence** [ˌsu:pə'si:dəns] → **supersession**.

ˌsu·per'sen·si·tive *adj.* 'überempfindlich.

ˌsu·per'ses·sion *s.* **1.** Ersetzung *f* (**by** durch); **2.** Abschaffung *f*, Aufhebung *f*;

3. Absetzung *f*; **4.** Verdrängung *f*.

ˌsu·per|ˈson·ic I *adj.* **1.** *phys.* Ultraschall…; **2.** ✈ Überschall…: ~ ***boom***, ~ ***bang*** → ***sonic bang***; ***at*** ~ ***speed*** mit Überschallgeschwindigkeit; **II** *s.* **3.** ✈, *phys.* ˈÜberschallflug(zeug *n*) *m*; ˌ~-ˈ**son·ics** *pl. phys.* a) Ultraschallwellen *pl.*, b) *mst sg. konstr.* Fachgebiet *n* des Ultraschalls; ˈ~·**star** *s.* Superstar *m*; ˈ~·**state** *s. pol.* Supermacht *f*.

su·per·sti·tion [ˌsuːpəˈstɪʃn] *s.* Aberglaube(n) *m*; ˌ**su·perˈsti·tious** [-ʃəs] *adj.* □ abergläubisch; ˌ**su·perˈsti·tious·ness** [-ʃəsnɪs] *s.* *das* Abergläubische, Aberglaube(n) *m*.

ˌ**su·per|ˈstra·tum** *s.* [*irr.*] **1.** *geol.* obere Schicht; **2.** *ling.* Superˈstrat *n*; ˈ~ˌ**struc·ture** *s.* **1.** Ober-, Aufbau *m*: ~ ***work*** Hochbau *m*; **2.** ⚓ (Decks)Aufbauten *pl.*; **3.** *fig.* Oberbau *m*; ˈ~·**tax** *s.* **1.** → ***surtax*** I; **2.** *Brit.* Einkommensteuerzuschlag *m*.

su·per·vene [ˌsuːpəˈviːn] *v/i.* **1.** (noch) hinˈzukommen ([***up***]***on*** zu); **2.** (unvermutet) eintreten, daˈzwischenkommen; **3.** (unmittelbar) folgen, sich ergeben; ˌ**su·perˈven·tion** [-ˈvenʃn] *s.* **1.** Hinˈzukommen *n* (***on*** zu); **2.** Daˈzwischenkommen *n*.

su·per·vise [ˈsuːpəvaɪz] *v/t.* beaufsichtigen, überˈwachen, die Aufsicht haben *od.* führen über (*acc.*), kontrollieren; ˌ**su·perˈvi·sion** [-ˈvɪʒn] *s.* **1.** Beaufsichtigung *f*; **2.** (Ober)Aufsicht *f*, Leitung *f*, Konˈtrolle *f* (***of*** über *acc.*): ***police*** ~ Polizeiaufsicht; **3.** *ped.* ˈSchulinspektiˈon *f*; ˈ**su·per·vi·sor** [-zə] *s.* **1.** Aufseher *m*, Aufsichtführende(r) *m*, Inˈspektor *m*, Kontrolˈleur *m*; **2.** *Am.* (leitender) Beamter e-s Stadt- *od.* Kreisverwaltungsvorstandes; **3.** *univ.* Doktorvater *m*; ˈ**su·per·vi·so·ry** [-zərɪ] *adj.* Aufsichts…: ***in a*** ~ ***capacity*** aufsichtführend.

su·pine¹ [ˈsjuːpaɪn] *s. ling.* Suˈpinum *n*.

su·pine² [sjuːˈpaɪn] *adj.* □ **1.** auf dem Rücken liegend, aus-, hingestreckt: ~ ***position*** Rückenlage *f*; **2.** *poet.* zuˈrückgelehnt; **3.** *fig.* (nach)lässig, untätig, träge.

sup·per [ˈsʌpə] *s.* **1.** Abendessen *n*: ***have*** ~ zu Abend essen; ~ ***club*** *Am.* exklusiver Nachtklub; **2.** ***the*** ♀ *eccl.* a) *a.* ***the Last*** ♀ das letzte Abendmahl, b) *a.* ***the Lord's*** ♀ das heilige Abendmahl, *R.C.* die heilige Kommunion.

sup·plant [səˈplɑːnt] *v/t. j-n od. et.* verdrängen, *Rivalen etc.* ausstechen.

sup·ple [ˈsʌpl] **I** *adj.* □ **1.** geschmeidig: a) biegsam, b) *fig.* beweglich (*Geist etc.*); **2.** unterˈwürfig; **II** *v/t.* **3.** geschmeidig machen.

sup·ple·ment I *s.* [ˈsʌplɪmənt] **1.** (***to***) Ergänzung *f* (*gen. od.* zu), Zusatz *m* (zu); **2.** Nachtrag *m*, Anhang *m* (*zu e-m Buch*), Ergänzungsband *m*; **3.** (*Zeitungs- etc.*)Beilage *f*; **4.** ⩘ Ergänzung (*auf 180 Grad*); **II** *v/t.* [ˈsʌplɪment] **5.** ergänzen; **sup·ple·ment·al** [ˌsʌplɪˈmentl] *adj.* □, **sup·ple·men·ta·ry** [ˌsʌplɪˈmentərɪ] *adj.* □ **1.** ergänzend, Ergänzungs…, Zusatz…, Nach(trags)…: ***be*** ~ ***to*** *et.* ergänzen; ~ ***agreement*** *pol.* Zusatzabkommen *n*; ~ ***budget***, ~ ***estimates*** Nachtragshaushalt *m*, -etat *m*; ~ ***order*** Nachbestellung *f*; ~ ***question*** Zusatzfrage *f*; ~ ***proceedings*** ⚖ (Zwangs)Vollstreckungsverfahren *n*; ***take a*** ~ ***ticket*** (e-e Fahrkarte) nachlösen; **2.** ⩘ supplemenˈtär; **3.** Hilfs…, Ersatz…, Zusatz…; **sup·ple·men·ta·tion** [ˌsʌplɪmenˈteɪʃn] *s.* Ergänzung *f*: a) Nachtragen *n*, b) Nachtrag *m*, Zusatz *m*.

sup·ple·ness [ˈsʌplnɪs] *s.* Geschmeidigkeit *f* (*a. fig.*).

sup·pli·ant [ˈsʌplɪənt] **I** *s.* (demütiger) Bittsteller; **II** *adj.* □ flehend, demütig (bittend).

sup·pli·cant [ˈsʌplɪkənt] → ***suppliant***; **sup·pli·cate** [ˈsʌplɪkeɪt] **I** *v/i.* **1.** demütig *od.* dringlich bitten, flehen (***for*** um); **II** *v/t.* **2.** anflehen, demütig bitten (***s.o. for s.th.*** j-n um et.); **3.** erbitten, erflehen, bitten um; **sup·pli·ca·tion** [ˌsʌplɪˈkeɪʃn] *s.* **1.** demütige Bitte (***for*** um), Flehen *n*; **2.** (Bitt)Gebet *n*; **3.** Bittschrift *f*, Gesuch *n*; ˈ**sup·pli·ca·to·ry** [-ətərɪ] *adj.* flehend, Bitt…

sup·pli·er [səˈplaɪə] *s.* Liefeˈrant(in), *a. pl.* Lieferfirma *f*.

sup·ply¹ [səˈplaɪ] **I** *v/t.* **1.** *Ware*, ⚡ *Strom etc.*, *a. fig. Beweis etc.* liefern; beschaffen, bereitstellen, zuführen; **2.** *j-n* beliefern, versorgen, -sehen, ausstatten; ⚙, ⚡ speisen (***with*** mit); **3.** *Fehlendes* ergänzen; *Verlust* ausgleichen, ersetzen; *Defizit* decken; **4.** *Bedürfnis* befriedigen; *Nachfrage* decken: ~ ***a want*** e-m Mangel abhelfen; **5.** *e-e Stelle* ausfüllen, einnehmen; *Amt* vorˈübergehend versehen: ~ ***the place of*** *j-n* vertreten; **II** *s.* **6.** Lieferung *f* (***to*** an *acc.*); Beschaffung *f*, Bereitstellung *f*; An-, Zufuhr *f*; **7.** Belieferung *f*, Versorgung *f* (***of*** mit): ~ ***of power*** Energie-, Stromversorgung; **8.** ⚙, ⚡ (Netz)Anschluß *m*; **9.** Ergänzung *f*; Beitrag *m*, Zuschuß *m*; **10.** ✝ Angebot *n*: ~ ***and demand*** Angebot und Nachfrage; ***be in short*** ~ knapp sein; **11.** *pl.* ✝ Arˈtikel *pl.*, Bedarf *m*: ***office supplies*** Bürobedarf; **12.** *mst pl.* Vorrat *m*, Lager *n*, Bestand *m*; **13.** *mst pl.* ⚔ Nachschub *m*, Verˈsorgung(smateriˌal *n*) *f*, Proviˈant *m*; **14.** *mst pl. parl.* bewilligter Eˈtat, (ˈAusgabe)Buˌdget *n*: ***Committee of*** ♀ Haushaltsausschuß *m*; **15.** (Amts-, Stell)Vertretung *f*: ***on*** ~ in Vertretung, als Ersatz; **16.** (Stell)Vertreter *m* (*Lehrer etc.*); **III** *adj.* **17.** Versorgungs…, Liefer(ungs)…: ~ ***house*** Lieferfirma *f*; ~-***side economics*** *pl.* angebotsorientierte Wirtschaftspolitik *sg.*; **18.** ⚔ Versorgungs…(*-bombe, -gebiet, -offizier, -schiff*), Nachschub…: ~ ***base*** Versorgungs-, Nachschubbasis *f*; ~ ***depot*** Nachschublager *n*; ~ ***lines*** Nachschubverbindungen; ~ ***sergeant*** Kammerunteroffizier *m*; **19.** ⚙, ⚡ Speise… (*-leitung, -stromkreis etc.*): ~ ***pipe*** Zuleitung(srohr *n*) *f*; **20.** Hilfs…, Ersatz…: ~ ***teacher*** Hilfslehrer *m*.

sup·ply² [ˈsʌplɪ] *adv.* → ***supple***.

sup·port [səˈpɔːt] **I** *v/t.* **1.** *Gewicht, Wand etc.* tragen, (ab)stützen, (aus)halten; **2.** ertragen, (er)dulden, aushalten; **3.** *j-n* unterˈstützen, stärken, *j-m* beistehen, *j-m* Rückendeckung geben; **4.** *sich, e-e Familie etc.* er-, unterˈhalten, sorgen für, ernähren (***on*** von): ~ ***o.s.*** für s-n Lebensunterhalt sorgen; **5.** *et.* finanzieren; **6.** *Debatte etc.* in Gang halten; **7.** eintreten für, unterˈstützen, fördern, befürworten; **8.** *Theorie etc.* vertreten; **9.** *Anklage, Anspruch etc.* beweisen, erhärten, begründen, rechtfertigen; **10.** ✝ *Währung* decken; **11.** a) *thea. Rolle* spielen, b) als Nebendarsteller auftreten mit *e-m Star etc.*; **II** *s.* **12.** *allg.* Stütze *f*: ***walk without*** ~; **13.** *bsd.* ⚙ Stütze *f*, Träger *m*, Ständer *m*, Strebe *f*, Absteifung *f*, Bettung *f*; Staˈtiv *n*; △ ˈDurchzug *m*; ⚔ (Gewehr-)Auflage *f*; **14.** *fig.* (*a.* ⚔ taktische) Unterˈstützung, Beistand *m*: ~ ***buying*** ✝ Stützungskäufe *pl.*; ***give*** ~ ***to*** → 3; ***in*** ~ ***of s.o.*** zur Unterstützung von j-m; **15.** (ˈLebens)ˌUnterhalt *m*; **16.** Unterˈhaltung *f e-r Einrichtung*; **17.** *fig.* Stütze *f*, (Rück)Halt *m*; **18.** Beweis *m*, Erhärtung *f*: ***in*** ~ ***of*** zur Bestätigung (*gen.*); **19.** ⚔ Reˈserve *f*, Verstärkung *f*; **20.** *thea.* a) Partner(in) *e-s Stars*, b) Unterˈstützung *f e-s Stars durch das Ensemble*, c) Enˈsemble *n*; **supˈport·a·ble** [-təbl] *adj.* □ **1.** haltbar, vertretbar (*Ansicht etc.*); **2.** erträglich, zu ertragen(d); **supˈport·er** [-tə] *s.* **1.** ⚙, △ Stütze *f*, Träger *m*; **2.** Stütze *f*, Beistand *m*, Helfer(in), Unterˈstützer(in); **3.** Erhalter(in); **4.** Anhänger(in), Verfechter (-in), Vertreter(in); **5.** ⚕ Tragbinde *f*, Stütze *f*; **supˈport·ing** [-tɪŋ] *adj.* **1.** tragend, stützend, Stütz…, Trag…, *fig. a.* Unterstützungs…: ~ ***actor*** *thea.* Nebendarsteller *m*; ~ ***cast*** *thea. etc.* Ensemble *n*; ~ ***bout*** *Boxen*: Rahmenkampf *m*; ~ ***fire*** ⚔ Unterstützungsfeuer *n*; ~ ***measures*** flankierende Maßnahmen; ~ ***part*** Nebenrolle *f*; ~ ***program(me)*** *Film*: Beiprogramm *n*; ~ ***purchases*** ✝ Stützungskäufe; ~ ***surfaces*** ✈ Tragwerk *n*; **2.** erhärtend: ~ ***document*** Beleg *m*, Unterlage *f*; ~ ***evidence*** ⚖ zusätzliche Beweise *pl.*

sup·pose [səˈpəʊz] **I** *v/t.* **1.** (als möglich *od.* gegeben) annehmen, sich vorstellen: ~ (*od.* ***supposing*** *od.* ***let us*** ~) angenommen, gesetzt den Fall; ***it is to be*** ~***d that*** es ist anzunehmen, daß; **2.** *imp.* (*e-n Vorschlag einleitend*) wie wäre es, wenn *wir e-n Spaziergang machten!*: ~ ***we went for a walk!***; ~ ***you meet me at 10 o'clock*** ich schlage vor, du triffst mich um 10 Uhr; **3.** vermuten, glauben, meinen: ***I don't*** ~ ***we shall be back*** ich glaube nicht, daß wir zurück sein werden; ***they are British, I*** ~ es sind wohl *od.* vermutlich Engländer; ***I*** ~ ***so*** ich nehme an, wahrscheinlich, vermutlich; **4.** (*mit acc. u. inf.*) halten für: ***I*** ~ ***him to be a painter***; ***he is*** ~***d to be rich*** er soll reich sein; **5.** (mit Notwendigkeit) vorˈaussetzen: ***creation*** ~***s a creator***; **6.** (*pass. mit inf.*) sollen: ***isn't he*** ~***d to be at home?*** sollte er nicht eigentlich zu Hause sein?; ***he is*** ~***d to do*** man erwartet *od.* verlangt von ihm, daß er *et.* tut; ***what is that*** ~***d to be*** (*od.* ***mean***) was soll das sein (*od.* heißen)?; **II** *v/i.* **7.** denken, glauben, vermuten; **supˈposed** [-zd] *adj.* □ **1.** angenommen: ***a*** ~ ***case***; **2.** vermutlich; **3.** vermeintlich, angeblich.

sup·po·si·tion [ˌsʌpəˈzɪʃn] *s.* **1.** Vorˈaussetzung *f*, Annahme *f*: ***on the*** ~ ***that*** unter der Voraussetzung, daß; **2.** Vermutung *f*, Mutmaßung *f*, Annahme *f*; ˌ**sup·poˈsi·tion·al** [-ʃənl] *adj.* □ angenommen, hypoˈthetisch; **sup·pos·i-**

ti·tious [sə͵pɒzɪˈtɪʃəs] *adj.* □ **1.** unecht, gefälscht; **2.** ˈuntergeschoben (*Kind, Absicht etc.*), erdichtet; **3.** → ***suppositional.***

sup·pos·i·to·ry [səˈpɒzɪtərɪ] *s.* ⚕ Zäpfchen *n*, Suppoˈsitorium *n*.

sup·press [səˈpres] *v/t.* **1.** *Aufstand etc., a. Gefühl, Lachen etc., a.* ϟ unterˈdrükken; **2.** *et.* abstellen, abschaffen; **3.** *Buch* verbieten *od.* unterˈdrücken; **4.** *Textstelle* streichen; **5.** *Skandal, Wahrheit etc.* verheimlichen, vertuschen, unterˈschlagen; **6.** ⚕ *Blutung* stillen, *Durchfall* stopfen; **7.** *psych.* verdrängen; **supˈpres·sant** [-sənt] *s. pharm.* Dämpfungsmittel *n*, (Appeˈtit- *etc.*) Zügler *m*; **supˈpres·sion** [-eʃn] *s.* **1.** Unterˈdrückung *f* (*a. fig. u.* ϟ); **2.** Aufhebung *f*, Abschaffung *f*; **3.** Verheimlichung *f*, Vertuschung *f*; **4.** ⚕ (Blut)Stillung *f*; Stopfung *f*, (Harn)Verhaltung *f*; **5.** *psych.* Verdrängung *f*; **supˈpres·sive** [-sɪv] *adj.* unterˈdrückend, Unterdrückungs…; **supˈpres·sor** [-sə] *s.* ϟ a) Sperrgerät *n*, b) Entstörer *m*: **~ *grid*** Bremsgitter *n*.

sup·pu·rate [ˈsʌpjʊəreɪt] *v/i.* ⚕ eitern; **sup·pu·ra·tion** [͵sʌpjʊəˈreɪʃn] *s.* Eiterung *f*; **ˈsup·pu·ra·tive** [-rətɪv] *adj.* eiternd, eitrig, Eiter…

su·pra [ˈsuːprə] (*Lat.*) *adv.* oben (*bei Verweisen in e-m Buch etc.*).

supra- [suːprə] *in Zssgn* über, supra…, Supra…

͵**supra|·conˈduc·tor** *s. phys.* Supraleiter *m*; ͵**~ˈmun·dane** *adj.* ˈüberweltlich; ͵**~ˈnas·al** *adj. anat.* über der Nase (befindlich); ͵**~ˈre·nal** *s. anat.* Nebenniere(ndrüse) *f*.

su·prem·a·cy [sʊˈpreməsɪ] *s.* **1.** Oberhoheit *f*: a) *pol.* höchste Gewalt, Souveräniˈtät *f*, b) Supreˈmat *m, n* (*in Kirchensachen*); **2.** *fig.* Vorherrschaft *f*, Überˈlegenheit *f*: ***air* ~** ⚔ Luftherrschaft *f*; **3.** Vorrang *m*; **su·preme** [sʊˈpriːm] **I** *adj.* □ **1.** höchst, oberst, Ober…: **~ *authority*** höchste (Regierungs)Gewalt; **~ *command*** ⚔ Oberbefehl *m*, -kommando *n*; **~ *commander*** ⚔ Oberbefehlshaber *m*; **𝔖 *Court*** *Am.* a) oberstes Bundesgericht, b) oberstes Gericht (*e-s Bundesstaates*); **𝔖 *Court* (*of Judicature*)** *Brit.* Oberster Gerichtshof; ***reign* ~** herrschen (*a. fig.*); **2.** höchst, größt, äußerst, überˈragend: **~ *courage***; **𝔖 *Being*** → 6; ***the* ~ *good*** *phls.* das höchste Gut; ***the* ~ *punishment*** die Todesstrafe; ***stand* ~ *among*** den höchsten Rang einnehmen unter (*dat.*); **3.** letzt: **~ *moment*** Augenblick *m* des Todes; **~ *sacrifice*** Hingabe *f* des Lebens; **4.** entscheidend, kritisch: ***the* ~ *hour in the history of a nation***; **II** *s.* **5. *the* ~** der *od.* die *od.* das Höchste; **6. *the* 𝔖** der Allerhöchste, Gott *m*; **su·preme·ly** [sʊˈpriːmlɪ] *adv.* höchst, aufs äußerste, ˈüberaus.

su·pre·mo [sʊˈpriːməʊ] *s. Brit.* F Oberboß *m*.

sur-¹ [sɜː] *in Zssgn* über, auf.

sur-² [sə] → ***sub-***.

sur·cease [sɜːˈsiːs] *obs.* **I** *v/i.* **1.** ablassen (***from*** von); **2.** aufhören; **II** *s.* **3.** Ende *n*, Aufhören *n*; **4.** Pause *f*.

sur·charge I *s.* [ˈsɜːtʃɑːdʒ] **1.** *bsd. fig.* Überˈlastung *f*; **2.** † a) Überˈforderung *f* (*a. fig.*), b) ˈÜberpreis *m*, (*a.* Steuer-) Zuschlag *m*, c) Strafporto *n*; **3.** ˈÜber-, Aufdruck *m* (*Briefmarke etc.*); **II** *v/t.* [sɜːˈtʃɑːdʒ] **4.** überˈlasten, -ˈfordern; **5.** † a) e-n Zuschlag *od.* ein Nachporto erheben auf (*acc.*), b) *Konto* zusätzlich belasten; **6.** *Briefmarken etc.* (*mit neuer Wertangabe*) überˈdrucken; **7.** überˈfüllen, -ˈsättigen.

sur·cingle [ˈsɜː͵sɪŋgl] *s.* Sattel-, Packgurt *m*.

sur·coat [ˈsɜːkəʊt] *s.* **1.** *hist.* a) Wappenrock *m*, b) ˈÜberrock *m* (*der Frauen*); **2.** Freizeitjacke *f*.

surd [sɜːd] **I** *adj.* **1.** 𝔄 ˈirratio͵nal (*Zahl*); **2.** *ling.* stimmlos; **II** *s.* **3.** 𝔄 ˈirratio͵nale Größe, *a.* Wurzelausdruck *m*; **4.** *ling.* stimmloser Laut.

sure [ʃʊə] **I** *adj.* □ → ***surely***; **1.** *pred.* (***of***) sicher, gewiß (*gen.*), überˈzeugt (von): ***I am* ~ *he is there***; ***are you* ~ (*about it*)?** bist du (dessen) sicher?; ***he is*** (*od.* ***feels***) **~ *of success*** er ist sich s-s Erfolges sicher; ***I'm* ~ *I didn't mean to hurt you*** ich wollte Sie ganz gewiß nicht verletzen; ***are you* ~ *you won't come?*** wollen Sie wirklich nicht kommen?; **2.** *pred.* sicher, gewiß, (ganz) bestimmt, zweifellos (*objektiver Sachverhalt*): ***he is* ~ *to come*** er kommt sicher *od.* bestimmt; ***man is* ~ *of death*** dem Menschen ist der Tod gewiß *od.* sicher; ***make* ~ *that* …** sich (davon) überzeugen, daß …; ***make* ~ *of s.th.*** a) sich von et. überzeugen, sich e-r Sache vergewissern, b) sich et. sichern; ***to make* ~** (*Redewendung*) um sicher zu gehen; ***be* ~ *to*** (*od.* ***and***) ***shut the window!*** vergiß nicht, das Fenster zu schließen!; ***to be* ~** (*Redewendung*) sicher(lich), natürlich (*a. einschränkend = freilich, allerdings*); **~ *thing*** *Am.* F (tod)sicher, klar; **3.** sicher, fest: ***a* ~ *footing***; **~ *faith*** *fig.* fester Glaube; **4.** sicher, untrüglich: ***a* ~ *proof***; **5.** verläßlich, zuverlässig; **6.** sicher, unfehlbar: ***a* ~ *cure* (*method*, *shot*)**; **II** *adv.* **7.** *obs. od.* F sicher(lich): (***as***) **~ *as eggs*** ‚bombensicher'; **~ *enough*** a) ganz bestimmt, sicher(lich), b) tatsächlich; **8.** F wirklich, ‚echt': ***it* ~ *was cold***; **9. ~!** *bsd. Am.* F sicher!, klar!; **ˈ~-͵fire** *adj.* F (tod)sicher, zuverlässig; ͵**~-ˈfoot·ed** *adj.* **1.** sicher (auf den Füßen *od.* Beinen; **2.** *fig.* sicher.

sure·ly [ˈʃʊəlɪ] *adv.* **1.** sicher(lich), zweifellos; **2.** (ganz) bestimmt *od.* gewiß, doch (wohl): **~ *something can be done to help him***; **3.** sicher: ***slowly but* ~**; **sure·ness** [ˈʃʊənɪs] *s.* Sicherheit *f*: a) Gewißheit *f*, b) feste Überˈzeugung, c) Zuverlässigkeit *f*; **sure·ty** [ˈʃʊərətɪ] *s.* **1.** *bsd.* ⚖ a) Bürge *m*, b) Bürgschaft *f*, Sicherheit *f*: ***stand* ~ *for*** bürgen *od.* Bürgschaft leisten (***for*** für *j-n*); **2.** Gewähr(leistung) *f*, Garanˈtie *f*; **3.** *obs.* Sicherheit *f*: ***of a* ~** sicher(lich), ohne Zweifel; **sure·ty·ship** [ˈʃʊərətɪʃɪp] *s. bsd.* ⚖ Bürgschaft(sleistung) *f*.

surf [sɜːf] **I** *s.* Brandung *f*; **II** *v/i. sport* surfen.

sur·face [ˈsɜːfɪs] **I** *s.* **1.** *allg.* Oberfläche *f*: **~ *of water*** Wasseroberfläche *f*; ***come*** (*od.* ***rise***) ***to the*** → 13; **2.** *fig.* Oberfläche *f*, *das* Äußere: ***on the* ~** a) äußerlich, b) vordergründig, c) oberflächlich betrachtet; → ***scratch*** 7; **3.** 𝔄 a) (Ober)Fläche *f*, b) Flächeninhalt *m*: ***lateral* ~** Seitenfläche; **4.** (Straßen)Belag *m*, (-)Decke *f*; **5.** ✈ (Trag)Fläche *f*; **6.** ⚒ Tag *m*: ***on the* ~** über Tag, im Tagebau; **II** *adj.* **7.** Oberflächen… (*a.* ⚙ *-härtung etc.*); **8.** *fig.* oberflächlich: a) flüchtig, b) vordergründig, äußerlich, Schein…; **III** *v/t.* **9.** ⚙ *allg.* die Oberfläche behandeln von; glätten; *Lackierung* spachteln; *Straße* mit e-m Belag versehen; **10.** ⚙ flach-, plandrehen; **11.** ⚓ *U-Boot* auftauchen lassen; **IV** *v/i.* **12.** ⚓ auftauchen (*U-Boot*); **13.** an die Oberfläche (*fig.* ans Tageslicht) kommen, sich zeigen; **~ *mail*** *s. Brit.* gewöhnliche Post (*Ggs. Luftpost*); **ˈ~·man** [-mən] *s.* [*irr.*] 🚂 Streckenarbeiter *m*; **~ *noise*** *s.* Rauschen *n* (*e-r Schallplatte*); **~ *print·ing*** *s. typ.* Reliˈef-, Hochdruck *m*.

sur·fac·er [ˈsɜːfɪsə] *s.* ⚙ **1.** Spachtelmasse *f*; **2.** ˈPlandreh- *od.* -hobelma͵schine *f*.

͵**sur·face|-to-ˈair mis·sile** *s.* ⚔ ˈBoden-ˈLuft-Ra͵kete *f*; **~ *work*** *s.* ⚒ Überˈtagearbeit *f*.

ˈsurf|·board *sport* **I** *s.* Surfbrett *n*; **II** *v/i.* surfen; **ˈ~·boat** *s.* ⚓ Brandungsboot *n*.

sur·feit [ˈsɜːfɪt] **I** *s.* **1.** ˈÜbermaß *n* (***of*** an *dat.*); **2.** *a. fig.* Überˈsättigung *f* (***of*** mit); **3.** ˈÜberdruß *m*: ***to* (*a*) ~** bis zum Überdruß; **II** *v/t.* **4.** überˈsättigen, -ˈfüttern (***with*** mit); **5.** überˈfüllen, -ˈladen; **III** *v/i.* **6.** sich überˈsättigen (***of***, ***with*** mit).

surf·er [ˈsɜːfə] *s. sport* Surfer(in); **surf·ing** [ˈsɜːfɪŋ] *s. sport* Surfen *n*.

surge [sɜːdʒ] **I** *s.* **1.** Woge *f*, Welle *f* (*beide a. fig.*); **2.** Brandung *f*; **3.** *a. fig.* Wogen *n*, (An)Branden *n*; Aufwallung *f der Gefühle*; **4.** ϟ Spannungsstoß *m*; **II** *v/i.* **5.** wogen: a) (hoch)branden (*a. fig.*), b) *fig.* (vorwärts)drängen (*Menge*), c) brausen (*Orgel, Verkehr etc.*); **6.** *fig.* (auf)wallen (*Blut, Gefühl etc.*); **7.** ϟ plötzlich ansteigen, heftig schwanken (*Spannung etc.*).

sur·geon [ˈsɜːdʒən] *s.* **1.** Chirˈurg *m*; **2.** ⚔ leitender Saniˈtätsoffi͵zier: **~ *general*** *Brit.* Stabsarzt *m*; **𝔖 *General*** *Am.* a) General(stabs)arzt *m*, b) ⚓ Marineadmiralarzt *m*; **~ *major*** *Brit.* Oberstabsarzt *m*; **3.** Schiffsarzt *m*; **4.** *hist.* Bader *m*; **ˈsur·ger·y** [-dʒərɪ] *s.* ⚕ **1.** Chirurˈgie *f*; **2.** chirˈurgische Behandlung, operaˈtiver Eingriff; **3.** Operatiˈonssaal *m*; **4.** *Brit.* Sprechzimmer *n*: **~ *hours*** Sprechstunden; **ˈsur·gi·cal** [-dʒɪkl] *adj.* □ ⚕ **1.** chirˈurgisch: **~ *cotton*** (Verband)Watte *f*; **2.** Operations…: **~ *wound***; **~ *fever*** septisches Fieber; **3.** mediˈzinisch: **~ *boot*** orthopädischer Schuh; **~ *stocking*** Stützstrumpf *m*; **~ *spirit*** Wundbenzin *n*.

surg·ing [ˈsɜːdʒɪŋ] **I** *s.* **1.** *a. fig.* Wogen *n*, Branden *n*; **2.** ϟ Pendeln *n* (*der Spannung etc.*); **II** *adj.* **3.** *a.* **ˈsurg·y** [-dʒɪ] *adj.* wogend, brandend (*a. fig.*).

sur·li·ness [ˈsɜːlɪnɪs] *s.* Verdrießlichkeit *f*, mürrisches Wesen; Bärbeißigkeit *f*; **sur·ly** [ˈsɜːlɪ] *adj.* □ **1.** verdrießlich, mürrisch; **2.** grob, bärbeißig; **3.** zäh (*Boden*).

sur·mise I *s.* [ˈsɜːmaɪz] Vermutung *f*, Mutmaßung *f*, Einbildung *f*; **II** *v/t.* [sɜːˈmaɪz] mutmaßen, vermuten, sich *et.* einbilden.

sur·mount [sɜːˈmaʊnt] *v/t.* **1.** überˈsteigen; **2.** *fig.* über'winden; **3.** bedecken, krönen: **~ed by** gekrönt *od.* überdeckt *od.* überragt von; **sur'mount·a·ble** [-təbl] *adj.* **1.** über'steigbar, ersteigbar; **2.** *fig.* über'windbar.

sur·name ['sɜːneɪm] **I** *s.* **1.** Fa'milien-, Nach-, Zuname *m*; **2.** *obs.* Beiname *m*; **II** *v/t.* **3.** *j-m* den Zu- *od. obs.* Beinamen ... geben: **~d** mit Zunamen.

sur·pass [sə'pɑːs] *v/t.* **1.** *j-n od. et.* über'treffen (*in* an *dat.*): **~ o.s.** sich selbst übertreffen; **2.** *et., j-s Kräfte etc.* über'steigen; **sur'pass·ing** [-sɪŋ] *adj.* □ her'vorragend, 'unüber,trefflich, unerreicht.

sur·plice ['sɜːplɪs] *s. eccl.* Chorhemd *n*, -rock *m*.

sur·plus ['sɜːpləs] **I** *s.* **1.** 'Überschuß *m*, Rest *m*; **2.** ✝ a) 'Überschuß *m*, Mehr (-betrag *m*) *n*, b) Mehrertrag *m*, 'überschüssiger Gewinn, c) (unverteilter) Reingewinn, d) Mehrwert *m*; **II** *adj.* **3.** 'überschüssig, Über(schuß)..., Mehr...: **~ population** Bevölkerungsüberschuß *m*; **~ weight** Mehr-, Übergewicht *n*; **'sur·plus·age** [-sɪdʒ] *s.* **1.** 'Überschuß *m*, -fülle *f* (*of* an *dat.*); **2.** *et.* 'Überflüssiges; **3.** ⚖ unerhebliches Vorbringen.

sur·prise [sə'praɪz] **I** *v/t.* **1.** über'raschen: a) ertappen, b) verblüffen, in Erstaunen (ver)setzen: **be ~d at s.th.** über et. erstaunt sein, sich über et. wundern, c) *bsd.* ⚔ über'rumpeln; **2.** befremden, empören; **3. ~ s.o. into (doing) s.th.** j-n zu et. verleiten, j-n dazu verleiten, et. zu tun; **II** *s.* **4.** Über'raschung *f*: a) Über'rump(e)lung *f*: **take by ~** *j-n, feindliche Stellung etc.* überrumpeln, *Festung etc.* im Handstreich nehmen, b) *et.* Über'raschendes: **it came as a great ~ (to him)** es kam (ihm) sehr überraschend, c) Verblüffung *f*, Erstaunen *n*, Verwunderung *f*, Bestürzung *f* (*at* über *acc.*): **to my ~** zu m-r Überraschung; **stare in ~** große Augen machen; **III** *adj.* **5.** über'raschend, Überraschungs...: **~ attack**; **~ visit**; **sur'pris·ed·ly** [-zɪdlɪ] *adv.* über'rascht; **sur'pris·ing** [-zɪŋ] *adj.* □ über'raschend, erstaunlich; **sur'pris·ing·ly** [-zɪŋlɪ] *adv.* über'raschend(erweise), erstaunlich(erweise).

sur·re·al·ism [sə'rɪəlɪzəm] *s.* Surrea'lismus *m*; **sur're·al·ist** [-ɪst] **I** *s.* Surrea'list(in); **II** *adj.* → **sur·re·al·is·tic** [sə,rɪə'lɪstɪk] *adj.* (□ **~ally**) surrea'listisch.

sur·re·but [,sʌrɪ'bʌt] *v/i.* ⚖ e-e Quintu'plik vorbringen; **,sur·re'but·ter** [-tə] *s.* ⚖ Quintu'plik *f*.

sur·re·join·der [,sʌrɪ'dʒɔɪndə] *s.* ⚖ Tri'plik *f*.

sur·ren·der [sə'rendə] **I** *v/t.* **1.** *et.* über'geben, ausliefern, -händigen (*to dat.*): **~ o.s. (to)** → 5, 6, 7; **2.** *Amt, Vorrecht, Hoffnung etc.* aufgeben; *et.* abtreten, verzichten auf (*acc.*); **3.** ⚖ a) *Sache, Urkunde* her'ausgeben, b) *Verbrecher* ausliefern; **4.** ✝ *Versicherungspolice* zum Rückkauf bringen; **II** *v/i.* **5.** ⚔ *u. fig.* sich ergeben (*to dat.*), kapitulieren; **6.** sich *der Verzweiflung etc.* hingeben *od.* über'lassen; **7.** ⚖ sich *der Polizei etc.* stellen; **III** *s.* **8.** 'Übergabe *f*, Auslieferung *f*, -händigung *f*; **9.** ⚔ 'Übergabe *f*, Kapitulati'on *f*; **10.** (*of*) Auf-, Preisgabe *f*, Abtretung *f* (*gen.*), Verzicht *m* (auf *acc.*); **11.** Hingabe *f*, Sich-über'lassen *n*; **12.** ⚖ Aufgabe *f* e-r Versicherung: **~ value** Rückkaufswert *m*; **13.** ⚖ a) Aufgabe *f e-s Rechts etc.*, b) Her'ausgabe *f*, c) Auslieferung *f e-s Verbrechers*.

sur·rep·ti·tious [,sʌrep'tɪʃəs] *adj.* □ **1.** erschlichen, betrügerisch; **2.** heimlich, verstohlen: **a ~ glance**; **~ edition** unerlaubter Nachdruck.

sur·ro·gate ['sʌrəgɪt] *s.* **1.** Stellvertreter *m* (*bsd. e-s Bischofs*); **2.** ⚖ *Am.* Nachlaß- u. Vormundschaftsrichter *m*; **3.** Ersatz *m*, Surro'gat *n* (*of*, *for* für).

sur·round [sə'raʊnd] **I** *v/t.* **1.** um'geben, -'ringen (*a. fig.*): **~ed by danger (luxury)** von Gefahr umringt *od.* mit Gefahr verbunden (von Luxus umgeben); **circumstances ~ing s.th.** (Begleit)Umstände e-r Sache; **2.** ⚔ *etc.* um'zingeln, -'stellen, einkreisen, -schließen; **II** *s.* **3.** Einfassung *f*, *bsd.* Boden(schutz)belag *m* zwischen Wand u. Teppich; **4.** *hunt. Am.* Treibjagd *f*; **sur'round·ing** [-dɪŋ] **I** *adj.* um'gebend, 'umliegend; **II** *s. pl.* Um'gebung *f*: a) 'Umgegend *f*, b) 'Umwelt *f*, c) 'Umfeld *n*.

sur·tax ['sɜːtæks] **I** *s.* (*a.* Einkommen-) Steuerzuschlag *m*; **II** *v/t.* mit e-m Steuerzuschlag belegen.

sur·veil·lance [sɜː'veɪləns] *s.* Über'wachung *f*, (*a.* Poli'zei)Aufsicht *f*: **be under ~** unter Polizeiaufsicht stehen; **keep under ~** überwachen.

sur·vey **I** *v/t.* [sə'veɪ] **1.** über'blicken, -'schauen; **2.** genau betrachten, (sorgfältig) prüfen, mustern; **3.** abschätzen, begutachten; **4.** besichtigen, inspizieren; **5.** *Land etc.* vermessen, aufnehmen; **6.** *fig.* e-n 'Überblick geben über (*acc.*); **II** *s.* ['sɜːveɪ] **7.** *bsd. fig.* 'Überblick *m*, -sicht *f* (*of* über *acc.*); **8.** Besichtigung *f*, Prüfung *f*; **9.** Schätzung *f*, Begutachtung *f*; **10.** Gutachten *n*, (Prüfungs)Bericht *m*; **11.** (Land)Vermessung *f*, Aufnahme *f*; **12.** (Lage)Plan *m*; **13.** (sta'tistische) Erhebung, 'Umfrage *f*; **14.** ⚕ 'Reihenunter,suchung *f*; **sur'vey·ing** [-eɪɪŋ] *s.* **1.** (Land-, Feld)Vermessung *f*, Vermessungsurkunde *f*, -wesen *n*; **2.** Vermessen *n*, Aufnehmen *n* (*von Land etc.*); **sur'vey·or** [-eɪə] *s.* **1.** Landmesser *m*, Geo'meter *m*: **~'s chain** Meßkette *f*; **2.** (amtlicher) In'spektor *od.* Verwalter *od.* Aufseher: **~ of highways** Straßenmeister *m*; **Board of** **~s** Baubehörde *f*; **3.** *Brit.* (ausführender) Archi'tekt; **4.** Sachverständige(r) *m*, Gutachter *m*.

sur·viv·al [sə'vaɪvl] *s.* **1.** Über'leben *n*: **~ of the fittest** *biol.* Überleben der Tüchtigsten; **~ kit** Überlebensausrüstung *f*; **~ rate** Überlebensquote *f*; **~ shelter** atomsicherer Bunker; **~ time** ⚔ Überlebenszeit *f*; **2.** Weiterleben *n*; **3.** Fortbestand *m*; **4.** 'Überbleibsel *n alten Brauchtums etc.*; **sur·vive** [sə'vaɪv] **I** *v/t.* **1.** *j-n od. et.* über'leben (*a. fig.* F *ertragen*), über'dauern, länger leben als; **2.** *Unglück etc.* über'leben, -'stehen; **II** *v/i.* **3.** am Leben bleiben, übrigbleiben, über'leben; **4.** noch leben *od.* bestehen; übriggeblieben sein; **5.** weiter-, fortleben *od.* -bestehen; **sur'viv·ing** [-vɪŋ] *adj.* **1.** über'lebend: **~ wife**; **2.** hinter'blieben: **~ dependents** Hinterbliebene; **3.** übrigbleibend: **~ debts** ✝ Restschulden; **sur'vi·vor** [-və] *s.* **1.** Über'lebende(r *m*) *f*; **2.** ⚖ Über'lebender, auf den nach dem Ableben der Miteigentümer das Eigentumsrecht 'übergeht.

sus·cep·ti·bil·i·ty [sə,septə'bɪlətɪ] *s.* **1.** Empfänglichkeit *f*, Anfälligkeit *f* (*to* für); **2.** Empfindlichkeit *f*; **3.** *pl.* (leicht verletzbare) Gefühle *pl.*, Feingefühl *n*; **sus·cep·ti·ble** [sə'septəbl] *adj.* □ **1.** anfällig (*to* für); **2.** empfindlich (*to* gegen); **3.** (*to*) empfänglich (für *Reize, Schmeicheleien etc.*), zugänglich (*dat.*); **4.** (leicht) zu beeindrucken(d); **5. be ~ of** (*od.* **to**) *et.* zulassen.

sus·cep·tive [sə'septɪv] *adj.* **1.** aufnehmend, aufnahmefähig, rezep'tiv; **2.** → **susceptible**.

sus·pect [sə'spekt] **I** *v/t.* **1.** *j-n* verdächtigen (*of gen.*), im Verdacht haben (*of doing et.* getan zu haben *od.* daß *j-d et.* tut): **be ~ed of doing s.th.** im Verdacht stehen *od.* verdächtigt werden, et. getan zu haben; **2.** argwöhnen, befürchten; **3.** für möglich halten, halb glauben; **4.** vermuten, glauben (*that* daß); **5.** *Echtheit, Wahrheit etc.* anzweifeln, miß'trauen (*dat.*); **II** *v/i.* **6.** (e-n) Verdacht hegen, argwöhnisch sein; **III** *s.* ['sʌspekt] **7.** Verdächtige(r *m*) *f*, verdächtige Per'son, Ver'dachtsper,son *f*: **smallpox ~** ⚕ Pockenverdächtige(r); **IV** *adj.* ['sʌspekt] **8.** verdächtig, su'spekt (*a. fig. fragwürdig*).

sus·pend [sə'spend] *v/t.* **1.** *a.* ⚙ aufhängen (*from* an *dat.*); **2.** *bsd.* ⚗ suspendieren, (*in Flüssigkeiten etc.*) schwebend halten; **3.** *Frage etc.* in der Schwebe *od.* unentschieden lassen; **4.** *einstweilen* auf-, verschieben; ⚖ *Verfahren, Vollstreckung* aussetzen: **~ a sentence** ⚖ e-e Strafe zur Bewährung aussetzen; **5.** *Verordnung etc.* zeitweilig aufheben *od.* außer Kraft setzen; **6.** *die Arbeit*, ⚔ *die Feindseligkeiten*, ✝ *Zahlungen etc.* (zeitweilig) einstellen; **7.** *j-n* (zeitweilig) des Amtes entheben, suspendieren; **8.** *Mitglied* zeitweilig ausschließen; **9.** *Sportler* sperren; **10.** mit *s-r Meinung etc.* zu'rückhalten; **11.** ♪ *Ton* vorhalten; **sus'pend·ed** [-dɪd] *adj.* **1.** hängend, Hänge...(*-decke, -lampe etc.*): **be ~** hängen (*by* an *dat.*, *from* von); **2.** schwebend; **3.** unter'brochen, ausgesetzt, zeitweilig eingestellt: **~ animation** ⚕ Scheintod *m*; **4.** ⚖ zur Bewährung ausgesetzt (*Strafe*): **~ sentence of two years** zwei Jahre mit Bewährung; **5.** suspendiert (*Beamter*); **sus'pend·er** [-də] *s.* **1.** *pl. bsd. Am.* Hosenträger *pl.*; **2.** *Brit.* Strumpf- *od.* Sockenhalter *m*: **~ belt** Hüftgürtel *m*, Straps *m*; **3.** Aufhängevorrichtung *f*.

sus·pense [sə'spens] *s.* **1.** Spannung *f*, Ungewißheit *f*: **anxious ~** Hangen u. Bangen *n*; **in ~** gespannt, voller Spannung; **be in ~** in der Schwebe sein; **keep in ~** a) *j-n* in Spannung halten, im ungewissen lassen, b) *et.* in der Schwebe lassen; **~ account** ✝ Interimskonto *n*; **~ entry** ✝ transitorische Buchung; **2.** → **suspension** 6; **sus'pense·ful** [-fʊl] *adj.* spannend; **su'spen·sion** [-nʃn] *s.* **1.** Aufhängen *n*; **2.** *bsd.* ⚙ Aufhängung *f*: **front-wheel ~**; **~ bridge** Hängebrükke *f*; **~ railway** Schwebebahn *f*; **3.** ⚙ Federung *f*: **~ spring** Tragfeder *f*; **4.** ⚗, *phys.* Suspensi'on *f*; *pl.* Aufschlämmungen *pl.*; **5.** (einstweilige) Einstellung (*der Feindseligkeiten etc.*): ~ ***of payment(s)*** ✝ Zahlungseinstellung; **6.** ⚖ Aufschub *m*, Aussetzung *f*; vor'übergehende Aufhebung *e-s Rechts*; Hemmung *f der Verjährung*; **7.** Aufschub *m*, Verschiebung *f*; **8.** Suspendierung *f* (***from*** von), (Dienst-, Amts)Enthebung *f*; **9.** zeitweiliger Ausschluß; **10.** *sport* Sperre *f*; **11.** ♪ Vorhalt *m*;

sus'pen·sive [-sɪv] *adj.* □ **1.** aufschiebend, suspen'siv: ~ ***condition***; ~ ***veto***; **2.** unter'brechend, hemmend; **3.** unschlüssig; **4.** unbestimmt; **sus'pen·so·ry** [-sərɪ] **I** *adj.* **1.** hängend, Schwebe…, Hänge…; **2.** *anat.* Aufhänge…; **3.** ⚖ → ***suspensive*** 1; **II** *s.* **4.** *anat.* a) *a.* ~ ***ligament*** Aufhängeband *n*, b) *a.* ~ ***muscle*** Aufhängemuskel *m*; **5.** ⚕ a) *a.* ~ ***bandage*** Suspen'sorium *n*, b) Bruchband *n*.

sus·pi·cion [sə'spɪʃn] *s.* **1.** Argwohn *m*, 'Mißtrauen *n* (***of*** gegen); **2.** (***of***) Verdacht *m* (gegen *j-n*), Verdächtigung *f* (*gen.*): ***above*** ~ über jeden Verdacht erhaben; ***on*** ~ ***of murder*** unter Mordverdacht *festgenommen werden*; ***be under*** ~ unter Verdacht stehen; ***cast a*** ~ ***on*** e-n Verdacht auf *j-n* werfen; ***have a*** ~ ***that*** e-n Verdacht haben *od.* hegen, daß; **3.** Vermutung *f*: ***no*** ~ keine Ahnung; **4.** *fig.* Spur *f*: ***a*** ~ ***of brandy*** (***arrogance***); ***a*** ~ ***of a smile*** der Anflug e-s Lächelns; **sus'pi·cious** [-ʃəs] *adj.* □ **1.** 'mißtrauisch, argwöhnisch (***of*** gegen): ***be*** ~ ***of s.th.*** et. befürchten; **2.** verdächtig, verdachterregend; **sus'pi·cious·ness** [-ʃəsnɪs] *s.* **1.** Mißtrauen *n*, Argwohn *m* (***of*** gegen); 'mißtrauisches Wesen; **2.** *das* Verdächtige.

sus·tain [sə'steɪn] *v/t.* **1.** stützen, tragen: ~***ing wall*** Stützmauer *f*; **2.** *Last, Druck, fig. den Vergleich etc.* aushalten; *e-m Angriff etc.* standhalten; **3.** *Niederlage, Schaden, Verletzungen, Verlust etc.* erleiden, da'vontragen; **4.** *et.* (aufrecht-)erhalten, in Gang halten; *Interesse* wachhalten: ~***ing program*** *Am. Radio, TV*: Programm *n* ohne Reklameeinblendungen; **5.** *j-n* er-, unter'halten, *Familie etc.* ernähren; *Heer* verpflegen; **6.** *Institution* unter'halten, -'stützen; **7.** *j-n, j-s Forderung* unter'stützen; **8.** ⚖ als rechtsgültig anerkennen, *e-m Antrag, Einwand etc.* stattgeben; **9.** *Behauptungen etc.* bestätigen, rechtfertigen, erhärten; **10.** *j-n* aufrecht halten; *j-m* Kraft geben; **11.** ♪ *Ton* (aus)halten; **12.** *Rolle* (gut) spielen; **sus'tained** [-nd] *adj.* **1.** anhaltend (*a. Interesse etc.*), Dauer…(*-feuer, -geschwindigkeit etc.*); **2.** ♪ a) (aus)gehalten (*Ton*), b) getragen; **3.** *phys.* ungedämpft.

sus·te·nance ['sʌstɪnəns] *s.* **1.** ('Lebens-)ˌUnterhalt *m*, Auskommen *n*; **2.** Nahrung *f*; **3.** Nährwert *m*; **4.** Erhaltung *f*, Ernährung *f*; **5.** *fig.* Beistand *m*, Stütze *f*; **sus·ten·ta·tion** [ˌsʌsten'teɪʃn] *s.* **1.** → ***sustenance*** 1, 2, 4; **2.** Unter'haltung *f e-s Instituts etc.*; **3.** (Aufrecht-)Erhaltung *f*; **4.** Unter'stützung *f*.

su·sur·rant [sjʊ'sʌrənt] *adj.* **1.** flüsternd, säuselnd; **2.** raschelnd.

sut·ler ['sʌtlə] *s.* ⚔ *hist.* Marke'tender(in).

su·ture ['sju:tʃə] **I** *s.* **1.** ⚕, ♀, *anat.* Naht *f*; **2.** ⚕ (Zs.-)Nähen *n*; **3.** ⚕ 'Nahtmateriˌal *n*, Faden *m*; **II** *v/t.* **4.** *bsd.* ⚕ (zu-, ver)nähen.

su·ze·rain ['su:zəreɪn] **I** *s.* **1.** Oberherr *m*, Suze'rän *m*; **2.** *pol.* Pro'tektorstaat *m*; **3.** *hist.* Oberlehensherr *m*; **II** *adj.* **4.** oberhoheitlich; **5.** *hist.* oberlehensherrlich; **'su·ze·rain·ty** [-tɪ] *s.* **1.** Oberhoheit *f*; **2.** *hist.* Oberlehensherrlichkeit *f*.

svelte [svelt] *adj.* schlank, gra'zil.

swab [swɒb] **I** *s.* **1.** a) Scheuerlappen *m*, b) Schrubber *m*, c) Mop *m*, d) Handfeger *m*, e) ⚓ Schwabber *m*; **2.** ⚕ a) Tupfer *m*, b) Abstrich *m*; **II** *v/t.* **3.** *a.* ~ ***down*** aufwischen, ⚓ *Deck* schrubben; **4.** ⚕ a) *Blut etc.* abtupfen, b) *Wunde* betupfen.

Swa·bi·an ['sweɪbjən] **I** *s.* Schwabe *m*, Schwäbin *f*; **II** *adj.* schwäbisch.

swad·dle ['swɒdl] **I** *adj.* **1.** *Säugling* wickeln, in Windeln legen; **2.** um'wickeln, einwickeln; **II** *s.* **3.** *Am.* Windel *f*.

swad·dling ['swɒdlɪŋ] *s.* Wickeln *n e-s Babys*; ~ **clothes** [kləʊðz] *s. pl.* Windeln *pl.*: ***be still in one's*** ~ *fig.* ‚noch in den Windeln liegen'.

swag [swæg] *s.* **1.** Gir'lande *f* (*Zierat*); **2.** *sl.* Beute *f*, Raub *m*.

swage [sweɪdʒ] **I** *s.* ⚙ **1.** Gesenk *n*; **2.** Präge *f*, Stanze *f*; **II** *v/t.* **3.** im Gesenk bearbeiten.

swag·ger ['swægə] **I** *v/i.* **1.** (ein'her)stolzieren; **2.** prahlen, aufschneiden, renommieren (***about*** mit); **II** *s.* **3.** stolzer Gang, Stolzieren *n*; **4.** Großtue'rei *f*, Prahle'rei *f*; **III** *adj.* **5.** F (tod)schick: ~ ***stick*** ⚔ Offi'ziersstöckchen *n*; **'swag·ger·er** [-ərə] *s.* Großtuer *m*, Aufschneider *m*; **'swag·ger·ing** [-ərɪŋ] *adj.* □ **1.** stolzierend; **2.** schwadronierend.

swain [sweɪn] *s.* **1.** *mst poet.* Bauernbursche *m*, Schäfer *m*; **2.** *poet. od. humor.* Liebhaber *m*, Verehrer *m*.

swal·low¹ ['swɒləʊ] **I** *v/t.* **1.** (ver)schlucken, verschlingen: ~ ***down*** hinunterschlucken; **2.** *fig. Buch etc.* verschlingen, *Ansicht etc.* begierig in sich aufnehmen; **3.** *Gebiet etc.* ‚schlucken', sich einverleiben; **4.** *mst* ~ ***up*** *fig. j-n, Schiff, Geld, Zeit etc.* verschlingen; **5.** ‚schlucken', für bare Münze nehmen; **6.** *Beleidigung etc.* schlucken, einstekken; **7.** *Tränen, Ärger* hin'unterschlukken; **8.** *Behauptung* zu'rücknehmen: ~ ***one's words***; **II** *v/i.* **9.** schlucken (*a. vor Erregung*): ~ ***hard*** *fig.* kräftig schlucken; ~ ***the wrong way*** sich verschlucken; **III** *s.* **10.** Schlund *m*, Kehle *f*; **11.** Schluck *m*.

swal·low² ['swɒləʊ] *s. orn.* Schwalbe *f*: ***one*** ~ ***does not make a summer*** eine Schwalbe macht noch keinen Sommer; **'~·tail** *s.* **1.** *orn.* Schwalbenschwanz-Kolibri *m*; **2.** *zo.* Schwalbenschwanz *m* (*Schmetterling*); **3.** ⚙ Schwalbenschwanz *m*; **4.** *a. pl.* Frack *m*; **'~-tailed** *adj.* Schwalbenschwanz…: ~ ***coat*** Frack *m*.

swam [swæm] *pret. von* ***swim***.

swa·mi ['swɑ:mɪ] *s.* **1.** Meister *m* (*bsd. Brahmane*); **2.** → ***pundit*** 2.

swamp [swɒmp] **I** *s.* **1.** Sumpf *m*; **2.** (Flach)Moor *n*; **II** *v/t.* **3.** über'schwemmen (*a. fig.*): ***be*** ~***ed with*** mit *Arbeit, Einladungen etc.* überhäuft werden *od.* sein, sich nicht mehr retten können vor (*dat.*); **4.** ⚓ *Boot* vollaufen lassen, zum Sinken bringen; **5.** *Am. pol. Gesetz* zu Fall bringen; **6.** *sport* ‚über'fahren'; **'swamp·y** [-pɪ] *adj.* sumpfig, mo'rastig, Sumpf…

swan [swɒn] *s.* **1.** *zo.* Schwan *m*: ♀ ***of Avon*** *fig.* der Schwan vom Avon (*Shakespeare*); **2.** ♀ *ast.* Schwan *m* (*Sternbild*).

swank [swæŋk] F **I** *s.* **1.** Protze'rei *f*, ‚Angabe' *f*; **2.** ‚Angeber' *m*; **II** *v/i.* **3.** protzen, ‚angeben'; **III** *adj.* **4.** → **'swank·y** [-kɪ] *adj.* F **1.** protzig; **2.** (tod)schick.

'swan|·like *adj. u. adv.* schwanengleich; ~ **maid·en** *s. myth.* Schwan(en)jungfrau *f*; **'~·neck** *s.* ⚙ Schwanenhals *m*.

swan·ner·y ['swɒnərɪ] *s.* Schwanenteich *m*.

swan| song *s. bsd. fig.* Schwanengesang *m*; **'~-ˌup·ping** *s. Brit. Einfangen u. Kennzeichnen der jungen Schwäne* (*bsd. auf der Themse*).

swap [swɒp] F **I** *v/t.* (aus-, ein)tauschen (***s.th. for*** et. für); *Pferde etc.* tauschen, wechseln: ***to*** ~ ***stories*** *fig.* Geschichten austauschen; **II** *v/i.* tauschen; **III** *s.* Tausch(handel) *m*; ✝ Swap(geschäft *n*) *m*.

sward [swɔ:d] *s.* Rasen *m*, Grasnarbe *f*; **'sward·ed** [-dɪd] *adj.* mit Rasen bedeckt.

swarm¹ [swɔ:m] **I** *s.* **1.** (Bienen- *etc.*) Schwarm *m*; **2.** Schwarm *m* (*Kinder, Soldaten etc.*); **3.** *fig.* Haufen *m*, Masse *f* (*Briefe etc.*); **II** *v/i.* **4.** schwärmen (*Bienen*); **5.** (um'her)schwärmen, (zs.-)strömen: ~ ***out*** a) ausschwärmen, b) hinausströmen; ~ ***to a place*** zu e-m Ort (hin)strömen; ***beggars*** ~ ***in that town*** in dieser Stadt wimmelt es von Bettlern; **6.** (***with***) wimmeln (von); **III** *v/t.* **7.** um'schwärmen, -'drängen; **8.** *Örtlichkeit* in Schwärmen über'fallen; **9.** *Bienen* ausschwärmen lassen.

swarm² [swɔ:m] **I** *v/t.* a) hochklettern an (*dat.*), b) hin'aufklettern auf (*acc.*); **II** *v/i.* klettern.

swarth·i·ness ['swɔ:ðɪnɪs] *s.* dunkle Gesichtsfarbe, Schwärze *f*, Dunkelbraun *n*; **swarth·y** ['swɔ:ðɪ] *adj.* □ dunkel (-häutig), schwärzlich.

swash [swɒʃ] **I** *v/i.* **1.** klatschen, schwappen (*Wasser etc.*); **2.** planschen (*im Wasser*); **II** *v/t.* **3.** *Wasser etc.* a) spritzen lassen, b) klatschen; **III** *s.* **4.** Platschen *n*, Schwappen *n*; **5.** Platsch *m*, Klatsch *m* (*Geräusch*); **'~ˌbuck·ler** [-ˌbʌklə] *s.* **1.** Schwadro'neur *m*, Bra'marbas *m*; **2.** verwegener Kerl; **3.** hi'storischer 'Abenteuerfilm *m od.* -roˌman *m*; **'~ˌbuck·ling** [-ˌbʌklɪŋ] **I** *s.* Bramarbasieren *n*, Prahlen *n*; **II** *adj.* schwadronierend, prahlerisch; ~ **plate** *s.* ⚙ Taumelscheibe *f*.

swas·ti·ka ['swɒstɪkə] *s.* Hakenkreuz *n*.

swat [swɒt] F **I** *v/t.* **1.** schlagen; **2.** *Fliege etc.* totschlagen; **II** *s.* **3.** (wuchtiger) Schlag; **4.** → ***swatter***.

swath [swɔ:θ] *s.* ✓ Grasnarbe *f*.

swathe¹ [sweɪð] **I** *v/t.* **1.** (um)'wickeln (***with*** mit), einwickeln; **2.** (*wie e-n Verband*) her'umwickeln; **3.** einhüllen; **II** *s.* **4.** Binde *f*, Verband *m*; **5.** (Wickel-)Band *n*; **6.** ⚕ 'Umschlag *m*.

swathe² [sweɪð] → ***swath***.

swat·ter ['swɒtə] *s.* Fliegenklatsche *f*.

sway [sweɪ] **I** *v/i.* **1.** schwanken, schaukeln, sich wiegen; **2.** sich neigen; **3.** (**to**) *fig.* sich zuneigen (*dat.*) (*öffentliche Meinung etc.*); **4.** herrschen; **II** *v/t.* **5.** *et.* schwenken, schaukeln, wiegen; **6.** neigen; **7.** ⚓ *mst* ~ **up** *Masten etc.* aufheißen; **8.** *fig.* beeinflussen, lenken; **9.** beherrschen, herrschen über (*acc.*); *Publikum* mitreißen; **10.** *rhet. Zepter etc.* schwingen; **III** *s.* **11.** Schwanken *n*, Schaukeln *n*, Wiegen *n*; **12.** Schwung *m*, Wucht *f*; **13.** 'Übergewicht *n*; **14.** Einfluß *m*: ***under the ~ of*** unter dem Einfluß *od.* im Banne (*gen.*) (→ 15); **15.** Herrschaft *f*, Gewalt *f*, Macht *f*: ***hold ~ over*** beherrschen, herrschen über (*acc.*); ***under the ~ of*** in der Gewalt *od.* unter der Herrschaft (*gen.*).

swear [sweə] **I** *v/i.* [*irr.*] **1.** schwören, e-n Eid leisten (***on the Bible*** auf die Bibel): ***~ by*** a) bei *Gott etc.* schwören, b) F schwören auf (*acc.*), felsenfest glauben an (*acc.*); ***~ by all that's holy*** Stein u. Bein schwören; ***~ off*** F *e-m Laster* abschwören; ***~ to*** a) *et.* beschwören, b) *et.* geloben; **2.** fluchen (***at*** auf *acc.*); **II** *v/t.* [*irr.*] **3.** *Eid* schwören, leisten; **4.** *et.* beschwören, eidlich bekräftigen; ***~ out*** ⚖ *Am. Haftbefehl* durch eidliche Strafanzeige erwirken; **5.** *Rache, Treue etc.* schwören; **6.** *a.* ***~ in*** *j-n* vereidigen: ***~ s.o. into an office*** j-n in ein Amt einschwören; ***~ s.o. to secrecy*** j-n eidlich zur Verschwiegenheit verpflichten; **III** *s.* **7.** F Fluch *m*; **'swear·ing** [-ərɪŋ] *s.* **1.** Schwören *n*: ***~-in*** ⚖ Vereidigung *f*; **2.** Fluchen *n*; **'swear-word** *s.* Fluch(wort *n*) *m*.

sweat [swet] **I** *s.* **1.** Schweiß *m*: ***cold ~*** kalter Schweiß, Angstschweiß; ***by the ~ of one's brow*** im Schweiße s-s Angesichts; ***be in a ~*** a) in Schweiß gebadet sein, b) F (vor Angst, Erregung *etc.*) schwitzen; ***get into a ~*** in Schweiß geraten; ***no ~!*** F kein Problem!; **2.** Schwitzen *n*, Schweißausbruch *m*; **3.** ⚙ Ausschwitzung *f*, Feuchtigkeit *f*; **4.** F Plakke'rei *f*; **5.** ***old ~*** ⚔ *sl.* alter Haudegen *m*; **II** *v/i.* [*Am. irr.*] **6.** schwitzen (***with*** vor *dat.*); **7.** ⚙, *phys. etc.* schwitzen, anlaufen; gären (*Tabak*); **8.** F schwitzen, sich schinden; **9.** ☤ für e-n Hungerlohn arbeiten; **III** *v/t.* [*Am. irr.*] **10.** schwitzen: ***~ blood*** Blut schwitzen; ***~ out*** a) *Krankheit etc.* (her)ausschwitzen, b) *fig. et.* mühsam hervorbringen; ***~ it out*** F durchhalten, es durchstehen; **11.** *Kleidung* 'durchschwitzen; **12.** *j-n* schwitzen lassen (*a.* F *fig. im Verhör etc.*); *fig.* schuften lassen, *Arbeiter* ausbeuten; F *j-n* ‚bluten lassen'; **13.** ⚙ schwitzen *od.* gären lassen; *metall.* (***~ out*** aus)seigern; (heiß-, weich)löten; *Kabel* schweißen; **'~·band** *s.* Schweißleder *n* (*im Hut*); *bsd. sport* Schweißband *n*.

sweat·ed ['swetɪd] *adj.* ☤ **1.** für Hungerlöhne hergestellt; **2.** ausgebeutet, 'unterbezahlt; **'sweat·er** [-tə] *s.* **1.** Sweater *m*, Pull'over *m*; **2.** ☤ Ausbeuter *m*.

sweat gland *s. physiol.* Schweißdrüse *f*.

sweat·i·ness ['swetɪnɪs] *s.* Verschwitztheit *f*, Schweißigkeit *f*.

sweat·ing ['swetɪŋ] *s.* **1.** Schwitzen *n*; **2.** ☤ Ausbeutung *f*; ***~ bath*** *s.* ⚕ Schwitzbad *n*; ***~ sys·tem*** *s.* ☤ 'Ausbeutungssy‚stem *n*.

'sweat|·shirt *s.* Sweatshirt *n*; **'~·shop** *s.* ☤ Ausbeutungsbetrieb *m*; **'~·suit** *s.* Trainingsanzug *m*.

sweat·y ['swetɪ] *adj.* □ **1.** schweißig, verschwitzt; **2.** anstrengend.

Swede [swi:d] *s.* **1.** Schwede *m*, Schwedin *f*; **2.** ⚘ *Brit.* → ***Swedish turnip***.

Swed·ish ['swi:dɪʃ] **I** *adj.* **1.** schwedisch; **II** *s.* **2.** *ling.* Schwedisch *n*; **3.** ***the ~*** *coll.* die Schweden *pl.*; ***~ tur·nip*** *s.* ⚘ *Brit.* Schwedische Rübe, Gelbe Kohlrübe.

sweep [swi:p] **I** *v/t.* [*irr.*] **1.** kehren, fegen: ***~ away*** (***off***, ***up***) weg-(fort-, auf-) kehren; **2.** freimachen, säubern (***of*** von; *a. fig.*); **3.** hin'wegstreichen über (*acc.*) (*Wind etc.*); **4.** *Flut etc.* jagen, treiben: ***~ before one*** *Feind* vor sich her treiben; ***~ all before one*** *fig.* auf der ganzen Linie siegen; **5.** *a.* ***~ away*** (*od.* ***off***) *fig.* fort-, mitreißen (*Flut etc.*): ***~ along with one*** *Zuhörer* mitreißen; ***~ s.o. off his feet*** j-s Herz im Sturm erobern; **6.** *a.* ***~ away*** *Hindernis etc.* (aus dem Weg) räumen, *e-m Übelstand etc.* abhelfen, aufräumen mit: ***~ aside*** *et.* abtun, beiseite schieben; ***~ off*** *j-n* hinwegraffen (*Tod*, *Krankheit*); **7.** *mit der Hand* streichen über (*acc.*); **8.** *Geld* einstreichen: ***~ the board*** *Kartenspiel u. fig.* alles gewinnen; **9.** a) *Gebiet* durch'streifen, b) *Horizont etc.* absuchen (*a.* ⚔ *mit Scheinwerfern*, *Radar*) (***for*** nach), c) hingleiten über (*acc.*) (*Blick etc.*); **10.** ⚔ *mit MG-Feuer* bestreichen; **11.** ♪ *Saiten*, *Tasten* (be)rühren, schlagen, (hin)gleiten über (*acc.*); **II** *v/i.* [*irr.*] **12.** kehren, fegen; **13.** fegen, stürmen, jagen (*Wind*, *Regen etc.*, *a. Krieg*, *Heer*), fluten (*Wasser*, *Truppen etc.*); *durchs Land* gehen (*Epidemie etc.*): ***~ along*** (***down***, ***over***) entlang- *od.* einher- (hernieder-, darüber hin)fegen *etc.*; ***~ down on*** sich (herab-) stürzen auf (*acc.*); ***fear swept over him*** Furcht überkam ihn; **14.** maje'stätisch ein'herschreiten: ***she swept from the room*** sie rauschte aus dem Zimmer; **15.** in weitem Bogen gleiten; **16.** sich da'hinziehen (*Küste*, *Straße etc.*); **17.** (***for***) ⚓ (nach *et.*) dreggen; ⚔ *Minen* suchen, räumen; **III** *s.* **18.** Kehren *n*, Fegen *n*: ***give s.th. a ~*** et. kehren; ***make a clean ~*** (***of***) *fig.* gründlich aufräumen (mit); **19.** *mst pl.* Müll *m*; **20.** *bsd. Brit.* Schornsteinfeger *m*; **21.** Da'hinfegen *n*, (Da'hin)Stürmen *n* (*des Windes etc.*); **22.** schwungvolle (Hand- *etc.*)Bewegung; Schwung *m* (*e-r Sense*, *Waffe etc.*); (Ruder)Schlag *m*; **23.** *fig.* Reichweite *f*, Bereich *m*, Spielraum *m*; weiter (geistiger) Hori'zont; **24.** Schwung *m*, Bogen *m* (*Straße etc.*); **25.** ausgedehnte Strecke, weite Fläche; **26.** Auffahrt *f zu e-m Haus*; **27.** Ziehstange *f*, Schwengel *m* (*Brunnen*); **28.** ⚓ langes Ruder; **29.** ♪ Tusch *m*; **30.** *Radar*: Abtaststrahl *m*; **31.** *Kartenspiel*: Gewinn *m* aller Stiche *od.* Karten; **IV** *adj.* **32.** ⚡ Kipp…

'sweep·back ✈ **I** *s.* Pfeilform *f*; **II** *adj.* pfeilförmig, Pfeil…

sweep·er ['swi:pə] *s.* **1.** (Straßen-) Kehrer *m*, Feger(in); **2.** 'Kehrma‚schine *f*; **3.** ⚓ Such-, Räumboot *n*; **4.** *Fußball*: Ausputzer *m*; **'sweep·ing** [-pɪŋ] **I** *adj.* □ **1.** kehrend, Kehr…; **2.** sausend, stürmisch (*Wind etc.*); **3.** ausgedehnt; **4.** schwungvoll (*a. fig. mitreißend*); **5.** 'durchschlagend, über'wältigend (*Sieg*, *Erfolg*); **6.** 'durchgreifend, radi'kal: ***~ changes***; **7.** um'fassend, weitreichend, *a.* (zu) stark verallgemeinernd, sum'marisch: ***~ statement***; **II** *s.* **8.** *pl.* a) → ***sweep*** 19, b) *fig. contp.* Abschaum *m*.

sweep| net *s.* **1.** ⚓ Schleppnetz *n*; **2.** Schmetterlingsnetz *n*; **'~·stake** *s. sport* **1.** *sg. od. pl.* a) *Pferderennen, dessen Dotierung rein aus Nenngeldern besteht*, b) *aus den Nenngeldern gebildete Dotierung*; **2.** *Lotterie, deren Gewinne sich ausschließlich aus den Einsätzen zs.-setzen*; **3.** *fig.* Rennen *n*, Kampf *m*.

sweet [swi:t] **I** *adj.* □ **1.** süß (*im Geschmack*); **2.** süß, lieblich (duftend): ***be ~ with*** duften nach; **3.** frisch (*Butter*, *Fleisch*, *Milch*); **4.** Frisch…, Süß…: ***~ water***; **5.** süß, lieblich (*Musik*, *Stimme*), **6.** süß, angenehm: ***~ dreams***; ***~ sleep***; **7.** süß, lieb: ***~ face***; ***at her own ~ will*** (ganz) nach ihrem Köpfchen; → ***seventeen*** II; **8.** (***to*** zu *od.* gegenüber *j-m*) lieb, nett, freundlich, sanft: ***~ nature*** *od.* ***temper***; ***be ~ on s.o.*** in j-n verliebt sein; **9.** F ‚süß', reizend, goldig (*alle a. iro.*): ***what a ~ dress!***; **10.** leicht, bequem; glatt, ruhig; **11.** ⚗ a) säurefrei (*Mineralien*), b) schwefelfrei, süß (*bsd. Benzin*, *Rohöl*); **12.** ✓ nicht sauer (*Boden*); **13.** *Jazz*: ‚sweet', melodi'ös; **II** *s.* **14.** Süße *f*; **15.** *Brit.* a) Bon'bon *m*, *n*, Süßigkeit *f*, b) *oft pl.* Nachtisch *m*, Süßspeise *f*; **16.** *mst pl. fig.* Freude *f*, Annehmlichkeit *f*: ***the ~(s) of life***; → ***sour*** 7; **17.** *mst in der Anrede*: Liebling *m*, Süße(r *m*) *f*; **‚~-and-'sour** *adj.* süß-sauer (*Soße etc.*); **'~·bread** *s.* Bries n; ***~ chest·nut*** *s.* 'Edelka‚stanie *f*; ***~ corn*** *s.* **1.** ⚘ Zuckermais *m*; **2.** grüne Maiskolben *pl.*

sweet·en ['swi:tn] **I** *v/t.* **1.** süßen; **2.** *fig.* versüßen, angenehm(er) machen; **II** *v/i.* **3.** süß(er) werden; **4.** milder *od.* sanfter werden; **'sweet·en·er** [-nə] *s.* Süßstoff *m*.

'sweet|·heart *s.* Liebste(r *m*) *f*, Schatz *m*; ***~ herbs*** *s. pl.* Küchen-, Gewürzkräuter *pl.*

sweet·ie ['swi:tɪ] *s.* **1.** F Schätzchen *n*, ‚Süße' *f*; **2.** *Brit.* Bon'bon *m*, *n*, *pl. a.* Süßigkeiten *pl.*

sweet·ing ['swi:tɪŋ] *s.* ⚘ Jo'hannisapfel *m*, Süßling *m*.

sweet·ish ['swi:tɪʃ] *adj.* süßlich.

'sweet|·meat *s.* Bon'bon *m*, *n*; **‚~-'na·tured** → ***sweet*** 8.

sweet·ness ['swi:tnɪs] *s.* **1.** Süße *f*, Süßigkeit *f*; **2.** süßer Duft; **3.** Frische *f*; **4.** *fig. et.* Angenehmes, Annehmlichkeit *f*, *das* Süße; **5.** Freundlichkeit *f*, Liebenswürdigkeit *f*.

sweet| oil *s.* O'livenöl *n*; ***~ pea*** *s.* ⚘ Gartenwicke *f*; ***~ po·ta·to*** *s.* ⚘ 'Süßkar‚toffel *f*, Ba'tate *f*; **‚~'scent·ed** *adj. bsd.* ⚘ wohlriechend, duftend; **'~·shop** *s. bsd. Brit.* Süßwarengeschäft *n*; **'~-talk** *v/t. Am.* F *j-m* schmeicheln; **‚~-'tem·pered** *adj.* sanft-, gutmütig; ***~ tooth*** *s.* F: ***she has a ~*** sie ißt gern Süßigkeiten; ***~ wil·liam*** *s.* ⚘ Stu'dentennelke *f*.

sweet·y ['swi:tɪ] → ***sweetie***.

swell [swel] **I** *v/i.* [*irr.*] **1.** *a.* ***~ up***, ***~ out*** (an-, auf)schwellen (***into***, ***to*** zu), dick werden; **2.** sich aufblasen *od.* -blähen (*a. fig.*); **3.** anschwellen, (an)steigen

(*Wasser etc.*, *a. fig. Preise*, *Anzahl etc.*); **4.** sich wölben: a) ansteigen (*Land etc.*), b) sich ausbauchen *od.* bauschen (*Mauerwerk*, *Möbel etc.*), c) ⚓ sich blähen (*Segel*); **5.** her'vorbrechen (*Quelle*, *Tränen*); **6.** *bsd.* ♪ a) anschwellen (***into*** zu), b) (an- u. ab-) schwellen (*Ton*, *Orgel etc.*); **7.** *fig.* bersten (wollen) (***with*** vor): ***his heart ~s with indignation***; **8.** aufwallen, sich steigern (***into*** zu) (*Gefühl*); **II** *v/t.* [*irr.*] **9.** ***~ up***, ***~ out*** *a.* ♪ *u. fig. Buch etc.* anschwellen lassen; **10.** aufblasen, -blähen, -treiben; **11.** *fig.* aufblähen (***with*** vor): ***~ed*** (***with pride***) stolzgeschwellt; **III** *s.* **12.** (An)Schwellen *n*; **13.** Schwellung *f*; **14.** ⚓ Dünung *f*; **15.** Wölbung *f*, Ausbauchung *f*; **16.** kleine Anhöhe, sanfte Steigung; **17.** *fig.* Anschwellen *n*, -wachsen *n*, (An)Steigen *n*; **18.** ♪ a) An- (u. Ab)Schwellen *n*, b) Schwellzeichen *n*, c) Schwellwerk *n* (*Orgel etc.*); **19.** F a) ‚hohes Tier', ‚Größe' *f*, b) ‚feiner Pinkel', c) ‚Ka'none' *f*, ‚Mordskerl' *m* (***at*** in *dat.*); **IV** *adj.* **20.** (*a. int.*) F ‚prima', ‚bombig'; **21.** F (tod)schick, ‚piekfein', feu'dal; **swelled** [-ld] *adj.* **1.** (an)geschwollen, aufgebläht: ***~ head*** F *fig.* Aufgeblasenheit *f*; **2.** geschweift (*Möbel*); '**swell·ing** [-lɪŋ] **I** *s.* **1.** (*a. fig. u.* ♪ An)Schwellen *n*; **2.** ⚕ Schwellung *f*, Geschwulst *f*, *a.* Beule *f*: ***hunger ~*** Hungerödem *n*; **3.** Wölbung *f*: a) Erhöhung *f*, b) ⚠ Ausbauchung *f*, ⚙ Schweifung *f*; **II** *adj.* □ **4.** (an)schwellend; **5.** ‚geschwollen' (*Stil etc.*).

swell| man·u·al *s.* ♪ 'Schwellmanu,al *n* (*Orgel*); **~ mob** *s. sl. die* Hochstapler *pl.*; **~ or·gan** *s.* ♪ Schwellwerk *n*.

swel·ter ['sweltə] **I** *v/i.* **1.** vor Hitze (fast) 'umkommen *od.* verschmachten; **2.** in Schweiß gebadet sein; **3.** (vor Hitze) kochen (*Stadt etc.*); **II** *s.* **4.** drückende Hitze, Schwüle *f*; **5.** F *fig.* Hexenkessel *m*; '**swel·ter·ing** [-tərɪŋ], '**swel·try** [-trɪ] *adj.* **1.** vor Hitze vergehend, verschmachtend; **2.** in Schweiß gebadet; **3.** drückend, schwül.

swept [swept] *pret. u. p.p. von* ***sweep***; '**~-back wing** → ***swept wing***; **~ vol·ume** *s. mot.* Hubraum *m*; **~ wing** *s.* ✈ Pfeilflügel *m*.

swerve [swɜːv] **I** *v/i.* **1.** ausbrechen (*Auto*, *Pferd*); **2.** *mot.* das Steuer her'umreißen; **3.** ausweichen; **4.** schwenken (*Straße*); **5.** *fig.* abweichen (***from*** von); **II** *v/t.* **6.** *sport Ball* anschneiden; **7.** *fig. j-n* abbringen (***from*** von); **III** *s.* **8.** Ausweichbewegung *f*, *mot.* Schlenker *m*.

swift [swɪft] **I** *adj.* □ **1.** *allg.* schnell, rasch; **2.** flüchtig (*Zeit*, *Stunde etc.*); **3.** geschwind, eilig; **4.** flink, hurtig, *a.* geschickt: ***a ~ worker***; ***~ wit*** rasche Auffassungsgabe; **5.** rasch, schnell bereit: ***~ to anger*** jähzornig; ***~ to take offence*** leicht beleidigt; **II** *adv.* **6.** *mst poet. od. in Zssgn* schnell, geschwind, rasch; **III** *s.* **7.** *orn.* (*bsd.* Mauer)Segler *m*; **8.** *e-e brit. Taubenrasse*; **9.** *zo.* → ***newt***; **10.** ⚙ Haspel *f*; ,**swift'foot·ed** *adj.* schnellfüßig, flink; '**swift·ness** [-nɪs] *s.* Schnelligkeit *f*.

swig [swɪg] F **I** *v/t. Getränk* ‚hin'unterkippen'; **II** *v/i.* e-n kräftigen Schluck nehmen (***at*** aus); **III** *s.* (kräftiger) Schluck.

swill [swɪl] **I** *v/t.* **1.** *bsd. Brit.* (ab)spülen: ***~ out*** ausspülen; **2.** *Bier etc.* ‚saufen'; **II** *v/i.* **3.** ‚saufen'; **III** *s.* **4.** (Ab)Spülen *n*; **5.** Schweinetrank *m*, -futter *n*; **6.** Spülicht *n* (*a. fig. contp.*); **7.** *fig. contp.* a) ‚Gesöff' *n*, b) ‚Saufraß' *m*.

swim [swɪm] **I** *v/i.* [*irr.*] **1.** schwimmen; **2.** schwimmen (*Gegenstand*), treiben; **3.** schweben, (sanft) gleiten; **4.** a) schwimmen (***in*** in *dat.*), b) über'schwemmt sein, 'überfließen (***with*** von): ***his eyes were ~ming with tears*** s-e Augen schwammen in Tränen; ***~ in*** *fig.* schwimmen in (*Geld etc.*); **5.** (ver-) schwimmen (***before one's eyes*** vor den Augen): ***my head ~s*** mir ist schwind(e)lig; **II** *v/t.* [*irr.*] **6.** *Strecke etc.* schwimmen, *Gewässer* durch'schwimmen; **7.** *Person*, *Pferd etc.* schwimmen lassen; **8.** F mit *j-m* um die Wette schwimmen; **III** *s.* **9.** Schwimmen *n*, Bad *n*: ***go for a ~*** schwimmen gehen; ***be in*** (***out of***) ***the ~*** F *fig.* a) (nicht) auf dem laufenden sein, b) (nicht) mithalten können; **10.** *Angelsport*: tiefe u. fischreiche Stelle (*e-s Flusses*); **11.** Schwindel(anfall) *m*; '**swim·mer** [-mə] *s.* **1.** Schwimmer(in); **2.** *zo.* 'Schwimmor,gan *n*.

swim·mer·et ['swɪmərət] *s. zo.* Schwimmfuß *m* (*Krebs*).

swim·ming ['swɪmɪŋ] **I** *s.* **1.** Schwimmen *n*; **2.** ***~ of the head*** Schwindelgefühl *n*; **II** *adj.* □ → ***swimmingly***; **3.** Schwimm…; **~ bath** *s.* Schwimmbad *n*; **~ blad·der** *s. zo.* Schwimmblase *f*.

swim·ming·ly ['swɪmɪŋlɪ] *adv. fig.* glatt, reibungslos.

swim·ming| pool *s.* **1.** Schwimmbecken *n*, Swimmingpool *m*; **2.** Schwimmbad *n*: a) Freibad *n*, b) *mst* ***indoor ~*** Hallenbad *n*; **~ trunks** *s. pl.* Badehose *f*.

swin·dle ['swɪndl] **I** *v/i.* **1.** betrügen, mogeln; **II** *v/t.* **2.** *j-n* beschwindeln, betrügen (***out of s.th.*** um et.); **3.** *et.* erschwindeln (***out of s.o.*** von j-m); **III** *s.* **4.** Schwindel *m*, Betrug *m*; '**swin·dler** [-lə] *s.* Schwindler(in), Betrüger(in).

swine [swaɪn] *pl.* **swine** *s. zo.*, *mst* ✓, *poet. od. obs.* Schwein *n* (*a. fig. contp.*); **~ fe·ver** *s. vet.* Schweinepest *f*; '**~·herd** *s. poet.* Schweinehirt *m*; '**~·pox** *s.* **1.** ⚕ *hist.* Wasserpocken *pl.*; **2.** *vet.* Schweinepocken *pl.*

swing [swɪŋ] **I** *v/t.* [*irr.*] **1.** *Stock*, *Keule*, *Lasso etc.* schwingen; **2.** *Glocke etc.* schwingen, (hin- u. her)schwenken: ***~ one's arms*** mit den Armen schlenkern; ***~ s.th. about*** et. (im Kreis) herumschwenken; **3.** *Beine etc.* baumeln lassen, *a. Tür etc.* pendeln lassen; *Hängematte etc.* aufhängen (***from*** an *dat.*): ***~ open*** (***to***) *Tor* auf-(zu)stoßen; **4.** *j-n in e-r Schaukel* schaukeln; **5.** *auf die Schulter etc.* (hoch)schwingen; **6.** ⚔ (***~ in*** *od.* ***out*** ein- *od.* aus)schwenken lassen; **7.** ⚓ (rund)schwojen; **8.** *bsd. Am.* F a) *et.* ‚schaukeln', ‚hinkriegen', b) *Wähler* her'umkriegen; **II** *v/i.* [*irr.*] **9.** (hin- u. her)schwingen, pendeln, ausschlagen (*Pendel*, *Zeiger*): ***~ into motion*** in Schwung *od.* Gang kommen; **10.** schweben, baumeln (***from*** an *dat.*) (*Glocke etc.*); **11.** (sich) schaukeln; **12.** F ‚baumeln' (*gehängt werden*): ***he must ~ for it***; **13.** sich (*in den Angeln*) drehen (*Tür etc.*): ***~ open*** (***to***) auffliegen (zuschlagen); ***~ round*** a) sich ruckartig umdrehen, b) sich drehen (*Wind etc.*), c) *fig.* umschlagen (*öffentliche Meinung etc.*); **14.** ⚓ schwojen; **15.** schwenken, mit schwungvollen Bewegungen gehen, (flott) marschieren: ***~ into line*** ⚔ einschwenken; **16.** *a.* ***~ it*** *sl.* a) ‚toll leben', b) ‚auf den Putz hauen'; **17.** schwanken; **18.** (zum Schlag) ausholen: ***~ at*** nach *j-m* schlagen; **19.** ♪ swingen; **III** *s.* **20.** (Hin- u. Her)Schwingen *n*, Pendeln *n*, Schwingung *f*; ⚙ Schwungweite *f*, Ausschlag *m* (*e-s Pendels od. Zeigers*): ***the ~ of the pendulum*** der Pendelschlag (*a. fig. od. pol.*); ***free ~*** Bewegungsfreiheit *f*, Spielraum *m* (*a. fig.*); ***in full ~*** in vollem Gange, im Schwung; ***give full ~ to*** a) *e-r Sache* freien Lauf lassen, b) *j-m* freie Hand lassen; **21.** Schaukeln *n*; **22.** a) Schwung *m beim Gehen*, *Skilauf etc.*, schwingender Gang, Schlenkern *n*, b) ♪ *etc.* Schwung *m*, (schwingender) Rhythmus: ***go with a ~*** a) Schwung haben, b) *fig.* wie am Schnürchen gehen; **23.** ♪ Swing *m* (*Jazz*); **24.** Schaukel *f*: ***lose on the ~s what you make on the roundabouts*** *fig.* genau so weit sein wie am Anfang; ***you make up on the ~s what you lose on the roundabouts*** was man hier verliert, macht man dort wieder wett; **25.** ✝ a) Swing *m*, Spielraum *m* für Kre'ditgewährung, b) *Am.* F Konjunk'turperi,ode *f*; **26.** *Boxen*: Schwinger *m*; **27.** Schwenkung *f*; '**~·back** *s.* **1.** *phot.* Einstellscheibe *f*; **2.** *fig.* (***to***) Rückkehr *f* (zu), Rückfall *m* (in *acc.*); '**~·boat** *s.* Schiffsschaukel *f*; **~ bridge** *s.* Drehbrücke *f*; **~ cred·it** *s.* ✝ 'Swingkre,dit *m*; **~ door** *s.* Pendeltür *f*.

swinge [swɪndʒ] *v/t. obs.* 'durchprügeln, (aus)peitschen; '**swinge·ing** [-dʒɪŋ] *adj. fig.* drastisch, ex'trem.

swing·er ['swɪŋə] *s. sl.* lebenslustige Per'son.

swing·ing ['swɪŋɪŋ] *adj.* □ **1.** schwingend, schaukelnd, pendelnd, Schwing…; **2.** Schwenk…; **3.** rhythmisch, schwungvoll; **4.** lebenslustig; **5.** schwankend: ***~ temperature*** ⚕ Temperaturschwankungen *pl.*

swin·gle [swɪŋgl] **I** *s.* ⚙ (Flachs-, Hanf-) Schwinge *f*; **II** *Flachs*, *Hanf* schwingeln; '**~·tree** *s.* Ortscheit *n*, Wagenschwengel *m*.

'**swing|-out** *adj.* ⚙ ausschwenkbar; **~ seat** *s.* Hollywoodschaukel *f*; **~ shift** *s. Am.* ✝ Spätschicht *f*; '**~-wing** *s.* ✈ **1.** Schwenkflügel *m*; **2.** Schwenkflügler *m*.

swin·ish ['swaɪnɪʃ] *adj.* □ schweinisch, säuisch.

swipe [swaɪp] **I** *v/i.* **1.** dreinschlagen, hauen; *sport* aus vollem Arm schlagen; **II** *v/t.* **2.** (hart) schlagen; **3.** *sl.* ‚klauen', stehlen; **III** *s.* **4.** *bsd. sport* harter Schlag, Hieb *m*; **5.** *pl. sl.* Dünnbier *n*.

swirl [swɜːl] **I** *v/i.* **1.** wirbeln (*Wasser*, *a. fig. Kopf*), e-n Strudel bilden; **2.** (her'um)wirbeln; **II** *v/t.* **3.** *et.* her'umwirbeln; **III** *s.* **4.** Wirbel *m*, Strudel *m*; **5.** *Am.* (Haar)Wirbel *m*; **6.** Wirbel(n *n*) *m* (*Drehbewegung*).

swish [swɪʃ] **I** *v/i.* **1.** schwirren, zischen, sausen; **2.** rascheln (*Seide*); **II** *v/t.* **3.** sausen *od.* schwirren lassen; **4.** *Brit.* 'durchprügeln; **III** *s.* **5.** Sausen *n*, Zischen *n*; **6.** Rascheln *n*; **7.** *Brit.* (Ruten-) Streich *m*, Peitschenhieb *m*; **IV** *adj.* **8.**

Brit. sl. ‚(tod)schick'.

Swiss [swɪs] **I** *pl.* **Swiss** *s.* **1.** Schweizer (-in); **2.** ⚙ ♀, *a.* ~ ***muslin*** 'Schweizermusse,lin *m* (*Stoff*); **II** *adj.* **3.** schweizerisch, Schweizer: ~ ***German*** Schweizerdeutsch *n*; ~ ***Guard*** *R.C.* a) Schweizergarde *f*, b) Schweizer *m*; ~ ***roll*** Biskuitrolle *f*.

switch [swɪtʃ] **I** *s.* **1.** Gerte *f*, Rute *f*; **2.** (Ruten)Streich *m*; **3.** falscher Zopf; **4.** ⚡, ⚙ Schalter *m*; **5.** 🚂 Weiche *f*; **6.** (***to***) *fig.* a) 'Umstellung *f* (auf *acc.*), Wechsel *m* (zu), b) Verwandlung *f* (in *acc.*), c) Vertauschung *f*; **II** *v/t.* **7.** peitschen; **8.** zucken mit; **9.** ⚡, ⚙ ('um)schalten: ~ ***on*** einschalten, *Licht* anschalten, *teleph. j-n* verbinden; ~ ***off*** *Gerät etc.* ab-, ausschalten, abstellen, *teleph. j-n* trennen; ~ ***to*** anschließen an (*acc.*); **10.** 🚂 a) *Zug* rangieren, b) *Waggons* 'umstellen; **11.** *fig. Produktion etc.* 'umstellen, *Methode, Thema etc.* wechseln, *Gedanken, Gespräch* 'überleiten (***to*** auf *acc.*); **III** *v/i.* **12.** 🚂 rangieren; **13.** ⚡, ⚙ (*a.* ~ ***over*** 'um)schalten; ~ ***off*** abschalten, *teleph.* trennen; **14.** *fig.* 'umstellen: ~ (***off*** *od.* ***over***) ***to*** übergehen zu, sich umstellen auf (*acc.*), *univ. etc.* umsatteln auf (*acc.*); '~·**back** *s. Brit.* **1.** *a.* ~ ***road*** Serpen'tinenstraße *f*; **2.** Achterbahn *f*; '~·**blade knife** *s.* Schnappmesser *n*; '~·**board** *s.* ⚡ **1.** Schaltbrett *n*, -tafel *f*; **2.** (Tele'fon)Zen,trale *f*, Vermittlung *f*: ~ ***operator*** Telefonist(in); ~ **box** *s.* **1.** ⚡ Schaltkasten *m*; **2.** 🚂 Stellwerk *n*.

switch·er·oo [,swɪtʃə'ru:] *s. Am. sl.* **1.** unerwartete Wendung; **2.** → ***switch*** 6 b u. c.

switch·ing ['swɪtʃɪŋ] **I** *s.* **1.** ⚡, ⚙ ('Um-) Schalten *n*; ~***-on*** Einschalten; ~***-off*** Ab-, Ausschalten; **2.** 🚂 Rangieren *n*; **II** *adj.* **3.** ⚡, ⚙ (Um)Schalt...; **4.** 🚂 Rangier...

switch| plug *s.* ⚡, ⚙ Schaltstöpsel *m*; '~·**yard** *s.* 🚂 *Am.* Rangier-, Verschiebebahnhof *m*.

swiv·el ['swɪvl] **I** *s.* Drehzapfen *m*, -ring *m*, -gelenk *n*, (⚓ Ketten)Wirbel *m*; **II** *v/t.* (*auf e-m Zapfen etc.*) drehen *od.* schwenken; **III** *v/i.* sich drehen; **IV** *adj.* dreh-, schwenkbar, Dreh..., Schwenk...; ~ **bridge** *s.* ⚙ Drehbrücke *f*; ~ **chair** *s.* Drehstuhl *m*; ~ **joint** *s.* ⚙ Drehgelenk *n*.

swiz·zle stick ['swɪzl] *s.* Sektquirl *m*.

swol·len ['swəʊlən] **I** *p.p. von* ***swell***; **II** *adj.* ⚕ geschwollen (*a. fig.*): ~***-headed*** aufgeblasen.

swoon [swu:n] **I** *v/i. oft* ~ ***away*** in Ohnmacht fallen (***with*** vor *dat.*); **II** *s.* Ohnmacht(sanfall *m*) *f*.

swoop [swu:p] **I** *v/i.* **1.** *oft* ~ ***down*** ([***up***]***on***, ***at***) her'abstoßen, sich stürzen (auf *acc.*), *fig.* zuschlagen, herfallen (über *acc.*); **II** *v/t.* **2.** *mst* ~ ***up*** F packen, ‚schnappen'; **III** *s.* **3.** Her'abstoßen *n* (*Raubvogel*); **4.** *fig.* a) 'Überfall *m*, b) Razzia *f*; **5.** ***at one*** (***fell***) ~ mit 'einem Schlag.

swop [swɒp] → ***swap***.

sword [sɔ:d] *s.* Schwert *n* (*a. fig.*); Säbel *m*, Degen *m*; *allg.* Waffe *f*: ***draw*** (***sheathe***) ***the*** ~ das Schwert ziehen (in die Scheide stecken), *fig.* den Kampf beginnen (beenden); ***put to the*** ~ über die Klinge springen lassen; → ***cross*** 11, ***measure*** 16; ~ **belt** *s.* **1.** Schwertgehenk *n*; **2.** ⚔ Degenkoppel *n*; ~ **cane** *s.* Stockdegen *m*; ~ **dance** *s.* Schwert(er)tanz *m*; '~·**fish** *s.* Schwertfisch *m*; ~ **knot** *s.* ⚔ Degen-, Säbelquaste *f*; ~ **lil·y** *s.* ⚘ Schwertel *m*, Siegwurz *f*; '~·**play** *s.* **1.** (Degen-, Säbel)Kampf *m*; **2.** Fechtkunst *f*; **3.** *fig.* Gefecht *n*, Du'ell *n*.

swords·man ['sɔ:dzmən] *s.* [*irr.*] Fechter *m*; Kämpfer *m*; '**swords·man·ship** [-ʃɪp] *s.* Fechtkunst *f*.

'**sword·stick** → ***sword cane***.

swore [swɔ:] *pret. von* ***swear***; **sworn** [swɔ:n] **I** *p.p. von* ***swear***; **II** *adj.* **1.** ⚖ (gerichtlich) vereidigt, beeidigt: ~ ***expert***; **2.** eidlich: ~ ***statement***; **3.** geschworen (*Gegner*): ~ ***enemies*** Todfeinde; **4.** verschworen (*Freunde*).

swot [swɒt] *ped. Brit.* F **I** *v/i.* **1.** büffeln, pauken; **II** *v/t.* **2.** *mst* ~ ***up*** *Lehrstoff* pauken, büffeln; **III** *s.* **3.** Büffler(in), Streber(in); **4.** Büffe'lei *f*, Pauke'rei *f*; *weitS.* hartes Stück Arbeit.

swung [swʌŋ] *pret. u. p.p. von* ***swing***.

syb·a·rite ['sɪbəraɪt] *s. fig.* Syba'rit *m*, Genußmensch *m*; **syb·a·rit·ic** [,sɪbə'rɪtɪk] *adj.* (□ ~***ally***) syba'ritisch, genußsüchtig; '**syb·a·rit·ism** [-rɪtɪzəm] *s.* Genußsucht *f*.

syc·a·more ['sɪkəmɔ:] *s.* ⚘ **1.** *Am.* Pla'tane *f*; **2.** *a.* ~ ***maple*** *Brit.* Bergahorn *m*; **3.** Syko'more *f*, Maulbeerfeigenbaum *m*.

syc·o·phan·cy ['sɪkəfənsɪ] *s.* Krieche'rei *f*, Speichellecke'rei *f*; '**syc·o·phant** [-nt] *s.* Schmeichler *m*, Kriecher *m*, Speichellecker *m*; **syc·o·phan·tic** [,sɪkəʊ'fæntɪk] *adj.* (□ ~***ally***) schmeichlerisch, kriecherisch.

syl·la·bar·y ['sɪləbərɪ] *s.* 'Silbenta,belle *f*; '**syl·la·bi** [-baɪ] *pl. von.* ***syllabus***.

syl·lab·ic [sɪ'læbɪk] *adj.* (□ ~***ally***) **1.** syl'labisch (*a.* ♪), Silben...: ~ ***accent***; **2.** silbenbildend, silbisch; **3.** *in Zssgn* ...silbig; **syl'lab·i·cate** [-keɪt], **syl'lab·i·fy** [-ɪfaɪ], **syl·la·bize** ['sɪləbaɪz] *v/t. ling.* syllabieren, in Silben teilen, Silbe für Silbe (aus)sprechen.

syl·la·ble ['sɪləbl] **I** *s.* **1.** *ling.* Silbe *f*: ***not a*** ~ *fig.* keine Silbe *od.* kein Sterbenswörtchen *sagen*; **2.** ♪ Tonsilbe *f*; **II** *v/t.* **3.** → ***syllabicate***; '**syl·la·bled** [-ld] *adj.* ...silbig.

syl·la·bus ['sɪləbəs] *pl.* **-bi** [-baɪ] *s.* **1.** Auszug *m*, Abriß *m*; zs.-fassende Inhaltsangabe; **2.** (*bsd.* Vorlesungs)Verzeichnis *n*; Lehr-, 'Unterrichtsplan *m*; **3.** ⚖ Kom'pendium *n von richtungweisenden Entscheidungen*; **4.** *R.C.* Syllabus *m*.

syl·lep·sis [sɪ'lepsɪs] *s. ling.* Syl'lepsis, Syl'lepse *f*.

syl·lo·gism ['sɪlədʒɪzəm] *s. phls.* Syllo'gismus *m*, (Vernunft)Schluß *m*; '**syl·lo·gize** [-dʒaɪz] *v/i.* syllogisieren, folgerichtig denken.

sylph [sɪlf] *s.* **1.** *myth.* Sylphe *m*, Luftgeist *m*; **2.** *fig.* Syl'phide *f*, gra'ziles Mädchen; '**sylph·ish** [-fɪʃ], '**sylph·like** [-laɪk], '**sylph·y** [-fɪ] *adj.* sylphenhaft, gra'zil.

syl·van ['sɪlvən] *adj. poet.* waldig, Wald...

sym·bi·o·sis [,sɪmbɪ'əʊsɪs] *s. biol. u. fig.* Symbi'ose *f*; ,**sym·bi'ot·ic** [-ɪ'ɒtɪk] *adj.* (□ ~***ally***) *biol.* symbi'o(n)tisch.

sym·bol ['sɪmbl] *s.* Sym'bol *n*, Sinnbild *n*, Zeichen *n*; **sym·bol·ic**, **sym·bol·i·cal** [sɪm'bɒlɪk(l)] *adj.* □ sym'bolisch, sinnbildlich (***of*** für): ***be*** ~ ***of s.th.*** et. versinnbildlichen; **sym·bol·ics** [sɪm'bɒlɪks] *s. pl. mst sg. konstr.* **1.** Studium *n* alter Sym'bole; **2.** *eccl.* Sym'bolik *f*; '**sym·bol·ism** [-bəlɪzəm] *s.* **1.** Sym'bolik *f* (*a. eccl.*), sym'bolische Darstellung; ⩘ Forma'lismus *m*; **2.** sym'bolische Bedeutung; **3.** *coll.* Sym'bole *pl.*; **4.** *paint. etc.* Symbo'lismus *m*; '**sym·bol·ize** [-bəlaɪz] *v/t.* **1.** symbolisieren: a) versinnbildlichen, b) sinnbildlich darstellen; **2.** sym'bolisch auffassen.

sym·met·ric, **sym·met·ri·cal** [sɪ'metrɪk(l)] *adj.* □ sym'metrisch, eben-, gleichmäßig: ~ ***axis*** ⩘ Symmetrieachse *f*; **sym·me·trize** ['sɪmɪtraɪz] *v/t.* sym'metrisch machen; **sym·me·try** ['sɪmɪtrɪ] *s.* Symme'trie *f* (*a. fig. Ebenmaß*).

sym·pa·thet·ic [,sɪmpə'θetɪk] **I** *adj.* (□ ~***ally***) **1.** mitfühlend, teilnehmend: ~ ***strike*** Sympathiestreik *m*; **2.** einfühlend, verständnisvoll; **3.** gleichgesinnt, geistesverwandt, kongeni'al; **4.** sym'pathisch; **5.** F wohlwollend (***to***[***ward***] gegen['über]); **6.** sympa'thetisch (*Kur, Tinte etc.*); **7.** ⚕, *physiol.* sym'pathisch (*Nervensystem etc.*); → 9a; **8.** ♪, *phys.* mitschwingend: ~ ***vibration*** Sympathieschwingung *f*; **II** *s.* **9.** a) *a.* ~ ***nerve*** *physiol.* Sym'pathikus(nerv) *m*, b) Sym'pathikussys,tem *n*.

sym·pa·thize ['sɪmpəθaɪz] *v/i.* **1.** (***with***) a) sympathisieren (mit), gleichgesinnt sein (*dat.*), b) über'einstimmen (mit), wohlwollend gegen'überstehen (*dat.*), c) mitfühlen (mit); **2.** sein Mitgefühl *od.* Beileid ausdrücken (***with*** *dat.*); **3.** ⚕ in Mitleidenschaft gezogen werden (***with*** von); '**sym·pa·thiz·er** [-zə] *s.* j-d, der *mit j-m od. e-r Sache* sympathisiert, Anhänger(in), *bsd. pol.* Sympathi'sant(in); '**sym·pa·thy** [-θɪ] *s.* **1.** Sympa'thie *f*, Zuneigung *f* (***for*** für): ~ ***strike*** Sympathiestreik *m*; **2.** Gleichgestimmtheit *f*; **3.** Mitleid *n*, -gefühl *n* (***with*** mit, ***for*** für): ***feel*** ~ ***for*** (*od.* ***with***) Mitleid haben mit *j-m*, Anteil nehmen an *e-r Sache*; **4.** *pl.* (An)Teilnahme *f*, Beileid *n*: ***letter of*** ~ Beileidschreiben *n*; ***offer one's sympathies to s.o.*** j-m sein Beileid bezeigen, j-m kondolieren; **5.** ⚕ Mitleidenschaft *f*; **6.** Wohlwollen *n*, Zustimmung *f*; **7.** Über'einstimmung *f*, Einklang *m*; **8.** *biol., psych.* Sympa'thie *f*, Wechselwirkung *f*.

sym·phon·ic [sɪm'fɒnɪk] *adj.* (□ ~***ally***) sin'fonisch, sym'phonisch, Sinfonie..., Symphonie...: ~ ***poem*** ♪ symphonische Dichtung; **sym'pho·ni·ous** [-'fəʊnjəs] *adj.* har'monisch (*a. fig.*); **sym·pho·nist** ['sɪmfənɪst] *s.* ♪ Sin'foniker *m*, Sym'phoniker *m*; **sym·pho·ny** ['sɪmfənɪ] **I** *s.* **1.** ♪ Sinfo'nie *f*, Sympho'nie *f*; **2.** *fig.* (*Farben- etc.*)Sympho'nie *f*, (*a. häusliche etc.*) Harmo'nie, Zs.-klang *m*; **II** *adj.* **3.** Sinfonie..., Symphonie...: ~ ***orchestra***.

sym·po·si·um [sɪm'pəʊzjəm] *pl.* **-si·a** [-zjə] *s.* **1.** *antiq.* Sym'posion *n*: a) Gastmahl *n*, b) *Titel philosophischer Dialoge*; **2.** *fig.* Sammlung *f* von Beiträgen (*über e-e Streitfrage*); **3.** Sym'posium *n*, (Fach)Tagung *f*.

symp·tom ['sɪmptəm] *s.* ⚕ *u. fig.* Sym-

ˈptom *n* (*of* für, von), (An)Zeichen *n*; **symp·to·mat·ic**, **symp·to·mat·i·cal** [ˌsɪmptəˈmætɪk(l)] *adj.* □ *bsd.* ⚕ sympˈtoˈmatisch (*a. fig. bezeichnend*) (***of*** für); **symp·tom·a·tol·o·gy** [ˌsɪmptəməˈtɒlədʒɪ] *s.* ⚕ Symptomatoloˈgie *f.*

syn- [sɪn] *in Zssgn* mit, zusammen.

syn·a·gogue [ˈsɪnəgɒg] *s. eccl.* Synaˈgoge *f.*

syn·a·l(o)e·pha [ˌsɪnəˈliːfə] *s. ling.* Synaˈloiphe *f*, Verschleifung *f.*

syn·an·ther·ous [sɪˈnænθərəs] *adj.* ⚘ synˈandrisch: **~ *plant*** Korbblüt(l)er *m*, Komposite *f.*

sync [sɪŋk] F *für* a) ***synchronization*** 1: ***in*** (***out of***) **~** (nicht) synchron, *fig.* (nicht) in Einklang, b) ***synchronize*** 5.

syn·carp [ˈsɪnkɑːp] *s.* ⚘ Sammelfrucht *f.*

ˌ**syn·chro**|ˈ**flash** [ˌsɪŋkrəʊ-] *s. phot.* Synˈchronblitz(licht *n*) *m*; ˌ**~**ˈ**mesh** [-ˈmeʃ] ⚙ **I** *adj.* Synchron…; **II** *s. a.* **~ *gear*** Synˈchrongetriebe *n.*

syn·chro·nism [ˈsɪŋkrənɪzəm] *s.* **1.** Synchroˈnismus *m*, Gleichzeitigkeit *f*; **2.** Synchronisatiˈon *f*; **3.** synchroˈnistische (Geˈschichts)Taˌbelle; **4.** *phys.* Gleichlauf *m*; **syn·chro·ni·za·tion** [ˌsɪŋkrənaɪˈzeɪʃn] *s.* **1.** *bsd. Film, TV*: Synchronisatiˈon *f*; **2.** Gleichzeitigkeit *f*, zeitliches Zs.-fallen; **syn·chro·nize** [ˈsɪŋkrənaɪz] **I** *v/i.* **1.** gleichzeitig sein, zeitlich zs.-fallen *od.* überˈeinstimmen; **2.** synˈchron gehen (*Uhr*) *od.* laufen (*Maschine*); **3.** synchronisiert sein (*Bild u. Ton e-s Films*); **II** *v/t.* **4.** *Uhren, Maschinen* synchronisieren: **~*d shifting*** *mot.* Synchron(gang)schaltung *f*; **5.** *Film, TV*: synchronisieren; **6.** *Ereignisse* synchroˈnistisch darstellen, *Gleichzeitiges* zs.-stellen; **7.** *Geschehnisse* (zeitlich) zs.-fallen lassen *od.* aufeinˈander abstimmen: **~*d swimming*** Synchronschwimmen *n*; **8.** ♪ a) *Ausführende* zum (genauen) Zs.-spiel bringen, b) *Stelle, Bogenstrich etc.* genau zuˈsammen ausführen (lassen); ˈ**syn·chro·nous** [-nəs] *adj.* □ **1.** gleichzeitig: ***be*** **~** (zeitlich) zs.-fallen; **2.** synˈchron: a) ⚙, ϟ gleichlaufend (*Maschine etc.*), gleichgehend (*Uhr*), b) ϟ, ⚙ von gleicher Phase u. Schwingungsdauer: **~ *motor*** Synchronmotor *m.*

syn·co·pal [ˈsɪŋkəpl] *adj.* **1.** synˈkopisch; **2.** ⚕ Ohnmachts…; ˈ**syn·co·pate** [-peɪt] *v/t.* **1.** *ling. Wort* synkopieren, zs.-ziehen; **2.** ♪ synkopieren; **syn·co·pa·tion** [ˌsɪŋkəˈpeɪʃn] *s.* **1.** → ***syncope*** 1; **2.** ♪ a) Synkopierung *f*, b) Synˈkope(n *pl.*) *f*, c) synˈkopische Muˈsik; **syn·co·pe** [ˈsɪŋkəpɪ] *s.* **1.** *ling.* a) Synˈkope *f*, kontrahiertes Wort, b) Kontraktiˈon *f*; **2.** ♪ Synˈkope *f*; **3.** ⚕ Synˈkope *f*, tiefe Ohnmacht.

syn·dic [ˈsɪndɪk] *s.* **1.** ⚖, ☤ Syndikus *m*, Rechtsberater *m*; **2.** *univ. Brit.* Seˈnatsmitglied *n*; ˈ**syn·di·cal·ism** [-kəlɪzəm] *s.* Syndikaˈlismus *m* (*radikaler Gewerkschaftssozialismus*); ˈ**syn·di·cate** **I** *s.* [-kɪt] **1.** ☤, ⚖ Syndiˈkat *n*, Konˈsortium *n*; **2.** ☤ a) Ring *m*, Verband *m*, ˈAbsatzkarˌtell *n*, b) ˈZeitungssyndiˌkat *n od.* -gruppe *f*; **3.** ˈPressezenˌtrale *f*; **4.** ‚Syndiˈkat' *n*, Verbrecherring *m*; **II** *v/t.* [-keɪt] **5.** ☤ zu e-m Syndiˈkat vereinigen; **6.** a) *Artikel etc.* in mehreren Zeitungen zuˈgleich veröffentlichen, b) über ein Syndiˈkat verkaufen, c) *Zeitungen* zu e-m Syndiˈkat zs.-schließen; **III** *v/i.* [-keɪt] **7.** ☤ sich zu e-m Syndiˈkat zs.-schließen; **IV** *adj.* [-kɪt] **8.** ☤ Konsortial…; **syn·di·ca·tion** [ˌsɪndɪˈkeɪʃn] *s.* ☤ Syndiˈkatsbildung *f.*

syn·drome [ˈsɪndrəʊm] *s.* ⚕ Synˈdrom *n* (*a. sociol. etc.*).

syn·od [ˈsɪnəd] *s. eccl.* Synˈode *f*; ˈ**syn·od·al** [-dl], **syn·od·ic**, **syn·od·i·cal** [sɪˈnɒdɪk(l)] *adj.* □ synˈodisch (*a. ast.*), Synoden…

syn·o·nym [ˈsɪnənɪm] *s. ling.* Synoˈnym *n*, bedeutungsgleiches *od.* -ähnliches Wort: ***be a*** **~ *for*** *fig.* gleichbedeutend sein mit; **syn·on·y·mous** [sɪˈnɒnɪməs] *adj.* □ **1.** *ling.* synoˈnym(isch), bedeutungsgleich *od.* -ähnlich; **2.** *allg.* gleichbedeutend (***with*** mit).

syn·op·sis [sɪˈnɒpsɪs] *pl.* **-ses** [-siːz] *s.* **1.** Synˈopse *f*: a) Zs.-fassung *f*, ˈÜbersicht *f*, Abriß *m*, b) *eccl.* (vergleichende) Zs.-schau; **synˈop·tic** [-ptɪk] *adj.* (□ **~*ally***) **1.** synˈoptisch, ˈübersichtlich, zs.-fassend: **~ *chart*** *meteor.* synoptische Karte; **2.** umˈfassend (*Genie*); **3.** *oft* 2 *eccl.* synˈoptisch; **Synˈop·tist**, *a.* 2 [-ptɪst] *s. eccl.* Synˈoptiker *m* (*Matthäus, Markus u. Lukas*).

syn·o·vi·a [sɪˈnəʊvɪə] *s. physiol.* Gelenkschmiere *f*; **synˈo·vi·al** [-əl] *adj.* Synovial…: **~ *fluid*** → ***synovia***; **syn·o·vi·tis** [ˌsɪnəˈvaɪtɪs] *s.* ⚕ Gelenkentzündung *f.*

syn·tac·tic, **syn·tac·ti·cal** [sɪnˈtæktɪk(l)] *adj.* □ *ling.* synˈtaktisch, Syntax…; **synˈtac·ti·cals** [-ɪklz] *s. pl. sg. konstr.* Synˈtaktik *f*; **syn·tax** [ˈsɪntæks] *s.* **1.** *ling.* Syntax *f*: a) Satzbau *m*, b) Satzlehre *f*; **2.** ∡, *phls.* Syntax *f*, Beˈweistheoˌrie *f.*

syn·the·sis [ˈsɪnθɪsɪs] *pl.* **-ses** [-siːz] *s. allg.* Synˈthese *f*; ˈ**syn·the·size** [-saɪz] *v/t.* **1.** zs.-fügen, (durch Synˈthese) aufbauen; **2.** ⚗, ⚙ synˈthetisch *od.* künstlich herstellen; **syn·thet·ic** [sɪnˈθetɪk] **I** *adj.* (□ **~*ally***) synˈthetisch: a) *bsd. ling., phls.* zs.-fügend: **~ *language***, b) ⚗ künstlich (*a. fig. unecht*), Kunst…: **~ *rubber***; **~ *trainer*** ✈ (Flug)Simulator *m*; **II** *s.* Kunststoff *m*; **syn·thet·i·cal** [sɪnˈθetɪkl] *adj.* □ → ***synthetic*** I; ˈ**syn·the·tize** [-ɪtaɪz] → ***synthesize***.

syn·ton·ic [sɪnˈtɒnɪk] *adj.* (□ **~*ally***) **1.** ϟ (auf gleiche Freˈquenz) abgestimmt; **2.** *psych.* extravertiert; **syn·to·nize** [ˈsɪntənaɪz] *v/t.* ϟ (***to*** auf *e-e bestimmte Frequenz*) abstimmen *od.* einstellen; **syn·to·ny** [ˈsɪntənɪ] *s.* **1.** ϟ (Freˈquenz-) Abstimmung *f*, Resoˈnanz *f*; **2.** *psych.* Extraversiˈon *f.*

syph·i·lis [ˈsɪfɪlɪs] *s.* ⚕ Syphilis *f*; **syph·i·lit·ic** [sɪfɪˈlɪtɪk] **I** *adj.* syphiˈlitisch; **II** *s.* Syphiˈlitiker(in).

sy·phon [ˈsaɪfn] → ***siphon***.

Syr·i·an [ˈsɪrɪən] **I** *adj.* syrisch; **II** *s.* Syr(i)er(in).

sy·rin·ga [sɪˈrɪŋgə] *s.* ⚘ Syˈringe *f*, Flieder *m.*

syr·inge [ˈsɪrɪndʒ] **I** *s.* **1.** ⚕, ⚙ Spritze *f*; **II** *v/t.* **2.** *Flüssigkeit etc.* (ein)spritzen; **3.** *Ohr* ausspritzen; **4.** *Pflanze etc.* ab-, bespritzen.

syr·inx [ˈsɪrɪŋks] *s.* **1.** *antiq.* Pan-, Hirtenflöte *f*; **2.** a) *anat.* Euˈstachische Röhre, b) ⚕ Fistel *f*; **3.** *orn.* Syrinx *f*, unterer Kehlkopf.

Syro- [saɪərəʊ] *in Zssgn* Syro…, syrisch.

syr·up [ˈsɪrəp] *s.* **1.** Sirup *m*, Zuckersaft *m*; **2.** *fig.* ‚süßliches Zeug', Kitsch *m*; ˈ**syr·up·y** [-pɪ] *adj.* **1.** sirupartig, dickflüssig, klebrig; **2.** *fig.* süßlich, sentimenˈtal.

sys·tem [ˈsɪstəm] *s.* **1.** *allg.* Syˈstem *n* (*a.* ∡, ♪, ⚗, ⚘, *zo.*): a) Gefüge *n*, Aufbau *m*, Anordnung *f*, b) Einheit *f*, geordnetes Ganzes, c) *phls., eccl.* Lehrgebäude *n*, d) ⚙ Anlage *f*, e) Verfahren *n*: **~ *of government*** Regierungssystem; **~ *of logarithms*** ∡ Logarithmensystem; ***electoral*** **~** *pol.* Wahlsystem, -verfahren; ***mountain*** **~** Gebirgssystem; ***savings-bank*** **~** Sparkassenwesen *n*; ***lack*** **~** kein System haben; **2.** *ast.* Syˈstem *n*: ***solar*** **~**; ***the*** **~** das Weltall; **3.** *geol.* Formatiˈon *f*; **4.** *pysiol.* a) (Orˈgan)Syˌstem *n*, b) ***the*** **~** der Organismus: ***digestive*** **~** Verdauungssystem; ***get s.th. out of one's*** **~** F et. loswerden; **5.** (*Eisenbahn-, Straßen-, Verkehrs- etc.*)Netz *n*: **~ *of roads***; **sys·tem·at·ic**, **sys·tem·at·i·cal** [ˌsɪstɪˈmætɪk(l)] *adj.* □ systeˈmatisch: a) plan-, zweckmäßig, -voll, b) meˈthodisch (*vorgehend od. geordnet*); ˈ**sys·tem·a·tist** [-mətɪst] *s.* Systeˈmatiker *m*; **sys·tem·a·ti·za·tion** [ˌsɪstɪmətaɪˈzeɪʃn] *s.* Systematisierung *f*; ˈ**sys·tem·a·tize** [-tɪmətaɪz] *v/t.* systematisieren, in ein Syˈstem bringen.

sys·tem·ic [sɪsˈtemɪk] *adj.* (□ **~*ally***) *physiol.* Körper…, Organ…: **~ *circulation*** großer Blutkreislauf; **~ *disease*** Systemerkrankung *f.*

sys·tems| **a·nal·y·sis** *s. Computer*: Syˈstemanaˌlyse *f*; **~ an·a·lyst** *s.* Syˈstemanaˌlytiker *m.*

sys·to·le [ˈsɪstəlɪ] *s.* Syˈstole *f*: a) ⚕ *Zs.-ziehung des Herzmuskels*, b) *Metrik*: *Verkürzung e-r langen Silbe.*

T

T, t [tiː] *pl.* **T's, Ts, t's, ts** *s.* **1.** T *n*, t *n* (*Buchstabe*): ***to a T*** haargenau; ***it suits me to a T*** das paßt mir ausgezeichnet; ***cross the T's*** a) peinlich genau sein, b) es klar u. deutlich sagen; **2.** *a.* ***flanged T*** ⚙ T-Stück *n*.
ta [tɑː] *int. Brit.* F danke.
Taal [tɑːl] *s. ling.* Afri'kaans *n*.
tab [tæb] *s.* **1.** Streifen *m*, *bsd.* a) Schlaufe *f*, (Mantel)Aufhänger *m*, b) Lappen *m*, Zipfel *m*, c) (Schuh)Lasche *f*, (Stiefel)Strippe *f*, d) Dorn *m am Schnürsenkel*, e) Ohrklappe *f* (*Mütze*); **2.** ⚔ (Kragen)Spiegel *m*; **3.** Schildchen *n*, Anhänger *m*, Eti'kett *n*; (Kar'tei)Reiter *m*; **4.** F a) Rechnung *f*, b) Kon'trolle *f*: ***keep ~(s) on*** *fig.* kontrollieren, beobachten, sich auf dem laufenden halten über (*acc.*); ***pick up the ~*** *Am.* (die Rechnung) bezahlen; **5.** ⚙ Nase *f*; **6.** ✈ Trimmruder *n*.
tab·by ['tæbɪ] **I** *s.* **1.** *obs.* Moi'ré *m*, *n* (*Stoff*); **2.** *mst* ***~ cat*** a) getigerte *od.* gescheckte Katze, b) (weibliche) Katze; **3.** F a) alte Jungfer, b) Klatschbase *f*; **II** *adj.* **4.** *obs.* Moiré…; **5.** gestreift; scheckig; **III** *v/t.* **6.** *Seide* moirieren.
tab·er·nac·le ['tæbənækl] *s.* **1.** *bibl.* Zelt *n*, Hütte *f*; **2.** 2 *eccl.* Stiftshütte *f der Juden*: ***Feast of 2s*** Laubhüttenfest *n*; **3.** *eccl.* a) (jüdischer) Tempel, b) 2 Mor'monentempel *m*, c) Bethaus *n der Dissenter*; **4.** Taber'nakel *n*: a) *R.C.* Sakra'mentshäuschen *n*, b) ⚠ Statuennische *f*; **5.** *fig.* Leib *m* (*als Wohnsitz der Seele*); **6.** ⚓ Mastbock *m*.
tab·la·ture ['tæblətʃə] *s.* **1.** Bild *n*: a) Tafelgemälde *n*, b) bildliche Darstellung (*a. fig.*); **2.** ♪ *hist.* Tabula'tur *f*.
ta·ble ['teɪbl] **I** *s.* **1.** *allg.* Tisch *m*: ***lay*** (*od.* ***put***) ***s.th. on the ~*** → 14 u. 15a; ***set*** (*od.* ***lay, spread***) ***the ~*** den Tisch decken; ***lay s.th. on the ~*** → 15a; ***turn the ~s*** (***on s.o.***) den Spieß umdrehen (gegenüber j-m); ***the ~s are turned*** das Blatt hat sich gewendet; **2.** Tafel *f*, Tisch *m*: a) gedeckter Tisch, b) Kost *f*, Essen *n*: ***at ~*** bei Tisch, beim Essen; ***keep*** (*od.* ***set***) ***a good ~*** e-e gute Küche führen; ***the Lord's ~*** der Tisch des Herrn, das Heilige Abendmahl; **3.** (Tisch-, Tafel)Runde *f*; → ***round table***; **4.** Komi'tee *n*, Ausschuß *m*; **5.** *geol.* Tafel(land *n*) *f*, Pla'teau *n*: ***~ mountain*** Tafelberg *m*; **6.** ⚠ a) Tafel *f*, Platte *f*, b) Sims *m*, *n*, Fries *m*; **7.** (Holz-, Stein-, *a.* Gedenk- *etc.*)Tafel *f*: ***the*** (***two***) ***~s of the law*** die Gesetzestafeln, die Zehn Gebote Gottes; **8.** Ta'belle *f*, Verzeichnis *n*: ***~ of contents*** Inhaltsverzeichnis; ***~ of wages*** Lohntabelle; **9.** ℞ Tabelle *f*: ***~ of logarithms*** Logarithmentafel *f*; ***learn one's ~s*** rechnen lernen; **10.** *anat.* Tafel *f*, Tabula *f* (ex'terna *od.* in'terna) (*Schädeldach*); **11.** ⚙ (Auflage)Tisch *m*; **12.** *opt.* Bildebene *f*; **13.** *Chiromantie*: Handteller *m*; **II** *v/t.* **14.** auf den Tisch legen (*a. fig. vorlegen*); **15.** *bsd. parl.* a) *Brit. Antrag etc.* einbringen, b) *Am.* zu'rückstellen, *bsd. Gesetzesvorlage* ruhen lassen; **16.** in e-e Tabelle eintragen, tabel'larisch verzeichnen.
ta·bleau ['tæbləʊ] *pl.* **'ta·bleaux** [-əʊz] *s.* **1.** Bild *n*: a) Gemälde *n*, b) anschauliche Darstellung; **2.** *Brit.* dra'matische Situati'on, über'raschende Szene: ***~!*** Tableau!, man stelle sich die Situation vor!; **3.** → ***~ vi·vant*** [viː'vɑ̃ːŋ] (*Fr.*) *s.* a) lebendes Bild, b) *fig.* malerische Szene.
'ta·ble|·cloth *s.* Tischtuch *n*, -decke *f*; **'~·cut** *adj.* mit Tafelschnitt (versehen) (*Edelstein*).
ta·ble d'hôte [ˌtɑːbl'dəʊt] (*Fr.*) *s.* *a.* ***~ meal*** Me'nü *n*.
ta·ble| knife *s.* [*irr.*] *Brit.* Tafel-, Tischmesser *n*; **'~·land** *s. geogr., geol.* Tafelland *n*, Hochebene *f*; **'~-ˌlift·ing** → ***table-turning***; **~ light·er** *s.* Tischfeuerzeug *n*; **~ lin·en** *s.* Tischwäsche *f*; **~ mat** *s.* Set *n*, *m*; **~ nap·kin** *s.* Servi'ette *f*; **'~-ˌrap·ping** *s. Spiritismus*: Tischklopfen *n*; **~ salt** *s.* Tafelsalz *n*; **~ set** *s. Radio, TV*: Tischgerät *n*; **'~·spoon** *s.* Eßlöffel *m*; **'~ˌspoon·ful** *s. ein* Eßlöffel(voll) *m*.
tab·let ['tæblɪt] *s.* **1.** Täfelchen *n*; **2.** (Gedenk-, Wand- *etc.*)Tafel *f*; **3.** *hist.* Schreibtafel *f*; **4.** (No'tiz-, Schreib-, Zeichen)Block *m*; **5.** a) Stück *n Seife*, b) Tafel *f Schokolade*; **6.** *pharm.* Ta'blette *f*; **7.** ⚠ Kappenstein *m*.
ta·ble| talk *s.* Tischgespräch *n*; **~ ten·nis** *s.* Tischtennis *n*; **~ top** *s.* Tischplatte *f*; **'~-ˌturn·ing** *s. Spiritismus*: Tischrücken *n*; **'~·ware** *s.* Tischgeschirr *n*; **~ wa·ter** *s.* Tafel-, Mine'ralwasser *n*.
tab·loid ['tæblɔɪd] **I** *s.* **1.** Bildzeitung *f*, Boule'vard-, Sensati'onsblatt *n*; *pl.* *a.* Boule'vardpresse *f*; **2.** *Am.* Informati'onsblatt *n*; **3.** *fig.* Kurzfassung *f*; **II** *adj.* **4.** konzentriert: ***in ~ form***.
ta·boo [tə'buː] **I** *adj.* ta'bu: a) unantastbar, b) verboten, c) verpönt; **II** *s.* Ta'bu *n*: ***put s.th. under*** (***a***) ***~*** → **III** *v/t.* für tabu erklären, tabuisieren.
tab·o(u)·ret ['tæbərɪt] *s.* **1.** Hocker *m*, Tabu'rett *n*; **2.** Stickrahmen *m*.
tab·u·lar ['tæbjʊlə] *adj.* ☐ **1.** tafelförmig, Tafel…, flach; **2.** dünn; **3.** blättrig; **4.** tabel'larisch, Tabellen…: ***~ standard*** ✝ Preisindexwährung *f*.
ta·bu·la ra·sa [ˌtæbjʊlə'rɑːsə] (*Lat.*) *s.* Tabula *f* rasa: a) unbeschriebenes Blatt, völlige Leere, b) reiner Tisch.
tab·u·late ['tæbjʊleɪt] **I** *v/t.* tabellarisieren, tabel'larisch (an)ordnen; **II** *adj.* → ***tabular***; **tab·u·la·tion** [ˌtæbjʊ'leɪʃn] *s.* **1.** Tabellarisierung *f*; **2.** Ta'belle *f*; **'tab·u·la·tor** [-tə] *s.* **1.** Tabellarisierer *m*; **2.** ⚙ Tabu'lator *m* (*Schreibmaschine*).
tach [tæk] F *für* ***tachometer***.
tach·o·graph ['tækəʊgrɑːf] *s.* ⚙ Tacho'graph *m*, Fahrtenschreiber *m*.
ta·chom·e·ter [tæ'kɒmɪtə] *s.* ⚙ Tacho'meter *n*, Geschwindigkeitsmesser *m*.
tac·it ['tæsɪt] *adj.* ☐ *bsd.* ⚖ stillschweigend: ***~ approval***.
tac·i·turn ['tæsɪtɜːn] *adj.* ☐ schweigsam, wortkarg; **tac·i·tur·ni·ty** [ˌtæsɪ'tɜːnətɪ] *s.* Schweigsamkeit *f*, Verschlossenheit *f*.
tack¹ [tæk] **I** *s.* **1.** (Nagel)Stift *m*, Reißnagel *m*, Zwecke *f*; **2.** *Näherei*: Heftstich *m*; **3.** ⚓ a) Halse *f*, b) Haltetau *n*; **4.** ⚓ Schlag *m*, Gang *m* (*beim Lavieren od. Kreuzen*): ***be on the port ~*** auf Backbordhalsen liegen; **5.** ⚓ Lavieren *n* (*a. fig.*); **6.** *fig.* Kurs *m*, Weg *m*, Richtung *f*: ***on the wrong ~*** auf dem Holzwege; ***try another ~*** es anders versuchen; **7.** *parl. Brit.* 'Zusatzantrag *m*, -arˌtikel *m*; **8.** ⚙ Klebrigkeit *f*; **II** *v/t.* **9.** heften (***to*** an *acc.*); **10.** *a.* ***~ down*** festmachen; **11.** *a.* ***~ together*** anein'anderfügen (*a. fig.*); **12.** (***on, to***) anfügen (an *acc.*): ***~ mortgages*** *Brit.* Hypotheken (verschiedenen Ranges) zs.-schreiben; ***~ securities*** ⚖ *Brit.* Sicherheiten zs.-fassen; ***~ a rider to a bill*** *parl. Brit.* e-e Vorlage mit e-m Zusatzantrag koppeln; **13.** ⚙ heftschweißen; **III** *v/i.* **14.** ⚓ a) wenden, b) lavieren (*a. fig.*).
tack² [tæk] *s.* F Nahrung *f*, ‚Fraß' *m*.
tack·le ['tækl] **I** *s.* **1.** Gerät *n*, (Werk-)Zeug *n*, Ausrüstung *f*; **2.** (Pferde)Geschirr *n*; **3.** *a.* ***block and ~*** ⚙ Flaschenzug *m*; **4.** ⚓ Talje *f*; **5.** ⚓ Takel-, Tauwerk *n*; **6.** *Fußball etc.*: Angreifen *n* (*e-s Gegners im Ballbesitz*); **7.** *amer. Fußball*: Halbstürmer *m*; **II** *v/t.* **8.** *et. od. j-n* packen; **9.** *Fußball etc.*: *Gegner im Ballbesitz* angreifen, stoppen; **10.** *j-n* angreifen, anein'andergeraten mit; **11.** *fig. j-n* (*mit Fragen etc.*) angehen (***on*** wegen); **12.** *fig.* a) *Problem etc.* anpacken, angehen, in Angriff nehmen, b) *Aufgabe etc.* lösen, fertig werden mit.
'tack-weld *v/t.* ⚙ heftschweißen.
tack·y ['tækɪ] *adj.* **1.** klebrig, zäh; **2.** *Am.* F a) schäbig, her'untergekommen, b) 'unmoˌdern, c) protzig.

tact [tækt] *s.* **1.** Takt *m*, Takt-, Zartgefühl *n*; **2.** Feingefühl *n* (**of** für); **3.** ♪ Takt(schlag) *m*; '**tact·ful** [-fʊl] *adj.* □ taktvoll; '**tact·ful·ness** [-fʊlnɪs] → ***tact*** 1.

tac·ti·cal ['tæktɪkl] *adj.* □ ⚔ taktisch (*a. fig. planvoll, klug*); **tac·ti·cian** [tæk'tɪʃn] *s.* ⚔ Taktiker *m* (*a. fig.*); '**tac·tics** [-ks] *s.* **1.** *sg. od. pl. konstr.* ⚔ Taktik *f*; **2.** *nur pl. konstr. fig.* Taktik *f*, planvolles Vorgehen.

tac·tile ['tæktaɪl] *adj.* **1.** tak'til, Tast...: ***~ sense*** Tastsinn *m*; ***~ hair*** *zo.*, ⚘ Tasthaar *n*; **2.** tast-, greifbar; **tac·til·i·ty** [tæk'tɪlətɪ] *s.* Greif-, Tastbarkeit *f*.

tact·less ['tæktlɪs] *adj.* □ taktlos; '**tact·less·ness** [-nɪs] *s.* Taktlosigkeit *f*.

tac·tu·al ['tæktjʊəl] *adj.* □ tastbar, Tast...: ***~ sense*** Tastsinn *m*.

tad·pole ['tædpəʊl] *s. zo.* Kaulquappe *f*.

taf·fe·ta ['tæfɪtə] *s.* Taft *m*.

taf·fy[1] ['tæfɪ] *s.* **1.** *Am.* → ***toffee***; **2.** F ‚Schmus' *m*, Schmeiche'lei *f*.

Taf·fy[2] ['tæfɪ] *s. sl.* Wa'liser *m*.

tag[1] [tæg] **I** *s.* **1.** (loses) Ende, Anhängsel *n*, Zipfel *m*, Fetzen *m*, Lappen *m*; **2.** Eti'kett *n*, Anhänger *m*, Schildchen *n*; Abzeichen *n*, Pla'kette *f*: ***~ day*** *Am.* Sammeltag *m*; **3.** a) Schlaufe *f am Stiefel*, b) (Schnürsenkel)Stift *m*; **4.** ⚙ a) Lötklemme *f*, b) Lötfahne *f*; **5.** a) Schwanzspitze *f* (*bsd. e-s Fuchses*), b) Wollklunker *f*, *m* (*Schaf*); **6.** (Schrift-) Schnörkel *m*; **7.** *ling.* Frageanhängsel *n*; **8.** Re'frain *m*, Kehrreim *m*; **9.** Schlußwort *n*, Po'inte *f*, Mo'ral *f*; **10.** stehende Redensart, bekanntes Zi'tat; **11.** Bezeichnung *f*, Beiname *m*; **12.** *Computer*: Identifizierungskennzeichen *n*; **13.** *Am.* Strafzettel *m*; **14.** → ***ragtag***; **II** *v/t.* **15.** mit e-m Etikett *etc.* versehen, etikettieren; *Waren* auszeichnen; *et.* markieren; **16.** mit e-m Schlußwort *od.* e-r Moral versehen; **17.** *Rede etc.* verbrämen; **18.** *et.* anhängen (**to** an *acc.*); **19.** *Schafen* Klunkerwolle abscheren; **20.** F hinter *j-m* ‚herlatschen'; **III** *v/i.* **21.** ***~ along*** F hinter'herlaufen: ***~ after*** → 20.

tag[2] [tæg] **I** *s.* Fangen *n*, Haschen *n* (*Kinderspiel*); **II** *v/t.* haschen.

tag end *s.* F **1.** ‚Schwanz' *m*, Schluß *m*; **2.** *Am.* a) (letzter) Rest, b) Fetzen *m* (*a. fig.*).

Ta·hi·ti·an [tɑː'hiːʃn] **I** *s.* **1.** Tahiti'aner (-in); **2.** *ling.* Ta'hitisch *n*; **II** *adj.* **3.** ta'hitisch.

tail[1] [teɪl] **I** *s.* **1.** *zo.* Schwanz *m*, (Pferde-) Schweif *m*: ***turn ~*** *fig.* ausreißen, davonlaufen; ***twist s.o.'s ~*** j-n piesacken; ***close on s.o.'s ~*** j-m dicht auf den Fersen; ***~s up*** fidel, hochgestimmt; ***keep your ~ up!*** laß dich nicht unterkriegen!; ***with one's ~ between one's legs*** *fig.* mit eingezogenem Schwanz; ***the ~ wags the dog*** *fig.* der Kleinste hat das Sagen; **2.** F Hinterteil *m*, Steiß *m*; **3.** *fig.* Schwanz *m*, Ende *n*, Schluß *m* (*e-r Marschkolonne*, *e-s Briefes etc.*): ***~ of a comet*** *ast.* Kometenschweif *m*; ***the ~ of the class*** *ped.* der ‚Schwanz' *od.* die Schlechtesten der Klasse; ***~ of a note*** ♪ Notenhals *m*; ***~ of a storm*** (ruhigeres) Ende e-s Sturms; ***out of the ~ of one's eye*** aus den Augenwinkeln; **4.** Haarzopf *m*, -schwanz *m*; **5.** a) Schleppe *f e-s Kleides*, b) (Rock-, Hemd)Schoß *m*, c) *pl.* Gesellschaftsanzug *m*, *bsd.* Frack *m*; **6.** ✈ Schwanz *m*, Heck *n*; **7.** *mst pl.* Rück-, Kehrseite *f e-r Münze*; **8.** a) Gefolge *n*, b) Anhang *m e-r Partei*, große Masse *e-r Gemeinschaft*; **9.** F ‚Beschatter' *m* (*Detektiv etc.*): ***put a ~ on s.o.*** j-n beschatten lassen; **10.** ✈ a) Leitwerk *n*, b) Heck *n*, Schwanz *m*; **II** *v/t.* **11.** mit e-m Schwanz versehen; **12.** *Marschkolonne etc.* beschließen; **13.** *a.* ***~ on*** befestigen, anhängen (**to** an *acc.*); **14.** *Tier* stutzen; **15.** *Beeren* zupfen, entstielen; **16.** F *j-n* ‚beschatten', verfolgen; **III** *v/i.* **17.** sich hinziehen: ***~ away*** (*od.* ***off***) a) abflauen, -nehmen, sich verlieren, b) zurückbleiben, -fallen, c) sich auseinanderziehen (*Marschkolonne etc.*); **18.** F hinter'herlaufen (***after s.o.*** j-m); **19.** ***~ back*** *mot. Brit.* e-n Rückstau bilden; **20.** △ eingelassen sein (***in*[*to*]** in *acc. od. dat.*).

tail[2] [teɪl] ⚖ **I** *s.* Beschränkung *f* (*der Erbfolge*), beschränktes Erb- *od.* Eigentumsrecht: ***heir in ~*** Vorerbe *m*; ***estate in ~ male*** Fideikommiß *m*; **II** *adj.* beschränkt: ***estate ~***.

'**tail|·back** *s. mot. Brit.* Rückstau *m*; '**~·board** *s.* Ladeklappe *f* (*a. mot.*); **~ coat** *s.* Frack *m*; **~ comb** *s.* Stielkamm *m*.

tailed [teild] *adj.* **1.** geschwänzt; **2.** *in Zssgn* ...schwänzig.

tail| end *s.* **1.** Schluß *m*, Ende *n*; **2.** → ***tail***[1] 2; ,**~'end·er** *s. sport* ‚Schlußlicht' *n*; **~ fin** *s.* **1.** *ichth.* Schwanzflosse *f*; **2.** ✈ Seitenflosse *f*; **~ fly** *s. Am.* (Angel-) Fliege *f*; '**~·gate I** *s.* **1.** a) → ***tailboard***, b) *mot.* Hecktür *f*; **2.** Niedertor *n* (*e-r Schleuse*); **II** *v/t. u. v/i. mot.* (zu) dicht auffahren (auf *acc.*); '**~-gun** *s.* ✈ Heckwaffe *f*; '**~-,heav·y** *adj.* ✈ schwanzlastig.

tail·ing ['teɪlɪŋ] *s.* **1.** △ eingelassenes Ende; **2.** *pl.* a) (*bsd.* Erz)Abfälle *pl.*, b) Ausschußmehl *n*.

tail lamp *s. mot. etc.* Rück-, Schlußlicht *n*.

tail·less ['teɪllɪs] *adj.* schwanzlos.

'**tail-light** → ***tail-lamp***.

tai·lor ['teɪlə] **I** *s.* **1.** Schneider *m*: ***the ~ makes the man*** Kleider machen Leute; **II** *v/t.* **2.** schneidern; **3.** schneidern für *j-n*; **4.** *j-n* kleiden; **5.** nach Maß arbeiten; **6.** *fig.* zuschneiden (**to** für *j-n*, auf *et.*); '**tai·lored** [-ləd] *adj.* maßgeschneidert, gut sitzend, tadellos gearbeitet: ***~ suit*** Maßanzug *m*; ***~ costume*** Schneiderkostüm *n*; ,**tai·lor'ess** [-ə'res] *s.* Schneiderin *f*.

'**tai·lor-made I** *adj.* **1.** → ***tailored*** 1; **2.** ele'gant gekleidet (*Dame*); **3.** auf Bestellung angefertigt; **4.** *fig.* (genau) zugeschnitten (**for** auf *acc.*); **II** *s.* **5.** 'Schneiderko,stüm *n*.

'**tail|·piece** *s.* **1.** ♪ Saitenhalter *m*; **2.** *typ.* 'Schlußvi,gnette *f*; **~ pipe** *s. mot.* Auspuffrohr(ende) *n*; **~ plane** *s.* ✈ Höhenflosse *f*; **~ skid** *s.* ✈ Schwanzsporn *m*; '**~·spin** *s.* **1.** ✈ (Ab)Trudeln *n*; **2.** *fig.* Panik *f*; '**~·stock** *s.* ⚙ Reitstock *m* (*Drehbank*); **~ u·nit** *s.* ✈ (Schwanz)Leitwerk *n*; **~ wind** *s.* ✈ Rückenwind *m*.

taint [teɪnt] **I** *s.* **1.** *bsd. fig.* Fleck *m*, Makel *m*; *fig.* a) *krankhafter etc.* Zug, b) Spur *f*: ***a ~ of suspicion*** ein Anflug von Mißtrauen; **2.** ⚕ a) (verborgene) Ansteckung, b) (verborgene) Anlage (**of** zu *e-r Krankheit*): ***hereditary ~*** erbliche Belastung; **3.** *fig.* verderblicher Einfluß, Gift *n*; **II** *v/t.* **4.** *a. fig.* verderben, -giften; **5.** anstecken; **6.** *fig.* verderben: ***be ~ed with*** behaftet sein mit; **7.** *bsd. fig.* beflecken, besudeln; **III** *v/i.* **8.** verderben, schlecht werden; '**taint·less** [-lɪs] *adj.* □ makellos.

take [teɪk] **I** *s.* **1.** a) *Fischerei*: Fang *m*, b) *hunt.* Beute *f* (*beide a.* F *fig.*); **2.** F Einnahme(n *pl.*) *f*; **3.** F Anteil *m* (**of** an *dat.*); **4.** *Film etc.*: Aufnahme *f*; **5.** *typ.* Porti'on *f* (*Manuskript*); **6.** ⚕ a) Reakti'on *f* (*a. fig.*), b) Anwachsen *n* (*e-s Transplantats*); **7.** *Schach etc.*: Schlagen *n* (*e-r Figur*); **II** *v/t.* [*irr.*] **8.** *allg.*, *a. Abschied*, *Partner*, *Unterricht etc.* nehmen: ***~ it or leave it*** *sl.* mach, was du willst; ***~n all in all*** im großen ganzen; ***taking one thing with another*** eins zum anderen gerechnet; → ***account*** 9, ***action*** 8, ***aim*** 6, ***care*** 4, ***consideration*** 1, ***effect*** 1 *etc.*; **9.** (weg)nehmen; **10.** nehmen, fassen, packen, ergreifen; **11.** *Fische etc.* fangen; **12.** *Verbrecher etc.* fangen, ergreifen; **13.** ⚔ gefangennehmen, *Gefangene* machen; **14.** ⚔ *Stadt*, *Stellung etc.* (ein)nehmen, *a. Land* erobern; *Schiff* kapern; **15.** *j-n* erwischen, ertappen (***stealing*** beim Stehlen, ***in a lie*** bei e-r Lüge); **16.** nehmen, sich aneignen, Besitz ergreifen von, sich bemächtigen (*gen.*); **17.** *Gabe etc.* (an-, entgegen)nehmen, empfangen; **18.** bekommen, erhalten; *Geld*, *Steuer etc.* einnehmen; *Preis etc.* gewinnen; **19.** (her'aus)nehmen (***from***, ***out of*** aus); *a. fig. Zitat etc.* entnehmen (***from*** *dat.*): ***I ~ it from s.o. who knows*** ich habe (*weiß*) es von j-m, der es genau weiß; **20.** *Speise etc.* zu sich nehmen; *Mahlzeit* einnehmen; *Gift*, *Medizin etc.* nehmen; **21.** sich *e-e Krankheit* holen *od.* zuziehen: ***be ~n ill*** krank werden; **22.** nehmen: a) auswählen: ***I am not taking any*** *sl.* ‚ohne mich'!, b) kaufen, c) mieten, d) *Eintritts-*, *Fahrkarte* lösen, e) *Frau* heiraten, f) *e-r Frau* beischlafen, g) *Weg* wählen; **23.** mitnehmen: ***~ me with you*** nimm mich mit; ***you can't ~ it with you*** *fig.* im Grabe nützt (dir) aller Reichtum nichts mehr; **24.** (hin- *od.* weg)bringen; *j-n wohin* führen: ***business took him to London***; ***he was ~n to the hospital*** er wurde in die Klinik gebracht; **25.** *j-n durch den Tod* nehmen, wegraffen; **26.** *A* abziehen (***from*** von); **27.** *j-n* treffen, erwischen (*Schlag*); **28.** *Hindernis* nehmen; **29.** *j-n* befallen, packen (*Empfindung*, *Krankheit*): ***be ~n with*** *e-e Krankheit* bekommen (→ 42); ***~n with fear*** von Furcht gepackt; **30.** *Gefühl* haben, bekommen, *Mitleid etc.* empfinden, *Mut* fassen, *Anstoß* nehmen; *Ab-*, *Zuneigung* fassen (**to** gegen, für): ***~ alarm*** beunruhigt sein (**at** über *acc.*); ***~ comfort*** sich trösten; → ***fancy*** 5, ***pride*** 1; **31.** *Feuer* fangen; **32.** *Bedeutung*, *Sinn*, *Eigenschaft*, *Gestalt* annehmen, bekommen: ***~ a new meaning***; **33.** *Farbe*, *Geruch*, *Geschmack* annehmen; **34.** *sport u. Spiele*: a) *Ball*, *Punkt*, *Figur*, *Stein* abnehmen (***from*** *dat.*), b) *Stein* schlagen, c) *Karte* stechen, d)

Spiel gewinnen; **35.** ⚖ *etc.* erwerben, *bsd.* erben; **36.** *Ware, Zeitung* beziehen; ☤ *Auftrag* her'einnehmen; **37.** nehmen, verwenden: **~ *4 eggs*** *Küche*: man nehme 4 Eier; **38.** *Zug, Taxi etc.* nehmen, benutzen; **39.** *Gelegenheit, Vorteil* ergreifen, wahrnehmen; → ***chance*** 2; **40.** (als Beispiel) nehmen; **41.** *Platz* einnehmen: **~*n*** besetzt; **42.** *fig. j-n, das Auge, den Sinn* gefangennehmen, fesseln, (für sich) einnehmen: ***be ~n with*** (*od.* ***by***) begeistert *od.* entzückt sein von (→ 29); **43.** *Befehl, Führung, Rolle, Stellung, Vorsitz* über'nehmen; **44.** *Mühe, Verantwortung* auf sich nehmen; **45.** leisten: a) *Arbeit, Dienst* verrichten, b) *Eid, Gelübde* ablegen, c) *Versprechen* (ab)geben; **46.** *Notiz, Aufzeichnung* machen, niederschreiben, *Diktat, Protokoll* aufnehmen; **47.** *phot. et. od. j-n* aufnehmen, *Bild* machen; **48.** *Messung, Zählung etc.* vornehmen, 'durchführen; **49.** *wissenschaftlich* ermitteln, *Größe, Temperatur etc.* messen; *Maß* nehmen; **50.** machen, tun: **~ *a look*** e-n Blick tun *od.* werfen; **~ *a swing*** schaukeln; **51.** *Maßnahme* ergreifen, treffen; **52.** *Auswahl* treffen; **53.** *Entschluß* fassen; **54.** *Fahrt, Spaziergang, a. Sprung, Verbeugung, Wendung etc.* machen; *Anlauf* nehmen; **55.** *Ansicht* vertreten; → ***stand*** 2, ***view*** 11; **56.** a) verstehen, b) auffassen, auslegen, c) *et. gut etc.* aufnehmen: ***do you ~ me?*** verstehen Sie(, was ich meine)?; ***I ~ it that*** ich nehme an, daß; **~ *s.th. ill of s.o.*** j-m et. übelnehmen; **~ *it seriously*** es ernst nehmen; **57.** ansehen *od.* betrachten (***as*** als); halten (***for*** für): ***I took him for an honest man***; **58.** sich *Rechte, Freiheiten* (her'aus)nehmen; **59.** a) *Rat, Auskunft* einholen, b) *Rat* annehmen, befolgen; **60.** *Wette, Angebot* annehmen; **61.** glauben: ***you may ~ it from me*** verlaß dich drauf!; **62.** *Beleidigung, Verlust etc., a. j-n* hinnehmen, *Strafe, Folgen* auf sich nehmen, sich *et.* gefallen lassen: **~ *people as they are*** die Leute nehmen, wie sie (eben) sind; **63.** *et.* ertragen, aushalten: ***can you ~ it?*** kannst du das aushalten?; **~ *it*** F es ‚kriegen', es ausbaden (müssen); **64.** ⚕ sich *e-r Behandlung etc.* unter'ziehen; **65.** *ped. Prüfung* machen, ablegen: **~ *French*** Examen im Französischen machen; → ***degree*** 3; **66.** *Rast, Ferien etc.* machen, *Urlaub, a. Bad* nehmen; **67.** *Platz, Raum* ein-, wegnehmen, beanspruchen; **68.** a) *Zeit, Material etc., a. fig. Geduld, Mut etc.* brauchen, erfordern, kosten, *gewisse Zeit* dauern: ***it took a long time*** es dauerte *od.* brauchte lange; ***it ~s brains and courage*** es erfordert Verstand u. Mut; ***it ~s a man to do that*** das kann nur ein Mann (fertigbringen), b) *j-n et.* kosten, *j-m et.* abverlangen: ***it took him*** (*od.* ***he took***) ***3 hours*** es kostete *od.* er brauchte 3 Stunden; → ***time*** 9; **69.** *Kleidergröße, Nummer* haben: ***which size in hats do you ~?***; **70.** *ling.* a) *grammatische Form* annehmen, im *Konjunktiv etc.* stehen, b) *Akzent, Endung, Objekt etc.* bekommen; **71.** aufnehmen, fassen, Platz bieten für; **III** *v/i.* [*irr.*] **72.** ⚘ *Wurzel* schlagen; **73.** ⚘, ⚕ anwachsen (*Pfropfreis, Steckling, Transplantat*); **74.** ⚕ wirken, anschlagen (*Droge etc.*); **75.** F ‚ankommen', ‚ziehen', ‚einschlagen', Anklang finden (*Buch, Theaterstück etc.*); **76.** ⚖ das Eigentumsrecht erlangen, *bsd.* erben, (als Erbe) zum Zuge kommen; **77.** sich *gut etc.* fotografieren (lassen); **78.** Feuer fangen; **79.** anbeißen (*Fisch*); **80.** ⚙ an-, eingreifen;

Zssgn mit prp.:

take| aft·er *v/i. j-m* nachschlagen, -geraten, ähneln (*dat.*); **~ for** *v/t.* **1.** halten für; **2.** auf *e-n Spaziergang etc.* mitnehmen; **~ from I** *v/t.* **1.** *j-m* wegnehmen; **2.** ⋔ abziehen von; **II** *v/i.* **3.** Abbruch tun (*dat.*), schmälern (*acc.*), her'absetzen (*acc.*); **4.** beeinträchtigen, mindern, (ab)schwächen; **~ in·to** *v/t.* **1.** (hin)'einführen in (*acc.*); **2.** bringen in (*acc.*); **~ to** *v/i.* **1.** a) sich begeben in (*acc.*) *od.* nach *od.* zu, b) sich flüchten in (*acc.*) *od.* zu, c) *fig.* Zuflucht nehmen zu: **~ *the stage*** zur Bühne gehen; → ***bed*** 1, ***heel***[1] *Redew.*, ***road*** 1; **2.** a) (her'an)gehen *od.* sich begeben an *e-e Arbeit etc.*, b) sich *e-r Sache* widmen, sich abgeben mit: **~ *doing s.th.*** dazu übergehen, et. zu tun; **3.** *et.* anfangen, sich ergeben (*dat.*), sich verlegen auf (*acc.*); *schlechte Gewohnheiten* annehmen: **~ *drink*(*ing*)** sich aufs Trinken verlegen, das Trinken anfangen; **4.** sich hingezogen fühlen zu, Gefallen finden an *j-m*; **~ up·on** *v/t.*: **~ *o.s. et.*** auf sich nehmen: ***take it upon o.s. to do s.th.*** a) es auf sich nehmen, et. zu tun, b) sich berufen fühlen, et. zu tun; **~ with** *v/i.* verfangen bei *j-m*: ***that won't ~ me*** das ‚zieht' bei mir nicht;

Zssgn mit adv.:

take| a·back *v/t.* verblüffen, über'raschen; → ***aback*** 3; **~ a·long** *v/t.* mitnehmen; **~ a·part** *v/t.* (*a.* F *fig. Gegner etc.*) ausein'andernehmen; **~ a·side** *v/t. j-n* bei'seite nehmen; **~ a·way** *v/t.* wegnehmen (***from s.o.*** j-m, ***from s.th.*** von et.): ***pizzas to ~*** (*Schild*) Pizzas zum Mitnehmen; **~ back** *v/t.* **1.** zu'rücknehmen (*a. fig. sein Wort*); **2.** *j-n im Geist* zu'rückversetzen (***to*** in *e-e Zeit*); **~ down** *v/t.* **1.** her'unter-, abnehmen; **2.** *Gebäude* abreißen, abtragen, *Gerüst* abnehmen; **3.** ⚙ *Motor etc.* zerlegen; **4.** *Baum* fällen; **5.** *Arznei etc.* (hin'unter-) schlucken; **6.** *j-n* demütigen, ‚ducken'; **7.** nieder-, aufschreiben, notieren; **~ for·ward** *v/t.* weiterführen, -bringen; **~ in** *v/t.* **1.** *Wasser etc.* (her)'einlassen; **2.** *Gast etc.* einlassen, aufnehmen; **3.** *Heimarbeit* annehmen; **4.** *Geld* einnehmen; **5.** ☤ *Waren* her'einnehmen; **6.** *Zeitung* halten; **7.** *fig.* in sich aufnehmen; *Lage* über'schauen; **8.** für bare Münze nehmen, glauben; **9.** her'einnehmen, einziehen, ⚓ *Segel* einholen; **10.** *Kleider* kürzer *od.* enger machen; **11.** einschließen (*a. fig. umfassen*); **12.** F *j-n* reinlegen: ***be taken in*** a) reinfallen, b) reingefallen sein; **~ off I** *v/t.* **1.** wegnehmen, -bringen, -schaffen; fortführen: ***take o.s. off*** sich fortmachen; **2.** *durch den Tod* hinraffen; **3.** *Verkehrsmittel* einstellen; **4.** *Hut etc.* abnehmen, *Kleidungsstück* ablegen, ausziehen; **5.** ⚕ abnehmen, amputieren; **6.** a) *Rabatt* abziehen, b) *Steuer etc.* senken; **7.** hin'unter-, austrinken; **8.** *thea. Stück* absetzen; **9.** ***take a day off*** sich e-n Tag freinehmen; **10.** *j-n* nachmachen, -äffen, imitieren; **II** *v/i.* **11.** *sport* abspringen; **12.** ✈ aufsteigen, starten; **13.** fortgehen, sich entfernen; **~ on I** *v/t.* **1.** *Arbeit* annehmen, über'nehmen; **2.** *Arbeiter* ein-, anstellen; *Mitglied* aufnehmen; **3.** a) *j-n* (als Gegner) annehmen, b) es aufnehmen mit *od.* gegen; **4.** *Wette* eingehen; **5.** *Eigenschaft, Gestalt, Farbe* annehmen; **II** *v/i.* **6.** F ‚sich haben', großes The'ater machen: ***don't ~ so!***; **~ out** *v/t.* **1.** a) her'ausnehmen, *a. Geld* abheben, b) wegnehmen, entfernen (***of*** von, aus); **2.** *Fleck* entfernen (***of*** aus); **3.** ☤, ⚖ *Patent, Vorladung etc.* erwirken; *Versicherung* abschließen; **4.** ***take it out*** sich schadlos halten (***in*** an *e-r Sache*); ***take it out of*** a) sich rächen *od.* schadlos halten für (*Beleidigung etc.*), b) *j-n* ‚kaputtmachen', erschöpfen, c) *sl. j-n* ‚wegputzen', liquidieren: ***take it out on s.o.*** s-n Zorn an j-m auslassen; **5.** (***of s.o.*** j-m) *den Unsinn etc.* austreiben; **6.** *j-n zum Abendessen etc.* ausführen; *Kinder* spazierenführen; **~ o·ver I** *v/t.* **1.** *Amt, Aufgabe, die Macht etc., a. Idee etc.* über'nehmen; **II** *v/i.* **2.** die Amtsgewalt, Leitung *etc.* über'nehmen; die Sache in die Hand nehmen: **~ *for s.o.*** j-s Stelle einnehmen; **3.** *fig.* in den Vordergrund treten; **~ up I** *v/t.* **1.** aufheben, -nehmen; **2.** *Pflaster* aufreißen; **3.** *Gerät, Waffe* erheben, ergreifen (***against*** gegen); **4.** *Reisende* mitnehmen; **5.** *Flüssigkeit* aufsaugen, -nehmen; **6.** *Tätigkeit* aufnehmen; sich befassen mit, sich verlegen auf (*acc.*); *Beruf* ergreifen; **7.** *Fall, Idee etc.* aufgreifen: ***take s.o. up on s.th.*** bei j-m wegen e-r Sache einhaken (→ 17); **8.** *Erzählung etc.* fortführen; **9.** *Platz, Zeit, Gedanken etc.* ausfüllen, beanspruchen, in Anspruch nehmen: ***taken up with*** in Anspruch genommen von; **10.** *Wohnsitz* aufschlagen; **11.** *Stelle* antreten; **12.** *Posten* einnehmen; **13.** *Verbrecher* aufgreifen, verhaften; **14.** *Masche* aufnehmen; **15.** ⚕ *Gefäß* abbinden; **16.** ☤ a) *Anleihe, Kapital* aufnehmen, b) *Aktien* zeichnen, c) *Wechsel* einlösen; **17.** *Wette, Herausforderung* annehmen: ***take s.o. up on it*** die Herausforderung annehmen; **18.** a) *e-m Redner* ins Wort fallen, b) *j-n* zu'rechtweisen, korrigieren; **II** *v/i.* **19.** **~ *with*** anbändeln *od.* sich einlassen mit.

'take|·a·way *Brit.* **I** *adj.* zum Mitnehmen: **~ *meals***; **II** *s.* Restau'rant *n* mit Straßenverkauf; **'~·down I** *adj.* zerlegbar; **II** *s.* Zerlegen *n*; **'~-home pay** *s.* Nettolohn *m*, -gehalt *n*; **'~-in** *s.* F **1.** Schwindel *m*, Betrug *m*; **2.** ‚Reinfall' *m*.

tak·en ['teɪkən] *p.p. von* ***take***.

'take|-off *s.* **1.** ✈ Start *m* (*a. mot.*), Abflug *m*; → ***assist*** 1; **2.** *sport* a) Absprung *m*, b) Absprungstelle *f*: **~ *board*** Absprungbalken *m*; **3.** *a.* **~ *point*** *fig.* Ausgangspunkt *m*; **4.** Nachahmung *f*, -äffung *f*, Karika'tur *f*; **'~·out** *Am.* **I** *adj.* **1.** → ***takeaway*** I; **II** *s.* **2.** → ***takeaway*** II; **3.** *sl.* Liquidierung *f*; **'~-‚o·ver** *s.* **1.** ☤ 'Übernahme *f e-r Firma*: **~ *bid*** Übernahmeangebot *n*; **2.** *pol.* 'Macht‚über-

nahme *f*.
tak·er ['teɪkə] *s.* **1.** Nehmer(in); **2.** ☤ Käufer(in); **3.** Wettende(r *m*) *f*.
tak·ing ['teɪkɪŋ] **I** *s.* **1.** (An-, Ab-, Auf-, Ein-, Ent-, Hin-, Weg- *etc.*)Nehmen *n* (*etc.* → ***take*** II); ⚖ Wegnahme *f*; **2.** Inbe'sitznahme *f*; **3.** ⚔ Einnahme *f*, Eroberung *f*; **4.** *pl.* ☤ Einnahmen *pl.*; **5.** F Aufregung *f*; **II** *adj.* □ **6.** fesselnd; **7.** anziehend, einnehmend, gewinnend; **8.** F ansteckend.
talc [tælk] *s.* Talk *m*.
tal·cum ['tælkəm] *s.* Talk *m*; ~ **pow·der** *s.* **1.** Talkum(puder *m*) *n*; **2.** Körperpuder *m*.
tale [teɪl] *s.* **1.** Erzählung *f*, Bericht *m*: ***it tells its own*** ~ es spricht für sich selbst; **2.** Erzählung *f*, Geschichte *f*: ***old wives'*** ~ Ammenmärchen *n*; ***thereby hangs a*** ~ damit ist e-e Geschichte verknüpft; **3.** Sage *f*, Märchen *n*; **4.** Lüge(ngeschichte) *f*, Unwahrheit *f*; **5.** Klatschgeschichte *f*: ***tell*** (*od.* ***carry, bear***) ~***s*** klatschen; ***tell*** ~***s*** (***out of school***) *fig.* aus der Schule plaudern; '~ˌ**bear·er** *s.* Klatschmaul *n*; '~ˌ**bear·ing** *s.* Zuträge'rei *f*, Klatsch(e'rei *f*) *m*.
tal·ent ['tælənt] *s.* **1.** Ta'lent *n*, Begabung *f* (*beide a. Person*): ~ ***for languages*** Sprachtalent; **2.** *coll.* Ta'lente *pl.* (*Personen*): ***engage the best*** ~ die besten Kräfte verpflichten; ~ ***scout*** Talentsucher *m*; ~ ***show*** ‚Talentschuppen' *m*; **3.** *bibl.* Pfund *n*; '**tal·ent·ed** [-tɪd] *adj.* talen'tiert, ta'lentvoll, begabt; '**tal·ent·less** [-lɪs] *adj.* 'untalenˌtiert, ta'lentlos.
ta·les·man ['teɪli:zmən] *s.* [*irr.*] Ersatzgeschworene(r) *m*.
'**taleˌtell·er** *s.* **1.** Märchen-, Geschichtenerzähler(in); **2.** Flunkerer *m*; **3.** Klatschmaul *n*.
tal·is·man ['tælɪzmən] *pl.* **-mans** *s.* 'Talisman *m*.
talk [tɔ:k] **I** *s.* **1.** Reden *n*; **2.** Gespräch *n*: a) Unter'haltung *f*, Plaude'rei *f*, b) *a. pol.* Unter'redung *f*: ***have a*** ~ ***with s.o.*** mit j-m reden *od.* plaudern, sich mit j-m unterhalten; **3.** Ansprache *f*; **4.** *bsd. Radio*: a) Plaude'rei *f*, b) Vortrag *m*; **5.** Gerede *n*, Geschwätz *n*: ***he is all*** ~ er ist ein großer Schwätzer; ***end in*** ~ im Sand verlaufen; ***there is*** ~ ***of his being bankrupt*** es heißt, daß er bank(e)rott ist; → ***small talk***; **6.** Gesprächsgegenstand *m*: ***be the*** ~ ***of the town*** Stadtgespräch sein; **7.** Sprache *f*, Art *f* zu reden; → ***baby talk***; **II** *v/i.* **8.** reden, sprechen: ~ ***big*** große Reden führen, ‚angeben'; ~ ***round s.th.*** um et. herumreden; **9.** reden, sprechen, plaudern, sich unter'halten (***about***, ***on*** über *acc.*, ***of*** von): ~ ***at*** *j-n* indirekt ansprechen, meinen; ~ ***to s.o.*** a) mit j-m sprechen *od.* reden, b) F j-m die Meinung sagen; ~ ***to o.s.*** Selbstgespräche führen; ~***ing of*** da wir gerade von … sprechen; ***you can*** ~***!*** F du hast gut reden!; ***now you are*** ~***ing!*** *sl.* das läßt sich eher hören!; **10.** *contp.* reden, schwatzen; **11.** *b.s.* reden, klatschen (***about*** über *acc.*); **III** *v/t.* **12.** *et.* reden: ~ ***nonsense***; ~ ***sense*** vernünftig reden; **13.** reden *od.* sprechen über (*acc.*): ~ ***business*** (***politics***); **14.** *Sprache* sprechen: ~ ***French***; **15.** reden: ~ ***o.s. hoarse*** sich heiser reden; ~ ***s.o. into believing s.th.*** j-n et. glauben machen; ~ ***s.o. into*** (***out of***) ***s.th.*** j-m et. ein- (aus-) reden;
Zssgn mit adv.:
talk| **a·way** *v/t.* *Zeit* verplaudern; ~ **back** *v/i.* e-e freche Antwort geben; ~ **down I** *v/t.* **1.** a) *j-n* unter den Tisch reden, b) niederschreien; **2.** *Flugzeug* ‚her'untersprechen'; **II** *v/i.* **3.** (***to***) sich dem (*niedrigen*) Ni'veau (*e-r Zuhörerschaft*) anpassen; ~ **o·ver** *v/t.* **1.** *j-n* über'reden; **2.** *et.* besprechen, 'durchsprechen; ~ **round** → ***talk over*** 1; ~ **up I** *v/i.* **1.** laut u. deutlich reden; **II** *v/t.* *Am.* F **2.** *et.* rühmen, anpreisen; **3.** *et.* frei her'aussagen.
talk·a·thon ['tɔ:kəθɒn] *s.* *Am.* F Marathonsitzung *f*.
talk·a·tive ['tɔ:kətɪv] *adj.* □ geschwätzig, gesprächig, redselig; '**talk·a·tive·ness** [-nɪs] *s.* Geschwätzigkeit *f etc.*
talk·ee-talk·ee [ˌtɔ:kɪ'tɔ:kɪ] *s.* F *contp.* Geschwätz *n*.
talk·er ['tɔ:kə] *s.* **1.** Schwätzer(in); **2.** Sprecher *m*, Sprechende(r *m*) *f*: ***he is a good*** ~ er kann (gut) reden.
talk·ie ['tɔ:kɪ] *s.* F Tonfilm *m*.
talk·ing ['tɔ:kɪŋ] **I** *s.* **1.** Sprechen *n*, Reden *n*: ***he did all the*** ~ er führte allein das Wort; ***let him do the*** ~ laß(t) ihn (für uns alle) sprechen; **II** *adj.* **2.** sprechend: ~ ***doll***; ~ ***parrot***; **3.** *teleph.* Sprech…: ~ ***current***; **4.** *fig.* sprechend: ~ ***eyes***; ~ **film**, ~ (**mo·tion**) **pic·ture** *s.* Tonfilm *m*; '~**-to** *s.* F: ***give s.o. a*** ~ j-m e-e Standpauke halten.
'**talk-show** *s.* *bsd. Am. TV*: Talk-Show *f*.
talk·y ['tɔ:kɪ] *adj.* F geschwätzig (*a. fig.*); '~**-talk** *s.* F Geschwätz *n*.
tall [tɔ:l] **I** *adj.* **1.** groß, hochgewachsen: ***he is six feet*** ~ er ist sechs Fuß groß; **2.** hoch: ~ ***house*** hohes Haus; **3.** F a) großsprecherisch, b) über'trieben, unglaublich (*Geschichte*): ***that's a*** ~ ***order*** das ist ein bißchen viel verlangt; **II** *adv.* **4.** F prahlerisch: ***talk*** ~ prahlen; '**tall·boy** *s.* hohe Kom'mode; '**tall·ish** [-lɪʃ] *adj.* ziemlich groß; '**tall·ness** [-nɪs] *s.* Größe *f*, Höhe *f*, Länge *f*.
tal·low ['tæləʊ] **I** *s.* **1.** *ausgelassener* Talg: ***vegetable*** ~ Pflanzenfett *n*; **2.** ⚙ Schmiere *f*; **3.** Talg-, Unschlittkerze *f*; **II** *v/t.* **4.** (ein)talgen, schmieren; **5.** *Tiere* mästen; '~**-faced** *adj.* bleich, käsig.
tal·low·y ['tæləʊɪ] *adj.* talgig.
tal·ly[1] ['tælɪ] **I** *s.* **1.** *hist.* Kerbholz *n*, -stock *m*; **2.** ☤ (Ab)Rechnung *f*; **3.** (Gegen)Rechnung *f*; **4.** ☤ Kontogegenbuch *n* (*e-s Kunden*); **5.** Seiten-, Gegenstück *n* (***of*** zu); **6.** Zählstrich *m*: ***by the*** ~ ☤ nach dem Stück *kaufen*; **7.** Eti'kett *n*, Marke *f*, Kennzeichen *n* (*auf Kisten etc.*); **8.** Ku'pon *m*; **II** *v/t.* **9.** (stückweise) nachzählen, buchen, kontrollieren; **10.** *oft* ~ ***up*** berechnen; **III** *v/i.* **11.** (***with***) über'einstimmen (mit), entsprechen (*dat.*); **12.** stimmen.
tal·ly[2] ['tælɪ] *v/t.* ⚓ *Schoten* beiholen.
tal·ly-ho [ˌtælɪ'həʊ] *hunt.* **I** *int.* hal'lo!, ho! (*Jagdruf*); **II** *pl.* **-hos** *s.* Hallo *n*; **III** *v/i.* ‚hallo' rufen.
'**tal·ly**|**-sheet** *s.* ☤ Kon'trolliste *f*; '~**-shop** *s.* ☤ *bsd. Brit.* Abzahlungsgeschäft *n*; ~ **sys·tem**, ~ **trade** *s.* ☤ *bsd. Brit.* 'Abzahlungsgeschäft *n*, -syˌstem *n*.
tal·mi gold ['tælmɪ] *s.* Talmigold *n*.
Tal·mud ['tælmʊd] *s.* Talmud *m*; **Tal·mud·ic** [tæl'mʊdɪk] *adj.* tal'mudisch; '**Tal·mud·ist** [-dɪst] *s.* Talmu'dist *m*.
tal·on ['tælən] *s.* **1.** *orn.* Klaue *f*, Kralle *f*; **2.** △ Kehlleiste *f*; **3.** *Kartenspiel*: Ta'lon *m*; **4.** ☤ Ta'lon *m*, 'Zinskuˌpon *m*.
ta·lus[1] ['teɪləs] *pl.* **-li** [-laɪ] *s.* **1.** *anat.* Talus *m*, Sprungbein *n*; **2.** Fußgelenk *n*; **3.** ⚕ Klumpfuß *m*.
ta·lus[2] ['teɪləs] *s.* **1.** Böschung *f*; **2.** *geol.* Geröll-, Schutthalde *f*.
tam [tæm] → ***tam-o'-shanter***.
tam·a·ble ['teɪməbl] *adj.* (be)zähmbar.
tam·a·rack ['tæmərӕk] *s.* ♀ **1.** Nordamer. Lärche *f*; **2.** Tamarakholz *n*;
tam·a·rind ['tæmərɪnd] *s.* ♀ Tama'rinde *f*; **tam·a·risk** ['tæmərɪsk] *s.* ♀ Tama'riske *f*.
tam·bour ['tæmˌbʊə] **I** *s.* **1.** (große) Trommel; **2.** *a.* ~ ***frame*** Stickrahmen *m*; **3.** Tambu'riersticke,rei *f*; **4.** △ a) Säulentrommel *f*, b) Tambour *m* (*Unterbau e-r Kuppel*); **5.** *Festungsbau*: Tambour *m*; **II** *v/t.* **6.** *Stoff* tamburieren.
tam·bou·rine [ˌtæmbə'ri:n] *s.* ♪ (flaches) Tamb(o)u'rin.
tame [teɪm] **I** *adj.* □ **1.** *allg.* zahm: a) gezähmt (*Tier*), b) friedlich, c) folgsam, d) harmlos (*Witz*), e) lahm, fad(e): ***a*** ~ ***affair***; **II** *v/t.* **2.** zähmen, bändigen (*a. fig.*); **3.** *Land* urbar machen; '**tame·ness** [-nɪs] *s.* **1.** Zahmheit *f* (*a. fig.*); **2.** Unter'würfigkeit *f*; **3.** Harmlosigkeit *f*; **4.** Lahmheit *f*, Langweiligkeit *f*; '**tam·er** [-mə] *s.* (Be)Zähmer(in), Bändiger(in).
Tam·ma·ny ['tæmənɪ] *s. pol. Am.* **1.** → a) ***Tammany Hall***, b) ***Tammany Society***; **2.** *fig.* po'litische Korrupti'on, ‚Filz' *m*; ~ **Hall** *s. pol. Am.* **1.** *Zentrale der* ***Tammany Society*** *in New York*; **2.** *fig. a.* ~ **So·ci·e·ty** *s. pol. Am. organisierte demokratische Partei in New York*.
tam-o'-shan·ter [ˌtæmə'ʃæntə] *s.* Schottenmütze *f*.
tamp [tæmp] *v/t.* ⚙ **1.** *Bohrloch* besetzen; zustopfen; **2.** *Sprengladung* verdämmen; **3.** *Lehm etc.* feststampfen; *Beton* rammen.
tamp·er[1] ['tæmpə] *s.* ⚙ Stampfer *m*.
tam·per[2] ['tæmpə] *v/i.* ~ ***with*** **1.** sich (unbefugt) zu schaffen machen mit, her'umbasteln *od.* -pfuschen an (*dat.*), *bsd. Urkunde etc.* verfälschen, ‚frisieren'; **2.** a) sich (ein)mischen in (*acc.*), b) hin'einpfuschen in (*acc.*); **3.** a) mit *j-m* intrigieren, b) *bsd. Zeugen* (zu) bestechen (suchen).
tam·pon ['tæmpən] **I** *s.* **1.** ⚕, *a. typ.* Tam'pon *m*; **2.** *allg.* Pfropfen *m*; **II** *v/t.* **3.** ⚕, *typ.* tamponieren.
tan [tæn] **I** *s.* **1.** ⚙ Lohe *f*; **2.** ⚗ Gerbstoff *m*; **3.** Lohfarbe *f*; **4.** (gelb)braunes Kleidungsstück (*bsd. Schuh*); **5.** (Sonnen)Bräune *f*; **II** *v/t.* **6.** ⚙ a) *Leder* gerben (*a. phot.*), b) beizen; **7.** *Haut* bräunen; **8.** F versohlen, *j-m* das Fell gerben; **III** *v/i.* **9.** a) sich bräunen (*Haut*), b) braun werden; **IV** *adj.* **10.** lohfarben, gelbbraun; **11.** Gerb…
tan·dem ['tændəm] **I** *adv.* **1.** hintereinander (angeordnet) (*bsd. Pferde, Maschinen etc.*); **II** *s.* **2.** Tandem *n* (*Gespann, Wagen, Fahrrad*): ***work in*** ~ ***with*** *fig.* zs.-arbeiten mit; **3.** ⚙ Reihe *f*,

Tandem *n*; **4.** ϟ Kas'kade *f*; **III** *adj.* **5.** Tandem..., hinterein'ander angeordnet; ~ ***bicycle*** Tandem *n*; ~ ***connection*** ϟ Kaskadenschaltung *f* ~ ***compound*** (***engine***) Reihenverbundmaschine *f*.

tang¹ [tæŋ] *s.* **1.** ⚙ a) Griffzapfen *m* (*Messer etc.*), b) Angel *f*, c) Dorn *m*; **2.** scharfer Geruch *od.* Geschmack; Beigeschmack *m* (***of*** von) (*a. fig.*).

tang² [tæŋ] **I** *s.* (scharfer) Klang; **II** *v/i. u. v/t.* (laut u. scharf) ertönen (lassen).

tang³ [tæŋ] *s.* ⚘ Seetang *m*.

tan·gent ['tændʒənt] **I** *s.* ⩘ Tan'gente *f*: ***fly*** (*od.* ***go***) ***off at a*** ~ *fig.* plötzlich (vom Thema) abspringen; **II** *adj.* → ***tangential*** 1; **tan·gen·tial** [tæn'dʒenʃl] *adj.* □ **1.** ⩘ berührend, tangenti'al, Berührungs..., Tangential...: ~ ***force*** Tangentialkraft *f*; ~ ***plane*** Berührungsebene *f*; ***be*** ~ ***to*** *et.* berühren; **2.** *fig.* a) sprunghaft, flüchtig, b) ziellos, c) 'untergeordnet, Neben...

tan·ge·rine [ˌtændʒə'riːn] *s.* ⚘ Manda'rine *f*.

tan·gi·ble ['tændʒəbl] *adj.* □ greifbar: a) fühlbar, b) *fig.* handgreiflich, c) ⚖ re'al: ~ ***assets*** materielle Vermögenswerte; ~ ***property*** Sachvermögen *n*.

tan·gle ['tæŋgl] **I** *v/t.* **1.** verwirren, -wikkeln, durchein'anderbringen (*alle a. fig.*); **2.** verstricken (*a. fig.*); **II** *v/i.* **3.** sich verheddern; **4.** ~ ***with*** sich mit *j-m* (in e-n Kampf *etc.*) einlassen; **III** *s.* **5.** Gewirr *n*, wirrer Knäuel; **6.** Verwirrung *f*, -wicklung *f*, Durchein'ander *n*.

tan·go ['tæŋgəʊ] **I** *pl.* **-gos** *s.* Tango *m* (*Tanz*); **II** *v/i. pret. u. p.p.* **-goed** Tango tanzen.

tank [tæŋk] **I** *s.* **1.** *mot. etc.* Tank *m*; **2.** (Wasser)Becken *n*, Zi'sterne *f*; **3.** 🚂 a) Wasserkasten *m*, b) 'Tenderlokomoˌtive *f*; **4.** *phot.* Bad *n*; **5.** ⚔ Panzer(wagen) *m*, Tank *m*; **6.** *Am. sl.* a) ,Kittchen' *n*, b) (Haft)Zelle *f*; **II** *v/t. u. v/i.* **7.** tanken; **8.** ~ ***up*** a) auf-, volltanken, b) *sl.* sich ,vollaufen' lassen: ~***ed*** besoffen; '**tank·age** [-kɪdʒ] *s.* **1.** Fassungsvermögen *n* e-s Tanks; **2.** (Gebühr *f* für) Aufbewahrung *f* in Tanks; **3.** ✓ Fleischmehl *n* (*Düngemittel*); '**tank·ard** [-kəd] *s.* (*bsd.* Bier)Krug *m*, Humpen *m*.

'**tank**|-ˌ**bust·er** *s.* ⚔ *sl.* **1.** Panzerknakker *m*; **2.** Jagdbomber *m* zur Panzerbekämpfung; ~ **car** *s.* 🚂 Kesselwagen *m*; ~ **de·stroy·er** *s.* ⚔ Sturmgeschütz *n*; ~ **dra·ma** *s. thea. Am.* F Sensati'onsstück *n*.

tank·er ['tæŋkə] *s.* **1.** ⚓ Tanker *m*, Tankschiff *n*; **2.** *a.* ~ ***aircraft*** ✈ Tankflugzeug *n*; **3.** *mot.* Tankwagen *m*; ~ **farm·ing** *s.* 'Hydrokulˌtur *f*.

tank top *s.* Pull'under *m*.

tan liq·uor *s.* ⚙ Beizbrühe *f*.

tanned [tænd] *adj.* braungebrannt.

tan·ner¹ ['tænə] *s. Brit. obs. sl.* Sixpencestück *n*.

tan·ner² ['tænə] *s.* ⚙ (Loh)Gerber *m*; '**tan·ner·y** [-ərɪ] *s.* Gerbe'rei *f*; '**tan·nic** [-nɪk] *adj.* Gerb...: ~ ***acid***; '**tan·nin** [-nɪn] *s.* ⚗ Tan'nin *n*.

tan·ning ['tænɪŋ] *s.* **1.** Gerben *n*; **2.** (Tracht *f*) Prügel *pl.*

tan| **ooze**, ~ **pick·le** → ***tan liquor***; '~-**pit** *s. Gerberei*: Lohgrube *f*.

tan·ta·li·za·tion [ˌtæntəlaɪ'zeɪʃn] *s.* **1.** Quälen *n*, Zappelnlassen *n*; **2.** (Tantalus)Qual *f*; **tan·ta·lize** ['tæntəlaɪz] *v/t. fig.* peinigen, quälen, zappeln lassen; **tan·ta·liz·ing** ['tæntəlaɪzɪŋ] *adj.* □ quälend, aufreizend, verlockend.

tan·ta·mount ['tæntəmaʊnt] *adj.* gleichbedeutend (***to*** mit): ***be*** ~ ***to*** *a.* gleichkommen (*dat.*).

tan·tiv·y [tæn'tɪvɪ] **I** *s.* **1.** schneller Ga'lopp; **2.** Hussa *n* (*Jagdruf*); **II** *adv.* **3.** eiligst, spornstreichs.

tan·trum ['tæntrəm] *s.* F **1.** schlechte Laune; **2.** Wut(anfall *m*) *f*, Koller *m*: ***fly into a*** ~ e-n Koller kriegen.

tap¹ [tæp] **I** *s.* **1.** Zapfen *m*, Spund *m* (Faß)Hahn *m*: ***on*** ~ a) angestochen, angezapft (*Faß*), b) vom Faß (*Bier etc.*), c) *fig.* (sofort) verfügbar; **2.** *Brit.* a) (Wasser-, Gas)Hahn *m*, b) Wasserleitung *f*: ***turn on the*** ~ F ,losflennen'; **3.** F (Getränke)Sorte *f*; **4.** *Brit.* → ***taproom***; **5.** ⚙ a) Gewindebohrer *m*, b) (Ab)Stich *m*, c) Abzweigung *f*; **6.** ϟ a) Stromabnehmer *m*, b) Zapfstelle *f*; **7.** ⚕ Punkti'on *f*; **II** *v/t.* **8.** mit e-m Zapfen *od.* Hahn versehen; **9.** *Flüssigkeit* abzapfen; **10.** *Faß* anstechen; **11.** ⚕ punktieren; **12.** ϟ *Telefonleitung etc.* anzapfen: ~ ***the wire***(***s***) a) Strom abzapfen, b) Telefongespräche *etc.* abhören; **13.** ϟ a) *Spannung* abgreifen, b) anschließen; **14.** ⚙ mit (e-m) Gewinde versehen; **15.** *metall. Schlacke* abstechen; **16.** *fig. Hilfsquellen etc.* erschließen; **17.** *fig. Vorräte etc.* angreifen, anbrechen; **18.** *sl. j-n* ,anpumpen' (***for*** um).

tap² [tæp] **I** *v/t.* **1.** (leicht) klopfen *od.* pochen an (*acc.*) *od.* auf (*acc.*) *od.* gegen, *et.* beklopfen; **2.** klopfen mit; **3.** *Schuh* flicken; **II** *v/i.* **4.** klopfen (***on***, ***at*** gegen, an *acc.*); **III** *s.* **5.** Klaps *m*, leichter Schlag; **6.** *pl.* ⚔ *Am.* Zapfenstreich *m*; **7.** Stück *n* Leder *m*, Flicken *m*.

tap| **dance** *s.* Steptanz *m*; '~-**dance** *v/i.* steppen; ~ **danc·er** *s.* Steptänzer(in); ~ **danc·ing** *s.* Steptanz *m*.

tape [teɪp] **I** *s.* **1.** schmales (Leinen-) Band, Zwirnband *n*; **2.** (Isolier-, Meß-, Me'tall- *etc.*)Band *n*, (Pa'pier-, Kleb- *etc.*)Streifen *m*; ⚕ Heftpflaster *n*; **3.** a) *Telegrafie*: Papierstreifen *m*, b) *Fernschreiber*, *Computer*: Lochstreifen *m*; **4.** ϟ (Video-, Ton)Band *n*; **5.** *sport* Zielband *n*: ***breast the*** ~ das Zielband durchreißen; **II** *v/t.* **6.** mit Band versehen; (mit Band) um'wickeln *od.* binden; **7.** mit Heftpflaster verkleben; **8.** *Buchteile* heften; **9.** mit dem Bandmaß messen: ***I've got him*** ~***d*** *sl.* ich habe ihn durchschaut, ich weiß genau Bescheid über ihn; **10.** mitschneiden: a) auf (Ton)Band aufnehmen, b) *TV* aufzeichnen; ~ **deck** *s.* ϟ Tapedeck *n*; ~ **li·brar·y** *s.* 'Bandarˌchiv *n*; ~ **line**, ~ **meas·ure** *s.* Meßband *n*, Bandmaß *n*; ~ **play·er** *s.* ϟ 'Bandˌwiedergabegerät *n*.

ta·per ['teɪpə] **I** *s.* **1.** (dünne) Wachskerze; **2.** ⚙ Verjüngung *f*; **3.** ϟ 'Widerstandsverteilung *f*; **II** *adj.* **4.** spitz zulaufend, verjüngt; **III** *v/t.* **5.** zuspitzen, verjüngen; **6.** ~ ***off*** *fig.* F *Produktion*, *a. den Tag etc.* auslaufen lassen; **IV** *v/i.* **7.** *oft* ~ ***off*** spitz zulaufen, sich verjüngen; all'mählich dünn werden; **8.** ~ ***off*** F allmählich aufhören, auslaufen.

'**tape**|-**reˌcord** *v/t.* → ***tape*** 10; ~ **re·cord·er** *s.* ϟ Tonbandgerät *n*; ~ **re·cord·ing** *s.* **1.** (Ton)Bandaufnahme *f*; **2.** *TV*: Aufzeichnung *f*.

ta·pered ['teɪpəd] *adj.*, '**ta·per·ing** [-ərɪŋ] → ***taper*** 4.

tap·es·tried ['tæpɪstrɪd] *adj.* gobe'lingeschmückt; **tap·es·try** ['tæpɪstrɪ] *s.* **1.** a) Gobe'lin *m*, Wandteppich *m*, gewirkte Ta'pete, b) Dekorati'onsstoff *m*; **2.** Tapisse'rie *f*.

'**tape·worm** *s. zo.* Bandwurm *m*.

tap·pet ['tæpɪt] *s.* ⚙ **1.** Daumen *m*, Mitnehmer *m*; **2.** (Ven'til- *etc.*)Stößel *m*; **3.** (Wellen)Nocke *f*; **4.** (Steuer)Knagge *f*.

'**tap**|·**room** [-rʊm] *s.* Schankstube *f*; '~-**root** *s.* ⚘ Pfahlwurzel *f*.

tar [tɑː] **I** *s.* **1.** Teer *m*; **2.** F ,Teerjacke' *f* (*Matrose*); **II** *v/t.* **3.** teeren: ~ ***and feather*** *j-n* teeren u. federn; ~***red with the same brush*** (*od.* ***stick***) kein Haar besser.

tar·a·did·dle ['tærədɪdl] *s.* F **1.** Flunke'rei *f*; **2.** Quatsch *m*.

ta·ran·tu·la [tə'ræntjʊlə] *s. zo.* Ta'rantel *f*.

'**tar**|·**board** *s.* Dach-, Teerpappe *f*; '~-**brush** *s.* Teerpinsel *m*: ***he has a touch of the*** ~ F er hat Neger- *od.* Indianerblut in den Adern.

tar·di·ness ['tɑːdɪnɪs] *s.* **1.** Langsamkeit *f*; **2.** Unpünktlichkeit *f*; **3.** Verspätung *f*; **tar·dy** ['tɑːdɪ] *adj.* □ **1.** langsam, träge; **2.** säumig, unpünktlich; **3.** spät, verspätet: ***be*** ~ (zu) spät kommen.

tare¹ [teə] *s.* **1.** ⚘ (*bsd.* Futter)Wicke *f*; **2.** *bibl.* Unkraut *n*.

tare² [teə] ⚖ **I** *s.* Tara *f*: ~ ***and tret*** Tara u. Gutgewicht *n*; **II** *v/t.* tarieren.

tar·get ['tɑːgɪt] **I** *s.* **1.** (Schieß-, Ziel-) Scheibe *f*; **2.** ⚔, *Radar etc.*: Ziel *n* (*a. fig.*): ***be off*** ~ das Ziel verfehlen, danebenschießen, *fig.* ,danebenhauen'; ***be on*** ~ a) das Ziel erfaßt haben, *a.* sich eingeschossen haben, *sport* aufs Tor gehen (*Schuß*), b) treffen, sitzen (*Schuß etc.*), c) *fig.* richtig geraten haben; **3.** *fig.* Zielscheibe *f des Spottes etc.*; **4.** *fig.* (Leistungs-, Produkti'ons- *etc.*)Ziel *n*, Soll *n*; **5.** 🚂 'Weichensiˌgnal *n*; **6.** ϟ a) 'Fangelekˌtrode *f*, b) 'Antikaˌthode *f von Röntgenröhren*, c) *Kernphysik*: Target *n*; **7.** *her.* runder Schild; **II** *adj.* **8.** Ziel...: ~ ***area*** ⚔ Zielbereich *m*, -raum *m*; ~ ***bombing*** gezielter Bombenwurf; ~ ***date*** Stichtag *m*, Termin *m*; ~ ***electrode*** → 6a; ~ ***group*** ⚖ Zielgruppe *f*; ~ ***language*** Zielsprache *f*; ~ ***pistol*** Übungspistole *f*; ~ ***practice*** Übungs-, Scheibenschießen *n*; ~-***seeking*** zielsuchend (*Rakete etc.*).

tar·iff ['tærɪf] **I** *s.* **1.** 'Zolltaˌrif *m*; **2.** Zoll (-gebühr *f*) *m*; **3.** (Ge'bühren-, 'Kosten- *etc.*)Taˌrif *m*; **4.** Preisverzeichnis *n* (*in e-m Hotel etc.*); **II** *v/t.* **5.** e-n Ta'rif aufstellen für; **6.** *Ware* mit Zoll belegen; ~ **rate** *s.* **1.** Ta'rifsatz *m*; **2.** Zollsatz *m*; ~ **wall** *s.* Zollschranke *f e-s Staates*.

tar·mac ['tɑːmæk] *s. Brit.* 'Teermakaˌdam(straße *f*, ✈ -rollfeld *n*) *m*, ✈ *a.* Hallenvorfeld *n*.

tar·nish ['tɑːnɪʃ] **I** *v/t.* **1.** trüben, matt *od.* blind machen, *e-r Sache* den Glanz nehmen; **2.** *fig.* besudeln, beflecken; **3.** ⚙ mattieren; **II** *v/i.* **4.** matt *od.* trübe werden; **5.** anlaufen (*Metall*); **III** *s.* **6.**

Trübung *f*; Beschlag *m*, Anlaufen *n* (*von Metall*); **7.** *fig.* Fleck *m*, Makel *m*.

tarp [tɑːp] *abbr.* → **tar·pau·lin** [tɑːˈpɔːlɪn] *s.* **1.** ⚓ a) Perˈsenning *f* (*geteertes Segeltuch*), b) Ölzeug *n* (*Hose*, *Mantel*); **2.** Plane *f*, Wagendecke *f*; **3.** Zeltbahn *f*.

tar·ra·did·dle → ***taradiddle***.

tar·ry¹ [ˈtɑːrɪ] *adj.* teerig.

tar·ry² [ˈtærɪ] **I** *v/i.* **1.** zögern, zaudern, säumen; **2.** (ver)weilen, bleiben; **II** *v/t.* **3.** *obs. et.* abwarten.

tar·sal [ˈtɑːsl] *anat.* **I** *adj.* **1.** Fußwurzel…; **2.** (Augen)Lidknorpel…; **II** *s.* **3.** *a.* ~ ***bone*** Fußwurzelknochen *m*; **4.** (Augen)Lidknorpel *m*.

tar·si·a [ˈtɑːsɪə] *s.* Inˈtarsia *f*, Einlegearbeit *f* in Holz.

tar·sus [ˈtɑːsəs] *pl.* **-si** [-saɪ] *s.* **1.** → ***tarsal*** 3 *u.* 4; **2.** *orn.* Laufknochen *m*; **3.** *zo.* Fußglied *n*.

tart¹ [tɑːt] *adj.* □ **1.** sauer, herb, scharf; **2.** *fig.* scharf, beißend: ~ ***reply***.

tart² [tɑːt] **I** *s.* **1.** a) (Obst)Torte *f*, Obstkuchen *m*, b) *bsd. Am.* (*Creme-*, Obst-) Törtchen *n*; **2.** *sl.* ‚Nutte' *f*; **II** *v/t.* ~ ***up*** *sl.* ‚aufputzen', ‚aufmotzen'.

tar·tan¹ [ˈtɑːtən] *s.* Tartan *m*: a) Schottentuch *n*, b) Schottenmuster *n*: ~ ***plaid*** Schottenplaid *n*.

tar·tan² [ˈtɑːtən] *s. sport* Tartan *n* (*Bahnbelag*).

Tar·tar¹ [ˈtɑːtə] **I** *s.* **1.** Taˈtar(in); **2.** *a.* ≈ Wüterich *m*, böser Kerl: ***catch a*** ~ an den Unrechten kommen; **II** *adj.* **3.** taˈtarisch.

tar·tar² [ˈtɑːtə] *s.* **1.** Weinstein *m*: ~ ***emetic*** ⚕ Brechweinstein; **2.** Zahnstein *m*; **tar·tar·ic** [tɑːˈtærɪk] *adj.*: ~ ***acid*** ⚗ Weinsäure *f*.

tart·ness [ˈtɑːtnɪs] *s.* Schärfe *f*: a) Säure *f*, Herbheit *f*, b) *fig.* Schroffheit *f*, Bissigkeit *f*.

task [tɑːsk] **I** *s.* **1.** Aufgabe *f*: ***take to*** ~ *fig. j-n* ins Gebet nehmen (***for*** wegen); **2.** Pflicht *f*, (auferlegte) Arbeit; **3.** *ped.* (Prüfungs)Aufgabe *f*; **II** *v/t.* **4.** *j-m* Arbeit zuweisen *od.* aufbürden, *j-n* beschäftigen; **5.** *fig. Kräfte etc.* stark beanspruchen, *sein Gedächtnis etc.* anstrengen; ~ **force** *s.* **1.** ⚔ *gemischter* Kampfverband (*für Sonderunternehmen*), Task force *f*; **2.** *Polizei*: a) Speziˈaleinheit *f*, Einsatzgruppe *f*, b) ˈSonderdezerˌnat *n*; **3.** ☤ Proˈjektgruppe *f*; ˈ~ˌ**mas·ter** *s.* **1.** (*bsd.* strenger) Arbeitgeber: ***severe*** ~ *fig.* strenger Zuchtmeister; **2.** ⚙ (Arbeit)Anweiser *m*; ~ **wag·es** *s. pl.* ☤ Akˈkord-, Stücklohn *m*; ˈ~·**work** *s.* **1.** ☤ Akˈkordarbeit *f*; **2.** harte Arbeit.

tas·sel [ˈtæsl] **I** *s.* Quaste *f*, Troddel *f*; **II** *v/t.* mit Quasten schmücken.

taste [teɪst] **I** *v/t.* **1.** *Speisen etc.* kosten, (ab)schmecken, probieren, versuchen (*a. fig.*); **2.** kosten, *Essen* anrühren: ***he had not ~d food for days***; **3.** *et.* (herˈaus)schmecken; **4.** *fig.* kosten, kennenlernen, erleben; **5.** *fig.* genießen; **II** *v/i.* **6.** schmecken (***of*** nach); **7.** kosten, versuchen (***of*** von *od. acc.*); **8.** ~ ***of*** → 4; **III** *s.* **9.** Geschmack *m*: ***a*** ~ ***of garlic*** ein Knoblauchgeschmack; ***leave a bad*** ~ ***in one's mouth*** *bsd. fig.* e-n üblen Nachgeschmack haben; **10.** Geschmackssinn *m*; **11.** (Kost)Probe *f* (***of*** von *od. gen.*): a) kleiner Bissen, b) Schlückchen *n*; **12.** *fig.* (Kost)Probe *f*, Vorgeschmack *m* (***of*** *gen.*); **13.** *fig.* Beigeschmack *m*, Anflug *m* (***of*** von); **14.** *fig.* (künstlerischer *od.* guter) Geschmack: ***in bad*** ~ geschmacklos (*a. weitS. unfein*, *taktlos*); ***in good*** ~ a) geschmackvoll, b) taktvoll; ***each to his*** (***own***) ~ jeder nach s-m Geschmack; **15.** Geschmacksrichtung *f*, Mode *f*; **16.** a) Neigung *f*, Sinn *m* (***for*** für), b) Geschmack *m*, Gefallen *n* (***for*** an *dat.*): ***not to my*** ~ nicht nach m-m Geschmack; **taste bud** *s. anat.* Geschmacksbecher *m*; ˈ**taste·ful** [-fʊl] *adj.* □ *fig.* geschmackvoll; ˈ**taste·ful·ness** [-fʊlnɪs] *s. fig.* guter Geschmack *e-r Sache*, *das* Geschmackvolle; ˈ**taste·less** [-lɪs] *adj.* □ **1.** unschmackhaft, fade; **2.** *fig.* geschmacklos; ˈ**taste·less·ness** [-lɪsnɪs] *s.* **1.** Unschmackhaftigkeit *f*; **2.** *fig.* Geschmack-, Taktlosigkeit *f*; ˈ**tast·er** [-tə] *s.* **1.** (berufsmäßiger Tee-, Wein- *etc.*)Koster *m*; **2.** *hist.* Vorkoster *m*; **3.** Proˈbiergläs-chen *n* (*für Wein*); **4.** (Käse)Stecher *m*; ˈ**tast·i·ness** [-tɪnɪs] *s.* **1.** Schmackhaftigkeit *f* (*Speise etc.*); **2.** *fig.* → ***tastefulness***; ˈ**tast·y** [-tɪ] *adj.* □ F **1.** schmackhaft; **2.** *fig.* geschmack-, stilvoll.

ta-ta [ˌtæˈtɑː] *int. Brit.* F ‚Tschüs'!, auf ˈWiedersehen!

Ta·tar [ˈtɑːtə] **I** *s.* Taˈtar(in); **II** *adj.* taˈtarisch; **Ta·tar·i·an** [tɑːˈteərɪən], **Ta·tar·ic** [tɑːˈtærɪk] *adj.* tatarisch.

tat·ter [ˈtætə] *s.* Lumpen *m*, Fetzen *m*: ***in ~s*** zerfetzt; ***tear to ~s*** (*a. fig. Argument etc.*) zerfetzen, -reißen; ˈ**tat·tered** [-təd] *adj.* **1.** zerlumpt, abgerissen; **2.** zerrissen, zerfetzt; **3.** ramponiert (*Ruf etc.*).

tat·tle [ˈtætl] **I** *v/i.* klatschen, ‚tratschen'; **II** *v/t.* ausplaudern; **III** *s.* Klatsch *m*, ‚Tratsch' *m*; ˈ**tat·tler** [-lə] *s.* Klatschbase *f*, -maul *n*.

tat·too¹ [təˈtuː] **I** *s.* **1.** ⚔ a) Zapfenstreich *m* (*Signal*), b) ˈAbendpaˌrade *f* mit Muˈsik; **2.** Trommeln *n*, Klopfen *n*: ***beat a*** (*od.* ***the devil's***) ~ ungeduldig mit den Fingern trommeln; **II** *v/i.* **3.** den Zapfenstreich blasen *od.* trommeln; **4.** trommeln, klopfen.

tat·too² [təˈtuː] **I** *v/t. pret. u. p.p.* **tat·ˈtooed** [-uːd] **1.** *Haut* tätowieren; **2.** *Muster* eintätowieren (***on*** in *acc.*); **II** *s.* **3.** Tätowierung *f*.

tat·ty [ˈtætɪ] *adj.* schäbig, schmuddelig, ‚billig'.

taught [tɔːt] *pret. u. p.p. von* ***teach***.

taunt [tɔːnt] **I** *v/t.* verhöhnen, -spotten: ~ ***s.o. with*** j-m *et.* (höhnisch) vorwerfen; **II** *v/i.* höhnen, spotten; **III** *s.* Spott *m*, Hohn *m*; ˈ**taunt·ing** [-tɪŋ] *adj.* □ spöttisch, höhnisch.

tau·rine [ˈtɔːraɪn] *adj.* **1.** *zo.* a) rinderartig, b) Rinder…, Stier…; **2.** *ast.* Stier…; **Tau·rus** [ˈtɔːrəs] *s. ast.* Stier *m* (*Sternbild u. Tierkreiszeichen*).

taut [tɔːt] *adj.* □ **1.** straff, stramm (*Seil etc.*), angespannt (*a. Nerven*, *Gesicht*, *Person*); **2.** schmuck (*Schiff etc.*); ˈ**taut·en** [-tən] **I** *v/t.* stramm ziehen, straff anspannen; **II** *v/i.* sich straffen *od.* spannen.

tau·to·log·ic, **tau·to·log·i·cal** [ˌtɔːtəˈlɒdʒɪk(l)] *adj.* □ tautoˈlogisch, unnötig dasˈselbe wiederˈholend; **tau·tol·o·gy** [tɔːˈtɒlədʒɪ] *s.* Tautoloˈgie *f*, Doppelaussage *f*.

tav·ern [ˈtævən] *s.* **1.** *obs.* Taˈverne *f*, Schenke *f*; **2.** *Am.* Gasthaus *n*.

taw¹ [tɔː] *v/t.* weißgerben.

taw² [tɔː] *s.* **1.** Murmel *f*; **2.** Murmelspiel *n*; **3.** Ausgangslinie *f*.

taw·dri·ness [ˈtɔːdrɪnɪs] *s.* **1.** Flitterhaftigkeit *f*, grelle Buntheit, Kitsch *m*; **2.** Wertlosigkeit *f*, Billigkeit *f*; **taw·dry** [ˈtɔːdrɪ] *adj.* □ **1.** flitterhaft, Flitter…; **2.** geschmacklos aufgemacht; **3.** grell, knallig; **4.** kitschig, billig.

tawed [tɔːd] *adj. Gerberei*: aˈlaungar (*Leder*); **taw·er** [ˈtɔːə] *s.* Weißgerber *m*; **taw·er·y** [ˈtɔːərɪ] *s.* Weißgerbeˈrei *f*.

taw·ny [ˈtɔːnɪ] *adj.* lohfarben, gelbbraun: ~ ***owl*** *orn.* Waldkauz *m*.

taws(e) [tɔːz] *s. Brit.* Peitsche *f*.

tax [tæks] **I** *s.* **1.** (Staats)Steuer *f* (***on*** auf *acc.*), Abgabe *f*: ~ ***on land*** Grundsteuer; **2.** Besteuerung *f* (***on*** *gen.*); ***after*** (***before***) ~ nach (vor) Abzug der Steuern, *a.* netto (brutto); **3.** Taxe *f*, Gebühr *f*; **4.** *fig.* a) Bürde *f*, Last *f*, b) Belastung *f*, Beanspruchung *f* (***on*** *gen. od.* von): ***a heavy*** ~ ***on his time*** e-e starke Inanspruchnahme s-r Zeit; **II** *v/t.* **5.** *j-n od. et.* besteuern, *j-m* e-e Steuer auferlegen; **6.** ⚖ *Kosten etc.* schätzen, taxieren, ansetzen (***at*** auf *acc.*); **7.** *fig.* belasten; **8.** *fig.* stark in Anspruch nehmen, anstrengen, strapazieren; **9.** auf e-e harte Probe stellen; **10.** *j-n* zuˈrechtweisen: ~ ***s.o. with*** j-n *e-r Sache* beschuldigen *od.* bezichtigen; **tax·a·ble** [ˈtæksəbl] **I** *adj.* □ **1.** besteuerbar; **2.** steuerpflichtig: ~ ***income***; **3.** Steuer…: ~ ***value***; **4.** ⚖ gebührenpflichtig; **II** *s. Am.* **5.** steuerpflichtiges Einkommen; **6.** Steuerpflichtige(r *m*) *f*; **tax·a·tion** [tækˈseɪʃn] *s.* **1.** Besteuerung *f*; **2.** *coll.* Steuern *pl.*; **3.** ⚖ Schätzung *f*, Taxierung *f*.

tax| al·low·ance *s.* Steuerfreibetrag *m*; ~ **a·void·ance** (leˈgale) ˈSteuerumˌgehung; ~ **brack·et** *s.* Steuerklasse *f*, -gruppe *f*; ~ **col·lec·tor** *s.* Steuereinnehmer *m*; ˈ**~-deˌduct·i·ble** *adj.* steuerabzugsfähig; ~ **dodg·er**, ~ **e·vad·er** *s.* ˈSteuerhinterˌzieher *m*; ~ **e·va·sion** *s.* ˈSteuerhinterˌziehung *f*; ˌ**~-exˈempt**, ˌ**~-ˈfree** *adj.* steuerfrei; ~ **ha·ven** *s.* ˈSteueroˌase *f*.

tax·i [ˈtæksɪ] **I** *pl.* ˈ**tax·is** *s.* **1.** → ***taxicab***; **II** *v/i.* **2.** mit e-m Taxi fahren; **3.** ✈ rollen; ˈ**~·cab** *s.* Taxi *n*; ~ **danc·er** *s. Am.* Taxigirl *n*.

tax·i·der·mal [ˌtæksɪˈdɜːml], **tax·iˈder·mic** [-mɪk] *adj.* taxiˈdermisch; **tax·i·der·mist** [ˈtæksɪdɜːmɪst] *s.* Präpaˈrator *m*, Ausstopfer *m* (*von Tieren*); **tax·i·der·my** [ˈtæksɪdɜːmɪ] *s.* Taxiderˈmie *f*.

ˈ**tax·i|-ˌdriv·er** *s.*, ˈ**~-man** [-mæn] *s.* [*irr.*] ˈTaxichaufˌfeur *m*, -fahrer *m*; ˈ**~ˌme·ter** *s.* Taxaˈmeter *m*, Zähler *m*, Fahrpreisanzeiger *m*; ˈ**~·plane** *s.* Lufttaxi *n*; ~ **rank** *s.* Taxistand *m*; ~ **strip**, ˈ**~·way** *s.* ✈ Rollbahn *f*.

ˈ**tax|ˌpay·er** *s.* Steuerzahler *m*; ~ **rate** *s.* Steuersatz *m*; ~ **re·fund** *s.* Steuerrückzahlung *f*; ~ **re·lief** *s.* Steuererleichterung(en *pl.*) *f*; ~ **re·turn** *s.* Steuererklärung *f*.

ˈ**T-bone steak** *s.* T-bone-Steak *n* (*Steak aus dem Rippenstück des Rinds*).

tea [tiː] *s.* **1.** Tee *m*; **2.** Tee(mahlzeit *f*) *m*: ***five-o'clock*** ~ Fünfuhrtee; **3.** *Am.*

sl. ‚Grass' *n* (*Marihuana*); ~ **bag** *s.* Teebeutel *m*; ~ **ball** *s. Am.* Tee-Ei *n*; ~ **bread** *s. ein* Teekuchen *m*; ~ **cad·dy** *s.* Teebüchse *f*; ~ **cake** *s.* Teekuchen *m*; '~**·cart** *s.* Teewagen *m.*

teach [tiːtʃ] *pret. u. p.p.* **taught** [tɔːt] **I** *v/t.* **1.** *Fach* lehren, 'Unterricht geben in (*dat.*); **2.** *j-n et.* lehren, *j-n* unter'richten, -'weisen in (*dat.*), *j-m* 'Unterricht geben in (*dat.*); **3.** *j-m et.* zeigen, beibringen: ~ ***s.o. to whistle*** j-m das Pfeifen beibringen; ~ ***s.o. better*** j-n e-s Besser(e)n belehren; ***I will ~ you to steal*** F dich werd' ich das Stehlen lehren!; ***that'll ~ you!*** F a) das wird dir e-e Lehre sein!, b) das kommt davon!; **4.** *Tier* dressieren, abrichten; **II** *v/i.* **5.** unter'richten, 'Unterricht geben, '**teach·a·ble** [-tʃəbl] *adj.* **1.** lehrbar (*Fach etc.*); **2.** gelehrig (*Person*); '**teach·er** [-tʃə] *s.* Lehrer(in): ~***s college*** *Am.* Pädagogische Hochschule.

'**teach-in** *s.* Teach-in *n.*

teach·ing ['tiːtʃɪŋ] **I** *s.* **1.** Unter'richten *n*, Lehren *n*; **2.** *oft pl.* Lehre *f*, Lehren *pl.*; **3.** Lehrberuf *m*; **II** *adj.* **4.** lehrend, unter'richtend: ~ ***aid*** Lehrmittel *n*; ~ ***machine*** Lehr-, Lernmaschine *f*; ~ ***profession*** Lehrberuf *m*; ~ ***staff*** Lehrkörper *m.*

tea| cloth *s.* **1.** kleine Tischdecke; **2.** *Am.* Geschirrtuch *n*; ~ **co·sy** *s., Am.* ~ **co·zy** *s.* Teewärmer *m*; '~**·cup** *s.* Teetasse *f*; → ***storm*** 1; '~**·cup,ful** [-ˌfʊl] *pl.* **-fuls** *s. e-e* Teetasse(voll); ~ **dance** *s.* Tanztee *m*; ~ **egg** *s.* Tee-Ei *n*; ~ **garden** *s.* 'Gartenrestauˌrant *n*; ~ **gown** *s.* Nachmittagskleid *n*; '~**·house** *s.* Teehaus *n* (*in China u. Japan*).

teak [tiːk] *s.* **1.** ⚘ Teakholzbaum *m*; **2.** Teak(holz) *n.*

teal [tiːl] *pl.* **teal** *s. orn.* Krickente *f.*

team [tiːm] **I** *s.* **1.** Gespann *n*; **2.** *bsd. sport u. fig.* Mannschaft *f*, Team *n*; **3.** (*Arbeits- etc.*)Gruppe *f*, Team *n*: ***by a ~ effort*** mit vereinten Kräften; **4.** Ab'teilung *f*, Ko'lonne *f von Arbeitern*; **5.** *orn.* Flug *m*, Zug *m*; **II** *v/t.* **6.** *Zugtiere* zs.-spannen; **7.** F *Arbeit* (an Unter'nehmer) vergeben; **III** *v/i.* **8.** ~ ***up*** *bsd. Am.* sich zs.-tun (***with*** mit); ~ **e·vent** *s. sport* Mannschaftswettbewerb *m*; '~**·mate** *s.* 'Mannschaftskameˌrad *m*; ~ **spir·it** *s.* **1.** *sport* Mannschaftsgeist *m*; **2.** *fig.* Gemeinschafts-, 'Korpsgeist *m.*

team·ster ['tiːmstə] *s.* **1.** Fuhrmann *m*; **2.** *Am.* Lastwagenfahrer *m.*

team| teach·ing *s. Am.* gemeinsamer 'Unterricht (*Fachlehrer*); '~**·work** *s.* **1.** *sport, thea.* Zs.-spiel *n*; **2.** *fig.* (gute) Zs.-arbeit, Teamwork *n.*

tea| par·ty *s.* Teegesellschaft *f*: ***the Boston*** ~ ~ *hist.* der Teesturm von Boston (*1773*); '~**·pot** *s.* Teekanne *f*; → ***tempest*** 1.

tear[1] [tɪə] *s.* **1.** Träne *f*: ***in ~s*** in Tränen (aufgelöst), unter Tränen; → ***fetch*** 3, ***squeeze*** 3; **2.** ⚙ (Harz- *etc.*)Tropfen *m*; (Glas)Träne *f.*

tear[2] [teə] **I** *s.* **1.** Riß *m*; **2.** ***at full ~*** in vollem Schwung; ***in a ~*** in wilder Hast; **II** *v/t.* [*irr.*] **3.** zerreißen: ~ ***in*** (*od.* ***to***) ***pieces*** in Stücke reißen; ~ ***open*** aufreißen; ~ ***out*** herausreißen; ***torn between hope and despair*** *fig.* zwischen Hoffnung u. Verzweiflung hin- u. hergerissen;: ***a country torn by civil war*** ein vom Bürgerkrieg zerrissenes Land; ***that's torn it!*** *sl.* jetzt ist es passiert!, damit ist alles ‚im Eimer'!; **4.** *Haut etc.* aufreißen; **5.** *Loch* reißen; **6.** zerren, (aus)reißen: ~ ***one's hair*** sich die Haare (aus)raufen; **7.** *a.* ~ ***away***, ~ ***off*** ab-, wegreißen (***from*** von): ~ ***o.s. away*** sich losreißen (*a. fig.*); ~ ***s.th. from s.o.*** j-m et. entreißen; **III** *v/i.* [*irr.*] **8.** (zer-) reißen; **9.** reißen, zerren (***at*** an *dat.*); **10.** F rasen, sausen, ‚fegen': ~ ***about*** herumsausen; ~ **up** *v/t.* **1.** aufreißen; **2.** *Baum etc.* ausreißen; **3.** zerreißen, in Stücke reißen; **4.** *fig.* unter'graben, zerstören.

tear·a·way ['teərəweɪ] **I** *adj.* ‚wild'; **II** *s.* ‚wilder' Kerl, Ra'bauke *m.*

tear| bomb [tɪə] Tränengasbombe *f*; '~**·drop** *s.* **1.** Träne *f*; **2.** Anhänger *m* (*Ohrring*).

tear·ful ['tɪəfʊl] *adj.* □ **1.** tränenreich; **2.** weinend, in Tränen; **3.** weinerlich; **4.** schmerzlich.

tear| gas [tɪə] *s.* ☤ Tränengas *n*; ~ **gland** *s. anat.* Tränendrüse *f.*

tear·ing ['teərɪŋ] *adj. fig.* F **1.** rasend, toll (*Tempo, Wut etc.*); **2.** ‚toll'; ~ **strength** *s.* ⚙ Zerreißfestigkeit *f.*

'**tear|ˌjerk·er** [tɪə] *s. Am.* F ‚Schnulze' *f*, ‚Schmachtfetzen' *m.*

'**tear-off** ['teərɒf] *adj.* Abreiß…: ~ ***calendar.***

'**tea|·room** [-rʊm] *s.* Teestube *f*, Ca'fé *n*; ~ **rose** *s.* ⚘ Teerose *f.*

tear sheet [teə] *s. Am.* Belegbogen *m.*

'**tear-stained** ['tɪə-] *adj.* **1.** tränennaß; **2.** verweint (*Augen*).

tease [tiːz] **I** *v/t.* **1.** ⚙ a) *Wolle* kämmen, krempeln, b) *Flachs* hecheln, c) *Werg* auszupfen; **2.** ⚙ *Tuch* krempeln, karden; **3.** *fig.* quälen: a) hänseln, aufziehen, b) ärgern, c) bestürmen, belästigen (***for*** wegen); **4.** (auf)reizen; **II** *s.* **5.** F a) → ***teaser*** 1, 2, b) Plage *f*, lästige Sache.

tea·sel ['tiːzl] **I** *s.* **1.** ⚘ Karde(ndistel) *f*; **2.** *Weberei*: Karde *f*; **II** *v/t.* **3.** → ***tease*** 2.

teas·er ['tiːzə] *s.* **1.** Necker *m*; **2.** Quälgeist, Plagegeist *m*; **3.** *sl.* Frau, die ‚alles verspricht und nichts hält'; **4.** F ‚harte Nuß', schwierige Sache; **5.** F et. Verlockendes.

tea| serv·ice, ~ **set** *s.* 'Teeserˌvice *n*; '~**·shop** → ***tearoom***; '~**·spoon** *s.* Teelöffel *m*; '~**·spoonˌful** [-ˌfʊl] *pl.* **-fuls** *s. ein* Teelöffel(voll) *m.*

teat [tiːt] *s.* **1.** *zo.* Zitze *f*; **2.** *anat.* Brustwarze *f*; **3.** (Gummi)Sauger *m*; **4.** ⚙ Warze *f.*

'**tea|-things** *s. pl.* Teegeschirr *n*; '~**·time** *s.* Teestunde *f*; ~ **tow·el** *s.* Geschirrtuch *n*; '~**-urn** *s.* **1.** 'Teemaˌschine *f*; **2.** Gefäß *n* zum Heißhalten des Teewassers.

tea·zel, tea·zle → ***teasel.***

tec [tek] *s. sl.* Detek'tiv *m.*

tech·nic ['teknɪk] **I** *adj.* → ***technical***; **II** *s. mst pl.* → a) ***technics***, b) ***technology***, c) ***technique***; '**tech·ni·cal** [-kl] *adj.* □ → ***technically***; **1.** ⚙ 'technisch: ~ ***bureau*** Konstruktionsbüro *n*; **2.** technisch (*a. sport*), fachlich, fachmännisch, Fach…, Spezial…: ~ ***book*** (technisches) Fachbuch; ~ ***dictionary*** Fachwörterbuch *n*; ~ ***school*** Fachhochschule *f*; ~ ***skill*** a) (technisches) Geschick, b) ♪ Technik *f*; ~ ***staff*** technisches Personal; ~ ***term*** Fachausdruck *m*; **3.** *fig.* technisch: a) sachlich, b) (rein) for'mal, c) theo'retisch: ~ ***knockout*** *Boxen*: technischer K. o.; ***on ~ grounds*** ⚖ aus formaljuristischen *od.* verfahrenstechnischen Gründen; **tech·ni·cal·i·ty** [ˌteknɪ'kælətɪ] *s.* **1.** *das* Technische; **2.** technische Besonderheit *od.* Einzelheit; **3.** Fachausdruck *m*; **4.** *bsd.* ⚖ (reine) Formsache, (for'male) Spitzfindigkeit; '**tech·ni·cal·ly** [-kəlɪ] *adv.* **1.** technisch *etc.*; **2.** genaugenommen, eigentlich; **tech·ni·cian** [tek'nɪʃn] *s.* **1.** Techniker(in) (*a. weitS. Virtuose etc.*), (technischer) Fachmann; **2.** ⚔ *Am.* Techniker *m* (*Dienstrang für Spezialisten*).

tech·nics ['teknɪks] *s. pl.* **1.** *mst sg. konstr.* Technik *f*, *bsd.* Ingeni'eurwissenschaft *f*; **2.** technische Einzelheiten *pl.*; **3.** Fachausdrücke *pl.*; **4.** → **technique** [tek'niːk] *s.* **1.** ⚙ (Arbeits)Verfahren *n*, (*Schweiß- etc.*)Technik *f*; **2.** ♪, *paint.*, *sport etc.* Technik *f*: a) Me'thode *f*, b) Art *f* der Ausführung, c) Geschicklichkeit *f*; **tech·noc·ra·cy** [tek'nɒkrəsɪ] *s.* Technokra'tie *f*; **tech·no·crat** ['teknəʊkræt] *s.* Techno'krat *m.*

tech·no·log·ic, tech·no·log·i·cal [ˌteknə'lɒdʒɪk(l)] *adj.* □ **1.** techno'logisch, technisch; **2.** ✝ techno'logisch (bedingt): ~ ***unemployment***; **tech·nol·o·gist** [tek'nɒlədʒɪst] *s.* Techno'loge *m*; **tech·nol·o·gy** [tek'nɒlədʒɪ] *s.* **1.** Technolo'gie *f*: ~ ***transfer*** Technologietransfer *m*; ***school of ~*** technische Universität; **2.** technische 'Fachterminoloˌgie.

tech·y ['tetʃɪ] → ***testy.***

tec·tol·o·gy [tek'tɒlədʒɪ] *s. biol.* Struk'turlehre *f.*

tec·ton·ic [tek'tɒnɪk] *adj.* (□ ~***ally***) **1.** △, *geol.* tek'tonisch; **2.** *biol.* struktu'rell; **tec'ton·ics** [-ks] *s. pl. mst sg. konstr.* **1.** △ *etc.* Tek'tonik *f*; **2.** *geol.* ('Geo)Tekˌtonik *f.*

tec·to·ri·al [tek'tɔːrɪəl] *adj. physiol.* Schutz…, Deck…: ~ ***membrane.***

tec·tri·ces [tek'traɪsiːz] *s. pl. zo.* Deckfedern *pl.*

ted·der ['tedə] *s.* ⚒ Heuwender *m.*

Ted·dy bear ['tedɪ] *s.* Teddybär *m.*

te·di·ous ['tiːdjəs] *adj.* □ **1.** langweilig, öde, ermüdend; **2.** weitschweifig; '**te·di·ous·ness** [-nɪs] *s.* **1.** Langweiligkeit *f*; **2.** Weitschweifigkeit *f*; '**te·di·um** [-jəm] *s.* **1.** Lang(e)weile *f*; **2.** Langweiligkeit *f.*

tee[1] [tiː] **I** *s.* ⚙ T-Stück *n*; **II** *adj.* T-…: ~ ***iron***; **III** *v/t.* ϟ abzweigen: ~ ***across*** (***together***) in Brücke (parallel)schalten.

tee[2] [tiː] **I** *s. sport* Tee *n*: a) *Curling*: Mittelpunkt *m* des Zielkreises, b) *Golf*: Abschlag(stelle *f*) *m*: ***to a ~*** *fig.* aufs Haar; **II** *v/t. Golf*: *Ball* auf die Abschlagstelle legen; **III** *v/i.* ~ ***off*** a) *Golf*: abschlagen, b) *fig.* anfangen.

teem[1] [tiːm] *v/i.* **1.** wimmeln, voll sein (***with*** von): ***the roads are ~ing with people***; ***this page ~s with mistakes*** diese Seite strotzt von Fehlern; **2.** reichlich vor'handen sein: ***fish ~ in that river*** in dem Fluß wimmelt es von Fischen; **3.** *obs.* a) schwanger sein, b) ⚘ Früchte tragen, c) *zo.* Junge gebären.

teem² [tiːm] **I** *v/t. bsd.* ⚙ *flüssiges Metall* (aus)gießen; **II** *v/i.* gießen (*a. fig. Regen*).
teen [tiːn] *Am.* → ***teenage(r)***; ˈ**teen·age** [-eɪdʒ] **I** *adj. a.* ***teenaged*** **1.** im Teenageralter; **2.** Teenager…; **II** *s.* **3.** → ***teens*** 1; ˈ**teenˌag·er** [-ˌeɪdʒə] *s.* Teenager *m.*
teens [tiːnz] *s. pl.* **1.** Teenageralter *n*: ***be in one's ~*** ein Teenager sein; **2.** Teenager *pl.*
tee·ny¹ [ˈtiːnɪ], *a.* ˌ**~-ˈwee·ny** [-ˈwiːnɪ] *adj.* F klitzeklein.
teen·y² [ˈtiːnɪ] *s.* F ‚Teeny' *m* (*jüngerer Teenager*).
ˈ**tee-shirt** [ˈtiː-] *s.* ˈT-Shirt *n.*
tee·ter [ˈtiːtə] *v/i. Am.* F **1.** (*a. v/t.*) schaukeln, wippen; **2.** (sch)wanken.
teeth [tiːθ] *pl. von* ***tooth.***
teethe [tiːð] *v/i.* zahnen, (die) Zähne bekommen: ***teething troubles*** a) Beschwerden beim Zahnen, b) *fig.* Kinderkrankheiten.
tee·to·tal [tiːˈtəʊtl] *adj.* abstiˈnent, Abstinenzler…; **teeˈto·tal·(l)er** [-tlə] *s.* Abstiˈnenzler(in), ˌAntialkoˈholiker (-in); **teeˈto·tal·ism** [-tlɪzəm] *s.* **1.** Abstiˈnenz *f*; **2.** Abstiˈnenzprinˌzip *n.*
tee·to·tum [ˌtiːtəʊˈtʌm] *s.* Drehwürfel *m.*
teg·u·ment [ˈtegjʊmənt] *etc.* → ***integument*** *etc.*
tele-¹ [telɪ] *in Zssgn* a) Fern…, b) Fernseh…
tele-² [telɪ] *in Zssgn* a) Ziel, b) Ende.
ˈ**tel·eˌcam·er·a** *s. TV* Fernsehkamera *f.*
ˈ**tel·e·cast I** *v/t.* [*irr.* → ***cast***] im Fernsehen überˈtragen *od.* bringen; **II** *s.* Fernsehsendung *f*; ˈ**tel·e·cast·er** *s.* (Fernseh)Ansager(in).
ˈ**tel·e·comˌmu·niˈca·tion I** *s.* **1.** Fernmeldeverbindung *f*, -verkehr *m*, ˈTelekommunikatiˌon *f*; **2.** *pl.* Fernmeldewesen *n*, -technik *f*; **II** *adj.* **3.** Fernmelde…
tel·e·con·fer·ence [ˈtelɪˌkɒnfərəns] *s.* Teleˈfonkonfeˌrenz *f.*
ˈ**tel·e·course** *s.* Fernsehlehrgang *m*, -kurs *m.*
tel·e·di·ag·no·sis [ˈtelɪˌdaɪəgˈnəʊsɪs] *s.* [*irr.*] ⚕ ˈFerndiagˌnose *f.*
ˈ**tel·e·film** *s.* Fernsehfilm *m.*
tel·e·gen·ic [ˌtelɪˈdʒenɪk] *adj. TV* teleˈgen.
tel·e·gram [ˈtelɪgræm] *s.* Teleˈgramm *n*: ***by ~*** telegrafisch.
tel·e·graph [ˈtelɪgrɑːf; -græf] **I** *s.* **1.** Teleˈgraf *m*; **2.** Teleˈgramm *n*; **3.** → ***telegraph board***; **II** *v/t.* **4.** telegrafieren; **5.** *j-n* teleˈgrafisch benachrichtigen; **6.** (*durch Zeichen*) zu verstehen geben, signalisieren; **7.** *sport Spielstand etc.* auf e-r Tafel anzeigen; **8.** *sl. Boxen: Schlag* ‚telegrafieren' (*erkennbar ansetzen*); **III** *v/i.* **9.** telegrafieren (***to*** *dat. od.* an *acc.*); **~ board** *s. bsd. sport* Anzeigetafel *f*; **~ code** *s.* Teleˈgrammschlüssel *m.*
te·leg·ra·pher [tɪˈlegrəfə] *s.* Telegraˈfist(in).
tel·e·graph·ese [ˌtelɪgrɑːˈfiːz] *s.* Teleˈgrammstil *m*; **tel·e·graph·ic** [ˌtelɪˈgræfɪk] *adj.* (□ ***~ally***) **1.** teleˈgrafisch: **~ *address*** Teleˈgrammadresse *f*, Drahtanschrift *f*; **2.** teleˈgrammartig (*Kürze, Stil*); **te·leg·ra·phist** [tɪˈlegrəfɪst] *s.* Telegraˈfist(in).
tel·e·graph| line *s.* Teleˈgrafenleitung *f*; **~ pole**, **~ post** *s.* Teleˈgrafenstange *f*, -mast *m.*
te·leg·ra·phy [tɪˈlegrəfɪ] *s.* Telegraˈfie *f.*
tel·e·ki·ne·sis [ˌtelɪkɪˈniːsɪs] *s. psych.* Telekiˈnese *f.*
tel·e·lens [ˈtelɪlens] *s. phot.* ˈTeleobjekˌtiv *n.*
te·lem·e·ter [ˈtelɪmiːtə] *s.* Teleˈmeter *n*: a) ⚙ Entfernungsmesser *m*, b) ⚡ Fernmeßgerät *n.*
tel·e·o·log·ic, **tel·e·o·log·i·cal** [ˌtelɪəˈlɒdʒɪk(l)] *adj.* □ *phls.* teleoˈlogisch: **~ *argument*** teleologischer Gottesbeweis; **tel·e·ol·o·gy** [ˌtelɪˈɒlədʒɪ] *s.* Teleoloˈgie *f.*
tel·e·path·ic [ˌtelɪˈpæθɪk] *adj.* (□ ***~ally***) teleˈpathisch; **te·lep·a·thy** [tɪˈlepəθɪ] *s.* Telepaˈthie *f*, Geˈdankenüberˌtragung *f.*
tel·e·phone [ˈtelɪfəʊn] **I** *s.* **1.** Teleˈfon *n*, Fernsprecher *m*: ***at the ~*** am Apparat; ***by ~*** telefonisch; ***on the ~*** telefonisch, durch das *od.* am Telefon; ***be on the ~*** a) Telefonanschluß haben, b) am Telefon sein; ***over the ~*** durch das *od.* per Telefon; **II** *v/t.* **2.** *j-n* anrufen, antelefonieren; **3.** *Nachricht etc.* telefonieren, teleˈfonisch überˈmitteln (***s.th. to s.o., s.o. s.th.*** j-m et.); **III** *v/i.* **4.** telefonieren; **~ booth**, *Brit.* **~ box** *s.* Teleˈfon-, Fernsprechzelle *f*; **~ call** *s.* Teleˈfongespräch *n*, (Teleˈfon)Anruf *m*; **~ connec·tion** *s.* Teleˈfonanschluß *m*; **~ direc·to·ry** *s.* Teleˈfon-, Fernsprechbuch *n*; **~ ex·change** *s.* Fernsprechamt *n*, Teleˈfonzenˌtrale *f*; **~ op·er·a·tor** *s.* Telefoˈnist(in); **~ re·ceiv·er** *s.* (Teleˈfon-)Hörer *m*; **~ sub·scrib·er** *s.* Fernsprechteilnehmer(in).
tel·e·phon·ic [ˌtelɪˈfɒnɪk] *adj.* (□ ***~ally***) teleˈfonisch, fernmündlich, Telefon…;
tel·e·pho·nist [tɪˈlefənɪst] *s.* Telefoˈnist(in); **te·leph·o·ny** [tɪˈlefənɪ] *s.* Telefoˈnie *f*, Fernsprechwesen *n.*
ˌ**tel·eˈpho·to** *phot.* **I** *adj.* **1.** Telefoto(grafie)…, Fernaufnahme…: **~ *lens*** → ***telelens***; **II** *s.* **2.** ˈTelefoto(graˌfie *f*) *n*, Fernbild *n*; **3.** ˈBildteleˌgramm *n*; **4.** Funkbild *n*; ˌ**tel·eˈpho·to·graph** → ***telephoto*** II; ˈ**tel·eˌpho·toˈgraph·ic** *adj.* (□ ***~ally***) **1.** ˈfernfotoˌgrafisch; **2.** ˈbildteleˌgrafisch; ˌ**tel·e·phoˈtog·ra·phy** *s.* **1.** ˈTele-, ˈFernfotograˌfie *f*; **2.** ˈBildtelegraˌfie *f.*
tel·e·play [ˈtelɪpleɪ] *s.* Fernsehspiel *n.*
ˈ**tel·eˌprint·er** *s.* Fernschreiber *m* (*Gerät*): **~ *message*** Fernschreiben *n*; **~ *operator*** Fernschreiber(in).
tel·e·prompt·er [ˈtelɪˌprɒmptə] *s. TV* Teleprompter *m* (*optisches Souffliergerät, Textband*).
ˈ**tel·e·reˌcord·ing** *s.* (Fernseh)Aufzeichnung *f.*
tel·e·scope [ˈtelɪskəʊp] **I** *s.* Teleˈskop *n*, Fernrohr *n*; **II** *v/t. u. v/i.* a) (sich) ineinˈanderschieben, b) (sich) verkürzen; **III** *adj.* → ***telescopic.***
tel·e·scop·ic [ˌtelɪˈskɒpɪk] *adj.* (□ ***~ally***) **1.** teleˈskopisch, Fernrohr…: **~ *sight*** ⚔ Zielfernrohr *n*; **2.** ineinˈanderschiebbar, ausziehbar, Auszieh…, Teleskop…
ˈ**tel·e·screen** *s. TV* Bildschirm *m.*
tel·e·text [ˈtelɪtekst] *s. TV* Videotext *m.*
ˌ**tel·e·therˈmom·e·ter** *s. phys.* ˈFern-, ˈTelethermoˌmeter *n.*
ˈ**tel·e·type**, ˌ**tel·eˈtypeˌwrit·er** *Am.* → ***teleprinter.***
ˈ**tel·e·view I** *v/t.* sich (im Fernsehen) ansehen; **II** *v/i.* fernsehen; ˈ**tel·eˌview·er** *s.* Fernsehzuschauer(in).
tel·e·vise [ˈtelɪvaɪz] → ***telecast*** I; ˈ**tel·eˌvi·sion I** *s.* **1.** Fernsehen *n*: ***watch ~*** fernsehen; ***on ~*** im Fernsehen; **2.** *a.* **~ *set*** Fernsehgerät *n*, Fernseher *m*; **II** *adj.* Fernseh…; ˈ**tel·e·vi·sor** *s.* **1.** → ***television*** 2; **2.** → ***telecaster***; **3.** → ***televiewer.***
tel·ex [ˈteleks] **I** *s.* **1.** Telex *n*, Fernschreibernetz *n*: ***be on the ~*** Telex- *od.* Fernschreibanschluß haben; **2.** Fernschreiber *m* (*Gerät*): **~ *operator*** Fernschreiber(in); **3.** Fernschreiben *n*: ***by ~*** per Telex *od.* Fernschreiben; **~ *operator*** Fernschreiber(in); **II** *v/t.* **4.** *j-m et.* telexen *od.* per Fernschreiben mitteilen.
tell [tel] [*irr.*] **I** *v/t.* **1.** sagen, erzählen (***s.o. s.th., s.th. to s.o.*** j-m et): ***I can ~ you that ...*** ich kann Sie *od.* Ihnen versichern, daß; ***I have been told*** mir ist gesagt worden; ***I told you so!*** ich habe es (dir) ja gleich gesagt!, ‚siehste'!; ***you are ~ing me!*** *sl.* wem sagen Sie das!; **~ *the world*** F (es) hinausposaunen; **2.** mitteilen, berichten, *a. die Wahrheit* sagen; *Neuigkeit* verkünden: **~ *a lie*** lügen; **3.** *Geheimnis* verraten; **4.** erkennen (***by, from*** an *dat.*), feststellen, sagen: **~ *by ear*** mit dem Gehör feststellen, hören; **5.** (mit Bestimmtheit) sagen: ***I cannot ~ what it is***; ***it is difficult to ~*** es ist schwer zu sagen; **6.** unterˈscheiden (***one from the other*** eines vom andern): **~ *apart*** auseinanderhalten; **7.** sagen, befehlen: **~ *s.o. to do s.th.*** j-m sagen, er solle et. tun; j-n et. tun heißen; ***do as you are told*** tu wie dir geheißen; **8.** *bsd. pol. Stimmen* zählen: ***all told*** alles in allem; **9.** **~ *off*** a) abzählen, b) ⚔ abkommandieren, c) F *j-m* ‚Bescheid stoßen'; **II** *v/i.* **10.** berichten, erzählen (***of*** von, ***about*** über *acc.*); **11.** *fig.* ein Zeichen *od.* Beweis sein (***of*** für, von); **12.** *et.* sagen können, wissen: ***how can you ~?, you never can ~*** man kann nie wissen; **13.** ‚petzen': **~ *on s.o.*** j-n verpetzen *od.* verraten; ***don't ~!*** nicht verraten!; **14.** sich auswirken (***on*** bei, auf *acc.*): ***the hard work began to ~ on him***; ***his troubles have told on him*** s-e Sorgen haben ihn sichtlich mitgenommen; ***every blow*** (***word***) **~*s*** jeder Schlag (jedes Wort) sitzt; ***that ~s against you*** das spricht gegen Sie; **15.** sich (deutlich) abheben (***against*** gegen, von); zur Geltung kommen (*Farbe etc.*); ˈ**tell·er** [-lə] *s.* **1.** Erzähler(in); **2.** Zähler (-in); *bsd. parl.* Stimmenzähler *m*; **3.** Kassierer(in), Schalterbeamte(r) *m* (*Bank*): **~*'s department*** Hauptkasse *f*; ***automatic ~*** Geldautomat *m*; ˈ**tell·ing** [-lɪŋ] *adj.* □ **1.** wirkungsvoll (*a. Schlag*), wirksam, eindrucksvoll; ˈdurchschlagend (*Erfolg, Wirkung*); **2.** *fig.* aufschlußreich; ˌ**tell·ing-ˈoff** *s.*: ***give s.o. a ~*** j-m ‚Bescheid stoßen'.
ˈ**tell·tale I** *s.* **1.** Klatschbase *f*, Zuträger (-in), ‚Petze' *f*; **2.** verräterisches (Kenn-)Zeichen; **3.** ⚙ (selbsttätige) Anzeigevorrichtung; **II** *adj.* **4.** *fig.* verräterisch: ***a ~ tear***; **5.** sprechend (*Ähnlichkeit*); **6.** ⚙ a) Anzeige…, b) Warnungs…: **~ *clock*** Kontrolluhr *f.*

tel·ly ['telɪ] *s. Brit.* F Fernseher *m* (*Gerät*): ***on the ~*** im Fernsehen.

tel·o·type ['teləʊtaɪp] *s.* **1.** e'lektrischer 'Schreib- *od.* 'Drucktele͵graph; **2.** auto'matisch gedrucktes Tele'gramm.

tel·pher ['telfə] **I** *s.* Wagen *m* e-r Hängebahn; **II** *adj.* (Elektro)Hängebahn…; **'tel·pher·age** [-ərɪdʒ] *s.* e'lektrische Lastenbeförderung; **'tel·pher·way** *s.* Telpherbahn *f*, E'lektrohängebahn *f*.

te·mer·i·ty [tɪ'merətɪ] *s.* **1.** (Toll)Kühnheit *f*, Verwegenheit *f*; *b.s.* Frechheit *f*.

temp [temp] *s. Brit.* F 'Zeitsekre͵tärin *f*.

tem·per ['tempə] **I** *s.* **1.** Tempera'ment *n*, Natu'rell *n*, Gemüt(sart *f*) *n*, Cha'rakter *m*, Veranlagung *f*: ***even ~*** Gleichmut *m*; ***have a quick ~*** ein hitziges Temperament haben; **2.** Stimmung *f*, Laune *f*: ***in a bad ~*** (in) schlechter Laune, schlecht gelaunt; **3.** Gereiztheit *f*, Zorn *m*, Wut *f*: ***be in a ~*** gereizt *od.* wütend sein; ***fly*** (*od.* ***get***) ***into a ~*** in Wut geraten; **4.** Gemütsruhe *f* (*obs. außer in den Redew.*): ***keep one's ~*** ruhig bleiben; ***lose one's ~*** in Wut geraten, die Geduld verlieren; ***out of ~*** übelgelaunt; ***put s.o. out of ~*** j-n wütend machen *od.* erzürnen; **5.** Zusatz *m*, Beimischung *f*, *metall.* Härtemittel *n*; **6.** *bsd.* ⚙ richtige Mischung; **7.** *metall.* Härte(grad *m*) *f*; **II** *v/t.* **8.** mildern (***with*** durch); **9.** *Farbe*, *Kalk*, *Mörtel* mischen, anmachen; **10.** ⚙ a) *Stahl* härten, anlassen, b) *Eisen* ablöschen, c) *Gußeisen* adouzieren, d) *Glas* rasch abkühlen; **11.** ♪ *Klavier etc.* temperieren; **III** *v/i.* **12.** ⚙ den richtigen Härtegrad erreichen *od.* haben.

tem·per·a ['tempərə] *s.* 'Tempera(male͵rei) *f*.

tem·per·a·ment ['tempərəmənt] *s.* **1.** → ***temper*** 1; **2.** Tempera'ment *n*, Lebhaftigkeit *f*; **3.** ♪ Tempera'tur *f*; **tem·per·a·men·tal** [͵tempərə'mentl] *adj.* □ **1.** tempera'mentvoll, veranlagungsmäßig, Temperaments…; **2.** a) reizbar, launisch, b) leicht erregbar; **3.** eigenwillig; **4.** ***be ~*** F (s-e) ‚Mucken' haben (*Gerät etc.*).

tem·per·ance ['tempərəns] *s.* **1.** Mäßigkeit *f*, Enthaltsamkeit *f*; **2.** Mäßigkeit *f* im *od.* Absti'nenz *f* vom Alkoholgenuß; **~ ho·tel** *s.* alkoholfreies Hotel; **~ move·ment** *s.* Absti'nenzbewegung *f*.

tem·per·ate ['tempərət] *adj.* □ **1.** gemäßigt, maßvoll: ***~ language***; **2.** zu'rückhaltend; **3.** mäßig: ***~ enthusiasm***; **4.** a) mäßig, enthaltsam (*bsd. im Essen u. Trinken*), b) absti'nent (*alkoholische Getränke meidend*); **5.** gemäßigt, mild (*Klima etc.*); **'tem·per·ate·ness** [-nɪs] *s.* **1.** Gemäßigtheit *f*; **2.** Beherrschtheit *f*, Zu'rückhaltung *f*; **3.** geringes Ausmaß; **4.** a) Mäßigkeit *f*, Enthaltsamkeit *f*, Mäßigung *f* (*bsd. im Essen u. Trinken*), b) Absti'nenz *f* (*von alkoholischen Getränken*); **5.** Milde *f* (*des Klimas etc.*).

tem·per·a·ture ['temprətʃə] *s.* **1.** *phys.* Tempera'tur *f*: ***at a ~ of*** bei e-r Temperatur von; **2.** *physiol.* ('Körper)Tempera͵tur *f*: ***to take s.o.'s ~*** j-s Temperatur messen; ***to have*** (*od.* ***run***) ***a ~*** ⚕ F Fieber *od.* (erhöhte) Temperatur haben.

tem·pest ['tempɪst] *s.* **1.** (wilder) Sturm: ***~ in a teapot*** *fig.* ‚Sturm im Wasserglas'; **2.** *fig.* Sturm *m*, Ausbruch *m*; **3.** Gewitter *n*; **tem·pes·tu·ous** [tem'pestjʊəs] *adj.* □ *a. fig.* stürmisch, ungestüm, heftig; **tem·pes·tu·ous·ness** [tem'pestjʊəsnɪs] *s.* Ungestüm *n*, Heftigkeit *f*.

Tem·plar ['templə] *s.* **1.** *hist.* Templer *m*, Tempelherr *m*, -ritter *m*; **2.** Tempelritter *m* (*Freimaurer*); **3.** *oft* ***Good ~*** Guttempler *m* (*ein Temperenzler*).

tem·plate ['templɪt] *s.* **1.** ⚙ Scha'blone *f*; **2.** ▲ a) 'Unterleger *m* (*Balken*), b) (Dach)Pfette *f*, c) Kragholz *n*; **3.** ⚓ Mallbrett *n*.

tem·ple¹ ['templ] *s.* **1.** *eccl.* Tempel *m* (*a. fig.*); **2.** *Am.* Syna'goge *f*; **3.** ~ ⚖ Temple *m* (*in London*, *Sitz zweier Rechtskollegien*: ***the Inner ~ u. the Middle ~***).

tem·ple² ['templ] *s. anat.* Schläfe *f*.

tem·ple³ ['templ] *s. Weberei*: Tömpel *m*.

tem·plet ['templɪt] → ***template***.

tem·po ['tempəʊ] *pl.* **-pi** *s.* ♪ Tempo *n* (*a. fig. Geschwindigkeit*): ***~ turn*** *Skisport*: Temposchwung *m*.

tem·po·ral¹ ['tempərəl] *adj.* □ **1.** zeitlich: a) Zeit… (*Ggs. räumlich*), b) irdisch; **2.** weltlich (*Ggs. geistlich*): ***~ courts***; **3.** *ling.* tempo'ral, Zeit…: ***~ adverb*** Umstandswort *n* der Zeit; ***~ clause*** Temporalsatz *m*.

tem·po·ral² ['tempərəl] *anat.* **I** *adj.* a) Schläfen…, b) Schläfenbein…; **II** *s.* Schläfenbein *n*.

tem·po·rar·i·ness ['tempərərɪnɪs] *s.* Einst-, Zeitweiligkeit *f*; **tem·po·rar·y** ['tempərərɪ] *adj.* □ provi'sorisch: a) vorläufig, einst-, zeitweilig, vor'übergehend, tempo'rär, b) behelfsmäßig, Not…, Hilfs…, Interims…: ***~ arrangement*** Übergangsregelung *f*; ***~ bridge*** Behelfs-, Notbrücke *f*; ***~ credit*** ✝ Zwischenkredit *m*.

tem·po·rize ['tempəraɪz] *v/i.* **1.** Zeit zu gewinnen suchen, abwarten, sich nicht festlegen, lavieren: ***~ with s.o.*** j-n hinhalten; **2.** mit dem Strom schwimmen, s-n Mantel nach dem Wind hängen; **'tem·po·riz·er** [-zə] *s.* **1.** j-d, der Zeit zu gewinnen sucht *od.* sich nicht festlegt; **2.** Opportu'nist(in); **'tem·po·riz·ing** [-zɪŋ] *adj.* □ **1.** hinhaltend, abwartend; **2.** opportu'nistisch.

tempt [tempt] *v/t.* **1.** *eccl.*, *a. allg. j-n* versuchen, in Versuchung führen; **2.** *j-n* verlocken, -leiten, da'zu bringen (***to do*** zu tun): ***be ~ed to do*** versucht *od.* geneigt sein, zu tun; **3.** reizen, locken (*Angebot*, *Sache*); **4.** *Gott*, *sein Schicksal* versuchen, her'ausfordern; **temp·ta·tion** [temp'teɪʃn] *s.* Versuchung *f*, -führung *f*, -lockung *f*: ***lead into ~*** in Versuchung führen; **'tempt·er** [-tə] *s.* Versucher *m*, -führer *m*: ***the ~*** *eccl.* der Versucher; **'tempt·ing** [-tɪŋ] *adj.* □ verführerisch, -lockend; **'tempt·ing·ness** [-tɪŋnɪs] *s. das* Verführerische; **'tempt·ress** [-trɪs] *s.* Versucherin *f*, Verführerin *f*.

ten [ten] **I** *adj.* **1.** zehn; **II** *s.* **2.** Zehn *f* (*Zahl*, *Spielkarte*): ***the upper ~*** *fig.* die oberen Zehntausend; **3.** F Zehner *m* (*Geldschein etc.*); **4.** zehn (Uhr).

ten·a·ble ['tenəbl] *adj.* **1.** haltbar (⚔ *Stellung*, *fig. Behauptung etc.*); **2.** verliehen (***for*** für, auf *acc.*): ***an office ~ for two years***; **'ten·a·ble·ness** [-nɪs] *s.* Haltbarkeit *f* (*a. fig.*).

te·na·cious [tɪ'neɪʃəs] *adj.* □ **1.** zäh(e), klebrig; **2.** *fig.* zäh(e), hartnäckig: ***be ~ of*** zäh an *et.* festhalten; ***~ of life*** zählebig; ***~ ideas*** zählebige Ideen; **3.** verläßlich, gut (*Gedächtnis*); **te'na·cious·ness** [-nɪs], **te·nac·i·ty** [tɪ'næsɪtɪ] *s.* **1.** *allg.* Zähigkeit *f*: a) Klebrigkeit *f*, b) *phys.* Zug-, Zähfestigkeit *f*, c) *fig.* Hartnäckigkeit *f*: ***~ of life*** zähes Leben; ***~ of purpose*** Zielstrebigkeit *f*; **2.** Verläßlichkeit *f* (*des Gedächtnisses*).

ten·an·cy ['tenənsɪ] *s.* ⚖ **1.** Pacht-, Mietverhältnis *n*: ***~ at will*** jederzeit beiderseits kündbares Pachtverhältnis; **2.** a) Pacht-, Mietbesitz *m*, b) Eigentum *n*: ***~ in common*** Miteigentum *n*; **3.** Pacht-, Mietdauer *f*; **'ten·ant** [-nt] **I** *s.* **1.** ⚖ Pächter(in), Mieter(in): ***~ farmer*** Gutspächter *m*; **2.** ⚖ Inhaber(in) (*von Realbesitz*, *Renten etc.*); **3.** Bewohner (-in); **4.** *hist.* Lehnsmann *m*; **II** *v/t.* **5.** bewohnen; **6.** *als Mieter etc.* beherbergen; **'ten·ant·a·ble** [-ntəbl] *adj.* **1.** ⚖ pacht-, mietbar; **2.** bewohnbar; **'ten·ant·less** *adj.* **1.** unverpachtet; **2.** unvermietet, leer(stehend); **'ten·ant·ry** [-trɪ] *s. coll.* Pächter *pl.*, Mieter *pl.*

tench [tenʃ] *pl.* **'tench·es**, *bsd. coll.* **tench** *s. ichth.* Schleie *f*.

tend¹ [tend] *v/i.* **1.** sich *in e-r bestimmten Richtung* bewegen; (hin)streben (***to*** [***-ward***] nach): ***~ from*** wegstreben von; **2.** *fig.* a) tendieren, neigen (***to***[***wards***] zu), b) da'zu neigen (***to do*** zu tun); **3.** abzielen, gerichtet sein (***to*** auf *acc.*); **4.** (da'zu) führen *od.* beitragen (***to*** [***do***] zu [tun]); hin'auslaufen (***to*** auf *acc.*); **5.** ⚓ schwoien.

tend² [tend] *v/t.* **1.** ⚙ *Maschine* bedienen; **2.** sich kümmern um, sorgen für, *Kranke* pflegen, *Vieh* hüten.

ten·den·cious → ***tendentious***.

tend·en·cy ['tendənsɪ] *s.* **1.** Ten'denz *f*: a) Richtung *f*, Strömung *f*, Hinstreben *n*, b) (bestimmte) Absicht, Zweck *m*, c) Hang *m* (***to***, ***toward*** zu), Neigung *f* (***to*** für); **2.** Gang *m*, Lauf *m*: ***the ~ of events***.

ten·den·tious [ten'denʃəs] *adj.* □ tendenzi'ös, Tendenz…; **ten'den·tious·ness** [-nɪs] *s.* tendenzi'öser Cha'rakter.

ten·der¹ ['tendə] *adj.* □ **1.** zart, weich, mürbe (*Fleisch etc.*); **2.** *allg.* zart (*a. Alter*, *Farbe*, *Gesundheit*): ***~ passion*** Liebe *f*; **3.** zart, zärtlich, sanft; **4.** zart, empfindlich (*Körperteil*, *a. Gewissen*): ***~ spot*** *fig.* wunder Punkt; **5.** heikel, kitzlig (*Thema*); **6.** bedacht (***of*** auf *acc.*).

ten·der² ['tendə] **I** *v/t.* **1.** (for'mell) anbieten; → ***oath*** 1, ***resignation*** 2; **2.** *s-e Dienste etc.* anbieten, zur Verfügung stellen; **3.** *s-n Dank*, *s-e Entschuldigung* zum Ausdruck bringen; **4.** ✝, ⚖ als Zahlung (*e-r Verpflichtung*) anbieten; **II** *v/i.* **5.** sich an e-r Ausschreibung beteiligen, ein Angebot machen: ***~ and contract for a supply*** e-n Lieferungsvertrag abschließen; **III** *s.* **6.** Anerbieten *n*, Angebot *n*: ***make a ~ of*** → 2; **7.** ✝ (***legal*** gesetzliches) Zahlungsmittel; **8.** ✝ Angebot *n*, Of'ferte *f bei Ausschreibung*: ***invite ~s for*** *ein Projekt* ausschreiben; ***put to ~*** in freier Ausschreibung vergeben; ***by ~*** in Submission; **9.** ✝ Kosten(vor)anschlag *m*; **10.**

⚖ Zahlungsangebot *n*; **11.** *~ **of resignation*** Rücktrittsgesuch *n*.
tend·er[3] ['tendə] *s.* **1.** Pfleger(in); **2.** 🚂 Tender *m*, Kohlewagen *m*; **3.** ⚓ Tender *m*, Begleitschiff *n*.
'ten·der|·foot *pl.* **-feet** *od.* **-foots** *s. Am.* F **1.** Anfänger(in), Greenhorn *n*; **2.** neuaufgenommener Pfadfinder; **ˌ~-'heart·ed** *adj.* □ weichherzig; **'~·loin** *s.* zartes Lendenstück, Fi'let *n*.
ten·der·ness ['tendənɪs] *s.* **1.** Zartheit *f*, Weichheit *f* (*a. fig.*); **2.** Empfindlichkeit *f* (*a. fig. des Gewissens etc.*); **3.** Zärtlichkeit *f*.
ten·di·nous ['tendɪnəs] *adj.* **1.** sehnig, flechsig; **2.** *anat.* Sehnen...; **ten·don** ['tendən] *s. anat.* Sehne *f*, Flechse *f*; **ten·do·vag·i·ni·tis** ['tendəʊˌvædʒɪ'naɪtɪs] *s.* ⚕ Sehnenscheidenentzündung *f*.
ten·dril ['tendrɪl] *s.* ⚘ Ranke *f*.
ten·e·brous ['tenɪbrəs] *adj.* dunkel, finster, düster.
ten·e·ment ['tenɪmənt] *s.* **1.** Wohnhaus *n*; **2.** *a.* *~ **house*** Miet(s)haus *n*, *bsd.* 'Mietskaˌserne *f*; **3.** Mietwohnung *f*; **4.** Wohnung *f*; **5.** ⚖ a) (Pacht)Besitz *m*, b) beständiger Besitz, beständiges Privi'legium.
te·nes·mus [tɪ'nezməs] *s.* ⚕ Te'nesmus *m*: ***rectal** ~* Stuhldrang *m*; ***vesical** ~* Harndrang *m*.
ten·et ['ti:net] *s.* (Grund-, Lehr)Satz *m*, Lehre *f*.
'ten·fold I *adj. u. adv.* zehnfach; **II** *s. das* Zehnfache.
ˌten-'gal·lon hat *s. Am.* breitrandiger Cowboyhut.
ten·ner ['tenə] *s.* F ‚Zehner' *m*: a) *Brit.* Zehn'pfundnote *f*, b) *Am.* Zehn'dollarnote *f*.
ten·nis ['tenɪs] *s. sport* Tennis *n*; *~ **arm*** *s.* ⚕ Tennisarm *m*; *~ **ball*** *s.* Tennisball *m*; *~ **court*** *s.* Tennisplatz *m*; *~ **rack·et*** *s.* Tennisschläger *m*.
ten·on ['tenən] ⚙ **I** *s.* Zapfen *m*; **II** *v/t.* verzapfen; *~ **saw*** *s.* ⚙ Ansatzsäge *f*, Fuchsschwanz *m*.
ten·or ['tenə] **I** *s.* **1.** Verlauf *m*; **2.** 'Tenor *m*, (wesentlicher) Inhalt, Sinn *m*; **3.** Absicht *f*; **4.** ✝ Laufzeit *f* (*Wechsel etc.*); **5.** ♪ Te'nor(stimme *f*, -parˌtie *f*, -sänger *m*, -instruˌment *n*) *m*; **II** *adj.* **6.** ♪ Tenor...
'ten·pin *s. Am.* **1.** Kegel *m*; **2.** *pl. sg. konstr. Am.* Bowling *n*.
tense[1] [tens] *s. ling.* Zeit(form) *f*, Tempus *n*: ***simple*** (***compound***) *~**s*** einfache (zs.-gesetzte) Zeiten.
tense[2] [tens] **I** *adj.* □ **1.** gespannt (*a. ling. Laut*); **2.** *fig.* a) (an)gespannt (*Person, Nerven*), b) spannungsgeladen: ***a** ~ **moment***; **II** *v/t.* **3.** straffen, (an)spannen; **III** *v/i.* **4.** sich straffen *od.* (an)spannen; **5.** *fig.* (vor Nervosi'tät *etc.*) starr werden; **'tense·ness** [-nɪs] *s.* **1.** Straffheit *f*; **2.** *fig.* (ner'vöse) Spannung; **'ten·si·ble** [-səbl] *adj.* dehnbar; **'ten·sile** [-saɪl] *adj.* dehn-, streckbar; *phys.* Dehn(ungs)..., Zug...: *~ **strength*** (***stress***) Zugfestigkeit *f* (-beanspruchung *f*); **ten·sim·e·ter** [ten'sɪmɪtə] *s.* ⚙ Gas-, Dampfdruckmesser *m*; **ten·si·om·e·ter** [tensɪ'ɒmɪtə] *s.* ⚙ Zugmesser *m*.
ten·sion ['tenʃn] *s.* **1.** Spannung *f* (*a.* ⚡); **2.** ⚕, *phys.* Druck *m*; **3.** *phys.* a) Dehnung *f*, b) Zug-, Spannkraft *f*: *~ **spring*** ⚙ Zug-, Spannfeder *f*; **4.** (ner'vöse) Spannung; **5.** *fig.* Spannung *f*, gespanntes Verhältnis: ***political** ~*; **'ten·sion·al** [-ʃənl] *adj.* Dehn..., Spann(ungs)...; **ten·sor** ['tensə] *s. anat.* Tensor *m* (*a.* ℞), Streck-, Spannmuskel *m*.
'ten|-spot *s. Am. sl.* **1.** *Kartenspiel*: Zehn *f*; **2.** → ***tenner*** b; **'~-strike** *s.* **1.** → ***strike*** 2 a; **2.** F *fig.* ‚Volltreffer' *m*.
tent[1] [tent] *s.* Zelt *n* (*a.* ⚕): ***pitch one's** ~**s*** s-e Zelte aufschlagen (*a. fig.*).
tent[2] [tent] ⚕ **I** *s.* Tam'pon *m*; **II** *v/t.* durch e-n Tampon offenhalten.
tent[3] [tent] *s. obs.* Tintowein *m*.
ten·ta·cle ['tentəkl] *s. zo.* **1.** Ten'takel *m*, *n* (*a.* ⚘), Fühler *m* (*a. fig.*); **2.** Fangarm *m e-s Polypen*; **'ten·ta·cled** [-ld] *adj.* ⚘, *zo.* mit Ten'takeln versehen; **ten·tac·u·lar** [ten'tækjʊlə] *adj.* Fühler..., Tentakel...
ten·ta·tive ['tentətɪv] **I** *adj.* □ **1.** versuchsweise, Versuchs...; **2.** provi'sorisch; **3.** vorsichtig; **II** *s.* **4.** Versuch *m*; **'ten·ta·tive·ly** [-lɪ] *adv.* versuchsweise.
ten·ter ['tentə] *s.* ⚙ Spannrahmen *m für Tuch*; **'~·hook** *s.* ⚙ Spannhaken *m*: ***be on** ~**s*** *fig.* auf die Folter gespannt sein, wie auf glühenden Kohlen sitzen; ***keep s.o. on** ~**s*** *fig.* j-n auf die Folter spannen.
tenth [tenθ] **I** *adj.* □ **1.** zehnt; **2.** zehntel; **II** *s.* **3.** *der* (*die, das*) Zehnte; **4.** Zehntel *n*: ***a** ~ **of a second*** e-e Zehntelsekunde; **5.** ♪ De'zime *f*; **'tenth·ly** [-lɪ] *adv.* zehntens.
tent| peg *s.* Zeltpflock *m*, Hering *m*; *~ **pole*** *s.* Zeltstange *f*; *~ **stitch*** *s. Stickerei*: Perlstich *m*.
ten·u·is ['tenjʊɪs] *pl.* **'ten·u·es** [-i:z] *s. ling.* Tenuis *f* (*stimmloser, nicht aspirierter Verschlußlaut*).
te·nu·ous ['tenjʊəs] *adj.* **1.** dünn; **2.** zart, fein; **3.** *fig.* dürftig.
ten·ure ['teˌnjʊə] *s.* **1.** (Grund-, *hist.* Lehens)Besitz *m*; **2.** ⚖ a) Besitzart *f*, b) Besitztitel *m*: *~ **by lease*** Pachtbesitz *m*; **3.** Besitzdauer *f*; **4.** (feste) Anstellung; **5.** Innehaben *n*, Bekleidung *f* (e-s Amtes): *~ **of office*** Amtsdauer *f*; **6.** *fig.* Genuß *m e-r Sache*.
te·pee ['ti:pi:] *s.* Indi'anerzelt *n*, Tipi *n*.
tep·id ['tepɪd] *adj.* □ lauwarm, lau (*a. fig.*); **te·pid·i·ty** [te'pɪdətɪ], **'tep·id·ness** [-nɪs] *s.* Lauheit *f* (*a. fig.*).
ter·cen·te·nar·y [ˌtɜ:sen'ti:nərɪ], **ˌter·cen'ten·ni·al** [-'tenjəl] **I** *adj.* **1.** dreihundertjährig; **II** *s.* **2.** dreihundertster Jahrestag; **3.** Dreihundert'jahrfeier *f*.
ter·cet ['tɜ:sɪt] *s.* **1.** *Metrik*: Ter'zine *f*; **2.** ♪ Tri'ole *f*.
ter·gi·ver·sate ['tɜ:dʒɪvɜ:seɪt] *v/i.* Ausflüchte machen; sich drehen und wenden; sich wider'sprechen; **ter·gi·ver·sa·tion** [ˌtɜ:dʒɪvɜ:'seɪʃn] *s.* **1.** Ausflucht *f*, Winkelzug *m*; **2.** Wankelmut *m*.
term [tɜ:m] **I** *s.* **1.** *bsd. fachlicher* Ausdruck, Bezeichnung *f*, Wort *n*: ***botanical** ~**s***; **2.** *pl.* a) Ausdrucksweise *f*, b) ('Denk)Kategoˌrien *pl.*: ***in** ~**s of*** a) in Form von (*od. gen.*), b) im Sinne (*gen.*), als, c) hinsichtlich (*gen.*), d) von ... her, vom Standpunkt (*gen.*), e) im Vergleich zu; ***in** ~**s of approval*** beifällig; ***in** ~**s of literature*** literarisch (betrachtet), vom Literarischen her; ***in plain** ~**s*** rundheraus (gesagt); ***in the strongest** ~**s*** schärfstens; ***think in** ~**s of money*** (nur) in Mark u. Pfennig denken; ***think in military** ~**s*** in militärischen Kategorien denken; **3.** Wortlaut *m*; **4.** a) Zeit *f*, Dauer *f*: *~ **of imprisonment*** Freiheitsstrafe *f*; *~ **of office*** Amtsdauer *f*, -periode *f*; ***on*** (*od.* ***in***) ***the long** ~* auf lange Sicht, langfristig (betrachtet); ***for a** ~ **of four years*** für die Dauer von vier Jahren, b) (*Zahlungs- etc.*)Frist *f*: *~ **deposit*** Termingeld *n*; **5.** ✝, ⚖ a) Laufzeit *f* (*Vertrag, Wechsel*), b) Ter'min *m*, c) *Brit.* Quar'talsterˌmin *m* (*vierteljährlicher Zahltag für Miete etc.*), d) *Brit. hist. halbjährlicher* Lohn-, Zahltag (*für Dienstboten*), e) ⚖ 'Sitzungsperiˌode *f*; **6.** *ped., univ.* Quar'tal *n*, Tri'mester *n*, Se'mester *n*: ***end of** ~* Schul- *od.* Semesterschluß *m*; ***keep** ~**s*** *Brit.* Jura studieren; **7.** *pl.* ✝, ⚖ (*Vertrags- etc.*)Bedingungen *pl.*: *~**s of delivery*** Lieferungsbedingungen; *~**s of trade*** Austauschverhältnis *n im* Außenhandel; ***on easy** ~**s*** zu günstigen Bedingungen; ***on equal** ~**s*** unter gleichen Bedingungen; ***come to** ~**s*** *a. fig.* handelseinig werden, sich einigen, *fig. a.* sich abfinden (***with*** mit); ***come to** ~**s with the past*** die Vergangenheit bewältigen; **8.** *pl.* Preise *pl.*, Hono'rar *n*: ***cash** ~**s*** Barpreis *m*; ***inclusive** ~**s*** Pauschalpreis *m*; **9.** *pl.* Beziehungen *pl.*: ***be on good*** (***bad***) *~**s with*** auf gutem (schlechtem) Fuße stehen mit; ***they are not on speaking** ~**s*** sie sprechen nicht (mehr) miteinander; **10.** *Logik*: Begriff *m*; → ***contradiction*** 2; **11.** ℞ a) Glied *n*: *~ **of a sum*** Summand *m*, b) *Geometrie*: Grenze *f*; **12.** ⛰ Terme *m*, Grenzstein *m*; **13.** *physiol.* a) Menstruati'on *f*, b) (nor'male) Schwangerschaftszeit: ***carry to*** (***full***) *~ **ein Kind*** austragen; ***she is near her** ~* ihre Niederkunft steht dicht bevor; **II** *v/t.* **14.** (be)nennen, bezeichnen als.
ter·ma·gant ['tɜ:məgənt] **I** *s.* Zankteufel *m*, (Haus)Drachen *m* (*Weib*); **II** *adj.* zänkisch, keifend.
ter·mi·na·ble ['tɜ:mɪnəbl] *adj.* □ **1.** begrenzbar; **2.** befristet, (zeitlich) begrenzt, kündbar (*Vertrag etc.*).
ter·mi·nal ['tɜ:mɪnl] **I** *adj.* □ → ***terminally***; **1.** letzt, Grenz..., End..., (Ab-)Schluß...: *~ **amplifier*** ⚡ Endverstärker *m*; *~ **station*** → *~ **value*** ℞ Endwert *m*; *~ **voltage*** ⚡ Klemmenspannung *f*; **2.** *univ.* Semester... *od.* Trimester...; **3.** ⚕ a) unheilbar (*a. fig.*), b) im Endstadium: *~ **case***, c) Sterbe...: *~ **clinic***, d) *fig.* verhängnisvoll (***to*** für); **4.** ⚘ gipfelständig; **II** *s.* **5.** Endstück *n*, -glied *n*, Spitze *f*; **6.** *ling.* Endsilbe *f od.* -buchstabe *m od.* -wort *n*; **7.** ⚡ a) (Anschluß-)Klemme *f*, (*Plus-, Minus*)Pol *m*, b) Klemmschraube *f*, c) Endstecker *m*; **8.** a) 🚂 'Endstatiˌon *f*, Kopfbahnhof *m*, b) ✈ Bestimmungsflughafen *m* (→ *a.* ***air terminal***), c) (zen'traler) 'Umschlagplatz, d) End- *od.* Ausgangspunkt *m*; **9.** *Computer*: Terminal *n*; **10.** *univ.* Se'mesterprüfung *f*; **'ter·mi·nal·ly** [-nəlɪ] *adv.* **1.** zum Schluß; **2.** ter'minweise; **3.** *~ **ill*** ⚕ unheilbar krank; **4.** *univ.* se'mesterweise; **'ter·mi·nate** [-neɪt] **I** *v/t.* **1.** *räumlich* begrenzen; **2.** beendigen, *Vertrag a.* aufheben, kündigen; **II** *v/i.* **3.** endigen (***in*** in *dat.*); **4.** *ling.* enden (***in***

auf *acc.*); **III** *adj.* [-nət] **5.** begrenzt; **6.** 𝔄 endlich; **ter·mi·na·tion** [ˌtɜːmɪˈneɪʃn] *s.* **1.** Aufhören *n*; **2.** Ende *n*, (Ab)Schluß *m*; **3.** Beendigung *f*: **~ of pregnancy** ⚕ Schwangerschaftsunterbrechung *f*; **4.** ⚖ Beendigung *f e-s Vertrags etc.*: a) Ablauf *m*, Erlöschen *n*, b) Aufhebung *f*, Kündigung *f*; **5.** *ling.* Endung *f*.

ter·mi·no·log·i·cal [ˌtɜːmɪnəˈlɒdʒɪkl] *adj.* □ terminoˈlogisch: **~ inexactitude** *humor.* Schwindelei *f*; **ter·mi·nol·o·gy** [ˌtɜːmɪˈnɒlədʒɪ] *s.* Terminoloˈgie *f*, Fachsprache *f*, -ausdrücke *pl.*

ter·mi·nus [ˈtɜːmɪnəs] *pl.* **-ni** [-naɪ], **-nus·es** *s.* **1.** Endpunkt *m*, Ziel *n*, Ende *n*; **2.** → **terminal** 8 a.

ter·mite [ˈtɜːmaɪt] *s. zo.* Terˈmite *f*.

ˈterm·time *s.* Schul- *od.* Seˈmesterzeit *f* (*Ggs. Ferien*).

tern¹ [tɜːn] *s. orn.* Seeschwalbe *f*.

tern² [tɜːn] *s.* Dreiergruppe *f*, -satz *m*; **ˈter·na·ry** [-nərɪ] *adj.* **1.** aus (je) drei bestehend, dreifältig; **2.** ⚘ dreizählig; **3.** *metall.* dreistoffig; **4.** 𝔄 terˈnär; **5.** aus drei Aˈtomen bestehend; **ˈter·nate** [-nɪt] *adj.* → **ternary** 1 *u.* 2.

ter·ra [ˈterə] (*Lat. u. Ital.*) *s.* Land *n*, Erde *f*.

ter·race [ˈterəs] **I** *s.* **1.** Terˈrasse *f* (*a.* △ *u. geol.*); **2.** *bsd. Brit.* Häuserreihe *f* an erhöht gelegener Straße; **3.** *Am.* Grünstreifen *m*, -anlage *f in der Straßenmitte*; **4.** *sport Brit.* (Zuschauer)Rang *m*: **the ~s** die Ränge (*a. die Zuschauer*); **II** *v/t.* **5.** terˈrassenförmig anlegen, terrassieren; **ˈter·raced** [-st] *adj.* **1.** terrassenförmig (angelegt); **2.** flach (*Dach*); **3. ~ house** *Brit.* Reihenhaus *n*.

ter·ra|-cot·ta [ˌterəˈkɒtə] **I** *s.* **1.** Terraˈkotta *f*; **2.** Terraˈkottafiˌgur *f*; **II** *adj.* **3.** Terrakotta...; **~ fir·ma** [ˈfɜːmə] (*Lat.*) *s.* festes Land.

ter·rain [teˈreɪn] *bsd.* ⚔ **I** *s.* Terˈrain *n*, Gelände *n*; **II** *adj.* Gelände...

ter·ra in·cog·ni·ta [ɪŋˈkɒgnɪtə] (*Lat.*) *s.* unerforschtes Land; *fig.* (völliges) Neuland.

ter·ra·ne·ous [təˈreɪnjəs] *adj.* ⚘ Land...

ter·ra·pin [ˈterəpɪn] *s. zo.* Dosenschildkröte *f*.

ter·raz·zo [teˈrætsəʊ] (*Ital.*) *s.* Terˈrazzo *m*, Zeˈmentmosaˌik *n*.

ter·rene [teˈriːn] *adj.* **1.** irdisch, Erd...; **2.** erdig, Erd...

ter·res·tri·al [tɪˈrestrɪəl] **I** *adj.* □ **1.** irdisch; **2.** Erd...: **~ globe** Erdball *m*; **3.** ⚘, *zo.*, *geol.* Land...; **II** *s.* **4.** Erdenbewohner(in).

ter·ri·ble [ˈterəbl] *adj.* □ schrecklich, furchtbar, fürchterlich (*alle a.* F *außerordentlich*); **ˈter·ri·ble·ness** [-nɪs] *s.* Schrecklichkeit *f etc.*

ter·ri·er¹ [ˈterɪə] *s.* **1.** *zo.* Terrier *m* (*Hunderasse*); **2.** F → **territorial** 4 a.

ter·ri·er² [ˈterɪə] *s.* ⚖ Flurbuch *n*.

ter·rif·ic [təˈrɪfɪk] *adj.* (□ **~ally**) **1.** furchtbar, fürchterlich, schrecklich (*alle a.* F *fig.*); **2.** F ‚toll', phanˈtastisch.

ter·ri·fied [ˈterɪfaɪd] *adj.* erschrocken, verängstigt, entsetzt: **be ~ of** schreckliche Angst haben vor (*dat.*); **ter·ri·fy** [ˈterɪfaɪ] *v/t.* erschrecken, *j-m* Angst und Schreck einjagen; **ˈter·ri·fy·ing** [-aɪɪŋ] *adj.* furchterregend, erschreckend, fürchterlich.

ter·ri·to·ri·al [ˌterɪˈtɔːrɪəl] **I** *adj.* □ **1.** Grund..., Land...: **~ property**; **2.** territoriˈal, Landes..., Gebiets...: **2 Army**, **2 Force** ⚔ Territorialarmee *f*, Landwehr *f*; **~ waters** *pol.* Hoheitsgewässer *pl.*; **3. 2** *pol.* Territorial..., ein Terriˈtorium (*der USA*) betreffend; **II** *s.* **4. 2** ⚔ a) Landwehrmann *m*, b) *pl.* Territoriˈaltruppen *pl.*; **ter·ri·to·ry** [ˈterɪtərɪ] *s.* **1.** (*a. fig.*) Gebiet *n*, Terriˈtorium *n*; **2.** *pol.* Hoheits-, Staatsgebiet *n*: **Federal ~** Bundesgebiet; **on British ~** auf britischem Gebiet; **3.** *pol.* Terriˈtorium *n* (*Schutzgebiet*); **4.** ☤ (Vertrags-, Vertreter)Gebiet *n*, (-)Bezirk *m*; **5.** *sport* F (Spielfeld)Hälfte *f*.

ter·ror [ˈterə] *s.* **1.** Schrecken *m*, Entsetzen *n*, schreckliche Furcht (**of** vor *dat.*); **2.** Schrecken *m* (**of** *od.* **to** *gen.*) (*schreckeneinflößende Person od. Sache*); **3.** Terror *m*: a) Gewalt-, Schreckensherrschaft *f*, b) Terrorakte *pl.*: **political ~** Politterror; **~ bombing** Bombenterror; **4.** F a) Ekel *n*, ‚Landplage' *f*, b) (schreckliche) Plage (**to** für), c) Alptraum *m*; **ˈter·ror·ism** [-ərɪzəm] *s.* **1.** → **terror** 3; **2.** Terroˈrismus *m*; **3.** Terrorisierung *f*; **ˈter·ror·ist** [-ərɪst] *s.* Terroˈrist(in); **ˈter·ror·ize** [-əraɪz] *v/t.* **1.** terrorisieren; **2.** einschüchtern.

ˈter·ror|-ˌstrick·en, **ˈ~-struck** *adj.* schreckerfüllt, starr vor Schreck.

ter·ry [ˈterɪ] *s.* **1.** ungeschnittener Samt *od.* Plüsch; **2.** Frotˈtiertuch *n*, Frotˈtee (-gewebe) *n*; **3.** Schlinge *f* (*des ungeschnittenen Samtes etc.*).

terse [tɜːs] *adj.* □ knapp, kurz u. bündig, markig; **ˈterse·ness** [-nɪs] *s.* Knappheit *f*, Kürze *f*, Bündigkeit *f*, Präˈgnanz *f*.

ter·tian [ˈtɜːʃn] ⚕ **I** *adj.* am dritten Tag wiederkehrend, Tertian...: **~ ague**, **~ fever**, **~ malaria** → **II** *s.* Tertiˈanfieber *n*.

ter·ti·ar·y [ˈtɜːʃərɪ] **I** *adj. allg.* tertiˈär, Tertiär...; **II** *s.* **2** *geol.* Tertiˈär *n*.

ter·zet·to [tɜːtˈsetəʊ] *pl.* **-tos**, **-ti** [-tɪ] (*Ital.*) *s.* ♪ Terˈzett *n*, Trio *n*.

tes·sel·late [ˈtesɪleɪt] *v/t.* tessellieren, mit Mosaˈiksteinen auslegen: **~d pavement** Mosaik(fuß)boden *m*; **tes·sel·la·tion** [ˌtesɪˈleɪʃn] *s.* Mosaˈik(arbeit *f*) *n*.

test [test] **I** *s.* **1.** *allg., a.* ⚙ Test *m*, Probe *f*, Versuch *m*; **2.** a) Prüfung *f*, Unterˈsuchung *f*, Stichprobe *f*, b) *fig.* Probe *f*, Prüfung *f*: **put to the ~** auf die Probe stellen; **stand the ~** die Probe bestehen, sich bewähren; **~ of strength** Kraftprobe *f*; → **acid test**, **crucial** 1; **3.** *fig.* Prüfstein *m*, Kriˈterium *n*: **success is not a fair ~**; **4.** *ped.*, *psych.* (Eignungs-, Leistungs)Prüfung *f*, Test *m*; **5.** *ped.* Klassenarbeit *f*; **6.** ⚕ (Blut- *etc.*)Probe *f*, (Haut- *etc.*)Test *m*; **7.** ⚗ a) Anaˈlyse *f*, b) Reaˈgens *n*; **8.** *metall.* a) Versuchstiegel *m*, Kaˈpelle *f*, b) Treibherd *m*; **9.** F → **test match**; **10.** *hist. Brit.* Testeid *m*; **II** *v/t.* **11.** (**for s.th.** auf et. [hin]) prüfen (*a. ped.*) *od.* unterˈsuchen, erproben, e-r Prüfung unterˈziehen, testen (*alle a.* ⚙): **~ out** ausprobieren; **12.** *fig. j-s Geduld etc.* auf die Probe stellen; **13.** *ped.*, *psych. j-n* testen; **14.** ⚗ analysieren; **15.** ⚡ *Leitung* prüfen *od.* abfragen; **16.** ⚔ *Waffe* anschießen; **III** *adj.* **17.** Probe..., Versuchs..., Prüf(ungs)..., Test...; → **test case**, **test flight** *etc.*

tes·ta·cean [teˈsteɪʃn] *zo.* **I** *adj.* hartschalig, Schal(tier)...; **II** *s.* Schaltier *n*; **tesˈta·ceous** [-ʃəs] *adj. zo.* hartschalig, Schalen...

tes·ta·ment [ˈtestəmənt] *s.* **1.** ⚖ Testaˈment *n*, letzter Wille; **2. 2** *bibl.* (*Altes od. Neues*) Testaˈment; **3.** *fig.* Zeugnis *n*, Beweis *m* (**to** *gen. od.* für); **tes·ta·men·ta·ry** [ˌtestəˈmentərɪ] *adj.* □ ⚖ testamenˈtarisch: a) letztwillig, b) durch Testaˈment (vermacht, bestimmt): **~ disposition** letztwillige Verfügung; **~ capacity** Testierfähigkeit *f*.

tes·tate [ˈtesteɪt] *adj.*: **die ~** ⚖ unter Hinterlassung e-s Testaments sterben, ein Testament hinterlassen; **tes·ta·tor** [teˈsteɪtə] *s.* ⚖ Erblasser *m*; **tes·ta·trix** [teˈsteɪtrɪks] *pl.* **-tri·ces** [-siːz] *s.* Erblasserin *f*.

ˈtest|-bed *s.* ⚙ Prüfstand *m*; **~ card** *s. TV* Testbild *n*; **~ case** *s.* **1.** ⚖ a) ˈMusterproˌzeß *m*, b) Präzeˈdenzfall *m*; **2.** *fig.* Muster-, Schulbeispiel *n*; **~ cir·cuit** *s.* ⚡ Meßkreis *m*; **~ drive** *s. mot.* Probefahrt *f*; **ˈ~-drive** *v/t.* [*irr.*] *Auto* probefahren.

test·ed [ˈtestɪd] *adj.* geprüft; erprobt (*a. weitS. bewährt*).

test·er¹ [ˈtestə] *s.* **1.** Prüfer *m*; **2.** Prüfgerät *n*.

tes·ter² [ˈtestə] *s.* **1.** △ Baldachin *m*; **2.** (Bett)Himmel *m*.

tes·tes [ˈtestiːz] *pl. von* **testis**.

test| flight *s.* ✈ Probeflug *m*; **ˈ~-glass** → **test tube**.

tes·ti·cle [ˈtestɪkl] *s. anat.* Hode *m*, *f*, Hoden *m*; **tesˈtic·u·lar** *adj.* Hoden...

tes·ti·fy [ˈtestɪfaɪ] **I** *v/t.* **1.** ⚖ aussagen, bezeugen; **2.** *fig.* bezeugen: a) zeugen von, b) kundtun; **II** *v/i.* **3.** ⚖ (als Zeuge) aussagen: **~ to** → 2; **refuse to ~** die Aussage verweigern; **tes·ti·mo·ni·al** [ˌtestɪˈməʊnjəl] *s.* **1.** (Führungs- *etc.*) Zeugnis *n*; **2.** Empfehlungsschreiben *n*; **3.** Zeichen *n* der Anerkennung, *bsd.* Ehrengabe *f*; **ˈtes·ti·mo·ny** [-ɪmənɪ] *s.* **1.** Zeugnis *n*: a) ⚖ (Zeugen)Aussage *f*, b) Beweis *m*: **in ~ whereof** ⚖ zu Urkund dessen; **bear ~ to** *et.* bezeugen (*a. fig.*); **call s.o. in ~** ⚖ j-n als Zeugen aufrufen, *fig.* j-n zum Zeugen anrufen; **have s.o.'s ~ for** j-n zum Zeugen haben für; **2.** *coll. od. pl.* Zeugnis(se *pl.*) *n*: **the ~ of history**; **3.** *bibl.* Zeugnis *n*: a) Gesetzestafeln *pl.*, b) *mst pl.* göttliche Offenbarung, *a.* Heilige Schrift.

tes·ti·ness [ˈtestɪnɪs] *s.* Gereiztheit *f*.

test·ing [ˈtestɪŋ] *adj. bsd.* ⚙ Probe..., Prüf..., Versuchs...: **~ engineer** ⚙ Prüfingenieur *m*; **~ ground** ⚙ a) Prüffeld *n*, b) Versuchsgelände *n*; **~ method** *psych.* Testmethode *f*.

tes·tis [ˈtestɪs] *pl.* **-tes** [-tiːz] (*Lat.*) → **testicle**.

test| match *s. Kricket*: internatioˈnaler Vergleichskampf; **~ pa·per** *s.* **1.** *ped.* a) schriftliche (Klassen)Arbeit, b) Prüfungsbogen *m*; **2.** ⚗ Reaˈgenzpaˌpier *n*; **~ pi·lot** *s.* ˈTestpiˌlot *m*; **~ print** *s. phot.* Probeabzug *m*; **~ run** *s.* ⚙ Probelauf *m*; **~ stand** *s.* ⚙ Prüfstand *m*; **~ tube** [-stt-] *s.* ⚗ Reaˈgenzglas *n*; **ˈ~-tube** *adj.*: **~ baby** ⚕ Retortenbaby *n*.

tes·ty [ˈtestɪ] *adj.* □ gereizt, reizbar.

tet·a·nus [ˈtetənəs] *s.* ⚕ Tetanus *m*, (*bsd.* Wund)Starrkrampf *m*.

tetch·y ['tetʃɪ] *adj.* ☐ reizbar.
tête-à-tête [ˌteɪtɑː'teɪt] (*Fr.*) **I** *adv.* **1.** vertraulich, unter vier Augen; **2.** ganz al'lein (***with*** mit); **II** *s.* **3.** Tête-à-tête *n.*
teth·er ['teðə] **I** *s.* Haltestrick *m*, -seil *n*: ***be at the end of one's ~*** *fig.* am Ende s-r (*a. finanziellen*) Kräfte sein, sich nicht mehr zu helfen wissen; **II** *v/t.* anbinden (***to*** an *acc.*).
tetra- [tetrə] *in Zssgn* vier.
tet·rad ['tetræd] *s.* **1.** Vierzahl *f*; **2.** ⚗ vierwertiges A'tom *od.* Ele'ment; **3.** *biol.* ('Sporen)Teˌtrade *f.*
tet·ra·gon ['tetrəgən] *s.* 𝔄 Tetra'gon *n*, Viereck *n*; **te·trag·o·nal** [te'trægənl] *adj.* 𝔄 tetrago'nal.
tet·ra·he·dral [ˌtetrə'hedrəl] *adj.* 𝔄 vierflächig, tetra'edrisch; ˌ**tet·ra'he·dron** [-drən] *pl.* **-'he·drons**, **-'he·dra** [-drə] *s.* 𝔄 Tetra'eder *n.*
tet·ter ['tetə] *s.* ⚕ (Haut)Flechte *f.*
Teu·ton ['tjuːtən] **I** *s.* **1.** Ger'mane *m*, Ger'manin *f*; **2.** Teu'tone *m*, Teu'tonin *f*; **3.** F Deutsche(r *m*) *f*; **II** *adj.* **4.** → ***Teutonic*** I; **Teu·ton·ic** [tjuː'tɒnɪk] **I** *adj.* **1.** ger'manisch; **2.** teu'tonisch; **3.** Deutschordens…: ***~ Order*** *hist.* Deutschritterorden *m*; **4.** F (typisch) deutsch; **II** *s.* **5.** *ling.* Ger'manisch *n*; '**Teu·ton·ism** [-tənɪzəm] *s.* **1.** Ger'manentum *n*, ger'manisches Wesen; **2.** *ling.* Germa'nismus *m.*
Tex·an ['teksən] **I** *adj.* te'xanisch, aus Texas; **II** *s.* Te'xaner(in).
text [tekst] *s.* **1.** (Ur)Text *m*, (genauer) Wortlaut; **2.** *typ.* a) Text(abdruck, -teil) *m* (*Ggs. Illustrationen, Vorwort etc.*), b) Text *m* (*Schriftgrad*), c) Frak'turschrift *f*; **3.** (Lied- *etc.*)Text *m*; **4.** a) Bibelspruch *m*, -stelle *f*, b) Bibeltext *m*; **5.** Thema *n*: ***stick to one's ~*** bei der Sache bleiben; **6.** → ***text hand***; '**~·book** *s.* Lehrbuch *n*, Leitfaden *m*: ***~ example*** *fig.* Paradebeispiel *n*; **~ hand** *s.* große Schreibschrift.
tex·tile ['tekstaɪl] **I** *s.* a) Gewebe *n*, Web-, Faserstoff *m*, b) *pl.* Web-, Tex'tilwaren *pl.*, Tex'tilien *pl.*; **II** *adj.* gewebt; Textil…, Stoff…, Gewebe…: ***~ goods*** → I b; ***~ industry*** Textilindustrie *f.*
tex·tu·al ['tekstjʊəl] *adj.* ☐ **1.** textlich, Text…; **2.** wortgetreu.
tex·tur·al ['tekstʃərəl] *adj.* ☐ **1.** Gewebe…; **2.** struktu'rell, Struktur…: ***~ changes***; **tex·ture** ['tekstʃə] *s.* **1.** Gewebe *n*; **2.** *biol.* Tex'tur *f* (*Gewebezustand*); **3.** Maserung *f* (*Holz*); **4.** Struk'tur *f*, Beschaffenheit *f*; **5.** *geol.*, *a. fig.* Struk'tur *f*, Gefüge *n.*
'**T-ˌgird·er** *s.* ⚙ T-Träger *m.*
Thai [taɪ] **I** *pl.* **Thais**, **Thai** *s.* **1.** Thai *m*, *f*, Thailänder(in); **2.** *ling.* a) Thai *n*, b) Thaisprachen *pl.*; **II** *adj.* **3.** Thai…, thailändisch.
thal·a·mus ['θæləməs] *pl.* **-mi** [-maɪ] *s.* *anat.* Sehhügel *m.*
thali·dom·i·de [θə'lɪdəmaɪd] *s. pharm.* Thalido'mid *n*: ***~ child*** Contergankind *n.*
Thames [temz] *npr.* Themse *f*: ***he won't set the ~ on fire*** *fig.* er hat das Pulver auch nicht erfunden.
than [ðæn; ðən] *cj.* (*nach e-m Komparativ*) als: ***more ~ was necessary*** mehr als nötig.
thane [θeɪn] *s.* **1.** *hist.* a) Gefolgsadlige(r) *m*, b) Than *m*, Lehensmann *m* (*der schottischen Könige*); **2.** *allg.* schottischer Adliger.
thank [θæŋk] **I** *v/t.* *j-m* danken, sich bedanken bei: (***I***) ***~ you*** danke; ***~ you*** bitte (*beim Servieren etc.*); (***yes,***) ***~ you*** ja, bitte; ***no, ~ you*** nein, danke; ***I will ~ you*** *oft iro.* ich wäre Ihnen sehr dankbar (***to do***, ***for doing*** wenn sie täten); ***~ you for nothing*** *iro.* ich danke (bestens); ***he has only himself to ~ for that*** das hat er sich selbst zuzuschreiben; **II** *s. pl.* a) Dank *m*, b) Dankesbezeigung(en *pl.*) *f*, Danksagung(en *pl.*) *f*: ***letter of ~s*** Dankesbrief *m*; ***in ~s for*** zum Dank für; ***with ~s*** dankend, mit Dank; ***~s to*** *a. fig. u. iro.* dank (*gen.*); ***small ~s to her*** sie hat sich nicht gerade über'anstrengt; (***many***) ***~s!*** vielen Dank!, danke!; ***no, ~s!*** nein, danke!; ***small ~s I got*** schlecht hat man es mir gedankt; '**thank·ful** [-fʊl] *adj.* ☐ dankbar (***to s.o.*** j-m): ***I am ~ that*** ich bin (heil)froh, daß; '**thank·less** [-lɪs] *adj.* ☐ undankbar (*a. fig. Aufgabe etc.*); '**thank·less·ness** [-lɪsnɪs] *s.* Undankbarkeit *f.*
thank of·fer·ing *s. bibl.* Sühneopfer *n der Juden.*
thanks·giv·ing ['θæŋksˌgɪvɪŋ] *s.* **1.** Danksagung *f*, *bsd.* Dankgebet *n*; **2.** ♀ (***Day***) (Ernte)Dankfest *n* (*4. Donnerstag im November*).
'**thank|ˌwor·thy** *adj.* dankenswert; '**~-you** [-jʊ] *s.* F Dankeschön *n.*
that[1] [ðæt] **I** *pron. u. adj.* (*hinweisend*) *pl.* **those** [ðəʊz] **1.** (*ohne pl.*) das: ***~'s all*** das ist alles; ***~'s it!*** a) das ist es ja (gerade)!, b) so ist's recht!; ***~'s what it is*** das ist es ja gerade; ***~'s that*** F das wäre erledigt, damit basta, das wär's; ***~ was ~!*** F das war's denn wohl!, aus der Traum!; ***~ is*** (***to say***) das heißt; ***and ~*** und zwar; ***at ~*** a) zudem, obendrein, b) F dabei; ***for all ~*** trotz alledem; ***like ~*** so; **2.** jener, jene, jenes, der, die, das, der-, die-, dasjenige: ***~ car over there*** das Auto da drüben; ***~ there man*** V der Mann da; ***those who*** diejenigen welche; ***~ which*** das, was; ***those are his friends*** das sind seine Freunde; **3.** solch: ***to ~ degree that*** in solchem Ausmaße *od.* so sehr, daß; **II** *adv.* **4.** F so (sehr), dermaßen: ***~ big***; ***not all ~ good*** (***much***) so gut (viel) auch wieder nicht.
that[2] [ðæt; ðət] *pl.* **that** *rel. pron.* **1.** (*bsd. in einschränkenden Sätzen*) der, die, das, welch: ***the book ~ he wanted*** das Buch, das er wünschte; ***any house ~*** jedes Haus, das; ***no one ~*** keiner, der; ***Mrs. Jones, Miss Black ~ was*** F Frau J., geborene B.; ***Mrs. Quilp ~ is*** die jetzige Frau Q.; **2.** (*nach* ***all***, ***everything***, ***nothing*** *etc.*) was: ***the best ~*** das Beste, was.
that[3] [ðæt; ðət] *cj.* **1.** (*in Subjekts- u. Objektssätzen*) daß: ***it is a pity ~ he is not here*** es ist schade, daß er nicht hier ist; ***it is 4 years ~ he went away*** es sind nun 4 Jahre her, daß *od.* seitdem er fortging; **2.** (*in Konsekutivsätzen*) daß: ***so ~*** so daß; **3.** (*in Finalsätzen*) da'mit, daß; **4.** (*in Kausalsätzen*) weil, da (ja), daß: ***not ~ I have any objection*** nicht, daß ich etwas dagegen hätte; ***it is rather ~*** es ist eher deshalb, weil; ***in ~*** a) darum, weil, b) insofern als; **5.** (*nach Adverbien der Zeit*) als, da.
thatch [θætʃ] **I** *s.* **1.** Dachstroh *n*; **2.** Strohdach *n*; **3.** F Haarwald *m*; **II** *v/t.* **4.** mit Stroh *od.* Binsen *etc.* decken: ***~ed roof*** → 2.
thaw [θɔː] **I** *v/i.* **1.** (auf)tauen, schmelzen; **2.** tauen (*Wetter*): ***it is ~ing*** es taut; **3.** *fig.* auftauen (*Person*); **II** *v/t.* **4.** schmelzen, auftauen; **5.** *a.* ***~ out*** *fig.* *j-n* zum Auftauen bringen; **III** *s.* **6.** (Auf-)Tauen *n*; **7.** Tauwetter *n* (*a. fig. pol.*); **8.** *fig.* ‚Auftauen' *n.*
the [*unbetont vor Konsonanten*: ðə; *unbetont vor Vokalen*: ðɪ; *betont od. alleinstehend*: ðiː] **I** *bestimmter Artikel* **1.** der, die, das, *pl.* die (*u. die entsprechenden Formen im acc. u. dat.*): ***~ book on ~ table*** das Buch auf dem Tisch; ***~ England of today*** das England von heute; ***~ Browns*** die Browns, die Familie Brown; **2.** *vor Maßangaben*: ***one dollar ~ pound*** einen Dollar das Pfund; ***wine at 2 pounds ~ bottle*** Wein zu 2 Pfund die Flasche; **3.** [ðiː] 'der, 'die, 'das (*hervorragende od. geeignete etc.*): ***he is ~ painter of the century*** er ist 'der Maler des Jahrhunderts; **II** *adv.* **4.** (*vor comp.*) desto, um so: ***~ … ~*** je … desto; ***~ sooner ~ better*** je eher, desto besser; ***so much ~ better*** um so besser.
the·a·ter *Am.*, **the·a·tre** *Brit.* ['θɪətə] *s.* **1.** The'ater *n* (*Gebäude u. Kunstgattung*); **2.** *coll.* Bühnenwerke *pl*; **3.** Hörsaal *m*: ***lecture ~***; (***operating***) ***~*** ⚕ Operationssaal *m*; ***~ nurse*** Operationsschwester *f*; **4.** *fig.* (***of war*** Kriegs-) Schauplatz *m*; '**~ˌgo·er** *s.* The'aterbesucher(in).
the·at·ri·cal [θɪ'ætrɪkl] **I** *adj.* ☐ **1.** Theater…, Bühnen…, bühnenmäßig; **2.** thea'tralisch: ***~ gestures***; **II** *s.* **3.** *pl.* The'ater-, *bsd.* Liebhaberaufführungen *pl.*; **the'at·rics** *s. pl.* **1.** *sg. konstr.* The'ater(reˌgie)kunst *f*; **2.** *fig.* Thea'tralik *f.*
thee [ðiː] *pron.* **1.** *obs. od. poet. od. bibl.* a) dich, b) dir: ***of ~*** dein; **2.** *dial.* (*u. in der Sprache der Quäker*) du.
theft [θeft] *s.* Diebstahl *m* (***from*** aus, ***from s.o.*** an j-m); '**~·proof** *adj.* diebstahlsicher.
the·in(e) ['θiːiːn; -ɪn] *s.* ⚗ The'in *n.*
their [ðeə; *vor Vokal* ðer] *pron.* (*besitzanzeigendes Fürwort der 3. pl.*) ihr, ihre: ***~ books*** ihre Bücher.
theirs [ðeəz] *pron.* der *od.* die *od.* das ihrige *od.* ihre: ***this book is ~*** dieses Buch gehört ihnen; ***a friend of ~*** ein Freund von ihnen.
the·ism[1] ['θiːɪzəm] *s.* ⚕ Teevergiftung *f.*
the·ism[2] ['θiːɪzəm] *s. eccl.* The'ismus *m*; **the·is·tic** [θiː'ɪstɪk] *adj.* the'istisch.
them [ðem; ðəm] *pron.* **1.** (*acc. u. dat. von* ***they***) a) sie (*acc.*), b) ihnen: ***they looked behind ~*** sie blickten hinter sich; **2.** F *od. dial.* sie (*nom.*): ***~ as*** diejenigen, die; **3.** *dial. od.* V diese: ***~ guys***; ***~ were the days!*** das waren (halt) noch Zeiten!
the·mat·ic [θɪ'mætɪk] *adj.* (☐ ***~ally***) **1.** *bsd.* ♪ the'matisch; **2.** *ling.* Stamm…, Thema…: ***~ vowel.***
theme [θiːm] *s.* **1.** Thema *n* (*a.* ♪): ***have s.th. for*** (***a***) ***~*** et. zum Thema haben; **2.** *bsd. Am.* (Schul)Aufsatz *m*, (-)Ar-

beit *f*; **3.** *ling.* (Wort)Stamm *m*; **4.** *Radio, TV*: 'Kennmelo,die *f*; **~ song** *s.* **1.** 'Titelmelo,die *f* (*Film etc.*); **2.** → ***theme*** 4.

them·selves [ðəm'selvz] *pron.* **1.** (*emphatisch*) (sie) selbst: ***they ~ said it***; **2.** *refl.* sich (selbst): ***the ideas in ~*** die Ideen an sich.

then [ðen] **I** *adv.* **1.** damals: ***long before ~*** lange vorher; **2.** dann: ***~ and there*** auf der Stelle, sofort; ***by ~*** bis dahin, inzwischen; ***from ~*** von da an; ***till ~*** bis dahin; **3.** dann, 'darauf, 'hierauf: ***what ~?*** was dann?; **4.** dann, außerdem: ***but ~*** aber andererseits *od.* freilich; **5.** dann, in dem Falle: ***if ... ~*** wenn ... dann; **6.** denn: ***well ~*** nun gut (denn); ***how ~ did he do it?*** wie hat er es denn (dann) getan?; **7.** also, folglich, dann: ***~ you did not expect me?*** du hast mich also nicht erwartet?; **II** *adj.* **8.** damalig: ***the ~ president***.

the·nar ['θi:nɑ:] *s. anat.* **1.** Handfläche *f*; **2.** Daumenballen *m*; **3.** Fußsohle *f*.

thence [ðens] *adv.* **1.** von da, von dort; **2.** (*zeitlich*) von da an, seit jener Zeit: ***a week ~*** e-e Woche darauf; **3.** 'daher, deshalb; **4.** 'daraus, aus dieser Tatsache: ***~ it follows***; **,~'forth**, **,~'for·ward(s)** *adv.* von da an, seit der Zeit, seit'dem.

the·oc·ra·cy [θɪ'ɒkrəsɪ] *s.* Theokra'tie *f*.

the·o·lo·gi·an [θɪə'ləʊdʒjən] *s.* Theo'loge *m*; **the·o'log·i·cal** [-'lɒdʒɪkl] *adj.* □ theo'logisch; **the·ol·o·gy** [θɪ'ɒlədʒɪ] *s.* Theolo'gie *f*.

the·oph·a·ny [θɪ'ɒfənɪ] *s.* Theopha'nie *f*, Erscheinung *f* (*e-s*) Gottes.

the·o·rem ['θɪərəm] *s.* ⩕, *phls.* Theo'rem *n*, (Grund-, Lehr)Satz *m*: ***~ of the cosine*** Kosinussatz.

the·o·ret·ic, **the·o·ret·i·cal** [θɪə'retɪk(l)] *adj.* □ **1.** theo'retisch; **2.** spekula'tiv; **the·o·rist** ['θɪərɪst] *s.* Theo'retiker(in); **the·o·rize** ['θɪəraɪz] *v/i.* **1.** theoretisieren, Theo'rien aufstellen; **2.** ***~ that*** die Theorie aufstellen, daß; annehmen, daß; **the·o·ry** ['θɪərɪ] *s.* Theo'rie *f*: a) Lehre *f*: ***~ of chances*** Wahrscheinlichkeitsrechnung *f*; ***~ of relativity*** Relativitätstheorie, b) theo'retischer Teil (*e-r Wissenschaft*): ***~ of music*** Musiktheorie, c) *Ggs. Praxis*: ***in ~*** theoretisch, d) Anschauung *f*: ***it is his pet ~*** es ist s-e Lieblingsidee.

the·o·soph·ic, **the·o·soph·i·cal** [θɪə'sɒfɪk(l)] *adj.* □ *eccl.* theo'sophisch; **the·os·o·phist** [θɪ'ɒsəfɪst] *s.* Theo'soph(in); **the·os·o·phy** [θɪ'ɒsəfɪ] *s.* Theoso'phie *f*.

ther·a·peu·tic, **ther·a·peu·ti·cal** [,θerə'pju:tɪk(l)] *adj.* □ thera'peutisch: ***~ exercises*** Bewegungstherapie *f*; **,ther·a'peu·tics** [-ks] *s. pl. mst sg. konstr.* Thera'peutik *f*, Thera'pie(lehre) *f*; **ther·a·pist** ['θerəpɪst] *s.* Thera'peut (-in): ***mental ~*** Psychotherapeut(in); **ther·a·py** ['θerəpɪ] *s.* Thera'pie *f*: a) Behandlung *f*, b) Heilverfahren *n*.

there [ðeə; ðə] **I** *adv.* **1.** da, dort: ***down*** (***up***, ***over***, ***in***) ***~*** da *od.* dort unten (oben, drüben, drinnen); ***have been ~*** *sl.* ‚dabeigewesen sein', genau Bescheid wissen; ***be not all ~*** *sl.* ‚nicht ganz richtig (im Oberstübchen) sein'; ***~ and then*** a) (gerade) hier u. jetzt, b) auf der Stelle, sofort; ***~ it is!*** a) da ist es!, b) *fig.* so steht es!; ***~ you are*** (*od.* ***go***)***!*** siehst du!, da hast du's; ***you ~!*** (*Anruf*) du da!, he!; **2.** ('da-, 'dort)hin: ***down*** (***up***, ***over***, ***in***) ***~*** (da- *od.* dort)hinunter (-hinauf, -hinüber, -hinein); ***~ and back*** hin u. zurück; ***get ~*** a) hingelangen, -kommen, b) *sl.* ‚es schaffen'; **3.** 'darin, in dieser Sache *od.* Hinsicht: ***~ I agree with you***; **4.** *fig.* da, an dieser Stelle (*in e-r Rede etc.*); **5.** es: ***~ is***, *pl.* ***~ are*** es gibt, ist, sind; ***~ was once a king*** es war einmal ein König; ***~ is no saying*** es läßt sich nicht sagen; ***~ was dancing*** es wurde getanzt; ***~'s a good boy*** (***girl***, ***fellow***)***!*** a) sei doch (so) lieb!, b) so bist du lieb!, brav!; **II** *int.* **6.** da!, schau (her)!, na!: ***~, ~!*** *tröstend*: (ganz) ruhig!; ***~ now*** na, bitte; **'~·a·bout**, *a.* **'~·bouts** ['ðeərə-] *adv.* **1.** da her'um, etwa da: ***somewhere ~*** da irgendwo; **2.** *fig.* so ungefähr, so etwa: ***500 people or ~s***; **,~'aft·er** [ðeər'ɑ:-] *adv.* **1.** da'nach, später; **2.** seit'her; **~·at** [,ðeər'æt] *adv. obs. od.* ⚖ **1.** da'selbst, dort; **2.** bei der Gelegenheit, 'dabei; **,~'by** *adv.* **1.** 'dadurch, auf diese Weise; **2.** da'bei, dar'an, da'von; **3.** nahe da'bei; **,~'for** *adv.* 'dafür; **'~·fore** *adv. u. cj.* **1.** deshalb, -wegen, 'daher, 'darum; **2.** demgemäß, folglich; **,~'from** *adv.* da'von, dar'aus, da'her; **~·in** [,ðeər'ɪn] *adv.* **1.** dar'in, da drinnen; **2.** *fig.* 'darin, in dieser Hinsicht; **,~·in'aft·er** [,ðeərɪn-] *adv. bsd.* ⚖ (*weiter*) unten, später (*in e-r Urkunde etc.*); **~·of** [,ðeər'ɒv] *adv. obs. od.* ⚖ **1.** da'von; **2.** dessen, deren; **~·on** [,ðeər'ɒn] *adv.* 'darauf, -über; **,~'to** *adv. obs.* **1.** da'zu, dar'an, da'für; **2.** außerdem, noch da'zu; **~·un·der** [,ðeər'ʌndə] *adv.* dar'unter; **~·up·on** [,ðeərə'pɒn] *adv.* **1.** dar'auf, 'hier'auf, da'nach; **2.** darauf'hin, demzufolge, 'darum; **,~'with** *adv.* **1.** 'damit; **2.** → ***thereupon***; **,~·with'al** *adv. obs.* **1.** über'dies, außerdem; **2.** 'damit.

therm [θɜ:m] *s. phys.* **1.** *unbestimmte Wärmeeinheit*; **2.** *Brit.* 100,000 Wärmeeinheiten *pl.* (*zur Messung des Gasverbrauchs*); **'ther·mae** [-mi:] (*Lat.*) *s. pl.* **1.** *antiq.* Thermen *pl.*; **2.** ⚕ Ther'malquellen *pl.*

ther·mal ['θɜ:ml] **I** *adj.* □ **1.** *phys.* thermisch, Wärme...: ***~ barrier*** ✈ Hitzemauer *f*; ***~ breeder*** thermischer Brüter; ***~ efficiency*** Wärmewirkungsgrad *m*; ***~ power-station*** Wärmekraftwerk *n*; ***~ reactor*** thermischer Reaktor; ***~ value*** Heizwert *m*; **2.** warm, heiß: ***~ water*** heiße Quelle; **3.** ⚕ ther'mal, Thermal...; **II** *s.* **4.** *pl.* ✈, *phys.* Thermik *f*; **'ther·mic** [-mɪk] *adj.* (□ ***~ally***) thermisch, Wärme..., Hitze...; **therm·i·on·ic** [,θɜ:mɪ'ɒnɪk] **I** *adj.* thermi'onisch: ***~ valve*** (*Am.* ***tube***) Elektronenröhre *f*; **II** *s. pl. mst sg. konstr.* Thermi'onik *f*, Lehre *f* von den Elektronenröhren.

thermo- [θɜ:məʊ] *in Zssgn* a) Wärme, Hitze, Thermo..., b) thermoe'lektrisch; **,ther·mo'chem·is·try** *s.* ⚗ Thermoche'mie *f*; **'ther·mo,cou·ple** *s.* ⚡ Thermoele'ment *n*; **,ther·mo·dy'nam·ics** *s. sg. u. pl. konstr. phys.* Thermody'namik *f*; **,ther·mo·e'lec·tric** *adj.* thermoe'lektrisch, 'wärmee,lektrisch: ***~ couple*** → ***thermocouple***.

ther·mom·e·ter [θə'mɒmɪtə] *s. phys.* Thermo'meter *n*: ***clinical ~*** ⚕ Fieberthermometer; ***~ reading*** Thermometerablesung *f*, -stand *m*; **ther·mo·met·ric**, **ther·mo·met·ri·cal** [,θɜ:məʊ'metrɪk(l)] *adj.* □ *phys.* thermo'metrisch, Thermometer...; **,ther·mo'nu·cle·ar** *adj. phys.* thermonukle'ar: ***~ bomb*** *a.* Fusionsbombe *f*; **'ther·mo·pile** *s. phys.* Thermosäule *f*; **,ther·mo'plas·tic** ⚗ **I** *adj.* thermo'plastisch; **II** *s.* Thermo'plast *m*.

Ther·mos (**bot·tle** *od.* **flask**) ['θɜ:mɒs] *s.* Thermosflasche *f*.

,ther·mo'set·ting *adj.* ⚗ ,thermostato'plastisch, hitzehärtbar.

ther·mo·stat ['θɜ:məʊstæt] *s.* ⚡, ⚙ Thermo'stat *m*; **ther·mo·stat·ic** [,θɜ:məʊ'stætɪk] *adj.* (□ ***~ally***) thermo'statisch.

the·sau·rus [θɪ'sɔ:rəs] *pl.* **-ri** [-raɪ] (*Lat.*) *s.* The'saurus *m*: a) Wörterbuch *n*, b) (Wort-, Wissens-, Sprach)Schatz *m*.

these [ði:z] *pl. von* **this**.

the·sis ['θi:sɪs] *pl.* **-ses** [-si:z] *s.* **1.** These *f*: a) Behauptung *f*, b) (Streit)Satz *m*, Postu'lat *n*; **2.** *univ.* Dissertati'on *f*; **3.** ['θesɪs] *Metrik*: unbetonte Silbe; **~ nov·el** *s.* Ten'denzro,man *m*; **~ play** *s. thea.* Pro'blemstück *n*.

Thes·pi·an ['θespɪən] **I** *adj. fig.* dra'matisch, Schauspiel...; **II** *s. oft humor.* Thespisjünger(in).

Thes·sa·lo·ni·ans [,θesə'ləʊnjənz] *s. pl. sg. konstr. bibl.* (Brief *m* des Paulus an die) Thessa'lonicher *pl.*

thews [θju:z] *s. pl.* **1.** Muskeln *pl.*, Sehnen *pl.*; **2.** *fig.* Kraft *f*.

they [ðeɪ; ðe] *pron.* **1.** (*pl. zu* ***he***, ***she***, ***it***) sie; **2.** man: ***~ say*** man sagt; **3.** es: ***who are ~? – ~ are Americans*** Wer sind sie? – Es (*od.* sie) sind Amerikaner; **4.** (*auf Kollektiva bezogen*) er, sie, es: ***the police ..., ~ ...*** die Polizei ..., sie (*sg.*); **5.** ***~ who*** diejenigen, welche.

they'd [ðeɪd] F *für* a) ***they would***, b) ***they had***.

thick [θɪk] **I** *adj.* □ **1.** *allg.* dick: ***a ~ neck***; ***a board 2 inches ~*** ein 2 Zoll starkes Brett; **2.** dicht (*Wald*, *Haar*, *Menschenmenge*, *a. Nebel etc.*); **3.** ***~ with*** über u. über bedeckt von; **4.** ***~ with*** voll von, voller, reich an (*dat.*): ***a tree ~ with leaves***; ***the air is ~ with snow*** die Luft ist voll(er) Schnee; **5.** dick(flüssig); **6.** neblig, trüb(e) (*Wetter*); **7.** schlammig, trübe; **8.** dumpf, belegt (*Stimme*); **9.** dumm; **10.** dicht (aufein'anderfolgend); **11.** F dick (befreundet): ***they are as ~ as thieves*** sie sind dicke Freunde, sie halten zusammen wie Pech u. Schwefel; **12.** *sl.* ‚stark', frech: ***that's a bit ~!*** das ist ein starkes Stück!; **II** *s.* **13.** dickster *od.* dichtester Teil; **14.** *fig.* Brennpunkt *m*: ***in the ~ of*** mitten in (*dat.*); ***in the ~ of it*** mittendrin; ***in the ~ of the fight*** im dichtesten Kampfgetümmel; ***the ~ of the crowd*** das dichteste Menschengewühl; ***through ~ and thin*** durch dick u. dünn; **15.** F Dummkopf *m*; **III** *adv.* **16.** dick: ***spread ~*** *Butter etc.* dick aufstreichen; ***lay it on ~*** F ‚dick auftragen'; **17.** dicht *od.* rasch (aufein'ander); *a.* ***fast and ~*** hageldicht (*Schläge*); **thick·en** ['θɪkən] **I** *v/t.* **1.** dick(er) machen, verdicken; **2.** *Sauce*, *Flüssigkeit* eindicken,

Suppe legieren; **3.** dicht(er) machen, verdichten; **4.** verstärken, -mehren; **5.** trüben; **II** *v/i.* **6.** dick(er) werden; **7.** dick(flüssig) werden; **8.** sich verdichten; **9.** sich trüben; **10.** sich verwirren: ***the plot ~s*** der Knoten (*im Drama etc.*) schürzt sich; **11.** zunehmen; **thick·en·er** [ˈθɪknə] *s.* ⚗ **1.** Eindicker *m*; **2.** Verdicker *m*, Absetzbehälter *m*; **3.** Verdickungsmittel *n*; **thick·en·ing** [ˈθɪknɪŋ] *s.* **1.** Verdickung *f*; **2.** Eindikkung *f*; **3.** Eindickmittel *n*; **4.** Verdichtung *f*; **5.** ⚕ Anschwellung *f*, Schwarte *f*.

thick·et [ˈθɪkɪt] *s.* Dickicht *n*; **ˈthick·et·ed** [-tɪd] *adj.* voller Dickicht(e).

ˈthick|·head *s.* Dummkopf *m*; **ˌ~-ˈhead·ed** *adj.* **1.** dickköpfig; **2.** *fig.* dumm.

thick·ness [ˈθɪknɪs] *s.* **1.** Dicke *f*, Stärke *f*; **2.** Dichte *f*; **3.** Verdickung *f*; **4.** ✝ Lage *f* (*Seide etc.*), Schicht *f*; **5.** Dickflüssigkeit *f*; **6.** Trübheit *f*: ***misty ~*** undurchdringlicher Nebel; **7.** Heiserkeit *f*, Undeutlichkeit *f*: ***~ of speech*** schwere Zunge.

ˌthick|ˈset *adj.* **1.** dicht (gepflanzt): ***a ~ hedge***; **2.** unterˈsetzt (*Person*); **ˌ~-ˈskinned** *adj.* **1.** dickhäutig; **2.** dickschalig; **3.** *zo.* Dickhäuter...; **4.** *fig.* dickfellig; **ˌ~-ˈskulled** [-ˈskʌld] *adj.* **1.** dickköpfig; **2.** → ***thick-witted***; **ˌ~-ˈwit·ted** *adj.* dumm, begriffsstutzig, schwer von Begriff.

thief [θiːf] *pl.* **thieves** [θiːvz] *s.* Dieb (-in): ***thieves' Latin*** Gaunersprache *f*; ***stop ~!*** haltet den Dieb!; ***one ought to set a ~ to catch a ~*** wenn man e-n Schlauen fangen will, muß man e-n Schlauen schicken; **thieve** [θiːv] *v/t. u. v/i.* stehlen; **thiev·er·y** [ˈθiːvərɪ] *s.* **1.** Diebeˈrei *f*, Diebstahl *m*; **2.** Diebesgut *n*; **thiev·ish** [ˈθiːvɪʃ] *adj.* □ **1.** diebisch, Dieb(e)s...; **2.** heimlich, verstohlen; **ˈthiev·ish·ness** [-nɪs] *s.* diebisches Wesen.

thigh [θaɪ] *s. anat.* (Ober)Schenkel *m*; **ˈ~·bone** *s. anat.* (Ober)Schenkelknochen *m*.

thill [θɪl] *s.* (Gabel)Deichsel *f*; **thill·er** [ˈθɪlə], *a.* **thill horse** *s.* Deichselpferd *n*.

thim·ble [ˈθɪmbl] *s.* **1.** *Näherei*: a) Fingerhut *m*, b) Nähring *m*; **2.** ⚙ a) Meˈtallring *m*, b) (Stock)Zwinge *f*; **ˈthim·ble·ful** [-fʊl] *pl.* **-fuls** *s.* **1.** Fingerhutvoll *m*, Schlückchen *n*; **2.** *fig.* Kleinigkeit *f*.

ˈthim·ble|·rig I *s.* Fingerhutspiel *n* (*Bauernfängerspiel*); **II** *v/t. a. allg.* betrügen; **ˈ~·rig·ger** *s.* **1.** Fingerhutspieler *m*; **2.** *allg.* Bauernfänger *m*.

thin [θɪn] **I** *adj.* □ **1.** *allg.* dünn: ***~ air***; ***~ blood***; ***~ clothes***; ***a ~ line*** e-e dünne *od.* schmale *od.* feine Linie; **2.** dünn, mager, schmächtig: ***as ~ as a lath*** spindeldürr; **3.** dünn, licht (*Wald, Haar etc.*): ***~ rain*** feiner Regen; **4.** dünn, schwach (*Getränk etc., a. Stimme, Ton*); **5.** ⚒ mager (*Boden*); **6.** *fig.* mager, spärlich, dürftig: ***a ~ house*** *thea.* e-e schwachbesuchte Vorstellung; ***he had a ~ time of it*** *sl.* es ging ihm ‚mies'; **7.** *fig.* fadenscheinig: ***a ~ excuse***; **8.** seicht, subˈstanzlos (*Buch etc.*); **II** *v/t.* **9.** *oft* ***~ down***, ***~ off***, ***~ out*** a) dünn(er) machen, b) *Flüssigkeit* verdünnen, c) *fig.* verringern, *Bevölkerung* dezimieren, *Schlachtreihe*, *Wald etc.* lichten; **III** *v/i.* **10.** *oft* ***~ down***, ***~ off***, ***~ out*** a) dünn(er) werden, b) sich verringern, c) sich lichten (*a. Haar*), d) *fig.* spärlicher werden, abnehmen: ***his hair is ~ning*** sein Haar lichtet sich.

thine [ðaɪn] *pron. obs. od. bibl. od. poet.* **1.** (*substantivisch*) der *od.* die *od.* das dein(ig)e, dein(e, er); **2.** (*adjektivisch vor Vokalen od. stummem h für* ***thy***) dein(e): ***~ eyes*** deine Augen.

thing [θɪŋ] *s.* **1.** *konkretes* Ding, Sache *f*, Gegenstand *m*: ***the law of ~s*** ⚖ das Sachenrecht; ***just the ~ I wanted*** genau (das), was ich wollte; **2.** *fig.* Ding *n*, Sache *f*, Angelegenheit *f*: ***~s political*** politische Dinge, alles Politische; ***above all ~s*** vor allen Dingen, vor allem; ***another ~*** etwas anderes; ***the best ~ to do*** das Beste(, was man tun kann); ***a foolish ~ to do*** e-e Torheit; ***for one ~*** (erstens) einmal; ***in all ~s*** in jeder Hinsicht; ***no small ~*** keine Kleinigkeit; ***no such ~*** nichts dergleichen; ***not a ~*** (rein) gar nichts; ***of all ~s*** ausgerechnet (*dieses etc.*); ***a pretty ~*** *iro.* e-e schöne Geschichte; ***taking one ~ with the other*** im großen (u.) ganzen; ***do great ~s*** große Dinge tun, Großes vollbringen; ***get ~s done*** et. zuwege bringen; ***do one's own ~*** F tun, was man will; ***know a ~ or two*** Bescheid wissen (***about*** über *acc.*); ***it's one of those ~s*** da kann man (halt) nichts machen; → ***first*** 1; **3.** *pl.* Sachen *pl.*, Zeug *n* (*Gepäck, Gerät, Kleider etc.*): ***swimming ~s*** Badesachen, -zeug; ***put on one's ~s*** sich anziehen; **4.** *pl.* Dinge *pl.*, ˈUmstände *pl.*, (Sach)Lage *f*: ***~s are improving*** die Dinge *od.* Verhältnisse bessern sich; ***~s look black for me*** es sieht schwarz aus für mich; **5.** Geschöpf *n*, Wesen *n*: ***dumb ~s***; **6.** a) Ding *n* (*Mädchen etc.*), b) Kerl *m*: (***the***) ***poor ~*** das arme Ding, der *od.* die Ärmste; ***poor ~!*** du *od.* Sie Ärmste(r)!; ***the dear old ~*** die gute alte Haut; **7.** ***the ~*** F a) die Hauptsache, b) das Richtige, richtig, c) das Schickliche, schicklich: ***the ~ was to*** das Wichtigste war zu; ***this is not the ~*** das ist nicht das Richtige; ***not to be*** (*od.* ***feel***) ***quite the ~*** nicht ganz auf dem Posten sein; ***that's not all the ~ to do*** so etwas tut man nicht; **ˌ~-in-itˈself** *s. phls. das* Ding an sich.

thing·um·a·bob [ˈθɪŋəmɪbɒb], **thing·um·a·jig** [ˈθɪŋəmɪdʒɪg], **thing·um·my** [ˈθɪŋəmɪ] *s.* F *der* (*die, das*) ‚Dings(da)' *od.* ‚Dingsbums'.

think [θɪŋk] [*irr.*] **I** *v/i.* **1.** denken (***of*** an *acc.*): ***~ ahead*** vorausdenken, *a.* vorsichtig sein; ***~ aloud*** laut denken; **2.** (***about***, ***over***) nachdenken (über *acc.*), sich (*e-e Sache*) überˈlegen; **3.** ***~ of*** a) sich besinnen auf (*acc.*), sich erinnern an (*acc.*): (***now that I***) ***come to ~ of it*** dabei fällt mir ein; b) *et.* bedenken: ***~ of it!*** denke daran!, c) sich *et.* denken *od.* vorstellen, d) *Plan etc.* ersinnen, ausdenken, e) halten von: ***~ much*** (*od.* ***highly***) ***of*** viel halten von, e-e hohe Meinung haben von; ***~ nothing of*** a) wenig halten von, b) nichts dabei finden (***to do s.th.*** et. zu tun); → ***better***[1] 4; **4.** meinen, denken: ***I ~ so*** ich glaube (schon), ich denke; ***I should ~ so*** ich denke doch, das will ich meinen; **5.** gedenken, vorhaben, beabsichtigen (***of doing***, ***to do*** zu tun); **II** *v/t.* **6.** *et.* denken: ***~ away*** *et.* wegdenken; ***~ out*** a) sich *et.* ausdenken, b) *Am. a.* ***~ through*** *Problem* zu Ende denken; ***~ s.th. over*** sich et. überlegen *od.* durch den Kopf gehen lassen; ***~ up*** F *Plan etc.* aushecken, sich ausdenken, sich *et.* einfallen lassen; **7.** sich *et.* denken *od.* vorstellen; **8.** halten für: ***~ o.s. clever***; ***~ it advisable*** es für ratsam halten *od.* erachten; ***I ~ it best to do*** ich halte es für das beste, *et.* zu tun; **9.** überˈlegen, nachdenken über (*acc.*); **10.** denken, vermuten: ***~ no harm*** nichts Böses denken; **III** *s.* F **11.** ***have a*** (***fresh***) ***~ about s.th.*** et. (noch einmal) überdenken; ***he has another ~ coming!*** da hat er sich aber schwer getäuscht!; **ˈthink·a·ble** [-kəbl] *adj.* denkbar: a) begreifbar, b) möglich; **ˈthink·er** [-kə] *s.* Denker(in); **ˈthink-in** *s.* F Konfeˈrenz *f*; **ˈthink·ing** [-kɪŋ] **I** *adj.* □ **1.** denkend, vernünftig: ***a ~ being*** ein denkendes Wesen; ***all ~ men*** jeder vernünftig Denkende; ***put on one's ~ cap*** F (mal) nachdenken; **2.** Denk...; **II** *s.* **3.** Denken *n*: ***way of ~*** Denkart *f*; ***do some hard*** (***quick***) ***~*** scharf nachdenken (schnell ‚schalten'); **4.** Meinung *f*: ***in*** (*od.* ***to***) ***my*** (***way of***) ***~*** m-r Meinung nach; **ˈthink-so** *s.*: ***on his*** (*etc.*) ***mere ~*** auf eine bloße Vermutung hin; **~ tank** *s.* F ‚ˈDenkfaˌbrik' *f*.

thin·ner[1] [ˈθɪnə] *s.* **1.** Verdünner *m* (*Arbeiter od. Gerät*); **2.** (*bsd.* Farben)Verdünnungsmittel *n*.

thin·ner[2] [ˈθɪnə] *comp. von* ***thin***.

thin·ness [ˈθɪnnɪs] *s.* **1.** Dünne *f*, Dünnheit *f*; **2.** Magerkeit *f*; **3.** Spärlichkeit *f*; **4.** *fig.* Dürftigkeit *f*, Seichtheit *f*.

ˌthin-ˈskinned *adj.* **1.** dünnhäutig; **2.** *fig.* (ˈüber)empfindlich.

third [θɜːd] **I** *adj.* □ → ***thirdly***; **1.** dritt: ***~ best*** *der* (*die, das*) Drittbeste; ***~ cousin*** Vetter *m* dritten Grades; ***~ degree*** dritter Grad; ***~ estate*** *pol. hist.* dritter Stand, Bürgertum *n*; ***~ party*** ⚖ Dritte(r *m*) *f*; **II** *s.* **2.** *der* (*die, das*) Dritte; **3.** ♪ Terz *f*; **4.** *mot.* F dritter Gang; **5.** Drittel *n*; **6.** *pl.* ✝ Waren *pl.* dritter Qualiˈtät, dritte Wahl; ***~ class*** *s.* 🚃 *etc.* dritte Klasse; **ˌ~-ˈclass** *adj. u. adv.* **1.** *allg.* drittklassig; **2.** 🚃 *etc. Abteil etc.* dritter Klasse: ***travel ~*** dritter Klasse reisen.

third·ly [ˈθɜːdlɪ] *adv.* drittens.

ˌthird|-ˈpar·ty *adj.* ⚖ Dritt...: ***~ debtor***, ***~ insurance*** Haftpflichtversicherung *f*; ***insured against ~ risks*** haftpflichtversichert; **ˌ~-ˈrate** *adj.* **1.** drittrangig; **2.** *fig.* minderwertig; ♀ **World** *s. pol. die* dritte Welt.

thirst [θɜːst] **I** *s.* **1.** Durst *m*; **2.** *fig.* Durst *m*, Gier *f*, Verlangen *n*, Sucht *f* (***for***, ***of***, ***after*** nach): ***~ for blood*** Blutdurst; ***~ for knowledge*** Wissensdurst; ***~ for power*** Machtgier; **II** *v/i.* **3.** *bsd. fig.* dürsten, lechzen (***for***, ***after*** nach *Rache etc.*); **ˈthirst·i·ness** [-tɪnɪs] *s.* Durst(igkeit *f*) *m*; **ˈthirst·y** [-tɪ] *adj.* □ **1.** durstig: ***be ~*** Durst haben, durstig sein; **2.** dürr, trocken (*Boden, Jahreszeit*); **3.** F ‚durstig', Durst verursachend: ***~ work***; **4.** *fig.* begierig, lechzend: ***be ~ for*** (*od.* ***after***) ***s.th.*** nach et. lechzen.

thir·teen [ˌθɜːˈtiːn] **I** *adj.* dreizehn; **II** *s.* Dreizehn *f*; ˌ**thirˈteenth** [-nθ] **I** *adj.* **1.** dreizehnt; **II** *s.* **2.** *der* (*die, das*) Dreizehnte; **3.** Dreizehntel *n*.

thir·ti·eth [ˈθɜːtɪɪθ] **I** *adj.* **1.** dreißigst; **II** *s.* **2.** *der* (*die, das*) Dreißigste; **3.** Dreißigstel *n*; **thir·ty** [ˈθɜːtɪ] **I** *adj.* **1.** dreißig: ***~ all***, F ***~ up*** *Tennis*: dreißig beide; **II** *s.* **2.** Dreißig *f*: ***the thirties*** a) die Dreißiger(jahre) (*des Lebens*): ***he is in his thirties*** er ist in den Dreißigern, b) die dreißiger Jahre (*e-s Jahrhunderts*); **3.** *Am. sl.* Ende *n* (*e-s Zeitungsartikels etc.*).

this [ðɪs] *pl.* **these** [ðiːz] **I** *pron.* **1.** a) dieser, diese, dieses, b) dies, das: ***all ~*** dies alles, all das; ***for all ~*** deswegen, darum; ***like ~*** so; ***~ is what I expected*** (genau) das habe ich erwartet; ***~ is what happened*** Folgendes geschah; **2.** dieses, dieser Zeitpunkt, dieses Ereignis: ***after ~*** danach; ***before ~*** zuvor; ***by ~*** bis dahin, mittlerweile; **II** *adj.* **3.** dieser, diese, dieses, ✝ *a.* laufend (*Monat, Jahr*): ***~ day week*** heute in e-r Woche; ***in ~ country*** hierzulande; ***~ morning*** heute morgen; ***~ time*** diesmal; ***these 3 weeks*** die letzten 3 Wochen, seit 3 Wochen; **III** *adv.* **4.** so: ***~ much*** so viel.

this·tle [ˈθɪsl] *s.* ⚘ Distel *f*; ˈ**~·down** *s.* ⚘ Distelwolle *f*.

this·tly [ˈθɪslɪ] *adj.* **1.** distelig; **2.** distelähnlich, stach(e)lig.

thith·er [ˈðɪðə] *obs. od. poet.* **I** *adv.* dort-, dahin; **II** *adj.* jenseitig.

ˈ**thole(-pin)** [θəʊl] *s.* ⚓ Dolle *f*.

thong [θɒŋ] **I** *s.* **1.** (Leder)Riemen *m* (*Halfter, Zügel, Peitschenschnur etc.*); **II** *v/t.* **2.** mit Riemen versehen *od.* befestigen; **3.** (mit e-m Riemen) peitschen.

tho·rac·ic [θɔːˈræsɪk] *adj. anat.* Brust...; **tho·rax** [ˈθɔːræks] *pl.* **-rax·es** [-ræksɪz] *s.* **1.** *anat.* Brust(korb *m*, -kasten *m*) *f*, Thorax *m*; **2.** *zo.* Mittelleib *m bei Gliederfüßlern.*

thorn [θɔːn] *s.* **1.** Dorn *m*: ***a ~ in the flesh*** (*od.* ***side***) *fig.* ein Pfahl im Fleische, ein Dorn im Auge; ***be*** (*od.* ***sit***) ***on ~s*** *fig.* (wie) auf glühenden Kohlen sitzen; **2.** *ling.* Dorn *m* (*altenglischer Buchstabe*); **~ ap·ple** *s.* ⚘ Stechapfel *m*.

thorn·y [ˈθɔːnɪ] *adj.* **1.** dornig, stach(e)lig; **2.** *fig.* dornenvoll, mühselig; **3.** *fig.* heikel: ***a ~ subject***.

thor·ough [ˈθʌrə] *adj.* □ → ***thoroughly***; **1.** gründlich: a) sorgfältig (*Person u. Sache*), b) genau, eingehend: ***a ~ inquiry***; ***a ~ knowledge***, c) ˈdurchgreifend: ***a ~ reform***; **2.** vollˈendet: a) vollˈkommen, meisterhaft, b) völlig, echt, durch u. durch: ***a ~ politician***, c) *contp.* ausgemacht: ***a ~ rascal***; ˌ**~-ˈbass** [-ˈbeɪs] *s.* ♪ Geneˈralbaß *m*; ˈ**~·bred I** *adj.* **1.** reinrassig, Vollblut...; **2.** *fig.* a) rassig, b) eleˈgant, c) kultiviert, d) schnittig (*Auto*); **II** *s.* **3.** Vollblut(pferd) *n*; **4.** rassiger *od.* kultivierter Mensch; **5.** *mot.* rassiger *od.* schnittiger Wagen; ˈ**~·fare** *s.* **1.** Hauptverkehrs-, ˈDurchgangsstraße *f*; **2.** ˈDurchfahrt *f*: ***no ~!***; **3.** Wasserstraße *f*; ˈ**~ˌgo·ing** *adj.* **1.** → ***thorough*** 1; **2.** exˈtrem, komproˈmißlos, durch u. durch.

thor·ough·ly [ˈθʌrəlɪ] *adv.* **1.** gründlich *etc.*; **2.** völlig, gänzlich, absoˈlut; ˈ**thor·ough·ness** [-ənɪs] *s.* **1.** Gründlichkeit *f*; **2.** Vollˈendung *f*, Vollˈkommenheit *f*.

ˈ**thor·ough·paced** *adj.* **1.** in allen Gangarten geübt (*Pferd*); **2.** *fig.* → ***thorough*** 2 b.

those [ðəʊz] *pron. pl. von* ***that***[1].

thou [ðaʊ] **I** *pron. poet. od. dial. od. bibl.* du; **II** *v/t.* mit ‚thou' anreden.

though [ðəʊ] **I** *cj.* **1.** obˈwohl, obˈgleich, obˈschon; **2.** *a.* ***even ~*** wenn auch, wennˈgleich, selbst wenn, zwar: ***important ~ it is*** so wichtig es auch ist; ***what ~ the way is long*** was macht es schon aus, wenn der Weg (auch) lang ist; **3.** jeˈdoch, doch; **4.** ***as ~*** als ob, wie wenn; **II** *adv.* **5.** F (*am Satzende*) aber, allerˈdings, dennoch, immerˈhin: ***I wish you had told me, ~.***

thought [θɔːt] **I** *pret. u. p.p. von* ***think***; **II** *s.* **1.** a) Gedanke *m*, Einfall *m*: ***a happy ~***, b) Gedankengang *m*, c) Gedanken *pl.*, Denken *n*: ***lost in ~*** in Gedanken (verloren); ***his one ~ was how to*** er dachte nur daran, wie er *es tun könnte*; ***it never entered my ~s*** es kam mir nie in den Sinn; **2.** *nur sg.* Denken *n*, Denkvermögen *n*; **3.** Überˈlegung *f*: ***give ~ to*** sich Gedanken machen über (*acc.*); ***take ~ how*** sich überlegen, wie *man es tun könnte*; ***after serious ~*** nach ernsthafter Erwägung; ***on second ~s*** a) nach reiflicher Überlegung, b) wenn ich es mir recht überlege; ***have second ~s about it*** (so seine) Zweifel darüber haben; ***without ~*** ohne zu überlegen; **4.** Absicht *f*: ***he had no ~ of coming***; ***we had*** (***some***) ***~s of going*** wir trugen uns mit dem Gedanken zu gehen; **5.** *mst pl.* Gedanke *m*, Meinung *f*, Ansicht *f*; **6.** (Für)Sorge *f*, Rücksicht *f*: ***give*** (*od.* ***have***) ***some ~ to*** Rücksicht nehmen auf (*acc.*); ***take ~ for*** Sorge tragen für *od.* um (*acc.*); ***take no ~ to*** nicht achten auf (*acc.*); **7.** *nur sg.* Denken *n*: a) Denkweise *f*: ***scientific ~***, b) Gedankenwelt *f*: ***Greek ~***; **8.** *fig.* Spur *f*: ***a ~ smaller*** e-e ‚Idee' kleiner; ***a ~ hesitant*** etwas zögernd; ˈ**thought·ful** [-fʊl] *adj.* □ **1.** gedankenvoll, nachdenklich, besinnlich (*a. Buch etc.*); **2.** achtsam (***of*** auf *acc.*); **3.** rücksichtsvoll, aufmerksam, zuˈvorkommend; ˈ**thought·ful·ness** [-fʊlnɪs] *s.* **1.** Nachdenklichkeit *f*, Besinnlichkeit *f*; **2.** Achtsamkeit *f*; **3.** Rücksichtnahme *f*, Aufmerksamkeit *f*; ˈ**thought·less** [-lɪs] *adj.* □ **1.** gedankenlos, unbesonnen, unbekümmert; **2.** rücksichtslos, unaufmerksam; ˈ**thought·less·ness** [-lɪsnɪs] *s.* **1.** Gedankenlosigkeit *f*, Unbekümmertheit *f*; **2.** Rücksichtslosigkeit *f*, Unaufmerksamkeit *f*.

ˌ**thought|-ˈout** *adj.* (***well ~*** wohl)durchdacht; **~ read·er** *s.* Gedankenleser (-in); **~ read·ing** *s.* Gedankenlesen *n*; **~ trans·fer·ence** *s.* Geˈdankenüberˌtragung *f*.

thou·sand [ˈθaʊznd] **I** *adj.* **1.** tausend (*a. fig. unzählige*): ***~ and one*** *fig.* zahllos, unzählig; ***The 𝔗 and One Nights*** Tausendundeine Nacht; ***a ~ times*** tausendmal; ***a ~ thanks*** tausend Dank; **II** *s.* **2.** Tausend *n*, *pl.* Tausende *pl.*: ***many ~s of times*** vieltausendmal; ***in their ~s, by the ~*** zu Tausenden; **3.** Tausend *f* (*Zahlzeichen*): ***one in a ~*** eine(r, s) unter tausend, ˈeine Ausnahme; ˈ**thou·sand·fold** [-ndf-] **I** *adj.* tausendfach, -fältig; **II** *adv. mst* ***a ~*** tausendfach, -mal; ˈ**thou·sandth** [-ntθ] **I** *s.* **1.** *der* (*die, das*) Tausendste; **2.** Tausendstel *n*; **II** *adj.* **3.** tausendst.

thral·dom [ˈθrɔːldəm] *s.* **1.** Leibeigenschaft *f*; **2.** *fig.* Knechtschaft *f*, Sklaveˈrei *f*; **thrall** [θrɔːl] *s.* **1.** *hist.* Leibeigene(r *m*) *f*, Hörige(r *m*) *f*; **2.** *fig.* Sklave *m*, Knecht *m*; **3.** → ***thraldom***; **thralldom** *Am.* → ***thraldom***.

thrash [θræʃ] **I** *v/t.* **1.** → ***thresh***; **2.** verdreschen, -prügeln; *fig.* (vernichtend) schlagen, ‚vermöbeln'; **II** *v/i.* **3.** *a.* ***~ about*** a) sich *im Bett etc.* ˈhin- u. ˈherwerfen, b) um sich schlagen, c) zappeln; **4.** ⚓ sich vorwärtsarbeiten; ˈ**thrash·er** [-ʃə] → ***thresher***; ˈ**thrash·ing** [-ʃɪŋ] *s.* Dresche *f*, Prügel *pl.*: ***give s.o. a ~*** → ***thrash*** 2.

thread [θred] **I** *s.* **1.** Faden *m*: a) Zwirn *m*, Garn *n*: ***hang by a ~*** *fig.* an e-m Faden hängen, b) *weitS.* Faser *f*, Fiber *f*, c) *fig.* (dünner) Strahl, Strich *m*, d) *fig.* Zs.-hang *m*: ***lose the ~*** (***of one's story***) den Faden verlieren; ***resume*** (*od.* ***take up***) ***the ~*** den Faden wieder aufnehmen; **2.** ⚙ Gewinde(gang *m*) *n*; **II** *v/t.* **3.** *Nadel* einfädeln; **4.** *Perlen etc.* aufreihen; **5.** mit Fäden durchˈziehen; **6.** *fig.* durchˈziehen, -ˈdringen; **7.** sich winden durch: ***~ one's way*** (***through***) sich (hindurch)schlängeln (durch); **8.** ⚙ Gewinde schneiden in (*acc.*): ***~ on*** anschrauben; ˈ**~·bare** *adj.* **1.** fadenscheinig, abgetragen; **2.** schäbig (gekleidet); **3.** *fig.* abgedroschen.

thread·ed [ˈθredɪd] *adj.* ⚙ Gewinde...: ***~ flange***; ˈ**thread·er** [-də] *s.* **1.** ˈEinfädelmaˌschine *f*; **2.** ⚙ Gewindeschneider *m*.

thread·ing lathe [ˈθredɪŋ] *s.* ⚙ Gewindeschneidbank *f*.

thread·y [ˈθredɪ] *adj.* **1.** fadenartig, faserig; **2.** Fäden ziehend; **3.** *fig.* schwach, dünn.

threat [θret] *s.* **1.** Drohung *f* (***of*** mit, ***to*** gegen); **2.** (***to***) Bedrohung *f* (*gen.*), Gefahr *f* (für): ***a ~ to peace***; ***there was a ~ of rain*** es drohte zu regnen; ˈ**threat·en** [-tn] **I** *v/t.* **1.** (***with***) *j-m* drohen (mit), *j-m* androhen (*acc.*), *j-n* bedrohen (mit); **2.** drohend ankündigen: ***the sky ~s a storm***; **3.** (damit) drohen (***to do*** zu tun); **4.** bedrohen, gefährden; **II** *v/i.* **5.** drohen; **6.** *fig.* drohen: a) drohend bevorstehen, b) Gefahr laufen (***to do*** zu tun); ˈ**threat·en·ing** [-tnɪŋ] *adj.* □ **1.** drohend, Droh...: ***~ letter*** Drohbrief *m*; **2.** *fig.* bedrohlich.

three [θriː] **I** *adj.* drei; **II** *s.* Drei *f* (*Zahl, Spielkarte etc.*); ˌ**~-ˈcol·o(u)r** *adj.* dreifarbig, Dreifarben...: ***~ process*** Dreifarbendruck(verfahren *n*) *m*; ˌ**~-ˈcor·nered** *adj.* **1.** dreieckig: ***~ hat*** Dreispitz *m*; **2.** zu dreien, Dreier...: ***a ~ discussion***; ˌ**~-ˈD** *adj.* ˈdreidimensioˌnal, 3-ˈD-...; ˈ**~-day e·vent** *s. Reitsport*: Military *f*; ˈ**~-day e·vent·er** *s.* Military-Reiter *m*; ˌ**~-ˈdeck·er** *s.* **1.** ⚓ *hist.* Dreidecker *m*; **2.** *et.* Dreiteiliges, *z.B.* F dreibändiger Roˈman; ˌ**~-di·ˈmen·sion·al** *adj.* ˈdreidimensioˌnal.

ˈ**three·fold I** *adj. u. adv.* dreifach; **II** *s. das* Dreifache.

ˈ**three|-lane** *adj.* dreispurig (*Autobahn etc.*); ˌ**~-ˈmast·er** *s.* ⚓ Dreimaster *m*;

ˈ**~-mile** *adj.* Dreimeilen...: **~ *zone*.**

three|·pence [ˈθrepəns] *s. Brit.* **1.** drei Pence *pl.*; **2.** *obs.* Dreiˈpencestück *n*; **~·pen·ny** [ˈθrepənɪ] *adj.* **1.** drei Pence wert, Dreipence...; **2.** *fig.* billig, wertlos.

ˈ**three|-phase** *adj.* ⚡ dreiphasig, Dreiphasen...: **~ *current*** Drehstrom *m*, Dreiphasenstrom *m*; ˈ**~-piece** *adj.* dreiteilig (*Anzug etc.*); ˈ**~-ply I** *adj.* **1.** dreifach (*Garn, Seil etc.*); **2.** dreischichtig (*Holz etc.*); **II** *s.* **3.** dreischichtiges Sperrholz; ˈ**~-point land·ing** *s.* ✈ Dreipunktlandung *f*; ˌ**~-ˈquar·ter I** *adj.* dreiviertel; **II** *s. a.* **~ *back*** *Rugby*: Dreiˈviertelspieler *m*; ˌ**~ˈscore** *adj. obs.* sechzig.

three·some [ˈθriːsəm] **I** *adj.* **1.** zu dreien, Dreier...; **II** *s.* **2.** Dreiergruppe *f*, ‚Trio' *n*; **3.** *Golf etc.*: Dreier(spiel *n*) *m*.

ˈ**three|-speed gear** *s.* ⚙ Dreiganggetriebe *n*; ˈ**~-stage** *adj.* ⚙ dreistufig (*Rakete, Verstärker etc.*); ˈ**~-way** *adj.* ⚙ Dreiwege...

thresh [θreʃ] *v/t. u. v/i.* dreschen: **~ (*over old*) *straw*** *fig.* leeres Stroh dreschen; **~ *out*** *fig. et.* gründlich erörtern, klären; ˈ**thresh·er** [-ʃə] *s.* **1.** Drescher *m*; **2.** ˈDreschmaˌschine *f*; ˈ**thresh·ing** [-ʃɪŋ] **I** *s.* Dreschen *n*; **II** *adj.* Dresch...: **~ *floor*** Dreschboden *m*, Tenne *f*.

thresh·old [ˈθreʃhəʊld] **I** *s.* **1.** (Tür-)Schwelle *f*; **2.** *fig.* Schwelle *f*, Beginn *m*; **3.** *psych.* (*Bewußtseins- etc.*)Schwelle *f*; **II** *adj.* **4.** *bsd.* ⚙ Schwellen...: **~ *frequency*; ~ *value*** Grenzwert *m*.

threw [θruː] *pret von* ***throw***.

thrice [θraɪs] *adv. obs.* **1.** dreimal; **2.** *fig.* sehr, ˈüberaus, höchst.

thrift [θrɪft] *s.* **1.** Sparsamkeit *f*: a) Sparsinn *m*, b) Wirtschaftlichkeit *f*; **2.** ♀ Grasnelke *f*; ˈ**thrift·i·ness** [-tɪnɪs] → ***thrift*** 1; ˈ**thrift·less** [-lɪs] *adj.* □ verschwenderisch; ˈ**thrift·less·ness** [-lɪsnɪs] *s.* Verschwendung *f*; ˈ**thrift·y** [-tɪ] *adj.* □ sparsam (***of, with*** mit): a) haushälterisch, b) wirtschaftlich (*a. Sachen*).

thrill [θrɪl] **I** *v/t.* **1.** erschauern lassen, erregen, packen, begeistern, elektrisieren, entzücken; **2.** *j-n* durchˈlaufen, -ˈschauern, überˈlaufen (*Gefühl*); **II** *v/i.* **3.** (er)beben, erschauern, zittern (***with*** vor *Freude etc.*); **4.** (***to***) sich begeistern (für), gepackt werden (von); **5.** durchˈlaufen, -ˈschauern, -ˈrieseln (***through*** *acc.*); **III** *s.* **6.** Zittern *n*, Erregung *f*, prickelndes Gefühl: ***a ~ of joy*** freudige Erregung; **7.** a) *das* Spannende *od.* Erregende, b) Nervenkitzel *m*, c) Sensatiˈon *f*; ˈ**thrill·er** [-lə] *s.* F ‚Reißer' *m*, ‚Krimi' *m*, Thriller *m* (*Kriminalroman, -film etc.*); ˈ**thrill·ing** [-lɪŋ] *adj.* □ **1.** erregend, packend, spannend, sensatioˈnell; **2.** hinreißend, begeisternd.

thrive [θraɪv] *v/i.* [*irr.*] **1.** gedeihen (*Pflanze, Tier etc.*); **2.** *fig.* gedeihen: a) blühen, Erfolg haben (*Geschäft etc.*), b) reich werden (*Person*), c) sich entwickeln (*Laster etc.*); **thriv·en** [ˈθrɪvn] *p.p. von* ***thrive***; ˈ**thriv·ing** [-vɪŋ] *adj.* □ *fig.* blühend.

thro' [θruː] *poet. für* ***through***.

throat [θrəʊt] *s.* **1.** *anat.* Kehle *f*, Gurgel *f*, Rachen *m*, Schlund *m*: ***sore ~*** Halsschmerzen *pl.*, rauher Hals; ***stick in one's ~*** j-m im Halse stecken bleiben (*Worte*); ***ram*** (*od.* ***thrust***) ***s.th. down s.o.'s ~*** j-m et. aufzwingen; **2.** Hals *m*, Kehle *f*: ***cut s.o.'s ~*** j-m den Hals abschneiden; ***cut one's own ~*** *fig.* sich selbst ruinieren; ***take s.o. by the ~*** j-n an der Gurgel packen; **3.** *fig.* ˈDurch-, Eingang *m*, verengte Öffnung, Schlund *m*, *z.B.* Hals *m e-r Vase*, Kehle *f e-s Kamins*, Gicht *f e-s Hochofens*; **4.** ∆ Hohlkehle *f*; ˈ**throat·y** [-tɪ] *adj.* □ **1.** kehlig, gutturˈral; **2.** rauh, heiser.

throb [θrɒb] **I** *v/i.* **1.** pochen, hämmern, klopfen (*Herz etc.*): **~*bing pains*** klopfende Schmerzen; **II** *s.* **2.** Pochen *n*, Klopfen *n*, Hämmern *n*, (Puls)Schlag *m*; **3.** *fig.* Erregung *f*, Erbeben *n*.

throe [θrəʊ] *s. mst pl.* heftiger Schmerz: a) *pl.* (Geburts)Wehen *pl.*, b) *pl.* Todeskampf *m*, Agoˈnie *f*: ***in the ~s of*** *fig.* mitten in *et. Unangenehmem*, im Kampfe mit.

throm·bo·sis [θrɒmˈbəʊsɪs] *s.* ⚕ Thromˈbose *f*; **thromˈbot·ic** [-ˈbɒtɪk] *adj.* ⚕ thromˈbotisch.

throne [θrəʊn] **I** *s.* **1.** Thron *m* (*König, Prinz*), Stuhl *m* (*Papst, Bischof*); **2.** *fig.* Thron *m*: a) Herrschaft *f*, b) Herrscher (-in); **II** *v/t.* **3.** auf den Thron setzen; **III** *v/i.* **4.** thronen.

throng [θrɒŋ] **I** *s.* **1.** (Menschen)Menge *f*; **2.** Gedränge *n*, Andrang *m*; **3.** Menge *f*, Masse *f* (*Sachen*); **II** *v/i.* **4.** sich drängen *od.* (zs.-)scharen, (herˈbei-, hinˈein- *etc.*)strömen; **III** *v/t.* **5.** sich drängen in (*dat.*): **~ *the streets***; **6.** bedrängen, umˈdrängen.

throt·tle [ˈθrɒtl] **I** *s.* **1.** F Kehle *f*; **2.** ⚙, *mot.* a) *a.* **~ *lever*** Gashebel *m*, b) *a.* **~ *valve*** Drosselklappe *f*: ***open*** (***close***) ***the ~*** Gas geben (wegnehmen); **II** *v/t.* **3.** erdrosseln; *fig.* ersticken, abwürgen, unterˈdrücken; **4.** *a.* **~ *down*** ⚙, *mot.* (ab)drosseln; **III** *v/i.* **5.** **~ *back*** (*od.* ***down***) *mot. etc.* drosseln, Gas wegnehmen.

through [θruː] **I** *prp.* **1.** *räumlich u. fig.* ˈdurch, durch ... hinˈdurch; **2.** durch, in (*überall umher in e-m Gebiet etc.*): **~ *all the country***; **3.** a) *e-n Zeitraum* hinˈdurch, während, b) *Am.* (von ...) bis; **4.** *bis zum Ende od. ganz* durch, fertig (mit): ***when will you get ~ your work?***; **5.** durch, mittels; **6.** aus, vor, durch, in-, zuˈfolge, wegen: **~ *fear*** aus *od.* vor Furcht; **~ *neglect*** infolge *od.* durch Nachlässigkeit; **II** *adv.* **7.** durch: **~ *and ~*** durch u. durch (*a. fig.*); ***push a needle ~*** e-e Nadel durchstechen; ***he would not let us ~*** er wollte uns nicht durchlassen; ***this train goes ~ to Boston*** dieser Zug fährt (durch) bis Boston; ***you are ~!*** *teleph.* Sie sind verbunden!; **8.** (ganz) durch (*von Anfang bis Ende*): ***read a letter ~*** e-n Brief ganz durchlesen; ***carry a matter ~*** e-e Sache durchführen; **9.** fertig (***with*** mit): ***I am ~ with him*** F er ist für mich erledigt; ***I'm ~ with it!*** ich habe es satt!; **III** *adj.* **10.** ˈdurchgehend, Durchgangs...: ***a ~ train*; ~ *carriage*** (*od.* ***coach***) Kurswagen *m*; **~ *dialing*** *teleph. Am.* ˈDurchwahl *f*; **~ *flight*** ✈ Direktflug *m*; **~ *traffic*** Durchgangsverkehr *m*; **~*way*** *Am.* Durchgangs- *od.* Schnellstraße *f*; **through·out** [θruːˈaʊt] **I** *prp.* **1.** überˈall in: **~ *the country*** im ganzen Land; **2.** während (*gen.*): **~ *the year*** das ganze Jahr hindurch; **II** *adv.* **3.** durch u. durch, ganz u. gar, ˈdurchweg; **4.** überall; **5.** die ganze Zeit; ˈ**through-put** *s. econ., a. Computer*: ˈDurchsatz *m*.

throve [θrəʊv] *pret. von* ***thrive***.

throw [θrəʊ] **I** *s.* **1.** Werfen *n*, (*Speer- etc.*)Wurf *m*; **2.** Wurf *m* (*a. Ringkampf, Würfelspiel*), *fig. a.* Coup *m*; **3.** ⚙ (Kolben)Hub *m*; **4.** ⚙ (Regler- *etc.*)Ausschlag *m*; **5.** ⚙ Kröpfung *f* (*Kurbelwelle*); **II** *v/t.* [*irr.*] **6.** werfen, schleudern; (*a. fig. Blick, Kußhand etc.*) zuwerfen (***s.o. s.th., s.th. to s.o.*** j-m et.); mit *Steinen etc.* werfen; *Wasser* schütten *od.* gießen: **~ *at*** werfen nach; **~ *o.s. at s.o.*** *fig.* sich j-m an den Hals werfen; **~ *a shawl over one's shoulders*** sich e-n Schal um die Schultern werfen; **~ *together*** zs.-werfen; ***be thrown*** (***together***) ***with*** *fig.* (*zufällig*) zs.-geraten mit; **7.** *Angel, Netz etc.* auswerfen; **8.** a) *Würfel* werfen, b) *Zahl* würfeln, c) *Karten* ausspielen *od.* ablegen; **9.** *Reiter* abwerfen; **10.** *Ringkampf*: *Gegner* werfen; **11.** *zo. Junge* werfen; **12.** *Brücke* schlagen (***over, across*** über *acc.*); **13.** *zo. Haut* abwerfen; **14.** ⚙ *Hebel* ˈumlegen, *Kupplung od. Schalter* ein-, ausrükken, ein-, ausschalten; **15.** *Töpferei*: formen, drehen; **16.** ⚙ *Seide* zwirnen, mulinieren; **17.** *fig.* in *Entzückung, Verwirrung etc.* versetzen; **18.** F *j-n* ‚ˈumwerfen' *od.* aus der Fassung bringen; **19.** F *e-e Gesellschaft* geben, *e-e Party* ‚schmeißen'; **20.** *Am.* F *Wettkampf* absichtlich verlieren; **21.** *sl. Wutanfall etc.* bekommen: **~ *a fit***; **III** *v/i.* [*irr.*] **22.** werfen; **23.** würfeln;

Zssgn mit prp.:

throw| in·to *v/t.* (hinˈein)werfen in (*acc.*): **~ *prison*** *j-n* ins Gefängnis werfen; **~ *the bargain*** (beim Kauf) dreingeben; ***throw o.s. into*** *fig.* sich in *die Arbeit, den Kampf etc.* stürzen; **~ (*up*·)*on*** *v/t.* **1.** werfen auf (*acc.*): ***be thrown upon o.s.*** (*od.* ***upon one's own resources***) auf sich selbst angewiesen sein; **2.** ***throw o.s.*** (***up***)***on*** a) sich auf *die Knie etc.* werfen, b) sich anvertrauen (*dat.*);

Zssgn mit adv.:

throw| a·way *v/t.* **1.** wegwerfen; **2.** *Geld etc.* verschwenden, -geuden ([***up***]***on*** an *acc.*); **3.** *Gelegenheit* verpassen, -schenken; **4.** *et.* verwerfen; **~ back I** *v/t.* **1.** zuˈrückwerfen (*a. fig. hemmen*): ***be thrown back upon*** angewiesen sein auf (*acc.*); **II** *v/i.* **2.** (***to***) zuˈrückkehren (zu), zuˈrückfallen (auf *acc.*, in *acc.*); **3.** nachgeraten (***to*** *dat.*); *biol.* rückarten; **~ down** *v/t.* **1.** (***o.s.*** sich) niederwerfen; **2.** ˈumstürzen, vernichten; **~ in** *v/t.* **1.** (hin)ˈeinwerfen; **2.** *Bemerkung etc.* einwerfen, -schalten; **3.** *et.* mit in den Kauf geben, dreingeben; **4.** ⚙ *Gang etc.* einrücken; **~ off I** *v/t.* **1.** *Kleider, Maske etc., a. fig. Schamgefühl etc.* abwerfen, ablegen; **2.** *Joch etc.* abwerfen, abschütteln, sich freimachen von; **3.** *Bekannte, Krankheit etc.* loswerden; **4.** *Verfolger, a. Hund* von der Fährte abbringen, abschütteln; **5.** *Gedicht etc.* hinwerfen, aus dem Ärmel schütteln; **6.** ⚙ a) kippen, ˈumlegen, b) auskuppeln, -rücken; **7.** *typ.* abziehen; **8.** *j-n* aus dem Konˈzept *od.* aus der

Fassung bringen; **II** *v/i.* **9.** (*hunt.* die Jagd) beginnen; **~ on** *v/t. Kleider* 'überwerfen, sich *et.* 'umwerfen; **~ o·pen** *v/t.* **1.** *Tür etc.* aufreißen, -stoßen; **2.** öffentlich zugänglich machen (***to*** *dat.* für); **~ out** *v/t.* **1.** (*a. j-n* hin)'auswerfen; **2.** *bsd. parl.* verwerfen; **3.** ⚠ vorbauen; anbauen (***to*** an *acc.*); **4.** *Bemerkung* fallenlassen, *Vorschlag etc.* äußern; *e-n Wink* geben; **5.** a) *et.* über den Haufen werfen, b) *j-n* aus dem Kon'zept bringen; **6.** ⚙ auskuppeln, -rücken; **7.** *Fühler etc.* ausstrecken: ***~ a chest*** F sich in die Brust werfen; **~ o·ver** *v/t.* **1.** über den Haufen werfen; **2.** *fig. Plan etc.* über Bord werfen, aufgeben; **3.** *Freund etc.* im Stich lassen, fallenlassen; **~ up I** *v/t.* **1.** in die Höhe werfen, hochwerfen; **2.** *et.* hastig errichten, *Schanze etc.* aufwerfen; **3.** *Karten, a. Amt etc.* hinwerfen, -schmeißen; **4.** erbrechen; **II** *v/i.* **5.** (sich er)brechen, sich über'geben.

'**throw|·a·way I** *s.* et. zum Wegwerfen, *z.B.* Re'klamezettel *m*; **II** *adj.* Wegwerf…: ***~ package***; ***~ bottle*** Einwegflasche *f*; ***~ prices*** † Schleuderpreise; '**~·back** *s.* **1.** *bsd. biol.* Ata'vismus *m*, *a. fig.* Rückkehr *f* (***to*** zu); **2.** *Film*: Rückblende *f*.

throw·er ['θrəʊə] *s.* **1.** Werfer(in); **2.** *Töpferei*: Dreher(in), Former(in); **3.** → ***throwster***.

'**throw-in** *s. sport* Einwurf *m*.

throw·ing ['θrəʊɪŋ] **I** *s.* Werfen *n*, (*Speer- etc.*)Wurf *m*: ***~ the javelin***; **II** *adj.* Wurf…: ***~ knife***.

thrown [θrəʊn] **I** *p.p. von **throw***; **II** *adj.* gezwirnt: ***~ silk*** Seidengarn *n*.

'**throw|·off** *s.* **1.** Aufbruch *m* (zur Jagd); **2.** *fig.* Beginn *m*; '**~-out** *s.* ⚙ **1.** Auswerfer *m*; **2.** Ausschalter *m*; **3.** *mot.* Ausrückvorrichtung *f*: ***~ lever*** (Kupplungs)Ausrückhebel *m*.

throw·ster ['θrəʊstə] *s.* Seidenzwirner(in).

thru [θruː] *Am.* F *für **through***.

thrum[1] [θrʌm] **I** *v/i.* **1.** ♪ klimpern (***on*** auf *dat.*); **2.** (mit den Fingern) trommeln; **II** *v/t.* **3.** ♪ klimpern auf (*dat.*); **4.** (mit den Fingern) trommeln auf (*dat.*).

thrum[2] [θrʌm] **I** *s.* **1.** *Weberei*: a) Trumm *n*, *m* (*am Ende der Kette*), b) *pl.* (Reihe *f* von) Fransen *pl.*, Saum *m*; **2.** Franse *f*; **3.** loser Faden; **4.** *oft pl.* Garnabfall *m*, Fussel *f*; **II** *v/t.* **5.** befransen.

thrush[1] [θrʌʃ] *s. orn.* Drossel *f*.

thrush[2] [θrʌʃ] *s.* **1.** ⚕ Soor *m*; **2.** *vet.* Strahlfäule *f*.

thrust [θrʌst] **I** *v/t.* [*irr.*] **1.** *Waffe etc.* stoßen; **2.** *allg.* stecken, schieben: ***~ o.s.*** (*od.* ***one's nose***) ***in*** *fig.* s-e Nase stecken *od.* sich einmischen in (*acc.*); ***~ one's hand into one's pocket*** die Hand in die Tasche stecken; ***~ on*** *et.* hastig anziehen, (sich) *et.* hastig überwerfen; **3.** stoßen, drängen, treiben, (*a. ins Gefängnis*) werfen: ***~ aside*** zur Seite stoßen; ***~ o.s. into*** sich werfen *od.* drängen in (*acc.*); ***~ out*** a) (her-, hin-) ausstoßen, b) *Zunge* herausstrecken, c) *Hand* ausstrecken; ***~ s.th. upon s.o.*** j-m et. aufdrängen; **4. *~ through*** *j-n* durch'bohren; **5. *~ in*** *Wort* einwerfen; **II** *v/i.* [*irr.*] **6.** stoßen (***at*** nach); **7.** sich *wohin* drängen *od.* schieben: ***~ into*** ⚔ hineinstoßen in *e-e Stellung etc.*; ***a ~ing politician*** ein ehrgeiziger *od.* aufstrebender Politiker; **III** *s.* **8.** Stoß *m*; **9.** Hieb *m* (*a. fig.*); **10.** *allg. u.* ⚙ Druck *m*; **11.** ✈, *phys.* Schub(kraft *f*) *m*; **12.** ⚙, ⚠ (Seiten)Schub *m*; **13.** *geol.* Schub *m*; **14.** ⚔ *u. fig.* a) Vorstoß *m*, b) Stoßrichtung *f*; **~ bear·ing** *s.* ⚙, ✈ Drucklager *n*; **~ per·form·ance** *s.* ⚙, ✈ Schubleistung *f*; **~ weap·on** *s.* ⚔ Stich-, Stoßwaffe *f*.

thud [θʌd] **I** *s.* dumpfer (Auf)Schlag, Bums *m*; **II** *v/i.* dumpf (auf)schlagen, bumsen.

thug [θʌg] *s.* **1.** (Gewalt)Verbrecher *m*, Raubmörder *m*; **2.** Rowdy *m*, ‚Schläger' *m*; **3.** *fig.* Gangster *m*, Halsabschneider *m*.

thumb [θʌm] **I** *s.* **1.** Daumen *m*: ***his fingers are all ~s, he is all ~s*** er hat zwei linke Hände; ***turn ~s down on*** *fig. et.* ablehnen, verwerfen; ***under s.o.'s ~*** unter j-s Fuchtel; ***that sticks out like a sore ~*** F a) das sieht ja ein Blinder, b) das fällt entsetzlich auf; ***it's ~s down on your offer!*** Ihr Angebot ist abgelehnt!; → ***rule*** 2; **II** *v/t.* **2.** *Buchseiten* 'durchblättern; **3.** *Buch* abgreifen, beschmutzen: (***well-***)***~ed*** abgegriffen; **4. *~ a lift*** (*od.* ***ride***) F per Anhalter fahren, trampen; ***~ a car*** e-n Wagen anhalten, sich mitnehmen lassen; **5. *~ one's nose at*** *j-m* e-e lange Nase machen; **~ in·dex** *s. typ.* Daumenindex *m*; '**~·mark** *s.* Daumenabdruck *m*; '**~·nail I** *s.* Daumennagel *m*; **II** *adj.*: ***~ sketch*** kleine (*fig.* kurze) Skizze; **~ nut** *s.* ⚙ Flügelmutter *f*; '**~·print** *s.* Daumenabdruck *m*; '**~·screw** *s.* **1.** *hist.* Daumenschraube *f*; **2.** ⚙ Flügelschraube *f*; '**~·stall** *s.* Däumling *m* (*Schutzkappe*); '**~·tack** *s. Am.* Reißnagel *m*.

thump [θʌmp] **I** *s.* **1.** dumpfer Schlag, Bums *m*; **2.** (Faust)Schlag *m*, Puff *m*; **II** *v/t.* **3.** schlagen auf (*acc.*), hämmern *od.* pochen gegen *od.* auf (*acc.*); *Kissen* aufschütteln; **4.** plumpsen gegen *od.* auf (*acc.*); **III** *v/i.* **5.** (auf)schlagen, (-) bumsen (***on*** auf *acc.*, ***at*** gegen); **6.** (laut) pochen (*Herz*); '**thump·er** [-pə] *s.* **1.** *sl.* Mordsding *n*, *e-e* ‚Wucht'; **2.** *sl.* faustdicke Lüge; '**thump·ing** [-pɪŋ] F **I** *adj.* kolos'sal, Mords…; **II** *adv.* mordsmäßig.

thun·der ['θʌndə] **I** *s.* **1.** Donner *m* (*a. fig. Getöse*): ***steal s.o.'s ~*** *fig.* j-m den Wind aus den Segeln nehmen; ***~s of applause*** donnernder Beifall; **II** *v/i.* **2.** donnern (*a. fig. Kanone, Zug etc.*); **3.** *fig.* wettern; **III** *v/t.* **4.** *et.* donnern; '**~·bolt** *s.* **1.** Blitz *m* (u. Donnerschlag *m*), Blitzstrahl *m* (*a. fig.*); **2.** *myth. u. geol.* Donnerkeil *m*; '**~·clap** *s.* Donnerschlag *m* (*a. fig.*); '**~·cloud** *s.* Gewitterwolke *f*.

thun·der·ing ['θʌndərɪŋ] **I** *adj.* □ **1.** donnernd (*a. fig.*); **2.** F kolos'sal, gewaltig: ***a ~ lie*** e-e faustdicke Lüge; **II** *adv.* **3.** F riesig, mächtig: ***~ glad***; '**thun·der·ous** [-rəs] *adj.* □ **1.** gewitterschwül; **2.** *fig.* donnernd; **3.** *fig.* gewaltig.

'**thun·der|,show·er** *s.* Gewitterschauer *m*; '**~·storm** *s.* Gewitter *n*, Unwetter *n*; '**~·struck** *adj.* (*fig.* wie) vom Blitz getroffen.

thun·der·y ['θʌndərɪ] *adj.* gewitterschwül: ***~ showers*** gewittrige Schauer.

Thu·rin·gi·an [θjʊə'rɪndʒɪən] **I** *adj.* Thüringer(…); **II** *s.* Thüringer(in).

Thurs·day ['θɜːzdɪ] *s.* Donnerstag *m*: ***on ~*** am Donnerstag; ***on ~s*** donnerstags.

thus [ðʌs] *adv.* **1.** so, folgendermaßen; **2.** so'mit, also, folglich, demgemäß; **3.** so, in diesem Maße: ***~ far*** soweit, bis jetzt; ***~ much*** so viel.

thwack [θwæk] **I** *v/t.* verprügeln, schlagen; **II** *s.* derber Schlag.

thwart [θwɔːt] **I** *v/t.* **1.** *Pläne etc.* durch'kreuzen, vereiteln, hinter'treiben; **2.** *j-m* entgegenarbeiten, *j-m* e-n Strich durch die Rechnung machen; **II** *s.* **3.** ⚓ Ruderbank *f*.

thy [ðaɪ] *adj. bibl., rhet., poet.* dein.

thyme [taɪm] *s.* ⚘ Thymian *m*.

thy·mus ['θaɪməs], *a.* **~ gland** *s. anat.* Thymus(drüse *f*) *m*.

thy·roid ['θaɪrɔɪd] ⚕ **I** *adj.* **1.** Schilddrüsen…; **2.** Schildknorpel…: ***~ cartilage*** → 4; **II** *s.* **3.** *a.* ***~ gland*** Schilddrüse *f*; **4.** Schildknorpel *m*.

thyr·sus ['θɜːsəs] *pl.* **-si** [-saɪ] *s. antiq. u.* ⚘ Thyrsus *m*.

thy·self [ðaɪ'self] *pron. bibl., rhet., poet.* **1.** du (selbst); **2.** *dat.* dir (selbst); **3.** *acc.* dich (selbst).

ti·ar·a [tɪ'ɑːrə] *s.* **1.** Ti'ara *f* (*Papstkrone u. fig. -würde*); **2.** Dia'dem *n*, Stirnreif *m* (*für Damen*).

tib·i·a ['tɪbɪə] *pl.* **-ae** [-iː] *s. anat.* Schienbein *n*, Tibia *f*; '**tib·i·al** [-əl] *adj. anat.* Schienbein…, Unterschenkel…

tic [tɪk] *s.* ⚕ Tic(k) *m*, (ner'vöses) Muskel- *od.* Gesichtszucken.

tick[1] [tɪk] **I** *s.* **1.** Ticken *n*: ***to*** (*od.* ***on***) ***the ~*** (auf die Sekunde) pünktlich; **2.** F Augenblick *m*; **3.** Häkchen *n*, Vermerkzeichen *n*; **II** *v/i.* **4.** ticken: ***~ over*** a) *mot.* im Leerlauf sein, b) *fig.* normal *od.* ganz gut laufen; ***what makes him ~?*** a) was hält ihn (so) in Schwung?, b) wie ‚funktioniert' er?; **III** *v/t.* **5.** *in e-r Liste* anhaken: ***to ~ off*** a) abhaken, b) F *j-n* ‚zs.-stauchen'.

tick[2] [tɪk] *s. zo.* Zecke *f*.

tick[3] [tɪk] *s.* **1.** (Kissen- *etc.*)Bezug *m*; **2.** Inlett *n*, Ma'tratzenbezug *m*; **3.** F Drillich *m*, Drell *m*.

tick[4] [tɪk] *s.* F Kre'dit *m*, Pump *m*: ***buy on ~*** auf Pump *od.* Borg kaufen.

tick·er ['tɪkə] *s.* **1.** *Börse*: Fernschreiber *m*; **2.** *sl.* a) ‚Wecker' *m* (*Uhr*), b) ‚Pumpe' *f* (*Herz*); **~ tape** *s. Am.* Lochstreifen *m*: ***~ parade*** Konfettiparade *f*.

tick·et ['tɪkɪt] **I** *s.* **1.** (Ausweis-, Eintritts-, Lebensmittel-, Mitglieds- *etc.*) Karte *f*; 🚂 *etc.* Fahrkarte *f*, -schein *m*; ✈ Flugschein *m*, Ticket *n*: ***take a ~*** e-e Karte lösen; **2.** (*bsd.* Gepäck-, Pfand-) Schein *m*; **3.** Lotte'rielos *n*; **4.** Eti'kett *n*, (*Preis- etc.*)Zettel *m*; **5.** *mot.* a) Strafzettel *m*, b) gebührenpflichtige Verwarnung; **6.** ⚓, ✈ Li'zenz *f*; **7.** *pol. bsd. Am.* a) (Wahl-, Kandi'daten)Liste *f*, b) ('Wahl-, Par'tei)Pro‚gramm *n*: ***split the ~*** panaschieren; ***vote a straight ~*** die Liste e-r Partei unverändert wählen; ***write one's own ~*** F (ganz) s-e eigenen Bedingungen stellen; **8. *~ of leave*** ⚖ *Brit.* (Schein *m* über) bedingte Freilassung: ***be on ~ of leave*** bedingt freigelassen sein; **9.** F *das* Richtige: ***that's the ~!***; **II** *v/t.* **10.** etikettieren, kennzeichnen, *Waren* auszeichnen; **~ a·gen·cy** *s. thea. etc.* Vorverkaufsstelle *f*; **~ col·lec·tor** *s.* 🚂 Bahnsteigschaffner *m*; **~ day** *s. Börse*: Tag *m* vor dem Abrechnungstag; **~ in·spec·tor** *s.* 'Fahrkartenkontrol,leur *m*; **~ of·fice** *s.* **1.** Fahrkartenschalter *m*; **2.** (The'ater)Kasse *f*; **~ punch** *s.* Lochzange *f*; **~ tout** *s.* Kartenschwarzhändler *m.*

tick·ing ['tɪkɪŋ] *s.* Drell *m*, Drillich *m*; **,~-'off** *s.* F ‚Anpfiff' *m.*

tick·le ['tɪkl] **I** *v/t.* **1.** kitzeln (*a. fig.*); **2.** *fig. j-s Eitelkeit etc.* schmeicheln; **3.** *fig.* amüsieren: ***~d pink*** F ‚ganz weg' (vor Freude); ***I'm ~d to death*** ich könnte mich totlachen (*a. iro.*); **4.** ***~ up*** (an-) reizen; **II** *v/i.* **5.** kitzeln; **6.** jucken; **III** *s.* **7.** Kitzel *m* (*a. fig.*); **8.** Juckreiz *m*; **'tick·ler** [-lə] *s.* **1.** kitzlige Sache, (schwieriges) Pro'blem; **2.** *Am.* No'tizbuch *n*: ***~ file*** Wiedervorlagemappe *f*; **3.** *a.* ***~ coil*** ⚡ Rückkopplungsspule *f*; **'tick·lish** [-lɪʃ] *adj.* □ **1.** kitz(e)lig; **2.** *fig.* a) kitzlig, heikel, schwierig, b) empfindlich (*Person*).

tick·tack ['tɪktæk] *s.* **1.** Ticktack *n*; **2.** *sl. Rennsport*: Zeichensprache *f* der Buchmacher: ***~ man*** Buchmachergehilfe *m.*

tid·al ['taɪdl] *adj.* **1.** Gezeiten…, den Gezeiten unter'worfen: ***~ basin*** ⚓ Tidebecken *n*; ***~ inlet*** Priel *m*; ***~ power plant*** Gezeitenkraftwerk *n*; **2.** Flut…: ***~ wave*** Flutwelle *f*, *fig. a.* Woge *f.*

tid·bit ['tɪdbɪt] *Am.* → ***titbit.***

tid·dly ['tɪdlɪ] *adj. Brit.* F **1.** winzig; **2.** ‚angesäuselt', beschwipst.

tid·dly·winks ['tɪdlɪwɪŋks] *s. pl.* Flohhüpfen *n.*

tide [taɪd] **I** *s.* **1.** a) Gezeiten *pl.*, Ebbe *f* u. Flut, b) Flut *f*, Tide *f*: ***high ~*** Flut; ***low ~*** Ebbe; ***the ~ is coming in*** (***going out***) die Flut kommt (die Ebbe setzt ein); ***the ~ is out*** es ist Ebbe; ***turn of the ~*** a) Gezeitenwechsel *m*, b) *fig.* Umschwung *m*; ***the ~ turns*** *fig.* das Blatt wendet sich; **2.** *fig.* Strom *m*, Strömung *f*: ***~ of events*** *der* Gang der Ereignisse; ***swim against*** (***with***) ***the ~*** gegen (mit) dem Strom schwimmen; **3.** *fig. die* rechte Zeit, günstiger Augenblick; **4.** *in Zssgn* Zeit *f*: ***winter~***; **II** *v/i.* **5.** (mit dem Strom) treiben, ⚓ bei Flut ein- *od.* auslaufen; **6.** ***~ over*** *fig.* hin'wegkommen über (*acc.*); **III** *v/t.* **7.** ***~ over*** *fig. j-m* hin'weghelfen über (*acc.*): ***~ it over*** ‚sich über Wasser halten'; **~ gate** *s.* Flut(schleusen)tor *n*; **~ ga(u)ge** *s.* (Gezeiten)Pegel *m*; **'~·land** *s.* Watt *n*; **'~·mark** *s.* **1.** Gezeitenmarke *f*; **2.** Pegelstand *m*; **3.** *bsd. Brit.* F schwarzer Rand (*am Hals etc.*); **~ ta·ble** *s.* Gezeitentafel *f*; **'~,wait·er** *s. hist.* Hafenzollbeamte(r) *m*; **'~,wa·ter** *s.* Flut-, Gezeitenwasser *n*: ***~ district*** Wattengebiet *n*; **'~·way** *s.* Priel *m.*

ti·di·ness ['taɪdɪnɪs] *s.* **1.** Sauberkeit *f*, Ordnung *f*; **2.** Nettigkeit *f.*

ti·dings ['taɪdɪŋz] *s. pl. sg. od. pl. konstr.* Nachricht(en *pl.*) *f*, Neuigkeit (-en *pl.*) *f*, Kunde *f.*

ti·dy ['taɪdɪ] **I** *adj.* □ **1.** sauber, reinlich, ordentlich (*Zimmer, Person, Aussehen etc.*); **2.** nett, schmuck; **3.** *fig.* F ordentlich, beträchtlich: ***a ~ penny*** e-e Stange Geld; **II** *s.* **4.** (Sofa- *etc.*)Schoner *m*; **5.** (Arbeits-, Flick- *etc.*)Beutel *m*; Fächerkasten *m*; **6.** Abfallkorb *m*; **III** *v/t.* **7.** *a.* ***~ up*** in Ordnung bringen, aufräumen, säubern: ***~ out*** ‚ausmisten'; ***~ o.s. up*** sich zurechtmachen; **IV** *v/i.* **8.** ***~ up*** aufräumen, saubermachen.

tie [taɪ] **I** *s.* **1.** (Schnür)Band *n*; **2.** a) Kra'watte *f*, b) Halstuch *n*; **3.** Schleife *f*, Masche *f*; **4.** *fig.* a) Band *n*: ***the ~(s) of friendship***, b) *pol.*, *psych.* Bindung *f*: ***mother ~***; **5.** *fig.* (lästige) Fessel, Last *f*; **6.** △, ⚙ a) Verbindung(sstück *n*) *f*, b) Anker *m*, c) → ***tie beam***; **7.** 🚂 *Am.* Schwelle *f*; **8.** *parl. pol.* Stimmengleichheit *f*: ***end in a ~*** stimmengleich enden; **9.** *sport* a) Punktgleichheit *f*, Gleichstand *m*, b) Unentschieden *n*, c) Ausscheidungsspiel *n*, d) Wieder'holung(sspiel *n*) *f*; **10.** ♪ Bindebogen *m*, Liga'tur *f*; **II** *v/t.* **11.** an-, festbinden (***to*** an *acc.*); **12.** binden, schnüren; *fig.* fesseln: ***~ s.o.'s hands*** (***tongue***) j-m die Hände (Zunge) binden; **13.** *Schleife, Schuhe etc.* binden; **14.** △, ⚙ verankern, befestigen; **15.** ♪ *Noten* (anein'ander)binden; **16.** (***to***) *fig. j-n* binden (an *acc.*), verpflichten (zu); **17.** hindern, hemmen; **18.** *j-n* in Anspruch nehmen (*Pflichten etc.*); **III** *v/i.* **19.** *sport* a) gleichstehen, punktgleich sein, b) unentschieden spielen *od.* kämpfen (***with*** gegen); **20.** *parl.*, *pol.* gleiche Stimmenzahl haben;

Zssgn mit adv.:

tie| down *v/t.* **1.** festbinden; **2.** niederhalten, fesseln; **3.** (***to***) *fig. j-n* binden (an *Pflichten, Regeln etc.*), *j-n* festlegen (auf *acc.*): ***be tied down*** (***by***) angebunden sein (durch *e-e Familie etc.*); **~ in** **I** *v/i.* (***with***) über'einstimmen (mit), passen (zu); **II** *v/t.* (***with***) verbinden *od.* koppeln (mit), einbauen (in *acc.*); **~ up** *v/t.* **1.** (an-, ein-, ver-, zs.-, zu)binden; **2.** *fig.* a) hemmen, fesseln, b) festhalten, beschäftigen; **3.** *fig.* lahmlegen; *Industrie, Produktion* stillegen; *Vorräte etc.* blockieren; **4.** ⚚, ⚖ festlegen: a) *Geld* fest anlegen, b) *bsd. Erbgut* e-r Verfügungsbeschränkung unter'werfen; **5.** ***tie it up*** *Am.* F die Sache erledigen.

tie| bar *s.* **1.** 🚂 a) Verbindungsstange *f* (*Weiche*), b) Spurstange *f*; **2.** *typ.* Bogen *m über 2 Buchstaben*; **~ beam** *s.* △ Zugbalken *m*; **'~,break(·er)** *s. Tennis*: Tie-Break *m, n.*

tied [taɪd] *adj.* ⚚ zweckgebunden; **~ house** *s. Brit.* Braue'reigaststätte *f.*

'tie|-in *s.* **1.** ⚚ *Am.* a) Gemeinschaftswerbung *f*, b) *a.* ***~ sale*** Kopplungsgeschäft *n*, -verkauf *m*; **2.** Zs.-hang *m*, Verbindung *f*; **'~-on** *adj.* zum Anbinden, Anhänge…

tier [tɪə] *s.* **1.** Reihe *f*, Lage *f*: ***in ~s*** in Reihen übereinander, lagenweise; **2.** *thea.* a) (Sitz)Reihe *f*, b) Rang *m*; **3.** *fig.* Rang *m*, Stufe *f.*

tierce [tɪəs] *s.* **1.** [*Kartenspiel*: tɜːs] ♪, *fenc.*, *eccl.*, *Kartenspiel*: Terz *f*; **2.** Weinfaß *n* (*mit 42 Gallonen*).

tie rod *s.* ⚙ **1.** Zugstange *f*; **2.** Kuppelstange *f*; **3.** 🚂 Spurstange *f.*

'tie-up *s.* **1.** a) Verbindung *f*, Zs.-hang *m*, b) Koppelung *f*; **2.** *Am.* Still-, Lahmlegung *f*; **3.** *bsd. Am.* (*a.* Verkehrs)Stockung *f*, Stillstand *m.*

tiff [tɪf] *s.* **1.** kleine Meinungsverschiedenheit, Kabbe'lei *f*; **2.** schlechte Laune: ***in a ~*** übelgelaunt.

tif·fin ['tɪfɪn] *s. Brit.* Mittagessen *n* (*in Indien*).

tige [tiːʒ] (*Fr.*) *s.* **1.** △ Säulenschaft *m*; **2.** ⚘ Stengel *m*, Stiel *m.*

ti·ger ['taɪgə] *s.* **1.** *zo.* Tiger *m* (*a. fig. Wüterich*): ***American ~*** Jaguar *m*: ***rouse the ~ in s.o.*** *fig.* j-n in kalte Wut versetzen; **2.** *hist. Brit. sl.* livrierter Bedienter, Page *m*; **~ cat** *s. zo.* **1.** Tigerkatze *f*; **2.** getigerte (Haus)Katze.

ti·ger·ish ['taɪgərɪʃ] *adj.* **1.** tigerartig; **2.** blutdürstig; **3.** wild, grausam.

tight [taɪt] **I** *adj.* □ **1.** dicht (*nicht leck*): ***a ~ barrel***; **2.** fest(sitzend) (*Kork, Knoten etc.*), stramm (*Schraube etc.*); **3.** straff, (an)gespannt (*Muskel, Seil etc.*); **4.** schmuck; **5.** a) (zu) eng, knapp, b) eng (anliegend) (*Kleid etc.*): ***~ fit*** knapper Sitz, ⚙ Feinpassung; **6.** a) eng, dicht (gedrängt), b) *fig.* F kritisch, ‚mulmig'; → ***corner*** 2; **7.** prall (voll); **8.** *fig.* a) komprimiert, straff (*Handlung etc.*), b) gedrängt, knapp (*Stil*), c) hieb- u. stichfest (*Argument*), d) straff, streng (*Sicherheitsmaßnahmen etc.*): ***a ~ schedule*** knappe Termine, *a.* ein voller Terminkalender; **9.** ⚚ a) knapp (*Geld*), b) angespannt (*Marktlage*); **10.** F knick(e)rig, geizig; **11.** eng, am Kleinen klebend (*Kunst etc.*); **12.** *sl.* ‚blau', besoffen; **II** *adv.* **13.** eng, knapp; *a.* ⚙ fest: ***hold ~*** festhalten; ***sit ~*** a) fest im Sattel sitzen, b) sich nicht (vom Fleck) rühren, c) *fig.* sich eisern behaupten, sich nicht beirren lassen, *a.* abwarten; **'tight·en** [-tn] **I** *v/t.* **1.** *a.* ***~ up*** zs.-ziehen; **2.** *Schraube, Zügel etc.* fest-, anziehen; *Feder, Gurt etc.* spannen; *Gürtel* enger schnallen; *Muskel, Seil etc.* straffen: ***~ one's grip*** fester zupacken, den Druck verstärken (*a. fig.*); **3.** *a.* ***~ up*** *fig.* a) *Manuskript, Handlung etc.* straffen, b) *Sicherheitsmaßnahmen etc.* verschärfen; **4.** (ab)dichten; **II** *v/i.* **5.** sich straffen; **6.** fester werden (*Griff*); **7.** *a.* ***~ up*** sich fest zs.-ziehen; **8.** ⚚ sich versteifen (*Markt*).

,tight|-'fist·ed → ***tight*** 10; **,~-'fit·ting** *adj.* **1.** → ***tight*** 5; **2.** ⚙ genau an- *od.* eingepaßt, Paß…; **,~-'laced** *adj.* sittenstreng, prüde, puri'tanisch; **,~-'lipped** *adj.* **1.** schmallippig; **2.** *fig.* verschlossen.

tight·ness ['taɪtnɪs] *s.* **1.** Dichtheit *f*; **2.** Festigkeit *f*, fester Sitz; **3.** Straffheit *f*; **4.** Enge *f*; **5.** Gedrängtheit *f*; **6.** Geiz *m*, Knicke'rei *f*; **7.** ⚚ a) (Geld)Knappheit *f*, b) angespannte Marktlage.

'tight·rope **I** *s.* (Draht)Seil *n* (*Zirkus*); **II** *adj.* (Draht)Seil…: ***~ walker*** Seiltänzer(in).

tights [taɪts] *s. pl.* **1.** ('Tänzer-, Ar'tisten)Tri,kot *n*; **2.** *bsd. Brit.* Strumpfhose *f.*

'tight·wad *s. Am.* F Geizkragen *m.*

ti·gress ['taɪgrɪs] *s.* **1.** Tigerin *f*; **2.** *fig.* Me'gäre *f*, (Weibs)Teufel *m.*

tike → ***tyke.***

til·de [tɪld] *s. ling.* Tilde *f.*

tile [taɪl] **I** *s.* **1.** (Dach)Ziegel *m*: ***he has a ~ loose*** *sl.* bei ihm ist eine Schraube locker; ***be*** (***out***) ***on the ~s*** *sl.* ‚herumsumpfen'; **2.** ([Kunst]Stein)Platte *f*, (Fußboden-, Wand-, Teppich)Fliese *f*, (Ofen-, Wand)Kachel *f*; **3.** *coll.* Ziegel *pl.*, Fliesen(fußboden *m*) *pl.*, Fliesen(ver)täfelung *f*; **4.** △ Hohlstein *m*; **5.** F

a) ‚Angströhre' *f* (*Zylinder*), b) ‚Deckel' *m* (*steifer Hut*); **II** *v/t.* **6.** (mit Ziegeln) decken; **7.** mit Fliesen *od.* Platten auslegen, fliesen, kacheln; **til·er** ['taɪlə] *s.* **1.** Dachdecker *m*; **2.** Fliesen-, Plattenleger *m*; **3.** Ziegelbrenner *m*; **4.** Logenhüter *m* (*Freimaurer*).

till¹ [tɪl] **I** *prp.* **1.** bis: ~ ***now*** bis jetzt, bisher; ~ ***then*** bis dahin *od.* dann *od.* nachher; **2.** bis zu: ~ ***death*** bis zum Tod, bis in den Tod; **3.** ***not*** ~ erst: ***not*** ~ ***yesterday***; **II** *cj.* **4.** bis; **5.** ***not*** ~ erst als (*od.* wenn).

till² [tɪl] *s.* **1.** Ladenkasse *f*: ~ ***money*** ☤ Kassenbestand *m*; **2.** Geldkasten *m*.

till³ [tɪl] ⚘ **I** *v/t.* *Boden* bebauen, bestellen, (be)ackern; **II** *v/i.* ackern, pflügen; **'till·a·ble** [-ləbl] *adj.* anbaufähig; **'tillage** [-lɪdʒ] *s.* **1.** Bodenbestellung *f*; **2.** Ackerbau *m*; **3.** Ackerland *n*.

till·er¹ ['tɪlə] *s.* **1.** (Acker)Bauer *m*; **2.** Ackerfräse *f*.

till·er² ['tɪlə] *s.* **1.** ⚓ Ruderpinne *f*; **2.** ⚙ Griff *m*; ~ **rope** *s.* ⚓ Steuerreep *n*.

tilt¹ [tɪlt] **I** *v/t.* **1.** kippen, neigen, schrägstellen; **2.** 'umkippen, 'umstoßen; **3.** ⚓ *Schiff* krängen; **4.** ⚙ recken (*schmieden*); **5.** *hist.* a) (mit eingelegter Lanze) anreiten gegen, b) *Lanze* einlegen; **II** *v/i.* **6.** *a.* ~ ***over*** a) sich neigen, kippen, b) ('um)kippen, 'umfallen; **7.** ⚓ krängen; **8.** *hist.* im Tur'nier kämpfen: ~ ***at*** a) anreiten gegen, b) (mit der Lanze) stechen nach, c) *fig.* losziehen gegen, attackieren; **III** *s.* **9.** Kippen *n*: ***give a*** ~ ***to*** → 1; **10.** Schräglage *f*, Neigung *f*: ***on the*** ~ auf der Kippe; **11.** *hist.* Tur'nier *n*, Lanzenbrechen *n*; **12.** *fig.* Strauß *m*, (Wort)Gefecht *n*; **13.** (Lanzen)Stoß *m*; **14.** (Angriffs)Wucht *f*: (***at***) ***full*** ~ mit voller Wucht *od.* Geschwindigkeit; **15.** *Am.* ‚Drall' *m*, Ten'denz *f*.

tilt² [tɪlt] **I** *s.* **1.** (Wagen- *etc.*)Plane *f*, Verdeck *n*; **2.** ⚓ Sonnensegel *n*; **3.** Sonnendach *n*; **II** *v/t.* (mit e-r Plane) bedecken.

tilt cart *s.* Kippwagen *m*.

tilt·er ['tɪltə] *s.* **1.** (*Kohlen-etc.*)Kipper *m*, Kippvorrichtung *f*; **2.** ⚙ *Walzwerk*: Wipptisch *m*.

tilth [tɪlθ] → ***tillage***.

tilt·ing ['tɪltɪŋ] *adj.* **1.** *hist.* Turnier…; **2.** ⚙ schwenk-, kippbar, Kipp…

'tilt·yard *s. hist.* Tur'nierplatz *m*.

tim·bal ['tɪmbl] *s.* ♪ *hist.* (Kessel)Pauke *f*.

tim·ber ['tɪmbə] **I** *s.* **1.** Bau-, Nutzholz *n*; **2.** *coll.* (Nutzholz)Bäume *pl.*, Baumbestand *m*, Wald(bestand) *m*; **3.** *Brit.* a) Bauholz *n*, b) Schnittholz *n*; **4.** ⚓ Inholz *n*; *pl.* Spantenwerk *n*; **5.** *Am. fig.* Holz *n*, Schlag *m*, Ka'liber *n*: ***a man of his*** ~; ***he is of presidential*** ~ er hat das Zeug zum Präsidenten; **II** *v/t.* **6.** (ver-)zimmern; **7.** *Holz* abvieren; **8.** *Graben etc.* absteifen; **III** *adj.* **9.** Holz…; **'timbered** [-əd] *adj.* **1.** gezimmert; **2.** Fachwerk…; **3.** bewaldet.

tim·ber| for·est *s.* Hochwald *m*; ~ **frame** ⚙ Bundsäge *f*; **'~-framed** *adj.* Fachwerk…

tim·ber·ing ['tɪmbərɪŋ] *s.* **1.** Zimmern *n*, Ausbau *m*; **2.** ⚙ Verschalung *f*; **3.** Bau-, Zimmerholz *n*; **4.** a) Gebälk *n*, b) Fachwerk *n*.

'tim·ber|·land *s. Am.* Waldland *n* (*für Nutzholz*); ~ **line** *s.* Baumgrenze *f*; **'~·man** [-mən] *s.* [*irr.*] **1.** Holzfäller *m*, -arbeiter *m*; **2.** ⚒ Stempelsetzer *m*; ~ **tree** Nutzholzbaum *m*; **'~·work** *s.* ⚙ Gebälk *n*; **'~·yard** *s.* Zimmerplatz *m*, Bauhof *m*.

tim·bre ['tæ̃mbrə] (*Fr.*) *s.* ♪, *ling.* Klangfarbe *f*, Timbre *n*.

tim·brel ['tɪmbrəl] *s.* Tambu'rin *n*.

time [taɪm] **I** *s.* **1.** Zeit *f*: ~ ***past, present, and to come*** Vergangenheit, Gegenwart und Zukunft; ***for all*** ~ für alle Zeiten; ~ ***will show*** die Zeit wird es lehren; **2.** Zeit *f*, Uhr(zeit) *f*: ***what's the*** ~***?, what*** ~ ***is it?*** wieviel Uhr *od.* wie spät ist es?; ***at this*** ~ ***of day*** a) zu dieser (späten) Tageszeit, b) *fig.* so spät, in diesem späten Stadium; ***bid*** (*od.* ***pass***) ***s.o. the*** ~ ***of*** (***the***) ***day***, ***pass the*** ~ ***of day with s.o.*** j-n grüßen; ***know the*** ~ ***of the day*** F wissen, was es geschlagen hat; ***some*** ~ ***about noon*** etwa um Mittag; ***this*** ~ ***tomorrow*** morgen um diese Zeit; ***this*** ~ ***twelve months*** heute übers Jahr; ***keep good*** ~ richtig gehen (*Uhr*); **3.** Zeit(dauer) *f*, Zeitabschnitt *m*, (*a. phys. Fall-, Schwingungs- etc.*)Dauer *f*; ☤ Laufzeit *f* (*Wechsel- etc.*); Arbeitszeit *f im Herstellungsprozeß etc.*: ***in three weeks'*** ~ in drei Wochen; ***a long*** ~ lange Zeit; ***be a long*** ~ ***in doing s.th.*** lange (Zeit) dazu brauchen, et. zu tun; **4.** Zeit(-punkt *m*) *f*: ~ ***of arrival*** Ankunftszeit; ***at the*** ~ a) zu dieser Zeit, damals, b) gerade; ***at the present*** ~ derzeit, gegenwärtig; ***at the same*** ~ a) zur selben Zeit, gleichzeitig, b) gleichwohl, zugleich, andererseits; (***at***) ***any*** ~, ***at all*** ~***s*** zu jeder Zeit; ***at no*** ~ nie; ***at that*** ~ zu der Zeit; ***at one*** ~ einst, früher (einmal); ***at some*** ~ irgendwann; ***for the*** ~ für den Augenblick; ***for the*** ~ ***being*** a) vorläufig, fürs erste, b) unter den gegenwärtigen Umständen; **5.** *oft pl.* Zeit(alter *n*) *f*, E'poche *f*: ~ ***immemorial***, ~ ***out of mind*** un(vor)denkliche Zeit; ***at*** (*od.* ***in***) ***the*** ~ ***of Queen Anne*** zur Zeit der Königin Anna; ***the good old*** ~***s*** die gute alte Zeit; **6.** *pl.* Zeiten *pl.*, (Zeit)Verhältnisse *pl.*: ***hard*** ~***s***; **7.** ***the*** ~***s*** die Zeit: ***behind the*** ~***s*** rückständig; ***move with the*** ~***s*** mit der Zeit gehen; **8.** Frist *f*, Ter'min *m*: ~ ***for payment*** Zahlungsfrist; ~ ***of delivery*** ☤ Lieferfrist, -zeit *f*; ***ask*** (***for a***) ~ ☤ um Frist(verlängerung) bitten; ***you must give me*** ~ Sie müssen mir Zeit geben *od.* lassen; **9.** (verfügbare) Zeit: ***have no*** ~ keine Zeit haben; ***have no*** ~ ***for s.o.*** *fig.* nichts übrig haben für j-n; ***buy a little*** ~ etwas Zeit (heraus)schinden; ***kill*** ~ die Zeit totschlagen; ***take*** (***the***) ~, ***take out*** ~ sich die Zeit nehmen (***to do*** zu tun); ***take one's*** ~ sich Zeit lassen; ~ ***is up!*** die Zeit ist um!; ~ ***gentlemen, please!*** (es ist bald) Polizeistunde! (*Lokal*); ~***!*** *sport* Zeit!: a) anfangen!, b) aufhören!; ~***!*** *parl.* Schluß!; → ***forelock***; **10.** Lehr-, Dienstzeit *f*: ***serve one's*** ~ s-e Lehre machen; **11.** a) (na'türliche *od.* nor'male) Zeit, b) Lebenszeit *f*: ~ ***of life*** Alter *n*; ***ahead of*** ~ vorzeitig; ***die before one's*** ~ vor der Zeit *od.* zu früh sterben; ***his*** ~ ***is drawing near*** sein Tod naht heran; **12.** a) Schwangerschaft *f*, b) Entbindung *f*, Niederkunft *f*: ***she is far on in her*** ~ sie ist hochschwanger; ***she is near her*** ~ sie steht kurz vor der Entbindung; **13.** (günstige) Zeit: ***now is the*** ~ nun ist die passende Gelegenheit, jetzt gilt es (***to do*** zu tun); ***at such*** ~***s*** bei solchen Gelegenheiten; ***bide one's*** ~ (s-e Zeit) abwarten; **14.** Mal *n*: ***the first*** ~ das erste Mal; ***for the last*** ~ zum letzten Mal; ***till next*** ~ bis zum nächsten Mal; ***every*** ~ jedesmal; ***many*** ~***s*** viele Male; ~ ***and again***, ~ ***after*** ~ immer wieder; ***at some other*** ~, ***at other*** ~***s*** ein anderes Mal; ***at a*** ~ auf einmal, zusammen, zugleich, jeweils; ***one at a*** ~ einzeln, immer nur eine(r, s); ***two at a*** ~ zu zweit, jeweils zwei; **15.** *pl.* mal, …mal: ***three*** ~***s four is twelve*** drei mal vier ist zwölf; ***twenty*** ~***s*** zwanzigmal; ***four*** ~***s the size of yours*** viermal so groß wie deines; **16.** *bsd. sport* (erzielte, gestoppte) Zeit; **17.** a) Tempo *n*, Zeitmaß *n* (*beide a.* ♪), b) ♪ Takt *m*: ***change of*** ~ Taktwechsel *m*; ***beat*** (***keep***) ~ den Takt schlagen (halten); **18.** ⚔ Marschtempo *n*, Schritt *m*: ***mark*** ~ a) ⚔ auf der Stelle treten (*a. fig.*), b) *fig.* nicht vom Fleck kommen;

Besondere Redewendungen:

against ~ gegen die Zeit *od.* Uhr, mit größter Eile; ***ahead of*** (*od.* ***before***) ***one's*** ~ s-r Zeit voraus; ***all the*** ~ a) die ganze Zeit (über), ständig, b) jederzeit; ***at*** ~***s*** zu Zeiten, gelegentlich; ***at all*** ~***s*** stets, zu jeder Zeit; ***at any*** ~ a) zu irgendeiner Zeit, jemals, b) jederzeit; ***behind*** ~ zu spät d(a)ran, verspätet; ***between*** ~***s*** in den Zwischenzeiten; ***by that*** ~ a) bis dahin, unterdessen, b) zu der Zeit; ***for a*** (*od.* ***some***) ~ e-e Zeitlang, einige Zeit; ***for a long*** ~ ***past*** schon seit langem; ***not for a long*** ~ noch lange nicht; ***from*** ~ ***to*** ~ von Zeit zu Zeit; ***in*** ~ a) rechtzeitig (***to do*** um zu tun), b) mit der Zeit, c) im (richtigen) Takt; ***in due*** ~ rechtzeitig, termingerecht; ***in good*** ~ (gerade) rechtzeitig; ***all in good*** ~ alles zu s-r Zeit; ***in one's own good*** ~ wenn es e-m paßt; ***in no*** ~ im Nu, im Handumdrehen; ***on*** ~ a) pünktlich, rechtzeitig, b) *bsd. Am.* für e-e (bestimmte) Zeit, c) ☤ *Am.* auf Zeit, *bsd.* auf Raten; ***out of*** ~ a) zur Unzeit, unzeitig, b) vorzeitig, c) zu spät, d) aus dem Takt *od.* Schritt; ***till such*** ~ ***as*** so lange bis; ***to*** ~ pünktlich; ***do*** ~ F *im Gefängnis* ‚sitzen'; ***have a good*** ~ es schön haben, es sich gutgehen lassen, sich gut amüsieren; ***have the*** ~ ***of one's life*** sich großartig amüsieren, leben wie ein Fürst; ***have a hard*** ~ Schlimmes durchmachen; ***he had a hard*** ~ ***getting up early*** es fiel ihm schwer, früh aufzustehen; ***with*** ~ mit der Zeit; ~ ***was, when*** die Zeit ist vorüber, als;

II *v/t.* **19.** (mit der Uhr) messen, (ab-)stoppen, die Zeit messen von; **20.** timen (*a. sport*), die Zeit *od.* den richtigen Zeitpunkt wählen *od.* bestimmen für, zur rechten Zeit tun; → ***timed***; **21.** zeitlich abstimmen; **22.** die Zeit festsetzen für: ***is*** ~***d to leave at 7*** *der Zug etc.* soll um 7 abfahren; **23.** ⚙ *Zündung etc.* einstellen; *Uhr* stellen; **24.** zeitlich regeln (***to*** nach); **25.** das Tempo *od.* den Takt angeben für; **III** *v/i.* **26.** Takt halten; **27.** zeitlich zs.- *od.* über'einstimmen (*with* mit); ˌ~**-and-**ˈ**mo·tion stud·y** *s.* ✝ Zeitstudie *f*; ~ **bar·gain** *s.* ✝ Terˈmingeschäft *n*; ˈ~**-base** *adj.* ϟ Kipp...; ~ **bill** *s.* ✝ Zeitwechsel *m*; ~ **bomb** *s.* Zeitbombe *f* (*a. fig.*); ˈ~**·card** *s.* **1.** Stech-, Stempelkarte *f*; **2.** Fahrplan *m*; ~ **clock** *s.* Stechuhr *f*; ~ **con·stant** *s. phys.* ˈZeitkonˌstante *f*; ˈ~**-conˌsum·ing** *adj.* zeitraubend.

timed [taɪmd] *adj.* zeitlich (genau) festgelegt *od.* reguliert, getimed: → ***ill-timed***; ***well-timed***.

time| de·pos·its *s. pl.* ✝ *Am.* Terˈmingelder *pl.*; ~ **draft** *s.* ✝ Zeitwechsel *m*; ˈ~**-exˌpired** *adj.* ⚔ *Brit.* ausgedient (*Soldat od. Unteroffizier*); ~ **ex·po·sure** *s. phot.* **1.** Zeitbelichtung *f*; **2.** Zeitaufnahme *f*; ~ **freight** *s.* ✝ *Am.* Eilfracht *f*; ~ **fuse** *s.* ⚔ Zeitzünder *m*; ˈ~**-ˌhon·o(u)red** *adj.* altˈehrwürdig; ˈ~ˌ**keep·er** *s.* **1.** Zeitmesser *m*; **2.** *sport u.* ✝ Zeitnehmer *m*; ~ **lag** *s. bsd.* ⚙ Verzögerung *f*, zeitliche Nacheilung *od.* Lücke; ˈ~**-lapse** *adj. phot.* Zeitraffer...

time·less [ˈtaɪmlɪs] *adj.* □ **1.** ewig; **2.** zeitlos (*a. Schönheit etc.*).

time lim·it *s.* Frist *f*, Terˈmin *m*.

time·li·ness [ˈtaɪmlɪnɪs] *s.* **1.** Rechtzeitigkeit *f*; **2.** günstige Zeit; **3.** Aktualiˈtät *f*.

time| loan *s.* ✝ Darlehen *n* auf Zeit; ~ **lock** *s.* ⚙ Zeitschloß *n*.

time·ly [ˈtaɪmlɪ] *adj.* **1.** rechtzeitig; **2.** (*zeitlich*) günstig, angebracht; **3.** aktuˈell.

ˌ**time|-ˈout** *pl.* **-ˈouts** *s.* **1.** *sport* Auszeit *f*; **2.** *Am.* Pause *f*; ~ **pay·ment** *s.* ✝ *Am.* Ratenzahlung *f*; ˈ~**·piece** *s.* Chronoˈmeter *n*, Uhr *f*.

tim·er [ˈtaɪmə] *s.* **1.** Zeitmesser *m* (*Apparat*); **2.** ⚙ Zeitgeber *m*, -schalter *m*; **3.** *mot.* Zündverteiler *m*; **4.** Stoppuhr *f*; **5.** *phot.* Zeitauslöser *m*; **6.** ⚙ *u. sport* Zeitnehmer *m* (*Person*).

ˈ**time|ˌsav·er** *s.* zeitsparendes Geˈrät *od.* Eleˈment; ˈ~ˌ**sav·ing** *adj.* zeit(er)sparend; ~ **sense** *s.* Zeitgefühl *n*; ˈ~**-ˌserv·er** *s.* Opportuˈnist(in), Gesinnungslump *m*; ˈ~ˌ**serv·ing I** *adj.* opportuˈnistisch; **II** *s.* Opportuˈnismus *m*, Gesinnungslumpeˈrei *f*; ~ **shar·ing** *s. Computer*: Time-sharing *n*; ~ **sheet** *s.* **1.** Arbeits(zeit)blatt *n*; **2.** Stechblatt *n*; ~ **sig·nal** *s. Radio*: Zeitzeichen *n*; ˈ~**-stud·y man** *s.* [*irr.*] ✝, ⚙ Zeitstudienfachmann *m*; ~ **switch** *s.* Zeitschalter *m*; ˈ~ˌ**ta·ble** *s.* **1.** a) Fahrplan *m*, b) Flugplan *m*; **2.** Stundenplan *m*; **3.** ‚Fahrplan' *m*, ˈZeittaˌbelle *f*; ˈ~**-ˌtest·ed** *adj.* (alt)bewährt; ˈ~**·work** *s.* ✝ nach Zeit bezahlte Arbeit; ˈ~**·worn** *adj.* **1.** abgenutzt (*a. fig.*); **2.** veraltet; **3.** abgedroschen.

tim·id [ˈtɪmɪd] *adj.* □ **1.** furchtsam, ängstlich (*of* vor *dat.*); **2.** schüchtern, zaghaft; **ti·mid·i·ty** [tɪˈmɪdətɪ], ˈ**tim·id·ness** [-nɪs] *s.* **1.** Ängstlichkeit *f*; **2.** Schüchternheit *f*.

tim·ing [ˈtaɪmɪŋ] *s.* **1.** Timing *n* (*a. sport*), zeitliche Abstimmung *od.* Berechnung; **2.** Wahl *f* des richtigen Zeitpunkts; **3.** (gewählter) Zeitpunkt; **4.** ⚙, *mot.* (zeitliche) Steuerung, (*Ventil-, Zündpunkt- etc.*)Einstellung *f*.

tim·or·ous [ˈtɪmərəs] *adj.* □ → ***timid***.

Tim·o·thy [ˈtɪməθɪ] *npr. u. s. bibl.* (Brief *m* des Paulus an) Tiˈmotheus *m*.

tim·pa·nist [ˈtɪmpənɪst] *s.* ♪ Pauker *m*; **tim·pa·no** [ˈtɪmpənəʊ] *pl.* **-ni** [-nɪ] *s.* (Kessel)Pauke *f*.

tin [tɪn] **I** *s.* **1.** ⚗, ⚙ Zinn *n*; **2.** (Weiß-)Blech *n*; **3.** (Blech-, *bsd. Brit.* Konˈserven)Dose *f*, (-)Büchse *f*; **4.** *sl.* ‚Piepen' *pl.* (*Geld*); **II** *adj.* **5.** zinnern, Zinn...; **6.** Blech..., blechern (*a. fig. contp.*); **III** *v/t.* **7.** verzinnen; **8.** *Brit.* eindosen, (in Büchsen) einmachen *od.* packen, konservieren; → ***tinned*** 2; ~ **can** *s.* **1.** Blechdose *f*; **2.** ⚓ *sl.* Zerstörer *m*; ˈ~**-coat** *v/t.* ⚙ feuerverzinnen; ~ **cry** *s.* ⚙ Zinngeschrei *n*.

tinc·ture [ˈtɪŋktʃə] **I** *s.* **1.** *pharm.* Tinkˈtur *f*; **2.** *poet.* Farbe *f*; **3.** *her.* Farbe *f*, Tinkˈtur *f*; **4.** *fig.* a) Spur *f*, Beigeschmack *m*, b) Anstrich *m*: ~ ***of education***; **II** *v/t.* **5.** färben; **6.** *fig.* a) → ***tinge*** 2, b) durchˈdringen (*with* mit).

tin·der [ˈtɪndə] *s.* Zunder *m*; ˈ~**·box** *s.* **1.** Zunderbüchse *f*; **2.** *fig.* Pulverfaß *n*.

tine [taɪn] *s.* **1.** Zinke *f*, Zacke *f* (*Gabel etc.*); **2.** *hunt.* (Geweih)Sprosse *f*.

tin| fish *s.* ⚓ *sl.* ‚Aal' *m* (*Torpedo*); ~ **foil** *s.* **1.** Stanniˈol *n*; **2.** Stanniˈolpaˌpier *n*; ˈ~**-foil I** *v/t.* **1.** mit Stanniˈol belegen; **2.** in Stanniˈol(paˌpier) verpacken; **II** *adj.* **3.** Stanniol...

ting [tɪŋ] **I** *s.* Klingeln *n*; **II** *v/t.* klingeln mit; **III** *v/i.* klingeln; ~**-a-ling** [ˌtɪŋəˈlɪŋ] *s.* Klingˈling *n*.

tinge [tɪndʒ] **I** *v/t.* **1.** tönen, (leicht) färben; **2.** *fig.* e-n Anstrich geben (*dat.*): ***be ~d with*** e-n Anflug haben von, et. von ... an sich haben; **II** *v/i.* **3.** sich färben; **III** *s.* **4.** leichter Farbton, Tönung *f*: ***have a ~ of red*** e-n Stich ins Rote haben, ins Rote spielen; **5.** *fig.* Anstrich *m*, Anflug *m*, Spur *f*.

tin·gle [ˈtɪŋgl] **I** *v/i.* **1.** prickeln, kribbeln, beißen, brennen (*Haut, Ohren etc.*) (***with cold*** vor Kälte); **2.** klingen, summen (*with* vor *dat.*): ***my ears are tingling*** mir klingen die Ohren; **3.** ~ ***with*** *fig.* ‚knistern' vor *Spannung, Erotik etc.*: ***the story ~s with suspense***; **4.** flirren (*Hitze, Licht*); **II** *s.* **5.** Prikkeln *n etc.*; **6.** Klingen *n in den Ohren*; **7.** (nerˈvöse) Erregung.

tin| god *s.* Götze *m*, Popanz *m*; ~ **hat** *s.* ⚔ F Stahlhelm *m*; ˈ~**·horn** *Am. sl.* **I** *adj.* angeberisch, hochstaplerisch; **II** *s.* Hochstapler *m*, Angeber *m*.

tink·er [ˈtɪŋkə] **I** *s.* **1.** Kesselflicker *m*: ***not worth a ~'s cuss*** keinen Pfifferling wert; **2.** a) Pfuscher *m*, Stümper *m*, b) Bastler *m*, Tüftler *m*; **3.** Pfuscheˈrei *f*: ***have a ~ at*** an *et.* herumpfuschen; **II** *v/i.* **4.** herˈumbasteln, -pfuschen (***at, with*** an *dat.*); **III** *v/t.* **5.** *mst* ~ ***up*** (rasch) zs.-flicken; zuˈrechtbasteln *od.* -pfuschen (*a. fig.*).

tin·kle [ˈtɪŋkl] **I** *v/i.* klingeln, hell (er-)klingen; **II** *v/t.* klingeln mit; **III** *s.* Klingeln *n*, (*a. fig.* Vers-, Wort)Geklingel *n*: ***give s.o. a.*** ~ *Brit.* F j-n ‚anklingeln'; ***have a*** ~ F ‚pinkeln'.

tin| Liz·zie [ˈlɪzɪ] *s. humor.* alter Klapperkasten (*Auto*); ˈ~**·man** [-mən] *s.* [*irr.*] **1.** Zinngießer *m*; **2.** → ***tinsmith***.

tinned [tɪnd] *adj.* **1.** verzinnt; **2.** *Brit.* konserviert, Dosen..., Büchsen...: ~ ***fruit*** Obstkonserven *pl.*; ~ ***meat*** Büchsenfleisch *n*; ~ ***music*** *humor.* ‚Musik *f* aus der Konserve'; **tin·ner** [ˈtɪnə] *s.* **1.** → ***tinsmith***; **2.** Verzinner *m*.

tin·ny [ˈtɪnɪ] *adj.* **1.** zinnern; **2.** zinnhaltig; **3.** blechern (*a. fig. Klang*).

tin o·pen·er *s. Brit.* Dosen-, Büchsenöffner *m*; ♀ **Pan Al·ley** [ˌtɪnpænˈælɪ] *s.* (Zentrum *n* der) ˈSchlagerinduˌstrie *f*; ~ **plate** *s.* Weiß-, Zinnblech *n*; ˈ~**-plate** *v/t.* verzinnen; ˈ~**·pot I** *s.* Blechtopf *m*; **II** *adj. sl.* ‚schäbig', ‚billig'.

tin·sel [ˈtɪnsl] **I** *s.* **1.** Flitter-, Rauschgold *n*, -silber *n*; **2.** Laˈmetta *n*; **3.** Glitzerschmuck *m*; **4.** *fig.* Flitterkram *m*, Kitsch *m*; **II** *adj.* **5.** Flitter...; **6.** *fig.* flitterhaft, kitschig, Flitter..., Schein...; **III** *v/t.* **7.** mit Flitterwerk verzieren.

ˈ**tin|·smith** *s.* Blechschmied *m*, Klempner *m*; ~ **sol·der** *s.* ⚙ Weichlot *n*, Lötzinn *n*.

tint [tɪnt] **I** *s.* **1.** (hellgetönte *od.* zarte) Farbe; **2.** (Farb)Ton *m*, Tönung *f*: ***autumnal ~s*** Herbstfärbung *f*; ***have a bluish ~*** ins Blaue spielen, e-n Stich ins Blaue haben; **3.** *paint.* Weißmischung *f*; **II** *v/t.* **4.** (leicht) färben: ***~ed glass*** Rauchglas *n*; ***~ed paper*** Tonpapier *n*; **5.** a) (ab)tönen, b) aufhellen.

tin·tin·nab·u·la·tion [ˈtɪntɪˌnæbjʊˈleɪʃn] *s.* Geklingel *n*.

ti·ny [ˈtaɪnɪ] **I** *adj.* winzig (*a. Geräusch etc.*); **II** *s.* Kleine(r *m*) *f* (*Kind*).

tip¹ [tɪp] **I** *s.* **1.** (Schwanz-, Stock- *etc.*) Spitze *f*, (Flügel- *etc.*)Ende *n*: ~ ***of the ear*** Ohrläppchen *n*; ~ ***of the finger*** (***nose, tongue***) Finger- (Nasen-, Zungen)spitze; ***have s.th. at the ~s of one's fingers*** et. ‚parat' haben, et. aus dem Effeff können; ***I have it on the ~ of my tongue*** es schwebt mir auf der Zunge; **2.** Gipfel *m*, (Berg)Spitze *f*; → ***iceberg***; **3.** ⚙ spitzes Endstück, *bsd.* a) (*Stock- etc.*)Zwinge *f*, b) Düse *f*, c) Tülle *f*, d) (Schuh)Kappe *f*; **4.** Filter *m e-r Zigarette*; **II** *v/t.* **5.** ⚙ mit e-r Spitze *etc.* versehen; beschlagen, bewehren; **6.** *Büsche etc.* stutzen.

tip² [tɪp] **I** *s.* **1.** Neigung *f*: ***give s.th. a ~*** → 3; **2.** (Schutt- *etc.*)Abladeplatz *m*, (*a.* Kohlen)Halde *f*; **II** *v/t.* **3.** kippen, neigen; → ***scale²*** 1; **4.** *mst* ~ ***over*** ˈumkippen; **5.** *Hut* abnehmen, an *den Hut* tippen (*zum Gruß*); **6.** *Brit. Müll etc.* abladen; **III** *v/i.* **7.** sich neigen; **8.** *mst* ~ ***over*** umkippen; ✈ auf den Kopf gehen (*beim Landen*); ~ **off** *v/t.* **1.** abladen; **2.** *sl. Glas Bier etc.* ‚hinˈunterkippen'; ~ **out I** *v/t.* ausschütten; **II** *v/i.* herˈausfallen; ~ **o·ver** → ***tip²*** 4 *u.* 8; ~ **up** *v/t. u. v/i.* **1.** hochkippen, -klappen; **2.** umkippen.

tip³ [tɪp] **I** *s.* **1.** Trinkgeld *n*; **2.** (Wett- *etc.*)Tip *m*; **3.** Tip *m*, Wink *m*, Fingerzeig *m*, Rat *m*; **II** *v/t.* **4.** *j-m* ein Trinkgeld geben; **5.** F *j-m* e-n Tip *od.* Wink geben: ~ ***s.o. off***, ~ ***s.o. the wink*** j-m (rechtzeitig) e-n Tip geben, j-n warnen; **6.** *sport* tippen auf (*acc.*); **III** *v/i.* **7.** Trinkgeld(er) geben.

tip⁴ [tɪp] **I** *s.* Klaps *m*; leichte Berührung; **II** *v/t.* leicht schlagen; antippen, antupfen.

tip| and run *s. Brit. Art* Kricket *n*; ˌ~**-and-ˈrun** *adj. fig.* Überraschungs..., blitzschnell: ~ ***raider*** ⚔ Einbruchsflieger *m*; ˈ~**·cart** *s.* Kippwagen *m*.

ˈ**tip-off** *s.* **1.** Tip *m*, Wink *m*; **2.** *sport* Sprungball *m*.

tipped [tɪpt] *adj.* **1.** mit e-m Endstück

od. e-r Zwinge, Spitze *etc.* versehen; **2.** mit Filter (*Zigarette*).
tip·per ['tɪpə] *s.* ⚙ Kippwagen *m.*
tip·pet ['tɪpɪt] *s.* **1.** Pele'rine *f*, (her'abhängender) Pelzkragen; **2.** *eccl.* (Seiden)Halsband *n*, (-)Schärpe *f.*
tip·ple ['tɪpl] **I** *v/t. u. v/i.* ‚picheln'; **II** *s.* (alko'holisches) Getränk; '**tip·pler** [-lə] *s.* ‚Pichler' *m*, Säufer *m.*
tip·si·fy ['tɪpsɪfaɪ] *v/t.* beduseln; '**tip·si·ness** [-ɪnɪs] *s.* Beschwipstheit *f.*
'**tip·staff** *pl.* **-staves** *s.* **1.** *hist.* Amtsstab *m*; **2.** Gerichtsdiener *m.*
tip·ster ['tɪpstə] *s.* **1.** *bsd. Rennsport u. Börse*: (berufsmäßiger) Tipgeber; **2.** Infor'mant *m.*
tip·sy ['tɪpsɪ] *adj.* □ **1.** angeheitert, beschwipst; **2.** wack(e)lig, schief; **~ cake** *s. mit Wein getränkter u. mit Eiercreme servierter Kuchen.*
'**tip**|-ˌ**tilt·ed** *adj.*: **~ *nose*** Stupsnase *f*; '**~·toe I** *s.*: ***on* ~** a) auf den Zehenspitzen, b) *fig.* neugierig, gespannt (***with*** vor *dat.*), c) darauf brennend (*et. zu tun*); **II** *adj. u. adv.* → I; **III** *v/i.* auf den Zehenspitzen gehen, schleichen; ˌ**~'top I** *s.* Gipfel *m*, *fig. a.* Höhepunkt *m*; **II** *adj. u. adv.* F 'tipp'topp, erstklassig; '**~-up** *adj.* aufklappbar: **~ *seat*** Klappsitz *m.*
ti·rade [taɪ'reɪd] *s.* **1.** Ti'rade *f* (*a.* ♪), Wortschwall *m*; **2.** 'Schimpfkanoˌnade *f.*
tire¹ ['taɪə] **I** *v/t.* ermüden (*a. fig. langweilen*): **~ *out*** erschöpfen; **~ *to death*** a) todmüde machen, b) *fig.* tödlich langweilen; **II** *v/i.* müde werden: a) ermüden, ermatten, b) *fig.* 'überdrüssig werden (***of*** *gen.*, ***of doing*** zu tun).
tire² ['taɪə] *mot. bsd. Am.* **I** *s.* (Rad-, Auto)Reifen *m*; **II** *v/t.* bereifen.
tire³ ['taɪə] *obs.* **I** *v/t.* schmücken; **II** *s.* a) (Kopf)Putz *m*, Schmuck *m*, b) (schöne) Kleidung, Kleid *n.*
tire| **cas·ing** *s. mot.* (Reifen)Mantel *m*, (-)Decke *f*; **~ chain** *s. mot.* Schneekette *f.*
tired¹ ['taɪəd] *adj.* **1.** müde: a) ermüdet (***by, with*** von): **~ *to death*** todmüde, b) 'überdrüssig (***of*** *gen.*); ***I am ~ of it*** *fig.* ich habe es satt; **2.** erschöpft, verbraucht; **3.** abgenutzt.
tired² ['taɪəd] *adj.* ⚙, *mot.* bereift.
tired·ness ['taɪədnɪs] *s.* **1.** Müdigkeit *f*; **2.** *fig.* 'Überdruß *m.*
tire| **ga(u)ge** *s. mot.* Reifendruckmesser *m*; **~ grip** *s.* ⚙ Griffigkeit *f* der Reifen.
tire·less¹ ['taɪəlɪs] *adj.* ⚙ unbereift.
tire·less² ['taɪəlɪs] *adj.* □ unermüdlich; '**tire·less·ness** [-nɪs] *s.* Unermüdlichkeit *f.*
tire| **le·ver** *s. mot.* ('Reifen)Monˌtierhebel *m*; **~ marks** *s. pl. mot.* Reifen-, Bremsspur(en *pl.*) *f*; **~ rim** *s.* Reifenwulst *m.*
tire·some ['taɪəsəm] *adj.* □ **1.** ermüdend (*a. fig.*); **2.** *fig.* unangenehm, lästig.
'**tireˌwom·an** *s.* [*irr.*] *obs.* **1.** Kammerzofe *f*; **2.** *thea.* Garderobi'ere *f.*
ti·ro → ***tyro.***
Tir·o·lese [ˌtɪrə'li:z] **I** *adj.* ti'rolerisch, ti'rolisch, Tiroler(…); **II** *s.* Ti'roler(in).
'**T-ˌi·ron** *s.* ⚙ T-Eisen *n.*
tis·sue ['tɪʃu:; 'tɪsju:] *s.* **1.** *biol.* (Zell-, Muskel- *etc.*)Gewebe *n*; **2.** ✝ feines Gewebe, Flor *m*; **3.** *a.* **~ *paper*** 'SeidenpaˌPier *n*; **4.** Pa'pier(taschen)tuch *n*; **5.** *phot.* 'KohlepaˌPier *n*; **6.** *fig.* (*Lügen- etc.*)Gewebe *n*, Netz *n.*
tit¹ [tɪt] *s. orn.* Meise *f.*
tit² [tɪt] *s.*: **~ *for tat*** wie du mir, so ich dir; ***give s.o. ~ for tat*** j-m mit gleicher Münze heimzahlen.
tit³ [tɪt] *s.* **1.** → ***teat***; **2.** *vulg.* ‚Titte' *f.*
Ti·tan ['taɪtən] *s.* Ti'tan *m*; '**Ti·tan·ess** [-tənɪs] *s.* Ti'tanin *f*; **ti·tan·ic** [taɪ'tænɪk] *adj.* **1.** ti'tanisch, gi'gantisch; **2.** ⚗ Titan…: **~ *acid***; **ti·ta·ni·um** [taɪ'teɪnjəm] *s.* ⚗ Ti'tan *n.*
tit·bit ['tɪtbɪt] *s.* Leckerbissen *m* (*a. fig.*).
tith·a·ble ['taɪðəbl] *adj.* zehntpflichtig.
tithe [taɪð] **I** *s.* **1.** *oft pl. bsd. eccl.* Zehnte *m*; **2.** Zehntel *n*: ***not a ~ of it*** *fig.* nicht ein bißchen davon; **II** *v/t.* **3.** den Zehnten bezahlen von; **4.** den Zehnten erheben von.
tit·il·late ['tɪtɪleɪt] *v/t. u. v/i.* kitzeln (*a. fig. angenehm erregen*); **tit·il·la·tion** [ˌtɪtɪ'leɪʃn] *s.* **1.** Kitzeln *n*; **2.** *fig.* Kitzel *m.*
tit·i·vate ['tɪtɪveɪt] *v/t. u. v/i. humor.* (sich) feinmachen, (sich) her'ausputzen.
tit·lark ['tɪtlɑ:k] *s. orn.* Pieper *m.*
ti·tle ['taɪtl] *s.* **1.** (*Buch- etc.*)Titel *m*; **2.** (Ka'pitel- *etc.*)ˌÜberschrift *f*; **3.** (Haupt)Abschnitt *m e-s Gesetzes etc.*; **4.** *Film*: 'Untertitel *m*; **5.** Bezeichnung *f*; **6.** (Adels-, Ehren-, Amts)Titel *m*: **~ *of nobility*** Adelsprädikat *n*; **7.** *sport* Titel *m*; **8.** ⚖ a) Rechtstitel *m*, -anspruch *m*, Recht *n* (***to*** auf *acc.*), b) dingliches Eigentum(srecht) (***to*** an *dat.*), c) Eigentumsurkunde *f*; **9.** *allg.* Recht *n* (***to*** auf *acc.*), Berechtigung *f* (***to do*** zu tun); **10.** *typ.* a) → ***title page***, b) Buchrücken *m*; '**ti·tled** [-ld] *adj.* **1.** betitelt, tituliert; **2.** ad(e)lig.
ti·tle| **deed** → ***title*** 8 c; '**~ˌhold·er** *s.* **1.** ⚖ (Rechts)Titelinhaber(in); **2.** *sport* Titelhalter(in), -verteidiger(in); **~ page** *s.* Titelblatt *n*; **~ role** *s. thea.* Titelrolle *f.*
'**tit·mouse** *s.* [*irr.*] *orn.* Meise *f.*
ti·trate ['taɪtreɪt] *v/t. u. v/i.* ⚗ titrieren.
tit·ter ['tɪtə] **I** *v/i.* kichern; **II** *s.* Gekicher *n*, Kichern *n.*
tit·tle ['tɪtl] *s.* **1.** Pünktchen *n*, (*bsd.* I-)Tüpfelchen *n*; **2.** *fig.* Tüttelchen *n*, *das* bißchen: ***to a ~*** aufs I-Tüpfelchen *od.* Haar, ganz genau; ***not a ~ of it*** nicht ein Iota (davon).
'**tit·tle-ˌtat·tle I** *s.* **1.** Schnickschnack *m*, Geschwätz *n*; **2.** Klatsch *m*, Tratsch *m*; **II** *v/i.* **3.** schwatzen, schwätzen; **4.** tratschen.
tit·u·lar ['tɪtjʊlə] **I** *adj.* □ **1.** Titel…; **2.** Titular…, nomi'nell: **~ *king*** Titularkönig *m*; **II** *s.* **3.** Titu'lar *m.*
Ti·tus ['taɪtəs] *npr. u. s. bibl.* (Brief *m* des Paulus an) Titus *m.*
tiz·zy ['tɪzɪ] *s.* F Aufregung *f.*
to [tu:; *im Satz mst* tʊ; *vor Konsonanten* tə] **I** *prp.* **1.** *Grundbedeutung*: zu; **2.** *Richtung u. Ziel, räumlich*: zu, nach, an (*acc.*), in (*acc.*), auf (*acc.*): **~ *bed*** zu Bett *gehen*; **~ *London*** nach London *reisen etc.*; **~ *school*** in die Schule *gehen*; **~ *the ground*** auf den *od.* zu Boden *fallen, werfen etc.*; **~ *the station*** zum Bahnhof; **~ *the wall*** an die Wand *nageln etc.*; **~ *the right*** auf der rechten Seite, rechts; ***back ~ back*** Rücken an Rücken; **3.** in (*dat.*): ***I have never been ~ London***; **4.** *Richtung, Ziel, Zweck, Wirkung*: zu, auf (*acc.*), an (*acc.*), in (*acc.*), für, gegen: ***pray ~ God*** zu Gott beten; ***our duty ~*** unsere Pflicht *j-m* gegenüber; **~ *dinner*** zum Essen *einladen etc.*; **~ *my surprise*** zu m-r Überraschung; ***pleasant ~ the ear*** angenehm für das Ohr; ***here's ~ you!*** F (auf) Ihre Gesundheit!, Prosit!; ***what is that ~ you?*** was geht das Sie an?; **~ *a large audience*** vor e-m großen Publikum *spielen*; **5.** *Zugehörigkeit*: zu, in (*acc.*), für, auf (*acc.*): ***cousin ~*** Vetter des *Königs etc.*, der *Frau N.*, von *N.*; ***he is a brother ~ her*** er ist ihr Bruder; ***secretary ~*** Sekretär des …, *j-s* Sekretär; ***that is all there is ~ it*** das ist alles; ***a cap with a tassel ~ it*** e-e Mütze mit e-r Troddel (daran); ***a room ~ myself*** ein eigenes Zimmer; ***a key ~ the trunk*** ein Schlüssel für den (*od.* zum) Koffer; **6.** *Gemäßheit*: nach: **~ *my feeling*** m-m Gefühl nach; ***not ~ my taste*** nicht nach m-m Geschmack; **7.** (im Verhältnis *od.* Vergleich) zu, gegen, gegen'über, auf (*acc.*), mit: ***you are but a child ~ him*** Sie sind nur ein Kind gegen ihn; ***nothing ~*** nichts im Vergleich zu; ***five ~ one*** fünf gegen eins, *sport etc.* fünf zu eins; ***three ~ the pound*** drei auf das Pfund; **8.** *Ausmaß, Grenze*: bis, (bis) zu, (bis) an (*acc.*), auf (*acc.*), in (*dat.*): **~ *the clouds***; ***goods ~ the value of*** Waren im Werte von; ***love ~ craziness*** bis zum Wahnsinn lieben; **9.** *zeitliche Ausdehnung od. Grenze*: bis, bis zu, bis gegen, auf (*acc.*), vor (*dat.*): ***a quarter ~ one*** ein Viertel vor eins; ***from three ~ four*** von drei bis vier (Uhr); **~ *this day*** bis zum heutigen Tag; **~ *the minute*** auf die Minute (genau); **10.** *Begleitung*: zu, nach: **~ *a guitar*** zu e-r Gitarre *singen*; **~ *a tune*** nach e-r Melodie *tanzen*; **11.** *zur Bildung des (betonten) Dativs*: **~ *me, you*** *etc.* mir, dir, Ihnen *etc.*; ***it seems ~ me*** es scheint mir; ***she was a good mother ~ him*** sie war ihm e-e gute Mutter; **12.** *zur Bezeichnung des Infinitivs*: **~ *be or not ~ be*** sein oder nicht sein; **~ *go*** gehen; ***I want ~ go*** ich möchte gehen; ***easy ~ understand*** leicht zu verstehen; ***years ~ come*** künftige Jahre; ***I want her ~ come*** ich will, daß sie kommt; **13.** *Zweck, Absicht*: um zu, zu: ***he only does it ~ earn money*** er tut es nur, um Geld zu verdienen; **14.** *zur Verkürzung des Nebensatzes*: ***I weep ~ think of it*** ich weine, wenn ich daran denke; ***he was the first ~ arrive*** er kam als erster; **~ *be honest, I should decline*** wenn ich ehrlich sein soll, muß ich ablehnen; **~ *hear him talk*** wenn man ihn (so) reden hört; **15.** *zur Andeutung e-s aus dem vorhergehenden zu ergänzenden Infinitivs*: ***I don't go because I don't want ~*** ich gehe nicht, weil ich nicht (gehen) will; **II** *adv.* [tu:] **16.** zu, geschlossen: ***pull the door ~*** die Tür zuziehen; **17.** *bei verschiedenen Verben*: dran; → ***fall to, put to*** *etc.*; **18.** zu Bewußtsein *od.* zu sich *kommen, bringen*; **19.** ⚓ nahe am Wind: ***keep her ~!***; **20.** **~ *and fro*** a) hin u. her, b) auf u. ab.
toad [təʊd] *s.* **1.** *zo.* Kröte *f*: ***a ~ under a***

harrow *fig.* ein geplagter Mensch; **2.** Ekel *n* (*Person*); **ˈ~ˌeat·ing I** *s.* Speichellecke'rei *f*; **II** *adj.* speichelleckerisch; **ˈ~·flax** *s.* ⚘ Leinkraut *n*; **ˌ~-in-the-ˈhole** *s. in Pfannkuchenteig gebakkene Würste*; **ˈ~·stool** *s. bot.* **1.** (größerer Blätter)Pilz; **2.** Giftpilz *m*.

toad·y [ˈtəʊdɪ] **I** *s.* Speichellecker *m*; **II** *v/i.* (*v/t.* vor *j-m*) kriechen *od.* scharˈwenzeln; **ˈtoad·y·ism** [-ɪɪzəm] *s.* Speichellecke'rei *f*.

to-and-fro [ˌtuːənˈfrəʊ] *s.* Hin u. Her *n*; Kommen u. Gehen *n*.

toast¹ [təʊst] **I** *s.* **1.** Toast *m*, geröstete (Weiß)Brotschnitte: ***have s.o. on ~*** *Brit. sl.* j-n ganz in der Hand haben; **II** *v/t.* **2.** toasten, rösten; **3.** sich *die Hände etc.* wärmen; **III** *v/i.* **4.** sich rösten *od.* toasten lassen; **5.** F sich *von der Sonne* braten lassen.

toast² [təʊst] **I** *s.* **1.** Trinkspruch *m*, Toast *m*: ***propose a ~ to s.o.*** e-n Toast auf j-n ausbringen; **2.** gefeierte Perˈson *od.* Sache; **II** *v/t.* **3.** toasten *od.* trinken auf (*acc.*); **III** *v/i.* **4.** toasten (***to*** auf *acc.*).

toast·er [ˈtəʊstə] *s.* Toaster *m*.

to·bac·co [təˈbækəʊ] *pl.* **-cos** *s.* **1.** *a.* ***~ plant*** Tabak(pflanze *f*) *m*; **2.** (Rauch-*etc.*)Tabak *m*: ***~ heart*** ⚕ Nikotinherz *n*; **toˈbac·co·nist** [-kənɪst] *s.* Tabak(waren)händler *m*: ***~'s*** (***shop***) Tabak(waren)laden *m*.

to·bog·gan [təˈbɒgən] **I** *s.* **1.** (Rodel-)Schlitten *m*; **2.** *Am.* Rodelhang *m*; **II** *v/i.* **3.** rodeln; **~ chute**, **~ slide** *s.* Rodelbahn *f*.

to·by [ˈtəʊbɪ] *s. a.* ***~ jug*** Bierkrug *m in Gestalt e-s dicken, alten Mannes*.

toc·sin [ˈtɒksɪn] *s.* **1.** Aˈlarm-, Sturmglocke *f*; **2.** Aˈlarm-, ˈWarnsiˌgnal *n*.

tod [tɒd] *s.*: ***on one's ~*** *Brit. sl.* allein.

to·day [təˈdeɪ] **I** *adv.* **1.** heute; **2.** heute, heutzutage; **II** *s.* **3.** heutiger Tag: ***~'s paper*** die heutige Zeitung, die Zeitung von heute; ***~'s rate*** † Tageskurs *m*; **4.** *das* Heute, heutige Zeit, Gegenwart *f*: ***of ~***, ***~'s*** von heute, heutig, Tages…, der Gegenwart.

tod·dle [ˈtɒdl] **I** *v/i.* **1.** watscheln (*bsd. kleine Kinder*); **2.** F (daˈhin)zotteln: ***~ off*** sich trollen, ‚abhauen'; **II** *s.* **3.** Watscheln *n*; **4.** F Bummel *m*; **5.** F → **ˈtod·dler** [-lə] *s.* Kleinkind *n*.

tod·dy [ˈtɒdɪ] *s.* Toddy *m*: a) *Art Grog*, b) Palmwein *m*.

to-do [təˈduː] *s.* F **1.** Lärm *m*; **2.** Geˈtue *n*, ‚Wirbel' *m*, ‚Theˈater' *n*: ***make much ~ about s.th.*** viel Wind um e-e Sache machen.

toe [təʊ] **I** *s.* **1.** *anat.* Zehe *f*: ***on one's ~s*** F ‚auf Draht'; ***turn one's ~s in*** (***out***) einwärts (auswärts) gehen; ***turn up one's ~s*** *sl.* ins Gras beißen; ***tread on s.o.'s ~s*** F *fig.* ‚j-m auf die Hühneraugen treten'; **2.** Vorderhuf *m* (*Pferd*); **3.** Spitze *f*, Kappe *f von Schuhen*, *Strümpfen etc.*; **4.** ⚙ a) (Well)Zapfen *m*, b) Nocken *m*, Daumen *m*, c) 🚂 Keil *m* (*Weiche*); **5.** *sport* Löffel *m* (*Golfschläger*); **II** *v/t.* **6.** a) *Strümpfe* mit neuen Spitzen versehen, b) *Schuhe* bekappen; **7.** mit den Zehen berühren: ***~ the line*** a) *a.* ***~ the mark*** in e-r Reihe (*sport* zum Start) antreten, b) *pol.* sich der Parteilinie unterwerfen, ‚spuren' (*a. weitS. gehorchen*); **8.** *sport den Ball* spitzeln; **9.** *sl. j-m* e-n (Fuß)Tritt versetzen; **10.** *Golf*: *Ball* mit dem Löffel schlagen; **ˈ~·board** *s. sport* Stoß-, Wurfbalken *m*; **ˈ~·cap** *s.* (Schuh)Kappe *f*.

-toed [təʊd] *in Zssgn* …zehig.

ˈtoe|ˌdanc·er *s.* Spitzentänzer(in); **ˈ~-hold** *s.* **1.** Halt *m* für die Zehen (*beim Klettern*); **2.** *fig.* a) Ansatzpunkt *m*, b) Brückenkopf *m*, ˈAusgangspositiˌon *f*: ***get a ~*** Fuß fassen; **3.** *Ringen*: Zehengriff *m*; **ˈ~·nail** *s.* Zehennagel *m*; **~ spin** *s.* ˈSpitzenpirouˌette *f*.

toff [tɒf] *s. Brit. sl.* ‚Fatzke' *m*.

tof·fee, **tof·fy** [ˈtɒfɪ] *s. Brit.* ˈSahnebonˌbon *m*, *n*, Toffee *n*: ***he can't shoot for ~*** F vom Schießen hat er keine Ahnung; ***not for ~*** F nicht für Geld u. gute Worte; **ˈ~-nosed** *adj.* F eingebildet.

tog [tɒg] F **I** *s. pl.* ‚Klaˈmotten' *pl*: ***golf ~s*** Golfdreß *m*; **II** *v/t.*: ***~ o.s. up*** sich ‚in Schale werfen'.

to·geth·er [təˈgeðə] **I** *adv.* **1.** zuˈsammen: ***call*** (***sew***) ***~*** zs.-rufen (-nähen); **2.** zu-, beiˈsammen, miteinˈander, gemeinsam; **3.** zusammen (genommen); **4.** miteinˈander *od.* gegeneinˈander: ***fight ~***; **5.** zuˈgleich, gleichzeitig, zusammen; **6.** *Tage etc.* nach-, hintereinˈander, *e-e Zeit* lang *od.* hinˈdurch: ***he talked for hours ~*** er sprach stundenlang; **7.** ***~ with*** zusammen *od.* gemeinsam mit, mit(samt); **II** *adj.* **8.** *Am. sl.* ausgeglichen (*Person*); **toˈgeth·er·ness** [-nɪs] *s. bsd. Am.* Zs.-gehörigkeit(sgefühl *n*) *f*; Einheit *f*; Nähe *f*.

tog·ger·y [ˈtɒgərɪ] → ***tog*** I.

tog·gle [ˈtɒgl] **I** *s.* **1.** ⚙, ⚓ Knebel *m*; **2.** *a.* ***~ joint*** ⚙ Knebel-, Kniegelenk *n*; **II** *v/t.* **3.** festknebeln; **~ switch** *s.* ↯ Kippschalter *m*.

toil¹ [tɔɪl] *s. mst pl. fig.* Schlingen *pl.*, Netz *n*: ***in the ~s of*** a) in den Schlingen *od.* Fängen *des Satans etc.*, b) in *Schulden etc.* verstrickt.

toil² [tɔɪl] **I** *s.* (mühselige) Arbeit, Mühe *f*, Plage *f*, Plackeˈrei *f*; **II** *v/i. a.* ***~ and moil*** sich abmühen *od.* abplacken *od.* quälen (***at***, ***on*** mit): ***~ up a hill*** e-n Berg mühsam erklimmen; **ˈtoil·er** [-lə] *s. fig.* Arbeitstier *n*, Schwerarbeiter *m*.

toi·let [ˈtɔɪlɪt] *s.* **1.** Toiˈlette *f*, Kloˈsett *n*; **2.** Friˈsier-, Toiˈlettentisch *m*; **3.** Toiˈlette *f* (*Ankleiden etc.*): ***make one's ~*** Toilette machen; **4.** Toiˈlette *f*, Kleidung *f*, *a.* (Abend)Kleid *n od.* (Gesellschafts)Anzug *m*; **~ bag** *s.* Kulˈturbeutel *m*; **~ case** *s.* ˈReiseneceˌssaire *n*; **~ pa·per** *s.* Toiˈletten-, Kloˈsettpaˌpier *n*; **~ pow·der** *s.* Körperpuder *m*; **~ roll** *s.* Rolle *f* Kloˈsettpaˌpier.

toi·let·ry [ˈtɔɪlɪtrɪ] *s.* Toiˈlettenarˌtikel *pl.*

toi·let| set *s.* Toiˈlettengarniˌtur *f*; **~ soap** *s.* Toiˈlettenseife *f*; **~ ta·ble** → ***toilet*** 2.

toil·ful [ˈtɔɪlfʊl], **ˈtoil·some** [-səm] *adj.* □ mühsam, -selig; **ˈtoil·some·ness** [-səmnɪs] *s.* Mühseligkeit *f*.

ˈtoil·worn *adj.* abgearbeitet.

To·kay [təʊˈkeɪ] *s.* Toˈkaier *m* (*Wein u. Traube*).

to·ken [ˈtəʊkən] **I** *s.* **1.** Zeichen *n*: a) Anzeichen *n*, Merkmal *n*, b) Beweis *m*: ***as a*** (*od.* ***in***) ***~ of*** als *od.* zum Zeichen (*gen.*); ***by the same ~*** a) aus dem gleichen Grunde, mit demselben Recht, umgekehrt, b) ferner, überdies; **2.** Andenken *n*, (Erinnerungs)Geschenk *n*, (ˈUnter)Pfand *n*; **3.** *hist.* Scheidemünze *f*; **4.** (Meˈtall)Marke *f* (*als Fahrausweis*); **5.** Spielmarke *f*; **6.** Gutschein *m*, Bon *m*; **II** *adj.* **7.** nomiˈnell: ***~ money*** a) Scheidemünzen *pl.*, b) Not-, Ersatzgeld *n*; ***~ payment*** symbolische Zahlung; ***~ strike*** (kurzer) Warnstreik; **8.** Alibi…: ***~ negro***; ***~ woman***; **9.** Schein…: ***~ raid*** Scheinangriff *m*.

told [təʊld] *pret. u. p.p. von* ***tell***.

tol·er·a·ble [ˈtɒlərəbl] *adj.* □ **1.** erträglich; **2.** *fig.* leidlich, mittelmäßig, erträglich; **3.** F ‚einigermaßen' (*gesund*), ‚so laˈla'; **ˈtol·er·a·ble·ness** [-nɪs] *s.* Erträglichkeit *f*; **ˈtol·er·ance** [-rəns] *s.* **1.** Toleˈranz *f*, Duldsamkeit *f*; **2.** (***of***) a) Duldung *f* (*gen.*), b) Nachsicht *f* (mit); **3.** ⚕ a) Toleˈranz *f*, ˈWiderstandsfähigkeit *f* (***for*** gegen), b) Verträglichkeit *f*; **4.** ⚙ Toleˈranz *f*, zulässige Abweichung, Spiel *n*, Fehlergrenze *f*; **ˈtol·er·ant** [-rənt] *adj.* □ **1.** toleˈrant, duldsam (***of*** gegen); **2.** geduldig, nachsichtig (***of*** mit); **3.** ⚕ ˈwiderstandsfähig (***of*** gegen); **tol·er·ate** [ˈtɒləreɪt] *v/t.* **1.** *j-n od. et.* dulden, tolerieren, *et. a.* zulassen, hinnehmen, *a. j-s Gesellschaft* ertragen; **2.** duldsam *od.* toleˈrant sein gegen; **3.** *bsd.* ⚕ vertragen; **tol·er·a·tion** [ˌtɒləˈreɪʃn] *s.* **1.** Duldung *f*; **2.** → ***tolerance*** 1.

toll¹ [təʊl] **I** *v/t.* **1.** *bsd. Totenglocke* läuten, erschallen lassen; **2.** *Stunde* schlagen; **3.** (durch Glockengeläut) verkünden; die Totenglocke läuten für *j-n*; **II** *v/i.* **4.** a) läuten, schallen, b) schlagen (*Glocke*); **III** *s.* **5.** Geläut *n*; **6.** Glokkenschlag *m*.

toll² [təʊl] *s.* **1.** *hist.* (*bsd.* Wege-, Brükken)Zoll *m*; **2.** Straßenbenutzungsgebühr *f*, Maut *f*; **3.** Standgeld *n auf dem Markt etc.*; **4.** *Am.* Hafengebühr *f*; **5.** *teleph. Am.* Gebühr *f* für ein Ferngespräch; **6.** *fig.* Triˈbut *m an Menschenleben etc.*, (Blut)Zoll *m*, (Zahl *f* der) Todesopfer *pl.*: ***the ~ of the road*** die Verkehrsopfer *od.* -unfälle; ***take its ~ of*** *fig. j-n* arg mitnehmen, s-n Tribut fordern von *j-m od. e-r Sache*, *Kräfte*, *Vorräte etc.* strapazieren; ***take a ~ of 100 lives*** 100 Todesopfer fordern (*Katastrophe*); **~ bar** → ***toll gate***; **~ call** *s. teleph.* **1.** *Am.* Ferngespräch *n*; **2.** *Brit. obs.* Nahverkehrsgespräch *n*; **~ gate** *s.* Schlagbaum *m e-r Mautstraße*; **ˈ~·house** *s.* Mautstelle *f*; **~ road** *s.*, **ˈ~·way** *s.* gebührenpflichtige Straße, Mautstraße *f*.

tol·u·ene [ˈtɒljʊiːn], **ˈtol·u·ol** [-jʊɒl] *s.* ⚗ Toluˈol *n*.

tom [tɒm] *s.* **1.** Männchen *n kleinerer Tiere*: ***~ turkey*** Truthahn *m*, Puter *m*; **2.** Kater *m*; **3.** ℒ *abbr. für* ***Thomas***: ***ℒ and Jerry*** *Am.* Eiergrog *m*; ***ℒ, Dick, and Harry*** Hinz u. Kunz; ***ℒ Thumb*** Däumling *m*.

tom·a·hawk [ˈtɒməhɔːk] **I** *s.* Tomahawk *m*, Kriegsbeil *n der Indianer*: ***bury*** (***dig up***) ***the ~*** *fig.* das Kriegsbeil begraben (ausgraben); **II** *v/t.* mit dem Tomahawk (er)schlagen.

to·ma·to [təˈmɑːtəʊ] *pl.* **-toes** *s.* ⚘ Toˈmate *f*.

tomb [tuːm] *s.* **1.** Grab(stätte *f*) *n*; **2.** Grabmal *n*, Gruft *f*; **3.** *fig. das* Grab, *der* Tod.

tom·bac, **tom·bak** ['tɒmbæk] *s. metall.* Tombak *m.*
tom·bo·la [tɒm'bəʊlə] *s.* Tombola *f.*
tom·boy ['tɒmbɔɪ] *s.* Wildfang *m*, Range *f* (*Mädchen*); '**tom·boy·ish** [-bɔɪɪʃ] *adj.* ausgelassen, wild.
'**tomb·stone** ['tu:m-] *s.* Grabstein *m.*
'**tom·cat** *s.* Kater *m.*
tome [təʊm] *s.* **1.** Band *m e-s Werkes*; **2.** (dicker) Wälzer (*Buch*).
tom·fool [ˌtɒm'fu:l] **I** *s.* Einfaltspinsel *m*, Narr *m*; **II** *adj.* dumm; **III** *v/i.* (he'rum-)albern; **tom·fool·er·y** [tɒm'fu:lərɪ] *s.* Albernheit *f*, Unsinn *m.*
tom·my ['tɒmɪ] *s.* **1.** a) *a.* ♀ ***Atkins*** Tommy *m* (*der brit. Soldat*), b) *a.* ♀ F Tommy *m*, *brit.* Landser *m* (*einfacher Soldat*); **2.** *dial.* ‚Fres'salien' *pl.*, Verpflegung *f*; **3.** ⚙ a) (verstellbarer) Schraubenschlüssel, b) *a.* ~ ***bar*** Knebelgriff *m*; ♀ **gun** *s.* ⚔ Ma'schinenpiˌstole *f*; ˌ~'**rot** *s.* F (purer) Blödsinn, Quatsch *m.*
to·mor·row [tə'mɒrəʊ] **I** *adv.* morgen: ~ ***week*** morgen in e-r Woche *od.* acht Tagen; ~ ***morning*** morgen früh; ~ ***night*** morgen abend; **II** *s. der* morgige Tag, *das* Morgen: ~***'s paper*** die morgige Zeitung; ~ ***never comes*** das werden wir nie erleben; ***the day after*** ~ übermorgen.
'**tom·tit** *s. orn.* (Blau)Meise *f.*
ton[1] [tʌn] *s.* **1.** *engl.* Tonne *f* (*Gewicht*): a) *a.* ***long*** ~ *bsd. Brit.* = *2240 lbs. od. 1016,05 kg*, b) *a.* ***short*** ~ *bsd. Am.* = *2000 lbs. od. 907,18 kg*, c) *a.* ***metric*** ~ metrische Tonne (= *2205 lbs. od. 1000 kg*); **2.** ⚓ Tonne *f* (*Raummaß*): a) ***register*** ~ Registertonne (= *100 cubic feet od. 2,83 m³*), b) ***gross register*** ~ Bruttoregistertonne (*Schiffsgrößenangabe*); **3.** ***weigh a*** ~ F ‚wahnsinnig' schwer sein; **4.** *pl.* e-e Unmenge (***of money*** Geld): ~***s of times*** ‚tausendmal'; **5.** ***do the*** ~ *Brit. sl.* a) mit 100 Meilen fahren, b) 100 Meilen schaffen (*Auto etc.*).
ton[2] [tɔ̃:ŋ] (*Fr.*) *s.* **1.** *die* (herrschende) Mode; **2.** Ele'ganz *f*: ***in the*** ~ modisch, elegant.
ton·al ['təʊnl] *adj.* □ ♪ **1.** Ton..., tonlich; **2.** to'nal; **to·nal·i·ty** [təʊ'nælətɪ] *s.* **1.** ♪ a) Tonali'tät *f*, Tonart *f*, b) 'Ton-, 'Klangchaˌrakter *m*; **2.** *paint.* Farbton *m*, Tönung *f.*
tone [təʊn] **I** *s.* **1.** *allg.* Ton *m*, Klang *m*: ***heart*** ~***s*** ⚕ Herztöne; **2.** Ton *m*, Stimme *f*: ***in an angry*** ~ in ärgerlichem Ton, mit zorniger Stimme; **3.** *ling.* a) Tonfall *m*, b) Tonhöhe *f*, Betonung *f*; **4.** ♪ a) Ton *m*, b) *Am.* Note *f*, c) Klang(farbe *f*) *m*; **5.** *paint.* (Farb)Ton *m*, Tönung *f* (*a. fig.*); **6.** ⚕ a) Tonus *m der Muskeln*, b) *fig.* Spannkraft *f*; **7.** *fig.* Geist *m*, Haltung *f*; **8.** Stimmung *f* (*a. Börse*); **9.** a) Ton *m*, Note *f*, Stil *m*, b) Ni'veau *n*: ***set the*** ~ ***of*** a) den Ton angeben für, b) den Stil *e-r Sache* bestimmen; ***raise*** (***lower***) ***the*** ~ (***of***) das Niveau (*gen.*) heben (senken); ***give*** ~ ***to*** Niveau verleihen (*dat.*); **II** *v/t.* **10.** e-n Ton verleihen (*dat.*), e-e Färbung geben (*dat.*); **11.** *Farbe etc.* abtönen: ~ ***down*** *Farbe*, *fig. Zorn etc.* dämpfen, mildern; ~ ***up*** *paint. u. fig.* (ver)stärken; **12.** *phot.* tonen; **13.** *fig.* a) 'umformen, -modeln, b) regeln; **III** *v/i.* **14.** *a.* ~ ***in*** (***with***) a) verschmelzen (mit), b) harmonieren (mit), passen (zu) (*bsd. Farbe*); **15.** ~ ***down*** sich mildern *od.* abschwächen; **16.** ~ ***up*** stärker werden; ~ **arm** *s.* Tonarm *m am Plattenspieler*; ~ **con·trol** *s.* ⚡ Klangregler *m.*
tone·less ['təʊnlɪs] *adj.* □ **1.** tonlos (*a. Stimme*); **2.** ausdruckslos.
tone po·em *s.* ♪ Tondichtung *f.*
tongs [tɒŋz] *s. pl. sg. konstr.* Zange *f*: ***a pair of*** ~ eine Zange; ***I would not touch that with a pair of*** ~ a) das würde ich nicht mal mit e-r Zange anfassen, b) *fig.* mit dieser Sache möchte ich nichts zu tun haben.
tongue [tʌŋ] **I** *s.* **1.** *anat.* Zunge *f* (*a. fig. Redeweise*): ***malicious*** ~***s*** böse Zungen; ***have a long*** (***ready***) ~ geschwätzig (schlagfertig) sein; ***find one's*** ~ die Sprache wiederfinden; ***give*** ~ a) sich laut u. deutlich äußern (***to*** zu), b) anschlagen (*Hund*), c) Laut geben (*Jagdhund*); ***hold one's*** ~ den Mund halten; ***keep a civil*** ~ ***in one's head*** höflich bleiben; ***put one's*** ~ ***out*** (***at s.o.***) (j-m) die Zunge herausstrecken; ***with*** (***one's***) ~ ***in*** (***one's***) ***cheek*** → ***tongue-in-cheek***; → ***wag*** 1; **2.** Sprache *f e-s Volkes*, Zunge *f*; **3.** *fig.* Zunge *f* (*Schuh*, *Flamme*, *Klarinette etc.*); **4.** (Glocken)Klöppel *m*; **5.** (Wagen-)Deichsel *f*; **6.** ⚙ Feder *f*, Spund *m*: ~ ***and groove*** Feder u. Nut; **7.** Dorn *m* (*Schnalle*); **8.** Zeiger *m* (*Waage*); **9.** ⚡ (Re'lais)Anker *m*; **10.** *geogr.* Landzunge *f*; **II** *v/t.* **11.** ♪ mit Flatterzunge blasen; **12.** ⚙ verzapfen; **tongued** [-ŋd] *adj.* **1.** *in Zssgn* ...züngig; **2.** ⚙ gefedert, gezapft.
ˌ**tongue**|**-in-'cheek** *adj.* **1.** i'ronisch; **2.** mit Hintergedanken; '~-ˌ**lash·ing** *s.* F Standpauke *f*; '~**-tied** *adj.* stumm, sprachlos (*vor Verlegenheit etc.*): ***be*** ~ keinen Ton herausbringen; ~ **twist·er** *s.* Zungenbrecher *m.*
ton·ic ['tɒnɪk] **I** *adj.* (□ ~***ally***) **1.** ⚕ tonisch: ~ ***spasm*** Starrkrampf *m*; **2.** ⚕ stärkend, belebend (*a. fig.*): ~ ***water*** Tonic *n*; **3.** *ling.* Ton...: ~ ***accent*** musikalischer Akzent; **4.** ♪ Tonika..., (Grund)Ton...: ~ ***chord*** Grundakkord *m*; ~ ***major*** gleichnamige Dur-Tonart; ~ ***sol-fa*** Tonika-Do-System *n*; **5.** *paint.* Tönungs..., Farbgebungs...; **II** *s.* **6.** ⚕ Stärkungsmittel *n*, Tonikum *n*; **7.** Tonic *n* (*Getränk*); **8.** *fig.* Stimulans *n*; **9.** ♪ Grundton *m*, Tonika *f*; **10.** *ling.* stimmhafter Laut; **to·nic·i·ty** [təʊ'nɪsətɪ] *s.* **1.** → ***tone*** 6; **2.** musi'kalischer Ton.
to·night [tə'naɪt] **I** *adv.* **1.** heute abend; **2.** heute nacht; **II** *s.* **3.** der heutige Abend; **4.** diese Nacht.
ton·nage ['tʌnɪdʒ] *s.* **1.** ⚓ Ton'nage *f*, Tonnengehalt *m*, Schiffsraum *m*; **2.** ⚓ Ge'samttonˌnage *f e-s Landes*; **3.** ⚓ Tonnengeld *n*; **4.** ⚙ (Ge'samt)Produktiˌon *f* (*Stahl etc.*).
tonne [tʌn] *s.* metrische Tonne.
ton·neau ['tɒnəʊ] *pl.* **-neaus** (*Fr.*) *s. mot.* hinterer Teil (*mit Rücksitzen*) e-s Autos.
ton·ner ['tʌnə] *s.* ⚓ *in Zssgn* ...tonner, *ein* Schiff von ... Tonnen.
to·nom·e·ter [təʊ'nɒmɪtə] *s.* **1.** ♪, *phys.* Tonhöhenmesser *m*; **2.** ⚕ Blutdruckmesser *m.*
ton·sil ['tɒnsl] *s. anat.* Mandel *f*; '**ton·sil·lar** [-sɪlə] *adj.* Mandel...; **ton·sil·lec·to·my** [ˌtɒnsɪ'lektəmɪ] *s.* ⚕ Mandelentfernung *f*; **ton·sil·li·tis** [ˌtɒnsɪ'laɪtɪs] *s.* ⚕ Mandelentzündung *f.*
ton·so·ri·al [tɒn'sɔ:rɪəl] *adj. mst humor.* Barbier...: ~ ***artist*** ‚Figaro' *m.*
ton·sure ['tɒnʃə] *eccl.* **I** *s.* **1.** Tonsurierung *f*; **2.** Ton'sur *f*; **II** *v/t.* **3.** tonsurieren.
to·ny ['təʊnɪ] *adj. Am.* F (tod)schick.
too [tu:] *adv.* **1.** (*vorangestellt*) zu, allzu: ***all*** ~ ***familiar*** allzu vertraut; ~ ***fond of comfort*** zu sehr auf Bequemlichkeit bedacht; ~ ***many*** zu viele; ***none*** ~ ***pleasant*** nicht gerade angenehm; **2.** F sehr, äußerst: ***it is*** ~ ***kind of you***; **3.** (*nachgestellt*) auch, ebenfalls.
took [tʊk] *pret. von* ***take***.
tool [tu:l] **I** *s.* **1.** Werkzeug *n*, Gerät *n*, Instru'ment *n*: ~***s*** *pl. a.* Handwerkszeug *n*; ***gardener's*** ~***s*** Gartengerät; **2.** ⚙ (Bohr-, Schneide- *etc.*)Werkzeug *n e-r Maschine*, *a.* Arbeits-, Drehstahl *m*; **3.** ⚙ a) 'Werkzeugmaˌschine *f*, b) Drehbank *f*; **4.** *typ.* a) 'Stempelfiˌgur *f* (*Punzarbeit*), b) (Präge)Stempel *m*; **5.** *pl. fig.* a) Handwerkszeug *n* (*Bücher etc.*), b) Rüstzeug *n* (*Fachwissen*); **6.** *fig. contp.* Werkzeug *n*, Handlanger *m*, Krea'tur *f e-s anderen*; **7.** V ‚Appa'rat' *m* (*Penis*); **II** *v/t.* **8.** ⚙ bearbeiten; **9.** *mst* ~ ***up*** *Fabrik* (maschi'nell) ausstatten, -rüsten; **10.** *Bucheinband* punzen; **11.** *sl.* ‚kutschieren' (*fahren*); **III** *v/i.* **12.** *mst* ~ ***up*** ⚙ sich (maschi'nell) ausrüsten (***for*** für); **13.** *a.* ~ ***along*** *sl.* (da'hin-, her'um)gondeln; ~ **bag** *s.* Werkzeugtasche *f*; ~ **bit** *s.* ⚙ Werkzeugspitze *f*; ~ **box** *s.* Werkzeugkasten *m*; ~ **car·ri·er** *s.* ⚙ Werkzeugschlitten *m*; ~ **en·gi·neer·ing** *s.* Arbeitsvorbereitung *f.*
tool·ing ['tu:lɪŋ] *s.* ⚙ **1.** Bearbeitung *f*; **2.** Einrichten *n e-r Werkzeugmaschine*; **3.** maschi'nelle Ausrüstung; **4.** *Buchbinderei*: Punzarbeit *f.*
'**tool**|ˌ**mak·er** *s.* Werkzeugmacher *m*; '~**-post** *s.* Schneidstahlhalter *m.*
toot [tu:t] *v/i.* **1.** (*a. v/t. et.*) tuten, blasen; **2.** hupen (*Auto*).
tooth [tu:θ] **I** *pl.* **teeth** [ti:θ] *s.* **1.** *anat.* Zahn *m*: ~ ***and nail*** *fig.* verbissen, erbittert (*be*)*kämpfen*; ***armed to the teeth*** bis an die Zähne bewaffnet; ***in the teeth of*** *fig.* a) gegen *Widerstand etc.* b) trotz *od.* ungeachtet *der Gefahr etc.*; ***cut one's teeth*** zahnen; ***draw the teeth of*** *fig.* a) *j-n* beruhigen, b) *j-n* ungefährlich machen, c) *e-r Sache* die Spitze nehmen, *et.* entschärfen; ***get one's teeth into*** sich an *e-e Arbeit etc.* ‚ranmachen'; ***have a sweet*** ~ gerne Süßigkeiten essen *od.* naschen; ***put teeth into*** (den nötigen) Nachdruck verleihen (*dat.*); ***set s.o.'s teeth on edge*** j-m auf die Nerven gehen *od.* ‚weh' tun; ***show one's teeth*** (***to***) a) die Zähne fletschen (gegen), b) *fig. j-m* die Zähne zeigen; **2.** Zahn *m e-s Kammes*, *e-r Säge*, *e-s Zahnrads etc.*; **3.** (Gabel)Zinke *f*; **II** *v/t.* **4.** *Rad etc.* bezahnen; **5.** *Brett* verzahnen; **III** *v/i.* **6.** inein'andergreifen (*Zahnräder*); '~**-ache** *s.* Zahnweh *n*; '~**-brush** *s.* Zahnbürste *f*; '~**-comb** *s.* Staubkamm *m*; ~ **de·cay** *s.* Zahnverfall *m.*
toothed [tu:θt] *adj.* **1.** mit Zähnen (versehen), Zahn..., gezahnt: ~ ***wheel*** Zahnrad *n*; **2.** ⚘ gezähnt, gezackt (*Blattrand*); **3.** ⚙ verzahnt; '**tooth·less**

[-θlɪs] *adj.* zahnlos.

ˈ**tooth|·paste** *s.* Zahnpasta *f*; ˈ**~·pick** *s.* Zahnstocher *m*; **~ pow·der** *s.* Zahnpulver *n*.

tooth·some [ˈtu:θsəm] *adj.* □ lecker (*a. fig.*).

too·tle [ˈtu:tl] *v/i.* **1.** tuten, dudeln; **2.** *Am.* F quatschen; **3.** F a) (herˈum)gondeln, b) ‚(daˈhin)zotteln': **~ *off*** sich trollen.

toot·sy(-woot·sy) [ˌtʊtsɪ(ˈwʊtsɪ)] *s. Kindersprache*: Füßchen *n*.

top¹ [tɒp] **I** *s.* **1.** ober(st)es Ende, Oberteil *n*; Spitze *f*, Gipfel *m e-s Berges etc.*; Krone *f*, Wipfel *m des Baumes*; (Haus-)Giebel *m*, Dach(spitze *f*) *n*; Kopf(ende *n*) *m des Tisches, e-r Buchseite etc.*: ***at the ~*** oben(an); ***at the ~ of*** oben an (*dat.*); ***at the ~ of one's speed*** mit höchster Geschwindigkeit; ***at the ~ of one's voice*** aus vollem Halse; ***page 20 at the ~*** auf Seite 20 oben; ***on ~*** oben (-auf); ***on (the) ~ of*** oben auf (*dat.*), über (*dat.*); ***on ~ of each other*** auf- *od.* übereinander; ***on (the) ~ of it*** obendrein; ***go over the ~*** a) ⚔ zum Sturmangriff (*aus dem Schützengraben*) antreten, b) *fig.* es maßlos übertreiben; **2.** *fig.* Spitze *f*, erste *od.* höchste Stelle; ˈSpitzenpositiˌon *f*: ***the ~ of the class*** der Primus der Klasse; ***the ~ of the tree*** (*od.* ***ladder***) *fig.* die höchste Stellung, der Gipfel des Erfolgs; ***at the ~*** an der Spitze; ***be on ~ (of the world)*** obenauf sein; ***come out on ~*** als Sieger *od.* Bester hervorgehen; ***come to the ~*** an die Spitze kommen, sich durchsetzen; ***get on ~ of s.th.*** e-r Sache Herr werden; **3.** *fig.* Gipfel *m*, *das* Äußerste *od.* Höchste; **4.** Scheitel *m*, Kopf *m*: ***from ~ to toe*** von Kopf bis Fuß; ***blow one's ~*** *sl.* ‚hochgehen', e-n Wutanfall haben; **5.** Oberfläche *f des Tisches, Wassers etc.*; **6.** *mot. etc.* Verdeck *n*; **7.** (Bett)Himmel *m*; **8.** (Möbel)Aufsatz *m*; **9.** ⚓ Mars *m, f*, Topp *m*; **10.** (Schuh)Oberleder *n*; **11.** Stulpe *f* (*Stiefel, Handschuh*); **12.** (Topf- *etc.*)Dekkel *m*; **13.** ⚘ a) (oberer Teil e-r) Pflanze *f* (*Ggs. Wurzel*), b) *mst pl.* (Rüben- *etc.*)Kraut *n*; **14.** Blume *f des Bieres*; **15.** *mot.* → ***top gear***; **II** *adj.* **16.** oberst: ***~ line*** Kopf-, Titelzeile *f*; ***the ~ rung*** *fig.* oberste Stelle, höchste Stellung; **17.** höchst: ***~ earner*** Spitzenverdiener(in); ***~ efficiency*** ⚙ Spitzenleistung *f*; ***~ price*** Höchstpreis *m*; ***~ speed*** Höchstgeschwindigkeit *f*; ***~ secret*** streng geheim; **18.** *der* (*die, das*) erste; **19.** Haupt...; **III** *v/t.* **20.** (oben) bedecken; krönen; **21.** überˈragen; **22.** *fig.* überˈtreffen, -ˈragen; **23.** die Spitze (*gen.*) erreichen; **24.** an der Spitze *der Klasse, e-r Liste etc.* stehen; **25.** überˈsteigen; **26.** ⚒ stutzen, kappen; **27.** *Hindernis* nehmen; **28.** *Golf*: *Ball* oben schlagen; **~ off** *v/t.* F *et.* abschließen *od.* krönen (***with*** mit); **~ out I** *v/i.* Richtfest feiern; **II** *v/t.* das Richtfest (*gen.*) feiern: ***~ a building***; **~ up** *v/t.* **1.** auf-, nachfüllen; **2.** F *j-m* nachschenken.

top² [tɒp] *s.* Kreisel *m* (*Spielzeug*).

to·paz [ˈtəʊpæz] *s. min.* Toˈpas *m*.

top| boot *s.* (kniehoher) Stiefel, Stulpenstiefel *m*; ˈ**~·coat** ˈÜberzieher *m*, Mantel *m*; **~ dog** *s.* F *fig.* **1.** *der* Herr *od.* Überˈlegene; *der* Sieger; **2.** ‚Chef' *m*, *der* Oberste; **3.** *der* (*die, das*) Beste; **~ draw·er** *s.* **1.** oberste Schublade; **2.** F *fig. die* oberen Zehntausend: ***he does not come from the ~*** er kommt nicht aus vornehmster Familie; ˌ**~-ˈdraw·er** *adj.* F **1.** vornehm; **2.** best; **~ dress·ing** *s.* **1.** ⚒ Kopfdüngung *f*; **2.** ⚙ Oberflächenbeschotterung *f*.

tope¹ [təʊp] *v/t. u. v/i.* ‚saufen'.

tope² [təʊp] *s. ichth.* Glatthai *m*.

to·pee [ˈtəʊpi:] *s.* Tropenhelm *m*.

top·er [ˈtəʊpə] *s.* Säufer *m*, Zecher *m*.

ˈ**top|·flight** *adj.* F erstklassig, prima; ˈ**~ˌflight·er** → ***topnotcher***; **~·gal·lant** [ˌtɒpˈgælənt; ⚓ təˈg-] ⚓ **I** *s.* Bramsegel *n*; **II** *adj.* Bram...: ***~ sail***; **~ gear** *s. mot.* höchster Gang; **~ hat** *s.* Zyˈlinder(hut) *m*; ˌ**~-ˈheav·y** *adj.* **1.** oberlastig (*Gefäß etc.*); **2.** ⚓ topplastig; **3.** ✈ kopflastig; **4.** ☤ a) ˈüberbewertet (*Wertpapiere*), b) ˈüberkapitalisiert (*Unternehmen*); ˌ**~-ˈhole** → ***topflight***.

top·ic [ˈtɒpɪk] *s.* **1.** Thema *n*, Gegenstand *m*; **2.** *phls.* Topik *f*; ˈ**top·i·cal** [-kl] **I** *adj.* □ **1.** örtlich, loˈkal (*a.* ⚕): ***~ colo(u)rs*** topische Farben; **2.** a) aktuˈell, b) zeitkritisch: ***~ song*** Lied *n* mit aktuellen Anspielungen; **3.** theˈmatisch; **II** *s.* **4.** aktuˈeller Film; **top·i·cal·i·ty** [ˌtɒpɪˈkælətɪ] *s.* aktuˈelle *od.* loˈkale Bedeutung.

top| kick *Am. sl. für* → ***top sergeant***; ˈ**~·knot** *s.* **1.** Haarknoten *m*; **2.** *orn.* (Feder)Haube *f*, Schopf *m*.

top·less [ˈtɒplɪs] *adj.* **1.** ohne Kopf; **2.** ˈOben-ˈohne...: ***~ dress*** (***night club, waitress***).

ˌ**top|-ˈline** *adj.* **1.** promiˈnent; **2.** wichtigst: ***~ news***; ˌ**~ˈlin·er** *s.* F Promiˈnente(r *m*) *f*; ˈ**~·mast** [-mɑ:st; -məst] *s.* ⚓ (Mars)Stenge *f*; ˈ**~·most** *adj.* höchst, oberst; ˌ**~ˈnotch** *adj.* F prima, erstklassig; ˌ**~ˈnotch·er** *s.* F ‚Kaˈnone' *f* (*Könner*).

to·pog·ra·pher [təˈpɒgrəfə] *s. geogr.* Topoˈgraph *m*; **top·o·graph·ic, top·o·graph·i·cal** [ˌtɒpəˈgræfɪk(l)] *adj.* □ topoˈgraphisch; **toˈpog·ra·phy** [-fɪ] *s.* **1.** *geogr., a.* ⚕ Topograˈphie *f*; **2.** ⚔ Geländekunde *f*.

top·per [ˈtɒpə] *s.* **1.** ⛏ oberer Stein; **2.** ☤ F (obenˈaufliegendes) Schaustück (*Obst etc.*); **3.** F Zyˈlinder *m* (*Hut*); **4.** F a) ‚(tolles) Ding', b) ‚Pfundskerl' *m*;

top·ping [ˈtɒpɪŋ] *adj.* □ F prima, fabelhaft.

top·ple [ˈtɒpl] **I** *v/i.* **1.** wackeln; **2.** kippen, stürzen, purzeln: ***~ down*** (*od.* ***over***) umkippen, hinpurzeln, niederstürzen; **II** *v/t.* **3.** ins Wanken bringen, stürzen: ***~ over*** *et.* umstürzen, -kippen; **4.** *fig. Regierung* stürzen.

tops [tɒps] *adj.* F prima, erstklassig, ‚super'.

top|·sail [ˈtɒpsl] *s.* ⚓ Marssegel *n*; **~ saw·yer** *s.* F *fig.* ‚hohes Tier'; ˌ**~-ˈse·cret** *adj.* streng geheim; **~ ser·geant** *s.* ⚔ *Am.* F Hauptfeldwebel *m*, ‚Spieß' *m*; ˈ**~·soil** *s.* ⚒ Ackerkrume *f*, Mutterboden *m*.

top·sy·tur·vy [ˌtɒpsɪˈtɜ:vɪ] **I** *adv.* **1.** das Oberste zuˈunterst, auf den Kopf: ***turn everything ~*** alles auf den Kopf stellen; **2.** kopfˈüber kopfˈunter *fallen*; **3.** drunter u. drüber, verkehrt; **II** *adj.* **4.** auf den Kopf gestellt, in wildem Durcheinˈander, chaˈotisch; **III** *s.* **5.** (wildes *od.* heilloses) Durcheinˈander, Kuddelmuddel *m, n*; ˌ**top·syˈtur·vy·dom** [-dəm] → ***topsyturvy*** 5.

toque [təʊk] *s.* **1.** *hist.* Baˈrett *n*; **2.** Toque *f* (*randloser Damenhut*).

tor [tɔ:] *s. Brit.* Felsturm *m*.

to·ra(h) [ˈtɔ:rə] *s.* **1.** ☩ *das* Gesetz Mosis; **2.** Thoˈra *f*.

torch [tɔ:tʃ] *s.* **1.** Fackel *f* (*a. fig. der Wissenschaft etc.*): ***carry a ~ for*** *Am. fig.* Mädchen (von ferne) verehren; **2.** *a.* ***electric ~*** *Brit.* Taschenlampe *f*; **3.** ⚙ a) Schweißbrenner *m*, b) → ***torch lamp***; **4.** *Am.* Brandstifter *m*; ˈ**~ˌbear·er** *s.* Fackelträger *m* (*a. fig.*); **~ lamp** *s.* ⚙ Lötlampe *f*; ˈ**~·light** *s.* Fackelschein *m*: ***~ procession*** Fackelzug *m*; **~ pine** *s.* ⚘ (Amer.) Pechkiefer *f*; **~ sing·er** *s.* Schnulzensänger(in); **~ song** *s.* ‚Schnulze' *f*, sentimenˈtales Liebeslied.

tore [tɔ:] *pret. von* ***tear²***.

tor·e·a·dor [ˈtɒrɪədɔ:] (*Span.*) *s.* Toreaˈdor *m*, berittener Stierkämpfer.

to·re·ro [tɒˈreərəʊ] *pl.* **-ros** (*Span.*) *s.* Toˈrero *m*, Stierkämpfer *m* (*zu Fuß*).

tor·ment I *v/t.* [tɔ:ˈment] **1.** *bsd. fig.* quälen, peinigen, foltern, plagen (***with*** mit): ***~ed with*** gequält *od.* gepeinigt von *Zweifel etc.*; **II** *s.* [ˈtɔ:ment] **2.** Qual *f*, Pein *f*, Marter *f*: ***be in ~*** Qualen ausstehen; **3.** Plage *f*; **4.** Quälgeist *m*; **torˈmen·tor** [-tə] *s.* **1.** Peiniger *m*; **2.** Quälgeist *m*; **3.** ⚓ lange Fleischgabel; **4.** *thea.* vordere Kuˈlisse; **torˈmen·tress** [-trɪs] *s.* Peinigerin *f*.

torn [tɔ:n] *p.p. von* ***tear²***.

tor·na·do [tɔ:ˈneɪdəʊ] *pl.* **-does** *s.* **1.** Torˈnado *m*: a) *Wirbelsturm in den USA*, b) *tropisches Wärmegewitter*; **2.** *fig.* a) (Beifall-, Proˈtest)Sturm *m*, b) Wirbelwind *m* (*Person*).

tor·pe·do [tɔ:ˈpi:dəʊ] **I** *pl.* **-does** *s.* **1.** ⚓ Torˈpedo *m*; **2.** *a.* ***aerial ~*** ✈ ˈLufttorˌpedo *m*; **3.** *a.* ***toy ~*** Knallerbse *f*; **4.** *ichth.* Zitterrochen *m*; **5.** *Am. sl.* ‚Killer' *m*; **II** *v/t.* **6.** torpedieren (*a. fig. vereiteln*); **~ boat** *s.* ⚓ Torˈpedoboot *n*; **~ plane** *s.* ⚔ Torˈpedoflugzeug *n*; **~ tube** *s.* Torˈpedorohr *n*.

tor·pid [ˈtɔ:pɪd] **I** *adj.* □ **1.** starr, erstarrt, betäubt; **2.** träge, schlaff; **3.** aˈpathisch, stumpf; **II** *s.* **4.** *mst* **tor·pid·i·ty** [tɔ:ˈpɪdətɪ], ˈ**tor·pid·ness** [-nɪs], ˈ**tor·por** [-pə] *s.* **1.** Erstarrung *f*, Betäubung *f*; **2.** Träg-, Schlaffheit *f*, ⚕ *a.* Torpor *m*; **3.** Apaˈthie *f*, Stumpfheit *f*.

torque [tɔ:k] *s.* ⚙, *phys.* ˈDrehmoˌment *n*; **~ shaft** *s.* ⚙ Dreh-, Torsiˈonsstab *m*.

tor·re·fy [ˈtɒrɪfaɪ] *v/t.* rösten, darren.

tor·rent [ˈtɒrənt] *s.* **1.** reißender Strom, *bsd.* Wild-, Sturzbach *m*; **2.** (Lava-) Strom *m*; **3.** ***~s of rain*** sintflutartige Regenfälle; ***it rains in ~s*** es gießt in Strömen; **4.** *fig.* Strom *m*, Schwall *m*, Sturzbach *m von Fragen etc.*; **tor·ren·tial** [təˈrenʃl] *adj.* □ **1.** reißend, strömend, sturzbachartig; **2.** sintflutartig: ***~ rain(s)***; **3.** *fig.* a) wortreich, b) wild, ungestüm.

tor·rid [ˈtɒrɪd] *adj.* **1.** sengend, brennend heiß (*a. fig. Leidenschaft etc.*): ***~ zone*** *geogr.* heiße Zone; **2.** ausgedörrt, verbrannt: ***~ plain***.

tor·sion [ˈtɔ:ʃn] *s.* **1.** *a.* ⚕ Drehung *f*; **2.** ⚙, *phys.* Torsiˈon *f*, Verdrehung *f*: ***~ balance*** Drehwaage *f*; **3.** ⚕ Abschnürung *f e-r Arterie*; ˈ**tor·sion·al** [-ʃənl] *adj.* Dreh…, (Ver)Drehungs…, Torsions…: *~ **force***.

tor·so ['tɔːsəʊ] *pl.* **-sos** *s.* Torso *m*: a) Rumpf *m*, b) *fig.* Bruchstück *n*, unvollendetes Werk.

tort [tɔːt] *s.* ⚖ unerlaubte Handlung, zi'vilrechtliches De'likt: ***law of ~s*** Schadenersatzrecht *n*; **'~-,fea·sor** [-ˌfiːzə] *s.* ⚖ rechtswidrig Handelnde(r) *m*.

tor·til·la [tɔː'tɪlə] (*Span.*) *s. Am.* Tor'tilla *f* (*Maiskuchen*).

tor·tious ['tɔːʃəs] *adj.* □ ⚖ rechtswidrig: ***~ act*** → ***tort***.

tor·toise ['tɔːtəs] **I** *s. zo.* Schildkröte *f*: ***as slow as a ~*** *fig.* (langsam) wie e-e Schnecke; **II** *adj.* Schildpatt…; **'~·shell** *s.* Schildpatt *n*: ***~ cat*** *zo.* Schildpattkatze *f*.

tor·tu·os·i·ty [ˌtɔːtjʊ'ɒsətɪ] *s.* **1.** Krümmung *f*, Windung *f*; **2.** Gewundenheit *f* (*a. fig.*); **3.** *fig.* 'Umständlichkeit *f*; **tor·tu·ous** ['tɔːtjʊəs] *adj.* □ **1.** gewunden, verschlungen, gekrümmt; **2.** *fig.* gewunden, 'umständlich; **3.** *fig.* ‚krumm', unehrlich.

tor·ture ['tɔːtʃə] **I** *s.* **1.** Folter(ung) *f*: ***put to the ~*** foltern; **2.** *fig.* Tor'tur *f*, Marter *f*, (Folter)Qual(en *pl.*) *f*; **II** *v/t.* **3.** foltern, martern, *fig. a.* quälen, peinigen; **4.** *Text etc.* entstellen; **'tor·tur·er** [-ərə] *s.* **1.** Folterknecht *m*; **2.** *fig.* Peiniger *m*.

to·rus ['tɔːrəs] *pl.* **-ri** [-raɪ] *s.* ⚠, ⩘, ⚙, ⚘, ✱ Torus *m*.

To·ry ['tɔːrɪ] **I** *s.* **1.** *pol. Brit.* Tory *m*, (*contp.* 'Ultra)Konserva'tive(r) *m*; **2.** *hist.* Tory *m* (*Loyalist in Amerika*); **II** *adj.* Tory…, konserva'tiv; **'To·ry·ism** [-ɪɪzəm] **1.** To'rysmus *m*; **2.** 'Ultrakonservaˌtismus *m*.

tosh [tɒʃ] *s. Brit. sl.* ‚Quatsch' *m*.

toss [tɒs] **I** *v/t.* **1.** werfen, schleudern: ***~ off*** a) *Reiter* abwerfen (*Pferd*), b) *Getränk* hinunterstürzen, c) *Arbeit* ‚hinhauen'; ***~ up*** hochschleudern, *in e-r Decke* prellen; **2.** *a.* ***~ up*** *Münze etc.*, *a. Kopf* hochwerfen: ***~ s.o. for*** mit j-m um *et.* losen (*durch Münzwurf*); **3.** *a.* ***~ about*** hin- u. herschleudern, schütteln; **4.** ⚓ *Riemen* pieken: ***~ oars!*** Riemen hoch!; **5.** *Am. sl. j-n* ‚filzen'; **II** *v/i.* **6.** *a.* ***~ about*** sich *im Schlaf etc.* hin- u. herwerfen *od.* -wälzen; **7.** *a.* ***~ about*** hin- u. hergeworfen werden, geschüttelt werden; hin- und herschwanken; flattern; **8.** rollen (*Schiff*); **9.** schwer gehen (*See*); **10.** *a.* ***~ up*** (durch Hochwerfen e-r Münze) losen (***for*** um); **III** *s.* **11.** Werfen *n*, Wurf *m*; **12.** Hoch-, Zu'rückwerfen *n des Kopfes*; **13.** a) Hochwerfen *n* e-r Münze, b) → ***toss-up***; **14.** Sturz *m vom Pferd etc.*: ***take a ~*** stürzen, *bsd.* abgeworfen werden; **'~-up** *s.* **1.** Losen *n mit e-r Münze*, Loswurf *m*; **2.** *fig.* ungewisse Sache: ***it is a ~ whether*** es ist völlig offen, ob.

tot¹ [tɒt] *s.* F **1.** Knirps *m*, Kerlchen *n*; **2.** *Brit.* Schlückchen *n* (*Alkohol*); **3.** *fig.* Häppchen *n*.

tot² [tɒt] F **I** *s.* **1.** (Gesamt)Summe *f*; **2.** a) Additi'onsaufgabe *f*, b) Additi'on *f*; **II** *v/t.* **3.** ***~ up*** zs.-zählen; **III** *v/i.* **4.** ***~ up*** sich belaufen (***to*** auf *acc.*); sich summieren.

to·tal ['təʊtl] **I** *adj.* □ **1.** ganz, gesamt, Gesamt…; **2.** to'tal, Total…, völlig, gänzlich; **II** *s.* **3.** (Gesamt)Summe *f*, Gesamtbetrag *m*, -menge *f*: ***a ~ of 20 cases*** insgesamt 20 Kisten; **4.** *die* Gesamtheit, *das* Ganze; **III** *v/t.* **5.** zs.-zählen; **6.** insgesamt betragen, sich belaufen auf (*acc.*): ***total(l)ing $70*** im Gesamtbetrag von 70 Dollar; **7.** *Am.* F *Auto* zu Schrott fahren; **to·tal·i·tar·i·an** [ˌtəʊtælɪ'teərɪən] *adj. pol.* totali'tär; **to·tal·i·tar·i·an·ism** [ˌtəʊtælɪ'teərɪənɪzəm] *s.* totali'täres Sy'stem; **to·tal·i·ty** [təʊ'tælətɪ] *s.* **1.** Gesamtheit *f*; **2.** Vollständigkeit *f*; **3.** *ast.* to'tale Verfinsterung; **'to·tal·i·za·tor** [-təlaɪzeɪtə] *s.* *Pferderennen*: Totali'sator *m*; **'to·tal·ize** [-təlaɪz] *v/t.* **1.** zs.-zählen; **2.** (zu e-m Ganzen) zs.-fassen; **'to·tal·iz·er** [-təlaɪzə] → ***totalizator***.

tote¹ [təʊt] *s. sl.* → ***totalizator***.

tote² [təʊt] *v/t.* F **1.** tragen (mit sich) schleppen; **2.** transportieren; ***~ bag*** *s. Am.* Einkaufs-, Tragtasche *f*.

to·tem ['təʊtəm] *s.* Totem *n*; ***~ pole***, ***~ post*** *s.* Totempfahl *m*.

tot·ter ['tɒtə] *v/i.* **1.** torkeln, wanken: ***~ to one's grave*** *fig.* dem Grabe zuwanken; **2.** (sch)wanken, wackeln: ***~ to its fall*** *fig.* (allmählich) zs.-brechen (*Reich etc.*); **'tot·ter·ing** [-ərɪŋ] *adj.* □, **'tot·ter·y** [-ərɪ] *adj.* wack(e)lig, (sch)wankend.

touch [tʌtʃ] **I** *s.* **1.** Berührung *f*: ***at a ~*** beim Berühren; ***on the slightest ~*** bei der leisesten Berührung; ***it has a velvety ~*** es fühlt sich wie Samt an; ***that was a*** (***near***) ***~*** F das hätte ins Auge gehen können; **2.** Tastsinn *m*: ***it is soft to the ~*** es fühlt sich weich an; **3.** (*Pinsel-etc.*)Strich *m*: ***put the finishing ~es to*** letzte Hand legen an (*acc.*), *e-r Sache* den letzten Schliff geben; **4.** ♪ a) Anschlag *m des Pianisten od. des Pianos*, b) Strich *m des Geigers*; **5.** *fig.* Fühlung(nahme) *f*, Verbindung *f*, Kon'takt *m*: ***get into ~ with*** sich in Verbindung setzen mit, Fühlung nehmen mit; ***please get in ~!*** bitte melden (Sie sich)!; ***keep in ~ with*** in Verbindung bleiben mit; ***lose ~ with*** den Kontakt mit *j-m od. e-r Sache* verlieren; ***put s.o. in ~ with*** j-n in Verbindung setzen mit; ***within ~*** in Reichweite; **6.** *fig.* Hand *f des Meisters etc.*, Stil *m*; (souve'räne) Ma'nier: ***light ~*** leichte Hand; ***with sure ~*** mit sicherer Hand; **7.** Einfühlungsvermögen *n*, Feingefühl *n*; **8.** *e-e Spur Pfeffer etc.*: ***a ~ of red*** ein rötlicher Hauch; **9.** Anflug *m von Sarkasmus etc.*, Hauch *m von Romantik etc.*: ***he has a ~ of genius*** er hat e-e geniale Ader; **10.** ✱ *etc.* (leichter) Anfall: ***a ~ of flu*** e-e leichte Grippe; ***a ~ of the sun*** ein leichter Sonnenstich; **11.** (besondere) Note, Zug *m*: ***the personal ~*** die persönliche Note; **12.** *fig.* Stempel *m*, Gepräge *n*; **13.** Probe *f*: ***put to the ~*** auf die Probe stellen; **14.** a) *Rugby etc.*: Mark *f*, b) *Fußball*: Seitenaus *n*; **15.** Fangspiel *n*; **16.** *sl.* a) Anpumpen *n*, b) gepumptes Geld: ***he is a soft ~*** er läßt sich leicht anpumpen, *weitS.* er ist ein leichtes Opfer; **II** *v/t.* **17.** an-, berühren (*a. weitS. Essen etc. mst neg.*); anfassen, angreifen: ***~ the spot*** das Richtige treffen; **18.** befühlen, betasten; **19.** *Hand etc.* legen (***to*** an *acc.*, auf *acc.*); **20.** mitein'ander in Berührung bringen; **21.** in Berührung kommen *od.* stehen mit; **22.** drücken auf (*acc.*), (leicht) anstoßen: ***to ~ the bell*** klingeln; ***to ~ glasses*** (mit den Gläsern) anstoßen; **23.** grenzen *od.* stoßen an (*acc.*); **24.** reichen an (*acc.*), erreichen; F *fig.* her'anreichen an (*acc.*), gleichkommen (*dat.*); **25.** erlangen, erreichen; **26.** ♪ *Saiten* rühren; *Ton* anschlagen; **27.** tönen, (leicht) färben; *fig.* färben, beeinflussen; **28.** beeindrucken; rühren, bewegen: ***~ed to tears*** zu Tränen gerührt; **29.** *fig.* verletzen, treffen; **30.** *fig.* berühren, betreffen; **31.** in Mitleidenschaft ziehen, mitnehmen: ***~ed*** a) angegangen (*Fleisch*), b) F ‚bekloppt', ‚nicht ganz bei Trost' (*Person*); **32.** *Ort* berühren, haltmachen in (*dat.*); *Hafen* anlaufen; **33.** *sl.* anpumpen (***for*** um); **III** *v/i.* **34.** sich berühren; **35.** ***~ at*** ⚓ anlegen bei *od.* in (*dat.*), anlaufen (*acc.*); **36.** ***~*** (***up***)***on*** *fig.* berühren: a) (kurz) erwähnen, b) betreffen;

Zssgn mit adv.:

touch| down *v/i.* **1.** *Rugby etc.*: e-n Versuch legen *od.* erzielen; **2.** ✈ aufsetzen; ***~ off*** *v/t.* **1.** skizzieren; **2.** *Skizze* flüchtig entwerfen; **3.** *e-e Explosion*, *fig. e-e Krise etc.* auslösen, *fig. a.* entfachen; ***~ up*** *v/t.* **1.** auffrischen (*a. fig.*), aufpolieren; verbessern; **2.** *phot.* retuschieren.

touch| and go *s.* ris'kante Sache, pre'käre Situati'on: ***it was ~*** es hing an e-m Haar, es stand auf des Messers Schneide; **ˌ~-and-'go** *adj.* **1.** ris'kant; **2.** flüchtig, oberflächlich: ***~ landing*** ✈ Aufsetz- u. Durchstartlandung; **'~·down** *s.* **1.** *Rugby etc.*: Versuch *m*; **2.** ✈ Aufsetzen *n*.

touch·i·ness ['tʌtʃɪnɪs] *s.* Empfindlichkeit *f*.

touch·ing ['tʌtʃɪŋ] *adj.* □ *fig.* rührend, ergreifend.

'touch|·line *s.* a) *Fußball*: Seitenlinie *f*, b) *Rugby*: Marklinie *f*; **'~-me-not** *s.* ⚘ (*fig.* F Blümlein *n*) Rührmichnichtan *n*; **'~ˌpa·per** *s.* 'Zündpaˌpier *n*; **'~·stone** *s.* **1.** *min.* Probierstein *m*; **2.** *fig.* Prüfstein *m*; ***~ sys·tem*** *s.* Zehn'fingersysˌtem *n*; ***~ tel·e·phone*** *s.* 'Tastenteleˌfon *n*; **'~-type** *v/i.* blindschreiben; **'~·wood** *s.* **1.** Zunder(holz *n*) *m*; **2.** ⚘ Feuerschwamm *m*.

touch·y ['tʌtʃɪ] *adj.* □ **1.** empfindlich, reizbar; **2.** a) ris'kant, b) heikel, kitzlig (*Thema*).

tough [tʌf] **I** *adj.* □ **1.** *allg.* zäh: a) hart, 'widerstandsfähig, b) ro'bust, stark (*Person*, *Körper etc.*), c) hartnäckig (*Kampf*, *Wille etc.*); **2.** *fig.* schwierig, unangenehm, ‚bös' (*Arbeit etc.*, *a.* F *Person*); F eklig, grob (*Person*): ***it was ~ going*** F es war ein hartes Stück Arbeit; ***he is a ~ customer*** mit ihm ist nicht gut Kirschen essen; ***if things get ~*** wenn es ‚mulmig' wird; ***~ luck*** F ‚Pech' *n*; **3.** rowdyhaft, bru'tal, übel, Verbrecher…: ***get ~ with s.o.*** j-m gegenüber massiv werden; **II** *s.* **4.** Rowdy *m*, Schläger(typ) *m*, ‚übler Kunde'; **tough·en** ['tʌfn] *v/t. u. v/i.* zäh(er) *etc.* machen (werden); **tough·ie** ['tʌfɪ] *s.* F **1.** ‚harte Nuß', schwierige Sache; **2.** → ***tough*** 4; **'tough·ness** [-nɪs] *s.* **1.** Zähigkeit *f*, Härte *f* (*a. fig.*); **2.** Ro'bustheit *f*; **3.** *fig.* Hartnäckigkeit *f*; **4.**

Schwierigkeit *f*; **5.** Brutali'tät *f*.

tou·pee, *a.* **tou·pet** ['tu:peɪ] (*Fr.*) *s.* Tou'pet *n* (*Haarersatzstück*).

tour [tʊə] **I** *s.* **1.** Tour *f* (**of** durch): a) (Rund)Reise *f*, (-)Fahrt *f*, b) Ausflug *m*, Wanderung *f*: ***conducted ~*** a) Führung *f*, b) Gesellschaftsreise *f*; ***the grand ~*** *hist.* (Bildungs)Reise durch Europa; ***~ operator*** Reiseveranstalter *m*; **2.** Rundgang *m* (**of** durch): ***~ of inspection*** Besichtigungsrundgang *od.* -rundfahrt *f*; **3.** *thea. etc.* Tour'nee *f*, Gastspielreise *f*: ***go on ~*** auf Tournee gehen; **4.** ⚔ (turnusmäßige) Dienstzeit; **II** *v/t.* **5.** bereisen; **III** *v/i.* **6.** e-e (*thea.* Gastspiel)Reise *od.* (*a. sport*) e-e Tour'nee machen (***through***, ***about*** durch); **~ de force** [ˌtʊədə'fɔ:s] (*Fr.*) *s.* **1.** Gewaltakt *m*; **2.** Glanzleistung *f*.

tour·ing ['tʊərɪŋ] *adj.* Touren..., Reise...: ***~ car*** *mot.* Tourenwagen *m*; ***~ company*** *thea.* Wanderbühne *f*; ***~ exhibition*** Wanderausstellung *f*; **tour·ism** ['tʊərɪzəm] *s.* Reise-, Fremdenverkehr *m*, Tou'rismus *m*; **tour·ist** ['tʊərɪst] **I** *s.* Tou'rist(in), (Ferien-, Vergnügungs-) Reisende(r *m*) *f*; **II** *adj.* Reise..., Fremden(verkehrs)..., Touristen...: ***~ agency***, ***~ bureau***, ***~ office*** a) Reisebüro *n*, b) Verkehrsamt *n*, -verein *m*; ***~ class*** ⚓, ✈ Touristenklasse *f*; ***~ industry*** Fremdenverkehr(sindustrie *f*) *m*; ***~ season*** Reisezeit *f*; ***~ ticket*** Rundreisekarte *f*; ***~ trap*** Touristenfalle *f*; **'tour·ist·y** *adj. contp.* tou'ristisch, Touristen...

tour·na·ment ['tʊənəmənt] *s.* (*hist. Ritter-*, *a. Tennis- etc.*)Tur'nier *n*.

tour·ney ['tʊənɪ] *bsd. hist.* **I** *s.* Tur'nier *n*; **II** *v/i.* turnieren.

tour·ni·quet ['tʊənɪkeɪ] *s.* ⚕ Aderpresse *f*.

tou·sle ['taʊzl] *v/t. Haar etc.* (zer)zausen, verwuscheln.

tout [taʊt] **I** *v/i.* **1.** (*bsd. aufdringliche* Kunden-, Stimmen)Werbung treiben (**for** für); **2.** *Pferderennen*: a) *Brit.* sich *durch Spionieren* gute Renntips verschaffen, b) Wettips geben *od.* verkaufen; **II** *s.* **3.** Kundenschlepper *m*, -werber *m*; **4.** *Pferderennen*: a) *Brit.* ,Spi'on' *m beim Pferdetraining*, b) Tipgeber *m*; **5.** (Karten)Schwarzhändler *m*.

tow¹ [təʊ] **I** *s.* **1.** a) Schleppen *n*, b) Schlepptau *n*: ***have in ~*** im Schlepptau haben (*a. fig.*); ***take ~*** sich schleppen lassen; ***take in ~*** *bsd. fig.* ins Schlepptau nehmen; **2.** *bsd.* ⚓ Schleppzug *m*; **II** *v/t.* **3.** (ab)schleppen, ins Schlepptau nehmen: ***~ away*** *Auto* abschleppen; ***~ed flight*** (***target***) Schleppflug *m* (-ziel *n*); **4.** *Schiff* treideln; **5.** *fig. j-n* ab-, mitschleppen, *wohin* bugsieren.

tow² [təʊ] *s.* (Schwing)Werg *n*.

tow·age ['təʊɪdʒ] *s.* **1.** Schleppen *n*, Bugsieren *n*; **2.** Schleppgebühr *f*.

to·ward I *adj.* ['təʊəd] **1.** *obs.* fügsam; **2.** *obs. od. Am.* vielversprechend; **3.** im Gange, am Werk; **4.** bevorstehend; **II** *prp.* [tə'wɔ:d] **5.** auf (*acc.*) ... zu, (nach) ... zu, nach ... hin, gegen *od.* zu ... (hin); **6.** *zeitlich*: gegen; **7.** *Gefühle etc.* gegen'über; **8.** *als Beitrag* zu, um *e-r Sache* willen, zum Zwecke (*gen.*): ***efforts ~ reconciliation*** Bemühungen um e-e Versöhnung; **to·wards** [tə'wɔ:dz] → ***toward*** II.

'tow|·a·way *adj.* Abschlepp...: ***~ zone***; **'~·boat** *s.* Schleppschiff *n*, Schlepper *m*.

tow·el ['taʊəl] **I** *s.* Handtuch *n*: ***throw in the ~*** *Boxen*: das Handtuch werfen (*a. fig. sich geschlagen geben*); **II** *v/t.* (mit e-m Handtuch) (ab)trocknen, (-)reiben; **~ horse**, **~ rack** *s.* Handtuchständer *m*.

tow·er ['taʊə] **I** *s.* **1.** Turm *m*: ***~ block*** *Brit.* (Büro-, Wohn)Hochhaus *n*; **2.** Feste *f*, Bollwerk *n*: ***~ of strength*** *fig.* Stütze *f*, Säule *f*; **3.** Zwinger *m*, Festung *f* (*Gefängnis*); **4.** ⚗ Turm *m* (*Reinigungsanlage*); **II** *v/i.* **5.** (hoch)ragen, sich (em'por)türmen (**to** zu): ***~ above*** *et. od. j-n* (weit) überragen (*a. fig. turmhoch überlegen sein* [*dat.*]); **'tow·ered** [-əd] *adj.* (hoch)getürmt; **'tow·er·ing** [-ərɪŋ] *adj.* **1.** (turm)hoch, hoch-, aufragend; **2.** *fig.* maßlos, gewaltig: ***~ ambition***; ***~ passion***; ***~ rage*** rasende Wut.

tow·ing ['təʊɪŋ] *adj.* (Ab)Schlepp...; **~ line**, **~ path**, **~ rope** → ***towline***, ***towpath***, ***towrope***.

'tow·line *s.* **1.** ⚓ Treidelleine *f*, Schlepptau *n*; **2.** Abschleppseil *n*.

town [taʊn] **I** *s.* **1.** Stadt *f* (*unter dem Rang e-r* ***city***); **2.** ***the ~*** *fig.* die Stadt: a) die Stadtbevölkerung, die Einwohnerschaft, b) das Stadtleben; **3.** *Brit.* Marktflecken *m*; **4.** *ohne art. die* (nächste) Stadt: a) Stadtzentrum *n*, b) *Brit. bsd.* London: ***to ~*** nach der *od.* in die Stadt, *Brit. bsd.* nach London; ***out of ~*** nicht in der Stadt, *Brit. bsd.* nicht in London, auswärts; ***go to ~*** F ,auf den Putz hauen'; → ***paint*** 2; **5.** *Brit.* Bürgerschaft *f e-r Universitätsstadt*; → ***gown*** 3; **II** *adj.* **6.** städtisch, Stadt..., Städte...; **'~·bred** *adj.* in der Stadt aufgewachsen; **~ cen·tre** *s. Brit.* Innenstadt *f*, City *f*; **~ clerk** *s.* 'Stadtdiˌrektor *m*; **~ coun·cil** *s.* Stadtrat *m* (*Gremium*); **~ coun·cil·(l)or** *s.* Stadtrat(smitglied *n*) *m*; **~ cri·er** *s.* Ausrufer *m*; **~ hall** *s.* Rathaus *n*; **~ house** *s.* Stadt-, *Am.* Reihenhaus *n*; **~ plan·ning** *s.* Städte-, Stadtplanung *f*; **'~·scape** [-skeɪp] *s.* Stadtbild *n*, *paint.* -ansicht *f*.

towns·folk ['taʊnzfəʊk] *s. pl.* Stadtleute *pl.*, Städter *pl*.

town·ship ['taʊnʃɪp] *s.* **1.** *hist.* (Dorf-, Stadt)Gemeinde *f od.* (-)Gebiet *n*; **2.** *Am.* Verwaltungsbezirk *m*; **3.** *surv. Am.* 6 Qua'dratmeilen großes Gebiet.

towns|·man ['taʊnzmən] *s.* [*irr.*] **1.** Städter *m*, Stadtbewohner *m*; **2.** *a.* ***fellow ~*** Mitbürger *m*; **'~ˌpeo·ple** [-nz-] → ***townsfolk***.

'tow|·path *s.* Treidelpfad *m*; **'~·rope** → ***towline***.

tox·(a)e·mi·a [tɒk'si:mɪə] *s.* ⚕ Blutvergiftung *f*.

tox·ic, **tox·i·cal** ['tɒksɪk(l)] *adj.* □ giftig, toxisch, Gift...; **'tox·i·cant** [-sɪkənt] **I** *adj.* giftig, toxisch; **II** *s.* Gift(-stoff *m*) *n*; **tox·i·co·log·i·cal** [ˌtɒksɪkə'lɒdʒɪkl] *adj.* □ toxiko'logisch; **tox·i·col·o·gist** [ˌtɒksɪ'kɒlədʒɪst] *s.* ⚕ Toxiko'loge *m*; **tox·i·col·o·gy** [ˌtɒksɪ'kɒlədʒɪ] *s.* ⚕ Toxikolo'gie *f*, Giftkunde *f*; **'tox·in** [-sɪn] *s.* ⚕ To'xin *n*, Gift(stoff *m*) *n*.

toy [tɔɪ] **I** *s.* **1.** (Kinder)Spielzeug *n* (*a. fig.*); *pl.* Spielwaren *pl.*, -sachen *pl.*; **2.** *fig.* Tand *m*, ,Kinkerlitzchen' *n*; **II** *v/i.* **3.** (***with***) spielen (mit *e-m Gegenstand*, *fig.* mit *e-m Gedanken*), *fig. a.* liebäugeln (mit); **III** *adj.* **4.** Spielzeug..., Kinder..., Zwerg...: ***~ dog*** Schoßhund *m*; ***~ train*** Miniatur-, Kindereisenbahn *f*; **~ book** *s.* Bilderbuch *n*; **'~-box** *s.* Spielzeugkiste *f*; **'~·shop** *s.* Spielwarenhandlung *f*.

trace¹ [treɪs] *s.* Zugriemen *m*, Strang *m* (*Pferdegeschirr*): ***in the ~s*** angespannt (*a. fig.*); ***kick over the ~s*** *fig.* über die Stränge schlagen.

trace² [treɪs] **I** *s.* **1.** (Fuß-, Wagen-, Wild- *etc.*)Spur *f*: ***hot on s.o.'s ~s*** j-m dicht auf den Fersen; ***without a ~*** spurlos; ***~ element*** ⚗ Spurenelement *n*; **2.** *fig.* Spur *f*: a) ('Über)Rest *m*: ***~s of ancient civilizations***, b) (An)Zeichen *n*: ***~s of fatigue***, c) geringe Menge, bißchen: ***not a ~ of fear*** keine Spur von Angst; ***a ~ of a smile*** der Anflug e-s Lächelns; **3.** ⚔ a) Leuchtspur *f*, b) *Radar*: Bildspur *f*; **4.** Linie *f*: a) Aufzeichnung *f* (*Meßgerät*), b) Zeichnung *f*, Skizze *f*, c) Pauszeichnung *f*, d) Grundriß *m*; **5.** *Am.* (markierter) Weg; **II** *v/t.* **6.** nachspüren (*dat.*), *j-s* Spur verfolgen; **7.** *Wild*, *Verbrecher* verfolgen, aufspüren; **8.** *a.* ***~ out*** *et. od. j-n* ausfindig machen *od.* aufspüren, *et.* auf-, her'ausfinden; **9.** *fig. e-r Entwicklung etc.* nachgehen, *e-e Sache* verfolgen: ***~ back*** *et.* zurückverfolgen (**to** bis zu); ***~ s.th. to*** et. zurückführen auf (*acc.*), et. herleiten von; **10.** erkennen; **11.** *Pfad* verfolgen; **12.** *a.* ***~ out*** (auf)zeichnen, skizzieren, entwerfen; **13.** *Buchstaben* sorgfältig (aus)ziehen, schreiben; **14.** ⚙ a) *a.* ***~ over*** ('durch)pausen, b) *Baufluch*t *etc.* abstecken, c) *Messung* aufzeichnen (*Gerät*); **'trace·a·ble** [-səbl] *adj.* □ **1.** auffindbar, nachweisbar; **2.** zu'rückzuführen(d) (**to** auf *acc.*); **'trac·er** [-sə] *s.* **1.** Aufspürer(in); **2.** ✉, 🚂 *Am.* Lauf-, Suchzettel *m*; **3.** *Schneiderei*: Kopierrädchen *n*; **4.** ⚙ Punzen *m*; **5.** ⚗ Iso'topenindiˌkator *m*; **6.** ⚔ a) *mst* ***~ bullet***, ***~ shell*** Leuchtspur-, Rauchspurgeschoß *n*, b) *mst* ***~ composition*** Leuchtspursatz *m*; **7.** a) technischer Zeichner, b) Pauser *m*; **'trac·er·y** [-sərɪ] *s.* **1.** ⚠ Maßwerk *n an gotischen Fenstern*; **2.** Flechtwerk *n*.

tra·che·a [trə'ki:ə] *pl.* **-che·ae** [-'ki:i:] *s.* **1.** *anat.* Tra'chea *f*, Luftröhre *f*; **2.** ⚘, *zo.* Tra'chee *f*; **tra'che·al** [-'ki:əl] *adj.* **1.** *anat.* Luftröhren...; **2.** *zo.* Tracheen...; **3.** ⚘ Gefäß...; **tra·che·i·tis** [ˌtrækɪ'aɪtɪs] *s.* ⚕ 'Luftröhrenkaˌtarrh *m*; **tra·che·ot·o·my** [ˌtrækɪ'ɒtəmɪ] *s.* ⚕ Luftröhrenschnitt *m*.

trac·ing ['treɪsɪŋ] *s.* **1.** Suchen *n*, Nachforschung *f*; **2.** ⚙ a) (Auf)Zeichnen *n*, b) 'Durchpausen *n*; **3.** ⚙ a) Zeichnung *f*, (Auf)Riß *m*, Plan *m*, b) Pause *f*; **4.** Aufzeichnung *f* (*e-s Kardiographen etc.*); **~ file** *s.* 'Suchkarˌtei *f*; **~ op·er·a·tion** *s.* Fahndung *f*; **~ pa·per** *s.* 'Pauspaˌpier *n*; **~ ser·vice** *s.* Suchdienst *m*.

track [træk] **I** *s.* **1.** (Fuß-, Wild- *etc.*) Spur *f* (*a. fig.*), Fährte *f*: ***on s.o.'s ~s*** j-m auf der Spur; ***be on the wrong ~*** auf der falschen Spur *od.* auf dem Holzweg sein; ***cover up one's ~s*** s-e Spuren verwischen; ***throw s.o. off the ~*** j-n von der (richtigen) Spur ablenken; ***keep ~ of*** *fig. et.* verfolgen, sich auf dem laufenden halten über (*acc.*); ***lose ~ of*** aus den Augen verlieren; ***make ~s*** *sl.* ‚abhauen'; ***make ~s for*** schnurstracks losgehen auf (*acc.*); ***stop in one's ~s*** wie festgewurzelt stehenbleiben; ***shoot s.o. in his ~s*** j-n auf der Stelle niederschießen; **2.** 🚂 Gleis *n*, Geleise *n u. pl.*, Schienenstrang *m*: ***off the ~*** entgleist, aus den Schienen; ***on ~*** ☤ auf (der) Achse, rollend; ***born on the wrong side of the ~s*** *fig. Am.* aus ärmlichen Verhältnissen stammend; **3.** ⚓ Fahrwasser *n*; **4.** ⚓ *übliche* Route; **5.** Weg *m*, Pfad *m*; **6.** (Ko'meten- *etc.*) Bahn *f*; **7.** *sport* a) (Renn-, Lauf-) Bahn *f*, b) *mst* ***~ events*** 'Laufdiszi,plinen *pl.*, c) *a.* ***~-and-field sports*** 'Leichtath,letik *f*; **8.** (Gleis-, Raupen-) Kette *f e-s Traktors etc.*; **9.** *mot.* a) Spurweite *f*, b) 'Reifenpro,fil *n*; **10.** *Computer, Tonband*: Spur *f*; **11.** *ped. Am.* Leistungsgruppe *f*; **II** *v/t.* **12.** nachspüren (*dat.*), *a. fig.* verfolgen (*acc.*); **13.** aufspüren: a) *a.* ***~ down*** *Wild, Verbrecher* zur Strecke bringen, b) ausfindig machen; **14.** *Weg* kennzeichnen; **15.** durch'queren; **16.** 🚂 *Am.* Gleise verlegen in (*dat.*); **17.** *Am.* (Schmutz)Spuren hinter'lassen auf (*dat.*); **18.** ⚙ mit Raupenketten versehen: ***~ed vehicle*** Ketten-, Raupenfahrzeug *n*; **III** *v/i.* **19.** Spur halten (*Räder*); **20.** *Film*: (mit der Kamera) fahren: ***~ing shot*** Fahraufnahme *f*; **IV** *adj.* **21.** 🚂 Gleis…, Schienen…; **22.** *sport* a) (Lauf)Bahn…, Lauf…, b) Leichtathletik…: **'track·age** [-kɪdʒ] *s.* 🚂 **1.** *coll.* Schienen *pl.*; **2.** Schienenlänge *f*; **3.** *Am.* Streckenbenutzungsrecht *n*, -gebühr *f*; **,track-and-'field** *adj.* Leichtathletik…; → ***track*** 7 c; **'track·er** [-kə] *s.* **1.** *bsd. hunt.* Spurenleser *m*: ***~ dog*** Spürhund *m*; **2.** *fig.* ‚Spürhund' *m* (*Person*); **3.** ⚔ Zielgeber *m* (*Gerät*).

'track|,lay·er *s.* **1.** 🚂 *Am.* Streckenarbeiter *m*; **2.** Raupenschlepper *m*; **'~,lay·ing** *adj.* ⚙ Raupen…, Gleisketten…: ***~ vehicle.***

track·less ['træklɪs] *adj.* ☐ **1.** unbetreten; **2.** weg-, pfadlos; **3.** schienenlos; **4.** spurlos.

track| meet *s. Am.* Leichtathletikveranstaltung *f*; **~ shoe** *s.* Rennschuh *m*; **~ suit** *s.* Trainingsanzug *m*; **~ walk·ing** *s. sport* Bahngehen *n*.

tract[1] [trækt] *s.* **1.** (ausgedehnte) Fläche, Strecke *f*, (Land)Strich *m*, Gebiet *n*, Gegend *f*; **2.** Zeitraum *m*; **3.** *anat.* Trakt *m*, (Ver'dauungs- *etc.*)Sy,stem *n*: ***respiratory ~*** Atemwege *pl.*; **4.** *physiol.* (Nerven)Strang *m*: ***optic ~*** Sehstrang.

tract[2] [trækt] *s. eccl.* Trak'tat *m, n*; *contp.* Trak'tätchen *n*.

trac·ta·ble ['træktəbl] *adj.* **1.** ☐ lenk-, folg-, fügsam; **2.** *fig.* gefügig, geschmeidig (*Material*).

trac·tion ['trækʃn] *s.* **1.** Ziehen *n*; **2.** ⚙, *phys.* a) Zug *m*, b) Zugleistung *f*: ***~ engine*** Zugmaschine *f*; **3.** *phys.* Reibungsdruck *m*; **4.** *mot.* a) Griffigkeit *f* (*Reifen*), b) *a.* ***~ of the road*** Bodenhaftung *f*; **5.** Trans'port *m*, Fortbewegung *f*; **6.** *physiol.* Zs.-ziehung *f* (*Muskeln*); **'trac·tion·al** [-ʃənl], **'trac·tive** [-tɪv] *adj.* ⚙ Zug…

trac·tor ['træktə] *s.* **1.** ⚙ 'Zugma,schine *f*, Traktor *m*, Schlepper *m*; **2.** ✈ a) Zugschraube *f*, b) *a.* ***~ airplane*** Flugzeug *n* mit Zugschraube; **~ truck** *s. Am. mot.* Sattelschlepper *m*.

trade [treɪd] **I** *s.* **1.** ☤ Handel *m*, (Handels)Verkehr *m*: ***foreign ~*** a) Außenhandel, b) ⚓ große Fahrt; ***home ~*** a) Binnenhandel, b) ⚓ kleine Fahrt; → ***board*** 9; **2.** ☤ Geschäft *n*: a) Gewerbe *n*, Geschäftszweig *m*, Branche *f*, b) (Einzel-, Groß)Handel *m*, c) Geschäftslage *f*, -gewinn *m*: ***be in ~*** (Einzel)Händler sein; ***do a good ~*** gute Geschäfte machen; ***sell to the ~*** an Wiederverkäufer abgeben; **3.** ☤ ***the ~*** a) *coll.* die Geschäftswelt, b) *Brit.* der Spiritu'osenhandel, c) die Kundschaft; **4.** Gewerbe *n*, Beruf *m*, Handwerk *n*: ***the ~*** *coll.* die Zunft *od.* Gilde; ***by ~*** *Bäcker etc.* von Beruf; ***every man to his ~*** jeder, wie er es gelernt hat; ***the ~ of war*** das Kriegshandwerk; **5.** *mst* ***the ~s*** *pl.* die Pas'satwinde *pl.*; **II** *v/i.* **6.** Handel treiben, handeln (***in*** mit *et.*); in Geschäftsverbindung stehen (***with*** mit *j-m*); *Am.* (ein)kaufen (***with*** bei *j-m*, ***at*** in *e-m Laden*); **7.** ***~ (up)on*** *fig.* spekulieren *od.* ‚reisen' auf (*acc.*), ausnutzen; **III** *v/t.* **8.** (aus)tauschen (***for*** gegen); **9.** ***~ in*** *bsd. Auto* in Zahlung geben; **~ ac·cept·ance** *s.* ☤ 'Handelsak,zept *n*; **~ ac·count** *s. Bilanz*: a) ***~s payable*** Warenschulden *pl.*, b) ***~s receivable*** Warenforderungen *pl.*; **~ as·so·ci·a·tion** *s.* **1.** Wirtschaftsverband *m*; **2.** Arbeitgeberverband *m*; **~ bal·ance** *s.* 'Handelsbi,lanz *f*; **~ bar·riers** *s. pl.* Handelsschranken *pl.*; **~ bill** *s.* Warenwechsel *m*; **~ cy·cle** *s.* Konjunk'turzyklus *m*; **~ di·rec·to·ry** *s.* Branchen-, Firmenverzeichnis *n*, 'Handelsa,dreßbuch *n*; **~ dis·count** *s.* 'Händlerra,batt *m*; **~ fair** *s.* (Handels)Messe *f*; **~ gap** *s.* 'Handelsbi,lanzdefizit *n*; **'~-in** *s.* in Zahlung gegebene Sache (*bsd. Auto*): ***~ value*** Eintausch-, Verrechnungswert *m*; **'~·mark I** *s.* **1.** Warenzeichen *n*: ***registered ~*** eingetragenes Warenzeichen; **2.** *fig.* Kennzeichen *n*; **II** *v/t.* **3.** *Ware* gesetzlich schützen lassen: ***~ed goods*** Markenartikel; **~ mis·sion** *s. pol.* 'Handelsmissi,on *f*; **~ name** *s.* **1.** Handelsbezeichnung *f*, Markenname *m*; **2.** Firmenname *m*, Firma *f*; **~ price** *s.* (Groß)Handelspreis *m*.

trad·er ['treɪdə] *s.* **1.** Händler *m*, Kaufmann *m*; **2.** *Börse*: 'Wertpa,pierhändler *m*; **3.** ⚓ Handelsschiff *n*.

trade| school *s.* Gewerbeschule *f*; **~ se·cret** *s.* Geschäftsgeheimnis *n*; **~ show** *s.* Filmvorführung *f* für Verleiher u. Kritiker.

trades|·man ['treɪdzmən] *s.* [*irr.*] **1.** (Einzel)Händler *m*; **2.** Ladeninhaber *m*; **3.** Handwerker *m*; **'~·peo·ple** [-zp-] *s. pl.* Geschäftsleute *pl.*

trade| sym·bol *s.* Bild *n* (*Warenzeichen*); **~ un·ion** *s.* Gewerkschaft *f*; **~ un·ion·ism** *s.* Gewerkschaftswesen *n*; **~ un·ion·ist** *s.* Gewerkschaftler(in); **~ wind** *s.* Pas'satwind *m*.

trad·ing ['treɪdɪŋ] **I** *s.* **1.** Handeln *n*; **2.** Handel *m* (***in*** mit *et.*, ***with*** mit *j-m*); **II** *adj.* **3.** Handels…; **~ a·re·a** *s.* ☤ Absatzgebiet *n*; **~ cap·i·tal** *s.* Be'triebska,pi,tal *n*; **~ com·pa·ny** *s.* Handelsgesellschaft *f*; **~ post** *s.* Handelsniederlassung *f*; **~ stamp** *s.* Ra'battmarke *f*.

tra·di·tion [trə'dɪʃn] *s.* **1.** Traditi'on *f*: a) (mündliche) Über'lieferung (*a. eccl.*), b) Herkommen *n*, (alter) Brauch, Brauchtum *n*: ***be in the ~*** sich im Rahmen der Tradition halten; **2.** ⚖ Auslieferung *f*, 'Übergabe *f*; **tra'di·tion·al** [-ʃənl] *adj.* ☐ traditio'nell, Traditions…: a) (mündlich) über'liefert, b) herkömmlich, brauchtümlich, (alt)hergebracht, üblich; **tra'di·tion·al·ism** [-ʃnəlɪzəm] *s. bsd. eccl.* Traditiona'lismus *m*, Festhalten *n* an der Über'lieferung.

tra·duce [trə'djuːs] *v/t.* verleumden.

traf·fic ['træfɪk] **I** *s.* **1.** (öffentlicher, Straßen-, Schiffs-, Eisenbahn- *etc.*) Verkehr; **2.** (Per'sonen-, Güter-, Nachrichten-, Fernsprech- *etc.*)Verkehr *m*; **3.** a) (Handels)Verkehr *m*, Handel *m* (***in*** in *dat.*, mit), b) *b.s.* ('ille,galer) Handel: ***drug ~***; **4.** *fig.* a) Verkehr *m*, Geschäft(e *pl.*) *n*, b) Austausch *m* (***in*** von): ***~ in ideas***; **II** *v/i. pret. u. p.p.* **'traf·ficked** [-kt] **5.** handeln, Handel treiben (***in*** in *dat.*, ***with*** mit); **6.** *fig.* verhandeln (***with*** mit).

traf·fi·ca·tor ['træfɪkeɪtə] *s. mot. Brit.* a) Blinker *m*, b) *hist.* Winker *m*.

traf·fic| cen·sus *s.* Verkehrszählung *f*; **~ cir·cle** *s. mot. Am.* Kreisverkehr *m*; **~ is·land** *s.* Verkehrsinsel *f*; **~ jam** *s.* Verkehrsstauung *f*, -stockung *f*, (Fahrzeug)Stau *m*.

traf·fick·er ['træfɪkə] *s.* (*a.* 'ille,galer) Händler.

traf·fic| lane *s. mot.* Spur *f*; **~ lights** *s. pl.* Verkehrsampel *f*; **~ man·a·ger** *s.* ☤ **1.** Versandleiter *m*; **2.** Be'triebsdi,rektor *m*; **~ of·fence** *s. Brit.*, **~ of·fense** *s. Am.* Ver'kehrsde,likt *n*; **~ of·fend·er** *s.* Verkehrssünder *m*; **~ reg·u·la·tions** *s. pl.* Verkehrsvorschriften *pl.*, (Straßen)Verkehrsordnung *f*; **~ sign** *s.* Verkehrszeichen *n*, -schild *n*; **~ ward·en** *s.* Poli'tesse *f*.

tra·ge·di·an [trə'dʒiːdjən] *s.* **1.** Tragiker *m*, Trauerspieldichter *m*; **2.** *thea.* Tra'göde *m*, tragischer Darsteller *m*; **tra·ge·di·enne** [trədʒiː'djen] *s. thea.* Tra'gödin *f*; **trag·e·dy** ['trædʒɪdɪ] *s.* **1.** Tra'gödie *f*: a) *thea.* Trauerspiel *n*, b) *fig.* tragische Begebenheit, *a.* Unglück *n*; **2.** *fig. das* Tragische; **tra·gic, trag·i·cal** ['trædʒɪk(l)] *adj.* ☐ *thea. u. fig.* tragisch: ***~ly*** tragischerweise; **trag·i·com·e·dy** [,trædʒɪ'kɒmɪdɪ] *s.* Tragiko'mödie *f* (*a. fig.*); **trag·i·com·ic** [,trædʒɪ'kɒmɪk] *adj.* (☐ ***~ally***) tragi'komisch.

trail [treɪl] **I** *v/t.* **1.** (nach)schleppen, (-) schleifen, hinter sich her ziehen: ***~ one's coat*** *fig.* Streit suchen; **2.** verfolgen (*acc.*), nachspüren (*dat.*), ‚beschatten' (*acc.*); **3.** zu'rückbleiben hinter (*dat.*); **II** *v/i.* **4.** schleifen (*Rock etc.*); **5.** wehen, flattern; her'unterhängen; **6.** ✿ kriechen, sich ranken; **7.** (sich da'hin-) ziehen (*Rauch etc.*); **8.** sich da'hinschleppen; **9.** nachhinken (*a. fig.*); **10.** ***~ off*** sich verlieren (*Klang, Stimme etc.*); **III** *s.* **11.** geschleppter Teil, *z.B.* Schleppe *f* (*Kleid*); **12.** *fig.* Schweif *m*, Schwanz *m* (*Meteor etc.*): ***~ of smoke*** Rauchfahne *f*; **13.** Spur *f*: ***~ of blood***; **14.** *hunt. u. fig.* Fährte *f*, Spur *f*: ***on s.o.'s ~*** j-m auf der Spur *od.* auf den Fersen; ***off the ~*** von der Spur abgekommen; **15.** (Trampel)Pfad *m*, Weg *m*: ***blaze the ~*** a) den Weg markieren, b) *fig.* den Weg bahnen (***for*** für), bahnbrechend sein; **'~,blaz·er** *s.* **1.** Pistensucher *m*; **2.** *fig.* Bahnbrecher *m*, Pio'nier *m*.

trail·er ['treɪlə] *s.* **1.** ⚘ Kriechpflanze *f*; rankender Ausläufer; **2.** *mot.* a) Anhänger *m*, b) *Am.* Wohnwagen *m*, Caravan *m*: ***~ camp***, ***~ park*** Platz *m* für Wohnwagen; **3.** *Film, TV*: (Pro'gramm-)Vorschau *f*; **'trail·er·ite** *s. Am.* Caravaner *m*.

trail·ing| a·e·ri·al ['treɪlɪŋ] *s.* ϟ 'Schleppan,tenne *f*; **~ ax·le** *s. mot.* nicht angetriebene Achse, Schleppachse *f*.

train [treɪn] **I** *s.* **1.** (Eisenbahn)Zug *m*: ***~ journey*** Bahnfahrt *f*; ***~ staff*** Zugpersonal *n*; ***by ~*** mit der Bahn; ***be on the ~*** im Zug sein *od.* sitzen; ***take a ~ to*** mit dem Zug fahren nach; **2.** Zug *m von Personen, Wagen etc.*, Kette *f*, Ko'lonne *f*: ***~ of barges*** Schleppzug (*Kähne*); **3.** Gefolge *n* (*a. fig.*): ***have*** (*od.* ***bring***) ***in its ~*** *et.* mit sich bringen, zur Folge haben; **4.** *fig.* Folge *f*, Kette *f*, Reihe *f von Ereignissen etc.*: ***~ of thought*** Gedankengang *m*; ***in ~*** a) im Gang, im Zuge, b) bereit (***for*** für); ***put in ~*** in Gang setzen; **5.** Schleppe *f am Kleid*; **6.** (Ko'meten)Schweif *m*; **7.** ⚒, ⚔ Zündlinie *f*; **8.** ⚙ Räder-, Triebwerk *n*; **II** *v/t.* **9.** auf-, erziehen; **10.** ⚘ ziehen; **11.** *j-n* ausbilden (*a.* ⚔), *a. Auge, Geist etc.* schulen: → ***trained***; **12.** *j-m et.* einexerzieren, beibringen; **13.** a) *Sportler, a. Pferde* trainieren, b) *Tiere* abrichten, dressieren (***to do*** zu tun), *Pferd* zureiten; **14.** ⚔ *Geschütz* richten (***on*** auf *acc.*); **III** *v/i.* **15.** sich ausbilden (***for*** zu, als); sich schulen *od.* üben; **16.** *sport* trainieren (***for*** für); **17.** *a.* ***~ it*** F mit der Bahn fahren; **~ down** *v/i. sport* abtrainieren, ‚abkochen'.

'train|,bear·er *s.* Schleppenträger *m*; **~ call** *s. teleph.* Zuggespräch *n*.

trained [treɪnd] *adj.* **1.** geübt, geschult (*Auge, Geist etc.*); **2.** (voll) ausgebildet, geschult, Fach...: ***~ men*** Fachkräfte;

train·ee [treɪ'ni:] *s.* **1.** a) Auszubildende(r *m*) *f*, Lehrling *m*, b) Prakti'kant (-in), c) *Management*: Trai'nee *m, f*: ***~ nurse*** Lernschwester *f*; **2.** ⚔ *Am.* Re'krut *m*; **'train·er** [-nə] *s.* **1.** Ausbilder *m*; **2.** *sport* Trainer *m*; **3.** a) Abrichter *m*, ('Hunde- *etc.*)Dres,seur *m*, b) Zureiter *m*; **4.** ✈ a) Schulflugzeug *n*, b) ('Flug)Simu,lator *m*.

train fer·ry *s.* Eisenbahnfähre *f*.

train·ing ['treɪnɪŋ] **I** *s.* **1.** Schulung *f*, Ausbildung *f*; **2.** Üben *n*; **3.** *sport* Training *n*: ***be in ~*** a) im Training stehen, b) (gut) in Form sein; ***go into ~*** das Training aufnehmen; ***out of ~*** nicht in Form; **4.** a) Abrichten *n von Tieren*, b) Zureiten *n*; **II** *adj.* **5.** Ausbildungs..., Schul(ungs)..., Lehr...; **6.** *sport* Trainings...; **~ camp** *s.* **1.** *sport* Trainingslager *n*; **2.** ⚔ Ausbildungslager *n*; **~ cen·ter** *Am.*, **~ cen·tre** *Brit. s.* Ausbildungszentrum *n*; **~ film** *s.* Lehrfilm *m*; **~ school** *s.* **1.** *ped.* Aufbauschule *f*; **2.** ⚖ Jugendstrafanstalt *f*; **~ ship** *s.* ⚓ Schulschiff *n*.

'train|·load *s.* Zugladung *f*; **~ oil** *s.* (Fisch)Tran *m*, *bsd.* Walöl *n*; **'~·sick** *adj.*: ***she gets ~*** ihr wird beim Zugfahren schlecht.

traipse [treɪps] → ***trapse***.

trait [treɪ] *s.* **1.** (Cha'rakter)Zug *m*, Merkmal *n*; **2.** *Am.* Gesichtszug *m*.

trai·tor ['treɪtə] *s.* Verräter *m* (***to*** an *dat.*); **'trai·tor·ous** [-tərəs] *adj.* □ verräterisch; **'trai·tress** [-trɪs] *s.* Verräterin *f*.

tra·jec·to·ry ['trædʒɪktərɪ] *s.* **1.** *phys.* Flugbahn *f*; Fallkurve *f e-r Bombe*; **2.** ⩓ Trajekto'rie *f*.

tram [træm] **I** *s.* **1.** *Brit.* (***by ~*** mit der) Straßenbahn *f*; **2.** ⚒ Förderwagen *m*, Hund *m*; **II** *v/i.* **3.** *a.* ***~ it*** *Brit.* mit der Straßenbahn fahren; **'~·car** *s. Brit.* Straßenbahnwagen *m*; **'~·line** *s.* **1.** *Brit.* Straßenbahnlinie *f*; **2.** *pl. Tennis etc.*: Seitenlinien *pl.* für Doppel; **3.** *pl. fig.* 'Leitprin,zipien *pl.*

tram·mel ['træml] **I** *s.* **1.** (Schlepp)Netz *n*; **2.** Spannriemen *m für Pferde*; **3.** *fig.* Fessel *f*; **4.** Kesselhaken *m*; **5.** ⩓ El'lipsenzirkel *m*; **6.** *a.* ***pair of ~s*** Stangenzirkel *m*; **II** *v/t.* **7.** *mst fig.* hemmen.

tra·mon·tane [trə'mɒnteɪn] *adj.* **1.** transal'pin(isch); **2.** *fig.* fremd, bar'barisch.

tramp [træmp] **I** *v/i.* **1.** trampeln (**[*up*]*on*** auf *acc.*); sta(m)pfen; **2.** *mst* ***~ it*** marschieren, wandern, ‚tippeln'; **3.** vagabundieren; **II** *v/t.* **4.** durch'wandern; **5.** ***~ down*** niedertrampeln; **III** *s.* **6.** Getrampel *n*; **7.** (schwerer) Tritt; **8.** (Fuß)Marsch *m*, Wanderung *f*: ***on the ~*** auf (der) Wanderschaft; **9.** Landstreicher *m*; **10.** F ‚Luder' *n*, ‚Flittchen' *n*; **11.** ⚓ Trampschiff *n*; **'tram·ple** [-pl] **I** *v/i.* **1.** (her'um)trampeln (**[*up*]*on*** auf *dat.*); **2.** *fig.* mit Füßen treten (**[*up*]*on*** *acc.*); **II** *v/t.* **3.** (zer)trampeln: ***~ down*** niedertrampeln; ***~ out*** *Feuer* austreten; ***~ under foot*** he'rumtrampeln auf (*dat.*); **III** *s.* **4.** Trampeln *n*.

tram·po·lin(e) ['træmpəlɪn] *s. sport* Trampo'lin *n*; **'tram·po·lin·er** *s.* Trampo'linspringer(in), -turner(in).

'tram·way *s.* **1.** *Brit.* Straßenbahn(linie) *f*; **2.** ⚒ Grubenbahn *f*.

trance [trɑ:ns] *s.* **1.** Trance(zustand *m*) *f*: ***go*** (***put***) ***into a ~*** in Trance fallen (versetzen); **2.** Verzückung *f*, Ek'stase *f*.

trank [træŋk] *s. Am.* F Beruhigungsmittel *n*.

tran·quil ['træŋkwɪl] *adj.* □ **1.** ruhig, friedlich; **2.** gelassen, heiter; **tran·quil·(l)i·ty** [træŋ'kwɪlətɪ] *s.* **1.** Ruhe *f*, Friede(n) *m*, Stille *f*; **2.** Gelassenheit *f*, Heiterkeit *f*; **'tran·quil·(l)ize** [-laɪz] *v/t.* (*v/i.* sich) beruhigen; **'tran·quil·(l)iz·er** [-laɪzə] *s.* Beruhigungsmittel *n*.

trans·act [træn'zækt] **I** *v/t. Geschäfte etc.* ('durch)führen, abwickeln; *Handel* abschließen; **II** *v/i.* ver-, unter'handeln (***with*** mit); **trans'ac·tion** [-kʃn] *s.* **1.** 'Durchführung *f*, Abwicklung *f*, Erledigung *f*; **2.** Ver-, Unter'handlung *f*; **3.** a) ✝ Transakti'on *f*, (Geschäfts)Abschluß *m*, Geschäft *n*, b) ⚖ Rechtsgeschäft *n*; **4.** *pl.* ✝ (Ge'schäfts),Umsatz *m*; **5.** *pl.* Proto'koll *n*, Sitzungsbericht *m*.

trans·al·pine [,trænz'ælpaɪn] *adj.* transal'pin(isch).

trans·at·lan·tic [,trænzət'læntɪk] *adj.* **1.** transat'lantisch, 'überseeisch; **2.** Übersee...: ***~ liner***; ***~ flight*** Ozeanflug *m*.

trans·ceiv·er [træn'si:və] *s.* ϟ Sender-Empfänger *m*.

tran·scend [træn'send] *v/t.* **1.** *bsd. fig.* über'schreiten, -'steigen; **2.** *fig.* über'treffen; **tran'scend·ence** [-dəns], **tran'scend·en·cy** [-dənsɪ] *s.* **1.** Über'legenheit *f*, Erhabenheit *f*; **2.** *phls., eccl., a.* ⩓ Transzen'denz *f*; **tran'scend·ent** [-dənt] *adj.* □ **1.** transzen'dent: a) *phls.* 'übersinnlich, b) *eccl.* 'überweltlich; **2.** her'vorragend.

tran·scen·den·tal [,trænsen'dentl] *adj.* □ **1.** *phls.* transzenden'tal: a) meta'physisch, b) *bei Kant*: apri'orisch: ***~ meditation*** transzendentale Meditation; **2.** 'überna,türlich; **3.** erhaben; **4.** ab'strus, verworren; **5.** ⩓ transzen'dent; **,tran·scen'den·tal·ism** [-təlɪzəm] *s.* Transzenden'talphiloso,phie *f*.

tran·scribe [træn'skraɪb] *v/t.* **1.** abschreiben; **2.** *Stenogramm etc.* über'tragen; **3.** ♪ transkribieren; **4.** *Radio, TV*: a) aufzeichnen, auf Band aufnehmen, b) (vom Band) über'tragen; **5.** *Computer*: 'umschreiben; **tran·script** ['trænskrɪpt] *s.* Abschrift *f*, Ko'pie *f*; **tran'scrip·tion** [-rɪpʃn] *s.* **1.** Abschreiben *n*; **2.** Abschrift *f*; **3.** 'Umschrift *f*; **4.** ♪ Transkripti'on *f*; **5.** *Radio, TV*: a) Aufnahme *f*, b) Aufzeichnung *f*.

trans·duc·er [trænz'dju:sə] *s.* **1.** ϟ ('Um)Wandler; **2.** ⚙ 'Umformer; **3.** *Computer*: Wandler *m*.

tran·sept ['trænsept] *s.* ⚠ Querschiff *n*.

trans·fer [træns'fɜ:] **I** *v/t.* **1.** hin'überbringen, -schaffen (***from ... to*** von ... nach *od.* zu); **2.** über'geben (***to*** *dat.*); **3.** *Betrieb, Truppen, Wohnsitz etc.* verlegen, *Beamten, Schüler in e-e andere Schule etc.* versetzen (***to*** nach, ***in***, ***into*** in *acc.*); *Technologie, a. sport Spieler* transferieren; ⚕ *Patienten* über'weisen; **4.** ⚖ (***to***) über'tragen (auf *acc.*), abtreten (an *acc.*); **5.** ✝ a) *Summe* vortragen, b) *Posten, Wertpapiere* 'umbuchen, c) *Aktien etc.* über'tragen; **6.** *Geld* über'weisen; **7.** *fig. Zuneigung etc.* über'tragen (***to*** auf *acc.*); **8.** *typ. Druck, Stich etc.* 'umdrucken, über'tragen; **II** *v/i.* **9.** 'übertreten (***to*** zu); **10.** verlegt *od.* versetzt werden (***to*** nach); **11.** 🚌 *etc.* 'umsteigen; **III** *s.* ['trænsfɜ:] **12.** (***to***) Über'tragung *f* (auf *acc.*), 'Übergabe *f* (an *acc.*); **13.** Wechsel *m* (***to*** zu); **14.** (***to***) a) Verlegung *f* (nach), b) Versetzung *f* (nach), c) *sport* Trans'fer *m od.* Wechsel *m* (zu); **15.** ⚖ (***to***) Über'tragung *f* (***to*** auf *acc.*), Abtretung *f* (an *acc.*); **16.** ('Geld)Über,weisung *f*: ***~ business*** ✝ Giroverkehr *m*; ***~ of foreign exchange*** Devisentransfer *m*; **17.** ✝ ('Wertpa,pier- *etc.*),Umbuchung *f*; **18.** ✝ ('Aktien- *etc.*)Über,tragung *f*; **19.** *typ.* a) Über'tragung *f*, 'Umdruck *m*, b) Abziehen *n*, Abzug *m*, c) Abziehbild *n*; **20.** 🚌 *etc.* a) 'Umsteigen *n*, b) 'Umsteigefahrkarte *f*, c) *a.* ⚓ 'Umschlagplatz *m*, d) Fährboot *n*; **trans'fer·a·ble** [-'fɜ:rəbl] *adj. bsd.* ✝, ⚖ über'tragbar (*a. Wahlstimme*).

trans·fer| bank *s.* ✝ Girobank *f*; **~ book** *s.* ✝ 'Umschreibungs-, Aktienbuch *n*; **~ day** *s.* ✝ 'Umschreibungstag *m*; **~ deed** *s.* Über'tragungsurkunde *f*.

trans·fer·ee [,trænsfɜ:'ri:] *s.* Zessio'nar *m*, Über'nehmer *m*; **trans·fer·ence** ['trænsfərəns] *s.* **1.** → ***transfer*** 14, 15, 17, 18; **2.** *psych.* Über'tragung *f*; **trans-**

fer·en·tial [ˌtrænsfəˈrenʃl] *adj.* Übertragungs…
trans·fer ink *s. typ.* ˈUmdrucktinte *f*, -farbe *f*.
trans·fer·or [trænsˈfɜːrə] *s.* ⚖ Zeˈdent *m*, Abtretende(r *m*) *f*.
trans·fer| pa·per *s. typ.* ˈUmdruckpaˌpier *n*; **~ pic·ture** *s.* Abziehbild *n*.
trans·fer·rer [trænsˈfɜːrə] *s.* **1.** Überˈtrager *m*; **2.** → ***transferor***.
trans·fer tick·et → ***transfer*** 20b.
trans·fig·u·ra·tion [ˌtrænsfɪgjʊˈreɪʃn] *s.* **1.** ˈUmgestaltung *f*; **2.** *eccl.* a) Verklärung *f*, b) ♎ Fest *n* der Verklärung (*6. August*); **trans·fig·ure** [trænsˈfɪgə] *v/t.* **1.** ˈumgestalten; **2.** *eccl. u. fig.* verklären.
trans·fix [trænsˈfɪks] *v/t.* **1.** durchˈstechen, -ˈbohren (*a. fig.*); **2.** *fig.* lähmen: **~*ed*** (wie) versteinert, starr (***with*** vor *dat.*).
trans·form [trænsˈfɔːm] **I** *v/t.* **1.** ˈumgestalten, -wandeln ([***in***]***to*** in *acc.*, zu); ˈumformen (*a.* ⚗); *a. j-n* verwandeln, verändern; **2.** ⚡ ˈumspannen; **II** *v/i.* **3.** sich verwandeln (***into*** zu); **trans·for·ma·tion** [ˌtrænsfəˈmeɪʃn] *s.* **1.** ˈUmgestaltung *f*, -bildung *f*; ˈUmwandlung *f*, -formung *f* (*a.* ⚗); Verwandlung *f*, (*a.* Chaˈrakter-, Sinnes)Änderung *f*; **~ *of energy*** *phys.* Energieumsetzung *f*; **~ (*scene*)** *thea.* Verwandlungsszene *f*; **2.** ⚡ ˈUmspannung *f*; **3.** ˈDamenpeˌrücke *f*; **transˈform·er** [-mə] *s.* **1.** ˈUmgestalter(in); **2.** ⚡ Transforˈmator *m*.
trans·fuse [trænsˈfjuːz] *v/t.* **1.** ˈumgießen; **2.** ⚕ a) *Blut* überˈtragen, b) e-e ˈBluttransfusiˌon machen bei, c) *Serum etc.* einspritzen; **3.** *fig.* einflößen (***into*** *dat.*); **4.** *fig.* durchˈdringen, erfüllen (***with*** mit, von); **transˈfu·sion** [-juːʒn] *s.* **1.** ˈUmgießen *n*; **2.** ⚕ (ˈBlut)Transfusiˌon *f*; **3.** *fig.* Erfüllung (***with*** mit).
trans·gress [trænsˈgres] **I** *v/t.* **1.** überˈschreiten (*a. fig.*); **2.** *fig. Gesetze etc.* überˈtreten; **II** *v/i.* **3.** (***against*** gegen) sich vergehen, sündigen; **transˈgres·sion** [-eʃn] *s.* **1.** Überˈschreitung *f* (*a. fig.*); **2.** Überˈtretung *f von Gesetzen etc.*; **3.** Vergehen *n*, Missetat *f*; **transˈgres·sor** [-sə] *s.* Missetäter(in).
tran·sience [ˈtrænzɪəns], **ˈtran·sien·cy** [-nsɪ] *s.* Vergänglichkeit *f*, Flüchtigkeit *f*; **ˈtran·sient** [-nt] **I** *adj.* ☐ **1.** *zeitlich* vorˈübergehend; **2.** vergänglich, flüchtig; **3.** *Am.* Durchgangs…: **~ *camp***; **~ *visitor*** → 5; **4.** ⚡ Einschalt…, Einschwing…; **II** *s.* **5.** *Am.* ˈDurchreisende(r *m*) *f*; **6.** ⚡ a) Einschaltstoß *m*, b) Einschwingvorgang, c) Wanderwelle *f*.
trans·i·re [trænzˈaɪərɪ] *s.* ✝ Zollbegleitschein *m*.
tran·sis·tor [trænˈsɪstə] *s.* ⚡ Tranˈsistor *m*; **tranˈsis·tor·ize** [-raɪz] *v/t.* ⚡ transistorisieren.
trans·it [ˈtrænsɪt] **I** *s.* **1.** ˈDurch-, ˈÜberfahrt *f*; **2.** *a. ast.* ˈDurchgang *m*; **3.** ✝ Tranˈsit *m*, ˈDurchfuhr *f*, Transˈport *m*: ***in* ~** unterwegs, auf dem Transport; **4.** ✝ ˈDurchgangsverkehr *m*; **5.** ˈDurchgangsstraße *f*; **6.** *Am.* öffentliche Verkehrsmittel *pl.*; **7.** *fig.* ˈÜbergang *m* (***to*** zu); **II** *adj.* **8.** *a.* ✝ Durchgangs… (*-lager, -verkehr etc.*): **~ *visa*** Durchreise-, Transitvisum *n*; **9.** ✝ Durchfuhr…, Transit…: **~ *trade*** Transithandel *m*.
tran·si·tion [trænˈsɪʒn] **I** *s.* **1.** ˈÜbergang *m* (*a.* ♪, *phys.*); **2.** ˈÜbergangszeit *f*: (***state of***) **~** Übergangsstadium *n*; **II** *adj.* **3.** → **tranˈsi·tion·al** [-ʒənl] *adj.* ☐ Übergangs…, Überleitungs…, Zwischen…
tran·si·tive [ˈtrænsɪtɪv] *adj.* ☐ **1.** *ling.* transitiv: **~ (*verb*)** Transitiv *n*, transitives Verb; **2.** Übergangs…
tran·si·to·ri·ness [ˈtrænsɪtərɪnɪs] *s.* Flüchtigkeit *f*, Vergänglichkeit *f*; **tran·si·to·ry** [ˈtrænsɪtərɪ] *adj.* ☐ **1.** *zeitlich* vorˈübergehend, transiˈtorisch; **2.** vergänglich, flüchtig.
trans·lat·a·ble [trænsˈleɪtəbl] *adj.* überˈsetzbar; **trans·late** [trænsˈleɪt] **I** *v/t.* **1.** *Buch etc.* überˈsetzen (*a. Computer*), -ˈtragen (***into*** in *acc.*); **2.** *fig. Grundsätze etc.* überˈtragen (***into*** in *acc.*, zu): **~ *ideas into action*** Gedanken in die Tat umsetzen; **3.** *fig.* a) auslegen, b) ausdrücken (***in*** in *dat.*); **4.** *eccl.* a) *Geistlichen* versetzen, b) *Reliquie etc.* ˈüberführen, verlegen (***to*** nach), c) *j-n* entrücken; **5.** *Brit. Schuhe etc.* ˈumarbeiten; **6.** ⚙ *Bewegung* überˈtragen (***to*** auf *acc.*); **II** *v/i.* **7.** sich *gut etc.* überˈsetzen lassen; **transˈla·tion** [-eɪʃn] *s.* **1.** Überˈsetzung *f*, -ˈtragung *f*; **2.** *fig.* Auslegung *f*; **3.** *eccl.* a) Versetzung *f*, b) Entrükkung *f*; **transˈla·tor** [-tə] *s.* **1.** Überˈsetzer(in); **2.** *Computer*: Überˈsetzer *m*.
trans·lit·er·ate [trænzˈlɪtəreɪt] *v/t.* transkribieren, ˈumschreiben; **trans·lit·er·a·tion** [ˌtrænzlɪtəˈreɪʃn] *s.* Transkriptiˈon *f*.
trans·lo·cate [ˌtrænzləʊˈkeɪt] *v/t.* verlagern.
trans·lu·cence [trænzˈluːsns], **transˈlu·cen·cy** [-sɪ] *s.* **1.** ˈDurchscheinen *n*; **2.** ˈLichtˌdurchlässigkeit *f*; **transˈlu·cent** *adj.* ☐ **1.** a) ˈlichtˌdurchlässig, b) halb ˈdurchsichtig; **2.** ˈdurchscheinend.
trans·ma·rine [ˌtrænzməˈriːn] *adj.* ˈüberseeisch, Übersee…
trans·mi·grant [trænzˈmaɪgrənt] *s.* ˈDurchreisende(r *m*) *f*, -wandernde(r *m*) *f*; **trans·mi·grate** [ˌtrænzmaɪˈgreɪt] *v/i.* **1.** fortziehen; **2.** ˈübersiedeln; **3.** auswandern; **4.** wandern (*Seele*); **trans·mi·gra·tion** [ˌtrænzmaɪˈgreɪʃn] *s.* **1.** Auswanderung *f*, ˈÜbersiedlung *f*; **2.** *a.* **~ *of souls*** Seelenwanderung *f*; **3.** ⚕ a) ˈÜberwandern *n* (*Ei-, Blutzelle etc.*), b) Diapeˈdese *f*.
trans·mis·si·ble [trænzˈmɪsəbl] *adj.* **1.** überˈsendbar; **2.** *a.* ⚕ *u. fig.* überˈtragbar (***to*** auf *acc.*).
trans·mis·sion [trænzˈmɪʃn] *s.* **1.** Überˈsendung *f*, -ˈmittlung *f*; ✝ Versand *m*; **2.** Überˈmittlung *f von Nachrichten etc.*; **3.** *ling.* (ˈText)Überˌlieferung *f*; **4.** ⚙ a) Transmissiˈon *f*, Überˈsetzung *f*, -ˈtragung *f*, b) Triebwelle *f*, -werk *n*: **~ *gear*** Wechselgetriebe *n*; **5.** Überˈtragung *f*: a) *biol.* Vererbung *f*, b) ⚕ Ansteckung *f*, c) *Radio, TV*: Sendung *f*, d) ⚖ Überˈlassung *f*, e) *phys.* Fortpflanzung *f*; **~ belt** *s.* ⚙ Treibriemen *m*; **~ gear·ing** *s.* ⚙ Überˈsetzungsgetriebe *n*; **~ ra·tio** *s.* ⚙ Überˈsetzungsverhältnis *n*; **~ shaft** *s.* ⚙ Karˈdanwelle *f*.
trans·mit [trænzˈmɪt] *v/t.* **1.** (***to***) überˈsenden, -ˈmitteln (*dat.*), (ver)senden (an *acc.*); *a. Telegramm etc.* weitergeben (an *acc.*), befördern; **2.** *Nachrichten etc.* mitteilen (***to*** *dat.*); **3.** *fig. Ideen etc.* überˈmitteln, weitergeben (***to*** an *acc.*); **4.** überˈtragen (*a.* ⚕): a) *biol.* vererben, b) ⚖ überˈschreiben, vermachen; **5.** *phys. Wellen, Wärme etc.* a) (weiter)leiten, b) *a. Kraft* überˈtragen, c) *Licht etc.* ˈdurchlassen; **transˈmit·tal** [-tl] → ***transmission*** 1–4a; **transˈmit·ter** [-tə] *s.* **1.** Überˈsender *m*, -ˈmittler *m*; **2.** *Radio*: a) Sendegerät *n*, b) Sender *m*; **3.** *teleph.* Mikroˈphon *n*; **4.** ⚙ (Meßwert)Geber *m*; **transˈmit·ting** [-tɪŋ] *adj.* Sende…(*-antenne, -stärke etc.*): **~ *station*** Sender *m*.
trans·mog·ri·fy [trænzˈmɒgrɪfaɪ] *v/t. humor.* (gänzlich) ˈummodeln.
trans·mut·a·ble [trænzˈmjuːtəbl] *adj.* ☐ ˈumwandelbar; **trans·mu·ta·tion** [ˌtrænzmjuːˈteɪʃn] *s.* **1.** ˈUmwandlung *f* (*a.* ⚗, *phys.*); **2.** *biol.* Transmutatiˈon *f*, ˈUmbildung *f*; **trans·mute** [trænzˈmjuːt] *v/t.* ˈumwandeln (***into*** in *acc.*).
trans·na·tion·al [trænzˈnæʃənl] *adj.* ˈüber-, ✝ ˈmultinatioˌnal.
trans·o·ce·an·ic [ˈtrænzˌəʊʃɪˈænɪk] *adj.* **1.** transozeˈanisch, ˈüberseeisch; **2.** a) Übersee…, b) Ozean…
tran·som [ˈtrænsəm] *s.* ⚠ a) Querbalken *m über e-r Tür*, b) (Quer)Blende *f e-s Fensters*.
tran·son·ic [trænˈsɒnɪk] *adj. phys.* Überschall…
trans·par·en·cy [trænsˈpærənsɪ] *s.* **1.** *a. fig.* ˈDurchsichtigkeit *f*, Transpaˈrenz *f*; **2.** Transpaˈrent *n*, Leuchtbild *n*; **3.** *phot.* Dia(posiˈtiv) *n*; **transˈpar·ent** [-nt] *adj.* ☐ **1.** ˈdurchsichtig (*a. fig. offenkundig*): **~ *colo(u)r*** ⚙ Lasurfarbe; **~ *slide*** Diapositiv *n*; **2.** *phys.* transpaˈrent, ˈlichtˌdurchlässig; **3.** *fig.* a) klar (*Stil etc.*), b) offen, ehrlich.
tran·spi·ra·tion [ˌtrænspɪˈreɪʃn] *s.* **1.** (*bsd.* Haut)Ausdünstung *f*; **2.** Schweiß *m*; **tran·spire** [trænˈspaɪə] **I** *v/i.* **1.** *physiol.* transpirieren, schwitzen; **2.** ausgedünstet werden; **3.** *fig.* ˈdurchsickern, bekannt werden; **4.** *fig.* passieren, sich ereignen; **II** *v/t.* **5.** ausdünsten, ausschwitzen.
trans·plant [trænsˈplɑːnt] **I** *v/t.* **1.** ⚘ ˈumpflanzen; **2.** ⚕ transplantieren, verpflanzen; **3.** *fig.* versetzen, -pflanzen (***to*** nach, ***into*** in *acc.*); **II** *v/i.* **4.** sich verpflanzen lassen; **III** *s.* [ˈtrænsplɑːnt] **5.** a) → ***transplantation***, b) ⚕ Transplanˈtat *n*; **trans·plan·ta·tion** [ˌtrænsplɑːnˈteɪʃn] *s.* Verpflanzung *f*: a) ⚘ ˈUmpflanzung *f*, b) *fig.* Versetzung *f*, ˈUmsiedlung *f*, c) ⚕ Transplantatiˈon *f*.
trans·port **I** *v/t.* [trænˈspɔːt] **1.** transportieren, befördern, versenden; **2.** *mst pass. fig.* a) *j-n* hinreißen, entzücken (***with*** vor *dat.*, von), b) heftig erregen: **~*ed with joy*** außer sich vor Freude; **3.** *bsd. hist.* deportieren; **II** *s.* [ˈtrænspɔːt] **4.** a) (ˈAb-, ˈAn)Transˌport *m*, Beförderung *f*, b) Versand *m*, c) Verschiffung *f*; **5.** Verkehr *m*; **6.** Beförderungsmittel *n od. pl.*; **7.** *a.* **~ *ship***, **~ *vessel*** a) Transˈport-, Frachtschiff *n*, b) ⚔ ˈTruppentransˌporter *m*; **8.** *a.* **~ *plane*** ✈ Transˈportflugzeug *n*; **9.** *fig.* a) Taumel *m der Freude etc.*, b) heftige Erregung: ***in a* ~ *of*** außer sich vor *Entzücken, Wut etc.*; **transˈport·a·ble** [-təbl] *adj.* transˈportfähig, versendbar; **trans·por·ta·tion** [ˌtrænspɔːˈteɪʃn] *s.* **1.** → ***transport*** 4; **2.** Transˈportsyˌstem *n*; **3.** *bsd. Am.* a) Beförderungsmittel *pl.*, b) Transˈportko-

sten *pl.*, c) Fahrausweis *m*; **4.** *bsd. hist.* Deportati'on *f*; **trans'port·er** [-tə] *s.* **1.** Beförderer *m*; **2.** ⚙ Förder-, Trans'portvorrichtung *f*.
trans·pose [træns'pəʊz] *v/t.* **1.** 'umstellen (*a. ling.*), ver-, 'umsetzen; **2.** ♪, ⅍, ⚗ transponieren; **trans·po·si·tion** [ˌtrænspə'zɪʃn] *s.* **1.** 'Umstellen *n*; **2.** 'Umstellung *f* (*a. ling.*); **3.** ♪, ⅍ Transpositi'on *f*; **4.** ⚡, ⚙ Kreuzung *f von Leitungen etc.*
trans·sex·u·al [trænz'seksjʊəl] **I** *adj.* transsexu'ell; **II** *s.* Transsexu'elle(r *m*) *f*.
trans·ship [træns'ʃɪp] *v/t.* ✝, ⚓ 'umladen, -schlagen; **trans'ship·ment** [-mənt] *s.* ⚓ 'Umladung *f*, 'Umschlag *m*: ~ **charge** Umladegebühr *f*; ~ **port** Umschlaghafen *m*.
tran·sub·stan·ti·ate [ˌtrænsəb'stænʃɪeɪt] *v/t.* 'umwandeln, (*a. eccl. Brot u. Wein*) verwandeln (**into**, **to** in *acc.*, zu); **tran·sub·stan·ti·a·tion** ['trænsəbˌstænʃɪ'eɪʃn] *s.* **1.** 'Stoffˌumwandlung *f*; **2.** *eccl.* Transsubstantiati'on *f*.
tran·sude [træn'sjuːd] *v/i.* **1.** *physiol.* 'durchschwitzen (*Flüssigkeiten*); **2.** ('durch)dringen, (-)sickern (**through** durch); **3.** abgesondert werden.
trans·ver·sal [trænz'vɜːsl] **I** *adj.* □ → **transverse** 1; **II** *s.* ⅍ Transver'sale *f*;
trans·verse ['trænzvɜːs] **I** *adj.* □ **1.** schräg, diago'nal, Quer…, quer(laufend) (**to** zu): ~ **flute** ♪ Querflöte *f*; ~ **section** ⅍ Querschnitt *m*; **II** *s.* **2.** Querstück *n*, -achse *f*, -muskel *m*; **3.** ⅍ große Achse e-r El'lipse.
trans·ves·tism [træns'vestɪzəm] *s. psych.* Transve'stismus *m*; **trans'ves·tite** [-taɪt] *s.* Transve'stit *m*.
trap¹ [træp] **I** *s.* **1.** *hunt.*, *a.* ⚔ *u. fig.* Falle *f*: **lay** (*od.* **set**) **a ~ for s.o.** j-m e-e Falle stellen; **walk** (*od.* **fall**) **into a ~** in e-e Falle gehen; **2.** ⚗ Abscheider *m*; **3.** a) Auffangvorrichtung *f*, b) Dampf-, Wasserverschluß *m*, c) Geruchverschluß *m* (*Klosett*); **4.** ⚡ (Funk)Sperrkreis *m*; **5.** *Tontaubenschießen*: 'Wurfmaˌschine *f*; **6.** *Golf*: Sandhindernis *n*; **7.** → **trapdoor**; **8.** *Brit.* Gig *n*, zweirädriger Einspänner; **9.** *mot.* offener Zweisitzer; **10.** *pl.* ♪ Schlagzeug *n*; **11.** *sl.* ‚Klappe' *f* (*Mund*); **II** *v/t.* **12.** fangen (*a. fig.*); (*a. phys. Elektronen*) einfangen; **13.** einschließen (*a.* ⚔); verschütten; **14.** *fig.* in e-e Falle locken, ‚fangen'; **15.** Fallen aufstellen in (*dat.*); **16.** ⚙ a) mit Wasserverschluß *etc.* versehen, verschließen, b) *Gase etc.* abfangen; **III** *v/i.* **17.** Fallen stellen (**for** *dat.*).
trap² [træp] *s. mst pl.* F ‚Kla'motten' *pl.*, Siebensachen *pl.*, Gepäck *n*.
trap³ [træp] *s. min.* Trapp *m*.
ˌ**trap**|'**door** *s.* **1.** Fall-, Klapptür *f*, (✈ Boden)Klappe *f*; **2.** *thea.* Versenkung *f*.
tra·peze [trə'piːz] *s.* Tra'pez *n*; **tra'pe·zi·form** [-zɪfɔːm] *adj.* tra'pezförmig; **tra'pe·zi·um** [-zjəm] *s.* **1.** ⅍ a) Tra'pez *n*, b) *bsd. Am.* Trapezo'id *n*; **2.** *anat.* großes Vieleckbein (*Handwurzel*); **trap·e·zoid** ['træpɪzɔɪd] **I** *s.* **1.** ⅍ a) *Brit.* Trapezo'id *n*, b) *bsd. Am.* Tra'pez *n*; **2.** *anat.* kleines Vieleckbein (*Handwurzel*); **II** *adj.* **3.** → **trap·e·zoi·dal** [ˌtræpɪ'zɔɪdl] ⅍ trapezo'id, *bsd. Am.* tra'pezförmig.

trap·per ['træpə] *s.* Trapper *m*, Pelztierjäger *m*.
trap·pings ['træpɪŋz] *s. pl.* **1.** Staatsgeschirr *n für Pferde*; **2.** *fig.* a) ‚Staat' *m*, Schmuck *m*, b) Drum u. Dran *n*, ‚Verzierungen' *pl.*
trapse [treɪps] *v/i.* **1.** (da'hin)latschen; **2.** (um'her)schlendern.
trap shoot·ing *s. sport* Trapschießen *n*.
trash [træʃ] *s.* **1.** *bsd. Am.* Abfall *m*, Müll *m*: ~ **can** Abfall-, Mülleimer *m od.* -tonne *f*; **2.** Plunder *m*, Schund *m*; **3.** *fig.* Schund *m*, Kitsch *m* (*Bücher etc.*); **4.** ‚Blech' *n*, Unsinn *m*; **5.** Ausschuß *m*, Gesindel *n*; → **white trash**; '**trash·i·ness** [-ʃɪnɪs] *s.* Wertlosigkeit *f*, Minderwertigkeit *f*; '**trash·y** [-ʃɪ] *adj.* □ wertlos, minderwertig, kitschig, Schund…, Kitsch…
trau·ma ['trɔːmə] *s.* Trauma *n*: a) ⚕ Wunde *f*, b) *psych.* seelische Erschütterung, (bleibender) Schock; **trau·mat·ic** [trɔː'mætɪk] *adj.* (□ **~ally**) ⚕, *psych.* trau'matisch: ~ **medicine** Unfallmedizin *f*.
trav·ail ['træveɪl] **I** *s.* **1.** *obs. od. rhet.* (mühevolle) Arbeit; **2.** (Geburts)Wehen *pl.*; **3.** *fig.* (Seelen)Qual *f*: **be in ~ with** schwer ringen mit; **II** *v/i.* **4.** sich abrackern; **5.** in den Wehen liegen.
trav·el ['trævl] **I** *s.* **1.** Reisen *n*: ~ **sickness** Reisekrankheit *f*; **2.** *mst pl.* (längere) Reise: **book of ~** Reisebeschreibung *f*; **3.** ⚙ Bewegung *f*, Lauf *m*, (Kolben- *etc.*)Hub *m*; **II** *v/i.* **4.** reisen, e-e Reise machen: ~ **light** mit leichtem Gepäck reisen; **5.** ✝ reisen (**in** in *e-r Ware*), als (Handels)Vertreter arbeiten (**for** für); **6.** *ast.*, *phys.*, *mot. etc.* sich bewegen; sich fortpflanzen (*Licht etc.*); **7.** ⚙ sich ('hin- u. 'her)bewegen, laufen (*Kolben etc.*); **8.** *bsd. fig.* schweifen, wandern (*Blick etc.*); **9.** F (da'hin)sausen; **III** *v/t.* **10.** *Land*, *a.* ✝ *Vertreterbezirk* bereisen, *Strecke* zu'rücklegen; ~ **a·gen·cy** *s.* 'Reisebüˌro *n*; ~ **al·low·ance** *s.* Reisekostenzuschuß *m*.
trav·el·la·tor ['trævəleɪtə] *s. Brit.* Rollsteig *m*.
trav·el(l)ed ['trævld] *adj.* **1.** (weit-, viel-) gereist; **2.** (viel)befahren (*Straße etc.*); '**trav·el·(l)er** [-lə] *s.* **1.** Reisende(r *m*) *f*; **2.** ✝ *bsd. Brit.* (Handlungs)Reisende(r) *m*, (Handels)Vertreter *m*; **3.** ⚙ Laufstück *n*, *bsd.* a) Laufkatze *f*, b) Hängekran *m*.
trav·el·(l)er's| **check** (*Brit.* **cheque**) *s.* Reisescheck *m*; ~ **joy** *s.* ⚘ Waldrebe *f*.
trav·el·(l)ing ['trævlɪŋ] *adj.* **1.** Reise… (*-koffer*, *-wecker*, *-kosten etc.*): ~ **agent**, *bsd. Am.* ~ **salesman** → **travel(l)er** 2; **2.** Wander…(*-ausstellung*, *-bücherei*, *-zirkus etc.*); fahrbar, auf Rädern: ~ **dental clinic**; ~ **crane** Laufkran *m*.
trav·e·log(ue) ['trævəlɒg] *s.* Reisebericht *m* (*Vortrag*, *mst mit Lichtbildern*), Reisefilm *m*.
trav·ers·a·ble ['trævəsəbl] *adj.* **1.** (leicht) durch- *od.* über'querbar; **2.** passierbar, befahrbar; **3.** ⚙ (aus-) schwenkbar; **trav·erse** ['trævəs] **I** *v/t.* **1.** durch-, über'queren; **2.** durch'ziehen, -'fließen; **3.** *Fluß etc.* über'spannen; **4.** *fig.* 'durchgehen, -sehen; **5.** ⚙, *a.* ⚔ *Geschütz* (seitwärts) schwenken, **6.** *Linie etc.* kreuzen, schneiden; **7.** *Plan etc.* durch'kreuzen; **8.** ⚓ kreuzen; **9.** ⚖ a) *Vorbringen* bestreiten, b) gegen *e-e Klage etc.* Einspruch erheben; **10.** *mount.*, *Skisport*: *Hang* queren; **II** *v/i.* **11.** ⚙ sich drehen; **12.** *fenc.*, *Reitsport*: traversieren; **13.** *mount.*, *Skisport*: queren; **III** *s.* **14.** Durch-, Über'querung *f*; **15.** ⚠ a) Quergitter *n*, b) Querwand *f*, c) Quergang *m*, d) Tra'verse *f*, Querstück *n*; **16.** ⅍ Schnittlinie *f*; **17.** ⚓ Koppelkurs *m*; **18.** ⚔ a) Traverse *f*, Querwall *m*, b) Schulterwehr *f*; **19.** ⚔ Schwenken *n* (*Geschütz*); **20.** ⚙ a) Schwenkung *f e-r Maschine*, b) schwenkbarer Teil; **21.** *surv.* Poly'gon(zug *m*) *n*; **22.** ⚖ a) Bestreitung *f*, b) Einspruch *m*; **23.** *mount.*, *Skisport*: a) Queren *n e-s Hanges*, b) Quergang *m*; **IV** *adj.* **24.** querlaufend, Quer…(*-bohrer etc.*): ~ **motion** Schwenkung *f*; **25.** Zickzack…: ~ **sailing** ⚓ Koppelkurs *m*; **26.** sich kreuzend (*Linien*).
trav·es·ty ['trævɪstɪ] **I** *s.* **1.** Trave'stie *f*; **2.** *fig.* Zerrbild *n*, Karika'tur *f*; **II** *v/t.* **3.** travestieren (*scherzhaft umgestalten*); **4.** *fig.* ins Lächerliche ziehen, verzerren.
trawl [trɔːl] ⚓ **I** *s. a.* ~ **net** (Grund-) Schleppnetz *n*; **II** *v/t. u. v/i.* mit dem Schleppnetz fischen; '**trawl·er** [-lə] *s.* (Grund)Schleppnetzfischer *m* (*Boot u. Person*).
tray [treɪ] *s.* **1.** Ta'blett *n*, (Ser'vier-, Tee)Brett *n*; **2.** a) Auslagekästchen *n*, b) ('umgehängtes) Verkaufsbrett, ‚Bauchladen' *m*; **3.** flache Schale; **4.** Ablagekorb *m im Büro*; **5.** (Koffer-) Einsatz *m*.
treach·er·ous ['tretʃərəs] *adj.* □ **1.** verräterisch, treulos (**to** gegen); **2.** (heim-) tückisch, 'hinterhältig; **3.** *fig.* tückisch, trügerisch (*Eis*, *Wetter etc.*), unzuverlässig (*a. Gedächtnis*); '**treach·er·ous·ness** [-nɪs] *s.* **1.** Treulosigkeit *f*, Verräte'rei *f*; **2.** *a. fig.* Tücke *f*; '**treach·er·y** [-rɪ] *s.* (**to**) Verrat *m* (an *dat.*), Verräte'rei *f*, Treulosigkeit *f* (gegen).
trea·cle ['triːkl] *s.* **1.** a) Sirup *m*, b) Me'lasse *f*; **2.** *fig.* a) Süßlichkeit *f*, b) süßliches Getue; '**trea·cly** [-lɪ] *adj.* **1.** sirupartig, Sirup…; **2.** *fig.* süßlich.
tread [tred] **I** *s.* **1.** Tritt *m*, Schritt *m*; **2.** a) Tritt(spur *f*) *m*, b) (Rad- *etc.*)Spur *f*; **3.** ⚙ Lauffläche *f* (*Rad*); *mot.* ('Reifen-) Proˌfil *n*; **4.** Spurweite *f*; **5.** Pe'dalabstand *m* (*Fahrrad*); **6.** a) Fußraste *f*, Trittbrett *n*, b) (Leiter)Sprosse *f*; **7.** Auftritt *m* (*Stufe*); **8.** *orn.* a) Treten *n* (*Begattung*), b) Hahnentritt *m* (*im Ei*); **II** *v/t.* [*irr.*] **9.** beschreiten: ~ **the boards** *thea.* (als Schauspieler) auftreten; **10.** *rhet. Zimmer etc.* durch'messen; **11.** *a.* ~ **down** zertreten, -trampeln: **to ~ out** *Feuer* austreten, *fig. Aufstand* niederwerfen; ~ **underfoot** niedertreten, *fig.* mit Füßen treten; **12.** *Pedale etc.*, *a. Wasser* treten; **13.** *orn.* treten, begatten; **III** *v/i.* [*irr.*] **14.** treten (**on** auf *acc.*): ~ **on air** (glück)selig sein; ~ **lightly** leise auftreten, *fig.* vorsichtig zu Werke gehen; **15.** (ein'her)schreiten; **16.** trampeln: ~ (**up**)**on** zertrampeln; **17.** unmittelbar folgen (**on** auf *acc.*); → **heel¹** *Redew.*; **18.** *orn.* a) treten (*Hahn*), b) sich paaren; **trea·dle** ['tredl] **I** *s.* **1.** ⚙ Tretkurbel *f*, Tritt *m*: ~

drive Fußantrieb *m*; **2.** Pe'dal *n*; **II** *v/i.* **3.** treten; '**tread·mill** *s.* Tretmühle *f* (*a. fig.*).

trea·son ['tri:zn] *s.* (⚖ Landes)Verrat *m* (***to*** an *dat.*): ***high ~, ~ felony*** Hochverrat *m*; '**trea·son·a·ble** [-nəbl] *adj.* □ (landes- *od.* hoch)verräterisch.

treas·ure ['treʒə] **I** *s.* **1.** Schatz *m* (*a. fig.*); **2.** Reichtum *m*, Reichtümer *pl.*, Schätze *pl.*: ***~s of the soil*** Bodenschätze; ***~ trove*** (herrenloser) Schatzfund, *fig.* Fundgrube *f*; **3.** F ,Perle' *f* (*Dienstmädchen etc.*); **4.** F Schatz *m*, Liebling *m*; **II** *v/t.* **5.** *oft* ***~ up*** *Schätze* (an)sammeln, aufhäufen; **6.** a) (hoch)schätzen, b) hegen, *a. Andenken* in Ehren halten; ***~ house*** *s.* **1.** Schatzhaus *n*, -kammer *f*; **2.** *fig.* Gold-, Fundgrube *f*.

treas·ur·er ['treʒərə] *s.* **1.** Schatzmeister (-in) (*a.* ☤); Kassenwart *m*; **2.** ☤ Leiter *m* der Fi'nanzab,teilung: ***city ~*** Stadtkämmerer *m*; **3.** Fis'kalbeamte(r) *m*: ***2 of the Household*** *Brit.* Fiskalbeamte(r) des königlichen Haushalts; '**treas·ur·er·ship** [-ʃɪp] *s.* Schatzmeisteramt *n*, Amt *n* e-s Kassenwarts.

treas·ur·y ['treʒərɪ] *s.* **1.** Schatzkammer *f*, -haus *n*; **2.** a) Schatzamt *n*, b) Staatsschatz *m*: ***Lords*** (*od.* ***Commissioners***) ***of the 2*** *das* brit. Finanzministerium; ***First Lord of the 2*** erster Schatzlord (*mst der Premierminister*); **3.** Fiskus *m*, Staatskasse *f*; **4.** *fig.* Schatz(kästlein *n*) *m*, Antholo'gie *f* (*Buchtitel*); **2 bench** *s. parl. Brit.* Regierungsbank *f*; ***~ bill*** *s.* ☤ (*kurzfristiger*) Schatzwechsel; **2 Board** *s. Brit.* Fi'nanzmini,sterium *n*; ***~ bond*** *s. Am.* (*langfristige*) Schatzanweisung; ***~ cer·tif·i·cate*** *s. Am.* (kurzfristiger) Schatzwechsel; **2 De·part·ment** *s. Am.* Fi'nanzmini,sterium *n*; ***~ note*** *s. Am.* (*mittelfristiger*) Schatzwechsel; **2 war·rant** *s. Brit.* Schatzanweisung *f*.

treat [tri:t] **I** *v/t.* **1.** behandeln, 'umgehen mit: ***~ s.o. brutally***; **2.** behandeln, betrachten (***as*** als); **3.** ⚕, ⚗, ⚙ behandeln (***for*** gegen, ***with*** mit); **4.** *fig. Thema etc.* behandeln; **5.** *j-m* e-n Genuß bereiten, *bsd. j-n* bewirten (***to*** mit): ***~ o.s. to*** sich *et.* gönnen *od.* leisten *od.* genehmigen; ***~ s.o. to s.th.*** j-m et. spendieren; ***be ~ed to s.th.*** in den Genuß e-r Sache kommen; **II** *v/i.* **6.** ***~ of*** handeln von, *Thema* behandeln; **7.** ***~ with*** verhandeln mit; **8.** (die Zeche) bezahlen, e-e Runde ausgeben; **III** *s.* **9.** (Extra)Vergnügen *n*, *bsd.* (Fest-) Schmaus *m*: ***school ~*** Schulfest *n od.* -ausflug *m*; **10.** *fig.* (Hoch)Genuß *m*, Wonne *f*; **11.** (Gratis)Bewirtung *f*: ***stand ~*** → 8; ***it is my ~*** das geht auf m-e Rechnung, diesmal bezahle ich; '**trea·tise** [-tɪz] *s.* (*wissenschaftliche*) Abhandlung; '**treat·ment** [-mənt] *s.* **1.** Behandlung *f* (*a.* ⚕, ⚗, *a. fig. e-s Themas etc.*): ***give s.th. the full ~*** *fig.* et. gründlich behandeln; ***give s.o. the ~*** F j-n ,in die Mangel nehmen'; **2.** ⚙ Bearbeitung *f*; **3.** *Film*: Treatment *n* (*erweitertes Handlungsschema*).

trea·ty ['tri:tɪ] *s.* **1.** (*bsd.* Staats)Vertrag *m*, Pakt *m*: ***~ powers*** Vertragsmächte; **2.** *obs.* Verhandlung *f*.

tre·ble ['trebl] **I** *adj.* □ **1.** dreifach; **2.** ⩘ dreistellig; **3.** ♪ Diskant..., Sopran...; **4.** hoch, schrill; **5.** *Radio*: Höhen...: ***~ control*** Höhenregler *m*; **II** *s.* **6.** ♪ *allg.* Dis'kant *m*; **III** *v/t. u. v/i.* **7.** (sich) verdreifachen.

tree [tri:] **I** *s.* **1.** Baum *m*: ***~ of life*** a) *bibl.* Baum des Lebens, b) ⚘ Lebensbaum; ***up a ~*** F in der Klemme; → ***top***[1] 2; **2.** (*Rosen- etc.*)Strauch *m*, (*Bananen- etc.*)Staude *f*; **3.** ⚙ Baum *m*, Welle *f*, Schaft *m*; (Holz)Gestell *n*; (Stiefel)Leisten *m*; **4.** → ***family tree***; **II** *v/t.* **5.** auf e-n Baum jagen; **6.** *j-n* in die Enge treiben; ***~ fern*** *s.* ⚘ Baumfarn *m*; ***~ frog*** *s. zo.* Laubfrosch *m*.

tree·less ['tri:lɪs] *adj.* baumlos, kahl.

tree| line *s.* Baumgrenze *f*; '**~·nail** *s.* ⚙ Holznagel *m*, Dübel *m*; ***~ nurs·er·y*** *s.* Baumschule *f*; ***~ sur·geon*** *s.* 'Baumchir,urg *m*; ***~ toad*** → ***tree frog***; '**~·top** *s.* Baumkrone *f*, -wipfel *m*.

tre·foil ['trefɔɪl] *s.* **1.** ⚘ Klee *m*; **2.** ⚠ Dreipaß *m*; **3.** *bsd. her.* Kleeblatt *n*.

trek [trek] **I** *v/i.* **1.** *Südafrika*: trecken, (im Ochsenwagen) reisen; **2.** ziehen, wandern; **II** *s.* **3.** Treck *m*.

trel·lis ['trelɪs] **I** *s.* **1.** Gitter *n*, Gatter *n*; **2.** ⚙ Gitterwerk *n*; **3.** ✓ Spa'lier *n*; **4.** Pergola *f*; **II** *v/t.* **5.** vergittern: ***~ed window*** Gitterfenster *n*; **6.** ✓ am Spalier ziehen; '**~·work** *s.* Gitterwerk *n* (*a.* ⚙).

trem·ble ['trembl] **I** *v/i.* **1.** (er)zittern, (-) beben (***at, with*** vor *dat.*): ***~ all over*** (*od.* ***in every limb***) am ganzen Leibe zittern; ***~ at the thought*** (*od.* ***to think***) bei dem Gedanken zittern; → ***balance*** 2; **2.** zittern, bangen (***for*** für, um): ***a trembling uncertainty*** e-e bange Ungewißheit; **II** *s.* **3.** Zittern *n*, Beben *n*: ***be all of a ~*** am ganzen Körper zittern; **4.** *pl. sg. konstr. vet.* Milchfieber *n*; '**trem·bler** [-lə] *s.* **1.** ⚡ ('Selbst)Unter,brecher *m*; **2.** e'lektrische Glocke *od.* Klingel; '**trem·bling** [-lɪŋ] *adj.* □ zitternd: ***~ grass*** ⚘ Zittergras *n*; ***~ poplar*** (*od.* ***tree***) ⚘ Zitterpappel *f*, Espe *f*.

tre·men·dous [trɪ'mendəs] *adj.* □ **1.** schrecklich, fürchterlich; **2.** F ungeheuer, e'norm, ,toll'.

trem·o·lo ['tremələʊ] *pl.* **-los** *s.* ♪ Tremolo *n*.

trem·or ['tremə] *s.* **1.** ⚕ Zittern *n*, Zukken *n*: ***~ of the heart*** Herzflackern *n*; **2.** Zittern *n*, Schau(d)er *m der Erregung*; **3.** Beben *n der Erde*; **4.** Angst (-gefühl *n*) *f*, Beben *n*.

trem·u·lous ['tremjʊləs] *adj.* □ **1.** zitternd, bebend; **2.** zitt(e)rig, ängstlich.

tre·nail ['trenl] → ***treenail***.

trench [trentʃ] **I** *v/t.* **1.** mit Gräben durch'ziehen *od.* (⚔) befestigen; **2.** ✓ tief 'umpflügen, ri'golen; **3.** zerschneiden, durch'furchen; **II** *v/i.* **4.** (⚔ Schützen)Gräben ausheben; **5.** *geol.* sich (ein)graben (*Fluß etc.*); **6.** ***~ (up)on*** beeinträchtigen, in *j-s Rechte* eingreifen; **7.** ***~ (up)on*** *fig.* hart grenzen an (*acc.*); **III** *s.* **8.** (⚔ Schützen)Graben *m*; **9.** Furche *f*, Rinne *f*; **10.** ⚒ Schramm *m*.

trench·an·cy ['trentʃənsɪ] *s.* Schärfe *f*; '**trench·ant** [-nt] *adj.* □ **1.** scharf, schneidend (*Witz etc.*); **2.** einschneidend, e'nergisch: ***a ~ policy***.

trench coat *s.* Trenchcoat *m*.

trench·er[1] ['trentʃə] *s.* ⚔ Schanzarbeiter *m*.

trench·er[2] ['trentʃə] *s.* **1.** Tranchier-, Schneidebrett *n*; **2.** *obs.* Speise *f*; ***~ cap*** → ***mortarboard*** 2; '**~·man** [-mən] *s.* [*irr.*] guter *etc.* Esser.

trench| fe·ver *s.* ⚕ Schützengrabenfieber *n*; ***~ foot*** *s.* ⚕ Schützengrabenfüße *pl.* (*Fußbrand*); ***~ mor·tar*** *s.* ⚔ Gra'natwerfer *m*; ***~ war·fare*** *s.* ⚔ Stellungskrieg *m*.

trend [trend] **I** *s.* **1.** Richtung *f* (*a. fig.*); **2.** *fig.* Ten'denz *f*, Entwicklung *f*, Trend *m* (*alle a.* ☤); Neigung *f*, Bestreben *n*: ***the ~ of his argument was*** s-e Beweisführung lief darauf hinaus; ***~ in*** *od.* ***of prices*** ☤ Preistendenz; **3.** *fig.* (Ver-) Lauf *m*: ***the ~ of events***; **II** *v/i.* **4.** sich neigen, streben, tendieren (***towards*** nach *e-r Richtung*); **5.** sich erstrecken, laufen (***towards*** nach *Süden etc.*); **6.** *geol.* streichen (***to*** nach); ***~ a·nal·y·sis*** *s.* ☤ Konjunk'turana,lyse *f*; '**~,set·ter** *s. Mode etc.*: j-d, der den Ton angibt, Schrittmacher *m*, Trendsetter *m*; '**~,set·ting** *adj.* tonangebend.

tren·dy ['trendɪ] *adj.* ('super)mo,dern, schick, modebewußt.

tre·pan [trɪ'pæn] **I** *s.* **1.** ⚕ *hist.* Schädelbohrer *m*; **2.** ⚙ 'Bohrma,schine *f*; **3.** *geol.* Stein-, Erdbohrer *m*; **II** *v/t.* **4.** ⚕ trepanieren.

trep·i·da·tion [,trepɪ'deɪʃn] *s.* **1.** ⚕ (Glieder-, Muskel)Zittern *n*; **2.** Beben *n*; **3.** Angst *f*, Bestürzung *f*.

tres·pass ['trespəs] **I** *s.* **1.** Über'tretung *f*, Vergehen *n*, Verstoß *m*, Sünde *f*; **2.** 'Übergriff *m*; **3.** 'Mißbrauch *m* (***on*** *gen.*); **4.** ⚖ *allg.* unerlaubte Handlung (*Zivilrecht*): a) unbefugtes Betreten, b) Besitzstörung *f*, c) 'Übergriff *m* gegen die Per'son (*z.B. Körperverletzung*); **5.** *a.* ***action for ~*** ⚖ Schadenersatzklage *f* aus unerlaubter Handlung, *z.B.* Besitzstörungsklage *f*; **II** *v/i.* **6.** ⚖ e-e unerlaubte Handlung begehen: ***~ (up)on*** a) widerrechtlich betreten, b) rechtswidrige Übergriffe gegen *j-s Eigentum* begehen; **7.** ***~ (up)on*** *fig.* a) 'übergreifen auf (*acc.*), b) hart grenzen an (*acc.*), c) *j-s Zeit etc.* über Gebühr in Anspruch nehmen; **8.** (***against***) verstoßen (gegen), sündigen (wider *od.* gegen); '**tres·pass·er** [-sə] *s.* **1.** ⚖ a) Rechtsverletzer *m*, b) Unbefugte(r *m*) *f*: ***~s will be prosecuted!*** Betreten bei Strafe verboten!; **2.** *obs.* Sünder(in).

tress [tres] *s.* **1.** (Haar)Flechte *f*, Zopf *m*; **2.** Locke *f*; **3.** *pl.* üppiges Haar; **tressed** [-st] *adj.* **1.** geflochten; **2.** gelockt.

tres·tle ['tresl] *s.* **1.** ⚙ Gestell *n*, Gerüst *n*, Bock *m*, Schragen *m*: ***~ table*** Zeichentisch *m*; **2.** ⚔ Brückenbock *m*: ***~ bridge*** Bockbrücke *f*; '**~·work** *s.* **1.** Gerüst *n*; **2.** *Am.* 'Bahnvia,dukt *m*.

trey [treɪ] *s.* Drei *f im Karten- od. Würfelspiel.*

tri·a·ble ['traɪəbl] *adj.* ⚖ a) justiti'abel, zu verhandeln(d) (*Sache*), b) belangbar, abzuurteilen(d) (*Person*).

tri·ad ['traɪəd] *s.* **1.** Tri'ade *f*: a) Dreizahl *f*, b) ⚗ dreiwertiges Ele'ment, c) ⩘ Dreiergruppe *f*, Trias *f*; **2.** ♪ Dreiklang *m*.

tri·al ['traɪəl] **I** *s.* **1.** Versuch *m* (***of*** mit), Probe *f*, Erprobung *f*, Prüfung *f* (*alle a.* ⚙): ***~ and error*** a) ⩘ Regula *f* falsi, b) empirische Methode; ***~ of strength*** Kraftprobe; ***on ~*** auf *od.* zur Probe; ***give a ~, make a ~ of*** e-n Versuch machen mit, erproben; ***be on ~*** a) erprobt werden, b) e-e Probezeit durchmachen (*Person*), c) *fig.* auf dem Prüfstand sein (→ *a.* 2); **2.** ⚖ ('Straf- *od.* Zi'vil)Pro,zeß *m*, (Gerichts)Verfahren *n*, (Haupt)Verhandlung *f*: **~ by jury** Schwurgerichtsverfahren; **be on** (*od.* **stand**) **~** unter Anklage stehen (**for** wegen); **bring** (*od.* **put**) **s.o. to ~** j-n vor Gericht bringen; **stand** (**one's**) **~** sich vor Gericht verantworten; **3.** (**to** für) *fig.* a) (Schicksals)Prüfung *f*, Heimsuchung *f*, b) Last *f*, Plage *f*, Stra'paze *f*; **4.** *sport* a) Vorlauf *m*, Ausscheidungsrennen *n*, b) Ausscheidungsspiel *n*; **II** *adj.* **5.** Versuchs…, Probe…: **~ balance** † Rohbilanz *f*; **~ balloon** *fig.* Versuchsballon *m*; **~ marriage** Ehe *f* auf Probe; **~ match** → 4 b; **~ order** † Probeauftrag *m*; **~ package** † Probepackung *f*; **~ period** Probezeit *f*; **~ run** Probefahrt *f*, -lauf *m*; **6.** ⚖ Verhandlungs…: **~ court** erstinstanzliches Gericht; **~ judge** Richter *m* der ersten Instanz; **~ lawyer** *Am.* Prozeßanwalt *m*.

tri·an·gle ['traɪæŋgl] *s.* **1.** ⊿ Dreieck *n*; **2.** ♪ Triangel *m*; **3.** ⚙ a) Reißdreieck *n*, b) Winkel *m*; **4.** *mst* **eternal ~** *fig.* Dreiecksverhältnis *n*; **tri·an·gu·lar** [traɪ'æŋgjʊlə] *adj.* dreieckig, -winkelig; *fig.* dreiseitig, Dreiecks…

Tri·as ['traɪəs] → **Tri·as·sic** [traɪ'æsɪk] *geol.* **I** *s.* 'Trias(formati,on) *f*; **II** *adj.* Trias…

trib·al ['traɪbl] *adj.* □ Stammes…; '**trib·al·ism** [-bəlɪzəm] *s.* 'Stammessy,stem *n od.* -gefühl *n*.

tri·bas·ic [traɪ'beɪsɪk] *adj.* ⚗ drei-, tribasisch.

tribe [traɪb] *s.* **1.** (Volks)Stamm *m*; **2.** ⚘, *zo.* Tribus *f*, Klasse *f*; **3.** *humor. u. contp.* Sippschaft *f*, ‚Verein' *m*; **tribes·man** ['traɪbzmən] *s.* [*irr.*] Stammesangehörige(r) *m*, -genosse *m*.

trib·u·la·tion [,trɪbjʊ'leɪʃn] *s.* Drangsal *f*, 'Widerwärtigkeit *f*.

tri·bu·nal [traɪ'bju:nl] *s.* **1.** ⚖ Gericht(shof *m*) *n*, Tribu'nal *n* (*a. fig.*); **2.** Richterstuhl *m* (*a. fig.*); **trib·une** ['trɪbju:n] *s.* **1.** *antiq.* ('Volks)Tri,bun *m*; **2.** Volksheld *m*; **3.** Tri'büne *f*; **4.** Rednerbühne *f*; **5.** Bischofsthron *m*.

trib·u·tar·y ['trɪbjʊtərɪ] **I** *adj.* □ **1.** tri'but-, zinspflichtig (**to** *dat.*); **2.** 'untergeordnet (**to** *dat.*); **3.** helfend, beisteuernd (**to** zu); **4.** *geogr.* Neben…: **~ stream**; **II** *s.* **5.** Tri'butpflichtige(r) *m*, *a.* tri'butpflichtiger Staat; **6.** *geogr.* Nebenfluß *m*; **trib·ute** ['trɪbju:t] *s.* Tri'but *m*: a) Zins *m*, Abgabe *f*, b) *fig.* Zoll *m*, Beitrag *m*, c) *fig.* Huldigung *f*, Achtungsbezeigung *f*, Anerkennung *f*: **~ of admiration** gebührende Bewunderung; **pay ~ to** *j-m* Hochachtung bezeigen *od.* Anerkennung zollen.

tri·car ['traɪkɑ:] *s. Brit.* Dreiradlieferwagen *m*.

trice [traɪs] *s.*: **in a ~** im Nu.

tri·ceps ['traɪseps] *pl.* '**tri·ceps·es** *s. anat.* Trizeps *m* (*Muskel*).

tri·chi·na [trɪ'kaɪnə] *pl.* **-nae** [-ni:] *s. zo.* Tri'chine *f*; **trich·i·no·sis** [,trɪkɪ'nəʊsɪs] *s.* ⚕ Trichi'nose *f*.

trich·o·mon·ad [,trɪkəʊ'mɒnæd] *s. zo.* Trichomo'nade *f*.

tri·chord ['traɪkɔ:d] *adj. u. s.* ♪ dreisaitig(es Instru'ment).

tri·chot·o·my [traɪ'kɒtəmɪ] *s.* Dreiheit *f*, -teilung *f*.

trick [trɪk] **I** *s.* **1.** Trick *m*, Kunstgriff *m*, Kniff *m*, List *f*; *pl. a.* Schliche *pl.*, Ränke *pl.*, Winkelzüge *pl.*: **full of ~s** raffiniert; **2.** (**dirty ~** gemeiner) Streich: **~s of fortune** Tücken des Schicksals; **the ~s of the memory** *fig.* die Tücken des Gedächtnisses; **be up to one's ~s** (wieder) Dummheiten machen; **be up to s.o.'s ~s** j-n *od.* j-s Schliche durchschauen; **what ~s have you been up to?** was hast du angestellt?; **play s.o. a ~, play a ~ on s.o.** j-m e-n Streich spielen; **none of your ~s!** keine Mätzchen!; **3.** Trick *m*, (*Karten- etc.*)Kunststück *n*: **do the ~** den Zweck erfüllen; **that did the ~** damit war es geschafft; **4.** (Sinnes)Täuschung *f*; **5.** (*bsd.* üble *od.* dumme) Angewohnheit, Eigenheit *f*; **6.** *Kartenspiel*: Stich *m*: **take** *od.* **win a ~** e-n Stich machen; **7.** ⚓ Rudertörn *m*; **8.** *Am. sl.* ‚Mieze' *f* (*Mädchen*); **9.** V ‚Nummer' *f* (*Koitus*); **II** *adj.* **10.** Trick…(*-dieb*, *-film*, *-szene*); **11.** Kunst…(*-flug*, *-reiten*); **III** *v/t.* **12.** über'listen, betrügen, prellen (**out of** um); **13.** *j-n* verleiten (**into doing** *et.* zu tun); **14.** *mst* **~ up** (*od.* **out**) schmükken, (her'aus)putzen; '**trick·er** [-kə] → **trickster**; '**trick·er·y** [-kərɪ] *s.* **1.** Betrüge'rei(en *pl.*) *f*, Gaune'rei(en *pl.*) *f*; **2.** Kniff *m*; '**trick·i·ness** [-kɪnɪs] *s.* **1.** Verschlagenheit *f*, Durch'triebenheit *f*; **2.** Kitzligkeit *f e-r Situation etc.*; **3.** Kompliziertheit *f*; '**trick·ish** [-kɪʃ] → **tricky**.

trick·le ['trɪkl] **I** *v/i.* **1.** tröpfeln (*a. fig.*); **2.** rieseln; kullern (*Tränen*); **3.** sickern: **~ out** *fig.* durchsickern; **4.** trudeln (*Ball etc.*); **II** *v/t.* **5.** tröpfeln (lassen), träufeln; **6.** rieseln lassen; **III** *s.* **7.** Tröpfeln *n*; Rieseln *n*; **8.** Rinnsal *n* (*a. fig.*); **~ charg·er** *s.* ϟ Kleinlader *m*.

trick·si·ness ['trɪksɪnɪs] *s.* **1.** → **trickiness**; **2.** 'Übermut *m*.

trick·ster ['trɪkstə] *s.* Gauner(in), Schwindler(in).

trick·sy ['trɪksɪ] *adj.* **1.** → **tricky** 1; **2.** 'übermütig.

trick·y ['trɪkɪ] *adj.* □ **1.** verschlagen, durch'trieben, raffiniert; **2.** heikel, kitzlig (*Lage*, *Problem*); **3.** kompliziert, knifflig; **4.** unzuverlässig.

tri·col·o(u)r ['trɪkələ] *s.* Triko'lore *f*.

tri·cot ['tri:kəʊ] *s.* Tri'kot *m* (*Stoff*).

tri·cy·cle ['traɪsɪkl] **I** *s.* Dreirad *n*; **II** *v/i.* Dreirad fahren.

tri·dent ['traɪdnt] *s.* Dreizack *m*.

tried [traɪd] **I** *p.p. von* **try**; **II** *adj.* erprobt, bewährt.

tri·en·ni·al [traɪ'enjəl] *adj.* □ **1.** dreijährig; **2.** alle drei Jahre stattfindend, dreijährlich.

tri·er·arch·y ['traɪərɑ:kɪ] *s. hist.* Trierar'chie *f*.

tri·fle ['traɪfl] **I** *s.* **1.** Kleinigkeit *f*: a) unbedeutender Gegenstand, b) Baga'telle *f*, Lap'palie *f*, c) Kinderspiel *n* (**to** für *j-n*), d) kleine Geldsumme, e) *das* bißchen: **a ~ expensive** etwas *od.* ein bißchen teuer; **not to stick at ~s** sich nicht mit Kleinigkeiten abgeben; **stand upon ~s** ein Kleinigkeitskrämer sein; **2.** a) *Brit.* Trifle *n* (*Biskuitdessert*), b) *Am.* 'Obstdes,sert *n* mit Sahne; **II** *v/i.* **3.** spielen (**with** mit *dem Bleistift etc.*); **4.** (**with**) *fig.* spielen (mit), sein Spiel treiben *od.* leichtfertig 'umgehen (mit): **he is not to be ~d with** er läßt nicht mit sich spaßen; **5.** tändeln, scherzen; leichtfertig da'herreden; **6.** (her'um-) trödeln; **III** *v/t.* **7.** **~ away** *Zeit* vertändeln, vertrödeln, *a. Geld* verplempern; '**tri·fler** [-lə] *s.* **1.** oberflächlicher *od.* fri'voler Mensch; **2.** Tändler *m*; **3.** Müßiggänger *m*; '**tri·fling** [-lɪŋ] *adj.* □ **1.** oberflächlich, leichtfertig; **2.** tändelnd; **3.** unbedeutend, geringfügig.

tri·fo·li·ate [traɪ'fəʊlɪət] *adj.* ⚘ **1.** dreiblätt(e)rig; **2.** → **tri·fo·li·o·late** [traɪ'fəʊlɪəleɪt] *adj.* ⚘ **1.** dreizählig (*Blatt*); **2.** mit dreizähligen Blättern (*Pflanze*).

trig [trɪg] F *für* **trigonometry**.

trig·ger ['trɪgə] **I** *s.* **1.** ϟ, *phot.*, ⚙ Auslöser *m* (*a. fig.*); **2.** Abzug *m* (*Feuerwaffe*), *am Gewehr*: *a.* Drücker *m*, *e-r Bombe*: Zünder *m*: **pull the ~** abdrükken; **quick on the ~** *fig.* ‚fix', ‚auf Draht' (*reaktionsschnell od. schlagfertig*); **II** *v/t.* **3.** ⚙ auslösen (*a. fig.*); **~ guard** *s.* ⚔ Abzugsbügel *m*; '**~-,hap·py** *adj.* **1.** schießwütig; **2.** *pol.* kriegslüstern; **3.** *fig.* kampflustig.

trig·o·no·met·ric, **trig·o·no·met·ri·cal** [,trɪgənə'metrɪk(l)] *adj.* □ ⊿ trigono'metrisch; **trig·o·nom·e·try** [,trɪgə'nɒmɪtrɪ] *s.* Trigonome'trie *f*.

tri·he·dral [,traɪ'hedrl] *adj.* ⊿ dreiflächig, tri'edrisch.

tri·lat·er·al [,traɪ'lætərəl] *adj.* **1.** ⊿ dreiseitig; **2.** *pol.* Dreier…: **~ talks**.

tril·by ['trɪlbɪ] *s.* **1.** *a.* **~ hat** *Brit.* F weicher Filzhut; **2.** *pl. sl.* ‚Haxen' *pl.* (*Füße*).

tri·lin·e·ar [,traɪ'lɪnɪə] *adj.* ⊿ dreilinig: **~ coordinates** Dreieckskoordinaten.

tri·lin·gual [,traɪ'lɪŋgwəl] *adj.* dreisprachig.

trill [trɪl] **I** *v/t. u. v/i.* **1.** ♪ *etc.* trillern, trällern; **2.** *ling.* (*bsd.* das r) rollen; **II** *s.* **3.** ♪ Triller *m*; **4.** *ling.* gerolltes r, gerollter Konso'nant.

tril·lion ['trɪljən] *s.* **1.** *Brit.* Trilli'on *f*; **2.** *Am.* Billi'on *f*.

tril·o·gy ['trɪlədʒɪ] *s.* Trilo'gie *f*.

trim [trɪm] **I** *v/t.* **1.** in Ordnung bringen, zu'rechtmachen; **2.** *Feuer* anschüren; **3.** *Haar*, *Hecken etc.* (be-, zu'recht-) schneiden, stutzen, *bsd. Hundefell* trimmen; **4.** *fig. Budget etc.* stutzen, beschneiden; **5.** ⚙ *Bauholz* behauen, zurichten; **6.** *a.* **~ up** (her'aus)putzen, schmücken, ausstaffieren, schönmachen; **7.** *Hüte etc.* besetzen, garnieren; **8.** F a) *j-n* ‚zs.-stauchen', b) ‚reinlegen', c) ‚vertrimmen' (*a. sport schlagen*); **9.** ✈, ⚓ trimmen: a) *Flugzeug*, *Schiff* in die richtige Lage bringen, b) *Segel* stellen, brassen: **~ one's sails to every wind** *fig.* sein Mäntelchen nach dem Wind hängen, c) *Kohlen* schaufeln, d) *Ladung* (richtig) verstauen; **10.** ϟ trimmen, (fein) abgleichen; **II** *v/i.* **11.** *fig.* e-n Mittelkurs steuern, *bsd. pol.* lavieren: **~ with the times** sich den Zeiten anpassen, Opportunitätspolitik treiben; **III** *s.* **12.** Ordnung *f*, (richtiger) Zustand, *a.* richtige (*körperliche od. seelische*) Verfassung *od.* Form: **in good** (**out of**) **~** in guter (schlechter) Verfassung (*a. Person*); **13.** ✈, ⚓ a) Trimm (-lage *f*) *m*, b) richtige Stellung *der Segel*, c) gute Verstauung *der Ladung*; **14.** Putz *m*, Staat *m*, Gala *f*; **15.** *mot.*

a) Innenausstattung *f*, b) Zierleiste(n *pl.*) *f*; **IV** *adj.* **16.** ordentlich; **17.** schmuck, sauber, a'drett; gepflegt (*a. Bart, Rasen etc.*); **18.** (gut) in Schuß.

tri·mes·ter [trɪ'mestə] *s.* **1.** Zeitraum *m* von drei Monaten, Vierteljahr *n*; **2.** *univ.* Tri'mester *n*.

trim·mer ['trɪmə] *s.* **1.** Aufarbeiter(in), Putzmacher(in); **2.** ⚓ a) (Kohlen)Trimmer *m*, b) Stauer *m*; **3.** *Zimmerei*: Wechselbalken *m*; **4.** *fig. bsd. pol.* Opportu'nist(in); '**trim·ming** [-mɪŋ] *s.* **1.** (Auf-, Aus)Putzen *n*, Zurichten *n*; **2.** a) (Hut-, Kleider)Besatz *m*, Borte *f*, b) *pl.* Zutaten *pl.*, Posa'menten *pl.*, c) *fig.* ‚Verzierung' *f*, ‚Garnierung' *f im Stil etc.*; **3.** *pl.* Garnierung *f*, Zutaten *pl.* (*Speise*); **4.** *pl.* Abfälle *pl.*, Schnipsel *pl.*; **5.** ⚓ a) Trimmen *n*, (Ver)Stauen *n*, b) Staulage *f*; **6.** (Tracht *f*) Prügel *pl.*; **7.** *bsd. sport* (böse) Abfuhr; '**trim·ness** [-mnɪs] *s.* **1.** gute Ordnung; **2.** gutes Aussehen, Gepflegtheit *f*.

trine [traɪn] **I** *adj.* **1.** dreifach; **II** *s.* **2.** Dreiheit *f*; **3.** *ast.* Trigo'nala͵spekt *m*.

Trin·i·tar·i·an [͵trɪnɪ'teərɪən] *eccl.* **I** *adj.* **1.** Dreieinigkeits...; **II** *s.* **2.** Bekenner (-in) der Drei'einigkeit; **3.** *hist.* Trini'tarier *m*; ͵**Trin·i'tar·i·an·ism** [-nɪzəm] *s.* Drei'einigkeitslehre *f*.

tri·ni·tro·tol·u·ene [traɪ͵naɪtrəʊ'tɒljʊiːn] *s.* ⚗ Trinitrotolu'ol *n*.

trin·i·ty ['trɪnɪtɪ] *s.* **1.** Dreiheit *f*; **2.** ⁓ *eccl.* Drei'einigkeit *f*; ⁓ **House** *s.* Verband *m* zur Aufsicht über See- u. Lotsenzeichen *etc.*; ⁓ **Sun·day** *s.* Sonntag *m* Trini'tatis; ⁓ **term** *s. univ.* 'Sommertri͵mester *n*.

trin·ket ['trɪŋkɪt] *s.* **1.** Schmuck *m*; (*bsd.* wertloses) Schmuckstück; **2.** *pl. fig.* Kram *m*, Plunder *m*.

tri·no·mi·al [traɪ'nəʊmjəl] **I** *adj.* **1.** A̷ tri'nomisch, dreigliedrig, -namig; **2.** *biol., zo.* dreigliedrig (*Artname*); **II** *s.* **3.** A̷ Tri'nom *n*, dreigliedrige (Zahlen-) Größe.

tri·o ['triːəʊ] *pl.* **-os** *s.* ♪ *u. fig.* Trio *n*.

tri·ode ['traɪəʊd] *s.* ⚡ Tri'ode *f*, 'Dreielek͵troden͵röhre *f*.

tri·o·let ['triːəʊlet] *s.* Trio'lett *n* (*Ringelgedicht*).

trip [trɪp] **I** *s.* **1.** (*bsd.* kurze, *a.* See)Reise; Ausflug *m*, Spritztour *f* (**to** nach); **2.** *weitS.* Fahrt *f*; **3.** Trippeln *n*; **4.** Stolpern *n*; **5.** Fehltritt *m* (*bsd. fig.*); **6.** *fig.* Fehler *m*; **7.** Beinstellen *n*; **8.** ⚙ Auslösung *f*: **~ cam** *od.* **dog** Schaltnocken *m*; **~ lever** Auslöse- *od.* Schalthebel *m*; **9.** *sl.* ‚Trip' *m* (*Drogenrausch*); **II** *v/i.* **10.** trippeln, tänzeln; **11.** stolpern, straucheln (*a. fig.*); **12.** *fig.* (e-n) Fehler machen: **catch s.o. ~ping** j-n bei e-m Fehler ertappen; **13.** *über ein Wort* stolpern, sich versprechen; **III** *v/t.* **14.** *oft* **~ up** *j-m* ein Bein stellen, *j-n* zu Fall bringen (*beide a fig.*); **15.** *fig.* vereiteln; **16.** (**in** bei *e-m Fehler etc.*) ertappen; **17.** ⚙ a) auslösen, b) schalten.

tri·par·tite [͵traɪ'pɑːtaɪt] *adj.* **1.** ⚘ dreiteilig; **2.** Dreier..., Dreimächte... (*Vertrag etc.*)

tripe [traɪp] *s.* **1.** Kal'daunen *pl.*, Kutteln *pl.*; **2.** *sl.* a) Schund *m*, Kitsch *m*, b) Quatsch *m*, Blödsinn *m*.

tri·phase ['traɪfeɪz] → **three-phase**.

tri·phib·i·ous [traɪ'fɪbɪəs] *adj.* ⚔ mit Einsatz von Land-, See- u. Luftstreitkräften ('durchgeführt).

triph·thong ['trɪfθɒŋ] *s. ling.* Tri'phthong *m*, Dreilaut *m*.

tri·plane ['traɪpleɪn] *s.* ✈ Dreidecker *m*.

tri·ple ['trɪpl] **I** *adj.* ☐ **1.** dreifach; **2.** dreimalig; **3.** Drei..., drei...: ⁓ **Alliance** *hist.* Tripelallianz *f*, Dreibund *m*; **~ fugue** ♪ Tripelfuge *f*; **~ jump** *sport* Dreisprung *m*; **~ time** ♪ Tripeltakt *m*; **II** *s.* **4.** *das* Dreifache; **III** *v/t. u. v/i.* **5.** (sich) verdreifachen.

tri·plet ['trɪplɪt] *s.* **1.** *biol.* Drilling *m*; **2.** Dreiergruppe *f*, Trio *n* (*drei Personen etc.*); **3.** ♪ Tri'ole *f*; **4.** *Verskunst*: Dreireim *m*.

tri·plex ['trɪpleks] **I** *adj.* **1.** dreifach: **~ glass** → 3; **II** *s.* **2.** ♪ Tripeltakt *m*; **3.** ⚙ Triplex-, Sicherheitsglas *n*.

trip·li·cate ['trɪplɪkət] **I** *adj.* **1.** dreifach; **2.** in dreifacher Ausfertigung (geschrieben *etc.*); **II** *s.* **3.** *das* Dreifache; **4.** dreifache Ausfertigung: **in ~** in dreifacher Ausfertigung; **5.** dritte Ausfertigung; **III** *v/t.* [-keɪt] **6.** verdreifachen; **7.** dreifach ausfertigen.

tri·pod ['traɪpɒd] *s.* **1.** Dreifuß *m*; **2.** *bsd. phot.* Sta'tiv *n*; **3.** ⚙, ⚔ Dreibein *n*.

tri·pos ['traɪpɒs] *s.* letztes Ex'amen *für* **honours** (*Cambridge*).

trip·per ['trɪpə] *s.* a) Ausflügler(in), b) Tou'rist(in).

trip·ping ['trɪpɪŋ] **I** *adj.* ☐ **1.** leicht(füßig), flink; **2.** flott, munter; **3.** strauchelnd (*a. fig.*); **4.** ⚙ Auslöse..., Schalt...; **II** *s.* **5.** Trippeln *n*; **6.** Beinstellen *n*.

trip·tych ['trɪptɪk] *s.* Triptychon *n*, dreiteiliges (Al'tar)Bild.

tri·sect [traɪ'sekt] *v/t.* in drei (gleiche) Teile teilen.

tri·syl·lab·ic [͵traɪsɪ'læbɪk] *adj.* (☐ **~ally**) dreisilbig; **tri·syl·la·ble** [͵traɪ'sɪləbl] *s.* dreisilbiges Wort.

trite [traɪt] *adj.* ☐ abgedroschen, platt, ba'nal; '**trite·ness** [-nɪs] *s.* Abgedroschenheit *f*, Plattheit *f*.

Tri·ton ['traɪtn] *s.* **1.** *antiq.* Triton *m* (*niederer Meergott*): **a ~ among (the) minnows** ein Riese unter Zwergen; **2.** ⁓ *zo.* Tritonshorn *n*; **3.** ⁓ *zo.* Molch *m*.

tri·tone ['traɪtəʊn] *s.* ♪ Tritonus *m*.

trit·u·rate ['trɪtjʊreɪt] *v/t.* zerreiben, -mahlen, -stoßen, pulverisieren.

tri·umph ['traɪəmf] **I** *s.* **1.** Tri'umph *m*: a) Sieg *m* (**over** über *acc.*), b) Siegesfreude *f* (**at** über *acc.*): **in ~** im Triumph, triumphierend; **2.** Tri'umph *m* (*Großtat, Erfolg*): **the ~s of science**; **II** *v/i.* **3.** triumphieren: a) den Sieg da'vontragen, b) jubeln, froh'lokken (*beide* **over** über *acc.*), c) Erfolg haben; **tri·um·phal** [traɪ'ʌmfl] *adj.* Triumph..., Sieges...: **~ arch** Triumphbogen *m*; **~ procession** Triumphzug *m*; **tri·um·phant** [traɪ'ʌmfənt] *adj.* ☐ **1.** triumphierend: a) den Sieg feiernd, b) sieg-, erfolg-, glorreich, c) froh'lokkend, jubelnd; **2.** *obs.* herrlich.

tri·um·vir [trɪ'ʌmvə] *pl.* **-virs** *od.* **-vi·ri** [trɪ'ʊmvɪriː] *s. antiq.* Tri'umvir *m* (*a. fig.*); **tri·um·vi·rate** [traɪ'ʌmvɪrət] *s.* **1.** *antiq.* Triumvi'rat *n* (*a. fig.*); **2.** *fig.* Dreigestirn *n*.

tri·une ['traɪjuːn] *adj. bsd. eccl.* drei'einig.

tri·va·lent [͵traɪ'veɪlənt] *adj.* ⚗ dreiwertig.

triv·et ['trɪvɪt] *s.* Dreifuß *m* (*bsd. für Kochgefäße*): (**as**) **right as a ~** *fig.* bei bester Gesundheit.

triv·i·a ['trɪvɪə] *s. pl.* Baga'tellen *pl.*; '**triv·i·al** [-əl] *adj.* ☐ **1.** trivi'al, ba'nal, all'täglich; **2.** gering(fügig), unbedeutend; **3.** oberflächlich (*Person*); **4.** volkstümlich (*Ggs. wissenschaftlich*); **triv·i·al·i·ty** [͵trɪvɪ'ælətɪ] *s.* **1.** Triviali'tät *f*, Plattheit *f*, Banali'tät *f* (*a. Ausspruch etc.*); **2.** Geringfügigkeit *f*, Belanglosigkeit *f*; '**triv·i·al·ize** *v/t.* bagatellisieren.

tri·week·ly [͵traɪ'wiːklɪ] **I** *adj.* **1.** dreiwöchentlich; **2.** dreimal wöchentlich erscheinend (*Zeitschrift etc.*); **II** *adv.* **3.** dreimal in der Woche.

troat [trəʊt] **I** *s.* Röhren *n des Hirsches*; **II** *v/i.* röhren.

tro·cha·ic [trəʊ'keɪɪk] *Metrik* **I** *adj.* tro'chäisch; **II** *s.* Tro'chäus *m* (*Vers*); **tro·chee** ['trəʊkiː] *s.* Tro'chäus *m* (*Versfuß*).

trod [trɒd] *pret. u. p.p. von* **tread**.

trod·den ['trɒdn] *p.p. von* **tread**.

trog·lo·dyte ['trɒglədaɪt] *s.* **1.** Troglo'dyt *m*, Höhlenbewohner *m*; **2.** *fig.* a) Einsiedler *m*, b) primi'tiver *od.* bru'taler Kerl; **trog·lo·dyt·ic** [͵trɒglə'dɪtɪk] *adj.* troglo'dytisch.

troi·ka ['trɔɪkə] (*Russ.*) *s.* Troika *f*, Dreigespann *n*.

Tro·jan ['trəʊdʒən] **I** *adj.* tro'janisch; **II** *s.* Tro'janer(in): **like a ~** F wie ein Pferd *arbeiten*.

troll[1] [trəʊl] **I** *v/t. u. v/i.* **1.** (fröhlich) trällern; **2.** (mit der Schleppangel) fischen (**for** nach); **II** *s.* **3.** Schleppangel *f*, künstlicher Köder.

troll[2] [trəʊl] *s.* Troll *m*, Kobold *m*.

trol·ley ['trɒlɪ] *s.* **1.** *Brit.* Hand-, Gepäck-, Einkaufswagen *m*; Kofferkuli *m*; (Schub)Karren *m*; **2.** ⚙ Förderwagen *m*; **3.** 🚂 *Brit.* Drai'sine *f*; **4.** ⚡ Kon'taktrolle *f bei Oberleitungsfahrzeugen*; **5.** *Am.* Straßenbahn(wagen *m*) *f*; **6.** *Brit.* Tee-, Servierwagen *m*; **~ bus** *s.* O(berleitungs)bus *m*; **~ car** *s. Am.* Straßenbahnwagen *m*; **~ pole** *s.* ⚡ Stromabnehmerstange *f*; **~ wire** *s.* Oberleitung *f*.

trol·lop ['trɒləp] **I** *s.* **1.** Schlampe *f*; **2.** ‚Flittchen' *n*; **II** *v/i.* **3.** schlampen; **4.** ‚latschen'.

trom·bone [trɒm'bəʊn] *s.* ♪ **1.** Po'saune *f*; **2.** → **trom'bon·ist** [-nɪst] *s.* ♪ Posau'nist *m*.

troop [truːp] **I** *s.* **1.** Trupp *m*, Schar *f*; **2.** *pl.* ⚔ Truppe(n *pl.*) *f*; **3.** ⚔ a) Schwa'dron *f*, b) ('Panzer)Kompa͵nie *f*, c) Batte'rie *f*; **II** *v/i.* **4.** *oft* **~ up**, **~ together** sich scharen, sich sammeln; **5.** (in Scharen) *wohin* ziehen, (her'ein- *etc.*) strömen, marschieren: **~ away**, **~ off** F abziehen, sich da'vonmachen; **III** *v/t.* **6.** **~ the colour(s)** *Brit.* ⚔ Fahnenparade abhalten; **~ car·ri·er** *s.* ⚔ **1.** ✈, ⚓ 'Truppentrans͵porter *m*; **2.** Mannschaftswagen *m*; '**~͵car·ry·ing** *adj.*: **~ vehicle** → **troop carrier** 2.

troop·er ['truːpə] *s.* **1.** ⚔ Reiter *m*, Kavalle'rist *m*: **swear like a ~** fluchen wie ein Landsknecht; **2.** 'Staatspoli͵zist *m*; **3.** *bsd. Am.* berittener Poli'zist; **4.** ⚔ Kavalle'riepferd *n*; **5.** *Brit.* → **troopship**.

'**troop·ship** *s.* ⚓ 'Truppentrans͵porter

m.

trope [trəʊp] *s.* Tropus *m* (*a.* ♪), bildlicher Ausdruck.

troph·ic [ˈtrɒfɪk] *adj. biol.* trophisch, Ernährungs…

tro·phy [ˈtrəʊfɪ] **I** *s.* **1.** Troˈphäe *f*, Siegeszeichen *n*, -beute *f* (*alle a. fig.*); **2.** Preis *m*, (*Jagd- etc.*)Troˈphäe *f*; **II** *v/t.* **3.** mit Troˈphäen schmücken.

trop·ic [ˈtrɒpɪk] **I** *s.* **1.** *ast., geogr.* Wendekreis *m*; **2.** *pl. geogr.* Tropen *pl.*; **II** *adj.* **3.** → ***tropical***[1].

trop·i·cal[1] [ˈtrɒpɪkl] *adj.* □ Tropen…, tropisch.

trop·i·cal[2] [ˈtrɒpɪkl] → ***tropological***.

trop·o·log·i·cal [ˌtrɒpəˈlɒdʒɪkl] *adj.* □ fiˈgürlich, metaˈphorisch.

trop·o·sphere [ˈtrɒpəˌsfɪə] *s. meteor.* Tropoˈsphäre *f*.

trot [trɒt] **I** *v/i.* **1.** traben, trotten, im Trab gehen *od.* reiten: **~ *along*** (*od.* ***off***) F ab-, losziehen; **II** *v/t.* **2.** *Pferd* traben lassen, *a. j-n* in Trab setzen; **3.** **~ *out*** a) *Pferd* vorreiten, -führen, b) *fig. et. od. j-n* vorführen, renommieren mit, *Argumente*, *Kenntnisse etc.*, *a. Wein etc.* auftischen, aufwarten mit; **4.** *a.* **~ *round*** *j-n* herˈumführen; **III** *s.* **5.** Trott *m*, Trab *m* (*a. fig.*): ***at a* ~** im Trab; ***keep s.o. on the* ~** j-n in Trab halten; **6.** F ‚Taps‘ *m* (*kleines Kind*); **7.** F ‚Tante‘ *f* (*alte Frau*); **8.** ***the* ~*s*** *pl.* F ‚Dünnpfiff‘ *m*; **9.** *ped. Am. sl.* a) Eselsbrücke *f*, ‚Klatsche‘ *f* (*Übersetzungshilfe*), b) Spickzettel *m*; **10.** F Trabrennen *n*.

troth [trəʊθ] *s. obs.* Treue(gelöbnis *n*) *f*: ***by my* ~*!*, *in* ~*!*** meiner Treu!, wahrlich!; ***pledge one's* ~** sein Wort verpfänden, ewige Treue schwören; ***plight one's* ~** sich verloben.

trot·ter [ˈtrɒtə] *s.* **1.** Traber *m* (*Pferd*); **2.** F Fuß *m*, Bein *n von Schlachttieren*: ***pigs* ~*s*** Schweinsfüße; **3.** *pl. humor.* ‚Haxen‘ *pl.*; **trot·ting race** [ˈtrɒtɪŋ] *s.* Trabrennen *n*.

trou·ble [ˈtrʌbl] **I** *v/t.* **1.** beunruhigen, stören, belästigen; **2.** *j-n* bemühen, bitten (***for*** um): ***may I* ~ *you to pass me the salt*** darf ich Sie um das Salz bitten; ***I will* ~ *you to hold your tongue*** *iro.* würden sie gefälligst den Mund halten; **3.** *j-m* ˈUmstände *od.* Unannehmlichkeiten bereiten, *j-m* Mühe machen; *j-n* behelligen (***about***, ***with*** mit); **4.** *j-n* plagen, quälen: ***be* ~*d with*** von *e-r Krankheit etc.* geplagt sein; **5.** *j-m* Sorge *od.* Verdruß *od.* Kummer machen *od.* bereiten, *j-n* beunruhigen: ***be* ~*d about*** sich Sorgen machen wegen; ***don't let it* ~ *you*** machen Sie sich deswegen keine Gedanken; **~*d face*** sorgenvolles *od.* gequältes Gesicht; **6.** *Wasser* trüben: **~*d waters*** *fig.* schwierige Situation, unangenehme Lage; ***fish in* ~*d waters*** *fig.* im trüben fischen; **II** *v/i.* **7.** sich beunruhigen (***about*** über *acc.*): ***I should not* ~ *if*** a) ich wäre beruhigt, wenn, b) es wäre mir gleichgültig, wenn; **8.** sich die Mühe machen, sich bemühen (***to do*** zu tun); sich ˈUmstände machen: ***don't* ~** (***yourself***) bemühen Sie sich nicht; ***don't* ~ *to write*** du brauchst nicht zu schreiben; **III** *s.* **9.** Mühe *f*, Plage *f*, Last *f*, Belästigung *f*, Störung *f*: ***give s.o.* ~** j-m Mühe verursachen; ***go to much* ~** sich besondere Mühe machen *od.* geben; ***put s.o. to* ~** j-m Umstände bereiten; ***save o.s. the* ~ *of doing*** sich die Mühe (er)sparen, zu tun; ***take*** (***the***) **~** sich (die) Mühe machen; ***take* ~ *over*** sich Mühe geben mit; (***it is***) ***no* ~** (***at all***) (es ist) nicht der Rede wert; **10.** Unannehmlichkeiten *pl.*, Schwierigkeiten *pl.*, Scherereien *pl.*, ‚Ärger‘ *m* (***with*** mit *der Polizei etc.*): ***ask*** *od.* ***look for* ~** unbedingt Ärger haben wollen; ***be in* ~** in Schwierigkeiten sein; ***get into* ~** in Schwierigkeiten geraten, Ärger bekommen; ***make* ~ *for s.o.*** j-n in Schwierigkeiten bringen; ***he is* ~** F er ist gefährlich, mit ihm wird es Ärger geben; **11.** Schwierigkeit *f*, Proˈblem *n*: ***the* ~ *is*** der Haken dabei ist, das Unangenehme ist (***that*** daß); ***what's the* ~*?*** wo(ran) fehlt's?, was ist los?; **12.** ⚕ Störung *f*, Leiden *n*: ***heart* ~** Herzleiden; **13.** a) *pol.* Unruhe(n *pl.*) *f*, Wirren *pl.*, b) *allg.* Afˈfäre *f*, Konˈflikt *m*; **14.** ⚙ Störung *f*, Deˈfekt *m*; ˈ**~ˌmak·er** *s.* Unruhestifter *m*; **~ man** [-mən] *s.* [*irr.*] ⚙ Störungssucher *m*; ˈ**~·proof** *adj.* störungsfrei; ˈ**~ˌshoot·er** *s. bsd. Am.* **1.** → ***trouble man***; **2.** *fig.* Friedensstifter *m*, ‚Feuerwehrmann‘ *m*.

trou·ble·some [ˈtrʌblsəm] *adj.* □ lästig, beschwerlich, unangenehm; ˈ**trou·ble·some·ness** [-nɪs] *s.* Lästigkeit *f*, Beschwerlichkeit *f*; *das* Unangenehme.

trouble spot *s.* **1.** ⚙ Schwachstelle *f*; **2.** *bsd. pol.* Unruheherd *m*.

trou·blous [ˈtrʌbləs] *adj.* □ *obs.* unruhig.

trough [trɒf] *s.* **1.** Trog *m*, Mulde *f*; **2.** Wanne *f*; **3.** Rinne *f*, Kaˈnal *m*; **4.** Wellental *n*: **~ *of the sea***; **5.** *a.* **~ *of low pressure*** *meteor.* Tief(druckrinne *f*) *n*; **6.** *bsd.* ⚚ Tiefpunkt *m*, ‚Talsohle‘ *f*.

trounce [traʊns] *v/t.* **1.** verprügeln; **2.** *fig.* herˈuntermachen; **3.** *sport* ‚überˈfahren‘, *j-m* e-e Abfuhr erteilen.

troupe [tru:p] *s.* (Schauspieler-, Zirkus-) Truppe *f*.

trou·sered [ˈtraʊzəd] *adj.* Hosen tragend, behost; ˈ**trou·ser·ing** [-zərɪŋ] *s.* Hosenstoff *m*; **trou·sers** [ˈtraʊzəz] *s. pl.* (***a pair of* ~** e-e) (lange) Hose; Hosen *pl.*; → ***wear***[1] 1.

trou·ser suit *s.* Hosenanzug *m*.

trousse [tru:s] *s.* ⚕ (chiˈrurgisches) Besteck.

trous·seau [ˈtru:səʊ] *pl.* **-seaus** (*Fr.*) *s.* Aussteuer *f*.

trout [traʊt] *ichth.* **I** *pl.* **-s**, *bsd. coll.* **trout** *s.* Foˈrelle *f*; **II** *v/i.* Foˈrellen fischen; **III** *adj.* Forellen…

trove [trəʊv] *s.* Fund *m*.

tro·ver [ˈtrəʊvə] *s.* ⚖ **1.** rechtswidrige Aneignung; **2.** *a.* ***action of* ~** Klage *f* auf Herˈausgabe des Wertes.

trow·el [ˈtraʊəl] **I** *s.* **1.** (Maurer)Kelle *f*: ***lay it on with a* ~** *fig.* (zu) dick auftragen; **2.** ✎ Hohlspatel *m*, Pflanzenheber *m*; **II** *v/t.* **3.** mit der Kelle auftragen, glätten.

troy (**weight**) [trɔɪ] *s.* ⚚ Troygewicht *n* (*für Edelmetalle, Edelsteine u. Arzneien*; *1 lb. = 373,24 g*).

tru·an·cy [ˈtru:ənsɪ] *s.* (Schul)Schwänzeˈrei *f*, unentschuldigtes Fernbleiben; ˈ**tru·ant** [-nt] **I** *s.* **1.** a) (Schul)Schwänzer(in), b) Bummler(in), Faulenzer (-in): ***play* ~** (*bsd.* die Schule) schwänzen, *a.* bummeln; **II** *adj.* **2.** träge, faul, pflichtvergessen; **3.** (schul)schwänzend; **4.** *fig.* (ab)schweifend (*Gedanken*).

truce [tru:s] *s.* **1.** ⚔ Waffenruhe *f*, -stillstand *m*: ***flag of* ~** Parlamentärflagge *f*; **~ *of God*** *hist.* Gottesfriede *m*; (***political***) **~** Burgfriede *m*; ***a* ~ *to talking!*** Schluß mit (dem) Reden!; **2.** *fig.* (Ruhe-, Atem)Pause *f* (***from*** von).

truck[1] [trʌk] **I** *s.* **1.** Tausch(handel) *m*; **2.** Verkehr *m*: ***have no* ~ *with s.o.*** mit j-m nichts zu tun haben; **3.** *Am.* Gemüse *n*: **~ *farm***, **~ *garden*** *Am.* Gemüsegärtnerei *f*; **~ *farmer*** *Am.* Gemüsegärtner *m*; **4.** *coll.* a) Kram(waren *pl.*) *m*, Hausbedarf *m*, b) *contp.* Plunder *m*; **5.** *mst* **~ *system*** ⚚ *hist.* Natuˈrallohn-, ˈTrucksyˌstem *n*; **II** *v/t.* **6.** (***for***) (aus-, ver)tauschen (gegen), eintauschen (für); **7.** verschachern; **III** *v/i.* **8.** Tauschhandel treiben; **9.** schachern, handeln (***for*** um).

truck[2] [trʌk] **I** *s.* **1.** ⚙ Block-, Laufrad *n*; **2.** Hand-, Gepäck-, Rollwagen *m*; **3.** Lore *f*: a) 🚂 *Brit.* offener Güterwagen, b) ⚒ Kippkarren *m*, Förderwagen *m*; **4.** *Am.* Lastauto *n*, -(kraft)wagen *m*: **~ *trailer*** a) Lastwagenanhänger *m*, b) Lastzug *m*; **5.** 🚂 Dreh-, ˈUntergestell *n*; **6.** ⚓ Flaggenknopf *m*; **II** *v/t.* **7.** auf Güter- *od.* Lastwagen *etc.* befördern; ˈ**truck·age** [-kɪdʒ] *s.* **1.** *Am.* ˈLastwagentransˌport *m*; **2.** Transˈportkosten *pl.*

truck·er[1] [ˈtrʌkə] *s. Am.* **1.** Lastwagen-, Fernlastfahrer *m*; **2.** ˈAutospediˌteur *m*.

truck·er[2] [ˈtrʌkə] *s. Am.* Gemüsegärtner *m*.

truck·le[1] [ˈtrʌkl] *v/i.* (zu Kreuze) kriechen (***to*** vor).

truck·le[2] [ˈtrʌkl] *s.* **1.** (Lauf)Rolle *f*; **2.** *mst* **~ *bed*** (niedriges) Rollbett.

truc·u·lence [ˈtrʌkjʊləns], ˈ**truc·u·len·cy** [-sɪ] *s.* Wildheit *f*; ˈ**truc·u·lent** [-nt] *adj.* □ **1.** wild, grausam; **2.** trotzig; **3.** gehässig.

trudge [trʌdʒ] **I** *v/i.* (*bsd.* mühsam) stapfen; sich (mühsam) (fort)schleppen: **~ *along***; **II** *v/t.* (mühsam) durchˈwandern; **III** *s.* mühseliger Marsch *od.* Weg.

true [tru:] **I** *adj.* □ → ***truly***; **1.** wahr, wahrheitsgetreu: ***a* ~ *story***; ***be* ~ *of*** zutreffen auf (*acc.*), gelten für; ***come* ~** sich bewahrheiten, sich erfüllen, eintreffen; **2.** wahr, echt, wirklich, (regel-) recht: ***a* ~ *Christian***; **~ *bill*** ⚖ begründete (*von den Geschworenen bestätigte*) Anklage(schrift); **~ *love*** wahre Liebe; (***it is***) **~** zwar, allerdings, freilich, zugegeben; **3.** (ge)treu (***to*** *dat.*): ***a* ~ *friend***; (***as***) **~ *as gold*** (*od.* ***steel***) treu wie Gold; **~ *to one's principles*** (***word***) s-n Grundsätzen (s-m Wort) getreu; **4.** (ge-) treu (***to*** *dat.*) (*von Sachen*): **~ *copy***; **~ *weight*** genaues *od.* richtiges Gewicht; **~ *to life*** lebenswahr, -echt; **~ *to nature*** naturgetreu; **~ *to size*** ⚙ maßgerecht, -haltig; **~ *to type*** artgemäß, typisch; **5.** rechtmäßig: **~ *heir*** (***owner***); **6.** zuverlässig: ***a* ~ *sign***; **7.** ⚙ genau, richtig eingestellt *od.* eingepaßt; **8.** ⚓, *phys.* rechtweisend (*Kurs, Peilung*): **~ *declination*** Ortsmißweisung *f*; **~ *north*** geographisch Nord; **9.** ♪ richtig gestimmt, rein; **10.** *biol.* reinrassig; **II** *adv.* **11.** wahr(ˈhaftig): ***speak* ~** die Wahrheit reden; **12.** (ge)treu (***to*** *dat.*); **13.** genau: ***shoot*** **~**; **III** *s.* **14.** ***the*** **~** das Wahre; **15.** ***out of*** **~** ⚙ unrund; **IV** *v/t.* **16.** *a.* **~ *up*** ⚙ *Lager* ausrichten; *Werkzeug* nachschleifen; *Rad* zentrieren; **~ blue** *s.* getreuer Anhänger; **ˌ~-ˈblue** *adj.* waschecht, treu; **ˈ~·born** *adj.* echt, gebürtig; **ˈ~·bred** *adj.* reinrassig; **ˌ~-ˈheart·ed** *adj.* aufrichtig, ehrlich; **ˌ~-ˈlife** *adj.* lebenswahr, -echt; **ˈ~·love** *s.* Geliebte(r *m*) *f.*

true·ness [ˈtruːnɪs] *s.* **1.** Wahrheit *f*; **2.** Echtheit *f*; **3.** Treue *f*; **4.** Richtigkeit *f*; **5.** Genauigkeit *f.*

truf·fle [ˈtrʌfl] *s.* ⚘ Trüffel *f.*

tru·ism [ˈtruːɪzəm] *s.* Binsenwahrheit *f*, Gemeinplatz *m.*

trull [trʌl] *s.* Dirne *f*, Hure *f.*

tru·ly [ˈtruːlɪ] *adv.* **1.** wahrheitsgemäß; **2.** aufrichtig: ***Yours*** (***very***) **~** (*als Briefschluß*) Hochachtungsvoll; ***yours*** **~** *humor.* meine Wenigkeit; **3.** wahrˈhaftig, in der Tat; **4.** genau.

trump¹ [trʌmp] *s. obs. od. poet.* Tromˈpete(nstoß *m*) *f*: ***the*** **~ *of doom*** die Posaune des Jüngsten Gerichts.

trump² [trʌmp] **I** *s.* **1.** a) Trumpf *m*, b) *a.* **~ *card*** Trumpfkarte *f* (*a. fig.*): ***play one's*** **~ *card*** *fig.* s-n Trumpf ausspielen; ***put s.o. to his*** **~** *fig.* j-n bis zum Äußersten treiben; ***turn up*** **~*s*** a) sich als das Beste erweisen, b) Glück haben; **2.** F *fig.* feiner Kerl; **II** *v/t.* **3.** (über-)ˈtrumpfen; **4.** *fig. j-n* überˈtrumpfen (***with*** mit); **III** *v/i.* **5.** Trumpf ausspielen, trumpfen.

trump³ [trʌmp] *v/t.* **~ *up*** *contp.* erdichten, erfinden, sich aus den Fingern saugen; **ˌtrumped-ˈup** [ˌtrʌmpt-] *adj.* erfunden, erlogen, falsch: **~ *charges.***

trump·er·y [ˈtrʌmpərɪ] **I** *s.* **1.** Plunder *m*, Schund *m*; **2.** *fig.* Gewäsch *n*, Quatsch *m*; **II** *adj.* **3.** Schund…, Kitsch…, kitschig, geschmacklos; **4.** *fig.* billig, nichtssagend: **~ *arguments.***

trum·pet [ˈtrʌmpɪt] **I** *s.* **1.** ♪ Tromˈpete *f*: **~ *call*** Trompetensignal *n*; ***blow one's own*** **~** *fig.* sein eigenes Lob singen; ***the last*** **~** die Posaune des Jüngsten Gerichts; **2.** Tromˈpetenstoß *m* (*a. des Elefanten*); **3.** ♪ Tromˈpete(nreˌgister *n*) *f* (*Orgel*); **4.** Schalltrichter *m*, Sprachrohr *n*; **5.** Hörrohr *n*; **II** *v/t. u. v/i.* **6.** tromˈpeten (*a. Elefant*): **~ (*forth*)** *fig.* ausposaunen; **ˈtrum·pet·er** [-tə] *s.* **1.** Tromˈpeter *m*; **2.** *fig.* a) ˈAuspoˌsauner(in), b) Lobredner *m*, c) ‚Sprachrohr' *n*; **3.** *orn.* Tromˈpetertaube *f*; **trum·pet ma·jor** *s.* ⚔ ˈStabstromˌpeter *m.*

trun·cate [trʌŋˈkeɪt] **I** *v/t.* **1.** *a. fig.* stutzen, beschneiden; **2.** ∡ abstumpfen; **3.** ⚙ *Gewinde* abflachen; **4.** *Computer*: beenden; **II** *adj.* **5.** abgestutzt, -stumpft (*Blätter, Muscheln*); **trunˈcat·ed** [-tɪd] *adj.* **1.** *a. fig.* gestutzt, beschnitten; **2.** ∡ abgestumpft: **~ *cone*** (***pyramid***) Kegel- (Pyramiden)stumpf *m*; **3.** ⚙ abgeflacht; **trun·ca·tion** [trʌŋˈkeɪʃn] *s.* **1.** *a. fig.* Stutzung *f*; **2.** ∡ Abstumpfung *f*; **3.** ⚙ Abflachung *f*; **4.** *Computer*: Beendigung *f.*

trun·cheon [ˈtrʌntʃən] *s.* **1.** *Brit.* (Gummi)Knüppel *m*, Schlagstock *m der Polizei*; **2.** Komˈmandostab *m.*

trun·dle [ˈtrʌndl] **I** *v/t.* *Faß etc.* trudeln, rollen; *Reifen* schlagen; *j-n im Rollstuhl etc.* fahren; **II** *v/i.* *oft* **~ *along*** rollen, sich wälzen, trudeln; **III** *s.* Rolle *f*, Walze *f*: **~ *bed*** → ***truckle²*** 2.

trunk [trʌŋk] *s.* **1.** (Baum)Stamm *m*; **2.** Rumpf *m*, Leib *m*, Torso *m*; **3.** *zo.* Rüssel *m*; **4.** (Schrank)Koffer *m*, Truhe *f*; **5.** △ (Säulen)Schaft *m*; **6.** *anat.* (*Nerven- etc.*)Strang *m*, Stamm *m*; **7.** *pl.* a) → ***trunk hose***, b) Badehose *f*, c) *sport* Shorts *pl.*, d) (ˈHerren)ˌUnterhose *f*; **8.** ⚙ Rohrleitung *f*, Schacht *m*; **9.** *teleph. bsd. Brit.* a) Fernleitung *f*, b) Fernverbindung *f*; **10.** 🚆 → ***trunk line*** 1; **11.** *mot. Am.* Kofferraum *m*; **12.** *Computer*: Anschlußstelle *f*; **~ call** *s. teleph. Brit.* Ferngespräch *n*; **~ hose** *s. hist.* Kniehose *f*; **~ line** *s.* **1.** 🚆 Hauptstrecke *f*, -linie *f*; **2.** → ***trunk*** 9 a; **~ road** *s.* Haupt-, Fernverkehrsstraße *f*; **~ route** *s. allg.* Hauptstrecke *f.*

trun·nion [ˈtrʌnjən] *s.* ⚙ (Dreh)Zapfen *m.*

truss [trʌs] **I** *v/t.* **1.** *oft* **~ *up*** a) bündeln, (fest)schnüren, zs.-binden, b) *j-n* fesseln; **2.** *Geflügel zum Braten* dressieren; **3.** △ absteifen, stützen; **4.** *oft* **~ *up*** *obs. Kleider etc.* aufschürzen, -stecken; **5.** *obs. j-n* aufhängen; **II** *s.* **6.** ⚕ Bruchband *n*; **7.** △ a) Träger *m*, Binder *m*, b) Fach-, Gitter-, Hängewerk *n*, Gerüst *n*; **8.** ⚓ Rack *n*; **9.** (Heu-, Stroh)Bündel *n*, (*a.* Schlüssel)Bund *n*; **10.** ⚘ Dolde *f*; **~ bridge** *s.* (Gitter)Fachwerkbrücke *f.*

trust [trʌst] **I** *s.* **1.** (***in***) Vertrauen *n* (auf *acc.*), Zutrauen *n* (zu *dat.*): ***place*** (*od.* ***put***) ***one's*** **~ *in*** → 13; ***position of*** **~** Vertrauensposten *m*; ***take s.th. on*** **~** et. (einfach) glauben; **2.** Zuversicht *f*, zuversichtliche Erwartung *od.* Hoffnung, Glaube *m*; **3.** Kreˈdit *m*: ***on*** **~** a) auf Kredit, b) auf Treu u. Glauben; **4.** Pflicht *f*, Verantwortung *f*; **5.** Verwahrung *f*, Obhut *f*: ***in*** **~** zu treuen Händen; **6.** Pfand *n*, anvertrautes Gut; **7.** ⚖ a) Treuhand(verhältnis *n*) *f*, b) Treuhandgut *n*, -vermögen *n*: ***breach of*** **~** Verletzung *f* der Treupflicht; **~ *territory*** *pol.* Treuhandgebiet *n*; ***hold s.th. in*** **~** et. treuhänderisch verwalten; **8.** ⚚ a) Trust *m*, b) Konˈzern *m*, c) Karˈtell *n*, Ring *m*; **9.** (*Familien- etc.*)Stiftung *f*; **II** *v/t.* **10.** *j-m* (ver)trauen, glauben, sich auf *j-n* verlassen: **~ *s.o. to do s.th.*** j-m zutrauen, daß er et. tut; **~ *him to do that!*** *iro.* a) das sieht ihm ähnlich!, b) verlaß dich drauf, er wird es tun!; **11.** (***s.o. with s.th., s.th. to s.o.*** j-m et.) anvertrauen; **12.** (zuversichtlich) hoffen *od.* erwarten, glauben; **III** *v/i.* **13.** (***in, to***) vertrauen (auf *acc.*), sein Vertrauen setzen (auf *acc.*); **14.** hoffen, glauben, denken; **~ com·pa·ny** *s. Am.* Treuhandgesellschaft *f od.* -bank *f*; **~ deed** *s.* Treuhandvertrag *m.*

trus·tee [ˌtrʌsˈtiː] *s.* **1.** Sachwalter *m* (*a. fig.*), (Vermögens)Verwalter *m*, Treuhänder *m*: **~ *in bankruptcy, official*** **~** Konkurs-, Masseverwalter; ***Public*** 𝔖 *Brit.* Öffentlicher Treuhänder; **~ *process*** *Am.* Beschlagnahme *f*, (*bsd.* Forderungs)Pfändung *f*; **~ *securities*, ~ *stock*** mündelsichere Wertpapiere; **2.** Kuˈrator *m*, Pfleger *m*: ***board of*** **~*s*** Kuratorium *n*; **ˌtrusˈtee·ship** [-ʃɪp] *s.* **1.** Treuhänderschaft *f*; **2.** Kuraˈtorium *n*; **3.** *pol.* a) Treuhandverwaltung *f*, b) Treuhandgebiet *n.*

trust·ful [ˈtrʌstfʊl] *adj.* □ vertrauensvoll, zutraulich.

trust fund *s.* ⚚ Treuhandvermögen *n.*

trust·i·fi·ca·tion [ˌtrʌstɪfɪˈkeɪʃn] *s.* ⚚ Verˈtrustung *f*, Trustbildung *f.*

trust·ing [ˈtrʌstɪŋ] *adj.* □ → ***trustful.***

ˈtrustˌwor·thi·ness [-ˌwɜːðɪnɪs] *s.* Vertrauenswürdigkeit *f*; **ˈtrustˌwor·thy** *adj.* □ vertrauenswürdig, zuverlässig.

trust·y [ˈtrʌstɪ] **I** *adj.* □ **1.** vertrauensvoll; **2.** treu, zuverlässig; **II** *s.* **3.** ‚Kalˈfakter' *m* (*privilegierter Sträfling*).

truth [truːθ] *s.* **1.** Wahrheit *f*: ***in*** **~**, *obs.* ***of a*** **~** in Wahrheit; ***the*** **~, *the whole*** **~ *and nothing but the*** **~** ⚖ die reine Wahrheit; ***to tell the*** **~, ~ *to tell*** um die Wahrheit zu sagen, ehrlich gesagt; ***there is no*** **~ *in it*** daran ist nichts Wahres; ***the*** **~ *is that I forgot it*** in Wirklichkeit *od.* tatsächlich habe ich es vergessen; **2.** *allgemein anerkannte* Wahrheit: ***historical*** **~**; **3.** Wahrˈhaftigkeit *f*; Aufrichtigkeit *f*; **4.** Wirklichkeit *f*, Echtheit *f*, Treue *f*; **5.** Richtigkeit *f*, Genauigkeit *f*: ***be out of*** **~** ⚙ nicht genau passen; **~ *to life*** Lebensechtheit *f*; **~ *to nature*** Naturtreue *f.*

truth·ful [ˈtruːθfʊl] *adj.* □ **1.** wahr (-heitsgemäß); **2.** wahrheitsliebend; **3.** echt, genau, getreu; **ˈtruth·ful·ness** [-nɪs] *s.* **1.** Wahrˈhaftigkeit *f*; **2.** Wahrheitsliebe *f*; **3.** Echtheit *f.*

try [traɪ] **I** *s.* **1.** Versuch *m*: ***have a*** **~** e-n Versuch machen, es versuchen (***at*** mit); **2.** *Rugby*: Versuch *m*; **II** *v/t.* **3.** versuchen, probieren: **~ *one's best*** sein Bestes tun; **~ *one's hand at s.th.*** sich an e-r Sache versuchen; **4.** *a.* **~ *out*** (aus-, ˈdurch)probieren, erproben, prüfen: **~ *a new method*** (***remedy, invention***); **~ *on*** *Kleid etc.* anprobieren, *Hut* aufprobieren; **~ *it on with s.o.*** *sl.* ‚es bei j-m probieren'; **5.** e-n Versuch machen mit, es versuchen mit: **~ *the door*** die Tür zu öffnen suchen; **~ *one's luck*** sein Glück versuchen (***with*** bei *j-m*); **6.** ⚖ a) verhandeln über *e-e Sache, Fall* unterˈsuchen, b) verhandeln gegen *j-n*, vor Gericht stellen; **7.** *Augen etc.* angreifen, (über)ˈanstrengen, *Geduld, Mut, Nerven etc.* auf e-e harte Probe stellen; **8.** *j-n* arg mitnehmen, plagen, quälen; **9.** *mst* **~ *out*** ⚙ a) *Metalle* raffinieren, scheiden, b) *Talg etc.* ausschmelzen, c) *Spiritus* rektifizieren; **III** *v/i.* **10.** versuchen (***at*** *acc.*), sich bemühen *od.* bewerben (***for*** um); **11.** versuchen, e-n Versuch machen: **~ *again!*** (versuch es) noch einmal!; **~ *and read!*** F versuche zu lesen!; **~ *hard*** sich große Mühe geben.

try·ing [ˈtraɪɪŋ] *adj.* □ **1.** schwierig, kritisch, unangenehm, nervtötend; **2.** anstrengend, ermüdend (***to*** für).

ˈtry|-on *s.* **1.** Anprobe *f*; **2.** F ˈSchwindelmaˌnöver *n*; **ˈ~-out** *s.* **1.** Probe *f*, Erprobung *f*; **2.** *sport* Ausscheidungskampf *m*, -spiel *n*; **~·sail** [ˈtraɪsl] *s.* ⚓ Gaffelsegel *n*; **~ square** *s.* ⚙ Richtscheit *n.*

tryst [trɪst] *obs.* **I** *s.* **1.** Stelldichein *n*, Rendezˈvous *n*; **2.** → ***trysting place***; **II** *v/t.* **3.** *j-n* (an e-n verabredeten Ort) bestellen; **4.** *Zeit, Ort* verabreden; **tryst·ing place** [-tɪŋ] *s.* Treffpunkt *m.*

tsar [zɑː] *etc.* → ***czar*** *etc.*

tset·se (fly) [ˈtsetsɪ] *s. zo.* Tsetsefliege *f.*

ˈT-shirt *s.* T-Shirt *n.*

ˈT-square *s.* ⚙ **1.** Reißschiene *f*; **2.** An-

schlagwinkel *m*.
tub [tʌb] **I** *s*. **1.** (Bade)Wanne *f*; **2.** *Brit.* F (Wannen)Bad *n*; **3.** Bottich *m*, Kübel *m*, Wanne *f*; **4.** (*Butter- etc.*)Faß *n*, Tonne *f*; **5.** Faß *n* (*als Maß*): ***a ~ of tea***; **6.** ⚓ *humor.* ‚Kahn' *m*, ‚Kasten' *m* (*Schiff*); **7.** *Rudern*: Übungsboot *n*; **8.** ⚒ Förderkorb *m*, -wagen *m*; **9.** *humor.* Kanzel *f*; **II** *v/t.* **10.** *bsd. Butter* in ein Faß tun; **11.** ⚘ in e-n Kübel pflanzen; **12.** F baden; **III** *v/i.* **13.** F (sich) baden; **14.** *Rudern*: im Übungsboot trainieren.
tu·ba [ˈtjuːbə] *s*. ♪ Tuba *f*.
tub·by [ˈtʌbɪ] **I** *adj.* **1.** faß-, tonnenartig; **2.** F rundlich, klein u. dick; **3.** dumpf, hohl (*klingend*); **II** *s*. **4.** F ‚Dickerchen' *n*.
tube [tjuːb] **I** *s*. **1.** Rohr(leitung *f*) *n*, Röhre *f*; (Glas- *etc.*)Röhrchen *n*: → ***test tube***; **2.** Schlauch *m*: (***inner***) ~ ⚙ (Luft)Schlauch *m*; **3.** (Meˈtall)Tube *f*: ~ ***colo(u)rs*** Tubenfarben; **4.** ♪ (Blas-)Rohr *n*; **5.** *anat.* (*Luft- etc.*)Röhre *f*, Kaˈnal *m*; **6.** ⚘ (Pollen)Schlauch *m*; **7.** ⚡ Röhre *f*: ***the*** ~ die ‚Röhre' *f* (*Fernseher*); ***on the*** ~ ‚in der Glotze'; **8.** a) (U-Bahn)Tunnel *m*, b) *a.* 2 *die* Londoner U-Bahn; **II** *v/t.* **9.** ⚙ mit Röhren versehen; **10.** (durch Röhren) befördern; **11.** (in Röhren *od.* Tuben) abfüllen; ˈ**tube-feed** [*irr.*] *v/t.* ⚕ künstlich (⚖ zwangs)ernähren; ˈ**tube·less** [-lɪs] *adj.* schlauchlos (*Reifen*).
tu·ber [ˈtjuːbə] *s*. **1.** ⚘ Knolle *f*, Knollen(-gewächs *n*) *m*; **2.** ⚕ Knoten *m*, Schwellung *f*, Tuber *n*.
tu·ber·cle [ˈtjuːbəkl] *s*. **1.** *biol.* Knötchen *n*; **2.** ⚕ a) Tuˈberkel(knötchen *n*) *m*, b) (*bsd.* ˈLungen)Tuˌberkel *m*; **3.** ⚘ kleine Knolle, Warze *f*; **tu·ber·cu·lar** [tjuːˈbɜːkjʊlə] → ***tuberculous***; **tu·ber·cu·lo·sis** [tjuːˌbɜːkjʊˈləʊsɪs] *s*. ⚕ Tuberkuˈlose *f*; **tu·ber·cu·lous** [tjuːˈbɜːkjʊləs] *adj.* **1.** ⚕ tuberkuˈlös, Tuberkel…; **2.** knotig.
tube·rose¹ [ˈtjuːbərəʊz] *s*. ⚘ Tubeˈrose *f*, ˈNachthyaˌzinthe *f*.
tu·ber·ose² [ˈtjuːbərəʊs] → ***tuberous***.
tu·ber·os·i·ty [ˌtjuːbəˈrɒsɪtɪ] → ***tuber*** 2.
tu·ber·ous [ˈtjuːbərəs] *adj.* **1.** *anat.*, ⚕ knotig, knötchenförmig; **2.** ⚘ a) knollentragend, b) knollig.
tub·ing [ˈtjuːbɪŋ] *s*. ⚙ **1.** ˈRöhrenmateriˌal *n*, Rohr *n*; **2.** *coll.* Röhren *pl.*, Röhrenanlage *f*; **3.** Rohr(stück) *n*.
ˈ**tub|-ˌthump·er** *s*. (g)eifernder *od.* schwülstiger Redner; ˈ**~-ˌthump·ing** *adj.* (g)eifernd, schwülstig.
tu·bu·lar [ˈtjuːbjʊlə] *adj.* rohrförmig, Röhren…, Rohr…: ~ ***boiler*** Heizrohrkessel *m*; ~ ***furniture*** Stahlrohrmöbel *pl.*; **tu·bule** [ˈtjuːbjuːl] *s*. **1.** Röhrchen *n*; **2.** *anat.* Kaˈnälchen *n*.
tuck [tʌk] **I** *s*. **1.** Falte *f*, Biese *f*, Einschlag *m*, Saum *m*; Lasche *f*; **2.** ⚓ Gilling *f*; **3.** *ped. Brit.* F Süßigkeiten *pl.*; **4.** *sport* Hocke *f*; **II** *v/t.* **5.** *mst* ~ ***in*** a) einnähen, b) *Falte* einschlagen; **6.** Biesen nähen in *ein Kleid*; **7.** *mst* ~ ***in*** (*od.* ***up***) ein-, ˈumschlagen: ~ ***up*** a) abnähen, b) hochstecken, -schürzen, c) raffen, d) *Ärmel* hochkrempeln; **8.** *et. wohin* stecken, *unter den Arm etc.* klemmen: ~ ***away*** a) wegstecken, verstauen, b) verstecken; ***~ed away*** versteckt (liegend) (*z.B. Dorf*); ~ ***in*** (*od.* ***up***) (warm) zudecken, (behaglich) einpacken; ~ ***up in bed*** ins Bett stecken; ~ ***up one's legs*** die Beine anziehen; **9.** ~ ***in*** *sl. Essen etc.* ‚verdrücken'; **III** *v/i.* **10.** sich falten: ~ ***away*** sich verstauen lassen; **11.** ~ ***in*** F *beim Essen* ‚einhauen': ~ ***into*** sich *et.* schmecken lassen.
tuck·er¹ [ˈtʌkə] *s*. **1.** Faltenleger *m* (*Nähmaschine*); **2.** *hist.* Brusttuch *n*: ***best bib and*** ~ *fig.* Sonntagsstaat *m*.
tuck·er² [ˈtʌkə] *v/t.* *mst* ~ ***out*** *Am.* F *j-n* ‚fertigmachen' (*völlig erschöpfen*): ***~ed out*** (total) erledigt.
ˈ**tuck|-in** *s*. *Brit. sl.* ‚Fresseˈrei' *f*, Schmaus *m*; ˈ**~-shop** *s*. *Brit. ped. sl.* Süßwarenladen *m*.
Tues·day [ˈtjuːzdɪ] *s*. Dienstag *m*: ***on*** ~ am Dienstag; ***on ~s*** dienstags.
tu·fa [ˈtjuːfə] *s*. *geol.* Kalktuff *m*, Tuff(-stein) *m*; **tu·fa·ceous** [tjuːˈfeɪʃəs] *adj.* (Kalk)Tuff…
tuff [tʌf] → ***tufa***.
tuft [tʌft] *s*. **1.** (*Gras-, Haar- etc.*)Büschel *n*, (*Feder- etc.*)Busch *m*, (*Haar-*)Schopf *m*; **2.** Quaste *f*, Troddel *f*; **3.** *anat.* Kapilˈlargefäßbündel *n*; ˈ**tuft·ed** [-tɪd] *adj.* **1.** büschelig; **2.** *orn.* Hauben…: ~ ***lark***; ˈ**tuftˌhunt·er** *s*. gesellschaftlicher Streber; **tuft·y** [ˈtʌftɪ] *adj.* büschelig.
tug [tʌg] **I** *v/t.* **1.** zerren, ziehen an (*dat.*); ⚓ schleppen; **II** *v/i.* **2.** ~ ***at*** zerren an (*dat.*); **3.** *fig.* sich (ab)placken; **III** *s*. **4.** Zerren *n*, (heftiger) Zug, Ruck *m*: ***give a ~ at*** → 2; ~ ***of war*** *sport u. fig.* Tauziehen *n*; **5.** *fig.* a) große Anstrengung, b) schwerer (*a. seelischer*) Kampf; **6.** *a.* ***~boat*** ⚓ Schleppdampfer *m*, Schlepper *m*.
tu·i·tion [tjuːˈɪʃn] *s*. ˈUnterricht *m*: ***private*** ~ Privatunterricht, -stunden *pl.*; **tuˈi·tion·al** [-ʃənl], **tuˈi·tion·ar·y** [-ʃnərɪ] *adj.* Unterrichts…, Studien…
tu·lip [ˈtjuːlɪp] *s*. ⚘ Tulpe *f*; ~ **tree** *s*. ⚘ Tulpenbaum *m*.
tulle [tjuːl] *s*. Tüll *m*.
tum·ble [ˈtʌmbl] **I** *s*. **1.** Fall *m*, Sturz *m* (*a.* ☿): ~ ***in prices*** ☿ Preissturz; **2.** Purzelbaum *m*; Salto *m*; **3.** *fig.* Wirrwarr *m*: ***all in a*** ~ kunterbunt durcheinander; **4.** ***give s.o. a.*** ~ *sl.* von j-m Notiz nehmen; **II** *v/i.* **5.** *a.* ~ ***down*** (ein-, ˈum-, hin-, hinˈab)fallen, (-)stürzen, (-)purzeln: ***to ~ over*** umkippen, sich überschlagen; **6.** purzeln, stolpern (***over*** über *acc.*); **7.** *wohin* stolpern (*eilen*): ~ ***into*** *fig.* a) *j-m in die Arme* laufen, b) in *e-n Krieg etc.* ‚hineinschlittern'; ~ ***to*** *sl. et.* plötzlich ‚kapieren' *od.* ‚spitzkriegen'; **8.** Luftsprünge *od.* Saltos *etc.* machen; *sport* Bodenübungen machen; **9.** sich wälzen; **10.** ⚔ taumeln (*Geschoß*); **11.** ☿ ‚purzeln' (*Aktien, Preise*); **III** *v/t.* **12.** zu Fall bringen, ˈumstürzen, -werfen; **13.** durchˈwühlen; **14.** schleudern, schmeißen; **15.** zerknüllen; *Haar* zerzausen; **16.** ⚙ schleudern; **17.** *hunt.* abschießen; ˈ**~-down** *adj.* baufällig; ~ **dri·er** *s*. Wäschetrockner *m*.
tum·bler [ˈtʌmblə] *s*. **1.** Trink-, Wasserglas *n*, Becher *m*; **2.** Parˈterreakroˌbat (-in); **3.** ⚙ a) Zuhaltung *f* (*Türschloß*), b) Richtwelle *f* (*Übersetzungsmotor*), c) Zahn *m*, d) Nocken, e) (Wasch-, Scheuer)Trommel *f*; **4.** *orn.* Tümmler *m*; **5.** *Am.* Stehaufmännchen *n*; ~ **switch** *s*. ⚡ Kippschalter *m*.
tum·brel [ˈtʌmbrəl], ˈ**tum·bril** [-rɪl] *s*. **1.** ⛏ Mistkarren *m*; **2.** *hist.* Schinderkarren *m*; **3.** ⚔ *hist.* Munitiˈonskarren *m*.
tu·me·fa·cient [ˌtjuːmɪˈfeɪʃnt] *adj.* ⚕ Schwellung erzeugend; ˌ**tu·meˈfac·tion** [-ˈfækʃn] *s*. ⚕ (An)Schwellung *f*, Geschwulst *f*; **tu·me·fy** [ˈtjuːmɪfaɪ] *v/i. u. v/t.* ⚕ (an)schwellen lassen; **tu·mes·cent** [tjuːˈmesnt] *adj.* (an)schwellend, geschwollen.
tu·mid [ˈtjuːmɪd] *adj.* □ geschwollen (*a. fig.*); **tu·mid·i·ty** [tjuːˈmɪdətɪ] *s*. **1.** ⚕ Schwellung *f*; **2.** *fig.* Geschwollenheit *f*.
tum·my [ˈtʌmɪ] *s*. *Kindersprache*: Bäuchlein *n*: ~ ***ache*** Bauchweh *n*.
tu·mo(u)r [ˈtjuːmə] *s*. ⚕ Tumor *m*.
tu·mult [ˈtjuːmʌlt] *s*. Tuˈmult *m*: a) Getöse *n*, Lärm *m*, b) (*a. seelischer*) Aufruhr *m*; **tu·mul·tu·ar·y** [tjuːˈmʌltjʊərɪ] *adj.* **1.** → ***tumultuous***; **2.** verworren; **3.** aufrührerisch; **tu·mul·tu·ous** [tjuːˈmʌltjʊəs] *adj.* □ **1.** tumultuˈarisch, lärmend; **2.** heftig, stürmisch, turbuˈlent.
tu·mu·lus [ˈtjuːmjʊləs] *s*. (*bsd. alter* Grab)Hügel.
tun [tʌn] *s*. **1.** Faß *n*; **2.** *Brit.* Tonne *f* (*altes Flüssigkeitsmaß*); **3.** *Brauerei*: Maischbottich *m*.
tune [tjuːn] **I** *s*. **1.** ♪ Meloˈdie *f*; Weise *f*, Lied *n*; *a.* Hymne *f*, Choˈral *m*: ***to the ~ of*** a) nach der Melodie von, b) *fig.* in Höhe von, von sage u. schreibe *£ 100*; ***call the*** ~ *fig.* das Sagen haben; ***change one's ~, sing another ~*** F e-n anderen Ton anschlagen, andere Saiten aufziehen; **2.** ♪ a) (richtige) (Ein)Stimmung e-s Instruˈments, b) richtige Tonhöhe: ***in*** ~ (richtig) gestimmt; ***out of*** ~ verstimmt; ***keep*** ~ a) Stimmung halten (*Instrument*), b) Ton halten; ***play out of*** ~ unrein *od.* falsch spielen; ***sing in*** ~ tonrein *od.* sauber singen; **3.** ⚡ Abstimmung *f*, (Scharf)Einstellung *f*; **4.** *fig.* Harmoˈnie *f*: ***in ~ with*** übereinstimmend mit, im Einklang (stehend) mit, harmonierend mit; ***be out of ~ with*** im Widerspruch stehen zu, nicht übereinstimmen mit; **5.** *fig.* Stimmung *f*: ***not in ~ for*** nicht aufgelegt zu; ***out of*** ~ verstimmt, mißgestimmt; **II** *v/t.* **6.** *a.* ~ ***up*** a) ♪ stimmen, b) *fig.* abstimmen (***to*** auf *acc.*); **7.** *Antenne, Radio, Stromkreis* abstimmen, einstellen (***to*** auf *acc.*); **8.** *fig.* a) (***to***) anpassen (an *acc.*), b) (***for***) bereitmachen (für); **III** *v/i.* **9.** ♪ stimmen; ~ **in** *v/i.* (das Radio *etc.*) einschalten: ~ ***to*** a) *e-n Sender, ein Programm* einschalten, b) *fig.* sich einstellen auf (*acc.*); ~ **up I** *v/t.* **1.** → ***tune*** 6; **2.** *mot.*, ✈ a) startbereit machen, b) *Motor* einfahren, c) *e-n Motor* tunen; **3.** *fig.* a) bereitmachen, b) in Schwung bringen, c) *das Befinden etc.* heben; **II** *v/i.* **4.** ♪ (die Instruˈmente) stimmen; **5.** F a) einsetzen, b) F losheulen.
tune·ful [ˈtjuːnfʊl] *adj.* □ **1.** meˈlodisch; **2.** *obs.* sangesfreudig: ~ ***birds***; ˈ**tune·less** [-nlɪs] *adj.* ˈunmeˌlodisch.
tun·er [ˈtjuːnə] *s*. **1.** ♪ (Instruˈmenten-)Stimmer *m*; **2.** ♪ a) Stimmpfeife *f*, b) Stimmvorrichtung *f* (*Orgel*); **3.** ⚡ Abstimmvorrichtung *f*; **4.** *Radio, TV*: Tuner *m*, Kaˈnalwähler *m*.
tune-up [ˈtjuːnʌp] *s*. **1.** *Am.* → ***warm-up*** 1 *u.* 3; **2.** ⚙ leistungsfördernde Maßnahmen *pl.*

tung·state ['tʌŋsteɪt] *s.* ⚗ Wolfra'mat *n*; '**tung·sten** [-stən] *s.* ⚗ Wolfram *n*: **~ steel** ⚙ Wolframstahl *m*; '**tung·stic** [-stɪk] *adj.* ⚗ Wolfram...: **~ acid**.

tu·nic ['tjuːnɪk] *s.* **1.** *antiq.* Tunika *f*; **2.** *bsd.* ⚔ *Brit.* Waffenrock *m*; **3.** a) 'Überkleid *n*, b) Kasack *m*; **4.** → ***tunicle***; **5.** *biol.* Häutchen *n*, Hülle *f*; '**tu·ni·ca** [-kə] *pl.* **-cae** [-siː] *s. anat.* Häutchen *n*, Mantel *m*; '**tu·ni·cate** [-kət] *s. zo.* Manteltier *n*; '**tu·ni·cle** [-kl] *s. R.C.* Meßgewand *n*.

tun·ing ['tjuːnɪŋ] **I** *s.* **1.** a) ♪ Stimmen *n*, b) *fig.* Ab-, Einstimmung *f* (**to** auf *acc.*); **2.** Anpassung *f* (**to** an *acc.*); **3.** ⚡ Abstimmung *f*, Einstellung *f* (**to** auf *acc.*); **II** *adj.* **4.** ♪ Stimm...: **~ fork**; **5.** ⚡ Abstimm...(*-kreis, -skala etc.*).

tun·nel ['tʌnl] **I** *s.* **1.** Tunnel *m*, Unter'führung *f* (*Straße, Bahn, Kanal*); **2.** *a. zo.* 'unterirdischer Gang, Tunnel *m*; **3.** ⚒ Stollen *m*; **4.** ✈ 'Windkaˌnal *m*; **II** *v/t.* **5.** unter'tunneln, e-n Tunnel bohren *od.* treiben durch; **III** *v/i.* **6.** e-n Tunnel anlegen *od.* treiben (**through** durch); '**tun·nel·(l)ing** [-lɪŋ] *s.* ⚙ Tunnelanlage *f*, -bau *m*.

tun·ny ['tʌnɪ] *s. bsd. coll.* Thunfisch *m*.

tup [tʌp] **I** *s.* **1.** *zo.* Widder *m*; **2.** ⚙ Hammerkopf *m*, Rammklotz *m*; **II** *v/t.* **3.** *zo.* bespringen, decken.

tup·pence ['tʌpəns], '**tup·pen·ny** [-pnɪ] *Brit.* F *für* ***twopence, twopenny***.

tur·ban ['tɜːbən] *s.* Turban *m*; '**tur·baned** [-nd] *adj.* turbantragend.

tur·bid ['tɜːbɪd] *adj.* ☐ **1.** dick(flüssig), trübe, schlammig; **2.** dick, dicht: **~ fog**; **3.** *fig.* verworren, wirr; **tur·bid·i·ty** [tɜː'bɪdətɪ], '**tur·bid·ness** [-nɪs] *s.* **1.** Trübheit *f*; **2.** Dicke *f*; **3.** *fig.* Verworrenheit *f*.

tur·bine ['tɜːbaɪn] **I** *s.* Tur'bine *f*; **II** *adj.* Turbinen...: **~ steamer**; **~-powered** mit Tur'binenantrieb.

turbo- [tɜːbəʊ] ⚙ *in Zssgn* Turbinen..., Turbo...; ˌ**tur·bo'jet (en·gine)** *s.* (Flugzeug *n* mit) Turbostrahltriebwerk *n*; ˌ**tur·bo'prop(-jet) (en·gine)** *s.* (Flugzeug *n* mit) ✈ 'Turbo-Pro'peller-Strahltriebwerk *n*; ˌ**tur·bo'ram-jet en·gine** *s.* ✈ Ma'schine *f* mit Staustrahltriebwerk.

tur·bot ['tɜːbət] *s. ichth.* Steinbutt *m*.

tur·bu·lence ['tɜːbjʊləns] *s.* **1.** Unruhe *f*, Aufruhr *m*, Ungestüm *n*, Sturm *m* (*a. meteor.*); **2.** *phys.* Turbu'lenz *f*, Wirbelbewegung *f*; '**tur·bu·lent** [-nt] *adj.* ☐ **1.** unruhig, ungestüm, stürmisch, turbu'lent; **2.** aufrührerisch; **3.** *phys.* verwirbelt, turbu'lent, Wirbel...

turd [tɜːd] *s.* V **1.** ‚Scheißhaufen' *m*; **2.** ‚Scheißer' *m*.

tu·reen [tə'riːn] *s.* Ter'rine *f*.

turf [tɜːf] **I** *s.* **1.** Rasen *m*; **2.** Rasenstück *n*, -sode *f*; **3.** Torf(ballen) *m*; **4.** *sport* Turf *m*: a) (Pferde)Rennbahn *f*, b) **the ~** *fig.* der Pferderennsport; **5.** *fig. j-s* Re'vier *n*; **II** *v/t.* **6.** mit Rasen bedekken; **7. ~ out** *Brit.* F *j-n* ‚rausschmeißen'; '**turf·ite** [-faɪt] *s.* (Pferde)Rennsportliebhaber *m*; '**turf·y** [-fɪ] *adj.* **1.** rasenbedeckt; **2.** torfartig; **3.** *fig.* (Pferde)Rennsport...

tur·ges·cence [tɜː'dʒesns] *s.* **1.** ⚕, ⚘ Schwellung *f*, Geschwulst *f*; **2.** *fig.* Schwulst *m*.

tur·gid ['tɜːdʒɪd] *adj.* ☐ **1.** ⚕ geschwollen; **2.** *fig.* schwülstig, ‚geschwollen'; **tur·gid·i·ty** [tɜː'dʒɪdətɪ], '**tur·gid·ness** [-nɪs] *s.* **1.** Geschwollensein *n*; **2.** *fig.* Geschwollenheit *f*, Schwülstigkeit *f*.

Turk [tɜːk] **I** *s.* **1.** Türke *m*, Türkin *f*: ***Young* ≈*s*** *pol.* Jungtürken *pl.*; **2.** *obs.* Ty'rann *m*; **II** *adj.* **3.** türkisch, Türken...

Tur·key[1] ['tɜːkɪ] **I** *s.* Tür'kei *f*; **II** *adj.* türkisch: **~ carpet** Orientteppich *m*; **~ red** *das* Türkischrot.

tur·key[2] ['tɜːkɪ] *s.* **1.** *orn.* Truthahn *m*, -henne *f*, Pute(r *m*) *f*: **talk ~** *Am. sl.* a) Fraktur reden (**with** mit), b) offen *od.* sachlich reden; **2.** *Am. sl. thea. etc.* ‚Pleite' *f*, ‚'Durchfall' *m*; **~ cock** *s.* **1.** Truthahn *m*, Puter *m*: (**as**) **red as a ~** puterrot (im Gesicht); **2.** *fig.* eingebildeter Fatzke.

Turk·ish ['tɜːkɪʃ] **I** *adj.* türkisch, Türken...; **II** *s. ling.* Türkisch *n*; **~ bath** *s.* türkisches Bad; **~ de·light** *s.* 'Fruchtgeˌleekonˌfekt *n*; **~ tow·el** *s.* Frottier-, Frot'tee(hand)tuch *n*.

Turko- [tɜːkəʊ, -kə] *in Zssgn* türkisch, Türken...

Tur·ko·man ['tɜːkəmən] *pl.* **-mans** *s.* **1.** Turk'mene *m*; **2.** *ling.* Turk'menisch *n*.

tur·mer·ic ['tɜːmərɪk] *s.* **1.** ⚘ Gelbwurz *f*; **2.** *pharm.* Kurkuma *f*; **3.** Kurkumagelb *n* (*Farbstoff*): **~ paper** ⚗ Kurkumapapier *n*.

tur·moil ['tɜːmɔɪl] *s.* **1.** *a. fig.* Aufruhr *m*, Tu'mult *m*: **in a ~** in Aufruhr; **2.** Getümmel *n*.

turn [tɜːn] **I** *s.* **1.** (Um)'Drehung *f*: **a single ~ of the handle**; **done to a ~** gerade richtig durchgebraten; **to a ~** *fig.* aufs Haar, vortrefflich; **2.** Turnus *m*, Reihe(nfolge) *f*: **by** (*od.* **in**) **~s** abwechselnd, wechselweise; **in ~** a) der Reihe nach, b) dann wieder; **in his ~** seinerseits; **speak out of ~** *fig.* unpassende Bemerkungen machen; **it is my ~** ich bin an der Reihe *od.* dran; **take ~s** (mit)einander *od.* sich abwechseln (**at** in *dat.*, bei); **take one's ~** handeln, wenn die Reihe an einen kommt; **wait your ~!** warte bis du dran bist!; **my ~ will come** *fig.* m-e Zeit kommt (auch) noch, ‚ich komme schon noch dran'; **3.** a) Drehung *f*, (**~ to the left** Links)Wendung *f*, b) *Schwimmen*: Wende *f*, c) *Skisport*: Wende *f*, Kehre *f*, Schwung *m*, d) *Eislauf etc.*: Kehre *f*; **4.** Wendepunkt *m* (*a. fig.*); **5.** Biegung *f*, Kurve *f*, Kehre *f*; **6.** Krümmung *f* (*a.* ⊿); **7.** Wendung *f*: a) 'Umkehr *f*: **be on the ~** ⚓ umschlagen (*Gezeit*) (→ *a.* 23); → ***tide*** 1, b) Richtung *f*, (Ver)Lauf *m*: **take a good** (**bad**) **~** sich zum Guten (Schlechten) wenden; **take a ~ for the better** (**worse**) sich bessern (verschlimmern); **take an interesting ~** e-e interessante Wendung nehmen (*Gespräch etc.*), c) (*Glücks-, Zeiten- etc.*) Wende *f*, Wechsel *m*, 'Umschwung *m*, Krise *f*: **~ of the century** Jahrhundertwende; **~ of life** Lebenswende, ⚕ Wechseljahre *pl. der Frau*; **8.** Ausschlag (-en *n*) *m e-r Waage*; **9.** (Arbeits-) Schicht *f*; **10.** Tour *f*, (einzelne) Windung (*Bandage, Kabel etc.*); **11.** (Rede-) Wendung *f*, Formulierung *f*; **12.** a) (kurzer) Spaziergang: **take a ~** e-n Spaziergang machen, b) kurze Fahrt, ‚Spritztour' *f*; **13.** (**for, to**) Neigung *f*, Hang *m*, Ta'lent *n* (zu), Sinn *m* (für); **14.** *a.* **~ of mind** Denkart *f*, -weise *f*; **15.** a) (*ungewöhnliche od. unerwartete*) Tat, b) Dienst *m*, Gefallen *m*: **a bad ~** e-e schlechte Tat *od.* ein schlechter Dienst; **a friendly ~** ein Freundschaftsdienst; **do s.o. a good ~** j-m e-n Gefallen tun; **one good ~ deserves another** e-e Liebe ist der andern wert; **16.** Anlaß *m*: **at every ~** auf Schritt u. Tritt; **17.** (kurze) Beschäftigung: **~** (**of work**) (Stück *n*) Arbeit *f*; **take a ~ at** rasch mal an *e-e Sache* gehen, sich kurz mit *e-r Sache* versuchen; **18.** F Schock *m*, Schrecken *m*: **give s.o. a. ~** j-n erschrecken; **19.** Zweck *m*: **this won't serve my ~** damit ist mir nicht gedient; **20.** ♪ Doppelschlag *m*; **21.** (Pro'gramm)Nummer *f*; **22.** ⚔ (Kehrt-) Wendung *f*: **left** (**right**) **~!** *Brit.* links- (rechts)um!; **about ~!** *Brit.* ganze Abteilung kehrt!; **23. on the ~** am Sauerwerden (*Milch*); **II** *v/t.* **24.** (*im Kreis od. um e-e Achse*) drehen; *Hahn, Schlüssel, Schraube, e-n Patienten etc.* ('um-, her'um)drehen; **25.** *a. Kleider* wenden; *et.* 'umkehren, -stülpen, -drehen; *Blatt, Buchseite* 'umdrehen, -wenden, *Buch* 'umblättern; *Boden* 'umpflügen, -graben; 🚂 *Weiche*, ⚙ *Hebel* 'umlegen: **it ~s my stomach** mir dreht sich dabei der Magen um; **~ s.o.'s head** *fig.* a) j-m den Kopf verdrehen, b) j-m zu Kopf steigen; **26.** zuwenden, -drehen, -kehren (**to** *dat.*); **27.** *Blick, Kamera, Schritte etc.* wenden, *a. Gedanken, Verlangen* richten, lenken (**against** gegen, **on** auf *acc.*, **to, toward**(**s**) nach, auf *acc.*): **~ the hose on the fire** den (Spritzen)Schlauch auf das Feuer richten; **28.** a) 'um-, ablenken, (-)leiten, (-) wenden, b) abwenden, abhalten, c) *j-n* 'umstimmen, abbringen (**from** von), d) *Richtung* ändern, e) *Gesprächsthema* wechseln; **29.** a) *Waage* zum Ausschlagen bringen, b) *fig.* ausschlaggebend sein bei: **~ an election** bei e-r Wahl den Ausschlag geben; → ***balance*** 2, ***scale***[2] 1; **30.** verwandeln (**into** in *acc.*): **~ water into wine**; **~ love into hate**; **~ into cash** ⚚ flüssigmachen, zu Geld machen; **31.** a) machen, werden lassen (**into** zu): **it ~ed her pale** es ließ sie erblassen; **~ colo**(**u**)**r** die Farbe wechseln, b) *a.* **~ sour** *Milch* sauer werden lassen, c) *Laub* verfärben; **32.** *Text* über'tragen, -'setzen (**into** ins *Italienische etc.*); **33.** her'umgehen um: **~ the corner** um die Ecke biegen, *fig.* über den Berg kommen; **34.** ⚔ a) um'gehen, -'fassen, b) aufrollen: **~ the enemy's flank**; **35.** hin'ausgehen *od.* hin'aus sein über *ein Alter, e-n Betrag etc.*: **he is just ~ing** (*od.* **has just ~ed**) **50** er ist gerade 50 geworden; **36.** ⚙ a) drehen, b) *Holzwaren, a. fig. Komplimente, Verse* drechseln; **37.** formen, *fig.* gestalten, bilden: **a well-~ed ankle**; **38.** *fig. Satz* formen, (ab)runden: **~ a phrase**; **39.** ⚚ verdienen, 'umsetzen; **40.** *Messerschneide etc.* verbiegen, *a.* stumpf machen: **~ the edge of** *fig. e-r Bemerkung etc.* die Spitze nehmen; **41.** *Purzelbaum etc.* schlagen; **42. ~ loose** los-, freilassen, -machen; **III** *v/i.* **43.** sich drehen (lassen), sich (im Kreis) (her'um)drehen; **44.** sich (ab-, hin-, zu-)

wenden; → ***turn to*** I; **45.** sich *stehend*, *liegend etc.* (ˈum-, herˈum)drehen; ⚓, *mot.* wenden, (⚓ ab)drehen; ✈, *mot.* kurven; **46.** (ab-, ein)biegen: ***I do not know which way to ~*** *fig.* ich weiß nicht, was ich machen soll; **47.** e-e Biegung machen (*Straße*, *Wasserlauf etc.*); **48.** sich krümmen *od.* winden (*Wurm etc.*): ***~ in one's grave*** sich im Grabe umdrehen; **49.** sich umdrehen, -stülpen (*Schirm etc.*): ***my stomach ~s at this sight*** bei diesem Anblick dreht sich mir der Magen um; **50.** schwind(e)lig werden: ***my head ~s*** mein Kopf dreht sich; **51.** sich (ver)wandeln (***into***, ***to*** in *acc.*), ˈumschlagen (*bsd. Wetter*): ***love has ~ed into hate***; **52.** *Kommunist*, *Soldat etc.*, *a. blaß*, *kalt etc.* werden: **~** (***sour***) sauer werden (*Milch*); **~** ***traitor*** zum Verräter werden; **53.** sich verfärben (*Laub*); **54.** sich wenden (*Gezeiten*); → ***tide*** 1;

Zssgn mit prp.:

turn| a·gainst I *v/i.* **1.** sich (*feindlich etc.*) wenden gegen; **II** *v/t.* **2.** *j-n* aufhetzen *od.* aufbringen gegen; **3.** *Spott etc.* richten gegen; **~ in·to** → ***turn*** 30, 31, 32, 51; **~ on I** *v/i.* **1.** sich drehen um *od.* in (*dat.*); **2.** → ***turn upon***; **3.** sich wenden *od.* richten gegen; **II** *v/t.* **4.** → ***turn*** 27; **~ to I** *v/i.* **1.** sich nach *links etc.* wenden (*Person*), nach *links etc.* abbiegen (*a. Fahrzeug*, *Straße etc.*); **2.** a) sich *der Musik*, *e-m Thema etc.* zuwenden, b) sich beschäftigen mit, c) sich anschicken (***doing s.th.*** et. zu tun); **3.** s-e Zuflucht nehmen zu: **~ *God***; **4.** sich an *j-n* wenden, *j-n od. et.* zu Rate ziehen; **5.** → ***turn*** 51; **II** *v/t.* **6.** *Hand* anlegen bei: ***turn a*** (*od.* ***one's***) ***hand to s.th.*** et. in Angriff nehmen; ***he can turn his hand to anything*** er ist zu allem zu gebrauchen; **7.** → ***turn*** 26, 27; **8.** verwandeln in (*acc.*); **9.** anwenden zu; → ***account*** 11; **~ up·on** *v/i.* **1.** *fig.* abhängen von; **2.** *fig.* sich drehen um, handeln von; **3.** → ***turn on*** 3;

Zssgn mit adv.:

turn| a·bout, ~ a·round I *v/t.* **1.** ˈumdrehen; **2.** ✓ *Heu*, *Boden* wenden; **II** *v/i.* **3.** sich ˈumdrehen; ⚔ kehrtmachen; *fig.* ˈumschwenken; **~ a·side** *v/t.* (*v/i.* sich) abwenden; **~ a·way I** *v/t.* **1.** abwenden (***from*** von); **2.** abweisen, wegschicken, -jagen; **3.** entlassen; **II** *v/i.* **4.** sich abwenden; **~ back I** *v/t.* **1.** ˈumkehren lassen; **2.** → ***turn down*** 3; **3.** *Uhr* zuˈrückdrehen; **II** *v/i.* **4.** zuˈrück-, ˈumkehren; **5.** zuˈrückgehen; **~ down I** *v/t.* **1.** ˈumkehren, -legen, -biegen; *Kragen* ˈumschlagen, *Buchseite etc.* ˈumknicken; **2.** *Gas*, *Lampe* kleiner stellen, *Radio etc.* leiser stellen; **3.** *Bett* aufdecken; *Bettdecke* zuˈrückschlagen; **4.** *j-n*, *Vorschlag etc.* ablehnen; *j-m* e-n Korb geben; **II** *v/i.* **5.** abwärts *od.* nach unten gebogen sein; **6.** sich ˈumlegen *od.* -schlagen lassen; **~ in I** *v/t.* **1.** a) einreichen, -senden, b) ab-, zuˈrückgeben; **2.** *Füße etc.* einwärts *od.* nach innen drehen *od.* biegen *od.* stellen; **3.** F *et.* zuˈstande bringen; **II** *v/i.* **4.** F zu Bett gehen; **5.** einwärts gebogen sein; **~ off I** *v/t.* **1.** *Wasser*, *Gas* abdrehen; *Licht*, *Radio etc.* ausschalten, abstellen; **2.** *Schlag etc.* abwenden, ablenken; **3.** F ˏrausschmeißenˈ, entlassen; **4.** F a) *j-m* die Lust nehmen, b) *j-n* anwidern; **II** *v/i.* **5.** abbiegen (*Person*, *a. Straße*); **~ on** *v/t.* **1.** *Gas*, *Wasser* aufdrehen, *a. Radio* anstellen; *Licht*, *Gerät* anmachen, einschalten; **2.** F a) *j-n* ˏantörnenˈ, b) *j-n* (*a. sexuell*) ˏanmachenˈ, ˏin Fahrtˈ bringen; **~ out I** *v/t.* **1.** hinˈauswerfen, wegjagen, vertreiben; **2.** entlassen (***of*** aus *e-m Amt etc.*); **3.** *Regierung* stürzen; **4.** *Vieh* auf die Weide treiben; **5.** *Taschen etc.* ˈumkehren, -stülpen; **6.** *Zimmer*, *Möbel* ausräumen; **7.** a) † *Waren* produzieren, herstellen, b) *contp. Bücher etc.* produzieren, c) *fig. Wissenschaftler etc.* herˈvorbringen (*Universität etc.*): ***Oxford has turned out many statesmen*** aus Oxford sind schon viele Staatsmänner hervorgegangen; **8.** → ***turn off*** 1; **9.** *Füße etc.* auswärts *od.* nach außen drehen *od.* biegen; **10.** ausstatten, herrichten, *bsd.* kleiden: ***well turned-out*** gutgekleidet; **11.** ⚔ antreten *od. die Wache* herˈaustreten lassen; **II** *v/i.* **12.** auswärts gebogen sein (*Füße etc.*); **13.** a) hinˈausziehen, herˈauskommen (***of*** aus), b) ⚔ ausrücken (*a. Feuerwehr etc.*), c) *zur Wahl etc.* kommen (*Bevölkerung*), d) ⚔ antreten, e) in Streik treten, f) F *aus dem Bett* aufstehen; **14.** *gut etc.* ausfallen, werden; **15.** sich gestalten, *gut etc.* ausgehen, ablaufen; **16.** sich erweisen *od.* entpuppen als, sich herˈausstellen: ***he turned out*** (***to be***) ***a good swimmer*** er entpuppte sich als guter Schwimmer; ***it turned out that he was*** (***had***), ***he turned out to be*** (***have***) es stellte sich heraus, daß er … war (hatte); **~ o·ver I** *v/t.* **1.** † *Geld*, *Ware* ˈumsetzen, e-n ˈUmsatz haben von; **2.** ˈumdrehen, -wenden, *Buch*, *Seite a.* ˈumblättern: ***please ~!*** bitte wenden!; → ***leaf*** 3; **3.** (***to***) a) überˈtragen (*dat. od.* auf *acc.*), überˈgeben (*dat.*), b) *j-n der Polizei etc.* ausliefern, überˈgeben; **4.** *a.* **~ *in one's mind*** überˈlegen, sich *et.* durch den Kopf gehen lassen; **II** *v/i.* **5.** sich *im Bett etc.* ˈumdrehen; **6.** ˈumkippen, -schlagen; **~ round I** *v/i.* **1.** sich (im Kreis *od.* herˈum)drehen; **2.** *fig.* s-n Sinn ändern, ˈumschwenken: ***but then he turned round and said*** doch dann sagte er plötzlich; **II** *v/t.* **3.** (herˈum)drehen; **~ to** *v/i.* sich ˏranmachenˈ (an die Arbeit), sich ins Zeug legen; **~ un·der** *v/t.* ✓ ˈunterpflügen; **~ up I** *v/t.* **1.** nach oben drehen *od.* richten *od.* biegen; *Kragen* hochschlagen, -klappen; → ***nose*** *Redew.*, ***toe*** 1; **2.** ausgraben, zuˈtage fördern; **3.** *Spielkarte* aufdecken; **4.** *Hose etc.* ˈum-, einschlagen; **5.** *Brit.* a) *Wort* nachschlagen, b) *Buch* zu Rate ziehen; **6.** *Gas*, *Licht* groß *od.* größer drehen, *Radio* lauter stellen; **7.** *Kind* übers Knie legen (*züchtigen*); **8.** F *j-m* den Magen ˈumdrehen (*vor Ekel*); **9.** *sl. Arbeit* ˏaufsteckenˈ; **II** *v/i.* **10.** sich nach oben drehen, nach oben gerichtet *od.* hochgeschlagen sein; **11.** *fig.* auftauchen: a) aufkreuzen, erscheinen (*Person*), b) zum Vorschein kommen, sich (ein)finden (*Sache*); **12.** geschehen, eintreten, passieren.

turn·a·ble [ˈtɜːnəbl] *adj.* drehbar.

ˈ**turn|·a·bout** *s.* **1.** *a. fig.* Kehrtwendung *f*; **2.** ⚓ Gegenkurs *m*; **3.** *fig.* ˈUmschwung *m*; **4.** *Am.* Karusˈsell *n*; ˈ**~·a·round** *s.* **1.** → ***turnabout*** 1, 3; **2.** *mot. etc.* Wendeplatz *m*; **3.** ⚙ (Geneˈral)Überˌholung *f*; ˈ**~·coat** *s.* Abtrünnige(r *m*) *f*, Reneˈgat *m*; ˈ**~·down I** *adj.* **1.** ˈumlegbar, Umleg…; **II** *s.* **2.** *a.* **~ *collar*** Umleg(e)kragen *m*; **3.** *fig.* Ablehnung *f*.

turned [tɜːnd] *adj.* **1.** ⚙ gedreht, gedrechselt; **2.** (ˈum)gebogen: **~*-back*** zurückgebogen; **~*-down*** a) abwärts gebogen, b) Umlege…; **~*-in*** einwärts gebogen; **3.** *typ.* auf dem Kopf stehend;

ˈ**turn·er** [-nə] *s.* **1.** ⚙ a) Dreher *m*, b) Drechsler *m*; **2.** *sport Am.* Turner(in);

ˈ**turn·er·y** [-nərɪ] *s.* ⚙ **1.** *coll.* a) Dreharbeit(en *pl.*) *f*, b) Drechslerarbeit(en *pl.*) *f*; **2.** a) Dreheˈrei *f*, b) Drechsleˈrei *f* (*Werkstatt*).

turn·ing [ˈtɜːnɪŋ] *s.* **1.** ⚙ Drehen *n*, Drechseln *n*; **2.** a) (Straßen-, Fluß)Biegung *f*, b) (Straßen)Ecke *f*, c) Querstraße *f*, Abzweigung *f*; **3.** *pl.* ⚙ Drehspäne *pl.*; **~ cir·cle** *s. mot.* Wendekreis *m*; **~ lathe** *s.* ⚙ Drehbank *f*; **~ ma·chine** *s.* ⚙ ˈDrehmaˌschine *f*; **~ point** *s.* **1.** ✈, *sport* Wendemarke *f*; **2.** *fig.* Wendepunkt *m*.

tur·nip [ˈtɜːnɪp] *s.* **1.** ⚘ (*bsd.* Weiße) Rübe; **2.** *sl.* ˏZwiebelˈ *f* (*Uhr*).

ˈ**turn|·key** *s.* Gefangenenwärter *m*, Schließer *m*; ˈ**~-off** *s.* **1.** Abzweigung *f*; **2.** Ausfahrt *f* (*Autobahn*); ˈ**~·out** *s.* **1.** † *Brit.* a) Streik *m*, Ausstand *m*, b) Streikende(r *m*) *f*; **2.** a) Besucher(zahl *f*) *pl.*, Zuschauer *pl.*, b) (Wahl- *etc.*) Beteiligung *f*; **3.** (Pferde)Gespann *n*, Kutsche *f*; **4.** Ausstattung *f*, *bsd.* Kleidung *f*; **5.** † Geˈsamtproduktiˌon *f*, Ausstoß *m*; **6.** a) Ausweichstelle *f* (*Autostraße*), b) → ***turn-off***; ˈ**~ˌo·ver** *s.* **1.** ˈUmstürzen *n*; **2.** † ˈUmsatz *m*: **~ *tax*** Umsatzsteuer *f*; **3.** Zu- u. Abgang *m* (*von Patienten in Krankenhäusern etc.*): ***labo***(***u***)***r ~*** Arbeitskräftebewegung *f*; **4.** † ˈUmgruppierung *f*, -schichtung *f*; **5.** *Brit.* (ˈZeitungs)Arˌtikel, der auf die nächste Seite übergreift; **6.** (Apfel- *etc.*) Tasche *f* (*Gebäck*); ˈ**~·pike** *s.* **1.** Schlagbaum *m* (*Mautstraße*); **2.** *a.* **~ *road*** gebührenpflichtige (*Am.* Schnell)Straße *f*, Mautstraße *f*; ˈ**~-round** *s.* **1.** †, ⚓ ˈUmschlag *m* (*Schiffsabfertigung*); **2.** Wendestelle *f*; **3.** → ***turnabout*** 3; ˈ**~·screw** *s.* ⚙ Schraubenzieher *m*; ˈ**~·spit** *s.* Drehspieß *m*; ˈ**~·stile** *s.* Drehkreuz *n an Durchgängen etc.*; ˈ**~ˌta·ble** *s.* **1.** 🚂 Drehscheibe *f*; **2.** Plattenteller *m* (*Plattenspieler*); ˈ**~·up I** *adj.* **1.** hochklappbar; **II** *s.* **2.** (ˈHosen- *etc.*)ˌUmschlag *m*; **3.** F Überˈraschung *f*, ˏDingˈ *n*.

tur·pen·tine [ˈtɜːpəntaɪn] *s.* ⚗ **1.** Terpenˈtin *n*; **2.** *a.* ***oil*** (*od.* ***spirits***) ***of ~*** Terpenˈtingeist *m*, -öl *n*.

tur·pi·tude [ˈtɜːpɪtjuːd] *s.* **1.** *a.* ***moral ~*** Verworfenheit *f*; **2.** Schandtat *f*.

turps [tɜːps] F → ***turpentine*** 2.

tur·quoise [ˈtɜːkwɔɪz] *s.* **1.** *min.* Türˈkis *m*; **2.** *a.* **~ *blue*** Türˈkisblau *n*: **~ *green*** Türkisgrün *n*.

tur·ret [ˈtʌrɪt] *s.* **1.** △ Türmchen *n*; **2.** ⚔, ⚓ Geschütz-, Panzer-, Gefechtsturm *m*: **~ *gun*** Turmgeschütz *n*; **3.** ✈ Kanzel *f*; **4.** ⚙ Reˈvolverkopf *m*: **~ *lathe*** Revolverdrehbank *f*; ˈ**tur·ret·ed** [-tɪd] *adj.* **1.** mit Türmchen; **2.** *zo.* spi-

ˈral-, türmchenförmig.

tur·tle¹ [ˈtɜːtl] *s. zo.* (See)Schildkröte *f*: ***turn ~*** a) ⚓ kentern, umschlagen, b) sich überschlagen, c) *Am.* F hilflos *od.* feige sein.

tur·tle² [ˈtɜːtl] *s. obs. für **turtledove**.*

ˈtur·tle|·dove *s. orn.* Turteltaube *f*; **ˈ~·neck** *s.* ˈRollkragen(pullˌover) *m.*

Tus·can [ˈtʌskən] **I** *adj.* tosˈkanisch; **II** *s.* Tosˈkaner(in).

tusk [tʌsk] *s. zo.* a) Fangzahn *m*, b) Stoßzahn *m des Elefanten etc.*, c) Hauer *m des Wildschweins*; **tusked** [-kt] *adj. zo.* mit Fangzähnen *etc.* (bewaffnet); **ˈtusk·er** [-kə] *s. zo.* Eleˈfant *m od.* Keiler *m* (*mit ausgebildeten Stoßzähnen*); **ˈtusk·y** [-kɪ] → ***tusked***.

tus·sle [ˈtʌsl] **I** *s.* **1.** Balgeˈrei *f*, Raufeˈrei *f* (*a. fig.*); **2.** *fig.* scharfe Kontroˈverse; **II** *v/i.* **3.** kämpfen, raufen, sich balgen (***for*** um *acc.*).

tus·sock [ˈtʌsək] *s.* (*bsd.* Gras)Büschel *n.*

tut(-tut) [tʌt] *int.* **1.** ach was!; **2.** pfui!; **3.** Unsinn!, Na, ˈna!

tu·te·lage [ˈtjuːtɪlɪdʒ] *s.* **1.** ⚖ Vormundschaft *f*; **2.** Unmündigkeit *f*; **3.** *fig.* a) Bevormundung *f*, b) Schutz *m*, c) (An-)Leitung *f*; **ˈtu·te·lar** [-lə], **ˈtu·te·lar·y** [-lərɪ] *adj.* **1.** schützend, Schutz…; **2.** ⚖ Vormunds…, Vormundschafts…

tu·tor [ˈtjuːtə] **I** *s.* **1.** Priˈvat-, Hauslehrer *m*; **2.** *ped.*, *univ. Brit.* Tutor *m*, Studienleiter *m*; **3.** *ped.*, *univ. Am.* Assiˈstent *m mit Lehrauftrag*; **4.** (Ein)Pauker *m*, Repeˈtitor *m*; **5.** ⚖ Vormund *m*; **II** *v/t.* **6.** *ped.* unterˈrichten, *j-m* Priˈvatˌunterricht geben; **7.** *j-n* schulen, erziehen; **8.** *fig. j-n* bevormunden; **ˈtu·tor·ess** *s.* **1.** *ped.* Priˈvatlehrerin *f*; **2.** *univ. Brit.* Tuˈtorin *f*; **tu·to·ri·al** [tjuːˈtɔːrɪəl] *ped.* **I** *adj.* Tutor…; **II** *s.* Tuˈtorenkurs (-us) *m*; **ˈtu·tor·ship** [-ʃɪp] *s.* **1.** Priˈvatlehrerstelle; **2.** *univ. Brit.* Amt *n* e-s Tutors.

tu·tu [ˈtuːtuː] *s.* (Balˈlett)Röckchen *n.*

tux·e·do [tʌkˈsiːdəʊ] *pl.* **-dos** *s. Am.* Smoking *m.*

TV [ˌtiːˈviː] F **I** *adj.* Fernseh…; **II** *s.* a) ˈFernsehappaˌrat *m*, b) (***on ~*** im) Fernsehen *n.*

twad·dle [ˈtwɒdl] **I** *v/i.* **1.** quasseln; **II** *s.* **2.** Gequassel *n*; **3.** Quatsch *m.*

twain [tweɪn] **I** *adj. obs.* zwei: ***in ~*** entzwei; **II** *s. die* Zwei *pl.*

twang [twæŋ] **I** *v/i.* **1.** schwirren, (scharf) klingen; **2.** näseln; **II** *v/t.* **3.** *Saiten etc.* schwirren (lassen), zupfen; klimpern *od.* kratzen auf (*dat.*); **4.** *et.* näseln, durch die Nase sprechen; **III** *s.* **5.** scharfer Ton *od.* Klang, Schwirren *n*; **6.** Näseln *n.*

tweak [twiːk] **I** *v/t.* zwicken, kneifen; **II** *s.* Zwicken *n.*

tweed [twiːd] *s.* **1.** Tweed *m* (*Wollgewebe*); **2.** *pl.* Tweedsachen *pl.*

Twee·dle·dum and Twee·dle·dee [ˌtwiːdlˈdʌmənˌtwiːdlˈdiː] *s.*: ***be*** (***alike***) ***as ~*** a) sich gleichen wie ein Ei dem andern, b) ‚Jacke wie Hose' sein.

'tween [twiːn] **I** *adv. u. prp.* → ***between***; **II** *in Zssgn* Zwischen…; **~ deck** *s.* ⚓ Zwischendeck *n.*

tween·y [ˈtwiːnɪ] *s. obs.* Hausmagd *f.*

tweet·er [ˈtwiːtə] *s. Radio*: Hochtonlautsprecher *m.*

tweez·ers [ˈtwiːzəz] *s. pl. a. **pair of ~*** Pinˈzette *f.*

twelfth [twelfθ] **I** *adj.* □ **1.** zwölft: ***ℒ Night*** Dreikönigsabend *m*; **II** *s.* **2.** *der* (*die*, *das*) Zwölfte; **3.** Zwölftel *n*; **ˈtwelfth·ly** [-lɪ] *adv.* zwölftens.

twelve [twelv] **I** *adj.* zwölf; **II** *s.* Zwölf *f*; **ˈtwelve·mo** [-məʊ] *s. typ.* Duoˈdez(forˌmat, -band *m*) *n.*

ˈtwelve-tone *adj.* ♪ Zwölfton…

twen·ti·eth [ˈtwentɪɪθ] **I** *adj.* **1.** zwanzigst; **II** *s.* **2.** *der* (*die*, *das*) Zwanzigste; **3.** Zwanzigstel *n.*

twen·ty [ˈtwentɪ] **I** *adj.* **1.** zwanzig; **II** *s.* **2.** Zwanzig *f*; **3.** ***in the twenties*** in den zwanziger Jahren (*e-s Jahrhunderts*); ***he is in his twenties*** er ist in den Zwanzigern.

twerp [twɜːp] *s. sl.* **1.** ‚(blöder) Heini'; **2.** ‚Niete' *f*, ‚Flasche' *f.*

twice [twaɪs] *adv.* zweimal: ***think ~ about s.th.*** *fig.* sich e-e Sache gründlich überlegen; ***he didn't think ~ about it*** er zögerte nicht lange; ***~ as much*** doppelt soviel, das Doppelte; ***~ the sum*** die doppelte Summe; **ˌ~-ˈtold** *adj. fig.* alt, abgedroschen: ***~ tales***.

twid·dle [ˈtwɪdl] *v/t.* (herˈum)spielen mit: ***~ one's thumbs*** *fig.* Däumchen drehen, die Hände in den Schoß legen.

twig¹ [twɪg] *s.* **1.** (dünner) Zweig, Rute *f*: ***hop the ~*** F ‚abkratzen' (*sterben*); **2.** Wünschelrute *f.*

twig² [twɪg] *Brit. sl.* **I** *v/t.* **1.** ‚kapieren' (*verstehen*); **2.** ‚spitzkriegen'; **II** *v/i.* **3.** ‚kapieren'.

twi·light [ˈtwaɪlaɪt] **I** *s.* **1.** (*mst* Abend-)Dämmerung *f*: ***~ of the gods*** *myth.* Götterdämmerung; **2.** Zwielicht *n* (*a. fig.*), Halbdunkel *n*; **3.** *fig. a.* ***~ state*** Dämmerzustand *m*; **II** *adj.* **4.** Zwielicht…, dämmerig, schattenhaft (*a. fig.*): ***~ sleep*** ⚕ *u. fig.* Dämmerschlaf *m.*

twill [twɪl] **I** *s.* Köper(stoff) *m*; **II** *v/t.* köpern.

twin [twɪn] **I** *s.* **1.** Zwilling *m*: ***the ℒs*** *ast.* die Zwillinge; **II** *adj.* **2.** Zwillings…, Doppel…, doppelt: ***~-bedded room*** Zweibettzimmer *n*; ***~ brother*** Zwillingsbruder *m*; ***~ engine*** ✈ Zwillingstriebwerk *n*; ***~-engined*** zweimotorig; ***~ town*** Partnerstadt *f*; ***~ track*** Doppelspur *f* (*Tonband*); **3.** ⚘ gepaart.

twine [twaɪn] **I** *s.* **1.** Bindfaden *m*, Schnur *f*; **2.** ⚙ Garn *n*, Zwirn *m*; **3.** Wick(e)lung *f*; **4.** Windung *f*; **5.** Geflecht *n*; **6.** ⚘ Ranke *f*; **II** *v/t.* **7.** *Fäden etc.* zs.-drehen, zwirnen; **8.** *Kranz* winden; **9.** *fig.* ineinˈanderschlingen, verflechten; **10.** schlingen, winden (***about***, ***around*** um); **11.** umˈschlingen, -ˈwinden, -ˈranken (***with*** mit); **III** *v/i.* **12.** sich verflechten (***with*** mit); **13.** sich winden *od.* schlingen; sich schlängeln; **ˈtwin·er** [-nə] *s.* **1.** ⚘ Kletter-, Schlingpflanze *f*; **2.** ⚙ ˈZwirnmaˌschine *f.*

twinge [twɪndʒ] **I** *s.* **1.** stechender Schmerz, Zwicken *n*, Stechen *n*, Stich *m* (*a. fig.*): ***~ of conscience*** Gewissensbisse *pl.*; **II** *v/t. u. v/i.* **2.** stechen; **3.** zwicken, kneifen.

twin·kle [ˈtwɪŋkl] **I** *v/i.* **1.** (auf)blitzen, glitzern, funkeln (*Sterne etc.*; *a. Augen*); **2.** huschen; **3.** (verschmitzt) zwinkern, blinzeln; **II** *s.* **4.** Blinken *n*, Blitzen *n*, Glitzern *n*; **5.** (Augen)Zwinkern *n*, Blinzeln *n*: ***a humorous ~***; **6.** → ***twinkling*** 2; **ˈtwin·kling** [-lɪŋ] *s.* **1.** → ***twinkle*** 4, 5; **2.** *fig.* Augenblick *m*: ***in the ~ of an eye*** im Nu, im Handumdrehen.

twirl [twɜːl] **I** *v/t.* **1.** (herˈum)wirbeln, quirlen; *Daumen*, *Locke etc.* drehen; *Bart* zwirbeln; → *a.* ***twiddle***; **II** *v/i.* **2.** (sich herˈum)wirbeln; **III** *s.* **3.** schnelle (Um)ˈDrehung, Wirbel *m*; **4.** Schnörkel *m.*

twist [twɪst] **I** *v/t.* **1.** drehen: ***~ off*** losdrehen, *Deckel* abschrauben; **2.** zs.-drehen, zwirnen; **3.** verflechten, -schlingen; **4.** *Kranz etc.* winden, *Schnur etc.* wickeln: ***~ s.o. round one's*** (***little***) ***finger*** j-n um den (kleinen) Finger wickeln; **5.** umˈwinden; **6.** wringen; **7.** (ver)biegen, (-)krümmen; *Fuß* vertreten; *Gesicht* verzerren: ***~ s.o.'s arm*** a) j-m den Arm verdrehen, b) *fig.* j-n unter Druck setzen; ***~ed mind*** *fig.* verbogener *od.* krankhafter Geist; ***~ed with pain*** schmerzverzerrt (*Züge*); **8.** *fig. Sinn*, *Bericht* verdrehen, entstellen; **9.** *dem Ball* Efˈfet geben; **II** *v/i.* **10.** sich drehen: ***~ round*** sich umdrehen; **11.** sich krümmen; **12.** sich winden (*a. fig.*); **13.** sich winden *od.* schlängeln (*Fluß etc.*); **14.** sich verziehen *od.* verzerren (*a. Gesicht*); **15.** sich verschlingen; **III** *s.* **16.** Drehung *f*, Windung *f*, Biegung *f*, Krümmung *f*; **17.** Drehung *f*, Rotatiˈon *f*; **18.** Geflecht *n*; **19.** Zwirnung *f*; **20.** Verflechtung *f*, Knäuel *m*, *n*; **21.** (Gesichts-)Verzerrung *f*; **22.** *fig.* Verdrehung *f*; **23.** *fig.* Veranlagung *od.* Neigung (***towards*** zu); **24.** *fig.* Trick *m*, ‚Dreh' *m*; **25.** *fig.* überˈraschende Wendung, ‚ˈKnallefˌfekt' *m*; **26.** ⚙ a) Drall *m* (*Schußwaffe*, *Seil etc.*), b) Torsiˈon *f*; **27.** Spiˈrale *f*: ***~ drill*** ⚙ Spiralbohrer *m*; **28.** ♪ Twist *m* (*Tanz*); **29.** a) (Seiden-, Baumwoll)Twist *m*, b) Zwirn *m*; **30.** Seil *n*, Schnur *f*; **31.** Rollentabak *m*; **32.** *Bäckerei*: Kringel *m*, Zopf *m*; **33.** *Wasserspringen*: Schraube *f*; **ˈtwist·er** [-tə] *s.* **1.** a) Dreher(in), Zwirner(in), b) Seiler(in); **2.** ⚙ ˈZwirn-, ˈDrehmaˌschine *f*; **3.** *sport* Efˈfetball *m*; **4.** F harte Nuß, knifflige Sache; **5.** F Gauner *m*; **6.** *Am.* Torˈnado *m*, Wirbel(wind) *m*; **ˈtwist·y** [-tɪ] *adj.* **1.** gewunden, kurvenreich; **2.** *fig.* falsch, verschlagen.

twit¹ [twɪt] *v/t.* **1.** *j-n* aufziehen (***with*** mit); **2.** *j-m* Vorwürfe machen (***with*** wegen).

twit² [twɪt] *s. Brit.* F Trottel *m.*

twitch [twɪtʃ] **I** *v/t.* **1.** zupfen, zerren, reißen; **2.** zucken mit; **II** *v/i.* **3.** zucken (***with*** vor); **III** *s.* **4.** Zucken *n*, Zuckung *f*; **5.** Ruck *m*; **6.** Stich *m* (*Schmerz*); **7.** Nasenbremse *f* (*Pferd*).

twit·ter [ˈtwɪtə] **I** *v/i.* **1.** zwitschern (*Vogel*), zirpen (*a. Insekt*); **2.** *fig.* a) (aufgeregt) schnattern, b) piepsen, c) kichern; **3.** F (vor Aufregung) zittern; **II** *v/t.* **4.** *et.* zwitschern; **III** *s.* **5.** Gezwitscher *n*; **6.** *fig.* Geschnatter *n* (*Person*); **7.** Kichern *n*; **8.** Nervosiˈtät *f*: ***in a ~*** aufgeregt.

two [tuː] **I** *s.* **1.** Zwei *f* (*Zahl*, *Spielkarte*, *Uhrzeit etc.*); **2.** Paar *n*: ***the ~*** die beiden, beide; ***the ~ of us*** wir beide; ***put ~ and ~ together*** *fig.* es sich zs.-reimen, s-e Schlüsse ziehen; ***in*** (*od.* ***by***) ***~s*** zu zweien, paarweise; ~ ***and*** ~ paarweise, zwei u. zwei; ~ ***can play at that game!*** das kann ich (*od.* ein anderer) auch! **II** *adj.* **3.** zwei: ***one or*** ~ einige; ***in a day or*** ~ in ein paar Tagen; ***in*** ~ entzwei; ***cut in*** ~ entzweischneiden; **4.** beide: ***the*** ~ ***cars***; **'~-bit** *adj. Am.* F **1.** 25-Cent-...; **2.** billig (*a. fig. contp.*); klein, unbedeutend; **'~ˌcy·cle** *adj.* ⚙ Zweitakt...: ~ ***engine***; **ˌ~-'edged** *adj.* zweischneidig (*a. fig.*); **ˌ~-'faced** *adj. fig.* falsch, heuchlerisch; **ˌ~-'fist·ed** *adj. Am.* F *fig.* ‚knallhart'; handfest; **'~·fold** *adj. u. adv.* zweifach, doppelt; **ˌ~-'four** *adj.* ♪ Zweiviertel...; **ˌ~-'hand·ed** *adj.* **1.** zweihändig; **2.** für zwei Per'sonen (*Spiel etc.*); **'~-horse** *adj.* zweispännig; **'~-job man** *s.* [*irr.*] Doppelverdiener *m*; **'~-lane** *adj.* zweispurig (*Straße*); **~·pence** ['tʌpəns] *s. Brit.* zwei Pence *pl.*: ***not to care*** ~ ***for*** *fig.* sich nicht scheren um; ***he didn't care*** ~ es war ihm völlig egal; **~·pen·ny** ['tʌpnɪ] *adj.* **1.** zwei Pence wert *od.* betragend, Zweipenny...; **2.** *fig.* armselig, billig; **~·pen·ny-half·pen·ny** [ˌtʌpnɪ'heɪpnɪ] *adj.* **1.** Zweieinhalbpenny...; **2.** *fig.* mise'rabel, schäbig; **'~-phase** *adj.* ⚡ zweiphasig, Zweiphasen...; **'~-piece I** *adj.* zweiteilig; **II** *s.* a) *a.* ~ ***dress*** Jakkenkleid *n*, b) *a.* ~ ***swimming suit*** Zweiteiler *m*; **'~-ply** *adj.* doppelt (*Stoff etc.*); zweischäftig (*Tau*); zweisträhnig (*Wolle etc.*); **ˌ~'seat·er** *s.* ✈, *mot.* Zweisitzer *m*; **'~·some** [-səm] *s.* **1.** *Golf*: Zweier(spiel *n*) *m*; **2.** *bsd. humor.* ‚Duo' *n*, ‚Pärchen' *n*; **'~-speed** *adj.* ⚙ Zweigang...; **'~-stage** *adj.* ⚙ zweistufig; **'~-step** *s.* Twostep *m* (*Tanz*); **'~-stroke** *adj. mot.* Zweitakt...; **'~-time** *v/t.* F **1.** *bsd. Ehepartner* betrügen; **2.** *j-n* ‚reinlegen'; **'~-way** *adj.* Zweiweg(e)..., Doppel...: ~ ***adapter*** (*od.* ***plug***) ⚡ Doppelstecker *m*; ~ ***cock*** Zweiwegehahn *m*; ~ ***communication*** ⚡ Doppelverkehr *m*, Gegensprechen *n*; ~ ***traffic*** Gegenverkehr *m*.

ty·coon [taɪ'kuːn] *s.* F **1.** Indu'striemaˌgnat *m*, -kapiˌtän *m*: ***oil*** ~ Ölmagnat; **2.** *pol.* ‚Oberbonze' *m*.

ty·ing ['taɪɪŋ] *pres. p. von* ***tie***.

tyke [taɪk] *s.* **1.** Köter *m*; **2.** Lümmel *m*, Kerl *m*; **3.** *Am.* F Kindchen *n*.

tym·pan ['tɪmpən] *s.* **1.** *typ.* Preßdeckel *m*; **2.** → ***tympanum*** 2; **tym·pan·ic** [tɪm'pænɪk] *adj. anat.* Mittelohr..., Trommelfell...: ~ ***membrane*** Trommelfell *n*; **tym·pa·ni·tis** [ˌtɪmpə'naɪtɪs] *s.* ⚕ Mittelohrentzündung *f*; **'tym·pa·num** [-nəm] *pl.* **-na** [-nə], **-nums** *s.* **1.** *anat.* a) Mittelohr *n*, b) Trommelfell *n*; **2.** △ Tympanon *n*: a) Giebelfeld *n*, b) Türbogenfeld *n*.

type [taɪp] **I** *s.* **1.** Typ(us) *m*: a) Urform *f*, b) typischer Vertreter, c) charakte'ristische Klasse; **2.** Ur-, Vorbild *n*, Muster *n*; **3.** ⚙ Typ *m*, Mo'dell *n*, Ausführung *f*, Baumuster *n*: ~ ***plate*** Typenschild *n*; **4.** Art *f*, Schlag *m*, Sorte *f* (*alle a.* F); ***out of*** ~ atypisch; ***he acted out of*** ~ das war sonst nicht s-e Art; → ***true*** 4; **5.** *typ.* a) Letter *f*, (Druck)Type *f*, b) *coll.* Lettern *pl.*, Schrift *f*, Druck *m*: ***in*** ~ (ab)gesetzt; ***set*** (***up***) ***in*** ~ setzen; **6.** *fig.* Sinnbild *n*, Sym'bol *n* (***of*** *gen. od.* für); **II** *v/t.* **7.** mit der Ma'schine (ab-)schreiben, (ab)tippen: ~***d*** maschinegeschrieben; ***typing pool*** Schreibsaal *m*, -büro *n*; **8.** ~ ***into*** in *e-n Computer* eingeben, -tippen; **III** *v/i.* **9.** ma'schineschreiben, tippen; ~ **a·re·a** *s. typ.* Satzspiegel *m*; **'~·cast** *v/t.* [*irr.* → ***cast***] *thea. etc.* a) *e-m Schauspieler* e-e s-m Typ entsprechende Rolle geben, b) *e-n Schauspieler* auf ein bestimmtes Rollenfach festlegen; **'~·face** *s. typ.* **1.** Schriftbild *n*; **2.** Schriftart *f*; ~ **found·er** *s. typ.* Schriftgießer *m*; ~ **found·ry** *s. typ.* Schriftgieße'rei *f*; ~ **met·al** *s. typ.* 'Letternmeˌtall *n*; ~ **page** *s. typ.* Satzspiegel *m*; **'~·script** *s.* Ma'schinenschrift(satz *m*) *f*, ma'schinengeschriebener Text; **'~ˌset·ter** *s. typ.* (Schrift)Setzer *m*; ~ **spec·i·men** *s.* **1.** ⚙ 'Musterexemˌplar *n*; **2.** *biol.* Typus *m*, Origi'nal *n*; **'~·write** *v/t. u. v/i.* [*irr.* → ***write***] → ***type*** 7, 9; **'~ˌwrit·er** *s.* **1.** 'Schreibmaˌschine *f*: ~ ***ribbon*** Farbband *n*; **2.** *a.* ~ ***face*** *typ.* 'Schreibmaˌschinenschrift *f*; **'~ˌwrit·ing** *s.* **1.** Ma'schineschreiben *n*; **2.** Ma'schinenschrift *f*; **'~ˌwrit·ten** *adj.* ma'schinegeschrieben, in Ma'schinenschrift.

ty·phoid ['taɪfɔɪd] ⚕ **I** *adj.* ty'phös, Typhus...: ~ ***fever*** → **II** *s.* ('Unterleibs-)Typhus *m*.

ty·phoon [taɪ'fuːn] *s.* Tai'fun *m*.

ty·phus ['taɪfəs] *s.* ⚕ Flecktyphus *m*, -fieber *n*.

typ·i·cal ['tɪpɪkl] *adj.* □ **1.** typisch: a) repräsenta'tiv, b) charakte'ristisch, bezeichnend, kennzeichnend (***of*** für): ***be*** ~ ***of*** *et.* kennzeichnen *od.* charakterisieren; **3.** sym'bolisch, sinnbildlich (***of*** für); **4.** a) vorbildlich, echt, b) hinweisend (***of*** auf *et. Künftiges*); **'typ·i·cal·ness** [-nɪs] *s.* **1.** *das* Typische; **2.** Sinnbildlichkeit *f*; **'typ·i·fy** [-ɪfaɪ] *v/t.* **1.** typisch *od.* ein typisches Beispiel sein für, verkörpern; **2.** versinnbildlichen.

typ·ist ['taɪpɪst] *s.* **1.** Ma'schinenschreiber(in); **2.** Schreibkraft *f*.

ty·pog·ra·pher [taɪ'pɒgrəfə] *s.* **1.** (Buch)Drucker *m*; **2.** (Schrift)Setzer *m*; **ty·po·graph·ic, ty·po·graph·i·cal** [ˌtaɪpə'græfɪk(l)] *adj.* □ **1.** Druck..., drucktechnisch: ~ ***error*** Druckfehler *m*; **2.** typo'graphisch, Buchdruck(er)...; **ty'pog·ra·phy** [-fɪ] *s.* **1.** Buchdruckerkunst *f*, Typogra'phie *f*; **2.** (Buch-)Druck *m*; **3.** Druckbild *n*.

ty·po·log·i·cal [ˌtaɪpə'lɒdʒɪkl] *adj.* typo'logisch; **ty·pol·o·gy** [taɪ'pɒlədʒɪ] *s.* Typolo'gie *f*.

ty·ran·nic, ty·ran·ni·cal [tɪ'rænɪk(l)] *adj.* □ ty'rannisch; **ty'ran·ni·cide** [-ɪsaɪd] *s.* **1.** Ty'rannenmord *m*; **2.** Ty'rannenmörder *m*; **tyr·an·nize** ['tɪrənaɪz] **I** *v/i.* ty'rannisch sein *od.* herrschen: ~ ***over*** → **II** *v/t.* tyrannisieren; **tyr·an·nous** ['tɪrənəs] *adj.* □ *rhet.* ty'rannisch; **tyr·an·ny** ['tɪrənɪ] *s.* **1.** Tyran'nei *f*: a) Despo'tismus, b) Gewalt-, Willkürherrschaft *f*; **2.** Tyran'nei *f* (*tyrannische Handlung etc.*); **3.** *antiq.* Ty'rannis *f*; **ty·rant** ['taɪərənt] *s.* Ty'rann(in).

tyre *etc. bsd. Brit.* → ***tire***[2] *etc.*

ty·ro ['taɪərəʊ] *pl.* **-ros** *s.* Anfänger(in), Neuling *m*.

Tyr·o·lese [ˌtɪrə'liːz] **I** *pl.* **-lese** *s.* Ti'roler(in); **II** *adj.* ti'rol(er)isch, Tiroler(...).

tzar *etc.* → ***czar*** *etc.*

U

U, u [juː] **I** *s.* **1.** U *n*, u *n* (*Buchstabe*); **2.** U *n*: ***U-bolt*** ⚙ U-Bolzen *m*; **II** *adj.* **3.** ***U*** *Brit.* F vornehm; **4.** *Brit.* jugendfrei: **~ *film.***

u·biq·ui·tous [juːˈbɪkwɪtəs] *adj.* ☐ allˈgegenwärtig, (gleichzeitig) ˈüberall zu finden(d); **uˈbiq·ui·ty** [-kwətɪ] *s.* Allˈgegenwart *f.*

ˈU-boat *s.* ⚓ U-Boot *n*, (deutsches) ˈUnterseeboot.

u·dal [ˈjuːdl] *s.* ⚖ *hist.* Alˈlod(ium) *n*, Freigut *n.*

ud·der [ˈʌdə] *s.* Euter *n.*

u·dom·e·ter [juːˈdɒmɪtə] *s. meteor.* Regenmesser *m*, Udoˈmeter *n.*

ugh [ʌx; ʊh; ɜːh] *int.* hu!, pfui!

ug·li·fy [ˈʌglɪfaɪ] *v/t.* häßlich machen, entstellen; **ˈug·li·ness** [-nɪs] *s.* Häßlichkeit *f*; **ug·ly** [ˈʌglɪ] **I** *adj.* ☐ **1.** häßlich, garstig (*beide a. fig.*); **2.** *fig.* gemein, schmutzig; **3.** unangenehm, ˈwiderwärtig, übel: ***an ~ customer*** ein unangenehmer Kerl, ‚ein übler Kunde'; **4.** bös, schlimm, gefährlich (*Situation*, *Wunde etc.*); **II** *s.* **5.** F häßlicher Mensch; ‚Ekel' *n.*

u·kase [juːˈkeɪz] *s. hist. u. fig.* Ukas *m*, Erlaß *m*, Befehl *m.*

U·krain·i·an [juːˈkreɪnjən] **I** *adj.* **1.** ukraˈinisch; **II** *s.* **2.** Ukraˈiner(in); **3.** *ling.* Ukraˈinisch *n.*

u·ku·le·le [ˌjuːkəˈleɪlɪ] *s.* ♪ Ukuˈlele *f*, *n.*

ul·cer [ˈʌlsə] *s.* **1.** ⚕ (*Magen- etc.*)Geschwür *n*; **2.** *fig.* a) (Eiter)Beule *f*, b) Schandfleck *m*; **ˈul·cer·ate** [-əreɪt] ⚕ **I** *v/t.* schwären lassen: **~*d*** eitrig, vereitert; **II** *v/i.* geschwürig werden, schwären; **ul·cer·a·tion** [ˌʌlsəˈreɪʃn] *s.* ⚕ Geschwür(bildung *f*) *n*; Schwären *n*, (Ver-)Eiterung *f*; **ul·cer·ous** [ˈʌlsərəs] *adj.* ☐ **1.** ⚕ geschwürig, eiternd; Geschwür(s)…, Eiter…; **2.** *fig.* korˈrupt, giftig.

ul·lage [ˈʌlɪdʒ] *s.* ☤ Schwund *m*: a) Lekˈkage *f*, Flüssigkeitsverlust *m*, b) Gewichtsverlust *m.*

ul·na [ˈʌlnə] *pl.* **-nae** [-niː] *s. anat.* Elle *f.*

ul·ster [ˈʌlstə] *s.* Ulster(mantel) *m.*

ul·te·ri·or [ʌlˈtɪərɪə] *adj.* ☐ **1.** (*räumlich*) jenseitig; **2.** später (folgend), weiter, anderweitig: **~ *action***; **3.** *fig.* tiefer(liegend), versteckt: **~ *motives*** tiefere Beweggründe, Hintergedanken.

ul·ti·mate [ˈʌltɪmət] **I** *adj.* ☐ **1.** äußerst, (aller)letzt; höchst; **2.** entferntest; **3.** endgültig, End…: **~ *consumer*** ☤ Endverbraucher *m*; **~ *result*** Endergebnis *n*; **4.** grundlegend, elemenˈtar, Grund…; **5.** ⚙, *phys.* Höchst…, Grenz…: **~ *strength*** Bruchfestigkeit *f*; **II** *s.* **6.** *das* Letzte, *das* Äußerste; **7.** *fig. der* Gipfel (***in*** an *dat.*); **ˈul·ti·mate·ly** [-lɪ] *adv.* schließlich, endlich, letzten Endes, im Grunde.

ul·ti·ma·tum [ˌʌltɪˈmeɪtəm] *pl.* **-tums**, **-ta** [-tə] *s. pol. u. fig.* Ultiˈmatum *n* (***to*** an *acc.*): ***deliver an ~ to*** *j-m* ein Ultimatum stellen.

ul·ti·mo [ˈʌltɪməʊ] (*Lat.*) *adv.* ☤ letzten *od.* vorigen Monats.

ul·tra [ˈʌltrə] **I** *adj.* **1.** exˈtrem, radiˈkal, Erz…, Ultra…; **2.** ˈübermäßig, überˈtrieben; ultra…, super…; **II** *s.* **3.** Extreˈmist *m*, Ultra *m*; **ˌ~ˈhigh fre·quen·cy** ↯ **I** *s.* Ultraˈhochfreˌquenz *f*, Ultraˈkurzwelle *f*; **II** *adj.* Ultrahochfrequenz…, Ultrakurzwellen…

ul·tra·ism [ˈʌltrəɪzəm] *s.* Extreˈmismus *m.*

ul·tra|·ma·rine [ˌʌltrəməˈriːn] **I** *adj.* **1.** ˈüberseeisch; **2.** ⛏, *paint.* ultramaˈrin: **~ *blue*** → **II** *s.* **3.** Ultramaˈrin(blau) *n*; **ˌ~ˈmod·ern** *adj.* ˈultra-, ˈhypermoˌdern; **ˌ~ˈmon·tane** [-ˈmɒnteɪn] **I** *adj.* **1.** jenseits der Berge (gelegen); **2.** südlich der Alpen (gelegen), italiˈenisch; **3.** *pol.*, *eccl.* ultramonˈtan, streng päpstlich; **II** *s.* **4.** → **ˌ~ˈmon·ta·nist** [-ˈmɒntənɪst] *s.* Ultramonˈtane(r *m*) *f*; **ˌ~ˈna·tion·al** *adj.* ˈultranatioˌnal; **ˌ~ˈshort wave** *s.* ↯ Ultraˈkurzwelle *f*; **ˌ~ˈson·ic** *phys.* **I** *adj.* Ultra-, Überschall…; **II** *s. pl. sg. konstr.* (Lehre *f* vom) Ultraschall *m*; **ˌ~ˈvi·o·let** *adj. phys.* ˈultravioˌlett.

ul·tra vi·res [ˌʌltrəˈvaɪəriːz] (*Lat.*) *adv. u. pred. adj.* ⚖ über j-s Macht *od.* Befugnisse (hinˈausgehend).

ul·u·late [ˈjuːljʊleɪt] *v/i.* heulen; **ul·u·la·tion** [ˌjuːljʊˈleɪʃn] *s.* Heulen *n*, (Weh-)Klagen *n.*

um·bel [ˈʌmbəl] *s.* ⚘ Dolde *f*; **ˈum·bel·late** [-leɪt] *adj.* doldenblütig, Dolden…; **um·bel·li·fer** [ʌmˈbelɪfə] *s.* Doldengewächs *n*; **um·bel·lif·er·ous** [ˌʌmbeˈlɪfərəs] *adj.* doldenblütig, -tragend.

um·ber [ˈʌmbə] *s.* **1.** *min.* Umber(erde *f*) *m*, Umbra *f*; **2.** *paint.* Erd-, Dunkelbraun *n.*

um·bil·i·cal [ˌʌmbɪˈlaɪkl] *adj. anat.* Nabel…: **~ (*cord*)** Nabelschnur *f*; **um·bil·i·cus** [ʌmˈbɪlɪkəs] *pl.* **-cus·es** *s.* **1.** *anat.* Nabel *m*; **2.** (nabelförmige) Delle; **3.** ⚘ (Samen)Nabel *m*; **4.** A Nabelpunkt *m.*

um·bra [ˈʌmbrə] *pl.* **-brae** [-briː], **-bras** *s. ast.* a) Kernschatten *m*, b) Umbra *f* (*dunkler Kern e-s Sonnenflecks*).

um·brage [ˈʌmbrɪdʒ] *s.* **1.** Anstoß *m*, Ärgernis *n*: ***give ~*** Anstoß erregen (***to*** bei); ***take ~ at*** Anstoß nehmen an (*dat.*); **2.** *poet.* Schatten *m von Bäumen*; **um·bra·geous** [ʌmˈbreɪdʒəs] *adj.* ☐ **1.** schattig, schattenspendend, -reich; **2.** *fig.* empfindlich, übelnehmerisch.

um·brel·la [ʌmˈbrelə] *s.* **1.** (*bsd.* Regen-)Schirm *m*: **~ *stand*** Schirmständer *m*; ***get*** (*od.* ***put***) ***under one ~*** *fig.* ‚unter ˈeinen Hut bringen'; **2.** ✈, ⚔ a) Jagdschutz *m*, Abschirmung *f*, b) *a.* **~ *barrage*** Feuervorhang *m*, -glocke *f*; **3.** *fig.* a) Schutz *m*, b) Rahmen *m*, c) Dach…: **~ *organization.***

um·laut [ˈʊmlaʊt] *ling.* **I** *s.* ˈUmlaut(zeichen *n*) *m*; **II** *v/t.* ˈumlauten.

um·pire [ˈʌmpaɪə] **I** *s.* **1.** *sport etc.* Schiedsrichter *m*, ˈUnparˌteiische(r *m*) *f*; **2.** ⚖ Obmann *m* e-s Schiedsgerichts; **II** *v/t.* **3.** als Schiedsrichter fungieren bei, *sport a. das Spiel* leiten.

ump·teen [ˌʌmpˈtiːn] *adj.* F ‚zig' (*viele*): **~ *times*** x-mal; **ˌumpˈteenth** [-nθ], **ˈump·ti·eth** [-tɪɪθ] *adj.* F ‚zigst', *der* (*die*, *das*) ˈsoundsoˈvielte: ***for the ~ time*** zum x-ten Mal.

'un [ən] *pron.* F *für* **one.**

un- [ʌn] *in Zssgn* **1.** Un…, un…, nicht…; **2.** ent…, los…, auf…, ver… (*bei Verben*).

ˌun·aˈbashed *adj.* **1.** unverfroren; **2.** unerschrocken.

un·a·bat·ed [ˌʌnəˈbeɪtɪd] *adj.* unvermindert; **ˌun·aˈbat·ing** [-tɪŋ] *adj.* unablässig, anhaltend.

ˌun·abˈbre·vi·at·ed *adj.* ungekürzt.

unˈa·ble *adj.* **1.** unfähig, außerˈstande (***to do*** zu tun): ***be ~ to work*** nicht arbeiten können, arbeitsunfähig sein; **~ *to pay*** zahlungsunfähig, insolvent; **2.** untauglich, ungeeignet (***for*** für).

ˌun·aˈbridged *adj.* ungekürzt.

ˌun·acˈcent·ed *adj.* unbetont.

ˌun·acˈcept·a·ble *adj.* **1.** unannehmbar (***to*** für); **2.** untragbar, unerwünscht (***to*** für).

ˌun·acˈcom·mo·dat·ing *adj.* **1.** ungefällig, **2.** unnachgiebig.

ˌun·acˈcom·pa·nied *adj.* unbegleitet, ohne Begleitung (*a.* ♪).

ˌun·acˈcom·plished *adj.* **1.** ˈunvollˌendet, unfertig; **2.** *fig.* ungebildet.

ˌun·acˈcount·a·ble *adj.* ☐ **1.** nicht verantwortlich; **2.** unerklärlich, seltsam; **ˌun·acˈcount·a·bly** *adv.* unerklärlicherweise.

ˌun·acˈcount·ed-for *adj.* **1.** unerklärt (geblieben); **2.** nicht belegt.

ˌun·acˈcus·tomed *adj.* **1.** ungewohnt; **2.** nicht gewöhnt (***to*** an *acc.*).

un·a·chiev·a·ble [ˌʌnəˈtʃiːvəbl] *adj.* **1.** unausführbar; **2.** unerreichbar; **ˌun·aˈchieved** [-vd] *adj.* unerreicht, ˈunvollˌendet.

ˌun·acˈknowl·edged *adj.* **1.** nicht anerkannt; **2.** uneingestanden; **3.** unbestätigt (*Brief etc.*).

ˌun·acˈquaint·ed *adj.* (***with***) unerfahren (in *dat.*), nicht vertraut (mit), unkundig (*gen.*): ***be ~ with*** *et.* nicht kennen.

ˌunˈact·a·ble *adj. thea.* nicht bühnengerecht, unaufführbar.

ˌun·aˈdapt·a·ble *adj.* **1.** nicht anpassungsfähig (***to*** an *acc.*); **2.** nicht anwendbar (***to*** auf *acc.*); **3.** ungeeignet (***for, to*** für, zu); **ˌun·aˈdapt·ed** *adj.* **1.** nicht angepaßt (***to*** *dat. od.* an *acc.*); **2.** ungeeignet, nicht eingerichtet (***to*** für).

ˌun·adˈdressed *adj.* ohne Anschrift.

ˌun·aˈdorned *adj.* schmucklos.

ˌun·aˈdul·ter·at·ed *adj.* rein, unverfälscht, echt.

ˌun·adˈven·tur·ous *adj.* **1.** ohne Unterˈnehmungsgeist; **2.** ereignislos (*Reise*).

ˈun·adˌvis·aˈbil·i·ty *s.* Unratsamkeit *f*; **ˌun·adˈvis·a·ble** *adj.* □ unratsam, nicht ratsam *od.* empfehlenswert; **ˌun·adˈvised** *adj.* □ **1.** unberaten; **2.** unbesonnen, ˈunüberˌlegt.

ˌun·afˈfect·ed *adj.* □ **1.** ungekünstelt, nicht affektiert (*Stil, Auftreten etc.*); **2.** echt, aufrichtig; **3.** unberührt, ungerührt, unbeeinflußt (***by*** von); **ˌun·afˈfect·ed·ness** [-nɪs] *s.* Naˈtürlichkeit *f*; Aufrichtigkeit *f*.

ˌun·aˈfraid *adj.* furchtlos: ***be ~ of*** keine Angst haben vor (*dat.*).

ˌunˈaid·ed *adj.* **1.** ohne Unterˈstützung, ohne Hilfe (***by*** von); (ganz) alˈlein; **2.** unbewaffnet, bloß (*Auge*).

ˌunˈal·ien·a·ble *adj.* □ unveräußerlich (*a. fig. Recht*).

ˌun·alˈloyed *adj.* **1.** ⚗ unvermischt, unlegiert; **2.** *fig.* ungetrübt, rein: ***~ happiness.***

unˈal·ter·a·ble *adj.* □ unveränderlich, unabänderlich; **ˌunˈal·tered** *adj.* unverändert.

ˌun·aˈmazed *adj.* nicht verwundert: ***be ~ at*** sich nicht wundern über (*acc.*).

un·am·big·u·ous [ˌʌnæmˈbɪgjʊəs] *adj.* □ unzweideutig; **ˌun·amˈbig·u·ous·ness** [-nɪs] *s.* Eindeutigkeit *f*.

ˌun·amˈbi·tious *adj.* □ **1.** nicht ehrgeizig, ohne Ehrgeiz; **2.** anspruchslos, schlicht (*Sache*).

ˌun·aˈme·na·ble *adj.* **1.** unzugänglich (***to*** *dat. od.* für); **2.** nicht verantwortlich (***to*** gegenüber).

ˌun·aˈmend·ed *adj.* unverbessert, unabgeändert; nicht ergänzt.

ˌun-Aˈmer·i·can *adj.* **1.** ˈunameriˌkanisch; **2.** ***~ activities*** *pol. Am.* staatsfeindliche Umtriebe.

ˌunˈa·mi·a·ble *adj.* □ unliebenswürdig, unfreundlich.

ˌun·aˈmus·ing *adj.* □ nicht unterˈhaltsam, langweilig, unergötzlich.

u·na·nim·i·ty [ˌjuːnəˈnɪmətɪ] *s.* **1.** Einstimmigkeit *f*; **2.** Einmütigkeit *f*; **u·nan·i·mous** [juːˈnænɪməs] *adj.* □ **1.** einmütig, einig; **2.** einstimmig (*Beschluß etc.*).

ˌun·anˈnounced *adj.* unangemeldet, unangekündigt.

ˌunˈan·swer·a·ble *adj.* □ **1.** nicht zu beantworten(d); unlösbar (*Rätsel*); **2.** ˈunwiderˌlegbar; **3.** nicht verantwortlich *od.* haftbar; **ˌunˈan·swered** *adj.* **1.** unbeantwortet; **2.** ˈunwiderˌlegt.

un·ap·peal·a·ble [ˌʌnəˈpiːləbl] *adj.* ⚖ nicht berufungs- *od.* rechtsmittelfähig, unanfechtbar.

un·ap·peas·a·ble [ˌʌnəˈpiːzəbl] *adj.* **1.** nicht zu besänftigen(d), unversöhnlich; **2.** nicht zuˈfriedenzustellen(d), unersättlich.

ˌunˈap·pe·tiz·ing *adj.* □ ˈunappeˌtitlich, *fig. a.* wenig reizvoll.

ˌun·apˈplied *adj.* nicht angewandt *od.* gebraucht: ***~ funds*** totes Kapital.

ˌun·apˈpre·ci·at·ed *adj.* nicht gebührend gewürdigt *od.* geschätzt, unbeachtet.

ˌun·apˈproach·a·ble *adj.* □ unnahbar.

ˌun·apˈpro·pri·at·ed *adj.* **1.** herrenlos; **2.** nicht verwendet *od.* gebraucht; **3.** ☤ nicht zugeteilt, keiner bestimmten Verwendung zugeführt.

ˌun·apˈproved *adj.* ungebilligt, nicht genehmigt.

ˌunˈapt *adj.* □ **1.** ungeeignet, untauglich (***for*** für, zu); **2.** unangebracht, unpassend; **3.** nicht geeignet (***to do*** zu tun); **4.** ungeschickt (***at*** bei, in *dat.*).

ˌunˈar·gued *adj.* **1.** unbesprochen; **2.** unbestritten.

ˌunˈarmed *adj.* **1.** unbewaffnet; **2.** unscharf (*Munition*).

ˌunˈar·mo(u)red *adj.* **1.** *bsd.* ⚔, ⚓ ungepanzert; **2.** ⚙ nicht bewehrt.

ˌun·as·cerˈtain·a·ble *adj.* nicht feststellbar; **ˌun·as·cerˈtained** *adj.* nicht (sicher) festgestellt.

ˌun·aˈshamed *adj.* □ **1.** nicht beschämt; **2.** schamlos.

ˌunˈasked *adj.* **1.** ungefragt; **2.** ungebeten, unaufgefordert; **3.** uneingeladen.

ˌun·asˈpir·ing *adj.* □ ohne Ehrgeiz, anspruchslos, bescheiden.

ˌun·asˈsail·a·ble *adj.* **1.** unangreifbar (*a. fig.*); **2.** *fig.* unanfechtbar.

ˌun·asˈsign·a·ble *adj.* ⚖ nicht überˈtragbar.

ˌun·asˈsist·ed *adj.* □ ohne Hilfe *od.* Unterˈstützung (***by*** von), (ganz) alˈlein.

ˌun·asˈsum·ing *adj.* □ anspruchslos, bescheiden.

ˌun·atˈtached *adj.* **1.** nicht befestigt (***to*** an *dat.*); **2.** nicht gebunden, unabhängig; **3.** ungebunden, frei, ledig; **4.** *ped., univ.* exˈtern, keinem College angehörend (*Student*); **5.** ⚔ zur Dispositiˈon stehend; **6.** ⚖ nicht mit Beschlag belegt.

ˌun·atˈtain·a·ble *adj.* □ unerreichbar.

ˌun·atˈtempt·ed *adj.* unversucht.

ˌun·atˈtend·ed *adj.* **1.** unbegleitet; **2.** *mst* ***~ to*** a) unbeaufsichtigt, b) vernachlässigt.

ˌun·atˈtest·ed *adj.* **1.** unbezeugt, unbestätigt; **2.** *Brit.* (behördlich) nicht überˈprüft.

ˌun·atˈtrac·tive *adj.* □ wenig anziehend, reizlos, ˈunattrakˌtiv.

ˌunˈau·thor·ized *adj.* **1.** nicht bevollmächtigt, unbefugt: ***~ person*** Unbefugte(r *m*) *f*; **2.** unerlaubt; unberechtigt (*Nachdruck etc.*).

un·a·vail·a·ble [ˌʌnəˈveɪləbl] *adj.* □ **1.** nicht verfügbar *od.* vorˈhanden; **2.** → **ˌun·aˈvail·ing** [-lɪŋ] *adj.* □ frucht-, nutzlos, vergeblich.

un·a·void·a·ble [ˌʌnəˈvɔɪdəbl] *adj.* □ **1.** unvermeidlich, unvermeidbar: ***~ cost*** notwendige Kosten; **2.** ⚖ unanfechtbar.

un·a·ware [ˌʌnəˈweə] *adj.* **1.** (***of***) nicht gewahr (*gen.*), in Unkenntnis (*gen.*): ***be ~ of*** sich *e-r Sache* nicht bewußt sein, *et.* nicht wissen *od.* bemerken; **2.** nichtsahnend: ***he was ~ that*** er ahnte nicht, daß; **ˌun·aˈwares** [-eəz] *adv.* **1.** versehentlich, unabsichtlich; **2.** unversehens, unerwartet, unvermutet: ***catch*** (*od.* ***take***) ***s.o. ~*** j-n überraschen; ***at ~*** unverhofft, überraschend.

ˌunˈbacked *adj.* **1.** ohne Rückhalt *od.* Unterˈstützung; **2.** ***~ horse*** Pferd, auf das nicht gesetzt wurde; **3.** ☤ ungedeckt, nicht indossiert.

ˌunˈbaked *adj.* **1.** ungebacken; **2.** *fig.* unreif.

ˌunˈbal·ance **I** *v/t.* **1.** aus dem Gleichgewicht bringen (*a. fig.*); **2.** *fig. Geist* verwirren; **II** *s.* **3.** gestörtes Gleichgewicht, *fig. a.* Unausgeglichenheit *f*; **4.** ↯, ⚙ Unwucht *f*; **ˌunˈbal·anced** *adj.* **1.** aus dem Gleichgewicht gebracht, nicht im Gleichgewicht (befindlich); **2.** *fig.* unausgeglichen (*a.* ☤); **3.** *psych.* laˈbil, ‚gestört'.

ˌun·bapˈtized *adj.* ungetauft.

ˌunˈbar *v/t.* aufriegeln.

ˌunˈbear·a·ble *adj.* □ unerträglich.

ˌunˈbeat·en *adj.* **1.** ungeschlagen, unbesiegt; **2.** *fig.* ˈunüberˌtroffen; **3.** unerforscht: ***~ region.***

ˌun·beˈcom·ing *adj.* □ **1.** unkleidsam: ***this hat is ~ to him*** dieser Hut steht ihm nicht; **2.** *fig.* unpassend, unschicklich, ungeziemend (***of, to, for*** für *j-n*).

ˌun·beˈfit·ting → ***unbecoming*** 2.

ˌun·beˈfriend·ed *adj.* ohne Freund(e).

un·be·known(st F) [ˌʌnbɪˈnəʊn(st)] *adj. u. adv.* **1.** (***to***) ohne *j-s* Wissen; **2.** unbekannt(erweise).

ˌun·beˈlief *s.* Unglaube *m*, Ungläubigkeit *f*; **ˌun·beˈliev·a·ble** *adj.* □ unglaublich; **ˌun·beˈliev·er** *s. eccl.* Ungläubige(r *m*) *f*, Glaubenslose(r *m*) *f*; **ˌun·beˈliev·ing** *adj.* □ ungläubig.

ˌunˈbend [*irr.* → ***bend***] **I** *v/t.* **1.** *Bogen etc., a. fig. Geist* entspannen; **2.** ⚙ geradebiegen, glätten; **3.** ⚓ a) *Tau etc.* losmachen, b) *Segel* abschlagen; **II** *v/i.* **4.** sich entspannen, sich lösen; **5.** *fig.* auftauen, freundlich(er) werden, s-e Förmlichkeit ablegen; **ˌunˈbend·ing** [-dɪŋ] *adj.* □ **1.** unbiegsam; **2.** *fig.* unbeugsam, entschlossen; **3.** *fig.* reserviert, steif.

un·be·seem·ing [ˌʌnbɪˈsiːmɪŋ] → ***unbecoming*** 2.

ˌunˈbi·as(s)ed *adj.* □ unvoreingenommen, *a.* ⚖ unbefangen.

ˌunˈbid(·den) *adj.* ungeheißen, unaufgefordert; ungebeten (*a. Gast*).

ˌunˈbind *v/t.* [*irr.* → ***bind***] **1.** *Gefangenen etc.* losbinden, befreien; **2.** *Haar, Knoten etc.* lösen.

ˌunˈbleached *adj.* ungebleicht.

ˌunˈblem·ished *adj. bsd. fig.* unbefleckt, makellos.

ˌunˈblink·ing *adj.* □ **1.** ungerührt; **2.** unerschrocken.

ˌunˈblush·ing *adj.* □ *fig.* schamlos.

ˌunˈbolt *v/t.* aufriegeln, öffnen.

ˌunˈborn *adj.* **1.** (noch) ungeboren; **2.** *fig.* (zu)künftig, kommend.

ˌunˈbos·om *v/t. Gedanken, Gefühle etc.* enthüllen, offenˈbaren (***to*** *dat.*): ***~ o.s.*** (***to s.o.***) sich (j-m) offenbaren, (j-m) sein Herz ausschütten.

ˌunˈbound *adj.* ungebunden: a) broschiert (*Buch*), b) *fig.* frei.

ˌ**unˈbound·ed** *adj.* □ **1.** unbegrenzt; **2.** *fig.* grenzen-, schrankenlos.
ˌ**unˈbrace** *v/t.* **1.** *Gurte etc.* lösen, losschnallen; **2.** entspannen (*a. fig.*): **~ o.s.** sich entspannen.
ˌ**unˈbreak·a·ble** *adj.* unzerbrechlich.
ˌ**unˈbrib·a·ble** *adj.* unbestechlich.
ˌ**unˈbri·dled** *adj.* **1.** ab-, ungezäumt; **2.** *fig.* ungezügelt, zügellos.
ˌ**unˈbro·ken** *adj.* □ **1.** ungebrochen (*a. fig. Eid etc.*), unzerbrochen, ganz, heil; **2.** ˈununterˌbrochen, ungestört; **3.** nicht zugeritten (*Pferd*); **4.** unbeeinträchtigt; **5.** ✓ ungepflügt; **6.** ungebrochen: **~ record.**
ˌ**unˈbroth·er·ly** *adj.* unbrüderlich.
ˌ**unˈbuck·le** *v/t.* auf-, losschnallen.
ˌ**unˈbuilt** *adj.* **1.** (noch) nicht gebaut; **2.** *a.* **~-on** unbebaut (*Gelände*).
ˌ**unˈbur·den** *v/t.* **1.** *bsd. fig.* entlasten, von e-r Last befreien, *Gewissen etc.* erleichtern: **~ o.s.** (**to s.o.**) (j-m) sein Herz ausschütten; **2.** a) *Geheimnis etc.* loswerden, b) *Sünden* bekennen, beichten: **~ one's troubles to s.o.** s-e Sorgen bei j-m abladen.
ˌ**unˈbur·ied** *adj.* unbegraben.
ˌ**unˈburnt** *adj.* **1.** unverbrannt; **2.** ⚙ ungebrannt (*Ziegel etc.*).
ˌ**unˈbur·y** *v/t.* ausgraben (*a. fig.*).
ˌ**unˈbusi·ness·like** *adj.* unkaufmännisch, nicht geschäftsmäßig.
ˌ**unˈbut·ton** *v/t.* aufknöpfen; ˌ**unˈbut·toned** *adj.* aufgeknöpft, *fig. a.* gelöst, zwanglos.
ˌ**unˈcalled** *adj.* **1.** unaufgefordert; **2.** ✝ nicht aufgerufen; ˌ**unˈcalled-for** *adj.* **1.** ungerufen, unerwünscht; unverlangt (*Sache*); **2.** unangebracht, unpassend: **~ remarks.**
unˈcan·ny *adj.* □ unheimlich (*a. fig.*).
ˌ**unˈcared-for** *adj.* **1.** unbeachtet; **2.** vernachlässigt; ungepflegt.
ˌ**unˈcase** *v/t.* auspacken.
un·ceas·ing [ʌnˈsi:sɪŋ] *adj.* □ unaufhörlich.
ˈ**unˌcer·eˈmo·ni·ous** *adj.* □ **1.** ungezwungen, zwanglos; **2.** a) unsanft, grob, b) unhöflich.
unˈcer·tain *adj.* □ **1.** unsicher, ungewiß, unbestimmt; **2.** nicht sicher: **be ~ of s.th.** e-r Sache nicht sicher *od.* gewiß sein; **3.** zweifelhaft, undeutlich, vage: **an ~ answer**; **4.** unzuverlässig: **an ~ friend**; **5.** unstet, unbeständig, veränderlich, launenhaft: **~ temper**, **~ weather**; **6.** unsicher, verunsichert; **unˈcer·tain·ty** [-tɪ] *s.* **1.** Unsicherheit *f*, Ungewißheit *f*; **2.** Zweifelhaftigkeit *f*; **3.** Unzuverlässigkeit *f*; **4.** Unbeständigkeit *f*.
ˌ**unˈcer·ti·fied** *adj.* nicht bescheinigt, unbeglaubigt.
ˌ**unˈchain** *v/t.* **1.** losketten; **2.** befreien (*a. fig.*).
ˌ**unˈchal·lenge·a·ble** *adj.* □ unanfechtbar, unbestreitbar; ˌ**unˈchal·lenged** *adj.* unbestritten, ˈunwiderˌsprochen, unangefochten.
un·change·a·ble [ˌʌnˈtʃeɪndʒəbl] *adj.* □ unveränderlich, unwandelbar; **un·changed** [ˌʌnˈtʃeɪndʒd] *adj.* unverändert; ˌ**unˈchang·ing** [-dʒɪŋ] *adj.* □ unveränderlich.
ˌ**unˈcharged** *adj.* **1.** nicht beladen; **2.** ⚖ nicht angeklagt; **3.** ⚡ nicht (auf)geladen; **4.** ungeladen (*Schußwaffe*); **5.** ✝ a) unbelastet (*Konto*), b) unberechnet.
ˌ**unˈchar·i·ta·ble** *adj.* □ lieblos, hartherzig, unfreundlich.
ˌ**unˈchart·ed** *adj.* auf keiner (Land)Karte verzeichnet, unbekannt, unerforscht (*a. fig.*).
ˌ**unˈchaste** *adj.* □ unkeusch; ˌ**unˈchas·ti·ty** *s.* Unkeuschheit *f*.
ˌ**unˈchecked** *adj.* **1.** ungehindert, ungehemmt; **2.** unkontrolliert, ungeprüft.
ˌ**unˈchiv·al·rous** *adj.* unritterlich, ˈungaˌlant.
ˌ**unˈchris·tened** *adj.* ungetauft.
ˌ**unˈchris·tian** *adj.* □ unchristlich.
un·ci·al [ˈʌnsɪəl] **I** *adj.* **1.** Unzial...; **II** *s.* **2.** Unziˈale *f* (*abgerundeter Großbuchstabe*); **3.** Unziˈalschrift *f*.
un·ci·form [ˈʌnsɪfɔ:m] **I** *adj.* hakenförmig; **II** *s. anat.* Hakenbein *n*.
ˌ**unˈcir·cum·cised** *adj.* unbeschnitten; ˈ**unˌcir·cumˈci·sion** *s. bibl. die* Unbeschnittenen *pl.*, *die* Heiden *pl.*
ˌ**unˈciv·il** *adj.* □ **1.** unhöflich, grob; **2.** *obs.* → ˌ**unˈciv·i·lized** *adj.* unzivilisiert.
ˌ**unˈclaimed** *adj.* **1.** nicht beansprucht, nicht geltend gemacht; **2.** nicht abgeholt *od.* abgehoben.
ˌ**unˈclasp** *v/t.* **1.** lösen, auf-, loshaken, -schnallen; öffnen; **2.** loslassen.
ˌ**unˈclas·si·fied** *adj.* **1.** nicht klassifiziert: **~ road** Landstraße *f*; **2.** ⚔ offen, nicht geheim.
un·cle [ˈʌŋkl] *s.* **1.** Onkel *m*: **cry ~** *Am.* F aufgeben; **2.** *sl.* Pfandleiher *m*.
ˌ**unˈclean** *adj.* □ unrein (*a. fig.*).
ˌ**unˈclean·li·ness** *s.* **1.** Unreinlichkeit *f*, Unsauberkeit *f*; **2.** *fig.* Unreinheit *f*; ˌ**unˈclean·ly** *adj.* **1.** unreinlich; **2.** *fig.* unrein, unkeusch.
ˌ**unˈclench I** *v/t.* **1.** *Faust* öffnen; **2.** *Griff* lockern; **II** *v/i.* **3.** sich öffnen *od.* lockern.
ˌ**unˈcloak** *v/t.* **1.** *j-m* den Mantel abnehmen; **2.** *fig.* enthüllen, -larven.
un·close [ˌʌnˈkləʊz] **I** *v/t.* **1.** öffnen; **2.** *fig.* enthüllen; **II** *v/i.* **3.** sich öffnen.
ˌ**unˈclothe** *v/t.* entkleiden, -blößen, -hüllen (*a. fig.*); ˌ**unˈclothed** *adj.* unbekleidet.
ˌ**unˈcloud·ed** *adj.* **1.** unbewölkt, wolkenlos; **2.** *fig.* ungetrübt.
un·co [ˈʌŋkəʊ] *Scot. od. dial.* **I** *adj.* ungewöhnlich, seltsam; **II** *adv.* äußerst, höchst: **the ~ guid** die ach so guten Menschen.
ˌ**unˈcock** *v/t.* *Gewehr(hahn) etc.* entspannen.
ˌ**unˈcoil** *v/t.* (*v/i.* sich) abwickeln *od.* abspulen *od.* aufrollen.
ˌ**un·colˈlect·ed** *adj.* **1.** nicht (ein)gesammelt; **2.** ✝ (noch) nicht erhoben (*Gebühren*); **3.** *fig.* nicht gefaßt *od.* gesammelt.
ˌ**unˈcol·o(u)red** *adj.* **1.** ungefärbt; **2.** *fig.* ungeschminkt, objekˈtiv.
un·come-at-a·ble [ˌʌnkʌmˈætəbl] *adj.* F unerreichbar; unzugänglich: **it's ~** ‚da ist nicht ranzukommen'.
ˌ**unˈcome·ly** *adj.* **1.** unschön, reizlos; **2.** *obs.* unschicklich.
unˈcom·fort·a·ble *adj.* □ **1.** unangenehm, beunruhigend; **2.** unbehaglich, ungemütlich (*beide a. fig. Gefühl etc.*), unbequem: **~ silence** peinliche Stille; **3.** *fig.* unangenehm berührt.
ˌ**un·comˈmit·ted** *adj.* **1.** nicht begangen (*Verbrechen etc.*); **2.** (**to**) nicht verpflichtet (zu), nicht gebunden (an *acc.*); **3.** ⚖ nicht inhaftiert *od.* eingewiesen; **4.** *parl.* nicht an e-n Ausschuß *etc.* verwiesen; **5.** *pol.* neuˈtral, blockfrei; **6.** nicht zweckgebunden: **~ funds.**
unˈcom·mon I *adj.* □ ungewöhnlich: a) selten, b) außergewöhnlich, -ordentlich; **II** *adv. obs.* äußerst, ungewöhnlich; **unˈcom·mon·ness** *s.* Ungewöhnlichkeit *f*.
ˌ**un·comˈmu·ni·ca·ble** *adj.* **1.** nicht mitteilbar; **2.** ⚕ nicht ansteckend; ˌ**un·comˈmu·ni·ca·tive** *adj.* □ nicht *od.* wenig mitteilsam, verschlossen.
ˌ**un·comˈpan·ion·a·ble** *adj.* ungesellig, nicht ˈumgänglich.
un·com·plain·ing [ˌʌnkəmˈpleɪnɪŋ] *adj.* □ klaglos, ohne Murren, geduldig; ˌ**un·comˈplain·ing·ness** [-nɪs] *s.* Klaglosigkeit *f*.
ˌ**un·comˈplai·sant** *adj.* □ ungefällig.
ˌ**un·comˈplet·ed** *adj.* ˈunvollˌendet.
ˌ**unˈcom·pli·cat·ed** *adj.* unkompliziert, einfach.
ˈ**unˌcom·pliˈmen·ta·ry** *adj.* **1.** nicht *od.* wenig schmeichelhaft; **2.** unhöflich.
un·com·pro·mis·ing [ʌnˈkɒmprəmaɪzɪŋ] *adj.* □ **1.** komproˈmißlos; **2.** unbeugsam, unnachgiebig; **3.** *fig.* entschieden, eindeutig.
ˌ**un·conˈcealed** *adj.* unverhohlen.
un·con·cern [ˌʌnkənˈsɜ:n] *s.* **1.** Sorglosigkeit *f*, Unbekümmertheit *f*; **2.** Gleichgültigkeit *f*; ˌ**un·conˈcerned** [-nd] *adj.* □ **1.** (**in**) unbeteiligt (an *dat.*), nicht verwickelt (in *acc.*); **2.** uninteressiert (**with** an *dat.*), gleichgültig; **3.** unbesorgt, unbekümmert (**about** um, wegen): **be ~ about** sich über *et.* keine Gedanken *od.* Sorgen machen; ˌ**un·conˈcern·ed·ness** [-nɪdnɪs] → **unconcern.**
ˌ**un·conˈdi·tion·al** *adj.* □ **1.** unbedingt, bedingungslos: **~ surrender** bedingungslose Kapitulation; **2.** uneingeschränkt, vorbehaltlos.
ˌ**un·conˈdi·tioned** *adj.* **1.** → **unconditional**; **2.** unbedingt: a) *phls.* absoˈlut, b) *psych.* angeboren: **~ reflex.**
ˌ**un·conˈfined** *adj.* □ unbegrenzt, unbeschränkt.
ˌ**un·conˈfirmed** *adj.* **1.** unbestätigt, nicht erhärtet, unverbürgt; **2.** *eccl.* a) nicht konfirmiert (*Protestanten*), b) nicht gefirmt (*Katholiken*).
ˌ**un·conˈgen·ial** *adj.* □ **1.** ungleichartig, nicht kongeniˈal; **2.** nicht zusagend, unangenehm, ˈunsymˌpathisch (**to** *dat.*); **3.** unfreundlich.
ˌ**un·conˈnect·ed** *adj.* **1.** unverbunden, getrennt; **2.** ˈunzuˌsammenhängend; **3.** ungebunden, ohne Anhang; **4.** nicht verwandt.
un·con·quer·a·ble [ˌʌnˈkɒŋkərəbl] *adj.* □ ˈunüberˌwindlich (*a. fig.*), unbesiegbar; ˌ**unˈcon·quered** [-kəd] unbesiegt, nicht erobert.
ˈ**unˌcon·sciˈen·tious** *adj.* □ nicht gewissenhaft, nachlässig.
un·con·scion·a·ble [ʌnˈkɒnʃnəbl] *adj.* □ **1.** gewissen-, skrupellos; **2.** unvernünftig, nicht zumutbar; **3.** ‚unverschämt', unglaublich, eˈnorm.
unˈcon·scious I *adj.* □ **1.** unbewußt: **be ~ of** nichts ahnen von, sich *e-r Sache* nicht bewußt sein; **2.** ⚕ bewußtlos, ohnmächtig; **3.** unbewußt, unwillkür-

lich; unfreiwillig (*a. Humor*); **4.** unabsichtlich; **5.** *psych.* unbewußt; **II** *s.* **6.** **the ~** *psych.* das Unbewußte; **un·ˈcon·scious·ness** *s.* **1.** Unbewußtheit *f*; **2.** ⚕ Bewußtlosigkeit *f*.

ˌunˈcon·se·crat·ed *adj.* ungeweiht.

ˌun·conˈsid·ered *adj.* **1.** unberücksichtigt; **2.** unbedacht, ˈunüberˌlegt.

ˈunˌcon·stiˈtu·tion·al *adj.* □ *pol.* verfassungswidrig.

ˌun·conˈstrained *adj.* □ zwanglos, ungezwungen; **ˌun·conˈstraint** *s.* Ungezwungenheit *f*, Zwanglosigkeit *f*.

ˌun·conˈtest·ed *adj.* unbestritten, unangefochten: **~ election** *pol.* Wahl *f* ohne Gegenkandidaten.

ˈunˌcon·traˈdict·ed *adj.* ˈunwiderˌsprochen, unbestritten.

ˌun·conˈtrol·la·ble *adj.* □ **1.** unkontrollierbar; **2.** unbändig, unbeherrscht: **an ~ temper**; **ˌun·conˈtrolled** *adj.* □ **1.** nicht kontrolliert, unbeaufsichtigt; **2.** unbeherrscht, zügellos.

ˌun·conˈven·tion·al *adj.* □ ˈunkonventioˌnell: a) unüblich, b) ungezwungen, form-, zwanglos; **ˈun·conˌven·tionˈal·i·ty** *s.* Zwanglosigkeit *f*, Ungezwungenheit *f*.

ˌun·conˈvert·ed *adj.* **1.** unverwandelt; **2.** *eccl.* unbekehrt (*a. fig. nicht überzeugt*); **3.** ✝ nicht konvertiert; **ˌun·conˈvert·i·ble** *adj.* **1.** nicht verwandelbar; **2.** nicht vertauschbar; **3.** ✝ nicht konvertierbar.

ˌun·conˈvinced *adj.* nicht überˈzeugt; **ˌun·conˈvinc·ing** *adj.* nicht überˈzeugend.

ˌunˈcooked *adj.* ungekocht, roh.

ˌunˈcord *v/t.* auf-, losbinden.

ˌunˈcork *v/t.* **1.** entkorken; **2.** *fig.* F *Gefühlen etc.* Luft machen; **3.** *Am.* F *et.* ‚vom Stapel lassen'.

ˌun·corˈrob·o·rat·ed *adj.* unbestätigt, nicht erhärtet.

un·count·a·ble [ˌʌnˈkaʊntəbl] *adj.* **1.** unzählbar; **2.** zahllos; **ˌunˈcount·ed** [-tɪd] *adj.* **1.** ungezählt; **2.** unzählig.

ˌunˈcouple *v/t.* **1.** *Hunde etc.* aus der Koppel (los)lassen; **2.** loslösen, trennen; **3.** ⚙ aus-, loskuppeln.

un·couth [ʌnˈku:θ] *adj.* □ **1.** ungeschlacht, unbeholfen, plump; **2.** grob, ungehobelt; **3.** *poet.* öde, wild (*Gegend*); **4.** *obs.* wunderlich.

ˌunˈcov·e·nant·ed *adj.* **1.** nicht vertraglich festgelegt; **2.** nicht vertraglich gebunden.

unˈcov·er I *v/t.* **1.** aufdecken, freilegen; *Körperteil, a. Kopf* entblößen: **~ o.s.** → 5; **2.** *fig.* aufdecken, enthüllen; **3.** ⚔ ohne Deckung lassen; **4.** *Boxen etc.*: ungedeckt lassen; **II** *v/i.* **5.** den Hut abnehmen; **unˈcov·ered** *adj.* **1.** unbedeckt (*a. barhäuptig*); **2.** unbekleidet, nackt; **3.** ⚔, *sport etc.* ungedeckt, ungeschützt; **4.** ✝ ungedeckt (*Wechsel etc.*).

ˌunˈcrit·i·cal *adj.* □ unkritisch, kriˈtiklos (**of** gegenüber).

ˌunˈcross *v/t. gekreuzte Arme od. Beine* geradelegen; **ˌunˈcrossed** *adj.* nicht gekreuzt: **~ cheque** (*Am.* **check**) ✝ Barscheck *m*.

unc·tion [ˈʌŋkʃn] *s.* **1.** Salbung *f*, Einreibung *f*; **2.** ⚕ Salbe *f*; **3.** *eccl.* a) (heiliges) Öl, b) Salbung *f* (*Weihe*), c) *a.* **extreme ~** Letzte Ölung; **4.** *fig.* Balsam *m* (*Linderung, Trost*) (**to** für); **5.** *fig.* Inbrunst *f*, Pathos *n*; **6.** *fig.* Salbung *f*, unechtes Pathos: **with ~** a) salbungsvoll, b) mit Genuß; **ˈunc·tu·ous** [-ktjʊəs] *adj.* □ **1.** ölig, fettig: **~ soil** fetter Boden; **2.** *fig.* salbungsvoll, ölig.

ˌunˈcul·ti·vat·ed *adj.* **1.** ⚘ unbebaut, unkultiviert; **2.** *fig.* brachliegend (*Talent etc.*); **3.** *fig.* ungebildet, unkultiviert.

ˌunˈcul·tured *adj.* unkultiviert (*a. fig. ungebildet*).

ˌunˈcurbed *adj.* **1.** abgezäumt; **2.** *fig.* ungezähmt, zügellos.

ˌunˈcured *adj.* **1.** ungeheilt; **2.** ungesalzen, ungepökelt.

ˌunˈcurl *v/t.* (*v/i.* sich) entkräuseln *od.* glätten.

ˌun·curˈtailed *adj.* ungekürzt, unbeschnitten.

ˌunˈcut *adj.* **1.** ungeschnitten; **2.** unzerschnitten; **3.** ⚘ ungemäht; **4.** ungeschliffen (*Diamant*); **5.** unbeschnitten (*Buch*); **6.** *fig.* ungekürzt.

ˌunˈdam·aged *adj.* unbeschädigt, unversehrt.

ˌunˈdamped *adj.* **1.** *bsd.* ♪, ⚡, *phys.* ungedämpft; **2.** unangefeuchtet; **3.** *fig.* nicht entmutigt.

un·date [ˈʌndeɪt] *adj.* wellig, wellenförmig.

un·dat·ed¹ [ˈʌndeɪtɪd] → **undate.**

ˌunˈdat·ed² *adj.* **1.** undatiert, ohne Datum; **2.** unbefristet.

un·daunt·ed [ˌʌnˈdɔ:ntɪd] *adj.* □ unerschrocken.

ˌun·deˈceive *v/t.* **1.** *j-m* die Augen öffnen, *j-n* desillusioˈnieren; **2.** aufklären (**of** über *acc.*), e-s Besser(e)n belehren; **ˌun·deˈceived** *adj.* **1.** nicht irregeführt; **2.** aufgeklärt, e-s Besser(e)n belehrt.

ˌun·deˈcid·ed *adj.* □ **1.** unentschieden, offen: **leave s.th. ~**; **2.** unbestimmt, vage; **3.** unentschlossen; **4.** unbeständig (*Wetter*).

ˌun·deˈci·pher·a·ble *adj.* **1.** nicht zu entziffern(d), nicht entzifferbar; **2.** unerklärlich, nicht enträtselbar.

ˌun·deˈclared *adj.* **1.** nicht bekanntgemacht, nicht erklärt: **~ war** Krieg *m* ohne Kriegserklärung; **2.** ✝ nicht deklariert.

ˌun·deˈfend·ed *adj.* **1.** unverteidigt; **2.** ⚖ a) unverteidigt, ohne Verteidiger, b) ˈunwiderˌsprochen (*Klage*).

ˌun·deˈfiled *adj.* unbefleckt, rein (*a. fig.*).

ˌun·deˈfin·a·ble *adj.* undefinierbar, unbestimmt.

ˌun·deˈfined *adj.* **1.** unbegrenzt; **2.** unbestimmt, vage.

ˌun·deˈmand·ing *adj.* **1.** anspruchslos (*a. fig.*); **2.** leicht: **~ task.**

ˌun·deˈmon·stra·tive *adj.* zuˈrückhaltend, reserviert, unaufdringlich.

ˌun·deˈni·a·ble *adj.* □ unleugbar, unbestreitbar.

ˈun·deˌnom·i·naˈtion·al *adj.* **1.** nicht konfessioˈnell gebunden; **2.** *ped.* interkonfessioˈnell, Gemeinschafts…, Simultan…: **~ school.**

un·der [ˈʌndə] **I** *prp.* **1.** *allg.* unter (*dat. od. acc.*); **2.** *Lage*: unter (*dat.*), ˈunterhalb von (*od. gen.*): **from ~ …** unter *dem Tisch etc.* hervor; **get out from ~** *Am. sl.* a) sich herauswinden, b) den Verlust wettmachen; **3.** *Richtung*: unter (*acc.*); **4.** unter (*dat.*), am Fuße von (*od. gen.*); **5.** *zeitlich*: unter (*dat.*), während: **~ his rule**; **~ the Stuarts** unter den Stuarts; **~ the date of** unter dem Datum vom *1. Januar etc.*; **6.** unter *der Autorität, Führung etc.*: **he fought ~ Wellington**; **7.** unter (*dat.*), unter dem Schutz von: **~ arms** unter Waffen; **~ darkness** im Schutz der Dunkelheit; **8.** unter (*dat.*), geringer als, weniger als: **persons ~ 40** (**years of age**) Personen unter 40 (Jahren); **in ~ an hour** in weniger als ˈeiner Stunde; **9.** *fig.* unter (*dat.*): **~ alcohol** unter Alkohol; **~ an assumed name** unter e-m angenommenen Namen; **~ supervision** unter Aufsicht; **10.** gemäß, laut, nach: **~ the terms of the contract**; **claims ~ a contract** Forderungen aus e-m Vertrag; **11.** in (*dat.*): **~ construction** im Bau; **~ repair** in Reparatur; **~ treatment** ⚕ in Behandlung; **12.** bei: **he studied physics ~ Maxwell**; **13.** mit: **~ s.o.'s signature** mit j-s Unterschrift, (eigenhändig) unterzeichnet von j-m; **~ separate cover** mit getrennter Post; **II** *adv.* **14.** darˈunter, unter; → **go** (**keep** *etc.*) **under**; **15.** unten: **as ~** wie unten (angeführt); **III** *adj.* **16.** unter, Unter…; **17.** unter, nieder, ˈuntergeordnet, Unter…; **18.** *nur in Zssgn* ungenügend, zu gering: **an ~dose**; **ˌ~ˈact** [-ərˈæ-] *v/t. u. v/i. thea. etc.* unterˈspielen, unterˈtreiben (*a. fig.*); **ˌ~·aˈchieve** [-ərə-] *v/i.* weniger leisten *od.* schlechter abschneiden als erwartet; **ˌ~ˈage** [-ərˈeɪ-] *adj.* minderjährig; **ˈ~ˌa·gent** [-ərˌeɪ-] *s.* ˈUntervertreter *m*; **ˈ~·arm** [-ərɑ:m] **I** *adj.* **1.** Unterarm…; **2.** → **underhand** 2; **II** *adv.* **3.** mit e-r ˈUnterarmbewegung; **ˌ~ˈbid** *v/t.* [*irr.* → **bid**] unterˈbieten; **ˌ~ˈbred** *adj.* unfein, ungebildet; **ˈ~·brush** *s.* ˈUnterholz *n*, Gestrüpp *n*; **ˈ~ˌcar·riage** *s.* **1.** ✈ Fahrwerk *n*; **2.** *mot. etc.* Fahrgestell *n*; **3.** ⚔ ˈUnterlaˌfette *f*; **ˌ~ˈcharge I** *v/t.* **1.** *j-m* zu wenig berechnen; **2.** *et.* zu gering berechnen; **3.** *Batterie etc.* unterˈladen; **4.** *Geschütz etc.* zu schwach laden; **II** *s.* **5.** zu geringe Berechnung *od.* Belastung; **6.** ungenügende (Auf)Ladung; **ˈ~·clothes** *s. pl.*, **ˈ~ˌcloth·ing** *s.* ˈUnterkleidung *f*, -wäsche *f*; **ˈ~·coat** *s.* **1.** ⚙, *paint.* Grundierung *f*; **2.** *zo.* Wollhaarkleid *n*; **ˈ~ˌcov·er** *adj.* **1.** Geheim…: **~ agent**, **~ man** (*bsd.* eingeschleuster) Geheimagent, Spitzel *m*; **ˈ~·croft** *s.* △ ˈunterirdisches Gewölbe, Krypta *f*; **ˈ~ˌcur·rent** *s.* ˈUnterströmung *f* (*a. fig.*); **ˌ~ˈcut I** *v/t.* [*irr.* → **cut**] **1.** unterˈhöhlen; **2.** (im Preis) unterˈbieten; **3.** *Golf, Tennis etc.*: *Ball* mit ˈUnterschnitt spielen; **II** *s.* ˈ**undercut 4.** Unterˈhöhlung *f*; **5.** *Golf, Tennis etc.*: unterˈschnittener Ball; **6.** *Küche*: *Brit.* Fiˈlet *n*, zartes Lendenstück; **ˌ~·deˈvel·oped** *adj. phot. u. fig.* ˈunterentwickelt: **~ child**; **~ country** Entwicklungsland *n*; **ˈ~·dog** *s. fig.* **1.** Verlierer *m*, Unterˈlegene(r *m*) *f*; **2.** a) *der* (soziˈal *etc.*) Schwächere *od.* Benachteiligte, b) *der* (zu Unrecht) Verfolgte; **ˌ~ˈdone** *adj.* nicht gar, nicht ˈdurchgebraten; **ˈ~·dose** ⚕ **I** *s.* **1.** zu geringe Dosis; **II** *v/t.* **ˌunderˈdose 2.** *j-m* e-e zu geringe Dosis geben; **3.** *et.* ˈunterdosieren; **ˌ~ˈdress** *v/t.* (*v/i.* sich) zu einfach kleiden; **ˌ~ˈes·ti·mate** [-ərˈestɪmeɪt] **I** *v/t.* unterˈschätzen; **II** *s.* [-mət] *a.* **ˈ~ˌes·tiˈma·tion** [-ərˌe-] Unterˈschätzung *f*; ˈUnterbewertung *f*; **ˌ~·exˈpose** [-dərɪ-] *v/t. phot.* ˈunterbelichten; **ˌ~·exˈpo·sure** [-dərɪ-] *s. phot.* ˈUnterbelichtung *f*; **ˌ~ˈfed** *adj.* ˈunterernährt; **ˌ~ˈfeed·ing** *s.* ˈUnterernährung *f*; **ˌ~ˈfoot** *adv.* **1.** unter den Füßen, unten, am Boden *zertrampeln etc.*; **2.** *fig.* in der Gewalt, unter Konˈtrolle; **ˈ~·frame** *s. mot. etc.* ˈUntergestell *n*, Rahmen *m*; **ˈ~ˌgar·ment** *s.* ˈUnterkleid(ung *f*) *n*; *pl.* ˈUnterwäsche *f*; **ˌ~ˈgo** *v/t.* [*irr.* → **go**] **1.** *e-n Wandel etc.* erleben, ˈdurchmachen; **2.** sich *e-r Operation etc.* unterˈziehen; **3.** erdulden; **ˌ~ˈgrad·u·ate** *univ.* **I** *s.* Stuˈdent(in); **II** *adj.* Studenten…; **ˈ~·ground I** *s.* **1.** *bsd. Brit.* ˈUntergrundbahn *f*, U-Bahn *f*; **2.** *pol.* ˈUntergrund(bewegung *f*) *m*; **3.** *Kunst*: Underground *m*; **II** *adj.* **4.** ˈunterirdisch: **~ cable** ⚙ Erdkabel *n*; **~ car park**, **~ garage** Tiefgarage *f*; **~ railway** (*Am.* **railroad**) → 1; **~ water** Grundwasser *n*; **5.** ⚒ unter Tag(e): **~ mining** Untertag(e)bau *m*; **6.** ⚙ Tiefbau…: **~ engineering** Tiefbau *m*; **7.** *fig.* Untergrund…, Geheim…, verborgen: **~ movement** *pol.* Untergrundbewegung *f*; **8.** *Kunst*: Underground…: **~ film**; **III** *adv.* **ˌunderˈground 9.** unter der *od.* die Erde, ˈunterirdisch; **10.** *fig.* im verborgenen, geheim: **go ~** a) *pol.* in den Untergrund gehen, b) untertauchen; **ˈ~·growth** *s.* ˈUnterholz *n*, Gestrüpp *n*; **ˌ~ˈhand** *adj. u. adv.* **1.** *fig.* a) heimlich, verstohlen, b) ˈhinterlistig; **2.** *sport* mit der Hand unter Schulterhöhe ausgeführt: **~ service** *Tennis*: Tiefaufschlag *m*; **ˌ~ˈhand·ed** *adj.* □ **1.** → **underhand** 1; **2.** † knapp an Arbeitskräften, ˈunterbelegt; **ˌ~·inˈsure** [-ərɪ-] *v/t.* (*v/i.* sich) ˈunterversichern; **ˌ~ˈlay I** *v/t.* [*irr.* → **lay¹**] **1.** (dar)ˈunterlegen; **2.** *et.* unterˈlegen, stützen; **3.** *typ. Satz* zurichten; **II** *v/i.* **4.** ⚒ sich neigen, einfallen; **III** *s.* **ˈunderlay 5.** ˈUnterlage *f*; **6.** *typ.* Zurichtebogen *m*; **7.** ⚒ schräges Flöz; **ˈ~·lease** *s.* ˈUnterverpachtung *f*, -miete *f*; **ˌ~ˈlet** *v/t.* [*irr.* → **let¹**] **1.** unter Wert verpachten *od.* vermieten; **2.** ˈunterverpachten, -vermieten; **ˌ~ˈlie** *v/t.* [*irr.* → **lie²**] **1.** liegen unter (*dat.*); **2.** zuˈgrunde liegen (*dat.*); **3.** † unterˈliegen (*dat.*), unterˈworfen sein (*dat.*); **ˌ~ˈline I** *v/t.* **1.** unterˈstreichen (*a. fig. betonen*); **II** *s.* **ˈunderline 2.** Unterˈstreichung *f*; **3.** *thea.* (Vor)Ankündigung *f* am Ende e-s Theˈaterplaˌkats; **4.** ˈBildˌunterschrift *f*.

un·der·ling [ˈʌndəlɪŋ] *s. contp.* Unterˈgebene(r *m*) *f*, (kleiner) Handlanger, ‚Kuli' *m*.

ˌun·der|ˈly·ing *adj.* **1.** darˈunterliegend; **2.** *fig.* zuˈgrundeliegend; **3.** † *Am.* Vorrangs…; **ˌ~ˈmanned** [-ˈmænd] *adj.* a) ⚓ ˈunterbemannt, b) (persoˈnell) ˈunterbesetzt; **ˌ~ˈmen·tioned** *adj.* unten erwähnt; **ˌ~ˈmine** *v/t.* **1.** ⚙ unterminieren (*a. fig.*); **2.** unterˈspülen, auswaschen; **3.** *fig.* unterˈgraben, (allˈmählich) zuˈgrunde richten; **ˈ~·most I** *adj.* unterst; **II** *adv.* zuˈunterst.

un·der·neath [ˌʌndəˈniːθ] **I** *prp.* **1.** unter (*dat. od. acc.*), ˈunterhalb (*gen.*); **II** *adv.* **2.** unten, darˈunter; **3.** auf der ˈUnterseite.

ˌun·der|ˈnour·ished *adj.* ˈunterernährt; **ˈ~·pants** *s. pl.* ˈUnterhose *f*; **ˈ~ˌpass** *s.* (ˈStraßen- *etc.*)Unterˌführung *f*; **ˌ~ˈpay** *v/t.* [*irr.* → **pay**] † ˈunterbezahlen; **ˌ~ˈpin** *v/t.* ⚠ (unter)ˈstützen, unterˈmauern (*beide a. fig.*); **ˌ~ˈpin·ning** *s.* **1.** ⚠ Unterˈmauerung *f*, ˈUnterbau *m* (*a. fig.*); **2.** F ‚Fahrgestell' *n* (*Beine*); **ˌ~ˈplay** *v/t. u. v/i.* **1.** → **underact**; **2. ~ one's hand** *fig.* nicht alle Trümpfe ausspielen; **ˈ~·plot** *s.* Nebenhandlung *f*, Epiˈsode *f* (*Roman etc.*); **ˌ~ˈpop·u·lat·ed** *adj.* ˈunterbevölkert; **ˌ~ˈprint** *v/t.* **1.** *typ.* a) gegendrucken, b) zu schwach drucken; **2.** *phot.* ˈunterkopieren; **ˌ~ˈpriv·i·leged** *adj.* †, *pol.* ˈunterpriviˌlegiert, schlechtergestellt; **ˌ~·proˈduc·tion** *s.* † ˈUnterproduktiˌon *f*; **ˌ~ˈproof** *adj.* † ˈunterproˌzentig (*Spirituosen*); **ˌ~ˈrate** *v/t.* **1.** unterˈschätzen, ˈunterbewerten (*a. sport*); **2.** † zu niedrig veranschlagen; **ˌ~·reˈac·tion** *s.* zu schwache Reaktiˈon; **ˈ~·seal** *mot.* **I** *s.* ˈUnterbodenschutz *m*; **II** *v/t.* mit Unterbodenschutz versehen; **ˌ~ˈscore** *v/t.* unterˈstreichen (*a. fig. betonen*); **ˌ~ˈsec·re·tar·y** *s. pol.* ˈStaatssekreˌtär *m*; **ˌ~ˈsell** *v/t.* [*irr.* → **sell**] † **1.** *j-n* unterˈbieten; **2.** *Ware* verschleudern, unter Wert verkaufen; **ˌ~ˈsexed** *adj.*: **be ~** e-n unterentwickelten Geschlechtstrieb haben; **ˈ~·shirt** *s.* ˈUnterhemd *n*; **ˌ~ˈshoot** *v/t.* [*irr.* → **shoot**]: **~ the runway** ✈ vor der Landebahn aufsetzen; **ˈ~·shot** *adj.* **1.** ⚙ ˈunterschlächtig (*Wasserrad*); **2.** mit vorstehendem ˈUnterkiefer; **ˌ~ˈsigned I** *adj.* unterˈzeichnet; **II** *s.*: **the undersigned** a) der (die) Unterˈzeichnete, b) die Unterˈzeichneten *pl.*; **ˌ~ˈsize(d)** *adj.* **1.** unter Norˈmalgröße; **2.** winzig; **ˈ~·skirt** *s.* ˈUnterrock *m*; **ˌ~ˈslung** *adj.* ⚙, *mot.* Hänge…(*-kühler etc.*), Unterzug…(*-rahmen*); unterˈbaut (*Feder etc.*); **ˈ~·soil** *s.* ˈUntergrund *m*; **ˌ~ˈstaffed** *adj.* ˈunterbesetzt.

un·der·stand [ˌʌndəˈstænd] [*irr.* → **stand**] **I** *v/t.* **1.** verstehen: a) begreifen, b) einsehen, c) *wörtlich etc.* auffassen, d) Verständnis haben für: **~ each other** *fig.* sich *od.* einander verstehen, *a.* zu e-r Einigung kommen; **give s.o. to ~** j-m zu verstehen geben; **make o.s. understood** sich verständlich machen; **do I** (*od.* **am I to**) **~ that ...** soll das etwa heißen, daß …; **be it understood** wohlverstanden; **what do you ~ by ...?** was verstehen Sie unter (*dat.*)?; **2.** sich verstehen auf (*acc.*), wissen (**how to** *inf.* wie man *et. macht*): **he ~s horses** er versteht sich auf Pferde; **she ~s children** sie kann mit Kindern umgehen; **3.** (als sicher) annehmen, vorˈaussetzen: **an understood thing** e-e ausgemachte Sache; **that is understood** das versteht sich (von selbst); **it is understood that** ⚖ es gilt als vereinbart, daß; **4.** erfahren, hören: **I ~ ...** wie ich höre; **I ~ that** ich hörte *od.* man sagte mir, daß; **it is understood** es heißt, wie verlautet; **5.** (**from**) entnehmen (*dat. od.* aus), schließen (aus); **6.** *bsd. ling.* sinngemäß ergänzen, hinˈzudenken; **II** *v/i.* **7.** verstehen: a) begreifen, b) *fig.* (volles) Verständnis haben; **8.** Verstand haben; **9.** hören: **..., so I ~** wie ich höre; **ˌun·derˈstand·a·ble** [-dəbl] *adj.* verständlich; **ˌun·derˈstand·a·bly** [-dəblɪ] *adv.* verständlich(erweise); **ˌun·derˈstand·ing** [-dɪŋ] **I** *s.* **1.** Verstehen *n*; **2.** Verstand *m*, Intelliˈgenz *f*; **3.** Verständnis *n* (**of** für); **4.** *gutes etc.* Einvernehmen (**between** zwischen); **5.** Verständigung *f*, Vereinbarung *f*, Überˈeinkunft *f*, Abmachung *f*: **come to an ~ with s.o.** zu e-r Einigung mit j-m kommen; **6.** Bedingung *f*: **on the ~ that** unter der Bedingung *od.* Voraussetzung, daß; **II** *adj.* □ **7.** verständig; **8.** verständnisvoll.

un·der|·state [ˌʌndəˈsteɪt] *v/t.* **1.** zu gering angeben; **2.** (bewußt) zuˈrückhaltend darstellen, unterˈtreiben; **3.** abschwächen, mildern; **ˌ~ˈstate·ment** *s.* **1.** zu niedrige Angabe; **2.** Unterˈtreibung *f*, Underˈstatement *n*; **ˌ~ˈsteer** *v/i.* *Auto* unterˈsteuern; **ˈ~ˌstrap·per** → **underling**; **ˈ~ˌstud·y** *thea.* **I** *v/t.* **1.** *Rolle* als zweite Besetzung einstudieren; **2.** für *e-n Schauspieler* einspringen; **II** *s.* **3.** zweite Besetzung; *fig.* Ersatzmann *m*; **ˌ~ˈtake** *v/t.* [*irr.* → **take**] **1.** *Aufgabe* überˈnehmen, *Sache* auf sich *od.* in die Hand nehmen; **2.** *Reise etc.* unterˈnehmen; **3.** *Risiko*, *Verantwortung etc.* überˈnehmen, eingehen; **4.** sich erbieten, sich verpflichten (**to do** zu tun); **5.** garantieren, sich verbürgen (**that** daß); **ˈ~ˌtak·er** *s.* Leichenbestatter *m*, Beˈstattungsinstiˌtut *n*; **ˌ~ˈtak·ing** *s.* **1.** ˈÜbernahme *f e-r Aufgabe*; **2.** Unterˈnehmung *f*, -ˈfangen *n*; **3.** † Unterˈnehmen *n*, Betrieb *m*: **industrial ~**; **4.** Verpflichtung *f*; **5.** Garanˈtie *f*; **6.** **ˈunderˌtaking** Leichenbestattung *f*; **ˌ~ˈten·ant** *s.* ˈUntermieter(in), -pächter(in); **ˌ~-the-ˈcount·er** *adj.* heimlich, dunkel, ˈilleˌgal; **ˌ~ˈtimed** *adj. phot.* ˈunterbelichtet; **ˈ~·tone** *s.* **1.** gedämpfter Ton, gedämpfte Stimme: **in an ~** halblaut; **2.** *fig.* ˈUnterton *m*; *Börse*: Grundton *m*; **3.** gedämpfte Farbe; **ˈ~·tow** *s.* ⚓ **1.** Sog *m*; **2.** ˈWidersee *f*; **ˌ~ˈval·ue** *v/t.* unterˈschätzen, ˈunterbewerten, zu gering ansetzen; **ˈ~·vest** *s.* *Brit.* ˈUnterhemd *n*; **ˈ~·wear** → **underclothes**; **ˈ~·weight I** *s.* ˈUntergewicht *n*; **II** *adj.* **ˌunderˈweight** ˈuntergewichtig: **be ~** Untergewicht haben; **ˈ~·wood** *s.* ˈUnterholz *n*, Gestrüpp *n* (*a. fig.*); **ˈ~·world** *s. allg.* ˈUnterwelt *f*; **ˈ~·write** *v/t.* [*irr.* → **write**] **1.** a) *et.* daˈrunterschreiben, b) *fig. et.* unterˈschreiben; **2.** † a) *Versicherungspolice* unterˈzeichnen, *Versicherung* überˈnehmen, b) *et.* versichern, c) die Haftung überˈnehmen für; **2.** *Aktienemission etc.* garantieren; **ˈ~ˌwrit·er** *s.* † **1.** Versicherer *m*, Versicherung(sgesellschaft) *f*; **2.** Mitglied *n e-s* Emissiˈonskonˌsortiums; **3.** Verˈsicherungsaˌgent *m*; **ˈ~ˌwrit·ing** *s.* † **1.** (See)Versicherung(sgeschäft *n*) *f*; **2.** Emissiˈonsgaranˌtie *f*: **~ syndicate** Emissionskonsortium *n*.

ˌun·deˈserved *adj.* unverdient; **ˌun·deˈserv·ed·ly** [-ɪdlɪ] *adv.* unverdientermaßen; **ˌun·deˈserv·ing** *adj.* □ unwert, unwürdig (**of** *gen.*): **be ~ of** kein *Mitgefühl etc.* verdienen.

ˌun·deˈsigned *adj.* □ unbeabsichtigt, unabsichtlich; **ˌun·deˈsign·ing** *adj.* ehrlich, aufrichtig.

ˈun·deˌsir·aˈbil·i·ty *s.* Unerwünschtheit *f*; **ˌun·deˈsir·a·ble I** *adj.* □ **1.** nicht wünschenswert; **2.** unerwünscht, lästig:

~ *alien*; II *s.* **3.** unerwünschte Per'son; ˌ**un·de'sired** *adj.* unerwünscht, 'unwillˌkommen; ˌ**un·de'sir·ous** *adj.* nicht begierig (***of*** nach): ***be ~ of*** *et.* nicht wünschen *od.* (haben) wollen.
ˌ**un·de'tach·a·ble** *adj.* nicht (ab)trennbar *od.* abnehmbar.
ˌ**un·de'tect·ed** *adj.* unentdeckt.
ˌ**un·de'ter·mined** *adj.* **1.** unentschieden, schwebend, offen: ***an ~ question***; **2.** unbestimmt, vage; **3.** unentschlossen, unschlüssig.
ˌ**un·de'terred** *adj.* nicht abgeschreckt, unbeeindruckt (***by*** von).
ˌ**un·de'vel·oped** *adj.* **1.** unentwickelt; **2.** unerschlossen (*Gebiet*).
un·de·vi·at·ing [ʌn'di:vɪeɪtɪŋ] *adj.* □ **1.** nicht abweichend; **2.** unentwegt, unbeirrbar.
un·dies ['ʌndɪz] *s. pl.* F ('Damen-) ˌUnterwäsche *f.*
'**unˌdif·fer'en·ti·at·ed** *adj.* undifferenziert.
ˌ**un·di'gest·ed** *adj.* unverdaut (*a. fig.*).
un'dig·ni·fied *adj.* würdelos.
ˌ**un·di'lut·ed** *adj.* unverdünnt, *a. fig.* unverwässert, unverfälscht.
ˌ**un·di'min·ished** *adj.* unvermindert.
ˌ**un·di'rect·ed** *adj.* **1.** ungeleitet, führungslos, ungelenkt; **2.** unadressiert; **3.** *phys.* ungerichtet.
ˌ**un·dis'cerned** *adj.* □ unbemerkt; ˌ**un·dis'cern·ing** *adj.* □ urteils-, einsichtslos, unkritisch.
ˌ**un·dis'charged** *adj.* **1.** unbezahlt; unbeglichen; **2.** (noch) nicht entlastet: ***~ debtor***; **3.** nicht abgeschossen (*Feuerwaffe*); **4.** nicht entladen (*Schiff etc.*).
un'dis·ci·plined *adj.* **1.** undiszipliniert, zuchtlos; **2.** ungeschult.
ˌ**un·dis'closed** *adj.* ungenannt, geheimgehalten, nicht bekanntgegeben.
ˌ**un·dis'cour·aged** *adj.* nicht entmutigt.
ˌ**un·dis'cov·er·a·ble** *adj.* unauffindbar, nicht zu entdecken(d); ˌ**un·dis'cov·ered** *adj.* **1.** unentdeckt; **2.** unbemerkt.
ˌ**un·dis'crim·i·nat·ing** *adj.* □ **1.** unterschiedslos; **2.** urteilslos, unkritisch.
ˌ**un·dis'cussed** *adj.* unerörtert.
ˌ**un·dis'guised** *adj.* □ **1.** unverkleidet, unmaskiert; **2.** *fig.* unverhüllt.
ˌ**un·dis'mayed** *adj.* unerschrocken.
ˌ**un·dis'posed** *adj.* **1.** ***~ of*** nicht verteilt *od.* vergeben, ☨ *a.* unverkauft; **2.** abgeneigt, nicht bereit *od.* (dazu) aufgelegt (***to do*** zu tun).
ˌ**un·dis'put·ed** *adj.* □ unbestritten.
ˌ**un·dis'tin·guish·a·ble** *adj.* □ **1.** nicht erkenn- *od.* wahrnehmbar; **2.** nicht unter'scheidbar, nicht zu unter'scheiden(d) (***from*** von); ˌ**un·dis'tinguished** *adj.* **1.** sich nicht unter'scheidend (***from*** von); **2.** 'durchschnittlich, nor'mal; **3.** → ***undistinguishable.***
ˌ**un·dis'turbed** *adj.* □ **1.** ungestört; **2.** unberührt, gelassen.
ˌ**un·di'vid·ed** *adj.* □ **1.** ungeteilt (*a. fig. Aufmerksamkeit etc.*); **2.** ☨ nicht verteilt: ***~ profits.***
un·do [ˌʌn'du:] *v/t.* [*irr.* → ***do***] **1.** *Paket, Knoten, a. Kragen, Mantel etc.* aufmachen, öffnen; aufknöpfen, -knüpfen, -lösen; losbinden; *j-m* den Reißverschluß *etc.* aufmachen; *Saum etc.* auftrennen; → ***undone***; **2.** *fig.* ungeschehen *od.* rückgängig machen, aufheben; **3.** *fig. et. od. j-n* ruinieren, zu'grunde richten; *Hoffnungen etc.* zu'nichte machen; ˌ**un'do·ing** *s.* **1.** *das* Aufmachen *etc.*; **2.** Ungeschehen-, Rückgängigmachen *n*; **3.** Zu'grunderichtung *f*; **4.** Unglück *n*, Verderben *n*, Ru'in *m*; ˌ**un'done I** *p.p. von* ***undo***; **II** *adj.* **1.** ungetan, unerledigt: ***leave s.th. ~*** et. unausgeführt lassen, et. unterlassen; ***leave nothing ~*** nichts unversucht lassen; **2.** offen: ***come ~*** aufgehen; **3.** ruiniert, ‚erledigt', ‚hin': ***he is ~*** es ist aus mit ihm.
un·doubt·ed [ʌn'daʊtɪd] *adj.* □ unbezweifelt, unbestritten; unzweifelhaft; **un'doubt·ed·ly** [-lɪ] *adv.* zweifellos, ohne (jeden) Zweifel.
un·dreamed, *a.* **un·dreamt** [*beide* ʌn'dremt] *adj. oft* ***~-of*** ungeahnt, nie erträumt, unerhört.
ˌ**un'dress I** *v/t.* **1.** (*v/i.* sich) entkleiden *od.* ausziehen; **II** *s.* **2.** Alltagskleid(ung *f*) *n*; **3.** Hauskleid *n*; **4.** ***in a state of ~*** a) halb bekleidet, im Negligé, b) unbekleidet; **5.** ⚔ 'Interimsuniˌform *f*; ˌ**un'dressed** *adj.* **1.** unbekleidet; **2.** *Küche*: a) ungarniert, b) unzubereitet; **3.** ⚙ a) ungegerbt (*Leder*), b) unbehauen (*Holz, Stein*); **4.** ⚕ unverbunden (*Wunde etc.*).
ˌ**un'drink·a·ble** *adj.* nicht trinkbar.
ˌ**un'due** *adj.* (□ → ***unduly***) **1.** 'übermäßig, über'trieben; **2.** ungehörig, unangebracht, ungebührlich; **3.** *bsd.* ⚖ unzulässig: ***~ influence*** unzulässige Beeinflussung; **4.** ☨ noch nicht fällig.
un·du·late ['ʌndjʊleɪt] **I** *v/i.* **1.** wogen, wallen, sich wellenförmig (fort)bewegen; **2.** wellenförmig verlaufen; **II** *v/t.* **3.** in wellenförmige Bewegung versetzen, wogen lassen; **4.** wellen; **III** *adj.* □ **5.** → '**un·du·lat·ed** [-tɪd] *adj.* wellenförmig, wellig, Wellen...: ***~ line*** Wellenlinie *f*; '**un·du·lat·ing** [-tɪŋ] *adj.* □ **1.** → ***undulated***; **2.** wallend, wogend; **un·du·la·tion** [ˌʌndjʊ'leɪʃn] *s.* **1.** wellenförmige Bewegung; Wallen *n*, Wogen *n*; **2.** *geol.* Welligkeit *f*; **3.** *phys.* Wellenbewegung *f*, -linie *f*; **4.** *phys.* Schwingung(sbewegung) *f*; **5.** ♪ Undulati'on *f*; '**un·du·la·to·ry** [-lətrɪ] *adj.* wellenförmig, Wellen...
ˌ**un'du·ly** *adv. von* ***undue*** 1–3: ***not ~ worried*** nicht übermäßig *od.* über Gebühr besorgt.
ˌ**un'du·ti·ful** *adj.* □ **1.** pflichtvergessen; **2.** ungehorsam; **3.** unehrerbietig.
un'dy·ing *adj.* □ **1.** unsterblich, unvergänglich (*Liebe, Ruhm etc.*); **2.** unendlich (*Haß etc.*).
ˌ**un'earned** *adj.* unverdient, nicht erarbeitet: ***~ income*** ☨ Einkommen *n* aus Vermögen, Kapitaleinkommen *n*.
ˌ**un'earth** *v/t.* **1.** *Tier* aus der Höhle treiben; **2.** ausgraben (*a. fig.*); **3.** *fig. et.* ans (Tages)Licht bringen, aufstöbern, ausfindig machen.
un'earth·ly *adj.* **1.** 'überirdisch; **2.** unirdisch, 'übernaˌtürlich; **3.** schauerlich, unheimlich; **4.** F unmöglich (*Zeit*): ***at an ~ hour.***
un'eas·i·ness *s.* **1.** (*körperliches u. geistiges*) Unbehagen; **2.** (innere) Unruhe; **3.** Unbehaglichkeit *f e-s Gefühls etc.*; **4.** Unsicherheit *f*; **un'eas·y** *adj.* □ **1.** unruhig, unbehaglich, besorgt, ner'vös: ***feel ~ about s.th.*** über et. beunruhigt sein; **2.** unbehaglich (*Gefühl*), beunruhigend (*Verdacht etc.*); **3.** unruhig: ***~ night***; **4.** unsicher (*im Sattel etc.*); **5.** gezwungen, unsicher (*Benehmen etc.*).
ˌ**un'eat·a·ble** *adj.* ungenießbar.
'**unˌe·co'nom·ic**, '**unˌe·co'nom·i·cal** *adj.* □ unwirtschaftlich.
ˌ**un'ed·i·fy·ing** *adj. fig.* wenig erbaulich, unerquicklich.
ˌ**un'ed·u·cat·ed** *adj.* ungebildet.
ˌ**un·em'bar·rassed** *adj.* **1.** nicht verlegen, ungeniert; **2.** unbehindert; **3.** von (Geld)Sorgen frei.
ˌ**un·e'mo·tion·al** *adj.* □ **1.** leidenschaftslos, nüchtern; **2.** teilnahmslos, passiv, kühl; **3.** gelassen.
ˌ**un·em'ploy·a·ble I** *adj.* **1.** nicht verwendbar, unbrauchbar; **2.** arbeitsunfähig (*Person*); **II** *s.* **3.** Arbeitsunfähige(r *m*) *f*; ˌ**un·em'ployed I** *adj.* **1.** arbeits-, erwerbs-, stellungslos; **2.** ungenützt, brachliegend: ***~ capital*** ☨ totes Kapital; **II** *s.* **3.** ***the ~*** *pl.* die Arbeitslosen *pl.*; ˌ**~·em'ploy·ment** *s.* Arbeitslosigkeit *f*: ***~ benefit*** Arbeitslosenunterstützung *f*; ***~ insurance*** Arbeitslosenversicherung *f*.
ˌ**un·en'cum·bered** *adj.* **1.** ⚖ unbelastet (*Grundbesitz*); **2.** (***by***) unbehindert (durch), frei (von).
un'end·ing *adj.* □ endlos, nicht enden wollend, unaufhörlich.
ˌ**un·en'dowed** *adj.* **1.** nicht ausgestattet (***with*** mit); **2.** nicht dotiert (***with*** mit), ohne Zuschuß; **3.** nicht begabt (***with*** mit).
ˌ**un·en'dur·a·ble** *adj.* □ unerträglich.
ˌ**un·en'gaged** *adj.* frei: a) nicht gebunden *od.* verpflichtet, b) nicht verlobt, c) unbeschäftigt.
ˌ**un-'Eng·lish** *adj.* unenglisch.
ˌ**un·en'light·ened** *adj. fig.* **1.** unerleuchtet; **2.** unaufgeklärt.
ˌ**un'en·ter·pris·ing** *adj.* □ nicht *od.* wenig unter'nehmungslustig, ohne Unter'nehmungsgeist.
ˌ**un'en·vi·a·ble** *adj.* □ nicht zu beneiden(d), wenig beneidenswert.
ˌ**un'e·qual** *adj.* □ **1.** ungleich (*a. Kampf*), 'unterschiedlich; **2.** nicht gewachsen (***to*** *dat.*); **3.** ungleichförmig; ˌ**un'e·qual(l)ed** *adj.* **1.** unerreicht, 'unüberˌtroffen (***by*** von, ***for*** in *od.* an *dat.*); **2.** beispiellos, *nachgestellt*: ohne'gleichen: ***~ ignorance.***
ˌ**un·e'quiv·o·cal** *adj.* □ **1.** unzweideutig, eindeutig; **2.** aufrichtig.
ˌ**un'err·ing** *adj.* □ unfehlbar, untrüglich.
ˌ**un·es'sen·tial I** *adj.* unwesentlich, unwichtig; **II** *s.* Nebensache *f*.
ˌ**un'e·ven** *adj.* □ **1.** uneben: ***~ ground***; **2.** ungerade (*Zahl*); **3.** ungleich(mäßig, -artig); **4.** unausgeglichen (*Charakter etc.*); ˌ**un'e·ven·ness** *s.* Unebenheit *f etc.*
ˌ**un·e'vent·ful** *adj.* □ ereignislos: ***be ~*** *a.* ohne Zwischenfälle verlaufen.
ˌ**un·ex'am·pled** *adj.* beispiellos, unvergleichlich, *nachgestellt*: ohne'gleichen: ***not ~*** nicht ohne Beispiel.
un·ex·celled [ˌʌnɪk'seld] *adj.* 'unüberˌtroffen.
ˌ**un·ex'cep·tion·a·ble** *adj.* □ untadelig, einwandfrei.
ˌ**un·ex'cep·tion·al** *adj.* □ **1.** nicht außergewöhnlich; **2.** ausnahmslos; **3.** →

unexceptionable.
ˌ**un·ex'cit·ing** *adj.* nicht *od.* wenig aufregend.
un·ex·pect·ed [ˌʌnɪk'spektɪd] *adj.* □ unerwartet, unvermutet.
ˌ**un·ex'pired** *adj.* (noch) nicht abgelaufen *od.* verfallen (*Frist etc.*), noch in Kraft.
ˌ**un·ex'plain·a·ble** *adj.* unerklärlich; ˌ**un·ex'plained** *adj.* unerklärt.
ˌ**un·ex'plored** *adj.* unerforscht.
ˌ**un·ex'pressed** *adj.* unausgesprochen.
ˌ**un'ex·pur·gat·ed** *adj.* nicht gereinigt, ungekürzt (*Bücher etc.*).
un'fad·ing *adj.* □ **1.** unverwelklich (*a. fig.*); **2.** *fig.* unvergänglich; **3.** nicht verblassend (*Farbe*).
un'fail·ing *adj.* □ **1.** unfehlbar; **2.** nie versagend; **3.** treu; **4.** unerschöpflich, unversiegbar.
ˌ**un'fair** *adj.* □ unfair: a) unbillig, ungerecht, b) unehrlich, *bsd.* ✝ unlauter, c) nicht anständig, d) unsportlich (*alle* ***to*** gegen'über): ~ ***competition*** unlauterer Wettbewerb; ˌ**un'fair·ly** *adv.* **1.** unfair, unbillig(erweise) *etc.*; zu Unrecht: ***not*** ~ nicht zu Unrecht; **2.** 'übermäßig; ˌ**un'fair·ness** *s.* Unfairneß *f*, Ungerechtigkeit *f etc.*
ˌ**un'faith·ful** *adj.* □ **1.** un(ge)treu, treulos; **2.** unaufrichtig; **3.** nicht wortgetreu, ungenau (*Abschrift, Übersetzung*); ˌ**un'faith·ful·ness** *s.* Untreue *f*, Treulosigkeit *f*.
un'fal·ter·ing *adj.* □ **1.** nicht schwankend, sicher (*Schritt etc.*); **2.** fest (*Stimme, Blick*); **3.** *fig.* unbeugsam, entschlossen.
ˌ**un·fa'mil·iar** *adj.* □ **1.** nicht vertraut, unbekannt (***to*** *dat.*); **2.** ungewohnt, fremd (***to*** *dat. od.* für).
ˌ**un'fash·ion·a·ble** *adj.* □ 'unmoˌdern, altmodisch.
ˌ**un'fas·ten I** *v/t.* aufmachen, losbinden, lösen, öffnen; **II** *v/i.* sich lösen, aufgehen; ˌ**un'fas·tened** *adj.* unbefestigt, lose.
ˌ**un'fa·ther·ly** *adj.* unväterlich, lieblos.
un·fath·om·a·ble [ʌn'fæðəməbl] *adj.* □ unergründlich (*a. fig.*); ˌ**un'fath·omed** *adj.* unergründet.
ˌ**un'fa·vo(u)r·a·ble** *adj.* □ **1.** unvorteilhaft (*a. Aussehen*), ungünstig (***for, to*** für); widrig (*Wetter, Umstände etc.*); **2.** ✝ passiv (*Zahlungsbilanz etc.*); ˌ**un'fa·vo(u)r·a·ble·ness** *s.* Unvorteilhaftigkeit *f*.
ˌ**un'fea·si·ble** *adj.* unausführbar.
un·feel·ing [ʌn'fiːlɪŋ] *adj.* □ gefühllos; **un'feel·ing·ness** [-nɪs] *s.* Gefühllosigkeit *f*.
un'feigned *adj.* □ **1.** ungeheuchelt, **2.** wahr, echt.
ˌ**un'felt** *adj.* ungefühlt.
ˌ**un·fer'ment·ed** *adj.* ungegoren.
ˌ**un'fet·ter** *v/t.* **1.** losketten; **2.** *fig.* befreien; ˌ**un'fet·tered** *adj. fig.* unbehindert, unbeschränkt, frei.
ˌ**un'fil·i·al** *adj.* □ lieb-, re'spektlos, pflichtvergessen (*Kind*).
ˌ**un'filled** *adj.* **1.** un(aus)gefüllt; **2.** unbesetzt (*Posten, Stelle*); **3.** ~ ***orders*** ✝ nicht ausgeführte Bestellungen, Auftragsbestand *m*.
ˌ**un'fin·ished** *adj.* **1.** unfertig (*a. fig. Stil etc.*); ⚙ unbearbeitet; **2.** 'unvollˌendet (*Symphonie etc.*); **3.** unerledigt: ~ ***business*** *parl.* unerledigte Punkte *pl.* (*der Geschäftsordnung*).
ˌ**un'fit I** *adj.* □ **1.** untauglich (*a.* ⚔), ungeeignet (***for*** für, zu): ~ ***for*** (***military***) ***service*** (wehr)dienstuntauglich; **2.** unfähig, unbefähigt (***for*** zu *et.*, ***to do*** zu tun); **II** *v/t.* **3.** ungeeignet *etc.* machen (***for*** für); ˌ**un'fit·ness** *s.* Untauglichkeit *f*; ˌ**un'fit·ted** *adj.* **1.** ungeeignet, untauglich; **2.** nicht (gut) ausgerüstet (***with*** mit); ˌ**un'fit·ting** *adj.* □ **1.** ungeeignet, unpassend; **2.** unschicklich.
ˌ**un'fix** *v/t.* losmachen, lösen: ~ ***bayonets!*** ⚔ Seitengewehr an Ort!; ˌ**un'fixed** *adj.* **1.** unbefestigt, lose; **2.** *fig.* schwankend.
ˌ**un'flag·ging** *adj.* □ unermüdlich.
ˌ**un'flap·pa·ble** *adj.* F unerschütterlich, nicht aus der Ruhe zu bringen.
ˌ**un'flat·ter·ing** *adj.* □ **1.** nicht *od.* wenig schmeichelhaft; **2.** ungeschminkt.
ˌ**un'fledged** *adj.* **1.** *orn.* ungefiedert, (noch) nicht flügge; **2.** *fig.* unreif.
un·flinch·ing [ʌn'flɪntʃɪŋ] *adj.* □ **1.** unerschütterlich, unerschrocken; **2.** entschlossen, unnachgiebig.
un·fly·a·ble [ˌʌn'flaɪəbl] *adj.* ✈ **1.** flugUntüchtig; **2.** ~ ***weather*** kein Flugwetter.
ˌ**un'fold I** *v/t.* **1.** entfalten, ausbreiten, öffnen; **2.** *fig.* a) enthüllen, darlegen, b) entwickeln; **II** *v/i.* **3.** sich entfalten *od.* öffnen; **4.** *fig.* sich entwickeln.
ˌ**un'forced** *adj.* □ ungezwungen.
ˌ**un·fore'see·a·ble** *adj.* 'unvorˌhersehbar; ˌ**un·fore'seen** *adj.* 'unvorˌhergesehen, unerwartet.
un·for·get·ta·ble [ˌʌnfə'getəbl] *adj.* □ unvergeßlich: ***of*** ~ ***beauty***.
un·for·giv·a·ble [ˌʌnfə'gɪvəbl] *adj.* unverzeihlich; ˌ**un·for'giv·en** *adj.* unverziehen; ˌ**un·for'giv·ing** *adj.* □ unversöhnlich, nachtragend.
ˌ**un·for'got·ten** *adj.* unvergessen.
ˌ**un'formed** *adj.* **1.** ungeformt, formlos; **2.** unfertig, unentwickelt; unausgebildet.
un'for·tu·nate I *adj.* □ **1.** unglücklich, Unglücks...; verhängnisvoll, un(glück)selig; **2.** bedauerlich; **II** *s.* **3.** Unglückliche(r *m*) *f*; **un'for·tu·nate·ly** *adv.* unglücklicherweise, bedauerlicherweise, leider.
ˌ**un'found·ed** *adj.* □ unbegründet, grundlos.
ˌ**un'freeze** *v/t.* **1.** auftauen; **2.** ✝ *Preise etc.* freigeben; **3.** *Gelder* zur Auszahlung freigeben.
ˌ**un·fre'quent·ed** *adj.* **1.** nicht *od.* wenig besucht; **2.** einsam.
ˌ**un'friend·ed** *adj.* ohne Freund(e).
ˌ**un'friend·li·ness** *s.* Unfreundlichkeit *f*; ˌ**un'friend·ly** *adj.* **1.** unfreundlich (*a. fig. Zimmer etc.*) (***to*** zu); **2.** ungünstig (***for, to*** für).
ˌ**un'frock** *v/t. eccl. j-m* das Priesteramt entziehen.
ˌ**un'fruit·ful** *adj.* □ **1.** unfruchtbar; **2.** *fig.* frucht-, ergebnislos; ˌ**un'fruit·ful·ness** *s.* **1.** Unfruchtbarkeit *f*; **2.** *fig.* Fruchtlosigkeit *f*.
ˌ**un'fund·ed** *adj.* ✝ unfundiert.
ˌ**un'furl I** *v/t. Fahne etc.* entfalten, -rollen; *Fächer* ausbreiten; ⚓ *Segel* losmachen; **II** *v/i.* sich entfalten.
ˌ**un'fur·nished** *adj.* **1.** nicht ausgerüstet *od.* versehen (***with*** mit); **2.** unmöbliert: ~ ***room***.
un·gain·li·ness [ʌn'geɪnlɪnɪs] *s.* Plumpheit *f*, Unbeholfenheit *f*; **un·gain·ly** [ʌn'geɪnlɪ] *adj.* unbeholfen, plump, linkisch.
ˌ**un'gal·lant** *adj.* □ **1.** 'ungaˌlant (***to*** zu, gegenüber); **2.** nicht tapfer.
ˌ**un'gear** *v/t.* ⚙ auskuppeln.
ˌ**un'gen·er·ous** *adj.* □ **1.** nicht freigebig, knauserig; **2.** kleinlich.
ˌ**un'gen·ial** *adj.* unfreundlich.
ˌ**un'gen·tle** *adj.* □ unsanft, unzart.
un'gen·tle·man·like → ***ungentlemanly***; **un'gen·tle·man·li·ness** *s.* **1.** unfeine Art; **2.** ungebildetes *od.* unfeines Benehmen; **un'gen·tle·man·ly** *adj.* unfein.
un·get-at-a·ble [ˌʌnget'ætəbl] *adj.* unnahbar.
ˌ**un'gird** *v/t.* losgürten.
ˌ**un'glazed** *adj.* **1.** unverglast; **2.** unglasiert.
ˌ**un'gloved** *adj.* ohne Handschuh(e).
ˌ**un'god·li·ness** *s.* Gottlosigkeit *f*; ˌ**un'god·ly** *adj.* **1.** gottlos (*a. weitS. verrucht*); **2.** F scheußlich, schrecklich, heillos.
un·gov·ern·a·ble [ˌʌn'gʌvənəbl] *adj.* □ **1.** unlenksam; **2.** zügellos, unbändig, wild; ˌ**un'gov·erned** *adj.* unbeherrscht.
ˌ**un'grace·ful** *adj.* □ 'ungraziˌös, ohne Anmut; plump, ungelenk.
ˌ**un'gra·cious** *adj.* □ ungnädig.
ˌ**un·gram'mat·i·cal** *adj.* □ *ling.* 'ungramˌmatisch.
un'grate·ful *adj.* □ undankbar (***to*** gegen) (*a. fig. unangenehm*); **un'grate·ful·ness** *s.* Undankbarkeit *f*.
ˌ**un'grat·i·fied** *adj.* unbefriedigt.
ˌ**un'ground·ed** *adj.* □ **1.** unbegründet; **2.** a) ungeschult, b) ohne sichere Grundlagen (*Wissen*).
ˌ**un'grudg·ing** *adj.* □ **1.** bereitwillig; **2.** neidlos, großzügig: ***be*** ~ ***in*** reichlich *Lob etc.* spenden.
un·gual ['ʌŋgwəl] *adj. zo.* Nagel..., Klauen..., Huf...
ˌ**un'guard·ed** *adj.* □ **1.** unbewacht (*a. fig. Moment etc.*); *a.* ⚙ ungeschützt; *a. sport, Schach*: ungedeckt; **2.** unbedacht.
un·guent ['ʌŋgwənt] *s.* Salbe *f*.
ˌ**un'guid·ed** *adj.* **1.** ungeleitet, führer-, führungslos; **2.** nicht (fern)gelenkt.
un·gu·late ['ʌŋgjʊleɪt] *zo.* **I** *adj.* hufförmig; mit Hufen; Huf...: ~ ***animal*** → **II** *s.* Huftier *n*.
ˌ**un'hal·lowed** *adj.* **1.** nicht geheiligt, ungeweiht; **2.** unheilig, pro'fan.
ˌ**un'ham·pered** *adj.* ungehindert.
ˌ**un'hand** *v/t. obs. j-n* loslassen.
ˌ**un'hand·i·ness** *s.* **1.** Unhandlichkeit *f*; **2.** Ungeschick(lichkeit *f*) *n*.
ˌ**un'hand·some** *adj.* □ unschön (*a. fig. Benehmen etc.*).
ˌ**un'hand·y** *adj.* □ **1.** unhandlich (*Sache*); **2.** unbeholfen, ungeschickt.
un'hap·pi·ly *adv.* unglücklicherweise, leider; **un'hap·pi·ness** *s.* Unglück(seligkeit *f*) *n*, Elend *n*; **un'hap·py** *adj.* □ unglücklich: a) traurig, elend, b) un(glück)selig, unheilvoll, c) unpassend, ungeschickt (*Bemerkung etc.*).
ˌ**un'harmed** *adj.* unversehrt.
ˌ**un·har'mo·ni·ous** *adj.* 'unharˌmonisch (*a. fig.*).
ˌ**un'har·ness** *v/t. Pferd* ausspannen.

un'health·i·ness *s.* Ungesundheit *f*; **un'health·y** *adj.* □ *allg.* ungesund: a) kränklich (*a. Aussehen etc.*), b) gesundheitsschädlich, c) (*moralisch*) schädlich, d) F gefährlich, e) *fig.* krankhaft.

ˌun'heard *adj.* **1.** ungehört: ***go ~*** unbeachtet bleiben; **2.** ⚖ ohne rechtliches Gehör; **ˌun'heard-of** *adj.* unerhört, beispiellos.

un·heed·ed [ˌʌn'hi:dɪd] *adj.* □ unbeachtet: ***go ~*** unbeachtet bleiben; **ˌun'heed·ful** *adj.* □ unachtsam, sorglos; nicht achtend (***of*** auf *acc.*); **ˌun'heed·ing** [-dɪŋ] *adj.* □ sorglos, unachtsam.

ˌun'help·ful *adj.* □ **1.** nicht hilfreich, ungefällig; **2.** (***to***) nutzlos (für), wenig dienlich (*dat.*).

un·hes·i·tat·ing [ʌn'hezɪteɪtɪŋ] *adj.* □ **1.** ohne Zaudern *od.* Zögern, unverzüglich; **2.** anstandslos, bereitwillig, *adv. a.* ohne weiteres.

ˌun'hin·dered *adj.* ungehindert.

ˌun'hinge *v/t.* **1.** *Tür etc.* aus den Angeln heben (*a. fig.*); **2.** die Angeln entfernen von; **3.** *fig. Nerven, Geist* zerrütten; **4.** *fig. j-n* aus dem Gleichgewicht bringen.

ˌun·his'tor·ic, **ˌun·his'tor·i·cal** *adj.* □ **1.** 'unhiˌstorisch; **2.** ungeschichtlich, legen'där.

ˌun'hitch *v/t.* **1.** loshaken, -machen; **2.** *Pferd* ausspannen.

ˌun'ho·ly *adj.* □ **1.** unheilig; **2.** ungeheiligt, nicht geweiht; **3.** gott-, ruchlos; **4.** F a) scheußlich, schrecklich, b) ‚unmöglich' (*Zeit*).

ˌun'hon·o(u)red *adj.* **1.** ungeehrt; unverehrt; **2.** ♆ nicht honoriert.

ˌun'hook I *v/t.* auf-, loshaken; **II** *v/i.* sich auf- *od.* loshaken (lassen).

un'hoped, **un'hoped-for** *adj.* unverhofft, unerwartet.

ˌun'horse *v/t.* aus dem Sattel heben *od.* werfen.

ˌun'house *v/t.* **1.** (aus dem Hause) vertreiben; **2.** obdachlos machen.

ˌun'hur·ried *adj.* □ gemütlich, gemächlich.

ˌun'hurt *adj.* **1.** unverletzt; **2.** unbeschädigt.

u·ni·cel·lu·lar [ˌju:nɪ'seljʊlə] *adj. biol.* einzellig: ***~ animal***, ***~ plant*** Einzeller *m.*

u·ni·col·o(u)r [ˌju:nɪ'kʌlə], **ˌu·ni'col·o(u)red** [-əd] *adj.* einfarbig.

u·ni·corn ['ju:nɪkɔ:n] *s.* Einhorn *n.*

un·i·de·aed [ˌʌnaɪ'dɪəd] *adj.* i'deenlos.

ˌun·i'den·ti·fied *adj.* nicht identifiziert, unbekannt: ***~ flying object*** unbekanntes Flugobjekt.

u·ni·di·men·sion·al [ˌju:nɪdɪ'menʃənl] *adj.* 'eindimensioˌnal.

u·ni·fi·ca·tion [ˌju:nɪfɪ'keɪʃn] *s.* **1.** Vereinigung *f*; **2.** Vereinheitlichung *f.*

u·ni·form ['ju:nɪfɔ:m] **I** *adj.* □ **1.** gleich (-förmig), uni'form; **2.** gleichbleibend, -mäßig, kon'stant; **3.** einheitlich, über'einstimmend, gleich, Einheits...; **4.** einförmig, -tönig; **II** *s.* **5.** Uni'form *f*, Dienstkleidung *f*; (Schwestern)Tracht *f*; **III** *v/t.* **6.** uniformieren (*a.* ⚔ *etc.*): ***~ed*** uniformiert, in Uniform; **u·ni·form·i·ty** [ju:nɪ'fɔ:mətɪ] *s.* **1.** Gleichförmigkeit *f*, -mäßigkeit *f*, Gleichheit *f*, Über'einstimmung *f*; **2.** Einheitlichkeit *f*; **3.** Einförmigkeit *f*, -tönigkeit *f.*

u·ni·fy ['ju:nɪfaɪ] *v/t.* **1.** verein(ig)en, zs.-schließen; **2.** vereinheitlichen.

u·ni·lat·er·al [ˌju:nɪ'lætərəl] *adj.* □ einseitig (*a.* ⚕ *u.* ⚖).

ˌun·il'lu·mi·nat·ed *adj.* **1.** unerleuchtet (*a. fig.*); **2.** *fig.* unwissend.

ˌun·im'ag·i·na·ble *adj.* □ unvorstellbar; **ˌun·im'ag·i·na·tive** *adj.* □ phantasielos, einfallslos; **ˌun·im'ag·ined** *adj.* ungeahnt.

ˌun·im'paired *adj.* unvermindert, unbeeinträchtigt, ungeschmälert.

ˌun·im'pas·sioned *adj.* leidenschaftslos.

ˌun·im'peach·a·ble *adj.* □ **1.** unanfechtbar; **2.** untad(e)lig.

ˌun·im'ped·ed *adj.* □ ungehindert.

ˌun·im'por·tant *adj.* unwichtig.

ˌun·im'pos·ing *adj.* nicht imponierend *od.* impo'sant, eindruckslos.

ˌun·im'pres·sion·a·ble *adj.* nicht zu beeindrucken(d), (für Eindrücke) unempfänglich.

ˌun·im'pres·sive → ***unimposing.***

ˌun·in'flect·ed *adj. ling.* unflektiert.

ˌun'in·flu·enced *adj.* unbeeinflußt (***by*** durch, von); **'unˌin·flu'en·tial** *adj.* ohne Einfluß, nicht einflußreich.

ˌun·in'formed *adj.* **1.** (***on***) nicht informiert *od.* unter'richtet (über *acc.*), nicht eingeweiht (in *acc.*); **2.** ungebildet.

ˌun·in'hab·it·a·ble *adj.* unbewohnbar; **ˌun·in'hab·it·ed** *adj.* unbewohnt.

ˌun·in'i·ti·at·ed *adj.* uneingeweiht, nicht eingeführt (***into*** in *acc.*).

ˌun'in·jured *adj.* **1.** unverletzt; **2.** unbeschädigt.

ˌun·in'spired *adj.* schwunglos, ohne Feuer; **ˌun·in'spir·ing** *adj.* nicht begeisternd, wenig anregend.

ˌun·in'struct·ed *adj.* **1.** nicht unter'richtet, unwissend; **2.** nicht instruiert, ohne Verhaltensmaßregeln; **ˌun·in'struc·tive** *adj.* nicht *od.* wenig instruk'tiv *od.* lehrreich.

ˌun·in'sured *adj.* unversichert.

ˌun·in'tel·li·gent *adj.* □ 'unintelliˌgent, beschränkt, geistlos, dumm.

'un·inˌtel·li·gi'bil·i·ty *s.* Unverständlichkeit *f*; **ˌun·in'tel·li·gi·ble** *adj.* □ unverständlich.

ˌun·in'tend·ed *adj.*, **ˌun·in'ten·tion·al** *adj.* □ unbeabsichtigt, unabsichtlich, ungewollt.

ˌun'in·ter·est·ed *adj.* □ inter'esselos, uninteressiert (***in*** an *dat.*), gleichgültig; **ˌun'in·ter·est·ing** *adj.* □ 'uninteresˌsant.

'unˌin·ter'rupt·ed *adj.* □ 'ununterˌbrochen: a) ungestört (***by*** von), b) kontinuierlich, fortlaufend, anhaltend: ***~ working hours*** durchgehende Arbeitszeit.

ˌun·in'vit·ed *adj.* un(ein)geladen; **ˌun·in'vit·ing** *adj.* □ nicht *od.* wenig einladend *od.* verlockend *od.* anziehend.

un·ion ['ju:njən] *s.* **1.** *allg.* Vereinigung *f*, (*a. eheliche*) Verbindung; **2.** Eintracht *f*, Harmo'nie *f*; **3.** *pol.* Zs.-schluß *m*; **4.** *pol. etc.* Uni'on *f*: a) (Staaten-) Bund *m*, *z.B. die U.S.A. pl.*, b) Vereinigung *f*, (Zweck)Verband *m*, Bund *m*, (*a. Post-, Zoll- etc.*)Verein *m*, c) *Brit. Vereinigung unabhängiger Kirchen*; **5.** Gewerkschaft *f*: ***~ dues*** *pl.* Gewerkschaftsbeitrag *m*; **6.** *Brit. hist.* a) *Kirchspielverband zur Armenpflege*, b) Armenhaus *n*; **7.** ⚙ Anschlußstück *n*, (Rohr)Verbindung *f*; **8.** ⚙ Mischgewebe *n*; **9.** ⚓ Gösch *f* (*Flaggenfeld mit Hoheitsabzeichen*): ***~ flag*** → ***union jack*** 1; **'un·ion·ism** [-nɪzəm] *s.* **1.** *pol.* Unio'nismus *m*, unio'nistische Bestrebungen *pl.*; **2.** Gewerkschaftswesen *n*; **'un·ion·ist** [-nɪst] *s.* **1.** ℒ *pol. hist.* Unio'nist *m*; **2.** Gewerkschaftler *m*; **'un·ion·ize** [-naɪz] *v/t.* gewerkschaftlich organisieren.

un·ion| jack *s.* **1.** ***Union Jack*** Union Jack *m* (*brit. Nationalflagge*); **2.** ⚓ → ***union*** 9; **~ joint** *s.* Rohrverbindung *f*; **~ shop** *s.* ♆ *bsd. Am. Betrieb, der nur Gewerkschaftsmitglieder einstellt od. Arbeitnehmer, die bereit sind, innerhalb von 30 Tagen der Gewerkschaft beizutreten*; **~ suit** *s. Am.* Hemdhose *f* mit langem Bein.

u·nip·a·rous [ju:'nɪpərəs] *adj.* **1.** ⚕ erst einmal geboren habend; **2.** *zo.* nur 'ein Junges gebärend (*bei e-m Wurf*); **2.** ⚘ nur 'eine Achse *od.* 'einen Ast treibend.

u·ni·par·tite [ˌju:nɪ'pɑ:taɪt] *adj.* einteilig.

u·ni·po·lar [ˌju:nɪ'pəʊlə] *adj.* **1.** *phys.*, ϟ einpolig, Einpol...; **2.** *anat.* monopo'lar (*Nervenzelle*).

u·nique [ju:'ni:k] **I** *adj.* □ **1.** einzig; **2.** einmalig, einzigartig; unerreicht, *nachgestellt*: ohne'gleichen; **3.** F außer-, ungewöhnlich; großartig; **4.** 𝔄 eindeutig; **II** *s.* **5.** Seltenheit *f*, Unikum *n*; **u'nique·ness** [-nɪs] *s.* Einzigartig-, Einmaligkeit *f.*

'u·ni·sex *adj.* Unisex...

ˌu·ni'sex·u·al *adj.* □ **1.** eingeschlechtig; **2.** *zo.*, ⚘ getrenntgeschlechtlich.

u·ni·son ['ju:nɪzn] *s.* **1.** ♪ Ein-, Gleichklang *m*, Uni'sono *n*: ***in ~*** unisono, einstimmig (*a. fig.*); **2.** *fig.* Einklang *m*, Über'einstimmung *f*: ***in ~ with*** in Einklang mit; **u·nis·o·nous** [ju:'nɪsənəs] *adj.* **1.** ♪ a) gleichklingend, b) einstimmig; **2.** *fig.* über'einstimmend.

u·nit ['ju:nɪt] *s.* **1.** *allg.* Einheit *f* (*Einzelding*): ***~ of account*** (***trade***, ***value***) ♆ (Ver)Rechnungs- (Handels-, Währungs)einheit; ***dwelling ~*** Wohneinheit; ***~ factor*** *biol.* Erbfaktor *m*; ***~ furniture*** Anbaumöbel *pl.*; ***~ price*** ♆ Einheitspreis *m*; ***~ wages*** ♆ Stück-, Akkordlohn *m*; **2.** *phys.* (Grund-, Maß-) Einheit *f*: ***~*** (***of***) ***power*** (***time***) Leistungs- (Zeit)einheit; **3.** 𝔄 Einer *m*, Einheit *f*; **4.** ⚔ Einheit *f*, Verband *m*, Truppenteil *m*; **5.** ⚙ a) (Bau)Einheit *f*, b) Aggre'gat *n*, Anlage *f*: ***~ construction*** Baukastenbauweise *f*; **6.** *fig.* Kern *m*, Zelle *f*: ***the family as the ~ of society.***

U·ni·tar·i·an [ˌju:nɪ'teərɪən] **I** *s. eccl.* Uni'tarier(in); **II** *adj.* uni'tarisch; **ˌU·ni'tar·i·an·ism** [-nɪzəm] *s. eccl.* Unita'rismus *m*; **u·ni·tar·y** ['ju:nɪtərɪ] *adj.* Einheits... (*a.* ϟ), 𝔄 *a.* uni'tär; einheitlich.

u·nite [ju:'naɪt] **I** *v/t.* **1.** verbinden (*a.* ⚗, ⚙), vereinigen; **2.** (ehelich) verbinden, verheiraten; **3.** *Eigenschaften* in sich vereinigen; **II** *v/i.* **4.** sich vereinigen; **5.** ⚗, ⚙ sich verbinden (***with*** mit); **6.** sich zs.-tun: ***~ in doing s.th.*** et. geschlossen *od.* vereint tun; **7.** sich anschließen (***with*** *dat. od.* an *acc.*); **8.** sich verheiraten; **u'nit·ed** [-tɪd] *adj.* vereinigt; vereint (*Kräfte etc.*), gemeinsam: ℒ ***Kingdom*** *das* Vereinigte König-

reich (*Großbritannien u. Nordirland*); ♀ ***Nations*** Vereinte Nationen; ♀ ***States*** *die* Vereinigten Staaten *von Nordamerika, die* U.S.A. *pl.*
u·nit·ize ['ju:nɪtaɪz] *v/t.* **1.** zu e-r Einheit machen; **2.** ⚙ nach dem 'Baukastenprin͵zip konstruieren; **3.** in Einheiten verpacken.
u·nit trust *s.* ✝ In'vestmenttrust *m.*
u·ni·ty ['ju:nətɪ] *s.* **1.** Einheit *f* (*a.* ⅌, ⚖): ***the dramatic unities*** *thea.* die drei Einheiten; **2.** Einheitlichkeit *f* (*a. e-s Kunstwerks*); **3.** Einigkeit *f*, Eintracht *f*: ~ (***of sentiment***) Einmütigkeit *f*; ***at*** ~ in Eintracht, im Einklang; **4.** *nationale etc.* Einheit.
u·ni·va·lent [͵ju:nɪ'veɪlənt] *adj.* ⚗ einwertig.
u·ni·ver·sal [͵ju:nɪ'vɜ:sl] **I** *adj.* □ **1.** ('all)um͵fassend, univer'sal, Universal…(*-genie, -erbe etc.*), gesamt, glo'bal: ~ ***knowledge*** umfassendes Wissen; ~ ***succession*** ⚖ Gesamtnachfolge *f*; **2.** allgemein (*a. Wahlrecht, Wehrpflicht etc.*): ~ ***partnership*** ⚖ allgemeine Gütergemeinschaft; ***the disappointment was*** ~ die Enttäuschung war allgemein; **3.** allgemein(gültig), univer'sell: ~ ***rule***; ~ ***remedy*** ⚕ Universalmittel *n*; **4.** allgemein, 'überall üblich *od.* anzutreffen(d); **5.** 'weltum͵fassend, Welt…: ~ ***language*** Weltsprache *f*; ♀ ***Postal Union*** Weltpostverein *m*; ~ ***time*** Weltzeit *f*; **6.** ⚙ Universal…(*-gerät etc.*): ~ ***current*** ⚡ Allstrom *m*; ~ ***joint*** Universal-, Kardangelenk *n*; **II** *s.* **7.** *das* Allgemeine; **8.** *Logik*: allgemeine Aussage; **9.** *phls.* Allgemeinbegriff *m*; ͵**u·ni'ver·sal·ism** [-səlɪzəm] *s. eccl., phls.* Universa'lismus *m*; **u·ni·ver·sal·i·ty** [͵ju:nɪvɜ:'sælətɪ] *s.* **1.** *das* 'Allum͵fassende, Allgemeinheit *f*; **2.** Universali'tät *f*, Vielseitigkeit *f*, um'fassende Bildung; **3.** Allgemeingültigkeit *f*; ͵**u·ni'ver·sal·ize** [-səlaɪz] *v/t.* allgemeingültig machen; allgemein verbreiten; **u·ni·verse** ['ju:nɪvɜ:s] *s.* **1.** Uni'versum *n*, (Welt)All *n*, Kosmos *m*; **2.** Welt *f*; ͵**u·ni'ver·si·ty** [-sətɪ] **I** *s.* Universi'tät *f*, Hochschule *f*: ***Open*** ♀, ♀ ***of the Air*** Fernsehuniversität *f*; ***at the*** ♀ ***of Oxford***, ***at Oxford*** ♀ auf *od.* an der Universität Oxford; **II** *adj.* Universitäts…, Hochschul…, aka'demisch: ~ ***education*** Hochschulbildung *f*; ~ ***extension*** *Art* Volkshochschule *f*; ~ ***man*** Akademiker *m*; ~ ***place*** Studienplatz *m*; ~ ***professor*** ordentlicher Professor.
u·ni·vo·cal [͵ju:nɪ'vəʊkl] **I** *adj.* □ eindeutig, unzweideutig; **II** *s.* Wort *n* mit nur 'einer Bedeutung.
͵**un'just** *adj.* □ ungerecht (***to*** gegen); **un'jus·ti·fi·a·ble** *adj.* □ nicht zu rechtfertigen(d), unverantwortlich; **un'jus·ti·fied** *adj.* ungerechtfertigt, unberechtigt; ͵**un'just·ness** *s.* Ungerechtigkeit *f.*
un·kempt [͵ʌn'kempt] *adj.* **1.** *obs.* ungekämmt, zerzaust; **2.** *fig.* ungepflegt, unordentlich, verwahrlost.
un'kind *adj.* □ **1.** unfreundlich (***to*** zu); **2.** rücksichtslos, herzlos (***to*** gegen); **un'kind·li·ness** *s.* Unfreundlichkeit *f*; **un'kind·ly** → ***unkind***; **un'kind·ness** *s.* Unfreundlichkeit *f etc.*
͵**un'know·ing** *adj.* □ **1.** unwissend; **2.** unwissentlich, unbewußt; **3.** nicht wissend, ohne zu wissen (***that*** daß, ***how*** wie *etc.*).
͵**un'known I** *adj.* **1.** unbekannt (***to*** *dat.*); → ***quantity*** 2; **2.** nie gekannt, beispiellos (*Entzücken etc.*); **II** *adv.* **3.** (***to s.o.***) ohne (j-s) Wissen; **III** *s.* **4.** *der* (*die, das*) Unbekannte; **5.** ⅌ Unbekannte *f.*
͵**un'la·bel(l)ed** *adj.* nicht etikettiert, ohne Eti'kett *od.* Aufschrift.
͵**un'la·bo(u)red** *adj.* mühelos (*a. fig. ungezwungen, leicht*).
͵**un'lace** *v/t.* aufschnüren.
͵**un'lade** *v/t.* [*irr.* → ***lade***] **1.** aus-, entladen; **2.** ⚓ *Ladung etc.* löschen; ͵**un'lad·en** *adj.* **1.** unbeladen: ~ ***weight*** Leergewicht *n*; **2.** *fig.* unbelastet (***with*** von).
͵**un'la·dy·like** *adj.* nicht damenhaft, unfein.
͵**un·la'ment·ed** *adj.* unbeklagt, unbeweint, unbetrauert.
͵**un'latch** *v/t.* aufklinken.
͵**un'law·ful** *adj.* □ **1.** ⚖ rechtswidrig, 'widerrechtlich, ungesetzlich, 'ille͵gal: ~ ***assembly*** Auflauf *m*, Zs.-rottung *f*; **2.** unerlaubt; **3.** unehelich; ͵**un'law·ful·ness** *s.* Ungesetzlichkeit *f etc.*
͵**un'learn** [*irr.* → ***learn***] **I** *v/t.* verlernen, vergessen; **II** *v/i.* 'umlernen.
un·learned[1] [͵ʌn'lɜ:nt] *adj.* nicht er- *od.* gelernt.
un·learn·ed[2] [͵ʌn'lɜ:nɪd] *adj.* ungelehrt.
͵**un'learnt** → ***unlearned***[1].
͵**un'leash** *v/t.* **1.** losbinden, *Hund* loskoppeln; **2.** *fig.* entfesseln, auslösen, loslassen.
͵**un'leav·ened** *adj.* ungesäuert (*Brot*).
un·less [ən'les] **I** *cj.* wenn … nicht; so'fern … nicht; es sei denn (, daß) …; außer wenn …; ausgenommen (wenn) …; vor'ausgesetzt, daß nicht …; **II** *prp.* außer.
͵**un'let·tered** *adj.* **1.** analpha'betisch; **2.** ungebildet, ungelehrt; **3.** unbeschriftet, unbedruckt.
͵**un'li·censed** *adj.* **1.** unerlaubt; **2.** nicht konzessioniert, (amtlich) nicht zugelassen, ohne Li'zenz.
͵**un'licked** *adj. fig.* a) ungehobelt, ungeschliffen, roh, b) unreif: ~ ***cub*** grüner Junge.
͵**un'lik·a·ble** *adj.* 'unsym͵pathisch.
͵**un'like I** *adj.* **1.** ungleich, (vonein'ander) verschieden; **2.** unähnlich; **II** *prp.* **3.** unähnlich (***s.o.*** j-m), verschieden von, anders als: ***that is very*** ~ ***him*** das sieht ihm gar nicht ähnlich; **4.** anders als, nicht wie; **5.** im Gegensatz zu.
͵**un'like·a·ble** → ***unlikable.***
un'like·li·hood, **un'like·li·ness** *s.* Unwahrscheinlichkeit *f*; **un'like·ly I** *adj.* **1.** unwahrscheinlich; **2.** (ziemlich) unmöglich: ~ ***place***; **3.** aussichtslos; **II** *adv.* **4.** unwahrscheinlich.
͵**un'lim·ber** *v/t. u. v/i.* **1.** ⚔ abprotzen; **2.** *fig.* (sich) bereitmachen.
un'lim·it·ed *adj.* **1.** unbegrenzt; unbeschränkt (*a. Haftung etc.*): ~ ***company*** ✝ *Brit.* Gesellschaft *f* mit unbeschränkter Haftung; **2.** ✝ *Börse*: nicht limitiert; **3.** *fig.* grenzen-, uferlos.
͵**un'lined**[1] *adj.* ungefüttert: ~ ***coat.***
͵**un'lined**[2] *adj.* **1.** unliniert, ohne Linien; **2.** faltenlos (*Gesicht*).
͵**un'link** *v/t.* **1.** losketten; **2.** *Kettenglieder* trennen; **3.** *Kette* ausein'andernehmen.
͵**un'liq·ui·dat·ed** *adj.* ✝ **1.** a) ungetilgt (*Schuld etc.*), b) nicht festgestellt (*Betrag etc.*); **2.** unliquidiert: ~ ***company.***
͵**un'list·ed** *adj.* **1.** nicht verzeichnet; **2.** *teleph. Am.* Geheim…: ~ ***number***; **3.** ✝ nicht notiert (*Wertpapier*).
͵**un'load I** *v/t.* **1.** ab-, aus-, entladen; ⚓ *Ladung* löschen; **2.** *fig.* (von e-r Last) befreien, erleichtern; **3.** *Waffe* entladen; **4.** *Börse*: *Aktien* (*massenhaft*) abstoßen, auf den Markt werfen; **5.** F (***on, onto***) a) *j-n, et.* ‚abladen' (bei), b) abwälzen (auf *acc.*), c) *Wut etc.* auslassen (an *dat.*); **II** *v/i.* **6.** aus-, abladen; **7.** gelöscht *od.* ausgeladen werden.
͵**un'lock** *v/t.* **1.** aufschließen, öffnen; **2.** *Waffe* entsichern; ͵**un'locked** *adj.* unverschlossen.
un'looked-for *adj.* unerwartet, 'unvor͵hergesehen, über'raschend.
͵**un'loose**, **un'loos·en** *v/t.* **1.** *Knoten etc.* lösen; **2.** *Griff etc.* lockern; **3.** losmachen, -lassen.
͵**un'lov·a·ble** *adj.* nicht *od.* wenig liebenswert; ͵**un'loved** *adj.* ungeliebt; ͵**un'love·ly** *adj.* unschön, reizlos; ͵**un'lov·ing** *adj.* □ kalt, lieblos.
un'luck·i·ly *adv.* unglücklicherweise; **un'luck·y** *adj.* □ unglücklich: a) vom Pech verfolgt: ***be*** ~ Pech *od.* kein Glück haben, b) fruchtlos: ~ ***effort***, c) ungünstig: ~ ***moment***, d) unheilvoll, Unglücks…: ~ ***day.***
͵**un'made** *adj.* ungemacht.
͵**un'make** *v/t.* [*irr.* → ***make***] **1.** aufheben, 'umstoßen, wider'rufen, rückgängig machen; **2.** *j-n* absetzen; **3.** vernichten; **4.** 'umbilden.
͵**un'man** *v/t.* **1.** entmannen; **2.** *j-n* s-r Kraft berauben; **3.** *j-n* verzagen lassen, entmutigen; **4.** verrohen (lassen); **5.** *e-m Schiff etc.* die Mannschaft nehmen: ~***ned*** unbemannt.
un'man·age·a·ble *adj.* □ **1.** schwer zu handhaben(d), unhandlich; **2.** *fig.* unfügsam, unlenksam, 'widerspenstig: ~ ***child***; **3.** unkontrollierbar (*Lage*).
͵**un'man·li·ness** *s.* Unmännlichkeit *f*; ͵**un'man·ly** *adj.* **1.** unmännlich; **2.** weibisch; **3.** feige.
un'man·ner·li·ness *s.* schlechtes Benehmen; **un'man·ner·ly** *adj.* ungezogen, 'unma͵nierlich.
͵**un'marked** *adj.* **1.** nicht markiert, unbezeichnet, ungezeichnet (*a. Gesicht*); **2.** unbemerkt; **3.** *sport* ungedeckt.
͵**un'mar·ket·a·ble** *adj.* ✝ **1.** nicht marktgängig *od.* -fähig; **2.** unverkäuflich.
͵**un'mar·riage·a·ble** *adj.* nicht heiratsfähig; ͵**un'mar·ried** *adj.* unverheiratet, ledig.
un·mask [͵ʌn'mɑ:sk] **I** *v/t.* **1.** *j-m* die Maske abnehmen, *j-n* demaskieren; **2.** *fig. j-n* entlarven, *j-m* die Maske her'unterreißen; **II** *v/i.* **3.** sich demaskieren; **4.** *fig.* die Maske fallen lassen; ͵**un'mask·ing** [-kɪŋ] *s. fig.* Entlarvung *f.*
͵**un'matched** *adj.* unvergleichlich, unerreicht, 'unüber͵troffen.
͵**un'mean·ing** *adj.* □ sinn-, bedeutungslos; nichtssagend (*a. Gesicht*); ͵**un'meant** *adj.* unbeabsichtigt.
͵**un'meas·ured** *adj.* **1.** ungemessen; **2.** unermeßlich, grenzenlos, unbegrenzt; **3.** unmäßig.
͵**un·me'lo·di·ous** *adj.* □ 'unme͵lodisch.

unˈmen·tion·a·ble I *adj.* **1.** unaussprechlich, taˈbu: ***an ~ topic*** ein Thema, über das man nicht spricht; **2.** → ***unspeakable***; **II** *s. pl. humor. die* Unaussprechlichen *pl.* (*Unterwäsche*); ˌ**unˈmen·tioned** *adj.* unerwähnt.
ˌ**unˈmer·chant·a·ble** → ***unmarketable***.
unˈmer·ci·ful *adj.* □ unbarmherzig.
ˌ**unˈmer·it·ed** *adj.* □ unverdient(ermaßen *adv.*).
ˌ**un·meˈthod·i·cal** *adj.* ˈunmeˌthodisch, sysˈtem-, planlos.
ˌ**unˈmil·i·tar·y** *adj.* **1.** ˈunmiliˌtärisch; **2.** nicht miliˈtärisch, Zivil...
unˈmind·ful *adj.* □ unachtsam; uneingedenk (***of*** *gen.*): ***be ~ of*** a) nicht achten auf (*acc.*), b) nicht denken an (*acc.*).
ˌ**un·misˈtak·a·ble** *adj.* □ **1.** ˈunˌmißverständlich; **2.** unverkennbar.
unˈmit·i·gat·ed *adj.* □ **1.** ungemildert, ganz; **2.** vollˈendet, Erz..., *nachgestellt*: durch u. durch: ***an ~ liar***.
ˌ**unˈmixed** *adj.* □ **1.** unvermischt; **2.** *fig.* ungemischt, rein, pur.
ˌ**unˈmod·i·fied** *adj.* unverändert, nicht abgeändert.
ˌ**un·moˈlest·ed** *adj.* unbelästigt, ungestört: ***live ~*** in Frieden leben.
ˌ**unˈmoor** ⚓ **I** *v/t.* **1.** abankern, losmachen; **2.** vor ˈeinem Anker liegen lassen; **II** *v/i.* **3.** den *od.* die Anker lichten.
ˌ**unˈmor·al** *adj.* ˈamoˌralisch.
ˌ**unˈmort·gaged** *adj.* ⚖ **1.** unverpfändet; **2.** hypoˈthekenfrei, unbelastet.
ˌ**unˈmount·ed** *adj.* **1.** unberitten: ***~ police***; **2.** nicht aufgezogen (*Bild etc.*); **3.** ⚙, ⚔ unmontiert; **4.** nicht gefaßt (*Stein*).
ˌ**unˈmourned** *adj.* unbetrauert.
ˌ**unˈmov·a·ble** *adj.* □ unbeweglich; ˌ**unˈmoved** *adj.* □ **1.** unbewegt; **2.** *fig.* ungerührt, unbewegt; **3.** *fig.* unerschütterlich, standhaft, gelassen; ˌ**unˈmov·ing** *adj.* regungslos.
ˌ**unˈmur·mur·ing** *adj.* □ ohne Murren, klaglos.
ˌ**unˈmu·si·cal** *adj.* □ **1.** ˈunmusiˌkalisch (*Person*); **2.** ˈunmeˌlodisch.
ˌ**unˈmuz·zle** *v/t.* **1.** *e-m Hund* den Maulkorb abnehmen: ***~d*** ohne Maulkorb; **2.** *fig. j-m* freie Meinungsäußerung gewähren.
ˌ**unˈnam·a·ble** *adj.* unsagbar.
ˌ**unˈnamed** *adj.* **1.** namenlos; **2.** nicht namentlich genannt, ungenannt.
unˈnat·u·ral *adj.* □ **1.** ˈunnaˌtürlich; **2.** künstlich, gekünstelt; **3.** ˈwidernaˌtürlich (*Laster*, *Verbrechen etc.*); **4.** ungeheuerlich, abˈscheulich; **5.** ungewöhnlich; **6.** anoˈmal.
ˌ**unˈnav·i·ga·ble** *adj.* nicht schiffbar, unbefahrbar.
unˈnec·es·sar·i·ly *adv.* unnötigerweise; **unˈnec·es·sar·y** *adj.* □ **1.** unnötig, nicht notwendig; **2.** nutzlos, ˈüberflüssig.
ˌ**unˈneed·ed** *adj.* nicht benötigt, nutzlos; ˌ**unˈneed·ful** *adj.* □ unnötig.
ˌ**unˈneigh·bo(u)r·ly** *adj.* nicht gutnachbarlich, unfreundlich.
ˌ**unˈnerve** *v/t.* entnerven, zermürben, *j-n* die Nerven *od.* den Mut verlieren lassen.
ˌ**unˈnot·ed** *adj.* **1.** unbeachtet, unberühmt; **2.** → ***unnoticed*** 1.
ˌ**unˈno·ticed** *adj.* **1.** unbemerkt, unbeobachtet; **2.** → ***unnoted*** 1.
ˌ**unˈnum·bered** *adj.* **1.** unnumeriert; **2.** *poet.* ungezählt, zahllos.
ˌ**un·obˈjec·tion·a·ble** *adj.* □ einwandfrei.
ˌ**un·obˈlig·ing** *adj.* ungefällig.
ˌ**un·obˈserv·ant** *adj.* unaufmerksam, unachtsam: ***be ~ of*** *et.* nicht beachten; ˌ**un·obˈserved** *adj.* □ unbeobachtet, unbemerkt.
ˌ**un·obˈstruct·ed** *adj.* **1.** unversperrt, ungehindert: ***~ view***; **2.** *fig.* unbehindert.
ˌ**un·obˈtain·a·ble** *adj.* **1.** ✝ nicht erhältlich; **2.** unerreichbar.
ˌ**un·obˈtru·sive** *adj.* □ unaufdringlich: a) zuˈrückhaltend, bescheiden, b) unauffällig; ˌ**un·obˈtru·sive·ness** *s.* Unaufdringlichkeit *f.*
ˌ**unˈoc·cu·pied** *adj.* frei: a) unbewohnt, leer(stehend), b) unbesetzt, c) unbeschäftigt.
ˌ**un·ofˈfend·ing** *adj.* **1.** nicht beleidigend; **2.** nicht anstößig.
ˌ**un·ofˈfi·cial** *adj.* □ **1.** nichtamtlich, ˈinoffiziˌell; **2.** ***~ strike*** ✝ wilder Streik.
ˌ**unˈop·ened** *adj.* **1.** ungeöffnet, verschlossen: ***~ letter***; **2.** ✝ unerschlossen: ***~ market***.
ˌ**un·opˈposed** *adj.* **1.** unbehindert; **2.** unbeanstandet: ***~ by*** ohne Widerstand *od.* Einspruch seitens (*gen.*).
ˌ**unˈor·gan·ized** *adj.* **1.** ˈunorˌganisch; **2.** unorganisiert, wirr; **3.** nicht organisiert.
ˌ**unˈor·tho·dox** *adj.* **1.** *eccl.* ˈunorthoˌdox; **2.** *fig.* ˈunorthoˌdox, unüblich, ˈunkonventioˌnell.
ˈ**unˌos·tenˈta·tious** *adj.* □ unaufdringlich, unauffällig: a) prunklos, schlicht, b) anspruchslos, zuˈrückhaltend, c) deˈzent (*Farben etc.*).
ˌ**unˈowned** *adj.* herrenlos.
ˌ**unˈpack** *v/t. u. v/i.* auspacken.
ˌ**unˈpaid** *adj.* **1.** *a.* ***~-for*** unbezahlt; rückständig (*Zinsen etc.*); **2.** ✝ noch nicht eingezahlt (*Kapital*); **3.** unbesoldet, unbezahlt, ehrenamtlich (*Stellung*).
unˈpal·at·a·ble *adj.* □ **1.** unschmackhaft, schlecht (schmeckend); **2.** *fig.* unangenehm, ˈwiderwärtig.
unˈpar·al·leled *adj.* einmalig, beispiellos, *nachgestellt*: ohneˈgleichen.
unˈpar·don·a·ble *adj.* □ unverzeihlich.
ˈ**unˌpar·liaˈmen·ta·ry** *adj. pol.* ˈunparlamenˌtarisch.
ˌ**unˈpat·ent·ed** *adj.* nicht patentiert.
ˈ**unˌpa·triˈot·ic** *adj.* (□ ***~ally***) ˈunpatriˌotisch.
ˌ**unˈpaved** *adj.* ungepflastert.
ˌ**unˈped·i·greed** *adj.* ohne Stammbaum.
ˌ**unˈpeo·ple** *v/t.* entvölkern.
ˌ**un·perˈceived** *adj.* □ unbemerkt.
ˌ**un·perˈformed** *adj.* **1.** nicht ausgeführt, ungetan, unverrichtet; **2.** *thea.* nicht aufgeführt (*Stück*).
ˈ**unˌper·son** *s. fig.* ˈUnperˌson *f.*
ˌ**un·perˈturbed** *adj.* nicht beunruhigt, gelassen, ruhig.
ˌ**unˈpick** *v/t. Naht etc.* (auf)trennen; ˌ**unˈpicked** *adj.* **1.** ungepflückt; **2.** ✝ unausgesucht, unsortiert (*Proben*).
ˌ**unˈpin** *v/t.* **1.** die Nadeln entfernen aus; **2.** losstecken, -machen.
ˌ**unˈpit·ied** *adj.* unbemitleidet; ˌ**unˈpit·y·ing** *adj.* □ mitleid(s)los.
ˌ**unˈplaced** *adj.* **1.** nicht ˈuntergebracht; nicht angestellt, ohne Stellung; **2.** *Rennsport*: unplaciert.
ˌ**unˈplait** *v/t.* **1.** glätten; **2.** *das Haar etc.* aufflechten.
ˌ**unˈplay·a·ble** *adj.* **1.** *sport* unbespielbar (*Boden*, *Platz*); **2.** ♪ unspielbar; **3.** *thea.* nicht bühnenreif.
unˈpleas·ant *adj.* □ *allg.* unangenehm: a) unerfreulich, b) unfreundlich, c) unwirsch (*Person*); **unˈpleas·ant·ness** *s.* **1.** *das* Unangenehme; **2.** Unannehmlichkeit *f*; **3.** ˈMißhelligkeit *f*, Unstimmigkeit *f.*
ˌ**unˈpledged** *adj.* **1.** nicht verpflichtet; **2.** ⚖ unverpfändet.
ˌ**unˈplug** *v/t.* den Pflock *od.* Stöpsel *od.* Stecker entfernen aus.
ˌ**unˈplumbed** *adj. fig.* unergründet, unergründlich.
ˌ**un·poˈet·ic**, ˌ**un·poˈet·i·cal** *adj.* □ ˈunpoˌetisch, undichterisch.
ˌ**unˈpol·ished** *adj.* **1.** unpoliert (*a. Reis*), ungeglättet, ungeschliffen; **2.** *fig.* unausgefeilt (*Stil etc.*); **3.** *fig.* ungeschliffen, ungehobelt.
ˌ**unˈpol·i·tic** → ***unpolitical*** 1; ˌ**un·poˈlit·i·cal** *adj.* **1.** (poˈlitisch) unklug; **2.** ˈunpoˌlitisch, an Poliˈtik uninteressiert; **3.** ˈunparˌteiisch.
ˌ**unˈpolled** *adj. pol.* **1.** nicht gewählt habend: ***~ elector*** Nichtwähler *m*; **2.** *Am.* nicht (in die Wählerliste) eingetragen.
ˌ**un·polˈlut·ed** *adj.* **1.** unverschmutzt, unverseucht (*Wasser etc.*); **2.** *fig.* unbefleckt.
ˌ**unˈpop·u·lar** *adj.* □ ˈunpopuˌlär, unbeliebt; ˈ**unˌpop·uˈlar·i·ty** *s.* ˈUnpopulariˌtät *f*, Unbeliebtheit *f.*
ˌ**un·posˈsessed** *adj.* **1.** herrenlos (*Sache*); **2.** ***~ of s.th.*** nicht im Besitz e-r Sache.
ˌ**unˈpost·ed** *adj.* **1.** nicht informiert, ˈununterˌrichtet; **2.** *Brit.* nicht aufgegeben (*Brief*).
ˌ**unˈprac·ti·cal** *adj.* □ unpraktisch; **unˈprac·ticed** *Am.*, **unˈprac·tised** *Brit. adj.* ungeübt (***in*** in *dat.*).
unˈprec·e·dent·ed *adj.* □ **1.** beispiellos, unerhört, noch nie dagewesen; **2.** ⚖ ohne Präzeˈdenzfall.
ˌ**un·preˈdict·a·ble** *adj.* unvorhersehbar, unberechenbar (*a. Person*): ***he is quite ~ a.*** er ist sehr schwer auszumachen.
ˌ**unˈprej·u·diced** *adj.* **1.** unvoreingenommen, vorurteilsfrei, *a.* ⚖ unbefangen; **2.** *a.* ⚖ unbeeinträchtigt.
ˌ**un·preˈmed·i·tat·ed** *adj.* □ **1.** ˈunüberˌlegt; **2.** unbeabsichtigt; **3.** ⚖ ohne Vorsatz.
ˌ**un·preˈpared** *adj.* □ **1.** unvorbereitet: ***an ~ speech***; **2.** (***for***) nicht vorbereitet *od.* gefaßt (auf *acc.*), nicht gerüstet (für).
ˈ**unˌpre·posˈsess·ing** *adj.* wenig anziehend, ˈunsymˌpathisch.
ˌ**un·preˈsent·a·ble** *adj.* nicht präsenˈtabel.
ˌ**un·preˈsum·ing** *adj.* nicht anmaßend *od.* vermessen, bescheiden.
ˌ**un·preˈtend·ing**, ˌ**un·preˈten·tious** *adj.* □ anspruchslos.
unˈprin·ci·pled *adj.* **1.** ohne (feste) Grundsätze, haltlos, chaˈrakterlos (*Person*); **2.** gewissenlos, charakterlos (*Benehmen*).
un·print·a·ble [ˌʌnˈprɪntəbl] *adj.* nicht druckfähig *od.* druckreif (*a. fig. anstößig*); ˌ**unˈprint·ed** [-tɪd] *adj.* **1.** unge-

druckt (*Schriften*); **2.** unbedruckt (*Stoffe etc.*).

ˌun'priv·i·leged *adj.* nicht privilegiert *od.* bevorrechtigt: **~ *creditor*** ⚖ Massegläubiger *m.*

ˌun·pro'duc·tive *adj.* □ 'unprodukˌtiv (*a. fig.*), unergiebig (***of*** an *dat.*), unfruchtbar (*a. fig.*), 'unrenˌtabel: **~ *capital*** † totes Kapital; **ˌun·pro'duc·tive·ness** *s.* 'Unproduktiviˌtät *f*, Unfruchtbarkeit *f*, Unergiebigkeit *f*, 'Unrentabiliˌtät *f*.

ˌun·pro'fes·sion·al *adj.* □ **1.** keiner freien Berufsgruppe zugehörig; **2.** nicht berufsmäßig; **3.** berufswidrig: **~ *conduct***; **4.** unfachmännisch.

ˌun'prof·it·a·ble *adj.* □ **1.** nicht einträglich *od.* gewinnbringend *od.* lohnend, 'unrenˌtabel; **2.** unvorteilhaft; **3.** nutz-, zwecklos; **ˌun'prof·it·a·ble·ness** *s.* **1.** Uneinträglichkeit *f*; **2.** Nutzlosigkeit *f*.

ˌun·pro'gres·sive *adj.* □ **1.** nicht fortschrittlich, rückständig; **2.** rückschrittlich, konserva'tiv, reaktio'när.

ˌun'prom·is·ing *adj.* □ nicht vielversprechend, ziemlich aussichtslos.

ˌun'prompt·ed *adj.* spon'tan.

ˌun·pro'nounce·a·ble *adj.* unaussprechlich.

ˌun·pro'pi·tious *adj.* □ ungünstig.

ˌun·pro'por·tion·al *adj.* □ unverhältnismäßig, 'unproportioˌnal.

ˌun·pro'tect·ed *adj.* **1.** ungeschützt, schutzlos; **2.** ungedeckt.

ˌun'proved, **ˌun'prov·en** *adj.* unerwiesen.

ˌun·pro'vid·ed *adj.* □ **1.** nicht versehen (***with*** mit): **~ *with*** ohne; **2.** unvorbereitet; **3. ~ *for*** unversorgt (*Kind*); **4. ~ *for*** nicht vorgesehen.

ˌun·pro'voked *adj.* □ **1.** unprovoziert; **2.** grundlos.

ˌun'pub·lish·a·ble *adj.* zur Veröffentlichung ungeeignet; **ˌun'pub·lished** *adj.* unveröffentlicht.

ˌun'punc·tu·al *adj.* □ unpünktlich; **'unˌpunc·tu'al·i·ty** *s.* Unpünktlichkeit *f*.

ˌun'pun·ished *adj.* unbestraft, ungestraft: ***go* ~** straflos ausgehen.

un·put·down·a·ble [ˌʌnpʊt'daʊnəbl] *adj.* F so faszinierend, daß man es nicht mehr aus der Hand legen kann (*Buch*).

ˌun'qual·i·fied *adj.* □ **1.** unqualifiziert: a) unbefähigt, ungeeignet (***for*** für), b) unberechtigt; **2.** uneingeschränkt, unbedingt, bedingungslos; **3.** F ausgesprochen (*Lügner etc.*).

un·quench·a·ble [ˌʌn'kwentʃəbl] *adj.* □ **1.** unlöschbar; **2.** *fig.* unstillbar.

un·ques·tion·a·ble [ʌn'kwestʃənəbl] *adj.* □ **1.** unzweifelhaft, fraglos; **2.** unbedenklich; **un'ques·tioned** [-tʃənd] *adj.* **1.** ungefragt; **2.** unbezweifelt, unbestritten; **un'ques·tion·ing** [-nɪŋ] *adj.* □ bedingungslos, blind: **~ *obedience***; **un'ques·tion·ing·ly** [-nɪŋlɪ] *adv.* ohne zu fragen, ohne Zögern.

ˌun'quote *v/i.*: **~!** Ende des Zitats!; **ˌun'quot·ed** *adj.* **1.** nicht zitiert; **2.** *Börse*: nicht notiert.

un'rav·el I *v/t.* **1.** *Gewebe* ausfasern; **2.** *Gestricktes* auftrennen; **3.** entwirren; **4.** *fig.* entwirren, enträtseln; **II** *v/i.* **5.** sich entwirren *etc.*

un·read [ˌʌn'red] *adj.* **1.** ungelesen; **2.** a) unbelesen, ungebildet, b) unbewandert (***in*** in *dat.*).

ˌun'read·a·ble *adj.* **1.** unleserlich (*Handschrift etc.*); **2.** schwer zu lesen (*Buch etc.*); **3.** nicht lesenswert (*Buch etc.*).

ˌun'read·i·ness *s.* mangelnde Bereitschaft; **ˌun'read·y** *adj.* □ nicht bereit *od.* fertig (***for*** zu).

ˌun'real *adj.* □ **1.** unwirklich; **2.** wesenlos; **3.** → **'unˌre·al'is·tic** *adj.* (□ **~*ally***) wirklichkeitsfremd, 'unreaˌlistisch; **ˌun·re'al·i·ty** *s.* **1.** Unwirklichkeit *f*; **2.** Wesenlosigkeit *f*.

ˌun're·al·iz·a·ble *adj.* nicht realisierbar: a) nicht zu verwirklichen(d), b) † nicht verwertbar, unverkäuflich; **ˌun're·al·ized** *adj.* **1.** nicht verwirklicht *od.* erfüllt; **2.** nicht vergegenwärtigt *od.* erkannt.

ˌun'rea·son *s.* **1.** Unvernunft *f*; **2.** Torheit *f*; **un'rea·son·a·ble** *adj.* □ **1.** unvernünftig; **2.** unvernünftig, unbillig, unmäßig, 'übermäßig; unzumutbar; **un'rea·son·a·ble·ness** *s.* **1.** Unvernunft *f*; **2.** Unbilligkeit *f*, Unmäßigkeit *f*; Unzumutbarkeit *f*; **un'rea·son·ing** *adj.* □ **1.** vernunftlos; **2.** unvernünftig, blind.

ˌun·re'ceipt·ed *adj.* † unquittiert.

ˌun·re'cep·tive *adj.* nicht aufnahmefähig, unempfänglich (***of***, ***to*** für).

ˌun·re'claimed *adj.* **1.** *fig.* ungebessert; **2.** ungezähmt; **3.** unkultiviert (*Land*).

ˌun'rec·og·niz·a·ble *adj.* □ nicht 'wiederzuerkennen(d); **ˌun'rec·og·nized** *adj.* **1.** nicht ('wieder)erkannt; **2.** nicht anerkannt.

ˌun'rec·on·ciled *adj.* unversöhnt (***to*** mit).

un·re·cord·ed [ˌʌnrɪ'kɔːdɪd] *adj.* **1.** (geschichtlich) nicht über'liefert *od.* aufgezeichnet *od.* belegt; **2.** nicht eingetragen *od.* registriert; **3.** ⚖ nicht beurkundet; **4.** a) nicht (auf Tonband *etc.*) aufgenommen, b) Leer…: **~ *tape***.

ˌun·re'deemed *adj.* **1.** *eccl.* unerlöst; **2.** † a) ungetilgt (*Schuld*), b) uneingelöst (*Wechsel*); **3.** uneingelöst (*Pfand*, *Versprechen*); **4.** *fig.* ungemildert (***by*** durch); Erz…: **~ *rascal***.

ˌun·re'dressed *adj.* **1.** nicht wiedergutgemacht; **2.** nicht abgestellt (*Mißstand*).

ˌun'reel *v/t.* (*v/i.* sich) abspulen.

ˌun·re'fined *adj.* **1.** ⚙ nicht raffiniert, ungeläutert, roh, Roh…; **2.** *fig.* ungebildet, unfein, unkultiviert.

ˌun·re'flect·ing *adj.* □ **1.** nicht reflektierend; **2.** gedankenlos, 'unüberˌlegt.

ˌun·re'formed *adj.* **1.** unverbessert; **2.** ungebessert (*Person*).

ˌun·re'fut·ed *adj.* 'unwiderˌlegt.

ˌun·re'gard·ed *adj.* unberücksichtigt, unbeachtet; **ˌun·re'gard·ful** *adj.* unachtsam, ohne Rücksicht (***of*** auf *acc.*).

un·re·gen·er·a·cy [ˌʌnrɪ'dʒenərəsɪ] *s.* *eccl.* Sündhaftigkeit *f*; **ˌun·re'gen·er·ate** [-rət] *adj.* **1.** *eccl.* nicht 'wiedergeboren; **2.** nicht gebessert.

ˌun'reg·is·tered *adj.* **1.** nicht registriert *od.* eingetragen (*a.* †, ⚖); **2.** (amtlich) nicht zugelassen (*Auto etc.*); nicht approbiert (*Arzt etc.*); **3.** nicht eingeschrieben (*Brief*).

ˌun·re'gret·ted *adj.* unbedauert, unbeklagt.

ˌun·re'hearsed *adj.* **1.** *thea.* ungeprobt; **2.** über'raschend, spon'tan.

ˌun·re'lat·ed *adj.* **1.** ohne Beziehung (***to*** zu); **2.** nicht verwandt (***to***, ***with*** mit) (*a. fig.*); **3.** nicht berichtet.

ˌun·re'lent·ing *adj.* □ **1.** unbeugsam, unerbittlich; **2.** unvermindert.

'un·reˌli·a'bil·i·ty *s.* Unzuverlässigkeit *f*; **ˌun·re'li·a·ble** *adj.* □ unzuverlässig.

ˌun·re'lieved *adj.* □ **1.** ungelindert; **2.** nicht unter'brochen, 'ununterˌbrochen; **3.** ⚔ a) nicht abgelöst (*Wache*), b) nicht entsetzt (*Festung etc.*).

un·re·mit·ting [ˌʌnrɪ'mɪtɪŋ] *adj.* □ unablässig, beharrlich.

ˌun·re'mu·ner·a·tive *adj.* nicht lohnend *od.* einträglich, 'unrenˌtabel.

ˌun·re'pair *s.* Baufälligkeit *f*, Verfall *m*: ***in*** (***a state of***) **~** in baufälligem Zustand.

ˌun·re'pealed *adj.* **1.** nicht wider'rufen; **2.** nicht aufgehoben.

ˌun·re'pent·ant *adj.* reuelos, unbußfertig; **ˌun·re'pent·ed** [-tɪd] *adj.* unbereut.

ˌun·rep·re'sent·ed *adj.* nicht vertreten.

ˌun·re'quit·ed *adj.* □ **1.** unerwidert: **~ *love***; **2.** unbelohnt (*Dienste*); **3.** ungesühnt (*Missetat*).

un·re·served [ˌʌnrɪ'zɜːvd] *adj.* □ **1.** uneingeschränkt, vorbehalt-, rückhaltlos, völlig; **2.** freimütig, offen(herzig); **3.** nicht reserviert; **ˌun·re'serv·ed·ness** [-vɪdnɪs] *s.* Offenheit *f*, Freimütigkeit *f*.

ˌun·re'sist·ed *adj.* ungehindert: ***be* ~** keinen Widerstand finden; **ˌun·re'sist·ing** *adj.* □ 'widerstandslos.

ˌun·re'solved *adj.* **1.** ungelöst: **~ *problem***; **2.** unschlüssig, unentschlossen; **3.** ♞, ♪ *etc.* unaufgelöst.

ˌun·re'spon·sive *adj.* □ **1.** unempfänglich (***to*** für): ***be* ~** (***to***) nicht reagieren *od.* ansprechen (auf *acc.*); **2.** teilnahmslos, kalt.

un·rest [ˌʌn'rest] *s.* Unruhe *f*, *pol. a.* Unruhen *pl.*; **ˌun'rest·ful** *adj.* □ **1.** ruhelos; **2.** ungemütlich; **3.** unbequem; **ˌun'rest·ing** *adj.* □ rastlos, unermüdlich.

ˌun·re'strained *adj.* □ **1.** ungehemmt (*a. fig. ungezwungen*); **2.** hemmungs-, zügellos; **3.** uneingeschränkt; **ˌun·re'straint** *s.* **1.** Ungehemmtheit *f*, *fig. a.* Ungezwungenheit *f*; **2.** Hemmungslosigkeit *f*.

ˌun·re'strict·ed *adj.* □ uneingeschränkt, unbeschränkt.

ˌun·re'turned *adj.* **1.** nicht zu'rückgegeben; **2.** unerwidert, unvergolten: ***be* ~** unerwidert bleiben; **3.** *pol.* nicht (*ins Parlament*) gewählt.

ˌun·re'vealed *adj.* nicht offen'bart, verborgen, geheim.

ˌun·re'vised *adj.* nicht revidiert (*a. fig. Ansicht etc.*).

ˌun·re'ward·ed *adj.* unbelohnt.

ˌun'rhymed *adj.* ungereimt, reimlos.

ˌun'rid·dle *v/t.* enträtseln.

ˌun'rig *v/t.* **1.** ⚓ abtakeln; **2.** abmontieren.

un'right·eous *adj.* □ **1.** nicht rechtschaffen; **2.** *eccl.* ungerecht, sündig; **un'right·eous·ness** *s.* Ungerechtigkeit *f*.

ˌun'rip *v/t.* aufreißen, -schlitzen.

ˌun'ripe *adj. allg.* unreif; **ˌun'ripe·ness** *s.* Unreife *f*.

un'ri·val(l)ed *adj.* **1.** ohne Ri'valen *od.*

Gegenspieler; **2.** unerreicht, unvergleichlich; ☨ konkur'renzlos.
ˌun'roll I *v/t.* **1.** entrollen, -falten; **2.** abwickeln; **II** *v/i.* **3.** sich entfalten; sich ausein'anderrollen.
ˌun·ro'man·tic *adj.* (□ ***~ally***) *allg.* 'unroˌmantisch.
ˌun'roof *v/t. Haus* abdecken.
ˌun'rope *v/t.* **1.** losbinden; **2.** *mount.* (*a. v/i.* sich) ausseilen.
ˌun'round *v/t. ling. Vokale* entrunden.
ˌun'ruf·fled *adj.* **1.** ungekräuselt, glatt; **2.** *fig.* gelassen, unerschüttert.
ˌun'ruled *adj.* **1.** *fig.* unbeherrscht; **2.** unliniert (*Papier*).
un·ru·li·ness [ʌn'ruːlɪnɪs] *s.* **1.** Unlenkbarkeit *f*, 'Widerspenstigkeit *f*; **2.** Ausgelassenheit *f*, Unbändigkeit *f*; **un·ru·ly** [ʌn'ruːlɪ] *adj.* **1.** unlenksam, aufsässig; **2.** ungebärdig; ausgelassen; **3.** ungestüm.
ˌun'sad·dle I *v/t.* **1.** *Pferd* absatteln; **2.** *j-n* aus dem Sattel werfen; **II** *v/i.* **3.** absatteln.
ˌun'safe *adj.* □ unsicher, gefährlich.
ˌun'said *adj.* ungesagt, unerwähnt.
ˌun'sal·a·ble *adj.* **1.** unverkäuflich; **2.** nicht gangbar (*Waren*).
ˌun'sal·a·ried *adj.* unbezahlt, ehrenamtlich: ***~ clerk*** ☨ Volontär *m*.
ˌun'sale·a·ble → ***unsalable***.
ˌun'sanc·tioned *adj.* nicht sanktioniert, nicht gebilligt *od.* geduldet.
ˌun'san·i·tar·y *adj.* **1.** ungesund; **2.** 'unhygiˌenisch.
'unˌsat·is'fac·to·ri·ness *s. das* Unbefriedigende, Unzulänglichkeit *f*; **'unˌsat·is'fac·to·ry** *adj.* □ unbefriedigend, ungenügend, unzulänglich; **ˌun'sat·is·fied** *adj.* **1.** unbefriedigt; **2.** unzufrieden; **3.** ☨ a) unbefriedigt (*Anspruch*, *Gläubiger*), b) unbezahlt, c) unerfüllt (*Bedingung*); **ˌun'sat·is·fy·ing** *adj.* → ***unsatisfactory***.
ˌun'sa·vo(u)r·i·ness *s.* **1.** Unschmackhaftigkeit *f*; **2.** Widerlichkeit *f*; **ˌun'sa·vo(u)r·y** *adj.* □ **1.** unschmackhaft; **2.** *a. fig.* 'unappeˌtitlich, unangenehm.
ˌun'say *v/t.* [*irr.* → ***say***] wider'rufen.
ˌun'scal·a·ble *adj.* unersteigbar.
ˌun'scathed [-'skeɪðd] *adj.* (völlig) unversehrt, unbeschädigt.
ˌun'sched·uled *adj.* **1.** nicht pro'grammgemäß; **2.** außerplanmäßig (*Abfahrt etc.*).
ˌun'schol·ar·ly *adj.* **1.** unwissenschaftlich; **2.** ungelehrt.
ˌun'schooled *adj.* **1.** ungeschult, nicht ausgebildet; **2.** unverbildet.
'unˌsci·en'tif·ic *adj.* (□ ***~ally***) unwissenschaftlich.
ˌun'scram·ble *v/t.* **1.** F entwirren; **2.** entschlüsseln, dechiffrieren; **3.** ϟ aussteuern.
ˌun'screened *adj.* **1.** ungeschützt, *a.* ϟ nicht abgeschirmt; **2.** ungesiebt (*Sand etc.*); **3.** nicht über'prüft.
ˌun'screw I *v/t.* ⚙ ab-, auf-, losschrauben; **II** *v/i.* sich her'aus- *od.* losdrehen; sich losschrauben lassen.
ˌun'script·ed *adj.* improvisiert (*Rede etc.*).
un'scru·pu·lous *adj.* □ skrupel-, bedenken-, gewissenlos.
ˌun'seal *v/t.* **1.** *Brief etc.* entsiegeln *od.* öffnen; **2.** *fig. j-m die Augen*, *Lippen* öffnen; **3.** *fig.* enthüllen; **ˌun'sealed** *adj.* **1.** a) unversiegelt, b) geöffnet; **2.** *fig.* nicht besiegelt.
un'search·a·ble *adj.* □ unerforschlich, unergründlich.
un'sea·son·a·ble *adj.* □ **1.** unzeitig; **2.** *fig.* unpassend, ungünstig.
ˌun'sea·soned *adj.* **1.** nicht (aus)gereift; **2.** nicht abgelagert (*Holz*); **3.** *fig.* nicht abgehärtet (***to*** gegen); **4.** *fig.* unerfahren; **5.** ungewürzt.
ˌun'seat *v/t.* **1.** *Reiter* abwerfen; **2.** *j-n* absetzen, des Postens entheben; **3.** *pol. j-m* s-n Sitz (im Parla'ment) nehmen; **ˌun'seat·ed** *adj.* ohne Sitz(gelegenheit): ***be ~*** nicht sitzen.
ˌun'seaˌwor·thy *adj.* ⚓ seeuntüchtig.
ˌun·se'cured *adj.* **1.** ungesichert (*a.* ☨ *Schuld*); **2.** unbefestigt; **3.** ☨ ungedeckt, nicht sichergestellt.
ˌun'seed·ed *sport* ungesetzt (*Spieler etc.*).
ˌun'see·ing *adj. fig.* blind: ***with ~ eyes*** mit leerem Blick, blind.
un'seem·li·ness *s.* Unziemlichkeit *f*; **un'seem·ly** *adj.* unziemlich, ungehörig.
ˌun'seen I *adj.* **1.** ungesehen, unbemerkt; **2.** unsichtbar; **3.** *ped.* unvorbereitet (*Übersetzungstext*); **II** *s.* **4.** ***the ~*** die Geisterwelt; **5.** *ped. Brit.* unvorbereitete 'Herüberˌsetzung *f*.
ˌun'self·ish *adj.* □ selbstlos, uneigennützig; **ˌun'self·ish·ness** *s.* Selbstlosigkeit *f*, Uneigennützigkeit *f*.
ˌun·sen'sa·tion·al *adj.* wenig sensatio'nell *od.* aufregend.
ˌun'ser·vice·a·ble *adj.* □ **1.** nicht verwendbar, unbrauchbar (*Gerät etc.*); **2.** betriebsunfähig.
ˌun'set·tle *v/t.* **1.** *et.* aus s-r (festen) Lage bringen; **2.** *fig.* beunruhigen; *a. j-n*, *j-s Glauben etc.* erschüttern, ins Wanken bringen; **3.** *fig.* verwirren, durchein'anderbringen; *j-n* aus dem (gewohnten) Gleis werfen; **4.** in Unordnung bringen; **ˌun'set·tled** *adj.* **1.** ohne festen Wohnsitz; **2.** unbesiedelt (*Land*); **3.** *fig.* unbestimmt, ungewiß, *a. allg.* unsicher (*Zeit etc.*); **4.** unentschieden, unerledigt (*Frage*); **5.** unbeständig, veränderlich (*Wetter*; ☨ *Markt*); **6.** schwankend, unentschlossen (*Person*); **7.** (geistig) gestört, aus dem (seelischen) Gleichgewicht; **8.** unstet (*Charakter*, *Leben*); **9.** ☨ unbezahlt, unerledigt; **10.** ⚖ nicht zugeschrieben; nicht reguliert (*Erbschaft*).
ˌun'sex *v/t. Frau* vermännlichen: ***~ o.s.*** alles Frauliche ablegen.
ˌun'shack·le *v/t. j-n* befreien (*a. fig.*); **ˌun'shack·led** *adj.* ungehemmt.
ˌun'shad·ed *adj.* **1.** unverdunkelt, unbeschattet; **2.** *paint.* nicht schattiert.
un'shak·a·ble *adj.* unerschütterlich; **ˌun'shak·en** *adj.* □ **1.** unerschüttert, fest; **2.** unerschütterlich.
ˌun'shape·ly *adj.* unförmig.
ˌun'shaved, **ˌun'shav·en** *adj.* unrasiert.
ˌun'sheathe *v/t. das Schwert* aus der Scheide ziehen.
ˌun'shed *adj.* unvergossen (*Tränen*).
ˌun'shell *v/t.* (ab)schälen, enthülsen.
ˌun'shel·tered *adj.* ungeschützt, schutz-, obdachlos.
ˌun'ship *v/t.* ⚓ a) *Ladung* löschen, ausladen, b) *Passagiere* ausschiffen, c) *Ruder*, *Mast etc.* abbauen.
ˌun'shod *adj.* **1.** unbeschuht, barfuß; **2.** unbeschlagen (*Pferd*).
ˌun'shorn *adj.* ungeschoren.
un·shrink·a·ble [ˌʌn'ʃrɪŋkəbl] *adj.* nicht einlaufend (*Stoffe*); **un'shrink·ing** *adj.* □ unverzagt, fest.
ˌun'sift·ed *adj.* **1.** ungesiebt; **2.** *fig.* ungeprüft.
ˌun'sight *adj.*: ***buy s.th. ~, unseen*** et. unbesehen kaufen; **ˌun'sight·ed** *adj.* **1.** nicht gesichtet; **2.** ungezielt (*Schuß*); **3.** ohne Vi'sier (*Gewehr etc.*).
un'sight·ly *adj.* unansehnlich, häßlich.
ˌun'signed *adj.* **1.** unsigniert, nicht unter'zeichnet; **2.** ♪ unbezeichnet.
ˌun'sized¹ *adj.* nicht nach Größe(n) geordnet *od.* sortiert.
ˌun'sized² *adj.* ⚙ **1.** ungrundiert; **2.** ungeleimt.
ˌun'skil·ful *adj.* □ ungeschickt.
ˌun'skilled *adj.* **1.** unerfahren, ungeschickt; **2.** ☨ ungelernt: ***~ worker***; ***the ~ labo(u)r*** *coll.* die Hilfsarbeiter *pl.*
ˌun'skill·ful *Am.* → ***unskilful***.
ˌun'skimmed *adj.* nicht entrahmt: ***~ milk*** Vollmilch *f*.
ˌun'slaked *adj.* **1.** ungelöscht (*Kalk*; *a. Durst*); **2.** *fig.* ungestillt.
ˌun'sleep·ing *adj.* **1.** schlaflos; **2.** *fig.* immer wach.
ˌun'smil·ing *adj.* □ ernst.
ˌun'smoked *adj.* **1.** ungeräuchert; **2.** nicht aufgeraucht: ***~ cigar***.
ˌun'snarl *v/t.* entwirren.
un'so·cia·ble *adj.* □ ungesellig, nicht 'umgänglich, reserviert.
ˌun'so·cial *adj.* □ **1.** 'unsoziˌal; **2.** 'asoziˌal, gesellschaftsfeindlich; **3.** ***work ~ hours*** *Brit.* außerhalb der normalen Arbeitszeit arbeiten.
ˌun'soiled *adj.* rein, sauber, *fig. a.* unbefleckt.
ˌun'sold *adj.* unverkauft; → ***subject*** 14.
ˌun'sol·der *v/t.* ⚙ ab-, loslöten.
ˌun'sol·dier·ly *adj.* 'unsolˌdatisch.
ˌun·so'lic·it·ed *adj.* **1.** unaufgefordert, unverlangt; **2.** freiwillig.
ˌun'solv·a·ble *adj.* unlösbar.
ˌun'solved *adj.* ungelöst.
ˌun·so'phis·ti·cat·ed *adj.* **1.** unverfälscht; **2.** lauter, rein; **3.** ungekünstelt, na'türlich, unverbildet; **4.** na'iv, harmlos; **5.** unverdorben.
ˌun'sought, **un'sought-for** *adj.* ungesucht, ungewollt.
ˌun'sound *adj.* □ **1.** ungesund (*a. fig.*): ***of ~ mind*** geistesgestört, unzurechnungsfähig; **2.** verdorben, schlecht (*Ware etc.*), faul (*Obst*); **3.** morsch, wurmstichig; **4.** brüchig, rissig; **5.** unzuverlässig; 'unsoˌlide (*a.* ☨); **6.** nicht stichhaltig, anfechtbar: ***~ argument***; **7.** falsch, verkehrt: ***~ doctrine*** Irrlehre *f*; ***~ policy*** verfehlte Politik; **ˌun'soundness** *s.* **1.** Ungesundheit *f* (*a. fig.*); **2.** Verdorbenheit *f*; **3.** *fig.* Unzuverlässigkeit *f*; **4.** Anfechtbarkeit *f*; **5.** Verfehltheit *f*, *das* Verkehrte.
un'spar·ing *adj.* □ **1.** freigebig, verschwenderisch (***in***, ***of*** mit): ***be ~ in*** nicht kargen mit *Lob etc.*; ***be ~ in one's efforts*** keine Mühe scheuen; **2.** reichlich, großzügig; **3.** schonungslos (***of*** gegen).
un'speak·a·ble *adj.* □ **1.** unsagbar, unsäglich, unbeschreiblich; **2.** F scheußlich, entsetzlich.

ˌunˈspec·i·fied *adj.* nicht (einzeln) angegeben, nicht spezifiziert.

ˌunˈspir·it·u·al *adj.* ☐ ungeistig.

ˌunˈspoiled, **ˌunˈspoilt** *adj.* **1.** *allg.* unverdorben; **2.** unbeschädigt; **3.** nicht verzogen (*Kind*).

ˌunˈspo·ken *adj.* un(aus)gesprochen, ungesagt; stillschweigend: **~-of** unerwähnt; **~-to** unangeredet.

ˌunˈsport·ing, **ˌunˈsports·man·like** *adj.* unsportlich, unfair.

ˌunˈspot·ted *adj.* **1.** fleckenlos; **2.** *fig.* makellos, unbefleckt; **3.** F unentdeckt.

ˌunˈsprung *adj.* ⚙ ungefedert.

ˌunˈsta·ble *adj.* **1.** *a. fig.* unsicher, nicht fest, schwankend, laˈbil; **2.** *fig.* unbeständig, unstet(ig); **3.** ⚗ ˈinstaˌbil.

ˌunˈstained *adj.* **1.** → ***unspotted*** 1, 2; **2.** ungefärbt.

ˌunˈstamped *adj.* ungestempelt; 📯 unfrankiert (*Brief*).

ˌunˈstates·man·like *adj.* unstaatsmännisch.

ˌunˈstead·i·ness *s.* **1.** Unsicherheit *f*; **2.** *fig.* Unstetigkeit *f*, Schwanken *n*; **3.** Unzuverlässigkeit *f*; **4.** Unregelmäßigkeit *f*; **ˌunˈstead·y** *adj.* ☐ **1.** unsicher, wack(e)lig; **2.** *fig.* unstet(ig); unbeständig, schwankend (*beide a.* ✝ *Kurse*, *Markt*); **3.** *fig.* ˈunsoˌlide; **4.** unregelmäßig.

ˌunˈstick *v/t.* [*irr.* → ***stick***[2]] lösen, losmachen.

unˈstint·ed *adj.* uneingeschränkt, unbegrenzt; **unˈstint·ing** [-tɪŋ] → ***unsparing*** 1, 2.

ˌunˈstitch *v/t.* auftrennen: **~ed** a) aufgetrennt, b) ungesteppt (*Falte*); ***come ~ed*** aufgehen (*Naht*).

ˌunˈstop *v/t.* **1.** entstöpseln, -korken, aufmachen; **2.** frei machen.

ˌunˈstrained *adj.* **1.** unfiltriert, ungefiltert; **2.** nicht angespannt (*a. fig.*); **3.** *fig.* ungezwungen.

ˌunˈstrap *v/t.* ab-, losschnallen.

ˌunˈstressed *adj.* **1.** *ling.* unbetont; **2.** ⚙ unbelastet.

ˌunˈstring *v/t.* [*irr.* → ***string***] **1.** *Perlen etc.* abfädeln; **2.** ♪ entsaiten; **3.** *Bogen*, *Saite* entspannen; **4.** *j-s Nerven* kaˈputtmachen, *j-n* (nervlich) ‚fertigmachen', demoralisieren.

ˌunˈstrung *adj.* **1.** ♪ a) saitenlos, unbezogen (*Saiteninstrument*), b) entspannt (*Saite*, *Bogen*); **2.** abgereiht (*Perlen*); **3.** *fig.* entnervt, mit den Nerven am Ende.

ˌunˈstuck *adj.* : ***come ~*** a) sich lösen, b) *fig.* scheitern.

ˌunˈstud·ied *adj.* ungesucht, ungekünstelt, naˈtürlich.

ˌun·subˈmis·sive *adj.* ☐ nicht unterˈwürfig, ˈwiderspenstig.

ˌun·subˈstan·tial *adj.* ☐ **1.** unstofflich, unkörperlich; **2.** unwesentlich; **3.** wenig stichhaltig *od.* fundiert: ***~ arguments***; **4.** gehaltlos (*Essen*).

ˌun·subˈstan·ti·at·ed *adj.* **1.** unbegründet; **2.** nicht erhärtet.

ˌun·sucˈcess *s.* ˈMißerfolg *m*, Fehlschlag *m*; **ˌun·sucˈcess·ful** *adj.* ☐ **1.** erfolglos: a) ohne Erfolg, b) mißˈglückt, mißˈlungen: ***be ~*** keinen Erfolg haben (***in doing s.th.*** bei *od.* mit et.); ***~ take-off*** ✈ Fehlstart *m*; **2.** ˈdurchgefallen (*Kandidat*); zuˈrückgewiesen (*Bewerber*); ⚖ unterˈlegen (*Partei*); **ˌun·sucˈcess·ful·ness** [-səkˈsesfʊlnɪs] *s.* Erfolglosigkeit *f*.

ˌunˈsuit·able *adj.* ☐ **1.** unpassend, ungeeignet (***to***, ***for*** für); **2.** unangemessen, unschicklich (***to***, ***for*** für); **ˌunˈsuit·ed** → ***unsuitable*** 1.

ˌunˈsul·lied *adj. mst fig.* unbefleckt.

ˌunˈsung *poet.* **I** *adj.* unbesungen; **II** *adv. fig.* sang- u. klanglos.

ˌun·supˈport·ed *adj.* **1.** ungestützt; **2.** *fig.* unbestätigt, ohne ˈUnterlagen; **3.** *fig.* nicht unterˈstützt (*Antrag etc.*, *a. Kinder etc.*).

ˌunˈsure *adj. allg.* unsicher, nicht sicher (***of*** *gen.*).

ˌun·surˈmount·a·ble *adj.* ˈunüberˌwindlich (*Hindernis etc.*) (*a. fig.*).

ˌun·surˈpass·a·ble *adj.* ☐ ˈunüberˌtrefflich; **ˌun·surˈpassed** *adj.* ˈunüberˌtroffen.

ˌun·susˈcep·ti·ble *adj.* **1.** unempfindlich (***to*** gegen); **2.** *fig.* unempfänglich (***to*** für).

un·sus·pect·ed [ˌʌnsəˈspektɪd] *adj.* ☐ **1.** unverdächtig(t); **2.** unvermutet, ungeahnt; **ˌun·susˈpect·ing** [-ɪŋ] *adj.* ☐ **1.** nichtsahnend, ahnungslos: ***~ of*** ohne *et.* zu ahnen; **2.** → ***unsuspicious*** 1.

ˌun·susˈpi·cious *adj.* ☐ **1.** arglos, nicht argwöhnisch; **2.** unverdächtig, harmlos.

ˌunˈsweet·ened *adj.* **1.** ungesüßt; **2.** *fig.* unversüßt.

un·swerv·ing [ʌnˈswɜːvɪŋ] *adj.* ☐ unbeirrbar, unerschütterlich.

ˌunˈsworn *adj.* **1.** unbeeidet; **2.** unvereidigt (*Zeuge etc.*).

ˌun·symˈmet·ri·cal *adj.* ☐ ˈunsymˌmetrisch.

ˈunˌsym·paˈthet·ic *adj.* (☐ ***~ally***) teilnahmslos, ohne Mitgefühl.

ˌun·sys·temˈat·ic *adj.* (☐ ***~ally***) ˈunsysteˌmatisch, planlos.

ˌunˈtaint·ed *adj.* ☐ **1.** fleckenlos (*a. fig.*); **2.** unverdorben: ***~ food***; **3.** *fig.* unbeeinträchtigt (***with*** von).

ˌunˈtal·ent·ed *adj.* untalentiert, unbegabt.

ˌunˈtam·a·ble *adj.* ☐ un(be)zähmbar; **ˌunˈtamed** *adj.* ungezähmt.

ˌunˈtan·gle *v/t.* **1.** entwirren (*a. fig.*); **2.** aus einer schwierigen Lage befreien.

ˌunˈtanned *adj.* **1.** ungegerbt (*Leder*); **2.** ungebräunt (*Haut*).

ˌunˈtapped *adj.* unangezapft (*a. fig.*): ***~ resources*** ungenützte Hilfsquellen.

ˌunˈtar·nished *adj.* **1.** ungetrübt; **2.** makellos, unbefleckt (*a. fig.*).

ˌunˈtast·ed *adj.* ungekostet (*a. fig.*).

ˌunˈtaught *adj.* **1.** ungelehrt, nicht unterˈrichtet; **2.** unwissend, ungebildet; **3.** ungelernt, selbstentwickelt (*Fähigkeit etc.*).

ˌunˈtaxed *adj.* unbesteuert.

ˌunˈteach·a·ble *adj.* **1.** unbelehrbar (*Person*); **2.** unlehrbar (*Sache*).

ˌunˈtem·pered *adj.* **1.** ⚙ ungehärtet, unvergütet (*Stahl*); **2.** *fig.* ungemildert (***with***, ***by*** durch).

ˌunˈten·a·ble *adj. fig.* unhaltbar.

ˌunˈten·ant·a·ble *adj.* unbewohn-, unvermietbar; **ˌunˈten·ant·ed** *adj.* **1.** unbewohnt, leer(stehend); **2.** ⚖ ungemietet, ungepachtet.

ˌunˈtend·ed *adj.* **1.** unbehütet, unbeaufsichtigt; **2.** vernachlässigt.

ˌunˈthank·ful *adj.* ☐ undankbar.

unˈthink·a·ble *adj.* undenkbar, unvorstellbar: ***the ~*** das Undenkbare; **ˌunˈthink·ing** *adj.* ☐ **1.** gedankenlos; **2.** nicht denkend.

ˌunˈthought *adj.* **1.** ˈunüberˌlegt; **2.** *mst* ***~-of*** a) unerwartet, unvermutet, b) unvorstellbar.

ˌunˈthread *v/t.* **1.** *Nadel* ausfädeln; den Faden herˈausziehen aus; **2.** *Perlen etc.* abfädeln; **3.** *a. fig.* sich hinˈdurchfinden durch, herˈausfinden aus; **4.** *mst fig.* entwirren.

ˌunˈthrift·y *adj.* ☐ **1.** verschwenderisch; **2.** unwirtschaftlich (*a. Sache*).

ˌunˈthrone *v/t. a. fig.* entthronen.

unˈti·di·ness *s.* Unordentlichkeit *f*; **unˈti·dy** *adj.* ☐ unordentlich.

ˌunˈtie *v/t.* aufknoten, auf-, losbinden, *Knoten* lösen.

un·til [ənˈtɪl] **I** *prp.* bis (*zeitlich*): ***not ~ Monday*** erst (am) Montag; **II** *cj.* bis: ***not ~*** erst als *od.* wenn, nicht eher als.

ˌunˈtilled *adj.* ⚒ unbebaut.

unˈtime·li·ness *s.* Unzeit *f*, falscher *od.* verfrühter Zeitpunkt; **unˈtime·ly** *adj. u. adv.* unzeitig: a) verfrüht, b) ungelegen, unpassend.

unˈtir·ing *adj.* ☐ unermüdlich.

un·to [ˈʌntʊ] *prp. obs. od. poet. od. bibl.* → ***to*** I.

ˌunˈtold *adj.* **1.** a) unerzählt, b) ungesagt: ***leave nothing ~*** nichts unerwähnt lassen; **2.** unsäglich (*Leiden etc.*); **3.** ungezählt, zahllos; **4.** unermeßlich.

unˈtouch·a·ble I *adj.* **1.** unberührbar; **2.** unantastbar, unangreifbar; **3.** unerreichbar, unnahbar; **II** *s.* **4.** Unberührbare(r *m*) *f* (*bei den Hindus*); **ˌunˈtouched** *adj.* **1.** unberührt (*a. Essen*) (*a. fig.*); unangetastet (*a. Vorrat*); **2.** *fig.* ungerührt, unbeeinflußt; **3.** nicht zuˈrechtgemacht, *fig.* ungeschminkt; **4.** *phot.* unretuschiert; **5.** *fig.* unerreicht.

un·to·ward [ˌʌntəˈwɔːd] *adj.* **1.** *obs.* ungefügig, ˈwiderspenstig; **2.** widrig, ungünstig, unglücklich (*Umstand etc.*); **ˌun·toˈward·ness** [-nɪs] *s.* **1.** *obs.* ˈWiderspenstigkeit *f*; **2.** Widrigkeit *f*, Ungunst *f*.

ˌunˈtrace·a·ble *adj.* unauffindbar, nicht ausfindig zu machen(d).

ˌunˈtrained *adj.* **1.** ungeschult (*a. fig.*), *a.* ⚔ unausgebildet; **2.** *sport* untrainiert; **3.** ungeübt; **4.** undressiert (*Tier*).

unˈtram·mel(l)ed *adj. bsd. fig.* ungebunden, ungehindert.

ˌun·transˈlat·a·ble *adj.* ☐ ˈunüberˌsetzbar.

ˌunˈtrav·el(l)ed *adj.* **1.** unbefahren (*Straße etc.*); **2.** nicht (weit) herˈumgekommen (*Person*).

ˌunˈtried *adj.* **1.** a) unerprobt, ungeprüft, b) unversucht; **2.** ⚖ a) unerledigt, (noch) nicht verhandelt (*Fall*), b) (noch) nicht vor Gericht gestellt.

ˌunˈtrimmed *adj.* **1.** unbeschnitten (*Bart*, *Hecke etc.*); **2.** ungepflegt, nicht (ordentlich) zuˈrechtgemacht; **3.** ungeschmückt.

ˌunˈtrod·den *adj.* unberührt (*Wildnis etc.*): ***~ paths*** *fig.* neue Wege.

ˌunˈtrou·bled *adj.* **1.** ungestört, unbelästigt; **2.** ruhig (*Geist*, *Zeiten etc.*); **3.** ungetrübt (*a. fig.*).

ˌunˈtrue *adj.* ☐ **1.** untreu (***to*** *dat.*); **2.** unwahr, falsch, irrig; **3.** (***to***) nicht in Überˈeinstimmung (mit), abweichend (von); **4.** ⚙ a) unrund, b) ungenau;

ˌ**unˈtru·ly** *adv.* fälschlich(erweise).
ˌ**unˈtrustˌwor·thi·ness** *s.* Unzuverlässigkeit *f*; ˌ**unˈtrustˌwor·thy** *adj.* □ unzuverlässig, nicht vertrauenswürdig.
ˌ**unˈtruth** *s.* **1.** Unwahrheit *f*; **2.** Falschheit *f*; ˌ**unˈtruth·ful** *adj.* □ **1.** unwahr (*Person od. Sache*); unaufrichtig; **2.** falsch, irrig.
ˌ**unˈtuned** *adj.* **1.** ♪ verstimmt; **2.** *fig.* verwirrt; **3.** → ˌ**unˈtune·ful** *adj.* □ ˈunmeˌlodisch.
ˌ**unˈturned** *adj.* nicht ˈumgedreht; → ***stone*** 1.
ˌ**unˈtu·tored** *adj.* **1.** ungebildet, ungeschult; **2.** unerzogen; **3.** unverbildet, naˈtürlich; **4.** unkultiviert.
ˌ**unˈtwine**, ˌ**unˈtwist I** *v/t.* **1.** aufdrehen, -flechten; **2.** *bsd. fig.* entwirren, lösen; **II** *v/i.* **3.** sich aufdrehen, aufgehen.
ˌ**unˈused** *adj.* **1.** unbenutzt, ungebraucht, nicht verwendet; **2.** a) ungewohnt, nicht gewöhnt (***to*** an *acc.*), b) nicht gewohnt (***to doing*** zu tun).
unˈu·su·al *adj.* □ un-, außergewöhnlich: ***it is ~ for him to*** es ist nicht s-e Art zu *inf.*
unˈut·ter·a·ble *adj.* □ **1.** unaussprechlich (*a. fig.*); **2.** → ***unspeakable*** 1; **3.** unglaublich, Erz...: ***~ scoundrel***; ˌ**unˈut·tered** *adj.* unausgesprochen, ungesagt.
ˌ**unˈval·ued** *adj.* **1.** nicht (ab)geschätzt, untaxiert; **2.** ✝ nennwertlos (*Aktien*); **3.** nicht geschätzt, wenig geachtet.
unˈvar·ied *adj.* unverändert, einförmig.
ˌ**unˈvar·nished** *adj.* **1.** ungefirnißt; **2.** *fig.* ungeschminkt: ***~ truth***; **3.** *fig.* schlicht, einfach.
unˈvar·y·ing *adj.* □ unveränderlich, gleichbleibend.
ˌ**unˈveil I** *v/t.* **1.** *Gesicht etc.* entschleiern, *Denkmal etc.* enthüllen (*a. fig.*): ***~ed*** a) unverschleiert, b) unverhüllt (*a. fig.*); **2.** sichtbar werden lassen; **II** *v/i.* **3.** den Schleier fallen lassen, sich enthüllen (*a. fig.*).
ˌ**unˈver·i·fied** *adj.* unbelegt, unbewiesen.
ˌ**unˈversed** *adj.* unbewandert (***in*** in *dat.*).
ˌ**unˈvoiced** *adj.* **1.** unausgesprochen, nicht geäußert; **2.** *ling.* stimmlos.
ˌ**unˈvouched**, *a.* **unˈvouched-for** *adj.* unverbürgt.
ˌ**unˈvouch·ered** *adj.* : ***~ fund*** *pol. Am.* Reptilienfonds *m.*
ˌ**unˈwant·ed** *adj.* unerwünscht.
unˈwar·i·ness *s.* Unvorsichtigkeit *f.*
ˌ**unˈwar·like** *adj.* unkriegerisch.
ˌ**unˈwarped** *adj.* **1.** nicht verzogen (*Holz*); **2.** *fig.* ˈunparˌteiisch.
unˈwar·rant·a·ble *adj.* □ unverantwortlich, ungerechtfertigt, nicht vertretbar, untragbar, unhaltbar; **unˈwar·rant·a·bly** *adv.* in unverantwortlicher *od.* ungerechtfertigter Weise; **unˈwar·rant·ed** *adj.* □ **1.** ungerechtfertigt, unberechtigt, unbefugt; **2.** ˌ***unˈwarranted*** unverbürgt, ohne Gewähr.
unˈwar·y *adj.* □ **1.** unvorsichtig; **2.** ˈunüberˌlegt.
ˌ**unˈwashed** *adj.* ungewaschen: ***the great ~*** *fig. contp.* der Pöbel.
ˌ**unˈwatched** *adj.* unbeobachtet.
ˌ**unˈwa·tered** *adj.* **1.** unbewässert; nicht begossen, nicht gesprengt (*Rasen etc.*); **2.** unverwässert (*Milch etc.*; *a.* ✝ *Kapital*).
unˈwa·ver·ing *adj.* □ unerschütterlich, standhaft, unentwegt.
un·wea·ried [ʌnˈwɪərɪd] *adj.* □ **1.** nicht ermüdet; **2.** unermüdlich; **unˈwea·ry·ing** [-ɪɪŋ] *adj.* □ unermüdlich.
ˌ**unˈwed(·ded)** *adj.* unverheiratet.
ˌ**unˈweighed** *adj.* **1.** ungewogen; **2.** nicht abgewogen, unbedacht.
unˈwel·come *adj.* □ ˈunwillˌkommen (*a. fig. unangenehm*).
ˌ**unˈwell** *adj.* unwohl, unpäßlich (*a. euphem.*).
ˌ**unˈwept** *adj.* **1.** unbeweint; **2.** unvergossen (*Tränen*).
ˌ**unˈwhole·some** *adj.* □ *allg.* ungesund (*a. fig.*); ˌ**unˈwhole·some·ness** *s.* Ungesundheit *f.*
un·wield·i·ness [ʌnˈwiːldɪnɪs] *s.* **1.** Unbeholfenheit *f*, Schwerfälligkeit *f*; **2.** Unhandlichkeit *f*; **unˈwield·y** *adj.* □ **1.** unbeholfen, plump, schwerfällig; **2.** a) unhandlich, b) sperrig.
ˌ**unˈwill·ing** *adj.* □ un-, ˈwiderwillig: ***be ~ to do*** abgeneigt sein, *et.* zu tun, *et.* nicht tun wollen; ***I am ~ to admit it*** ich gebe es ungern zu; **unˈwill·ing·ly** *adv.* ungern, ˈwiderwillig; **unˈwill·ing·ness** *s.* ˈWiderwille *m*, Abgeneigtheit *f.*
un·wind [ˌʌnˈwaɪnd] [*irr.* → ***wind***[2]] **I** *v/t.* **1.** ab-, auf-, loswickeln, abspulen; **II** *v/i.* **2.** sich ab- *od.* loswickeln; **3.** F sich entspannen.
un·wink·ing [ˌʌnˈwɪŋkɪŋ] *adj.* □ unverwandt, starr (*Blick*).
ˌ**unˈwis·dom** *s.* Unklugheit *f*; ˌ**unˈwise** *adj.* □ unklug, töricht.
ˌ**unˈwished** *adj.* **1.** ungewünscht; **2.** *a.* ***~-for*** unerwünscht.
unˈwit·ting *adj.* □ unwissentlich, unabsichtlich.
unˈwom·an·li·ness *s.* Unweiblichkeit *f*; **unˈwom·an·ly** *adj.* unweiblich, unfraulich.
unˈwont·ed *adj.* □ **1.** nicht gewöhnt (***to*** an *acc.*), ungewohnt (***to*** *inf.* zu *inf.*); **2.** ungewöhnlich.
ˌ**unˈwork·a·ble** *adj.* **1.** unaus-, ˈunˌdurchführbar (*Plan*); **2.** ⚙ nicht bearbeitungsfähig; **3.** ⚙ a) nicht betriebsfähig, b) ⚒ nicht abbauwürdig.
ˌ**unˈworked** *adj.* **1.** unbearbeitet (*Boden etc.*), roh (*a.* ⚙); **2.** ⚒ unverritzt: ***~ coal*** anstehende Kohle.
ˌ**unˈwork·man·like** *adj.* unfachmännisch, unfachgemäß, stümperhaft.
ˌ**unˈworld·li·ness** *s.* **1.** Weltfremdheit *f*; **2.** Uneigennützigkeit *f*; **3.** Geistigkeit *f*; ˌ**unˈworld·ly** *adj.* **1.** unweltlich, nicht weltlich (gesinnt), weltfremd; **2.** uneigennützig; **3.** unirdisch, geistig.
ˌ**unˈworn** *adj.* **1.** ungetragen (*Kleid etc.*); **2.** nicht abgetragen.
unˈwor·thi·ness *s.* Unwürdigkeit *f*; **unˈwor·thy** *adj.* □ unwürdig (***of*** *gen.*): ***he is ~ of it*** er verdient es nicht, er ist es nicht wert; ***he is ~ of respect*** er verdient keine Achtung.
un·wound [ˌʌnˈwaʊnd] *adj.* **1.** abgewickelt; **2.** abgelaufen, nicht aufgezogen (*Uhr*).
ˌ**unˈwrap** *v/t.* auswickeln, -packen.
ˌ**unˈwrin·kled** *adj.* nicht gerunzelt *od.* zerknittert, faltenlos, glatt.
ˌ**unˈwrit·ten** *adj.* **1.** ungeschrieben: ***~ law*** a) ⚖ ungeschriebenes Recht, b) *fig.* ungeschriebenes Gesetz; **2.** *a.* ***~-on*** unbeschrieben.
ˌ**unˈwrought** *adj.* unbe-, unverarbeitet, roh: ***~ goods*** Rohstoffe.
unˈyield·ing *adj.* □ **1.** nicht nachgebend (***to*** *dat.*), fest (*a. fig.*), unbiegsam, starr; **2.** *fig.* unnachgiebig, hart, unbeugsam.
ˌ**unˈyoke** *v/t.* **1.** aus-, losspannen; **2.** *fig.* (los)trennen, lösen.
ˌ**unˈzip** *v/t.* den Reißverschluß aufmachen an (*dat.*).
up [ʌp] **I** *adv.* **1.** a) nach oben, hoch, (her-, hin)ˈauf, aufwärts, in die Höhe, emˈpor, b) oben (*a. fig.*): ***... and ~*** u. (noch) höher *od.* mehr, von ... aufwärts; ***~ and ~*** immer höher; ***three stor(e)ys ~*** drei Stock hoch, oben im dritten Stock(werk); ***~ and down*** auf u. ab, hin u. her; *fig.* überall; ***~ from the country*** vom Lande; ***~ till now*** bis jetzt; **2.** nach *od.* im Norden: ***~ from Cuba*** von Cuba aus in nördlicher Richtung; **3.** a) in der *od.* in die (*bsd.* Haupt)Stadt, b) *Brit. bsd.* in *od.* nach London; **4.** am *od.* zum Studienort, im College *etc.*: ***he stayed ~ for the vacation***; **5.** *Am.* F in (*dat.*): ***~ north*** im Norden; **6.** aufrecht, gerade: ***sit ~***; **7.** herˈan, her, auf ... (*acc.*) zu, hin: ***he went straight ~ to the door*** er ging geradewegs auf die Tür zu *od.* zur Tür; **8.** ***~ to*** a) hinˈauf nach *od.* zu, b) bis (zu), bis an *od.* auf (*acc.*), c) gemäß, entsprechend; → ***date***[2] 5; ***~ to town*** in die Stadt, *Brit. bsd.* nach London; ***~ to the chin*** bis ans *od.* zum Kinn; ***~ to death*** bis zum Tode; ***be ~ to*** F a) *et.* vorhaben, *et.* im Schilde führen, b) gewachsen sein (*dat.*), c) entsprechen (*dat.*), d) *j-s* Sache sein, abhängen von *j-m*, e) fähig *od.* bereit sein zu, f) vorbereitet *od.* gefaßt sein auf (*acc.*), g) vertraut sein mit, bewandert sein in (*dat.*); ***what are you ~ to?*** was hast du vor?, was machst du (***there*** da)?; → ***trick*** 2; ***he is ~ to no good*** er führt nichts Gutes im Schilde; ***it is ~ to him*** es liegt an ihm, es hängt von ihm ab, es ist s-e Sache; ***it is not ~ to much*** es taugt nicht viel; ***he is not ~ to much*** mit ihm ist nicht viel los; **9.** *mit Verben* (*siehe jeweils diese*): a) auf..., aus..., ver..., b) zuˈsammen...: ***add ~*** zs.-zählen; ***eat ~*** aufessen; **II** *adj.* **10.** aufwärts..., nach oben gerichtet; **11.** im Innern (des Landes *etc.*); **12.** nach der *od.* zur Stadt: ***~ train***; ***~ platform*** Bahnsteig *m* für Stadtzüge; **13.** a) oben (befindlich), b) hoch (*a. fig.*): ***be ~*** *fig.* an der Spitze sein, obenauf sein; ***he is ~ in*** (*od.* ***on***) ***that subject*** F in diesem Fach ist er gut beschlagen *od.* weiß er (gut) Bescheid; ***prices are ~*** die Preise sind hoch *od.* gestiegen; ***wheat is ~*** ✝ Weizen steht hoch (im Kurs), der Weizenpreis ist gestiegen; **14.** auf(gestanden), auf den Beinen (*a. fig.*): ***~ and about*** F (wieder) auf den Beinen; ***~ and coming*** → ***up-and-coming***; ***~ and doing*** a) auf den Beinen, b) rührig, tüchtig; ***be ~ late*** lange aufbleiben; ***be ~ against*** F *e-r Schwierigkeit etc.* gegenüberstehen; ***be ~ against it*** F ‚dran' sein, in der Klemme sein *od.* sitzen; ***be ~ to*** → 8; **15.** *parl. Brit.* geschlossen: ***Parliament is ~*** das Parlament hat s-e Sitzungen beendet *od.* hat

sich vertagt; **16.** (zum Sprechen) aufgestanden: ***the Home Secretary is ~*** der Innenminister spricht; **17.** (*bei verschiedenen Substantiven*) a) aufgegangen (*Sonne, Samen*), b) hochgeschlagen (*Kragen*), c) hochgekrempelt (*Ärmel etc.*), d) aufgespannt (*Schirm*), e) aufgeschlagen (*Zelt*), f) hoch-, aufgezogen (*Vorhang etc.*), g) aufgestiegen (*Ballon etc.*), h) aufgeflogen (*Vogel*), i) angeschwollen (*Fluß etc.*); **18.** schäumend (*Apfelwein etc.*); **19.** in Aufregung, in Aufruhr: ***his temper is ~*** er ist aufgebracht; ***the whole country was ~*** das ganze Land befand sich in Aufruhr; **20.** F ‚los', im Gange: ***what's ~?*** was ist los?; ***is anything ~?*** ist (irgend et-) was los?; ***the hunt is ~*** die Jagd ist eröffnet; → ***arm***² 1, ***blood*** 2; **21.** abgelaufen, vor'bei, um (*Zeit*): ***the game is ~*** *fig.* das Spiel ist aus; ***it's all ~*** alles ist aus; ***it's all ~ with him*** es ist aus mit ihm; **22.** ***~ with*** *j-m* ebenbürtig *od.* gewachsen; **23.** ***~ for*** bereit zu: ***be ~ for discussion*** zur Diskussion stehen; ***be ~ for election*** auf der Wahlliste stehen; ***be ~ for examination*** sich e-r Prüfung unterziehen; ***be ~ for sale*** zum Kauf stehen; ***be ~ for trial*** ⚖ a) vor Gericht stehen, b) verhandelt werden; ***be*** (***had***) ***~ for*** F vorgeladen werden wegen; ***the case is ~ before the court*** der Fall wird (vor Gericht) verhandelt; **24.** *sport etc. um e-n Punkt etc.* vor'aus: ***be one ~; one ~ for you!*** eins zu null für dich! (*a. fig.*); **25.** *Baseball*: am Schlag; **26.** *sl.* a) hoffnungsvoll, opti'mistisch, b) in Hochstimmung; **III** *int.* **27.** ***~!*** auf!, hoch!, her'auf!, hin'auf!, her'an!; ***~*** (***with you***)***!*** (steh) auf!; ***~ ...!*** hoch (lebe) ...!; **IV** *prp.* **28.** auf ... (*acc.*) (hinauf), hinauf, em'por (*a. fig.*): ***~ the hill*** (***river***) den Berg (Fluß) hinauf, bergauf (flußaufwärts); ***~ the street*** die Straße hinauf *od.* entlang; ***~ yours!*** V ‚leck mich'!; **29.** in das Innere *e-s Landes etc.*: ***~*** (***the***) ***country*** landeinwärts; **30.** oben an *od.* auf (*dat.*): ***~ the tree*** (oben) auf dem Baum; ***~ the road*** weiter oben an der Straße; **V** *s.* **31.** ***the ~s and downs*** das Auf u. Ab, die Höhen u. Tiefen *des Lebens*; ***on the ~ and ~*** F a) im Steigen (begriffen), im Kommen, b) in Ordnung, ehrlich; **32.** F Preisanstieg *m*; **33.** *sl.* Aufputschmittel *n*; **34.** F Höhergestellte(r *m*) *f*; **VI** *v/i.* **35.** ***~ with*** *sl. et.* hochreißen: ***he ~ped with his gun***; **36.** *Am. sl.* Aufputschmittel nehmen; **VII** *v/t.* **37.** *Preis, Produktion etc.* erhöhen; **38.** *Am.* F *j-n* (im Rang) befördern (***to*** zu).

ˌup-and-'com·ing *adj.* aufstrebend.

ˌup-and-'down *adj.* auf- und ab gehend: ***~ looks*** kritisch musternde Blicke; ***~ motion*** Aufundabbewegung *f*; ***~ stroke*** ⚙ Doppelhub *m*.

u·pas ['ju:pəs] *s.* **1.** *a.* ***~-tree*** ⚘ Upasbaum *m*; **2.** a) Upassaft *m* (*Pfeilgift*), b) *fig.* Gift, verderblicher Einfluß.

'up·beat I *s.* **1.** ♪ Auftakt *m*; **2.** ***on the ~*** *fig.* im Aufschwung; **II** *adj.* **3.** F beschwingt.

'up-bow [-bəʊ] *s.* ♪ Aufstrich *m*.

up'braid *v/t. j-m* Vorwürfe machen, *j-n, a. et.* tadeln, rügen: ***~ s.o. with*** (*od.* ***for***) ***s.th.*** j-m et. vorwerfen, j-m wegen e-r Sache Vorwürfe machen; **up'braid·ing I** *s.* Vorwurf *m*, Tadel *m*, Rüge *f*; **II** *adj.* □ vorwurfsvoll, tadelnd.

'upˌbring·ing *s.* **1.** Erziehung *f*; **2.** Groß-, Aufziehen *n*.

'up·cast I *adj.* em'porgerichtet (*Blick etc.*), aufgeschlagen (*Augen*); **II** *s. a.* ***~ shaft*** ⚒ Wetter-, Luftschacht *m*.

'up·chuck I *v/i.* (sich er)brechen; **II** *v/t. et.* erbrechen.

'upˌcom·ing *adj. Am.* kommend, be'vorstehend.

ˌup'coun·try I *adv.* land'einwärts; **II** *adj.* im Inneren des Landes (gelegen *od.* lebend), binnenländisch; *contp.* bäurisch; **III** *s.* *das* (Landes)Innere, Binnen-, Hinterland *n*.

'upˌcur·rent *s.* ✈ Aufwind *m*.

up'date I *v/t.* **1.** auf den neuesten Stand bringen; **II** *s.* ***'update*** **2.** 'Unterlage(n *pl.*) *f etc.* über den neuesten Stand; **3.** auf den neuesten Stand gebrachte Versi'on *etc.*, neuester Bericht (***on*** über *acc.*).

'up·do *s.* F 'Hochfriˌsur *f*.

'up·draft *Am.*, **'up·draught** *Brit. s.* Aufwind *m*.

up'end *v/t.* F **1.** hochkant stellen, *Faß etc.* aufrichten; **2.** *Gefäß* 'umstülpen; **3.** *fig.* ‚auf den Kopf stellen'.

'up·front *adj. Am.* F **1.** freimütig, di'rekt; **2.** vordringlich; **3.** führend; **4.** Voraus...

'up·grade I *s.* **1.** Steigung *f*: ***on the ~*** *fig.* im (An)Steigen (begriffen); **II** *adj.* **2.** *Am.* ansteigend; **III** *adv.* **3.** *Am.* berg'auf; **IV** *v/t.* ***up'grade*** **4.** höher einstufen; **5.** *j-n* (im Rang) befördern: ***~ s.o.'s status*** *fig.* j-n ‚aufwerten'; **6.** ☤ a) (die Quali'tät *gen.*) verbessern, b) *Produkt* durch ein besseres Erzeugnis ersetzen.

up·heav·al [ʌp'hi:vl] *s.* **1.** *geol.* Erhebung *f*; **2.** *fig.* 'Umwälzung *f*, 'Umbruch *m*: ***social ~s***.

up'heave *v/t. u. v/i.* [*irr.* → ***heave***] (sich) heben.

ˌup'hill I *adv.* **1.** den Berg hin'auf, berg'auf; **2.** aufwärts; **II** *adj.* **3.** bergauf führend, ansteigend; **4.** hochgelegen, oben (auf dem Berg) gelegen; **5.** *fig.* mühselig, hart: ***~ work***.

up'hold *v/t.* [*irr.* → ***hold***²] **1.** hochhalten, aufrecht halten; **2.** halten, stützen (*a. fig.*); **3.** *fig.* aufrechterhalten, unter'stützen; **4.** ⚖ *Urteil* (in zweiter In'stanz) bestätigen; **5.** *fig.* beibehalten; **6.** *Brit.* in'stand halten; **up'hold·er** *s.* Erhalter *m*, Verteidiger *m*, Wahrer *m*: ***~ of public order*** Hüter *m* der öffentlichen Ordnung.

up·hol·ster [ʌp'həʊlstə] *v/t.* **1.** a) (auf-, aus)polstern, b) beziehen: ***~ed goods*** Polsterware(n *pl.*) *f*; **2.** *Zimmer* (mit Teppichen, Vorhängen *etc.*) ausstatten; **up'hol·ster·er** [-tərə] *s.* Polsterer *m*; **up'hol·ster·y** [-tərɪ] *s.* **1.** 'Polstermateriˌal *n*, Polsterung *f*, (Möbel)Bezugsstoff *m*; **2.** Polstern *n*.

'up·keep *s.* **1.** a) In'standhaltung *f*, b) In'standhaltungskosten *pl.*; **2.** 'Unterhalt(skosten *pl.*) *m*.

up·land ['ʌplənd] **I** *s. mst pl.* Hochland *n*; **II** *adj.* Hochland(s)...

up'lift I *v/t.* **1.** em'porheben; **2.** *Augen, Stimme, a. fig. Stimmung, Niveau* heben; **3.** *fig.* a) aufrichten, Auftrieb verleihen (*dat.*), b) erbauen; **II** *s.* ***'uplift*** **4.** *fig.* a) (innerer) Auftrieb, b) Erbauung *f*; **5.** *fig.* a) Aufschwung *m*, b) Hebung *f*, (Ver)Besserung *f*; **6.** ***~ brassiere*** Stützbüstenhalter *m*.

up·on [ə'pɒn] *prp.* → ***on*** (***upon*** *ist bsd. in der Umgangssprache weniger geläufig als* ***on***, *jedoch in folgenden Fällen üblich*): a) *in verschiedenen Redewendungen*: ***~ this*** hierauf, darauf(hin), b) *in Beteuerungen*: ***~ my word*** (***of hono***[***u***]***r***)***!*** auf mein Wort!, c) *in kumulativen Wendungen*: ***loss ~ loss*** Verlust auf Verlust, dauernde Verluste; ***petition ~ petition*** ein Gesuch nach dem anderen, d) *als Märchenanfang*: ***once ~ a time there was*** es war einmal.

up·per ['ʌpə] **I** *adj.* **1.** ober, höher, Ober...(*-arm, -deck, -kiefer, -leder etc.*): ***~ case*** *typ.* a) Oberkasten *m*, b) Versal-, Großbuchstaben *pl.*; ***~ circle*** *thea.* zweiter Rang; ***~ class*** *sociol.* Oberschicht *f*; ***~ crust*** F *die* Spitzen *pl.* der Gesellschaft; ***get the ~ hand*** *fig.* die Oberhand gewinnen; ***⁂ House*** *parl.* Oberhaus *n*; ***~ stor***(***e***)***y*** oberes Stockwerk; ***there is something wrong in his ~ stor***(***e***)***y*** F *fig.* er ist nicht ganz richtig im Oberstübchen; **II** *s.* **2.** *mst pl.* Oberleder *n* (*Schuh*): ***be*** (***down***) ***on one's ~s*** F a) die Schuhe durchgelaufen haben, b) *fig.* ‚total abgebrannt' *od.* ‚auf dem Hund' sein; **3.** F a) Oberzahn *m*, b) obere ('Zahn)ProˌTHese, c) (Py'jama- *etc.*)Oberteil *n*; **4.** *sl.* Aufputschmittel *n*; **'~·cut** *Boxen*: **I** *s.* Aufwärts-, Kinnhaken *m*; **II** *v/t.* [*irr.* → ***cut***] *j-m* e-n Aufwärtshaken versetzen.

'up·per·most I *adj.* oberst, höchst; **II** *adv.* ganz oben, oben'an, zu'oberst; an erster Stelle: ***say whatever comes ~*** sagen, was e-m gerade einfällt.

up·pish ['ʌpɪʃ] *adj.* □ F **1.** hochnäsig; **2.** anmaßend.

up·pi·ty ['ʌpətɪ] → ***uppish***.

up'raise *v/t.* erheben: ***with hands ~d*** mit erhobenen Händen.

up·right I *adj.* □ [ˌʌp'raɪt] **1.** auf-, senkrecht, gerade: ***~ piano*** → 7; ***~ size*** Hochformat *n*; **2.** aufrecht (sitzend, stehend, gehend); **3.** ['ʌpraɪt] *fig.* aufrecht, rechtschaffen; **II** *adv.* [ˌʌp'raɪt] **4.** aufrecht, gerade; **III** *s.* ['ʌpraɪt] **5.** (senkrechte) Stütze, Träger *m*, Ständer *m*, Pfosten *m*, (Treppen)Säule *f*; **6.** *pl. sport* (Tor)Pfosten *pl.*; **7.** ♪ ('Wand-) KlaˌVier *n*, Pi'ano *n*; **up·right·ness** ['ʌpraɪtnɪs] *s. fig.* Geradheit *f*, Rechtschaffenheit *f*.

'upˌris·ing *s.* **1.** Aufstehen *n*; **2.** *fig.* Aufstand *m*, (Volks)Erhebung *f*.

ˌup'riv·er → ***upstream***.

'up·roar *s. fig.* Aufruhr *m*, Tu'mult *m*, Toben *n*, Lärm *m*: ***in*** (***an***) ***~*** in Aufruhr; **up·roar·i·ous** [ʌp'rɔ:rɪəs] *adj.* □ **1.** lärmend, laut, stürmisch (*Begrüßung etc.*), tosend (*Beifall*), schallend (*Gelächter*); **2.** tumultu'arisch, tobend; **3.** ‚toll', zum Brüllen (komisch).

up'root *v/t.* **1.** ausreißen; *Baum etc.* entwurzeln (*a. fig.*); **2.** *fig.* her'ausreißen (***from*** aus); **3.** *fig.* ausmerzen, -rotten.

up'set¹ **I** *v/t.* [*irr.* → ***set***] **1.** 'umwerfen, -kippen, -stoßen; *Boot* zum Kentern bringen; **2.** *fig. Regierung* stürzen; **3.** *fig. Plan* 'umstoßen, über den Haufen werfen, vereiteln; → ***apple-cart***; **4.** *fig. j-n* umwerfen, aus der Fassung bringen, bestürzen, durchein'anderbringen; **5.** in Unordnung bringen; *Magen* verderben; **6.** ⚙ stauchen; **II** *v/i.* [*irr.* → ***set***] **7.** 'umkippen, -stürzen; 'umschlagen, kentern (*Boot*); **III** *s.* **8.** 'Umkippen *n*; ⚓ 'Umschlagen *n*, Kentern *n*; **9.** Sturz *m*, Fall *m*; **10.** 'Umsturz *m*; **11.** Unordnung *f*, Durchein'ander *n*; **12.** Bestürzung *f*, Verwirrung *f*; **13.** Vereitelung *f*; **14.** (*a.* ⚕ Magen)Verstimmung *f*, Ärger *m*; **15.** Streit *m*, Meinungsverschiedenheit *f*; **16.** *sport* Über'raschung *f* (*unerwartete Niederlage etc.*).

'up·set² *adj. attr.* **1.** verdorben (*Magen*): *~ **stomach*** Magenverstimmung *f*; **2.** *~ **price*** Anschlagspreis *m* (*Auktion*).

'up·shot *s.* (End)Ergebnis *n*, Ende *n*, Ausgang *m*, Fazit *n*: ***in the ~*** am Ende, schließlich.

'up·side *s.* Oberseite *f*; *~* **down** *adv.* **1.** das Oberste zu'unterst, mit dem Kopf *od.* Oberteil nach unten, verkehrt (her-'um); **2.** *fig.* drunter u. drüber, vollkommen durchein'ander: ***turn everything ~*** alles auf den Kopf stellen; **ˌ~-'down** *adj.* auf den Kopf gestellt, 'umgekehrt: *~ **flight*** ✈ Rückenflug *m*; *~ **world*** *fig.* verkehrte Welt.

up·si·lon [ju:p'saılən] *s.* Ypsilon *n* (*Buchstabe*).

ˌup'stage I *adv. thea.* **1.** im *od.* in den 'Hintergrund der Bühne; **II** *adj.* **2.** zum 'Bühnenˌhintergrund gehörig; **3.** F hochnäsig; **III** *v/t.* **4.** *fig. j-m* ‚die Schau stehlen', *j-n* in den 'Hintergrund drängen; **5.** F *j-n* hochnäsig behandeln; **IV** *s.* **6.** *thea.* 'Bühnenˌhintergrund *m*.

ˌup'stairs I *adv.* **1.** die Treppe hin'auf, nach oben; → ***kick*** 9; **2.** e-e Treppe höher; **3.** oben, in e-m oberen Stockwerk: ***a bit weak ~*** F leicht ‚behämmert'; **4.** im oberen Stockwerk (gelegen), ober; **II** *s. pl. a. sg. konstr.* **5.** oberes Stockwerk, Obergeschoß *n*.

up'stand·ing *adj.* **1.** aufrecht (*a. fig. ehrlich, tüchtig*); **2.** großgewachsen, (groß u.) kräftig.

'up·start I *s.* Em'porkömmling *m*, Parve'nü *m*; **II** *adj.* em'porgekommen, Parvenü…, neureich.

'up·state *Am.* **I** *s.* 'Hinterland *n e-s Staates*; **II** *adj. u. adv.* aus dem *od.* in den *od.* im ländlichen *od.* nördlichen Teil des Staates, in *od.* aus der *od.* in die Pro'vinz.

ˌup'stream I *adv.* **1.** strom'aufwärts; **2.** gegen den Strom; **II** *adj.* **3.** strom'aufwärts gerichtet; **4.** (weiter) strom'aufwärts gelegen.

'up·stroke *s.* **1.** Aufstrich *m beim Schreiben*; **2.** ⚙ (Aufwärts)Hub *m*.

up'surge I *v/i.* aufwallen; **II** *s.* **'*upsurge*** Aufwallung *f*; *fig. a.* Aufschwung *m*.

'up·sweep *s.* **1.** Schweifung *f* (*Bogen etc.*); **2.** 'Hochfriˌsur *f*; **up'swept** *adj.* **1.** nach oben gebogen *od.* gekrümmt; **2.** hochgekämmt (*Frisur*).

'up·swing *s. fig.* Aufschwung *m*.

up·sy-dai·sy [ˌʌpsı'deızı] *int.* F hoppla!

'up·take *s.* **1.** Auffassungsvermögen *n*: ***be quick on the ~*** schnell begreifen, ‚schnell schalten'; ***be slow on the ~*** schwer von Begriff sein, e-e ‚lange Leitung' haben; **2.** Aufnahme *f*; **3.** ⚙ a) Steigrohr *n*, -leitung *f*, b) 'Fuchs(kaˌnal) *m*.

'up·throw *s.* **1.** 'Umwälzung *f*; **2.** *geol.* Verwerfung *f* (ins Hangende).

'up·thrust *s.* **1.** Em'porschleudern *n*, Stoß *m* nach oben; **2.** *geol.* Horstbildung *f*.

'up·tight *adj.* **1.** *sl.* ner'vös (***about*** wegen); **2.** ‚zickig'; **3.** steif, verklemmt; **4.** ‚pleite'.

ˌup-to-'date *adj.* **1.** a) mo'dern, neuzeitlich, b) zeitnah, aktu'ell (*Thema etc.*); **2.** a) auf der Höhe (*der Zeit*), auf dem laufenden, auf dem neuesten Stand, b) modisch; **ˌup-to-'date·ness** [-nıs] *s.* **1.** Neuzeitlichkeit *f*, Moderni'tät *f*; **2.** Aktuali'tät *f*.

ˌup-to-the-'min·ute *adj.* allerneuest, allerletzt.

up'town I *adv.* **1.** im *od.* in den oberen Stadtteil; **2.** in den Wohnvierteln, in die Wohnviertel; **II** *adj.* **3.** im oberen Stadtteil (gelegen); **4.** in den Wohnvierteln (gelegen *od.* lebend).

'up·trend *s.* Aufschwung *m*, steigende Ten'denz.

up'turn I *v/t.* **1.** 'umdrehen; **2.** (*v/i.* sich) nach oben richten *od.* kehren; *Blick* in die Höhe richten; **II** *s.* **'*upturn*** **3.** (An-)Steigen *n* (*der Kurse etc.*); **4.** *fig.* Aufschwung *m*; **ˌup'turned** *adj.* **1.** nach oben gerichtet *od.* gebogen: *~ **nose*** Stupsnase *f*; **2.** 'umgeworfen, 'umgekippt, ⚓ gekentert.

up·ward ['ʌpwəd] **I** *adv. a.* **'up·wards** [-dz] **1.** aufwärts (*a. fig.*): ***from five dollars ~*** von 5 Dollar an (aufwärts); **2.** nach oben (*a. fig.*); **3.** mehr, dar'über (hin'aus): *~ **of 10 years*** mehr als *od.* über 10 Jahre; **II** *adj.* **4.** nach oben gerichtet; (an)steigend (*Tendenz etc.*): *~ **glance*** Blick *m* nach oben; *~ **movement*** ☤ Aufwärtsbewegung *f*.

u·rae·mi·a [ˌjʊə'ri:mjə] *s.* ⚕ Urä'mie *f*;

u·ra·nal·y·sis [ˌjʊərə'næləsıs] *s.* ⚕ U'rin-, 'Harnunterˌsuchung *f*.

u·ra·nite ['jʊərənaıt] *s. min.* Ura'nit *n*, U'ranglimmer *m*.

u·ra·ni·um [jʊ'reınjəm] *s.* U'ran *n*.

u·ra·nog·ra·phy [ˌjʊərə'nɒgrəfı] *s.* Himmelsbeschreibung *f*.

u·ra·nous ['jʊərənəs] *adj.* ⚗ Uran…, u'ranhaltig.

U·ra·nus ['jʊərənəs] *s. ast.* Uranus *m* (*Planet*).

ur·ban ['ɜ:bən] *adj.* städtisch, Stadt…: *~ **district*** Stadtbezirk *m*; *~ **guerilla*** Stadtguerilla *m*; *~ **planning*** Stadtplanung *f*; *~ **renewal*** Stadtsanierung *f*; *~ **sprawl***, *~ **spread*** unkontrollierte Ausdehnung e-r Stadt; **ur·bane** [ɜ:'beın] *adj.* ☐ **1.** ur'ban: a) weltgewandt, -männisch, b) kulti'viert, gebildet; **2.** höflich, liebenswürdig; **ur·bane·ness** [ɜ:'beınıs] *s.* **1.** (Welt)Gewandtheit *f*; Bildung *f*; **2.** Höflichkeit *f*, Liebenswürdigkeit *f*; **'ur·ban·ism** [-nızəm] *s. Am.* **1.** Stadtleben *n*; **2.** Urba'nistik *f*; **3.** → ***urbanization***; **'ur·ban·ite** [-naıt] *s. Am.* Städter(in); **ur·ban·i·ty** [ɜ:'bænətı] → ***urbaneness***; **ur·ban·i·za·tion** [ˌɜ:bənaı'zeıʃn] *s.* **1.** Verstädterung *f*; **2.** Verfeinerung *f*; **'ur·ban·ize** [-naız] *v/t.* urbanisieren: a) verstädtern, städtischen Cha'rakter verleihen (*dat.*), b) verfeinern.

ur·chin ['ɜ:tʃın] *s.* **1.** Bengel *m*, Balg *m*, *n*; **2.** *zo.* a) *dial.* Igel *m*, b) *mst* ***sea ~*** Seeigel *m*.

u·re·a ['jʊərıə] *s.* ⚗, *biol.* Harnstoff *m*, Karba'mid *n*; **'ure·al** [-əl] *adj.* Harnstoff…

u·re·mi·a → ***uraemia***.

u·re·ter [ˌjʊə'ri:tə] *s. anat.* Harnleiter *m*; **ˌu're·thra** [-'ri:θrə] *s. anat.* Harnröhre *f*; **ˌu'ret·ic** [-'retık] *adj. physiol.* **1.** harntreibend, diu'retisch; **2.** Harn…

urge [ɜ:dʒ] **I** *v/t.* **1.** *a.* *~ **on*** (*od.* ***forward***) (an-, vorwärts)treiben, anspornen (*a. fig.*); **2.** *fig. j-n* drängen, dringend bitten *od.* auffordern, dringen in *j-n*, *j-m* (heftig) zusetzen: ***be ~d to do*** sich genötigt sehen zu tun; ***~d by necessity*** der Not gehorchend; **3.** drängen *od.* dringen auf (*acc.*); (hartnäckig) bestehen auf (*dat.*); Nachdruck legen auf (*acc.*): *~ **s.th. on s.o.*** j-m et. eindringlich vorstellen *od.* vor Augen führen, j-m et. einschärfen; ***he ~d the necessity for immediate action*** er drängte auf sofortige Maßnahmen; **4.** *als Grund* geltend machen, *Einwand etc.* ins Feld führen; **5.** *Sache* vor'an-, betreiben, beschleunigen; **II** *v/i.* **6.** drängen: *~ **against*** sich nachdrücklich aussprechen gegen; **III** *s.* **7.** Drang *m*, (An)Trieb *m*: ***creative ~*** Schaffensdrang; ***sexual ~*** Geschlechtstrieb; **8.** Inbrunst *f*: ***religious ~***; **'ur·gen·cy** [-dʒənsı] *s.* **1.** Dringlichkeit *f*; **2.** (dringende) Not, Druck *m*; **3.** Drängen *n*; **4.** *parl. Brit.* Dringlichkeitsantrag *m*; **5.** Eindringlichkeit *f*; **'ur·gent** [-dʒənt] *adj.* ☐ **1.** dringend (*a. Mangel*; *a. teleph. Gespräch*), dringlich, eilig: ***the matter is ~*** die Sache eilt; ***be in ~ need of*** *et.* dringend brauchen; **2.** drängend: ***be ~ about*** (*od.* ***for***) ***s.th.*** zu et. drängen, auf et. dringen; ***be ~ with s.o.*** j-n drängen, in j-n dringen (***for*** wegen, ***to do*** zu tun); **3.** zu-, aufdringlich; **4.** hartnäckig.

u·ric ['jʊərık] *adj.* Urin…, Harn…: *~ **acid*** Harnsäure *f*.

u·ri·nal ['jʊərınl] *s.* **1.** U'rinflasche *f* (*für Kranke*); **2.** Harnglas *n*; **3.** a) U'rinbekken *n* (*in Toiletten*), b) Pis'soir *n*; **u·ri·nal·y·sis** [ˌjʊərı'næləsıs] *pl.* **-ses** [-si:z] → ***uranalysis***; **u·ri·nar·y** ['jʊərınərı] *adj.* Harn…, Urin…: *~ **bladder*** Harnblase *f*; *~ **calculus*** ⚕ Blasenstein *m*; **u·ri·nate** ['jʊərıneıt] *v/i.* urinieren; **u·rine** ['jʊərın] *s.* U'rin *m*, Harn *m*.

urn [ɜ:n] *s.* **1.** Urne *f*; **2.** 'Tee- *od.* 'Kaffeemaˌschine *f*.

u·ro·gen·i·tal [ˌjʊərəʊ'dʒenıtl] *adj.* ⚕ urogeni'tal.

u·rol·o·gy [ˌjʊə'rɒlədʒı] *s.* ⚕ Urolo'gie *f*.

ur·sine ['ɜ:saın] *adj. zo.* bärenartig, Bären…

U·ru·guay·an [ˌjʊərʊ'gwaıən] **I** *adj.* urugu'ayisch; **II** *s.* Urugu'ayer(in).

us [ʌs; əs] *pron.* **1.** uns (*dat. od. acc.*): ***all of ~*** wir alle; ***both of ~*** wir beide; **2.** *dial.* wir: *~ **poor people***.

us·a·ble ['ju:zəbl] *adj.* brauch-, verwendbar.

us·age ['ju:zıdʒ] *s.* **1.** Brauch *m*, Gepflogenheit *f*, Usus *m*: (***commercial***) *~* Handelsbrauch, Usance *f*; **2.** übliches Verfahren, Praxis *f*; **3.** Sprachgebrauch *m*: ***English ~***; **4.** Gebrauch *m*, Verwendung *f*; **5.** Behandlung(sweise) *f*.

us·ance ['ju:zns] *s.* ☤ **1.** (übliche) Wechselfrist, Uso *m*: ***at ~*** nach Uso; ***bill at ~*** Usowechsel *m*; **2.** Uso *m*,

U'sance *f*, Handelsbrauch *m*.

use **I** *s.* [ju:s] **1.** Gebrauch *m*, Benutzung *f*, Benützung *f*, An-, Verwendung *f*: ***for ~*** zum Gebrauch; ***for ~ in schools*** für den Schulgebrauch; ***directions for ~*** Gebrauchsanweisung *f*; ***in ~*** in Gebrauch, gebräuchlich; ***be in daily ~*** täglich gebraucht werden; ***in common ~*** allgemein gebräuchlich; ***come into ~*** in Gebrauch kommen; ***out of ~*** nicht in Gebrauch; ***fall*** (*od.* ***go*** *od.* ***pass***) ***out of ~*** außer Gebrauch kommen, ungebräuchlich werden; ***with ~*** durch (ständigen) Gebrauch; ***make ~ of*** Gebrauch machen von, benutzen; ***make*** (***a***) ***bad ~ of*** (e-n) schlechten Gebrauch machen von; **2.** a) Verwendung(szweck *m*) *f*, b) Brauchbarkeit *f*, Verwendbarkeit *f*, c) Zweck *m*, Sinn *m*, Nutzen *m*, Nützlichkeit *f*: ***of ~*** (***to***) brauchbar (für), nützlich (*dat.*), von Nutzen (für); ***it is of no ~ doing*** *od.* ***to do*** es ist unnütz *od.* nutz- *od.* zwecklos zu tun, es hat keinen Zweck zu tun; ***is this of ~ to you?*** können Sie das (ge-) brauchen?; ***crying is no ~*** Weinen führt zu nichts; ***what is the ~*** (***of it***)***?*** was hat es (überhaupt) für einen Zweck?; ***put to*** (***good***) ***~*** (gut) an- *od.* verwenden; ***have no ~ for*** a) nicht brauchen können, mit *et. od. j-m* nichts anfangen können, b) *bsd. Am.* F nichts übrig haben für; **3.** Fähigkeit *f*, *et.* zu gebrauchen, Gebrauch *m*: ***he lost the ~ of his right eye*** er kann auf dem rechten Auge nicht mehr sehen; ***have the ~ of one's limbs*** sich bewegen können; **4.** Gewohnheit *f*, Brauch *m*, Übung *f*, Praxis *f*: ***once a ~ and ever a custom*** jung gewohnt, alt getan; **5.** Benutzungsrecht *n*; **6.** ⚖ a) Nutznießung *f*, b) Nutzen *m*; **II** *v/t.* [ju:z] **7.** gebrauchen, Gebrauch machen von (*a. von e-m Recht etc.*), benutzen, benützen, *a. Gewalt* anwenden, *a. Sorgfalt* verwenden, sich bedienen (*gen.*), *Gelegenheit etc.* nutzen, sich zu'nutze machen: ***~ one's brains*** den Verstand gebrauchen, s-n Kopf anstrengen; ***~ one's legs*** zu Fuß gehen; **8.** ***~ up*** a) *et.* auf-, verbrauchen, b) F *j-n* erschöpfen, ‚fertigmachen'; → ***used*** 2; **9.** behandeln, verfahren mit: ***~ s.o. ill*** j-n schlecht behandeln; ***how has the world ~d you?*** wie ist es dir ergangen?; **III** *v/i.* **10.** *nur pret.* [ju:st] pflegte (***to do*** zu tun): ***it ~d to be said*** man pflegte zu sagen; ***he ~d to live here*** er wohnte früher hier; ***he does not come as often as he ~d*** (***to***) er kommt nicht mehr so oft wie früher *od.* sonst; **use·a·ble** ['ju:zəbl] → ***usable***; **used** [ju:zd] *adj.* **1.** gebraucht, getragen (*Kleidung*): ***~ car*** *mot.* Gebrauchtwagen *m*; **2.** ***~ up*** a) aufgebraucht, verbraucht (*a. Luft*), b) F ‚erledigt', ‚fertig', erschöpft; **3.** [ju:st] a) gewohnt (***to*** zu *od. acc.*), b) gewöhnt (***to*** an *acc.*): ***he is ~ to working late*** er ist gewohnt, lange zu arbeiten; ***get ~ to*** sich gewöhnen an (*acc.*); **use·ful** ['ju:sfʊl] *adj.* □ **1.** nützlich, brauchbar, (zweck)dienlich, (gut) verwendbar: ***~ tools***; ***a ~ man*** ein brauchbarer Mann; ***~ talks*** nützliche Gespräche; ***make o.s. ~*** sich nützlich machen; **2.** *bsd.* ⚙ nutzbar, Nutz…: ***~ efficiency*** Nutzleistung *f*; ***~ load*** Nutzlast *f*; ***~ plant*** Nutzpflanze *f*; '**use·ful·ness** [-fʊlnɪs] *s.* Nützlichkeit *f*, Brauchbarkeit *f*, Zweckmäßigkeit *f*; **use·less** ['ju:slɪs] *adj.* □ **1.** nutz-, sinn-, zwecklos, unnütz, vergeblich: ***it is ~ to*** es erübrigt sich zu; **2.** unbrauchbar; '**use·less·ness** [-lɪsnɪs] *s.* Nutz-, Zwecklosigkeit *f*; Unbrauchbarkeit *f*; **us·er** ['ju:zə] *s.* **1.** Benutzer (-in); **2.** ✝ Verbraucher(in); **3.** ⚖ Nießbrauch *m*, Benutzungsrecht *n*.

'**U-shaped** *adj.* U-förmig: ***~ iron*** ⚙ U-Eisen *n*.

ush·er ['ʌʃə] **I** *s.* **1.** Türhüter *m*; **2.** Platzanweiser(in); **3.** a) ⚖ Gerichtsdiener *m*, b) *allg.* 'Aufsichtsper,son *f*; **4.** Zere'monienmeister *m*; **5.** *Brit. obs.* Hilfslehrer *m*; **II** *v/t.* **6.** (*mst* ***~ in***) her'ein-, hin'ein)führen, (-)geleiten; **7.** ***~ in*** *a. fig.* ankündigen, *e-e Epoche etc.* einleiten; **ush·er·ette** [,ʌʃə'ret] *s.* Platzanweiserin *f*.

u·su·al ['ju:ʒʊəl] *adj.* □ üblich, gewöhnlich, gebräuchlich: ***as ~*** wie gewöhnlich, wie sonst; ***the ~ thing*** das Übliche; ***it has become the ~ thing*** (***with us***) es ist (bei uns) gang u. gäbe geworden; ***it is ~ for shops to close at 6 o'clock*** die Geschäfte schließen gewöhnlich um 6 Uhr; ***the ~ pride with her*** ihr üblicher Stolz; '**u·su·al·ly** [-əlɪ] *adv.* (für) gewöhnlich, in der Regel, meist(ens).

u·su·fruct ['ju:sju:frʌkt] *s.* ⚖ Nießbrauch *m*, Nutznießung *f*; **u·su·fruc·tu·ar·y** [,ju:sju:'frʌktjʊərɪ] **I** *s.* Nießbraucher(in); **II** *adj.* Nutzungs…: ***~ right***.

u·su·rer ['ju:ʒərə] *s.* Wucherer *m*; **u·su·ri·ous** [ju:'zjʊərɪəs] *adj.* □ wucherisch, Wucher…: ***~ interest*** → ***usury*** 2; **u·su·ri·ous·ness** [ju:'zjʊərɪəsnɪs] *s.* Wuche'rei *f*.

u·surp [ju:'zɜ:p] *v/t.* **1.** an sich reißen, sich 'widerrechtlich aneignen, sich bemächtigen (*gen.*); **2.** sich ('widerrechtlich) anmaßen; **3.** *Aufmerksamkeit etc.* mit Beschlag belegen; **u·sur·pa·tion** [,ju:zɜ:'peɪʃn] *s.* **1.** Usurpati'on *f*: a) 'widerrechtliche Machtergreifung *od.* Aneignung, Anmaßung *f e-s Rechts etc.*, b) ***~ of the throne*** Thronraub *m*; **2.** unberechtigter Eingriff (***on*** in *acc.*); **u'surp·er** [-pə] *s.* **1.** Usur'pator *m*, unrechtmäßiger Machthaber, Thronräuber *m*; **2.** unberechtigter Besitzergreifer; **3.** *fig.* Eindringling *m* (***on*** in *acc.*); **u'surp·ing** [-pɪŋ] *adj.* □ usurpa'torisch.

u·su·ry ['ju:ʒʊrɪ] *s.* **1.** (Zins)Wucher *m*: ***practise ~*** Wucher treiben; **2.** Wucherzinsen *pl.* (***at*** auf *acc.*): ***return s.th. with ~*** *fig. et.* mit Zins u. Zinseszins heimzahlen.

u·ten·sil [ju:'tensl] *s.* **1.** (*a. Schreib- etc.*) Gerät *n*, Werkzeug *n*; Gebrauchs-, Haushaltsgegenstand *m*: (***kitchen***) ***~*** Küchengerät; **2.** Geschirr *n*, Gefäß *n*; **3.** *pl.* Uten'silien *pl.*, Geräte *pl.*; (Küchen)Geschirr *n*.

u·ter·ine ['ju:təraɪn] *adj.* **1.** *anat.* Gebärmutter…, Uterus…; **2.** von der'selben Mutter stammend: ***~ brother*** Halbbruder mütterlicherseits; **u·ter·us** ['ju:tərəs] *pl.* **-ter·i** [-təraɪ] *s. anat.* Uterus *m*, Gebärmutter *f*.

u·til·i·tar·i·an [,ju:tɪlɪ'teərɪən] **I** *adj.* **1.** utilita'ristisch, Nützlichkeits…; **2.** praktisch, zweckmäßig; **3.** *contp.* gemein; **II** *s.* **4.** Utilita'rist(in); **,u·til·i'tar·i·an·ism** [-nɪzəm] *s.* Utilita'rismus *m*.

u·til·i·ty [ju:'tɪlətɪ] **I** *s.* **1.** *a.* ✝ Nutzen *m* (***to*** für), Nützlichkeit *f*; **2.** *et.* Nützliches, nützliche Einrichtung; **3.** a) *a. **public ~*** (***company*** *od.* ***corporation***) öffentlicher Versorgungsbetrieb, *pl. a.* Stadtwerke *pl.*, b) *pl.* Leistungen *pl.* der öffentlichen Versorgungsbetriebe, *bsd.* Strom-, Gas- u. Wasserversorgung *f*; **4.** ⚙ Zusatzgerät *n*; **II** *adj.* **5.** ✝, ⚙ Gebrauchs…(*-güter*, *-möbel*, *-wagen etc.*); **6.** Mehrzweck…; ***~ man*** *s.* [*irr.*] **1.** *bsd. Am.* Fak'totum *n*; **2.** *thea.* vielseitig einsetzbarer Chargenspieler.

u·ti·liz·a·ble ['ju:tɪlaɪzəbl] *adj.* verwendbar, verwertbar, nutzbar; **u·ti·li·za·tion** [,ju:tɪlaɪ'zeɪʃn] *s.* Nutzbarmachung *f*, Verwertung *f*, (Aus)Nutzung *f*, An-, Verwendung *f*; **u·ti·lize** ['ju:tɪlaɪz] *v/t.* **1.** (aus)nutzen, verwerten, sich *et.* nutzbar *od.* zu'nutze machen; **2.** verwenden.

ut·most ['ʌtməʊst] **I** *adj.* äußerst: a) entlegenst, fernst, b) *fig.* höchst, größt; **II** *s. das* Äußerste: ***the ~ that I can do***; ***do one's ~*** sein äußerstes *od.* möglichstes tun; ***at the ~*** allerhöchstens; ***to the ~*** aufs äußerste; ***to the ~ of my powers*** nach besten Kräften.

U·to·pi·a [ju:'təʊpjə] *s.* **1.** U'topia *n* (*Idealstaat*); **2.** *oft* 2 *fig.* Uto'pie *f*; **U'to·pi·an** [-jən], *a.* 2 **I** *adj.* u'topisch, phan'tastisch; **II** *s.* Uto'pist(in), Phan'tast (-in); **U'to·pi·an·ism** [-jənɪzəm], *a.* 2 *s.* Uto'pismus *m*.

u·tri·cle ['ju:trɪkl] *s.* **1.** *zo.*, ⚘ Schlauch *m*, bläs-chenförmiges Luft- *od.* Saftgefäß; **2.** ⚕ U'triculus *m* (*Säckchen im Ohrlabyrinth*).

ut·ter ['ʌtə] **I** *adj.* □ → ***utterly***; **1.** äußerst, höchst, völlig; **2.** endgültig, entschieden: ***~ denial***; **3.** *contp.* ausgesprochen, voll'endet (*Schurke*, *Unsinn etc.*); **II** *v/t.* **4.** *Gedanken*, *Gefühle* äußern, ausdrücken, aussprechen; **5.** *Laute etc.* ausstoßen, von sich geben, her'vorbringen; **6.** *Falschgeld etc.* in 'Umlauf setzen, verbreiten; **ut·ter·ance** ['ʌtərəns] *s.* **1.** (stimmlicher) Ausdruck, Äußerung *f*: ***give ~ to*** *e-m Gefühl etc.* Ausdruck verleihen; **2.** Sprechweise *f*, Aussprache *f*, Vortrag *m*; **3.** *a. pl.* Äußerung *f*, Aussage *f*, Worte *pl.*; '**ut·ter·er** [-ərə] *s.* **1.** Äußernde(r *m*) *f*; **2.** Verbreiter(in); '**ut·ter·ly** [-lɪ] *adv.* äußerst, abso'lut, völlig, ganz, to'tal; '**ut·ter·most** [-məʊst] → ***utmost***.

'**U-turn** *s.* **1.** *mot.* Wende *f*; **2.** *fig.* Kehrtwende *f*.

u·vu·la ['ju:vjʊlə] *pl.* **-lae** [-li:] *s. anat.* Zäpfchen *n*; '**u·vu·lar** [-lə] **I** *adj.* Zäpfchen…, *ling. a.* uvu'lar; **II** *s. ling.* Zäpfchenlaut *m*, Uvu'lar *m*.

ux·o·ri·ous [ʌk'sɔ:rɪəs] *adj.* □ treuliebend, -ergeben; **ux'o·ri·ous·ness** [-nɪs] *s.* treue Ergebenheit (*des Gatten*).

V

V, v [viː] *s.* V *n*, v *n* (*Buchstabe*).

vac [væk] *Brit.* F *für* ***vacation***.

va·can·cy [ˈveɪkənsɪ] *s.* **1.** Leere *f* (*a. fig.*): ***stare into ~*** ins Leere starren; **2.** leerer *od.* freier Platz; Lücke *f* (*a. fig.*); **3.** leer(stehend)es *od.* unbewohntes Haus; **4.** freie *od.* offene Stelle, unbesetztes Amt, Vaˈkanz *f*; *univ.* freier Studienplatz *m*; *pl. Zeitung*: Stellenangebote *pl.*; **5.** a) Geistesabwesenheit *f*, b) geistige Leere, c) Geistlosigkeit *f*; **6.** Untätigkeit *f*, Muße *f*; **ˈva·cant** [-nt] *adj.* □ **1.** leer, frei, unbesetzt (*Sitz, Zimmer, Zeit etc.*); **2.** leer(stehend), unbewohnt, unvermietet (*Haus*); unbebaut (*Grundstück*): ***~ possession*** sofort beziehbar; **3.** frei, offen (*Stelle*), vaˈkant, unbesetzt (*Amt*); **4.** a) geistesabwesend, b) leer: ***~ mind***; ***~ stare***, c) geistlos.

va·cate [vəˈkeɪt] *v/t.* **1.** *Wohnung etc.*, ⚔ *Stellung etc.* räumen; *Sitz etc.* freimachen; **2.** *Stelle* aufgeben, aus *e-m Amt* scheiden: ***be ~d*** freiwerden (*Stelle*); **3.** *Truppen etc.* evakuieren; **4.** ⚖ *Vertrag, Urteil etc.* aufheben; **vaˈca·tion** [-eɪʃn] **I** *s.* **1.** Räumung *f*; **2.** Niederlegung *f od.* Erledigung *f e-s Amtes*; **3.** (Gerichts-, *univ.* Seˈmester-, *Am.* Schul)Ferien *pl.*: ***the long ~*** die großen Ferien, die Sommerferien; **4.** *bsd. Am.* Urlaub *m*: ***on ~*** im Urlaub; ***~ shutdown*** Betriebsferien *pl.*; **II** *v/i.* **5.** *bsd. Am.* in Ferien sein, Urlaub machen; **vaˈca·tion·ist** [-eɪʃnɪst] *s. Am.* Urlauber(in).

vac·ci·nal [ˈvæksɪnl] *adj.* ⚕ Impf…; **vac·ci·nate** [ˈvæksɪneɪt] *v/t. u. v/i.* impfen (***against*** gegen); **vac·ci·na·tion** [ˌvæksɪˈneɪʃn] *s.* (Schutz)Impfung *f*; **ˈvac·ci·na·tor** [-neɪtə] *s.* **1.** Impfarzt *m*; **2.** Impfnadel *f*; **ˈvac·cine** [-siːn] ⚕ **I** *adj.* Impf…, Kuhpocken…: ***~ matter*** → II; **II** *s.* Impfstoff *m*, Vakˈzine *f*: ***bovine ~*** Kuhlymphe *f*; **vac·cin·i·a** [vækˈsɪnjə] *s.* ⚕ Kuhpocken *pl.*

vac·il·late [ˈvæsɪleɪt] *v/i. mst fig.* schwanken; **ˈvac·il·lat·ing** [-tɪŋ] *adj.* □ schwankend (*mst fig. unschlüssig*); **vac·il·la·tion** [ˌvæsɪˈleɪʃn] *s.* Schwanken *n* (*mst fig. Unschlüssigkeit, Wankelmut*).

va·cu·i·ty [væˈkjuːətɪ] *s.* **1.** → ***vacancy*** 1, 5; **2.** *fig.* Nichtigkeit *f*, Plattheit *f*; **vac·u·ous** [ˈvækjʊəs] *adj.* □ **1.** → ***vacant*** 4; **2.** nichtssagend (*Redensart*); **3.** müßig (*Leben*); **vac·u·um** [ˈvækjʊəm] **I** *pl.* **-ums** [-z] *s.* **1.** ⚙, *phys.* Vakuum *n*, (*bsd.* luft)leerer Raum; **2.** *fig.* Vakuum *n*, Leere *f*, Lücke *f*; **II** *adj.* **3.** Vakuum…: ***~ bottle*** (*od.* ***flask***) Thermosflasche *f*; ***~ brake*** ⚙ Unterdruckbremse *f*; ***~ can***, ***~ tin*** Vakuumdose *f*; ***~ cleaner*** Staubsauger *m*; ***~ drier*** Vakuumtrockner *m*; ***~ ga(u)ge*** Unterdruckmesser *m*; ***~-packed*** vakuumverpackt; ***~-sealed*** vakuumdicht; ***~ tube***, ***~ valve*** ϟ Vakuumröhre *f*; **III** *v/t.* **4.** (mit dem Staubsauger) saugen *od.* reinigen.

va·de me·cum [ˌveɪdɪˈmiːkəm] *s.* Vadeˈmekum *n*, Handbuch *n*.

vag·a·bond [ˈvægəbɒnd] **I** *adj.* **1.** vagabundierend (*a.* ϟ); **2.** Vagabunden…, vagaˈbundenhaft; **3.** nomadisierend; **4.** Wander…, unstet: ***a ~ life***; **II** *s.* **5.** Vagaˈbund(in), Landstreicher(in); **6.** F Strolch *m*; **III** *v/i.* **7.** vagabundieren; **ˈvag·a·bond·age** [-dɪdʒ] *s.* **1.** Landstreicheˈrei *f*, Vagaˈbundenleben *n*; **2.** *coll.* Vagaˈbunden *pl.*; **ˈvag·a·bond·ism** [-dɪzəm] → ***vagabondage*** 1; **ˈvag·a·bond·ize** [-daɪz] → ***vagabond*** 7.

va·gar·y [ˈveɪgərɪ] *s.* **1.** wunderlicher Einfall; *pl. a.* Phantasteˈreien *pl.*; **2.** Kaˈprice *f*, Grille *f*, Laune *f*; **3.** *mst pl.* Extravaˈganzen *pl.*: ***the vagaries of fashion***.

va·gi·na [vəˈdʒaɪnə] *pl.* **-nas** *s.* **1.** *anat.* Vaˈgina *f*, Scheide *f*; **2.** ⚘ Blattscheide *f*; **vagˈi·nal** [-nl] *adj.* vagiˈnal, Vaginal…, Scheiden…: ***~ spray*** Intimspray *n*.

va·gran·cy [ˈveɪgrənsɪ] *s.* **1.** Landstreicheˈrei *f* (*a.* ⚖); **2.** *coll.* Landstreicher *pl.*; **ˈva·grant** [-nt] **I** *adj.* □ **1.** wandernd (*a. weitS. Zelle etc.*), vagabundierend; **2.** → ***vagabond*** 3 *u.* 4; **3.** *fig.* kapriziˈös, launisch; **II** *s.* **4.** → ***vagabond*** 5.

vague [veɪg] *adj.* □ **1.** vage: a) undeutlich, nebelhaft, verschwommen (*alle a. fig.*), b) unbestimmt (*Gefühl, Verdacht, Versprechen etc.*), dunkel (*Ahnung, Gerücht etc.*), c) unklar (*Antwort etc.*): ***~ hope*** vage Hoffnung; ***not the ~st idea*** nicht die leiseste Ahnung; ***be ~ about s.th.*** sich unklar ausdrücken über (*acc.*); **2.** → ***vacant*** 4a; **ˈvague·ness** [-nɪs] *s.* Unbestimmtheit *f*, Verschwommenheit *f*.

vain [veɪn] *adj.* □ **1.** eitel, eingebildet (***of*** auf *acc.*); **2.** *fig.* eitel, leer (*Vergnügen etc.*; *a. Drohung, Hoffnung etc.*), nichtig; **3.** vergeblich, fruchtlos: ***~ efforts***; **4.** ***in ~*** vergeblich: a) vergebens, umˈsonst, b) unnütz; **ˌ~ˈglo·ri·ous** *adj.* □ prahlerisch, großsprecherisch, -spurig.

vain·ness [ˈveɪnnɪs] *s.* **1.** Vergeblichkeit *f*; **2.** Hohl-, Leerheit *f*.

vale[1] [veɪl] *s. poet. od. in Namen*: Tal *n*: ***~ of tears*** Jammertal *n*.

va·le[2] [ˈveɪlɪ] (*Lat.*) **I** *int.* lebe wohl!; **II** *s.* Lebeˈwohl *n*.

val·e·dic·tion [ˌvælɪˈdɪkʃn] *s.* **1.** Abschied(nehmen *n*) *m*; **2.** Abschiedsworte *pl.*; **val·e·dic·to·ri·an** [ˌvælɪdɪkˈtɔːrɪən] *s. Am. ped., univ.* Abschiedsredner *m*; **ˌval·eˈdic·to·ry** [-ktərɪ] **I** *adj.* Abschieds…: ***~ address*** → II; **II** *s. bsd. Am. ped., univ.* Abschiedsrede *f*.

va·lence [ˈveɪləns], **ˈva·len·cy** [-sɪ] ⚗, ⚛, *biol., phys.* Wertigkeit *f*, Vaˈlenz *f*.

val·en·tine [ˈvæləntaɪn] *s.* **1.** Valentinsgruß *m* (*zum Valentinstag, 14. Februar, dem od. der Liebsten gesandt*); **2.** am Valentinstag erwählte(r) Liebste(r), *a. allg.* Schatz *m*.

va·le·ri·an [vəˈlɪərɪən] *s.* ⚘, *pharm.* Baldrian *m*; **va·le·ri·an·ic** [vəˌlɪərɪˈænɪk], **vaˈler·ic** [-ˈlerɪk] *adj.* ⚗ Baldrian…, Valerian…

val·et [ˈvælɪt] **I** *s.* a) (Kammer)Diener *m*, b) Hausdiener *m im Hotel*; **II** *v/t. j-n* bedienen, versorgen; **III** *v/i.* Diener sein.

val·e·tu·di·nar·i·an [ˌvælɪtjuːdɪˈneərɪən] **I** *adj.* **1.** kränklich, kränkelnd; **2.** rekonvalesˈzent; **3.** a) geˈsundheitsfaˌnatisch, b) hypoˈchondrisch; **II** *s.* **4.** kränkliche Perˈson; **5.** Rekonvalesˈzent(in); **6.** ‚Geˈsundheitsaˌpostel' *m*; **7.** Hypoˈchonder *m*; **ˌval·e·tu·diˈnar·i·an·ism** [-nɪzəm] *s.* **1.** Kränklichkeit *f*; **2.** Hypochonˈdrie *f*; **ˌval·eˈtu·di·nar·y** [-nərɪ] → ***valetudinarian***.

Val·hal·la [vælˈhælə], **Valˈhall** [-ˈhæl] *s. myth.* Walˈhalla *f*.

val·iant [ˈvæljənt] *adj.* □ tapfer, mutig, heldenhaft, heˈroisch.

val·id [ˈvælɪd] *adj.* □ **1.** gültig: a) stichhaltig, triftig (*Beweis, Grund*), b) begründet, berechtigt (*Anspruch, Argument etc.*), c) richtig (*Entscheidung etc.*); **2.** ⚖ (rechts)gültig, rechtskräftig; **3.** wirksam (*Methode etc.*); **ˈval·i·date** [-deɪt] *v/t.* ⚖ a) für (rechts)gültig erklären, rechtswirksam machen, b) bestätigen; **val·i·da·tion** [ˌvælɪˈdeɪʃn] *s.* Gültigkeit(serklärung) *f*; **va·lid·i·ty** [vəˈlɪdətɪ] *s.* **1.** Gültigkeit *f*: a) Triftigkeit *f*, Stichhaltigkeit *f*, b) Richtigkeit *f*; **2.** ⚖ Rechtsgültigkeit *f*, -kraft *f*; **3.** Gültigkeit(sdauer) *f*.

va·lise [vəˈliːz] *s.* Reisetasche *f*.

Val·kyr [ˈvælkɪə], **Val·kyr·i·a** [vælˈkɪərjə], **Val·kyr·ie** [-ˈkɪərɪ] *s. myth.* Walküre *f*.

val·ley [ˈvælɪ] *s.* **1.** Tal *n*: ***down the ~*** talabwärts; **2.** △ Dachkehle *f*.

val·or *Am.* → ***valour***.

val·or·i·za·tion [ˌvæləraɪˈzeɪʃn] *s.* ☿ Valorisatiˈon *f*, Aufwertung *f*; **val·or·ize** [ˈvæləraɪz] *v/t.* ☿ valorisieren, aufwerten, den Preis *e-r Ware* heben *od.* stützen.

val·or·ous [ˈvælərəs] *adj.* □ *rhet.* tapfer, mutig, heldenhaft, -mütig; **val·our**

['vælə] *s.* Tapferkeit *f*, Heldenmut *m.*

val·u·a·ble ['væljʊəbl] **I** *adj.* ☐ **1.** wertvoll: a) kostbar, teuer, b) *fig.* nützlich: ***for ~ consideration*** ⚖ entgeltlich; **2.** abschätzbar; **II** *s.* **3.** *pl.* Wertsachen *pl.*, -gegenstände *pl.*

val·u·a·tion [ˌvæljʊ'eɪʃn] *s.* **1.** Bewertung *f*, (Ab)Schätzung *f*, Wertbestimmung *f*, Taxierung *f*, Veranschlagung *f*; **2.** a) Schätzungswert *m* (festgesetzter) Wert *od.* Preis, Taxe *f*, b) Gegenwartswert *m* e-r 'Lebensverˌsicherungspoˌlice; **3.** Wertschätzung *f*, Würdigung *f*: ***we take him at his own ~*** wir beurteilen ihn so, wie er sich selbst sieht; **val·u·a·tor** ['væljʊeɪtə] *s.* ⚚ (Ab)Schätzer *m*, Ta'xator *m.*

val·ue ['vælju:] **I** *s.* **1.** *allg.* Wert *m* (*a.* ⅍, ⚗, *phys. u. fig.*): ***moral ~s*** *fig.* sittliche Werte; ***be of ~ to*** *j-m* wertvoll *od.* nützlich sein; **2.** Wert *m*, Einschätzung *f*: ***set a high ~ (up)on*** a) großen Wert legen auf (*acc.*), b) *et.* hoch einschätzen; **3.** ⚚ Wert *m*: ***assessed ~*** Taxwert; ***at ~*** zum Tageskurs; ***book ~*** Buchwert; ***commercial ~*** Handelswert; **4.** ⚚ a) (Verkehrs)Wert *m*, Kaufkraft *f*, Preis *m*, b) Gegenwert *m*, -leistung *f*, c) Währung *f*, Va'luta *f*, d) *a.* ***good ~*** re'elle Ware, Quali'tätsware *f*, e) → ***valuation*** 1 *u.* 2, f) Wert *m*, Preis *m*, Betrag *m*: ***for ~ received*** Betrag erhalten; ***to the ~ of*** im *od.* bis zum Betrag von; ***give (get) good ~ (for one's money)*** reell bedienen (bedient werden); ***it is excellent ~ for money*** es ist äußerst preiswert, es ist ausgezeichnet; **5.** *fig.* Wert *m*, Gewicht *n e-s Wortes etc.*; **6.** *paint.* Verhältnis *n* von Licht u. Schatten, Farb-, Grauwert *m*; **7.** ♪ Noten-, Zeitwert *m*; **8.** *ling.* Lautwert *m*; **II** *v/t.* **9.** a) den Wert *od.* Preis *e-r Sache* bestimmen *od.* festsetzen, b) (ab-) schätzen, veranschlagen, taxieren (***at*** auf *acc.*); **10.** ⚚ *Wechsel* ziehen (***[up]on*** auf *j-n*); **11.** *Wert, Nutzen, Bedeutung* schätzen, (*vergleichend*) bewerten; **12.** (hoch)schätzen, achten; **ˌ~-'add·ed tax** *s.* ⚚ Mehrwertsteuer *f.*

val·ued ['vælju:d] *adj.* **1.** (hoch)geschätzt; **2.** taxiert, veranschlagt (***at*** auf *acc.*): ***~ at £ 100*** £ 100 wert.

'val·ue|-free *adj.* wertfrei; **~ judg(e)·ment** *s.* Werturteil *n.*

val·ue·less ['væljulɪs] *adj.* wertlos; **'val·u·er** [-juə] → ***valuator.***

val·ue stress *s. Phonetik*: Sinnbetonung *f.*

va·lu·ta [və'lu:tə] (*Ital.*) *s.* ⚚ Va'luta *f.*

valve [vælv] *s.* **1.** ⚙ Ven'til *n*, Absperrvorrichtung *f*, Klappe *f*, Hahn *m*, Regu'lierorˌgan *n*: ***~ gear*** Ventilsteuerung *f*; ***~-in-head engine*** kopfgesteuerter Motor; **2.** ♪ Klappe *f* (*Blasinstrument*); **3.** ⚕ (*Herz- etc.*)Klappe *f*: ***cardiac ~***; **4.** *zo.* (Muschel)Klappe *f*; **5.** ⚘ a) Klappe *f*, b) Kammer *f* (*beide e-r Fruchtkapsel*); **6.** ⚡ *Brit.* (Elek'tronen-, Fernseh-, Radio)Röhre *f*: ***~ amplifier*** Röhrenverstärker *m*; **7.** ⚙ Schleusentor *n*; **8.** *obs.* Türflügel *m*; **'valve·less** [-lɪs] *adj.* ven'tillos; **'val·vu·lar** [-vjʊlə] *adj.* **1.** klappenförmig, Klappen...: ***~ defect*** ⚕ Klappenfehler *m*; **2.** mit Klappe(n) *od.* Ven'til(en) (versehen); **3.** ⚘ klappig; **'val·vule** [-vju:l] *s.* kleine Klappe; **val·vu·li·tis** [ˌvælvjʊ'laɪtɪs] *s.* ⚕ (Herz-) Klappenentzündung *f.*

va·moose [və'mu:s], **va'mose** [-'məʊs] *Am. sl.* **I** *v/i.* ‚verduften', ‚Leine ziehen'; **II** *v/t.* fluchtartig verlassen.

vamp¹ [væmp] **I** *s.* **1.** a) Oberleder *n*, b) (Vorder)Klappe *f* (*Schuh*), c) (aufgesetzter) Flicken; **2.** ♪ (improvisierte) Begleitung; **3.** *fig.* Flickwerk *n*; **II** *v/t.* **4.** *mst* ***~ up*** a) flicken, reparieren, b) vorschuhen; **5.** ***~ up*** F a) *et.* ‚aufpolieren', ‚aufmotzen', b) *Zeitungsartikel etc.* zs.-stoppeln; **6.** ♪ (aus dem Stegreif) begleiten; **III** *v/i.* **7.** ♪ improvisieren.

vamp² [væmp] F **I** *s.* Vamp *m*; **II** *v/t.* a) *Männer* verführen, ‚ausnehmen', b) *j-n* becircen.

vam·pire ['væmpaɪə] *s.* **1.** Vampir *m*: a) *blutsaugendes Gespenst*, b) *fig.* Erpresser(in), Blutsauger(in); **2.** *a.* ***~ bat*** *zo.* Vampir *m*, Blattnase *f*; **3.** *thea.* kleine Falltür auf der Bühne; **'vam·pir·ism** [-ərɪzəm] *s.* **1.** Vampirglaube *m*; **2.** Blutsaugen *n* (*e-s Vampirs*); **3.** *fig.* Ausbeutung *f.*

van¹ [væn] *s.* **1.** ⚔ Vorhut *f*, Vor'ausabˌteilung *f*, Spitze *f*; **2.** ⚓ Vorgeschwader *n*; **3.** *fig.* vorderste Reihe, Spitze *f.*

van² [væn] *s.* **1.** Last-, Lieferwagen *m*; **2.** Gefangenenwagen *m* (*Polizei*); **3.** F a) Wohnwagen *m*: ***gipsy's ~*** Zigeunerwagen *m*, b) *Am.* 'Wohnmoˌbil *n*; **4.** 🚃 *Brit.* (geschlossener) Güterwagen; Dienst-, Gepäckwagen *m.*

van³ [væn] *s.* **1.** *obs. od. poet.* Schwinge *f*, Fittich *m*; **2.** *Brit.* Getreideschwinge *f*; **3.** ⚒ *Brit.* Schwingschaufel *od.* -probe *f.*

va·na·di·um [və'neɪdjəm] *s.* ⚗ Va'nadium *n.*

Van·dal ['vændl] **I** *s.* **1.** *hist.* Van'dale *m*, Van'dalin *f*; **2.** ♀ *fig.* Van'dale *m*; **II** *adj.* *a.* **Van·dal·ic** [væn'dælɪk] **3.** *hist.* van'dalisch, Vandalen...; **4.** ♀ *fig.* van'dalenhaft, zerstörungswütig; **'van·dal·ism** [-dəlɪzəm] *s. fig.* Vanda'lismus *m*: a) Zerstörungswut *f*, b) *a.* ***act(s) of ~*** mutwillige Zerstörung; **'van·dal·ize** *v/t.* **1.** mutwillig zerstören, verwüsten; **2.** wie die Van'dalen hausen in (*dat.*).

Van·dyke [ˌvæn'daɪk] **I** *adj.* **1.** von Van Dyck, in Van Dyckscher Ma'nier; **II** *s.* **2.** *oft* ♀ *abbr. für* a) ***~ beard***, b) ***~ collar***; **3.** Zackenmuster *n*; **~ beard** *s.* Spitz-, Knebelbart *m*; **~ col·lar** *s.* Van'dyckkragen *m.*

vane [veɪn] *s.* **1.** Wetterfahne *f*, -hahn *m*; **2.** Windmühlenflügel *m*; **3.** (Pro'peller-, Venti'lator- *etc.*)Flügel *m*; (Tur'binen-, ✈ Leit)Schaufel *f*; **4.** *surv.* Di'opter *n*; **5.** *zo.* Fahne *f* (*Feder*); **6.** (Pfeil)Fiederung *f.*

van·guard ['vængɑ:d] → ***van¹.***

va·nil·la [və'nɪlə] *s.* ⚘, ⚚ Va'nille *f.*

van·ish ['vænɪʃ] *v/i.* **1.** (plötzlich) verschwinden; **2.** (langsam) (ver-, ent-) schwinden, da'hinschwinden, sich verlieren (***from*** von, aus); **3.** (spurlos) verschwinden: ***~ into (thin) air*** sich in Luft auflösen; **4.** ⅍ verschwinden, Null werden.

van·ish·ing| cream ['vænɪʃɪŋ] *s.* (*rasch eindringende*) Tagescreme; **~ line** *s.* Fluchtlinie *f*; **~ point** *s.* **1.** Fluchtpunkt *m* (*Perspektive*); **2.** *fig.* Nullpunkt *m.*

van·i·ty ['vænətɪ] *s.* **1.** *persönliche* Eitelkeit; **2.** *j-s* Stolz *m* (*Sache*); **3.** Leer-, Hohlheit *f*, Eitel-, Nichtigkeit *f*: ♀ ***Fair*** *fig.* Jahrmarkt *m* der Eitelkeit; **4.** *Am.* Toi'lettentisch *m*; **5.** *a.* ***~ bag*** (*od.* ***box, case***) Hand-, Kos'metiktäschchen *n*, -koffer *m.*

van·quish ['væŋkwɪʃ] **I** *v/t.* besiegen, über'wältigen, *a. fig. Stolz etc.* über'winden, bezwingen; **II** *v/i.* siegreich sein, siegen; **'van·quish·er** [-ʃə] *s.* Sieger *m*, Bezwinger *m.*

van·tage ['vɑ:ntɪdʒ] *s.* **1.** *Tennis*: Vorteil *m*; **2.** ***coign*** (*od.* ***point***) ***of ~*** günstiger (Angriffs- *od.* Ausgangs)Punkt; **~ ground** *s.* günstige Lage *od.* Stellung (*a. fig.*); **~ point** *s.* **1.** Aussichtspunkt *m*; **2.** günstiger (Ausgangs)Punkt; **3.** → ***vantage ground.***

vap·id ['væpɪd] *adj.* ☐ **1.** schal: ***~ beer***; **2.** *fig.* a) schal, seicht, leer, b) öd(e), fad(e); **va·pid·i·ty** [væ'pɪdətɪ], **'vap·id·ness** [-nɪs] *s.* **1.** Schalheit *f* (*a. fig.*); **2.** *fig.* a) Fadheit, b) Leere *f.*

va·por *Am.* → ***vapour.***

va·por·i·za·tion [ˌveɪpəraɪ'zeɪʃn] *s. phys.* Verdampfung *f*, -dunstung *f.*

va·por·ize ['veɪpəraɪz] **I** *v/t.* **1.** ⚗, *phys.* ver-, eindampfen, verdunsten (lassen); **2.** ⚙ vergasen; **II** *v/i.* **3.** verdampfen, verdunsten; **'va·por·iz·er** [-zə] *s.* ⚙ **1.** Ver'dampfungsappaˌrat *m*, Zerstäuber *m*; **2.** Vergaser *m*; **'va·por·ous** [-rəs] *adj.* ☐ **1.** dampfig, dunstig; **2.** *fig.* nebelhaft; **3.** duftig (*Gewebe*).

va·pour ['veɪpə] **I** *s.* **1.** Dampf *m* (*a. phys.*), Dunst *m* (*a. fig.*): ***~ bath*** Dampfbad *n*; ***~ trail*** ✈ Kondensstreifen; **2.** a) ⚙ Gas *n*, b) *mot.* Gemisch *n*: ***~ motor*** Gasmotor *m*; **3.** ⚕ a) (Inhalati'ons)Dampf *m*, b) *obs.* (*innere*) Blähung; **4.** *fig.* Phan'tom *n*, Hirngespinst *n*; **5.** *pl. obs.* Schwermut *f*; **II** *v/i.* **6.** (ver)dampfen; **7.** *fig.* schwadronieren, prahlen.

var·an ['værən] *s. zo.* Wa'ran *m.*

var·ec ['verek] *s.* **1.** Seetang *m*; **2.** ⚗ Varek *m*, Seetangasche *f.*

var·i·a·bil·i·ty [ˌveərɪə'bɪlətɪ] *s.* **1.** Veränderlichkeit *f*, Schwanken *n*, Unbeständigkeit *f* (*a. fig.*); **2.** ⅍, *phys.*, *a. biol.* Variabili'tät *f.*

var·i·a·ble ['veərɪəbl] **I** *adj.* ☐ **1.** veränderlich, 'unterschiedlich, wechselnd; schwankend (*a. Person*): ***~ cost*** ⚚ bewegliche Kosten *pl.*; ***~ wind*** *meteor.* Wind aus wechselnder Richtung; **2.** *bsd.* ⅍, *ast.*, *biol.*, *phys.* vari'abel, wandelbar, ⅍, *phys. a.* ungleichförmig; **3.** ⚙ regelbar, ver-, einstellbar: ***~ capacitor*** Drehkondensator *m*; ***~ gear*** Wechselgetriebe *n*; ***infinitely ~*** stufenlos regelbar; ***~-speed*** mit veränderlicher Drehzahl; **II** *s.* **4.** veränderliche Größe, *bsd.* ⅍ Vari'able *f*, Veränderliche *f*; **5.** *ast.* vari'abler Stern; **'var·i·a·ble·ness** [-nɪs] → ***variability***; **'var·i·ance** [-ɪəns] *s.* **1.** Veränderung *f*; **2.** Abweichung *f* (*a.* ⚖ *zwischen Klage u. Beweisergebnis*); **3.** Uneinigkeit *f*, Meinungsverschiedenheit *f*, Streit *m*: ***be at ~ (with)*** uneinig sein (mit *j-m*); → 4; ***set at ~*** entzweien; **4.** *fig.* 'Widerstreit *m*, -spruch *m*, Unvereinbarkeit *f*: ***be at ~ (with)*** unvereinbar sein (mit *et.*), im Widerspruch stehen (zu); → 3; **'var·i·ant** [-ɪənt] **I** *adj.* abweichend, verschieden; 'unterschiedlich; **II** *s.* Vari'ante *f*: a) Spielart *f*, b) abweichende

Lesart; **var·i·a·tion** [ˌveərɪˈeɪʃn] *s.* **1.** Veränderung *f*, Wechsel *m*, Schwankung *f*; **2.** Abweichung *f*; **3.** ♪, ⨁, *ast.*, *biol. etc.* Variatiˈon *f*; **4.** (ˈOrts)ˌMißweisung *f*, magˈnetische Deklinatiˈon *f* (*Kompaß*).

var·i·col·o(u)red [ˈveərɪkʌləd] *adj.* bunt: a) vielfarbig, b) *fig.* mannigfaltig.

var·i·cose [ˈværɪkəʊs] *adj.* ⚕ krampfad(e)rig, variˈkös: ~ ***vein*** Krampfader *f*; ~ ***bandage*** Krampfaderbinde *f*; **var·i·co·sis** [ˌværɪˈkəʊsɪs], **var·i·cos·i·ty** [ˌværɪˈkɒsətɪ] *s.* Krampfaderleiden *n*, Krampfader(n *pl.*) *f*.

var·ied [ˈveərɪd] *adj.* □ verschieden(artig); mannigfaltig, abwechslungsreich, bunt.

var·i·e·gate [ˈveərɪgeɪt] *v/t.* **1.** bunt gestalten (*a. fig.*); **2.** *fig.* (durch Abwechslung) beleben, variieren; ˈ**var·i·e·gat·ed** [-tɪd] *adj.* **1.** bunt(scheckig, -gefleckt), vielfarbig; **2.** → ***varied***; **var·i·e·ga·tion** [ˌveərɪˈgeɪʃn] *s.* Buntheit *f*.

va·ri·e·ty [vəˈraɪətɪ] *s.* **1.** Verschieden-, Buntheit *f*, Mannigfaltigkeit *f*, Vielseitigkeit *f*, Abwechslung *f*; **2.** Vielfalt *f*, Reihe *f*, Anzahl *f*, *bsd.* ✝ Auswahl *f*: ***owing to a ~ of causes*** aus verschiedenen Gründen; **3.** Sorte *f*, Art *f*; **4.** *allg.*, *a.* ⚘, *zo.* Ab-, Spielart *f*; **5.** ⚘, *zo.* a) Varieˈtät *f* (*Unterabteilung e-r Art*), b) Variˈante *f*; **6.** Varieˈté *n*: ~ ***artist*** Varietékünstler *m*; ~ **meat** *s. Am.* Inneˈreien *pl.*; ~ **show** *s.* Varieˈté(vorstellung *f*) *n*; ~ **store** *s.* ✝ *Am.* Kleinkaufhaus *n*; ~ **the·a·tre** *s.* Varieˈté(theˌater) *n*.

var·i·form [ˈveərɪfɔːm] *adj.* vielgestaltig (*a. fig.*).

va·ri·o·la [vəˈraɪələ] *s.* ⚕ Pocken *pl.*

var·i·om·e·ter [ˌveərɪˈɒmɪtə] *s.* ⚙, ⚡, *phys.* Varioˈmeter *n*.

var·i·o·rum [ˌveərɪˈɔːrəm] **I** *adj.* ~ ***edition*** → **II** *s.* Ausgabe *f* mit Anmerkungen verschiedener Kommentaˈtoren *od.* mit verschiedenen Lesarten.

var·i·ous [ˈveərɪəs] *adj.* □ **1.** verschieden(artig); **2.** mehrere, verschiedene; **3.** → ***varied***.

var·ix [ˈveərɪks] *pl.* **-i·ces** [ˈværɪsiːz] *s.* ⚕ Krampfader(knoten *m*) *f*.

var·let [ˈvɑːlɪt] *s.* **1.** *hist.* Knappe *m*, Page *m*; **2.** *obs.* Schelm *m*, Schuft *m*.

var·mint [ˈvɑːmɪnt] *s.* **1.** *zo.* Schädling *m*; **2.** F Haˈlunke *m*.

var·nish [ˈvɑːnɪʃ] **I** *s.* ⚙ **1.** Lack *m*: ***oil*** ~ Öllack *m*; **2.** *a.* ***clear*** ~ Klarlack *m*, Firnis *m*; **3.** (ˈMöbel)Poliˌtur *f*; **4.** *Töpferei*: Glaˈsur *f*; **5.** *fig.* Firnis *m*, Tünche *f*, äußerer Anstrich; **II** *v/t.* *a.* ~ ***over*** **6.** a) lackieren, firnissen, b) glasieren; **7.** *Möbel* (auf)polieren; **8.** *fig.* überˈtünchen, beschönigen.

var·si·ty [ˈvɑːsətɪ] *s.* F **1.** ‚Uniˈ *f* (*Universität*); **2.** *a.* ~ ***team*** *sport Am.* Universiˈtäts- *od.* College- *od.* Schulmannschaft *f*.

var·y [ˈveərɪ] **I** *v/t.* **1.** (ver-, *a.* ⚖ ab)ändern; **2.** variieren, ˈunterschiedlich gestalten, Abwechslung bringen in (*acc.*), wechseln mit *et.*, *a.* ♪ abwandeln; **II** *v/i.* **3.** sich (ver)ändern, variieren (*a. biol.*), wechseln, schwanken; **4.** verschieden sein, abweichen (***from*** von); ˈ**var·y·ing** [-ɪɪŋ] *adj.* wechselnd, ˈunterschiedlich, verschieden.

vas·cu·lar [ˈvæskjʊlə] *adj.* ⚘, *physiol.* Gefäß...(*-pflanzen, -system etc.*): ~ ***tissue*** ⚘ Stranggewebe *n*.

vase [vɑːz] *s.* Vase *f*.

vas·ec·to·my [væˈsektəmɪ] *s.* ⚕ Vasektoˈmie *f*.

vas·e·line [ˈvæsɪliːn] *s.* ⚗ Vaseˈlin *n*.

vas·sal [ˈvæsl] **I** *s.* **1.** Vaˈsall(in), Lehnsmann *m*; **2.** *fig.* ˈUntertan *m*, Unterˈgebene(r *m*) *f*; **3.** *fig.* Sklave *m* (***to*** *gen.*); **II** *adj.* **4.** Vasallen...; ˈ**vas·sal·age** [-səlɪdʒ] *s.* **1.** *hist.* Vaˈsallentum *n*, Lehnspflicht *f*, (***to*** gegenüber); **2.** *coll.* Vaˈsallen *pl.*; **3.** *fig.* a) Abhängigkeit *f* (***to*** von), b) ˈUnterwürfigkeit *f*.

vast [vɑːst] **I** *adj.* □ **1.** weit, ausgedehnt, unermeßlich; **2.** *a. fig.* ungeheuer, (riesen)groß, riesig, gewaltig: ~ ***difference***; ~ ***quantity***; **II** *s.* **3.** *poet.* Weite *f*; ˈ**vast·ly** [-lɪ] *adv.* gewaltig, in hohem Maße; ungemein, äußerst: ~ ***superior*** haushoch überlegen, weitaus besser; ˈ**vast·ness** [-nɪs] *s.* **1.** Weite *f*, Unermeßlichkeit *f* (*a. fig.*); **2.** ungeheure Größe, riesige Zahl, Unmenge *f*.

vat [væt] **I** *s.* ⚙ **1.** großes Faß, Bottich *m*, Kufe *f*; **2.** a) *Färberei*: Küpe *f*, b) *a.* ***tan*** ~ *Gerberei*: Lohgrube *f*; **II** *v/t.* **3.** (ver)küpen, in ein Faß *etc.* füllen; **4.** in e-m Faß *etc.* behandeln: ~***ted*** faßreif (*Wein etc.*).

Vat·i·can [ˈvætɪkən] *s.* Vatiˈkan *m*: ~ ***council*** Vatikanisches Konzil.

vaude·ville [ˈvəʊdəvɪl] *s.* **1.** *Brit.* heiteres Singspiel (mit Tanzeinlagen); **2.** *Am.* Varieˈté *n*.

vault[1] [vɔːlt] **I** *s.* **1.** ⚠ (*a. poet.* Himmels)Gewölbe *n*, Wölbung *f*; **2.** Kellergewölbe *n*; **3.** Grabgewölbe *n*, Gruft *f*: ***family*** ~; **4.** Treˈsorraum *m*; **5.** *anat.* Wölbung *f*, (Schädel)Dach *n*; (Gaumen)Bogen *m*; (Zwerchfell)Kuppel *f*; **II** *v/t.* **6.** (über)ˈwölben; **III** *v/i.* **7.** sich wölben.

vault[2] [vɔːlt] **I** *v/i.* **1.** springen, sich schwingen, setzen (***over*** über *acc.*); **2.** *Reitsport*: kurbettieren; **II** *v/t.* **3.** überˈspringen; **III** *s.* **4.** *bsd. sport* Sprung *m*; **5.** *Reitsport*: Kurˈbette *f*.

vault·ed [ˈvɔːltɪd] *adj.* **1.** gewölbt, Gewölbe...; **2.** überˈwölbt.

vault·er [ˈvɔːltə] *s.* Springer *m*.

vault·ing[1] [ˈvɔːltɪŋ] *s.* ⚠ **1.** Spannen *n* e-s Gewölbes; **2.** Wölbung *f*; **3.** Gewölbe *n* (*od. pl. coll.*).

vault·ing[2] [ˈvɔːltɪŋ] *s.* Springen *n*; ~ **horse** *s. Turnen*: (Lang-, Sprung)Pferd *n*; ~ **pole** *s. sport* Sprungstab *m*.

vaunt [vɔːnt] **I** *v/t.* sich rühmen (*gen.*), sich brüsten mit; **II** *v/i.* (***of***) sich rühmen (*gen.*), sich brüsten (mit); **III** *s.* Prahleˈrei *f*; ˈ**vaunt·er** [-tə] *s.* Prahler(in); ˈ**vaunt·ing** [-tɪŋ] *adj.* □ prahlerisch.

ˈ**V-Day** *s.* Tag *m* des Sieges (*im 2. Weltkrieg*; *8. 5. 1945*).

've [v] F *abbr. für* ***have***.

veal [viːl] *s.* Kalbfleisch *n*: ~ ***chop*** Kalbskotelett *n*; ~ ***cutlet*** Kalbsschnitzel *n*.

vec·tor [ˈvektə] **I** *s.* **1.** ⨁, *a.* ✈ Vektor *m*; **2.** ⚕, *vet.* Bakˈterienüberˌträger *m*; **II** *v/t.* **3.** *Flugzeug* (mittels Funk *od.* Raˈdar) leiten, (auf Ziel) einweisen.

V-E Day → ***V-Day***.

vee [viː] **I** *s.* V *n*, v *n*, Vau *n* (*Buchstabe*), **II** *adj.* V-förmig, V-...: ~ ***belt*** Keilriemen *m*; ~ ***engine*** V-Motor *m*.

veep [viːp] *s. Am.* F ‚Vizeˈ *m* (*Vizepräsident*).

veer [vɪə] **I** *v/i.* *a.* ~ ***round*** **1.** sich (ˈum-) drehen; ˈumspringen, sich drehen (*Wind*); *fig.* ˈumschwenken (***to*** zu); **2.** ⚓ (ab)drehen, wenden; **II** *v/t.* **3.** *a.* ~ ***round*** *Schiff etc.* wenden, drehen, schwenken; **4.** ⚓ *Tauwerk* fieren, abschießen: ~ ***and haul*** fieren u. holen; **III** *s.* **5.** Wendung *f*, Drehung *f*, Richtungswechsel *m*.

veg·e·ta·ble [ˈvədʒtəbl] **I** *s.* **1.** *allg.* (*bsd.* Gemüse-, Futter)Pflanze *f*: ***be a mere*** ~, ***live like a*** ~ *fig.* (nur noch) dahinvegetieren; **2.** *a. pl.* Gemüse *n*; **3.** ✓ Grünfutter *n*; **II** *adj.* **4.** pflanzlich, vegetaˈbilisch, Pflanzen...: ~ ***diet*** Pflanzenkost *f*; ~ ***kingdom*** Pflanzenreich *n*; ~ ***marrow*** Kürbis(frucht *f*) *m*; **5.** Gemüse...: ~ ***garden***; ~ ***soup***.

veg·e·tal [ˈvedʒɪtl] *adj.* **1.** ⚘ → ***vegetable*** 4 *u.* 5; **2.** *physiol.* vegetaˈtiv; **veg·e·tar·i·an** [ˌvedʒɪˈteərɪən] **I** *s.* **1.** Vegeˈtarier(in); **II** *adj.* **2.** vegeˈtarisch; **3.** Vegetarier...; **veg·e·tar·i·an·ism** [ˌvedʒɪˈteərɪənɪzəm] *s.* Vegetaˈrismus *m*, vegeˈtarische Lebensweise; ˈ**veg·e·tate** [-teɪt] *v/i.* **1.** (*wie e-e Pflanze*) wachsen; vegetieren; **2.** *contp.* (daˈhin)vegetieren; **veg·e·ta·tion** [ˌvedʒɪˈteɪʃn] *s.* **1.** Vegetatiˈon *f*, Pflanzenwelt *f*, -decke *f*: ***luxuriant*** ~; **2.** Vegetieren *n*, Pflanzenwuchs *m*; **3.** *fig.* (Daˈhin)Vegetieren *n*; **4.** ⚕ Wucherung *f*; ˈ**veg·e·ta·tive** [-tətɪv] *adj.* □ *biol.* **1.** vegetaˈtiv: a) wie Pflanzen wachsend, b) wachstumsfördernd, c) Wachstums...; **2.** Vegetations..., pflanzlich.

ve·he·mence [ˈviːɪməns] *s.* **1.** *a. fig.* Heftigkeit *f*, Veheˈmenz *f*, Gewalt *f*, Wucht *f*; **2.** *fig.* Ungestüm *n*, Leidenschaft *f*; ˈ**ve·he·ment** [-nt] *adj.* □ *a. fig.* heftig, gewaltig, veheˈment, *fig. a.* ungestüm, leidenschaftlich, hitzig.

ve·hi·cle [ˈviːɪkl] *s.* **1.** Fahrzeug *n*, Beförderungsmittel *n*, *engS.* Wagen *m*; **2.** a) *a.* ***space*** ~ Raumfahrzeug *n*, b) ˈTrägeraˌkete *f*; **3.** *fig.* a) Ausdrucksmittel *n*, Medium *n*, Veˈhikel *n*, b) Träger *m*, Vermittler *m*; **4.** ⚗, *biol.* Trägerflüssigkeit *f*; **5.** *pharm.*, ⚗, ⚙ Bindemittel *n*; **ve·hic·u·lar** [vɪˈhɪkjʊlə] *adj.* Fahrzeug..., Wagen...: ~ ***traffic***.

veil [veɪl] **I** *s.* **1.** (Gesichts- *etc.*)Schleier *m*: ***take the*** ~ *eccl.* den Schleier nehmen (*Nonne werden*); **2.** *phot.* (*a.* Nebel-, Dunst)Schleier *m*; **3.** *fig.* Schleier *m*, Maske *f*, Deckmantel *m*: ***draw a ~ over*** den Schleier des Vergessens breiten über (*acc.*); ***under the ~ of darkness*** im Schutze der Dunkelheit; ***under the ~ of charity*** unter dem Deckmantel der Nächstenliebe; **4.** ⚘, *anat.* → ***velum***; **5.** *eccl.* a) (Tempel)Vorhang *m*, b) Velum *n* (*Kelchtuch*); **6.** Verschleierung *f der Stimme*; **II** *v/t.* **7.** verschleiern, -hüllen (*a. fig.*); **III** *v/i.* **8.** sich verschleiern; **veiled** [-ld] *adj.* verschleiert (*a. phot.*, *fig.*) (*a. Stimme*); ˈ**veil·ing** [-lɪŋ] *s.* **1.** Verschleierung *f* (*a. phot. u. fig.*); **2.** ✝ Schleier(stoff) *m*.

vein [veɪn] *s.* **1.** *anat.* Vene *f*; **2.** *allg.* Ader *f*: a) *anat.* Blutgefäß *n*, b) ⚘ Blattnerv *m*, c) Maser *f* (*Holz, Marmor*), d) *geol.* (Erz)Gang *m*, e) Wasserader *f*; **3.** *fig.* a) *poetische etc.* Ader, Veranlagung *f*, Hang *m* (***of*** zu), b) (Ton)Art *f*, c)

Stimmung *f*: ***be in the ~ for*** in Stimmung sein zu; **veined** [-nd] *adj.* **1.** *allg.* geädert; **2.** gemasert; **'vein·ing** [-nɪŋ] *s.* Äderung *f*, Maserung *f*; **'vein·let** [-lɪt] *s.* **1.** Äderchen *n*; **2.** ⚘ Seitenrippe *f*.

ve·la ['viːlə] *pl. von* ***velum***.

ve·lar ['viːlə] **I** *adj. anat.*, *ling.* ve'lar, Gaumensegel..., Velar...; **II** *s. ling.* Gaumensegellaut *m*, Ve'lar(laut) *m*; **'ve·lar·ize** [-əraɪz] *v/t. ling. Laut* velarisieren.

veld(t) [velt] *s. geogr.* Gras- *od.* Buschland *n* (*Südafrika*).

vel·le·i·ty [ve'liːətɪ] *s.* kraftloses, zögerndes Wollen.

vel·lum ['veləm] *s.* **1.** ('Kalbs-, 'Schreib-) Perga͵ment *n*, Ve'lin *n*: ***~ cloth*** Pausleinen *n*; **2.** *a.* ***~ paper*** Ve'linpa͵pier *n*.

ve·loc·i·pede [vɪ'lɒsɪpiːd] *s.* **1.** *hist.* Velozi'ped *n* (*Lauf-*, *Fahrrad*); **2.** *Am.* (Kinder)Dreirad *n*.

ve·loc·i·ty [vɪ'lɒsətɪ] *s. bsd.* ⚙, *phys.* Geschwindigkeit *f*: ***at a ~ of*** mit e-r Geschwindigkeit von; ***initial ~*** Anfangsgeschwindigkeit.

ve·lour(s) [və'lʊə] *s.* ✝ Ve'lours *m*.

ve·lum ['viːləm] *pl.* **-la** [-lə] *s.* **1.** ⚘, *anat.* Hülle *f*, Segel *n*; **2.** *anat.* Gaumensegel *n*, weicher Gaumen; **3.** ⚘ Schleier *m an Hutpilzen*.

vel·vet ['velvɪt] **I** *s.* **1.** Samt *m*: ***be on ~*** *sl.* glänzend dastehen; **2.** *zo.* Bast *m an jungen Geweihen etc.*; **II** *adj.* **3.** samten, aus Samt, Samt...; **4.** samtartig, -weich, samten (*a. fig.*): ***an iron hand in a ~ glove*** *fig.* e-e eiserne Faust unter dem Samthandschuh; ***handle s.o. with ~ gloves*** *fig.* j-n mit Samthandschuhen anfassen; **vel·vet·een** [͵velvɪ'tiːn] *s.* Man'(s)chester *m*, Baumwollsamt *m*; **'vel·vet·y** [-tɪ] → ***velvet*** 4.

ve·nal ['viːnl] *adj.* □ käuflich, bestechlich, kor'rupt; **ve·nal·i·ty** [viː'nælətɪ] *s.* Käuflichkeit *f*, Kor'ruptheit *f*, Bestechlichkeit *f*.

ve·na·tion [viː'neɪʃn] *s.* ⚘, *zo.* Geäder *n*.

vend [vend] *v/t.* a) *bsd.* ⚖ verkaufen, b) zum Verkauf anbieten, c) hausieren mit; **vend·ee** [ven'diː] *s.* ⚖ Käufer *m*; **'vend·er** [-də] *s.* **1.** (Straßen)Verkäufer *m*, (-)Händler *m*; **2.** → ***vendor***.

ven·det·ta [ven'detə] *s.* Blutrache *f*.

vend·i·ble ['vendəbl] *adj.* □ verkäuflich.

vend·ing ma·chine ['vendɪŋ] *s.* (Ver'kaufs)Auto͵mat *m*.

ven·dor ['vendɔː] *s.* **1.** ⚖ Verkäufer(in); **2.** (Ver'kaufs)Auto͵mat *m*.

ven·due ['vendjuː] *s. bsd. Am.* Aukti'on *f*, Versteigerung *f*.

ve·neer [və'nɪə] **I** *v/t.* **1.** ⚙ a) *Holz* furnieren, einlegen, b) *Stein* auslegen, c) *Töpferei*: (mit dünner Schicht) über'ziehen; **2.** *fig.* um'kleiden, e-n äußeren Anstrich geben; **3.** *fig. Eigenschaften etc.* über'tünchen, verdecken; **II** *s.* **4.** ⚙ Fur'nier(holz, -blatt) *n*; **5.** *fig.* Tünche *f*, äußerer Anstrich; **ve'neer·ing** [-ərɪŋ] *s.* **1.** ⚙ a) Furnierholz *n*, b) Furnierung *f*, c) Fur'nierarbeit *f*; **2.** *fig.* → ***veneer*** 5.

ven·er·a·bil·i·ty [͵venərə'bɪlətɪ] *s.* Ehrwürdigkeit *f*; **ven·er·a·ble** ['venərəbl] *adj.* □ **1.** ehrwürdig (*a. R.C.*) (*a. fig. Bauwerk etc.*), verehrungswürdig; **2.** *Anglikanische Kirche*: Hoch(ehr)würden *m* (*Archidiakon*): ***2 Sir***; **ven·er·a·ble·ness** ['venərəblnɪs] *s.* Ehrwürdigkeit *f*.

ven·er·ate ['venəreɪt] *v/t.* **1.** verehren; **2.** in Ehren halten; **ven·er·a·tion** [͵venə'reɪʃn] *s.* (***of***) a) Verehrung *f* (*gen.*), b) Ehrfurcht *f* (vor *dat.*); **'ven·er·a·tor** [-tə] *s.* Verehrer(in).

ve·ne·re·al [və'nɪərɪəl] *adj.* **1.** geschlechtlich, Geschlechts..., Sexual...; **2.** ⚕ a) ve'nerisch, Geschlechts..., b) geschlechtskrank: ***~ disease*** Geschlechtskrankheit *f*; **ve·ne·re·ol·o·gist** [və͵nɪərɪ'ɒlədʒɪst] *s.* ⚕ Venero'loge *m*, Facharzt *m* für Geschlechtskrankheiten.

Ve·ne·tian [və'niːʃn] **I** *adj.* venezi'anisch: ***~ blind*** (Stab)Jalousie *f*; ***~ glass*** Muranoglas *n*; **II** *s.* Venezi'aner(in).

Ven·e·zue·lan [͵vene'zweɪlən] **I** *adj.* venezo'lanisch; **II** *s.* Venezo'laner(in).

venge·ance ['vendʒəns] *s.* Rache *f*, Vergeltung *f*: ***take ~ (up)on*** Vergeltung üben *od.* sich rächen an (*dat.*); ***with a ~*** F a) mächtig, mit Macht, wie besessen, wie der Teufel, b) *jetzt* erst recht, c) im Exzess, übertrieben; **'venge·ful** [-fʊl] *adj.* □ *rhet.* rachsüchtig, -gierig.

ve·ni·al ['viːnjəl] *adj.* □ verzeihlich: ***~ sin*** *R.C.* läßliche Sünde.

ven·i·son ['venzn] *s.* Wildbret *n*.

ven·om ['venəm] *s.* **1.** *zo.* (Schlangen-*etc.*)Gift *n*; **2.** *fig.* Gift *n*, Gehässigkeit *f*; **'ven·omed** [-md], **'ven·om·ous** [-məs] *adj.* □ **1.** giftig: ***~ snake*** Giftschlange *f*; **2.** *fig.* giftig, gehässig; **'ven·om·ous·ness** [-məsnɪs] *s.* Giftigkeit *f*, *fig. a.* Gehässigkeit *f*.

ve·nose ['viːnəʊs] → ***venous***; **ve·nos·i·ty** [vɪ'nɒsətɪ] *s. biol.* **1.** Äderung *f*; **2.** ⚕ Venosi'tät *f*; **ve·nous** ['viːnəs] *adj.* □ *biol.* **1.** Venen..., Adern...; **2.** ve'nös: ***~ blood***; **3.** ⚘ geädert.

vent [vent] **I** *s.* **1.** (Luft)Loch *n*, (Abzugs)Öffnung *f*, Schlitz *m*, ⚙ *a.* Entlüfter(stutzen) *m*: ***~ window*** → ***ventipane***; **2.** Spundloch *n* (*Faß*); **3.** ⚔ *hist.* Schießscharte *f*; **4.** Fingerloch *n* (*Flöte etc.*); **5.** (Vul'kan)Schlot *m*; **6.** *orn.*, *ichth.* After *m*; **7.** *zo.* Aufstoßen *n* zum Luftholen (*Otter etc.*); **8.** Auslaß *m* (*a. fig.*): ***find (a) ~*** *fig.* sich entladen (*Gefühl*); ***give ~ to*** → 9; **II** *v/t.* **9.** *fig. e-m Gefühl* Luft machen, *Wut etc.* auslassen (***on*** an *dat.*); **10.** ⚙ a) e-e Abzugsöffnung *etc.* anbringen an (*dat.*), b) *Rauch etc.* abziehen lassen, c) ventilieren; **III** *v/i.* **11.** *hunt.* aufstoßen (zum Luftholen) (*Otter etc.*); **'vent·age** [-tɪdʒ] → ***vent*** 1, 4, 8.

ven·ter ['ventə] *s.* **1.** *anat.* a) Bauch (-höhle *f*) *m*, b) (Muskel- *etc.*)Bauch *m*; **2.** *zo.* (In'sekten)Magen *m*; **3.** ⚖ Mutter(leib *m*) *f*: ***child of a second ~*** Kind *n* von e-r zweiten Frau.

'vent·hole → ***vent*** 1.

ven·ti·late ['ventɪleɪt] *v/t.* **1.** ventilieren, (be-, ent-, 'durch)lüften; **2.** *physiol.* Sauerstoff zuführen (*dat.*); **3.** *fig.* ventilieren: a) zur Sprache bringen, erörtern, b) *Meinung etc.* äußern; **4.** → ***vent*** 9; **'ven·ti·lat·ing** [-tɪŋ] *adj.* Ventilations..., Lüftungs...; **ven·ti·la·tion** [͵ventɪ'leɪʃn] *s.* **1.** Ventilati'on *f*, (Be-, Ent)Lüftung *f* (*beide a. Anlage*), Luftzufuhr *f*; ⚒ Bewetterung *f*; **2.** a) (freie) Erörterung, öffentliche Diskussi'on, b) Äußerung *f e-s Gefühls etc.*, Entladung *f*; **'ven·ti·la·tor** [-tə] *s.* Venti'lator *m*, Entlüfter *m*, Lüftungsanlage *f*.

ven·ti·pane ['ventɪpeɪn] *s. mot.* Ausstellfenster *n*.

ven·tral ['ventrəl] *adj.* □ *biol.* ven'tral, Bauch...

ven·tri·cle ['ventrɪkl] *s. anat.* Ven'trikel *m*, (Körper)Höhle *f*, *bsd.* (Herz-, Hirn-) Kammer *f*; **ven·tric·u·lar** [ven'trɪkjʊlə] *adj. anat.* ventriku'lär, Kammer...

ven·tri·lo·qui·al [͵ventrɪ'ləʊkwɪəl] *adj.* bauchrednerisch, Bauchrede...

ven·tril·o·quism [ven'trɪləkwɪzəm] *s.* Bauchreden *n*; **ven'tril·o·quist** [-ɪst] *s.* Bauchredner(in); **ven'tril·o·quize** [-kwaɪz] **I** *v/i.* bauchreden; **II** *v/t. et.* bauchrednerisch sagen; **ven'tril·o·quy** [-kwɪ] *s.* Bauchreden *n*.

ven·ture ['ventʃə] **I** *s.* **1.** Wagnis *n*: a) Risiko *n*, b) (gewagtes) Unter'nehmen; **2.** ✝ a) (geschäftliches) Unter'nehmen, Operati'on *f*, b) Spekulati'on *f*; **3.** Spekulati'onsob͵jekt *n*, Einsatz *m*; **4.** *obs.* Glück *n*: ***at a ~*** aufs Geratewohl, auf gut Glück; **II** *v/t.* **5.** *et.* riskieren, wagen, aufs Spiel setzen: ***nothing ~ nothing have*** (*od.* ***gain[ed]***) wer nicht wagt, der nicht gewinnt; **6.** *Bemerkung etc.* (zu äußern) wagen; **III** *v/i.* **7.** (es) wagen, sich erlauben (***to do*** zu tun); **8.** ***~ (up)on*** sich an *e-e Sache* wagen; **9.** sich *wohin* wagen; **'ven·ture·some** [-səm] *adj.* □ waghalsig: a) kühn, verwegen (*Person*), b) gewagt, ris'kant (*Tat*); **'ven·ture·some·ness** [-səmnɪs] *s.* Waghalsigkeit *f*; **'ven·tur·ous** [-ərəs] *adj.* □ → ***venturesome***.

ven·ue ['venjuː] *s.* **1.** ⚖ a) Gerichtsstand *m*, zuständiger Verhandlungsort *m*, *Brit. a.* zuständige Grafschaft, b) örtliche Zuständigkeit; **2.** a) Schauplatz *m*, b) Treffpunkt *m*, Tagungsort *m*, c) *sport* Austragungsort *m*.

Ve·nus ['viːnəs] *s. allg.* Venus *f*.

ve·ra·cious [və'reɪʃəs] *adj.* □ **1.** wahr'haftig, wahrheitsliebend; **2.** wahr (-heitsgetreu): ***~ account***; **ve·rac·i·ty** [və'ræsətɪ] *s.* **1.** Wahr'haftigkeit *f*, Wahrheitsliebe *f*; **2.** Richtigkeit *f*; **3.** Wahrheit *f*.

ve·ran·da(h) [və'rændə] *s.* Ve'randa *f*.

verb [vɜːb] *s. ling.* Zeitwort *n*, Verb(um) *n*; **'ver·bal** [-bl] **I** *adj.* □ **1.** Wort... (*-fehler*, *-gedächtnis*, *-kritik etc.*); **2.** mündlich (*a. Vertrag etc.*): ***~ message***; **3.** (wort)wörtlich: ***~ copy***; ***~ translation***; **4.** wörtlich, Verbal...: ***~ note*** *pol.* Verbalnote *f*; **5.** *ling.* ver'bal, Verbal..., Zeitwort...: ***~ noun*** → 6; **II** *s.* **6.** *ling.* Ver'bal͵substantiv *n*; **'ver·bal·ism** [-bəlɪzəm] *s.* **1.** Ausdruck *m*; **2.** Verba'lismus *m*, Wortemache'rei *f*; **3.** Wortklaube'rei *f*; **'ver·bal·ist** [-bəlɪst] *s.* **1.** *bsd. ped.* Verba'list(in); **2.** wortgewandte Per'son; **'ver·bal·ize** [-bəlaɪz] **I** *v/t.* **1.** in Worte fassen, formulieren; **2.** *ling.* in ein Verb verwandeln; **II** *v/i.* **3.** viele Worte machen; **ver·ba·tim** [vɜː'beɪtɪm] **I** *adv.* ver'batim, (wort)wörtlich, Wort für Wort; **II** *adj.* → ***verbal*** 3; **III** *s.* wortgetreuer Bericht; **'ver·bi·age** [-bɪɪdʒ] *s.* **1.** Wortschwall *m*; **2.** Dikti'on *f*; **ver·bose** [vɜː'bəʊs] *adj.* □ wortreich, weitschweifig; **ver·bos·i·ty** [vɜː'bɒsətɪ] *s.* Wortreichtum *m*.

ver·dan·cy ['vɜːdənsɪ] *s.* **1.** (frisches)

Grün; **2.** *fig.* Unerfahrenheit *f*; Unreife *f*; ˈ**ver·dant** [-nt] *adj.* □ **1.** grün, grünend; **2.** *fig.* grün, unreif.
ver·dict [ˈvɜːdɪkt] *s.* **1.** ⚖ (Wahr)Spruch *m* der Geschworenen, Verˈdikt *n*: **~ *of not guilty*** Erkennen *n* auf „nicht schuldig"; ***bring in*** (*od.* ***return***) ***a ~ of guilty*** auf schuldig erkennen; **2.** *fig.* Urteil *n* (***on*** über *acc.*).
ver·di·gris [ˈvɜːdɪgrɪs] *s.* Grünspan *m.*
ver·dure [ˈvɜːdʒə] *s.* **1.** (frisches) Grün; **2.** Vegetatiˈon *f*, saftiger Pflanzenwuchs; **3.** *fig.* Frische *f*, Kraft *f*.
verge [vɜːdʒ] **I** *s.* **1.** *mst fig.* Rand *m*, Grenze *f*: ***on the ~ of*** am Rande *der Verzweiflung etc.*, dicht vor (*dat.*); ***on the ~ of tears*** den Tränen nahe; ***on the ~ of doing*** nahe daran, zu tun; **2.** ✓ (Beet)Einfassung *f*, (Gras)Streifen *m*; **3.** ⚖ *Brit. hist.* Gerichtsbezirk *m* rund um den Königshof; **4.** ⚙ a) ˈüberstehende Dachkante, b) Säulenschaft *m*, c) Schwungstift *m* (*Uhrhemmung*), d) Zugstab *m* (*Setzmaschine*); **5.** a) *bsd. eccl.* Amtsstab *m*, b) *hist.* Belehnungsstab *m*; **II** *v/i.* **6.** *mst fig.* grenzen *od.* streifen (***on*** an *acc.*); **7.** (***on, into***) sich nähern (*dat.*), (in *e-e Farbe etc.*) ˈübergehen; **8.** sich (hin)neigen (***to[wards]*** nach); ˈ**ver·ger** [-dʒə] *s.* **1.** Kirchendiener *m*, Küster *m*; **2.** *bsd. Brit. eccl.* (Amts)Stabträger *m*.
ver·i·est [ˈverɪɪst] *adj.* (*sup. von* ***very*** II) *obs.* äußerst: ***the ~ child*** (selbst) das kleinste Kind; ***the ~ nonsense*** der reinste Unsinn; ***the ~ rascal*** der ärgste *od.* größte Schuft.
ver·i·fi·a·ble [ˈverɪfaɪəbl] *adj.* nachweis-, nachprüfbar, verifizierbar; **ver·i·fi·ca·tion** [ˌverɪfɪˈkeɪʃn] *s.* **1.** Nachprüfung *f*; **2.** Echtheitsnachweis *m*, Richtigbefund *m*; **3.** Beglaubigung *f*, Beurkundung *f*; (⚖ eidliche) Bestätigung; **ver·i·fy** [ˈverɪfaɪ] *v/t.* **1.** *auf die Richtigkeit hin* (nach)prüfen; **2.** die Richtigkeit *od.* Echtheit *e-r Angabe etc.* feststellen *od.* nachweisen, verifizieren; **3.** *Urkunde etc.* beglaubigen; beweisen, belegen; **4.** ⚖ eidlich beteuern; **5.** bestätigen; **6.** *Versprechen etc.* erfüllen, wahrmachen.
ver·i·ly [ˈverəlɪ] *adv. bibl.* wahrlich.
ver·i·si·mil·i·tude [ˌverɪsɪˈmɪlɪtjuːd] *s.* Wahrˈscheinlichkeit *f*.
ver·i·ta·ble [ˈverɪtəbl] *adj.* □ wahr (-haft), wirklich, echt.
ver·i·ty [ˈverətɪ] *s.* **1.** (Grund)Wahrheit *f*: ***of a ~*** wahrhaftig; ***eternal verities*** ewige Wahrheiten; **2.** Wahrheit *f*; **3.** (*j-s*) Wahrˈhaftigkeit *f*.
ver·juice [ˈvɜːdʒuːs] *s.* **1.** Obst-, Traubensaft *m* (*bsd. von unreifen Früchten*); **2.** Essig *m* (*a. fig.*).
ver·meil [ˈvɜːmeɪl] **I** *s.* **1.** *bsd. poet. für* ***vermilion***; **2.** ⚙ Verˈmeil *n*: a) feuervergoldetes Silber *od.* Kupfer, vergoldete Bronze, b) hochroter Graˈnat; **II** *adj.* **3.** *poet.* purpur-, scharlachrot.
ver·mi·cel·li [ˌvɜːmɪˈselɪ] (*Ital.*) *s. pl.* Fadennudeln *pl*.
ver·mi·cide [ˈvɜːmɪsaɪd] *s. pharm.* Wurmmittel *n*; **ver·mic·u·lat·ed** [vɜːˈmɪkjʊleɪtɪd] *adj.* **1.** wurmstichig; **2.** △ geschlängelt; **ver·mi·form** [ˈvɜːmɪfɔːm] *adj. biol.* wurmförmig: ***~ appendix*** *anat.* Wurmfortsatz *m*; **ver·mi·fuge** [ˈvɜːmɪfjuːdʒ] → ***vermicide***.
ver·mil·ion [vəˈmɪljən] **I** *s.* **1.** Zinˈnober *m*; **2.** Zinˈnoberrot *n*; **II** *adj.* **3.** zinˈnoberrot; **III** *v/t.* **4.** mit Zinˈnober *od.* zinˈnoberrot färben.
ver·min [ˈvɜːmɪn] *s. mst pl. konstr.* **1.** *zo. coll.* a) Ungeziefer *n*, b) Schädlinge *pl.*, Paraˈsiten *pl.*, c) *hunt.* Raubzeug *n*; **2.** *fig. contp.* Geschmeiß *n*, Pack *n*; ˈ**~-ˌkill·er** *s.* **1.** Kammerjäger *m*; **2.** Ungeziefervertilgungsmittel *n*.
ver·min·ous [ˈvɜːmɪnəs] *adj.* □ **1.** voller Ungeziefer; verlaust, verwanzt, verseucht; **2.** durch Ungeziefer verursacht: ***~ disease***; **3.** *fig.* a) schädlich, b) niedrig, gemein.
ver·mo(u)th [ˈvɜːməθ] *s.* Wermut(wein) *m*.
ver·nac·u·lar [vəˈnækjʊlə] **I** *adj.* □ **1.** einheimisch, Landes...(*-sprache*); **2.** mundartlich, Volks..., Heimat...: ***~ poetry***; **3.** ⚕ enˈdemisch, loˈkal: ***~ disease***; **II** *s.* **4.** Landes-, Mutter-, Volkssprache *f*; **5.** Mundart *f*, Diaˈlekt *m*; **6.** Jarˈgon *m*; **7.** Fachsprache *f*; **8.** → **verˈnac·u·lar·ism** [-ərɪzəm] *s.* volkstümlicher *od.* mundartlicher Ausdruck; **verˈnac·u·lar·ize** [-əraɪz] *v/t.* **1.** *Ausdrücke etc.* einbürgern; **2.** in Volkssprache *od.* Mundart überˈtragen, mundartlich ausdrücken.
ver·nal [ˈvɜːnl] *adj.* □ **1.** Frühlings...; **2.** *fig.* frühlingshaft, Jugend...; **~ e·qui·nox** *s. ast.* ˈFrühlingsäquiˌnoktium *n* (*21. März*).
ver·ni·er [ˈvɜːnjə] *s.* ⚙ **1.** Nonius *m* (*Gradteiler*); **2.** Fein(ein)steller *m*, Verniˈer *m*; **~ cal·(l)i·per(s)** *s.* ⚙ Schublehre *f* mit Nonius.
Ver·o·nese [ˌverəˈniːz] **I** *adj.* veroˈnesisch, aus Veˈrona; **II** *s.* Veroˈneser(in).
ve·ron·i·ca [vɪˈrɒnɪkə] *s.* **1.** ⚘ Veˈronika *f*, Ehrenpreis *m*; **2.** *R.C. u. paint.* Schweißtuch *n* der Veˈronika.
ver·sa·tile [ˈvɜːsətaɪl] *adj.* □ **1.** vielseitig (begabt *od.* gebildet); gewandt, wendig, beweglich; **2.** unbeständig, wandelbar; **3.** ⚘, *zo.* (frei) beweglich; **ver·sa·til·i·ty** [ˌvɜːsəˈtɪlətɪ] *s.* **1.** Vielseitigkeit *f*, Gewandtheit *f*, Wendigkeit *f*, geistige Beweglichkeit; **2.** Unbeständigkeit *f*.
verse [vɜːs] **I** *s.* **1.** a) Vers(zeile *f*) *m*, b) (Gedicht)Zeile *f*, c) *allg.* Vers *m*, Strophe *f*: ***~ drama*** Versdrama *n*; → ***chapter*** 1; **2.** *coll. ohne art.* a) Verse *pl.*, b) Poeˈsie *f*, Dichtung *f*; **3.** Vers (-maß *n*) *m*: ***blank ~*** a) Blankvers, b) reimloser Vers; **II** *v/t.* **4.** in Verse bringen; **III** *v/i.* **5.** dichten, Verse machen.
versed[1] [vɜːst] *adj.* bewandert, beschlagen, versiert (***in*** in *dat.*).
versed[2] [vɜːst] *adj.* Ꭿ ˈumgekehrt: ***~ sine*** Sinusversus *m*.
ver·si·fi·ca·tion [ˌvɜːsɪfɪˈkeɪʃn] *s.* **1.** Verskunst *f*, Versemachen *n*; **2.** Versbau *m*; **ver·si·fi·er** [ˈvɜːsɪfaɪə] *s.* Verseschmied *m*, Dichterling *m*; **ver·si·fy** [ˈvɜːsɪfaɪ] → ***verse*** 4 *u.* 5.
ver·sion [ˈvɜːʃn] *s.* **1.** (*a.* ˈBibel)Überˌsetzung *f*; **2.** *thea. etc.* (*Bühnen- etc.*) Fassung *f*; **3.** Darstellung *f*, Fassung *f*, Lesart *f*, Versiˈon *f*; **4.** Spielart *f*, Variˈante *f*; **5.** ⚙ (*Export- etc.*)Ausführung *f*, Moˈdell *n*.
ver·sus [ˈvɜːsəs] *prp.* ⚖, *a. sport u. fig.* gegen, kontra.
vert [vɜːt] *eccl.* F **I** *v/i.* ˈübertreten, konvertieren; **II** *s.* Konverˈtit(in).
ver·te·bra [ˈvɜːtɪbrə] *pl.* **-brae** [-briː] *s. anat.* **1.** (Rücken)Wirbel *m*; **2.** *pl.* Wirbelsäule *f*; ˈ**ver·te·bral** [-rəl] *adj.* □ verteˈbral, Wirbel(säulen)...: ***~ column*** Wirbelsäule *f*; ˈ**ver·te·brate** [-rɪt] **I** *adj.* **1.** mit e-r Wirbelsäule (versehen), Wirbel...(*-tier*); **2.** *zo.* zu den Wirbeltieren gehörig; **II** *s.* **3.** Wirbeltier *n*; ˈ**ver·te·brat·ed** [-reɪtɪd] → ***vertebrate*** I.
ver·tex [ˈvɜːteks] *pl. mst* **-ti·ces** [-tɪsiːz] *s.* **1.** *biol.* Scheitel *m*; **2.** Ꭿ Scheitelpunkt *m*, Spitze *f* (*beide a. fig.*); **3.** *ast.* a) Zeˈnith *m*, b) Vertex *m*; **4.** *fig.* Gipfel *m*; ˈ**ver·ti·cal** [-tɪkl] **I** *adj.* □ **1.** senk-, lotrecht, vertiˈkal: ***~ clearance*** ⚙ lichte Höhe; ***~ engine*** ⚙ stehender Motor; ***~ section*** △ Aufriß *m*; ***~ take-off*** ✈ Senkrechtstart *m*; ***~ take-off plane*** *od.* ***aircraft*** ✈ Senkrechtstarter *m*; **2.** *ast.*, Ꭿ Scheitel..., Höhen..., Vertikal...: ***~ angle*** Scheitelwinkel *m*; ***~ circle*** *ast.* Vertikalkreis *m*; ***~ section*** △ Aufriß *m*; **II** *s.* **3.** Senkrechte *f*.
ver·tig·i·nous [vɜːˈtɪdʒɪnəs] *adj.* □ **1.** wirbelnd; **2.** schwindlig, Schwindel...; **3.** schwindelerregend, schwindelnd: ***~ height***; **ver·ti·go** [ˈvɜːtɪgəʊ] *pl.* **-goes** *s.* ⚕ Schwindel(gefühl *n*, -anfall *m*) *m*.
ver·tu [vɜːˈtuː] → ***virtu***.
ver·vain [ˈvɜːveɪn] *s.* ⚘ Eisenkraut *n*.
verve [vɜːv] *s.* (künstlerische) Begeisterung, Schwung *m*, Feuer *n*, Verve *f*.
ver·y [ˈverɪ] **I** *adv.* **1.** sehr, äußerst, außerordentlich: ***~ good*** a) sehr gut, b) einverstanden, sehr wohl; ***~ well*** a) sehr gut, b) meinetwegen, na schön; ***not ~ good*** nicht sehr *od.* besonders *od.* gerade gut; **2.** ***~ much*** (*in Verbindung mit Verben*) sehr, außerordentlich: ***he was ~ much pleased***; **3.** (*vor sup.*) aller...: ***the ~ last drop*** der allerletzte Tropfen; **4.** völlig, ganz; **II** *adj.* **5.** gerade, genau: ***the ~ opposite*** genau das Gegenteil; ***the ~ thing*** genau *od.* gerade das (Richtige); ***at the ~ edge*** ganz am Rand, am äußersten Rand; **6.** bloß: ***the ~ fact of his presence***; ***the ~ thought*** der bloße Gedanke, schon der Gedanke; **7.** rein, pur, schier: ***from ~ egoism***; ***the ~ truth*** die reine Wahrheit; **8.** frisch: ***in the ~ act*** auf frischer Tat; **9.** wahr, wirklich: ***~ God of ~ God*** *bibl.* wahrer Gott vom wahren Gott; ***the ~ heart of the matter*** der Kern der Sache; ***in ~ deed*** (***truth***) tatsächlich (wahrhaftig); **10.** (*nach* ***this***, ***that***, ***the***) (der-, die-, das)ˈselbe, (der, die, das) gleiche *od.* nämliche: ***that ~ afternoon***; ***the ~ same words***; **11.** selbst, soˈgar: ***his ~ servants***; **12.** → ***veriest***.
ver·y| high fre·quen·cy [ˈverɪ] *s.* ϟ ˈHochfreˌquenz *f*, Ultraˈkurzwelle *f*.
Ver·y| light [ˈvɪərɪ; ˈverɪ] *s.* ⚔ ˈLeuchtpaˌtrone *f*; **~ pis·tol** *s.* ⚔ ˈLeuchtpiˌstole *f*; **~'s night sig·nals** *s.* ⚔ Siˈgnalschießen *n* mit ˈLeuchtmuniˌtion.
ve·si·ca [ˈvesɪkə] *pl.* **-cas** (*Lat.*) *s.* **1.** *biol.* Blase *f*, Zyste *f*; **2.** *anat.*, *zo.* (Harn-, Gallen-, *ichth.* Schwimm)Blase *f*; ˈ**ves·i·cal** [-kl] *adj.* Blasen...; ˈ**ves·i·cant** [-kənt] **I** *adj.* **1.** ⚕ blasenziehend; **II** *s.* **2.** ⚕ blasenziehendes Mittel, Zugpflaster *n*; **3.** ⚔ ätzender Kampfstoff; ˈ**ves·i·cate** [-keɪt] **I** *v/i.* Blasen ziehen; **II** *v/t.* Blasen ziehen auf (*dat.*); **ves·i-**

ca·tion [ˌvesɪˈkeɪʃn] *s.* Blasenbildung *f*; ˈ**ves·i·ca·to·ry** [-keɪtərɪ] → ***vesicant***; ˈ**ves·i·cle** [-kl] *s.* Bläs-chen *n*; **ve·sic·u·lar** [vɪˈsɪkjʊlə] *adj.* **1.** Bläs-chen..., Blasen...; **2.** blasenförmig, blasig; **3.** blasig, Bläs-chen aufweisend.

ves·per [ˈvespə] *s.* **1.** ♀ *ast.* Abendstern *m*; **2.** *poet.* Abend *m*; **3.** *pl. eccl.* Vesper *f*, Abendgottesdienst *m*, -andacht *f*; **4.** *a.* ~ ***bell*** Abendglocke *f*, -läuten *n*.

ves·sel [ˈvesl] *s.* **1.** Gefäß *n* (*a. anat.*, ⚘ *u. fig.*); **2.** ⚓ (*a.* ✈ Luft)Schiff *n*, (Wasser)Fahrzeug *n*.

vest [vest] **I** *s.* **1.** *Brit.* ˈUnterhemd *n*; **2.** *Brit.* † *od. Am.* Weste *f*; **3.** a) Damenweste *f*, b) Einsatzweste *f*; **4.** *poet.* Gewand *n*; **II** *v/t.* **5.** *bsd. eccl.* bekleiden; **6.** (***with***) *fig. j-n* bekleiden, ausstatten (mit *Befugnissen etc.*), bevollmächtigen; *j-n* einsetzen (in *Eigentum*, *Rechte etc.*); **7.** *Recht etc.* überˈtragen, verleihen (***in s.o.*** j-m): ~***ed interest***, ~***ed right*** sicher begründetes Anrecht, unabdingbares Recht; ~***ed interests*** *die* maßgeblichen Kreise (*e-r Stadt etc.*); **8.** *Am. Feindvermögen* mit Beschlag belegen: ~***ing order*** Beschlagnahmeverfügung *f*; **III** *v/i.* **9.** *bsd. eccl.* sich bekleiden; **10.** ˈübergehen (***in*** auf *acc.*) (*Vermögen etc.*); **11.** (***in***) zustehen (*dat.*), liegen (bei) (*Recht etc.*).

ves·ta [ˈvestə] *s. Brit. a.* ~ ***match*** kurzes Streichholz.

ves·tal [ˈvestl] **I** *adj.* **1.** *antiq.* veˈstalisch; **2.** *fig.* keusch, rein; **II** *s.* **3.** *antiq.* Veˈstalin *f*; **4.** Jungfrau *f*; **5.** Nonne *f*.

ves·ti·bule [ˈvestɪbjuːl] *s.* **1.** (Vor)Halle *f*, Vorplatz *m*, Vestiˈbül *n*; **2.** 🚃 *Am.* (Harˈmonika)Verbindungsgang *m zwischen zwei D-Zug-Wagen*; **3.** *anat.* Vorhof *m*; ~ ***school*** *s. Am.* Lehrwerkstatt *f* (*e-s Industriebetriebs*); ~ ***train*** *s. bsd. Am.* D-Zug *m*.

ves·tige [ˈvestɪdʒ] *s.* **1.** *obs. od. poet.* Spur *f*; **2.** *bsd. fig.* Spur *f*, ˈÜberrest *m*, -bleibsel *n*; **3.** *fig.* Spur *f*, *ein* bißchen; **4.** *biol.* Rudiˈment *n*, verkümmertes Orˈgan *od.* Glied; **ves·tig·i·al** [veˈstɪdʒɪəl] *adj.* **1.** spurenhaft, restlich; **2.** *biol.* rudimenˈtär, verkümmert.

vest·ment [ˈvestmənt] *s.* **1.** Amtstracht *f*, Robe *f*, *a. eccl.* Orˈnat *m*; **2.** *eccl.* Meßgewand *n*; **3.** Gewand *n*, Kleid *n* (*beide a. fig.*).

ˌ**vest-ˈpock·et** *adj. fig.* im ˈWestentaschenforˌmat, Westentaschen..., Klein..., Miniatur...

ves·try [ˈvestrɪ] *s. eccl.* **1.** Sakriˈstei *f*; **2.** Bet-, Gemeindesaal *m*; **3.** *Brit.* a) *a.* ***common*** ~, ***general*** ~, ***ordinary*** ~ Gemeindesteuerpflichtige *pl.*, b) *a.* ***select*** ~ Kirchenvorstand *m*; ~ ***clerk*** *s. Brit.* Rechnungsführer *m* der Kirchgemeinde; ˈ~**man** [-mən] *s.* [*irr.*] Gemeindevertreter *m*.

ves·ture [ˈvestʃə] *s. obs. od. poet.* a) Gewand *n*, Kleid(ung *f*) *n*, b) Hülle *f* (*a. fig.*), Mantel *m*.

ve·su·vi·an [vɪˈsuːvjən] **I** *adj.* **1.** ♀ *geogr.* veˈsuvisch; **2.** vulˈkanisch; **II** *s.* **3.** *obs.* Windstreichhölzchen *n*.

vet[1] [vet] F **I** *s.* **1.** Tierarzt *m*; **II** *v/t.* **2.** *Tier* unterˈsuchen *od.* behandeln; **3.** *humor.* a) *j-n* verarzten, b) *j-n* auf Herz u. Nieren prüfen, (*a.* poˈlitisch) überˈprüfen.

vet[2] [vet] *Am.* F *für* ***veteran***.

vetch [vetʃ] *s.* ⚘ Wicke *f*; ˈ**vetch·ling** [-lɪŋ] *s.* ⚘ Platterbse *f*.

vet·er·an [ˈvetərən] **I** *s.* **1.** Veteˈran *m* (*alter Soldat od. Beamter*); **2.** ⚔ *Am.* ehemaliger Kriegsteilnehmer; **3.** *fig.* ‚alter Hase'; **II** *adj.* **4.** alt-, ausgedient; **5.** kampferprobt: ~ ***troops***; **6.** *fig.* erfahren: ~ ***golfer***; **7.** ~ ***car*** *mot.* Oldtimer *m*.

vet·er·i·nar·i·an [ˌvetərɪˈneərɪən] → **vet·er·i·nar·y** [ˈvetərɪnərɪ] **I** *s.* Tierarzt *m*, Veteriˈnär *m*; **II** *adj.* tierärztlich: ~ ***medicine*** Tiermedizin *f*; ~ ***surgeon*** → I.

ve·to [ˈviːtəʊ] *pol.* **I** *pl.* **-toes** *s.* **1.** Veto *n*, Einspruch *m*: ***put a*** (*od.* ***one's***) ~ (***up***)***on*** → 3; **2.** *a.* ~ ***power*** Veto-, Einspruchsrecht *n*; **II** *v/t.* **3.** sein Veto einlegen gegen, Einspruch erheben gegen; **4.** unterˈsagen, verbieten.

vet·ting [ˈvetɪŋ] *s. pol.* F ˈSicherheitsüberˌprüfung *f*.

vex [veks] *v/t.* **1.** *j-n* ärgern, belästigen, aufbringen, irritieren; → ***vexed***; **2.** quälen, bedrücken, beunruhigen; **3.** schikanieren; **4.** *j-n* verwirren, *j-m* ein Rätsel sein; **5.** *obs. od. poet. Meer* aufwühlen.

vex·a·tion [vekˈseɪʃn] *s.* **1.** Ärger *m*, Verdruß *m*; **2.** Plage *f*, Qual *f*; **3.** Belästigung *f*; **4.** Schiˈkane *f*; **5.** Beunruhigung *f*, Sorge *f*; **vex·a·tious** [vekˈseɪʃəs] *adj.* □ **1.** lästig, verdrießlich, ärgerlich, leidig; **2.** ⚖ schikaˈnös: ***a*** ~ ***suit***; **vex·a·tious·ness** [vekˈseɪʃəsnɪs] *s.* Ärgerlich-, Verdrießlich-, Lästigkeit *f*; **vexed** [vekst] *adj.* □ **1.** ärgerlich (***at s.th.***, ***with s.o.*** über *acc.*); **2.** beunruhigt (***with*** durch, von); **3.** (ˈviel)umˌstritten, strittig: ~ ***question***; **vex·ing** [ˈveksɪŋ] → ***vexatious*** 1.

vi·a [ˈvaɪə] (*Lat.*) **I** *prp.* via, über (*acc.*): ~ ***London***; ~ ***air mail*** per Luftpost; **II** *s.* Weg *m*: ~ ***media*** *fig.* Mittelding *od.* -weg.

vi·a·ble [ˈvaɪəbl] *adj. a. fig.* lebensfähig: ~ ***child***; ~ ***industry***.

vi·a·duct [ˈvaɪədʌkt] *s.* Viaˈdukt *m*.

vi·al [ˈvaɪəl] *s.* (Glas)Fläschchen *n*, Phiˈole *f*: ***pour out the*** ~***s of one's wrath*** *bibl. u. fig.* die Schalen s-s Zornes ausgießen (***upon*** über *acc.*).

vi·and [ˈvaɪənd] *s. pl.* **1.** Lebensmittel *pl.*; **2.** (ˈReise)Proviˌant *m*.

vi·at·i·cum [vaɪˈætɪkəm] *pl.* **-cums** *s. eccl.* Viˈatikum *n* (*bei der letzten Ölung gereichte Eucharistie*).

vibes [vaɪbz] *s. pl.* F **1.** *mst sg konstr.* ♪ Vibraˈphon *n*; **2.** Ausstrahlung *f* (*e-r Person*).

vi·bran·cy [ˈvaɪbrənsɪ] *s.* Resoˈnanz *f*, Schwingen *n*; **vi·brant** [ˈvaɪbrənt] *adj.* **1.** vibrierend: a) schwingend (*Saite etc.*), b) laut schallend (*Ton*); **2.** zitternd, bebend (***with*** vor *dat.*): ~ ***with energy***; **3.** pulsierend (***with*** von): ~ ***cities***; **4.** kraftvoll, lebensprühend: ***a*** ~ ***personality***; **5.** erregt; **6.** *ling.* stimmhaft (*Laut*).

vi·bra·phone [ˈvaɪbrəfəʊn] *s.* ♪ Vibraˈphon *n*.

vi·brate [vaɪˈbreɪt] **I** *v/i.* **1.** vibrieren: a) zittern (*a. phys.*), b) (nach)klingen, (-)schwingen (*Töne*); **2.** pulsieren (***with*** von); **3.** zittern, beben (***with*** vor *Erregung etc.*); **II** *v/t.* **4.** in Schwingungen versetzen; **5.** vibrieren *od.* schwingen *od.* zittern lassen, rütteln; **viˈbra·tion** [-eɪʃn] *s.* **1.** Schwingen *n*, Vibrieren *n*, Zittern *n*: ~**-*proof*** erschütterungsfrei; **2.** *phys.* Vibratiˈon *f*: a) Schwingung *f*, b) Oszillatiˈon *f*; **3.** *fig.* a) Pulsieren *n*, b) *pl.* Ausstrahlung *f e-r Person*; **viˈbra·tion·al** [-eɪʃənl] *adj.* Schwingungs...; **viˈbra·tor** [-eɪtə] *s.* **1.** ⚙ Viˈbrator *m* (*a.* ⚕), ˈRüttelappaˌrat *m*; **2.** ⚡ Oszilˈlator *m*: a) Summer *m*, b) Zerhacker *m*; **3.** ♪ Zunge *f*, Blatt *n*; **vi·bra·to·ry** [ˈvaɪbrətərɪ] *adj.* **1.** schwingungsfähig; **2.** vibrierend; **3.** Vibrations..., Schwingungs...

vic·ar [ˈvɪkə] *s. eccl.* **1.** *Brit.* Viˈkar *m*, (ˈUnter)Pfarrer *m*; **2.** *Protestantische Episkopalkirche in den USA*: a) (ˈUnter)Pfarrer *m*, b) Stellvertreter *m* des Bischofs; **3.** *R.C.* a) ***cardinal*** ~ Kardinalvikar *m*, b) ♀ ***of*** (***Jesus***) ***Christ*** Statthalter *m* Christi (*Papst*); **4.** Ersatz *m*; ˈ**vic·ar·age** [-ərɪdʒ] *s.* **1.** Pfarrhaus *n*; **2.** Vikariˈat *n* (*Amt des Vikars*); ˈ**vic·ar gen·er·al** *s. eccl.* Geneˈralviˌkar *m*.

vi·car·i·ous [vaɪˈkeərɪəs] *adj.* □ **1.** stellvertretend; **2.** *fig.* mit-, nachempfunden, *Erlebnis etc.* aus zweiter Hand: ~ ***pleasure***.

vice[1] [vaɪs] *s.* **1.** Laster *n*: a) Untugend *f*, b) schlechte (An)Gewohnheit; **2.** Lasterhaftigkeit *f*, Verderbtheit *f*: ~ ***squad*** Sittenpolizei *f*, ˈSittendezerˌnat *n*; **3.** körperlicher Fehler, Gebrechen *n*; **4.** *fig.*, *a.* ⚖ Mangel *m*, Fehler *m*; **5.** Verirrung *f*, Auswuchs *m*; **6.** Unart *f* (*Pferd*).

vice[2] [vaɪs] *s.* ⚙ Schraubstock *m* (*a. fig.*).

vi·ce[3] [ˈvaɪsɪ] *prp.* an Stelle von.

vice[4] [vaɪs] *s.* F ‚Vize' *m* (*abbr. für* ***vice admiral*** *etc.*).

vice- [vaɪs] *in Zssgn* stellvertretend, Vize...

vice| ad·mi·ral *s.* ⚓ ˈVizeadmiˌral *m*; ˌ~-ˈ**chair·man** *s.* [*irr.*] stellvertretender Vorsitzender, ˈVizepräsiˌdent *m*; ˌ~-ˈ**chan·cel·lor** *s.* **1.** ˈVizekanzler *m*; **2.** *Brit. univ.* (geschäftsführender) Rektor; ˌ~-ˈ**con·sul** *s.* ˈVizeˌkonsul *m*; ˌ~-ˈ**ge·rent** [-ˈdʒerənt] **I** *s.* Stellvertreter *m*, Statthalter *m*; **II** *adj.* stellvertretend; ˌ~-ˈ**pres·i·dent** *s.* ˈVizepräsiˌdent *m*: a) stellvertretender Vorsitzender, b) † *Am.* Diˈrektor *m*, Vorstandsmitglied *n*; ˌ~ˈ**re·gal** *adj.* vizeköniglich; ~·**reine** [ˌvaɪsˈreɪn] *s.* Gemahlin *f* des Vizekönigs; ~·**roy** [ˈvaɪsrɔɪ] *s.* Vizekönig *m*; ˌ~ˈ**roy·al** *adj.* vizeköniglich.

vi·ce ver·sa [ˌvaɪsɪˈvɜːsə] (*Lat.*) *adv.* ˈumgekehrt, vice versa.

vic·i·nage [ˈvɪsɪnɪdʒ] → ***vicinity***; ˈ**vic·i·nal** [-nl] *adj.* benachbart, ˈumliegend, nah; **vi·cin·i·ty** [vɪˈsɪnətɪ] *s.* **1.** Nähe *f*, Nachbarschaft *f*: ***in close*** ~ ***to*** in unmittelbarer Nähe von; ***in the*** ~ ***of 40*** *fig.* um (die) 40 herum; **2.** Nachbarschaft *f*, (nähere) Umˈgebung: ***the*** ~ ***of London***.

vi·cious [ˈvɪʃəs] *adj.* □ **1.** lasterhaft, verderbt, ˈunmoˌralisch; **2.** verwerflich: ~ ***habit***; **3.** bösartig, boshaft, gemein: ~ ***attack***; **4.** bös-, unartig (*Tier*); **5.** heftig, ‚bös': ***a*** ~ ***blow***; **6.** F scheußlich, schlimm: ~ ***headache***; **7.** *a.* ⚖ fehler-, mangelhaft; **8.** *obs.* schädlich: ~ ***air***; ~ **cir·cle** *s.* **1.** Circulus *m* vitiˈosus, Teufelskreis *m*; **2.** *phls.* Zirkel-, Trugschluß

m.
vi·cious·ness ['vɪʃəsnɪs] *s.* **1.** Lasterhaftigkeit *f*, Verderbtheit *f*; **2.** Verwerflichkeit *f*; **3.** Bösartigkeit *f*, Gemeinheit *f*; **4.** Fehlerhaftigkeit *f*.
vi·cis·si·tude [vɪ'sɪsɪtju:d] *s.* **1.** Wandel *m*, Wechsel *m*; **2.** *pl.* Wechselfälle *pl.*, *das* Auf u. Ab: ***the ~s of life***; **3.** *pl.* Schicksalsschläge *pl.*; **vi·cis·si·tu·di·nous** [vɪˌsɪsɪ'tju:dɪnəs] *adj.* wechselvoll.
vic·tim ['vɪktɪm] *s.* **1.** Opfer *n*: a) (Unfall- *etc.*)Tote(r *m*) *f*, b) Leidtragende(r *m*) *f*, c) Betrogene(r *m*) *f*: ***fall a ~ to*** zum Opfer fallen (*dat.*); **2.** Opfer(tier) *n*; **'vic·tim·ize** [-maɪz] *v/t.* **1.** *j-n* (auf-)opfern; **2.** quälen, schikanieren, belästigen; **3.** prellen, betrügen.
vic·tor ['vɪktə] **I** *s.* Sieger(in); **II** *adj.* siegreich, Sieger...
vic·to·ri·a [vɪk'tɔ:rɪə] *s.* Vik'toria *f* (*zweisitziger Einspänner*); **2 Cross** *s.* Vik'toriakreuz *n* (*brit. Tapferkeitsauszeichnung*).
Vic·tor·i·an [vɪk'tɔ:rɪən] **I** *adj.* **1.** Vikto'ri'anisch: ***~ Period***; **2.** viktori'anisch: ***~ habits***; **II** *s.* **3.** Viktori'aner(in).
vic·to·ri·ous [vɪk'tɔ:rɪəs] *adj.* ☐ **1.** siegreich (***over*** über *acc.*): ***be ~*** den Sieg davontragen, siegen; **2.** Sieges...; **vic·to·ry** ['vɪktərɪ] *s.* **1.** Sieg *m* (*a. fig.*): ***~ ceremony*** Siegerehrung *f*; ***~ rostrum*** Siegespodest *n*; **2.** *fig.* Tri'umph *m*, Erfolg *m*, Sieg *m*: ***moral ~***.
vict·ual ['vɪtl] **I** *s. mst pl.* Eßwaren *pl.*, Lebensmittel *pl.*, Provi'ant *m*; **II** *v/t.* (*v/i.* sich) verpflegen *od.* verproviantieren *od.* mit Lebensmitteln versorgen; **'vict·ual·(l)er** [-lə] *s.* **1.** ('Lebensmittel-)Liefeˌrant *m*; **2.** *a.* ***licensed ~*** *Brit.* Schankwirt *m*; **3.** ⚓ Provi'antschiff *n*; **'vict·ual·(l)ing** [-lɪŋ] *s.* Verproviantierung *f*: ***~ ship*** Proviantschiff *n*.
vi·de ['vaɪdi:] (*Lat.*) *int.* siehe!
vi·de·li·cet [vɪ'di:lɪset] (*Lat.*) *adv.* nämlich, das heißt (*abbr.* ***viz***; *lies*: ***namely, that is***).
vid·e·o ['vɪdɪəʊ] **I** *pl.* **-os** *s.* F **1.** ,Video' *n* (*Videotechnik*); **2.** *Computer*: Bildschirm-, Datensichtgerät *n*; **3.** *Am.* (***on*** im) Fernsehen *n*; **II** *adj.* **4.** Video...: ***~ cassette*** (***recorder***); ***~ disc*** Bildplatte *f*; **5.** *Computer*: Bildschirm...: ***~ terminal*** → 2; **6.** *Am.* F Fernseh...: ***~ program***; **'~·phone** F *für* ***videotelephone***; **'~·tape I** *s.* Videoband *n*; **II** *v/t.* auf Videoband aufnehmen, aufzeichnen; **'~ˌtel·e·phone** *s.* 'Bildteleˌfon *n*.
vie [vaɪ] *v/i.* wetteifern: ***~ with s.o. in*** (*od.* ***for***) ***s.th.*** mit j-m in *od.* um et. wetteifern.
Vi·en·nese [ˌvɪe'ni:z] **I** *s. sg. u. pl.* **1.** a) Wiener(in), b) Wiener(innen) *pl.*; **2.** *ling.* Wienerisch *n*; **II** *adj.* **3.** wienerisch, Wiener(...).
view [vju:] **I** *v/t.* **1.** (sich) ansehen, betrachten, besichtigen, in Augenschein nehmen, prüfen; **2.** *fig.* ansehen, auffassen, betrachten, beurteilen; **3.** über'blicken, -'schauen; **4.** *obs.* sehen; **II** *s.* **5.** (An-, Hin)Sehen *n*, Besichtigung *f*: ***at first ~*** auf den ersten Blick; ***on nearer ~*** bei näherer Betrachtung; **6.** Sicht *f* (*a. fig.*): ***in ~*** a) in Sicht, sichtbar, b) *fig.* in (Aus)Sicht; ***in ~ of*** *fig.* im Hinblick auf (*acc.*), in Anbetracht *od.* angesichts (*gen.*); ***in full ~ of*** direkt vor *j-s* Augen; ***on ~*** zu besichtigen(d), ausgestellt; ***on the long ~*** *fig.* auf weite Sicht; ***out of ~*** außer Sicht, nicht zu sehen; ***come in ~*** in Sicht kommen, sichtbar werden; ***have in ~*** *fig.* im Auge haben, beabsichtigen; ***keep in ~*** *fig.* im Auge behalten; **7.** Aussicht *f*, (Aus-)Blick *m* (***of, over*** auf *acc.*); Szene'rie *f*; **8.** *paint.*, *phot.* Ansicht *f*, Bild *n*: ***~s of London***; ***sectional ~*** ⚙ Ansicht im Schnitt; **9.** *fig.* 'Überblick *m* (***of*** über *acc.*); **10.** Absicht *f*: ***with a ~ to*** a) (*ger.*) mit *od.* in der Absicht zu (*tun*), zu dem Zweck (*gen.*), b) im Hinblick auf (*acc.*); **11.** *fig.* Ansicht *f*, Auffassung *f*, Urteil *n* (***of, on*** über *acc.*): ***in my ~*** in m-n Augen, m-s Erachtens; ***form a ~ on*** sich ein Urteil bilden über (*acc.*); ***take the ~ that*** die Ansicht *od.* den Standpunkt vertreten, daß; ***take a bright*** (***dim, grave***) ***~ of*** *et.* optimistisch (pessimistisch, ernst) beurteilen; **12.** Vorführung *f*: ***private ~ of a film***; **view·a·ble** ['vju:əbl] *adj.* **1.** sichtbar; **2.** *fig.* sehenswert; **view data** *s. pl.* Bildschirmtext *m*; **view·er** ['vju:ə] *s.* **1.** Betrachter(in); **2.** Fernsehzuschauer (-in); **'view·er·ship** *s.* Fernsehpublikum *n*.
'view|ˌfind·er *s. phot.* (Bild)Sucher *m*; **~ hal·loo** *s. hunt.* Hal'lo(ruf *m*) *n* (*beim Erscheinen des Fuchses*).
'view|·phone *s.* 'Bildteleˌfon *n*; **'~·point** *s. fig.* Gesichts-, Standpunkt *m*.
view·y ['vju:ɪ] *adj.* F verstiegen, über'spannt, ,fimmelig'.
vig·il ['vɪdʒɪl] *s.* **1.** Wachsein *n*, Wachen *n* (*zur Nachtzeit*); **2.** Nachtwache *f*: ***keep ~*** wachen (***over*** bei); **3.** *eccl.* a) *mst pl.* Vi'gilie(n *pl.*) *f*, Nachtwache *f* (*vor Kirchenfesten*), b) Vi'gil *f* (*Vortag e-s Kirchenfests*): ***on the ~ of*** am Vorabend von (*od. gen.*); **'vig·i·lance** [-ləns] *s.* **1.** Wachsamkeit *f*: ***~ committee*** *od.* ***group*** *bsd. Am.* Bürgerwehr *f*, Selbstschutzgruppe *f*; **2.** ⚕ Schlaflosigkeit *f*; **'vig·i·lant** [-lənt] *adj.* ☐ wachsam, 'umsichtig, aufmerksam; **vig·i·lan·te** [ˌvɪdʒɪ'læntɪ] *s.* Mitglied *n* e-s ***vigilance committee***.
vi·gnette [vɪ'njet] **I** *s. typ.*, *phot. etc.* Vi'gnette *f*; **II** *v/t.* vignettieren.
vig·or *Am.* → ***vigour***.
vig·or·ous ['vɪgərəs] *adj.* ☐ **1.** *allg.* kräftig; **2.** kraftvoll, vi'tal; **3.** lebhaft, ak'tiv, tatkräftig; **4.** e'nergisch, nachdrücklich; wirksam; **vig·our** ['vɪgə] *s.* **1.** (Körper-, Geistes)Kraft *f*, Vitali'tät *f*; **2.** Ener'gie *f*; **3.** *biol.* Lebenskraft *f*; **4.** *fig.* Nachdruck *m*, Wirkung *f*.
Vi·king, *a.* **2** ['vaɪkɪŋ] *hist.* **I** *s.* Wiking (-er) *m*; **II** *adj.* Wikinger...
vile [vaɪl] *adj.* ☐ **1.** *obs.* wertlos; **2.** gemein, schändlich, abstoßend, schmutzig; **3.** F scheußlich, ab'scheulich, mise'rabel: ***a ~ hat***; ***~ weather***; **'vile·ness** [-nɪs] *s.* **1.** Gemeinheit *f*, Schändlichkeit *f*; **2.** F Scheußlichkeit *f*.
vil·i·fi·ca·tion [ˌvɪlɪfɪ'keɪʃn] *s.* **1.** Schmähung *f*, Verleumdung *f*, -unglimpfung *f*; **2.** Her'absetzung *f*; **vil·i·fi·er** ['vɪlɪfaɪə] *s.* Verleumder(in); **vil·i·fy** ['vɪlɪfaɪ] *v/t.* **1.** schmähen, verleumden, verunglimpfen; **2.** her'absetzen.
vil·la ['vɪlə] *s.* **1.** Villa *f*, Landhaus *n*; **2.** *Brit.* a) Doppelhaushälfte *f*, b) 'Einfaˌmilienhaus *n*.
vil·lage ['vɪlɪdʒ] **I** *s.* Dorf *n*; **II** *adj.* dörflich, Dorf...; **'vil·lag·er** [-dʒə] *s.* Dorfbewohner(in), Dörfler(in).
vil·lain ['vɪlən] *s.* **1.** *a. thea. u. humor.* Schurke *m*, Bösewicht *m*; **2.** *humor.* Schlingel *m*; **3.** → ***villein***; **vil·lain·age** ['vɪlɪnɪdʒ] → ***villeinage***; **'vil·lain·ous** [-nəs] *adj.* ☐ **1.** schurkisch, Schurken..., schändlich; **2.** F → ***vile*** 2, 3; **'vil·lain·y** [-nɪ] *s.* **1.** Schurke'rei *f*; **2.** → ***vileness***.
vil·lein ['vɪlɪn] *s. hist.* **1.** Leibeigene(r) *m*; **2.** *später*: Zinsbauer *m*; **'vil·lein·age** [-nɪdʒ] *s.* **1.** Leibeigenschaft *f*; **2.** 'Hintersassengut *n*.
vil·li·form ['vɪlɪfɔ:m] *adj. biol.* zottenförmig; **vil·lose** ['vɪləʊs], **vil·lous** ['vɪləs] *adj. biol.* zottig; **'vil·lus** [-ləs] *pl.* **-li** [-laɪ] *s.* **1.** *anat.* (Darm)Zotte *f*; **2.** ⚘ Zottenhaar *n*.
vim [vɪm] *s.* F Schwung *m*, ,Schmiß' *m*: ***full of ~*** ,toll in Form'.
vin·ai·grette [ˌvɪneɪ'gret] *s.* **1.** Riechfläschchen *n*, -dose *f*; **2.** *a.* ***~ sauce*** *Küche*: Vinai'grette *f* (*Soße*).
vin·ci·ble ['vɪnsɪbl] *adj.* besiegbar, über'windbar.
vin·cu·lum ['vɪŋkjʊləm] *pl.* **-la** [-lə] *s.* **1.** ⅍ Strich *m* (*über mehreren Zahlen*), Über'streichung *f* (*an Stelle von Klammern*); **2.** *bsd. fig.* Band *n*.
vin·di·ca·ble ['vɪndɪkəbl] *adj.* haltbar, zu rechtfertigen(d); **vin·di·cate** ['vɪndɪkeɪt] *v/t.* **1.** in Schutz nehmen, verteidigen (***from*** vor *dat.*, gegen); **2.** rechtfertigen (***o.s.*** sich), bestätigen; **3.** ⚖ a) Anspruch erheben auf (*acc.*), beanspruchen, b) *Recht, Anspruch* geltend machen, c) *Recht etc.* behaupten; **vin·di·ca·tion** [ˌvɪndɪ'keɪʃn] *s.* **1.** Verteidigung *f*, Rechtfertigung *f*: ***in ~ of*** zur Rechtfertigung von (*od. gen.*); **2.** ⚖ a) Behauptung *f*, b) Geltendmachung *f*; **'vin·di·ca·to·ry** [-keɪtərɪ] *adj.* ☐ **1.** rechtfertigend, Rechtfertigungs...; **2.** rächend, Straf...
vin·dic·tive [vɪn'dɪktɪv] *adj.* ☐ **1.** rachsüchtig; **2.** als Strafe: ***~ damages*** ⚖ tatsächlicher Schadensersatz zuzüglich e-r Buße; **vin'dic·tive·ness** [-nɪs] *s.* Rachsucht *f*.
vine [vaɪn] ⚘ **I** *s.* **1.** (*Hopfen- etc.*)Rebe *f*, Kletterpflanze *f*; **2.** Wein(stock) *m*, (Wein)Rebe *f*; **II** *adj.* **3.** Wein..., Reb (-en)...; **'~-clad** *adj. poet.* weinlaubbekränzt; **'~ˌdress·er** *s.* Winzer *m*; **~ fret·ter** *s.* Reblaus *f*.
vin·e·gar ['vɪnɪgə] **I** *s.* **1.** (Wein)Essig *m*: ***aromatic ~*** aromatischer Essig, Gewürzessig; **2.** *pharm.* Essig *m*; **3.** *fig.* Verdrießlichkeit *f*; **4.** *Am.* F → ***vim***; **II** *v/t.* **5.** Essig tun an (*acc.*); **'vin·e·gar·y** [-ərɪ] *adj.* **1.** (essig)sauer (*a. fig.*); **2.** a) griesgrämig, b) ätzend.
'vine|ˌgrow·er *s.* Weinbauer *m*, Winzer *m*; **'~ˌgrow·ing** *s.* Weinbau *m*; **~ leaf** *s.* [*irr.*] Wein-, Rebenblatt *n*: ***vine leaves*** Weinlaub *n*; **~ louse** *s.* [*irr.*] Reblaus *f*; **~ mil·dew** *s.* ⚘ Traubenfäule *f*.
vin·er·y ['vaɪnərɪ] *s.* **1.** Treibhaus *n* für Reben; **2.** → **vine·yard** ['vɪnjəd] *s.* Weinberg *m od.* -garten *m*.
vin·i·cul·tur·al [ˌvɪnɪ'kʌltʃərəl] *adj.* weinbaukundlich; **vin·i·cul·ture** ['vɪnɪkʌltʃə] *s.* Weinbau *m* (*Fach*).
vi·nos·i·ty [vaɪ'nɒsətɪ] *s.* **1.** Weinartigkeit *f*; **2.** Weinseligkeit *f*; **vi·nous** ['vaɪnəs] *adj.* **1.** weinartig, Wein...; **2.**

weinhaltig; **3.** *fig.* weinselig; **4.** weingerötet: ~ ***face***; **5.** weinrot.

vin·tage ['vɪntɪdʒ] *s.* **1.** Weinertrag *m*, -ernte *f*; **2.** Weinlese(zeit) *f*; **3.** (guter) Wein, (her'vorragender) Jahrgang: ~ ***wine*** Spitzenwein *m*; **4.** F a) Jahrgang *m*, b) Herstellung *f*, *mot. etc. a.* Baujahr *n*: ~ ***car*** *mot.* Oldtimer *m*; '**vin·tag·er** [-dʒə] *s.* Weinleser(in).

vint·ner ['vɪntnə] *s.* Weinhändler *m*.

vi·nyl ['vaɪnɪl] ⚗ **I** *s.* Vi'nyl *n*; **II** *adj.* Vinyl…: ~ ***polymers*** Vinylpolymere *pl.*

vi·ol ['vaɪəl] *s.* ♪ *hist.* Vi'ole *f*: ***bass*** ~ Viola *f* da gamba, Gambe *f*.

vi·o·la[1] [vɪ'əʊlə] *s.* ♪ **1.** Vi'ola *f*, Bratsche *f*; **2.** → ***viol***.

vi·o·la[2] ['vaɪələ] *s.* ⚘ Veilchen *n*, Stiefmütterchen *n*.

vi·o·la·ble ['vaɪələbl] *adj.* □ verletzbar (*bsd. Gesetz, Vertrag*); **vi·o·late** ['vaɪəleɪt] *v/t.* **1.** *Eid, Vertrag, Grenze etc.* verletzen, *Gesetz* über'treten, *bsd. Versprechen* brechen, *e-m Gebot, dem Gewissen* zu'widerhandeln; **2.** *Frieden, Stille, Schlaf* (grob) stören; **3.** *a. fig.* Gewalt antun (*dat.*); **4.** *Frau* schänden, vergewaltigen; **5.** *Heiligtum etc.* entweihen, schänden; **vi·o·la·tion** [ˌvaɪə'leɪʃn] *s.* **1.** Verletzung *f*, Über'tretung *f*, Bruch *m e-s Eides, Gesetzes*; Zu'widerhandlung *f*: ***in*** ~ ***of*** unter Verletzung von; **2.** (grobe) Störung; **3.** Vergewaltigung *f* (*a. fig.*), Schändung *f e-r Frau*; **4.** Entweihung *f*, Schändung *f*; '**vi·o·la·tor** [-leɪtə] *s.* **1.** Verletzer(in), Über'treter (-in); **2.** Schänder(in).

vi·o·lence ['vaɪələns] *s.* **1.** Gewalt(tätigkeit) *f*; **2.** ⚖ Gewalt(tat, -anwendung) *f*: ***by*** ~ gewaltsam; ***crimes of*** ~ Gewaltverbrechen *pl.*; **3.** Verletzung *f*, Unrecht *n*, Schändung *f*: ***do*** ~ ***to*** Gewalt antun (*dat.*), *Gefühle etc.* verletzen, *Heiliges* entweihen; **4.** *bsd. fig.* Heftigkeit *f*, Ungestüm *n*; '**vi·o·lent** [-nt] *adj.* □ **1.** heftig, gewaltig, stark: ~ ***blow***; ~ ***tempest***; **2.** gewaltsam, -tätig (*Person od. Handlung*), Gewalt…: ~ ***death*** gewaltsamer Tod; ~ ***interpretation*** *fig.* gewaltsame Auslegung; ~ ***measures*** Gewaltmaßnahmen *pl.*; ***lay*** ~ ***hands on*** Gewalt antun (*dat.*); **3.** *fig.* heftig, ungestüm, hitzig; **4.** grell, laut (*Farben, Töne*).

vi·o·let ['vaɪəlɪt] **I** *s.* **1.** ⚘ Veilchen *n*: ***shrinking*** ~ F scheues Wesen (*Person*); **2.** Veilchenblau *n*, Vio'lett *n*; **II** *adj.* **3.** veilchenblau, vio'lett.

vi·o·lin [ˌvaɪə'lɪn] *s.* ♪ Vio'line *f*, Geige *f*: ***play the*** ~ Geige spielen, geigen; ***first*** ~ erste(r) Geige(r); ~ ***case*** Geigenkasten *m*; ~ ***clef*** Violinschlüssel *m*; **vi·o·lin·ist** ['vaɪəlɪnɪst] *s.* Violi'nist(in), Geiger(in).

vi·ol·ist ['vaɪəlɪst] *s.* ♪ **1.** *hist.* Vi'olenspieler(in); **2.** [vɪ'əʊlɪst] Brat'schist(in).

vi·o·lon·cel·list [ˌvaɪələn'tʃelɪst] *s.* ♪ (Violon)Cel'list(in); **vi·o·lon'cel·lo** [-ləʊ] *pl.* **-los** *s.* (Violon)'Cello *n*.

VIP [ˌviːaɪ'piː] *s. sl.* ‚hohes' *od.* ‚großes Tier' (*aus **Very Important Person***).

vi·per ['vaɪpə] *s.* **1.** *zo.* Viper *f*, Otter *f*, Natter *f*; **2.** *zo. a.* ***common*** ~ Kreuzotter *f*; **3.** *allg.* Giftschlange *f* (*a. fig.*): ***cherish a*** ~ ***in one's bosom*** *fig.* e-e Schlange an s-m Busen nähren; ***generation of*** ~***s*** *bibl.* Natterngezücht *n*; '**vi·per·ine** [-əraɪn] *adj. zo.* a) vipernartig, b) Vipern…; '**vi·per·ish** [-ərɪʃ] *adj.*, '**vi·per·ous** [-ərəs] *adj.* □ **1.** → ***viperine***; **2.** *fig.* giftig, tückisch.

vi·per's grass *s.* ⚘ Schwarzwurzel *f*.

vi·ra·go [vɪ'rɑːgəʊ] *pl.* **-gos** *s.* **1.** Mannweib *n*; **2.** Zankteufel *m*, ‚Drachen' *m*, Xan'thippe *f*.

vi·res ['vaɪəriːz] *pl. von* ***vis***.

vir·gin ['vɜːdʒɪn] **I** *s.* **1.** a) Jungfrau *f* (*a. ast.*), b) ‚Jungfrau' *f* (*Mann*); **2.** a) *eccl.* ***the*** (***Blessed***) ♀ (***Mary***) die Heilige Jungfrau, b) *Kunst*: Ma'donna *f*; **II** *adj.* **3.** jungfräulich, unberührt (*beide a. fig. Schnee etc.*): ~ ***forest*** Urwald *m*; ♀ ***Mother*** *eccl.* Mutter *f* Gottes; ***the*** ♀ ***Queen*** *hist.* die jungfräuliche Königin (*Elisabeth I von England*); ~ ***queen*** *zo.* unbefruchtete (Bienen)Königin; ~ ***soil*** a) jungfräulicher Boden, ungepflügtes Land, b) *fig.* Neuland *n*, c) *fig.* unberührter Geist; **4.** rein, keusch, jungfräulich: ~ ***modesty***; **5.** ⚙ a) rein, unvermischt (*Stoffe etc.*), b) jungfräulich, gediegen (*Metalle*): ~ ***gold*** (***oil***) Jungferngold *n* (-öl *n*); ~ ***wool*** Schurwolle *f*; **6.** *fig.* Jungfern…: ~ ***cruise*** Jungfernfahrt *f*; '**vir·gin·al** [-nl] *adj.* □ **1.** jungfräulich, Jungfern…: ~ ***membrane*** *anat.* Jungfernhäutchen *n*; **2.** → ***virgin*** 4; **3.** *zo.* unbefruchtet; '**vir·gin·hood** [-hʊd] *s.* Jungfräulichkeit *f*, Jungfernschaft *f*.

Vir·gin·i·a [və'dʒɪnjə] *s. a.* ~ ***tobacco*** Virginia(tabak) *m*; ~ ***creep·er*** *s.* ⚘ Wilder Wein, Jungfernrebe *f*.

Vir·gin·i·an [və'dʒɪnjən] **I** *adj.* Virginia…; **II** *s.* Vir'ginier(in).

vir·gin·i·ty [və'dʒɪnətɪ] *s.* **1.** Jungfräulichkeit *f*, Jungfernschaft *f*; **2.** Reinheit *f*, Keuschheit *f*, Unberührtheit *f* (*a. fig.*).

Vir·go ['vɜːgəʊ] *s. ast.* Jungfrau *f*.

vir·i·des·cent [ˌvɪrɪ'desnt] *adj.* grün (-lich); **vi·rid·i·ty** [vɪ'rɪdətɪ] *s.* **1.** *biol.* grünes Aussehen; **2.** *fig.* Frische *f*.

vir·ile ['vɪraɪl] *adj.* **1.** männlich, kräftig (*beide a. fig. Stil etc.*), Männer…, Mannes…: ~ ***voice***; **2.** *physiol.* po'tent: ~ ***member*** männliches Glied; **vi·ril·i·ty** [vɪ'rɪlətɪ] *s.* **1.** Männlichkeit *f*; **2.** Mannesalter *n*, -jahre *pl.*; **3.** *physiol.* Po'tenz *f*, Zeugungskraft *f*; **4.** *fig.* Kraft *f*.

vi·rol·o·gy [ˌvaɪə'rɒlədʒɪ] *s.* ⚕ Virolo'gie *f*, Virusforschung *f*.

vir·tu [vɜː'tuː] *s.* **1.** Kunst-, Liebhaberwert *m*: ***article of*** ~ Kunstgegenstand *m*; **2.** *coll.* Kunstgegenstände *pl.*; **3.** → ***virtuosity*** 2.

vir·tu·al ['vɜːtʃʊəl] *adj.* □ **1.** tatsächlich, praktisch, eigentlich; **2.** ⚙, *phys.* virtu'ell; '**vir·tu·al·ly** [-əlɪ] *adv.* eigentlich, praktisch, im Grunde (genommen).

vir·tue ['vɜːtjuː] *s.* **1.** Tugend(haftigkeit) *f*: ***woman of*** ~ tugendhafte Frau; ***lady of easy*** ~ leichtes Mädchen; **2.** Rechtschaffenheit *f*; **3.** Tugend *f*: ***make a*** ~ ***of necessity*** aus der Not e-e Tugend machen; **4.** Wirksamkeit *f*, Wirkung *f*, Erfolg *m*; **5.** (gute) Eigenschaft, Vorzug *m*; (hoher) Wert; **6.** ***by*** (*od.* ***in***) ~ ***of*** kraft *e-s Gesetzes, e-r Vollmacht etc.*, auf Grund von (*od. gen.*), vermöge (*gen.*).

vir·tu·os·i·ty [ˌvɜːtjʊ'ɒsətɪ] **I** *s.* **1.** Virtuosi'tät *f*, blendende Technik, meisterhaftes Können; **2.** Kunstsinn *m*, -liebhabe'rei *f*; **II** *adj.* **3.** virtu'os, meisterhaft; **vir·tu·o·so** [ˌvɜːtjʊ'əʊzəʊ] *pl.* **-si** [-siː] *s.* **1.** Virtu'ose *m*; **2.** Kunstkenner *m*.

vir·tu·ous ['vɜːtʃʊəs] *adj.* □ **1.** tugendhaft; **2.** rechtschaffen.

vir·u·lence ['vɪrʊləns], '**vir·u·len·cy** [-sɪ] *s.* ⚕ *u. fig.* Viru'lenz *f*, Giftigkeit *f*, Bösartigkeit *f*; '**vir·u·lent** [-nt] *adj.* □ **1.** giftig, bösartig (*Gift, Krankheit*) (*a. fig.*); **2.** ⚕ viru'lent (*a. fig.*), sehr ansteckend.

vi·rus ['vaɪərəs] *s.* **1.** ⚕ Virus *n*: a) Krankheitserreger *m*, b) Gift-, Impfstoff *m*; **2.** *fig.* Gift *n*, Ba'zillus *m*: ***the*** ~ ***of hatred***.

vis [vɪs] *pl.* **vi·res** ['vaɪəriːz] (*Lat.*) *s. bsd. phys.* Kraft *f*: ~ ***inertiae*** Trägheitskraft; ~ ***mortua*** tote Kraft; ~ ***viva*** kinetische Energie; ~ ***major*** ⚖ höhere Gewalt.

vi·sa ['viːzə] **I** *s.* Visum *n*: a) Sichtvermerk *m* (*im Paß etc.*), b) Einreisebewilligung *f*; **II** *v/t.* ein Visum eintragen in (*acc.*).

vis·age ['vɪzɪdʒ] *s. poet.* Antlitz *n*.

vis-à-vis ['viːzɑːviː; vizavi] (*Fr.*) **I** *adv.* gegen'über (***to, with*** von); **II** *s.* Gegen'über *n*: a) Visa'vis *n*, b) *fig.* ('Amts-) Kolˌlege *m*.

vis·cer·a ['vɪsərə] *s. pl. anat.* Eingeweide *pl.*: ***abdominal*** ~ Bauchorgane *pl.*; '**vis·cer·al** [-rəl] *adj. anat.* Eingeweide…

vis·cid ['vɪsɪd] *adj.* **1.** klebrig (*a.* ⚘); **2.** *bsd. phys.* vis'kos, dick-, zähflüssig; **vis·cid·i·ty** [vɪ'sɪdətɪ] *s.* **1.** Klebrigkeit *f*; **2.** → ***viscosity***.

vis·cose ['vɪskəʊs] *s.* ⚙ Vis'kose *f* (*Art Zellulose*): ~ ***silk*** Viskose-, Zellstoffseide *f*; **vis·cos·i·ty** [vɪs'kɒsətɪ] *s. phys.* Viskosi'tät *f*, (Grad *m* der) Zähflüssigkeit *f*, Konsi'stenz *f*.

vis·count ['vaɪkaʊnt] *s.* Vi'comte *m* (*brit. Adelstitel zwischen* **baron** *u.* **earl**); '**vis·count·cy** [-sɪ] *s.* Rang *m od.* Würde *f* e-s Vi'comte; '**vis·count·ess** [-tɪs] *s.* Vicom'tesse *f*; '**vis·count·y** [-tɪ] → ***viscountcy***.

vis·cous ['vɪskəs] → ***viscid***.

vi·sé ['viːzeɪ] **I** *s.* → ***visa*** I; **II** *v/t. pret. u. p.p.* **-séd** → ***visa*** II.

vise [vaɪs] *Am.* → ***vice***[2].

vis·i·bil·i·ty [ˌvɪzɪ'bɪlətɪ] *s.* **1.** Sichtbarkeit *f*; **2.** *meteor.* Sicht(weite) *f*: ***high*** (***low***) ~ gute (schlechte) Sicht; ~ (***conditions***) Sichtverhältnisse *pl.*; **vis·i·ble** ['vɪzəbl] *adj.* □ **1.** sichtbar; **2.** *fig.* (er-, offen-) sichtlich, merklich, deutlich, erkennbar; **3.** ⚙ sichtbar (gemacht), graphisch dargestellt; **4.** *pred.* a) zu sehen (*Sache*), b) zu sprechen (*Person*).

Vis·i·goth ['vɪzɪgɒθ] *s. hist.* Westgote *m*, -gotin *f*.

vi·sion ['vɪʒn] **I** *s.* **1.** Sehkraft *f*, -vermögen *n*: ***field of*** ~ Blickfeld *n*; **2.** *fig.* a) visio'näre Kraft, (Seher-, Weit)Blick *m*, b) Phanta'sie *f*, Vorstellungsvermögen *n*, Einsicht *f*: ***bold*** ~ kühne (Zukunfts)Ideen; **3.** Visi'on *f*: a) Traum-, Wunschbild *n*, b) *oft pl. psych.* Halluzinati'onen *pl.*, Gesichte *pl.*; **4.** a) Anblick *m*, Bild *n*, b) Traum *m*, et. Schönes; **II** *adj.* **5.** *TV* Bild…: ~ ***mixer***; ~ ***control*** Bildregie *f*; **III** *v/t.* **6.** *fig.* (er-) schauen; '**vi·sion·ar·y** [-nərɪ] **I** *adj.* **1.** visio'när, (hell)seherisch; **2.** phan'tastisch, verstiegen, ‚traumtänzerisch': ***a***

~ scheme; **3.** unwirklich, eingebildet; **4.** Visions...; **II** *s.* **5.** Visio'när *m*, Hellseher *m*; **6.** Phan'tast *m*, Träumer *m*, Schwärmer *m*, ‚Traumtänzer' *m*.

vis·it ['vɪzɪt] **I** *v/t.* **1.** besuchen: a) *j-n, Arzt, Kranke, Lokal etc.* aufsuchen, b) inspizieren, in Augenschein nehmen, c) *Stadt, Museum etc.* besichtigen; **2.** ⚖ durch'suchen; **3.** heimsuchen (**s.th. upon** *j-n* mit et.): a) befallen (*Krankheit, Unglück*), b) *bibl. u. fig.* (be-)strafen, *Sünden* vergelten (**upon** an *dat.*); **4.** *bibl.* belohnen, segnen; **II** *v/i.* **5.** e-n Besuch *od.* Besuche machen; **6.** *Am.* F plaudern; **III** *s.* **7.** Besuch *m*: **on a ~** auf Besuch (**to** bei *j-m*, in *e-r Stadt etc.*); **make** (*od.* **pay**) **a ~** e-n Besuch machen; **~ to the doctor** Konsultation *f* beim Arzt, Arztbesuch *m*; **8.** (for'meller) Besuch, *bsd.* Inspekti'on *f*; **9.** ⚖, ⚓ Durch'suchung *f*; **10.** *Am.* F Plausch *m*; **'vis·it·ant** [-tənt] **I** *s.* **1.** *rhet.* Besucher (-in); **2.** *orn.* Strichvogel *m*; **II** *adj.* **3.** *rhet.* auf Besuch; **vis·it·a·tion** [ˌvɪzɪ'teɪʃn] *s.* **1.** Besuchen *n*; **2.** offizi'eller Besuch, Besichtigung *f*, Visitati'on *f*: **right of ~** ⚓ Durchsuchungsrecht *n* (*auf See*); **~ (of the sick)** *eccl.* Krankenbesuch; **3.** *fig.* Heimsuchung: a) (gottgesandte) Prüfung *f*, Strafe *f* (Gottes), b) himmlischer Beistand: **2 of our Lady** *R.C.* Heimsuchung Mariae; **4.** *zo.* massenhaftes Auftreten; **5.** F langer Besuch; **vis·it·a·to·ri·al** [ˌvɪzɪtə'tɔːrɪəl] *adj.* Visitations..., Überwachungs..., Aufsichts...: **~ power** Aufsichtsbefugnis *f*; **'vis·it·ing** [-tɪŋ] *adj.* Besuchs..., Besucher...: **~ book** Besuchsliste *f*; **~ card** Visitenkarte *f*; **~ hours** Besuchszeit *f*; **~ nurse** *Am.* Gemeindeschwester *f*; **~ professor** *univ.* Gastprofessor *m*; **~ team** *sport* Gastmannschaft *f*; **be on ~ terms with s.o.** j-n so gut kennen, daß man ihn besucht; **'vis·i·tor** [-tə] *s.* **1.** Besucher(in) (**to** *gen.*), (*a.* Kur)Gast *m*; *pl.* Besuch *m*: **summer ~s** Sommergäste *pl.*; **~s' book** a) Fremdenbuch *n*, b) Gästebuch *n*; **2.** Visi'tator *m*, In'spektor *m*; **vis·i·to·ri·al** [ˌvɪzɪ'tɔːrɪəl] → **visitatorial**.

vi·sor ['vaɪzə] *s.* **1.** *hist. u. fig.* Vi'sier *n*; **2.** (Mützen)Schirm *m*; **3.** *mot.* Sonnenblende *f*.

vis·ta ['vɪstə] *s.* **1.** (Aus-, 'Durch)Blick *m*, Aussicht *f*; **2.** Al'lee *f*; **3.** ⚠ Gale'rie *f*, Korridor *m*; **4.** (lange) Reihe, Kette *f*: **a ~ of years**; **5.** *fig.* Ausblick *m*, -sicht *f* (**of** auf *acc.*), Möglichkeit *f*, Perspek'tive *f*: **his words opened up new ~s**.

vis·u·al ['vɪzjʊəl] **I** *adj.* □ **1.** Seh..., Gesichts...: **~ acuity** Sehschärfe *f*; **~ angle** Gesichtswinkel *m*; **~ nerve** Sehnerv *m*; **~ test** Augentest *m*; **2.** visu'ell (*Eindruck, Gedächtnis etc.*): **~ aid(s)** *ped.* Anschauungsmaterial *n*; **~ arts** bildende Künste; **~ display unit** *Computer*: Datensichtgerät *n*; **~ instruction** *ped.* Anschauungsunterricht *m*; **3.** sichtbar: **~ objects**; **4.** optisch, Sicht...(*-anzeige, -bereich, -zeichen etc.*); **II** *s.* **5.** *typ.*, ✝ a) (Roh)Skizze *f* e-s Layouts, b) 'Bildeleˌment *n* e-r Anzeige; **vis·u·al·i·za·tion** [ˌvɪzjʊəlaɪ'zeɪʃn] *s.* Vergegenwärtigung *f*; **'vis·u·al·ize** [-laɪz] *v/t.* sich vergegenwärtigen *od.* vor Augen stellen, sich vorstellen, sich ein Bild machen von; **'vis·u·al·iz·er** [-laɪzə] *s.* ✝ graphischer I'deengestalter.

vi·ta ['viːtə] (*Lat.*) *pl.* **-tae** [-taɪ] *s. Am.* Lebenslauf *m*.

vi·tal ['vaɪtl] **I** *adj.* **1.** Lebens...(*-frage, -funktion, -funke etc.*): **~ energy** (*od.* **power**) Lebenskraft *f*; **~ statistics** a) Bevölkerungsstatistik *f*, b) *humor.* Körpermaße *pl.*; **Bureau of 2 Statistics** *Am.* Personenstandsregister *n*; **2.** lebenswichtig (*Industrie, Organ etc.*): **~ parts** → 8; **3.** (hoch)wichtig, entscheidend (**to** für): **~ problems**; **of ~ importance** von entscheidender Bedeutung; **4.** wesentlich, grundlegend; **5.** *mst fig.* le'bendig: **~ style**; **6.** vi'tal, lebensprühend; **7.** lebensgefährlich: **~ wound**; **II** *s.* **8.** *pl.* a) *anat.* ‚edle Teile' *pl.*, lebenswichtige Or'gane *pl.*, b) *fig. das* Wesentliche, wichtige Bestandteile *pl.*; **vi·tal·i·ty** [vaɪ'tælətɪ] *s.* **1.** Vitali'tät *f*, Lebenskraft *f*; **2.** Lebensfähigkeit *f*, -dauer *f* (*a. fig.*); **vi·tal·i·za·tion** [ˌvaɪtəlaɪ'zeɪʃn] *s.* Belebung *f*, Aktivierung *f*; **'vi·tal·ize** [-təlaɪz] *v/t.* **1.** beleben, kräftigen; **2.** mit Lebenskraft erfüllen; **3.** *fig.* a) verle'bendigen, b) le'bendig gestalten.

vi·ta·min(e) ['vɪtəmɪn] *s.* Vita'min *n*.

vi·ti·ate ['vɪʃɪeɪt] *v/t.* **1.** *allg.* verderben; **2.** beeinträchtigen; **3.** a) *Luft etc.* verunreinigen, b) *fig. Atmosphäre* vergiften; **4.** *Argument etc.* wider'legen; **5.** *bsd.* ⚖ ungültig machen, aufheben; **vi·ti·a·tion** [ˌvɪʃɪ'eɪʃn] *s.* **1.** Verderben *n*, Verderbnis *f*; **2.** Beeinträchtigung *f*; **3.** Verunreinigung *f*; **4.** Wider'legung *f*; **5.** ⚖ Aufhebung *f*.

vit·i·cul·ture ['vɪtɪkʌltʃə] *s.* Weinbau *m*.

vit·re·ous ['vɪtrɪəs] *adj.* **1.** Glas..., aus Glas, gläsern; **2.** glasartig, glasig: **~ body** *anat.* Glaskörper *m des Auges*; **~ electricity** positive Elektrizität; **3.** *geol.* glasig; **vi·tres·cent** [vɪ'tresnt] *adj.* **1.** verglasend; **2.** verglasbar.

vit·ri·fac·tion [ˌvɪtrɪ'fækʃn], **vit·ri·fi·ca·tion** [ˌvɪtrɪfɪ'keɪʃn] *s.* ⚙ Ver-, Über'glasung *f*, Sinterung *f*; **vit·ri·fy** ['vɪtrɪfaɪ] ⚙ **I** *v/t.* ver-, über'glasen, glasieren, sintern; *Keramik*: dicht brennen; **II** *v/i.* (sich) verglasen.

vit·ri·ol ['vɪtrɪəl] *s.* **1.** ⚗ Vitri'ol *n*: **blue ~**, **copper ~** Kupfervitriol, -sulfat *n*; **green ~** Eisenvitriol, Ferrosulfat *n*; **white ~** Zinksulfat *n*; **2.** ⚗ a) Vitri'olsäure *f*, b) **oil of ~** Vitriolöl *n*, rauchende Schwefelsäure; **3.** *fig.* a) Gift *n*, Säure *f*, b) Giftigkeit *f*, Schärfe *f*; **vit·ri·ol·ic** [ˌvɪtrɪ'ɒlɪk] *adj.* **1.** vitri'olisch, Vitriol...: **~ acid** → **vitriol** 2b; **2.** *fig.* ätzend, beißend: **~ remark**; **'vit·ri·ol·ize** [-laɪz] *v/t.* **1.** ⚗ vitriolisieren; **2.** *j-n* mit Vitriol bespritzen *od.* verletzen.

vi·tu·per·ate [vɪ'tjuːpəreɪt] *v/t.* **1.** beschimpfen, schmähen; **2.** scharf tadeln; **vi·tu·per·a·tion** [vɪˌtjuːpə'reɪʃn] *s.* **1.** Schmähung *f*, (wüste) Beschimpfung; *pl.* Schimpfworte *pl.*; **2.** scharfer Tadel *m*; **vi'tu·per·a·tive** [-pərətɪv] *adj.* □ **1.** schmähend, Schmäh...; **2.** tadelnd.

vi·va¹ ['viːvə] (*Ital.*) **I** *int.* Hoch!; **II** *s.* Hoch(ruf *m*) *n*.

vi·va² ['vaɪvə] → **viva voce**.

vi·va·cious [vɪ'veɪʃəs] *adj.* □ lebhaft, munter; **vi·vac·i·ty** [vɪ'væsətɪ] *s.* Lebhaftigkeit *f*, Munterkeit *f*.

vi·var·i·um [vaɪ'veərɪəm] *pl.* **-i·a** [-ɪə] *s.* Vi'varium *n* (*Aquarium, Terrarium etc.*).

vi·va vo·ce [ˌvaɪvə'vəʊsɪ] **I** *adj. u. adv.* mündlich; **II** *s.* mündliche Prüfung; **vi·va-vo·ce** [ˌvaɪvə'vəʊsɪ] *v/t.* mündlich prüfen.

viv·id ['vɪvɪd] *adj.* □ **1.** *allg.* lebhaft: a) impul'siv (*Mensch*), b) inten'siv (*Gefühle, Phantasie*), c) leuchtend (*Farbe etc.*), d) deutlich, klar (*Schilderung etc.*); **2.** le'bendig (*Porträt etc.*); **'viv·id·ness** [-nɪs] *s.* **1.** Lebhaftigkeit *f*; **2.** Le'bendigkeit *f*.

viv·i·fy ['vɪvɪfaɪ] *v/t.* **1.** 'wiederbeleben; **2.** *fig.* Leben geben (*dat.*), beleben, anregen; **3.** *fig.* intensivieren; **4.** *biol.* in lebendes Gewebe verwandeln; **vi·vip·a·rous** [vɪ'vɪpərəs] *adj.* □ **1.** *zo.* lebendgebärend; **2.** ⚘ noch an der Mutterpflanze keimend (*Samen*); **viv·i·sect** [ˌvɪvɪ'sekt] *v/t. u. v/i.* vivisezieren, lebend sezieren; **viv·i·sec·tion** [ˌvɪvɪ'sekʃn] *s.* Vivisekti'on *f*.

vix·en ['vɪksn] *s.* **1.** *zo.* Füchsin *f*; **2.** *fig.* ‚Drachen' *m*, Xan'thippe *f*; **'vix·en·ish** [-nɪʃ] *adj.* zänkisch.

vi·zier [vɪ'zɪə] *s.* We'sir *m*.

vi·zor → **visor**.

V-J Day *s.* Tag *m* des Sieges der Alli'ierten über Japan (*im 2. Weltkrieg*; *2. 9. 1945*).

vo·ca·ble ['vəʊkəbl] *s.* Vo'kabel *f*.

vo·cab·u·lar·y [vəʊ'kæbjʊlərɪ] *s.* Voka-bu'lar *n*: a) Wörterverzeichnis *n*, b) Wortschatz *m*.

vo·cal ['vəʊkl] **I** *adj.* □ → **vocally**; **1.** stimmlich, mündlich, Stimm..., Sprech...: **~ c(h)ords** Stimmbänder *pl.*; **2.** ♪ Vokal..., Gesang(s)..., gesanglich: **~ music** Vokalmusik *f*; **~ part** Singstimme *f*; **~ recital** Liederabend *m*; **3.** klingend, 'widerhallend (**with** von); **4.** stimmbegabt, der Sprache mächtig; **5.** laut, vernehmbar, *a.* gesprächig: **become ~** *fig.* laut werden, sich vernehmen lassen; **6.** *ling.* a) vo'kalisch, b) stimmhaft; **II** *s.* **7.** (gesungener) Schlager; **vo·cal·ic** [vəʊ'kælɪk] *adj.* vo'kalisch; **'vo·cal·ism** [-kəlɪzəm] *s.* **1.** Vokalisati'on *f* (*Vokalbildung u. -aussprache*); **2.** Vo'kalsyˌstem *n e-r Sprache*; **'vo·cal·ist** [-kəlɪst] *s.* ♪ Sänger(in); **vo·cal·i·za·tion** [ˌvəʊkəlaɪ'zeɪʃn] *s.* **1.** *bsd.* ♪ Stimmgebung *f*; **2.** *ling.* a) Vokalisati'on *f*, b) stimmhafte Aussprache; **'vo·cal·ize** [-kəlaɪz] **I** *v/t.* **1.** *Laut* aussprechen, *a.* singen; **2.** *ling.* a) *Konsonanten* vokalisieren, b) stimmhaft aussprechen; **3.** → **vowelize** 1; **II** *v/i.* **4.** (*beim Singen*) vokalisieren.

vo·ca·tion [vəʊ'keɪʃn] *s.* **1.** (*eccl.* göttliche, *allg.* innere) Berufung (**for** zu); **2.** Begabung *f*, Eignung *f* (**for** für); **3.** Beruf *m*, Beschäftigung *f*; **vo'ca·tion·al** [-ʃənl] *adj.* □ beruflich, Berufs... (*-ausbildung, -krankheit, -schule etc.*): **~ guidance** Berufsberatung *f*.

voc·a·tive ['vɒkətɪv] **I** *adj. ling.* vokativisch, Anrede...: **~ case** → **II** *s.* Vokativ *m*.

vo·cif·er·ate [vəʊ'sɪfəreɪt] *v/i.* schreien, brüllen; **vo·cif·er·a·tion** [vəʊˌsɪfə'reɪʃn] *s. a. pl.* Schreien *n*, Brüllen *n*, Geschrei *n*; **vo'cif·er·ous** [-fərəs] *adj.* □ **1.** laut schreiend, brüllend; **2.** lärmend, laut; **3.** lautstark: **~ protest**.

vod·ka ['vɒdkə] *s.* Wodka *m*.

vogue [vəʊg] *s.* **1.** *allg.* (herrschende) Mode: ***all the ~*** (die) große Mode, der letzte Schrei; ***be in ~*** (in) Mode sein; ***come into ~*** in Mode kommen; **2.** Beliebtheit *f*: ***be in full ~*** großen Anklang finden, sehr im Schwange sein; ***have a short-lived ~*** sich e-r kurzen Beliebtheit erfreuen; **~ word** *s.* Modewort *n*.

voice [vɔɪs] **I** *s.* **1.** Stimme *f* (*a. fig. des Gewissens etc.*): ***the still, small ~ (within)*** *fig.* die leise Stimme des Gewissens; ***in (good) ~*** ♪ (gut) bei Stimme; ***in a low ~*** mit leiser Stimme; **~ box** Kehlkopf *m*; **~ radio** ⚡ Sprechfunk *m*; **~ range** ♪ Stimmumfang *m*; **2.** *fig.* Ausdruck *m*, Äußerung *f*: ***find ~ in*** Ausdruck finden in (*dat.*); ***give ~ to*** → 7; **3.** *fig. allg.* Stimme *f*: a) Entscheidung *f*: ***give one's ~ for*** stimmen für; ***with one ~*** einstimmig, b) Stimmrecht *n*: ***have a (no) ~ in*** et. (nichts) zu sagen haben bei *od.* in (*dat.*), c) Sprecher(in), Sprachrohr *n*; **4.** ♪ a) *a.* **~ *quality*** Stimmton *m*, b) (Orgel)Stimme *f*; **5.** *ling.* a) stimmhafter Laut, b) Stimmton *m*; **6.** *ling.* Genus *n* des Verbs: ***active ~*** Aktiv *n*; ***passive ~*** Passiv *n*; **II** *v/t.* **7.** Ausdruck geben *od.* verleihen (*dat.*), *Meinung etc.* äußern, in Worte fassen; **8.** ♪ *Orgelpfeife etc.* regulieren; **9.** *ling.* (stimmhaft) (aus)sprechen; **voiced** [-st] *adj.* **1.** *in Zssgn* mit *leiser etc.* Stimme: ***low-~***; **2.** *ling.* stimmhaft; **'voice·less** [-lɪs] *adj.* **1.** ohne Stimme, stumm; **2.** sprachlos; **3.** *parl.* nicht stimmfähig; **4.** *ling.* stimmlos; **'voice-ˌo·ver** *s. Film, TV*: 'Off-Kommenˌtar *n*.

void [vɔɪd] **I** *adj.* □ **1.** leer; **2.** **~ *of*** ohne, bar (*gen.*), arm an (*dat.*), frei von; **3.** unbewohnt; **4.** unbesetzt, frei (*Amt*); **5.** ⚖ nichtig, ungültig, -wirksam; → ***null*** 1; **II** *s.* **6.** (*fig.* Gefühl *n* der) Leere *f*, leerer Raum; **7.** *fig.* Lücke *f*: ***fill the ~*** die Lücke schließen; **8.** ⚖ unbewohntes Gebäude; **III** *v/t.* **9.** räumen (***of*** von); **10.** ⚖ a) aufheben, b) anfechten; **11.** *physiol. Urin etc.* ausscheiden; **'void·a·ble** [-dəbl] *adj.* ⚖ aufheb- *od.* anfechtbar; **'void·ance** [-dəns] *s.* Räumung *f*; **'void·ness** [-nɪs] *s.* **1.** Leere *f*; **2.** ⚖ Nichtigkeit *f*, Ungültigkeit *f*.

voile [vɔɪl] *s.* Voile *m*, Schleierstoff *m*.

vo·lant ['vəʊlənt] *adj.* **1.** *zo.* fliegend (*a. her.*); **2.** *poet.* flüchtig.

vol·a·tile ['vɒlətaɪl] *adj.* **1.** *phys.* verdampfbar, (leicht) flüchtig, vola'til, ä'therisch (*Öl etc.*); **2.** *fig.* flüchtig, vergänglich; **3.** *fig.* a) le'bendig, lebhaft, b) launisch, unbeständig, flatterhaft; **vol·a·til·i·ty** [ˌvɒlə'tɪlətɪ] *s.* **1.** *phys.* Verdampfbarkeit *f*, Flüchtigkeit *f* (*a. fig.*); **2.** *fig.* a) Lebhaftigkeit *f*, b) Unbeständig-, Flatterhaftigkeit *f*; **vol·a·til·i·za·tion** [vɒˌlætɪlaɪ'zeɪʃn] *s. phys.* Verflüchtigung *f*, Verdampfung *f*; **vol·a·til·ize** [vɒ'lætɪlaɪz] *v/t.* (*v/i.* sich) verflüchtigen, verdunsten, verdampfen.

vol-au-vent ['vɒləʊvɑ̃:ŋ; vɔlovɑ̃] (*Fr.*) *s.* Vol-au-'vent *m* (*gefüllte Blätterteigpastete*).

vol·can·ic [vɒl'kænɪk] *adj.* (□ **~*ally***) **1.** *geol.* vul'kanisch, Vulkan…; **2.** *fig.* ungestüm, explo'siv; **vol·ca·no** [vɒl'keɪnəʊ] *pl.* **-no(e)s** *s.* **1.** *geol.* Vul'kan *m*; **2.** *fig.* Vul'kan *m*, Pulverfaß *n*: ***sit on the top of a ~*** (wie) auf e-m Pulverfaß sitzen; **vol·can·ol·o·gy** [ˌvɒlkə'nɒlədʒɪ] *s.* Vulkanolo'gie *f*.

vole[1] [vəʊl] *s. zo.* Wühlmaus *f*.

vole[2] [vəʊl] *s. Kartenspiel*: Gewinn *m* aller Stiche.

vo·li·tion [vəʊ'lɪʃn] *s.* **1.** Willensäußerung *f*, -akt *m*, (Willens)Entschluß *m*: ***on one's own ~*** aus eigenem Entschluß; **2.** Wille *m*, Wollen *n*, Willenskraft *f*; **vo'li·tion·al** [-ʃənl] *adj.* □ Willens…, willensmäßig; **vol·i·tive** ['vɒlɪtɪv] *adj.* **1.** Willens…; **2.** *ling.* voli'tiv.

vol·ley ['vɒlɪ] **I** *s.* **1.** (Gewehr-, Geschütz)Salve *f*; (Pfeil-, Stein- *etc.*)Hagel *m*; *Artillerie, Flak*: Gruppe *f*: **~ *bombing*** ✈ Reihenwurf *m*; **2.** *fig.* Schwall *m*, Strom *m*, Flut *f*: ***a ~ of oaths***; **3.** *sport*: a) *Tennis*: Volley *m* (*Schlag*), (*Ball a.*) Flugball *m*, b) *Fußball*: Volleyschuß *m*: ***take a ball at*** *od.* ***on the ~*** → 6; **4.** *Badminton*: Ballwechsel *m*; **II** *v/t.* **5.** in e-r Salve abschießen; **6.** *sport*: *den Ball* volley nehmen, (*Fußball a.*) (di'rekt) aus der Luft nehmen; **7.** *mst* **~ *out*** *od.* ***forth*** e-n Schwall von *Worten etc.* von sich geben; **III** *v/i.* **8.** e-e Salve *od.* Salven abgeben; **9.** hageln (*Geschosse*), krachen (*Geschütze*); **10.** *sport*: a) *Tennis*: volieren, b) *Fußball*: volley schießen; **'~·ball** *s. sport* **1.** Volleyball(spiel *n*) *m*; **2.** Volleyball *m*.

vol·plane ['vɒlpleɪn] ✈ **I** *s.* Gleitflug *m*; **II** *v/i.* im Gleitflug niedergehen.

volt[1] [vɒlt] *s. fenc. u. Reitsport*: Volte *f*.

volt[2] [vəʊlt] *s.* ⚡ Volt *n*; **'volt·age** [-tɪdʒ] *s.* ⚡ (Volt)Spannung *f*; **vol·ta·ic** [vɒl'teɪɪk] *adj.* ⚡ vol'taisch, gal'vanisch (*Batterie, Element, Strom etc.*): **~ *couple*** Elektrodenmetalle *pl.*

volte-face [ˌvɒlt'fɑ:s; vɔltəfas] (*Fr.*) *s. fig.* (to'tale) (Kehrt)Wendung.

volt·me·ter ['vəʊltˌmi:tə] *s.* ⚡ Voltmeter *m*, Spannungsmesser *m*.

vol·u·bil·i·ty [ˌvɒljʊ'bɪlətɪ] *s. fig.* a) glatter Fluß (*der Rede*), b) Zungenfertigkeit *f*, Redegewandtheit *f*, c) Redseligkeit *f*, d) Wortreichtum *m*; **vol·u·ble** ['vɒljʊbl] *adj.* □ **1.** a) geläufig (*Zunge*), fließend (*Rede*), b) zungenfertig, (rede-)gewandt, c) redselig, d) wortreich; **2.** ⚘ windend.

vol·ume ['vɒlju:m] *s.* **1.** Band *m e-s Buches*; Buch *n* (*a. fig.*): ***a three-~ novel*** ein dreibändiger Roman; ***speak ~s (for)*** *fig.* Bände sprechen (für); **2.** Ⱥ, ⚗, *phys. etc.* Vo'lumen *n*, (Raum)Inhalt *m*; **3.** *fig.* 'Umfang *m*, Vo'lumen *n*: **~ *of imports***; **~ *of traffic*** Verkehrsaufkommen *n*; **4.** *fig.* Masse *f*, Schwall *m*; **5.** ♪ Klangfülle *f*, 'Stimmvoˌlumen *n*, -ˌumfang *m*; **6.** ⚡ Lautstärke *f*: **~ *control*** Lautstärkeregler *m*; **'vol·umed** [-md] *adj. in Zssgn* …bändig: ***a three-~ book***; **vol·u·met·ric** [ˌvɒljʊ'metrɪk] *adj.* (□ **~*ally***) Ⱥ, ⚗ volu'metrisch: **~ *analysis*** ⚗ volumetrische Analyse, Maßanalyse *f*; **~ *density*** Raumdichte *f*; **vol·u·met·ri·cal** [ˌvɒljʊ'metrɪkl] *adj.* □ → ***volumetric***; **vo·lu·mi·nous** [və'lju:mɪnəs] *adj.* □ **1.** vielbändig (*literarisches Werk*); **2.** produk'tiv: ***a ~ author***; **3.** massig, 'umfangreich, volumi'nös: **~ *correspondence***; **4.** bauschig; **5.** ♪ voll: **~ *voice***.

vol·un·tar·i·ness ['vɒləntərɪnɪs] *s.* **1.** Freiwilligkeit *f*; **2.** (Willens)Freiheit *f*; **vol·un·tar·y** ['vɒləntərɪ] **I** *adj.* □ **1.** freiwillig, spon'tan: **~ *contribution***; **~ *death*** Freitod *m*; **2.** frei, unabhängig; **3.** ⚖ a) vorsätzlich, schuldhaft, b) freiwillig, unentgeltlich, c) außergerichtlich, gütlich: **~ *settlement***; **~ *jurisdiction*** freiwillige Gerichtsbarkeit; **4.** durch freiwillige Spenden unter'halten (*Schule etc.*); **5.** *physiol.* willkürlich: **~ *muscles***; **6.** *psych.* volunta'ristisch; **II** *s.* **7.** a) freiwillige *od.* wahlweise Arbeit, b) *a.* **~ *exercise*** *sport* Kür(übung) *f*; **8.** ♪ Orgelsolo *n*.

vol·un·teer [ˌvɒlən'tɪə] **I** *s.* **1.** Freiwillige(r *m*) *f* (*a.* ⚔); **2.** ⚖ unentgeltlicher Rechtsnachfolger; **II** *adj.* **3.** freiwillig, Freiwilligen…; **4.** ⚘ wildwachsend; **III** *v/i.* **5.** sich freiwillig melden *od.* erbieten (***for*** für, zu), als Freiwilliger eintreten *od.* dienen; **IV** *v/t.* **6.** *Dienste etc.* freiwillig anbieten *od.* leisten; **7.** sich *e-e Bemerkung* erlauben; **8.** (freiwillig) zum besten geben: ***he ~ed a song***.

vo·lup·tu·ar·y [və'lʌptjʊərɪ] *s.* Lüstling *m*, sinnlicher Mensch; **vo'lup·tu·ous** [-tʃʊəs] *adj.* □ **1.** wollüstig, sinnlich; geil, lüstern; **2.** üppig, sinnlich: **~ *body***; **vo'lup·tu·ous·ness** [-jʊəsnɪs] *s.* **1.** Wollust *f*, Sinnlichkeit *f*, Geilheit *f*, Lüsternheit *f*; **2.** Üppigkeit *f*.

vo·lute [və'lju:t] *s.* **1.** Schnörkel *m*, Spi'rale *f*; **2.** △ Vo'lute *f*, Schnecke *f*; **3.** *zo.* Windung *f* (*Schneckengehäuse*); **vo'lut·ed** [-tɪd] *adj.* **1.** gewunden, spi'ral-, schneckenförmig; **2.** △ mit Vo'luten (versehen); **vo'lu·tion** [-ju:ʃn] *s.* **1.** Drehung *f*; **2.** *anat., zo.* Windung *f*.

vom·it ['vɒmɪt] **I** *v/t.* **1.** (er)brechen; **2.** *fig. Feuer etc.* (aus)speien; *Rauch, a. Flüche etc.* ausstoßen; **II** *v/i.* **3.** (sich er)brechen, sich über'geben; **4.** Rauch ausstoßen; Lava auswerfen, Feuer speien (*Vulkan*); **III** *s.* **5.** Erbrechen *n*; **6.** *das* Erbrochene; **7.** ⚕ Brechmittel *n*; **8.** *fig.* Unflat *m*; **'vom·i·tive** [-tɪv], **'vom·i·to·ry** [-tərɪ] **I** *s.* ⚕ Brechmittel *n*; **II** *adj.* Erbrechen verursachend, Brech…

voo·doo ['vu:du:] **I** *s.* **1.** Wodu *m*, Zauberkult *m*; **2.** Zauber *m*, Hexe'rei *f*; **3.** *a.* **~ *doctor***, **~ *priest*** (Wodu)Zauberer *m*, Medi'zinmann *m*; **4.** Fetisch *m*, Götze *m*; **II** *v/t.* **5.** behexen; **'voo·doo·ism** *s.* Wodukult *m*.

vo·ra·cious [və'reɪʃəs] *adj.* □ gefräßig, gierig, unersättlich (*a. fig.*); **vo'ra·cious·ness** [-nɪs], **vo·rac·i·ty** [vɒ'ræsətɪ] *s.* Gefräßigkeit *f*, Unersättlichkeit *f*, Gier *f* (***of*** nach).

vor·tex ['vɔ:teks] *pl.* **-ti·ces** [-tɪsi:z] *s.* Wirbel *m*, Strudel *m* (*a. phys. fig.*); **'vor·ti·cal** [-tɪkl] *adj.* □ **1.** wirbelnd, kreisend, Wirbel…; **2.** wirbel-, strudelartig.

vo·ta·ress ['vəʊtərɪs] *s.* Geweihte *f* (*etc.*, → ***votary***); **vo·ta·ry** ['vəʊtərɪ] *s.* **1.** *eccl.* Geweihte(r *m*) *f*; **2.** *fig.* Verfechter(in), (Vor)Kämpfer(in); **3.** *fig.* Anhänger (-in), Verehrer(in), Jünger(in), Enthusi'ast(in).

vote [vəʊt] **I** *s.* **1.** (Wahl)Stimme *f*, Votum *n*: **~ *of censure***, **~ *of no confidence*** *parl.* Mißtrauensvotum; **~ *of confidence*** *parl.* Vertrauensvotum; ***give one's ~ to*** (*od.* ***for***) s-e Stimme geben (*dat.*), stimmen für; **2.** Abstimmung *f*, Wahl *f*: ***put s.th. to the ~***, ***take a ~ on s.th.*** über e-e Sache abstimmen lassen; ***take the ~*** abstimmen; **3.** Stimmzettel *m*, Stimme *f*: ***cast one's ~***

s-e Stimme abgeben; **4.** ***the ~*** das Stimm-, Wahlrecht; **5.** a) Stimme *f*, Stimmzettel *m*, b) ***the ~*** *coll.* die Stimmen *pl.*: ***the Labour ~***, c) Wahlergebnis *n*; **6.** Beschluß *m*: ***a unanimous ~***; **7.** (Geld)Bewilligung *f*; **II** *v/i.* **8.** (ab-)stimmen, wählen, s-e Stimme abgeben: ***~ against*** stimmen gegen; ***~ for*** stimmen für (*a.* F *für et. sein*); **III** *v/t.* **9.** abstimmen über (*acc.*), wählen, stimmen für: ***~ down*** niederstimmen; ***~ s.o. in*** j-n wählen; ***~ s.o. out*** (***of office***) j-n abwählen; ***~ s.th. through*** et. durchbringen; ***~ that*** dafür sein, daß, vorschlagen, daß; **10.** (durch Abstimmung) wählen *od.* beschließen *od. Geld* bewilligen; **11.** allgemein erklären für *od.* halten für; **'vote-ˌcatch·er** *s.*, **'vote-ˌget·ter** *s.* ,'Wahllokomoˌtive' *f*, Stimmenfänger *m*; **'vote·less** [-lɪs] *adj.* ohne Stimmrecht *od.* Stimme; **'vot·er** [-tə] *s.* Wähler(in), Wahl-, Stimmberechtigte(r *m*) *f*.

vot·ing ['vəʊtɪŋ] **I** *s.* (Ab)Stimmen *n*, Abstimmung *f*; **II** *adj.* Stimm..., Wahl...; **~ age** *s.* Wahlalter *n*; **~ machine** *s.* 'Wahlmaˌschine *f*; **~ pa·per** *s.* Stimmzettel *m*; **~ share** *s.* ✝ Stimmrechtaktie *f*; **~ stock** *s.* ✝ **1.** stimmberechtigtes 'Aktienkapiˌtal; **2.** *bsd. Am.* 'Stimmrechtsˌaktie *f*; **~ pow·er** *s.* ✝ Stimmrecht *n*.

vo·tive ['vəʊtɪv] *adj.* Weih..., Votiv..., Denk...: ***~ medal*** (Ge)Denkmünze *f*; ***~ tablet*** Votivtafel *f*.

vouch [vaʊtʃ] **I** *v/i.* **1.** ***~ for*** (sich ver-)bürgen für; **2.** ***~ that*** dafür bürgen, daß; **II** *v/t.* **3.** bezeugen; bestätigen, (urkundlich) belegen; **4.** (sich ver)bürgen für; **'vouch·er** [-tʃə] *s.* **1.** Zeuge *m*, Bürge *m*; **2.** 'Unterlage *f*, Doku'ment *n*: ***support by ~*** dokumentarisch belegen; **3.** (Rechnungs)Beleg *m*, Quittung *f*: ***~ check*** ✝ *Am.* Verrechnungsscheck; ***~ copy*** Belegdoppel *n*; **4.** Gutschein *m*; **5.** Eintrittskarte *f*; **vouch'safe** [-'seɪf] *v/t.* **1.** (gnädig) gewähren; **2.** geruhen zu *tun*; **3.** sich her'ablassen zu: ***he ~d me no answer*** er würdigte mich keiner Antwort.

vow [vaʊ] **I** *s.* **1.** Gelübde *n* (*a. eccl.*); *oft pl.* (feierliches) Versprechen, (Treu-)Schwur *m*: ***be under a ~*** ein Gelübde abgelegt haben, versprochen haben (***to do*** zu tun); ***take*** (*od.* ***make***) ***a ~*** ein Gelübde ablegen; ***take ~s*** *eccl.* Profeß ablegen, in ein Kloster eintreten; **II** *v/t.* **2.** geloben; **3.** (sich) schwören, (sich) geloben, hoch u. heilig versprechen (***to do*** zu tun); **4.** feierlich erklären.

vow·el ['vaʊəl] **I** *s. ling.* **1.** Vo'kal *m*, Selbstlaut *m*; **II** *adj.* **2.** vo'kalisch; **3.** Vokal..., Selbstlaut...: ***~ gradation*** Ablaut *m*; ***~ mutation*** Umlaut *m*; **vow·el·ize** ['vaʊəlaɪz] *v/t.* **1.** *hebräischen od. kurzschriftlichen Text* mit Vo'kalzeichen versehen; **2.** *Laut* vokalisieren.

voy·age ['vɔɪɪdʒ] **I** *s. längere* (See-, Flug-)Reise: ***~ home*** Rück-, Heimreise; ***~ out*** Hinreise *f*; **II** *v/i.* (*bsd.* zur See) reisen; **III** *v/t.* reisen durch, bereisen; **voy·ag·er** ['vɔɪədʒə] *s.* (See)Reisende(r *m*) *f*.

vo·yeur·ism [vwɑː'jɜːrɪzəm] *s.* Voy'eurtum *n*.

'V|-sign *s.* **1.** Siegeszeichen *n* (*mit gespreizten Fingern*), *Am. a.* Zeichen der Zustimmung; **2.** *Brit.* ,Vogel' *m*; **'~-type en·gine** *s. mot.* V-Motor *m*.

vul·can·ite ['vʌlkənaɪt] *s.* Ebo'nit *n*, Vulka'nit *n* (*Hartgummi*); **'vul·can·ize** [-aɪz] *v/t. Kautschuk* vulkanisieren: ***~d fibre*** (*Am.* ***fiber***) ⚗ Vulkanfiber *f*.

vul·gar ['vʌlgə] **I** *adj.* □ → ***vulgarly***; **1.** (all)gemein, Volks...: ***~ herd*** *die* Masse, *das* gemeine Volk; ***2 Era*** *die* christlichen Jahrhunderte; **2.** volkstümlich: ***~ superstitions***; **3.** vul'gärsprachlich, in der Volkssprache (verfaßt *etc.*): ***~ tongue*** Volkssprache *f*; ***2 Latin*** Vulgärlatein *n*; **4.** ungebildet, ungehobelt; **5.** vul'gär, unfein, ordi'när, gewöhnlich, unanständig, pöbelhaft; **6.** ⩘ gemein, gewöhnlich: ***~ fraction***; **II** *s.* **7.** ***the ~*** *pl.* das (gemeine) Volk; **vul·gar·i·an** [vʌl'geərɪən] *s.* **1.** vul'gärer Mensch, Ple'bejer *m*; **2.** Parve'nü *m*, Protz *m*; **'vul·gar·ism** [-ərɪzəm] *s.* **1.** Unfeinheit *f*, vul'gäres Benehmen; **2.** Gemeinheit *f*, Unanständigkeit *f*; **3.** *ling.* Vulga'rismus *m*, vul'gärer Ausdruck; **vul·gar·i·ty** [vʌl'gærətɪ] *s.* **1.** ungehobeltes Wesen, vul'gäre Art; **2.** Gewöhnlichkeit *f*, Pöbelhaftigkeit *f*; **3.** Unsitte *f*, Ungezogenheit *f*; **'vul·gar·ize** [-əraɪz] *v/t.* **1.** popularisieren, popu'lär machen, verbreiten; **2.** her'abwürdigen, vulgarisieren; **'vul·gar·ly** [-lɪ] *adv.* **1.** allgemein, gemeinhin, landläufig; **2.** → ***vulgar*** 4, 5.

vul·ner·a·bil·i·ty [ˌvʌlnərə'bɪlətɪ] *s.* Verwundbarkeit *f*; **vul·ner·a·ble** ['vʌlnərəbl] *adj.* **1.** verwundbar (*a. fig.*); **2.** angreifbar; **3.** anfällig (***to*** für); **4.** ⚔, *sport* ungeschützt, offen; **vul·ner·ar·y** ['vʌlnərərɪ] **I** *adj.* Wund..., Heil...; **II** *s.* Wundmittel *n*.

vul·pine ['vʌlpaɪn] *adj.* **1.** fuchsartig, Fuchs...; **2.** *fig.* füchsisch, verschlagen.

vul·ture ['vʌltʃə] *s. zo.* Geier *m* (*a. fig.*).

vul·va ['vʌlvə] *pl.* **-vae** [-viː] *s. anat.* Vulva *f*, (äußere) weibliche Scham.

vy·ing ['vaɪɪŋ] *adj.* □ wetteifernd.

W

W, w ['dʌblju:] *s.* W *n*, w *n* (*Buchstabe*).
Waac [wæk] *s.* ⚔ F *Brit.* Ar'meehelferin *f* (*aus* ***Women's Army Auxiliary Corps***).
Waaf [wæf] *s.* ⚔ F *Brit.* Luftwaffenhelferin *f* (*aus* ***Women's Auxiliary Air Force***).
WAC, ***Wac*** [wæk] *s.* ⚔ F *Am.* Ar'meehelferin *f* (*aus* ***Women's Army Corps***).
wack·y ['wækɪ] *adj.* ‚blöd'.
wad [wɒd] **I** *s.* **1.** Pfropf(en) *m*, (*Watte- etc.*)Bausch *m*, Polster *n*; **2.** Pa'pierknäuel *m*, *n*; **3.** a) (Banknoten)Bündel *n*, (-)Rolle *f*, b) *Am.* F Haufen *m* Geld, c) Stoß *m* Pa'piere; **4.** ⚔ *hist.* Ladepfropf *m*; **II** *v/t.* **5.** zu e-m Bausch *etc.* zs.-pressen; **6.** *~ up Am.* fest zs.-rollen; **7.** *Öffnung* ver-, zustopfen; **8.** *Kleidungsstück etc.* wattieren, auspolstern, füttern; **wad·ding** ['wɒdɪŋ] **I** *s.* **1.** Einlage *f* (*zum Polstern od. Verpacken*); **2.** Watte *f*; **3.** Wattierung *f*; **II** *adj.* **4.** Wattier…
wad·dle ['wɒdl] **I** *v/i.* watscheln; **II** *s.* watschelnder Gang.
wade [weɪd] **I** *v/i.* waten: ***~ through*** F *fig.* sich durchkämpfen durch; ***~ in(to)*** F *fig.* a) ‚hin'einsteigen', sich einmischen (in *acc.*), b) sich ‚reinknien' (in *e-e Arbeit etc.*): ***~ into a problem*** ein Problem anpacken *od.* angehen; **II** *v/t.* durch'waten; **III** *s.* Waten *n*; '**wad·er** [-də] *s.* **1.** *orn.* Wat-, Stelzvogel *m*; **2.** *pl.* (hohe) Wasserstiefel *pl.*
wa·fer ['weɪfə] *s.* **1.** Ob'late *f* (*a.* ⚕ *u. Siegelmarke*); **2.** (*bsd.* Eis)Waffel *f*: ***as thin as a ~, ~-thin*** hauchdünn (*a. fig.*); **3.** *a.* ***consecrated ~*** *eccl.* Hostie *f*, Ob'late *f*; **4.** ⚡ Mikroplättchen *n*.
waf·fle ['wɒfl] **I** *s.* Waffel *f*; **II** *v/i.* F ‚quasseln'; '**~-,i·ron** *s.* Waffeleisen *n*.
waft [wɑ:ft] **I** *v/t.* **1.** *wohin* wehen, tragen; **II** *v/i.* **2.** (her'an)getragen werden, schweben; **III** *s.* **3.** Flügelschlag *m*; **4.** Wehen *n*; **5.** (Duft)Hauch *m*, (-)Welle *f*; **6.** *fig.* Anwandlung *f*, Welle *f* (*von Freude, Neid etc.*); **7.** ⚓ Flagge *f* im Schau (*Notsignal*).
wag [wæg] **I** *v/i.* **1.** wackeln; wedeln, wippen (*Schwanz*): ***~ one's tongue*** tratschen; ***set tongues ~ging*** viel Gerede verursachen; → ***tail*** 1; **II** *v/t.* **2.** wackeln *od.* wedeln *od.* wippen mit *dem Schwanz etc.*; *den Kopf* schütteln *od.* wiegen: ***~ one's finger at*** *j-m* mit dem Finger drohen; **3.** (hin- u. her)bewegen, schwenken; **III** *s.* **4.** Wackeln *n*; Wedeln *n*, (Kopf)Schütteln *n*; **5.** Witzbold *m*, Spaßvogel *m*.
wage¹ [weɪdʒ] *v/t. Krieg* führen, *Feldzug* unter'nehmen (***on, against*** gegen): ***~ effective war on*** *fig. e-r Sache* wirksam zu Leibe gehen.
wage² [weɪdʒ] *s.* **1.** *mst pl.* ✝ (Arbeits-)Lohn *m*: ***~s per hour*** Stundenlohn; **2.** *pl.* ✝ Lohnanteil *m* (*an der Produktion*); **3.** *pl. sg. konstr. fig.* Lohn *m*: ***the ~s of sin*** *bibl.* der Sünde Sold; ***~ a·gree·ment*** *s.* ✝ Ta'rifvertrag *m*; ***~ bill*** *s.* (aus)bezahlte (Gesamt)Löhne *pl.*; ***~ claim*** *s.* Lohnforderung *f*; ***~ dis·pute*** *s.* Lohnkampf *m*; ***~ earn·er*** *s.* Lohnempfänger(in); ***~ freeze*** *s.* Lohnstopp *m*; ***~ fund*** *s.* Lohnfonds *m*; ***~ in·cen·tive*** *s.* Lohnanreiz *m*; '**~-in·ten·sive** *adj.* 'lohninten,siv; ***~ lev·el*** *s.* 'Lohnni,veau *n*; ***~ pack·et*** *s.* Lohntüte *f*.
wa·ger ['weɪdʒə] **I** *s.* **1.** Wette *f*; **II** *v/t.* **2.** wetten um, setzen auf (*acc.*); wetten mit (***that*** daß); **3.** *fig. Ehre etc.* aufs Spiel setzen; **III** *v/i.* **4.** wetten, e-e Wette eingehen.
wage| rate *s.* Lohnsatz *m*; ***~ scale*** *s.* ✝ **1.** Lohnskala *f*; **2.** ('Lohn)Ta,rif *m*; ***~ set·tle·ment*** *s.* Lohnabschluß *m*; ***~ slave*** *s.* Lohnsklave *m*; ***~ slip*** *s.* Lohnstreifen *m*, -zettel *m*.
wag·ger·y ['wægərɪ] *s.* Schelme'rei *f*, Schalkhaftigkeit *f*; **wag·gish** ['wægɪʃ] *adj.* □ schalkhaft, schelmisch, spaßig, lose; **wag·gish·ness** ['wægɪʃnɪs] → ***waggery***.
wag·gle ['wægl] → ***wag*** I *u.* II.
wag·gon ['wægən] *s.* **1.** (Last-, Roll-)Wagen *m*; **2.** 🚃 *Brit.* (offener) Güterwagen, Wag'gon *m*: ***by ~*** ✝ per Achse; **3.** *Am.* a) (Liefer-, Verkaufs-, Poli'zei- *etc.*)Wagen *m*, b) *mot.* Kombi(wagen) *m*; **4.** ***the*** ♀ *ast.* der Große Wagen; **5.** F *fig.* → ***water wag(g)on***.
wag·gon·er ['wægənə] *s.* **1.** (Fracht-)Fuhrmann *m*; **2.** ♀ *ast.* Fuhrmann *m*.
'**wag·gon|·load** *s.* **1.** Wagenladung *f*, Fuhre *f*; **2.** Wag'gonladung *f*: ***by the ~*** waggonweise; ***~ train*** *s.* **1.** ⚔ Ar'meetrain *m*; **2.** 🚃 *Am.* Güterzug *m*; ***~ vault*** *s.* ⚠ Tonnengewölbe *n*.
Wag·ne·ri·an [vɑ:g'nɪərɪən] ♪ **I** *adj.* wagnerisch, wagneri'anisch, Wagner…; **II** *s. a.* **Wag·ner·ite** ['vɑ:gnəraɪt] Wagneri'aner(in).
wag·on *etc. bsd. Am.* → ***waggon*** *etc.*
wa·gon-lit ['vægɔ̃:n'li:; vagɔ̃li] (*Fr.*) *s.* 🚃 Schlafwagen(abteil *n*) *m*.
'**wag·tail** *s. orn.* Bachstelze *f*.
waif [weɪf] *s.* **1.** ⚖ a) *Brit.* weggeworfenes Diebesgut, b) herrenloses Gut, *bsd.* Strandgut *n* (*a. fig.*); **2.** a) Heimatlose(r *m*) *f*, b) verlassenes *od.* verwahrlostes Kind: ***~s and strays*** verwahrloste Kinder, c) streunendes *od.* verwahrlostes Tier; **3.** *fig.* 'Überrest *m*.
wail [weɪl] **I** *v/i.* (weh)klagen, jammern (***for*** um, ***over*** über *acc.*); schreien, wimmern, heulen (*a. Sirene, Wind*) (***with*** vor *Schmerz etc.*); **II** *v/t.* bejammern; **III** *s.* (Weh)Klagen *n*, Jammern *n*; (Weh)Geschrei *n*, Wimmern *n*; '**wail·ing** [-lɪŋ] **I** *s.* → ***wail*** III; **II** *adj.* □ (weh)klagend *etc.*; Klage…: ♀ ***Wall*** Klagemauer *f*.
wain [weɪn] *s.* **1.** *poet.* Karren *m*, Wagen *m*; **2.** ♀ → ***Charles's Wain***.
wain·scot ['weɪnskət] **I** *s.* (*bsd. untere*) (Wand)Täfelung, Tafelwerk *n*, Holzverkleidung *f*; **II** *v/t. Wand etc.* verkleiden, (ver)täfeln; '**wain·scot·ing** [-tɪŋ] *s.* **1.** → ***wainscot*** I; **2.** Täfelholz *n*.
waist [weɪst] *s.* **1.** Taille *f*; **2.** a) Mieder *n*, b) *bsd. Am.* Bluse *f*; **3.** Mittelstück *n*, schmalste Stelle (*e-s Dinges*), Schweifung *f* (*e-r Glocke etc.*); **4.** ⚓ Mitteldeck *n*, Kuhl *f*; '**~·band** [-sb-] *s.* (Hosen-, Rock)Bund *m*; ***~·coat*** ['weɪskəʊt] *s.* (*a.* Damen)Weste *f*, (ärmellose) Jacke; *hist.* Wams *n*; **,~-'deep** *adj. u. adv.* bis zur Taille *od.* Hüfte, hüfthoch.
waist·ed ['weɪstɪd] *adj.* mit e-r … Taille: ***short-~***.
,waist|-'high → ***waist-deep***; '**~·line** *s.* **1.** Gürtellinie *f*, Taille *f*; **2.** 'Taille(n-,umfang *m*) *f*: ***watch one's ~*** auf s-e Linie achten.
wait [weɪt] **I** *v/i.* **1.** warten (***for*** auf *acc.*): ***~ for s.o. to come*** warten, daß *od.* bis j-d kommt; ***~ up for s.o.*** aufbleiben u. auf j-n warten; ***keep s.o. ~ing*** j-n warten lassen; ***that can ~*** *fig.* das kann warten, das hat Zeit; ***dinner is ~ing*** das Essen wartet *od.* ist bereit; ***you just ~!*** F na warte!; ***~ for it!*** F *Brit.* a) immer mit der Ruhe, b) du wirst's kaum glauben!; **2.** (ab)warten, sich gedulden: ***~ and see!*** ‚abwarten u. Tee trinken'!; ***I can't ~ to see him*** ich kann es kaum noch erwarten, bis ich ihn sehe; **3.** ***~ (up)on*** a) *j-m* dienen, b) *j-m* aufwarten, *j-n* bedienen, c) *j-m* s-e Aufwartung machen, d) *fig. e-r Sache* folgen, *et.* begleiten (*Umstand*); **4.** *a.* ***~ at table*** (bei Tisch) bedienen; **II** *v/t.* **5.** warten auf (*acc.*), abwarten: ***~ one's opportunity*** e-e günstige Gelegenheit abwarten; ***~ out*** das Ende (*gen.*) abwarten; **6.** F aufschieben, mit *dem Essen etc.* warten (***for s.o.*** auf j-n); **III** *s.* **7.** a) Warten *n*, b) Wartezeit *f*: ***have a long ~*** lange warten müssen; **8.** Lauer *f*: ***lay a ~ for*** *j-m* e-n Hinterhalt legen; ***lie in ~*** im Hinterhalt liegen; ***lie in ~ for*** *j-m* auflauern; **9.** *pl.* a) Weihnachtssänger *pl.*, b) *hist.* 'Stadtmusi,kanten *pl.*; '**wait·er** [-tə] *s.* **1.** Kellner *m*, *in der*

Anrede: (Herr) Ober *m*; **2.** Servier-, Präsentierteller *m*.

wait·ing [ˈweɪtɪŋ] **I** *s.* **1.** → ***wait*** 7; **2.** Dienst *m bei Hofe etc.*, Aufwarten *n*: ***in ~*** a) diensttuend; → ***lady-in-waiting*** *etc.*, b) ⚔ *Brit.* in Bereitschaft; **II** *adj.* **3.** (ab)wartend; → ***game***[1] 4; **4.** Warte…: ***~ list, ~ period*** *allg.* Wartezeit *f*; ***~ room*** a) 🚂 Wartesaal *m*, b) ⚕ *etc.* Wartezimmer *n*; **~ girl** *s.*, **~ maid** *s.* Kammerzofe *f*.

wait·ress [ˈweɪtrɪs] *s.* Kellnerin *f*; *in der Anrede*: Fräulein *n*.

waive [weɪv] *v/t. bsd.* ⚖ **1.** verzichten auf (*acc.*), sich *e-s Rechtes, Vorteils* begeben; **2.** *Frage* zuˈrückstellen; ˈ**waiv·er** [-və] *s.* ⚖ **1.** Verzicht *m* (***of*** auf *acc.*), Verzichtleistung *f*; **2.** Verzichterklärung *f*.

wake[1] [weɪk] *s.* **1.** ⚓ Kielwasser *n* (*a. fig.*): ***in the ~ of*** a) im Kielwasser *e-s Schiffes*, b) *fig.* im Gefolge (*gen.*); ***follow in s.o.'s ~*** *fig.* in j-s Kielwasser segeln; ***bring s.th. in its ~*** et. nach sich ziehen, et. zur Folge haben; **2.** ✈ Luftschraubenstrahl *m*; **3.** Sog *m*.

wake[2] [weɪk] **I** *v/i.* [*irr.*] **1.** *oft* ***~ up*** aufwachen, wach werden (*alle a. fig. Person, Gefühl etc.*); **2.** wachen, wach sein *od.* bleiben; **3.** ***~ to*** sich *e-r Gefahr etc.* bewußt werden; **4.** *vom Tode od. von den Toten* auferstehen; **II** *v/t.* [*irr.*] **5.** *a.* ***~ up*** (auf)wecken, wachrütteln (*a. fig.*); **6.** *fig.* erwecken, *Erinnerungen, Gefühle* wachrufen, *Streit etc.* erregen; **7.** *fig. j-n, j-s Geist etc.* aufrütteln; **8.** (*von den Toten*) auferwecken; **III** *s.* **9.** *bsd. Irish* a) Totenwache *f*, b) Leichenschmaus *m*; **10.** *hist.* Kirchweih(fest *n*) *f*, Kirmes *f*; **11.** *Brit.* Betriebsferien *pl.*; ˈ**wake·ful** [-fʊl] *adj.* □ **1.** wachend; **2.** schlaflos; **3.** *fig.* wachsam; ˈ**wak·en** [-kən] → ***wake***[2] 1, 3, 5, 6 *u.* 7; ˈ**wak·ing** [-kɪŋ] **I** *s.* **1.** (Er)Wachen *n*; **2.** (Nacht-)Wache *f*; **II** *adj.* **3.** wach: ***~ dream*** Tagtraum *m*; ***in his ~ hours*** in s-n wachen Stunden, *a.* von früh bis spät.

wale [weɪl] *s.* **1.** → ***weal***[2]; **2.** *Weberei*: a) Rippe *f* (*e-s Gewebes*), b) Salleiste *f*, feste Webkante; **3.** ⚙ a) Verbindungsstück *n*, b) Gurtholz *n*; **4.** ⚓ a) Berg-, Krummholz *n*, b) Dollbord *m* (*e-s Boots*).

walk [wɔːk] **I** *s.* **1.** Gehen *n*: ***go at a ~*** im Schritt gehen; **2.** Gang(art *f*) *m*, Schritt *m*: ***a dignified ~***; **3.** Spaziergang *m*: ***go for*** (*od.* ***take***) ***a ~*** e-n Spaziergang machen; ***take s.o. for a ~*** j-n spazierenführen, mit j-m spazierengehen; **4.** (Spazier)Weg *m*: a) Promeˈnade *f*, b) Strecke *f*: ***a ten minutes' ~ to the station*** zehn (Geh)Minuten zum Bahnhof; ***quite a ~*** ein gutes Stück zu gehen; **5.** Alˈlee *f*; **6.** (Geflügel)Auslauf *m*; → ***sheepwalk***; **7.** Route *f e-s Hausierers etc.*, Runde *f e-s Polizisten etc.*; **8.** *fig.* a) (Arbeits)Gebiet *n*, b) *mst* ***~ of life*** (soziˈale) Schicht *od.* Stellung, *a.* Beruf *m*; **II** *v/i.* **9.** gehen (*a. sport*), zu Fuß gehen; **10.** im Schritt gehen (*a. Pferd*); **11.** spazierengehen, wandern; **12.** ˈumgehen (*Geist*): ***~ in one's sleep*** nachtwandeln; **III** *v/t.* **13.** *Strecke* zuˈrücklegen, (zu Fuß) gehen; **14.** *Bezirk* durchˈwandern, *Raum* durchˈschreiten; **15.** auf u. ab (*od.* umˈher)gehen in *od.* auf (*dat.*); **16.** *Pferd* a) führen, b) im Schritt gehen lassen; **17.** *j-n wohin* führen: ***~ s.o. off his feet*** j-n abhetzen; **18.** spazierenführen; **19.** um die Wette gehen mit;

Zssgn mit adv. u. prp.:

walk| a·bout, ~ a·round I *v/i.* umˈhergehen, -wandern; **II** *v/t. j-n* umˈherführen; **~ a·way** *v/i.* **1.** weg-, fortgehen: ***~ from*** *sport j-m* (einfach) davonlaufen, *j-n* ‚stehenlassen'; **2.** ***~ with*** a) mit *et.* durchbrennen, b) *et.* ‚mitgehen' lassen, c) *e-n Kampf etc.* spielend gewinnen; **~ off I** *v/i.* **1.** daˈvon-, fortgehen; **2.** → ***walk away*** 2; **II** *v/t.* **3.** *j-n* abführen; **4.** *s-n Rausch, Zorn etc.* durch e-n Spaziergang vertreiben; **~ out I** *v/i.* **1.** hinˈausgehen: ***~ on*** F *j-n* im Stich lassen, verlassen; **2.** ***~ with s.o.*** F mit j-m ‚gehen' *od.* ein Verhältnis haben; **3.** ✝ in (den) Streik treten; **4.** *pol.* zuˈrücktreten; **II** *v/t.* **5.** *Hund etc.* ausführen; **6.** *j-n* auf e-n Spaziergang mitnehmen; **~ o·ver** *v/i. fig.* spielend gewinnen; **~ up** *v/i.* **1.** hinˈaufgehen, herˈaufkommen: ***~ to s.o.*** auf j-n zugehen; **2.** *Straße* entlanggehen.

ˈ**walk·a·bout** *s.* **1.** Wanderung *f*; **2.** ‚Bad *n* in der Menge' (*e-s Politikers etc.*).

walk·a·thon [ˈwɔːkəθɒn] **1.** *sport* Marathongehen *n*; **2.** ˈDauertanzturˌnier *n*.

ˈ**walk·a·way** → ***walkover*** 2.

walk·er [ˈwɔːkə] *s.* **1.** Spaziergänger(in): ***be a good ~*** gut zu Fuß sein; **2.** *sport* Geher *m*; **3.** *orn. Brit.* Laufvogel *m*; ˌ**~-ˈon** [-ərɒn] *s.* → ***walk-on*** 1.

walk·ie-talk·ie [ˌwɔːkɪˈtɔːkɪ] *s.* tragbares Funksprechgerät, Walkie-talkie *n*.

ˈ**walk-in I** *adj.* **1.** begehbar: ***~ closet*** → 2; **II** *s.* **2.** begehbarer Schrank; **3.** Kühlraum *m*; **4.** *Am.* F leichter Wahlsieg.

walk·ing [ˈwɔːkɪŋ] **I** *adj.* **1.** gehend, wandernd; *bsd. fig.* wandelnd (*Leiche, Lexikon*): ***~ wounded*** ⚔ Leichtverwundete *pl.*; **2.** Geh…, Marsch…, Spazier…: ***drive at a ~ speed*** *mot.* (im) Schritt fahren; ***within ~ distance*** zu Fuß erreichbar; **II** *s.* **3.** (Spazieren)Gehen *n*; Wandern *n*; **4.** *sport* Gehen *n*; **~ boots** *s. pl.* Wanderstiefel *pl.*; **~ chair** → ***gocart*** 1; **~ del·e·gate** *s.* Gewerkschaftsbeauftragte(r) *m*; **~ gen·tle·man** *s.* [*irr.*], **~ la·dy** → ***walk-on*** 1; **~ pa·pers** *s. pl. sl.* **1.** Entˈlassung(spaˌpiere *pl.*) *f*; **2.** ‚Laufpaß' *m*; **~ part** *s. thea.* Staˈtistenrolle *f*; **~ stick** *s.* Spazierstock *m*; **~ tick·et** → ***walking papers***; **~ tour** *s.* Wanderung *f*.

ˈ**walk|-on** *s. Film, thea.* **1.** Staˈtist(in), Komˈparse *m*, Komˈparsin *f*; **2.** *a.* ***~ part*** Staˈtisten-, Komˈparsenrolle *f*; ˈ**~-out** *s.* **1.** ✝ Ausstand *m*, Streik *m*; **2.** Auszug *m*; ˈ**~ˌo·ver** *s. sport* **1.** einseitiger Wettbewerb; **2.** ‚Spaziergang' *m*, leichter Sieg (*a. fig.*); ˈ**~-ˌup** *Am.* F **I** *adj.* ohne Fahrstuhl (*Haus*); **II** *s.* (Wohnung *f* in e-m) Haus ohne Fahrstuhl; ˈ**~·way** *s.* **1.** Laufgang *m*; **2.** *Am.* Gehweg *m*.

wall [wɔːl] **I** *s.* **1.** Wand *f* (*a. fig.*): ***up against the ~, with one's back to the ~*** in e-r aussichtslosen Lage; ***drive*** (*od.* ***push***) ***s.o. to the ~*** *fig.* a) j-n an die Wand drücken, b) j-n in die Enge treiben; ***go to the ~*** a) an die Wand gedrückt werden, b) ✝ Konkurs machen; ***drive*** (*od.* ***send***) ***s.o. up the ~*** F j-n ‚auf die Palme bringen'; ***run*** (*od.* ***bang***) ***one's head against a ~*** F mit dem Kopf durch die Wand wollen; **2.** ⚙ (Innen)Wand *f*; **3.** Mauer *f* (*a. fig.*): ***a ~ of silence***; ***the* ♀** a) die (Berliner) Mauer, b) die Klagemauer (*in Jerusalem*); **4.** Wall *m* (*a. fig.*), (Stadt-, Schutz)Mauer *f*: ***within the ~s*** in den Mauern (e-r Stadt); **5.** *anat.* (*Brust-, Zell- etc.*)Wand *f*; **6.** Häuserseite *f*: ***give s.o. the ~*** a) j-n auf der Häuserseite gehen lassen (*aus Höflichkeit*), b) *fig.* j-m den Vorrang lassen; **7.** ⚒ (Abbau-, Orts)Stoß *m*; **II** *v/t.* **8.** *a.* ***~ in*** mit e-r Mauer *od.* e-m Wall umˈgeben, umˈmauern: ***~ in*** (*od.* ***up***) einmauern; **9.** *a.* ***~ up*** a) ver-, zumauern, b) (aus)mauern, umˈwanden; **10.** *fig.* ab-, einschließen, *den Geist* verschließen (***against*** gegen).

wal·la·by [ˈwɒləbɪ] *pl.* **-bies** [-bɪz] *s. zo.* Wallaby *n* (*kleineres Känguruh*).

wal·lah [ˈwɒlə] *s.* F ‚Knülch' *m*.

wall| bars *s. pl. sport* Sprossenwand *f*; **~ brack·et** *s.* ˈWandarm *m*, -konˌsole *f*; **~ creep·er** *s. orn.* Mauerläufer *m*; **~ cress** *s.* ⚘ Acker-, *Brit. a.* Gänsekresse *f*.

wal·let [ˈwɒlɪt] *s.* **1.** kleine Werkzeugtasche; **2.** a) Brieftasche *f*, b) (*flache*) Geldtasche.

ˈ**wall-eye** *s.* **1.** *vet.* Glasauge *n*; **2.** ⚕ a) Hornhautfleck *m*, b) auswärtsschielendes Auge; ˈ**wall-eyed** *adj.* **1.** *vet.* glasäugig (*Pferd etc.*); **2.** ⚕ a) mit Hornhautflecken, b) (auswärts)schielend.

ˈ**wall|ˌflow·er** *s.* **1.** ⚘ Goldlack *m*; **2.** F *fig.* ‚Mauerblümchen' *n* (*Mädchen*); **~ fruit** *s.* Spaˈlierobst *n*; **~ map** *s.* Wandkarte *f*.

Wal·loon [wɒˈluːn] **I** *s.* **1.** Walˈlone *m*, Walˈlonin *f*; **2.** *ling.* Walˈlonisch *n*; **II** *adj.* **3.** walˈlonisch.

wal·lop [ˈwɒləp] **I** *v/t.* **1.** F a) (ver)prügeln, verdreschen, b) j-m eine ‚knallen', c) *sport* ‚überˈfahren' (*besiegen*); **II** *v/i.* **2.** F rasen, sausen; **3.** brodeln; **III** *s.* **4.** F a) wuchtiger Schlag, b) Schlagkraft *f*, c) *Am.* Mordsspaß *m*; ˈ**wal·lop·ing** [-pɪŋ] **I** *adj.* F riesig, Mords…; **II** *s.* F ‚Dresche' *f*, Tracht *f* Prügel.

wal·low [ˈwɒləʊ] **I** *v/i.* **1.** sich wälzen *od.* suhlen (*Schweine etc.*) (*a. fig.*): ***~ in money*** *fig.* in Geld schwimmen; ***~ in pleasure*** im Vergnügen schwelgen; ***~ in vice*** dem Laster frönen; **II** *s.* **2.** Sichˈwälzen *n*; **3.** Schwelgen *n*; **4.** *hunt.* Suhle *f*; **5.** *fig.* Sumpf *m*.

wall| paint·ing *s.* Wandgemälde *n*; ˈ**~ˌpa·per I** *s.* Taˈpete *f*; **II** *v/t. u. v/i.* tapezieren; **~ plug** *s.* ⚡ Netzstecker *m*; **~ sock·et** *s.* ⚡ (Wand)Steckdose *f*; ♀ **Street** *s.* Wall Street *f*: a) *Bank- u. Börsenstraße in New York*, b) *fig.* der amer. Geld- u. Kapiˈtalmarkt, c) *fig.* die amer. ˈHochfiˌnanz; **~ tent** *s.* Steilwandzelt *n*; ˌ**~-to-ˈ~** *adj.*: ***~ carpet*** Spannteppich *m*; ***~ carpeting*** Teppichboden *m*; **~ tree** *s.* Spaˈlierbaum *m*.

wal·nut [ˈwɔːlnʌt] *s.* ⚘ **1.** Walnuß *f* (*Frucht*); **2.** Walnuß(baum *m*) *f*; **3.** Nußbaumholz *n*.

wal·rus [ˈwɔːlrəs] *s.* **1.** *zo.* Walroß *n*; **2.** *a.* ***~ m(o)ustache*** Schnauzbart *m*.

waltz [wɔːls] **I** *s.* **1.** Walzer *m*; **II** *v/i.* **2.** (*v/t.* mit *j-m*) Walzer tanzen, walzen; **3.** *vor Freude etc.* herˈumtanzen; **~ time** *s.* ♪ Walzertakt *m*.

wan [wɒn] *adj.* ☐ **1.** bleich, blaß, fahl; **2.** schwach, matt (*Lächeln etc.*).

wand [wɒnd] *s.* **1.** Rute *f*; **2.** Zauberstab *m*; **3.** (Amts-, Komˈmando)Stab *m*; **4.** ♪ Taktstock *m*.

wan·der [ˈwɒndə] *v/i.* **1.** wandern: a) ziehen, streifen, b) schlendern, bummeln, c) *fig.* schweifen, irren, gleiten (*Auge*, *Gedanken etc.*): **~ *in*** hereinschneien (*Besucher*); **~ *off*** a) davonziehen, b) sich verlieren (***into*** in *acc.*) (*a. fig.*); **2.** *a.* **~ *about*** umˈherwandern, -ziehen, -irren, -schweifen (*a. fig.*); **3.** *a.* **~ *away*** irregehen, sich verirren (*a. fig.*); **4.** abirren, -weichen (***from*** von) (*a. fig.*): **~ *from the subject*** vom Thema abschweifen; **5.** phantasieren: a) irrereden, faseln, b) im Fieber reden; **6.** geistesabwesend sein; **ˈwan·der·ing** [-dərɪŋ] **I** *s.* **1.** Wandern *n*; **2.** Heˈrumziehen *n*; **3.** *mst pl.* a) Wanderung(en *pl.*) *f*, b) Wanderschaft *f*; **4.** *mst pl.* Phantasieren *n*: a) Irrereden *n*, Faseln *n*, b) Fieberwahn *m*; **II** *adj.* ☐ **5.** wandernd, Wander…; **6.** umˈherschweifend, Nomaden…; **7.** unstet: ***the ♀ Jew*** der Ewige Jude; **8.** irregehend, abirrend (*a. fig.*): **~ *bullet*** verirrte Kugel; **9.** ⚘ Kriech…, Schling…; **10.** ✱ Wander…(*-niere*, *-zelle*).

wan·der·lust [ˈwɒndəlʌst] (*Ger.*) *s.* Wanderlust *f*, Fernweh *n*.

wane [weɪn] **I** *v/i.* **1.** abnehmen (*a. Mond*), nachlassen, schwinden (*Einfluß*, *Kräfte*, *Interesse etc.*); **2.** schwächer werden, verblassen (*Licht*, *Farben etc.*); **3.** zu Ende gehen; **II** *s.* **4.** Abnehmen *n*, Abnahme *f*, Schwinden *n*: ***be on the ~*** → 1 *u.* 3; ***in the ~ of the moon*** bei abnehmendem Mond.

wan·gle [ˈwæŋgl] *sl.* **I** *v/t.* **1.** *et.* ‚drehen' *od.* ‚deichseln' *od.* ‚schaukeln'; **2.** *et.* ‚organisieren' (*beschaffen*): **~ *o.s. s.th.*** et. für sich ‚herausschlagen'; **3.** ergaunern: **~ *s.th. out of s.o.*** j-m et. abluchsen; **~ *s.o. into doing s.th.*** j-n dazu bringen, et. zu tun; **4.** ‚frisieren' (*fälschen*); **II** *v/i.* **5.** mogeln, ‚schieben'; **6.** sich herˈauswinden (***out of*** aus *dat.*); **III** *s.* **7.** Kniff *m*, Trick *m*; **8.** Schiebung *f*, Mogeˈlei *f*; **ˈwan·gler** [-lə] *s.* Gauner *m*, Schieber *m*, Mogler *m*.

wank [wæŋk] *v/i. Brit.* V ‚wichsen' (*masturbieren*).

wan·na [ˈwɒnə] F *für* ***want to***: ***I ~ go***.

want [wɒnt] **I** *v/t.* **1.** wünschen: a) (haben) wollen, b) *vor inf.* (*et. tun*) wollen: ***I ~ to go*** ich möchte gehen; ***I ~ed to go*** ich wollte gehen; ***what do you ~ (with me)?*** was hab' ich damit zu tun?; ***I ~ you to try*** ich möchte, daß du es versuchst; ***I ~ it done*** ich wünsche *od.* möchte, daß es getan wird; ***~ed*** gesucht (*in Annoncen*; *a. von der Polizei*); ***you are ~ed*** du wirst gewünscht *od.* gesucht, man will dich sprechen; **2.** ermangeln (*gen.*), nicht (genug) haben, es fehlen lassen an (*dat.*): *obs.* ***he ~s judg(e)ment*** es fehlt ihm an Urteilsvermögen; **3.** a) brauchen, nötig haben, erfordern, benötigen, bedürfen (*gen.*), b) müssen, sollen: ***you ~ some rest*** du hast etwas Ruhe nötig; ***this clock ~s repairing*** (*od.* ***to be repaired***) diese Uhr müßte *od.* sollte repariert werden; ***it ~s doing*** es muß getan werden; ***you don't ~ to be rude*** Sie brauchen nicht grob zu werden; ***you ~ to see a doctor*** du solltest e-n Arzt aufsuchen; **II** *v/i.* **4.** ermangeln (***for*** *gen.*): ***he does not ~ for talent*** es fehlt ihm nicht an Begabung; ***he ~s for nothing*** es fehlt ihm an nichts; **5.** (***in***) es fehlen lassen (an *dat.*), ermangeln (*gen.*); → ***wanting*** 2; **6.** Not leiden; **III** *s.* **7.** *pl.* Bedürfnisse *pl.*, Wünsche *pl.*: ***a man of few ~s*** ein Mann mit geringen Bedürfnissen *od.* Ansprüchen; **8.** Notwendigkeit *f*, Bedürfnis *n*, Erfordernis *n*; Bedarf *m*; **9.** Mangel *m*, Ermangelung *f*: ***a (long-)felt ~*** → ***feel*** 2; **~ *of care*** Achtlosigkeit *f*; **~ *of sense*** Unvernunft *f*; ***from*** (*od.* ***for***) **~ *of*** aus Mangel an (*dat.*), in Ermang(e)lung (*gen.*); ***be in (great) ~ of s.th.*** et. (dringend) brauchen *od.* benötigen; ***in ~ of repair*** reparaturbedürftig; **10.** Bedürftigkeit *f*, Armut *f*, Not *f*: ***be in ~*** Not leiden; **want ad** *s.* F **1.** Stellengesuch *n*; **2.** Stellenangebot *n*;

want·age [ˈwɒntɪdʒ] *s.* ✝ Fehlbetrag *m*, Defizit *n*; **ˈwant·ing** [-tɪŋ] **I** *adj.* **1.** fehlend, mangelnd; **2.** ermangelnd (***in*** *gen.*): ***be ~ in*** es fehlen lassen an (*dat.*); ***be ~ to*** *j-n* im Stich lassen, *e-r Erwartung* nicht gerecht werden, *e-r Lage* nicht gewachsen sein; ***he is never found ~*** auf ihn ist immer Verlaß; **3.** nachlässig (***in*** in *dat.*); **II** *prp.* **4.** ohne: ***a book ~ a cover***.

wan·ton [ˈwɒntən] **I** *adj.* ☐ **1.** mutwillig: a) ausgelassen, wild, b) leichtfertig, c) böswillig (*a.* ⚖), d) rücksichtslos; **~ *negligence*** ⚖ grobe Fahrlässigkeit; **2.** liederlich, ausschweifend; **3.** wollüstig, geil; **4.** üppig (*Haar*, *Phantasie etc.*); **II** *s.* **5.** *obs.* a) Buhlerin *f*, Dirne *f*, b) Wüstling *m*; **III** *v/i.* **6.** umˈhertollen; **7.** ⚘ wuchern; **ˈwan·ton·ness** [-nɪs] *s.* **1.** Mutwille *m*; **2.** Böswilligkeit *f*; **3.** Liederlichkeit *f*; **4.** Geilheit *f*, Lüsternheit *f*.

wap·en·take [ˈwæpənteɪk] *s.* Hundertschaft *f*, Bezirk *m* (*Unterteilung der nördlichen Grafschaften Englands*).

war [wɔː] **I** *s.* **1.** Krieg *m*: **~ *of aggression*** (***attrition***, ***independence***, ***nerves***, ***succession***) Angriffs- (Zermürbungs-, Unabhängigkeits-, Nerven-, Erbfolge)krieg; ***be at ~*** (***with***) a) Krieg führen (gegen *od.* mit), b) *fig.* im Streit liegen *od.* auf (dem) Kriegsfuß stehen (mit); ***make ~*** Krieg führen, kämpfen (***on***, ***upon***, ***against*** gegen, ***with*** mit); ***go to ~*** (***with***) Krieg beginnen (mit); ***carry the ~ into the enemy's country*** (*od.* ***camp***) a) den Krieg ins feindliche Land *od.* Lager tragen, b) *fig.* zum Gegenangriff ˈübergehen; ***he has been in the ~s*** *fig. Brit.* es hat ihn arg mitgenommen; → ***declare*** 1; **2.** Kampf *m*, Streit *m* (*a. fig.*); **3.** Feindseligkeit *f*; **II** *v/i.* **4.** kämpfen, streiten (***against*** gegen, ***with*** mit); **5.** → ***warring*** 2; **III** *adj.* **6.** Kriegs…

war·ble [ˈwɔːbl] **I** *v/t. u. v/i.* trillern, schmettern (*Singvögel od. Person*); **II** *s.* Trillern *n*; **ˈwar·bler** [-lə] *s.* **1.** trillernder Vogel; **2.** a) Grasmücke *f*, b) Teichrohrsänger *m*.

ˈwar|-ˌblind·ed *adj.* kriegsblind; **~ bond** *s.* Kriegsschuldverschreibung *f*; **~ cloud** *s. mst pl.* (drohende) Kriegsgefahr; **~ crime** *s.* Kriegsverbrechen *n*; **~ crim·i·nal** *s.* Kriegsverbrecher *m*; **~ cry** *s.* Schlachtruf *m* (*der Soldaten*) (*a. fig.*), Kriegsruf *m* (*der Indianer*).

ward [wɔːd] **I** *s.* **1.** (Stadt-, Wahl)Bezirk *m*: **~ *heeler*** *pol. Am.* F (Wahl)Bezirksleiter *m* (*e-r Partei*); **2.** a) (ˈKrankenhaus)Statiˌon *f*: **~ *sister*** Stationsschwester *f*, b) (Kranken)Saal *m od.* (-)Zimmer *n*; **3.** a) (Gefängnis)Trakt *m*, b) Zelle *f*; **4.** *obs.* Gewahrsam *m*, Haft *f*; **5.** ⚖ a) Mündel *n*: **~ *of court***, **~ *in chancery*** Mündel unter Amtsvormundschaft, b) Vormundschaft *f*: ***in ~*** unter Vormundschaft (stehend); **6.** Schützling *m*; **7.** ⚙ a) Gewirre *n* (*e-s Schlosses*), b) (Einschnitt *m* im) Schlüsselbart *m*; **8.** ***keep watch and ~*** Wache halten; **II** *v/t.* **9.** **~ *off*** *Schlag etc.* parieren, abwehren, *Gefahr* abwenden.

war| dance *s.* Kriegstanz *m*; **~ debt** *s.* Kriegsschuld *f*.

ward·en [ˈwɔːdn] *s.* **1.** *obs.* Wächter *m*; **2.** Aufseher *m*, (*bsd.* Luftschutz)Wart *m*; Herbergsvater *m*; → ***game warden***; **3.** *mst hist.* Gouverˈneur *m*; **4.** (*Brit.* ˈAnstalts-, *Am.* Geˈfängnis)Diˌrektor *m*, (*a.* Kirchen)Vorsteher *m*; *Brit. univ.* Rektor *m e-s College*: ***♀ of the Mint*** *Brit.* Münzwardein *m*.

ward·er [ˈwɔːdə] *s.* **1.** *obs.* Wächter *m*; **2.** *Brit.* a) (Muˈseums- *etc.*)Wärter *m*, b) Aufsichtsbeamte(r) *m* (*Strafanstalt*); **ˈward·ress** [-drɪs] *s. Brit.* Aufsichtsbeamtin *f*.

ward·robe [ˈwɔːdrəub] *s.* **1.** Gardeˈrobe *f*, Kleiderbestand *m*; **2.** Kleiderschrank *m*; **3.** Gardeˈrobe *f* (*a. thea.*): a) Kleiderkammer *f*, b) Ankleidezimmer *n*; **~ bed** *s.* Schrankbett *n*; **~ trunk** *s.* Schrankkoffer *m*.

ward·room [ˈwɔːdrum] *s.* ⚓ Offiˈziersmesse *f*.

ward·ship [ˈwɔːdʃɪp] *s.* Vormundschaft *f* (***of***, ***over*** über *acc.*).

ware[1] [weə] *s.* **1.** *mst pl.* Ware(n *pl.*) *f*, Arˈtikel *m* (*od. pl.*), Erzeugnis(se *pl.*) *n*: ***peddle one's ~s*** *fig. contp.* mit s-m Kram hausieren gehen; **2.** Geschirr *n*, Porzelˈlan *n*, Töpferware *f*.

ware[2] [weə] *v/i. u. v/t. obs.* sich vorsehen (vor *dat.*): ***~!*** Vorsicht!

ˈware·house I *s.* [-haus] **1.** Lagerhaus *n*, Speicher *m*: ***customs ~*** ✝ Zollniederlage *f*; **2.** (Waren)Lager *n*, Niederlage *f*; **3.** *bsd. Brit.* Großhandelsgeschäft *n*; **4.** *Am. contp.* ‚Bude' *f*, ‚Schuppen' *m*; **II** *v/t.* [-hauz] **5.** auf Lager nehmen, (ein)lagern; **6.** *Möbel etc.* zur Aufbewahrung geben *od.* nehmen; **7.** unter Zollverschluß bringen; **~ ac·count** *s.* Lagerkonto *n*; **~ bond** *s.* **1.** Lagerschein *m*; **2.** Zollverschlußbescheinigung *f*; **ˈ~·man** [-mən] *s.* [*irr.*] ✝ **1.** Lageˈrist *m*, Lagerverwalter *m*; **2.** Lagerarbeiter *m*; **3.** *Brit.* Großhändler *m*.

ˈwar·fare *s.* **1.** Kriegführung *f*; **2.** (*a. Wirtschafts- etc.*)Krieg *m*; **3.** *fig.* Kampf *m*, Fehde *f*, Streit *m*.

war| game *s.* ⚔ **1.** Kriegs-, Planspiel *n*; **2.** Maˈnöver *n*; **~ god** *s.* Kriegsgott *m*; **~ grave** *s.* Kriegs-, Solˈdatengrab *n*; **~ guilt** *s.* Kriegsschuld *f*; **ˈ~·head** *s.* ⚔ Spreng-, Gefechtskopf *m* (*e-s Torpedos etc.*); **ˈ~·horse** *s.* **1.** *poet.* Schlachtroß *n* (*a. fig.* F); **2.** F alter Haudegen *od.* Kämpe (*a. fig.*).

war·i·ness [ˈweərɪnɪs] *s.* Vorsicht *f*, Behutsamkeit *f*.

ˈwar·like *adj.* **1.** kriegerisch; **2.** Kriegs…
war·lock [ˈwɔːlɒk] *s. obs.* Zauberer *m.*
ˈwar·lord *s. rhet.* Kriegsherr *m.*
warm [wɔːm] **I** *adj.* ☐ **1.** *allg.* warm (*a. Farbe etc.*; *a. fig. Herz, Interesse etc.*): ***a ~ corner*** *fig.* e-e ‚ungemütliche Ecke' (*gefährlicher Ort*); ***a ~ reception*** ein warmer Empfang (*a. iro. von Gegnern*); ***~ work*** a) schwere Arbeit, b) gefährliche Sache, c) heißer Kampf; ***keep s.th. ~*** (F *fig.* sich) et. warmhalten; ***make it*** (*od.* ***things***) ***~ for s.o.*** j-m die Hölle heiß machen; ***this place is too ~ for me*** *fig.* hier brennt mir der Boden unter den Füßen; **2.** erhitzt, heiß; **3.** a) glühend, leidenschaftlich, eifrig, b) herzlich; **4.** erregt, hitzig; **5.** *hunt.* frisch (*Fährte etc.*); **6.** F ‚warm', nahe (dran) (*im Suchspiel*): ***you are getting ~er*** *fig.* du kommst der Sache (schon) näher; **II** *s.* **7.** *et.* Warmes, warmes Zimmer *etc.*; **8.** ***give*** (***have***) ***a ~*** *et.* (sich) (auf)wärmen; **III** *v/t.* **9.** *a.* ***~ up*** (an-, auf-, er)wärmen, *Milch etc.* warm machen: ***~ over*** *Am. Speisen etc.*, *a. fig. alte Geschichten etc.* aufwärmen; ***~ one's feet*** sich die Füße wärmen; **10.** *fig. Herz etc.* (er)wärmen; **11.** ***~ up*** *fig.* a) Schwung bringen in (*acc.*), b) *Zuschauer etc.* einstimmen; **12.** F verprügeln, -sohlen; **IV** *v/i.* **13.** *a.* ***~ up*** warm werden, sich erwärmen; *Motor etc.* warmlaufen; **14.** ***~ up*** *fig.* in Schwung kommen (*Party etc.*); **15.** *fig.* (***to***) a) sich erwärmen (für), b) warm werden (mit *j-m*); **16.** (***for***) a) *sport* sich aufwärmen (für), b) sich vorbereiten (auf *acc.*); **ˌ~-ˈblood·ed** *adj.* **1.** *zo.* warmblütig: ***~ animals*** Warmblüter *pl.*; **2.** *fig.* heißblütig; **ˌ~-ˈheart·ed** *adj.* ☐ warmherzig.
warm·ing [ˈwɔːmɪŋ] *s.* **1.** (Auf-, An-)Wärmen *n*, Erwärmung *f*; **2.** F Tracht *f* Prügel, ‚Senge' *f*; ***~ pad*** *s.* ↯ Heizkissen *n.*
warm·ish [ˈwɔːmɪʃ] *adj.* lauwarm.
war|·mon·ger [ˈwɔːˌmʌŋgə] *s.* Kriegshetzer *m*; **ˈ~ˌmon·ger·ing** [-ərɪŋ] *s.* Kriegshetze *f*, -treibeˈrei *f.*
warmth [wɔːmθ] *s.* **1.** Wärme *f*; **2.** *fig.* Wärme *f*: a) Herzlichkeit *f*, b) Eifer *m*, Begeisterung *f*; **3.** Heftigkeit *f*, Erregtheit *f.*
ˈwarm-up *s.* **1.** a) *sport* Aufwärmen *n*, b) *fig.* Vorbereitung (***for*** auf *acc.*); **2.** Warmlaufen *n* (*des Motors etc.*); **3.** *TV etc.*: Einstimmung *f* (*des Publikums*).
warn [wɔːn] *v/t.* **1.** warnen (***of, against*** vor *dat.*): ***~ s.o. against doing s.th.*** j-n davor warnen, et. zu tun; **2.** *j-n* (warnend) hinweisen, aufmerksam machen (***of*** auf *acc.*, ***that*** daß); **3.** ermahnen *od.* auffordern (***to do*** zu tun); **4.** *j-m* (dringend) raten, nahelegen (***to do*** zu tun); **5.** (***of***) *j-n* in Kenntnis setzen *od.* verständigen (von), *j-n* wissen lassen (*acc.*), *j-m* ankündigen (*acc.*); **6.** verwarnen; **7.** ***~ off*** (***from***) a) abweisen, -halten (von), b) hinˈausweisen (aus); **ˈwarn·ing** [-nɪŋ] **I** *s.* **1.** Warnen *n*, Warnung *f*: ***give s.o.*** (***fair***) ***~, give*** (***fair***) ***~ to s.o.*** j-n (rechtzeitig) warnen (***of*** vor *dat.*); ***take ~ by*** (*od.* ***from***) sich *et.* zur Warnung dienen lassen; **2.** a) Verwarnung *f*, b) (Er)Mahnung *f*; **3.** *fig.* Warnung *f*, warnendes Beispiel; **4.** warnendes An- *od.* Vorzeichen (***of*** für); **5.** ˈWarnsiˌgnal *n*; **6.** Benachrichtigung *f*, (Vor)Anzeige *f*, Ankündigung *f*: ***give ~*** (***of***) *j-m* ankündigen (*acc.*), Bescheid geben (über *acc.*); ***without any ~*** völlig unerwartet; **7.** a) Kündigung *f*, b) (Kündigungs)Frist *f*: ***give ~*** (***to***) (*j-m*) kündigen; ***at a minute's ~*** a) ✝ auf jederzeitige Kündigung, b) ✝ fristlos, c) in kürzester Frist, jeden Augenblick; **II** *adj.* ☐ **8.** warnend, Warn…(*-glocke, -meldung, -schuß etc.*): ***~ colo***(***u***)***r, ~ coloration*** *zo.* Warn-, Trutzfarbe *f*; ***~ light*** a) ⚙ Warnlicht *n*, b) ⚓ Warn-, Signalfeuer *n*; ***~ strike*** ✝ Warnstreik *m*; ***~ triangle*** *mot.* Warndreieck *n.*
warn't [wɑːnt] *dial. für* a) ***wasn't***, b) ***weren't***.
War| Of·fice *s. Brit. hist.* ˈKriegsminiˌsterium *n*; ♀ **or·phan** *s.* Kriegswaise *f.*
warp [wɔːp] **I** *v/t.* **1.** *Holz etc.* verziehen, werfen, krümmen; ✈ *Tragflächen* verwinden; **2.** *j-n, j-s Geist* nachteilig beeinflussen, verschroben machen; *j-s Urteil* verfälschen; → ***warped*** 3; **3.** a) verleiten (***into*** zu), b) abbringen (***from*** von); **4.** *Tatsache etc.* entstellen, verdrehen, -zerren; **5.** ⚓ *Schiff* bugsieren, verholen; **6.** *Weberei*: *Kette* anscheren, anzetteln; **7.** ✓ a) mit Schlamm düngen, b) *a.* ***~ up*** verschlammen; **II** *v/i.* **8.** sich werfen *od.* verziehen *od.* krümmen, krumm werden (*Holz etc.*); **9.** entstellt *od.* verdreht werden; **III** *s.* **10.** Verziehen *n*, Verkrümmung *f*, -werfung *f* (*von Holz etc.*); **11.** *fig.* Neigung *f*; **12.** *fig.* a) Entstellung *f*, Verzerrung *f*, b) Verschrobenheit *f*; **13.** *Weberei*: Kette(nfäden *pl.*) *f*, Zettel *m*: ***~ and woof*** Kette u. Schuß; **14.** ⚓ Bugsiertau *n*, Warpleine *f*; **15.** ✓, *geol.* Schlamm (-ablagerung *f*) *m*, Schlick *m.*
war| paint *s.* **1.** Kriegsbemalung *f* (*der Indianer*); **2.** F a) ‚volle Kriegsbemalung', b) große Gala; ***~ path*** *s.* Kriegspfad *m* (*der Indianer*): ***be on the ~*** a) auf dem Kriegspfad sein (*a. fig.*), b) *fig.* kampflustig sein.
warped [wɔːpt] *adj.* **1.** verzogen (*Holz etc.*), krumm (*a.* ⩚); **2.** *fig.* verzerrt, verfälscht; **3.** *fig.* ‚verbogen', verschroben: ***~ mind***; **4.** parˈteiisch.
war plane *s.* Kampfflugzeug *n.*
war·rant [ˈwɒrənt] **I** *s.* **1.** *a.* ***~ of attorney*** Vollmacht *f*; Befugnis *f*, Berechtigung *f*; **2.** Rechtfertigung *f*: ***not without ~*** nicht ohne gewisse Berechtigung; **3.** Garanˈtie *f*, Gewähr *f* (*a. fig.*); **4.** Berechtigungsschein *m*: ***dividend ~*** ✝ Dividenden-, Gewinnanteilschein *m*; **5.** ⚖ (Vollˈziehungs- *etc.*)Befehl *m*: ***~ of apprehension*** a) Steckbrief *m*, b) *a.* ***~ of arrest*** Haftbefehl *m*; ***~ of attachment*** Beschlagnahmeverfügung *f*; ***a ~ is out against him*** er wird steckbrieflich gesucht; **6.** ⚔ Paˈtent *n*, Beförderungsurkunde *f*: ***~*** (***officer***) a) ⚓ (Ober)Stabsbootsmann *m*, Deckoffizier *m*, b) ⚔ *etwa*: (Ober)Stabsfeldwebel *m*; **7.** ✝ (Lager-, Waren)Schein *m*: ***bond ~*** Zollgeleitschein; **8.** ✝ (Rück-)Zahlungsanweisung *f*; **II** *v/t.* **9.** *bsd.* ⚖ bevollmächtigen, autorisieren; **10.** rechtfertigen, berechtigen zu; **11.** *a.* ✝ garantieren, zusichern, haften für, gewährleisten: ***I can't ~ that*** das kann ich nicht garantieren; ***~ed for three years*** drei Jahre Garantie; ***I'll ~*** (***you***) F a) mein Wort darauf, b) ich könnte schwören; **12.** bestätigen, erweisen; **ˈwar·rant·a·ble** [-təbl] *adj.* ☐ **1.** vertretbar, gerechtfertigt, berechtigt; **2.** *hunt.* jagdbar (*Hirsch*); **ˈwar·rant·a·bly** [-təblɪ] *adv.* mit Recht, berechtigterweise; **war·ran·tee** [ˌwɒrənˈtiː] *s.* ✝, ⚖ Sicherheitsempfänger *m*; **ˈwar·rant·er** [-tə], **ˈwar·ran·tor** [-tɔː] *s.* Sicherheitsgeber *m*; **ˈwar·ran·ty** [-tɪ] *s.* **1.** ✝, ⚖ Ermächtigung *f*, Vollmacht *f* (***for*** zu); **2.** Rechtfertigung *f*; **3.** *bsd.* ⚖ Bürgschaft *f*, Garanˈtie *f*; **4.** *a.* ***~ deed*** ⚖ a) ˈRechtsgaranˌtie *f*, b) *Am.* ˈGrundstücksüberˌtragungsurkunde *f.*
war·ren [ˈwɒrən] *s.* **1.** Kaˈninchengehege *n*; **2.** *hist. Brit.* Wildgehege *n*; **3.** *fig.* Labyˈrinth *n*, *bsd.* a) ˈMietskaˌserne *f*, b) enges Straßengewirr.
war·ring [ˈwɔːrɪŋ] *adj.* **1.** sich bekriegend, (sich) streitend; **2.** *fig.* ˈwiderstreitend, entgegengesetzt.
war·ri·or [ˈwɒrɪə] *s. poet.* Krieger *m.*
war| risk in·sur·ance *s.* ✝ Kriegsversicherung *f*; **ˈ~·ship** *s.* Kriegsschiff *n.*
wart [wɔːt] *s.* **1.** ⚕, ♀, *zo.* Warze *f*: ***~s and all*** *fig.* mit all s-n Fehlern u. Schwächen; **2.** ♀ Auswuchs *m*; **ˈwart·ed** [-tɪd] *adj.* warzig.
ˈwar·time **I** *s.* Kriegszeit *f*; **II** *adj.* Kriegs…
wart·y [ˈwɔːtɪ] *adj.* warzig.
war|·wea·ry [ˈwɔːˌwɪərɪ] *adj.* kriegsmüde; ***~ whoop*** *s.* Kriegsgeheul *n* (*der Indianer*); ***~ wid·ow*** *s.* Kriegerwitwe *f*; **ˈ~·worn** *adj.* **1.** kriegszerstört, vom Krieg verwüstet; **2.** kriegsmüde.
war·y [ˈweərɪ] *adj.* ☐ vorsichtig: a) wachsam, *a.* argwöhnisch, b) ˈumsichtig, c) behutsam: ***be ~*** sich hüten (***of*** vor *dat.*, ***of doing*** et. zu tun).
was [wɒz; wəz] *1. u. 3. sg. pret. ind. von* ***be***; *im pass.* wurde: ***he ~ killed***; ***he ~ to have come*** er hätte kommen sollen; ***he didn't know what ~ to come*** er ahnte nicht, was noch kommen sollte; ***he ~ never to see his mother again*** er sollte seine Mutter nie mehr wiedersehen.
wash [wɒʃ] **I** *s.* **1.** Waschen *n*, Wäsche *f*: ***at the ~*** in der Wäsche(rei); ***give s.th. a ~*** et. (ab)waschen; ***have a ~*** sich waschen; ***come out in the ~*** a) herausgehen (*Flecken*), b) *fig.* F in Ordnung kommen, c) *fig.* F sich zeigen; **2.** (*zu waschende od. gewaschene*) Wäsche: ***in the ~*** in der Wäsche; **3.** Spülwasser *n* (*a. fig. dünne Suppe etc.*); **4.** Spülicht *n*, Küchenabfälle *pl.*; **5.** *fig. contp.* Gewäsch *n*, leeres Gerede; **6.** ⚕ Waschung *f*; **7.** (*Augen-, Haar- etc.*)Wasser *n*; **8.** Wellenschlag *m*, (Tosen *n* der) Brandung *f*; **9.** ⚓ Kielwasser *n* (*a. fig.*); **10.** ✈ a) Luftstrudel *m*, b) glatte Strömung; **11.** *geol.* a) (Alluviˈal)Schutt *m*, b) Schwemmland *n*; **12.** seichtes Gewässer; **13.** ˈFarbˌüberzug *m*: a) dünn aufgetragene (Wasser)Farbe, b) △ Tünche *f*; **14.** ⚙ a) Bad *n*, Abspritzung *f*, b) Plattierung *f*; **II** *adj.* **15.** waschbar, -echt, Wasch…: ***~ glove*** Waschlederhandschuh *m*; ***~ silk*** Waschseide *f*; **III** *v/t.* **16.** waschen: ***~*** (***up***) ***dishes*** Geschirr (ab)spülen; → ***hand*** *Redew.*; **17.** (ab)spülen; (-)spritzen; **18.** be-, um-, überˈspülen (*Fluten*); **19.** (fort-, weg-)

spülen, (-)schwemmen: **~ *ashore***; **20.** *geol.* graben (*Wasser*); → ***wash away*** 2, ***wash out*** 1; **21.** a) tünchen, b) dünn anstreichen, c) tuschen; **22.** *Erze* waschen, schlämmen; **23.** ⚙ plattieren; **IV** *v/i.* **24.** sich waschen; waschen (*Wäscherin etc.*); **25.** sich *gut etc.* waschen (lassen), waschecht sein; **26.** *bsd. Brit.* F a) standhalten, b) ‚ziehen', stichhaltig sein: ***that won't ~*** (***with me***) das zieht nicht (bei mir); **27.** (*vom Wasser*) gespült *od.* geschwemmt werden; **28.** fluten, spülen (***over*** über *acc.*); branden, schlagen (***against*** gegen), plätschern; *Zssgn mit adv.*:

wash| a·way I *v/t.* **1.** ab-, wegwaschen; **2.** weg-, fortspülen, -schwemmen; **II** *v/i.* **3.** weggeschwemmt werden; **~ down** *v/t.* **1.** abwaschen, -spritzen; **2.** hin'unterspülen (*a. Essen mit e-m Getränk*); **~ off** → ***wash away***; **~ out I** *v/t.* **1.** auswaschen, ausspülen, unter'spülen (*a. geol. etc.*); **2.** F *Plan etc.* fallenlassen, aufgeben; **3. *washed out*** a) → ***washed-out***, b) wegen Regens abgesagt *od.* abgebrochen (*Veranstaltung*); **II** *v/i.* **4.** sich auswaschen, verblassen; **5.** sich wegwaschen lassen (*Farbe*); **~ up I** *v/t.* **1.** *Geschirr* spülen; **2.** → ***washed-up***; **II** *v/i.* **3.** F sich (Gesicht u. Hände) waschen; **4.** Geschirr spülen.

wash·a·ble ['wɒʃəbl] *adj.* waschecht, -bar; *Tapete*: abwaschbar.

wash|·ba·sin ['wɒʃˌbeɪsn] *s.* Waschbecken *n*, -schüssel *f*; **'~·board** *s.* **1.** Waschbrett *n*; **2.** Fuß-, Scheuerleiste *f* (*an der Wand*); **~ bot·tle** *s.* ⚗ **1.** Spritzflasche *f*; **2.** (Gas)Waschflasche *f*; **'~·bowl** → ***washbasin***; **'~ˌcloth** *s. Am.* Waschlappen *m*.

washed|-out [ˌwɒʃt'aʊt] *adj.* **1.** verwaschen, verblaßt; **2.** F ‚fertig', ‚erledigt' (*erschöpft*); **ˌ~-'up** *adj.* F ‚erledigt', ‚fertig': a) erschöpft, b) völlig ruiniert.

wash·er ['wɒʃə] *s.* **1.** Wäscher(in); **2.** 'Waschmaˌschine *f*; **3.** (Ge'schirr)Spülmaˌschine *f*; **4.** *Papierherstellung*: Halb(zeug)holländer *m*; **5.** ⚙ 'Unterlegscheibe *f*, Dichtungsring *m*; **'~ˌwom·an** *s.* [*irr.*] Waschfrau *f*, Wäscherin *f*.

wash·e·te·ri·a [ˌwɒʃə'tɪərɪə] *s. Brit.* **1.** 'Waschsaˌlon *m*; **2.** (Auto)Waschanlage *f*.

'wash·hand *adj. Brit.* Handwasch…: **~ *basin*** (Hand)Waschbecken *n*; **~ *stand*** (Hand)Waschständer *m*.

wash·i·ness ['wɒʃɪnɪs] *s.* **1.** Wässerigkeit *f* (*a. fig.*); **2.** Verwaschenheit *f*.

wash·ing ['wɒʃɪŋ] **I** *s.* **1.** → ***wash*** 1, 2; **2.** *oft pl.* Spülwasser *n*; **3.** ⚙ nasse Aufbereitung, Erzwäsche *f*; **4.** 'Farbˌüberzug *m*; **II** *adj.* **5.** Wasch…, Wäsche…; **~ ma·chine** *s.* 'Waschmaˌschine *f*; **~ so·da** *s.* (Bleich)Soda *f*, *n*; **ˌ~-'up** *s.* Abwasch *m* (*a. Geschirr*): ***do the ~*** Geschirr spülen; **~ *liquid*** Spülmittel *n*.

wash| leath·er *s.* **1.** Waschleder *n*; **2.** Fenster(putz)leder *n*; **'~·out** *s.* **1.** *geol.* Auswaschung *f*; **2.** Unter'spülung *f* (*e-r Straße etc.*); **3.** *sl.* a) ‚Niete' *f*, Versager *m* (*Person*), b) ‚Pleite' *f*, ‚Reinfall' *m*, c) ⚔ ‚Fahrkarte' *f* (*Fehlschuß*); **'~·rag** *s. Am.* Waschlappen *m*; **'~·room** *s. Am.* (öffentliche) Toi'lette; **~ sale** *s.* ✝ *Börse*: Scheinverkauf *m*; **'~·stand** *s.* **1.** Waschständer *m*; **2.** Waschbecken *n* (*mit fließendem Wasser*); **'~·tub** *s.* Waschwanne *f*.

wash·y ['wɒʃɪ] *adj.* □ **1.** verwässert, wässerig (*beide a. fig. kraftlos, seicht*); **2.** verwaschen, blaß (*Farbe*).

WASP [wɒsp] *s. Am.* prote'stantischer weißer Angelsachse (*aus* ***White Anglo-Saxon Protestant***).

wasp [wɒsp] *s. zo.* Wespe *f*; **'wasp·ish** [-pɪʃ] *adj.* □ *fig.* a) reizbar, b) gereizt, giftig.

was·sail ['wɒseɪl] *s. obs.* **1.** (Trink)Gelage *n*; **2.** Würzbier *n*.

wast [wɒst; wəst] *obs. 2. sg. pret. ind. von* ***be***: ***thou ~*** du warst.

wast·age ['weɪstɪdʒ] *s.* **1.** Verlust *m*, Abgang *m*, Verschleiß *m*; **2.** Vergeudung *f*: **~ *of energy*** a) Energieverschwendung *f*, b) *fig.* Leerlauf *m*.

waste [weɪst] **I** *adj.* **1.** öde, wüst, unfruchtbar, unbebaut (*Land*): ***lie ~*** brachliegen; ***lay ~*** verwüsten; **2.** a) nutzlos, 'überflüssig, b) ungenutzt, 'überschüssig: **~ *energy***; **3.** unbrauchbar, Abfall…; **4.** ⚙ a) abgängig, Abgangs…, Ab…(*-gas etc.*), b) Abfluß…, Ablauf…; **II** *s.* **5.** Verschwendung *f*, Vergeudung *f*: **~ *of energy*** (***money***, ***time***) Kraft- (Geld-, Zeit)verschwendung; ***go*** (*od.* ***run***) ***to ~*** a) brachliegen, verwildern, b) vergeudet werden, c) verlottern, -fallen; **6.** Verfall *m*, Verschleiß *m*, Abgang *m*, Verlust *m*; **7.** Wüste *f*, (Ein)Öde *f*: **~ *of water*** Wasserwüste; **8.** Abfall *m*; ⚙ *a.* Abgänge *pl.*, *bsd.* a) Ausschuß *m*, b) Putzbaumwolle *f*, c) Wollabfälle *pl.*, d) Werg *n*, e) *typ.* Makula'tur *f*, f) Gekrätz *n*; **9.** ⚒ Abraum *m*; **10.** ⚖ Wertminderung *f* (*e-s Grundstücks durch Vernachlässigung*); **III** *v/t.* **11.** *Geld*, *Worte*, *Zeit etc.* verschwenden, vergeuden (***on*** an *acc.*): ***you are wasting your breath*** du kannst dir deine Worte sparen; ***a ~d talent*** ein ungenutztes Talent; **12. *be ~d*** nutzlos sein, ohne Wirkung bleiben (***on*** auf *acc.*), am falschen Platz stehen; **13.** zehren an (*dat.*), aufzehren, schwächen; **14.** verwüsten, verheeren; **15.** ⚖ Vermögensschaden verursachen bei, *Besitztum* verkommen lassen; **16.** a) F *Sportler etc.* ‚verheizen', b) *Am. sl. j-n* ‚'umlegen'; **IV** *v/i.* **17.** *fig.* vergeudet *od.* verschwendet werden; **18.** sich verzetteln (***in*** in *dat.*); **19.** vergehen, (ungenutzt) verstreichen (*Zeit*, *Gelegenheit etc.*); **20.** *a.* **~ *away*** a) abnehmen, schwinden, b) da'hinsiechen, verfallen; **21.** verschwenderisch sein: **~ *not, want not*** spare in der Zeit, so hast du in der Not; **'~ˌbas·ket** *s.* Abfall-, *bsd.* Pa'pierkorb *m*; **~ dis·pos·al** *s.* Müllbeseitigung *f*.

waste·ful ['weɪstfʊl] *adj.* □ **1.** kostspielig, unwirtschaftlich, verschwenderisch; **2.** verschwenderisch (***of*** mit): ***be ~ of*** verschwenderisch umgehen mit; **3.** *poet.* wüst, öde; **'waste·ful·ness** [-nɪs] *s.* Verschwendung(ssucht) *f*.

waste| gas *s.* ⚙ Abgas *n*; **~ heat** *s.* ⚙ Abwärme *f*; **'~·land** *s.* Ödland *n* (*a. fig.*); **~ oil** *s.* Altöl *n*; **ˌ~'pa·per** *s.* **1.** 'Abfallpaˌpier *n*, Makula'tur *f* (*a. fig.*); **2.** 'Altpaˌpier *n*; **ˌ~'pa·per bas·ket** *s.* Pa'pierkorb *m*; **~ pipe** *s.* ⚙ Abfluß-, Abzugsrohr *n*; **~ prod·uct** *s.* **1.** ⚙ 'Abfallproˌdukt *n*; **2.** *biol.* Ausscheidungsstoff *m*.

wast·er ['weɪstə] *s.* **1.** → ***wastrel*** 1 *u.* 3; **2.** *metall.* a) Fehlguß *m*, b) Schrottstück *n*.

waste| steam *s.* ⚙ Abdampf *m*; **~ wa·ter** *s.* Abwasser *n*; **~ wool** *s.* Twist *m*.

wast·ing ['weɪstɪŋ] *adj.* **1.** zehrend, schwächend: **~ *disease***; → ***palsy*** 1; **2.** schwindend, abnehmend.

wast·rel ['weɪstrəl] *s.* **1.** a) Verschwender *m*, b) Taugenichts *m*; **2.** He'rumtreiber *m*; **3.** ✝ 'Ausschuß(arˌtikel *m*, -ware *f*) *m*, fehlerhaftes Exem'plar.

watch [wɒtʃ] **I** *s.* **1.** Wache *f*, Wacht *f*: ***be*** (***up***)***on the ~*** a) wachsam *od.* auf der Hut sein, b) (***for***) Ausschau halten (nach), lauern (auf *acc.*), achthaben (auf *acc.*); ***keep*** (***a***) **~** (***on*** *od.* ***over***) Wache halten, wachen (über *acc.*), aufpassen (auf *acc.*); → ***ward*** 8; **2.** (Schild-)Wache *f*, Wachtposten *m*; **3.** *mst pl. hist.* (Nacht)Wache *f* (*Zeiteinteilung*): ***in the silent ~es of the night*** in den stillen Stunden der Nacht; **4.** ⚓ (Schiffs)Wache *f* (*Zeitabschnitt u. Mannschaft*); **5.** *hist.* Nachtwächter *m*; **6.** *obs.* a) Wachen *n*, wache Stunden *pl.*, b) Totenwache *f*; **7.** (Taschen-, Armband)Uhr *f*; **II** *v/i.* **8.** zusehen, zuschauen; **9.** (***for***) warten, lauern (auf *acc.*), Ausschau halten (nach); **10.** wachen (***with*** bei), wach sein; **11. ~ *over*** wachen über (*acc.*), bewachen, aufpassen auf (*acc.*); **12.** ⚔ Posten stehen, Wache halten; **13. ~ *out*** (***for***) a) → 9, b) aufpassen, achtgeben: **~ *out!*** Vorsicht!, paß auf!; **III** *v/t.* **14.** beobachten: a) *j-m* zuschauen (***working*** bei der Arbeit), b) ein wachsames Auge haben auf (*acc.*), *a. Verdächtigen* über'wachen, c) *Vorgang etc.* verfolgen, im Auge behalten, d) ⚖ *den Verlauf e-s Prozesses* verfolgen; **15.** *Vieh* hüten, bewachen; **16.** *Gelegenheit* abwarten, abpassen, wahrnehmen: **~ *one's time***; **17.** achthaben auf (*acc.*) (*od.* ***that*** daß): **~ *one's step*** a) vorsichtig gehen, b) F sich vorsehen; **~ *your step!*** Vorsicht!; **'~·boat** *s.* ⚓ Wach(t)boot *n*; **~ box** *s.* **1.** ⚔ Schilderhaus *n*; **2.** 'Unterstand *m* (*für Wachmänner etc.*); **'~·case** *s.* Uhrgehäuse *n*; **'~·dog** *s.* Wachhund *m* (*a. fig.*): **~ *committee*** Überwachungsausschuß *m*.

watch·er ['wɒtʃə] *s.* **1.** Wächter *m*; **2.** Beobachter(in); **3.** j-d, der Kranken- *od.* Totenwache hält.

watch·ful ['wɒtʃfʊl] *adj.* □ wachsam, aufmerksam, *a.* lauernd (***of*** auf *acc.*); **'watch·ful·ness** [-nɪs] *s.* **1.** Wachsamkeit *f*; **2.** Vorsicht *f*; **3.** Wachen *n* (***over*** über *dat.*).

watch|·house ['wɒtʃhaʊs] *s.* (Poli'zei-)Wache *f*; **'~ˌmak·er** *s.* Uhrmacher *m*; **'~ˌmak·ing** *s.* Uhrmache'rei *f*; **'~·man** [-mən] *s.* [*irr.*] **1.** (Nacht)Wächter *m*; **2.** *hist.* Nachtwächter *m* (*e-r Stadt etc.*); **~ night** *s. eccl.* Sil'vestergottesdienst *m*; **~ of·fi·cer** *s.* ⚓ 'Wachoffiˌzier *m*; **~ pock·et** *s.* Uhrtasche *f*; **~ spring** *s.* Uhrfeder *f*; **'~·strap** *s.* Uhr(arm)band *n*; **'~ˌtow·er** *s.* ⚔ Wach(t)turm *m*; **'~·word** *s.* **1.** Losung *f*, Pa'role *f* (*a. fig. e-r Partei etc.*); **2.** *fig.* Schlagwort *n*.

wa·ter ['wɔːtə] **I** *v/t.* **1.** bewässern, *Rasen*, *Straße etc.* sprengen, *Pflanzen* (be-)gießen; **2.** *Vieh* tränken; **3.** mit Wasser versorgen; **4.** *oft* **~ down** verwässern: a) verdünnen, *Wein* panschen, b) *fig. Erklärung etc.* abschwächen, c) *fig.* mundgerecht machen: ***a ~ed-down liberalism*** ein verwässerter Liberalismus; **5.** † *Aktienkapital* verwässern; **6.** ⚙ *Stoff* wässern, moirieren; **II** *v/i.* **7.** wässern (*Mund*), tränen (*Augen*): ***his mouth ~ed*** das Wasser lief ihm im Mund zusammen (***for***, ***after*** nach); ***make s.o.'s mouth ~*** j-m den Mund wässerig machen; **8.** ⚓ Wasser einnehmen; **9.** trinken, zur Tränke gehen (*Vieh*); **10.** ✈ wassern; **III** *s.* **11.** Wasser *n*: ***in deep ~(s)*** *fig.* in Schwierigkeiten, in der Klemme; ***hold ~*** *fig.* stichhaltig sein; ***keep one's head above ~*** *fig.* sich (gerade noch) über Wasser halten; ***make the ~*** ⚓ vom Stapel laufen; ***throw cold ~ on*** *fig. e-r Sache* e-n Dämpfer aufsetzen, wie e-e kalte Dusche wirken auf (*acc.*); ***still ~s run deep*** stille Wasser sind tief; → ***hot*** 13, ***oil*** 1, ***trouble*** 6; **12.** *oft pl.* Brunnen *m*, Wasser *n* (*e-r Heilquelle*): ***drink*** (*od.* ***take***) ***the ~s*** (***at***) e-e Kur machen (in *dat.*); **13.** *oft pl.* Wasser *n od. pl.*, Gewässer *n od. pl.*, *a.* Fluten *pl.*: ***by ~*** zu Wasser, auf dem Wasserweg; ***on the ~*** a) zur See, b) zu Schiff; ***the ~s*** *poet.* das Meer, die See; **14.** Wasserstand *m*; → ***low water***; **15.** (Toi'letten)Wasser *n*; **16.** Wasserlösung *f*; **17.** *physiol.* Wasser *n* (*Sekret, z. B. Speichel, a. Urin*): ***the ~(s)*** das Fruchtwasser; ***make*** (*od.* ***pass***) ~ Wasser lassen, urinieren; ***~ on the brain*** Wasserkopf *m*; ***~ on the knee*** Kniegelenkerguß *m*; **18.** Wasser *n* (*reiner Glanz e-s Edelsteins*): ***of the first ~*** reinsten Wassers (*a. fig.*); **19.** Wasser(glanz *m*) *n*, Moi'ré *n* (*Stoff*); **~ bath** *s.* Wasserbad *n* (*a.* ⚗); **~ bed** *s.* ⚕ Wasserbett *n*, -kissen *n*; **~ bird** *s. zo. allg.* Wasservogel *m*; **~ blis·ter** *s.* ⚕ Wasserblase *f*; **'~·borne** *adj.* **1.** auf dem Wasser schwimmend; **2.** zu Wasser befördert (*Ware*), auf dem Wasser stattfindend (*Verkehr*), Wasser…; **~ bot·tle** *s.* **1.** Wasserflasche *f*; **2.** Feldflasche *f*; **'~-bound** *adj.* vom Wasser eingeschlossen *od.* abgeschnitten; **~ bus** *s.* (Linien)Flußboot *n*; **~ butt** *s.* Wasserfaß *n*, Regentonne *f*; **~ can·non** *s.* Wasserwerfer *m*; **~ car·riage** *s.* Trans'port *m* zu Wasser, 'Wassertrans,port *m*; ♒ **Car·ri·er** → ***Aquarius***; **'~-cart** *s.* Wasserwagen *m*, *bsd.* Sprengwagen *m*; **~ chute** *s.* Wasserrutschbahn *f*; **~ clock** *s.* ⚙ Wasseruhr *f*; **~ clos·et** *s.* ('Wasser)Klo,sett *n*; **'~,col·o(u)r I** *s.* **1.** Wasser-, Aqua'rellfarbe *f*; **2.** Aqua'rellmale,rei *f*; **3.** Aqua'rell *n* (*Bild*); **II** *adj.* **4.** Aquarell…; **'~,col·o(u)r·ist** *s.* Aqua'rellmaler(in); **'~-cooled** *adj.* ⚙ wassergekühlt; **'~-,cool·ing** *s.* ⚙ Wasserkühlung *f*; **'~·course** *s.* **1.** Wasserlauf *m*; **2.** Fluß-, Strombett *n*; **3.** Ka'nal *m*; **'~·craft** *s.* Wasserfahrzeug(e *pl.*) *n*; **'~·cress** *s. oft pl.* ⚘ Brunnenkresse *f*; **~ cure** *s.* ⚕ **1.** Wasserkur *f*; **2.** Wasserheilkunde *f*; **'~·fall** *s.* Wasserfall *m*; **'~,find·er** *s.* (Wünschel)Rutengänger *m*; **'~·fog** *s.* Tröpfchennebel *m*; **'~·fowl** *s. zo.* **1.** Wasservogel *m*; **2.** *coll.* Wasservögel *pl.*; **'~·front** *s.* Hafengebiet *n*, -viertel *n*; an ein Gewässer grenzendes (Stadt)Gebiet; **~ gage** *Am.* → ***water gauge***; **~ gate** *s.* **1.** Schleuse *f*; **2.** Fluttor *n*; **~ gauge** *s.* ⚙ **1.** Wasserstands(an)zeiger *m*; **2.** Pegel *m*, Peil *m*, hy'draulischer Wasserdruckmesser; **3.** *Wasserdruck, gemessen in* ***inches*** *Wassersäule*; **~ glass** *s.* Wasserglas *n* (*a.* ⚗); **~ egg** Kalkei *n*; **~ gru·el** *s.* (dünner) Haferschleim; **~ heat·er** *s.* Warmwasserbereiter *m*; **~ hose** *s.* Wasserschlauch *m*; **~ ice** *s.* Fruchteis *n*.

wa·ter·i·ness ['wɔːtərɪnɪs] *s.* Wäßrigkeit *f*.

wa·ter·ing ['wɔːtərɪŋ] **I** *s.* **1.** (Be)Wässern *n etc.*; **II** *adj.* **2.** Bewässerungs…; **3.** Kur…, Bade…; **~ can** *s.* Gießkanne *f*; **~ cart** *s.* Sprengwagen *m*; **~ place** *s.* **1.** *bsd. Brit.* a) Bade-, Kurort *m*, Bad *n*, b) (See)Bad *n*; **2.** (Vieh)Tränke *f*, Wasserstelle *f*; **~ pot** *s. Am.* Gießkanne *f*.

wa·ter| jack·et *s.* ⚙ (Wasser)Kühlmantel *m*; **~ jump** *s. sport* Wassergraben *m*; **~ lev·el** *s.* **1.** Wasserstand *m*, -spiegel *m*; **2.** ⚙ a) Pegelstand *m*, b) Wasserwaage *f*; **3.** *geol.* (Grund)Wasserspiegel *m*; **~ lil·y** *s.* ⚘ Seerose *f*, Wasserlilie *f*; **'~·line** *s.* ⚓ Wasserlinie *f e-s Schiffs od. als Wasserzeichen*; **'~·logged** *adj.* **1.** voll Wasser (*Boot etc.*); **2.** vollgesogen (*Holz etc.*).

Wa·ter·loo [,wɔːtə'luː] *s.*: ***meet one's ~*** *fig.* sein Waterloo erleben.

wa·ter| main *s.* Haupt(wasser)rohr *n*; **'~·man** [-mən] *s.* [*irr.*] **1.** ⚓ Fährmann *m*; **2.** *sport* Ruderer *m*; **3.** *myth.* Wassergeist *m*; **'~·mark I** *s.* **1.** Wasserzeichen *n* (*in Papier*); **2.** ⚓ Wassermarke *f*, *bsd.* Flutzeichen *n*; → ***high*** (***low***) ***watermark***; **II** *v/t.* **3.** *Papier* mit Wasserzeichen versehen; **'~,mel·on** *s.* ⚘ 'Wasserme,lone *f*; **~ me·ter** *s.* Wasserzähler *m*, -uhr *f*; **~ pipe** *s.* **1.** ⚙ Wasser(leitungs)rohr *n*; **2.** orien'talische Wasserpfeife; **~ plane** *s.* Wasserflugzeug *n*; **~ plate** *s.* Wärmeteller *m*; **~ po·lo** *s. sport* Wasserballspiel *n*; **'~·proof I** *adj.* wasserdicht; **II** *s.* wasserdichter Stoff *od.* Mantel *etc.*, Regenmantel *m*; **III** *v/t.* imprägnieren; **~ re·cyc·ling** *s.* Wasseraufbereitung *f*; **,~-re'pel·lent** *adj.* wasserabstoßend; **'~·scape** [-skeɪp] *s. paint.* Seestück *n*; **~ seal** *s.* ⚙ Wasserverschluß *m*; **'~·shed** *s. geogr.* **1.** *Brit.* Wasserscheide *f*; **2.** Einzugs-, Stromgebiet *n*; **3.** *fig.* a) Trennungslinie *f*, b) Wendepunkt *m*; **'~·side I** *s.* Küste *f*, See-, Flußufer *n*; **II** *adj.* Küsten…, (Fluß)Ufer…; **'~-ski** *v/i.* Wasserski laufen; **,~-'sol·u·ble** *adj.* ⚗ wasserlöslich; **'~·spout** *s.* **1.** Abtraufe *f*; **2.** *meteor.* Wasserhose *f*; **~ sup·ply** *s.* Wasserversorgung *f*; **~ ta·ble** *s.* **1.** △ Wasserabflußleiste *f*; **2.** *geol.* Grundwasserspiegel *m*; **'~·tight** *adj.* **1.** wasserdicht: ***keep s.th. in ~ compartments*** *fig.* et. isoliert halten *od.* betrachten; **2.** *fig.* a) unanfechtbar, b) sicher, c) stichhaltig (*Argument*); **~ vole** *s. zo.* Wasserratte *f*; **~ wag·(g)on** *s.* Wasser(versorgungs)wagen *m*: ***be on*** (***off***) ***the ~*** F nicht mehr (wieder) trinken; ***go on the ~*** F das Trinken sein lassen; **~ wag·tail** *s. orn.* Bachstelze *f*; **'~-wave I** *s.* Wasserwelle *f* (*im Haar*); **II** *v/t.* in Wasserwellen legen; **'~·way** *s.* **1.** Wasserstraße *f*, Schiffahrtsweg *m*; **2.** ⚓ Wassergang *m* (*Decksrinne*); **'~·works** *s. pl. oft sg. konstr.* **1.** Wasserwerk *n*; **2.** a) Fon'täne(n *pl.*) *f*, b) Wasserspiel *n*: ***turn on the ~*** F (los-)heulen; **3.** F (Harn)Blase *f*.

wa·ter·y ['wɔːtərɪ] *adj.* **1.** Wasser…: ***a ~ grave*** ein nasses Grab; **2.** wässerig: a) feucht (*Boden*), b) regenverkündend (*Sonne etc.*): ***~ sky*** Regenhimmel *m*; **3.** triefend: a) *allg.* voll Wasser, naß (*Kleider*), b) tränend (*Auge*); **4.** verwässert: a) fad(e) (*Speise*), b) wässerig, blaß (*Farbe*), c) *fig.* seicht (*Stil*).

watt [wɒt] *s.* ↯ Watt *n*; **watt·age** ['wɒtɪdʒ] *s.* ↯ Wattleistung *f*.

wat·tle ['wɒtl] **I** *s.* **1.** *Brit. dial.* Hürde *f*; **2.** *a. pl.* Flecht-, Gitterwerk *n*: ***~ and daub*** △ mit Lehm beworfenes Flechtwerk; **3.** ⚘ (au'stralische) A'kazie; **4.** a) *orn.* Kehllappen *pl.*, b) *ichth.* Bartfäden *pl.*; **II** *v/t.* **5.** aus Flechtwerk herstellen; **6.** *Ruten* zs.-flechten; **'wat·tling** [-lɪŋ] *s.* Flechtwerk *n*.

waul [wɔːl] *v/i.* jämmerlich schreien, jaulen.

wave [weɪv] **I** *s.* **1.** Welle *f* (*a. phys.*; *a. im Haar etc.*), Woge *f* (*beide a. fig. von Gefühl etc.*): ***the ~s*** *poet.* die See; ***~ of indignation*** Woge der Entrüstung; ***make ~s*** *fig. Am.* ‚Wellen schlagen'; **2.** (*Angriffs-, Einwanderer- etc.*)Welle *f*: ***in ~s*** in aufeinanderfolgenden Wellen; **3.** ⚙ a) Flamme *f* (*im Stoff*), b) *typ.* Guil'loche *f* (*Zierlinie auf Wertpapieren etc.*); **4.** Wink(en *n*) *m*, Schwenken *n*; **II** *v/i.* **5.** wogen (*a. Kornfeld etc.*); **6.** wehen, flattern, wallen; **7.** (***to s.o.*** j-m zu)winken, Zeichen geben; **8.** sich wellen (*Haar*); **III** *v/t.* **9.** *Fahne, Waffe etc.* schwenken, schwingen, hin- u. herbewegen: ***~ one's arms*** mit den Armen fuchteln; ***~ one's hand*** (mit der Hand) winken (***to*** *j-m*); **10.** *Haar etc.* wellen, in Wellen legen; **11.** ⚙ a) *Stoff* flammen, b) *Wertpapiere etc.* guillochieren; **12.** *j-m* zuwinken: ***~ aside*** *j-n* beiseite winken, *fig. j-n od. et.* mit e-r Handbewegung abtun; **13.** *et.* zuwinken: ***~ a farewell*** nachwinken (***to s.o.*** j-m); **~ band** *s.* ↯ Wellenband *n*; **'~·length** *s.* ↯, *phys.* Wellenlänge *f*: ***be on the same ~*** *fig.* auf der gleichen Wellenlänge liegen.

wa·ver ['weɪvə] *v/i.* **1.** (sch)wanken, taumeln; flackern (*Licht*); zittern (*Hände, Stimme etc.*); **2.** *fig.* wanken: a) unschlüssig sein, schwanken (***between*** zwischen), b) zu weichen beginnen.

wa·ver·er ['weɪvərə] *s. fig.* Unentschlossene(r *m*) *f*; **'wa·ver·ing** [-vərɪŋ] *adj.* ☐ **1.** flackernd; **2.** zitternd; **3.** (sch)wankend (*a. fig.*).

wave trap *s.* ↯ Sperrkreis *m*.

wav·y ['weɪvɪ] *adj.* ☐ **1.** wellig, gewellt (*Haar, Linie etc.*); **2.** wogend.

wax¹ [wæks] **I** *v/i.* **1.** wachsen, zunehmen (*bsd. Mond*) (*a. fig. rhet.*): ***~ and wane*** zu- u. abnehmen; **2.** *vor adj.*: *alt, frech, laut etc.* werden; **II** *s.* **3.** ***be in a ~*** F e-e Stinkwut haben.

wax² [wæks] **I** *s.* **1.** (Bienen-, Pflanzen- *etc.*)Wachs *n*: ***like ~*** *fig.* (wie) Wachs *in j-s Händen*; **2.** Siegellack *m*; **3.** *a.* ***cobbler's ~*** Schusterpech *n*; **4.** Ohrenschmalz *n*; **II** *v/t.* **5.** (ein)wachsen, bohnern; **6.** verpichen; **7.** (auf Schallplatte) aufnehmen; **'~·cloth** *s.* **1.** Wachstuch *n*; **2.** Bohnertuch *n*; **~ doll** *s.* Wachspuppe *f*.

wax·en [ˈwæksən] → ***waxy***.

wax| light *s.* Wachskerze *f*; **~ pa·per** *s.* ˈWachspaˌpier *n*; **ˈ~·work** *s.* **1.** ˈWachsfiˌgur *f*; **2.** *a. pl. sg. konstr.* ˈWachsfiˌgurenkabiˌnett *n*.

wax·y [ˈwæksɪ] *adj.* □ **1.** wächsern (*a. Gesichtsfarbe*), wie Wachs; **2.** *fig.* weich (wie Wachs), nachgiebig; **3.** ⚕ Wachs…: ***~ liver***.

way¹ [weɪ] *s.* **1.** Weg *m*, Pfad *m*, Straße *f*, Bahn *f* (*a. fig.*): ***~ back*** Rückweg; ***~ home*** Heimweg; ***~ in*** Eingang *m*; ***~ out*** *bsd. fig.* Ausweg; ***~ through*** Durchfahrt *f*, -reise *f*; ***~s and means*** Mittel u. Wege, *bsd. pol.* Geldbeschaffung(smaßnahmen) *f*; ***Committee of ~s and Means*** *parl.* Finanz-, Haushaltsausschuß *m*; ***the ~ of the Cross*** *R.C.* der Kreuzweg; ***over*** (*od.* ***across***) ***the ~*** gegenüber; ***ask the*** (*od.* ***one's***) ***~*** nach dem Weg fragen; ***find a ~*** *fig.* e-n (Aus-)Weg finden; ***lose one's ~*** sich verirren *od.* verlaufen; ***take one's ~*** sich aufmachen (***to*** nach); **2.** *fig.* Gang *m*, (üblicher) Weg: ***that is the ~ of the world*** das ist der Lauf der Welt; ***go the ~ of all flesh*** den Weg allen Fleisches gehen (*sterben*); **3.** Richtung *f*, Seite *f*: ***which ~ is he looking?*** wohin schaut er?; ***this ~*** a) hierher, b) hier entlang, c) → 6; ***the other ~ round*** umgekehrt; **4.** Weg *m*, Entfernung *f*, Strecke *f*: ***a long ~ off*** weit (von hier) entfernt; ***a long ~ off perfection*** alles andere als vollkommen; ***a little ~*** ein kleines Stück (Wegs); **5.** (freie) Bahn, Platz *m*: ***be*** (*od.* ***stand***) ***in s.o.'s ~*** j-m im Weg sein (*a. fig.*); ***give ~*** a) nachgeben, b) (zurück)weichen, c) sich *der Verzweiflung etc.* hingeben; **6.** Art *f* u. Weise *f*, Weg *m*, Meˈthode *f*: ***any ~*** auf jede *od.* irgendeine Art; ***any ~ you please*** ganz wie Sie wollen; ***in a big*** (***small***) ***~*** im großen (kleinen); ***one ~ or another*** irgendwie, so oder so; ***some ~ or other*** auf die eine oder andere Weise, irgendwie; ***~ of living*** (***thinking***) Lebens-(Denk)weise; ***to my ~ of thinking*** nach m-r Meinung; ***in a polite*** (***friendly***) ***~*** höflich (freundlich); ***in its ~*** auf s-e Art; ***in what*** (*od.* ***which***) ***~*** inwiefern, wieso; ***the right*** (***wrong***) ***~*** (***to do it***) richtig (falsch); ***the same ~*** genauso; ***the ~ he does it*** so wie er es macht; ***this*** (*od.* ***that***) ***~*** so; ***that's the ~ to do it*** so macht man das; **7.** Brauch *m*, Sitte *f*: ***the good old ~s*** die guten alten Bräuche; **8.** Eigenart *f*: ***funny ~s*** komische Manieren; ***it is not his ~*** es ist nicht s-e Art *od.* Gewohnheit; ***she has a winning ~ with her*** sie hat e-e gewinnende Art; ***that is always the ~ with him*** so macht er es (*od.* geht es ihm) immer; **9.** Hinsicht *f*, Beziehung *f*: ***in a ~*** in gewisser Hinsicht; ***in one ~*** in ˈeiner Beziehung; ***in some ~s*** in mancher Hinsicht; ***in the ~ of food*** an Lebensmitteln, was Nahrung anbelangt; ***no ~*** keineswegs; **10.** (*bsd.* Gesundheits)Zustand *m*, Lage *f*: ***in a bad ~*** in e-r schlimmen Lage; ***live in a great*** (***small***) ***~*** auf großem Fuß (in kleinen Verhältnissen *od.* sehr bescheiden) leben; **11.** Berufszweig *m*, Fach *n*: ***it is not in his ~*** es schlägt nicht in sein Fach; ***he is in the oil ~*** er ist im Ölhandel (beschäftigt); **12.** F Umˈgebung *f*, Gegend *f*: ***somewhere London ~*** irgendwo in der Gegend von London; **13.** ⚙ a) (Hahn)Weg *m*, Bohrung *f*, b) *pl.* Führungen *pl.* (*bei Maschinen*); **14.** Fahrt(geschwindigkeit) *f*: ***gather*** (***lose***) ***~*** Fahrt vergrößern (verlieren); **15.** *pl. Schiffbau*: a) Helling *f*, b) Stapelblöcke *pl.*;

Besondere Redewendungen:

by the ~ a) im Vorbeigehen, unterwegs; b) am Weg(esrand), an der Straße, c) *fig.* übrigens, nebenbei (bemerkt); ***but that is by the ~!*** doch dies nur nebenbei; ***by ~ of*** a) (auf dem Weg) über (*acc.*), durch, b) *fig.* in der Absicht zu, um … zu, c) als *Entschuldigung etc.*; ***by ~ of example*** beispielsweise; ***by ~ of exchange*** auf dem Tauschwege; ***be by ~ of being angry*** im Begriff sein aufzubrausen; ***be by ~ of doing*** (***s.th.***) a) dabei sein(, et.) zu tun, b) pflegen *od.* gewohnt sein *od.* die Aufgabe haben(, et.) zu tun; → ***family*** 5; ***in the ~ of*** a) auf dem Weg *od.* dabei zu, b) hinsichtlich (*gen.*); ***in the ~ of business*** auf dem üblichen Geschäftsweg; ***put s.o. in the ~*** (***of doing***) j-m die Möglichkeit geben (zu tun); ***no ~!*** F nichts da!; ***on the*** (*od.* ***one's***) ***~*** unterwegs, auf dem Wege; ***be well on one's ~*** im Gange sein, schon weit vorangekommen sein (*a. fig.*); ***out of the ~*** a) abgelegen, b) *fig.* ungewöhnlich, ausgefallen, c) *fig.* abwegig; ***nothing out of the ~*** nichts Ungewöhnliches; ***go out of one's ~*** ein übriges tun, sich besonders anstrengen; ***put s.o. out of the ~*** *fig.* j-n aus dem Wege räumen (*töten*); → ***harm*** 1; ***under ~*** a) ⚓ in Fahrt, unterwegs, b) *fig.* im *od.* in Gang; ***be in a fair*** (*od.* ***good***) ***~*** auf dem besten Wege sein, die besten Möglichkeiten haben; ***come*** (***in***) ***s.o.'s ~*** *bsd. fig.* j-m über den Weg laufen, j-m begegnen; ***go a long ~ to***(***wards***) viel dazu beitragen zu, ein gutes Stück weiterhelfen bei; ***go s.o.'s ~*** a) den gleichen Weg gehen wie j-d, b) j-n begleiten; ***go one's ~***(***s***) seinen Weg gehen, *fig.* s-n Lauf nehmen; ***have a ~ with*** mit *j-m* umzugehen wissen; ***have one's own ~*** s-n Willen durchsetzen; ***if I had my*** (***own***) ***~*** wenn es nach mir ginge; ***have it your ~!*** du sollst recht haben!; ***you can't have it both ~s*** du kannst nicht beides haben; ***know one's ~ about*** sich auskennen (*fig.* ***in*** mit); ***lead the ~*** (*a. fig.* mit gutem Beispiel) vorangehen; ***learn the hard ~*** Lehrgeld bezahlen müssen; ***make ~*** a) Platz machen (***for*** für), b) vorwärtskommen (*a. fig. Fortschritte machen*); ***make one's ~*** sich durchsetzen, s-n Weg machen; → ***mend*** 2, ***pave***, ***pay*** 3; ***see one's ~ to do s.th.*** e-e Möglichkeit sehen, et. zu tun; ***work one's ~ through college*** sich sein Studium durch Nebenarbeit verdienen, Werkstudent sein; ***work one's ~ up*** *a. fig.* sich hocharbeiten.

way² [weɪ] *adv.* F weit *oben, unten etc.*: ***~ back*** weit entfernt; ***~ back in 1902*** (schon) damals im Jahre 1902.

ˈway|·bill *s.* **1.** Passaˈgierliste *f*; **2.** ⚚ Frachtbrief *m*, Begleitschein *m*; **ˈ~ˌfar·er** [-ˌfeərə] *s. obs.* Reisende(r) *m*, Wandersmann *m*; **ˈ~ˌfar·ing** [-ˌfeərɪŋ] *adj.* reisend, wandernd; **ˌ~ˈlay** *v/t.* [*irr.* → ***lay¹***] *j-m* auflauern; **ˈ~·leave** *s.* ⚖ *Brit.* Wegerecht *n*; **ˌ~-ˈout** *adj.* F **1.** exˈzentrisch, ausgefallen, ‚irr(e)'; **2.** ‚toll', ‚super'; **ˈ~·side I** *s.* Straßen-, Wegrand *m*: ***by the ~*** am Wege, am Straßenrand; ***fall by the ~*** *fig.* auf der Strecke bleiben; **II** *adj.* am Wege (stehend), an der Straße (gelegen): ***a ~ inn***.

way| sta·tion *s.* 🚂 *Am.* ˈZwischenstatiˌon *f*; **~ train** *s. Am.* Bummelzug *m*.

way·ward [ˈweɪwəd] *adj.* □ **1.** launisch, unberechenbar; **2.** eigensinnig, ˈwiderspenstig; ⚖ verwahrlost (*Jugendliche[r]*); **3.** ungeraten: ***a ~ son***; **ˈway·ward·ness** [-nɪs] *s.* **1.** ˈWiderspenstigkeit *f*, Eigensinn *m*; **2.** Launenhaftigkeit *f*.

ˈway·worn *adj.* reisemüde.

we [wiː; wɪ] *pron. pl.* wir *pl.*

weak [wiːk] *adj.* □ **1.** *allg.* schwach (*a. zahlenmäßig*) (*a. fig. Argument, Spieler, Stil, Stimme etc.*; *a. ling.*): ***~ in Latin*** *fig.* schwach in Latein; → ***sex*** 2; **2.** ⚕ schwach: a) empfindlich, b) kränklich; **3.** (chaˈrakter)schwach, laˈbil, schwächlich: ***~ point*** (*od.* ***side***) schwacher Punkt, schwache Seite, Schwäche *f*; **4.** schwach, dünn (*Tee etc.*); **5.** ⚚ schwach, flau (*Markt*); **ˈweak·en** [-kən] **I** *v/t.* **1.** *j-n od. et.* schwächen; **2.** *Getränk etc.* verdünnen; **3.** *fig. Beweis etc.* abschwächen, entkräften; **II** *v/i.* **4.** schwach *od.* schwächer werden, nachlassen, erlahmen; **ˈweak·en·ing** [-knɪŋ] *s.* (Ab)Schwächung *f*.

ˌweak-ˈkneed *adj.* F **1.** feig; **2.** → ***weak-minded*** 2.

weak·ling [ˈwiːklɪŋ] *s.* Schwächling *m*; **ˈweak·ly** [-lɪ] **I** *adj.* schwächlich; **II** *adv. von* ***weak***; **ˌweak-ˈmind·ed** *adj.* **1.** schwachsinnig; **2.** chaˈrakterschwach.

weak·ness [ˈwiːknɪs] *s.* **1.** *allg.* (*a.* Chaˈrakter)Schwäche *f*; **2.** Schwächlichkeit *f*, Kränklichkeit *f*; **3.** schwache Seite, schwacher Punkt; **4.** Nachteil *m*, Schwäche *f*, Mangel *m*; **5.** F Schwäche *f*, Vorliebe *f* (***for*** für); **6.** ⚚ Flauheit *f*.

ˌweak|-ˈsight·ed *adj.* ⚕ schwachsichtig; **ˌ~-ˈspir·it·ed** *adj.* kleinmütig.

weal¹ [wiːl] *s.* Wohl *n*: ***~ and woe*** *das* Wohl u. Wehe, gute u. schlechte Tage; ***the public*** (*od.* ***common*** *od.* ***general***) ***~*** das Allgemeinwohl.

weal² [wiːl] *s.* Schwiele *f*, Strieme(n *m*) *f* (*auf der Haut*).

wealth [welθ] *s.* **1.** Reichtum *m* (*a. fig. Fülle*) (***of*** an *dat.*, von); **2.** Reichtümer *pl.*; **3.** ⚚ a) Besitz *m*, Vermögen *n*: ***~ tax*** Vermögenssteuer *f*, b) *a.* ***personal ~*** Wohlstand *m*; **ˈwealth·y** [-θɪ] *adj.* □ reich (*a. fig.* ***in*** an *dat.*), wohlhabend.

wean [wiːn] *v/t.* **1.** *Kind, junges Tier* entwöhnen; **2.** *a.* ***~ away from*** *fig. j-n* abbringen von, *j-m et.* abgewöhnen.

weap·on [ˈwepən] *s.* Waffe *f* (*a.* ⚘, *zo. u. fig.*); **ˈweap·on·less** [-lɪs] *adj.* wehrlos, unbewaffnet; **ˈweap·on·ry** [-rɪ] *s.* Waffen *pl.*

wear¹ [weə] **I** *v/t.* [*irr.*] **1.** *am Körper* tragen (*a. Bart, Brille, a. Trauer*), *Kleidungsstück a.* anhaben, *Hut a.* aufhaben: ***~ the breeches*** (*od.* ***trousers*** *od.* ***pants***) F *fig.* die Hosen anhaben (*Ehefrau*); ***she ~s her years well*** *fig.* sie sieht jung aus für ihr Alter; ***~ one's hair long*** das Haar lang tragen; **2.** *Lächeln, Miene etc.* zur Schau tragen, zeigen; **3.** ***~ away*** (*od.* ***down***, ***off***, ***out***)

Kleid etc. abnutzen, abtragen, *Absätze* abtreten, *Stufen etc.* austreten; *Löcher* reißen (***in*** in *acc.*): ***~ into holes*** ganz abtragen, *Schuhe* durchlaufen; **4.** eingraben, nagen: ***a groove worn by water***; **5.** *a.* ***~ away*** *Gestein etc.* auswaschen, -höhlen; *Farbe etc.* verwischen; **6.** *a.* ***~ out*** ermüden, *a. Geduld* erschöpfen; → ***welcome*** 1; **7.** *a.* ***~ down*** zermürben: a) entkräften, b) *fig.* niederringen, *Widerstand* brechen: ***worn to a shadow*** nur noch ein Schatten (*Person*); **II** *v/i.* [*irr.*] **8.** halten, haltbar sein: ***~ well*** a) sehr haltbar sein (*Stoff etc.*), sich gut tragen (*Kleid etc.*), b) *fig.* sich gut halten, wenig altern (*Person*); **9.** *a.* ***~ away*** (*od.* ***down***, ***off***, ***out***) sich abtragen *od.* abnutzen, verschleißen: ***~ away*** *a.* sich verwischen; ***~ off*** *fig.* sich verlieren (*Eindruck*, *Wirkung*); ***~ out*** *fig.* sich erschöpfen; ***~ thin*** a) fadenscheinig werden, b) sich erschöpfen (*Geduld etc.*); **10.** *a.* ***~ away*** langsam vergehen, da'hinschleichen (*Zeit*): ***~ to an end*** schleppend zu Ende gehen; **11.** ***~ on*** sich da'hinschleppen (*Zeit*, *Geschichte etc.*); **III** *s.* **12.** Tragen *n*: ***clothes for everyday ~*** Alltagskleidung *f*; ***have in constant ~*** ständig tragen; **13.** (Be)Kleidung *f*, Mode *f*: ***be the ~*** Mode sein, getragen werden; **14.** Abnutzung *f*, Verschleiß *m*: ***~ and tear*** a) ⚙ Abnutzung, Verschleiß (*a. fig.*), b) ✝ Abschreibung *f* für Wertminderung; ***for hard ~*** strapazierfähig; ***the worse for ~*** abgetragen, mitgenommen (*a. fig.*); **15.** Haltbarkeit *f*: ***there is still a great deal of ~ in it*** das läßt sich noch gut tragen.

wear² [weə] ⚓ **I** *v/t.* [*irr.*] *Schiff* halsen; **II** *v/i.* [*irr.*] vor dem Wind drehen (*Schiff*).

wear·a·ble ['weərəbl] *adj.* tragbar (*Kleid*).

wea·ri·ness ['wɪərɪnɪs] *s.* **1.** Müdigkeit *f*; **2.** *fig.* 'Überdruß *m*.

wear·ing ['weərɪŋ] *adj.* **1.** Kleidungs...; **2.** abnützend; **3.** ermüdend, zermürbend.

wea·ri·some ['wɪərɪsəm] *adj.* □ ermüdend (*mst fig. langweilig*).

ˌ**wear-re'sist·ant** *adj.* strapa'zierfähig.

wea·ry ['wɪərɪ] **I** *adj.* □ **1.** müde, matt (***with*** von, vor *dat.*); **2.** müde, 'überdrüssig (***of*** *gen.*): ***~ of life*** lebensmüde; **3.** ermüdend: a) beschwerlich, b) langweilig; **II** *v/t.* **4.** ermüden (*a. fig. langweilen*); **III** *v/i.* **5.** überdrüssig *od.* müde werden (***of*** *gen.*).

wea·sel ['wi:zl] *s.* **1.** *zo.* Wiesel *n*; **2.** F *contp.* ,Schlange' *f*, ,Ratte' *f*.

weath·er ['weðə] **I** *s.* **1.** a) Wetter *n*, Witterung *f*, b) Unwetter *n*: ***in fine ~*** bei schönem Wetter; ***make good*** (*od.* ***bad***) ***~*** ⚓ auf gutes (schlechtes) Wetter stoßen; ***make heavy ~ of s.th.*** *fig.* ,viel Wind machen' um et.; ***under the ~*** F a) nicht in Form (*unpäßlich*), b) e-n Katzenjammer habend, c) ,angesäuselt'; **2.** ⚓ Luv-, Windseite *f*; **II** *v/t.* **3.** dem Wetter aussetzen, *Holz etc.* auswittern; *geol.* verwittern (lassen); **4.** a) ⚓ *den Sturm* abwettern, b) *a.* ***~ out*** *fig. Sturm*, *Krise etc.* über'stehen; **5.** ⚓ luvwärts um'schiffen; **III** *v/i.* **6.** *geol.* verwittern; '**~-ˌbeat·en** *adj.* **1.** vom Wetter mitgenommen; **2.** verwittert; **3.** wetterhart; '**~·board** *s.* **1.** ⚙ a) Wasserschenkel *m*, b) Schal-, Schindelbrett *n*, c) *pl.* Verschalung *f*; **2.** ⚓ Waschbord *n*; '**~·board·ing** *s.* Verschalung *f*; '**~-bound** *adj.* schlechtwetterbehindert; **~ bureau** *s.* Wetteramt *n*; **~ chart** *s.* Wetterkarte *f*; '**~·cock** *s.* **1.** Wetterhahn *m*; **2.** *fig.* wetterwendische Per'son; '**~-eye** [-aɪ] *s.*: ***keep one's ~ open*** *fig.* gut aufpassen; **~ fore·cast** *s.* 'Wetterbericht *m*, -vorˌhersage *f*; '**~·man** [-mæn] *s.* [*irr.*] F **1.** Meteoro'loge *m*; **2.** Wetteransager *m*; '**~·proof** *adj.* wetterfest; **~ sat·el·lite** *s.* 'Wettersatelˌlit *m*; **~ side** *s.* **1.** → ***weather*** 2; **2.** Wetterseite *f*; **~ sta·tion** *s.* Wetterwarte *f*; **~ strip** *s.* Dichtungsleiste *f*; **~ vane** *s.* Wetterfahne *f*; '**~-worn** → ***weather-beaten***.

weave [wi:v] **I** *v/t.* [*irr.*] **1.** weben, wirken; **2.** zs.-weben, flechten; **3.** (ein-)flechten (***into*** in *acc.*), verweben, -flechten (***with*** mit, ***into*** zu) (*a. fig.*); **4.** *fig.* ersinnen, erfinden; **II** *v/i.* [*irr.*] **5.** weben; **6.** hin- u. herpendeln (*a. Boxer*), sich schlängeln *od.* winden; **7.** ***get weaving*** *Brit.* F ,sich ranhalten'; **III** *s.* **8.** Gewebe *n*; **9.** Webart *f*; '**weav·er** [-və] *s.* **1.** Weber(in); Wirker(in); **2.** *a.* ***~-bird*** *orn.* Webervogel *m*; '**weav·ing** [-vɪŋ] **I** *s.* Weben *n*, Webe'rei *f*; **II** *adj.* Web...: ***~ loom*** Webstuhl *m*; ***~ mill*** Weberei *f*.

wea·zen ['wi:zn] → ***wizen***.

web [web] *s.* **1.** a) Gewebe *n*, Gespinst *n*, b) Netz *n* (*der Spinne etc.*) (*alle a. fig.*): ***a ~ of lies*** ein Lügengewebe; **2.** Gurt(band *n*) *m*; **3.** *zo.* a) Schwimm-, Flughaut *f*, b) Bart *m e-r Feder*; **4.** ⚙ Sägeblatt *n*; **5.** (Pa'pier- *etc.*)Bahn *f*, (-)Rolle *f*; **webbed** [webd] *adj. zo.* schwimmhäutig: ***~ foot*** Schwimmfuß *m*; **web·bing** ['webɪŋ] *s.* **1.** Gewebe *n*; **2.** → ***web*** 2.

'**web|·foot** *s.* [*irr.*] *zo.* Schwimmfuß *m*; '**~-ˌfoot·ed**, '**~-toed** *adj.* schwimmfüßig.

wed [wed] **I** *v/t.* **1.** *rhet.* ehelichen, heiraten: ***~ded bliss*** eheliches Glück; **2.** vermählen (***to*** mit); **3.** *fig.* eng verbinden (***with***, ***to*** mit): ***be ~ded to s.th.*** a) an et. fest gebunden *od.* gekettet sein, b) sich e-r Sache verschrieben haben; **II** *v/i.* **4.** sich vermählen.

we'd [wi:d; wɪd] F *für* a) ***we would***, ***we should***, b) ***we had***.

wed·ding ['wedɪŋ] *s.* Hochzeit *f*, Trauung *f*; **~ an·ni·ver·sa·ry** *s.* (*dritter etc.*) Hochzeitstag; **~ break·fast** *s.* Hochzeitsessen *n*; **~ cake** *s.* Hochzeitskuchen *m*; **~ day** *s.* Hochzeitstag *m*; **~ dress** *s.* Hochzeits-, Brautkleid *n*; **~ ring** *s.* Trauring *m*.

we·del ['wedl] *v/i. Skisport*: wedeln.

wedge [wedʒ] **I** *s.* **1.** ⚙ Keil *m* (*a. fig.*): ***~ writing*** Keilschrift *f*; ***the thin end of the ~*** *fig.* ein erster kleiner Anfang; **2.** a) keilförmiges Stück (*Land etc.*), b) Ecke *f* (*Käse etc.*), c) Stück *n* (*Kuchen*); **3.** ⚔ 'Keil(formatiˌon *f*) *m*; **4.** *Golf*: Wedge *m* (*Schläger*); **II** *v/t.* **5.** ⚙ a) verkeilen, festklemmen, b) (mit e-m Keil) spalten: ***~ off*** abspalten; **6.** (ein-)keilen, (-)zwängen (***in*** in *acc.*): ***~ o.s. in*** sich hineinzwängen; **~ (fric·tion) gear** *s.* ⚙ Keilrädergetriebe *n*; **~ heel** *s.* (Schuh *m* mit) Keilabsatz *m*; '**~-shaped** *adj.* keilförmig.

wed·lock ['wedlɒk] *s.* Ehe(stand *m*) *f*: ***born in lawful*** (***out of***) ***~*** ehelich (unehelich) geboren.

Wednes·day ['wenzdɪ] *s.* Mittwoch *m*: ***on ~*** am Mittwoch; ***on ~s*** mittwochs.

wee¹ [wi:] *adj.* klein, winzig: ***a ~ bit*** ein klein wenig; ***the ~ hours*** die frühen Morgenstunden.

wee² [wi:] F **I** *s.* ,Pi'pi' *n*; **II** *v/i.* ,Pi'pi machen'.

weed [wi:d] **I** *s.* **1.** Unkraut *n*: ***ill ~s grow apace*** Unkraut verdirbt nicht; ***~ killer*** Unkrautvertilgungsmittel *n*; **2.** F a) ,Glimmstengel' *m* (*Zigarre*, *Zigarette*), b) ,Kraut' *n* (*Tabak*), c) ,Grass' *n* (*Marihuana*); **3.** *sl.* Kümmerling *m* (*schwächliches Tier*, *a. Person*); **II** *v/t.* **4.** *Unkraut od. Garten etc.* jäten; **5.** ***~ out***, ***~ up*** *fig.* aussondern, -merzen; **6.** *fig.* säubern; **III** *v/i.* **7.** (Unkraut) jäten; '**weed·er** [-də] *s.* **1.** Jäter *m*; **2.** ⚙ Jätwerkzeug *n*; **weed kil·ler** *s.* Unkrautvertilgungsmittel *n*.

weeds [wi:dz] *s. pl. mst* ***widow's ~*** Witwen-, Trauerkleidung *f*.

weed·y ['wi:dɪ] *adj.* **1.** voll Unkraut; **2.** unkrautartig; **3.** F a) schmächtig, b) schlaksig, c) klapperig.

week [wi:k] *s.* Woche *f*: ***by the ~*** wochenweise; ***for ~s*** wochenlang; ***today ~***, ***this day ~*** a) heute in 8 Tagen, b) heute vor 8 Tagen; '**~·day** **I** *s.* Wochen-, Werktag *m*: ***on ~s*** werktags; **II** *adj.* Werktags...; ˌ**~'end** **I** *s.* Wochenende *n*; **II** *adj.* Wochenend...: ***~ speech*** Sonntagsrede *f*; ***~ ticket*** Sonntags(rückfahr)karte *f*; **III** *v/i.* das Wochenende verbringen; ˌ**~'end·er** [-'endə] *s.* Wochenendausflügler(in); '**~-ends** *adv. Am.* an Wochenenden.

week·ly ['wi:klɪ] **I** *adj. u. adv.* wöchentlich; **II** *s. a.* ***~ paper*** Wochenzeitung *f*, -(zeit)schrift *f*.

wee·ny ['wi:nɪ] *adj.* F winzig.

weep [wi:p] **I** *v/i.* [*irr.*] **1.** weinen, Tränen vergießen (***for*** vor *Freude etc.*, um *j-n*): ***~ at*** (*od.* ***over***) weinen über (*acc.*); **2.** a) triefen, b) tröpfeln, c) ⚕ nässen (*Wunde etc.*); **3.** trauern (*Baum*); **II** *v/t.* [*irr.*] **4.** *Tränen* vergießen, weinen; **5.** beweinen; **III** *s.* **6.** ***have a good ~*** F sich tüchtig ausweinen; '**weep·er** [-pə] *s.* **1.** Weinende(r *m*) *f*, *bsd.* Klageweib *n*; **2.** a) Trauerbinde *f od.* -flor *m*, b) *pl.* Witwenschleier *m*; '**weep·ie** → ***weepy*** 3; '**weep·ing** [-pɪŋ] **I** *adj.* □ **1.** weinend; **2.** ⚘ Trauer...: ***~ willow*** Trauerweide *f*; **3.** triefend, tropfend; **4.** ⚕ nässend; **II** *s.* **5.** Weinen *n*; '**wee·py** ['wi:pɪ] F **I** *adj.* **1.** weinerlich; **2.** rührselig; **II** *s.* **3.** ,Schnulze' *f*.

wee·vil ['wi:vɪl] *s. zo.* **1.** Rüsselkäfer *m*; **2.** *allg.* Getreidekäfer *m*.

'**wee·wee** → ***wee²***.

weft [weft] *s. Weberei*: a) Einschlag(faden) *m*, Schuß(faden) *m*, b) Gewebe *n* (*a. poet.*).

weigh¹ [weɪ] **I** *s.* **1.** Wiegen *n*; **II** *v/t.* **2.** (ab)wiegen (***by*** nach); **3.** (*in der Hand*) wiegen; **4.** *fig.* (sorgsam) er-, abwägen (***with***, ***against*** gegen): ***~ one's words*** s-e Worte abwägen; **5.** ***~ anchor*** ⚓ a) den Anker lichten, b) auslaufen (*Schiff*); **6.** (nieder)drücken; **III** *v/i.* **7.** wiegen, *2 Kilo etc.* schwer sein; **8.** *fig. schwer etc.* wiegen, ins Gewicht fallen, ausschlaggebend sein (***with s.o.*** bei j-m): **~ *against s.o.*** a) gegen j-n sprechen, b) gegen j-n ins Feld geführt werden; **9.** *fig.* lasten (**on**, **upon** auf *dat.*); *Zssgn mit adv.*:

weigh| down *v/t.* niederdrücken (*a. fig.*); **~ in I** *v/t.* **1.** ✈ *sein Gepäck* wiegen lassen; **2.** *sport* a) *Jockei* nach dem Rennen wiegen, b) *Boxer, Gewichtheber etc.* vor dem Kampf wiegen; **II** *v/i.* **3.** ✈ sein Gepäck wiegen lassen; **4.** *sport* gewogen werden: ***he ~ed in at 200 pounds*** er brachte 200 Pfund auf die Waage; **5.** a) eingreifen, sich einschalten, b) **~ *with*** *Argument etc.* vorbringen; **~ out I** *v/t.* **1.** *Ware* auswiegen; **2.** *sport Jockei* vor dem Rennen wiegen; **II** *v/i.* **3.** *sport* gewogen werden.

weigh² [weɪ] *s.*: ***get under ~*** ⚓ unter Segel gehen.

ˈweigh·bridge *s.* Brückenwaage *f.*

weigh·er [ˈweɪə] *s.* **1.** Wäger *m*, Waagemeister *m*; **2.** → **weigh·ing ma·chine** [ˈweɪɪŋ] *s.* ⚙ Waage *f.*

weight [weɪt] **I** *s.* **1.** Gewicht *n* (*a. Maß u. Gegenstand*): ***~s and measures*** Maße u. Gewichte; ***by ~*** nach Gewicht; ***under ~*** ⚒ untergewichtig, zu leicht; ***lose*** (***put on***) **~** *an Körpergewicht* ab-(zu)nehmen; ***pull one's ~*** *fig.* sein(en) Teil leisten; ***throw one's ~ about*** F sich aufspielen *od.* ‚breitmachen'; ***that takes a ~ off my mind*** da fällt mir ein Stein vom Herzen; **2.** *fig.* Gewicht *n*: a) Last *f*, Wucht *f*, b) (*Sorgen- etc.*)Last *f*, Bürde *f*, c) Bedeutung *f*, d) Einfluß *m*, Geltung *f*: ***of ~*** gewichtig, schwerwiegend; ***men of ~*** bedeutende *od.* einflußreiche Leute; ***the ~ of evidence*** die Last des Beweismaterials; ***add ~ to*** *e-r Sache* Gewicht verleihen; ***carry*** (*od.* ***have***) **~ *with*** viel gelten bei; ***give ~ to*** *e-r Sache* große Bedeutung beimessen; **3.** *sport* a) *a.* **~ *category*** Gewichtsklasse *f*, b) Gewicht *n* (*Gerät*), c) (Stoß)Kugel *f*; **II** *v/t.* **4.** a) beschweren, b) belasten (*a. fig.*): **~ *the scales in favo(u)r of s.o.*** j-m e-n (unerlaubten) Vorteil verschaffen; **5.** ⚒ *Stoffe etc.* durch Beimischung *von Mineralien etc.* schwerer machen; **ˈweight·i·ness** [-tɪnɪs] *s.* Gewicht *n*, *fig. a.* (Ge)Wichtigkeit *f.*

weight·less [ˈweɪtlɪs] *adj.* schwerelos; **ˈweight·less·ness** [-nɪs] *s.* Schwerelosigkeit *f.*

weight| lift·er *s. sport* Gewichtheber *m*; **~ lift·ing** *s. sport* Gewichtheben *n*; **~ watch·er** *s.* j-d, der auf sein Gewicht achtet.

weight·y [ˈweɪtɪ] *adj.* □ **1.** schwer, gewichtig, *fig. a.* schwerwiegend; **2.** *fig.* einflußreich, gewichtig (*Person*).

weir [wɪə] *s.* **1.** (Stau)Wehr *n*; **2.** Fischreuse *f.*

weird [wɪəd] *adj.* □ **1.** *poet.* Schicksals...: **~ *sisters*** Schicksalsschwestern, Nornen; **2.** unheimlich; **3.** F ulkig, ‚verrückt'; **weir·do** [ˈwɪədəʊ] *pl.* **-dos** *s.* F ‚irrer Typ'.

welch [welʃ] → ***welsh²***.

wel·come [ˈwelkəm] **I** *s.* **1.** Willkomm(-en *n*) *m*, Empfang *m* (*a. iro.*): ***bid s.o. ~*** → 2; ***outstay*** (*od.* ***overstay*** *od.* ***wear out***) ***one's ~*** länger bleiben als man erwünscht ist; **II** *v/t.* **2.** bewillkommnen, willˈkommen heißen; **3.** *fig.* begrüßen: a) *et.* gutheißen, b) gern annehmen; **III** *adj.* **4.** willkommen, angenehm (*Gast, a. Nachricht etc.*): ***make s.o. ~*** j-n herzlich empfangen *od.* aufnehmen; **5.** ***you are ~ to it*** Sie können es gerne behalten *od.* nehmen, es steht zu Ihrer Verfügung; ***you are ~ to do it*** es steht Ihnen frei, es zu tun; das können Sie gerne tun; ***you are ~ to your own opinion*** *iro.* meinetwegen können Sie denken, was Sie wollen; (***you are***) **~!** nichts zu danken!, keine Ursache!, bitte (sehr)!; ***and ~*** *iro.* meinetwegen, wenn's Ihnen Spaß macht; **IV** *int.* **6.** willˈkommen (***to*** in *England etc.*).

weld [weld] **I** *v/t.* ⚙ (ver-, zs.-)schweißen: **~ *on*** anschweißen (***to*** an *acc.*); **~ *together*** zs.-schweißen, *fig. a.* zs.-schmieden; **II** *v/i.* ⚙ sich schweißen lassen; **III** *s.* ⚙ Schweißstelle *f*, -naht *f*; **ˈweld·a·ble** [-dəbl] *adj.* schweißbar; **ˈweld·ed** [-dɪd] *adj.* geschweißt, Schweiß...: **~ *joint*** Schweißverbindung *f*; **ˈweld·er** [-də] *s.* ⚙ **1.** Schweißer *m*; **2.** Schweißbrenner *m*, -gerät *n*; **ˈweld·ing** [-dɪŋ] *adj.* Schweiß...

wel·fare [ˈwelfeə] *s.* **1.** Wohl *n*, *e-r Person*: *a.* Wohlergehen *n*; **2.** a) (***public***) **~** (öffentliche) Wohlfahrt, b) *Am.* Soziˈalhilfe *f*: ***be on ~*** Sozialhilfe beziehen; **~ state** *s. pol.* Wohlfahrtsstaat *m*; **~ stat·ism** [ˈsteɪtɪzəm] → ***welfarism***; **~ work** *s. Am.* Soziˈalarbeit *f*; **~ work·er** *s. Am.* Soziˈalarbeiter(in).

wel·far·ism [ˈwelfeərɪzəm] *s.* wohlfahrtsstaatliche Poliˈtik.

wel·kin [ˈwelkɪn] *s. poet.* Himmelszelt *n*: ***make the ~ ring with shouts*** die Luft mit Geschrei erfüllen.

well¹ [wel] **I** *adv.* **1.** gut, wohl: ***be ~ off*** a) gut versehen sein (***for*** mit), b) wohlhabend *od.* gut daran sein; ***do o.s.*** (*od.* ***live***) **~** gut leben, es sich wohl sein lassen; ***be ~ up in*** bewandert sein in *e-m Fach etc.*; **2.** gut, recht, geschickt: ***do ~*** gut *od.* recht daran tun (***to do*** zu tun); ***sing ~*** gut singen; **~ *done!*** gut gemacht!, bravo!; **~ *roared, lion!*** gut gebrüllt, Löwe!; **3.** gut, freundschaftlich: ***think*** (*od.* ***speak***) **~ *of*** gut denken (*od.* sprechen) über (*acc.*); **4.** gut, sehr: ***love s.o. ~*** j-n sehr lieben; ***it speaks ~ for him*** es spricht sehr für ihn; **5.** wohl, mit gutem Grund: ***one may ~ ask this question*** man kann wohl *od.* mit gutem Grund so fragen; ***you cannot very ~ do that*** das kannst du nicht gut tun; ***not very ~*** wohl kaum; **6.** recht, eigentlich: ***he does not know ~ how*** er weiß nicht recht wie; **7.** gut, genau, gründlich: ***know s.o. ~*** j-n gut kennen; ***he knows only too ~*** er weiß nur zu gut; **8.** gut, ganz, völlig: ***he is ~ out of sight*** er ist völlig außer Sicht; **9.** gut, beträchtlich, weit: **~ *away*** weit weg; ***he walked ~ ahead of them*** er ging ihnen ein gutes Stück voraus; ***until ~ past midnight*** bis lange nach Mitternacht; **10.** gut, tüchtig, gründlich: ***stir ~***; **11.** gut, mit Leichtigkeit: ***you could ~ have done it*** du hättest es leicht tun können; ***it is very ~ possible*** es ist durchaus *od.* sehr wohl möglich; ***as ~*** ebenso, außerdem; (***just***) ***as ~*** ebenso (-gut), genauso(gut); ***as ~ ... as*** sowohl ... als auch, nicht nur ... sondern auch; ***as ~ as*** ebensogut wie; **II** *adj.* **12.** wohl, gesund: ***be*** (*od.* ***feel***) **~** sich wohl fühlen; **13.** in Ordnung, richtig, gut: ***I am very ~ where I am*** ich fühle mich hier sehr wohl; ***it is all very ~ but*** *iro.* das ist ja alles schön u. gut, aber; **14.** gut, günstig: ***that is just as ~*** das ist schon gut so; ***very ~*** sehr wohl, nun gut; **~ *and good*** schön und gut; **15.** ratsam, richtig, gut: ***it would be ~*** es wäre angebracht *od.* ratsam; **III** *int.* **16.** nun, na, schön: **~!** (*empört*) na, hör mal!; **~ *then*** nun (also); **~ *then?*** (*erwartend*) na, und?; **~, ~!** so, so!, (*beruhigend*) schon gut; **17.** (*überlegend*) (t)ja, hm; **IV** *s.* **18.** *das* Gute: ***let ~ alone!*** laß gut sein!, laß die Finger davon!

well² [wel] **I** *s.* **1.** (*gegrabener*) Brunnen, Ziehbrunnen *m*; **2.** *a. fig.* Quelle *f*; **3.** a) Mineˈralbrunnen *m*, b) *pl.* (*in Ortsnamen*) Bad *n*; **4.** *fig.* (Ur)Quell *m*; **5.** ⚙ a) (Senk-, Öl- *etc.*)Schacht *m*, b) Bohrloch *n*; **6.** Δ a) Fahrstuhl-, Luft-, Lichtschacht *m*, b) (Raum *m* für das) Treppenhaus *n*; **7.** ⚓ a) Pumpensod *m*, b) Fischbehälter *m*; **8.** ⚙ eingelassener Behälter: a) *mot.* Kofferraum *m*, b) Tintenbehälter *m*; **9.** ⚖ *Brit.* eingefriedigter Platz für Anwälte; **II** *v/i.* **10.** quellen (***from*** aus): **~ *up*** (*od.* ***forth***, ***out***) hervorquellen; **~ *over*** überfließen.

ˌwell|-adˈvised *adj.* ˈwohlüberˌlegt, klug; **ˌ~-apˈpoint·ed** *adj.* gutausgestattet; **ˌ~-ˈbal·anced** *adj. fig.* **1.** ausgewogen: **~ *diet***; **2.** (innerlich) ausgeglichen; **ˌ~-beˈhaved** *adj.* wohlerzogen, artig; **ˌ~-ˈbe·ing** *s.* **1.** Wohl(ergehen) *n*; **2.** *mst* ***sense of ~*** Wohlgefühl *n*; **ˌ~-beˈlov·ed** *adj.* vielgeliebt; **ˌ~-ˈborn** *adj.* von vornehmer Herkunft, aus guter Faˈmilie; **ˌ~-ˈbred** *adj.* **1.** wohlerzogen; **2.** gebildet, fein; **ˌ~-ˈcho·sen** *adj.* (gut-) gewählt, treffend: **~ *words***; **ˌ~-conˈnect·ed** *adj.* mit guten Beziehungen *od.* mit vornehmer Verwandtschaft; **ˌ~-diˈrect·ed** *adj.* wohl-, gutgezielt (*Schlag etc.*); **ˌ~-disˈposed** *adj.* wohlgesinnt; **ˌ~-ˈdone** *adj.* **1.** gutgemacht; **2.** ˈdurchgebraten (*Fleisch*); **ˌ~-ˈearned** *adj.* wohlverdient; **ˌ~-ˈfa·vo(u)red** *adj. obs.* gutaussehend, hübsch; **ˌ~-ˈfed** *adj.* gut-, wohlgenährt; **ˌ~-ˈfound·ed** *adj.* wohlbegründet; **ˌ~-ˈgroomed** *adj.* gepflegt; **ˌ~-ˈground·ed** *adj.* **1.** → ***well-founded***; **2.** mit guter Vorbildung (*in e-m Fach*).

ˈwell·head *s.* **1.** → ***wellspring***; **2.** Brunneneinfassung *f.*

ˌwell|-ˈheeled *adj.* F ‚(gut)betucht'; **ˌ~-inˈformed** *adj.* **1.** ˈgutunterˌrichtet; **2.** (vielseitig) gebildet.

Wel·ling·ton (**boot**) [ˈwelɪŋtən] *s.* Schaft-, Gummi-, Wasserstiefel *m.*

well|-in·ten·tioned [ˌwelɪnˈtenʃnd] *adj.* **1.** gut, wohlgemeint; **2.** wohlmeinend (*Person*); **ˌ~-ˈjudged** *adj.* wohlberechnet, angebracht; **ˌ~-ˈkept** *adj.* **1.** gepflegt; **2.** streng gehütet: **~ *secret***; **ˌ~-ˈknit** *adj.* **1.** drahtig (*Figur, Person*); **2.** ˈgutdurchˌdacht; **ˌ~-ˈknown** *adj.* **1.** weithin bekannt; **2.** wohlbekannt; **ˌ~-ˈmade** *adj.* **1.** gutgemacht; **2.** gutgewachsen, gutgebaut (*Person od. Tier*); **ˌ~-ˈman·nered** *adj.* wohlerzogen, mit guten Maˈnieren; **ˌ~-ˈmatched** *adj.* **1.** *sport* gleich stark; **2.** ***a ~ couple*** ein Paar, das gut zs.-paßt; **ˌ~-ˈmean·ing** → ***well-intentioned***; **ˌ~-ˈmeant** *adj.* gutgemeint; ˈ~-**nigh** *adv.* fast, so gut wie: ~ ***impossible***; ˌ~-ˈ**off** *adj.* wohlhabend, gutsituiert; ˌ~-ˈ**oiled** *adj. fig.* F **1.** gutfunktionierend; **2.** ziemlich ‚angesäuselt'; ˌ~-**proˈpor·tioned** *adj.* wohlproportioniert, gutgebaut; ˌ~-ˈ**read** [-ˈred] *adj.* (sehr) belesen; ˌ~-ˈ**reg·u·lat·ed** *adj.* wohlgeregelt, -geordnet; ˌ~-ˈ**round·ed** *adj.* **1.** (wohl)beleibt; **2.** *fig.* a) abgerundet, eleˈgant (*Stil*, *Form etc.*), b) ausgeglichen, c) vielseitig (*Bildung etc.*); ˌ~-ˈ**spent** *adj.* **1.** gutgenützt (*Zeit*); **2.** sinnvoll ausgegeben (*Geld*); ˌ~-ˈ**spo·ken** *adj.* **1.** redegewandt; **2.** höflich im Ausdruck.

ˈ**well·spring** *s.* Quelle *f*, *fig. a.* (Ur-)Quell *m*.

ˌ**well**|-ˈ**tem·pered** *adj.* **1.** gutmütig; **2.** ♪ wohltemperiert (*Klavier*, *Stimmung*); ˈ~-ˌ**thought-ˈout** *adj.* ˈwohlerwogen, -durchˌdacht; ˌ~-ˈ**timed** *adj.* (zeitlich) wohlberechnet; *sport* gutgetimed; ˌ~-**to-ˈdo** *adj.* wohlhabend; ˌ~-ˈ**tried** *adj.* (wohl)erprobt, bewährt; ˌ~-ˈ**turned** *adj. fig.* wohlgesetzt, eleˈgant (*Worte*); ˈ~-ˌ**wish·er** *s.* **1.** Gönner(in); **2.** Befürworter(in); **3.** *pl.* jubelnde Menge; ˌ~-ˈ**worn** *adj.* **1.** abgetragen, abgenutzt; **2.** *fig.* abgedroschen.

Welsh[1] [welʃ] **I** *adj.* **1.** waˈlisisch; **II** *s.* **2.** ***the*** ~ die Waˈliser *pl.*; **3.** *ling.* Waˈlisisch *n*.

welsh[2] [welʃ] *v/i.* F **1.** mit den (Wett-)Gewinnen ˈdurchgehen (*Buchmacher*): ~ ***on*** a) *j-n* um s-n (Wett)Gewinn betrügen, b) *j-n* ‚verschaukeln'; **2.** sich ‚drücken' (***on*** vor *dat.*).

Welsh cor·gy *s.* Welsh Corgi *m* (*walisische Hunderasse*).

welsh·er [ˈwelʃə] *s.* F **1.** betrügerischer Buchmacher; **2.** ‚falscher Hund'.

Welsh|·**man** [ˈwelʃmən] *s.* [*irr.*] Waˈliser *m*; ~ **rab·bit**, ~ **rare·bit** *s.* überˈbackene Käseschnitte.

welt [welt] **I** *s.* **1.** Einfassung *f*, Rand *m*; **2.** *Schneiderei*: a) (Zier)Borte *f*, b) Rollsaum *m*, c) Stoßkante *f*; **3.** Rahmen *m* (*Schuh*); **4.** a) Strieme(n *m*) *f*, b) F (heftiger) Schlag; **II** *v/t.* **5.** a) *Kleid etc.* einfassen, b) *Schuh* auf Rahmen arbeiten, c) *Blech* falzen: ~***ed*** randgenäht (*Schuh*); **6.** F ‚verdreschen'.

wel·ter [ˈweltə] **I** *v/i.* **1.** *poet.* sich wälzen (***in*** in *s-m Blut etc.*) (*a. fig.*); **II** *s.* **2.** Wogen *n*, Toben *n* (*Wellen etc.*); **3.** *fig.* Tuˈmult *m*, Durcheinˈander *n*, Wirrwarr *m*, Chaos *n*.

ˈ**wel·ter·weight** *s. sport* Weltergewicht (-ler *m*) *n*.

wen [wen] *s.* ⚕ (Balg)Geschwulst *f*, *bsd.* Grützbeutel *m am Kopf*: ***the great*** ~ *fig.* London *n*.

wench [wentʃ] **I** *s.* **1.** *obs. od. humor.* (*bsd.* Bauern)Mädchen *n*, Weibsbild *n*; **2.** *obs.* Hure *f*, Dirne *f*; **II** *v/i.* **3.** huren.

wend [wend] *v/t.* ~ ***one's way*** sich wenden, s-n Weg nehmen (***to*** nach, zu).

went [went] *pret. von* **go**.

wept [wept] *pret u. p.p. von* ***weep***.

were [wɜː; wə] **1.** *pret. von* **be**: *du* warst, *Sie* waren; *wir*, *sie* waren, *ihr* wart; **2.** *pret. pass.*: wurde(n); **3.** *subj. pret.* wäre(n).

were·wolf [ˈwɪəwʊlf] *s.* [*irr.*] Werwolf *m*.

west [west] **I** *s.* **1.** Westen *m*: ***the wind is coming from the*** ~ der Wind kommt von Westen; **2.** Westen *m* (*Landesteil*); **3.** ***the*** ♀ *geogr.* der Westen: a) Westengland *n*, b) die *amer.* Weststaaten *pl.*, c) das Abendland; **4.** *poet.* West (-wind) *m*; **II** *adj.* **5.** westlich, West...; **III** *adv.* **6.** westwärts, nach Westen: ***go*** ~ a) nach Westen *od.* westwärts gehen *od.* ziehen, b) *sl.* ‚draufgehen' (*sterben*, *kaputt- od. verlorengehen*); **7.** ~ ***of*** westlich von; ˈ**west·er·ly** [-təlɪ] **I** *adj.* westlich, West...; **II** *adv.* westwärts, gegen Westen.

west·ern [ˈwestən] **I** *adj.* **1.** westlich, West...: ***the*** ♀ ***Empire*** *hist.* das weströmische Reich; **2.** *oft* ♀ westlich, abendländisch; **3.** ♀ ˈwestameriˌkanisch, (Wild)West...; **II** *s.* **4.** → ***westerner***; **5.** Western *m*: a) Wildˈwestfilm *m*, b) Wildˈwestroˌman *m*; ˈ**west·ern·er** [-nə] *s.* **1.** Westländer *m*; **2.** *a.* ♀ *Am.* Weststaatler *m*; **3.** *oft* ♀ Abendländer *m*; ˈ**west·ern·ize** [-naɪz] *v/t.* verwestlichen; ˈ**west·ern·most** [-məʊst] *adj.* westlichst.

West In·di·an I *adj.* westˈindisch; **II** *s.* Westˈindier(in).

West·pha·li·an [westˈfeɪljən] **I** *adj.* westˈfälisch; **II** *s.* Westˈfale *m*, Westˈfälin *f*.

west·ward [ˈwestwəd] *adj. u. adv.* westlich, westwärts, nach Westen; ˈ**west·wards** [-dz] *adv.* → ***westward***.

wet [wet] **I** *adj.* **1.** naß, durchˈnäßt (***with*** von): ~ ***through*** durchnäßt; ~ ***to the skin*** naß bis auf die Haut; ~ ***blanket*** *fig.* a) Dämpfer *m*, kalte Dusche, b) Störenfried *m*, Spielverderber(in); fader Kerl; ***throw a*** ~ ***blanket on*** *e-r Sache* e-n Dämpfer aufsetzen; ~ ***paint!*** frisch gestrichen!; ~ ***steam*** ⚙ Naßdampf *m*; **2.** regnerisch, feucht (*Klima*); **3.** ⚙ naß, Naß...(*-gewinnung etc.*); **4.** *Am.* ‚feucht' (*nicht unter Alkoholverbot stehend*); **5.** F feuchtfröhlich; **6.** a) blöd, ‚doof', b) ***all*** ~ falsch, verkehrt: ***you are all*** ~***!*** du irrst dich gewaltig!; **II** *s.* **7.** Flüssigkeit *f*, Feuchtigkeit *f*, Nässe *f*; **8.** Regen(wetter *n*) *m*; **9.** F Drink *m*: ***have a*** ~ ‚einen heben'; **10.** *Am.* F Gegner *m* der Prohibitiˈon; **11.** F a) Blödmann *m*, b) *Brit.* Weichling *m*; **III** *v/t.* [*irr.*] **12.** benetzen, anfeuchten, naßmachen, nässen: ~ ***through*** durchnässen; → ***whistle*** 7; **13.** F *ein Ereignis etc.* ‚begießen': ~ ***a bargain***; ˈ~·**back** *s. Am. sl. illegaler Einwanderer aus Mexiko*; ~ **cell** *s.* ϟ ˈNaßeleˌment *n*; ~ **dock** *s.* ⚓ Flutbecken *n*.

weth·er [ˈweðə] *s. zo.* Hammel *m*.

wet·ness [ˈwetnɪs] *s.* Nässe *f*, Feuchtigkeit *f*.

ˈ**wet**| **nurse** *s.* (Säug)Amme *f*; ˈ~-**nurse** *v/t.* **1.** säugen; **2.** *fig.* verhätscheln; ~ **pack** *s.* ⚕ feuchter ˈUmschlag; ~ **suit** *s. sport* Kälteschutzanzug *m*.

wey [weɪ] *s. obs. ein Trockengewicht.*

whack [wæk] F **I** *v/t.* **1.** a) *j-m* e-n (knallenden) Schlag versetzen, b) *sport* F haushoch schlagen: ~***ed*** F ‚fertig', ‚geschafft'; **2.** ~ ***up*** F (auf)teilen; **3.** ~ ***up*** *Am.* F a) et. organisieren, b) *j-n* antreiben; **II** *s.* **4.** (knallender) Schlag; **5.** (An)Teil *m* (***of*** an *dat.*); **6.** Versuch *m*: ***take a*** ~ ***at*** e-n Versuch machen mit; **7.** ***out of*** ~ nicht in Ordnung; ˈ**whack·er** [-kə] *s. sl.* **1.** Mordsding *n*; **2.** faustdicke Lüge; ˈ**whack·ing** [-kɪŋ] **I** *adj. u. adv.* F Mords...; **II** *s.* F (Tracht *f*) Prügel *pl.*

whale [weɪl] **I** *pl.* **whales** *bsd. coll.* **whale** *s. zo.* Wal *m*: ***a*** ~ ***of*** F Riesen..., Mords...; ***a*** ~ ***of a lot*** e-e Riesenmenge; ***a*** ~ ***of a fellow*** F ein Riesenkerl; ***be a*** ~ ***for*** (*od.* ***on***) F ganz versessen sein auf (*acc.*); ***be a*** ~ ***at*** F e-e ‚Kanone' sein in (*dat.*); ***we had a*** ~ ***of a time*** wir hatten e-n Mordsspaß; **II** *v/i.* Walfang treiben; **III** *v/t.* F ‚verdreschen'; ˈ~·**bone** *s.* Fischbein(stab *m*) *n*; ~ **calf** *s.* [*irr.*] *zo.* junger Wal; ~ **fish·er·y** *s.* **1.** Walfang *m*; **2.** Walfanggebiet *n*; ~ **oil** *s.* Walfischtran *m*.

whal·er [ˈweɪlə] *s.* Walfänger *m* (*Person u. Boot*).

whal·ing[1] [ˈweɪlɪŋ] **I** *s.* Walfang *m*; **II** *adj.* Walfang...: ~ ***gun*** Harpunengeschütz *n*.

whal·ing[2] [ˈweɪlɪŋ] F **I** *adj. u. adv.* eˈnorm, Mords...; **II** *s.* (Tracht *f*) Prügel *pl.*

wham·my [ˈwæmɪ] *s.* F **1.** böser Blick; **2.** ‚Hammer' *m*: a) böse Sache, b) knallharter Schlag *etc.*

whang [wæŋ] F **I** *s.* Knall *m*, Krach *m*, Bums *m*; **II** *v/t.* knallen, hauen; **III** *v/i.* knallen (*a. schießen*), krachen, bumsen; **IV** *int.* krach!, bums!

wharf [wɔːf] ⚓ **I** *pl.* **wharves** [-vz] *od.* **wharfs** *s.* **1.** Kai *m*; **II** *v/t.* **2.** *Waren* löschen; **3.** *Schiff* am Kai festmachen; ˈ**wharf·age** [-fɪdʒ] *s.* **1.** Kaianlage(n *pl.*) *f*; **2.** Kaigeld *n*; ˈ**wharf·in·ger** [-fɪndʒə] *s.* ⚓ **1.** Kaimeister *m*; **2.** Kaibesitzer *m*.

what [wɒt] **I** *pron. interrog.* **1.** was, wie: ~ ***is her name?*** wie ist ihr Name?; ~ ***did he do?*** was hat er getan?; ~ ***is he?*** was ist er (von Beruf)?; ~***'s for lunch?*** was gibt's zum Mittagessen?; **2.** was für ein, welcher, *vor pl.* was für: ~ ***an idea!*** was für e-e Idee!; ~ ***book?*** was für ein Buch?; ~ ***luck!*** welch ein Glück!; **3.** was (*um Wiederholung e-s Wortes bittend*): ***he claims to be*** ~***?*** was will er sein?; **II** *pron. rel.* **4.** (das) was: ***this is*** ~ ***we hoped for*** (gerade) das erhofften wir; ***I don't know*** ~ ***he said*** ich weiß nicht, was er sagte; ***it is nothing compared to*** ~ ***...*** es ist nichts im Vergleich zu dem, was ...; **5.** was (auch immer); **III** *adj.* **6.** was für ein, welch: ***I don't know*** ~ ***decision you have taken*** ich weiß nicht, was für e-n Entschluß du gefaßt hast; **7.** alle *od.* jede die, alles was: ~ ***money I had*** was ich an Geld hatte, all mein Geld; **8.** soviel(e) ... wie;

Besondere Redewendungen:

and ~ ***not, and*** ~ ***have you*** F und was nicht sonst noch alles; ~ ***about?*** wie wär's mit *od.* wenn?, wie steht's mit?; ~ ***for?*** wozu?, wofür?; ~ ***if?*** und wenn nun?, (und) was geschieht, wenn?; ~ ***next?*** a) was sonst noch?, b) *iro.* sonst noch was?, das fehlte noch!; ~ ***news?*** was gibt es Neues?; (***well,***) ~ ***of it?, so*** ~***?*** na, und?, na, wenn schon?; ~ ***though?*** was tut's, wenn?; ~ ***with*** infolge, durch, in Anbetracht (*gen.*); ~ ***with ..., ~ with*** ... teils durch ..., teils durch ...; ***but*** ~ F daß (*nicht*); ***I know*** ~ F ich weiß was, ich habe e-e Idee; ***she knows*** ~***'s*** ~ F sie weiß Bescheid; sie weiß, was los ist; ***I'll tell you ~*** ich will dir (mal) was sagen.

what|-d'you-call-it [ˈwɒtdjʊˌkɔːlɪt] (*od.* **-'em** [-em] *od.* **-him** *od.* **-her**), **ˈ~-d'ye-ˌcall-it** [-djəˌkɔːlɪt] (*od.* **-'em** [-em] *od.* **-him** *od.* **-her**) *s.* F Dings(da, -bums) *m, f, n*; **~ˈe'er** *poet.* → ***whatever***; **~ˈev·er I** *pron.* **1.** was (auch immer), alles was: ***take ~ you like!***; ***~ you do*** was du auch tust; **2.** was auch; trotz allem, was: ***do it ~ happens!***; **3.** F was denn, was in aller Welt: ***~ do you want?*** was willst du denn?; **II** *adj.* **4.** welch … auch (immer): ***for ~ reasons he is angry*** aus welchen Gründen er auch immer ärgerlich ist; **5.** *mit neg.*: überˈhaupt, gar *nichts*, *niemand etc.*: ***no doubt ~*** überhaupt *od.* gar kein Zweifel; **ˈ~·not** *s.* Etaˈgere *f.*

what's [wɒts] F *für* ***what is***; **ˈ~-her-name** [-sənem], **ˈ~-his-name** [-sɪzneɪm], **ˈ~-its-name** *s.* F Dings(da) *m, f, n*: ***Mr. what's-his-name*** Herr Dingsda, Herr Soundso.

what·soˈev·er → ***whatever***.

wheal [wiːl] → ***wale***.

wheat [wiːt] *s.* ⚘ Weizen *m*: ***~ belt*** *geogr. Am.* Weizengürtel *m.*

whee·dle [ˈwiːdl] **I** *v/t.* **1.** *j-n* umˈschmeicheln; **2.** *j-n* beschwatzen, überˈreden (***into doing s.th.*** et. zu tun); **3.** ***~ s.th. out of s.o.*** j-m et. abschwatzen *od.* abschmeicheln; **II** *v/i.* **4.** schmeicheln; **ˈwhee·dling** [-lɪŋ] *adj.* □ schmeichlerisch.

wheel [wiːl] **I** *s.* **1.** *allg.* Rad *n* (*a.* ⚙): ***the ~s of government*** die Regierungsmaschinerie; ***the ~ of Fortune*** *fig.* das Glücksrad; ***~s within ~s*** *fig.* a) ein kompliziertes Räderwerk, b) e-e äußerst komplizierte *od.* schwer durchschaubare Sache; ***a big ~*** *Am.* F ein ‚großes Tier'; → ***fifth wheel, shoulder*** 1, ***spoke***[1] 4; **2.** ⚙ Scheibe *f*; **3.** Lenkrad *n*: ***at the ~*** a) am Steuer, b) *fig.* am Ruder; **4.** F a) (Fahr)Rad *n*, b) Auto *n*, ‚fahrbarer ˈUntersatz'; **5.** *hist.* Rad *n* (*Folterinstrument*): ***break s.o. on the ~*** j-n rädern *od.* aufs Rad flechten; ***break a (butter)fly (up)on the ~*** *fig.* mit Kanonen nach Spatzen schießen; **6.** *pl. fig.* Räder(werk *n*) *pl.*, Getriebe *n*; **7.** Drehung *f*, Kreis(bewegung *f*) *m*; ⚔ Schwenkung *f*: ***right (left) ~!*** rechts (links) schwenkt!; **II** *v/t.* **8.** *j-n od. et.* fahren, schieben, *et. a.* rollen; **9.** ⚔ schwenken lassen; **III** *v/i.* **10.** sich (im Kreis) drehen; **11.** *a.* ***~ about*** *od.* ***(a)round*** sich (rasch) ˈumwenden *od.* -drehen; **12.** ⚔ schwenken; **13.** rollen, fahren; **14.** F radeln; **ˈ~ˌbar·row** *s.* Schubkarre(n *m*) *f*; **ˈ~·base** *s.* ⚙ Radstand *m*; **~ brake** *s.* Radbremse *f*; **ˈ~·chair** *s.* Rollstuhl *m.*

wheeled [wiːld] *adj.* **1.** fahrbar, Roll…, Räder…: ***~ bed*** ⚕ Rollbett *n*; **2.** *in Zssgn* …räd(e)rig: ***three-~***.

wheel·er [ˈwiːlə] *s.* **1.** *in Zssgn* Fahrzeug *n* mit … Rädern: ***four-~*** Vierradwagen *m*, Zweiachser *m*; **2.** → ***wheel horse***; **3.** → **ˌ~-ˈdeal·er** *s. Am.* F ‚ausgekochter' Bursche, *a.* (raffinierter) Geschäftemacher; **ˌ~-ˈdeal·ing** *s.* F **1.** Machenschaften *pl.*; **2.** Geschäftemacheˈrei *f.*

wheel horse *s.* Stangen-, Deichselpferd *n.*

wheel·ing and deal·ing [ˈwiːlɪŋ] → ***wheeler-dealing***.

ˈwheel·wright [-raɪt] *s.* ⚙ Stellmacher *m.*

wheeze [wiːz] **I** *v/i.* **1.** keuchen, schnaufen; **II** *v/t.* **2.** *a.* ***~ out*** *et.* keuchen(d herˈvorstoßen); **III** *s.* **3.** Keuchen *n*, Schnaufen *n*, pfeifendes Atmen *od.* Geräusch; **4.** *sl.* a) *thea.* (improvisierter) Scherz, Gag *m*, b) Jux *m*, Ulk *m*, c) alter Witz; **ˈwheez·y** [-zɪ] *adj.* □ keuchend, asthˈmatisch (*a. humor. Orgel etc.*).

whelk[1] [welk] *s. zo.* Wellhorn(schnecke *f*) *n.*

whelk[2] [welk] *s.* ⚕ Pustel *f.*

whelm [welm] *v/t. poet.* **1.** ver-, überˈschütten, versenken, -schlingen; **2.** *fig.* a) überˈschütten *od.* -ˈhäufen (***in, with*** mit), b) überˈwältigen.

whelp [welp] **I** *s.* **1.** *zo.* a) Welpe *m* (*junger Hund, Fuchs od. Wolf*), b) *allg.* Junge(s) *n*; **2.** Balg *m, n* (*ungezogenes Kind*); **II** *v/t. u. v/i.* **3.** (Junge) werfen.

when [wen] **I** *adv.* **1.** *fragend*: wann; **2.** *relativ*: als, wo, da: ***the years ~ we were poor*** die Jahre, als wir arm waren; ***the day ~*** der Tag, an dem *od.* als; **II** *cj.* **3.** wann: ***she doesn't know ~ to be silent*** sie weiß nicht, wann sie schweigen muß; **4.** zu der Zeit *od.* in dem Augenblick, als: ***~ (he was) young, he lived in M.*** als er noch jung war, wohnte er in M.; ***we were about to start ~ it began to rain*** wir wollten gerade fortgehen, als es anfing zu regnen *od.* da fing es an zu regnen; ***say ~!*** F sag halt!, sag, wenn du genug hast! (*bsd. beim Eingießen*); **5.** (dann,) wenn; **6.** (immer) wenn, soˈbald, soˈoft; **7.** woraufˈhin, und dann; **8.** obˈwohl, wo … (doch), da … doch; **III** *pron.* **9.** wann, welche Zeit: ***from ~ does it date?*** aus welcher Zeit stammt es?; ***since ~?*** seit wann?; ***till ~?*** bis wann?; **10.** *relativ*: ***since ~*** und seitdem; ***till ~*** und bis dahin; **IV** *s.* **11.** ***the ~ and where of s.th.*** das Wann und Wo e-r Sache.

whence [wens] *bsd. poet.* **I** *adv.* **1.** woˈher: a) von wo(her), *obs.* von wannen, b) *fig.* woˈvon, woˈdurch, wie: ***~ comes it that*** wie kommt es, daß; **II** *cj.* **2.** von woˈher; **3.** *fig.* wesˈhalb, und deshalb.

ˌwhen(·so)ˈev·er I *cj.* wann (auch) immer, einerlei wann, (immer) wenn, soˈoft (als), jedesmal wenn; **II** *adv. fragend*: wann denn (nur).

where [weə] **I** *adv.* (*fragend u. relativ*) **1.** wo; **2.** woˈhin; **3.** worˈin, inwieˈfern, in welcher Hinsicht; **II** *cj.* **4.** (da) wo; **5.** daˈhin *od.* irgendwoˈhin wo, woˈhin; **III** *pron.* **6.** (*relativ*) (da *od.* dort,) wo: ***he lives not far from ~ it happened*** er wohnt nicht weit von dort, wo es geschah; **7.** (*fragend*) wo: ***~ … from?*** woher?, von wo?; ***~ … to?*** wohin?; **~·a·bouts I** *adv. od. cj.* [ˌweərəˈbaʊts] wo ungefähr *od.* etwa; **II** *s. pl.* [ˈweərəbaʊts] *sg. konstr.* Aufenthalt(sort) *m*, Verbleib *m*; **~·as** [weərˈæz] *cj.* **1.** wohinˈgegen, während, wo … doch; **2.** ⚖ da; in Anbetracht dessen, daß (*im Deutschen mst unübersetzt*); **~·at** [weərˈæt] *adv. u. cj.* **1.** worˈan, woˈbei, worˈauf; **2.** (*relativ*) an welchem (welcher) *od.* dem (der), wo; **~ˈby** *adv. u. cj.* **1.** woˈdurch, woˈmit; **2.** (*relativ*) durch welchen (welche[s]); **ˈ~·fore I** *adv. od. cj.* **1.** wesˈhalb, woˈzu, warˈum; **2.** (*relativ*) wesˈwegen, und deshalb; **II** *s. oft pl.* **3.** *das* Weshalb, *die* Gründe *pl.*; **~ˈfrom** *adv. u. cj.* woˈher, von wo; **~·in** [weərˈɪn] *adv.* worˈin, in welchem (welcher); **~·of** [weərˈɒv] *adv. u. cj.* woˈvon; **~·on** [weərˈɒn] *adv. od. cj.* **1.** worˈauf; **2.** (*relativ*) auf dem (der) *od.* den (die, das), auf welchem (welcher) *od.* welchen (welche, welches); **ˌ~·soˈev·er** → ***wherever*** 1; **~ˈto** *adv. od. cj.* woˈhin; **~·up·on** [weərəˈpɒn] *adv. od. cj.* **1.** worauf(ˈhin); **2.** (*als Satzanfang*) daraufˈhin.

wher·ev·er [weərˈevə] *adv. od. cj.* **1.** wo (-ˈhin) auch immer, ganz gleich, wo (-hin); **2.** F wo(hin) denn (nur)?

where|ˈwith *adv. od. cj.* woˈmit; **ˈ~·with·al** *s.* Mittel *pl.*, *das* Nötige, *das* nötige (Klein)Geld.

wher·ry [ˈwerɪ] ⚓ *s.* **1.** Jolle *f*; **2.** Skullboot *n*; **3.** Fährboot *n*; **4.** *Brit.* Frachtsegler *m.*

whet [wet] **I** *v/t.* **1.** wetzen, schärfen, schleifen; **2.** *fig. Appetit* anregen; *Neugierde etc.* anstacheln; **II** *s.* **3.** Wetzen *n*, Schärfen *n*; **4.** *fig.* Ansporn *m*, Anreiz *m*; **5.** (Appeˈtit)Anreger *m*, Aperiˈtif *m.*

wheth·er [ˈweðə] *cj.* **1.** ob (***or not*** oder nicht); ***~ or no*** auf jeden Fall, so oder so; **2.** ***~ … or*** entweder *od.* sei es, daß … oder.

ˈwhet·stone *s.* **1.** Wetz-, Schleifstein *m*; **2.** *fig.* Anreiz *m*, Ansporn *m.*

whew [hwuː] *int.* **1.** *erstaunt*: (h)ui!, Mann!; **2.** *angeekelt, erleichtert, erschöpft*: puh!

whey [weɪ] *s.* Molke *f*; **ˈ~·faced** *adj.* käsig, käseweiß.

which [wɪtʃ] **I** *interrog.* **1.** welch (*aus e-r bestimmten Gruppe od. Anzahl*): ***~ of you?*** welcher *od.* wer von euch?; **II** *pron.* (*relativ*) **2.** welch, der (die, das) (*bezogen auf Dinge, Tiere od. obs. Personen*); **3.** (*auf den vorhergehenden Satz bezüglich*) was; **4.** (*in eingeschobenen Sätzen*) (etwas,) was; **III** *adj.* **5.** (*fragend od. relativ*) welch: ***~ place will you take?*** auf welchem Platz willst du sitzen?; **~ˈev·er, ˌ~·soˈev·er** *pron. u. adj.* welch (auch) immer; ganz gleich, welch.

whiff [wɪf] **I** *s.* **1.** Luftzug *m*, Hauch *m*; **2.** Duftwolke *f* (*a.* übler) Geruch; **3.** Zug *m* (*beim Rauchen*); **4.** Schuß *m Chloroform etc.*; **5.** *fig.* Anflug *m*; **6.** F Zigaˈrillo *n, m*; **II** *v/i. u. v/t.* **7.** blasen, wehen; **8.** paffen, rauchen; **9.** (*nur v/i.*) ‚duften', (unangenehm) riechen.

whif·fle [ˈwɪfl] *v/i. u. v/t.* wehen.

Whig [wɪg] *pol. hist.* **I** *s.* **1.** *Brit.* Whig *m* (*Liberaler*); **2.** *Am.* Whig *m*: a) Natioˈnal(republiˌkan)er *m* (*Unterstützer der amer. Revolution*), b) *Anhänger e-r Oppositionspartei gegen die Demokraten um 1840*); **II** *adj.* **3.** Whig…, whigˈgistisch; **Whig·gism** [ˈwɪgɪzəm] *s. pol.* Whigˈgismus *m.*

while [waɪl] **I** *s.* **1.** Weile *f*, Zeit(spanne) *f*: ***a long ~ ago*** vor e-r ganzen Weile; ***(for) a ~*** e-e Zeitlang; ***for a long ~*** lange (Zeit), seit langem; ***in a little ~*** bald, binnen kurzem; ***the ~*** derweil, währenddessen; ***between ~s*** zwischendurch; ***worth (one's) ~*** der Mühe wert, (sich) lohnend; ***it is not worth*** (***one's***) ~ es ist nicht der Mühe wert, es lohnt sich nicht; → ***once*** 1; **II** *cj.* **2.** (*zeitlich*) während; **3.** so'lange (wie); **4.** während, wo(hin)'gegen; **5.** wenn auch, ob'wohl, zwar; **III** *v/t.* **6.** *mst* ***~ away*** sich *die Zeit* vertreiben; **whilst** [waɪlst] → ***while*** II.

whim [wɪm] *s.* **1.** Laune *f*, Grille *f*, wunderlicher Einfall, Ma'rotte *f*: ***at one's own ~*** ganz nach Laune; **2.** ⚒ Göpel *m*.

whim·per ['wɪmpə] **I** *v/t. u. v/i.* wimmern, winseln; **II** *s.* Wimmern *n*, Winseln *n*.

whim·sey → ***whimsy***.

whim·si·cal ['wɪmzɪkl] *adj.* □ **1.** launen-, grillenhaft, wunderlich; **2.** schrullig, ab'sonderlich, seltsam; **3.** hu'morig, launig; **whim·si·cal·i·ty** [wɪmzɪ'kælətɪ], '**whim·si·cal·ness** [-nɪs] *s.* **1.** Grillenhaftigkeit *f*, Wunderlichkeit *f*; **2.** → ***whim*** 1; **whim·sy** ['wɪmzɪ] **I** *s.* Laune *f*, Grille *f*, Schrulle *f*; **II** *adj.* → ***whimsical***.

whin¹ [wɪn] *s.* ♀ *bsd. Brit.* Stechginster *m*.

whin² [wɪn] → ***whinstone***.

whine [waɪn] **I** *v/i.* **1.** winseln, wimmern; **2.** greinen, quengeln, jammern; **II** *v/t.* **3.** *et.* weinerlich sagen, winseln; **III** *s.* **4.** Gewinsel *n*; **5.** Gejammer *n*, Gequengel *n*; '**whin·ing** [-nɪŋ] *adj.* □ weinerlich, greinend; winselnd.

whin·ny ['wɪnɪ] **I** *v/i.* wiehern; **II** *s.* Wiehern *n*.

whin·stone ['wɪnstəʊn] *s. geol.* Ba'salt(-tuff) *m*, Trapp *m*.

whip [wɪp] **I** *s.* **1.** Peitsche *f*, Geißel *f*; **2.** ***be a good*** (***poor***) ~ gut (schlecht) kutschieren; **3.** *hunt.* Pi'kör *m*; **4.** *parl.* a) Einpeitscher *m*, b) parlamen'tarischer Geschäftsführer, c) Rundschreiben *n*, Aufforderung(sschreiben *n*) *f* (*bei e-r Versammlung etc. zu erscheinen*): ***three-line ~*** a) Aufforderung, unbedingt zu erscheinen, b) (abso'luter) Fraktionszwang (***on a vote*** bei e-r Abstimmung); **5.** ⚙ a) Wippe *f* (*a.* ⚡), b) *a.* ***~-and-derry*** Flaschenzug *m*; **6.** *Näherei*: über'wendliche Naht; **7.** *Küche*: Creme(speise) *f*; **II** *v/t.* **8.** peitschen; **9.** (aus)peitschen, geißeln (*a. fig.*); **10.** *a.* ***~ on*** antreiben; **11.** schlagen: a) verprügeln: ***~ s.th. into*** (***out of***) ***s.o.*** j-m et. einbleuen (mit Schlägen austreiben), b) *bsd. sport* F besiegen, ‚über'fahren'; **12.** reißen, raffen: ***~ away*** wegreißen; ***~ from*** wegreißen *od.* fegen von; ***~ off*** a) weg-, herunterreißen, b) *j-n* entführen; ***~ on*** *Kleidungsstück* überwerfen; ***~ out*** (plötzlich) zücken, (schnell) *aus der Tasche* ziehen; **13.** *Gewässer* abfischen; **14.** a) *Schnur etc.* um'wickeln, ⚓ *Tau* betakeln, b) *Schnur* wickeln (***about*** um *acc.*); **15.** über'wendlich nähen, über'nähen, um'säumen; **16.** *Eier*, *Sahne* (schaumig) schlagen: ***~ped cream*** Schlagsahne *f*; ***~ped eggs*** Eischnee *m*; **17.** *Brit.* F ‚klauen'; **III** *v/i.* **18.** sausen, flitzen, schnellen; ***~ in*** *v/t.* **1.** *hunt. Hunde* zs.-treiben; **2.** *parl.* zs.-trommeln; ***~ round*** *v/i.* **1.** sich ruckartig 'umdrehen; **2.** F den Hut her'umgehen lassen; ***~ up*** *v/t.* **1.** antreiben; **2.** *fig.* aufpeitschen; **3.** a) *Leute* zs.-trommeln, b) *Essen etc.* ‚herzaubern'.

whip| aer·i·al (*bsd. Am.* **an·ten·na**) *s.* ⚡ 'Staban,tenne *f*; '**~·cord** *s.* **1.** Peitschenschnur *f*; **2.** Whipcord *m* (*schräggeripptes Kammgarn*); **~ hand** *s.* rechte Hand *des Reiters etc.*: ***get the ~ of s.o.*** die Oberhand gewinnen über j-n; ***have the ~ of*** *j-n* an der Kandare *od.* in der Gewalt haben; '**~·lash** *s.* **1.** → ***whipcord*** 1; **2.** *a.* ***~ injury*** ⚕ 'Peitschenschlagsyn,drom *n*.

whip·per ['wɪpə] *s.* Peitschende(r *m*) *f*; **,~-'in**, *pl.* **,~s-'in** → ***whip*** 3 *u.* 4; '**~,snap·per** *s.* **1.** Drei'käsehoch *m*; **2.** Gernegroß *m*, Gelbschnabel *m*, Springinsfeld *m*.

whip·pet ['wɪpɪt] *s.* **1.** *zo.* Whippet *m* (*kleiner englischer Rennhund*); **2.** ✕ *hist.* leichter Panzerkampfwagen.

whip·ping ['wɪpɪŋ] *s.* **1.** (Aus)Peitschen *n*; **2.** (Tracht *f*) Prügel *pl.*, Hiebe *pl.* (*a. fig.* F *Niederlage*); **3.** 'Garnum,wick(e)lung *f*; **~ boy** *s. hist.* Prügelknabe *m*, *fig. a.* Sündenbock *m*; **~ cream** *s.* Schlagsahne *f*; **~ post** *s. hist.* Schandpfahl *m*; **~ top** *s.* Kreisel *m* (*der mit Peitsche getrieben wird*).

whip·ple·tree ['wɪpltri:] *s.* Ortscheit *n*, Wagenschwengel *m*.

whip| ray *s. ichth.* Stechrochen *m*; '**~-round** *s. Brit.* F spon'tane (Geld-) Sammlung: ***have a ~*** → ***whip round*** 2; '**~·saw I** *s.* (zweihändige) Schrotsäge; **II** *v/t.* mit der Schrotsäge sägen; **III** *v/i. bsd. Poker*: *Am.* zs.-spielen mit.

whir → ***whirr***.

whirl [wɜ:l] **I** *v/i.* **1.** wirbeln, sich drehen: ***~ about*** (*od.* ***round***) a) herumwirbeln, b) sich rasch umdrehen; **2.** sausen, hetzen, eilen; **3.** wirbeln, sich drehen (*Kopf*): ***my head ~s*** mir ist schwindelig; **II** *v/t.* **4.** *allg.* wirbeln: ***~ up dust*** Staub aufwirbeln; **III** *s.* **5.** Wirbeln *n*; **6.** Wirbel *m*: a) schnelle Kreisbewegung, b) Strudel *m*: ***give s.th. a ~*** a) et. herumwirbeln, b) F et. (aus)probieren; **7.** *fig.* Wirbel *m*: a) Trubel *m*, wirres Treiben, b) Schwindel *m* (*der Sinne etc.*): ***a ~ of passion***; ***her thoughts were in a ~*** ihre Gedanken wirbelten durcheinander; '**~·blast** *s.* Wirbelsturm *m*.

whirl·i·gig ['wɜ:lɪgɪg] *s.* **1.** a) Windrädchen *n*, b) Kreisel *m etc.* (*Spielzeug*); **2.** Karus'sell *n* (*a. fig. der Zeit*); **3.** *fig.* Wirbel *m der Ereignisse etc.*

'**whirl|·pool** *s.* Strudel *m* (*a. fig.*); '**~·wind** *s.* Wirbelwind *m* (*a. fig. Person*): ***a ~ romance*** e-e stürmische Romanze.

'**whirl·y·bird** ['wɜ:lɪ-] *s. Am.* F Hubschrauber *m*.

whirr [wɜ:] **I** *v/i.* schwirren, surren; **II** *v/t.* schwirren lassen; **III** *s.* Schwirren *n*, Surren *n*.

whisk [wɪsk] **I** *s.* **1.** Wischen *n*, Fegen *n*; **2.** Wischer *m*: a) leichter Schlag, b) schnelle Bewegung (*bsd. Tierschwanz*); **3.** Husch *m*: ***in a ~*** im Nu; **4.** (*Stroh- etc.*)Wisch *m*, Büschel *n*; **5.** (Staub-, Fliegen)Wedel *m*; **6.** *Küche*: Schneebesen *m*; **II** *v/t.* **7.** *Staub etc.* (weg)wischen, (-)fegen; **8.** fegen, *mit dem Schwanz* schlagen; **9.** ***~ away*** (*od.* ***off***) schnell verschwinden lassen, wegzaubern, -nehmen; *j-n* schnellstens wegbringen, entführen; **10.** *Sahne*, *Eischnee* schlagen; **III** *v/i.* **11.** wischen, huschen, flitzen: ***~ away*** forthuschen; '**whisk·er** [-kə] *s.* **1.** *pl.* Backenbart *m*; **2.** a) Barthaar *n*, b) F Schnurrbart *m*; **3.** *zo.* Schnurr-, Barthaar *n* (*von Katzen etc.*); '**whisk·ered** [-kəd] *adj.* **1.** e-n Backenbart tragend; **2.** *zo.* mit Schnurrhaaren versehen.

whis·key ['wɪskɪ] *s.* **1.** (*bsd.* in den USA u. Irland hergestellter) Whisky; **2.** → **whis·ky** *s.* Whisky *m*: ***~ and soda*** Whisky Soda *m*; ***~ sour*** Whisky mit Zitrone.

whis·per ['wɪspə] **I** *v/i. u. v/t.* **1.** wispern, flüstern, raunen (*alle a. poet. Baum, Wind etc.*): ***~ s.th. to s.o.*** j-m et. zuflüstern; **2.** *fig. b.s.* flüstern, tuscheln, munkeln; **II** *s.* **3.** Flüstern *n*, Wispern *n*, Geflüster *n*: ***in a ~***, ***in ~s*** im Flüsterton; **4.** Getuschel *n*; **5.** a) geflüsterte *od.* heimliche Bemerkung, b) Gerücht *n*; **6.** Raunen *n*; '**whis·per·er** [-ərə] *s.* **1.** Flüsternde(r *m*) *f*; **2.** Zuträger(in), Ohrenbläser(in); '**whis·per·ing** [-pərɪŋ] **I** *adj.* □ **1.** flüsternd; **2.** Flüster…: ***~ baritone***; ***~ campaign*** Flüsterkampagne *f*; ***~ gallery*** Flüstergalerie *f*; **II** *s.* **3.** → ***whisper*** 3.

whist¹ [wɪst] *int. dial.* pst!, st!, still!

whist² [wɪst] *s.* Whist *n* (*Kartenspiel*): ***~ drive*** Whistrunde *f*.

whis·tle ['wɪsl] **I** *v/i.* **1.** pfeifen (*Person, Vogel, Lokomotive etc.*; *a. Kugel, Wind etc.*) (***to s.o.*** j-m); ***~ for*** *j-m*, *s-m Hund etc.* pfeifen; ***he may ~ for it*** F darauf kann er lange warten, das kann er sich in den Kamin schreiben; ***~ in the dark*** *fig.* den Mutigen markieren; **II** *v/t.* **2.** *Melodie etc.* pfeifen; **3.** ***~ back*** *Hund etc.* zurückpfeifen; ***~ up*** *fig.* a) herbeordern, b) ins Spiel bringen; **III** *s.* **4.** Pfeife *f*: ***blow the ~ on*** F a) *j-n, et.* ‚verpfeifen', b) *et.* ausplaudern, c) *j-n, et.* stoppen; ***pay for one's ~*** den Spaß teuer bezahlen; **5.** (*sport a.* Ab)Pfiff *m*; Pfeifton *m*; **6.** Pfeifen *n* (*des Windes etc.*); **7.** F Kehle *f*: ***wet one's ~*** ‚einen heben'; '**~·stop** *s. Am.* **1.** 🚂 Bedarfshaltestelle *f*; **2.** *fig.* Kleinstadt *f*, ‚Kaff' *n*; **3.** *pol.* kurzer Besuch (*e-s Kandidaten*); '**~-stop** *v/i. Am. pol.* von Ort zu Ort reisen u. Wahlreden halten.

whis·tling ['wɪslɪŋ] *s.* Pfeifen *n*; **~ buoy** *s.* ⚓ Pfeifboje *f*; **~ thrush** *s. orn.* Singdrossel *f*.

whit [wɪt] *s.* (*ein*) bißchen: ***no ~***, ***not a ~*** keinen Deut, kein Jota, kein bißchen.

white [waɪt] **I** *adj.* **1.** *allg.* weiß: ***as ~ as snow*** schneeweiß; **2.** blaß, bleich: ***as ~ as a sheet*** leichenblaß; → ***bleed*** 10; **3.** weiß(rassig): ***~ supremacy*** Vorherrschaft der Weißen; **4.** *fig.* a) rechtschaffen, b) harmlos, c) *Am.* F anständig: ***that's ~ of you***; **II** *s.* **5.** Weiß *n*, weiße Farbe: ***dressed in ~*** weiß *od.* in Weiß gekleidet; **6.** Weiße *f*, weiße Beschaffenheit; **7.** Weiße(r *m*) *f*, Angehörige(r *m*) *f* der weißen Rasse; **8.** *a.* ***~ of egg*** Eiweiß *n*; **9.** *a.* ***~ of the eye*** *das* Weiße im Auge; **10.** *typ.* Lücke *f*; **11.** *zo.* Weißling *m*; **12.** *pl.* ⚕ Weißfluß *m*, Leukor'rhöe *f*; **~ ant** *s. zo.* Ter'mite *f*; '**~·bait** *s. ein* Weißfisch *m*, Breitling *m*; **~ bear** *s. zo.* Eisbär *m*; **2 Book** *s. pol.* Weißbuch *n*; **~ bronze** *s.* 'Weißme,tall *n*; '**~·cap** *s.* schaumgekrönte Welle; **~ coal** *s.* ⚙ weiße Kohle, Wasserkraft *f*; **,~-'col·lar** *adj.* Büro…: ***~ worker*** (Büro)Angestellte(r *m*) *f*; ~ ***crime*** Weiße-Kragen-Kriminalität *f*; ~ **el·e·phant** *s.* **1.** *zo.* weißer Ele'fant; **2.** F lästiger Besitz; ♀ **En·sign** *s.* ⚓ *Brit.* Kriegsflagge *f*; '~**-faced** *adj.* blaß: ~ ***horse*** Blesse *f*; ~ **feath·er** *s.*: ***show the*** ~ sich feige zeigen, ‚kneifen'; ♀ **Fri·ar** *s. R.C.* Karme'liter(mönch) *m*; ~ **frost** *s.* (Rauh-)Reif *m*; ~ **goods** *s. pl.* **1.** Weißwaren *pl.*; **2.** Haushaltswäsche *f*; '~**-haired** *adj.* weiß- *od.* hellhaarig: ~ ***boy*** *Am.* F Liebling *m* (*des Chefs etc.*).

ˌ**White'hall** *s. Brit.* Whitehall *n*: a) *Straße in Westminster, London, Sitz der Ministerien*, b) *fig. die brit. Regierung od. ihre Politik.*

white| heat *s.* Weißglut *f* (*a. fig. Zorn*): ***work at a*** ~ mit fieberhaftem Eifer arbeiten; ~ **hope** *s.* **1.** *Am. sl.* weißer Boxer, der Aussicht auf den Meistertitel hat; **2.** F ‚*die* große Hoffnung' (*Person*); ~ **horse** *s.* **1.** *zo.* Schimmel *m*, weißes Pferd; **2.** → ***whitecap***; ˌ~**-'hot** *adj.* **1.** weißglühend (*a. fig. vor Zorn etc.*); **2.** *fig.* rasend (*Eile etc.*); ♀ **House** *s. das* Weiße Haus (*Regierungssitz des Präsidenten der USA in Washington*); ~ **lie** *s.* Notlüge *f*; ~ **line** *s.* weiße Linie, Fahrbahnbegrenzung *f*; '~**-ˌliv·ered** *adj.* feig(e); ~ **mag·ic** *s.* weiße Ma'gie (*Gutes bewirkende Zauberkunst*); ~ **man** *s.* [*irr.*] **1.** → ***white*** 7; **2.** F ‚feiner Kerl'; ~ **man's bur·den** *s. fig. die* Bürde des weißen Mannes; ~ **meat** *s.* weißes Fleisch (*vom Geflügel, Kalb etc.*); ~ **met·al** *s.* ⚙ a) Neusilber *n*, b) 'Weißmeˌtall *n*.

whit·en ['waɪtn] **I** *v/i.* **1.** weiß werden; **2.** bleich *od.* blaß werden; **II** *v/t.* **3.** weiß machen; **4.** bleichen; '**white·ness** [-nɪs] *s.* **1.** Weiße *f*; **2.** Blässe *f*; '**whit·en·ing** [-nɪŋ] *s.* **1.** Weißen *n*; **2.** Schlämmkreide *f*.

white| noise *s.* ⚡ weißes Rauschen; ~ **sale** *s.* ✝ Weiße Woche; ~ **sauce** *s.* helle Sauce; ~ **sheet** *s.* Büßerhemd *n*: ***stand in a*** ~ *fig.* s-e Sünden bekennen; ˌ~**-'slave** *adj.*: ~ ***agent*** → ~ **slav·er** *s.* Mädchenhändler *m*; '~**·smith** *s.* ⚙ **1.** Klempner *m*; **2.** *metall.* Feinschmied *m*; '~**·thorn** *s.* ⚘ Weißdorn *m*; '~**·throat** *s. orn.* (Dorn)Grasmücke *f*; ~ **tie** *s.* **1.** weiße Fliege; **2.** Abendanzug *m*; ~ **trash** *s. Am.* F **1.** arme weiße Bevölkerung; **2.** arme(r) Weiße(r) (*in den amer. Südstaaten*); '~**·wash I** *s.* **1.** Tünche *f*; **2.** flüssiges Hautbleichmittel; **3.** *fig.* F a) Tünche *f*, Beschönigung *f*, b) Ehrenrettung *f*, *contp.* ‚Mohrenwäsche' *f*, c) ✝ *Brit.* Schuldentlastung *f*; **4.** *sport* F ‚Zu-'Null-Niederlage' *f*; **II** *v/t.* **5.** a) tünchen, b) weißen, kalken; **6.** *fig.* a) über'tünchen, b) reinwaschen, rehabilitieren, c) ✝ *Brit. Bankrotteur* wieder zahlungsfähig erklären; **7.** *sport* F *Gegner* zu Null schlagen; ~ **wine** *s.* Weißwein *m*.

whit·ey ['waɪtɪ] *s. Am. contp.* **1.** Weiße(r) *m*; **2.** *oft* ♀ *coll.* die Weißen.

whith·er ['wɪðə] *adv. poet.* **1.** (*fragend*) wo'hin: ~ ***England?*** (*Schlagzeile*) England, wohin *od.* was nun?; **2.** (*relativ*) wohin: a) (*verbunden*) in welchen *etc.*, zu welchem *etc.*, b) (*unverbunden*) da'hin, wo.

whit·ing[1] ['waɪtɪŋ] *s. ichth.* Weißfisch *m*, Mer'lan *m*.

whit·ing[2] ['waɪtɪŋ] *s.* Schlämmkreide *f*.

whit·ish ['waɪtɪʃ] *adj.* weißlich.

whit·low ['wɪtləʊ] *s.* ⚕ 'Umlauf *m*, Nagelgeschwür *n*.

Whit [wɪt] *in Zssgn* Pfingst…: ~ ***Monday***; ~ ***Sunday***.

Whit·sun ['wɪtsn] **I** *adj.* Pfingst…, pfingstlich; **II** *s.* → '~**·tide** *s.* Pfingsten *n od. pl.*, Pfingstfest *n*.

whit·tle ['wɪtl] *v/t.* **1.** (zu'recht)schnitzen; **2.** ~ ***away*** *od.* ***off*** wegschnitze(l)n, -schnippeln; **3.** ~ ***down***, ~ ***away***, ~ ***off*** *fig.* a) (Stück für Stück) beschneiden, stutzen, verringern, b) *Gesundheit etc.* schwächen.

whiz(z) [wɪz] **I** *v/i.* **1.** zischen, schwirren, sausen (*Geschoß etc.*); **II** *s.* **2.** Zischen *n*, Sausen *n*; **3.** *Am.* F a) ‚Ka'none' *f* (*Könner*), b) tolles Ding; **III** *adj.* **4.** F ‚toll', ‚super'; ~ **kid** *s.* F ‚Wunderkind' *n*, Ge'nie *n*, *a.* ‚Senkrechtstarter' *m*.

who [hu:; hʊ] **I** *interrog.* **1.** wer: ♀***'s*** ♀ Wer ist Wer? (*Verzeichnis prominenter Persönlichkeiten*); ~ ***goes there?*** ⚔ (halt,) wer da?; **2.** F (*für* ***whom***) wen, wem; **II** *pron.* (*relativ*) **3.** (*unverbunden*) wer: ***I know*** ~ ***has done it***; **4.** (*verbunden*): welch, der (die, das): ***the man*** ~ ***arrived yesterday***.

whoa [wəʊ] *int.* brr!, halt!

who·dun·(n)it [ˌhu:'dʌnɪt] *s.* F ‚Krimi' *m* (*Kriminalroman etc.*).

who·ev·er [hu:'evə] **I** *pron.* (*relativ*) wer (auch) immer, jeder der; **II** *interrog.* F (*für* ***who ever***) wer denn nur.

whole [həʊl] **I** *adj.* □ → ***wholly***; **1.** ganz, voll(kommen, -ständig): ~ ***number*** ℞ ganze Zahl; ***a*** ~ ***lot of*** F e-e ganze Menge; **2.** heil: a) unversehrt: ***with a*** ~ ***skin*** mit heiler Haut, b) unbeschädigt, ‚ganz'; **3.** Voll(wert)…: ~ ***food***; ~ ***meal*** Vollweizenmehl *n*; ~ ***milk*** Vollmilch *f*; ***(made) out of*** ~ ***cloth*** *Am.* F völlig aus der Luft gegriffen, frei erfunden; **II** *s.* **4.** *das* Ganze, Gesamtheit *f*: ***the*** ~ ***of London*** ganz London; ***the*** ~ ***of my property*** mein ganzes Vermögen; **5.** Ganze(s) *n*, Einheit *f*: ***in*** ~ ***or in part*** ganz oder teilweise; ***on the*** ~ im (großen u.) ganzen, alles in allem; '~**-bound** *adj.* in Ganzleder (gebunden); ˌ~**-'col·o(u)red** *adj.* einfarbig; ˌ~**-'heart·ed** *adj.* □ aufrichtig, rückhaltlos, voll, von ganzem Herzen; ˌ~**-'hog·ger** [-'hɒgə] *s. sl.* kompro'mißloser Mensch; *pol.* ‚'Hundert-('fünfzig)proˌzentige(r)' *m*; ˌ~**-'length I** *adj.* Ganz…, Voll…: ~ ***portrait*** Vollporträt *n*, Ganzbild *n*; **II** *s.* Por'trät *n od.* Statue *f* in voller Größe; ~ **life in·sur·ance** *s.* Erlebensfall-Versicherung *f*; '~**·meal** *adj.* Vollkorn…

whole·ness ['həʊlnɪs] *s.* **1.** Ganzheit *f*; **2.** Vollständigkeit *f*.

'**whole·sale I** *s.* **1.** ✝ Großhandel *m*: ***by*** ~ → 4; **II** *adj.* **2.** ✝ Großhandels…, Engros…: ~ ***dealer*** → ***wholesaler***; ~ ***purchase*** Einkauf *m* im großen, Engroseinkauf *m*; ~ ***trade*** Großhandel *m*; **3.** *fig.* a) Massen…, b) 'unterschiedslos, pau'schal: ~ ***slaughter*** Massenmord *m*; **III** *adv.* **4.** ✝ im großen, en gros; **5.** a) *fig.* in Bausch u. Bogen, 'unterschiedslos, b) massenhaft; '**wholeˌsal·er** [-ˌseɪlə] *s.* ✝ Großhändler *m*; Gros'sist *m*.

whole·some ['həʊlsəm] *adj.* □ **1.** gesund (*bsd. heilsam, bekömmlich*) (*a. fig. Humor, Strafe etc.*); **2.** gut, nützlich, zuträglich; '**whole·some·ness** [-nɪs] *s.* **1.** Gesundheit *f*, Bekömmlichkeit *f*; **2.** Nützlichkeit *f*.

ˌ**whole|-'time** → ***full-time***; ~ **tone** *s.* ♪ Ganzton *m*; '~**-wheat** *adj.* Vollkorn…

whol·ly ['həʊllɪ] *adv.* ganz, gänzlich, völlig.

whom [hu:m] **I** *pron.* (*interrog.*) **1.** wen; **2.** (*Objekt-Kasus von* ***who***): ***of*** ~ von wem; ***to*** ~ wem; **II** *pron.* (*relativ*) **3.** (*verbunden*) welchen, welche, welches, den (die, das); **4.** (*unverbunden*) wen; den(jenigen), welchen; die(jenige), welche; *pl.* die(jenigen), welche; **5.** (*Objekt-Kasus von* ***who***): ***of*** ~ von welchem *etc.*, dessen, deren; ***to*** ~ dem (der, denen); ***all of*** ~ ***were dead*** welche alle tot waren; **6.** welchem, welcher, welchen, dem (der, denen): ***the master*** ~ ***she serves*** der Herr, dem sie dient.

whoop [hu:p] **I** *s.* **1.** a) Schlachtruf *m*, b) (*bsd.* Freuden)Schrei *m*: ***not worth a*** ~ F keinen Pfifferling wert; **2.** ⚕ Keuchen *n* (*bei Keuchhusten*); **II** *v/i.* **3.** schreien, brüllen, *a.* jauchzen; **4.** ⚕ keuchen; **III** *v/t.* **5.** *et.* brüllen; **6.** ~ ***it up*** *Am. sl.* a) ‚auf den Putz hauen', ‚toll feiern'; b) die Trommel rühren (***for*** für).

whoop·ee ['wʊpi:] *Am.* F **I** *s.*: ***make*** ~ ‚auf den Putz hauen', ‚toll feiern', *a.* Sauf- *od.* Sexparties feiern; **II** *int.* [wʊ'pi:] juch'hu!

whoop·ing cough ['hu:pɪŋ] *s.* ⚕ Keuchhusten *m*.

whoops [wʊps] *int.* hoppla!

woosh [wʊʃ; wu:ʃ] *v/i.* zischen, sausen.

whop [wɒp] *v/t.* F vertrimmen (*a. fig. besiegen*); **whop·per** ['wɒpə] *s. sl.* **1.** Mordsding *n*; **2.** (faust)dicke Lüge; **whop·ping** ['wɒpɪŋ] *adj. u. adv.* F e'norm, Mords…

whore [hɔ:] **I** *s.* Hure *f*; **II** *v/i.* huren; '~**·house** *s.* Bor'dell *n*.

whorl [wɜ:l] *s.* **1.** ⚘ Quirl *m*; **2.** *anat.*, *zo.* Windung *f*; **3.** ⚙ Wirtel *m*.

whor·tle·ber·ry ['wɜ:tlˌberɪ] *s.* **1.** ⚘ Heidelbeere *f*: ***red*** ~ Preiselbeere *f*; **2.** → ***huckleberry***.

whose [hu:z] *pron.* **1.** (*fragend*) wessen: ~ ***is it?*** wem gehört es?; **2.** (*relativ*) dessen, deren.

who·sit ['hu:zɪt] *s.* F ‚Dingsda' *m, f, n*.

ˌ**who·so'ev·er** → ***whoever***.

why [waɪ] **I** *adv.* **1.** (*fragend u. relativ*) war'um, wes'halb, wo'zu: ~ ***so?*** wieso?, warum das?; ***the reason*** ~ (der Grund) weshalb; ***that is*** ~ deshalb; **II** *int.* **2.** nun (gut); **3.** (ja) na'türlich; **4.** ja doch (*als Füllwort*); **5.** na'nu; aber (… doch): ~***, that's Peter!*** aber das ist ja *od.* doch Peter!; **III** *s.* **6.** *das* War'um, Grund *m*: ***the*** ~ ***and wherefore*** das Warum u. Weshalb.

wick [wɪk] *s.* Docht *m*.

wick·ed ['wɪkɪd] *adj.* □ **1.** böse, gottlos, schlecht, sündhaft, verrucht: ***the*** ~ ***one*** *bibl.* der Böse, Satan *m*; **2.** böse, schlimm (*ungezogen, a. humor. schalkhaft*) (*a.* F *Schmerz, Wunde etc.*); **3.** boshaft, bösartig (*a. Tier*); **4.** gemein; **5.** *sl.* ‚toll', großartig; '**wick·ed·ness** [-nɪs] *s.* Gottlosigkeit *f*; Schlechtigkeit *f*, Verruchtheit *f*; Bosheit *f*.

wick·er ['wɪkə] **I** *s.* a) Weidenrute *f*, b) Korbweide *f*, c) → ***wickerwork***; **II** *adj.*

aus Weiden geflochten, Weiden..., Korb..., Flecht...: ~ ***basket*** Weidenkorb *m*; ~ ***chair*** Rohrstuhl *m*; ~ ***furniture*** Korbmöbel *pl.*; '~**·work** *s.* **1.** Flechtwerk *n*; **2.** Korbwaren *pl.*

wick·et ['wɪkɪt] *s.* **1.** Pförtchen *n*; **2.** (Tür *f* mit) Drehkreuz *n*; **3.** (*mst vergittertes*) Schalterfenster; **4.** *Kricket*: a) Dreistab *m*, Tor *n*, b) Spielfeld *n*: ***be on a good*** (***sticky***) ~ gut (schlecht) stehen (*a. fig.*); ***take a*** ~ e-n Schläger ausmachen; ***keep*** ~ Torwart sein; ***win by 2 ~s*** das Spiel gewinnen, obwohl 2 Schläger noch nicht geschlagen haben; ***first*** (***second*** *etc.*) ~ ***down*** nachdem der erste (zweite *etc.*) Schläger ausgeschieden ist; '~**ˌkeep·er** *s.* Torhüter *m.*

wide [waɪd] **I** *adj.* □ → ***widely***; **1.** breit (*a. bei Maßangaben*): ***a*** ~ ***forehead*** (***ribbon***, ***street***); ~ ***screen*** (*Film*) Breitwand *f*; ***5 feet*** ~ 5 Fuß breit; **2.** weit, ausgedehnt: ~ ***distribution***; ~ ***difference*** großer Unterschied; ***a*** ~ ***public*** ein breites Publikum; ***the*** ~ ***world*** die weite Welt; **3.** *fig.* a) ausgedehnt, um'fassend, 'umfangreich, weitreichend, b) reich (*Erfahrung*, *Wissen etc.*): ~ ***culture*** umfassende Bildung; ~ ***reading*** große Belesenheit; **4.** a) weit (-gehend, -läufig), b) weitherzig, großzügig: ***take*** ~ ***views*** weitherzig *od.* großzügig sein; **5.** weit offen, aufgerissen: ~ ***eyes***; **6.** weit, lose, nicht anliegend: ~ ***clothes***; **7.** weit entfernt (***of*** von *der Wahrheit etc.*), weit'ab *vom Ziel*; → ***mark***[1] 11; **II** *adv.* **8.** weit: ~ ***apart*** weit auseinander; ~ ***open*** a) weit offen, b) völlig ungedeckt (*Boxer*), c) *fig.* schutzlos, d) → ***wide-open*** 2; ***far and*** ~ weit u. breit; **9.** weit'ab (*vom Ziel*, *der Wahrheit etc.*): ***go*** ~ weit danebengehen; ˌ~**-'an·gle** *adj. phot.* Weitwinkel...: ~ ***lens***; ˌ~**-a'wake I** *adj.* **1.** hellwach (*a. fig.*); **2.** *fig.* aufgeweckt, ‚hell'; **3.** *fig.* wachsam, aufmerksam; voll bewußt (***to*** *gen.*); **II** *s.* '***wide-awake*** **4.** Kala'breser *m* (*Schlapphut*); ˌ~**-'eyed** *adj.* **1.** mit (weit) aufgerissenen Augen; **2.** *fig.* na'iv, kindlich.

wide·ly ['waɪdlɪ] *adv.* weit: ~ ***scattered*** weitverstreut; ~ ***known*** weit u. breit *od.* in weiten Kreisen bekannt; ~ ***discussed*** vieldiskutiert; ***be*** ~ ***read*** sehr belesen sein; ***differ*** ~ a) sehr verschieden sein, b) sehr unterschiedlicher Meinung sein.

wid·en ['waɪdn] *v/t. u. v/i.* **1.** breiter machen (werden); **2.** (sich) erweitern (*a. fig.*); **3.** (sich) vertiefen (*Kluft*, *Zwist*); '**wide·ness** [-nɪs] *s.* **1.** Breite *f*; **2.** Ausdehnung *f* (*a. fig.*).

ˌ**wide|-'o·pen** *adj.* **1.** weitgeöffnet; **2.** *Am.* äußerst ‚großzügig' (*Stadt etc.*, *bezüglich Glücksspiel etc.*); '~**·spread** *adj.* **1.** weitausgebreitet, ausgedehnt; **2.** weitverbreitet.

widg·eon ['wɪdʒən] *pl.* **-eons**, *coll.* **-eon** *s. orn.* Pfeifente *f.*

wid·ow ['wɪdəʊ] *s.* Witwe *f*: ~***'s mite*** *bibl.* Scherflein *n* der (armen) Witwe; '**wid·owed** [-əʊd] *adj.* **1.** verwitwet; **2.** verwaist, verlassen; '**wid·ow·er** [-əʊə] *s.* Witwer *m*; '**wid·ow·hood** [-əʊhʊd] *s.* Witwenstand *m.*

width [wɪdθ] *s.* **1.** Breite *f*, Weite *f*: ***2 feet in*** ~ 2 Fuß breit; **2.** (Stoff-, Ta'peten-, Rock)Bahn *f.*

wield [wi:ld] *v/t.* **1.** *Macht*, *Einfluß etc.* ausüben (***over*** über *acc.*); **2.** *rhet.* *Werkzeug*, *Waffe* handhaben, führen, schwingen: ~ ***the pen*** die Feder führen, schreiben; → ***sceptre***.

wie·ner ['wi:nə] *s. Am.*, '**wie·nie** ['wi:nɪ] *s.* F Wiener Würstchen *n.*

wife [waɪf] *pl.* **wives** [waɪvz] *s.* **1.** (Ehe-) Frau *f*, Gattin *f*: ***wedded*** ~ angetraute Gattin; ***take to*** ~ zur Frau nehmen; **2.** Weib *n*; '**wife·hood** [-hʊd] *s.* Ehestand *m e-r Frau*; '**wife·like** [-laɪk], '**wife·ly** [-lɪ] *adj.* (haus)fraulich; **wife swapping** *s.* F Partnertausch *m*; **wif·ie** ['waɪfɪ] *s.* F Frauchen *n.*

wig [wɪg] *s.* Pe'rücke *f*; **wigged** [wɪgd] *adj.* mit Perücke (versehen); **wig·ging** ['wɪgɪŋ] *s. Brit.* F Standpauke *f.*

wig·gle ['wɪgl] **I** *v/i.* **1.** → ***wriggle*** 1; **2.** wackeln, schwänzeln; **II** *v/t.* **3.** wackeln mit.

wight [waɪt] *s. obs. od. humor.* Wicht *m*, Kerl *m.*

wig·wam ['wɪgwæm] *s.* Wigwam *m*, Indi'anerzelt *n*, -hütte *f.*

wild [waɪld] **I** *adj.* □ **1.** *allg.* wild: a) *zo.* ungezähmt, in Freiheit lebend, gefährlich, b) ⚘ wildwachsend, c) verwildert, 'wildroˌmantisch, verlassen (*Land*), d) unzivilisiert, bar'barisch (*Volk*, *Stamm*), e) stürmisch: ***a*** ~ ***coast***, f) wütend, heftig (*Sturm*, *Streit etc.*), g) irr, verstört: ***a*** ~ ***look***, h) scheu (*Tier*), i) rasend (***with*** vor *dat.*): ~ ***with fear***, j) F wütend (***about*** über *acc.*): ***drive s.o.*** ~ F j-n wild machen, j-n ‚auf die Palme bringen', k) ungezügelt (*Person*, *Gefühl*), l) unbändig: ~ ***delight***, m) F toll, verrückt, n) ausschweifend, o) (***about***) versessen *od.* scharf (auf *acc.*), wild (nach), p) hirnverbrannt, unsinnig, abenteuerlich: ~ ***plan***, q) plan-, ziellos: ***a*** ~ ***guess*** e-e wilde Vermutung; ***a*** ~ ***shot*** ein Schuß ins Blaue, r) wirr, wüst: ~ ***disorder***; **II** *adv.* **2.** aufs Gerate'wohl: ***run*** ~ a) ⚘ ins Kraut schießen, b) verwildern (*Garten etc.*, *a. fig.*); ***shoot*** ~ ins Blaue schießen; ***talk*** ~ a) (wild) drauflosreden, b) sinnloses Zeug reden; **III** *s. rhet.* **3.** *a. pl.* Wüste *f*; **4.** *a. pl.* Wildnis *f*; ~ ***boar*** *s. zo.* Wildschwein *n*; '~**·cat I** *s.* **1.** *zo.* Wildkatze *f*; **2.** *fig.* Wilde(r *m*) *f*; **3.** → ***wildcatting*** 2; **4.** ✝ 'Schwindelunterˌnehmen *n*; **5.** ✝ wilder Streik; **II** *adj.* **6.** ✝ a) unsicher, spekula'tiv, b) Schwindel...: ~ ***company***, c) ungesetzlich, wild: ~ ***strike***; '~**ˌcat·ting** [-ˌkætɪŋ] *s.* **1.** wildes Spekulieren; **2.** wilde *od.* spekula'tive Ölbohrung.

wil·der·ness ['wɪldənɪs] *s.* **1.** Wildnis *f*, Wüste *f* (*a. fig.*): ***voice*** (***crying***) ***in the*** ~ a) *bibl.* Stimme des Predigers in der Wüste, b) *fig.* Rufer *m* in der Wüste; ***be sent into the*** ~ *fig. pol.* in die Wüste geschickt werden; **2.** wildwachsendes Gartenstück; **3.** *fig.* Masse *f*, Gewirr *n.*

ˌ**wild|-'eyed** *adj.* mit wildem Blick; '~**-ˌfire** *s.* **1.** verheerendes Feuer: ***spread like*** ~ sich wie ein Lauffeuer verbreiten (*Nachricht etc.*); **2.** ⚔ *hist.* griechisches Feuer; '~**·fowl** *s. coll.* Wildvögel *pl.*; ~ **goose** *s.* [*irr.*] Wildgans *f*; ˌ~**-'goose chase** *s. fig.* vergebliche Mühe, fruchtloses Unterfangen.

wild·ing ['waɪldɪŋ] *s.* ⚘ a) Wildling *m* (*unveredelte Pflanze*), *bsd.* Holzapfelbaum *m*, b) *Frucht e-r solchen Pflanze.*

'**wild·life** *s. coll.* wildlebende Tiere *pl.*: ~ ***park*** Naturpark *m.*

wild·ness ['waɪldnɪs] *s. allg.* Wildheit *f.*

'**wildˌwa·ter** *s.* Wildwasser *n*: ~ ***sport***.

wile [waɪl] **I** *s.* **1.** *mst pl.* List *f*, Trick *m*; *pl.* Kniffe *pl.*, Schliche *pl.*, Ränke *pl.*; **II** *v/t.* **2.** verlocken, *j-n wohin* locken; **3.** → ***while*** 6.

wil·ful ['wɪlfʊl] *adj.* □ **1.** *bsd.* ⚖ vorsätzlich: ~ ***deceit*** arglistige Täuschung; ~ ***murder*** Mord *m*; **2.** eigenwillig, -sinnig, halsstarrig; '**wil·ful·ness** [-nɪs] *s.* **1.** Vorsätzlichkeit *f*; **2.** Eigenwille *m*, -sinn *m*, Halsstarrigkeit *f.*

wil·i·ness ['waɪlɪnɪs] *s.* (Arg)List *f*, Verschlagenheit *f*, Gerissenheit *f.*

will[1] [wɪl] **I** *v/aux.* [*irr.*] **1.** (*zur Bezeichnung des Futurs*, *Brit. mst nur 2. u. 3. sg. u. pl.*) werden: ***he*** ~ ***come*** er wird kommen; **2.** wollen, werden, willens sein zu: ~ ***you pass me the bread, please?*** reichen Sie mir doch bitte das Brot!; ~ ***do!*** *sl.* wird gemacht!; **3.** (*immer*, *bestimmt*, *unbedingt*) werden (*oft a. unübersetzt*): ***birds*** ~ ***sing*** Vögel singen; ***boys*** ~ ***be boys*** Jungen sind nun einmal so; ***accidents*** ~ ***happen*** Unfälle wird es immer geben; ***you*** ~ ***get in my light!*** du mußt mir natürlich (immer) im Licht stehen!; **4.** *Erwartung*, *Vermutung od. Annahme*: werden: ***they*** ~ ***have gone now*** sie werden *od.* dürften jetzt (wohl) gegangen sein; ***this*** ~ ***be your train, I suppose*** das ist wohl dein Zug, das dürfte dein Zug sein; **5.** → ***would***; **II** *v/i. u. v/t.* **6.** wollen, wünschen: ***as you*** ~***!*** wie du willst!; → ***would*** 3, ***will***[2] II.

will[2] [wɪl] **I** *s.* **1.** Wille *m* (*a. phls.*): a) Wollen *n*, b) Wunsch *m*, Befehl *m*, c) (Be)Streben *n*, d) Willenskraft *f*: ***an iron*** ~ ein eiserner Wille; ***good*** ~ guter Wille (→ *a.* ***goodwill***); ~ ***to peace*** Friedenswille; ~ ***to power*** Machtwille, -streben; ***at*** ~ nach Wunsch *od.* Belieben *od.* Laune; ***of one's own*** (***free***) ~ aus freien Stücken; ***with a*** ~ mit Lust u. Liebe, mit Macht; ***have one's*** ~ s-n Willen haben *od.* durchsetzen; **2.** *a.* ***last*** ~ ***and testament*** ⚖ letzter Wille, Testa'ment *n*; **II** *v/t.* **3.** wollen, entscheiden; **4.** ernstlich *od.* fest wollen; **5.** *j-n* (durch Willenskraft) zwingen (***to do*** zu tun): ~ ***o.s.*** (***in***)***to*** sich zwingen zu; **6.** ⚖ (letzt)willig a) verfügen, b) vermachen (***to*** *dat.*); **III** *v/i.* **7.** wollen.

willed [wɪld] *adj.* ...willig, mit e-m ... Willen; → ***strong-willed*** *etc.*

will·ful, **will·ful·ness** *bsd. Am.* → ***wilful***, ***wilfulness***.

wil·lies ['wɪlɪz] *s. pl.* F: ***get the*** ~ ‚Zustände' bekommen; ***it gives me the*** ~ dabei wird mir ganz anders, dabei läuft es mir eiskalt den Rücken runter.

will·ing ['wɪlɪŋ] *adj.* □ **1.** *pred.* gewillt, willens, bereit: ***I am*** ~ ***to believe*** ich glaube gern; **2.** (bereit)willig; **3.** gern geschehen *od.* geleistet: ***a*** ~ ***gift*** ein gern gegebenes Geschenk; '**will·ing·ly** [-lɪ] *adv.* bereitwillig, gern; '**will·ing·ness** [-nɪs] *s.* (Bereit)Willigkeit *f*, Bereitschaft *f*, Geneigtheit *f.*

will-less ['wɪllɪs] *adj.* willenlos.

will-o'-the-wisp [ˌwɪləðə'wɪsp] *s.* **1.** Irrlicht *n* (*a. fig.*); **2.** *fig.* Illusi'on *f*, Phan'tom *n.*

wil·low¹ ['wɪləʊ] *s.* **1.** ⚘ Weide *f*: ***wear the ~*** *fig.* um den Geliebten trauern; **2.** F *Kricket*: Schlagholz *n*.

wil·low² ['wɪləʊ] **I** *s. Spinnerei*: Reißwolf *m*; **II** *v/t. Baumwolle etc.* wolfen, reißen.

wil·low·y ['wɪləʊɪ] *adj.* **1.** weidenbestanden *od.* -artig; **2.** *fig.* a) biegsam, geschmeidig, b) gertenschlank.

'will,pow·er *s.* Willenskraft *f*.

wil·ly-nil·ly [,wɪlɪ'nɪlɪ] *adv.* wohl oder übel, nolens volens.

wilt¹ [wɪlt] *obs. od. poet. du* willst.

wilt² [wɪlt] *v/i.* **1.** (ver)welken, welk *od.* schlaff werden; **2.** F *fig.* a) schlappmachen, ‚eingehen', b) nachlassen.

wil·y ['waɪlɪ] *adj.* □ gerissen.

wim·ple ['wɪmpl] *s.* **1.** *hist.* Rise *f*; **2.** (Nonnen)Schleier *m*.

win [wɪn] **I** *v/t.* [*irr.*] **1.** *Kampf, Spiel etc., a. Sieg, Preis* gewinnen: ***~ s.th. from*** (*od.* ***of***) ***s.o.*** j-m et. abgewinnen; ***~ one's way*** *fig.* s-n Weg machen; → ***day*** 5, ***field*** 6; **2.** *Reichtum, Ruhm etc.* erlangen, *Lob* ernten; zu *Ehren* gelangen; → ***spur*** 1; **3.** *j-m Lob etc.* einbringen, -tragen; **4.** *Liebe, Sympathie, a. e-n Freund, j-s Unterstützung* gewinnen; **5.** *a.* ***~ over*** *j-n* für sich gewinnen, auf s-e Seite ziehen, *a. j-s Herz* erobern; **6.** *j-n* dazu bringen (***to do*** zu tun): ***~ s.o. round*** j-n ‚rumkriegen'; **7.** *Stelle, Ziel* erreichen: ***~ the shore***; **8.** *sein Brot, s-n Lebensunterhalt* verdienen; **9.** ⚔ *sl.* ‚organisieren'; **10.** ⚒, *min.* a) *Erz, Kohle* gewinnen, b) erschließen; **II** *v/i.* [*irr.*] **11.** gewinnen, siegen: ***~ hands down*** F spielend gewinnen; ***~ out*** F sich durchsetzen (***over*** gegen); ***~ through*** a) durchkommen, b) ans Ziel gelangen (*a. fig.*), c) *fig.* sich durchsetzen; **III** *s.* **12.** *bsd. sport* Sieg *m*.

wince [wɪns] **I** *v/i.* (zs.-)zucken, zs.-, zu'rückfahren (***at*** bei, ***under*** unter *dat.*); **II** *s.* (Zs.-)Zucken *n*.

winch [wɪntʃ] ⚙ **I** *s.* **1.** Winde *f*, Haspel *f*; **2.** Kurbel *f*; **II** *v/t.* **3.** hochwinden.

wind¹ [wɪnd; *poet. a.* waɪnd] **I** *s.* **1.** Wind *m*: ***before the ~*** vor dem *od.* im Wind; ***between ~ and water*** a) ⚓ zwischen Wind u. Wasser, b) in der *od.* die Magengrube, c) *fig.* an e-r empfindlichen Stelle; ***in***(***to***) ***the ~'s eye*** gegen den Wind; ***like the ~*** wie der Wind (*schnell*); ***to the four ~s*** in alle (vier) Winde, in alle (Himmels)Richtungen; ***under the ~*** ⚓ in Lee; ***be in the ~*** *fig.* (heimlich) im Gange sein, in der Luft liegen; ***cast*** (*od.* ***fling, throw***) ***to the ~s*** *fig. Rat etc.* in den Wind schlagen, *Klugheit etc.* außer acht lassen; ***get*** (***have***) ***the ~ up*** *sl.* ‚Manschetten' *od.* ‚Schiß' kriegen (haben); ***know how the ~ blows*** *fig.* wissen, woher der Wind weht; ***put the ~ up s.o.*** F j-n ins Bockshorn jagen; ***raise the ~*** F (das nötige) Geld auftreiben; ***sail close to the ~*** a) ⚓ hart am Wind segeln, b) *fig.* mit e-m Fuß im Zuchthaus stehen, sich hart an der Grenze des Erlaubten bewegen; ***sow the ~ and reap the whirlwind*** Wind säen u. Sturm ernten; ***have*** (*od.* ***take***) ***the ~ of*** a) *e-m Schiff* den Wind abgewinnen, b) *fig.* e-n Vorteil *od.* die Oberhand haben über (*acc.*); ***take the ~ out of s.o.'s sails*** *fig.* j-m den Wind aus den Segeln nehmen; ***~ and weather permitting*** bei gutem Wetter; → ***ill*** 4; **2.** ⚙ a) (*Gebläse- etc.*) Wind *m*, b) Luft *f in e-m Reifen etc.*; **3.** ⚕ (Darm)Wind(e *pl.*) *m*, Blähung(en *pl.*) *f*: ***break ~*** e-n Wind abgehen lassen; **4.** ♪ ***the ~*** *coll.* die Blasinstrumente *pl.*, *a.* die Bläser *pl.*; **5.** *hunt.* Wind *m*, Witterung *f* (*a. fig.*): ***get ~ of*** a) wittern, b) *fig.* Wind bekommen von; **6.** Atem *m*: ***have a good ~*** e-e gute Lunge haben; ***have a long ~*** e-n langen Atem haben (*a. fig.*); ***get one's second ~*** den zweiten Wind bekommen, den toten Punkt überwunden haben; ***sound in ~ and limb*** kerngesund; ***have lost one's ~*** außer Atem sein; **7.** Wind *m*, leeres Geschwätz; **II** *v/t.* **8.** *hunt.* wittern; **9.** ***be ~ed*** außer Atem *od.* erschöpft sein; **10.** verschnaufen lassen.

wind² [waɪnd] **I** *s.* **1.** Windung *f*, Biegung *f*; **2.** Um'drehung *f*; **II** *v/t.* [*irr.*] **3.** winden, wickeln, schlingen (***round*** um *acc.*): ***~ off*** (***on to***) ***a reel*** *et.* ab- (auf-) spulen; **4.** *oft* ***~ up*** a) auf-, hochwinden, b) *Garn etc.* aufwickeln, -spulen, c) *Uhr etc.* aufziehen, d) *Saite etc.* spannen; **5.** a) *Kurbel* drehen, b) kurbeln: ***~ forward*** (***back***) *Film* weiter- (zurück-) spulen; ***~ up*** (***down***) *Autofenster* hoch- (herunter)kurbeln; **6.** ⚓ *Schiff* wenden; **7.** (sich) *wohin* schlängeln: ***~ o.s.*** (*od.* ***one's way***) ***into s.o.'s affection*** *fig.* sich j-s Zuneigung erschleichen; **III** *v/i.* [*irr.*] **8.** sich winden *od.* schlängeln (*a. Straße etc.*); **9.** sich winden *od.* wickeln *od.* schlingen (***round*** um *acc.*); ***~ off*** *v/t.* abwickeln, -spulen; ***~ up*** **I** *v/t.* **1.** → ***wind²*** 4, 5; **2.** *fig.* anspannen, erregen, (hin'ein)steigern; **3.** *bsd. Rede* (ab-) schließen; **4.** ✝ a) *Geschäft* abwickeln, b) *Unternehmen* auflösen, liquidieren; **II** *v/i.* **5.** (*bsd.* s-e Rede) schließen (***by saying*** mit den Worten); **6.** F *wo* enden, ‚landen': ***he'll ~ in prison***; **7.** ✝ Kon'kurs machen.

wind·bag ['wɪndbæg] *s.* F *contp.* Schwätzer *m*, Schaumschläger *m*.

'wind|·blown ['wɪnd-] *adj.* **1.** windig; **2.** windschief; **3.** (vom Wind) zerzaust; **4.** Windstoß...: ***~ hairdo***; **'~·break** *s.* **1.** Windschutz *m* (*Hecke etc.*); **2.** Windbruch *m*; **'~,bro·ken** *adj. vet.* kurzatmig (*Pferd*); **'~,cheat·er** *s. Brit.* Windjacke *f*; **~ cone** *s.* ✈ Luftsack *m*.

wind·ed ['wɪndɪd] *adj.* **1.** außer Atem; **2.** *in Zssgn* ...atmig: ***short-~***.

wind egg [wɪnd] *s.* Windei *n*.

wind·er ['waɪndə] *s.* **1.** Spuler(in); **2.** ⚙ Winde *f*; **3.** ⚘ Schlingpflanze *f*; **4.** a) Schlüssel *m* (*zum Aufziehen*), b) Kurbel *f*.

'wind|·fall ['wɪnd-] *s.* **1.** Fallobst *n*; **2.** Windbruch *m*; **3.** *fig.* (unverhoffter) Glücksfall *od.* Gewinn; **'~,flow·er** *s.* ⚘ Ane'mone *f*; **~ force** *s.* Windstärke *f*; **~ ga(u)ge** *s.* Wind(stärke-, -geschwindigkeits)messer *m*, Anemo'meter *n*.

wind·i·ness ['wɪndɪnɪs] *s.* Windigkeit *f* (*a. fig. contp.*).

wind·ing ['waɪndɪŋ] **I** *s.* **1.** Winden *n*, Spulen *n*; **2.** (Ein-, Auf)Wickeln *n*, (Um)'Wickeln *n*; **3.** Windung *f*, Biegung *f*; **4.** Um'wick(e)lung *f*; **5.** ⚡ Wicklung *f*; **II** *adj.* □ **6.** gewunden: a) sich windend *od.* schlängelnd, b) Wendel...(*-treppe*); **7.** krumm, schief (*a. fig.*); **~ sheet** *s.* Leichentuch *n*; **~ tack·le** *s.* ⚓ Gien *n* (*Flaschenzug*); **,~-'up** *s.* **1.** Aufziehen *n* (*Uhr etc.*): ***~ mechanism*** Aufziehwerk *n*; **2.** ✝ a) Abwicklung *f*, Erledigung *f* (*e-s Geschäfts*), b) Liquidati'on *f*, Auflösung *f* (*e-r Firma*); ***~ sale*** (Total)Ausverkauf *m*.

wind| in·stru·ment [wɪnd] *s.* ♪ 'Blasinstru,ment *n*; **'~,jam·mer** [-,dʒæmə] *s.* **1.** ⚓ Windjammer *m* (*Schiff*); **2.** *Am. sl.* → ***windbag***.

wind·lass ['wɪndləs] **I** *s.* **1.** ⚙ Winde *f*; **2.** ⚒ Förderhaspel *f*; **3.** ⚓ Ankerspill *n*; **II** *v/t.* hochwinden.

wind·less ['wɪndlɪs] *adj.* windstill.

wind·mill ['wɪnmɪl] *s.* **1.** Windmühle *f*: ***tilt at*** (*od.* ***fight***) ***~s*** *fig.* gegen Windmühlen kämpfen; ***throw one's cap over the ~*** a) Luftschlösser bauen, b) jede Vorsicht außer acht lassen; **2.** Windrädchen *n*.

win·dow ['wɪndəʊ] *s.* **1.** Fenster *n* (*a.* ⚙, *geol.*; *a. im Briefumschlag*): ***look out of*** (*od.* ***at***) ***the ~*** zum Fenster hinaussehen; **2.** Fensterscheibe *f*; **3.** Schaufenster *n*, Auslage *f*; **4.** (Bank- *etc.*)Schalter *m*; **5.** ⚔ *Radar*: Störfolie *f*.

win·dow| box *s.* Blumenkasten *m*; **~ clean·er** *s.* Fensterputzer *m*; **~ dis·play** *s.* 'Schaufensterauslage *f*, -re,klame *f*; **'~-dress** *v/t.* **1.** ✝ *Bilanz* verschleiern, ‚frisieren'; **2.** ‚aufputzen'; **~ dress·er** *s.* 'Schaufensterdekora,teur *m*; **~ dress·ing** *s.* **1.** 'Schaufensterdekorati,on *f*; **2.** *fig.* Aufmachung *f*, Mache *f*; **3.** ✝ Bi'lanzverschleierung *f*, ‚Frisieren' *n*.

win·dowed ['wɪndəʊd] *adj.* mit Fenster(n) (versehen).

win·dow| en·ve·lope *s.* 'Fenster,brief-,umschlag *m*; **~ gar·den·ing** *s.* Blumenzucht *f* am Fenster; **~ jam·ming** *s.* ⚔ *Radar*: Folienstörung *f*; **'~·pane** *s.* Fensterscheibe *f*; **'~·screen** *s.* **1.** Fliegenfenster *n*; **2.** Zierfüllung *f* e-s Fensters (*aus Buntglas, Gitter etc.*); **~ seat** *s.* Fensterplatz *m*; **~ shade** *s. Am.* Rou'leau *n*, Jalou'sie *f*; **'~-,shop·per** *s.* j-d, der e-n Schaufensterbummel macht; **'~-,shop·ping** *s.* Schaufensterbummel *m*: ***go ~*** e-n Schaufensterbummel machen; **~ shut·ter** *s.* Fensterladen *m*; **'~·sill** *s.* Fensterbrett *n*, -bank *f*.

'wind|·pipe ['wɪnd-] *s. anat.* Luftröhre *f*.

wind| pow·er [wɪnd] *s.* Windkraft *f*; **~ rose** *s. meteor.* Windrose *f*; **'~·sail** *s.* **1.** Windflügel *m*; **2.** ⚓ Windsack *m*; **'~·screen** *s. Brit.*, **'~,shield** *s. Am. mot.* Windschutzscheibe *f*: ***~ washer*** Scheibenwaschanlage *f*; ***~ wiper*** Scheibenwischer *m*; **'~·sleeve** *s.*, **'~·sock** *s.* ✈ Luftsack *m*; **'~·swept** ['wɪnd-] *adj.* **1.** vom Wind gepeitscht; **2.** *fig.* Windstoß...(*-frisur*); **'~,surf·ing** *s.* Windsurfen *n*; **~ tun·nel** *s.* ✈, *phys.* 'Windka,nal *m*; **'~·up** ['waɪnd-] *s.* **1.** → ***winding-up*** 2; **2.** Schluß *m*, Ende *n*.

wind·ward ['wɪndwəd] **I** *adv.* wind-, luvwärts; **II** *adj.* windwärts, Luv..., Wind...; **III** *s.* Windseite *f*, Luv(seite) *f*.

wind·y ['wɪndɪ] *adj.* □ **1.** windig: a) stürmisch (*Wetter*), b) zugig (*Ort*); **2.** *fig.* a) windig, hohl, leer, b) geschwätzig; **3.** ⚕ blähend; **4.** *Brit. sl.* ner'vös, ängstlich.

wine [waɪn] **I** *s.* **1.** Wein *m*: ***new ~ in old bottles*** *bibl.* junger Wein in alten

Schläuchen (*a. fig.*); **2.** *Brit. univ.* Weinabend *m*; **II** *v/t.*: ~ **and dine s.o.** j-n fürstlich bewirten; **'~ˌbib·ber** [-ˌbɪbə] *s.* Weinsäufer(in); **'~ˌbot·tle** *s.* Weinflasche *f*; ~ **cool·er** *s.* Weinkühler *m*; ~ **cra·dle** *s.* Weinkorb *m*; **'~·glass** *s.* Weinglas *n*; **'~ˌgrow·er** *s.* Weinbauer *m*; **'~ˌgrow·ing** *s.* Wein(an)bau *m*: ~ **area** Weinbaugebiet *n*; ~ **list** *s.* Weinkarte *f*; ~ **mer·chant** *s.* Weinhändler *m*; **'~·press** *s.* Weinpresse *f*, -kelter *f*.

win·er·y ['waɪnərɪ] *s.* Weinkelle'rei *f*.

'wine|·skin *s.* Weinschlauch *m*; ~ **stone** *s.* ⚗ Weinstein *m*; **'~ˌtast·er** *s.* Weinprüfer *m*; **'~ˌtast·ing** *s.* Weinprobe *f*.

wing [wɪŋ] **I** *s.* **1.** *orn.* Flügel *m* (*a.* ⚘, *zo.*, *a.* ⚙, ⚠, *a. pol.*); *rhet.* Schwinge *f*, Fittich *m* (*a. fig.*): **on the ~** a) im Fluge, b) *fig.* auf Reisen; **on the ~s of the wind** mit Windeseile; **under s.o.'s ~(s)** *fig.* unter j-s Fittichen *od.* Schutz; **clip s.o.'s ~s** j-m die Flügel stutzen; **lend ~s to** a) *Hoffnung etc.* beflügeln, b) j-m Beine machen; **spread** (*od.* **try**) **one's ~s** versuchen, auf eigenen Beinen zu stehen *od.* sich durchzusetzen; **singe one's ~s** *fig.* sich die Finger verbrennen; **take ~** a) aufsteigen, davonfliegen, b) aufbrechen, c) *fig.* beflügelt werden; **2.** Federfahne *f* (*Pfeil*); **3.** *humor.* Arm *m*; **4.** (Tür-, Fenster- *etc.*) Flügel *m*; **5.** *mst pl. thea.* ('Seiten)Kuˌlisse *f*: **wait in the ~s** *fig.* sich bereithalten; **6.** ✈ Tragfläche *f*; **7.** *mot.* Kotflügel *m*; **8.** ⚔, ⚓ Flügel *m* (*Aufstellung*); **9.** ✈ a) *brit. Luftwaffe*: Gruppe *f*, b) *amer. Luftwaffe*: Geschwader *n*, c) *pl.* F ,Schwinge' *f* (*Pilotenabzeichen*); **10.** *sport* a) Flügel *m* (*Spielfeldteil*), b) → **winger**; **II** *v/t.* **11.** mit Flügeln *etc.* versehen; **12.** *fig.* beflügeln (*beschleunigen*); **13.** *Strecke* (durch)'fliegen; **14.** a) *Vogel* anschießen, flügeln, b) F *j-n* (*bsd.* am Arm) verwunden; **III** *v/i.* **15.** fliegen; ~ **as·sem·bly** *s.* ✈ Tragwerk *n*; **'~·beat** *s.* Flügelschlag *m*; ~ **case** *s. zo.* Flügeldecke *f*; ~ **chair** *s.* Ohrensessel *m*; ~ **com·mand·er** *s.* ✈, ⚔ **1.** *Brit.* Oberst'leutnant *m* der Luftwaffe; **2.** *Am.* Ge'schwaderkommoˌdore *m*; ~ **cov·ert** *s. zo.* Deckfeder *f*.

wing·ding ['wɪŋdɪŋ] *s. sl.* **1.** (*a.* Wut-) Anfall *m*; **2.** ,tolles Ding'.

winged [wɪŋd] *adj.* □ **1.** *orn.*, *a.* ⚘ geflügelt; Flügel... ; *in Zssgn* ...flügelig: **the ~ horse** *fig.* der Pegasus; ~ **screw** ⚙ Flügelschraube *f*; ~ **words** *fig.* geflügelte Worte; **2.** *fig.* a) beflügelt, schnell, b) beschwingt.

wing·er ['wɪŋə] *s. sport* Außen-, Flügelstürmer *m*.

wing| feath·er *s. orn.* Schwungfeder *f*; **'~ˌheav·y** *adj.* ✈ querlastig; ~ **nut** *s.* ⚙ Flügelmutter *f*; **'~ˌo·ver** *s.* ✈ Immelmann-Turn *m*; ~ **sheath** → **wing case**; **'~·span** ✈, **'~·spread** *s. orn.*, ✈ Spannweite *f*.

wink [wɪŋk] **I** *v/i.* **1.** blinzeln, zwinkern: ~ **at** a) *j-m* zublinzeln, b) *fig.* ein Auge zudrücken bei, *et.* ignorieren; **as easy as ~ing** *Brit.* F kinderleicht; **like ~ing** F wie der Blitz; **2.** blinken, flimmern (*Licht*); **II** *v/t.* **3.** mit *den Augen* blinzeln *od.* zwinkern; **III** *s.* **4.** Blinzeln *n*, Zwinkern *n*, Wink *m* (*mit den Augen*): **forty ~s** Nickerchen *n*; **not to sleep a ~, not to get a ~ of sleep** kein Auge zutun; → **tip**³ 5; **in a ~** im Nu.

win·kle ['wɪŋkl] **I** *s. zo.* (eßbare) Strandschnecke; **II** *v/t.* ~ **out** a) her'ausziehen (*a. fig.* F), b) F *j-n* aussieben, -sondern.

win·ner ['wɪnə] *s.* **1.** Gewinner(in), *sport a.* Sieger(in); **2.** sicherer Gewinner; **3.** ,todsichere' Sache; **4.** ,Schlager' *m*.

win·ning ['wɪnɪŋ] **I** *adj.* □ **1.** *bsd. sport* siegreich, Sieger..., Sieges...; **2.** entscheidend: ~ **hit**; **3.** *fig.* gewinnend, einnehmend; **II** *s.* **4.** ⚒ Abbau *m*, Gewinnung *f*; **5.** *pl.* Gewinn *m* (*bsd. im Spiel*); **6.** Gewinnen *n*, Sieg *m*; ~ **post** *s. sport* Zielpfosten *m*.

win·now ['wɪnəʊ] **I** *v/t.* **1.** a) *Getreide* schwingen, b) *Spreu* trennen (**from** von); **2.** *fig.* sichten; **3.** *fig.* trennen, (unter)'scheiden (**from** von); **II** *s.* **4.** Wanne *f*, Futterschwinge *f*.

wi·no ['waɪnəʊ] *pl.* **-nos** *s. Am. sl.* ,Weinsüffel' *m*, Weinsäufer(in).

win·some ['wɪnsəm] *adj.* □ **1.** gewinnend: ~ **smile**; **2.** (lieb)reizend.

win·ter ['wɪntə] **I** *s.* **1.** Winter *m*; **2.** *poet.* Lenz *m*, (Lebens)Jahr *n*: **a man of fifty ~s**; **II** *v/i.* **3.** (*a. v/t. Tiere, Pflanzen*) über'wintern; **III** *adj.* **4.** winterlich; Winter...: ~ **crop** 🌾 Winterfrucht *f*; ~ **garden** Wintergarten *m*; ~ **sleep** Winterschlaf *m*; ~ **sports** Wintersport *m*; **win·ter·ize** ['wɪntəraɪz] *v/t.* auf den Winter vorbereiten, *bsd.* ⚙ winterfest machen; **'win·ter·tide** *s.* Winter(zeit *f*) *m*; **'~·weight** *adj.* Winter...: ~ **clothes**.

win·tri·ness ['wɪntrɪnɪs] *s.* Kälte *f*, Frostigkeit *f*; **win·try** ['wɪntrɪ] *adj.* **1.** winterlich, frostig; **2.** *fig.* a) trüb(e), b) alt, c) frostig: ~ **smile**.

wipe [waɪp] **I** *s.* **1.** (Ab)Wischen *n*: **give s.th. a ~** et. abwischen; **2.** F a) (harter) Schlag, b) *fig.* Seitenhieb *m*; **II** *v/t.* **3.** (ab-, sauber-, trocken)wischen, abreiben, reinigen: ~ **s.o.'s eye** (**for him**) *sl.* j-n ausstechen; ~ **one's lips** sich den Mund wischen; → **floor** 1; ~ **off** *v/t.* **1.** ab-, wegwischen; **2.** *fig.* bereinigen, auslöschen; *Rechnung* begleichen: **wipe s.th. off the slate** et. begraben *od.* vergessen; ~ **out** *v/t.* **1.** auswischen; **2.** wegwischen, (aus)löschen, tilgen (*a. fig.*): ~ **a disgrace** e-n Schandfleck tilgen, e-e Scharte auswetzen; **3.** *Armee, Stadt etc.* vernichten, ,ausradieren'; *Rasse etc.* ausrotten; ~ **up** *v/t.* **1.** aufwischen; **2.** (ab)trocknen.

wip·er ['waɪpə] *s.* **1.** Wischer *m* (*Person od. Vorrichtung*); **2.** Wischtuch *n*; **3.** ⚙ a) Hebedaumen *m*, b) Abstreifring *m*, c) ⚡ Kon'takt-, Schleifarm *m*; **4.** → **wipe** 2.

wire ['waɪə] **I** *s.* **1.** Draht *m*; **2.** ⚡ Leitung(sdraht *m*) *f*; → **live**² 3; **3.** ⚡ (Kabel)Ader *f*; **4.** F Tele'gramm *n*: **by ~** telegraphisch; **5.** *pl.* a) Drähte *pl. e-s Marionettenspiels*, b) *fig.* geheime Fäden *pl.*, Beziehungen *pl.*: **pull the ~** a) der Drahtzieher sein, b) s-e Beziehungen spielen lassen; **6.** *opt.* Faden *m im Okular*; **7.** ♪ Drahtsaite(n *pl.*) *f*; **II** *adj.* **8.** Draht...: ~ **brush**; **III** *v/t.* **9.** mit Draht(geflecht) versehen; **10.** mit Draht zs.-binden *od.* befestigen; **11.** ⚡ Leitungen legen in, (be)schalten, verdrahten: ~ **to** anschließen an (*acc.*); **12.** F *e-e Nachricht od. j-m* telegraphieren; **13.** *hunt.* mit Drahtschlingen fangen; **IV** *v/i.* **14.** F telegraphieren: ~ **away** *od.* **in** *sl.* loslegen, sich ins Zeug legen; ~ **cloth** → **wire gauze**; ~ **cut·ter** *s.* ⚙ Drahtschere *f*; **'~·draw** *v/t.* [*irr.* → **draw**] **1.** ⚙ *Metall* drahtziehen; **2.** *fig.* a) in die Länge ziehen, b) *Argument* über'spitzen; **'~·drawn** *adj. fig.* a) langatmig, b) über'spitzt; ~ **en·tan·gle·ment** *s.* ⚔ Drahtverhau *m*; ~ **ga(u)ge** *s.* ⚙ Drahtlehre *f*; ~ **gauze** *s.* Drahtgaze *f*, -gewebe *n*, -netz *n*; **'~·haired** *adj. zo.* Drahthaar...: ~ **terrier**.

wire·less ['waɪəlɪs] ⚡ **I** *adj.* **1.** drahtlos, Funk...: ~ **message** Funkspruch *m*; **2.** *Brit.* Radio..., Rundfunk...: ~ **set** → 3; **II** *s.* **3.** *Brit.* 'Radio(appaˌrat *m*) *n*: **on the ~** im Radio *od.* Rundfunk; **4.** *abbr. für* ~ **telegraphy**, ~ **telephony** *etc.*; **III** *v/t. Brit.* **5.** *Nachricht etc.* funken; ~ **car** *s. Brit.* Funkstreifenwagen *m*; ~ **op·er·a·tor** *s.* ✈ (Bord)Funker *m*; ~ **pi·rate** *s.* Schwarzhörer *m*; ~ (**re·ceiv·ing**) **set** *s.* (Funk)Empfänger *m*; ~ **sta·tion** *s.* (*a.* 'Rund)Funkstatiˌon *f*; ~ **te·leg·ra·phy** *s.* drahtlose Telegra'phie, 'Funktelegraˌphie *f*; ~ **te·leph·o·ny** *s.* drahtlose Telepho'nie, Sprechfunk *m*.

'wire|·man [-mən] *s.* [*irr.*] **1.** Tele'graphen-, Tele'phonarbeiter *m*; **2.** E'lektroinstallaˌteur *m*; **3.** 'Abhörspeziaˌlist *m*; ~ **net·ting** *s.* ⚙ **1.** Drahtnetz *n*; **2.** *pl.* Maschendraht *m*; **'~ˌpho·to** *s.* 'Bildteleˌgramm *n*; **'~ˌpull·er** *s. fig.* ,Drahtzieher' *m*; **'~ˌpull·ing** *s. bsd. pol.* ,Drahtziehe'rei *f*; ~ **rod** *s.* ⚙ Walz-, Stabdraht *m*; ~ **rope** *s.* Drahtseil *n*; ~ **rope·way** *s.* Drahtseilbahn *f*; ~ **ser·vice** *s. Am.* 'Nachrichtenagenˌtur *f*; **'~·tap** *v/t. u. v/i.* (*j-s*) Tele'fongespräche abhören, (*j-s*) Leitung(en) anzapfen; **'~ˌtap·ping** *s.* Abhören *n*, Anzapfen *n* (von Tele'phonleitungen); **'~ˌwalk·er** *s.* 'Drahtseilakroˌbat(in), Seiltänzer(in); **'~·worm** *s. zo.* Drahtwurm *m*; **'~·wove** *adj.* **1.** Velin...(*-papier*); **2.** aus Draht geflochten.

wir·ing ['waɪərɪŋ] *s.* **1.** Verdrahtung *f* (*a.* ⚡); **2.** ⚡ a) (Be)Schaltung *f*, b) Leitungsnetz *n*: ~ **diagram** Schaltplan *m*, -schema *n*.

wir·y ['waɪərɪ] *adj.* □ **1.** Draht...; **2.** drahtig (*Haar, Muskeln, Person etc.*); **3.** a) vibrierend, b) me'tallisch (*Ton*).

wis·dom ['wɪzdəm] *s.* Weisheit *f*, Klugheit *f*; ~ **tooth** *s.* [*irr.*] Weisheitszahn *m*: **cut one's ~ teeth** *fig.* vernünftig werden.

wise¹ [waɪz] **I** *adj.* □ → **wisely**; **1.** weise, klug, erfahren, einsichtig; **2.** gescheit, verständig; **3.** wissend, unter'richtet: **be none the ~r** (**for it**) nicht klüger sein als zuvor; **without anybody being the ~r for it** ohne daß es j-d gemerkt hätte; **~r after the event** um e-e Erfahrung klüger; **be ~ to** F Bescheid wissen über (*acc.*); **get ~ to** F *et.* ,spitzkriegen', *j-n od. et.* durch'schauen; **put s.o. ~ to** F j-m *et.* ,stecken'; **4.** schlau, gerissen; **5.** F neunmalklug: ~ **guy** ,Klugscheißer' *m*; **6.** *obs.* ~ **man** Zauberer *m*; ~ **woman** a) Hexe *f*, b) Wahrsagerin *f*, c) weise Frau (*Hebamme*); **II** *v/t.* **7.** ~ **up** *Am.* F *j-n* informieren (**to** über *acc.*); **III** *v/i.* **8.** ~ **up** *Am.* F a) ,schlau' werden, b) ~ **up to** *et.* ,spitzkriegen'.

wise² [waɪz] *s. obs.* Art *f*, Weise *f*: **in**

any ~ auf irgendeine Weise; *in no* ~ in keiner Weise, keineswegs; *in this* ~ auf diese Art u. Weise.

-wise [waɪz] *in Zssgn* a) …artig, nach Art von, b) …weise, c) F …mäßig.

'wise|ˌa·cre [-ˌeɪkə] *s.* Neunmalkluge(r) *m*, Besserwisser *m*; **'~·crack** F **I** *s.* witzige *od.* treffende Bemerkung; Witze'lei *f*; **II** *v/i.* witzeln, ‚flachsen'; **'~-ˌcrack·er** *s.* F Witzbold *m*.

wise·ly ['waɪzlɪ] *adv.* **1.** weise (*etc.*; → *wise*[1] 1 *u.* 2); **2.** klug, kluger-, vernünftigerweise; **3.** (wohl)weislich.

wish [wɪʃ] **I** *v/t.* **1.** (sich) wünschen; **2.** wollen, wünschen: *I ~ I were rich* ich wollte, ich wäre reich; *I ~ you to come* ich möchte, daß du kommst; *~ s.o. further* (*od. at the devil*) j-n zum Teufel wünschen; *~ o.s. home* sich nach Hause sehnen; **3.** hoffen: *I ~ it may prove true*; *it is to be ~ed* es ist zu hoffen *od.* wünschen; **4.** *j-m Glück, Spaß etc.* wünschen: *~ s.o. well* (*ill*) j-m wohl- (übel)wollen; *~ s.th. on s.o.* j-m et. (*Böses*) wünschen, j-m et. aufhalsen; → *joy* 1; **5.** *j-m guten Morgen etc.* wünschen; *j-m Adieu etc.* sagen: *~ s.o. farewell*; **II** *v/i.* **6.** wünschen: *~ for* sich *et.* wünschen, sich sehnen nach; *he cannot ~ for anything better* er kann sich nichts Besseres wünschen; **III** *s.* **7.** Wunsch *m*: a) Verlangen *n* (*for* nach), b) Bitte *f* (*for* um *acc.*), c) *das* Gewünschte: *you shall have your ~* du sollst haben, was du dir wünschst; → *father* 5; **8.** *pl. gute* Wünsche *pl.*, Glückwünsche *pl.*: *good ~es*; **'wish·bone** *s.* **1.** *orn.* Brust-, Gabelbein *n*; **2.** *mot.* Dreiecklenker *m*: *~ suspension* Schwingarmfederung *f*; **wish·ful** ['wɪʃfʊl] *adj.* □ **1.** vom Wunsch erfüllt, begierig (*to do* zu tun); **2.** sehnsüchtig: *~ thinking* Wunschdenken *n*.

wish·ing| bone ['wɪʃɪŋ] → *wishbone* 1; *~ cap* *s.* Zauber-, Wunschkappe *f*.

wish-wash ['wɪʃwɒʃ] *s.* **1.** labberiges Zeug (*a. fig. Geschreibsel*); **2.** *fig.* Geschwätz *n*; **wish·y-wash·y** ['wɪʃɪˌwɒʃɪ] *adj.* labberig: a) wäßrig, b) *fig.* saft- u. kraftlos, seicht.

wisp [wɪsp] *s.* **1.** (*Stroh- etc.*)Wisch *m*, (*Heu-, Haar*)Büschel *n*; (*Haar*)Strähne *f*; **2.** Handfeger *m*; **3.** Strich *m*, Zug *m* (*Vögel*); **4.** Fetzen *m*, Streifen *m*: *~ of smoke* Rauchfetzen *m*; *a ~ of a boy* ein schmächtiges Bürschchen; **'wisp·y** [-pɪ] *adj.* **1.** büschelig (*Haar etc.*); **2.** dünn, schmächtig.

wist·ful ['wɪstfʊl] *adj.* □ **1.** sehnsüchtig, wehmütig; **2.** nachdenklich, versonnen.

wit[1] [wɪt] *s.* **1.** *oft pl.* geistige Fähigkeiten *pl.*, Intelli'genz *f*; **2.** *oft pl.* Verstand *m*: *be at one's ~s' end* mit s-r Weisheit zu Ende sein; *have one's ~s about one* s-e fünf Sinne beisammen haben; *keep one's ~s about one* e-n klaren Kopf behalten; *live by one's ~s* sich mehr oder weniger ehrlich durchs Leben schlagen; *out of one's ~s* von Sinnen, verrückt; *frighten s.o out of his ~s* j-n zu Tode erschrecken; **3.** Witz *m*, Geist *m*, Es'prit *m*; **4.** witziger Kopf, geistreicher Mensch; **5.** *obs.* Witz *m*, witziger Einfall.

wit[2] [wɪt] *v/t. u. v/i.* [*irr.*] *obs.* wissen: *to ~ bsd.* ⚖ das heißt, nämlich.

witch [wɪtʃ] **I** *s.* **1.** Hexe *f*, Zauberin *f*: *~es' sabbath* Hexensabbat *m*; **2.** *fig.* alte Hexe; **3.** F betörendes Wesen, bezaubernde Frau; **II** *v/t.* **4.** be-, verhexen; **'~·craft** *s.* **1.** Hexe'rei *f*, Zaube'rei *f*; **2.** Zauber(kraft *f*) *m*; *~* **doc·tor** *s.* Medi'zinmann *m*.

witch·er·y ['wɪtʃərɪ] *s.* **1.** → *witchcraft*; **2.** *fig.* Zauber *m*.

witch hunt *s. bsd. pol.* Hexenjagd *f* (*for*, *against* auf *acc.*).

witch·ing ['wɪtʃɪŋ] *adj.* □ **1.** Hexen…: *~ hour* Geisterstunde *f*; **2.** → *bewitching*.

wit·e·na·ge·mot [ˌwɪtɪnəgɪ'məʊt] *s. hist. gesetzgebende Versammlung im Angelsachsenreich.*

with [wɪð] *prp.* **1.** mit (*vermittels*): *cut ~ a knife*; *fill ~ water*; **2.** (zs.) mit: *he went ~ his friends*; **3.** nebst, samt: *~ all expenses*; **4.** mit (*besitzend*): *a coat ~ three pockets*; *~ no hat* ohne Hut; **5.** mit (*Art u. Weise*): *~ care*; *~ a smile*; *~ the door open* bei offener Tür; **6.** in Über'einstimmung mit: *I am quite ~ you* ich bin ganz Ihrer Ansicht *od.* ganz auf Ihrer Seite; **7.** mit (*in derselben Weise, im gleichen Grad, zur selben Zeit*): *the sun changes ~ the seasons*; *rise ~ the sun*; **8.** bei: *sit* (*sleep*) *~ s.o.*; *work ~ a firm*; *I have no money ~ me*; **9.** (*kausal*) durch, vor (*dat.*), von, an (*dat.*): *die ~ cancer* an Krebs sterben; *stiff ~ cold* steif vor Kälte; *wet ~ tears* von Tränen naß, tränennaß; *tremble ~ fear* vor Furcht zittern; **10.** bei, für: *~ God all things are possible* bei Gott ist kein Ding unmöglich; **11.** gegen, mit: *fight ~ s.o.*; **12.** bei, auf seiten (von): *it rests ~ you to decide* die Entscheidung liegt bei dir; **13.** trotz, bei: *~ all her brains* bei all ihrer Klugheit; **14.** angesichts; in Anbetracht der Tatsache, daß: *you can't leave ~ your mother so ill* du kannst nicht weggehen, wenn deine Mutter so krank ist; **15.** *~ it sl.* a) ‚auf Draht', ‚schwer auf der Höhe', b) modebewußt, c) up to date, modern: *get ~ it!* mach mit!, sei kein Frosch!

with·al [wɪ'ðɔːl] *obs.* **I** *adv.* außerdem, 'oben'drein, da'bei; **II** *prp.* (*nachgestellt*) mit.

with·draw [wɪð'drɔː] [*irr.* → *draw*] **I** *v/t.* **1.** (*from*) zu'rückziehen, -nehmen (von, aus): a) wegnehmen, entfernen (von, aus), *Schlüssel etc., a.* ⚔ *Truppen* abziehen, her'ausziehen (aus), b) entziehen (*dat.*), c) einziehen, d) *fig. Auftrag, Aussage etc.* wider'rufen, *Wort etc.* zu'rücknehmen: *~ a motion* e-n Antrag zurückziehen; **2.** † a) *Geld* abheben, *a. Kapital* entnehmen, b) *Kredit* kündigen; **II** *v/i.* **3.** (*from*) sich zu'rückziehen (von, aus): a) sich entfernen, b) zu'rückgehen, ⚔ *a.* sich absetzen, c) zu'rücktreten (von *e-m Posten, Vertrag*), d) austreten (aus *e-r Gesellschaft*), e) *fig.* sich distanzieren (von *j-m, e-r Sache*): *~ within o.s. fig.* sich in sich selbst zurückziehen; **with'draw·al** [-ɔːəl] *s.* **1.** Zu'rückziehung *f*, -nahme *f* (*a. fig. Widerrufung*) (*a.* ⚔ *von Truppen*): *~* (*from circulation*) Einziehung, Außerkurssetzung *f*; **2.** † (Geld)Abhebung *f*, Entnahme *f*; **3.** *bsd.* ⚔ Ab-, Rückzug *m*; **4.** (*from*) Rücktritt *m* (von *e-m Amt, Vertrag etc.*), Ausscheiden *n* (aus); **5.** Entzug *m*; **6.** ⚕ Entziehung *f*: *~ cure*; *~ symptoms* Entziehungs-, Ausfallserscheinungen *pl.*; **7.** *sport* Startverzicht *m*; **with'drawn** [-ɔːn] **I** *pp von withdraw*; **II** *adj.* **1.** *psych.* in sich gekehrt; **2.** zu'rückgezogen.

with·er ['wɪðə] **I** *v/i.* **1.** *oft ~ up* (ver-)welken, verdorren, austrocknen; **2.** *fig.* a) vergehen (*Schönheit etc.*), b) ‚eingehen' (*Firma etc.*), c) *oft ~ away* schwinden (*Hoffnung etc.*); **II** *v/t.* **3.** (ver)welken lassen, ausdörren, -trocknen: *~ed fig.* verhutzelt; **4.** *fig. j-n mit e-m Blick etc., a. j-s Ruf* vernichten; **with·er·ing** ['wɪðərɪŋ] *adj.* □ **1.** ausdörrend; **2.** *fig.* vernichtend: *a ~ look* (*remark*).

with·ers ['wɪðəz] *s. pl. zo.* 'Widerrist *m* (*Pferd etc.*): *my ~ are unwrung fig.* das trifft mich nicht.

with'hold *v/t.* [*irr.* → *hold*[2]] **1.** zu'rück-, abhalten (*s.o. from* j-n von *et.*): *~ o.s. from s.th.* sich e-r Sache enthalten; *~ing tax* Quellensteuer *f*; **2.** vorenthalten, versagen (*s.th. from s.o.* j-m et.).

with·in [wɪ'ðɪn] **I** *prp.* **1.** innerhalb von (*od. gen.*), in (*dat.*) (*beide a. zeitlich binnen*): *~ 3 hours* binnen *od.* in nicht mehr als 3 Stunden; *~ a week of his arrival* e-e Woche nach *od.* vor s-r Ankunft; **2.** im *od.* in den Bereich von: *~ call* (*hearing, reach, sight*) in Ruf- (Hör-, Reich-, Sicht)weite; *~ the meaning of the Act* im Rahmen des Gesetzes; *~ my powers* a) im Rahmen m-r Befugnisse, b) soweit es in m-n Kräften steht; *~ o.s. sport* ohne sich zu verausgaben (*laufen etc.*); *live ~ one's income* nicht über s-e Verhältnisse leben; **3.** im 'Umkreis von, nicht weiter (entfernt) als: *~ a mile of* bis auf e-e Meile von; → *ace* 3; **II** *adv.* **4.** (dr)innen, drin, im Innern: *~ and without* innen u. außen; *from ~* von innen; **5.** a) im *od.* zu Hause, drinnen, b) ins Haus, hi'nein; **6.** *fig.* innerlich, im Innern; **III** *s.* **7.** *das* Innere.

with·out [wɪ'ðaʊt] **I** *prp.* **1.** ohne (*doing* zu tun): *~ difficulty*; *~ his finding me* ohne daß er mich fand *od.* findet; *~ doubt* zweifellos; → *do without*, *go without*; **2.** außerhalb, jenseits, vor (*dat.*); **II** *adv.* **3.** (dr)außen, äußerlich; **4.** ohne: *go ~* leer ausgehen; **III** *s.* **5.** *das* Äußere: *from ~* von außen; **IV** *cj.* **6.** *a. ~ that obs. od.* F a) wenn nicht, außer wenn, b) ohne daß.

with'stand [*irr.* → *stand*] *v/t.* wider'stehen (*dat.*): a) sich wider'setzen (*dat.*), b) aushalten (*acc.*), standhalten (*dat.*).

wit·less ['wɪtlɪs] *adj.* □ **1.** geist-, witzlos; **2.** dumm, einfältig; **3.** verrückt; **4.** ahnungslos.

wit·ness ['wɪtnɪs] **I** *s.* **1.** Zeuge *m*, Zeugin *f* (*a.* ⚖ *u. fig.*): *be a ~ of s.th.* Zeuge von et. sein; *call s.o. to ~* j-n als Zeugen anrufen; *a living ~ to* ein lebender Zeuge (*gen.*); *~ for the prosecution* (*Brit. a. for the Crown*) Belastungszeuge; *prosecuting ~* a) Nebenkläger(in), b) Belastungszeuge; *~ for the defence* (*Am. defense*) Entlastungszeuge; ≈ *eccl.* Zeuge Je'hovas; **2.** Zeugnis *n*, Bestätigung *f*, Beweis *m* (*of, to gen. od.* für): *bear ~ to* (*od. of*) Zeugnis ablegen von, *et.* bestätigen; *in ~ whereof* zum Zeugnis *od.* urkundlich

dessen; **II** *v/t.* **3.** bezeugen, beweisen: **~ *Shakespeare*** als Beweis dient Shakespeare; **4.** Zeuge sein von, zu'gegen sein bei, (mit)erleben (*a. fig.*); **5.** *fig.* zeugen von, Zeuge sein von; **6.** ⚖ *j-s Unterschrift* beglaubigen, *Dokument* als Zeuge unter'schreiben; **III** *v/i.* **7.** zeugen, Zeuge sein, Zeugnis ablegen, ⚖ *a.* aussagen (***against*** gegen, ***for, to*** für): ***~ to s.th.*** *fig.* et. bezeugen; ***this agreement ~eth*** ⚖ dieser Vertrag be-inhaltet; **~ box** *bsd. Brit.*, **~ stand** *Am. s.* ⚖ Zeugenstand *m.*

wit·ted ['wɪtɪd] *adj. in Zssgn* ...denkend, ...sinnig; → ***half-witted*** *etc.*

wit·ti·cism ['wɪtɪsɪzəm] *s.* witzige Bemerkung.

wit·ti·ness ['wɪtɪnɪs] *s.* Witzigkeit *f.*

wit·ting·ly ['wɪtɪŋlɪ] *adv.* wissentlich.

wit·ty ['wɪtɪ] *adj.* □ witzig, geistreich.

wives [waɪvz] *pl. von* ***wife***.

wiz [wɪz] F *für* ***wizard*** 2.

wiz·ard ['wɪzəd] **I** *s.* **1.** Zauberer *m*, Hexenmeister *m* (*beide a. fig.*); **2.** *fig.* Ge'nie *n*, Leuchte *f*, ‚Ka'none' *f*; **II** *adj.* **3.** magisch, Zauber...; **4.** F ‚phan'tastisch'; '**wiz·ard·ry** [-drɪ] *s.* Zaube'rei *f*, Hexe'rei *f* (*a. fig.*).

wiz·en ['wɪzn], '**wiz·ened** [-nd] *adj.* verhutzelt, schrump(e)lig.

wo, woa [wəʊ] *int.* brr! (*zum Pferd*).

wob·ble ['wɒbl] **I** *v/i.* **1.** wackeln; schwanken (*a. fig.* ***between*** zwischen); **2.** schlottern (*Knie etc.*); **3.** ⚙ a) flattern (*Rad*), b) ‚eiern' (*Schallplatte*); **II** *s.* **4.** Wackeln *n*; Schwanken *n* (*a. fig.*); ⚙ Flattern *n*; '**wob·bly** [-lɪ] *adj.* wack(e)lig.

woe [wəʊ] **I** *int.* wehe!, ach!; **II** *s.* Weh *n*, Leid *n*, Kummer *m*, Not *f*: ***face of ~*** jämmerliche Miene; ***tale of ~*** Leidensgeschichte *f*; ***~ is me!*** wehe mir!; ***~ (be) to ...!, ~ betide ...!*** wehe (*dat.*)!, verflucht sei(en) ...!; → ***weal***¹; **woe·begone** ['wəʊbɪˌgɒn] *adj.* **1.** leid-, jammervoll, vergrämt; **2.** verwahrlost; **woe·ful** ['wəʊfʊl] *adj.* □ *rhet. od. humor.* **1.** kummer-, sorgenvoll; **2.** elend, jammervoll; **3.** *contp.* erbärmlich, jämmerlich.

wog [wɒg] *s. sl. contp.* farbiger Ausländer.

woke [wəʊk] *pret. von* ***wake***².

wold [wəʊld] *s.* **1.** hügeliges Land; **2.** Hochebene *f.*

wolf [wʊlf] **I** *pl.* **wolves** [-vz] *s.* **1.** *zo.* Wolf *m*: ***a ~ in sheep's clothing*** *fig.* ein Wolf im Schafspelz; ***lone ~*** *fig.* Einzelgänger *m*; ***cry ~*** *fig.* blinden Alarm schlagen; ***keep the ~ from the door*** *fig.* sich über Wasser halten; **2.** *fig.* a) Wolf *m*, räuberische *od.* gierige Per'son, b) F ‚Casa'nova' *m*, Schürzenjäger *m*; **3.** ♪ Disso'nanz *f*; **II** *v/t.* **4.** *a.* ***~ down*** *Speisen* (gierig) verschlingen; **~ call** *s. Am.* F *bewundernder Pfiff od. Ausruf* (*beim Anblick e-r attraktiven Frau*); **~ cub** *s. zo.* junger Wolf.

wolf·ish ['wʊlfɪʃ] *adj.* □ **1.** wölfisch (*a. fig.*), Wolfs...; **2.** *fig.* wild, gefräßig: ***~ appetite*** Wolfshunger *m.*

wolf pack *s.* **1.** Wolfsrudel *n*; **2.** ⚓, ⚔ Rudel *n* U-Boote.

wolf·ram ['wʊlfrəm] *s.* **1.** ⚗ Wolfram *n*; **2.** → '**wolf·ram·ite** [-maɪt] *s. min.* Wolfra'mit *m.*

wol·ver·ine ['wʊlvəri:n] *s. zo.* (Amer.) Vielfraß *m.*

wolves [wʊlvz] *pl. von* ***wolf***.

wom·an ['wʊmən] **I** *pl.* **wom·en** ['wɪmɪn] *s.* **1.** Frau *f*, Weib *n*: ***~ of the world*** Frau von Welt; ***play the ~*** empfindsam *od.* ängstlich sein; → ***women***; **2.** a) Hausangestellte *f*, b) Zofe *f*; **3.** (*ohne Artikel*) das weibliche Geschlecht, die Frauen *pl.*, das Weib: ***born of ~*** vom Weibe geboren (*sterblich*); ***~'s reason*** weibliche Logik; **4.** ***the ~*** *fig.* das Weib, die Frau, das typisch Weibliche; **5.** F a) (Ehe)Frau *f*, b) Freundin *f*, Geliebte *f*; **II** *adj.* **6.** weiblich, Frauen...: ***~ doctor*** Ärztin *f*; ***~ student*** Studentin *f.*

wom·an·hood ['wʊmənhʊd] *s.* **1.** Stellung *f* der (erwachsenen) Frau: ***reach ~*** e-e Frau werden; **2.** Weiblich-, Fraulichkeit *f*; **3.** → ***womankind*** 1; '**wom·an·ish** [-nɪʃ] *adj.* □ **1.** *contp.* weibisch; **2.** → ***womanly***; '**wom·an·ize** [-naɪz] **I** *v/t.* weibisch machen; **II** *v/i.* F hinter den Weibern her sein; '**wom·an·iz·er** [-naɪzə] *s.* F Schürzenjäger *m.*

ˌ**wom·an**|'**kind** *s.* **1.** *coll.* Frauen(welt *f*) *pl.*, Weiblichkeit *f*; **2.** → ***womenfolk*** 2; '**~·like** *adj.* wie e-e Frau, fraulich, weiblich.

wom·an·li·ness ['wʊmənlɪnɪs] *s.* Fraulich-, Weiblichkeit *f*; **wom·an·ly** ['wʊmənlɪ] *adj.* fraulich, weiblich (*a. weitS.*).

womb [wu:m] *s. anat.* Gebärmutter *f*; *weitS.* (Mutter)Leib *m*, Schoß *m* (*a. fig. der Erde, der Zukunft etc.*); **~ en·vy** *s. psych.* Gebärneid *m*; ˌ**~-to-'tomb** *adj.* von der Wiege bis zur Bahre.

wom·en ['wɪmɪn] *pl. von* ***woman***: ***~'s rights*** Frauenrechte; ***~'s team*** *sport* Damenmannschaft *f*; '**~·folk** *s. pl.* **1.** → ***womankind*** 1; **2.** *die* Frauen *pl.* (*in e-r Familie*), *mein etc.* ‚Weibervolk' *n* (da'heim).

Wom·en's| **Lib** [lɪb] F, **~ Lib·e·ra·tion (Move·ment)** *s.* 'Frauenemanzipatiˌonsbewegung *f*; **~ Lib·ber** ['lɪbə] *s.* F Anhängerin *f* der Emanzipati'onsbewegung, *contp.* ‚E'manze' *f.*

won [wʌn] *pret. u. p.p. von* ***win***.

won·der ['wʌndə] **I** *s.* **1.** Wunder *n*, et. Wunderbares, Wundertat *f*, -werk *n*: ***a ~ of skill*** ein (wahres) Wunder an Geschicklichkeit (*Person*); ***the 7 ~s of the world*** die 7 Weltwunder; ***work*** (*od.* ***do***) ***~s*** Wunder wirken; ***promise ~s*** *j-m* goldene Berge versprechen; (***it is***) ***no*** (*od.* ***small***) ***~ that*** kein Wunder, daß; ***~s will never cease*** es gibt immer noch Wunder; → ***nine*** 1, ***sign*** 8; **2.** Verwunderung *f*, (Er)Staunen *n*: ***filled with ~*** von Staunen erfüllt; ***for a ~*** a) erstaunlicherweise, b) ausnahmsweise; ***in ~*** erstaunt, verwundert; **II** *v/i.* **3.** sich (ver)wundern, erstaunt sein (***at, about*** über *acc.*): ***not to be ~ed at*** nicht zu verwundern; **4.** a) neugierig *od.* gespannt sein, gern wissen mögen (***if, whether, what*** *etc.*), b) sich fragen *od.* über'legen: ***I ~ whether I might ...?*** dürfte ich vielleicht ...?, ob ich wohl ... kann?; ***I ~ if you could help me*** vielleicht können Sie mir helfen; ***well, I ~!*** na, ich weiß nicht (recht)!; **~ boy** *s.* ‚Wunderknabe' *m*; **~ child** *s.* [*irr.*] *Am.* Wunderkind *n*; **~ drug** *s.* Wunderdroge *f*, -mittel *n.*

won·der·ful ['wʌndəfʊl] *adj.* □ wunderbar, -voll, herrlich: ***not so ~*** F nicht so toll.

won·der·ing ['wʌndərɪŋ] *adj.* □ verwundert, erstaunt, staunend.

'**won·der·land** *s.* Wunder-, Märchenland *n* (*a. fig.*).

won·der·ment ['wʌndəmənt] *s.* Verwunderung *f*, Staunen *n.*

'**won·der**|**-struck** *adj.* von Staunen ergriffen (***at*** über *acc.*); '**~-ˌwork·er** *s.* Wundertäter(in); '**~-ˌwork·ing** *adj.* wundertätig.

won·drous ['wʌndrəs] *rhet.* **I** *adj.* □ wundersam, -bar; **II** *adv.* a) wunderbar(erweise), b) außerordentlich.

won·ky ['wɒŋkɪ] *adj. Brit. sl.* wack(e)lig (*a. fig.*).

won't [wəʊnt] F *für* ***will not***.

wont [wəʊnt] **I** *adj.*: ***be ~ to do*** gewohnt sein *od.* pflegen zu tun; **II** *s.* Gewohnheit *f*, Brauch *m*; '**wont·ed** [-tɪd] *adj.* **1.** *obs.* gewohnt; **2.** gewöhnlich, üblich; **3.** *Am.* eingewöhnt (***to*** in *dat.*).

woo [wu:] *v/t.* **1.** werben *od.* freien um, *j-m* den Hof machen; **2.** *fig.* trachten nach, buhlen um; **3.** *fig.* a) *j-n* um'werben, b) locken, drängen (***to*** zu).

wood [wʊd] **I** *s.* **1.** *oft pl.* Wald *m*, Waldung *f*, Gehölz *n*: ***be out of the ~*** (*Am.* ***~s***) F über den Berg sein; ***he cannot see the ~ for the trees*** er sieht den Wald vor lauter Bäumen nicht; → ***halloo*** III; **2.** Holz *n*: ***touch ~!*** unberufen!; **3.** (Holz)Faß *n*: ***wine from the ~*** Wein (direkt) vom Faß; **4.** ***the ~*** ♪ → ***woodwind*** 2; **5.** → ***wood block*** 2; **6.** *Bowling*: (*bsd.* abgeräumter) Kegel; **7.** *pl. Skisport*: ‚Bretter' *pl.*; **8.** *Golf*: Holz (-schläger *m*) *n*; **II** *adj.* **9.** hölzern, Holz...; **10.** Wald...; **~ al·co·hol** *s.* ⚗ Holzgeist *m*; **~ a·nem·o·ne** *s.* ⚘ Buschwindrös-chen *n*; '**~·bind**, '**~·bine** *s.* **1.** ⚘ Geißblatt *n*; **2.** *Am.* wilder Wein; **~ block** *s.* **1.** Par'kettbrettchen *n*; **2.** *typ.* a) Druckstock *m*, b) Holzschnitt *m*; **~ carv·er** *s.* Holzschnitzer *m*; **~ carv·ing** *s.* Holzschnitze'rei *f* (*a. Schnitzwerk*); '**~·chuck** *s. zo.* (amer.) Waldmurmeltier *n*; **~ coal** *s.* **1.** *min.* Braunkohle *f*; **2.** Holzkohle *f*; '**~·cock** *s. orn.* Waldschnepfe *f*; '**~·craft** *s.* **1.** die Fähigkeit, im Wald zu (über)leben; **2.** Holzschnitze'rei *f*; '**~·cut** *s. typ.* **1.** Holzstock *m* (*Druckform*); **2.** Holzschnitt *m* (*Druckerzeugnis*); 'ˌ**~ˌcut·ter** *s.* **1.** Holzfäller *m*; **2.** *Kunst*: Holzschneider *m.*

wood·ed ['wʊdɪd] *adj.* bewaldet, waldig, Wald...

wood·en ['wʊdn] *adj.* □ **1.** hölzern, Holz...: ***♀ Horse*** *das* Trojanische Pferd; ***~ spoon*** a) Holzlöffel *m*, b) *bsd. sport* Trostpreis *m*; **2.** *fig.* hölzern, steif (*a. Person*); **3.** *fig.* ausdruckslos (*Gesicht etc.*); **4.** stumpf(sinnig).

wood| **en·grav·er** *s.* Holzschneider *m*; **~ en·grav·ing** *s.* **1.** Holzschneiden *n*; **2.** Holzschnitt *m.*

'**wood·en**|ˌ**head·ed** *adj.* F dumm.

wood| **gas** *s.* ⚙ Holzgas *n*; **~ grouse** *s. orn.* Auerhahn *m.*

wood·i·ness ['wʊdɪnɪs] *s.* **1.** Waldreichtum *m*; **2.** Holzigkeit *f.*

wood| **king·fish·er** *s. orn.* Königsfischer *m*; '**~·land I** *s.* Waldland *n*, Waldung *f*; **II** *adj.* Wald...; **~ lark** *s. orn.* Heidelerche *f*; **~ louse** *s.* [*irr.*] *zo.*

Bohrassel *f*; **ˈ~·man** [-mən] *s.* [*irr.*] **1.** *Brit.* Förster *m*; **2.** Holzfäller *m*; **3.** Jäger *m*; **4.** Waldbewohner *m*; **~ naph·tha** *s.* ⚗ Holzgeist *m*; **~ nymph** *s.* **1.** *myth.* Waldnymphe *f*; **2.** *zo. eine* Motte; **3.** *orn. ein* Kolibri *m*; **ˈ~ˌpeck·er** *s. orn.* Specht *m*; **~ pi·geon** *s. orn.* Ringeltaube *f*; **ˈ~·pile** *s.* Holzhaufen *m*, -stoß *m*; **~ pulp** *s.* ⚙ Holz(zell)stoff *m*, Holzschliff *m*; **ˈ~·ruff** *s.* ✿ Waldmeister *m*; **~·print** → ***woodcut*** 2; **ˈ~·shav·ings** *s. pl.* Hobelspäne *pl.*; **ˈ~·shed** *s.* Holzschuppen *m*.

woods·man [ˈwʊdzmən] *s.* [*irr.*] *s.* Waldbewohner *m*.

wood| sor·rel *s.* ✿ Sauerklee *m*; **~ spir·it** *s.* ⚗ Holzgeist *m*; **~ tar** *s.* ⚗ Holzteer *m*; **~ tick** *s. zo.* Holzbock *m*; **ˈ~·wind** [-wɪnd] ♪ **I** *s.* **1.** ˈHolzblasinstruˌment *n*; **2.** *oft pl.* ˈHolzblasinstruˌmente *pl.* (*e-s Orchesters*), Holz(bläser *pl.*) *n*; **II** *adj.* **3.** Holzblas…; **~ wool** *s.* ⚕ Zellstoffwatte *f*; **ˈ~·work** *s.* ⚠ **1.** Holz-, Balkenwerk *n*; **2.** Holzarbeit(en *pl.*) *f*; **ˈ~ˌwork·ing I** *s.* Holzbearbeitung *f*; **II** *adj.* holzbearbeitend, Holzbearbeitungs…: **~ *machine***; **ˈ~·worm** *s. zo.* Holzwurm *m*.

wood·y [ˈwʊdɪ] *adj.* **1.** a) waldig, Wald…, b) waldreich; **2.** holzig, Holz…

ˈwood·yard *s.* Holzplatz *m*.

woo·er [ˈwuːə] *s.* Freier *m*, Anbeter *m*.

woof¹ [wuːf] *s.* **1.** *Weberei*: a) Einschlag *m*, (Ein)Schuß *m*, b) Schußgarn *n*; **2.** Gewebe *n*.

woof² [wʊf] *v/i.* bellen.

woof·er [ˈwuːfə] *s.* ⚡ Tieftonlautsprecher *m*.

woo·ing [ˈwuːɪŋ] *s.* (*a. fig.* Liebes)Werben *n*, Freien *n*, Werbung *f*.

wool [wʊl] **I** *s.* **1.** Wolle *f*: ***dyed in the ~*** in der Wolle gefärbt, *bsd. fig.* waschecht; → ***cry*** 2; **2.** Wollfaden *m*, -garn *n*; **3.** Wollstoff *m*, -tuch *n*; **4.** Zell-, Pflanzenwolle *f*; **5.** (*Baum-, Glas- etc.*)Wolle *f*; **6.** F ‚Wolle' *f*, (kurzes) wolliges Kopfhaar: ***lose one's ~*** ärgerlich werden; ***pull the ~ over s.o.'s eyes*** F j-n hinters Licht führen; **II** *adj.* **7.** wollen, Woll…; **~ card** *s.* Wollkrempel *m*, -kratze *f*; **~ clip** *s.* † (jährlicher) Wollertrag; **~ comb·ing** *s.* Wollkämmen *n*; **ˈ~-dyed** *adj.* in der Wolle gefärbt.

wool·en *Am.* → ***woollen***.

ˈwool|ˌgath·er·ing I *s. fig.* Verträumtheit *f*, Spintisieren *n*; **II** *adj.* verträumt, spintisierend; **ˈ~ˌgrow·er** *s.* Schafzüchter *m*; **~ hall** *s.* † *Brit.* Wollbörse *f*.

wool·i·ness *Am.* → ***woolliness***.

wool·len [ˈwʊlən] **I** *s.* **1.** Wollstoff *m*; **2.** *pl.* Wollsachen *pl.* (*a. wollene Unterwäsche*), Wollkleidung *f*; **II** *adj.* **3.** wollen, Woll…: **~ *goods*** Wollwaren; **~ drap·er** *s.* Wollwarenhändler *m*.

wool·li·ness [ˈwʊlɪnɪs] *s.* **1.** Wolligkeit *f*; **2.** *paint. u. fig.* Verschwommenheit *f*; **wool·ly** [ˈwʊlɪ] **I** *adj.* **1.** wollig, weich, flaumig; **2.** Wolle tragend, Woll…; **3.** *paint. u. fig.* verschwommen; belegt (*Stimme*); **II** *s.* **4.** wollenes Kleidungsstück, *bsd.* Wolljacke *f*; *pl.* → ***woollen*** 2.

ˈwool|·pack *s.* **1.** Wollsack *m* (*Verpackung*); **2.** Wollballen *m* (*240 englische Pfund*); **3.** *meteor.* Haufenwolke *f*; **ˈ~·sack** *s. pol.* a) Wollsack *m* (*Sitz des Lordkanzlers im englischen Oberhaus*), b) *fig.* Amt *n* des Lordkanzlers; **ˈ~ˌsort·er** *s.* Wollsortierer *m* (*Person od. Maschine*): **~'s *disease*** ⚕ Lungenmilzbrand; **ˈ~ˌsta·pler** *s.* † **1.** Woll(groß)händler *m*; **2.** Wollsortierer *m*; **ˈ~-work** *s.* Wollsticke'rei *f*.

wool·y *Am.* → ***woolly***.

woo·pies [ˈwuːpɪz] *s. pl.* wohlhabende Seniˈoren *pl.* (= ***well-off older people***).

wooz·y [ˈwuːzɪ] *adj. Am. sl.* **1.** (*von Alkohol etc.*) benebelt; **2.** a) wirr (im Kopf, b) ‚komisch' (im Magen).

wop [wɒp] *s. sl. contp.* ‚Itaker' *m*, ‚Spaˈghetti(fresser)' *m*.

word [wɜːd] **I** *s.* **1.** Wort *n*: **~s** a) Worte, b) *ling.* Wörter; ***~ for ~*** Wort für Wort, (wort)wörtlich; ***at a ~*** sofort, aufs Wort; ***in a ~*** mit ˈeinem Wort, kurz (-um); ***in other ~s*** mit anderen Worten; ***in so many ~s*** wörtlich, ausdrücklich; ***the last ~*** a) das letzte Wort (***on*** in *e-r Sache*), b) das Allerneueste *od.* -beste (***in*** an *dat.*); ***have the last ~*** das letzte Wort haben; ***have no ~s for*** nicht wissen, was man zu *e-r Sache* sagen soll; ***put into ~s*** in Worte fassen; ***too silly for ~s*** unsagbar dumm; ***cold's not the ~ for it!*** F kalt ist gar kein Ausdruck!; ***he is a man of few ~s*** er macht nicht viele Worte, er ist ein schweigsamer Mensch; ***he hasn't a ~ to throw at a dog*** er macht den Mund nicht auf; **2.** Wort *n*, Ausspruch *m*: **~s** Worte, Rede, Äußerung; ***by ~ of mouth*** mündlich; ***have a ~ with s.o.*** (kurz) mit j-m sprechen; ***have a ~ to say*** et. (Wichtiges) zu sagen haben; ***put in*** (*od.* ***say***) ***a*** (***good***) ***~ for*** ein (gutes) Wort einlegen für; ***I take your ~ for it*** ich glaube es dir; **3.** *pl.* Text *m e-s Lieds etc.*; **4.** *pl.* Wortwechsel *m*, Streit *m*: ***have ~s*** (***with***) sich streiten *od.* zanken mit; **5.** a) Befehl *m*, Komˈmando *n*, b) Losung *f*, Paˈrole *f*, c) Zeichen *n*, Siˈgnal *n*: ***give the ~*** (***to do***); ***pass the ~*** durch-, weitersagen; ***sharp's the ~!*** (jetzt aber) dalli!; **6.** Bescheid *m*, Nachricht *f*: ***leave ~*** Bescheid hinterlassen (***with*** bei); ***send ~ to*** *j-m* Nachricht geben; **7.** Wort *n*, Versprechen *n*: ***~ of hono(u)r*** Ehrenwort; ***break*** (***give*** *od.* ***pass, keep***) ***one's ~*** sein Wort brechen (geben, halten); ***take s.o. at his ~*** j-n beim Wort nehmen; ***he is as good as his ~*** er ist ein Mann von Wort; er hält, was er verspricht; (***up***)***on my ~!*** auf mein Wort!; **8. *the* 𝔚** *eccl.* das Wort Gottes, das Evanˈgelium; **II** *v/t.* **9.** in Worte fassen, (in Worten) ausdrücken, formulieren: ***~ed as follows*** mit folgendem Wortlaut; **~ ac·cent** *s. ling.* ˈWortakˌzent *m*; **ˈ~-blind** *adj.* ⚕ wortblind; **ˈ~·book** *s.* **1.** Vokabuˈlar *n*; **2.** Wörterbuch *n*; **3.** ♪ Textbuch *n*, Liˈbretto *n*; **ˈ~-ˌcatch·er** *s. contp.* Wortklauber *m*; **ˈ~-deaf** *adj. psych.* worttaub; **~ for·ma·tion** *s. ling.* Wortbildung *f*; **ˌ~-for-ˈword** *adj.* (wort)wörtlich.

word·i·ness [ˈwɜːdɪnɪs] *s.* Wortreichtum *m*, Langatmigkeit *f*; **ˈword·ing** [-ɪŋ] *s.* Fassung *f*, Formulierung *f*, Wortlaut *m*.

word·less [ˈwɜːdlɪs] *adj.* **1.** wortlos, stumm; **2.** schweigsam.

ˌword|-of-ˈmouth *adj.* mündlich: ***~ advertising*** Mundwerbung *f*; **~ or·der** *s. ling.* Wortstellung *f* (*im Satz*); **~ paint·ing** anschauliche Schilderung; **ˌ~-ˈper·fect** *adj.* **1.** *thea. etc.* textsicher; **2.** perˈfekt auswendig gelernt: ***~ text***; ***~ picture*** → ***word painting***; **ˈ~·play** *s.* Wortspiel *n*; **~ pow·er** *s.* Wortschatz *m*; **~ pro·cess·ing** *s. Computer*: Textverarbeitung *f*; **ˈ~ˌsplit·ting** *s.* Wortklaubeˈrei *f*.

word·y [ˈwɜːdɪ] *adj.* ☐ **1.** Wort…: ***~ warfare*** Wortkrieg *m*; **2.** wortreich, langatmig.

wore [wɔː] *pret. von* ***wear¹***, *pret. u. p.p. von* ***wear²***.

work [wɜːk] **I** *s.* **1.** Arbeit *f*: a) Tätigkeit *f*, Beschäftigung *f*, b) Aufgabe *f*, c) Hand-, Nadelarbeit *f*, Stickeˈrei *f*, Näheˈrei *f*, d) Leistung *f*, e) Erzeugnis *n*: ***~ done*** geleistete Arbeit; ***a beautiful piece of ~*** e-e schöne Arbeit; ***good ~!*** gut gemacht!; ***total ~ in hand*** † Gesamtaufträge *pl.*; ***~ in process material*** † Material in Fabrikation; ***at ~*** a) bei der Arbeit, b) in Tätigkeit, in Betrieb; ***be at ~ on*** arbeiten an (*dat.*); ***do ~*** arbeiten; ***be in*** (***out of***) ***~*** (keine) Arbeit haben; (***put***) ***out of ~*** arbeitslos (machen); ***set to ~*** an die Arbeit gehen; ***have one's ~ cut out*** (***for one***) (‚schwer) zu tun' haben; ***make ~*** Arbeit verursachen; ***make sad ~ of*** arg wirtschaften mit; ***make short ~ of*** kurzen Prozeß *od.* nicht viel Federlesens machen mit; ***it's all in the day's ~*** das ist nichts Besonderes, das gehört alles (mit) dazu; **2.** *phys.* Arbeit *f*: ***convert heat into ~***; **3.** *künstlerisches etc.* Werk (*a. coll.*): ***the ~(s) of Bach***; **4.** a) Werk *n* (*Tat u. Resultat*): ***the ~ of a moment*** *es war* das Werk e-s Augenblicks, b) *bsd. pl. eccl.* (gutes) Werk; **5.** ⚙ → ***workpiece***; **6.** *pl.* a) (*bsd.* öffentliche) Bauten *pl. od.* Anlagen *pl.*, b) ⚔ Befestigungen *pl.*, (Festungs)Werk *n*; **7.** *pl. sg. konstr.* Werk *n*, Faˈbrik(anlagen *pl.*) *f*, Betrieb *m*: ***iron~s*** Eisenhütte *f*; ***~s council*** (***engineer, outing, superintendent***) Betriebsrat (-ingenieur, -ausflug, -direktor) *m*; ***~ manager*** Werkleiter *m*; **8.** *pl.* (Trieb-, Uhr- *etc.*)Werk *n*, Getriebe *n*; **9. *the ~s*** *sl.* alles, der ganze Krempel; ***give s.o. the ~s*** j-n ‚fertigmachen'; ***shoot the ~s*** *Kartenspiel od. fig.* aufs Ganze gehen; **II** *v/i.* **10.** (***at***) arbeiten (an *dat.*), sich beschäftigen (mit): ***~ to rule*** Dienst nach Vorschrift tun; **11.** arbeiten (*fig. kämpfen* ***against*** gegen, ***for*** für *e-e Sache*), sich anstrengen; **12.** ⚙ a) funktionieren, gehen (*beide a. fig.*), b) in Betrieb *od.* in Gang sein; **13.** *fig.* ‚klappen', gehen, gelingen, sich machen lassen: ***it won't ~*** es geht nicht; **14.** (*p.p. oft* ***wrought***) wirken (*a. Gift etc.*), sich auswirken ([***up***]***on, with*** auf *acc.*, bei); **15.** sich bearbeiten lassen; **16.** sich (*hindurch-, hoch- etc.*)arbeiten: ***~ into*** eindringen in (*acc.*); ***~ loose*** sich losarbeiten, sich lockern; **17.** in (heftiger) Bewegung sein; **18.** arbeiten, zucken (*Gesichtszüge etc.*), mahlen (*Kiefer*) (***with*** vor *Erregung etc.*); **19.** ⚓ *gegen den Wind etc.* fahren, segeln; **20.** gären; arbeiten (*a. fig. Gedanken etc.*); **21.** (hand)arbeiten, stricken, nähen; **III** *v/t.* **22.** *a.* ⚙ a) bearbeiten, *Teig* kneten, b) verarbeiten, (ver)formen, gestalten (***into*** zu);

23. *Maschine etc.* bedienen, *Wagen* führen, lenken; **24.** ⚙ (an-, be)treiben: ***~ed by electricity***; **25.** ⚘ *Boden* bearbeiten, bestellen; **26.** *Betrieb* leiten, *Fabrik etc.* betreiben, *Gut etc.* bewirtschaften; **27.** ⚒ *Grube* abbauen, ausbeuten; **28.** *geschäftlich* bereisen, bearbeiten; **29.** *j-n, Tiere tüchtig* arbeiten lassen, antreiben; **30.** *fig. j-n* bearbeiten, *j-m* zusetzen; **31.** arbeiten mit, bewegen: ***he ~ed his jaws*** s-e Kiefer mahlten; **32.** a) ***~ one's way*** sich (*hindurch- etc.*)arbeiten, b) verdienen, erarbeiten; → ***passage*** 6; **33.** sticken, nähen, machen; **34.** gären lassen; **35.** errechnen, lösen; **36.** (*p.p. oft* ***wrought***) her'vorbringen, -rufen, *Veränderung etc.* bewirken, *Wunder* wirken *od.* tun, führen zu, verursachen: ***~ hardship***; **37.** (*p.p. oft* ***wrought***) fertigbringen, zu'stande bringen: ***~ it*** F es ‚deichseln'; **38.** *sl. et.* ‚her'ausschlagen', ‚organisieren'; **39.** *in e-n Zustand* versetzen, erregen: ***~ o.s. into a rage*** sich in e-e Wut hineinsteigern;
Zssgn mit adv.:
work| a·round → ***work round***; **~ a·way** *v/i.* (flott) arbeiten (***at*** an *dat.*); **~ in I** *v/t.* einarbeiten, -flechten, -fügen; **II** *v/i.* ***~ with*** harmonieren mit, passen zu; **~ off** *v/t.* **1.** weg-, aufarbeiten; **2.** *überflüssige Energie* loswerden; **3.** *Gefühl* abreagieren (***on*** an *dat.*); **4.** *typ.* abdrucken, -ziehen; **5.** *Ware etc.* loswerden, abstoßen (***on*** an *acc.*); **6.** *Schuld* abarbeiten; **~ out I** *v/t.* **1.** ausrechnen, *Aufgabe* lösen; **2.** *Plan* ausarbeiten; **3.** bewerkstelligen; **4.** ⚒ abbauen, (*a. fig. Thema etc.*) erschöpfen; **II** *v/i.* **5.** sich her'ausarbeiten, zum Vorschein kommen (***from*** aus); **6.** ***~ at*** sich belaufen auf (*acc.*); **7.** ‚klappen', *gut etc.* gehen, sich *gut etc.* anlassen: ***~ well*** (***badly***); **8.** *sport* trainieren; **~ o·ver** *v/t.* **1.** über'arbeiten; **2.** *sl. j-n* ‚in die Mache nehmen'; **~ round** *v/i.* **1.** ***~ to*** a) *ein Problem etc.* angehen, b) sich 'durchringen zu; **2.** ***~ to*** kommen zu, Zeit finden für; **3.** drehen (*Wind*); **~ to·geth·er** *v/i.* **1.** zs.-arbeiten; **2.** inein'andergreifen (*Zahnräder*); **~ up I** *v/t.* **1.** verarbeiten (***into*** zu); **2.** ausarbeiten, entwickeln; **3.** *Thema* bearbeiten; sich einarbeiten in (*acc.*), gründlich studieren; **4.** *Geschäft etc.* auf- *od.* ausbauen; **5.** a) *Interesse etc.* entwickeln, b) sich *Appetit etc.* holen; **6.** *Gefühl, Nerven, a. Zuhörer etc.* aufpeitschen, -wühlen, *Interesse* wecken: ***work o.s. up*** sich aufregen; ***~ a rage, work o.s. up into a rage*** sich in e-e Wut hineinsteigern; ***worked up*** aufgebracht; **II** *v/i.* **7.** *fig.* sich steigern (***to*** zu).

work·a·ble ['wɜːkəbl] *adj.* ☐ **1.** bearbeitungsfähig, (ver)formbar; **2.** betriebsfähig; **3.** 'durch-, ausführbar (*Plan etc.*); **4.** ⚒ abbauwürdig.

work·a·day ['wɜːkədeɪ] *adj.* **1.** Alltags…; **2.** *fig.* all'täglich.

work·a·hol·ic [ˌwɜːkə'hɒlɪk] *s.* Arbeitssüchtige(r *m*) *f*; Arbeitstier *n*.

'work|·bench *s.* ⚙ Werkbank *f*; **'~·book** *s.* **1.** ⚙ Betriebsanleitung *f*; **2.** *ped.* Arbeitsheft *n*; **'~·box** *s.* Nähkasten *m*; **~ camp** *s.* Arbeitslager *n*; **'~·day** *s.* Arbeits-, Werktag *m*: ***on ~s*** werktags.

work·er ['wɜːkə] *s.* **1.** a) Arbeiter(in), b) Angestellte(r *m*) *f*, c) Fachmann *m*, d) *allg.* Arbeitskraft *f*: ***~s*** Belegschaft *f*, Arbeiterschaft *f*; **2.** *fig.* Urheber(in); **3.** *a.* ***~ ant, ~ bee*** *zo.* Arbeiterin *f* (*Ameise, Biene*); **~ di·rec·tor** *s.* ✝ 'Arbeitsdiˌrektor *m*; **~ par·tic·i·pa·tion** *s.* ✝ Mitbestimmung *f*.

'work|ˌfel·low *s.* 'Arbeitskameˌrad *m*; **~ force** *s.* ✝ **1.** Belegschaft *f*; **2.** 'Arbeitskräftepotentiˌal *n*; **'~·girl** *s.* Fa'brikarbeiterin *f*; **'~·horse** *s.* Arbeitspferd *n* (*a. fig.*); **'~·house** *s.* **1.** *Brit. obs.* Armenhaus *n* (mit Arbeitszwang); **2.** ⚖ *Am.* Arbeitshaus *n*.

work·ing ['wɜːkɪŋ] **I** *s.* **1.** Arbeiten *n*; **2.** *a. pl.* Tätigkeit *f*, Wirken *n*; **3.** ⚙ Be-, Verarbeitung *f*; **4.** ⚙ a) Funktionieren *n*, b) Arbeitsweise *f*; **5.** Lösen *n e-s Problems*; **6.** mühsame Arbeit, Kampf *m*; **7.** Gärung *f*; **8.** *mst pl.* ⚒, *min.* a) Abbau *m*, b) Grube *f*; **II** *adj.* **9.** arbeitend, berufs-, werktätig: ***~ population***; ***~ student*** Werkstudent *m*; **10.** Arbeits…: ***~ method*** Arbeitsverfahren *n*; **11.** ⚙, ✝ Betriebs…(*-kapital, -kosten,* ⚡ *-spannung etc.*); **12.** grundlegend, Ausgangs…, Arbeits…: ***~ hypothesis***; ***~ title*** Arbeitstitel *m* (*e-s Buchs etc.*); **13.** brauchbar, praktisch: ***~ knowledge*** ausreichende Kenntnisse; **~ class** *s.* Arbeiterklasse *f*; **ˌ~-'class** *adj.* der Arbeiterklasse, Arbeiter…; **~ con·di·tion** *s.* **1.** ⚙ a) Betriebszustand *m*, b) *pl.* Betriebsbedingungen *pl.*; **2.** Arbeitsverhältnis *n*; **~ day** → ***workday***; **~ draw·ing** *s.* ⚙ Werk(statt)zeichnung *f*; **~ hour** *s.* Arbeitsstunde *f*; *pl.* Arbeitszeit *f*; **~ˌload** *s.* **1.** ⚡ Betriebsbelastung *f*; **2.** ⚙ Nutzlast *f*; **~ lunch** *s.* Arbeitsessen *n*; **~ ma·jor·i·ty** *s. pol.* arbeitsfähige Mehrheit; **'~·man** *s.* [*irr.*] → ***workman***; **~ mod·el** *s.* ⚙ Ver'suchsmoˌdell *n*; **~ or·der** *s.* ⚙ Betriebszustand *m*: ***in ~*** in betriebsfähigem Zustand; **ˌ~-'out** *s.* **1.** Ausarbeitung *f*; **2.** Lösung *f* (*e-r Aufgabe*); **~ stroke** *s. mot.* Arbeitstakt *m*; **~ sur·face** *s.* ⚙ Arbeits-, Lauffläche *f*.

work·less ['wɜːklɪs] *adj.* arbeitslos.

'work|·load *s.* Arbeitspensum *n*; **'~·man** [-mən] *s.* [*irr.*] **1.** Arbeiter *m*; **2.** Handwerker *m*; **'~·man·like** [-laɪk], **'~·ly** [-lɪ] *adj.* kunstgerecht, fachmännisch; **'~·man·ship** [-ʃɪp] *s.* **1.** *j-s* Werk *n*; **2.** Kunst(fertigkeit) *f*; **3.** *gute etc.* Ausführung; Verarbeitungsgüte *f*; Quali'tätsarbeit *f*; **'~·men's com·pen·sa·tion act** [-mənz] *s.* Arbeiterunfallversicherungsgesetz *n*; **'~·out** *s.* **1.** F *sport* (Konditi'ons)Training *n*; **2.** Versuch *m*, Erprobung *f*; **'~ˌpeo·ple** *s. pl.* Belegschaft *f*; **~ per·mit** *s.* Arbeitserlaubnis *f*; **'~·piece** *s.* ⚙ Arbeits-, Werkstück *n*; **'~·place** *s. Am.* Arbeitsplatz *m*; **~ shar·ing** *s.* ✝ Arbeitsaufteilung *f*; **~ sheet** *s.* **1.** 'Arbeitsbogen *m*, -ˌunterlage *f*; **2.** *Am.* ✝ 'Rohbiˌlanz *f*; **'~·shop** *s.* **1.** Werkstatt *f*: ***~ drawing*** ⚙ Werkstatt-, Konstruktionszeichnung *f*; **2.** *ped.* Werkraum *m*; **3.** *fig.* a) Werkstatt *f* (*e-r Künstlergruppe etc.*): ***~ theatre*** (*Am.* ***theater***) Werkstatttheater *n*, b) Workshop *m*, Kurs *m*, Semi'nar *n*; **'~·shy** *adj.* arbeitsscheu; **'~ˌta·ble** *s.* Werktisch *m*; **ˌ~-to-'rule** *s.* Dienst *m* nach Vorschrift; **'~·wear** *s.* Arbeitskleidung *f*; **'~ˌwom·an** *s.* [*irr.*] Arbeiterin *f*.

world [wɜːld] **I** *s.* **1.** *allg.* Welt *f*: a) Erde *f*, b) Himmelskörper *m*, c) (Welt)All *n*, d) *fig. die* Menschen *pl.*, *die* Leute *pl.*, e) Sphäre *f*, Mili'eu *n*, f) (Na'tur)Reich *n*: (***animal***) ***vegetable ~*** (Tier-) Pflanzenreich, -welt; ***lower ~*** Unterwelt; ***the commercial ~, the ~ of commerce*** die Handelswelt; ***the ~ of letters*** die gelehrte Welt; ***a ~ of difference*** ein himmelweiter Unterschied; ***other ~s*** andere Welten; ***all the ~*** die ganze Welt, jedermann; ***all the ~ over*** in der ganzen Welt; ***all the ~ and his wife*** F Gott u. die Welt; alles, was Beine hatte; ***for all the ~*** in jeder Hinsicht; ***for all the ~ like*** (*od.* ***as if***) genauso wie (*od.* als ob); ***for all the ~ to see*** vor aller Augen; ***from all over the ~*** aus aller Herren Länder; ***not for the ~*** nicht um die (*od.* alles in der) Welt; ***in the ~*** (auf) der Welt; ***out of this*** (*od.* ***the***) ***~*** *sl.* phantastisch; ***bring*** (***come***) ***into the ~*** zur Welt bringen (kommen); ***carry the ~ before one*** glänzenden Erfolg haben; ***have the best of both ~s*** die Vorteile beider Seiten genießen; ***put into the ~*** in die Welt setzen; ***think the ~ of*** große Stücke halten auf (*acc.*); ***she is all the ~ to him*** sie ist sein ein u. alles; ***how goes the ~ with you?*** wie geht's, wie steht's?; ***what*** (***who***) ***in the ~?*** was (wer) in aller Welt?; ***it's a small ~!*** die Welt ist ein Dorf!; **2.** ***a ~ of*** e-e Welt von, e-e Unmenge *Schwierigkeiten etc.*; **II** *adj.* **3.** Welt…: ***~ champion*** (***language, literature, politics, record*** *etc.*); **≈ Court** *s.* Internationaler Ständiger Gerichtshof; **≈ Cup** *s.* **1.** *Skisport etc.*: Weltcup *m*; **2.** Fußballweltmeisterschaft *f*; **'~-ˌfa·mous** *adj.* weltberühmt.

world·li·ness ['wɜːldlɪnɪs] *s.* Weltlichkeit *f*, weltlicher Sinn.

world·ling ['wɜːldlɪŋ] *s.* Weltkind *n*.

world·ly ['wɜːldlɪ] *adj. u. adv.* **1.** weltlich, irdisch, zeitlich: ***~ goods*** irdische Güter; **2.** weltlich (gesinnt): ***~ innocence*** Weltfremdheit *f*; ***~ wisdom*** Weltklugheit *f*; **ˌ~-'wise** *adj.* weltklug.

world| pow·er *s. pol.* Weltmacht *f*; **~ se·ries** *s. Baseball*: US-Meisterschaftsspiele *pl.*; **'~ˌshak·ing** *adj. a. iro.* welterschütternd: ***it isn't ~ after all***; **~ view** *s.* Weltanschauung *f*; **≈ War** *s.* Weltkrieg *m*: ***~ I*** (***II***) erster (zweiter) Weltkrieg; **'~-ˌwea·ry** *adj.* weltverdrossen; **'~·wide** *adj.* weltweit, auf der ganzen Welt: ***~ reputation*** Weltruf *m*; ***~ strategy*** ⚔ Großraumstrategie *f*.

worm [wɜːm] **I** *s.* **1.** *zo.* Wurm *m* (*a. fig. contp. Person*): ***even a ~ will turn*** *fig.* auch der Wurm krümmt sich, wenn er getreten wird; **2.** *pl.* ⚕ Würmer *pl.*; **3.** ⚙ a) (Schrauben-, Schnecken)Gewinde *n*, b) (Förder-, Steuer- *etc.*)Schnecke *f*, c) (Rohr-, Kühl)Schlange *f*; **II** *v/t.* **4.** ***~ one's way*** (*od.* ***o.s.***) a) sich *wohin* schlängeln, b) *fig.* sich einschleichen (***into*** in *j-s Vertrauen etc.*); **5.** ***~ a secret out of s.o.*** j-m ein Geheimnis entlocken; **6.** ⚕ von Würmern befreien; **III** *v/i.* **7.** sich schlängeln, kriechen; **8.** sich winden; **~ drive** *s.* ⚙ Schneckenantrieb *m*; **'~-ˌeat·en** *adj.* **1.** wurmstichig; **2.** *fig.* veraltet; **~ gear** *s.* ⚙ **1.** Schneckengetriebe *n*; **2.** → ***worm wheel***; **'~'s-eye view** *s.* 'Froschperspeķtive *f*; **~ thread** *s.* ⚙ Schneckengewinde *n*; **~ wheel** *s.* ⚙ Schneckenrad *n*; **ˈ~wood** *s.* **1.** ⚘ Wermut *m*; **2.** *fig.* Bitterkeit *f*: ***be (gall and) ~ to*** *j-n* bitter ankommen.

worm·y [ˈwɜːmɪ] *adj.* **1.** wurmig, voller Würmer; **2.** wurmstichig; **3.** wurmartig; **4.** *fig.* kriecherisch.

worn [wɔːn] **I** *p.p. von* ***wear***[1]; **II** *adj.* **1.** getragen (*Kleider*); **2.** → ***worn-out*** 1; **3.** erschöpft, abgespannt; **4.** *fig.* abgedroschen: ***~ joke***; **ˌ~-ˈout** *adj.* **1.** abgetragen, -genutzt; **2.** völlig erschöpft, todmüde, zermürbt; **3.** → ***worn*** 4.

wor·ried [ˈwʌrɪd] *adj.* **1.** gequält; **2.** sorgenvoll, besorgt; **3.** beunruhigt, ängstlich; **ˈwor·ri·er** [-ɪə] *s.* j-d, der sich ständig Sorgen macht; **ˈwor·ri·ment** [-ɪmənt] *s.* F **1.** Plage *f*, Quäleˈrei *f*; **2.** Angst *f*, Sorge *f*; **ˈwor·ri·some** [-ɪsəm] *adj.* **1.** quälend; **2.** lästig; **3.** beunruhigend; **4.** unruhig.

wor·ry [ˈwʌrɪ] **I** *v/t.* **1.** a) zausen, schütteln, beuteln, b) *Tier* (ab)würgen (*Hund etc.*); **2.** quälen, plagen (*a. fig. belästigen*); *fig. j-m* zusetzen: ***~ s.o. into a decision*** j-n so lange quälen, bis er e-e Entscheidung trifft; ***~ s.o. out of s.th.*** a) j-n mühsam von et. abbringen, b) j-n durch unablässiges Quälen um et. bringen; **3.** a) ärgern, b) beunruhigen, quälen, *j-m* Sorgen machen: ***~ o.s.*** → 7; **4.** ***~ out*** *Plan etc.* ausknobeln; **II** *v/i.* **5.** zerren, reißen (***at*** an *dat.*); **6.** sich quälen *od.* plagen; **7.** sich beunruhigen, sich Gedanken *od.* Sorgen machen (***about***, ***over*** um, wegen); **8.** ***~ along*** sich mühsam *od.* mit knapper Not durchschlagen; ***~ through s.th.*** sich durch et. hindurchquälen; **III** *s.* **9.** Kummer *m*, Besorgnis *f*, Sorge *f*, (innere) Unruhe; **10.** (Ursache *f* von) Ärger *m*, Aufregung *f*; **11.** Quälgeist *m*; **12.** a) Schütteln *n*, Beuteln *n*, b) Abwürgen *n* (*bsd. vom Hund*); **ˈwor·ry·ing** [-ɪɪŋ] *adj.* ☐ beunruhigend, quälend.

worse [wɜːs] **I** *adj.* (*comp. von* ***bad***, ***evil***, ***ill***) **1.** schlechter, schlimmer (*beide a.* ⚕), übler, ärger: ***~ and ~*** immer schlechter *od.* schlimmer; ***the ~*** desto schlimmer; ***so much*** (*od.* ***all***) ***the ~*** um so schlimmer; ***~ luck!*** leider!, unglücklicherweise!, um so schlimmer!; ***to make it ~*** (*Redew.*) um das Unglück vollzumachen; → ***wear***[1] 14; ***he is ~ than yesterday*** es geht ihm schlechter als gestern; **2.** schlechter gestellt: (***not***) ***to be the ~ for*** (keinen) Schaden gelitten haben durch, (nicht) schlechter gestellt sein wegen; ***he is none the ~*** (***for it***) er ist darum nicht übler dran; ***you would be none the ~ for a walk*** ein Spaziergang würde dir gar nichts schaden; ***be*** (***none***) ***the ~ for drink*** (nicht) betrunken sein; **II** *adv.* **3.** schlechter, schlimmer, ärger: ***none the ~*** nicht schlechter; ***be ~ off*** schlechter daran sein; ***you could do ~ than …*** du könntest ruhig …; **III** *s.* **4.** Schlechtere(s) *n*, Schlimmere(s) *n*: ***~ followed*** Schlimmeres folgte; → ***better***[1] 2; ***from bad to ~*** vom Regen in die Traufe; ***a change for the ~*** e-e Wendung zum Schlechten; **ˈwors·en** [-sn] **I** *v/t.* **1.** schlechter machen, verschlechtern; **2.** *Unglück etc.* verschlimmern; **3.** *j-n* schlechter stellen; **II** *v/i.* **4.** sich verschlechtern *od.* verschlimmern; **ˈwors·en·ing** [-snɪŋ] *s.* Verschlechterung *f*, -schlimmerung *f*.

wor·ship [ˈwɜːʃɪp] **I** *s.* **1.** *eccl.* a) (*a. fig.*) Anbetung *f*, Verehrung *f*, Kult(us) *m*, b) (***public ~*** öffentlicher) Gottesdienst, Ritus *m*: ***place of ~*** Kultstätte *f*, Gotteshaus *n*; ***the ~ of wealth*** *fig.* die Anbetung des Reichtums; **2.** (*der*, *die*, *das*) Angebetete; **3.** ***his*** (***your***) ℒ *bsd. Brit.* Seiner (Euer) Hochwürden (*Anrede, jetzt bsd. für Bürgermeister u. Richter*); **II** *v/t.* **4.** anbeten, verehren, huldigen (*dat.*) (*alle a. fig. vergöttern*); **III** *v/i.* **5.** beten, s-e Andacht verrichten; **wor·ship·er** *Am.* → ***worshipper***; **ˈwor·ship·ful** [-fʊl] *adj.* ☐ **1.** verehrend, anbetend (*Blick etc.*); **2.** *obs.* (ehr)würdig, achtbar; **3.** (*in der Anrede*) hochwohllöblich, hochverehrt; **ˈwor·ship·per** [-pə] *s.* **1.** Anbeter(in), Verehrer(in): ***~ of idols*** Götzendiener *m*; **2.** Beter(in): ***the ~s*** die Andächtigen, die Kirchgänger.

worst [wɜːst] **I** *adj.* (*sup. von* ***bad***, ***evil***, ***ill***) schlechtest, schlimmst, übelst, ärgst: ***and, which is ~*** und, was das schlimmste ist; **II** *adv.* am schlechtesten *od.* übelsten, am schlimmsten *od.* ärgsten; **III** *s. der* (*die*, *das*) Schlechteste *od.* Schlimmste *od.* Ärgste: ***at*** (***the***) ***~*** schlimmstenfalls; ***be prepared for the ~*** aufs Schlimmste gefaßt sein; ***do one's ~*** es so schlecht *od.* schlimm wie möglich machen; ***do your ~!*** mach, was du willst!; ***let him do his ~!*** soll er nur!; ***get the ~ of it*** den kürzeren ziehen; ***if*** (*od.* ***when***) ***the ~ comes to the ~*** wenn es zum Schlimmsten kommt, wenn alle Stricke reißen; ***he was at his ~*** er zeigte sich von seiner schlechtesten Seite, er war in denkbar schlechter Form; ***see s.o.*** (***s.th.***) ***at his*** (***its***) ***~*** j-n (et.) von der schlechtesten *od.* schwächsten Seite sehen; ***the illness is at its ~*** die Krankheit ist auf ihrem Höhepunkt; ***the ~ of it is*** das Schlimmste daran ist; **IV** *v/t.* überˈwältigen, schlagen.

wor·sted [ˈwʊstɪd] ⚙ **I** *s.* **1.** Kammgarn *n*, -wolle *f*; **2.** Kammgarnstoff *m*; **II** *adj.* **3.** wollen, Woll…: ***~ wool*** Kammwolle *f*; ***~ yarn*** Kammgarn *n*; **4.** Kammgarn…

wort[1] [wɜːt] *in Zssgn* …kraut *n*, …wurz *f*.

wort[2] [wɜːt] *s.* (Bier)Würze *f*: ***original ~*** Stammwürze.

worth [wɜːθ] **I** *adj.* **1.** (*e-n bestimmten Betrag*) wert (***to*** *dat. od.* für): ***he is ~ a million*** er besitzt *od.* verdient e-e Million, er ist e-e Million wert; ***for all you are ~*** F so sehr du kannst, ‚auf Teufel komm raus'; ***my opinion for what it may be ~*** m-e unmaßgebliche Meinung; ***take it for what it is ~!*** *fig.* nimm es für das, was es wirklich ist!; **2.** *fig.* würdig, wert (*gen.*): ***~ doing*** wert getan zu werden; ***~ mentioning*** (***reading***, ***seeing***) erwähnens- (lesens-, sehens-) wert; ***be ~ the trouble***, ***be ~ it*** F sich lohnen, der Mühe wert sein; → ***powder*** 1, ***while*** 1; **II** *s.* **3.** Wert *m* (*a. fig. Bedeutung, Verdienst*): ***of no ~*** wertlos; ***get the ~ of one's money*** für sein Geld et. (Gleichwertiges) bekommen; ***20 pence's ~ of stamps*** Briefmarken im Wert von 20 Pence, für 20 Pence Briefmarken; ***men of ~*** verdiente *od.* verdienstvolle Leute.

wor·thi·ly [ˈwɜːðɪlɪ] *adv.* **1.** nach Verdienst, angemessen; **2.** mit Recht; **3.** würdig; **ˈwor·thi·ness** [-ɪnɪs] *s.* Wert *m*; **worth·less** [ˈwɜːθlɪs] *adj.* ☐ **1.** wertlos; **2.** *fig.* un-, nichtswürdig.

ˌworthˈwhile *adj.* lohnend, der Mühe wert.

wor·thy [ˈwɜːðɪ] **I** *adj.* ☐ → ***worthily***; **1.** würdig, achtbar, angesehen; **2.** würdig, wert (***of*** *gen.*): ***be ~ of*** *e-r Sache* wert *od.* würdig sein, *et.* verdienen; ***he is not ~ of her*** er ist ihrer nicht wert *od.* würdig; ***~ of credit*** a) glaubwürdig, b) ☤ kreditwürdig; ***~ of a better cause*** e-r besseren Sache würdig; **3.** würdig (*Gegner*, *Nachfolger etc.*), angemessen (*Belohnung*); **4.** *humor.* trefflich, wakker (*Person*); **II** *s.* **5.** große Perˈsönlichkeit, Größe *f*, Held(in) (*mst pl.*); **6.** *humor. der* Wackere.

would [wʊd; wəd] **1.** *pret. von* ***will***[1] I: a) wollte(st), wollten: ***he ~ not go*** er wollte durchaus nicht gehen, b) pflegte(st), pflegten zu (*oft unübersetzt*): ***he ~ take a walk every day*** er pflegte täglich e-n Spaziergang zu machen; ***now and then a bird ~ call*** ab u. zu ertönte ein Vogelruf; ***you ~ do that!*** du mußtest das natürlich tun!, das sieht dir ähnlich!, c) *fragend*: würdest *du*?, würden *Sie*?: ***~ you pass me the salt, please?***, d) *vermutend*: ***that ~ be 3 dollars*** das wären (dann) 3 Dollar; ***it ~ seem that*** es scheint fast, daß; **2.** *konditional*: würde(st), würden: ***she ~ do it if she could***; ***he ~ have come if …*** er wäre gekommen, wenn …; **3.** *pret. von* ***will***[1] II: *ich* wollte *od.* wünschte *od.* möchte: ***I ~ it were otherwise***; ***~*** (***to***) ***God*** wollte Gott; ***I ~ have you know*** ich muß Ihnen (schon) sagen.

would-be [ˈwʊdbiː] **I** *adj.* **1.** Möchtegern…: ***~ critic*** Kritikaster *m*; ***~ painter*** Farbenkleckser *m*; ***~ poet*** Dichterling *m*; ***~ huntsman*** Sonntagsjäger *m*; ***~ witty*** geistreich sein sollend (*Bemerkung etc.*); **2.** angehend, zukünftig: ***~ author***, ***~ wife***; **II** *s.* **3.** Gernegroß *m*, Möchtegern *m*.

wound[1] [waʊnd] *pret. u. p.p. von* ***wind***[2] *u.* ***wind***[3].

wound[2] [wuːnd] **I** *s.* **1.** Wunde *f* (*a. fig.*), Verletzung *f*, -wundung *f*: ***~ of entry*** (***exit***) ⚔ Einschuß *m* (Ausschuß *m*); **2.** *fig.* Verletzung *f*, Kränkung *f*; **II** *v/t.* **3.** verwunden, verletzen (*beide a. fig. kränken*); **ˈwound·ed** [-dɪd] *adj.* verwundet, verletzt (*beide a. fig. gekränkt*): ***~ veteran*** Kriegsversehrte(r) *m*; ***the ~*** die Verwundeten; ***~ vanity*** gekränkte Eitelkeit.

wove [wəʊv] *pret. u. obs. p.p. von* ***weave***; **ˈwo·ven** [-vən] *p.p. von* ***weave***: ***~ goods*** Web-, Wirkwaren.

wove pa·per *s.* ⚙ Veˈlinpaˌpier *n*.

wow [waʊ] **I** *int.* Mann!, toll!; **II** *s. bsd. Am. sl.* a) Bombenerfolg *m*, b) ‚tolles Ding', c) ‚toller Kerl', ‚tolle Frau' *etc.*: ***he*** (***it***) ***is a ~*** er (es) ist 'ne Wucht; **III** *v/t. j-n* hinreißen.

wrack[1] [ræk] *s.* **1.** → ***wreck*** 1 *u.* 2; **2.** ***~ and ruin*** Untergang u. Verderben; ***go to ~*** untergehen; **3.** Seetang *m*.

wrack[2] → ***rack***[4] I.

wraith [reɪθ] *s.* **1.** Geistererscheinung *f* (*bsd. von gerade Gestorbenen*); **2.** Geist *m*, Gespenst *n*.

wran·gle ['ræŋgl] **I** *v/i.* (sich) zanken *od.* streiten, sich in den Haaren liegen; **II** *s.* Streit *m*, Zank *m*; '**wran·gler** [-lə] *s.* **1.** Zänker(in), streitsüchtige Per'son; **2.** *univ. Brit. Student in Cambridge, der bei der höchsten mathematischen Abschlußprüfung den 1. Grad erhalten hat*; **3.** guter Debattierer; **4.** *Am.* Cowboy *m*.

wrap [ræp] **I** *v/t.* [*irr.*] **1.** wickeln, hüllen; *a. Arme* schlingen (***round*** um *acc.*); **2.** *mst* **~ *up*** (ein)wickeln, (-)packen, (-)hüllen, (-)schlagen (***in*** in *acc.*): **~ *o.s. up*** (***well***) sich warm anziehen; **3.** **~ *up*** F a) *et.* glücklich ‚über die Bühne' bringen, b) abschließen, beenden; **~ *it up*** die Sache (erfolgreich) zu Ende führen; ***that ~s it up*** (***for today***)***!*** das wär's (für heute)!; **4.** *oft* **~ *up*** *fig.* (ein)hüllen, verbergen, *Tadel etc.* (ver)kleiden (***in*** in *acc.*): ***~ped up in mystery*** *fig.* geheimnisvoll, rätselhaft; ***~ped*** (*od.* ***wrapt***) ***in silence*** in Schweigen gehüllt; ***be ~ped up in*** a) völlig in Anspruch genommen sein von (*e-r Arbeit etc.*), ganz aufgehen in (*s-r Arbeit, s-n Kindern etc.*), b) versunken sein in (*acc.*); **5.** *fig.* verwickeln, -stricken (***in*** in *acc.*); **II** *v/i.* [*irr.*] **6.** sich einhüllen: **~ *up well!*** zieh dich warm an!; **7.** sich legen *od.* wickeln *od.* schlingen (***round*** um); **8.** sich legen (***over*** um) (*Kleider*); **9.** **~ *up!*** *sl.* halt's Maul!; **III** *s.* **10.** Hülle *f*, *bsd.* a) Decke *f*, b) Schal *m*, Pelz *m*, c) 'Umhang *m*, Mantel *m*: ***keep s.th. under ~s*** *fig.* et. geheimhalten; '**~·a·round I** *adj.* ⚙ Rundum…, Vollsicht…(*-verglasung*): **~ *windshield*** (*Brit.* ***windscreen***) *mot.* Panoramascheibe *f*; **II** *s.* Wickelbluse *f*, -kleid *n*.

wrap·per ['ræpə] *s.* **1.** (Ein)Packer(in); **2.** Hülle *f*, Decke *f*, 'Überzug *m*, Verpackung *f*; **3.** ('Buch),Umschlag *m*, Schutzhülle *f*; **4.** *a.* ***postal ~*** ✉ Kreuz-, Streifband *n*; **5.** a) Schal *m*, b) 'Überwurf *m*, c) Morgenrock *m*; **6.** Deckblatt *n* (*der Zigarre*); '**wrap·ping** [-pɪŋ] *s.* **1.** *mst pl.* Um'hüllung *f*, Hülle *f*, Verpakkung *f*; **2.** Ein-, Verpacken *n*: ***~-paper*** Einwickel-, Packpapier *n*.

wrapt [ræpt] *pret. u. p.p. von* ***wrap***.

wrath [rɒθ] *s.* Zorn *m*, Wut *f*: ***the ~ of God*** der Zorn Gottes; ***he looked like the ~ of god*** F er sah gräßlich aus; '**wrath·ful** [-fʊl] *adj.* ☐ zornig, grimmig, wutentbrannt; '**wrath·y** [-θɪ] *adj.* ☐ *bsd.* F → ***wrathful***.

wreak [ri:k] *v/t.* *Rache* (aus)üben, *Wut etc.* auslassen ([***up***]***on*** an *dat.*).

wreath [ri:θ] *pl.* **wreaths** [-ðz] *s.* **1.** Kranz *m* (*a. fig.*), Gir'lande *f*, (Blumen-)Gewinde *n*; **2.** (*Rauch- etc.*)Ring *m*; **3.** Windung *f* (*e-s Seiles etc.*); **4.** (Schnee- *etc.*)Wehe *f*; **wreathe** [ri:ð] **I** *v/t.* **1.** winden, wickeln (***round***, ***about*** um); **2.** a) *Kranz etc.* flechten, winden, b) (zu Kränzen) flechten; **3.** um'kränzen, -'geben, -'winden; **4.** bekränzen, schmücken; **5.** kräuseln: ***~d in smiles*** lächelnd; **II** *v/i.* **6.** sich winden *od.* wikkeln; **7.** sich ringeln *od.* kräuseln (*Rauchwolke etc.*).

wreck [rek] **I** *s.* **1.** ⚓ a) (Schiffs)Wrack *n*, b) Schiffbruch *m*, Schiffsunglück *n*, c) ⚖ Strandgut *n*; **2.** Wrack *n* (*mot. etc.*, *a. fig. bsd. Person*), Ru'ine *f*, Trümmerhaufen *m* (*a. fig.*): ***nervous ~*** *fig.* Nervenbündel *n*; ***she is the ~ of her former self*** sie ist nur (noch) ein Schatten ihrer selbst; **3.** *pl.* Trümmer *pl.* (*oft fig.*); **4.** *fig.* a) Ru'in *m*, 'Untergang *m*, b) Zerstörung *f*, Vernichtung *f von Hoffnungen etc.*; **II** *v/t.* **5.** *allg.* zertrümmern, -stören, *Schiff* zum Scheitern bringen (*a. fig.*): ***be ~ed*** a) → 8, b) in Trümmer gehen, c) entgleisen (*Zug*); **6.** *fig.* zu'grunde richten, ruinieren, ka'puttmachen, *Gesundheit a.* zerrütten, *Pläne, Hoffnungen etc.* vernichten, zerstören; **7.** ⚓, ⚙ abwracken; **III** *v/i.* **8.** Schiffbruch erleiden, scheitern (*a. fig.*); **9.** verunglücken; **10.** zerstört *od.* vernichtet werden (*mst fig.*); '**wreck·age** [-kɪdʒ] *s.* **1.** Wrack(teile *pl.*) *n*, (Schiffs-, *allg.* Unfall)Trümmer *pl.*; **2.** *fig.* Strandgut *n* (des Lebens); **3.** → ***wreck*** 4; **wrecked** [-kt] *adj.* **1.** gestrandet, gescheitert (*a. fig.*); **2.** schiffbrüchig (*Person*); **3.** zertrümmert, zerstört, vernichtet (*alle a. fig.*); zerrüttet (*Gesundheit etc.*): **~ *car*** Schrottauto *n*; '**wreck·er** [-kə] *s.* **1.** Strandräuber *m*; **2.** Sabo'teur *m*, Zerstörer *m* (*beide a. fig.*); **3.** ⚓ a) Bergungsschiff *n*, b) Bergungsarbeiter *m*; **4.** ⚙ Abbrucharbeiter *m*; **5.** *mot. Am.* Abschleppwagen *m*; '**wreck·ing** [-kɪŋ] *adj.* **1.** *Am.* Bergungs…: **~ *crew***; **~ *service*** (***truck***) *mot.* Abschleppdienst *m* (-wagen *m*); **2.** *Am.* Abbruch…: **~ *company*** Abbruchfirma *f*.

wren[1] [ren] *s. orn.* Zaunkönig *m*.

Wren[2] [ren] *s.* ⚔ *Brit.* F Angehörige *f* des ***Women's Royal Naval Service***, Ma'rinehelferin *f*.

wrench [rentʃ] **I** *s.* **1.** (drehender *od.* heftiger) Ruck, heftige Drehung; **2.** ⚕ Verzerrung *f*, -renkung *f*, -stauchung *f*: ***give a ~ to*** → 7; **3.** *fig.* Verdrehung *f*, -zerrung *f*; **4.** *fig.* (Trennungs)Schmerz *m*: ***it was a great ~*** der Abschied tat sehr weh; **5.** ⚙ Schraubenschlüssel *m*; **II** *v/t.* **6.** (mit e-m Ruck) reißen, zerren, ziehen: **~ *s.th.*** (***away***) ***from s.o.*** j-m et. entwinden *od.* -reißen (*a. fig.*); **~ *open*** *Tür etc.* aufreißen; **7.** ⚕ verrenken, verstauchen; **8.** verdrehen, verzerren (*a. fig. entstellen*).

wrest [rest] **I** *v/t.* **1.** (gewaltsam) reißen: **~ *from*** *j-m et.* entreißen, -winden, *fig. a.* abringen; **2.** *fig. Sinn, Gesetz etc.* verdrehen; **II** *s.* **3.** Ruck *m*, Reißen *n*; **4.** ♪ Stimmhammer *m*.

wres·tle ['resl] **I** *v/i.* **1.** *a. sport* ringen (*a. fig.* ***for*** um, ***with God*** mit Gott); **2.** *fig.* sich abmühen, kämpfen (***with*** mit); **II** *v/t.* **3.** ringen *od.* kämpfen mit; **III** *s.* **4.** → ***wrestling*** I; **5.** *fig.* Ringen *n*, schwerer Kampf; '**wres·tler** [-lə] *s.* *sport* Ringer *m*, Ringkämpfer *m*; '**wres·tling** [-lɪŋ] **I** *s. bsd. sport u. fig.* Ringen *n*; **II** *adj.* Ring…: **~ *match*** Ringkampf *m*.

wretch [retʃ] **1.** *a.* ***poor ~*** armes Wesen, armer Kerl *od.* Teufel (*a. iro.*); **2.** Schuft *m*; **3.** *iro.* Wicht *m*, ‚Tropf' *m*; **wretch·ed** ['retʃɪd] *adj.* ☐ **1.** elend, unglücklich, *a.* deprimiert (*Person*); **2.** erbärmlich, mise'rabel, schlecht, dürftig; **3.** scheußlich, ekelhaft, unangenehm; **4.** *gesundheitlich* elend: ***feel ~*** sich elend *od.* schlecht fühlen; **wretch·ed·ness** ['retʃɪdnɪs] *s.* **1.** Elend *n*, Unglück *n*; **2.** Erbärmlichkeit *f*, Gemeinheit *f*.

wrig·gle ['rɪgl] **I** *v/i.* **1.** sich winden (*a. fig. verlegen od. listig*), sich schlängeln, zappeln: **~ *along*** sich dahinschlängeln; **~ *out*** sich herauswinden (***of s.th.*** aus e-r Sache) (*a. fig.*); **II** *v/t.* **2.** wackeln *od.* zappeln mit; mit *den Hüften* schaukeln; **3.** schlängeln, winden, ringeln: **~ *o.s.*** (***along***, ***through***) sich (entlang-, hindurch)winden; **~ *o.s. into*** *fig.* sich einschleichen in (*acc.*); **~ *o.s. out of*** sich herauswinden aus; **III** *s.* **4.** Windung *f*, Krümmung *f*; **5.** schlängelnde Bewegung, Schlängeln *n*, Ringeln *n*, Wackeln *n*; '**wrig·gler** [-lə] *s.* **1.** Ringeltier *n*, Wurm *m*; **2.** *fig.* aalglatter Kerl.

wright [raɪt] *s. in Zssgn* …verfertiger *m*, …macher *m*, …bauer *m*.

wring [rɪŋ] **I** *v/t.* [*irr.*] **1.** **~ *out*** *Wäsche etc.* (aus)wringen, auswinden; **2.** a) *e-m Tier den Hals* abdrehen, b) *j-m den Hals* 'umdrehen: ***I'll ~ your neck***; **3.** verdrehen, -zerren (*a. fig.*); **4.** a) *Hände* (*verzweifelt*) ringen, b) *j-m die Hand* (kräftig) drücken, pressen; **5.** *j-n* drükken (*Schuh etc.*); **6.** **~ *s.o.'s heart*** *fig.* j-m sehr zu Herzen gehen, j-m ans Herz greifen; **7.** abringen, entreißen, -winden (***from s.o.*** j-m): **~ *admiration from*** *j-m* Bewunderung abnötigen; **8.** *fig. Geld, Zustimmung* erpressen (***from***, ***out of*** von); **II** *s.* **9.** Wringen *n*, (Aus)Winden *n*; Pressen *n*, Druck *m*: ***give s.th. a ~*** → 1 *u.* 4b; **wring·er** ['rɪŋə] *s.* 'Wringma,schine *f*: ***go through the ~*** F ‚durch den Wolf gedreht werden'; **wring·ing** ['rɪŋɪŋ] *adj.* **1.** Wring…: **~ *machine*** → ***wringer***; **2.** *a.* **~ *wet*** F klatschnaß.

wrin·kle[1] ['rɪŋkl] **I** *s.* **1.** Runzel *f*, Falte *f* (*im Gesicht*); *a.* Kniff *m* (*in Papier etc.*); **2.** Unebenheit *f*, Vertiefung *f*, Furche *f*; **II** *v/t.* **3.** *oft* **~ *up*** a) *Stirn, Augenbrauen* runzeln, b) *Nase* rümpfen; **4.** *Stoff, Papier etc.* falten, kniffen, zerknittern; **III** *v/i.* **5.** Falten werfen, Runzeln bekommen, sich runzeln, runz(e)lig werden, knittern.

wrin·kle[2] ['rɪŋkl] *s.* F **1.** Kniff *m*, Trick *m*; **2.** Wink *m*, Tip *m*; **3.** Neuheit *f*; **4.** Fehler *m*.

wrin·kly ['rɪŋklɪ] *adj.* **1.** faltig, runz(e)lig (*Gesicht etc.*); **2.** leicht knitternd (*Stoff*); **3.** gekräuselt.

wrist [rɪst] *s.* **1.** Handgelenk *n*; **2.** ⚙ → ***wrist pin***; '**~·band** [-stb-] *s.* **1.** Bündchen *n*, ('Hemd)Man,schette *f*; **2.** Armband *n*; '**~·drop** *s.* ⚕ Handgelenkslähmung *f*.

wrist·let ['rɪstlɪt] *s.* **1.** Pulswärmer *m*; **2.** Armband *n*: **~ *watch*** → ***wristwatch***; **3.** *sport* Schweißband *n*; **4.** *humor. od. sl.* Handschelle *f*.

wrist| pin *s.* ⚙ Zapfen *m*, *bsd.* Kolbenbolzen *m*; '**~·watch** *s.* Armbanduhr *f*.

writ [rɪt] *s.* **1.** ⚖ a) behördlicher Erlaß, b) gerichtlicher Befehl, c) *a.* **~ *of summons*** (Vor)Ladung *f*: **~ *of attachment*** a) Haftbefehl *m*, b) *dinglicher* Arrest(befehl); **~ *of execution*** Vollstreckungsbefehl; ***take out a ~ against s.o.***, ***serve a ~ on s.o.*** j-n vorladen (lassen); **2.** ⚖ *hist. Brit.* Urkunde *f*; **3.** *pol. Brit.* Wahlausschreibung *f* für das Parla'ment; **4.** ***Holy*** (*od.* ***Sacred***) 2 *die*

Heilige Schrift.

write [raɪt] [*irr.*] **I** *v/t.* **1.** *et.* schreiben: ***writ(ten) large*** *fig.* deutlich, leicht erkennbar; **2.** (auf-, nieder)schreiben, schriftlich niederlegen, notieren, aufzeichnen: ***it is written that*** es steht geschrieben, daß; ***it is written on*** (*od.* ***all over***) ***his face*** es steht ihm im Gesicht geschrieben; **3.** *Scheck etc.* ausschreiben, -füllen; **4.** *Papier etc.* vollschreiben; **5.** *j-m et.* schreiben, schriftlich mitteilen: **~ *s.o. s.th.***; **6.** *Buch etc.* verfassen, *a. Musik* schreiben: **~ *poetry*** dichten, Gedichte schreiben; **7. ~ *o.s.*** sich bezeichnen als; **II** *v/i.* **8.** schreiben; **9.** schreiben, schriftstellern; **10.** schreiben, schriftliche Mitteilung machen: ***it's nothing to ~ home about*** *fig.* das ist nichts Besonderes, darauf brauchst du dir (braucht er sich *etc.*) nichts einzubilden; **~ *to ask*** schriftlich anfragen; **~ *for s.th.*** et. anfordern, sich et. kommen lassen;

Zssgn mit adv.:

write| down *v/t.* **1.** → ***write*** 2; **2.** *fig.* a) (schriftlich) her'absetzen, herziehen über (*acc.*), b) nennen, bezeichnen *od.* hinstellen als; **3.** ✝ abschreiben; **~ in** *v/t.* einfügen, -tragen; **~ off** *v/t.* **1.** (schnell) her'unterschreiben, ‚hinhauen'; **2.** ✝ (vollständig) abschreiben (*a. fig.*); **~ out** *v/t.* **1.** *Namen etc.* ausschreiben; **2.** abschreiben: **~ *fair*** ins reine schreiben; **3.** ***write o.s. out*** sich ausschreiben (*Autor*); **~ up** *v/t.* **1.** ausführlich darstellen *od.* beschreiben; **2.** *ergänzend* nachtragen, *Text* weiterführen; **3.** loben(d erwähnen), her'ausstreichen, anpreisen; **4.** ✝ e-n zu hohen Buchwert angeben für.

'write|-down *s.* ✝ Abschreibung *f*: **'~-off** *s.* a) ✝ (gänzliche) Abschreibung, b) *mot.* F To'talschaden: ***it's a ~*** F das können wir abschreiben.

writ·er ['raɪtə] *s.* **1.** Schreiber(in): ***~'s cramp*** (*od.* ***palsy***) Schreibkrampf *m*; **2.** Schriftsteller(in), Verfasser(in), Autor *m*, Au'torin *f*: ***the ~*** der Verfasser (= *ich*); **~ *for the press*** Journalist(in); **3. ~ *to the signet*** *Scot.* No'tar *m*, Rechtsanwalt *m*; **'writ·er·ship** [-ʃɪp] *s. Brit.* Schreiberstelle *f*.

'write-up *s.* **1.** lobender Pressebericht *od.* Ar'tikel; **2.** ✝ zu hohe Buchwertangabe.

writhe [raɪð] *v/i.* **1.** sich krümmen, sich winden (***with*** vor *dat.*); **2.** *fig.* sich winden, leiden (***under***, ***at*** unter *e-r Kränkung etc.*).

writ·ing ['raɪtɪŋ] **I** *s.* **1.** Schreiben *n* (*Tätigkeit*); **2.** Schriftstelle'rei *f*; **3.** schriftliche Ausfertigung *od.* Abfassung; **4.** Schreiben *n*, Schriftstück *n*, *et.* Geschriebenes, *a.* Urkunde *f*: ***in ~*** schriftlich; ***the ~ on the wall*** *fig.* die Schrift an der Wand, das Menetekel; **5.** Schrift *f*, *literarisches* Werk; Aufsatz *m*, Ar'tikel *m*; **6.** Brief *m*; **7.** Inschrift *f*; **8.** Schreibweise *f*, Stil *m*; **9.** (Hand)Schrift *f*; **II** *adj.* **10.** schreibend, *bsd.* schriftstellernd: **~ *man*** Schriftsteller *m*; **11.** Schreib...; **~ book** *s.* Schreibheft *n*; **~ case** *s.* Schreibmappe *f*; **~ desk** *s.* Schreibtisch *m*; **~ pad** *s.* 'Schreibˌunterlage *f*, -block *m*; **~ pa·per** *s.* 'Schreib-, 'Briefpaˌpier *n*; **~ ta·ble** *s.* Schreibtisch *m*.

writ·ten ['rɪtn] **I** *p.p. von* ***write***; **II** *adj.* **1.** schriftlich: **~ *examination***; **~ *evidence*** ⚖ Urkundenbeweis *m*; **~ *language*** Schriftsprache *f*; **2.** geschrieben: **~ *law***; **~ *question*** *parl.* kleine Anfrage.

wrong [rɒŋ] **I** *adj.* ☐ → ***wrongly***; **1.** falsch, unrichtig, verkehrt, irrig: ***be ~*** *a.* a) unrecht haben, sich irren (*Person*), b) falsch gehen (*Uhr*); ***you are ~ in believing*** du irrst dich, wenn du glaubst; ***prove s.o. ~*** beweisen, daß j-d im Irrtum ist; **2.** verkehrt, falsch: ***bring the ~ book***; ***do the ~ thing*** das Falsche tun, es verkehrt machen; ***get hold of the ~ end of the stick*** *fig.* es völlig mißverstehen, es verkehrt ansehen; ***the ~ side*** die verkehrte *od.* falsche (*von Stoff*: linke) Seite; (***the***) **~ *side out*** das Innere nach außen (gekehrt) (*Kleidungsstück etc.*); ***be on the ~ side of 40*** über 40 (Jahre alt) sein; ***he will laugh on the ~ side of his mouth*** das Lachen wird ihm schon vergehen; ***have got out of bed*** (***on***) ***the ~ side*** F mit dem linken Bein zuerst aufgestanden sein; → ***blanket*** 1; **3.** nicht in Ordnung: ***s.th. is ~ with it*** es stimmt et. daran nicht; ***what is ~ with you?*** was ist los mit dir?, was hast du?; ***what's ~ with ...?*** a) was gibt es auszusetzen an (*dat.*)?, b) F wie wär's mit...?; **4.** unrecht: ***it is ~ of you to laugh***; **II** *adv.* **5.** falsch, unrichtig, verkehrt: ***get it ~*** es ganz falsch verstehen; ***go ~*** a) nicht richtig funktionieren *od.* gehen (*Uhr etc.*), b) schiefgehen (*Vorhaben etc.*), c) auf Abwege *od.* die schiefe Bahn geraten (*bsd. Frau*), d) fehlgehen; ***where did we go ~?*** was haben wir falsch gemacht?; ***get in ~ with s.o.*** *Am.* F es mit j-m verderben; ***get s.o. in ~*** *Am.* F j-n in Mißkredit bringen (***with*** bei); ***take s.th. ~*** et. übelnehmen; **III** *s.* **6.** Unrecht *n*: ***do s.o. ~*** j-m ein Unrecht zufügen; **7.** Irrtum *m*, Unrecht *n*: ***be in the ~*** unrecht haben; ***put s.o. in the ~*** j-n ins Unrecht setzen; **8.** Kränkung *f*, Beleidigung *f*; **9.** ⚖ Rechtsverletzung *f*: ***private ~*** Privatdelikt *n*; ***public ~*** öffentliches Delikt; **IV** *v/t.* **10.** *j-m* Unrecht tun (*a. in Gedanken etc.*), *j-n* ungerecht behandeln: ***I am ~ed*** mir geschieht Unrecht; **11.** *j-m* schaden, Schaden zufügen, *j-n* benachteiligen; **ˌ~'do·er** *s.* Übel-, Missetäter(in), Sünder(in); **ˌ~'do·ing** *s.* **1.** Missetat *f*, Sünde *f*; **2.** Vergehen *n*, Verbrechen *n*.

wrong·ful ['rɒŋfʊl] *adj.* ☐ **1.** ungerecht; **2.** beleidigend, kränkend; **3.** ⚖ unrechtmäßig, 'widerrechtlich, ungesetzlich.

ˌwrong'head·ed *adj.* ☐ **1.** querköpfig, verbohrt (*Person*); **2.** verschroben, verdreht, hirnverbrannt.

wrong·ly ['rɒŋlɪ] *adv.* **1.** → ***wrong*** II; **2.** ungerechterweise, zu *od.* mit Unrecht; **3.** irrtümlicher-, fälschlicherweise; **wrong·ness** ['rɒŋnɪs] *s.* **1.** Unrichtigkeit *f*, Verkehrtheit *f*, Fehlerhaftigkeit *f*; **2.** Unrechtmäßigkeit *f*; **3.** Ungerechtigkeit *f*.

wrote [rəʊt] *pret. u. obs. p.p. von* ***write***.

wroth [rəʊθ] *adj.* zornig, erzürnt.

wrought [rɔːt] **I** *pret. u. p.p. von* ***work***; **II** *adj.* **1.** be-, ge-, verarbeitet: **~ *goods*** Fertigwaren; **2.** a) gehämmert, geschmiedet, b) schmiedeeisern; **3.** gewirkt; **~ i·ron** *s.* Schmiedeeisen *n*; **ˌ~-'i·ron** *adj.* schmiedeeisern; **~ steel** *s.* Schmiede-, Schweißstahl *m*; **ˌ~-'up** *adj.* aufgebracht, erregt.

wrung [rʌŋ] *pret. u. p.p. von* ***wring***.

wry [raɪ] *adj.* ☐ **1.** schief, krumm, verzerrt: ***make*** (*od.* ***pull***) ***a ~ face*** e-e Grimasse schneiden; **2.** *fig.* a) verschroben: **~ *notion***, b) gequält: **~ *smile***, c) sar'kastisch: **~ *humo(u)r***; **'~-mouthed** *adj.* **1.** schiefmäulig; **2.** *fig.* a) wenig schmeichelhaft, b) sar'kastisch; **'~-neck** *s. orn.* Wendehals *m*.

X

X, x [eks] **I** *pl.* **X's, x's, Xs, xs** ['eksɪz] *s.* **1.** X *n*, x *n* (*Buchstabe*); **2.** A a) x *n* (*1. unbekannte Größe od. abhängige Variable*), b) x-Achse *f*, Ab'szisse *f* (*im Koordinatensystem*); **3.** *fig.* X *n*, unbekannte Größe; **4.** → 6; **II** *adj.* **5.** X-..., X-förmig; **6. ~ *film*** nicht jugendfreier Film (*ab 18*).

Xan·thip·pe [zæn'θɪpɪ] *s. fig.* Xan'thippe *f*, Hausdrachen *m*.

xe·nog·a·my [ziː'nɒgəmɪ] *s.* ♀ Fremdbestäubung *f*.

xen·o·pho·bi·a [ˌzenə'fəʊbjə] *s.* Xenopho'bie *f*, Fremdenfeindlichkeit *f*; **ˌxen·o'pho·bic** [-bɪk] *adj.* xeno'phob, fremdenfeindlich.

xe·ra·si·a [zɪ'reɪzɪə] *s.* ⚕ Trockenheit *f* des Haares.

xe·ro·phyte ['zɪərəʊfaɪt] *s.* ♀ Trockenheitspflanze *f*.

xiph·oid ['zɪfɔɪd] *adj. anat.* **1.** schwertförmig; **2.** Schwertfortsatz...: **~ *appendage***, **~ *process*** Schwertfortsatz *m*.

Xmas ['krɪsməs] F *für* ***Christmas***.

X-ray [ˌeks'reɪ] **I** *s.* ⚕, *phys.* **1.** X-Strahl *m*, Röntgenstrahl *m*; **2.** Röntgenaufnahme *f*, -bild *n*; **II** *v/t.* **3.** röntgen: a) ein Röntgenbild machen von, b) durch'leuchten; **4.** bestrahlen; **III** *adj.* **5.** Röntgen...

xy·lene ['zaɪliːn] *s.* ⚗ Xy'lol *n*.

xy·lo·graph ['zaɪləgrɑːf] *s.* Holzschnitt *m*; **xy·log·ra·pher** [zaɪ'lɒgrəfə] *s.* Holzschneider *m*; **xy·lo·graph·ic** [ˌzaɪlə'græfɪk] *adj.* Holzschnitt...; **xy·log·ra·phy** [zaɪ'lɒgrəfɪ] *s.* Xylogra'phie *f*, Holzschneidekunst *f*.

xy·lo·phone ['zaɪləfəʊn] *s.* ♪ Xylo'phon *n*.

xy·lose ['zaɪləʊs] *s.* ⚗ Xy'lose *f*, Holzzucker *m*.

Y

Y, y [waɪ] **I** *pl.* **Y's, y's, Ys, ys** [waɪz] *s.* **1.** Y *n*, y *n*, Ypsilon *n* (*Buchstabe*); **2.** A a) y *n* (*2. unbekannte Größe od. abhängige Variable*), b) y-Achse *f*, Ordi'nate *f* (*im Koordinatensystem*); **II** *adj.* **3.** Y-..., Y-förmig, gabelförmig.

y- [ɪ] *obs. Präfix zur Bildung des p.p., entsprechend dem deutschen* ge-.

yacht [jɒt] ⚓ **I** *s.* **1.** (Segel-, Motor-) Jacht *f*: **~ club** Jachtklub *m*; **2.** (Renn-) Segler *m*; **II** *v/i.* **3.** auf e-r Jacht fahren; **4.** (sport)segeln; **yacht·er** ['jɒtə] → ***yachtsman***; **yacht·ing** ['jɒtɪŋ] **I** *s.* **1.** Jacht-, Segelsport *m*; **2.** (Sport)Segeln *n*; **II** *adj.* **3.** Segel..., Jacht...

yachts·man ['jɒtsmən] *s.* [*irr.*] **1.** Jachtfahrer *m*; **2.** (Sport)Segler *m*; **'yachts·man·ship** [-ʃɪp] *s.* Segelkunst *f*.

yah [jɑː] *int.* a) puh!, b) ätsch!

ya·hoo [jə'huː] *s.* **1.** bru'taler Kerl; **2.** Saukerl *m*.

yak¹ [jæk] *v/i.* F quasseln.

yak² [jæk] *s.* Yak *m*, Grunzochs *m*.

yank¹ [jæŋk] F **I** *v/t.* (mit e-m Ruck her'aus)ziehen, (*hoch- etc.*)reißen; **II** *v/i.* reißen, heftig ziehen; **III** *s.* (heftiger) Ruck.

Yank² [jæŋk] F *für* ***Yankee***.

Yan·kee ['jæŋkɪ] *s.* Yankee *m* (*Spitzname*): a) Neu-'Engländer(in), b) Nordstaatler(in) (*der USA*), c) (*allg., von Nichtamerikanern gebraucht*) ('Nord-) Ameri,kaner(in): **~ *Doodle*** *amer. Volkslied.*

yap [jæp] **I** *s.* **1.** Kläffen *n*, Gekläff *n*; **2.** F a) Gequassel *n*, b) ,Schnauze' *f* (*Mund*); **II** *v/i.* **3.** kläffen; **4.** F a) quasseln, b) ,meckern'.

yard¹ [jɑːd] *s.* **1.** Yard *n* (*= 0,914 m*); **2.** → ***yardstick*** 1: ***by the ~*** yardweise; **~ *goods*** Kurzwaren; **3.** ⚓ Rah(e) *f*.

yard² [jɑːd] *s.* **1.** Hof(raum) *m*; **2.** Arbeits-, Bau-, Stapel)Platz *m*; **3.** 🚂 *Brit.* Rangier-, Verschiebebahnhof *m*; **4.** ***the*** **~** → ***Scotland Yard***; **5.** ✓ Hof *m*, Gehege *n*: ***poultry ~***; **6.** *Am.* Winterweideplatz *m* (*für Elche u. Rotwild*).

yard·age ['jɑːdɪdʒ] *s.* in Yards angegebene Zahl *od.* Länge, Yards *pl.*

'yard·man [-mən] *s.* [*irr.*] **1.** 🚂 Rangier-, Bahnhofsarbeiter *m*; **2.** ⚓ Werftarbeiter *m*; **3.** ✓ Stall-, Viehhofarbeiter *m*; **~ mas·ter** *s.* 🚂 Rangiermeister *m*; **'~·stick** *s.* **1.** Yard-, Maßstock *m*; **2.** *fig.* Maßstab *m*.

yarn [jɑːn] **I** *s.* **1.** Garn *n*; **2.** ⚓ Kabelgarn *n*; **3.** F abenteuerliche (*a. weitS. erlogene*) Geschichte, (Seemanns)Garn *n*: ***spin a ~*** e-e Abenteuergeschichte erzählen, ein (Seemanns)Garn spinnen; **II** *v/i.* **4.** F (Geschichten) erzählen, ein Garn spinnen, (mitein'ander) klönen.

yar·row ['jærəʊ] *s.* ♀ Schafgarbe *f*.

yaw [jɔː] *v/i.* **1.** ⚓ gieren (*vom Kurs abkommen*); **2.** ✈ (*um Hochachse*) gieren, scheren; **3.** *fig.* schwanken.

yawl [jɔːl] *s.* ⚓ **1.** Segeljolle *f*; **2.** Be'sankutter *m*.

yawn [jɔːn] **I** *v/i.* **1.** gähnen (*a. fig. Abgrund etc.*); **2.** *fig.* a) sich weit u. tief auftun, b) weit offenstehen; **II** *v/t.* **3.** gähnen(d sagen); **III** *s.* **4.** Gähnen *n*; **'yawn·ing** [-nɪŋ] *adj.* □ gähnend (*a. fig.*).

y·clept [ɪ'klept] *adj. obs. od. humor.* genannt, namens.

ye¹ [jiː] *pron. obs. od. bibl. od. humor.* **1.** ihr, Ihr; **2.** euch, Euch, dir, Dir; **3.** du, Du; **4.** F *für* ***you***: ***how d'ye do?***

ye² [jiː] *archaisierend für* ***the***.

yea [jeɪ] **I** *adv.* **1.** ja; **2.** für'wahr, wahr'haftig; **3.** *obs.* ja so'gar; **II** *s.* **4.** Ja *n*; **5.** *parl. etc.* Ja(stimme *f*) *n*: ***~s and nays*** Stimmen für u. wider; ***the ~s have it!*** der Antrag ist angenommen!

yeah [jeə] *adv.* F ja, klar: ***~?*** so?, na, na!

yean [jiːn] *zo.* **I** *v/t.* werfen (*Lamm, Zicklein*); **II** *v/i.* a) lammen (*Schaf*), b) zickeln (*Ziege*); **'yean·ling** [-lɪŋ] *s.* a) Lamm *n*, b) Zicklein *n*.

year [jɜː] *s.* **1.** Jahr *n*: **~ *of grace*** Jahr des Heils; ***for ~s*** jahrelang, seit Jahren, auf Jahre hinaus; **~ *in*, ~ *out*** jahrein, jahraus; **~ *by* ~, *from* ~ *to* ~, ~ *after* ~** Jahr für Jahr; ***in the ~ one*** *humor.* vor undenklichen Zeiten; ***take ~s off s.o.*** j-n um Jahre jünger machen; **2.** *pl.* Alter *n*: ***~s of discretion*** gesetztes *od.* vernünftiges Alter; ***well on in ~s*** hochbetagt; ***be getting on in ~s*** in die Jahre kommen; ***he bears his ~s well*** er ist für sein Alter noch recht rüstig; **3.** *ped. univ.* Jahrgang *m*; **'~·book** *s.* Jahrbuch *n*.

year·ling ['jɜːlɪŋ] **I** *s.* **1.** Jährling *m*: a) einjähriges Tier, b) einjährige Pflanze; **2.** *Pferdesport*: Einjährige(s) *n*; **II** *adj.* **3.** einjährig.

'year·long *adj.* einjährig.

year·ly ['jɜːlɪ] **I** *adj.* jährlich, Jahres...; **II** *adv.* jährlich, jedes Jahr (einmal).

yearn [jɜːn] *v/i.* **1.** sich sehnen, Sehnsucht haben (***for, after*** nach, ***to do*** danach, zu tun); **2.** (*bsd.* Mitleid, Zuneigung) empfinden (***to*[*wards*]** für, mit); **'yearn·ing** [-nɪŋ] **I** *s.* Sehnsucht *f*, Sehnen *n*, Verlangen *n*; **II** *adj.* □ sehnsüchtig, sehnend, verlangend.

yeast [jiːst] **I** *s.* **1.** (Bier-, Back)Hefe *f*; **2.** Gischt *f*, Schaum *m*; **3.** *fig.* Triebkraft *f*; **II** *v/i.* **4.** gären; **~ pow·der** *s.* Backpulver *n*.

yeast·y ['jiːstɪ] *adj.* **1.** heftig; **2.** gärend; **3.** schäumend; **4.** *fig. contp.* leer, hohl; **5.** *fig.* a) unstet, b) 'überschäumend.

yegg(·man) ['jeg(mən)] *s.* [*irr.*] *Am. sl.* ,Schränker' *m*, Geldschrankknacker *m*.

yell [jel] **I** *v/i.* **1.** schreien, brüllen (***with*** vor *dat.*); **II** *v/t.* **2.** gellen(d ausstoßen), schreien; **III** *s.* **3.** gellender (Auf-) Schrei; **4.** *Am. univ.* (rhythmischer) Anfeuerungs- *od.* Schlachtruf.

yel·low ['jeləʊ] **I** *adj.* **1.** gelb (*a. Rasse*): ***~-haired*** flachshaarig; ***the ~ peril*** die gelbe Gefahr; **2.** *fig.* a) *obs.* neidisch, mißgünstig, b) F feig: **~ *streak*** feiger Zug; **3.** sensati'onslüstern; → ***yellow paper, yellow press***; **II** *s.* **4.** Gelb *n*: ***at ~*** *Am.* bei (*od.* auf) Gelb (*Verkehrsampel*); **5.** Eigelb *n*; **6.** ♀, ⚕ *od. vet.* Gelbsucht *f*; **III** *v/t.* **7.** gelb färben; **IV** *v/i.* **8.** sich gelb färben, vergilben; **~ card** *s.*: ***be shown the ~*** *Fußball*: die gelbe Karte (gezeigt) bekommen; **'~-dog I** *s.* **1.** Köter *m*, ,Prome'nadenmischung' *f*; **2.** *fig.* gemeiner *od.* feiger Kerl; **II** *adj.* **3.** a) hundsgemein, b) feig; **4.** *Am.* gewerkschaftsfeindlich; **~ earth** *s. min.* **1.** Gelberde *f*; **2.** → ***yellow ochre***; **~ fe·ver** *s.* ⚕ Gelbfieber *n*; **'~,ham·mer** *s. orn.* Goldammer *f*.

yel·low·ish ['jeləʊɪʃ] *adj.* gelblich.

yel·low| jack *s.* **1.** ⚕ Gelbfieber *n*; **2.** ⚓ Quaran'täneflagge *f*; **~ met·al** *s.* 'Muntzme,tall *n*; **~ o·chre** (*Am.* **o·cher**) *s. min.* gelber Ocker, Gelberde *f*; **~ pag·es** *s. pl. teleph.* (*die*) gelben Seiten, Branchenverzeichnis *n*; **~ pa·per** *s.* Sensati'ons-, Re'volverblatt *n*; **~ press** *s.* Sensati'ons-, Boule'vardpresse *f*; **~ soap** *s.* Schmierseife *f*.

yelp [jelp] **I** *v/i.* **1.** a) (auf)jaulen, b) aufschreien; **2.** (*a. v/t.*) kreischen; **II** *s.* **3.** a) (Auf)Jaulen *n*, b) Aufschrei *m*.

yen¹ [jen] *s.* Yen *m* (*japanische Münzeinheit*).

yen² [jen] F *für* ***yearning*** I.

yeo·man ['jəʊmən] *s.* [*irr.*] **1.** *Brit. hist.* a) Freisasse *m*, b) ⚔ berittener Mi'lizsol,dat: **~ *service*** *fig.* treue Dienste *pl.*; **2.** *a.* **~ *of the Guard*** 'Leibgar,dist *m*; **3.** ⚓ Ver'waltungs,unteroffi,zier *m*; **'yeo·man·ry** [-rɪ] *s. coll. hist.* **1.** Freisassen *pl.*; **2.** ⚔ berittene Mi'liz.

yep [jep] *adv.* F ja.

yes [jes] **I** *adv.* **1.** ja, ja'wohl: ***say ~*** (***to***) a) ja sagen (zu), (*e-e Sache*) bejahen (*beide a. fig.*), b) einwilligen (in *acc.*); **2.** ja, gewiß, aller'dings; **3.** (ja) doch; **4.** ja so'gar; **5.** *fragend od. anzweifelnd*: ja?, wirklich?; **II** *s.* **6.** Ja *n*; **7.** *fig.* Ja (-wort) *n*; **8.** *parl.* Ja(stimme *f*) *n*; **~ man** *s.* [*irr.*] F Jasager *m*.

yes·ter ['jestə] *adj.* **1.** *obs. od. poet.* gestrig; **2.** *in Zssgn* → ***yesterday*** 2; **ˈ~·day** [-dɪ] **I** *adv.* **1.** gestern: ***I was not born ~*** *fig.* ich bin (doch) nicht von gestern; **II** *adj.* **2.** gestrig, vergangen, letzt: ***~ morning*** gestern früh; **III** *s.* **3.** der gestrige Tag: ***the day before ~*** vorgestern; ***~'s paper*** die gestrige Zeitung; ***of ~*** von gestern; ***~s*** vergangene Tage *od.* Zeiten; **4.** *fig. das* Gestern; **ˌ~-ˈyear** *adv. u. s. obs. od. poet.* voriges Jahr.

yet [jet] **I** *adv.* **1.** (immer) noch, jetzt noch: ***not ~*** noch nicht; ***nothing ~*** noch nichts; ***~ a moment*** (nur) noch einen Augenblick; **2.** schon (jetzt), jetzt: (***as***) ***~*** bis jetzt, bisher; ***have you finished ~?*** bist du schon fertig?; ***not just ~*** nicht gerade jetzt; **3.** (doch) noch, schon (noch): ***he will win ~***; **4.** noch, soˈgar (*beim Komparativ*): ***~ better*** noch besser; ***~ more important*** sogar noch wichtiger; **5.** noch (daˈzu), außerdem: ***another and ~ another*** noch einer u. noch einer dazu; ***~ again*** immer wieder; ***nor ~*** (und) auch nicht; **6.** dennoch, trotzdem, jeˈdoch, aber: ***but ~*** aber doch *od.* trotzdem; **II** *cj.* **7.** aber (dennoch *od.* zuˈgleich), doch.

yew [ju:] ⚘ **I** *s.* **1.** *a.* ***~ tree*** Eibe *f*; **2.** Eibenholz *n*; **II** *adj.* **3.** Eiben...

Yid [jɪd] *s. sl.* Jude *m*; **Yid·dish** [ˈjɪdɪʃ] *ling.* **I** *s.* Jiddisch *n*; **II** *adj.* jiddisch.

yield [ji:ld] **I** *v/t.* **1.** *als Ertrag* ergeben, (ein-, herˈvor)bringen, *a. Ernte* erbringen, *bsd. Gewinn* abwerfen, *Früchte*, *a. Zinsen etc.* tragen, *Produkte etc.* liefern: ***~ 6 %*** ✝ 6 % (Rendite) abwerfen; **2.** *Resultat* ergeben, liefern; **3.** *fig.* gewähren, zugestehen, einräumen (***s.th. to s.o.*** j-m et.): ***~ consent*** einwilligen; ***~ the point*** sich (*in e-r Debatte*) geschlagen geben; ***~ precedence to*** *j-m* den Vorrang einräumen; **4.** *a.* ***~ up*** a) auf-, hergeben, b) (***to***) abtreten (an *acc.*), überˈlassen, -ˈgeben (*dat.*), ausliefern (*dat. od.* an *acc.*): ***~ o.s. to*** *fig.* sich *e-r Sache* überlassen; ***~ a secret*** ein Geheimnis preisgeben; ***~ the palm*** (***to s.o.***) sich (j-m) geschlagen geben; ***~ place to*** Platz machen (*dat.*); → ***ghost*** 2; **II** *v/i.* **5.** *guten etc.* Ertrag geben *od.* liefern, *bsd.* ✓ tragen; **6.** nachgeben, weichen (*Sache u. Person*): ***~ to despair*** sich der Verzweiflung hingeben; ***~ to force*** der Gewalt weichen; ***I ~ to none*** ich stehe keinem nach (***in*** in *dat.*); **7.** sich fügen (***to*** *dat.*); **8.** einwilligen (***to*** in *acc.*); **III** *s.* **9.** Ertrag *m*: a) Ernte *f*, b) Ausbeute *f* (*a.* ⚙, *phys.*), Gewinn *m*: ***~ of tax***(***es***) Steueraufkommen *n*, -ertrag *m*; **10.** ✝ a) Zinsertrag *m*, b) Renˈdite *f*; **11.** ⚙ a) Meˈtallgehalt *m von Erz*, b) Ausgiebigkeit *f von Farben etc.*, c) Nachgiebigkeit *f von Material*; **ˈyield·ing** [-dɪŋ] *adj.* ☐ **1.** ergiebig, einträglich: ***~ interest*** ✝ verzinslich; **2.** nachgebend, dehnbar, biegsam; **3.** *fig.* nachgiebig, gefügig; **yield point** *s.* ⚙ Fließ-, Streckgrenze *f*, -punkt *m*.

yip [jɪp] *Am.* F *für* ***yelp***; **yip·pee** [jɪˈpi:; ˈjɪpɪ] *int.* hurˈra!

yob [jɒb] *s. Brit.* F Rowdy *m*.

yo·del [ˈjəʊdl] **I** *v/t. u. v/i.* jodeln; **II** *s.* Jodler *m* (*Gesang*).

yo·ga [ˈjəʊgə] *s.* Joga *m*, *n*, Yoga *m*, *n*.

yo·gh(o)urt [ˈjɒgət] *s.* Joghurt *m*, *n*.

yo·gi [ˈjəʊgɪ] *s.* Jogi *m*, Yogi *m*.

yo-heave-ho [ˌjəʊhi:vˈhəʊ], **yo-ho** [jəʊˈhəʊ] *int.* ⚓ hau-ˈruck!

yoicks [jɔɪks] *hunt.* **I** *int.* hussa!; **II** *s.* Hussa(ruf *m*) *n*.

yoke [jəʊk] **I** *s.* **1.** ✓, *antiq. u. fig.* Joch *n*: ***~ of matrimony*** Joch der Ehe; ***pass under the ~*** sich unter das Joch beugen; **2.** *sg. od. pl.* Paar *n*, Gespann *n*: ***two ~ of oxen***; **3.** ⚙ a) Schultertrage *f* (*für Eimer etc.*), b) Glockengerüst *n*, c) Bügel *m*, d) ϟ (Maˈgnet-, Pol)Joch *n*, e) *mot.* Gabelgelenk *n*, f) doppeltes Achslager, g) ⚓ Ruderjoch *n*; **4.** Passe *f*, Sattel *m* (*an Kleidern*); **II** *v/t.* **5.** *Tiere* anschirren, anjochen; **6.** *fig.* paaren, verbinden (***with***, ***to*** mit); **III** *v/i.* **7.** verbunden sein (***with*** mit *j-m*): ***~ together*** zs.-arbeiten; ***~ bone*** *s. anat.* Jochbein *n*; **ˈ~ˌfel·low** *s. obs.* **1.** Mitarbeiter *m*; **2.** (Lebens)Gefährte *m*, (-)Gefährtin *f*.

yo·kel [ˈjəʊkl] *s.* Bauer(ntrampel) *m*.

ˈyoke·mate → ***yokefellow***.

yolk [jəʊk] *s.* **1.** *zo.* Eidotter *m*, *n*, Eigelb *n*; **2.** Woll-, Fettschweiß *m* (*der Schafwolle*).

yon [jɒn] *obs. od. dial.* **I** *adj. u. pron.* jene(r, s) dort (drüben); **II** *adv.* → ***yonder*** I; **ˈyon·der** [-də] **I** *adv.* **1.** da *od.* dort drüben; **2.** *obs.* da drüben hin; **II** *adj. u. pron.* **3.** → ***yon*** I.

yore [jɔ:] *s.*: ***of ~*** vorzeiten, ehedem, vormals; ***in days of ~*** in alten Zeiten.

York·shire [ˈjɔ:kʃə] *adj.* aus der Grafschaft Yorkshire, Yorkshire...: ***~ flannel*** ✝ *feiner Flanell aus ungefärbter Wolle*; ***~ pudding*** *gebackener Eierteig, der zum Rinderbraten gegessen wird.*

you [ju:; jʊ; jə] *pron.* **1.** a) (*nom.*) du, ihr, Sie, b) (*dat.*) dir, euch, Ihnen, c) (*acc.*) dich, euch, Sie: ***don't ~ do that!*** tu das ja nicht!; ***that's a wine for ~!*** das ist vielleicht ein (gutes) Weinchen!; **2.** man: ***that does ~ good*** das tut einem gut; ***what should ~ do?*** was soll man tun?

you'd [ju:d; jʊd; jəd] F *für* a) ***you would***, b) ***you had***.

young [jʌŋ] **I** *adj.* jung (*a. fig. frisch, neu, unerfahren*): ***~ ambition*** jugendlicher Ehrgeiz; ***~ animal*** Jungtier *n*; ***~ children*** kleine Kinder; ***~ love*** junge Liebe; ***her ~ man*** F ihr Schatz; ***~ Smith*** Smith junior; ***a ~ state*** ein junger Staat; ***~ person*** ⚖ Jugendliche(r), Heranwachsende(r) (*14 bis 17 Jahre alt*); ***the ~ person*** *fig.* die (unverdorbene) Jugend; ***~ in one's job*** unerfahren in s-r Arbeit; **II** *s. coll.* (Tier)Junge *pl.*: ***with ~*** trächtig; **young·ish** [ˈjʌŋɪʃ] *adj.* ziemlich jung; **ˈyoung·ster** [-stə] *s.* **1.** Bursch(e) *m*, Junge *m*, Kleine(r *m*) *f*; **2.** *sport* Youngster *m*.

your [jɔ:] *pron. u. adj.* **1.** a) *sg.* dein(e), b) *pl.* euer, eure, c) *sg. od. pl.* Ihr(e); **2.** *impers.* F a) so ein(e), b) der (die, das) vielgepriesene *od.* -gerühmte.

yours [jɔ:z] *pron.* **1.** a) *sg.* dein, der (die, das) dein(ig)e, die dein(ig)en, b) *pl.* euer, eure(s), der (die, das) eur(ig)e, die eur(ig)en, c) *Höflichkeitsform*, *sg. od. pl.* Ihr, der (die, das) Ihr(ig)e, die Ihr(ig)en: ***this is ~*** das gehört dir (euch, Ihnen); ***what is mine is ~*** was mein ist, ist (auch) dein; ***my sister and ~*** meine u. deine Schwester; → ***truly*** 2; **2.** a) die Dein(ig)en (Euren, Ihren), b) das Dein(ig)e, deine Habe: ***you and ~***; **3.** ✝ Ihr Schreiben.

yourˈself *pl.* **-ˈselves** [-vz] *pron.* (*in Verbindung mit* ***you*** *od. e-m Imperativ*) **1.** a) *sg.* (du, Sie) selbst, b) *pl.* (ihr, Sie) selbst: ***by ~*** a) selbst, selber, selbständig, allein, b) allein, für sich; ***be ~!*** F nimm dich zusammen!; ***you are not ~ today*** du bist (Sie sind) heute ganz anders als sonst *od.* nicht auf der Höhe; ***what will you do with ~ today?*** was wirst du (werden Sie) heute anfangen?; **2.** *refl.* a) *sg.* dir, dich, sich, b) *pl.* euch, sich: ***did you hurt ~?*** hast du dich (haben Sie sich) verletzt?

youth [ju:θ] **I** *s.* **1.** *allg.* Jugend *f*: a) Jungsein *n*, b) Jugendfrische *f*, c) Jugendzeit *f*, d) *coll. sg. od. pl. konstr.* junge Leute *pl. od.* Menschen *pl.*; **2.** Frühstadium *n*; **3.** *pl.* **youths** [-ðz] junger Mann, Jüngling *m*; **II** *adj.* **4.** Jugend...: ***~ hostel*** Jugendherberge *f*; **ˈyouth·ful** [-fʊl] *adj.* ☐ **1.** jung (*a. fig.*); **2.** jugendlich; **3.** Jugend...: ***~ days***; **ˈyouth·ful·ness** [-fʊlnɪs] *s.* Jugend(lichkeit) *f*.

yowl [jaʊl] **I** *v/t. u. v/i.* jaulen, heulen; **II** *s.* Jaulen *n*, Heulen *n*.

yuck [jʌk] *int. sl.* pfui Teufel!

Yu·go·slav → ***Jugoslav***.

yule [ju:l] *s.* Weihnachts-, Julfest *n*; ***~ log*** *s.* Weihnachtsscheit *n im Kamin*; **ˈ~·tide** *s.* Weihnachtszeit *f*.

yum·my [ˈjʌmɪ] F **I** *adj.* a) *allg.* ‚prima', ‚toll', b) lecker (*Mahlzeit etc.*); **II** *int.* → ***yum-yum***.

yum-yum [ˌjʌmˈjʌm] *int.* F mm!, lecker!

yup·pie [ˈjʌpɪ] *s. junger, karrierebewußter und ausgabefreudiger Mensch mit urbanem Lebensstil* (*häufig bestimmten Modetrends folgend*) (= ***young urban*** *od.* ***upwardly mobile professional***).

Z

Z, z [*Brit.* zed; *Am.* ziː] *s.* Z *n*, z *n* (*Buchstabe*).

za·ny [ˈzeɪnɪ] **I** *s.* **1.** *hist.* Hansˈwurst *m*; **2.** *fig. contp.* Blödmann *m*; **II** *adj.* **3.** närrisch; **4.** *fig.* ‚blöd'.

zap [zæp] **I** *v/t. sl.* **1.** *j-n* abknallen; **2.** *j-m* ein Ding verpassen (*Kugel, Schlag etc.*): ~**!** zack!; **3.** *fig. j-n* ‚fertigmachen'; **II** *s.* **4.** ‚Schmiß' *m*.

zeal [ziːl] *s.* **1.** (Dienst-, Arbeits-, Glaubens- *etc.*)Eifer *m*: ***full of*** ~ (dienst- *etc.*)eifrig; **2.** Begeisterung *f*, Hingabe *f*, Inbrunst *f*.

zeal·ot [ˈzelət] *s.* (*bsd.* Glaubens)Eiferer *m*, Zeˈlot *m*, Faˈnatiker(in); **ˈzeal·ot·ry** [-trɪ] *s.* Zeloˈtismus *m*, faˈnatischer (Glaubens- *etc.*)Eifer.

zeal·ous [ˈzeləs] *adj.* □ **1.** (dienst)eifrig; **2.** eifernd, faˈnatisch; **3.** eifrig bedacht (***to do*** darauf, zu tun, ***for*** auf *acc.*); **4.** heiß, innig; **5.** begeistert; **ˈzeal·ous·ness** [-nɪs] → ***zeal***.

ze·bra [ˈziːbrə] *pl.* **-bras** *od. coll.* **-bra** *s. zo.* Zebra *n*; ~ **cross·ing** *s. Verkehr*: Zebrastreifen *m*.

zed [zed] *s. Brit.* **1.** Zet *n* (*Buchstabe*); **2.** ⚙ Z-Eisen *n*.

Zen (**Bud·dhism**) [zen] *s.* ˈZen(-Budˌdhismus *m*) *n*.

ze·ner di·ode [ˈziːnə] *s.* ↯ ˈZenerdiˌode *f*.

ze·nith [ˈzenɪθ] *s.* Zeˈnit *m*: a) *ast.* Scheitelpunkt *m* (*a. Ballistik*), b) *fig.* Höhe-, Gipfelpunkt *m*: ***be at one's*** (*od.* ***the***) ~ den Zenit erreicht haben, im Zenit stehen.

Zeph·a·ni·ah [ˌzefəˈnaɪə] *npr. u. s. bibl.* (das Buch) Zeˈphanja *m*.

zeph·yr [ˈzefə] *s.* **1.** *poet.* Zephir *m*, Westwind *m*, laues Lüftchen; **2.** sehr leichtes Gewebe, *a.* leichter Schal *etc.*; **3.** ✝ a) *a.* ~ ***cloth*** Zephir *m* (*Gewebe*), b) *a.* ~ ***worsted*** Zephirwolle *f*, c) *a.* ~ ***yarn*** Zephirgarn *n*.

ze·ro [ˈzɪərəʊ] **I** *pl.* **-ros** *s.* **1.** Null *f* (*Zahl od. Zeichen*); **2.** *phys.* Null (-punkt *m*) *f*, Ausgangspunkt *m* (*Skala*), *bsd.* Gefrierpunkt *m*; **3.** ⩚ Null (-punkt *m*, -stelle) *f*; **4.** *fig.* Null-, Tiefpunkt *m*: ***at*** ~ auf dem Nullpunkt (angelangt); **5.** *fig.* Null *f*, Nichts *n*; **6.** ⚔ → ***zero hour***; **7.** ✈ Höhe *f* unter 1000 Fuß: ***at*** ~ in Bodennähe; **II** *v/t.* **8.** ⚙ auf Null (ein)stellen; **III** *v/i.* **9.** ~ ***in on*** a) ⚔ sich einschießen auf (*acc.*) (*a. fig.*), b) *a. fig.* immer dichter herˈankommen an (*acc.*), einkreisen, c) *fig.* sich konzentrieren auf (*acc.*); **IV** *adj.* **10.** *bsd. Am.* F null; ~ ***option*** *pol.* Nullösung *f*; ~ **con·duc·tor** *s.* ↯ Nulleiter *m*; ~ **grav·i·ty** *s. phys.* (Zustand *m* der) Schwerelosigkeit *f*; ~ **growth** *s.* **1.** ✝ Nullwachstum *n*; **2.** *a.* ***zero population growth*** Bevölkerungsstillstand *m*; ~ **hour** *s.* **1.** ⚔ X-Zeit *f*, Stunde *f* X (*festgelegter Zeitpunkt des Beginns e-r Operation*); **2.** *fig.* genauer Zeitpunkt, kritischer Augenblick.

zest [zest] **I** *s.* **1.** Würze *f* (*a. fig. Reiz*): ***add*** ~ ***to*** *e-r Sache* Würze *od.* Reiz verleihen; **2.** *fig.* (***for***) Genuß *m*, Lust *f*, Freude *f* (an *dat.*), Begeisterung *f* (für), Schwung *m*: ~ ***for life*** Lebenshunger *m*; **II** *v/t.* **3.** würzen (*a. fig.*); **ˈzest·ful** [-fʊl] *adj.* □ **1.** reizvoll; **2.** schwungvoll, begeistert.

zig·zag [ˈzɪgzæg] **I** *s.* **1.** Zickzack *m*; **2.** Zickzacklinie *f*, -bewegung *f*, -kurs *m* (*a. fig.*); **3.** Zickzackweg *m*, Serpenˈtine(nstraße) *f*; **II** *adj.* **4.** zickzackförmig, Zickzack…; **III** *adv.* **5.** im Zickzack; **IV** *v/i.* **6.** im Zickzack fahren, laufen *etc.*, *a.* verlaufen (*Weg etc.*).

zilch [zɪltʃ] *s. Am. sl.* Null *f*, Nichts *n*.

zinc [zɪŋk] **I** *s.* ⚗ Zink *n*; **II** *v/t. pret. u. p.p.* **zinc(k)ed** [-kt] verzinken; **zin·cog·ra·pher** [zɪŋˈkɒgrəfə] *s.* Zinkoˈgraph *m*, Zinkstecher *m*; **ˈzinc·ous** [-kəs] *adj.* ⚗ Zink…; **zinc white** *s.* Zinkweiß *n*.

zing [zɪŋ] F **I** *s.* → ***zip*** 1 *u.* 2; **II** *v/i.* → ***zip*** 4; **III** *v/t.* → ***zip*** 8.

Zi·on [ˈzaɪən] *s. bibl.* Zion *m*; **ˈZi·on·ism** [-nɪzəm] *s.* Zioˈnismus *m*; **ˈZi·on·ist** [-nɪst] **I** *s.* Zioˈnist(in); **II** *adj.* zioˈnistisch, Zionisten…

zip [zɪp] **I** *s.* **1.** Schwirren *n*, Zischen *n*; **2.** F ‚Schmiß' *m*, Schwung *m*; **3.** F → ***zip fastener***; **II** *v/i.* **4.** schwirren, zischen; **5.** F ‚Schmiß' haben; **III** *v/t.* **6.** schwirren lassen; **7.** mit e-m Reißverschluß schließen *od.* öffnen; **8.** *a.* ~ ***up*** F a) ‚schmissig' machen, b) Schwung bringen in (*acc.*); ~ **ar·e·a** *s. Am.* Postleitzone *f*; ~ **code** *s. Am.* Postleitzahl *f*; ~ **fas·ten·er** *s.* Reißverschluß *m*.

zip·per [ˈzɪpə] **I** *s.* Reißverschluß *m*: ~ ***bag*** Reißverschlußtasche *f*; **II** *v/t.* mit Reißverschluß versehen; **zip·py** [ˈzɪpɪ] *adj.* F ‚schmissig'.

zith·er [ˈzɪθə] *s.* ♪ Zither *f*; **ˈzith·er·ist** [-ərɪst] *s.* Zitherspieler(in).

zo·di·ac [ˈzəʊdɪæk] *s. ast.* Tierkreis *m*: ***signs of the*** ~ Tierkreiszeichen *pl.*; **zo·di·a·cal** [zəʊˈdaɪəkl] *adj.* Tierkreis…, Zodiakal…

zom·bi(e) [ˈzɒmbɪ] *s.* **1.** Schlangengottheit *f*; **2.** Zombie *m* (*wiederbeseelte Leiche*); **3.** F a) ‚Monster' *n*, b) ‚Roboter' *m*, c) Trottel *m*; **4.** *Am.* (*ein*) Cocktail *m*.

zon·al [ˈzəʊnl] *adj.* □ **1.** zonenförmig; **2.** Zonen…; **zone** [zəʊn] **I** *s.* **1.** *allg.* Zone *f*: a) *geogr.* (Erd)Gürtel *m*, b) Gebietsstreifen *m*, Gürtel *m*, c) *fig.* Bereich *m*, (*a.* Körper)Gegend *f*, d) *poet.* Gürtel *m*: ***torrid*** ~ heiße Zone; ***wheat*** ~ Weizengürtel; ~ ***of occupation*** Besatzungszone; **2.** a) (Verkehrs)Zone *f*, *a.* Teilstrecke *f*, b) 🚂, ☏ *Am.* (Gebühren)Zone *f*, c) ☏ Post(zustell)bezirk *m*; **II** *v/t.* **3.** in Zonen aufteilen.

zonked [zɒŋkt] *adj. sl.* **1.** ‚high' (*im Drogenrausch*); **2.** ‚stinkbesoffen'.

zoo [zuː] *s.* Zoo *m*.

zo·o·blast [ˈzəʊəblæst] *s. zo.* tierische Zelle.

zo·o·chem·is·try [ˌzəʊəˈkemɪstrɪ] *s. zo.* Zoocheˈmie *f*.

zo·og·a·my [zəʊˈɒgəmɪ] *s. zo.* geschlechtliche Fortpflanzung.

zo·og·e·ny [zəʊˈɒdʒənɪ] *s. zo.* Zoogeˈnese *f*, Entstehung *f* der Tierarten.

zo·og·ra·phy [zəʊˈɒgrəfɪ] *s.* beschreibende Zooloˈgie.

zo·o·lite [ˈzəʊəlaɪt] *s.* fosˈsiles Tier.

zo·o·log·i·cal [ˌzəʊəˈlɒdʒɪkl] *adj.* □ zooˈlogisch: ~ ***garden(s)*** [zʊˈlɒdʒɪkl] zoologischer Garten; **zo·ol·o·gist** [zəʊˈɒlədʒɪst] *s.* Zooˈloge *m*, Zooˈlogin *f*; **zoˈol·o·gy** [-dʒɪ] *s.* Zooloˈgie *f*, Tierkunde *f*.

zoom [zuːm] **I** *v/i.* **1.** surren; **2.** sausen; **3.** ✈ steil hochziehen; **4.** *phot., Film*: zoomen: ~ ***in on s.th.*** a) et. heranholen, b) *fig.* et. ‚einkreisen'; **II** *v/t.* **5.** surren; **6.** *Flugzeug* hochreißen; **III** *s.* **7.** ✈ Steilflug *m*; **8.** *fig.* Hochschnellen *n*; **9.** *phot., Film*: a) *a.* ~ ***lens*** ˈZoom (-objekˌtiv) *n*, b) *a.* ~ ***travel*** Zoomfahrt *f*; **10.** *Am.* (*ein*) Cocktail *m*; **ˈzoom·er** [-mə] *s.* → ***zoom*** 9a.

zo·o·phyte [ˈzəʊəfaɪt] *s. zo.* Zooˈphyt *m*, Pflanzentier *n*.

zo·ot·o·my [zəʊˈɒtəmɪ] *s.* Zootoˈmie *f*, ˈTieranatoˌmie *f*.

zos·ter [ˈzɒstə] *s.* ⚕ Gürtelrose *f*.

zounds [zaʊndz] *int. obs.* sapperˈlot!

zy·go·ma [zaɪˈgəʊmə] *pl.* **-ma·ta** [-mətə] *s. anat.* **1.** Jochbogen *m*; **2.** Jochbein(fortsatz *m*) *n*.

zy·mo·sis [zaɪˈməʊsɪs] *pl.* **-ses** [-siːz] *s.* **1.** ⚗ Gärung *f*; **2.** ⚕ Infektiˈonskrankheit *f*; **zyˈmot·ic** [-ˈmɒtɪk] *adj.* (□ ~***ally***); **1.** ⚗ gärend, Gärungs…; **2.** ⚕ Infektions…

British and American Abbreviations

Britische und amerikanische Abkürzungen

a ***acre*** Acre *m*.
AA ***anti-aircraft*** Fla, Flugabwehr *f*; *Brit.* ***Automobile Association*** Automo'bilklub *m*; ***Alcoholics Anonymous*** Ano'nyme Alko'holiker *pl*.
AAA *Brit.* ***Amateur Athletic Association*** 'Leichtath,letikverband *m*; ***American Automobile Association*** Amer. Automo'bilklub *m*.
a.a.r. ***against all risks*** gegen jede Gefahr.
AB ***able(-bodied) seaman*** 'Vollma,trose *m*; *Am.* ***Bachelor of Arts*** (*siehe* ***BA***).
abbr., abbrev. ***abbreviated*** abgekürzt; ***abbreviation*** Abk., Abkürzung *f*.
ABC ***American Broadcasting Company*** Amer. Rundfunkgesellschaft *f*.
ABM ***antiballistic missile*** Anti-Ra'keten Ra'kete *f*.
abr. ***abridged*** (ab)gekürzt; ***abridg(e)ment*** (Ab-, Ver)Kürzung *f*.
AC ***alternating current*** Wechselstrom *m*.
a/c ***account current*** Kontokor'rent *n*; ***account*** Kto., Konto *n*; Rechnung *f*.
AD ***Anno Domini*** im Jahre des Herrn.
add(r). ***address*** Adr., A'dresse *f*.
Adm. ***Admiral*** Adm., Admi'ral *m*.
addnl. ***additional*** zusätzlich.
advt. ***advertisement*** Anz., Anzeige *f*, Ankündigung *f*.
AEC *Am.* ***Atomic Energy Commission*** A'tomener,gie-Kommissi,on *f*.
AFC ***automatic frequency control*** auto'matische Fre'quenz(fein)abstimmung *f*.
AFEX ['eɪfeks] ***Air Force Exchange*** (*Verkaufsläden für Angehörige der amer. Luftstreitkräfte*).
AFL-CIO ***American Federation of Labor & Congress of Industrial Organizations*** (*größter amer. Gewerkschaftsverband*).
AFN ***American Forces Network*** (*Rundfunkanstalt der amer. Streitkräfte*).
aft(n). ***afternoon*** Nachmittag *m*.
Aids [eɪdz] ***Acquired Immune Deficiency Syndrome*** Aids *n*, Im'munschwächekrankheit *f*.
AK ***Alaska*** (*Staat der USA*).
AL., Ala. ***Alabama*** (*Staat der USA*).
Alas. ***Alaska*** (*Staat der USA*).
Alta. ***Alberta*** (*Kanad. Provinz*).
AM ***amplitude modulation*** (*Frequenzbereich der Kurz-, Mittel- u. Langwellen*); *Am.* ***Master of Art*** (*siehe* ***MA***).
Am. ***America*** A'merika *n*; ***American*** ameri'kanisch.
a.m. ***ante meridiem*** (*Lat.* = ***before noon***) morgens, vormittags.
AMA ***American Medical Association*** Amer. Ärzteverband *m*.
amp. ***ampere*** A., Am'pere *n*.
AP ***Associated Press*** (*amer. Nachrichtenagentur*).
approx. ***approximate(ly)*** annähernd, etwa.
appx. ***appendix*** Anh., Anhang *m*.
Apr. ***April*** April *m*.
APT *Brit.* ***Advanced Passenger Train*** (*Hochgeschwindigkeitszug*).
AR ***Arkansas*** (*Staat der USA*).
ARC ***American Red Cross*** *das* Amer. Rote Kreuz.
Ariz. ***Arizona*** (*Staat der USA*).
Ark. ***Arkansas*** (*Staat der USA*).
ARP ***Air-Raid Precautions*** Luftschutz *m*.
arr. ***arrival*** Ankunft *f*.
art. ***article*** Art., Ar'tikel *m*; ***artificial*** künstlich.
AS ***Anglo-Saxon*** Angelsächsisch *n*, angelsächsisch; ***anti-submarine*** U-Boot--Abwehr...
ASA ***American Standards Association*** Amer. 'Normungs-Organisati,on *f*.
ASCII ['æski:] ***American Standard Code for Information Interchange*** (*standardisierter Code zur Darstellung alphanumerischer Zeichen*).
asst. ***assistant*** Asst., Assi'stent(in).
asst'd ***assorted*** assor'tiert, gem., gemischt.
ATC ***air traffic control*** Flugsicherung *f*.
Aug. ***August*** Aug., Au'gust *m*.
auth. ***author(ess)*** Verfasser(in).
av. ***average*** 'Durchschnitt *m*; Hava'rie *f*.
avdp. ***avoirdupois*** Handelsgewicht *n*.
Ave. ***Avenue*** Al'lee *f*, Straße *f*.
AWACS ['eɪwæks] ***Airborne Warning and Control System*** (*luftgestütztes Frühwarn- und Überwachungssystem*).
AWOL ***absence without leave*** unerlaubte Entfernung von der Truppe.
AZ ***Arizona*** (*Staat der USA*).

b. ***born*** geboren.
BA ***Bachelor of Arts*** Bakka'laureus *m* der Philoso'phie; ***British Academy*** Brit. Akade'mie *f*; ***British Airways*** Brit. Luftverkehrsgesellschaft *f*.
BAgr(ic) ***Bachelor of Agriculture*** Bakka'laureus *m* der Landwirtschaft.
b&b ***bed and breakfast*** Über'nachtung *f* mit Frühstück.
BAOR ***British Army of the Rhine*** Brit. 'Rheinar,mee *f*.
Bart. ***Baronet*** Baronet *m*.
BBC ***British Broadcasting Corporation*** Brit. Rundfunkgesellschaft *f*.
bbl. ***barrel*** Faß *n*.
BC ***before Christ*** vor Christus; ***British Columbia*** (*Kanad. Provinz*).
BCom(m) ***Bachelor of Commerce*** Bakka'laureus *m* der Wirtschaftswissenschaften.
BD ***Bachelor of Divinity*** Bakka'laureus *m* der Theolo'gie.
bd. ***bound*** gebunden (*Buchbinderei*).
BDS ***Bachelor of Dental Surgery*** Bakka'laureus *m* der 'Zahnmedi,zin.
bds. ***boards*** karto'niert (*Buchbinderei*).
BE ***Bachelor of Education*** Bakka'laureus *m* der Erziehungswissenschaft; ***Bachelor of Engineering*** Bakka'laureus *m* der Inge'nieurwissenschaft(en); (*siehe* ***B/E***).
B/E ***Bill of Exchange*** Wechsel *m*.
Beds. ***Bedfordshire*** (*engl. Grafschaft*).
b/f ***brought forward*** 'Übertrag *m*.
BFBS ***British Forces Broadcasting Service*** (*Rundfunkanstalt der brit. Streitkräfte*).
B'ham ***Birmingham*** (*Stadt in England*).
b.h.p. ***brake horse-power*** Brems-PS *f od. pl.*, Bremsleistung *f* in PS.
BIF ***British Industries Fair*** Brit. Indu'striemesse *f*.
BIS ***Bank for International Settlements*** BIZ, Bank *f* für internatio'nalen Zahlungsausgleich.
bk. ***book*** Buch *n*.
BL ***Bachelor of Law*** Bakka'laureus *m* des Rechts.
B/L ***bill of lading*** (See)Frachtbrief *m*.
bl. ***barrel*** Faß *n*.
bldg. ***building*** Geb., Gebäude *n*.
BLit(t) ***Bachelor of Literature*** Bakka'laureus *m* der Litera'tur.
bls. ***bales*** Ballen *pl*.; ***barrels*** Faß *pl*.
Blvd. ***Boulevard*** Boule'vard *m*.
BM ***Bachelor of Medicine*** Bakka'laureus *m* der Medi'zin; ***British Museum*** Britisches Mu'seum.
BMA ***British Medical Association*** Brit. Ärzteverband *m*.
BMus ***Bachelor of Music*** Bakka'laureus *m* der Mu'sik.
b.o. ***branch office*** Zweigstelle *f*, Fili'ale *f*; ***body odo(u)r*** Körpergeruch *m*; ***buyer's option*** 'Kaufopti,on *f*; ***box office*** (The'ater)Kasse *f*.
B.o.T. ***Board of Trade*** Brit. 'Handelsmini,sterium *n*.
bot. ***bought*** gekauft; ***bottle*** Flasche *f*.
BPharm ***Bachelor of Pharmacy*** Bakka'laureus *m* der Pharma'zie.
BPhil ***Bachelor of Philosophy*** Bakka'laureus *m* der Philoso'phie.
BR ***British Rail*** (*Eisenbahn in Großbritannien*).
B/R ***bills receivable*** Wechselforderungen *pl*.
Br. ***Britain*** Großbri'tannien *n*; ***British*** britisch.
BRCS ***British Red Cross Society*** *das* Brit. Rote Kreuz.
Brit. ***Britain*** Großbri'tannien *n*; ***British*** britisch.
Bros. ***brothers*** Gebr., Gebrüder *pl*. (*in Firmenbezeichnungen*).

BS *Am.* ***Bachelor of Science*** Bakka'laureus *m* der Na'turwissenschaften; ***British Standard*** Brit. Norm *f.*
B/S ***bill of sale*** Über'eignungsvertrag *m.*
BSc *Brit.* ***Bachelor of Science*** Bakka'laureus *m* der Na'turwissenschaften.
BSG ***British Standard Gauge*** (*brit. Norm*).
B.S.I. ***British Standards Institution*** Brit. 'Normungs-Organisati,on *f.*
BST ***British Summer Time*** Brit. Sommerzeit *f.*
BT. ***Baronet*** Baronet *m.*
BTA ***British Tourist Authority*** Brit. Fremdenverkehrsbehörde *f.*
bt. fwd. ***brought forward*** 'Übertrag *m.*
B.th.u. Btu ***British Thermal Unit(s)*** Brit. Wärmeeinheit(en *pl.*) *f.*
bu. ***bushel*** Scheffel *m.*
Bucks. ***Buckinghamshire*** (*engl. Grafschaft*).
bus. *Am.* ***business*** Arbeit *f, die* Geschäfte *pl.*

C ***Celsius, centigrade*** Celsius, hundertgradig (*Thermometer*).
c ***cent(s)*** Cent *m* (*amer. Münze*); ***century*** Jahr'hundert *n*; ***circa*** ca., circa, ungefähr; ***cubic*** Kubik...
CA ***California*** (*Staat der USA*); ***chartered accountant*** beeidigter 'Bücherre,visor *od.* Wirtschaftsprüfer; ***current account*** Girokonto *n.*
CAB *Brit.* ***Citizens' Advice Bureau*** (*Bürgerberatungsorganisation*).
c.a.d. ***cash against documents*** Zahlung *f* gegen Doku'mentenaushändigung.
Cal(if). ***California*** (*Staat der USA*).
Cambs. ***Cambridgeshire*** (*engl. Grafschaft*).
Can. ***Canada*** Kanada *n*; ***Canadian*** ka'nadisch.
C & W. ***country and western*** (*Musik*).
Cantab. ***Cantabrigiensis*** (*Titel etc.*) der Universi'tät Cambridge.
Capt. ***Captain*** Kapi'tän *m*, Hauptmann *m*, Rittmeister *m.*
Card. ***Cardinal*** Kardi'nal *m.*
CARE [keə] ***Cooperative for American Relief Everywhere*** (*amer. Organisation, die Hilfsgüter an Bedürftige in aller Welt versendet*).
Cath. ***Catholic*** kath., ka'tholisch.
CB ***Citizens' Band*** CB-Funk *m* (*Wellenbereich für privaten Funkverkehr*); ***Companion of (the Order of) the Bath*** Ritter *m* des Bath-Ordens; (*a.* ***C/B***) ***cash book*** Kassabuch *n.*
CBC ***Canadian Broadcasting Corporation*** Ka'nadische Runkdfunkgesellschaft.
CBS ***Columbia Broadcasting System*** (*amer. Rundfunkgesellschaft*).
CC ***City Council*** Stadtrat *m*; *Brit.* ***County Council*** Grafschaftsrat *m.*
cc *Brit.* ***cubic centimetre(s)***, *Am.* ***cubic centimeter(s)*** ccm, Ku'bikzenti,meter *m, n od. pl.*
CD ***compact disc*** CD(-Platte) *f*; ***Corps Diplomatique*** (*Fr.* = ***Diplomatic Corps***) CD *n*, Diplo'matisches Korps.
CE ***Church of England*** angli'kanische Kirche; ***civil engineer*** 'Bauinge,nieur *m.*
cert. ***certificate*** Bescheinigung *f.*
CET ***Central European Time*** MEZ, 'mitteleuro,päische Zeit.
cf. ***confer*** vgl., vergleiche.

Ch. ***chapter*** Kap., Ka'pitel *n.*
ch. ***chain*** (*Länge einer*) Meßkette *f*; ***chapter*** Kap., Ka'pitel *n*; ***chief*** ltd., leitende(r) ..., oberste(r) ...
c.h. ***central heating*** ZH, Zen'tralheizung *f.*
ChB ***Chirurgiae Baccaleureus*** (*Lat.* = ***Bachelor of Surgery***) Bakka'laureus *m* der Chirur'gie.
Ches. ***Cheshire*** (*engl. Grafschaft*).
C.I. ***Channel Islands*** Ka'nalinseln *pl.*
C/I ***certificate of insurance*** Ver'sicherungspo,lice *f.*
CIA ***Central Intelligence Agency*** (*Geheimdienst der USA*).
CID ***Criminal Investigation Department*** (*brit. Kriminalpolizei*).
c.i.f. ***cost, insurance, freight*** Kosten, Versicherung und Fracht einbegriffen.
C.-in-C. ***Commander-in-Chief*** 'Oberkomman,dierende(r) *m* (*dem Land-, Luft- und Seestreitmächte unterstehen*).
cir(c). ***circa*** ca., circa, ungefähr; ***circular*** Rundschreiben *n*; ***circulation*** 'Umlauf *m*, Auflage *f* (*Zeitung etc.*).
ck(s)., ***cask*** Faß *n*; ***casks*** Fässer *pl.*
cl. ***class*** Klasse *f.*
cm *Brit.* ***centimetre(s)***, *Am.* ***centimeter(s)*** cm, Zenti'meter *m, n od. pl.*
CND ***Campaign for Nuclear Disarmament*** Feldzug *m* für ato'mare Abrüstung.
CO ***Colorado*** (*Staat der USA*); ***Commanding Officer*** Komman'deur *m*; ***conscientious objector*** Kriegsdienstverweigerer *m.*
Co. ***Company*** Gesellschaft *f*; ***county*** *Brit.* Grafschaft *f*, (Verwaltungs)Bezirk *m.*
c/o ***care of*** p.A., per A'dresse, bei.
COD, c.o.d. ***cash*** (*Am.* ***collection***) ***on delivery*** zahlbar bei Lieferung, per Nachnahme.
C. of E. ***Church of England*** angli'kanische Kirche; ***Council of Europe*** ER, Eu'roparat *m.*
COI *Brit.* ***Central Office of Information*** (*staatliches Auskunftsbüro zur Verbreitung amtlicher Publikationen etc.*).
Col. ***Colorado*** (*Staat der USA*); ***Colonel*** Oberst *m.*
conc. ***concerning*** betr., betreffend, betrifft.
Conn. ***Connecticut*** (*Staat der USA*).
Cons. ***Conservative*** konserva'tiv (*Brit. pol.*); ***Consul*** Konsul *m.*
cont., contd. ***continued*** fortgesetzt.
Corn. ***Cornwall*** (*engl. Grafschaft*).
Corp. ***Corporal*** Korpo'ral *m*, 'Unteroffi,zier *m*; ***Corporation*** (*siehe Wörterverzeichnis*).
corr. ***corresponding*** entspr., entsprechend.
cp. ***compare*** vgl., vergleiche.
CPA *Am.* ***certified public accountant*** beeidigter 'Bücherre,visor *od.* Wirtschaftsprüfer.
c.p.s. ***cycles per second*** Hertz *pl.*
CT ***Connecticut*** (*Staat der USA*).
ct(s) ***cent(s)*** (*amer. Münze*).
cu(b). ***cubic*** Ku'bik...
cu.ft. ***cubic foot*** Ku'bikfuß *m.*
cu.in. ***cubic inch*** Ku'bikzoll *m.*
Cumb. ***Cumberland*** (*ehemalige engl. Grafschaft*).
cum d(iv) ***cum dividend*** mit Divi'dende.
CUP ***Cambridge University Press*** Verlag *m* der Universi'tät Cambridge.

c.w.o. ***cash with order*** Barzahlung *f* bei Bestellung.
cwt ***hundredweight*** (*etwa 1*) Zentner *m.*

d. *Brit.* ***penny, pence*** (*bis 1971 verwendete Abkürzung*); ***died*** gest., gestorben.
DA ***deposit account*** Depo'sitenkonto *n*; *Am.* ***district attorney*** Staatsanwalt *m.*
DAR *Am.* ***Daughters of the American Revolution*** (*patriotische Frauenvereinigung*).
DAT ***digital audio tape*** (*in Cassetten befindliches Tonband für Digitalaufnahmen mit DAT-Recordern*).
DB ***daybook*** Jour'nal *n.*
DC ***direct current*** Gleichstrom *m*; ***District of Columbia*** Di'strikt Columbia (*mit der amer. Hauptstadt Washington*).
DCL ***Doctor of Civil Law*** Doktor *m* des Zi'vilrechts.
DD ***Doctor of Divinity*** Dr. theol., Doktor *m* der Theolo'gie.
d-d *euphem. für* ***damned*** verdammt.
DDS ***Doctor of Dental Surgery*** Dr. med. dent., Doktor *m* der 'Zahnmedi,zin.
DDT ***dichlorodiphenyltrichloroethane*** DDT, Di'chlordiphe'nyltrichlorä,than *n* (*Insekten- und Seuchenbekämpfungsmittel*).
DE ***Delaware*** (*Staat der USA*).
Dec. ***December*** Dez., De'zember *m.*
dec. ***deceased*** gest., gestorben.
DEd ***Doctor of Education*** Dr. paed., Doktor *m* der Päda'gogik.
def. ***defendant*** Beklagte(r *m*) *f.*
deg. ***degree(s)*** Grad *m od. pl.*
Del. ***Delaware*** (*Staat der USA*).
DEng ***Doctor of Engineering*** Dr.-Ing., Doktor *m* der Inge'nieurwissenschaften.
dep. ***departure*** Abf., Abfahrt *f.*
Dept. ***Department*** Ab'teilung *f.*
Derby. ***Derbyshire*** (*engl. Grafschaft*).
dft. ***draft*** Tratte *f.*
diff. ***different*** versch., verschieden; ***difference*** 'Unterschied *m.*
Dir. ***Director*** Dir., Di'rektor *m.*
disc. ***discount*** Dis'kont *m*, Abzug *m.*
dist. ***distance*** Entfernung *f*; ***district*** Bez., Bezirk *m.*
div. ***dividend*** Divi'dende *f*; ***divorced*** gesch., geschieden.
DIY ***do-it-yourself*** „mach es selber!"; (*in Zssgn*) Heimwerker...
DJ ***disc jockey*** Diskjockey *m*; ***dinner jacket*** Smoking(jacke *f*) *m.*
DLit(t) ***Doctor of Letters, Doctor of Literature*** Doktor *m* der Litera'turwissenschaft.
do. ***ditto*** do., dito; dgl., desgleichen.
doc. ***document*** Doku'ment *n*, Urkunde *f.*
dol. ***dollar(s)*** Dollar *m od. pl.*
Dors. ***Dorsetshire*** (*engl. Grafschaft*).
doz. ***dozen(s)*** Dutzend *n od. pl.*
DP ***displaced person*** Verschleppte(r *m*) *f*; ***data processing*** DV, Datenverarbeitung *f.*
d/p ***documents against payment*** Doku'mente *pl.* gegen Zahlung.
DPh(il) ***Doctor of Philosophy*** Dr. phil., Doktor *m* der Philoso'phie.
Dpt. ***Department*** Ab'teilung *f.*
Dr. ***Doctor*** Dr., Doktor *m*; ***debtor*** Schuldner *m.*
dr. ***dra(ch)m*** Dram *m*, Drachme *f* (*Handelsgewicht*); ***drawer*** Tras'sant *m.*
d.s., d/s ***days after sight*** Tage nach Sicht (*bei Wechseln*).
DSc ***Doctor of Science*** Dr. rer. nat., Doktor *m* der Na'turwissenschaften.

DST ***Daylight-Saving Time*** Sommerzeit *f.*
DTh(eol) ***Doctor of Theology*** Dr. theol., Doktor *m* der Theolo'gie.
Dur. ***Durham*** *(engl. Grafschaft)*
dwt. ***pennyweight*** Pennygewicht *n.*
dz. ***dozen(s)*** Dutzend *n od. pl.*

E ***east*** O, Ost(en *m*); ***east(ern)*** ö, östlich; ***English*** engl., englisch.
E. & O. E. ***errors and omissions excepted*** Irrtümer und Auslassungen vorbehalten.
EC ***European Community*** EG, Euro'päische Gemeinschaft; ***East Central*** London Mitte-Ost (*Postbezirk*).
ECE ***Economic Commission for Europe*** 'Wirtschaftskommissi,on *f* für Eu'ropa (*des Wirtschafts- u. Sozialrates der UN*).
ECG ***electrocardiogram*** EKG, E'lektrokardio,gramm *n.*
ECOSOC ***Economic and Social Council*** Wirtschafts- und Sozi'alrat *m* (*der UN*).
ECSC ***European Coal and Steel Community*** EGKS, Euro'päische Gemeinschaft für Kohle und Stahl.
ECU ***European Currency Unit(s)*** Euro'päische Währungseinheit(en *pl.*) *f.*
Ed., ed. ***edition*** Aufl., Auflage *f*; ***edited*** hrsg., her'ausgegeben; ***editor*** Hrsg., Her'ausgeber *m.*
EDP ***electronic data processing*** EDV, elek'tronische Datenverarbeitung.
E.E., E./E. ***errors excepted*** Irrtümer vorbehalten.
EEC ***European Economic Community*** *hist.* EWG, Euro'päische Wirtschaftsgemeinschaft.
EFTA ['eftə] ***European Free Trade Association*** EFTA, Euro'päische Freihandelsgemeinschaft.
e.g. ***exempli gratia*** (*Lat.* = ***for instance***) z.B., zum Beispiel.
EMA ***European Monetary Agreement*** EWA, Euro'päisches Währungsabkommen.
enc(l). ***enclosure(s)*** Anl., Anlage(n *pl.*) *f.*
Eng(l). ***England*** Engl., England *n*; ***English*** engl., englisch.
ESA ***European Space Agency*** Euro'päische Weltraumbehörde.
ESP ***extrasensory perception*** außersinnliche Wahrnehmung.
Esq(r). ***Esquire*** (*in Briefadressen, nachgestellt*) Herrn.
ESRO ***European Space Research Organization*** ESRO, Euro'päische Organisati'on für Weltraumforschung.
Ess. ***Essex*** (*engl. Grafschaft*).
est. ***established*** gegr., gegründet; ***estimated*** gesch., geschätzt.
ESx ***East Sussex*** (*engl. Grafschaft*).
ETA ***estimated time of arrival*** vor'aussichtliche Ankunft(szeit).
etc., &c. ***et cetera, and the rest, and so on*** etc., usw., und so weiter.
ETD ***estimated time of departure*** vor'aussichtliche Abflugzeit *bzw.* Abfahrtszeit.
EU ***European Union*** EU, Euro'päische Uni'on.
Euratom [juər'ætəm] ***European Atomic Energy Community*** Eura'tom *f*, Euro'päische A'tomgemeinschaft.
excl. ***exclusive, excluding*** ausschl., ausschließlich, ohne.
ex. div. ***ex dividend*** ohne (*od.* ausschließlich) Divi'dende.
ex. int. ***ex interest*** ohne (*od.* ausschließlich) Zinsen.

F ***Fahrenheit*** (*Thermometereinteilung*); *univ.* ***Fellow*** (*siehe Wörterverzeichnis* ***fellow*** 6).
f. ***farthing*** (*ehemalige brit. Münze*); ***fathom*** Faden *m*, Klafter *m, n, f*; ***feminine*** w., weiblich; ***foot, feet*** Fuß *m od. pl.*; ***following*** folgend.
FA *Brit.* ***Football Association*** Fußballverband *m.*
f.a.a. ***free of all average*** frei von Beschädigung.
Fah(r). ***Fahrenheit*** (*Thermometereinteilung*).
FAO ***Food and Agriculture Organization*** Organisati'on *f* für Ernährung und Landwirtschaft (*der UN*).
f.a.s. ***free alongside ship*** frei Längsseite (See)Schiff.
FBI ***Federal Bureau of Investigation*** Amer. Bundeskrimi'nalamt *n*; ***Federation of British Industries*** Brit. Indu'strieverband *m.*
FCC ***Federal Communications Commission*** Amer. 'Bundeskommissi,on *f* für das Nachrichtenwesen.
Feb. ***February*** Febr., Februar.
fig. ***figure(s)*** Abb., Abbildung(en *pl.*) *f.*
FL, Fla. ***Florida*** (*Staat der USA*).
FM ***frequency modulation*** UKW (*Frequenzbereich der Ultrakurzwellen*).
fm ***fathom(s)*** Faden *m od. pl.*, Klafter *m, n, f od. pl.*
FO *Brit.* ***Foreign Office*** Auswärtiges Amt.
fo(l). ***folio*** Folio *n*, Seite *f.*
f.o.b. ***free on board*** frei Schiff.
f.o.r. ***free on rail*** frei Wag'gon.
FP ***freezing point*** Gefrierpunkt *m*; ***fireplug*** Hy'drant *m.*
Fr. ***France*** Frankreich *n*; ***French*** franz., fran'zösisch.
fr. ***franc(s)*** Franc(s *pl.*) *m*, Franken *m od. pl.*
Fri. ***Friday*** Fr., Freitag *m.*
ft. ***foot, feet*** Fuß *m od. pl.*
FTC ***Federal Trade Commission*** Amer. Bundes'handelskommissi,on *f* (*zur Verhinderung unlauteren Wettbewerbs*).
fur. ***furlong(s)*** (*Längenmaß*).

g ***gram(s), gramme(s)*** g., Gramm *n od. pl.*; ***gallon(s)*** Gal'lone(n *pl.*) *f.*
g. ***ga(u)ge*** Nor'malmaß *n*; 🚂 Spur *f*; ***guinea*** Gui'nee *f* (*105 p.*).
GA ***general agent*** Gene'ralvertreter *m*; ***general assembly*** Hauptversammlung *f*; *siehe* **Ga.**
Ga. ***Georgia*** (*Staat der USA*).
gal(l). ***gallon(s)*** Gal'lone(n *pl.*) *f.*
GATT [gæt] ***General Agreement on Tariffs and Trade*** Allgemeines Zoll- und Handelsabkommen.
GB ***Great Britain*** GB, Großbri'tannien *n.*
G.B.S. ***George Bernard Shaw*** (*irischer Dramatiker*).
GCB ***(Knight) Grand Cross of the Bath*** (Ritter *m* des) Großkreuz(es) *n* des Bath-Ordens.
GCE ***General Certificate of Education*** (*siehe Wörterverzeichnis*).
GCSE ***General Certificate of Secondary Education*** (*schulische Abschlußprüfung, die seit 1988 u.a. die „O-levels" des GCE ersetzt*).
Gen. ***General*** Gene'ral *m.*
gen. ***general(ly)*** allgemein.
Ger. ***German*** deutsch, Deutsche(r *m*) *f*; ***Germany*** Deutschland *n.*
GI ***government issue*** von der Re'gierung ausgegeben, Staatseigentum *n*; *der* amer. Sol'dat.
gi. ***gil(s)*** Viertelpinte(n *pl.*) *f.*
GLC ***Greater London Council*** (*ehemaliger*) Stadtrat von Groß-London (*bis 1985*).
Glos. ***Gloucestershire*** (*engl. Grafschaft*).
GMT ***Greenwich Mean Time*** WEZ, 'westeuro,päische Zeit.
GNP ***gross national product*** Bruttosozi'alpro,dukt *n.*
gns. ***guineas*** Gui'neen *pl.*
GOP *Am.* ***Grand Old Party*** Republi'kanische Par'tei.
Gov. ***Government*** Re'gierung *f*; ***Governor*** Gouver'neur *m.*
GP ***general practitioner*** Arzt *m* (Ärztin *f*) für Allge'meinmedi,zin; ***Gallup Poll*** 'Meinungs,umfrage *f* (*insbesondere zum Wählerverhalten*).
GPO ***General Post Office*** Hauptpostamt *n.*
gr. ***grain(s)*** Gran *n od. pl.*; ***gross*** brutto; Gros *n od. pl.* (*12 Dutzend*).
gr. wt ***gross weight*** Bruttogewicht *n.*
gs. ***guineas*** Gui'neen *pl.*
gtd., guar. ***guaranteed*** garan'tiert.

h. ***hour(s)*** Std., Stunde(n *pl.*) *f*, Uhr *f* (*bei Zeitangaben*); ***height*** Höhe *f.*
h&c ***hot and cold*** warm u. kalt (*Wasser*).
Hants. ***Hampshire*** (*engl. Grafschaft*).
HBM ***His (Her) Britannic Majesty*** Seine (Ihre) Bri'tannische Maje'stät.
HC *Brit.* ***House of Commons*** 'Unterhaus *n.*
hdbk ***handbook*** Handbuch *n.*
HE ***high explosive*** 'hochexplo,siv; ***His Eminence*** Seine Emi'nenz *f*; ***His (Her) Excellency*** Seine (Ihre) Exzel'lenz *f.*
Heref. ***Herefordshire*** (*ehemalige engl. Grafschaft*).
Herts. ***Hertfordshire*** (*engl. Grafschaft*).
HF ***high frequency*** 'Hochfre,quenz *f*; *Brit.* ***Home Fleet*** Flotte *f* in den Heimatgewässern.
hf. ***half*** halb.
hf.bd ***half bound*** in Halbfranz gebunden (*Halbleder*).
hhd ***hogshead*** (*Hohlmaß, etwa 240 Liter*); großes Faß.
HI ***Hawaii*** (*Staat der USA*).
HL. *Brit.* ***House of Lords*** Oberhaus *n.*
HM ***His (Her) Majesty*** Seine (Ihre) Maje'stät.
HMS ***His (Her) Majesty's Service*** Dienst *m*, 📯 Dienstsache *f*; ***His (Her) Majesty's Ship (Steamer)*** Seiner (Ihrer) Maje'stät Schiff *n* (Dampfschiff *n*).
HMSO ***His (Her) Majesty's Stationery Office*** (*Brit. Staatsdruckerei*).
HO ***Head Office*** Hauptgeschäftsstelle *f*, Zen'trale *f*; *Brit.* ***Home Office*** 'Innenmini,sterium *n.*
Hon. ***Honorary*** ehrenamtlich; ***Hono(u)rable*** (der *od.* die) Ehrenwerte (*Anrede und Titel*).
HP, hp ***horsepower*** PS, Pferdestärke *f*; ***high pressure*** Hochdruck *m*; ***hire purchase*** Ratenkauf *m.*
HQ, Hq. ***Headquarters*** 'Stab(squar,tier *n*) *m*, 'Hauptquar,tier *n.*
HR *Am.* ***House of Representatives*** Repräsen'tantenhaus *n.*

hr ***hour(s)*** Stunde(n *pl.*) *f.*
HRH ***His (Her) Royal Highness*** Seine (Ihre) Königliche Hoheit.
hrs. ***hours*** Std., Stunden *pl.*
HT, h.t. ***high tension*** Hochspannung *f.*
ht ***height*** H., Höhe *f.*
Hunts. ***Huntingdonshire*** (*ehemalige engl. Grafschaft*).
HWM ***high-water mark*** Hochwasserstandsmarke *f.*

I. ***island(s), isle(s)*** Insel(n *pl.*) *f.*
IA, Ia. ***Iowa*** (*Staat der USA*).
IATA [aɪˈɑːtə] ***International Air Transport Association*** Internatio'naler Luftverkehrsverband.
IBA ***Independent Broadcasting Authority*** (*Dachorganisation der brit. privaten Fernseh- u. Rundfunkanstalten*).
ib(id). ***ibidem*** (*Lat.* = ***in the same place***) ebd.,ebenda.
IBRD ***International Bank for Reconstruction and Development*** Internatio'nale Bank für Wieder'aufbau und Entwicklung, Weltbank *f.*
IC ***integrated circuit*** inte'grierter Schaltkreis.
ICAO ***International Civil Aviation Organization*** Internatio'nale Zi'villuftfahrt-Organisatiˌon.
ICBM ***intercontinental ballistic missile*** interkontinen'taler bal'listischer Flugkörper, Interkontinen'talraˌkete *f.*
ICFTU ***International Confederation of Free Trade Unions*** Internatio'naler Bund Freier Gewerkschaften.
ICJ ***International Court of Justice*** IG, Internatio'naler Gerichtshof.
ICU ***intensive care unit*** Inten'sivstatiˌon *f.*
ID ***Idaho*** (*Staat der USA*); ***identity*** Identi'tät *f*; ***Intelligence Department*** Nachrichtenamt *n.*
Id(a). ***Idaho*** (*Staat der USA*).
i.e. ***id est*** (*Lat.* = ***that is to say***) d.h., das heißt.
IHP, ihp ***indicated horsepower*** i. PS, indi'zierte Pferdestärke.
Il, Ill. ***Illinois*** (*Staat der USA*).
ILO ***International Labo(u)r Organization*** Internatio'nale 'Arbeitsorganisatiˌon.
ILS ***instrument landing system*** Instru'mentenˌlandesyˌstem *n.*
IMF ***International Monetary Fund*** IWF, Internatio'naler Währungsfonds.
Imp. ***Imperial*** Reichs..., Empire...
IN ***Indiana*** (*Staat der USA*).
in. ***inch(es)*** Zoll *m od. pl.*
Inc. ***Incorporated*** (amtlich) eingetragen.
incl. ***inclusive, including*** einschl., einschließlich.
incog. ***incognito*** in'kognito (*unter anderem Namen*).
Ind. ***Indiana*** (*Staat der USA*).
inst. ***instant*** d.M., dieses Monats.
IOC ***International Olympic Committee*** Internatio'nales O'lympisches Komi'tee.
I. of M. ***Isle of Man*** (*engl. Insel*).
I. of W. ***Isle of Wight*** (*engl. Insel, Grafschaft*).
IOM *siehe* ***I. of M.***
IOU ***I owe you*** Schuldschein *m.*
IOW *siehe* ***I. of W.***
IPA ***International Phonetic Association*** Internatio'nale Pho'netische Gesellschaft.
IW ***intelligence quotient*** Intelli'genzquotiˌent *m.*
Ir. ***Ireland*** Irland *n*; ***Irish*** irisch.
IRA ***Irish Republican Army*** IRA, 'Irisch-Republi'kanische Ar'mee.
IRBM ***intermediate-range ballistic missile*** 'Mittelstreckenraˌkete *f.*
ISBN ***international standard book number*** ISBN-Nummer *f.*
ISDN ***integrated services digital network*** 'dienste-inteˌgrierendes digi'tales Fernmeldenetz.
ISO ***International Organization for Standardization*** IOS, Internatio'nale Organisati'on für Standardi'sierung, Internatio'nale 'Normenorganisatiˌon.
ITV ***Independent Television*** (*unabhängige brit. kommerzielle Fernsehanstalten*).
IUD ***intrauterine device*** Intraute'rinpesˌsar *n*, -spiˌrale *f.*
IYHF ***International Youth Hostel Federation*** Internatio'naler Jugendherbergsverband.

J. ***Judge*** Richter *m*; ***justice*** Ju'stiz *f*; Richter *m.*
Jan. ***January*** Jan., Januar *m.*
JATO [ˈdʒeɪtəʊ] ***jet-assisted takeoff*** Start *m* mit 'Startraˌkete.
JC ***Jesus Christ*** Jesus Christus *m.*
JCB ***Juris Civilis Baccalaureus*** (*Lat.* = ***Bachelor of Civil Law***) Bakka'laureus *m* des Zi'vilrechts.
JCD ***Juris Civilis Doctor*** (*Lat.* = ***Doctor of Civil Law***) Doktor *m* des Zi'vilrechts.
Jnr ***junior*** *siehe* ***Jr, jun(r).***
JP ***Justice of the Peace*** Friedensrichter *m.*
Jr ***junior*** (*Lat.* = ***the younger***) jr., jun., der Jüngere.
JUD ***Juris Utriusque Doctor*** (*Lat.* = ***Doctor of Civil and Canon Law***) Doktor *m* beider Rechte.
Jul. ***July*** Jul., Juli *m.*
Jun. ***June*** Jun., Juni *m.*
jun(r). ***junior*** (*Lat.* = ***the younger***) jr., jun., der Jüngere.

Kan(s). ***Kansas*** (*Staat der USA*).
KC ***Knight Commander*** Kom'tur *m*, Großmeister *m*; *Brit.* ***King's Counsel*** Kronanwalt *m.*
KCB ***Knight Commander of the Bath*** Großmeister *m* des Bath-Ordens.
Ken. ***Kentucky*** (*Staat der USA*).
kg ***kilogram(s), kilogramme(s)*** kg., Kilo'gramm *n.*
kHz ***kilohertz*** kHz, Kilo'hertz *n od. pl.*
KIA ***killed in action*** gefallen.
KKK ***Ku Klux Klan*** (*geheime Terrororganisation in den USA*).
km *Brit.* ***kilometre(s)***, *Am.* ***kilometer(s)*** km, Kilo'meter *m od. pl.*
KO, k.o. ***knockout*** K.o., Knock-out *m.*
k.p.h. *Brit.* ***kilometre(s) per hour***, *Am.* ***kilometer(s) per hour*** 'Stundenkiloˌmeter *m od. pl.*
KS ***Kansas*** (*Staat der USA*).
kV ***kilovolt(s)*** kV, Kilo'volt *n od. pl.*
kW ***kilowatt(s)*** kW, Kilo'watt *n od. pl.*
KY, Ky ***Kentucky*** (*Staat der USA*).

L *Brit.* ***learner (driver)*** Fahrschüler(in) (*Plakette an Kraftfahrzeugen*).
l. ***left*** l., links; ***length*** Länge *f*; ***line*** Z., Zeile *f*; Lin., Linie *f*; (*meist* **l**) *Brit.* ***litre(s)***, *Am.* ***liter(s)*** l., Liter *m*, *n od. pl.*
£ ***pound(s) sterling*** Pfund *n od. pl.* Sterling (*Währung*).
LA ***Los Angeles*** (*Stadt in Kalifornien*); ***Louisiana*** (*Staat der USA*).
£A ***Australian pound*** au'stralisches Pfund (*Währung*).
Lab. ***Labrador*** (*Kanad. Halbinsel*).
Lancs. ***Lancashire*** (*engl. Grafschaft*).
lang. ***language*** Spr., Sprache *f.*
lat. ***latitude*** geo'graphische Breite.
lb. ***pound(s)*** Pfund *n od. pl.* (*Gewicht*).
L/C ***letter of credit*** Kre'ditbrief *m.*
LCJ *Brit.* ***Lord Chief Justice*** Lord'oberrichter *m.*
Ld. ***Lord*** Lord *m.*
£E ***Egyptian pound*** ä'gyptisches Pfund (*Währung*).
Leics. ***Leicestershire*** (*engl. Grafschaft*).
Lincs. ***Lincolnshire*** (*engl. Grafschaft*).
LJ *Brit.* ***Lord Justice*** Lordrichter *m.*
ll. ***lines*** Zeilen *pl.*; Linien *pl.*
LL D ***Legum Doctor*** (*Lat.* = ***Doctor of Laws***) Dr. jur., Doktor *m* der Rechte.
LMT ***local mean time*** mittlere Ortszeit (*in USA*).
loc. cit. ***loco citato*** (*Lat.* = ***in the place cited***) a. a. O., am angeführten Ort.
lon(g). ***longitude*** geo'graphische Länge.
LP ***long-playing record*** LP, Langspielplatte *f*; ***Labour Party*** (*brit. Linkspartei*); *siehe* **l.p.**
l.p. ***low pressure*** Tiefdruck *m.*
L'pool ***Liverpool*** *n.*
LSD ***lysergic acid diathylamide*** LSD, Lysergsäurediäthylamid *n.*
LSE ***London School of Economics*** (*renommierte Londoner Wirtschaftshochschule*).
LSO ***London Symphony Orchestra*** *das* Londoner Sinfo'nie-Orˌchester.
Lt. ***Lieutenant*** Leutnant *m.*
l.t. ***low tension*** Niederspannung *f.*
Lt.-Col. ***Lieutenant-Colonel*** Oberst'leutnant *m.*
Ltd. ***limited*** mit beschränkter Haftung.
Lt.-Gen. ***Lieutenant-General*** Gene'ralleutnant *m.*

m ***male*** m, männlich; ***masculine*** m, männlich; ***married*** verh., verheiratet; *Brit.* ***metre(s)***, *Am.* ***meter(s)*** m, Meter *m*, *n od. pl.*; ***mile(s)*** M., Meile(n *pl.*) *f*; ***minute(s)*** min, Min., Mi'nute(n *pl.*) *f.*
MA ***Master of Arts*** Ma'gister *m* der Philoso'phie; ***Massachusetts*** (*Staat der USA*); ***military academy*** Mili'tärakaˌdeˌmie *f.*
Maj. ***Major*** Ma'jor *m.*
Maj.-Gen. ***Major-General*** Gene'ralmaˌjor *m.*
Man. ***Manitoba*** (*Kanad. Provinz*).
Mar. ***March*** März *m.*
Mass. ***Massachusetts*** (*Staat der USA*).
max. ***maximum*** Max., Maximum *n.*
MB ***Medicinae Baccalaureus*** (*Lat.* = ***Bachelor of Medicine***) Bakka'laureus *m* der Medi'zin.
MC ***Master of Ceremonies*** Zere'monienmeister *m*, *Am.* Conféren'cier *m*; *Am.* ***Member of Congress*** Parla'mentsmitglied *n.*
MD ***Maryland*** (*Staat der USA*); ***Managing Director*** geschäftsführender Di'rektor; ***Medicinae Doctor*** (*Lat.* = ***Doctor of Medicine***) Dr. med., Doktor *m* der Medi'zin.
M/D ***months' date*** Monate nach heute.
Md. ***Maryland*** (*Staat der USA*).
MDS ***Master of Dental Surgery*** Ma'gister *m* der 'Zahnmediˌzin.

ME, Me. ***Maine*** (*Staat der USA*).
med. ***medical*** med., medi'zinisch; ***medicine*** Med., Medi'zin *f*; ***medieval*** mittelalterlich.
mg ***milligramme(s), milligram(s)*** mg, Milligramm *n od. pl.*
MI ***Michigan*** (*Staat der USA*).
mil. ***mile(s)*** M., Meile(n *pl.*) *f*.
Mich. ***Michigan*** (*Staat der USA*).
Middx. ***Middlesex*** (*ehemalige engl. Grafschaft*).
min. ***minute(s)*** min., Min., Mi'nute(n *pl.*) *f*; ***minimum*** Min., Minimum *n*.
Minn. ***Minnesota*** (*Staat der USA*).
Miss. ***Mississippi*** (*Staat der USA*).
mm *Brit.* ***millimetre(s)***, *Am.* ***millimeter(s)*** mm, Milli'meter *m, n od. pl.*
MN ***Minnesota*** (*Staat der USA*).
MO ***Missouri*** (*Staat der USA*); ***mail order*** *siehe Wörterverzeichnis*; ***money order*** *siehe Wörterverzeichnis*.
Mo. ***Missouri*** (*Staat der USA*).
Mon. ***Monday*** Mo., Montag *m*.
Mont. ***Montana*** (*Staat der USA*).
MP *Brit.* ***Member of Parliament*** Abgeordnete(r *m*) *f* des 'Unterhauses; ***Military Police*** Mili'tärpoli,zei *f*.
mph ***miles per hour*** Stundenmeilen *pl.*
MPharm ***Master of Pharmacy*** Ma'gister *m* der Pharma'zie.
Mr ['mɪstə] ***Mister*** Herr *m*.
Mrs ['mɪsɪz] *ursprünglich* ***Mistress*** Frau *f*.
MS ***Mississippi*** (*Staat der USA*); ***manuscript*** Mskr(pt)., Manu'skript *n*; ***motorship*** Motorschiff *n*.
Ms [mɪz] Frau *f* (*neutrale Anredeform für unverheiratete und verheiratete Frauen*).
MSc ***Master of Science*** Ma'gister *m* der Na'turwissenschaften.
MSL ***mean sea level*** mittlere (See)Höhe, Nor'malnull *n*.
MSS ***manuscripts*** Manu'skripte *pl.*
MT ***Montana*** (*Staat der USA*).
Mt ***Mount*** Berg *m*.
mt ***megaton*** Megatonne *f*.
M'ter ***Manchester*** *n*.
MTh ***Master of Theology*** Ma'gister *m* der Theolo'gie.
Mx ***Middlesex*** (*ehemalige engl. Grafschaft*).

N ***North*** N, Nord(en *m*); ***north(ern)*** n, nördlich.
n ***neuter*** n, Neutrum *n*, neu'tral; ***noun*** Subst., Substantiv *n*; ***noon*** Mittag *m*.
Naafi ['næfɪ] *Brit.* ***Navy, Army and Air Force Institutes*** (*Truppenbetreuungsinstitution der brit. Streitkräfte, u. a. für Kantinen u. Geschäfte zuständig*).
NASA ['næsə] *Am.* ***National Aeronautics and Space Administration*** Natio'nale Luft- u. Raumfahrtbehörde *f*.
nat. ***national*** nat., natio'nal; ***natural*** nat., na'türlich.
NATO ['neɪtəʊ] ***North Atlantic Treaty Organization*** Nordat'lantikpakt-Organisati,on *f*.
NB ***New Brunswick*** (*Kanad. Provinz*).
NBC *Am.* ***National Broadcasting Corporation*** Natio'nale Rundfunkgesellschaft.
NC ***North Carolina*** (*Staat der USA*).
N.C.B. *Brit.* ***National Coal Board*** Natio'nale Kohlenbehörde.
n.d. ***no date*** ohne Datum.
ND, N Dak ***North Dakota*** (*Staat der USA*).
NE ***Nebraska*** (*Staat der USA*); ***northeast*** NO, Nord'ost(en *m*); ***northeast(ern)*** nö, nord'östlich.
Neb(r). ***Nebraska*** (*Staat der USA*).
neg. ***negative*** neg., negativ.
Nev. ***Nevada*** (*Staat der USA*).
NF ***Newfoundland*** (*Kanad. Provinz*).
NH ***New Hampshire*** (*Staat der USA*).
NHS ***National Health Service*** Staatlicher Gesundheitsdienst.
NJ ***New Jersey*** (*Staat der USA*).
NM, N Mex. ***New Mexico*** (*Staat der USA*).
No. ***North*** N, Nord(en *m*); ***numero*** Nr., Nummer *f*; ***number*** Zahl *f*.
Norf. ***Norfolk*** (*engl. Grafschaft*).
Northants. ***Northamptonshire*** (*engl. Grafschaft*).
Notts. ***Nottinghamshire*** (*engl. Grafschaft*).
Nov. ***November*** Nov., No'vember *m*.
n.p. or d. ***no place or date*** ohne Ort oder Datum.
NS ***Nova Scotia*** (*Kanad. Provinz*).
NSB *Brit.* ***National Savings Bank*** *etwa* Postsparkasse *f*.
NSPCC ***National Society for the Prevention of Cruelty to Children*** (*brit. Kinderschutzverein*).
NSW ***New South Wales*** (*Bundesstaat Australiens*).
NT ***New Testament*** NT, Neues Testa'ment; ***Northern Territory*** (*Verwaltungsbezirk Australiens*).
nt.wt. ***net weight*** Nettogewicht *n*.
NV ***Nevada*** (*Staat der USA*).
NW ***northwest*** NW, Nord'west(en *m*); ***northwest(ern)*** nw, nord'westlich.
NWT ***Northwest Territories*** (*N-Kanada östl. des Yukon Territory*).
NY ***New York*** (*Staat der USA*).
NYC ***New York City*** (die Stadt) New York.
N Yorks. ***North Yorkshire*** (*engl. Grafschaft*).

O. ***Ohio*** (*Staat der USA*); ***order*** Auftr., Auftrag *m*.
o/a ***on account of*** auf Rechnung von.
OAP ***old-age pensioner*** (Alters)Rentner(in), Ruhegeldempfänger(in).
OAS ***Organization of American States*** Organisati'on *f* ameri'kanischer Staaten.
OAU ***Organization of African Unity*** Organisati'on *f* für Afri'kanische Einheit.
ob. ***obiit*** (*Lat.* = ***died***) gest., gestorben.
Oct. ***October*** Okt., Ok'tober *m*.
OECD ***Organization for Economic Cooperation and Development*** Organisati'on *f* für wirtschaftliche Zu'sammenarbeit und Entwicklung.
OH ***Ohio*** (*Staat der USA*).
OHMS ***On His (Her) Majesty's Service*** im Dienste Seiner (Ihrer) Maje'stät; ✆ Dienstsache *f*.
OJ *Am.* ***orange juice*** O'rangensaft *m*.
OK ***Oklahoma*** (*Staat der USA*); *siehe* ***O.K.***
O.K. (*möglicherweise aus:*) ***all correct*** in Ordnung.
Okla. ***Oklahoma*** (*Staat der USA*).
o.n.o. ***or near(est) offer*** VB, Verhandlungsbasis *f*.
Ont. ***Ontario*** (*Kanad. Provinz*).
OPEC ['əʊpek] ***Organization of Petroleum Exporting Countries*** Organisati'on *f* der Erdöl expor'tierenden Länder.
OR ***Oregon*** (*Staat der USA*).
o.r. ***owner's risk*** auf Gefahr des Eigentümers.
Ore(g). ***Oregon*** (*Staat der USA*).
OT ***Old Testament*** AT, Altes Testa'ment.
OUP ***Oxford University Press*** Verlag *m* der Universi'tät Oxford.
Oxon. ***Oxfordshire*** (*engl. Grafschaft*); ***Oxoniensis*** (*Titel etc.*) der Universi'tät Oxford.
oz. ***ounce(s)*** Unze(n *pl.*) *f*.

p. ***penny, pence*** (*brit. Münze*).
p. ***page*** S., Seite *f*; ***part*** T., Teil *m*.
PA, Pa. ***Pennsylvania*** (*Staat der USA*).
p.a. ***per annum*** (*Lat.* = ***yearly***) jährlich.
p&p ***postage and packing*** (Kosten *pl.* für) Porto *n* und Verpackung *f*.
par(a). ***paragraph*** Par., Para'graph *m*, Abschnitt *m*.
PAYE ***pay as you earn*** (*Brit. Quellenabzugsverfahren. Arbeitgeber zieht Lohn- bzw. Einkommensteuer direkt vom Lohn bzw. Gehalt ab*).
PC *Brit.* ***police constable*** Schutzmann *m*; ***Personal Computer*** PC, Perso'nalcom,puter *m*; *Am.* ***Peace Corps*** Friedenscorps *n*.
p.c. ***per cent*** %, Pro'zent *n od. pl.*; ***postcard*** Postkarte *f*.
p/c ***price current*** Preisliste *f*.
pcl. ***parcel*** Pa'ket *n*.
pcs. ***pieces*** Stück(e *pl.*) *n*.
PD ***Police Department*** Poli'zeibehörde *f*; ***per diem*** (*Lat.* = ***by the day***) pro Tag.
pd. ***paid*** bez., bezahlt.
PEI ***Prince Edward Island*** (*Kanad. Provinz*).
PEN [pen], *mst* **PEN Club** (***International Association of) Poets, Playwrights, Editors, Essayists and Novelists*** PEN-Club *m* (*Internationaler Verband von Dichtern, Dramatikern, Redakteuren, Essayisten und Romanschriftstellern.*
Penn(a). ***Pennsylvania*** (*Staat der USA*).
per pro(c). ***per procurationem*** (*Lat.* = ***by proxy***) pp., ppa., per Pro'kura.
PhD ***Philosophiae Doctor*** (*Lat.* = ***Doctor of Philosophy***) Dr. phil., Doktor *m* der Philoso'phie.
Pk ***Park*** Park *m*; ***Peak*** Spitze *f*, (Berg-) Gipfel *m*.
Pl. ***Place*** Platz *m*.
PLC, Plc, plc *Brit.* ***public limited company*** AG, Aktiengesellschaft *f*.
p.m. ***post meridiem*** (*Lat.* = ***after noon***) nachm., nachmittags, ab., abends.
PO ***post office*** Postamt *n*; ***postal order*** Postanweisung *f*.
POB ***post-office box*** Postschließfach *n*.
p.o.d. ***pay on delivery*** Nachnahme *f*.
POO ***post-office order*** Postanweisung *f*.
pos(it). ***positive*** pos., positiv.
POW ***prisoner of war*** Kriegsgefangene(r) *m*.
p.p. ***per procurationem*** (*Lat.* = ***by proxy***) pp., ppa., per Pro'kura.
pp. ***pages*** Seiten *pl.*
PR ***public relations*** PR, Öffentlichkeitsarbeit *f*.
pref. ***preface*** Vw., Vorwort *n*.
Pres. ***President*** Präsi'dent *m*.
pro. ***professional*** professio'nell, Berufs...
Prof. ***Professor*** Pro'fessor *m*.
prol. ***prologue*** Pro'log *m*.
Prot. ***Protestant*** Prot., Prote'stant *m*.
prox. ***proximo*** (*Lat.* = ***next month***) n. M., nächsten Monats.

PS ***postscript*** PS, Post'skript *n*, Nachschrift *f*.
PT ***physical training*** Leibeserziehung *f*.
pt. ***part*** Teil *m*; ***payment*** Zahlung *f*; ***pint*** (*Brit. 0,57 l, Am. 0,47 l*); ***point*** *siehe Wörterverzeichnis*.
PTA ***Parent-Teacher Association*** Eltern-Lehrer-Vereinigung *f*.
Pte. *Brit.* ***Private*** Sol'dat *m* (*Dienstgrad*).
PTO, p.t.o. ***please turn over*** b.w., bitte wenden.
Pvt. *Am.* ***Private*** Sol'dat *m* (*Dienstgrad*).
PW ***prisoner of war*** Kriegsgefangene(r) *m*.
PX ***Post Exchange*** (*Verkaufsläden für Angehörige der amer. Streitkräfte*).

QC *Brit.* ***Queen's Counsel*** Kronanwalt *m*.
Qld. ***Queensland*** (*Bundesstaat Australiens*).
qr ***quarter*** (*etwa 1*) Viertelzentner *m* (*Handelsgewicht*).
qt ***quart*** Quart *n* (*Brit. 1,14 l, Am. 0,95 l*).
Que. ***Quebec*** (*Kanad. Provinz*).
quot. ***quotation*** Kurs-, 'Preisno,tierung *f*.

R. ***Réaumur*** (*Thermometereinteilung*); ***River*** Strom *m*, Fluß *m*.
r. ***right*** r., rechts.
RA *Brit.* ***Royal Academy*** Königliche Akade'mie.
RAC *Brit.* ***Royal Automobile Club*** Königlicher Automo'bilklub.
RAF ***Royal Air Force*** Königlich-Brit. Luftwaffe *f*.
RAM *Computer*: ***random access memory*** Speicher *m* mit wahlfreiem Zugriff, Arbeitsspeicher *m*.
RC ***Roman Catholic*** r.-k., römisch--ka'tholisch.
Rd ***Road*** Str., Straße *f*.
recd ***received*** erhalten.
ref(c). **(*in*) *reference* (*to*)** (mit) Bezug *m* (auf); Empf., Empfehlung *f*.
regd ***registered*** eingetragen; ✆ eingeschrieben.
reg. tn ***register ton*** RT, Re'gistertonne *f*.
res. ***residence*** Wohnsitz *m*, -ort *m*; ***research*** Forschung *f*; ***reserve*** Re'serve *f*, Reserve...
ret(d). ***retired*** i.R., im Ruhestand.
Rev(d). ***Reverend*** Ehrwürden (*Titel u. Anrede*).
RI ***Rhode Island*** (*Staat der USA*).
rm ***room*** Zi., Zimmer *n*.
RMA *Brit.* ***Royal Military Academy*** Königliche Mili'tärakade,mie (*Sandhurst*).
RN ***Royal Navy*** Königlich-Brit. Ma'rine *f*.
ROM *Computer*: ***read only memory*** Nur-Lese-Speicher *m*, Fest(wert)speicher *m*.
RP ***received pronunciation*** Standardaussprache *f* (*des Englischen in Südengland*); ***reply paid*** Rückantwort bezahlt (*bei Telegrammen*).
r.p.m. ***revolutions per minute*** U/min., Um'drehungen *pl.* pro Mi'nute.
RR *Am.* ***Railroad*** Eisenbahn *f*.
RS *Brit.* ***Royal Society*** Königliche Gesellschaft (*traditionsreicher u. bedeutendster naturwissenschaftlicher Verein Großbritanniens*).
RSPCA ***Royal Society for the Prevention of Cruelty to Animals*** (*brit. Tierschutzverein*).
RSVP ***répondez s'il vous plaît*** (*Fr.* = ***please reply***) u. A. w. g., um Antwort wird gebeten; Antwort erbeten.
rt ***right*** r., rechts.
Rt Hon. ***Right Honourable*** (*der od. die*) Sehr Ehrenwerte (*Titel u. Anrede*).
RU ***Rugby Union*** 'Rugby-Uni,on *f*.
Ry *Brit.* ***Railway*** Eisenbahn *f*.

S ***south*** S., Süd(en *m*); ***south(ern)*** s., südlich.
s ***second(s)*** s, sec., sek., Sek., Se'kunde(n *pl.*) *f*; ***shilling(s)*** Schilling(e *pl.*) *m*.
SA ***South Africa*** 'Süd'afrika *n*; ***South America*** S.A., 'Süda'merika *n*; ***South Australia*** (*Bundesstaat Australiens*); ***Salvation Army*** H.A., 'Heilsar,mee *f*.
s.a.e. ***stamped addressed envelope*** fran'kierter, mit (eigener) Anschrift versehener 'Brief,umschlag.
Salop ***Shropshire*** (*engl. Grafschaft*).
Salt [sɔːlt] ***Strategic Arms Limitation Talks*** (*Verhandlungen zwischen der Sowjetunion und den USA über einen Vertrag zur Begrenzung und zum Abbau strategischer Waffensysteme*).
Sask. ***Saskatchewan*** (*Kanad. Provinz*).
Sat. ***Saturday*** Sa., Samstag *m*, Sonnabend *m*.
S Aus(tr). ***South Australia*** (*Bundesstaat Australiens*).
SB ***sales book*** Verkaufsbuch *n*.
SC ***South Carolina*** (*Staat der USA*); ***Security Council*** Sicherheitsrat *m* (*der UN*).
Sch. ***school*** Sch., Schule *f*.
SD, S Dak. ***South Dakota*** (*Staat der USA*).
SPD *Brit.* ***Social Democratic Party*** Sozi'aldemo,kratische Par'tei.
SE ***southeast*** SO., Süd'ost(en *m*); ***southeast(ern)*** sö, süd'östlich; ***Stock Exchange*** Börse *f*.
SEATO ['siːtəʊ] ***South-East Asia Treaty Organization*** Südost'asienpakt-Organisati,on *f* (*1977 aufgelöst*).
Sec. ***Secretary*** Sekr., Sekre'tär *m*; Mi'nister *m*.
sec. ***second(s)*** s, sec, sek., Sek., Se'kunde(n *pl.*) *f*; ***secondary*** *siehe Wörterverzeichnis*.
sen(r). ***senior*** (*Lat.* = ***the elder***) sen., der Ältere.
Sep(t). ***September*** Sep(t)., Sep'tember *m*.
Serg(t). ***Sergeant*** Fw, Feldwebel *m*; Wachtmeister *m*.
SF ***science fiction*** Science-'fiction *f* (*Literatur*).
Sgt. *siehe* **Serg(t).**
sh ***share*** Aktie *f*; ***sheet*** Druckbogen *m* (*Buchdruck*); ***shilling(s)*** Schilling(e *pl.*) *m*.
SHAPE [ʃeɪp] ***Supreme Headquarters Allied Powers Europe*** 'Oberkom,mando *n* der Alli'ierten Streitkräfte in Eu'ropa.
SM ***Sergeant-Major*** Oberfeldwebel *m*; Oberwachtmeister *m*.
S/N ***shipping note*** Frachtannahmeschein *m*, Schiffszettel *m*.
Soc. ***Society*** Gesellschaft *f*; Verein *m*.
Som(s). ***Somerset(shire)*** (*engl. Grafschaft*).
SOS SOS (*Internationales Seenotzeichen*).
sp.gr. ***specific gravity*** sp.G., spe'zifisches Gewicht.
S.P.Q.R. ***small profits, quick returns*** kleine Gewinne, rasche 'Umsätze.
Sq. ***Square*** Platz *m*.
sq. ***square*** Qua'drat...
sq.ft ***square foot*** Qua'dratfuß *m*.
sq. in. ***square inch*** Qua'dratzoll *m*.
Sr ***senior*** (*Lat.* = ***the elder***) sen., der Ältere.
SS ***steamship*** Dampfer *m*; ***saints*** *die* Heiligen *pl*.
St. ***Saint ...*** St., Sankt ...; ***Street*** Str., Straße *f*; ***Station*** B(h)f., Bahnhof *m*.
st. ***stone*** (*Gewicht*).
STA ***scheduled time of arrival*** planmäßige Ankunft(szeit).
Sta. ***Station*** B(h)f., Bahnhof *m*.
Staffs. ***Staffordshire*** (*engl. Grafschaft*).
STD *Brit.* ***subscriber trunk dialling*** Selbstwählfernverkehr *m*; ***scheduled time of departure*** planmäßige Abflugzeit *bzw.* Abfahrtszeit.
stg ***sterling*** Sterling *m* (*brit. Währungseinheit*).
STOL [stɒl] ***short takeoff and landing (aircraft)*** STOL-, Kurzstart(-Flugzeug *n*) *m*.
Str. ***Strait*** Straße *f* (*Meerenge*).
sub. ***substitute*** Ersatz *m*.
Suff. ***Suffolk*** (*engl. Grafschaft*).
Sun. ***Sunday*** So., Sonntag *m*.
supp(l). ***supplement*** Nachtrag *m*.
Suss. ***Sussex*** (*ehemalige engl. Grafschaft*).
SW ***southwest*** SW, Süd'west(en *m*).
Sx ***Sussex*** (*ehemalige engl. Grafschaft*).
Sy ***Surrey*** (*engl. Grafschaft*).
S Yorks. ***South Yorkshire*** (*engl. Grafschaft*).

t ***ton(s)*** Tonne(n *pl.*) *f* (*Handelsgewicht*).
Tas. ***Tasmania*** (*Bundesstaat Australiens*).
TB ***tuberculosis*** Tb, Tbc, Tuberku'lose *f*.
TC ***Trusteeship Council*** Treuhandschaftsrat *m* (*der UN*).
TD ***Treasury Department*** Fi'nanzmini,sterium *n* der USA.
TEFL ***Teaching English as a Foreign Language*** das Unter'richten von Englisch als Fremdsprache.
tel. ***telephone*** Tel., Tele'fon *n*.
Tenn. ***Tennessee*** (*Staat der USA*).
Ter(r). ***Terrace*** (*in Straßennamen*) Häuserreihe *f* (*in Hanglage od. über einem Hang gelegen*); ***Territory*** (Hoheits)Gebiet *n*, Terri'torium *n*.
Tex. ***Texas*** (*Staat der USA*).
tgm. ***telegram*** Tele'gramm *n*.
TGWU *Brit.* ***Transport and General Workers' Union*** Trans'portarbeitergewerkschaft *f*.
Th., Thu(r)., Thurs. ***Thursday*** Do., Donnerstag *m*.
TN ***Tennessee*** (*Staat der USA*).
tn ***ton(s)*** Tonne(n *pl.*) *f* (*Handelsgewicht*).
TO ***Telegraph (Telephone) Office*** Tele'grafenamt *n* (Fernsprechamt *n*); ***turnover*** 'Umsatz *m*.
TRH *Brit.* ***Their Royal Highnesses*** Ihre Königlichen Hoheiten.
TU ***Trade(s) Union(s)*** Gew., Gewerkschaft(en *pl.*) *f*.
Tu. ***Tuesday*** Di., Dienstag *m*.
TUC *Brit.* ***Trades Union Congress*** Gewerkschaftsverband *m*.
Tue(s). ***Tuesday*** Di., Dienstag *m*.
TV ***television*** FS, Fernsehen *n*; Fernseh...
TX ***Texas*** (*Staat der USA*).

U ***universal*** allgemein (*zugelassen*); für alle Altersstufen geeignet (*Kinoprogramm ohne Jugendverbot*).

UFO ***unidentified flying object*** Ufo *n.*
UHF ***ultrahigh frequency*** UHF, Ultra'hochfre,quenz(-Bereich *m*) *f*, Dezi'meterwellenbereich *m.*
UK ***United Kingdom*** Vereinigtes Königreich (*England, Schottland, Wales u. Nordirland*).
ult(o). ***ultimo*** (*Lat.* = ***in the last*** [***month***]) v. Mts., vorigen Monats.
UMW ***United Mine Workers*** Vereinigte Bergarbeiter *pl.* (*amer. Gewerkschaftsverband*).
UN ***United Nations*** Vereinte Nati'onen *pl.*
UNESCO [juːˈneskəʊ] ***United Nations Educational, Scientific and Cultural Organization*** Organisati'on *f* der Vereinten Nati'onen für Wissenschaft, Erziehung und Kul'tur.
UNICEF [ˈjuːnɪsef] ***United Nations Children's Fund*** (*früher* ***United Nations International Children's Emergency Fund***) Kinderhilfswerk *n* der Vereinten Nati'onen.
UNO ***United Nations Organization*** UNO *f.*
UNSC ***United Nations Security Council*** Sicherheitsrat *m* der Vereinten Nati'onen.
UPI ***United Press International*** (*amer. Nachrichtenagentur*).
US ***United States*** Vereinigte Staaten *pl.*
USA ***United States of America*** Vereinigte Staaten *pl.* von A'merika; ***United States Army*** Heer *n* der Vereinigten Staaten.
USAF(E) ***United States Air Force*** (***Europe***) Luftwaffe *f* der Vereinigten Staaten (in Eu'ropa).
USN ***United States Navy*** Ma'rine *f* der Vereinigten Staaten.
USS ***United States Senate*** Se'nat *m* der Vereinigten Staaten; ***United States Ship*** (Kriegs)Schiff *n* der Vereinigten Staaten.
USSR *hist.* ***Union of Soviet Socialist Republics*** UdSSR, Uni'on *f* der Sozia'listischen So'wjetrepu,bliken.
UT, Ut. ***Utah*** (*Staat der USA*).
UV ***ultraviolet*** UV, 'ultravio,lett.

V ***volt(s)*** V., Volt *n od. pl.*
v. ***very*** sehr; ***verse*** V., Vers *m*; ***versus*** (*Lat.* = ***against***) gegen; ***vide*** (*Lat.* = ***see***) s., siehe; ***volt(s)*** V, Volt *n od. pl.*
VA, Va. ***Virginia*** (*Staat der USA*).
VAT ***value added tax*** Mwst., Mehrwertsteuer *f.*
VCR ***video cassette recorder*** 'Videore,corder *m.*
VD ***venereal disease*** Geschlechtskrankheit *f.*
VHF ***very high frequency*** VHF, UKW, Ultrakurzwelle(n *pl.*) *f*, Meterwellenbereich *m.*
Vic. ***Victoria*** (*Bundesstaat Australiens*).
VIP ***very important person*** VIP *m*, ‚hohes Tier'.
Vis(c). ***Viscount(ess)*** Vi'comte *m* (Vicom'tesse *f*).
viz. ***videlicet*** (*Lat.* = ***namely***) nämlich.
vol. ***volume*** Bd., Band *m* (*eines Buches*).
vols. ***volumes*** Bde., Bände *pl.*
VP(res.) ***Vice President*** 'Vizepräsi,dent *m* (*stellvertretender Vorsitzender, Vorstandsmitglied etc.*).
vs. ***versus*** (*Lat.* = ***against***) gegen.
VSOP ***very superior old pale*** (*Bezeichnung für 20-25 Jahre alten Branntwein, Portwein etc.*).
VT, Vt. ***Vermont*** (*Staat der USA*).
VTOL [ˈviːtɒl] ***vertical takeoff and landing*** (***aircraft***) Senkrechtstarter *m.*
v.v. ***vice versa*** (*Lat.* = ***conversely***) 'umgekehrt.

W ***west*** West(en *m*); ***west(ern)*** w., westlich; ***watt(s)*** W., Watt *n od. pl.*
w ***watt(s)*** W., Watt *n od. pl.*; ***week*** Wo., Woche *f*; ***width*** Weite *f*, Breite *f*; ***wife*** (Ehe)Frau *f*; ***with*** mit.
WA ***Washington*** (*Staat der USA*); *siehe* ***W Aus(tr)***.
War(ks) ***Warwickshire*** (*engl. Grafschaft*).
Wash. ***Washington*** (*Staat der USA*).
WASP [wɒsp] ***White Anglo-Saxon Protestant*** (*protestantischer Amerikaner britischer od. nordeuropäischer Abstammung*).
W Aus(tr). ***Western Australia*** (*Bundesstaat Australiens*).
WC ***West Central*** London Mitte-West (*Postbezirk*); ***water closet*** WC, 'Wasserklo,sett *n.*
Wed(s). ***Wednesday*** Mi., Mittwoch *m.*
w.e.f. ***with effect from*** mit Wirkung vom.
WEU ***Western European Union*** 'Westeuro,päische Uni'on.
WFTU ***World Federation of Trade Unions*** Weltgewerkschaftsbund *m.*
WHO ***World Health Organization*** 'Weltgesundheitsorganisati,on *f* (*der UN*).
WI ***West Indies*** Westindien *n*; *siehe* ***Wis(c)***.
Wilts. ***Wiltshire*** (*engl. Grafschaft*).
Wis(c). ***Wisconsin*** (*Staat der USA*).
wk ***week*** Wo., Woche *f*; ***work*** Arbeit *f.*
wkly ***weekly*** wöchentlich.
wks. ***weeks*** Wo., Wochen *pl.*
w/o ***without*** o., ohne.
Worc. ***Worcestershire*** (*ehemalige engl. Grafschaft*).
WP, w.p. ***weather permitting*** (nur) bei gutem Wetter.
w.p.a. ***with particular average*** mit Teilschaden (*Versicherung inklusive Teilschaden*).
w.p.m. ***words per minute*** Wörter *pl.* pro Mi'nute.
w.r.t. ***with reference to*** bezüglich.
W Sx ***West Sussex*** (*engl. Grafschaft*).
wt ***weight*** Gewicht *n.*
WV, W Va. ***West Virginia*** (*Staat der USA*).
WW I (*od.* **II**) ***World War I*** (*od.* ***II***) der erste (*od.* zweite) Weltkrieg.
WY, Wyo. ***Wyoming*** (*Staat der USA*).
W Yorks. ***West Yorkshire*** (*engl. Grafschaft*).

x-d ***ex dividend*** ohne Divi'dende.
x-i. ***ex interest*** ohne Zinsen.
Xm., Xmas [ˈkrɪsməs] ***Christmas*** Weihnacht(en *n*) *f.*
Xn ***Christian*** christlich.
Xroads ***crossroads*** Straßenkreuzung *f.*
Xt ***Christ*** Christus *m.*
Xtian ***Christian*** christlich.

yd(s) ***yard(s)*** Elle(n *pl.*) *f* (*Längenmaß*).
YHA ***Youth Hostels Association*** Jugendherbergsverband *m.*
YMCA ***Young Men's Christian Association*** CVJM, Christlicher Verein Junger Männer.
Yorks. ***Yorkshire*** (*ehemalige engl. Grafschaft*).
yr ***year*** Jahr *n*; ***your*** *siehe Wörterverzeichnis*; ***younger*** jünger(e, -es); junior.
yrs ***years*** Jahre *pl.*; ***yours*** *siehe Wörterverzeichnis.*
YWCA ***Young Women's Christian Association*** Christlicher Verein Junger Frauen und Mädchen.

Proper Names
Eigennamen

Ab·er·deen [ˌæbəˈdiːn] *Stadt in Schottland*; ˌ**Ab·erˈdeen·shire** [-ʃə] *schottische Grafschaft (bis 1975).*
Ab·er·yst·wyth [ˌæbəˈrɪstwɪθ] *Stadt in Wales.*
A·bra·ham [ˈeɪbrəhæm] Abraham *m.*
A·chil·les [əˈkɪliːz] Aˈchilles *m.*
A·da [ˈeɪdə] Ada *f*, Adda *f.*
Ad·am [ˈædəm] Adam *m.*
Ad·di·son [ˈædɪsn] *englischer Autor.*
Ad·e·laide [ˈædəleɪd] *Stadt in Australien*; Adelheid *f.*
A·den [ˈeɪdn] Aden *n* (*Hauptstadt des Südjemen*).
Ad·i·ron·dacks [ˌædɪˈrɒndæks] *pl. Gebirgszug im Staat New York* (*USA*).
Ad·olf [ˈædɒlf], **A·dol·phus** [əˈdɒlfəs] Adolf *m.*
A·dri·an [ˈeɪdrɪən] Adrian *m*, Adriˈane *f.*
A·dri·at·ic Sea [ˌeɪdrɪˈætɪk ˈsiː] *das* Adriˈatische Meer.
Ae·ge·an Sea [iːˈdʒiːən ˈsiː] *das* Äˈgäische Meer, *die* Äˈgäis.
Aes·chy·lus [ˈiːskɪləs] Äschylus *m.*
Ae·sop [ˈiːsɒp] Äˈsop *m.*
Af·gha·nis·tan [æfˈgænɪstæn] Afˈghanistan *n.*
Af·ri·ca [ˈæfrɪkə] Afrika *n.*
Ag·a·tha [ˈægəθə] Aˈgathe *f.*
Ag·gie [ˈægɪ] *Koseform für* ***Agatha, Agnes.***
Ag·nes [ˈægnɪs] Agnes *f.*
Aix-la-Cha·pelle [ˌeɪkslɑːʃæˈpel] Aachen *n.*
Al·a·ba·ma [ˌæləˈbæmə] *Staat der USA.*
Al·an [ˈælən] *m.*
A·las·ka [əˈlæskə] *Staat der USA.*
Al·ba·ni·a [ælˈbeɪnjə] Alˈbanien *n.*
Al·ba·ny [ˈɔːlbənɪ] *Hauptstadt des Staates New York* (*USA*).
Al·bert [ˈælbət] Albert *m.*
Al·ber·ta [ælˈbɜːtə] *Provinz in Kanada.*
Al·bu·quer·que [ˈælbəkɜːkɪ] *Stadt in New Mexiko* (*USA*).
Al·der·ney [ˈɔːldənɪ] *brit. Kanalinsel.*
Al·der·shot [ˈɔːldəʃɒt] *Stadt in Südengland.*
A·leu·tian Is·lands [əˌluːʃjənˈaɪləndz] *pl. die* Aleˈuten *pl.*
Al·ex [ˈælɪks] *abbr. für* ***Alexander.***
Al·ex·an·der [ˌælɪgˈzɑːndə] Alexˈander *m.*
Al·ex·an·dra [ˌælɪgˈzɑːndrə] Alexˈandra *f.*
Alf [ælf] *abbr. für* ***Alfred.***
Al·fred [ˈælfrɪd] Alfred *m.*
Al·ge·ri·a [ælˈdʒɪərɪə] Alˈgerien *n.*
Al·ger·non [ˈældʒənən] *m.*
Al·giers [ˈældʒɪəz] Algier *n.*
Al·ice [ˈælɪs] Aˈlice *f*, Else *f.*
Al·i·son [ˈælɪsn] *f.*
Al·lan [ˈælən] *m.*
Al·le·ghe·nies [ælɪˈgenɪs; *Am.* ˌælɪˈgeɪnɪz] *pl. Gebirge im Osten der USA.*
Al·le·ghe·ny [ælɪˈgenɪ; *Am.* ˌælɪˈgeɪnɪ] *Fluß in Pennsylvania* (*USA*); **~ Mountains** *siehe* ***Allgehenies.***
Al·len [ˈælən] *m.*
Al·sace [ælˈsæs], **Al·sa·ti·a** [ælˈseɪʃjə] das Elsaß.
A·man·da [əˈmændə] Aˈmanda *f.*
Am·a·zon [ˈæməzən] Amaˈzonas *m.*
A·me·lia [əˈmiːljə] Aˈmalie *f.*
A·mer·i·ca [əˈmerɪkə] Aˈmerika *n.*
A·my [ˈeɪmɪ] *f.*
An·chor·age [ˈæŋkərɪdʒ] *Stadt in Alaska* (*USA*).
An·des [ˈændiːz] *pl. die* Anden *pl.*
An·dor·ra [ænˈdɔːrə] Anˈdorra *n.*
An·drew [ˈændruː] Anˈdreas *m.*
An·dy [ˈændɪ] *abbr. für* ***Andrew.***
An·ge·la [ˈændʒələ] Angela *f.*
An·gle·sey [ˈæŋglsɪ] *walisische Grafschaft (bis 1974).*
An·gli·a [ˈæŋglɪə] *lateinischer Name für England.*
An·go·la [æŋˈgəʊlə] Anˈgola *n.*
An·gus [ˈæŋgəs] *schottische Grafschaft (bis 1975); Vorname m.*
A·ni·ta [əˈniːtə] Aˈnita *f.*
Ann [æn], **An·na** [ˈænə] Anna *f*, Anne *f.*
An·na·belle [ˈænəbel] Annaˈbella *f.*
An·na·po·lis [əˈnæpəlɪs] *Hauptstadt von Maryland* (*USA*).
Anne [æn] Anna *f*, Anne *f.*
Ant·arc·ti·ca [æntˈɑːktɪkə] *die* Antˈarktis.
An·the·a [ˈænθɪə; ænˈθɪə] *f.*
An·tho·ny [ˈæntənɪ; ˈænθənɪ] Anton *m.*
An·til·les [ænˈtɪliːz] *pl. die* Anˈtillen *pl.*
An·to·ny [ˈæntənɪ] Anton *m.*
An·trim [ˈæntrɪm] *nordirische Grafschaft.*
Ant·werp [ˈæntwɜːp] Antˈwerpen *n.*
Ap·en·nines [ˈæpɪnaɪnz] *pl. der* Apenˈnin, *die* Apenˈninen *pl.*
Ap·pa·la·chians [ˌæpəˈleɪtʃjənz] *pl. die* Appaˈlachen *pl.*
A·ra·bi·a [əˈreɪbjə] Aˈrabien *n.*
Ar·chi·bald [ˈɑːtʃɪbəld] Archibald *m.*
Ar·chi·me·des [ˌɑːkɪˈmiːdiːz] Archiˈmedes *m.*
Arc·tic [ˈɑːktɪk] *die* Arktis.
Ar·den [ˈɑːdn] *Familienname.*
Ar·gen·ti·na [ˌɑːdʒənˈtiːnə] Argenˈtinien *n.*
Ar·gen·tine [ˈɑːdʒəntaɪn]: ***the*** ~ Argenˈtinien *n*
Ar·gyll(shire) [ɑːˈgaɪl(ʃə)] *schottische Grafschaft (bis 1975).*
Ar·is·toph·an·es [ˌærɪˈstɒfəniːz] Ariˈstophanes *m.*
Ar·is·to·tle [ˈærɪstɒtl] Ariˈstoteles *m.*
Ar·i·zo·na [ˌærɪˈzəʊnə] *Staat der USA.*
Ar·kan·sas [ˈɑːkənsɔː] *Fluß in USA; Staat der USA.*
Ar·ling·ton [ˈɑːlɪŋtən] *Ehrenfriedhof bei Washington (D.C.).*
Ar·magh [ɑːˈmɑː] *nordirische Grafschaft.*
Ar·me·ni·a [ɑːˈmiːnjə] Arˈmenien *n.*
Ar·nold [ˈɑːnəld] Arnold *m.*
Art [ɑːt] *abbr. für* ***Arthur.***
Ar·thur [ˈɑːθə] Art(h)ur *m*; ***King*** ~ König Artus.
As·cot [ˈæskət] *Ort in Südengland (Pferderennen).*
A·sia [ˈeɪʃə] Asien *n*; ~ ***Minor*** Kleinˈasien *n.*
As·syr·i·a [əˈsɪrɪə] Asˈsyrien *n.*
Ath·ens [ˈæθɪnz] Aˈthen *n.*
At·lan·ta [ətˈlæntə] *Hauptstadt von Georgia* (*USA*).
At·lan·tic (O·cean) [ətˈlæntɪk (ətˌlæntɪkˈəʊʃən)] *der* Atˈlantik, *der* Atˈlantische Ozean.
Auck·land [ˈɔːklənd] *Hafenstadt in Neuseeland.*
Au·den [ˈɔːdn] *englischer Dichter.*
Au·drey [ˈɔːdrɪ] *f.*
Au·gus·ta [ɔːˈgʌstə] *Hauptstadt von Maine* (*USA*).
Au·gus·tus [ɔːˈgʌstəs] August *m.*
Aus·ten [ˈɒstɪn] *Familienname.*
Aus·tin [ˈɒstɪn] *Hauptstadt von Texas* (*USA*).
Aus·tra·lia [ɒˈstreɪljə] Auˈstralien *n.*
Aus·tri·a [ˈɒstrɪə] Österreich *n.*
A·von [ˈeɪvən] *Fluß in Mittelengland; englische Grafschaft.*
Ax·min·ster [ˈæksmɪnstə] *Stadt in Südwest-England.*
Ayr(shire) [ˈeə(ʃə)] *schottische Grafschaft (bis 1975).*
A·zores [əˈzɔːz] *pl. die* Aˈzoren *pl.*

Bab·y·lon [ˈbæbɪlən] Babylon *n.*
Ba·con [ˈbeɪkən] *englischer Philosoph.*
Ba·den-Pow·ell [ˌbeɪdnˈpəʊəl] *Gründer der Boy Scouts.*
Ba·ha·mas [bəˈhɑːməz] *pl. die* Baˈhams *pl.*
Bah·rain [bɑːˈreɪn] Bahˈrain *n.*
Bai·le A·tha Cli·ath [ˌblɔːˈkliː] *gälischer Name für* ***Dublin.***
Bald·win [ˈbɔːldwɪn] Balduin *m*; *amer. Autor.*
Bâle [bɑːl] Basel *n.*
Bal·four [ˈbælfə] *brit. Staatsmann.*
Bal·kans [ˈbɔːlkənz] *pl. der* Balkan.
Bal·mo·ral [bælˈmɒrəl] *Residenz des englischen Königshauses in Schottland.*
Bal·tic Sea [ˌbɔːltɪkˈsiː] *die* Ostsee.
Bal·ti·more [ˈbɔːltɪmɔː] *Hafenstadt in Maryland* (*USA*).
Banff(shire) [ˈbænf(ʃə)] *schottische Grafschaft (bis 1975).*
Bang·la·desh [ˌbæŋgləˈdeʃ] Bangladesch *n.*
Bar·ba·dos [bɑːˈbeɪdəʊz] Barˈbados *n.*
Bar·ba·ra [ˈbɑːbərə] Barbara *f.*
Bark·ing [ˈbɑːkɪŋ] *Stadtbezirk von Groß-London.*

Bar·net ['bɑːnɪt] *Stadtbezirk von Groß-London.*
Bar·ry ['bærɪ] *m.*
Bart [bɑːt] *abbr. für* ***Bartholomew.***
Bar·thol·o·mew [bɑː'θɒləmjuː] Bartholo'mäus *m.*
Bas·il ['bæzl] Ba'silius *m.*
Bath [bɑːθ] *Badeort in Südengland.*
Bat·on Rouge [ˌbætən'ruːʒ] *Hauptstadt von Louisiana.*
Bat·ter·sea ['bætəsiː] *Stadtteil von London.*
Ba·var·i·a [bə'veərɪə] Bayern *n.*
Bea·cons·field ['biːkənzfiːld] *Adelsname Disraelis.*
Beards·ley ['bɪədzlɪ] *englischer Zeichner u. Illustrator.*
Be·a·trice ['bɪətrɪs] Bea'trice *f.*
Bea·ver·brook ['biˈvəbrʊk] *brit. Zeitungsverleger.*
Beck·et ['bekɪt]: ***Saint Thomas à*** ~ der heilige Thomas Becket.
Beck·ett ['bekɪt] *irischer Dichter und Dramatiker.*
Beck·y ['bekɪ] *f.*
Bed·ford ['bedfəd] *Stadt in Mittelengland; a.* **Bed·ford·shire** [-ʃə] *englische Grafschaft.*
Beer·bohm ['bɪəbəʊm] *englischer Kritiker und Karikaturist.*
Bel·fast [ˌbel'fɑːst; 'belfɑːst] Belfast *n.*
Bel·gium ['beldʒəm] Belgien *n.*
Bel·grade [ˌbel'greɪd] Belgrad *n.*
Bel·gra·vi·a [bel'greɪvjə] *Stadtteil von London.*
Be·lin·da [bɪ'lɪndə; bə-] Be'linda *f.*
Be·lize [be'liːz] Be'lize *n.*
Bell, Bel·la ['bel(ə)] *abbr. für* ***Isabel.***
Ben [[ben] *abbr. für* ***Benjamin.***
Ben·e·dict ['benɪdɪkt] Benedikt *m.*
Ben·gal [ˌbeŋ'gɔːl] Ben'galen *n.*
Be·nin [be'nɪn] Be'nin *n.*
Ben·ja·min ['bendʒəmɪn] Benjamin *m.*
Ben Nev·is [ˌben'nevɪs] *höchster Berg Schottlands u. Großbritanniens.*
Berke·ley ['bɜːklɪ] *Stadt in Kalifornien;* ['bɑːklɪ] *irischer Bischof u. Philosoph.*
Berk·shire ['bɑːkʃə] *englische Grafschaft;* ~ **Hills** [ˌbɜːkʃɪə'hɪlz] *pl. Gebirgszug in Massachusetts (USA).*
Ber·lin [bɜː'lɪn] Ber'lin *n.*
Ber·mu·das [bə'mjuːdəs] *pl. die* Ber'mudas *pl., die* Ber'mudainseln *pl.*
Ber·nard ['bɜːnəd] Bernhard *m.*
Bern(e) [bɜːn] Bern *n.*
Ber·nie ['bɜːnɪ] *abbr. für* ***Bernard.***
Bern·stein ['bɜːnstaɪn; -stiːn] *amer. Dirigent und Komponist.*
Bert [bɜːt] *abbr. für* ***Albert, Bertram, Bertrand, Gilbert, Hubert.***
Ber·tha ['bɜːθə] Berta *f.*
Ber·tram ['bɜːtrəm], **Ber·trand** ['bɜːtrənd] Bertram *m.*
Ber·wick(shire) ['berɪk(ʃə)] *schottische Grafschaft (bis 1975).*
Ber·yl ['berɪl] *f.*
Bess, Bes·sy ['bes(ɪ)], **Bet·s(e)y** ['betsɪ], **Bet·ty** ['betɪ] *abbr. für* ***Elizabeth.***
Bex·ley ['bekslɪ] *Stadtbezirk von Groß--London.*
Bhu·tan [buː'tɑːn] Bhu'tan *n.*
Bill, Bil·ly ['bɪl(ɪ)] Willi *m.*
Bir·ken·head ['bɜːkənhed] *Hafenstadt in Nordwest-England.*
Bir·ming·ham ['bɜːmɪŋəm] *Industriestadt in Mittelengland; Stadt in Alabama (USA).*
Bis·cay ['bɪskeɪ; -kɪ]: ***Bay of*** ~ *der* Golf von Bis'caya.
Bis·marck ['bɪzmɑːk] *Hauptstadt von North Dakota (USA).*
Blooms·bur·y ['bluːmzbərɪ] *Stadtteil von London.*
Bo·ad·i·cea [ˌbəʊədɪ'sɪə] *Königin in Britannien.*
Bob [bɒb] *abbr. für* ***Robert.***
Bo·he·mi·a [bəʊ'hiːmjə] Böhmen *n.*
Boi·se ['bɔɪzɪ; -sɪ] *Hauptstadt von Idaho (USA).*
Bol·eyn ['bʊlɪn]: ***Anne*** ~ *zweite Frau Heinrichs VIII. von England.*
Bo·liv·i·a [bə'lɪvjə] Bo'livien *n.*
Bom·bay [ˌbɒm'beɪ] Bombay *n.*
Bo·na·parte ['bəʊnəpɑːt] Bona'parte *(Familienname zweier französischer Kaiser).*
Booth [buːð] *Gründer der Heilsarmee.*
Bor·ders ['bɔːdəz] *Verwaltungsregion in Schottland.*
Bor·is ['bɒrɪs] Boris *m.*
Bos·ton ['bɒstən] *Hauptstadt von Massachusetts (USA).*
Bo·tswa·na [bɒ'tswɑːnə] Bo'tswana *n.*
Bourne·mouth ['bɔːnməθ] *Seebad in Südengland.*
Brad·ford ['brædfəd] *Industriestadt in Nordengland.*
Bra·zil [brə'zɪl] Bra'silien *n.*
Breck·nock(shire) ['breknɒk(ʃə)], **Brec·on(shire)** ['brekən(ʃə)] *walisische Grafschaft (bis 1974).*
Bren·da ['brendə] *f.*
Brent [brent] *Stadtbezirk von Groß-London.*
Bri·an ['braɪən] *m.*
Bridg·et ['brɪdʒɪt] Bri'gitte *f.*
Brigh·ton ['braɪtn] *Seebad in Südengland.*
Bris·bane ['brɪsbən] *Hauptstadt von Queensland (Australien).*
Bris·tol ['brɪstl] *Hafenstadt in Südengland.*
Bri·tain ['brɪtn] Bri'tannien *n.*
Bri·tan·ni·a [brɪ'tænjə] *poet.* Bri'tannien *n.*
Brit·ish Co·lum·bi·a [ˌbrɪtɪʃkə'lʌmbɪə] *Provinz in Kanada.*
Brit·ta·ny ['brɪtənɪ] die Bre'tagne.
Brit·ten ['brɪtn] *englischer Komponist.*
Broad·way ['brɔːdweɪ] *Straße in Manhatten, New York City (USA). Zentrum des amer. kommerziellen Theaters.*
Brom·ley ['brɒmlɪ] *Stadtbezirk von Groß--London.*
Bron·të ['brɒntɪ] *Name dreier englischer Autorinnen.*
Bronx [brɒŋks] *Stadtbezirk von New York (USA).*
Brook·lyn ['brʊklɪn] *Stadtbezirk von New York (USA).*
Brow·ning ['braʊnɪŋ] *englischer Dichter.*
Bruce [bruːs] *m.*
Bruges [bruːʒ] Brügge *n.*
Bru·nei ['bruːnaɪ] Brunei *n.*
Bruns·wick [brʌnzwɪk] Braunschweig *n.*
Brus·sels ['brʌslz] Brüssel *n.*
Bry·an ['braɪən] *m.*
Bu·chn·an [bjuː'kænən] *Familienname.*
Bu·ch·rest [ˌbjuːkə'rest] Bukarest *n.*
Buck·ing·ham(shire) ['bʌkɪŋəm(ʃə)] *englische Grafschaft.*
Bu·da·pest [ˌbjuːdə'pest] Budapest *n.*
Bud·dha ['bʊdə] Buddha *m.*
Bul·gar·i·a [bʌl'geərɪə] Bul'garien *n.*
Bur·gun·dy ['bɜːgəndɪ] Bur'gund *n.*
Bur·ki·na Fas·o [buəˌkiːnə'fæsəʊ] Bur'kina Faso *n (Staat in Westafrika, frühere Bezeichnung Obervolta).*
Bur·ma ['bɜːmə] Birma *n.*
Burns [bɜːnz] *schottischer Dichter.*
Bu·run·di [bʊ'rʊndɪ] Bu'rundi *n.*
Bute(shire) ['bjuːt(ʃə)] *schottische Grafschaft (bis 1975).*
By·ron ['baɪərən] *englischer Dichter.*

Caer·nar·von(shire) [kə'nɑːvən(ʃə)] *walisische Grafschaft (bis 1974).*
Cae·sar ['siːzə] Cäsar *m.*
Cain [keɪn] Kain *m.*
Cai·ro ['kaɪərəʊ] Kairo *n.*
Caith·ness ['keɪθnes] *schottische Grafschaft (bis 1975).*
Ca·lais ['kæleɪ] Ca'lais *n.*
Cal·cut·ta [kæl'kʌtə] Kal'kutta *n.*
Cal·e·do·nia [ˌkælɪ'dəʊnjə] Kale'donien *n (poet. für Schottland).*
Cal·ga·ry ['kælgərɪ] *Stadt in Alberta (Kanada).*
Cal·i·for·nia [ˌkælɪ'fɔːnjə] Kali'fornien *n (Staat der USA).*
Cam·bo·dia [kæm'bəʊdjə] Kam'bodscha *n.*
Cam·bridge ['keɪmbrɪdʒ] *englische Universitätsstadt; Stadt in Massachusetts (USA), Sitz der Harvard University; a.* **Cam·bridge·shire** [-ʃə] *englische Grafschaft.*
Cam·den ['kæmdən] *Stadtbezirk von Groß-London.*
Cam·er·oon ['kæməruːn; *bsd. Am.* ˌkæmə'ruːn] Kamerun *n.*
Camp·bell ['kæmbl] *Familienname.*
Can·a·da ['kænədə] Kanada *n.*
Ca·nar·y Is·lands [kəˌneərɪ'aɪləndz] *pl. die* Ka'narischen Inseln *pl.*
Can·ber·ra ['kænbərə] *Hauptstadt von Australien.*
Can·ter·bur·y ['kæntəbərɪ] *Stadt in Südengland.*
Cape Ca·nav·er·al [ˌkeɪpkə'nævərəl] *Raketenversuchszentrum in Florida (USA).*
Cape Town ['keɪptaʊn] Kapstadt *n.*
Cape Verde Is·lands [keɪp'vɜːd 'aɪləndz] *pl. die* Kap'verden *pl.*
Ca·pri ['kæprɪ; 'kɑː-; *Am. a.* kæ'priː] Capri *n.*
Car·diff ['kɑːdɪf] *Hauptstadt von Wales.*
Car·di·gan(shire) ['kɑːdɪgən(ʃə)] *walisische Grafschaft (bis 1974).*
Ca·rin·thi·a [kə'rɪnθɪə] Kärnten *n.*
Carl [kɑːl] Karl *m*, Carl *m.*
Car·lisle [kɑː'laɪl] *Stadt in Nordwestengland.*
Car·mar·then(shire) [kə'mɑːðn(ʃə)] *walisische Grafschaft (bis 1974).*
Car·ne·gie [kɑː'negɪ] *amer. Industrieller.*
Car·ol(e) ['kærəl] Ka'rola *f.*
Car·o·line ['kærəlaɪn], **Car·o·lyn** ['kærəlɪn] Karo'line *f.*
Car·pa·thi·ans [kɑː'peɪθjənz] *pl. die* Kar'paten *pl.*
Car·rie ['kærɪ] *abbr. für* ***Caroline.***
Car·son Cit·y [ˌkɑːsn'sɪtɪ] *Hauptstadt von Nevada (USA).*
Car·ter ['kɑːtə] *39. Präsident der USA.*
Cath·er·ine ['kæθərɪn] Katha'rina *f*, Kat(h)rin *f.*
Cath·y ['kæθɪ] *abbr. für* ***Catherine.***
Cav·an ['kævən] *Grafschaft im der Republik Irland zugehörigen Teil der Provinz Ulster; Hauptstadt dieser Grafschaft.*
Cax·ton ['kækstən] *erster englischer Buchdrucker.*
Ce·cil ['sesl; 'sɪsl] *m.*
Ce·cile ['sesɪl; *Am.* sɪ'siːl], **Ce·cil·ia** [sɪ'sɪljə; sɪ'siːljə], **Cec·i·ly** ['sɪsɪlɪ; 'seslɪ] Cä'cilie *f.*

Ced·ric ['si:drɪk; 'sedrɪk] *m.*
Cel·ia ['si:ljə] *f.*
Cen·tral ['sentrəl] *Verwaltungsregion in Schottland.*
Cen·tral Af·ri·can Re·pub·lic ['sentrəl-ˌæfrɪkənrɪ'pʌblɪk] *die* Zen'tralafriˌkanische Repu'blik.
Cey·lon [sɪ'lɒn] Ceylon *n.*
Chad [tʃæd] *der* Tschad.
Cham·ber·lain ['tʃeɪmbəlɪn] *Name mehrerer britischer Staatsmänner.*
Char·ing Cross [ˌtʃærɪŋ'krɒs] *Stadtteil von London.*
Char·le·magne ['ʃɑ:ləmeɪn] Karl der Große.
Charles [tʃɑ:lz] Karl *m.*
Charles·ton ['tʃɑ:lstən] *Hauptstadt von West Virginia (USA).*
Char·lotte ['ʃɑ:lət] Char'lotte *f.*
Chas [tʃæz] *abbr. für* **Charles.**
Chau·cer ['tʃɔ:sə] *englischer Dichter.*
Chel·sea ['tʃelsɪ] *Stadtteil von London.*
Chel·ten·ham ['tʃeltnəm] *Stadtteil von London.*
Chesh·ire ['tʃeʃə] *englische Grafschaft.*
Ches·ter·field ['tʃestəfi:ld] *Industriestadt in Mittelengland.*
Chev·i·ot Hills [ˌtʃevɪət'hɪlz] *pl. Grenzgebirge zwischen England und Schottland.*
Chey·enne [ʃaɪ'æn] *Hauptstadt von Wyoming.*
Chi·ca·go [ʃɪ'kɑ:gəʊ; *bsd. Am.* ʃɪ'kɔ:gəʊ] *Industriestadt in USA.*
Chil·e ['tʃɪlɪ] Chile *n.*
Chi·na ['tʃaɪnə] China *n*; ***Republic of*** ~ *die* Repu'blik China; ***People's Republic of*** ~ *die* 'Volksrepuˌblik China.
Chip·pen·dale ['tʃɪpəndeɪl] *englischer Kunsttischler.*
Chlo·e ['kləʊɪ] Chloe *f.*
Chris [krɪs] *abbr. für* ***Christina, Christine, Christian, Christopher.***
Christ·church ['kraɪstʃɜ:tʃ] *Stadt in Neuseeland; Stadt in Hampshire (England).*
Chris·tian ['krɪstjən] Christian *m.*
Chris·ti·na [krɪ'sti:nə], **Chris·tine** ['krɪsti:n; krɪ'sti:n] Chri'stine *f.*
Chris·to·pher ['krɪstəfə] Christoph *m.*
Chrys·ler ['kraɪzlə] *amer. Industrieller.*
Church·ill ['tʃɜ:tʃɪl] *brit. Staatsmann.*
Cin·cin·na·ti [ˌsɪnsɪ'nætɪ] *Stadt in Ohio.*
Cis·sie ['sɪsɪ] *abbr. für* **Cecily.**
Clack·man·nan(shire) [klæk'mænən(ʃə)] *schottische Grafschaft (bis 1975).*
Clap·ham ['klæpəm] *Stadtteil von London.*
Clar·a ['kleərə], **Clare** [kleə] Klara *f.*
Clare [kleə] *Grafschaft in der Provinz Munster (Irland).*
Clar·en·don ['klærəndən] *Name mehrerer englischer Staatsmänner.*
Claud(e) [klɔ:d] Claudius *m.*
Clem·ent ['klemənt] Klemens *m*; Clemens *m.*
Cle·o·pat·ra [klɪə'pætrə] Kle'opatra *f.*
Cleve·land ['kli:vlənd] *Industriestadt in USA; englische Grafschaft.*
Cliff [klɪf] *abbr. für* **Clifford.**
Clif·ford ['klɪfəd] *m.*
Clive [klaɪv] *Begründer der brit. Herrschaft in Indien; Vorname m.*
Clwyd ['klu:ɪd] *walisische Grafschaft.*
Clyde [klaɪd] *Fluß in Schottland.*
Cole·ridge ['kəʊlərɪdʒ] *englischer Dichter.*
Col·in ['kɒlɪn] *m.*
Co·logne [kə'ləʊn] Köln *n.*
Co·lom·bi·a [kə'lɒmbɪə] Ko'lumbien *n.*
Co·lom·bo [kə'lʌmbəʊ] *Hauptstadt von Sri Lanka.*
Col·o·ra·do [ˌkɒlə'rɑ:dəʊ] *Staat der USA; Name zweier Flüsse in USA.*
Co·lum·bi·a [kə'lʌmbɪə] *Fluß in USA; Hauptstadt von South Carolina (USA);* ***District of*** ~ (***DC***) *Bundesdistrikt (mit der Hauptstadt Washington) der USA.*
Co·lum·bus [kə'lʌmbəs] *Entdecker Amerikas; Hauptstadt von Ohio (USA).*
Com·o·ro Is·lands [ˌkɒmərəʊ'aɪləndz] *pl. die* Ko'moren *pl.*
Con·cord ['kɒŋkəd] *Hauptstadt von New Hampshire (USA).*
Con·fu·cius [kən'fju:ʃjəs; -ʃəs] Kon'fuzius *m (chinesischer Philosoph).*
Con·go ['kɒŋgəʊ] der Kongo.
Con·nacht ['kɒnət], *früher* **Con·naught** ['kɒnɔ:t] *Provinz in Irland.*
Con·nect·i·cut [kə'netɪkət] *Staat der USA.*
Con·nie ['kɒnɪ] *abbr. für* ***Conrad, Constance, Cornelia.***
Con·rad ['kɒnræd] Konrad *m.*
Con·stance ['kɒnstəns] Kon'stanze *f*; ***Lake*** ~ *der* Bodensee.
Con·stan·ti·no·ple [ˌkɒnstæntɪ'nəʊpl] Konstanti'nopel *n.*
Cook [kʊk] *englischer Weltumsegler.*
Coo·per ['ku:pə] *amer. Autor.*
Co·pen·ha·gen [ˌkəʊpn'heɪgən] Kopen'hagen *n.*
Cor·dil·le·ras [ˌkɔ:dɪ'ljeərəs] *pl. die* Kordil'leren *pl.*
Cor·inth ['kɒrɪnθ] Ko'rinth *n.*
Cork [kɔ:k] *Grafschaft in der Provinz Munster (Irland); Hauptstadt dieser Grafschaft u. der Provinz Munster.*
Cor·ne·lia [kɔ:'ni:ljə] Cor'nelia *f.*
Corn·wall ['kɔ:nwəl] *englische Grafschaft.*
Cos·ta Ri·ca [ˌkɒstə'ri:kə] Costa Rica *n.*
Cov·ent Gar·den [ˌkɒvənt'gɑ:dn] *die Londoner Oper.*
Cov·en·try ['kɒvəntrɪ] *Industriestadt in Mittelengland.*
Craig [kreɪg] *m.*
Crete [kri:t] Kreta *n.*
Cri·me·a [kraɪ'mɪə] die Krim.
Crom·well ['krɒmwəl] *englischer Staatsmann.*
Croy·don ['krɔɪdn] *Stadtbezirk von London.*
Cru·soe ['kru:səʊ]: ***Robinson*** ~ *Romanheld.*
Cu·ba ['kju:bə] Kuba *n.*
Cum·ber·land ['kʌmbələnd] *englische Grafschaft (bis 1975).*
Cum·bri·a ['kʌmbrɪə] *englische Grafschaft.*
Cyn·thi·a ['sɪnθɪə] *f.*
Cy·prus ['saɪprəs] Zypern *n.*
Cy·rus ['saɪərəs] Cyrus *m.*
Czech·o·slo·va·ki·a [ˌtʃekəʊsləʊ'vækɪə] *hist.* die Tschechoslowa'kei.
Czech Re·pub·lic [ˌtʃekrɪ'pʌblɪk] Tschechische Repu'blik, Tschechien *n.*

Dag·en·ham ['dægənəm] *Stadtteil von London.*
Da·ho·mey [də'həʊmɪ] Da'home *n (früherer Name von* **Benin***).*
Dal·las ['dæləs] *Stadt in Texas (USA).*
Dal·ma·ti·a [dæl'meɪʃjə] Dal'matien *n.*
Dam·o·cles ['dæməkli:z] Damokles *m.*
Dan·iel ['dænjəl] Daniel *m.*
Dan·ube ['dænju:b] Donau *f.*
Daph·ne ['dæfnɪ] Daphne *f.*
Dar·da·nelles [ˌdɑ:də'nelz] *pl. die* Darda'nellen *pl.*
Dar·jee·ling [dɑ:'dʒi:lɪŋ] *Stadt in Indien.*
Dart·moor ['dɑ:t:ˌmʊə] *Landstrich in Südwest-England.*
Dart·mouth ['dɑ:tməθ] *Stadt in Devon (England).*
Dar·win ['dɑ:wɪn] *englischer Naturforscher.*
Dave [deɪv] *abbr. für* **David.**
Da·vid ['deɪvɪd] David *m.*
Dawn [dɔ:n] *f.*
Dean [di:n] *m.*
Deb·by ['debɪ] *abbr. für* **Deborah.**
Deb·o·rah ['debərə] *f.*
Dee [di:] *Fluß in England; Fluß in Schottland.*
De·foe [dɪ'fəʊ] *englischer Autor.*
Deir·dre ['dɪədrɪ] *(Ir.) f.*
Del·a·ware ['deləweə] *Staat der USA; Fluß in USA.*
Den·bigh(shire) ['denbɪ(ʃə)] *walisische Grafschaft (bis 1974).*
Den·is ['denɪs] *m.*
De·nise [də'ni:z; də'ni:s] De'nise *f.*
Den·mark ['denmɑ:k] Dänemark *n.*
Den·nis ['denɪs] *m.*
Den·ver ['denvə] *Hauptstadt von Colorado (USA).*
Dept·ford ['detfəd] *Stadtteil von Groß-London.*
Der·by(shire) ['dɑ:bɪ(ʃə)] *englische Grafschaft.*
Der·ek, Der·rick ['derɪk] *m.*
Des Moines [dɪ'mɔɪn] *Hauptstadt von Iowa (USA).*
Des·mond ['dezmənd] *m.*
De·troit [də'trɔɪt] *Industriestadt in Michigan (USA).*
De·vis·es [dɪ'vaɪzɪz] *Stadt in Wiltshire (England).*
Dev·on(shire) ['devn(ʃə)] *englische Grafschaft.*
Dew·ey ['dju:ɪ] *amer. Philosoph.*
Di·an·a [daɪ'ænə] Di'ana *f.*
Dick [dɪk] *abbr. für* **Richard.**
Dick·ens ['dɪkɪnz] *englischer Autor.*
Dis·rae·li [dɪs'reɪlɪ] *brit. Staatsmann.*
Dol·ly ['dɒlɪ] *abbr. für* **Dorothy.**
Do·lo·mites ['dɒləmaɪts] *pl. die* Dolo'miten *pl. (Teil der Ostalpen).*
Dom·i·nic ['dɒmɪnɪk] Domi'nik *m.*
Do·min·i·can Re·pub·lic [dəˌmɪnɪkənrɪ'pʌblɪk] *die* Domini'kanische Repu'blik.
Don [dɒn] *abbr. für* **Donald.**
Don·ald ['dɒnld] *m.*
Don·cas·ter ['dɒŋkəstə] *Stadt in South Yorkshire (England).*
Don·e·gal ['dɒnɪgɔ:l; *Ir.* ˌdʌnɪ'gɔ:l] *Grafschaft im der Republik Irland zugehörigen Teil der Provinz Ulster.*
Don Ju·an [ˌdɒn'dʒu:ən] Don Ju'an *m.*
Donne [dʌn; dɒn] *englischer Dichter.*
Don Quix·ote [ˌdɒn'kwɪksət] Don Qui'chotte *m.*
Do·reen [dɔ:'ri:n; 'dɔ:ri:n] *f.*
Dor·is ['dɒrɪs] Doris *f.*
Dor·o·thy ['dɒrəθɪ] Doro'thea *f.*
Dor·set(shire) ['dɔ:sɪt(ʃə)] *englische Grafschaft.*
Dos Pas·sos [ˌdɒs'pæsɒs] *amer. Autor.*
Doug [dʌg] *abbr. für* **Douglas.**
Doug·las ['dʌgləs] *Vorname m; schottische Adelsfamilie.*
Do·ra ['dɔ:rə] Dora *f.*
Do·ver ['dəʊvə] *Hafenstadt in Südengland; Hauptstadt von Delaware (USA).*
Down [daʊn] *nordirische Grafschaft.*
Down·ing Street ['daʊnɪŋstri:t] *Straße in*

London mit der Amtswohnung der Premierministers.
Drei·ser ['draɪzə] *amer. Autor.*
Dry·den ['draɪdn] *engl. Dichter.*
Dub·lin ['dʌblɪn] *Hauptstadt von Irland; Grafschaft in der Provinz Leinster (Irland).*
Du·luth [dju:'lu:θ; *Am.* də'lu:θ] *Stadt in Minnesota (USA).*
Dul·wich ['dʌlɪdʒ] *Stadtteil von Groß--London.*
Dum·bar·ton(shire) [dʌm'bɑ:tn(ʃə)] *schottische Grafschaft (bis 1975).*
Dum·fries and Gal·lo·way [dʌmˌfri:sən-'gæləweɪ] *Verwaltungsregion in Schottland;* **Dum'fries·shire** [-ʃə] *schottische Grafschaft (bis 1975).*
Dun·can ['dʌŋkən] *m.*
Dun·e·din [dʌ'ni:dɪn] *Hafenstadt in Neuseeland.*
Dun·ge·ness [dʌndʒɪ'nes; dʌndʒ'nes] *Landspitze in Kent (England).*
Dun·kirk [dʌn'kɜ:k] Dün'kirchen *n.*
Dur·ban ['dɜ:bən] *Hafenstadt in Südafrika.*
Dur·ham ['dʌrəm] *englische Grafschaft.*
Dyf·ed ['dʌvɪd] *walisische Grafschaft.*

Ea·ling ['i:lɪŋ] *Stadtbezirk von Groß-London.*
East Lo·thi·an [ˌi:st'ləʊðjən] *schottische Grafschaft (bis 1975).*
East Sus·sex [ˌi:st'sʌsɪks] *englische Grafschaft.*
Ec·ua·dor ['ekwədɔ:] Ecua'dor *n.*
Ed·die ['edɪ] *abbr. für* ***Edward.***
Ed·gar ['edgə] Edgar *m.*
Ed·in·burgh ['edɪnbərə] Edinburg *n.*
Ed·i·son ['edɪsn] *amer. Erfinder.*
E·dith ['i:dɪθ] Edith *f.*
Ed·mon·ton ['edməntən] *Hauptstadt von Alberta (Kanada).*
Ed·mund ['edmənd] Edmund *m.*
Ed·ward ['edwəd] Eduard *m.*
E·gypt ['i:dʒɪpt] Ä'gypten *n.*
Ei·leen ['aɪli:n; *Am.* aɪ'li:n] *f.*
Ei·re ['eərə] *Name der Republik Irland.*
Ei·sen·how·er ['aɪznˌhaʊə] *34. Präsident der USA.*
E·laine [e'leɪn; ɪ'leɪn] *siehe* ***Helen.***
El·ea·nor ['elɪnə] Eleo'nore *f.*
El·i·jah [ɪ'laɪdʒə] E'lias *m.*
El·i·nor ['elɪnə] Eleo'nore *f.*
El·i·ot ['eljət] *englischer Dichter.*
E·li·za [ɪ'laɪzə] *abbr. für* ***Elizabeth.***
E·liz·a·beth [ɪ'lɪzəbəθ] E'lisabeth *f.*
El·len ['elɪn] *siehe* ***Helen.***
El·lis Is·land [ˌelɪs'aɪlənd] *Insel im Hafen von New York (USA).*
El Sal·va·dor [el'sælvədɔ:] El Salva'dor *n.*
El·sa ['elsə], **El·sie** ['elsɪ] Elsa *f*, Else *f.*
Em·er·son ['emәsn] *amer. Dichter und Philosoph.*
Em·i·ly ['emɪlɪ] E'milie *f.*
Em·ma ['emə] Emma *f.*
Em·mie, Em·my ['emɪ] *Koseform für* ***Emma.***
En·field ['enfi:ld] *Stadtbezirk von Groß-London.*
Eng·land ['ɪŋglənd] England *n.*
E·nid ['i:nɪd] *f.*
E·noch ['i:nɒk] *m.*
Ep·som ['epsəm] *Stadt in Südengland (Pferderennen).*
Equa·to·ri·al Guin·ea [ˌekwə'tɔ:rɪəl 'gɪnɪ] Äquatori'algui,nea *n.*
Er·ic ['erɪk] Erich *m.*
Er·i·ca ['erɪkə] Erika *f.*
E·rie ['ɪərɪ] *Hafenstadt in Pennsylvania (USA);* **Lake ~** der Eriesee *(in Nordamerika).*
Er·nest ['ɜ:nɪst] Ernst *m.*
Er·nie ['ɜ:nɪ] *abbr. für* ***Ernest.***
Es·sex ['esɪks] *englische Grafschaft.*
Es·to·nia [e'stəʊnjə] Estland *n.*
Eth·el ['eθl] *f.*
E·thi·o·pi·a [ˌi:θɪ'əʊpjə] Äthi'opien *n.*
E·ton ['i:tn] *Stadt in Berkshire (England) mit berühmter Public School.*
Eu·gene ['ju:dʒi:n] Eugen *m.*
Eu·ge·ni·a [ju:'dʒi:njə] Eu'genie *f.*
Eu·nice ['ju:nɪs] Eu'nice *f.*
Eu·phra·tes [ju:'freɪti:z] Euphrat *m.*
Eur·a·sia [jʊə'reɪʃə; -ʒə] Eu'rasien *n.*
Eu·rip·i·des [jʊə'rɪpɪdi:z] Eu'ripides *m.*
Eu·rope ['jʊərəp] Eu'ropa *n.*
Eus·tace ['ju:stəs] Eu'stachius *m.*
E·va ['i:və] Eva *f.*
Ev·ans ['evənz] *Familienname.*
Eve [i:v] Eva *f.*
Ev·e·lyn ['i:vlɪn; 'evlɪn] *m, f.*
Ev·er·glades ['evəgleɪdz] *pl. Sumpfgebiet in Florida (USA).*
Ex·e·ter ['eksɪtə] *Hauptstadt von Devonshire (England).*

Faer·oes ['feərəʊz] *pl. die* Färöer *pl.*
Falk·land Is·lands [ˌfɔ:(l)klənd'aɪləndz] *pl. die* Falklandinseln *pl.*
Fal·staff ['fɔ:lstɑ:f] *Bühnenfigur bei Shakespeare.*
Fan·ny ['fænɪ] *abbr. für* ***Frances.***
Far·a·day ['færədɪ] *englischer Chemiker und Physiker.*
Farn·bor·ough ['fɑ:nbərə] *Stadt in Hampshire (England).*
Far·oes ['feərəʊz] *siehe* ***Faeroes.***
Faulk·ner ['fɔ:knə] *amer. Autor.*
Fawkes [fɔ:ks] *Haupt der Pulververschwörung (1605).*
Fed·er·al Re·pub·lic of Ger·ma·ny ['fedərəlrɪˌpʌblɪkəv'dʒɜ:mənɪ] *die* 'Bundesrepu,blik Deutschland.
Fe·li·ci·a [fə'lɪsɪə] Fe'lizia *f.*
Fe·lic·i·ty [fə'lɪsətɪ] Fe'lizitas *f.*
Fe·lix ['fi:lɪks] Felix *m.*
Fe·lix·stowe ['fi:lɪkstəʊ] *Stadt in Suffolk (England).*
Felt·ham ['feltəm] *Stadtteil von Groß--London.*
Fer·man·ash [fə'mænə] *nordirische Grafschaft.*
Fiel·ding ['fi:ldɪŋ] *englischer Autor.*
Fife [faɪf] *Verwaltungsregion in Schottland; a.* **'Fife·shire** [-ʃə] *schottische Grafschaft (bis 1975).*
Fi·ji [ˌfi:'dʒi:; *bsd. Am.* 'fi:dʒi:] Fidschi *n.*
Finch·ley ['fɪntʃlɪ] *Stadtteil von London.*
Fin·land ['fɪnlənd] Finnland *n.*
Fi·o·na [fɪ'əʊnə] *f.*
Firth of Forth [ˌfɜ:θəv'fɔ:θ] *Meeresbucht an der schottischen Ostküste.*
Fitz·ger·ald [fɪts'dʒerəld] *Familienname.*
Flan·ders ['flɑ:ndəz] Flandern *n.*
Flem·ing ['flemɪŋ] *brit. Bakteriologe.*
Flint(shire) ['flɪnt(ʃə)] *walisische Grafschaft (bis 1974).*
Flo·ra ['flɔ:rə] Flora *f.*
For·ence ['flɒrəns] Flo'renz *n;* Flo-ren'tine *f.*
Flor·i·da ['flɒrɪdə] *Staat der USA.*
Flush·ing ['flʌʃɪŋ] *Stadtteil von New York;* Vlissingen *n.*
Folke·stone ['fəʊkstən] *Seebad in Südengland.*
Ford [fɔ:d] *amer. Industrieller; 38. Präsident der USA.*
For·syth [fɔ:'saɪθ] *Familienname.*
Fort Lau·der·dale [ˌfɔ:t'lɔ:dədeɪl] *Stadt in Florida (USA).*
Fort Worth [ˌfɔ:t'wɜ:θ] *Stadt in Texas (USA).*
Foth·er·in·ghay ['fɒðərɪŋgeɪ] *Schloß in Nordengland.*
Fow·ler ['faʊlə] *Familienname.*
France [frɑ:ns] Frankreich *n.*
Fran·ces ['frɑ:nsɪs] Fran'ziska *f.*
Fran·cis ['frɑ:nsɪs] Franz *m.*
Frank [fræŋk] Frank *m.*
Frank·fort ['fræŋkfət] *Hauptstadt von Kentucky (USA); seltene englische Schreibweise für Frankfurt.*
Frank·lin ['fræŋklɪn] *amer. Staatsmann; Verwaltungsbezirk der Northwest Territories (Kanada).*
Fred [fred] *abbr. für* ***Alfred, Frederic(k).***
Fre·da ['fri:də] Frieda *f.*
Fred·die, Fred·dy ['fredɪ] *Koseformen für* ***Frederic(k), Alfred.***
Fred·er·ic(k) ['fredrɪk] Friedrich *m.*
Fres·no ['freznəʊ] *Stadt in Kalifornien (USA).*
Fris·co ['frɪskəʊ] *umgangssprachliche Bezeichnung für* ***San Francisco.***
Frost [frɒst] *amer. Dichter.*
Ful·bright ['fʊlbraɪt] *amer. Politiker.*
Ful·ham ['fʊləm] *Stadtteil von London.*
Ful·ton ['fʊltən] *amer. Erfinder.*

Ga·bon ['gæbən] Ga'bun *n.*
Gains·bor·ough ['geɪnzbərə] *englischer Maler.*
Gal·a·gher ['gæləhə] *Familienname.*
Gal·lup ['gæləp] *amer. Statistiker.*
Gals·wor·thy ['gɔ:lzwɜ:ðɪ] *englischer Autor.*
Gal·way ['gɔ:lweɪ] *Grafschaft in der Provinz Connaught (Irland); Hauptstadt dieser Grafschaft.*
Gam·bia ['gæmbɪə] Gambia *n.*
Gan·ges ['gændʒi:z] Ganges *m.*
Gar·eth ['gærəθ] *m.*
Gar·ry, Gar·y ['gærɪ] *m.*
Gaul [gɔ:l] Gallien *n.*
Ga·vin ['gævɪn] *m.*
Ga·za Strip ['gɑ:zəstrɪp] *der* Gazastreifen.
Gene [dʒi:n] *abbr. für* ***Eugene, Eugenia.***
Ge·ne·va [dʒɪ'ni:və] Genf *n.*
Gen·o·a ['dʒenəʊə] Genua *n.*
Geoff [dʒef] *abbr. für* ***Geoffr(e)y.***
Geof·fr(e)y ['dʒefrɪ] Gottfried *m.*
George [dʒɔ:dʒ] Georg *m.*
Geor·gia ['dʒɔ:dʒjə; *Am.* -dʒə] *Staat der USA.*
Ger·ald ['dʒerəld] Gerald *m*, Gerold *m.*
Ger·al·dine ['dʒerəldi:n] Geral'dine *f.*
Ger·ard ['dʒerɑ:d; *bsd. Am.* dʒe'rɑ:d] Gerhard *m.*
Ger·man Dem·o·crat·ic Re·pub·lic ['dʒɜ:məndeməˌkrætɪkrɪ'pʌblɪk] *hist. die* Deutsche Demo'kratische Repu'blik.
Ger·ma·ny ['dʒɜ:mənɪ] Deutschland *n.*
Ger·ry ['dʒerɪ] *abbr. für* ***Gerald, Geraldine.***
Gersh·win ['gɜ:ʃwɪn] *amer. Komponist.*
Ger·tie ['gɜ:tɪ] Gertie *f.*
Ger·trude ['gɜ:tru:d] Gertrud *f.*
Get·tys·burgh ['getɪzbɜ:g] *Stadt in Pennsylvania (USA).*
Gha·na ['gɑ:nə] Ghana *n.*
Ghent [gent] Gent *n.*
Gi·bral·tar [dʒɪ'brɔ:ltə] Gi'braltar *n.*

Giel·gud ['gi:lgʊd]: ***Sir John*** ~ *berühmter englischer Schauspieler.*
Gil·bert ['gɪlbət] Gilbert *m.*
Giles [dʒaɪlz] Julius *m.*
Gil [dʒɪl; gɪl] *abbr. für* **Gillian.**
Gil·li·an ['dʒɪlɪən; 'gɪlɪən] *f.*
Glad·stone ['glædstən] *brit. Staatsmann.*
Gla·dys ['glædɪs] *f.*
Gla·mor·gan·shire [glə'mɔ:gənʃə] *walisische Graftschaft.*
Glas·gow ['glɑ:sgəʊ] *Stadt in Schottland.*
Glen [glen] *m.*
Glo·ri·a ['glɔ:rɪə] Gloria *f.*
Glouces·ter ['glɒstə] *Stadt in Südengland; a.* **Glouces·ter·shire** [-ʃə] *englische Grafschaft.*
Glynde·bourne ['glaɪndbɔ:n] *kleiner Ort in East Sussex (England) mit Opernfestspielen.*
God·frey ['gɒdfrɪ] Gottfried *m.*
Go·li·ath [gəʊ'laɪəθ] Goliath *m.*
Gor·don ['gɔ:dn] *Familienname; Vorname m.*
Go·tham ['gəʊtəm] *Ortsname; fig.* ‚Schilda' *n.*
Grace [greɪs] Gracia *f,* Grazia *f.*
Gra·ham ['greɪəm] *Familienname, Vorname m.*
Gram·pi·an ['græmpjən] *Verwaltungsregion in Schottland.*
Grand Can·yon [ˌgrænd'kænjən] *Durchbruchstal des Colorado in Arizona (USA).*
Great Brit·ain [ˌgreɪt'brɪtn] Großbri'tannien *n.*
Great·er Lon·don [ˌgreɪtə'lʌndən] *der Großraum London.*
Great·er Man·ches·ter [ˌgreɪtə'mæntʃɪstə] *der Großraum Manchester in Nordengland.*
Greece [gri:s] Griechenland *n.*
Greene [gri:n] *englischer Autor.*
Green·land ['gri:nlənd] Grönland *n.*
Green·wich ['grɪnɪdʒ] *Stadtbezirk Groß-Londons;* ~ ***Village*** *Stadtteil von New York (USA).*
Greg [greg] *abbr. für* **Gregory.**
Greg·o·ry ['gregərɪ] Gregor *m.*
Gre·na·da [gre'neɪdə] Gre'nada *n.*
Gre·ta ['gri:tə; 'gretə] *abb. für* **Margaret.**
Grims·by ['grɪmzbɪ] *Hafenstadt in Humberside (England).*
Gri·sons ['gri:zɔ̃:ŋ] Grau'bünden *n.*
Gros·ve·nor ['grəʊvnə] *Platz und Straße in London.*
Gua·te·ma·la [gwætɪ'mɑ:lə] Guate'mala *n.*
Guern·sey ['gɜ:nzɪ] *brit. Kanalinsel.*
Guin·ea ['gɪnɪ] Gui'nea *n;* **Guin·ea-Bis·sau** [ˌgɪnɪbɪ'saʊ] Gui'nea-Bis'sau *n.*
Guin·e·vere ['gwɪnɪˌvɪə] *Gemahlin des König Artus.*
Guin·ness ['gɪnɪs; gɪ'nes] *Familienname.*
Gul·li·ver ['gʌlɪvə] *Romanheld.*
Guy [gaɪ] Guido *m.*
Guy·ana [gaɪ'ænə] Gu'yana *n.*
Gwen [gwen] *abb. für* ***Gwendolen, Gwendoline, Gwendoly.***
Gwen·do·len, Gwen·do·line, Gwen·do·lyn ['gwendəlɪn] *f.*
Gwent [gwent] *walisische Grafschaft.*
Gwy·nedd ['gwɪnəð; -eð] *walisische Grafschaft.*

Hack·ney ['hæknɪ] *Stadtbezirk von Groß--London.*
Hague [heɪg]: ***the*** ~ Den Haag.
Hai·ti ['heɪtɪ] Ha'iti *n.*
Hal [hæl] *abbr. für* **Harold, Henry.**
Hal·i·fax ['hælɪfæks] *Hauptstadt von Neuschottland (Kanada); Stadt in West Yorkshire (England).*
Hal·ley ['hælɪ] *englischer Astronom.*
Ham·il·ton ['hæmltən] *Familienname; Stadt in der Provinz Ontario (Kanada).*
Ham·let ['hæmlɪt] *Bühnenfigur bei Shakespeare.*
Ham·mer·smith ['hæməsmɪθ] *Stadtbezirk von Groß-London.*
Hamp·shire ['hæmpʃə] *englische Grafschaft.*
Hamp·stead ['hæmpstɪd] *Stadtteil von Groß-London.*
Han·o·ver ['hænəʊvə] Han'nover *n.*
Ha·ra·re [hə'rɑ:reɪ] *Hauptstadt von Zimbabwe.*
Har·dy ['hɑ:dɪ] *englischer Autor.*
Ha·rin·gey ['hærɪŋgeɪ] *Stadtbezirk von Groß-London.*
Har·lem ['hɑ:ləm] *Stadtteil von New York.*
Har·old ['hærəld] Harald *m.*
Har·ri·et, Har·ri·ot ['hærɪət] *f.*
Har·ris·burg ['hærɪsbɜ:g] *Hauptstadt von Pennsylvania (USA).*
Har·row ['hærəʊ] *Stadtbezirk Groß-Londons mit berühmter Public School.*
Har·ry ['hærɪ] *abbr. für* **Harold, Henry.**
Hart·ford ['hɑ:tfəd] *Hauptstadt von Connecticut (USA).*
Har·tle·pool ['hɑ:tlɪpu:l] *Hafenstadt in Cleveland (England).*
Har·vard U·ni·ver·si·ty ['hɑ:vədˌju:nɪ'vɜ:sətɪ] *Universität in Cambridge, Massachusetts (USA).*
Har·vey ['hɑ:vɪ] *Vorname m; Familienname.*
Har·wich ['hærɪdʒ] *Hafenstadt in Südost-England.*
Has·tings ['heɪstɪŋz] *Stadt in Südengland.*
Ha·van·a [hə'vænə] Ha'vanna *n.*
Ha·ver·ing ['heɪvərɪŋ] *Stadtbezirk von Groß-London.*
Ha·wai·i [hə'waɪi:] *Staat der USA.*
Haw·thorne ['hɔ:θɔ:n] *amer. Autor.*
Ha·zel ['heɪzl] *f.*
Heath·row ['hi:θrəʊ] *Großflughafen von London.*
Heb·ri·des ['hebrɪdi:z] *pl. die* He'briden *pl.*
Hel·en ['helɪn] He'lene *f.*
Hel·e·na ['helɪnə] *Hauptstadt von Montana (USA).*
Hel·i·go·land ['helɪgəʊlænd] Helgoland *n.*
Hel·sin·ki ['helzɪŋkɪ] Helsinki *n.*
Hem·ing·way ['hemɪŋweɪ] *amer. Autor.*
Hen·ley ['henlɪ] *Stadt an der Themse (Ruderregatta).*
Hen·ry ['henrɪ] Heinrich *m.*
Hep·burn ['hebɜ:n; 'hepbɜ:n] *amer. Filmschauspielerin.*
Her·bert ['hɜ:bət] Herbert *m.*
Her·e·ford and Worces·ter [ˌherɪfədn'wʊstə] *englische Grafschaft;* **Her·e·ford·shire** [-ʃə] *englische Grafschaft (bis 1974).*
Hert·ford(shire) ['hɑ:tfəd(ʃə)] *englische Grafschaft.*
Hesse ['hesɪ] Hessen *n.*
High·land ['haɪlənd] *Verwaltungsregion in Schottland.*
Hil·a·ry ['hɪlərɪ] Hi'laria *f,* Hi'larius *m.*
Hil·da ['hɪldə] Hilda *f,* Hilde *f.*
Hil·ling·don ['hɪlɪŋdən] *Stadtbezirk von Groß-London.*
Hi·ma·la·ya [ˌhɪmə'leɪə] *der* Hi'malaya.
Hi·ro·shi·ma [hɪ'rɒʃɪmə] *Hafenstadt in Japan.*
Ho·bart ['həʊbɑ:t] *Hauptstadt des australischen Bundesstaates Tasmanien.*
Ho·garth ['həʊgɑ:θ] *englischer Maler.*
Hol·born ['həʊbən] *Stadtteil von London.*
Hol·land ['hɒlənd] Holland *n.*
Hol·ly·wood ['hɒlɪwʊd] *Filmstadt in Kalifornien (USA).*
Holmes [həʊmz] *Familienname.*
Ho·mer ['həʊmə] Ho'mer *m.*
Hon·du·ras [hɒn'djʊərəs] Hon'duras *n.*
Hong Kong [ˌhɒŋ'kɒŋ] Hongkong *m.*
Ho·no·lu·lu [ˌhɒnə'lu:lu:] *Hauptstadt von Hawaii (USA).*
Hor·ace ['hɒrəs] Ho'raz *m (römischer Dichter und Satiriker), Vorname m.*
Houns·low ['haʊnzləʊ] *Stadtbezirk von Groß-London.*
Hous·ton ['hju:stən; 'ju:stən] *Stadt in Texas (USA).*
How·ard ['haʊəd] *m.*
Hu·bert ['hju:bət] Hubert *m,* Hu'bertus *m.*
Hud·son ['hʌdsn] *Familienname; Fluß im Staat New York (USA).*
Hugh [hju:] Hugo *m.*
Hughes [hju:z] *Familienname.*
Hull [hʌl] *Hafenstadt in Humberside (England).*
Hum·ber ['hʌmbə] *Fluß in England;* **'Hum·ber·side** [-saɪd] *englische Grafschaft.*
Hume [hju:m] *englischer Philosoph.*
Hum·phr(e)y ['hʌmfrɪ] *m.*
Hun·ga·ry ['hʌŋgərɪ] Ungarn *n.*
Hun·ting·don(shire) ['hʌntɪŋdən(ʃə)] *englische Grafschaft (bis 1974).*
Hux·ley ['hʌkslɪ] *englischer Autor; englischer Biologe.*
Hyde Park [ˌhaɪd'pɑ:k] *Park in London.*

I·an [ɪən; 'i:ən] Jan *m.*
I·be·ri·an Pen·in·su·la [aɪˌbɪərɪənpɪ'nɪnsjʊlə] *die* I'berische Halbinsel.
Ice·land ['aɪslənd] Island *n.*
I·da ['aɪdə] Ida *f.*
I·da·ho ['aɪdəhəʊ] *Staat der USA.*
Il·ford ['ɪlfəd] *Stadtteil von Groß-London.*
Il·li·nois [ˌɪlɪ'nɔɪ] *Staat der USA; Fluß in USA.*
In·di·a ['ɪndjə] Indien *n.*
In·di·an·a [ˌɪndɪ'ænə] *Staat der USA.*
In·di·an·a·po·lis [ˌɪndɪə'næpəlɪs] *Hauptstadt von Indiana (USA).*
In·do·ne·sia [ˌɪndəʊ'ni:zjə] Indo'nesien *n.*
In·dus ['ɪndəs] Indus *m.*
In·ver·ness(shire) [ˌɪnvə'nes(ʃə)] *schottische Grafschaft (bis 1974).*
I·o·wa ['aɪəʊə; 'aɪəwə] *Staat der USA.*
Ips·wich ['ɪpswɪtʃ] *Hauptstadt von Suffolk (England).*
I·ran [ɪ'rɑ:n] I'ran *m.*
I·raq [ɪ'rɑ:k] I'rak *m.*
Ire·land ['aɪələnd] Irland *n.*
I·rene [aɪ'ri:nɪ; 'aɪri:n] I'rene *f.*
I·ris ['aɪərɪs] Iris *f.*
Ir·ving ['ɜ:vɪŋ] *amer. Autor.*
I·saac ['aɪzək] Isaak *m.*
Is·a·bel ['ɪzəbəl] Isa'bella *f.*
Ish·er·wood ['ɪʃəwʊd] *englisch-amerikanischer Schriftsteller und Dramatiker.*
Is·lam·a·bad [ɪz'lɑ:məbɑ:d] *Hauptstadt von Pakistan.*
Isle of Man [ˌaɪləv'mæn] *Insel in der Irischen See, die unmittelbar der englischen Krone untersteht, aber nicht zum Vereinigten Königreich gehört.*

Isle of Wight [ˌaɪləv'waɪt] *englische Grafschaft, Insel im Ärmelkanal.*
I·sle·worth ['aɪzlwəθ] *Stadtteil von Groß-London.*
Is·ling·ton ['ɪzlɪŋtən] *Stadtbezirk von Groß-London.*
Is·o·bel ['ɪzəbəl] Isa'bella *f.*
Is·ra·el ['ɪzreɪəl] Israel *n.*
Is·tan·bul [ˌɪstən'buːl] Istanbul *n.*
It·a·ly ['ɪtəlɪ] I'talien *n.*
I·van ['aɪvən] Iwan *m.*
Ivor ['aɪvə] *m.*
I·vo·ry Coast ['aɪvərɪkəʊst] *die* Elfenbeinküste.

Jack [dʒæk] Hans *m.*
Jack·ie ['dʒækɪ] *abbr. für* **Jacqueline.**
Jack·son ['dʒæksn] *Hauptstadt von Mississippi (USA).*
Jack·son·ville ['dʒæksnvɪl] *Hafenstadt in Florida (USA).*
Ja·cob ['dʒeɪkəb] Jakob *m.*
Jac·que·line ['dʒækIɪn] *f.*
Jaf·fa ['dʒæfə] *Hafenstadt in Israel.*
Ja·mai·ca [dʒə'meɪkə] Ja'maika *n.*
James [dʒeɪmz] Jakob *m.*
Jane [dʒeɪn] Jo'hanna *f.*
Jan·et ['dʒænɪt] Jo'hanna *f.*
Jan·ice ['dʒænɪs] *f.*
Ja·pan [dʒə'pæn] Japan *n.*
Ja·son ['dʒeɪsn] *m.*
Jas·per ['dʒæspə] Kaspar *m.*
Ja·va ['dʒɑːvə] Java *n.*
Jean [dʒiːn] Jo'hanna *f.*
Jeff [dʒef] *abbr. für* **Jeffrey.**
Jef·fer·son ['dʒefəsn] *3. Präsident der USA.*
Jef·fer·son Cit·y [ˌdʒefəsn'sɪtɪ] *Hauptstadt von Missouri (USA).*
Jef·frey ['dʒefrɪ] Gottfried *m.*
Je·ho·vah [dzɪ'həʊvə] Je'hova *m.*
Jen·ni·fer ['dʒenɪfə] *f.*
Jen·ny ['dʒenɪ; 'dʒɪnɪ] *Koseform für* **Jane.**
Jer·e·my ['dʒerɪmɪ] Jere'mias *m.*
Je·rome [dʒə'rəʊm] Hie'ronymus *m.*
Jer·ry ['dʒerɪ] *abbr. für* **Jeremy, Jerome, Gerald, Gerard.**
Jer·sey ['dʒɜːzɪ] *brit. Kanalinsel.*
Je·ru·sa·lem [dʒə'ruːsələm] Je'rusalem *n.*
Jes·si·ca ['dʒesɪkə] *f.*
Je·sus ['dʒiːzəs] Jesus *m.*
Jill [dʒɪl] *abbr. für* **Gillian.**
Jim(my) ['dʒɪmɪ] *abbr. für* **James.**
Jo [dʒəʊ] *abbr. für* **Joanna, Joseph, Josephine.**
Joan [dʒəʊn], **Jo·an·na** [dʒəʊ'ænə] Jo'hanna *f.*
Job [dʒɒb] Hiob *m.*
Joc·e·lin(e), Joc·e·lyn ['dʒɒslɪn] *f.*
Joe [dʒəʊ] *abbr. für* **Joseph, Josephine.**
Jo·han·nes·burg [dʒəʊ'hænɪsbɜːg] *Stadt in Südafrika.*
John [dʒɒn] Jo'hannes *m*, Johann *m.*
John·ny ['dʒɒnɪ] Häns-chen *n.*
John o'Groats [ˌdʒɒnə'grəʊts] *Dorf an der Nordostspitze des schottischen Festlandes. Gilt volkstümlich als nördlichster Punkt des festländischen Großbritannien.*
John·son ['dʒɒnsn] *36. Präsident der USA; englischer Lexikograph.*
Jon·a·than ['dʒɒnəθən] Jonathan *m.*
Jon·son ['dʒɒnsn] *englischer Dichter.*
Jor·dan ['dʒɔːdn] Jor'danien *n.*
Jo·seph ['dʒəʊzɪf] Joseph *m.*
Jo·se·phine [dʒəʊzɪ'fiːn] Jose'phine *f.*
Josh·u·a ['dʒɒʃwə] Josua *m.*
Joule [dʒuːl] *englischer Physiker.*
Joy [dʒɔɪ] *f.*
Joyce [dʒɔɪs] *irischer Autor; Vorname f.*
Ju·dith ['dʒuːdɪθ] Judith *f.*
Ju·dy ['dʒuːdɪ] *abbr. für* **Judith.**
Jul·ia ['dʒuːljə] Julia *f.*
Jul·ian ['dʒuːljən] Julius *m*, Juli'anus *m.*
Jul·i·et ['dʒuːljət; -ljet] Julia *f*, Juli'ette *f.*
Jul·ius ['dʒuːljəs] Julius *m.*
June [dʒuːn] *f.*
Ju·neau ['dʒuːnəʊ] *Hauptstadt von Alaska (USA).*
Jus·tin ['dʒʌstɪn] Ju'stin(us) *m.*

Kam·pu·che·a [ˌkæmpʊ'tʃɪə] *hist.* Kam'bodscha *n.*
Kan·sas ['kænzəs] *Staat der USA; Fluß in USA.*
Kan·sas Cit·y [kænzəs'sɪtɪ] *Stadt in Missouri (USA); Stadt in Kansas (USA).*
Ka·ra·chi [kə'rɑːtʃɪ] Ka'ratschi *n.*
Kar·en ['kɑːrən; 'kærən] Karin *f.*
Kash·mir [ˌkæʃ'mɪə] Kaschmir *n.*
Ka·tar [kæ'tɑː] Katar *n (Scheichtum am Persischen Golf).*
Kate [keɪt] Käthe *f.*
Kath·a·rine, Kath·er·ine ['kæθərɪn] Katha'rina *f*, Kat(h)rin *f.*
Kath·leen ['kæθlɪn] *f.*
Kath·y ['kæθɪ] *abbr. für* **Katharine, Katherine.**
Kay [keɪ] Kai *m*, Kay *m, f.*
Keats [kiːts] *englischer Dichter.*
Kee·wa·tin [kiː'wɒtɪn; *Am.* kiː'weɪtn] *Verwaltungsbezirk der Northwest Territories (Kanada).*
Keith [kiːθ] *m.*
Kel·vin ['kelvɪn] *brit. Mathematiker und Physiker.*
Ken [ken] *abbr. für* **Kenneth.**
Ken·ne·dy ['kenɪdɪ] *35. Präsident der USA;* ~ **International Airport** *Großflughafen von New York (USA).*
Ken·neth ['kenɪθ] *m.*
Ken·sing·ton ['kenzɪŋtən] *Stadtteil von London.*
Ken·sing·ton and Chel·sea [ˌkenzɪŋtənən'tʃelsɪ] *Stadtbezirk von Groß-London.*
Kent [kent] *englische Grafschaft.*
Ken·tuck·y [ken'tʌkɪ] *Staat der USA; Fluß in USA.*
Ken·ya ['kenjə] Kenia *n.*
Ker·ry ['kerɪ] *Grafschaft in der Provinz Munster (Irland).*
Kev·in ['kevɪn] *m.*
Kew [kjuː] *Stadtteil von Groß-London. Botanischer Garten.*
Keynes [keɪnz] *englischer Wirtschaftwissenschaftler.*
Kil·dare [kɪl'deə] *Grafschaft in der Provinz Leinster (Irland).*
Kil·ken·ny [kɪl'kenɪ] *Grafschaft in der Provinz Leinster (Irland); Hauptstadt dieser Grafschaft.*
Kin·car·dine(shire) [kɪn'kɑːdɪn(ʃə)] *schottische Grafschaft (bis 1975).*
King·ston up·on Hull [ˌkɪŋstənəpɒn'hʌl] *offizielle Bezeichnung für* **Hull.**
King·ston up·on Thames [ˌkɪŋstənəpɒn'temz] *Stadtbezirk von Groß-London; Hauptstadt von Surrey (England).*
Kin·ross ['kɪnrɒs] *schottische Grafschaft (bis 1975).*
Kir·cud·bright(shire) [kɜː'kuːbrɪ(ʃə)] *schottische Grafschaft (bis 1975).*
Kit(ty) ['kɪt(tɪ)] *abbr. für* **Catherine, Katherine.**
Klon·dyke ['klɒndaɪk] *Fluß in Kanada; Landschaft in Kanada.*
Knox [nɒks] *schottischer Reformator.*
Knox·ville [nɒksvɪl] *Stadt in Tennessee (USA).*
Ko·re·a [kə'rɪə] Ko'rea *n;* ***Democratic People's Republic of*** ~ *die* Demo'kratische 'Volksrepuˌblik Ko'rea; ***Republic of*** ~ *die* Repu'blik Ko'rea.
Kos·ci·us·ko [ˌkɒsɪ'ʌskəʊ]: ***Mount*** ~ *höchster Berg Australiens, im Bundesstaat New South Wales.*
Krem·lin ['kremlɪn] *der* Kreml.
Ku·wait [kʊ'weɪt] Ku'wait *n.*

Lab·ra·dor ['læbrədɔː] *Provinz in Kanada.*
La Guar·dia [lə'gwɑːdɪə; lə'gɑːdɪə] *ehemaliger Bürgermeister von New York;* ~ ***Airport*** *Flughafen in New York (USA).*
Laing [læŋ; leɪŋ] *Familienname.*
Lake Huron [ˌleɪk'hjʊərən] der Huronsee *(in Nordamerika).*
Lake Su·pe·ri·or [ˌleɪksuː'pɪərɪə] der Obere See *(in Nordamerika).*
Lam·beth ['læmbəθ] *Stadtbezirk von Groß-London;* ~ **Palace** *Londoner Residenz des Erzbischofs von Canterbury.*
Lan·ark(shire) ['lænək(ʃə)] *schottische Grafschaft (bis 1975).*
Lan·ca·shire ['læŋkəʃə] *englische Grafschaft.*
Lan·cas·ter ['læŋkəstə] *Stadt in Nordwest-England; Stadt in USA.*
Land's End [ˌlændz'end] *westlichster Punkt Englands, in Cornwall.*
La·nier [lə'nɪə] *amer. Dichter.*
Lan·sing ['lænsɪŋ] *Hauptstadt von Michigan (USA).*
Laoigh·is [liːʃ; 'leɪʃ] *siehe* **Leix.**
La·os ['lɑːɒs; laʊs] Laos *n.*
Lar·ry ['lærɪ] *abbr. für* **Laurence, Lawrence.**
La·tham ['leɪθəm; 'leɪðəm] *Familienname.*
Lat·in A·mer·i·ca [ˌlætɪnə'merɪkə] La'teinaˌmerika *n.*
Lat·via ['lætvɪə] Lettland *n.*
Laugh·ton ['lɔːtn] *Familienname.*
Lau·ra ['lɔːrə] Laura *f.*
Lau·rence ['lɒrəns] Lorenz *m.*
Law·rence ['lɒrəns] Lorenz *m; Familienname.*
Lear [lɪə] *Bühnenfigur bei Shakespeare.*
Leb·a·non ['lebənən] *der* Libanon.
Leeds [liːdz] *Industriestadt in Ostengland.*
Le·fe·vre [lə'fiːvə; lə'feɪvə] *Familienname.*
Legge [leg] *Familienname.*
Leices·ter ['lestə] *Hauptstadt der englischen Grafschaft* **'Leices·ter·shire** [-ʃə].
Leigh [liː] *Familienname; Vorname m.*
Lein·ster ['lenstə] *Provinz in Irland.*
Lei·trim ['liːtrɪm] *Grafschaft in der Provinz Connacht.*
Leix [liːʃ] *Grafschaft in der Provinz Leinster (Irland).*
Le·o ['liːəʊ] Leo *m.*
Leon·ard ['lenəd] Leonhard *m.*
Les·ley ['lezlɪ; *Am.* 'leslɪ] *f.*
Les·lie ['lezlɪ; *Am.* 'leslɪ] *m.*
Le·so·tho [lə'suːtuː; lə'səʊtəʊ] Le'sotho *n.*
Lew·is ['luːɪs] Ludwig *m; amer. Autor.*
Lew·i·sham ['luːɪʃəm] *Stadtbezirk von Groß-London.*
Lex·ing·ton ['leksɪŋtən] *Stadt in Massachusetts (USA).*
Li·be·ria [laɪ'bɪərɪə] Li'beria *n.*
Lib·y·a ['lɪbɪə] Libyen *n.*
Liech·ten·stein ['lɪktənstaɪn] Liechtenstein *n.*
Lil·i·an ['lɪlɪən] *f.*
Lil·y ['lɪlɪ] Lilli *f*, Lili *f*, Lilly *f*, Lily *f.*

Lim·er·ick ['lɪmərɪk] *Grafschaft in der Provinz Munster (Irland); Hauptstadt dieser Grafschaft.*
Lin·coln ['lɪŋkən] *16. Präsident der USA; Hauptstadt von Nebraska (USA); Stadt in der englischen Grafschaft* **'Lin·coln·shire** [-ʃə].
Lin·da ['lɪndə] Linda *f.*
Lind·bergh ['lɪndbɜːg] *amer. Flieger.*
Li·o·nel ['laɪənl] *m.*
Li·sa ['liːzə; 'laɪzə] Lisa *f.*
Lis·bon ['lɪzbən] Lissabon *n.*
Lith·u·a·nia [ˌlɪθjuː'eɪnjə] Litauen *n.*
Lit·tle Rock ['lɪtlrɒk] *Hauptstadt von Arkansas (USA).*
Liv·er·pool ['lɪvəpuːl] *Hafenstadt in Nordwest-England; Verwaltungszentrum von* **Merseyside.**
Live·sey ['lɪvsɪ; -zɪ] *Familienname.*
Liv·ing·stone ['lɪvɪŋstən] *englischer Afrikaforscher.*
Li·vo·nia [lɪ'vəʊnjə] Livland *n.*
Liv·y ['lɪvɪ] Livius *m.*
Liz [lɪz] *abbr. für* **Elizabeth.**
Li·za ['laɪzə] Lisa *f.*
Lloyd [lɔɪd] *Familienname; Vorname m.*
Loch Lo·mond [ˌlɒk'ləʊmənd], **Loch Ness** [ˌlɒk'nes] *Seen in Schottland.*
Locke [lɒk] *englischer Philosoph.*
Lo·is ['ləʊɪs] *f.*
Lom·bar·dy ['lɒmbədɪ] die Lombar'dei.
Lon·don ['lʌndən] London *n;* **City of ~** *London im engeren Sinn; Zentraler Stadtbezirk von Groß-London und eines der größten Finanzzentren der Welt.*
Lon·don·der·ry [ˌlʌndən'derɪ] *nordirische Grafschaft.*
Long·ford ['lɒŋfəd] *Grafschaft in der Provinz Leinster (Irland).*
Lor·na ['lɔːnə] *f.*
Lor·raine [lɒ'reɪn] Lothringen *n.*
Los Al·a·mos [ˌlɒs'æləmɒs] *Stadt in New Mexico (USA); Atomforschungszentrum.*
Los An·ge·les [ˌlɒs'ændʒɪliːz] *Stadt in Kalifornien (USA).*
Lo·thi·an ['ləʊðjən] *Verwaltungsregion in Schottland.*
Lou [luː] *abbr. für* **Louis, Louisa, Louise.**
Lou·is ['luːɪ; 'lʊɪ; *bsd. Am.* 'luːɪs] Ludwig *m.*
Lou·i·sa [luː'iːzə] Lu'ise *f.*
Lou·ise [luː'iːz] Lu'ise f.
Lou·i·si·a·na [luːˌiːzɪ'ænə] *Staat der USA.*
Lou·is·ville ['luːɪvɪl] *Stadt in Kentucky (USA).*
Louth [laʊð] *Grafschaft in der Provinz Leinster (Irland).*
Lowes [ləʊz] *Familienname.*
Lowes·toft ['ləʊstɒft] *Hafenstadt in Suffolk (England).*
Low·ry ['laʊərɪ; 'laʊrɪ] *Familienname.*
Lu·cia ['luːsjə] Lucia *f,* Luzia *f.*
Lu·cius ['luːsjəs] *m.*
Lu·cy ['luːsɪ] *abbr. für* **Lucia.**
Lud·gate ['lʌdgɪt; -geɪt] *Familienname.*
Luke [luːk] Lukas *m.*
Lux·em·b(o)urg ['lʌksəmbɜːg] Luxemburg *n.*
Lyd·i·a ['lɪdɪə] Lydia *f.*
Lynn [lɪn] *f.*
Ly·ons ['laɪənz] Lyon *n; Familienname.*

Mab [mæb] *Feenkönigin.*
Ma·bel ['meɪbl] *f.*
Ma·cau·ley [mə'kɔːlɪ] *englischer Historiker.*
Mac·beth [mək'beθ] *Bühnenfigur bei Shakespeare.*
Mac·Car·thy [mə'kɑːθɪ] *Familienname.*
Mac·Gee [mə'giː] *Familienname.*
Mac·Ken·zie [mə'kenzɪ] *Strom in Nordwestkanada; Verwaltungsbezirk der Northwest Territories (Kanada).*
Mac·Leish [mə'kliːʃ] *amer. Dichter.*
Mac·leod [mə'kləʊd] *Familienname.*
Mad·a·gas·car [ˌmædə'gæskə] Mada'gaskar *n.*
Mad·e·leine ['mædlɪn; -leɪn] Magda'lena *f,* Magda'lene *f.*
Ma·dei·ra [mə'dɪərə] Ma'deira *n.*
Madge [mædʒ] *abbr. für* **Margaret.**
Mad·ison ['mædɪsn] *4. Präsident der USA; Hauptstadt von Wisconsin (USA).*
Ma·dras [mə'drɑːs] Madras *n.*
Mag·da·len ['mægdəlɪn] Magda'lena *f,* Magda'lene *f;* **~ College** ['mɔːdlɪn] *College in Cambridge*
Mag·gie ['mægɪ] *abbr. für* **Margaret.**
Ma·ho·met [mə'hɒmɪt] Mohammed *m.*
Maine [meɪn] *Staat der USA.*
Ma·jor·ca [mə'dʒɔːkə] Mal'lorca *n.*
Ma·la·wi [mə'lɑːwɪ] Ma'lawi *n.*
Ma·lay·sia [mə'leɪzɪə] Ma'laysia *n.*
Mal·colm ['mælkəm] *m.*
Mal·dives ['mɔːldɪvz] *pl. die* Male'diven *pl.*
Ma·li ['mɑːlɪ] Mali *n.*
Mal·ta ['mɔːltə] Malta *n.*
Ma·mie ['meɪmɪ] *abbr. für* **Mary, Margaret.**
Man·ches·ter ['mæntʃɪstə] *Industriestadt in Nordwest-England. Früher wichtiges Zentrum der Woll- u. Baumwollindustrie.*
Man·chu·ri·a [mæn'tʃʊərɪə] die Mandschu'rei.
Man·dy ['mændɪ] *abbr. für* **Amanda.**
Man·hat·tan [mæn'hætn] *Stadtbezirk von New York (USA).*
Man·i·to·ba [ˌmænɪ'təʊbə] *Provinz in Kanada.*
Mar·ga·ret ['mɑːgərɪt] Marga'reta *f,* Marga'rete *f.*
Mar·ge·ry ['mɑːdʒərɪ] *siehe* **Margaret.**
Mar·gie ['mɑːdʒɪ] *abbr. für* **Margaret.**
Ma·ri·a [mə'raɪə; mə'rɪə] Ma'ria *f.*
Mar·i·an ['meərɪən; :mærɪən] Mari'anne *f.*
Ma·rie ['mɑːrɪ; mə'riː] Ma'rie *f.*
Mar·i·lyn ['mærɪlɪn] *f.*
Mar·i·on ['mærɪən; 'meərɪən] Marion *f.*
Mar·jo·rie, Mar·jo·ry ['mɑːdʒərɪ] *f.*
Mar·lowe ['mɑːləʊ] *englischer Dichter.*
Mar·tha ['mɑːθə] Mart(h)a *f.*
Mar·tin ['mɑːtɪn; *Am.* 'mɑːrtn] Martin *m.*
Mar·y ['meərɪ] Ma'ria *f,* Ma'rie *f.*
Mar·y·land ['meərɪlənd; *bsd. Am.* 'merɪlənd] *Staat der USA.*
Mar·y·le·bone ['mærələbən] *Stadtteil von London.*
Mas·sa·chu·setts [ˌmæsə'tʃuːsɪts] *Staat der USA.*
Ma(t)·thew ['mæθjuː] Mat'thäus *m.*
Maud [mɔːd] *abbr. für* **Magdalen(e).**
Maugham [mɔːm] *englischer Autor.*
Mau·reen ['mɔːriːn; *bsd. Am.* mɔː'riːn] *f.*
Mau·rice ['mɒrɪs] Moritz *m.*
Mau·ri·ta·nia [ˌmɒrɪ'teɪnjə] Maure'tanien *n.*
Mau·ri·ti·us [mə'rɪʃəs] Mau'ritius *n.*
Ma·vis ['meɪvɪs] *f.*
Max [mæks] Max *m.*
Max·ine ['mæksiːn; *bsd. Am.* mæk'siːn] *f.*
May [meɪ] *abbr. für* **Mary.**
May·o ['meɪəʊ] *Name zweier amer. Chirurgen; Grafschaft in der Provinz Connacht (Irland).*
Mc·Cart·ney [mə'kɑːtnɪ] *englischer Musiker u. Komponist. Mitglied der „Beatles".*
Meath [miːð; miːθ] *Grafschaft in der Provinz Leinster (Irland).*
Med·i·ter·ra·ne·an (Sea) [ˌmedɪtə'reɪnjən('siː)] *das* Mittelmeer.
Meg [meg] *abbr. für* **Margaret.**
Mel·bourne ['melbən] *Stadt in Australien.*
Mel·ville ['melvɪl] *amer. Autor.*
Mem·phis ['memfɪs] *Stadt in Tennessee (USA); antike Ruinenstadt am Nil, Nordägypten.*
Mer·i·on·eth(shire) [ˌmerɪ'ɒnɪθ(ʃə)] *walisische Grafschaft (bis 1975).*
Mer·sey·side ['mɜːzɪsaɪd] *Stadtgrafschaft in Nordwest-England.*
Mer·ton ['mɜːtn] *Stadtbezirk von Groß-London.*
Me·thu·en ['meθjʊɪn] *Familienname.*
Mex·i·co ['meksɪkəʊ] Mexiko *n.*
Mi·am·i [maɪ'æmɪ] *Badeort in Florida (USA).*
Mi·chael ['maɪkl] Michael *m.*
Mi·chelle [miː'ʃel; mɪ'ʃel] Mi'chèle *f,* Mi'chelle *f.*
Mich·i·gan ['mɪʃɪgən] *Staat der USA;* **Lake ~** der Michigansee *(in Nordamerika).*
Mick [mɪk] *abbr. für* **Michael.**
Mid·les·brough ['mɪdlzbrə] *Hauptstadt von Cleveland (England).*
Mid·dle·sex ['mɪdlseks] *englische Grafschaft (bis 1974).*
Mid Gla·mor·gan [ˌmɪdglə'mɔːgən] *walisische Grafschaft.*
Mid·lands ['mɪdləndz] *pl. die* Midlands *pl. (die zentral gelegenen Grafschaften Mittelenglands: Warwickshire, Northamptonshire, Leicestershire, Nottinghamshire; Derbyshire; Staffordshire, West Midlands u. der Ostteil von Hereford and Worcester).*
.**Mid·lo·thi·an** [mɪd'ləʊðɪən] *schottische Grafschaft (bis 1975).*
Mid·west [ˌmɪd'west] *der* Mittlere Westen *(USA).*
Mi·ers ['maɪəz] *Familienname.*
Mike [maɪk] *abbr. für* **Michael.**
Mi·lan [mɪ'læn] Mailand *n.*
Mil·dred ['mɪldrɪd] Miltraud *f,* Miltrud *f.*
Miles [maɪlz] *m.*
Mil·li·cent ['mɪlɪsnt] *f.*
Mil·lie, Mil·ly ['mɪlɪ] *abbr. für* **Amelia, Emily, Mildred, Millicent.**
Mil·ton ['mɪltən] *englischer Dichter u. Verfechter des Parlamentarismus.*
Mil·wau·kee [mɪl'wɔːkɪ] *Industriestadt in Wisconsin (USA).*
Min·ne·ap·o·lis [ˌmɪnɪ'æpəlɪs] *Stadt in Minnesota (USA).*
Min·ne·so·ta [ˌmɪnɪ'səʊtə] *Staat der USA.*
Mi·ran·da [mɪ'rændə] Mi'randa *f.*
Mir·i·am ['mɪrɪəm] *f.*
Mis·sis·sip·pi [ˌmɪsɪ'sɪpɪ] *Staat der USA; Fluß in USA.*
Mis·sou·ri [mɪ'zʊərɪ] *Staat der USA; Fluß in USA.*
Mitch·ell ['mɪtʃl] *Familienname; Vorname m.*
Moi·ra ['mɔɪərə] *f.*
Moll [mɒl], **Mol·ly** ['mɒlɪ] *Koseformen für* **Mary.**
Mo·na·co ['mɒnəkəʊ] Mo'naco *n.*
Mon·a·ghan ['mɒnəhən] *Grafschaft im der Republik Irland zugehörigen Teil der Provinz Ulster.*

Mon·go·lia [mɒŋ'gəʊljə] die Mongo'lei.
Mon·i·ca ['mɒnɪkə] Monika *f.*
Mon·mouth(shire) ['mɒnməθ(ʃə)] *walisische Grafschaft (bis 1974).*
Mon·roe [mən'rəʊ] *5. Präsident der USA; amer. Filmschauspielerin.*
Mon·ta·na [mɒn'tænə] *Staat der USA.*
Mont·gom·er·y [mənt'gʌmərɪ] *brit. Feldmarschall; Hauptstadt von Alabama (USA); a.* **Mont'gom·er·y·shire** [-ʃə] *walisische Grafschaft (bis 1974).*
Mont·pe·lier [mɒnt'piːljə] *Hauptstadt von Vermont (USA).*
Mont·re·al [ˌmɒntrɪ'ɔːl] *Stadt in Kanada.*
Mo·ra·vi·a [mə'reɪvjə] Mähren *n.*
Mor·ay(shire) ['mʌrɪ(ʃə)] *schottische Grafschaft (bis 1975).*
More [mɔː]: ***Thomas*** ~ Thomas Morus.
Mo·roc·co [mə'rɒkəʊ] Ma'rokko *n.*
Mos·cow ['mɒskəʊ] Moskau *n.*
Mo·selle [məʊ'zel] Mosel *f.*
Mount Ev·er·est [ˌmaʊnt'evərɪst] *höchster Berg der Erde.*
Mount Mc·Kin·ley [ˌmaʊntmə'kɪnlɪ] *höchster Berg der USA, in Alaska.*
Mo·zam·bique [məʊzəm'biːk] Moçam'bique *n.*
Mu·nich ['mjuːnɪk] München *n.*
Mun·ster ['mʌnstə] *Provinz in Irland.*
Mu·ri·el ['mjʊərɪəl] *f.*
Mur·ray ['mʌrɪ] *Familienname; Fluß in Australien.*
Myan·mar ['mjænmɑː] Myanmar *n (offizieller Name für* ***Birma****).*
My·ra ['maɪərə] *f.*

Nab·o·kov [nə'bəʊkɒf] *amer. Autor russischer Herkunft.*
Nairn(shire) ['neən(ʃə)] *schottische Grafschaft (bis 1975).*
Na·mib·ia [nə'mɪbɪə] Na'mibia *n.*
Nan·cy ['nænsɪ] *f.*
Nan·ga Par·bat [ˌnʌŋgə'pɑːbət] *Berg im Himalaya.*
Na·o·mi ['neɪəmɪ] *f.*
Na·ples ['neɪplz] Ne'apel *n.*
Na·po·le·on [nə'pəʊljən] Na'poleon *m.*
Nash·ville ['næʃvɪl] *Hauptstadt von Tennessee (USA).*
Na·tal [nə'tæl] Natal *n.*
Nat·a·lie ['nætəlɪ] Na'talia *f,* Na'talie *f.*
Na·than·iel [nə'θænjəl] Na't(h)anael *m.*
Na·u·ru [nɑː'uːruː] Na'uru *n.*
Naz·a·reth ['næzərɪθ] Nazareth *n.*
Neal [niːl] *m.*
Ne·bras·ka [nɪ'bræskə] *Staat der USA.*
Neil(l) [niːl] *Vorname m; Familienname.*
Nell, Nel·ly ['nel(lɪ)] *abbr. für* ***Eleanor, Ellen, Helen.***
Nel·son ['nelsn] *brit. Admiral.*
Ne·pal [nɪ'pɔːl] Nepal *n.*
Neth·er·lands ['neðələndz] *pl. die* Niederlande *pl.*
Ne·va·da [ne'vɑːdə] *Staat der USA.*
Nev·il, Nev·ille ['nevɪl] *m.*
New·ark ['njuːək; *Am.* 'nuːərk] *Stadt in New Jersey (USA).*
New Bruns·wick [ˌnjuː'brʌnzwɪk] *Provinz in Kanada.*
New·bur·y ['njuːbərɪ] *Stadt in Berkshire (England).*
New·cas·tle ['njuːˌkɑːsl] *siehe* ***Newcastle-upon-Tyne****; Stadt in New South Wales (Australien).*
New·cas·tle-up·on-Tyne ['njuːˌkɑːsl-əˌpɒn'taɪn] *Hauptstadt von Tyne and Wear (England).*
New Del·hi [ˌnjuː'delɪ] *Hauptstadt von Indien.*
New Eng·land [ˌnjuː'ɪŋglənd] Neu-'England *n (USA).*
New·found·land ['njuːfəndlənd] Neu'fundland *n (Provinz in Kanada).*
New Guin·ea [ˌnjuː'gɪnɪ] Neugui'nea *n.*
New·ham ['njuːəm] *Stadtbezirk von Groß-London.*
New Hamp·shire [ˌnjuː'hæmpʃə] *Staat der USA.*
New Jer·sey [ˌnjuː'dʒɜːzɪ] *Staat der USA.*
New Mex·i·co [ˌnjuː'meksɪkəʊ] *Staat der USA.*
New Or·le·ans [ˌnjuː'ɔːlɪənz] *Hafenstadt in Louisiana (USA).*
New South Wales [ˌnjuːsaʊθ'weɪlz] Neusüd'wales *n (Bundesstaat Australiens).*
New·ton ['njuːtn] *englischer Physiker.*
New York [ˌnjuː'jɔːk; *Am.* ˌnuː'jɔːrk] *Staat der USA; größte Stadt der USA.*
New Zea·land [ˌnjuː'ziːlənd] Neu'seeland *n.*
Ni·ag·a·ra [naɪ'ægərə] Nia'gara *m.*
Nic·a·ra·gua [ˌnɪkə'rægjʊə] Nica'ragua *n.*
Nich·o·las ['nɪkələs] Nikolaus *m.*
Nick [nɪk] *abbr. für* ***Nicholas.***
Ni·gel ['naɪdʒəl] *m.*
Ni·ger ['naɪdʒə] Niger *m (Fluß in Westafrika);* [niː'ʒeə] Niger *n (Republik in Westafrika).*
Ni·ge·ri·a [naɪ'dʒɪərɪə] Ni'geria *n.*
Nile [naɪl] Nil *m.*
Nix·on ['nɪksən] *37. Präsident der USA.*
No·bel [nəʊ'bel] *schwedischer Industrieller; Stifter des Nobelpreises.*
No·el ['nəʊəl] *m.*
No·ra ['nɔːrə] Nora *f.*
Nor·folk ['nɔːfək] *englische Grafschaft; Hafenstadt in Virginia (USA) u. Hauptstützpunkt der US-Atlantikflotte.*
Nor·man ['nɔːmən] *m.*
Nor·man·dy ['nɔːməndɪ] die Norman'die.
North·amp·ton [nɔ'θæmptən] *Stadt in Mittelengland; a.* **North'amp·ton·shire** [-ʃə] *englische Grafschaft.*
North Cape ['nɔːθkeɪp] *das* Nordkap.
North Car·o·li·na [ˌnɔːθkærə'laɪnə] *Staat der USA.*
North Da·ko·ta [ˌnɔːθdə'kəʊtə] *Staat der USA.*
North·ern Ire·land [ˌnɔːðn'aɪələnd] Nord'irland *n.*
North·ern Ter·ri·to·ry [ˌnɔːðn'terɪtərɪ] 'Nordterriˌtorium *n (Australien).*
North Sea [ˌnɔːθ'siː] *die* Nordsee.
Norh·um·ber·land [nɔː'θʌmbələnd] *englische Grafschaft.*
North·west Ter·ri·to·ries [ˌnɔːθ'west'terɪtərɪz] Nord'westterriˌtorien *pl. (Australien).*
North York·shire [ˌnɔːθ'jɔːkʃə] *englische Grafschaft.*
Nor·way ['nɔːweɪ] Norwegen *n.*
Nor·wich ['nɒrɪdʒ] *Stadt in Ostengland.*
Not·ting·ham ['nɒtɪŋəm] *Industriestadt in Mittelengland; a.* **'Not·ting·ham·shire** [-ʃə-[*englische Grafschaft.*
No·va Sco·tia [ˌnəʊvə'skəʊʃə] Neu'schottland *n.*
Nu·rem·berg ['njʊərəmbɜːg] Nürnberg *n.*

Oak·land ['əʊklənd] *Hafenstadt in Kalifornien (USA).*
O'Ca·sey [əʊ'keɪsɪ] *irischer Dramatiker.*
O'Con·nor [əʊ'kɒnə] *Familienname.*
O·ce·an·i·a [ˌəʊsɪ'eɪnjə] Oze'anien *n.*
O·dets [əʊ'dets] *amer. Dramatiker.*
Of·fa·ly ['ɒfəlɪ] *Grafschaft in der Provinz Leinster (Irland).*
O'Fla·her·ty [əʊ'fleətɪ; *Am.* əʊ'flæhətɪ] *irischer Romanschriftsteller.*
O'Har·a [əʊ'hɑːrə; *Am.* əʊ'hærə] *Familienname.*
O·hi·o [əʊ'haɪəʊ] *Staat der USA; Fluß in den USA.*
O·kla·ho·ma [ˌəʊklə'həʊmə] *Staat der USA;* ~ ***City*** *Hauptstadt von Oklahoma (USA).*
O'Lear·y [əʊ'lɪərɪ] *Familienname.*
Ol·ive ['ɒlɪv] O'livia *f.*
Ol·i·ver ['ɒlɪvə] Oliver *m.*
O·liv·i·a [ɒ'lɪvɪə] *f.*
O·livi·er [ə'lɪvɪeɪ]: ***Sir Laurence*** ~ *berühmter englischer Schauspieler.*
O·lym·pia [əʊ'lɪmpɪə] *Hauptstadt von Washington (USA).*
O·ma·ha ['əʊməhə; *Am. a.* -hɔː] *Stadt in Nebraska (USA).*
O·man [əʊ'mɑːn] O'man *n.*
O'Neill [əʊ'niːl] *amer. Dramatiker.*
On·ta·ri·o [ɒn'teərɪəʊ] *Provinz in Kanada;* ***Lake*** ~ der Ontariosee *(in Nordmerika).*
Or·ange ['ɒrɪndʒ] O'ranien *n (Herrscherfamilie);* O'ranje *m (Fluß in Südafrika).*
Or·e·gon ['ɒrɪgən] *Staat der USA.*
Ork·ney ['ɔːknɪ] *insulare Verwaltungsregion Schottlands (bis 1975 schottische Graftschaft);* ~ **Is·lands** [ˌɔːknɪ'aɪləndz] *pl. die* Orkneyinseln *pl.*
Or·well ['ɔːwəl] *englischer Autor.*
Os·borne ['ɒzbən] *englischer Dramatiker.*
Os·car ['ɒskə] Oskar *m.*
O'Shea [əʊ'ʃeɪ] *Familienname.*
Ost·end [ɒ'stend] Ost'ende *n.*
O'Sul·li·van [əʊ'sʌlɪvən] *Familienname.*
Os·wald ['ɒzvəld] Oswald *m.*
Ot·ta·wa ['ɒtəwə] *Hauptstadt von Kanada.*
Ouach·i·ta ['wɒʃɪtɔː] *Fluß in Arkansas u. Louisiana.*
Oug·ham ['əʊkəm] *Familienname.*
Ouze [uːz] *englischer Flußname.*
Ow·en ['əʊɪn] *Familienname.*
Ow·ens ['əʊɪnz] *amer. Leichtathlet.*
Ox·ford ['ɒksfəd] *englische Universitätsstadt; a.* **'Ox·ford·shire** [-ʃə] *englische Grafschaft.*
O·zark Moun·tains [ˌəʊzɑːk'maʊntɪnz] *pl.,* **O·zark Pla·teau** [ˌəʊzɑːk'plætəʊ] *Plateau westlich des Mississippi in Missouri, Arkansas u. Oklahoma (USA).*

Pa·cif·ic (O·cean) [pə'sɪfɪk; pəˌsɪfɪk'əʊʃn] *der* Pa'zifik, *der* Pa'zifische Ozean.
Pad·ding·ton ['pædɪŋtən] *Stadtteil von London.*
Pad·dy ['pædɪ] *abbr. für* ***Patricia, Patrick.***
Paign·ton ['peɪntən] *Teilstadt von* ***Torbay*** *in Devon (England.*
Paine [peɪn] *amer. Staatstheoretiker.*
Pais·ley ['peɪzlɪ] *radikaler nordirischer protestantischer Politiker; Industriestadt in Schottland.*
Pak·i·stan [ˌpɑːkɪs'tɑːn] Pakistan *n.*
Pal·es·tine ['pæləstaɪn] Palä'stina *n.*
Pall Mall [ˌpæl'mæl] *Straße in London.*
Palm Beach [ˌpɑːm'biːtʃ; *Am. a.* ˌpɑːlm-] *Seeband in Florida (USA).*
Pal·mer ['pɑːmə; *Am. a.* 'pɑːlmə] *Familienname.*
Pam [pæm] *abbr. für* ***Pamela.***
Pam·e·la ['pæmələ] Pa'mela *f.*
Pan·a·ma [ˌpænə'mɑː; 'pænəmɑː] Panama *n.*

Pa·pua New Guin·ea ['pɑ:pʊə,nju:'gɪnɪ; 'pæpjʊə-] Papua-Neugui'nea *n.*
Par·a·guay ['pærəgwaɪ] Para'guay *n.*
Par·is ['pærɪs] Pa'ris *n.*
Pat [pæt] *abbr. für* ***Patricia, Patrick.***
Pa·tience ['peɪʃəns] *f.*
Pa·tri·cia [pə'trɪʃə] Pa'trizia *f.*
Pat·rick ['pætrɪk] Pa'trizius *m.*
Paul [pɔ:l] Paul *m.*
Pau·la ['pɔ:lə] Paula *f.*
Pau·line [pɔ:'li:n; 'pɔ:li:n] Pau'line *f.*
Pearl [pɜ:l] *f.*
Pearl Har·bor [,pɜ:l'hɑ:bə] *Hafenstadt auf Hawaii (USA).*
Pears [pɪəz; peəz] *Familienname.*
Pear·sall ['pɪəsɔ:l; -səl] *Familienname.*
Pear·son ['pɪəsn] *Familienname.*
Peart [pɪət] *Familienname.*
Pee·bles(shire) ['pi:blz(ʃə)] *schottische Grafschaft (bis 1975).*
Peg(gy) ['peg(ɪ)] *abbr. für* ***Margaret.***
Pe·king [,pi:'kɪŋ] Peking *n.*
Pem·broke(shire) ['pembrʊk(ʃə)] *walisische Grafschaft (bis 1974).*
Pe·nel·o·pe [pɪ'neləpɪ] Pe'nelope *f.*
Penn·syl·va·nia [,pensɪl'veɪnjə] *Staat der USA.*
Pen·ny ['penɪ] *abbr. für* ***Penelope.***
Pen·zance [pen'zæns] *westlichste Stadt Englands, in Cornwall.*
Pepys [pi:ps] *Verfasser berühmter Tagebücher.*
Per·cy ['pɜ:sɪ] *m.*
Per·sia ['pɜ:ʃə; *Am.* 'pɜrʒə] Persien *n.*
Perth [pɜ:θ] *Hauptstadt von West-Australien; Stadt in Tayside (Schottland); siehe* ***Perthshire.***
Perth·shire ['pɜ:θʃə] *schottische Grafschaft (bis 1975).*
Pe·ru [pə'ru:] Pe'ru *n.*
Pete [pi:t] *abbr. für* ***Peter.***
Pe·ter ['pi:tə] Peter *m*, Petrus *m.*
Pe·ter·bor·ough ['pi:təbrə] *Stadt in Cambridgeshire (England).*
Phil·a·del·phia [,fɪlə'delfjə] *Stadt in Pennsylvania (USA).*
Phil·ip ['fɪlɪp] Philipp *m.*
Phi·lip·pa ['fɪlɪpə] Phi'lippa *f.*
Phil·ip·pines ['fɪlɪpi:nz] *pl. die* Philip'pinen *pl.*
Phoe·be ['fi:bɪ] Phöbe *f.*
Phoe·nix ['fi:nɪks] *Hauptstadt von Arizona (USA).*
Phyl·lis ['fɪlɪs] Phyllis *f.*
Pic·ca·dil·ly [pɪkə'dɪlɪ] *Straße in London.*
Pied·mont ['pi:dmənt] Pie'mont *n.*
Pierce [pɪəs] *Familienname; Vorname m.*
Pierre [pɪə; *Am.* pɪər] *Hauptstadt von South Dakota (USA).*
Pin·ter ['pɪntə] *englischer Dramatiker.*
Pitts·burgh ['pɪtsbɜ:g] *Stadt in Pennsylvania (USA).*
Plan·tag·e·net [plæn'tædʒənɪt] *englisches Herrschergeschlecht.*
Pla·to ['pleɪtəʊ] Plato *m.*
Plym·outh ['plɪməθ] *Hafenstadt in Südengland.*
Poe [pəʊ] *amer. Dichter u. Schriftsteller.*
Po·land ['pəʊlənd] Polen *n.*
Pol·ly ['pɒlɪ] *Koseform von* ***Mary.***
Pol·y·ne·sia [,pɒlɪ'ni:zjə; *Am.* -'ni:ʒə] Poly'nesien *n.*
Pom·er·a·nia [,pɒmə'reɪnjə] Pommern *n.*
Pope [pəʊp] *englischer Dichter.*
Port-au-Prince [,pɔ:təʊ'prɪns] *Hauptstadt von Haiti.*
Port E·liz·a·beth [,pɔ:tɪ'lɪzəbəθ] *Hafenstadt in Südafrika.*
Port·land ['pɔ:tlənd] *Hafenstadt in Maine (USA); Stadt in Oregon (USA).*
Ports·mouth ['pɔ:tsməθ] *Hafenstadt in Südengland; Hafenstadt in Virginia (USA).*
Por·tu·gal ['pɔ:tjʊgl; 'pɔ:tʃʊgl] Portugal *n.*
Po·to·mac [pə'təʊmək] *Fluß in USA.*
Pound [paʊnd] *amer.Dichter.*
Pow·ell ['pəʊəl; 'paʊəl] *Familienname.*
Pow·lett [pɔ:lɪt] *Familienname.*
Pow·ys ['pəʊɪs; 'paʊɪs] *walisische Grafschaft; Familienname.*
Prague [prɑ:g] Prag *n.*
Pre·to·ria [prɪ'tɔ:rɪə] *Hauptstadt von Südafrika.*
Priest·ley ['pri:stlɪ] *englischer Autor.*
Prince Ed·ward Is·land [prɪns,edwəd-'aɪlənd] *Provinz in Kanada.*
Prince·ton ['prɪnstən] *Universitätsstadt in New Jersey (USA).*
Pris·cil·la [prɪ'sɪlə] Pris'cilla *f.*
Prit·chard ['prɪtʃəd] *Familienname.*
Prov·i·dence ['prɒvɪdəns] *Hauptstadt von Rhode Island (USA).*
Pru·dence ['pru:dns] Pru'dentia *f.*
Prus·sia ['prʌʃə] Preußen *n.*
Puer·to Ri·co [,pwɜ:təʊ'ri:kəʊ] Puerto Rico *n.*
Pugh [pju:] *Familienname.*
Pul·itz·er ['pʊlɪtsə; 'pju:-] *amer. Journalist, Stifter des Pulitzerpreises.*
Pun·jab [,pʌn'dʒɑ:b] Pan'dschab *n.*
Pur·cell ['pɜ:sl] *englischer Komponist.*
Pyr·e·nees [,pɪrɪ'ni:z; *Am.* 'pɪrəni:z] *pl. die* Pyre'näen *pl.*

Qua·tar [kæ'tɑ:; *Am.* 'kɑ:tər] Quatar *n.*
Que·bec [kwɪ'bek] *Provinz u. Stadt in Kanada.*
Queen·ie ['kwi:nɪ] *f.*
Queens [kwi:nz] *Stadtbezirk von New York (USA).*
Queens·land ['kwi:nzlənd] *Bundesstaat Australiens.*
Quen·tin ['kwentɪn; *Am.* -tn] Quin'tin(us) *m.*
Qui·nault ['kwɪnlt] *Familienname.*
Quin·c(e)y ['kwɪnsɪ] *Familienname.*

Ra·chel ['reɪtʃəl] Ra(c)hel *f.*
Rad·nor(shire) ['rædnə(ʃə)] *walisische Grafschaft (bis 1974).*
Rae [reɪ] *Familienname; Vorname m, f.*
Ra·leigh ['rɔ:lɪ; 'rɑ:lɪ] *englischer Seefahrer; Hauptstadt von North Carolina (USA).*
Ralph [reɪf; rælf] Ralf *m.*
Ran·dolph ['rændɒlf] *m.*
Ran·dy ['rændɪ] *abbr. für* ***Randolph.***
Rat·is·bon ['rætɪzbɒn] Regensburg *n.*
Ra·wal·pin·di [,rɑ:wəl'pɪndɪ] *Stadt in Pakistan.*
Ray [reɪ] *m, f.*
Ray·mond ['reɪmənd] Raimund *m.*
Read·ing ['redɪŋ] *Stadt in Südengland.*
Rea·gan ['reɪgən] *40. Präsident der USA.*
Re·bec·ca [rɪ'bekə] Re'bekka *f.*
Red·bridge ['redbrɪdʒ] *Stadtbezirk von Groß-London.*
Reg [redʒ] *abbr. für* ***Reginald.***
Re·gi·na [rɪ'dʒaɪnə] Re'gina *f*, Re'gine *f; Hauptstadt von Saskatchewan (Kanada).*
Reg·i·nald ['redʒɪnld] Re(g)inald *m.*
Reid [ri:d] *Familienname.*
Ren·frew(shire) ['renfru:(ʃə)] *schottische Grafschaft (bis 1975).*
Rhine [raɪn] Rhein *m.*
Rhode Is·land [,rəʊd'aɪlənd] *Staat der USA.*
Rhodes [rəʊdz] *britisch-südafrikanischer Staatsmann;* Rhodos *n.*
Rho·de·sia [rəʊ'di:zjə; *Am.* -ʒə] Rho'desien *n (heutiger Name:* ***Zimbabwe).***
Rhon·dda ['rɒndə] *Stadt in Mid Glamorgan (Wales).*
Rich·ard ['rɪtʃəd] Richard *m.*
Rich·ard·son ['rɪtʃədsn] *englischer Autor.*
Rich·mond ['rɪtʃmənd] *Hauptstadt von Virginia (USA); Stadtbezirk von New York (USA), heute üblicherweise* ***Staten Island*** *genannt; siehe* ***Richmond-upon--Thames.***
Rich·mond-up·on-Thames ['rɪtʃmənd-ə,pɒn'temz] *Stadtbezirk von Groß-London.*
Ri·ta ['ri:tə] Rita *f.*
Ro·a·noke [,rəʊə'nəʊk] *Fluß in Virginia u. North Carolina (USA); Stadt in Virginia (USA);* ~ ***Island*** *Insel vor der Küste von North Carolina (USA).*
Rob·ert ['rɒbət] Robert *m.*
Rob·in ['rɒbɪn] *abbr. für* ***Robert.***
Rob·in Hood [,rɒbɪn'hʊd] *legendärer englischer Geächteter, Bandenführer und Wohltäter der Armen zur Zeit Richards I.*
Roch·es·ter ['rɒtʃɪstə] *Stadt im Staat New York (USA); Stadt in Kent (England).*
Rock·e·fel·ler ['rɒkɪfelə] *amer. Industrieller.*
Rock·y Moun·tains [,rɒkɪ'maʊntɪnz] *pl. Gebirge in USA.*
Rod [rɒd] *abbr. für* ***Rodney.***
Rod·ney ['rɒdnɪ] *m.*
Rog·er ['rɒdʒə] Rüdiger *m*, Roger *m.*
Ro·ma·nia [ru:'meɪnjə; rʊ-; *Am.* rəʊ-] Ru'mänien *n.*
Rome [rəʊm] Rom *n.*
Ro·me·o ['rəʊmɪəʊ] *Bühnenfigur bei Shakespeare.*
Ron [rɒn] *abbr. für* ***Ronald.***
Ron·ald ['rɒnld] Ronald *m.*
Roo·se·velt ['rəʊzəvelt] *Name zweier Präsidenten der USA.*
Ros·a·lie ['rəʊzəlɪ; 'rɒz-] Ro'salia *f*, Ro'salie *f.*
Ros·a·lind ['rɒzəlɪnd] Rosa'linde *f.*
Ros·com·mon [rɒs'kɒmən] *Grafschaft in der Provinz Connacht (Irland); Hauptstadt dieser Grafschaft.*
Rose [rəʊz] Rosa *f.*
Rose·mar·y ['rəʊzmərɪ; *Am.* -merɪ] 'Rosema,rie *f.*
Ross and Cro·mar·ty [,rɒsən'krɒmətɪ] *schottische Grafschaft (bis 1975).*
Rouse [raʊs; ru:s] *Familienname.*
Routh [raʊθ] *Familienname.*
Rox·burg(shire) ['rɒksbərə(ʃə)] *schottische Grafschaft (bis 1975).*
Roy [rɔɪ] *m.*
Ru·dolf, Ru·dolph ['ru:dɒlf] Rudolf *m*, Rudolph *m.*
Rud·yard ['rʌdjəd] *m.*
Rug·by ['rʌgbɪ] *berühmte Public School.*
Ru·pert ['ru:pət] Rupert *m.*
Rus·sell ['rʌsl] *englischer Philosoph.*
Rus·sia ['rʌʃə] Rußland *n.*
Ruth [ru:θ] Ruth *f.*
Rut·land(shire) ['rʌtlənd(ʃə)] *englische Grafschaft (bis 1974).*
Rwan·da [rʊ'ændə] Ru'anda *n.*

Sac·ra·men·to [,sækrə'mentəʊ] *Hauptstadt von Kalifornien (USA).*

Sa·ha·ra [sə'hɑːrə; *Am. a.* sə'hærə; sə'heərə] Sa'hara *f.*
Sa·lem ['seɪləm] *Hauptstadt von Oregon (USA).*
Salis·bur·y ['sɔːlzbərɪ] *früherer Name von* **Harare**; *Stadt in Südengland.*
Sal·ly ['sælɪ] *abbr. für* **Sara(h).**
Salt Lake Cit·y [ˌsɔːltleɪk'sɪtɪ] *Hauptstadt von Utah (USA).*
Sam [sæm] *abbr. für* **Samuel.**
Sa·man·tha [sə'mænθə] *f.*
Sa·moa [sə'məʊə] Sa'moa *n (Inselgruppe im Pazifik);* **Western** ~ West-Sa'moa *n (unabhängiger Inselstaat).*
Sam·son ['sæmsn] Samson *m*, Simson *m.*
Sam·u·el ['sæmjʊəl] Samuel *m.*
San An·to·nio [ˌsænæn'təʊnɪəʊ] *Stadt in Texas (USA).*
San Ber·nar·di·no [sænˌbɜːnə'diːnəʊ] *Stadt in Kalifornien (USA).*
Sand·hurst ['sændhɜːst] *Ort in Berkshire (England) mit berühmter Militärakademie.*
San Die·go [ˌsændɪ'eɪgəʊ] *Hafenstadt u. Flottenstützpunkt in Kalifornien (USA).*
San·dra ['sændrə] *abbr. für* **Alexandra.**
San·dy ['sændɪ] *abbr. für* **Alexander, Alexandra.**
San Fran·cis·co [ˌsænfrən'sɪskəʊ] San Fran'zisko *n.*
San Ma·ri·no [ˌsænmə'riːnəʊ] San Ma'rino *n.*
San·ta Fe [ˌsæntə'feɪ] *Hauptstadt von New Mexico (USA).*
Sar·a(h) ['seərə] Sara *f.*
Sar·di·nia [sɑː'dɪnjə] Sar'dinien *n.*
Sas·katch·e·wan [səs'kætʃɪwən] *Provinz in Kanada.*
Sas·ka·toon [ˌsæskə'tuːn] *Stadt in Saskatchewan (Kanada).*
Sau·di A·ra·bi·a [ˌsaʊdɪə'reɪbɪə] Saudi-A'rabien *n.*
Sa·voy [sə'vɔɪ] Sa'voyen *n.*
Saw·yer ['sɔːjə] *Familienname.*
Sax·o·ny ['sæksnɪ] Sachsen *n.*
Scan·di·na·vi·a [ˌskændɪ'neɪvjə] Skandi'navien *n.*
Sche·nec·ta·dy [skɪ'nektədɪ] *Stadt im Staat New York (USA).*
Scot·land ['skɒtlənd] Schottland *n.*
Scott [skɒt] *schottischer Autor; englischer Polarforscher.*
Seam·us ['ʃeɪməs] *siehe* **James.**
Sean [ʃɔːn] *siehe* **John.**
Searle [sɜːl] *Familienname.*
Se·at·tle [sɪ'ætl] *Hafenstadt im Staat Washington (USA).*
Sedg·wick ['sedʒwɪk] *Familienname.*
Sel·kirk(shire) ['selkɜːk(ʃə)] *schottische Grafschaft (bis 1975).*
Sen·e·gal [ˌsenɪ'gɔːl] Senegal *n.*
Seoul [səʊl] Se'oul *n.*
Sev·ern ['sevən] *Fluß in Wales u. West-England.*
Sew·ell ['sjuːəl; *Am.* 'suːəl] *Familienname.*
Sey·chelles [seɪ'ʃelz] *pl. die* Sey'chellen(-Inseln) *pl.*
Sey·mour ['siːmə; *schottisch* 'seɪmɔː] *m.*
Shake·speare ['ʃeɪkˌspɪə] *englischer Dichter und Dramatiker.*
Shar·jah ['ʃɑːdʒə] Schardscha *n (Mitglied der Vereinigten Arabischen Emirate).*
Shaw [ʃɔː] *irischer Dramatiker.*
Shef·field ['ʃefiːld] *Industriestadt in Mittelengland.*
Shei·la ['ʃiːlə] *siehe* **Celia.**
Shel·ley ['ʃelɪ] *englischer Dichter.*
Sher·lock ['ʃɜːlɒk] *m.*
Shet·land ['ʃetlənd] *insulare Verwaltungsregion Schottlands;* ~ **Is·lands** [ˌʃetlənd'aɪləndz] *pl. die* Shetlandinseln *pl.*
Shir·ley ['ʃɜːlɪ] *f.*
Shrop·shire ['ʃrɒpʃə] *englische Grafschaft.*
Shy·lock ['ʃaɪlɒk] *Bühnenfigur bei Shakespeare.*
Si·am [ˌsaɪ'æm; 'saɪæm] Siam *n (früherer Name Thailands).*
Si·be·ri·a [saɪ'bɪərɪə] Si'birien *n.*
Sib·yl ['sɪbɪl] Si'bylle *f.*
Sic·i·ly ['sɪsɪlɪ] Si'zilien *n.*
Sid [sɪd] *abbr. für* **Sidney** *(Vorname).*
Sid·ney ['sɪdnɪ] *Familienname; Vorname m,f.*
Si·er·ra Le·one [sɪˌerəlɪ'əʊn] Sierra Le'one *n.*
Sik·kim ['sɪkɪm] Sikkim *n.*
Si·le·sia [saɪ'liːzjə] Schlesien *n.*
Sil·vi·a ['sɪlvɪə] Silvia *f.*
Si·mon ['saɪmən] Simon *m.*
Si·nai (Pen·in·su·la) ['saɪnɪaɪ (ˌsaɪnɪaɪpɪ'nɪnsjʊlə)] Sinai(halbinsel *f*) *n.*
Sin·clair ['sɪŋkleə] *amer. Autor; Vorname m.*
Sin·ga·pore [ˌsɪŋgə'pɔː] Singapur *n.*
Sing Sing ['sɪŋsɪŋ] *Staatsgefängnis von New York (USA).*
Sli·go ['slaɪgəʊ] *Grafschaft in der Provinz Connacht (Irland); Hauptstadt dieser Grafschaft.*
Sloan [sləʊn] *amer. Maler.*
Slough [slaʊ] *Stadt in Berkshire (England).*
Snow·don ['snəʊdn] *Berg in Wales.*
Soc·ra·tes ['sɒkrətiːz] Sokrates *m.*
Sol·o·mon ['sɒləmən] Salomo *m.*
So·ma·lia [səʊ'mɑːlɪə] So'malia *n.*
So·mers ['sʌməz] *Familienname.*
Som·er·set(shire) ['sʌməsɪt(ʃə)] *englische Grafschaft.*
So·nia ['sɒnɪə] Sonja *f.*
So·phi·a [səʊ'faɪə] So'phia *f*, So'fia *f.*
So·phie, So·phy ['səʊfɪ] So'phie *f*, So'fie *f.*
Soph·o·cles ['sɒfəkliːs] Sophokles *m.*
South Af·ri·ca [ˌsaʊθ'æfrɪkə] Süd'afrika *n.*
South·amp·ton [saʊθ'æmptən] *Hafenstadt in Südengland.*
South Aus·tra·lia [ˌsaʊθɒ'streɪljə] 'Süd-auˌstralien *n (Bundesstaat Australiens).*
South Car·o·li·na [ˌsaʊθkærə'laɪnə] *Staat der USA.*
South Da·ko·ta [ˌsaʊθdə'kəʊtə] *Staat der USA.*
South Gla·mor·gan [ˌsaʊθglə'mɔːgən] *walisische Grafschaft.*
South·ey ['saʊðɪ; 'sʌðɪ] *englischer Dichter.*
South·wark ['sʌðək; 'saʊθwək] *Stadtbezirk von Groß-London.*
South York·shire [ˌsaʊθ'jɔːkʃə] *Stadtgrafschaft in Nordengland.*
So·viet Un·ion [ˌsəʊvɪət'juːnjən] *hist. die* So'wjetuniˌon *f.*
Spain [speɪn] Spanien *n.*
Spring·field ['sprɪŋfiːld] *Hauptstadt von Illinois (USA); Stadt in Massachusetts (USA); Stadt in Missouri (USA).*
Sri Lan·ka [ˌsriː'læŋkə] Sri Lanka *n.*
Staf·ford(shire) ['stæfəd(ʃə)] *englische Grafschaft.*
Stan [stæn] *abbr. für* **Stanley** *(Vorname).*
Stan·ley ['stænlɪ] *englischer Afrika-Forscher; Vorname m.*
Stat·en Is·land [ˌstætn'aɪlənd] *Insel an der Mündung des Hudson River in New York; Stadtbezirk von New York (USA).*
Stein·beck ['staɪnbek] *amer. Autor.*
Stel·la ['stelə] Stella *f.*
Steph·a·nie ['stefənɪ] Stephanie *f*, Stefanie *f.*
Ste·phen ['stiːvn] Stephan *m*, Stefan *m.*
Ste·phen·son ['stiːvnsn] *englischer Erfinder.*
Steu·ben ['stjuːbən; 'stuː-, 'ʃtɔɪ-] *amer. General preußischer Herkunft im amer. Unabhängigkeitskrieg.*
Steve [stiːv] *abbr. für* **Stephen, Steven.**
Ste·ven ['stiːvn] *siehe* **Stephen.**
Ste·ven·son ['stiːvnsn] *englischer Autor.*
Stew·art [stjʊət; 'stjuːət; *Am.* 'stuːərt] *Familienname; Vorname m.*
Stir·lin(shire) ['stɜːlɪŋ(ʃə)] *schottische Grafschaft (bis 1975).*
St. John [snt'dʒɒn] *Hafenstadt an der Mündung des gleichnamigen Flusses in New Brunswick (Kanada);* ['sɪndʒən] *Familienname.*
St. John's [snt'dʒɒnz] *Hauptstadt von Neufundland (Kanada).*
St. Law·rence [snt'lɔːrəns] Sankt-'Lorenz-Strom *m.*
St. Louis [snt'lʊɪs; *Am.* ˌseɪnt'luːɪs] *Industriestadt in Missouri (USA).*
Stone·henge [ˌstəʊn'hendʒ] *prähistorisches megalithisches Bauwerk bei Salisbury in Wiltshire (England).*
St. Pan·cras [snt'pæŋkrəs] *Stadtteil von London.*
St. Paul [snt'pɔːl; *Am.* ˌseɪnt-] *Hauptstadt von Minnesota (USA).*
Stra·chey ['streɪtʃɪ] *englischer Biograph.*
Strat·ford on A·von [ˌstrætfədɒn'eɪvn] *Stadt in Mittelengland.*
Strath·clyde [stræθ'klaɪd] *Verwaltungsregion in Schottland.*
Stu·art [stjʊət; 'stjuːət; *Am.* 'stuːərt] *schottisch-englisches Herrschergeschlecht; Vorname m.*
Styr·i·a ['stɪrɪə] *die* Steiermark.
Su·dan [suː'dɑːn] *der* Su'dan *m.*
Sud·bur·y ['sʌdbərɪ] *Stadt in Ontario (Kanada); Ort in Suffolk (England).*
Sue [sjuː; suː] *abbr. für* **Susan.**
Su·ez ['sʊɪz; *Am.* suː'ez; 'suːez] Suez *n.*
Suf·folk ['sʌfək] *englische Grafschaft.*
Sul·li·van ['sʌlɪvən] *Familienname.*
Su·ri·nam [ˌsʊərɪ'næm] Suri'nam *n.*
Su·ri·na·me [ˌsʊərɪ'nɑːmə] Suri'nam *n.*
Sur·rey ['sʌrɪ] *englische Grafschaft.*
Su·san ['suːzn] Su'sanne *f.*
Su·sie ['suːzɪ] Susi *f.*
Sus·que·han·na [ˌsʌskwɪ'hænə] *Fluß im Osten der USA.*
Sus·sex ['sʌsɪks] *englische Grafschaft.*
Suth·er·land ['sʌðələnd] *schottische Grafschaft (bis 1975).*
Sut·ton ['sʌtn] *Stadtbezirk von Groß-London.*
Su·zanne [suː'zæn] Su'sanne *f*, Su'sanna *f.*
Swan·sea ['swɒnzɪ] *Hafenstadt in Wales.*
Swa·zi·land ['swɑːzɪlænd] Swasiland *n.*
Swe·den ['swiːdn] Schweden *n.*
Swift [swɪft] *irischer Autor.*
Swit·zer·land ['swɪtsələnd] die Schweiz.
Syd·ney ['sɪdnɪ] *Hauptstadt von New South Wales (Australien) und größte Stadt Australiens.*
Syl·vi·a ['sɪlvɪə] Silvia *f*, Sylvia *f.*
Synge [sɪŋ] *irischer Dichter und Dramatiker.*
Syr·a·cuse ['sɪrəkjuːs] *Stadt im Staat*

New York (*USA*); [*Brit.* 'saɪərəkjuːz] Syrakus *n* (*Stadt auf Sizilien*).
Syr·ia ['sɪrɪə] Syrien *n*.

Ta·hi·ti [tɑː'hiːtɪ; tə-] Ta'hiti *n*.
Tai·wan [ˌtaɪ'wɑːn] Taiwan *n*.
Tal·la·has·see [ˌtælə'hæsɪ] *Hauptstadt von Florida* (*USA*).
Tam·pa ['tæmpə] *Stadt in Florida* (*USA*).
Tan·gier [tæn'dʒɪə] Tanger *n*.
Tan·za·nia [ˌtænzə'nɪə] Tansa'nia *n*.
Tas·ma·nia [tæz'meɪnjə] Tas'manien *n*.
Tay·lor ['teɪlə] *Familienname*.
Tay·side ['teɪsaɪd] *Verwaltungsregion in Schottland*.
Ted(dy) ['ted(ɪ)] *abbr. für* ***Edward, Theodore.***
Tees·side ['tiːzsaɪd] *frühere Bezeichnung der Industrieregion um Middlesbrough* (*Nordengland*), *heute zu* ***Cleveland*** *gehörig*.
Teign·mouth ['tɪnməθ] *Stadt in Devon* (*England*).
Ten·e·rife, *früher* **Ten·e·riffe** [ˌtenə'riːf] Tene'riffa *n*.
Ten·nes·see [ˌtenə'siː] *Staat der USA*; *Fluß in USA*.
Ten·ny·son ['tenɪsn] *englischer Dichter*.
Ter·ence ['terəns] *m*.
Te·re·sa [tə'riːzə] Te'resa *f*, Te'rese *f*.
Ter·ry ['terɪ] *abbr. für* ***Terence, T(h)eresa.***
Tex·as ['teksəs] *Staat der USA*.
Thack·er·ay ['θækərɪ] *englischer Romanschriftsteller*.
Thai·land ['taɪlænd] Thailand *n*.
Thames [temz] Themse *f* (*Fluß in Südengland*).
That·cher ['θætʃə] *englische Premierministerin*.
The·a [θɪə; 'θiːə] Thea *f*.
The·o ['θiːəʊ; 'θɪəʊ] Theo *m*.
The·o·bald ['θɪəʊbɔːld] Theobald *m*.
The·o·dore ['θɪədɔː] Theodor *m*.
The·re·sa [tɪ'riːzə] The'resa *f*, The'rese *f*.
Tho·mas ['tɒməs] Thomas *m*.
Tho·reau ['θɔːrəʊ; *Am.* θə'rəʊ] *amer. Schriftsteller, Philosoph und Sozialkritiker*.
Thu·rin·gia [θjʊə'rɪndʒɪə] Thüringen *n*.
Thu·ron [tʊ'rɒn] *Familienname*.
Ti·bet [tɪ'bet] Tibet *n*.
Ti·gris ['taɪgrɪs] Tigris *m*.
Tim [tɪm] *abbr. für* ***Timothy.***
Tim·o·thy ['tɪməθɪ] Ti'motheus *m*.
Ti·na ['tiːnə] *abbr. für* ***Christina, Christine.***
Tin·dale ['tɪndeɪl] *Familienname*.
Tip·per·ar·y [ˌtɪpə'reərɪ] *Grafschaft in der Provinz Munster* (*Irland*).
To·bi·as [tə'baɪəs] To'bias *m*.
To·by ['təʊbɪ] *abbr. für* ***Tobias.***
To·go ['təʊgəʊ] Togo *n*.
To·kyo ['təʊkjəʊ] Tokio *n*.
To·le·do [tə'liːdəʊ] *Stadt in Ohio* (*USA*); [*Brit.* tɒ'leɪdəʊ] *Stadt in Zentralspanien*.
Tol·kien ['tɒlkiːn] *englischer Schriftsteller und Philologe*.
Tom(my) ['tɒm(ɪ)] *abbr. für* ***Thomas.***
Ton·ga ['tɒŋə] Tonga *n* (*Inselgruppe u. Königreich im südwestlichen Pazifik*).
To·ny ['təʊnɪ] Toni *m*.
To·pe·ka [təʊ'piːkə] *Hauptstadt von Kansas* (*USA*).
Tor·bay [ˌtɔː'beɪ] *Stadt in Devon* (*England*); *a.* ***Tor Bay*** *Bucht des Ärmelkanals an der Küste von Devon*.
To·ron·to [tə'rɒntəʊ] *Stadt in Kanada*.
Tor·quay [ˌtɔː'kiː] *Teilstadt von* ***Torbay*** *in Devon* (*England*).
Tot·ten·ham ['tɒtnəm] *Stadtteil von Groß-London*.
Tour·neur ['tɜːnə] *Familienname*.
Tow·er Ham·lets ['taʊəˌhæmlɪts] *Stadtbezirk von Groß-London*.
Toyn·bee ['tɔɪnbɪ] *englischer Historiker*.
Tra·cy ['treɪsɪ] *amer. Filmschauspieler*; *Vorname f*, (*seltener*) *m*.
Tra·fal·gar [trə'fælgə]: ***Cape*** ~ Kap *n* Tra'falgar (*an der Südwestküste Spaniens*); ~ ***Square*** *Platz in London*.
Trans·vaal ['trænzvɑːl] Trans'vaal *n*.
Trans·syl·va·nia ˌtrænsɪl'veɪnjə] Sieben'bürgen *n*.
Trent [trent] *Fluß in Mittelengland*.
Tren·ton [trentən] *Hauptstadt von New Jersey* (*USA*).
Tre·vel·yan [trɪ'veljən; -'vɪl-] *Name zweier englischer Historiker*.
Treves [triːvz] Trier *n*.
Trev·or ['trevə] *m*.
Tri·e·ste [triː'est] Tri'est *n*.
Trin·i·dad and To·ba·go [ˌtrɪnɪdædntəʊ'beɪgəʊ] Trinidad und To'bago *n*.
Trol·lope ['trɒləp] *englischer Romanschriftsteller*.
Troy [trɔɪ] Troja *n* (*antike Stadt in Kleinasien am Eingang der Dardanellen*); *Name mehrerer Sädte in USA* (*im Staat New York*; *in Michigan*; *in Ohio*).
Tru·man ['truːmən] *33. Präsident der USA*.
Tuc·son [tuː'sɒn; 'tuːsɒn] *Stadt in Arizona* (*USA*).
Tu·dor ['tjuːdə] *englisches Herrschergeschlecht*.
Tu·ni·sia [tjuː'nɪzɪə; *Am.* tuː'niːʒə; -'nɪʒə] Tu'nesien *n*.
Tur·key ['tɜːkɪ] die Tür'kei.
Tur·ner ['tɜːnə] *englischer Landschaftsmaler*.
Tus·ca·ny ['tʌskənɪ] die Tos'kana.
Twain [tweɪn] *amer. Autor*.
Twick·en·ham ['twɪknəm] *Stadtteil von Groß-London*.
Tyn·dale ['tɪndl] *englischer Bibelübersetzer*.
Tyne and Wear [ˌtaɪnənd'wɪə] *Stadtgrafschaft in Nordengland*.
Ty·rol [tɪ'rəʊl] Ti'rol *n*.
Ty·rone [tɪ'rəʊn] *nordirische Grafschaft*.
U·gan·da [juː'gændə] U'ganda *n*.
U·ist ['juːɪst: ***North*** ~, ***South*** ~ *zwei Inseln der Äußeren Hebriden* (*Schottland*).
U·kraine ['juːkreɪn] *die* Ukra'ine.
Ul·ster ['ʌlstə] *Provinz im Norden Irlands, seit 1921 zweigeteilt. 3 Grafschaften gehören heute zur Republik Irland, die restlichen 6 bilden das heutige Nordirland, Teil des Vereinigten Königreichs von Großbritannien u. Nordirland*.
U·lys·ses [juː'lɪsiːz] *m*.
Un·ion of So·viet So·cial·ist Re·pub·lics [ˌjuːnjənəfˌsəʊvɪətˌsəʊʃəlɪstrɪ'pʌblɪks] *hist. die* Uni'on der Sozia'listischen So'wjetrepuˌbliken.
U·nit·ed Ar·ab E·mir·ates [juː'naɪtɪdˌærəbe'mɪrəts] *pl. die* Vereinigten A'rabischen Emi'rate *pl*.
U·nit·ed King·dom [juːˌnaɪtɪd'kɪŋdəm] *das* Vereinigte Königreich (*Großbritannien und Nordirland*).
U·nit·ed States of A·mer·i·ca [juːˌnaɪtɪdsteɪtsəvə'merɪkə] *die* Vereinigten Staaten von A'merika *pl*.
Up·dike ['ʌpdaɪk] *amer. Schriftsteller*.
Up·per Vol·ta [ˌʌpə'vɒltə] Ober'volta *n* (*ehemalige Bezeichnung von* ***Burkina Faso***).
U·ri·ah [ˌjʊə'raɪə] U'ria(s) *m*, Uriel *m*.
Ur·quhart ['ɜːkət] *schottischer Schriftsteller und Übersetzer*.
Ur·su·la ['ɜːsjʊlə] Ursula *f*.
U·ru·guay [jʊərʊgwaɪ; 'ʊrə-] Uruguay *n*.
U·tah ['juːtɑː; -tɔː] *Staat der USA*.
Ut·tox·e·ter [juː'tɒksɪtə; ʌ'tɒksɪtə] *Ort in Staffordshire* (*England*).

Val·en·tine ['væləntaɪn] Valentin *m*; Valen'tine *f*.
Va(l)·let·ta [və'letə] *Hauptstadt von Malta*.
Van·brugh ['vænbrə; væn'bruː] *englischer Dramatiker und Baumeister*.
Van·cou·ver [væn'kuːvə] *Hafenstadt in Kanada*.
Van·der·bilt ['vændəbɪlt] *amer. Finanzier*.
Va·nes·sa [və'nesə] *f*.
Vat·i·can ['vætɪkən] *der* Vati'kan; ~ **Cit·y** [ˌvætɪkən'sɪtɪ] Vati'kanstadt *f*.
Vaughan [vɔːn] *Familienname*; ~ **Williams** [ˌvɔːn'wɪljəmz] *englischer Komponist*.
Vaux [vɔːz; vɒks; vɔːks; vəʊks] *Familienname*; **de** ~ [dɪ'vəʊ] *Familienname*.
Vaux·hall [ˌvɒks'hɔːl] *Stadtteil von London*.
Ven·e·zu·e·la [ˌvene'zweɪlə] Venezu'ela *n*.
Ven·ice ['venɪs] Ve'nedig *n*.
Ve·ra ['vɪərə] Vera *f*.
Ver·gil ['vɜːdʒɪl] *siehe* ***Virgil.***
Ver·mont [vɜː'mɒnt] *Staat der USA*.
Ver·ner ['vɜːnə] *Familienname*.
Ver·non ['vɜːnən] *m*.
Ve·ron·i·ca [vɪ'rɒnɪkə; və-] Ve'ronika *f*.
Vick·y ['vɪkɪ] *abbr. für* ***Victoria.***
Vic·tor ['vɪktə] Viktor *m*.
Vic·to·ri·a [vɪk'tɔːrɪə] Vik'toria *f*; *Bundesstaat Australiens*; *Hauptstadt von British Columbia* (*Kanada*); *Hauptstadt der brit. Kronkolonie Hongkong*.
Vi·en·na [vɪ'enə] Wien *n*.
Viet·nam, Viet Nam [ˌvjet'næm] Viet'nam *n*.
Vi·o·la ['vaɪələ; 'vɪəʊlə] Vi'ola *f*.
Vi·o·let ['vaɪələt] Vio'letta *f*, Vio'lette *f*.
Vir·gil ['vɜːdʒɪl] Ver'gil *m* (*römischer Dichter*).
Vir·gin·ia [və'dʒɪnjə] *Staat der USA*; *Vorname f*.
Vis·tu·la ['vɪstjʊlə] Weichsel *f* (*Fluß*).
Viv·i·an ['vɪvɪən] *m*, (*seltener*) *f*.
Viv·i·en ['vɪvɪən] *f*.
Viv·i·enne ['vɪvɪən; vɪvɪ'en] *f*.
Vol·ga ['vɒlgə] Wolga *f*.
Vosges [vəʊʒ] *pl. die* Vo'gesen *pl*.

Wa·bash ['wɔːbæʃ] *Nebenfluß des Ohio in Indiana u. Illinois* (*USA*).
Wad·dell [wɒ'del; 'wɒdl] *Familienname*.
Wad·ham ['wɒdəm] *Familienname*.
Wales [weɪlz] Wales *n*.
Wal·lace ['wɒlɪs] *englischer Autor*.
Wal·la·sey ['wɒləsɪ] *Stadt in Merseyside* (*England*).
Wal·pole ['wɔːlpəʊl] *Name zweier englischer Schriftsteller*.
Walter ['wɔːltə] Walter *m*.
Wal·tham For·est [ˌwɔːlθəm'fɒrɪst] *Stadtbezirk von Groß-London*.
Wands·worth ['wɒndzwəθ] *Stadtbezirk von Groß-London*.
War·hol ['wɔːhɔːl; 'wɔːhəʊl] *amer. Pop-Art-Künstler u. Filmregisseur*.

War·saw ['wɔːsɔː] Warschau *n.*
War·wick(shire) ['wɒrɪk(ʃə)] *englische Grafschaft.*
Wash·ing·ton ['wɒʃɪŋtən] *1. Präsident der USA; Staat der USA; a.* ~ **DC** *Bundeshauptstadt der USA.*
Wa·ter·ford ['wɔːtəfəd] *Grafschaft in der Provinz Munster (Irland); Hauptstadt dieser Grafschaft.*
Wa·ter·loo [ˌwɔːtə'luː] *Ort in Belgien.*
Wat·son ['wɒtsn] *Familienname.*
Watt [wɒt] *schottischer Erfinder.*
Waugh [wɔː] *englischer Romanschriftsteller.*
Wayne [weɪn] *amer. Filmschauspieler.*
Weald [wiːld]: ***the*** ~ *Landschaft im südöstlichen England. Früher ausgedehntes Waldgebiet.*
Web·ster ['webstə] *amer. Lexikograph.*
Wedg·wood ['wedʒwʊd] *englischer Keramiker.*
Wel·ling·ton ['welɪŋtən] *brit. Feldherr; Hauptstadt von Neuseeland.*
Wem·bley ['wemblɪ] *Stadtteil von Groß--London.*
Wen·dy ['wendɪ] *f.*
Went·worth ['wentwəθ] *Familienname.*
West Brom·wich [ˌwest'brɒmɪdʒ] *Stadt in West Midlands (England).*
West·ern Aus·tra·lia [ˌwestənɒ'streɪljə] 'Westauˌstralien *n.*
West·ern Isles [ˌwestən'aɪlz] *Insulare Verwaltungsregion Schottlands.*
West·ern Sa·moa [ˌwestənsə'məʊə] Westsa'moa *n.*
West Gla·mor·gan [ˌwestglə'mɔːgən] *walisische Grafschaft.*
West In·dies [ˌwest'ɪndiːz] *pl.*: ***the*** ~ *die* West'indischen Inseln *pl.*
West Lo·thi·an [ˌwest'ləʊðjən] *schottische Grafschaft (bis 1975).*
West·meath [west'miːð] *Grafschaft in der Provinz Leinster (Irland).*
West Mid·lands [ˌwest'mɪdləndz] *pl. Stadtgrafschaft in Mittelengland.*
West·min·ster ['wesᵗmɪnstə] *a.* **City of** ~ *Stadtbezirk von Groß-London.*
West·mor·land ['wesᵗmələnd] *englische Grafschaft (bis 1974).*
West·pha·lia [west'feɪljə] West'falen *n.*
West Vir·gin·ia [ˌwestvə'dʒɪnjə] *Staat der USA.*
West York·shire [ˌwest'jɔːkʃə] *Stadtgrafschaft in Nordengland.*
Wex·ford ['weksfəd] *Grafschaft in der Provinz Leinster (Irland); Hauptstadt dieser Grafschaft.*
Wey·mouth ['weɪməθ] *Badeort in Dorset (Südengland); Stadt in Massachusetts (USA).*
Whal·ley ['weɪlɪ; 'wɔːlɪ] *Familienname.*
Whar·am ['weərəm] *Familienname.*
Whar·ton ['wɔːtn] *amer. Romanschriftstellerin.*
Whi·tack·er ['wɪtəkə] *Familienname.*
Whit·a·ker ['wɪtəkə] *Familienname.*
Whit·by ['wɪtbɪ] *Fischereihafen in North Yorkshire (England); Stadt in Ontario (Kanada).*
White·hall [ˌwaɪt'hɔːl] *Straße in London.*
Whit·man ['wɪtmən] *amer. Dichter.*
Whit·ta·ker ['wɪtəkə] *Familienname.*
Wick·low ['wɪkləʊ] *Grafschaft in der Provinz Leinster (Irland).*
Wig·town(shire) ['wɪgtən(ʃə)] *schottische Grafschaft (bis 1974).*
Wilde [waɪld] *irischer Schriftsteller.*
Wil·der ['waɪldə] *amer. Autor.*
Wil·fred ['wɪlfrɪd] Wilfried *m.*
Will [wɪl] *abbr. für* ***William.***
Wil·liam ['wɪljəm] Wilhelm *m.*
Wil·ming·ton ['wɪlmɪŋtən] *Hafenstadt in Delaware (USA); Hafenstadt in North Carolina (USA).*
Wil·son ['wɪlsn] *Familienname.*
Wilt·shire ['wɪltʃə] *englische Grafschaft.*
Wim·ble·don ['wɪmbldən] *Stadtteil von Groß-London (Tennisturniere).*
Win·ches·ter ['wɪnᵗʃɪstə] *Hauptstadt von Hampshire (England) mit berühmter Public School.*
Wind·sor ['wɪnzə] *Stadt in Berkshire (England); Stadt in Ontario (Kanada).*
Win·i·fred ['wɪnɪfrɪd] *f.*
Win·nie ['wɪnɪ] *abbr. für* ***Winifred.***
Win·ni·peg ['wɪnɪpeg] *Hauptstadt von Manitoba (Kanada).*
Win·ston ['wɪnstən] *m.*
Wis·con·sin [wɪs'kɒnsɪn] *Staat der USA; Fluß in Wisconsin (USA).*
Wit·ham ['wɪðəm] *Stadt in Essex (England).*
Wolds [wəʊldz]: ***the*** ~ *Höhenzug in Nordostengland.*
Wolfe [wʊlf] *amer. Autor.*
Wol·lon·gong ['wʊləŋgɒŋ] *Industrie- u. Hafenstadt in New South Wales (Australien).*
Wol·sey ['wʊlzɪ] *englischer Kardinal u. Staatsmann.*
Wol·ver·hamp·ton ['wʊlvəˌhæmᵖtən] *Industriestadt in West Midlands (England).*
Woolf [wʊlf] *englische Autorin.*
Wool·wich ['wʊlɪdʒ] *Stadtteil von Groß-London.*
Wor·ces·ter ['wʊstə] *Industriestadt in Mittelengland; a.* **'Wor·ces·ter·shire** [-ʃə] *englische Grafschaft (bis 1974).*
Words·worth ['wɜːdzwəθ] *englischer Dichter.*
Wren [ren] *englischer Architekt.*
Wright [raɪt] *Name zweier amer. Flugpioniere.*
Wyc·liffe ['wɪklɪf] *englischer Reformator und Bibelübersetzer.*
Wy·man ['waɪmən] *Familienname.*
Wy·o·ming [waɪ'əʊmɪŋ] *Staat der USA.*

Xan·thip·pe [zæn'tɪpɪ] Xan'thippe *f.*

Yale [jeɪl] *hoher britischer Kolonialbeamter und Förderer der Yale University in New Haven, Connecticut (USA).*
Yeat·man ['jiːtmən; 'jeɪt-; 'jet-] *Familienname.*
Yeats [jeɪts] *irischer Dichter.*
Yel·low·stone ['jeləʊstəʊn] *Fluß im Nordwesten der USA; Nationalpark in Wyoming, Montana und Idaho (USA).*
Ye·men ['jemən] *der* Yemen.
Yeo·vil ['jəʊvɪl] *Stadt in Somersetshire (England).*
Yonge [jʌŋ] *Familienname.*
Yon·kers ['jɒŋkəz; *Am.* 'jɑːŋkərz] *Stadt im Staat New York (USA).*
York [jɔːk] *Stadt in Nordost-England;* **'York·shire** [-ʃə]: (***North, South, West***) ~ *Grafschaften in England.*
Yo·sem·i·te Na·tion·al Park [jəʊ'semɪtɪˌnæʃnl'pɑːk] *Nationalpark in Kalifornien (USA).*
Yu·go·sla·via [ˌjuːgəʊ'slɑːvjə] Jugo'slawien *n.*
Yu·ill ['juːɪl] *Familienname.*
Yu·kon ['juːkɒn] *Strom im nordwestlichen Nordamerika; a.* ***the*** ~ *siehe* ***Yukon Territory;*** **Yu·kon Ter·ri·to·ry** [ˌjuːkɒn'terɪtərɪ] *Territorium im äußersten Nordwesten Kanadas.*
Y·vone [ɪ'vɒn] I'vonne *f,* Y'vonne *f.*

Zach·a·ri·ah [ˌzækə'raɪə], **Zach·a·ry** ['zækərɪ] Zacha'rias *m.*
Za·ire [zɑː'ɪə; *Am. a.* 'zaɪər] Za'ire *n.*
Zam·bia ['zæmbɪə] Sambia *n.*
Zan·zi·bar [ˌzænzɪ'bɑː; *Am.* 'zænzəbɑːr] Sansibar *n (zu Tansania gehörige Insel vor der Ostküste Afrikas).*
Zel·da ['zeldə] *f.*
Zet·land ['zetlənd] *schottische Grafschaft (bis 1975).*
Zim·ba·bwe [zɪm'bɑːbwɪ; -weɪ] Sim'babwe *n (seit 1980 Name für* **Rhodesia).**
Zo·e ['zəʊɪ] Zoe *f.*
Zu·rich ['zjʊərɪk] Zürich *n.*